Washington Representatives ONLINE

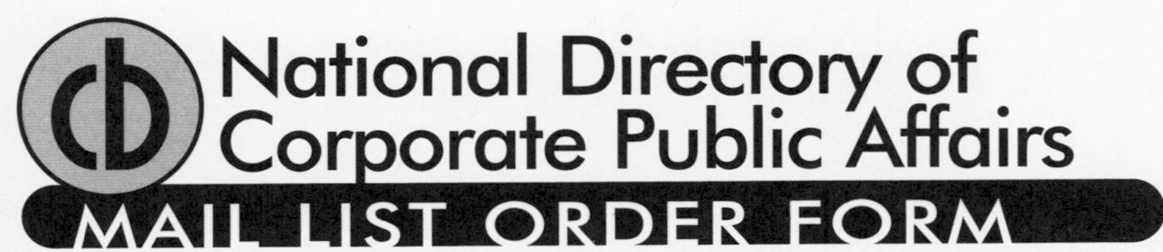

PRICES:

$150 per thousand ($250 minimum)
Additional charges for selects may apply.
Multiple use license also available.
For breakdowns and exact counts/prices, call (202) 464-1662, ext. 26.

ORDER FORM: (Please use a separate form for each list ordered.)

PLEASE SEND ME:

☐ **Your list of all 13,000 Corporate Public Affairs Officers.**
☐ **Officers with primary responsibility in the following categories:** (Check all that apply.)

☐ Public Affairs/Corporate Affairs
☐ Government Relations/Lobbying
☐ Regulatory Affairs
☐ Political Action (PAC)
☐ Communications/Public Relations
☐ Issues Management/Policy Planning
☐ Foreign Affairs
☐ Chairman of the Board
☐ Community Affairs
☐ Philanthropy/Corporate Giving
☐ Investor Relations
☐ Employee Relations
☐ Consumer Affairs
☐ Educational Affairs
☐ Environmental Affairs
☐ Chief Executive Officer

☐ **Companies by Industry Index category** (call for available categories):

____

☐ **Type of Office** (Headquarters, DC Government Affairs Office, PACs, etc. Call for available categories):

____

LIST FORMAT (Check One)

☐ Pressure Sensitive Labels (add $30/M)
☐ 3 1/2" Diskette ($20 disk fee)
☐ Email ($20 fee)

NOTE: Check, money order, or credit card information MUST accompany orders.

SEND TO: Columbia Books, Inc.,
1825 Connecticut Ave, NW, Suite 625
Washington, DC 20009
PHONE: (202) 464-1662, ext 26
FAX: (202) 464-1775
E-MAIL: info@columbiabooks.com

NAME: ____________________
TITLE: ____________________ EMAIL: ____________________
ORGANIZATION: ____________________
ADDRESS: ____________________
CITY/STATE/ZIP CODE: ____________________
TELEPHONE (required): ____________________
FAX: ____________________

☐ **Check enclosed**
☐ **Charge to credit card #**
☐ Visa ☐ M/C ☐ AMEX **Exp. Date:** ____________________

SIGNATURE (required): ____________________
DATE: ____________________

2006 NATIONAL DIRECTORY OF

Corporate Public Affairs

A profile of the public and government affairs programs and executives in America's largest and most influential corporations

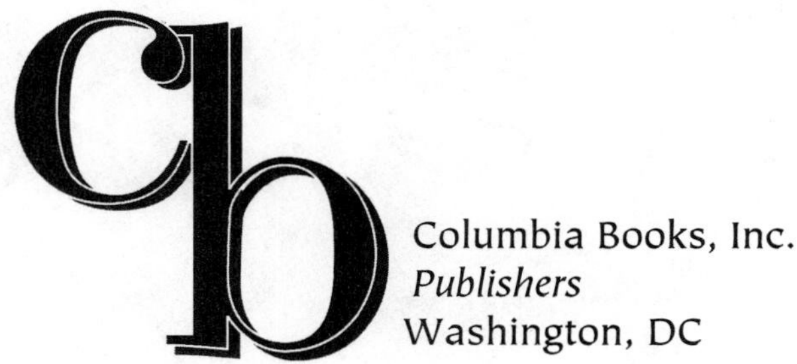

Columbia Books, Inc.
Publishers
Washington, DC

Senior Editor: Valerie S. Sheridan
Assistant Editor: LarShone Jemmott
Assistant Editor: Anthony St. Clair

Twenty-fourth Edition – 2006

ISBN 0-9747322-7-3
ISSN 0749-9736

Columbia Books, Inc.

Debra Mayberry, President

2006 National Directory of Corporate Public Affairs

Table Of Contents

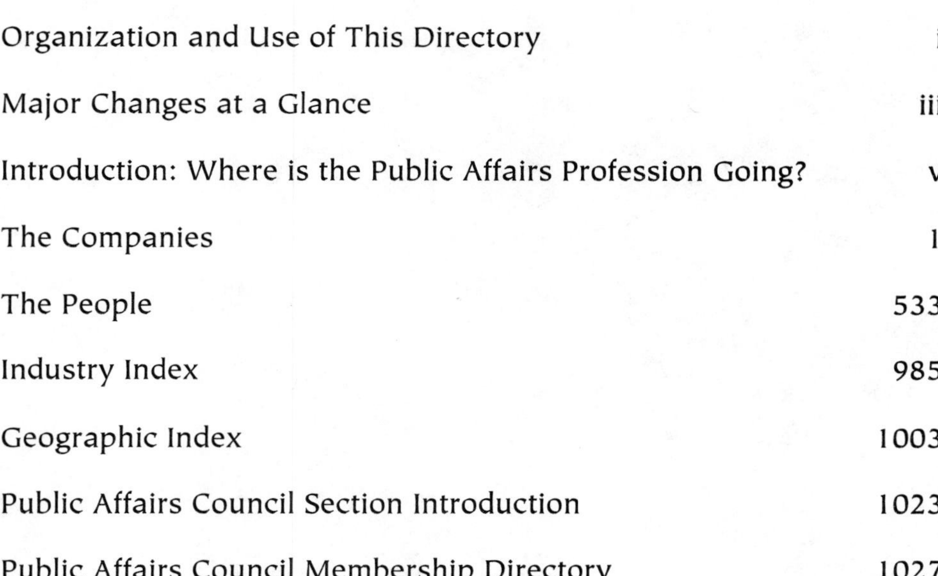

Organization and Use of This Directory	i
Major Changes at a Glance	iii
Introduction: Where is the Public Affairs Profession Going?	v
The Companies	1
The People	533
Industry Index	985
Geographic Index	1003
Public Affairs Council Section Introduction	1023
Public Affairs Council Membership Directory	1027

2006 National Directory of Corporate Public Affairs

Organization and Use of This Directory

This book provides a profile of the corporate public affairs profession in the United States — identifying the key people in that important community and including the principal corporate offices from which the many forms of public affairs activities are conducted.

The contents have been compiled from a continuous, year-long review of government, press and other sources accessible to the public. The information is updated and amplified from responses to questionnaires that are sent annually to every company listed in the directory or by telephone interviews with company representatives.

This volume is organized into two sections: The first is *The Companies*, an alphabetized catalogue of the approximately 1,500 major companies in the United States that have been identified as having public and/or government affairs programs. It includes the address of corporate headquarters and (where applicable) the address of the company's Washington, DC area office; its political action committee; and its foundation or corporate giving program. Key facts and figures on corporate philanthropic activity and political action committee involvement are also summarized. Finally, a roster of each company's public affairs and related activities personnel is included, with an indication as to whether they are located at the main headquarters office, in the nation's capital, or at some other office. Company Chairmen and Chief Executive Officers have also been included, as have annual revenues figures.

The second section of this book, designated *The People*, is an alphabetized listing of the approximately 13,000 corporate employees engaged in the informational, political and philanthropic aspects of public affairs throughout this country.

The *Industry Index* and *Geographic Index* provide further assistance in finding company listings by subject or by location.

Cross-references assist the user in locating listings for companies who have recently merged or changed names, are also known by a nickname or acronym, or whose public affairs personnel appear in the listings of their parent companies. Recent merger and name-change information is also included in the quick-reference guide titled *Major Changes at a Glance*, which appears on the following pages.

Publisher's Note: Columbia Books, Inc. is pleased to continue our collaboration with the Public Affairs Council with an Introduction composed by the Council's President, Douglas G. Pinkham. We have also included again this year their membership directory and information on their programs and services in a special section at the back of this directory. The Public Affairs Council is the premier professional association for public affairs executives. With this additional feature, we are able to provide our readers with a more comprehensive guide to the public affairs industry.

2006 National Directory of Corporate Public Affairs

Major Changes at a Glance

This feature enables readers to quickly track recent mergers, name changes, and spin-offs affecting the corporations listed or previously listed in the *National Directory of Corporate Public Affairs.*

Name Changes

Old Name	New Name
Allied Domecq Quick Service Restaurants	Dunkin'Brands Inc.
American Express Financial Advisors, Inc.	Ameriprise Financial Services Inc.
American United Life Insurance Co.	OneAmerica Financial Partners Inc.
Anthem Inc.	Wellpoint, Inc.
Arch Wireless, Inc.	USA Mobility, Inc.
ATOFINA Chemicals Inc.	Arkema Inc.
ATOFINA Petrochemicals, Inc.	Total Petrochemicals USA Inc.
Aventis Pasteur	Sanofi Pasteur Inc.
ChevronTexaco Corp.	Chevron Corp.
PTEK Holdings, Inc.	Premiere Global Services, Inc.
UNOVA, Inc.	Intermec
Wabtec Corp.	Westinghouse Air Brake Technologies
Wausau Insurance Companies	Employers Insurance Co. of Wausau

Recent Acquisitions

Company Acquired	Acquired by
7-Eleven, Inc.	Seven-Eleven Japan
Advanced Fibre Communications, Inc.	Tellabs
America West Airlines	USAirways Group
American Household, Inc.	Jarden Corp.
AT&T Wireless Services	Cingular Wireless
The Gillette Co.	The Procter & Gamble Co.
The KRONE Group	ADC
Mandalay Resort Group	MGM Mirage
May Department Stores Co.	Federated Department Stores, Inc.
Mississippi Chemical Corp.	Terra Industries Inc.
NUI Corp.	AGL Resources, Inc.
PeopleSoft	Oracle Corporation
Pulitzer Inc.	Lee Enterprises
SouthTrust Corp.	Wachovia Corp.
StorageTek	Sun Microsystems
Titan Corp. (now L-3 Comunications Titan Group)	L-3 Communications Corp.
Wellpoint Health Networks Inc.	Anthem Inc.
Wyndham Internat'l (now Wyndham World-wide)	Cendant Corp.

Recent Mergers

Merging Companies		New Company
Adolph Coors Co.	Molson Inc.	Molson Coors Brewing Co. (see Coors Brewing Co.)
Dimon Incorporated	Standard Commercial Corp.	Alliance One Internat'l Inc.
Great Lakes Chemical Corp.	Crompton Corp.	Chemtura
Kmart Holding Corp.	Sears, Roebuck & Co.	Sears Holding Corp.
Sprint Communications Corp.	Nextel Communications Inc.	Sprint Nextel

Pending Mergers and Acquisitions

The companies listed below have announced their intention to merge, however further information was not available at the time this edition went to press.

AT&T	SBC Communications Inc.
Bank of America Corp.	MBNA Corp.
Capital One Financial Corp.	Hibernia Corp.
Cinergy Corp.	Duke Energy Corp.
Lincoln Nat'l Corp. (see Lincoln Financial Group)	Jefferson-Pilot Corp.
MCI Inc.	Verizon Communications Inc.
PSE&G	Exelon Corp.

Recent and Pending-Spin-offs

Original Company	Company/Division Spun Off	New Company Name
American Express Co.	American Express Financial Advisors	Ameriprise Financial Services Inc.
Viacom Inc.	CBS	CBS Corp.

2006 National Directory of Corporate Public Affairs

Where is the Public Affairs Profession Going?

Douglas G. Pinkham
President, Public Affairs Council

Public affairs departments are becoming increasingly sophisticated – both in their ties to business management and in the strategies they employ to advance public policy agendas. But this is to be expected. Government at all levels – local, state, national and international – is growing in size and influence. And it is government, after all, that decides the rules of business. These include: who sells and exports products, who acquires other companies, who owns intellectual property, and who pays taxes.

At the same time, companies are facing pressures from other directions. Three-quarters of the general public now believe that Corporate America's reputation is either "not good" or "terrible." Corporate scandals, globalization and growing environmental concerns have provided an opening for labor unions and activist groups to launch anti-brand campaigns targeting shareholders and customers. Wall Street, meanwhile, has its own set of expectations.

And yet, companies have never had so many opportunities to build rapport with employees, local communities and other stakeholders. And they've never had so many opportunities to take a leadership role on issues such as human rights, environmental sustainability and corporate ethics.

The challenge for companies everywhere is to focus on business priorities, but with a wider peripheral vision that sees and reacts to the shifting landscape. It's not good enough to just be profitable, or just be on a list of "most admired companies." Corporations need to understand their business environments as well as they understand their financing and operations.

A new study from the Foundation for Public Affairs illustrates the changes occurring in the field. The report, called *The State of Corporate Public Affairs*, notes that this higher level of sophistication is reflected in the growing involvement of public affairs in corporate management, in the adoption of new approaches to political involvement, and in the increased emphasis on performance measurement.

Earning a Seat at the Table

More and more corporations are realizing the value of public affairs. Fifty-three percent of the public affairs executives responding to the survey sat on their companies' senior management committees. In addition, 30 percent maintained Board-level public affairs or public policy committees. Just three years ago (when the study was last conducted), only 50 percent served on management teams and only 21 percent had public affairs or public policy committees.

One of best indicators of the new linkage between public affairs and business management was the level of involvement in corporate strategic planning. In the 2005 survey, more than 75 percent of respondents rated the degree of involvement as a "4" or higher on a scale of 1 to 5. The most common ways in which public affairs influenced corporate strategy and business planning were: (1) identifying/prioritizing public policy issues for senior management; (2) commenting on corporate, operating unit and other strategic plans for sensitivity to emerging political and social trends; and (3) providing forecasts of political and social trends for senior management.

Other data also indicated a greater appreciation for the role of public affairs. The number of companies who operated Washington, DC, offices jumped dramatically over the last three years. In 2002, only 44 percent of responding companies maintained Washington offices; however, that number has now risen to 57 percent. In particular, companies in the technology sector have expanded their involvement in national politics.

In the international arena, 46 percent of those surveyed have increased their public affairs activities over the past three years and most of the rest have maintained their current workload. When asked why they were devoting more resources to global public affairs, two-thirds said it was because their companies were entering new markets. Yet, despite these rising numbers, most companies felt they had lots of room for growth. When it came to their international public affairs capabilities, 62 percent gave themselves a rating of "2" or lower on a scale of 1 to 5.

Despite the progress that has been made, public affairs departments still struggled in two areas: reporting relationships to the CEO and the coordination between public relations and government affairs. While 42 percent of respondents in the 2005 survey said they reported directly to the CEO, this number has dropped slightly since 2002. As new positions have been added to the C-suite (e.g., chief ethics officer, chief privacy/security officer), maintaining a direct line to the boss has become more difficult.

Similarly, while most companies gave themselves high marks for the level of coordination between public relations and government affairs, only 44 percent of respondents said these two functions were co-located in the same department. This was a surprising finding because the percentage was 56 percent in 2002 and it's even higher in other regions of the world. (According to a previous Public Affairs Council study on management models, the most common reason for this phenomenon is that companies lack an executive with the right skills and experiences to head up both functions.) Nevertheless, even if departments weren't integrated on the organization chart, it was encouraging that nearly three-fourths believed they have successfully integrated their PR and government affairs strategies.

New Approaches to Advocacy

The media use the terms "public affairs," "government relations" and "lobbying" interchangeably, but it's wrong to assume that direct lobbying is the only strategy used in legislative or regulatory disputes. Make no mistake about it; lobbying is still a growth industry. In fact, there are now about 35,000 lobbyists in Washington, D.C., (more than double the number registered back in 2000). However, our research shows that companies are taking a much more comprehensive approach to advocacy.

When asked to list the three most important political involvement activities at the federal level, the top vote-getters were: direct lobbying by public affairs executives, maintaining a PAC, lobbying or relationship-building by CEOs, and participation in coalitions. At the state level the answers were much the same, though CEO involvement was considered a bit less important and grassroots/grasstops activism was considered a more valuable strategy.

Overall, CEO involvement in public affairs programs is on the upswing throughout Corporate America. The share of CEOs that endorsed "Get-out-the-vote" activities in 2004 was 22 percent higher than in 2002 (a non-presidential election year). In addition, the percentage of top executives who actively participated in trade/business associations and endorsed the company's PAC grew by 9 percent over the three-year period.

While impressive, these numbers pale in comparison to the growth experienced by corporate PACs. According to the Public Affairs Council's recent *Corporate PAC Benchmarking Project*, the median corporate PAC increased its receipts by 17 percent during this past election cycle. One of the main reasons was passage of the Bipartisan Campaign Reform Act (BCRA), which greatly reduced the prevalence of soft money contributions. As a result, "hard dollar" contributions – through PACs and individual donations – have received renewed attention. While many campaign finance experts predicted that corporate dollars would flow into the so-called section 527 groups, most companies have chosen to stay clear of these organizations.

When companies have felt they lack the resources internally to address public policy issues, they haven't hesitated to look outside for extra help, said *The State of Corporate Public Affairs* report. In addition to hiring state and federal lobbyists, companies often have hired legislative tracking services, communications firms, and PAC/grassroots management vendors. They also have relied more on their trade associations. In fact, said the study, more than 90 percent of those surveyed used their trade associations for issue monitoring, issue advocacy and direct lobbying. And 57 percent took part in association grassroots campaigns.

Improvements in information technology have enabled companies and associations to use a complex mix of strategies to support advocacy goals. More than 60 percent of those surveyed maintained their own public affairs Internet or Intranet sites and – remarkably – 54 percent of them were linked to the company's primary Web site. Public affairs sites were most often used for providing legislative updates, publishing position papers and issue briefs, and for offering computerized matching of zip codes and legislative districts. All of these services have helped to keep employees and other stakeholders informed about important public policy issues.

Demonstrating Impact

Public affairs executives have an increasingly well-developed capability to measure the effectiveness of their efforts. Back in 2002, only 42 percent gave themselves a score of "4" or higher on a scale of 1-5. But in 2005, 56 percent earned high marks for their ability to evaluate their own performance.

The most common methods noted were: objectives achieved (mentioned by 99% of respondents), internal customer satisfaction (78%), legislative wins and losses (67%) and costs reduced or avoided (62%). Other yardsticks included surveys of external customer attitudes, benchmarking, revenue created, and the level of employee political involvement.

What's more, companies noted that they were systematically evaluating the usefulness of their trade and business association memberships. Nearly two-thirds gave themselves a high rating for this capability. The most common evaluation criteria included: program alignment with company goals, response to issues important to the company, effectiveness with key government decision-makers, staff responsiveness and credibility, results achieved, and reputation in Washington, DC, or state capitals.

What Comes Next?

It's always tempting to look for trends and assume that they will be magnified in the future. In the case of information technology, it's fair to say that the Internet and email will continue to revolutionize the way companies and associations communicate with employees and supporters. It's also safe to assume that the public affairs profession will continue to expand – especially at the international level.

Technology and globalization will also make the field of public affairs more challenging, however. And that means some of the current trends will need to be reversed in order for companies to maximize their effectiveness. In a world of 24-hour-a-day news and constant crises, companies who have resisted the integration (either structural or strategic) of public relations and government relations will find themselves at a severe disadvantage. Similarly, companies who rely too heavily on contract lobbyists and trade associations may find they don't have enough people looking out for their specific interests.

Leading companies thoroughly understand threats and opportunities, and approach each new issue like a start-up company with a new product. What resources do we need to get to market? What's our most effective strategy? What are our competitors doing? Should we go it alone or should we form a partnership? What could go wrong and how can we increase our chances for success?

Public affairs professionals who have a strong relationship with senior management, have experience in all forms of communication, know their stakeholders, and bring an entrepreneurial spirit to work each day will be the ones who achieve the most success. Their public affairs operations will expand and they'll have a major impact at all levels.

On the other hand, those who are hesitant to try new approaches, or who view their role one-dimensionally, will find it tougher to stay relevant. Eventually they will face staff cutbacks and – because they lack sufficient resources – they will have diminished impact.

So, when someone asks you where the public affairs business is going, say, "It depends. Where would you like to take it?"

Douglas G. Pinkham is president of the Washington, D.C.-based Public Affairs Council. The Council's 550 corporate, association and consultant members work together to enhance the value and professionalism of the public affairs practice, and to provide thoughtful leadership as corporate citizens.

The Council's annual membership directory is published within this edition of the National Directory of Corporate Public Affairs. Whenever a Council member is listed elsewhere in the book, it is identified by the Council logo.

2006 National Directory of Corporate Public Affairs

The Companies

The companies listed here include many of America's largest corporations, as well as some smaller companies with active public/government affairs programs. The information about their public affairs offices and personnel was originally collected from public records and submitted to the companies for verification. Most responded in writing. Those that did not were contacted by phone in an effort to confirm as much of their listings as possible. More recent information, collected since consultation with the companies, has also been included. Every effort has been made to insure its accuracy.

3Com Corp.

Designs and manufactures communications products.

www.3com.com
Annual Revenues: $2.82 billion

Chairman of the Board
BENHAMOU, Eric A.
Tel: (508) 323 - 5000
Fax: (508) 323 - 1111

President and Chief Exec. Officer
CLAFLIN, Bruce
Tel: (508) 323 - 5000
Fax: (508) 323 - 1111

Main Headquarters
Mailing: 350 Campus Dr.
Marlborough, MA 01752-3064
Tel: (508) 323 - 5000
Fax: (508) 323 - 1111

Public Affairs and Related Activities Personnel

At Headquarters

BOWMAN, Susan
Senior V. President, Human Resources
Tel: (508) 323 - 5000
Fax: (508) 323 - 1111

VUCKSON, Joe
Manager, Corporate Public Relations
Tel: (508) 323 - 5000
Fax: (508) 323 - 1111

3M Company

A manufacturer of health care products, abrasives, adhesives, traffic control and safety products, electronic and telecommunications products and services, and a wide variety of other products for home and work.

www.mmm.com
Annual Revenues: $20.1 billion

Chairman and Chief Exec. Officer
MCNERNEY, W. James, Jr.
Tel: (651) 733 - 1110
Fax: (651) 733 - 9973

Main Headquarters
Mailing: 3M Center
St. Paul, MN 55144-1000
Tel: (651) 733 - 1110
Fax: (651) 733 - 9973

Washington Office
Contact: Thomas F. Beddow
Mailing: 1425 K St. NW
Suite 300
Washington, DC 20005
Tel: (202) 414 - 3000
Fax: (202) 414 - 3037

Political Action Committees

Minnesota Mining and Manufacturing Co. PAC (3M PAC)
Contact: Katen K. Martodam
3M Center
St. Paul, MN 55144-1000
Tel: (651) 733 - 1110
Fax: (651) 733 - 9973

Contributions to Candidates: $41,250 (01/05 - 09/05)
Democrats: $4,500; Republicans: $34,750; Other: $2,000.

Principal Recipients

SENATE REPUBLICANS		HOUSE REPUBLICANS	
Kennedy, Mark (MN)	$3,000	Hastert, Dennis J. (IL)	$2,000
		Kline, John P (MN)	$2,000

Corporate Foundations and Giving Programs

Minnesota Mining and Manufacturing Foundation
Contact: B. W. Kaufmann
3M Center
St. Paul, MN 55144-1000
Tel: (651) 733 - 1110
Fax: (651) 733 - 9973

Annual Grant Total: over $5,000,000

Significant additional financial, in-kind and volunteer service donations are made through direct giving program.

Geographic Preference: National; Area(s) in which the company operates

Primary Interests: Arts and Culture; Community Affairs; Education; Environment/Conservation; Health and Human Services

Recent Recipients: Junior Achievement; Massachusetts Institute of Technology; United Way

Public Affairs and Related Activities Personnel

At Headquarters

BEAR, Peter D.
Manager, International Government Affairs and Government Markets
Mailstop: Bldg. 225-15-15
Tel: (651) 733 - 3374
Fax: (651) 737 - 2901

CIRILLO, Alex
Staff V. President, Community Affairs and Workforce Diversity
Tel: (651) 733 - 1110
Fax: (651) 733 - 9973

COLIN, Mark
Director, Investor Relations
Tel: (651) 733 - 1110
Fax: (651) 733 - 9973

GAHLON, Dan E.
V. President, Public Relations and Corporate Communications
Mailstop: Bldg. 225-15-15
Tel: (651) 733 - 1880
Fax: (651) 737 - 2901

GARRY, Daniel B.
Manager, Public Issues
Mailstop: Bldg. 225-1S-05
Tel: (651) 736 - 6198
Fax: (651) 736 - 2133

HAGMEIER, Katherine L.
Media Representative
Mailstop: Bldg. 225-1S-15
Tel: (651) 575 - 4368
Fax: (651) 737 - 2901

KAUFMANN, B. W.
Manager, Contributions and Community Affairs
Tel: (651) 733 - 1110
Fax: (651) 733 - 9973

KLEVEN, C. F.
Manager, Contributions and Secretary, 3M Foundation
Tel: (651) 733 - 1110
Fax: (651) 733 - 9973

LALOR, Angela
Exec. Director, Human Resources
Tel: (651) 733 - 1110
Fax: (651) 733 - 9973

MARTODAM, Katen K.
PAC Treasurer
Tel: (651) 733 - 1110
Fax: (651) 733 - 9973

NELSON, William M.
Regional Manager, State Government Affairs
Mailstop: Bldg. 225-1S-15
wmnelson@mmm.com
Tel: (651) 733 - 6516
Fax: (651) 737 - 2901

RAGETH, Jeffrey K.
National Manager, State Government Affairs
Mailstop: Bldg. 225-1S-15
jkrageth@mmm.com
Tel: (651) 575 - 3556

At Washington Office

BEDDOW, Thomas F.
Staff V. President, Corporate Public Affairs
tfbeddow@mmm.com
Registered Federal Lobbyist.
Tel: (202) 414 - 3000
Fax: (202) 414 - 3037

3M Company

** continued from previous page*

BOWLDEN, Taylor R. — Tel: (202) 414 - 3000
Manager, Federal Government Affairs, Traffic Control Materials Division — Fax: (202) 414 - 3037
Registered Federal Lobbyist.

HAYNES, Mildred W. — Tel: (202) 414 - 3000
Manager, Government Relations — Fax: (202) 414 - 3037
mwhaynes@mmm.com
Registered Federal Lobbyist.

HUTTON, Helena — Tel: (202) 414 - 3000
Manager, Government Relations — Fax: (202) 414 - 3037
Registered Federal Lobbyist.

WITORT, Stephen F. — Tel: (202) 414 - 3000
Director, Public Affairs — Fax: (202) 414 - 3037
Registered Federal Lobbyist.

At Other Offices

BRIDGES, Russell B. — Tel: (512) 984 - 6561
State Government Affairs Manager — Fax: (512) 984 - 3556
6801 River Place Blvd.
Mailstop: A130-5N-07
Austin, TX 78726-9000

7-Eleven, Inc.

PUBLIC AFFAIRS COUNCIL

A member of the Public Affairs Council. An operator of convenience stores. A subsidiary of Seven-Eleven Japan.

www.7-Eleven.com
Annual Revenues: $10.21 billion

Chairman, President and Chief Exec. Officer
KEYES, James M. — Tel: (214) 828 - 7011 — Fax: (214) 828 - 7090

Main Headquarters
Mailing: 2711 N. Haskell Ave. — Tel: (214) 828 - 7011
Dallas, TX 75204 — Fax: (214) 828 - 7090

Political Action Committees

US 7-Eleven Employees' Political Action Committee (US SEPAC)
Contact: Sherri Durst
2711 N. Haskell Ave. — Tel: (214) 828 - 7011
Dallas, TX 75204 — Fax: (214) 828 - 7090

Contributions to Candidates: none reported (01/05 - 09/05)

Corporate Foundations and Giving Programs

7-Eleven Corporate Giving Program
Contact: Nancy Lear
2711 N. Haskell Ave. — Tel: (214) 828 - 7480
Dallas, TX 75204 — Fax: (214) 828 - 7090

Annual Grant Total: $1,000,000 - $2,000,000
Geographic Preference: Area(s) in which the company operates
Primary Interests: Arts and Culture; Education; Hunger; Literacy
Recent Recipients: American Red Cross; Education Is Freedom; Muscular Dystrophy Ass'n

Public Affairs and Related Activities Personnel

At Headquarters

ANDREWS, Michael A. — Tel: (214) 828 - 7011 — Fax: (214) 828 - 7090

CHABRIS, Margaret A. — Tel: (214) 828 - 7345
Director, 7-Eleven Public Relations — Fax: (214) 828 - 7090

DAVIDSON, Carole — Tel: (214) 828 - 7021
V. President, Investor Relations — Fax: (214) 828 - 7090
cdavid01@7-11.com

DURST, Sherri — Tel: (214) 828 - 7011
PAC Treasurer — Fax: (214) 828 - 7090

LEAR, Nancy — Tel: (214) 828 - 7480
Manager, Community Affairs — Fax: (214) 828 - 7090

ROSTRON, Paul — Tel: (214) 828 - 7011
Senior V. President, Human Resources — Fax: (214) 828 - 7090

VOLKENING, Ronnie R. — Tel: (214) 841 - 6598
Director, Government Affairs — Fax: (214) 841 - 6727

WILKIE, Jack — Tel: (214) 828 - 7011
V. President, Corporate Communications — Fax: (214) 828 - 7090

99 Cents Only Stores

A discount retailer.

www.99only.com
Annual Revenues: $972.2 million

Chairman and Chief Exec. Officer
GOLD, David — Tel: (323) 980 - 8145 — Fax: (323) 980 - 8160

Main Headquarters
Mailing: 4000 E. Union Pacific Ave. — Tel: (323) 980 - 8145
City of Commerce, CA 90023 — Fax: (323) 980 - 8160

Public Affairs and Related Activities Personnel

At Headquarters

CASTANIA, Jennifer — Tel: (323) 980 - 8145
V. President, Human Resources — Fax: (323) 980 - 8160
jenniferc@99only.com

LEE, Albert — Tel: (323) 980 - 8145
Secretary to the President and Manager, Investor Relations — Fax: (323) 980 - 8160

AAI Corp.

Products and services include unmanned aerial vehicle systems, training and simulation systems, automated aircraft test and maintenance equipment, armament systems, logistical and engineering services, and other leading-edge technology solutions for defense needs.

www.aaicorp.com
Annual Revenues: $350 million

President and Chief Exec. Officer
STRADER, Frederick M. — Tel: (410) 666 - 1400 — TF: (800) 626 - 2616

Main Headquarters
Mailing: P.O. Box 126 — Tel: (410) 666 - 1400
Hunt Valley, MD 21030-0126 — TF: (800) 626 - 2616
Street: 124 Industry Ln.
Cockeysville, MD 21030

Washington Office
Contact: Albert P. Barry
Mailing: 1235 S. Clark St. — Tel: (703) 412 - 4170
Suite 1100 — Fax: (703) 416 - 4820
Arlington, VA 22202

Political Action Committees

AAI Corp. PAC
Contact: Marc L. Ehudin
1235 S. Clark St. — Tel: (703) 412 - 4170
Suite 1100 — Fax: (703) 416 - 4820
Arlington, VA 22202

Contributions to Candidates: $25,500 (01/05 - 09/05)
Democrats: $10,500; Republicans: $15,000.

Principal Recipients

SENATE DEMOCRATS		HOUSE DEMOCRATS	
Mikulski, Barbara (MD)	$2,000	Murtha, John P Mr. (PA)	$2,500
		Ruppersberger, Dutch (MD)	$2,000
SENATE REPUBLICANS		**HOUSE REPUBLICANS**	
Cochran, Thad (MS)	$2,000	Brown, Henry (SC)	$2,500
Santorum, Richard (PA)	$2,000	Crenshaw, Ander (FL)	$1,500
Specter, Arlen (PA)	$2,000		

Public Affairs and Related Activities Personnel

At Headquarters

CHRIST, Richard — Tel: (410) 628 - 3406
Treasurer, AAI Corp. Political Action Committee — Fax: (410) 628 - 8740
christ@aaicorp.com — TF: (800) 626 - 6283

CORONA, Sharon — Tel: (410) 666 - 1400
Manager, Corporate Communications — Fax: (410) 628 - 3199
corona@aaicorp.com — TF: (800) 626 - 2616

GONZALEZ PALMER, Anna-Maria — Tel: (410) 628 - 8550
V. President, Human Resources — Fax: (410) 628 - 8661 — TF: (800) 626 - 2616

At Washington Office

BARRY, Albert P. — Tel: (703) 412 - 4170
V. President, Washington Operations — Fax: (703) 416 - 4820
Barry@aaicorp.com
Registered Federal Lobbyist.

EHUDIN, Marc L. — Tel: (703) 412 - 4170
Director, Legislative Affairs — Fax: (703) 416 - 4820
ehudin@aaicorp.com
Registered Federal Lobbyist.

HOTSENPILLER, Susan — Tel: (703) 412 - 4170
Director, Legislative Affairs — Fax: (703) 416 - 4820
hotsenps@aaicorp.com
Registered Federal Lobbyist.

AAR Corp.

A supplier of parts and equipment for the aerospace and aviation industries. Also performs technical services and manufactures proprietary products.

www.aarcorp.com
Annual Revenues: $874.3 million

Chairman of the Board
EICHNER, Ira A. — Tel: (630) 227 - 2000; Fax: (630) 227 - 2019

President and Chief Exec. Officer
STORCH, David P. — Tel: (630) 227 - 2000; Fax: (630) 227 - 2019
aarceo@aarcorp.com

Main Headquarters
Mailing: One AAR Pl.
1100 N. Wood Dale Rd.
Wood Dale, IL 60191
Tel: (630) 227 - 2000; Fax: (630) 227 - 2019

Public Affairs and Related Activities Personnel

At Headquarters

BOWMAN, John
Investor Relations Contact
Tel: (630) 227 - 2145; Fax: (630) 227 - 2019

MASON, Chris
Director, Corporate Communications
chris.mason@aarcorp.com
Tel: (630) 227 - 2062; Fax: (630) 227 - 2019

ABB Inc.

PUBLIC AFFAIRS COUNCIL

A member of the Public Affairs Council. Serves customers in power transmission and distribution; automation; oil, gas, and petrochemicals; industrial products and contracting; and financial services.

www.abb.us

Chief Exec. Officer Designate
KINDLE, Fred — Tel: (203) 750 - 2200; Fax: (203) 750 - 2263; TF: (800) 626 - 4999

Main Headquarters
Mailing: 501 Merritt Seven
Norwalk, CT 06851
Tel: (203) 750 - 2200; Fax: (203) 750 - 2263; TF: (800) 626 - 4999

Washington Office
Mailing: 1455 Pennsylvania Ave. NW
Suite 210
Washington, DC 20004
Tel: (202) 638 - 1256; Fax: (202) 737 - 1311

Political Action Committees

Asea Brown Boveri (ABB) Employees' Fund for Effective Government
Contact: Bruce B. Talley
1455 Pennsylvania Ave. NW
Suite 210
Washington, DC 20004
Tel: (202) 639 - 4062; Fax: (202) 737 - 1311

Contributions to Candidates: $4,500 (01/05 - 09/05)
Democrats: $1,500; Republicans: $3,000.

Principal Recipients

SENATE DEMOCRATS		HOUSE DEMOCRATS	
		Boucher, Fredrick (VA)	$500
		Etheridge, Bob (NC)	$500
		Pascrell, William (NJ)	$500

SENATE REPUBLICANS		HOUSE REPUBLICANS	
Burr, Richard (NC)	$1,000	LaTourette, Steve (OH)	$1,000
		Shays, Christopher (CT)	$1,000

Corporate Foundations and Giving Programs

ABB Inc. Corporate Giving
501 Merritt Seven
Norwalk, CT 06851
Tel: (203) 750 - 2200; Fax: (203) 750 - 2263; TF: (800) 626 - 4999

Annual Grant Total: under $100,000
Geographic Preference: Connecticut
Primary Interests: Education; Environment/Conservation
Recent Recipients: American Cancer Society; Special Olympics

Public Affairs and Related Activities Personnel

At Headquarters

CHIRONNA, John G.
Director, Investor Relations
john.g.chironna@us.abb.com
Tel: (203) 750 - 7743; Fax: (203) 750 - 2262; TF: (800) 626 - 4999

KURTZ, Ronald
Director, Media Relations
Tel: (203) 750 - 2407; Fax: (203) 750 - 7788; TF: (800) 626 - 4999

OPPERMAN, Jeffrey
Manager, Corporate Communications
Tel: (203) 750 - 2448; Fax: (203) 750 - 7788; TF: (800) 626 - 4999

At Washington Office

TALLEY, Bruce B.
V. President, Government Affairs
Registered Federal Lobbyist.
Responsibilities include political action.
Tel: (202) 639 - 4062; Fax: (202) 737 - 1311

Abbott Laboratories

A global, broad-based healthcare company devoted to the discovery, development,manufacture and marketing of pharmaceuticals and medical products, including nutritionals, devices and diagnostics.

www.abbott.com
Annual Revenues: $19.7 billion

Main Headquarters
Mailing: 100 Abbott Park Rd.
Abbott Park, IL 60064-3500
Tel: (847) 937 - 6100

Washington Office
Contact: Elaine Leavenworth
Mailing: 1399 New York Ave. NW
Suite 200
Washington, DC 20005
Tel: (202) 378 - 2020; Fax: (202) 783 - 6631

Political Action Committees

Abbott Employee PAC
1399 New York Ave. NW
Suite 200
Washington, DC 20005
Tel: (202) 378 - 2020; Fax: (202) 783 - 6631

Contributions to Candidates: $157,775 (01/05 - 09/05)
Democrats: $25,775; Republicans: $131,000; Other: $1,000.

Principal Recipients

SENATE DEMOCRATS		HOUSE DEMOCRATS	
Carper, Thomas R (DE)	$5,000		
Nelson, Benjamin (NE)	$5,000		

SENATE REPUBLICANS		HOUSE REPUBLICANS	
Santorum, Richard (PA)	$8,000	Barton, Joe L (TX)	$5,000
Kyl, Jon L (AZ)	$6,000	Blunt, Roy (MO)	$5,000
Dewine, Richard (OH)	$5,500	Deal, Nathan (GA)	$5,000
Allen, George (VA)	$5,000	Ferguson, Mike (NJ)	$5,000
Hatch, Orrin (UT)	$5,000	Hastert, Dennis J. (IL)	$5,000
Smith, Gordon (OR)	$4,500	Johnson, Nancy (CT)	$5,000
Talent, James (MO)	$4,500	Kirk, Mark Steven (IL)	$5,000
		DeLay, Tom (TX)	$4,000

Corporate Foundations and Giving Programs

Abbott Fund
Contact: Cindy Schwab
100 Abbott Park Rd.
Abbott Park, IL 60064-3500
Tel: (847) 937 - 7075; Fax: (847) 935 - 5051

Annual Grant Total: over $5,000,000
Geographic Preference: Area(s) in which the company operates
Primary Interests: Arts and Culture; Civic and Public Affairs; Health and Human Services; Higher Education
Recent Recipients: American Red Cross; Big Brothers/Big Sisters; Nat'l Merit Scholarship; United Way; Urban League

Public Affairs and Related Activities Personnel

At Headquarters

BABINGTON, Catherine V.
V. President, Public Affairs
Mailstop: Dept. 383, AP6D
Tel: (847) 937 - 3931

BEATRICE, Michael G.
V. President, Corporate Regulatory and Quality Science
Tel: (847) 937 - 6100

BROTZ, Melissa
Divisional V. President, External Communications
Tel: (847) 935 - 3456

BRYAN, Catherine
Director, External Communications
Tel: (847) 936 - 6722

HAMILTON, Jonathon
Senior Manager, External Communications
Tel: (847) 937 - 8646

MORRISON, Kelly
Manager, External Communications
Tel: (847) 937 - 3802

SCHWAB, Cindy
V. President, Abbott Fund
Tel: (847) 937 - 7075; Fax: (847) 935 - 5051

SMOTER, Jennifer
Director, External Communications
Tel: (847) 935 - 8865; Fax: (847) 937 - 9555

At Washington Office

BURCKY, Claude
Divisional V. President, Global Government Affairs and Policy
Tel: (202) 378 - 2020; Fax: (202) 783 - 6631

CALVERT, Barbara
Director, Medical Products Reimbursement
Tel: (202) 378 - 2020; Fax: (202) 783 - 6631

Abbott Laboratories

• continued from previous page

HAAS, Rosemary T. — Tel: (202) 378 - 2020
Senior Director, Federal Government Affairs — Fax: (202) 783 - 6631
Registered Federal Lobbyist.

LEAVENWORTH, Elaine — Tel: (202) 378 - 2020
V. President, Government Affairs — Fax: (202) 783 - 6631
Registered Federal Lobbyist.

LURAY, Jennifer M. — Tel: (202) 378 - 2020
Senior Director, Government Affairs and Policy — Fax: (202) 783 - 6631

SCHOLNICK, Howard D. — Tel: (202) 378 - 2020
Director, Federal Government Affairs — Fax: (202) 783 - 6631

SENSIBAUGH, Cynthia B. — Tel: (202) 378 - 2020
Senior Director, Federal Government Affairs — Fax: (202) 783 - 6631
Registered Federal Lobbyist.

TAYLOR, John, III — Tel: (202) 378 - 2020
Divisional V. President, Federal Government Affairs — Fax: (202) 783 - 6631

WHITE, James J. — Tel: (202) 378 - 2020
Director, Federal Government Affairs — Fax: (202) 783 - 6631

WITENSTEIN, Adele — Tel: (202) 378 - 2020
Senior Director, Policy and Government Affairs — Fax: (202) 783 - 6631

ABC Television Network

See listing on page 4 under ABC, Inc.

ABC, Inc.

A subsidiary of Walt Disney (see separate listing). Operates the ABC Television Network, the ABC Radio Network, and various television and radio stations. Provides programming for cable television and publishes trade magazines, involved in international production/distribution and multimedia activities.

www.abc.go.com
Annual Revenues: $9.56 billion

Main Headquarters
Mailing: 77 W. 66th St. — Tel: (212) 456 - 7777
New York, NY 10023 — Fax: (212) 456 - 1424
TF: (800) 221 - 7386

Public Affairs and Related Activities Personnel

At Headquarters

SEWELL, Susan — Tel: (212) 456 - 7777
V. President, Media Relations-Network Communications (ABC Television Network) — Fax: (212) 456 - 7909
sewells@abc.com — TF: (800) 221 - 7386

SNYDER, Jeffrey — Tel: (212) 456 - 7777
V. President, ABC News--Media Relations — TF: (800) 221 - 7386

Abercrombie & Fitch Co.

A retailer of casual apparel.
www.abercrombie.com

Chairman and Chief Exec. Officer — Tel: (614) 283 - 6500
JEFFRIES, Michael S. — Fax: (614) 283 - 6710

Main Headquarters
Mailing: 6301 Fitch Path — Tel: (614) 283 - 6500
New Albany, OH 43054 — Fax: (614) 283 - 6710

Public Affairs and Related Activities Personnel

At Headquarters

LENNOX, Thomas D. — Tel: (614) 283 - 6751
Director, Investor Relations and Corporate Communications — Fax: (614) 283 - 6710
tom_lennox@abercrombie.com

ABX Air, Inc.

A cargo airline with a fleet of 115 aircraft operating out of Wilmington, OH and 11 hubs throughout the U.S. Provides airlift capacity and sort facility staffing to DHL, as well as charter and maintenance services to a diverse group of customers.

www.abxair.com

President and Chief Exec. Officer — Tel: (937) 382 - 5591
HETE, Joe — Fax: (937) 382 - 0896

Main Headquarters
Mailing: 145 Hunter Dr. — Tel: (937) 382 - 5591
Wilmington, OH 45177 — Fax: (937) 382 - 0896

Political Action Committees

ABX Air PAC
Contact: Robert Gray
145 Hunter Dr. — Tel: (937) 382 - 5591
Wilmington, OH 45177 — Fax: (937) 382 - 0896

Contributions to Candidates: none reported (01/05 - 09/05)

Public Affairs and Related Activities Personnel

At Headquarters

GRAY, Robert — Tel: (937) 382 - 5591
PAC Contact — Fax: (937) 382 - 0896

HUBER, Beth — Tel: (937) 382 - 5591
Supervisor, Community Relations — Ext: 2536
Mailstop: 2061 G — Fax: (937) 382 - 0896
beth.huber@abxair.com
Responsibilities include media relations and investor relations.

RHODES, Gene — Tel: (937) 382 - 5591
V. President, Human Resources — Fax: (937) 382 - 0896

Accenture

Formerly Andersen Consulting. A global management consulting and technology services company.

www.accenture.com
Annual Revenues: $13.3 billion

Chairman of the Board — Tel: (917) 452 - 4400
FOREHAND, Joe W. — Fax: (917) 527 - 9915

Chief Exec. Officer — Tel: (917) 452 - 4400
GREEN, William D. "Bill" — Fax: (917) 527 - 9915

Main Headquarters
Mailing: 1345 Ave. of the Americas — Tel: (917) 452 - 4400
New York, NY 10105 — Fax: (917) 527 - 9915

Washington Office
Contact: James M. Carroll
Mailing: 800 Connecticut Ave. NW — Tel: (202) 533 - 1100
Suite 600 — Fax: (202) 533 - 1134
Washington, DC 20006

Political Action Committees

Accenture PAC
Contact: James M. Carroll
800 Connecticut Ave. NW — Tel: (202) 533 - 1174
Suite 600 — Fax: (202) 533 - 1111
Washington, DC 20006

Contributions to Candidates: $104,680 (01/05 - 09/05)
Democrats: $44,180; Republicans: $60,500.

Principal Recipients

SENATE DEMOCRATS		HOUSE DEMOCRATS	
Carper, Thomas R (DE)	$5,580	Emanuel, Rahm (IL)	$5,000
Ford, Harold E Jr (TN)	$1,500	Tanner, John S. (TN)	$3,500
		Murtha, John P Mr. (PA)	$2,500
SENATE REPUBLICANS		**HOUSE REPUBLICANS**	
Allen, George (VA)	$6,000	Blunt, Roy (MO)	$5,000
Santorum, Richard (PA)	$2,500	Davis, Tom (VA)	$4,000
Smith, Gordon (OR)	$2,000	Sessions, Pete (TX)	$2,500
DeMint, James (SC)	$1,500		

Public Affairs and Related Activities Personnel

At Headquarters

COLE, Martin L. — Tel: (917) 452 - 4400
Group Chief Exec., Government — Fax: (917) 527 - 9915

MEYER, Carol — Tel: (917) 452 - 4400
Managing Partner, Investor Relations — Fax: (917) 527 - 9915

MURPHY, James E. — Tel: (917) 452 - 4400
Global Managing Director, Marketing and Communications — Fax: (917) 527 - 9915

SMART, Jill — Tel: (917) 452 - 4400
Managing Partner, Human Resources — Fax: (917) 527 - 9915

STRAUBE, David — Tel: (917) 452 - 2349
Director, Investor Relations (New York) — Fax: (917) 527 - 9915

TAYLOR, Roxanne — Tel: (917) 452 - 5106
Managing Partner, Corporate Communications — Fax: (917) 527 - 9915
roxanne.taylor@accenture.com

VISCONTI, Diego — Tel: (917) 452 - 4400
Group Chief Exec., Communications and High Tech — Fax: (917) 527 - 9915

At Washington Office

ARKY, M. Elizabeth — Tel: (202) 533 - 1100
Director, Government Relations — Fax: (202) 533 - 1111
m.elizabeth.arky@accenture.com
Registered Federal Lobbyist.

CARROLL, James M. — Tel: (202) 533 - 1174
Associate Partner, Government Relations — Fax: (202) 533 - 1111
james.m.carroll@accenture.com
Registered Federal Lobbyist.
Responsibilities also include political action.

Accenture

** continued from previous page*

DERGE, M. Jennie — Tel: (202) 533 - 1100 Fax: (202) 533 - 1134
Registered Federal Lobbyist.

DYSON, Caryn L. — Tel: (202) 533 - 1100 Fax: (202) 533 - 1134
Registered Federal Lobbyist.

KOONCE, Thomas — Tel: (202) 533 - 1100 Fax: (202) 533 - 1134
Registered Federal Lobbyist.

SPIGELMYER, Sharon
Associate, Government Relations — Tel: (202) 533 - 1100 Fax: (202) 533 - 1134
Registered Federal Lobbyist.

ZOMER, Binyamin A. — Tel: (202) 533 - 1100 Fax: (202) 533 - 1134
Registered Federal Lobbyist.

Ace Hardware Corp.

A retailer-owned hardware cooperative.
www.acehardware.com
Annual Revenues: $3.289 billion

Chairman of the Board
GLENN, J. Thomas — Tel: (423) 899 - 6306 Ext: 20 Fax: (423) 892 - 1744

President and Chief Exec. Officer
GRIFFITH, Ray A. — Tel: (630) 990 - 6635 Fax: (630) 571 - 0573
rgriff@acehardware.com

Main Headquarters
Mailing: 2200 Kensington Ct.
Oak Brook, IL 60523-2100 — Tel: (630) 990 - 6600 Fax: (630) 990 - 3145

Corporate Foundations and Giving Programs

Ace Hardware Foundation
Contact: Sarah Gniadek
2200 Kensington Ct.
Oak Brook, IL 60523-2100 — Tel: (630) 990 - 6523 Fax: (630) 990 - 1742

Annual Grant Total: $2,000,000 - $5,000,000
Geographic Preference: National
Primary Interests: Children; Human Welfare; Medicine and Health Care
Recent Recipients: American Red Cross; Children's Miracle Network

Public Affairs and Related Activities Personnel

At Headquarters

ALEXANDER, Jimmy
V. President, Human Resources — Tel: (630) 990 - 6620 Fax: (630) 990 - 1742

ERICKSON, Paula K.
Manager, Corporate Communications and Public Relations — Tel: (630) 990 - 6920 Fax: (630) 990 - 3145
erickson@acehardware.com
Responsibilities include corporate philanthropy.

GNIADEK, Sarah
Coordinator Ace Hardware Foundation — Tel: (630) 990 - 6523 Fax: (630) 990 - 1742

Acme Cleveland

See listing on page 151 under Danaher Corp.

Activision, Inc.

Publishes entertainment software.
www.activision.com
Annual Revenues: $864.1 million

Co-Chairman of the Board
KELLY, Brian G. — Tel: (310) 255 - 2000 Fax: (310) 255 - 2100

Chairman, Chief Exec. Officer and Director
KOTICK, Robert A. — Tel: (310) 255 - 2000 Fax: (310) 255 - 2100

Main Headquarters
Mailing: 3100 Ocean Park Blvd.
Santa Monica, CA 90405-3032 — Tel: (310) 255 - 2000 Fax: (310) 255 - 2100

Public Affairs and Related Activities Personnel

At Headquarters

LATAIF, Maryanne
V. President, Corporate Communications — Tel: (310) 255 - 2704 Fax: (310) 255 - 2100

MULVIHILL SOUTHEY, Kristen
V. President, Investor Relations — Tel: (310) 255 - 2635 Fax: (310) 255 - 2100
kmulvihill@activision.com

ROWE, Michael
Exec. V. President, Human Resources — Tel: (310) 255 - 2000 Fax: (310) 255 - 2100

Acxiom Corporation

Customer data integration products and services.
www.acxiom.com
Annual Revenues: $866.1 million

Chairman and Company Leader
MORGAN, Charles D. — Tel: (501) 342 - 6161 Fax: (501) 342 - 3913

Main Headquarters
Mailing: One Information Way
Little Rock, AR 72202 — Tel: (501) 342 - 1000 Fax: (501) 342 - 3913 TF: (888) 322 - 9466

Political Action Committees

The Acxiom Corp. Associates
One Information Way
Little Rock, AR 72202 — Tel: (501) 342 - 1000 Fax: (501) 342 - 3913 TF: (888) 322 - 9466

Contributions to Candidates: $9,000 (01/05 - 09/05)
Democrats: $5,000; Republicans: $4,000.

Principal Recipients

SENATE DEMOCRATS		HOUSE DEMOCRATS	
Pryor, Mark (AR)	$1,000	Boucher, Fredrick (VA)	$1,000
		Frank, Barney (MA)	$1,000
		Moore, Dennis (KS)	$1,000
		Ross, Michael Avery (AR)	$1,000
SENATE REPUBLICANS		**HOUSE REPUBLICANS**	
Ensign, John Eric (NV)	$2,000	Bachus, Spencer (AL)	$1,000
Allen, George (VA)	$1,000		

Public Affairs and Related Activities Personnel

At Headquarters

INGRAM, Dale
Public Relations Leader — Tel: (501) 342 - 4346 Fax: (501) 342 - 3913 TF: (888) 322 - 9466

RAYMOND, Katharine
Investor Relations Coordinator — Tel: (501) 342 - 3545 Fax: (501) 342 - 3913 TF: (888) 322 - 9466

Adaptec, Inc.

Provides computer software and hardware storage solutions.
www.adaptec.com
Annual Revenues: $419 million

Chairman of the Board
CONTI, Carl J. — Tel: (408) 945 - 8600 Fax: (408) 262 - 2533

Interim Chief Exec. Officer
MERCER, D. Scott — Tel: (408) 945 - 8600 Fax: (408) 262 - 2533

Main Headquarters
Mailing: 691 S. Milpitas Blvd.
Milpitas, CA 95035-5473 — Tel: (408) 945 - 8600 Fax: (408) 262 - 2533

Corporate Foundations and Giving Programs

Adaptec Foundation
Contact: Linda Thompson
691 S. Milpitas Blvd.
Milpitas, CA 95035-5473 — Tel: (408) 945 - 8600 Fax: (408) 262 - 2533

Assets: $1,342,495 (2002)
Annual Grant Total: $500,000 - $750,000
Geographic Preference: California
Primary Interests: Education; Housing; Human Welfare; Medicine and Health Care
Recent Recipients: Salvation Army; YMCA; YWCA

Public Affairs and Related Activities Personnel

At Headquarters

CAMARATA, Mary
Director, Corporate Communications — Tel: (408) 957 - 1630 Fax: (408) 262 - 2533
mary_camarata@adeptec.com

MOHR, Marshall
Chief Financial Officer — Tel: (408) 957 - 6773 Fax: (408) 262 - 2533
marshall_mohr@adaptec.com
Responsibilities include investor relations.

OLERICH, Shirley
V. President, Human Resources — Tel: (408) 945 - 8600 Fax: (408) 262 - 2533

THOMPSON, Linda
Foundation Contact — Tel: (408) 945 - 8600 Fax: (408) 262 - 2533

ADC

A supplier of broadband communications services. Acquired The KRONE Group in 2004.
www.adc.com
Annual Revenues: $1.05 billion

Chairman of the Board
BLANCHARD, John A. — Tel: (952) 938 - 8080 Fax: (952) 917 - 1717

ADC

• continued from previous page

President and Chief Exec. Officer
SWITZ, Robert E.
Tel: (952) 938 - 8080
Fax: (952) 917 - 1717

Main Headquarters
Mailing: P.O. Box 1101
Minneapolis, MN 55440-1101
Tel: (952) 938 - 8080
Fax: (952) 917 - 1717
TF: (800) 366 - 3889

Street: 13625 Technology Dr.
Eden Prairie, MN 55344-2252

Corporate Foundations and Giving Programs

ADC Foundation
Contact: Bill Linder-Scholer
P.O. Box 1101
Minneapolis, MN 55440-1101
Tel: (952) 915 - 0580
Fax: (952) 917 - 0965

Annual Grant Total: none reported
Geographic Preference: Santa Teresa, NM; Westborough, MA; Minneapolis, MN; Canada; Marietta, GA; St. Paul, MN
Primary Interests: Education; Math and Science; Technology

Public Affairs and Related Activities Personnel

At Headquarters

BORMAN, Mark P.
V. President, Investor Relations
mark.borman@adc.com
Tel: (952) 917 - 0590
Fax: (952) 946 - 2147

GROTHAUS, Chuck
Director, Corporate Public Relations
chuck.grothaus@adc.com
Tel: (952) 917 - 0306
Fax: (952) 917 - 0647

LINDER-SCHOLER, Bill
Exec. Director, ADC Foundation
bill.linder-scholer@adc.com
Tel: (952) 915 - 0580
Fax: (952) 917 - 0965

OWEN, Laura N.
V. President, Human Resources
laura.owen@adc.com
Tel: (952) 914 - 6188
Fax: (952) 946 - 3292

SCHMITT, Glenda
Community Relations Specialist
glenda.schmitt@adc.com
Tel: (952) 917 - 0445
Fax: (952) 917 - 0965
TF: (800) 366 - 3889

Adelphia Communications Corp.

A cable television operator.
www.adelphia.com
Annual Revenues: $4.0 billion

Chairman and Chief Exec. Officer
SCHLEYER, William T.
Tel: (303) 268 - 6300

Main Headquarters
Mailing: 5619 DTC Pkwy.
Greenwood, CO 80111
Tel: (303) 268 - 6300
TF: (877) 496 - 6704

Political Action Committees

Adelphia Communications Corp. PAC
Contact: Randall D. Fisher
5619 DTC Pkwy.
Greenwood, CO 80111
Tel: (303) 268 - 6300
TF: (877) 496 - 6704

Contributions to Candidates: $2,000 (01/05 - 09/05)
Republicans: $2,000.

Principal Recipients

SENATE REPUBLICANS
Santorum, Richard (PA) $2,000

HOUSE REPUBLICANS

Corporate Foundations and Giving Programs

Adelphia Communications Community Affairs Program
5619 DTC Pkwy.
Greenwood, CO 80111
Tel: (303) 268 - 6300
TF: (877) 496 - 6704

Annual Grant Total: none reported
Special programs include Cable in the Classroom, through which the company provides local schools with free basic cable service and more than 525 hours of commercial-free, educational programming each month.

Public Affairs and Related Activities Personnel

At Headquarters

BRUNICK, David
Senior V. President, Human Resources
Tel: (303) 268 - 6300
TF: (877) 496 - 6704

FISHER, Randall D.
Treasurer, Adelphia Communications Corp. PAC
Tel: (303) 268 - 6300
TF: (877) 496 - 6704

JACOBSON, Paul
V. President, Corporate Communications
paul.jacobson@adelphia.com
Tel: (303) 268 - 6426

STULL, Eric
Director, External Communications
erica.stull@adelphia.com
Tel: (303) 268 - 6502
TF: (877) 496 - 6704

Administaff, Inc.

A professional employer organization that serves as an outsourced, full-service human resources department for thousands of small and medium-sized companies throughout the United States.
www.administaff.com
Annual Revenues: $892 million

Chairman and Chief Exec. Officer
SARVADI, Paul J.
Tel: (281) 358 - 8986
TF: (800) 237 - 3170

Main Headquarters
Mailing: 19001 Crescent Springs Dr.
Kingwood, TX 77339-3802
Tel: (281) 358 - 8986
TF: (800) 237 - 3170

Public Affairs and Related Activities Personnel

At Headquarters

DODD, Alan
Director, Corporate Communications
alan_dodd@administaff.com
Tel: (281) 348 - 3105
Fax: (281) 348 - 2849
TF: (800) 237 - 3170

PRICE, Corinn
Director, Community Relations
corinn_price@administaff.com
Tel: (281) 348 - 3893
TF: (800) 237 - 3170

SHARP, Douglas S.
V. President, Finance and Chief Financial Officer
douglas_sharp@administaff.com
Responsibilities include investor relations.
Tel: (281) 348 - 3232
TF: (800) 237 - 3170

Adobe Systems Inc.

A manufacturer of computer software.
www.adobe.com

Co-Chairman of the Board
GESCHKE, Dr. Charles M.
Tel: (408) 536 - 6000
Fax: (408) 537 - 6000

Co-Chairman of the Board
WARNOCK, Dr. John E.
Tel: (408) 536 - 6000
Fax: (408) 537 - 6000

President and Chief Exec. Officer
CHIZEN, Bruce
Tel: (408) 536 - 6000
Fax: (408) 537 - 6000

Main Headquarters
Mailing: 345 Park Ave.
San Jose, CA 95110-2704
Tel: (408) 536 - 6000
Fax: (408) 537 - 6000

Washington Office
Contact: Michael Engelhardt
Mailing: 8201 Greensboro Dr., Suite 1000
McLean, VA 22102
Tel: (703) 883 - 2831

Corporate Foundations and Giving Programs

Adobe Corporate Affairs/Community Relations
Contact: Michelle Mann
151 Almaden Blvd.
San Jose, CA 95110-2704
Tel: (408) 536 - 3993
Fax: (408) 537 - 6313

Annual Grant Total: $2,000,000 - $5,000,000
In 2003, Adobe's philanthropic programs contributed more than U.S. $3.5 million to non-profit organizations and schools in the form of cash, grants, scholarships, and matching gifts, and approximately U.S. $2.5 million in software donations. Adobe also provided in-kind support to many charitable causes, with employees coordinating more than 80 volunteer events for a variety of community organizations.
Geographic Preference: Area in which the company is headquartered; Canada; India; Japan; Area(s) in which employees live and work
Primary Interests: Education; Human Welfare; Hunger
Recent Recipients: Children's Discovery Museum of San Jose; City Year, Inc.; Habitat for Humanity; Meals on Wheels; U.S. Fund for UNICEF; YMCA

Public Affairs and Related Activities Personnel

At Headquarters

BURR, Kevin
V. President, Corporate Communications
Mailstop: M/S WT-18
Tel: (408) 536 - 6000
Fax: (408) 537 - 6000

DEMO, Murray
Senior V. President and Chief Financial Officer
Responsibilities include investor relations.
Tel: (408) 536 - 6000
Fax: (408) 537 - 6000

DYRDAHL, Melissa
Senior V. President, Corporate Marketing and Communications
Tel: (408) 536 - 6000
Fax: (408) 537 - 6000

HUGHES, Paul
Public Policy Advisor
Tel: (408) 536 - 6000
Fax: (408) 537 - 6000

TOWNSLEY, Theresa
Senior V. President, Human Resources
Tel: (408) 536 - 6000
Fax: (408) 537 - 6000

At Washington Office

ENGELHARDT, Michael
Senior Director, Public Policy
mengelha@adobe.com
Registered Federal Lobbyist.
Tel: (703) 883 - 2831

Adobe Systems Inc.

** continued from previous page*

At Other Offices

MANN, Michelle — Tel: (408) 536 - 3993
Group Manager, Corporate Affairs/Community Relations — Fax: (408) 537 - 6313
151 Almaden Blvd.
Mailstop: M/S A11
San Jose, CA 95110-2704

Advance Auto Parts, Inc.

An automotive retailer.
www.advanceautoparts.com
Annual Revenues: $3.288 billion

President and Chief Exec. Officer
COPPOLA, Michael N. — Tel: (540) 362 - 4911

Main Headquarters
Mailing: 5673 Airport Rd.
Roanoke, VA 24012 — Tel: (540) 362 - 4911

Public Affairs and Related Activities Personnel

At Headquarters

BERGMAN, Adam — Tel: (540) 362 - 4911
V. President, Investor and Media Relations

GRAY, Jeffrey — Tel: (540) 362 - 4911
Exec. V. President and Chief Financial Officer
Responsibilities include investor relations.

ORESON, Keith — Tel: (540) 362 - 4911
Senior V. President, Human Resources and Benefits

Advanced Fibre Communications, Inc.

See listing on page 468 under Tellabs.

Advanced Micro Devices, Inc.

A manufacturer of electronic computer components.
www.amd.com
Annual Revenues: $2.7 billion

Chairman, President and Chief Exec. Officer
RUIZ, Hector de J., Ph.D. — Tel: (408) 749 - 4000; TF: (800) 538 - 8450

Main Headquarters
Mailing: One AMD Pl.
P.O. Box 3453
Sunnyvale, CA 94088 — Tel: (408) 749 - 4000; TF: (800) 538 - 8450

Political Action Committees

Advanced Micro Devices Inc. PAC
Contact: Steven J. Kester
5204 E. Ben White Blvd.
M/S 500
Austin, TX 78741

Contributions to Candidates: $3,000 (01/05 - 09/05)
Republicans: $3,000.

Principal Recipients

SENATE REPUBLICANS		HOUSE REPUBLICANS	
Allen, George (VA)	$1,000	Smith, Lamar (TX)	$1,000
		Carter, John (TX)	$500
		Sweeney, John E. (NY)	$500

Corporate Foundations and Giving Programs

Advanced Micro Devices Contributions Program
One AMD Pl. — Tel: (408) 749 - 4000
P.O. Box 3453 — TF: (800) 538 - 8450
Sunnyvale, CA 94088

Assets: $4,000 (1999)
Annual Grant Total: none reported
Geographic Preference: Area(s) in which the company operates
Primary Interests: Community Development; Early Childhood Education; Employment; Higher Education; Housing; Hunger; Medicine and Health Care
Recent Recipients: Girlstart; Housing Trust of Santa Clara County; Project Hope

Public Affairs and Related Activities Personnel

At Headquarters

ANIXTER, Benjamin M. — Tel: (408) 749 - 4000
V. President, External Affairs — Fax: (408) 749 - 3127; TF: (800) 538 - 8450

HURLEY, Bill — Tel: (408) 749 - 4000
Assistant General Counsel and Director, Government Relations — TF: (800) 538 - 8450

KROLL, Dave — Tel: (408) 749 - 4000
Director, Corporate Communications — TF: (800) 538 - 8450

LYMAN, Kevin — Tel: (408) 749 - 4000
Senior V. President, Human Resources — TF: (800) 538 - 8450

PEERMAN, Allyson — Tel: (408) 749 - 4000
Manager, Corporate Community Affairs — TF: (800) 538 - 8450

At Other Offices

KESTER, Steven J.
5204 E. Ben White Blvd.
M/S 500
Austin, TX 78741

AdvancePCS

See listing on page 101 under Caremark Rx, Inc.

Advanta Corp.

Financial services for small businesses and business professionals.
www.advanta.com
Annual Revenues: $348.9 million

Chairman and Chief Exec. Officer
ALTER, Dennis — Tel: (215) 657 - 4000; Fax: (215) 444 - 5101

Main Headquarters
Mailing: P.O. Box 844
Spring House, PA 19477-0844 — Tel: (215) 657 - 4000; Fax: (215) 444 - 5101
Street: Welsh & McKean Rds.
Spring House, PA 19477

Washington Office
Contact: Frank M. Salinger
Mailing: 1301 Pennsylvania Ave. NW — Tel: (202) 347 - 1289
Suite 500 — Fax: (202) 347 - 6876
Washington, DC 20004-1701

Political Action Committees

Advanta Corp. Employees' Political Involvement Fund
Contact: Devon C. Dorman
One Righter Pkwy., Second Floor — Tel: (302) 529 - 6565
Brandywine Corporate Center
Wilmington, DE 19803

Contributions to Candidates: $24,940 (01/05 - 09/05)
Democrats: $8,940; Republicans: $16,000.

Principal Recipients

SENATE DEMOCRATS		HOUSE DEMOCRATS	
Carper, Thomas R (DE)	$1,440	Matheson, James (UT)	$3,500
Ford, Harold E Jr (TN)	$1,000	Crowley, Joseph (NY)	$2,000
SENATE REPUBLICANS		**HOUSE REPUBLICANS**	
Santorum, Richard (PA)	$2,500	Oxley, Michael (OH)	$3,000
Talent, James (MO)	$1,000	Feeney, Tom (FL)	$2,000
		Pryce, Deborah (OH)	$2,000
		Royce, Ed Mr (CA)	$2,000

Corporate Foundations and Giving Programs

Advanta Foundation
Contact: Linda Brecht Marr
P.O. Box 844 — Tel: (215) 444 - 5073
Spring House, PA 19477-0844 — Fax: (215) 444 - 5075

Annual Grant Total: none reported
Geographic Preference: Pennsylvania; Delaware; Salt Lake City, UT
Primary Interests: Children; Cultural Education; Health and Human Services; Housing; Urban Affairs; Youth Services

Public Affairs and Related Activities Personnel

At Headquarters

BRECHT MARR, Linda — Tel: (215) 444 - 5073
Director, Sponsorships — Fax: (215) 444 - 5075
lbrechtmarr@advanta.com

CURRAN, Christopher — Tel: (215) 657 - 4000
V. President, Investor Relations — Fax: (215) 444 - 5101
ccurran@advanta.com

GOODMAN, David — Tel: (215) 444 - 5073
Director, Communications — Fax: (215) 444 - 5075
AdvantaCommunications@advanta.com

WILF, Marcia — Tel: (215) 657 - 4000
V. President, Human Resources — Fax: (215) 444 - 5075

At Washington Office

SALINGER, Frank M. — Tel: (202) 347 - 1289
V. President, Government Relations — Fax: (202) 347 - 6876
Mailstop: M/S DCC
fsalinger@advanta.com

At Other Offices

DORMAN, Devon C. — Tel: (302) 529 - 6565
PAC Administrator
One Righter Pkwy., Second Floor
Brandywine Corporate Center
Wilmington, DE 19803
ddorman@advanta.com

Advantica Restaurant Group, Inc.

See listing on page 156 under Denny's Corp.

Advo Inc.

A direct mail/advertising company.
www.advo.com
Annual Revenues: $1.18 billion

Chairman of the Board
MAHONEY, John
Tel: (860) 285 - 6100
Fax: (860) 285 - 1567
TF: (800) 559 - 2386

Chief Exec. Officer
HARDING, Scott
Tel: (860) 285 - 6100
Fax: (860) 285 - 1567
TF: (800) 559 - 2386

Main Headquarters
Mailing: One Targeting Centre
Windsor, CT 06095
Tel: (860) 285 - 6100
Fax: (860) 285 - 1567
TF: (800) 559 - 2386

Political Action Committees

Advo Inc. PAC (ADVOPAC)
Contact: Vincent Giuliano
One Targeting Centre
Windsor, CT 06095
Tel: (860) 285 - 6126
Fax: (860) 285 - 6230
TF: (800) 559 - 2386

Contributions to Candidates: $2,750 (01/05 - 09/05)
Democrats: $2,750.

Principal Recipients

SENATE DEMOCRATS		HOUSE DEMOCRATS
Carper, Thomas R (DE)	$2,500	
Wetterling, Patty (MN)	$250	

Corporate Foundations and Giving Programs

Advo Inc. Corporate Giving Program
Contact: Susan O'Dell
One Targeting Centre
Windsor, CT 06095
Tel: (860) 285 - 6100
Fax: (860) 285 - 1567
TF: (800) 559 - 2386

Annual Grant Total: none reported

Public Affairs and Related Activities Personnel

At Headquarters

DLUGOLENSKI, Mary Lou
Director, Communications
mldlugol@advoc.com
Tel: (860) 285 - 6197
Fax: (860) 285 - 1567
TF: (800) 559 - 2386

GIULIANO, Vincent
Senior V. President, Government Relations
Tel: (860) 285 - 6126
Fax: (860) 285 - 6230
TF: (800) 559 - 2386

Responsibilities include political action.

HUTTER, Christopher T.
V. President, Investor Relations; and Treasurer
cthutter@advo.com
Tel: (860) 285 - 6424
Fax: (860) 285 - 6245
TF: (800) 559 - 2386

O'DELL, Susan
Contact, Advo-System Inc. Corporate Giving Program
Tel: (860) 285 - 6100
Fax: (860) 285 - 1567
TF: (800) 559 - 2386

AEGON USA, Inc.

PUBLIC AFFAIRS COUNCIL

A member of the Public Affairs Council. An insurance holding company. A U.S. subsidiary of AEGON N.V. of the Netherlands which is also the parent company of Transamerica Corp.
www.aegonins.com
Annual Revenues: $16 billion

President and Chief Exec. Officer
BAIRD, Patrick S.
Tel: (410) 576 - 4501
Fax: (410) 374 - 8685

Main Headquarters
Mailing: 1111 N. Charles St.
Baltimore, MD 21201
Tel: (410) 576 - 4501
Fax: (410) 374 - 8685

Political Action Committees

AEGON USA, Inc. PAC
Contact: Jeanne de Cervens
1111 N. Charles St.
Baltimore, MD 21201
Tel: (410) 576 - 4529
Fax: (410) 374 - 8621

Contributions to Candidates: $50,500 (01/05 - 09/05)
Democrats: $20,500; Republicans: $30,000.

Principal Recipients

SENATE DEMOCRATS		HOUSE DEMOCRATS	
Baucus, Max (MT)	$1,500	Cardin, Ben (MD)	$5,000
Feinstein, Dianne (CA)	$1,500		

SENATE REPUBLICANS		HOUSE REPUBLICANS	
Santorum, Richard (PA)	$5,000	Latham, Thomas P (IA)	$5,000
		Johnson, Nancy (CT)	$2,000
		Northup, Anne M. (KY)	$2,000

Corporate Foundations and Giving Programs

AEGON Transamerica Foundation
1111 N. Charles St.
Baltimore, MD 21201
Tel: (410) 576 - 4501
Fax: (410) 374 - 8685

Annual Grant Total: none reported

Public Affairs and Related Activities Personnel

At Headquarters

DE CERVENS, Jeanne
Assistant General Counsel and Director, Government Relations
jdecervens@aegonusa.com
Tel: (410) 576 - 4529
Fax: (410) 374 - 8621

TUCKER, Gregory
Public Relations Officer
gtucker@aegonusa.com
Tel: (410) 576 - 4751
Fax: (410) 374 - 8685

AEP Public Service Co. of Oklahoma

See listing on page 30 under American Electric Power Co Inc.

Aerojet

See listing on page 210 under GenCorp.

The Aerospace Corp.

A private non-profit company which provides engineering support for launch and satellite systems.
www.aero.org

Main Headquarters
Mailing: P.O. Box 92957
Los Angeles, CA 90009-2957
Tel: (310) 336 - 5000
Fax: (310) 336 - 7055
Street: 2350 E. El Segundo Blvd.
El Segundo, CA 90245-4691

Public Affairs and Related Activities Personnel

At Headquarters

BRILL, Linda F.
Principal Director, Corporate Communications
Mailstop: M1-447
linda.f.brill@aero.org
Tel: (310) 336 - 1192
Fax: (310) 336 - 8249

JONTA, David L.
Media Relations Specialist
dave.l.jonta@aero.org
Tel: (310) 336 - 5041
Fax: (310) 336 - 7055

WORTMAN, Mary
Director, Internal Communications
Mailstop: 450
mary.f.wortman@aero.org
Tel: (310) 336 - 0128
Fax: (310) 336 - 7055

The AES Corp.

PUBLIC AFFAIRS COUNCIL

A member of the Public Affairs Council. A global power company.
www.aes.com
Annual Revenues: $10.3 billion

Chairman of the Board
DARMAN, Richard G.
Tel: (202) 347 - 2626
Fax: (202) 347 - 1818

President and Chief Exec. Officer
HANRAHAN, Paul T.
Tel: (703) 522 - 1315
Fax: (703) 528 - 4510

Main Headquarters
Mailing: 4300 Wilson Blvd.
11th Floor
Arlington, VA 22203
Tel: (703) 522 - 1315
Fax: (703) 528 - 4510

Political Action Committees

Aes Corp./AES Shady Point Political Action Committee
Contact: Lundy Kiger
P.O. Box 1740
Panama, OK 74951
Tel: (918) 962 - 9451

Contributions to Candidates: none reported (01/05 - 09/05)

Public Affairs and Related Activities Personnel

At Headquarters

CUNNINGHAM, Scott
V. President, Investor Relations
Tel: (703) 682 - 6336
Fax: (703) 528 - 4510

KLOOSTERBOER, Jay
V. President and Chief Human Resources Officer
Tel: (703) 522 - 1315
Fax: (703) 528 - 4510

PENCE, Robin
V. President, Communications
Tel: (703) 682 - 6552
Fax: (703) 528 - 4510

At Other Offices

KIGER, Lundy
PAC Treasurer
P.O. Box 1740
Panama, OK 74951
Tel: (918) 962 - 9451

Aetna Inc.

An insurance and financial services company.
www.aetna.com
Annual Revenues: $25.19 billion

Chairman and Chief Exec. Officer
ROWE, John W., M.D. — Tel: (860) 273 - 0123; TF: (800) 872 - 3862

Main Headquarters
Mailing: 151 Farmington Ave.
Hartford, CT 06156 — Tel: (860) 273 - 0123; TF: (800) 872 - 3862

Washington Office
Contact: Jonathan M. Topodas
Mailing: 1331 F St. NW
Suite 450
Washington, DC 20004 — Tel: (202) 223 - 2821; Fax: (202) 223 - 4424

Political Action Committees

Aetna Inc. Political Action Committee
Contact: Jonathan M. Topodas
1331 F St. NW
Suite 450
Washington, DC 20004 — Tel: (202) 419 - 7042; Fax: (202) 223 - 4424

Contributions to Candidates: $59,000 (01/05 - 09/05)
Democrats: $16,000; Republicans: $43,000.

Principal Recipients

SENATE DEMOCRATS		HOUSE DEMOCRATS	
Lieberman, Joe (CT)	$5,000		
Carper, Thomas R (DE)	$2,000		
Conrad, Kent (ND)	$2,000		
Nelson, Benjamin (NE)	$2,000		
SENATE REPUBLICANS		**HOUSE REPUBLICANS**	
Ensign, John Eric (NV)	$3,000	Johnson, Nancy (CT)	$5,000
Santorum, Richard (PA)	$3,000	Cantor, Eric (VA)	$2,000
Snowe, Olympia (ME)	$3,000	Hart, Melissa (PA)	$2,000
Kyl, Jon L (AZ)	$2,000	Deal, Nathan (GA)	$1,500
Talent, James (MO)	$2,000	Kelly, Sue W (NY)	$1,500

Corporate Foundations and Giving Programs

Aetna Foundation
Contact: Marilda L. Gandara
151 Farmington Ave.
Hartford, CT 06156 — Tel: (860) 273 - 4770; Fax: (860) 273 - 4764

Annual Grant Total: over $5,000,000
Contributed over $15 million in 2002.
Geographic Preference: Connecticut
Primary Interests: Arts and Culture; Civic and Public Affairs; Community Affairs; Education; Medicine and Health Care

Public Affairs and Related Activities Personnel

At Headquarters

BOLTON, Roger — Tel: (860) 273 - 1704; Fax: (860) 273 - 1624
Senior V. President, Communications

CARTER, David W. — Tel: (860) 273 - 3658; TF: (800) 872 - 3862
V. President, Public Relations
carterdw@aetna.com

ENTREKIN, David — Tel: (860) 273 - 7830; Fax: (860) 273 - 3971; TF: (800) 872 - 3862
V. President, Investor Relations
Mailstop: MS RW3H
entrekind@aetna.com

GANDARA, Marilda L. — Tel: (860) 273 - 4770; Fax: (860) 273 - 4764
President, Aetna Foundation

GRIFFITHS, Jill — Tel: (860) 273 - 8162; TF: (800) 872 - 3862
V. President, Business Communications
(Aetna U.S. Healthcare, Inc.)
griffithsjb@aetna.com

LABERGE, Alfred — Tel: (860) 273 - 4788; Fax: (860) 273 - 6675
Assistant V. President, Corporate Public Relations
Mailstop: MS RWAK
labergear@aetna.com

OAKES, Dennis — Tel: (860) 273 - 6184; Fax: (860) 372 - 3971; TF: (800) 872 - 3862
V. President, Public Policy
Mailstop: RW3H
oakesd@aetna.com

WRIGHT, Elease E. — Tel: (860) 273 - 8371; Fax: (860) 560 - 8721
Senior V. President, Human Resources

At Washington Office

IOVINO, Charlyn A. — Tel: (202) 419 - 7047; Fax: (202) 223 - 4424
V. President and Counsel
iovinoca@aetna.com
Registered Federal Lobbyist.

TOPODAS, Jonathan M. — Tel: (202) 419 - 7042; Fax: (202) 223 - 4424
V. President and Counsel; PAC Treasurer
jonathan.topodas@aetna.com
Registered Federal Lobbyist.

Aetna U.S. Healthcare, Inc.

See listing on page 9 under Aetna Inc.

AFC Enterprises

Parent company of restaurants including Church's Chicken and Popeyes Chicken & Biscuits.
www.afce.com
Annual Revenues: $2.6 billion

Chairman and Chief Exec. Officer
BELATTI, Frank J. — Tel: (404) 459 - 4450
fbelatti@afce.com

Chief Exec. Officer
KEYMER, Kenneth L. — Tel: (404) 459 - 4450

Main Headquarters
Mailing: 555 Glenridge Connector NE
Suite 300
Atlanta, GA 30342 — Tel: (404) 459 - 4450

Corporate Foundations and Giving Programs

AFC Enterprises Foundation
555 Glenridge Connector NE
Suite 300
Atlanta, GA 30342 — Tel: (404) 459 - 4450

Annual Grant Total: $750,000 - $1,000,000
Geographic Preference: National
Primary Interests: Arts and Culture; Education; Environment/Conservation; Housing
Recent Recipients: Habitat for Humanity

Public Affairs and Related Activities Personnel

At Headquarters

KISSELL, Felise G. — Tel: (404) 459 - 4450
V. President, Investor Relations and Finance
fkissell@afce.com

STOUT, Stan — Tel: (404) 459 - 4450
V. President and Chief People Services Officer

THOMPSON, Alicia — Tel: (404) 459 - 4572
V. President, Communications and Public Relations
(Popeyes Chicken & Biscuits)

Affiliated Computer Services, Inc. (ACS)

A member of the Public Affairs Council. Business process and technology outsourcing provider.
www.acs-inc.com
Annual Revenues: $3.06 billion

Chairman of the Board
DEASON, Darwin — Tel: (214) 841 - 6111
darwin.deason@acs-inc.com

Chief Exec. Officer
RICH, Jeffrey A. — Tel: (214) 841 - 6111
jeff.rich@acs-inc.com

Main Headquarters
Mailing: 2828 N. Haskell Ave.
Dallas, TX 75204 — Tel: (214) 841 - 6111

Washington Office
Mailing: 1200 K St., NW
Washington, DC 20005 — Tel: (202) 414 - 3720; Fax: (202) 289 - 8274

Political Action Committees

Affiliated Computer Services Inc. PAC
Contact: John Coleman
1200 K St., NW
Washington, DC 20005 — Tel: (202) 414 - 3720; Fax: (202) 289 - 8274

Contributions to Candidates: $14,000 (01/05 - 09/05)
Democrats: $9,000; Republicans: $5,000.

Principal Recipients

SENATE DEMOCRATS		HOUSE DEMOCRATS	
Clinton, Hillary Rodham (NY)	$5,000	Menendez, Robert (NJ)	$1,000
Kennedy, John Neely (LA)	$2,000		
Baucus, Max (MT)	$1,000		
SENATE REPUBLICANS		**HOUSE REPUBLICANS**	
Chambliss, Saxby (GA)	$500	Pence, Mike (IN)	$2,500
Santorum, Richard (PA)	$500	Deal, Nathan (GA)	$1,000
		Norwood, Charles (GA)	$500

Public Affairs and Related Activities Personnel

At Headquarters

DELANEY, Keenan — Tel: (214) 841 - 6111
V. President, Public Affairs

EDWARDS, Warren — Tel: (214) 841 - 6111
Exec. V. President and Chief Financial Officer
Responsibilities include investor relations.

Affiliated Computer Services, Inc. (ACS)

• continued from previous page

POOL, Lesley — Tel: (214) 841 - 6111
Senior V. President and Chief Marketing Officer
Responsibilities include media relations.

At Washington Office

COLEMAN, John — Tel: (202) 414 - 3720
PAC Treasurer — Fax: (202) 289 - 8274

AFLAC Incorporated

Formerly American Family Life Assurance Co. A supplemental life and health insurance provider.

www.aflac.com
Annual Revenues: $9.6 billion

Chairman and Chief Exec. Officer — Tel: (706) 323 - 3431
AMOS, Daniel P. — Fax: (706) 660 - 7333
TF: (800) 992 - 3522

Main Headquarters
Mailing: 1932 Wynnton Rd. — Tel: (706) 323 - 3431
Columbus, GA 31999 — Fax: (706) 660 - 7333
TF: (800) 992 - 3522

Political Action Committees

AFLAC Inc. Political Action Committee (AFLACPAC)
Contact: Joey M. Loudermilk
1932 Wynnton Rd. — Tel: (706) 323 - 3431
Columbus, GA 31999 — Fax: (706) 660 - 7333
TF: (800) 992 - 3522

Contributions to Candidates: $436,600 (01/05 - 09/05)
Democrats: $188,600; Republicans: $248,000.

Principal Recipients

SENATE DEMOCRATS
Clinton, Hillary Rodham (NY) $5,000
Ford, Harold E Jr (TN) $5,000

HOUSE DEMOCRATS
Marshall, Jim (GA) $10,000
Scott, David (GA) $10,000
Bean, Melissa (IL) $5,000
Bishop, Sanford (GA) $5,000
Lewis, John (GA) $5,000
Matsui, Doris (CA) $5,000
Neal, Richard E Mr. (MA) $5,000
Pomeroy, Earl (ND) $5,000

SENATE REPUBLICANS
Allen, George (VA) $5,000
Enzi, Michael B (WY) $5,000
Harris, Katherine (FL) $5,000
Santorum, Richard (PA) $5,000

HOUSE REPUBLICANS
McCrery, Jim (LA) $11,000
Price, Thomas (GA) $8,000
Westmoreland, Lynn (GA) $8,000
Bachus, Spencer (AL) $5,000
Barrett, James (SC) $5,000
Barton, Joe L (TX) $5,000
Blunt, Roy (MO) $5,000
Bonner, Josiah (AL) $5,000
Brown-Waite, Virginia (FL) $5,000
Duncan, John (TN) $5,000
English, Philip S (PA) $5,000
Foley, Mark (FL) $5,000
Gingrey, Phillip (GA) $5,000
Hart, Melissa (PA) $5,000
Hastert, Dennis J. (IL) $5,000
Hayworth, J D (AZ) $5,000
Herger, Wally (CA) $5,000
Johnson, Nancy (CT) $5,000
Kingston, John (GA) $5,000
Linder, John (GA) $5,000
Norwood, Charles (GA) $5,000
Reynolds, Thomas (NY) $5,000
Shaw, Clay (FL) $5,000
Thomas, William M (CA) $5,000

Corporate Foundations and Giving Programs

AFLAC Corporate Giving Program
Contact: Angela S. Hart
1932 Wynnton Rd. — Tel: (706) 323 - 3431
Columbus, GA 31999 — Fax: (706) 660 - 7333
TF: (800) 992 - 3522

Annual Grant Total: none reported
Geographic Preference: Columbus, OH
Primary Interests: Arts and Culture; Education; Health; Youth Services
Recent Recipients: American Cancer Society

Public Affairs and Related Activities Personnel

At Headquarters

CLARK, Mechelle — Tel: (706) 243 - 8004
Media Contact — Fax: (706) 660 - 7333
meclark@aflac.com — TF: (800) 992 - 3522

FRIOU, Phillip J. "Jack — Tel: (706) 323 - 3431
Senior V. President, Governmental Relations — Fax: (706) 660 - 7333
TF: (800) 992 - 3522

HART, Angela S. — Tel: (706) 323 - 3431
Senior V. President, Community Relations — Fax: (706) 660 - 7333
TF: (800) 992 - 3522

JANKE, Kenneth S., Jr. — Tel: (706) 323 - 3431
Senior V. President, Investor Relations — Fax: (706) 660 - 7333
TF: (800) 992 - 3522

KANE, Laura — Tel: (706) 596 - 3493
Manager, Corporate Communications — Fax: (706) 660 - 7333
lkane@aflac.com — TF: (800) 992 - 3522

LOUDERMILK, Joey M. — Tel: (706) 323 - 3431
Exec. V. President, General Counsel and Corporate Secretary — Fax: (706) 660 - 7333
TF: (800) 992 - 3522
Responsibilities include political action.

PRINGLE, David L. — Tel: (706) 596 - 3985
V. President, Federal Relations — Fax: (706) 660 - 7333
TF: (800) 992 - 3522

RIGBY, Gina J. — Tel: (706) 323 - 3431
Director, Federal Relations — Fax: (706) 660 - 7333
TF: (800) 992 - 3522

TILLMAN, Audrey B. — Tel: (706) 323 - 3431
Senior V. President; and Director, Human Resources, Facilities and Health Services — Fax: (706) 660 - 7333
TF: (800) 992 - 3522

Aftermarket Technology Corp.

A manufacturer of aftermarket automotive products.

www.goatc.com
Annual Revenues: $416 million

Chairman, President and Chief Exec. Officer — Tel: (630) 271 - 8100
JOHNSON, Don T.

Main Headquarters
Mailing: 1400 Opus Place — Tel: (630) 271 - 8100
Suite 600
Downers Grove, IL 60515

Public Affairs and Related Activities Personnel

At Headquarters

MACHOTA, John J. — Tel: (630) 271 - 8100
V. President, Human Resources

RYAN, Mary T. — Tel: (630) 663 - 8283
V. President, Communications and Investor Relations
maryan@corpatc.com

AG Processing Inc

A grains processing cooperative.

www.agp.com
Annual Revenues: $1.8 billion

Chairman of the Board — Tel: (402) 496 - 7809
DAVIS, Bradley T. — Fax: (402) 498 - 2215
TF: (800) 247 - 1345

Chief Exec. Officer — Tel: (402) 496 - 7809
REAGAN, Marty P. — Fax: (402) 498 - 2215
TF: (800) 247 - 1345

Main Headquarters
Mailing: P.O. Box 2047 — Tel: (402) 496 - 7809
Omaha, NE 68103-2047 — Fax: (402) 498 - 2215
TF: (800) 247 - 1345

Street: 12700 W. Dodge Rd.
Omaha, NE 68154

Political Action Committees

AG Processing Inc. PAC (AGPAC)
Contact: Judy Ford
P.O. Box 2047 — Tel: (402) 496 - 7809
Omaha, NE 68103-2047 — Fax: (402) 498 - 5548
TF: (800) 247 - 1345

Contributions to Candidates: $21,000 (01/05 - 09/05)

AG Processing Inc

** continued from previous page*

Democrats: $1,000; Republicans: $20,000.

Principal Recipients

SENATE DEMOCRATS		HOUSE DEMOCRATS	
Johnson, Tim (SD)	$1,000		
SENATE REPUBLICANS		**HOUSE REPUBLICANS**	
Talent, James (MO)	$5,000	Kennedy, Mark (MN)	$4,000
Coleman, Norm (MN)	$4,000	Kline, John P (MN)	$4,000
		Fortenberry, Jeffrey (NE)	$2,000
		Latham, Thomas P (IA)	$1,000

Corporate Foundations and Giving Programs

AG Processing Corporate Contributions
Contact: Mike Maranell
P.O. Box 2047
Omaha, NE 68103-2047
Tel: (402) 496 - 2279
Fax: (402) 498 - 5552

Annual Grant Total: none reported

Public Affairs and Related Activities Personnel

At Headquarters

CAMPBELL, John
V. President, Government Relations and Industrial Products
Tel: (402) 496 - 5546
Fax: (402) 498 - 2215

FORD, Judy
Senior V. President, Human Resources
Tel: (402) 496 - 7809
Fax: (402) 498 - 5548
TF: (800) 247 - 1345

Responsibilities include political action.

JORGENSEN, Kelly
Director, Environmental Affairs
Tel: (402) 496 - 7809
Fax: (402) 498 - 2208

MARANELL, Mike
Senior V. President, Corporate and Member Relations
Tel: (402) 496 - 2279
Fax: (402) 498 - 5552

AGCO Corp.

A manufacturer, designer, and distributor of agricultural equipment and replacement parts.

www.agcocorp.com
Annual Revenues: $5.273 billion

Chairman of the Board
RATLIFF, Robert J.
Tel: (770) 813 - 9200
Fax: (770) 813 - 6118

President and Chief Exec. Officer
RICHENHAGEN, Martin
Tel: (770) 813 - 6101
Fax: (770) 813 - 6118

Main Headquarters
Mailing: 4205 River Green Pkwy.
Duluth, GA 30096-2568
Tel: (770) 813 - 9200
Fax: (770) 813 - 6118

Corporate Foundations and Giving Programs

AGCO Corp. Community Affairs
4205 River Green Pkwy.
Duluth, GA 30096-2568
Tel: (770) 813 - 9200
Fax: (770) 813 - 6118

Annual Grant Total: none reported

Recent Recipients: American Red Cross; Future Farmers of America; Junior Achievement; United Way

Public Affairs and Related Activities Personnel

At Headquarters

BOYD, Norm
Senior V. President, Human Resources
Tel: (770) 813 - 6144
Fax: (770) 813 - 6118

DYE, Molly
V. President, Corporate Relations
Tel: (770) 813 - 6044
Fax: (770) 813 - 6118

Agere Systems Inc.

Provides computer and internet services.

www.agere.com
Annual Revenues: $2.2 billion

Chairman of the Board
WAGNER, Harold A.
Tel: (610) 712 - 4323
Fax: (610) 712 - 4106

President and Chief Exec. Officer
DICKSON, John T.
Tel: (610) 712 - 4323
Fax: (610) 712 - 4106

Main Headquarters
Mailing: 1110 American Parkway NE
Allentown, PA 18109-3229
Tel: (610) 712 - 4323
Fax: (610) 712 - 4106

Corporate Foundations and Giving Programs

Agere Systems Community Involvement Councils
Contact: Stephanie Polak
1110 American Parkway NE
Allentown, PA 18109-3229
Tel: (610) 712 - 7292
Fax: (610) 712 - 4106

Annual Grant Total: none reported

Geographic Preference: Area(s) in which employees live and work
Primary Interests: Community Development; Environment/Conservation; K-12 Education

Public Affairs and Related Activities Personnel

At Headquarters

BECKER, Kay
Media Relations Contact
kabecker@agere.com
Tel: (610) 712 - 3689
Fax: (610) 712 - 4106

HALEY, Glen
Media Relations Contact
glenhaley@agere.com
Tel: (610) 712 - 1747
Fax: (610) 712 - 4106

LONGFELLOW, David
V. President, Investor and Government Relations
Tel: (610) 712 - 6011
Fax: (610) 712 - 4106

PENNINGTON, Kevin P.
Senior V. President, Human Resources and Real Estate
Tel: (610) 712 - 4323
Fax: (610) 712 - 4106

POLAK, Stephanie
Contact, Lehigh Valley Community Involvement Council
spolak@agere.com
Tel: (610) 712 - 7292
Fax: (610) 712 - 4106

Agilent Technologies, Inc.

Manufacturer of technical instruments, systems and solutions.

www.agilent.com
Annual Revenues: $7.2 billion

President and Chief Exec. Officer
SULLIVAN, William P.
Tel: (650) 752 - 5300
Fax: (650) 752 - 5633

Main Headquarters
Mailing: P.O. Box 10395
Palo Alto, CA 94303-0395
Street: 395 Page Mill Rd.
Palo Alto, CA 94303
Tel: (650) 752 - 5300
Fax: (650) 752 - 5633

Washington Office
Contact: Frank Orlandella
Mailing: 1666 K St. NW
Suite 420
Washington, DC 20006
Tel: (202) 416 - 6210
Fax: (202) 416 - 6253

Corporate Foundations and Giving Programs

Agilent Foundation
Contact: Karen Lewis
P.O. Box 10395
Palo Alto, CA 94303-0395
Tel: (650) 752 - 5153
Fax: (650) 752 - 5633

Annual Grant Total: none reported

Public Affairs and Related Activities Personnel

At Headquarters

DRAKE, Michele
Manager, Public Relations
michele_drake@agilent.com
Tel: (650) 752 - 5296
Fax: (650) 752 - 5633

FLORES, Amy
Manager, Public Relations
amy_flores@agilent.com
Tel: (650) 752 - 5303
Fax: (650) 752 - 5633

FROMEN, Peter
Investor Relations Associate
Tel: (650) 752 - 5300
Fax: (650) 752 - 5633

HALLORAN, Jean M.
Senior V. President, Human Resources
jean_halloran@agilent.com
Tel: (650) 752 - 5000
Fax: (650) 752 - 5633

LEWIS, Karen
Exec. Director, Agilent Foundation
karen_lewis@agilent.com
Tel: (650) 752 - 5153
Fax: (650) 752 - 5633

SMITH, Janet
Media Relations Contact
janet_smith@agilent.com
Tel: (970) 679 - 5397

TERRY, Hilliard
Director, Investor Relations
Tel: (650) 752 - 5300
Fax: (650) 752 - 5633

At Washington Office

ORLANDELLA, Frank
Director, Federal Public Policy
frank_orlandella@agilent.com
Tel: (202) 416 - 6210
Fax: (202) 416 - 6253
Registered Federal Lobbyist.

PANCAKE, R. Robbins
Tel: (202) 416 - 6210
Fax: (202) 416 - 6253
Registered Federal Lobbyist.

PORTER, Catherine
Tel: (202) 416 - 6210
Fax: (202) 416 - 6253
Registered Federal Lobbyist.

Agilysys, Inc.

Formerly known as Pioneer-Standard Electronics, Inc. A provider of enterprise computer technology solutions.

www.agilysys.com
Annual Revenues: $1.6 billion

Agilysys, Inc.

* continued from previous page

Chairman, President and Chief Exec. Officer
RHEIN, Arthur
arthur.rhein@agilysys.com
Tel: (440) 720 - 8500
Fax: (440) 720 - 8501
TF: (800) 422 - 2400

Main Headquarters
Mailing: 6065 Parkland Blvd.
Cleveland, OH 44124
Tel: (440) 720 - 8500
Fax: (440) 720 - 8501
TF: (800) 422 - 2400

Corporate Foundations and Giving Programs

Agilysys, Inc. Corporate Giving Program
6065 Parkland Blvd.
Cleveland, OH 44124
Tel: (440) 720 - 8500
Fax: (440) 720 - 8501
TF: (800) 422 - 2400

Annual Grant Total: none reported

Public Affairs and Related Activities Personnel

At Headquarters

ELLIS, Martin
Exec. V. President, Treasurer, and Chief Financial Officer
martin.ellis@agilysys.com
Tel: (440) 720 - 8682
Fax: (440) 720 - 8677
TF: (800) 422 - 2400

SAYERS, Richard
Exec. V. President, Chief Human Resources Officer
rick.sayers@agilysys.com
Tel: (440) 720 - 8675
Fax: (440) 720 - 8501
TF: (800) 422 - 2400

YOUNG, Julie
Director, Corporate Communications
julie.young@agilysys.com
Tel: (440) 720 - 8602
Fax: (440) 720 - 8720
TF: (800) 422 - 2400

AGL Resources, Inc.

A regional energy holding company whose core business is natural gas distribution. Acquired NUI Corp. in 2004.
www.aglresources.com
Annual Revenues: $1.05 billion

Chairman, President and Chief Exec. Officer
REYNOLDS, Paula
Tel: (404) 584 - 9470
Fax: (404) 584 - 3479

Main Headquarters
Mailing: P.O. Box 4569
Atlanta, GA 30302-4569
Tel: (404) 584 - 4000
Fax: (404) 584 - 3479
Street: 817 W. Peachtree St., N.W.
Atlanta, GA 30308

Political Action Committees

AGL Resources Inc. Political Action Committee Inc.
Contact: Christine Williams
P.O. Box 4569
Atlanta, GA 30302-4569
Tel: (404) 584 - 4000
Fax: (404) 584 - 3479

Contributions to Candidates: $16,500 (01/05 - 09/05)
Democrats: $7,000; Republicans: $9,500.

Principal Recipients

SENATE DEMOCRATS		HOUSE DEMOCRATS	
Lautenberg, Frank (NJ)	$5,000	Lewis, John (GA)	$2,000
SENATE REPUBLICANS		**HOUSE REPUBLICANS**	
Chambliss, Saxby (GA)	$2,000	Cantor, Eric (VA)	$1,000
Allen, George (VA)	$1,000	Garrett, E Scott (NJ)	$1,000
Isakson, John (GA)	$1,000	Kingston, John (GA)	$1,000
Corker Jr, Robert P (TN)	$500	Linder, John (GA)	$1,000
		Norwood, Charles (GA)	$1,000

Virginia Natural Gas Inc. Committee for Effective Government
Contact: James C. Balderson
5100 E. Virginia Beach Blvd.
Norfolk, VA 23502

Contributions to Candidates: $500 (01/05 - 09/05)
Republicans: $500.

Principal Recipients

SENATE REPUBLICANS	HOUSE REPUBLICANS	
	Drake, Thelma Day (VA)	$500

Corporate Foundations and Giving Programs

AGL Resources Private Foundation, Inc.
P.O. Box 4569
Atlanta, GA 30302-4569
Tel: (404) 584 - 4000
Fax: (404) 584 - 3479

Assets: $3,685,182 (2002)
Annual Grant Total: none reported
Primary Interests: Education; Environment/Conservation; Literacy; Math and Science
Recent Recipients: United Negro College Fund

Public Affairs and Related Activities Personnel

At Headquarters

BATSON, Bryan
Senior V. President, External Affairs
Tel: (404) 584 - 4000
Fax: (404) 584 - 3479

GOLD, Nick
Director, Media Relations
ngold@aglresources.com
Tel: (404) 584 - 3457
Fax: (404) 584 - 3479

LITTLE, Brian
Director, Investor Relations
blittle@aglresources.com
Tel: (404) 584 - 4414
Fax: (404) 584 - 3479

MADDEN, Kevin P.
Exec. V. President, Distribution Operations and External Affairs
Tel: (404) 584 - 4000
Fax: (404) 584 - 3479

MONFRIED, Martha J.
Director, Public Affairs
Tel: (404) 584 - 4000
Fax: (404) 584 - 3479

MOORE, Richard
Director, Government Affairs and Economic Development
rmoore@aglresources.com
Tel: (404) 584 - 9470
Fax: (404) 584 - 3479

PLATT, Melanie M.
Senior V. President, Human Resources
Tel: (404) 584 - 4000
Fax: (404) 584 - 3479

QUINN, Matthew C.
Planning Director, Investor Relations
mcquinn@aglresources.com
Tel: (404) 584 - 3192
Fax: (404) 584 - 3479

THOMAS, R. Lindsay
Senior V. President, Governmental Affairs
Tel: (404) 584 - 4000
Fax: (404) 584 - 3479

WILLIAMS, Christine
PAC Treasurer
Tel: (404) 584 - 4000
Fax: (404) 584 - 3479

At Other Offices

BALDERSON, James C.
Treasurer, Virginia Natural Gas Committee for Effective Government
5100 E. Virginia Beach Blvd.
Norfolk, VA 23502

AgrEvo

See listing on page 66 under Bayer CropScience.

Agrilink Foods, Inc.

See listing on page 75 under Birds Eye Foods.

AIG American General Corp.

A consumer financial services organization. A subsidiary of American Internat'l Group, Inc. (see separate listing).
www.americangeneral.com
Annual Revenues: $11.06 billion

President and Chief Exec. Officer
MARTIN, Rodney O., Jr.
Tel: (713) 831 - 8500
Fax: (713) 523 - 8531

President and Chief Exec. Officer
SULLIVAN, Martin J.

Main Headquarters
Mailing: 2929 Allen Pkwy.
Houston, TX 77019
Tel: (713) 522 - 1111
Fax: (713) 523 - 8531

Political Action Committees

American General Corp. Political Action Committee (AGCPAC)
Contact: Robert A. Gender
70 Pine St.
19th Floor
New York, NY 10270
Tel: (212) 770 - 7000
Fax: (212) 509 - 9705

Contributions to Candidates: none reported (01/05 - 09/05)

Corporate Foundations and Giving Programs

American General Corp. Charitable Trust
Contact: Cindy Wieties
2929 Allen Pkwy.
Houston, TX 77019
Tel: (713) 522 - 1111
Fax: (713) 523 - 8531

Annual Grant Total: $2,000,000 - $5,000,000
Geographic Preference: National
Primary Interests: Arts and Culture; Education; Health and Human Services
Recent Recipients: Anti-Defamation League; United Negro College Fund; United Way

Public Affairs and Related Activities Personnel

At Headquarters

JENNINGS, Thomas
Director, State Government Relations
Tel: (713) 342 - 7489
Fax: (713) 523 - 8531

WIETIES, Cindy
Director, Community Relations
Tel: (713) 522 - 1111
Fax: (713) 523 - 8531

At Other Offices

GENDER, Robert A.
PAC Treasurer
70 Pine St.
19th Floor
New York, NY 10270
Tel: (212) 770 - 7000
Fax: (212) 509 - 9705

AIG Hawaii Insurance Co., Inc.

See listing on page 32 under American Internat'l Group, Inc.

AIG SunAmerica Inc.

A life insurance and financial services company. A subsidiary of American Internat'l Group, Inc. (see separate listing).

www.aigsunamerica.com
Annual Revenues: $537 million

Chairman of the Board
BROAD, Eli
Tel: (310) 772 - 6000
TF: (800) 871 - 2000

President and Chief Exec. Officer
WINTROB, Jay S.
Tel: (310) 772 - 6000
TF: (800) 871 - 2000

Main Headquarters
Mailing: One SunAmerica Center
Los Angeles, CA 90067-6022
Tel: (310) 772 - 6000
TF: (800) 871 - 2000

Public Affairs and Related Activities Personnel

At Headquarters

BOGGS, Casey
Director, Public Relations
Tel: (310) 772 - 6775
TF: (800) 871 - 2000

TREITLER, Betsy
V. President, Marketing/Communications
Tel: (310) 772 - 6000
TF: (800) 871 - 2000

At Other Offices

PLUHOWSKI, John E.
V. President, Corporate Communications
2929 Allen Pkwy.
Houston, TX 77019-2155
Tel: (713) 522 - 1111
Fax: (713) 523 - 8531

Air Liquide America Corp.

A manufacturer and distributor of industrial gases and gas applications technology. A U.S. subsidiary of Air Liquide S.A. of Paris, France.

www.airliquide.com
Annual Revenues: $2.18 billion

President and Chief Exec. Officer
DUFOUR, Pierre
Tel: (713) 624 - 8000
Fax: (713) 624 - 8085

Main Headquarters
Mailing: 2700 Post Oak Blvd.
Suite 1800
Houston, TX 77056
Tel: (713) 624 - 8000
Fax: (713) 624 - 8085
TF: (877) 820 - 2522

Political Action Committees

Air Liquide America Corp. PAC
Contact: James W. Clinton
12800 W. Little York
Houston, TX 77041

Contributions to Candidates: none reported (01/05 - 09/05)

Public Affairs and Related Activities Personnel

At Headquarters

LABELLE, Diane
Director, Corporate Communications
Tel: (713) 624 - 8000
Fax: (713) 624 - 8085
TF: (877) 820 - 2522

At Other Offices

CLINTON, James W.
PAC Treasurer
12800 W. Little York
Houston, TX 77041

Air Products and Chemicals, Inc.

A member of the Public Affairs Council. Producer and distributor of atmospheric gases, process and specialty gases, performance materials and chemical intermediates.

www.airproducts.com
Annual Revenues: $6.3 billion

Chairman, President and Chief Exec. Officer
JONES, John P., III
Tel: (610) 481 - 4911
Fax: (610) 841 - 5900

Main Headquarters
Mailing: 7201 Hamilton Blvd.
Allentown, PA 18195-1501
Tel: (610) 481 - 4911
Fax: (610) 841 - 5900

Washington Office
Contact: Richard Goodstein
Mailing: 1101 Pennsylvania Ave. NW
Suite 510
Washington, DC 20004
Tel: (202) 659 - 1324
Fax: (202) 659 - 1328

Political Action Committees

Air Products and Chemicals Inc. Political Alliance
Contact: Lynn Long
P.O. Box 441
Trexlertown, PA 18087

Contributions to Candidates: $41,000 (01/05 - 09/05)
Democrats: $23,000; Republicans: $18,000.

Principal Recipients

SENATE DEMOCRATS		HOUSE DEMOCRATS	
Conrad, Kent (ND)	$1,000	Murtha, John P Mr. (PA)	$10,000
Ford, Harold E Jr (TN)	$1,000	Green, Gene (TX)	$2,500
Lieberman, Joe (CT)	$1,000	Holden, Timothy (PA)	$2,000
Kennedy, Ted (MA)	$500		
SENATE REPUBLICANS		**HOUSE REPUBLICANS**	
Santorum, Richard (PA)	$1,500	Dent, Charles W (PA)	$5,000
Alexander, Lamar (TN)	$1,000	Gerlach, Jim (PA)	$2,500
Crapo, Michael D (ID)	$1,000		

Corporate Foundations and Giving Programs

Air Products and Chemicals, Inc. Foundation
Contact: Timothy J. Holt
7201 Hamilton Blvd.
Allentown, PA 18195-1501
Tel: (610) 481 - 4453
Fax: (610) 841 - 5900

Annual Grant Total: $2,000,000 - $5,000,000
Annual grant total given is for the Foundation and direct corporate contributions combined.
Geographic Preference: Area(s) in which the company operates; Florida; Kentucky; Louisiana; Pennsylvania; Texas; California
Primary Interests: Arts and Culture; Community Development; Diversity; Economic Development; Education; Health; Health and Human Services

Public Affairs and Related Activities Personnel

At Headquarters

ALLEN, Larry W.
V. President, Environment, Health, Safety and Quality
allenlw@airproducts.com
Tel: (610) 481 - 6289
Fax: (610) 841 - 5900

BAUER, Debbie A.
Coordinator, Communications
bauerd@airproducts.com
Tel: (610) 481 - 8061
Fax: (610) 841 - 5900

HILGERT, Kassie
Manager, Community Relations and Philanthropy
hilgerk@airproducts.com
Tel: (610) 481 - 8527
Fax: (610) 841 - 5900

HOLT, Timothy J.
Director, Corporate Relations
holttj@airproducts.com
Tel: (610) 481 - 4453
Fax: (610) 841 - 5900

KLEBE, Elizabeth L.
V. President, Corporate Communications
klebeel@airproducts.com
Tel: (610) 481 - 4697
Fax: (610) 841 - 5900

MCDONALD, Catherine E.
Manager, Financial Communications
mcdonace@airproducts.com
Tel: (610) 481 - 3673
Fax: (610) 481 - 6642

MENTESANA, Beth K.
Manager, Corporate Public Relations
mentesbk@airproducts.com
Tel: (610) 481 - 2459
Fax: (610) 841 - 5900

MINELLA, Lynn C.
V. President, Human Resouces
minelllc@airproducts.com
Tel: (610) 481 - 6667
Fax: (610) 841 - 5900

MYERS, David
Manager, Government Relations
myersdj@airproducts.com
Tel: (610) 481 - 8185
Fax: (610) 841 - 5900

SNYDER, Peter L.
Manager, Government Relations
snyderpl@airproducts.com
Tel: (610) 481 - 3278
Fax: (610) 841 - 5900

SPROGER, Philip C.
Director, Investor Relations
sprogepc@airproducts.com
Tel: (610) 481 - 7461
Fax: (610) 841 - 5900

WALCK, Ken M.
Manager, Investor Relations
walckkm@airproducts.com
Tel: (610) 481 - 8315
Fax: (610) 481 - 2729

At Washington Office

GOODSTEIN, Richard
Federal Relations Representative
goodstrf@airproducts.com
Tel: (202) 659 - 1324
Fax: (202) 659 - 1328

WINKLER, Philip
Tel: (202) 659 - 1324
Fax: (202) 659 - 1328

Registered Federal Lobbyist.

At Other Offices

LONG, Lynn
Treasurer, Air Products and Chemicals Inc. Political Action Committee
P.O. Box 441
Trexlertown, PA 18087
longl@airproducts.com

Airborne, Inc.

See listing on page 158 under DHL Holdings (USA), Inc.

Airbus North America Holdings, Inc.

U.S. marketing subsidiary of an airplane manufacturing consortium headquartered in Blagnac, France.

www.airbusnorthamerica.com

Chairman of the Board
MCARTOR, T. Allen — Tel: (703) 834 - 3400; Fax: (703) 834 - 3567

President and Chief Exec. Officer
ECCLESTON, Barry — Tel: (703) 834 - 3400; Fax: (703) 834 - 3567

Main Headquarters
Mailing: 198 Van Buren St.
Suite 300
Herndon, VA 20170
Tel: (703) 834 - 3400; Fax: (703) 834 - 3567

Public Affairs and Related Activities Personnel

At Headquarters

GRECZYN, Mary Anne
Manager, Communications
Tel: (703) 834 - 3400; Fax: (703) 834 - 3340

LUGINBILL, Mark
Manager, Communications
Tel: (703) 834 - 3400; Fax: (703) 834 - 3340

MCCONNELL, Clay
V. President, Communications
Tel: (703) 834 - 3400; Fax: (703) 834 - 3567

MOXLEY, Jodie
Government Affairs
Tel: (703) 834 - 3400; Fax: (703) 834 - 3567

WRIGLEY, Robert E.
Director, Governmental Affairs
Tel: (703) 834 - 3400; Fax: (703) 834 - 3567

Airgas, Inc.

A distributor of industrial, medical, and specialty gases, related equipment, and safety supplies.

www.airgas.com
Annual Revenues: $2.411 billion

President, Chairman and Chief Exec. Officer
MCCAUSLAND, Peter — Tel: (610) 687 - 5253; Fax: (610) 687 - 1052; TF: (800) 255 - 2165

Main Headquarters
Mailing: P.O. Box 6675
Radnor, PA 19087-8675
Tel: (610) 687 - 5253; Fax: (610) 687 - 1052; TF: (800) 255 - 2165

Street: 259 N. Radnor-Chester Rd.
Radnor, PA 19087-5283

Corporate Foundations and Giving Programs

Airgas, Inc., Corporate Contributions Program
P.O. Box 6675
Radnor, PA 19087-8675
Tel: (610) 687 - 5253; Fax: (610) 687 - 1052; TF: (800) 255 - 2165

Annual Grant Total: none reported

McCausland Foundation
Contact: Connie Gross
P.O. Box 6675
Radnor, PA 19087-8675
Tel: (610) 902 - 6240; Fax: (610) 687 - 1058; TF: (800) 255 - 2165

Annual Grant Total: none reported

Public Affairs and Related Activities Personnel

At Headquarters

ELY, James S.
V. President, Communications
jim.ely@airgas.com
Tel: (610) 902 - 6010; Fax: (610) 687 - 1052; TF: (800) 255 - 2165

GROSS, Connie
Administrator, McCausland Foundation
connie.gross@airgas.com
Tel: (610) 902 - 6240; Fax: (610) 687 - 1058; TF: (800) 255 - 2165

NIGRO, Melissa B.
Director, Investor Relations
melissa.nigro@airgas.com
Tel: (610) 902 - 6206; Fax: (610) 687 - 1052; TF: (800) 255 - 2165

WILSON, Dwight T.
Senior V. President, Human Resources
Tel: (610) 687 - 5253; Fax: (610) 687 - 1052; TF: (800) 255 - 2165

AirTran Airways

Provides airline services.

www.airtran.com
Annual Revenues: $1.041 billion

Chairman and Chief Exec. Officer
LEONARD, Joseph B. — Tel: (407) 251 - 5600; Fax: (407) 251 - 5727

Main Headquarters
Mailing: 9955 Airtran Blvd.
Orlando, FL 32827-5330
Tel: (407) 251 - 5600; Fax: (407) 251 - 5727

Political Action Committees

AirTran Airways PAC
Contact: Stanley Gadek
9955 Airtran Blvd.
Orlando, FL 32827-5330
Tel: (407) 251 - 5600; Fax: (407) 251 - 5727

Contributions to Candidates: $13,000 (01/05 - 09/05)
Democrats: $1,000; Republicans: $11,000; Other: $1,000.

Principal Recipients

SENATE DEMOCRATS
Nelson, Benjamin (NE) $1,000

SENATE REPUBLICANS
Chambliss, Saxby (GA) $4,000
Stevens, Ted (AK) $2,000

HOUSE DEMOCRATS

HOUSE OTHER
Oberstar, James L (MN) $1,000

HOUSE REPUBLICANS
Burns, Othell (GA) $3,000
Gingrey, Phillip (GA) $1,000
Kuhl, John R Jr (NY) $1,000

Corporate Foundations and Giving Programs

AirTran Airways Charitable Contributions
Contact: Tad Hutcheson
9955 Airtran Blvd.
Orlando, FL 32827-5330
Tel: (407) 254 - 7442; Fax: (407) 251 - 5727

Annual Grant Total: none reported

Public Affairs and Related Activities Personnel

At Headquarters

BLINDE, Loral
V. President, Human Resources
Tel: (407) 251 - 5600; Fax: (407) 251 - 5727

GADEK, Stanley
Senior V. President, Finance; Chief Financial Officer; and PAC Treasurer
Tel: (407) 251 - 5600; Fax: (407) 251 - 5727

GRAHAM-WEAVER, Judy
Manager, Public Relations
judy.graham-weave@airtran.com
Tel: (407) 254 - 7448; Fax: (407) 251 - 5727

HAAK, Arnie
Director, Financial Analysis
Responsibilities include investor relations.
Tel: (407) 251 - 3618; Fax: (407) 251 - 5727

HUTCHESON, Tad
Director, Corporte Communications
tad.hutcheson@airtran.com
Responsibilities include corporate giving.
Tel: (407) 254 - 7442; Fax: (407) 251 - 5727

AK Steel Corp.

A producer of flat-rolled steel. Acquired Armco Inc. in 1999.

www.aksteel.com
Annual Revenues: $5.2 billion

President and Chief Exec. Officer
WAINSCOTT, James L. — Tel: (513) 425 - 5392; Fax: (513) 425 - 2676; TF: (800) 331 - 5050

Main Headquarters
Mailing: 703 Curtis St.
Middletown, OH 45043
Tel: (513) 425 - 5000; Fax: (513) 425 - 2676; TF: (800) 331 - 5050

Political Action Committees

AK Steel Political Action Committee
Contact: Albert Ferrara, Jr.
703 Curtis St.
Middletown, OH 45043
Tel: (513) 425 - 5000; Fax: (513) 425 - 2676; TF: (800) 331 - 5050

Contributions to Candidates: $10,500 (01/05 - 09/05)
Democrats: $1,000; Republicans: $9,500.

Principal Recipients

SENATE DEMOCRATS
Cardin, Benjamin (MD) $1,000

SENATE REPUBLICANS
Santorum, Richard (PA) $2,500

HOUSE DEMOCRATS

HOUSE REPUBLICANS
Boehner, John (OH) $2,500
English, Philip S (PA) $2,500
Ney, Robert W (OH) $1,000
Sodrel, Michael (IN) $1,000

Corporate Foundations and Giving Programs

AK Steel Foundation
Contact: Alan H. McCoy
703 Curtis St.
Middletown, OH 45043
Tel: (513) 425 - 2826; Fax: (513) 425 - 2676

Assets: $14,450,013 (2002)
Annual Grant Total: $1,000,000 - $2,000,000
Geographic Preference: Ohio
Primary Interests: Higher Education; Medicine and Health Care
Recent Recipients: Catholic Charities; Habitat for Humanity; Junior Achievement; United Way

AK Steel Corp.

* continued from previous page

Public Affairs and Related Activities Personnel

At Headquarters

FERRARA, Albert, Jr. — Tel: (513) 425 - 5000
V. President, Finance, Chief Financial Officer and PAC Treasurer — Fax: (513) 425 - 2676; TF: (800) 331 - 5050
Responsibilities include investor relations.

MCCOY, Alan H. — Tel: (513) 425 - 2826
V. President, Government and Public Relations — Fax: (513) 425 - 2676

ZIZZO, Lawrence F. — Tel: (513) 425 - 5000
V. President, Human Resources — Fax: (513) 425 - 2676; TF: (800) 331 - 5050

Alabama Gas Corp.

See listing on page 180 under Energen Corp.

Alabama Power Co.

An electric utility subsidiary of Southern Co. (see separate listing).

President and Chief Exec. Officer
MCCRARY, Charles D. — Tel: (205) 257 - 1000; Fax: (205) 257 - 5100

Main Headquarters
Mailing: P.O. Box 2641, Birmingham, AL 35291 — Tel: (205) 257 - 1000; Fax: (205) 257 - 1860
Street: 600 N. 18th St., Birmingham, AL 35291

Washington Office
Contact: Joseph A. "Buzz" Miller
Mailing: 601 Pennsylvania Ave., NW, Suite 800, Washington, DC 20004 — Tel: (202) 261 - 5000; Fax: (202) 296 - 7937

Political Action Committees

Alabama Power Co. Employees Federal PAC
Contact: Rex Neil Boyd
P.O. Box 2641
Birmingham, AL 35291 — Tel: (205) 257 - 2596; Fax: (205) 257 - 2622

Contributions to Candidates: $19,000 (01/05 - 09/05)
Democrats: $5,000; Republicans: $14,000.

Principal Recipients

SENATE DEMOCRATS

HOUSE DEMOCRATS
Davis, Artur (AL) $5,000

HOUSE OTHER
Rogers, Michael (AL) $10,000
Everett, Terry (AL) $3,000
Aderholt, Robert B (AL) $1,000

Corporate Foundations and Giving Programs

Alabama Power Foundation, Inc.
Contact: William B. Johnson
P.O. Box 2641
Birmingham, AL 35291 — Tel: (205) 257 - 1000; Fax: (205) 257 - 1860

Annual Grant Total: over $5,000,000
Geographic Preference: Alabama
Primary Interests: Education; Health and Human Services
Recent Recipients: Junior Achievement; United Way

Public Affairs and Related Activities Personnel

At Headquarters

BOWERS, Willard L. — Tel: (205) 257 - 1000
V. President, Environmental Affairs — Fax: (205) 257 - 1860

BOYD, Rex Neil — Tel: (205) 257 - 2596
Manager, Governmental Projects - Government Relations — Fax: (205) 257 - 2622

GROGAN, John D. — Tel: (205) 257 - 1000
Manager, Environmental Compliance — Fax: (205) 257 - 1860

JOHNSON, William B. — Tel: (205) 257 - 1000
President, Alabama Power Foundation, Inc. — Fax: (205) 257 - 1860

MARTIN, C. Alan — Tel: (205) 257 - 1000
Exec. V. President, Customer Service and Satisfaction — Fax: (205) 257 - 1860

SELLERS, Nick — Tel: (205) 257 - 3111
Director, Federal Legislative Relations — Fax: (205) 257 - 2622

SMITH, Julian H., Jr. — Tel: (205) 257 - 2187
V. President, Corporate Relations — Fax: (205) 257 - 2622

SMITH, Zeke W. — Tel: (205) 257 - 2167
Director, Regulatory and Pricing — Fax: (205) 257 - 1860

SPENCER, Steve R. — Tel: (205) 257 - 1000
Exec. V. President, External Affairs — Fax: (205) 257 - 2176

WORMLEY, Harry J. — Tel: (205) 257 - 2602
Director, Corporate Relations — Fax: (205) 257 - 2622

At Washington Office

MCCOOL, James M., Jr. — Tel: (202) 775 - 0944
Washington Representative — Fax: (202) 296 - 7937

MILLER, Joseph A. "Buzz" — Tel: (202) 775 - 0944
V. President, Government Relations — Fax: (202) 296 - 7937

At Other Offices

PAYNE, John H. — Tel: (334) 223 - 5446
Manager, State Legislative Affairs
Two N. Jackson St.
Montgomery, AL 36104

REESE, Donald W. — Tel: (334) 223 - 5440
V. President, State Relations
Two N. Jackson St.
Montgomery, AL 36104

SANDERS, Leslie D. — Tel: (334) 223 - 5405
Director, Constituency Relations
Two N. Jackson St.
Montgomery, AL 36104

Alaska Air Group, Inc.

A regional airline holding company. Subsidiaries include Alaska Airlines, Inc. and Horizon Air Industries.

www.alaskaair.com
Annual Revenues: $2.826 billion

Chairman, President and Chief Exec. Officer
AYER, William S. — Tel: (206) 433 - 3200; Fax: (206) 431 - 5558

Main Headquarters
Mailing: P.O. Box 68900, Seattle, WA 98168-0947 — Tel: (206) 433 - 3200; Fax: (206) 431 - 5558
Street: 19300 Pacific Hwy. South, Seattle, WA 98188

Washington Office
Contact: Megan Lawrence
Mailing: 1201 Pennsylvania Ave. NW, Washington, DC 20004 — Tel: (202) 626 - 6781

Political Action Committees

Alaska Air Group Inc. Political Action Committee
Contact: William L. MacKay
P.O. Box 68900
Seattle, WA 98168-0947 — Tel: (206) 433 - 3200; Fax: (206) 431 - 5558

Contributions to Candidates: $18,000 (01/05 - 09/05)
Democrats: $6,000; Republicans: $11,000; Other: $1,000.

Principal Recipients

SENATE DEMOCRATS
Baucus, Max (MT) $1,000

HOUSE DEMOCRATS
Defazio, Peter A (OR) $1,000
Dicks, Norm D (WA) $1,000
Honda, Mike (CA) $1,000
Larsen, Rick (WA) $1,000
Smith, Adam (WA) $1,000

HOUSE OTHER
Oberstar, James L (MN) $1,000

SENATE REPUBLICANS
Burns, Conrad (MT) $2,000
Smith, Gordon (OR) $1,000

HOUSE REPUBLICANS
Young, Don E (AK) $2,000
Hastings, Doc (WA) $1,000
McMorris, Cathy (WA) $1,000
Rehberg, Dennis (MT) $1,000
Reichert, Dave (WA) $1,000
Simpson, Michael (ID) $1,000
Walden, Gregory (OR) $1,000

Corporate Foundations and Giving Programs

Alaska Airlines, Inc. Foundation
Contact: Susan Bramstedt
4750 International Airport Rd.
Anchorage, AK 99502 — Tel: (907) 266 - 7230; Fax: (907) 266 - 7229

Annual Grant Total: $1,000,000 - $2,000,000
Guidelines are available.
Geographic Preference: Area(s) in which the company operates
Primary Interests: Arts and Culture; Education; Medical Research; Social Services
Recent Recipients: Make-A-Wish Foundation

Alaska Air Group, Inc.

** continued from previous page*

Public Affairs and Related Activities Personnel

At Headquarters

CANCELMI, Louis G. — Tel: (206) 433 - 5170; Fax: (206) 431 - 5558
Staff V. President, Corporate Communications
(Alaska Airlines, Inc.)

CONIFF, Bill — Tel: (206) 431 - 4626; Fax: (206) 431 - 5558
Director, Corporate Communications
(Horizon Air Industries)

GAMMON, Jeanne — Tel: (206) 433 - 3200
Administrator, Corporate Affairs
(Alaska Airlines, Inc.)
jeanne.gammon@alaskaair.com

HARTMAN, Donna — Tel: (206) 392 - 5383; Fax: (206) 431 - 5558
Corporate Contributions Administrator
(Alaska Airlines, Inc.)
donna.hartman@alaskaair.com
Responsibilities include corporate philanthropy.

MACKAY, William L. — Tel: (206) 433 - 3200; Fax: (206) 431 - 5558
V. President, Public and Government Affairs
(Alaska Airlines, Inc.)
Responsibilities include corporate philanthropy, corporate communications, and political action.

MCSKIMMING, Jen — Tel: (206) 431 - 4672; Fax: (206) 431 - 5558
Manager, Media Relations
(Horizon Air Industries)
jen.mcskimming@horizonair.com

RUSSO, Dan — Tel: (206) 431 - 4513; Fax: (206) 431 - 5558
Director, Marketing and Communications
(Horizon Air Industries)

SPERRY, Sam R. — Tel: (206) 392 - 5038; Fax: (206) 431 - 5558
Director, Corporate Communications
(Alaska Airlines, Inc.)

TILDEN, Bradley — Tel: (206) 433 - 3200; Fax: (206) 431 - 5558
Divisional Exec. V. President and Chief Financial Officer
Responsibilities include political action.

At Washington Office

LAWRENCE, Megan — Tel: (202) 626 - 6781
Director, Government Affairs

SPRAGUE, Joseph — Tel: (202) 626 - 6781
Senior V. President, Public and Government Affairs
joe.sprague@alaskaair.com
(Alaska Airlines, Inc.)
Registered Federal Lobbyist.

At Other Offices

BRAMSTEDT, Susan — Tel: (907) 266 - 7230; Fax: (907) 266 - 7229
Director, Public Affairs-Alaska
(Alaska Airlines, Inc.)
4750 International Airport Rd.
Anchorage, AK 99502
susan.bramstedt@alaskaair.com

Alaska Airlines, Inc.

See listing on page 15 under Alaska Air Group, Inc.

Albany Internat'l Corp.

A manufacturer of fabrics for the paper machine industry.
www.albint.com
Annual Revenues: $816 million

Chairman and Chief Exec. Officer — Tel: (518) 445 - 2200; Fax: (518) 445 - 2265
SCHMELER, Frank R.

Main Headquarters — Tel: (518) 445 - 2200; Fax: (518) 445 - 2265
Mailing: P.O. Box 1907
Albany, NY 12201-1907
Street: 1373 Broadway
Albany, NY 12204-1907

Corporate Foundations and Giving Programs

Albany Internat'l Corporate Contributions
Contact: Kenneth C. Pulver
P.O. Box 1907 — Tel: (518) 445 - 2214
Albany, NY 12201-1907 — Fax: (518) 447 - 6343

Annual Grant Total: none reported
Geographic Preference: Area(s) in which the company operates
Primary Interests: Arts and Culture; Community Development; Higher Education

Public Affairs and Related Activities Personnel

At Headquarters

PULVER, Kenneth C. — Tel: (518) 445 - 2214; Fax: (518) 447 - 6343
V. President, Global Marketing and Communications
Responsibilities include government relations.

SIEGEL, Susan — Tel: (518) 445 - 2284; Fax: (518) 447 - 6343
Manager, Corporate Communications

Albemarle Corp.

Supplier of specialty and fine performance chemicals that enhance consumer products.
www.albemarle.com
Annual Revenues: $916.9 million

Chairman of the Board — Tel: (804) 788 - 6000; Fax: (804) 788 - 6094
GOTTWALD, William M., M.D.
bill_gottwald@albemarle.com

President and Chief Exec. Officer — Tel: (804) 788 - 6000; Fax: (804) 788 - 5688
ROHR, Mark C.

Main Headquarters — Tel: (225) 388 - 3030; Fax: (225) 388 - 7848
Mailing: 451 Florida St.
Baton Rouge, LA 70801-1765

Washington Office — Tel: (202) 223 - 1848; Fax: (202) 388 - 7848
Contact: Barbara A. Little
Mailing: 1155 15th St. NW
Suite 611
Washington, DC 20005

Political Action Committees

Albemarle Corp. PAC
Contact: Luther Kissam, IV
330 S. Fourth St. — Tel: (804) 788 - 6000
Richmond, VA 23219 — Fax: (804) 788 - 5688

Contributions to Candidates: $1,000 (01/05 - 09/05)
Republicans: $1,000.

Principal Recipients

SENATE REPUBLICANS
Santorum, Richard (PA) $1,000

HOUSE REPUBLICANS

Public Affairs and Related Activities Personnel

At Headquarters

MILLIGAN, Rene — Tel: (225) 288 - 7106; Fax: (225) 388 - 7848
Marketing Communications Representative
rene_milligan@albemarle.com

ZUMSTEIN, Ron — Tel: (225) 388 - 3030; Fax: (225) 388 - 7848
V. President, Health, Safety and Environment
ron_zumstein@albemarle.com

At Washington Office

LITTLE, Barbara A. — Tel: (202) 223 - 1848; Fax: (202) 388 - 7848
V. President, Government Relations
Registered Federal Lobbyist.

At Other Offices

GREER, Carson — Tel: (804) 788 - 6092; Fax: (804) 788 - 5688
Manager, Corporate Communications
330 S. Fourth St.
Richmond, VA 23219
carson_greer@albemarle.com

HARSH, Jack P. — Tel: (804) 788 - 6000; Fax: (804) 788 - 6094
V. President, Human Resources
330 S. Fourth St.
Richmond, VA 23219
jack_harsh@albemarle.com

KISSAM, Luther, IV — Tel: (804) 788 - 6000; Fax: (804) 788 - 5688
PAC Treasurer
330 S. Fourth St.
Richmond, VA 23219

RUIZ, Laura M. — Tel: (804) 778 - 6005; Fax: (804) 788 - 5688
Corporate Director, Investor Relations and Consumer Advocacy
330 S. Fourth St.
Richmond, VA 23219
laura_ruiz@albemarle.com

Alberto-Culver Co.

A manufacturer and distributor of hair and beauty-care and household consumer products.
www.alberto.com
Annual Revenues: $2.5 billion

Chairman of the Board — Tel: (708) 450 - 3000; Fax: (708) 450 - 3435
BERNICK, Carol L.

President and Chief Exec. Officer — Tel: (708) 450 - 3000; Fax: (708) 450 - 3435
BERNICK, Howard B.
hbernick@alberto.com

Main Headquarters — Tel: (708) 450 - 3000; Fax: (708) 450 - 3435
Mailing: 2525 Armitage Ave.
Melrose Park, IL 60160

Corporate Foundations and Giving Programs

Alberto-Culver Corporate Contributions Program
Contact: Daniel B. Stone

Alberto-Culver Co.

• continued from previous page

2525 Armitage Ave.
Melrose Park, IL 60160
Tel: (708) 450 - 3005
Fax: (708) 450 - 3435

Annual Grant Total: none reported
Geographic Preference: Area(s) in which the company operates; Illinois
Primary Interests: Civic and Public Affairs; Education; Youth Services

Public Affairs and Related Activities Personnel

At Headquarters

DAVIDSON, Wesley C.
V. President, Corporate Development and Investor Relations
wdavidson@alberto.com
Tel: (708) 450 - 3145
Fax: (708) 450 - 3435

STONE, Daniel B.
V. President, Corporate Communications
dstone@alberto.com
Responsibilities include corporate philanthropy.
Tel: (708) 450 - 3005
Fax: (708) 450 - 3435

Albertson's, Inc.

A supermarket chain.
www.albertsons.com
Annual Revenues: $37.9 billion

Chairman and Chief Exec. Officer
JOHNSTON, Lawrence R.
Tel: (208) 395 - 6200
Fax: (208) 395 - 6631

Main Headquarters
Mailing: 250 E. Parkcenter Blvd.
Boise, ID 83706
Tel: (208) 395 - 6200
Fax: (208) 395 - 6631
TF: (877) 932 - 7948

Political Action Committees

Albertson's Inc. Political Action Committee
Contact: Renee Bergquist
250 E. Parkcenter Blvd.
Boise, ID 83706
Tel: (208) 395 - 6200
Fax: (208) 395 - 6631

Contributions to Candidates: $21,500 (01/05 - 09/05)
Democrats: $1,000; Republicans: $20,500.

Principal Recipients

HOUSE OTHER
Rush, Bobby (IL) $1,000

SENATE REPUBLICANS
Santorum, Richard (PA) $5,000
Chambliss, Saxby (GA) $1,000

HOUSE REPUBLICANS
Hastert, Dennis J. (IL) $5,000
Thomas, William M (CA) $5,000
Bonilla, Henry (TX) $2,500
Miller, Gary (CA) $1,000
Renzi, Richard (AZ) $1,000

Corporate Foundations and Giving Programs

Albertson's Corporate Contributions Program
Contact: Susan Neumann
250 E. Parkcenter Blvd.
Boise, ID 83706
Tel: (208) 395 - 6200
Fax: (208) 395 - 6631
TF: (877) 932 - 7948

Annual Grant Total: none reported
Geographic Preference: Area(s) in which the company operates
Primary Interests: Education; Health and Human Services; Hunger; Youth Services

Public Affairs and Related Activities Personnel

At Headquarters

BERGQUIST, Renee
PAC Contact
Tel: (208) 395 - 6200
Fax: (208) 395 - 6631

FALLOW, Kerianne
Corporate Director, Government Relations
Tel: (208) 395 - 6200
Fax: (208) 395 - 6631
TF: (877) 932 - 7948

HERBERT, Kathy
Exec. V. President, Human Resources
Tel: (208) 395 - 6200
Fax: (208) 395 - 6631

NEUMANN, Susan
Senior V. President, Education, Communications and Public Affairs
Tel: (208) 395 - 6200
Fax: (208) 395 - 6631
TF: (877) 932 - 7948

PARKER, Dave
V. President, Investor Relations
david.parker@albertsons.com
Tel: (208) 395 - 6622
Fax: (208) 395 - 6631
TF: (877) 932 - 7948

Alco Standard Corp.

See listing on page 255 under Ikon Office Solutions, Inc.

Alcoa Inc.

A member of the Public Affairs Council. A producer of primary aluminum, fabricated aluminum, and alumina. Active in all major aspects of the industy including, mining, refining, smelting, fabricating and recycling. Related businesses include packaging machinery, precision castings, vinyl siding, plastic bottles and closures, electrical distribution systems for cars and trucks, and fiber optic cable. Acquired Cordant Technologies, Howmet, and Reynolds Metals in 2000.
www.alcoa.com
Annual Revenues: $22.9 billion

Chairman and Chief Exec. Officer
BELDA, Alain J. P.
alain.belda@alcoa.com
Tel: (412) 553 - 4545
Fax: (412) 553 - 4498

Main Headquarters
Mailing: 201 Isabella St.
Pittsburgh, PA 15212-5858
Tel: (412) 553 - 4545
Fax: (412) 553 - 4498

Washington Office
Contact: Russell C. Wisor
Mailing: 1909 K St. NW
Suite 750
Washington, DC 20006-1171
Tel: (202) 956 - 5306
Fax: (202) 956 - 5305

Corporate Foundations and Giving Programs

Alcoa Foundation
Contact: Kathleen W. Buechel
201 Isabella St.
Pittsburgh, PA 15212-5858
Tel: (412) 553 - 2348

Assets: $441,245,083 (2000)
Annual Grant Total: none reported
Guidelines are available. Annual grants in 2000 totaled $21.3 million worldwide. Grants of a local nature will be considered only if located in or near a corporate facility.
Geographic Preference: Area(s) in which the company operates
Primary Interests: Education; Engineering; Environment/Conservation; Families; Health; Safety; Security; Technology

Public Affairs and Related Activities Personnel

At Headquarters

BUECHEL, Kathleen W.
President and Treasurer, Alcoa Foundation
kathleen.buechel@alcoa.com
Tel: (412) 553 - 2348

HITCHERY, Regina M.
V. President, Human Resources
Tel: (412) 553 - 4545
Fax: (412) 553 - 4498

LOWERY, Kevin G.
Director, Corporate Communications
kevin.lowery@alcoa.com
Tel: (412) 553 - 1424
Fax: (412) 553 - 4498

SALTZMAN, Joyce
Media Contact
joyce.saltzman@alcoa.com
Tel: (412) 553 - 4467
Fax: (412) 553 - 4498

At Washington Office

CALIFF, Lee H.
Director, Government Affairs
lee.califf@alcoa.com
Registered Federal Lobbyist.
Tel: (202) 956 - 5306
Fax: (202) 956 - 5305

WISOR, Russell C.
V. President, Government Affairs
russell.wisor@alcoa.com
Registered Federal Lobbyist.
Tel: (202) 956 - 5306
Fax: (202) 956 - 5305

At Other Offices

OPLINGER, William F.
Director, Investor Relations
390 Park Ave.
New York, NY 10022
Tel: (212) 826 - 2674

SIEWERT, Richard L. "Jake"
V. President, Environment, Health and Safety and Global Communications and Public Strategy
390 Park Ave.
New York, NY 10022
jake.siewert@alcoa.com
Tel: (212) 836 - 2733

Alcon Inc.

A manufacturer of ophthalmic pharmaceuticals, contact lens care solutions, ophthalmic surgical instruments and accessory products.
www.alconlabs.com
Annual Revenues: $3.4 billion

Chairman, President and Chief Exec. Officer
RAYMENT, Cary
Tel: (817) 293 - 0450
Fax: (817) 551 - 4615

Main Headquarters
Mailing: 6201 South Fwy.
Fort Worth, TX 76134
Tel: (817) 293 - 0450
Fax: (817) 551 - 4615

Political Action Committees

Alcon Laboratories Inc. PAC AKA Alcon PAC
Contact: Brette McClellan
6201 South Fwy.
Fort Worth, TX 76134
Tel: (817) 293 - 0450
Fax: (817) 551 - 4615

Contributions to Candidates: $12,202 (01/05 - 09/05)

Alcon Inc.

** continued from previous page*

Democrats: $500; Republicans: $11,702.

Principal Recipients

SENATE DEMOCRATS		HOUSE DEMOCRATS	
		Thompson, Mike (CA)	$500

SENATE REPUBLICANS		HOUSE REPUBLICANS	
Santorum, Richard (PA)	$3,202	Barton, Joe L (TX)	$2,000
Cornyn, John (TX)	$2,000	Granger, Kay N (TX)	$1,500
Hutchison, Kay Bailey (TX)	$500	Jindal, Bobby (LA)	$1,000
		Johnson, Nancy (CT)	$1,000
		Herger, Wally (CA)	$500

Corporate Foundations and Giving Programs

Alcon Foundation
Contact: Winona Edwards
6201 South Fwy. — Tel: (817) 293 - 0450
Fort Worth, TX 76134 — Fax: (817) 568 - 7000

Annual Grant Total: $400,000 - $500,000
Geographic Preference: Area(s) in which the company operates; Texas
Primary Interests: Medicine and Health Care
Recent Recipients: Ass'n for Research in Vision and Ophthalmology

Public Affairs and Related Activities Personnel

At Headquarters

BRAZELL, Wes — Tel: (817) 293 - 0450
Director, Investor Relations — Fax: (817) 551 - 4615

CAGLE, Gerald D., Ph.D. — Tel: (817) 293 - 0450
Senior V. President, Research and Development — Fax: (817) 551 - 4615
Responsibilities include regulatory affairs.

COX, Kay — Tel: (817) 293 - 0450
V. President, Human Resources — Fax: (817) 551 - 4615

DUVALL, Carol — Tel: (817) 293 - 0450
PAC Treasurer — Fax: (817) 551 - 4615
(Alcon Laboratories, Inc.)

EDWARDS, Winona — Tel: (817) 293 - 0450
President, Alcon Foundation — Fax: (817) 568 - 7000

MACHATTON, Doug — Tel: (817) 293 - 0450
V. President, Investor Relations and Strategic Corporate Communications — Fax: (817) 551 - 4615

MCCLELLAN, Brette — Tel: (817) 293 - 0450
Director, Governmental Relations — Fax: (817) 551 - 4615
Responsibilities include political action.

RAY, Dick — Tel: (817) 293 - 0450
Director, Safety and Environmental Affairs — Fax: (817) 551 - 4615
Mailstop: M/S AM-16

Alcon Laboratories, Inc.

See listing on page 17 under Alcon Inc.

Alexander & Baldwin, Inc.

A diversified company in ocean transportation, food products (coffee and sugar), and property development and management.
www.alexanderbaldwin.com
Annual Revenues: $1.05 billion

Chairman of the Board — Tel: (808) 525 - 6611
STOCKHOLM, Charles M. — Fax: (808) 525 - 6652

President and Chief Exec. Officer — Tel: (808) 525 - 6611
DOANE, Allen — Fax: (808) 525 - 6652

Main Headquarters
Mailing: P.O. Box 3440 — Tel: (808) 525 - 6611
Honolulu, HI 96801-3440 — Fax: (808) 525 - 6652
Street: 822 Bishop St.
Honolulu, HI 96813

Political Action Committees

Alexander & Baldwin Inc. FEDPAC (A&B FEDPAC)
Contact: Paul T. Oshiro
P.O. Box 3440 — Tel: (808) 525 - 6611
Honolulu, HI 96801-3440 — Fax: (808) 525 - 6652

Contributions to Candidates: $18,000 (01/05 - 09/05)
Democrats: $16,500; Republicans: $1,500.

Principal Recipients

SENATE DEMOCRATS		HOUSE DEMOCRATS	
Akaka, Daniel (HI)	$4,000	Abercrombie, Neil (HI)	$3,000
Conrad, Kent (ND)	$500	Becerra, Xavier (CA)	$1,000
Nelson, Benjamin (NE)	$500	Melancon, Charlie (LA)	$1,000
Nelson, Bill (FL)	$500	Millender-McDonald, Juanita (CA)	$1,000
Stabenow, Debbie (MI)	$500	Pomeroy, Earl (ND)	$1,000

SENATE REPUBLICANS		HOUSE REPUBLICANS	
Burns, Conrad (MT)	$500		

Corporate Foundations and Giving Programs

Alexander & Baldwin Foundation
Contact: Meredith J. Ching
P.O. Box 3440 — Tel: (808) 525 - 6611
Honolulu, HI 96801-3440 — Fax: (808) 525 - 6677

Annual Grant Total: $1,000,000 - $2,000,000
Geographic Preference: Hawaii; California
Primary Interests: Community Affairs; Education; Health and Human Services
Recent Recipients: United Way

Public Affairs and Related Activities Personnel

At Headquarters

CHING, Meredith J. — Tel: (808) 525 - 6611
V. President, Government and Community Relations — Fax: (808) 525 - 6677
mching@abinc.com

HOWE, Linda — Tel: (808) 525 - 6642
Manager, Community Relations; and V. President, Alexander & Baldwin Foundation — Fax: (808) 525 - 6677
lhowe@abinc.com

KELLEY, John B. — Tel: (808) 525 - 8422
V. President, Investor Relations — Fax: (808) 525 - 6651
jkelley@abinc.com

O'KEEFE, Sean M. — Tel: (808) 877 - 0081
Director, Environmental Affairs — Fax: (808) 871 - 7663

OSHIRO, Paul T. — Tel: (808) 525 - 6611
Treasurer, A&B FEDPAC — Fax: (808) 525 - 6652

YAMANAKA, Ruthann S. — Tel: (808) 525 - 8425
V. President, Human Resources — Fax: (808) 525 - 6611

Algonquin Gas Transmission, LLC/Duke Energy

www.duke-energy.com

Main Headquarters
Mailing: 890 Winter St., Suite 300 — Tel: (617) 254 - 4050
Waltham, MA 02451 — Fax: (617) 560 - 1580

Public Affairs and Related Activities Personnel

At Headquarters

SHERIDAN, John P. — Tel: (617) 560 - 1444
Regional Director, Public and Government Relations — Fax: (617) 560 - 1580
jpsheridan@duke-energy.com

Allegheny Energy Inc.

A member of the Public Affairs Council. A diversified energy company.
www.alleghenyenergy.com
Annual Revenues: $4 billion

Chairman, President and Chief Exec. Officer — Tel: (724) 837 - 3000
EVANSON, Paul J.

Main Headquarters
Mailing: 800 Cabin Hill Dr. — Tel: (724) 837 - 3000
Greensburg, PA 15601

Washington Office
Contact: J. Michael Eckard
Mailing: 1301 Pennsylvania Ave. NW — Tel: (202) 824 - 0404
Suite 1030 — Fax: (202) 347 - 0132
Washington, DC 20004

Political Action Committees

Allegheny Energy Inc. Federal PAC
Contact: Michael Kriner
800 Cabin Hill Dr. — Tel: (724) 837 - 3000
Greensburg, PA 15601

Contributions to Candidates: $27,000 (01/05 - 09/05)
Democrats: $14,000; Republicans: $13,000.

Principal Recipients

SENATE DEMOCRATS		HOUSE DEMOCRATS	
Byrd, Robert C (WV)	$1,000	Murtha, John P Mr. (PA)	$5,000
Conrad, Kent (ND)	$1,000		
Mikulski, Barbara (MD)	$1,000		

SENATE REPUBLICANS		HOUSE REPUBLICANS	
Santorum, Richard (PA)	$1,000	Murphy, Tim (PA)	$3,000

Allegheny Energy Inc. PAC
Contact: Brenda S. Lampard
10802 Bower Ave.
Williamsport, MD 21795

Contributions to Candidates: none reported (01/05 - 09/05)

Corporate Foundations and Giving Programs

Allegheny Energy Corporate Contributions Program

Allegheny Energy Inc.

• continued from previous page

800 Cabin Hill Dr.
Greensburg, PA 15601
Tel: (724) 837 - 3000

Annual Grant Total: none reported

Public Affairs and Related Activities Personnel

At Headquarters

KRINER, Michael
Treasurer, Allegheny Energy Inc. Federal PAC
Tel: (724) 837 - 3000

KUNIANSKY, Max
Director, Investor Relations
Tel: (724) 838 - 6895

PAVLIK, Paul J.
Manager, State Governmental Affairs
ppavlik@alleghenyenergy.com
Tel: (724) 837 - 3000

SCHAUB, Patricia A.
V. President, External Affairs
pschaub@alleghenyenergy.com
Tel: (724) 837 - 3000

SOLOMON, Fred
Media Contact
fsolomo@alleghenyenergy.com
Tel: (724) 838 - 6650

At Washington Office

CAMPBELL, John P.
Tel: (202) 824 - 0404
Fax: (202) 347 - 0132
Registered Federal Lobbyist.

CANNON, David C., Jr.
Tel: (202) 824 - 0404
Fax: (202) 347 - 0132
Registered Federal Lobbyist.

ECKARD, J. Michael
Director, Federal Government Affairs
jeckard@alleghenyenergy.com
Registered Federal Lobbyist.
Tel: (202) 824 - 0404
Fax: (202) 347 - 0132

GARDNER, Thomas R.
Tel: (202) 824 - 0404
Fax: (202) 347 - 0132
Registered Federal Lobbyist.

GRABIAK, Terri J.
Tel: (202) 824 - 0404
Fax: (202) 347 - 0132
Registered Federal Lobbyist.

HAMMER, Jeannine M.
Tel: (202) 824 - 0404
Fax: (202) 347 - 0132
Registered Federal Lobbyist.

RICHARDSON, Joseph H.
Tel: (202) 824 - 0404
Fax: (202) 347 - 0132
Registered Federal Lobbyist.

SERKES, Jeffrey D.
Tel: (202) 824 - 0404
Fax: (202) 347 - 0132
Registered Federal Lobbyist.

At Other Offices

LAMPARD, Brenda S.
Treasurer, Allegheny Energy Inc. PAC
10802 Bower Ave.
Williamsport, MD 21795

MASON, Jay
Manager, State Governmental Affairs (MD)
68 State Circle
Annapolis, MD 21401
Tel: (410) 268 - 0858
Fax: (410) 268 - 0506

MINARDI, Samuel A.
Manager, State Government Affairs (WV)
Seven Greenbrier St.
Charleston, WV 25311
Tel: (304) 345 - 4695
Fax: (304) 345 - 4571

RIGGLEMAN, David L.
Director, State Affairs (WV)
1310 Fairmont Ave.
Fairmont, WV 26551-0392
driggle@alleghenyenergy.com
Tel: (304) 367 - 3430
Fax: (304) 367 - 3156

Allegheny Technologies Incorporated

A manufacturer of stainless steel and specialty steel alloys.

www.alleghenytechnologies.com
Annual Revenues: $2.1 billion

Chairman, President and Chief Exec. Officer
HASSEY, L. Patrick
Tel: (412) 394 - 2800
Fax: (412) 394 - 2805

Main Headquarters
Mailing: 1000 Six PPG Pl.
Pittsburgh, PA 15222-5479
Tel: (412) 394 - 2800
Fax: (412) 394 - 3034

Political Action Committees

Allegheny Technologies Corp. PAC
Contact: Dale G. Reid
1000 Six PPG Pl.
Pittsburgh, PA 15222-5479
Tel: (412) 394 - 2800
Fax: (412) 394 - 3034

Contributions to Candidates: $5,000 (01/05 - 09/05)
Democrats: $500; Republicans: $4,500.

Principal Recipients

SENATE DEMOCRATS

HOUSE DEMOCRATS
Murtha, John P Mr. (PA) $500

SENATE REPUBLICANS

HOUSE REPUBLICANS
English, Philip S (PA) $2,000
Murphy, Tim (PA) $1,500
Hart, Melissa (PA) $1,000

Corporate Foundations and Giving Programs

Allegheny Technologies Charitable Trust
Contact: Jon D. Walton
1000 Six PPG Pl.
Pittsburgh, PA 15222-5479
Tel: (412) 394 - 2800
Fax: (412) 394 - 3035

Assets: $733,723,000 (2002)
Annual Grant Total: $1,000,000 - $2,000,000
In addition to the charitable trust, the company also makes direct donations.
Geographic Preference: Area(s) in which the company operates; Connecticut; Illinois; Indiana; New York; Pennsylvania; Oklahoma
Primary Interests: Civic and Public Affairs; Higher Education; Medicine and Health Care
Recent Recipients: Junior Achievement; United Way; YMCA

Public Affairs and Related Activities Personnel

At Headquarters

GREENFIELD, Dan
Director, Investor Relations and Corporate Communications
Tel: (412) 394 - 3004
Fax: (412) 394 - 3034

HARSHMAN, Richard J.
Senior V. President, Finance and Chief Financial Officer
rharshman@alleghenytechnologies.com
Responsibilities include investor relations.
Tel: (412) 394 - 2861
Fax: (412) 394 - 3034

REID, Dale G.
V. President, Controller, Chief Accounting Officer and Treasurer
dreid@alleghenytechnologies.com
Responsibilities include political action.
Tel: (412) 394 - 2800
Fax: (412) 394 - 3034

WALTON, Jon D.
Exec. V. President, Human Resources; Chief Legal and Compliance Officer; General Counsel; and Secretary
jwalton@alleghenytechnologies.com
Responsibilities include corporate philanthropy.
Tel: (412) 394 - 2800
Fax: (412) 394 - 3035

Allegiance Healthcare

See listing on page 100 under Cardinal Health Inc.

Allegiance Telecom, Inc.

See listing on page 529 under XO Communications, Inc.

Allergan Inc.

A member of the Public Affairs Council. A global healthcare company providing specialty pharmaceutical products in the eye care, neuromodulator and skin care markets.

www.allergan.com
Annual Revenues: $1.7 billion

Chairman, President and Chief Exec. Officer
PYOTT, David E. I.
Tel: (714) 246 - 4500
Fax: (714) 246 - 4971
TF: (800) 347 - 4500

Main Headquarters
Mailing: P.O. Box 19534
Irvine, CA 92623-9534
Tel: (714) 246 - 4500
Fax: (714) 246 - 4971
TF: (800) 347 - 4500

Street: 2525 DuPont Dr.
Irvine, CA 92612

Washington Office
Contact: W. Bradford Gary
Mailing: 2201 N St. NW
Suite 113
Washington, DC 20037
Tel: (202) 822 - 0982

Political Action Committees

Allergan Inc. Political Action Committee for Employees (APACE)
Contact: Edith Bennett
2148 E. Orangeview Ln.
Orange, CA 92857

Contributions to Candidates: $38,000 (01/05 - 09/05)

Allergan Inc.

** continued from previous page*

Democrats: $6,500; Republicans: $31,500.

Principal Recipients

SENATE DEMOCRATS		HOUSE DEMOCRATS	
Kennedy, Ted (MA)	$1,000	Sanchez, Loretta (CA)	$3,500
		Eshoo, Anna (CA)	$2,000

SENATE REPUBLICANS		HOUSE REPUBLICANS	
Hatch, Orrin (UT)	$3,000	Issa, Darrell (CA)	$6,000
Enzi, Michael B (WY)	$1,000	Barton, Joe L (TX)	$5,000
		Cox, Christopher (CA)	$5,000
		Royce, Ed Mr (CA)	$3,500
		Campbell, John (CA)	$3,000
		Thomas, William M (CA)	$2,000

Corporate Foundations and Giving Programs

Allergan Foundation
P.O. Box 19534 — Tel: (714) 246 - 4500
Irvine, CA 92623-9534 — Fax: (714) 246 - 4971
TF: (800) 347 - 4500

Annual Grant Total: none reported
Primary Interests: Arts and Culture; Civic and Cultural Activities; Education; Health and Human Services

Public Affairs and Related Activities Personnel

At Headquarters

HINDMAN, John — Tel: (714) 246 - 4636
Senior V. President, Treasury and Investor Relations — Fax: (714) 246 - 4971
hindman_jim@allergan.com — TF: (800) 347 - 4500

VAN HOVE, Caroline — Tel: (714) 245 - 5134
Media Contact — Fax: (714) 246 - 4971
TF: (800) 347 - 4500

WILSON, Roy J. — Tel: (714) 246 - 4500
Exec. V. President, Human Resources and Information Technology — Fax: (714) 246 - 4971
TF: (800) 347 - 4500

At Washington Office

GARY, W. Bradford — Tel: (202) 822 - 0982
V. President, Government Operations
gary_brad@allergan.com
Registered Federal Lobbyist.

At Other Offices

BENNETT, Edith
Contact, Allergan Inc. Political Action Committee
2148 E. Orangeview Ln.
Orange, CA 92857

ALLETE

ALLETE provides energy services in the upper Midwest and has significant real estate holdings in Florida.

www.allete.com
Annual Revenues: $1.5 billion

President and Chief Exec. Officer — Tel: (218) 279 - 5000
SHIPPAR, Donald J. — Fax: (218) 279 - 5050

Main Headquarters
Mailing: 30 W. Superior St. — Tel: (218) 279 - 5000
Duluth, MN 55802 — Fax: (218) 279 - 5050

Washington Office
Contact: William J. Libro
Mailing: 122 C St. NW — Tel: (202) 638 - 7707
Suite 840 — Fax: (202) 638 - 7710
Washington, DC 20001

Political Action Committees

Allete PAC
Contact: Margaret A. Robare
30 W. Superior St. — Tel: (218) 722 - 5642
Duluth, MN 55802 — Ext: 3654
Fax: (218) 279 - 5050

Contributions to Candidates: $17,000 (01/05 - 09/05)
Democrats: $6,000; Republicans: $9,000; Other: $2,000.

Principal Recipients

SENATE DEMOCRATS		HOUSE DEMOCRATS	
Bingaman, Jeff (NM)	$1,000	Obey, David R (WI)	$2,000
Conrad, Kent (ND)	$1,000		
Nelson, Benjamin (NE)	$1,000		

Corporate Foundations and Giving Programs

Minnesota Power Corporate Contributions Program
Contact: Peggy Hanson
30 W. Superior St. — Tel: (218) 722 - 2641
Duluth, MN 55802 — Fax: (218) 279 - 5050

Annual Grant Total: $750,000 - $1,000,000
Geographic Preference: Area(s) in which the company operates
Primary Interests: Arts and Culture; Civic and Public Affairs; Environment/Conservation; Health and Human Services; K-12 Education

Public Affairs and Related Activities Personnel

At Headquarters

HANSON, Peggy — Tel: (218) 722 - 2641
Community Relations Representative — Fax: (218) 279 - 5050
phanson@mnpower.com
Responsibilities include corporate contributions.

HODNIK, Margaret L. — Tel: (218) 723 - 3966
Director, Public Affairs — Fax: (218) 723 - 3966

MCMILLAN, David — Tel: (218) 279 - 5000
Senior V. President, Marketing and Public Affairs (Minnesota Power) — Fax: (218) 279 - 5050
dmcmillan@mnpower.com

NIEMI, Dennis L. — Tel: (218) 723 - 3945
Director, Environmental Services — Fax: (218) 279 - 5050
dniemi@mnpower.com

PAGEL, Craig R. — Tel: (218) 722 - 5642
Senior Government Affairs Representative (Minnesota Power) — Ext: 3759
cpagel@mnpower.com — Fax: (218) 279 - 5050

ROBARE, Margaret A. — Tel: (218) 722 - 5642
Government Relations Representative — Ext: 3654
mrobare@mnpower.com — Fax: (218) 279 - 5050

STENDER, Bruce W. — Tel: (218) 279 - 5000
Chairman of the Board — Fax: (218) 279 - 5050

THORP, Timothy J. — Tel: (218) 279 - 5000
V. President, Investor Relations — Fax: (218) 279 - 5050
tthorp@allete.com

At Washington Office

LIBRO, William J. — Tel: (202) 638 - 7707
Director, Federal Affairs — Fax: (202) 638 - 7710
blibro@exchange1.mnpower.com
Registered Federal Lobbyist.

At Other Offices

GARVEY, Stephen J. — Tel: (612) 225 - 1009
Manager, State Legislative Affairs (Minnesota Power) — Fax: (612) 224 - 1004
P.O. Box One, 161 St. Anthony St.
St. Paul, MN 55103
sgarvey@mnpower.com

Alliance Gaming Corp.

A supplier of slot machines and casino management systems.

www.alliancegaming.com
Annual Revenues: $500 million

President and Chief Exec. Officer — Tel: (702) 270 - 7600
HADDRILL, Richard — Fax: (702) 270 - 7699

Main Headquarters
Mailing: 6601 Bermuda Rd. — Tel: (702) 270 - 7600
Las Vegas, NV 89119-3605 — Fax: (702) 270 - 7679

Public Affairs and Related Activities Personnel

At Headquarters

DES CHAMPS, Steve — Tel: (702) 270 - 7600
Senior V. President and Chief Financial Officer — Fax: (702) 270 - 7679
Responsibilities include investor and media relations.

LERNER, Mark — Tel: (702) 270 - 7600
Senior V. President, Law and Government; General Counsel and Secretary — Fax: (702) 270 - 7699

Alliance One Internat'l Inc.

Formed by the merger of Dimon Incorporated and Standard Commercial Corp. in May 2005.

www.dimon.com

Chairman and Chief Exec. Officer — Tel: (434) 792 - 7511
HARKER, Brian J. — Fax: (434) 791 - 0415

Main Headquarters
Mailing: 512 Bridge St. — Tel: (434) 792 - 7511
Danville, VA 24541 — Fax: (434) 791 - 0415

Political Action Committees

Alliance One Internat'l Inc. PAC
Contact: Carol Whitehead
2201 Miller Rd.
Wilson, NC 27893

Contributions to Candidates: $3,000 (01/05 - 09/05)

Alliance One Internat'l Inc.

• continued from previous page

Republicans: $3,000.

Principal Recipients

SENATE REPUBLICANS		HOUSE REPUBLICANS	
Allen, George (VA)	$2,000	Jones, Walter (NC)	$1,000

Public Affairs and Related Activities Personnel

At Headquarters

BOND, Ritchie L. — Tel: (434) 791 - 6952
Senior V. President and Treasurer — Fax: (434) 791 - 0415

Responsibilities include investor and media relations.

At Other Offices

BABB, Henry C. — Tel: (252) 237 - 1106
Senior V. President, Chief Legal Officer and Secretary — Fax: (252) 237 - 0018
2201 Miller Rd.
Wilson, NC 27893
Responsibilities include public affairs and media relations.

WHITEHEAD, Carol
Treasurer, Alliance One Internat'l Inc. PAC
2201 Miller Rd.
Wilson, NC 27893

Alliant Energy Corp.

A member of the Public Affairs Council. Formed in 1998 from the merger of Interstate Power Co., Wisconsin Power & Light Co. and IES Industries, Inc.

www.alliantenergy.com
Annual Revenues: $2.61 billion

Chairman of the Board — Tel: (608) 458 - 3311
DAVIS, Erroll B., Jr. — Fax: (608) 458 - 3397

President and Chief Exec. Officer — Tel: (608) 458 - 3311
HARVEY, William D. — Fax: (608) 458 - 4820

Main Headquarters

Mailing: P.O. Box 77007, Madison, WI 53707-1007 — Tel: (608) 458 - 3311; Fax: (608) 458 - 3397
Street: 4902 N. Biltmore Ln., Madison, WI 53718

Washington Office

Contact: Phil Moeller
Mailing: Market Square, 801 Pennsylvania Ave., NW, Suite 640, West Tower, Washington, DC 20004-2615 — Tel: (202) 347 - 8132; Fax: (202) 347 - 8136

Political Action Committees

Alliant Energy Employees' PAC (Federal)
Contact: Phil Moeller
Market Square, 801 Pennsylvania Ave., NW — Tel: (202) 347 - 8132
Suite 640, West Tower — Fax: (202) 347 - 8136
Washington, DC 20004-2615

Contributions to Candidates: $11,250 (01/05 - 09/05)
Democrats: $2,750; Republicans: $8,500.

Principal Recipients

SENATE DEMOCRATS		HOUSE DEMOCRATS	
Nelson, Benjamin (NE)	$500	Baldwin, Tammy (WI)	$1,000
		Boucher, Fredrick (VA)	$1,000
SENATE REPUBLICANS		**HOUSE REPUBLICANS**	
Allen, George (VA)	$1,000	Nussle, Jim (IA)	$1,500
Thomas, Craig (WY)	$1,000	Kennedy, Mark (MN)	$1,000
		King, Steven (IA)	$1,000
		Latham, Thomas P (IA)	$1,000
		McSweeney, David (IL)	$1,000
		Shimkus, John (IL)	$1,000

Corporate Foundations and Giving Programs

Alliant Energy Foundation, Inc.
Contact: Tim Heinrich
P.O. Box 77007 — Tel: (608) 458 - 3221
Madison, WI 53707-1007 — Fax: (608) 458 - 0133

Assets: $27,000,000 (2004)
Annual Grant Total: $1,000,000 - $2,000,000
Donated approximately $1.8 million in 2004.
Geographic Preference: Wisconsin; Iowa; Illinois; Minnesota
Primary Interests: Arts and Culture; Civic and Cultural Activities; Education; Environment/Conservation
Recent Recipients: United Way; University of Wisconsin; YWCA

Public Affairs and Related Activities Personnel

At Headquarters

AESCHBACH, Joni — Tel: (608) 458 - 3407
Manager, Shareowner Services — Fax: (608) 458 - 3321
joniaeschbach@alliantenergy.com

HEINRICH, Tim — Tel: (608) 458 - 3221
Director, Community Affairs — Fax: (608) 458 - 0133
timheinrich@alliantenergy.com

HELBACH, David W. — Tel: (608) 458 - 5718
Director, Corporate Public Affairs — Fax: (608) 458 - 3481
davidhelbach@alliantenergy.com

JORDAHL, William — Tel: (608) 458 - 4814
Manager, Public Affairs — Fax: (608) 458 - 3481
billjordahl@alliantenergy.com

LIPP, Kathy — Tel: (608) 458 - 4812
Chief Environmental, Health and Safety Officer

At Washington Office

MOELLER, Phil — Tel: (202) 347 - 8132
Washington Representative and PAC Contact — Fax: (202) 347 - 8136
philmoeller@alliantenergy.com
Registered Federal Lobbyist.

At Other Offices

HARRMANN, Terry O. — Tel: (515) 284 - 5699
Manager, Public Affairs — Fax: (515) 284 - 7130
321 E. Walnut, Suite 373
Des Moines, IA 50309
terryharrmann@alliant-energy.com

PETERSEN, Tom — Tel: (319) 786 - 4490
Director, Corporate Communications — Fax: (319) 786 - 4796
200 First St. SE
Cedar Rapids, IA 52401
tompetersen@alliantenergy.com

Alliant Exchange, Inc.

See listing on page 485 under US Foodservice.

Alliant Techsystems

Alliant Techsystems (ATK) is an aerospace and defense company involved in propulsion, composite structures, munitions, and precision capabilities. The Company has three business groups: Aerospace, Precision Systems, and Ammunition.

www.atk.com
Annual Revenues: $2.4 billion

Chairman and Chief Exec. Officer — Tel: (952) 351 - 3000
MURPHY, Daniel J. — Fax: (952) 351 - 3009

Main Headquarters

Mailing: 5050 Lincoln Dr., Edina, MN 55436 — Tel: (952) 351 - 3000; Fax: (952) 351 - 3009

Washington Office

Contact: John E. "Ted" Gordon
Mailing: Crystal Gateway 3, 1215 S. Clark St., Suite 1510, Arlington, VA 22202 — Tel: (703) 412 - 5977; Fax: (703) 412 - 5970

Political Action Committees

Alliant Techsystems Inc. Employee Citizenship Fund
Contact: Lynn W. Heninger
Crystal Gateway 3, 1215 S. Clark St. — Tel: (703) 412 - 5960
Suite 1510 — Fax: (703) 412 - 5970
Arlington, VA 22202

Contributions to Candidates: $83,500 (01/05 - 09/05)
Democrats: $27,500; Republicans: $55,000; Other: $1,000.

Principal Recipients

SENATE DEMOCRATS		HOUSE DEMOCRATS	
Nelson, Bill (FL)	$2,000	Murtha, John P Mr. (PA)	$4,000
		Skelton, Ike (MO)	$2,000
SENATE REPUBLICANS		**HOUSE REPUBLICANS**	
Allen, George (VA)	$5,000	Granger, Kay N (TX)	$2,500
Talent, James (MO)	$3,500	Cunningham, Duke (CA)	$2,000
Kennedy, Mark (MN)	$2,500	Graves, Sam (MO)	$2,000
Hatch, Orrin (UT)	$2,000	Tiahrt, Todd W. (KS)	$2,000
		Wicker, Roger (MS)	$2,000
		Wilson, Heather (NM)	$2,000
		Wolf, Frank R (VA)	$2,000

Corporate Foundations and Giving Programs

ATK Foundation
Contact: Karen Engelbret

Alliant Techsystems

** continued from previous page*

5050 Lincoln Dr.
Edina, MN 55436
Tel: (952) 351 - 2778
Fax: (952) 351 - 3009

Annual Grant Total: $1,000,000 - $2,000,000

Contributions from the ATK Community Investment Foundation are focused in four areas: employee programs, community programs, military and customer programs, and The United Way. The information below applies to one or more of the above listed programs.

Geographic Preference: Area(s) in which the company operates; Area in which the company is headquartered

Recent Recipients: Junior Achievement; ROTC (Reserved Officer Training Corps); U.S. First; United Negro College Fund; United Way

Public Affairs and Related Activities Personnel

At Headquarters

ENGELBRET, Karen
Foundation Contact
karen.engelbret@atk.com
Tel: (952) 351 - 2778
Fax: (952) 351 - 3009

HALLOWELL, Bryce
Director, External Communications
bryce.hallowell@atk.com
Tel: (952) 351 - 3087
Fax: (952) 351 - 3009

PATINEAU, Paula J.
Senior V. President, Human Resources and Administrative Services
paula_patineau@atk.com
Responsibilities include corporate philanthropy.
Tel: (952) 351 - 3000
Fax: (952) 351 - 3053

WOLD, Steve
V. President, Investor Relations
steve_wold@atk.com
Tel: (952) 351 - 3056
Fax: (952) 351 - 3009

At Washington Office

CHENEY, Gregory S.
Registered Federal Lobbyist.
Tel: (703) 412 - 5977
Fax: (703) 412 - 5970

GORDON, John E. "Ted"
V. President, Washington Operations
Registered Federal Lobbyist.
Tel: (703) 412 - 5961
Fax: (703) 412 - 5970

HENINGER, Lynn W.
Director, Legislative Liaison, Space
Registered Federal Lobbyist.
Responsibilities include political action.
Tel: (703) 412 - 5960
Fax: (703) 412 - 5970

LUMME, Dale A.
Registered Federal Lobbyist.
Tel: (703) 412 - 5977
Fax: (703) 412 - 5970

MASCH, Donald
Director, Government Relations
donald_masch@atk.com
Registered Federal Lobbyist.
Tel: (703) 412 - 5977
Fax: (703) 412 - 5970

NEAL, Erin
Senior Manager, Congressional Relations
Registered Federal Lobbyist.
Tel: (703) 412 - 5977
Fax: (703) 412 - 5970

Allied Domecq Quick Service Restaurants

See listing on page 169 under Dunkin' Brands.

Allied Waste Industries, Inc.

Provides waste collection, transfer, recycling, and disposal services for residential, commercial and industrial customers. Acquired Browning-Ferris Industries in 1999.

www.alliedwaste.com
Annual Revenues: $5.4 billion

Chairman and Chief Exec. Officer
ZILLMER, John J.
Tel: (480) 627 - 2700
Fax: (480) 627 - 2701

Main Headquarters
Mailing: 15880 N. Greenway-Hayden Loop
Suite 100
Scottsdale, AZ 85260
Tel: (480) 627 - 2700
Fax: (480) 627 - 2701

Public Affairs and Related Activities Personnel

At Headquarters

BURNETT, Michael S.
V. President, Investor Relations and Corporate Communications
Tel: (480) 627 - 2785
Fax: (480) 627 - 2701

EVANS, Edward A.
Exec. V. President, Human Resources and Organizational Development
Tel: (480) 627 - 2700
Fax: (480) 627 - 2701

Allina Health System

See listing on page 22 under Allina Hospitals and Clinics.

Allina Hospitals and Clinics

Formerly known as Allina Health System. An integrated provider of medical services.

www.allina.com
Annual Revenues: $2 billion

Chairman of the Board
CRAWFORD, Rollin H.
Tel: (612) 775 - 5000

President and Chief Exec. Officer
PETTINGILL, Richard
Mailstop: M.R. 43303
dick.pettingill@allina.com
Tel: (612) 775 - 9732
Fax: (612) 775 - 9723

Main Headquarters
Mailing: 710 E. 24th St.
Minneapolis, MN 55404
Tel: (612) 775 - 5000

Public Affairs and Related Activities Personnel

At Headquarters

JOHNSON, Todd M.
V. President, Government Affairs
Mailstop: M. R. 43400
todd.johnson@allina.com
Tel: (612) 775 - 9658
Fax: (612) 775 - 9634

JONES, Patricia
Exec. V. President, Human Resources
Mailstop: M. R. 43303
patricia.jones@allina.com
Tel: (612) 775 - 9727

ORBUCH, David B.
Exec. V. President, Corporate Responsibility and Community Relations
Mailstop: M. R. 43202
david.orbuch@allina.com
Tel: (612) 775 - 5819
Fax: (612) 775 - 9739

PHENIX, Amy
V. President, Communications
Mailstop: M. R. 43202
amy.phenix@allina.com
Tel: (612) 775 - 9767
Fax: (612) 775 - 9739

Allison Transmission Division

See listing on page 214 under General Motors Corp.

Allmerica Property & Casualty Companies, Inc.

An insurance and financial services company. Stock is traded under the name of the holding corporation, Allmerica Financial Corp.

www.allmerica.com

Chairman of the Board
ANGELINI, Michael P.
Tel: (508) 855 - 1000

President and Chief Exec. Officer
EPPINGER, Frederick H.
Tel: (508) 855 - 1000

Main Headquarters
Mailing: 440 Lincoln St.
Worcester, MA 01653
Tel: (508) 855 - 1000

Political Action Committees

First Allmerica Financial Life Insurance Co. Federal PAC
Contact: John L. McDonough
440 Lincoln St.
Worcester, MA 01653
Tel: (508) 855 - 1000

Contributions to Candidates: $1,000 (01/05 - 09/05)
Democrats: $1,000.

Principal Recipients

SENATE DEMOCRATS	HOUSE DEMOCRATS
	Mcgovern, James (MA) $1,000

Corporate Foundations and Giving Programs

Allmerica Charitable Foundation
Contact: Cheryl Lapriore
440 Lincoln St.
Worcester, MA 01653
Tel: (508) 855 - 1000

Annual Grant Total: none reported
Geographic Preference: Worcester, MA; Howell, MI
Primary Interests: Education; Youth Services

Public Affairs and Related Activities Personnel

At Headquarters

BUCKLEY, Michael F.
Director, Public Information
mibuckley@allmerica.com
Tel: (508) 855 - 3099
Fax: (508) 855 - 3675

HAASE, Bonnie K.
V. President an Chief Human Resources Officer
Tel: (508) 855 - 1000

LAPRIORE, Cheryl
V. President, Corporate Community Relations
Tel: (508) 855 - 1000

MCDONOUGH, John L.
Treasurer, First Allmerica Financial Life Insurance Co. PAC
Tel: (508) 855 - 1000

MUTALIK, Sujata
V. President, Investor Relations
smutalik@allmerica.com
Tel: (508) 855 - 3457

Allmerica Property & Casualty Companies, Inc.

• continued from previous page

At Other Offices

BEST, Becky E.
Manager, Corporate Community Relations
(Citizens Insurance Co.)
645 W. Grand River
Howell, MI 48843

Allstate Insurance Co.

PUBLIC AFFAIRS COUNCIL

A member of the Public Affairs Council. Provides insurance and financial services.
www.allstate.com
Annual Revenues: $28.8 billion

Chairman, President and Chief Exec. Officer
LIDDY, Edward M. — Tel: (847) 402 - 5000
eliddy@allstate.com — Fax: (847) 402 - 5448 — TF: (800) 574 - 3553

Main Headquarters
Mailing: 2775 Sanders Rd. — Tel: (847) 402 - 5000
Northbrook, IL 60062-6127 — Fax: (847) 326 - 7519 — TF: (800) 574 - 3553

Washington Office
Contact: J. Charles Bruse
Mailing: 1615 L St. NW — Tel: (202) 626 - 8240
Suite 650 — Fax: (202) 626 - 8575
Washington, DC 20036

Political Action Committees

Allstate Insurance Co. Political Action Committee (ALLPAC)
Contact: Steven Verney
2775 Sanders Rd. — Tel: (847) 402 - 5000
Northbrook, IL 60062-6127 — Fax: (847) 326 - 7519 — TF: (800) 574 - 3553

Contributions to Candidates: $53,500 (01/05 - 09/05)
Democrats: $16,000; Republicans: $37,500.

Principal Recipients

SENATE DEMOCRATS		HOUSE DEMOCRATS	
Carper, Thomas R (DE)	$3,000	Davis, Danny K (IL)	$1,500
Nelson, Benjamin (NE)	$2,000		
Nelson, Bill (FL)	$2,000		
SENATE REPUBLICANS		**HOUSE REPUBLICANS**	
DeMint, James (SC)	$2,000	Johnson, Nancy (CT)	$2,000
Lugar, Richard G (IN)	$2,000	Kirk, Mark Steven (IL)	$2,000
Santorum, Richard (PA)	$1,500	Pryce, Deborah (OH)	$1,500

Corporate Foundations and Giving Programs

The Allstate Foundation
Contact: Jan Epstein
2775 Sanders Rd. — Tel: (847) 402 - 2794
Northbrook, IL 60062-6127 — TF: (800) 574 - 3553

Annual Grant Total: over $5,000,000
Maintains a website at www.allstate.com/foundation. Contributed $7.1 million in 2001.
Primary Interests: Community Development; Disaster Relief; Diversity; Financial Planning; Housing; Safety; Security; Youth Services
Recent Recipients: Boys and Girls Club

Public Affairs and Related Activities Personnel

At Headquarters

CROCKETT, Joan M. — Tel: (847) 402 - 5000
Senior V. President, Human Resources — Fax: (847) 402 - 5448
jcrockett@allstate.com — TF: (800) 574 - 3553

DEBRECENY, Peter — Tel: (847) 402 - 3111
V. President, Corporate Relations — Fax: (847) 326 - 7519
pdebreceny@allstate.com — TF: (800) 574 - 3553

DOYLE, Karen — Tel: (847) 402 - 5000
National Media Contact — Fax: (847) 326 - 7519 — TF: (800) 574 - 3553

DUDAS, Jim — Tel: (847) 402 - 5000
National Media Contact — Fax: (847) 326 - 7519 — TF: (800) 574 - 3553

EPSTEIN, Jan — Tel: (847) 402 - 2794
Exec. Director, Allstate Foundation — TF: (800) 574 - 3553
jepstein@allstate.com

HIRSCH, Rebecca — Tel: (847) 402 - 5000
National Media Contact — Fax: (847) 326 - 7519 — TF: (800) 574 - 3553

HORSTMAN, Mary Alice — Tel: (847) 402 - 5000
Director, Corporate Relations — Fax: (847) 326 - 7519 — TF: (800) 574 - 3553

MARGOLIS, Laura — Tel: (847) 402 - 5000
National Media Contact — Fax: (847) 326 - 7519 — TF: (800) 574 - 3553

MCCABE, E. James — Tel: (847) 402 - 5889
Manager, Government Relations — Fax: (847) 326 - 7524
Mailstop: Suite A3

MELLANDER, William — Tel: (847) 402 - 5000
National Media Contact — Fax: (847) 326 - 7519 — TF: (800) 574 - 3553

NOLAN, George — Tel: (847) 402 - 5000
National Media Contact — Fax: (847) 326 - 7519 — TF: (800) 574 - 3553

QUILES, Marissa — Tel: (847) 402 - 5000
National Media Contact — Fax: (847) 326 - 7519 — TF: (800) 574 - 3553

TOPOLEWSKI, Jen — Tel: (847) 402 - 5000
National Media Contact — Fax: (847) 326 - 7519 — TF: (800) 574 - 3553

TREVINO, Michael — Tel: (847) 402 - 5000
National Media Contact — Fax: (847) 326 - 7519 — TF: (800) 574 - 3553

VERNEY, Steven — Tel: (847) 402 - 5000
PAC Treasurer — Fax: (847) 326 - 7519 — TF: (800) 574 - 3553

At Washington Office

BRUSE, J. Charles — Tel: (202) 626 - 8240
V. President and Assistant General Counsel
cbruse@allstate.com
Registered Federal Lobbyist.

PAPPAS, Dean T. — Tel: (202) 626 - 8240
Counsel — Fax: (202) 626 - 8575
Registered Federal Lobbyist.

ALLTEL

A communications company.
www.alltel.com
Annual Revenues: $8 billion

Chairman of the Board — Tel: (501) 905 - 8000
FORD, Joe T.
joe.t.ford@alltel.com

President and Chief Exec. Officer — Tel: (501) 905 - 8000
FORD, Scott T.
scott.t.ford@alltel.com

Main Headquarters
Mailing: One Allied Dr. — Tel: (501) 905 - 8000
Little Rock, AR 72202 — Fax: (501) 905 - 6018

Washington Office
Mailing: 601 Pennsylvania Ave. NW — Tel: (202) 783 - 3970
Suite 720 — Fax: (202) 783 - 3982
Washington, DC 20004

Political Action Committees

ALLTEL Corp. Political Action Committee (APAC)
Contact: John A. Ebner
One Allied Dr. — Tel: (501) 905 - 8000
Little Rock, AR 72202 — Fax: (501) 905 - 6018

Contributions to Candidates: $12,500 (01/05 - 09/05)
Democrats: $6,000; Republicans: $6,500.

Principal Recipients

SENATE DEMOCRATS		HOUSE DEMOCRATS	
Inouye, Daniel K (HI)	$1,000	Watt, Melvin (NC)	$2,000
Nelson, Benjamin (NE)	$1,000	Boucher, Fredrick (VA)	$1,000
Pryor, Mark (AR)	$1,000		
SENATE REPUBLICANS		**HOUSE REPUBLICANS**	
Ensign, John Eric (NV)	$2,000	Terry, Lee (NE)	$1,500
		Alexander, Rodney (LA)	$1,000
		Pickering, Chip (MS)	$1,000
		Shimkus, John (IL)	$1,000

Corporate Foundations and Giving Programs

ALLTEL Corp., Corporate Giving Program
Contact: Jessica Brogdon
One Allied Dr. — Tel: (501) 905 - 8000
Little Rock, AR 72202 — Fax: (501) 905 - 6018

Annual Grant Total: none reported
Primary Interests: Arts and Culture; Disaster Relief; Education; Health and Human Services

ALLTEL

** continued from previous page*

Public Affairs and Related Activities Personnel

At Headquarters

AVERY, David — Tel: (501) 905 - 5876
Staff Manager, Corporate Communications — Fax: (501) 905 - 6018
david.avery@alltel.com

BROGDON, Jessica — Tel: (501) 905 - 8000
Contact, Corporate Contributions — Fax: (501) 905 - 6018

CLANCY, Rob — Tel: (501) 905 - 8991
V. President, Investor Relations
rob.clancy@alltel.com

DUVALL, C. J. — Tel: (501) 905 - 8000
Senior V. President, Human Resources

EBNER, John A. — Tel: (501) 905 - 8000
PAC Treasurer — Fax: (501) 905 - 6018

FRANTZ, Francis X. — Tel: (501) 905 - 5615
Exec. V. President, External Affairs, General Counsel and Secretary

Responsibilities include federal and state government affairs and corporate communications.

MOREAU, Andrew — Tel: (501) 905 - 7962
V. President, Corporate Communications — Fax: (501) 905 - 6018
andrew.moreau@alltel.com

WHITE, Larry D. — Tel: (501) 905 - 5590
Manager, Corporate Communications — Fax: (501) 905 - 6018
larry.d.white@alltel.com

At Washington Office

BARTLETT, David — Tel: (202) 783 - 3970
Assistant V. President, Federal Regulatory Affairs — Fax: (202) 783 - 3982
Registered Federal Lobbyist.

JOHANNS, Stephanie — Tel: (202) 783 - 3970
Senior V. President, Federal Regulatory Affairs — Fax: (202) 783 - 3982

PARANDIAN, Chris — Tel: (202) 783 - 3970
V. President, Federal Legislative Affairs — Fax: (202) 783 - 3982
Registered Federal Lobbyist.

RABIN, Glenn S. — Tel: (202) 783 - 3973
V. President, Federal Communications Counsel — Fax: (202) 783 - 3982
glenn.rabin@alltel.com
Registered Federal Lobbyist.

SETTELMYER, Scott — Tel: (202) 783 - 3970
PAC Treasurer — Fax: (202) 783 - 3982

Aloha Airlines, Inc.

A scheduled airline, providing passenger and air cargo service.

www.alohaairlines.com

Chairman of the Board — Tel: (808) 539 - 5909
CHING, Han H.

President and Chief Exec. Officer — Tel: (808) 539 - 5909
BANMILLER, David A. — Fax: (808) 836 - 0303

Main Headquarters
Mailing: Two Waterfront Plaza — Tel: (808) 539 - 5909
Suite 500 — Fax: (808) 836 - 0303
Honolulu, HI 96813

Political Action Committees

Aloha Airlines, Inc. PAC
Contact: Stephanie Ackerman
Two Waterfront Plaza — Tel: (808) 836 - 4172
Suite 500 — Fax: (808) 836 - 0303
Honolulu, HI 96813

Contributions to Candidates: none reported (01/05 - 09/05)

Public Affairs and Related Activities Personnel

At Headquarters

ACKERMAN, Stephanie — Tel: (808) 836 - 4172
Senior V. President, Public Relations and Government Affairs — Fax: (808) 836 - 0303
sackerman@alohaairlines.com

GLAUBERMAN, Stu — Tel: (808) 539 - 5947
Director, Corporate Communications — Fax: (808) 836 - 0303
sglauberman@alohaairlines.com

Alpharma Inc.

A pharmaceutical company.

www.alpharma.com
Annual Revenues: $975 million

Chairman of the Board — Tel: (201) 947 - 7774
SISSENER, Einar W. — Fax: (201) 947 - 5541
TF: (800) 445 - 4216

President and Chief Exec. Officer — Tel: (201) 947 - 7774
WIIK, Ingrid — Fax: (201) 947 - 5541
TF: (800) 445 - 4216

Main Headquarters
Mailing: One Executive Dr. — Tel: (201) 947 - 7774
Fort Lee, NJ 07024 — Fax: (201) 947 - 5541
TF: (800) 445 - 4216

Public Affairs and Related Activities Personnel

At Headquarters

MAKRAKIS, Kathleen — Tel: (201) 228 - 5085
V. President, Investor Relations — Fax: (201) 947 - 5541
investorrelations@alpharma.com — TF: (800) 445 - 4216

ROSE, George P. — Tel: (201) 947 - 7774
Exec. V. President, Human Resources and Communications — Fax: (201) 947 - 5541
TF: (800) 445 - 4216

Altera Corp.

Provides programmable logic technology.

www.altera.com
Annual Revenues: $1.02 billion

Chairman, President and Chief Exec. Officer — Tel: (408) 544 - 7000
DAANE, John P. — Fax: (408) 544 - 7740

Main Headquarters
Mailing: 101 Innovation Dr. — Tel: (408) 544 - 7000
San Jose, CA 95134-1941 — Fax: (408) 544 - 7740

Corporate Foundations and Giving Programs

Altera Corporate Giving Program
101 Innovation Dr. — Tel: (408) 544 - 7000
San Jose, CA 95134-1941 — Fax: (408) 544 - 7740

Annual Grant Total: none reported
Geographic Preference: Area(s) in which employees live and work; Area in which the company is headquartered
Primary Interests: Education; Health and Human Services; Youth Services
Recent Recipients: American Heart Ass'n; Habitat for Humanity; Salvation Army; Toys for Tots

Public Affairs and Related Activities Personnel

At Headquarters

FIENBERG, Bruce — Tel: (408) 544 - 6397
Senior Manager, Public Relations — Fax: (408) 544 - 7740

FITZHENRY, Jack R. — Tel: (408) 544 - 7000
V. President, Human Resources — Fax: (408) 544 - 7740

ST. DENIS, Kelly — Tel: (408) 544 - 6397
Media Relations Contact — Fax: (408) 544 - 7740

WYLIE, Scott — Tel: (408) 544 - 6996
V. President, Investor Relations — Fax: (408) 544 - 7740
swylie@altera.com

Alticor Inc.

Engaged in direct selling, e-commerce, and business-to-business services through its subsidiaries, Amway Corp., Quixtar Inc. and Access Business Group.

www.alticor.com

Chairman of the Board — Tel: (616) 787 - 6000
VANANDEL, Steve — Fax: (616) 787 - 6177

President — Tel: (616) 787 - 6000
DEVOS, Doug — Fax: (616) 787 - 6177

Main Headquarters
Mailing: 7575 Fulton St. East — Tel: (616) 787 - 6000
Ada, MI 49355-0001 — Fax: (616) 787 - 6177

Washington Office
Contact: Michael J. Zarrelli
Mailing: 214 Massachusetts Ave. NE — Tel: (202) 547 - 5005
Suite 210 — Fax: (202) 547 - 5008
Washington, DC 20002

Political Action Committees

Alticor Inc. Political Action Committee (ALTIPAC)
Contact: Michael J. Zarrelli
214 Massachusetts Ave. NE — Tel: (202) 547 - 5005
Suite 210 — Fax: (202) 547 - 5008
Washington, DC 20002

Contributions to Candidates: $3,500 (01/05 - 09/05)
Republicans: $3,500.

Principal Recipients

SENATE REPUBLICANS	HOUSE REPUBLICANS	
	Hastert, Dennis J. (IL)	$1,500
	Hoekstra, Peter (MI)	$1,000
	Rogers, Michael J (MI)	$1,000

Alticor Inc.

** continued from previous page*

Corporate Foundations and Giving Programs

Alticor Corporate Contributions
Contact: Erin L. Rowe-Graves
7575 Fulton St. East — Tel: (616) 787 - 7144
Ada, MI 49355-0001 — Fax: (616) 787 - 4764

Annual Grant Total: none reported

Public Affairs and Related Activities Personnel

At Headquarters

BAIN, Mark — Tel: (616) 787 - 8636
V. President, Corporate Communications — Fax: (616) 787 - 5669
Mailstop: M/S 49-2N

BLOEMENDAAL, Dirk C. — Tel: (616) 787 - 7560
Senior Corporate Counsel, North American Government Affairs — Fax: (616) 787 - 5624
Mailstop: M/S 78-2G

BOLAND, Mary Kathryn "Kati" — Tel: (616) 787 - 6972
Supervisor, External Affairs — Fax: (616) 787 - 4764
Mailstop: M/S 49-2N

DORNAN, Beth A. — Tel: (616) 787 - 6445
Director, Quixtar Communications — Fax: (616) 787 - 7102
(Quixtar Inc.)
Mailstop: M/S SC-2P

HARRISON, Brian — Tel: (616) 787 - 7560
Government Affairs Specialist — Fax: (616) 787 - 5624
Mailstop: M/S 78-2G

HORDER-KOOP, Robin — Tel: (616) 787 - 7717
V. President, Worldwide Human Resources — Fax: (616) 787 - 6177
Mailstop: M/S 78-1M

KAZEMIER, Jeanie A. — Tel: (616) 787 - 8584
Senior Legislative Analyst — Fax: (616) 787 - 5624
Mailstop: M/S 78-2G

ROWE-GRAVES, Erin L. — Tel: (616) 787 - 7144
Manager, Industry and Community Affairs — Fax: (616) 787 - 4764
Mailstop: M/S 49-2N

At Washington Office

HOLWILL, Richard N. — Tel: (202) 547 - 0300
V. President, Public Policy — Fax: (202) 547 - 5008

(Amway Corp.)
Responsibilities include worldwide government affairs.

ZARRELLI, Michael J. — Tel: (202) 547 - 5005
Manager, Federal Affairs — Fax: (202) 547 - 5008
Registered Federal Lobbyist.

Altria Corporate Services, Inc.

See listing on page 25 under Altria Group, Inc.

Altria Group, Inc.

PUBLIC AFFAIRS COUNCIL

A member of the Public Affairs Council. Formerly known as Philip Morris Companies Inc. A diversified corporation active in the tobacco and food products industries. Subsidiaries include Kraft Foods Inc. and Philip Morris U.S.A. (see separate listings). Brands include Marlboro cigarettes, Tombstone pizza, Oscar Mayer and Kraft foods, among others.

www.altria.com
Annual Revenues: $89.924 billion

Chairman and Chief Exec. Officer
CAMILLERI, Louis C. — Tel: (917) 663 - 2121 — Fax: (917) 663 - 2167

Main Headquarters
Mailing: 120 Park Ave. — Tel: (917) 663 - 4000
New York, NY 10017 — Fax: (917) 663 - 2167

Washington Office
Contact: John F. Scruggs
Mailing: 101 Constitution Ave. NW — Tel: (202) 354 - 1500
Suite 400 West — Fax: (202) 354 - 1505
Washington, DC 20001

Political Action Committees

Altria Group Inc. Political Action Committee
Contact: Mel Raines
101 Constitution Ave. NW — Tel: (202) 354 - 1500
Suite 400 West — Fax: (202) 354 - 1505
Washington, DC 20001

Contributions to Candidates: $255,500 (01/05 - 09/05)
Democrats: $82,500; Republicans: $173,000.

Principal Recipients

SENATE DEMOCRATS		HOUSE DEMOCRATS	
Clinton, Hillary Rodham (NY)	$3,000	Jefferson, William (LA)	$6,000
		Rangel, Charles B (NY)	$5,000
		Towns, Edolphus (NY)	$5,000
SENATE REPUBLICANS		**HOUSE REPUBLICANS**	
Ensign, John Eric (NV)	$8,000	Cantor, Eric (VA)	$9,000
Allen, George (VA)	$6,500	Bonilla, Henry (TX)	$6,000
Hatch, Orrin (UT)	$6,000	Blunt, Roy (MO)	$5,000
Chambliss, Saxby (GA)	$5,000	Hayes, Robert (NC)	$5,000
Lott, Trent (MS)	$5,000		

Corporate Foundations and Giving Programs

Altria Group, Inc. Contributions
Contact: Jennifer Goodale
120 Park Ave. — Tel: (917) 663 - 2081
New York, NY 10017 — Fax: (917) 663 - 5396

Annual Grant Total: over $5,000,000
Geographic Preference: Area(s) in which the company operates
Primary Interests: Arts and Humanities; Hunger

Public Affairs and Related Activities Personnel

At Headquarters

CAPPELLO, Christine — Tel: (917) 663 - 4000
Manager, Employee Giving — Fax: (914) 272 - 0349

COLLAMORE, Thomas J. — Tel: (917) 663 - 3924
V. President, Public Affairs — Fax: (917) 663 - 5464
Mailstop: 17th Floor

DISABATO, Michelle — Tel: (917) 663 - 3346
Manager, Planning and Analysis — Fax: (917) 663 - 5431

DONINI, Marilynn J. — Tel: (917) 663 - 4171
Manager, Contributions Program — Fax: (917) 663 - 5874
(Altria Corporate Services, Inc.)
Mailstop: 17th Floor

EIDMAN, Diane — Tel: (917) 663 - 2845
Director, Corporate Contributions — Fax: (917) 663 - 5874

GOODALE, Jennifer — Tel: (917) 663 - 2081
V. President, Corporate Contributions — Fax: (917) 663 - 5396

GRIZZAFFI, Elizabeth M. "Betty" — Tel: (917) 663 - 3544
Supervisor, Internal Communications — Fax: (917) 663 - 5739
(Altria Corporate Services, Inc.)
Mailstop: 25th Floor

LAMPE, Kathy — Tel: (917) 663 - 3044
Assistant Corporate Secretary — Fax: (917) 663 - 2167
Responsibilities include investor relations.

MCNAMARA, Kathleen — Tel: (917) 663 - 3046
Manager, Contributions Programs — Fax: (917) 663 - 5475
(Altria Corporate Services, Inc.)
Mailstop: 17th Floor

NEKOLA, Kathleen — Tel: (917) 663 - 3686
Director, Corporate Affairs Planning — Fax: (917) 663 - 5513

PARRISH, Steven C. — Tel: (917) 663 - 3074
Senior V. President, Corporate Affairs — Fax: (917) 663 - 2395
Mailstop: 22nd Floor

ROGERS, Ralph L., Jr. — Tel: (917) 663 - 2206
Director, Corporate Responsibility Planning — Fax: (917) 663 - 5431
(Altria Corporate Services, Inc.)

ROLLI, Nicholas M. — Tel: (917) 663 - 4000
V. President, Investor Relations and Financial Communications — Fax: (917) 663 - 5430
(Altria Corporate Services, Inc.)

WALKER, Lisa — Tel: (917) 663 - 2878
Director, Corporate Contributions — Fax: (917) 663 - 5874

YESKO, Diane M. — Tel: (917) 663 - 3457
Supervisor, External Communications — Fax: (917) 663 - 5439
(Altria Corporate Services, Inc.)
Mailstop: 25th Floor

At Washington Office

BLUNT, Abigail — Tel: (202) 354 - 1500
Director, Government Affairs- Food — Fax: (202) 354 - 1505

COLEGROVE, Dan — Tel: (202) 354 - 1500
District Director — Fax: (202) 354 - 1505
dan.colegrove@altria.com
(Altria Corporate Services, Inc.)

CONDON, Leonard W. — Tel: (202) 354 - 1500
Director, International Business Relations — Fax: (202) 354 - 1505
len.condon@altria.com

Altria Group, Inc.

** continued from previous page*

FOLKERTS, Brian — Tel: (202) 354 - 1500
V. President, Government Affairs - Food — Fax: (202) 354 - 1505
brian.folkerts@altria.com
Registered Federal Lobbyist.

GIMBEL, Tod I. — Tel: (202) 354 - 1500
Regional Director, East — Fax: (202) 354 - 1505
tod.gimbel@altria.com

HOEL, John — Tel: (202) 354 - 1500
V. President, Federal Government Affairs- Tobacco — Fax: (202) 354 - 1505
Registered Federal Lobbyist.

LOMBARD, Tanya — Tel: (202) 354 - 1500
Director, Government Affairs- Tobacco — Fax: (202) 354 - 1505
tanya.lombard@altria.com

MCKITTRICK, Beverly E. — Tel: (202) 354 - 1500
Director, Federal Policy- Tobacco — Fax: (202) 354 - 1505
beverly.mckittrick@altria.com
(Altria Corporate Services, Inc.)
Registered Federal Lobbyist.

NELSON, Donald M., Jr. — Tel: (202) 354 - 1500
V. President, International Business Relations — Fax: (202) 354 - 1505
donald.nelson@altria.com
(Altria Corporate Services, Inc.)
Registered Federal Lobbyist.

OSTRONIC, John — Tel: (202) 354 - 1500
Manager, Political Outreach — Fax: (202) 354 - 1505
john.ostronic@altria.com

PLESSALA DUPERIER, Laurie — Tel: (202) 354 - 1500
V. President and Associate General Counsel, Government Affairs — Fax: (202) 354 - 1505

PORTNOY, James — Tel: (202) 354 - 1500
Senior Legislative Counsel — Fax: (202) 354 - 1505
james.portnoy@altria.com

RAINES, Mel — Tel: (202) 354 - 1500
Director, GA Outreach and Communications — Fax: (202) 354 - 1505

SCOTT, Gregory R. — Tel: (202) 354 - 1500
Director, Federal Affairs - Tobacco — Fax: (202) 354 - 1505
gregory.scott@altria.com
(Altria Corporate Services, Inc.)
Registered Federal Lobbyist.

SCRUGGS, John F. — Tel: (202) 354 - 1500
V. President, Government Affairs — Fax: (202) 354 - 1505
john.scruggs@altria.com
Registered Federal Lobbyist.

SORRELLS, John — Tel: (202) 354 - 1500
Director, Corporate Communications — Fax: (202) 354 - 1505
john.sorrells@altria.com
(Altria Corporate Services, Inc.)

TURNER, Henry — Tel: (202) 354 - 1500
V. President, State Government Affairs — Fax: (202) 354 - 1505
henry.turner@altria.com

WASHINGTON, Shaunise — Tel: (202) 354 - 1500
V. President, Government Affairs Policy Outreach — Fax: (202) 354 - 1505
shaunise.washington@altria.com

WESTFALL, Linda "Tuckie" — Tel: (202) 354 - 1500
Director, Government Affairs - Food — Fax: (202) 354 - 1505
tuckie.westfall@altria.com
(Altria Corporate Services, Inc.)
Registered Federal Lobbyist.

At Other Offices

CRAWFORD, Derek L. — Tel: (847) 646 - 0534
Regional Director, State Government Affairs — Fax: (847) 646 - 0979
(Altria Corporate Services, Inc.)
Three Lakes Dr. West
Northfield, IL 60093

DILLARD, Jack K. — Tel: (512) 478 - 3394
Regional Director, State Government Affairs (IX) — Fax: (512) 478 - 0647
(Altria Corporate Services, Inc.)
1005 Congress Ave.
Suite 850
Austin, TX 78702

FISHER, Scott S. — Tel: (800) 554 - 9406
Regional Director, State Government Affairs — Fax: (513) 831 - 7219
(Altria Corporate Services, Inc.)
400 Technecenter Dr.
Suite 302
Milford, OH 45150

GILES, Betsy — Tel: (512) 478 - 3394
Regional Director, State Government Affairs — Fax: (512) 478 - 0657
(Altria Corporate Services, Inc.)
1005 Congress Ave.
Suite 850
Austin, TX 78702

POOLE, Jay — Tel: (804) 484 - 2313
V. President, Agricultural Policy and Programs
615 Maury St.
Richmond, VA 23224

RAINEY, John — Tel: (804) 484 - 6292
Regional Director, State Government Affairs — Fax: (804) 274 - 2841
615 Maury St.
Richmond, VA 23224

SMITH, Dan — Tel: (678) 297 - 9365
Regional Director, State Government Affairs — Fax: (678) 297 - 9393
333 N. Point Center East
Suite 15
Alpharetta, GA 30022

SULLIVAN, Marcia — Tel: (800) 525 - 5680
Director, Public Affairs — Fax: (512) 478 - 0647
(Altria Corporate Services, Inc.)
1005 Congress Ave.
Suite 850
Austin, TX 78702

VARGAS, Cesar — Tel: (916) 441 - 2288
Regional Director, State Government Affairs — Fax: (916) 441 - 2897
915 L St., Suite 1410
Sacramento, CA 95814

Alyeska Pipeline Service Co.

Operator of the trans-Alaska pipeline.
www.alyeska-pipe.com

President and Chief Exec. Officer — Tel: (907) 787 - 8700
WIGHT, David — Fax: (907) 787 - 8611

Main Headquarters
Mailing: P.O. Box 196660 — Tel: (907) 787 - 8700
Anchorage, AK 99519-6660

Washington Office
Contact: William L. Hensley
Mailing: 1667 K St. NW — Tel: (202) 466 - 3866
Suite 430 — Fax: (202) 466 - 3886
Washington, DC 20006

Corporate Foundations and Giving Programs

Alyeska Pipeline Service Co. Contributions Program
Contact: Janie Leask
P.O. Box 196660 — Tel: (907) 787 - 8870
Anchorage, AK 99519-6660 — Fax: (907) 787 - 8240

Annual Grant Total: $750,000 - $1,000,000
Geographic Preference: Alaska

Public Affairs and Related Activities Personnel

At Headquarters

BLACK, Ruth — Tel: (907) 787 - 8700
Manager, Valdez Communications — Fax: (907) 834 - 7585

HEATWOLE, Mike — Tel: (907) 787 - 8870
Manager, Corporate Communications — Fax: (907) 787 - 8240
Mailstop: MS 542

LEASK, Janie — Tel: (907) 787 - 8870
Manager, Community Relations — Fax: (907) 787 - 8240
Mailstop: MS 542

THOMAS, Curtis — Tel: (907) 450 - 5857
Manager, Fairbanks Communications — Fax: (907) 450 - 5894
Mailstop: MS 815

At Washington Office

HENSLEY, William L. — Tel: (202) 466 - 3866
Manager, Federal Government Relations — Fax: (202) 466 - 3886
Registered Federal Lobbyist.

Amazon.com, Inc.

An online retailer. Offers such items as books, CDs, Video and Audiotapes, DVDs, software, computer and video games, and household products. Also offers online auctions and electronic greeting cards.
www.amazon.com
Annual Revenues: $3.122 billion

Chairman, President and Chief Exec. Officer — Tel: (206) 266 - 1000
BEZOS, Jeffrey P. — Fax: (206) 266 - 1821

Main Headquarters
Mailing: P.O. Box 81226 — Tel: (206) 266 - 1000
Seattle, WA 98108-1226 — Fax: (206) 266 - 1821
Street: 1200 12th Ave. South, Bldg. 1200
Seattle, WA 98144

Washington Office
Contact: Unique Morris
Mailing: 126 C St. NW — Tel: (202) 347 - 7390
Suite Three
Washington, DC 20001

Amazon.com, Inc.

** continued from previous page*

Political Action Committees

Amazon.com Holdings Inc. Separate Segregated Fund
Contact: Jim Hill
126 C St. NW — Tel: (202) 347 - 7390
Suite Three
Washington, DC 20001

Contributions to Candidates: $13,000 (01/05 - 09/05)
Democrats: $6,500; Republicans: $6,500.

Principal Recipients

SENATE DEMOCRATS		HOUSE DEMOCRATS	
Carper, Thomas R (DE)	$2,000	Boucher, Fredrick (VA)	$1,500
		Pomeroy, Earl (ND)	$1,000
		Chandler, Ben (KY)	$500
		Larsen, Rick (WA)	$500
SENATE REPUBLICANS		**HOUSE REPUBLICANS**	
Ensign, John Eric (NV)	$2,500		
Allen, George (VA)	$2,000		

Public Affairs and Related Activities Personnel

At Headquarters

INGLE, Molly — Tel: (206) 266 - 1000; Fax: (206) 266 - 1821
Media Contact
ingle@amazon.com

LEINWEAVER, Jeff — Tel: (206) 266 - 1000; Fax: (206) 266 - 1821
Coordinator, Public Relations

WILSON, Michelle — Tel: (206) 266 - 1000; Fax: (206) 266 - 1821
Senior V. President, Human Resources, General Counsel and Secretary

At Washington Office

HILL, Jim — Tel: (202) 347 - 7390
Treasurer, Amazon.com Holdings Inc. Separate Segregated Fund

MISENER, Paul E. — Tel: (202) 347 - 7390
V. President, Global Public Policy
Registered Federal Lobbyist.

MORRIS, Unique — Tel: (202) 347 - 7389
Coordinator, Public Policy
morris@amazon.com

RINGLEY, Sharon — Tel: (202) 347 - 7390
Registered Federal Lobbyist.

Ambac Financial Group, Inc.

A holding company that provides, through its subsidiaries, financial guarantee insurance and other financial services to both public and private clients worldwide.
www.ambac.com
Annual Revenues: $1.406 billion

President and Chief Exec. Officer
GENADER, Robert J. — Tel: (212) 668 - 0340; Fax: (212) 509 - 9190; TF: (800) 221 - 1854

Chairman of the Board
LASSITER, Phillip B. — Tel: (212) 668 - 0340; Fax: (212) 509 - 9190; TF: (800) 221 - 1854
plassiter@ambac.com

Main Headquarters
Mailing: One State St. Plaza, New York, NY 10004 — Tel: (212) 668 - 0340; Fax: (212) 509 - 9190; TF: (800) 221 - 1854

Corporate Foundations and Giving Programs

Ambac Financial Group, Inc. Corporate Contributions Program
Contact: Susan Oehrig
One State St. Plaza — Tel: (212) 668 - 0340
New York, NY 10004 — Fax: (212) 509 - 9190; TF: (800) 221 - 1854

Annual Grant Total: $500,000 - $750,000
Primary Interests: Arts and Culture; Community Affairs; Education; Youth Services
Recent Recipients: Alzheimer's Ass'n; American Cancer Society; American Diabetes Ass'n; American Foundation for AIDS Research; American Lung Ass'n; American Red Cross; Amnesty Internat'l; Anti-Defamation League; Boy Scouts of America; Common Sense for Animals; Doctors Without Borders; Habitat for Humanity; Jackie Robinson Foundation; Junior Achievement; Make-A-Wish Foundation; March of Dimes; Museum of Modern Art, The; Nat'l Audubon Soc.; Nat'l Park Foundation; Planned Parenthood Federation of America; Salvation Army; Seeing Eye Inc.; United Negro College Fund; YMCA

Public Affairs and Related Activities Personnel

At Headquarters

DOYLE, Kevin J. — Tel: (212) 208 - 3283; Fax: (212) 208 - 3558; TF: (800) 221 - 1854
Senior V. President, General Counsel and Internal Audit
kdoyle@ambac.com
Responsibilities include government relations.

GANDOLFO, Thomas J. — Tel: (212) 208 - 3349; Fax: (212) 509 - 9190; TF: (800) 221 - 1854
Senior V. President and Chief Financial Officer
tgandolfo@ambac.com
Responsibilities include investor relations.

OEHRIG, Susan — Tel: (212) 668 - 0340; Fax: (212) 509 - 9190; TF: (800) 221 - 1854
Chairman, Contributions Committee

POILLON, Peter R. — Tel: (212) 208 - 3333; Fax: (212) 208 - 3108; TF: (800) 221 - 1854
Managing Director, Investor Relations and Media Contact
ppoillon@ambac.com

AMBAC Inc.

See listing on page 27 under Ambac Financial Group, Inc.

AMC Entertainment Inc.

Owns and operates cinemas in the U.S., Japan, Portugal and Spain. Also known as American Multi-Cinema, Inc.
www.amctheatres.com
Annual Revenues: $1.34 billion

Chairman, President and Chief Exec. Officer
BROWN, Peter C. — Tel: (816) 221 - 4000; Fax: (816) 480 - 4617

Main Headquarters
Mailing: 920 Main St., Kansas City, MO 64105-2017 — Tel: (816) 221 - 4000; Fax: (816) 480 - 4617

Corporate Foundations and Giving Programs

AMC Corporate Contributions
P.O. Box 219430 — Tel: (816) 221 - 4000
Kansas City, MO 64121 — Fax: (816) 480 - 4725

Annual Grant Total: none reported
The company is in the process of establishing a new corporate charitable giving policy.

Public Affairs and Related Activities Personnel

At Headquarters

BELL, Melanie — Tel: (816) 480 - 2560; Fax: (816) 480 - 4617
Director, Corporate Communications
mbell@amctheatres.com

KOLEGA, Andra — Tel: (816) 221 - 4000; Fax: (816) 480 - 4617
V. President, Community Relations

RAMSEY, Craig R. — Tel: (816) 221 - 4000; Fax: (816) 480 - 4617
Chief Financial Officer
Responsibilities include investor relations.

Amcast Industrial Corporation

A manufacturer of light-alloy wheels, aluminum auto components, copper and brass fittings.
www.amcast.com
Annual Revenues: $423.9 million

Chairman, President and Chief Exec. Officer
POND, Byron O., Jr. — Tel: (937) 291 - 7000; Fax: (937) 291 - 7007
byron.pond@amcast.com

Main Headquarters
Mailing: 7887 Washington Village Dr., Dayton, OH 45459 — Tel: (937) 291 - 7000; Fax: (937) 291 - 7005

Corporate Foundations and Giving Programs

Amcast Industrial Foundation
Contact: Jo Francis
7887 Washington Village Dr. — Tel: (937) 291 - 7023
Dayton, OH 45459 — Fax: (937) 291 - 7007

Assets: $185,000 (2004)
Annual Grant Total: under $100,000
Geographic Preference: Area(s) in which the company operates
Primary Interests: Civic and Public Affairs; Higher Education
Recent Recipients: United Way

Public Affairs and Related Activities Personnel

At Headquarters

FRANCIS, Jo — Tel: (937) 291 - 7023; Fax: (937) 291 - 7007
Exec. Secretary
jo.francis@amcast.com
Responsibilities include corporate philanthropy.

HIGGINS, Michael R. — Tel: (937) 291 - 7015; Fax: (937) 291 - 7005
Treasurer
michael.higgins@amcast.com
Responsibilities include investor relations.

Amerada Hess Corp.

A producer, refiner and marketer of petroleum products.
www.hess.com
Annual Revenues: $13.4 billion

Amerada Hess Corp.

* continued from previous page

Chairman and Chief Exec. Officer
HESS, John B.
Tel: (212) 997 - 8500
Fax: (212) 536 - 8390

Main Headquarters
Mailing: 1185 Ave. of the Americas
New York, NY 10036
Tel: (212) 997 - 8500
Fax: (212) 536 - 8390

Corporate Foundations and Giving Programs

Amerada Hess Corporate Contributions Program
1185 Ave. of the Americas
New York, NY 10036
Tel: (212) 997 - 8500
Fax: (212) 536 - 8390

Annual Grant Total: none reported

Public Affairs and Related Activities Personnel

At Headquarters

BOHLING, B. J.
Senior V. President, Human Resources
Tel: (212) 536 - 8147
Fax: (212) 536 - 8318

BRESNICK, G. I.
V. President, Health, Safety and Environment
Tel: (212) 997 - 8500
Fax: (212) 536 - 8390

WILSON, Jay R.
V. President, Investor Relations
Responsbilities include corporate relations.
Tel: (212) 536 - 8940
Fax: (212) 536 - 8390

AMERCO

Holding company. Subsidiaries include U-Haul Internat'l, Oxford Life Insurance Co., Republic Western Insurance Co. and Amerco Real Estate Co.

www.amerco.com

Chairman and President
SHOEN, Edward "Joe"
Tel: (775) 688 - 6300
Fax: (775) 688 - 6338

Main Headquarters
Mailing: 1325 Airmotive Way, Suite 100
Reno, NV 89502-3239
Tel: (775) 688 - 6300
Fax: (775) 688 - 6338

Corporate Foundations and Giving Programs

Corporate Contributions Program
Contact: Joanne Fried
2727 N. Central Ave.
P.O. Box 21502
Phoenix, AZ 85004
Tel: (602) 263 - 6194
Fax: (602) 263 - 6772

Annual Grant Total: none reported
Primary Interests: Housing; Hunger; Social Services

Public Affairs and Related Activities Personnel

At Headquarters

KELLY, Henry P.
V. President, Human Resources
Tel: (775) 688 - 6300
Fax: (775) 688 - 6338

At Other Offices

CRAHAN, Pat
Director, Government Relations
(U-Haul Internat'l, Inc.)
2727 N. Central Ave.
P.O. Box 21502
Phoenix, AZ 85004
Tel: (602) 263 - 6804
Fax: (602) 263 - 6889

FLACHMAN, Jennifer
Director, Investor Relations
2727 N. Central Ave.
P.O. Box 21502
Phoenix, AZ 85004
Tel: (602) 263 - 6568
Fax: (602) 263 - 6772

FRIED, Joanne
Director, Media and Public Relations
(U-Haul Internat'l, Inc.)
2727 N. Central Ave.
P.O. Box 21502
Phoenix, AZ 85004
Tel: (602) 263 - 6194
Fax: (602) 263 - 6772

HEULE, Amber
Media and Public Relations Specialist
2727 N. Central Ave.
P.O. Box 21502
Phoenix, AZ 85004
Tel: (602) 263 - 6815
Fax: (602) 263 - 6889

Ameren Corp.

An electric utility formed from the merger of Union Electric Co. and CIPSCO Inc. Acquired Illinois Power Co. in October, 2004.

www.ameren.com
Annual Revenues: $5.16 billion

Chairman and Chief Exec. Officer
RAINWATER, Gary L.
Tel: (314) 621 - 3222
Fax: (314) 554 - 3066
TF: (800) 552 - 7583

Main Headquarters
Mailing: P.O. Box 66149
St. Louis, MO 63166-6149
Tel: (314) 621 - 3222
TF: (800) 552 - 7583

Street: One Ameren Plaza, 1901 Chouteau Ave.
St. Louis, MO 63103

Washington Office
Contact: Susan LaBombard
Mailing: 101 Constitution Ave. NW
Suite 800
Washington, DC 20001
Tel: (202) 742 - 4459
Fax: (202) 742 - 4458

Political Action Committees

Ameren Federal Political Action Committee (Ameren FedPAC)
Contact: Donna Bailey
607 E. Adams St.
Springfield, IL 62739
Tel: (217) 535 - 5025
Fax: (217) 535 - 5095

Contributions to Candidates: $30,000 (01/05 - 09/05)
Democrats: $5,500; Republicans: $24,500.

Principal Recipients

SENATE DEMOCRATS

HOUSE DEMOCRATS
Carnahan, Russ (MO) $2,000

SENATE REPUBLICANS
Talent, James (MO) $5,000

HOUSE REPUBLICANS
Blunt, Roy (MO) $5,000
Shimkus, John (IL) $4,000
Hulshof, Kenny (MO) $3,500
Akin, William Todd (MO) $2,000
LaHood, Ray (IL) $2,000

Corporate Foundations and Giving Programs

Ameren Corporate Giving Program
Contact: Otis Cowan
P.O. Box 66149
St. Louis, MO 63166-6149
Tel: (314) 554 - 4740
Fax: (314) 554 - 2888
TF: (800) 552 - 7583

Assets: $8,417,609 (2004)
Annual Grant Total: over $5,000,000
Geographic Preference: Illinois; Missouri
Primary Interests: Civic and Cultural Activities; Community Affairs; Education; Senior Citizens; Youth Services
Recent Recipients: St. Louis Symphony; United Way; YMCA

Public Affairs and Related Activities Personnel

At Headquarters

COWAN, Otis
Manager, Community Relations
Mailstop: MC100
Tel: (314) 554 - 4740
Fax: (314) 554 - 2888
TF: (800) 552 - 7583

GALLAGHER, Susan
Director, Corporate Communications
Mailstop: M/S 100
Tel: (314) 554 - 2175
Fax: (314) 554 - 2888
TF: (800) 552 - 7583

MARTIN, Donna
Senior V. President and Chief Human Resources Officer
Mailstop: MC 500
Tel: (314) 554 - 2454
Fax: (314) 992 - 6693
TF: (800) 552 - 7583

MENNE, Mike
V. President, Environmental Safety and Health
Tel: (314) 554 - 2816
Fax: (314) 554 - 4182
TF: (800) 552 - 7583

At Washington Office

LABOMBARD, Susan
Manager, Federal Legislative Affairs
Registered Federal Lobbyist.
Tel: (202) 742 - 4459
Fax: (202) 742 - 4458

At Other Offices

BAILEY, Donna
Legislative and Community Relations Supervisor, Contact, Ameren Federal Political Action Committee
607 E. Adams St.
Springfield, IL 62739
Tel: (217) 535 - 5025
Fax: (217) 535 - 5095

CLEARY, Michael B.
Supervisor, Corporate Communications
101 Madison St.
P.O. Box 780
Jefferson City, MO 65102
Tel: (573) 681 - 7137
Fax: (573) 681 - 7296

DUNCAN, Drue
Manager, Legislative Affairs
(AmerenUE)
101 Madison St.
P.O. Box 780
Jefferson City, MO 65102
Tel: (573) 681 - 7124
Fax: (573) 681 - 7296

MITCHELSON, Randy K.
Director, Government Relations
(AmerenCIPS)
607 E. Adams St.
Springfield, IL 62739
Tel: (217) 535 - 5059
Fax: (217) 535 - 5095

Ameren Corp.

• continued from previous page

O'BRIEN, Dan
Public Affairs Representative
(AmerenCIPS)
607 E. Adams St.
Springfield, IL 62739
Tel: (217) 535 - 5489
Fax: (217) 535 - 5095

SHEPPARD, George N.
Public Affairs Representative
(AmerenCIPS)
607 E. Adams St.
Springfield, IL 62739
Tel: (618) 993 - 4628
Fax: (618) 993 - 4610

SULLIVAN, Michael T.
Manager, Govenmental Relations
607 E. Adams St.
Springfield, IL 62739
Tel: (217) 535 - 5489
Fax: (217) 535 - 5095

AmerenCIPS

See listing on page 28 under Ameren Corp.

AmerenUE

See listing on page 28 under Ameren Corp.

America Online, Inc.

See listing on page 475 under Time Warner Inc.

America West Airlines

See listing on page 496 under US Airways Group, Inc.

American Airlines, Inc.

See listing on page 37 under AMR Corp.

American Axle and Manufacturing, Inc.

Specializes in automotive parts and accessories.

www.aam.com
Annual Revenues: $3.107 billion

Co-Founder, Chairman and Chief Exec. Officer
DAUCH, Richard E.
Tel: (313) 974 - 2000
Fax: (313) 758 - 3929

Main Headquarters
Mailing: One Dauch Dr.
Detroit, MI 48211
Tel: (313) 974 - 2000
Fax: (313) 758 - 3929

Public Affairs and Related Activities Personnel

At Headquarters

GRAY, Carrie L. P.
Director, Corporate Relations
grayc@aam.com
Tel: (313) 758 - 4880
Fax: (313) 758 - 3929

SON, Christopher M.
Director, Investor Relations
chris.son@aam.com
Tel: (313) 758 - 4814
Fax: (313) 758 - 3929

American Bankers Insurance Group

See listing on page 50 under Assurant.

American Century Cos., Inc.

A member of the Public Affairs Council. A financial investments firm.

www.americancentury.com
Annual Revenues: $1.11 billion

Chairman of the Board
STOWERS, James E., III
Tel: (816) 531 - 5575
Fax: (816) 340 - 7962
TF: (800) 345 - 2021

President and Chief Exec. Officer
LYONS, William M.
Tel: (816) 531 - 5575
Fax: (816) 340 - 7962
TF: (800) 345 - 2021

Main Headquarters
Mailing: 4500 Main St.
Kansas City, MO 64111
Tel: (816) 340 - 4200
Fax: (816) 340 - 7962
TF: (800) 345 - 2021

Political Action Committees

American Century Cos., Inc. PAC (AKA American Century Investments PAC)
Contact: William B. Bates
4500 Main St.
Kansas City, MO 64111
Tel: (816) 340 - 4066
Fax: (816) 344 - 4816
TF: (800) 345 - 2021

Contributions to Candidates: $7,000 (01/05 - 09/05)
Democrats: $3,000; Republicans: $4,000.

Principal Recipients

SENATE DEMOCRATS		HOUSE DEMOCRATS	
Carper, Thomas R (DE)	$1,000	Cleaver, Emanuel (MO)	$1,000
		Menendez, Robert (NJ)	$1,000

SENATE REPUBLICANS		HOUSE REPUBLICANS	
		Baker, Hugh (LA)	$1,000
		Blunt, Roy (MO)	$1,000
		Hulshof, Kenny (MO)	$1,000
		Royce, Ed Mr (CA)	$1,000

Corporate Foundations and Giving Programs

American Century Co. Foundation
Contact: Mary Jo Browne
4500 Main St.
Kansas City, MO 64111
Tel: (816) 531 - 5575
Fax: (816) 340 - 7962
TF: (800) 345 - 2021

Annual Grant Total: none reported

Primary Interests: Arts and Culture; Civic and Public Affairs; Education; Health and Human Services

Public Affairs and Related Activities Personnel

At Headquarters

BATES, William B.
V. President, Government Affairs
wbb@americancentury.com
Responsibilities include political action.
Tel: (816) 340 - 4066
Fax: (816) 344 - 4816
TF: (800) 345 - 2021

BROWNE, Mary Jo
Contact, American Century Co. Foundation
Tel: (816) 531 - 5575
Fax: (816) 340 - 7962
TF: (800) 345 - 2021

DOYLE, Chris
V. President, Public Relations
Tel: (816) 531 - 5575
TF: (800) 345 - 2021

WILLIAMS, Randy
Community Relations
Tel: (816) 531 - 5575
Fax: (816) 340 - 7962
TF: (800) 345 - 2021

American Crystal Sugar Co.

A member of the Public Affairs Council. An agricultural cooperative that specializes in sugar and sugar-based products and by-products.

www.crystalsugar.com
Annual Revenues: $866.4 million

Chairman of the Board
STADSTAD, G. Terry
Tel: (218) 236 - 4400
Fax: (218) 236 - 4485

Chief Exec. Officer
HORVATH, James
jhorvath@crystalsugar.com
Tel: (218) 236 - 4400
Fax: (218) 236 - 4718

Main Headquarters
Mailing: 101 N. Third St.
Moorhead, MN 56560-1990
Tel: (218) 236 - 4400
Fax: (218) 236 - 4485

Washington Office
Contact: Kevin S. Price
Mailing: 50 F St., NW
Suite 900
Washington, DC 20001
Tel: (202) 879 - 0804
Fax: (202) 626 - 8896

Political Action Committees

American Crystal Sugar PAC
Contact: Sam S. M. Wai
101 N. Third St.
Moorhead, MN 56560-1990
Tel: (218) 236 - 4400
Ext: 4430
Fax: (218) 236 - 4485

Contributions to Candidates: $278,681 (01/05 - 09/05)
Democrats: $169,500; Republicans: $106,000; Other: $3,181.

Principal Recipients

SENATE DEMOCRATS		HOUSE DEMOCRATS	
Casey, Bob (PA)	$5,000	Herseth, Stephanie (SD)	$10,000
Byrd, Robert C (WV)	$4,000	Melancon, Charlie (LA)	$10,000
Nelson, Bill (FL)	$2,500	Pomeroy, Earl (ND)	$7,000

SENATE REPUBLICANS		HOUSE REPUBLICANS	
Chambliss, Saxby (GA)	$5,000	Rehberg, Dennis (MT)	$10,000
Martinez, Mel (FL)	$5,000	Gutknecht, Gil (MN)	$9,000
Burns, Conrad (MT)	$3,500	Simpson, Michael (ID)	$6,000

Corporate Foundations and Giving Programs

American Crystal Sugar Corporate Contributions Program
Contact: Jeff Schweitzer
101 N. Third St.
Moorhead, MN 56560-1990
Tel: (218) 236 - 4400
Ext: 4492
Fax: (218) 236 - 4718

Annual Grant Total: none reported

American Crystal Sugar Co.

** continued from previous page*

Public Affairs and Related Activities Personnel

At Headquarters

SCHWEITZER, Jeff
Manager, Public Relations
Tel: (218) 236 - 4400 Ext: 4492
Fax: (218) 236 - 4718

Responsibilities include corporate philanthropy.

SMITH, Joel
Manager, Regulatory Affairs
jsmith@crystalsugar.com
Tel: (218) 236 - 4400 Ext: 4347
Fax: (218) 236 - 4388

WAI, Sam S. M.
Treasurer, American Crystal PAC
swai@crystalsugar.com
Tel: (218) 236 - 4400 Ext: 4430
Fax: (218) 236 - 4485

At Washington Office

PRICE, Kevin S.
Director, Government Affairs
kprice@crystalsugar.com
Registered Federal Lobbyist.
Tel: (202) 879 - 0804
Fax: (202) 626 - 8896

American Electric Power Co. Inc.

A multinational energy company. Acquired Central and South West Corp. in 2000.

www.aep.com
Annual Revenues: $61.25 billion

Chairman, President and Chief Exec. Officer
MORRIS, Michael G.
Tel: (614) 223 - 1000
Fax: (614) 223 - 1823

Main Headquarters
Mailing: One Riverside Plaza
Columbus, OH 43215-2373
Tel: (614) 223 - 1000
Fax: (614) 223 - 1823

Washington Office
Contact: Anthony P. Kavanagh
Mailing: 801 Pennsylvania Ave. NW
Suite 320
Washington, DC 20004
Tel: (202) 383 - 3430
Fax: (202) 383 - 3459

Political Action Committees

The American Electric Power Committee for Responsible Government
Contact: Doreen W. Hohl
One Riverside Plaza
Columbus, OH 43215-2373
Tel: (614) 223 - 1000
Fax: (614) 223 - 1823

Contributions to Candidates: $179,750 (01/05 - 09/05)

Democrats: $45,500; Republicans: $132,750; Other: $1,500.

Principal Recipients

SENATE DEMOCRATS		HOUSE DEMOCRATS	
		Boucher, Fredrick (VA)	$4,000
		Stupak, Bart (MI)	$4,000
		Towns, Edolphus (NY)	$3,000

SENATE REPUBLICANS		HOUSE REPUBLICANS	
Dewine, Richard (OH)	$5,000	Sullivan, John (OK)	$4,000
Inhofe, James M (OK)	$3,000	Barton, Joe L (TX)	$3,500
Talent, James (MO)	$3,000	McCrery, Jim (LA)	$3,000
Allen, George (VA)	$2,000	Pryce, Deborah (OH)	$3,000
Lugar, Richard G (IN)	$2,000		
Sununu, John (NH)	$2,000		
McConnell, Mitch (KY)	$1,500		

Corporate Foundations and Giving Programs

American Electric Power Contributions Program
Contact: Rody Woischke McCool
One Riverside Plaza
Columbus, OH 43215-2373
Tel: (614) 223 - 1697
Fax: (614) 223 - 1682

Annual Grant Total: $2,000,000 - $5,000,000

Geographic Preference: Arkansas; Indiana; Kentucky; Louisiana; Michigan; Ohio; Oklahoma; Tennessee; Texas; Virginia; West Virginia

Primary Interests: Community Development; Education; Environment/Conservation; Housing; Hunger; Safety; United Way Campaigns

Public Affairs and Related Activities Personnel

At Headquarters

FLORA, Terry
Public Affairs Contact
(AEP Ohio)
Tel: (614) 883 - 7999
Fax: (614) 223 - 1823

HAGELIN, David
Corporate Media Relations
Tel: (614) 223 - 1938
Fax: (614) 223 - 1823

HEMLEPP, Pat D.
Director, Corporate Media Relations
Tel: (614) 223 - 1620
Fax: (614) 223 - 1823

HOHL, Doreen W.
PAC Treasurer
Tel: (614) 223 - 1000
Fax: (614) 223 - 1823

MCCOOL, Rody Woischke
Contributions Administrator
Tel: (614) 223 - 1697
Fax: (614) 223 - 1682

MCHENRY, Melissa
Corporate Media Relations Contact
Tel: (614) 716 - 1120
Fax: (614) 223 - 1823

ROZSA, Bette Jo
Managing Director, Investor Relations
bjrozsa@aep.com
Tel: (614) 223 - 2840
Fax: (614) 223 - 2807

SLOAT, Julie
V. President, Investor Relations
Tel: (614) 716 - 2885
Fax: (614) 223 - 1823

At Washington Office

CAMPBELL, Sabrina V.
Director, Federal Agency Relations
Registered Federal Lobbyist.
Tel: (202) 628 - 1645
Fax: (202) 628 - 4276

HARTSOE, Joseph R.
V. President and Associate General Counsel, Federal Policy
Registered Federal Lobbyist.
Tel: (202) 383 - 3430
Fax: (202) 383 - 3459

KAVANAGH, Anthony P.
V. President, Governmental Affairs
Registered Federal Lobbyist.
Tel: (202) 383 - 3430
Fax: (202) 628 - 4276

MCBROOM, Marty
Director, Federal Environmental Affairs
Registered Federal Lobbyist.
Tel: (202) 383 - 3430
Fax: (202) 383 - 3459

At Other Offices

BRIAN, Mike
Public Affairs Contact
(Indiana Michigan Power Co.)
110 E. Wayne St.
Fort Wayne, IN 46802
Tel: (260) 425 - 2137

JONES, Larry
Public Affairs Contact
(AEP Texas)
400 W. 15th St.
Suite 1500
Austin, TX 78701
Tel: (512) 391 - 2970
Fax: (512) 391 - 2965

ROBINSON, Ronn
Manager, Corporate Communications
(Kentucky Power)
101A Enterprise Dr.
P.O. Box 5190
Frankfort, KY 40602
Tel: (502) 696 - 7003

SCHALK, Bill
Public Affairs Contact
(Indiana Michigan Power Co.)
110 E. Wayne St.
Fort Wayne, IN 46802
Tel: (269) 465 - 6101

WHITEFORD, Stan
Communications Consultant
(AEP Public Service Co. of Oklahoma)
P.O. Box 201
Tulsa, OK 74102
Tel: (918) 599 - 2574

American Express Co.

A member of the Public Affairs Council. American Express Co., founded in 1850, is a global travel, financial and network services provider.

www.americanexpress.com
Annual Revenues: $29.1 billion

Chairman and Chief Exec. Officer
CHENAULT, Kenneth I.
Tel: (212) 640 - 2000

Main Headquarters
Mailing: Three World Financial Center
200 Vesey St.
New York, NY 10285
Tel: (212) 640 - 2000

Washington Office
Mailing: 801 Pennsylvania Ave. NW
Suite 650
Washington, DC 20004
Tel: (202) 624 - 0761
Fax: (202) 624 - 0775

Political Action Committees

American Express Co. Political Action Committee
Three World Financial Center
200 Vesey St.
New York, NY 10285
Tel: (212) 640 - 2000

Contributions to Candidates: $79,500 (01/05 - 09/05)

Democrats: $40,500; Republicans: $39,000.

American Express Co.

** continued from previous page*

Principal Recipients

SENATE DEMOCRATS		HOUSE DEMOCRATS	
Carper, Thomas R (DE)	$5,000	Menendez, Robert (NJ)	$4,500
Lieberman, Joe (CT)	$5,000	Crowley, Joseph (NY)	$3,000
Nelson, Bill (FL)	$2,500	Matheson, James (UT)	$2,500
Conrad, Kent (ND)	$2,000	Meeks, Gregory W (NY)	$2,000
SENATE REPUBLICANS		**HOUSE REPUBLICANS**	
Santorum, Richard (PA)	$5,000	Oxley, Michael (OH)	$5,000
Bennett, Robert F (UT)	$4,000	Royce, Ed Mr (CA)	$4,000
Kyl, Jon L (AZ)	$4,000	Cantor, Eric (VA)	$2,500

Corporate Foundations and Giving Programs

American Express Philanthropic Program and Foundation
Contact: Connie Higginson
Three World Financial Center
200 Vesey St.
New York, NY 10285
Tel: (212) 640 - 4649
Fax: (212) 640 - 0325

Annual Grant Total: over $5,000,000

The American Express Philanthropic Program focuses on three themes: economic independence, cultural heritage, and community service. Guidelines and grant lists are available at www.americanexpress.com/corp/philanthropy

Geographic Preference: Area(s) in which the company operates; International; Arizona; Florida; North Carolina; New York; Utah

Primary Interests: Arts and Culture; Disaster Relief; Employment; Financial Planning; Historic Preservation

Recent Recipients: American Red Cross; Boys and Girls Club; United Negro College Fund

Public Affairs and Related Activities Personnel

At Headquarters

BAEZ, Diana
Coordinator, Corporate and Financial Public Relations
Tel: (212) 640 - 2000

HIGGINSON, Connie
President, American Express Philanthropic Program and Foundation
connie.higgenson@aexp.com
Tel: (212) 640 - 4649
Fax: (212) 640 - 0325

LEMSON, Steve D.
V. President, State Government Affairs
steve.lemson@aexp.com
Tel: (212) 640 - 5028

O.NEILL, Mike
Senior V. President, Corporate and Financial Public Relations
Tel: (212) 640 - 5951
Fax: (212) 640 - 0332

STOVALL, Ronald
Senior V. President, Investor Relations
ronald.stovall@aexp.com
Tel: (212) 640 - 5574

At Washington Office

CHRISTENSON, Arne L.
Senior V. President, Government Affairs
Registered Federal Lobbyist.
Tel: (202) 624 - 0761
Fax: (202) 624 - 0775

American Express Financial Advisors, Inc.

See listing on page 35 under Ameriprise Financial Services Inc.

American Express Travel Related Services

See listing on page 30 under American Express Co.

American Family Insurance

See listing on page 31 under American Family Insurance Group.

American Family Insurance Group

www.amfam.com
Annual Revenues: $6.6 billion

Chairman and Chief Exec. Officer
PIERCE, Harvey R.
Tel: (608) 249 - 4100 Ext: 30451
Fax: (608) 243 - 4928

Main Headquarters
Mailing: 6000 American Pkwy.
Madison, WI 53783
Tel: (608) 249 - 2111
Fax: (608) 243 - 4921

Political Action Committees

American Family Mutual Insurance Co. Federal PAC (AMFAM Federal PAC)
Contact: Mark Afable
6000 American Pkwy.
Madison, WI 53783
Tel: (608) 249 - 2111
Fax: (608) 245 - 8619

Contributions to Candidates: $7,000 (01/05 - 09/05)
Democrats: $3,000; Republicans: $4,000.

Principal Recipients

SENATE DEMOCRATS		HOUSE DEMOCRATS	
		Baldwin, Tammy (WI)	$1,000
		Kind, Ron (WI)	$1,000
		Moore, Gwen (WI)	$1,000
SENATE REPUBLICANS		**HOUSE REPUBLICANS**	
Talent, James (MO)	$1,000	Hulshof, Kenny (MO)	$1,000
		Petri, Thomas (WI)	$1,000
		Ryan, Paul D (WI)	$1,000

Corporate Foundations and Giving Programs

American Family Insurance Corporate Contributions
Contact: Judy K. Lowell
6000 American Pkwy.
Madison, WI 53783
Tel: (608) 242 - 4100
Fax: (608) 243 - 4928

Annual Grant Total: none reported

Public Affairs and Related Activities Personnel

At Headquarters

AFABLE, Mark
V. President, Government Affairs and Compliance
mafable@amfam.com
Responsibilities include political action.
Tel: (608) 249 - 2111
Fax: (608) 245 - 8619

CHVALA, Vicki
V. President, Human Resources
vchvala@amfam.com
Tel: (608) 249 - 2111
Fax: (608) 243 - 4928

FANSHAW, Lee
Counsel, Government Affairs
lfanshaw@amfam.com
Tel: (608) 249 - 2111
Fax: (608) 245 - 8619

LOWELL, Judy K.
Manager, Community Relations
jpowell@amfam.com
Tel: (608) 242 - 4100
Fax: (608) 243 - 4928

MOSLEY, Vanessa
Director, Consumer Affairs
Tel: (608) 249 - 2111
Fax: (608) 245 - 8619

MUTH, Ken
Director, Media Relations
Tel: (608) 242 - 4100
Fax: (608) 243 - 4921

American Financial Group Inc.

A financial services company specializing in private passenger automobile and specialty property casualty insurance; the sale of tax-deferred annuities; and life and health insurance products.
www.amfnl.com
Annual Revenues: $3.9 billion

Chairman of the Board
LINDNER, Carl H.
Tel: (513) 579 - 2121
Fax: (513) 579 - 2580

Co-Chief Exec. Officer
LINDNER, Carl H., III
Tel: (513) 579 - 2121
Fax: (513) 579 - 2580

Co-Chief Exec. Officer
LINDNER, S. Craig
Tel: (513) 579 - 2121
Fax: (513) 579 - 2580

Main Headquarters
Mailing: One E. Fourth St.
Cincinnati, OH 45202
Tel: (513) 579 - 2121
Fax: (513) 579 - 2580

Public Affairs and Related Activities Personnel

At Headquarters

WATSON, Anne N.
V. President, Investor Relations
(Great American Insurance Co.)
Tel: (513) 579 - 6652
Fax: (513) 579 - 2580

American Freightways

See listing on page 193 under FedEx Freight.

American General Corp.

See listing on page 12 under AIG American General Corp.

American General Life & Accident Insurance Co.

See listing on page 12 under AIG American General Corp.

American Greetings Corp.

A manufacturer and distributor of greeting cards and other consumer products.
www.americangreetings.com
Annual Revenues: $2.355 billion

Chairman of the Board
WEISS, Morry
Tel: (216) 252 - 7300
Fax: (216) 252 - 6778

Chief Exec. Officer
WEISS, Zev
Tel: (216) 252 - 7300
Fax: (216) 252 - 6778

Main Headquarters
Mailing: One American Rd.
Cleveland, OH 44144-2398
Tel: (216) 252 - 7300
Fax: (216) 252 - 6778

Corporate Foundations and Giving Programs

American Greetings Corp. Contributions Program

American Greetings Corp.

* continued from previous page

One American Rd. Tel: (216) 252 - 7300
Cleveland, OH 44144-2398 Fax: (216) 252 - 6778

Annual Grant Total: $1,000,000 - $2,000,000
Geographic Preference: Area(s) in which the company operates
Primary Interests: Community Development; Health; Higher Education; Women

Public Affairs and Related Activities Personnel

At Headquarters

HENRICHSEN, Laurie — Tel: (216) 252 - 4943
Consumer Media and Public Relations — Fax: (216) 252 - 6778
laurie.henrichsen@amgreetings.com

HOLIDAY, Sue — Tel: (800) 777 - 4891
Manager, Consumer Relations — Fax: (216) 252 - 6778

LEWIS, Jaye — Tel: (216) 252 - 7300
Trade Media and Public Relations Contact — Fax: (216) 252 - 6778

SMITH, Stephen J. — Tel: (216) 252 - 4864
V. President, Treasurer and Investor Relations — Fax: (216) 252 - 6778

American Home Products Corp.

See listing on page 526 under Wyeth.

American Honda Motor Co., Inc.

A member of the Public Affairs Council. Importer, distributor, and manufacturer of automobiles, motorcycles and power equipment.
www.honda.com

President and Chief Exec. Officer — Tel: (310) 783 - 2000
KONDO, Koichi — Fax: (310) 783 - 3900

Main Headquarters
Mailing: 1919 Torrance Blvd. — Tel: (310) 783 - 2000
Torrance, CA 90501-2746 — Fax: (310) 783 - 3900

Washington Office
Contact: Ed Cohen
Mailing: 1001 G St., NW — Tel: (202) 661 - 4400
Suite 950 — Fax: (202) 661 - 4459
Washington, DC 20001

Corporate Foundations and Giving Programs

American Honda Foundation
1919 Torrance Blvd. — Tel: (310) 783 - 2000
Torrance, CA 90501-2746 — Fax: (310) 783 - 3900

Annual Grant Total: none reported

Public Affairs and Related Activities Personnel

At Headquarters

ANTONIUS, Kurt — Tel: (310) 783 - 3170
Assistant V. President, Public Relations — Fax: (310) 783 - 3622
Mailstop: M/S 100-3C-2A
kurt_antonius@ahm.honda.com

CAREY, Kathryn — Tel: (310) 783 - 2000
Foundation Manager — Fax: (310) 783 - 3900
kathryn_carey@ahm.honda.com

SMITH, Jeffrey A. — Tel: (310) 781 - 5062
Assistant V. President, Corporate Affairs and Communications — Fax: (310) 787 - 4417
Mailstop: 100-3C-2A
jeffrey_smith@ahm.honda.com

At Washington Office

BRILLHART, Ember A. — Tel: (202) 661 - 4400
Senior Legislative Coordinator — Fax: (202) 661 - 4459
ember_brillhart@hma.honda.com
(Honda North America, Inc.)

CALPIN, Patrick — Tel: (202) 661 - 4400
Analyst, Government Relations — Fax: (202) 661 - 4459
patrick_calpin@hna.honda.com
(Honda North America, Inc.)
Registered Federal Lobbyist.

COHEN, Ed — Tel: (202) 661 - 4400
V. President, Government and Industry Relations — Fax: (202) 661 - 4459
Registered Federal Lobbyist.

DELLINGER, Kent — Tel: (202) 661 - 4400
Manager, Government Relations — Fax: (202) 661 - 4459
kent_dellinger@hna.honda.com
(Honda North America, Inc.)

GERKE, Scott A. — Tel: (202) 661 - 4400
Senior Analyst, Government Relations — Fax: (202) 661 - 4459
scott_gerke@hna.honda.com
(Honda North America, Inc.)
Registered Federal Lobbyist.

HARRINGTON, Toni — Tel: (202) 661 - 4400
Assistant V. President, Government and Industry Relations — Fax: (202) 661 - 4459
toni_harrington@hna.honda.com
(Honda North America, Inc.)
Registered Federal Lobbyist.

At Other Offices

MILLER, Ed — Tel: (937) 645 - 8789
Manager, Corporate Communications, Government Trade and Community — Fax: (937) 645 - 8787
(Honda of America Manufacturing, Inc.)
24000 Honda Pkwy.
Marysville, OH 43040

MORRISON, Mark — Tel: (205) 355 - 5000
Manager, Corporate Affairs and Communications — Fax: (205) 355 - 5020
(Honda Manufacturing of Alabama LLC)
1800 Honda Dr.
Lincoln, AL 35096

American Household, Inc.

See listing on page 267 under Jarden Corp.

American Internat'l Group, Inc.

A member of the Public Affairs Council. Major insurance industry holding company. Subsidiaries include Hartford Steam Boiler Inspection and Insurance Co. (see separate listing). Acquired American General Corp. in 2001.
www.aigcorporate.com
Annual Revenues: $97.9 billion

Interim Chairman of the Board — Tel: (212) 770 - 7000
ZARB, Frank G. — Fax: (212) 509 - 9705

President and Chief Executive Officer — Tel: (212) 770 - 7000
SULLIVAN, Martin J. — Fax: (212) 770 - 7821

Main Headquarters
Mailing: 70 Pine St. — Tel: (212) 770 - 7000
New York, NY 10270 — Fax: (212) 509 - 9705

Washington Office
Contact: L. Oakley Johnson
Mailing: 1399 New York Ave. NW — Tel: (202) 585 - 5800
Suite 900 — Fax: (202) 585 - 5820
Washington, DC 20005

Political Action Committees

American Internat'l Group, Inc. Employee Political Action Committee (AIG-EPAC)
Contact: Robert A. Gender
70 Pine St. — Tel: (212) 770 - 7000
New York, NY 10270 — Fax: (212) 509 - 9705

Contributions to Candidates: $56,100 (01/05 - 09/05)
Democrats: $40,100; Republicans: $16,000.

Principal Recipients

SENATE DEMOCRATS		HOUSE DEMOCRATS	
Clinton, Hillary Rodham (NY)	$7,000	Larson, John B (CT)	$5,000
Lieberman, Joe (CT)	$7,000	Weiner, Anthony (NY)	$2,500
Conrad, Kent (ND)	$5,000	Israel, Steve (NY)	$1,000
Nelson, Benjamin (NE)	$5,000	Matsui, Doris (CA)	$1,000
SENATE REPUBLICANS		**HOUSE REPUBLICANS**	
Kyl, Jon L (AZ)	$5,000	Biggert, Judy (IL)	$1,000
		Brady, Kevin Patrick (TX)	$1,000
		Cubin, Barbara L (WY)	$1,000
		Dewine, R. Pat (OH)	$1,000
		LaHood, Ray (IL)	$1,000
		Manzullo, Donald (IL)	$1,000

Corporate Foundations and Giving Programs

American International Group Corporate Giving Program
70 Pine St. — Tel: (212) 770 - 7000
New York, NY 10270 — Fax: (212) 509 - 9705

Annual Grant Total: none reported

Public Affairs and Related Activities Personnel

At Headquarters

CLOONAN, Edward T. — Tel: (212) 770 - 7887
V. President, Corporate Affairs — Fax: (212) 770 - 6786

FREUDMANN, Axel I. — Tel: (212) 770 - 7000
Senior V. President, Human Resources — Fax: (212) 742 - 2115

GENDER, Robert A. — Tel: (212) 770 - 7000
PAC Treasurer — Fax: (212) 509 - 9705

HAMRAH, Charlene M. — Tel: (212) 770 - 7070
V. President and Director, Investor Relations — Fax: (212) 425 - 3499

LEE, Edmund — Tel: (212) 770 - 6698
Assistant V. President, International and Corporate Affairs — Fax: (212) 770 - 6786

American Internat'l Group, Inc.

• continued from previous page

NORAT, Cecelia — Tel: (212) 770 - 7000
V. President, State Relations — Fax: (212) 770 - 7821

NORTON, Joe — Tel: (212) 770 - 3144
Director, Public Relations — Fax: (212) 770 - 7821

WINANS, Christopher — Tel: (212) 770 - 7000
V. President, Media Relations — Fax: (212) 509 - 9705

WISNER, Frank G. — Tel: (212) 770 - 7000
V. Chairman, External Affairs — Fax: (212) 770 - 7821

At Washington Office

CHIN, James — Tel: (202) 585 - 5800 — Fax: (202) 585 - 5820
Registered Federal Lobbyist.

DETMER, Kyra L. — Tel: (202) 585 - 5800
Director, Federal Government Affairs — Fax: (202) 585 - 5820
Registered Federal Lobbyist.

GALLAGHER, Shawn — Tel: (202) 585 - 5800 — Fax: (202) 585 - 5820
Registered Federal Lobbyist.

JOHNSON, L. Oakley — Tel: (202) 585 - 5800
Senior V. President, Corporate Affairs — Fax: (202) 585 - 5820
Registered Federal Lobbyist.

KEEGAN, Diana — Tel: (202) 585 - 5800 — Fax: (202) 585 - 5820
Registered Federal Lobbyist.

MERSKI, Richard P. — Tel: (202) 585 - 5807
V. President, Corporate Affairs — Fax: (202) 585 - 5820
Registered Federal Lobbyist.

MULVEY, Kevin C. W. — Tel: (202) 585 - 5800
Assistant V. President, International Government Affairs — Fax: (202) 585 - 5820
Registered Federal Lobbyist.

WELLING, Brad G. — Tel: (202) 585 - 5800
Assistant V. President, Federal Government Affairs — Fax: (202) 585 - 5820
Registered Federal Lobbyist.

American Medical Security Group, Inc.

A health-care benefits provider.
www.eams.com

Chairman, President and Chief Exec. Officer
MILLER, Samuel V. — Tel: (920) 661 - 1111 — Fax: (920) 661 - 2222 — TF: (800) 232 - 5432

Main Headquarters
Mailing: PO Box 19032, Green Bay, WI 54307 — Tel: (920) 661 - 1111 — Fax: (920) 661 - 2222 — TF: (800) 232 - 5432

Washington Office
Contact: Kristen Freites
Mailing: 4201 Wilson Blvd., Suite 110-492, Arlington, VA 22203 — Tel: (703) 243 - 0973 — Fax: (703) 243 - 5790

Political Action Committees

American Medical Security Group, Inc. PAC
Contact: James Prochnow
PO Box 19032
Green Bay, WI 54307 — Tel: (920) 661 - 1353 — Fax: (920) 661 - 2025 — TF: (800) 232 - 5432

Contributions to Candidates: none reported (01/05 - 09/05)

Corporate Foundations and Giving Programs

American Medical Security Group, Inc. Charitable Contributions
PO Box 19032
Green Bay, WI 54307 — Tel: (920) 661 - 1111 — Fax: (920) 661 - 2222 — TF: (800) 232 - 5432

Annual Grant Total: none reported
Recent Recipients: American Red Cross; Boys and Girls Club; Junior Achievement; United Way; YMCA

Public Affairs and Related Activities Personnel

At Headquarters

PROCHNOW, James — Tel: (920) 661 - 1353
PAC Treasurer — Fax: (920) 661 - 2025 — TF: (800) 232 - 5432

STEIL, Robert J. — Tel: (920) 661 - 1353
National Director, Government Affairs — Fax: (920) 661 - 2025 — TF: (800) 232 - 5432

WIRCH, John R. — Tel: (920) 661 - 1111
V. President, Human Resources — Fax: (920) 661 - 2222 — TF: (800) 232 - 5432

At Washington Office

FREITES, Kristen — Tel: (703) 243 - 0973
Senior Government Affairs Specialist — Fax: (703) 243 - 5790
Registered Federal Lobbyist.

American Multi-Cinema, Inc.

See listing on page 27 under AMC Entertainment Inc.

American Nat'l Insurance Co.

A whollyowned subsiy of PacifiCare HEalth Systems.
www.anico.com
Annual Revenues: $2.13 billion

Chairman and Chief Exec. Officer
MOODY, Robert L. — Tel: (409) 763 - 4661 — Fax: (409) 766 - 6933 — TF: (800) 899 - 6502

Main Headquarters
Mailing: One Moody Plaza, Galveston, TX 77550-7999 — Tel: (409) 763 - 4661 — Fax: (409) 766 - 6663 — TF: (800) 899 - 6502

Political Action Committees

American Nat'l Insurance Co. Employee PAC
Contact: Mark Flippin
One Moody Plaza
Galveston, TX 77550-7999 — Tel: (409) 766 - 6537 — Fax: (409) 766 - 6663 — TF: (800) 899 - 6502

Contributions to Candidates: none reported (01/05 - 09/05)

Public Affairs and Related Activities Personnel

At Headquarters

FLIPPIN, Mark — Tel: (409) 766 - 6537
Secretary — Fax: (409) 766 - 6663
mark.flippin@anico.com — TF: (800) 899 - 6502
Responsibilities include political action.

PAVLICEK, Steve — Tel: (409) 766 - 6447
Senior V. President and Controller — Fax: (409) 766 - 6933 — TF: (800) 899 - 6502
Responsibilities include investor relations.

TOLMAN, Gareth W. — Tel: (409) 766 - 6560
Senior V. President, Corporate Affairs — Fax: (409) 766 - 6663
gary.tolman@anico.com — TF: (800) 899 - 6502
Responsibilities include political action.

American Power Conversion Corp.

www.apcc.com
Annual Revenues: $1.7 billion

Chairman, President and Chief Exec. Officer
DOWDELL, Rodger B., Jr. — Tel: (401) 789 - 5735 — Fax: (401) 789 - 3710 — TF: (800) 788 - 2208

Main Headquarters
Mailing: 132 Fairgrounds Rd., West Kingston, RI 02892 — Tel: (401) 789 - 5735 — Fax: (401) 789 - 3710 — TF: (800) 788 - 2208

Corporate Foundations and Giving Programs

American Power Conversion Corp. Corporate Contributions Program
132 Fairgrounds Rd.
West Kingston, RI 02892 — Tel: (401) 789 - 5735 — Fax: (401) 789 - 3710 — TF: (800) 788 - 2208

Annual Grant Total: none reported
Grants made only to 501(c)(3) organizations. Guidelines and an application can be obtained at www.apcc.com/corporate/contributions.cfm.
Geographic Preference: Area(s) in which the company operates
Primary Interests: Education; Math and Science; Technology

Public Affairs and Related Activities Personnel

At Headquarters

DAVIS, Aaron L. — Tel: (401) 789 - 5735
V. President, Marketing Communications — Fax: (401) 789 - 3710 — TF: (800) 788 - 2208
Responsibilities include media relations.

American President Cos., Ltd.

See listing on page 42 under APL Americas.

American Savings Bank, F.S.B.

See listing on page 236 under Hawaiian Electric Industries, Inc.

American Security Group

See listing on page 50 under Assurant.

American Standard Companies Inc.

A diversified manufacturer of plumbing, air conditioning, and transportation equipment.
www.americanstandard.com
Annual Revenues: $9.5 billion

Chairman and Chief Exec. Officer
POSES, Frederic M. — Tel: (732) 980 - 6000 Fax: (732) 980 - 3340

Main Headquarters
Mailing: One Centennial Ave.
PO Box 6820
Piscataway, NJ 08854
Tel: (732) 980 - 6000 Fax: (732) 980 - 3340

Washington Office
Contact: James E. Wolf
Mailing: 1501 Lee Hwy.
Suite 140
Arlington, VA 22209-1109
Tel: (703) 525 - 4015 Fax: (703) 525 - 0327

Corporate Foundations and Giving Programs
American Standard Foundation
Contact: R. Scott Massengill
One Centennial Ave.
PO Box 6820
Piscataway, NJ 08854
Tel: (732) 980 - 6000 Fax: (732) 980 - 3340

Annual Grant Total: $2,000,000 - $5,000,000
Giving includes employee matching gifts aid to educational programs and scholarships for children of employees under the Nat'l Merit Scholarship program.
Geographic Preference: Area(s) in which the company operates
Primary Interests: Health; Social Services; United Way Campaigns
Recent Recipients: American Red Cross; Nat'l Merit Scholarship

Public Affairs and Related Activities Personnel

At Headquarters

COSTELLO, Lawrence B.
Senior V. President, Human Resources
Tel: (732) 980 - 3000 Fax: (732) 980 - 3335

FISHER, R. Bruce
V. President, Strategic Planning and Investor Relations
bfisher@americanstandard.com
Tel: (732) 980 - 6095 Fax: (732) 980 - 3335

GLOVER, Lisa
Director, Media Relations
lglover@americanstandard.com
Tel: (732) 980 - 6048 Fax: (732) 980 - 3335

LONDON, Shelly J.
V. President and Chief Communications Officer
slondon@americanstandard.com
Tel: (732) 980 - 6175 Fax: (732) 980 - 3335

MASSENGILL, R. Scott
V. President, Treasurer and Contact, Corporate Foundation
Tel: (732) 980 - 6000 Fax: (732) 980 - 3340

At Washington Office

MODI, David T.
V. President, Government and Public Affairs
Registered Federal Lobbyist.
Tel: (703) 525 - 4015 Fax: (703) 525 - 0327

WOLF, James E.
V. President
asdwolf@aol.com
Tel: (703) 525 - 4015 Fax: (703) 525 - 0327

American Stock Exchange

A wholly-owned subsidiary of the Nat'l Ass'n of Securities Dealers, Inc. (NASD).
www.amex.com
Annual Revenues: $287.1 million

Chairman and Chief Executive Officer
WOLKOFF, Neal L. — Tel: (212) 306 - 1000 Fax: (212) 306 - 1152

Main Headquarters
Mailing: 86 Trinity Pl.
New York, NY 10006
Tel: (212) 306 - 1000 Fax: (212) 306 - 1152

Political Action Committees
American Stock Exchange Federal PAC
Contact: J. Bruce Ferguson
86 Trinity Pl.
New York, NY 10006
Tel: (212) 306 - 1403 Fax: (212) 306 - 1152

Contributions to Candidates: none reported (01/05 - 09/05)

Corporate Foundations and Giving Programs
American Stock Exchange Corporate Giving Program
86 Trinity Pl.
New York, NY 10006
Tel: (212) 306 - 1000 Fax: (212) 306 - 1152

Annual Grant Total: $300,000 - $400,000
Donations are made primarily to causes and organizations in New York City.
Primary Interests: Arts and Culture; Community Development; Education; Minority Opportunities; Urban Affairs; Women; Youth Services

Public Affairs and Related Activities Personnel

At Headquarters

CHUNG, Mary
Media Contact
mary.chung@amex.com
Tel: (212) 306 - 1641 Fax: (212) 306 - 1152

DAVID, Javier
Media Contact
Tel: (212) 306 - 1440 Fax: (212) 306 - 1152

FERGUSON, J. Bruce
Associate General Counsel
Responsibilities include political action.
Tel: (212) 306 - 1403 Fax: (212) 306 - 1152

American United Life Insurance Co.

See listing on page 34 under American United Life Insurance Co.

American United Life Insurance Co.

Formerly American United Life Insurance Co.
www.oneamerica.com
Annual Revenues: $1.004 billion

Chairman of the Board
SEMLER, Jerry D. — Tel: (317) 285 - 1877 Fax: (317) 285 - 1979

President and Chief Exec. Officer
MOLENDORP, Dayton H. — Tel: (317) 285 - 1370 Fax: (317) 285 - 1979

Main Headquarters
Mailing: P.O. Box 368
Indianapolis, IN 46206-0368
Tel: (317) 285 - 1877 Fax: (317) 285 - 1979
Street: One American Square
Indianapolis, IN 46282

Political Action Committees
American United Life Insurance Co. PAC
Contact: Ron Fritz
P.O. Box 368
Indianapolis, IN 46206-0368
Tel: (317) 285 - 1877 Fax: (317) 285 - 1979

Contributions to Candidates: none reported (01/05 - 09/05)

Corporate Foundations and Giving Programs
OneAmerica Foundation
Contact: Jerry D. Semler
P.O. Box 368
Indianapolis, IN 46206-0368
Tel: (317) 285 - 1877 Fax: (317) 285 - 1979

Annual Grant Total: $1,000,000 - $2,000,000
Primary Interests: Education; Health and Human Services

Public Affairs and Related Activities Personnel

At Headquarters

FREEMAN, James W.
V. President, Community Affairs
jim_freeman@aul.com
Tel: (317) 285 - 1609 Fax: (317) 285 - 1979

FRITZ, Ron
PAC Contact
Tel: (317) 285 - 1877 Fax: (317) 285 - 1979

YAMASAKI, Vicki
V. President, Planning and Communications
Tel: (317) 285 - 1877 Fax: (317) 285 - 1979

AmeriCredit Corp.

An auto finance company.
www.americredit.com
Annual Revenues: $1.2 billion

Chairman and Chief Exec. Officer
MORRIS, Clifton H., Jr. — Tel: (817) 302 - 7000 Fax: (817) 302 - 7479 TF: (800) 644 - 2297

Main Headquarters
Mailing: 801 Cherry St.
Suite 3900
Fort Worth, TX 76102-6803
Tel: (817) 302 - 7000 Fax: (817) 302 - 7479 TF: (800) 644 - 2297

Political Action Committees
AmeriCredit Corp. PAC
Contact: Chris A. Choate
801 Cherry St.
Suite 3900
Fort Worth, TX 76102-6803
Tel: (817) 302 - 7000 Fax: (817) 302 - 7479 TF: (800) 644 - 2297

Contributions to Candidates: none reported (01/05 - 09/05)

Corporate Foundations and Giving Programs
AmeriCredit Community Investment
Contact: John Hoffmann
801 Cherry St.
Suite 3900
Fort Worth, TX 76102-6803
Tel: (817) 302 - 7627 Fax: (817) 302 - 7479 TF: (800) 644 - 2297

Annual Grant Total: none reported
Geographic Preference: Canada; National
Recent Recipients: March of Dimes; Salvation Army; Susan G. Komen Breast Cancer Foundation; United Way

AmeriCredit Corp.

* continued from previous page

Public Affairs and Related Activities Personnel

At Headquarters

ALLEN, Amy
Manager, Public Relations
amy.allen@americredit.com
Tel: (817) 302 - 7423
Fax: (817) 302 - 7479
TF: (800) 644 - 2297

CHOATE, Chris A.
Chief Financial Officer, Chief Legal Officer, and PAC Treasurer
Tel: (817) 302 - 7000
Fax: (817) 302 - 7479
TF: (800) 644 - 2297

DEYOUNG, Caitlin
V. President, Investor Relations
Tel: (817) 302 - 7394
Fax: (817) 302 - 7479
TF: (800) 644 - 2297

HOFFMANN, John
V. President, Public Relations and Communication
john.hoffmann@americredit.com
Tel: (817) 302 - 7627
Fax: (817) 302 - 7479
TF: (800) 644 - 2297

LANDKAMER, Jason
Assistant V. President, Investor Relations
Tel: (817) 302 - 7811
Fax: (817) 302 - 7479
TF: (800) 644 - 2297

Ameriprise Financial Services Inc.

American Express Financial Advisors, Inc., the company spun off from American Express in September 2005. A financial services company.

www.ameriprise.com
Annual Revenues: $6.172 billion

Chairman and Chief Exec. Officer
CRACCHIOLO, James C.
Tel: (612) 671 - 3131
Fax: (612) 671 - 2741
TF: (800) 328 - 8300

Main Headquarters
Mailing: 50606 AXP Financial Center
Minneapolis, MN 55474
Tel: (612) 671 - 3131
Fax: (612) 671 - 2741
TF: (800) 328 - 8300

Washington Office
Mailing: 801 Pennsylvania Ave. NW
Suite 650
Washington, DC 20004
Tel: (202) 624 - 0761
Fax: (202) 624 - 0775

Political Action Committees

Ameriprise Financial PAC
Contact: Brian Pietsch
801 Pennsylvania Ave. NW
Suite 650
Washington, DC 20004
Tel: (202) 624 - 0761
Fax: (202) 624 - 0775

Contributions to Candidates: none reported (01/05 - 09/05)

Corporate Foundations and Giving Programs

Ameriprise Minnesota Philanthropic Program
Contact: Terry Williams
50606 AXP Financial Center
Minneapolis, MN 55474
Tel: (612) 671 - 3131
Fax: (612) 671 - 5112
TF: (800) 328 - 8300

Annual Grant Total: over $5,000,000
Geographic Preference: Minnesota
Primary Interests: Arts and Culture; Community Affairs; Economic Development
Recent Recipients: Minneapolis Institute of Arts; Minnesota Orchestra; WomenVenture; YouthLink

Public Affairs and Related Activities Personnel

At Headquarters

AUSTIN, Susan
Manager, Public Affairs and Communications
susan.2.austin@ameriprise.com
Tel: (612) 671 - 1359
Fax: (612) 671 - 5112
TF: (800) 328 - 8300

CONNOLLY, Steven
Manager, Public Affairs and Communications
steven.x.connolly@ameriprise.com
Tel: (612) 671 - 4146
Fax: (612) 671 - 5112
TF: (800) 328 - 8300

HUNTER, Kelli A.
Exec. V. President, Human Resources
Tel: (612) 671 - 3131
Fax: (612) 671 - 2741
TF: (800) 328 - 8300

JOHNSON, Paul
Director, Public Affairs and Communications
paul.w.johnson@ameriprise.com
Tel: (612) 671 - 0625
Fax: (612) 671 - 5112
TF: (800) 328 - 8300

MILLER, Jean
Manager, Public Affairs and Communications
jean.m.miller@ameriprise.com
Tel: (612) 671 - 1933
Fax: (612) 671 - 5112
TF: (800) 328 - 8300

VANDRISSE, Peg
Manager, Regulatory Affairs
Tel: (612) 671 - 3541
Fax: (612) 671 - 2741
TF: (800) 328 - 8300

WILLIAMS, Terry
Director, Community Relations Program
Tel: (612) 671 - 3131
Fax: (612) 671 - 5112
TF: (800) 328 - 8300

At Washington Office

PIETSCH, Brian
V. President, State Government Relations
Mailstop: Unit 53
Responsibilities include political action.
Tel: (202) 624 - 0761
Fax: (202) 624 - 0775

AmeriSource Bergen Corp.

A member of the Public Affairs Council. Formed from the merger of Bergen Brunswig Corp. and AmeriSource Health Corp. A wholesale distributor of specialty healthcare products and pharmaceuticals.

www.amerisourcebergen.net
Annual Revenues: $21 billion

Chief Exec. Officer
YOST, R. David
Tel: (610) 727 - 7000
Fax: (610) 727 - 3600
TF: (800) 829 - 3132

Main Headquarters
Mailing: 1300 Morris Dr.
Suite 100
Chesterbrook, PA 19087-5594
Tel: (610) 727 - 7000
Fax: (610) 727 - 3600
TF: (800) 829 - 3132

Washington Office
Mailing: 1666 K St. NW
Suite 500
Washington, DC 20006
Tel: (202) 887 - 1469

Political Action Committees

AmeriSource Bergen PAC (ABC PAC)
Contact: Jack Quinn
1300 Morris Dr.
Suite 100
Chesterbrook, PA 19087-5594
Tel: (610) 727 - 7000
Fax: (610) 727 - 3600
TF: (800) 829 - 3132

Contributions to Candidates: $22,750 (01/05 - 09/05)
Republicans: $22,750.

Principal Recipients

SENATE REPUBLICANS		HOUSE REPUBLICANS	
Santorum, Richard (PA)	$3,500	Johnson, Nancy (CT)	$5,000
Grassley, Charles (IA)	$2,500	Whitfield, Ed (KY)	$5,000
Hatch, Orrin (UT)	$1,000	Deal, Nathan (GA)	$2,500
		Gerlach, Jim (PA)	$2,250
		Hart, Melissa (PA)	$1,000

Public Affairs and Related Activities Personnel

At Headquarters

BRUNGESS, Barbara A.
Manager, Corporate and Investor Relations
bbrungess@amerisourcebergen.com
Tel: (610) 727 - 7199
Fax: (610) 727 - 3603
TF: (800) 829 - 3132

FISHER, Jeanne
Senior V. President, Human Resources
Tel: (610) 727 - 7000
Fax: (610) 727 - 3600
TF: (800) 829 - 3132

KILPATRIC, Mike N.
V. President, Corporate and Investor Relations
mkilpatric@amerisourcebergen.com
Tel: (610) 727 - 7118
Fax: (610) 727 - 3603
TF: (800) 829 - 3132

LORD, Nat
Director, Legislative Government Affairs
Tel: (610) 727 - 7000
Fax: (610) 727 - 3600
TF: (800) 829 - 3132

QUINN, Jack
PAC Treasurer
Tel: (610) 727 - 7000
Fax: (610) 727 - 3600
TF: (800) 829 - 3132

At Washington Office

JOHNSON, Melinda
Director, Government Affairs
Registered Federal Lobbyist.
Tel: (202) 887 - 1469

NORTON, Rita
V. President, Government Affairs
Registered Federal Lobbyist.
Tel: (202) 887 - 1469

Ameristar Casinos, Inc.

A hotel and casino operator.

www.ameristarcasinos.com
Annual Revenues: $698 million

Ameristar Casinos, Inc.
* continued from previous page

Chairman, President, and Chief Exec. Officer Tel: (702) 567 - 7000
NEILSEN, Craig H. Fax: (702) 369 - 8860

Main Headquarters
Mailing: 3773 Howard Hughes Pkwy. Tel: (702) 567 - 7000
Suite 490 Fax: (702) 369 - 8860
Las Vegas, NV 89109-0949

Public Affairs and Related Activities Personnel

At Headquarters

CALLAHAN, Kathleen B. Tel: (702) 567 - 7053
Director, Communications Fax: (702) 369 - 8860
kathy.callahan@ameristar.com

KANOFSKY, Gordon R. Tel: (702) 567 - 7000
Exec. V. President Fax: (702) 369 - 8860
Responsibilities include government and legal affairs.

STEINBAUER, Tom Tel: (702) 567 - 7000
Senior V. President, Finance and Chief Financial Officer Fax: (702) 369 - 8860
Responsibilities include investor relations.

AmeriSteel Corp.
See listing on page 219 under Gerdau Ameristeel Corp.

Ameritech Illinois
See listing on page 423 under SBC Illinois.

Ameritrade Holding Corp.
Provides brokerage products and services.
www.ameritradeholding.com
Annual Revenues: $880 million

Chairman of the Board Tel: (402) 597 - 5658
RICKETTS, J. Joe Fax: (402) 597 - 7789
TF: (800) 237 - 8692

Chief Exec. Officer Tel: (402) 597 - 5658
MOGLIA, Joseph H. Fax: (402) 597 - 7789
TF: (800) 237 - 8692

Main Headquarters
Mailing: 4211 S. 102nd St. Tel: (402) 597 - 5658
Omaha, NE 68127-1031 Fax: (402) 597 - 7789
TF: (800) 237 - 8692

Political Action Committees

Ameritrad PAC
Contact: Phylis M. Esposito
4211 S. 102nd St. Tel: (402) 597 - 5658
Omaha, NE 68127-1031 Fax: (402) 597 - 7789
TF: (800) 237 - 8692

Contributions to Candidates: $2,000 (01/05 - 09/05)
Democrats: $2,000.

Principal Recipients

SENATE DEMOCRATS		HOUSE DEMOCRATS	
Nelson, Benjamin (NE)	$2,000		

Public Affairs and Related Activities Personnel

At Headquarters

ESPOSITO, Phylis M. Tel: (402) 597 - 5658
Chief Stategy Officer Fax: (402) 597 - 7789
TF: (800) 237 - 8692

KUSH, Donna Tel: (402) 827 - 8931
Managing Director, Corporate Communications Fax: (402) 597 - 7789
dkush@ameritrade.com TF: (800) 237 - 8692

PLEISS, Dave Tel: (402) 597 - 5658
Director, Investor Relations Fax: (402) 597 - 7789
dpleiss@ameritrade.com TF: (800) 237 - 8692

AmerUs Group
www.amerus.com
Annual Revenues: $1.615 billion

Chairman and Chief Exec. Officer Tel: (515) 362 - 3600
BROOKS, Roger K.

Main Headquarters
Mailing: 699 Walnut St. Tel: (515) 362 - 3600
Des Moines, IA 50309

Political Action Committees

AmerUs Group PAC
Contact: James A. Smallenberger
699 Walnut St. Tel: (515) 362 - 3600
Des Moines, IA 50309

Contributions to Candidates: $2,000 (01/05 - 09/05)
Democrats: $2,000.

Principal Recipients

SENATE DEMOCRATS		HOUSE DEMOCRATS	
Nelson, Benjamin (NE)	$1,000	Pomeroy, Earl (ND)	$1,000

Corporate Foundations and Giving Programs

AmerUs Group Charitable Foundation
699 Walnut St. Tel: (515) 362 - 3600
Des Moines, IA 50309

Assets: $5,785,3590
Annual Grant Total: none reported
More information on the foundation is available at www.amerus.com.
Geographic Preference: Iowa

Public Affairs and Related Activities Personnel

At Headquarters

CELANDER, Jeananne Tel: (515) 362 - 3600
Director, Corporate Relations and Assistant Corporate Secretary
Mailstop: Suite 2000

SMALLENBERGER, James A. Tel: (515) 362 - 3600
Contact, Political Action

Ametek, Inc.
A manufacturer of electric motors for vacuum cleaners and related appliances; instruments for aerospace, process control and industrial markets; and specialty metals.
www.ametek.com
Annual Revenues: $1.04 billion

Chairman and Chief Exec. Officer Tel: (610) 647 - 2121
HERMANCE, Frank S. Fax: (610) 323 - 9337
TF: (800) 473 - 1286

Main Headquarters
Mailing: 37 N. Valley Rd., Bldg. Four Tel: (610) 647 - 2121
P.O. Box 1764 Fax: (610) 323 - 9337
Paoli, PA 19301 TF: (800) 473 - 1286

Corporate Foundations and Giving Programs

The Ametek Foundation
Contact: Kathy Londra
37 N. Valley Rd., Bldg. Four Tel: (610) 647 - 2121
P.O. Box 1764 Fax: (610) 323 - 9337
Paoli, PA 19301 TF: (800) 473 - 1286

Assets: $8,000,000 (2001)
Annual Grant Total: $750,000 - $1,000,000
Geographic Preference: Area(s) in which the company operates; National
Primary Interests: Arts and Culture; Community Affairs; Higher Education; Medical Research; Medicine and Health Care; Youth Services

Public Affairs and Related Activities Personnel

At Headquarters

BURKE, William F. Tel: (610) 647 - 2121
V. President, Investor and Corporate Relations Fax: (610) 323 - 9337
bill.burke@ametek.com TF: (800) 473 - 1286

LONDRA, Kathy Tel: (610) 647 - 2121
Administrator, The Ametek Foundation Fax: (610) 323 - 9337
kathy.londra@ametek.com TF: (800) 473 - 1286

MCKINLEY, James P. Tel: (610) 889 - 5234
Manager, Corporate Communications Fax: (610) 323 - 9337
jim.mckinley@ametek.com TF: (800) 473 - 1286

WEAVER, John Tel: (610) 647 - 2121
V. President, Human Resources Fax: (610) 323 - 9337
john.weaver@ametek.com TF: (800) 473 - 1286

Amgen Inc.
A biotechnology company. Acquired Immunex Corp. in July of 2002.
www.amgen.com
Annual Revenues: $3.763 billion

Chairman, President and Chief Exec. Officer Tel: (805) 447 - 1000
SHARER, Kevin Fax: (805) 499 - 3507
kevins@amgen.com

Main Headquarters
Mailing: One Amgen Center Dr. Tel: (805) 447 - 1000
Thousand Oaks, CA 91320-1799 Fax: (805) 447 - 1010

Washington Office
Mailing: 555 13th St. NW Tel: (202) 585 - 9610
Suite 600 West
Washington, DC 20004

Political Action Committees

Amgen Inc. Political Action Committee
Contact: Rodger Currie
555 13th St. NW Tel: (202) 585 - 9610
Suite 600 West
Washington, DC 20004

Amgen Inc.

• continued from previous page

Contributions to Candidates: $155,500 (01/05 - 09/05)

Democrats: $48,000; Republicans: $107,500.

Principal Recipients

SENATE DEMOCRATS		HOUSE DEMOCRATS	
Kennedy, Ted (MA)	$8,000		
Carper, Thomas R (DE)	$5,000		
Conrad, Kent (ND)	$5,000		
Feinstein, Dianne (CA)	$5,000		

SENATE REPUBLICANS		HOUSE REPUBLICANS	
Dewine, Richard (OH)	$10,000	Cantor, Eric (VA)	$10,000
Santorum, Richard (PA)	$8,000	DeLay, Tom (TX)	$8,000
Thomas, Craig (WY)	$5,000	Feeney, Tom (FL)	$5,000
		Hastert, Dennis J. (IL)	$5,000
		Johnson, Nancy (CT)	$5,000
		McCrery, Jim (LA)	$5,000
		Rogers, Michael J (MI)	$5,000

Corporate Foundations and Giving Programs

Amgen Foundation
One Amgen Center Dr.
Thousand Oaks, CA 91320-1799
Tel: (805) 447 - 1000
Fax: (805) 447 - 1010

Annual Grant Total: $750,000 - $1,000,000

Gives mainly to non-profit organizations in Ventura County, California.

Geographic Preference: California

Primary Interests: Arts and Culture; Education; Environment/Conservation; Math and Science; Medicine and Health Care; Social Services

Public Affairs and Related Activities Personnel

At Headquarters

DAVIS, Kristin
Media Relations Contact
Tel: (805) 447 - 1000
Fax: (805) 447 - 1010

MCNAMEE, Brian
Senior V. President, Human Resources
brianm@amgen.com
Tel: (805) 447 - 1000
Fax: (805) 499 - 3507

PIANO, Phyllis J.
V. President, Corporate Communications and Philanthropy
Tel: (805) 447 - 1000
Fax: (805) 447 - 1010

SOOD, Arvind
V. President, Investor Relations
Tel: (805) 447 - 1060
Fax: (805) 447 - 1010

SPEAR, Jonathan B.
V. President, Public Policy
Tel: (805) 447 - 1000
Fax: (805) 447 - 1010

At Washington Office

ATORCHA, L. Nicole
Manager, Federal Government Affairs
nickiea@amgen.com
Registered Federal Lobbyist.
Tel: (202) 585 - 9610

BEIER, David W.
Senior V. President, Global Government Affairs
Registered Federal Lobbyist.
Tel: (202) 585 - 9610

CHEN, Kenneth
Director, Advocacy and Allied Development
Tel: (202) 585 - 9610

CURRIE, Rodger
V. President, Federal Government Affairs
Registered Federal Lobbyist.
Responsibilities include political action.
Tel: (202) 585 - 9610

GUARDUCCI, Mara
Director, Government Affairs
Registered Federal Lobbyist.
Tel: (202) 585 - 9610

LINTHICUM, Kimberly
Registered Federal Lobbyist.
Tel: (202) 585 - 9610

NOGUCHI, Phil
Director, Regulatory Development
Tel: (202) 585 - 9610

OFMAN, Joshua J.
V. President, Reimbursement and Payment Policy
Registered Federal Lobbyist.
Tel: (202) 585 - 9610

OLSEN, Scott
Director, Government Affairs
Registered Federal Lobbyist.
Tel: (202) 585 - 9610

SWIRE, Andrew
Associate Director, Government Relations
Registered Federal Lobbyist.
Tel: (202) 585 - 9610

Amkor Technology, Inc.

A supplier of outsourced packaging and test semiconductor interconnect services.

www.amkor.com

Annual Revenues: $1.517 billion

Chairman and Chief Exec. Officer
KIM, James J.
Tel: (480) 821 - 5000
Fax: (480) 821 - 8276

Main Headquarters
Mailing: 1900 S. Price Rd.
Chandler, AZ 85248-1604
Tel: (480) 821 - 5000
Fax: (480) 821 - 8276

Public Affairs and Related Activities Personnel

At Headquarters

LUTH, Jeff
V. President, Corporate Communications
jluth@amkor.com
Responsibilities include investor relations.
Tel: (480) 821 - 2408
Ext: 5130
Fax: (480) 821 - 1713

AMP Incorporated

See listing on page 483 under Tyco Electronics Corp.

Ampco-Pittsburgh Corp.

A manufacturer of air handling equipment and steel products.

www.ampcopgh.com

Annual Revenues: $219.2 million

Chairman and Chief Exec. Officer
PAUL, Robert A.
rpaul@ampcopgh.com
Tel: (412) 456 - 4453
Fax: (412) 456 - 4404

Main Headquarters
Mailing: 600 Grant St., Suite 4600
Pittsburgh, PA 15219
Tel: (412) 456 - 4400
Fax: (412) 456 - 4404

Corporate Foundations and Giving Programs

Fair Oaks Foundation, Inc.
Contact: Rose Hoover
600 Grant St., Suite 4600
Pittsburgh, PA 15219
Tel: (412) 456 - 4418
Fax: (412) 456 - 4404

Assets: $5,511,230 (2002)

Annual Grant Total: $400,000 - $500,000

Geographic Preference: New York; Pennsylvania; Virginia

Primary Interests: Arts and Humanities; Community Development; Education; Health and Human Services; Religion

Recent Recipients: Cornell University; Harvard University; United Way

Public Affairs and Related Activities Personnel

At Headquarters

HOOVER, Rose
V. President and Corporate Secretary
rhoover@ampcopgh.com
Responsibilities include corporate philanthropy.
Tel: (412) 456 - 4418
Fax: (412) 456 - 4404

SCHULTZ, Robert F.
V. President, Industrial Relations; and Senior Counsel
rschultz@ampcopgh.com
Tel: (412) 456 - 4491
Fax: (412) 456 - 4404

AMR Corp.

The parent company of American Airlines, Inc.

www.aa.com

Annual Revenues: $18.9 billion

Chairman, President and Chief Exec. Officer
ARPEY, Gerard J.
Tel: (817) 963 - 1234
Fax: (817) 967 - 2523

Main Headquarters
Mailing: P.O. Box 619616
Dallas-Fort Worth Airport, TX 75261
Street: 4333 Amon Carter Blvd.
Fort Worth, TX 76155
Tel: (817) 963 - 1234
Fax: (817) 967 - 2523

Washington Office
Contact: William K. Ris, Jr.
Mailing: 1101 17th St. NW
Suite 600
Washington, DC 20036
Tel: (202) 496 - 5654
Fax: (202) 496 - 5660

Political Action Committees

American Airlines PAC
Contact: Norma H. Kaehler
1101 17th St. NW
Suite 600
Washington, DC 20036
Tel: (202) 496 - 5654
Fax: (202) 496 - 5660

Contributions to Candidates: $81,500 (01/05 - 09/05)

Democrats: $26,000; Republicans: $54,500; Other: $1,000.

AMR Corp.

• continued from previous page

Principal Recipients

SENATE DEMOCRATS		HOUSE DEMOCRATS	
Nelson, Bill (FL)	$2,500	Carnahan, Russ (MO)	$3,000
		Johnson, Eddie (TX)	$3,000
		Meeks, Gregory W (NY)	$2,500
SENATE REPUBLICANS		**HOUSE REPUBLICANS**	
Burns, Conrad (MT)	$5,000	Graves, Sam (MO)	$3,000
Hutchison, Kay Bailey (TX)	$3,000	Knollenberg, Joe (MI)	$3,000
Talent, James (MO)	$2,000		

Corporate Foundations and Giving Programs

AMR/American Airlines Foundation
Contact: Kathy Andersen
P.O. Box 619616 — Tel: (817) 967 - 3545
Dallas-Fort Worth Airport, TX 75261 — Fax: (817) 967 - 9784

Annual Grant Total: $1,000,000 - $2,000,000
Geographic Preference: Area(s) in which the company operates; Dallas, TX; Chicago, IL; Miami, FL; Ft. Worth, TX; San Juan, PR
Primary Interests: Arts and Culture; Environment/Conservation; Health and Human Services; Higher Education
Recent Recipients: Cystic Fibrosis Foundation; Susan G. Komen Breast Cancer Foundation; United Negro College Fund

Public Affairs and Related Activities Personnel

At Headquarters

ANDERSEN, Kathy — Tel: (817) 967 - 3545
Administrator, AMR/American Airlines Foundation — Fax: (817) 967 - 9784
Mailstop: MD 5575
kathy.andersen@aa.com

BECKER, Alton W. — Tel: (817) 967 - 1577
Managing Director, Corporate Communications — Fax: (817) 967 - 3816
al.becker@aa.com

BONANNO, Kathy — Tel: (817) 963 - 1234
Director, Investor Relations — Fax: (817) 967 - 2523

BRUNDAGE, Jeffrey J. — Tel: (817) 963 - 1234
Senior V. President, Human Resources — Fax: (817) 967 - 2523
(American Airlines, Inc.)

CARPENTER, John A. — Tel: (817) 967 - 1575
V. President, Corporate Affairs — Fax: (817) 967 - 1477
(American Airlines, Inc.)
Mailstop: MD 5575

FRIZZELL, Roger — Tel: (817) 963 - 1234
V. President, Corporate Communications — Fax: (817) 967 - 2523
(American Airlines, Inc.)

HAGAN, Daniel B. — Tel: (817) 967 - 2340
Managing Director, Corporate Affairs — Fax: (817) 967 - 1477
Mailstop: MD 5575
dan.hagan@aa.com

HOTARD, John — Tel: (817) 967 - 1577
Manager, Corporate Communications — Fax: (817) 967 - 3816
Mailstop: MD 5575
john.hotard@aa.com

At Washington Office

ELWELL, Dan — Tel: (202) 496 - 5654
Managing Director, International and Government Affairs — Fax: (202) 496 - 5660
(American Airlines, Inc.)
Registered Federal Lobbyist.

FISHER, Kevin — Tel: (202) 496 - 5654
Legislative Coordinator — Fax: (202) 496 - 5660
(American Airlines, Inc.)
Registered Federal Lobbyist.

KAEHLER, Norma H. — Tel: (202) 496 - 5654
Managing Director, Government Affairs and Contact, American Airlines PAC — Fax: (202) 496 - 5660
(American Airlines, Inc.)
Registered Federal Lobbyist.

LE POCHAT, Joe — Tel: (202) 496 - 5654
Managing Director, International and Government Affairs — Fax: (202) 496 - 5660
(American Airlines, Inc.)
Registered Federal Lobbyist.

NELSON, Carl A. — Tel: (202) 496 - 5654
Associate General Counsel — Fax: (202) 496 - 5660

RIS, William K., Jr. — Tel: (202) 496 - 5666
Senior V. President, Government Affairs — Fax: (202) 496 - 5660
(American Airlines, Inc.)
Registered Federal Lobbyist.

At Other Offices

FAGAN, Mary Frances — Tel: (773) 686 - 5614
Manager, Corporate Communications
(American Airlines, Inc.)
Box 66065, O'Hare Airport
Chicago, IL 60666
mary.frances.fagan@aa.com

HOOD, William L. — Tel: (847) 928 - 5437
Managing Director, Corporate Affairs — Fax: (847) 928 - 5695
(American Airlines, Inc.)
9525 W. Bryn Mawr Ave.
Suite 700
Rosemont, IL 60018
bill.hood@aa.com

WHITE, Dawn B. — Tel: (305) 520 - 3233
Managing Director, Corporate Affairs — Fax: (305) 520 - 3404
(American Airlines, Inc.)
999 Ponce de Leon Blvd.
Suite 610
Coral Gables, FL 33134
dawn.white@aa.com

Amsted Industries Inc.

A diversified manufacturer of products for the railroad, construction and building markets and general industry.
www.amsted.com
Annual Revenues: $1.65 billion

Chairman, President, and Chief Exec. Officer — Tel: (312) 645 - 1700
REUM, W. Robert — Fax: (312) 819 - 8420

Main Headquarters
Mailing: 180 N. Stetson St. — Tel: (312) 645 - 1700
Suite 1800 — Fax: (312) 819 - 8420
Chicago, IL 60601

Corporate Foundations and Giving Programs

Amsted Industries Foundation
Contact: Shirley J. Whitesell
180 N. Stetson St. — Tel: (312) 819 - 8515
Suite 1800 — Fax: (312) 819 - 8423
Chicago, IL 60601

Assets: $1,620,457 (2003)
Annual Grant Total: $300,000 - $400,000
Beginning in 1993, Amsted changed its foundation focus, emphasizing its Matching Gifts program. Therefore, the Foundation is no longer accepting proposals for funding.
Geographic Preference: National; Area(s) in which the company operates
Primary Interests: Arts and Culture; Education; Health and Human Services

Public Affairs and Related Activities Personnel

At Headquarters

WHITESELL, Shirley J. — Tel: (312) 819 - 8515
V. President, People — Fax: (312) 819 - 8423
Responsibilities include corporate philanthropy.

Amtrak

An intercity passenger rail company.
www.amtrak.com
Annual Revenues: $2.1 billion

Chairman of the Board — Tel: (202) 906 - 3000
LANEY, David M. — Fax: (202) 906 - 3865

President and Chief Exec. Officer — Tel: (202) 906 - 3960
GUNN, David L. — Fax: (202) 906 - 3865

Main Headquarters
Mailing: 60 Massachusetts Ave. NE — Tel: (202) 906 - 3000
Washington, DC 20002 — Fax: (202) 906 - 3865

Public Affairs and Related Activities Personnel

At Headquarters

BOURNE, Frances — Tel: (202) 906 - 3000
Director, Intergovernmental Relations — Fax: (202) 906 - 3865

BRESS, Joseph M. — Tel: (202) 906 - 3000
V. President, Labor Relations — Fax: (202) 906 - 3865

GREEN, Lorraine A. — Tel: (202) 906 - 3000
V. President, Human Resources — Fax: (202) 906 - 3865

LEONARD, Scott — Tel: (202) 906 - 3000
Government Affairs Specialist — Fax: (202) 906 - 3865

MASON, Marcus — Tel: (202) 906 - 3000
Senior Director, Government Affairs - House — Fax: (202) 906 - 3865

MCHUGH, Joseph H. — Tel: (202) 906 - 3867
V. President, Government Affairs and Policy — Fax: (202) 906 - 3865

NIELSON, Caroline — Tel: (202) 906 - 3000
Senior Director, Government Affairs - Senate — Fax: (202) 906 - 3865

SABIN, Joshua — Tel: (202) 906 - 3000
Senior Government Affairs Officer-Midwest — Fax: (202) 906 - 3865

Amtrak

** continued from previous page*

SCHULZ, William — Tel: (202) 906 - 3000
Chief, Corporate Communications — Fax: (202) 906 - 3865

WARREN, Mitch — Tel: (202) 906 - 3000
Senior Director, National State Relations — Fax: (202) 906 - 3865

At Other Offices

COHEN, Peter — Tel: (212) 630 - 6373
Director, Government Affairs - Northeast
(AMTRAK Northeast)
400 W. 31st St.
PSCC Bldg. 5 North
New York, NY 10001

CUBE, Antonio — Tel: (510) 238 - 4360
Director, Government Affairs - West
(AMTRAK West)
530 Water St.
Fifth Floor
Oakland, CA 94607

LANG, Ray — Tel: (312) 880 - 5233
Director, Government Affairs - Midwest — Fax: (312) 880 - 5167
525 W. Van Buren St.
Chicago, IL 60607

AMTRAK Northeast

See listing on page 38 under Amtrak.

AMTRAK West

See listing on page 38 under Amtrak.

Amway Corp.

See listing on page 24 under Alticor Inc.

Anacomp, Inc.

A provider of technology outsourcing services and document imaging solutions.

www.anacomp.com
Annual Revenues: $184 million

President and Chief Exec. Officer — Tel: (858) 716 - 3400
CRAMER, Jeffrey R. — Fax: (858) 716 - 3775
TF: (800) 350 - 3044

Main Headquarters
Mailing: 15378 Ave. of Science — Tel: (858) 716 - 3400
San Diego, CA 92128 — Fax: (858) 716 - 3775
TF: (800) 350 - 3044

Public Affairs and Related Activities Personnel

At Headquarters

FOX, Linster — Tel: (858) 716 - 3400
Chief Financial Officer — Fax: (858) 716 - 3775
lfox@anacomp.com — TF: (800) 350 - 3044

ROCHE, Martin J. "Frank" — Tel: (858) 716 - 3400
Exec. V. President and General Manager, International — Fax: (858) 716 - 3775
TF: (800) 350 - 3044

Anadarko Petroleum Corp.

A petroleum exploration and production company. Merged with Union Pacific Resources Co. in 2000.

www.anadarko.com
Annual Revenues: $5 billion

Chairman of the Board — Tel: (832) 636 - 1000
ALLISON, Robert J., Jr.
robert_allison@anadarko.com

President and Chief Exec. Officer — Tel: (832) 636 - 1000
HACKETT, James T.

Main Headquarters
Mailing: 1201 Lake Robbins Dr. — Tel: (832) 636 - 1000
The Woodlands, TX 77380

Washington Office
Contact: Gregory M. Pensabene
Mailing: 800 Connecticut Ave. NW — Tel: (202) 861 - 8064
Suite 700 — Fax: (202) 861 - 8065
Washington, DC 20006

Political Action Committees

Anadarko Petroleum Corp. Political Action Committee
Contact: Albert L. Richey
1201 Lake Robbins Dr. — Tel: (832) 636 - 1000
The Woodlands, TX 77380

Contributions to Candidates: $44,500 (01/05 - 09/05)
Democrats: $2,000; Republicans: $42,500.

Principal Recipients

SENATE REPUBLICANS		HOUSE REPUBLICANS	
Lott, Trent (MS)	$5,000	Barton, Joe L (TX)	$5,000
Burns, Conrad (MT)	$4,000	Pombo, Richard (CA)	$4,000
Thomas, Craig (WY)	$4,000	DeLay, Tom (TX)	$2,500
Hutchison, Kay Bailey (TX)	$3,000		
Talent, James (MO)	$3,000		

Corporate Foundations and Giving Programs

Anadarko Petroleum Corp. Contributions Program
Contact: Margaret Cooper
1201 Lake Robbins Dr. — Tel: (832) 636 - 8355
The Woodlands, TX 77380

Annual Grant Total: none reported

Public Affairs and Related Activities Personnel

At Headquarters

COOPER, Margaret — Tel: (832) 636 - 8355
Senior Community and Public Affairs Coordinator
margaret_cooper@anadarko.com
Responsibilities include corporate philanthropy and media relations.

LARSON, David R. — Tel: (832) 636 - 3265
V. President, Investor Relations
david_larson@anadarko.com

LAWRENCE, Stewart — Tel: (832) 636 - 3326
Manager, Investor Relations
stewart_lawrence@anadarko.com

LEONARD, K. — Tel: (832) 636 - 3594
Senior Corporate Communications Advisor

LEWIS, Richard A. — Tel: (832) 636 - 1000
V. President, Human Resources
richard_lewis@anadarko.com

REEVES, Robert K. — Tel: (832) 636 - 1000
Senior V. President, Corporate Affairs and Law

RICHEY, Albert L. — Tel: (832) 636 - 1000
V. President and Treasurer; Treasurer, Anadarko Petroleum Corp. Political Action Committee

WONG, Teresa — Tel: (832) 636 - 1203
Manager, Public Affairs and Corporate Communications
teresa_wong@anadarko.com

At Washington Office

PENSABENE, Gregory M. — Tel: (202) 861 - 5918
V. President, Government Relations — Fax: (202) 861 - 8065
Registered Federal Lobbyist.

At Other Offices

HANLEY, Mark — Tel: (907) 273 - 6310
Manager, Public Affairs - Alaska
3201 C St.
Suite 603
Anchorage, AK 99503

ROBITAILLE, Rick — Tel: (307) 232 - 9505
Manager, Public Affairs - Western Division
P.O. Box 50648
Casper, WY 82605

Analog Devices, Inc.

A manufacturer of precision, high-performance linear, digital and mixed signal integrated circuits used in analog and digital signal processing applications.

www.analog.com
Annual Revenues: $2.6 billion

Chairman of the Board — Tel: (781) 329 - 4700
STATA, Ray — Fax: (781) 326 - 8703
TF: (800) 262 - 5643

President and Chief Exec. Officer — Tel: (781) 329 - 4700
FISHMAN, Jerald G. — Fax: (781) 326 - 8703
TF: (800) 262 - 5643

Main Headquarters
Mailing: One Technology Way — Tel: (781) 329 - 4700
P.O. Box 9106 — Fax: (781) 326 - 8703
Norwood, MA 02062-9106 — TF: (800) 262 - 5643

Corporate Foundations and Giving Programs

Analog Devices Corporate Contributions Program

Analog Devices, Inc.
* continued from previous page

One Technology Way — Tel: (781) 329 - 4700
P.O. Box 9106 — Fax: (781) 326 - 8703
Norwood, MA 02062-9106 — TF: (800) 262 - 5643

Annual Grant Total: $1,000,000 - $2,000,000
Geographic Preference: Area(s) in which the company operates
Primary Interests: Arts and Culture; Community Affairs; Health; Higher Education

Public Affairs and Related Activities Personnel

At Headquarters

TAGLIAFERRO, Maria — Tel: (781) 461 - 3282
Director, Corporate Communications — Fax: (781) 461 - 3638
maria.tagliaferra@analog.com — TF: (800) 262 - 5643

Andersen Corp.
Manufacturer of vinyl-clad wood window units and patio doors.
www.andersenwindows.com
Annual Revenues: $2 billion

Chairman of the Board — Tel: (651) 264 - 5150
GAROFALO, Donald L.

President and Chief Exec. Officer — Tel: (651) 264 - 5150
HUMPHREY, James E.

Main Headquarters
Mailing: 100 Fourth Ave. North — Tel: (651) 264 - 5150
Bayport, MN 55003-1096

Corporate Foundations and Giving Programs

Bayport Foundation
Contact: Susan Roeder
100 Fourth Ave. North — Tel: (651) 264 - 7432
Bayport, MN 55003-1096

Annual Grant Total: none reported
Geographic Preference: Area in which the company is headquartered; Minnesota
Recent Recipients: Habitat for Humanity; Minnesota Children's Museum

Public Affairs and Related Activities Personnel

At Headquarters

EINCK, Stacy — Tel: (651) 264 - 5150
Manager, Public Affairs

MCDONOUGH, Maureen — Tel: (651) 264 - 5287
Director, Corporate Communications
maureen.mcdonough@andersencorp.com

ROEDER, Susan — Tel: (651) 264 - 7432
Manager, Community Relations and Public Affairs
susan.roeder@andersencorp.com

SNYDER, Cameron — Tel: (651) 264 - 5881
Manager, Brand Public Relations
cameron.snyder@andersencorp.com

Anderson Exploration
See listing on page 157 under Devon Energy Corp.

The Andersons, Inc.
www.andersonsinc.com

Chairman of the Board — Tel: (419) 893 - 5050
ANDERSON, Richard P. — Fax: (419) 891 - 6670

President and Chief Exec. Officer — Tel: (419) 893 - 5050
ANDERSON, Michael J. — Fax: (419) 891 - 6670

Main Headquarters
Mailing: P.O. Box 119 — Tel: (419) 893 - 5050
Maumee, OH 43537 — Fax: (419) 891 - 6655
Street: 480 W. Dussel Dr.
Maumee, OH 43537

Corporate Foundations and Giving Programs

Anderson Foundation
Contact: Dale W. Fallat
P.O. Box 119 — Tel: (419) 891 - 6474
Maumee, OH 43537 — Fax: (419) 891 - 6695

Annual Grant Total: $500,000 - $750,000
Geographic Preference: Illinois; Indiana; Michigan; Ohio; Area(s) in which the company operates
Primary Interests: Arts and Culture; Higher Education; Youth Services
Recent Recipients: United Way; YMCA

Public Affairs and Related Activities Personnel

At Headquarters

ANDERSON, Thomas H. — Tel: (419) 891 - 6405
Chairman, Anderson Foundation — Fax: (419) 891 - 6695

FALLAT, Dale W. — Tel: (419) 891 - 6474
V. President, Corporate Services — Fax: (419) 891 - 6695
dale_fallat@andersoninc.com
Responsibilities include corporate contributions.

GALLAGHER, Charles E. — Tel: (419) 893 - 5050
V. President, Human Resources — Fax: (419) 891 - 6655

SMITH, Gary L. — Tel: (419) 891 - 6417
V. President, Finance and Treasurer, Anderson Foundation — Fax: (419) 891 - 6655
gary_smith@andersonsinc.com
Responsibilities include investor relations.

Andrew Corp.
A leading supplier of communications equipment, systems and service, Andrew serves its global customer base by managing a network of manufacturing, sales and distribution facilities with 71 locations in 29 countries. Major markets are wireless communications (cellular, personal communications services and land mobile radio), fixed-line and broadband wireless telecommunication networks, broadcast and government.
www.andrew.com
Annual Revenues: $1.84 billion

Chairman of the Board — Tel: (708) 349 - 3300
NICHOLAS, Charles R. — Fax: (708) 349 - 5444

President and Chief Exec. Officer — Tel: (708) 349 - 3300
FAISON, Ralph E. — Fax: (708) 349 - 5444

Main Headquarters
Mailing: 10500 W. 153rd St. — Tel: (708) 349 - 3300
Orland Park, IL 60462 — Fax: (708) 349 - 5444

Public Affairs and Related Activities Personnel

At Headquarters

ASPAN, Rick — Tel: (708) 349 - 5166
Director, Public Relations — Fax: (708) 349 - 5444
rick.aspan@andrew.com

QUINN-QUINTIN, Karen A. — Tel: (708) 349 - 3300
V. President and Chief Human Resources Officer — Fax: (708) 349 - 5444

Andrx Corp.
Manufactures and distributes oral and injectible pharmaceuticals.
www.andrx.com

Chairman of the Board — Tel: (954) 584 - 0300
DUBOW, Lawrence J. — Fax: (954) 382 - 7729
TF: (800) 621 - 7143

Chief Exec. Officer and Director — Tel: (954) 584 - 0300
RICE, Thomas P. — Fax: (954) 792 - 1034
TF: (800) 621 - 7143

Main Headquarters
Mailing: 4955 Orange Dr. — Tel: (954) 584 - 0300
Davie, FL 33314 — Fax: (954) 382 - 7729
TF: (800) 621 - 7143

Public Affairs and Related Activities Personnel

At Headquarters

WATKINS, Ian J. — Tel: (954) 584 - 0300
Senior V. President, Human Resources — Fax: (954) 792 - 1034
TF: (800) 621 - 7143

At Other Offices

TOMEK, Allison — Tel: (954) 382 - 7696
Manager, Investor Relations — Fax: (954) 382 - 7729
8151 Peters Rd.
Fourth Floor
Plantation, FL 33324
allison.tomek@andrx.com
Responsibilities include media relations.

Angelica Corp.
Provides textile services to healthcare institutions.
www.angelica.com
Annual Revenues: $316.1 million

Chairman of the Board — Tel: (314) 854 - 3800
HUBBLE, Don W. — Fax: (314) 854 - 3890

Chief Exec. Officer — Tel: (314) 854 - 3800
O'HARA, Stephen M. — Fax: (314) 854 - 3890

Main Headquarters
Mailing: 424 S. Woods Mill Rd. — Tel: (314) 854 - 3800
Chesterfield, MO 63017 — Fax: (314) 854 - 3890

Public Affairs and Related Activities Personnel

At Headquarters

SHAFFER, James W. — Tel: (314) 854 - 3800
V. President and Chief Financial Officer — Fax: (314) 854 - 3890
Serves as the senior public affairs executive at company headquarters.

Anheuser-Busch Cos., Inc.

A member of the Public Affairs Council. A brewing company.
www.anheuser-busch.com
Annual Revenues: $14.9 billion

Chairman of the Board
BUSCH, August A., III — Tel: (314) 577 - 2000 Fax: (314) 577 - 2900

President and Chief Exec. Officer
STOKES, Patrick T. — Tel: (314) 577 - 2000 Fax: (314) 577 - 2900

Main Headquarters
Mailing: One Busch Pl.
St. Louis, MO 63118-1852 — Tel: (314) 577 - 2000 Fax: (314) 577 - 2900

Washington Office
Contact: Michael F. Roche
Mailing: 1401 I St. NW
Suite 200
Washington, DC 20005 — Tel: (202) 293 - 9494 Fax: (202) 223 - 9594

Political Action Committees

Anheuser-Busch Cos. Inc. Political Action Committee (AB-PAC)
Contact: William E. Kimmins, Jr.
One Busch Pl.
St. Louis, MO 63118-1852 — Tel: (314) 577 - 2329 Fax: (314) 577 - 7622

Contributions to Candidates: $273,774 (01/05 - 09/05)
Democrats: $81,825; Republicans: $190,949; Other: $1,000.

Principal Recipients

SENATE DEMOCRATS		HOUSE DEMOCRATS	
Baucus, Max (MT)	$5,000	Menendez, Robert (NJ)	$5,000
Nelson, Bill (FL)	$5,000	Sanchez, Loretta (CA)	$5,000
		Sires, Albio (NJ)	$5,000
SENATE REPUBLICANS		**HOUSE REPUBLICANS**	
Hatch, Orrin (UT)	$10,000	Hastert, Dennis J. (IL)	$10,000
Talent, James (MO)	$10,000	Akin, William Todd (MO)	$5,500
Harris, Katherine (FL)	$5,000	Boehner, John (OH)	$5,000
Martinez, Mel (FL)	$5,000	Bonilla, Henry (TX)	$5,000
Thomas, Craig (WY)	$5,000	Hulshof, Kenny (MO)	$5,000
Vitter, David (LA)	$5,000	Tiberi, Patrick (OH)	$5,000

Corporate Foundations and Giving Programs

Anheuser-Busch Charitable Trust & Anheuser-Busch Foundation
Contact: Carol Hennemann
One Busch Pl.
St. Louis, MO 63118-1852 — Tel: (314) 577 - 2000 Fax: (314) 577 - 2900

Annual Grant Total: over $5,000,000
Geographic Preference: Area(s) in which the company operates
Primary Interests: Arts and Culture; Environment/Conservation; Health and Human Services; Higher Education; Minority Opportunities; Youth Services
Recent Recipients: Boys and Girls Club; United Way; YWCA

Public Affairs and Related Activities Personnel

At Headquarters

BROWN, JoBeth — Tel: (314) 577 - 3314 Fax: (314) 577 - 3251
V. President; Corporate Secretary and; Chair, Contributions Committee

CASTELLANO, Joseph P. — Tel: (314) 577 - 2000 Fax: (314) 577 - 2900
V. President, Corporate Human Resources

FORTH, Rodney D. — Tel: (314) 577 - 4618 Fax: (314) 765 - 9190
Region V. President, Government Affairs

HENNEMANN, Carol — Tel: (314) 577 - 2000 Fax: (314) 577 - 2900
Contact, Charitable Contributions

JACOB, John E. — Tel: (314) 577 - 2000 Fax: (314) 577 - 2900
Exec. V. President, Global Communications

KATZ, Francine I. — Tel: (314) 577 - 9744 Fax: (314) 577 - 3194
V. President, Communications and Consumer Affairs

KIMMINS, William E., Jr. — Tel: (314) 577 - 2329 Fax: (314) 577 - 7622
V. President and Treasurer
Responsibilities include political action.

LAMBRIGHT, Stephen K. — Tel: (314) 577 - 2000 Fax: (314) 577 - 2900
Group V. President and Senior Counsel
Responsibilities include public affairs.

MCKINNEY, Lewis P. — Tel: (314) 577 - 7066 Fax: (314) 577 - 7616
Region Director, Government Affairs

MCLOUGHLIN, Peter C. — Tel: (314) 577 - 2000 Fax: (314) 577 - 2900
V. President, Corporate Media

VOGT, Terry — Tel: (314) 577 - 2000 Fax: (314) 577 - 2900
V. President, Communications

At Washington Office

HEFFERNAN, Barbara D. — Tel: (202) 293 - 9494 Fax: (202) 223 - 9594
Director, National Government Affairs
Registered Federal Lobbyist.

LOPEZ, Johann — Tel: (202) 293 - 9494 Fax: (202) 223 - 9594
Region Director, Government Affairs

MCCARTHY, Daniel M. — Tel: (202) 293 - 9494 Fax: (202) 223 - 9594
Director, National Government Affairs
Registered Federal Lobbyist.

ROCHE, Michael F. — Tel: (202) 293 - 9494 Fax: (202) 223 - 9594
V. President, National Affairs
Registered Federal Lobbyist.

ZASTROW, Katja — Tel: (202) 293 - 9494 Fax: (202) 223 - 9594
Region Director, Government Affairs

At Other Offices

BALDONADO, Andrew — Tel: (818) 908 - 5507 Fax: (818) 908 - 5695
Region V. President, Government Affairs
15800 Roscoe Blvd.
Van Nuys, CA 91406-1379

GREER, Curtis — Tel: (973) 424 - 5341 Fax: (973) 994 - 2286
Region Director, Government Affairs
300 U.S. Hwy. One
Newark, NJ 07114

Anixter Internat'l, Inc.

A distributor of communications components.
www.anixter.com
Annual Revenues: $2.5 billion

Chairman of the Board
ZELL, Samuel — Tel: (224) 521 - 8000

President and Chief Exec. Officer
GRUBBS, Robert W. — Tel: (224) 521 - 8000

Main Headquarters
Mailing: 2301 Patriot Blvd.
Glenview, IL 60025-8020 — Tel: (224) 521 - 8000

Political Action Committees

Anixter Internat'l/ANTEC PAC
Contact: Lawrence A. Margolis
11450 Technology Circle
Duluth, GA 30097

Contributions to Candidates: none reported (01/05 - 09/05)

Public Affairs and Related Activities Personnel

At Headquarters

GARLAND, Patricia — Tel: (224) 521 - 8000
Director, Human Resources

LETHAM, Dennis J. — Tel: (224) 521 - 8601
Chief Financial Officer and Senior V. President, Finance
Responsibilities include investor relations.

MARKS, Dawn — Tel: (224) 521 - 8484
Media Relations Contact

At Other Offices

MARGOLIS, Lawrence A.
PAC Treasurer
11450 Technology Circle
Duluth, GA 30097

ANR Pipeline

See listing on page 177 under El Paso Corp.

Anthem Blue Cross and Blue Shield

See listing on page 516 under Wellpoint, Inc.

Anthem, Inc.

See listing on page 516 under Wellpoint, Inc.

AOL Time Warner Inc.

See listing on page 475 under Time Warner Inc.

Aon Corp.

An insurance holding company. Subsidiaries include Aon Risk Services, Inc. Acquired Alexander and Alexander Services in 1997.
www.aon.com

Executive Chairman
RYAN, Patrick G. — Tel: (312) 381 - 1000 Fax: (312) 381 - 0240

President and Chief Exec. Officer
CASE, Gregory C. — Tel: (312) 381 - 1000 Fax: (312) 381 - 0240

Main Headquarters
Mailing: 200 E.Randolph St.
Chicago, IL 60601 — Tel: (312) 381 - 1000 Fax: (312) 381 - 0240

Political Action Committees

Aon Corp. PAC
Contact: Diane M. Aigotti
200 E.Randolph St.
Chicago, IL 60601 — Tel: (312) 381 - 1000 Fax: (312) 381 - 0240

Aon Corp.

* continued from previous page

Contributions to Candidates: $16,000 (01/05 - 09/05)
Democrats: $10,000; Republicans: $6,000.

Principal Recipients

SENATE DEMOCRATS		HOUSE DEMOCRATS	
Nelson, Bill (FL)	$5,000	Andrews, Robert (NJ)	$1,000
Obama, Barack (IL)	$3,000	Pomeroy, Earl (ND)	$1,000
SENATE REPUBLICANS		**HOUSE REPUBLICANS**	
Dewine, Richard (OH)	$1,000	Baker, Hugh (LA)	$5,000

Corporate Foundations and Giving Programs

Aon Foundation
Contact: Carolyn E. Labutka
200 E.Randolph St. Tel: (312) 381 - 3549
Chicago, IL 60601 Fax: (312) 381 - 0240

Annual Grant Total: $2,000,000 - $5,000,000
Geographic Preference: Area(s) in which the company operates
Primary Interests: Arts and Culture; Education; Youth Services
Recent Recipients: Anti-Defamation League; Boys and Girls Club; Nat'l Merit Scholarship

Public Affairs and Related Activities Personnel

At Headquarters

AIGOTTI, Diane M. Tel: (312) 381 - 1000
Senior V. President and Treasurer; PAC Treasurer Fax: (312) 381 - 0240

FARMER, Jeremy G. O. Tel: (312) 381 - 1000
Senior V. President, Human Resources Fax: (312) 381 - 0240

LABUTKA, Carolyn E. Tel: (312) 381 - 3549
V. President and Exec. Director, Aon Foundation Fax: (312) 381 - 0240

ORENDORFF, Al Tel: (312) 381 - 3153
Director, Public Relations Fax: (312) 381 - 0240
al_orendorff@aon.com

RIVKIN, Robert S. Tel: (312) 381 - 1000
V. President, Deputy General Counsel, Litigation and Government Affairs Fax: (312) 381 - 0240

STREEM, Craig A. Tel: (312) 381 - 1000
V. President, Investor Relations Fax: (312) 381 - 0240

SULLIVAN, Gary Tel: (312) 381 - 1000
V. President, Corporate Communications Fax: (312) 381 - 0240

VAN DE WALLE, Dave Tel: (312) 381 - 5028
V. President, Global Public Relations Fax: (312) 381 - 0240
dave_vandewalle@aon.com

Apache Corp.

An independent energy company engaged in exploration, development, production and marketing of natural gas and crude oil.
www.apachecorp.com
Annual Revenues: $2.56 billion

Chairman of the Board Tel: (713) 296 - 6000
PLANK, Raymond Fax: (713) 296 - 6480
raymond.plank@apachecorp.com TF: (800) 874 - 3262

President and Chief Exec. Officer Tel: (713) 296 - 6000
FARRIS, G. Steven Fax: (713) 296 - 6480
TF: (800) 874 - 3262

Main Headquarters
Mailing: 2000 Post Oak Blvd., Suite 100 Tel: (713) 296 - 6000
Houston, TX 77056-4400 Fax: (713) 296 - 6480
TF: (800) 874 - 3262

Political Action Committees

Apache Corp. PAC
Contact: Urban F. "Obie" O'Brien, III
2000 Post Oak Blvd., Suite 100 Tel: (713) 296 - 6150
Houston, TX 77056-4400 Fax: (713) 296 - 6480
TF: (800) 874 - 3262

Contributions to Candidates: none reported (01/05 - 09/05)

Corporate Foundations and Giving Programs

Apache Corporate Giving Program
Contact: Urban F. "Obie" O'Brien, III
2000 Post Oak Blvd., Suite 100 Tel: (713) 296 - 6150
Houston, TX 77056-4400 Fax: (713) 296 - 6480
TF: (800) 874 - 3262

Annual Grant Total: none reported
Geographic Preference: Area(s) in which the company operates
Primary Interests: Arts and Culture; Community Affairs; Education; Social Services; Urban Affairs

Public Affairs and Related Activities Personnel

At Headquarters

BATTON, Anne Tel: (713) 296 - 6253
Manager, e-Commerce Fax: (713) 296 - 6480
anne.batton@apachecorp.com TF: (800) 874 - 3262

BENDER, Jeffrey M. Tel: (713) 296 - 6159
V. President, Human Resources Fax: (713) 296 - 6480
jeffrey.bender@apachecorp.com TF: (800) 874 - 3262

DYE, Robert J. Tel: (713) 296 - 6662
V. President, Investor Relations Fax: (713) 296 - 6480
TF: (800) 874 - 3262

HIGGINS, David Tel: (713) 296 - 6690
Director, Strategic Communications Fax: (713) 296 - 6480
david.higgins@apachecorp.com TF: (800) 874 - 3262

LENTINI, Anthony R., Jr. Tel: (713) 296 - 6107
V. President, Public and International Affairs Fax: (713) 296 - 6480
tony.lentini@apachecorp.com TF: (800) 874 - 3262

MINTZ, Bill Tel: (713) 296 - 7276
Director, Public and International Affairs Fax: (713) 296 - 6452
bill.mintz@apachecorp.com TF: (800) 874 - 3262

NUTTING, Lisa Tel: (713) 296 - 7279
Manager, Corporate Communications Fax: (713) 296 - 6480
lisa.nutting@apachecorp.com TF: (800) 874 - 3262

O'BRIEN, Urban F. "Obie", III Tel: (713) 296 - 6150
Director, Governmental, Regulatory and Community Affairs Fax: (713) 296 - 6480
obie.obrien@apachecorp.com TF: (800) 874 - 3262

Apache Nitrogen Products Inc.

See listing on page 42 under Apache Corp.

APL Americas

Formerly American President Lines, Ltd. A major intermodal container transportation and distribution services company. A wholly owned subsidiary of NOL Group.
www.apl.com
Annual Revenues: $3.6 billion

Main Headquarters
Mailing: 1111 Broadway Tel: (510) 272 - 8000
Oakland, CA 94607-5500 Fax: (510) 272 - 7421

Washington Office
Contact: Roy Bowman
Mailing: 1667 K St. NW Tel: (202) 331 - 1424
Suite 400 Fax: (202) 775 - 8427
Washington, DC 20006

Political Action Committees

APL Ltd. PAC
Contact: Timothy J. Windle
1111 Broadway Tel: (510) 272 - 8000
Oakland, CA 94607-5500 Fax: (510) 272 - 7421

Contributions to Candidates: $6,500 (01/05 - 09/05)
Democrats: $1,000; Republicans: $5,500.

Principal Recipients

SENATE DEMOCRATS		HOUSE DEMOCRATS	
		Tauscher, Ellen O (CA)	$1,000
SENATE REPUBLICANS		**HOUSE REPUBLICANS**	
Vitter, David (LA)	$1,000	Pombo, Richard (CA)	$1,500
		Hunter, Duncan (CA)	$1,000
		Reichert, Dave (WA)	$1,000
		Young, Don E (AK)	$1,000

Corporate Foundations and Giving Programs

APL Limited Foundation
Contact: John Pachtner
1111 Broadway Tel: (510) 272 - 8000
Oakland, CA 94607-5500 Fax: (510) 272 - 7421

Annual Grant Total: $500,000 - $750,000
Emphasis is placed on matching grants and community volunteer service organizations.
Geographic Preference: California; Area in which the company is headquartered; Area(s) in which the company operates
Primary Interests: Community Affairs; Environment/Conservation
Recent Recipients: Boys and Girls Club; Nat'l Arts Council; Nature Conservancy; Project Hope

Public Affairs and Related Activities Personnel

At Headquarters

PACHTNER, John Tel: (510) 272 - 8000
Community Affairs Contact Fax: (510) 272 - 7421
john.pachtner@apl.com

WINDLE, Timothy J. Tel: (510) 272 - 8000
General Counsel and Treasurer, APL Ltd. PAC Fax: (510) 272 - 7421
timothy_windle@apl.com

APL Americas
** continued from previous page*

ZAMPA, Mike — Tel: (510) 272 - 7380
Director, Corporate Communications — Fax: (510) 272 - 7421
michael_zampa@apl.com

At Washington Office

BOWMAN, Roy — Tel: (202) 331 - 1424
V. President, Government Affairs — Fax: (202) 775 - 8427
roy_bowman@apl.com
Registered Federal Lobbyist.

DECROSTA, John — Tel: (202) 331 - 1424
Director, Legislative Affairs — Fax: (202) 775 - 8427

PERRY, Tim C. — Tel: (202) 496 - 2482
Trade and Regulatory Afffairs — Fax: (202) 775 - 8427
Registered Federal Lobbyist.

Apogee Enterprises, Inc.
Manufacturer of windows and glass.
www.apog.com
Annual Revenues: $800 million

Chairman, President and Chief Exec. Officer — Tel: (952) 835 - 1874
HUFFER, Russell — Fax: (952) 835 - 3196

Main Headquarters
Mailing: 7900 Xerxes Ave. South — Tel: (952) 835 - 1874
Suite 1800 — Fax: (952) 835 - 3196
Minneapolis, MN 55431-1159

Corporate Foundations and Giving Programs

ASIST: Apogee and Subsidiaries In-Service Team
7900 Xerxes Ave. South — Tel: (952) 835 - 1874
Suite 1800 — Fax: (952) 835 - 3196
Minneapolis, MN 55431-1159

Annual Grant Total: none reported
Provides volunteer participation opportunities to Apogee employees.
Primary Interests: Children; Hunger; Youth Services

Public Affairs and Related Activities Personnel

At Headquarters

JACKSON, Mary Ann — Tel: (952) 487 - 7538
Director, Investor Relations — Fax: (952) 835 - 3196
mjackson@apog.com
Responsibilities include media relations.

Apollo Group, Inc.
Provides higher education programs for working adults.
www.apollogrp.edu
Annual Revenues: $1 billion

Chairman, Chief Exec. Officer and President — Tel: (480) 966 - 5394
NELSON, Todd S. — Fax: (480) 379 - 3503
todd.nelson@apollogrp.edu — TF: (800) 990 - APOL

Main Headquarters
Mailing: 4615 E. Elwood St. — Tel: (480) 966 - 5394
Phoenix, AZ 85040-1958 — Fax: (480) 379 - 3503
TF: (800) 990 - APOL

Political Action Committees

Apollo Group, Inc. Political Organization for Legislative Leadership
Contact: Sherryl Gibson
4615 E. Elwood St. — Tel: (480) 966 - 5394
Phoenix, AZ 85040-1958 — Fax: (480) 379 - 3503
TF: (800) 990 - APOL

Contributions to Candidates: $23,000 (01/05 - 09/05)
Democrats: $11,000; Republicans: $12,000.

Principal Recipients

SENATE DEMOCRATS		HOUSE DEMOCRATS	
Pallone, Frank (NJ)	$1,000	Andrews, Robert (NJ)	$10,000
SENATE REPUBLICANS		**HOUSE REPUBLICANS**	
Enzi, Michael B (WY)	$2,000	McKeon, Howard (CA)	$2,500
McConnell, Mitch (KY)	$500		

Public Affairs and Related Activities Personnel

At Headquarters

DICKEY, Ayla — Tel: (480) 966 - 5394 Ext: 2952
Associate V. President, Public Relations — Fax: (480) 379 - 3503
ayla.dickey@apollogrp.edu — TF: (800) 990 - APOL

GIBSON, Sherryl — Tel: (480) 966 - 5394
PAC Treasurer — Fax: (480) 379 - 3503
TF: (800) 990 - APOL

PASINSKI, Janess — Tel: (480) 966 - 5394
Manager, Investor Relations — Fax: (480) 379 - 3503
janess.pasinski@apollogrp.edu — TF: (800) 990 - APOL

THOMPSON, Diane — Tel: (480) 966 - 5394
V. President/Counsel, Human Resources — Fax: (480) 379 - 3503
TF: (800) 990 - APOL

Apple Computer, Inc.
A member of the Public Affairs Council. A personal computer manufacturer.
www.apple.com
Annual Revenues: $5.36 billion

Chairman of the Board — Tel: (408) 996 - 1010
CAMPBELL, William B. — Fax: (408) 996 - 0275

Chief Exec. Officer — Tel: (408) 996 - 1010
JOBS, Steve — Fax: (408) 996 - 0275

Main Headquarters
Mailing: One Infinite Loop — Tel: (408) 996 - 1010
Cupertino, CA 95014 — Fax: (408) 996 - 0275

Corporate Foundations and Giving Programs

Apple Education Grants Program
Contact: Don Zundel
One Infinite Loop — Tel: (707) 546 - 7966
Cupertino, CA 95014 — Fax: (707) 695 - 1857

Annual Grant Total: over $5,000,000
Focuses on gifts of computer equipment and training. No cash grants are awarded. Call or write for latest guidelines.
Geographic Preference: National
Primary Interests: Arts and Culture; K-12 Education; Social Services
Recent Recipients: Nat'l AIDS Council; Nat'l Center for Family Literacy

Public Affairs and Related Activities Personnel

At Headquarters

BYER, David — Tel: (408) 996 - 1010
Fax: (408) 996 - 0275

COTTON, Katie — Tel: (408) 972 - 7269
V. President, Worldwide Corporate Communications — Fax: (408) 996 - 0275
katiec@apple.com

DOWLING, Steve — Tel: (408) 974 - 1896
Senior Manager, Corporate Media Relations — Fax: (408) 996 - 0275
dowling@apple.com

FOSTER, Catherine H. — Tel: (408) 996 - 1010
Director, Government Affairs — Fax: (408) 996 - 0275

PAXTON, Nancy — Tel: (408) 996 - 1010
Director, Investor Relations — Fax: (408) 996 - 0275
paxton1@apple.com

TENUTA, Joshua P. — Tel: (408) 996 - 1010
Attorney — Fax: (408) 996 - 0275

WILDER, Todd — Tel: (408) 974 - 8335
Education and Government Media Relations — Fax: (408) 996 - 0275
wilder@apple.com

ZUNDEL, Don — Tel: (707) 546 - 7966
Contact, Apple Education Grants Program — Fax: (707) 695 - 1857

Applebee's Internat'l, Inc.
An operator of casual dining restaurants.
www.applebees.com
Annual Revenues: $827 million

Chairman and Chief Exec. Officer — Tel: (913) 967 - 4000
HILL, Lloyd L. — Fax: (913) 341 - 1694

Main Headquarters
Mailing: 4551 W. 107th St. — Tel: (913) 967 - 4000
Overland Park, KS 66207-4037 — Fax: (913) 341 - 1694

Public Affairs and Related Activities Personnel

At Headquarters

DIRAIMO, Carol — Tel: (913) 967 - 4109
V. President, Investor Relations — Fax: (913) 341 - 1694
ca.diraimo@applebees.com

ELLISON, Laurie — Tel: (913) 967 - 2718
Exec. Director, Corporate Communications — Fax: (913) 341 - 1694
laurie.ellison@applebees.com

KAUCIC, Louis A. — Tel: (913) 967 - 4000
Exec. V. President and Chief People Officer — Fax: (913) 341 - 1694

YBARRA, Frank — Tel: (913) 967 - 4159
Senior Communications Manager — Fax: (913) 341 - 1694
frank.ybarra@applebees.com

Applera Corp.
Formerly The PE Corp. A worldwide manufacturer of life science systems for research and related applications.
www.applera.com
Annual Revenues: $1.8 billion

Applera Corp.

* continued from previous page

Chairman, President and Chief Exec. Officer
WHITE, Tony L. — Tel: (203) 840 - 2000; TF: (800) 761 - 5381

Main Headquarters
Mailing: 301 Merritt Seven
P.O. Box 5435
Norwalk, CT 06856-5435
Tel: (203) 840 - 2000; TF: (800) 761 - 5381

Corporate Foundations and Giving Programs

Applera Charitable Foundation
Contact: Ugo DeBlasi
301 Merritt Seven
P.O. Box 5435
Norwalk, CT 06856-5435
Tel: (203) 840 - 2000; TF: (800) 761 - 5381

Annual Grant Total: $750,000 - $1,000,000
Geographic Preference: Area in which the company is headquartered; Area(s) in which the company operates

Public Affairs and Related Activities Personnel

At Headquarters

DEBLASI, Ugo
Exec. Director, Applera Charitable Foundation
Tel: (203) 840 - 2000; TF: (800) 761 - 5381

At Other Offices

DWORKIN, Peter
V. President, Investor Relations and Corporate Communications
850 Lincoln Center Dr.
Foster City, CA 94404-1128
dworkipg@appliedbiosystems.com
Tel: (650) 554 - 2479; Fax: (650) 554 - 2810

KAPOR, Ana
Manager, Corporate Communications and Investor Relations
850 Lincoln Center Dr.
Foster City, CA 94404-1128
kapora1@appliedbiosystems.com
Tel: (650) 638 - 6227; Fax: (650) 554 - 2920

KERR, Barbara J.
V. President, Human Resources
850 Lincoln Center Dr.
Foster City, CA 94404-1128
kerrbj@appliedbiosystems.com
Tel: (650) 638 - 6310

SPEECHLY, David
Senior Director, Investor Relations and Corporate Communications
(Celara Genomics)
1401 Harbor Bay Pkwy.
Alameda, CA 94502
david.speechly@celera.com
Tel: (510) 749 - 7853; Fax: (510) 749 - 6200

Appleton

A producer of carbonless, thermal, coated free sheet and specialty coated papers.
www.appletonideas.com
Annual Revenues: $1.1 billion

President and Chief Exec. Officer
RICHARDS, Mark R. — Tel: (920) 734 - 9841; Fax: (920) 991 - 8080; TF: (800) 558 - 8390

Main Headquarters
Mailing: P.O. Box 359
Appleton, WI 54912-0359
Tel: (920) 734 - 9841; Fax: (920) 991 - 8080; TF: (800) 558 - 8390

Street: 825 E. Wisconsin Ave.
Appleton, WI 54912

Corporate Foundations and Giving Programs

Appleton Papers Contributions Program
P.O. Box 359
Appleton, WI 54912-0359
Tel: (920) 734 - 9841; Fax: (920) 991 - 8080; TF: (800) 558 - 8390

Annual Grant Total: $500,000 - $750,000
Geographic Preference: Area(s) in which the company operates; Wisconsin; Ohio; Pennsylvania
Primary Interests: Arts and Culture; Community Affairs; Health and Human Services; Substance Abuse Prevention; Youth Services

Public Affairs and Related Activities Personnel

At Headquarters

KARCH, Paul J.
V. President, Human Resources and Law; Secretary; and General Counsel
Tel: (920) 734 - 9841; Fax: (920) 991 - 8080; TF: (800) 558 - 8390

VAN DEN BRANDT, Bill
Manager, Corporate Communications
bvandenbrandt@appletonpapers.com
Tel: (920) 991 - 8613; Fax: (920) 991 - 8506; TF: (800) 558 - 8390

Applied Industrial Technologies

Formerly known as Bearings, Inc. A North American industrial distributor serving the Maintenance Repair Operations (MRO) and Original Equipment Manufacturing (OEM) markets with products including bearings, power transmission components, fluid power components and systems, industrial rubber products, linear components, and general maintenance, safety and mill supply products.
www.appliedindustrial.com
Annual Revenues: $1.46 billion

Chairman and Chief Exec. Officer
PUGH, David L.
dpugh@applied.com
Tel: (216) 426 - 4000 Ext: 4447; Fax: (216) 426 - 4804; TF: (877) 279 - 2799

Main Headquarters
Mailing: One Applied Plaza
Cleveland, OH 44115
Tel: (216) 426 - 4000; Fax: (216) 426 - 4804; TF: (877) 279 - 2799

Corporate Foundations and Giving Programs

Applied Industrial Technologies Corporate Contributions Program
One Applied Plaza
Cleveland, OH 44115
Tel: (216) 426 - 4000; Fax: (216) 426 - 4804; TF: (877) 279 - 2799

Annual Grant Total: none reported

Public Affairs and Related Activities Personnel

At Headquarters

COTICCHIA, Michael L.
V. President, Human Resources and Administration
mcoticchia@applied.com
Tel: (216) 426 - 4511 Ext: 4511; Fax: (216) 426 - 4844; TF: (877) 279 - 2799

EISELE, Mark O.
V. President, Chief Financial Officer and Treasurer
Tel: (216) 426 - 4000; Fax: (216) 426 - 4804; TF: (877) 279 - 2799

Responsibilities include investor relations.

SHAW, Richard C.
V. President, Communications and Learning
rshaw@applied.com
Tel: (216) 426 - 4343; Fax: (216) 426 - 4808; TF: (877) 279 - 2799

Applied Materials, Inc.

A member of the Public Affairs Council. A supplier of water fabrication systems and services to the global semiconductor industry.
www.appliedmaterials.com
Annual Revenues: $7.34 billion

Chairman of the Board
MORGAN, James C. — Tel: (408) 727 - 5555; Fax: (408) 748 - 5119

President and Chief Exec. Officer
SPLINTER, Michael R. — Tel: (408) 727 - 5555; Fax: (408) 748 - 9943

Main Headquarters
Mailing: 3050 Bowers Ave.
P.O. Box 58039
Santa Clara, CA 95054-3299
Tel: (408) 727 - 5555; Fax: (408) 748 - 9943

Washington Office
Contact: William G. Morin
Mailing: 1400 I St. NW
Suite 540
Washington, DC 20005
Tel: (202) 638 - 4434

Political Action Committees

Applied Materials Inc. PAC
Contact: Russell H. Miller
20 Park Rd., Suite E
Burlingame, CA 94010

Contributions to Candidates: none reported (01/05 - 09/05)

Corporate Foundations and Giving Programs

Applied Materials Community and University Affairs
Contact: Michael K. O'Farrell
3050 Bowers Ave.
P.O. Box 58039
Santa Clara, CA 95054-3299
Tel: (408) 727 - 5555; Fax: (408) 748 - 5119

Annual Grant Total: over $5,000,000
Geographic Preference: Area(s) in which the company operates
Primary Interests: Arts and Culture; Civic and Public Affairs; Education; Health and Human Services

Public Affairs and Related Activities Personnel

At Headquarters

BOWMAN, Paul
Managing Director, Investor Relations
Tel: (408) 563 - 1698; Fax: (408) 748 - 9943

DUNCAN, Connie
Manager, Product Public Relations
connie_duncan@appliedmaterials.com
Tel: (408) 563 - 6209; Fax: (408) 986 - 2855

LIEBMAN, Jeanette
Group V. President, Global Human Resources
Tel: (408) 727 - 5555; Fax: (408) 748 - 9943

Applied Materials, Inc.

• continued from previous page

MILLER, David
Senior Manager, Worldwide Media Relations
david_miller@appliedmaterials.com
Tel: (408) 563 - 9582
Fax: (408) 986 - 7115

NEWBOE, Betty
Director, Product Public Relations
betty_x_newboe@appliedmaterials.com
Tel: (408) 563 - 0647
Fax: (408) 986 - 2855

O'FARRELL, Michael K.
V. President, Community and University Relations
Tel: (408) 727 - 5555
Fax: (408) 748 - 5119

PON, Joe
Director, Corporate and Government Affairs
Mailstop: MS 2710
joe_pon@appliedmaterials.com
Tel: (408) 748 - 5508
Fax: (408) 986 - 7115

TAYLOR, Steve
Director, North American Corporate Affairs
steve_taylor@appliedmaterials.com
Tel: (512) 272 - 2120
Fax: (512) 272 - 3041

ZEPEDA VERA, Patricia
Specialist, Worldwide Media Relations
patricia_zepeda_vera@appliedmaterials.com
Tel: (408) 563 - 8160
Fax: (408) 986 - 7115

At Washington Office

BEHRNS, Eric
Registered Federal Lobbyist.
Tel: (202) 638 - 4434

MORIN, William G.
Director, Government Affairs
william_morin@amat.com
Registered Federal Lobbyist.
Tel: (202) 638 - 4434

At Other Offices

MILLER, Russell H.
Treasurer, Applied Materials Inc. PAC
20 Park Rd., Suite E
Burlingame, CA 94010

AptarGroup, Inc.

A manufacturer of personal care and household products.

www.aptar.com
Annual Revenues: $927 million

Chairman of the Board
HARRIS, King
Tel: (815) 477 - 0424
Fax: (815) 477 - 0481

President and Chief Exec. Officer
SIEBEL, Carl A.
Tel: (815) 477 - 0424
Fax: (815) 477 - 0481

Main Headquarters
Mailing: 475 W. Terra Cotta Ave.
Suite E
Crystal Lake, IL 60014-9695
Tel: (815) 477 - 0424
Fax: (815) 477 - 0481

Public Affairs and Related Activities Personnel

At Headquarters

DELLAMARIA, Matt
Director, Corporate Communications
Tel: (815) 477 - 0424
Fax: (815) 477 - 0481

HAGGE, Stephen
Chief Financial Officer
Responsibilities include investor relations.
Tel: (815) 477 - 0424
Fax: (815) 477 - 0481

LOWRIMORE, Lawrence
V. President, Human Resources
Tel: (815) 477 - 0424
Fax: (815) 477 - 0481

Aquila, Inc.

PUBLIC AFFAIRS COUNCIL

A member of the Public Affairs Council. Operates electricity and natural gas distribution utilities in Colorado, Iowa, Kansas, Michigan, Minnesota, Missouri and Nebraska. The company also owns and operates power generation assets.

www.aquila.com

Chairman, President and Chief Exec. Officer
GREEN, Richard C.
Tel: (816) 421 - 6600
Fax: (816) 467 - 3005

Main Headquarters
Mailing: P.O. Box 13287
Kansas City, MO 64199-3287
Tel: (816) 421 - 6600
Fax: (816) 467 - 3005
Street: 20 W. Ninth St.
Kansas City, MO 64105

Political Action Committees

Aquila Employee PAC
Contact: Kimberly Gencur
P.O. Box 13287
Kansas City, MO 64199-3287
Tel: (816) 467 - 3411
Fax: (816) 467 - 9411

Contributions to Candidates: $7,000 (01/05 - 09/05)
Democrats: $3,000; Republicans: $4,000.

Principal Recipients

SENATE DEMOCRATS
Nelson, Benjamin (NE) $2,000

SENATE REPUBLICANS
Talent, James (MO) $2,000

HOUSE DEMOCRATS
Skelton, Ike (MO) $1,000

HOUSE REPUBLICANS
Fortenberry, Jeffrey (NE) $1,000
Hulshof, Kenny (MO) $500
Terry, Lee (NE) $500

Corporate Foundations and Giving Programs

Aquila Charitable Contributions Program
Contact: Lynn Wilson
P.O. Box 13287
Kansas City, MO 64199-3287
Tel: (816) 467 - 3776
Fax: (816) 467 - 9776

Annual Grant Total: none reported

Geographic Preference: Area in which the company is headquartered

Primary Interests: Community Development; Economic Development; Education; Literacy; Youth Services

Public Affairs and Related Activities Personnel

At Headquarters

ARNALL, Maurice
Director, Regulatory Services - Analytical Support
maurice.arnall@aquila.com
Tel: (816) 737 - 7751
Fax: (816) 743 - 3751

BUTKUS, Al
V. President, Corporate Communications
al.butkus@aquila.com
Tel: (816) 467 - 3616
Fax: (816) 467 - 3005

CLARK, Neala
Director, Investor Relations
neala.clark@aquila.com
Tel: (816) 467 - 3562
Fax: (816) 467 - 3435

DUNN, Norma F.
Senior V. President, Corporate Communications
norma.dunn@aquila.com
Tel: (816) 467 - 3143
Fax: (816) 467 - 9143

GENCUR, Kimberly
Legislative Services-Colorado/Kansas
kimberly.gencur@aquila.com
Tel: (816) 467 - 3411
Fax: (816) 467 - 9411

MINTER, George A.
V. President, Corporate Communications
george.minter@aquila.com
Tel: (816) 467 - 3772
Fax: (816) 467 - 3005

MURRAY, Stephen D.
Legislative Services - Missouri
steve.murray@aquila.com
Tel: (816) 467 - 3434
Fax: (816) 467 - 9434

RUSSELL, Gene
Director, Environmental Services
gene.russell@aquila.com
Tel: (816) 467 - 3865
Fax: (816) 467 - 9865

SMITH, Brandee
Communications Coordinator
brandee.smith@aquila.com
Tel: (816) 467 - 3304
Fax: (816) 467 - 3005

WALKER, Diane
Corporate Communications
diane.walker@aquila.com
Tel: (816) 467 - 3686
Fax: (816) 467 - 9686

WILSON, Lynn
Contact, Corporate Giving Program
Tel: (816) 467 - 3776
Fax: (816) 467 - 9776

At Other Offices

DAVIS, Jan L.
Director, Community Services
1815 Capitol Ave.
Omaha, NE 68102
jan.davis@aquila.com
Tel: (402) 221 - 2234
Fax: (402) 221 - 2601

EMPSON, Jon R.
Senior V. President, Regulated Operations
1815 Capitol Ave.
Omaha, NE 68102
jon.empson@aquila.com
Tel: (402) 221 - 2375
Fax: (402) 221 - 2501

FUJII, Stacey
Legislative Services - Minnesota/Michigan
161 St. Anthony St.
Suite 815
St. Paul, MN 55103
Tel: (651) 222 - 4314
Fax: (651) 222 - 4372

JUREK, Steve
V. President, Regulatory Services-Gas
1815 Capitol Ave.
Omaha, NE 68102
steve.jurek@aquila.com
Tel: (402) 221 - 2262
Fax: (402) 221 - 2501

NESS, Judith L.
Director, Community Services-Missouri
10700 E. 350 Hwy.
Kansas City, MO 64138
judy.ness@aquila.com
Tel: (816) 737 - 7528
Fax: (816) 737 - 7921

Aquila, Inc.

* continued from previous page

WALTER, Susan J. Tel: (515) 270 - 6336
Director, Government Affairs-Iowa Fax: (515) 270 - 6384
2190 N.W. 82nd St., Suite Three
Clive, IA 50325
susan.walter@aquila.com

WILLIAM, Dennis Tel: (816) 737 - 7857
V. President, Regulatory Services-Electric Fax: (816) 737 - 7505
10700 E. 350 Hwy.
Kansas City, MO 64138
denny.williams@aquila.com

ARAMARK

Provider of service management to institutions and the public in such areas as child care and education, food and support services, health care, and uniform and career apparel.
www.aramark.com
Annual Revenues: $10.2 billion

Chairman and Chief Exec. Officer
NEUBAUER, Joseph Tel: (215) 238 - 3000 Fax: (215) 238 - 3333 TF: (800) 999 - 8989

Main Headquarters
Mailing: The ARAMARK Tower
1101 Market St.
Philadelphia, PA 19107
Tel: (215) 238 - 3000 Fax: (215) 238 - 3333 TF: (800) 999 - 8989

Political Action Committees

ARAMARK Political Action Committee (ARAMARK PAC)
Contact: Erin Frey
The ARAMARK Tower
1101 Market St.
Philadelphia, PA 19107
Tel: (215) 238 - 3000 Fax: (215) 238 - 3333 TF: (800) 999 - 8989

Contributions to Candidates: $1,300 (01/05 - 09/05)
Republicans: $1,300.

Principal Recipients

SENATE REPUBLICANS	HOUSE REPUBLICANS	
	Gingrey, Phillip (GA)	$1,300

Corporate Foundations and Giving Programs

ARAMARK Corporate Contributions Program
Contact: Donna Irvin
The ARAMARK Tower
1101 Market St.
Philadelphia, PA 19107
Tel: (215) 238 - 3271 TF: (800) 999 - 8989

Annual Grant Total: none reported
Primary Interests: Arts and Culture; Community Affairs; Education; Health; Youth Services

Public Affairs and Related Activities Personnel

At Headquarters

ALBERT, Debbie Tel: (215) 238 - 3614
Senior Communications Director Fax: (215) 415 - 8511
albert_debbie@aramark.com TF: (800) 999 - 8989

CHAVILLE, Bobbi Tel: (215) 238 - 3726
Associate V. President, Investor Relations Fax: (215) 238 - 3333
TF: (800) 999 - 8989

COST, Tim Tel: (215) 238 - 7101
Exec. V. President, Corporate Affairs Fax: (215) 238 - 3333
TF: (800) 999 - 8989

FREY, Erin Tel: (215) 238 - 3000
PAC Contact Fax: (215) 238 - 3333
TF: (800) 999 - 8989

IRVIN, Donna Tel: (215) 238 - 3271
Exec. Director, Corporate Contributions TF: (800) 999 - 8989

MCKEE, Lynn B. Tel: (215) 238 - 3000
Exec. V. President, Human Resources Fax: (215) 238 - 3333
TF: (800) 999 - 8989

Arch Chemicals, Inc.

A member of the Public Affairs Council. A chemicals company.
www.archchemicals.com
Annual Revenues: $939.4 million

Chairman, President and Chief Exec. Officer
CAMPBELL, Michael E. Tel: (203) 229 - 2900 Fax: (203) 229 - 3213 TF: (877) 275 - 6973

Main Headquarters
Mailing: P.O. Box 5204
Norwalk, CT 06856-5204
Tel: (203) 229 - 2900 Fax: (203) 229 - 3652 TF: (877) 275 - 6973

Street: 501 Merritt Seven
Norwalk, CT 06851

Political Action Committees

Arch Chemicals, Inc. Government Participation Fund
Contact: W. Paul Bush
P.O. Box 5204
Norwalk, CT 06856-5204
Tel: (203) 229 - 2900 Fax: (203) 229 - 3213 TF: (877) 275 - 6973

Contributions to Candidates: $1,000 (01/05 - 09/05)
Republicans: $1,000.

Principal Recipients

SENATE REPUBLICANS	HOUSE REPUBLICANS	
	Reynolds, Thomas (NY)	$1,000

Corporate Foundations and Giving Programs

Arch Chemicals Corporate Contributions
P.O. Box 5204
Norwalk, CT 06856-5204
Tel: (203) 229 - 2900 Fax: (203) 229 - 3652 TF: (877) 275 - 6973

Annual Grant Total: none reported
Provides support through its Employee Matching Contributions, Local Community Contributions, In-Kind Donations, Scholarship Program and Grants.

Public Affairs and Related Activities Personnel

At Headquarters

ANDERSON, Hayes Tel: (203) 229 - 2900
V. President, Human Resources Fax: (203) 229 - 3213
TF: (877) 275 - 6973

BUSH, W. Paul Tel: (203) 229 - 2900
PAC Treasurer Fax: (203) 229 - 3213
TF: (877) 275 - 6973

FAFORD, Mark E. Tel: (203) 229 - 2654
Director, Investor Relations and Communications Fax: (203) 229 - 3507
mefaford@archchemicals.com TF: (877) 275 - 6973

WALTER, Dale N. Tel: (203) 229 - 3033
Manager, Corporate Communications Fax: (203) 229 - 3213
dnwalter@archchemicals.com TF: (877) 275 - 6973

Arch Coal, Inc.

Engaged in the mining, production and sale of coal.
www.archcoal.com
Annual Revenues: $1.46 billion

Chairman of the Board
BOYD, James R. Tel: (314) 994 - 2700 Fax: (314) 994 - 2719

President and Chief Exec. Officer
LEER, Steven F. Tel: (314) 994 - 2700 Fax: (314) 994 - 2719

Main Headquarters
Mailing: One CityPlace Dr.
Suite 300
St. Louis, MO 63141
Tel: (314) 994 - 2700 Fax: (314) 994 - 2719

Political Action Committees

ARCHPAC
Contact: James E. Florczak
One CityPlace Dr.
Suite 300
St. Louis, MO 63141
Tel: (314) 994 - 2700 Fax: (314) 994 - 2719

Contributions to Candidates: $38,000 (01/05 - 09/05)
Democrats: $4,000; Republicans: $34,000.

Principal Recipients

SENATE DEMOCRATS		HOUSE DEMOCRATS	
		Boucher, Fredrick (VA)	$2,000
SENATE REPUBLICANS		**HOUSE REPUBLICANS**	
Talent, James (MO)	$5,000	Cubin, Barbara L (WY)	$5,000
Burns, Conrad (MT)	$2,000	DeLay, Tom (TX)	$5,000
Thomas, Craig (WY)	$2,000	Capito, Shelley (WV)	$2,000
		Pombo, Richard (CA)	$2,000

Corporate Foundations and Giving Programs

Arch Coal Corporate Contributions
Contact: Deck S. Slone
One CityPlace Dr.
Suite 300
St. Louis, MO 63141
Tel: (314) 994 - 2700 Fax: (314) 994 - 2719

Annual Grant Total: none reported
Primary Interests: Community Affairs; Economic Development; Environment/Conservation

Public Affairs and Related Activities Personnel

At Headquarters

FELDMAN, Sheila B. Tel: (314) 994 - 2700
V. President, Human Resources Fax: (314) 994 - 2719

FLORCZAK, James E. Tel: (314) 994 - 2700
PAC Treasurer Fax: (314) 994 - 2719

SLONE, Deck S. Tel: (314) 994 - 2700
V. President, Investor Relations and Public Affairs Fax: (314) 994 - 2719

Arch Wireless, Inc.

See listing on page 497 under USA Mobility, Inc.

Archer Daniels Midland Co. (ADM)

A member of the Public Affairs Council. Major agri-business engaged in milling and other processing of food and feed products.
www.admworld.com
Annual Revenues: $20.05 billion

Chairman and Chief Executive
ANDREAS, G. Allen — Tel: (217) 424 - 5200; Fax: (217) 424 - 5839

Main Headquarters
Mailing: P.O. Box 1470, Decatur, IL 62525 — Tel: (217) 424 - 5200; TF: (800) 637 - 5843
Street: 4666 Faries Pkwy., Decatur, IL 62526

Political Action Committees

Archer Daniels Midland Co. PAC (ADM PAC)
Contact: Steven R. Mills
P.O. Box 1470
Decatur, IL 62525 — Tel: (217) 424 - 5200; TF: (800) 637 - 5843

Contributions to Candidates: $20,000 (01/05 - 09/05)
Democrats: $6,000; Republicans: $14,000.

Principal Recipients

SENATE DEMOCRATS		HOUSE DEMOCRATS	
Nelson, Benjamin (NE)	$4,000		
Bayh, Evan (IN)	$2,000		
SENATE REPUBLICANS		**HOUSE REPUBLICANS**	
Talent, James (MO)	$10,000	Shaw, Clay (FL)	$2,000
Lugar, Richard G (IN)	$1,000	LaHood, Ray (IL)	$1,000

Public Affairs and Related Activities Personnel

At Headquarters

AUSURA, Maureen K.
V. President, Human Resources — Tel: (217) 424 - 5200; Fax: (217) 424 - 5839

GRIMESTAD, Dwight E.
V. President, Investor Relations — Tel: (217) 424 - 5200; Fax: (217) 424 - 5839

HERZFELD, Shannon
V. President, Government Relations — Tel: (217) 424 - 5200; TF: (800) 637 - 5843

MILLER, Karla
V. President, Public Relations — Tel: (217) 424 - 5200; Fax: (217) 424 - 5839
Responsibilities include investor relations.

MILLS, Steven R.
PAC Treasurer — Tel: (217) 424 - 5200; TF: (800) 637 - 5843

PETERSON, Brian
Senior V. President, Corporate Affairs — Tel: (217) 424 - 5413; Fax: (217) 424 - 5839; TF: (800) 637 - 5843

REED, John G., Jr.
V. President, Governmental Affairs — Tel: (217) 424 - 5200; TF: (800) 637 - 5843

ARCO Chemical Co.

See listing on page 301 under Lyondell Chemical Co.

AREVA Enterprises, Inc.

Engaged in supply and service of the nuclear fuel cycle.
www.areva.com

Co-Chief Exec. Officer
CHRISTOPHER, Tom — Tel: (301) 841 - 1600; Fax: (301) 841 - 1611

Co-Chief Exec. Officer
MCMURPHY, Michael A. — Tel: (301) 841 - 1600; Fax: (301) 841 - 1611

Main Headquarters
Mailing: 4800 Hampden Ln., Suite 1100, Bethesda, MD 20814 — Tel: (301) 841 - 1600; Fax: (301) 841 - 1611

Political Action Committees

AREVA COGEMA Framatome ANP PAC
Contact: Katherine Crocker Williams
4800 Hampden Ln.
Suite 1100
Bethesda, MD 20814 — Tel: (301) 841 - 1600; Fax: (301) 841 - 1611

Contributions to Candidates: $13,000 (01/05 - 09/05)
Democrats: $4,000; Republicans: $9,000.

Principal Recipients

SENATE DEMOCRATS		HOUSE DEMOCRATS	
Bingaman, Jeff (NM)	$1,000	Clyburn, James (SC)	$1,000
		Spratt, John (SC)	$1,000
		Visclosky, Peter (IN)	$1,000
SENATE REPUBLICANS		**HOUSE REPUBLICANS**	
Allen, George (VA)	$1,000	Barrett, James (SC)	$1,000
Graham, Lindsey (SC)	$1,000	Biggert, Judy (IL)	$1,000
Inhofe, James M (OK)	$1,000	Norwood, Charles (GA)	$1,000
Santorum, Richard (PA)	$1,000	Wamp, Zach (TN)	$1,000
		Wilson, Heather (NM)	$1,000

Public Affairs and Related Activities Personnel

At Headquarters

HARRISON, Laurie
V. President, Government Relations — Tel: (301) 841 - 1600; Fax: (301) 841 - 1611

LANG, Nancy
Public Relations Contact — Tel: (301) 841 - 1693; Fax: (301) 841 - 1611

MCHALE, Erin
Manager, Federal Affairs — Tel: (301) 841 - 1600; Fax: (301) 841 - 1611

WILLIAMS, Katherine Crocker
PAC Treasurer — Tel: (301) 841 - 1600; Fax: (301) 841 - 1611

Arizona Public Service Co.

See listing on page 384 under Pinnacle West Capital Corp.

Arkansas Best Corporation

A diversified transportation holding company.
www.arkbest.com
Annual Revenues: $1.28 billion

Chairman, President and Chief Exec. Officer
YOUNG, Robert A., III — Tel: (479) 785 - 6000; Fax: (479) 785 - 6004

Main Headquarters
Mailing: P.O. Box 10048, Fort Smith, AR 72917 — Tel: (479) 785 - 6000; Fax: (479) 785 - 6004
Street: 3801 Old Greenwood Rd., Fort Smith, AR 72903

Political Action Committees

Arkansas Best Corp. PAC
Contact: Richard F. Cooper
P.O. Box 10048
Fort Smith, AR 72917 — Tel: (479) 785 - 6130; Fax: (479) 785 - 6124

Contributions to Candidates: $5,000 (01/05 - 09/05)
Democrats: $1,000; Republicans: $4,000.

Principal Recipients

SENATE DEMOCRATS		HOUSE DEMOCRATS	
Pryor, Mark (AR)	$1,000		
SENATE REPUBLICANS		**HOUSE REPUBLICANS**	
Dewine, Richard (OH)	$1,000	Boozman, John (AR)	$1,000
		Johnson, Samuel (TX)	$1,000
		Kline, John P (MN)	$1,000

Corporate Foundations and Giving Programs

Arkansas Best Corp. Contributions Program
P.O. Box 10048
Fort Smith, AR 72917 — Tel: (479) 785 - 6186; Fax: (479) 785 - 6004

Annual Grant Total: none reported

Public Affairs and Related Activities Personnel

At Headquarters

BOYD, Jennifer
Public Relations/Corporate Communications Contact — Tel: (479) 785 - 8892; Fax: (479) 785 - 8992

COOPER, Richard F.
V. President, Administration; Treasurer, Arkansas Best Corp. PAC — Tel: (479) 785 - 6130; Fax: (479) 785 - 6124

HUMPHREY, David
Director, Investor Relations — Tel: (479) 785 - 6200; Fax: (479) 785 - 6004

Arkansas Blue Cross and Blue Shield

www.arkansasbluecross.com

Chairman of the Board
MCCLERKIN, Hayes C. — Tel: (501) 378 - 2000

Chief Exec. Officer
SHOPTAW, Robert L. — Tel: (501) 378 - 2000

Main Headquarters
Mailing: P.O. Box 2181, 320 W. Capitol, Little Rock, AR 72203-2181 — Tel: (501) 378 - 2000

Public Affairs and Related Activities Personnel

At Headquarters

ANDERSON, Michael D.
Governmental Relations Representative — Tel: (501) 378 - 2220

Arkansas Blue Cross and Blue Shield
** continued from previous page*

CANTERBURY, Norman — Tel: (501) 378 - 2000
Director, Managed Pharmacy Program
Responsibilities include lobbying.

DOUGLASS, J. Lee — Tel: (501) 378 - 2000
Senior V. President, Law and Government Relations

HEUER, Maxine — Tel: (501) 378 - 2000
Manager, Public Policy Issues Analysis

O'SULLIVAN, Patrick — Tel: (501) 378 - 2221
V. President, Advertising and Communications — Fax: (501) 378 - 2969

SEWALL, Frank B. — Tel: (501) 378 - 3297
Senior Counsel, Regulatory

WHITEHORN, Kelly M. — Tel: (501) 378 - 2344
Communications Coordinator — Fax: (501) 378 - 2969

Arkansas Power and Light Co.
See listing on page 182 under Entergy Arkansas, Inc.

Armstrong Holdings, Inc.
The parent company of Armstrong World Industries, Inc., a manufacturer and designer of floors, ceilings, and cabinets.
www.armstrong.com
Annual Revenues: $3 billion

Chairman and Chief Exec. Officer — Tel: (717) 397 - 3371
LOCKHART, Michael D.
mdlockhart@armstrong.com

Main Headquarters
Mailing: P.O. Box 3001, Lancaster, PA 17604-3001 — Tel: (717) 397 - 0611
Street: 2500 Columbia Ave., Lancaster, PA 17603

Corporate Foundations and Giving Programs

Armstrong Foundation
Contact: Jan Biagio
P.O. Box 3001 — Tel: (717) 397 - 2416
Lancaster, PA 17604-3001

Annual Grant Total: none reported

Public Affairs and Related Activities Personnel

At Headquarters

ANGELLO, Matthew J. — Tel: (717) 397 - 0611
Senior V. President, Human Resources
(Armstrong World Industries)

BIAGIO, Jan — Tel: (717) 397 - 2416
Foundation Coordinator

RILEY, Beth — Tel: (717) 396 - 6354
Director, Investor Relations

SMITH, Dorothy Brown — Tel: (717) 396 - 5696
V. President, Corporate Communications and Diversity

Armstrong World Industries
See listing on page 48 under Armstrong Holdings, Inc.

ARRIS Group, Inc.
A communications technology company.
www.arrisi.com
Annual Revenues: $652 million

Chairman, President and Chief Exec. Officer — Tel: (770) 622 - 8400
STANZIONE, Robert J. — Fax: (770) 622 - 8770

Main Headquarters
Mailing: 3871 Lakefield Dr., Suwanee, GA 30024 — Tel: (770) 622 - 8400 — Fax: (770) 622 - 8770

Public Affairs and Related Activities Personnel

At Headquarters

BAUER, James A. — Tel: (770) 622 - 8400
Investor Relations Contact — Fax: (847) 615 - 8924
jim.bauer@arrisi.com

SWAN, Alex — Tel: (770) 622 - 8400
Director, Media Relations — Fax: (770) 622 - 8770
alex.swan@arrisi.com

Arrow Electronics, Inc.
Arrow Electronics is a global provider of products, services, and solutions to industrial and commercial users of electronic components and computer products.
www.arrow.com
Annual Revenues: $10.6 billion

Chairman of the Board — Tel: (631) 847 - 2000
DUVAL, Daniel

Chief Exec. Officer — Tel: (631) 847 - 2000
MITCHELL, William

Main Headquarters
Mailing: 50 Marcus Dr., Melville, NY 11747 — Tel: (631) 847 - 2000

Corporate Foundations and Giving Programs

Arrow Electronics, Inc. Corporate Contributions Program
Contact: Marianne Carlton
50 Marcus Dr. — Tel: (631) 847 - 2000
Melville, NY 11747

Annual Grant Total: none reported

Public Affairs and Related Activities Personnel

At Headquarters

BIRNS, Ira — Tel: (631) 847 - 2000
V. President and Treasurer

CARLTON, Marianne — Tel: (631) 847 - 2000
Director, Internal Communications and Charitable Giving

ROBERTS, Jeff — Tel: (631) 847 - 2000
Director, Media Relations

STRAYER, Jaqueline F. — Tel: (631) 847 - 2000
V. President, Corporate Communications

ArvinMeritor
Supplies components for medium and heavy-duty vehicles and light vehicles.
www.arvinmeritor.com
Annual Revenues: $7 billion

Chairman, Chief Exec. Officer and President — Tel: (248) 435 - 1000
MCCLURE, Charles G. "Chip" — Fax: (248) 435 - 1393 — TF: (800) 535 - 5560

Main Headquarters
Mailing: 2135 W. Maple Rd., Troy, MI 48084 — Tel: (248) 435 - 1000 — Fax: (248) 435 - 1393 — TF: (800) 535 - 5560

Political Action Committees

ArvinMeritor Automotive Inc. Employees for Good Government
Contact: Wendy Siegel
124 W. Allegan, Suite 800
Lansing, MI 48933

Contributions to Candidates: none reported (01/05 - 09/05)

Corporate Foundations and Giving Programs

ArvinMeritor Fund
2135 W. Maple Rd. — Tel: (248) 435 - 1000
Troy, MI 48084 — Fax: (248) 435 - 1393 — TF: (800) 535 - 5560

Annual Grant Total: none reported

Public Affairs and Related Activities Personnel

At Headquarters

CUMMINS, Lin M. — Tel: (248) 435 - 7112
Senior V. President, Communications — Fax: (248) 435 - 1393
linda.cummins@arvinmeritor.com — TF: (800) 535 - 5560

HANLEY, Colleen — Tel: (248) 435 - 1417
Senior Director, Global Marketing Communications — Fax: (313) 551 - 2894
colleen.hanley@arvinmeritor.com — TF: (800) 535 - 5560

MCCLURE, Krista — Tel: (248) 435 - 7115
Senior Director, Corporate Communications and Media Relations — Fax: (248) 435 - 1031
krista.mclure@arvinmeritor.com — TF: (800) 535 - 5560

MCGUIRE, Alice — Tel: (248) 655 - 2159
V. President, Investor Relations — Fax: (248) 435 - 1189
alice.mcguire@arvinmeritor.com — TF: (800) 535 - 5560

PENNINGTON, D. Mike — Tel: (248) 435 - 1933
Senior Director, Global Marketing Communications — Fax: (248) 435 - 9946
david.pennington@arvinmeritor.com — TF: (800) 535 - 5560

RUSH, Jerry — Tel: (248) 435 - 7907
Senior Director, Government Affairs and Community Relations — Fax: (248) 435 - 1031
jerry.rush@arvinmeritor.com — TF: (800) 535 - 5560

WHITUS, Ernie — Tel: (248) 435 - 1060
Senior V. President, Human Resources — Fax: (248) 435 - 1393 — TF: (800) 535 - 5560

At Other Offices

SIEGEL, Wendy
PAC Treasurer
124 W. Allegan, Suite 800
Lansing, MI 48933

Asbury Automotive Group
An automotive retailer.
www.asburyauto.com
Annual Revenues: $5.3 billion

Asbury Automotive Group

** continued from previous page*

President and Chief Exec. Officer
GILMAN, Kenneth B. Tel: (212) 885 - 2500

Main Headquarters
Mailing: 622 Third Ave., 37th Floor, New York, NY 10017 Tel: (212) 885 - 2500

Public Affairs and Related Activities Personnel

At Headquarters

JOHNSON, Philip R. Tel: (212) 885 - 2500
V. President, Human Resources

LEVENSON, Allen Tel: (212) 885 - 2500
V. President, Sales and Marketing
Responsibilities include public relations.

ROOKS, John M. Tel: (203) 356 - 4400
V. President, Risk Management

YONKUS, Stacey Tel: (212) 885 - 2512
Director, Investor Relations
syonkus@asburyauto.com

Asea Brown Boveri Inc.

See listing on page 3 under ABB Inc.

Ashland Inc.

PUBLIC AFFAIRS COUNCIL

A member of the Public Affairs Council. A diversified energy company with operations in petroleum refining, transportation and marketing; retail gasoline marketing; motor oil and lubricant marketing; chemicals; and construction.

www.ashland.com

Annual Revenues: $7.719 billion

Chairman and Chief Exec. Officer
O'BRIEN, James J. Tel: (859) 815 - 3333 Fax: (859) 815 - 4795

Main Headquarters
Mailing: P.O. Box 391, Covington, KY 41012-0391 Tel: (859) 815 - 3333 Fax: (859) 815 - 4795
Street: 50 E. River Center Blvd., Covington, KY 41012

Washington Office
Contact: Michael J. Toohey
Mailing: 555 12th St. NW, Suite 620 North, Washington, DC 20004 Tel: (202) 223 - 8290 Fax: (202) 293 - 2913

Political Action Committees

Ashland Inc. Political Action Committee for Employees (PACE)
Contact: Brenda G. Anderson
555 12th St. NW, Suite 620 North, Washington, DC 20004 Tel: (202) 223 - 8290 Fax: (202) 293 - 2913

Contributions to Candidates: $64,740 (01/05 - 09/05)
Democrats: $13,240; Republicans: $50,500; Other: $1,000.

Principal Recipients

SENATE DEMOCRATS		HOUSE DEMOCRATS	
Carper, Thomas R (DE)	$3,740		
Baucus, Max (MT)	$2,000		

SENATE REPUBLICANS		HOUSE REPUBLICANS	
Burns, Conrad (MT)	$3,500	Northup, Anne M. (KY)	$4,000
Chambliss, Saxby (GA)	$2,000	Hobson, David (OH)	$2,500
Smith, Gordon (OR)	$2,000	Davis, Geoffrey (KY)	$2,000
Talent, James (MO)	$2,000	Dewine, R. Pat (OH)	$2,000
Santorum, Richard (PA)	$1,500	Linder, John (GA)	$2,000
		Sensenbrenner, Jim (WI)	$2,000
		Sessions, Pete (TX)	$2,000
		Wolf, Frank R (VA)	$2,000

Corporate Foundations and Giving Programs

Ashland Inc. Corporate Giving Progam
Contact: Deborah George
3499 Blazer Pkwy., Lexington, KY 40509 Tel: (859) 357 - 3409

Annual Grant Total: $2,000,000 - $5,000,000
The company also maintains an employee matching gifts program.
Geographic Preference: Area(s) in which the company operates
Primary Interests: Community Affairs; Environment/Conservation; Health and Human Services; Higher Education

Public Affairs and Related Activities Personnel

At Headquarters

ESLER, Susan B. Tel: (859) 815 - 3333 Fax: (859) 815 - 4795
V. President, Human Resources

JOHNSON, Martha C. Tel: (859) 815 - 3333 Fax: (859) 815 - 4795
V. President, Communications and Corporate Affairs
mcjohnson@ashland.com

PORTER, Daragh Tel: (859) 815 - 3825 Fax: (859) 815 - 5056
V. President, Finance and Treasurer

TREON, Julie C. Tel: (859) 815 - 3333 Fax: (859) 815 - 4795
Director, Communications

At Washington Office

ANDERSON, Brenda G. Tel: (202) 223 - 8290 Fax: (202) 293 - 2913
Representative, Federal Government Relations
bfleming@ashland.com
Registered Federal Lobbyist.

FONES, Linda L. Tel: (202) 223 - 8290 Fax: (202) 293 - 2913
Adminstrative Coordinator and Grassroots Manager

TOOHEY, Michael J. Tel: (202) 223 - 8290 Fax: (202) 293 - 2913
Director, Government Relations
mjtoohey@ashland.com
Registered Federal Lobbyist.

At Other Offices

GEORGE, Deborah Tel: (859) 357 - 3409
Contact, Corporate Giving
3499 Blazer Pkwy., Lexington, KY 40509

LOVE, Daryl Tel: (859) 357 - 3136
Community Relations Manager
3499 Blazer Pkwy., Lexington, KY 40509

Asplundh Tree Expert Co.

Provides line clearance services to the utility industry.

www.asplundh.com

Chairman and Chief Exec. Officer
ASPLUNDH, Christopher Tel: (215) 784 - 4200 Fax: (215) 784 - 4493

Main Headquarters
Mailing: 708 Blair Mill Rd., Willow Grove, PA 19090 Tel: (215) 784 - 4200 Fax: (215) 784 - 4493 TF: (800) 248 - TREE

Political Action Committees

Asplundh Tree Expert Co. PAC (ATE PAC)
Contact: Joseph P. Dwyer
708 Blair Mill Rd., Willow Grove, PA 19090 Tel: (215) 784 - 4200 Fax: (215) 784 - 4493

Contributions to Candidates: none reported (01/05 - 09/05)

Corporate Foundations and Giving Programs

Asplundh Tree Expert Co. Charitable Contributions
Contact: Christopher Asplundh
708 Blair Mill Rd., Willow Grove, PA 19090 Tel: (215) 784 - 4200 Fax: (215) 784 - 4493

Annual Grant Total: none reported
Contributions are done at the discretion of various company executives.

Public Affairs and Related Activities Personnel

At Headquarters

CHIPMAN, Patti Tel: (215) 784 - 4214 Fax: (215) 784 - 4405 TF: (800) 248 - TREE
Manager, Corporate Communications
pchip@asplundh.com

DWYER, Joseph P. Tel: (215) 784 - 4200 Fax: (215) 784 - 4493
Secretary-Treasurer
Responsibilities include political action.

Associated Banc-Corp.

A multibank holding company.

www.associatedbank.com

Chairman of the Board
GALLAGHER, Robert C. Tel: (920) 491 - 7000 Fax: (920) 491 - 7090 TF: (800) 236 - 2722

President and Chief Exec. Officer
BEIDEMAN, Paul S. Tel: (920) 491 - 7000 Fax: (920) 491 - 7090 TF: (800) 236 - 2722

Main Headquarters
Mailing: 1200 Hansen Rd., Green Bay, WI 54304 Tel: (920) 491 - 7000 Fax: (920) 491 - 7090 TF: (800) 236 - 2722

Associated Banc-Corp.

* continued from previous page

Public Affairs and Related Activities Personnel

At Headquarters

DRAYNA, Jonathan E. — Tel: (920) 491 - 7006
Director, Corporate Communications — Fax: (920) 491 - 7010
jon.drayna@associatedbank.com — TF: (800) 236 - 2722

JOHNSON, Robert J. — Tel: (920) 491 - 7170
Director, Human Resources — Fax: (920) 491 - 7090
TF: (800) 236 - 2722

SELNER, Joseph B. — Tel: (920) 491 - 7120
Exec. V. President and Chief Financial Officer — Fax: (920) 491 - 7090
joe.selner@associatedbank.com — TF: (800) 236 - 2722
Responsibilities include shareholder relations.

Associated Milk Producers, Inc.

See listing on page 150 under Dairy Farmers of America, Inc.

Associated Press

www.ap.org

Chairman of the Board — Tel: (212) 621 - 1500
OSBORNE, Burl — Fax: (212) 621 - 5447

President and Chief Exec. Officer — Tel: (212) 621 - 1500
CURLEY, Tom — Fax: (212) 621 - 5447

Main Headquarters
Mailing: 450 W. 33rd St. — Tel: (212) 621 - 1500
New York, NY 10001 — Fax: (212) 621 - 5447

Public Affairs and Related Activities Personnel

At Headquarters

HALE, Ellen — Tel: (212) 621 - 1500
Director, Corporate Communications — Fax: (212) 621 - 5447

STOKES, Jack — Tel: (212) 621 - 1720
Director, Media Relations — Fax: (212) 621 - 5447

Associates Corp. of North America

See listing on page 122 under Citigroup, Inc.

Assurant

Formerly Fortis, Inc. A provider of specialized insurance products, financial services and banking in North America and selected other markets.

www.assurant.com
Annual Revenues: $7.4 billion

Chairman of the Board — Tel: (212) 859 - 7000
PALMS, John Michael — Fax: (212) 859 - 7010

President, Chief Exec. Officer and Director — Tel: (212) 859 - 7000
CLAYTON, J. Kerry — Fax: (212) 859 - 7010

Main Headquarters
Mailing: One Chase Manhattan Plaza — Tel: (212) 859 - 7000
41st Floor — Fax: (212) 859 - 7010
New York, NY 10005

Washington Office
Contact: Edwin L. Harper
Mailing: 1101 Pennsylvania Ave. NW — Tel: (202) 756 - 2469
Washington, DC 20004

Political Action Committees

Assurant Political Action Committee
Contact: Amy Newgard
501 W. Michigan St. — Tel: (414) 299 - 7722
Milwaukee, WI 53201 — Fax: (414) 299 - 6168

Contributions to Candidates: $127,105 (01/05 - 09/05)
Democrats: $36,500; Republicans: $90,605.

Principal Recipients

SENATE DEMOCRATS		HOUSE DEMOCRATS	
Carper, Thomas R (DE)	$5,000	Scott, David (GA)	$3,500
Nelson, Benjamin (NE)	$4,000		
Lieberman, Joe (CT)	$2,500		

SENATE REPUBLICANS		HOUSE REPUBLICANS	
Santorum, Richard (PA)	$5,750	Cantor, Eric (VA)	$3,500
Kyl, Jon L (AZ)	$5,000	Kelly, Sue W (NY)	$3,500
Kennedy, Mark (MN)	$2,500	Ney, Robert W (OH)	$3,000
Martinez, Mel (FL)	$2,500	McCrery, Jim (LA)	$2,500
Vitter, David (LA)	$2,500		

Corporate Foundations and Giving Programs

Assurant Foundation
11222 Quail Roost Dr. — Tel: (305) 253 - 2244
Miami, FL 33157-6596 — Fax: (305) 252 - 6987

Annual Grant Total: $1,000,000 - $2,000,000
Geographic Preference: Area(s) in which the company operates; New York
Primary Interests: Arts and Humanities; Education; Health and Human Services; Religion
Recent Recipients: American Red Cross; Share Our Strength; United Way

Assurant Solutions Charitable Giving Program
One Chase Manhattan Plaza — Tel: (212) 859 - 7000
41st Floor — Fax: (212) 859 - 7010
New York, NY 10005

Annual Grant Total: $1,000,000 - $2,000,000
Geographic Preference: Area(s) in which the company operates
Primary Interests: Arts and Culture; Education; Health and Human Services

Public Affairs and Related Activities Personnel

At Headquarters

CAINS, Larry — Tel: (212) 859 - -704
Senior V. President, Investor Relations — Fax: (212) 859 - 7010
larry.cains@assurant.com

CALL, Laurel — Tel: (212) 859 - 7000
Fax: (212) 859 - 7010

GUTHRIE, Drew — Tel: (212) 859 - 7002
Manager, Communications and Media Relations — Fax: (212) 859 - 7010
drew.guthrie@assurant.com

HALL, Kristy — Tel: (212) 859 - 7026
Foundation Administrator — Fax: (212) 859 - 7010

KIVETT, Melissa — Tel: (212) 859 - 7029
V. President, Investor Relations — Fax: (212) 859 - 7010
melissa.kivett@assurant.com

WALKER, Allen — Tel: (212) 859 - 7000
V. President, Development and Corporate Communications — Fax: (212) 859 - 7010
allen.walker@assurant.com

At Washington Office

HARPER, Edwin L. — Tel: (202) 756 - 2225
Senior V. President, Public Affairs/Government Relations
ed.harper@assurant.com
Registered Federal Lobbyist.

LANCASTER, Ronnie B. — Tel: (202) 756 - 2469
Senior V. President, Federal Government Relations

At Other Offices

BASSETT, Harry — Tel: (770) 763 - 1000
Senior V. President, Government Relations — Fax: (770) 859 - 4403
(Assurant Solutions)
260 Interstate N. Circle NW
Atlanta, GA 30339
harry_bassett@assurant.com

NEWGARD, Amy — Tel: (414) 299 - 7722
Treasurer, Assurant Political Action Committee — Fax: (414) 299 - 6168
501 W. Michigan St.
Milwaukee, WI 53201

RICHARDS, Joyce — Tel: (816) 474 - 2314
Community Relations Contact
2323 Grand
Kansas City, MO 64108

SYKES, James A. — Tel: (770) 763 - 1015
Director, Corporate Communications — Fax: (770) 859 - 4325
(Assurant Solutions)
260 Interstate N. Circle NW
Atlanta, GA 30339
james.sykes@assurant.com

TYCZKOWSKI, Sue — Tel: (414) 299 - 7722
Contact, Assurant Political Action Committee — Fax: (414) 299 - 6168
501 W. Michigan St.
Milwaukee, WI 53201

AstraZeneca Pharmaceuticals

A member of the Public Affairs Council. A global research and development based ethical pharmaceutical company.

www.astrazeneca-us.com
Annual Revenues: $9.38 billion

President and Chief Exec. Officer — Tel: (302) 886 - 3000
BRENNAN, David R. — Fax: (302) 886 - 1889
Mailstop: A2C — TF: (800) 456 - 3669
davidms.brennan@astrazeneca.com

Main Headquarters
Mailing: P.O. Box 15437 — Tel: (302) 886 - 3000
Wilmington, DE 19850-5437 — Fax: (302) 886 - 2972
TF: (800) 456 - 3669

Street: 1800 Concord Pike
Wilmington, DE 19803

AstraZeneca Pharmaceuticals

** continued from previous page*

Washington Office
Contact: Richard Buckley
Mailing: 701 Pennsylvania Ave. NW
Suite 500
Washington, DC 20004
Tel: (202) 350 - 5571
Fax: (202) 350 - 5510

Political Action Committees

Zeneca Inc. Political Action Committee
Contact: Kelly Rollison
P.O. Box 15437
Wilmington, DE 19850-5437
Tel: (302) 886 - 3000
Fax: (302) 886 - 2972
TF: (800) 456 - 3669

Contributions to Candidates: $71,320 (01/05 - 09/05)
Democrats: $20,320; Republicans: $51,000.

Principal Recipients

SENATE DEMOCRATS		HOUSE DEMOCRATS	
Carper, Thomas R (DE)	$4,320		
Nelson, Benjamin (NE)	$4,000		
Ford, Harold E Jr (TN)	$2,000		
SENATE REPUBLICANS		**HOUSE REPUBLICANS**	
Santorum, Richard (PA)	$7,000	Ferguson, Mike (NJ)	$3,000
Allen, George (VA)	$3,500	Johnson, Nancy (CT)	$2,500
Kyl, Jon L (AZ)	$2,000	Barton, Joe L (TX)	$2,000
		Feeney, Tom (FL)	$2,000
		Jindal, Bobby (LA)	$2,000
		Wilson, Joe (SC)	$2,000

Corporate Foundations and Giving Programs

AstraZeneca Corporate Donations
P.O. Box 15437
Wilmington, DE 19850-5437
Tel: (302) 886 - 3000
Fax: (302) 886 - 2972
TF: (800) 456 - 3669

Annual Grant Total: over $5,000,000
Donated more than $7 million to 501(c)(3) organizations.
Geographic Preference: Area(s) in which the company operates
Primary Interests: Arts and Culture; Civic and Public Affairs; Community Affairs; Education; Health and Human Services

Public Affairs and Related Activities Personnel

At Headquarters

BLOOM-BAGLIN, Rachel
Exec. Director, Corporate External Communications
Mailstop: A1C-320
rachel.bloom-baglin@astrazeneca.com
Tel: (302) 886 - 7858
Fax: (302) 886 - 5973
TF: (800) 456 - 3669

BOUROGIANNIS, Angela
Manager, Corporate and Community Affairs
Mailstop: M/S FOC 3C/W
Tel: (302) 886 - 7855
Fax: (302) 886 - 3029
TF: (800) 456 - 3669

BURIGATTO, Carla
Director, Media Relations
Tel: (302) 886 - 5953
Fax: (302) 886 - 2972
TF: (800) 456 - 3669

DAVIS, Chester "Chip", Jr.
V. President, Government Affairs
chip.davis@astrazeneca.com
Tel: (302) 886 - 5650
Fax: (302) 886 - 5015
TF: (800) 456 - 3669

FICK, Irene T.
Senior Manager, Corporate and Community Affairs
Mailstop: FOC 3C/W
irene.fick@astrazeneca.com
Tel: (302) 886 - 3278
Fax: (302) 886 - 3029
TF: (800) 456 - 3669

LAMPERT, Steven B.
Exec. Director, Brand Communications
Mailstop: FOC 3C/W
steve.lampert@astrazeneca.com
Tel: (302) 886 - 7862
Fax: (302) 886 - 3119
TF: (800) 456 - 3669

NICOLI, David P.
V. President, Communications and External Relations
Tel: (302) 886 - 3771
Fax: (302) 886 - 3029
TF: (800) 456 - 3669

ROLLISON, Kelly
Treasurer, Zeneca Inc. Political Action Committee
Tel: (302) 886 - 3000
Fax: (302) 886 - 2972
TF: (800) 456 - 3669

STOKER, Penny
V. President, Human Resources
Tel: (302) 886 - 3000
Fax: (302) 886 - 2972
TF: (800) 456 - 3669

At Washington Office

BUCKLEY, Richard
V. President, Federal Government Affairs
Registered Federal Lobbyist.
Tel: (202) 350 - 5571
Fax: (202) 350 - 5510

DESCHENES, Elise
Senior Manager, Federal Government Affairs
elise.deschenes@astrazeneca.com
Registered Federal Lobbyist.
Tel: (202) 350 - 5572
Fax: (202) 350 - 5510

ESPOSITO, Anne
Director, Federal Government Affairs
Tel: (202) 350 - 5571
Fax: (202) 350 - 5510

MCCOURT, Marion EE.
V. President, Government, Policy and Managed Markets
Tel: (202) 350 - 5571
Fax: (202) 350 - 5510

MCMILLAN, Stephen
Director, Pharmaceutical Federal Government Affairs
stephen.s.d.mcmillan@astrazeneca.com
Registered Federal Lobbyist.
Tel: (202) 350 - 5577
Fax: (202) 350 - 5510

POMFRET, Jacqueline M.
Senior Manager, Federal Government Affairs
Registered Federal Lobbyist.
Tel: (202) 350 - 5578
Fax: (202) 350 - 5510

At Other Offices

ANDERSON, David
Director, State Government Affairs
23 Hunter Run Blvd.
Cohoes, NY 12047
david.anderson@az.com
Tel: (518) 785 - 4589
Fax: (518) 785 - 0883
TF: (877) 893 - 0390
Ext: 41877
Ext: 41877

BENAVIDEZ, Troy
Manager, State Government Affairs
501 Laguna Blvd. SW
Alburquerque, NM 87104
troy.benavidez@astrazeneca.com
Tel: (505) 246 - 2030
Fax: (505) 246 - 8788
TF: (800) 822 - 9209
Ext: 60031
Ext: 60031

BOWERS, William L.
Regional Director, State Government Affairs
6568 Oasis Dr.
Loveland, OH 45140
william.bowers2@astrazeneca.com
Tel: (513) 583 - 0264
Fax: (513) 583 - 1481
TF: (800) 822 - 9209
Ext: 60779
Ext: 60779

BOWMAN, Karen Rhodes
Director, State Government Affairs (Western Region)
5301 S. Superstition Mountain Dr.
Gield Canyon, AZ 85218
karen.bowman@astrazeneca.com
Tel: (480) 288 - 6907
Fax: (480) 288 - 6909
TF: (800) 822 - 9209
Ext: 60839
Ext: 60839

CURTIS, Carol A.
Director, State Government Affairs
P.O. Box 901-435
Kansas City, MO 64190
carol.curtis2@astrazeneca.com
Tel: (816) 436 - 5152
Fax: (816) 436 - 8385
TF: (800) 822 - 9209
Ext: 60077
Ext: 60077

DIMAIO, Mark A.
Director, State Government Affairs
19 Lonacre Ct.
Hockessin, DE 19707
mark.dimaio2@astrazeneca.com
Tel: (302) 234 - 3179
Fax: (302) 234 - 3159
TF: (800) 822 - 9209
Ext: 60068
Ext: 60068

EDDY, Julie
Director, State Government Affairs
3753 Ivy Green Trail
Tallahassee, FL 32311
julie.eddy@astrazeneca.com
Tel: (850) 219 - 9011
Fax: (850) 219 - 9013
TF: (800) 822 - 9209
Ext: 60201
Ext: 60201

FULLER, Joseph H.
Director, State Government Affairs
8923 Eighth Ave., N.E.
Seattle, WA 98115
joe.fuller@astrazeneca.com
Tel: (206) 526 - 5195
Fax: (206) 526 - 5196
TF: (800) 822 - 9209
Ext: 60024
Ext: 60024

LEVESQUE, Gerald R. "Gerry"
Associate Director, State Government Affairs
19 Sugar Maple Dr.
Coventry, RI 02816
gerard.levesque@az.com
Tel: (401) 827 - 0558
Fax: (401) 827 - 0574
TF: (800) 822 - 9209
Ext: 69022
Ext: 69022

MCCORMICK, Ellen
Manager, State Government Affairs
P.O. Box 1222
Sacramento, CA 95812
ellen.mccormick@astrazeneca.com
Tel: (916) 457 - 3703
Fax: (916) 457 - 3413
TF: (800) 893 - 0390
Ext: 41981
Ext: 41981

NAKAISHI, Drake
Director, State Government Affairs Operation
541 Colonel Dewees Rd.
Wayne, PA 19087
drake.nakaishi@astrazeneca.com
Tel: (610) 688 - 2345
Fax: (610) 989 - 0109
TF: (866) 672 - 6155
Ext: 70212
Ext: 70212

O'BRIEN, Christine Davis
Director, State Government Affairs
4205 Lonesome Valley Ct.
Austin, TX 78731
christine.daviso'brien@astrazeneca.com
Tel: (512) 419 - 0455
Fax: (512) 419 - 0456
TF: (800) 822 - 9209
Ext: 60012
Ext: 60012

SHANK, Brian
Associate Director, State Government Affairs
104 Mancino Ct.
Cary, NC 27519
brian.shank@az.com
Tel: (919) 462 - 1847
Fax: (919) 462 - 1856
TF: (877) 893 - 0390
Ext: 43428
Ext: 43428

SPENCER, Adriane
Director, State Government Affairs
7516 Jeannette St.
New Orleans, LA 70118
adriane.spencer2@astrazeneca.com
Tel: (504) 866 - 0990
Fax: (504) 866 - 3991
TF: (800) 822 - 9209
Ext: 60886
Ext: 60886

AT&T

A member of the Public Affairs Council. A provider of long-distance and internet services. The company has announced plans to merge with SBC (see separate listing). Completion of the merger is expected in the first half of 2006.

www.att.com

Chairman and Chief Exec. Officer Tel: (908) 234 - 3020
DORMAN, David W.

Main Headquarters
Mailing: One AT&T Way
Bedminster, NJ 07921-0752 Tel: (908) 234 - 3020

Washington Office
Contact: James W. Cicconi
Mailing: 1120 20th St. NW Tel: (202) 457 - 3810
Suite 1000 Fax: (202) 457 - 2008
Washington, DC 20036-3406

Political Action Committees

AT&T Corp. Political Action Committee (AT&T PAC)
Contact: Patrick Moletteri
One AT&T Way Tel: (908) 234 - 3020
Bedminster, NJ 07921-0752

Contributions to Candidates: $170,000 (01/05 - 09/05)
Democrats: $78,000; Republicans: $89,500; Other: $2,500.

Principal Recipients

SENATE DEMOCRATS
Nelson, Benjamin (NE) $5,000
Kennedy, Ted (MA) $4,000
Pryor, Mark (AR) $2,500

SENATE REPUBLICANS
Allen, George (VA) $7,000
Burns, Conrad (MT) $3,000

HOUSE DEMOCRATS
Conyers, John Jr. (MI) $7,500
Markey, Edward (MA) $5,000

HOUSE REPUBLICANS
Cannon, Christopher (UT) $7,500
Pickering, Chip (MS) $7,500
Ferguson, Mike (NJ) $5,000
Rogers, Michael J (MI) $5,000
Wilson, Heather (NM) $5,000

Corporate Foundations and Giving Programs

AT&T Foundation
Contact: Marilyn Reynick
32 Ave. of the Americas, Room S606
New York, NY 10013-2412

Annual Grant Total: over $5,000,000
Guidelines are available. The company donates approximately $48 million through the Foundation. Maintains a web site at http://www.att.com/foundation.
Geographic Preference: National
Primary Interests: Arts and Culture; Children; Families; Health and Human Services; Higher Education; Minority Opportunities

Public Affairs and Related Activities Personnel

At Headquarters

BYRNES, Jim Tel: (908) 234 - 8754
Corporate Media Relations Contact
jbyrnes@att.com

GRADDICK-WEIR, Mirian M. Tel: (908) 234 - 3020
Exec. V. President, Human Resources
Mailstop: 4353K2
mgraddick@att.com

MOLETTERI, Patrick Tel: (908) 234 - 3020
Treasurer, AT&T PAC

OLIVER, William H. Tel: (908) 234 - 5090
V. President, Public Affairs Fax: (908) 532 - 1332
Mailstop: Room 5B210
wholiver@att.com

SCHAUER, Robert Tel: (908) 234 - 3020
V. President, Public Relations - Public Policy
Mailstop: 2347H3
rschauer@att.com

SCHWEDER, J. Michael Tel: (908) 234 - 3020
Director, Government Relations Regional
Mailstop: 3161C3
schweder@att.com

At Washington Office

ALVAREZ, Amy Tel: (202) 457 - 3810
V. President, Federal Regulatory Affairs Fax: (202) 457 - 2008
Registered Federal Lobbyist.

BORRELLI, Alice Tel: (202) 457 - 3810
V. President, Congressional Relations Fax: (202) 457 - 2267
aborrelli@att.com
Registered Federal Lobbyist.

CALI, Leonard J. Tel: (202) 457 - 2120
V. President - Law and Director, Federal Government Affairs Fax: (202) 457 - 2545
lcali@att.com
Registered Federal Lobbyist.

CARPENTER, Jot D., Jr. Tel: (202) 457 - 3810
V. President, Congressional Affairs Fax: (202) 457 - 2267
jdcjr@att.com
Registered Federal Lobbyist.

CICCONI, James W. Tel: (202) 457 - 3810
General Counsel and Exec. V. President, Law and Government Affairs Fax: (202) 457 - 2244
jcicconi@att.com
Registered Federal Lobbyist.

CONDIT, David Tel: (202) 457 - 3810
V. President, Law and State Government Affairs Fax: (202) 457 - 2008
dcondit@att.com

DELCASINO, Michael Tel: (202) 457 - 3810
V. President, Federal Regulatory Affairs Fax: (202) 457 - 2008

JACOBY, Peter G. Tel: (202) 457 - 3810
V. President and Director, Congressional Relations Fax: (202) 457 - 2267
pgjacoby@att.com
Registered Federal Lobbyist.

JOHNSON, Broderick D. Tel: (202) 457 - 3810
V. President, Congressional Relations Fax: (202) 457 - 2267
broderickdjohns@att.com

LUBIN, Joel Tel: (202) 457 - 3810
V. President, Federal Public Policy Fax: (202) 457 - 2545
lubin@att.com
Registered Federal Lobbyist.

MACOMBER, Debbie Tel: (202) 457 - 3810
Staff Manager, Federal Government Affairs Fax: (202) 457 - 2008

MARKIEWICZ, Stephanie J. Tel: (202) 457 - 3810
V. President, Congressional Relations Fax: (202) 263 - 2640
smarkiewicz@att.com
Registered Federal Lobbyist.

MARSH, Joan M. Tel: (202) 457 - 3810
V. President, Federal Regulatory Affairs Fax: (202) 457 - 2716
joanmariemarsh@att.com

QUINN, Robert W. Tel: (202) 457 - 3810
V. President and Director Federal Regulatory Affairs Fax: (202) 263 - 2655
rquinn@att.com
Registered Federal Lobbyist.

SCHOENBERGER, Douglas Tel: (202) 457 - 3810
V. President, International Government Affairs Fax: (202) 457 - 2008
Registered Federal Lobbyist.

SIMONE, Frank S. Tel: (202) 457 - 3810
V. President, Federal Regulatory Affairs Fax: (202) 457 - 2545
fsimone@att.com

WILNER, Carol W. Tel: (202) 457 - 3810
V. President and Director, Executive Branch Relations Fax: (202) 457 - 2258
cwilner@att.com
Registered Federal Lobbyist.

At Other Offices

BARRY, Robert Tel: (312) 230 - 2560
State Director, Government Affairs Fax: (312) 230 - 8835
222 W. Adams
Suite 1500
Chicago, IL 60606

DEVINE, William H. Tel: (916) 448 - 2853
State Director, Government Affairs Fax: (916) 443 - 6021
1121 L St., Suite 801
Sacramento, CA 95814
bdevine@att.com

FINNERTY, Elizabeth Tel: (614) 228 - 7959
State Director, Government Affairs Fax: (614) 228 - 7965
65 E. State St.
Columbus, OH 43215
bfinnerty@att.com

REYNICK, Marilyn
Director, AT&T Foundation
32 Ave. of the Americas, Room S606
New York, NY 10013-2412

ROOS, David E. Tel: (518) 463 - 3107
State Director, Government Affairs Fax: (518) 463 - 5943
111 Washington Ave., Suite 706
Albany, NY 12210-2213
droos@att.com

WINGO, Patrick T. Tel: (404) 810 - 4769
Director, Law and Government Affairs - Georgia Fax: (404) 810 - 5901
1230 Peachtree St., N.E.
Room 400
Atlanta, GA 30309
wingo@att.com

AT&T Communications

See listing on page 52 under AT&T.

AT&T Communications of California

See listing on page 52 under AT&T.

AT&T Communications of Delaware, Inc.

See listing on page 52 under AT&T.

AT&T Communications of the Midwest, Inc.

See listing on page 52 under AT&T.

AT&T Wireless Services

See listing on page 120 under Cingular Wireless.

ATA Holdings Corp.

Formerly known as Amtran, Inc. A holding company whose major subsidiary is ATA Airlines, Inc.

www.ata.com

Chairman, President and Chief Exec. Officer
MIKELSONS, J. George
Tel: (317) 247 - 4000
Fax: (317) 243 - 4169

Main Headquarters
Mailing: P.O. Box 51609
Indianapolis, IN 46251-0609
Tel: (317) 247 - 4000
Fax: (317) 243 - 4169
Street: 7337 W. Washington St.
Indianapolis, IN 46231

Political Action Committees

ATA Airlines, Inc. PAC
Contact: Gilbert F. Viets
P.O. Box 51609
Indianapolis, IN 46251-0609
Tel: (317) 247 - 4000
Fax: (317) 243 - 4169

Contributions to Candidates: none reported (01/05 - 09/05)

Public Affairs and Related Activities Personnel

At Headquarters

FOLEY, Michelle
Media Contact
Tel: (317) 282 - 2659
Fax: (317) 243 - 4169

MEYER, Richard W., Jr.
Senior V. President, Employee Relations
Tel: (317) 247 - 4000
Fax: (317) 243 - 4169

VIETS, Gilbert F.
PAC Treasurer
Tel: (317) 247 - 4000
Fax: (317) 243 - 4169

Atlanta Hawks

See listing on page 482 under Turner Broadcasting System, Inc.

Atlanta Journal Constitution

A newspaper publishing company.

www.ajc.com

Main Headquarters
Mailing: 72 Marietta St. NW
Atlanta, GA 30303
Tel: (404) 526 - 5151
Fax: (404) 526 - 5199

Corporate Foundations and Giving Programs

Atlanta Journal Constitution Corporate Giving Program
Contact: Reed Kimbrough
72 Marietta St. NW
Atlanta, GA 30303
Tel: (404) 526 - 5151
Fax: (404) 526 - 5199

Annual Grant Total: none reported
Geographic Preference: Georgia
Primary Interests: Arts and Culture; Education; Literacy; Minority Opportunities; Social Services

Public Affairs and Related Activities Personnel

At Headquarters

KIMBROUGH, Reed
V. President, Community Affairs and Workforce Diversity
Tel: (404) 526 - 5151
Fax: (404) 526 - 5199
Responsibilities include corporate philanthropy.

MURRAY, Alice
Director of Marketing Administration
Tel: (404) 526 - 5151
Fax: (404) 526 - 5199
Responsibilities include corporate communications.

RATTRAY, Paula
V. President, Marketing
prattray@ajc.com
Tel: (404) 526 - 5151
Fax: (404) 526 - 5199
Responsibilities include public affairs.

Atlanta Thrashers

See listing on page 482 under Turner Broadcasting System, Inc.

Atlantic Coast Airlines Holdings, Inc.

See listing on page 199 under FLYi, Inc.

Atmel Corp.

A manufacturer of complex integrated circuits.

www.atmel.com
Annual Revenues: $1.47 billion

Chairman, President and Chief Exec. Officer
PERLEGOS, George
gperlegos@atmel.com
Tel: (408) 441 - 0311
Fax: (408) 436 - 4200

Main Headquarters
Mailing: 2325 Orchard Pkwy.
San Jose, CA 95131
Tel: (408) 441 - 0311
Fax: (408) 436 - 4200

Public Affairs and Related Activities Personnel

At Headquarters

HORWITZ, Steve
Director, Investor Relations
shorowitz@atmel.com
Tel: (408) 487 - 2677
Fax: (408) 436 - 4200

LA PLANTE, Bobbi
V. President, Global Human Resources
blaplante@atmel.com
Tel: (408) 441 - 0311
Fax: (408) 436 - 4200

OVER, Clive
Corporate Communications Contact
cliveover@atmel.com
Tel: (408) 441 - 0311
Fax: (408) 436 - 4200

THOMPSON, Wendy
Corporate Communications Contact
wthompson@atmel.com
Tel: (408) 441 - 0311
Fax: (408) 436 - 4200

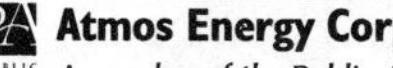

Atmos Energy Corp.

A member of the Public Affairs Council. A natural gas distribution company.

www.atmosenergy.com

Chairman, President and Chief Exec. Officer
BEST, Robert W.
robert.best@atmosenergy.com
Tel: (972) 934 - 9227
Fax: (972) 855 - 3030
TF: (800) 382 - 8667

Main Headquarters
Mailing: P.O. Box 650205
Dallas, TX 75265-0205
Tel: (972) 934 - 9227
Fax: (972) 855 - 3030
TF: (800) 382 - 8667

Political Action Committees

Atmost Energy Corp. PAC
Contact: Tom D. Stephens
P.O. Box 650205
Dallas, TX 75265-0205
Tel: (972) 855 - 3789
Fax: (972) 855 - 3030
TF: (800) 382 - 8667

Contributions to Candidates: $6,000 (01/05 - 09/05)
Republicans: $6,000.

Principal Recipients

SENATE REPUBLICANS		HOUSE REPUBLICANS	
Allen, George (VA)	$1,000	Carter, John (TX)	$2,000
Bryant, Edward (TN)	$1,000	Gohmert, Louis (TX)	$1,000
Talent, James (MO)	$500		
Vitter, David (LA)	$500		

Corporate Foundations and Giving Programs

Atmos Energy Community Relations Program
P.O. Box 650205
Dallas, TX 75265-0205
Tel: (972) 934 - 9227
Fax: (972) 855 - 3030
TF: (800) 382 - 8667

Annual Grant Total: none reported
Geographic Preference: Dallas, TX
Primary Interests: Arts and Culture; Economic Development; Education; Health and Human Services
Recent Recipients: Boy Scouts of America; Junior Achievement; Susan G. Komen Breast Cancer Foundation; United Way

Public Affairs and Related Activities Personnel

At Headquarters

ASTON, Verlon R., Jr.
V. President, Governmental and Public Affairs
Tel: (972) 934 - 9227
Fax: (972) 855 - 3030
TF: (800) 382 - 8667

HUNTER, Gerald R.
Director, Corporate Communications
gerald.hunter@atmosenergy.com
Tel: (972) 855 - 3116
Fax: (972) 855 - 3040
TF: (800) 382 - 8667

KAPPES, Susan C.
V. President, Investor Relations and Corporate Communications
Tel: (972) 855 - 3729
Fax: (972) 855 - 3030
TF: (800) 382 - 8667

MCGREGOR, Wynn D.
V. President, Human Resources
wynn.mcgregor@atmosenergy.com
Tel: (972) 934 - 9227
Fax: (972) 855 - 3030
TF: (800) 382 - 8667

STEPHENS, Tom D.
Director, Governmental Affairs
Tom.Stephens@atmosenergy.com
Tel: (972) 855 - 3789
Fax: (972) 855 - 3030
TF: (800) 382 - 8667
Responsibilities include political action.

Atmos Energy Corp.
** continued from previous page*

At Other Offices

BARTLING, James W. — Tel: (913) 764 - 0531 Ext: 225
Manager, Public Affairs - Kansas Division — Fax: (913) 764 - 1610
730 N. Ridgeview
Olathe, KS 66061
James.Bartling@atmosenergy.com

ATOFINA Chemicals, Inc.
A manufacturer of high performance chemicals and polymers.
www.atofemachemicals.com
Annual Revenues: $17.68 billion

Chairman and Chief Exec. Officer
LE HENAFF, Thierry — Tel: (215) 419 - 7000; Fax: (215) 419 - 7591; TF: (800) 225 - 7788

Main Headquarters
Mailing: 2000 Market St.
Philadelphia, PA 19103-9000 — Tel: (215) 419 - 7000; Fax: (215) 419 - 7591; TF: (800) 225 - 7788

Washington Office
Contact: Charles A. Kitchen
Mailing: 1200 N. Nash St.
Suite 1150
Arlington, VA 22209 — Tel: (703) 527 - 2099; Fax: (703) 527 - 2092

Political Action Committees

Arkema Corporation PAC
Contact: Joseph Urbani
2000 Market St.
Philadelphia, PA 19103-9000 — Tel: (215) 419 - 7000; Fax: (215) 419 - 7591; TF: (800) 225 - 7788

Contributions to Candidates: $7,000 (01/05 - 09/05)
Democrats: $1,000; Republicans: $6,000.

Principal Recipients

SENATE DEMOCRATS		HOUSE DEMOCRATS	
		Green, Gene (TX)	$1,000
SENATE REPUBLICANS		**HOUSE REPUBLICANS**	
Santorum, Richard (PA)	$1,500	Fitzpatrick, Michael (PA)	$2,000
		Gerlach, Jim (PA)	$1,000
		Peterson, John Mr. (PA)	$1,000
		Weldon, Curt (PA)	$500

Corporate Foundations and Giving Programs

Arkema Inc. Foundation
Contact: Jane C. Crawford
2000 Market St.
Philadelphia, PA 19103-9000 — Tel: (215) 419 - 7614; Fax: (215) 419 - 5229; TF: (800) 225 - 7788

Annual Grant Total: $400,000 - $500,000
Geographic Preference: Area(s) in which the company operates
Primary Interests: Arts and Culture; Civic and Public Affairs; Education; United Way Campaigns
Recent Recipients: Pennsylvania Ballet; Philadelphia Art Museum; United Way

Public Affairs and Related Activities Personnel

At Headquarters

BELL, Jim — Tel: (215) 419 - 5293; Fax: (215) 419 - 7591; TF: (800) 225 - 7788
Senior Communications Manager

BOSSHART, Amy — Tel: (215) 419 - 7230; Fax: (215) 419 - 7591; TF: (800) 225 - 7788
Manager Employee Communications/Communications Manager

CRAWFORD, Jane C. — Tel: (215) 419 - 7614; Fax: (215) 419 - 5229; TF: (800) 225 - 7788
Chief Public Affairs Officer and President, Arkema Inc. Foundation

GIANGRASSO, Chris — Tel: (215) 419 - 7714; Fax: (215) 419 - 7591; TF: (800) 225 - 7788
V. President, Human Resources and Communications

HOWARD, Stan — Tel: (215) 419 - 7027; Fax: (215) 419 - 7591; TF: (800) 225 - 7788
Senior Communications Manager

KRAMER, Walter — Tel: (215) 419 - 7149; Fax: (215) 419 - 7591; TF: (800) 225 - 7788
Manager, Community Relations

PALMIERI, Anita — Tel: (215) 419 - 5013; Fax: (215) 419 - 7591; TF: (800) 225 - 7788
Senior Communications Manager

URBANI, Joseph — Tel: (215) 419 - 7000; Fax: (215) 419 - 7591; TF: (800) 225 - 7788
Treasurer, ATOFINA PAC

At Washington Office

KITCHEN, Charles A. — Tel: (703) 527 - 2099; Fax: (703) 527 - 2092
Director, Government Relations
ckitchen@ato.com
Registered Federal Lobbyist.

ATOFINA Petrochemicals Inc.
See listing on page 478 under Total Petrochemicals USA, Inc.

The Austin Co.
An international organization of consultants, designers, engineers and constructors specializing in industrial, governmental and commercial facilities.
www.theaustin.com
Annual Revenues: $500 million

Chairman and Chief Exec. Officer
MELSOP, J. William — Tel: (440) 544 - 2600; Fax: (440) 544 - 2616

Main Headquarters
Mailing: 6095 Parkland Blvd.
Cleveland, OH 44124 — Tel: (440) 544 - 2600; Fax: (440) 544 - 2616

Public Affairs and Related Activities Personnel

At Headquarters

PIERCE, Michael G. — Tel: (440) 544 - 2600; Fax: (440) 544 - 2616
Manager, Marketing and Communication Services

Austin Industries
A diverse construction company.
www.austin-ind.com
Annual Revenues: $1.27 billion

Chairman of the Board
SOLOMON, William T. — Tel: (214) 443 - 5500

President and Chief Exec. Officer
GAFFORD, Ronald J. — Tel: (214) 443 - 5500

Main Headquarters
Mailing: P.O. Box 1590
Dallas, TX 75221-1590 — Tel: (214) 443 - 5500
Street: 3535 Travis Rd., Suite 300
Dallas, TX 75204-1466

Political Action Committees

Austin Industries Cos. PAC
Contact: Charles Hardy
P.O. Box 1590
Dallas, TX 75221-1590 — Tel: (214) 443 - 5500 Ext: 575; Fax: (214) 443 - 5516

Contributions to Candidates: $5,500 (01/05 - 09/05)
Democrats: $2,500; Republicans: $3,000.

Principal Recipients

SENATE DEMOCRATS		HOUSE DEMOCRATS	
Lincoln, Blanche (AR)	$1,000	Johnson, Eddie (TX)	$1,000
		Cardin, Ben (MD)	$500
SENATE REPUBLICANS		**HOUSE REPUBLICANS**	
Hutchison, Kay Bailey (TX)		Marchant, Kenny (TX)	$1,000
	$1,000	Hensarling, Jeb (TX)	$500
		Ramstad, Jim (MN)	$500

Corporate Foundations and Giving Programs

Austin Industries Corporate Giving Program
P.O. Box 1590 — Tel: (214) 443 - 5500
Dallas, TX 75221-1590

Annual Grant Total: none reported

Public Affairs and Related Activities Personnel

At Headquarters

ELISE, Lori — Tel: (214) 443 - 5500; Fax: (214) 443 - 5622
Director, Corporate Communications

HARDY, Charles — Tel: (214) 443 - 5500 Ext: 575; Fax: (214) 443 - 5516
Corporate Attorney; PAC Treasurer

SCHRANZ, James E. — Tel: (214) 443 - 5500
V. President, Human Resources and Treasurer

Auto-Owners Insurance Group
A property, casualty and life insurance company.
www.auto-owners.com
Annual Revenues: $4.54 billion

Chairman of the Board
ARENDS, Herman J. — Tel: (517) 323 - 1200; Fax: (517) 323 - 8796

Auto-Owners Insurance Group

* continued from previous page

Chief Exec. Officer
LOOYENGA, Roger — Tel: (517) 323 - 1200 Fax: (517) 323 - 8796

Main Headquarters
Mailing: 6101 Anacapri Blvd.
Lansing, MI 48917 — Tel: (517) 323 - 1200 Fax: (517) 323 - 8796

Public Affairs and Related Activities Personnel

At Headquarters

MCKAY, Eugenie M.
Director, Corporate Communications — Tel: (517) 323 - 1200 Fax: (517) 323 - 8796

MCKENZIE, Sherry
Manager, Education and Training — Tel: (517) 323 - 1200 Fax: (517) 323 - 8796

THELEN, Dan
V. President, Personnel — Tel: (517) 323 - 1200 Fax: (517) 323 - 8796

Autodesk Inc.

A software manufacturer.
www.autodesk.com
Annual Revenues: $947.5 million

Chairman, President and Chief Exec. Officer
BARTZ, Carol — Tel: (415) 507 - 5000 Fax: (415) 507 - 5100

Main Headquarters
Mailing: 111 McInnis Pkwy.
San Rafael, CA 94903 — Tel: (415) 507 - 5000 Fax: (415) 507 - 5100

Corporate Foundations and Giving Programs

Autodesk, Inc. Foundation
111 McInnis Pkwy.
San Rafael, CA 94903 — Tel: (415) 507 - 5000 Fax: (415) 507 - 5100

Annual Grant Total: $500,000 - $750,000
Geographic Preference: California
Primary Interests: Arts and Culture; Civic and Public Affairs; Education; Environment/Conservation; Health and Human Services; Technology
Recent Recipients: Project Open Hand

Public Affairs and Related Activities Personnel

At Headquarters

BECKER, Jan
V. President, Human Resources — Tel: (415) 507 - 5000 Fax: (415) 507 - 5100

HOLSTEIN, Dawn
Global Communications Contact
dawn.holstein@autodesk.com — Tel: (415) 507 - 6554 Fax: (415) 507 - 5100

PACK, Nicole
Corporate Communications Contact
nicole.pack@autodesk.com — Tel: (415) 507 - 6282 Fax: (415) 507 - 5100

PIRRI, Sue
V. President, Investor Relations
sue.pirri@autodesk.com — Tel: (415) 507 - 6705 Fax: (415) 507 - 6129

Automatic Data Processing, Inc.

A computing and information service company.
www.adp.com
Annual Revenues: $8.5 billion

Chairman and Chief Exec. Officer
WEINBACH, Arthur F.
arthur_weinbach@adp.com — Tel: (973) 974 - 5000 TF: (800) 225 - 5237

Main Headquarters
Mailing: One ADP Blvd.
Roseland, NJ 07068-1728 — Tel: (973) 974 - 5000 TF: (800) 225 - 5237

Corporate Foundations and Giving Programs

Automatic Data Processing Foundation
One ADP Blvd.
Roseland, NJ 07068-1728 — Tel: (973) 974 - 5000 TF: (800) 225 - 5237

Annual Grant Total: $1,000,000 - $2,000,000
Program emphasizes matching funds for contributions of Automatic Data Processsing employees.

Public Affairs and Related Activities Personnel

At Headquarters

BERKE, Richard
V. President, Human Resources
richard_burke@adp.com — Tel: (973) 994 - 5000 Fax: (973) 974 - 3302 TF: (800) 225 - 5237

CORALLO, Terry
Director, Public Relations and Advertising
terrym_corallo@adp.com — Tel: (973) 974 - 7640 TF: (800) 225 - 5237

AutoNation, Inc.

An automobile retail company.
www.autonation.com
Annual Revenues: $20 billion

Chairman and Chief Exec. Officer
JACKSON, Michael
jacksonm@autonation.com — Tel: (954) 769 - 7200 Fax: (954) 769 - 6494

Main Headquarters
Mailing: AutoNation Tower
110 SE Sixth St.
Fort Lauderdale, FL 33301 — Tel: (954) 769 - 7200 Fax: (954) 769 - 6494

Corporate Foundations and Giving Programs

AutoNation Corporate Contributions Program
Contact: Gale M. Butler
AutoNation Tower
110 SE Sixth St.
Fort Lauderdale, FL 33301 — Tel: (954) 769 - 7209 Fax: (954) 769 - 6494

Annual Grant Total: $1,000,000 - $2,000,000
Geographic Preference: Florida
Primary Interests: Education; Health and Human Services
Recent Recipients: Take Stock in Children; United Way

Public Affairs and Related Activities Personnel

At Headquarters

BUTLER, Gale M.
V. President, Corporate Affairs
Mailstop: 20th Floor
butlerg@AutoNation.com — Tel: (954) 769 - 7209 Fax: (954) 769 - 6494

CANNON, Marc
V. President, Corporate Communications
Mailstop: 20th Floor
cannonm@autonation.com — Tel: (954) 769 - 7208 Fax: (954) 679 - 6398

EVANS, James D.
Senior V. President, Industry Relations
evansj@autonation.com — Tel: (954) 769 - 7200 Fax: (954) 769 - 6494

FERRANDO, Jon
Chief Counsel
ferrandoj@autonation.com — Tel: (954) 769 - 7200 Fax: (954) 769 - 6494
Responsibilities include corporate public affairs.

RING, Audrey
Director, Corporate Communications
Mailstop: 20th Floor
ringa@autonation.com — Tel: (954) 769 - 4687 Fax: (954) 769 - 6389

ZIMMERMAN, John M.
V. President, Investor Relations
Mailstop: 29th Floor
zimmermanj@autonation.com — Tel: (954) 769 - 6000 Fax: (954) 769 - 6398

AutoZone, Inc.

A member of the Public Affairs Council. An auto parts chain.
www.autozone.com
Annual Revenues: $5.67 billion

Chairman of the Board
MCKENNA, W. Andrew — Tel: (901) 495 - 6500 Fax: (901) 495 - 8300

President and Chief Exec. Officer
RHODES, William C. — Tel: (901) 495 - 6500 Fax: (901) 495 - 8300

Main Headquarters
Mailing: 123 S. Front St.
Memphis, TN 38103 — Tel: (901) 495 - 6500 Fax: (901) 495 - 8300

Political Action Committees

AutoZone Inc. Committee for Better Government
Contact: Ray Pohlman
123 S. Front St.
Memphis, TN 38103 — Tel: (901) 495 - 7962 Fax: (901) 495 - 8300

Contributions to Candidates: $5,000 (01/05 - 09/05)
Republicans: $5,000.

Principal Recipients

SENATE REPUBLICANS		HOUSE REPUBLICANS
Alexander, Lamar (TN)	$5,000	

Corporate Foundations and Giving Programs

AutoZone Corporate Contributions Program
Contact: Trina Atkins
123 S. Front St.
Memphis, TN 38103 — Tel: (901) 495 - 6500 Fax: (901) 495 - 8300

Annual Grant Total: none reported
Geographic Preference: Area(s) in which employees live and work
Primary Interests: Education; Health and Human Services

Public Affairs and Related Activities Personnel

At Headquarters

ATKINS, Trina
Manager, Communications — Tel: (901) 495 - 6500 Fax: (901) 495 - 8300

CAMPBELL, Brian
Investor Relations Contact
brian.campbell@autozone.com — Tel: (901) 495 - 7005 Fax: (901) 495 - 8300

AutoZone, Inc.

• continued from previous page

POHLMAN, Ray — Tel: (901) 495 - 7962; Fax: (901) 495 - 8300
Director, Government Affairs and Media Contact
ray.pohlman@autozone.com
Responsibilities include political action.

VANDERLINDE, Daisy L. — Tel: (901) 495 - 6500; Fax: (901) 495 - 8300
Senior V. President, Human Resources and Loss Prevention

Avaya Inc.

A provider of communications networks and services.

www.avaya.com
Annual Revenues: $5 billion

Chairman and Chief Exec. Officer
PETERSON, Donald K. — Tel: (908) 953 - 6000; Fax: (908) 953 - 7609
dpeterson@avaya.com

Main Headquarters
Mailing: 211 Mount Airy Rd.
Basking Ridge, NJ 07920 — Tel: (908) 953 - 6000; Fax: (908) 953 - 7609

Washington Office
Contact: Chuck E. Crowders
Mailing: 490 L'Enfant Plaza SW — Tel: (202) 378 - 2375
Suite 511
Washington, DC 20024

Political Action Committees

Avaya Inc. PAC
Contact: Chuck E. Crowders
490 L'Enfant Plaza SW — Tel: (202) 378 - 2374
Suite 511 — Fax: (202) 220 - 7093
Washington, DC 20024

Contributions to Candidates: $15,500 (01/05 - 09/05)
Democrats: $9,000; Republicans: $6,500.

Principal Recipients

SENATE DEMOCRATS		HOUSE DEMOCRATS	
Feinstein, Dianne (CA)	$1,000	Eshoo, Anna (CA)	$1,000
		Holden, Timothy (PA)	$1,000
		Menendez, Robert (NJ)	$1,000
		Obey, David R (WI)	$1,000
		Price, David E (NC)	$1,000
		Rangel, Charles B (NY)	$1,000
SENATE REPUBLICANS		**HOUSE REPUBLICANS**	
		Barton, Joe L (TX)	$1,000
		Brady, Kevin Patrick (TX)	$1,000
		Dreier, David (CA)	$1,000
		Hoekstra, Peter (MI)	$1,000
		Istook, Ernest (OK)	$1,000
		Sessions, Pete (TX)	$1,000

Public Affairs and Related Activities Personnel

At Headquarters

DIMARZO, Maryanne — Tel: (908) 953 - 6000; Fax: (908) 953 - 7609
Senior V. President, Human Resources
mdimarzo@avaya.com

HORNE, W. Scott — Tel: (908) 953 - 3476; Fax: (908) 953 - 7609
Corporate Communications Contact
horne@avaya.com

KLINE, Deb — Tel: (908) 953 - 6179; Fax: (908) 953 - 7609
Corporate Communications, Eastern North America and Canada
klined@avaya.com

NEWMAN, Lynn — Tel: (908) 953 - 8692; Fax: (908) 953 - 7609
Financial Media and Corporate Issues
lynnnewman@avaya.com

THIELE, Mary — Tel: (908) 953 - 6152; Fax: (908) 953 - 7609
Corporate Communications, Western North America
mthiele@avaya.com

At Washington Office

CROWDERS, Chuck E. — Tel: (202) 378 - 2374; Fax: (202) 220 - 7093
V. President and Head, Government Affairs
crowders@avaya.com
Registered Federal Lobbyist.

KEEFE, Kenneth — Tel: (202) 378 - 2373; Fax: (202) 220 - 7093
Director, Government Affairs, Federal/State
klkeefe@avaya.com
Registered Federal Lobbyist.

Aventis CropScience

See listing on page 66 under Bayer CropScience.

Aventis Pasteur

See listing on page 420 under Sanofi Pasteur, Inc.

Aventis Pharmaceuticals

See listing on page 421 under Sanofi-Aventis Inc.

Avery Dennison Corp.

A worldwide manufacturer of self-adhesive materials, tapes and labels, office products, tags, retail systems and specialty chemicals. Consumer brands include AVERY brand office labels and card products, indexes, binders and software, and FASSON brand self-adhesive materials for industrial markets.

www.averydennison.com
Annual Revenues: $5.34 billion

Chairman of the Board
NEAL, Philip M. — Tel: (626) 304 - 2000; Fax: (626) 792 - 7312

President and Chief Exec. Officer
SCARBOROUGH, Dean A. — Tel: (626) 304 - 2000; Fax: (626) 792 - 7312

Main Headquarters
Mailing: 150 N. Orange Grove Blvd. — Tel: (626) 304 - 2000
Pasadena, CA 91103 — Fax: (626) 792 - 7312

Corporate Foundations and Giving Programs

Avery Dennison Corporate Contributions
150 N. Orange Grove Blvd. — Tel: (626) 304 - 2000
Pasadena, CA 91103 — Fax: (626) 792 - 7312

Assets: $8,000,000 (1999)
Annual Grant Total: $300,000 - $400,000

Public Affairs and Related Activities Personnel

At Headquarters

COLEMAN, Charles E. — Tel: (626) 304 - 2014; Fax: (626) 577 - 9587
Director, Media Relations and Financial Communications
charles.coleman@averydennison.com

DIXON, Diane B. — Tel: (626) 304 - 2118; Fax: (626) 792 - 7312
Senior V. President, Worldwide Communications and Advertising
diane.dixon@averydennison.com

GUENTHER, Cynthia S. — Tel: (626) 304 - 2204; Fax: (626) 792 - 7312
Investor Relations Contact

SCHULER, J. Terry — Tel: (626) 304 - 2000; Fax: (626) 792 - 7312
Senior V. President, Human Resources
terry.schuler@averydennison.com

Avid Technology, Inc.

A digital media company.

www.avid.com
Annual Revenues: $419 million

President and Chief Exec. Officer
KRALL, David A. — Tel: (978) 640 - 6789; Fax: (978) 640 - 1366

Main Headquarters
Mailing: Avid Technology Park — Tel: (978) 640 - 6789
One Park West — Fax: (978) 640 - 1366
Tewksbury, MA 01876

Public Affairs and Related Activities Personnel

At Headquarters

BAKER, Patricia A. — Tel: (978) 640 - 6789; Fax: (978) 640 - 1366
V. President, Human Resources

GRAY, Steve — Tel: (978) 640 - 6789; Fax: (978) 640 - 1366
V. President, Corporate and Marketing Communications

HOLLAND, Carter — Tel: (978) 640 - 3172; Fax: (978) 640 - 1366
Director, Corporate Communications
carter_holland@avid.com

PALADINO, Amy — Tel: (978) 640 - 3051; Fax: (978) 640 - 1366
Manager, Public Relations
amy_paladino@avid.com

RIDLON, Dean — Tel: (978) 640 - 5309; Fax: (978) 640 - 3166
Director, Investor Relations
investor_relations@avid.com

Avista Corp.

An energy, information and technology company.

www.avistacorp.com
Annual Revenues: $6 billion

Avista Corp.

* continued from previous page

Chairman, President and Chief Exec. Officer
ELY, Gary
Mailstop: MSC-12
gary.ely@avistacorp.com
Tel: (509) 489 - 0500
Fax: (509) 495 - 8725

Main Headquarters
Mailing: P.O. Box 3727
Spokane, WA 99220-3727
Tel: (509) 489 - 0500
Fax: (509) 495 - 8725
TF: (800) 727 - 9170

Street: 1411 E. Mission Ave.
Spokane, WA 99202

Political Action Committees

Avista Employees for Effective Government Political Action Committee
Contact: Susan Barry
P.O. Box 3727
Spokane, WA 99220-3727
Tel: (509) 489 - 0500
Fax: (509) 495 - 8725
TF: (800) 727 - 9170

Contributions to Candidates: $8,900 (01/05 - 09/05)
Democrats: $1,500; Republicans: $7,400.

Principal Recipients

SENATE DEMOCRATS		HOUSE DEMOCRATS	
Murray, Patty (WA)	$1,000		
Nelson, Benjamin (NE)	$500		
SENATE REPUBLICANS		**HOUSE REPUBLICANS**	
Smith, Gordon (OR)	$1,400	McMorris, Cathy (WA)	$3,000
Craig, Larry (ID)	$1,000	Simpson, Michael (ID)	$1,000
		Walden, Gregory (OR)	$1,000

Corporate Foundations and Giving Programs

Avista Foundation
Contact: Debbie Simock
P.O. Box 3727
Spokane, WA 99220-3727
Tel: (509) 489 - 0500
Fax: (509) 495 - 8725
TF: (800) 727 - 9170

Annual Grant Total: $100,000 - $200,000
More information about the foundation can be found on their website: www.avistafoundation.org
Geographic Preference: California; Idaho; Montana; Oregon; Washington State
Primary Interests: Cultural Education; Economic Development; K-12 Education

Public Affairs and Related Activities Personnel

At Headquarters

BARRY, Susan
PAC Treasurer
Tel: (509) 489 - 0500
Fax: (509) 495 - 8725
TF: (800) 727 - 9170

FELTES, Karen S.
V. President, Human Resources and Corporate Secretary
Tel: (509) 489 - 0500
Fax: (509) 495 - 8725
TF: (800) 727 - 9170

IMHOF, Hugh
Manager, Media and Information
hugh.imhof@avistacorp.com
Tel: (509) 495 - 4264
Fax: (509) 495 - 8725
TF: (800) 727 - 9170

MEYER, David J.
V. President and Chief Counsel, Regulatory and Government Affairs
Tel: (509) 489 - 0500
Fax: (509) 495 - 8725
TF: (800) 727 - 9170

SIMOCK, Debbie
Foundation Contact
Tel: (509) 489 - 0500
Fax: (509) 495 - 8725
TF: (800) 727 - 9170

WUERST, Jessie
Investor Relations Contact
jessie.wuerst@avistacorp.com
Tel: (509) 495 - 8578
Fax: (509) 495 - 8725
TF: (800) 727 - 9170

At Other Offices

COLWELL, Neil V.
Director, State Government Relations-ID and MT
802 W. Bannock
Suite 306
Boise, ID 83702
ncolwell1@mindspring.com
Tel: (208) 343 - 3821
Fax: (208) 385 - 7328

SPRAGUE, K. Collins
Director, State Government Relations-WA
Savings League Bldg., Suite 101
1501 S. Capitol Way
Olympia, WA 98501
csprague@hctc.com
Tel: (360) 956 - 7436
Fax: (360) 754 - 7465

Avnet Electronics Marketing

See listing on page 57 under Avnet Inc.

Avnet Inc.

A distributor of electronic components, computer products and services, and embedded systems.
www.avnet.com
Annual Revenues: $8.9 billion

Chairman and Chief Exec. Officer
VALLEE, Roy
roy.vallee@avnet.com
Tel: (480) 463 - 2000

Main Headquarters
Mailing: 2211 S. 47th St.
Phoenix, AZ 85034
Tel: (480) 643 - 2000

Corporate Foundations and Giving Programs

Avnet, Inc. Corporate Contributions Program
Contact: Teri Radosevich
2211 S. 47th St.
Phoenix, AZ 85034
Tel: (480) 643 - 2000

Annual Grant Total: $300,000 - $400,000
Primary Interests: Children; Community Affairs; Education

Public Affairs and Related Activities Personnel

At Headquarters

FANNING, Sean
Senior V. President, Global Communications
(Avnet Electronics Marketing)
sean.fanning@avnet.com
Tel: (480) 643 - 7824

GOREL, Michelle
Director, Communications
(Avnet Technology Solutions)
michelle.gorel@avnet.com
Tel: (480) 794 - 6943

JURCY, Jan
V. President, Public Relations
jan.jurcy@avnet.com
Tel: (480) 643 - 7642
Fax: (480) 643 - 7415

KEENAN, Vince
V. President and Director, Investor Relations
Tel: (480) 643 - 7053
Fax: (480) 643 - 7370

MAAG, Allen
Chief Communications Officer
al.maag@avnet.com
Tel: (480) 643 - 7651
Fax: (480) 643 - 7240
Responsibilities include corporate communications public affairs and community relations.

MILLER, Janice
V. President, Organizational Development and Human Resources
janice.miller@avnet.com
Tel: (480) 643 - 2000

RADOSEVICH, Teri
Director, Community Relations
teri.radosevich@avnet.com
Tel: (480) 643 - 2000
Responsibilities include government affairs.

Avon Products, Inc.

PUBLIC AFFAIRS COUNCIL

A member of the Public Affairs Council. Manufacturer and distributor of cosmetics, fragrances, toiletries and costume jewelry.
www.avon.com
Annual Revenues: $5.99 billion

Chairman and Chief Exec. Officer
JUNG, Andrea
Tel: (212) 282 - 5000
Fax: (212) 282 - 6220

Main Headquarters
Mailing: 1345 Ave. of the Americas
New York, NY 10020
Tel: (212) 282 - 7000
Fax: (212) 282 - 6220

Political Action Committees

Avon Products, Inc. Fund for Responsible Government
Contact: Josephine Mills
1345 Ave. of the Americas
New York, NY 10020
Tel: (212) 282 - 5609
Fax: (212) 282 - 6086

Contributions to Candidates: none reported (01/05 - 09/05)

Corporate Foundations and Giving Programs

Avon Products Foundation Inc.
Contact: Susan Arnot Heaney
1345 Ave. of the Americas
New York, NY 10020
Tel: (212) 282 - 5668
Fax: (212) 282 - 6220

Assets: $38,437,478 (2000)
Annual Grant Total: over $5,000,000
Groups may apply to New York corporate headquarters for support. The company also makes substantial grants in the form of direct corporate contributions to organizations that support economic opportunity for women and that promote breast cancer awareness and early detection. Donations totalled over $31 million in 2000.
Primary Interests: Arts and Humanities; Community Affairs; Education; Medical Research; Medicine and Health Care; Social Services; Women's Health
Recent Recipients: New York Presbyterian Hospital

Public Affairs and Related Activities Personnel

At Headquarters

ALZIARI, Lucien
Senior V. President, Human Resources
Tel: (212) 282 - 7000
Fax: (212) 282 - 6220

BEAUDET, Victor
Exec. Director, Financial Communications and Corporate Communications
Tel: (212) 282 - 5344
Fax: (212) 282 - 6220

Avon Products, Inc.

* continued from previous page

CASTELLANO, Laura — Tel: (212) 282 - 5345
Corporate Social Responsibility Contact — Fax: (212) 282 - 6220

COFFEY, Debora — Tel: (212) 282 - 5660
V. President, Public Relations and Promotions — Fax: (212) 282 - 6220

FORESTI, Rob — Tel: (212) 282 - 5320
Investor Relations Contact — Fax: (212) 282 - 6035

GLASER, Nancy — Tel: (212) 282 - 7000
Senior V. President, Communications — Fax: (212) 282 - 6220

HEANEY, Susan Arnot — Tel: (212) 282 - 5668
Foundation Contact — Fax: (212) 282 - 6220
susan.heaney@avonfoundation.com

JOHANSEN, Renee — Tel: (212) 282 - 5320
V. President, Investor Relations — Fax: (212) 282 - 6035

MILLS, Josephine — Tel: (212) 282 - 5609
Director, Global Government Affairs — Fax: (212) 282 - 6086
Mailstop: 27th Floor
Responsibilities include political action.

QUIRAMA, Luis — Tel: (212) 282 - 7000
Shareholder Relations Contact — Fax: (212) 282 - 6220

WALAS, Kathleen — Tel: (212) 282 - 5140
President, Avon Products Foundation
Mailstop: 27th Floor

AXA Financial, Inc.

A financial services organization. Its parent company AXA Group is headquartered in Paris, France. Acquired The MONY Group in July, 2004.

www.axa-financial.com

Chairman of the Board — Tel: (212) 554 - 1234
DE CASTRIES, Henri — TF: (888) AXA - INFO

President and Chief Exec. Officer — Tel: (212) 314 - 3788
CONDRON, Christopher M. "Kip" — TF: (888) AXA - INFO
christopher.condron@axa-financial.com

Main Headquarters
Mailing: 1290 Ave. of the Americas — Tel: (212) 554 - 1234
New York, NY 10104 — TF: (888) AXA - INFO

Political Action Committees

AXA Equitable Life Insurance Co. PAC
Contact: Paul J. Flora
1290 Ave. of the Americas — Tel: (212) 554 - 1234
New York, NY 10104 — TF: (888) AXA - INFO

Contributions to Candidates: $41,000 (01/05 - 09/05)
Democrats: $12,500; Republicans: $28,500.

Principal Recipients

SENATE DEMOCRATS		HOUSE DEMOCRATS	
Carper, Thomas R (DE)	$3,000	Becerra, Xavier (CA)	$2,000
Baucus, Max (MT)	$1,500	Kanjorski, Paul (PA)	$2,000
		Tubbs-Jones, Stephanie (OH)	$2,000

SENATE REPUBLICANS		HOUSE REPUBLICANS	
Bennett, Robert F (UT)	$5,000	Beauprez, Robert (CO)	$2,500
Snowe, Olympia (ME)	$5,000	Chocola, Christopher (IN)	$2,000
Crapo, Michael D (ID)	$3,000	Johnson, Nancy (CT)	$2,000
		Lewis, Ron (KY)	$2,000
		Royce, Ed Mr (CA)	$2,000

Corporate Foundations and Giving Programs

The AXA Foundation
1290 Ave. of the Americas — Tel: (212) 554 - 1234
New York, NY 10104 — TF: (888) AXA - INFO

Assets: $37,464,9920
Annual Grant Total: over $5,000,000
Geographic Preference: National
Primary Interests: Higher Education
Recent Recipients: Scholarship America

Public Affairs and Related Activities Personnel

At Headquarters

BLEVINS, Jennifer C. — Tel: (212) 554 - 1234
Exec. V. President, Human Resources — TF: (888) AXA - INFO

FLORA, Paul J. — Tel: (212) 554 - 1234
PAC Treasurer — TF: (888) AXA - INFO

JOSEPH, Rosalind — Tel: (212) 314 - 4295
Manager, AXA Group Communications and Media Relations — TF: (888) AXA - INFO
rosalind.joseph@axa-financial.com

TAYLOR, Mary — Tel: (212) 314 - 5845
Corporate Communications Contact — TF: (888) AXA - INFO

TOLVIN, Jeff — Tel: (212) 314 - 2811
Assistant V. President, Public Relations — TF: (888) AXA - INFO
jeffrey.tolvin@axa-financial.com

Aztar Corp.

A gaming operator with major casino properties in New Jersey and Nevada.

www.aztar.com
Annual Revenues: $813.1 million

Chairman and Chief Exec. Officer — Tel: (602) 381 - 4100
HADDOCK, Robert M. — Fax: (602) 381 - 4107

Main Headquarters
Mailing: 2390 E. Camelback Rd. — Tel: (602) 381 - 4100
Suite 400 — Fax: (602) 381 - 4107
Phoenix, AZ 85016-3452

Corporate Foundations and Giving Programs

Aztar Corp. Contributions Program
Contact: Joe C. Cole
2390 E. Camelback Rd. — Tel: (602) 381 - 4100
Suite 400 — Fax: (602) 381 - 4107
Phoenix, AZ 85016-3452

Annual Grant Total: none reported

Public Affairs and Related Activities Personnel

At Headquarters

COLE, Joe C. — Tel: (602) 381 - 4100
V. President, Corporate Communications — Fax: (602) 381 - 4107
joecole@aztar.com

The Babcock & Wilcox Company

Designs, engineers, manufactures, constructs and services steam generating and environmental equipment for utilities and industries worldwide. A subsidiary of McDermott Internat'l, Inc. (see separate listing).

www.babcock.com
Annual Revenues: $1.4 billion

Main Headquarters
Mailing: P.O. Box 351 — Tel: (330) 753 - 4511
Barberton, OH 44203 — Fax: (330) 860 - 1886
Street: 20 S. Van Buren Ave.
Barberton, OH 44203-0351

Washington Office
Contact: Julius L. "Bud" Piland
Mailing: McDermott Internat'l / Babcock & Wilcox — Tel: (703) 529 - 7238
1820 N. Fort Myer Dr., Suite 804 — Fax: (703) 351 - 6417
Arlington, VA 22209

Political Action Committees

The Babcock & Wilcox Co. Good Government Fund
Contact: David S. Black
2016 Mount Athios Rd.
Lynchburg, VA 24504

Contributions to Candidates: $12,000 (01/05 - 09/05)
Democrats: $2,000; Republicans: $10,000.

Principal Recipients

SENATE REPUBLICANS		HOUSE REPUBLICANS	
Dewine, Richard (OH)	$1,500	Barton, Joe L (TX)	$2,500
Santorum, Richard (PA)	$1,000	Foley, Mark (FL)	$2,000
		Hobson, David (OH)	$2,000

Public Affairs and Related Activities Personnel

At Headquarters

MCCAULLEY, Sharyn L. — Tel: (330) 860 - 1326
Manager, Communications — Fax: (330) 860 - 6362
slmccaulley@babcock.com

MONTER, Cathy — Tel: (330) 860 - 2620
Manager, Human Resources — Fax: (330) 860 - 1886

At Washington Office

PILAND, Julius L. "Bud" — Tel: (703) 351 - 6304
Manager, Government Programs — Fax: (703) 351 - 6417

At Other Offices

BLACK, David S.
PAC Treasurer
2016 Mount Athios Rd.
Lynchburg, VA 24504
dsblack@mcdermott.com

BAE Systems North America

A member of the Public Affairs Council. A high-technology company specializing in defense electronics, information technology and services.
www.na.baesystems.com
Annual Revenues: $5 billion

President and Chief Exec. Officer — Tel: (301) 838 - 6000
RONALD, Mark

Main Headquarters
Mailing: 1601 Research Blvd., Rockville, MD 20850 — Tel: (301) 838 - 6000; Fax: (301) 838 - 6925

Washington Office
Contact: Robert J. Fitch
Mailing: 1300 N. 17th St., Suite 1400, Arlington, VA 22209 — Tel: (703) 907 - 8200; Fax: (703) 907 - 8300

Political Action Committees

BAE Systems USA PAC
Contact: Sydelle Lyon
1300 N. 17th St.
Suite 1400
Arlington, VA 22209
Tel: (703) 907 - 8200
Fax: (703) 907 - 8300

Contributions to Candidates: $225,499 (01/05 - 09/05)
Democrats: $92,500; Republicans: $132,999.

Principal Recipients

SENATE DEMOCRATS		HOUSE DEMOCRATS	
Kennedy, Ted (MA)	$5,000	Murtha, John P Mr. (PA)	$10,000
Nelson, Bill (FL)	$5,000	Skelton, Ike (MO)	$10,000
Lieberman, Joe (CT)	$3,500	Moran, James (VA)	$8,000
Clinton, Hillary Rodham (NY)	$3,000	Israel, Steve (NY)	$5,500

SENATE REPUBLICANS		HOUSE REPUBLICANS	
Stevens, Ted (AK)	$9,000	Bradley, Joseph (NH)	$12,000
Cochran, Thad (MS)	$8,000	Cunningham, Duke (CA)	$10,000
Santorum, Richard (PA)	$5,000	Hunter, Duncan (CA)	$10,000
Allen, George (VA)	$3,000	Lewis, Jerry (CA)	$10,000
Lugar, Richard G (IN)	$3,000	Young, C. W. Bill (FL)	$10,000

Public Affairs and Related Activities Personnel

At Headquarters

GRAY, Curt — Tel: (301) 838 - 6000; Fax: (301) 838 - 6925
Senior V. President, Human Resources

HASTINGS, Robert — Tel: (301) 838 - 6712; Fax: (301) 838 - 6925
V. President, Public Affairs and Communications
robert.hastings@baesystems.com

At Washington Office

FITCH, Robert J. — Tel: (703) 907 - 8200; Fax: (703) 907 - 8300
Senior V. President, Government Relations and Marketing

FRASER, James H. — Tel: (703) 907 - 8200; Fax: (703) 907 - 8300
Director, Government Affairs

LENOVER, Susan — Tel: (703) 907 - 8200; Fax: (703) 907 - 8300
Assistant to the V. President, Coporate Communications

LYON, Sydelle — Tel: (703) 907 - 8200; Fax: (703) 907 - 8300
PAC Manager

MEASELL, John H. — Tel: (703) 907 - 8261; Fax: (703) 465 - 0329
Director, Public Relations
john.h.measell@baesystems.com

VESSELLA, Candace C. — Tel: (703) 907 - 8200; Fax: (703) 907 - 8300
V. President, Government Affairs
Responsibilities include political action.

Baker Hughes Inc.

A provider of products and services for the worldwide oil, gas and continuous process industries.
www.bakerhughes.com
Annual Revenues: $5.382 billion

Chairman and Chief Exec. Officer — Tel: (713) 439 - 8600; Fax: (713) 439 - 8699
DEATON, Chad C.

Main Headquarters
Mailing: 3900 Essex Ln., Suite 1200, Houston, TX 77027-5177 — Tel: (713) 439 - 8600; Fax: (713) 439 - 8699

Corporate Foundations and Giving Programs

Baker Hughes Foundation
Contact: Ike Kerridge
3900 Essex Ln., Suite 1200
Houston, TX 77027-5177
Tel: (713) 439 - 8662
Fax: (713) 439 - 8699

Annual Grant Total: none reported
Primary Interests: Children
Recent Recipients: Child Advocates

Public Affairs and Related Activities Personnel

At Headquarters

BITTO, Ron — Tel: (713) 439 - 8391; Fax: (713) 439 - 8280
Director, Communications

FLAHARTY, Gary R. — Tel: (713) 439 - 8039; Fax: (713) 439 - 8472
Director, Investor Relations
gary.flaharty@bakerhughes.com

KERRIDGE, Ike — Tel: (713) 439 - 8662; Fax: (713) 439 - 8699
Exec. Director, Baker Hughes Foundation

NAKANISHI, Greg — Tel: (713) 439 - 8737; Fax: (713) 439 - 8699
V. President, Human Resources

Ball Aerospace & Technologies

See listing on page 59 under Ball Corp.

Ball Corp.

A producer of rigid packaging products for food and beverages, and a provider of aerospace and other technology products and services to government and commercial customers.
www.ball.com
Annual Revenues: $5 billion

Chairman, President and Chief Exec. Officer — Tel: (303) 469 - 3131; Fax: (303) 460 - 2127
HOOVER, R. David

Main Headquarters
Mailing: P.O. Box 5000, Broomfield, CO 80038-5000 — Tel: (303) 469 - 3131; Fax: (303) 460 - 5256
Street: Ten Longs Peak Dr., Broomfield, CO 80021-2510

Washington Office
Contact: Carol Lane
Mailing: 2200 Clarendon Blvd., Suite 1202, Arlington, VA 22201 — Tel: (703) 284 - 5400; Fax: (703) 284 - 5449

Political Action Committees

Ball Corp. Political Action Committee (Ball PAC)
Contact: Harold L. Sohn
P.O. Box 5000
Broomfield, CO 80038-5000
Tel: (303) 460 - 2126
Fax: (303) 460 - 2127

Contributions to Candidates: none reported (01/05 - 09/05)

Corporate Foundations and Giving Programs

Ball Corporate Contributions Program
Contact: Harold L. Sohn
P.O. Box 5000
Broomfield, CO 80038-5000
Tel: (303) 460 - 2126
Fax: (303) 460 - 2127

Annual Grant Total: none reported
Geographic Preference: Area(s) in which the company operates
Primary Interests: Civic and Public Affairs; Health and Human Services; Higher Education

Public Affairs and Related Activities Personnel

At Headquarters

BAILEY, Joette — Tel: (303) 469 - 5511; Fax: (303) 460 - 5256
Director, Environmental Services
jbailey@ball.com

MCCARTY, S. Scott — Tel: (303) 460 - 2103; Fax: (303) 460 - 2663
Director, Corporate Relations
smccarty@ball.com

SCOTT, Ann — Tel: (303) 460 - 3537; Fax: (303) 460 - 2127
Manager, Investor Relations and Pension Plans
ascott@ball.com

SOHN, Harold L. — Tel: (303) 460 - 2126; Fax: (303) 460 - 2127
V. President, Corporate Relations
hsohn@ball.com
Responsibilities include government relations, corporate communications, corporate philanthropy, and political action.

At Washington Office

CAMPBELL, John D. — Tel: (703) 284 - 5400; Fax: (703) 284 - 5449
Manager, Legislative Affairs
Registered Federal Lobbyist.

LANE, Carol — Tel: (703) 284 - 5400; Fax: (703) 284 - 5449
V. President, Washington Operations
(Ball Aerospace & Technologies)

Bally Manufacturing Corp.

See listing on page 59 under Bally Total Fitness Holding Corp.

Bally Total Fitness Holding Corp.

A holding company for Bally Total Fitness, an owner and operator of health and fitness club facilities.
www.ballyfitness.com
Annual Revenues: $852 million

Bally Total Fitness Holding Corp.

** continued from previous page*

Chairman and Chief Exec. Officer
TOBACK, Paul A. Tel: (773) 380 - 3000 Fax: (773) 399 - 0476

Main Headquarters
Mailing: 8700 W. Bryn Mawr Ave.
Chicago, IL 60631
Tel: (773) 380 - 3000 Fax: (773) 399 - 0476

Corporate Foundations and Giving Programs

Bally Total Fitness "Stronger Communities" Campaign
Contact: Matt Messinger
8700 W. Bryn Mawr Ave.
Chicago, IL 60631
Tel: (773) 380 - 3000 Fax: (773) 399 - 0476

Annual Grant Total: over $5,000,000

Public Affairs and Related Activities Personnel

At Headquarters

MESSINGER, Matt
Senior Director, Public Director
mmessinger@ballyfitness.com
Tel: (773) 380 - 3000 Fax: (773) 399 - 0476

BancWest Corp.

A bank holding company. Formed by the merger of First Hawaiian, Inc. and Banc of the West in 1998.
www.bancwestcorp.com
Annual Revenues: $2.187 billion

Chairman of the Board
DODS, Walter A., Jr. Tel: (808) 525 - 7000 Fax: (808) 557 - 086

Chief Exec. Officer
MCGRATH, Don J. Tel: (808) 525 - 7000 Fax: (808) 557 - 086

Main Headquarters
Mailing: P.O. Box 3200
Honolulu, HI 96847
Tel: (808) 525 - 7000 Fax: (808) 557 - 086
Street: 999 Bishop St.
Honolulu, HI 96813

Corporate Foundations and Giving Programs

First Hawaiian Foundation
Contact: Sharon Shiroma Brown
P.O. Box 3200
Honolulu, HI 96847
Tel: (808) 525 - 7777 Fax: (808) 557 - 086

Annual Grant Total: $1,000,000 - $2,000,000
Geographic Preference: Hawaii
Primary Interests: Arts and Culture; Education; Families; United Way Campaigns
Recent Recipients: St. Francis Healthcare Foundation; United Way; YMCA

Public Affairs and Related Activities Personnel

At Headquarters

BROWN, Sharon Shiroma
President, First Hawaiian Foundation
(First Hawaiian Bank)
Tel: (808) 525 - 7777 Fax: (808) 557 - 086

KEIR, Gerry
Exec. V. President, Corporate Communications
Tel: (808) 525 - 7086 Fax: (808) 557 - 086

SHEPHERD, Michael
Exec. V. President and General Counsel
Tel: (808) 525 - 7000 Fax: (808) 557 - 086

Bandag, Inc.

A manufacturer of tread rubber and supplies for tire retreaders; also provides equipment rental and leasing services.
www.bandag.com
Annual Revenues: $964.9 million

Chairman and Chief Exec. Officer
CARVER, Martin Tel: (563) 262 - 1400 Fax: (563) 262 - 1263

Main Headquarters
Mailing: Bandag Center
2905 N. Hwy. 61
Muscatine, IA 52761-5886
Tel: (563) 262 - 1400 Fax: (563) 262 - 1263

Corporate Foundations and Giving Programs

Bandag Corporate Contributions Program
Bandag Center
2905 N. Hwy. 61
Muscatine, IA 52761-5886
Tel: (563) 262 - 1400 Fax: (563) 262 - 1263

Annual Grant Total: $500,000 - $750,000
Geographic Preference: Iowa
Primary Interests: Children; Community Affairs; Youth Services
Recent Recipients: Boy Scouts of America; United Way; YMCA; YWCA

Public Affairs and Related Activities Personnel

At Headquarters

BLOCK, Bill
Director, Corporate Communications
Tel: (563) 262 - 1400 Fax: (563) 262 - 1263

HEIDBREDER, Warren W.
V. President, Chief Financial Officer and Corporate Secretary
Responsibilities include investor relations.
Tel: (563) 262 - 1260 Fax: (563) 262 - 1263

Bank of America Corp.

A member of the Public Affairs Council. A bank holding company. Formed by the merger of NationsBank, BankAmerica and Seafirst Bank in 1998. Acquired FleetBoston Financial in April, 2004. In July of 2005, the company announced plans to merge with MBNA (see separate listing)
www.bankofamerica.com
Annual Revenues: $53.1 billion

Chairman, President and Chief Exec. Officer
LEWIS, Kenneth D. Tel: (704) 386 - 4343 Fax: (704) 386 - 6699

Main Headquarters
Mailing: Bank of America Corporate Center
100 N. Tryon St.
Charlotte, NC 28255-0001
Tel: (704) 386 - 4343 Fax: (704) 386 - 6699

Washington Office
Contact: Jeanne-Marie Murphy
Mailing: 730 15th St. NW
Washington, DC 20005
Tel: (202) 624 - 4134 Fax: (202) 383 - 3475

Political Action Committees

Bank of America Corp. Federal Political Action Committee
Contact: Jeanne-Marie Murphy
730 15th St. NW
Washington, DC 20005
Tel: (202) 624 - 4134 Fax: (202) 383 - 3475

Contributions to Candidates: $19,750 (01/05 - 09/05)
Democrats: $7,000; Republicans: $12,750.

Principal Recipients

SENATE REPUBLICANS		HOUSE REPUBLICANS	
Thomas, Craig (WY)	$1,000	Bachus, Spencer (AL)	$3,000

Bank of America State and Federal Corp. PAC
Contact: Gregory E. Swanson
Bank of America Plaza
600 Peachtree St. NE
Atlanta, GA 30308
Tel: (404) 607 - 5267

Contributions to Candidates: $464,250 (01/05 - 09/05)
Democrats: $153,500; Republicans: $310,750.

Principal Recipients

SENATE DEMOCRATS		HOUSE DEMOCRATS	
Ford, Harold E Jr (TN)	$5,000	Markey, Edward (MA)	$5,000
Stabenow, Debbie (MI)	$4,000	Scott, David (GA)	$5,000
SENATE REPUBLICANS		**HOUSE REPUBLICANS**	
Bennett, Robert F (UT)	$9,000	Baker, Hugh (LA)	$6,000
Santorum, Richard (PA)	$9,000	McHenry, Patrick (NC)	$6,000
Burns, Conrad (MT)	$5,500	Shaw, Clay (FL)	$6,000
McConnell, Mitch (KY)	$5,000	Reynolds, Thomas (NY)	$5,500
Talent, James (MO)	$3,500	Cantor, Eric (VA)	$5,000
		DeLay, Tom (TX)	$5,000
		Hensarling, Jeb (TX)	$5,000
		Myrick, Sue (NC)	$5,000
		Ney, Robert W (OH)	$5,000
		Oxley, Michael (OH)	$5,000

Corporate Foundations and Giving Programs

Bank of America Foundation
Bank of America Corporate Center
100 N. Tryon St.
Charlotte, NC 28255-0001
Tel: (704) 386 - 4343 Fax: (704) 386 - 6699

Annual Grant Total: over $5,000,000
Solicitors should contact the state president or city executive of the bank in their area.
Geographic Preference: Washington, DC; Florida; Georgia; Kentucky; Maryland; North Carolina; South Carolina; Tennessee; Texas; Virginia
Primary Interests: Arts and Culture; Civic and Public Affairs; Education; Social Services

Public Affairs and Related Activities Personnel

At Headquarters

ALPHIN, Steele
Global Personnel Executive
steele.alphin@bankofamerica.com
Tel: (704) 386 - 4343 Fax: (704) 386 - 6699

FRANCISCO, Terry
Media Contact
Tel: (704) 386 - 4343 Fax: (704) 386 - 6699

MCALISTER, Sheryl
Public Relations
sheryl.mcalister@bankofamerica.com
Tel: (704) 386 - 4343 Fax: (704) 386 - 6699

PLEPLER, Andrew
President, Foundation
Tel: (704) 386 - 4343 Fax: (704) 386 - 6699

STICKLER, Bob
Investor Communications
Tel: (704) 386 - 4343 Fax: (704) 386 - 6699

Bank of America Corp.

** continued from previous page*

STITT, Kevin — Tel: (704) 386 - 4343; Fax: (704) 386 - 6699
Investor Relations Executive
kevin.stitt@bankofamerica.com

TURNER, Betty — Tel: (704) 386 - 4343; Fax: (704) 386 - 6699
V. President, State/Local Lobbyist and State Government Relations

At Washington Office

HILL, Edward J. — Tel: (202) 624 - 4134 Ext: 85; Fax: (202) 383 - 3475
V. President, Government Relations
Mailstop: DCI-701-05-11
edward.j.hill@bankofamerica.com
Registered Federal Lobbyist.

MARSHALL, Patricia Warr — Tel: (202) 624 - 4134; Fax: (202) 383 - 3475
Senior V. President, State Government Relations

MURPHY, Jeanne-Marie — Tel: (202) 624 - 4134; Fax: (202) 383 - 3475
Senior V. President, Federal Government Relations
Mailstop: DCI-701-05-11
jeanne-marie.murphy@bankofamerica.com
Registered Federal Lobbyist.
Responsibilities include political action.

At Other Offices

SWANSON, Gregory E. — Tel: (404) 607 - 5267
Treasurer, Bank of America Corp. State and Federal PAC
Bank of America Plaza
600 Peachtree St. NE
Atlanta, GA 30308

Bank of America Illinois

See listing on page 60 under Bank of America Corp.

Bank of America Texas, N.A.

See listing on page 60 under Bank of America Corp.

Bank of Hawaii

See listing on page 61 under Bank of Hawaii Corp.

Bank of Hawaii Corp.

Formerly known as Pacific Century Financial Corp. A banking and financial services company. Parent company of the Bank of Hawaii.
www.boh.com

Chairman, Chief Exec. Officer, and President — Fax: (808) 537 - 8440; TF: (888) 643 - 3888
LANDON, Allan R.

Main Headquarters
Mailing: P.O. Box 2900, Honolulu, HI 96846 — Fax: (808) 537 - 8440; TF: (888) 643 - 3888

Political Action Committees

Pacific Century Corp. Special Political Education Committee
Contact: Lance N. Tanaka
P.O. Box 2900
Honolulu, HI 96846 — Tel: (808) 537 - 8351; Fax: (808) 537 - 8440; TF: (888) 643 - 3888

Contributions to Candidates: $12,000 (01/05 - 09/05)
Democrats: $12,000.

Principal Recipients

SENATE DEMOCRATS
Akaka, Daniel (HI) $10,000

HOUSE DEMOCRATS
Case, Edward (HI) $2,000

Corporate Foundations and Giving Programs

Bank of Hawaii Charitable Foundation
Contact: Paula Boyce
P.O. Box 3170
Honolulu, HI 96802-3170 — Tel: (808) 538 - 4945

Annual Grant Total: under $100,000
Contributes to charitable organizations which are working to improve the quality of life, health, and well-being of our communities.
Geographic Preference: Hawaii; American Samoa; Guam
Primary Interests: Arts and Culture; Community Development; Education; Health and Human Services
Recent Recipients: Meals on Wheels

Public Affairs and Related Activities Personnel

At Headquarters

CROWELL, Robert I. — Tel: (808) 538 - 4636; Fax: (808) 538 - 1788; TF: (888) 643 - 3888
Treasurer, Pacific Century Financial Corp. Special Political Education Committee

HOCKLANDER, Neal C. — Tel: (808) 537 - 8366; Fax: (808) 537 - 8063; TF: (888) 643 - 3888
V. Chairman, Human Resources and Security

KIGUCHI, Stafford — Tel: (808) 537 - 8246; Fax: (808) 537 - 8440; TF: (888) 643 - 3888
Senior V. President and Manager, Corporate Communications
skiguchi@boh.com

TANAKA, Lance N. — Tel: (808) 537 - 8351; Fax: (808) 537 - 8440; TF: (888) 643 - 3888
V. President and Manager, Government Affairs

WYRICK, Cindy — Tel: (808) 537 - 8430; Fax: (808) 538 - 4445; TF: (888) 643 - 3888
Senior V. President, Investor Relations/Corporate Secretary
cwyrick@boh.com

At Other Offices

BOYCE, Paula — Tel: (808) 538 - 4945
Foundation Contact
P.O. Box 3170
Honolulu, HI 96802-3170

The Bank of New York Co., Inc.

A bank holding company.
www.bankofny.com

Chairman and Chief Exec. Officer — Tel: (212) 495 - 1784; Fax: (212) 635 - 1799
RENYI, Thomas A.

Main Headquarters
Mailing: One Wall St., New York, NY 10286 — Tel: (212) 495 - 1784; Fax: (212) 635 - 1799

Political Action Committees

Bank of New York Co. Political Action Committee (BNY PAC)
Contact: Thomas J. Mastro
One Wall St.
New York, NY 10286 — Tel: (212) 495 - 1784; Fax: (212) 635 - 1799

Contributions to Candidates: $4,200 (01/05 - 09/05)
Republicans: $4,200.

Principal Recipients

SENATE REPUBLICANS

HOUSE REPUBLICANS
Reynolds, Thomas (NY) $4,200

Corporate Foundations and Giving Programs

The Bank of New York Co., Inc. Corporate Contributions Program
One Wall St.
New York, NY 10286 — Tel: (212) 495 - 1784; Fax: (212) 635 - 1799

Annual Grant Total: $2,000,000 - $5,000,000
Recent Recipients: Big Brothers/Big Sisters; Girl Scouts of America; Junior Achievement; March of Dimes; Salvation Army; Toys for Tots; United Way

Public Affairs and Related Activities Personnel

At Headquarters

HEINE, Kevin — Tel: (212) 635 - 1569; Fax: (212) 635 - 1799
V. President, Corporate Communications
kheine@bankofny.com

MASTRO, Thomas J. — Tel: (212) 495 - 1784; Fax: (212) 635 - 1799
Comptroller and PAC Treasurer
Mailstop: Tenth Floor

MURPHY, Joseph F. — Tel: (212) 635 - 7740; Fax: (212) 635 - 1799
Managing Director, Investor Relations
jfmurphy@bankofny.com

Bank of Oklahoma, N.A.

See listing on page 85 under BOK Financial Corp.

Bank One Corp.

See listing on page 332 under J P Morgan Chase & Co.

Bankers Trust Co.

See listing on page 157 under Deutsche Banc AlexBrown.

Banta Corp.

A provider of printing and digital imaging services and supply-chain management outsourcing services.
www.banta.com
Annual Revenues: $1.45 billion

Chairman, President and Chief Exec. Officer — Tel: (920) 751 - 7777; Fax: (920) 751 - 7790
STREETER, Stephanie A.

Main Headquarters
Mailing: P.O. Box 8003, Menasha, WI 54952-8003 — Tel: (920) 751 - 7777; Fax: (920) 751 - 7790
Street: 225 Main St., Menasha, WI 54952

Corporate Foundations and Giving Programs

Banta Corp. Foundation
Contact: Frank W. Rudolph

Banta Corp.

** continued from previous page*

P.O. Box 8003
Menasha, WI 54952-8003
Tel: (920) 751 - 7777
Fax: (920) 751 - 7790

Annual Grant Total: $500,000 - $750,000

The Foundation does not make grants to individuals.

Geographic Preference: Area(s) in which the company operates

Primary Interests: Higher Education; Medicine and Health Care; Performing Arts; Youth Services

Public Affairs and Related Activities Personnel

At Headquarters

FLEMING, Mark A.
Director, Investor and Corporate Communications
Tel: (920) 751 - 7713
Fax: (920) 751 - 7790

RUDOLPH, Frank W.
V. President, Human Resources
Also serves as President, Banta Foundation.
Tel: (920) 751 - 7777
Fax: (920) 751 - 7790

Barclays Bank PLC

See listing on page 62 under Barclays Capital.

Barclays Capital

The investment banking division of Barclays Bank PLC.

www.barcap.com

Main Headquarters

Mailing: 200 Park Ave.
New York, NY 10166
Tel: (212) 412 - 4000

Washington Office

Contact: Marlene Nicholson

Mailing: 1501 K St., NW
Suite 500
Washington, DC 20005
Tel: (202) 736 - 8653

Corporate Foundations and Giving Programs

Barclays Charitable Giving Committee
Contact: Karina Byrne
200 Park Ave.
New York, NY 10166
Tel: (212) 412 - 7561

Annual Grant Total: $200,000 - $300,000

Provides educational gift matching up to $2,000 per employee per calendar year. Lump sum donations considered to employee involved charities/client charities.

Geographic Preference: New York; New Jersey; Connecticut

Primary Interests: Arts and Humanities; Education; Math and Science; Social Services

Public Affairs and Related Activities Personnel

At Headquarters

BYRNE, Karina
Corporate Communications Contact
karina.byrne@barcap.com
Tel: (212) 412 - 7561

FRIEL, Kristin
Corporate Communications Contact
Tel: (212) 412 - 7521

TRUELL, Peter
Corporate Communications Contaact
Tel: (212) 412 - 7576

At Washington Office

NICHOLSON, Marlene
Director, Government Relations
marlene.nicholson@barcap.com
Registered Federal Lobbyist.
Tel: (202) 736 - 8653

Barnes & Noble, Inc.

A retailer of books.

www.barnesandnobleinc.com

Annual Revenues: $40 billion

Chairman
RIGGIO, Leonard
Tel: (212) 633 - 3333
Fax: (212) 366 - 5186

Chief Exec. Officer
RIGGIO, Stephen
Tel: (212) 633 - 3444
Fax: (212) 675 - 0413

Main Headquarters

Mailing: 122 Fifth Ave.
New York, NY 10011
Tel: (212) 633 - 3300
Fax: (212) 675 - 0413

Corporate Foundations and Giving Programs

Barnes & Noble Corporate Contributions
Contact: Mary Ellen Keating
122 Fifth Ave.
New York, NY 10011
Tel: (212) 633 - 3323
Fax: (212) 807 - 6033

Annual Grant Total: none reported

Public Affairs and Related Activities Personnel

At Headquarters

BROWN, Carolyn
Director, Corporate Communications
cbrown@bn.com
Tel: (212) 633 - 4062
Fax: (212) 807 - 6033

KEATING, Mary Ellen
Senior V. President, Corporate Communications and Public Affairs
Tel: (212) 633 - 3323
Fax: (212) 807 - 6033

MILEVOJ, Andy
Manager, Investor Relations
amilevoj@bn.com
Tel: (212) 633 - 3489
Fax: (212) 675 - 0413

SMITH, Michelle
V. President, Human Resources
msmith@bn.com
Tel: (212) 633 - 3280
Fax: (212) 645 - 1828

Barnes Group Inc.

Manufacturer and distributor of precision metal parts and supplies.

www.barnesgroupinc.com

Annual Revenues: $768.8 million

Chairman of the Board
BARNES, Thomas O.
Tel: (860) 583 - 7070
Fax: (860) 589 - 3507

President and Chief Exec. Officer
CARPENTER, Edmund M.
Tel: (860) 583 - 7070
Fax: (860) 589 - 3507

Main Headquarters

Mailing: P.O. Box 489
Bristol, CT 06011-0489
Tel: (860) 583 - 7070
Fax: (860) 589 - 3507

Street: 123 Main St.
Bristol, CT 06011

Corporate Foundations and Giving Programs

Barnes Group Foundation
Contact: John R. Arrington
P.O. Box 489
Bristol, CT 06011-0489
Tel: (860) 583 - 7070
Fax: (860) 589 - 3507

Assets: $1,183,670 (2002)

Annual Grant Total: $750,000 - $1,000,000

The Foundation does not accept unsolicited applications for funds.

Geographic Preference: Area in which the company is headquartered

Primary Interests: Education; Environment/Conservation; Higher Education

Recent Recipients: Boy Scouts of America; United Way

Public Affairs and Related Activities Personnel

At Headquarters

ARRINGTON, John R.
Senior V. President, Human Resources
Tel: (860) 583 - 7070
Fax: (860) 589 - 3507

KOPPY, Brian D.
Investor Relations Contact
Tel: (860) 973 - 2126
Fax: (860) 589 - 3507

MCKELVEY, Stephen J.
Associate Director, Corporate Communications
Tel: (860) 973 - 2132
Fax: (860) 585 - 7795

Baroid Drilling Fluids Division

See listing on page 230 under Halliburton Company.

Barr Pharmaceuticals, Inc.

A specialty pharmaceutical company engaged in the development, manufacture and marketing of proprietary and generic pharmaceuticals.

www.barrlabs.com

Annual Revenues: $509.7 million

Chairman and Chief Exec. Officer
DOWNEY, Bruce L.
bdowney@barrlabs.com
Tel: (201) 930 - 3300
Fax: (201) 930 - 3330
TF: (800) 222 - 0190

Main Headquarters

Mailing: 400 Chesnut Ridge Rd.
Woodcliff Lake, NJ 07677
Tel: (201) 930 - 3300
Fax: (201) 930 - 3330
TF: (800) 222 - 0190

Washington Office

Contact: Jake Hansen

Mailing: 444 N. Capitol St. NW
Suite 722
Washington, DC 20001
Tel: (202) 393 - 6599
Fax: (202) 638 - 3386

Corporate Foundations and Giving Programs

Barr Laboratories, Inc. Corporate Contributions Program
400 Chesnut Ridge Rd.
Woodcliff Lake, NJ 07677
Tel: (201) 930 - 3300
Fax: (201) 930 - 3330
TF: (800) 222 - 0190

Annual Grant Total: none reported

Barr Pharmaceuticals, Inc.

* continued from previous page

Public Affairs and Related Activities Personnel

At Headquarters

MUNDKUR, Christine
Senior V. President, Quality and Regulatory Counsel
(Barr Laboratories, Inc.)
Tel: (201) 930 - 3300
Fax: (201) 930 - 3330
TF: (800) 222 - 0190

At Washington Office

HANSEN, Jake
V. President, Government Affairs
jhansen@barrlabs.com
(Barr Laboratories, Inc.)
Registered Federal Lobbyist.
Tel: (202) 393 - 6599
Fax: (202) 638 - 3386

BASF Corporation

Chemical and chemical-related business including basic, intermediate and specialty chemicals; polymers and fibers; dispersions; automotive and industrial coatings; agricultural products; plant biotechnology and vitamins.

www.basf-corp.com
Annual Revenues: $6.78 billion

Chairman and Chief Exec. Officer
LOBBE, Klaus Peter
Tel: (973) 245 - 6000
Fax: (973) 245 - 6002

Main Headquarters
Mailing: 100 Campus Dr.
Florham Park, NJ 07932
Tel: (973) 245 - 6000
Fax: (973) 245 - 6002

Washington Office
Contact: E. Thomas Coleman
Mailing: 601 13th St. NW
Suite 200 North
Washington, DC 20005
Tel: (202) 682 - 9462
Fax: (202) 682 - 9459

Political Action Committees

BASF Corp. Employees Political Action Committee
Contact: Philip E. Kaplan
100 Campus Dr.
Florham Park, NJ 07932
Tel: (973) 245 - 6000
Fax: (973) 245 - 6002

Contributions to Candidates: $23,500 (01/05 - 09/05)
Democrats: $1,000; Republicans: $21,500; Other: $1,000.

Principal Recipients

SENATE DEMOCRATS
Carper, Thomas R (DE) $1,000

HOUSE DEMOCRATS

HOUSE OTHER
Oberstar, James L (MN) $1,000

SENATE REPUBLICANS
Talent, James (MO) $9,000
Alexander, Lamar (TN) $1,000
Domenici, Pete (NM) $1,000
Santorum, Richard (PA) $1,000

HOUSE REPUBLICANS
Ferguson, Mike (NJ) $1,500
Deal, Nathan (GA) $1,000
Hart, Melissa (PA) $1,000
Hobson, David (OH) $1,000
McCrery, Jim (LA) $1,000
McHenry, Patrick (NC) $1,000
Poe, Ted (TX) $1,000
Wamp, Zach (TN) $1,000
Weller, Jerry (IL) $1,000

Corporate Foundations and Giving Programs

BASF Corp. Contributions Program
Contact: Glenn Majeski
100 Campus Dr.
Florham Park, NJ 07932
Tel: (973) 245 - 6070
Fax: (973) 245 - 6714

Annual Grant Total: none reported
Geographic Preference: Area(s) in which the company operates
Primary Interests: Math and Science

Public Affairs and Related Activities Personnel

At Headquarters

BUKLAD, Barbara Ann
Tel: (973) 245 - 6000
Fax: (973) 245 - 6002

GOLDBERG, Steven J.
V. President and Associate General Counsel, Regulatory Law and Government Affairs
goldbes@basf-corp.com
Tel: (973) 245 - 6057
Fax: (973) 245 - 6002

GUENTHER, Bob
Media Relations Contact
guenthr@basf-corp.com
Tel: (973) 245 - 6013
Fax: (973) 245 - 6715

KAPLAN, Philip E.
PAC Treasurer
Tel: (973) 245 - 6000
Fax: (973) 245 - 6002

MAAS, Norman H.
Senior V. President, Human Resources
Tel: (973) 245 - 6000
Fax: (973) 245 - 6002

MAJESKI, Glenn
Manager, Corporate Donations
Mailstop: M/S 3-045
majeskg@basf-corp.com
Tel: (973) 245 - 6070
Fax: (973) 245 - 6714

MAURER, Jack
Manager, Media Relations
maurerjl@basf.com
Tel: (973) 245 - 6072
Fax: (973) 245 - 6714

MCGRATH, Don
V. President, Corporate Communications
Tel: (973) 245 - 6000
Fax: (973) 245 - 6002

STRYKER, David
Senior V. President and General Counsel
Responsibilities include legal and government affairs.
Tel: (973) 245 - 6000
Fax: (973) 245 - 6002

At Washington Office

COLEMAN, E. Thomas
V. President, Government Relations
colemae@basf.com
Registered Federal Lobbyist.
Tel: (202) 682 - 9462
Fax: (202) 682 - 9459

DESETA, Anne
Manager, Grassroots Program
desetaa@basf-corp.com
Registered Federal Lobbyist.
Tel: (202) 414 - 6340
Fax: (202) 682 - 9459

THIES, Gregory A.
Director, Government Affairs
thiesg@basf-corp.com
Registered Federal Lobbyist.
Tel: (202) 414 - 6337
Fax: (202) 682 - 9459

At Other Offices

ELLIOTT, David A.
Manager, Communications NAFTA II (Coatings, Polymers and Fine Chemicals)
1609 Biddle Ave.
W. Administration Bldg. 1-114
Wyandotte, MI 48192
elliotd1@basf-corp.com
Tel: (734) 324 - 6148
Fax: (734) 324 - 6549

Basin Cooperative Serivces

See listing on page 63 under Basin Electric Power Cooperative.

Basin Electric Power Cooperative

www.basinelectric.com
Annual Revenues: $500.8 million

Chief Exec. Officer
HARPER, Ronald R.
rharper@bepc.com
Tel: (701) 223 - 0441
Fax: (701) 224 - 5336

Main Headquarters
Mailing: 1717 E. Interstate Ave.
Bismarck, ND 58503
Tel: (701) 223 - 0441
Fax: (701) 224 - 5336

Political Action Committees

Basin Electric Power Cooperative PAC (Basin Electric PAC)
Contact: Sheryl R. Massey
1717 E. Interstate Ave.
Bismarck, ND 58503
Tel: (701) 223 - 0441
Fax: (701) 224 - 5336

Contributions to Candidates: $3,500 (01/05 - 09/05)
Democrats: $2,500; Other: $1,000.

Principal Recipients

SENATE DEMOCRATS
Conrad, Kent (ND) $2,000

HOUSE DEMOCRATS
Pomeroy, Earl (ND) $500

HOUSE OTHER
Oberstar, James L (MN) $1,000

Public Affairs and Related Activities Personnel

At Headquarters

EDWARDS, Alan
V. President, External Relations and Communications
Tel: (701) 223 - 0441
Fax: (701) 224 - 5336

EGGL, Mike
V. President, Government Relations
meggl@bepc.com
Tel: (701) 223 - 0441
Fax: (701) 224 - 5336

HILL, Daryl R.
Coordinator, News Media
dhill@bepc.com
Tel: (701) 223 - 0441
Fax: (701) 224 - 5315

MASSEY, Sheryl R.
Treasurer, Basin Electric PAC
(Basin Cooperative Serivces,
Basin Telecommunication, Inc., Dakota Coal Co.,
Dakota Gasification Co.)
smassey@bepc.com
Tel: (701) 223 - 0441
Fax: (701) 224 - 5336

Basin Electric Power Cooperative

* continued from previous page

POLING, Fletcher H. — Tel: (701) 223 - 0441
Legislative Representative — Fax: (701) 224 - 5336
(Basin Cooperative Serivces,
Basin Telecommunication, Inc., Dakota Coal Co.,
Dakota Gasification Co.)
fpoling@bepc.com

ROBB, Floyd — Tel: (701) 223 - 0441
V. President, Communications and Marketing Support — Fax: (701) 255 - 5142
frobb@bepc.com

At Other Offices

STAFFORD, Bill — Tel: (307) 322 - 9121
Director, Government Relations — Fax: (307) 322 - 3823
1560 Johnston St.
Wheatland, WY 82201
bstafford@bepc.com

Basin Telecommunication, Inc.

See listing on page 63 under Basin Electric Power Cooperative.

Baskin Robins

See listing on page 169 under Dunkin' Brands.

Bassett Furniture Industries, Inc.

www.bassettfurniture.com
Annual Revenues: $305.7 million

Chairman of the Board — Tel: (276) 629 - 6000
FULTON, Paul — Fax: (276) 629 - 6333

President and Chief Exec. Officer — Tel: (276) 629 - 6000
SPILLMAN, Robert — Fax: (276) 629 - 6332
rspillman@bassettfurniture.com

Main Headquarters
Mailing: 3525 Fairystone Park Hwy. — Tel: (276) 629 - 6000
Bassett, VA 24055 — Fax: (276) 629 - 6333

Corporate Foundations and Giving Programs

Bassett Furniture Industries, Inc. Corporate Contributions
Contact: Jay S. Moore
3525 Fairystone Park Hwy. — Tel: (276) 629 - 6450
Bassett, VA 24055 — Fax: (276) 629 - 6418

Annual Grant Total: none reported

Public Affairs and Related Activities Personnel

At Headquarters

MOORE, Jay S. — Tel: (276) 629 - 6450
Director, Corporate and Community Affairs — Fax: (276) 629 - 6418
jsmoore@bassettfurniture.com

SAFRIT, Barry — Tel: (276) 629 - 6757
V. President and Chief Financial Officer — Fax: (276) 629 - 6332
Responsibilities include investor relations.

Bath Iron Works Corp.

A subsidiary of General Dynamics Corp. (see separate listing). Specializes in shipbuilding and repairing.
www.gdbiw.com
Annual Revenues: $1 billion

Main Headquarters
Mailing: 700 Washington St. — Tel: (207) 443 - 3311
Bath, ME 04530 — Fax: (207) 442 - 1567

Washington Office
Contact: Tom Bowler
Mailing: 1201 M St. SE — Tel: (202) 454 - 2900
Suite 100 — Fax: (202) 454 - 2901
Washington, DC 20003

Public Affairs and Related Activities Personnel

At Headquarters

GILDART, Kevin P. — Tel: (207) 442 - 2025
V. President, Human Resources — Fax: (207) 442 - 5592

LESKO, Dirk A. — Tel: (207) 442 - 2072
Director, Strategic Planning and Communications — Fax: (207) 442 - 1009
dirk.lesko@gdbiw.com

NADEAU, Dan — Tel: (207) 442 - 1635
Director, Environmental Health and Safety — Fax: (207) 442 - 3356
dan.nadeau@gdbiw.com

STERGIO, Gerald — Tel: (207) 443 - 3311
Director, Labor Relations — Fax: (207) 442 - 1567

At Washington Office

BOWLER, Tom — Tel: (202) 454 - 2900
V. President, Programs and Strategic Planning — Fax: (202) 454 - 2901

Battelle

Provides technology development, management and commercialization.
www.battelle.org
Annual Revenues: $1.029 billion

President and Chief Exec. Officer — Tel: (614) 424 - 6424
KOHRT, Carl F. — Fax: (614) 424 - 3260
TF: (800) 201 - 2011

Main Headquarters
Mailing: 505 King Ave. — Tel: (614) 424 - 6424
Columbus, OH 43201-2693 — Fax: (614) 424 - 3260
TF: (800) 201 - 2011

Washington Office
Contact: John F. "Jack" Bagley
Mailing: 901 D St. SW — Tel: (202) 646 - 5255
Suite 900 — Fax: (202) 646 - 5233
Washington, DC 20024

Corporate Foundations and Giving Programs

Battelle Memorial Institute Giving Program
Contact: Karen Hollern
505 King Ave. — Tel: (614) 424 - 7361
Columbus, OH 43201-2693 — Fax: (614) 424 - 3301
TF: (800) 201 - 2011

Annual Grant Total: $1,000,000 - $2,000,000
Geographic Preference: Area(s) in which the company operates
Primary Interests: Community Affairs; Education
Recent Recipients: United Way; YMCA

Public Affairs and Related Activities Personnel

At Headquarters

BERRY, Mark — Tel: (614) 424 - 5544
Manager, Media Relations — Fax: (614) 424 - 3260
berrym@battelle.org — TF: (800) 201 - 2011

DELANEY, Katy — Tel: (410) 306 - 8638
Manager, National Media Relations
delaneyk@battelle.org

HOLLERN, Karen — Tel: (614) 424 - 7361
Director, Corporate Community Relations — Fax: (614) 424 - 3301
TF: (800) 201 - 2011

LYNCH, Robin Abruzere — Tel: (614) 424 - 6424
Fax: (614) 424 - 3260
TF: (800) 201 - 2011

MCCLAIN, Thomas E. — Tel: (614) 424 - 7728
V. President, Corporate Communications — Fax: (614) 424 - 3260
TF: (800) 201 - 2011

At Washington Office

BAGLEY, John F. "Jack" — Tel: (202) 479 - 0500
V. President, External Relations — Fax: (202) 646 - 5271
Registered Federal Lobbyist.

BARNES, Rudy — Tel: (202) 646 - 5255
Director, Government Relations for Dept. of Energy Programs — Fax: (202) 646 - 5271
Registered Federal Lobbyist.

DESMOND, Carrie E. — Tel: (202) 646 - 5255
Assistant Director, Congressional Affairs — Fax: (202) 646 - 5271
Registered Federal Lobbyist.

TOLER, Mary M. — Tel: (202) 646 - 5255
Assistant Director, Congressional Affairs — Fax: (202) 646 - 5271
Registered Federal Lobbyist.

Bausch & Lomb

A member of the Public Affairs Council. A manufacturer of contact lenses, lens care products, and ophthalmic surgical and pharmaceutical products.
www.bausch.com
Annual Revenues: $2.2 billion

Chairman and Chief Exec. Officer — Tel: (585) 338 - 6000
ZARRELLA, Ronald L. — Fax: (585) 338 - 6007
TF: (800) 344 - 8815

Main Headquarters
Mailing: One Bausch & Lomb Pl. — Tel: (585) 338 - 6000
Rochester, NY 14604-0054 — Fax: (585) 338 - 6007
TF: (800) 344 - 8815

Corporate Foundations and Giving Programs

Bausch & Lomb Corporate Giving
Contact: Barbara M. Kelley

Bausch & Lomb

** continued from previous page*

One Bausch & Lomb Pl.
Rochester, NY 14604-0054
Tel: (585) 338 - 5386
Fax: (585) 338 - 8551
TF: (800) 344 - 8815

Annual Grant Total: none reported
Primary Interests: Community Affairs; Health and Human Services; United Way Campaigns
Recent Recipients: Int'l Agency for the Prevention of Blindness; Rochester Institute of Technology

Public Affairs and Related Activities Personnel

At Headquarters

GRAHAM, Margaret
Director, Corporate Communications
mgraham@bausch.com
Tel: (585) 338 - 5469
Fax: (585) 338 - 8551
TF: (800) 344 - 8815

KELLEY, Barbara M.
V. President, Communications and Investor Relations
barbara_m_kelley@bausch.com
Tel: (585) 338 - 5386
Fax: (585) 338 - 8551
TF: (800) 344 - 8815

RITZ, Daniel L.
Director, Investor Relations
dritz@bausch.com
Tel: (585) 338 - 5802
Fax: (585) 338 - 8551
TF: (800) 344 - 8815

Baxter Healthcare Corp.

A member of the Public Affairs Council. See listing on page 65 under Baxter Internat'l Inc.

Baxter Internat'l Inc.

www.baxter.com
Annual Revenues: $9.509 billion

Chairman and Chief Exec. Officer
PARKINSON, Robert L., Jr.
Tel: (847) 948 - 2025
Fax: (847) 948 - 3642

Main Headquarters
Mailing: One Baxter Pkwy.
Deerfield, IL 60015-4633
Tel: (847) 948 - 2025
Fax: (847) 948 - 3642

Washington Office
Mailing: 1501 K St. NW
Suite 375
Washington, DC 20005
Tel: (202) 508 - 8200

Political Action Committees

BAXPAC
Contact: Sarah M. Gregg
1501 K St. NW
Suite 375
Washington, DC 20005
Tel: (202) 508 - 8206
Fax: (202) 296 - 7177

Contributions to Candidates: $37,000 (01/05 - 09/05)
Democrats: $6,000; Republicans: $31,000.

Principal Recipients

SENATE DEMOCRATS		HOUSE DEMOCRATS	
Lieberman, Joe (CT)	$2,000		
Feinstein, Dianne (CA)	$1,000		
Kennedy, Ted (MA)	$1,000		
Nelson, Benjamin (NE)	$1,000		

SENATE REPUBLICANS		HOUSE REPUBLICANS	
Hatch, Orrin (UT)	$2,000	Dreier, David (CA)	$4,000
Lugar, Richard G (IN)	$1,000	Ferguson, Mike (NJ)	$3,000
Santorum, Richard (PA)	$1,000	Jindal, Bobby (LA)	$2,000
		Johnson, Nancy (CT)	$2,000
		Thomas, William M (CA)	$2,000

Corporate Foundations and Giving Programs

Baxter Internat'l Foundation
Contact: Celene Peurye
One Baxter Pkwy.
Deerfield, IL 60015-4633
Tel: (847) 948 - 4604
Fax: (847) 948 - 4026

Assets: $37,878,241 (2003)
Annual Grant Total: $2,000,000 - $5,000,000
Geographic Preference: National; International
Primary Interests: Medicine and Health Care
Recent Recipients: Indiana University

Public Affairs and Related Activities Personnel

At Headquarters

CREVISTON, Sarah
V. President, Government Affairs
sarah_creviston@baxter.com
Tel: (847) 948 - 4278
Fax: (847) 948 - 2896

CYNKAR, Amy
Senior Communications Associate, External Communications
Tel: (847) 948 - 5166
Fax: (847) 948 - 2016

GARDINER, Erin
Manager, External Communications
erin_gardiner@baxter.com
Tel: (847) 948 - 4210
Fax: (847) 948 - 2016

MAY, Karen J.
Corporate V. President, Human Resources
Tel: (847) 948 - 2025
Fax: (847) 948 - 3642

PEURYE, Celene
Exec. Director, Foundation
Tel: (847) 948 - 4604
Fax: (847) 948 - 4026

RESMAN, Cindy
Director, External Communications
cindy_resman@baxter.com
Tel: (847) 948 - 2815
Fax: (847) 948 - 2016

SPAK, Deborah G.
Director, External Communications
deborah_spak@baxter.com
Tel: (847) 948 - 2349
Fax: (847) 948 - 2016

YOUNG, Sally
V. President, Corporate Communications
sally_young@baxter.com
Tel: (847) 948 - 2304
Fax: (847) 948 - 3216

At Washington Office

GREGG, Sarah M.
V. President, Federal Legislative Affairs and Payment Planning
greggs@baxter.com
(Baxter Healthcare Corp.)
Registered Federal Lobbyist.
Tel: (202) 508 - 8206
Fax: (202) 296 - 7177

At Other Offices

VOEPEL, David
Director, State Government Affairs
625 S. Second St.
Suite 103B
Springfield, IL 62704
david_voepel@baxter.com
Tel: (217) 753 - 9626
Fax: (217) 753 - 9627

Bayer Corporation

A member of the Public Affairs Council. The North American subsidiary of Bayer AG. It is a research-based company with major businesses in health care and life sciences.

www.bayer.com
Annual Revenues: $11.5 billion

Chairman of the Board
WENNING, Werner
Tel: (412) 777 - 2000
TF: (800) 662 - 2927

President and Chief Exec. Officer
MOLNAR, Dr. Attila
Tel: (412) 777 - 2000
TF: (800) 662 - 2927

Main Headquarters
Mailing: 100 Bayer Rd.
Pittsburgh, PA 15205-9741
Tel: (412) 777 - 2000
Fax: (412) 777 - 2034
TF: (800) 662 - 2927

Washington Office
Contact: Ronald F. Docksai, Ph.D.
Mailing: 1275 Pennsylvania Ave. NW
Suite 801
Washington, DC 20004-2404
Tel: (202) 737 - 8900
Fax: (202) 737 - 8909

Political Action Committees

Bayer Corp. PAC
Contact: Tracy Spagnol
100 Bayer Rd.
Pittsburgh, PA 15205-9741
Tel: (412) 777 - 2000
TF: (800) 662 - 2927

Contributions to Candidates: $96,000 (01/05 - 09/05)
Democrats: $18,500; Republicans: $76,500; Other: $1,000.

Principal Recipients

SENATE DEMOCRATS		HOUSE DEMOCRATS	
Lieberman, Joe (CT)	$4,000		
Nelson, Benjamin (NE)	$3,500		

SENATE REPUBLICANS		HOUSE REPUBLICANS	
Santorum, Richard (PA)	$4,000	Murphy, Tim (PA)	$5,000
Hatch, Orrin (UT)	$3,000	Johnson, Nancy (CT)	$4,000
Alexander, Lamar (TN)	$2,500	Bonilla, Henry (TX)	$3,500
Allen, George (VA)	$2,500	English, Philip S (PA)	$3,500
		Gerlach, Jim (PA)	$3,500

Corporate Foundations and Giving Programs

Bayer Foundation
Contact: Rebecca Lucore

Bayer Corporation
** continued from previous page*

100 Bayer Rd.
Pittsburgh, PA 15205-9741
Tel: (412) 777 - 5791
Fax: (412) 778 - 4432
TF: (800) 662 - 2927

Assets: $54,459,000 (2000)
Annual Grant Total: $2,000,000 - $5,000,000
Website address: www.bayerus.com/community/charity/index.html
Geographic Preference: Area(s) in which employees live and work
Primary Interests: Arts and Culture; Community Affairs; International Affairs; Math and Science; United Way Campaigns

Public Affairs and Related Activities Personnel

At Headquarters

LUCORE, Rebecca — Tel: (412) 777 - 5791
Exec. Director, Bayer Foundation — Fax: (412) 778 - 4432; TF: (800) 662 - 2927

RYAN, Mark — Tel: (412) 777 - 2000
Senior V. President, Communications — TF: (800) 662 - 2927

SPAGNOL, Tracy — Tel: (412) 777 - 2000
Treasurer, Bayer Corp. PAC — TF: (800) 662 - 2927

At Washington Office

DOCKSAI, Ronald F., Ph.D. — Tel: (202) 737 - 8900
V. President, Federal Government Relations — Fax: (202) 737 - 8909
Registered Federal Lobbyist.

LILBURN, Tom — Tel: (202) 737 - 8900
Director, Federal Government Relations, Healthcare — Fax: (202) 737 - 8909

REIMERS, Jean D. — Tel: (202) 737 - 8900
Director, Federal Government Relations — Fax: (202) 737 - 8909
Registered Federal Lobbyist.

SPAGNOLI, Julie — Tel: (202) 737 - 8900
Director, Federal Government Relations — Fax: (202) 737 - 8909

VAN EGMOND, Juliane H. — Tel: (202) 737 - 8900
Director, Federal Government Relations — Fax: (202) 737 - 8909
Registered Federal Lobbyist.

At Other Offices

OLIVER, Sandra — Tel: (203) 812 - 3804
Director, Public Policy and State Government Affairs — Fax: (203) 812 - 6570
(Bayer Corporation Pharmaceutical Division)
400 Morgan Ln.
West Haven, CT 06516

PHAN, Stacie — Tel: (203) 812 - 3804
Manager, Public Policy and Communications, Pharmaceutical Division — Fax: (203) 812 - 6570
400 Morgan Ln.
West Haven, CT 06516

STEPHENS, Donna — Tel: (410) 263 - 8756
Manager, State Government Affairs
3102 Riverwalk Dr.
Annapolis, MD 21403

Bayer Corporation Pharmaceutical Division
See listing on page 65 under Bayer Corporation.

Bayer Crop Protection
See listing on page 66 under Bayer CropScience.

Bayer CropScience
Formed by the merger of Aventis CropScience and Bayer Crop Protection in 2001. Specializes in crop protection products and technology, animal nutrition, and health products. Based in Rhein, Germany. A subsidiary of Bayer AG.
www.bayercropscience.com
Annual Revenues: $3.798 billion

Chairman of the Board — Tel: (919) 549 - 2000
BERSCHAUER, Dr. Friedrich

President and Chief Exec. Officer — Tel: (919) 549 - 2000
ZIRAKPARUAR, Esmail, Ph.D.

Main Headquarters
Mailing: Two T.W. Alexander Dr. — Tel: (919) 549 - 2000
P.O. Box 12
Research Triangle Park, NC 27009

Washington Office
Contact: Jean D. Reimers
Mailing: 1275 Pennsylvania Ave. NW — Tel: (202) 756 - 3779
Suite 801 — Fax: (202) 628 - 6622
Washington, DC 20004

Public Affairs and Related Activities Personnel

At Headquarters

CHERNY, Margaret — Tel: (919) 549 - 2000
V. President, Government Relations and Communications

GADSBY, Margaret — Tel: (919) 549 - 2000
Director, Public and Government Affairs, Communications, and Stewardship

SEITZ, Andrew — Tel: (919) 549 - 2000
Media Contact
andrew.seitz@bayercropscience.com

At Washington Office

REIMERS, Jean D. — Tel: (202) 756 - 3779
Director, Government Relations — Fax: (202) 737 - 8909

BB&T Corp.
A financial holding company. Acquired First Virginia Banks, Inc. in July, 2003.
www.bbandt.com
Annual Revenues: $6.13 billion

Chairman and Chief Exec. Officer — Tel: (336) 733 - 2000
ALLISON, John A., IV

Main Headquarters
Mailing: 200 W. Second St. — Tel: (336) 733 - 2000
Winston-Salem, NC 27101

Political Action Committees

Branch Banking and Trust Co. PAC
Contact: Chris L. Henson
200 W. Second St. — Tel: (336) 733 - 2000
Winston-Salem, NC 27101

Contributions to Candidates: $28,600 (01/05 - 09/05)
Democrats: $4,000; Republicans: $24,600.

Principal Recipients

SENATE DEMOCRATS		HOUSE DEMOCRATS	
Carper, Thomas R (DE)	$3,000	McIntyre, Mike (NC)	$1,000
SENATE REPUBLICANS		**HOUSE REPUBLICANS**	
Dole, Elizabeth (NC)	$8,000	Foxx, Virginia (NC)	$5,000
McConnell, Mitch (KY)	$5,000	McHenry, Patrick (NC)	$2,000
Allen, George (VA)	$1,000	Myrick, Sue (NC)	$1,000
Graham, Lindsey (SC)	$1,000	Oxley, Michael (OH)	$1,000

Corporate Foundations and Giving Programs

BB&T Contributions Committee
Contact: Rodney Hughes
200 W. Second St. — Tel: (336) 733 - 2000
Winston-Salem, NC 27101
Annual Grant Total: none reported

Public Affairs and Related Activities Personnel

At Headquarters

HENSON, Chris L. — Tel: (336) 733 - 2000
Senior Exec. V. President and Chief Financial Officer
Responsibilities include political action and investor relations.

HUGHES, Rodney — Tel: (336) 733 - 2000
Contact, BB&T Contributions Committee

KEEL, Clarence — Tel: (336) 733 - 2000
V. President, Shareholder Relations

NICHOLSON, Thomas A., Jr. — Tel: (336) 733 - 3058
Exec. V. President, Investor Relations

At Other Offices

DENHAM, Robert — Tel: (910) 914 - 9073
Senior V. President, Public Relations
127 W. Webster St.
Whiteville, NC 28472

BBDO New York
An advertising firm.
www.bbdo.com

Chief Exec. Officer — Tel: (212) 459 - 5000
ROSENSHIN, Allen — Fax: (212) 459 - 6645

Main Headquarters
Mailing: 1285 Ave. of the Americas — Tel: (212) 459 - 5000
New York, NY 10019-6095 — Fax: (212) 459 - 6645

Corporate Foundations and Giving Programs

BBDO New York Corporate Contributions Program
Contact: Marc Sigle
1285 Ave. of the Americas — Tel: (212) 459 - 5000
New York, NY 10019-6095 — Fax: (212) 459 - 6645
Annual Grant Total: none reported

Public Affairs and Related Activities Personnel

At Headquarters

BEN-HAIM, Laurie — Tel: (212) 459 - 5000
Press Relations — Fax: (212) 459 - 6645
laurie.ben-haim@bbdo.com

ELVOVE, Roy — Tel: (212) 459 - 5797
Exec. V. President, Director of Corp. Communications — Fax: (212) 459 - 6645

BBDO New York

** continued from previous page*

SIGLE, Marc
Exec. V. President and Treasurer
Responsibilities include corporate giving.
Tel: (212) 459 - 5000
Fax: (212) 459 - 6645

BCI Coca-Cola Bottling Co. of Los Angeles

See listing on page 128 under Coca-Cola Enterprises Inc.

Bcom3 Group, Inc.

See listing on page 95 under Leo Burnett Worldwide.

BD

See listing on page 68 under Becton, Dickinson and Co.

BEA Systems, Inc.

An e-business infrastructure software company.
www.bea.com
Annual Revenues: $979.5 million

Chairman and Chief Exec. Officer
CHUANG, Alfred S.
alfred.chuang@bea.com
Tel: (408) 570 - 8000
Fax: (408) 570 - 8901

Main Headquarters
Mailing: 2315 N. First St.
San Jose, CA 95131
Tel: (408) 570 - 8000
Fax: (408) 570 - 8901

Corporate Foundations and Giving Programs

BEA Foundation
2315 N. First St.
San Jose, CA 95131
Tel: (408) 570 - 8000
Fax: (408) 570 - 8901

Annual Grant Total: none reported
Geographic Preference: Area(s) in which the company operates; California; Boston, MA; New Jersey; Denver, CO; Seattle, WA
Primary Interests: Early Childhood Education; Youth Services

Public Affairs and Related Activities Personnel

At Headquarters

FAULKNER, Kevin
V. President, Investor Relations
kevin.faulkner@bea.com
Tel: (408) 570 - 8000
Fax: (408) 570 - 8901

MCGEE, Karesh
Public Relations Contact
Tel: (408) 570 - 8288
Fax: (408) 570 - 8901

PETRY, May
Public Relations Contact
may.petry@bea.com
Tel: (408) 570 - 8704
Fax: (408) 570 - 8901

THACKER, Michael
Public Relations Contact
Tel: (408) 570 - 8040
Fax: (408) 570 - 8901

WU, Jeanne
Senior V. President, Human Resources
Tel: (408) 570 - 8000
Fax: (408) 570 - 8901

Bear, Stearns and Co. Inc.

An investment and financial services company.
www.bearstearns.com
Annual Revenues: $8.7 billion

Chairman and Chief Exec. Officer
CAYNE, James E.
Tel: (212) 272 - 2000
Fax: (212) 272 - 5143
TF: (800) 417 - 2327

Main Headquarters
Mailing: 383 Madison Ave.
New York, NY 10179
Tel: (212) 272 - 2000
Fax: (212) 272 - 5143
TF: (800) 417 - 2327

Political Action Committees

Bear, Stearns and Co. Inc. Political Campaign Committee
Contact: Michael Abatemarco
383 Madison Ave.
New York, NY 10179
Tel: (212) 272 - 2000
Fax: (212) 272 - 5143
TF: (800) 417 - 2327

Contributions to Candidates: $52,500 (01/05 - 09/05)
Democrats: $9,000; Republicans: $43,500.

Principal Recipients

SENATE DEMOCRATS		HOUSE DEMOCRATS	
Ford, Harold E Jr (TN)	$2,000	Kanjorski, Paul (PA)	$3,000
SENATE REPUBLICANS		**HOUSE REPUBLICANS**	
Santorum, Richard (PA)	$5,000	Oxley, Michael (OH)	$5,000
Hatch, Orrin (UT)	$3,000	Thomas, William M (CA)	$5,000
Bennett, Robert F (UT)	$2,500	Bachus, Spencer (AL)	$2,500
Crapo, Michael D (ID)	$2,500	Baker, Hugh (LA)	$2,500
Hagel, Charles T (NE)	$2,500	Pryce, Deborah (OH)	$2,500
		Kelly, Sue W (NY)	$2,000

Corporate Foundations and Giving Programs

Bear, Stearns and Co. Corporate Contributions Program
383 Madison Ave.
New York, NY 10179
Tel: (212) 272 - 2000
Fax: (212) 272 - 5143
TF: (800) 417 - 2327

Annual Grant Total: none reported

Public Affairs and Related Activities Personnel

At Headquarters

ABATEMARCO, Michael
PAC Treasurer
Tel: (212) 272 - 2000
Fax: (212) 272 - 5143
TF: (800) 417 - 2327

O'NEILL, Mary Lynn
PAC Administrator and Managing Director, Equity Research
Tel: (212) 272 - 2000
Fax: (212) 272 - 5143
TF: (800) 417 - 2327

VENTURA, Elizabeth
Director, Investor Relations
Tel: (212) 272 - 9251
Fax: (212) 272 - 5143
TF: (800) 417 - 2327

Bear Stearns Asset Management

See listing on page 67 under Bear, Stearns and Co Inc.

Bearings, Inc.

See listing on page 44 under Applied Industrial Technologies.

Bechtel Group, Inc.

An international engineering and construction company.
www.bechtel.com
Annual Revenues: $13.4 billion

Chairman and Chief Exec. Officer
BECHTEL, Riley P.
Tel: (415) 768 - 1234
Fax: (415) 768 - 9038

Main Headquarters
Mailing: 50 Beale St.
San Francisco, CA 94105-1895
Tel: (415) 768 - 1234
Fax: (415) 768 - 9038

Washington Office
Contact: Robert H. Ragan
Mailing: 1015 15th St. NW
Suite 700
Washington, DC 20005-2605
Tel: (202) 828 - 5200
Fax: (202) 785 - 2645

Political Action Committees

Bechtel Group Inc. PAC
Contact: Robert H. Ragan
1015 15th St. NW
Suite 700
Washington, DC 20005-2605
Tel: (202) 828 - 5200
Fax: (202) 785 - 2645

Contributions to Candidates: $28,000 (01/05 - 09/05)
Democrats: $7,000; Republicans: $21,000.

Principal Recipients

SENATE DEMOCRATS		HOUSE DEMOCRATS	
Bingaman, Jeff (NM)	$1,000	Skelton, Ike (MO)	$2,000
SENATE REPUBLICANS		**HOUSE REPUBLICANS**	
Dewine, Richard (OH)	$1,000	Knollenberg, Joe (MI)	$3,000
Lugar, Richard G (IN)	$1,000	Young, Don E (AK)	$2,500
Thomas, Craig (WY)	$1,000	Wamp, Zach (TN)	$2,000
		Hastings, Doc (WA)	$1,500

Corporate Foundations and Giving Programs

Bechtel Foundation
Contact: Susan Grisso
50 Beale St.
San Francisco, CA 94105-1895
Tel: (415) 768 - 1234
Fax: (415) 768 - 9038

Assets: $20,000,000 (1999)
Annual Grant Total: $2,000,000 - $5,000,000
Geographic Preference: Area(s) in which the company operates
Primary Interests: Education; Math and Science

Public Affairs and Related Activities Personnel

At Headquarters

COVEY, Jock
Manager, Corporate Affairs
Tel: (415) 768 - 1234
Fax: (415) 768 - 0263

GRISSO, Susan
Foundation Manager
Tel: (415) 768 - 1234
Fax: (415) 768 - 9038

MORETON, Mary
Manager, Human Resources
Tel: (415) 768 - 1234
Fax: (415) 768 - 9038

At Washington Office

DEEGAN, Colleen A.
Manager, Government Programs
(Bechtel National, Inc.)
Registered Federal Lobbyist.
Tel: (202) 828 - 5200
Fax: (202) 785 - 2645

Bechtel Group, Inc.

** continued from previous page*

HOWARD, Jane A.
Manager, Global Market Access - BCorp
jahoward@bechtel.com
Registered Federal Lobbyist.
Tel: (202) 828 - 5200
Fax: (202) 785 - 2645

KENNEDY, Daniel E.
V. President and Manager, Government Affairs
(Bechtel National, Inc.)
Registered Federal Lobbyist.
Tel: (202) 828 - 5200
Fax: (202) 785 - 2645

MENAKER, Howard M.
Manager, Public Affairs
(Bechtel Systems and Infrastructure)
Tel: (202) 828 - 5200
Fax: (202) 785 - 2645

RAGAN, Robert H.
Principal V. President and Manager
(Bechtel Systems and Infrastructure)
Registered Federal Lobbyist.
Tel: (202) 828 - 5200
Fax: (202) 785 - 2645

WARNER, Ann D.
V. President, Government Programs
(Bechtel Systems and Infrastructure)
Registered Federal Lobbyist.
Tel: (202) 828 - 5200
Fax: (202) 785 - 2645

Bechtel National, Inc.

See listing on page 67 under Bechtel Group, Inc.

Bechtel Systems and Infrastructure

See listing on page 67 under Bechtel Group, Inc.

Beckman Coulter, Inc.

A manufacturer of biomedical testing instrument systems, tests and supplies that simplify and automate laboratory processes.

www.beckmancoulter.com
Annual Revenues: $2.5 billion

Chairman of the Board
WOODS, Betty
Tel: (714) 871 - 4848
Fax: (714) 773 - 8283
TF: (800) 742 - 2345

Chief Executive Officer
GARRETT, Scott
Tel: (714) 871 - 4848
Fax: (714) 773 - 8283
TF: (800) 742 - 2345

Main Headquarters

Mailing: P.O. Box 3100
Fullerton, CA 92834
Tel: (714) 871 - 4848
Fax: (714) 773 - 8283
TF: (800) 742 - 2345

Street: 4300 N. Harbor Blvd.
Fullerton, CA 92835

Corporate Foundations and Giving Programs

Beckman Coulter Corporate Contributions Program
Contact: Sarah Nessl
4300 N. Harbor Blvd.
Fullerton, CA 92835
Tel: (714) 773 - 8763
Fax: (714) 773 - 7743
TF: (800) 742 - 2345

Annual Grant Total: none reported
Primary Interests: Education

Public Affairs and Related Activities Personnel

At Headquarters

HERDERT, Jeanie D.
Director, Investor Relations
Mailstop: C-30-B
jdherbert@beckman.com
Tel: (714) 773 - 8762
Fax: (714) 773 - 7743
TF: (800) 742 - 2345

HURLEY, Bob
V. President, Human Resources and Corporate Communications
Tel: (714) 773 - 7987
Fax: (714) 773 - 7743
TF: (800) 742 - 2345

SKOGLUND, Cynthia
Investor Relations Specialist
Tel: (714) 773 - 8213
Fax: (714) 773 - 8111
TF: (800) 742 - 2345

WARDE, Anne M.
Manager, Communications
amwarde@beckman.com
Tel: (714) 773 - 7655
Fax: (714) 773 - 7743
TF: (800) 742 - 2345

At Other Offices

NESSL, Sarah
Community Relations
4300 N. Harbor Blvd.
Mailstop: c-30-b
Fullerton, CA 92835
Responsibilities include corporate philanthropy.
Tel: (714) 773 - 8763
Fax: (714) 773 - 7743
TF: (800) 742 - 2345

Becton, Dickinson and Co.

A member of the Public Affairs Council. A manufacturer of a broad range of medical supplies and devices and diagnostic systems for use by health care professionals, medical research institutions, industry and the general public.

www.bd.com

Chairman, President and Chief Exec. Officer
LUDWIG, Edward J.
edward_ludwig@bd.com
Tel: (201) 847 - 6800
Fax: (201) 847 - 6475

Main Headquarters

Mailing: One Becton Dr.
Franklin Lakes, NJ 07417-1880
Tel: (201) 847 - 6800
Fax: (201) 847 - 6475

Political Action Committees

Becton Dickinson and Co. Political Action Committee (BD PAC)
Contact: Richard K. Berman
One Becton Dr.
Franklin Lakes, NJ 07417-1880
Tel: (201) 847 - 6800
Fax: (201) 847 - 6475

Contributions to Candidates: $14,000 (01/05 - 09/05)
Democrats: $6,000; Republicans: $8,000.

Principal Recipients

SENATE DEMOCRATS
Lautenberg, Frank (NJ) $1,000
Nelson, Benjamin (NE) $1,000

HOUSE DEMOCRATS
Menendez, Robert (NJ) $2,000
Hoyer, Steny (MD) $1,000
Rothman, Steven R (NJ) $1,000

SENATE REPUBLICANS
Burr, Richard (NC) $2,000
Hatch, Orrin (UT) $1,000

HOUSE REPUBLICANS
Dreier, David (CA) $1,000
Frelinghuysen, Rod (NJ) $1,000
Issa, Darrell (CA) $1,000
Jindal, Bobby (LA) $1,000
Ramstad, Jim (MN) $1,000

Corporate Foundations and Giving Programs

BD Community Partnerships
Contact: Jennifer Farrington
One Becton Dr.
Franklin Lakes, NJ 07417-1880
Tel: (201) 847 - 7065
Fax: (201) 847 - 5305

Annual Grant Total: $2,000,000 - $5,000,000
Primary Interests: Disaster Relief; Health and Human Services; Medicine and Health Care

Public Affairs and Related Activities Personnel

At Headquarters

BERMAN, Richard K.
PAC Treasurer
richard_berman@bd.com
Tel: (201) 847 - 6800
Fax: (201) 847 - 6475

BOLES, Donna M.
V. President, Human Resources
Tel: (201) 847 - 6800
Fax: (201) 847 - 6475

FARRINGTON, Jennifer
Manager, Community Relations
jennifer_farrington@bd.com
Tel: (201) 847 - 7065
Fax: (201) 847 - 5305

PARANICAS, Dean J.
V. President, Corporate Secretary and Public Policy
paranicas@bd.com
Tel: (201) 847 - 6800
Fax: (201) 847 - 6475

SHRADER, Patricia B.
V. President, Corporate Regulatory, Public Policy and Communications
patricia_shrader@bd.com
Tel: (201) 847 - 7429
Fax: (201) 847 - 6475

SPINELLA, Patricia A.
Investor Relations Contact
Tel: (201) 847 - 5453
Fax: (201) 847 - 6475

WHITE, Colleen T.
Corporate Communications Contact
Tel: (201) 847 - 5369
Fax: (201) 847 - 6475

Bed Bath & Beyond Inc.

A nationwide chain of stores selling domestic merchandise and home furnishings.

www.bedbathandbeyond.com
Annual Revenues: $2.93 billion

Co-Chairman of the Board
EISENBERG, Warren
Tel: (908) 688 - 0888
Ext: 4500
Fax: (908) 688 - 6483

Co-Chairman of the Board
FEINSTEIN, Leonard
Tel: (908) 688 - 0888
Fax: (908) 688 - 6483

President and Chief Exec. Officer
TEMARES, Steven H.
Tel: (908) 688 - 0888
Fax: (908) 688 - 6483

Main Headquarters

Mailing: 650 Liberty Ave.
Union, NJ 07083
Tel: (908) 688 - 0888
Fax: (908) 688 - 6483

Bed Bath & Beyond Inc.

* continued from previous page

Public Affairs and Related Activities Personnel

At Headquarters

CURWIN, Ron — Tel: (908) 688 - 0888 Ext: 4550
Chief Financial Officer and Investor Relations Contact — Fax: (908) 688 - 6483

VAN DYKE, Concetta — Tel: (908) 688 - 0888
V. President, Human Resources — Fax: (908) 688 - 6483

Belden CDT Inc.

Formed from the merger of Cable Design Technologies Corp. and Belden, Inc. in July, 2004.

www.beldencdt.com
Annual Revenues: $966.2 million

Chairman of the Board
CRESSY, Bryan C. — Tel: (314) 854 - 8000 Fax: (314) 854 - 8001

President and Chief Exec. Officer
CUNNINGHAM, C. Baker — Tel: (314) 854 - 8000 Fax: (314) 854 - 8001

Main Headquarters
Mailing: 7701 Forsyth Blvd.
Suite 800
St. Louis, MO 63105-1861 — Tel: (314) 854 - 8000 Fax: (314) 854 - 8001

Public Affairs and Related Activities Personnel

At Headquarters

JOHNSON, Dee — Tel: (314) 854 - 8045
Director, Investor Relations — Fax: (314) 854 - 8003

Responsibilities include public affairs.

STAPLES, Cathy — Tel: (314) 854 - 8000
V. President, Human Resources — Fax: (314) 854 - 8001

Belden, Inc.

See listing on page 69 under Belden CDT Inc.

Belk, Inc.

Owns and operates fashion department stores.

www.belk.com
Annual Revenues: $2.4 billion

Chairman and Chief Exec. Officer
BELK, Thomas M., Jr. — Tel: (704) 357 - 1064 Fax: (704) 357 - 1876

Main Headquarters
Mailing: 2801 W. Tyvola Rd.
Charlotte, NC 28217-4500 — Tel: (704) 357 - 1064 Fax: (704) 357 - 1876

Corporate Foundations and Giving Programs

The Belk Foundation
Contact: M. C. Belk Pilon
2801 W. Tyvola Rd.
Charlotte, NC 28217-4500 — Tel: (704) 426 - 8396 Fax: (704) 357 - 1876

Assets: $60,000,000 (1999)
Annual Grant Total: $2,000,000 - $5,000,000
Geographic Preference: North Carolina; South Carolina
Primary Interests: Arts and Culture; Higher Education; Medicine and Health Care; United Way Campaigns; Youth Services
Recent Recipients: Boy Scouts of America; Salvation Army; United Way; YMCA

Public Affairs and Related Activities Personnel

At Headquarters

PERNOTTO, Steve — Tel: (704) 426 - 1890
Exec. V. President, Human Resources — Fax: (704) 357 - 1876
steve_pernotto@belk.com
Responsibilities include corporate communications.

PILON, M. C. Belk — Tel: (704) 426 - 8396
Foundation Administrator — Fax: (704) 357 - 1876
m_c_belk@belk.com

STARCHER, Darlene — Tel: (704) 357 - 1000
Director, Communications — Fax: (704) 357 - 1876
darlene_starcher@belk.com

WYCHE, Paul B., Jr. — Tel: (704) 426 - 8404
Senior V. President and Associate Counsel — Fax: (704) 357 - 1876
paul_wyche@belk.com
Responsibilitites include corporate philanthropy.

Bell Helicopter Textron

A helicopter manufacturing subsidiary of Textron, Inc. (see separate listing).

www.bellhelicopter.textron.com
Annual Revenues: $1.8 billion

Chief Exec. Officer
REDENBAUGH, Mike A. — Tel: (817) 280 - 5000 Fax: (817) 280 - 3299

Main Headquarters
Mailing: P.O. Box 482
Fort Worth, TX 76101 — Tel: (817) 280 - 2011 Fax: (817) 280 - 2321
Street: 600 E. Hurst Blvd.
Hurst, TX 76053

Corporate Foundations and Giving Programs

Bell Helicopter Textron Corporate Giving Program
Contact: Carl L. Harris
P.O. Box 482
Fort Worth, TX 76101 — Tel: (817) 280 - 2425 Fax: (817) 280 - 8221

Annual Grant Total: $1,000,000 - $2,000,000
Geographic Preference: Texas
Primary Interests: Arts and Culture; Early Childhood Education; Law Enforcement; Medicine and Health Care; Minority Opportunities

Public Affairs and Related Activities Personnel

At Headquarters

COX, Mike — Tel: (817) 280 - 8416
Manager, Advertising and Media Relations — Fax: (817) 280 - 2321
mcox@bellhelicopter.textron.com

DICK, Erin — Tel: (817) 280 - 8416
Press Contact — Fax: (817) 280 - 2321
edick@bellhelicopter.textron.com

HARRIS, Carl L. — Tel: (817) 280 - 2425
Director, Public Affairs and Advertising — Fax: (817) 280 - 8221

LEDER, Bob — Tel: (817) 280 - 6440
Manager, Communications Operations — Fax: (817) 280 - 8221
bleder@bellhelicopter.textron.com

Bell Microproducts, Inc.

Markets and distributes semiconductor and computer products to original equipment manufacturers.

www.bellmicro.com
Annual Revenues: $2.827 billion

Chairman, President and Chief Exec. Officer
BELL, W. Donald — Tel: (408) 451 - 9400 Fax: (408) 451 - 1632

Main Headquarters
Mailing: 1941 Ringwood Ave.
San Jose, CA 95131-1721 — Tel: (408) 451 - 9400 Fax: (408) 451 - 1600

Public Affairs and Related Activities Personnel

At Headquarters

JACQUET, Richard J. "Dick" — Tel: (408) 451 - 9400
Senior V. President, Human Resources — Fax: (408) 451 - 1632

SAYEGH, Eli — Tel: (408) 451 - 1865
Director, Investor Relations — Fax: (408) 451 - 1694

BellSouth Corp.

PUBLIC AFFAIRS COUNCIL

A member of the Public Affairs Council. BellSouth Corp. is a parent company of Cingular Wireless (see separate listing), a wireless voice and data provider. The company offers voice and data services, and residential and small business services such as local and long distance service, dial up and high speed DSL internet acess, and satellite television. For businesses, BellSouth provides local and long distance voice and data networking solutions.

www.bellsouth.com
Annual Revenues: $22.44 billion

Chairman and Chief Exec. Officer
ACKERMAN, F. Duane — Tel: (404) 249 - 2000 Fax: (404) 249 - 3839

Main Headquarters
Mailing: 1155 Peachtree St. NE
Atlanta, GA 30309-3610 — Tel: (404) 249 - 2000 Fax: (404) 249 - 2071

Washington Office
Contact: Herschel L. Abbott, Jr.
Mailing: 1133 21st St. NW
Suite 900
Washington, DC 20036 — Tel: (202) 463 - 4100 Fax: (202) 463 - 4141

Political Action Committees

BellSouth Corp. Employees' Federal Political Action Committee
Contact: J. Pittman
1155 Peachtree St. NE
Atlanta, GA 30309-3610 — Tel: (404) 249 - 2000 Fax: (404) 249 - 2071

Contributions to Candidates: $387,350 (01/05 - 09/05)
Democrats: $165,600; Republicans: $221,750.

BellSouth Corp.

** continued from previous page*

Principal Recipients

SENATE DEMOCRATS		HOUSE DEMOCRATS	
Conrad, Kent (ND)	$4,500	Melancon, Charlie (LA)	$7,000
Clinton, Hillary Rodham (NY)	$3,500	Gordon, Barton (TN)	$5,000
		Menendez, Robert (NJ)	$4,250
SENATE REPUBLICANS		**HOUSE REPUBLICANS**	
Martinez, Mel (FL)	$5,000	Bachus, Spencer (AL)	$7,500
McConnell, Mitch (KY)	$5,000	Pickering, Chip (MS)	$7,000
Santorum, Richard (PA)	$5,000	Northup, Anne M. (KY)	$5,000
Harris, Katherine (FL)	$4,000	Blackburn, Marsha (TN)	$4,500
Lott, Trent (MS)	$4,000	Linder, John (GA)	$4,500
		Myrick, Sue (NC)	$4,500

Corporate Foundations and Giving Programs

BellSouth Foundation
Contact: Mary Boehm
1155 Peachtree St. NE — Tel: (404) 249 - 2329
Atlanta, GA 30309-3610 — Fax: (404) 249 - 2071

Annual Grant Total: $2,000,000 - $5,000,000
Significant other contributions are made under a corporate donation program.
Geographic Preference: Alabama; Florida; Georgia; Kentucky; Louisiana; Mississippi; North Carolina; South Carolina; Tennessee; Area(s) in which the company operates
Primary Interests: Education

BellSouth Telecommunications Corporate Contributions Program
Contact: Barbara Foston
1155 Peachtree St. NE — Tel: (404) 249 - 2417
Atlanta, GA 30309-3610 — Fax: (404) 249 - 5696

Assets: $17,600,000 (2003)
Annual Grant Total: none reported
Geographic Preference: Alabama; Florida; Kentucky; Louisiana; Mississippi; North Carolina; Tennessee; South Carolina; Georgia

Public Affairs and Related Activities Personnel

At Headquarters

BATTCHER, Jeff — Tel: (404) 249 - 2793
Director, Senior Corporate Media Relations — Fax: (404) 249 - 3839
Mailstop: 19G03 Campanile
jeff.battcher@bellsouth.com

BETZ, Dennis M. — Tel: (404) 249 - 3170
Assistant V. President, Media Relations — Fax: (404) 249 - 0149
Mailstop: 1917 Campanile
dennis.betz@bellsouth.com

BOEHM, Mary — Tel: (404) 249 - 2329
President, BellSouth Foundation — Fax: (404) 249 - 2071
Mailstop: 7H08 Campanile
mary.boehm@bellsouth.com

DAVIS, Nancy J. — Tel: (404) 249 - 3491
V. President, Investor Relations — Fax: (404) 249 - 3839
Mailstop: 14K10 Campanile
nancy.davis@bellsouth.com

FOSTON, Barbara — Tel: (404) 249 - 2417
Specialist, Corporate Contributions Program — Fax: (404) 249 - 5696
Mailstop: 7H08 Campanile
barbara.foston@bellsouth.com

PATE, William C. — Tel: (404) 249 - 2400
V. President, Advertising and Public Relations — Fax: (404) 249 - 2866
Mailstop: 1915 Campanile
william.pate@bellsouth.com

PITTMAN, J. — Tel: (404) 249 - 2000
Treasurer, BellSouth Corp. Employees' Federal PAC — Fax: (404) 249 - 2071
Mailstop: 14D03

SIBBERNSEN, Richard D. — Tel: (404) 249 - 2000
V. President, Human Resources — Fax: (404) 249 - 2071

At Washington Office

ABBOTT, Herschel L., Jr. — Tel: (202) 463 - 4104
V. President, Governmental Affairs — Fax: (202) 463 - 4141
herschel.abbott@bellsouth.com
Registered Federal Lobbyist.

BANKS, Jonathan — Tel: (202) 463 - 4182
V. President, Exec. and Regulatory Affairs - BellSouth D.C. — Fax: (202) 463 - 4141
jonathan.banks@bellsouth.com

BARRON, David M. — Tel: (202) 463 - 4100
Assistant V. President, Federal Relations/National Security — Fax: (202) 463 - 4141
david.barron@bellsouth.com
Registered Federal Lobbyist.

BOOZER, Lyndon K. — Tel: (202) 463 - 4100
Assistant V. President, Federal Relations — Fax: (202) 463 - 4196
lyndon.boozer@bellsouth.com
Registered Federal Lobbyist.

CORONADO, Troup — Tel: (202) 463 - 4100
Fax: (202) 463 - 4141
Registered Federal Lobbyist.

MCCAUGHEY, Eileen — Tel: (202) 463 - 4100
Director, Planning and Political Operations — Fax: (202) 463 - 4141
Registered Federal Lobbyist.

MCCLOSKEY, William J. — Tel: (202) 463 - 4129
Director, Media Relations — Fax: (202) 463 - 4612
bill.mccloskey@bellsouth.com

MORTON, Gregg F. — Tel: (202) 463 - 4100
Fax: (202) 463 - 4141
Registered Federal Lobbyist.

POSSNER, Karen B. — Tel: (202) 463 - 4100
V. President, National Security and Strategic Policy — Fax: (202) 463 - 4637
karen.possner@bellsouth.com
Registered Federal Lobbyist.

REYNOLDS, Glenn — Tel: (202) 463 - 4100
V. President, Federal Regulatory — Fax: (202) 463 - 4142
glenn.reynolds@bellsouth.com

WHITE, Ward H. — Tel: (202) 463 - 4100
V. President, Federal Relations — Fax: (202) 463 - 8070
ward.white@bellsouth.com
Registered Federal Lobbyist.

At Other Offices

BLACKBURN, Kenneth E., II
Assistant V. President, External Affairs
333 Commerce St., Suite 2102
Nashville, TN 37201-3300
kenny.blackburn@bellsouth.com

CHANDLER, Joe — Tel: (404) 829 - 8700
Director, Media Relations
2180 Lake Blvd.
Suite 11C18
Atlanta, GA 30319
joe.chandler@bellsouth.net

FLYNT, Roger M., III — Tel: (205) 714 - 0714
V. President, Regulatory and External Affairs — Fax: (205)
600 19th St.
Room 28B3
Birmingham, AL 35203
flynt.mayo@bsi.bls.com

GEOGHEGAN, J. Ronald — Tel: (502) 582 - 3156
Exec. Director, Regulatory and External Affairs — Fax: (502) 875 - 6517
601 W. Chestnut St.
Louisville, KY 40203
ron.geoghegan@bellsouth.com

GREENE, Margaret H. — Tel: (404) 335 - 0851
President, Regulatory and External Affairs — Fax: (404) 524 - 1937
BellSouth Center
675 W. Peachtree St. NE
Mailstop: Room 4516
Atlanta, GA 30375
margaret.greene@bellsouth.com

HATHCOCK, C. Don — Tel: (704) 417 - 8764
V. President, Legislative Affairs
1522 BellSouth Plaza
300 S. Brevard St.
Charlotte, NC 28202
don.hathcock@bellsouth.com

HOWORTH, Charles — Tel: (615) 214 - 6520
V. President, Regulatory Affairs
333 Commerce St.
Suite 2104
Nashville, TN 37201
charles.howorth@bellsouth.com

LAWRENCE, Ted — Tel: (404) 986 - 1738
Exec. Director, Regulatory and External Affairs
1025 Lenox Park Blvd.
Suite 6B648
Atlanta, GA 30319

PLEDGER, Gary L. — Tel: (205) 714 - 0222
Director, Corporate and External Affairs — Fax: (205) 321 - 2699
600 19th St. North
Birmingham, AL 35203
gary.pledger@bellsouth.com
Responsibilities include state government relations.

RAYNOR, Michael S. — Tel: (850) 577 - 5500
V. President, Public Affairs
150 S. Monroe St., Suite 400
Tallahassee, FL 32301-1556
michael.raynor@bellsouth.com

SPEARS, James B. — Tel: (615) 214 - 3800
Exec. Director, Regulatory and External Affairs
333 Commerce St., Suite 2102
Nashville, TN 37201-3300
jim.spears@bellsouth.com

STOWE, Paige — Tel: (601) 961 - 3800; Fax: (601) 961 - 0415
V. President, Regulatory
175 E. Capitol St.
P.O. Box 811
Jackson, MS 39205
paige.stowe@bellsouth.net

VAN DYKE, Jeff A. — Tel: (919) 821 - 6016
Exec. Director, Regulatory and External Affairs
121 W. Morgan St.
First Floor
Raleigh, NC 27601
jeff.vandyke@bellsouth.com

WILLIAMS, T. E. — Tel: (504) 528 - 2200; Fax: (504) 528 - 7556
V. President, Regulatory
365 Canal St., Suite 3000
New Orleans, LA 70130
tommy.williams@bellsouth.com

Belo Corp.

A newspaper publishing and television broadcasting company.
www.belo.com
Annual Revenues: $1.5 billion

Chairman, President, and Chief Exec. Officer
DECHERD, Robert W. — Tel: (214) 977 - 6606; Fax: (214) 977 - 6603

Main Headquarters
Mailing: P.O. Box 655237
Dallas, TX 75265-5237 — Tel: (214) 977 - 6606; Fax: (214) 977 - 6603
Street: 400 S. Record St.
Dallas, TX 75202-4841

Corporate Foundations and Giving Programs

Belo Foundation
Contact: Amy Meadows
P.O. Box 655237 — Tel: (214) 977 - 6661
Dallas, TX 75265-5237 — Fax: (214) 977 - 6620

Annual Grant Total: none reported
Interests include capital or endowment campaigns of qualified organizations.

Public Affairs and Related Activities Personnel

At Headquarters

DEL REGNO, Nancy — Tel: (214) 977 - 6606; Fax: (214) 977 - 7051
Manager, Corporate Communications and Investor Relations
ndelregno@belo.com

HENDRICKSON, Carey P. — Tel: (214) 977 - 6626; Fax: (214) 977 - 7051
V. President/Investor Relations and Corporate Communications
chendrickson@belo.com

KERR, Guy H. — Tel: (214) 977 - 6606; Fax: (214) 977 - 6603
Senior V. President, Law and Government

MEADOWS, Amy — Tel: (214) 977 - 6661; Fax: (214) 977 - 6620
Exec. Director, Belo Foundation

SPITZBERG, Marian — Tel: (214) 977 - 6627; Fax: (214) 977 - 6603
Senior V. President, Human Resources
mspitzberg@belo.com

WILLIAMSON, Dennis A. — Tel: (214) 977 - 6606; Fax: (214) 977 - 6603
Senior Corporate V. President and Chief Financial Officer

Bemis Company, Inc.

A supplier of flexible packaging and pressure sensitive materials.
www.bemis.com
Annual Revenues: $2.834 billion

President, Chief Exec. Officer, and Chairman of the Board
CURLER, Jeffrey H. — Tel: (612) 376 - 3000; Fax: (612) 376 - 3150

Main Headquarters
Mailing: 222 S. Ninth St.
Suite 2300
Minneapolis, MN 55402-4099 — Tel: (612) 376 - 3000; Fax: (612) 376 - 3180

Corporate Foundations and Giving Programs

Bemis Company Foundation
Contact: Audrey Kirchner
222 S. Ninth St. — Tel: (612) 376 - 3007
Suite 2300 — Fax: (612) 376 - 3150
Minneapolis, MN 55402-4099

Assets: $995,0280
Annual Grant Total: $2,000,000 - $5,000,000
Geographic Preference: Area(s) in which the company operates; National
Primary Interests: Arts and Culture; Higher Education; Social Services
Recent Recipients: Boys and Girls Club; Citizen's Scholarship Foundation of America; Habitat for Humanity; United Negro College Fund; United Way; University of Wisconsin

Public Affairs and Related Activities Personnel

At Headquarters

KIRCHNER, Audrey — Tel: (612) 376 - 3007; Fax: (612) 376 - 3150
Administrative Assistant
Responsibilities include corporate contributions.

MILLER, Melanie E. R. — Tel: (612) 376 - 3000
V. President and Treasurer
Responsibilities include investor relations.

Ben & Jerry's Homemade Inc.

Manufacturer and distributor of frozen dairy products. Acquired by Unilever United States (see separate listing) in 2000, although the company continues to operate separately from Unilever's current U.S. ice cream business.
www.benjerry.com

Main Headquarters
Mailing: 30 Community Dr.
South Burlington, VT 05403-6828 — Tel: (802) 846 - 1500

Corporate Foundations and Giving Programs

Ben & Jerry's Foundation
Contact: Debbie Kessler
30 Community Dr. — Tel: (802) 846 - 1500
South Burlington, VT 05403-6828

Assets: $5,772,927 (2002)
Annual Grant Total: $2,000,000 - $5,000,000
The foundation only considers proposals from grassroots, constituent-led organizations that are organizing for systemic social change.
Geographic Preference: National
Primary Interests: Children; Environment/Conservation; Families; Minority Opportunities; Women

Public Affairs and Related Activities Personnel

At Headquarters

HEIMERT, Chrystie — Tel: (802) 846 - 1500 Ext: 7700; Fax: (802) 846 - 1536
Director, Public Relations
chrystieh@benjerry.com

HOLDEN, Lee — Tel: (802) 846 - 1500 Ext: 7701; Fax: (802) 846 - 1536
Senior Public Relations Specialist
lee@benjerry.com

KESSLER, Debbie — Tel: (802) 846 - 1500
Foundation Contact

Benchmark Electronics

Provides electronics design and manufacturing services.
www.bench.com
Annual Revenues: $1.277 billion

Chairman of the Board
NIGBOR, Donald E. — Tel: (979) 849 - 6550; Fax: (979) 848 - 5270

President and Chief Exec. Officer
FU, Cary T. — Tel: (979) 849 - 6550; Fax: (979) 848 - 5270

Main Headquarters
Mailing: 3000 Technology Dr.
Angleton, TX 77515 — Tel: (979) 849 - 6550; Fax: (979) 848 - 5270

Public Affairs and Related Activities Personnel

At Headquarters

DELLY, Gayla J. — Tel: (979) 849 - 6550 Ext: 1304; Fax: (979) 848 - 5270
Exec. V. President, Chief Financial Officer and Treasurer
gayla.delly@bench.com
Responsibilities include investor relations.

ODOM, Kevin — Tel: (979) 849 - 6550 Ext: 1360; Fax: (979) 848 - 5270
Corporate Communications Contact
kevin.odom@bench.com

Beneficial Life Insurance Co.

See listing on page 249 under HSBC North America Holdings Inc.

Beneficial Management Corp.

See listing on page 249 under HSBC North America Holdings Inc.

Berkshire Gas Co., The (Berkshire)

See listing on page 181 under Energy East Corp.

Berkshire Hathaway

A conglomerate with subsidiaries in property and casualty insurance, shoe and uniform and candy manufacturing, publishing, and home cleaning systems. Subsidiaries include FlightSafety Internat'l Inc. and GEICO Corp. (see separate listings.) Acquired Johns Manville and Shaw Industries (see separate listings) in 2001, Fruit of the Loom, Inc. in April of 2002, and McLane Company, Inc. and Clayton Homes, Inc. in 2003 (see separate listings).
www.berkshirehathaway.com
Annual Revenues: $37.668 billion

Chairman and Chief Exec. Officer
BUFFETT, Warren E. — Tel: (402) 346 - 1400; Fax: (402) 346 - 3375

Main Headquarters
Mailing: 1440 Kiewit Plaza
Omaha, NE 68131 — Tel: (402) 346 - 1400; Fax: (402) 346 - 3375

Berkshire Hathaway

** continued from previous page*

Corporate Foundations and Giving Programs

Berkshire Hathaway Corporate Contributions
Contact: Marc D. Hamburg
1440 Kiewit Plaza — Tel: (402) 346 - 1400
Omaha, NE 68131 — Fax: (402) 346 - 3375

Annual Grant Total: none reported
Corporate contributions of Berkshire Hathaway are directed by corporate shareholders. They do not accept or consider grant applications.

Public Affairs and Related Activities Personnel

At Headquarters

HAMBURG, Marc D. — Tel: (402) 346 - 1400
V. President, Chief Financial Officer and Treasurer — Fax: (402) 346 - 3375
Responsibilities include investor relations and corporate philanthropy.

At Other Offices

SHIVEL, John — Tel: (270) 781 - 6400
V. President, Advertising and Corporate Communications — Fax: (270) 781 - 6588
(Fruit of the Loom, Inc.)
One Fruit of the Loom Dr.
Bowling Green, KY 42102

Berlex, Inc.

A member of the Public Affairs Council. The U.S. affiliate of Schering AG, Germany. A specialty pharmaceutical company.
www.berlex.com

Main Headquarters
Mailing: P.O. Box 1000, Montville, NJ 07045 — Tel: (973) 487 - 2000; TF: (800) 237 - 5392
Street: 340 Changebridge Rd., Montville, NJ 07045

Corporate Foundations and Giving Programs

Berlex Corporate Giving
Contact: Anne King
P.O. Box 1000 — Fax: (973) 487 - 2005
Montville, NJ 07045 — TF: (800) 237 - 5392

Annual Grant Total: $300,000 - $400,000
Geographic Preference: New Jersey; California
Primary Interests: Community Affairs; Education

Public Affairs and Related Activities Personnel

At Headquarters

JORDAN, Kimberley — TF: (800) 237 - 5392
Manager, Product Public Relations

KING, Anne — Fax: (973) 487 - 2005
Manager, Public Affairs — TF: (800) 237 - 5392
anne_king@berlex.com

MARION, Joanne — TF: (800) 237 - 5392
Director, Investor Relations

SALEM, Richard — Fax: (973) 487 - 2052
V. President, Public Relations and Marketing Services — TF: (800) 237 - 5392
richard_salem@berlex.com

SCHILLACE, Kim — TF: (800) 237 - 5392
Manager, Product Public Relations
kimberly_schillace@berlex.com

SHILLABER, James — Fax: (973) 487 - 2003
Director, Human Resources — TF: (800) 237 - 5392

Berwind Group

A company with subsidiaries active in such varied industries as coal mining, specialty chemicals, automotive parts, real estate investment and property management.
www.berwind.com
Annual Revenues: $1 billion

President and Chief Exec. Officer — Tel: (215) 563 - 2800
HAMLING, James L. — Fax: (215) 575 - 2314

Main Headquarters
Mailing: 3000 Centre Square West, 1500 Market St., Philadelphia, PA 19102 — Tel: (215) 563 - 2800; Fax: (215) 575 - 2314

Corporate Foundations and Giving Programs

Berwind Corporate Contributions
Contact: Mary La Rue
3000 Centre Square West — Tel: (215) 563 - 2800
1500 Market St. — Fax: (215) 575 - 2314
Philadelphia, PA 19102

Annual Grant Total: $750,000 - $1,000,000
All requests for contributions are reviewed by a contributions committee.
Primary Interests: Civic and Cultural Activities; Education; Environment/Conservation; Health and Human Services

Public Affairs and Related Activities Personnel

At Headquarters

LA RUE, Mary — Tel: (215) 563 - 2800
Chairperson, Corporate Contributions — Fax: (215) 575 - 2314

Best Buy Co., Inc.

A member of the Public Affairs Council. A specialty retailer of consumer electronics, personal computers, entertainment software and appliances.
www.bestbuy.com
Annual Revenues: $27.4 billion

Chairman of the Board — Tel: (612) 291 - 1000
SCHULZE, Richard M.
richard.schulze@bestbuy.com

V. Chairman and Chief Exec. Officer — Tel: (612) 291 - 1000
ANDERSON, Bradbury H. — Fax: (612) 292 - 2195
brad.anderson@bestbuy.com

Main Headquarters
Mailing: 7601 Penn Ave. South, Richfield, MN 55423 — Tel: (612) 291 - 1000; Fax: (612) 292 - 4001

Political Action Committees

Best Buy Co., Inc. Employee Political Forum
Contact: Paula J. Prahl
P.O. Box 9312 — Tel: (612) 291 - 6120
Minneaplois, MN 55440-9312 — Fax: (612) 292 - 4001

Contributions to Candidates: $2,000 (01/05 - 09/05)
Democrats: $1,000; Republicans: $1,000.

Principal Recipients

SENATE DEMOCRATS	HOUSE DEMOCRATS	
	Mccollum, Betty (MN)	$1,000
SENATE REPUBLICANS	**HOUSE REPUBLICANS**	
	Ramstad, Jim (MN)	$1,000

Corporate Foundations and Giving Programs

Best Buy Children's Foundation/ Corporate Contributions
7601 Penn Ave. South — Tel: (612) 291 - 1000
Richfield, MN 55423 — Fax: (612) 292 - 4001

Assets: $17,072,761 (2003)
Annual Grant Total: over $5,000,000
The Best Buy Children's Foundation supports and strenthens communities by contributing to a variety of national organizations that foster engaged, fun learning experiences for children through integrating innovative, interactive technology into those experiences.
Geographic Preference: National
Primary Interests: Children; K-12 Education; Youth Services
Recent Recipients: Junior Achievement

Public Affairs and Related Activities Personnel

At Headquarters

BISHOP, Laura — Tel: (612) 291 - 1000
Director, Government Relations — Fax: (612) 292 - 4001
laura.bishop@bestbuy.com

BRYANT, Dawn — Tel: (612) 292 - 4000
Senior Corporate Public Relations Specialist — Fax: (612) 292 - 4001
dawn.bryant@bestbuy.com

BUSCH, Susan — Tel: (612) 292 - 4000
Director, Corporate Public Relations — Fax: (612) 292 - 4001
susan.busch@bestbuy.com

DRISCOLL, Jennifer — Tel: (612) 291 - 1000
V. President, Investor Relations — Fax: (612) 292 - 4001
jennifer.driscoll@bestbuy.com

GREV, Jason — Tel: (612) 291 - 1000
Senior Government Relations Specialist — Fax: (612) 292 - 4001
jason.grev@bestbuy.com

HAWKS, Lisa — Tel: (612) 292 - 4000
Director, Consumer Public Relations — Fax: (612) 292 - 4001
lisa.hawks@bestbuy.com

HILTNER, Mike — Tel: (612) 291 - 1000
Senior Government Relations Specialist — Fax: (612) 292 - 4001

HOFF, Susan S. — Tel: (612) 291 - 6100
Senior V. President and Chief Communication Officer — Fax: (612) 292 - 4001
susan.hoff@bestbuy.com
Responsibilities also include corporate contributions and government affairs.

SLUSS, Jessica — Tel: (612) 291 - 6108
Community Relations Specialist — Fax: (612) 292 - 4001

WALDEN, John — Tel: (612) 291 - 1000

WELDON, Amy — Tel: (612) 291 - 1000
Public Affairs Specialist — Fax: (612) 292 - 4001
amy.weldon@bestbuy.com

Best Buy Co., Inc.

* continued from previous page

At Other Offices

PRAHL, Paula J. — Tel: (612) 291 - 6120
V. President, Public Affairs; PAC Treasurer — Fax: (612) 292 - 4001
P.O. Box 9312
Minneaplois, MN 55440-9312
paula.prahl@bestbuy.com

Best Western Internat'l

An international hotel chain.

www.bestwestern.com
Annual Revenues: $157.2 million

Chairman of the Board — Tel: (602) 957 - 4200
MCRAE, Larry — TF: (800) 528 - 1234

President and Chief Exec. Officer — Tel: (602) 957 - 4200
KONG, David — TF: (800) 528 - 1234

Main Headquarters
Mailing: 6201 N. 24th Pkwy. — Tel: (602) 957 - 4200
Phoenix, AZ 85016-2023 — TF: (800) 528 - 1234

Public Affairs and Related Activities Personnel

At Headquarters

SEOMIN, Denise — Tel: (602) 957 - 5668
Manager, Consumer Media Relations — Fax: (602) 957 - 5641
denise.seomin@bestwestern.com — TF: (800) 528 - 1234

TRUMBLE, David — Tel: (602) 957 - 5753
Director, External Communications — Fax: (602) 957 - 5641
david.trumble@bestwestern.com — TF: (800) 528 - 1234

BET

See listing on page 505 under Viacom Inc/CBS Corp.

Beverly Enterprises, Inc.

A provider of post-acute healthcare.

www.beverlycorp.com
Annual Revenues: $2.709 billion

Chairman, President and Chief Exec. Officer — Tel: (479) 201 - 2000
FLOYD, William R. — Fax: (479) 201 - 1101
bill_floyd@beverlycorp.com

Main Headquarters
Mailing: 1000 Beverly Way — Tel: (479) 201 - 2000
Fort Smith, AR 72919-5273 — Fax: (479) 201 - 1101

Washington Office
Contact: Jack A. McDonald
Mailing: 1250 H St. NW, Suite 555 — Tel: (202) 393 - 2800
Washington, DC 20005 — Fax: (202) 783 - 5411

Political Action Committees

Beverly Enterprises, Inc. PAC
Contact: Jack A. McDonald
1250 H St. NW, Suite 555 — Tel: (202) 393 - 2800
Washington, DC 20005 — Fax: (202) 783 - 5411

Contributions to Candidates: $70,720 (01/05 - 09/05)
Democrats: $27,000; Republicans: $43,720.

Principal Recipients

SENATE DEMOCRATS		HOUSE DEMOCRATS	
Pryor, Mark (AR)	$6,000	Berry, Marion (AR)	$5,000
Baucus, Max (MT)	$5,000	Ross, Michael Avery (AR)	$3,500
Conrad, Kent (ND)	$4,500		

SENATE REPUBLICANS		HOUSE REPUBLICANS	
Santorum, Richard (PA)	$5,000	Hastert, Dennis J. (IL)	$10,000
Hatch, Orrin (UT)	$2,500	Johnson, Nancy (CT)	$3,500
Smith, Gordon (OR)	$2,500	Barton, Joe L (TX)	$2,500
		English, Philip S (PA)	$2,500
		Thomas, William M (CA)	$2,500
		Gerlach, Jim (PA)	$2,220

Public Affairs and Related Activities Personnel

At Headquarters

DEANS, Lawrence — Tel: (479) 201 - 2000
Senior V. President, Human Resources — Fax: (479) 201 - 1101

GRIFFITH, James M. "Jim" — Tel: (479) 201 - 5273
Senior V. President, Investor Relations and Corporate Communications — Fax: (479) 201 - 1101

JACKSON, Blair — Tel: (479) 201 - 5263
V. President, Corporate Communications — Fax: (479) 201 - 1101

At Washington Office

MCDONALD, Jack A. — Tel: (202) 393 - 2800
Senior V. President, Government Relations — Fax: (202) 783 - 5411
jack_mcdonald@beverlycorp.org
Registered Federal Lobbyist.

BGE

See listing on page 137 under Constellation Energy.

BIC Corp.

The U.S. subsidiary of Societe Bic of Clichy, France, manufacturer of writing instruments, shavers, lighters, and correction fluids.

www.bicworld.com

Chairman and Chief Exec. Officer — Tel: (203) 783 - 2000
BICH, Bruno — Fax: (203) 783 - 2081

Main Headquarters
Mailing: 500 Bic Dr. — Tel: (203) 783 - 2000
Milford, CT 06460 — Fax: (203) 783 - 2081

Public Affairs and Related Activities Personnel

At Headquarters

KWONG, Linda K. — Tel: (203) 783 - 2049
Director, Corporate Communications — Fax: (203) 783 - 2684

Big Lots Inc.

Formerly known as Consolidated Stores Corp. A broadline closeout retailer.

www.biglots.com
Annual Revenues: $3.433 billion

Chairman and Chief Exec. Officer — Tel: (614) 278 - 6800
FISHMAN, Steven S. — Fax: (614) 278 - 6676

Main Headquarters
Mailing: 300 Phillipi Rd. — Tel: (614) 278 - 6800
Columbus, OH 43228-5311 — Fax: (614) 278 - 6676

Corporate Foundations and Giving Programs

Big Lots Inc. Corporate Contributions Program
300 Phillipi Rd. — Tel: (614) 278 - 6800
Columbus, OH 43228-5311 — Fax: (614) 278 - 6676

Annual Grant Total: none reported
Primary Interests: Children; Education; Youth Services
Recent Recipients: Boys and Girls Club

Public Affairs and Related Activities Personnel

At Headquarters

JOHNSON, Timothy A. — Tel: (614) 278 - 6622
V. President, Strategic Planning and Investor Relations — Fax: (614) 278 - 6666

MCMASTERS, Beth — Tel: (614) 278 - 6974
Public Relations Contact — Fax: (614) 278 - 6676

ZIEGLER, Pat — Tel: (614) 278 - 6820
Public Relations Contact — Fax: (614) 278 - 6676

Big Three Industries

See listing on page 13 under Air Liquide America Corp.

Big Y Foods Inc.

A grocery store holding company

www.bigy.com
Annual Revenues: $1.2 billion

Chairman and Chief Exec. Officer — Tel: (413) 784 - 0600
D'AMOUR, Donald H. — Fax: (413) 732 - 7350
ddamour@bigy.com

Main Headquarters
Mailing: P.O. Box 7840 — Tel: (413) 784 - 0600
Springfield, MA 01102 — Fax: (413) 732 - 7350
Street: 2145 Roosevelt Ave.
Springfield, MA 01104

Public Affairs and Related Activities Personnel

At Headquarters

D'AMOUR-DALEY, Claire M. — Tel: (413) 784 - 0600
V. President, Corporate Communications — Fax: (413) 732 - 7350

HENRY, Jack — Tel: (413) 784 - 0600
V. President, Human Resources — Fax: (413) 732 - 7350
jhenry@bigy.com

Binney and Smith Inc.

A manufacturer of children's art products and professional artist materials. A wholly-owned subsidiary of Hallmark Cards, Inc. (see separate listing). Major brand names include Crayola, Silly Putty and Model Magic.

www.binney-smith.com
Annual Revenues: $500 million

President and Chief Exec. Officer
SCHWAB, Mark J. — Tel: (610) 253 - 6271; Fax: (610) 250 - 5768

Main Headquarters
Mailing: P.O. Box 431, Easton, PA 18044-0431 — Tel: (610) 253 - 6271; Fax: (610) 250 - 5768
Street: 1100 Church Ln., Easton, PA 18040

Corporate Foundations and Giving Programs

Binney and Smith Corporate Contributions Program
Contact: Margaret Heckman
P.O. Box 431
Easton, PA 18044-0431 — Tel: (610) 559 - 6660

Annual Grant Total: $300,000 - $400,000
Geographic Preference: Pennsylvania
Primary Interests: Arts and Culture; Education

Public Affairs and Related Activities Personnel

At Headquarters

HECKMAN, Margaret — Tel: (610) 559 - 6660
Corporate Contributions Contact

TUCKER, Susan — Tel: (610) 253 - 6272 Ext: 4293; Fax: (610) 250 - 5768
Media Contact

WOODS, Steven — Tel: (610) 253 - 6271; Fax: (610) 250 - 5768
V. President, Human Resources

Bio-Rad Laboratories, Inc.

A scientific services provider.

www.bio-rad.com
Annual Revenues: $1.09 billion

Chairman of the Board
SCHWARTZ, David — Tel: (510) 724 - 7000; Fax: (510) 741 - 5817; TF: (800) 424 - 6723

President and Chief Exec. Officer
SCHWARTZ, Norman — Tel: (510) 724 - 7000; Fax: (510) 741 - 5817; TF: (800) 424 - 6723

Main Headquarters
Mailing: 1000 Alfred Nobel Dr., Hercules, CA 94547-1811 — Tel: (510) 724 - 7000; Fax: (510) 741 - 5817; TF: (800) 424 - 6723

Public Affairs and Related Activities Personnel

At Headquarters

ANDERSON, Dick — Tel: (510) 724 - 7000; Fax: (510) 741 - 5817; TF: (800) 424 - 6723
Director, Human Resources

BERG, Susan — Tel: (510) 741 - 6063; Fax: (510) 741 - 5817; TF: (800) 424 - 6723
Corporate Communications Manager
susan_berg@bio-rad.com

HUTTON, Ron — Tel: (510) 741 - 6142; Fax: (510) 741 - 5817; TF: (800) 424 - 6723
Treasurer and Manager, Investor Relations
ron_hutton@bio-rad.com

Biogen Idec Inc.

Formed from the merger of Biogen, Inc. and IDEC Pharmaceuticals Corp. in November, 2003. A biopharmaceutical company.

www.biogen.com
Annual Revenues: $1.043 billion

Exec. Chairman of the Board
RASTETTER, William H., Ph.D. — Tel: (617) 679 - 2000; Fax: (617) 679 - 2617

President and Chief Exec. Officer
MULLEN, James C. — Tel: (617) 679 - 2000; Fax: (617) 679 - 2617

Main Headquarters
Mailing: 14 Cambridge Center, Cambridge, MA 02142 — Tel: (617) 679 - 2000; Fax: (617) 679 - 2617

Washington Office
Contact: David Foster
Mailing: 801 Pennsylvania Ave. NW, Suite 710, Washington, DC 20004 — Tel: (202) 383 - 1440

Political Action Committees

Biogen Idec PAC
Contact: David Foster
801 Pennsylvania Ave. NW
Suite 710
Washington, DC 20004 — Tel: (202) 383 - 1440

Contributions to Candidates: $14,200 (01/05 - 09/05)
Democrats: $2,000; Republicans: $12,200.

Principal Recipients

SENATE DEMOCRATS
Kennedy, Ted (MA) $2,000

HOUSE DEMOCRATS

SENATE REPUBLICANS
Dewine, Richard (OH) $2,100
Santorum, Richard (PA) $1,000

HOUSE REPUBLICANS
Barton, Joe L (TX) $2,100
Deal, Nathan (GA) $2,000
Issa, Darrell (CA) $2,000
Ferguson, Mike (NJ) $1,000
Hart, Melissa (PA) $1,000
Upton, Fred (MI) $1,000

Corporate Foundations and Giving Programs

Biogen Idec Corporate Giving Program
14 Cambridge Center
Cambridge, MA 02142 — Tel: (617) 679 - 2000; Fax: (617) 679 - 2617

Annual Grant Total: none reported
Geographic Preference: Area(s) in which employees live and work
Primary Interests: Arts and Culture; Community Development; Education; Medicine and Health Care

Public Affairs and Related Activities Personnel

At Headquarters

BROCKELMAN, Amy — Tel: (617) 914 - 6524; Fax: (617) 679 - 2617
Senior Manager, Public Affairs

HUNT, Tim — Tel: (617) 914 - 6524; Fax: (617) 679 - 2617
Senior Director, Public Affairs

JUVES, Jose — Tel: (617) 914 - 6524; Fax: (617) 679 - 2617
Associate Director, Public Affairs

MATSUI, Connie L. — Tel: (617) 679 - 2000; Fax: (617) 679 - 2617
Exec. V. President, Corporate Strategy and Communications

PAGLIARO, Kara — Tel: (617) 914 - 6524; Fax: (617) 679 - 2617
Associate, Public Affairs

RYAN, Amy — Tel: (617) 914 - 6524; Fax: (617) 679 - 2617
Associate Director, Public Affairs

SCHNEIER, Craig Eric — Tel: (617) 679 - 2000; Fax: (617) 679 - 2617
Exec. V. President, Human Resources

At Washington Office

FOSTER, David — Tel: (202) 383 - 1440
V. President, Government Affairs
david_foster@biogen.com

Biomet Inc.

A manufacturer of orthopedic and surgical equipment and supplies.

www.biomet.com
Annual Revenues: $1.879 billion

Chairman of the Board
NOBLITT, Niles L. — Tel: (574) 267 - 6639; Fax: (574) 267 - 8137
niles.noblitt@biometmail.com

President and Chief Exec. Officer
MILLER, Dane A., Ph.D. — Tel: (574) 267 - 6639; Fax: (574) 267 - 8137
dane.miller@biometmail.com

Main Headquarters
Mailing: P.O. Box 587, Warsaw, IN 46581-0587 — Tel: (574) 267 - 6639; Fax: (574) 267 - 8137
Street: 56 E. Bell Dr., Warsaw, IN 46580

Corporate Foundations and Giving Programs

Biomet Foundation
P.O. Box 587
Warsaw, IN 46581-0587 — Tel: (574) 267 - 6639; Fax: (574) 267 - 8137

Annual Grant Total: none reported
Primary Interests: Arts and Humanities; Math and Science; Social Services

Public Affairs and Related Activities Personnel

At Headquarters

GOSLEE, Barbara — Tel: (574) 372 - 1514; Fax: (574) 267 - 8137
Manager, Corporate Communications

NIEMIER, Charles E. — Tel: (574) 267 - 6639; Fax: (574) 267 - 8137
Senior V. President, International Operations
charles.niemier@biometmail.com

SASSO, Greg W. — Tel: (574) 372 - 1528; Fax: (574) 267 - 8137
V. President, Corporate Development and Communications
greg.sasso@biometmail.com

Birds Eye Foods

Formerly known as Agrilink Foods, Inc. A food processing company.
www.birdseyefoods.com
Annual Revenues: $1 billion

Chairman, President and Chief Exec. Officer
MULLEN, Dennis M. Tel: (585) 383 - 1850
dmullen@birdseyefoods.com Fax: (585) 385 - 2857
TF: (800) 999 - 5044

Main Headquarters
Mailing: P.O. Box 20670 Tel: (585) 383 - 1850
Rochester, NY 14602-0670 Fax: (585) 385 - 2857
TF: (800) 999 - 5044

Street: 90 Linden Oaks
Rochester, NY 14625

Political Action Committees

Birds Eye Foods, Inc. PAC
Contact: Timothy Benjamin
P.O. Box 20670 Tel: (585) 383 - 1850
Rochester, NY 14602-0670 Fax: (585) 383 - 1281
TF: (800) 999 - 5044

Contributions to Candidates: none reported (01/05 - 09/05)

Corporate Foundations and Giving Programs

Birds Eye Foods Foundation
Contact: Sue Riker
P.O. Box 20670 Tel: (585) 264 - 3155
Rochester, NY 14602-0670 Fax: (585) 383 - 1606
TF: (800) 999 - 5044

Annual Grant Total: $200,000 - $300,000
Geographic Preference: Area(s) in which the company operates; Georgia; Michigan; New York; Ohio; Pennsylvania; Texas; Washington State
Primary Interests: Arts and Culture; Higher Education; Social Services
Recent Recipients: Salvation Army; United Way

Public Affairs and Related Activities Personnel

At Headquarters

BENJAMIN, Timothy Tel: (585) 383 - 1850
PAC Contact Fax: (585) 383 - 1281
tbenjamin@birdseyefoods.com TF: (800) 999 - 5044

RIKER, Sue Tel: (585) 264 - 3155
Contact, Birds Eye Foods Foundation Fax: (585) 383 - 1606
sriker@birdseyefoods.com TF: (800) 999 - 5044

SLIZEWSKI, Beatrice B. Tel: (585) 264 - 3189
V. President, Corporate Communications Fax: (585) 383 - 5609
bslizewski@birdseyefoods.com TF: (800) 999 - 5044
Responsibilities include corporate contributions.

WARLICK-JARVIE, Lois Tel: (585) 264 - 3136
V. President, Human Resources Fax: (585) 383 - 1281
TF: (800) 999 - 5044

Birmingham Steel Corp.

See listing on page 358 under Nucor Corp.

The BISYS Group, Inc.

Provides outsourcing services for the financial services industry.
www.bisys.com
Annual Revenues: $865.7 million

Chairman of the Board Tel: (212) 907 - 6000
CARSDALE, Robert J. Fax: (212) 907 - 6014

President and Chief Exec. Officer Tel: (212) 907 - 6000
FRADIN, Russell P. Fax: (212) 907 - 6014

Main Headquarters
Mailing: 90 Park Ave. Tel: (212) 907 - 6000
Tenth Floor Fax: (212) 907 - 6014
New York, NY 10016-1301

Public Affairs and Related Activities Personnel

At Headquarters

BRIGGS, Daniel J. Tel: (212) 907 - 6134
V. President, Finance and Investor Relations Fax: (212) 907 - 6001
daniel.briggs@bisys.com
Responsibilities include media relations.

RYBARCZYK, Mark J. Tel: (212) 907 - 6000
Exec. V. President, Human Resources Fax: (212) 907 - 6001

BJ Services Co.

Provides pumping, cementing and sand control servicing to the petroleum industry.
www.bjservices.com
Annual Revenues: $2.233 billion

Chairman, President and Chief Exec. Officer Tel: (713) 462 - 4239
STEWART, J. W. Fax: (713) 895 - 5851

Main Headquarters
Mailing: P.O. Box 4442 Tel: (713) 462 - 4239
Houston, TX 77210-4442 Fax: (713) 895 - 5851

Street: 5500 N.W. Central Dr.
Houston, TX 77092

Public Affairs and Related Activities Personnel

At Headquarters

COONS, Robert C. Tel: (713) 895 - 5873
Director, Corporate Communications Fax: (713) 895 - 5851
rcoons@bjservices.com

DOUGET, Susan E. Tel: (713) 462 - 4239
Director, Human Resources Fax: (713) 895 - 5897
Responsibilities include corporate philanthropy.

BJ's Wholesale Club, Inc.

Operates a chain of membership warehouse clubs in the eastern United States.
www.bjs.com
Annual Revenues: $5.28 billion

Chairman of the Board Tel: (508) 651 - 7400
ZARKIN, Herbert J. Fax: (508) 651 - 6167
TF: (800) 257 - 2582

President and Chief Exec. Officer Tel: (508) 651 - 7400
WEDGE, Michael T. Fax: (508) 651 - 6167
TF: (800) 257 - 2582

Main Headquarters
Mailing: One Mercer Rd. Tel: (508) 651 - 7400
Natick, MA 01760 Fax: (508) 651 - 6167
TF: (800) 257 - 2582

Public Affairs and Related Activities Personnel

At Headquarters

BREAULT, Sandra Tel: (508) 651 - 7400
Public Relations and Corporate Communications Fax: (508) 651 - 6167
Contact TF: (800) 257 - 2582

DAVIS, Thomas, III Tel: (508) 651 - 7400
Senior V. President and Director, Human Resources Fax: (508) 651 - 6167
TF: (800) 257 - 2582

MALONEY, Cathleen M. Tel: (508) 651 - 6650
V. President and Manager, Investor Relations Fax: (508) 651 - 6167
cmaloney@bjs.com TF: (800) 257 - 2582

The Black & Decker Corp.

A global marketer and manufacturer of power tools, security hardware and other home improvement products, small household appliances and commercial products.
www.blackanddecker.com
Annual Revenues: $4.2 billion

Chairman, President, and Chief Exec. Officer Tel: (410) 716 - 3900
ARCHIBALD, Nolan D. Fax: (410) 716 - 2933
nolan.archibald@bdk.com

Main Headquarters
Mailing: 701 E. Joppa Rd. Tel: (410) 716 - 3900
Towson, MD 21286 Fax: (410) 716 - 2933

Corporate Foundations and Giving Programs

Black & Decker Corporate Contributions Program
Contact: Barbara B. Lucas
701 E. Joppa Rd. Tel: (410) 716 - 2980
Towson, MD 21286 Fax: (410) 716 - 2933

Annual Grant Total: none reported

Public Affairs and Related Activities Personnel

At Headquarters

LUCAS, Barbara B. Tel: (410) 716 - 2980
Senior V. President, Public Affairs; and Corporate Fax: (410) 716 - 2933
Secretary
barbara.lucas@bdk.com
Responsibilities include corporate philanthropy.

MCBRIDE, Paul F. Tel: (410) 716 - 3900
Senior V. President, Human Resources and Corporate Fax: (410) 716 - 2933
Initiatives

ROTHLEITNER, Mark M. Tel: (410) 716 - 3076
V. President, Investor Relations and Treasurer Fax: (410) 716 - 2933
mark.rothleitner@bdk.com

Black & Veatch

A global engineering, construction and consulting firm. Specializes in infrastucture development in the fields of energy, water, and information.
www.bv.com
Annual Revenues: $2.5 billion

Chairman, President and Chief Exec. Officer Tel: (913) 458 - 2000
RODMAN, Len C. Fax: (913) 458 - 3730
rodmanlc@bv.com

Main Headquarters
Mailing: 11401 Lamar Ave. Tel: (913) 458 - 2000
Overland Park, KS 66211 Fax: (913) 458 - 2934

Black & Veatch

• continued from previous page

Political Action Committees

Black & Veatch Good Government Fund
Contact: Robert F. Riordan
11401 Lamar Ave. Tel: (913) 458 - 7867
Overland Park, KS 66211 Fax: (913) 458 - 3730

Contributions to Candidates: none reported (01/05 - 09/05)

Public Affairs and Related Activities Personnel

At Headquarters

ITEIL, Linda — Tel: (913) 458 - 4629
Communications Specialist — Fax: (913) 458 - 2934

PETZ, Carl — Tel: (913) 458 - 4685
Director, Corporate Communications — Fax: (913) 458 - 2934

RIORDAN, Robert F. — Tel: (913) 458 - 7867
V. President, Government Affairs and PAC Contact — Fax: (913) 458 - 3730
riordanrf@bv.com

SMITH, Corrine — Tel: (913) 458 - 3500
V. President, Brand Management and Communications
smithco@bv.com

Black Hills Corp.

An energy and communications company.
www.blackhillscorp.com
Annual Revenues: $1 billion

Chief Exec. Officer and President — Tel: (605) 721 - 1700
EMERY, David R. — Fax: (605) 721 - 2599
demery@bh-corp.com

Main Headquarters
Mailing: P.O. Box 1400 — Tel: (605) 721 - 1700
Rapid City, SD 57709-1400 — Fax: (605) 721 - 2599
Street: 625 Ninth St.
Rapid City, SD 57701-2428

Political Action Committees

Black Hills Corporation PAC
Contact: Marlena J. Parr
P.O. Box 1400 — Tel: (605) 721 - 1700
Rapid City, SD 57709-1400 — Fax: (605) 721 - 2599

Contributions to Candidates: $2,000 (01/05 - 09/05)
Democrats: $2,000.

Principal Recipients

SENATE DEMOCRATS	HOUSE DEMOCRATS	
	Visclosky, Peter (IN)	$2,000

Public Affairs and Related Activities Personnel

At Headquarters

ALEXANDER, Nancy — Tel: (605) 721 - 1700
Director, Human Resources

EVANS, Linden — Tel: (605) 721 - 1700
President and Chief Operating Officer, Retail Business Segment — Fax: (605) 721 - 2599

JAHR, Dale T. — Tel: (605) 721 - 2326
Investor Relations Director — Fax: (605) 721 - 2568
djahr@bh-corp.com

PARR, Marlena J. — Tel: (605) 721 - 1700
PAC Treasurer — Fax: (605) 721 - 2599
mparr@bh-corp.com

THIRSTRUP-ZAR, Barbara — Tel: (605) 721 - 1700
Manager, Governmental and Public Affairs — Fax: (605) 721 - 2568
bthirstrup@bh-corp.com

WHITE, Kyle D. — Tel: (605) 721 - 1700
V. President, Corporate Affairs — Fax: (605) 721 - 2568

Bloomberg L.P.

A multimedia company.
www.bloomberg.com
Annual Revenues: $3.5 billion

Chairman of the Board — Tel: (212) 318 - 2000
GRAUER, Peter T. — Fax: (917) 369 - 5000

Chief Exec. Officer — Tel: (212) 318 - 2000
SENWICK, Lex — Fax: (917) 369 - 5000

Main Headquarters
Mailing: 499 Park Ave. — Tel: (212) 318 - 2000
New York, NY 10022 — Fax: (917) 369 - 5000

Washington Office
Contact: Gregory R. Babyak
Mailing: 1399 New York Ave. NW — Tel: (202) 624 - 1952
11th Floor — Fax: (202) 624 - 1300
Washington, DC 20005-4711

Public Affairs and Related Activities Personnel

At Washington Office

BABYAK, Gregory R. — Tel: (202) 624 - 1952
Counsel — Fax: (202) 624 - 1300
Registered Federal Lobbyist.

Bloomingdale's

A retail store chain. A division of Federated Department Stores (see separate listing).
www.bloomingdales.com
Annual Revenues: $1.747 billion

Chairman and Chief Exec. Officer — Tel: (212) 705 - 2000
GOULD, Michael — Fax: (212) 705 - 2805

Main Headquarters
Mailing: 1000 Third Ave. — Tel: (212) 705 - 2000
New York, NY 10022 — Fax: (212) 705 - 2805

Corporate Foundations and Giving Programs

Bloomingdale Corporate Giving Program
Contact: Anne Keating
1000 Third Ave. — Tel: (212) 705 - 2434
New York, NY 10022 — Fax: (212) 705 - 2805

Annual Grant Total: none reported
Primary Interests: Children; Medicine and Health Care; Women

Public Affairs and Related Activities Personnel

At Headquarters

KEATING, Anne — Tel: (212) 705 - 2434
Senior V. President, Public Relations — Fax: (212) 705 - 2805
Responsibilities include corporate philanthropy.

MCKAY, Kelly — Tel: (212) 705 - 2443
Press Contact — Fax: (212) 705 - 2805
kelly.mckay@fds.com

QUARTA, Elizabeth — Tel: (212) 705 - 2349
Press Contact — Fax: (212) 705 - 2805
elizabethquarta@fdw.com

Blue Cross and Blue Shield of Alabama

www.bcbsal.org
Annual Revenues: $2.147 billion

President and Chief Exec. Officer — Tel: (205) 220 - 2100
POPE, Gary Philip — Fax: (205) 220 - 4841

Main Headquarters
Mailing: 450 Riverchase Pkwy. East — Tel: (205) 220 - 2100
Birmingham, AL 35244 — Fax: (205) 220 - 4841

Corporate Foundations and Giving Programs

Caring Foundation
Contact: James M. Brown
450 Riverchase Pkwy. East — Tel: (205) 220 - 2100
Birmingham, AL 35244 — Fax: (205) 220 - 4841

Annual Grant Total: $2,000,000 - $5,000,000
Geographic Preference: Area in which the company is headquartered
Primary Interests: Children; Disaster Relief; Education; Medicine and Health Care; Safety

Public Affairs and Related Activities Personnel

At Headquarters

BROWN, James M. — Tel: (205) 220 - 2100
Senior V. President, Caring Foundation — Fax: (205) 220 - 4841

ESTOCK, Larry — Tel: (205) 220 - 2100
Communications Coordinator — Fax: (205) 220 - 4841

HARTSELL, Charles R. — Tel: (205) 988 - 2126
Senior V. President, Government Programs, Claims and Public Affairs — Fax: (205) 220 - 4841
chartsell@bcbsal.org

Blue Cross and Blue Shield of Arizona

www.bcbsaz.com

President and Chief Exec. Officer — Tel: (602) 864 - 4400
BOALS, Richard L. — Fax: (602) 864 - 4242
TF: (800) 232 - 2345

Main Headquarters
Mailing: P.O. Box 13466 — Tel: (602) 864 - 4400
Phoenix, AZ 85002-3466 — Fax: (602) 864 - 4242
TF: (800) 232 - 2345
Street: 2444 W. Las Palmaritas Dr.
Phoenix, AZ 85021

Political Action Committees

Healthy Government Committee - The PAC/Blue Cross & Blue Shield/Arizona
Contact: Kate Baker
P.O. Box 13466 — Tel: (602) 864 - 4616
Phoenix, AZ 85002-3466 — Fax: (602) 864 - 4242
TF: (800) 232 - 2345

Blue Cross and Blue Shield of Arizona

* continued from previous page

Contributions to Candidates: $2,750 (01/05 - 09/05)
Democrats: $500; Republicans: $2,250.

Principal Recipients

SENATE DEMOCRATS		HOUSE DEMOCRATS	
		Grijalva, Raul (AZ)	$500
SENATE REPUBLICANS		**HOUSE REPUBLICANS**	
Kyl, Jon L (AZ)	$2,000	Renzi, Richard (AZ)	$250

Corporate Foundations and Giving Programs

Blue Cross and Blue Shield of Arizona Community Affairs
P.O. Box 13466
Phoenix, AZ 85002-3466
Tel: (602) 864 - 4400
Fax: (602) 864 - 4242
TF: (800) 232 - 2345

Annual Grant Total: none reported
Geographic Preference: Arizona
Primary Interests: Children; Families

Public Affairs and Related Activities Personnel

At Headquarters

BAKER, Kate
Contact, Healthy Government Committee
Tel: (602) 864 - 4616
Fax: (602) 864 - 4242
TF: (800) 232 - 2345

BASSETT, Charles
Director, Government Relations
Tel: (602) 864 - 4350
Fax: (602) 864 - 4242
TF: (800) 232 - 2345

HANNON, Richard M.
Senior V. President, Marketing and Provider Affairs
Tel: (602) 864 - 4418
Fax: (602) 864 - 4242
TF: (800) 232 - 2345

Blue Cross and Blue Shield of Delaware

A subsidiary of CareFirst Blue Cross and Blue Shield (see separate listing).
www.bcbsde.com
Annual Revenues: $815.5 million

President
CONSTANTINE, Timothy J.
Tel: (302) 421 - 3000
Fax: (302) 421 - 2592

Main Headquarters
Mailing: P.O. Box 1991
One Brandywine Gateway
Wilmington, DE 19899-1991
Tel: (302) 421 - 3000
Fax: (302) 421 - 2592

Public Affairs and Related Activities Personnel

At Headquarters

RIABOV, Darelle L
Director, Corporate Communications
Tel: (302) 421 - 3300
Fax: (302) 421 - 2592

Blue Cross and Blue Shield of Florida

www.bcbsfl.com
Annual Revenues: $5.99 billion

Chairman and Chief Exec. Officer
LUFANO, Dr. Robert
Tel: (904) 791 - 6111
Fax: (904) 905 - 4486
TF: (800) 477 - 3736

Main Headquarters
Mailing: 4800 Deerwood Campus Pkwy.
Jacksonville, FL 32246-8273
Tel: (904) 791 - 6111
Fax: (904) 905 - 4486
TF: (800) 477 - 3736

Political Action Committees

Florida Health PAC
Contact: James Mandeville
P.O. Box 6936
Jacksonville, FL 32236

Contributions to Candidates: $4,000 (01/05 - 09/05)
Republicans: $4,000.

Principal Recipients

SENATE REPUBLICANS	HOUSE REPUBLICANS	
	Brown-Waite, Virginia (FL)	$1,000
	Diaz-Balart, Lincoln (FL)	$1,000
	Mack, Connie (FL)	$1,000
	Stearns, Clifford (FL)	$1,000

Corporate Foundations and Giving Programs

The Blue Foundation for a Healthy Florida, Inc.
Contact: Michael S. Hutton
4800 Deerwood Campus Pkwy.
Jacksonville, FL 32246-8273
Tel: (904) 791 - 6111
Fax: (904) 905 - 4486
TF: (800) 477 - 3736

Annual Grant Total: $1,000,000 - $2,000,000
The foundation is primarily interested in helping uninsured and underserved Floridians.
Geographic Preference: Florida
Primary Interests: Health and Human Services

Public Affairs and Related Activities Personnel

At Headquarters

COSTON, Sandra
Tel: (904) 791 - 6111
Fax: (904) 905 - 4486
TF: (800) 477 - 3736

EASTERLING-CHARLES, Deborah
Government Relations Representative
Mailstop: DCC3-4
Tel: (904) 905 - 6647
Fax: (904) 905 - 4486
TF: (800) 477 - 3736

HIGHTOWER, Michael R.
V. President, Governmental and Legislative Relations
Tel: (904) 905 - 6072
Fax: (904) 905 - 4486
TF: (800) 477 - 3736

HUTTON, Michael S.
Grants Manager
michael.hutton@bcbsfl.com
Tel: (904) 791 - 6111
Fax: (904) 905 - 4486
TF: (800) 477 - 3736

JOLLIVETTE, Cyrus
Senior V. President, Public Affairs
Tel: (904) 791 - 6111
Fax: (904) 905 - 4486
TF: (800) 477 - 3736

KAMMER, Randy M.
V. President, Regulatory Affairs and Public Policy
Tel: (904) 905 - 6661
Fax: (904) 905 - 4486
TF: (800) 477 - 3736

LORD, Curtis
Tel: (904) 791 - 6111
Fax: (904) 905 - 4486
TF: (800) 477 - 3736

LUTHER, Lisa Acheson
Senior Consultant, Public Relations
Tel: (904) 905 - 3402
Fax: (904) 905 - 4486
TF: (800) 477 - 3736

MCCABE, Patrick
V. President, Corporate Communications
Tel: (904) 905 - 6123
Fax: (904) 905 - 4486
TF: (800) 477 - 3736

SMITH, Steven D.
Director, State Government/Legislation Relations
Mailstop: DCC3-4
Tel: (904) 905 - 6742
Fax: (904) 905 - 4486
TF: (800) 477 - 3736

TOWLER, Susan
V. President, Community Relations
Tel: (904) 905 - 6803
Fax: (904) 905 - 4486
TF: (800) 477 - 3736

WOLLITZ, Jeffry R.
Director, Federal Government/Legislation Relations
Mailstop: DCC3-4
Tel: (904) 905 - 6072
Fax: (904) 905 - 4486
TF: (800) 477 - 3736

At Other Offices

MANDEVILLE, James
Treasurer, Florida Health Political Action Committee
P.O. Box 6936
Jacksonville, FL 32236

Blue Cross and Blue Shield of Kansas City

www.bcbskc.com

President and Chief Exec. Officer
BOWSER, Tom
Tel: (816) 395 - 2222

Main Headquarters
Mailing: One Pershing Square
2301 Main St.
Kansas City, MO 64108
Tel: (816) 395 - 2222

Political Action Committees

Blue Cross & Blue Shield of Kansas City Federal PAC
Contact: Steven R. Bledsoe
One Pershing Square
2301 Main St.
Kansas City, MO 64108
Tel: (816) 395 - 2086
Fax: (816) 395 - 2379

Contributions to Candidates: $4,500 (01/05 - 09/05)
Democrats: $500; Republicans: $4,000.

Principal Recipients

SENATE DEMOCRATS	HOUSE DEMOCRATS	
	Cleaver, Emanuel (MO)	$500
SENATE REPUBLICANS	**HOUSE REPUBLICANS**	
	Graves, Sam (MO)	$2,000
	Hulshof, Kenny (MO)	$2,000

Blue Cross and Blue Shield of Kansas City

** continued from previous page*

Corporate Foundations and Giving Programs

The Caring Program for Children
Contact: Alice Ellison
One Pershing Square — Tel: (816) 395 - 2222
2301 Main St.
Kansas City, MO 64108

Annual Grant Total: none reported
Primary Interests: Children's Health

Public Affairs and Related Activities Personnel

At Headquarters

BLEDSOE, Steven R. — Tel: (816) 395 - 2086
V. President, Government Affairs — Fax: (816) 395 - 2379
Responsibilities include political action.

ELLISON, Alice — Tel: (816) 395 - 2222
V. President, Community Relations

JOHNSON, Susan M. — Tel: (816) 395 - 3566
Director, Corporate Communications
susan.johnson@bcbskc.com

Blue Cross and Blue Shield of Kansas, Inc.

www.bcbsks.com

Chariman of the Board — Tel: (785) 291 - 8700
ALLEY, John M., III — Fax: (785) 291 - 8216

President and Chief Exec. Officer — Tel: (785) 291 - 8700
MATTOX, Michael M. — Fax: (785) 291 - 8216
mike.mattox@bcbsks.com

Main Headquarters
Mailing: 1133 S.W. Topeka Blvd. — Tel: (785) 291 - 7000
Topeka, KS 66629 — Fax: (785) 291 - 8216

Political Action Committees

Blue Cross and Blue Shield of Kansas Employee PAC
Contact: Lisa Berke
1133 S.W. Topeka Blvd. — Tel: (785) 291 - 8860
Topeka, KS 66629 — Fax: (785) 291 - 8216

Contributions to Candidates: none reported (01/05 - 09/05)

Public Affairs and Related Activities Personnel

At Headquarters

BAILEY, S. Graham — Tel: (785) 291 - 8846
V. President, Corporate Communications and Public Relations — Fax: (785) 291 - 7664
Mailstop: MS 510
graham.bailey@bcbsks.com

BERKE, Lisa — Tel: (785) 291 - 8860
PAC Treasurer — Fax: (785) 291 - 8216
lisa.berke@bcbsks.com

BRUTTON, Mary Beth — Tel: (785) 291 - 8869
Public Information Coordinator — Fax: (785) 291 - 7664
Mailstop: MS 548

PALENSKE, Fred — Tel: (785) 291 - 7810
Director, Legislative and Regulatory Relations — Fax: (785) 291 - 8216
fred.palenske@bcbsks.com

ROWELL, Susan M. — Tel: (785) 291 - 8698
Manager, Communications — Fax: (785) 291 - 7664
Mailstop: MS 502
susan.rowell@bcbsks.com

Blue Cross and Blue Shield of Louisiana

www.bcbsla.com

President and Chief Exec. Officer — Tel: (225) 295 - 3307
BARRY, Gery J. — Fax: (225) 295 - 2054
TF: (800) 599 - 2583

Main Headquarters
Mailing: P.O. Box 98029 — Tel: (225) 295 - 3307
Baton Rouge, LA 70898-9029 — Fax: (225) 295 - 2054
TF: (800) 599 - 2583

Street: 5525 Reitz Ave.
Baton Rouge, LA 70809

Corporate Foundations and Giving Programs

Louisiana Child Care Foundation, Inc.
Contact: Pat Robinson
P.O. Box 98029 — Tel: (225) 295 - 2206
Baton Rouge, LA 70898-9029 — Fax: (225) 298 - 1812
TF: (800) 599 - 2583

Annual Grant Total: none reported
Primary Interests: Children; Education
Recent Recipients: Boys and Girls Club; Girl Scouts of America; Salvation Army; YMCA

Public Affairs and Related Activities Personnel

At Headquarters

MAGINNIS, John H., Jr. — Tel: (225) 295 - 2405
V. President, Corporate Communications — Fax: (225) 295 - 2583
TF: (800) 599 - 2583

MCINTYRE, Pamela — Tel: (225) 295 - 3307
Interim V. President, Human Resources — Fax: (225) 295 - 2054
TF: (800) 599 - 2583

ROBINSON, Pat — Tel: (225) 295 - 2206
Foundation Contact — Fax: (225) 298 - 1812
TF: (800) 599 - 2583

Blue Cross and Blue Shield of Maryland

See listing on page 101 under CareFirst BlueCross and BlueShield.

Blue Cross and Blue Shield of Massachusetts

www.bcbsma.com
Annual Revenues: $3.725 billion

President and Chief Exec. Officer — Tel: (617) 246 - 5000
KILLINGSWORTH, Cleve — TF: (800) 325 - 2583

Main Headquarters
Mailing: 401 Park Dr. — Tel: (617) 246 - 5000
Boston, MA 02215 — TF: (800) 325 - 2583

Political Action Committees

FED CAREPAC, The Blue Cross & Blue Shield of MA PAC
Contact: Meghan Driscoll
401 Park Dr. — Tel: (617) 246 - 5000
Boston, MA 02215 — TF: (800) 325 - 2583

Contributions to Candidates: $200 (01/05 - 09/05)
Democrats: $200.

Principal Recipients

SENATE DEMOCRATS	HOUSE DEMOCRATS	
	Obey, David R (WI)	$200

Corporate Foundations and Giving Programs

Blue Cross and Blue Shield of Massachusetts Foundation
Contact: Andrew Dreyfus
401 Park Dr. — Tel: (617) 246 - 5000
Boston, MA 02215 — TF: (800) 325 - 2583

Annual Grant Total: $1,000,000 - $2,000,000
Primary Interests: Children; Children's Health; Families

Public Affairs and Related Activities Personnel

At Headquarters

CURLEY, Jay — Tel: (617) 246 - 5000
Director, Government, Public and Regulatory Affairs — TF: (800) 325 - 2583

DREYFUS, Andrew — Tel: (617) 246 - 5000
President, Blue Cross and Blue Shield of Massachusetts Foundation — TF: (800) 325 - 2583
andrew.dreyfus@bcbsmafoundation.org

DRISCOLL, Meghan — Tel: (617) 246 - 5000
Treasurer, Fed CarePAC — TF: (800) 325 - 2583

LEAHY, Susan — Tel: (617) 246 - 4823
Director, Public Relations and Media — TF: (800) 325 - 2583
susan.leahy-schuh@bcbsma.com

LEE, Celeste Reid — Tel: (617) 246 - 5000
Director, Community Partnerships — TF: (800) 325 - 2583
celeste.lee@bcbsmafoundation.org

MEADE, Peter — Tel: (617) 246 - 5000
Exec. V. President, Corporate Affairs — TF: (800) 325 - 2583

SCHOENBAUM, John A. — Tel: (617) 246 - 4356
V. President, Corporate Affairs — TF: (800) 325 - 2583
Schoenbaum_John_A/bos1_bcbsma@bcbsma.com

STEVENS-EDOUARD, Sylvia — Tel: (617) 246 - 4845
Director, Community Relations — TF: (800) 325 - 2583

Blue Cross and Blue Shield of Minnesota

A member of the Public Affairs Council. A health insurance company.
www.bluecrossmn.com

President and Chief Exec. Officer — Tel: (651) 662 - 8000
BANKS, Mark W., M.D. — TF: (800) 382 - 2000

Main Headquarters
Mailing: 3535 Blue Cross Rd. — Tel: (651) 662 - 8000
Eagan, MN 55122--115 — TF: (800) 382 - 2000

Blue Cross and Blue Shield of Minnesota

** continued from previous page*

Corporate Foundations and Giving Programs

Blue Cross and Blue Shield of Minnesota Foundation
Contact: Daniel S. Johnson
3535 Blue Cross Rd. — Tel: (651) 662 - 1580
Eagan, MN 55122--115 — Fax: (651) 662 - 1570
TF: (800) 382 - 2000

Annual Grant Total: $1,000,000 - $2,000,000
A priority of the foundation is to help communities take action to prevent youth tobacco use.
Geographic Preference: Minnesota
Primary Interests: Health; Youth Services

Public Affairs and Related Activities Personnel

At Headquarters

GOFF, Cynthia — Tel: (651) 662 - 2872
Director, Public Policy — Fax: (651) 662 - 6201
Mailstop: MS 3-27 — TF: (800) 382 - 2000
cynthia.goff@bluecrossmn.com

HENNINGS, Janice — Tel: (651) 662 - 6139
Policy and Legislative Affairs Media Contact — TF: (800) 382 - 2000

JOHNSON, Daniel S. — Tel: (651) 662 - 1580
Exec. Director, Blue Cross and Blue Shield of Minnesota Foundation and Community Affairs — Fax: (651) 662 - 1570
TF: (800) 382 - 2000

KLEPPE, Roger — Tel: (651) 662 - 8000
Senior V. President, Human Resources — TF: (800) 382 - 2000

MOCK, Kathleen A. — Tel: (651) 662 - 2580
V. President, Policy and Legislative Affairs — Fax: (651) 662 - 6201
TF: (800) 382 - 2000

NIEMIEC, Richard — Tel: (651) 662 - 8550
Senior V. President, Corporate Affairs — Fax: (651) 662 - 1989
TF: (800) 382 - 2000

OESTREICH, Karl W. — Tel: (651) 662 - 1502
Director, Media and Public Relations — Fax: (651) 662 - 1570
Mailstop: Route 4-59 — TF: (800) 382 - 2000
karl_w_oestreich@bluecrossmn.com

PATTERSON, Shawn — Tel: (651) 662 - 8766
V. President, Marketing and Communications — Fax: (651) 662 - 1570
TF: (800) 382 - 2000

STALBOERGER, Philip G. — Tel: (651) 662 - 2151
Director, Legislative Affairs — Fax: (651) 662 - 6201
Mailstop: MS 3-27 — TF: (800) 382 - 2000

STROM, Monika — Tel: (651) 662 - 6889
Community Affairs, Media Contact — TF: (800) 382 - 2000
monika_strom@bluecrossmn.com

Blue Cross and Blue Shield of Mississippi

www.bcbsms.com

President and Chief Exec. Officer — Tel: (601) 932 - 3704
HALE, Rick — Fax: (601) 939 - 7035
TF: (800) 222 - 8046

Main Headquarters
Mailing: P.O. Box 1043 — Tel: (601) 932 - 3704
Jackson, MS 39215-1043 — Fax: (601) 939 - 7035
TF: (800) 222 - 8046

Street: 3545 Lakeland Dr.
Flowood, MS 39232-9799

Corporate Foundations and Giving Programs

Blue Cross and Blue Shield of Mississippi Foundation
Contact: John Sewell
P.O. Box 1043 — Tel: (601) 932 - 3704
Jackson, MS 39215-1043 — Fax: (601) 939 - 7035
TF: (800) 222 - 8046

Annual Grant Total: none reported
Geographic Preference: Mississippi
Primary Interests: Medicine and Health Care
Recent Recipients: American Heart Ass'n; American Red Cross; March of Dimes

Public Affairs and Related Activities Personnel

At Headquarters

PACE, Charles D. — Tel: (601) 644 - 5026
Governmental Affairs and Compliance — Fax: (601) 939 - 7035
cpace@bcbsms.com — TF: (800) 222 - 8046

SEWELL, John — Tel: (601) 932 - 3704
Contact, Blue Cross and Blue Shield of Missisippi Foundation — Fax: (601) 939 - 7035
TF: (800) 222 - 8046

Blue Cross and Blue Shield of Montana

www.bcbsmt.com
Annual Revenues: $478.3 million

Chairman of the Board — Tel: (406) 444 - 8200
LUSK, Jerry E. — Fax: (406) 447 - 3454
TF: (800) 447 - 7828

President and Chief Exec. Officer — Tel: (406) 444 - 8200
CLADOUHOS, Sherry L. — Fax: (406) 447 - 3454
TF: (800) 447 - 7828

Main Headquarters
Mailing: P.O. Box 4309 — Tel: (406) 444 - 8200
Helena, MT 59604-4309 — Fax: (406) 447 - 3454
TF: (800) 447 - 7828

Street: 560 N. Park Ave.
Helena, MT 59601

Corporate Foundations and Giving Programs

Caring Foundation of Montana
P.O. Box 4309 — Tel: (406) 444 - 8200
Helena, MT 59604-4309 — Fax: (406) 447 - 3454
TF: (800) 447 - 7828

Annual Grant Total: none reported
Geographic Preference: Area(s) in which the company operates
Primary Interests: Children; Medicine and Health Care
Recent Recipients: United Way

Public Affairs and Related Activities Personnel

At Headquarters

ASK, Tanya — Tel: (406) 444 - 8975
Senior V. President, Government and Public Affairs — Fax: (406) 447 - 8607
TF: (800) 447 - 7828

MCGILLEN, Linda — Tel: (406) 444 - 8931
Director, Corporate Communications — Fax: (406) 447 - 3454
lmcgillen@bcbsmt.com — TF: (800) 447 - 7828

Blue Cross and Blue Shield of Nebraska

www.bcbsne.com
Annual Revenues: $705.6 million

President and Chief Exec. Officer — Tel: (402) 390 - 1800
MARTIN, Steven S. — Fax: (402) 398 - 3736

Main Headquarters
Mailing: 7261 Mercy Rd. — Tel: (402) 390 - 1820
P.O. Box 3248 — Fax: (402) 398 - 3736
Omaha, NE 68180

Political Action Committees

Blue Cross and Blue Shield of Nebraska PAC
Contact: Adrian D. Wilson
7261 Mercy Rd. — Tel: (402) 390 - 1800
P.O. Box 3248 — Fax: (402) 398 - 3736
Omaha, NE 68180

Contributions to Candidates: none reported (01/05 - 09/05)

Corporate Foundations and Giving Programs

Blue Cross and Blue Shield of Nebraska Giving
7261 Mercy Rd. — Tel: (402) 390 - 1820
P.O. Box 3248 — Fax: (402) 398 - 3736
Omaha, NE 68180

Annual Grant Total: none reported
Geographic Preference: Northeastern United States
Primary Interests: Arts and Humanities; Civic and Cultural Activities; Education; Health

Public Affairs and Related Activities Personnel

At Headquarters

LAGRECA, Celia A. — Tel: (402) 390 - 1838
Senior V. President, Corporate Communications — Fax: (402) 398 - 3736

PICKERING, Brian — Tel: (402) 398 - 3694
Manager, Public Relations and Communications — Fax: (402) 398 - 3736
brian.pickering@bcbsne.com

WILSON, Adrian D. — Tel: (402) 390 - 1800
PAC Treasurer — Fax: (402) 398 - 3736

Blue Cross and Blue Shield of New Jersey

See listing on page 248 under Horizon Blue Cross Blue Shield of New Jersey.

Blue Cross and Blue Shield of North Carolina

A health insurance company.
www.bcbsnc.com
Annual Revenues: $3.15 billion

President and Chief Exec. Officer — Tel: (919) 489 - 7431
GRECZYN, Robert J. — Fax: (919) 765 - 4837

Main Headquarters
Mailing: P.O. Box 2291 — Tel: (919) 489 - 7431
Durham, NC 27702-2291 — Fax: (919) 765 - 4837

Political Action Committees

Blue Cross and Blue Shield of North Carolina Employee PAC - Federal
Contact: Bradley T. Adcock
P.O. Box 2291 — Tel: (919) 765 - 4119
Durham, NC 27702-2291 — Fax: (919) 765 - 4837

Blue Cross and Blue Shield of North Carolina

* continued from previous page

Contributions to Candidates: $3,500 (01/05 - 09/05)

Democrats: $2,000; Republicans: $1,500.

Principal Recipients

SENATE DEMOCRATS	HOUSE DEMOCRATS	
	Etheridge, Bob (NC)	$2,000
SENATE REPUBLICANS	**HOUSE REPUBLICANS**	
	Myrick, Sue (NC)	$1,500

Corporate Foundations and Giving Programs

BCBSNC Foundation
Contact: Danielle Breslin
P.O. Box 2291 Tel: (919) 765 - 4114
Durham, NC 27702-2291 Fax: (919) 765 - 4837

Annual Grant Total: over $5,000,000
The foundation has donated over $14 million since 2000.
Geographic Preference: North Carolina
Primary Interests: Medicine and Health Care

Public Affairs and Related Activities Personnel

At Headquarters

ADCOCK, Bradley T. Tel: (919) 765 - 4119
V. President, Government Affairs Fax: (919) 765 - 4837
brad.adcock@bcbsnc.com
Responsibilities include political action.

BRESLIN, Danielle Tel: (919) 765 - 4114
Manager, BCBSNC Foundation Fax: (919) 765 - 4837
danielle.breslin@bcbsnc.com

GARRISON, Lynne G. Tel: (919) 765 - 7256
V. President, Corporate Communications Fax: (919) 765 - 4837
Mailstop: M/S HQ4
lynne.garrison@bcbsnc.com

HIGGINS, Kathy Tel: (919) 765 - 4104
V. President and V. Chairman, BCBSNC Foundation Fax: (919) 765 - 4837
Mailstop: M/S HQ4
kathy.higgins@bcbsnc.com

POWELL, Susanne Tel: (919) 765 - 4897
Director, Corporate Communications Fax: (919) 765 - 4837
Mailstop: M/S HQ4
susanne.powell@bcbsnc.com

STINNEFORD, Mark Tel: (919) 765 - 3745
Manager, Public Affairs Fax: (919) 765 - 4837
Mailstop: M/S HQ4
mark.stinneford@bcbsnc.com

TUTTLE, Gayle Tel: (919) 765 - 3747
Media Contact Fax: (919) 765 - 4837

VAVRINA, Robert T., Jr. Tel: (919) 489 - 7431
Senior V. President, Human Resources Fax: (919) 765 - 4837

WRIGHT, Kenneth D. Tel: (919) 765 - 7582
Director, State and Federal Relations Fax: (919) 765 - 4837
Mailstop: M/S HQ4
ken.wright@bcbsnc.com

Blue Cross and Blue Shield of North Dakota

www.bcbsnd.com
Annual Revenues: $859.3 million

Chairman of the Board Tel: (701) 282 - 1100
KEOGH, Frank Fax: (701) 282 - 1469
TF: (800) 342 - 4718

President and Chief Exec. Officer Tel: (701) 282 - 1100
UNHJEM, Michael B. Fax: (701) 282 - 1469
TF: (800) 342 - 4718

Main Headquarters
Mailing: 4510 13th Ave. SW Tel: (701) 282 - 1100
Fargo, ND 58121-0001 Fax: (701) 282 - 1469
TF: (800) 342 - 4718

Public Affairs and Related Activities Personnel

At Headquarters

GAUPER, Larry L. Tel: (701) 282 - 1160
V. President, Communications Fax: (701) 282 - 1469
larry.gauper@noridian.com TF: (800) 342 - 4718

SORENSEN, Jim Tel: (701) 282 - 1485
Assistant V. President, Communications Fax: (701) 282 - 1469
jim.sorensen@noridian.com TF: (800) 342 - 4718

At Other Offices

ULMER, Daniel P. Tel: (701) 223 - 6348
Director, Government Relations Fax: (701) 255 - 5595
107 W. Main St.
P.O. Box 2657
Bismarck, ND 58501

Blue Cross and Blue Shield of Oregon

See listing on page 406 under Regence BlueCross BlueShield of Oregon.

Blue Cross & Blue Shield of Rhode Island

www.bcbsri.com

Acting President and Chief Exec. Officer Tel: (401) 459 - 2500
PURCELL, James E. Fax: (401) 459 - 1290
purcell.j@bcbsri.org TF: (800) 637 - 3718

Main Headquarters
Mailing: 444 Westminster St. Tel: (401) 459 - 1000
Providence, RI 02903-3279 TF: (800) 637 - 3718

Public Affairs and Related Activities Personnel

At Headquarters

GASBARRO, Eric Tel: (401) 459 - 5169
Assistant V. President, Human Resources Fax: (401) 455 - 6990
gasbarro.e@bcbsri.org TF: (800) 637 - 3718

HUFF, Dale Tel: (401) 459 - 1232
Chief Communications Officer Fax: (401) 459 - 1333
huff.d@bcbsri.org TF: (800) 637 - 3718

KEOUGH, Kim Tel: (401) 459 - 5601
Assistant V. President, Public Relations Fax: (401) 459 - 1333
keough.k@bcbsri.org TF: (800) 637 - 3718

TAYLOR, Jeff Tel: (401) 459 - 1241
Director, Legislative Affairs Fax: (401) 459 - 1333
taylor.j@bcbsri.org TF: (800) 637 - 3718

Blue Cross and Blue Shield of Tennessee

www.bcbst.com

Chief Exec. Officer Tel: (423) 755 - 5600
GREGG, Vicky B. TF: (800) 565 - 9140

Main Headquarters
Mailing: 801 Pine St. Tel: (423) 755 - 5600
Chattanooga, TN 37402-2555 TF: (800) 565 - 9140

Public Affairs and Related Activities Personnel

At Other Offices

GARY, Tim Tel: (615) 386 - 8524
General Counsel, VSHP, Inc./Chief Compliance and Risk Officer, Governmental Programs Fax: (615) 386 - 8509
3200 West End Ave.
Suite 102
Nashville, TN 37203-1332

LOCKE, David R. Tel: (615) 386 - 8524
Director, State Government Relations Fax: (615) 386 - 8509
3200 West End Ave.
Suite 102
Nashville, TN 37203-1332

Blue Cross and Blue Shield of Texas, Inc.

A division of Health Care Service Corp.
www.bcbstx.com

Main Headquarters
Mailing: 901 S. Central Exwy. Tel: (972) 766 - 6900
Richardson, TX 75080 Fax: (972) 766 - 5298

Public Affairs and Related Activities Personnel

At Headquarters

HUNT, Sue Tel: (972) 766 - 6900
V. President, Human Resources Fax: (972) 766 - 5298

TAYLOR, Ronald Tel: (972) 766 - 6900
V. President and General Counsel, Legal and Government Affairs Fax: (972) 766 - 5298

At Other Offices

SIMONTON, Kay Tel: (512) 472 - 2721
Government Relations Representative Fax: (512) 472 - 3256
206 W. 13th St.
Austin, TX 78701

Blue Cross and Blue Shield of Utah

See listing on page 406 under Regence BlueCross BlueShield of Utah.

Blue Cross and Blue Shield of Vermont
www.bcbsvt.com
Annual Revenues: $440 million

Chairman of the Board
GRANDQUIST, Deborah
Tel: (802) 223 - 6131
Fax: (802) 223 - 4229
TF: (800) 255 - 4550

President and Chief Exec. Officer
MILNES, William R.
milnesw@bcbsvt.com
Tel: (802) 223 - 6131
Fax: (802) 223 - 4229
TF: (800) 255 - 4550

Main Headquarters
Mailing: P.O. Box 186
Montpelier, VT 05601
Tel: (802) 223 - 6131
Fax: (802) 223 - 4229
TF: (800) 255 - 4550

Corporate Foundations and Giving Programs

Blue Cross and Blue Shield of Vermont Corporate Contributions
P.O. Box 186
Montpelier, VT 05601
Tel: (802) 223 - 6131
Fax: (802) 223 - 4229
TF: (800) 255 - 4550

Annual Grant Total: none reported
Primary Interests: Health
Recent Recipients: American Heart Ass'n; American Red Cross; Arthritis Foundation; March of Dimes

Public Affairs and Related Activities Personnel

At Headquarters

GODDARD, Kevin
V. President, External Affairs
goddardk@bcbsvt.com
Tel: (802) 223 - 6131
Fax: (802) 223 - 4229
TF: (800) 255 - 4550

PARRY, Kathy
Coordinator, External Affairs
parryk@bcbsvt.com
Tel: (802) 371 - 3205
Fax: (802) 223 - 4229
TF: (800) 255 - 4550

TOFFERI, Mr. Leigh J.
Director, Government, Public and Community Relations
tofferil@bcbsvt.com
Tel: (802) 371 - 3205
Fax: (802) 223 - 4229
TF: (800) 255 - 4550

Blue Cross and Blue Shield of Wyoming
www.bcbswy.com

Chairman of the Board
BONNER, Dave
Tel: (307) 634 - 1393
Fax: (307) 638 - 5742
TF: (800) 442 - 2376

President and Chief Exec. Officer
CRILLY, Tim J.
tim.crilly@bcbswy.com
Tel: (307) 634 - 1393
Fax: (307) 638 - 6927

Main Headquarters
Mailing: 4000 House Ave.
Cheyenne, WY 82000-1
Tel: (307) 634 - 1393
Fax: (307) 638 - 5742
TF: (800) 442 - 2376

Corporate Foundations and Giving Programs

Caring Foundation of Wyoming Inc.
Contact: Karen Rich
4000 House Ave.
Cheyenne, WY 82001
Tel: (307) 432 - 2829
Fax: (307) 638 - 6927

Annual Grant Total: none reported
Primary Interests: Children's Health

Public Affairs and Related Activities Personnel

At Other Offices

RICH, Karen
Contact, Caring Program for Children
4000 House Ave.
Cheyenne, WY 82001
Tel: (307) 432 - 2829
Fax: (307) 638 - 6927

Blue Cross and Blue Shield, Highmark
See listing on page 243 under Highmark Inc.

Blue Cross Blue Shield of Central New York
See listing on page 187 under Exellus Blue Cross Blue Shield.

Blue Cross Blue Shield of Georgia
A subsidiary of Wellpoint Inc. (see separate listing).
www.bcbsga.com

President and Chief Exec. Officer
MATTHEWS, Caz
Tel: (404) 842 - 8000
Fax: (404) 842 - 8801

Main Headquarters
Mailing: 3350 Peachtree Rd. NE
Atlanta, GA 30326
Tel: (404) 842 - 8000
Fax: (404) 842 - 8801

Public Affairs and Related Activities Personnel

At Headquarters

HARMAN, Charles E.
V. President, Public Affairs
charman@bcbsga.com
Tel: (404) 842 - 8980
Fax: (404) 842 - 8451

HOLLEY, Caroline E.
Legislative Affairs Specialist
caroline.holley@bcbsga.com
Tel: (404) 842 - 8207
Fax: (404) 842 - 8287

ODOM, Amy M.
Director, Public Affairs
amy.odom@bcbsga.com
Tel: (404) 842 - 8132
Fax: (404) 842 - 8801

Blue Cross Blue Shield of Michigan
www.bcbsm.com
Annual Revenues: $11.83 billion

President and Chief Exec. Officer
WHITMER, Richard E.
Mailstop: M/S 2001
rwhitmer@bcbsm.com
Tel: (313) 225 - 9000
Fax: (313) 225 - 6250

Main Headquarters
Mailing: 600 Lafayette East
Detroit, MI 48226
Tel: (313) 225 - 9000

Political Action Committees

Blue Cross Blue Shield of Michigan Politicial Action Committee (BCBSM PAC)
Contact: Dan Loepp
600 Lafayette East
Detroit, MI 48226
Tel: (313) 225 - 6841
Fax: (313) 225 - 6250

Contributions to Candidates: $7,000 (01/05 - 09/05)
Democrats: $4,000; Republicans: $3,000.

Principal Recipients

SENATE DEMOCRATS
Stabenow, Debbie (MI) $4,000

HOUSE DEMOCRATS

SENATE REPUBLICANS

HOUSE REPUBLICANS
McCotter, Thaddeus (MI) $2,000
Knollenberg, Joe (MI) $1,000

Corporate Foundations and Giving Programs

Blue Cross Blue Shield of Michigan Foundation
Contact: Ira Strumwasser, Ph.D.
600 Lafayette East
Detroit, MI 48226
Tel: (313) 225 - 6399
Fax: (313) 225 - 7730

Assets: $60,000,000 (2000)
Annual Grant Total: $2,000,000 - $5,000,000
Gives $3,000,000 in grants annually.
Geographic Preference: Michigan
Primary Interests: Health; Medicine and Health Care

Public Affairs and Related Activities Personnel

At Headquarters

JONES, Diana
V. President, Community Affairs
Mailstop: M/S 0250
djones@bcbsm.com
Tel: (313) 225 - 7230
Fax: (313) 225 - 9693

KASPEREK, Robert W.
V. President, Regulatory Affairs
Mailstop: M/S 2028
rkasperek@bcbsm.com
Tel: (313) 225 - 8135
Fax: (313) 225 - 8020

LOEPP, Dan
Senior V. President and Chief of Staff
Mailstop: M/S 2003
dloepp@bcbsm.com
Responsibilities include governmental affairs and political action.
Tel: (313) 225 - 6841
Fax: (313) 225 - 6250

STOJIC, Helen
Director, Media Relations
Mailstop: M/S 0221
hstojic@bcbsm.com
Tel: (313) 225 - 8113
Fax: (313) 225 - 6764

STRUMWASSER, Ira, Ph.D.
Exec. Director, Blue Cross Blue Shield of Michigan Foundation
Mailstop: M/S X520
istrumwasser@bcbsm.com
Tel: (313) 225 - 6399
Fax: (313) 225 - 7730

At Other Offices

COOK, Mark
Director, State Government Relations
602 W. Ionia
Lansing, MI 48933
mcook@bcbsm.com
Tel: (517) 371 - 7908
Fax: (517) 371 - 7979

PENDELL-LEAVITT, Cami
Manager, Executive Branch Relations and Legislative Affairs
602 W. Ionia
Lansing, MI 48933
Tel: (517) 371 - 7905
Fax: (517) 372 - 7979

Blue Cross of Idaho
www.bcidaho.com

Blue Cross of Idaho
** continued from previous page*

President and Chief Exec. Officer
FLACHBART, Ray
rflachbart@bcidaho.com
Tel: (208) 345 - 4550
Fax: (208) 331 - 7311

Main Headquarters
Mailing: P.O. Box 7408
Boise, ID 83707
Tel: (208) 345 - 4550
Fax: (208) 331 - 7311

Corporate Foundations and Giving Programs

Blue Cross of Idaho Community Involvement
P.O. Box 7408
Boise, ID 83707
Tel: (208) 345 - 4550
Fax: (208) 331 - 7311

Annual Grant Total: none reported
Recent Recipients: Boys and Girls Club; United Way

Public Affairs and Related Activities Personnel

At Headquarters

BASSLER, Thomas B.
General Counsel, Senior V. President, Legal Services and Government Affairs
tbassler@bcidaho.com
Tel: (208) 331 - 7385
Fax: (208) 331 - 7320

HENRY, Debra M.
V. President, Human Resources and Administrative Services
dhenry@bcidaho.com
Tel: (208) 345 - 4550
Fax: (208) 331 - 7311

MCKAY, Tod
Corporate and Media Relations Specialist
tmckay@bcidaho.com
Tel: (208) 331 - 7465
Fax: (208) 331 - 7335

TAYLOR, Julie M.
Director, Governmental Affairs
jtaylor@bcidaho.com
Tel: (208) 331 - 7357
Fax: (208) 331 - 7320

Blue Cross of Northeastern Pennsylvania
www.bcnepa.com

President and Chief Exec. Officer
CESARE, Denise S.
denise.cesare@bcnepa.com
Tel: (570) 200 - 6300

Main Headquarters
Mailing: 19 N. Main St.
Wilkes-Barre, PA 18711-0302
Tel: (570) 200 - 6300

Political Action Committees

Blue Cross Voice
Contact: Kimberly Kockler
19 N. Main St.
Wilkes-Barre, PA 18711-0302
Tel: (570) 200 - 6300

Contributions to Candidates: none reported (01/05 - 09/05)

Corporate Foundations and Giving Programs

Blue Ribbon Foundation
Contact: Lisa Baker
19 N. Main St.
Wilkes-Barre, PA 18711-0302
Tel: (570) 200 - 6305
Fax: (570) 200 - 6699

Assets: $7,705,171 (2003)
Annual Grant Total: $750,000 - $1,000,000
Geographic Preference: Pennsylvania
Primary Interests: Children; Education; Families; Health and Human Services
Recent Recipients: Boy Scouts of America; Salvation Army; United Way

Public Affairs and Related Activities Personnel

At Headquarters

BAKER, Lisa
Exec. Director, Foundation for Funding Community-Based Health Initiatives
lisa.baker@bcnepa.com
Tel: (570) 200 - 6305
Fax: (570) 200 - 6699

DAVIS, James
State Government Affairs Representative
Tel: (570) 200 - 6300

DAVIS, Mike
Director, External Affairs
Tel: (570) 200 - 6300

KOCKLER, Kimberly
Director, Policy Management
Tel: (570) 200 - 6300

Responsibilities include political action.

SNYDER, Gerard
Manager, Public Relations
gerard.snyder@bcnepa.com
Tel: (570) 200 - 6310
Fax: (570) 200 - 6699

Blue Cross, Independence
See listing on page 256 under Independence Blue Cross (Pennsylvania).

Blue Diamond Growers
A wholesaler of almonds.
www.bluediamondgrowers.com
Annual Revenues: $410.2 million

Chairman of the Board
ISOM, W. Howard
hisom@bdgrowers.com
Tel: (916) 442 - 0771
Fax: (916) 325 - 2880

President and Chief Exec. Officer
YOUNGDAHL, Douglas D.
dyoungdahl@bdgrowers.com
Tel: (916) 442 - 0771
Fax: (916) 325 - 2880

Main Headquarters
Mailing: P.O. Box 1768
Sacramento, CA 95812-1768
Tel: (916) 442 - 0771
Fax: (916) 325 - 2880
Street: 1802 C St.
Sacramento, CA 95814

Political Action Committees

Blue Diamond Growers PAC
Contact: Susan Brauner
P.O. Box 1768
Sacramento, CA 95812-1768
Tel: (916) 446 - 8354
Fax: (916) 325 - 2880

Contributions to Candidates: $22,900 (01/05 - 09/05)
Democrats: $8,000; Republicans: $14,900.

Principal Recipients

SENATE DEMOCRATS

HOUSE DEMOCRATS
Costa, Jim (CA) $3,000
Matsui, Robert (CA) $3,000

SENATE REPUBLICANS

HOUSE REPUBLICANS
Lungren, Daniel E (CA) $3,500
Thomas, William M (CA) $3,000
Doolittle, John (CA) $2,400

Corporate Foundations and Giving Programs

Blue Diamond Growers Charitable Contributions Program
Contact: Susan Brauner
P.O. Box 1768
Sacramento, CA 95812-1768
Tel: (916) 446 - 8354
Fax: (916) 325 - 2880

Annual Grant Total: under $100,000
Geographic Preference: Sacramento, CA
Primary Interests: Youth Services

Public Affairs and Related Activities Personnel

At Headquarters

BRAUNER, Susan
Director, Communications
sbrauner@bdgrowers.com
Responsibilities include political action.
Tel: (916) 446 - 8354
Fax: (916) 325 - 2880

PFANNER, Jennifer
Media Relations Contact
jpfanner@bdgrowers.com
Tel: (916) 325 - 2859
Fax: (916) 325 - 2880

Blue Shield of California
A member of the Public Affairs Council. A health insurer.
www.mylifepath.com

Chairman, President and Chief Exec. Officer
BODAKEN, Bruce G.
Tel: (415) 229 - 5000
Fax: (415) 229 - 5070
TF: (800) 200 - 3242

Main Headquarters
Mailing: 50 Beale St.
San Francisco, CA 94105-1808
Tel: (415) 229 - 5000
Fax: (415) 229 - 5070
TF: (800) 200 - 3242

Political Action Committees

Blue Shield of California PAC
Contact: Steven Sturman
50 Beale St.
San Francisco, CA 94105-1808
Tel: (415) 229 - 5000
Fax: (415) 229 - 5070
TF: (800) 200 - 3242

Contributions to Candidates: $12,600 (01/05 - 09/05)
Democrats: $6,100; Republicans: $6,500.

Principal Recipients

SENATE DEMOCRATS
Bayh, Evan (IN) $1,600
Carper, Thomas R (DE) $1,500
Clinton, Hillary Rodham (NY) $1,000

HOUSE DEMOCRATS
Costa, Jim (CA) $1,000
Matsui, Doris (CA) $1,000

SENATE REPUBLICANS

HOUSE REPUBLICANS
Lewis, Jerry (CA) $2,500
Thomas, William M (CA) $2,000
Cunningham, Duke (CA) $1,000
Jindal, Bobby (LA) $1,000

Blue Shield of California

* continued from previous page

Corporate Foundations and Giving Programs

Blue Shield Foundation
Contact: Andrew McFarland
50 Beale St.
San Francisco, CA 94105-1808
Tel: (415) 229 - 5000
Fax: (415) 229 - 5070
TF: (800) 200 - 3242

Annual Grant Total: none reported
Primary Interests: Math and Science; Medicine and Health Care; Technology; Women

Public Affairs and Related Activities Personnel

At Headquarters

EPSTEIN, Tom
V. President, Public Affairs
Tel: (415) 229 - 5110
Fax: (415) 229 - 5070
TF: (800) 200 - 3242

FARNAN, Lisa
V. President, Provider Relations and Network Development
Tel: (415) 229 - 5000
Fax: (415) 229 - 5070
TF: (800) 200 - 3242

HAYLING, Crystal
President and Chief Exec. Officer, Blue Shield of California Foundation
Tel: (415) 229 - 5000
Fax: (415) 229 - 5070
TF: (800) 200 - 3242

JACKSON, Marianne
Senior V. President, Human Resources
Tel: (415) 229 - 5000
Fax: (415) 229 - 5070
TF: (800) 200 - 3242

MCFARLAND, Andrew
Grants Administrator
andrew.mcfarland@blueshieldfoundation.org
Tel: (415) 229 - 5000
Fax: (415) 229 - 5070
TF: (800) 200 - 3242

STURMAN, Steven
PAC Treasurer
Tel: (415) 229 - 5000
Fax: (415) 229 - 5070
TF: (800) 200 - 3242

Blue Shield of Idaho

See listing on page 407 under Regence BlueShield of Idaho.

BlueCross BlueShield of Oklahoma

A member of the Public Affairs Council. A health insurance provider.
www.bcbsok.com

Chairman, President and Chief Exec. Officer
KING, Ron
Tel: (918) 560 - 3500
Fax: (918) 592 - 9492

Main Headquarters
Mailing: P.O. Box 3283
Tulsa, OK 74102-3283
Tel: (918) 560 - 3500
Fax: (918) 592 - 9492

Corporate Foundations and Giving Programs

Blue Cross and Blue Shield of Oklahoma Caring Program for Children
Contact: Mary Jane Lindman
P.O. Box 3283
Tulsa, OK 74102-3283
Tel: (918) 592 - 9484
Fax: (918) 592 - 9492

Annual Grant Total: none reported
Primary Interests: Children's Health

Public Affairs and Related Activities Personnel

At Headquarters

LINDMAN, Mary Jane
Contact, Blue Cross and Blue Shield of Oklahoma Caring Program for Children
Tel: (918) 592 - 9484
Fax: (918) 592 - 9492

RUTTMAN, David C.
V. President, Human Resources
Tel: (918) 560 - 3500
Fax: (918) 592 - 9492

SPONSLER, Linda L.
V. President, Advertising and Public Communications; and V. President and Director, Caring Program
Tel: (918) 560 - 3500
Fax: (918) 592 - 9492

At Other Offices

AZAR, Barbara
Public Affairs
3401 N.W. 63rd St
Oklahoma City, Ok 73116
bazar@bcbsok.com
Tel: (405) 841 - 9597
Fax: (405) 841 - 9663

BINKOWSKI, Beverly
Public Affairs
3401 N.W. 63rd St.
Oklahoma City, OK 73116
bbinkowski@bcbsok.com
Tel: (405) 841 - 9597
Fax: (405) 841 - 9663

BlueCross BlueShield of South Carolina

A member of the Public Affairs Council. A health insurance company.
www.southcarolinablues.com

Main Headquarters
Mailing: I-20 at Alpine Rd.
Columbia, SC 29219-0001
Tel: (803) 788 - 0222
Fax: (803) 264 - 5520
TF: (800) 288 - 2227

Public Affairs and Related Activities Personnel

At Headquarters

CLOSE, Carol
Manager, Public Affairs
Mailstop: AX-215
carol.close@bcbssc.com
Tel: (803) 264 - 3451
Fax: (803) 264 - 0204
TF: (800) 288 - 2227
Ext: 43451
Ext: 43451

GRADDICK, Joan
Senior Public Affairs Specialist
Mailstop: AX-215
joan.graddick@bcbssc.com
Tel: (803) 264 - 3452
Fax: (803) 264 - 5520
TF: (800) 288 - 2227
Ext: 43452
Ext: 43452

HAMMOND, Elizabeth
Media Contact
Tel: (803) 264 - 4626
Fax: (803) 264 - 5520
TF: (800) 288 - 2227

JOHNSON, George L.
V. President, Corporate Communications and Public Affairs
Mailstop: AX-210
george.johnson@bcbssc.com
Tel: (803) 264 - 2021
Fax: (803) 264 - 5522
TF: (800) 288 - 2227
Ext: 42021
Ext: 42021

THORNE, Donna M.
Director, Corporate Communications
Mailstop: AX-210
donna.thorne@bcbssc.com
Tel: (803) 264 - 2437
Fax: (803) 264 - 5522
TF: (800) 288 - 2227
Ext: 42437
Ext: 42437

At Other Offices

O'NEIL, William B., Jr.
Federal Affairs Representative
3010 Stonehurst Dr.
Emmitsburg, MD 21727
william.oneil@bcbssc.com
Tel: (301) 447 - 1926
Fax: (301) 447 - 1928

BlueCross, Capital

See listing on page 100 under Capital BlueCross (Pennsylvania).

BMC Software

System software products.
www.bmc.com
Annual Revenues: $1.3 billion

Chairman of the Board
CUPP, Garland
garland_cupp@bmc.com
Tel: (713) 918 - 8800
Fax: (713) 918 - 8000
TF: (800) 841 - 2031

President and Chief Exec. Officer
BEAUCHAMP, Robert E.
bob_beauchamp@bmc.com
Tel: (713) 918 - 8800
Fax: (713) 918 - 8000
TF: (800) 841 - 2031

Main Headquarters
Mailing: 2101 City West Blvd.
Houston, TX 77042-2827
Tel: (713) 918 - 8800
Fax: (713) 918 - 8000
TF: (800) 841 - 2031

Corporate Foundations and Giving Programs

BMC Software Community Relations
2101 City West Blvd.
Houston, TX 77042-2827
Tel: (713) 918 - 8800
Fax: (713) 918 - 8000
TF: (800) 841 - 2031

Annual Grant Total: none reported
Primary Interests: Health; Higher Education; Social Services
Recent Recipients: Habitat for Humanity; Race for the Cure; Special Olympics

Public Affairs and Related Activities Personnel

At Headquarters

FOSTER, Andrew
Director, Public Relations
Tel: (650) 930 - 5550
Fax: (713) 918 - 8000
TF: (800) 841 - 2031

SOLCHER, Steve
Investor Relations Contact
Tel: (713) 918 - 8800
Fax: (713) 918 - 8000
TF: (800) 841 - 2031

BMW (U.S.) Holding Corp.

The American import and sales subsidiary of the German manufacturer of automobiles and motorcycles.
www.bmwusa.com

Chairman and Chief Exec. Officer
PURVES, Tom
Tel: (201) 307 - 3501

Main Headquarters
Mailing: 300 Chestnut Ridge Rd
Woodcliff Lake, NJ 07677
Street: 300 Chestnut Ridge Rd
Woodcliff Lake, NJ 07677
Tel: (201) 307 - 4000
Fax: (201) 307 - 3607

BMW (U.S.) Holding Corp.

* continued from previous page

Washington Office
Mailing: The Executive Tower
1399 New York Ave. NW, Suite 425
Washington, DC 20005
Tel: (202) 393 - 2150
Fax: (202) 393 - 2151

Corporate Foundations and Giving Programs

BMW of North American Charitable Contributions
Contact: Michael McHale
300 Chestnut Ridge Rd
Woodcliff Lake, NJ 07677
Tel: (201) 307 - 3814
Fax: (201) 573 - 8416

Annual Grant Total: none reported
Primary Interests: Education; Environment/Conservation; Safety

Public Affairs and Related Activities Personnel

At Headquarters

BRUNNER, John
Manager, Human Resources
Tel: (201) 307 - 4000
Fax: (201) 573 - 8416

MCHALE, Michael
Group Communications Manager
Tel: (201) 307 - 3814
Fax: (201) 573 - 8416

MCKINLEY, Martha
Manager, Business Communications
Tel: (201) 307 - 3786
Fax: (201) 307 - 3607

MITCHELL, Robert D.
Manager, Corporate Communications
Tel: (201) 307 - 3701
Fax: (201) 307 - 3607

At Washington Office

HELSING, Craig R.
V. President, Government Relations
Responsibilities include corporate public affairs.
Tel: (202) 393 - 2150
Fax: (202) 393 - 2151

Bob Evans Farms, Inc.

A producer of food products and owner and operator of a chain of family restaurants.
www.bobevans.com
Annual Revenues: $1.061 billion

Chairman of the Board
RABOLD, Robert E. H.
Tel: (614) 491 - 2225
Fax: (614) 492 - 4949
TF: (800) 272 - 7675

President and Chief Exec. Officer
CORBIN, Larry C.
Tel: (614) 491 - 2225
Fax: (614) 492 - 4949
TF: (800) 272 - 7675

Main Headquarters
Mailing: 3776 S. High St.
Columbus, OH 43207-0863
Tel: (614) 491 - 2225
Fax: (614) 492 - 4949
TF: (800) 272 - 7675

Corporate Foundations and Giving Programs

Bob Evans Farms Corporate Contributions
Contact: Mary L. Cusick
3776 S. High St.
Columbus, OH 43207-0863
Tel: (614) 492 - 4920
Fax: (614) 492 - 4934
TF: (800) 272 - 7675

Annual Grant Total: none reported
The annual giving budget is determined by pre-tax profits.
Geographic Preference: Ohio
Primary Interests: Children; Community Affairs; Education; Families; Youth Services
Recent Recipients: Boy Scouts of America; Children's Defense Fund; Ohio State University; United Negro College Fund

Public Affairs and Related Activities Personnel

At Headquarters

CUSICK, Mary L.
Senior V. President, Investor Relations and Corporate Communications
Tel: (614) 492 - 4920
Fax: (614) 492 - 4934
TF: (800) 272 - 7675

ROBERTS-MYERS, Tammy M.
Director, Corporate Communications
Tel: (614) 492 - 4954
Fax: (614) 497 - 4330
TF: (800) 272 - 7675

Boehringer Ingelheim Corp.

A manufacturer and marketer of prescription medicines, consumer healthcare products, and animal health products.
us.boehringer-ingelheim.com

Chief Exec. Officer
CARROLL, J. Martin
Tel: (203) 798 - 9988
Fax: (203) 791 - 6234

Main Headquarters
Mailing: 900 Ridgebury Rd.
P.O. Box 368
Ridgefield, CT 06877
Tel: (203) 798 - 9988
Fax: (203) 791 - 6234

Corporate Foundations and Giving Programs

Boehringer Ingelheim Cares Foundation
Contact: Ralph Craft
900 Ridgebury Rd.
P.O. Box 368
Ridgefield, CT 06877
Tel: (203) 798 - 9988
Fax: (203) 791 - 6234

Annual Grant Total: none reported
For more information about the foundation, please contact the Secretariat at the address and contact numbers shown above.

Public Affairs and Related Activities Personnel

At Headquarters

CRAFT, Ralph
President, Foundation
Tel: (203) 798 - 9988
Fax: (203) 791 - 6234

CRISSEY, Lara
Media Contact
lcrissey@rdg.boehringer-ingelheim.com
Tel: (203) 798 - 4740
Fax: (203) 791 - 6234

FRY, Amy
Corporate Director, Communications and Public Relations
Tel: (203) 798 - 9988
Fax: (203) 791 - 6234

SLESINGER, Arthur E.
Corporate Director, Environmental Affairs/Health Safety
Tel: (203) 798 - 5075
Fax: (203) 791 - 6476

The Boeing Co.

PUBLIC AFFAIRS COUNCIL

A member of the Public Affairs Council. The Boeing Co. is a global aerospace company, with its heritage that mirrors the history of flight. It specializes in satellites, commercial jetliners, launch systems and services, human space flight and military aircraft.
www.boeing.com
Annual Revenues: $50.5 billion

Chairman of the Board
PLATT, Lewis E.
Tel: (312) 544 - 2000
Fax: (312) 544 - 2082

Interim President and Chief Exec. Officer
BELL, James A.
Tel: (312) 544 - 2000
Fax: (312) 544 - 2082

Main Headquarters
Mailing: World Headquarters
100 N. Riverside
Chicago, IL 60606-1596
Tel: (312) 544 - 2000
Fax: (312) 544 - 2082

Washington Office
Contact: Rudy F. de Leon
Mailing: 1200 Wilson Blvd.
Arlington, VA 22209-2305
Tel: (703) 465 - 3500

Political Action Committees

The Boeing Co. PAC (BPAC)
Contact: Kristine B. Miller
1200 Wilson Blvd.
Arlington, VA 22209-2305
Tel: (703) 465 - 3232
Fax: (703) 465 - 3362

Contributions to Candidates: $346,500 (01/05 - 09/05)
Democrats: $135,000; Republicans: $210,500; Other: $1,000.

Principal Recipients

SENATE DEMOCRATS		HOUSE DEMOCRATS	
Conrad, Kent (ND)	$4,500	Harman, Jane (CA)	$10,000
Clinton, Hillary Rodham (NY)	$4,000	Murtha, John P Mr. (PA)	$10,000
Kennedy, Ted (MA)	$4,000	Skelton, Ike (MO)	$10,000
		Matsui, Doris (CA)	$5,000
		Pelosi, Nancy (CA)	$5,000

SENATE REPUBLICANS		HOUSE REPUBLICANS	
Talent, James (MO)	$10,000	Tiahrt, Todd W. (KS)	$7,000
Burns, Conrad (MT)	$8,000	DeLay, Tom (TX)	$5,000
Santorum, Richard (PA)	$5,500		
Stevens, Ted (AK)	$5,500		

Corporate Foundations and Giving Programs

Boeing Community and Education Relations
Contact: Antoinette Bailey
World Headquarters
100 N. Riverside
Chicago, IL 60606-1596
Tel: (312) 544 - 2000
Fax: (312) 544 - 2304

Annual Grant Total: over $5,000,000
The company also sponsors educational and cultural gift matching programs.
Geographic Preference: Area(s) in which the company operates
Primary Interests: Arts and Culture; Education; Health and Human Services

Public Affairs and Related Activities Personnel

At Headquarters

BAILEY, Antoinette
V. President, Community and Education Relations
Tel: (312) 544 - 2000
Fax: (312) 544 - 2304

DERN, John
V. President, Media Relations
Tel: (312) 544 - 2002
Fax: (312) 544 - 2082

The Boeing Co.

** continued from previous page*

DOHNALEK, David
V. President, Investor Relations
investor.relations@boeing.com
Tel: (312) 544 - 2000
Fax: (312) 544 - 2099

HULLIN, Tod
Senior V. President, Communications
Tel: (312) 544 - 2002
Fax: (312) 544 - 2082

JOHNSON, James C.
V. President, Associate General Counsel and Corporate Secretary
Responsibilities include investor relations.
Tel: (312) 544 - 2000
Fax: (312) 544 - 2829

MCCRACKEN, Larry
V. President, Corporate Communications
Tel: (312) 544 - 2002
Fax: (312) 544 - 2955

At Washington Office

AUSTELL, Theodore "Ted"
V. President, International Policy
Tel: (703) 465 - 3876
Fax: (703) 465 - 3018

BACHELLER, Burt P.
Director, International Programs
Tel: (703) 465 - 3500

BAUERLEIN, Robert D.
V. President, International Operations
Tel: (703) 465 - 3505
Fax: (703) 465 - 3041

COON, James W.
Director, Legislative Affairs
Registered Federal Lobbyist.
Tel: (703) 465 - 3264
Fax: (703) 465 - 3004

CRAGIN, Maureen P.
V. President, Communications
Tel: (703) 465 - 3252
Fax: (703) 465 - 3032

DE LEON, Rudy F.
Senior V. President, Washington DC Operations
Registered Federal Lobbyist.
Tel: (703) 465 - 3500

DOLE, Gregory S.
Director, Commercial Trade Policy
Tel: (703) 465 - 3619
Fax: (703) 465 - 3009

DUNN, Loretta L.
V. President, Satellite Systems, Boeing Satellite Systems, Inc.
Registered Federal Lobbyist.
Tel: (703) 465 - 3282
Fax: (703) 465 - 3341

ELLIS, Andrew K.
V. President, Integrated Defense Systems
Tel: (703) 465 - 3405
Fax: (703) 465 - 3985

FALLON, Willard G.
Registered Federal Lobbyist.
Tel: (703) 465 - 3500

GLEASON, Donna
Director, Corporate Legislation
Registered Federal Lobbyist.
Tel: (703) 465 - 3263
Fax: (703) 465 - 3004

GOFF, Donald G.
Director, Legislative Affairs, Corporate Programs
Registered Federal Lobbyist.
Tel: (703) 465 - 3218
Fax: (703) 465 - 3004

HANNA, Christine E.
Manager, Legislative Affairs, International Programs
Registered Federal Lobbyist.
Tel: (703) 465 - 3213
Fax: (703) 465 - 3003

HANNA, Elizabeth
Tel: (703) 465 - 3500

HAZERA, Ramona B.
Director, Export-Import Management and Compliance
Tel: (703) 465 - 3312

HEILIG, Paul T.
Manager, Legislative Affairs, Homeland Security, Phantom Works
Registered Federal Lobbyist.
Tel: (703) 465 - 3666
Fax: (703) 465 - 3004

HOFGARD, Jefferson F.
Director, International Operations Policy
Tel: (703) 465 - 3219
Fax: (703) 465 - 3041

HURT, Michael
Tel: (703) 465 - 3500

IARROBINO, Paul
Manager, Legislative Affairs, Missile Defense
Registered Federal Lobbyist.
Tel: (703) 465 - 3304

JANS, Megan C.
Manager, Legislative Affairs, Army Programs
Registered Federal Lobbyist.
Tel: (703) 465 - 3687
Fax: (703) 465 - 3004

KENNETT, Doug
Director, Communications
Tel: (703) 465 - 3532
Fax: (703) 465 - 3033

MATTON, Mike
V. President, Legislative Affairs
Registered Federal Lobbyist.
Tel: (703) 465 - 3625
Fax: (703) 465 - 3002

MCSWEENY, Thomas
Registered Federal Lobbyist.
Tel: (703) 465 - 3500

MILLER, Kristine B.
PAC Manager
Registered Federal Lobbyist.
Tel: (703) 465 - 3232
Fax: (703) 465 - 3362

MOLONEY, John M.
Director, Legislative Affairs
Tel: (703) 465 - 3500

PICKERING, Thomas R.
Senior V. President, International Relations
Tel: (703) 465 - 3471

REESE, David K.
Tel: (703) 465 - 3500

ROBERTS, Roselee N.
Director, Legislative Affairs -- Space and Legislation
Registered Federal Lobbyist.
Tel: (703) 465 - 3681

ROMAN, George C.
V. President and Chief of Staff, Washington Operations
Tel: (703) 465 - 3434
Fax: (703) 465 - 3134

RUPINSKI, Walter F.
V. President, Export Management and Compliance
Tel: (703) 465 - 3500

RUSSELL, Cheryl
Director, EXIM, OMB and Federal Affairs
Tel: (703) 465 - 3610

RUTER, Philip E.
Deputy Legislative Affairs Director
Registered Federal Lobbyist.
Tel: (703) 465 - 3665

SCHWAB, Richard F.
Legislative Affairs, Navy and USMC Programs
Registered Federal Lobbyist.
Tel: (703) 465 - 3686

SCHWARTZ, Elizabeth Nash
Director, Legislative Affairs
Registered Federal Lobbyist.
Tel: (703) 465 - 3668

TAPPAN, Joan S.
Director, Constituent Relations
Tel: (703) 465 - 3258
Fax: (703) 465 - 3045

TRAYNHAM, David
Director, Strategy and Policy, Commercial Airplane Programs
Tel: (703) 465 - 3652

VILHAUER, Robert J.
Director, Air Traffic Management
Tel: (703) 465 - 3671

WAGNER, Brian
Legislative Affairs -- Space Issues
Registered Federal Lobbyist.
Tel: (703) 465 - 3241
Fax: (703) 465 - 3003

WEAVER, Frank C.
Director, Telecommunications Policy
Tel: (703) 465 - 3448

WILSON, John K.
Manager, Legislative Affairs, Air Force Programs
Registered Federal Lobbyist.
Tel: (703) 465 - 3608

Boise Cascade Corp.

A major distributor of office products and building materials and an integrated manufacturer of paper and wood products.

www.bc.com
Annual Revenues: $7.422 billion

Chairman and Chief Exec. Officer
STEPHENS, W. Thomas
Tel: (208) 384 - 6161
Fax: (208) 384 - 4841

Main Headquarters
Mailing: P.O. Box 50
Boise, ID 83728-0001
Street: 1111 W. Jefferson St.
Boise, ID 83728
Tel: (208) 384 - 6161
Fax: (208) 384 - 4841

Public Affairs and Related Activities Personnel

At Headquarters

ALDEN, Linda
Communications Manager - Boise Paper
Tel: (208) 384 - 7037
Fax: (208) 384 - 7224

MCNUTT, Rob
Investor Relations Contact
Tel: (208) 384 - 7023
Fax: (208) 384 - 4841

MOSER, Mike
Media Contact
Tel: (208) 384 - 6016
Fax: (208) 384 - 4841

NUXOLL, Erin
V. President, Human Resources
Tel: (208) 384 - 394
Fax: (208) 384 - 4841

At Other Offices

ANDERSON, Bob
Public Affairs Manager - Boise Paper
523 Third Ave.
International Falls, MN 56649-2387
Tel: (218) 285 - 5312
Fax: (218) 285 - 5528

VOEGELE, Craig C.
Public Policy Manager - Washington and California
1501 S. Capitol Way, Suite 307
Olympia, WA 98501-2296
Tel: (360) 352 - 5270
Fax: (360) 357 - 3124

BOK Financial Corp.

A multi-bank holding company.

www.bokf.com
Annual Revenues: $918 million

Chairman of the Board
KAISER, George B.
Tel: (918) 588 - 6000
Fax: (918) 588 - 6300

President and Chief Exec. Officer
LYBARGER, Stanley A.
Tel: (918) 588 - 6000
Fax: (918) 588 - 6300

Main Headquarters
Mailing: P.O. Box 2300
Tulsa, OK 74192
Street: Bank of Oklahoma Tower
One Williams Center
Tulsa, OK 74192
Tel: (918) 588 - 6000
Fax: (918) 588 - 6300

BOK Financial Corp.

** continued from previous page*

Political Action Committees

BOK Financial Corp. Political Action Committee (BOKF PAC)
Contact: Joyce Thedford
201 Robert S. Kerr Ave.
Mezzanine
Oklahoma City, OK 73102

Contributions to Candidates: none reported (01/05 - 09/05)

Corporate Foundations and Giving Programs

Bank of Oklahoma Corporate Contributions Program/Bank of Oklahoma Foundation
Contact: Leslie Paris
P.O. Box 2300 — Tel: (918) 588 - 6000
Tulsa, OK 74192 — Fax: (918) 588 - 6853

Annual Grant Total: none reported
Excludes religious, political, and fraternal organizations or groups.
Geographic Preference: Arkansas; Oklahoma; New Mexico; Texas

Public Affairs and Related Activities Personnel

At Headquarters

NEIL, Steven E. — Tel: (918) 588 - 6752
Investor Relations Contact — Fax: (918) 588 - 6300

PARIS, Leslie — Tel: (918) 588 - 6000
V. President, Community Relations — Fax: (918) 588 - 6853

At Other Offices

THEDFORD, Joyce
PAC Treasurer
201 Robert S. Kerr Ave.
Mezzanine
Oklahoma City, OK 73102

Bombardier

An airplane and rail transportation systems manufacturer headquartered in Quebec, Canada.
www.bombardieraerospace.com

Main Headquarters
Mailing: One Learjet Way — Tel: (316) 946 - 2000
Wichita, KS 67209 — Fax: (316) 946 - 2220

Washington Office
Contact: Oakley Brooks
Mailing: 1808 I St. NW, Suite 400 — Tel: (202) 414 - 8980
Washington, DC 20006 — Fax: (202) 955 - 8389

Political Action Committees

Bombardier Transportation Holdings USA Employee Political Fund
Contact: Paul Overby
1501 Lebanon Church Rd
Pittsburgh, PA 15236

Contributions to Candidates: $1,500 (01/05 - 09/05)
Democrats: $1,000; Republicans: $500.

Learjet Inc. PAC
Contact: Ane G. Beaurivage
One Learjet Way — Tel: (316) 946 - 2000
Wichita, KS 67209 — Fax: (316) 946 - 2220

Contributions to Candidates: none reported (01/05 - 09/05)

Public Affairs and Related Activities Personnel

At Headquarters

BEAURIVAGE, Ane G. — Tel: (316) 946 - 2000
Treasurer, Learjet Inc. PAC — Fax: (316) 946 - 2220

FOX, William J. — Tel: (316) 946 - 2000
Senior V. President, Public Affairs

At Washington Office

BROOKS, Oakley — Tel: (202) 414 - 8989
V. President, Government Affairs — Fax: (202) 789 - 0076

At Other Offices

OVERBY, Paul
Treasurer, Bombardier Transportation Holdings USA Employee Political Fund
1501 Lebanon Church Rd
Pittsburgh, PA 15236

The Bon Ton Stores, Inc.

A regional department store chain.
www.bonton.com
Annual Revenues: $1.310 billion

Chairman of the Board
GRUMBACHER, Tim — Tel: (717) 757 - 7660; Fax: (717) 751 - 3196

President and Chief Exec. Officer
BERGREN, Byron L. — Tel: (717) 757 - 7660; Fax: (717) 751 - 3196

Main Headquarters
Mailing: P.O. Box 2821 — Tel: (717) 757 - 7660
York, PA 17405-2821 — Fax: (717) 751 - 3196
Street: 2801 E. Market St.
York, PA 17402-2406

Corporate Foundations and Giving Programs

The Bon Ton Stores Foundation
Contact: Ryan J. Sattler
P.O. Box 2821 — Tel: (717) 757 - 7660
York, PA 17405-2821 — Fax: (717) 751 - 3196

Annual Grant Total: none reported

Public Affairs and Related Activities Personnel

At Headquarters

KERR, Mary — Tel: (717) 751 - 3071
V. President, Corporate Communications — Fax: (717) 751 - 3037

SATTLER, Ryan J. — Tel: (717) 757 - 7660
Senior V. President, Human Resources — Fax: (717) 751 - 3196
Responsibilities include corporate philanthropy.

Booz Allen Hamilton Inc.

A global management and technology consulting firm.
www.boozallen.com
Annual Revenues: $3.3 billion

Chairman and Chief Exec. Officer
SHRADER, Ralph W. — Tel: (703) 902 - 5000; Fax: (703) 902 - 3333

Main Headquarters
Mailing: 8283 Greensboro Dr. — Tel: (703) 902 - 5000
McLean, VA 22102-3802 — Fax: (703) 902 - 3333

Public Affairs and Related Activities Personnel

At Headquarters

LERCH, Marie — Tel: (703) 902 - 5559
Senior Director, Marketing and Communications — Fax: (703) 902 - 3323
lerch_marie@bah.com

ROZANSKI, Horacio — Tel: (703) 902 - 5000
V. President and Chief Human Resources Officer — Fax: (703) 902 - 3333

VON BOSTEL, Sylvia — Tel: (703) 902 - 5518
Manager, Government Relations — Fax: (703) 902 - 3333

Borden Chemical, Inc.

See listing on page 243 under Hexion Specialty Chemicals, Inc.

Borders Group, Inc.

A retailer of books, music, video, and other products.
www.bordersgroupinc.com
Annual Revenues: $3.9 billion

Chairman, President and Chief Exec. Officer
JOSEFOWICZ, Gregory P. — Tel: (734) 477 - 1100; Fax: (734) 477 - 1901
gjosefow@bordersgroupinc.com

Main Headquarters
Mailing: 100 Phoenix Dr. — Tel: (734) 477 - 1100
Ann Arbor, MI 48108 — Fax: (734) 477 - 1517

Corporate Foundations and Giving Programs

Borders Group Foundation
Contact: Thom Bales
100 Phoenix Dr. — Tel: (734) 477 - 1100
Ann Arbor, MI 48108 — Fax: (734) 477 - 1517

Annual Grant Total: none reported
Recipients are all employee-based.
Geographic Preference: Area(s) in which employees live and work
Primary Interests: Employment

Public Affairs and Related Activities Personnel

At Headquarters

BALES, Thom — Tel: (734) 477 - 1100
Administrator, Borders Group Foundation — Fax: (734) 477 - 1517

RACKLYEFT, Jamie — Tel: (734) 477 - 1622
Manager, Corporate Communications — Fax: (734) 477 - 4730
jracklye@bordersgroupinc.com

ROMAN, Anne — Tel: (734) 477 - 1392
Director, Public Relations — Fax: (734) 477 - 1517
aroman@bordersgroupinc.com

SMITH, Dan — Tel: (734) 477 - 1798
Senior V. President, Human Resources — Fax: (734) 477 - 1899
dsmith@bordersgroupinc.com

Borg-Warner Automotive, Inc.

See listing on page 87 under BorgWarner Inc.

BorgWarner Inc.

A manufacturer of auto components and systems.
www.bwauto.com
Annual Revenues: $3.5 billion

Chairman and Chief Exec. Officer Tel: (248) 754 - 9200
MANGANELLO, Timothy M.

Main Headquarters
Mailing: 3850 Hamlin Rd. Tel: (248) 754 - 9200
Auburn Hills, MI 48326

Corporate Foundations and Giving Programs

Borg Warner Inc. Corporate Contributions Program
Contact: Mary E. Brevard
3850 Hamlin Rd. Tel: (248) 754 - 9200
Auburn Hills, MI 48326

Annual Grant Total: none reported

Public Affairs and Related Activities Personnel

At Headquarters

BREVARD, Mary E. Tel: (248) 754 - 9200
V. President, Investor Relations and Communications
Responsibilities include corporate contributions and government affairs.

D'AVERSA, Angela Tel: (248) 754 - 9200
Acting V. President, Human Resources

FEIKENS, Beth Tel: (248) 754 - 0883
Manager, Corporate Communications

Bose Corp.

A stereo speaker manufacturer.
www.bose.com
Annual Revenues: $1.7 billion

Chairman and Chief Exec. Officer Tel: (508) 879 - 7330
BOSE, Amar G. Fax: (508) 766 - 7543
amar_bose@bose.com

Main Headquarters
Mailing: The Mountain Tel: (508) 879 - 7330
Framingham, MA 01701-9168 Fax: (508) 766 - 7543

Public Affairs and Related Activities Personnel

At Headquarters

BERTHIAUME, Joanne Tel: (508) 766 - 7882
Media Contact Fax: (508) 766 - 7543

CINOTTI, Carolyn Tel: (508) 879 - 7330
Director, Public Relations Fax: (508) 766 - 7543

FREEDMAN, Jodi S. Tel: (508) 766 - 7051
Senior Communications Specialist Fax: (508) 620 - 5523
jodi_freedman@bose.com

Boston Gas

See listing on page 279 under KeySpan Corp.

Boston Globe Newspaper

See listing on page 221 under Globe Newspaper Co.

Boston Scientific Corp.

PUBLIC AFFAIRS COUNCIL
A member of the Public Affairs Council. A medical device company.
www.bsci.com
Annual Revenues: $3.5 billion

Chairman of the Board Tel: (508) 650 - 8000
ABELE, John E. Fax: (508) 647 - 2200

President and Chief Exec. Officer Tel: (508) 650 - 8000
TOBIN, James R. Fax: (508) 647 - 2200

Main Headquarters
Mailing: One Boston Scientific Pl. Tel: (508) 650 - 8000
Natick, MA 01760-1537 Fax: (508) 647 - 2200

Washington Office
Contact: Sarah E. Wells
Mailing: 1331 Pennsylvania Ave. NW Tel: (202) 637 - 8020
Suite 550 South Fax: (202) 637 - 8028
Washington, DC 20004

Political Action Committees

Boston Scientific Corp. Political Action Committee (BSC PAC)
Contact: Lawrence C. Best
One Boston Scientific Pl. Tel: (508) 650 - 8000
Natick, MA 01760-1537 Fax: (508) 647 - 2200

Contributions to Candidates: $35,538 (01/05 - 09/05)
Democrats: $12,000; Republicans: $22,538; Other: $1,000.

Principal Recipients

SENATE DEMOCRATS		**HOUSE DEMOCRATS**	
Kennedy, Ted (MA)	$5,000	Cardin, Ben (MD)	$2,000
SENATE REPUBLICANS		**HOUSE REPUBLICANS**	
Burr, Richard (NC)	$2,000	DeLay, Tom (TX)	$2,500
Ensign, John Eric (NV)	$2,000	Lewis, Ron (KY)	$2,000
Hatch, Orrin (UT)	$2,000	Sweeney, John E. (NY)	$2,000
Santorum, Richard (PA)	$1,000	Ferguson, Mike (NJ)	$1,038

Public Affairs and Related Activities Personnel

At Headquarters

BEST, Lawrence C. Tel: (508) 650 - 8000
Senior V. President and Chief Financial Officer; PAC Treasurer Fax: (508) 647 - 2200
bestl@bsci.com

DONOVAN, Paul Tel: (508) 650 - 8541
Senior V. President, Corporate Communications Fax: (508) 647 - 2200

KOFOL, Milan Tel: (508) 650 - 8595
V. President, Investor Relations and Treasurer Fax: (508) 647 - 2200
kofolm@bsci.com

QUINN, Lucia Tel: (508) 650 - 8000
Senior V. President, Human Resources Fax: (508) 647 - 2200

RICHNER, Ms. Randel, BSN, MPH Tel: (508) 650 - 7410
V. President, Federal Affairs, Reimbursement and Outcomes Planning Fax: (508) 647 - 5348

At Washington Office

BARRY, Paul E. Tel: (202) 637 - 8020
Director, International Health Policy Fax: (202) 637 - 8028
Registered Federal Lobbyist.

BIEBUYCK, Beatrice Tel: (202) 637 - 8020
Fax: (202) 637 - 8028
Registered Federal Lobbyist.

BLANK, Tony Tel: (202) 637 - 8020
Fax: (202) 637 - 8028
Registered Federal Lobbyist.

LAPIERRE, Steven N. Tel: (202) 637 - 8020
Director, Legislative Affairs Fax: (202) 637 - 8028
Registered Federal Lobbyist.

NEUMANN, Larry Tel: (202) 637 - 8020
Fax: (202) 637 - 8028
Registered Federal Lobbyist.

WELLS, Sarah E. Tel: (202) 637 - 8020
Director, Health Policy and Payment Fax: (202) 637 - 8028
Registered Federal Lobbyist.

Bourns, Inc.

A manufacturer of electronic components and scientific instruments.
www.bourns.com

Chairman and Chief Exec. Officer Tel: (909) 781 - 5690
BOURNS, Gordon L. Fax: (909) 781 - 5273

Main Headquarters
Mailing: 1200 Columbia Ave. Tel: (909) 781 - 5690
Riverside, CA 92507-2114 Fax: (909) 781 - 5006

Corporate Foundations and Giving Programs

Bourns Foundation
Contact: Karen J. Smarr
1200 Columbia Ave. Tel: (909) 781 - 5690
Riverside, CA 92507-2114 Fax: (909) 781 - 5006

Assets: $321,804,000 (2003)
Annual Grant Total: $100,000 - $200,000
Geographic Preference: California; Utah
Primary Interests: Education; Engineering; Math and Science
Recent Recipients: University of California - Riverside

Public Affairs and Related Activities Personnel

At Headquarters

BRIDGES, Mike Tel: (909) 781 - 5397
Manager, Marketing Services Fax: (909) 781 - 5122
mike_bridges@bourns.com
Responsibilities include public relations.

SMARR, Karen J. Tel: (909) 781 - 5690
Secretary-Treasurer, Foundation Fax: (909) 781 - 5006

Bowater Incorporated

A manufacturer of newsprint, coated and uncoated mechanical papers, bleached kraft pulp and lumber products.

www.bowater.com
Annual Revenues: $3.190 billion

Chairman, President and Chief Exec. Officer
NEMIROW, Arnold M.
Tel: (864) 271 - 7733
Fax: (864) 282 - 9482

Main Headquarters
Mailing: P.O. Box 1028
Greenville, SC 29602
Tel: (864) 271 - 7733
Fax: (864) 282 - 9482
Street: 55 E. Camperdown Way
Greenville, SC 29601

Corporate Foundations and Giving Programs

Bowater Contributions Program
Contact: Gordon R. Manuel
P.O. Box 1028
Greenville, SC 29602
Tel: (864) 282 - 9448
Fax: (864) 282 - 9594

Annual Grant Total: none reported
Geographic Preference: Area(s) in which the company operates

Public Affairs and Related Activities Personnel

At Headquarters

MANUEL, Gordon R.
Director, Government Affairs
Tel: (864) 282 - 9448
Fax: (864) 282 - 9594
Responsibilities include corporate contributions and communications.

WRIGHT, James T.
Senior V. President, Human Resources
Tel: (864) 271 - 7733
Fax: (864) 282 - 9482

Boyd Gaming Corp.

A casino entertainment company.

www.boydgaming.com
Annual Revenues: $1.3 billion

Chairman and Chief Exec. Officer
BOYD, William S.
Tel: (702) 792 - 7200
Fax: (702) 792 - 7266
TF: (800) 695 - 2455

Main Headquarters
Mailing: 2950 Industrial Rd.
Las Vegas, NV 89109-1100
Tel: (702) 792 - 7200
Fax: (702) 792 - 7266
TF: (800) 695 - 2455

Political Action Committees

Boyd PAC
Contact: Richard Alan Darnold
2950 Industrial Rd.
Las Vegas, NV 89109-1100
Tel: (702) 792 - 7200
Fax: (702) 792 - 7266
TF: (800) 695 - 2455

Contributions to Candidates: $9,000 (01/05 - 09/05)
Democrats: $3,000; Republicans: $6,000.

Principal Recipients

SENATE DEMOCRATS	HOUSE DEMOCRATS	
	Berkley, Shelley (NV)	$3,000
SENATE REPUBLICANS	**HOUSE REPUBLICANS**	
	Porter, Jon (NV)	$5,000
	Sessions, Pete (TX)	$1,000

Corporate Foundations and Giving Programs

Boyd Foundation
Contact: William S. Boyd
2950 Industrial Rd.
Las Vegas, NV 89109-1100
Tel: (702) 792 - 7200
Fax: (702) 792 - 7266
TF: (800) 695 - 2455

Annual Grant Total: under $100,000
Geographic Preference: Nevada
Primary Interests: Higher Education; Human Welfare; Medicine and Health Care; Religion

Public Affairs and Related Activities Personnel

At Headquarters

DARNOLD, Richard Alan
PAC Treasurer
Tel: (702) 792 - 7200
Fax: (702) 792 - 7266
TF: (800) 695 - 2455

PALMER, Mr. Cass
V. President, Human Resources
Tel: (702) 792 - 7200
Fax: (702) 792 - 7266
TF: (800) 695 - 2455

POLOVINA, Gina B.
V. President, Government and Community Affairs
Tel: (702) 792 - 7200
Fax: (702) 792 - 7266
TF: (800) 695 - 2455

STILLWELL, Robert D.
V. President, Corporate Communications
Tel: (702) 792 - 7200
Fax: (702) 792 - 7266
TF: (800) 695 - 2455

BP

A member of the Public Affairs Council. A wholly-owned subsidiary of BP p.l.c. Its core businesses are petroleum exploration and production, refining and marketing, chemicals, and solar. Completed its acquisition of ARCO (Atlantic Richfield Co.) in 2000. The company changed its name from BP Amoco Corp. to BP in the summer of 2000.

www.bp.com

Chairman of the Board
SUTHERLAND, P. D.
Tel: (212) 421 - 5010
Fax: (212) 421 - 5084

Group Chief Executive
BROWNE, John
Tel: (312) 856 - 6111
Fax: (312) 856 - 2460

Main Headquarters
Mailing: 535 Madison Ave.
New York, NY 10022
Tel: (212) 421 - 5010
Fax: (212) 421 - 5084

Washington Office
Contact: Michael P. Brien
Mailing: 1776 I St. NW
Suite 1000
Washington, DC 20006-3707
Tel: (202) 785 - 4888
Fax: (202) 457 - 6597

Corporate Foundations and Giving Programs

BP Foundation, Inc.
Contact: Brian Dinges
4101 Winfield Rd.
Warrenville, IL 60555
Tel: (630) 821 - 3174

Annual Grant Total: over $5,000,000
Geographic Preference: International; National
Primary Interests: Disaster Relief
Recent Recipients: United Way

Public Affairs and Related Activities Personnel

At Headquarters

MCLARE, Rachael
Director, Investor Relations
Tel: (212) 421 - 5010
Fax: (212) 421 - 5084

At Washington Office

BRIEN, Michael P.
Chief of Staff, U.S. Government and Public Affairs
brienmp@bp.com
Registered Federal Lobbyist.
Tel: (202) 457 - 6573
Fax: (202) 457 - 6597

CANNON, Ben
Director, Government Affairs
Tel: (202) 785 - 4888
Ext: 6595
Fax: (202) 457 - 6597

HEROLD, Richard
Director, International Affairs
heroldra@bp.com
Registered Federal Lobbyist.
Tel: (202) 785 - 4888
Fax: (202) 457 - 6597

HOWELL, Sarah
Director, Environmental and Corporate Communications
Tel: (202) 457 - 6603
Fax: (202) 457 - 6597

HUDSON, Margaret R. "Peggy"
V. President, Federal and International Affairs
hudspr@bp.com
Registered Federal Lobbyist.
Tel: (202) 785 - 6581
Fax: (202) 457 - 6597

MILLER, Brian W.
Director, U.S. Government and International Affairs
millerbw@bp.com
Registered Federal Lobbyist.
Tel: (202) 785 - 4888
Fax: (202) 457 - 6597

REICHERTS, Elizabeth "Liz"
Director,US Government and International Affairs
reicheea@bp.com
Registered Federal Lobbyist.
Tel: (202) 785 - 4888
Fax: (202) 457 - 6597

ROGERS, Susan
Director, Tax Policy
rogerssl@bp.com
Registered Federal Lobbyist.
Tel: (202) 785 - 4888
Fax: (202) 457 - 6597

SANDERS, Greg
Director, International Affairs
Tel: (202) 785 - 4888
Fax: (202) 457 - 6597

At Other Offices

BAILEY, Cindy
Associate Director, Local Government Affairs
(BP Exploration - Alaska, Inc.)
P.O. Box 196612
Anchorage, AK 99519-6612
Tel: (907) 564 - 5537
Fax: (907) 564 - 4124

DAGIAN, Glenn A.
Senior Government Affairs Representative
1005 Congress Ave., Suite 830
Austin, TX 78701
Tel: (512) 477 - 3901

DINGES, Brian
Contact, BP Foundation, Inc
4101 Winfield Rd.
Warrenville, IL 60555
Tel: (630) 821 - 3174

BP

* continued from previous page

GRETHER, C. Heidi
Director, Government Affairs
435 Mill St.
Williamston, MI 48895
Tel: (517) 371 - 4560
Fax: (517) 485 - 8856

QUESNEL, Paul A.
Director, Government Affairs
(BP Exploration - Alaska, Inc.)
P.O. Box 196612
Anchorage, AK 99519-6612
Tel: (907) 564 - 5585

RANDALL, Kathleen A.
Government Affairs Representative
P.O. Box 369
Summerville, SC 39484
Tel: (843) 871 - 1543

BP Exploration - Alaska, Inc.

See listing on page 88 under BP.

Brady Corp.

Manufactures identification products and specialty tapes.
www.bradycorp.com
Annual Revenues: $671 million

President and Chief Exec. Officer
JAEHNERT, Frank M.
Tel: (414) 358 - 6600
Fax: (800) 292 - 2289

Main Headquarters
Mailing: P.O. Box 571
Milwaukee, WI 53201-0571
Tel: (414) 358 - 6600
Fax: (800) 292 - 2289

Corporate Foundations and Giving Programs

W. H. Brady Foundation
Contact: Dr. Elizabeth Pungello
P.O. Box 571
Milwaukee, WI 53201-0571
Tel: (414) 358 - 6600
Fax: (800) 292 - 2289

Annual Grant Total: none reported
Geographic Preference: Area(s) in which employees live and work
Primary Interests: Education

Public Affairs and Related Activities Personnel

At Headquarters

BOLENS, Barbara G.
V. President, Treasurer and Director, Investor Relations
Tel: (414) 358 - 6600
Fax: (800) 292 - 2289

HERBSTREIT, Carol
Manager, Corporate Communications
Tel: (414) 438 - 6882
Fax: (414) 358 - 6798

OLIVER, Michael O.
Senior V. President, Human Resources
Tel: (414) 358 - 6600
Fax: (800) 292 - 2289

PUNGELLO, Dr. Elizabeth
President, Foundation
Tel: (414) 358 - 6600
Fax: (800) 292 - 2289

Bridgestone Americas Holding, Inc.

A subsidiary of Bridgestone Corp., a tire and rubber company.
www.bridgestone-firestone.com
Annual Revenues: $16.27 billion

Chairman and Chief Exec. Officer
EMKES, Mark A.
Tel: (615) 937 - 0088
Fax: (615) 937 - 3612

Main Headquarters
Mailing: 535 Marriott Dr.
Nashville, TN 37214-8900
Tel: (615) 937 - 0088
Fax: (615) 937 - 3621

Washington Office
Mailing: 607 14th St. NW
Suite 500
Washington, DC 20005
Tel: (202) 354 - 8220
Fax: (202) 354 - 8201

Political Action Committees

Bridgestone/Firestone PAC
535 Marriott Dr.
Nashville, TN 37214-8900
Tel: (615) 937 - 0088
Fax: (615) 937 - 3621

Contributions to Candidates: $36,000 (01/05 - 09/05)
Democrats: $10,000; Republicans: $26,000.

Principal Recipients

SENATE REPUBLICANS		HOUSE REPUBLICANS	
Burr, Richard (NC)	$5,000	Burton, Danny (IN)	$2,000
Coburn, Thomas (OK)	$2,000	Stearns, Clifford (FL)	$2,000
Stevens, Ted (AK)	$2,000		

Corporate Foundations and Giving Programs

Bridgestone/Firestone Trust Fund
Contact: Bernice Csaszar
535 Marriott Dr.
Nashville, TN 37214-8900
Tel: (615) 937 - 0088
Fax: (615) 937 - 1414

Annual Grant Total: $2,000,000 - $5,000,000
Geographic Preference: Area(s) in which the company operates
Primary Interests: Arts and Culture; Community Affairs; Education; Environment/Conservation; Medicine and Health Care; Social Services

Public Affairs and Related Activities Personnel

At Headquarters

CSASZAR, Bernice
Administrator, Bridgetone/Firestone Trust Fund
Tel: (615) 937 - 0088
Fax: (615) 937 - 1414

KARBOWIAK, Christine
V. President, Public Affairs
Tel: (615) 937 - 0088
Fax: (615) 937 - 1414

SMITH, Perry L.
Community and Public Relations Coordinator
Tel: (615) 937 - 0088
Fax: (615) 937 - 3612

At Washington Office

CARLIN, J. David
Tel: (202) 354 - 8220
Fax: (202) 354 - 8201

Briggs and Stratton Corp.

A manufacturer of gasoline engines and automotive locking devices.
www.briggsandstratton.com
Annual Revenues: $1.312 billion

Chairman, President and Chief Exec. Officer
SHIELY, John S.
Tel: (414) 259 - 5333
Fax: (414) 479 - 1245

Main Headquarters
Mailing: P.O. Box 702
Milwaukee, WI 53201-0702
Tel: (414) 259 - 5333
Fax: (414) 479 - 1245
Street: 12301 W. Wirth St.
Wauwatosa, WI 53222

Corporate Foundations and Giving Programs

Briggs and Stratton Corp. Foundation
Contact: Robert Heath
P.O. Box 702
Milwaukee, WI 53201-0702
Tel: (414) 259 - 5333
Fax: (414) 479 - 1245

Annual Grant Total: $1,000,000 - $2,000,000
Geographic Preference: Area in which the company is headquartered
Primary Interests: Arts and Culture; Community Development; Higher Education; United Way Campaigns
Recent Recipients: Big Brothers/Big Sisters; United Performing Arts Fund; United Way

Public Affairs and Related Activities Personnel

At Headquarters

BRENN, James E.
Senior V. President and Chief Financial Officer
Responsibilities include investor relations.
Tel: (414) 259 - 5333
Fax: (414) 479 - 1245

HEATH, Robert
Secretary and Treasurer, Briggs and Stratton Corp. Foundation
Tel: (414) 259 - 5333
Fax: (414) 479 - 1245

MAHLOCH, Jeffrey G.
V. President, Human Resources
Tel: (414) 259 - 5333
Fax: (414) 479 - 1245

THOMPSON, George R., III
V. President, Community Relations and Corporate Communications
Tel: (414) 259 - 5333
Fax: (414) 479 - 1245

The Brink's Co.

Formerly known as The Pittston Co. A diversified firm with interests in business services in the form of worldwide security transportation services through Brink's, Inc.; home security services through Brink's Home Security, Inc.; global air freight and logistics management services through BAX Global, Inc.
www.brinkscompany.com

Chairman, President and Chief Exec. Officer
DAN, Michael T.
Tel: (804) 289 - 9600
Fax: (804) 289 - 9770

Main Headquarters
Mailing: P.O. Box 18100
Richmond, VA 23226-8100
Tel: (804) 289 - 9600
Fax: (804) 289 - 9758
Street: 1801 Bayberry Ct.
Richmond, VA 23226

Political Action Committees

The Brink's Co. Political Action Committee
Contact: James B. Hartough
P.O. Box 18100
Richmond, VA 23226-8100
Tel: (804) 289 - 9645
Fax: (804) 289 - 9753

Contributions to Candidates: $6,000 (01/05 - 09/05)
Republicans: $6,000.

Principal Recipients

SENATE REPUBLICANS		HOUSE REPUBLICANS	
Santorum, Richard (PA)	$2,500	Bonilla, Henry (TX)	$1,000
Dewine, Richard (OH)	$1,000	Cantor, Eric (VA)	$1,000
		Pombo, Richard (CA)	$500

Corporate Foundations and Giving Programs

The Brink's Co. Corporate Contributions
Contact: Frank T. Lennon

The Brink's Co.

** continued from previous page*

P.O. Box 18100 — Tel: (804) 289 - 9660
Richmond, VA 23226-8100 — Fax: (804) 289 - 9753

Annual Grant Total: none reported
Geographic Preference: Area(s) in which the company operates

Public Affairs and Related Activities Personnel

At Headquarters

DUDLEY, Scott W. — Tel: (804) 289 - 9708
Director, Investor Relations — Fax: (804) 289 - 9770
sdudley@brinkscompany.com
Responsibilities include media relations.

HARTOUGH, James B. — Tel: (804) 289 - 9645
V. President, Corporate Finance and Treasurer; Treasurer, Brink's Co. Political Action Committee — Fax: (804) 289 - 9753

LENNON, Frank T. — Tel: (804) 289 - 9660
V. President and Chief Administrative Officer — Fax: (804) 289 - 9753
Responsibilities include corporate philanthropy.

VEROSTIC, Joseph R. — Tel: (804) 289 - 9600
Director, Human Resources — Fax: (804) 289 - 9770
Responsibilities include corporate giving.

Brinker Internat'l, Inc.

Operating company for co-owned, franchised and joint-venture theme restaurants including Chili's Grill and Bar, Romano's Macaroni Grill, On The Border Mexican Grill & Cantina Cafe, Maggiano's Little Italy, Corner Bakery Cafe, and Big Bowl.

www.brinker.com
Annual Revenues: $3.2 billion

Chairman and Chief Exec. Officer — Tel: (972) 980 - 9917
BROOKS, Douglas

Main Headquarters
Mailing: 6820 LBJ Fwy. — Tel: (972) 980 - 9917
Dallas, TX 75240

Political Action Committees

Brinker Internat'l Inc. Political Action Committee
Contact: Joe Taylor
6820 LBJ Fwy. — Tel: (972) 980 - 9917
Dallas, TX 75240 — Fax: (972) 770 - 9400

Contributions to Candidates: $49,600 (01/05 - 09/05)
Democrats: $12,000; Republicans: $37,600.

Principal Recipients

SENATE DEMOCRATS		HOUSE DEMOCRATS	
		Boyd, F Allen Jr (FL)	$2,500
		Hoyer, Steny (MD)	$2,500
		Napolitano, Grace (CA)	$2,000
SENATE REPUBLICANS		**HOUSE REPUBLICANS**	
Hatch, Orrin (UT)	$5,000	Sessions, Pete (TX)	$5,000
Butler, Keith (MI)	$3,000	Granger, Kay N (TX)	$4,000
Santorum, Richard (PA)	$2,500	Johnson, Samuel (TX)	$2,100
Smith, Gordon (OR)	$2,000	Barton, Joe L (TX)	$2,000
		Keller, Richard (FL)	$2,000
		Marchant, Kenny (TX)	$2,000

Corporate Foundations and Giving Programs

Brinker Internat'l Corporate Giving Program
Contact: Melissa Ward
6820 LBJ Fwy. — Tel: (972) 980 - 9917
Dallas, TX 75240 — Fax: (972) 770 - 5977

Annual Grant Total: $2,000,000 - $5,000,000

Public Affairs and Related Activities Personnel

At Headquarters

ADAMS, Louis — Tel: (972) 770 - 4967
Director, Public Relations
louis.adams@brinker.com

GOLDEN, Nan — Tel: (972) 770 - 9510
Director, Public Affairs
nan.golden@brinker.com
Responsibilities include government affairs.

SCHWEINFURTH, Lynn — Tel: (972) 770 - 7228
V. President, Investor Relations — Fax: (972) 770 - 8815

TAYLOR, Joe — Tel: (972) 980 - 9917
V. President Corporate Affairs and PAC Contact — Fax: (972) 770 - 9400

WARD, Melissa — Tel: (972) 980 - 9917
Community Relations Manager, Brinker International Corporate Giving Program — Fax: (972) 770 - 5977

Bristol-Myers Squibb Co.

A manufacturer of pharmaceuticals, nutritionals, and medical devices.

www.bms.com
Annual Revenues: $19.4 billion

Chairman and Chief Exec. Officer — Tel: (212) 546 - 4000
DOLAN, Peter R. — Fax: (212) 546 - 4020
peter.dolan@bms.com

Main Headquarters
Mailing: 345 Park Ave. — Tel: (212) 546 - 4000
New York, NY 10154-0037 — Fax: (212) 546 - 4020

Washington Office
Contact: Richard L. Thompson
Mailing: 655 15th St. NW — Tel: (202) 783 - 0900
Suite 300 — Fax: (202) 783 - 2308
Washington, DC 20005

Political Action Committees

Bristol-Myers Squibb Co. Employee PAC
Contact: Peter Cheng
345 Park Ave. — Tel: (212) 546 - 4000
New York, NY 10154-0037 — Fax: (212) 546 - 4020

Contributions to Candidates: $64,500 (01/05 - 09/05)
Democrats: $27,500; Republicans: $37,000.

Principal Recipients

SENATE DEMOCRATS		HOUSE DEMOCRATS	
Nelson, Benjamin (NE)	$4,000	Menendez, Robert (NJ)	$2,500
Baucus, Max (MT)	$2,500	Scott, David (GA)	$2,500
Lieberman, Joe (CT)	$2,000		
SENATE REPUBLICANS		**HOUSE REPUBLICANS**	
Santorum, Richard (PA)	$2,500	Barton, Joe L (TX)	$2,500
		Blunt, Roy (MO)	$2,500
		Bonilla, Henry (TX)	$2,500
		DeLay, Tom (TX)	$2,500
		Reynolds, Thomas (NY)	$1,500

Corporate Foundations and Giving Programs

Bristol-Myers Squibb Foundation
Contact: John Damonti
345 Park Ave. — Tel: (212) 546 - 4566
New York, NY 10154-0037 — Fax: (212) 546 - 4020

Annual Grant Total: over $5,000,000
Annual grants total is $34 million.
Geographic Preference: Area(s) in which the company operates; National
Primary Interests: Community Affairs; Education; Health; Medical Research
Recent Recipients: American Heart Ass'n; Baylor College of Medicine; Salvation Army; United Way; YMCA

Bristol-Myers Squibb Patient Assistance Foundation, Inc.
Contact: John Damonti
345 Park Ave. — Tel: (212) 546 - 4566
New York, NY 10154-0037 — Fax: (212) 546 - 4020

Annual Grant Total: none reported
National and international giving is handled by the Bristol-Myers Squibb Foundation.
Geographic Preference: Area(s) in which the company operates

Public Affairs and Related Activities Personnel

At Headquarters

BEAR, Stephen E. — Tel: (212) 546 - 4000
Senior V. President, Human Resources — Fax: (212) 546 - 4020
steve.bear@bms.com

BODNAR, Andrew G., M.D. — Tel: (212) 546 - 4000
Senior V. President, Strategy, Medical and External Affairs — Fax: (212) 546 - 4020

CHENG, Peter — Tel: (212) 546 - 4000
PAC Treasurer — Fax: (212) 546 - 4020

DAMONTI, John — Tel: (212) 546 - 4566
President, Bristol-Myers Squibb Foundation — Fax: (212) 546 - 4020
john.damonti@bms.com

ELICKER, John — Tel: (212) 546 - 3775
V. President, Investor Relations — Fax: (212) 546 - 4020
john.elicker@bms.com

PLOHOROS, Tony — Tel: (212) 546 - 4379
Corporate and Business Communications Contact — Fax: (212) 546 - 9711
tony.plohoros@bms.com

SCHOENBORN, Jeffrey — Tel: (212) 546 - 2846
Corporate Communications Contact — Fax: (212) 546 - 4020
jeffrey@schoenborn@bms.com

Bristol-Myers Squibb Co.

* continued from previous page

ZITO, Robert T.
Senior V. President, Corporate Affairs
Tel: (212) 546 - 4000
Fax: (212) 546 - 4020

At Washington Office

CAROZZA, Michael C.
V. President, Federal Government Affairs
michael.carozza@bms.com
Registered Federal Lobbyist.
Tel: (202) 783 - 8659
Fax: (202) 783 - 2308

PERNIE, Chris
Registered Federal Lobbyist.
Tel: (202) 783 - 0900
Fax: (202) 783 - 2308

RYAN, John G.
Senior Counsel and Director, Government Affairs
john.ryan@bms.com
Registered Federal Lobbyist.
Tel: (202) 783 - 0900
Fax: (202) 783 - 2308

SUMPTER-JOHNSON, Mary
Manager, Government Affairs
Registered Federal Lobbyist.
Tel: (202) 783 - 0900
Fax: (202) 783 - 2308

THOMPSON, Richard L.
Senior V. President, Policy and Government Affairs
dick.thompson@bms.com
Registered Federal Lobbyist.
Tel: (202) 783 - 8618
Fax: (202) 638 - 3709

WARR, David E.
Director, International Government Affairs
david.warr@bms.com
Registered Federal Lobbyist.
Tel: (202) 783 - 0900
Fax: (202) 783 - 2308

At Other Offices

BOND, Jeff
V. President, State Government Affairs
777 Scuddersmill Rd.
Plainsboro, NJ 08536
Tel: (609) 897 - 3850

BRUNET, Pam M.
Manager, Community Affairs
P.O. Box 4755, Bldg. 22
Syracuse, NY 13221-4755
pam.brunet@bms.com
Tel: (315) 432 - 2709

FUREY, Tracy
V. President, Corporate Affairs
P.O. Box 4000
Princeton, NJ 08543
tracy.furey@bms.com
Tel: (609) 252 - 3208
Fax: (609) 252 - 7830

GILLESPIE, Karen Sue
Associate Director, State Government Affairs
950 E. Paces Ferry Rd., Suite 2003
Atlanta, GA 30326
karen.gillespie@bms.com
Tel: (404) 231 - 6460
Fax: (404) 231 - 6464

PACOTTI, Linda
Associate Director, Government Affairs
777 Scuddersmill Rd.
Plainsboro, NJ 08536
linda.pacotti@bms.com
Tel: (609) 897 - 5214

PARADOSSI, Pete
Associate Director, Public Affairs and Communications
(Mead Johnson Nutritionals)
2400 W. Lloyd Exwy.
Evansville, IN 47721
pete.paradossi@bms.com
Tel: (812) 429 - 7413
Fax: (812) 429 - 8994

VANDEVEER, Michael D.
Associate Director, State Government Affairs
2400 W. Lloyd Exwy.
Mailstop: M/S B216
Evansville, IN 47711-0001
michael.vandeveer@bms.com
Tel: (812) 429 - 7418

British Airways

A commerical air carrier.
www.britishairways.com
Annual Revenues: $11.887 billion

Main Headquarters
Mailing: 7520 Astoria Blvd.
Jackson Heights, NY 11370
Tel: (347) 418 - 4000
Fax: (347) 397 - 4204

Corporate Foundations and Giving Programs

British Airways Corporate Giving Program
7520 Astoria Blvd.
Jackson Heights, NY 11370
Tel: (347) 418 - 4000
Fax: (347) 397 - 4204

Annual Grant Total: none reported

Public Affairs and Related Activities Personnel

At Headquarters

LAMPL, John W.
V. President, Corporate Communications (The Americas)
Tel: (347) 418 - 4729
Fax: (347) 397 - 4204

RUDIWITZ, Irv
Senior V. President, Human Resources
Tel: (347) 418 - 4000
Fax: (347) 397 - 4204

Broadcom Corp.

Designs and develops semiconductor solutions that enable broadband communications and networking of voice, video and data services.
www.broadcom.com
Annual Revenues: $2.4 billion

Chairman of the Board
SAMUELI, Henry, Ph.D.
Tel: (949) 450 - 8700
Fax: (949) 450 - 8710

President and Chief Executive Officer
MCGREGOR, Scott A.
Tel: (949) 450 - 8700
Fax: (949) 450 - 8710

Main Headquarters
Mailing: P.O. Box 57013
Irvine, CA 92619-7013
Street: 16215 Alton Pkwy.
Irvine, CA 92618
Tel: (949) 450 - 8700
Fax: (949) 450 - 8710

Public Affairs and Related Activities Personnel

At Headquarters

ANDREW, T. Peter
Senior Director, Investor Relations
andrewtp@broadcom.com
Tel: (949) 926 - 5663
Fax: (949) 450 - 8710

BLANNING, Bill
V. President, Corporate Communications
blanning@broadcom.com
Tel: (949) 926 - 5555
Fax: (949) 450 - 0754

BRANDLIN, Laura
Director, Marketing Communications
lbrandlin@broadcom.com
Tel: (949) 450 - 8700
Fax: (949) 450 - 8710

DYER-BRUGGEMAN, Dianne
V. President, Human Resources
Tel: (949) 450 - 8700
Fax: (949) 450 - 8710

BroadVision, Inc.

Supplies application solutions for large-scale, personalized business on the Internet.
www.broadvision.com

Chairman, President and Chief Exec. Officer
CHEN, Dr. Pehong
pehong.chen@broadvision.com
Tel: (650) 542 - 5100
Fax: (650) 542 - 5900

Main Headquarters
Mailing: 585 Broadway
Redwood City, CA 94063
Tel: (650) 542 - 5100
Fax: (650) 542 - 5900

Public Affairs and Related Activities Personnel

At Headquarters

HERRICK, Bill
Investor and Media Relations Contact
Tel: (650) 542 - 3865
Fax: (650) 542 - 5900

Brooklyn Union

See listing on page 279 under KeySpan Corp.

Brookshire Grocery Co.

www.brookshires.com
Annual Revenues: $1.9 billion

Chairman and Chief. Exec. Officer
MASSEY, Marvin S., Jr.
Tel: (903) 534 - 3000
Fax: (903) 534 - 2206

Main Headquarters
Mailing: P.O. Box 1411
Tyler, TX 75710-1411
Street: 1600 W. South West Loop 323
Tyler, TX 75701
Tel: (903) 534 - 3000
Fax: (903) 534 - 2206

Corporate Foundations and Giving Programs

Brookshire Grocery Corporate Contributions
Contact: Allison White
P.O. Box 1411
Tyler, TX 75710-1411
Tel: (903) 534 - 3000
Fax: (903) 534 - 2206

Annual Grant Total: none reported
Recent Recipients: Boys and Girls Club; Children's Miracle Network; Girl Scouts of America; United Way

Public Affairs and Related Activities Personnel

At Headquarters

ANDERSON, Sam
Director, Public Relations
samanderson@brookshires.com
Tel: (903) 534 - 3112
Fax: (903) 534 - 2198

BROOKSHIRE, Tim
President, Human Resources and Financial Group
timbrookshire@brookshires.com
Tel: (903) 534 - 3000
Fax: (903) 534 - 2198

GEE, Jim
Manager, Public Relations
jimgee@brookshires.com
Tel: (903) 534 - 3000
Fax: (903) 534 - 2198

WHITE, Allison
Foundation Contact
Tel: (903) 534 - 3000
Fax: (903) 534 - 2206

Brown & Brown, Inc.

An insurance agency.
www.bbinsurance.com
Annual Revenues: $647 million

Chairman and Chief Exec. Officer
BROWN, J. Hyatt — Tel: (386) 252 - 9601; TF: (800) 877 - 2769

Main Headquarters
Mailing: 220 S. Ridgewood Ave.
Daytona Beach, FL 32114
Tel: (386) 252 - 9601; TF: (800) 877 - 2769

Public Affairs and Related Activities Personnel

At Headquarters

HUDSON, Douglas K — Tel: (352) 732 - 6522; TF: (800) 877 - 2769
Director, Communications and Investor Relations
dhudson@bbinsurance.com

WALKER, Cory T. — Tel: (386) 239 - 7250; Fax: (386) 239 - 7252; TF: (800) 877 - 2769
Senior V. President, Treasurer and Chief Financial Officer
cwalker@bbins.com
Responsibilities include media and investor relations.

Brown and Sons, Inc., Alex

See listing on page 157 under Deutsche Banc AlexBrown.

Brown and Williamson Tobacco Corp.

See listing on page 410 under Reynolds American Inc.

Brown-Forman Corp.

A member of the Public Affairs Council. A diversified producer and marketer of quality consumer products, including wine and spirits, and consumer durable goods.
www.brown-forman.com
Annual Revenues: $2.208 billion

Chairman of the Board
BROWN, Owsley, II — Tel: (502) 585 - 1100; Fax: (502) 774 - 6633
owsley_brown@b-f.com

Main Headquarters
Mailing: 850 Dixie Hwy.
Louisville, KY 40210
Tel: (502) 585 - 1100; Fax: (502) 774 - 6633

Political Action Committees

Brown-Forman/Lenox Political Action Committee
Contact: Mark H. Smith
850 Dixie Hwy.
Louisville, KY 40210
Tel: (502) 774 - 7152; Fax: (502) 774 - 6720

Contributions to Candidates: $44,408 (01/05 - 09/05)
Democrats: $21,568; Republicans: $22,840.

Principal Recipients

SENATE DEMOCRATS		HOUSE DEMOCRATS	
Carper, Thomas R (DE)	$3,000	Chandler, Ben (KY)	$5,000
Conrad, Kent (ND)	$3,000	Davis, Lincoln (TN)	$5,000
		Thompson, Mike (CA)	$3,068
		Gordon, Barton (TN)	$2,500
SENATE REPUBLICANS		**HOUSE REPUBLICANS**	
Alexander, Lamar (TN)	$5,000	Northup, Anne M. (KY)	$5,000
Burns, Conrad (MT)	$5,000	Whitfield, Ed (KY)	$3,000
Kennedy, Mark (MN)	$2,000	Lewis, Ron (KY)	$2,840

Corporate Foundations and Giving Programs

Brown-Forman Corporate Contributions
Contact: Lois Mateus
850 Dixie Hwy.
Louisville, KY 40210
Tel: (502) 774 - 7682; Fax: (502) 774 - 7185

Annual Grant Total: none reported
Geographic Preference: Area in which the company is headquartered

Public Affairs and Related Activities Personnel

At Headquarters

BUBENHOFER, Rick — Tel: (502) 585 - 1100; Fax: (502) 774 - 6633
Assistant V. President and Director, Public Relations

GRAVEN, T. J. — Tel: (502) 585 - 7442; Fax: (502) 774 - 6633
Assistant V. President and Director, Investor Relations

LYNCH, Philip J. — Tel: (502) 774 - 7928; Fax: (502) 774 - 7185
V. President and Director, Corporate Communications

MATEUS, Lois — Tel: (502) 774 - 7682; Fax: (502) 774 - 7185
Senior V. President, Corporate Communications and Services
lois_mateus@b-f.com
Responsibilities include corporate philanthropy.

MEADE, Sharon — Tel: (502) 585 - 1100; Fax: (502) 774 - 6633
Manager, Internal Strategic Communications
sharon_meade@b-f.com

SMITH, Mark H. — Tel: (502) 774 - 7152; Fax: (502) 774 - 6720
V. President/Director, Government Relations and Public Policy
mark_smith@b-f.com

WELCH, James S., Jr. — Tel: (502) 774 - 7351; Fax: (502) 774 - 7185
V. Chairman, Strategy and Human Resources

Brown Shoe Co., Inc.

A footwear company with worldwide operations.
www.brownshoe.com
Annual Revenues: $1.84 billion

Chairman and Chief Exec. Officer
FROMM, Ronald A. — Tel: (314) 854 - 4101; Fax: (314) 854 - 4274
rfromm@brownshoe.com

Main Headquarters
Mailing: P.O. Box 29
St. Louis, MO 63166-0029
Tel: (314) 854 - 4000; Fax: (314) 854 - 4274; TF: (800) 766 - 6465

Street: 8300 Maryland Ave.
St. Louis, MO 63105

Corporate Foundations and Giving Programs

Brown Shoe Inc. Charitable Trust
Contact: Thomas G. Malecek
P.O. Box 29
St. Louis, MO 63166-0029
Tel: (314) 854 - 4084; Fax: (314) 854 - 2016

Annual Grant Total: none reported
Geographic Preference: Area(s) in which the company operates
Primary Interests: Civic and Cultural Activities; Health and Human Services; Higher Education

Public Affairs and Related Activities Personnel

At Headquarters

FAGAN, Elizabeth A. "Beth" — Tel: (314) 854 - 4093; Fax: (314) 854 - 4091
V. President, Public Affairs
bfagan@brownshoe.com

KOCH, Douglas — Tel: (314) 854 - 4120; Fax: (314) 854 - 4274
Senior V. President, Human Resources
dkoch@brownshoe.com

MALECEK, Thomas G. — Tel: (314) 854 - 4084; Fax: (314) 854 - 2016
Director, Security; and Contact, Brown Shoe Charitable Trust
tmalecek@brownshoe.com

ROSEN, Andrew M. — Tel: (314) 854 - 4124; Fax: (314) 854 - 4274
Senior V. President, Treasurer and Chief Financial Officer
arosen@brownshoe.com
Responsibilities include investor relations.

Bruno's Inc.

A grocery store chain.
www.brunos.com
Annual Revenues: $1.9 billion

Chief Exec. Officer
COHAGEN, Dean — Tel: (205) 940 - 9400; Fax: (205) 912 - 4628

Main Headquarters
Mailing: P.O. Box 2486
Birmingham, AL 35201-2486
Tel: (205) 940 - 9400; Fax: (205) 912 - 4628
Street: 800 Lakeshore Pkwy.
Birmingham, AL 35211

Corporate Foundations and Giving Programs

Bruno's Charitable Giving
P.O. Box 2486
Birmingham, AL 35201-2486
Tel: (205) 940 - 9400; Fax: (205) 912 - 4628

Annual Grant Total: none reported

Public Affairs and Related Activities Personnel

At Headquarters

JACKSON, Debbie — Tel: (205) 940 - 9400; Fax: (205) 912 - 4628
Senior V. President, Human Resources

Brunswick Corp.

A manufacturer of marine and recreational products.
www.brunswick.com
Annual Revenues: $4.128 billion

Chairman and Chief Exec. Officer
BUCKLEY, George W. — Tel: (847) 735 - 4700; Fax: (847) 735 - 4765
george.buckley@brunswick.com

Main Headquarters
Mailing: One N. Field Ct.
Lake Forest, IL 60045-4811
Tel: (847) 735 - 4700; Fax: (847) 735 - 4765

Political Action Committees

Brunswick Corp. Good Government Fund
Contact: William Metzger

Brunswick Corp.

** continued from previous page*

One N. Field Ct.
Lake Forest, IL 60045-4811
Tel: (847) 735 - 4700
Fax: (847) 735 - 4765

Contributions to Candidates: $17,000 (01/05 - 09/05)
Democrats: $1,500; Republicans: $13,500; Other: $2,000.

Principal Recipients

SENATE REPUBLICANS

HOUSE REPUBLICANS

Vitter, David (LA)	$2,500
Duncan, John (TN)	$2,000
Kirk, Mark Steven (IL)	$2,000
Petri, Thomas (WI)	$2,000

Corporate Foundations and Giving Programs

Brunswick Foundation
Contact: Homer Stewart
One N. Field Ct.
Lake Forest, IL 60045-4811
Tel: (847) 735 - 4214
Fax: (847) 735 - 4765

Annual Grant Total: none reported

Public Affairs and Related Activities Personnel

At Headquarters

CHIEGER, Kathryn J.
V. President, Corporate and Investor Relations
kathryn.chieger@brunswick.com
Tel: (847) 735 - 4612
Fax: (847) 735 - 4750

KUBERA, Dan
Director, Public and Financial Relations
daniel.kubera@brunswick.com
Tel: (847) 735 - 4617
Fax: (847) 735 - 4750

LOCKRIDGE, B. Russell
V. President and Chief Human Resources Officer
russell.lockridge@brunswick.com
Tel: (847) 735 - 4214
Fax: (847) 735 - 4050

METZGER, William
PAC Treasurer
Tel: (847) 735 - 4700
Fax: (847) 735 - 4765

STEWART, Homer
President, Brunswick Foundation; Manager, Human Resources
homer.stewart@brunswick.com
Tel: (847) 735 - 4214
Fax: (847) 735 - 4765

Brush Engineered Materials Inc.

A member of the Public Affairs Council. A producer of engineered materials, including beryllium, beryllium alloys, beryllia ceramic, precious metal products and specialty metal systems.
www.beminc.com
Annual Revenues: $472.6 million

Chairman, President and Chief Exec. Officer
HARNETT, Gordon D.
Tel: (216) 486 - 4200
Fax: (216) 383 - 4091
TF: (800) 321 - 2076

Main Headquarters
Mailing: 17876 St. Clair Ave.
Cleveland, OH 44110
Tel: (216) 486 - 4200
Fax: (216) 383 - 4091
TF: (800) 321 - 2076

Political Action Committees

Brush Wellman Good Government Fund
Contact: Scott V. Raymont
17876 St. Clair Ave.
Cleveland, OH 44110
Tel: (216) 486 - 4200
Fax: (216) 383 - 4091
TF: (800) 321 - 2076

Contributions to Candidates: $500 (01/05 - 09/05)
Republicans: $500.

Principal Recipients

SENATE REPUBLICANS

Kyl, Jon L (AZ)	$500

HOUSE REPUBLICANS

Corporate Foundations and Giving Programs

Brush Wellman Corporate Contributions Program
Contact: Daniel A. Skoch
17876 St. Clair Ave.
Cleveland, OH 44110
Tel: (216) 486 - 4200
Fax: (216) 383 - 4091
TF: (800) 321 - 2076

Annual Grant Total: none reported

Public Affairs and Related Activities Personnel

At Headquarters

CARPENTER, Patrick S.
Press Contact
Tel: (216) 383 - 6835
Fax: (216) 383 - 4091
TF: (800) 321 - 2076

HASYCHAK, Michael C.
V. President, Treasurer and Secretary
Responsibilities include investor relations.
Tel: (216) 383 - 6823
Fax: (216) 383 - 4091
TF: (800) 321 - 2076

RAYMONT, Scott V.
Treasurer, Brush Wellman Good Government Fund
Tel: (216) 486 - 4200
Fax: (216) 383 - 4091
TF: (800) 321 - 2076

SKOCH, Daniel A.
Senior V. President, Administration and Human Resources
Responsibilities include corporate philanthropy.
Tel: (216) 486 - 4200
Fax: (216) 383 - 4091
TF: (800) 321 - 2076

BT Alex.Brown Inc.

See listing on page 157 under Deutsche Banc AlexBrown.

Budd Company, The

See listing on page 474 under Thyssenkrupp Budd Company.

Bunge Ltd.

A global agribusiness and food company. Acquired Cereol of France, parent company of the U.S.-based Central Soya Company, Inc., in 2003.
www.bunge.com
Annual Revenues: $11.5 billion

Chairman and Chief Exec. Officer
WEISSER, Alberto
Tel: (914) 684 - 2800

Main Headquarters
Mailing: 50 Main St.
Sixth Floor
White Plains, NY 10606-1901
Tel: (914) 684 - 2800

Washington Office
Contact: Thomas J. Erickson
Mailing: 750 First St. NE
suite 1070
Washington, DC 20002
Tel: (202) 216 - 1780

Political Action Committees

Bunge North America Inc. PAC
Contact: Robert D. Scarry
750 First St. NE
suite 1070
Washington, DC 20002
Tel: (202) 216 - 1780

Contributions to Candidates: none reported (01/05 - 09/05)

Corporate Foundations and Giving Programs

Bunge Corp. Foundation
Contact: Philip W. Staggs
11720 Borman Dr.
St. Louis, MO 63146
Tel: (314) 292 - 2000

Assets: $558,768 (2001)
Annual Grant Total: $400,000 - $500,000
Geographic Preference: National
Primary Interests: Arts and Humanities; Higher Education; Performing Arts
Recent Recipients: Harvard University; Missouri Botanical Gardens; New York Public Library

Public Affairs and Related Activities Personnel

At Headquarters

LINDSAY, Stewart
Media Contact
stewart.lindsay@binge.com
Tel: (914) 684 - 3369

TER-JUNG, Susie
Communications and Investor Relations Contact
susie.ter-jung@bunge.com
Tel: (914) 684 - 3398

At Washington Office

ERICKSON, Thomas J.
V. President, Government and Industry Affairs
terickson@bunge.com
Registered Federal Lobbyist.
Tel: (202) 216 - 1780

SCARRY, Robert D.
PAC Treasurer
Tel: (202) 216 - 1780

SCHANTZ, Victoria
Registered Federal Lobbyist.
Tel: (202) 216 - 1780

At Other Offices

STAGGS, Philip W.
V. President, Human Resources; and V. President, Foundation
11720 Borman Dr.
St. Louis, MO 63146
Tel: (314) 292 - 2000

Burger King Corporation

A fast-food chain. Acquired by a group of investors that include Texas Pacific Group, Bain Capital and Goldman Sachs Capital Partners in December, 2002.
www.burgerking.com

Chairman and Chief Exec. Officer
BRENNEMAN, Greg
Tel: (305) 378 - 3000
Fax: (305) 378 - 7910

Main Headquarters
Mailing: 5505 Blue Lagoon Dr.
Miami, FL 33126
Tel: (305) 378 - 3000
Fax: (305) 378 - 7910

Political Action Committees

Burger King Corp. Political Action Committee
Contact: Craig S. Prusher

Burger King Corporation

• continued from previous page

5505 Blue Lagoon Dr.
Miami, FL 33126
Tel: (305) 378 - 3066
Fax: (305) 378 - 7910

Contributions to Candidates: $13,000 (01/05 - 09/05)
Democrats: $1,500; Republicans: $11,500.

Principal Recipients

SENATE DEMOCRATS
Carper, Thomas R (DE) $1,000

HOUSE DEMOCRATS
Melancon, Charlie (LA) $500

SENATE REPUBLICANS
Santorum, Richard (PA) $5,000
Hatch, Orrin (UT) $2,500
Brownback, Sam (KS) $1,000
Talent, James (MO) $1,000

HOUSE REPUBLICANS
Keller, Richard (FL) $1,000
Cannon, Christopher (UT) $500
Hobson, David (OH) $500

Corporate Foundations and Giving Programs

Burger King Corporate Contributions Program
5505 Blue Lagoon Dr.
Miami, FL 33126
Tel: (305) 378 - 3000
Fax: (305) 378 - 7910

Annual Grant Total: none reported
Not currently accepting applications for grants.
Primary Interests: Children; Diversity; Youth Services
Recent Recipients: United Way; Urban League

Burger King/McLamore Foundation
9300 S. Dadeland Blvd.
Miami, FL 33156

Annual Grant Total: $1,000,000 - $2,000,000
Geographic Preference: National
Primary Interests: Education

Public Affairs and Related Activities Personnel

At Headquarters

JOHNSON, Edna Boone
Senior V. President, Global Communications
Tel: (305) 378 - 3000
Fax: (305) 378 - 7910

PRUSHER, Craig S.
V. President, Assistant General Counsel; PAC Treasurer
cprusher@whopper.com
Tel: (305) 378 - 3066
Fax: (305) 378 - 7910

SMITH, Peter C.
Chief Human Resources Officer
Tel: (305) 378 - 3000
Fax: (305) 378 - 7910

Burlington Coat Factory Warehouse Corp.

A retailer of clothing and home fashions.

www.coat.com
Annual Revenues: $3.171 billion

Chairman, President and Chief Exec. Officer
MILSTEIN, Monroe G.
monroe.milstein@coat.com
Tel: (609) 387 - 7800
Ext: 1201
Fax: (609) 239 - 8242

Main Headquarters
Mailing: 1830 Route 130
Burlington, NJ 08016
Tel: (609) 387 - 7800
Fax: (609) 239 - 8242

Public Affairs and Related Activities Personnel

At Headquarters

LAPENTA, Robert
Chief Financial Officer
bob.lapenta@coat.com
Tel: (609) 387 - 7800
Ext: 1216
Fax: (609) 239 - 8242
Responsibilities include investor relations.

MASCIO, Judy
Director, Human Resources
judy.mascio@coat.com
Tel: (609) 387 - 7800
Ext: 2217
Fax: (609) 239 - 8242

Burlington Industries LLC

See listing on page 262 under Internat'l Textiles Group.

Burlington Northern Santa Fe Corporation

PUBLIC AFFAIRS COUNCIL

A member of the Public Affairs Council. Formed in 1995 by the merger of Burlington Northern Inc. and Santa Fe Pacific Corp.

www.bnsf.com
Annual Revenues: $10.9 billion

Chairman, President, and Chief Exec. Officer
ROSE, Matthew K.
Tel: (817) 867 - 6100
Fax: (817) 352 - 7924

Main Headquarters
Mailing: P.O. Box 961057
Fort Worth, TX 76161-2830
Fax: (817) 352 - 7924
TF: (800) 795 - 2673
Street: 2650 Lou Menk Dr.
Fort Worth, TX 76131-2185

Washington Office
Contact: Arthur P. Endres, Jr.
Mailing: 700 13th St. NW
Suite 220
Washington, DC 20005
Tel: (202) 347 - 8662
Fax: (202) 347 - 8675

Political Action Committees

Burlington Northern Santa Fe Corp. RAILPAC
Contact: Patricia A. Murphy
700 13th St. NW
Suite 220
Washington, DC 20005
Tel: (202) 347 - 8662
Fax: (202) 347 - 8675

Contributions to Candidates: $273,000 (01/05 - 09/05)
Democrats: $68,500; Republicans: $202,500; Other: $2,000.

Principal Recipients

SENATE DEMOCRATS
Carper, Thomas R (DE) $8,000
Conrad, Kent (ND) $8,000

HOUSE DEMOCRATS
Thompson, Mike (CA) $5,000

SENATE REPUBLICANS
Burns, Conrad (MT) $9,000
Allen, George (VA) $8,000
Ensign, John Eric (NV) $5,000
Santorum, Richard (PA) $5,000
Kyl, Jon L (AZ) $4,000
Talent, James (MO) $4,000

HOUSE REPUBLICANS
Blunt, Roy (MO) $10,000
Barton, Joe L (TX) $5,000
Bonilla, Henry (TX) $5,000
Cantor, Eric (VA) $5,000
DeLay, Tom (TX) $5,000
Hastert, Dennis J. (IL) $5,000
LaTourette, Steve (OH) $5,000

Corporate Foundations and Giving Programs

Burlington Northern Santa Fe Foundation
Contact: Richard A. Russack
P.O. Box 961057
Fort Worth, TX 76161-2830
Tel: (817) 867 - 6425
Fax: (817) 352 - 7924

Annual Grant Total: none reported
Geographic Preference: Area(s) in which the company operates
Primary Interests: Arts and Culture; Education; Youth Services

Public Affairs and Related Activities Personnel

At Headquarters

HIATTE, Patrick D.
General Director, Corporate Communications
patrick.hiatte@bnsf.com
Tel: (817) 867 - 6418
Fax: (817) 352 - 7924

MICHALSKI, Jeanne
V. President, Human Resources
jeanne.michalski@bnsf.com
Tel: (817) 352 - 6460
Fax: (817) 352 - 7924

MORELAND, Jeffrey R.
Exec. V. President, Law and Government Affairs and Secretary
jeffrey.moreland@bnsf.com
Tel: (817) 352 - 1350
Fax: (817) 352 - 7111
TF: (800) 795 - 2673

MORGAN, Marsha K.
V. President, Investor Relations
marsha.morgan@bnsf.com
Tel: (817) 352 - 6452
Fax: (817) 352 - 7171

RUSSACK, Richard A.
V. President, Corporate Relations; and President, Burlington Northern Santa Fe Foundation
richard.russack@bnsf.com
Tel: (817) 867 - 6425
Fax: (817) 352 - 7924

At Washington Office

BASQUIN, Ashley
Director, Government Affairs
ashley.basquin@bnsf.com
Registered Federal Lobbyist.
Tel: (202) 347 - 8662
Fax: (202) 347 - 8675

ENDRES, Arthur P., Jr.
V. President, Government Affairs
skip.endres@bnsf.com
Registered Federal Lobbyist.
Tel: (202) 347 - 8662
Fax: (202) 347 - 8675

HENDERSON-HAWKINS, Amy C.
Assistant V. President, Federal Government Affairs
amy.hawkins@bnsf.com
Tel: (202) 347 - 8662
Fax: (202) 347 - 8675

HORNBACHER, Mickey
Manager, Government Affairs
(BNSF Railway Company)
Tel: (202) 347 - 8662
Fax: (202) 347 - 8675

MURPHY, Patricia A.
PAC Contact
Tel: (202) 347 - 8662
Fax: (202) 347 - 8675

At Other Offices

ACOSTA, Juan M.
Director, Government Affairs
1127 11th St., Suite 242
Sacramento, CA 95814-3883
juan.acosta@bnsf.com
Tel: (916) 448 - 4086
Fax: (916) 448 - 8937

Burlington Northern Santa Fe Corporation

** continued from previous page*

DICAMILLO, LaDonna V.
Director, Government Affairs
3770 E. 26th St.
Los Angeles, CA 90023-4506
ladonna.dicamillo@bnsf.com
Tel: (323) 267 - 4041
Fax: (909) 946 - 0490

HOWARD, Roger W.
Director, Government Affairs
3253 E. Chestnut Epwy.
Springfield, MO 65802
roger.howard@bnsf.com
Tel: (417) 829 - 4902
Fax: (417) 829 - 4903

KEARNS, Dennis A.
Legislative Counsel and Exec. Director, Government Affairs
1001 Congress, Suite 250
Austin, TX 78701
dennis.kearns@bnsf.com
Tel: (512) 473 - 2823
Fax: (512) 473 - 8570

KEIM, Patrick C.
Director, Government Affairs
139 N. Last Chance Gulch
Helena, MT 59601
patrick.keim@bnsf.com
Tel: (406) 447 - 2301
Fax: (406) 449 - 8610

MUNGUIA, Roberto F.
Director, Government Affairs
201 N. Seventh St.
Lincoln, NE 68508-1309
roberto.munguia@bnsf.com
Tel: (402) 458 - 7738
Fax: (402) 458 - 7739

NORRIS, Cathy J.
Director, Government Affairs
P.O. Box 260317
Littleton, CO 80163
cathy.norris@bnsf.com
Tel: (303) 480 - 7406
Fax: (303) 480 - 7407

NOWICKI, Paul E.
Assistant V. President, Government and Public Policy
547 W. Jackson Blvd., Suite 1509
Chicago, IL 60661-5717
paul.nowicki@bnsf.com
Tel: (312) 850 - 5678
Fax: (312) 850 - 5677

SWEENEY, Brian J.
Legislative Counsel and Exec. Director, Government Affairs
325 Cedar St., Suite 620
St. Paul, MN 55101
brian.sweeney@bnsf.com
Tel: (651) 298 - 2458
Fax: (651) 298 - 7352

WHITE, Pamela S.
Manager, Government Affairs
P.O. Box 961039
Ft. Worth, TX 76161-0039
pamela.white@bnsf.com
Tel: (817) 352 - 2326
Fax: (817) 352 - 2392

Burlington Resources Inc.

An independent oil and gas exploration and production company.

www.br-inc.com
Annual Revenues: $3.326 billion

Chairman, President, Chief Exec. Officer
SHACKOULS, Bobby S.
Tel: (713) 624 - 9000
Fax: (713) 624 - 9645
TF: (800) 262 - 3456

Main Headquarters
Mailing: 717 Texas Ave.
Suite 2100
Houston, TX 77002-2712
Tel: (713) 624 - 9000

Political Action Committees

Burlington Resources Inc. Political Action Committee (BRPAC)
Contact: Gavin H. Smith
717 Texas Ave.
Suite 2100
Houston, TX 77002-2712
Tel: (713) 624 - 9898
Fax: (713) 624 - 9955
TF: (800) 262 - 3456

Contributions to Candidates: $15,000 (01/05 - 09/05)
Democrats: $1,000; Republicans: $14,000.

Principal Recipients

SENATE DEMOCRATS

HOUSE DEMOCRATS

Boren, David (OK)	$500
Cuellar, Henry (TX)	$500

SENATE REPUBLICANS

Allen, George (VA)	$2,000
Hutchison, Kay Bailey (TX)	$2,000
Vitter, David (LA)	$1,500
Burns, Conrad (MT)	$1,000
Craig, Larry (ID)	$1,000
Thomas, Craig (WY)	$1,000

HOUSE REPUBLICANS

Hastert, Dennis J. (IL)	$2,500
Pearce, Steve (NM)	$1,000
Pombo, Richard (CA)	$1,000
Peterson, John Mr. (PA)	$500
Sessions, Pete (TX)	$500

Corporate Foundations and Giving Programs

Burlington Resources/Meridian Oil Foundation
Contact: Gavin H. Smith
717 Texas Ave.
Suite 2100
Houston, TX 77002-2712
Tel: (713) 624 - 9898
Fax: (713) 624 - 9955
TF: (800) 262 - 3456

Annual Grant Total: $2,000,000 - $5,000,000
Geographic Preference: Colorado; Washington State; Texas; New Mexico; Arizona
Primary Interests: Arts and Culture; Education; Medicine and Health Care
Recent Recipients: Louisiana State University; Texas A & M University; United Way

Public Affairs and Related Activities Personnel

At Headquarters

AHLSTROM, Lee
Director, Investor Relations
Tel: (713) 624 - 9548
Fax: (713) 624 - 9645

BARTLETT, James
Director, Corporate Communications
Tel: (713) 624 - 9354
Fax: (713) 624 - 9645

DESANCTIS, Ellen R.
V. President, Investor Relations and Corporate Communications
edesanctis@br-inc.com
Tel: (713) 624 - 9256
Fax: (713) 624 - 9645
TF: (800) 262 - 3456

SMITH, Gavin H.
V. President, Corporate Affairs; President, Burlington Resources/Meridian Oil Foundation; BRPAC Director and Treasurer
(Burlington Resources Oil & Gas Co.)
gsmith@br-inc.com
Responsibilities include government affairs.
Tel: (713) 624 - 9898
Fax: (713) 624 - 9955
TF: (800) 262 - 3456

USHER, William
V. President, Human Resources and Administration
wusher@br-inc.com
Tel: (713) 624 - 9500
Fax: (713) 624 - 9645
TF: (800) 262 - 3456

Burlington Resources Oil & Gas Co.

See listing on page 95 under Burlington Resources Inc.

Leo Burnett Worldwide

A marketing communications agency.

www.leoburnett.com
Annual Revenues: $1.0723 billion

Chairman and Chief Exec. Officer
BERNADINE, Thomas
Tel: (312) 220 - 5959
Fax: (312) 220 - 3299

Main Headquarters
Mailing: 35 W. Wacker Dr.
Chicago, IL 60601
Tel: (312) 220 - 5959
Fax: (312) 220 - 3299

Corporate Foundations and Giving Programs

Leo Burnett Co. Charitable Foundation
Contact: Kristin Anderson
35 W. Wacker Dr.
Chicago, IL 60601
Tel: (312) 220 - 5959
Fax: (312) 220 - 3299

Annual Grant Total: $1,000,000 - $2,000,000
Gives to programs supporting the socio-economic structure of the Chicago metropolitan area.
Geographic Preference: Chicago, IL
Primary Interests: Community Affairs; Education; Urban Affairs; Youth Services

Public Affairs and Related Activities Personnel

At Headquarters

ANDERSON, Kristin
Senior V. President and Director, Community Affairs
Tel: (312) 220 - 5959
Fax: (312) 220 - 3299

FLETCHER, Kristin
Manager, Corporate Communications
kristin.fletcher@chi.leoburnett.com
Tel: (312) 220 - 4795
Fax: (312) 220 - 3299

NELSON, Karlyn
Associate Manager, Corporate Public Relations
karlyn.nelson@chi.leoburnett.com
Tel: (312) 220 - 3921
Fax: (312) 220 - 3299

THOMPSON, Julie
Senior V. President and Director, Corporate Communications
julie.thompson@chi.leoburnett.com
Tel: (312) 220 - 5995
Fax: (312) 220 - 6599

At Other Offices

HAAS, Lawrence J.
Director, Public Affairs
(Manning Selvage & Lee)
Two Lafayette Center
1133 21st St., NW, Suite 300
Washington, DC 20036
Tel: (202) 467 - 6600
Fax: (202) 467 - 5187

Butler Manufacturing Co.

A manufacturer of pre-engineered buildings and of construction materials for non-residential structures. A wholly-owned subsidiary of BlueScope Steel Co., based in Australia.

www.butlermfg.com
Annual Revenues: $896.6 million

Main Headquarters
Mailing: 1540 Genesee St.
Kansas City, MO 64102
Tel: (816) 968 - 3000
Fax: (816) 968 - 3720

Butler Manufacturing Co.

** continued from previous page*

Corporate Foundations and Giving Programs

Butler Manufacturing Co. Foundation
Contact: Pamela Bird Yeater
1540 Genesee St. Tel: (816) 968 - 3000
Kansas City, MO 64102 Fax: (816) 968 - 3720

Annual Grant Total: $500,000 - $750,000
Guidelines are available.
Geographic Preference: Area(s) in which the company operates
Primary Interests: Civic and Cultural Activities; Community Affairs; Health and Human Services; Higher Education; United Way Campaigns
Recent Recipients: United Way; University of Wisconsin

Public Affairs and Related Activities Personnel

At Headquarters

BIRD YEATER, Pamela Tel: (816) 968 - 3000
Foundation Administrator Fax: (816) 968 - 3720

CLARK, Leslie Tel: (816) 968 - 3525
Manager, Marketing Communications Fax: (816) 968 - 6503

MILLER, Larry C. Tel: (816) 968 - 3216
Chief Financial Officer and V. President, Finance Fax: (816) 968 - 6503
lcmiller@butlermfg.org
Responsibilities include corporate communications and investor relations.

Buzzi Unicem USA

Formed by the merger of Lone Star Industries and RC Cement in 2004. A subsidiary of Buzzi Unicem SpA of Italy.
www.lonestarind.com

President and Chief Exec. Officer Tel: (610) 866 - 4400
NEPERENY, David Fax: (610) 866 - 9430

Main Headquarters
Mailing: 100 Brodhead Rd. Tel: (610) 882 - 5000
Suite 230 Fax: (610) 866 - 9430
Bethlehem, PA 18017

Political Action Committees

Buzzi Unicom USA, Inc.
Contact: Michael Berlin
100 Brodhead Rd. Tel: (610) 866 - 4400
Suite 230 Fax: (610) 866 - 9430
Bethlehem, PA 18017

Contributions to Candidates: $3,000 (01/05 - 09/05)
Republicans: $2,500; Other: $500.

Principal Recipients

HOUSE OTHER
Oberstar, James L (MN) $500

SENATE REPUBLICANS
Talent, James (MO) $500

HOUSE REPUBLICANS
Tiahrt, Todd W. (KS) $1,000
Dent, Charles W (PA) $500
Shuster, William (PA) $500

Public Affairs and Related Activities Personnel

At Headquarters

BERLIN, Michael Tel: (610) 866 - 4400
Senior V President, Marketing/Promotions and Governement Affairs Fax: (610) 866 - 9430

BWX Technologies

See listing on page 312 under McDermott Internat'l, Inc.

C. R. Bard, Inc.

A member of the Public Affairs Council. A medical device manufacturer of vascular, urological, oncological and surgical health care products.
www.crbard.com
Annual Revenues: $1.165 billion

Chairman and Chief Exec. Officer Tel: (908) 277 - 8000
RING, Timothy M. Fax: (908) 277 - 8078
TF: (800) 367 - 2273

Main Headquarters
Mailing: 730 Central Ave. Tel: (908) 277 - 8000
Murray Hill, NJ 07974 Fax: (908) 277 - 8240
TF: (800) 367 - 2273

Political Action Committees

C.R. Bard Inc. Active Citizenship Committee (BardACC)
Contact: Todd C. Schermerhorn
730 Central Ave. Tel: (908) 277 - 8139
Murray Hill, NJ 07974 Fax: (908) 277 - 8078
TF: (800) 367 - 2273

Contributions to Candidates: $15,499 (01/05 - 09/05)
Democrats: $1,000; Republicans: $14,499.

Principal Recipients

SENATE DEMOCRATS

HOUSE DEMOCRATS
Menendez, Robert (NJ) $1,000

SENATE REPUBLICANS
Hatch, Orrin (UT) $2,000

HOUSE REPUBLICANS
Ferguson, Mike (NJ) $6,499
Dreier, David (CA) $2,000
Bonilla, Henry (TX) $1,000
Burton, Danny (IN) $1,000
Johnson, Nancy (CT) $1,000
Ramstad, Jim (MN) $1,000

Corporate Foundations and Giving Programs

C. R. Bard Foundation, Inc. and Corporate Giving Program
Contact: Linda A. Hrevnack
730 Central Ave. Tel: (908) 277 - 8182
Murray Hill, NJ 07974 Fax: (908) 277 - 8098
TF: (800) 367 - 2273

Assets: $900,233 (2004)
Annual Grant Total: $2,000,000 - $5,000,000
Geographic Preference: Area(s) in which the company operates
Primary Interests: Education; Health

Public Affairs and Related Activities Personnel

At Headquarters

BARRY, Brian R. Tel: (908) 277 - 8000
V. President, Regulatory and Clinical Affairs Fax: (908) 277 - 8078
TF: (800) 367 - 2273

HREVNACK, Linda A. Tel: (908) 277 - 8182
Manager, Community Affairs and Contributions Fax: (908) 277 - 8098
linda.hrevnack@crbard.com TF: (800) 367 - 2273

KELLY, Bronwen K. Tel: (908) 277 - 8000
V. President, Human Resources Fax: (908) 277 - 8078
TF: (800) 367 - 2273

SCHERMERHORN, Todd C. Tel: (908) 277 - 8139
Senior V. President and Chief Financial Officer Fax: (908) 277 - 8078
todd.schermerhorn@crbard.com TF: (800) 367 - 2273
Responsibilities include corporate communications, investor relations, and political action.

At Other Offices

GLASS, Holly P. Tel: (703) 754 - 2848
V. President, Government and Public Relations Fax: (703) 754 - 7889
14241 Clubhouse Rd.
Gainesville, VA 20155

Cable Design Technologies Corp.

See listing on page 69 under Belden CDT Inc.

Cablevision Systems Corp.

A cable television programming and broadcasting company.
www.cablevision.com
Annual Revenues: $4.2 billion

Chairman of the Board Tel: (516) 803 - 2300
DOLAN, Charles F. Fax: (516) 803 - 1186

President and Chief Exec. Officer Tel: (516) 803 - 2300
DOLAN, James L. Fax: (516) 803 - 1186

Main Headquarters
Mailing: 1111 Stewart Ave. Tel: (516) 803 - 2300
Bethpage, NY 11714-3581 Fax: (516) 803 - 1186

Political Action Committees

Cablevision Systems Corp. Political Action Committee
Contact: Lisa Rosenblum
1111 Stewart Ave. Tel: (516) 803 - 2580
Bethpage, NY 11714-3581 Fax: (516) 803 - 1186

Contributions to Candidates: $30,700 (01/05 - 09/05)
Democrats: $17,200; Republicans: $13,500.

Cablevision Systems Corp.

* continued from previous page

Principal Recipients

SENATE DEMOCRATS		HOUSE DEMOCRATS	
		Pallone, Frank (NJ)	$3,500
		Menendez, Robert (NJ)	$2,500
		Bishop, Timothy (NY)	$2,000
		Mccarthy, Carolyn (NY)	$1,200
SENATE REPUBLICANS		**HOUSE REPUBLICANS**	
Burns, Conrad (MT)	$5,000	Fossella, Vito (NY)	$1,500
Sununu, John (NH)	$5,000		

Public Affairs and Related Activities Personnel

At Headquarters

HRYBENKO, Elizabeth — Tel: (516) 803 - 2300
Director, Investor Relations — Fax: (516) 803 - 1186
ehrybenk@cablevision.com

KERNS, Kim — Tel: (516) 803 - 2300
V. President, Corporate Communications — Fax: (516) 803 - 1186

LANFANT, Katya — Tel: (516) 803 - 2539
Manager, Corporate Communications — Fax: (516) 803 - 2368

ROSENBLUM, Lisa — Tel: (516) 803 - 2580
Senior V. President, Government Relations and Education — Fax: (516) 803 - 1186
lrosenbl@cablevision.com
Responsibilities include political action.

SCHROEDER, Lee — Tel: (516) 803 - 2534
V. President, Government and Regulatory Strategy — Fax: (516) 803 - 1186

SCHUELER, Charles — Tel: (516) 803 - 1013
Senior V. President, Media and Community Relations — Fax: (516) 803 - 1186
cschuele@cablevision.com

Cabot Corp.

Manufacturer of carbon black and other specialty chemicals and materials.

www.cabot-corp.com
Annual Revenues: $1.7 billion

Chairman, President and Chief Exec. Officer
BURNES, Kennett F. — Tel: (617) 345 - 0100 — Fax: (617) 342 - 6103

Main Headquarters
Mailing: Two Seaport Ln.
Suite 1300
Boston, MA 02210-2019
Tel: (617) 345 - 0100 — Fax: (617) 342 - 6103

Corporate Foundations and Giving Programs

Cabot Corp. Foundation
Contact: Peter S. Gregory
Two Seaport Ln.
Suite 1300
Boston, MA 02210-2019
Tel: (617) 342 - 6105 — Fax: (617) 342 - 6159

Assets: $1,360,964 (2002)
Annual Grant Total: $1,000,000 - $2,000,000

Contributions are limited to non-profit organizations that are qualified to receive tax-deductible charitable contributions under section 501 (c)(3) of the Internal Revenue Code. Guidelines are available.

Geographic Preference: Area(s) in which the company operates; Georgia; Louisiana; Massachusetts; Pennsylvania; Texas; West Virginia

Primary Interests: Community Affairs; Environment/Conservation; Health; Higher Education; Math and Science

Recent Recipients: Special Olympics; United Way

Public Affairs and Related Activities Personnel

At Headquarters

GREGORY, Peter S. — Tel: (617) 342 - 6105
Managing Director, Corporate Giving — Fax: (617) 342 - 6159
peter_gregory@cabot-corp.com

MORRISSEY, Karen M. — Tel: (617) 342 - 6221
V. President, Corporate Affairs — Fax: (617) 342 - 6312
Responsibilities include corporate communications.

O'NEILL, Martin — Tel: (617) 345 - 0100
V. President, Safety, Health and Environmental Affairs — Fax: (617) 342 - 6103

ROBINSON, Susannah — Tel: (617) 345 - 0100
Director, Investor Relations — Fax: (617) 342 - 6103

SHEPARD, Ethel — Tel: (617) 342 - 6254
Manager, Corporate Communications — Fax: (617) 342 - 6312

SISCO, Robby D. — Tel: (617) 342 - 6004
V. President, Human Resources — Fax: (617) 342 - 6089

CACI Internat'l Inc.

A network solutions provider.

www.caci.com
Annual Revenues: $642 million

Chairman, President and Chief Exec. Officer
LONDON, Dr. J. P. — Tel: (703) 841 - 7800 — Fax: (703) 841 - 7882

Main Headquarters
Mailing: 1100 N. Glebe Rd.
Arlington, VA 22201-4798
Tel: (703) 841 - 7800 — Fax: (703) 841 - 7882

Public Affairs and Related Activities Personnel

At Headquarters

BROWN, Jody — Tel: (703) 841 - 7801
Exec. V. President, Public Relations — Fax: (703) 841 - 7882
jbrown@caci.com

DRAGICS, David L. — Tel: (703) 841 - 7835
V. President, Investor Relations — Fax: (703) 841 - 7882
ddragics@caci.com

PEEVY, Mary — Tel: (703) 841 - 3719
Coordinator, Investor Relations — Fax: (703) 841 - 7882
mpeevy@caci.com

Cadbury Schweppes Americas Beverages

Formerly operated under the names Dr Pepper/Seven Up Inc., Motts, or Snapple. Maintains alternate website addresses at www.7up.com and www.drpepper.com.

www.dpsu.com
Annual Revenues: $3.225 billion

President and Chief Exec. Officer
CASSAGNE, Gil M. — Tel: (972) 673 - 7000 — Fax: (972) 673 - 7980 — TF: (800) 696 - 5891

Chief Exec. Officer
STITZER, Todd — Tel: (972) 673 - 7000 — Fax: (972) 673 - 7980 — TF: (800) 696 - 5891

Main Headquarters
Mailing: P.O. Box 869077
Plano, TX 75086-9077
Tel: (972) 673 - 7000 — Fax: (972) 673 - 7980 — TF: (800) 696 - 5891

Street: 5301 Legacy Dr.
Plano, TX 75024

Washington Office
Contact: Deborah Louison
Mailing: 1225 I St. NW
Washington, DC 20005
Tel: (202) 661 - 6189 — Fax: (202) 464 - 0431

Public Affairs and Related Activities Personnel

At Washington Office

LOUISON, Deborah — Tel: (202) 661 - 6189
V. President, Government Affairs — Fax: (202) 464 - 0431

At Other Offices

ALFARO, Charles — Tel: (973) 909 - 2585
V. President, Corporate Communications
389 Interpace
Parsippany, NJ 07054
charles.alfaro@am.csplc.com

Cadence Design Systems, Inc.

Develops and markets electronic design automation software products.

www.cadence.com
Annual Revenues: $1.2 billion

President and Chief Exec. Officer
FISTER, Michael J. — Tel: (408) 943 - 1234 — Fax: (408) 943 - 0513 — TF: (800) 862 - 4522

Main Headquarters
Mailing: 2655 Seely Ave.
San Jose, CA 95134
Tel: (408) 943 - 1234 — Fax: (408) 943 - 0513 — TF: (800) 862 - 4522

Corporate Foundations and Giving Programs

Cadence Design Systems Community Involvement Program
Contact: Kathy Wheeler
2655 Seely Ave.
San Jose, CA 95134
Tel: (408) 943 - 1234 — Fax: (408) 943 - 0513

Annual Grant Total: none reported

The company also maintains an employee matching gifts program.

Primary Interests: Animal Protection; Arts and Culture; Education; Environment/Conservation; Health and Human Services

Cadence Design Systems, Inc.

* continued from previous page

Public Affairs and Related Activities Personnel

At Headquarters

ERKANAT, Judy
Senior Public Relations Manager
Mailstop: Bldg. 8
jerkanat@cadence.com
Tel: (408) 894 - 2302
Fax: (408) 944 - 0747

HUNTER, Adolph
Director, Corporate Communications
Mailstop: Bldg. 8
adolph@cadence.com
Tel: (408) 948 - 1234
Fax: (408) 944 - 0747
TF: (800) 862 - 4522

JORDAN, Jennifer
Corporate V. President, Investor Relations
Tel: (408) 943 - 1234
Fax: (408) 943 - 0513
TF: (800) 862 - 4522

LINDSTROM, Alan H.
Senior Manager, Investor Relations
Mailstop: Bldg. 5
Tel: (408) 943 - 1234
Fax: (408) 943 - 0513

MUCHOW, Debi
Corporate V. President, Human Resources and Organizational Development
Tel: (408) 943 - 1234
Fax: (408) 943 - 0513
TF: (800) 862 - 4522

SZYMANSKI, Nancy
Senior Manager, Corporate Public Relations
Mailstop: Bldg. 8
nancy@cadence.com
Tel: (408) 473 - 8382
Fax: (408) 944 - 0747
TF: (800) 862 - 4522

WHEELER, Kathy
Community Involvement Contact
Tel: (408) 943 - 1234
Fax: (408) 943 - 0513

California Federal Bank

See listing on page 122 under Citigroup, Inc.

Callaway Golf Co.

Markets and designs golf products.
www.callawaygolf.com
Annual Revenues: $792.1 million

Chairman of the Board
BEARD, Ronald S.
Tel: (760) 931 - 1771
Fax: (760) 930 - 5015
TF: (800) 228 - 2767

President and Chief Exec. Officer
FELLOWS, George
Tel: (760) 931 - 1771
Fax: (760) 930 - 5015
TF: (800) 228 - 2767

Main Headquarters
Mailing: 2180 Rutherford Rd.
Carlsbad, CA 92008-7328
Tel: (760) 931 - 1771
Fax: (760) 930 - 5015
TF: (800) 228 - 2767

Corporate Foundations and Giving Programs

Callaway Golf Company Foundation
Contact: Paul B. Thompson
2180 Rutherford Rd.
Carlsbad, CA 92008-7328
Tel: (760) 931 - 1771
Fax: (760) 930 - 5015
TF: (800) 228 - 2767

Assets: $4,798,070 (2002)
Annual Grant Total: $500,000 - $750,000
More information can be found about the foundation at the following website: www.callawaygolf.com/corporate/community/foundation.asp
Geographic Preference: California
Primary Interests: Domestic Violence; Families; Medicine and Health Care; Persons with Disabilities; Youth Services

Public Affairs and Related Activities Personnel

At Headquarters

DORMAN, Larry
Senior V. President, Global Press and Public Relations
Tel: (760) 931 - 1771
Fax: (760) 804 - 4154
TF: (800) 228 - 2767

KAPTAIN, Donna L.
Senior V. President, Human Resources
Tel: (760) 931 - 1771
Fax: (760) 930 - 5015
TF: (800) 228 - 2767

THOMPSON, Paul B.
Exec. Director, Foundation
Tel: (760) 931 - 1771
Fax: (760) 930 - 5015
TF: (800) 228 - 2767

Calpine Corp.

A member of the Public Affairs Council. A provider of low-cost electricity and thermal energy.
www.calpine.com
Annual Revenues: $7.59 billion

Chairman, President and Chief Exec. Officer
CARTWRIGHT, Peter
petec@calpine.com
Tel: (408) 995 - 5115
Fax: (408) 297 - 9688
TF: (800) 359 - 5115

Main Headquarters
Mailing: 50 W. San Fernando St.
San Jose, CA 95113
Tel: (408) 995 - 5115
Fax: (408) 297 - 9688
TF: (800) 359 - 5115

Washington Office
Contact: Jeannie Connelly
Mailing: 1401 H St. NW
Suite 510
Washington, DC 20005
Tel: (202) 589 - 0909
Fax: (202) 589 - 0922

Political Action Committees

Calpine Corp. PAC
Contact: Joseph E. Ronan, Jr.
50 W. San Fernando St.
San Jose, CA 95113
Tel: (408) 794 - 2607
Fax: (408) 975 - 4648
TF: (800) 359 - 5115

Contributions to Candidates: $55,750 (01/05 - 09/05)
Democrats: $19,250; Republicans: $36,500.

Principal Recipients

SENATE DEMOCRATS		HOUSE DEMOCRATS	
Bingaman, Jeff (NM)	$2,000	Thompson, Mike (CA)	$1,250
Carper, Thomas R (DE)	$2,000		

SENATE REPUBLICANS		HOUSE REPUBLICANS	
Chafee, Lincoln (RI)	$2,000	Barton, Joe L (TX)	$2,500
Santorum, Richard (PA)	$1,500	Issa, Darrell (CA)	$2,000
		DeLay, Tom (TX)	$1,500

Corporate Foundations and Giving Programs

Calpine Foundation
Contact: Janice M. Stewart
50 W. San Fernando St.
San Jose, CA 95113
Tel: (408) 792 - 1180
Fax: (408) 975 - 4648

Annual Grant Total: none reported
Geographic Preference: San Jose, CA
Primary Interests: Arts and Culture; Civic and Public Affairs; Community Affairs; Education; Environment/Conservation; Health and Human Services; Youth Services

Public Affairs and Related Activities Personnel

At Headquarters

BARRAZA, Richard D.
Senior V. President, Investor Relations
rickb@calpine.com
Tel: (408) 792 - 1125
Fax: (408) 294 - 2877
TF: (800) 359 - 5115

BUNTON, Karen
Investor Relations Contact
investor-relations@calpine.com
Tel: (408) 792 - 1121
Fax: (408) 297 - 9688
TF: (800) 359 - 5115

HIGHLANDER, Bill
V. President, Public Relations
highlander@calpine.com
Tel: (408) 792 - 1244
Fax: (408) 297 - 9688
TF: (800) 359 - 5115

MILLER, John
Senior V. President, Human Resources and Safety
Tel: (408) 995 - 5115
Fax: (408) 297 - 9688
TF: (800) 359 - 5115

POTTER, Katherine
Manager, Public Relations
katherip@calpine.com
Tel: (408) 792 - 1168
Fax: (408) 297 - 9688
TF: (800) 359 - 5115

ROBERTSON, Kent
Manager, Public Relations
kentr@calpine.com
Tel: (408) 794 - 2416
Fax: (408) 297 - 9688
TF: (800) 359 - 5115

RONAN, Joseph E., Jr.
Senior V. President, Government and Regulatory Affairs
joer@calpine.com
Responsibilities include political action.
Tel: (408) 794 - 2607
Fax: (408) 975 - 4648
TF: (800) 359 - 5115

STEWART, Janice M.
President and Chief Exec. Officer, Calpine Foundation
Tel: (408) 792 - 1180
Fax: (408) 975 - 4648

At Washington Office

CONNELLY, Jeannie
V. President, Government Affairs
jconnelly@calpine.com
Registered Federal Lobbyist.
Tel: (202) 589 - 0909

DUXBURY, Peggy
Registered Federal Lobbyist.
Tel: (202) 589 - 0909
Fax: (202) 589 - 0922

HENNEBERRY, Brian
Registered Federal Lobbyist.
Tel: (202) 589 - 0909
Fax: (202) 589 - 0922

MCINTYRE, Yvonne A.
Registered Federal Lobbyist.
Tel: (202) 589 - 0909
Fax: (202) 589 - 0922

Calpine Corp.

• continued from previous page

At Other Offices

FLUMERFELT, John
Director, Public Relations
Two Atlantic Ave.
Third Floor
Boston, MA 02110
jflumert@calpine.com
Tel: (617) 557 - 5381
Fax: (617) 723 - 7635

LAIDLAW, Meg
Director, Public Relations
717 Texas Ave.
Houston, TX 77002
mlaidlaw@calpine.com
Tel: (713) 830 - 8655

WALKER, Crystal
Manager, Government and Public Affairs
Island Center
2701 N. Rocky Point
Tampa, FL 33607
cwalker@calpine.com
Tel: (813) 637 - 7333

Campbell Soup Co.

A manufacturer of processed prepared foods. Subsidiaries include Pepperidge Farm.

www.campbellsoup.com
Annual Revenues: $6.66 billion

Chairman of the Board
GOLUB, Harvey
harvey_golub@campbellsoup.com
Tel: (856) 342 - 4800
Fax: (856) 342 - 3878
TF: (800) 257 - 8443

President and Chief Exec. Officer
CONANT, Douglas R.
douglas_conant@campbellsoup.com
Tel: (856) 342 - 4800
Fax: (856) 342 - 3878
TF: (800) 257 - 8443

Main Headquarters
Mailing: One Campbell Pl.
Camden, NJ 08103-1701
Tel: (856) 342 - 4800
Fax: (856) 342 - 3878
TF: (800) 257 - 8443

Corporate Foundations and Giving Programs

Campbell Soup Foundation
Contact: Wendy Milanese
One Campbell Pl.
Camden, NJ 08103-1701
Tel: (856) 342 - 6423
Fax: (856) 541 - 8185
TF: (800) 257 - 8443

Annual Grant Total: $1,000,000 - $2,000,000
Geographic Preference: Area(s) in which the company operates
Primary Interests: Community Affairs
Recent Recipients: Big Brothers/Big Sisters; United Way

Pepperidge Farm, Inc. Corporate Giving Program
595 Westport Ave.
Norwalk, CT 06851
Tel: (203) 846 - 7000

Annual Grant Total: none reported
Pepperidge Farm also participates in Campbell community support efforts.
Recent Recipients: Habitat for Humanity; United Way

Public Affairs and Related Activities Personnel

At Headquarters

BUCKLEY, Jerry D.
Senior V. President, Public Affairs; and Chairman, Campbell Soup Foundation
jerry_buckley@campbellsoup.com
Tel: (856) 342 - 6007
Fax: (856) 342 - 6314
TF: (800) 257 - 8443

FAULKNER, John W.
Director, Brand Communications
john_w_faulkner@campbellsoup.com
Tel: (856) 342 - 3738
Fax: (856) 541 - 8185
TF: (800) 257 - 8443

FREEDMAN, Judy K.
Group Director, Public Affairs
judy_freedman@campbellsoup.com
Tel: (856) 342 - 3892
Fax: (856) 541 - 8185
TF: (800) 257 - 8443

GONZALEZ-JOSEPH, Jessica
Manager, Community Relations
jessica_gonzalez@campbellsoup.com
Tel: (856) 342 - 3789
Fax: (856) 541 - 8185
TF: (800) 257 - 8443

GRIEHS, Leonard F.
V. President, Investor Relations
len_griehs@campbellsoup.com
Tel: (856) 342 - 6428
Fax: (856) 342 - 3878
TF: (800) 257 - 8443

HENDERSON, Lisa
Director, Organization Communications
lisa_henderson@campbellsoup.com
Tel: (856) 968 - 5891
Fax: (856) 541 - 8185
TF: (800) 257 - 8443

JOHNSTON, Mr. Kelly D.
V. President, Government Relations
kelly_johnston@campbellsoup.com
Tel: (856) 968 - 4367
Fax: (856) 342 - 3889
TF: (800) 257 - 8443

KADEN, Ellen O.
Senior V. President, Law and Government Affairs
ellen_kaden@campbellsoup.com
Tel: (856) 342 - 6125
Fax: (856) 342 - 5216
TF: (800) 257 - 8443

MILANESE, Wendy
Grant Administrator, Campbell Soup Foundation
wendy_milanese@campbellsoup.com
Tel: (856) 342 - 6423
Fax: (856) 541 - 8185
TF: (800) 257 - 8443

PIZARRO, Anne
Director, Campbell's Labels for Education Program
anne_pizarro@campbellsoup.com
Tel: (856) 342 - 6390
Fax: (856) 968 - 2976
TF: (800) 257 - 8443

REARDON, Nancy A.
Senior V. President; Chief Human Resources and Communications Officer
nancy_reardon@cambellsoup.com
Tel: (856) 342 - 6440
Fax: (856) 342 - 4782
TF: (800) 257 - 8443

At Other Offices

REDMOND, Nancy
Director, Corporate and Brand Communications (Pepperidge Farm, Inc.)
595 Westport Ave.
Norwalk, CT 06851
nancy_redmond@pepperidgefarm.com
Tel: (203) 846 - 7395
Fax: (203) 846 - 7130

Canadian Nat'l / Illinois Central

Holding company; rail transportation.

www.cn.ca

Main Headquarters
Mailing: 601 Pennsylvania Ave. NW, Suite 500
Washington, DC 20004
Tel: (202) 347 - 7196
Fax: (202) 347 - 8237

Political Action Committees

Grand Trunk Rail -- Illinois Central Railroad Co. PAC (GTR-ICR PAC)
Contact: Roger A. Cobb
17641 S. Ashland Ave.
P.O. Box 5025
Homewood, IL 60430

Contributions to Candidates: $9,950 (01/05 - 09/05)
Democrats: $4,750; Republicans: $4,200; Other: $1,000.

Principal Recipients

SENATE DEMOCRATS
Stabenow, Debbie (MI) $1,250
Conrad, Kent (ND) $500
Nelson, Benjamin (NE) $500

HOUSE DEMOCRATS
Dingell, John D (MI) $1,000

HOUSE OTHER
Oberstar, James L (MN) $1,000

SENATE REPUBLICANS
Lott, Trent (MS) $1,000
Santorum, Richard (PA) $500

HOUSE REPUBLICANS
Knollenberg, Joe (MI) $1,200
LaTourette, Steve (OH) $1,000

Public Affairs and Related Activities Personnel

At Headquarters

COMBE, Gloria
Washington Representative
gloria.combe@cn.ca
Tel: (202) 347 - 7196
Fax: (202) 347 - 8237

PHILLIPS, Karen Borlaug
V. President, North American Public and Government Affairs
karen.phillips@cn.ca
Tel: (202) 347 - 7816
Fax: (202) 347 - 8237

At Other Offices

COBB, Roger A.
PAC Treasurer
17641 S. Ashland Ave.
P.O. Box 5025
Homewood, IL 60430

Canandaigua Wine Co. Inc.

See listing on page 137 under Constellation Brands, Inc.

Canon U.S.A., Inc.

Imports, markets and distributes photographic products and equipment. A subsidiary of Canon, Inc. of Tokyo, Japan.

www.usa.canon.com

President and Chief Exec. Officer
ADACHI, Yoroku
Tel: (516) 328 - 5000
Fax: (516) 328 - 5069

Main Headquarters
Mailing: One Canon Plaza
Lake Success, NY 11042-1198
Tel: (516) 328 - 5000
Fax: (516) 328 - 5069

Corporate Foundations and Giving Programs

Canon Community Relations Program
Contact: Debra Epstein

Canon U.S.A., Inc.

* continued from previous page

One Canon Plaza
Lake Success, NY 11042-1198
Tel: (516) 488 - 6700
Fax: (516) 328 - 5069

Annual Grant Total: none reported

Geographic Preference: Atlanta, GA; Chicago, IL; Dallas, TX; Washington, DC; Honolulu, HI; Irvine, CA; San Jose, CA

Primary Interests: Environment/Conservation; Health and Human Services

Recent Recipients: American Red Cross; Give the Gift of Sight; March of Dimes

Public Affairs and Related Activities Personnel

At Headquarters

EPSTEIN, Debra
V. President and General Manager, Corporate Communications
Tel: (516) 488 - 6700
Fax: (516) 328 - 5069
Responsibilities include investor relations and corporate philanthropy.

GILBERT, William
Senior V. President, Human Resources
Tel: (516) 488 - 6700
Fax: (516) 328 - 5069

Capital BlueCross (Pennsylvania)

A member of the Public Affairs Council. A health insurer.

www.capbluecross.com

Chairman of the Board
LEHR, William, Jr.
Tel: (717) 541 - 7000
Fax: (717) 541 - 6072

President and Chief Exec. Officer
SMITH, Anita M.
Tel: (717) 541 - 7000
Fax: (717) 541 - 6072

Main Headquarters

Mailing: P.O. Box 772531
Harrisburg, PA 17177-2531
Tel: (717) 541 - 7000
Fax: (717) 541 - 6072

Street: 2500 Elmerton Ave.
Harrisburg, PA 17177

Public Affairs and Related Activities Personnel

At Headquarters

ABRAHAM, Aji
Director, Government Liaison
Tel: (717) 541 - 6134
Fax: (717) 541 - 6072

BUTERA, Joseph
Media Relations Specialist
Tel: (717) 541 - 6139
Fax: (717) 541 - 6696

FITZPATRICK, Barclay
V. President, Corporate Communications
Tel: (717) 541 - 7752
Fax: (717) 651 - 8424

JONES, Krista
Marketing Communications Specialist
Tel: (717) 541 - 6768
Fax: (717) 541 - 6696

MELUSKY, Linda M.
Government Relations Representative/ PAC
Tel: (717) 541 - 6135
Fax: (717) 541 - 6696

TALBOT, Andrea
Senior Consultant, Health Education
Tel: (717) 703 - 8574
Fax: (717) 651 - 4325

VAN VALKENBURGH, Lee H.
V. President, Corporate Services
Mailstop: Dept. 2531
Tel: (717) 541 - 6137
Fax: (717) 541 - 6696

Capital One Financial Corp.

In March of 2005, the company announced plans to acquire Hibernia Corp. Completion of the merger is expected in the final quarter of 2005.

www.capitalone.com
Annual Revenues: $7.25 billion

Chairman and Chief Exec. Officer
FAIRBANK, Richard D.
Tel: (703) 875 - 1000

Main Headquarters

Mailing: 1680 Capital One Dr.
12th Floor
McLean, VA 22102
Tel: (703) 875 - 1000

Political Action Committees

Capital One Financial Corp. Associates Political Fund
Contact: Scott Silverthorne
1680 Capital One Dr.
12th Floor
McLean, VA 22102
Tel: (703) 875 - 1000

Contributions to Candidates: $121,450 (01/05 - 09/05)
Democrats: $40,450; Republicans: $81,000.

Principal Recipients

SENATE DEMOCRATS

Johnson, Tim (SD)	$10,000
Carper, Thomas R (DE)	$3,450

HOUSE DEMOCRATS

Green, Alexander (TX)	$2,500

SENATE REPUBLICANS

Allen, George (VA)	$4,500
Ensign, John Eric (NV)	$4,000
McConnell, Mitch (KY)	$2,500

HOUSE REPUBLICANS

DeLay, Tom (TX)	$5,000
Davis, Tom (VA)	$3,000
Barton, Joe L (TX)	$2,500
Sessions, Pete (TX)	$2,500

Corporate Foundations and Giving Programs

Capital One Financial Corp. Corporate Giving Program
1680 Capital One Dr.
12th Floor
McLean, VA 22102
Tel: (703) 875 - 1000

Annual Grant Total: none reported

Primary Interests: Community Development; Education; Housing; Youth Services

Public Affairs and Related Activities Personnel

At Headquarters

BRESEE, Elizabeth
Tel: (703) 875 - 1000

OLSON, Rick
Tel: (703) 875 - 1000

ROWEN, Michael
Investor Relations Contact
Tel: (703) 720 - 2455

SILVERTHORNE, Scott
Director, Government Relations
Tel: (703) 875 - 1000
Responsibilities include political action.

STEIN, Larry
Tel: (703) 875 - 1000

At Other Offices

STEAD, Tatiana
Director, Corporate Media
1680 Capital One Dr.
Suite 1300
McLean, VA 22102
Tel: (703) 720 - 2352
Fax: (703) 720 - 2315

Caraustar Industries, Inc.

Manufactures recyled paperboard products.

www.caraustar.com
Annual Revenues: $1 billion

Chairman of the Board
ROGERS, James E.
Fax: (770) 732 - 3401

President and Chief Exec. Officer
KEOUGH, Michael J.
Tel: (770) 948 - 3101
Fax: (770) 732 - 3401

Main Headquarters

Mailing: P.O. Box 115
Austell, GA 30168-0115
Tel: (770) 948 - 3101
Fax: (770) 732 - 3401

Street: 5000 Austell-Powder Springs Rd.
Suite 300
Austell, GA 30106-3227

Public Affairs and Related Activities Personnel

At Headquarters

HEILMAN, Janet B.
Investor Relations Contact
Tel: (770) 948 - 3101
Ext: 3779
Fax: (770) 732 - 3401

SMEDSTAD, Barry
V. President, Human Resources and Public Relations
Tel: (770) 948 - 3101
Fax: (770) 732 - 3401

Cardinal Health Inc.

A member of the Public Affairs Council. As a provider of products and services supporting the health-care industry, Cardinal companies develop, manufacture, package and market products for patient care, develop drug-delivery technologies, distribute pharmaceuticals, medical-surgical and laboratory supplies, and offer consulting and other services that improve quality and efficiency in health-care.

www.cardinal.com
Annual Revenues: $75 billion

Chairman and Chief Exec. Officer
WALTER, Robert D.
Tel: (614) 757 - 5000
Fax: (614) 757 - 6000
TF: (800) 234 - 8701

Main Headquarters

Mailing: 7000 Cardinal Pl.
Dublin, OH 43017
Tel: (614) 757 - 5000
Fax: (614) 757 - 6000
TF: (800) 234 - 8701

Political Action Committees

Cardinal Health Inc. PAC
Contact: Gary Dolch
7000 Cardinal Pl.
Dublin, OH 43017
Tel: (614) 757 - 5000
Fax: (614) 757 - 6000
TF: (800) 234 - 8701

Contributions to Candidates: $36,000 (01/05 - 09/05)
Democrats: $4,000; Republicans: $32,000.

Cardinal Health Inc.

** continued from previous page*

Principal Recipients

SENATE DEMOCRATS		HOUSE DEMOCRATS	
Bingaman, Jeff (NM)	$1,000		
SENATE REPUBLICANS		**HOUSE REPUBLICANS**	
Dewine, Richard (OH)	$2,000	DeLay, Tom (TX)	$5,000
Santorum, Richard (PA)	$2,000	Hastert, Dennis J. (IL)	$5,000
		Hobson, David (OH)	$2,500
		Pryce, Deborah (OH)	$2,500
		Boehner, John (OH)	$2,000
		Deal, Nathan (GA)	$2,000
		Thomas, William M (CA)	$2,000
		Tiberi, Patrick (OH)	$2,000

Corporate Foundations and Giving Programs

Cardinal Health Foundation
Contact: Debra Hadley
7000 Cardinal Pl.
Dublin, OH 43017
Tel: (614) 757 - 7481
Fax: (614) 757 - 8450
TF: (800) 234 - 8701

Annual Grant Total: none reported

Public Affairs and Related Activities Personnel

At Headquarters

DOLCH, Gary
Exec. V. President, Quality and Regulatory Affairs
Tel: (614) 757 - 5000
Fax: (614) 757 - 6000
TF: (800) 234 - 8701

GARDNER, Angela
Manager, Media Relations
Tel: (614) 757 - 5000
Fax: (614) 757 - 6000
TF: (800) 234 - 8701

HADLEY, Debra
Exec. Director, Cardinal Health Foundation
debra.hadley@cardinal.com
Tel: (614) 757 - 7481
Fax: (614) 757 - 8450
TF: (800) 234 - 8701

MAZZOLA, Jim
V. President, Public Relations and Corporate Communications
jim.mazzola@cardinal.com
Tel: (614) 757 - 5000
Fax: (614) 757 - 6000
TF: (800) 234 - 8701

STROHM, Jason
V. President, Investor Relations
jason.strohm@cardinal.com
Tel: (614) 757 - 5000
Fax: (614) 757 - 6000
TF: (800) 234 - 8701

WATKINS, Carole S.
Exec. V. President, Human Resources
Tel: (614) 757 - 5000
Fax: (614) 757 - 6000
TF: (800) 234 - 8701

WOODBURN, Connie R.
Senior V. President, Government Relations
connie.woodburn@cardinal.com
Tel: (614) 757 - 7769
Fax: (614) 757 - 5115
TF: (800) 234 - 8701

At Other Offices

FENTON, Geoffrey D.
V. President, Communications
(Cardinal Health Medical Products and Services)
1430 Waukegan Rd.
McGaw Park, IL 60085
Tel: (847) 578 - 4432
Fax: (847) 578 - 4438

GAIDAMAK, Donna
Manager, Media Relations
(Cardinal Health Medical Products and Services)
1430 Waukegan Rd.
McGaw Park, IL 60085
Tel: (847) 578 - 4434
Fax: (847) 578 - 4438

Cardinal Health Medical Products and Services

See listing on page 100 under Cardinal Health Inc.

CareFirst BlueCross and BlueShield

Formerly known as Blue Cross and Blue Shield of Maryland.
www.carefirst.com

Chairman of the Board
MERSON, Michael
Tel: (410) 581 - 3000
Fax: (410) 998 - 5351

President and Chief Exec. Officer
JEWS, William L.
Tel: (410) 581 - 3000

Main Headquarters
Mailing: 10455 Mill Run Circle
Owings Mills, MD 21117
Tel: (410) 581 - 3000
Fax: (410) 998 - 5351

Washington Office
Mailing: 840 First St. NE
Washington, DC 20002
Tel: (202) 479 - 8000
Fax: (202) 479 - 8323

Political Action Committees

CareFirst Associates' Federal PAC
Contact: Livio Broccolino
10455 Mill Run Circle
Owings Mills, MD 21117
Tel: (410) 581 - 3000
Fax: (410) 998 - 5133

Contributions to Candidates: $2,500 (01/05 - 09/05)
Democrats: $2,500.

Principal Recipients

		HOUSE OTHER	
Mikulski, Barbara (MD)	$2,000	Cummings, Elijah (MD)	$500

Corporate Foundations and Giving Programs

BlueCross Blue Shield Corporate Giving
Contact: Lawanda Jenkins
10455 Mill Run Circle
Owings Mills, MD 21117
Tel: (410) 998 - 6010
Fax: (410) 998 - 5351

Annual Grant Total: none reported
Geographic Preference: Washington, DC metropolitan area (including Northern Virginia and Suburban Maryland); Maryland; Delaware
Primary Interests: Health; Medical Research

Public Affairs and Related Activities Personnel

At Headquarters

BROCCOLINO, Livio
Deputy General Counsel
Responsibilities include political action.
Tel: (410) 581 - 3000
Fax: (410) 998 - 5133

DOHERTY, Frances P.
V. President, Government Affairs
Tel: (410) 998 - 5496
Fax: (410) 998 - 4500

GALLANT, Ann T.
V. President, Corporate Communications
Tel: (410) 998 - 6001
Fax: (410) 998 - 5351

JENKINS, Lawanda
Manager, Community Relations
Tel: (410) 998 - 6010
Fax: (410) 998 - 5351

KENNEDY, Jeanne
V. President, Business Risk Management
Tel: (410) 581 - 3000
Fax: (410) 998 - 5351

MCSHANE, Michael A.
V. President, Human Resources
Tel: (410) 581 - 3000

At Washington Office

DEUTERMAN, Pamela
V. President, Federal Programs
Tel: (202) 479 - 8000
Fax: (202) 479 - 8323

Caremark Rx, Inc.

PUBLIC AFFAIRS COUNCIL

A member of the Public Affairs Council. A pharmaceutical services company. Acquired AdvancePCS in March, 2004.
www.caremarkrx.com

Chairman, Chief Exec. Officer, and President
CRAWFORD, E. Mac
Tel: (615) 743 - 6600

Main Headquarters
Mailing: 211 Commerce St.
Suite 800
Nashville, TN 37201
Tel: (615) 743 - 6600

Washington Office
Contact: Russell C. Ring
Mailing: 1300 I St. NW
Suite 525 West
Washington, DC 20005
Tel: (202) 772 - 3500
Fax: (202) 772 - 3535

Political Action Committees

Caremark RX, Inc. Employees Political Action Committee
Contact: James C. Luthin
2211 Sanders Rd.
Northbrook, IL 60062

Contributions to Candidates: $62,000 (01/05 - 09/05)
Democrats: $23,500; Republicans: $38,500.

Principal Recipients

SENATE DEMOCRATS		HOUSE DEMOCRATS	
Baucus, Max (MT)	$5,000	Capps, Lois G (CA)	$2,000
Clinton, Hillary Rodham (NY)	$3,000		
Lieberman, Joe (CT)	$2,000		
Nelson, Benjamin (NE)	$2,000		
SENATE REPUBLICANS		**HOUSE REPUBLICANS**	
Kyl, Jon L (AZ)	$4,000	Barton, Joe L (TX)	$5,000
Ensign, John Eric (NV)	$2,000	Cantor, Eric (VA)	$5,000
Talent, James (MO)	$2,000	Deal, Nathan (GA)	$2,000
Santorum, Richard (PA)	$1,500	English, Philip S (PA)	$2,000
		Hart, Melissa (PA)	$2,000
		Lewis, Ron (KY)	$2,000
		Shadegg, John (AZ)	$2,000

Public Affairs and Related Activities Personnel

At Headquarters

GALLAGHER, Joan M.
Senior V. President, Corporate Communications
Tel: (615) 743 - 6600

Caremark Rx, Inc.

* continued from previous page

HARDIN, Edward L., Jr. — Tel: (615) 743 - 6600
Exec. V. President and General Counsel
Responsibilities include government affairs.

At Washington Office

PARKER, Wendy — Tel: (202) 772 - 3500; Fax: (202) 772 - 3535
V. President, Federal Affairs
Registered Federal Lobbyist.

RING, Russell C. — Tel: (202) 772 - 3500; Fax: (202) 772 - 3535
Senior V. President, Government Relations
Registered Federal Lobbyist.

At Other Offices

ERICKSON, Kelly Carper — Tel: (469) 524 - 7304
V. President, External Communications
750 W. John Carpenter Fwy.
Irving, TX 75039

LUTHIN, James C.
PAC Treasurer
2211 Sanders Rd.
Northbrook, IL 60062

THOMAS, Dale — Tel: (480) 614 - 7212
Manager, Public Relations
9501 Shea Blvd.
Scottsdale, AZ 85260

Cargill Crop Nutrition

See listing on page 334 under Mosaic Co.

Cargill, Incorporated

A member of the Public Affairs Council. A commodity processing and marketing company.
www.cargill.com
Annual Revenues: $49 billion

Chairman and Chief Exec. Officer — Tel: (952) 742 - 7575; Fax: (952) 742 - 7393
STALEY, Warren R.
warren_staley@cargill.com

Main Headquarters
Mailing: P.O. Box 9300, Minneapolis, MN 55440-9300 — Tel: (952) 742 - 7575; Fax: (952) 742 - 7393
Street: 15407 McGinty Rd. West, Wayzata, MN 55391-2399

Washington Office
Contact: Van Yeutter
Mailing: 1101 15th St. NW, Suite 1000, Washington, DC 20005 — Tel: (202) 530 - 8160; Fax: (202) 530 - 8180

Political Action Committees

Cargill, Inc. Political Action Committee
Contact: Jane Allen
P.O. Box 9300 — Tel: (952) 742 - 7110
Minneapolis, MN 55440-9300

Contributions to Candidates: $34,000 (01/05 - 09/05)
Democrats: $5,000; Republicans: $29,000.

Principal Recipients

SENATE DEMOCRATS
Nelson, Benjamin (NE) $1,000

HOUSE DEMOCRATS

SENATE REPUBLICANS
Bennett, Robert F (UT) $3,000
Santorum, Richard (PA) $2,500
Lugar, Richard G (IN) $2,000
Talent, James (MO) $1,000

HOUSE REPUBLICANS
Kennedy, Mark (MN) $5,000
Neugebauer, Randy (TX) $3,000
Latham, Thomas P (IA) $2,500
Hastert, Dennis J. (IL) $2,000
King, Steven (IA) $2,000

Corporate Foundations and Giving Programs

Cargill Foundation
Contact: Mark Murphy
P.O. Box 9300 — Tel: (952) 742 - 2792; Fax: (952) 742 - 7224
Minneapolis, MN 55440-9300

Annual Grant Total: over $5,000,000
Guidelines are available
Geographic Preference: Area in which the company is headquartered
Primary Interests: Arts and Culture; Community Affairs; Education; Social Services
Recent Recipients: America's Second Harvest; United Way

Public Affairs and Related Activities Personnel

At Headquarters

ALLEN, Jane — Tel: (952) 742 - 7110
Treasurer, Cargill Inc. Political Action Committee
Mailstop: MS 5
jane_allen@cargill.com

JOHNSON, Robbin S. — Tel: (952) 742 - 6206; Fax: (952) 742 - 7209
Senior V. President and Director, Corporate Affairs
robbin_johnson@cargill.com

MURPHY, Mark — Tel: (952) 742 - 2792; Fax: (952) 742 - 7224
Exec. Director, Cargill Foundation; and Manager, Stakeholder Relations
Mailstop: MS 50
mark_murphy@cargill.com
Responsibilities include corporate communications.

SISKA, Nancy P. — Tel: (952) 742 - 5172; Fax: (952) 742 - 6215
Corporate V. President, Human Resources
nancy_siska@cargill.com

ZUMWINKLE, Michael — Tel: (952) 742 - 2982; Fax: (952) 742 - 7393
Director, State Government Relations
michael_zumwinkle@cargill.com

At Washington Office

BOUGHNER, Derry — Tel: (202) 530 - 8160; Fax: (202) 530 - 8180
Registered Federal Lobbyist.

EDWARDSON, Bryan B. — Tel: (202) 530 - 8160; Fax: (202) 530 - 8180
Director, Public Policy
bryan_edwardson@cargill.com
Registered Federal Lobbyist.

FAY, Elizabeth — Tel: (202) 530 - 8160; Fax: (202) 530 - 8180
Director, Public Policy
Registered Federal Lobbyist.

MUENZMAIER, Marty — Tel: (202) 530 - 8160; Fax: (202) 530 - 8180
Registered Federal Lobbyist.

MULLINS, Mike — Tel: (202) 530 - 8160; Fax: (202) 530 - 8180
Assistant V. President, Public Affairs
mike_mullins@cargill.com
Registered Federal Lobbyist.

YEUTTER, Van — Tel: (202) 530 - 8160; Fax: (202) 530 - 8180
Assistant V. President, Public Affiars
v_yeutter@cargill.com

At Other Offices

BRADY, Bill — Tel: (952) 742 - 6608; Fax: (952) 742 - 6208
Public Affairs Counselor
P.O. Box 5625
MS25
Minneapolis, MN 55440-5625
bill_brady@cargill.com

CLEMENS, Lisa — Tel: (952) 742 - 6405; Fax: (952) 742 - 6208
Public Affairs Counselor
P.O. Box 5625
MS25
Minneapolis, MN 55440-5625

DALEY, Candice — Tel: (952) 742 - 6193; Fax: (952) 742 - 6208
Public Affairs Counselor
P.O. Box 5625
MS25
Minneapolis, MN 55440-5625

FEIDER, David — Tel: (952) 742 - 6910; Fax: (952) 742 - 6208
Public Affairs Counselor
P.O. Box 5625
MS25
Minneapolis, MN 55440-5625
david_feider@cargill.com

FLIGGE, Lori — Tel: (952) 742 - 2275; Fax: (952) 742 - 6208
Public Affairs Counselor
P.O. Box 5625
MS25
Minneapolis, MN 55440-5625

JOHNSON, Lori — Tel: (952) 742 - 6194; Fax: (952) 742 - 6208
Public Affairs Counselor
P.O. Box 5625
MS25
Minneapolis, MN 55440-5625

KLEIN, Mark — Tel: (952) 742 - 6211; Fax: (952) 742 - 7393
Public Affairs Counselor
P.O. Box 5625
Minneapolis, MN 55440-5625
mark_klein@cargill.com

RAQUET, Bonnie — Tel: (952) 742 - 5215; Fax: (952) 742 - 7209
Corporate V. President, Public Affairs
P.O. Box 5625
MS25
Minneapolis, MN 55440-5625
bonnie_raquet@cargill.com

Carlisle Companies Inc.

Operating units include construction materials and transportation products companies.
www.carlisle.com
Annual Revenues: $2.108 billion

Chief Exec. Officer
MCKINNISH, Richmond — Tel: (704) 501 - 1100 Fax: (704) 501 - 1190

Main Headquarters
Mailing: 13925 Ballantyne Corp. Pl., Suite 400, Charlotte, NC 28277 — Tel: (704) 501 - 1100 Fax: (704) 501 - 1190

Public Affairs and Related Activities Personnel

At Headquarters

LOWE, Carol P.
V. President and Chief Financial Officer — Tel: (704) 501 - 1100 Fax: (704) 501 - 1191

Carlson Companies

A privately-held company with subsidiaries active in hotels, resorts, restaurants, travel, loyalty programs, promotional and sales marketing and incentives. Its restaurant and hotel division, Carlson Hospitality Worldwide, includes T.G.I.Friday's and Pick Up Stix restaurants, Radisson Hotels & Resorts Worldwide, Regent International Hotels, Country Inns & Suites By Carlson, Park Inn Hotels, Park Plaza Hotels & Resorts, and Radisson Seven Seas Cruises.
www.carlson.com
Annual Revenues: $6.8 billion

Chairman and Chief Exec. Officer
CARLSON NELSON, Marilyn — Tel: (763) 212 - 5000 Fax: (763) 212 - 2219

Main Headquarters
Mailing: P.O. Box 59159, Minneapolis, MN 55459-8212 — Tel: (763) 212 - 1000 Fax: (763) 212 - 2219
Street: 701 Carlson Pkwy., Minnetonka, MN 55305

Political Action Committees

Carlson Restaurants Worldwide Political Action Committee
Contact: Leslie Sharman
4201 Marsh Ln.
Carrolton, TX 75007 — Tel: (972) 662 - 4621 Fax: (972) 662 - 5588

Contributions to Candidates: $1,000 (01/05 - 09/05)
Republicans: $1,000.

Principal Recipients

SENATE REPUBLICANS	HOUSE REPUBLICANS	
	Keller, Richard (FL)	$1,000

Corporate Foundations and Giving Programs

Curtis L. Carlson Family Foundation
Contact: Donna Snyder
301 Carlson Pkwy., Suite 100
Plymouth, MN 55447 — Tel: (952) 404 - 5051 Fax: (952) 404 - 5601

Annual Grant Total: none reported

Public Affairs and Related Activities Personnel

At Headquarters

CODY, Douglas
V. President, Exec. Communications
drcody@carlson.com — Tel: (763) 212 - 2488 Fax: (763) 212 - 2219

CRONSON, Joan
Director, Public Relations (Hospitality Group)
jcronson@carlson.com — Tel: (763) 212 - 1418 Fax: (763) 212 - 3400

MACALUS, Sam
Director, Public Relations
smacalus@carlson.com — Tel: (763) 212 - 2477 Fax: (763) 212 - 2219

NEWPERSON, Deborah Cundy
V. President, Community Affairs — Tel: (763) 212 - 1000 Fax: (763) 212 - 2219

POLSKI, Thomas J.
V. President, Public Relations and Communications (Hospitality Group)
tpolski@carlson.com — Tel: (763) 212 - 5616 Fax: (763) 212 - 3400

PORTER, Jim
Exec. V. President, Human Resources — Tel: (763) 212 - 1915 Fax: (763) 212 - 2219

At Other Offices

FRESHWATER, Amy H.
Senior Director, Public Relations
(Friday's Hospitality Worldwide)
4201 Marsh Ln.
Carrolton, TX 75007
afreshwater@crww.com — Tel: (972) 662 - 5549 Fax: (972) 307 - 2811

SHARMAN, Leslie
Treasurer, Carlson Restaurants Worldwide Political Action Committee
4201 Marsh Ln.
Carrolton, TX 75007 — Tel: (972) 662 - 4621 Fax: (972) 662 - 5588

SNYDER, Donna
Contact, Curtis L. Carlson Family Foundation
301 Carlson Pkwy., Suite 100
Plymouth, MN 55447
dds@carlson.com — Tel: (952) 404 - 5051 Fax: (952) 404 - 5601

YOUNG, April
Government Affairs Manager
(Carlson Restaurants Worldwide, Inc.)
4201 Marsh Ln.
Carrolton, TX 75007 — Tel: (972) 662 - 5685 Fax: (972) 307 - 2820

Carlson Restaurants Worldwide, Inc.

PUBLIC AFFAIRS COUNCIL

A member of the Public Affairs Council. *See listing on page 103 under Carlson Companies.*

Carmike Cinemas, Inc.

Constructs and operates movie theatres.
www.carmike.com

Chairman, President and Chief Exec. Officer
PATRICK, Michael W. — Tel: (706) 576 - 3400 Fax: (706) 576 - 2812 TF: (800) 241 - 0431

Main Headquarters
Mailing: P.O. Box 391, Columbus, GA 31902-0391 — Tel: (706) 576 - 3400 TF: (800) 241 - 0431
Street: Carmike Plaza, 1301 First Ave., Columbus, GA 31901

Public Affairs and Related Activities Personnel

At Headquarters

RUSSELL, Judy
Director, Investor and Public Relations — Tel: (706) 576 - 2737 Fax: (775) 310 - 5435 TF: (800) 241 - 0431

Carnival Corp.

Multiple-night cruise line company.
www.carnivalcorp.com
Annual Revenues: $4.37 billion

Chairman and Chief Exec. Officer
ARISON, Micky
marison@carnival.com — Tel: (305) 599 - 2600 Fax: (305) 406 - 4700

Main Headquarters
Mailing: Carnival Pl., 3655 N.W. 87th Ave., Miami, FL 33178-2428 — Tel: (305) 599 - 2600 Fax: (305) 406 - 4700

Corporate Foundations and Giving Programs

Carnival Foundation
Contact: Linda Coll
Carnival Pl.
3655 N.W. 87th Ave.
Miami, FL 33178-2428 — Tel: (305) 599 - 2600 Ext: 10113 Fax: (305) 406 - 8630

Annual Grant Total: none reported
Geographic Preference: Miami, FL
Primary Interests: Arts and Culture; Children; Education; Health
Recent Recipients: Nat'l Foundation for the Advancement of the Arts; New World Symphony; U.S. Middle East Foundation for Academic Exchange

Public Affairs and Related Activities Personnel

At Headquarters

COLL, Linda
Director, Carnival Foundation
(Carnival Cruise Lines)
lcoll@carnival.com — Tel: (305) 599 - 2600 Ext: 10113 Fax: (305) 406 - 8630

GALLAGHER, Tim J.
V. President, Public Relations
(Carnival Cruise Lines)
tgallagher@carnival.com — Tel: (305) 599 - 2600 Ext: 16000 Fax: (305) 406 - 8630

ROBERTS, Beth
V. President, Investor Relations — Tel: (305) 406 - 5539 Fax: (305) 406 - 4700

Carnival Cruise Lines

See listing on page 103 under Carnival Corp.

Carolina Group

See listing on page 299 under Lorillard Tobacco Co.

Carolina Power and Light Co.

See listing on page 395 under Progress Energy.

Carpenter Technology Corp.

A manufacturer of specialty metals. Acquired Talley Industries, Inc. in 1998.
www.cartech.com
Annual Revenues: $1.324 billion

Carpenter Technology Corp.

* continued from previous page

Chairman, President and Chief Exec. Officer
TORCOLINI, Robert J. — Tel: (610) 208 - 2000 Fax: (610) 208 - 3716

Main Headquarters
Mailing: P.O. Box 14662, Reading, PA 19612-4662 — Tel: (610) 208 - 2000 Fax: (610) 208 - 3716
Street: Two Meridian Blvd., Wyomissing, PA 19610-1339

Political Action Committees

Carpenter Technology Corp. Federal PAC
Contact: David Christiansen
P.O. Box 14662
Reading, PA 19612-4662 — Tel: (610) 208 - 2000 Fax: (610) 208 - 3716

Contributions to Candidates: none reported (01/05 - 09/05)

Corporate Foundations and Giving Programs

Carpenter Technology Corp. Contributions
P.O. Box 14662
Reading, PA 19612-4662 — Tel: (610) 208 - 2000 Fax: (610) 208 - 3716

Annual Grant Total: $400,000 - $500,000
Geographic Preference: California; Pennsylvania; South Carolina
Primary Interests: Arts and Culture; Community Affairs; Education; United Way Campaigns
Recent Recipients: Nat'l Merit Scholarship; United Way

Public Affairs and Related Activities Personnel

At Headquarters

CHRISTIANSEN, David
PAC Treasurer — Tel: (610) 208 - 2000 Fax: (610) 208 - 3716

THAMES, John E.
V. President, Human Resources — Tel: (610) 208 - 2000 Fax: (610) 208 - 3716

VASQUEZ, Jaime
V. President and Treasurer, Investor Relations — Tel: (610) 208 - 2165 Fax: (610) 208 - 2989
jvasquez@cartech.com
Responsibilities include communications.

CarrAmerica Realty Corp.

An owner and operator of office properties.
www.carramerica.com
Annual Revenues: $528 million

Chairman and Chief Exec. Officer
CARR, Thomas A. — Tel: (202) 729 - 1700 Fax: (202) 729 - 1150 TF: (800) 417 - 2277

Main Headquarters
Mailing: 1850 K St. NW, Suite 500, Washington, DC 20006-2213 — Tel: (202) 729 - 1700 Fax: (202) 729 - 1150 TF: (800) 417 - 2277

Public Affairs and Related Activities Personnel

At Headquarters

SIMON, Darryl A.
Senior V. President, Human Resources and Risk Management — Tel: (202) 729 - 1700 Fax: (202) 729 - 1150 TF: (800) 417 - 2277

WALSH, Stephen
Senior V. President, Capital Markets — Tel: (202) 729 - 1764 Fax: (202) 729 - 1150 TF: (800) 417 - 2277
stephen.walsh@carramerica.com
Responsibilities include investor relations.

WIDMAYER, Karen L.
Senior V. President, Corporate Communications — Tel: (202) 729 - 1789 Fax: (202) 729 - 1150 TF: (800) 417 - 2277
karen.widmayer@carramerica.com

Carrier Corp.

A manufacturer of heating, air conditioning and refrigeration equipment for commercial, residential, and transportation applications. A wholly-owned subsidiary of United Technologies Corp. (see separate listing).
www.carrier.com
Annual Revenues: $8.895 billion

Main Headquarters
Mailing: One Carrier Pl., Farmington, CT 06034-4015 — Tel: (860) 674 - 3000 Fax: (860) 674 - 3193

Corporate Foundations and Giving Programs

Carrier Corp. Community Relations Department Contributions
One Carrier Pl.
Farmington, CT 06034-4015 — Tel: (860) 674 - 3000 Fax: (860) 674 - 3193

Annual Grant Total: $1,000,000 - $2,000,000
Guidelines are available.
Geographic Preference: Georgia; Indiana; New York; Tennessee; Texas; Illinois; Michigan; North Carolina
Primary Interests: Civic and Cultural Activities; Education; Health and Human Services

Public Affairs and Related Activities Personnel

At Headquarters

BAILEY, Gerald E.
V. President, Environmental Health and Safety — Tel: (860) 674 - 3398 Fax: (860) 674 - 3193
gerald.bailey@carrier.utc.com

LINTNER, Nancy T.
V. Presiden, Community Affairs — Tel: (860) 674 - 3000 Fax: (860) 674 - 3193

MANDYCK, John M.
V. President, Government and International Relations — Tel: (860) 674 - 3006 Fax: (860) 674 - 3193
john.mandyck@carrier.utc.com

PREUX, Patrick
V. President, Human Resources — Tel: (860) 674 - 3000 Fax: (860) 674 - 3193

Carter-Wallace, Inc.

See listing on page 318 under MedPointe Inc.

Case Corp.

See listing on page 104 under Case New Holland Inc.

Case New Holland Inc.

A manufacturer of agricultural and construction machinery. Formed by the merger of Case Corp. and New Holland N.V. in 1999.
www.cnh.com
Annual Revenues: $12 billion

Chairman of the Board
HUDSON, Katherine M. — Tel: (847) 735 - 9200

President and Chief Exec. Officer
BOYANOVSKY, Harold — Tel: (847) 735 - 9200

Main Headquarters
Mailing: 100 S. Saunders Rd., Lake Forest, IL 60045 — Tel: (847) 735 - 9200

Washington Office
Contact: Joseph E. Samora, Jr.
Mailing: 1001 G St. NW, Suite 100 East, Washington, DC 20001 — Tel: (202) 737 - 7575 Fax: (202) 737 - 9090

Political Action Committees

Case New Holland Excellence in Government Committee
Contact: Joseph E. Samora, Jr.
1001 G St. NW
Suite 100 East
Washington, DC 20001 — Tel: (202) 737 - 7575 Fax: (202) 737 - 9090

Contributions to Candidates: $15,000 (01/05 - 09/05)
Republicans: $10,000; Other: $5,000.

Principal Recipients

HOUSE OTHER
Pitts, Joseph R (PA) $5,000

Public Affairs and Related Activities Personnel

At Headquarters

TREFTS, Al
Senior Director, Investor Relations and Corporate Finance — Tel: (847) 955 - 3821 Fax: (847) 955 - 3961

At Washington Office

KINZEL, Will C.
Manager, Government Affairs — Tel: (202) 737 - 7575 Fax: (202) 737 - 9090
Registered Federal Lobbyist.

NADHERNY, Steven T.
Director, Government Affairs — Tel: (202) 737 - 7575 Fax: (202) 737 - 9090
Registered Federal Lobbyist.

SAMORA, Joseph E., Jr.
Senior V. President; PAC Treasurer — Tel: (202) 737 - 7575 Fax: (202) 737 - 9090
Registered Federal Lobbyist.

Cash America Internat'l, Inc.

A member of the Public Affairs Council. A diversified specialty finance company.
www.cashamerica.com
Annual Revenues: $355.9 million

Chairman of the Board
DAUGHERTY, Jack R. — Tel: (817) 335 - 1100 Fax: (817) 570 - 1645
jdaugherty@casham.com

President and Chief Exec. Officer
FEEHAN, Daniel R. — Tel: (817) 335 - 1100 Fax: (817) 570 - 1645
dfeehan@casham.com

Main Headquarters
Mailing: Cash America Bldg., 1600 W. Seventh St., Fort Worth, TX 76102-2599 — Tel: (817) 335 - 1100 Fax: (817) 570 - 1645

Cash America Internat'l, Inc.

** continued from previous page*

Political Action Committees

Cash American Internat'l, Inc. PAC
Contact: John Linscott
Cash America Bldg.
1600 W. Seventh St.
Fort Worth, TX 76102-2599
Tel: (817) 335 - 1100
Fax: (817) 570 - 1645

Contributions to Candidates: $56,350 (01/05 - 09/05)
Democrats: $15,000; Republicans: $41,350.

Principal Recipients

SENATE DEMOCRATS		HOUSE DEMOCRATS	
Stabenow, Debbie (MI)	$3,000	Kanjorski, Paul (PA)	$4,000
Ford, Harold E Jr (TN)	$1,000		
SENATE REPUBLICANS		**HOUSE REPUBLICANS**	
Burns, Conrad (MT)	$1,000	DeLay, Tom (TX)	$5,000
Cornyn, John (TX)	$1,000	Hensarling, Jeb (TX)	$5,000
		Sessions, Pete (TX)	$3,000
		Bachus, Spencer (AL)	$2,500
		Blasdel, Chuck (OH)	$2,500

Public Affairs and Related Activities Personnel

At Headquarters

BESSANT, Thomas, Jr.
Media Contact
Tel: (817) 335 - 1100
Fax: (817) 570 - 1645

JACKSON, Mary L.
V. President, Public and Government Relations
mjackson@casham.com
Tel: (817) 570 - 1616
Fax: (817) 570 - 1645

LINSCOTT, John
PAC Treasurer
Tel: (817) 335 - 1100
Fax: (817) 570 - 1645

LITTRELL, Dee
Manager, Investor Relations
dlittrell@casham.com
Tel: (817) 335 - 1100
Fax: (817) 570 - 1645

Catalina Marketing Corp.

A targeted marketing services company. Works to meet the needs of manufacturers, retailers, and consumers.
www.catalinamarketing.com
Annual Revenues: $410 million

Chairman of the Board
BEINECKE, Frederick W.
Tel: (727) 579 - 5000
Fax: (727) 556 - 2700

Chief Exec. Officer
BUELL, L. Dick
Tel: (727) 579 - 5000
Fax: (727) 556 - 2700

Main Headquarters
Mailing: 200 Carillon Pkwy.
St. Petersburg, FL 33716
Tel: (727) 579 - 5000
Fax: (727) 556 - 2700

Corporate Foundations and Giving Programs

The Catalina Marketing Charitable Foundation
Contact: William Protz
200 Carillon Pkwy.
St. Petersburg, FL 33716
Tel: (727) 579 - 5069
Fax: (727) 556 - 2700

Assets: $331,171 (2002)
Annual Grant Total: under $100,000
Geographic Preference: Florida
Primary Interests: Education; Medicine and Health Care; Youth Services
Recent Recipients: Salvation Army

Public Affairs and Related Activities Personnel

At Headquarters

ANDRIANO, Nicole
Manager, Public Relations
nicole.andriso@catalinamarketing.com
Tel: (727) 579 - 5000
Fax: (727) 556 - 2700

COOVERT, Crystal
Exec. Director, Communications
Tel: (727) 579 - 5452
Fax: (727) 556 - 2700

FRIAR, Rick
Exec. V. President and Chief Finacial Officer
rick.friar@catalinamarketing.com
Tel: (727) 579 - 5218
Fax: (727) 556 - 2700

PROTZ, William
Exec. Director, Community Relations
bill.protz@catalinamarketing.com
Responsibilities include corporate philanthropy.
Tel: (727) 579 - 5069
Fax: (727) 556 - 2700

Caterpillar Inc.

A member of the Public Affairs Council. Manufacturer of mining and construction equipment, diesel and natural gas engines and turbines.
www.cat.com
Annual Revenues: $30.25 billion

Chairman and Chief Exec. Officer
OWENS, James W.
Tel: (309) 675 - 1000
Fax: (309) 675 - 6155

Main Headquarters
Mailing: 100 NE Adams St.
Peoria, IL 61629-1465
Tel: (309) 675 - 1000
Fax: (309) 675 - 6155

Washington Office
Contact: William C. Lane
Mailing: 818 Connecticut Ave. NW
Suite 600
Washington, DC 20006-2702
Tel: (202) 466 - 0672
Fax: (202) 466 - 0684

Political Action Committees

CATPAC
Contact: Douglas P. Crew
100 NE Adams St.
Peoria, IL 61629-1465
Tel: (309) 675 - 5248
Fax: (309) 675 - 5815

Contributions to Candidates: $122,000 (01/05 - 09/05)
Democrats: $19,500; Republicans: $102,500.

Principal Recipients

SENATE DEMOCRATS		HOUSE DEMOCRATS	
Baucus, Max (MT)	$2,500		
SENATE REPUBLICANS		**HOUSE REPUBLICANS**	
Lugar, Richard G (IN)	$5,000	Hastert, Dennis J. (IL)	$5,000
Burns, Conrad (MT)	$2,500	Kennedy, Mark (MN)	$5,000
Santorum, Richard (PA)	$2,500	LaHood, Ray (IL)	$5,000
		Wilson, Heather (NM)	$4,000
		Boozman, John (AR)	$3,000
		Emerson, Jo Ann (MO)	$3,000
		Kirk, Mark Steven (IL)	$3,000
		Northup, Anne M. (KY)	$3,000
		Wilson, Joe (SC)	$3,000

Corporate Foundations and Giving Programs

Caterpillar Inc. Foundation
Contact: Henry W. Holling
100 NE Adams St.
Peoria, IL 61629-1465
Tel: (309) 675 - 4418
Fax: (309) 675 - 5815

Annual Grant Total: none reported
Geographic Preference: Area(s) in which the company operates
Primary Interests: Arts and Culture; Economic Development; Education; United Way Campaigns
Recent Recipients: Pennsylvania State University; United Way

Caterpillar Corporate Giving Program
100 NE Adams St.
Peoria, IL 61629-1465
Tel: (309) 675 - 1000
Fax: (309) 675 - 6155

Annual Grant Total: none reported
Geographic Preference: Area(s) in which the company operates; National
Primary Interests: Civic and Public Affairs; Economic Development

Public Affairs and Related Activities Personnel

At Headquarters

ALFORD, Chip
Coordinator, Corporate Communications
Tel: (309) 675 - 1464
Fax: (309) 675 - 6155

BANWART, Sidney C.
V. President, Human Services Division
Tel: (309) 675 - 5222
Fax: (309) 675 - 5330

CREW, Douglas P.
Manager, Governmental Affairs
crew_douglas_p@cat.com
Tel: (309) 675 - 5248
Fax: (309) 675 - 5815

DEWALT, Michael
Director, Investor Relations
Tel: (309) 675 - 1000
Fax: (309) 675 - 6155

DOOLITTLE, Thomas M.
Manager, Corporate Communications
Tel: (309) 675 - 6058
Fax: (309) 675 - 5815

ELDER, Timothy L.
Director, Corporate Public Affairs
Tel: (309) 675 - 4872
Fax: (309) 675 - 5815

HAUSSER, Marsha
Senior Public Information Representative
Tel: (309) 675 - 1307
Fax: (309) 675 - 5588

HENNINGSEN, Anker B.
Manager, Marketing Communications
Tel: (309) 578 - 9889
Fax: (309) 675 - 6155

HOLLING, Henry W.
Manager, Community and Corporate Support; V. President and Manager, Foundation
Tel: (309) 675 - 4418
Fax: (309) 675 - 5815

MORRISON, Maryann
Corporate Contributions
Tel: (309) 675 - 4464
Fax: (309) 675 - 6155

VEST, Gary L.
PAC Treasurer
Tel: (309) 675 - 1000
Fax: (309) 675 - 6155

At Washington Office

BRENT, Richard
Washington Manager, Solar
Registered Federal Lobbyist.
Tel: (202) 466 - 0655
Fax: (202) 466 - 0684

HIMES, Kathryn S.
Manager, Government Affairs
Tel: (202) 466 - 0683
Fax: (202) 466 - 0684

LANE, William C.
Washington Director, Governmental Affairs
Registered Federal Lobbyist.
Tel: (202) 466 - 0672
Fax: (202) 466 - 0684

Caterpillar Inc.

** continued from previous page*

VOLZ, Carl M. — Tel: (202) 466 - 0670
Manager, Government Affairs Issue Analysis — Fax: (202) 466 - 0684
Registered Federal Lobbyist.

At Other Offices

DEFOE, Donald H. — Tel: (217) 753 - 8050
Manager, State Governmental Affairs — Fax: (217) 753 - 3618
600 S. Second St., Suite 101
Springfield, IL 62704

WALTERS, Thomas P. — Tel: (217) 753 - 8050
Illinois Government Affairs Representative — Fax: (217) 753 - 3618
600 S. Second St., Suite 101
Springfield, IL 62704

CB Richard Ellis Services, Inc.

A commercial real estate firm.

www.cbre.com

Annual Revenues: $1.2 billion

Chief Exec. Officer — Tel: (310) 606 - 4720
WHITE, Brett — Fax: (310) 606 - 4701

Main Headquarters

Mailing: 100 N. Sepulveda Blvd. — Tel: (310) 606 - 4700
Suite 1050 — Fax: (310) 606 - 4701
El Segundo, CA 90245

Public Affairs and Related Activities Personnel

At Other Offices

DOMINGUEZ, Victor — Tel: (310) 354 - 5064
Managing Director, Corporate Communications — Fax: (310) 380 - 5896
970 W. 190th St.
Suite 100
Torrance, CA 90502
victor.dominguez@cbre.com

IACO, Steve — Tel: (212) 984 - 6535
Senior Managing Director, Corporate Communications
200 Park Ave.
New York, NY 10166

KEENAN, Melanie — Tel: (212) 284 - 8073
Director, Communications
560 Lexington Ave.
20th Floor
New York, NY 10022
melanie.keenan@cbre.com

MCGRATH, Robert — Tel: (212) 984 - 8267
Senior Director, Corporate Communications — Fax: (212) 984 - 8207
200 Park Ave.
New York, NY 10166
robert.mcgrath@cbre.com

VAN BERKEL, Jack — Tel: (949) 809 - 4229
Senior V. President, Human Resources — Fax: (949) 809 - 4799
4400 MacArthur Blvd.
Suite 600
Newport Beach, CA 92660
jack.vanberkel@cbre.com

YOUNG, Shelley — Tel: (212) 984 - 8359
Director, Investor Relations
200 Park Ave.
New York, NY 10166

CBRL Group, Inc.

A member of the Public Affairs Council. A holding company whose principal subsidary is Cracker Barrel Old Country Store, Inc., a combination restaurant and gift shops company serving the motoring public.

www.cbrlgroup.com

Annual Revenues: $1.96 billion

Chairman, President and Chief Exec. Officer — Tel: (615) 444 - 5533
WOODHOUSE, Michael A. — Fax: (615) 443 - 9511

Main Headquarters

Mailing: 305 Hartman Dr. — Tel: (615) 444 - 5533
Lebanon, TN 37088 — Fax: (615) 443 - 9476

Political Action Committees

CBRL Group PAC

Contact: Dwayne Evans

305 Hartman Dr. — Tel: (615) 444 - 5533
Lebanon, TN 37088 — Fax: (615) 443 - 9511

Contributions to Candidates: $11,250 (01/05 - 09/05)

Democrats: $250; Republicans: $11,000.

Principal Recipients

SENATE REPUBLICANS		HOUSE REPUBLICANS	
Burns, Conrad (MT)	$1,000	Cannon, Christopher (UT)	$1,000
Chafee, Lincoln (RI)	$1,000	Gard, John G (WI)	$1,000
Hatch, Orrin (UT)	$1,000	Northup, Anne M. (KY)	$1,000
Kyl, Jon L (AZ)	$1,000	Petri, Thomas (WI)	$1,000
Santorum, Richard (PA)	$1,000	Whalen, Michael (IA)	$1,000
Talent, James (MO)	$1,000		

Corporate Foundations and Giving Programs

CBRL Group Foundation

Contact: Penny D. Carroll

305 Hartman Dr. — Tel: (615) 443 - 9807
Lebanon, TN 37088 — Fax: (615) 443 - 9511

Annual Grant Total: none reported

Public Affairs and Related Activities Personnel

At Headquarters

CARROLL, Penny D. — Tel: (615) 443 - 9807
Foundation Director, CBRL Group Foundation — Fax: (615) 443 - 9511

COTTON, Bruce — Tel: (615) 444 - 5533
V. President, Government Relations — Fax: (615) 443 - 9511

DAVIS, Julie K. — Tel: (615) 443 - 9266
Director, Corporate Communications — Fax: (615) 443 - 9322
(Cracker Barrel Old Country Store, Inc.)

EVANS, Dwayne — Tel: (615) 444 - 5533
PAC Treasurer — Fax: (615) 443 - 9511

HILL, Norman J. — Tel: (615) 444 - 5533
Senior V. President, Human Resources — Fax: (615) 443 - 9511
(Cracker Barrel Old Country Store, Inc.)

SHEEHY, Pat — Tel: (615) 444 - 5533
Manager, Government Relations — Fax: (615) 443 - 9511
(Cracker Barrel Old Country Store, Inc.)

TAYLOR, Jim — Tel: (615) 444 - 5533
Manager, Communications — Fax: (615) 443 - 9322
(Cracker Barrel Old Country Store, Inc.)

CBS Corp.

See listing on page 505 under Viacom Inc/CBS Corp.

CBS Television

See listing on page 505 under Viacom Inc/CBS Corp.

CDI Corp.

A search and recruitment organization. Provides staffing, outsourcing and engineering services to the automotive, electronics and petrochemicals industries.

www.cdicorp.com

Annual Revenues: $1.045 billion

Chairman of the Board — Tel: (215) 569 - 2200
GARRISON, Walter R. — Fax: (215) 569 - 1452

President and Chief Exec. Officer — Tel: (215) 569 - 2200
BALLOU, Roger H. — Fax: (215) 569 - 1452

Main Headquarters

Mailing: 1717 Arch St. — Tel: (215) 569 - 2200
35th Floor — Fax: (215) 569 - 1452
Philadelphia, PA 19103-2768

Public Affairs and Related Activities Personnel

At Headquarters

VENGLARIK, Cecilia — Tel: (215) 569 - 2200
Senior V. President, Human Resources — Fax: (215) 569 - 1452

WEBB, Vincent — Tel: (215) 636 - 1240
V. President, Corporate Communications and Marketing — Fax: (215) 569 - 1452
vince.webb@cdicorp.com
Responsibilities include investor relations.

CDW Corp.

Formerly known as CDW Computer Centers, Inc. A distributor of computers and computer related products to business customers. Purchased the Canadian operations and selected North American assets of Micro Warehouse, Inc. in September, 2003.

www.cdw.com

Annual Revenues: $3.8 billion

CDW Corp.

* continued from previous page

Chairman and Chief Exec. Officer
EDWARDSON, John A.
Tel: (847) 465 - 6000
Fax: (847) 465 - 3444

Main Headquarters
Mailing: 200 N. Milwaukee Ave.
Vernon Hills, IL 60061
Tel: (847) 465 - 6000
Fax: (847) 465 - 3444
TF: (800) 800 - 4239

Public Affairs and Related Activities Personnel

At Headquarters

CARAHER, Kelly
Public Relations Coordinator
Tel: (847) 968 - 0729
Fax: (847) 465 - 3444
TF: (800) 800 - 4239

KLIMSTRA, Cindy T.
Director, Investor Relations
cklimstra@cdw.com
Tel: (847) 968 - 0268
Fax: (847) 465 - 3444
TF: (800) 800 - 4239

ROSS, Gary
General Manager, Corporate Communications
Tel: (847) 371 - 5048
Fax: (847) 465 - 3444
TF: (800) 800 - 4239

WALTER, Clark
Senior Program Manager, Investor Relations
cwalter@cdw.com
Tel: (847) 968 - 0728
Fax: (847) 465 - 3444
TF: (800) 800 - 4239

Celanese

An industrial company with business lines in commodity chemicals, acetate fibers and technical polymers. A subsidiary of Germany-based Celanese, A.G. Formerly known as Hoechst Celanese Corp.

www.celanese.com
Annual Revenues: $5 billion

Chairman of the Board
CHU, Chinh E.
Tel: (972) 443 - 4000

President and Chief Exec. Officer
WEIDMAN, David N.
Tel: (972) 443 - 4000

Main Headquarters
Mailing: 1601 W. LBJ Fwy.
Dallas, TX 75234
Tel: (972) 443 - 4000

Washington Office
Contact: Eugene Steadman, Jr.
Mailing: 1331 Pennsylvania Ave. NW
Suite 600
Washington, DC 20004-1790
Tel: (202) 637 - 3468
Fax: (703) 358 - 9786

Political Action Committees

Celanese Americas Corp. PAC
Contact: Andrew Spathakis
550 U.S. Hwy. 202/206
Suite 310
Bedminster, NJ 07921

Contributions to Candidates: $22,000 (01/05 - 09/05)
Democrats: $6,500; Republicans: $15,500.

Principal Recipients

SENATE DEMOCRATS

HOUSE DEMOCRATS

Boucher, Fredrick (VA)	$3,500
McIntyre, Mike (NC)	$1,000
Ortiz, Solomon (TX)	$1,000
Tanner, John S. (TN)	$1,000

SENATE REPUBLICANS

Alexander, Lamar (TN)	$2,500
Allen, George (VA)	$1,000
Santorum, Richard (PA)	$1,000

HOUSE REPUBLICANS

Sessions, Pete (TX)	$3,000
Barton, Joe L (TX)	$1,000
DeLay, Tom (TX)	$1,000
Ferguson, Mike (NJ)	$1,000
Goode, Virgil H. Jr. (VA)	$1,000
Gutknecht, Gil (MN)	$1,000
Hall, Ralph (TX)	$1,000
Marchant, Kenny (TX)	$1,000
Whitfield, Ed (KY)	$1,000

Public Affairs and Related Activities Personnel

At Headquarters

CULLERS, Jeanne
Media Contact
Tel: (972) 443 - 4847
Fax: (972) 443 - 8519

FERRARA, Gerald P.
V. President, Governmental Affairs
gpferrara@celanese.com
Tel: (972) 443 - 3848
Fax: (972) 443 - 8476

OBERLE, Mark
Investor Relations Contact
mark.oberle@celanese.com
Tel: (972) 443 - 4464
Fax: (972) 332 - 9373

At Washington Office

CARPENTER, Robert R.
Director, State and Governmental Affairs
RRCarpenter@celanese.com
Registered Federal Lobbyist.
Tel: (703) 637 - 3469
Fax: (972) 443 - 8685

STEADMAN, Eugene, Jr.
Director, Governmental Relations
esteadman@celanese.com
Registered Federal Lobbyist.
Tel: (703) 637 - 3468
Fax: (972) 443 - 8684

At Other Offices

SPATHAKIS, Andrew
PAC Treasurer
550 U.S. Hwy. 202/206
Suite 310
Bedminster, NJ 07921

Celara Genomics

See listing on page 43 under Applera Corp.

CellStar Corp.

A global provider of wireless communications products.

www.cellstar.com
Annual Revenues: $1.793 billion

Chief Exec. Officer
KAISER, Robert A.
Tel: (972) 466 - 5000
TF: (800) 723 - 9040

Main Headquarters
Mailing: 1730 Briercroft Ct.
Carrollton, TX 75006
Tel: (972) 466 - 5000
TF: (800) 723 - 9040

Public Affairs and Related Activities Personnel

At Headquarters

GUNN, Sherrian
Director, Investor Relations and Corporate Communications
sgunn@cellstar.com
Tel: (972) 466 - 5031
Fax: (972) 466 - 0288
TF: (800) 723 - 9040

Cemex USA

A manufacturer of cement, concrete and producer of aggregates and minerals. A subsidiary of Cemex S.A. de C.V. of Mexico.

www.cemexusa.com

President and Chief Exec. Officer
PEREZ, Gilberto
Tel: (713) 650 - 6200
Fax: (713) 653 - 6815

Main Headquarters
Mailing: 840 Gessner
Suite 1400
Houston, TX 77024
Tel: (713) 650 - 6200
Fax: (713) 653 - 6815

Political Action Committees

Cemex Inc. Employees Political Action Committee
Contact: Claire Dai-McGaughy
840 Gessner
Suite 1400
Houston, TX 77024
Tel: (713) 650 - 6200
Fax: (713) 653 - 6815

Contributions to Candidates: $4,500 (01/05 - 09/05)
Republicans: $4,500.

Principal Recipients

SENATE REPUBLICANS

Talent, James (MO)	$1,000

HOUSE REPUBLICANS

Hobson, David (OH)	$1,500
Miller, Gary (CA)	$1,000
Shuster, William (PA)	$1,000

Public Affairs and Related Activities Personnel

At Headquarters

DAI-MCGAUGHY, Claire
Treasurer, Cemex Inc. Employees Political Action Committee
Tel: (713) 650 - 6200
Fax: (713) 653 - 6815

MILLER, Andrew M.
Exec. V. President, Human Resources
Tel: (713) 650 - 6200
Fax: (713) 653 - 6815

SHAPIRO, Richard
Exec. V. President, Public Affairs and Marketing
Tel: (713) 650 - 6200
Fax: (713) 653 - 6815

Cendant Car Rental Group

See listing on page 108 under Cendant Corp.

Cendant Corp.

A business and consumer services company, operating in four main areas: travel, real estate, direct marketing, and other business and consumer services. Acquired the management and franchise business of Wyndham International (now Wyndham Worldwide) in October of 2005.

www.cendant.com
Annual Revenues: $8.882 billion

Chairman, President and Chief Exec. Officer Tel: (212) 413 - 1800
SILVERMAN, Henry R.
henry.silverman@cendant.com

Main Headquarters
Mailing: Nine W. 57th St. Tel: (973) 428 - 9700
37th Floor
New York, NY 10019

Washington Office
Mailing: 101 Constitution Ave. NW Tel: (202) 742 - 4270
Suite 800 Fax: (202) 742 - 4271
Washington, DC 20001

Political Action Committees

Cendant Corp. Political Action Committee
Contact: Samuel H. Wright
101 Constitution Ave. NW Tel: (202) 742 - 4270
Suite 800 Fax: (202) 742 - 4271
Washington, DC 20001

Contributions to Candidates: $47,500 (01/05 - 09/05)
Democrats: $13,500; Republicans: $34,000.

Principal Recipients

SENATE DEMOCRATS		HOUSE DEMOCRATS	
Lieberman, Joe (CT)	$1,000	Ackerman, Gary (NY)	$2,500
Nelson, Bill (FL)	$1,000		

SENATE REPUBLICANS		HOUSE REPUBLICANS	
Santorum, Richard (PA)	$2,500	Hastert, Dennis J. (IL)	$5,000
Kyl, Jon L (AZ)	$2,000	Garrett, E Scott (NJ)	$2,000
Hagel, Charles T (NE)	$1,500	Lobiondo, Frank (NJ)	$2,000
Chafee, Lincoln (RI)	$1,000	Shaw, Clay (FL)	$2,000
Talent, James (MO)	$1,000	Shays, Christopher (CT)	$2,000
Vitter, David (LA)	$1,000		

Corporate Foundations and Giving Programs

Cendant Corporate Giving Program
Nine W. 57th St. Tel: (973) 428 - 9700
37th Floor
New York, NY 10019

Annual Grant Total: none reported
Recent Recipients: Inner City Games

Public Affairs and Related Activities Personnel

At Headquarters

BLOOM, Elliot Tel: (973) 496 - 8414
Senior V. President, Corporate Communications
elliot.bloom@cendant.com

DIAMOND, Henry A. Tel: (212) 413 - 1920
V. President, Investor Relations

LEVENSON, Sam Tel: (212) 413 - 1834
Senior V. President, Investor Relations
sam.levenson@cendant.com

At Washington Office

DIMASI, Steven Tel: (202) 742 - 4270
Senior Director, Government Relations Fax: (202) 742 - 4271
Registered Federal Lobbyist.

HUNTER-TURNER, Kimberly Tel: (202) 742 - 4270
V. President, Government Relations Fax: (202) 742 - 4271
Registered Federal Lobbyist.

LIN, Kenneth Tel: (202) 742 - 4270
Policy and Information Analysis Fax: (202) 742 - 4271

WRIGHT, Samuel H. Tel: (202) 742 - 4270
Senior V. President, Government Relations Fax: (202) 742 - 4271
samuel.wright@cendant.com
Registered Federal Lobbyist.

At Other Offices

BARROWS, John Tel: (973) 496 - 7865
V. President, Corporate Communications and Public Affairs Fax: (973) 496 - 3585
(Cendant Car Rental Group)
Six Sylvan Way
Parsippany, NJ 07054
john.barrows@cendant.com

CONLEY, Terence P. Tel: (973) 428 - 9700
Exec. V. President, Human Resources and Corporate Services
One Campus Dr.
Parsippany, NJ 07054

MCCLAIN, John Tel: (973) 428 - 9700
Treasurer, Cendant Corp. PAC
Six Sylvan Way
Parsippany, NJ 07054

PANUS, Mark Tel: (973) 496 - 7215
V. President, Communications and Public Affairs
One Campus Dr.
Parsippany, NJ 07054
mark.panus@cendant.com

Cenex Harvest States Cooperatives

See listing on page 116 under CHS Inc.

CenterPoint Energy

A member of the Public Affairs Council. An electric and natural gas energy delivery company, operations including electric transmission and distribution, natural gas distribution and sales, and pipeline and gathering operations. Formerly known as the regulated operations of Reliant Energy. The unregulated operations of Reliant Energy were spun off to form a separate company called Reliant Resources (see separate listing).

www.centerpointenergy.com

Chairman of the Board Tel: (713) 207 - 1111
CARROLL, Milton

President and Chief Exec. Officer Tel: (713) 207 - 1111
MCCLANAHAN, David M.

Main Headquarters
Mailing: 1111 Louisiana St. Tel: (713) 207 - 1111
Houston, TX 77002 Fax: (713) 207 - 3169

Political Action Committees

CenterPoint Energy, Inc. Political Action Committee
Contact: Dan Cromack
P.O. Box 4567
Houston, TX 77210

Contributions to Candidates: $18,250 (01/05 - 09/05)
Democrats: $5,000; Republicans: $13,250.

Principal Recipients

SENATE DEMOCRATS		HOUSE DEMOCRATS	
Bingaman, Jeff (NM)	$1,000	Green, Gene (TX)	$2,000
Conrad, Kent (ND)	$1,000	Cuellar, Henry (TX)	$1,000

SENATE REPUBLICANS		HOUSE REPUBLICANS	
Cornyn, John (TX)	$1,000	Barton, Joe L (TX)	$2,000
Inhofe, James M (OK)	$1,000	Bonilla, Henry (TX)	$1,000
		Brady, Kevin Patrick (TX)	$1,000
		Carter, John (TX)	$1,000
		Culberson, John (TX)	$1,000
		Gohmert, Louis (TX)	$1,000
		Johnson, Samuel (TX)	$1,000
		McCaul, Michael (TX)	$1,000
		Smith, Lamar (TX)	$1,000
		Terry, Lee (NE)	$1,000

Public Affairs and Related Activities Personnel

At Headquarters

JOHNSON, Preston Tel: (713) 207 - 1111
Senior V. President, Human Resources and Shared Services

LOWE, Leticia Tel: (713) 207 - 7702
Manager, Media Relations

OWENS, Sharon Tel: (713) 207 - 1111
V. President, Community Relations

PAULSEN, Marianne Tel: (713) 207 - 6500
Investor Relations Contact

ROZZELL, Scott Tel: (713) 207 - 1111
Exec. V. President and General Counsel
Responsibilities include legislative and regulatory affairs and corporate communications.

WHITLOCK, Gary Tel: (713) 207 - 1111
Exec. V. President and Chief Financial Officer
Responsibilities include investor relations.

CenterPoint Energy

** continued from previous page*

At Other Offices

BRIDGE, Mr. Tracy B.
Director, Government and Public Relations
(CenterPoint Energy Minnegasco)
800 LaSalle Ave.
Minneapolis, MN 55402-2006
Tel: (612) 372 - 4664
Fax: (612) 321 - 5137

CROMACK, Dan
PAC Treasurer
P.O. Box 4567
Houston, TX 77210

HARGEST, Connie
Senior Specialist, Local Government Relations
(CenterPoint Energy Minnegasco)
800 LaSalle Ave.
Minneapolis, MN 55402-2006
Tel: (612) 372 - 4664
Fax: (612) 321 - 5137

HENDRICKSON, Arnold
Senior Specialist, Local Government Relations
(CenterPoint Energy Minnegasco)
800 LaSalle Ave.
Minneapolis, MN 55402-2006
Tel: (612) 372 - 4664
Fax: (612) 321 - 5137

LUND, Rolf
Manager, Public Relations
(CenterPoint Energy Minnegasco)
800 LaSalle Ave.
Minneapolis, MN 55402-2006
Tel: (612) 372 - 4664
Fax: (612) 321 - 5137

PEDERSON, Patty
Associate Director, Public Relations
(CenterPoint Energy Minnegasco)
800 LaSalle Ave.
Minneapolis, MN 55402-2006
Tel: (612) 372 - 4664
Fax: (612) 321 - 5137

SWINTEK, Albert
Manager, Local Government Relations
(CenterPoint Energy Minnegasco)
800 LaSalle Ave.
Minneapolis, MN 55402-2006
Tel: (612) 372 - 4664
Fax: (612) 321 - 5137

TURBES, Susan M.
Associate Director, State Government Relations
(CenterPoint Energy Minnegasco)
800 LaSalle Ave.
Mailstop: FL 14
Minneapolis, MN 55402-2006
Tel: (612) 321 - 4850
Fax: (612) 321 - 5137

CenterPoint Energy Minnegasco

See listing on page 108 under CenterPoint Energy.

Centex Corporation

A home building, financial services, and construction company.

www.centex.com

Annual Revenues: $12.859 billion

Chairman and Chief Exec. Officer
ELLER, Timothy
Tel: (214) 981 - 5000
Fax: (214) 981 - 6859

Main Headquarters
Mailing: P.O. Box 199000
Dallas, TX 75219-9000
Tel: (214) 981 - 5000
Fax: (214) 981 - 6859
Street: 2728 N. Harwood
Dallas, TX 75201-1516

Political Action Committees

CentexPac
Contact: Kathleen Weiss
P.O. Box 199000
Dallas, TX 75219-9000
Tel: (214) 981 - 5000
Fax: (214) 981 - 6859

Contributions to Candidates: $1,000 (01/05 - 09/05)
Republicans: $1,000.

Principal Recipients

SENATE REPUBLICANS	HOUSE REPUBLICANS	
	Ney, Robert W (OH)	$1,000

Corporate Foundations and Giving Programs

Centex Corporate Contributions Program
Contact: Joan Saynor
P.O. Box 199000
Dallas, TX 75219-9000
Tel: (214) 981 - 6636
Fax: (214) 981 - 6859

Annual Grant Total: none reported

Geographic Preference: Dallas, TX

Recent Recipients: American Heart Ass'n; Boys and Girls Club; Goodwill Industries; Habitat for Humanity; Junior League; Nature Conservancy; United Way

Public Affairs and Related Activities Personnel

At Headquarters

DEVROY, Neil J.
V. President, Corporate Communications and Public Affairs
ndevroy@centex.com
Tel: (214) 981 - 6154
Fax: (214) 981 - 6859

GOODMAN, Gayle A.
Public Relations Manager
ggoodman@centex.com
Tel: (214) 981 - 6034
Fax: (214) 981 - 6859

MOYER, Matthew G.
V. President, Investor Relations
Tel: (214) 981 - 5000
Fax: (214) 981 - 6859

NESSER, Anita
PAC Treasurer
Tel: (214) 981 - 5000
Fax: (214) 981 - 6859

SAYNOR, Joan
Manager, Community Relations
jsaynor@centex.com
Tel: (214) 981 - 6636
Fax: (214) 981 - 6859

WEISS, Kathleen
Director, Government and Public Affairs
Tel: (214) 981 - 5000
Fax: (214) 981 - 6859

Centocor, Inc.

A wholly-owned subsidiary of Johnson & Johnson (see separate listing).

www.centocor.com

Annual Revenues: $1.1 billion

Main Headquarters
Mailing: 800/850 Ridgeview Dr.
Horsham, PA 19044
Tel: (610) 651 - 6000
Fax: (610) 651 - 6100

Public Affairs and Related Activities Personnel

At Headquarters

CUNNINGHAM, Larry
V. President, Human Resources
Tel: (610) 651 - 6000
Fax: (610) 651 - 6100

JONES, Stella
V. President, Regulatory Affairs
Tel: (610) 651 - 6000
Fax: (610) 651 - 6100

PARKS, Michael
Media and Public Relations Contact
Tel: (215) 983 - 8000
Fax: (610) 651 - 6100

Central Louisiana Electric Co. Inc.

See listing on page 124 under Cleco Corp.

Central Maine Power Co. (CMP)

See listing on page 181 under Energy East Corp.

Central Soya Company, Inc.

See listing on page 93 under Bunge Ltd.

Central States Coca-Cola Bottling Co.

See listing on page 128 under Coca-Cola Enterprises Inc.

Central Vermont Public Service Corp.

An electric utility.

www.cvps.com

Annual Revenues: $302.5 million

Chairman of the Board
BERTRAND, Frederic H.
Tel: (802) 773 - 2711
Fax: (802) 747 - 2199
TF: (800) 649 - 2877

President and Chief Exec. Officer
YOUNG, Robert
Tel: (802) 773 - 2711
Fax: (802) 747 - 2199
TF: (800) 649 - 2877

Main Headquarters
Mailing: 77 Grove St.
Rutland, VT 05701
Tel: (802) 773 - 2711
Fax: (802) 747 - 2199
TF: (800) 649 - 2877

Corporate Foundations and Giving Programs

Central Vermont Public Service Community Giving Program
77 Grove St.
Rutland, VT 05701
Tel: (802) 773 - 2711
Fax: (802) 747 - 2199
TF: (800) 649 - 2877

Annual Grant Total: none reported

The company suspended its giving program in July 2005 until its financial circumstances improve.

Public Affairs and Related Activities Personnel

At Headquarters

COSTELLO, Steve
Director, Public Affairs
scostel@cvps.com
Tel: (802) 747 - 5427
Fax: (802) 747 - 2199
TF: (800) 649 - 2877

DEEHAN, William J.
V. President, Power Planning and Regulatory Affairs
Tel: (800) 649 - 2877
Fax: (802) 747 - 2199
TF: (800) 649 - 2877

Central Vermont Public Service Corp.

** continued from previous page*

GIBSON, Jean H.
Senior V. President, Chief Financial Officer and Treasurer
jgibson@cvps.com
Responsibilities include investor relations.
Tel: (802) 747 - 5435
Fax: (802) 747 - 2199
TF: (800) 649 - 2877

ROCHELEAU, Dale A.
Senior V. President, Legal and Public Affairs; and Corporate Secretary
Tel: (802) 773 - 2711
Fax: (802) 747 - 2199
TF: (800) 649 - 2877

At Other Offices

JOHNSON, Kerrick
Director, Governmental Affairs
P.O. Box 39
Montpelier, VT 05601-0039
Tel: (802) 229 - 9448
Fax: (802) 229 - 9541

Century Aluminum Co.

www.centuryaluminum.com
Annual Revenues: $1.06 billion

Chairman and Chief Exec. Officer
DAVIS, Craig A.
Tel: (831) 642 - 9300
Fax: (831) 642 - 9399
TF: (888) 642 - 9300

Main Headquarters
Mailing: 2511 Garden Rd.
Monterey, CA 93940-5330
Tel: (831) 642 - 9300
Fax: (831) 642 - 9399
TF: (888) 642 - 9300

Public Affairs and Related Activities Personnel

At Headquarters

DILDINE, Steven M.
Director, Corporate Communications
mdildine@centuryca.com
Responsibilities include investor relations.
Tel: (831) 642 - 9364
Fax: (831) 642 - 9328
TF: (888) 642 - 9300

CenturyTel, Inc.

A provider of communications services, primarily to rural and small to mid-size cities in 26 states.
www.centurytel.com
Annual Revenues: $2.41 billion

Chairman and Chief Exec. Officer
POST, Glen F., III
Tel: (318) 388 - 9000
Fax: (318) 340 - 5520

Main Headquarters
Mailing: P.O. Box 4065
Monroe, LA 71211-4065
Street: 100 CenturyTel Dr.
Monroe, LA 71203
Tel: (318) 388 - 9000
Fax: (318) 340 - 5520

Political Action Committees

CenturyTel Fed PAC
Contact: John Jones
P.O. Box 4065
Monroe, LA 71211-4065
Tel: (318) 362 - 1583
Fax: (318) 388 - 9602

Contributions to Candidates: $11,700 (01/05 - 09/05)
Democrats: $7,750; Republicans: $3,950.

Principal Recipients

SENATE DEMOCRATS
Kennedy, John Neely (LA) $1,000

HOUSE DEMOCRATS
Baldwin, Tammy (WI) $2,750
Ross, Michael Avery (AR) $2,000
Berry, Marion (AR) $1,000
Gordon, Barton (TN) $1,000

SENATE REPUBLICANS

HOUSE REPUBLICANS
Gutknecht, Gil (MN) $1,200
Jindal, Bobby (LA) $1,000
Pickering, Chip (MS) $1,000

Public Affairs and Related Activities Personnel

At Headquarters

CAMERON, Patricia M.
V. President, Corporate Communications
patricia.cameron@centurytel.com
Tel: (318) 388 - 9674
Fax: (318) 340 - 5520

DAVIS, Tony
V. President, Investor Relations
tony.davis@centurytel.com
Fax: (318) 388 - 9064
TF: (800) 833 - 1188

HUGHES, Ivan
V. President, Human Resources
ivan.hughes@centurytel.com
Tel: (318) 388 - 9000
Fax: (318) 388 - 9799

JONES, John
V. President, Federal Government Relations
john.jones@centurytel.com
Tel: (318) 362 - 1583
Fax: (318) 388 - 9602

Cephalon, Inc.

A member of the Public Affairs Council. A biopharmaceutical company.
www.cephalon.com
Annual Revenues: $506.9 million

Chairman and Chief Exec. Officer
BALDINO, Frank, Jr., Ph.D.
Tel: (610) 344 - 0200
Fax: (610) 344 - 6590

Main Headquarters
Mailing: 41 Moores Rd.
Frazer, PA 19355
Tel: (610) 344 - 0200
Fax: (610) 344 - 6590

Washington Office
Mailing: 1101 Pennsylvania Ave. NW
Washington, DC 20004
Tel:

Political Action Committees

Cephalon, Inc. Employees PAC
Contact: Robert W. Grupp
41 Moores Rd.
Frazer, PA 19355
Tel: (610) 738 - 6402
Fax: (610) 344 - 0981

Contributions to Candidates: $8,500 (01/05 - 09/05)
Democrats: $1,000; Republicans: $7,500.

Principal Recipients

SENATE DEMOCRATS

HOUSE DEMOCRATS
Matheson, James (UT) $1,000

SENATE REPUBLICANS
Hatch, Orrin (UT) $2,500
Lott, Trent (MS) $1,000

HOUSE REPUBLICANS
Murphy, Tim (PA) $2,000
Cannon, Christopher (UT) $1,000
Nussle, Jim (IA) $1,000

Public Affairs and Related Activities Personnel

At Headquarters

BECKHARDT, Stacey
Senior Manager, Public Relations
sbeckhar@cephalon.com
Tel: (610) 738 - 6198
Fax: (610) 344 - 0981

BENDER, Jeannine M.
Director, Government Relations
jbender@cephalon.com
Tel: (610) 344 - 6527
Fax: (610) 344 - 6590

GRUPP, Robert W.
V. President, Public Affairs; PAC Treasurer
rgrupp@cephalon.com
Tel: (610) 738 - 6402
Fax: (610) 344 - 0981

MERRITT, Robert S. "Chip"
Senior Director, Investor Relations
cmerritt@cephalon.com
Tel: (610) 738 - 6376
Fax: (610) 344 - 0981

WILLIAMS, Sheryl
Senior Director, Public Relations
swilliam@cephalon.com
Tel: (610) 738 - 6493
Fax: (610) 344 - 0981

WRIGHT, Yvonne Klemets
Manager, Corporate Communications
ywright@cephalon.com
Tel: (610) 738 - 6340
Fax: (610) 344 - 0981

Ceres Group, Inc.

Provides insurance services through its subsidiaries.
www.ceresgp.com
Annual Revenues: $534.2 million

Chairman of the Board
RUH, William J.
Tel: (440) 572 - 2400
Fax: (440) 878 - 2959
TF: (800) 321 - 3997

President and Chief Exec. Officer
KILIAN, Thomas J.
Tel: (440) 572 - 2400
Fax: (440) 878 - 2959
TF: (800) 321 - 3997

Main Headquarters
Mailing: 17800 Royalton Rd.
Cleveland, OH 44136-5149
Tel: (440) 572 - 2400
Fax: (440) 878 - 2959
TF: (800) 321 - 3997

Public Affairs and Related Activities Personnel

At Headquarters

BENTKOWSKI, Gayle V.
Senior V. President, Corporate Communications
gmvixler@ceresgp.com
Responsibilities include investor relations.
Tel: (440) 572 - 8848
Fax: (440) 878 - 2959
TF: (800) 643 - 2474

PARENTE, Joseph A.
V. President and Director, Consumer Relations
Tel: (440) 572 - 2400
Fax: (440) 878 - 2959
TF: (800) 321 - 3997

Ceridian Corp.

An information services company.
www.ceridian.com
Annual Revenues: $1.3 billion

Chairman, President and Chief Exec. Officer
TURNER, Ronald L. — Tel: (952) 853 - 8100 / Fax: (952) 853 - 7272

Main Headquarters
Mailing: 3311 E. Old Shakopee Rd., Minneapolis, MN 55425-1640 — Tel: (952) 853 - 8100 / Fax: (952) 853 - 7272

Washington Office
Contact: James J. O'Connell
Mailing: 1300 I St. NW, Suite 420 East, Washington, DC 20005 — Tel: (202) 789 - 6525 / Fax: (202) 789 - 6593

Political Action Committees

Ceridian Corp. Political Action Committee (Ceridian PAC)
Contact: Anne G. Kominek
1300 I St. NW
Suite 420 East
Washington, DC 20005
Tel: (202) 789 - 6525
Fax: (202) 789 - 6593

Contributions to Candidates: $9,500 (01/05 - 09/05)
Republicans: $9,500.

Principal Recipients

SENATE REPUBLICANS		HOUSE REPUBLICANS	
Ensign, John Eric (NV)	$2,000	Hunter, Duncan (CA)	$2,000
DeMint, James (SC)	$1,000	Cantor, Eric (VA)	$1,000
Santorum, Richard (PA)	$1,000	Johnson, Nancy (CT)	$1,000
		Ramstad, Jim (MN)	$1,000
		Kline, John P (MN)	$500

Corporate Foundations and Giving Programs

Ceridian Corp. Contributions Program
Contact: Kathy Fahnhorst
3311 E. Old Shakopee Rd.
Minneapolis, MN 55425-1640
Tel: (952) 853 - 3457
Fax: (952) 853 - 5082

Annual Grant Total: none reported
Recent Recipients: Children's Defense Fund

Public Affairs and Related Activities Personnel

At Headquarters

FAHNHORST, Kathy
Manager, Employee/Community Affairs
kathleen.p.fahnhorst@ceridian.com
Tel: (952) 853 - 3457 / Fax: (952) 853 - 5082

HUGHES, Shirley
Senior V. President, Human Resources
Tel: (952) 853 - 3301 / Fax: (952) 853 - 7272

MANSON, Craig G.
V. President, Investor Relations
Tel: (952) 853 - 6022 / Fax: (952) 853 - 7272

At Washington Office

DEMBECK, Allison L.
Manager, Government Relations
Registered Federal Lobbyist.
Tel: (202) 789 - 6524 / Fax: (202) 789 - 6593

KOMINEK, Anne G.
PAC Contact
Tel: (202) 789 - 6525 / Fax: (202) 789 - 6593

O'CONNELL, James J.
V. President, Government Relations and HR Policy
james.j.oconnell@ceridian.com
Registered Federal Lobbyist.
Tel: (202) 789 - 6525 / Fax: (202) 789 - 6593

CertainTeed Corp.

See listing on page 419 under Saint-Gobain Corp.

Cessna Aircraft Co.

A manufacturer of general aviation aircraft. A subsidiary of Textron, Inc. (see separate listing).
www.cessna.com

President, Chief Exec. Officer and Chairman of the Board
PELTON, Jack J. — Tel: (316) 517 - 6000 / Fax: (316) 517 - 6640

Main Headquarters
Mailing: P.O. Box 7706, Wichita, KS 67277-7706 — Tel: (316) 517 - 6000 / Fax: (316) 517 - 6640
Street: One Cessna Blvd., Wichita, KS 67215-8716

Corporate Foundations and Giving Programs

Cessna Foundation, Inc.
P.O. Box 7706
Wichita, KS 67277-7706
Tel: (316) 517 - 6000
Fax: (316) 517 - 6640

Annual Grant Total: none reported
All requests must be submitted in writing. Grants are not awarded to individuals.
Geographic Preference: Area(s) in which the company operates
Primary Interests: Civic and Cultural Activities; Education; Health; Religion

Public Affairs and Related Activities Personnel

At Headquarters

FULLERTON, Rhonda
Manager, Community and Corporate Affairs
Tel: (316) 517 - 1602 / Fax: (316) 517 - 7812

MEYER, Russell W., Jr.
Chairman Emeritus
Tel: (316) 517 - 6000 / Fax: (316) 517 - 6640

STANGARONE, Bob
V. President, Communications
Tel: (316) 517 - 6131 / Fax: (316) 517 - 6640

WALTERS, Jim
Senior V. President, Human Resources
Tel: (316) 517 - 1287 / Fax: (316) 517 - 6640

C F Industries, Inc.

A member of the Public Affairs Council. A manufacturer of chemical fertilizers.
www.cfindustries.com
Annual Revenues: $1.087 billion

President and Chief Exec. Officer
WILSON, Stephen R. — Tel: (847) 438 - 9500 / Fax: (847) 438 - 0211

Main Headquarters
Mailing: One Salem Lake Dr., Long Grove, IL 60047 — Tel: (847) 438 - 9500 / Fax: (847) 438 - 0211

Washington Office
Contact: Rosemary L. O'Brien
Mailing: 1401 I St., N.W., Suite 340, Washington, DC 20005-2225 — Tel: (202) 371 - 9279 / Fax: (202) 371 - 9169

Political Action Committees

C F Industries, Inc. PAC
Contact: Dennis W. Baker
One Salem Lake Dr.
Long Grove, IL 60047
Tel: (847) 438 - 9500
Fax: (847) 438 - 0211

Contributions to Candidates: $6,200 (01/05 - 09/05)
Democrats: $1,000; Republicans: $4,200; Other: $1,000.

Principal Recipients

SENATE DEMOCRATS		HOUSE DEMOCRATS	
		Pomeroy, Earl (ND)	$1,000
		HOUSE OTHER	
		Peterson, Collin (MN)	$1,000
SENATE REPUBLICANS		**HOUSE REPUBLICANS**	
Vitter, David (LA)	$2,000	Goodlatte, Robert (VA)	$1,000
Harris, Katherine (FL)	$200	Putnam, Adam (FL)	$1,000

Public Affairs and Related Activities Personnel

At Headquarters

BAKER, Dennis W.
Treasurer and Contact, C F Industries, Inc. PAC
dbaker@cfindustries.com
Tel: (847) 438 - 9500 / Fax: (847) 438 - 0211

EPPEL, W.G.
V. President, Human Resources
weppel@cfindustries.com
Tel: (847) 438 - 9500 Ext: 3232 / Fax: (847) 438 - 0211

At Washington Office

O'BRIEN, Rosemary L.
V. President, Public Affairs
Registered Federal Lobbyist.
Tel: (202) 371 - 9279 / Fax: (202) 371 - 9169

PERALTA, Jesus
Policy Manager
Tel: (202) 371 - 9279 / Fax: (202) 371 - 9169

At Other Offices

BUZZANCA, Frank N.
V. President, Environmental, Health, Safety and Engineering
P.O. Box 1849
Bartow, FL 33831
Tel: (941) 533 - 0926

MANN, Larry E.
Manager, Industrial Relations
P.O. Box 468
Donaldsonville, LA 70346
Tel: (504) 473 - 8291 / Fax: (504) 473 - 1864

CH Energy Group, Inc.

A family of energy supply and service businesses.
www.chenergygroup.com
Annual Revenues: $791.5 million

CH Energy Group, Inc.

** continued from previous page*

Chairman, President and Chief Exec. Officer
LANT, Steven V.
Tel: (845) 452 - 2000
Fax: (845) 486 - 5465
TF: (800) 527 - 2714

Main Headquarters
Mailing: 284 South Ave.
Poughkeepsie, NY 12601-4879
Tel: (845) 452 - 2000
Fax: (845) 486 - 5465
TF: (800) 527 - 2714

Corporate Foundations and Giving Programs

Central Hudson Gas & Electric Corp. Contributions Program
Contact: Denise Doring VanBuren
284 South Ave.
Poughkeepsie, NY 12601-4879
Tel: (845) 452 - 2000
Fax: (845) 471 - 8323
TF: (800) 527 - 2714

Annual Grant Total: $200,000 - $300,000
Geographic Preference: New York; Area(s) in which the company operates
Primary Interests: Community Affairs; Education; Health; Human Welfare

Public Affairs and Related Activities Personnel

At Headquarters

CLOCK, Jeffrey A.
Director, Environmental Affairs
Tel: (845) 452 - 5534
Fax: (845) 486 - 5465
TF: (800) 527 - 2714

RENNER, Stacey A.
Assistant Treasurer, Investor Relations
srenner@cenhud.com
Tel: (845) 486 - 5730
Fax: (845) 486 - 5465
TF: (800) 527 - 2714

ROYCE, Susan M.
Director, Community Outreach
Tel: (845) 452 - 2000
Fax: (845) 486 - 5465
TF: (800) 527 - 2714

VANBUREN, Denise Doring
V. President, Corporate Communications and Community Relations
Tel: (845) 452 - 2000
Fax: (845) 471 - 8323
TF: (800) 527 - 2714
Responsibilities include corporate philanthropy.

CH2M Hill Companies, Inc.

A member of the Public Affairs Council. An employee-owned firm providing comprehensive services in engineering, planning, economics, and environmental sciences to both the public and private sectors. Specializes in water, wastewater, transportation, energy, the environment, telecommunications, information technology, and construction.
www.ch2mhill.com
Annual Revenues: $1.94 billion

Chairman, President and Chief Exec. Officer
PETERSON, Ralph R.
Tel: (303) 771 - 0900
Fax: (720) 286 - 9250

Main Headquarters
Mailing: 9191 S. Jamaica St.
Englewood, CO 80112
Tel: (303) 771 - 0900
Fax: (720) 286 - 9250

Washington Office
Mailing: 555 11th St. NW
Suite 525
Washington, DC 20004
Tel: (202) 393 - 2426
Fax: (202) 783 - 8410

Political Action Committees

CH2M Hill Companies, Ltd. PAC
Contact: L. L. Nelson
9191 S. Jamaica St.
Englewood, CO 80112
Tel: (303) 771 - 0900
Fax: (720) 286 - 9250

Contributions to Candidates: $89,250 (01/05 - 09/05)
Democrats: $27,250; Republicans: $61,000; Other: $1,000.

Principal Recipients

SENATE DEMOCRATS		HOUSE DEMOCRATS	
Carper, Thomas R (DE)	$1,000	Defazio, Peter A (OR)	$2,000
Conrad, Kent (ND)	$1,000		
Lieberman, Joe (CT)	$1,000		
Nelson, Benjamin (NE)	$1,000		
Nelson, Bill (FL)	$1,000		

SENATE REPUBLICANS		HOUSE REPUBLICANS	
Burns, Conrad (MT)	$1,500	LaHood, Ray (IL)	$3,000
Snowe, Olympia (ME)	$1,500	Duncan, John (TN)	$2,000
Allen, George (VA)	$1,000	Feeney, Tom (FL)	$2,000
Chafee, Lincoln (RI)	$1,000	Hobson, David (OH)	$2,000
Crapo, Michael D (ID)	$1,000	Ros-Lehtinen, Ileana (FL)	$2,000
DeMint, James (SC)	$1,000	Taylor, Charles H (NC)	$2,000
Dewine, Richard (OH)	$1,000	Thomas, William M (CA)	$2,000
Kyl, Jon L (AZ)	$1,000	Turner, Mike (OH)	$2,000
Thomas, Craig (WY)	$1,000	Wamp, Zach (TN)	$2,000
		Young, Don E (AK)	$2,000

Corporate Foundations and Giving Programs

CH2M Hill Foundation/Corporate Contributions
Contact: L. L. Nelson
9191 S. Jamaica St.
Englewood, CO 80112
Tel: (303) 771 - 0900
Fax: (720) 286 - 9250

Annual Grant Total: none reported
Primary Interests: Education; Environment/Conservation; Math and Science

Public Affairs and Related Activities Personnel

At Headquarters

ARMSTRONG, Andre
Media Relations Contact
andre.armstrong@ch2m.com
Tel: (303) 286 - 2425
Fax: (720) 286 - 9250

KECK, Patty
Manager, Public Relations
patty.keck@ch2m.com
Tel: (720) 286 - 2596
Fax: (720) 286 - 9250

NELSON, L. L.
Treasurer, Foundation; PAC Treasurer
Tel: (303) 771 - 0900
Fax: (720) 286 - 9250

At Washington Office

BRANICK, Robert C.
Director, Federal Affairs
Tel: (202) 393 - 2426
Fax: (202) 783 - 8410

CORRIGAN, Richard L.
Senior V. President, Governmental Affairs
rcorriga@ch2m.com
Tel: (202) 393 - 2426
Fax: (202) 783 - 8410

STIFFLER-CLAUS, Vanessa
Federal Affairs Associate
Tel: (202) 393 - 2426
Fax: (202) 783 - 8410

Champion Enterprises, Inc.

Produces manufactured homes.
championhomes.net
Annual Revenues: $1.548 billion

Chairman of the Board
ISAKOW, Selwyn
Tel: (248) 340 - 9090
Fax: (248) 340 - 9345

President and Chief Exec. Officer
GRIFFITHS, William C.
Tel: (248) 340 - 9090
Fax: (248) 340 - 9345

Main Headquarters
Mailing: 2701 Cambridge Ct.
Suite 300
Auburn Hills, MI 48326
Tel: (248) 340 - 9090
Fax: (248) 340 - 9345

Public Affairs and Related Activities Personnel

At Headquarters

LETTIERI, Lisa D.
V. President, Investor Relations
llettieri@championhomes.net
Tel: (248) 340 - 7731
Fax: (248) 340 - 9345

NUGENT, Jeffrey L.
V. President, Human Resources
Tel: (248) 340 - 9090
Fax: (248) 340 - 9345

Charming Shoppes, Inc.

Operates a chain of ladies' apparel shops under the names Fashion Bug, Fashion Bug Plus, Catherines, Accessorize and Lane Bryant.
www.charmingshoppes.com
Annual Revenues: $1.993 billion

Chairman, President and Chief Exec. Officer
BERN, Dorrit J.
Tel: (215) 245 - 9100
Fax: (215) 638 - 6759

Main Headquarters
Mailing: 450 Winks Ln.
Bensalem, PA 19020
Tel: (215) 245 - 9100
Fax: (215) 638 - 6759

Public Affairs and Related Activities Personnel

At Headquarters

COOLICK, Gayle M.
Director, Investor Relations
Tel: (215) 638 - 6955
Fax: (215) 638 - 6759

DESABATO, Anthony A.
Exec. V. President, Corporate and Labor Relations
Tel: (215) 638 - 6636
Fax: (215) 638 - 6759

VARMA, Gale H.
Exec. V. President, Human Resources
Tel: (215) 245 - 9100
Fax: (215) 638 - 6759

Charter Communications, Inc.

A communications company.
www.chartercom.com
Annual Revenues: $476.3 million

Chairman of the Board
ALLEN, Paul G.
pallen@chartercom.com
Tel: (314) 965 - 0555
Fax: (314) 965 - 5761

Charter Communications, Inc.
** continued from previous page*

President and Chief Exec. Officer
SMIT, Neil
Tel: (314) 965 - 0555
Fax: (314) 965 - 9745

Main Headquarters
Mailing: 12405 Powerscourt Dr.
St. Louis, MO 63131
Tel: (314) 965 - 0555
Fax: (314) 965 - 9745

Public Affairs and Related Activities Personnel

At Headquarters

ANDERSEN, David C.
Senior V. President, Communications
dandersen@chartercom.com
Responsibilities include political action.
Tel: (314) 543 - 2213
Fax: (314) 965 - 8793

MOEHLE, Mary Jo
Senior Director, Investor Relations
mmoehle@chartercom.com
Tel: (314) 543 - 2397
Fax: (314) 965 - 0571

PHILPOTT, Joy
V. President, Government Affairs and Franchise Relations
jphilpott1@charter.com
Tel: (770) 754 - 5275

RAMSEY, Lynne F.
Senior V. President, Human Resources
lramsey@chartercom.com
Tel: (314) 543 - 5687
Fax: (314) 965 - 5761

Charter One Financial, Inc.
See listing on page 123 under Citizens Financial Group, Inc.

CheckFree Corp.
A member of the Public Affairs Council. A provider of financial electronic commerce services.
www.checkfreecorp.com
Annual Revenues: $606.5 million

Chairman and Chief Exec. Officer
KIGHT, Peter J.
Tel: (678) 375 - 3000
Fax: (678) 375 - 1477

Main Headquarters
Mailing: 4411 E. Jones Bridge Rd.
Norcross, GA 30092-1615
Tel: (678) 375 - 3000
Fax: (678) 375 - 1477

Political Action Committees

CheckFree Corp. PAC
Contact: Brenda C. Jones
4411 E. Jones Bridge Rd.
Norcross, GA 30092-1615
Tel: (678) 375 - 3430
Fax: (678) 375 - 2025

Contributions to Candidates: $16,000 (01/05 - 09/05)
Democrats: $2,000; Republicans: $14,000.

Principal Recipients

SENATE DEMOCRATS		HOUSE DEMOCRATS	
Carper, Thomas R (DE)	$1,000	Frank, Barney (MA)	$1,000
SENATE REPUBLICANS		**HOUSE REPUBLICANS**	
Chambliss, Saxby (GA)	$2,500	Tiberi, Patrick (OH)	$3,000
Ensign, John Eric (NV)	$1,500	Barton, Joe L (TX)	$2,000
Santorum, Richard (PA)	$1,000	Bachus, Spencer (AL)	$1,000
		Gingrey, Phillip (GA)	$1,000
		Ney, Robert W (OH)	$1,000
		Price, Thomas (GA)	$1,000

Public Affairs and Related Activities Personnel

At Headquarters

FONTAINE, David
Media Relations Director
Tel: (678) 375 - 1682
Fax: (678) 375 - 3304

GABLE, Deborah N.
Senior V. President, Human Resources
Tel: (678) 375 - 3000
Fax: (678) 375 - 1477

JONES, Brenda C.
Director, Government Affairs; and PAC Treasurer
Tel: (678) 375 - 3430
Fax: (678) 375 - 2025

WICKS, Judy DeRango
V. President, Media Strategy
Tel: (678) 375 - 3000
Fax: (678) 375 - 1477

Checkpoint Systems, Inc.
Manufactures products for retail.
www.checkpointsystems.com
Annual Revenues: $778.7 million

Chairman of the Board
ADERS, Robert O.
Tel: (856) 848 - 1800
Fax: (856) 848 - 0937
TF: (800) 257 - 5540

Chief Exec. Officer
OFF, George W.
Tel: (856) 848 - 1800
Fax: (856) 848 - 0937
TF: (800) 257 - 5540

Main Headquarters
Mailing: 101 Wolf Dr.
Thorofare, NJ 08086
Tel: (856) 848 - 1800
Fax: (856) 848 - 0937
TF: (800) 257 - 5540

Public Affairs and Related Activities Personnel

At Headquarters

BURNS, W. Craig
Chief Financial Officer, Exec. V. President and Treasurer
craig.burns@checkpt.com
Responsibilities include investor relations.
Tel: (856) 384 - 3174
Fax: (856) 848 - 2042
TF: (800) 257 - 5540

LAUDISIO, Glenda
Director, Corporate Communications
glenda.laudisio@checkpt.com
Tel: (856) 384 - 2411
Fax: (856) 384 - 1480
TF: (800) 257 - 5540

Cheesecake Factory Inc.
Operates casual dining restaurants.
www.thecheesecakefactory.com
Annual Revenues: $652 million

Chairman, President and Chief Exec. Officer
OVERTON, David
Tel: (818) 871 - 3000
Fax: (818) 871 - 3100

Main Headquarters
Mailing: 26950 Agoura Rd.
Calabasas Hills, CA 91301-5335
Tel: (818) 871 - 3000
Fax: (818) 871 - 3100

Corporate Foundations and Giving Programs

Cheesecake Factory Oscar and Evelyn Overton Charitable Foundation
Contact: David Overton
26950 Agoura Rd.
Calabasas Hills, CA 91301-5335
Tel: (818) 871 - 3000
Fax: (818) 871 - 3100

Assets: $21,523 (2001)
Annual Grant Total: $100,000 - $200,000
Primary Interests: Arts and Culture; Disaster Relief; Medicine and Health Care
Recent Recipients: Salvation Army

Public Affairs and Related Activities Personnel

At Headquarters

EYNON, Edward T.
Senior V. President, Human Resources
Tel: (818) 871 - 3000
Fax: (818) 871 - 3100

GORDON, Howard R.
Senior V. President, Public Relations and Marketing
Tel: (818) 871 - 3000
Fax: (818) 871 - 3100

VALLAIRE, Jane
Manager, Investor Relations
Responsibilities include media relations.
Tel: (818) 871 - 3000
Fax: (818) 871 - 3100

The Chemed Corporation
A diversified corporation with strategic positions in plumbing, drain cleaning, and appliance and air-conditioning repair and maintenance; and (in Iowa only) janitorial supply products and services. Subsidiaries include VITAS Healthcare Corp. (see separate listing).
www.chemed.com
Annual Revenues: $477.1 million

Chairman of the Board
HUTTON, Edward L.
Tel: (513) 762 - 6900
Fax: (513) 762 - 6919

President and Chief Exec. Officer
MCNAMARA, Kevin J.
Tel: (513) 762 - 6900
Fax: (513) 762 - 6919

Main Headquarters
Mailing: 2600 Chemed Center
255 E. Fifth St.
Cincinnati, OH 45202-4726
Tel: (513) 762 - 6900
Fax: (513) 762 - 6919
TF: (800) 438 - 7686

Corporate Foundations and Giving Programs

The Chemed Foundation
Contact: Sandra E. Laney
2600 Chemed Center
255 E. Fifth St.
Cincinnati, OH 45202-4726
Tel: (513) 762 - 6900
Fax: (513) 762 - 6919

Annual Grant Total: none reported
Recent local recipients include the Community Land Cooperative of Cincinnati and Cumberland College.
Primary Interests: Arts and Humanities; Education; Social Services

Public Affairs and Related Activities Personnel

At Headquarters

LANEY, Sandra E.
President, The Chemed Foundation
Tel: (513) 762 - 6900
Fax: (513) 762 - 6919

WARNER, Sherri L.
Director, Investor Relations
Responsibilities include media relations.
Tel: (513) 762 - 6900
Fax: (513) 762 - 6919
TF: (800) 438 - 7686

WILLIAMS, David
Exec. V. President, Chief Financial Officer and Spokesperson
Responsibilities include investor relations.
Tel: (513) 762 - 6901
Fax: (513) 762 - 6919
TF: (800) 438 - 7686

Chemtura

A member of the Public Affairs Council. A chemical and plastic additives manufacturer. Formed in 2005 by the merger of Great Lakes Chemical Corp. and Crompton Corp.
www.chemtura.com
Annual Revenues: $3.7 billion

Chairman, President and Chief Exec. Officer — Tel: (203) 573 - 2000
WOOD, Robert L. — Fax: (203) 573 - 3711

Main Headquarters
Mailing: 199 Benson Rd. — Tel: (203) 573 - 2000
Middlebury, VT 06749 — Fax: (203) 573 - 3711

Political Action Committees

Chemtura Corporate PAC
Contact: Steven E. Brokaw
199 Benson Rd. — Tel: (203) 573 - 2000
Middlebury, VT 06749 — Fax: (203) 573 - 3711

Contributions to Candidates: none reported (01/05 - 09/05)

Public Affairs and Related Activities Personnel

At Headquarters

BROKAW, Steven E. — Tel: (203) 573 - 2000
PAC Treasurer — Fax: (203) 573 - 3711

DUNNELL, Mary Ann — Tel: (203) 573 - 3034
Media Contact — Fax: (203) 573 - 3711

KUSER, William — Tel: (203) 573 - 2213
Investor Relations Contact — Fax: (203) 573 - 3711

Chesapeake Corp.

A specialty packaging company.
www.cskcorp.com
Annual Revenues: $822 million

Chairman and Chief Exec. Officer — Tel: (804) 697 - 1000
JOHNSON, Thomas H. — Fax: (804) 697 - 1199

Main Headquarters
Mailing: 1021 E. Cary St. — Tel: (804) 697 - 1000
Richmond, VA 23217 — Fax: (804) 697 - 1199

Corporate Foundations and Giving Programs

Chesapeake Corp. Foundation
Contact: J. P. Causey, Jr.
1021 E. Cary St. — Tel: (804) 697 - 1166
Richmond, VA 23217 — Fax: (804) 697 - 1199

Assets: $1,800,000 (2000)
Annual Grant Total: $300,000 - $400,000
Geographic Preference: Area(s) in which employees live and work; Area(s) in which the company operates; North Carolina; Virginia
Primary Interests: Higher Education; Social Services
Recent Recipients: University of Virginia; Virginia Foundation of Independent Colleges

Public Affairs and Related Activities Personnel

At Headquarters

CAUSEY, J. P., Jr. — Tel: (804) 697 - 1166
President, Chesapeake Corp. Foundation — Fax: (804) 697 - 1199

MOSTROM, Joel K. — Tel: (804) 697 - 1147
Senior V. President and Chief Financial Officer — Fax: (804) 697 - 1199
joel.mostrom@cskcorp.com
Responsibilities include investor relations.

VAGI, Joseph C. — Tel: (804) 697 - 1110
Manager, Corporate Communications — Fax: (804) 697 - 1197
joe.vaggi@cskcorp.com

WINTER, David — Tel: (804) 697 - 1000
Director, Human Resources — Fax: (804) 697 - 1199

Chevron Corp.

A member of the Public Affairs Council. Formerly ChevronTexaco Corp. A petroleum company formed by the merger of Chevron Corp. and Texaco Inc.
www.chevrontexaco.com
Annual Revenues: $120 billion

Chairman and Chief Exec. Officer — Tel: (925) 842 - 1000
O'REILLY, David J.

Main Headquarters
Mailing: 6001 Bollinger Canyon Rd. — Tel: (925) 842 - 1000
San Ramon, CA 94583
Street: 575 Market St.
San Francisco, CA 94105

Washington Office
Contact: Lisa B. Barry
Mailing: 1401 I St. NW — Tel: (202) 408 - 5800
Suite 1200 — Fax: (202) 408 - 5845
Washington, DC 20005-2225

Political Action Committees

Chevron Employees PAC
Contact: Ramiro G. Estrada
6001 Bollinger Canyon Rd. — Tel: (925) 842 - 1000
San Ramon, CA 94583

Contributions to Candidates: $96,000 (01/05 - 09/05)
Democrats: $28,000; Republicans: $68,000.

Principal Recipients

SENATE DEMOCRATS		HOUSE DEMOCRATS	
Feinstein, Dianne (CA)	$10,000	Cuellar, Henry (TX)	$3,000
Bingaman, Jeff (NM)	$2,000		
Conrad, Kent (ND)	$2,000		
SENATE REPUBLICANS		**HOUSE REPUBLICANS**	
Lott, Trent (MS)	$5,000	DeLay, Tom (TX)	$5,000
Ensign, John Eric (NV)	$4,000	Hastert, Dennis J. (IL)	$5,000
Thomas, Craig (WY)	$3,000	Barton, Joe L (TX)	$3,000
Allen, George (VA)	$2,000	Pombo, Richard (CA)	$3,000

Corporate Foundations and Giving Programs

ChevronTexaco Foundation
6001 Bollinger Canyon Rd. — Tel: (925) 842 - 1000
San Ramon, CA 94583

Annual Grant Total: none reported
The foundation is currently not accepting unsolicited applications for grants.
Primary Interests: Diversity; Education

Public Affairs and Related Activities Personnel

At Headquarters

ESTRADA, Ramiro G. — Tel: (925) 842 - 1000
Treasurer, Chevron PAC

PRESTON, Alan — Tel: (925) 842 - 1000
V. President, Human Resources

RICHARDS, Randy — Tel: (925) 842 - 3523
Manager, Investor Relations

YARRINGTON, Patricia E. — Tel: (925) 842 - 1000
V. President, Policy, Government and Public Affairs

ZYGOCKI, Rhonda I. — Tel: (925) 842 - 1000
V. President, Health, Environment and Safety

At Washington Office

BARRY, Lisa B. — Tel: (202) 408 - 5800
V. President and General Manager, Government Affairs — Fax: (202) 408 - 5845
Registered Federal Lobbyist.

BLANCHARD, Judith A. — Tel: (202) 408 - 5800
Manager, Federal Relations — Fax: (202) 408 - 5845
Registered Federal Lobbyist.

FAGER, Dan L. — Tel: (202) 408 - 5800
Manager, Federal Relations — Fax: (202) 408 - 5845
Registered Federal Lobbyist.

HAYDEN, Ludwig — Tel: (202) 408 - 5800
Manager, Federal Relations — Fax: (202) 408 - 5845
Registered Federal Lobbyist.

HOPKINS, Mark D. — Tel: (202) 408 - 5800
Manager, Federal Relations — Fax: (202) 408 - 5845
Registered Federal Lobbyist.

IRWIN, William T. — Tel: (202) 408 - 5800
Manager, International Relations — Fax: (202) 408 - 5845
Registered Federal Lobbyist.

SEDNEY, Diana — Tel: (202) 408 - 5800
Manager, International Relations — Fax: (202) 408 - 5845
Registered Federal Lobbyist.

WASHINGTON, Greg J. — Tel: (202) 408 - 5800
Manager, Federal Relations — Fax: (202) 408 - 5845
Registered Federal Lobbyist.

ChevronTexaco Corp.

See listing on page 114 under Chevron Corp.

Chicago Mercantile Exchange Inc.

A member of the Public Affairs Council. A wholly owned subsidiary of Chicago Mercantile Exchange Holdings Inc. The largest futures exchange in the U.S.
www.cme.com
Annual Revenues: $753 million

Chairman of the Board — Tel: (312) 930 - 1000
DUFFY, Terrence A.

Chief Exec. Officer — Tel: (312) 930 - 1000
DONOHUE, Craig S.

Main Headquarters
Mailing: 20 S. Wacker Dr. — Tel: (312) 930 - 1000
Chicago, IL 60606-7499

Chicago Mercantile Exchange Inc.

** continued from previous page*

Washington Office
Mailing: 701 Pennsylvania Ave. NW
Plaza Suit O1
Washington, DC 20004
Tel: (202) 638 - 3838
Fax: (202) 638 - 5799

Political Action Committees

Chicago Mercantile Exchange PAC (CME PAC)
Contact: Lanae Clarke
701 Pennsylvania Ave. NW
Plaza Suit O1
Washington, DC 20004
Tel: (202) 638 - 3838
Fax: (202) 638 - 5799

Contributions to Candidates: none reported (01/05 - 09/05)

Corporate Foundations and Giving Programs

CME Foundation
Contact: Kristin Wood
20 S. Wacker Dr.
Chicago, IL 60606-7499
Tel: (312) 930 - 4510
Fax: (312) 930 - 3439

Annual Grant Total: none reported
Primary Interests: Child Welfare; Education; Health and Human Services

Public Affairs and Related Activities Personnel

At Headquarters

LISKEY, Anita
Director, Corporate Communications
aliskey@cme.com
Tel: (312) 466 - 4613
Fax: (312) 930 - 3439

PROSPERI, David P.
Director, Public Relations
dprosper@cme.com
Tel: (312) 634 - 8770
Fax: (312) 930 - 3439

SCHOENBERG, Allan
Associate Director, Technology Communications
aschoenb@cme.com
Tel: (312) 930 - 8189
Fax: (312) 930 - 3439

WOOD, Kristin
Foundation Contact
kwood@cme.com
Tel: (312) 930 - 4510
Fax: (312) 930 - 3439

At Washington Office

CHAMBLISS, C. Saxby "Bo", Jr.
Associate Director, Government Relations
Tel: (202) 638 - 3838
Fax: (202) 638 - 5799

CLARKE, Lanae
Manager, Government Relations
Tel: (202) 638 - 3838
Fax: (202) 638 - 5799

Chicago Sun-Times

Daily and weekly newspaper company owned by Hollinger International.
www.suntimes.com

Chairman of the Board
PARIS, Gordon
Tel: (312) 321 - 3000

Chief Exec. Officer
CRUICKSHANK, John
Tel: (312) 321 - 3000

Main Headquarters
Mailing: 350 N. Orleans
Chicago, IL 60654
Tel: (312) 321 - 3000

Corporate Foundations and Giving Programs

Chicago Sun-Times Charity Trust
Contact: Patricia Dudek
350 N. Orleans
Chicago, IL 60654
Tel: (312) 321 - 3000

Assets: $2,175,0000
Annual Grant Total: $100,000 - $200,000
Guidelines are available.
Geographic Preference: Chicago, IL; Area in which the company is headquartered
Primary Interests: Arts and Culture; Literacy; Social Services; Youth Services
Recent Recipients: Big Brothers/Big Sisters; Junior Achievement

Public Affairs and Related Activities Personnel

At Headquarters

DUDEK, Patricia
Foundation President
pdudek@suntimes.com
Responsibilities include community affairs.
Tel: (312) 321 - 3000

Chicago Title and Trust Co.

See listing on page 193 under Fidelity Nat'l Financial, Inc.

The Children's Place Retail Stores, Inc.

The Children's Place Retail Stores, Inc. is a specialty retailer of value-priced apparel and accessories for children, newborn to age ten.
www.childrensplace.com

Chairman and Chief Exec. Officer
DABAH, Ezra
edabah@childrensplace.com
Tel: (201) 558 - 2400
Fax: (201) 558 - 2837
TF: (800) 527 - 5355

Main Headquarters
Mailing: 915 Secaucus Rd.
Secaucus, NJ 07094
Tel: (201) 558 - 2400
TF: (800) 527 - 5355

Public Affairs and Related Activities Personnel

At Headquarters

LABAR, Susan
Director, Investor Relations
Tel: (201) 453 - 6955
TF: (800) 527 - 5355

Chiquita Brands Internat'l, Inc.

An international marketer and distributor of fresh and processed food products.
www.chiquita.com
Annual Revenues: $2.242 billion

Chairman, President and Chief Exec. Officer
AGUIRRE, Fernando
Tel: (513) 784 - 8000
Fax: (513) 784 - 8030

Main Headquarters
Mailing: 250 E. Fifth St.
Cincinnati, OH 45202
Tel: (513) 784 - 8000
Fax: (513) 564 - 2920

Corporate Foundations and Giving Programs

Chiquita Brands Internat'l, Inc. Corporate Giving
250 E. Fifth St.
Cincinnati, OH 45202
Tel: (513) 784 - 8000
Fax: (513) 564 - 2920

Annual Grant Total: none reported
Maintains an employee matching gifts program for educational institutions.
Geographic Preference: Area(s) in which employees live and work
Primary Interests: Children's Health; Education; Environment/Conservation

Public Affairs and Related Activities Personnel

At Headquarters

MITCHELL, Michael
Director, Corporate Communications
mmitchell@chiquita.com
Tel: (513) 784 - 8959
Fax: (513) 784 - 8030

MORRIS, Barry
V. President, Human Resources
bmorris@chiquita.com
Tel: (513) 784 - 8000
Fax: (513) 784 - 8030

Chiron Corp.

PUBLIC AFFAIRS COUNCIL

A member of the Public Affairs Council. A biotechnology company specializing in biopharmaceuticals, blood testing, and vaccines. Involved in research and development of products for preventing and treating cancer, infectious diseases, and cardiovascular diseases.
www.chiron.com
Annual Revenues: $1.14 billion

Chairman, President and Chief Exec. Officer
PIEN, Howard
Tel: (510) 655 - 8730
Fax: (510) 655 - 9910

Main Headquarters
Mailing: 4560 Horton St.
Emeryville, CA 94608-2916
Tel: (510) 655 - 8730
Fax: (510) 655 - 9910

Washington Office
Contact: Marguerite D. Baxter
Mailing: 1300 I St. NW
Suite 1090
Washington, DC 20005
Tel: (202) 962 - 8640
Fax: (202) 289 - 6819

Corporate Foundations and Giving Programs

Chiron Corporate Contributions Program
Contact: Jay Grover
4560 Horton St.
Emeryville, CA 94608-2916
Tel: (510) 655 - 8730
Fax: (510) 655 - 9910

Annual Grant Total: none reported

Public Affairs and Related Activities Personnel

At Headquarters

FORREST, Martin
V. President, Corporate Communications and Investor Relations
Tel: (510) 655 - 8730
Fax: (510) 655 - 9910

GROVER, Jay
Director, Government and Community Relations
Responsibilities include corporate philanthropy.
Tel: (510) 655 - 8730
Fax: (510) 655 - 9910

HILL, Anne
V. President, Human Resources
Tel: (510) 655 - 8730
Fax: (510) 655 - 9910

At Washington Office

BAXTER, Marguerite D.
V. President, Government Relations
Registered Federal Lobbyist.
Tel: (202) 962 - 8640
Fax: (202) 289 - 6819

KEANEY, David
Registered Federal Lobbyist.
Tel: (202) 962 - 8640
Fax: (202) 289 - 6819

ChoicePoint Inc.

Provides data services to the insurance industry, businesses, government, non-profit organizations and individuals.
www.choicepoint.com
Annual Revenues: $919 million

ChoicePoint Inc.

* continued from previous page

Chairman and Chief Exec. Officer
SMITH, Derek V.
Tel: (770) 752 - 6000
Fax: (770) 752 - 6005

Main Headquarters
Mailing: 1000 Alderman Dr.
Alpharetta, GA 30005-4101
Tel: (770) 752 - 6000
Fax: (770) 752 - 5939

Corporate Foundations and Giving Programs

ChoicePoint Cares
1000 Alderman Dr.
Alpharetta, GA 30005-4101
Tel: (770) 752 - 6000
Fax: (770) 752 - 5939

Annual Grant Total: $100,000 - $200,000
Focuses on volunteer background screening and support of youth organizations.
Primary Interests: Youth Services
Recent Recipients: Boys and Girls Club; Georgia Innocence Project; Habitat for Humanity

Public Affairs and Related Activities Personnel

At Headquarters

COLBY, Ansley
V. President, ChoicePoint Cares
Mailstop: Suite 71-E
Tel: (770) 752 - 6000
Fax: (770) 752 - 6005

DAVIS, David W.
Corporate Secretary; and V. President, Government Affairs
Tel: (770) 752 - 6000
Fax: (770) 752 - 5939

DETLEFTS, Suzanne
Chief People Officer
Tel: (770) 752 - 6000
Fax: (770) 752 - 5939

JONES, Chuck
Director, External Affairs
chuck.jones@choicepoint.com
Tel: (770) 752 - 3594
Fax: (770) 752 - 6062

KAMERSCHEN, Robert W.
V. President, Law and Public Policy
Tel: (770) 752 - 6000
Fax: (770) 752 - 5939

MONGELLI, John M.
V. President, Corporate Investor Relations
Tel: (770) 752 - 6000
Fax: (770) 752 - 6167

CHS Inc.

Formerly known as Cenex Harvest States Cooperatives. Farm supply cooperative.
www.chsinc.com
Annual Revenues: $11 billion

President and Chief Exec. Officer
JOHNSON, John D.
Tel: (651) 355 - 6000
Fax: (651) 355 - 6432
TF: (800) 232 - 3639

Main Headquarters
Mailing: P.O. Box 64089
St. Paul, MN 55164-0089
Tel: (651) 355 - 6000
Fax: (651) 355 - 6432
TF: (800) 232 - 3639

Street: 5500 Cenex Dr.
Inver Grove Heights, MN 55077

Washington Office
Contact: Robert J. Looney
Mailing: 1745 S. Clark St., Suite 404
Arlington, VA 22202
Tel: (703) 413 - 9620

Political Action Committees

CHS Inc. - Agrilance PAC
Contact: James Bareksten
P.O. Box 64089
St. Paul, MN 55164-0089
Tel: (651) 355 - 6000
Fax: (651) 355 - 6432
TF: (800) 232 - 3639

Contributions to Candidates: $4,500 (01/05 - 09/05)
Democrats: $2,000; Republicans: $1,500; Other: $1,000.

Principal Recipients

SENATE DEMOCRATS		HOUSE DEMOCRATS	
Conrad, Kent (ND)	$1,000	Herseth, Stephanie (SD)	$500
		Pomeroy, Earl (ND)	$500
		HOUSE OTHER	
		Peterson, Collin (MN)	$1,000
SENATE REPUBLICANS		**HOUSE REPUBLICANS**	
		Goodlatte, Robert (VA)	$1,000
		Graves, Sam (MO)	$500

Corporate Foundations and Giving Programs

CHS Foundation
P.O. Box 64089
St. Paul, MN 55164-0089
Tel: (651) 355 - 6000
Fax: (651) 355 - 6432
TF: (800) 232 - 3639

Annual Grant Total: $500,000 - $750,000
Geographic Preference: Area(s) in which the company operates
Primary Interests: Education; Rural Affairs
Recent Recipients: University of Minnesota

CHS Corporate Giving Program
Contact: Mary Kaste
P.O. Box 64089
St. Paul, MN 55164-0089
Tel: (651) 355 - 6000
Fax: (651) 355 - 6432
TF: (800) 232 - 3639

Annual Grant Total: under $100,000
Geographic Preference: Midwest; Pacific Northwest
Primary Interests: Agriculture; Health; Human Welfare; Youth Services
Recent Recipients: U.S. Fund for UNICEF; United Way

Public Affairs and Related Activities Personnel

At Headquarters

ANDERSON, Allen J.
V. President, Governmental Affairs
al.anderson@chsinc.com
Tel: (651) 355 - 6000
Fax: (651) 355 - 6432
TF: (800) 232 - 3639

BAREKSTEN, James
PAC Treasurer
Tel: (651) 355 - 6000
Fax: (651) 355 - 6432
TF: (800) 232 - 3639

JORDAN, Lani
Director, Corporate Communications
lani.jordan@chsinc.com
Tel: (651) 355 - 6000
Fax: (651) 355 - 6432
TF: (800) 232 - 3639

KASTE, Mary
Manager, Corporate Contributions; and Manager, CHS Cooperative Foundation
mary.kaste@chsinc.com
Tel: (651) 355 - 6000
Fax: (651) 355 - 6432
TF: (800) 232 - 3639

LARSON, Tom
Exec. V. President, Public Affairs and Chief Operating Officer
tlarson@cenexharveststates.com
Tel: (651) 355 - 6000
Fax: (651) 355 - 6432
TF: (800) 232 - 3639
Responsibilities include communications, public and government affairs and the CHS Foundation.

TRAUB, Tom
V. President, Human Resources
Tel: (651) 355 - 6000
Fax: (651) 355 - 6432
TF: (800) 232 - 3639

At Washington Office

LOONEY, Robert J.
Director, Federal Affairs
bob.looney@chsinc.com
Tel: (703) 413 - 9620
Fax: (703) 413 - 9626

The Chubb Corp.

An insurance holding company.
www.chubb.com
Annual Revenues: $7.754 billion

Chaiman, President and Chief Exec. Officer
FINNEGAN, John D.
Tel: (908) 903 - 2000
Fax: (908) 903 - 2027

Main Headquarters
Mailing: P.O. Box 1615
Warren, NJ 07061-1615
Tel: (908) 903 - 2000
Fax: (908) 903 - 2027
Street: 15 Mountain View Rd.
Warren, NJ 07059

Washington Office
Contact: Daniel J. Conway
Mailing: One Massachusetts Ave. NW
Suite 350
Washington, DC 20001
Tel: (202) 408 - 8123
Fax: (202) 296 - 7683

Political Action Committees

Chubb Corp. PAC (CHUBBPAC)
P.O. Box 1615
Warren, NJ 07061-1615
Tel: (908) 903 - 2000
Fax: (908) 903 - 2027

Contributions to Candidates: $39,109 (01/05 - 09/05)
Democrats: $5,750; Republicans: $33,359.

Principal Recipients

SENATE DEMOCRATS		HOUSE DEMOCRATS	
Carper, Thomas R (DE)	$1,000	Frank, Barney (MA)	$1,000
Nelson, Benjamin (NE)	$1,000	Green, Alexander (TX)	$1,000
		Israel, Steve (NY)	$1,000
SENATE REPUBLICANS		**HOUSE REPUBLICANS**	
Bennett, Robert F (UT)	$5,000	Kelly, Sue W (NY)	$2,500
Kyl, Jon L (AZ)	$4,271	Ferguson, Mike (NJ)	$2,000
Allen, George (VA)	$3,136	Oxley, Michael (OH)	$2,000
Santorum, Richard (PA)	$2,000	Price, Thomas (GA)	$2,000
Chambliss, Saxby (GA)	$1,000	Kingston, John (GA)	$1,000
Sununu, John (NH)	$1,000	Manzullo, Donald (IL)	$1,000
		Pryce, Deborah (OH)	$1,000
		Renzi, Richard (AZ)	$1,000

Corporate Foundations and Giving Programs

Chubb Foundation

The Chubb Corp.

* continued from previous page

P.O. Box 1615
Warren, NJ 07061-1615
Tel: (908) 903 - 2000
Fax: (908) 903 - 2027

Annual Grant Total: $750,000 - $1,000,000
Provides scholarship support for dependants of qualified current, retired and deceased employees.

Public Affairs and Related Activities Personnel

At Headquarters

GREENBERG, Mark
Senior V. President, Corporate Communications
mgreenberg@chubb.com
Tel: (908) 903 - 2682
Fax: (908) 903 - 3134

MARZOCCHI, Robert A.
PAC Treasurer
Tel: (908) 903 - 2000
Fax: (908) 903 - 2027

MONTGOMERY, Glenn A.
Financial Information Contact
gmontgomery@chubb.com
Tel: (908) 903 - 2365
Fax: (908) 903 - 2027

SCHUSSEL, Mark
Manager, Public Relations
mschussel@chubb.com
Tel: (908) 903 - 2107
Fax: (908) 903 - 2027

At Washington Office

CONWAY, Daniel J.
Senior V. President, External Affairs
dconway@chubb.com
Registered Federal Lobbyist.
Tel: (202) 408 - 8123
Ext: 112
Fax: (202) 296 - 7683

FREE, Brant
Senior V. President, International External Affairs
bfree@chubb.com
Tel: (202) 408 - 8123
Ext: 114
Fax: (202) 296 - 7683

FULLER, Stephen A.
V. President, International External Affairs
sfuller@chubb.com
Tel: (202) 408 - 8123
Fax: (202) 296 - 7683

KORKUCH, Marylu
V. President and Director, Government Affairs
mkorkuch@chubb.com
Registered Federal Lobbyist.
Tel: (202) 408 - 8123
Fax: (202) 296 - 7683

MULLIGAN, Robert J.
V. President, International External Affairs
rmulligan@chubb.com
Registered Federal Lobbyist.
Tel: (202) 408 - 8123
Fax: (202) 296 - 7683

Church & Dwight Co., Inc.

A manufacturer of specialty chemicals and consumer products. Brands include Arm & Hammer.
www.churchdwight.com
Annual Revenues: $1.462 billion

Chairman of the Board
DAVIES, Robert A., II
Tel: (609) 683 - 5900
Fax: (609) 497 - 7177

President and Chief Exec. Officer
CRAIGIE, James R.
Tel: (609) 683 - 5900
Fax: (609) 497 - 7269

Main Headquarters
Mailing: 469 N. Harrison St.
Princeton, NJ 08543-5297
Tel: (609) 683 - 5900
Fax: (609) 497 - 7269

Corporate Foundations and Giving Programs

Church & Dwight Co. Contributions
469 N. Harrison St.
Princeton, NJ 08543-5297
Tel: (609) 683 - 5900
Fax: (609) 497 - 7269

Annual Grant Total: $300,000 - $400,000

Public Affairs and Related Activities Personnel

At Headquarters

EIREF, Zvi
Media and Investor Relations Contact
Tel: (609) 279 - 7666
Fax: (609) 497 - 7269

MOORE, Dennis M.
V. President, Human Resources
Tel: (609) 683 - 5900
Fax: (609) 497 - 7269

Church's Chicken

See listing on page 9 under AFC Enterprises.

Churchill Downs, Inc.

An owner of horse-racing tracks, including the Kentucky Derby.
www.churchilldowns.com
Annual Revenues: $463 million

Chairman of the Board
POLLARD, Carl F.
Tel: (502) 636 - 4400
Fax: (502) 636 - 4430
TF: (800) 283 - 3729

President and Chief Exec. Officer
MEEKER, Thomas H.
Tel: (502) 636 - 4400
Fax: (502) 636 - 4430
TF: (800) 283 - 3729

Main Headquarters
Mailing: 700 Central Ave.
Louisville, KY 40208
Tel: (502) 636 - 4400
Fax: (502) 636 - 4430
TF: (800) 283 - 3729

Political Action Committees

Churchill Down Inc. FPAC
Contact: Vicki L. Baumgardner
700 Central Ave.
Louisville, KY 40208
Tel: (502) 636 - 4400
Fax: (502) 636 - 4430
TF: (800) 283 - 3729

Contributions to Candidates: none reported (01/05 - 09/05)

Corporate Foundations and Giving Programs

Churchill Downs Foundation
Contact: Vicki L. Baumgardner
700 Central Ave.
Louisville, KY 40208
Tel: (502) 636 - 4400
Fax: (502) 636 - 4430
TF: (800) 283 - 3729

Assets: $1,758,914 (2001)
Annual Grant Total: $200,000 - $300,000
Geographic Preference: Kentucky
Primary Interests: Arts and Culture; Human Welfare

Public Affairs and Related Activities Personnel

At Headquarters

ASHER, John
V. President, Racing Communications
Tel: (502) 636 - 4400
Fax: (502) 636 - 4430
TF: (800) 283 - 3729

BAUMGARDNER, Vicki L.
PAC Treasurer; and Foundation Treasurer
Tel: (502) 636 - 4400
Fax: (502) 636 - 4430
TF: (800) 283 - 3729

JOHNSON, Dana
Director, Community Relations
Tel: (502) 636 - 4400
Fax: (502) 636 - 4430
TF: (800) 283 - 3729

KOENIG, Julie
Director, Communications
Tel: (502) 636 - 4502
Fax: (502) 636 - 4430
TF: (800) 283 - 3729

Ciba Specialty Chemicals

PUBLIC AFFAIRS COUNCIL

A member of the Public Affairs Council. A manufacturer of specialty chemicals.
www.cibasc.com
Annual Revenues: $5.7 billion

Chairman and Chief Exec. Officer
MEYER, Armin
Tel: (914) 785 - 2000
Fax: (914) 785 - 2211
TF: (800) 431 - 1900

Main Headquarters
Mailing: 540 White Plains Rd.
Tarrytown, NY 10591-2005
Tel: (914) 785 - 2000
Fax: (914) 785 - 2211
TF: (800) 431 - 1900

Washington Office
Mailing: 1825 I St., N.W., Suite 400
Washington, DC 20006
Tel: (202) 857 - 5200
Fax: (202) 857 - 5219

Political Action Committees

Ciba Specialty Chemicals Corp. Employee Good Government Fund
Contact: John L. Deming
1825 I St., N.W., Suite 400
Washington, DC 20006
Tel: (202) 857 - 5200
Fax: (202) 857 - 5219

Contributions to Candidates: $6,000 (01/05 - 09/05)
Democrats: $2,000; Republicans: $4,000.

Principal Recipients

SENATE DEMOCRATS
Carper, Thomas R (DE) $1,000

HOUSE DEMOCRATS
Berry, Marion (AR) $1,000

SENATE REPUBLICANS
Chafee, Lincoln (RI) $1,000

HOUSE REPUBLICANS
Bonner, Josiah (AL) $1,000
Castle, Michael (DE) $1,000
Myrick, Sue (NC) $1,000

Corporate Foundations and Giving Programs

Ciba Specialty Chemicals Foundation
Contact: W. Scott Tew
540 White Plains Rd.
Tarrytown, NY 10591-2005
Tel: (914) 785 - 4578
Fax: (914) 785 - 2211
TF: (800) 431 - 1900

Annual Grant Total: none reported
Geographic Preference: Area(s) in which the company operates
Primary Interests: Civic and Cultural Activities; Education; Environment/Conservation; Health and Human Services; Math and Science

Ciba Specialty Chemicals

* continued from previous page

Public Affairs and Related Activities Personnel

At Headquarters

ROSSMAN, Patricia
Head, Corporate Communications
pat.rossman@cibase.com
Tel: (914) 785 - 2000
Fax: (914) 785 - 2211
TF: (800) 431 - 1900

TEW, W. Scott
Head, Public Affairs
scott.tew@cibase.com
Tel: (914) 785 - 4578
Fax: (914) 785 - 2211
TF: (800) 431 - 1900

At Washington Office

DEMING, John L.
V. President, Government Relations
john.deming@cibasc.com
Registered Federal Lobbyist.
Tel: (202) 857 - 5200
Fax: (202) 857 - 5219

CIBER, Inc.

Provides consulting services for internet strategy and development.

www.ciber.com
Annual Revenues: $608.3 million

Chairman of the Board
STEVENSON, Bobby G.
Tel: (303) 220 - 0100
Fax: (303) 220 - 7100
TF: (800) 242 - 3799

President and Chief Exec. Officer
SLINGERLEND, Mac J.
Tel: (303) 220 - 0100
Fax: (303) 220 - 7100
TF: (800) 242 - 3799

Main Headquarters
Mailing: 5251 DTC Pkwy.
Suite 1400
Greenwood Village, CO 80111-2742
Tel: (303) 220 - 0100
Fax: (303) 220 - 7100
TF: (800) 242 - 3799

Public Affairs and Related Activities Personnel

At Headquarters

BIRDSEYE, Wally
President, Federal Solutions
Tel: (303) 220 - 0100
Fax: (303) 220 - 7100
TF: (800) 242 - 3799

BURNS, Ed
President, State Government Solutions
Tel: (303) 220 - 0100
Fax: (303) 220 - 7100
TF: (800) 242 - 3799

CAPUTO, Robin
V. President, Marketing and Public Relations
Tel: (303) 220 - 0100
Fax: (303) 220 - 7100
TF: (800) 242 - 3799

MATUSCHEK, Jennifer
V. President, Investor Relations
jmatuschek@ciber.com
Tel: (303) 220 - 0100
Fax: (303) 220 - 7100
TF: (800) 242 - 3799

STONER, Diane
Manager, Public Relations/Marketing Communications
dstoner@ciber.com
Tel: (303) 874 - 2112
Fax: (303) 220 - 7100
TF: (800) 242 - 3799

CIENA Corp.

A global provider of network solutions for service providers, cable operators and enterprises.

www.ciena.com
Annual Revenues: $283.1 million

Exec. Chairman of the Board
NETTLES, Patrick H.
pnettles@ciena.com
Tel: (410) 694 - 5700
Fax: (410) 694 - 5750

President and Chief Exec. Officer
SMITH, Gary B.
Tel: (410) 694 - 5700
Fax: (410) 694 - 5750

Main Headquarters
Mailing: 1201 Winterson Rd.
Linthicum, MD 21090
Tel: (410) 694 - 5700
Fax: (410) 694 - 5750

Public Affairs and Related Activities Personnel

At Headquarters

ANDERSON, Nicole
Public Relations Contact
Tel: (410) 694 - 5786
Fax: (410) 865 - 8929

DULONG, Suzanne
Chief Communications Officer
ir@ciena.com
Tel: (410) 694 - 5700
Fax: (410) 694 - 5750

MOORE, Lynn
V. President, Global Human Resources
Tel: (410) 694 - 5700
Fax: (410) 694 - 5750

TOWNS, Jessic
Investor Relations Contact
Tel: (410) 694 - 5700
Fax: (410) 694 - 5750

CIGNA Corp.

The CIGNA companies are providers of insurance, health care, employee benefits, pension and investment management, and related financial services to businesses and individuals worldwide.

www.cigna.com
Annual Revenues: $19.115 billion

Chairman and Chief Exec. Officer
HANWAY, H. Edward
Tel: (215) 761 - 1000

Main Headquarters
Mailing: One Liberty Pl.
1650 Market St.
Philadelphia, PA 19192
Tel: (215) 761 - 1000

Washington Office
Contact: Arthur Lifson
Mailing: 601 Pennsylvania Ave. NW
Suite 500 South Bldg.
Washington, DC 20004
Tel: (202) 861 - 1451
Fax: (202) 861 - 6363

Political Action Committees

CIGNA PAC
Contact: Mordecai Schwartz
Two Liberty Pl.
1601 Chestnut St.
Philadelphia, PA 19192
Tel: (215) 761 - 1000

Contributions to Candidates: $130,980 (01/05 - 09/05)
Democrats: $23,980; Republicans: $107,000.

Principal Recipients

SENATE DEMOCRATS		HOUSE DEMOCRATS	
Nelson, Benjamin (NE)	$4,000		
Lieberman, Joe (CT)	$3,000		
SENATE REPUBLICANS		**HOUSE REPUBLICANS**	
Kyl, Jon L (AZ)	$9,000	Cantor, Eric (VA)	$9,000
Smith, Gordon (OR)	$3,000	Gerlach, Jim (PA)	$7,000
Burns, Conrad (MT)	$2,000	Hastert, Dennis J. (IL)	$5,000
Ensign, John Eric (NV)	$2,000	Oxley, Michael (OH)	$5,000
Enzi, Michael B (WY)	$2,000	Fitzpatrick, Michael (PA)	$4,000
		Barton, Joe L (TX)	$3,500
		Johnson, Nancy (CT)	$3,000
		Renzi, Richard (AZ)	$3,000
		Ryan, Paul D (WI)	$3,000

Corporate Foundations and Giving Programs

CIGNA Foundation
Contact: Arnold W. Wright, Jr.
Two Liberty Pl.
1601 Chestnut St.
Philadelphia, PA 19192
Tel: (215) 761 - 6055
Fax: (215) 761 - 5515

Annual Grant Total: over $5,000,000
Guidelines are available. Supports employee volunteerism in areas of interest.
Geographic Preference: Hartford, CT; Philadelphia, PA
Primary Interests: Arts and Culture; Children's Health; Civic and Public Affairs; Education; Health and Human Services; Women's Health
Recent Recipients: Philadelphia Art Museum; United Way

Public Affairs and Related Activities Personnel

At Headquarters

CANNON, John, III
Senior V. President, Public Affairs; and Associate General Counsel
Tel: (215) 761 - 1000

DETRICK, Edwin J.
V. President, Investor Relations
edwin.detrick@cigna.com
Tel: (215) 761 - 1414

MURABITO, John M.
Exec. V. President, Human Resources
Tel: (215) 761 - 1000

At Washington Office

JULASON, Kristin P.
V. President, Federal Affairs Communications
kristin.julason@cigna.com
Registered Federal Lobbyist.
Tel: (202) 861 - 1451
Fax: (202) 296 - 2521

LIFSON, Arthur
V. President, Federal Affairs
arthur.lifson@cigna.com
Tel: (202) 296 - 7174
Ext: 689
Fax: (202) 296 - 2521

At Other Offices

BARONE, Gloria
Director, CIGNA Group Insurance Communications
Two Liberty Pl.
1601 Chestnut St.
Philadelphia, PA 19192-1553
gloria.barone@cigna.com
Tel: (215) 761 - 4758

CIGNA Corp.

** continued from previous page*

POTTER, Wendell — Tel: (215) 761 - 4450 Fax: (215) 761 - 5351
V. President, Corporate and Executive Communications
Two Liberty Pl.
1601 Chestnut St.
Philadelphia, PA 19192-1553
wendell.potter@cigna.com

SCHWARTZ, Mordecai — Tel: (215) 761 - 1000
PAC Treasurer
Two Liberty Pl.
1601 Chestnut St.
Philadelphia, PA 19192

WRIGHT, Arnold W., Jr. — Tel: (215) 761 - 6055 Fax: (215) 761 - 5515
V. President, Contributions and Exec. Director, CIGNA Foundation
Two Liberty Pl.
1601 Chestnut St.
Philadelphia, PA 19192
woodie.wright@cigna.com

Cincinnati Bell Inc.

A member of the Public Affairs Council. Formerly part of Broadwing Communications. An integrated provider of advanced local, long distance, directory, wireless, Internet, and broadband communications services and equipment to residents and businesses.

www.cincinnatibell.com
Annual Revenues: $2.35 billion

President and Chief Exec. Officer
CASSIDY, John F. — Tel: (513) 397 - 9900 Fax: (513) 723 - 9815

Main Headquarters
Mailing: P.O. Box 2301, Cincinnati, OH 45201-2301 — Tel: (513) 397 - 9900 Fax: (513) 723 - 9815
Street: 201 E. Fourth St., Cincinnati, OH 45202

Political Action Committees

Cincinnati Bell Inc. Federal Political Action Committee
Contact: Mark W. Peterson
P.O. Box 2301
Cincinnati, OH 45201-2301 — Tel: (513) 397 - 9900 Fax: (513) 723 - 9815

Contributions to Candidates: $2,750 (01/05 - 09/05)
Democrats: $250; Republicans: $2,500.

Principal Recipients

SENATE DEMOCRATS		HOUSE DEMOCRATS	
		Baldwin, Tammy (WI)	$250
SENATE REPUBLICANS		**HOUSE REPUBLICANS**	
Dewine, Richard (OH)	$1,000	Boehner, John (OH)	$1,000
		Gutknecht, Gil (MN)	$500

Public Affairs and Related Activities Personnel

At Headquarters

COLWELL, Christopher S. — Tel: (513) 397 - 7540 Fax: (513) 723 - 9815
V. President, Government Relations
Mailstop: M/S 102-890
chris.colwell@cinbell.com

KEATING, Brian G. — Tel: (513) 397 - 9900 Fax: (513) 723 - 9815
V. President, Human Resources and Administration

PETERSON, Mark W. — Tel: (513) 397 - 9900 Fax: (513) 723 - 9815
V. President and Treasurer; PAC Treasurer

RINGO, D. Scott — Tel: (513) 397 - 1354 Fax: (513) 723 - 9815
Government Relations Contact
scott.ringo@cinbell.com

ROMITO, Mark — Tel: (513) 397 - 1366 Fax: (513) 723 - 9815
Federal and State Regulatory Affairs
mark.romito@cinbell.com

VANDERWOUDE, Michael — Tel: (513) 397 - 9900 Fax: (513) 723 - 9815
V. President, Investor Relations and Corporate Communications

Cincinnati Financial Corp.

www.cinfin.com
Annual Revenues: $3.61 billion

Chairman, President and Chief Exec. Officer
SCHIFF, John J., Jr. — Tel: (513) 870 - 2000 Fax: (513) 870 - 2935

Main Headquarters
Mailing: P.O. Box 145496, Cincinnati, OH 45250 — Tel: (513) 870 - 2000
Street: 6200 S. Gilmore Rd., Fairfield, OH 45014

Corporate Foundations and Giving Programs

Cincinnati Financial Corp. Contributions
Contact: Gregory J. Ziegler
P.O. Box 145496
Cincinnati, OH 45250 — Tel: (513) 870 - 2000 Fax: (513) 870 - 2911

Annual Grant Total: none reported
Geographic Preference: Cincinnati, OH

Public Affairs and Related Activities Personnel

At Headquarters

GILLIAM, Scott A. — Tel: (513) 870 - 2000 Fax: (513) 870 - 2985
Assistant V. President and Government Relations Officer
scott_gilliam@cinfin.com

SHEVCHIK, Joan O. — Tel: (513) 870 - 2198 Fax: (513) 870 - 2935
Senior V. President, Corporate Communications

ZIEGLER, Gregory J. — Tel: (513) 870 - 2000 Fax: (513) 870 - 2911
V. President and Director, Personnel
greg_ziegler@cinfin.com
Responsibilities include corporate philanthropy.

Cincinnati Gas and Electric Co.

See listing on page 119 under Cinergy Corp.

Cincinnati Industrial Machinery

See listing on page 171 under Eagle-Picher Industries, Inc.

Cincinnati Milacron, Inc.

See listing on page 326 under Milacron Inc.

Cinergy Corp.

A member of the Public Affairs Council. A diversified energy company. In May 2005, the company announced plans to merge with Duke Energy Corp. (see separate listing).

www.cinergy.com
Annual Revenues: $12.922 billion

Chairman, President and Chief Exec. Officer
ROGERS, James E. — Tel: (513) 421 - 9500 Fax: (513) 651 - 9196

Main Headquarters
Mailing: P.O. Box 960, Cincinnati, OH 45201-0960 — Tel: (513) 421 - 9500
Street: 139 E. Fourth St., Cincinnati, OH 45202

Washington Office
Contact: Mary Kenkel
Mailing: 1301 Pennsylvania Ave., N.W., Suite 1030, Washington, DC 20004 — Tel: (202) 824 - 0400 Fax: (202) 824 - 0418

Political Action Committees

Cinergy Corp. Political Action Committee
Contact: Mary Kenkel
1301 Pennsylvania Ave., N.W., Suite 1030
Washington, DC 20004 — Tel: (202) 824 - 0400 Fax: (202) 824 - 0418

Contributions to Candidates: $49,750 (01/05 - 09/05)
Democrats: $17,000; Republicans: $32,750.

Principal Recipients

SENATE DEMOCRATS		HOUSE DEMOCRATS	
Bingaman, Jeff (NM)	$3,500	Boucher, Fredrick (VA)	$2,000
Carper, Thomas R (DE)	$3,500	Dingell, John D (MI)	$2,000
Byrd, Robert C (WV)	$2,000		
SENATE REPUBLICANS		**HOUSE REPUBLICANS**	
Lugar, Richard G (IN)	$5,250	Pryce, Deborah (OH)	$3,500
Dewine, Richard (OH)	$2,500	Barton, Joe L (TX)	$2,500
		Chocola, Christopher (IN)	$2,000
		Schmidt, Jeannette (OH)	$2,000

Corporate Foundations and Giving Programs

Cinergy Foundation
Contact: Karol King
P.O. Box 960
Cincinnati, OH 45201-0960 — Tel: (513) 287 - 1251 Fax: (513) 651 - 9196

Annual Grant Total: $2,000,000 - $5,000,000

Public Affairs and Related Activities Personnel

At Headquarters

ARNETT, Bradley C. — Tel: (513) 287 - 3024
Managing Director, Investor Relations and Assistant Treasurer
bradley.arnett@cinergy.com

AUMILLER, Wendy L. — Tel: (513) 421 - 9500
PAC Treasurer

BLACK, Keith — Tel: (513) 287 - 3704 Fax: (513) 287 - 2513
General Manager, State Government Affairs
Mailstop: M/S 28AT

Cinergy Corp.

** continued from previous page*

BRASH, Steven L.
Manager, External Communications
Tel: (513) 287 - 2226
Fax: (513) 651 - 9196

HALE, J. Joseph, Jr.
V. President, Corporate Communications; and President, Cinergy Foundation
Tel: (513) 287 - 2410
Fax: (513) 287 - 4030

KING, Karol
Manager, Cinergy Foundation
Tel: (513) 287 - 1251
Fax: (513) 651 - 9196

NEEDHAM, Victor, III
Manager, Regional Government Affairs
Mailstop: M/S 28AT
Tel: (513) 287 - 2609

STOWELL, John L.
V. President, Environmental Strategy, Federal Affairs and Sustainability
Mailstop: Suite 2801
jstowell@cinergy.com
Tel: (513) 287 - 3540
Fax: (513) 287 - 3412

VERHAGEN, Timothy J.
V. President, Human Resources
Tel: (513) 421 - 9500

At Washington Office

KENKEL, Mary
General Manager, Federal Government Affairs and National Media
Registered Federal Lobbyist.
Tel: (202) 824 - 0400
Fax: (202) 824 - 0418

At Other Offices

CELONA, David
Manager, Government Affairs - Ohio
155 E. Broad St.
21st Floor
Columbus, OH 43215
Tel: (614) 221 - 7551
Fax: (614) 221 - 7556

GRIFFITH, Julie
General Manager, Government Affairs - Indiana
251 N. Illinois St., Suite 1600
Indianapolis, IN 46204
Tel: (317) 488 - 3507
Fax: (317) 588 - 3519

Cingular Wireless

A joint venture between the domestic wireless divisions of SBC and BellSouth (see separate listings). Acquired AT&T Wireless Services in 2004.

www.cingular.com
Annual Revenues: $14.7 billion

President and Chief Exec. Officer
SIGMAN, Stanley T.
Tel: (404) 236 - 6000
Fax: (866) 246 - 4852
TF: (800) 331 - 0500

Main Headquarters
Mailing: 5565 Glenridge Connector
Atlanta, GA 30342
Tel: (404) 236 - 6000
Fax: (866) 246 - 4852
TF: (800) 331 - 0500

Washington Office
Mailing: 1818 N St. NW
Suite 800
Washington, DC 20036
Tel: (202) 419 - 3000
Fax: (202) 419 - 3030

Political Action Committees

Cingular Wireless LLC Employee Political Action Committee
Contact: James Hoeberling
5565 Glenridge Connector
Atlanta, GA 30342
Tel: (404) 236 - 6000
Fax: (866) 246 - 4852
TF: (800) 331 - 0500

Contributions to Candidates: $61,500 (01/05 - 09/05)
Democrats: $21,000; Republicans: $40,500.

Principal Recipients

SENATE DEMOCRATS		HOUSE DEMOCRATS	
Nelson, Benjamin (NE)	$2,000	Dingell, John D (MI)	$2,000
		Menendez, Robert (NJ)	$2,000
		Towns, Edolphus (NY)	$2,000
		Gonzalez, Charles A (TX)	$1,500

SENATE REPUBLICANS		HOUSE REPUBLICANS	
DeMint, James (SC)	$5,000	Reynolds, Thomas (NY)	$2,500
Stevens, Ted (AK)	$2,500	Shimkus, John (IL)	$2,000
Vitter, David (LA)	$2,500	Pombo, Richard (CA)	$1,500
Santorum, Richard (PA)	$2,000		
Smith, Gordon (OR)	$2,000		
Sununu, John (NH)	$2,000		

Corporate Foundations and Giving Programs

Cingular Wireless Charitable Contributions
5565 Glenridge Connector
Atlanta, GA 30342
Tel: (404) 236 - 6000
Fax: (866) 246 - 4852
TF: (800) 331 - 0500

Annual Grant Total: none reported
Geographic Preference: Area(s) in which the company operates
Primary Interests: Arts and Culture; Education; Social Services

Public Affairs and Related Activities Personnel

At Headquarters

BOWCOCK, Jennifer
Director, Public Relations
jennifer.bowcock@cingular.com
Tel: (404) 236 - 6319
Fax: (866) 236 - 6323
TF: (800) 331 - 0500

BRADLEY, Rickford D.
Exec. V. President, Human Resources
Tel: (404) 236 - 6000
Fax: (866) 246 - 4852
TF: (800) 331 - 0500

BURLESON, Ron
V. President, State Relations, Regulatory and Legal
Tel: (404) 236 - 6000
Fax: (866) 236 - 6015
TF: (800) 331 - 0500

CARBONELL, Joaquin R., III
Senior V. President and General Counsel, Regulatory and Legal
Mailstop: 2094 W
joaquin.carbonell@cingular.com
Responsibilities include federal and state legislative affairs.
Tel: (404) 236 - 6000
Ext: 6141
Fax: (404) 236 - 6145
TF: (800) 331 - 0500

HOEBERLING, James
Treasurer, Cingular Wireless LLC Employee PAC
Tel: (404) 236 - 6000
Fax: (866) 246 - 4852
TF: (800) 331 - 0500

OWEN, Clay
Senior Director, Media Relations
clay.owen@cingular.com
Tel: (404) 236 - 6153
Fax: (866) 246 - 4852
TF: (800) 331 - 0500

ROTH, Paul R.
Exec. V. President, External Affairs and Public Relations
Tel: (404) 236 - 6000
Fax: (866) 246 - 4852
TF: (800) 331 - 0500

SCHNABEL, Maria
Director, Hispanic Public Relations
maria.schnabel@cingular.com
Tel: (404) 236 - 6432
Fax: (866) 246 - 4852
TF: (800) 331 - 0500

SIEGEL, Mark
Exec. Director, Media Relations
mark.a.siegel@cingular.com
Tel: (404) 236 - 6312
Fax: (866) 246 - 4852
TF: (800) 331 - 0500

At Washington Office

BUGEL, James
Exec. Director, External Affairs
Registered Federal Lobbyist.
Tel: (202) 419 - 3000
Ext: 3004
Fax: (202) 419 - 3030

COHEN, Rochelle
Senior Director, Media Relations
rochelle.cohen@cingular.com
Tel: (202) 419 - 3007
Fax: (202) 419 - 3030

FONTES, Brian F.
V. President, Federal Relations
brian.fontes@cingular.com
Registered Federal Lobbyist.
Tel: (202) 419 - 3000
Ext: 3010
Fax: (202) 419 - 3030

HERNDON, Heather
Manager, Congressional Affairs
Registered Federal Lobbyist.
Tel: (202) 419 - 3000
Fax: (202) 419 - 3030

PALMER, Susan K.
Manager, Regulatory Affairs
susan.k.palmer@cingular.com
Tel: (202) 419 - 3000
Ext: 3009

WELLS, Kent M.
V. President, Congressional Affairs
Mailstop: 800
kent.wells@cingular.com
Registered Federal Lobbyist.
Tel: (202) 419 - 3000
Ext: 3025

Circuit City Stores, Inc.

A retailer of brand-name consumer electronics, major appliances, and used cars and trucks in the United States.

www.circuitcity.com
Annual Revenues: $12.791 billion

Chairman and Chief Exec. Officer
MCCOLLOUGH, W. Alan
alan_mccollough@circuitcity.com
Tel: (804) 527 - 4000
Fax: (804) 527 - 4164

Main Headquarters
Mailing: 9950 Mayland Dr.
Richmond, VA 23233
Tel: (804) 527 - 4000
Fax: (804) 527 - 4164

Political Action Committees

Circuit City Stores Inc. PAC
Contact: William P. Cimino
9950 Mayland Dr.
Richmond, VA 23233
Tel: (804) 418 - 8163
Fax: (804) 527 - 4164

Contributions to Candidates: none reported (01/05 - 09/05)

Circuit City Stores, Inc.

* continued from previous page

Corporate Foundations and Giving Programs

Circuit City Foundation
Contact: Ms. Sandy Stoddart
9950 Mayland Dr. — Tel: (804) 527 - 4000
Richmond, VA 23233 — Fax: (804) 527 - 4164

Assets: $2,680,884 (2002)
Annual Grant Total: $2,000,000 - $5,000,000
The Foundation does not accept unsolicited applications for funding.
Geographic Preference: Area(s) in which employees live and work; Area(s) in which the company operates
Primary Interests: Education
Recent Recipients: Achievable Dream; United Way

Public Affairs and Related Activities Personnel

At Headquarters

CANNON, W. Steven — Tel: (804) 527 - 4014
Senior V. President and General Counsel — Fax: (804) 527 - 4164
steve_cannon@circuitcity.com

CIMINO, William P. — Tel: (804) 418 - 8163
Director, Corporate Communications — Fax: (804) 527 - 4164
Responsibilities include political action.

JONAS, Eric A. — Tel: (804) 527 - 4000
Senior V. President, Human Resources — Fax: (804) 527 - 4164

STODDART, Ms. Sandy — Tel: (804) 527 - 4000
Exec. Director, Circuit City Foundation — Fax: (804) 527 - 4164
sandy_stoddart@circuitcity.com

TATE, Amanda — Tel: (804) 418 - 8298
Senior Public Relations Representative — Fax: (804) 527 - 4164

Cirrus Logic, Inc.

Provides digital technology for consumer electronics.
www.cirrus.com
Annual Revenues: $418 million

Chairman of the Board
HACKWORTH, Michael L. — Tel: (512) 851 - 4000; TF: (800) 888 - 5016

President and Chief Exec. Officer
FRENCH, David D. — Tel: (512) 851 - 4000; TF: (800) 888 - 5016

Main Headquarters
Mailing: 2901 Via Fortuna — Tel: (512) 851 - 4000
Austin, TX 78746 — TF: (800) 888 - 5016

Public Affairs and Related Activities Personnel

At Headquarters

ALLEN, David — Tel: (512) 851 - 4000
V. President, Investor Relations; and Treasurer — TF: (800) 888 - 5016

BENSON, Jo-Dee — Tel: (512) 851 - 4653
V. President, Integrated Communications — TF: (800) 888 - 5016

SCHNELL, Bill — Tel: (512) 851 - 4000
Manager, Public Relations — TF: (800) 888 - 5016
bill.schnell@cirrus.com

Cisco Systems, Inc.

A member of the Public Affairs Council. A worldwide leader in networking for the internet.
www.cisco.com
Annual Revenues: $24.8 billion

Chairman of the Board
MORGRIDGE, John P. — Tel: (408) 526 - 4000
jmorgridge@cisco.com — Fax: (408) 526 - 4100; TF: (800) 553 - 6387

President and Chief Exec. Officer
CHAMBERS, John T. — Tel: (408) 526 - 4000; Fax: (408) 526 - 4100; TF: (800) 553 - 6387

Main Headquarters
Mailing: 170 W. Tasman Dr. — Tel: (408) 526 - 4000
San Jose, CA 95134-1706 — Fax: (408) 526 - 4100; TF: (800) 553 - 6387

Washington Office
Contact: Michael Timmeny
Mailing: 601 Pennsylvania Ave. NW — Tel: (202) 661 - 4000
Suite 520, N. Bldg. — Fax: (202) 661 - 4041
Washington, DC 20004

Corporate Foundations and Giving Programs

Cisco Systems Foundation
Contact: Tae Yoo
170 W. Tasman Dr. — Tel: (408) 526 - 7659
San Jose, CA 95134-1706 — Fax: (408) 526 - 6310; TF: (800) 553 - 6387

Annual Grant Total: over $5,000,000
The Foundation has an employee matching gifts program.
Geographic Preference: Area(s) in which the company operates
Primary Interests: Community Affairs; Education; Health and Human Services

Public Affairs and Related Activities Personnel

At Headquarters

BRUCE, Penny — Tel: (408) 853 - 9188
Media Contact, Public Affairs — Fax: (408) 526 - 4100
pebruce@cisco.com — TF: (800) 553 - 6387

CHRISTIE, Blair — Tel: (408) 526 - 4000
Director, Investor Relations — Fax: (408) 526 - 4100; TF: (800) 553 - 6387

DCAMP, Kate — Tel: (408) 527 - 9530
Senior V. President, Human Resources — Fax: (408) 526 - 4100
kdcamp@cisco.com — TF: (800) 553 - 6387

EARNHARDT, John — Tel: (408) 527 - 2180
Manager, Communications — Fax: (408) 526 - 4100
john.earnhardt@cisco.com — TF: (800) 553 - 6387

HADULCO, Ray — Tel: (408) 853 - 6054
Media Contact, Public Affairs — Fax: (408) 526 - 4100
rayh@cisco.com — TF: (800) 553 - 6387

YOO, Tae — Tel: (408) 526 - 7659
V. President and Contact, Cisco Foundation — Fax: (408) 526 - 6310; TF: (800) 553 - 6387

At Washington Office

CAMPBELL, Jeffrey — Tel: (202) 661 - 4000
Director, Technology Policy — Fax: (202) 661 - 4041
Registered Federal Lobbyist.

CUNNINGHAM, Bryan — Tel: (202) 661 - 4000; Fax: (202) 661 - 4041
Registered Federal Lobbyist.

TANIELIAN, Matthew — Tel: (202) 661 - 4000
Senior Policy Counsel — Fax: (202) 661 - 4041
Registered Federal Lobbyist.

TIMMENY, Michael — Tel: (202) 661 - 4040
Director, Federal Government Affairs — Fax: (202) 661 - 4041
mtimmeny@cisco.com
Registered Federal Lobbyist.

The CIT Group, Inc.

Offers commerical and consumer financing solutions.
www.cit.com

Chairman, President and Chief Exec. Officer
PEEK, Jeffrey M. — Tel: (212) 536 - 1390; Fax: (212) 536 - 1912

Main Headquarters
Mailing: 1211 Avenue of the Americas — Tel: (212) 536 - 1390
New York, NY 10036 — Fax: (212) 536 - 1912

Corporate Foundations and Giving Programs

CIT Corporate Giving Program
Contact: Anita F. Contini
1211 Avenue of the Americas — Tel: (212) 536 - 1390
New York, NY 10036 — Fax: (212) 536 - 1912

Annual Grant Total: none reported
Geographic Preference: Area in which the company is headquartered; National
Primary Interests: Arts and Humanities; Diversity; Education; Social Services
Recent Recipients: American Red Cross; United Way

Public Affairs and Related Activities Personnel

At Headquarters

CONTINI, Anita F. — Tel: (212) 536 - 1390
Senior V. President and Director, Public and Corporate Affairs — Fax: (212) 536 - 1912

GERARD, Valerie L. — Tel: (212) 422 - 3284
Senior V. President, Investor Relations — Fax: (212) 536 - 1912

GIPSON, Kelley J. — Tel: (212) 536 - 1390
Exec. V. President, Marketing and Corporate Communications — Fax: (212) 536 - 1912

MITCHELL, Susan P. — Tel: (212) 536 - 1390
Exec. V. President, Human Resources — Fax: (212) 536 - 1912
susan.mitchell@cit.com

CITGO Petroleum Corporation

A petroleum refining and marketing corporation.
www.citgo.com
Annual Revenues: $32.027 billion

Chairman of the Board
GRANADO, Alejandro — Tel: (832) 486 - 4000; Fax: (832) 486 - 1814

Main Headquarters
Mailing: P.O. Box 4689 — Tel: (832) 486 - 4000
Houston, TX 77210 — Fax: (832) 486 - 1814
Street: 1293 Eldridge Pkwy.
Houston, TX 77077

CITGO Petroleum Corporation

** continued from previous page*

Corporate Foundations and Giving Programs

CITGO Corporate Contributions
Contact: Carolyn Stewart
P.O. Box 4689 — Tel: (832) 486 - 4000
Houston, TX 77210 — Fax: (832) 486 - 1814

Annual Grant Total: none reported
Recent Recipients: Muscular Dystrophy Ass'n; Nature Conservancy; United Way

Public Affairs and Related Activities Personnel

At Headquarters

ABREU, Rafael Gomez — Tel: (832) 486 - 4000
V. President, Strategic Shareholder Relations, Government and Public Affairs — Fax: (832) 486 - 1814

DOWE, Tammy — Tel: (832) 486 - 4000
Manager, Corporate Legislative Issues — Fax: (832) 486 - 1814

GARAY, Fernando — Tel: (832) 486 - 1489
Manager, Public Affairs — Fax: (832) 486 - 1843
Responsibilities include investor relations.

MCCOLLUM, David — Tel: (832) 486 - 4260
Investor Relations Contact — Fax: (832) 486 - 1843

STEWART, Carolyn — Tel: (832) 486 - 4000
Corporate Contributions Contact — Fax: (832) 486 - 1814

CitiCorp

See listing on page 122 under Citigroup, Inc.

Citigroup, Inc.

Citigroup is a global financial services company that provides consumers, corporations, governments and institutions with a broad range of financial products and services, including consumer banking and credit, corporate and investment banking, insurance, securities brokerage, and asset management. Major brand names under Citigroup's trademark red umbrella include Citibank, CitiFinancial, Primerica (see separate listing), Citigroup Global Markets, Inc. (see separate listing), Banamex, and Travelers Life and Annuity. Spun off Travelers Property Casualty Corp. (see separate listing) and acquired Golden State Bancorp, the parent company of California Federal Bank, in 2002.

www.citigroup.com
Annual Revenues: $108.2 billion

Chairman of the Board
WEILL, Sanford I. — Tel: (212) 559 - 1000; Fax: (212) 793 - 3946; TF: (800) 285 - 3000

Chief Exec. Officer
PRINCE, Charles O., III — Tel: (212) 559 - 1000; Fax: (212) 793 - 3946; TF: (800) 285 - 3000

Main Headquarters
Mailing: 399 Park Ave.
New York, NY 10043
Tel: (212) 559 - 1000; Fax: (212) 793 - 3946; TF: (800) 285 - 3000

Washington Office
Contact: Nicholas E. Calio
Mailing: 1101 Pennsylvania Ave. NW
Suite 1000
Washington, DC 20004
Tel: (202) 879 - 6871; Fax: (202) 783 - 4460

Political Action Committees

Citigroup Inc. Federal Political Action Committee
Contact: Mike Conway
1101 Pennsylvania Ave. NW — Tel: (202) 879 - 6871
Suite 1000 — Fax: (202) 783 - 4460
Washington, DC 20004

Contributions to Candidates: $181,500 (01/05 - 09/05)
Democrats: $46,500; Republicans: $135,000.

Principal Recipients

SENATE DEMOCRATS		HOUSE DEMOCRATS	
Carper, Thomas R (DE)	$4,000	Crowley, Joseph (NY)	$4,000
SENATE REPUBLICANS		**HOUSE REPUBLICANS**	
Hatch, Orrin (UT)	$6,000	Bachus, Spencer (AL)	$5,000
Kyl, Jon L (AZ)	$6,000	Blunt, Roy (MO)	$5,000
Ensign, John Eric (NV)	$5,000	Oxley, Michael (OH)	$5,000
Talent, James (MO)	$4,500	Reynolds, Thomas (NY)	$5,000
Crapo, Michael D (ID)	$3,500		
Allen, George (VA)	$3,000		

Citigroup Inc. Federal/State Political Action Committee
Contact: Theresa A. Russell
1101 Pennsylvania Ave. NW — Tel: (202) 879 - 6871
Suite 1000 — Fax: (202) 783 - 4460
Washington, DC 20004

Contributions to Candidates: $3,000 (01/05 - 09/05)
Republicans: $3,000.

Principal Recipients

SENATE REPUBLICANS		HOUSE REPUBLICANS	
		Dewine, R. Pat (OH)	$2,000
		Bilirakis, Michael (FL)	$1,000

Corporate Foundations and Giving Programs

Citigroup Foundation
Contact: Rebecca Van Sickle
850 Third Ave. — Tel: (212) 559 - 9163
13th Floor
New York, NY 10022-6211

Annual Grant Total: over $5,000,000
The Foundation does not encourage unsolicited proposals, preferring to seek proposals from organizations with successful track records in its priority areas of interest.
Primary Interests: Arts and Humanities; Community Development; Education; Environment/Conservation; Health and Human Services
Recent Recipients: Operation Smile; United Negro College Fund

Public Affairs and Related Activities Personnel

At Headquarters

JOHNSON, Leah — Tel: (212) 559 - 9446
Director, Public Affairs — Fax: (212) 793 - 3946; TF: (800) 285 - 3000

SCHLEIN, Michael — Tel: (212) 793 - 0141
Senior V. President, Global Corporate Affairs, Human Resources and Business Practices — Fax: (212) 793 - 3946; TF: (800) 285 - 3000
schleinm@citi.com

TILDESLEY, Arthur — Tel: (212) 559 - 1000
Director, Investor Relations — Fax: (212) 793 - 3946; TF: (800) 285 - 3000

At Washington Office

ANDERSON, Karen — Tel: (202) 879 - 6871
V. President, Deputy Director - State and Local Government Relations — Fax: (202) 783 - 4460
andersonk@citigroup.com

ANDREWS, Michael P. — Tel: (202) 879 - 6810
V. President and Director, International Business Affairs — Fax: (202) 783 - 4460
andrewsm@citigroup.com
Registered Federal Lobbyist.

BURGESON, Christine McCarlie — Tel: (202) 879 - 6871
V. President, Federal Government Affairs — Fax: (202) 783 - 4460
Registered Federal Lobbyist.

CALIO, Nicholas E. — Tel: (202) 879 - 6871
Senior V. President, Global Government Affairs — Fax: (202) 783 - 4460
Registered Federal Lobbyist.

CALLAHAN, Patrick — Tel: (202) 879 - 6871
Chief of Staff, State and Local Government — Fax: (202) 783 - 4460
callahanp@citi.com

CONWAY, Mike — Tel: (202) 879 - 6871
Treasurer, Citigroup Federal PAC — Fax: (202) 783 - 4460
Registered Federal Lobbyist.

DOWLING, S. Colin — Tel: (202) 879 - 6871
Senior V. President and Director, State and Local Government Relations — Fax: (202) 783 - 4460
dowlingc@citigroup.com

GRUBBS, Wendy — Tel: (202) 879 - 6871
V. President, Federal Government Affairs, Global Consumer Investment Bank — Fax: (202) 783 - 4460
Registered Federal Lobbyist.

JOHNSON, Lionel — Tel: (202) 879 - 6855
V. President, International Government Relations — Fax: (202) 783 - 4460
johnsonli@citi.com
Registered Federal Lobbyist.

LEVEY, Jeffrey R. — Tel: (202) 879 - 6818
V. President, Tax Legislation — Fax: (202) 783 - 1873
jeffrey.levey@citicorp.com
Registered Federal Lobbyist.

NOKES, Sara — Tel: (202) 879 - 6849
Manager, Political and External Affairs — Fax: (202) 783 - 4460
nokess@citigroup.com
Registered Federal Lobbyist.

RUSSELL, Theresa A. — Tel: (202) 879 - 6871
Treasurer, Citigroup Inc. Federal/State PAC — Fax: (202) 783 - 4460

RYAN, Jimmy — Tel: (202) 879 - 6871
V. President, Federal Government Relations — Fax: (202) 783 - 4460
Registered Federal Lobbyist.

SCHELLHAS, Robert — Tel: (202) 879 - 6814
V. President, Federal Government Affairs — Fax: (202) 783 - 4460
Registered Federal Lobbyist.

Citigroup, Inc.

** continued from previous page*

SOLOMON, Maura — Tel: (202) 879 - 6820
V. President and Counsel, Federal Government Relations — Fax: (202) 783 - 4460
solomonma@citigroup.com
Registered Federal Lobbyist.

SWEENEY, Robert — Tel: (202) 879 - 6871
V. President, Mid-Atlantic Region, State and Local Government Relations — Fax: (202) 783 - 4460
sweeneyr@citi.com

WINGATE, Heather — Tel: (202) 879 - 6845
V. President, Global Government Affairs — Fax: (202) 783 - 4460
Registered Federal Lobbyist.

At Other Offices

BANTHAM, Jim W. — Tel: (972) 652 - 4626
V. President, Central Region - State and Local Government Relations
P.O. Box 660237
Dallas, TX 75266-0237
banthamj@citi.com

GRIFFIN, Mary — Tel: (518) 432 - 1286
V. President, New York Region - State and Local Government Relations
95 Columbia St.
Albany, NY 12210
griffinm@citi.com

OLSEN, Lynnea — Tel: (916) 321 - 5529
V. President and Counsel, West Region - State and Local Government Relations
11115 11th St., Suite 205
Sacramento, CA 95814
olsenl@citigroup.com

VAN SICKLE, Rebecca — Tel: (212) 559 - 9163
Grants Manager, Citigroup Foundation
850 Third Ave.
13th Floor
New York, NY 10022-6211

Citizens Communications Co.

A telecom company. Formerly known as Citizens Utilities Company.
www.czn.net
Annual Revenues: $2.193 billion

President and Chief Exec. Officer
WILDEROTTER, Maggie — Tel: (203) 614 - 5600 — Fax: (203) 614 - 4602

Main Headquarters
Mailing: Three High Ridge Park, Stamford, CT 06905 — Tel: (203) 614 - 5600 — Fax: (203) 614 - 4602

Political Action Committees

Citizens Utilities Co. Political Action Committee
Contact: Robert Binder
180 S. Clinton Ave.
Rochester, NY 14646-0500

Contributions to Candidates: none reported (01/05 - 09/05)

Public Affairs and Related Activities Personnel

At Headquarters

DISTURCO, Jean M. — Tel: (203) 614 - 5600
Senior V. President, Human Resources — Fax: (203) 614 - 4602

SMITH, Brigid M. — Tel: (203) 614 - 5600
Assistant V. President, Corporate Communications — Fax: (203) 614 - 4602
bsmith@czn.com

At Other Offices

BINDER, Robert
PAC Treasurer
180 S. Clinton Ave.
Rochester, NY 14646-0500

Citizens Financial Group, Inc.

Acquired Charter One Financial, Inc. in August, 2004.
www.citizensbank.com
Annual Revenues: $691 million

Chairman, President and Chief Exec. Officer
FISH, Lawrence K. — Tel: (401) 456 - 7000 — Fax: (401) 456 - 7819

Main Headquarters
Mailing: One Citizens Plaza, Providence, RI 02903 — Tel: (401) 456 - 7000 — Fax: (401) 456 - 7819

Political Action Committees

Citizens Financial Group PAC
Contact: Ken Robinson
One Citizens Plaza — Tel: (401) 455 - 5934
Providence, RI 02903 — Fax: (401) 456 - 7644

Contributions to Candidates: $30,500 (01/05 - 09/05)

Democrats: $18,500; Republicans: $12,000.

Principal Recipients

SENATE DEMOCRATS		HOUSE DEMOCRATS	
Kennedy, Ted (MA)	$5,000	Lynch, Stephen (MA)	$2,000
Stabenow, Debbie (MI)	$1,500	Markey, Edward (MA)	$2,000
Carper, Thomas R (DE)	$1,000	Maloney, Carolyn (NY)	$1,500
Johnson, Tim (SD)	$1,000		
Ford, Harold E Jr (TN)	$500		

SENATE REPUBLICANS		HOUSE REPUBLICANS	
Santorum, Richard (PA)	$2,000	Bachus, Spencer (AL)	$2,000
Sununu, John (NH)	$2,000	Baker, Hugh (LA)	$2,000
Chafee, Lincoln (RI)	$1,500		

Corporate Foundations and Giving Programs

Citizens Charitable Foundation
Contact: Blake Jordan
One Citizens Plaza — Tel: (617) 725 - 5841
Providence, RI 02903 — Fax: (617) 725 - 5807

Annual Grant Total: under $100,000
Primary Interests: Community Affairs; Economic Development; Housing

Public Affairs and Related Activities Personnel

At Headquarters

CAMPION, Heather P. — Tel: (401) 456 - 7000
Group Exec. V. President, Corporate Affairs — Fax: (401) 456 - 7819

COTTAM, Barbara S. — Tel: (401) 456 - 7000
Senior V. President; and Director, Corporate Communications — Fax: (401) 456 - 7644

JORDAN, Blake — Tel: (617) 725 - 5841
Senior V. President; and Director, Corporate Giving — Fax: (617) 725 - 5807

MCKENZIE, Katherine F. — Tel: (401) 456 - 7000
Group Exec. V. President, Human Resources — Fax: (401) 456 - 7819

O'DONNELL, Kathy — Tel: (401) 455 - 5507
V. President and Director, Public Relations — Fax: (401) 456 - 7819
kathy.o'donnell@citizensbank.com

ROBINSON, Ken — Tel: (401) 455 - 5934
Senior V. President and Manager, Government Relations — Fax: (401) 456 - 7644

Citizens Utilities Company

See listing on page 123 under Citizens Communications Co.

Citrix Systems, Inc.

Supplies access infrastructure solutions.
www.citrix.com

Chairman of the Board
BOGAN, Thomas S. — Tel: (954) 267 - 3000 — Fax: (954) 267 - 9319 — TF: (800) 424 - 8749

President and Chief Exec. Officer
TEMPLETON, Mark B. — Tel: (954) 267 - 3000
mark.templeton@citrix.com — Fax: (954) 267 - 3100 — TF: (800) 424 - 8749

Main Headquarters
Mailing: 851 W. Cypress Creek Rd., Fort Lauderdale, FL 33309 — Tel: (954) 267 - 3000 — Fax: (954) 267 - 9319 — TF: (800) 424 - 8749

Corporate Foundations and Giving Programs

Citrix Systems Corporate Giving Program
851 W. Cypress Creek Rd. — Tel: (954) 267 - 3000
Fort Lauderdale, FL 33309 — Fax: (954) 267 - 9319 — TF: (800) 424 - 8749

Annual Grant Total: none reported
Primary Interests: Economic Development; Education; Technology

Public Affairs and Related Activities Personnel

At Headquarters

ARMSTRONG, Eric — Tel: (954) 267 - 2977
Director, Public and Analyst Relations — Fax: (954) 267 - 2525
eric.armstrong@citrix.com — TF: (800) 424 - 8749

GRANT, Bruce — Tel: (954) 267 - 3000
V. President, Human Resources — Fax: (954) 267 - 9319 — TF: (800) 424 - 8749

JONES, David — Tel: (954) 267 - 3000
Corporate V. President, Business Development and Corporate Affairs — Fax: (954) 267 - 9319 — TF: (800) 424 - 8749

LILLY, Jeff — Tel: (954) 267 - 2886
Manager, Investor Relations — Fax: (954) 267 - 3101
jeff.lilly@citrix.com — TF: (800) 424 - 8749

RIOS, Sabrina — Tel: (954) 267 - 2529
Manager, Product Public Relations — Fax: (954) 267 - 2525
sabrina.rios@citrix.com — TF: (800) 424 - 8749

City Nat'l Bank

See listing on page 124 under City Nat'l Corp.

City Nat'l Corp.

A regional bank holding company.
www.cnb.com
Annual Revenues: $691.8 million

Chairman of the Board TF: (800) 773 - 7100
GOLDSMITH, Bram

President and Chief Exec. Officer TF: (800) 773 - 7100
GOLDSMITH, Russell

Main Headquarters
Mailing: City National Center TF: (800) 773 - 7100
400 N. Roxbury Dr.
Beverly Hills, CA 90210

Public Affairs and Related Activities Personnel

At Headquarters

CAREY, Christopher J. Tel: (310) 888 - 6777
Exec. V. President and Chief Financial Officer TF: (800) 773 - 7100
(City Nat'l Bank)
chris.carey@cnb.com
Responsibilities include investor relations.

DWYER, Kate TF: (800) 773 - 7100
Exec. V. President, Human Resources

At Other Offices

WALKER, Cary Tel: (213) 833 - 4715
Senior V. President and Manager, Corporate Public Relations Fax: (213) 833 - 4702
TF: (800) 773 - 7100
(City Nat'l Bank)
606 S. Olive St.
Los Angeles, CA 90014
cary.walker@cnb.com

Clarity Vision, Inc.

See listing on page 243 under Highmark Inc.

Clear Channel Communications

A diversified media company with operations in radio and television broadcasting, outdoor advertising, and live entertainment.
www.clearchannel.com
Annual Revenues: $7.97 billion

Chairman of the Board Tel: (210) 822 - 2828
MAYS, Lowry Fax: (210) 822 - 2299
llowrymays@clearchannel.com

President and Chief Exec. Officer Tel: (210) 822 - 2828
MAYS, Mark Fax: (210) 822 - 2299
markpmays@clearchannel.com

Main Headquarters
Mailing: 200 E. Basse Rd. Tel: (210) 822 - 2828
San Antonio, TX 78209 Fax: (210) 822 - 2299

Washington Office
Contact: Jessica Wallace Marventano
Mailing: 1401 I St., NW Tel: (202) 289 - 3230
Suite 401 Fax: (202) 289 - 0050
Washington, DC 20005

Political Action Committees

Clear Channel Communications Inc. Political Action Committee
Contact: Andrew W. Levin
1401 I St., NW Tel: (202) 289 - 3230
Suite 401 Fax: (202) 289 - 0050
Washington, DC 20005

Contributions to Candidates: $138,500 (01/05 - 09/05)
Democrats: $42,000; Republicans: $96,500.

Principal Recipients

SENATE DEMOCRATS		HOUSE DEMOCRATS	
Nelson, Benjamin (NE)	$4,500	Gonzalez, Charles A (TX)	$3,000
		Markey, Edward (MA)	$3,000
		Conyers, John Jr. (MI)	$2,500

SENATE REPUBLICANS		HOUSE REPUBLICANS	
Burns, Conrad (MT)	$8,000	Cantor, Eric (VA)	$5,000
Dewine, Richard (OH)	$5,000	Bachus, Spencer (AL)	$3,000
Ensign, John Eric (NV)	$5,000	Bonilla, Henry (TX)	$3,000
Hutchison, Kay Bailey (TX)	$5,000	Whitfield, Ed (KY)	$3,000
		Upton, Fred (MI)	$2,500
Santorum, Richard (PA)	$5,000		
Kyl, Jon L (AZ)	$3,500		

Public Affairs and Related Activities Personnel

At Headquarters

DOLLINGER, Lisa Tel: (210) 822 - 2828
Senior V. President and Chief Communications Officer Fax: (210) 822 - 2299
lisadollinger@clearchannel.com

HAMERSLY, Bill Tel: (210) 822 - 2828
Senior V. President, Human Resources Fax: (210) 822 - 2299
billhamersly@clearchannel.com

HILL, Julie Tel: (210) 822 - 2828
Senior V. President, Finance and Strategic Development Fax: (210) 822 - 2299
juliehill@clearchannel.com

JOHNSON, Kathryn Tel: (210) 822 - 2828
Senior V. President, Corporate Relations Fax: (210) 822 - 2299
kathrynmaysjohnson@clearchannel.com

PALMER, Randy Tel: (210) 822 - 2828
V. President, Investor Relations Fax: (210) 822 - 2299
randypalmer@clearchannel.com

WARREN, Diane D. Tel: (210) 822 - 2828
Senior V. President, Corporate Affairs Fax: (210) 822 - 2299
dianedwarren@clearchannel.com

At Washington Office

FISHER, Robert Tel: (202) 289 - 3230
Director, Government Affairs Fax: (202) 289 - 0050
robertfisher@clearchannel.com
Registered Federal Lobbyist.

KELSAY, Brendan Tel: (202) 289 - 3230
Director, Government Affairs Fax: (202) 289 - 0050
brendankelsay@clearchannel.com
Registered Federal Lobbyist.

LEVIN, Andrew W. Tel: (202) 289 - 3230
Fax: (202) 289 - 0050
Registered Federal Lobbyist.
Responsibilities include political action.

MARVENTANO, Jessica Wallace Tel: (202) 289 - 3224
Senior V. President, Government Affairs Fax: (202) 289 - 0050
jessicaamarventano@clearchannel.com
Registered Federal Lobbyist.
Responsibilities include political action.

Cleco Corp.

A member of the Public Affairs Council. A midstream energy company. Formerly known as the Central Louisiana Electric Co.
www.cleco.com
Annual Revenues: $1.058 billion

Chairman of the Board Tel: (318) 484 - 7400
GARRETT, J. Patrick Fax: (318) 484 - 7465

President and Chief Exec. Officer Tel: (318) 484 - 7400
EPPLER, David M. Fax: (318) 484 - 7465

Main Headquarters
Mailing: P.O. Box 5000 Tel: (318) 484 - 7400
Pineville, LA 71361-5000 Fax: (318) 484 - 7465
Street: 2030 Donahue Ferry Rd.
Pineville, LA 71360

Political Action Committees

United Employees' PAC, Central Louisiana Electric Co. Inc. (CLECO PAC)
Contact: Melissa Henry
P.O. Box 5000 Tel: (318) 484 - 7400
Pineville, LA 71361-5000 Fax: (318) 484 - 7465

Contributions to Candidates: $6,000 (01/05 - 09/05)
Democrats: $1,500; Republicans: $4,500.

Principal Recipients

SENATE DEMOCRATS		HOUSE DEMOCRATS	
Kennedy, John Neely (LA)	$500	Jefferson, William (LA)	$1,000

SENATE REPUBLICANS		HOUSE REPUBLICANS	
Vitter, David (LA)	$2,000	Alexander, Rodney (LA)	$2,000
		Jindal, Bobby (LA)	$500

Corporate Foundations and Giving Programs

Cleco Corporate Contributions
Contact: Robin Cooper
P.O. Box 5000 Tel: (318) 484 - 7400
Pineville, LA 71361-5000 Fax: (318) 484 - 7465

Annual Grant Total: none reported

Public Affairs and Related Activities Personnel

At Headquarters

BAUSEWINE, George W. Tel: (318) 484 - 7400
V. President, Regulatory Affairs and Rates Fax: (318) 484 - 7465
george.bausewine@cleco.com

Cleco Corp.

* continued from previous page

BROUSSARD, Susan
Manager, Corporate and Strategic Communications
Tel: (318) 484 - 7773
Fax: (318) 484 - 7465

BURNS, Mike
Investor Relations Contact
Tel: (318) 484 - 7663
Fax: (318) 484 - 7465

COOPER, Robin
Advertising, Corporate Contributions Contact
Tel: (318) 484 - 7400
Fax: (318) 484 - 7465

FREDERIC, Christy
General Manager, Safety and Public Affairs
christy.frederic@cleco.com
Tel: (318) 484 - 7400
Fax: (318) 484 - 7465

HENRY, Melissa
Treasurer, United Employees' PAC
Tel: (318) 484 - 7400
Fax: (318) 484 - 7465

SHAW, Michiele
V. President, Human Resources, Communications and Ethics
Tel: (318) 484 - 7400
Fax: (318) 484 - 7465

WILLIAMS, James D. "Dennie"
Director, State and Federal Affairs
dennie.williams@cleco.com
Tel: (318) 484 - 7688
Fax: (318) 484 - 7106

Cleveland-Cliffs Inc

A natural resource production and service company with interests in iron ore.

www.cleveland-cliffs.com
Annual Revenues: $330.4 million

Chairman, President and Chief Exec. Officer
BRINZO, John S.
jsbrinzo@cleveland-cliffs.com
Tel: (216) 694 - 5700
Fax: (216) 694 - 4880

Main Headquarters
Mailing: 1100 Superior Ave.
Cleveland, OH 44114-2589
Tel: (216) 694 - 5700
Fax: (216) 694 - 4880

Political Action Committees

Cleveland-Cliffs Inc Political Action Committee (CLIFFSPAC)
Contact: Mr. Dana W. Byrne
1100 Superior Ave.
Cleveland, OH 44114-2589
Tel: (216) 694 - 5700
Fax: (216) 694 - 5537

Contributions to Candidates: $14,000 (01/05 - 09/05)
Democrats: $3,000; Republicans: $10,000; Other: $1,000.

Principal Recipients

SENATE DEMOCRATS
Stabenow, Debbie (MI) $500

HOUSE DEMOCRATS
Stupak, Bart (MI) $2,500

HOUSE OTHER
Oberstar, James L (MN) $1,000

SENATE REPUBLICANS
Kennedy, Mark (MN) $5,000
Dewine, Richard (OH) $2,000

HOUSE REPUBLICANS
Rogers, Michael J (MI) $2,000
Murphy, Tim (PA) $500
Pombo, Richard (CA) $500

Corporate Foundations and Giving Programs

Cleveland-Cliffs Foundation
Contact: Mr. Dana W. Byrne
1100 Superior Ave.
Cleveland, OH 44114-2589
Tel: (216) 694 - 5700
Fax: (216) 694 - 5537

Annual Grant Total: $300,000 - $400,000
Geographic Preference: Area(s) in which the company operates
Primary Interests: Education; Health and Human Services
Recent Recipients: Case Western Reserve University; Cleveland Orchestra; Michigan Technological University; Nature Conservancy; United Way

Public Affairs and Related Activities Personnel

At Headquarters

BYRNE, Mr. Dana W.
V. President, Public Affairs
dwbyrne@cleveland-cliffs.com
Responsibilities include political action.
Tel: (216) 694 - 5700
Fax: (216) 694 - 5537

CROUCH, David B.
Director, Environmental Affairs
dbcrouch@cleveland-cliffs.com
Tel: (216) 694 - 5700
Fax: (216) 694 - 4880

KUMMER, Randy L.
Senior V. President, Human Resources
rlkummer@cleveland-cliffs.com
Tel: (216) 694 - 5700
Fax: (216) 694 - 4880

RICE, Fred B.
Director, Investor Relations
fbrice@cleveland-cliffs.com
Tel: (216) 694 - 5459
Fax: (216) 694 - 6741

The Clorox Co.

A member of the Public Affairs Council. A diversified manufacturer of household grocery products and products for the food service industry.

www.clorox.com
Annual Revenues: $4.3 billion

Chairman, Chief Exec. Officer, and President
JOHNSTON, Gerald E. "Jerry"
Tel: (510) 271 - 7000
Fax: (510) 832 - 1463

Main Headquarters
Mailing: P.O. Box 24305
Oakland, CA 94623-1305
Street: 1221 Broadway
Oakland, CA 94612-1837
Tel: (510) 271 - 7000
Fax: (510) 832 - 1463

Political Action Committees

Clorox Employees' Political Action Committee (ClorPAC)
Contact: Victoria Jones
P.O. Box 24305
Oakland, CA 94623-1305
Tel: (510) 271 - 2971
Fax: (510) 271 - 6583

Contributions to Candidates: $7,500 (01/05 - 09/05)
Democrats: $3,500; Republicans: $4,000.

Principal Recipients

SENATE DEMOCRATS

HOUSE DEMOCRATS
Eshoo, Anna (CA) $1,000
Roybal-Allard, Lucille (CA) $1,000
Sanchez, Linda (CA) $1,000

SENATE REPUBLICANS
Allen, George (VA) $1,000

HOUSE REPUBLICANS
Goodlatte, Robert (VA) $1,000
Hastert, Dennis J. (IL) $1,000
McHugh, John (NY) $1,000

Corporate Foundations and Giving Programs

The Clorox Co. Foundation
Contact: Victoria Jones
P.O. Box 24305
Oakland, CA 94623-1305
Tel: (510) 271 - 2971
Fax: (510) 271 - 6583

Annual Grant Total: $2,000,000 - $5,000,000
Geographic Preference: California; Area(s) in which the company operates
Primary Interests: K-12 Education; Youth Services

Public Affairs and Related Activities Personnel

At Headquarters

AUSTENFELD, Steve
V. President, Investor Relations
Tel: (510) 271 - 2270
Fax: (510) 208 - 1546

GENTZ, Robin M.
Manager, Government Affairs Issues
robin.gentz@clorox.com
Tel: (510) 271 - 7081
Fax: (510) 271 - 6583

HEINRICH, Daniel J.
Senior V. President and Chief Financial Officer
heinrich@clorox.com
Responsibilities include investor relations.
Tel: (510) 271 - 7377
Fax: (510) 832 - 1463

IYER, Suzanne
Government Affairs Issues Manager
suzanne.iyer@clorox.com
Tel: (510) 271 - 7739
Fax: (510) 271 - 6583

JONES, Victoria
Director, Government Affairs and Community Relations
victoria.jones@clorox.com
Tel: (510) 271 - 2971
Fax: (510) 271 - 6583

KANE, Jacqueline P.
Senior V. President, Human Resources
Tel: (510) 271 - 7503
Fax: (510) 208 - 1556

RANDOLPH, Beverly
Consumer Services Manager
beverly.randolph@clorox.com
Tel: (510) 271 - 7283
Fax: (510) 208 - 2682

ClubCorp Internat'l Inc.

An operator of private clubs, resorts and public golf courses.

www.clubcorp.com

Chairman of the Board
DEDMAN, Robert H., Jr.
Tel: (972) 243 - 6191
Fax: (972) 888 - 7555

President and Chief Exec. Officer
BECKERT, John A.
Tel: (972) 243 - 6191
Fax: (972) 888 - 7555

Main Headquarters
Mailing: 3030 LBJ Frwy.
Suite 700
Dallas, TX 75234
Tel: (972) 243 - 6191
Fax: (972) 888 - 7555

Public Affairs and Related Activities Personnel

At Headquarters

BALDWIN, Patricia
V. President, Corporate Communications
Tel: (972) 243 - 6191
Fax: (972) 888 - 7555

LONGSTREET, John H.
Senior V. President, Human Resources
Tel: (972) 243 - 6191
Fax: (972) 888 - 7555

CMS Energy Corp.

An integrated energy company.
www.cmsenergy.com
Annual Revenues: $8.7 billion

Chairman of the Board
WHIPPLE, Kenneth — Tel: (517) 788 - 0550

President and Chief Exec. Officer
JOOS, David W. — Tel: (517) 788 - 0550

Main Headquarters
Mailing: One Energy Plaza
Jackson, MI 49201 — Tel: (517) 788 - 0550

Washington Office
Contact: George A. Pickart
Mailing: 1016 16th St. NW
Suite 500
Washington, DC 20036
Tel: (202) 293 - 5794
Fax: (202) 223 - 6178

Political Action Committees

Consumers Energy Co. Employees for Better Government
Contact: Carrie Schneider
One Energy Plaza
Jackson, MI 49201
Tel: (517) 788 - 2322
Fax: (517) 788 - 1315

Contributions to Candidates: $51,720 (01/05 - 09/05)
Democrats: $10,500; Republicans: $41,220.

Principal Recipients

SENATE DEMOCRATS		HOUSE DEMOCRATS	
Bingaman, Jeff (NM)	$1,000	Stupak, Bart (MI)	$5,000
Stabenow, Debbie (MI)	$1,000		

SENATE REPUBLICANS		HOUSE REPUBLICANS	
Inhofe, James M (OK)	$2,000	Schwarz, John (MI)	$13,000
Talent, James (MO)	$1,000	Hoekstra, Peter (MI)	$5,000
Thomas, Craig (WY)	$1,000	McCotter, Thaddeus (MI)	$3,500
		Miller, Candice S. (MI)	$2,100
		Rogers, Michael J (MI)	$2,000
		Ehlers, Vernon J (MI)	$1,620

Corporate Foundations and Giving Programs

Consumers Energy Foundation & CMS Energy Foundation
Contact: Carolyn A. Bloodworth
One Energy Plaza
Jackson, MI 49201
Tel: (517) 788 - 0432
Fax: (517) 788 - 2281

Annual Grant Total: $2,000,000 - $5,000,000
Geographic Preference: Area(s) in which the company operates
Primary Interests: Arts and Culture; Community Development; Environment/Conservation; Higher Education; Social Services; United Way Campaigns

Public Affairs and Related Activities Personnel

At Headquarters

BLOODWORTH, Carolyn A.
Director, Corporate Giving
cbloodworth@cmsenergy.com
Tel: (517) 788 - 0432
Fax: (517) 788 - 2281

EDELSON, Howard J.
Director, Political Affairs
hjedelso@cmsenergy.com
Tel: (517) 788 - 0091
Fax: (517) 788 - 1315

HOLYFIELD, Jeff
Director, News and Information
Tel: (517) 788 - 2396

MATTESON, Richard A., Jr.
Director, Corporate Communications
rmatteson@cmsenergy.com
Tel: (517) 788 - 2258
Fax: (517) 788 - 0940

MENGEBIER, David G.
Senior V. President, Governmental and Public Affairs/Community Services
Tel: (517) 788 - 1818
Fax: (517) 788 - 0953

MOUNTCASTLE, Laura L.
V. President, Investor Relations and Treasurer
llmountc@cmsenergy.com
Tel: (517) 788 - 0123
Fax: (517) 788 - 1006

SCHNEIDER, Carrie
Contact, Consumers Energy Co. Employees for Better Employment
Tel: (517) 788 - 2322
Fax: (517) 788 - 1315

At Washington Office

PICKART, George A.
Director, International Affairs
Registered Federal Lobbyist.
Tel: (202) 293 - 5794
Fax: (202) 223 - 6178

At Other Offices

HADDEN, Jacalyn Hart
Director, State Governmental Affairs
(Consumers Energy Co.)
124 W. Allegan St.
Suite 1900
Lansing, MI 48933
jhhadden@cmsenergy.com
Tel: (517) 702 - 2820

CNA Financial Corp.

A member of the Public Affairs Council. The holding company for CNA Insurance Companies.
www.cna.com
Annual Revenues: $11 billion

Chairman and Chief Exec. Officer
LILIENTHAL, Stephen W.
Tel: (312) 822 - 5000
Fax: (312) 822 - 6419

Main Headquarters
Mailing: CNA Center
333 S. Wabash Ave.
Chicago, IL 60685
Tel: (312) 822 - 5000
Fax: (312) 822 - 6419

Political Action Committees

CNA Financial Corp. Citizens for Good Government
CNA Center
333 S. Wabash Ave.
Chicago, IL 60685
Tel: (312) 822 - 5000
Fax: (312) 822 - 6419

Contributions to Candidates: $23,500 (01/05 - 09/05)
Democrats: $5,000; Republicans: $18,500.

Principal Recipients

SENATE DEMOCRATS		HOUSE DEMOCRATS	
Nelson, Benjamin (NE)	$2,000		
Carper, Thomas R (DE)	$1,000		
Conrad, Kent (ND)	$1,000		
Leahy, Patrick (VT)	$1,000		

SENATE REPUBLICANS		HOUSE REPUBLICANS	
Dewine, Richard (OH)	$5,000	Hastert, Dennis J. (IL)	$5,000
Santorum, Richard (PA)	$2,000	Gard, John G (WI)	$1,500
		Baker, Hugh (LA)	$1,000
		Kirk, Mark Steven (IL)	$1,000
		Manzullo, Donald (IL)	$1,000
		McCrery, Jim (LA)	$1,000
		Weller, Jerry (IL)	$1,000

Corporate Foundations and Giving Programs

CNA Foundation
Contact: Sarah Pang
CNA Center
333 S. Wabash Ave.
Chicago, IL 60685
Tel: (312) 822 - 6394
Fax: (312) 817 - 2042

Assets: $12,139,000 (2004)
Annual Grant Total: $2,000,000 - $5,000,000
Geographic Preference: Area(s) in which the company operates; Illinois; Chicago, IL
Primary Interests: Arts and Culture; Education; Health and Human Services; Social Services

Public Affairs and Related Activities Personnel

At Headquarters

BORON, Andrew
Director, State Government Relations
Tel: (312) 822 - 1739
Fax: (312) 822 - 1186

DAVIS, Heather
Senior V. President, Government Relations
Tel: (312) 822 - 1740
Fax: (312) 822 - 1186

MANERO, Joseph
Director, State Government Relations
Tel: (312) 822 - 2894
Fax: (312) 822 - 1186

MELCHERT, Karen E.
Director, State Government Relations
(CNA Insurance Cos.)
Mailstop: 43rd Floor
Tel: (312) 822 - 2718
Fax: (312) 822 - 1186

PANG, Sarah
Foundation Executive Director
Tel: (312) 822 - 6394
Fax: (312) 817 - 2042

POWERS, Linda M.
Director, State Government Relations
Mailstop: 43 South
Tel: (312) 822 - 4212
Fax: (312) 822 - 1186

STERN, Michael
Director, State Government Relations
Tel: (312) 822 - 4641
Fax: (312) 822 - 1186

CNA Insurance Cos.

See listing on page 126 under CNA Financial Corp.

CNF Inc.

A global supply chain management company.
www.cnf.com
Annual Revenues: $4.9 billion

Chairman of the Board
KENNEDY, Dr. W. Keith, Jr.
Tel: (650) 494 - 2900
Fax: (650) 813 - 0160

President and Chief Exec. Officer
STOTLAR, Douglas
Tel: (650) 494 - 2900
Fax: (650) 813 - 0160

Main Headquarters
Mailing: 3240 Hillview Ave.
Palo Alto, CA 94304
Tel: (650) 494 - 2900
Fax: (650) 813 - 0160

CNF Inc.

** continued from previous page*

Political Action Committees

CNF Inc. PAC
Contact: Mark C. Thickpenny
3240 Hillview Ave.
Palo Alto, CA 94304
Tel: (650) 494 - 2900
Fax: (650) 813 - 0160

Contributions to Candidates: $10,500 (01/05 - 09/05)
Democrats: $5,000; Republicans: $4,500; Other: $1,000.

Principal Recipients

SENATE DEMOCRATS		HOUSE DEMOCRATS	
Lincoln, Blanche (AR)	$1,000	Eshoo, Anna (CA)	$2,000
		Rahall, Nick J Ii (WV)	$1,000
		Tauscher, Ellen O (CA)	$1,000
		HOUSE OTHER	
		Oberstar, James L (MN)	$1,000
SENATE REPUBLICANS		**HOUSE REPUBLICANS**	
Talent, James (MO)	$1,500	Lungren, Daniel E (CA)	$2,000
		Duncan, John (TN)	$1,000

Corporate Foundations and Giving Programs

CNF Inc. Contributions Program
3240 Hillview Ave.
Palo Alto, CA 94304
Tel: (650) 494 - 2900
Fax: (650) 813 - 0160

Annual Grant Total: $500,000 - $750,000

Grants awarded to both national groups and local organizations in the communities where the company has facilities.

Geographic Preference: Area(s) in which the company operates

Primary Interests: Community Development; Higher Education; Social Services

Recent Recipients: Harvard University; Stanford University

Public Affairs and Related Activities Personnel

At Headquarters

ALLEN, James R.
V. President, Public Affairs and Corporate Communications
allen.jim@cnf.com
Responsibilities include government affairs.
Tel: (650) 813 - 5335
Fax: (650) 813 - 0158

FENIMORE, Jamie
Public Relations Contact
Tel: (650) 494 - 2900
Fax: (650) 813 - 0158

FOSSENIER, Patrick
Director, Investor Relations
fossenier.patrick@cnf.com
Tel: (650) 813 - 5353
Fax: (650) 813 - 0160

MULLETT, Charles
Tel: (650) 494 - 2900
Fax: (650) 813 - 0160

SLATE, David L.
V. President, Human Resources and Deputy General Counsel
Tel: (650) 494 - 2900
Fax: (650) 813 - 0160

THICKPENNY, Mark C.
V. President and Treasurer
Responsibilities include political action.
Tel: (650) 494 - 2900
Fax: (650) 813 - 0160

CNF Transportation Inc.

See listing on page 126 under CNF Inc.

CNG

See listing on page 162 under Dominion Resources, Inc.

Coachmen Industries, Inc.

A manufacturer of recreational vehicles and modular homes.

www.coachmen.com
Annual Revenues: $665.1 million

Chairman and Chief Exec. Officer
SKINNER, Claire C.
cskinner@coachmen.com
Tel: (574) 262 - 0123
Fax: (574) 262 - 8823

Main Headquarters
Mailing: P.O. Box 3300
Elkhart, IN 46515
Street: 2831 Dexter Dr.
Elkhart, IN 46514
Tel: (574) 262 - 0123
Fax: (574) 262 - 8823

Corporate Foundations and Giving Programs

Coachmen Industries Corporate Contributions Program
Contact: William G. Lenhart
P.O. Box 3300
Elkhart, IN 46515
Tel: (574) 262 - 0123
Fax: (574) 262 - 8823

Annual Grant Total: $400,000 - $500,000

Public Affairs and Related Activities Personnel

At Headquarters

LENHART, William G.
Senior V. President, Human Resources
blenhart@coachmen.com
Responsibilities also include corporate philanthropy.
Tel: (574) 262 - 0123
Fax: (574) 262 - 8823

TRYKA, Jeffrey
Director, Planning and Investor Relations
jtryka@coachmen.com
Responsibilities include media relations.
Tel: (574) 262 - 0123
Fax: (574) 262 - 8823

Coca-Cola Bottling Co. Consolidated

Bottles, cans, and markets products of The Coca-Cola Co. (see separate listing).

www.cokeconsolidated.com
Annual Revenues: $1.25 billion

Chairman and Chief Exec. Officer
HARRISON, J. Frank, III
Tel: (704) 551 - 4400
Fax: (704) 551 - 4646

Main Headquarters
Mailing: 4100 Coca-Cola Plaza
Charlotte, NC 28211
Tel: (704) 551 - 4400
Fax: (704) 551 - 4646

Political Action Committees

Coca-Cola Bottling Co. United Inc. Committee for Good Government
Contact: Virginia Walker Jones
P.O. Box 2006
Birmingham, AL 35201

Contributions to Candidates: $2,000 (01/05 - 09/05)
Democrats: $2,000.

Principal Recipients

SENATE DEMOCRATS	HOUSE DEMOCRATS	
	Davis, Artur (AL)	$2,000

Public Affairs and Related Activities Personnel

At Headquarters

HENRY, Kevin A.
V. President, Human Resources
Tel: (704) 551 - 4400
Fax: (704) 551 - 4646

STEELE, Lauren C.
V. President, Corporate Affairs
Responsibilities include corporate communications.
Tel: (704) 551 - 4551
Fax: (704) 551 - 4646

At Other Offices

JONES, Virginia Walker
Treasurer, Coca-Cola Bottling Co. United Inc. Committee for Good Government
P.O. Box 2006
Birmingham, AL 35201

Coca-Cola Bottling Co. of Kentucky

See listing on page 128 under Coca-Cola Enterprises Inc.

Coca-Cola Bottling Co. of New York, Inc., The

See listing on page 128 under Coca-Cola Enterprises Inc.

The Coca-Cola Co.

PUBLIC AFFAIRS COUNCIL

www.cocacola.com
Annual Revenues: $20.092 billion

Chairman and Chief Exec. Officer
ISDELL, E. Neville
Tel: (404) 676 - 2121
Fax: (404) 676 - 6792

Main Headquarters
Mailing: P.O. Box 1734
Atlanta, GA 30301
Street: One Coca-Cola Plaza
Atlanta, GA 30313
Tel: (404) 676 - 2121
Fax: (404) 676 - 6792

Washington Office
Contact: Barclay T. Resler
Mailing: 800 Connecticut Ave. NW
Suite 711
Washington, DC 20006
Tel: (202) 466 - 5310

Political Action Committees

The Coca-Cola Co. Non-partisan Committee for Good Government
Contact: David M. Taggart
P.O. Box 1734
Atlanta, GA 30301
Tel: (404) 676 - 2121
Fax: (404) 676 - 6792

Contributions to Candidates: $67,000 (01/05 - 09/05)

The Coca-Cola Co.

* continued from previous page

Democrats: $23,000; Republicans: $44,000.

Principal Recipients

SENATE DEMOCRATS		HOUSE DEMOCRATS	
Clinton, Hillary Rodham (NY)	$2,500	Lewis, John (GA)	$3,000
		Scott, David (GA)	$2,500
		Hoyer, Steny (MD)	$2,000
SENATE REPUBLICANS		**HOUSE REPUBLICANS**	
Ensign, John Eric (NV)	$2,000	Linder, John (GA)	$3,000
Gregg, Judd (NH)	$2,000	Price, Thomas (GA)	$3,000
Smith, Gordon (OR)	$2,000	Bonilla, Henry (TX)	$2,000
Burns, Conrad (MT)	$1,500	Keller, Richard (FL)	$2,000
		Kingston, John (GA)	$2,000
		Northup, Anne M. (KY)	$2,000

Corporate Foundations and Giving Programs

The Coca-Cola Foundation, Inc.
P.O. Box 442 — Tel: (800) 306 - 2653
Atlanta, GA 30301-0442

Annual Grant Total: over $5,000,000

Guidelines are available.

Geographic Preference: Atlanta, GA; Area(s) in which the company operates
Primary Interests: Arts and Culture; Education

Coca-Cola Scholars Foundation
P.O. Box 1734 — Tel: (404) 676 - 2121
Atlanta, GA 30301 — Fax: (404) 676 - 6792

Annual Grant Total: none reported

Annually awards fifty $20,000 and one hundred $4,000 post-secondary scholarships to promising high school seniors around the country. Selection is based on a number of factors, with special emphasis on character, personal merit, and leadership skills.

Geographic Preference: National
Primary Interests: Higher Education

Public Affairs and Related Activities Personnel

At Headquarters

DEUTSCH, Ben — Tel: (404) 676 - 2121
Director, Financial Communications — Fax: (404) 676 - 6428

ECHOLS, Matthew T. — Tel: (404) 676 - 2251
Director, State Government Relations — Fax: (404) 676 - 6792
Mailstop: USA 644
mechols@na.ko.com

HOPKINS, Douglas W. — Tel: (404) 676 - 7733
Manager, Corporate Affairs, Finance, and Administration — Fax: (404) 515 - 2272
Mailstop: USA 19
dhopkins@na.ko.com

JONES, Ingrid Saunders — Tel: (404) 676 - 2121
Senior V. President, Corporate External Affairs — Fax: (404) 676 - 6792
ijones@na.ko.com

MARK, Larry — Tel: (404) 676 - 2121
Director, Investor Relations — Fax: (404) 676 - 6792
lmark@na.ko.com

MCCRAGUE, Cynthia — Tel: (404) 676 - 2121
Senior V. President and Director, Human Resources — Fax: (404) 676 - 6792

PACE, Amanda — Tel: (404) 676 - 2121
Director, Consumer Affairs — Fax: (404) 676 - 6792
apace@na.ko.com

SCHAFER, Dan A. — Tel: (404) 676 - 2121
Director, North American Communications — Fax: (404) 676 - 6792

SOUTUS, Sonya — Tel: (404) 676 - 2121
Assistant V. President and Director, Media Relations — Fax: (404) 515 - 6428
ssoutus@na.ko.com

SUTLIVE, Charles — Tel: (404) 676 - 5451
Manager, State Government Relations — Fax: (404) 676 - 8265
Mailstop: USA 645
csutlive@na.ko.com

TAGGART, David M. — Tel: (404) 676 - 2121
Treasurer, Coca-Cola Co. Non-Partisan Committee for Good Government — Fax: (404) 676 - 6792
dtaggart@na.ko.com

TUGGLE, Clyde C. — Tel: (404) 676 - 2121
Senior V. President and Director, Worldwide Public Affairs and Communications — Fax: (404) 676 - 6792
ctuggle@na.ko.com

At Washington Office

ANDERSON, Bryan D. — Tel: (202) 973 - 2663
Assistant V. President, Government Relations — Fax: (202) 466 - 2262
banderson@na.ko.com
Registered Federal Lobbyist.

BROWNLEE, John T. — Tel: (202) 973 - 2667
Manager, Government Relations — Fax: (202) 466 - 2262
jbrownlee@na.ko.com
Registered Federal Lobbyist.

RESLER, Barclay T. — Tel: (202) 973 - 2660
V. President, Governmental Relations — Fax: (202) 466 - 2262
bresler@na.ko.com
Registered Federal Lobbyist.

Coca-Cola Enterprises Inc.

A member of the Public Affairs Council. Bottler of Coca-Cola products.

www.cokecce.com
Annual Revenues: $16.8 billion

Chairman of the Board — Tel: (770) 989 - 3000
KLINE, Lowry F. — Fax: (770) 989 - 3363

President and Chief Exec. Officer — Tel: (770) 989 - 3000
ALM, John R. — Fax: (770) 989 - 3363

Main Headquarters

Mailing: P.O. Box 723040 — Tel: (770) 989 - 3000
Atlanta, GA 31139-0040 — Fax: (770) 989 - 3363
Street: 2500 Windy Ridge Pkwy.
Suite 900
Atlanta, GA 30339

Political Action Committees

Coca-Cola Enterprises Employee PAC
Contact: Eugene M. "Gene" Rackley
P.O. Box 723040 — Tel: (770) 989 - 3000
Atlanta, GA 31139-0040 — Fax: (770) 989 - 3788

Contributions to Candidates: $71,350 (01/05 - 09/05)

Democrats: $28,100; Republicans: $43,250.

Principal Recipients

SENATE DEMOCRATS		HOUSE DEMOCRATS	
Clinton, Hillary Rodham (NY)	$2,500	Hoyer, Steny (MD)	$7,500
		Vargas, Juan (CA)	$5,000
		Scott, David (GA)	$3,000
		Boyd, F Allen Jr (FL)	$2,500
		Nation, Joe (CA)	$2,100
SENATE REPUBLICANS		**HOUSE REPUBLICANS**	
Smith, Gordon (OR)	$6,000	Boehner, John (OH)	$2,500
Martinez, Mel (FL)	$5,000	Bonilla, Henry (TX)	$2,000
McConnell, Mitch (KY)	$5,000		

Public Affairs and Related Activities Personnel

At Headquarters

ANTHONY, Scott — Tel: (770) 989 - 3105
V. President, Investor Relations — Fax: (770) 989 - 3788

ASMAN, Laura Brightwell — Tel: (770) 989 - 3023
Corporate Director, Public Affairs — Fax: (770) 989 - 3790

BOWLING, Dan — Tel: (770) 989 - 3000
Senior V. President, Human Resources — Fax: (770) 989 - 3781

DOWNS, John H., Jr. — Tel: (770) 989 - 3775
Senior V. President, Public Affairs and Communications — Fax: (770) 989 - 3781
Responsibilities include government relations.

RACKLEY, Eugene M. "Gene" — Tel: (770) 989 - 3000
Corporate Manager, Government Relations — Fax: (770) 989 - 3788

At Other Offices

ETHERLY, Curtis — Tel: (410) 290 - 3024
V. President, Public Affairs
9770 Patuxent Woods Dr.
Columbia, MD 21046

KIENER, Ashlie — Tel: (636) 443 - 6150
Director, Public Affairs — Fax: (636) 443 - 7208
(Central States Coca-Cola Bottling Co.)
3800 Mueller Rd.
St. Charles, MO 63301

LANZ, Robert J. "Bob" — Tel: (914) 789 - 1193
V. President, Public Affairs — Fax: (914) 345 - 3944
(Coca-Cola Bottling Co. of New York, Inc., The)
Three Skyline Dr.
Hawthorne, NY 10532

PHILLIPS, Robert W. "Bob" — Tel: (213) 744 - 8653
V. President, Public Affairs — Fax: (213) 744 - 8903
(BCI Coca-Cola Bottling Co. of Los Angeles)
1334 S. Central Ave.
Los Angeles, CA 90021

Coca-Cola Enterprises Inc.

* *continued from previous page*

POTTS, Roy — Tel: (502) 775 - 4692, Fax: (502) 775 - 4691
Manager, Public Affairs
(Coca-Cola Bottling Co. of Kentucky)
1661 W. Hill St.
Louisville, KY 40210

SORDS, David — Tel: (512) 832 - 2518
Director, Public Affairs
9600 Burnet Rd.
Austin, TX 78758

VILLARRUBIA, Kel P. — Tel: (504) 818 - 7360, Fax: (504) 826 - 7258
V. President, Public Affairs
(Louisiana Coca-Cola Bottling Co. Ltd.)
5601 Citrus Blvd.
Harahan, LA 70123

The Coleman Company, Inc.

Manufactures and distributes widely diversified product lines for camping and leisure time at hardware/home center markets throughout the U.S., Canada and more than 100 other countries. A subsidiary of American Household, Inc.

www.coleman.com

President and Chief Exec. Officer — Tel: (316) 832 - 2700
KIEDAISCH, Gary A.

Main Headquarters
Mailing: 3600 N. Hydraulic, Wichita, KS 67219 — Tel: (316) 832 - 2700

Public Affairs and Related Activities Personnel

At Headquarters

PAULSON, Nancy — Tel: (316) 832 - 2700
Senior V. President, Global Human Resources

REID, Jim — Tel: (316) 832 - 2700
Senior Director, Public Relations

WALDEN, Ann — Tel: (316) 832 - 2700
Manager, Public Relations

Colgate-Palmolive Co.

A worldwide manufacturer and distributor of consumer products for personal and household care.

www.colgate.com
Annual Revenues: $9.428 billion

Chairman and Chief Exec. Officer — Tel: (212) 310 - 2000, Fax: (212) 310 - 3284
MARK, Reuben

Main Headquarters
Mailing: 300 Park Ave., New York, NY 10022 — Tel: (212) 310 - 2000, Fax: (212) 310 - 2475

Corporate Foundations and Giving Programs

Colgate-Palmolive Corporate Giving Program
300 Park Ave.
New York, NY 10022 — Tel: (212) 310 - 2000, Fax: (212) 310 - 2475

Annual Grant Total: over $5,000,000
Geographic Preference: Area(s) in which the company operates; New York City; National
Primary Interests: Education; Minority Opportunities; Women; Youth Services

Public Affairs and Related Activities Personnel

At Headquarters

GORKEN, Stephen S. — Tel: (212) 310 - 2000, Fax: (212) 310 - 2475
V. President, Global Labor Relations

KIRKPATRICK, Robert K. — Tel: (212) 310 - 2000, Fax: (212) 310 - 3284
V. President, Global Media

THOMPSON, Bina H. — Tel: (212) 310 - 3072, Fax: (212) 310 - 3302
V. President, Investor Relations

ZERBE, Julie A. — Tel: (212) 310 - 2000, Fax: (212) 310 - 3284
V. President, Corporate Communications

Collins & Aikman Corp.

A manufacturer of textile, noise abatement and plastic interior trim and convertible top systems to the North American automotive industry.

www.collinsaikman.com
Annual Revenues: $1.823 billion

Chairman and Chief Exec. Officer — Tel: (248) 824 - 2500
STOCKMAN, David A.

Main Headquarters
Mailing: 250 Stephenson Hwy., Troy, MI 48083 — Tel: (248) 824 - 2500, Fax: (248) 824 - 1532

Political Action Committees

Collins and Aikman Corp. PAC
Contact: Jonathan Peisner
250 Stephenson Hwy. — Tel: (248) 824 - 2500
Troy, MI 48083

Contributions to Candidates: none reported (01/05 - 09/05)

Corporate Foundations and Giving Programs

Collins & Aikman Foundation
Contact: J. Michael Stepp
P.O. Box 32665 — Tel: (704) 547 - 8500, Fax: (704) 547 - 2360
Charlotte, NC 28232-2665

Annual Grant Total: $200,000 - $300,000
Geographic Preference: Area(s) in which the company operates
Primary Interests: Arts and Culture; Education; Health
Recent Recipients: Nat'l Merit Scholarship; United Way; YMCA

Public Affairs and Related Activities Personnel

At Headquarters

KRAUSE, Robert A. — Tel: (248) 733 - 4355
V. President, Treasurer; and Head, Investor Relations
robert.krause@colaik.com

PEISNER, Jonathan — Tel: (248) 824 - 2500
PAC Treasurer

TINNELL, Greg L. — Tel: (248) 824 - 1629
Senior V. President, Human Resources
greg.tinnell@colaik.com

YOUNGMAN, David — Tel: (248) 824 - 1562, Fax: (248) 824 - 1532
Director, Corporate Communications
david.youngman@colaik.com

At Other Offices

STEPP, J. Michael — Tel: (704) 547 - 8500, Fax: (704) 547 - 2360
President, Foundation
P.O. Box 32665
Charlotte, NC 28232-2665

The Colonial Bancgroup, Inc.

A bank holding company.

www.colonialbank.com

Chairman and Chief Exec. Officer — Tel: (334) 240 - 5000, TF: (800) 285 - 5886
LOWDER, Robert E.

Main Headquarters
Mailing: Colonial Financial Center, One Commerce St., Montgomery, AL 36104 — Tel: (334) 240 - 5000, TF: (800) 285 - 5886

Political Action Committees

Colonial Bancgroup Inc. Federal Political Action Committee (Colonial Fed PAC)
Colonial Financial Center — Tel: (334) 240 - 5000, TF: (800) 285 - 5886
One Commerce St.
Montgomery, AL 36104

Contributions to Candidates: $3,000 (01/05 - 09/05)
Republicans: $3,000.

Principal Recipients

SENATE REPUBLICANS	HOUSE REPUBLICANS	
	Everett, Terry (AL)	$3,000

Public Affairs and Related Activities Personnel

At Headquarters

ALLRED, Glenda — Tel: (334) 240 - 5000, TF: (800) 285 - 5886
Investor Relations

PARRISH, Harlan — Tel: (334) 240 - 5000, TF: (800) 285 - 5886
PAC Treasurer

Colonial Gas

See listing on page 279 under KeySpan Corp.

Colonial Life & Accident Insurance Co.

Provides benefits communication, service, enrollment, and supplemental insurance to employees and their families at the worksite. A subsidiary of UnumProvident Corp. (see separate listing).

www.coloniallife.com

President and Chief Exec. Officer — Tel: (803) 798 - 7000, TF: (800) 325 - 4368
HORN, Randall C. "Randy"

Main Headquarters
Mailing: P.O. Box 1365, Columbia, SC 29202 — Tel: (803) 798 - 7000, TF: (800) 325 - 4368
Street: 1200 Colonial Life Blvd., Columbia, SC 29210

Political Action Committees

COLPAC
Contact: Jacqueline B. Winston
P.O. Box 1365 — Tel: (803) 798 - 7000, TF: (800) 325 - 4368
Columbia, SC 29202

Contributions to Candidates: none reported (01/05 - 09/05)

Colonial Life & Accident Insurance Co.

* continued from previous page

Corporate Foundations and Giving Programs

Colonial Life & Accident Insurance Co. Corp. Giving Program
Contact: Donna Northam
P.O. Box 1365 — Tel: (803) 213 - 5634
Columbia, SC 29202 — Fax: (803) 213 - 7461
TF: (800) 325 - 4368

Annual Grant Total: $400,000 - $500,000

Public Affairs and Related Activities Personnel

At Headquarters

NORTHAM, Donna — Tel: (803) 213 - 5634
Assistant V. President, Corporate and External Communications — Fax: (803) 213 - 7461
TF: (800) 325 - 4368
Responsibilities include community affairs.

REYNOLDS, Jeanne — Tel: (803) 213 - 6274
Media Relations — Fax: (803) 213 - 7433
jdreynolds@unum.com — TF: (800) 325 - 4368

WINSTON, Jacqueline B. — Tel: (803) 798 - 7000
PAC Treasurer — TF: (800) 325 - 4368

Colonial Pipeline Co.

A joint venture of the following major oil companies - CITGO Petroleum, ConocoPhillips, Shell, Koch Industries, and UNOCAL Corp. (see separate listings).

www.colpipe.com

Chairman of the Board — Tel: (678) 762 - 2211
CAFFEY, Bill — Fax: (678) 762 - 2883
TF: (800) 275 - 3004

President and Chief Exec. Officer — Fax: (678) 762 - 2883
LEMMON, David L. — TF: (800) 275 - 3004

Main Headquarters

Mailing: P.O. Box 1624 — Tel: (678) 762 - 2211
Alpharetta, GA 30009-9934 — Fax: (678) 762 - 2883
TF: (800) 275 - 3004

Street: 1185 Sanctuary Pkwy., Suite 100
Alpharetta, GA 30004-4738

Public Affairs and Related Activities Personnel

At Headquarters

BAKER, Steve — Fax: (678) 762 - 2315
Manager, Media and Marketing — TF: (800) 275 - 3004

BARANSKI, Susan Castiglione — Tel: (678) 762 - 2211
Senior Manager, Corporate and Public Affairs — Fax: (678) 762 - 2883
TF: (800) 275 - 3004

BRANDON, Rhonda S. — Fax: (678) 762 - 2883
V. President, Human Resources — TF: (800) 275 - 3004

BURNS, Dona Harrington — Fax: (678) 762 - 2315
Manager, Corporate Communications — TF: (800) 275 - 3004

MCDOUGALD, Grace E. — Fax: (678) 762 - 2315
Manager, Community Relations — TF: (800) 275 - 3004

WHITEHEAD, Samuel W. — Fax: (678) 762 - 2315
Manager, Government Affairs — TF: (800) 275 - 3004

Colonial Supplemental Insurance

See listing on page 129 under Colonial Life & Accident Insurance Co.

Columbia Energy Group

See listing on page 349 under NiSource Inc.

Columbia Gas Transmission Corp.

See listing on page 349 under NiSource Inc.

Columbia/HCA Healthcare Corp.

See listing on page 237 under HCA.

Comcast Corporation

A company engaged in wireline (cable) communications, commerce and content. Acquired AT&T Broadband in November, 2002.

www.comcast.com
Annual Revenues: $20 billion

Chairman and Chief Exec. Officer — Tel: (215) 665 - 1700
ROBERTS, Brian L. — Fax: (215) 981 - 7790

Main Headquarters

Mailing: 1500 Market St. — Tel: (215) 665 - 1700
Philadelphia, PA 19102 — Fax: (215) 981 - 7790

Washington Office

Contact: Kerry Knott

Mailing: 2001 Pennsylvania Ave. NW — Tel: (202) 379 - 7100
Suite 500 — Fax: (202) 466 - 7718
Washington, DC 20006

Political Action Committees

Comcast Corp. Political Action Committee
Contact: Joseph W. Waz, Jr.
1500 Market St. — Tel: (215) 981 - 7607
Philadelphia, PA 19102 — Fax: (215) 981 - 7712

Contributions to Candidates: $277,200 (01/05 - 09/05)
Democrats: $113,500; Republicans: $163,700.

Principal Recipients

SENATE DEMOCRATS		**HOUSE DEMOCRATS**	
Lautenberg, Frank (NJ)	$10,000	Markey, Edward (MA)	$7,500
Nelson, Bill (FL)	$8,500	Eshoo, Anna (CA)	$6,500
Kennedy, Ted (MA)	$6,000		
SENATE REPUBLICANS		**HOUSE REPUBLICANS**	
Snowe, Olympia (ME)	$7,500	Upton, Fred (MI)	$10,000
Allen, George (VA)	$7,000	Pickering, Chip (MS)	$9,000

Corporate Foundations and Giving Programs

The Comcast Foundation
Contact: Joseph W. Waz, Jr.
1500 Market St. — Tel: (215) 981 - 7607
Philadelphia, PA 19102 — Fax: (215) 981 - 7712

Annual Grant Total: over $5,000,000
The company also provides substantial corporate and in-kind support, which totals over $30 million per year.
Geographic Preference: Area(s) in which the company operates
Primary Interests: Education

Public Affairs and Related Activities Personnel

At Headquarters

COHEN, David L. — Tel: (215) 981 - 7585
Exec. V. President — Fax: (215) 981 - 7790
david_cohen@comcast.com

DOONER, Marlene S. — Tel: (215) 981 - 7392
V. President, Investor Relations — Fax: (215) 981 - 7790
marlene_dooner@comcast.com

FITZPATRICK, Tim — Tel: (215) 981 - 8515
Director, Corporate Communications — Fax: (215) 981 - 7790

KHOURY, Jennifer — Tel: (215) 320 - 7408
Senior Director, Corporate Communications — Fax: (215) 981 - 7790

MIKALAUSKAS, Kenneth — Tel: (215) 665 - 1700
Treasurer, Comcast Corp. Political Action Committee — Fax: (215) 981 - 7712

MOYER, Jenni — Tel: (215) 851 - 3311
Director, Corporate Communications — Fax: (215) 981 - 7790

RUDNAY, D'Arcy — Tel: (215) 981 - 8582
V. President, Corporate Communications — Fax: (215) 981 - 7790

RUSSO, Jeanne — Tel: (215) 981 - 8552
Director, Corporate Communications — Fax: (215) 981 - 7790

WAZ, Joseph W., Jr. — Tel: (215) 981 - 7607
V. President, External Affairs and Public Policy Counsel — Fax: (215) 981 - 7712
jww@comcast.com
Responsibilities include corporate contributions and government affairs.

At Washington Office

CLARKE, Victoria "Tori" — Tel: (202) 379 - 7100
Senior Advisor, Communications and Government Affairs — Fax: (202) 466 - 7718

COLTHARP, James R. — Tel: (202) 379 - 7100
Chief Policy Advisor, FCC and Regulatory — Fax: (202) 466 - 7718
jim_coltharp@comcast.com
Registered Federal Lobbyist.

KELLY, Brian — Tel: (202) 379 - 7100
Senior Director, Government Affairs — Fax: (202) 466 - 7718
Registered Federal Lobbyist.

KNOTT, Kerry — Tel: (202) 379 - 7105
V. President, Federal Government Affairs — Fax: (202) 466 - 7718
kerry_knott@comcast.com
Registered Federal Lobbyist.

MAXFIELD, Melissa — Tel: (202) 379 - 7100
Senior Director, Federal Government Affairs — Fax: (202) 466 - 7718
Registered Federal Lobbyist.

MORABITO, John S. — Tel: (202) 379 - 7100
Senior Director and Policy Counsel, Federal Affairs — Fax: (202) 466 - 7718
Registered Federal Lobbyist.

Comdisco, Inc.

See listing on page 460 under SunGard Data Systems, Inc.

ComEd

See listing on page 187 under Exelon Corp.

Comerica Incorporated

A member of the Public Affairs Council. Formed by a merger in September 1992 of Comerica Bank and Manufacturers Bank, N.A.

www.comerica.com
Annual Revenues: $4.197 billion

Chairman, President and Chief Exec. Officer
BABB, Ralph W., Jr. — Tel: (313) 222 - 6918; Fax: (313) 964 - 0638; TF: (800) 521 - 1190

Main Headquarters
Mailing: P.O. Box 75000, Detroit, MI 48275 — Tel: (313) 222 - 4000; TF: (800) 521 - 1190
Street: Comerica Tower at Detroit Center, 500 Woodward Ave., Detroit, MI 48226

Political Action Committees

Comerica Inc. Committee for Responsible Political Action (Comerica PAC)
Contact: Michael D. McLauchlan
P.O. Box 75000
Detroit, MI 48275 — Tel: (313) 222 - 7496; Fax: (313) 222 - 8720; TF: (800) 521 - 1190

Contributions to Candidates: $1,000 (01/05 - 09/05)
Democrats: $1,000.

Principal Recipients

SENATE DEMOCRATS		HOUSE DEMOCRATS	
		Bell, Christopher (TX)	$1,000

Comerica Inc. PAC
Contact: James M. Garavaglia
P.O. Box 75000
Detroit, MI 48275 — Tel: (313) 222 - 3688; Fax: (313) 222 - 8720; TF: (800) 521 - 1190

Contributions to Candidates: $18,600 (01/05 - 09/05)
Democrats: $7,000; Republicans: $11,600.

Corporate Foundations and Giving Programs

Comerica Incorporated Corporate Contributions Program
Contact: Caroline Chambers
P.O. Box 75000
Detroit, MI 48275 — Tel: (313) 222 - 3571; Fax: (313) 222 - 5555; TF: (800) 521 - 1190

Annual Grant Total: $2,000,000 - $5,000,000
Geographic Preference: Michigan; California; Florida; Texas
Primary Interests: Economic Development; Education; Housing

Public Affairs and Related Activities Personnel

At Headquarters

ARSENAULT, Helen
First V. President, Investor Relations
Mailstop: mc 3015
Tel: (313) 222 - 2840; Fax: (313) 965 - 4648; TF: (800) 521 - 1190

CHAMBERS, Caroline
Corporate Contributions Manager, Exec. Admin.
Mailstop: mc 3390
Tel: (313) 222 - 3571; Fax: (313) 222 - 5555; TF: (800) 521 - 1190

COLE, Charlene
Educational Relations Officer, Civic Affairs
Mailstop: mc 3352
Tel: (313) 222 - 3882; Fax: (313) 222 - 8720; TF: (800) 521 - 1190

GARAVAGLIA, James M.
Senior V. President, Public Affairs
Mailstop: mc 3352
Tel: (313) 222 - 3688; Fax: (313) 222 - 8720; TF: (800) 521 - 1190

GUYTON, Louise G.
V. President, Public Affairs
Mailstop: mc 3352
Tel: (313) 222 - 8620; Fax: (313) 222 - 8720; TF: (800) 521 - 1190

HUGHES, Coleen R.
CRA Coordinator, Public Affairs
Mailstop: mc 3352
Tel: (313) 222 - 8618; Fax: (313) 222 - 8720; TF: (800) 521 - 1190

KOSAIAN, Rebecca
Employee Communications Representative
Mailstop: mc 3350
Tel: (313) 222 - 7300; Fax: (313) 222 - 6040; TF: (800) 521 - 1190

MCLAUCHLAN, Michael D.
First V. President, Government Relations
Mailstop: mc 3352
Tel: (313) 222 - 7496; Fax: (313) 222 - 8720; TF: (800) 521 - 1190

MCMURRAY, Sharon R.
Senior V. President, Corporate Communications
Mailstop: mc 3350
Tel: (313) 222 - 4881; Fax: (313) 222 - 3240; TF: (800) 521 - 1190

MIELKE, Wayne J.
V. President, Corporate Communications
Mailstop: mc 3350
Tel: (313) 222 - 4732; Fax: (313) 222 - 3240; TF: (800) 521 - 1190

ODOM, Melanie
V. President, Public Affairs
Mailstop: MC 3352
Tel: (313) 222 - 4105; TF: (800) 521 - 1190

PITTON, Kathleen A.
V. President, Corporate Communications
Mailstop: mc 3350
Tel: (313) 222 - 4916; Fax: (313) 222 - 3240; TF: (800) 521 - 1190

REID, Kathryn A.
First V. President, Affiliate CRA/Public Affairs
Mailstop: mc 3352
Tel: (313) 222 - 7276; Fax: (313) 222 - 8720; TF: (800) 521 - 1190

SMITH, Loretta G.
V. President, Community Relations
Mailstop: mc 3352
Tel: (313) 222 - 6987; Fax: (313) 222 - 8720; TF: (800) 521 - 1190

At Other Offices

HEANY, Sandra K.
Assistant V. President and CRA Coordinator, Community Affairs
101 N. Washington Square
Mailstop: mc 7816
Lansing, MI 48933
Tel: (517) 342 - 5765; Fax: (517) 342 - 5969; TF: (800) 521 - 1190

Commerce Bancshares Inc.

Bank holding company.

www.commercebank.com
Annual Revenues: $1.028 billion

Chairman, President, and Chief Exec. Officer
KEMPER, David W. — Fax: (314) 746 - 8514; TF: (800) 892 - 7100

Main Headquarters
Mailing: P.O. Box 419248, Kansas City, MO 64141-6248 — Tel: (816) 234 - 2000; TF: (800) 892 - 7100
Street: 1000 Walnut St., Kansas City, MO 64106

Political Action Committees

Commerce Bancs PAC
Contact: Robert Lay
P.O. Box 419248
Kansas City, MO 64141-6248 — Tel: (816) 234 - 2000; TF: (800) 892 - 7100

Contributions to Candidates: $3,000 (01/05 - 09/05)
Democrats: $250; Republicans: $2,750.

Principal Recipients

SENATE DEMOCRATS		HOUSE DEMOCRATS	
		Skelton, Ike (MO)	$250
SENATE REPUBLICANS		**HOUSE REPUBLICANS**	
Talent, James (MO)	$2,500	Emerson, Jo Ann (MO)	$250

Corporate Foundations and Giving Programs

Commerce Bancshares Foundation
Contact: Michael D. Fields
P.O. Box 419248
Kansas City, MO 64141-6248 — Tel: (816) 234 - 2000; TF: (800) 892 - 7100

Annual Grant Total: $1,000,000 - $2,000,000
Geographic Preference: Kansas; Illinois; Missouri
Primary Interests: Arts and Culture; Education; Health; Human Welfare
Recent Recipients: United Way; YMCA

Public Affairs and Related Activities Personnel

At Headquarters

ABERDEEN, Jeffery D.
Controller
jeff.aberdeen@commercebank.com
Responsibilities include investor relations.
Tel: (816) 234 - 2081; TF: (800) 892 - 7100

FIELDS, Michael D.
President, Foundation
Tel: (816) 234 - 2000; TF: (800) 892 - 7100

LAY, Robert
Treasurer, Commerce Bancs PAC
Tel: (816) 234 - 2000; TF: (800) 892 - 7100

At Other Offices

FOSTER, Sara E.
Senior V. President, Human Resources
8000 Forsyth Blvd.
Clayton, MO 63105
Tel: (314) 746 - 8542

HOWARD, Jeanne
Director, Regional Marketing
8000 Forsyth Blvd.
Clayton, MO 63105
jeanne.howard@commercebank.com
Responsibilities include media relations.
TF: (800) 892 - 7100

Commercial Federal Corp.

A provider of financial services, including Commercial Federal Bank.
www.comfedbank.com
Annual Revenues: $797.4 million

Chairman and Chief Exec. Officer
FITZGERALD, William A.
Tel: (402) 554 - 9200
Fax: (402) 514 - 5486
TF: (800) 228 - 5023

Main Headquarters
Mailing: 13220 California St.
Omaha, NE 68154
Tel: (402) 554 - 9200
Fax: (402) 514 - 5486
TF: (800) 228 - 5023

Political Action Committees

Commercial Federal PAC
Contact: John J. Griffith
13220 California St.
Omaha, NE 68154
Tel: (402) 514 - 5445
Fax: (402) 514 - 5484
TF: (800) 228 - 5023

Contributions to Candidates: $3,000 (01/05 - 09/05)
Republicans: $3,000.

Principal Recipients

SENATE REPUBLICANS		HOUSE REPUBLICANS	
		Fortenberry, Jeffrey (NE)	$1,000
		Latham, Thomas P (IA)	$1,000
		Terry, Lee (NE)	$1,000

Corporate Foundations and Giving Programs

Commercial Federal Corp. Contributions Program
Contact: Roger L. Lewis
13220 California St.
Omaha, NE 68154
Tel: (402) 514 - 5306
Fax: (402) 514 - 5486
TF: (800) 228 - 5023

Annual Grant Total: $1,000,000 - $2,000,000

Public Affairs and Related Activities Personnel

At Headquarters

FERREL, Celia Clinch
Manager, Public Relations
Tel: (402) 514 - 5306
Fax: (402) 514 - 5486
TF: (800) 228 - 5023

GARYN, Hal
Director, Audit, Risk Management, and Investor Relations
Tel: (402) 554 - 5336
Fax: (402) 514 - 5487
TF: (800) 228 - 5023

GRIFFITH, John J.
Director, Human Resources
Tel: (402) 514 - 5445
Fax: (402) 514 - 5484
TF: (800) 228 - 5023

LEWIS, Roger L.
Senior V. President and Director, Marketing
Tel: (402) 514 - 5306
Fax: (402) 514 - 5486
TF: (800) 228 - 5023

Responsibilities include corporate philanthropy.

Commercial Metals Co.

www.commercialmetals.com
Annual Revenues: $2.441 billion

Chairman and Chief Exec. Officer
RABIN, Stanley A.
Tel: (214) 689 - 4300
Fax: (214) 689 - 5886

Main Headquarters
Mailing: 6565 N. MacArthur Blvd.
Suite 800
Irving, TX 75039
Tel: (214) 689 - 4300
Fax: (214) 689 - 5886

Corporate Foundations and Giving Programs

Commercial Metals Corporate Giving
6565 N. MacArthur Blvd.
Suite 800
Irving, TX 75039
Tel: (214) 689 - 4300
Fax: (214) 689 - 5886

Annual Grant Total: $1,000,000 - $2,000,000
Most giving is directed to Jewish welfare organizations in New York, Texas, and Israel.
Geographic Preference: International; New York; Texas
Primary Interests: Children; Education; Health; Women

Public Affairs and Related Activities Personnel

At Headquarters

BARNES, Jesse
Manager, Human Resources
jbarnes@commercialmetals.com
Tel: (214) 689 - 4300
Fax: (214) 689 - 5886

LARSON, William B.
V. President and Chief Financial Officer
Tel: (214) 689 - 4325
Fax: (214) 689 - 4326
Responsibilities include corporate contributions and investor relations.

NASH, Mr. Kelly
Manager, Environment
Tel: (214) 689 - 4300
Fax: (214) 689 - 5886

SUDBURY, David M.
V. President, General Counsel and Secretary
dsudbury@commercialmetals.com
Tel: (214) 689 - 4367
Fax: (214) 689 - 5886
Responsibilities include shareholder relations.

At Other Offices

OKLE, Debbie L.
Director, Public Relations
P.O. Box 1046
Dallas, TX 75221-1046
dokle@commercialmetals.com
Tel: (214) 689 - 4354
Fax: (214) 689 - 5886

Commercial Union Insurance Companies

See listing on page 363 under OneBeacon Insurance.

Commonwealth Energy System

See listing on page 357 under NSTAR.

CommScope

Formed in 1997 as a spin-off of General Instruments Corp.
www.commscope.com
Annual Revenues: $738.5 million

Chairman and Chief Exec. Officer
DRENDEL, Frank M.
frendel@commscope.com
Tel: (828) 324 - 2200

Main Headquarters
Mailing: 1100 CommScope Pl. SE
Hickory, NC 28603
Tel: (828) 324 - 2200
Fax: (828) 982 - 1708

Public Affairs and Related Activities Personnel

At Headquarters

ARMSTRONG, Phil M., Jr.
V. President, Investor Relations and Corporate Communications
parmstro@commscope.com
Tel: (828) 323 - 4848
Fax: (828) 323 - 4849

LAMBERT, Betsy H.
Manager, Corporate Communications and Media Relations
blambert@commscope.com
Tel: (828) 323 - 4873
Fax: (828) 982 - 1708

WRIGHT, James L.
Senior V. President, Human Resources and Environment
Tel: (828) 324 - 2200
Fax: (828) 982 - 1708

Compass Bancshares, Inc.

A financial holding company. Banking subsidiaries include Compass Bank and Central Bank of the South.
www.compassweb.com
Annual Revenues: $1.436 billion

Chairman and Chief Exec. Officer
JONES, D. Paul
paul.jones@compassbnk.com
Tel: (205) 297 - 3529
TF: (800) 239 - 2265

Main Headquarters
Mailing: P.O. Box 10566
Birmingham, AL 35296
Street: 15 S. 20th St.
Birmingham, AL 35233
Tel: (205) 297 - 3000
TF: (800) 239 - 2265

Political Action Committees

Compass Bancshares PAC
Contact: Sue Brewis
P.O. Box 10566
Birmingham, AL 35296
Tel: (205) 297 - 5738
Fax: (205) 297 - 5030
TF: (800) 239 - 2265

Contributions to Candidates: $49,000 (01/05 - 09/05)
Democrats: $1,000; Republicans: $48,000.

Principal Recipients

SENATE DEMOCRATS		HOUSE DEMOCRATS	
Nelson, Bill (FL)	$1,000		
SENATE REPUBLICANS		**HOUSE REPUBLICANS**	
Martinez, Mel (FL)	$5,000	Biggert, Judy (IL)	$6,000
		Aderholt, Robert B (AL)	$2,500
		Everett, Terry (AL)	$2,500
		Rogers, Michael (AL)	$2,500
		Sessions, Pete (TX)	$2,500

Corporate Foundations and Giving Programs

Compass Bank Foundation
Contact: Joye Hehn

Compass Bancshares, Inc.

* continued from previous page

P.O. Box 10566
Birmingham, AL 35296
Tel: (205) 297 - 3554
Fax: (205) 297 - 3043
TF: (800) 239 - 2265

Annual Grant Total: none reported
Geographic Preference: Alabama
Primary Interests: Health; Higher Education; Social Services; Youth Services
Recent Recipients: United Way

Public Affairs and Related Activities Personnel

At Headquarters

BILEK, Edward J.
Director, Investor Relations
ed.bilek@compassbnk.com
Tel: (205) 297 - 3331
Fax: (205) 297 - 4239
TF: (800) 239 - 2265

BREWIS, Sue
Treasurer, Compass Bancshares PAC
sue.brewis@compassbnk.com
Tel: (205) 297 - 5738
Fax: (205) 297 - 5030
TF: (800) 239 - 2265

HARRIS, E. Lee
Exec. V. President, Human Resources (Compass Bank)
lee.harris@compassbnk.com
Tel: (205) 297 - 3466
Fax: (205) 297 - 3336
TF: (800) 239 - 2265

HEHN, Joye
Contact, Compass Bank Foundation
Tel: (205) 297 - 3554
Fax: (205) 297 - 3043
TF: (800) 239 - 2265

Compass Bank

See listing on page 132 under Compass Bancshares, Inc.

Computer Associates Internat'l, Inc.

Specializes in mission-critical business computing. Provides software, support, and integration services.
www.ca.com
Annual Revenues: $2.964 billion

Chairman of the Board
RANERI, Lewis S.
Tel: (631) 342 - 6000
Fax: (631) 342 - 4295
TF: (800) 225 - 5224

President and Chief Exec. Officer
SWAINSON, John
Tel: (631) 342 - 6000
Fax: (631) 342 - 6800
TF: (800) 225 - 5224

Main Headquarters
Mailing: One Computer Associates Plaza
Islandia, NY 11749
Tel: (631) 342 - 6000
Fax: (631) 342 - 6800
TF: (800) 225 - 5224

Washington Office
Mailing: 2291 Wood Oak Dr.
Herndon, VA 20171
Tel: (703) 709 - 4621

Corporate Foundations and Giving Programs

Computer Associates Matching Charitable Gifts Program
One Computer Associates Plaza
Islandia, NY 11749
Tel: (631) 342 - 6000
Fax: (631) 342 - 6800
TF: (800) 225 - 5224

Annual Grant Total: $2,000,000 - $5,000,000
Geographic Preference: International
Primary Interests: Children; Education
Recent Recipients: Habitat for Humanity; Make-A-Wish Foundation

Public Affairs and Related Activities Personnel

At Headquarters

GOODMAN, Andy
Exec. V. President, Human Resources
Tel: (631) 342 - 6000
Fax: (631) 342 - 4295
TF: (800) 225 - 5224

GORDON, Robert
Business Unit V. President, Public Relations
bobg@ca.com
Tel: (631) 342 - 2391
Fax: (631) 342 - 4295
TF: (800) 225 - 5224

KAFERLE, Dan
Senior V. President, Corporate Communications
daniel.kaferle@ca.com
Tel: (631) 342 - 2111
Fax: (631) 342 - 4295
TF: (800) 225 - 5224

LAPIERRE, Shannon
V. President, Corporate Media Relations
shannon.lapierr@ca.com
Tel: (631) 342 - 3839
Fax: (631) 342 - 4295
TF: (800) 225 - 5224

WARREN, Bill
Senior V. President, Executive Communications and Public Affairs
william.warren@ca.com
Tel: (631) 342 - 6344
Fax: (631) 342 - 4295
TF: (800) 225 - 5224

At Washington Office

HERBERT, Allen
Director, Government Affairs
Registered Federal Lobbyist.
Tel: (703) 709 - 4621

Computer Sciences Corp.

A provider of computer services. Acquired DynCorp in March, 2003.
www.csc.com
Annual Revenues: $11.426 billion

Chairman and Chief Exec. Officer
HONEYCUTT, Van B.
vhoneycutt@csc.com
Tel: (310) 615 - 1726

Main Headquarters
Mailing: 2100 E. Grand Ave.
El Segundo, CA 90245
Tel: (310) 615 - 0311

Washington Office
Contact: Lance B. Swann
Mailing: 3170 Fairview Park Dr.
Falls Church, VA 22042
Tel: (703) 876 - 1000

Political Action Committees

Computer Sciences Corp. PAC (CSC PAC)
Contact: Donald DeBuck
2100 E. Grand Ave.
El Segundo, CA 90245
Tel: (310) 615 - 0311

Contributions to Candidates: $16,000 (01/05 - 09/05)
Democrats: $4,000; Republicans: $11,000; Other: $1,000.

Principal Recipients

SENATE DEMOCRATS
Carper, Thomas R (DE) $1,000
Lieberman, Joe (CT) $1,000

HOUSE DEMOCRATS
Hoyer, Steny (MD) $1,000
Ruppersberger, Dutch (MD) $1,000

HOUSE OTHER
Oberstar, James L (MN) $1,000

SENATE REPUBLICANS
Lott, Trent (MS) $2,000
Allen, George (VA) $1,000
Ensign, John Eric (NV) $1,000

HOUSE REPUBLICANS
Davis, Tom (VA) $2,000
Weldon, Curt (PA) $2,000
Knollenberg, Joe (MI) $1,000
Sensenbrenner, Jim (WI) $1,000
Wilson, Heather (NM) $1,000

Dyncorp Internat'l Corp. Federal PAC (DIPAC)
Contact: Mike Thorne
8445 Freeport Pkwy.
Suite 400
Irving, TX 75063

Contributions to Candidates: none reported (01/05 - 09/05)

Corporate Foundations and Giving Programs

Computer Sciences Corporate Giving Program
Contact: Linda Johnson
2100 E. Grand Ave.
El Segundo, CA 90245
Tel: (310) 615 - 1722
Fax: (310) 322 - 9805

Annual Grant Total: under $100,000
Geographic Preference: California; Massachusetts; Michigan; Virginia; Area(s) in which the company operates
Primary Interests: Health; Human Welfare

Public Affairs and Related Activities Personnel

At Headquarters

DEBUCK, Donald
PAC Treasurer
Tel: (310) 615 - 0311

DICKERSON, Mike
Director, Corporate Communications
mdickers@csc.com
Tel: (310) 615 - 1647
Fax: (310) 615 - 1699

HERIN, Janet
Senior Media Relations Representative
jherin@csc.com
Tel: (310) 615 - 1693
Fax: (310) 615 - 1699

JOHNSON, Linda
Senior Manager, Corporate Communications and Marketing
ljohnson@csc.com
Responsibilities also include corporate philanthropy.
Tel: (310) 615 - 1722
Fax: (310) 322 - 9805

LACKEY, William "Bill"
Director, Investor Relations
blackey3@csc.com
Tel: (310) 615 - 1700
Fax: (310) 647 - 1801

MANERI, K. Peter
V. President, Corporate Communications and Marketing
pmaneri@csc.com
Tel: (310) 615 - 1783

RUNGE, Lisa
Manager, Investor Relations
lrunge@csc.com
Tel: (310) 615 - 1680
Fax: (310) 647 - 1801

VENN, Rich
Media Relations Representative
rvenn@csc.com
Tel: (310) 615 - 3926

VOLLRATH, Fred
V. President, Human Resources
fvollrat@csc.com
Tel: (310) 615 - 1785
Fax: (310) 322 - 9767

Computer Sciences Corp.

** continued from previous page*

At Washington Office

OLIVIER, Robert — Tel: (703) 876 - 1000
Senior Director, Corporate Communications — Fax: (703) 849 - 1005

SWANN, Lance B. — Tel: (703) 876 - 1000
V. President, Government Relations — Fax: (703) 849 - 1005
lswann@csc.com

TAYLOR, Chuck — Tel: (703) 641 - 3430
Director, Communications Federal Sector
ctaylor@csc.com

At Other Offices

THORNE, Mike
Treasurer, DIPAC
8445 Freeport Pkwy.
Suite 400
Irving, TX 75063

Compuware Corp.

Data processing professional services and system software products.

www.compuware.com
Annual Revenues: $1.264 billion

Chairman and Chief Exec. Officer
KARMANOS, Peter, Jr. — Tel: (313) 227 - 7300; Fax: (313) 227 - 7555; TF: (800) 292 - 7432

Main Headquarters
Mailing: One Campus Martius, Detroit, MI 48226 — Tel: (313) 227 - 7300; Fax: (313) 227 - 7555; TF: (800) 292 - 7432

Public Affairs and Related Activities Personnel

At Headquarters

DEITCH, Penny — Tel: (313) 227 - 7883
Contact, Diversity and Community Relations — Fax: (313) 227 - 7555; TF: (800) 292 - 7432

ELKIN, Lisa — Tel: (313) 227 - 7345
V. President, Corporate Communications and Investor Relations — Fax: (313) 227 - 7555; TF: (800) 292 - 7432
lisa.elkin@compuware.com

Comverse Technology, Inc.

Designs, manufactures and markets computer and telecommunications systems and software.

www.cmvt.com
Annual Revenues: $959.4 million

Chairman and Chief Exec. Officer
ALEXANDER, Kobi — Tel: (516) 677 - 7200; Fax: (516) 677 - 7355
kobi_alexander@comverse.com

Main Headquarters
Mailing: 170 Crossways Park Dr., Woodbury, NY 11797 — Tel: (516) 677 - 7200; Fax: (516) 677 - 7355

Public Affairs and Related Activities Personnel

At Headquarters

BAKER, Paul D. — Tel: (516) 677 - 7226
V. President, Corporate Marketing and Communications — Fax: (516) 677 - 7323
paul_baker@comverse.com
Responsibilities also include investor relations.

ConAgra Foods, Inc.

A packaged food company that serves consumer grocery retailers as well as foodservice establishments.

www.conagrafoods.com
Annual Revenues: $exceeds 14.5 billion

Main Headquarters
Mailing: One ConAgra Dr., Omaha, NE 68102-5001 — Tel: (402) 595 - 4000

Washington Office
Contact: Brent A. Baglien
Mailing: 1627 I St. NW, Suite 950, Washington, DC 20006 — Tel: (202) 223 - 5115; Fax: (202) 223 - 5118

Political Action Committees

ConAgra Foods Good Government Association
Contact: Brent A. Baglien
1627 I St. NW, Suite 950
Washington, DC 20006 — Tel: (202) 223 - 5115; Fax: (202) 223 - 5118

Contributions to Candidates: $46,000 (01/05 - 09/05)
Democrats: $9,500; Republicans: $36,500.

Principal Recipients

SENATE DEMOCRATS

Conrad, Kent (ND)	$3,000
Nelson, Benjamin (NE)	$2,500

HOUSE DEMOCRATS

SENATE REPUBLICANS

Talent, James (MO)	$5,000
Kennedy, Mark (MN)	$2,000
Lugar, Richard G (IN)	$2,000
Smith, Gordon (OR)	$2,000

HOUSE REPUBLICANS

Boehner, John (OH)	$2,500
Blunt, Roy (MO)	$2,000
Bonilla, Henry (TX)	$2,000
Goodlatte, Robert (VA)	$2,000
Gutknecht, Gil (MN)	$2,000
Latham, Thomas P (IA)	$2,000
Terry, Lee (NE)	$2,000

Corporate Foundations and Giving Programs

ConAgra Foods Foundation
Contact: Nancy Peck
One ConAgra Dr.
Omaha, NE 68102-5001 — Tel: (402) 595 - 4215; Fax: (402) 595 - 4595

Annual Grant Total: none reported
Geographic Preference: Area(s) in which the company operates
Primary Interests: Arts and Culture; Civic and Cultural Activities; Community Affairs; Food Safety; Health and Human Services; Higher Education; Hunger; Nutrition; Youth Services
Recent Recipients: America's Second Harvest; American Dietetic Ass'n Foundation; Boys and Girls Club; Salvation Army; United Negro College Fund; United Way; Urban League; YMCA; YWCA

ConAgra Foods Feeding Children Better Foundation
One ConAgra Dr.
Omaha, NE 68102-5001 — Tel: (402) 595 - 4000

Annual Grant Total: none reported
Primary Interests: Children; Hunger; Nutrition
Recent Recipients: America's Second Harvest; Center on Hunger and Poverty

Public Affairs and Related Activities Personnel

At Headquarters

FERNANDEZ, Michael — Tel: (402) 595 - 4000
Senior V. President, Corporate Affairs; and Chief Communications Officer

KIRCHER, Christopher P. — Tel: (402) 595 - 4000
V. President, Communications

KLINEFELTER, Chris W. — Tel: (402) 595 - 4154
V. President, Investor Relations — Fax: (402) 595 - 4083

PECK, Nancy — Tel: (402) 595 - 4215
Contact, ConAgra Foods Foundation — Fax: (402) 595 - 4595

WHEELER, Anita L. — Tel: (402) 595 - 4215
President, ConAgra Foods Foundation — Fax: (402) 595 - 4595

At Washington Office

BAGLIEN, Brent A. — Tel: (202) 223 - 5115
V. President, Government Affairs — Fax: (202) 223 - 5118
Registered Federal Lobbyist.

Cone Mills Corp.

See listing on page 262 under Internat'l Textiles Group.

Conectiv

Provides energy, services and essential products to homes and businesses. A subsidiary of Pepco Holdings, Inc. (see separate listing).

www.conectiv.com

Chief Exec. Officer
WRAASE, Dennis R. — Tel: (302) 283 - 6064; Fax: (302) 283 - 6015

Main Headquarters
Mailing: P.O. Box 9239, Newark, DE 19714-9239 — Tel: (302) 283 - 6064; Fax: (302) 283 - 6015
Street: 401 Eagle Run Rd., Newark, DE 19702

Corporate Foundations and Giving Programs

Conectiv Corporate Giving Program
Contact: Bridget A. Shelton
P.O. Box 9239
Newark, DE 19714-9239 — Tel: (302) 283 - 5808; Fax: (302) 283 - 6015

Annual Grant Total: $750,000 - $1,000,000
Geographic Preference: Area(s) in which the company operates
Primary Interests: Education; Emergency Services; Employment; Environment/Conservation; Safety

Public Affairs and Related Activities Personnel

At Headquarters

BROWN, Tim — Tel: (302) 283 - 5803
Director, Corporate Communications — TF: (800) 266 - 3284
Mailstop: 79NC62
tim.brown@conectiv.com

Conectiv

* continued from previous page

SHELTON, Bridget A. — Tel: (302) 283 - 5808; Fax: (302) 283 - 6015
Public Affairs Coordinator
(Delmarva Power)

YINGLING, Bill — Tel: (302) 283 - 5811
Senior Public Relations Consultant - Delmarva Power

At Other Offices

KENNEDY, Elizabeth — Tel: (609) 625 - 5567; Fax: (609) 625 - 6944
Senior Public Affairs Consultant - NJ
(Atlantic City Electric)
5100 Harding Hwy.
Mays Landing, NJ 08330
betty.kennedy@conectiv.com

Conexant Systems, Inc.

Provides semiconductor solutions. Spun-off Mindspeed Technologies, Inc. (see separate listing) in June of 2003.

www.conexant.com
Annual Revenues: $901.9 million

Chairman and Chief Exec. Officer — Tel: (949) 483 - 4600
DECKER, Dwight W.

Main Headquarters
Mailing: 4000 MacArthur Blvd.
Newport Beach, CA 92660 — Tel: (949) 483 - 4600

Public Affairs and Related Activities Personnel

At Headquarters

ALLEN, Scott — Tel: (949) 483 - 4600
Senior V. President, Communications

CARLSON, Gwen — Tel: (949) 483 - 7363
Media Relations Contact

THOMAS, Bruce — Tel: (949) 483 - 2698
Director, Investor Relations

VISHNY, Michael — Tel: (949) 483 - 4600
Senior V. President, Human Resources

Connecticut Natural Gas Corp. (CNG)

See listing on page 181 under Energy East Corp.

ConocoPhillips

A member of the Public Affairs Council. Formed from the merger between Conoco Inc. and Phillips Petroleum Co. in August of 2002. An international integrated energy company with operations in some 49 countries.

www.conocophillips.com
Annual Revenues: $38.737 billion

Chairman and Chief Exec. Officer — Tel: (281) 293 - 1000
MULVA, James J. "Jim"

Main Headquarters
Mailing: P.O. Box 2197
Houston, TX 77252-2197 — Tel: (281) 293 - 1000; Fax: (281) 293 - 1440
Street: 600 N. Dairy Ashford Rd.
Houston, TX 77079

Washington Office
Mailing: 1776 I St. NW
Suite 700
Washington, DC 20006 — Tel: (202) 833 - 0900; Fax: (202) 785 - 0639

Political Action Committees

ConocoPhillips Spirit PAC
Contact: Julie Bryant
1400 B Plaza Office Bldg.
Bartlesville, OK 74004

Contributions to Candidates: $39,500 (01/05 - 09/05)
Democrats: $5,000; Republicans: $34,500.

Principal Recipients

SENATE DEMOCRATS		HOUSE DEMOCRATS	
		Boren, David (OK)	$4,000
SENATE REPUBLICANS		**HOUSE REPUBLICANS**	
Anthony, Bob (OK)	$4,000	Hastert, Dennis J. (IL)	$2,500
Thomas, Craig (WY)	$3,000	Barton, Joe L (TX)	$2,000
DeMint, James (SC)	$2,000	McHenry, Patrick (NC)	$2,000

Corporate Foundations and Giving Programs

ConocoPhillips Contributions Program
Contact: Clara Bradley
P.O. Box 2197
Houston, TX 77252-2197 — Tel: (281) 293 - 1000

Annual Grant Total: none reported
Annual grants total approximately $35 million. No endowments or "bricks and mortar" grants. Guidelines available.
Primary Interests: Arts and Culture; Education; Environment/Conservation; Health; Safety; Youth Services

Public Affairs and Related Activities Personnel

At Headquarters

BRADLEY, Clara — Tel: (281) 293 - 1000
Manager, Community Relations

FALCONA, Samuel — Tel: (281) 293 - 5966; Fax: (281) 293 - 2152
V. President, Corporate Communications
Mailstop: MA3158
sfalco@ppco.com

KNICKEL, Carin S. — Tel: (281) 293 - 1000; Fax: (281) 293 - 1440
V. President, Human Resources

LOWE, John E. — Tel: (281) 293 - 1000; Fax: (281) 293 - 1440
Exec. V. President, Planning Strategy and Corporate Affairs

MEADOWS, Steve — Tel: (281) 293 - 1000; Fax: (281) 293 - 1440
V. President, State Government Affairs

RIDGE, Robert A. — Tel: (281) 293 - 1000
V. President, Health, Safety and Environment

At Washington Office

DUNCAN, Don — Tel: (202) 833 - 0907; Fax: (202) 785 - 0639
V. President, Federal and International Affairs
drdunca@ppco.com
Registered Federal Lobbyist.

GODLOVE, Jim — Fax: (202) 785 - 0639
Manager, Federal Affairs - International
jwgodlo@ppco.com
Registered Federal Lobbyist.

LARCOM, M. Kay — Fax: (202) 785 - 0639
Director, Federal Affairs - International
m.kay.larcom@conoco.com
Registered Federal Lobbyist.

REAMY, Jeff M. — Tel: (202) 833 - 0922; Fax: (202) 785 - 0639
Manager, Federal Affairs - Downstream
jmreamy@ppco.com
Registered Federal Lobbyist.

RUDD, Dana R. — Tel: (202) 833 - 0914; Fax: (202) 785 - 0639
Manager, Federal Affairs - Upstream
drrudd@ppco.com
Registered Federal Lobbyist.

At Other Offices

BRYANT, Julie
Treasurer, ConocoPhillips Spirit PAC
1400 B Plaza Office Bldg.
Bartlesville, OK 74004

Conseco, Inc.

A financial services company.

www.conseco.com
Annual Revenues: $4.33 billion

Chairman of the Board — Tel: (317) 817 - 6100; TF: (800) 888 - 4918
HILLIARD, R. Glenn

President and Chief Exec. Officer — Tel: (317) 817 - 6100; TF: (800) 888 - 4918
KIRSCH, William S.

Main Headquarters
Mailing: 11825 N. Pennsylvania St.
Carmel, IN 46032 — Tel: (317) 817 - 6100; TF: (800) 888 - 4918

Political Action Committees

Conseco Concerned Citizens PAC
Contact: Stephen W. Robertson
11825 N. Pennsylvania St.
Carmel, IN 46032 — Tel: (317) 817 - 3539; TF: (800) 888 - 4918

Contributions to Candidates: $13,500 (01/05 - 09/05)
Democrats: $1,000; Republicans: $12,500.

Principal Recipients

SENATE DEMOCRATS		HOUSE DEMOCRATS	
Nelson, Bill (FL)	$1,000		
SENATE REPUBLICANS		**HOUSE REPUBLICANS**	
		Burton, Danny (IN)	$5,000
		King, Peter (NY)	$5,000
		Davis, Geoffrey (KY)	$2,500

Public Affairs and Related Activities Personnel

At Headquarters

ROBERTSON, Stephen W. — Tel: (317) 817 - 3539; TF: (800) 888 - 4918
Senior V. President, Chief Compliance and Regulatory Affairs Officer
steve_robertson@conseco.com
Responsibilities include political action.

Conseco, Inc.

** continued from previous page*

ROSENSTEELE, James — Tel: (317) 817 - 4418
Senior V. President, Marketing Communications — TF: (800) 888 - 4918
james_rosensteele@conseco.com
Responsibilities include public affairs.

ZEHNDER, Anthony — Tel: (317) 817 - 6100
Exec. V. President, Corporate Communications — TF: (800) 888 - 4918

CONSOL Coal Group

See listing on page 136 under CONSOL Energy Inc.

CONSOL Energy Inc.

A publicly-held coal and natural gas producer listed on the New York Stock Exchange as CNX.
www.consolenergy.com
Annual Revenues: $2.8 billion

Chairman of the Board
WHITMIRE, John — Tel: (412) 831 - 4000, Fax: (412) 831 - 4103

President and Chief Exec. Officer
HARVEY, J. Brett — Tel: (412) 831 - 4000, Fax: (412) 831 - 4103

Main Headquarters
Mailing: Consol Plaza
1800 Washington Rd.
Pittsburgh, PA 15241-1421
Tel: (412) 831 - 4000, Fax: (412) 831 - 4103

Political Action Committees

CONSOL Coal Group PAC
Consol Plaza
1800 Washington Rd.
Pittsburgh, PA 15241-1421
Tel: (412) 831 - 4000, Fax: (412) 831 - 4103

Contributions to Candidates: $8,000 (01/05 - 09/05)
Democrats: $2,000; Republicans: $6,000.

Principal Recipients

SENATE DEMOCRATS

HOUSE DEMOCRATS
Boucher, Fredrick (VA) $1,000
Mollohan, Alan (WV) $1,000

SENATE REPUBLICANS
Santorum, Richard (PA) $2,000
Dewine, Richard (OH) $1,000

HOUSE REPUBLICANS
English, Philip S (PA) $1,000
Hart, Melissa (PA) $1,000
Pombo, Richard (CA) $1,000

Corporate Foundations and Giving Programs

CONSOL Corporate Contributions Program
Contact: Joyce Stewart
Consol Plaza
1800 Washington Rd.
Pittsburgh, PA 15241-1421
Tel: (412) 831 - 4068, Fax: (412) 831 - 4103

Annual Grant Total: $400,000 - $500,000

Public Affairs and Related Activities Personnel

At Headquarters

HOFFMAN, Thomas F. — Tel: (412) 831 - 4060
V. President, External Affairs — Fax: (412) 831 - 4103

HOLT, Jack — Tel: (412) 831 - 4053
Senior V. President, Safety — Fax: (412) 831 - 4004

SLAGEL, Gary E. — Tel: (412) 831 - 4532
Director, Government Affairs — Fax: (412) 831 - 4574

STEWART, Joyce — Tel: (412) 831 - 4068
Coordinator, Public Relations — Fax: (412) 831 - 4103

YOUNG, Stephen G. — Tel: (412) 831 - 4043
V. President, Government Affairs — Fax: (412) 831 - 4574

Consolidated Edison Co. of New York, Inc.

A member of the Public Affairs Council. An electric, gas and steam utility.
www.coned.com
Annual Revenues: $9.8 billion

Chairman of the Board
MCGRATH, Eugene R. — Tel: (212) 460 - 4600, Fax: (212) 677 - 0734

President and Chief Exec. Officer
BURKE, Kevin — Tel: (212) 460 - 4600, Fax: (212) 477 - 2536

Main Headquarters
Mailing: Four Irving Pl.
New York, NY 10003
Tel: (212) 460 - 4600, Fax: (212) 477 - 2536

Washington Office
Contact: Hilary S. Wehner
Mailing: 420 Seventh St. NW
Suite 918
Washington, DC 20004
Tel: (202) 628 - 6515, Fax: (202) 628 - 6947

Political Action Committees

Consolidated Edison Inc. Employees PAC (CEI PAC)
Contact: Edward J. Rasmussen
Four Irving Pl.
New York, NY 10003
Tel: (212) 460 - 4600, Fax: (212) 677 - 0734

Contributions to Candidates: $3,250 (01/05 - 09/05)
Democrats: $2,000; Republicans: $1,250.

Principal Recipients

SENATE DEMOCRATS
Bingaman, Jeff (NM) $1,000

HOUSE DEMOCRATS
Towns, Edolphus (NY) $1,000

SENATE REPUBLICANS

HOUSE REPUBLICANS
Reynolds, Thomas (NY) $1,000
Sweeney, John E. (NY) $250

Corporate Foundations and Giving Programs

ConEdison Strategies Partnerships
Four Irving Pl.
New York, NY 10003
Tel: (212) 460 - 4600, Fax: (212) 477 - 2536

Annual Grant Total: over $5,000,000
For program guidelines, please visit our website: www.coned.com/partnerships.
Geographic Preference: Area(s) in which the company operates
Primary Interests: Community Affairs; Education; Environment/Conservation

Public Affairs and Related Activities Personnel

At Headquarters

BANKS, John H. — Tel: (212) 460 - 2706
V. President, Government Relations — Fax: (212) 460 - 3730

CHILDRESS, Mr. Jan — Tel: (212) 460 - 6611
Investor Relations Contact — Fax: (212) 677 - 0734

CLENDENIN, Michael — Tel: (212) 460 - 4111
Director, Media Relations — Fax: (212) 477 - 2536

GMACH, David — Tel: (212) 460 - 6427
Director, Public Affairs (Manhattan) — Fax: (212) 614 - 1453

MCCARTNEY, Mary S. — Tel: (212) 460 - 4571
Director, Corporate Communications — Fax: (212) 614 - 1821

RASMUSSEN, Edward J. — Tel: (212) 460 - 4600
PAC Treasurer — Fax: (212) 677 - 0734

RESHESKE, Frances A. — Tel: (212) 460 - 3882
Senior V. President, Public Affairs — Fax: (212) 353 - 2501
resheskef@coned.com

At Washington Office

WEHNER, Hilary S. — Tel: (202) 628 - 6515
Manager, Federal Government Affairs — Fax: (202) 628 - 6947
Registered Federal Lobbyist.

At Other Offices

CONSLATO, Carol — Tel: (718) 275 - 5657
Director, Public Affairs (Queens) — Fax: (718) 575 - 3769
118-29 Queens Blvd.
Forrest Hills, NY 11375

IRVING, Mark — Tel: (718) 390 - 6368
Director, Public Affairs (Staten Island) — Fax: (718) 720 - 3802
One Davis Ave.
Staten Island, NY 10310

MCMILLAN, Gail — Tel: (718) 904 - 4841
Director, Public Affairs (Bronx) — Fax: (718) 904 - 4860
511 Theodore Fremd
Mailstop: Bldg. 21
Bronx, NY 10580

MILLER, Sandra — Tel: (914) 925 - 6047
Director, Public Affairs (Westchester) — Fax: (914) 921 - 3758
511 Theodore Fremd Ave.
Rye, NY 10580

YUILLE, Antonia — Tel: (718) 802 - 5066
Director, Public Affairs (Brooklyn) — Fax: (718) 802 - 5554
30 Flatbush Ave.
Brooklyn, NY 11217

Consolidated Freightways, Inc.

See listing on page 126 under CNF Inc.

Consolidated Natural Gas

See listing on page 162 under Dominion Resources, Inc.

Consolidated Papers, Inc.

See listing on page 458 under Stora Enso North America.

Constellation Brands, Inc.

A member of the Public Affairs Council. A producer and marketer of beer, wine, and distilled spirits in North America and the United Kingdom.

www.cbrands.com
Annual Revenues: $3.634 billion

Chairman and Chief Exec. Officer
SANDS, Richard — Tel: (585) 218 - 3669; TF: (888) 724 - 2169
richard.sands@cbrands.com

Main Headquarters
Mailing: 370 Woodcliff Dr.
Suite 300
Fairport, NY 14450
Tel: (585) 218 - 3600; TF: (888) 724 - 2169

Political Action Committees

Constellation Brands Inc. PAC
Contact: Perry Humphrey
300 Willbrook Office Park
Fairport, NY 14450
Tel: (585) 218 - 3600

Contributions to Candidates: $24,500 (01/05 - 09/05)
Democrats: $18,500; Republicans: $6,000.

Principal Recipients

SENATE DEMOCRATS
- Clinton, Hillary Rodham (NY) $5,000
- Nelson, Benjamin (NE) $5,000
- Carper, Thomas R (DE) $2,000
- Feinstein, Dianne (CA) $1,000

HOUSE DEMOCRATS
- Thompson, Mike (CA) $5,000
- Bishop, Timothy (NY) $500

SENATE REPUBLICANS
- Alexander, Lamar (TN) $1,000

HOUSE REPUBLICANS
- Reynolds, Thomas (NY) $5,000

Public Affairs and Related Activities Personnel

At Headquarters

CZUDAK, Bob
Director, Investor Relations
bob.czudak@cbrands.com
Tel: (585) 218 - 3668; TF: (888) 724 - 2169

DWORKIN, Philippa M.
Senior V. President, Corporate Communications
philippa.dworkin@cbrands.com
Tel: (585) 218 - 3733; TF: (888) 724 - 2169

FINKLE, James P.
Senior V. President, External Affairs
james.finkle@cbrands.com
Responsibilities include government relations and political action.
Tel: (585) 218 - 3600; Fax: (585) 218 - 2155; TF: (888) 724 - 2169

HARWOOD, Kevin
Manager, Corporate Communications
kevin.harwood@cbrands.com
Tel: (585) 218 - 3600; TF: (888) 724 - 2169

MARTIN, Michael A.
V. President, Corporate Communications
mike.martin@cbrands.com
Tel: (585) 218 - 3669; TF: (888) 724 - 2169

SCHNORR, Lisa
V. President, Investor Relations
lisa.schnorr@cbrands.com
Tel: (585) 218 - 3677; TF: (888) 724 - 2169

WILSON, W. Keith
Exec. V. President and Chief Human Resources Officer
Tel: (585) 218 - 3600; TF: (888) 724 - 2169

At Other Offices

HUMPHREY, Perry
PAC Treasurer
300 Willbrook Office Park
Fairport, NY 14450
Tel: (585) 218 - 3600

Constellation Energy

A member of the Public Affairs Council. A holding company whose subsidiaries include energy-related businesses focused on power marketing, generation, portfolio management, and BGE.

www.constellation.com
Annual Revenues: $12.5 billion

Chairman, President and Chief Exec. Officer
SHATTUCK, Mayo A., III
Mailstop: 18th Floor
Tel: (410) 783 - 2800; TF: (888) 460 - 2002

Main Headquarters
Mailing: 750 E. Pratt St.
Baltimore, MD 21202
Tel: (410) 783 - 2800

Washington Office
Contact: David M. Gilbert
Mailing: 101 Constitution Ave., NW
Suite 980 East
Washington, DC 20001
Tel: (202) 942 - 9840; Fax: (202) 942 - 9847; TF: (888) 460 - 2002

Political Action Committees

Constellation Energy PAC
Contact: Kelly Nowlan
47 State Circle
Suite 402
Annapolis, MD 21401
Tel: (410) 269 - 5195; Fax: (410) 269 - 5289; TF: (888) 460 - 2002

Contributions to Candidates: $80,500 (01/05 - 09/05)
Democrats: $50,000; Republicans: $30,500.

Principal Recipients

SENATE DEMOCRATS
- Cardin, Benjamin (MD) $4,000
- Bingaman, Jeff (NM) $3,500
- Baucus, Max (MT) $2,500
- Mikulski, Barbara (MD) $2,000

HOUSE DEMOCRATS
- Ruppersberger, Dutch (MD) $5,000
- Wynn, Albert (MD) $3,500
- Hoyer, Steny (MD) $3,000
- Boren, David (OK) $2,500
- Boswell, Leonard (IA) $2,500
- Edwards, Chet (TX) $2,500
- Herseth, Stephanie (SD) $2,500
- Matheson, James (UT) $2,500

SENATE REPUBLICANS
- Thomas, Craig (WY) $3,000
- Allen, George (VA) $2,500
- Santorum, Richard (PA) $2,500

HOUSE REPUBLICANS
- DeLay, Tom (TX) $2,500

Corporate Foundations and Giving Programs

Constellation Energy Corporate Contributions Program
750 E. Pratt St.
Baltimore, MD 21202
Tel: (888) 460 - 2002; Fax: (410) 783 - 3279

Assets: $2,900,000 (2002)
Annual Grant Total: $2,000,000 - $5,000,000
Makes grants to non-profit groups in the geographic preferences and primary interests listed.
Geographic Preference: Area(s) in which the company operates; Central Maryland
Primary Interests: Economic Development; Education; Environment/Conservation
Recent Recipients: Baltimore Museum of Art; Baltimore Symphony Orchestra; Chesapeake Bay Foundation; Clean Air Partners

Public Affairs and Related Activities Personnel

At Headquarters

ALLEN, Paul J.
Senior V. President, Corporate Affairs
Mailstop: 18th Floor
paul.j.allen@constellation.com
Tel: (410) 783 - 3024; Fax: (410) 783 - 3029; TF: (888) 460 - 2002

BRANSON, Milton R., Jr.
Senior Government Relations Representative
Mailstop: 5th Floor
milton.r.branson@constellation.com
Tel: (410) 783 - 5201; Fax: (410) 230 - 4703; TF: (888) 460 - 2002

GOULD, Robert L.
Managing Director, Corporate Communications
Mailstop: #200, Candler
rob.gould@constellation.com
Tel: (410) 230 - 9840; Fax: (410) 230 - 9849; TF: (888) 460 - 2002

RUSZIN, Thomas E., Jr.
V. President, Total Rewards and HR Services
Mailstop: 16th Floor
thomas.e.ruszin@constellation.com
Responsibilities include investor relations.
Tel: (410) 783 - 3610; Fax: (410) 783 - 3610; TF: (888) 460 - 2002

SMALL, Malinda B.
Managing Director, Brand Implementation
Mailstop: Fifth Floor
malinda.b.small@constellation.com
Responsibilities include corporate philanthropy.
Tel: (410) 783 - 3266; Fax: (410) 783 - 3279; TF: (888) 460 - 2002

SNEAD, Michael C.
Manager, Occupational Health and Environmental Management
Tel: (410) 234 - 6302; Fax: (410) 234 - 5487; TF: (888) 460 - 2002

UGOL, Marc L.
V. President, CEG Human Resources
Mailstop: Fifth Floor
Tel: (410) 783 - 2800; TF: (888) 460 - 2002

WALLS, Patricia
Manager, BGE Human Resources (BGE)
Mailstop: G&E Bldg., #700
Tel: (410) 234 - 6151; Fax: (410) 234 - 6858; TF: (888) 460 - 2002

WELSH, Charles B.
Manager, Marketing Communications and Research
Mailstop: # 200, Candler
Tel: (410) 230 - 9860; Fax: (410) 783 - 3269; TF: (888) 460 - 2002

At Washington Office

CHERRY, Jan E.
Legislative Administrator
jan.e.cherry@constellation.com
Tel: (202) 942 - 9840; Fax: (202) 942 - 9847; TF: (888) 460 - 2002

GILBERT, David M.
Managing Director, Federal Affairs
Registered Federal Lobbyist.
Tel: (202) 942 - 9840; Fax: (202) 942 - 9847; TF: (888) 460 - 2002

Constellation Energy

* continued from previous page

At Other Offices

DEMPSEY, Mary E. — Tel: (410) 269 - 5283
Manager, Public Affairs — Fax: (410) 269 - 5288
47 State Circle, Suite 403 — TF: (888) 460 - 2002
Annapolis, MD 21401
mary.e.dempsey@constellation.com

FOWLER, Michael L. — Tel: (410) 269 - 5279
Senior Government Relations Representative — Fax: (410) 269 - 5289
47 State Circle, Suite 403 — TF: (888) 460 - 2002
Annapolis, MD 21401
michael.l.fowler@constellation.com

JOHANSON, Bonnie L. — Tel: (410) 269 - 5282
Senior Government Relations Representative — Fax: (410) 269 - 5289
47 State Circle, Suite 403 — TF: (888) 460 - 2002
Annapolis, MD 21401
bonnie.l.johansen@constellation.com

NOWLAN, Kelly — Tel: (410) 269 - 5195
Government Relations Administrator — Fax: (410) 269 - 5289
47 State Circle — TF: (888) 460 - 2002
Suite 402
Annapolis, MD 21401
kelly.nowlan@constellation.com

NUNEZ, Alexander G. — Tel: (410) 269 - 5193
Senior Public Affairs Representative and Annapolis Counsel — Fax: (410) 269 - 5289
47 State Circle, Suite 403 — TF: (888) 460 - 2002
Annapolis, MD 21401
alexander.g.nunez@constellation.com

Consumers Energy Co.

See listing on page 126 under CMS Energy Corp.

ContiGroup Companies, Inc.

An international agribusiness company with interests in commodity marketing, feed and flour milling and livestock and poultry production and processing. The company also provides consumer and commercial financial services.

www.contigroup.com
Annual Revenues: $4 billion

Chairman and Chief Exec. Officer — Tel: (212) 207 - 5100
FRIBOURG, Paul J. — Fax: (212) 207 - 5181
paul.fribourg@conti.com

Main Headquarters
Mailing: 277 Park Ave. — Tel: (212) 207 - 5617
New York, NY 10172 — Fax: (212) 207 - 5181

Political Action Committees

ContiGroup Companies Political Action Committee
Contact: Michael Mayberry
277 Park Ave. — Tel: (212) 207 - 5100
New York, NY 10172 — Fax: (212) 207 - 5181

Contributions to Candidates: $1,000 (01/05 - 09/05)
Republicans: $1,000.

Principal Recipients

SENATE REPUBLICANS		HOUSE REPUBLICANS	
		Bonilla, Henry (TX)	$1,000

Corporate Foundations and Giving Programs

ContiGroup Foundation
Contact: Susan McIntyre
277 Park Ave. — Tel: (212) 207 - 5879
New York, NY 10172 — Fax: (212) 207 - 5043

Annual Grant Total: $300,000 - $400,000
Primary Interests: Arts and Humanities; Community Affairs; Education; Youth Services
Recent Recipients: Columbia University; Nat'l Merit Scholarship

Public Affairs and Related Activities Personnel

At Headquarters

MAYBERRY, Michael — Tel: (212) 207 - 5100
Treasurer, ContiGroup Companies Political Action Committee — Fax: (212) 207 - 5181
michael.mayberry@conti.com

MCCASLIN, Teresa E. — Tel: (212) 207 - 5560
Exec. V. President, Human Resources and Information Systems — Fax: (212) 207 - 5043

MCINTYRE, Susan — Tel: (212) 207 - 5879
Assistant Secretary, ContiGroup Companies Foundation — Fax: (212) 207 - 5043
susan.mcintyre@conti.com

Continental Airlines

www.continental.com
Annual Revenues: $9.744 billion

Main Headquarters
Mailing: P.O. Box 4607 — Tel: (713) 324 - 5000
Houston, TX 77210-4607 — Fax: (713) 324 - 2087

Street: 1600 Smith St.
Houston, TX 77002

Washington Office
Contact: Nancy H. Van Duyne
Mailing: 1350 I St. NW — Tel: (202) 289 - 6060
Suite 1250 — Fax: (202) 289 - 1546
Washington, DC 20005

Political Action Committees

Continental Airlines, Inc. Employee Fund For A Better America
Contact: Rebecca G. Cox
1350 I St. NW — Tel: (202) 715 - 5433
Suite 1250 — Fax: (202) 289 - 1546
Washington, DC 20005

Contributions to Candidates: $52,000 (01/05 - 09/05)
Democrats: $11,500; Republicans: $40,500.

Principal Recipients

SENATE DEMOCRATS		HOUSE DEMOCRATS	
Stabenow, Debbie (MI)	$1,000	Menendez, Robert (NJ)	$2,500
SENATE REPUBLICANS		**HOUSE REPUBLICANS**	
Dewine, Richard (OH)	$7,000	DeLay, Tom (TX)	$4,000
Burns, Conrad (MT)	$3,000	Blunt, Roy (MO)	$2,500
Stevens, Ted (AK)	$2,000	Dewine, R. Pat (OH)	$2,500
Cornyn, John (TX)	$1,000	LaTourette, Steve (OH)	$2,500

Public Affairs and Related Activities Personnel

At Headquarters

BONDS, Mike — Tel: (713) 324 - 5000
Senior V. President, Human Resources and Labor Relations

DELEON, Martin — Tel: (713) 324 - 5000
Manager, Public Relations — Fax: (713) 324 - 2087
martin.deleon@coair.com

FOXHALL, Irene E. "Nene" — Tel: (713) 324 - 5140
V. President, State and Civic Affairs — Fax: (713) 324 - 6329
nfoxha@coair.com

GABEL, DeAnne — Tel: (713) 324 - 5152
Investor Relations Contact — Fax: (713) 324 - 2637

HIRSCH, Susan — Tel: (713) 324 - 5080
Director, Community Affairs — Fax: (713) 324 - 2087

KING, Julie — Tel: (713) 324 - 5080
Manager, Public Relations — Fax: (713) 324 - 2087
jking05@coair.com

MESSING, David J. — Tel: (713) 324 - 5080
Managing Director, Public Relations — Fax: (713) 324 - 2087
dmessi@coair.com

OSORIO, Macky — Tel: (713) 324 - 5080
Manager, Public Relations — Fax: (713) 324 - 2087
mosori@coair.com

WALKER, John E. "Ned" — Tel: (713) 324 - 5080
Senior V. President, Worldwide Corporate Communications — Fax: (713) 324 - 2087
nwalke@coair.com

WILCOX, Courtney — Tel: (713) 324 - 5080
Senior Specialist, Public Relations — Fax: (713) 324 - 2087
courtney.wilcox@coair.com

At Washington Office

COX, Rebecca G. — Tel: (202) 715 - 5433
Senior V. President, Government Affairs — Fax: (202) 289 - 1546
rcox01@coair.com
Registered Federal Lobbyist.

VAN DUYNE, Nancy H. — Tel: (202) 289 - 6060
Staff V. President, Congressional Affairs — Fax: (202) 289 - 1546
nvandu@coair.com
Registered Federal Lobbyist.

Continental Casualty Co.

See listing on page 126 under CNA Financial Corp.

Convergys Corp.

A member of the Public Affairs Council. An integrated outsourced billing and customer service corporation.

www.convergys.com
Annual Revenues: $2.32 billion

Chairman, President, and Chief Exec. Officer — Tel: (513) 723 - 7000
ORR, James F. — Fax: (513) 458 - 1315
TF: (800) 344 - 3000

Main Headquarters
Mailing: 201 E. Fourth St. — Tel: (513) 723 - 7000
Cincinnati, OH 45202 — Fax: (513) 458 - 1315
TF: (800) 344 - 3000

Convergys Corp.

* continued from previous page

Political Action Committees

Convergys Political Action Committee
Contact: Tim M. Wesolowski
201 E. Fourth St.
Cincinnati, OH 45202
Tel: (513) 723 - 7000
Fax: (513) 458 - 1315
TF: (800) 344 - 3000

Contributions to Candidates: $10,750 (01/05 - 09/05)
Republicans: $10,750.

Principal Recipients

SENATE REPUBLICANS		HOUSE REPUBLICANS	
Shelby, Richard (AL)	$1,000	Davis, Tom (VA)	$3,000
		Chabot, Steven J (OH)	$1,000
		Dewine, R. Pat (OH)	$1,000
		Feeney, Tom (FL)	$1,000
		Ney, Robert W (OH)	$1,000
		Schmidt, Jeannette (OH)	$1,000
		Tiahrt, Todd W. (KS)	$1,000

Corporate Foundations and Giving Programs

Convergys Foundation
201 E. Fourth St.
Cincinnati, OH 45202
Tel: (513) 723 - 7000
Fax: (513) 458 - 1315
TF: (800) 344 - 3000

Annual Grant Total: $750,000 - $1,000,000
The foundation does not accept unsolicited applications for grants.
Geographic Preference: Area in which the company is headquartered
Primary Interests: Arts and Culture; Children; Education; Health and Human Services; Performing Arts

Public Affairs and Related Activities Personnel

At Headquarters

CRUZ, Thomas A.
Senior V. President, Human Resources and Administration
tom.cruz@convergys.com
Tel: (513) 723 - 7000
Fax: (513) 451 - 8624
TF: (800) 344 - 3000

GARVEY, Jane
V. President, Corporate Communications
Tel: (513) 723 - 7000
Fax: (513) 458 - 1315
TF: (800) 344 - 3000

GREENWALD, Taylor
Director, Investor Relations
taylor.greenwald@convergys.com
Tel: (513) 723 - 3961
Fax: (513) 458 - 1315
TF: (800) 344 - 3000

KIRKHORN, Erik
Director, Government Relations
erik.kirkhorn@convergys.com
Tel: (513) 723 - 4900
Fax: (513) 421 - 8624
TF: (800) 344 - 3000

MORRIS, Renea
Director, Public Relations
Tel: (513) 723 - 7000
Fax: (513) 458 - 1315
TF: (800) 344 - 3000

PRATT, John
Corporate Public Relations
john.pratt@convergys.com
Tel: (513) 723 - 3333
Fax: (513) 458 - 1315
TF: (800) 344 - 3000

WESOLOWSKI, Tim M.
PAC Contact
Tel: (513) 723 - 7000
Fax: (513) 458 - 1315
TF: (800) 344 - 3000

Cooper Cameron Corp.

Manufacturer of oil and gas pressure control equipment.
www.coopercameron.com
Annual Revenues: $1.563 billion

Chairman, President and Chief Exec. Officer
ERIKSON, Sheldon R.
Tel: (713) 513 - 3312
Fax: (713) 513 - 3456

Main Headquarters
Mailing: 1333 West Loop South
Suite 1700
Houston, TX 77027
Tel: (713) 513 - 3300
Fax: (713) 513 - 3456

Corporate Foundations and Giving Programs

Cooper Cameron Corporate Contributions Program
Contact: Sheldon R. Erikson
1333 West Loop South
Suite 1700
Houston, TX 77027
Tel: (713) 513 - 3312
Fax: (713) 513 - 3456

Annual Grant Total: none reported

Public Affairs and Related Activities Personnel

At Headquarters

AMANN, R. Scott
V. President, Investor Relations
Responsibilities also include corporate communications.
Tel: (713) 513 - 3344
Fax: (713) 513 - 3456

SCHMITT, Jane C.
V. President, Human Resources
Tel: (713) 513 - 3300
Fax: (713) 513 - 3456

Cooper Industries

A member of the Public Affairs Council. A diversified, worldwide manufacturer of electrical products, tools and hardware.
www.cooperindustries.com
Annual Revenues: $4.2 billion

Chairman of the Board
RILEY, H. John, Jr.
riley@cooperindustries.com
Tel: (713) 209 - 8401
Fax: (713) 209 - 8977

President and Chief Exec. Officer
HACHIGIAN, Kirk S.
Tel: (713) 209 - 8400
Fax: (713) 209 - 8995

Main Headquarters
Mailing: P.O. Box 4446
Houston, TX 77210-4446
Tel: (713) 209 - 8400
Fax: (713) 209 - 8995
Street: Chase Tower, 58th Floor
600 Travis St.
Houston, TX 77002-1001

Political Action Committees

Cooper Industries Political Action Committee (CIPAC)
Contact: Alan J. Hill
P.O. Box 4446
Houston, TX 77210-4446
Tel: (713) 209 - 8414
Fax: (713) 209 - 8983

Contributions to Candidates: $9,500 (01/05 - 09/05)
Republicans: $9,500.

Principal Recipients

SENATE REPUBLICANS		HOUSE REPUBLICANS	
Burns, Conrad (MT)	$2,500	Blunt, Roy (MO)	$2,500
Talent, James (MO)	$2,500	Bonilla, Henry (TX)	$2,000

Corporate Foundations and Giving Programs

Cooper Industries Foundation
P.O. Box 4446
Houston, TX 77210-4446
Tel: (713) 209 - 8400
Fax: (713) 209 - 8995

Annual Grant Total: $2,000,000 - $5,000,000
Geographic Preference: Area(s) in which the company operates
Primary Interests: Adult Education and Training; Civic and Cultural Activities
Recent Recipients: Nature Conservancy; United Way

Public Affairs and Related Activities Personnel

At Headquarters

BAJENSKI, Richard J.
V. President, Investor Relations and Public Affairs
bajenski@cooperindustries.com
Tel: (713) 209 - 8610
Fax: (713) 209 - 8981

BREED, John S.
Director, Media and Government Relations
breed@cooperindustries.com
Tel: (713) 209 - 8835
Fax: (713) 209 - 8982

HILL, Alan J.
V. President and Treasurer
hilla@cooperindustries.com
Responsibilities include political action.
Tel: (713) 209 - 8414
Fax: (713) 209 - 8983

SHEIL, David R.
Senior V. President, Human Resources
sheil@cooperindustries.com
Tel: (713) 209 - 8418
Fax: (713) 209 - 8989

TEETS, Robert
V. President, Environmental Affairs and Risk Management
teets@cooperindustries.com
Tel: (713) 209 - 8635
Fax: (713) 209 - 8990

Cooper Tire & Rubber Company

A tire and rubber products company.
www.coopertire.com
Annual Revenues: $2.081 billion

Chairman and Chief Exec. Officer
DATTILO, Thomas
Tel: (419) 423 - 1321
Fax: (419) 424 - 4108

Main Headquarters
Mailing: P.O. Box 550
Findlay, OH 45839-0550
Tel: (419) 423 - 1321
Fax: (419) 424 - 4108
Street: 701 Lima Ave.
Findlay, OH 45840

Political Action Committees

Cooper Tire & Rubber Co. Political Action Committee
Contact: Stephen O. Schroeder
P.O. Box 550
Findlay, OH 45839-0550
Tel: (419) 423 - 1321
Fax: (419) 424 - 4212

Contributions to Candidates: $6,000 (01/05 - 09/05)

Cooper Tire & Rubber Company

** continued from previous page*

Republicans: $6,000.

Principal Recipients

SENATE REPUBLICANS		HOUSE REPUBLICANS	
Dewine, Richard (OH)	$1,000	Wicker, Roger (MS)	$2,000
Lott, Trent (MS)	$1,000	Bonilla, Henry (TX)	$1,000
		Pickering, Chip (MS)	$1,000

Corporate Foundations and Giving Programs

Cooper Tire & Rubber Foundation
Contact: Patricia J. Brown
P.O. Box 550 — Tel: (419) 424 - 4370
Findlay, OH 45839-0550

Annual Grant Total: none reported
No grants made to individuals.
Geographic Preference: Area(s) in which the company operates
Primary Interests: Arts and Culture; Education; Health

Public Affairs and Related Activities Personnel

At Headquarters

BROWN, Patricia J. — Tel: (419) 424 - 4370
V. President, Global Branding and Communications
pjbrown@coopertire.com

CROW, Debbie — Tel: (419) 427 - 4857
Manager, Internal Communications — Fax: (419) 427 - 4719

GEERS, James H. — Tel: (419) 423 - 1321
V. President, Human Resources — Fax: (419) 424 - 4108
jhgeers@coopertire.com

HENDRIKSEN, Roger S. — Tel: (419) 427 - 4768
Director, Investor Relations — Fax: (419) 424 - 4108
rshendriksen@coopertire.com

SCHROEDER, Stephen O. — Tel: (419) 423 - 1321
V. President-Treasurer — Fax: (419) 424 - 4212
soschroeder@coopertire.com
Responsibilities include public affairs and political action.

WEAVER, Philip G. — Tel: (419) 423 - 1321
V. President and Chief Financial Officer — Fax: (419) 424 - 4212
pgweaver@coopertire.com
Responsibilities include corporate philanthropy.

Coors Brewing Co.

A member of the Public Affairs Council. A subsidiary of Molson Coors Brewing Company. Molson Coors Brewing Company was formed by the 2005 merger of Molson Inc. and Adolph Coors Company.

www.coors.com
Annual Revenues: $2.43 billion

Chairman of the Board — Tel: (303) 277 - 2410
COORS, Peter H. — Fax: (303) 277 - 6517
Mailstop: M/S NH300

President and Chief Exec. Officer — Tel: (303) 279 - 6565
VAN PAASSCHEN, Frits

Main Headquarters

Mailing: P.O. Box 4030 — Tel: (303) 279 - 6565
Golden, CO 80401-0030
Street: Corporate Headquarters
17735 W. 32nd Ave.
Golden, CO 80401-1295

Washington Office

Contact: Richard C. Crawford
Mailing: 801 Pennsylvania Ave. NW — Tel: (202) 737 - 4444
Suite 252 North Bldg. — Fax: (202) 737 - 0951
Washington, DC 20004-2604

Political Action Committees

Political Action Coors Employees (PACE)
Contact: Richard C. Crawford
801 Pennsylvania Ave. NW — Tel: (202) 737 - 4444
Suite 252 North Bldg. — Fax: (202) 737 - 0951
Washington, DC 20004-2604

Contributions to Candidates: none reported (01/05 - 09/05)

Corporate Foundations and Giving Programs

Coors Brewing Co. Corporate Contributions Program
Contact: Buck Boze
P.O. Box 4030 — Tel: (303) 277 - 5953
Golden, CO 80401-0030 — Fax: (303) 277 - 6132

Annual Grant Total: none reported
Guidelines are available.
Geographic Preference: Colorado; Tennessee; Virginia
Primary Interests: Community Affairs

Public Affairs and Related Activities Personnel

At Headquarters

ALEXANDER, Bart — Tel: (303) 277 - 6401
Director, Corporate Responsibility — Fax: (303) 277 - 5723
Mailstop: M/S NH250

BOZE, Buck — Tel: (303) 277 - 5953
Manager, Corporate Contributions — Fax: (303) 277 - 6132
Mailstop: M/S NH420

DUNNEWALD, David A. — Tel: (303) 277 - 5308
Director, Investor Relations — Fax: (303) 277 - 7666
Mailstop: M/S NH370

GOLDMAN, Cindy — Tel: (303) 277 - 3002
Director and Assistant General Counsel — Fax: (303) 277 - 7373
Mailstop: M/S NH335

MENOGAN, Annita — Tel: (303) 277 - 5919
V. President and Corporate Secretary — Fax: (303) 277 - 2601
Responsibilities include investor relations.

MILLS, Vonda — Tel: (303) 277 - 5816
Chief People Officer — Fax: (303) 277 - 6082
Mailstop: M/S NH345

RAZEE, Sher — Tel: (303) 277 - 2813
Government Affairs — Fax: (303) 277 - 5723
Mailstop: M/S NH280

TIMOTHY, Alan R. — Tel: (303) 277 - 6240
V. President, Government Affairs — Fax: (303) 277 - 5723
Mailstop: M/S NH280

WALKER, Samuel D. — Tel: (303) 277 - 2164
Global Chief Legal Officer — Fax: (303) 277 - 6212
Mailstop: M/S MCCC

At Washington Office

CRAWFORD, Richard C. — Tel: (202) 737 - 4444
Director, Federal Government Affairs — Fax: (202) 737 - 0951
Mailstop: RR 896
Registered Federal Lobbyist.

At Other Offices

HICKS, Robin Y. — Tel: (901) 375 - 2086
Guest Relations Supervisor — Fax: (901) 375 - 2848
5151 E. Raines Rd.
Memphis, TN 38118

HUNT, Bob — Tel: (678) 393 - 2563
Manager, Government Affairs (Southern Region) — Fax: (678) 393 - 9631
1185 Sanctuary Pkwy.
Suite 250
Alpharetta, GA 30004

KAWULOK, Donald W. — Tel: (303) 825 - 7661
Manager, Government Affairs — Fax: (303) 825 - 4629
216 16th St. Mall
Suite 860
Denver, CO 80202

LIVINGSTON, Bob — Tel: (916) 786 - 2666
Manager, Government Affairs (Western Region) — Fax: (916) 786 - 9396
3001 Douglas Blvd.
Suite 200
Roseville, CA 95661

MILLER, Bonnie R. — Tel: (303) 825 - 7661
Manager, Colorado Government Affairs — Fax: (303) 825 - 4629
216 16th St. Mall, Suite 860
Denver, CO 80202

TRETIAK, Stan — Tel: (804) 782 - 9441
Manager, Government Affairs, Eastern Region — Fax: (804) 225 - 8356
1001 E. Broad St., 230 Old City Hall
Richmond, VA 23219

WENDELKEN, Janet T. — Tel: (540) 289 - 8211
Manager, Public Relations (Shenandoah Brewery) — Fax: (540) 289 - 8405
P.O. Box 25, Rte. 340 South
Elkton, VA 22827

The Copley Press, Inc.

A newspaper publishing company.

www.copleynews.com

Chairman, President, and Chief Exec. Officer — Tel: (858) 454 - 0411
COPLEY, David C.

Main Headquarters

Mailing: P.O. Box 1530 — Tel: (858) 454 - 0411
La Jolla, CA 92038-1530
Street: 7776 Ivanhoe Ave.
La Jolla, CA 92037-4574

Corporate Foundations and Giving Programs

Copley Foundation, James S.
Contact: Terry L. Gilbert

The Copley Press, Inc.

** continued from previous page*

P.O. Box 1530
La Jolla, CA 92038-1530
Tel: (858) 454 - 0411
Fax: (858) 729 - 7672

Assets: $20,000,000 (2003)
Annual Grant Total: $1,000,000 - $2,000,000
Geographic Preference: Area(s) in which the company operates; Illinois; California; Ohio
Primary Interests: Arts and Culture; Education; Medicine and Health Care; Social Services; Youth Services
Recent Recipients: Boys and Girls Club; United Way; YMCA; YWCA

Public Affairs and Related Activities Personnel

At Headquarters

FUSON, Harold W., Jr.
V. President and Chief Legal Officer
Tel: (858) 454 - 0411

GILBERT, Terry L.
Foundation Administrator
Tel: (858) 454 - 0411
Fax: (858) 729 - 7672

VARGAS, James F.
V. President and Chief Human Resources Officer
Tel: (858) 454 - 0411

Corn Products Internat'l, Inc.

A supplier of food and industrial ingredients derived from the processing of corn and other starch-based materials.

www.cornproducts.com
Annual Revenues: $2.3 billion

Chairman, President and Chief Exec. Officer
SCOTT, Samuel C., III
Tel: (708) 551 - 2600
Fax: (708) 551 - 2700

Main Headquarters
Mailing: P.O. Box 7100
Westchester, IL 60154
Tel: (708) 551 - 2600
Fax: (708) 551 - 2700
Street: Five Westbrook Corporate Center
Westchester, IL 60154

Public Affairs and Related Activities Personnel

At Headquarters

HIRCHAK, James J.
V. President, Human Resources
Tel: (708) 551 - 2600
Fax: (708) 551 - 2700

LINDLEY, Mark C.
Director, Corporate Communications
Tel: (708) 551 - 2602
Fax: (708) 551 - 2601

VANDERVOORT, Richard M.
V. P., Strategic Business Dev., Investor Relations, and Gov. and Regulatory Affairs
ir@cornproducts.com
Tel: (708) 551 - 2595
Fax: (708) 551 - 2700

Corning Incorporated

A manufacturer of optical fiber, cable and components, high-performance glass and components for televisions and other electronic displays for communications and communications-related industries; and advanced materials for the scientific, life sciences, and environmental markets.

www.corning.com
Annual Revenues: $6.272 billion

Chairman of the Board
HOUGHTON, James R.
houghtonjr@corning.com
Tel: (607) 974 - 8668
Fax: (607) 974 - 8444

President and Chief Exec. Officer
WEEKS, Wendell P.
Tel: (607) 974 - 9000
Fax: (607) 974 - 8551

Main Headquarters
Mailing: One Riverfront Plaza
Corning, NY 14831-0001
Tel: (607) 974 - 9000
Fax: (607) 974 - 8551

Washington Office
Contact: Timothy J. Regan
Mailing: 1350 I St. NW
Suite 500
Washington, DC 20005-3305
Tel: (202) 682 - 3200
Fax: (202) 682 - 3130

Political Action Committees

Corning Incorporated Employees PAC (CorePAC)
Contact: Timothy J. Regan
1350 I St. NW
Suite 500
Washington, DC 20005-3305
Tel: (202) 682 - 3140
Fax: (202) 682 - 3130

Contributions to Candidates: $55,500 (01/05 - 09/05)
Democrats: $12,000; Republicans: $43,500.

Principal Recipients

SENATE DEMOCRATS

Pryor, Mark (AR)	$5,000
Byrd, Robert C (WV)	$1,000
Rockefeller, John (WV)	$1,000

HOUSE DEMOCRATS

Boucher, Fredrick (VA)	$1,500
Levin, Sander (MI)	$1,500

SENATE REPUBLICANS

Burns, Conrad (MT)	$8,500
Snowe, Olympia (ME)	$5,000
Allen, George (VA)	$1,500

HOUSE REPUBLICANS

Kuhl, John R Jr (NY)	$5,500
Upton, Fred (MI)	$2,500
Bass, Charles (NH)	$2,000
Camp, David Lee (MI)	$2,000
Schwarz, John (MI)	$2,000
Barton, Joe L (TX)	$1,500

Corporate Foundations and Giving Programs

Corning Foundation
Contact: Kristin A. Swain
One Riverfront Plaza
Corning, NY 14831-0001
Tel: (607) 974 - 8722
Fax: (607) 974 - 8551

Annual Grant Total: $2,000,000 - $5,000,000
Guidelines are available.
Geographic Preference: Area(s) in which the company operates; Michigan; New York; Ohio; Pennsylvania
Primary Interests: Civic and Cultural Activities; Education; Engineering; Math and Science
Recent Recipients: Harvard University; Metropolitan Museum of Art; United Way

Public Affairs and Related Activities Personnel

At Headquarters

COLLINS, Dan F.
V. President, Corporate Communications
collinsdf@corning.com
Tel: (607) 974 - 4197
Fax: (607) 974 - 8509

DIETZ, Katherine M.
V. President, Investor Relations
dietzkm@corning.com
Tel: (607) 974 - 8217
Fax: (607) 974 - 8551

PORTER, Pam
Director, Corporate Media Relations
Tel: (607) 974 - 9000
Fax: (607) 974 - 8551

SWAIN, Kristin A.
President, Corning Foundation
Mailstop: MP-LB-C
swainka@corning.com
Tel: (607) 974 - 8722
Fax: (607) 974 - 8551

At Washington Office

FENDLEY, Stanley G.
Director, Legislative and Regulatory Affairs
fendleysg@corning.com
Registered Federal Lobbyist.
Tel: (202) 682 - 3133
Fax: (202) 682 - 3130

REGAN, Timothy J.
Senior V. President, Government Affairs
regantj@corning.com
Registered Federal Lobbyist.
Responsibilities include political action.
Tel: (202) 682 - 3140
Fax: (202) 682 - 3130

TRANTER, G. Thomas
Registered Federal Lobbyist.
Tel: (202) 682 - 3200
Fax: (202) 682 - 3130

WAGGONER, Debra
Director, Public Policy
Registered Federal Lobbyist.
Tel: (202) 682 - 3200
Fax: (202) 682 - 3130

Corporation for Public Broadcasting

Non-commercial radio and television.

www.cpb.org
Annual Revenues: $397.9 million

Chairman of the Board
HALPERN, Cheryl
Tel: (202) 879 - 9600
Fax: (202) 879 - 9700

President and Chief Exec. Officer
DE STACY HARRISON, Patricia
Tel: (202) 879 - 9600
Fax: (202) 879 - 9700

Main Headquarters
Mailing: 401 Ninth St. NW
Washington, DC 20004-2129
Tel: (202) 879 - 9600
Fax: (202) 879 - 9700

Public Affairs and Related Activities Personnel

At Headquarters

LEVY, Michael
Corporate and Public Affairs Contact
Tel: (202) 879 - 9758
Fax: (202) 879 - 9700

Corrections Corp. of America

Management of prisons and detention institutions for government agencies.

www.correctionscorp.com
Annual Revenues: $1.148 billion

Chairman of the Board
ANDREWS, William F.
Tel: (615) 263 - 3000
Fax: (615) 263 - 3140
TF: (800) 624 - 2931

Corrections Corp. of America
** continued from previous page*

President and Chief Exec. Officer
FERGUSON, John D.
john.ferguson@correctionscorp.com
Tel: (615) 263 - 3000
Fax: (615) 263 - 3140
TF: (800) 624 - 2931

Main Headquarters
Mailing: 10 Burton Hills Blvd.
Nashville, TN 37215
Tel: (615) 263 - 3000
Fax: (615) 263 - 3140
TF: (800) 624 - 2931

Washington Office
Mailing: 444 N. Capitol St. NW
Suite 545
Washington, DC 20001
Tel: (202) 347 - 8717

Political Action Committees

Corrections Corp. of American PAC
Contact: Gus Puryear
444 N. Capitol St. NW
Suite 545
Washington, DC 20001
Tel: (202) 347 - 8717

Contributions to Candidates: $32,293 (01/05 - 09/05)
Democrats: $7,500; Republicans: $24,793.

Principal Recipients

SENATE DEMOCRATS		HOUSE DEMOCRATS	
Carper, Thomas R (DE)	$2,500		
SENATE REPUBLICANS		**HOUSE REPUBLICANS**	
Dewine, Richard (OH)	$5,000	Cannon, Christopher (UT)	$2,000
Graham, Lindsey (SC)	$2,614		
Coburn, Thomas (OK)	$1,179	Dewine, R. Pat (OH)	$2,000

Corporate Foundations and Giving Programs

Corrections Corp. of America Corporate Giving Program
Contact: Louise Chickering
10 Burton Hills Blvd.
Nashville, TN 37215
Tel: (615) 263 - 3106
Fax: (615) 263 - 3140
TF: (800) 624 - 2931

Annual Grant Total: none reported
Geographic Preference: Area(s) in which the company operates
Primary Interests: Early Childhood Education

Public Affairs and Related Activities Personnel

At Headquarters

ADELMAN, Dean
V. President, Human Resources
dean.adelman@correctionscorp.com
Tel: (615) 263 - 3017
Fax: (615) 263 - 3140
TF: (800) 624 - 2931

CHICKERING, Louise
V. President, Marketing and Communications
louise.chickering@correctionscorp.com
Tel: (615) 263 - 3106
Fax: (615) 263 - 3140
TF: (800) 624 - 2931

DEMLER, Karin
Director, Investor Relations
karin.demler@correctionscorp.com
Tel: (615) 263 - 3005
Fax: (615) 263 - 3140
TF: (800) 624 - 2931

OWEN, Steve
Director, Marketing and Communications
steve.owen@correctionscorp.com
Tel: (615) 263 - 3107
Fax: (615) 263 - 3140
TF: (800) 624 - 2931

At Washington Office

BOULDIN, Ken
Registered Federal Lobbyist.
Tel: (202) 347 - 8717

HININGER, Damon
Registered Federal Lobbyist.
Tel: (202) 347 - 8717

PURYEAR, Gus
Registered Federal Lobbyist.
Tel: (202) 347 - 8717

QUINLAN, Mike
Registered Federal Lobbyist.
Tel: (202) 347 - 8717

WILEY, Jeremy
Legislative Affairs
Registered Federal Lobbyist.
Tel: (202) 347 - 8717

Costco Wholesale Corp.
Operator of chain membership warehouse stores.
www.costco.com
Annual Revenues: $34.797 billion

Chairman of the Board
BROTMAN, Jeffrey H.
Tel: (425) 313 - 8100
Fax: (425) 313 - 6593

President, Chief Exec. Officer
SINEGAL, James D.
Tel: (425) 313 - 8100
Fax: (425) 313 - 6593

Main Headquarters
Mailing: 999 Lake Dr.
Issaquah, WA 98027
Tel: (425) 313 - 8100
Fax: (425) 313 - 6593

Public Affairs and Related Activities Personnel

At Headquarters

COOPER, Muriel
Contact, Community Relations and Administration
Tel: (425) 313 - 8100
Fax: (425) 313 - 6593

ELLIOTT, Jeffrey
Director, Financial Planning and Investor Relations
Tel: (425) 313 - 8264
Fax: (425) 313 - 6430

MATTHEWS, John
Senior V. President, Human Resources and Risk Management
Tel: (425) 313 - 8100
Fax: (425) 313 - 6593

NELSON, Robert E.
V. President, Financial Planning and Investor Relations
Tel: (425) 313 - 8255
Fax: (425) 313 - 6430

Country Insurance and Financial Services
www.countryfinancial.com

Chief Exec. Officer
BLACKBURN, John D.

Main Headquarters
Mailing: P.O. Box 2020
Bloomington, IL 61701-2020
Street: 1701 N. Towanda Ave.
Bloomington, IL 61701
Tel: (309) 821 - 3000

Public Affairs and Related Activities Personnel

At Headquarters

FRAUTSCHI, Deanna L.
Senior V. President, Communications and Human Resources

OLOFFSON, Cathy
Media Relations Coordinator
Tel: (309) 821 - 2171

ZEHR, Melinda
Manager, Public Relations
Tel: (309) 821 - 2009

Country Music Television
See listing on page 505 under Viacom Inc/CBS Corp.

Countrywide Home Loans Inc.
A banking, financial and insurance holding company.
www.countrywide.com

Chairman and Chief Exec. Officer
MOZILO, Angelo R.
Tel: (818) 225 - 3000
TF: (800) 556 - 9568

Main Headquarters
Mailing: 4500 Park Granada
Calabasas, CA 91302
Tel: (818) 225 - 3000
TF: (800) 556 - 9568

Washington Office
Contact: Gordon R. "Pete" Mills
Mailing: 1717 Pennsylvania Ave. NW
Suite 700
Washington, DC 20006
Tel: (202) 974 - 1100
Fax: (202) 974 - 1128

Political Action Committees

Countrywide Financial Corp. PAC
Contact: Gordon R. "Pete" Mills
1717 Pennsylvania Ave. NW
Suite 700
Washington, DC 20006
Tel: (202) 293 - 8550
Fax: (202) 974 - 1128

Contributions to Candidates: $38,500 (01/05 - 09/05)
Democrats: $22,000; Republicans: $16,500.

Principal Recipients

SENATE DEMOCRATS		HOUSE DEMOCRATS	
Carper, Thomas R (DE)	$6,000	Sherman, Brad (CA)	$2,000
Ford, Harold E Jr (TN)	$5,000		
Conrad, Kent (ND)	$1,000		
Johnson, Tim (SD)	$1,000		
SENATE REPUBLICANS		**HOUSE REPUBLICANS**	
Bennett, Robert F (UT)	$2,000	Royce, Ed Mr (CA)	$7,000
		Ney, Robert W (OH)	$2,500

Public Affairs and Related Activities Personnel

At Washington Office

CARLISLE, Corey C.
Registered Federal Lobbyist.
Tel: (202) 974 - 1100
Fax: (202) 974 - 1128

MILLS, Gordon R. "Pete"
Senior V. President, Legislative/Regulatory Affairs
pete_mills@countrywide.com
Tel: (202) 293 - 8550
Fax: (202) 974 - 1128

Countrywide Home Loans Inc.

• continued from previous page

WILLIAMS, Jimmie L. — Tel: (202) 974 - 1100
V. President, Legislative/Regulatory Affairs — Fax: (202) 974 - 1128
jimmie_williams@countrywide.com
Registered Federal Lobbyist.

The Courier-Journal

A newspaper publishing company.
www.courier-journal.com

President and Publisher
MANASSAH, Edward E. — Tel: (502) 582 - 4101; TF: (800) 765 - 4011
emanassa@louisvil.gannett.com

Main Headquarters
Mailing: P.O. Box 740031, Louisville, KY 40201-7431 — Tel: (502) 582 - 4011; TF: (800) 765 - 4011
Street: 525 W. Broadway, Louisville, KY 40202

Corporate Foundations and Giving Programs

The Courier-Journal Corporate Giving
Contact: Mary Ann Stinson
P.O. Box 740031
Louisville, KY 40201-7431
Tel: (502) 582 - 4011; Fax: (502) 582 - 4066; TF: (800) 765 - 4011

Annual Grant Total: none reported

Public Affairs and Related Activities Personnel

At Headquarters

CHAPMAN, Barry — Tel: (502) 582 - 4225; TF: (800) 765 - 4011
V. President, Human Resources
bchapman@louisvil.gannett.com

STINSON, Mary Ann — Tel: (502) 582 - 4011; Fax: (502) 582 - 4066; TF: (800) 765 - 4011
Exec. Assistant to the Publisher
Responsibilities include corporate philanthropy.

Covance, Inc.

A pharmaceutical development company.
www.covance.com
Annual Revenues: $1.02 billion

Chairman of the Board
KUEBLER, Christopher A. — Tel: (609) 452 - 4440; Fax: (609) 452 - 9375; TF: (800) 621 - 8901

President and Chief Exec. Officer
HERRING, Joseph — Tel: (609) 452 - 4440; Fax: (609) 452 - 9375; TF: (800) 621 - 8901

Main Headquarters
Mailing: 210 Carnegie Center, Princeton, NJ 08540-6233 — Tel: (609) 452 - 4440; Fax: (609) 452 - 9375; TF: (800) 621 - 8901

Public Affairs and Related Activities Personnel

At Headquarters

ISIP, Laurene — Tel: (609) 452 - 4440; Fax: (609) 452 - 9375; TF: (800) 621 - 8901
Senior Director, Corporate Communications

SURDEZ, Paul — Tel: (609) 452 - 4440; Fax: (609) 452 - 9375; TF: (800) 621 - 8901
Director, Investor Relations

Covansys

An information technology services provider.
www.covansys.com

Chairman, President and Chief Exec. Officer
VATTIKUTI, Rejendra B. — Tel: (248) 488 - 2088; Fax: (248) 488 - 2089; TF: (800) 688 - 2088

Main Headquarters
Mailing: 32605 W. Twelve Mile Rd., Farmington Hills, MI 48334-3339 — Tel: (248) 488 - 2088; Fax: (248) 488 - 2089; TF: (800) 688 - 2088

Public Affairs and Related Activities Personnel

At Headquarters

JONES, Michelle — Tel: (248) 848 - 2269; Fax: (248) 488 - 2089; TF: (800) 688 - 2088
V. President, Marketing
mjones@covansys.com
Responsibilities include corporate communications.

TROUBA, James S. — Tel: (248) 848 - 2267; Fax: (248) 488 - 2089; TF: (800) 688 - 2088
Chief Financial Officer and Investor Relations Contact

Covanta Energy Corp.

Offers power and related infrastructure services. A subsidiary of Danielson Holding Corp.
www.covantaenergy.com
Annual Revenues: $984.7 million

Director, President and Chief Exec. Officer
ORLANDO, Anthony J. — Tel: (973) 882 - 9000

Main Headquarters
Mailing: 40 Lane Rd., Fairfield, NJ 07004 — Tel: (973) 882 - 9000

Political Action Committees

Covanta Energy Corp. PAC
Contact: Paula C. Soos
40 Lane Rd.
Fairfield, NJ 07004
Tel: (973) 882 - 7081; Fax: (973) 882 - 7251

Contributions to Candidates: $500 (01/05 - 09/05)
Democrats: $500.

Principal Recipients

SENATE DEMOCRATS		HOUSE DEMOCRATS
Nelson, Bill (FL)	$500	

Public Affairs and Related Activities Personnel

At Headquarters

MONTELEONE, Robert — Tel: (973) 882 - 9000
V. President, Human Resources

SOOS, Paula C. — Tel: (973) 882 - 7081; Fax: (973) 882 - 7251
Senior Director, Government Relations

Coventry Health Care

A health care company.
www.cvty.com
Annual Revenues: $5.35 billion

Chairman of the Board
WISE, Allen F. — Tel: (301) 581 - 0600; Fax: (301) 493 - 0705

Chief Exec. Officer
WOLF, Dale B. — Tel: (301) 581 - 0600; Fax: (301) 493 - 0705

Main Headquarters
Mailing: 6705 Rockledge Dr., Suite 100, Bethesda, MD 20817 — Tel: (301) 581 - 0600; Fax: (301) 493 - 0705

Corporate Foundations and Giving Programs

Coventry Health Care Corporate Contributions Program
6705 Rockledge Dr.
Suite 100
Bethesda, MD 20817
Tel: (301) 581 - 0600; Fax: (301) 493 - 0705

Annual Grant Total: none reported

Public Affairs and Related Activities Personnel

At Headquarters

DAVIS, Patricia — Tel: (301) 581 - 0600; Fax: (301) 493 - 0705
Chief Human Resources Officer

GUERTIN, Shawn M. — Tel: (301) 581 - 5701; Fax: (301) 493 - 0705
Exec. V. President and Chief Financial Officer
Responsibilities include investor relations.

Cox Communications, Inc.

See listing on page 143 under Cox Enterprises, Inc.

Cox Enterprises, Inc.

A diversified communications company involved in newspaper publishing, radio and TV broadcasting, cable TV and programming. Parent company of Cox Communications.
www.coxenterprises.com
Annual Revenues: $8.693 billion

Chairman and Chief Exec. Officer
KENNEDY, James C. — Tel: (678) 645 - 0000

Main Headquarters
Mailing: 6205 Peachtree Dunwoody Rd., Atlanta, GA 30328 — Tel: (678) 645 - 0000

Washington Office
Contact: Alexander V. Netchvolodoff
Mailing: 1225 19th St. NW, Suite 450, Washington, DC 20036 — Tel: (202) 296 - 4933; Fax: (202) 296 - 4951

Corporate Foundations and Giving Programs

James M. Cox Foundation

Cox Enterprises, Inc.

** continued from previous page*

6205 Peachtree Dunwoody Rd. Tel: (678) 645 - 0000
Atlanta, GA 30328

Annual Grant Total: $1,000,000 - $2,000,000
Geographic Preference: Georgia
Primary Interests: Arts and Culture; Civic and Public Affairs; Education; Health
Recent Recipients: American Red Cross

Cox Communications Corporate Contributions
6205 Peachtree Dunwoody Rd. Tel: (678) 645 - 0000
Atlanta, GA 30328

Annual Grant Total: none reported
Provides a variety of contributions, both financially and in volunteer time.
Geographic Preference: Area(s) in which the company operates
Primary Interests: Education; Technology; Youth Services

Public Affairs and Related Activities Personnel

At Headquarters

COHN, Amy Tel: (678) 645 - 0000
Exec. Director, Public Affairs
(Cox Communications, Inc.)
amy.cohn@cox.com

EAST, Ellen M. Tel: (678) 645 - 0000
V. President, Corporate Communications and Public Affairs
(Cox Communications, Inc.)
ellen.east@cox.com

JIMENEZ, Roberto I. Tel: (678) 645 - 0000
V. President, Corporate Communications and Public Affairs

LEAMER, Marybeth H. Tel: (678) 645 - 0000
V. President, Human Resources
marybeth.leamer@cox.com

SURRATT, Anthony Tel: (678) 645 - 0000
Exec. Director, Public Relations
(Cox Communications, Inc.)
anthony.surratt@cox.com

At Washington Office

HUBBARD, Sherry L. Tel: (202) 296 - 4933
Director, Operations Fax: (202) 296 - 4951
sherry.hubbard@cox.com
Registered Federal Lobbyist.

NETCHVOLODOFF, Alexander V. Tel: (202) 296 - 4933
Senior V. President, Public Policy Fax: (202) 296 - 4951
alexander.netchvolodoff@cox.com
Registered Federal Lobbyist.

WILSON, Alexandra M. Tel: (202) 296 - 4933
V. President, Public Policy Fax: (202) 296 - 4951
alexandra.wilson@cox.com
Registered Federal Lobbyist.

At Other Offices

BALL, Mary Tel: (619) 266 - 5203
V. President, Government and Community Relations Fax: (619) 266 - 5555
5159 Federal Blvd.
San Diego, CA 92105
mary.ball@cox.com

BENNETT, Vickie Tel: (806) 771 - 6221
Manager, Community Relations
(Cox Communications, Inc.)
6710 Hartford Ave.
Lubbock, TX 79413
vickie.bennett@cox.com

BREWSTER, Joe Tel: (850) 314 - 8101
Director, Community Affairs
(Cox Communications, Inc.)
320 Racetrack Rd., N.W.
Ft. Walton Beach, FL 32549
joe.brewster@cox.com

DE SOLLER, Marty Z. Tel: (949) 546 - 2596
V. President, Public Relations
29947 Avenida De Las Banderas
Rancho Santa Margarita, CA 92688
marty.zajic@cox.com

FREDERICK, Christy Tel: (216) 535 - 3357
Director, Public Relations and Government Affairs Fax: (216) 676 - 8689
12221 Plaza Dr.
Parma, OH 44130

JOHNSON, Ivan D. Tel: (623) 328 - 3250
V. President, Community Relations/Televideo Fax: (623) 328 - 3580
(Cox Communications, Inc.)
1550 W. Deer Valley Rd.
Phoenix, AZ 85027
ivan.johnson@cox.com

MURPHEY, Lynn Tel: (478) 784 - 5106
Director, Public Relations Fax: (478) 784 - 5100
(Cox Communications, Inc.)
6601 Hawkinsville Rd.
Macon, GA 31297-0278
lynn.murphey@cox.com

TECK, Kristin Tel: (402) 934 - 0256
V. President, Government and Public Affairs Fax: (402) 933 - 0010
11505 W. Dodge Rd.
Omaha, NE 68154

WOLFE, John Tel: (860) 432 - 5008
V. President, Government and Public Affairs Fax: (860) 512 - 5115
(Cox Communications, Inc.)
170 Utopia St.
Manchester, CT 06040-0310
john.wolfe@cox.com

Cracker Barrel Old Country Store, Inc.

See listing on page 106 under CBRL Group, Inc.

Crane Co.

Manufactures and sells vending machines, airplane braking devices, pumps, valves, and other industrial goods.
www.craneco.com
Annual Revenues: $1.587 billion

Chairman of the Board Tel: (203) 363 - 7300
EVANS, Robert S. Fax: (203) 363 - 7295

President and Chief Exec. Officer Tel: (203) 363 - 7300
FAST, Eric C. Fax: (203) 363 - 7295

Main Headquarters
Mailing: 100 First Stamford Pl. Tel: (203) 363 - 7300
Stamford, CT 06902 Fax: (203) 363 - 7295

Corporate Foundations and Giving Programs

Crane Foundation
Contact: Gil Dickoff
100 First Stamford Pl. Tel: (203) 363 - 7277
Stamford, CT 06902 Fax: (203) 363 - 7295

Annual Grant Total: $200,000 - $300,000
Primary Interests: Education; Math and Science; Religion
Recent Recipients: Carnegie Mellon University; Junior Achievement

The Crane Fund
140 Sylvan Ave. Tel: (201) 585 - 0888
Englewood Cliffs, NJ 07632

Annual Grant Total: none reported
Grants aid to former employees who are unable to be self-supporting due to age or disability.

Crane Fund for Widows and Children
100 First Stamford Pl. Tel: (203) 363 - 7300
Stamford, CT 06902 Fax: (203) 363 - 7295

Annual Grant Total: $1,000,000 - $2,000,000
Geographic Preference: Area(s) in which the company operates

Public Affairs and Related Activities Personnel

At Headquarters

DICKOFF, Gil Tel: (203) 363 - 7277
Treasurer, Crane Foundation Fax: (203) 363 - 7295
gdickoff@craneco.com

KOPCZICK, Elise M. Tel: (203) 363 - 7349
V. President, Human Resources Fax: (203) 363 - 7295
ekopczick@craneco.com

PANTALEONI, Anthony D. Tel: (203) 363 - 7214
V. President, Environment, Health and Safety Fax: (203) 363 - 7295
apantaleoni@craneco.com

VIPOND, J. Robert Tel: (203) 363 - 7301
V. President, Finance and Chief Financial Officer Fax: (203) 363 - 7303

Credit Suisse First Boston

A member of the Public Affairs Council. Provides investment banking, securities brokerage and other financial services. Merged with Donaldson, Lufkin and Jenrette, Inc. in 2000.
www.csfb.com

Chief Exec. Officer Tel: (212) 325 - 2000
DOUGAN, Brady W. Fax: (212) 538 - 4633
brady.dougan@csfb.com

Main Headquarters
Mailing: 11 Madison Ave. Tel: (212) 325 - 2000
New York, NY 10010-3629 Fax: (212) 538 - 4633

Washington Office
Contact: Joseph L. Seidel
Mailing: 1201 F St. NW Tel: (202) 626 - 3301
Suite 450
Washington, DC 20004

Political Action Committees

Credit Suisse First Boston Corp. Government Action Fund
Contact: Mary Lynne Whalen
1201 F St. NW Tel: (202) 626 - 3301
Suite 450
Washington, DC 20004

Credit Suisse First Boston

* continued from previous page

Contributions to Candidates: $107,720 (01/05 - 09/05)
Democrats: $32,220; Republicans: $75,500.

Principal Recipients

SENATE DEMOCRATS		HOUSE DEMOCRATS	
Ford, Harold E Jr (TN)	$4,220		
Conrad, Kent (ND)	$2,500		
Nelson, Bill (FL)	$2,500		
Stabenow, Debbie (MI)	$2,000		
SENATE REPUBLICANS		**HOUSE REPUBLICANS**	
Santorum, Richard (PA)	$5,000	Dreier, David (CA)	$10,000
Allen, George (VA)	$2,500	McCrery, Jim (LA)	$5,000
Hagel, Charles T (NE)	$2,500	Oxley, Michael (OH)	$5,000
Crapo, Michael D (ID)	$2,000	Sweeney, John E. (NY)	$5,000
		Bachus, Spencer (AL)	$3,500
		Baker, Hugh (LA)	$3,500
		Tiberi, Patrick (OH)	$3,500

Corporate Foundations and Giving Programs

Credit Suisse First Boston Foundation Trust
Contact: Alison Johnson
11 Madison Ave. Tel: (212) 325 - 2000
New York, NY 10010-3629 Fax: (212) 538 - 4633

Annual Grant Total: $2,000,000 - $5,000,000
The foundation is currently not accepting unsolicited proposals.
Geographic Preference: Metro New York/New Jersey
Primary Interests: Education; Urban Affairs; Youth Services
Recent Recipients: Habitat for Humanity

Public Affairs and Related Activities Personnel

At Headquarters

JOHNSON, Alison — Tel: (212) 325 - 2000, Fax: (212) 538 - 4633
Contact, CSFB Foundation
alison.johnson@csfb.com

MCFADDEN, Jeanmarie — Tel: (212) 325 - 2000, Fax: (212) 538 - 4633
Director, Corporate Communications

PACE, Joanne — Tel: (212) 325 - 2000, Fax: (212) 538 - 4633
Global Head, Human Resources

VON BARGEN, Christina — Tel: (212) 325 - 2802, Fax: (212) 538 - 4633
Media Contact

At Washington Office

LANDERS, David M. — Tel: (202) 626 - 3301
Registered Federal Lobbyist.

SEIDEL, Joseph L. — Tel: (202) 626 - 3301
Director
Registered Federal Lobbyist.

WHALEN, Mary Lynne — Tel: (202) 626 - 3301
Managing Director
mary.whalen@csfb.com
Registered Federal Lobbyist.
Responsibilities include political action.

Crompton Corp.

See listing on page 114 under Chemtura.

Crowley Maritime Corp.

An ocean transportation operating company.
www.crowley.com
Annual Revenues: $800 million

Chairman, President and Chief Exec. Officer — Tel: (510) 251 - 7500, Fax: (510) 251 - 7788
CROWLEY, Thomas B., Jr.

Main Headquarters
Mailing: 155 Grand Ave., Oakland, CA 94612 — Tel: (510) 251 - 7500, Fax: (510) 251 - 7788

Washington Office
Mailing: 575 Seventh St. NW, Suite 600, Washington, DC 20004 — Tel:

Political Action Committees

Crowley Maritime Federal Political Action Committee
Contact: Albert M. Marucco
575 Seventh St. NW
Suite 600
Washington, DC 20004

Contributions to Candidates: $15,500 (01/05 - 09/05)
Democrats: $5,500; Republicans: $8,000; Other: $2,000.

Principal Recipients

SENATE DEMOCRATS		HOUSE DEMOCRATS	
		Abercrombie, Neil (HI)	$1,000
		Baird, Brian N (WA)	$1,000
		Filner, Bob (CA)	$1,000
		Jefferson, William (LA)	$1,000
		Menendez, Robert (NJ)	$1,000
		HOUSE OTHER	
		Oberstar, James L (MN)	$2,000
SENATE REPUBLICANS		**HOUSE REPUBLICANS**	
Stevens, Ted (AK)	$1,000	Young, Don E (AK)	$3,500
		Hunter, Duncan (CA)	$1,000
		Pickering, Chip (MS)	$1,000
		Vitter, David (LA)	$1,000

Public Affairs and Related Activities Personnel

At Washington Office

MARUCCO, Albert M.
PAC Treasurer
Mailstop: Ninth Floor

At Other Offices

KIMBLE, Jenifer — Tel: (904) 727 - 2513
Senior Specialist, Corporate Communications
9487 Regency Square Blvd.
Jacksonville, FL 32225
jenifer.kimble@crowley.com

MILLER, Mark — Tel: (904) 727 - 4295
Director, Corporate Communications
9487 Regency Square Blvd.
Jacksonville, FL 32225
mark.miller@crowley.com

RODGERS, Susan — Tel: (904) 727 - 2291
V. President, Human Resources
9487 Regency Square Blvd.
Jacksonville, FL 32225
susan.rodgers@crowley.com

Crown Cork and Seal Co.

See listing on page 145 under Crown Holdings, Inc.

Crown Equipment Corp.

Manufacturer of industrial trucks, tractors, and trailers.
www.crown.com

Chairman and Chief Exec. Officer — Tel: (419) 629 - 2311, Fax: (419) 629 - 3796
DICKE, James F., II

Main Headquarters
Mailing: 44 S. Washington St., New Bremen, OH 45869 — Tel: (419) 629 - 2311, Fax: (419) 629 - 3796

Public Affairs and Related Activities Personnel

At Headquarters

CORNER, Greg — Tel: (419) 629 - 2311, Fax: (419) 629 - 3796
Manager, Marketing and Communications

HELMSTETTER, Dave — Tel: (419) 629 - 2311, Fax: (419) 629 - 3067
Publicity Administrator
dave.helmstetter@crown.com

NIEKAMP, Randy — Tel: (419) 629 - 2311, Fax: (419) 629 - 3796
V. President, Human Resources
randy.niekamp@crown.com

Crown Holdings, Inc.

Formerly known as Crown Cork and Seal Co. A manufacturer of packaging products for consumer marketing companies worldwide.
www.crowncork.com
Annual Revenues: $7.187 billion

Chairman, President and Chief Exec. Officer — Tel: (215) 698 - 5170, Fax: (215) 698 - 5201
CONWAY, John W.
jconway@crowncork.com

Main Headquarters
Mailing: One Crown Way, Philadelphia, PA 19154-4599 — Tel: (215) 698 - 5100, Fax: (215) 698 - 5201

Political Action Committees

Crown Cork and Seal Co. PAC
Contact: Michael F. Dunleavy
One Crown Way Tel: (215) 698 - 5351
Philadelphia, PA 19154-4599 Fax: (215) 698 - 5201

Crown Holdings, Inc.

** continued from previous page*

Contributions to Candidates: $11,200 (01/05 - 09/05)
Republicans: $11,200.

Principal Recipients

SENATE REPUBLICANS		HOUSE REPUBLICANS	
Santorum, Richard (PA)	$3,000	Dewine, R. Pat (OH)	$4,000
Allen, George (VA)	$2,000	Hastert, Dennis J. (IL)	$1,200
Talent, James (MO)	$1,000		

Corporate Foundations and Giving Programs

Crown Cork and Seal Corporate Contributions
One Crown Way
Philadelphia, PA 19154-4599
Tel: (215) 698 - 5100
Fax: (215) 698 - 5201

Annual Grant Total: none reported

Public Affairs and Related Activities Personnel

At Headquarters

ABRAMOWICZ, Daniel A.
Exec. V. President, Corporate Technologies and Regulatory Affairs
Tel: (215) 698 - 5100
Fax: (215) 698 - 5201

DONAHUE, Timothy J.
Senior V. President, Finance
tdonahue@crowncork.com
Responsibilities include investor relations.
Tel: (215) 698 - 5351
Fax: (215) 698 - 5201

DUNLEAVY, Michael F.
V. President, Corporate Affairs and Public Relations/PAC Treasurer
mdunleavy@crowncork.com
Tel: (215) 698 - 5351
Fax: (215) 698 - 5201

CS First Boston

See listing on page 144 under Credit Suisse First Boston.

CSK Auto, Inc.

A retailer of automotive parts and accessories.
www.cskauto.com
Annual Revenues: $1.577 billion

Chairman and Chief Exec. Officer
JENKINS, Maynard, Jr.
Tel: (602) 265 - 9200
Fax: (602) 631 - 7321

Main Headquarters
Mailing: 645 E. Missouri Ave., Suite 400
Phoenix, AZ 85012
Tel: (602) 265 - 9200
Fax: (602) 631 - 7321

Public Affairs and Related Activities Personnel

At Headquarters

METCALF, Wendy
Director, Media
Tel: (602) 265 - 9200
Fax: (602) 631 - 7321

MYERS, Jim
Director, Creative/Broadcast Production and Public Relations
Tel: (602) 265 - 9200
Fax: (602) 631 - 7321

WATSON, Don W.
Senior V. President and Chief Financial Officer
Responsibilities include investor relations.
Tel: (602) 631 - 7224
Fax: (602) 631 - 7321

CSX Corp.

A member of the Public Affairs Council. Major subsidiaries include CSX Transportation, CSX Intermodal, and CSX World Terminals LLC.
www.csx.com
Annual Revenues: $8.11 billion

Chairman, President, and Chief Exec. Officer
WARD, Michael J.
Tel: (904) 359 - 3200

Main Headquarters
Mailing: 500 Water St.
Jacksonville, FL 32203
Tel: (904) 359 - 3200

Washington Office
Mailing: 1331 Pennsylvania Ave. NW
Suite 560
Washington, DC 20004
Tel: (202) 783 - 8124
Fax: (202) 783 - 5929

Political Action Committees

CSX Corp. Good Government Fund
Contact: J. Anne Chettle
1331 Pennsylvania Ave. NW
Suite 560
Washington, DC 20004
Tel: (202) 783 - 8124
Fax: (202) 783 - 5929

Contributions to Candidates: $123,500 (01/05 - 09/05)
Democrats: $27,000; Republicans: $94,500; Other: $2,000.

Principal Recipients

SENATE DEMOCRATS		HOUSE DEMOCRATS	
Nelson, Bill (FL)	$5,000	Brown, Corrine (FL)	$2,000
		Clyburn, James (SC)	$2,000
		Hoyer, Steny (MD)	$2,000
		Jefferson, William (LA)	$2,000
		Thompson, Bennie (MS)	$2,000

HOUSE OTHER	
Oberstar, James L (MN)	$2,000

SENATE REPUBLICANS		HOUSE REPUBLICANS	
Lott, Trent (MS)	$5,000	Whitfield, Ed (KY)	$5,000
Smith, Gordon (OR)	$5,000	Crenshaw, Ander (FL)	$2,500
Allen, George (VA)	$3,000	Bachus, Spencer (AL)	$2,000
Santorum, Richard (PA)	$3,000	Cantor, Eric (VA)	$2,000
		Cox, Christopher (CA)	$2,000
		DeLay, Tom (TX)	$2,000
		Duncan, John (TN)	$2,000
		Hulshof, Kenny (MO)	$2,000
		Knollenberg, Joe (MI)	$2,000
		LaTourette, Steve (OH)	$2,000
		Mica, John (FL)	$2,000
		Shaw, Clay (FL)	$2,000
		Young, Don E (AK)	$2,000

Corporate Foundations and Giving Programs

CSX Corporate Contributions Program
500 Water St.
Jacksonville, FL 32203
Tel: (904) 359 - 3200

Annual Grant Total: $2,000,000 - $5,000,000
Geographic Preference: National

Public Affairs and Related Activities Personnel

At Headquarters

BAGGS, David
Assistant V. President, Treasury and Investor Relations
Mailstop: C110
david_baggs@csx.com
Tel: (904) 359 - 4812
Fax: (904) 359 - 1899

CASELLINI, John P.
V. President, State Relations
john_casellini@csx.com
Tel: (904) 359 - 3200

FITZSIMMONS, Ellen M.
Senior V. President, Law and Public Affairs
Tel: (904) 359 - 3200

HAULTER, Robert J.
Senior V. President, Human Resources and Labor Relations
Tel: (904) 359 - 3200
Fax: (904) 359 - 1899

MEYER, Vance
V. President, Corporate Communications
Tel: (904) 359 - 3161
Fax: (904) 359 - 1899

SCHEV, Meg
Regional Media Contact
Tel: (904) 366 - 2949

SEASE, Gary T.
Managing Director, Employee Communications
gary_sease@csx.com
Tel: (904) 359 - 1719
Fax: (904) 359 - 1899

SKIPPER, Misty
Regional Media Contact
Tel: (904) 366 - 2949

SKORNIAK, Kim
Regional Media Contact
Tel: (904) 366 - 2949

At Washington Office

CHETTLE, J. Anne
Director, Federal Affairs
Registered Federal Lobbyist.
Responsibilities include political action.
Tel: (202) 783 - 8124
Fax: (202) 783 - 5929

FLIPPIN, Stephen R.
Director, Government Relations
Registered Federal Lobbyist.
Tel: (202) 783 - 8124
Fax: (202) 783 - 5929

RUEHLING, Michael J.
Senior V. President, Federal Legislation
mike_ruehling@csx.com
Registered Federal Lobbyist.
Tel: (202) 783 - 8124
Fax: (202) 783 - 5929

SHUDTZ, Peter J.
Senior V. President, Regulatory Affairs and Washington Counsel
peter_shudtz@csx.com
Registered Federal Lobbyist.
Tel: (202) 783 - 1343
Fax: (202) 783 - 5929

CSX Corp.

* continued from previous page

At Other Offices

CAMUSO, G. Craig — Tel: (404) 350 - 5227
Regional V. President, State Relations-Georgia — Fax: (404) 350 - 5131
1590 Marietta Blvd.
Atlanta, GA 30318-3699

CHEETHAM, J. Randolph — Tel: (304) 522 - 5146
Regional V. President, State Relations - West Virginia — Fax: (304) 522 - 5714
935 Seventh Ave.
Huntington, WV 25701

DRAKE, Thomas G. — Tel: (734) 464 - 4948
Regional V. President, State Relations - Michigan/Indiana
12780 Levan Rd.
Livonia, MI 48150

SULLIVAN, Robert T. — Tel: (215) 209 - 4580
Director, Media Relations and Public Affairs
(CSX Transportation)
2001 Market St.
Philadelphia, PA 19101
robert_sullivan@csx.com

CSX Transportation

See listing on page 146 under CSX Corp.

CTS Corp.

Designs, manufactures, and sells automotive electronic components, electronic assemblies and provides electronics manufacturing services (EMS) primarily for original equipment manufacturers in the communications and computer industries.
www.ctscorp.com
Annual Revenues: $463 million

President and Chief Exec. Officer
SCHWANZ, Donald K. — Tel: (574) 293 - 7511; Fax: (574) 293 - 6146
dschwanz@ctscorp.com

Main Headquarters
Mailing: 905 West Blvd., North
Elkhart, IN 46514 — Tel: (574) 293 - 7511; Fax: (574) 293 - 6146

Corporate Foundations and Giving Programs

CTS Corp. Foundation
Contact: James L. Cummins
905 West Blvd., North — Tel: (574) 293 - 7511 Ext: 278
Elkhart, IN 46514 — Fax: (574) 293 - 6146

Annual Grant Total: none reported

Public Affairs and Related Activities Personnel

At Headquarters

CUMMINS, James L. — Tel: (574) 293 - 7511 Ext: 278
Trustee, CTS Corp. Foundation — Fax: (574) 293 - 6146
jcummins@ctscorp.com

WALORSKI, Mitchell J. — Tel: (574) 293 - 7511
Director, Investor Relations — Fax: (574) 293 - 6146

Cubic Corp.

Manufacturer of electronic equipment.
www.cubic.com
Annual Revenues: $501.7 million

Chairman, President and Chief Exec. Officer
ZABLE, Walter J. — Tel: (858) 277 - 6780; Fax: (858) 505 - 1523
walter.zable@cubic.com

Main Headquarters
Mailing: P.O. Box 85587
San Diego, CA 92186-5587 — Tel: (858) 277 - 6780; Fax: (858) 505 - 1523
Street: 9333 Balboa Ave.
San Diego, CA 92123

Washington Office
Contact: Jack W. Liddle
Mailing: Crystal Gateway One, Suite 1102 — Tel: (703) 415 - 1600
1235 S. Clark St. — Fax: (703) 415 - 1608
Arlington, VA 22202

Political Action Committees

Cubic Corp. Employees' Political Action Committee
Contact: Brian D. Loya
P.O. Box 85587 — Tel: (858) 277 - 6780
San Diego, CA 92186-5587 — Fax: (858) 505 - 1523

Contributions to Candidates: $18,500 (01/05 - 09/05)
Democrats: $5,500; Republicans: $13,000.

Principal Recipients

SENATE DEMOCRATS		HOUSE DEMOCRATS	
Lieberman, Joe (CT)	$1,000	Dicks, Norm D (WA)	$1,000
Nelson, Bill (FL)	$1,000	Moran, James (VA)	$1,000
		Tauscher, Ellen O (CA)	$1,000

SENATE REPUBLICANS		HOUSE REPUBLICANS	
Ensign, John Eric (NV)	$1,000	Hunter, Duncan (CA)	$3,000
Talent, James (MO)	$1,000	Cunningham, Duke (CA)	$2,000
		Kingston, John (GA)	$2,000
		LaTourette, Steve (OH)	$1,000
		Lewis, Jerry (CA)	$1,000
		Ryun, Jim R (KS)	$1,000

Corporate Foundations and Giving Programs

Cubic Corp. Community Outreach
Contact: Jae Lande
P.O. Box 85587 — Tel: (858) 277 - 6780
San Diego, CA 92186-5587 — Fax: (858) 505 - 1523

Annual Grant Total: none reported

Public Affairs and Related Activities Personnel

At Headquarters

LANDE, Jae — Tel: (858) 277 - 6780
Director, Public Relations — Fax: (858) 505 - 1523

LOYA, Brian D. — Tel: (858) 277 - 6780
PAC Treasurer — Fax: (858) 505 - 1523

At Washington Office

LIDDLE, Jack W. — Tel: (703) 415 - 1600
V. President, Legislative Affairs — Fax: (703) 415 - 1608
jack.liddle@cubic.com
(Cubic Defense Systems)
Registered Federal Lobbyist.

Cubic Defense Systems

See listing on page 147 under Cubic Corp.

Cullen/Frost Bankers, Inc.

See listing on page 207 under Frost Nat'l Bank.

Cumberland Farms, Inc.

Operator of convenience stores and gas service stations.
www.cumberlandfarms.com

Chairman and Chief Exec. Officer
BENTAS, Lilly — Tel: (781) 828 - 4900 Ext: 3385; Fax: (781) 828 - 5246; TF: (800) 225 - 9702

Main Headquarters
Mailing: 777 Dedham St.
Canton, MA 02021 — Tel: (781) 828 - 4900; Fax: (781) 828 - 9624; TF: (800) 225 - 9702

Corporate Foundations and Giving Programs

Cumberland Farms Corporate Giving
Contact: Foster G. Macrides
777 Dedham St. — Tel: (781) 828 - 4900 Ext: 5266
Canton, MA 02021 — Fax: (781) 828 - 9012; TF: (800) 225 - 9702

Annual Grant Total: none reported
Primary Interests: Children's Health; Health and Human Services; Hunger; Safety
Recent Recipients: Muscular Dystrophy Ass'n; Toys for Tots

Public Affairs and Related Activities Personnel

At Headquarters

MACRIDES, Foster G. — Tel: (781) 828 - 4900 Ext: 5266
V. President, Human Resources — Fax: (781) 828 - 9012; TF: (800) 225 - 9702
Responsibilities also include corporate communications.

Cummins Engine Co.

See listing on page 147 under Cummins, Inc.

Cummins, Inc.

Formerly Cummins Engine Co., Inc. A manufacturer of diesel engines.
www.cummins.com
Annual Revenues: $8.4 billion

Chairman and Chief Exec. Officer
SOLSO, Theodore M. "Tim" — Tel: (812) 377 - 5000; Fax: (812) 342 - 9288
tim.m.solso@cummins.com

Main Headquarters
Mailing: P.O. Box 3005
Columbus, IN 47202-3005 — Tel: (812) 377 - 5000; Fax: (812) 377 - 3334
Street: 500 Jackson St.
Columbus, IN 47201

Cummins, Inc.

* continued from previous page

Washington Office
Contact: Steven L. May
Mailing: 601 Pennsylvania Ave. NW
North Bldg., Suite 625
Washington, DC 20004
Tel: (202) 393 - 8585
Ext: `
Fax: (202) 393 - 8111

Political Action Committees

Cummins, Inc. Political Action Committee (CIPAC)
Contact: Catherine Van Way
601 Pennsylvania Ave. NW
North Bldg., Suite 625
Washington, DC 20004
Tel: (202) 393 - 8585
Fax: (202) 393 - 8111

Contributions to Candidates: $21,500 (01/05 - 09/05)
Democrats: $5,000; Republicans: $15,500; Other: $1,000.

Principal Recipients

SENATE DEMOCRATS
Bayh, Evan (IN) $1,000
Clinton, Hillary Rodham (NY) $1,000
Durbin, Richard J (IL) $1,000
Ford, Harold E Jr (TN) $1,000

HOUSE DEMOCRATS

SENATE REPUBLICANS
Lugar, Richard G (IN) $2,000
Burns, Conrad (MT) $1,000
Inhofe, James M (OK) $1,000
Thomas, Craig (WY) $1,000

HOUSE REPUBLICANS
Pence, Mike (IN) $3,000
Blunt, Roy (MO) $2,000
Dreier, David (CA) $1,500

Corporate Foundations and Giving Programs

Cummins Foundation
Contact: Gale Dudley Nay
P.O. Box 3005
Columbus, IN 47202-3005
Tel: (812) 377 - 3114
Fax: (812) 377 - 7897

Annual Grant Total: $2,000,000 - $5,000,000
Most grants are small (rarely exceeding $25,000) and are granted to local plant communities. Guidelines are available.
Geographic Preference: Area(s) in which the company operates
Primary Interests: Arts and Humanities; Community Development; Education; Minority Opportunities; Youth Services

Public Affairs and Related Activities Personnel

At Headquarters

CANTRELL, Dean
Director, Investor Relations
Tel: (812) 377 - 0162
Fax: (812) 377 - 3334

COOK, Jill
V. President, Human Resources
Tel: (812) 377 - 5000
Fax: (812) 377 - 3334

HANAFEE, Susan
Exec. Director, Communications and Information
Tel: (317) 610 - 2494
Fax: (812) 377 - 3334

LAND, Mark
Director, Public Relations
mark.d.land@cummins.com
Tel: (317) 610 - 2456
Fax: (812) 377 - 3613

NAY, Gale Dudley
Foundation Contact
Tel: (812) 377 - 3114
Fax: (812) 377 - 7897

At Washington Office

FOSTER, Emily Diedrich
Washington Representative
Tel: (202) 393 - 8585
Ext: `
Fax: (202) 393 - 8111
Registered Federal Lobbyist.

MAY, Steven L.
V. President, Government Relations
steven.may@cummins.com
Registered Federal Lobbyist.
Tel: (202) 393 - 8585
Fax: (202) 393 - 8111

RENJEL, Louis E.
Director, Legislative and Regulatory Affairs
Tel: (202) 393 - 8585
Ext: `
Fax: (202) 393 - 8111
Registered Federal Lobbyist.

VAN WAY, Catherine
Director, Legislative and Regulatory Affairs
Registered Federal Lobbyist.
Responsibilities also include political action.
Tel: (202) 393 - 8585
Fax: (202) 393 - 8111

VUJOVICH, Christine M.
V. President, Marketing and Environmental Policy
christine.m.vujovich@cummins.com
Registered Federal Lobbyist.
Tel: (202) 393 - 8585
Fax: (202) 393 - 8111

CUNA Mutual Group

A financial services provider to credit unions and their members worldwide, offering insurance, investment and technological solutions through strategic relationships and multiple service channels.
www.cunamutual.com

Chairman of the Board
BURD, Loretta
Tel: (608) 238 - 5851
Fax: (608) 238 - 0830
TF: (800) 356 - 2644

Chief Exec. Officer
POST, Jeff
Tel: (608) 238 - 5851
Fax: (608) 238 - 0830
TF: (800) 356 - 2644

Main Headquarters
Mailing: P.O. Box 391
Madison, WI 53701
Tel: (608) 238 - 5851
Fax: (608) 238 - 0830
TF: (800) 356 - 2644

Street: 5910 Mineral Point Rd.
Madison, WI 53705

Washington Office
Mailing: 6408 Grove Dale Dr.
Suite 204
Alexandria, VA 22310
Tel: (703) 822 - 0200
Fax: (703) 822 - 0304

Corporate Foundations and Giving Programs

CUNA Mutual Group Foundation
Contact: Steve Goldberg
P.O. Box 391
Madison, WI 53701
Tel: (608) 231 - 7755
Fax: (608) 236 - 775
TF: (800) 356 - 2644

Annual Grant Total: none reported
Only 501(c)(3) organizations are considered for grants.
Geographic Preference: Area(s) in which the company operates
Primary Interests: Social Services; United Way Campaigns

Public Affairs and Related Activities Personnel

At Headquarters

BURTON, Tom
Senior Manager, Editorial
tom.burton@cunamutual.com
Tel: (608) 231 - 7272
Fax: (608) 236 - 7272
TF: (800) 356 - 2644

EICH, Jack
Manager, Media Relations
jack.eich@cunamutual.com
Tel: (608) 232 - 6539
Fax: (608) 236 - 8685
TF: (800) 356 - 2644

GOLDBERG, Steve
Exec. Director, CUNA Mutual Foundation
steven.goldberg@cunamutual.com
Tel: (608) 231 - 7755
Fax: (608) 236 - 775
TF: (800) 356 - 2644

TSCHUDY, Phil
Manager, Media Relations
philip.tschudy@cunamutual.com
Tel: (608) 231 - 7188
Fax: (608) 236 - 7188
TF: (800) 356 - 2644

UHLMANN, Rick
Senior Manager, Media Relations
rick.uhlmann@cunamutual.com
Tel: (608) 231 - 8940
Fax: (608) 236 - 8940
TF: (800) 356 - 2644

CUNA Mutual Insurance Co.

See listing on page 148 under CUNA Mutual Group.

Curtice Burns Foods

See listing on page 75 under Birds Eye Foods.

CVS

Retail chain involved in sale of health/beauty aids and prescription drugs.
www.cvs.com
Annual Revenues: $22.241 billion

Chairman, President and Chief Exec. Officer
RYAN, Thomas M.
Tel: (401) 765 - 1500
Fax: (401) 769 - 4488

Main Headquarters
Mailing: One CVS Dr.
Woonsocket, RI 02895
Tel: (401) 765 - 1500
Fax: (401) 769 - 4488

Political Action Committees

CVS Corporation Federal Political Action Fund
Contact: Edward J. Sturgeon
One CVS Dr.
Woonsocket, RI 02895
Tel: (401) 765 - 1500
Fax: (401) 769 - 4488

Contributions to Candidates: $8,250 (01/05 - 09/05)
Democrats: $5,250; Republicans: $3,000.

Principal Recipients

SENATE DEMOCRATS
Whitehouse, Sheldon Ii (RI) $2,500
Clinton, Hillary Rodham (NY) $2,000
Kennedy, Ted (MA) $500

HOUSE DEMOCRATS
Langevin, James (RI) $250

SENATE REPUBLICANS

HOUSE REPUBLICANS
Deal, Nathan (GA) $2,500
Cantor, Eric (VA) $500

CVS

* continued from previous page

Corporate Foundations and Giving Programs

CVS Corporate Community Grants
Contact: Jack Kramer
One CVS Dr.
Woonsocket, RI 02895
Tel: (401) 765 - 1500
Ext: 3005
Fax: (401) 769 - 6012

Annual Grant Total: none reported

Innovations grants program for schools; volunteer challenge grants for CVS employees; and scholarship programs for children of CVS employees.

Primary Interests: Children's Health; K-12 Education; Literacy; Women's Health; Youth Services

Public Affairs and Related Activities Personnel

At Headquarters

ANDREWS, Todd G.
Director, Corporate Communications
tgandrews@cvs.com
Tel: (401) 770 - 5717
Fax: (401) 762 - 9227

BUSH, Lucille
Director, Community Relations
Tel: (401) 765 - 1500
Fax: (401) 769 - 4488

FERDINANDI, Michael
Senior V. President, Human Resources and Corporate Communications
Tel: (401) 765 - 1500
Fax: (401) 769 - 4488

KRAMER, Jack
Senior V. President, Governmental Affairs and Corporate Relations
Tel: (401) 765 - 1500
Ext: 3005
Fax: (401) 769 - 6012

MCGUIRE, Mike
Director, Investor Relations
Tel: (401) 765 - 1500
Fax: (401) 769 - 4488

ORTIZ, Carlos
V. President, Governmental Affairs
Tel: (401) 765 - 1500
Fax: (401) 762 - 9227

STURGEON, Edward J.
PAC Treasurer
Tel: (401) 765 - 1500
Fax: (401) 769 - 4488

VEILLEUX, Jennifer
Director, Community Relations
Tel: (401) 765 - 1500
Fax: (401) 769 - 4488

At Other Offices

CHRISTAL, Nancy R.
V. President, Investor Relations
670 White Plains Rd.
Suite 210
Scarsdale, NY 10583
nrchristal@cvs.com
Tel: (914) 722 - 4704
Fax: (914) 722 - 0847

Cypress Semiconductor Corp.

Designs, manufactures and assembles semiconductor devices.

www.cypress.com
Annual Revenues: $819.2 million

Chairman of the Board
BENHAMOU, Eric A.
eab@cypress.com
Tel: (408) 943 - 2600
Fax: (408) 943 - 4730

President and Chief Exec. Officer
RODGERS, T. J.
Tel: (408) 943 - 2600
Fax: (408) 943 - 4730

Main Headquarters
Mailing: 198 Champion Ct.
San Jose, CA 95134
Tel: (408) 943 - 2600
Fax: (408) 943 - 6841

Public Affairs and Related Activities Personnel

At Headquarters

MCCARTHY, Joseph L.
V. President, Corporate Communications
jmy@cypress.com
Tel: (408) 943 - 2902
Fax: (408) 456 - 1910

MINOR, Bill
V. President, Human Resources
Tel: (408) 943 - 2600
Fax: (408) 943 - 4730

Cyprus Amax Minerals Co.

See listing on page 381 under Phelps Dodge Corp.

Cytec Industries Inc.

A specialty chemicals and materials company. Serves a broad group of end users, including the water treatment, mining, coatings, plastics, aerospace, and automotive industries.

www.cytec.com
Annual Revenues: $1.39 billion

Chairman, President and Chief Exec. Officer
LILLEY, David
david_lilley@gm.cytec.com
Tel: (973) 357 - 3100
Fax: (973) 357 - 3054
TF: (800) 652 - 6013

Main Headquarters
Mailing: Five Garret Mountain Plaza
West Paterson, NJ 07424
Tel: (973) 357 - 3100
Fax: (973) 357 - 3065
TF: (800) 652 - 6013

Corporate Foundations and Giving Programs

Cytec Industries Corporate Contributions Program
Five Garret Mountain Plaza
West Paterson, NJ 07424
Tel: (973) 357 - 3100
Fax: (973) 357 - 3065
TF: (800) 652 - 6013

Annual Grant Total: none reported

Public Affairs and Related Activities Personnel

At Headquarters

DRILLOCK, David M.
V. President, Investor Relations and Controller
Tel: (973) 357 - 3249
Fax: (973) 357 - 3088
TF: (800) 652 - 6013

MAROSITS, Joseph E.
V. President, Human Resources
joseph_marosits@gm.cytec.com
Tel: (973) 357 - 3290
Fax: (973) 357 - 3060
TF: (800) 652 - 6013

PETERSEN, Gail L.
Director, Communications and Public Affairs
Tel: (973) 357 - 3100
Fax: (973) 357 - 3065
TF: (800) 652 - 6013

DaimlerChrysler Corp.

A member of the Public Affairs Council. An automobile manufacturer. Formed by the merger of Daimler-Benz and Chrysler Corp. in 1998.

www.daimlerchrysler.com
Annual Revenues: $136 million

Chairman of the Board
SCHREMPP, Jurgen E.
Tel: (248) 576 - 5741
Fax: (248) 576 - 4742
TF: (800) 992 - 1997

President and Chief Exec. Officer
ZETSCHE, Dieter
Tel: (248) 576 - 5741
Fax: (248) 576 - 4742
TF: (800) 992 - 1997

Main Headquarters
Mailing: 1000 Chrysler Dr.
Auburn Hills, MI 48326-2766
Tel: (248) 576 - 5741
Fax: (248) 576 - 4742
TF: (800) 992 - 1997

Washington Office
Contact: Robert G. Liberatore
Mailing: 1401 H St. NW
Suite 700
Washington, DC 20005
Tel: (202) 414 - 6700
Fax: (202) 414 - 6716

Political Action Committees

DaimlerChrysler Corp. Political Support Committee
Contact: Brenda T. Day
1401 H St. NW
Suite 700
Washington, DC 20005
Tel: (202) 414 - 6714
Fax: (202) 414 - 6743

Contributions to Candidates: $188,330 (01/05 - 09/05)
Democrats: $64,330; Republicans: $124,000.

Principal Recipients

SENATE DEMOCRATS		HOUSE DEMOCRATS	
Carper, Thomas R (DE)	$5,580	Levin, Sander (MI)	$5,000
Byrd, Robert C (WV)	$5,000	Dingell, John D (MI)	$4,500
Conrad, Kent (ND)	$4,500		
SENATE REPUBLICANS		**HOUSE REPUBLICANS**	
Dewine, Richard (OH)	$10,000	Cantor, Eric (VA)	$5,000
Talent, James (MO)	$10,000	Barton, Joe L (TX)	$4,500
Kyl, Jon L (AZ)	$5,000	DeLay, Tom (TX)	$4,000
		Manzullo, Donald (IL)	$4,000

Corporate Foundations and Giving Programs

DaimlerChrysler Corp. Fund
Contact: Brian G. Glowiak
1000 Chrysler Dr.
Auburn Hills, MI 48326-2766
Tel: (248) 512 - 2500
Fax: (248) 512 - 2503
TF: (800) 992 - 1997

Annual Grant Total: over $5,000,000

Encourages employee and DaimlerChrysler involvement. DaimlerChrysler's Physically Challenged Resource Center offers information and rebates on adaptive driving aids and conversion equipment for the disabled. Guidelines are available.

Geographic Preference: Area(s) in which the company operates; Alabama; Delaware; Illinois; Indiana; Michigan; Missouri; New York; Ohio; Wisconsin

Primary Interests: Adult Education and Training; Community Development

Recent Recipients: Detroit Symphony Orchestra; Nat'l Public Radio; United Way

Public Affairs and Related Activities Personnel

At Headquarters

COOK, Maura Rhea
Senior Manager, International Affairs and Public Policy
Mailstop: CIMS 485-10-95
Tel: (248) 512 - 3348
Fax: (248) 512 - 3919
TF: (800) 992 - 1997

DaimlerChrysler Corp.

** continued from previous page*

FOUNTAIN, W. Frank
Senior V. President, Internal Affairs and Public Policy
Mailstop: CIMS 485-10-96
wff3@daimlerchrysler.com
Tel: (248) 512 - 4218
Fax: (248) 512 - 1762
TF: (800) 992 - 1997

GLOWIAK, Brian G.
Senior Manager, DaimlerChrysler Corp. Fund
Mailstop: CIMS 485-10-94
Tel: (248) 512 - 2500
Fax: (248) 512 - 2503
TF: (800) 992 - 1997

HOFFMAN, Frederick W.
Director, State Relations
Mailstop: CIMS 485-10-95
Tel: (248) 512 - 3352
Fax: (248) 512 - 3919
TF: (800) 992 - 1997

VINES, Jason
V. President, Corporate Communications
Tel: (248) 576 - 5741
Fax: (248) 576 - 4742
TF: (800) 992 - 1997

WEISS, Leven C.
Senior Manager, Civic and Community Relations
Mailstop: CIMS 485-10-95
Tel: (248) 512 - 3360
Fax: (248) 512 - 3919
TF: (800) 992 - 1997

At Washington Office

BECKER, Linda M.
Senior Manager, Public Policy and Communications
Registered Federal Lobbyist.
Tel: (202) 414 - 6757
Fax: (202) 414 - 6741

CRAVEN, William
Program Management Specialist
Registered Federal Lobbyist.
Tel: (202) 414 - 6711
Fax: (202) 414 - 6738

DAY, Brenda T.
Director, Congressional Affairs
Registered Federal Lobbyist.
Tel: (202) 414 - 6714
Fax: (202) 414 - 6743

ELDRIDGE, Earle
Senior Manager, Washington Public Affairs
Tel: (202) 414 - 6700
Fax: (202) 414 - 6716

FELRICE, Barry
Director, Regulatory Affairs
Registered Federal Lobbyist.
Tel: (202) 414 - 6730
Fax: (202) 414 - 6738

FERRY, Holly
Grassroots Program Manager
Registered Federal Lobbyist.
Tel: (202) 414 - 6713
Fax: (202) 414 - 6743

FITZGIBBONS, Dennis B.
Director, Public Policy
Registered Federal Lobbyist.
Tel: (202) 414 - 6764
Fax: (202) 414 - 6741

JONES, Jake
Senior Manager, Legislative Affairs
jj91@daimlerchrysler.com
Registered Federal Lobbyist.
Tel: (202) 414 - 6746
Fax: (202) 414 - 6743

KISSEL, Marie
Senior Manager, Trade Policy
Registered Federal Lobbyist.
Tel: (202) 414 - 6732
Fax: (202) 414 - 6741

LIBERATORE, Robert G.
Senior V. President, External Affairs and Public Policy
Registered Federal Lobbyist.
Tel: (202) 414 - 6747
Fax: (202) 414 - 6716

SCHLAISS, Karl-Heinz
Senior Manager, Corporate Relations
Tel: (202) 414 - 6744
Fax: (202) 414 - 6738

Dain Rauscher Corp.

See listing on page 405 under RBC Dain Rauscher Corp.

Dairy Farmers of America, Inc.

www.dfamilk.com
Annual Revenues: $7.902 billion

Chairman of the Board
CAMERLO, Tom
jcamerlo@dfamilk.com
Tel: (816) 801 - 6455
Fax: (816) 801 - 6590

President and Chief Exec. Officer
HANMAN, Gary E.
ghanman@dfamilk.com
Tel: (816) 801 - 6455
Fax: (816) 801 - 6590

Main Headquarters
Mailing: P.O. Box 909700
Kansas City, MO 64190-9700
Tel: (816) 801 - 6455
Fax: (816) 801 - 6590

Political Action Committees

Dairy Farmers of America, Inc. PAC
Contact: J. Sam Stone
P.O. Box 909700
Kansas City, MO 64190-9700
Tel: (816) 801 - 6455
Fax: (816) 801 - 6590

Contributions to Candidates: $160,500 (01/05 - 09/05)
Democrats: $48,500; Republicans: $109,000; Other: $3,000.

Principal Recipients

SENATE DEMOCRATS
Bingaman, Jeff (NM) $2,000

HOUSE DEMOCRATS
Boyd, F Allen Jr (FL) $4,500

HOUSE OTHER
Peterson, Collin (MN) $3,000

SENATE REPUBLICANS
Talent, James (MO) $5,000
Vitter, David (LA) $4,000
Allen, George (VA) $2,000
Bennett, Robert F (UT) $2,000
Chambliss, Saxby (GA) $2,000
Coburn, Thomas (OK) $2,000

HOUSE REPUBLICANS
Blunt, Roy (MO) $5,000
Graves, Sam (MO) $5,000
Sherwood, Donald L (PA) $5,000
Bonilla, Henry (TX) $3,000
Carter, John (TX) $3,000
Conaway, K Michael (TX) $3,000

Corporate Foundations and Giving Programs

Associated Milk Producers, Inc. Contributions Program
Contact: Donald H. Schriver
P.O. Box 909700
Kansas City, MO 64190-9700
Tel: (816) 801 - 6470
Fax: (816) 801 - 6471

Annual Grant Total: none reported
Geographic Preference: Central United States
Primary Interests: Agriculture; Youth Services

Public Affairs and Related Activities Personnel

At Headquarters

GRIEB, Patsy
Coordinator, Public and Media Relations
Tel: (816) 801 - 6488
Fax: (816) 801 - 6590

PAPEN, Harold
Corporate V. President, Human Resources and Administration
hpapen@dfamilk.com
Tel: (816) 801 - 6490
Fax: (816) 801 - 6590

SCHAFER, Agnes
V. President, Communications and Public Relations
Tel: (816) 801 - 6455
Fax: (816) 801 - 6590

SCHRIVER, Donald H.
Exec. V. President; Contact, Associated Milk Producers, Inc. Contributions Program
dschriver@dfamilk.com
Tel: (816) 801 - 6470
Fax: (816) 801 - 6471

STONE, J. Sam
V. President, Government and Member Relations; PAC Treasurer
Tel: (816) 801 - 6455
Fax: (816) 801 - 6590

Dairylea Cooperative Inc.

www.dairylea.com

Chief Exec. Officer
SMITH, Richard P.
Tel: (315) 433 - 0100
Fax: (315) 433 - 2345
TF: (800) 654 - 8838

Main Headquarters
Mailing: P.O. Box 4844
Syracuse, NY 13221-4844
Tel: (315) 433 - 0100
Fax: (315) 433 - 2345
TF: (800) 654 - 8838

Political Action Committees

Dairylea Cooperative PAC (LEAPAC)
Contact: Alexander Baruch
P.O. Box 4844
Syracuse, NY 13221-4844
Tel: (315) 433 - 0100
Fax: (315) 433 - 2345
TF: (800) 654 - 8838

Contributions to Candidates: $2,000 (01/05 - 09/05)
Republicans: $2,000.

Principal Recipients

SENATE REPUBLICANS
Chambliss, Saxby (GA) $1,000

HOUSE REPUBLICANS
Boehlert, Sherwood (NY) $500
Kelly, Sue W (NY) $500

Public Affairs and Related Activities Personnel

At Headquarters

BARUCH, Alexander
PAC Treasurer
Tel: (315) 433 - 0100
Fax: (315) 433 - 2345
TF: (800) 654 - 8838

PECKHAM, Katie
Communications Contact
Tel: (315) 433 - 0100
Ext: 5594
Fax: (315) 433 - 2345
TF: (800) 654 - 8838

TRUDELL, Tracy
Communications Contact
Tel: (315) 433 - 0100
Ext: 5598
Fax: (315) 433 - 2345
TF: (800) 654 - 8838

Dakota Coal Co.

See listing on page 63 under Basin Electric Power Cooperative.

Dakota Gasification Co.

See listing on page 63 under Basin Electric Power Cooperative.

Dan River, Inc.

A textile manufacturer.
www.danriver.com
Annual Revenues: $631.1 million

Chairman and Chief Exec. Officer
LANIER, Joseph L., Jr. Tel: (434) 799 - 7000 Fax: (434) 799 - 7276

Main Headquarters
Mailing: P.O. Box 261, Danville, VA 24543 Tel: (434) 799 - 7000 Fax: (434) 799 - 7276
Street: 700 Lanier Ave., Danville, VA 24543

Corporate Foundations and Giving Programs

Dan River Foundation
Contact: Barry F. Shea
P.O. Box 261
Danville, VA 24543 Tel: (434) 799 - 7000 Fax: (434) 799 - 7276

Annual Grant Total: $100,000 - $200,000
Geographic Preference: Area(s) in which the company operates
Primary Interests: Community Affairs; Health and Human Services; Higher Education; Youth Services
Recent Recipients: United Way; Virginia Foundation of Independent Colleges

Public Affairs and Related Activities Personnel

At Headquarters

LAUSSADE, Denise
V. President, Finance Tel: (434) 799 - 4113 Fax: (434) 799 - 7276
Responsibilities include investor relations.

SHEA, Barry F.
Treasurer, Dan River Foundation Tel: (434) 799 - 7000 Fax: (434) 799 - 7276

Dana Corp.

A member of the Public Affairs Council. A manufacturer of automotive systems equipment, both original and aftermarket parts.
www.dana.com
Annual Revenues: $9.1 billion

Chairman, Chief Exec. Officer and President
BURNS, Michael J. Tel: (419) 535 - 4500 Fax: (419) 535 - 4756

Main Headquarters
Mailing: Box 1000, Toledo, OH 43697-1000 Tel: (419) 535 - 4500 Fax: (419) 535 - 4756
Street: 4500 Dorr St., Toledo, OH 43615

Political Action Committees

Dana Corp. PAC
Contact: Edward C. McNeal
Box 1000
Toledo, OH 43697-1000 Tel: (419) 535 - 4662 Fax: (419) 535 - 4756

Contributions to Candidates: $1,000 (01/05 - 09/05)
Republicans: $1,000.

Principal Recipients

SENATE REPUBLICANS
Cornyn, John (TX) $1,000

HOUSE REPUBLICANS

Corporate Foundations and Giving Programs

Dana Corp. Foundation
Contact: Edward C. McNeal
Box 1000
Toledo, OH 43697-1000 Tel: (419) 535 - 4662 Fax: (419) 535 - 4756

Annual Grant Total: $2,000,000 - $5,000,000
Geographic Preference: Area(s) in which the company operates
Recent Recipients: Junior Achievement; United Way

Public Affairs and Related Activities Personnel

At Headquarters

HARDS, Michelle
Director, Investor Relations Tel: (419) 535 - 4500 Fax: (419) 535 - 4756

MCNEAL, Edward C.
V. President, Government Relations Tel: (419) 535 - 4662 Fax: (419) 535 - 4756
Responsibilities also include corporate philanthropy.

Danaher Corp.

Designs, manufactures and markets products and services with strong brand names, proprietary technologies, and major market positions that improve the way we live and work.
www.danaher.com
Annual Revenues: $5.2 billion

Chairman of the Board
RALES, Steven M. Tel: (202) 828 - 0850 Fax: (202) 828 - 0860

President and Chief Exec. Officer
CULP, H. Lawrence, Jr. Tel: (202) 828 - 0850 Fax: (202) 828 - 0860

Main Headquarters
Mailing: 2099 Pennsylvania Ave. NW, Washington, DC 20006 Tel: (202) 828 - 0850 Fax: (202) 828 - 0860

Corporate Foundations and Giving Programs

Danaher Foundation
Contact: Patrick W. Allender
2099 Pennsylvania Ave. NW
Washington, DC 20006 Tel: (202) 828 - 0850 Fax: (202) 828 - 0860

Assets: $1,309,507 (2002)
Annual Grant Total: $100,000 - $200,000
Geographic Preference: Area(s) in which the company operates
Primary Interests: Education; Health
Recent Recipients: American Cancer Society; Habitat for Humanity; Make-A-Wish Foundation

Public Affairs and Related Activities Personnel

At Headquarters

ALLENDER, Patrick W.
Exec. V. President, Chief Financial Officer , Secretary; and President, Foundation Tel: (202) 828 - 0850 Fax: (202) 828 - 0860

WILSON, Andy
V. President, Investor Relations Tel: (202) 828 - 0850 Fax: (202) 828 - 0860

Darden Restaurants, Inc.

A member of the Public Affairs Council. A casual dining company. Restaurant divisions include Red Lobster, Olive Garden, Bahama Breeze and Smokey Bones.
www.darden.com
Annual Revenues: $5.36 billion

Chairman
LEE, Joe R. Tel: (407) 245 - 4000 Fax: (407) 245 - 4462

Chief Exec. Officer
OTIS, Clarence Tel: (407) 245 - 4000 Fax: (407) 245 - 4462

Main Headquarters
Mailing: P.O. Box 593330, Orlando, FL 32859 Tel: (407) 245 - 4000 Fax: (407) 245 - 4462
Street: 5900 Lake Ellenor Dr., Orlando, FL 32809

Political Action Committees

Darden Restaurants Employees Good Government Fund
Contact: Betty Salvas
P.O. Box 593330
Orlando, FL 32859 Tel: (407) 245 - 6734 Fax: (407) 245 - 4462

Contributions to Candidates: $38,500 (01/05 - 09/05)
Democrats: $4,500; Republicans: $34,000.

Principal Recipients

SENATE DEMOCRATS
Ford, Harold E Jr (TN) $2,500
Nelson, Bill (FL) $2,000

HOUSE DEMOCRATS

SENATE REPUBLICANS
Santorum, Richard (PA) $7,500
Hatch, Orrin (UT) $5,000

HOUSE REPUBLICANS
Blunt, Roy (MO) $5,000
Feeney, Tom (FL) $5,000
Keller, Richard (FL) $3,500
Cantor, Eric (VA) $2,500
Mack, Connie (FL) $2,500
Weldon, David (FL) $2,000
Pombo, Richard (CA) $1,000

Corporate Foundations and Giving Programs

Darden Restaurants Foundation
Contact: Patty DeYoung
P.O. Box 593330
Orlando, FL 32859 Tel: (407) 245 - 5213 Fax: (407) 245 - 4310

Annual Grant Total: none reported

Public Affairs and Related Activities Personnel

At Headquarters

CIPPOLLONE, Tom
Director, Risk Management Tel: (407) 245 - 4969 Fax: (407) 245 - 6678
tcippollone@darden.com

DESIMONE, Jim
V. President, Media and Communications Tel: (407) 245 - 4567 Fax: (407) 245 - 4462

DEYOUNG, Patty
Representative, Foundation/Community Affairs Tel: (407) 245 - 5213 Fax: (407) 245 - 4310
pdeyoung@darden.com

DIMOPOULOS, Linda, Jr.
Exec. V. President and Chief Financial Officer Tel: (407) 245 - 4000
Responsibilities include investor relations.

LYONS, Daniel M.
Senior V. President, Human Resources Tel: (407) 245 - 5217 Fax: (407) 245 - 5114
dlyons@darden.com

Darden Restaurants, Inc.

* continued from previous page

SALVAS, Betty — Tel: (407) 245 - 6734
Corporate Relations Representative — Fax: (407) 245 - 4462
bsalvas@darden.com

SMITH, Joe — Tel: (407) 245 - 5530
Director, Communications and Travel Services — Fax: (407) 245 - 4325
jsmith@darden.com

STROUD, Matthew — Tel: (407) 245 - 5144
V. President, Investor Relations — Fax: (407) 245 - 5510
mstroud@darden.com

WALSH, Richard J. — Tel: (407) 245 - 5366
Senior V. President, Corporate Affairs — Fax: (407) 245 - 5310
rwalsh@darden.com
Responsibilities include government affairs.

WILLIAMS, George — Tel: (407) 245 - 5312
V. President, Government and Environmental Relations — Fax: (407) 245 - 5135

DaVita, Inc.

Provides dialysis services for diagnosed kidney problems.
www.davita.com
Annual Revenues: $2.3 billion

Chairman and Chief Exec. Officer
THIRY, Kent J. — Tel: (310) 536 - 2400

Main Headquarters
Mailing: 601 Hawaii St.
El Segundo, CA 90245 — Tel: (310) 536 - 2400

Political Action Committees

DaVita PAC
Contact: Tom Weinberg
601 Hawaii St. — Tel: (202) 393 - 4060
El Segundo, CA 90245

Contributions to Candidates: $50,700 (01/05 - 09/05)
Democrats: $14,700; Republicans: $36,000.

Principal Recipients

SENATE DEMOCRATS		HOUSE DEMOCRATS	
Conrad, Kent (ND)	$5,000	Jefferson, William (LA)	$2,500
Wyden, Ronald Lee (OR)	$4,000		
Cardin, Benjamin (MD)	$1,000		

SENATE REPUBLICANS		HOUSE REPUBLICANS	
Smith, Gordon (OR)	$5,000	Camp, David Lee (MI)	$5,000
		Cantor, Eric (VA)	$5,000
		Hayworth, J D (AZ)	$5,000
		Johnson, Nancy (CT)	$5,000
		Thomas, William M (CA)	$5,000
		English, Philip S (PA)	$2,500
		Hulshof, Kenny (MO)	$2,000

Public Affairs and Related Activities Personnel

At Headquarters

WEINBERG, Tom — Tel: (202) 393 - 4060
PAC Treasurer

ZUMWALT, LeAnne — Tel: (650) 696 - 8910
V. President, Investor Relations

Day & Zimmerman

www.dayzim.com
Annual Revenues: $1.3 billion

Chairman and Chief Exec. Officer
YOH, Harold L., III — Tel: (215) 299 - 8000; TF: (800) 523 - 0786

Main Headquarters
Mailing: 1818 Market St.
Philadelphia, PA 19103 — Tel: (215) 299 - 8000; Fax: (215) 299 - 8030; TF: (800) 523 - 0786

Political Action Committees

Day & Zimmerman Inc. Federal PAC (DayPAC - Federal)
Contact: Joseph Ritzel
1818 Market St. — Tel: (215) 299 - 8000
Philadelphia, PA 19103 — TF: (800) 523 - 0786

Contributions to Candidates: $12,500 (01/05 - 09/05)
Democrats: $6,500; Republicans: $6,000.

Principal Recipients

SENATE DEMOCRATS		HOUSE DEMOCRATS	
		Murtha, John P Mr. (PA)	$5,500
		Bordallo, Madeleine (GU)	$1,000

SENATE REPUBLICANS		HOUSE REPUBLICANS	
Allen, George (VA)	$1,000	English, Philip S (PA)	$1,000
Santorum, Richard (PA)	$1,000	Frelinghuysen, Rod (NJ)	$1,000
Talent, James (MO)	$1,000	Weldon, Curt (PA)	$1,000

Public Affairs and Related Activities Personnel

At Headquarters

GOSDECK, Sharon — Tel: (215) 299 - 8000
V. President, Corporate Communications — Fax: (215) 299 - 8033; TF: (800) 523 - 0786

HICKEY, James J. — Tel: (215) 299 - 8000
V. President, Government Affairs — Fax: (215) 299 - 8030; TF: (800) 523 - 0786

RITZEL, Joseph — Tel: (215) 299 - 8000
Chief Financial Officer; Treasurer, DayPAC - Federal — TF: (800) 523 - 0786
Mailstop: 22nd Floor

Dayton Power and Light Co.

See listing on page 166 under DPL Inc.

Dean Foods Company

A dairy and specialty food distributor producing a full line of branded and private label products, including fluid milk, ice cream, and extended shelf life products. Merged with Suiza Foods Corp. in December of 2001.
www.deanfoods.com
Annual Revenues: $8.23 billion

Chairman and Chief Exec. Officer
ENGLES, Gregg L. — Tel: (214) 303 - 3400; Fax: (214) 303 - 3499

Main Headquarters
Mailing: 2515 McKinney Ave., Suite 1200 — Tel: (214) 303 - 3400
Dallas, TX 75201 — Fax: (214) 303 - 3499

Washington Office
Contact: Bill Tinklepaugh
Mailing: 2111 Wilson Blvd., Suite 700 — Tel: (703) 351 - 5022
Arlington, VA 22201 — Fax: (703) 351 - 9772

Political Action Committees

Dean Foods Co. Political Action Committee
Contact: Bill Tinklepaugh
2111 Wilson Blvd., Suite 700 — Tel: (703) 351 - 5022
Arlington, VA 22201 — Fax: (703) 351 - 9772

Contributions to Candidates: $83,500 (01/05 - 09/05)
Democrats: $22,500; Republicans: $59,000; Other: $2,000.

Principal Recipients

SENATE REPUBLICANS		HOUSE REPUBLICANS	
Chambliss, Saxby (GA)	$5,000	Hastert, Dennis J. (IL)	$5,000
Allen, George (VA)	$2,000	Bonilla, Henry (TX)	$4,000
Lott, Trent (MS)	$2,000	DeLay, Tom (TX)	$2,500
Lugar, Richard G (IN)	$2,000	Dreier, David (CA)	$2,500
		Sessions, Pete (TX)	$2,500

Public Affairs and Related Activities Personnel

At Headquarters

CALADO, Miguel — Tel: (214) 303 - 3400
Exec. V. President and President, International — Fax: (214) 303 - 3499

DUNN, Robert — Tel: (214) 303 - 3400
Senior V. President, Human Resources — Fax: (214) 303 - 3499

SIBERT, Rich — Tel: (214) 303 - 3400
Director,Investor Relations — Fax: (214) 303 - 3499

At Washington Office

TINKLEPAUGH, Bill — Tel: (703) 351 - 5022
Senior V. President, Government and Industry Relations — Fax: (703) 351 - 9772
Registered Federal Lobbyist.

Deere & Company

A member of the Public Affairs Council. A manufacturer and distributor of agricultural, forestry, construction, and lawn and turf care equipment.
www.deere.com
Annual Revenues: $19.986 billion

Chairman and Chief Exec. Officer
LANE, Robert W. — Tel: (309) 765 - 4114; Fax: (309) 765 - 5772

Main Headquarters
Mailing: One John Deere Pl. — Tel: (309) 765 - 8000
Moline, IL 61265-8098 — Fax: (309) 765 - 5772

Deere & Company

* *continued from previous page*

Washington Office
Contact: Charles R. Stamp, Jr.
Mailing: 1808 I St. NW, Eighth Floor, Washington, DC 20006 — Tel: (202) 223 - 4817; Fax: (202) 296 - 0011

Political Action Committees

Deere & Co. Civic Action Fund
One John Deere Pl.
Moline, IL 61265-8098
Tel: (309) 765 - 8000
Fax: (309) 765 - 5772

Contributions to Candidates: $98,000 (01/05 - 09/05)
Democrats: $15,000; Republicans: $83,000.

John Deere Political Action Committee
Contact: Candace Schnoor
One John Deere Pl.
Moline, IL 61265-8098
Tel: (309) 765 - 8000
Fax: (309) 765 - 5772

Contributions to Candidates: none reported (01/05 - 09/05)

Corporate Foundations and Giving Programs

John Deere Foundation
Contact: James H. Collins
One John Deere Pl.
Moline, IL 61265-8098
Tel: (309) 765 - 4311
Fax: (309) 765 - 9855

Annual Grant Total: over $5,000,000
Primary Interests: Community Development; Education; Human Welfare

Deere & Company Contributions Committee
One John Deere Pl.
Moline, IL 61265-8098
Tel: (309) 765 - 8000
Fax: (309) 765 - 5772

Annual Grant Total: $100,000 - $200,000
Primary Interests: Community Development; Education; Human Welfare

Public Affairs and Related Activities Personnel

At Headquarters

COLLINS, James H.
Director, Community Relations and President, John Deere Foundation
Tel: (309) 765 - 4311
Fax: (309) 765 - 9855

EHLERT, Carolyn J.
Director, Public Affairs Policy and Program Support
Tel: (309) 765 - 4954
Fax: (309) 765 - 5183

EMERSON, Frances B.
V. President, Corporate Communications and Chairman, John Deere Foundation
Tel: (309) 765 - 4634
Fax: (309) 765 - 5772

GOLDEN, Kenneth B.
Manager, Public Relations
Tel: (309) 765 - 5678
Fax: (309) 765 - 5682

HORNBUCKLE, Mertroe B.
V. President, Human Resources
Tel: (309) 765 - 4252
Fax: (309) 765 - 5066

LEONARD, Mary
Communications Manager, Public Relations
Tel: (309) 765 - 4106
Fax: (309) 765 - 5682

SCHNOOR, Candace
PAC Treasurer
Tel: (309) 765 - 8000
Fax: (309) 765 - 5772

ZIEGLER, Marie Z.
V. President, Investor Relations
Tel: (309) 765 - 4491
Fax: (309) 765 - 4663

At Washington Office

BEHAN, William M.
Director, Agricutural Affairs
behanwilliamm@johndeere.com
Registered Federal Lobbyist.
Tel: (202) 223 - 4817
Fax: (202) 296 - 0011

RAUBER, John W., Jr.
Director, Washington Public Affairs
Registered Federal Lobbyist.
Tel: (202) 223 - 4817
Fax: (202) 296 - 0011

SANDHERR, Cynthia C.
Director, Washington Public Affairs
Registered Federal Lobbyist.
Tel: (202) 223 - 4817
Fax: (202) 296 - 0011

STAMP, Charles R., Jr.
V. President, Public Affairs Worldwide (Global AgServices)
Registered Federal Lobbyist.
Tel: (202) 223 - 4817
Fax: (202) 296 - 0011

At Other Offices

ILES, Thom
Director, Public Affairs
2000 John Deere Run
Raleigh, NC 27513
Tel: (919) 804 - 2795

PARKIN, Jerry D.
Director, State Public Affairs
666 Grand Ave.
Suite 1707
Des Moines, IA 50309
Tel: (515) 244 - 9377

Del Monte Foods

A producer of canned fruits and vegetables.
www.delmonte.com
Annual Revenues: $1.512 billion

Chairman, President and Chief Exec. Officer
WOLFORD, Richard G.
Tel: (415) 247 - 3000
Fax: (415) 247 - 3565

Main Headquarters
Mailing: P.O. Box 193575, San Francisco, CA 94119-3575 — Tel: (415) 247 - 3000; Fax: (415) 247 - 3565
Street: One Market Plaza, San Francisco, CA 94105

Public Affairs and Related Activities Personnel

At Headquarters

GIBBONS, Thomas E.
Senior V. President and Treasurer
Responsibilities include investor relations.
Tel: (415) 247 - 3382
Fax: (415) 247 - 3565

Delaware North Companies

Operates in the foodservice, hospitality, retail and entertainment industries.
www.delawarenorth.com
Annual Revenues: $2 billion

Chairman and Chief Exec. Officer
JACOBS, Jeremy J., Sr.
Tel: (716) 858 - 5000
Fax: (716) 858 - 5125

Main Headquarters
Mailing: 40 Fountain Plaza, Buffalo, NY 14202 — Tel: (716) 858 - 5000; Fax: (716) 858 - 5125

Political Action Committees

Delaware North Companies PAC
Contact: Terry C. Burton
40 Fountain Plaza
Buffalo, NY 14202
Tel: (716) 858 - 5000
Fax: (716) 858 - 5125

Contributions to Candidates: none reported (01/05 - 09/05)

Corporate Foundations and Giving Programs

Delaware North Cos., Inc. Contributions Program
40 Fountain Plaza
Buffalo, NY 14202
Tel: (716) 858 - 5000
Fax: (716) 858 - 5125

Annual Grant Total: none reported
Geographic Preference: Continental United States; Canada; Australia; United Kingdom
Primary Interests: Education; Health and Human Services
Recent Recipients: Habitat for Humanity; Mid-South County Community College; United Way; University of Buffalo

Public Affairs and Related Activities Personnel

At Headquarters

BISSETT, William J.
V. President, External Affairs
Tel: (716) 858 - 5000
Fax: (716) 858 - 5479

BURTON, Terry C.
PAC Treasurer
Tel: (716) 858 - 5000
Fax: (716) 858 - 5125

HOBEL, Candace
Coordinator, Public Relations
chobel@dncinc.com
Tel: (716) 858 - 5503
Fax: (716) 858 - 5125

MORGAN, Eileen
V. President, Human Resources
Tel: (716) 858 - 5000
Fax: (716) 858 - 5125

WATKINS, Wendy A.
V. President, Corporate Communications and Public Relations
wwatkins@dncinc.com
Tel: (716) 858 - 5092
Fax: (716) 858 - 5125

Delco Remy Internat'l Inc.

A manufacturing holding company. A subsidiary of Citicorp Venture Capital Ltd., a Citigroup (see separate listing) company.
www.delcoremy.com

Chairman of the Board
SPERLICH, Harold K.
Tel: (765) 778 - 6499
Fax: (765) 778 - 6404
TF: (800) 372 - 5131

Main Headquarters
Mailing: 2902 Enterprise Dr., Anderson, IN 46013 — Tel: (765) 778 - 6499; Fax: (765) 778 - 6404; TF: (800) 372 - 5131

Corporate Foundations and Giving Programs

Delco Remy Corporate Giving

Delco Remy Internat'l Inc.

* continued from previous page

2902 Enterprise Dr.
Anderson, IN 46013
Tel: (765) 778 - 6499
Fax: (765) 778 - 6404
TF: (800) 372 - 5131

Annual Grant Total: none reported
Primary Interests: Education; Health
Recent Recipients: American Cancer Society; American Red Cross; Big Brothers/Big Sisters; Junior Achievement; Salvation Army

Public Affairs and Related Activities Personnel

At Headquarters

CAMPBELL, Leah
Manager, Public Relations
Tel: (765) 778 - 6848
Fax: (765) 778 - 6404
TF: (800) 372 - 5131

ENGLISH, Roderick
Senior V. President, Human Resources
Tel: (765) 778 - 6499
Fax: (765) 778 - 6404
TF: (800) 372 - 5131

WEBB, Keri
Investor Relations Contact
Tel: (765) 778 - 6523
Fax: (765) 778 - 6404
TF: (800) 372 - 5131

Dell Inc.

A member of the Public Affairs Council. Provider of products and services required for customers worldwide to build their information technology and internet infrastructures.
www.dell.com
Annual Revenues: $31.168 billion

Chairman of the Board
DELL, Michael S.
Tel: (512) 338 - 4400
Fax: (512) 728 - 3653
TF: (800) 289 - 3355

President and Chief Exec. Officer
ROLLINS, Kevin B.
Tel: (512) 338 - 4400
Fax: (512) 728 - 3653
TF: (800) 289 - 3355

Main Headquarters
Mailing: One Dell Way
Round Rock, TX 78682
Tel: (512) 338 - 4400
Fax: (512) 728 - 3653
TF: (800) 289 - 3355

Washington Office
Contact: Becca Gould
Mailing: 1225 I St. NW
Suite 920
Washington, DC 20005
Tel: (202) 408 - 5538
Fax: (202) 408 - 7664

Political Action Committees

Dell Inc. Employees PAC
Contact: Becca Gould
1225 I St. NW
Suite 920
Washington, DC 20005
Tel: (202) 408 - 3355
Fax: (202) 408 - 7664

Contributions to Candidates: $41,000 (01/05 - 09/05)
Democrats: $9,000; Republicans: $32,000.

Principal Recipients

SENATE DEMOCRATS
Baucus, Max (MT) $1,000
Ford, Harold E Jr (TN) $1,000

HOUSE DEMOCRATS

SENATE REPUBLICANS
Allen, George (VA) $2,000
Alexander, Lamar (TN) $1,000
Ensign, John Eric (NV) $1,000
Burr, Richard (NC) $500

HOUSE REPUBLICANS
Carter, John (TX) $5,000
Hastert, Dennis J. (IL) $5,000
Gohmert, Louis (TX) $3,000
Cantor, Eric (VA) $2,500
Barton, Joe L (TX) $2,000
Foxx, Virginia (NC) $1,500

Corporate Foundations and Giving Programs

Michael and Susn Dell Foundation
Contact: Janet Mountain
One Dell Way
Round Rock, TX 78682
Tel: (512) 338 - 4400
Fax: (512) 728 - 3653
TF: (800) 289 - 3355

Annual Grant Total: none reported
Primary focus is on preparing youth for the digital world. www.dell.com/dellfoundation.
Geographic Preference: Tennessee; Texas; Idaho; Oregon
Primary Interests: Youth Services

Public Affairs and Related Activities Personnel

At Headquarters

EVERETT, Brenda
Investor Relations Contact
Tel: (512) 728 - 7800
Fax: (512) 728 - 3653
TF: (800) 289 - 3355

MCKINNON, Paul
Senior V. President, Human Resources
Tel: (512) 338 - 4400
Fax: (512) 728 - 3653
TF: (800) 289 - 3355

MOUNTAIN, Janet
Exec. Director, Foundation
Tel: (512) 338 - 4400
Fax: (512) 728 - 3653
TF: (800) 289 - 3355

TYSON, Lynn A.
V. President, Investor Relations and Corporate Communications
Mailstop: M/S 9006
lynn_tyson@dell.com
Tel: (512) 723 - 1130
Fax: (512) 728 - 4238
TF: (800) 289 - 3355

At Washington Office

BROWNELL, Paul
Manager, Federal Government Relations
Registered Federal Lobbyist.
Tel: (202) 408 - 5538
Fax: (202) 408 - 7664

GOULD, Becca
V. President, Government Relations; and PAC Treasurer
becca_gould@dell.com
Registered Federal Lobbyist.
Tel: (202) 408 - 3355
Fax: (202) 408 - 7664

Deloitte & Touche LLP

The nation's fourth largest professional services firm. Provides assurance and advisory, tax and management consulting services.
www.us.deloitte.com

Chairman of the Board
ALLEN, Sharon L.
Tel: (212) 489 - 1600
Fax: (212) 489 - 1687

Chief Exec. Officer
QUIGLEY, James H.
Tel: (212) 489 - 1600
Fax: (212) 489 - 1687

Main Headquarters
Mailing: 1633 Broadway
New York, NY 10019
Tel: (212) 489 - 1600
Fax: (212) 489 - 1687

Washington Office
Contact: Cindy M. Stevens
Mailing: 555 12th St. NW
Suite 500
Washington, DC 20004
Tel: (202) 879 - 5600
Fax: (202) 638 - 7857

Political Action Committees

Deloitte & Touche LLP Federal Political Action Committee
Contact: Cindy M. Stevens
555 12th St. NW
Suite 500
Washington, DC 20004
Tel: (202) 879 - 5978
Fax: (202) 638 - 7845

Contributions to Candidates: $284,532 (01/05 - 09/05)
Democrats: $47,000; Republicans: $234,532; Other: $3,000.

Principal Recipients

SENATE DEMOCRATS
Carper, Thomas R (DE) $7,000
Feinstein, Dianne (CA) $4,000

HOUSE DEMOCRATS
Schultz, Debbie (FL) $4,500

SENATE REPUBLICANS
Lott, Trent (MS) $5,000
Talent, James (MO) $4,500
Santorum, Richard (PA) $4,000

HOUSE REPUBLICANS
Price, Thomas (GA) $17,000
Bonilla, Henry (TX) $10,000
Baker, Hugh (LA) $8,421
Bachus, Spencer (AL) $5,000
Camp, David Lee (MI) $5,000
Fitzpatrick, Michael (PA) $5,000
Gerlach, Jim (PA) $5,000
Oxley, Michael (OH) $5,000

Corporate Foundations and Giving Programs

Deloitte & Touche Foundation
Contact: Janet Butchko
Ten Westport Rd.
Wilton, CT 06897
Tel: (203) 761 - 3474

Annual Grant Total: $2,000,000 - $5,000,000
Contributions are made to higher education in the form of matching gifts of employee and partner contributions to academic programs at degree-granting institutions.
Primary Interests: Adult Education and Training; Higher Education

Public Affairs and Related Activities Personnel

At Headquarters

HARRINGTON, Deborah
Director, Public Relations
(Deloitte Services LP)
Tel: (212) 489 - 1600
Fax: (212) 489 - 1687

LINDENBERG, Keith
National Director
Tel: (212) 489 - 2000
Fax: (212) 489 - 1687

Deloitte & Touche LLP

* continued from previous page

SCHUTZMAN, David
Director, Public Relations Industries and Functions (Deloitte Services LP)
Tel: (212) 489 - 1600
Fax: (212) 489 - 1687

At Washington Office

GENOSI, Courtney
Manager
Tel: (202) 879 - 5978
Fax: (202) 638 - 7857
Registered Federal Lobbyist.
Responsibilities include government affairs.

HEETER, Charles P.
Principal
Tel: (202) 879 - 5978
Fax: (202) 638 - 7857
Registered Federal Lobbyist.
Responsibilities include government affairs.

STEVENS, Cindy M.
Director, Federal Programs
Tel: (202) 879 - 5978
Fax: (202) 638 - 7845
Registered Federal Lobbyist.

At Other Offices

BUTCHKO, Janet
Manager, Academic Development
Ten Westport Rd.
Wilton, CT 06897
Tel: (203) 761 - 3474
Responsibilities include corporate philanthropy.

Delphi Automotive Corp.

See listing on page 155 under Delphi Corp.

Delphi Corp.

Designs, engineers and manufactures automobile components and vehicle electronics.

www.delphi.com

Annual Revenues: $29 billion

Chairman and Chief Exec. Officer
MILLER, Rodney S. "Steve"
Tel: (248) 813 - 2000
Fax: (248) 813 - 2670

Main Headquarters
Mailing: 5725 Delphi Dr.
Troy, MI 48098-2815
Tel: (248) 813 - 2000
Fax: (248) 813 - 2670

Washington Office
Contact: John T. Anderson
Mailing: 1301 Pennsylvania Ave. NW
Suite 1030
Washington, DC 20004
Tel: (202) 824 - 0401
Fax: (202) 628 - 5815

Political Action Committees

Delphi Corporation Political Action Committee
Contact: Thomas Woods
5725 Delphi Dr.
Troy, MI 48098-2815
Tel: (248) 813 - 2620
Fax: (248) 813 - 3253

Contributions to Candidates: $17,000 (01/05 - 09/05)
Democrats: $5,000; Republicans: $12,000.

Principal Recipients

SENATE DEMOCRATS
Stabenow, Debbie (MI) $2,000

HOUSE DEMOCRATS
Kildee, Dale E (MI) $1,000
Reyes, Silvestre (TX) $1,000
Slaughter, Louise M (NY) $1,000

SENATE REPUBLICANS
Dewine, Richard (OH) $1,000
Lott, Trent (MS) $1,000

HOUSE REPUBLICANS
Knollenberg, Joe (MI) $2,000
Pickering, Chip (MS) $2,000
Rogers, Michael J (MI) $2,000
Ehlers, Vernon J (MI) $1,000
Ferguson, Mike (NJ) $1,000
Hoekstra, Peter (MI) $1,000
Tiberi, Patrick (OH) $1,000

Corporate Foundations and Giving Programs

Delphi Foundation
5725 Delphi Dr.
Troy, MI 48098-2815
Tel: (248) 813 - 2000
Fax: (248) 813 - 2670

Annual Grant Total: $500,000 - $750,000
For more information, please refer to www.delphi.com.
Geographic Preference: Area in which the company is headquartered
Primary Interests: Arts and Humanities; Education; Engineering; Health and Human Services; Minority Opportunities

Public Affairs and Related Activities Personnel

At Headquarters

BAUCUS, Claudia
Manager, Financial Communications
claudia.baucus@delphi.com
Tel: (248) 813 - 2942
Fax: (248) 813 - 2670

BEEBER, Ronald
Corporate Director, Government and Community Relations
Mailstop: 483-400-501
Tel: (248) 813 - 2595
Fax: (248) 813 - 3253

BODKIN, Dave
Director, Media Relations
david.g.bodkin@delphi.com
Tel: (248) 813 - 2532
Fax: (248) 813 - 2670

BUTLER, Kevin M.
V. President, Human Resources Management
Mailstop: M/S 483-400-606
Tel: (248) 813 - 2000
Fax: (248) 813 - 2523

HEALY, Karen L.
V. President, Corporate Affairs, Marketing Communications, and Facilities
Mailstop: M/S 483-400-501
Tel: (248) 813 - 2529
Fax: (248) 813 - 2530

MARENTETTE, Charles
Director, Investor Relations
Tel: (248) 813 - 2495
Fax: (248) 813 - 2670

WEBER, Mark R.
Exec. V. President, Operations, Human Resources Management and Corporate Affairs
Tel: (248) 813 - 2000
Fax: (248) 813 - 2670

WOODS, Thomas
Regional Director, Government and Community Relations
Mailstop: 483-400-501
Tel: (248) 813 - 2620
Fax: (248) 813 - 3253

At Washington Office

ANDERSON, John T.
Director, Corporate Affairs
john.t.anderson@delphi.com
Tel: (202) 824 - 0401
Fax: (202) 628 - 5815
Registered Federal Lobbyist.

VIZZACCARO, Dina
Director, Federal Relations
dina.vizzaccaro@delphi.com
Tel: (202) 824 - 0412
Fax: (202) 628 - 5815
Registered Federal Lobbyist.

Delta Air Lines, Inc.

A commercial air carrier.

www.delta.com

Annual Revenues: $13.879 billion

Non-Exec. Chairman of the Board
SMITH, John F.
Tel: (404) 715 - 2600
Fax: (404) 715 - 2731

Chief Exec. Officer
GRINSTEIN, Gerald
Tel: (404) 715 - 2600
Fax: (404) 715 - 2731

Main Headquarters
Mailing: P.O. Box 20706
Atlanta, GA 30320-6001
Street: 1030 Delta Blvd.
Atlanta, GA 30320-6001
Tel: (404) 715 - 2600
Fax: (404) 715 - 2731

Washington Office
Contact: D. Scott Yohe
Mailing: 1275 K St. NW
Suite 1200
Washington, DC 20005
Tel: (202) 216 - 0700
Fax: (202) 216 - 0824

Political Action Committees

Delta Air Lines Inc. Political Action Committee (DELTA-PAC)
Contact: Delores Gallego
P.O. Box 20706
Atlanta, GA 30320-6001
Tel: (404) 715 - 2458
Fax: (404) 715 - 4779

Contributions to Candidates: $25,500 (01/05 - 09/05)
Democrats: $4,000; Republicans: $21,500.

Principal Recipients

SENATE DEMOCRATS
Baucus, Max (MT) $2,000

HOUSE DEMOCRATS

SENATE REPUBLICANS
Hatch, Orrin (UT) $4,000
Burns, Conrad (MT) $3,000
Dewine, Richard (OH) $2,000
Lott, Trent (MS) $1,000

HOUSE REPUBLICANS
Norwood, Charles (GA) $2,000
Boustany, Jr, Charles (LA) $1,500

Corporate Foundations and Giving Programs

The Delta Air Lines Foundation
Contact: Lee Macenczak

Delta Air Lines, Inc.

** continued from previous page*

P.O. Box 20706
Atlanta, GA 30320-6001
Tel: (404) 715 - 2600
Fax: (404) 715 - 2731

Annual Grant Total: $2,000,000 - $5,000,000

Also sponsors an employee matching gifts program, which matches contributions to institutions of higher education.

Primary Interests: Civic and Cultural Activities; Community Development; Families; Higher Education

Recent Recipients: United Way

Public Affairs and Related Activities Personnel

At Headquarters

BLISSIT, Doug
V. President, Public Affairs
Tel: (404) 715 - 2455
Fax: (404) 715 - 4779

GALLEGO, Delores
General Manager, Public Affairs; PAC Treasurer
Mailstop: Dept. 976
Tel: (404) 715 - 2458
Fax: (404) 715 - 4779

GRIMMETT, Gail
V. President, Revenue and Investor Relations
Tel: (404) 715 - 2600
Fax: (404) 715 - 2731

KENNEDY, John
General Manager, Media Relations
Tel: (404) 715 - 2600
Fax: (404) 715 - 2731

MACENCZAK, Lee
Executive V. President and Chief Human Resources Officer
Tel: (404) 715 - 2600
Fax: (404) 715 - 2731

RIGGS, Greg
Senior V. President, General Counsel and Chief Corporate Affairs Officer
Tel: (404) 715 - 2600
Fax: (404) 715 - 2731
Responsibilities include corporate communications and government affairs.

At Washington Office

KENNEDY, Sharlene D.
Manager, Government Affairs
sharlene.kennedy@delta.com
Tel: (202) 216 - 0700
Fax: (202) 216 - 0824
Registered Federal Lobbyist.

KLINETOB, Sametta
Director, Government Affairs
Tel: (202) 216 - 0700
Fax: (202) 216 - 0824

YOHE, D. Scott
Senior V. President, Government Affairs
Tel: (202) 296 - 6464
Fax: (202) 466 - 2610
Registered Federal Lobbyist.

Deluxe Corp.

Subsidiaries provide personal and business checks; business forms and self-inking stamps; and fraud prevention services and customer retention programs to banks, credit unions, financial services companies, consumers, and small businesses. Services are distributed via direct mail, the Internet, telephone, and the company's national sales force.

www.deluxe.com

Chairman and Chief Exec. Officer
MOSNER, Lawrence J.
Tel: (651) 483 - 7111
Fax: (651) 481 - 4163

Main Headquarters
Mailing: P.O. Box 64235
St. Paul, MN 55164-0235
Tel: (651) 483 - 7111
Fax: (651) 481 - 4477
Street: 3680 Victoria St., North
Shoreview, MN 55126-2966

Corporate Foundations and Giving Programs

Deluxe Corp. Foundation
P.O. Box 64235
St. Paul, MN 55164-0235
Tel: (651) 787 - 5124
Fax: (651) 481 - 4371

Assets: $30,876,019 (2003)
Annual Grant Total: $2,000,000 - $5,000,000

Guidelines are available at www.deluxe.com. Total corporate giving in 2003, including subsidiaries, was more than $2 million.

Geographic Preference: Area(s) in which the company operates

Primary Interests: Arts and Culture; Education; Financially Disadvantaged; Persons with Disabilities; Youth Services

Recent Recipients: Minnesota Council on Foundations

Public Affairs and Related Activities Personnel

At Headquarters

ALEXANDER, Stuart
V. President, Investor Relations and Public Affairs; President, Deluxe Corp. Foundation
stu.alexander@deluxe.com
Tel: (651) 483 - 7358
Fax: (651) 481 - 4477

ANDERSON, Jennifer A.
Director, Foundations
jenny.anderson@deluxe.com
Tel: (651) 483 - 7842
Fax: (651) 481 - 4477

HANSON, Debra
Senior Communications Specialist
debra.hanson@deluxe.com
Tel: (651) 483 - 7111
Ext: 7367
Fax: (651) 481 - 4477

Demoulas Market Basket

Retail grocery chain.

Main Headquarters
Mailing: 875 East St.
Tewksbury, MA 01876
Tel: (978) 851 - 8000
Fax: (978) 640 - 8390

Corporate Foundations and Giving Programs

Demoulas Foundation
Contact: T. A. Demoulas
286 Chelmsford St.
Chelmsford, MA 01824
Tel: (978) 851 - 8000
Fax: (978) 851 - 3942

Annual Grant Total: $2,000,000 - $5,000,000

Geographic Preference: Area in which the company is headquartered

Primary Interests: Arts and Humanities; Education; Health

Recent Recipients: Boston College; Boston Police Department; United Negro College Fund

Public Affairs and Related Activities Personnel

At Other Offices

DEMOULAS, T. A.
Foundation Contact
286 Chelmsford St.
Chelmsford, MA 01824
Tel: (978) 851 - 8000
Fax: (978) 851 - 3942

Denny's Corp.

America's largest full-service family restaurant chain.

www.dennys.com
Annual Revenues: $960 million

Chairman of the Board
MARKS, Robert E.
Tel: (864) 597 - 8000

Chief Exec. Officer and President
MARCHIOLI, Nelson J.
Tel: (864) 597 - 8000

Main Headquarters
Mailing: 203 E. Main St.
Spartanburg, SC 29319-0001
Tel: (864) 597 - 8000

Public Affairs and Related Activities Personnel

At Headquarters

ATKINS, Debbie
Director, Public Relations
Tel: (864) 597 - 8361
Fax: (864) 597 - 7538

LEWIS, Alex
Assistant Treasurer and Director, Investor Relations
Tel: (877) 784 - 7167
Fax: (864) 597 - 8216

PARISH, Rhonda
Senior V. President, Human Resources
Tel: (864) 597 - 8000

Dentsply Internat'l

A manufacturer of dental equipment and supplies.

www.dentsply.com

Chairman and Chief Exec. Officer
KUNKLE, Gary, Jr.
Tel: (717) 845 - 7511
Fax: (717) 849 - 4762
TF: (800) 877 - 0020

Main Headquarters
Mailing: P.O. Box 872
York, PA 17405-0872
Tel: (717) 845 - 7511
Fax: (717) 849 - 4762
TF: (800) 877 - 0020
Street: 221 W. Philadelphia St.
York, PA 17405

Corporate Foundations and Giving Programs

Dentsply Internat'l Foundation
Contact: William E. Reardon
P.O. Box 872
York, PA 17405-0872
Tel: (717) 845 - 7511
Fax: (717) 849 - 4762
TF: (800) 877 - 0020

Annual Grant Total: $200,000 - $300,000

Primary Interests: Adult Education and Training; Community Affairs; Health; Higher Education

Public Affairs and Related Activities Personnel

At Headquarters

MCKINNEY, Rachel P.
Corporate V. President, Human Resources
Tel: (717) 845 - 7511
Fax: (717) 849 - 4762
TF: (800) 877 - 0020

MILES, John C., II
Director
jmiles@dentsply.com
Tel: (717) 845 - 7511
Fax: (717) 849 - 4762
TF: (800) 877 - 0020

REARDON, William E.
Corporate Treasurer, Dentsply Internat'l Foundation
wreardon@dentsply.com
Tel: (717) 845 - 7511
Fax: (717) 849 - 4762
TF: (800) 877 - 0020

RHODES, George R.
V. President, Professional Relations and Corporate Communications
grhodes@dentsply.com
Tel: (717) 845 - 7511
Fax: (717) 849 - 4762
TF: (800) 877 - 0020

The Depository Trust & Clearing Corp.

Provides clearance, settlement and information services for equities, corporate and municipal bonds, government and mortgage-backed securities, over-the-counter credit derivatives and emerging market debt. Also provides custody and asset servicing for more than two million securities issues from the U.S. and 100 other countries and territories. Also processes mutual funds and insurance transactions.

www.dtcc.com

Chairman and Chief Exec. Officer
CONSIDINE, Jill M. — Tel: (212) 855 - 1000

Main Headquarters
Mailing: 55 Water St.
49th Floor
New York, NY 10041-0099
Tel: (212) 855 - 1000
Fax: (212) 855 - 8440

Public Affairs and Related Activities Personnel

At Headquarters

ARGENTO, Lisa
Director, Corporate Communications
largento@dtcc.com
Tel: (212) 855 - 5302
Fax: (212) 785 - 9681

CAREY, Kevin P.
Chief Administrative Officer
kcarey@dtcc.com
Tel: (212) 855 - 3230

GOLDSTEIN, Stuart Z.
Managing Director, Corporate Communications
sgoldstein@dtcc.com
Tel: (212) 855 - 5470
Fax: (212) 785 - 9681

INOSANTO, Judith
Director, Corporate Communications
jinosanto@dtcc.com
Tel: (212) 855 - 5479
Fax: (212) 855 - 5424

JENKINS, Rosalie
Director, Corporate Communications
rjenkins@dtcc.com
Tel: (212) 855 - 5468
Fax: (212) 908 - 2327

KELLEHER, Edward C.
Director, Corporate Communications
eckelleher@dtcc.com
Tel: (212) 855 - 5301
Fax: (212) 785 - 9681

LETZLER, Steve
Director, Corporate Communications
sletzler@dtcc.com
Tel: (212) 855 - 5469
Fax: (212) 908 - 2366

LEVY-BUENO, Crystal
Director, Corporate Communications
clevy-bueno@dtcc.com
Tel: (212) 855 - 5473
Fax: (212) 908 - 2224

Detroit Edison

See listing on page 167 under DTE Energy Co.

Deutsche Banc Alex.Brown

A bank holding company.

www.alexbrown.db.com

President and Chief Exec. Officer
WAUGH, Seth H. — Tel: (212) 469 - 8000

Main Headquarters
Mailing: 60 Wall St.
New York, NY 10005
Tel: (212) 250 - 2500

Corporate Foundations and Giving Programs

Alex Brown and Sons Charitable Foundation, Inc.
Contact: Margaret Preston
P.O. Box 2257
Baltimore, MD 21203
Tel: (410) 237 - 5862

Annual Grant Total: $1,000,000 - $2,000,000
Geographic Preference: Baltimore, MD
Primary Interests: Community Development; Education; Health
Recent Recipients: American Red Cross; Johns Hopkins University; United Way

Public Affairs and Related Activities Personnel

At Other Offices

PRESTON, Margaret
Secretary, Foundation
P.O. Box 2257
Baltimore, MD 21203
Tel: (410) 237 - 5862

Devon Energy Corp.

Engaged in oil and gas exploration, production and property acquisitions. Devon is an independent oil and gas producer and processor of natural gas and natural gas liquids in North America. The company also has operations in selected international areas. Acquired Santa Fe Snyder Corp. in 2000, Mitchell Energy & Development Corp. in January of 2002, Anderson Exploration in 2001, and Ocean Energy in 2004.

www.devonenergy.com
Annual Revenues: $9.189 billion

Chairman and Chief Exec. Officer
NICHOLS, J. Larry
nicholsl@dvn.com
Tel: (405) 235 - 3611
Fax: (405) 552 - 4667

Main Headquarters
Mailing: 20 N. Broadway, Suite 1500
Oklahoma City, OK 73102
Tel: (405) 235 - 3611
Fax: (405) 552 - 4667

Political Action Committees

Devon Energy Corp. Political Action Committee
Contact: Duke Ligon
20 N. Broadway, Suite 1500
Oklahoma City, OK 73102
Tel: (405) 552 - 4604
Fax: (405) 552 - 4667

Contributions to Candidates: $8,000 (01/05 - 09/05)
Democrats: $2,000; Republicans: $6,000.

Principal Recipients

SENATE DEMOCRATS		HOUSE DEMOCRATS	
Bingaman, Jeff (NM)	$1,000	Boren, David (OK)	$1,000
SENATE REPUBLICANS		**HOUSE REPUBLICANS**	
Inhofe, James M (OK)	$1,000	Barton, Joe L (TX)	$1,000
		Cannon, Christopher (UT)	$1,000
		Cole, Tom (OK)	$1,000
		Gibbons, James A (NV)	$1,000
		Sullivan, John (OK)	$1,000

Public Affairs and Related Activities Personnel

At Headquarters

BOUGHMAN, Melany
Investor Relations Analyst
Tel: (405) 552 - 4578
Fax: (405) 552 - 4667

ENGEL, Brian E.
Public Affairs Manager
brian.engel@dvn.com
Tel: (405) 228 - 7750
Fax: (405) 552 - 7818

HOWARD, Jaren J.
Tel: (405) 235 - 3611
Fax: (405) 552 - 4667

LIGON, Duke
Senior V. President, General Counsel; and PAC Contact
Tel: (405) 552 - 4604
Fax: (405) 552 - 4667

POLEY, Paul R.
V. President, Human Resources
Tel: (405) 235 - 3611
Fax: (405) 552 - 4667

ROBERTS, Judy
Shareholder Services Administrator
judy.roberts@dvn.com
Tel: (405) 235 - 3611
Fax: (405) 552 - 7818

WHITE, Vincent W.
V. President, Communications and Investor Relations
Tel: (405) 552 - 4505
Fax: (405) 552 - 7818

WILLIAMSON, Wendi
Supervisor, Communications
wendi.williamson@dvn.com
Tel: (405) 228 - 4494
Fax: (405) 552 - 7818

DeVry Inc.

A higher education company.

www.devry.com
Annual Revenues: $648 million

Chairman of the Board
KELLER, Dennis J.
Tel: (630) 571 - 7700
Fax: (630) 571 - 0317
TF: (800) 225 - 8000

Chief Exec. Officer
TAYLOR, Ronald L.
Tel: (630) 571 - 7700
Fax: (630) 571 - 0317
TF: (800) 225 - 8000

Main Headquarters
Mailing: One Tower Ln.
Suite 1000
Oakbrook Terrace, IL 60181-4624
Tel: (630) 571 - 7700
Fax: (630) 571 - 0317
TF: (800) 225 - 8000

Political Action Committees

DeVry Inc. PAC
Contact: Norman M. Levine
One Tower Ln.
Suite 1000
Oakbrook Terrace, IL 60181-4624
Tel: (630) 571 - 7700
Fax: (630) 571 - 0317
TF: (800) 225 - 8000

Contributions to Candidates: $1,450 (01/05 - 09/05)
Democrats: $1,000; Republicans: $450.

Principal Recipients

SENATE DEMOCRATS		HOUSE DEMOCRATS	
Durbin, Richard J (IL)	$500	Jackson, Jesse (IL)	$250
		Schakowsky, Janice (IL)	$250
SENATE REPUBLICANS		**HOUSE REPUBLICANS**	
Alexander, Lamar (TN)	$200	McKeon, Howard (CA)	$250

Public Affairs and Related Activities Personnel

At Headquarters

BATES, Joan
Director, Investor Relations
Tel: (630) 571 - 7700
Fax: (630) 571 - 0317
TF: (800) 225 - 8000

DeVry Inc.

** continued from previous page*

CALABRO, Jack L. — Tel: (630) 571 - 7700
V. President, Human Resources — Fax: (630) 571 - 0317
TF: (800) 225 - 8000

LEVINE, Norman M. — Tel: (630) 571 - 7700
Senior V. President,PAC Treasurer — Fax: (630) 571 - 0317
TF: (800) 225 - 8000

MCCLURE, Jennifer — Tel: (630) 706 - 3118
Director, Government and Association Relations — TF: (800) 225 - 8000

NIFFENEGGER, Jonelle — Tel: (630) 571 - 7700
Director, Public Relations — Fax: (630) 571 - 0317
TF: (800) 225 - 8000

PARROTT, Sharon Thomas — Tel: (630) 571 - 7700
Senior V. President, Chief Compliance Officer — Fax: (630) 571 - 1991
TF: (800) 225 - 8000

Dexter Corp.

See listing on page 264 under Invitrogen Corp.

DHL Holdings (USA), Inc.

Provides international air express services. A wholly owned subsidiary of Deutsche Post World Net, headquarterd in Bonn, Germany. Acquired Airborne, Inc. (ground operations only) in August, 2003.
www.dhl-usa.com
Annual Revenues: $3.2 billion

Main Headquarters
Mailing: 1200 S. Pine Island Rd. — Tel: (954) 888 - 7000
Suite 61000 — Fax: (954) 888 - 7310
Plantation, FL 33324

Public Affairs and Related Activities Personnel

At Headquarters

MULLEN, John — Tel: (954) 888 - 7000
Chief Exec. Officer — Fax: (954) 888 - 7310

NORTHCUTT, Scott M. — Tel: (954) 888 - 7000
Exec. V. President, Human Resources — Fax: (954) 888 - 7310

At Other Offices

MINTZ, Robert — Tel: (425) 605 - 6165
Manager, Public Relations — Fax: (425) 914 - 2967
12015 115th Ave. NE
Building E, Suite 220
Kirkland, WA 98034

Diageo North America

A member of the Public Affairs Council. Formerly known as Guinness/UDV. Producer and distributor of alcoholic beverages.
www.diageo.com

Main Headquarters
Mailing: Six Landmark Sq. — Tel: (203) 359 - 7100
Stamford, CT 06901 — Fax: (203) 359 - 7402

Washington Office
Mailing: 1301 K St. NW — Tel: (202) 715 - 1105
Suite 1000 East Tower — Fax: (202) 715 - 1114
Washington, DC 20005

Political Action Committees

Diageo North America Employees' Political Participation Committee
Contact: James Ricci
Six Landmark Sq. — Tel: (203) 359 - 7100
Stamford, CT 06901

Contributions to Candidates: $12,000 (01/05 - 09/05)
Democrats: $4,000; Republicans: $8,000.

Principal Recipients

SENATE DEMOCRATS		HOUSE DEMOCRATS	
Carper, Thomas R (DE)	$1,000	Cardoza, Dennis (CA)	$1,000
Nelson, Bill (FL)	$1,000	Rangel, Charles B (NY)	$1,000
SENATE REPUBLICANS		**HOUSE REPUBLICANS**	
Burns, Conrad (MT)	$2,500	Dreier, David (CA)	$2,000
Ensign, John Eric (NV)	$2,500	Reynolds, Thomas (NY)	$1,000

Corporate Foundations and Giving Programs

Diageo Foundation
Contact: Barry Becton
1301 K St. NW — Tel: (202) 715 - 1111
Suite 1000 East Tower — Fax: (202) 715 - 1114
Washington, DC 20005

Annual Grant Total: $750,000 - $1,000,000
Recipients must be 501(c)(3) non-profit organizations.
Geographic Preference: Area in which the company is headquartered; Area(s) in which the company operates
Primary Interests: Civic and Cultural Activities; Minority Opportunities; Youth Services

Public Affairs and Related Activities Personnel

At Headquarters

DOWLING, Jeannine — Tel: (203) 359 - 7100
V. President, Corporate Communications and External Affairs

GALANIS, Gary — Tel: (203) 359 - 7100
Director, Media Relations and External Affairs

MCPHEE, Jessica — Tel: (203) 359 - 7100
Manager, Corporate Communications

RICCI, James — Tel: (203) 359 - 7100
PAC Treasurer

SMITH, Guy — Tel: (203) 359 - 7100
Exec. V. President, External Affairs and Corporate Strategy

At Washington Office

BECTON, Barry — Tel: (202) 715 - 1111
Foundation Contact — Fax: (202) 715 - 1114

BERTMAN, Michael — Tel: (202) 715 - 1115
Director, Federal Affairs — Fax: (202) 715 - 1114
Registered Federal Lobbyist.

LANE, Kenneth F. — Tel: (202) 715 - 1118
V. President, State Government Relations — Fax: (202) 715 - 1114

PANZER, Carolyn — Tel: (202) 715 - 1105
Senior V. President, Public Policy — Fax: (202) 715 - 1114

Diagnostic/Retrieval Systems, Inc.

See listing on page 166 under DRS Technologies, Inc.

The Dial Corporation

A consumer products manufacturer.
www.dialcorp.com

Chairman and Chief Exec. Officer
CASPER, Bradley A. — Tel: (480) 754 - 3425
Fax: (480) 754 - 1098

Main Headquarters
Mailing: 15501 N. Dial Blvd. — Tel: (480) 754 - 3425
Scottsdale, AZ 85260 — Fax: (480) 754 - 1098

Political Action Committees

Dial Corp. Employees' Political Action Committee
Contact: David Riddiford
15501 N. Dial Blvd. — Tel: (480) 754 - 3425
Scottsdale, AZ 85260 — Fax: (480) 754 - 1098

Contributions to Candidates: $1,000 (01/05 - 09/05)
Republicans: $1,000.

Principal Recipients

SENATE REPUBLICANS	HOUSE REPUBLICANS	
	Hastert, Dennis J. (IL)	$1,000

Corporate Foundations and Giving Programs

The Dial Corporation Contributions Program
Contact: Cynthia A. Demers
15501 N. Dial Blvd. — Tel: (480) 754 - 4090
Scottsdale, AZ 85260 — Fax: (480) 754 - 8003

Annual Grant Total: none reported
Geographic Preference: Arizona
Primary Interests: Children; Education
Recent Recipients: Habitat for Humanity; Juvenile Diabetes Foundation; United Way

Public Affairs and Related Activities Personnel

At Headquarters

BLUM, Steven — Tel: (480) 754 - 3425
Senior V. President, Investor Relations
Mailstop: M/S 2125
blum@dialcorp.com

DEMERS, Cynthia A. — Tel: (480) 754 - 4090
V. President, Corporate and Government Affairs — Fax: (480) 754 - 8003
Mailstop: Suite 2160
demers@dialcorp.com
Responsibilities include corporate philanthropy.

PRICE-EDWARDS, Tonsa — Tel: (480) 754 - 3425
Director, Human Resources International and Employment Services — Fax: (480) 754 - 1098

RIDDIFORD, David — Tel: (480) 754 - 3425
PAC Treasurer — Fax: (480) 754 - 1098

At Other Offices

DAIL, Betsy — Tel: (480) 754 - 6172
Director, Regulatory and Product Safety
15101 N. Scottsdale Rd.
Suite 5033
Scottsdale, AZ 85254

Dictaphone Corp.
www.dictaphone.com

Chairman and Chief Exec. Officer
SCHWAGER, Rob — Tel: (203) 381 - 7000

Main Headquarters
Mailing: 3191 Broadbridge Ave.
Stratford, CT 06614-2559 — Tel: (203) 381 - 7000

Public Affairs and Related Activities Personnel

At Headquarters

FALLATI, Donald — Tel: (203) 381 - 7218
Executive V. President, Marketing and Strategic Planning
dfal@dictaphone.com
Responsibilities include media relations.

LEDWICK, Tim — Tel: (203) 381 - 7000
Financial Information Contact
tim.ledwick@dictaphone.com

QAMAR, Robert K. — Tel: (203) 381 - 7000
Responsibilities include public relations.

Diebold, Inc.
Manufacturer of financial self-service transaction systems and security products.
www.diebold.com

Chairman and Chief Exec. Officer
O'DELL, Waldon W. — Tel: (330) 490 - 4000, Fax: (330) 490 - 3794
odellw@diebold.com

Main Headquarters
Mailing: 5995 Mayfair Rd.
P.O. Box 3077
North Canton, OH 44720-8077 — Tel: (330) 490 - 4000, Fax: (330) 490 - 3794

Corporate Foundations and Giving Programs

Diebold Corporate Contributions Program
Contact: Sheila M. Rutt
5995 Mayfair Rd.
P.O. Box 3077
North Canton, OH 44720-8077 — Tel: (330) 490 - 4000, Fax: (330) 490 - 3794

Annual Grant Total: $300,000 - $400,000
Geographic Preference: Area(s) in which the company operates

Public Affairs and Related Activities Personnel

At Headquarters

BAKO, Jennifer — Tel: (330) 490 - 4000, Fax: (330) 490 - 3794
Senior Specialist, Investor Relations and Communications

KANDES, Carrie — Tel: (330) 490 - 4000, Fax: (330) 490 - 3794
Manager, Media Relations

KRISTOFF, John — Tel: (330) 490 - 5900, Fax: (330) 490 - 3794
V. President, Global Communication and Investor Relations
kristoj@diebold.com

RUTT, Sheila M. — Tel: (330) 490 - 4000, Fax: (330) 490 - 3794
V. President, Chief Human Resources Officer

Dillard's Inc.
Formerly known as Dillard Department Stores, Inc.
www.dillards.com
Annual Revenues: $7.8 billion

Chairman and Chief Exec. Officer
DILLARD, William T., II — Tel: (501) 376 - 5200, Fax: (501) 376 - 5885, TF: (800) 643 - 8274

Main Headquarters
Mailing: P.O. Box 486
Little Rock, AR 72203 — Tel: (501) 376 - 5200, Fax: (501) 376 - 5885, TF: (800) 643 - 8274
Street: 1600 Cantrell Rd.
Little Rock, AR 72201

Corporate Foundations and Giving Programs

Dillard Department Stores Corporate Contributions Program
Contact: Ken Eaton
P.O. Box 486
Little Rock, AR 72203 — Tel: (501) 376 - 5200, Fax: (501) 376 - 5885, TF: (800) 643 - 8274

Annual Grant Total: none reported

Public Affairs and Related Activities Personnel

At Headquarters

BULL, Julie — Tel: (501) 376 - 5965, Fax: (501) 376 - 5885, TF: (800) 643 - 8274
Director, Investor Relations
investor.relations@dillards.com

EATON, Ken — Tel: (501) 376 - 5200, Fax: (501) 376 - 5885, TF: (800) 643 - 8274
V. President, Advertising
Responsibilities include corporate philanthropy.

RICHARDS, Steven — Tel: (501) 376 - 5550, Fax: (501) 376 - 5885, TF: (800) 643 - 8274
Manager, Communications

Dime Bancorp, Inc.
See listing on page 512 under Washington Mutual, Inc.

Dimon Incorporated
See listing on page 20 under Alliance One Internat'l Inc.

The DIRECTV Group, Inc.
Formerly known as Hughes Electronics Corp. A subsidiary of News Corporation Ltd. (see separate listing). A provider of digital television entertainment, broadband services, satellite-based private business networks, and global video and data broadcasting.
www.directv.com

Chairman of the Board
MURDOCH, K. Rupert — Tel: (310) 964 - 0700, Fax: (310) 647 - 6212

President and Chief Exec. Officer
CAREY, Chase — Tel: (310) 964 - 0700, Fax: (310) 647 - 6212

Main Headquarters
Mailing: P.O. Box 956
El Segundo, CA 90245-0956 — Tel: (310) 964 - 0700, Fax: (310) 647 - 6212
Street: 2230 E. Imperial Hwy.
El Segundo, CA 90245

Political Action Committees

DIRECTV Group Inc. Fund--Federal
Contact: Cary Davidson
520 S. Grand Ave.
Suite 700
Los Angeles, CA 90071

Contributions to Candidates: $12,000 (01/05 - 09/05)
Democrats: $2,000; Republicans: $10,000.

Principal Recipients

SENATE DEMOCRATS		HOUSE DEMOCRATS	
		Boucher, Fredrick (VA)	$1,000
		Pallone, Frank (NJ)	$1,000
SENATE REPUBLICANS		**HOUSE REPUBLICANS**	
Burns, Conrad (MT)	$1,000	Sensenbrenner, Jim (WI)	$2,500
Dewine, Richard (OH)	$1,000	Pickering, Chip (MS)	$1,000
McConnell, Mitch (KY)	$1,000	Sullivan, John (OK)	$1,000
Santorum, Richard (PA)	$1,000	Dewine, R. Pat (OH)	$500
Snowe, Olympia (ME)	$1,000		

Corporate Foundations and Giving Programs

Directv Goes to School
P.O. Box 956
El Segundo, CA 90245-0956 — Tel: (310) 964 - 0700, Fax: (310) 647 - 6212

Annual Grant Total: none reported
Primary Interests: Children; Education

Public Affairs and Related Activities Personnel

At Headquarters

EIDS, Susan — Tel: (310) 964 - 0700, Fax: (310) 647 - 6212

MARSOCCI, Bob — Tel: (310) 964 - 0700, Fax: (310) 535 - 5225
Senior Director, Public Relations

MERCER, Robert — Tel: (310) 726 - 4683, Fax: (310) 535 - 5225
Director, Public Relations

READ, Joslyn — Tel: (310) 964 - 0700, Fax: (310) 647 - 6212

VALINE, Jade — Tel: (310) 964 - 3429, Fax: (310) 535 - 5225
Public Relations Specialist

At Other Offices

DAVIDSON, Cary
PAC Treasurer
520 S. Grand Ave.
Suite 700
Los Angeles, CA 90071

The Walt Disney Company
A family entertainment company.
http://corporate.disney.go.com/index.html

Chairman of the Board
MITCHELL, George J. — Tel: (818) 560 - 1000, Fax: (818) 560 - 1930

The Walt Disney Company

• continued from previous page

Chief Exec. Officer
EISNER, Michael D. — Tel: (818) 560 - 6180; Fax: (818) 560 - 1930
michael.eisner@corp.disney.com

Main Headquarters
Mailing: 500 S. Buena Vista St.
Burbank, CA 91521 — Tel: (818) 560 - 1000; Fax: (818) 560 - 1930

Washington Office
Contact: Preston R. Padden
Mailing: 1150 17th St. NW
Suite 400
Washington, DC 20036 — Tel: (202) 222 - 4700; Fax: (202) 222 - 4799

Political Action Committees

Walt Disney Productions Employees PAC (Disney Employees Political Action Committee)
Contact: Richard M. Bates
1150 17th St. NW — Tel: (202) 222 - 4700
Suite 400
Washington, DC 20036

Contributions to Candidates: $105,500 (01/05 - 09/05)
Democrats: $39,000; Republicans: $66,500.

Principal Recipients

SENATE DEMOCRATS		HOUSE DEMOCRATS	
Conrad, Kent (ND)	$5,000	Markey, Edward (MA)	$5,000
Nelson, Benjamin (NE)	$2,000	Schiff, Adam (CA)	$5,000
		Dingell, John D (MI)	$2,500
		Wynn, Albert (MD)	$2,500

SENATE REPUBLICANS		HOUSE REPUBLICANS	
Martinez, Mel (FL)	$5,000	Hastert, Dennis J. (IL)	$10,000
Santorum, Richard (PA)	$5,000	Dewine, R. Pat (OH)	$5,000
Stevens, Ted (AK)	$5,000	Pence, Mike (IN)	$5,000
Smith, Gordon (OR)	$2,500	DeLay, Tom (TX)	$2,500
Burns, Conrad (MT)	$2,000	Dreier, David (CA)	$2,500
Graham, Lindsey (SC)	$2,000	Goodlatte, Robert (VA)	$2,500

Corporate Foundations and Giving Programs

The Walt Disney Company Foundation
Contact: Ms. Tillie J. Baptie
500 S. Buena Vista St. — Tel: (818) 560 - 5025
Burbank, CA 91521 — Fax: (818) 560 - 1930

Annual Grant Total: $2,000,000 - $5,000,000
Geographic Preference: California; Florida
Primary Interests: Arts and Humanities; Children's Health; Education; Health and Human Services; Youth Services
Recent Recipients: Arts United; California Institute of the Arts; Central Florida Capital Funds Committee; Metro Orlando Urban League; Nat'l Ass'n for the Advancement of Colored People; United Negro College Fund; United Way

Public Affairs and Related Activities Personnel

At Headquarters

BAPTIE, Ms. Tillie J. — Tel: (818) 560 - 5025
V. President, Corporate Relations — Fax: (818) 560 - 1930
tillie.baptie@corp.disney.com

LONGFORD, Bernadette L. — Tel: (818) 560 - 1000
Manager, Corporate Community Relations — Fax: (818) 560 - 1930

MUCHA, Zenia — Tel: (818) 560 - 1000
Senior V. President, Corporate Communications — Fax: (818) 560 - 1930
zenia.mucha@corp.disney.com

RENFRO, John M. — Tel: (818) 560 - 1000
Senior V. President and Chief Human Resources Officer — Fax: (818) 560 - 1930

SPELICH, John W. — Tel: (818) 560 - 8543
Corporate Communications — Fax: (818) 560 - 1930

WEBB, Wendy — Tel: (818) 560 - 5758
Senior V. President, Investor Relations — Fax: (818) 560 - 1930

At Washington Office

BATES, Richard M. — Tel: (202) 222 - 4700
V. President, Government Relations

Registered Federal Lobbyist.

DOW, Troy — Tel: (202) 222 - 4700; Fax: (202) 222 - 4799

Registered Federal Lobbyist.

FOX, Susan — Tel: (202) 222 - 4700
V. President, Government Relations
susan.fox@corp.disney.com
Registered Federal Lobbyist.

MOORE, Jessica — Tel: (202) 222 - 4735
Manager, Government Relations — Fax: (202) 222 - 4799
jessica.moore@disney.com

PADDEN, Preston R. — Tel: (202) 222 - 4700
Exec. V. President, Government Relations
preston.padden@corp.disney.com
Registered Federal Lobbyist.

ROSE, Mitch F. — Tel: (202) 222 - 4700
V. President, Government Relations

Registered Federal Lobbyist.

The Dixie Group, Inc.

A manufacturer of carpet yarns and floor coverings. Changed its name from Dixie Yarns, Inc. in 1997.
www.thedixiegroup.com

Chairman and Chief Exec. Officer
FRIERSON, Daniel K. — Tel: (423) 510 - 7000; Fax: (423) 510 - 7015; TF: (866) 606 - 7475

Main Headquarters
Mailing: P.O. Box 25107
Chattanooga, TN 37422-5107 — Tel: (423) 510 - 7000; Fax: (423) 510 - 7015; TF: (888) 695 - 2470

Street: 345-B Nowlin Ln.
Chattanooga, TN 37421

Corporate Foundations and Giving Programs

Dixie Group Foundation
Contact: Starr T. Klein
P.O. Box 25107
Chattanooga, TN 37422-5107 — Tel: (423) 510 - 7005; Fax: (423) 510 - 7015; TF: (866) 695 - 2470

Annual Grant Total: under $100,000
Contributions in 2001 were $15,000.
Geographic Preference: Area in which the company is headquartered; Area(s) in which employees live and work
Primary Interests: Community Affairs; Education; Youth Services
Recent Recipients: United Way

Public Affairs and Related Activities Personnel

At Headquarters

KLEIN, Starr T. — Tel: (423) 510 - 7005
Secretary — Fax: (423) 510 - 7015; TF: (866) 695 - 2470

Responsibilities include corporate philanthropy.

At Other Offices

DAVIS, W. Derek — Tel: (706) 876 - 5804
V. President, Human Resources — Fax: (706) 876 - 5898
2208 S. Hamilton St. — TF: (866) 606 - 7475
Dalton, GA 30721

Dixie Yarns, Inc.

See listing on page 160 under The Dixie Group, Inc.

Dole Food Company, Inc.

www.dole.com
Annual Revenues: $4.8 billion

Chairman and Chief Exec. Officer
MURDOCK, David H. — Tel: (818) 879 - 6600; Fax: (818) 879 - 6890

Main Headquarters
Mailing: One Dole Dr.
Westlake Village, CA 91362-7300 — Tel: (818) 879 - 6600; Fax: (818) 879 - 6890

Political Action Committees

Dole Food Co., Inc. PAC
Contact: Beth Potillo
One Dole Dr. — Tel: (818) 879 - 6600
Westlake Village, CA 91362-7300 — Fax: (818) 879 - 6628

Contributions to Candidates: none reported (01/05 - 09/05)

Corporate Foundations and Giving Programs

Dole Food Co., Inc. Charitable Contribution Program
Contact: Marty Ordman
One Dole Dr. — Tel: (818) 879 - 6600
Westlake Village, CA 91362-7300 — Fax: (818) 879 - 6890

Annual Grant Total: none reported
Focuses on nutrition education programs for children as a way to prevent diseases in future generations.
Primary Interests: Children's Health

Public Affairs and Related Activities Personnel

At Headquarters

HAGEN, Sue — Tel: (818) 879 - 6600
V. President, Human Resources — Fax: (818) 879 - 6890

MANEKI, Freya — Tel: (818) 879 - 6600
Corporate Communications — Fax: (818) 879 - 6890
Responsibilities include investor relations.

Dole Food Company, Inc.

** continued from previous page*

ORDMAN, Marty — Tel: (818) 879 - 6600
V. President, Marketing Services — Fax: (818) 879 - 6890
Responsibilities include corporate contributions.

POTILLO, Beth — Tel: (818) 879 - 6600
Treasurer, Dole Food Co. Inc. PAC — Fax: (818) 879 - 6628

Dollar General Corp.

Company-owned and franchised discount stores located in Eastern and Southeastern states.

www.dollargeneral.com
Annual Revenues: $5.323 billion

Chairman and Chief Exec. Officer
PERDUE, David A. — Tel: (615) 855 - 4000

Main Headquarters
Mailing: 100 Mission Ridge
Goodlettsville, TN 37072 — Tel: (615) 855 - 4000

Corporate Foundations and Giving Programs

Dollar General Literacy Foundation
Contact: Denine Torr
100 Mission Ridge
Goodlettsville, TN 37072 — Tel: (615) 855 - 4000

Annual Grant Total: $2,000,000 - $5,000,000
Geographic Preference: Area(s) in which employees live and work; Area(s) in which the company operates
Primary Interests: Literacy

Public Affairs and Related Activities Personnel

At Headquarters

KAUFMAN, Emma Jo — Tel: (615) 855 - 5525
Senior Director, Investor Relations
ekauffman@dollargeneral.com

MARTIN, Andrea — Tel: (615) 855 - 4228
Media Contact
amartin@dollargeneral.com

MOSS, Karen — Tel: (615) 855 - 5210
Director, Corporate Communications — Fax: (615) 855 - 5527
kmoss@dollargeneral.com

RICE, Jeff — Tel: (615) 855 - 4000
V. President, Human Resources

TORR, Denine — Tel: (615) 855 - 4000
Coordinator, Charitable Contributions
dtorr@dollargeneral.com

Dollar Rent A Car, Inc.

See listing on page 161 under Dollar Thrifty Automotive Group, Inc.

Dollar Thrifty Automotive Group, Inc.

A car rental and leasing company. Operates separately under the names of Dollar Rent A Car and Thrifty Car Rental.

www.dtag.com
Annual Revenues: $1.1 billion

Chairman of the Board
CAPO, Joseph E. — Tel: (918) 660 - 7700 / Fax: (918) 669 - 2934

President and Chief Exec. Officer
PAXTON, Gary L. — Tel: (918) 660 - 7700 / Fax: (918) 669 - 2934

Main Headquarters
Mailing: P.O. Box 35985
Tulsa, OK 74153-0985 — Tel: (918) 660 - 7700 / Fax: (918) 669 - 2934
Street: 5330 E. 31st St.
Tulsa, OK 74153-0985

Political Action Committees

Dollar Thrifty Automotive Group, Inc. PAC
Contact: Pamela S. Peck
P.O. Box 35985
Tulsa, OK 74153-0985 — Tel: (918) 660 - 7700 / Fax: (918) 669 - 2934

Contributions to Candidates: $19,000 (01/05 - 09/05)
Democrats: $2,000; Republicans: $17,000.

Principal Recipients

SENATE DEMOCRATS		HOUSE DEMOCRATS	
Lieberman, Joe (CT)	$1,000	Holden, Timothy (PA)	$1,000
SENATE REPUBLICANS		**HOUSE REPUBLICANS**	
Inhofe, James M (OK)	$7,000	Hastert, Dennis J. (IL)	$5,000
		Young, Don E (AK)	$2,500
		Graves, Sam (MO)	$1,500
		Cole, Tom (OK)	$1,000

Public Affairs and Related Activities Personnel

At Headquarters

GILL, Emily — Tel: (918) 669 - 2949
Staff Manager, Public Relations — Fax: (918) 669 - 2934
(Dollar Rent A Car, Inc.)
egill@dollar.com

PAYNE, Christopher — Tel: (918) 660 - 7700
Manager, Corporate Communications — Fax: (918) 669 - 2934
(Thrifty Inc.)
chris.payne@thrifty.com

PECK, Pamela S. — Tel: (918) 660 - 7700
PAC Treasurer — Fax: (918) 669 - 2934

SNOW, Terry Wilson — Tel: (918) 660 - 7700
Exec. Director, Corporate Communications — Fax: (918) 669 - 2934
tsnow@dtag.com

Dollar Tree Stores, Inc.

A discount retail chain.

www.dollartreestoresinc.com

Chairman of the Board
BROCK, Macon F., Jr. — Tel: (757) 321 - 5000 / Fax: (757) 321 - 5292

Chief Exec. Officer
SASSER, Bob — Tel: (757) 321 - 5000 / Fax: (757) 321 - 5292

Main Headquarters
Mailing: 500 Volvo Pkwy.
Chesapeake, VA 23320 — Tel: (757) 321 - 5000 / Fax: (757) 321 - 5292

Public Affairs and Related Activities Personnel

At Headquarters

FOTHERGILL, James E. — Tel: (757) 321 - 5000
Chief People Officer — Fax: (757) 321 - 5292

ROBB, Erica — Tel: (757) 321 - 5000
Director, Investor Relations — Fax: (757) 321 - 5292

Dominick's Finer Foods, Inc.

A food and drug store chain. A subsidiary of Safeway Inc. (see separate listing).

www.dominicks.com

Main Headquarters
Mailing: 711 Jorie Blvd
Oak Brook, IL 60523 — Tel: (630) 891 - 5000 / Fax: (630) 891 - 5180

Public Affairs and Related Activities Personnel

At Headquarters

REDMOND, Wynona — Tel: (630) 891 - 5175
Director, Public Affairs — Fax: (630) 891 - 5180

Dominion

See listing on page 162 under Dominion Resources, Inc.

Dominion Peoples

A natural gas utility subsidiary of Dominion Resources, Inc. (see separate listing).

Main Headquarters
Mailing: P.O. Box 26666
Richmond, PA 23261-2666 — Tel: (412) 244 - 2626

Corporate Foundations and Giving Programs

The Dominion Foundation
Contact: James C. Mesloh
Dominion Tower
625 Liberty Ave.
Pittsburgh, PA 15222 — Tel: (412) 690 - 1200

Annual Grant Total: none reported

Public Affairs and Related Activities Personnel

At Headquarters

JONES, Robert D. — Tel: (412) 497 - 6578
Senior External Affairs Manager - PA
robert_d_jones@dom.com

At Other Offices

LOCKLEY, Elmore, Jr. — Tel: (412) 497 - 6742
Manager, Media Relations - PA
Dominion Tower
625 Liberty Ave.
Pittsburgh, PA 15222
elmore_lockley@dom.com

Dominion Resources, Inc.

* continued from previous page

MESLOH, James C. | Tel: (412) 690 - 1200
Foundation Contact
Dominion Tower
625 Liberty Ave.
Pittsburgh, PA 15222
james_mesloh@dom.com

Dominion Resources, Inc.

A member of the Public Affairs Council. An energy company. Acquired Consolidated Natural Gas in 1999. Subsidiaries include Dominion Virginia Power, Dominion North Carolina Power, Dominion East Ohio (formerly East Ohio Gas Co.), Dominion Hope, Dominion Peoples (formerly Peoples Natural Gas Co.), Dominion Exploration & Production, and Dominion Transmission (formerly CNG Transmission), among others.

www.dom.com
Annual Revenues: $10.558 billion

Chairman, President and Chief Exec. Officer
CAPPS, Thos. E.
Tel: (804) 819 - 2000
Fax: (804) 819 - 2233

Main Headquarters
Mailing: P.O. Box 26532
Richmond, VA 23261
Tel: (804) 819 - 2000
Fax: (804) 819 - 2233
Street: 120 Tredegar St.
Richmond, VA 23219

Washington Office
Contact: Jayne L. Victor
Mailing: 444 N. Capitol St. NW
Suite 729
Washington, DC 20001
Tel: (202) 585 - 4211
Fax: (202) 737 - 3874

Political Action Committees

Dominion PAC
Contact: William C. Hall, Jr.
P.O. Box 26532
Richmond, VA 23261
Tel: (804) 819 - 2040
Fax: (804) 819 - 2233

Contributions to Candidates: $112,176 (01/05 - 09/05)
Democrats: $34,501; Republicans: $77,675.

Principal Recipients

SENATE DEMOCRATS		HOUSE DEMOCRATS	
Bingaman, Jeff (NM)	$2,000	Boucher, Fredrick (VA)	$5,000
Landrieu, Mary (LA)	$1,001		

SENATE REPUBLICANS		HOUSE REPUBLICANS	
Santorum, Richard (PA)	$3,500	Barton, Joe L (TX)	$6,000
Dewine, Richard (OH)	$3,000	Capito, Shelley (WV)	$5,000
Allen, George (VA)	$2,500	Simmons, Rob (CT)	$5,000
Burns, Conrad (MT)	$2,000	Boustany, Jr, Charles (LA)	$2,000
Thomas, Craig (WY)	$2,000	Murphy, Tim (PA)	$2,000
		Reynolds, Thomas (NY)	$2,000
		Wilson, Heather (NM)	$2,000

Corporate Foundations and Giving Programs

Dominion Resources Foundation
Contact: Marjorie N. Grier
P.O. Box 26532
Richmond, VA 23261
Tel: (804) 819 - 2578
Fax: (804) 819 - 2217

Annual Grant Total: $1,000,000 - $2,000,000
Geographic Preference: Area(s) in which the company operates; North Carolina; Virginia; Connecticut; Louisiana; Ohio; Oklahoma; Pennsylvania; Texas; West Virginia
Primary Interests: Community Affairs; Education; Human Welfare

Public Affairs and Related Activities Personnel

At Headquarters

BLUE, Robert M.
Managing Director, State Affairs and Corporate Public Policy
Tel: (804) 771 - 4517
Fax: (804) 771 - 3643

GRIER, Marjorie N.
Director, Corporate Philanthropy
marjorie_grier@dom.com
Tel: (804) 819 - 2578
Fax: (804) 819 - 2217

HALL, William C., Jr.
V. President, External Affairs and Corporate Communications
Tel: (804) 819 - 2040
Fax: (804) 819 - 2233

LAZENBY, Mark
Corporate Communications
mark_lazenby@dom.com
Tel: (804) 819 - 2042
Fax: (804) 819 - 2233

NORVELLE, James W.
Director, Media Relations (Electric)
Jim_Norvelle@dom.com
Tel: (804) 771 - 6115
Fax: (804) 771 - 3054

PITCHFORD, Barbara F.
Assistant Corporate Secretary
barbara_pitchford@dom.com
Responsibilities include investor relations.
Tel: (804) 819 - 2000
Fax: (804) 819 - 2233

At Washington Office

CHAPMAN, Kelly G.
Manager, Federal Policy
kelly_chapman@dom.com
Registered Federal Lobbyist.
Tel: (202) 585 - 4211
Fax: (202) 737 - 3874

MCKAY, Bruce
Manager, Federal Policy
bruce_mckay@dom.com
Tel: (202) 585 - 4207
Fax: (202) 737 - 3874

VICTOR, Jayne L.
Director, Corporate Federal Affairs
Jayne_Victor@dom.com
Tel: (202) 585 - 4203
Fax: (202) 737 - 3874

At Other Offices

BAAB, Carl F.
Director, Media Relations and Internet Communications
P.O. Box 26666
Richmond, VA 23261-6666
Carl_Baab@dom.com
Tel: (804) 771 - 4557

BOARD, Virginia M.
Director, Community Affairs
P.O. Box 26666
Richmond, VA 23261-6666
Virginia_Board@dom.com
Tel: (804) 771 - 4491

DONOVAN, Daniel E., Jr.
Manager Media Relations (Gas)
Dominion CNG Tower
625 Liberty Ave.
Pittsburgh, PA 15222-3199
Daniel_E_Donovan@dom.com
Tel: (412) 690 - 1370
Fax: (412) 690 - 1020

HARDY, Eva S.
Senior V. President, External Affairs and Corporate Communications
P.O. Box 26666
Richmond, VA 23261-6666
eva_s_hardy@dom.com
Tel: (804) 771 - 4741

POWELL, Anita W.
PAC and Grassroots Manager
P.O. Box 26666
Mailstop: 20th Floor
Richmond, VA 23261-6666
Anita_Powell@dom.com
Tel: (804) 771 - 4442
Fax: (804) 771 - 3643

THOMPSON, Michael A.
Manager, State Government Affairs, North Carolina and Ohio
P.O. Box 26666 OJRP 20
Richmond, VA 23261-6666
Michael_Thompson@dom.com
Tel: (804) 771 - 3655

VARLEY, Robert W.
Director, State and Local Affairs
1201 E. 55th St.
Cleveland, OH 44103
robert_w_varley@dom.com
Tel: (216) 736 - 6207

WADE, Chet G.
Director Employee Communications
P.O. Box 2666
Richmond, VA 23261
Chet_Wade@dom.com
Tel: (804) 771 - 5697

WEEKLEY, Daniel A.
Director, State and Local Affairs
Rope Ferry Rd.
Waterford, CT 06385
daniel_a_weekley@dom.com
Tel: (860) 444 - 5271
TF: (800) 552 - 4034

WHEARY, Herbert S.
Public Policy Director
P.O. Box 26666
Richmond, VA 23261-6666
Herbert_Wheary@dom.com
Tel: (804) 771 - 3611

WILLIAMS, Junius H., Jr.
Director, State and Local Affairs
2700 Cromwell Rd.
Norfolk, VA 23501
Junius_Williams@dom.com
Tel: (757) 857 - 2690

Domino's Pizza, LLC

A pizza delivery company.
www.dominos.com

Chairman and Chief Exec. Officer
BRANDON, David A.
brandod@dominos.com
Tel: (734) 930 - 3030
Fax: (734) 930 - 4346

Main Headquarters
Mailing: P.O. Box 997
Ann Arbor, MI 48106-0997
Tel: (734) 930 - 3030
Fax: (734) 930 - 4346
Street: 30 Frank Lloyd Wright Dr.
Ann Arbor, MI 48106

Political Action Committees

Domino's Pizza LLC Political Action Committee (Domino's Pizza PAC)
Contact: Jeffrey D. Lawrence

Domino's Pizza, LLC

** continued from previous page*

P.O. Box 997 Tel: (734) 930 - 3030
Ann Arbor, MI 48106-0997 Fax: (734) 930 - 4346

Contributions to Candidates: none reported (01/05 - 09/05)

Corporate Foundations and Giving Programs

Domino's Pizza Community Relations Program
Contact: Angie Torango
P.O. Box 997 Tel: (734) 930 - 3565
Ann Arbor, MI 48106-0997 Fax: (734) 930 - 4346

Annual Grant Total: none reported
The company has an exclusive grantmaking relationship with the Make-A-Wish Foundation.

Public Affairs and Related Activities Personnel

At Headquarters

GARCIA, Elisa D. Tel: (734) 930 - 3678
Exec. V. President and General Counsel Fax: (734) 930 - 4346
garciae@dominos.com
Responsibilties include legal and government affairs.

LAWRENCE, Jeffrey D. Tel: (734) 930 - 3030
Contact, Domino's Pizza PAC Fax: (734) 930 - 4346
lawrenj@dominos.com

LIDDLE, Lynn M. Tel: (734) 930 - 3563
Executive V. President, Corporate Communications and Investor Relations Fax: (734) 668 - 1946

RYAN, Holly Tel: (734) 930 - 3030
Manager, Public Relations Fax: (734) 930 - 4346
ryanh@dominos.com
Responsibilities also include corporate philanthropy.

TORANGO, Angie Tel: (734) 930 - 3565
Domino's Pizza Community Relations Program Contact Fax: (734) 930 - 4346

Donaldson Company, Inc.

A worldwide manufacturer of filtration systems and replacement parts.
www.donaldson.com

Chairman of the Board
VAN DYKE, William G. Tel: (952) 887 - 3131
Fax: (952) 887 - 3005
TF: (800) 887 - 3131

President and Chief Exec. Officer
COOK, William Tel: (952) 887 - 3131
Fax: (952) 887 - 3155
TF: (800) 887 - 3131

Main Headquarters
Mailing: P.O. Box 1299 Tel: (952) 887 - 3131
Minneapolis, MN 55440-1299 Fax: (952) 887 - 3155
TF: (800) 887 - 3131

Corporate Foundations and Giving Programs

The Donaldson Foundation
Contact: Norman C. Linnell
P.O. Box 1299 Tel: (952) 703 - 4999
Minneapolis, MN 55440-1299 Fax: (952) 887 - 3005
TF: (800) 887 - 3131

Annual Grant Total: $750,000 - $1,000,000
Focuses on programs that help to foster the transition to economic self-sufficiency. Guidelines are available.
Geographic Preference: Area(s) in which the company operates
Primary Interests: Education
Recent Recipients: Citizen's Scholarship Foundation of America; United Way; University of Minnesota

Public Affairs and Related Activities Personnel

At Headquarters

KAHN, Becky Tel: (952) 887 - 3131
Manager, Corporate Communications Fax: (952) 887 - 3155
TF: (800) 887 - 3131

LINNELL, Norman C. Tel: (952) 703 - 4999
President, The Donaldson Foundation Fax: (952) 887 - 3005
Mailstop: MS 101 TF: (800) 887 - 3131
donaldsonfoundation@mail.donaldson.com

MCMURRAY, Charles Tel: (952) 887 - 3131
V. President, Human Resources Fax: (952) 887 - 3155
TF: (800) 887 - 3131

PRIADKA, Nicholas Tel: (952) 887 - 3131
Senior V. President, International Fax: (952) 887 - 3155
TF: (800) 887 - 3131

SHEFFER, Rich Tel: (952) 887 - 3753
Assistant Treasurer and Director, Investor Relations Fax: (952) 887 - 3005
rscheffer@mail.donaldson.com TF: (800) 887 - 3131

R R Donnelley

PUBLIC AFFAIRS COUNCIL

A member of the Public Affairs Council. A commercial printing company.
www.rrdonnelley.com
Annual Revenues: $5.298 billion

Chairman of the Board
WOLF, Stephen M. Tel: (312) 326 - 8000

Chief Exec. Officer
ANGELSON, Mark A. Tel: (312) 326 - 8000
Fax: (312) 326 - 8494

Main Headquarters
Mailing: 111 S. Wacker Dr. Tel: (312) 326 - 8000
Chicago, IL 60606 Fax: (312) 326 - 8494

Political Action Committees

R R Donnelley Good Government Fund
Contact: Lucie F. Naphin
111 S. Wacker Dr. Tel: (312) 326 - 8030
Chicago, IL 60606 Fax: (312) 326 - 8494

Contributions to Candidates: $30,000 (01/05 - 09/05)
Democrats: $17,000; Republicans: $13,000.

Principal Recipients

SENATE DEMOCRATS		HOUSE DEMOCRATS	
Carper, Thomas R (DE)	$3,000	Emanuel, Rahm (IL)	$5,000
Bayh, Evan (IN)	$2,000	Davis, Danny K (IL)	$3,000
Lieberman, Joe (CT)	$2,000	Hoyer, Steny (MD)	$2,000
SENATE REPUBLICANS		**HOUSE REPUBLICANS**	
Ensign, John Eric (NV)	$2,000	Hastert, Dennis J. (IL)	$5,000
Lugar, Richard G (IN)	$2,000	Davis, Tom (VA)	$2,000
Dewine, Richard (OH)	$1,000	Biggert, Judy (IL)	$1,000

Corporate Foundations and Giving Programs

R R Donnelley Corporate Contributions Program
Contact: Susan M. Levy
111 S. Wacker Dr. Tel: (312) 326 - 8102
Chicago, IL 60606 Fax: (312) 326 - 8262

Annual Grant Total: $2,000,000 - $5,000,000
Geographic Preference: Area in which the company is headquartered
Primary Interests: Education; Human Welfare; Literacy

Public Affairs and Related Activities Personnel

At Headquarters

BOHABOY, Scott A. Tel: (312) 326 - 7730
V. President, Investor Relations Fax: (312) 326 - 7748
scott.a.bohaboy@rrd.com

FITZGERALD, Doug Tel: (630) 322 - 6830
Senior V. President, Marketing and Communications
doug.fizgerald@rrd.com
Responsibilities include media relations.

GLADNEY, Carrie L. Tel: (312) 326 - 8031
Coordinator, Government Relations Fax: (312) 326 - 8494
carrie.gladney@rrd.com

LEVY, Susan M. Tel: (312) 326 - 8102
Director, Community Relations Fax: (312) 326 - 8262
susan.levy@rrd.com

MANZELLA, Michael Tel: (312) 326 - 8038
V. President, Environmental Affairs Fax: (630) 322 - 6711
michael.manzella@rrd.com

NAPHIN, Lucie F. Tel: (312) 326 - 8030
V. President, Government Relations Fax: (312) 326 - 8494
lucie.naphin@rrd.com
Responsibilities include political action.

PANEGA, Andrew Tel: (312) 326 - 8990
Senior V. President, Human Resources Fax: (312) 326 - 7660

DoubleClick, Inc.

A global internet advertising company.
www.doubleclick.com

Chief Exec. Officer
ROSENBLATT, David Tel: (212) 683 - 0001
Fax: (212) 287 - 1203

Main Headquarters
Mailing: 111 Eighth Ave. Tel: (212) 683 - 0001
Tenth Floor Fax: (212) 287 - 1203
New York, NY 10011

Public Affairs and Related Activities Personnel

At Headquarters

CONNORTON, Jennifer Tel: (212) 381 - 5183
Director, Public Relations Fax: (212) 287 - 1203

Dow AgroSciences LLC

A wholly-owned subsidiary of Dow Chemical Co. (see separate listing). Formerly known as DowElanco, a joint venture between Dow Chemical and Eli Lilly and Co. The company changed its name to Dow AgroSciences when Dow Chemical acquired 100% of DowElanco in 1997.
www.dowagro.com
Annual Revenues: $3 billion

Dow AgroSciences LLC

* continued from previous page

President and Chief Exec. Officer
PERIBERE, Jerome — Tel: (317) 337 - 3000

Main Headquarters
Mailing: 9330 Zionsville Rd.
Indianapolis, IN 46268 — Tel: (317) 337 - 3000

Washington Office
Contact: C. Thomas Campbell
Mailing: 1776 I St. NW
Suite 1050
Washington, DC 20006
Tel: (202) 429 - 3438
Fax: (202) 429 - 3467

Political Action Committees

Dow Chemical Agricultural Executive Political Action Committee
Contact: Jacob Secor, Ph.D.
9330 Zionsville Rd.
Indianapolis, IN 46268
Tel: (317) 337 - 4751
Fax: (317) 337 - 4880

Contributions to Candidates: $5,500 (01/05 - 09/05)
Democrats: $1,500; Republicans: $3,000; Other: $1,000.

Principal Recipients

SENATE DEMOCRATS

HOUSE DEMOCRATS
Case, Edward (HI) $1,000
Costa, Jim (CA) $500

HOUSE OTHER
Peterson, Collin (MN) $1,000

SENATE REPUBLICANS
Burns, Conrad (MT) $500

HOUSE REPUBLICANS
Pence, Mike (IN) $1,000
Taylor, Charles H (NC) $1,000
Lucas, Frank D (OK) $500

Corporate Foundations and Giving Programs

Dow AgroSciences Corporate Giving Program
Contact: Tim Maniscalo
9330 Zionsville Rd.
Indianapolis, IN 46268
Tel: (317) 337 - 4359
Fax: (317) 337 - 4880

Annual Grant Total: none reported

Public Affairs and Related Activities Personnel

At Headquarters

GIESSELMAN, Janet
V. President, Corporate Affairs
jgiesselman@dow.com
Tel: (317) 337 - 3000
Fax: (317) 337 - 4880

HAMLIN, Garry
Manager, Public Policy Resources
Tel: (317) 337 - 4799

MANISCALO, Tim
Manager, Corporate Contributions
tmmaniscalo@dow.com
Tel: (317) 337 - 4359
Fax: (317) 337 - 4880

SECOR, Jacob, Ph.D.
Leader, State Government and Public Affairs, Midwest and South
jsecor@dow.com
Tel: (317) 337 - 4751
Fax: (317) 337 - 4880

At Washington Office

CAMPBELL, C. Thomas
Manager, Federal Government Relations
tcampbell@dow.com
Registered Federal Lobbyist.
Tel: (202) 429 - 3438
Fax: (202) 429 - 3467

SHURDUT, Bradley A.
Global Leader, Government and Regulatory Affairs, Biotechnology
bshurdut@dow.com
Registered Federal Lobbyist.
Tel: (202) 429 - 3434
Fax: (202) 429 - 3467

At Other Offices

STUART, Bryan, Ph.D.
Leader, State Government and Public Affairs, Western States
P.O. Box 2710
Carmichael, CA 95609-2710
blstuart@dow.com
Tel: (916) 944 - 0278
Fax: (916) 791 - 6800

The Dow Chemical Company

A member of the Public Affairs Council. A science and technology company providing innovative chemical, plastic and agricultural products and services to many consumer markets. With annual sales of $33 billion, Dow serves customers in more than 180 countries and a wide range of markets that are vital to human progress including food, transportation, health and medicine, personal and home care, and building and construction, among others. Committed to the principles of sustainable develoment, Dow and its approximately 46,000 employees seek to balance economic, environmental and social responsibilities.

www.dow.com
Annual Revenues: $33 billion

Chairman and Chief Exec. Officer
STAVROPOULOS, William S.
Tel: (989) 636 - 1000
Fax: (989) 638 - 1740

Main Headquarters
Mailing: 2030 Dow Center
Midland, MI 48674-0001
Tel: (989) 636 - 1000

Washington Office
Contact: Peter A. Molinaro
Mailing: 1776 I St. NW
Suite 1050
Washington, DC 20006
Tel: (202) 429 - 3400
Fax: (202) 429 - 3467

Political Action Committees

Political Action Committee of Employees of the Dow Chemical Co. (PACE)
Contact: Peter A. Molinaro
1776 I St. NW
Suite 1050
Washington, DC 20006
Tel: (202) 429 - 3400
Fax: (202) 429 - 3467

Contributions to Candidates: $52,250 (01/05 - 09/05)
Democrats: $12,000; Republicans: $40,250.

Principal Recipients

SENATE DEMOCRATS
Carper, Thomas R (DE) $4,500

HOUSE DEMOCRATS
Melancon, Charlie (LA) $1,500

SENATE REPUBLICANS
Alexander, Lamar (TN) $2,500
Cornyn, John (TX) $2,500
Santorum, Richard (PA) $2,500
Domenici, Pete (NM) $2,000
McConnell, Mitch (KY) $1,500

HOUSE REPUBLICANS
Hastert, Dennis J. (IL) $5,000
Camp, David Lee (MI) $3,250
DeLay, Tom (TX) $2,500
Thomas, William M (CA) $1,500

Corporate Foundations and Giving Programs

The Dow Chemical Co. Foundation
Contact: Lynne Glynn
2030 Dow Center
Midland, MI 48674-0001
Tel: (989) 636 - 9846
Fax: (989) 638 - 1727

Annual Grant Total: over $5,000,000
Geographic Preference: National
Primary Interests: Community Development; Environment/Conservation; Higher Education; Math and Science

Public Affairs and Related Activities Personnel

At Headquarters

DAVIS, R. Matthew
Public Affairs Director, Plastics
rmdavis@dow.com
Tel: (989) 636 - 1000
Fax: (989) 638 - 2359

GLYNN, Lynne
Foundation Contact
Tel: (989) 636 - 9846
Fax: (989) 638 - 1727

GRAHAM, David W.
Global V. President, Environment, Health and Safety
dwgraham@dow.com
Tel: (989) 636 - 1000
Fax: (989) 636 - 0389

HAWKINS, Neil C.
Director, Issues Management
nchawkins@dow.com
Tel: (989) 636 - 1000
Fax: (989) 636 - 3518

HAYES, Michael D.
Global V. President, Public Affairs, Public Policy and Advocacy
mdhayes@dow.com
Tel: (989) 636 - 1000
Fax: (989) 638 - 1727

MAXEY, Catherine C.
Public Affairs Director, Chemicals and Intermediates and Performance Chemicals and Thermosets
ccmaxey@dow.com
Tel: (989) 636 - 1000
Fax: (989) 638 - 1727

NEWMAN, Cindy C.
Director, Corporate Communications
ccnewman@dow.com
Tel: (989) 636 - 1000
Fax: (989) 636 - 3518

OPPERMAN, Sarah R.
Global V. President, Public Affairs, Communications and Reputation
sropperman@dow.com
Tel: (989) 636 - 1000
Fax: (989) 638 - 1727

WASHINGTON, Lawrence J., Jr.
Corporate V. President, Environment, Health and Safety, Human Resources and Public Affairs
Tel: (989) 636 - 1000

At Washington Office

BARROW, Craig S.
Director, Science Policy
Registered Federal Lobbyist.
Tel: (202) 429 - 3400
Fax: (202) 429 - 3467

BOYD, Janet C.
Director, Government Relations-Tax and Benefits
Registered Federal Lobbyist.
Tel: (202) 429 - 3400
Fax: (202) 429 - 3467

The Dow Chemical Company

• continued from previous page

MOLINARO, Peter A. — Tel: (202) 429 - 3400
V. President, Federal and State Government Affairs — Fax: (202) 429 - 3467
Registered Federal Lobbyist.
Responsibilities include political action.

SCHOENBERGER, Jeff — Tel: (202) 429 - 3400
Legislative Assistant — Fax: (202) 429 - 3467

SCHROETER, Lisa — Tel: (202) 429 - 3400
Director, International Government Affairs — Fax: (202) 429 - 3467
Registered Federal Lobbyist.

VEGA, Louis A. — Tel: (202) 429 - 3400
Director, Federal and State Government Affairs — Fax: (202) 429 - 3467
Registered Federal Lobbyist.

VERHEGGEN, Ted — Tel: (202) 429 - 3400
Legislative Counsel — Fax: (202) 429 - 3467
Registered Federal Lobbyist.

Dow Corning Corp.

A member of the Public Affairs Council. A 50/50 joint venture of Dow Chemical and Corning Inc. A manufacturer of specialty chemicals.
www.dowcorning.com

Chairman and Chief Exec. Officer
BURNS, Stephanie A. — Tel: (989) 496 - 4000
Mailstop: C01301 — Fax: (989) 496 - 8240

Main Headquarters
Mailing: P.O. Box 994 — Tel: (989) 496 - 4000
Midland, MI 48686-0994 — Fax: (989) 496 - 8240
Street: 2200 W. Salzburg Rd.
Midland, MI 48686

Washington Office
Contact: Faye Graul
Mailing: 7105 Park Point Ct. — Tel: (703) 440 - 4071
Fairfax Station, VA 22039 — Fax: (703) 440 - 4072

Political Action Committees

Dow Corning Legislative Action Team
Contact: Chris Velasquez
P.O. Box 994 — Tel: (989) 496 - 4000
Midland, MI 48686-0994 — Fax: (989) 496 - 8240

Contributions to Candidates: $1,795 (01/05 - 09/05)
Republicans: $1,795.

Principal Recipients

SENATE REPUBLICANS	HOUSE REPUBLICANS	
	Camp, David Lee (MI)	$1,795

Corporate Foundations and Giving Programs

Dow Corning Foundation
Contact: Anne M. DeBoer
P.O. Box 994 — Tel: (989) 496 - 4000
Midland, MI 48686-0994 — Fax: (989) 496 - 8240

Annual Grant Total: $500,000 - $750,000
Geographic Preference: Area(s) in which the company operates
Primary Interests: Animal Protection; Community Affairs; Education; Environment/Conservation; Higher Education; Math and Science
Recent Recipients: Michigan State University; Michigan Technological University

Dow Corning Contributions Program
Contact: Anne M. DeBoer
P.O. Box 994 — Tel: (989) 496 - 4000
Midland, MI 48686-0994 — Fax: (989) 496 - 8240

Annual Grant Total: $1,000,000 - $2,000,000
Geographic Preference: Area(s) in which the company operates; College and university communities where the company actively recruits employees; Michigan; Kentucky; North Carolina
Primary Interests: Arts and Culture; Community Affairs; Environment/Conservation; Higher Education; K-12 Education
Recent Recipients: Junior Achievement; United Way

Public Affairs and Related Activities Personnel

At Headquarters

BENECKE, Mary Lou — Tel: (989) 496 - 8689
Manager, Media Relations — Fax: (989) 496 - 8240
Mailstop: C1252

BOTZ, Jan — Tel: (989) 496 - 6470
Exec. Director, Communications — Fax: (989) 496 - 8240
Mailstop: C01306
jan.botz@dowcorning.com

DEBOER, Anne M. — Tel: (989) 496 - 4000
Exec. Director, Foundation — Fax: (989) 496 - 8240
anne.deboer@dowcorning.com

GAGLIARDI, Bill — Tel: (989) 496 - 6393
Manager, Environmental Health and Safety Communications — Fax: (989) 496 - 8240
bill.gagliardi@dowcorning.com

MARCELA, Paul — Tel: (989) 496 - 6365
Chairman, Dow Corning Legislative Action Team — Fax: (989) 496 - 1709
paul.marcela@dowcorning.com

SWANTEK, Rosemary V. — Tel: (989) 496 - 4000
Manager, Internal Communications — Fax: (989) 496 - 8240
Mailstop: #C02100

VELASQUEZ, Chris — Tel: (989) 496 - 4000
PAC Treasurer — Fax: (989) 496 - 8240

At Washington Office

GRAUL, Faye — Tel: (703) 440 - 4071
V. President, Government Relations - U.S. Area — Fax: (703) 440 - 4072
faye.graul@dowcorning.com
Registered Federal Lobbyist.

Dow Jones and Co.

A publisher of business news, information services and community newspapers.
www.dj.com
Annual Revenues: $1.773 billion

Chairman and Chief Exec. Officer — Tel: (212) 416 - 3055
KANN, Peter R.
peter.kann@dowjones.com

Main Headquarters
Mailing: World Financial Center — Tel: (609) 420 - 4000
200 Liberty St.
New York, NY 10281

Corporate Foundations and Giving Programs

Dow Jones Foundation
Contact: Tom McGuirl
P.O. Box 300 — Tel: (609) 520 - 5143
Princeton, NJ 08543 — Fax: (609) 520 - 5180

Assets: $300,000 (2000)
Annual Grant Total: $1,000,000 - $2,000,000
Geographic Preference: Area(s) in which the company operates
Primary Interests: Community Affairs; Education; Journalism
Recent Recipients: Columbia University; Nat'l Merit Scholarship; Nat'l Urban League

Dow Jones Newspaper Fund
Contact: Richard Holden
P.O. Box 300 — Tel: (609) 520 - 5930
Princeton, NJ 08543

Assets: $675,000 (2001)
Annual Grant Total: $400,000 - $500,000
Principal recipients are college students who receive summer internships and colleges and universities that sponsor workshops for high school students and for high school journalism teachers and advisors. The Dow Jones Newspaper Fund also provides publications for students interested in considering careers in journalism. The Fund puts a special emphasis on helping to promote diversity in the newspaper industry. Email richard.holden@dowjones.com to request a copy of the annual report for program and proposal guidelines. Information is also available on the company's website at www.dowjones.com/newsfund.

Public Affairs and Related Activities Personnel

At Headquarters

WOLFCALE, Amy — Tel: (609) 420 - 4000
V. President, Corporate Communications

At Other Offices

CHRISTIE, Robert — Tel: (609) 520 - 5143
Director, Corporate Communications — Fax: (609) 520 - 5180
P.O. Box 300
Princeton, NJ 08543

DONOHUE, Mark — Tel: (609) 520 - 5660
Director, Investor Relations
P.O. Box 300
Princeton, NJ 08543
mark.donohue@dowjones.com

HOLDEN, Richard — Tel: (609) 520 - 5930
Exec. Director, Dow Jones Newspaper Fund
P.O. Box 300
Princeton, NJ 08543
richard.holden@dowjones.com

MCGUIRL, Tom — Tel: (609) 520 - 5143
Administrative Officer, Dow Jones Foundation, Treasurer, Dow Jones and Co. — Fax: (609) 520 - 5180
P.O. Box 300
Princeton, NJ 08543
tom.mcguirl@dowjones.com

PYHEL, Nicole C. — Tel: (609) 520 - 4057
Director, Corporate Communications
P.O. Box 300
Princeton, NJ 08543
nicole.pyhel@dowjones.com

SCADUTO, James A. — Tel: (609) 520 - 4701
V. President, Human Resources
P.O. Box 300
Princeton, NJ 08543

Downey Savings and Loan Ass'n, F.A.

www.downeysavings.com

Chairman of the Board
MCALISTER, Maurice L. — Tel: (949) 854 - 3100 Fax: (949) 854 - 8162

President and Chief Executive Officer
ROSENTHAL, Daniel D. — Tel: (949) 854 - 3100 Fax: (949) 854 - 8162

Main Headquarters
Mailing: P.O. Box 6000, Newport Beach, CA 92658-6000 — Tel: (949) 854 - 3100 Fax: (949) 854 - 8162
Street: 3501 Jamboree Rd., Newport Beach, CA 92660

Political Action Committees

Downey Savings and Loan Ass'n PAC
Contact: Kent Smith
P.O. Box 6000
Newport Beach, CA 92658-6000 — Tel: (949) 854 - 3100 Fax: (949) 854 - 4560

Contributions to Candidates: none reported (01/05 - 09/05)

Corporate Foundations and Giving Programs

Downey Savings and Loan Ass'n Corporate Contributions
Contact: Lilia Villasenor
P.O. Box 6000
Newport Beach, CA 92658-6000 — Tel: (949) 854 - 3100 Fax: (949) 823 - 5375

Annual Grant Total: none reported

Public Affairs and Related Activities Personnel

At Headquarters

BRIGGS, Kendice
Senior V. President and Director, Human Resources — Tel: (949) 854 - 3100 Fax: (949) 854 - 4979

SMITH, Kent
Contact, Downey Savings and Loan Ass'n PAC — Tel: (949) 854 - 3100 Fax: (949) 854 - 4560

VILLASENOR, Lilia
Manager, Community Development and Investment — Tel: (949) 854 - 3100 Fax: (949) 823 - 5375
Responsibilities include corporate philanthropy.

DPL Inc.

Subsidiaries include Dayton Power & Light Co.
www.dplinc.com
Annual Revenues: $1.199 billion

Chairman of the Board
BIGGS, Robert D. — Tel: (937) 224 - 6000 Fax: (937) 259 - 7813

President and Chief Exec. Officer
MAHONEY, James V. — Tel: (937) 224 - 6000 Fax: (937) 259 - 7813

Main Headquarters
Mailing: 1065 Woodman Dr., Dayton, OH 45432 — Tel: (937) 224 - 6000 Fax: (937) 259 - 7813

Political Action Committees

Dayton Power and Light Co. Employees' Fund for Responsible Citizenship
Contact: Timothy G. Rice
1065 Woodman Dr.
Dayton, OH 45432 — Tel: (937) 224 - 6000 Fax: (937) 259 - 7813

Contributions to Candidates: none reported (01/05 - 09/05)

Corporate Foundations and Giving Programs

Dayton Power & Light Co. Foundation
Contact: Ginny Strausburg
1065 Woodman Dr.
Dayton, OH 45432 — Tel: (937) 259 - 7924 Fax: (937) 259 - 7923

Annual Grant Total: $750,000 - $1,000,000
Geographic Preference: Area(s) in which the company operates
Primary Interests: Adult Education and Training; Arts and Humanities; Education; Energy Conservation; Engineering; Environment/Conservation; Minority Opportunities; Youth Services
Recent Recipients: American Red Cross; Boy Scouts of America; United Way

Public Affairs and Related Activities Personnel

At Headquarters

MEYER, Arthur G. "Art"
V. President and Corporate Secretary
(Dayton Power and Light Co.) — Tel: (937) 259 - 7208 Fax: (937) 259 - 7386
Responsibilities include legal and corporate affairs.

RICE, Timothy G.
PAC Treasurer — Tel: (937) 224 - 6000 Fax: (937) 259 - 7813

STRAUSBURG, Ginny
Exec. Director, Dayton Power & Light Foundation — Tel: (937) 259 - 7924 Fax: (937) 259 - 7923

TATHAM, Tom
Manager, Corporate Communications and Community Relations
(Dayton Power and Light Co.) — Tel: (937) 259 - 7347 Fax: (937) 259 - 7813

DQE, Inc.

See listing on page 170 under Duquesne Light Holdings.

Dr Pepper/Seven Up Inc.

See listing on page 97 under Cadbury Schweppes Americas Beverages.

Dreyer's Grand Ice Cream Holdings, Inc.

Formed from the merger of Dreyer's Grand Ice Cream, Inc. and Nestle Ice Cream Co., LLC in June of 2003. A manufacturer and distributor of premium ice cream, super-premium ice cream, yogurt and sherbet products.
www.dreyers.com
Annual Revenues: $1.399 billion

Chairman and Chief Exec. Officer
ROGERS, T. Gary — Tel: (510) 652 - 8187

Main Headquarters
Mailing: 5929 College Ave., Oakland, CA 94618 — Tel: (510) 652 - 8187

Corporate Foundations and Giving Programs

Dreyer's Grand Ice Cream Foundation
Contact: Kelly Su'a
5929 College Ave.
Oakland, CA 94618 — Tel: (510) 652 - 8187 Fax: (510) 601 - 4400

Annual Grant Total: $300,000 - $400,000
Contributions total 1.5 percent of the company's pre-tax earnings.
Geographic Preference: Area in which the company is headquartered
Primary Interests: K-12 Education

Public Affairs and Related Activities Personnel

At Headquarters

BAILY, Dori Sera
Director, Corporate Communications — Tel: (510) 601 - 4241 Fax: (510) 601 - 4400
dsbaily@dreyers.com

GOELLER-JOHNSON, Kim
Manager, Public Relations--Premium Brands — Tel: (510) 601 - 4211 Fax: (510) 601 - 4400
kagvelle@dreyers.com

MCINTYRE, Diane
Manager, Public Relations--Superpremium Brands — Tel: (510) 652 - 4338 Fax: (510) 450 - 4592
dmmcinty@dreyers.com

SU'A, Kelly
Secretary-Treasurer, Charitable Foundation — Tel: (510) 652 - 8187 Fax: (510) 601 - 4400

WEBSTER, Scott
Assistant Treasurer, Investor Relations — Tel: (510) 450 - 4545
cswebste@dreyers.com

The Dreyfus Corp.

Mutual funds and other financial services. A subsidiary of Mellon Financial Corp. (see separate listing).
www.dreyfus.com

Chairman and Chief Exec. Officer
CANTER, Stephen E. — Tel: (212) 922 - 6360 Fax: (212) 922 - 6585

Main Headquarters
Mailing: 200 Park Ave., New York, NY 10166 — Tel: (212) 922 - 6000 Fax: (212) 922 - 6585

Corporate Foundations and Giving Programs

Dreyfus Corporate Contributions Program
Contact: Patrice M. Kozlowski
200 Park Ave.
New York, NY 10166 — Tel: (212) 922 - 6030 Fax: (212) 922 - 6585

Annual Grant Total: none reported
Geographic Preference: New York City
Primary Interests: Arts and Culture; Education; Social Services
Recent Recipients: Cystic Fibrosis Foundation

Public Affairs and Related Activities Personnel

At Headquarters

DEMPSEY, Maureen
Communications Specialist — Tel: (212) 922 - 6648 Fax: (212) 922 - 6585
dempsey.m@dreyfus.com

HOEY, Richard
Chief Economist and Chief Investment Strategist — Tel: (212) 922 - 6000 Fax: (212) 922 - 6038
Responsibilities include investor relations.

KOZLOWSKI, Patrice M.
Senior V. President, Corporate Communications — Tel: (212) 922 - 6030 Fax: (212) 922 - 6585
kozlowski.pm@dreyfus.com

DRS Technologies, Inc.

A supplier of defense technology systems.
www.drs.com
Annual Revenues: $1 billion

Chairman, President and Chief Exec. Officer
NEWMAN, Mark S. — Tel: (973) 898 - 1500 Fax: (973) 898 - 4730
msn@drs.com

Main Headquarters
Mailing: Five Sylvan Way, Parsippany, NJ 07054 — Tel: (973) 898 - 1500 Fax: (973) 898 - 4730 TF: (866) 898 - 1500

DRS Technologies, Inc.

• continued from previous page

Washington Office
Contact: Mike Bowman
Mailing: 1755 S. Clark St.
Suite 1100
Arlington, VA 22202
Tel: (703) 416 - 8000
Fax: (703) 416 - 8010

Political Action Committees

DRS Technologies Good Government Fund
Contact: Richard A. Schneider
Five Sylvan Way
Parsippany, NJ 07054
Tel: (973) 898 - 1500
Fax: (973) 898 - 4730

Contributions to Candidates: $106,000 (01/05 - 09/05)
Democrats: $36,500; Republicans: $69,500.

Principal Recipients

SENATE DEMOCRATS		HOUSE DEMOCRATS	
Clinton, Hillary Rodham (NY)	$2,000	Murtha, John P Mr. (PA)	$5,000
		Skelton, Ike (MO)	$4,500
Kennedy, Ted (MA)	$2,000	Rothman, Steven R (NJ)	$4,000
Feinstein, Dianne (CA)	$1,000		

SENATE REPUBLICANS		HOUSE REPUBLICANS	
Allen, George (VA)	$5,000	Frelinghuysen, Rod (NJ)	$5,000
Santorum, Richard (PA)	$5,000	Granger, Kay N (TX)	$5,000
Cochran, Thad (MS)	$2,000	Sessions, Pete (TX)	$5,000
Dewine, Richard (OH)	$2,000	Hunter, Duncan (CA)	$4,000
		Hobson, David (OH)	$3,500

Public Affairs and Related Activities Personnel

At Headquarters

SCHNEIDER, Richard A.
Exec. V. President and Chief Financial Officer
Tel: (973) 898 - 1500
Fax: (973) 898 - 4730

Also serves as PAC contact.

WILLIAMSON, Patricia M.
V. President, Corporate Communications and Investor Relations
p.williamson@drs.com
Tel: (973) 898 - 1500 Ext: 6025
Fax: (973) 898 - 4730

At Washington Office

ANSLEY, Robert
V. President, Congressional Affairs
Tel: (703) 416 - 8000
Fax: (703) 416 - 8010

ATWELL, Robert
V. President, Army Programs
atwell@drs-esg.com
Tel: (703) 416 - 8000
Fax: (703) 416 - 8010

BOWMAN, Mike
Executive V. President, Washington Operations
bowman@drs-esg.com
Tel: (703) 416 - 8000
Fax: (703) 416 - 8010

CROCKER, Michael
V. President, Navy Programs
mdcrocker@drs-esg.com
Tel: (703) 416 - 8000
Fax: (703) 416 - 8010

HANSEN, Kip L.
V. President, Government Relations
khansen@drs-esg.com
Registered Federal Lobbyist.
Tel: (703) 416 - 8000
Fax: (703) 416 - 8010

REYNARD, Richard
V. President
Registered Federal Lobbyist.
Tel: (703) 416 - 8000
Fax: (703) 416 - 8010

Drummond Co., Inc.

A company engaged in coal mining and production of coke and coal-based chemicals.
www.drummondco.com

Chairman and Chief Exec. Officer
DRUMMOND, Garry
Tel: (205) 945 - 6300
Fax: (205) 945 - 6521

Main Headquarters
Mailing: P.O. Box 10246
Birmingham, AL 35202
Tel: (205) 945 - 6300
Fax: (205) 945 - 6570

Political Action Committees

Drummond Co. Inc. Political Action Committee (DPAC)
Contact: E. Bruce Windham
P.O. Box 10246
Birmingham, AL 35202
Tel: (205) 387 - 0501
Fax: (205) 945 - 6570

Contributions to Candidates: $3,000 (01/05 - 09/05)
Democrats: $1,000; Republicans: $2,000.

Principal Recipients

SENATE DEMOCRATS		HOUSE DEMOCRATS	
Byrd, Robert C (WV)	$1,000		

SENATE REPUBLICANS		HOUSE REPUBLICANS	
		Everett, Terry (AL)	$2,000

Corporate Foundations and Giving Programs

Drummond Co., Inc. Contributions Program
Contact: Walter F. Johnsey
P.O. Box 10246
Birmingham, AL 35202
Tel: (205) 945 - 6300
Fax: (205) 945 - 6570

Annual Grant Total: none reported
Geographic Preference: Alabama; Area(s) in which the company operates

Public Affairs and Related Activities Personnel

At Headquarters

JOHNSEY, Walter F.
Senior Exec. V. President, External Affairs
Tel: (205) 945 - 6300
Fax: (205) 945 - 6570

TRACY, Mike
Manager, Public Relations; President, Mining Division
Tel: (205) 945 - 6518
Fax: (205) 945 - 6522

WINDHAM, E. Bruce
Director, Regulatory and Governmental Relations
Tel: (205) 387 - 0501
Fax: (205) 945 - 6570

DST Systems, Inc.

A computer software services provider.
www.dstsystems.com
Annual Revenues: $2.4 billion

President and Chief Exec. Officer
MCDONNELL, Thomas A.
Tel: (816) 435 - 1000
Fax: (816) 435 - 8630
TF: (888) 378 - 4636

Main Headquarters
Mailing: 333 W. 11th St.
Kansas City, MO 64105
Tel: (816) 435 - 1000
Fax: (816) 435 - 8630
TF: (888) 378 - 4636

Public Affairs and Related Activities Personnel

At Headquarters

METZLER, Jill
Media Relations Contact
jdmetzler@dstsystems.com
Tel: (816) 843 - 9087
Fax: (816) 843 - 9245
TF: (888) 378 - 4636

SCHLATTER, Julie A.
Director, Corporate Marketing and Technology Communications
Tel: (816) 435 - 1000
Fax: (816) 435 - 8630
TF: (888) 378 - 4636

DTE Energy Co.

A member of the Public Affairs Council. Provides energy through its two principal subsidiaries, Detroit Edison and Michigan Consolidated Gas Co. Acquired MCN Energy Group Inc. in 2001.
www.dteenergy.com
Annual Revenues: $7.114 billion

Chairman and Chief Exec. Officer
EARLEY, Anthony F., Jr.
Tel: (313) 235 - 8000

Main Headquarters
Mailing: 2000 Second Ave.
Detroit, MI 48226
Tel: (313) 235 - 8000

Washington Office
Contact: Renze Hoeksema
Mailing: 601 Pennsylvania Ave. NW
Suite 350, North Bldg.
Washington, DC 20004-3613
Tel: (202) 347 - 8420
Fax: (202) 347 - 8423

Political Action Committees

DTE Energy PAC (EDPAC-Federal)
Contact: Douglas Ziemnick
2000 Second Ave.
Detroit, MI 48226
Tel: (313) 235 - 8000
Fax: (313) 235 - 0327

Contributions to Candidates: $112,830 (01/05 - 09/05)
Democrats: $47,250; Republicans: $65,580.

Principal Recipients

SENATE DEMOCRATS		HOUSE DEMOCRATS	
Stabenow, Debbie (MI)	$3,500	Stupak, Bart (MI)	$5,000
Bingaman, Jeff (NM)	$2,000	Conyers, John Jr. (MI)	$2,500

SENATE REPUBLICANS		HOUSE REPUBLICANS	
Santorum, Richard (PA)	$2,000	Hastert, Dennis J. (IL)	$5,000
Thomas, Craig (WY)	$2,000	Knollenberg, Joe (MI)	$5,000
		DeLay, Tom (TX)	$4,000
		Camp, David Lee (MI)	$3,000
		Rogers, Michael J (MI)	$3,000

Corporate Foundations and Giving Programs

DTE Energy Foundation
Contact: Karla Hall

DTE Energy Co.

* continued from previous page

2000 Second Ave.
Detroit, MI 48226
Tel: (313) 235 - 9271
Fax: (313) 235 - 0285

Annual Grant Total: over $5,000,000

Geographic Preference: Area in which the company is headquartered

Primary Interests: Community Affairs; Economic Development; Engineering; Environment/Conservation; Minority Opportunities

Recent Recipients: Detroit Institute of Arts; Habitat for Humanity; United Way; University of Detroit; West Shore Symphony

Public Affairs and Related Activities Personnel

At Headquarters

HALL, Karla
V. President and Foundation Secretary
Tel: (313) 235 - 9271
Fax: (313) 235 - 0285

HILLEGONDS, Paul
Senior V. President, Corporate Affairs and Communications
Mailstop: 2476WCB
Tel: (313) 235 - 8000

KESSLER, Lorie
Director, Media Relations
kesslerl@dteenergy.com
Tel: (313) 235 - 5555

PORTER, Michael C.
V. President, Corporate Communications
Tel: (313) 235 - 8850

SHELL, Fred
V. President, Corporate and Governmental Affairs
Tel: (313) 235 - 8000

ZIEMNICK, Douglas
PAC Treasurer
Tel: (313) 235 - 8000
Fax: (313) 235 - 0327

At Washington Office

BRITTO, Karen
Manager, Federal Affairs
brittok@dteenergy.com
Registered Federal Lobbyist.
Tel: (202) 347 - 8420
Fax: (202) 347 - 8423

DEANNA, Jennifer
Legislative Assistant
deanna@dteenergy.com
(Detroit Edison)
Registered Federal Lobbyist.
Tel: (202) 347 - 8420
Fax: (202) 347 - 8423

HOEKSEMA, Renze
Director, Federal Affairs
Registered Federal Lobbyist.
Tel: (202) 347 - 8420
Fax: (202) 347 - 8423

JONES, Mark
Regional Manager, Federal Affairs
Tel: (202) 347 - 8420
Fax: (202) 347 - 8423

At Other Offices

MOODY, Nancy
Director, State Government Affairs
101 S. Washington Square, Suite 700
Lansing, MI 48933-1708
Tel: (517) 371 - 2350
Fax: (517) 371 - 1016

Duchossois Industries, Inc.

A diversified manufacturing and services organization involved in transportation, consumer products, defense, and entertainment.

Chairman of the Board
DUCHOSSOIS, Richard L.
Tel: (630) 279 - 3600
Fax: (630) 530 - 6091
TF: (800) 282 - 6225

President and Chief Exec. Officer
DUCHOSSOIS, Craig J.
cjd@duch.com
Tel: (630) 279 - 3600
Fax: (630) 530 - 6057
TF: (800) 282 - 6225

Main Headquarters
Mailing: 845 Larch Ave.
Elmhurst, IL 60126
Tel: (630) 279 - 3600
Fax: (630) 530 - 6091
TF: (800) 528 - 5880

Political Action Committees

Duchossois Industries Inc. Political Action Committee
Contact: Robert L. Fealy
845 Larch Ave.
Elmhurst, IL 60126
Tel: (630) 279 - 3600
Fax: (630) 993 - 8644
TF: (800) 282 - 6225

Contributions to Candidates: $6,500 (01/05 - 09/05)
Democrats: $1,000; Republicans: $5,500.

Principal Recipients

SENATE DEMOCRATS		HOUSE DEMOCRATS	
		Bean, Melissa (IL)	$1,000
SENATE REPUBLICANS		**HOUSE REPUBLICANS**	
Santorum, Richard (PA)	$3,000	McSweeney, David (IL)	$2,500

Corporate Foundations and Giving Programs

Duchossois Family Foundation
Contact: Kimberly T. Duchossois
845 Larch Ave.
Elmhurst, IL 60126
Tel: (630) 279 - 3600
Fax: (630) 530 - 6057
TF: (800) 282 - 6225

Annual Grant Total: $300,000 - $400,000

Geographic Preference: Chicago, IL

Primary Interests: Arts and Culture; Medical Research; Mental Health; Youth Services

Public Affairs and Related Activities Personnel

At Headquarters

DUCHOSSOIS, Kimberly T.
President, Duchossois Family Foundation
Tel: (630) 279 - 3600
Fax: (630) 530 - 6057
TF: (800) 282 - 6225

FEALY, Robert L.
Treasurer, Duchossois Industries Inc. Political Action Committee
rfealy@duch.com
Tel: (630) 279 - 3600
Fax: (630) 993 - 8644
TF: (800) 282 - 6225

Duke Energy Corp.

A member of the Public Affairs Council. An electric utility. Duke Power Co. merged with PanEnergy in 1996 and became Duke Energy Corp. in 1997. In May 2005, the company announced its intention to merge with Cinergy Corp. (see separate listing).

www.duke-energy.com
Annual Revenues: $59.503 billion

Chairman and Chief Exec. Officer
ANDERSON, Paul M.
Mailstop: M/S EC3XB
pmanderson@duke-energy.com
Tel: (704) 382 - 3525
Fax: (704) 382 - 3588

Main Headquarters
Mailing: P.O. Box 1244
Charlotte, NC 28201-1244
Street: 526 S. Church St.
Charlotte, NC 28202-1904
Tel: (704) 594 - 6200
Fax: (704) 382 - 3588

Washington Office
Contact: Beverly K. Marshall
Mailing: 401 Ninth St. NW
Suite 1100
Washington, DC 20004
Tel: (202) 331 - 8090
Fax: (202) 331 - 1181

Corporate Foundations and Giving Programs

The Duke Energy Foundation
P.O. Box 1244
Charlotte, NC 28201-1244
Tel: (704) 594 - 6200
Fax: (704) 382 - 3588

Annual Grant Total: over $5,000,000

Geographic Preference: North Carolina; South Carolina

Primary Interests: Community Affairs; Education

Recent Recipients: Art Council; Independent College Fund; United Way

Public Affairs and Related Activities Personnel

At Headquarters

ADAMS, Susie C.
V. President, Public Affairs/Duke Power
Mailstop: M/S EC12X
sadams@duke-energy.com
Tel: (704) 382 - 8978
Fax: (704) 382 - 4629

BOWMAN, Roberta B.
V. President, External Relations
Mailstop: M/S PB040
rbowman@duke-energy.com
Tel: (704) 382 - 8347
Fax: (704) 382 - 3800

CLAUNCH, Charles K.
Regional Director, State Government Affairs-South Carolina
Mailstop: M/S PB05D
cclaunch@duke-energy.com
Tel: (704) 373 - 6622
Fax: (704) 382 - 3588

DILL, Julie
V. President, Investor Relations
Mailstop: EC3XK
jadill@duke-energy.com
Tel: (704) 382 - 4332
Fax: (704) 382 - 3588

EBEL, Gregory L.
V. President, Investor and Shareholder Relations
Mailstop: M/S PB03E
glebel@duke-energy.com
Tel: (704) 382 - 8118
Fax: (704) 382 - 0084

EVERETT, George T.
V. President, Environment and Public Policy/Duke Power
Mailstop: M/S EC12H
gteverett@duke-energy.com
Tel: (704) 373 - 4363
Fax: (704) 373 - 5393

HAGER, Janice
V. President, Rates and Regulatory Affairs
Mailstop: EC12H
jdhager@duke-energy.com
Tel: (704) 382 - 6963
Fax: (704) 382 - 3588

Duke Energy Corp.

* continued from previous page

HARWOOD, Joseph E. — Tel: (704) 382 - 8194
V. President, State Government Affairs — Fax: (704) 382 - 3588
Mailstop: M/S PB05D
jharwood@duke-energy.com

HAUSER, David L. — Tel: (704) 382 - 5963
Chief Financial Officer — Fax: (704) 382 - 3588
Mailstop: EC3XF
dhauser@duke-energy.com

HENDRICKS, James R., Jr. — Tel: (704) 382 - 8203
V. President, Corporate Environment, Health, and Safety — Fax: (704) 382 - 3588
Mailstop: M/S EC12ZA
jhendricks@duke-energy.com

KELLEY, Winston R. — Tel: (704) 382 - 5783
V. President, Government and Business Relations/Duke Power — Fax: (704) 382 - 3264
Mailstop: M/S EC12B
wrkelley@duke-energy.com

MCALISTER, John W. — Tel: (704) 382 - 8346
Regional Director, North Carolina Governmental Affairs — Fax: (704) 382 - 3588
Mailstop: M/S PB05D
jwmcalister@duke-energy.com

OSBORNE, Richard J. — Tel: (704) 382 - 5159
Group V. President, Public and Regulatory Policy
Mailstop: M/S EC3XG
rosborne@duke-energy.com

RHYNE, Lisa A. — Tel: (704) 382 - 8357
PAC Contact — Fax: (704) 382 - 3558

ROCHE, Cathy S. — Tel: (704) 373 - 4860
V. President, Corporate Communications — Fax: (704) 382 - 8375
Mailstop: M/S EC06G
csroche@duke-energy.com

ROLFE, Christopher C. — Tel: (704) 382 - 4343
V. President, Human Resources — Fax: (704) 382 - 3588
Mailstop: M/S PB04M
crolfe@duke-energy.com

SHEFFIELD, Peter — Tel: (704) 373 - 4503
Manager, Media — Fax: (704) 382 - 8375
Mailstop: M/S ECO6G
pysheffield@duke-energy.com

WHEELESS, Charles Randy — Tel: (704) 382 - 8979
Senior Communications Specialist (General Corporate Info, Human Resources, E-business, IT/IM, Environment) — Fax: (704) 382 - 8375
Mailstop: M/S ECO6G
crwheele@duke-energy.com

At Washington Office

HAYWOOD, Michael S. — Tel: (202) 331 - 8090
Director, Federal Government Affairs — Fax: (202) 331 - 1181
mshaywood@duke-energy.com

HYDE, Richard W. — Tel: (202) 331 - 8090
Director, Federal Governmental Affairs-Washington — Fax: (202) 331 - 1181
rwhyde@duke-energy.com

MARSHALL, Beverly K. — Tel: (202) 331 - 8090
V. President, Federal Government Affairs — Fax: (202) 331 - 1181
bkmarshall@duke-energy.com

MITCHELL, David F. — Tel: (202) 331 - 8090
Director, EHS Federal Government Affairs — Fax: (202) 331 - 1181
dmitchel@duke-energy.com

At Other Offices

BECK, Toni — Tel: (713) 627 - 5720
V. President, Public Affairs, DEGT
P.O. Box 1642
Houston, TX 77251-1642

BISHOP, Russell E. — Tel: (303) 605 - 1765
V. President, Governmental Affairs — Fax: (303) 893 - 2613
370 17th St., Suite 900
Denver, CO 80202
rbishop@duke-energy.com

FAHRENTHOLD, Brian C. — Tel: (713) 627 - 4814
Regional Director, State Governmental Affairs — Fax: (713) 989 - 3076
P.O. Box 1642
Houston, TX 77251-1642
bcfahren@duke-energy.com

HANLEY, Marylee — Tel: (617) 560 - 1573
Manager, Government and Public Affairs, DEGT/Maritimes
1284 Soldiers Field Rd.
Boston, MA 02135
mhanley@duke-energy.com

MCGUIRE-HECKMAN, Laura — Tel: (713) 627 - 4332
Regional Director, State Governmental Affairs — Fax: (713) 989 - 3076
P.O. Box 1642
Mailstop: M/S W0-9C60
Houston, TX 77251-1642
lmcguireheckman@duke-energy.com

PEREZ, Katherine C. — Tel: (713) 627 - 6527
Director, Public Affairs/DENA — Fax: (713) 627 - 5767
P.O. Box 1642
Houston, TX 77251-1642
kperez@duke-energy.com

SHERIDAN, John P. — Tel: (617) 560 - 1444
Regional Director, State Governmental Affairs — Fax: (617) 560 - 1580
1284 Soldiers Field Rd.
Mailstop: M/S WO-6P41
Boston, MA 02135
jpsheridan@duke-energy.com

The Dun & Bradstreet Corp.

Provides business-to-business credit, marketing, and purchasing information and related services.

www.dnb.com
Annual Revenues: $1.4 billion

Chairman and Chief Exec. Officer
ALESIO, Steven W. — Tel: (973) 921 - 5500

Main Headquarters
Mailing: 103 JFK Pkwy.
Short Hills, NJ 07078 — Tel: (973) 921 - 5500

Corporate Foundations and Giving Programs

The Dun & Bradstreet Corp. Foundation
Contact: Eileen Baker
103 JFK Pkwy.
Short Hills, NJ 07078 — Tel: (973) 921 - 5500

Assets: $1,132,364 (1999)
Annual Grant Total: $750,000 - $1,000,000
Geographic Preference: National
Primary Interests: Arts and Culture; Community Affairs; Health and Human Services; Higher Education
Recent Recipients: Junior Achievement; Nat'l Urban League

Public Affairs and Related Activities Personnel

At Headquarters

BAKER, Eileen — Tel: (973) 921 - 5500
Manager, The Dun & Bradstreet Corp. Foundation
bakere@dnb.com

CLIFFORD, Patricia A. — Tel: (973) 921 - 5500
V. President, Human Resources
cliffordp@dnb.com
Responsibilities include corporate communications.

GUINNESSEY, Kathleen M. — Tel: (973) 921 - 5665
Vice President, Treasury and Investor Relations
guinnesseyk@dnb.com

RUDICH, Yvette — Tel: (973) 921 - 5986
Leader, Global External Communications

Dunkin' Brands

Formerly operated as Allied Domecq Quick Service Restaurants. Includes Dunkin' Donuts, Baskin Robbins, and Togo's. A division of Allied Domecq plc of Bristol, England.

www.dunkinbrands.com

Chief Exec. Officer
LUTHER, Jon — Tel: (781) 737 - 5200; Fax: (781) 986 - 6987

Main Headquarters
Mailing: 130 Royall St.
Canton, MA 02021 — Tel: (781) 737 - 5200; Fax: (781) 986 - 6987

Public Affairs and Related Activities Personnel

At Headquarters

DECHANTAL, RoJean — Tel: (781) 737 - 5200
People Services Officer — Fax: (781) 986 - 6987

KING, Michelle — Tel: (781) 737 - 3585
Media Contact — Fax: (781) 986 - 6987
michelle.king@dunkinbrands.com

KRAVETZ, Carolyn — Tel: (781) 737 - 3602
Media Contact — Fax: (781) 986 - 6987

DuPont

A member of the Public Affairs Council. A science company that develops science-based solutions to meet human needs worldwide.

www.dupont.com
Annual Revenues: $24.726 billion

Chairman and Chief Exec. Officer
HOLLIDAY, Charles O., Jr. — Tel: (302) 773 - 2495; Fax: (302) 773 - 2919; TF: (800) 441 - 7515

Main Headquarters
Mailing: 1007 Market St.
Wilmington, DE 19898 — Tel: (302) 774 - 1000; Fax: (302) 773 - 2919; TF: (800) 441 - 7515

DuPont

* *continued from previous page*

Washington Office

Contact: Nancie S. Johnson

Mailing: 601 Pennsylvania Ave. NW, North Bldg., Suite 325, Washington, DC 20004 — Tel: (202) 728 - 3600; Fax: (202) 728 - 3649

Political Action Committees

DuPont Good Government Fund
Contact: Mr. Marc Legere
1007 Market St.
Wilmington, DE 19898
Tel: (302) 774 - 1000
Fax: (302) 773 - 2919
TF: (800) 441 - 7515

Contributions to Candidates: $86,750 (01/05 - 09/05)

Democrats: $17,500; Republicans: $69,250.

Principal Recipients

SENATE DEMOCRATS		HOUSE DEMOCRATS	
Carper, Thomas R (DE)	$4,500	Clyburn, James (SC)	$2,500
SENATE REPUBLICANS		**HOUSE REPUBLICANS**	
Allen, George (VA)	$9,000	Castle, Michael (DE)	$5,000
Burns, Conrad (MT)	$5,000	Lewis, Jerry (CA)	$3,000
Ensign, John Eric (NV)	$5,000	Jindal, Bobby (LA)	$2,500
Talent, James (MO)	$5,000	Poe, Ted (TX)	$2,250
Alexander, Lamar (TN)	$3,000		
Corker Jr, Robert P (TN)	$2,500		

Corporate Foundations and Giving Programs

DuPont Contributions
DuPont External Affairs
1007 Market St., N-9520
Wilmington, DE 19898
Tel: (302) 774 - 2416
Fax: (302) 773 - 2919

Annual Grant Total: over $5,000,000

Assistance in higher education administered by Committee on Educational Aid; other grants made through Contributions Committee. Giving totalled approximately $28 million in 1999.

Geographic Preference: Area in which the company is headquartered; Area(s) in which the company operates; National; International

Primary Interests: Education; Environment/Conservation; Health and Human Services; Medicine and Health Care

Public Affairs and Related Activities Personnel

At Headquarters

BANKS, Sylvia
Team Leader, Corporate Contributions and Community Affairs
Mailstop: D-11046
Tel: (302) 773 - 2731
Fax: (302) 773 - 2919
TF: (800) 441 - 7515

BOREL, Jam
Senior V. President, Human Resources
Tel: (302) 774 - 1000
Fax: (302) 773 - 2919
TF: (800) 441 - 7515

CAPTAIN, Lorie
Manager, Public Affairs and Human Resources Communications
Tel: (302) 774 - 1000
Fax: (302) 773 - 2919
TF: (800) 441 - 7515

FISHER, Linda
V. President, Safety, Health and Environment
Tel: (302) 774 - 4060
Fax: (302) 773 - 2919
TF: (800) 441 - 7515

FORTE, Kathleen H.
V. President, DuPont Global Public Affairs
Mailstop: D-11030
kathleen.h.forte@usa.dupont.com
Tel: (302) 773 - 4418
Fax: (302) 773 - 0188
TF: (800) 441 - 7515

LEGERE, Mr. Marc
PAC Treasurer
Mailstop: Room D-11078
Tel: (302) 774 - 1000
Fax: (302) 773 - 2919
TF: (800) 441 - 7515

LUKACH, Carol
V. President, Investor Relations
Tel: (302) 774 - 0583
Fax: (302) 774 - 7321
TF: (800) 441 - 7515

WEBB, Clif
Director, Corporate Media Relations
Mailstop: D-11028-1
r-clifton.webb@usa.dupont.com
Tel: (302) 774 - 4005
Fax: (302) 774 - 9560
TF: (800) 441 - 7515

At Washington Office

BOYKIN, Clete
Senior Manager, Government Affairs
Registered Federal Lobbyist.
Tel: (202) 728 - 3645
Fax: (202) 728 - 3649

JACKSON, Tami S.
Manager, State Government and Public Affairs
tami.s.jackson@usa.dupont.com
Tel: (202) 728 - 3645
Fax: (202) 728 - 3649

JOHNSON, Nancie S.
V. President, Government Affairs
nancie.s.johnson@usa.dupont.com
Tel: (202) 728 - 3645
Fax: (202) 728 - 3649

PARR, Michael
Sr.Manager, Government Affairs
Tel: (202) 728 - 3661
Fax: (202) 728 - 3649

PUGLIESE, Frank P., Jr.
Managing Director, Government Affairs
Registered Federal Lobbyist.
Tel: (202) 728 - 3600
Fax: (202) 728 - 3649

Duquesne Light Co.

See listing on page 170 under Duquesne Light Holdings.

Duquesne Light Holdings

Formerly known as DQE, Inc. A utility holding company.

www.dqe.com

Annual Revenues: $1.3 billion

Chairman of the Board
BOZZONE, Robert P.
Tel: (412) 393 - 6000
Fax: (412) 393 - 6448

President and Chief Exec. Officer
O'BRIEN, Morgan K.
mobrien@dqe.com
Tel: (412) 393 - 6000
Fax: (412) 393 - 6448

Main Headquarters

Mailing: 411 Seventh Ave., Pittsburgh, PA 15219 — Tel: (412) 393 - 6000; Fax: (412) 393 - 6448

Political Action Committees

Duquesne Light Co. Federal PAC
Contact: Anthony Pekny
411 Seventh Ave.
Pittsburgh, PA 15219
Tel: (412) 393 - 6000
Fax: (412) 393 - 6448

Contributions to Candidates: $500 (01/05 - 09/05)

Republicans: $500.

Principal Recipients

SENATE REPUBLICANS	HOUSE REPUBLICANS	
	Hart, Melissa (PA)	$500

Corporate Foundations and Giving Programs

Duquesne Light Co. Contributions Program
411 Seventh Ave.
Pittsburgh, PA 15219
Tel: (412) 393 - 6000
Fax: (412) 393 - 6448

Annual Grant Total: $500,000 - $750,000

Giving limited to Allegheny and Beaver counties, PA.

Geographic Preference: Pennsylvania

Public Affairs and Related Activities Personnel

At Headquarters

COATES, Pam
Manager, Community Relations
pcoates@dqe.com
Tel: (412) 393 - 6000
Fax: (412) 393 - 6448

HENLEY, Maria
Public Involvement Specialist
Tel: (412) 393 - 1405
Fax: (412) 393 - 6110

LAUDENSLAGER, John
Senior Manager, Media and Government Relations
jlaudenslager@dqe.com
Tel: (412) 393 - 1502
Fax: (412) 393 - 5517

LUCCI, Jerry
General Manager, Corporate Communications
jlucci@dqe.com
Tel: (412) 393 - 1258
Fax: (412) 393 - 1412

PEKNY, Anthony
PAC Treasurer
Tel: (412) 393 - 6000
Fax: (412) 393 - 6448

ROSS, Thomas E.
Manager, Shareholder Relations
tross@dqe.com
Tel: (412) 393 - 1191
Fax: (412) 393 - 1263

SIEBER, Rich
Manager, Marketing Communications (Duquesne Light Co.)
rsieber@dqe.com
Tel: (412) 393 - 6393
Fax: (412) 393 - 6825

Dura Automotive Systems, Inc.

Manufacturer of automotive components.

www.duraauto.com

Chairman of the Board
RUED, Scott D.
Tel: (248) 299 - 7500
Fax: (248) 299 - 7501

President and Chief Exec. Officer
DENTON, Lawrence A.
Tel: (248) 299 - 7500
Fax: (248) 299 - 7501

Main Headquarters

Mailing: 2791 Research Dr., Rochester Hills, MI 48309-3575 — Tel: (248) 299 - 7500; Fax: (248) 299 - 7501

Dura Automotive Systems, Inc.

** continued from previous page*

Public Affairs and Related Activities Personnel

At Headquarters

GRISHAM, Marlene — Tel: (248) 299 - 7500
Marketing — Fax: (248) 299 - 7501
Responsibilities include corporate communications.

SKOTAK, Theresa L. — Tel: (248) 299 - 7500
V. President, Human Resources — Fax: (248) 299 - 7501

Dynegy, Inc.

Produces and delivers energy, including natural gas, power, natural gas liquids, and coal through its owned and contractually controlled network of pipelines and other physical assets. Subsidiaries include Illinois Power Co. (see separate listing). Merged with Illinova Corp. in 2000.
www.dynegy.com
Annual Revenues: $42.242 billion

Chairman, President and Chief Exec. Officer
WILLIAMSON, Bruce A. — Tel: (713) 507 - 6400 — Fax: (713) 507 - 3871

Main Headquarters
Mailing: 1000 Louisiana St.
Suite 5800
Houston, TX 77002-5050
Tel: (713) 507 - 6400
Fax: (713) 507 - 3871

Political Action Committees

Dynegy Inc. Political Action Committee
Contact: Steven Dalhoff
1000 Louisiana St.
Suite 5800
Houston, TX 77002-5050
Tel: (713) 507 - 6400
Fax: (713) 507 - 3871

Contributions to Candidates: $2,000 (01/05 - 09/05)
Democrats: $2,000.

Principal Recipients

SENATE DEMOCRATS		HOUSE DEMOCRATS	
Bingaman, Jeff (NM)	$1,000	Costello, Jerry F (IL)	$1,000

Corporate Foundations and Giving Programs

Dynegy Corporate Giving Program
Contact: David Byford
1000 Louisiana St.
Suite 5800
Houston, TX 77002-5050
Tel: (713) 507 - 6400
Fax: (713) 507 - 3871

Annual Grant Total: none reported

Public Affairs and Related Activities Personnel

At Headquarters

BYFORD, David — Tel: (713) 507 - 6400
Director, Public Relations — Fax: (713) 507 - 3871
david.byford@dynegy.com
Responsibilities include corporate philanthropy

DALHOFF, Steven — Tel: (713) 507 - 6400
Treasurer, Dynegy Inc. PAC — Fax: (713) 507 - 3871

JOHNSON, Linda — Tel: (713) 507 - 6400
V. President, Human Resources — Fax: (713) 507 - 3871

SOUSA, John — Tel: (713) 507 - 6400
V. President, Public Relations — Fax: (713) 507 - 3871
john.sousa@dynegy.com
Responsibilities include corporate philanthropy.

WILT, Peter J. — Tel: (713) 507 - 6400
V. President, Investor Relations — Fax: (713) 507 - 3871

E.I. du Pont de Nemours & Co.

See listing on page 169 under DuPont.

Eagle-Picher Industries, Inc.

A diversified manufacturer of chemicals, electronic and precision products, machinery, plastic coatings and rubber products for automotive, industrial and machinery use.
www.epcorp.com

President and Chief Exec. Officer
WEBER, John H. — Tel: (602) 794 - 9600 — Fax: (602) 794 - 9601

Main Headquarters
Mailing: 3402 E. University Dr.
Phoenix, AZ 85034
Tel: (602) 794 - 9600
Fax: (602) 794 - 9601

Public Affairs and Related Activities Personnel

At Headquarters

BLOOM, Cyndi — Tel: (602) 794 - 9604
Manager, Marketing Communications — Fax: (602) 794 - 9601

HARPER, Paul D. — Tel: (602) 794 - 9600
Director, Environmental Affairs and Safety — Fax: (602) 794 - 9601

MILLS, Gerald T. — Tel: (602) 794 - 9600
Senior V. President, Human Resources — Fax: (602) 794 - 9601

Earthlink, Inc.

An internet service provider.
www.earthlink.com

President and Chief Exec. Officer
BETTY, Charles Garry — Tel: (404) 815 - 0770 — Fax: (404) 815 - 8805

Main Headquarters
Mailing: 1375 Peachtree St.
Atlanta, GA 30309
Tel: (404) 815 - 0770
Fax: (404) 815 - 8805

Political Action Committees

Earthlink, Inc. PAC
Contact: James Hoeberling
1375 Peachtree St.
Atlanta, GA 30309
Tel: (404) 815 - 0770
Fax: (404) 815 - 8805

Contributions to Candidates: none reported (01/05 - 09/05)

Public Affairs and Related Activities Personnel

At Headquarters

GALLENTINE, Mike — Tel: (404) 748 - 7153
V. President, Investor Relations — Fax: (404) 815 - 8805

GARBERTH, Deisha — Tel: (404) 815 - 0770
Media Relations Contact — Fax: (404) 815 - 8805

GREENFIELD, Daniel — Tel: (404) 815 - 0770
V. President, Corporate Communications — Fax: (404) 815 - 8805

HOEBERLING, James — Tel: (404) 815 - 0770
Contact, Earthlink, Inc. PAC — Fax: (404) 815 - 8805

UHLIG, Ken — Tel: (404) 815 - 0770
Chief People Officer — Fax: (404) 815 - 8805

Eastern Enterprises

See listing on page 279 under KeySpan Corp.

Eastern Utilities Associates

See listing on page 339 under Nat'l Grid USA.

Eastman Chemical Co.

A member of the Public Affairs Council. A producer of chemicals, fibers and plastics.
www.eastman.com
Annual Revenues: $6.6 billion

Chairman and Chief Exec. Officer
FERGUSON, J. Brian — Tel: (423) 229 - 5901
ferguson@eastman.com — Fax: (423) 224 - 0323 — TF: (800) 327 - 8626

Main Headquarters
Mailing: P.O. Box 511
Kingsport, TN 37662-5075
Tel: (423) 229 - 2000
Fax: (423) 224 - 0323
TF: (800) 327 - 8626

Street: 200 S. Wilcox
Kingsport, TN 37662

Washington Office
Contact: Rodney D. Irvin
Mailing: 1300 Wilson Blvd.
Suite 900
Arlington, VA 22209-2307
Tel: (703) 524 - 7700
Fax: (703) 524 - 7707

Political Action Committees

EASTPAC, Political Action Committee of Eastman Chemical Co.
Contact: Rodney D. Irvin
1300 Wilson Blvd.
Suite 900
Arlington, VA 22209-2307
Tel: (703) 524 - 7647
Fax: (703) 524 - 7707

Contributions to Candidates: $20,000 (01/05 - 09/05)
Democrats: $6,500; Republicans: $13,500.

Principal Recipients

SENATE DEMOCRATS		HOUSE DEMOCRATS	
Pryor, Mark (AR)	$1,500	Boucher, Fredrick (VA)	$1,000
Baucus, Max (MT)	$1,000	Davis, Lincoln (TN)	$1,000
		Gordon, Barton (TN)	$1,000
		Tanner, John S. (TN)	$1,000

SENATE REPUBLICANS		HOUSE REPUBLICANS	
DeMint, James (SC)	$2,500	Wamp, Zach (TN)	$2,000
Allen, George (VA)	$2,000	Duncan, John (TN)	$1,000
Graham, Lindsey (SC)	$1,000	Gohmert, Louis (TX)	$1,000
Santorum, Richard (PA)	$1,000	Hall, Ralph (TX)	$1,000
Talent, James (MO)	$1,000	Wilson, Joe (SC)	$1,000

Corporate Foundations and Giving Programs

Eastman Chemical Corporate Contributions
Contact: Paul Montgomery

Eastman Chemical Co.

** continued from previous page*

P.O. Box 431 Tel: (423) 229 - 1413
Kingsport, TN 37662 Fax: (423) 229 - 8280

Annual Grant Total: $2,000,000 - $5,000,000

Public Affairs and Related Activities Personnel

At Headquarters

BLEDSOE, Tracy
Communications Representative
tracyb@eastman.com
Tel: (423) 224 - 0498
Fax: (423) 229 - 1004
TF: (800) 327 - 8626

BRINKLEY, Teresa
Advanced Community Relations Representative
Tel: (423) 229 - 6811
Fax: (423) 229 - 1008
TF: (800) 327 - 8626

DEAN, C. Fletcher
Principal Communications Representative
Tel: (423) 229 - 3880
Fax: (423) 229 - 1008
TF: (800) 327 - 8626

HARRIS, Sandy
Corporate Information Center
eastman1@eastman.com
Tel: (423) 229 - 2196
Fax: (423) 224 - 0323
TF: (800) 327 - 8626

HUGHES, Vickie
Senior Exec. Assistant, Communications and Public Affairs
vhughes@eastman.com
Tel: (423) 229 - 1302
Fax: (423) 229 - 1679
TF: (800) 327 - 8626

LAWSON, Martha G.
Director, Communications and Brand Management
mglawson@eastman.com
Tel: (423) 229 - 6574
Fax: (423) 229 - 1008
TF: (800) 327 - 8626

LEDFORD, Nancy
Manager, Disclosure Communications
nledford@eastman.com
Tel: (423) 229 - 5264
Fax: (423) 229 - 1008
TF: (800) 327 - 8626

RIDDLE, Gregory A.
Director, Investor Relations
griddle@eastman.com
Tel: (423) 229 - 8692
Fax: (423) 229 - 1351
TF: (800) 327 - 8626

SCHURGER, Marc
Director, Product Safety and Health
Tel: (423) 229 - 5921
Fax: (423) 224 - 0208
TF: (800) 327 - 8626

Responsibilities include environmental affairs.

SHAFFER, Teresa
Community Relations Representative
shaffert@eastman.com
Tel: (423) 229 - 6962
Fax: (423) 224 - 0847
TF: (800) 327 - 8626

SNEED, Norris P.
Senior V. President, Communications, Public Affairs, Human Resources and Organizational Effectiveness
npsneed@eastman.com
Tel: (423) 229 - 8498
Fax: (423) 229 - 1679
TF: (800) 327 - 8626

SORRELLS, J. Charles
Government Relations Fellow
Tel: (423) 229 - 8111
Fax: (423) 229 - 8280
TF: (800) 327 - 8626

VALENTINE, Wanda
Community Relations Associate
wandav@eastman.com
Tel: (423) 229 - 4406
Fax: (423) 229 - 8280
TF: (800) 327 - 8626

WAGNER, Anna
Senior Administrative Assistant, Government Relations
awagner@eastman.com
Tel: (423) 229 - 2030
Fax: (423) 229 - 8280
TF: (800) 327 - 8626

WATKINS, Katherine R.
Manager, Marketing Communications
Tel: (423) 229 - 3078
Fax: (423) 229 - 1525
TF: (800) 327 - 8626

At Washington Office

IRVIN, Rodney D.
Director, Government Relations
rodirvin@eastman.com
Registered Federal Lobbyist.
Tel: (703) 524 - 7647
Fax: (703) 524 - 7707

SCHLOESSER, Lynn L.
Manager, Federal Government Relations
Registered Federal Lobbyist.
Tel: (703) 524 - 7661
Fax: (703) 524 - 7707

At Other Offices

CHILDRESS, Mike
Manager, Communication and Public Affairs (Texas)
P.O. Box 7444
Longview, TX 75607-7444
Tel: (903) 237 - 5082
Fax: (903) 237 - 5704

MONTGOMERY, Paul
Director, Community Relations and Corporate Travel
P.O. Box 431
Kingsport, TN 37662
pmontgomery@eastman.com
Responsibilities include corporate philanthropy.
Tel: (423) 229 - 1413
Fax: (423) 229 - 8280

Eastman Kodak Company

PUBLIC AFFAIRS COUNCIL

A member of the Public Affairs Council. A manufacturer of photographic equipment and materials. Also manufactures health care products and office equipment.

www.kodak.com
Annual Revenues: $13.317 billion

Chairman of the Board
CARP, Daniel A.
Tel: (585) 724 - 4000
Fax: (585) 724 - 1724

Chief Exec. Officer and President
PEREZ, Antonio
Tel: (585) 724 - 4000
Fax: (585) 724 - 1724

Main Headquarters
Mailing: 343 State St.
Rochester, NY 14650-0516
Tel: (585) 724 - 4000
Fax: (585) 724 - 1724

Washington Office
Contact: Stephen J. Ciccone
Mailing: 1250 H St. NW
Suite 800
Washington, DC 20005
Tel: (202) 857 - 3400
Fax: (202) 857 - 3401

Political Action Committees

Eastman Kodak Co. Employee PAC
Contact: Celeste Amaral
343 State St.
Rochester, NY 14650-0516
Tel: (585) 724 - 4000
Fax: (585) 724 - 1724

Contributions to Candidates: $42,000 (01/05 - 09/05)
Democrats: $18,000; Republicans: $24,000.

Principal Recipients

SENATE DEMOCRATS

Clinton, Hillary Rodham (NY)	$5,000
Baucus, Max (MT)	$1,000
Carper, Thomas R (DE)	$1,000
Ford, Harold E Jr (TN)	$1,000
Kennedy, Ted (MA)	$1,000

HOUSE DEMOCRATS

Jefferson, William (LA)	$2,000
Meeks, Gregory W (NY)	$2,000

SENATE REPUBLICANS

Dewine, Richard (OH)	$2,000
Snowe, Olympia (ME)	$1,000

HOUSE REPUBLICANS

Reynolds, Thomas (NY)	$5,000
Johnson, Nancy (CT)	$3,000
Sweeney, John E. (NY)	$3,000
Kuhl, John R Jr (NY)	$2,000
Walden, Gregory (OR)	$2,000

Corporate Foundations and Giving Programs

Eastman Kodak Charitable Trust
Contact: Essie L. Calhoun
343 State St.
Rochester, NY 14650-0516
Tel: (585) 724 - 1980
Fax: (585) 724 - 1376

Annual Grant Total: over $5,000,000
Geographic Preference: Area(s) in which the company operates; New York; Colorado
Primary Interests: Arts and Culture; Health and Human Services; Higher Education; Minority Opportunities
Recent Recipients: Massachusetts Institute of Technology; United Negro College Fund; United Way

Public Affairs and Related Activities Personnel

At Headquarters

AMARAL, Celeste
Treasurer, Eastman Kodak Co. Employee PAC
Tel: (585) 724 - 4000
Fax: (585) 724 - 1724

BENARD, Michael
V. President, Communications and Public Affairs
Tel: (585) 724 - 4000
Fax: (585) 724 - 4854

CALHOUN, Essie L.
Director, Community Relations and Contributions
Tel: (585) 724 - 1980
Fax: (585) 724 - 1376

FLICK, Donald
Director, Investor Relations
donald.flick@kodak.com
Tel: (585) 724 - 4683
Fax: (585) 724 - 1089

HICKMAN, Jan
Director, Employee Communications
jan.hickman@kodak.com
Tel: (585) 724 - 4408
Fax: (585) 724 - 9610

KISER, David
V. President and Director, Corporate Health, Safety and Environment
david.kiser@kodak.com
Tel: (585) 724 - 4000
Fax: (585) 724 - 1724

At Washington Office

CHENGALUR, Soma
Director, Health, Safety and Environmental Policy
Tel: (202) 857 - 3400
Fax: (202) 857 - 3401

CICCONE, Stephen J.
Director and V. President, Public Affairs
stephen.ciccone@kodak.com
Tel: (202) 857 - 3400
Fax: (202) 857 - 3401

DEOL, Jasprit
Director, Technology Policy
jasprit.deol@kodak.com
Tel: (202) 857 - 3400
Fax: (202) 857 - 3401

HARRINGTON, W. Brendan
Director, International Trade Relations
brendan.harrington@kodak.com
Tel: (202) 857 - 3400
Fax: (202) 857 - 3401

JARMAN, Richard B.
Director, Advanced Manufacturing Affairs
richard.jarman@kodak.com
Registered Federal Lobbyist.
Tel: (202) 857 - 3400
Fax: (202) 857 - 3401

Eastman Kodak Company

** continued from previous page*

JONES, Diane R. — Tel: (202) 857 - 3462 / Fax: (202) 857 - 3401
Director, Public Affairs - Health Imaging
diane.jones@kodak.com
Registered Federal Lobbyist.

POWELL, Aquila — Tel: (202) 857 - 3465 / Fax: (202) 857 - 3401
Director, Workforce Policy
aquila.powell@kodak.com

At Other Offices

HICKERSON, David B. — Tel: (773) 867 - 3570 / Fax: (773) 867 - 3571
Manager, State and Local Government Relations - Midwest Region
8600 W. Bryn Mawr Ave.
Suite 800 South
Chicago, IL 60631
david.hickerson@kodak.com

MANTELLI, Lucille M. — Tel: (970) 686 - 4102 / Fax: (970) 686 - 4154
Director, Communications and Public Affairs (Kodak Division)
9952 Eastman Park Dr.
Windsor, CO 80551-1334
lucille.mantelli@kodak.com

Eaton Corp.

A member of the Public Affairs Council. A global manufacturer of highly engineered products that serve the vehicle, industrial, construction, commercial and aerospace markets.
www.eaton.com
Annual Revenues: $9.8 billion

Chairman and Chief Exec. Officer
CUTLER, Alexander M. "Sandy" — Tel: (216) 523 - 4092 / Fax: (216) 523 - 4787

Main Headquarters
Mailing: Eaton Center
1111 Superior Ave.
Cleveland, OH 44114-2584
Tel: (216) 523 - 5000 / Fax: (216) 523 - 4787

Political Action Committees

Eaton Corp. Public Policy Association (EPPA)
Contact: Robert A. Elliott
Eaton Center
1111 Superior Ave.
Cleveland, OH 44114-2584
Tel: (216) 523 - 5000 / Fax: (216) 523 - 4787

Contributions to Candidates: $500 (01/05 - 09/05)
Republicans: $500.

Principal Recipients

SENATE REPUBLICANS		HOUSE REPUBLICANS	
		Dewine, R. Pat (OH)	$500

Corporate Foundations and Giving Programs

Eaton Charitable Fund
Contact: William B. "Barry" Doggett
Eaton Center
1111 Superior Ave.
Cleveland, OH 44114-2584
Tel: (216) 523 - 4664 / Fax: (216) 479 - 7013

Assets: $9,979,741 (2002)
Annual Grant Total: $2,000,000 - $5,000,000
Geographic Preference: Area(s) in which the company operates
Primary Interests: Arts and Culture; Education; United Way Campaigns
Recent Recipients: Habitat for Humanity; Junior Achievement; YMCA

Public Affairs and Related Activities Personnel

At Headquarters

COOK, Susan J. — Tel: (216) 523 - 4651 / Fax: (216) 523 - 4787
V. President, Human Resources
susancook@eaton.com

DOGGETT, William B. "Barry" — Tel: (216) 523 - 4664 / Fax: (216) 479 - 7013
V. President, Public and Community Affairs

ELLIOTT, Robert A. — Tel: (216) 523 - 5000 / Fax: (216) 523 - 4787
PAC Treasurer

HARTMAN, William C. — Tel: (216) 523 - 4501 / Fax: (216) 479 - 7020
V. President, Investor Relations
WilliamHartman@eaton.com

HESS, Christopher D. — Tel: (216) 523 - 4198 / Fax: (216) 479 - 7013
Manager, Public Affairs
christopherdhess@eatonm.com

RUNCIS, Veronica M. — Tel: (216) 523 - 4835 / Fax: (216) 479 - 7013
Manager, Corporate Contributions
veronicaruncis@eaton.com

STITT, Emily A. — Tel: (216) 523 - 4450 / Fax: (216) 479 - 7013
Administrator, Matching Gifts
emmystitt@eaton.com

WEIDNER, Tim J. — Tel: (216) 523 - 4744 / Fax: (216) 479 - 7080
Manager, Digital Communications
TimWeidner@eaton.com

eBay, Inc.

An online trading community with an auction-style format. Enables individuals and businesses to trade items at the local, national, and international levels.
www.ebay.com
Annual Revenues: $748.8 million

Founder and Chairman
OMIDYAR, Pierre M. — Tel: (408) 558 - 7400 / Fax: (408) 558 - 7401 / TF: (800) 322 - 9266
pomidyar@ebay.com

President and Chief Exec. Officer
WHITMAN, Margaret C. "Meg" — Tel: (408) 558 - 7400 / Fax: (408) 558 - 7401 / TF: (800) 322 - 9266
mwhitman@ebay.com

Main Headquarters
Mailing: 2145 Hamilton Ave.
San Jose, CA 95125
Tel: (408) 558 - 7400 / Fax: (408) 558 - 7401 / TF: (800) 322 - 9266

Political Action Committees

eBay Inc.-Committee for Responsible Internet Commerce
Contact: Sharon McBride
228 S. Washington St., Suite 115
Alexandria, VA 22314

Contributions to Candidates: $27,717 (01/05 - 09/05)
Democrats: $8,153; Republicans: $19,564.

Principal Recipients

SENATE DEMOCRATS		HOUSE DEMOCRATS	
Nelson, Benjamin (NE)	$2,000	Boucher, Fredrick (VA)	$1,000
		Cooper, James (TN)	$1,000
		Eshoo, Anna (CA)	$1,000
		Matheson, James (UT)	$1,000
		Smith, Adam (WA)	$1,000
		Towns, Edolphus (NY)	$1,000

SENATE REPUBLICANS		HOUSE REPUBLICANS	
Cornyn, John (TX)	$1,000	Cannon, Christopher (UT)	$3,564
DeMint, James (SC)	$1,000	Dreier, David (CA)	$2,000
Ensign, John Eric (NV)	$1,000	Fortenberry, Jeffrey (NE)	$1,000
Hagel, Charles T (NE)	$1,000	Goodlatte, Robert (VA)	$1,000
Hutchison, Kay Bailey (TX)	$1,000	Hart, Melissa (PA)	$1,000
		Manzullo, Donald (IL)	$1,000
		Northup, Anne M. (KY)	$1,000
		Pickering, Chip (MS)	$1,000
		Terry, Lee (NE)	$1,000
		Upton, Fred (MI)	$1,000

Corporate Foundations and Giving Programs

The eBay Foundation
Contact: Irene Wong
60 S. Market St.
Suite 1000
San Jose, CA 95113

Annual Grant Total: none reported
Community grants given only to 501(c)3 organizations in San Jose, CA and Salt Lake City, UT. See website for guidelines.
Geographic Preference: Area(s) in which the company operates
Primary Interests: Technology
Recent Recipients: Junior Achievement; Net Corps Americas

Public Affairs and Related Activities Personnel

At Headquarters

AXELROD, Beth — Tel: (408) 558 - 7400 / Fax: (408) 558 - 7401 / TF: (800) 322 - 9266
Senior V. President, Human Resources

BARRETT, Nancy E. — Tel: (408) 558 - 7400 / Fax: (408) 558 - 7401 / TF: (800) 322 - 9266
V. President, Human Resources

GOMEZ, Henry — Tel: (408) 558 - 7400 / Fax: (408) 558 - 7401 / TF: (800) 322 - 9266
Senior V. President, Corporate Communications and Government Relations

JACOBSON, Michael R. — Tel: (408) 558 - 7400 / Fax: (408) 558 - 7401 / TF: (800) 322 - 9266
V. President, Legal Affairs, General Counsel and Secretary
mjacobson@ebay.com

eBay, Inc.

** continued from previous page*

At Other Offices

MCBRIDE, Sharon
PAC Director
228 S. Washington St., Suite 115
Alexandria, VA 22314

TEMMINS, Amy
Program Coordinator, eBay Foundation
60 S. Market St.
Suite 1000
San Jose, CA 95113

WONG, Irene
Exec. Director, eBay Foundation
60 S. Market St.
Suite 1000
San Jose, CA 95113

Contributions to Candidates: $10,357 (01/05 - 09/05)

Democrats: $6,000; Republicans: $4,357.

Principal Recipients

SENATE DEMOCRATS		HOUSE DEMOCRATS	
		Boucher, Fredrick (VA)	$1,000
		Conyers, John Jr. (MI)	$1,000
		Dingell, John D (MI)	$1,000
		Doyle, Mike (PA)	$1,000
		Lofgren, Zoe (CA)	$1,000
		Udall, Mark (CO)	$1,000
SENATE REPUBLICANS		**HOUSE REPUBLICANS**	
Ensign, John Eric (NV)	$857	Upton, Fred (MI)	$1,500
		Bass, Charles (NH)	$1,000
		Terry, Lee (NE)	$1,000

Public Affairs and Related Activities Personnel

At Headquarters

CAULK, Stece
Director, Public Relations and Investor Relations
Tel: (303) 723 - 1000
Fax: (303) 723 - 1399

LUMPKIN, Marc
Director, Communications
marc.lumpkin@echostar.com
Contractor
Tel: (303) 723 - 2020
Fax: (303) 723 - 1399

At Washington Office

LIEBERMAN, Ross J.
Government Relations
Registered Federal Lobbyist.
Tel: (202) 293 - 0981
Fax: (202) 293 - 0984

WATSON, Karen E.
Director, Government Relations
Registered Federal Lobbyist.
Tel: (202) 293 - 0981
Fax: (202) 293 - 0984

EBSCO Industries, Inc.

A global sales, service, and manufacturing corporation.

www.ebscoind.com

Chairman of the Board
STEPHENS, J. T.
Tel: (205) 991 - 6600
Fax: (205) 995 - 1517

Chief Exec. Officer
BROOKE, F. Dixon, Jr.
dbrooke@ebsco.com
Tel: (205) 991 - 6600
Fax: (205) 995 - 1517

Main Headquarters
Mailing: P.O. Box 1943
Birmingham, AL 35201-1943
Street: 5724 Hwy. 280 East
Birmingham, AL 35242
Tel: (205) 991 - 6600
Fax: (205) 995 - 1517

Corporate Foundations and Giving Programs

EBSCO Industries, Inc. Corporate Giving Program

Contact: Wanda Dimon

P.O. Box 1943
Birmingham, AL 35201-1943
Tel: (205) 991 - 6600
Fax: (205) 995 - 1517

Annual Grant Total: none reported

Public Affairs and Related Activities Personnel

At Headquarters

BONNETT, Madelyn C.
Assistant General Manager, Corporate Communications
Tel: (205) 991 - 6600
Fax: (205) 995 - 1517

DIMON, Wanda
Contact, EBSCO Industries, Inc. Corporate Giving Program
Tel: (205) 991 - 6600
Fax: (205) 995 - 1517

THOMPSON, John
Director, Human Resources
jthompson@ebsco.com
Tel: (205) 991 - 6600
Ext: 1100
Fax: (205) 995 - 1517

THOMPSON, Sheri C.
Manager, Public Relations
scthompson@ebsco.com
Tel: (205) 991 - 1278
Fax: (205) 995 - 1636

EchoStar Communications Corp.

A communications company. Known for the broadcast t.v. services it provides through its brand name DISH Network.

www.dishnetwork.com

Annual Revenues: $4.8 billion

Chairman and Chief Exec. Officer
ERGEN, Charles W.
Tel: (303) 723 - 1000
Fax: (303) 723 - 1399

Main Headquarters
Mailing: 9601 S. Meridian Blvd.
Englewood, CO 80112
Tel: (303) 723 - 1000
Fax: (303) 723 - 1399

Washington Office
Contact: Karen E. Watson
Mailing: 1233 20th St., NW
Suite 701
Washington, DC 20036
Tel: (202) 293 - 0981
Fax: (202) 293 - 0984

Political Action Committees

EchoStar Communications Corp. PAC

Contact: Karen E. Watson

1233 20th St., NW
Suite 701
Washington, DC 20036
Tel: (202) 293 - 0981
Fax: (202) 293 - 0984

Ecolab Inc.

A worldwide developer and marketer of cleaning and sanitizing products, systems and services for the hospitality, foodservice, and healthcare industries.

www.ecolab.com

Chairman of the Board
SCHUMAN, Allan L.
Tel: (651) 293 - 2233
Fax: (651) 225 - 2092

Chief Exec. Officer
BAKER, Douglas
Tel: (651) 293 - 2233
Fax: (651) 225 - 2092

Main Headquarters
Mailing: Ecolab Center
370 N. Wabasha St.
St. Paul, MN 55102
Tel: (651) 293 - 2233
Fax: (651) 225 - 2092

Political Action Committees

Ecolab Inc. PAC

Contact: Jeffrey K. Peterson

Ecolab Center
370 N. Wabasha St.
St. Paul, MN 55102
Tel: (651) 293 - 2557
Fax: (651) 225 - 3274

Contributions to Candidates: $8,000 (01/05 - 09/05)

Democrats: $1,000; Republicans: $6,000; Other: $1,000.

Principal Recipients

SENATE DEMOCRATS		HOUSE DEMOCRATS	
Conrad, Kent (ND)	$1,000		
		HOUSE OTHER	
		Peterson, Collin (MN)	$1,000
SENATE REPUBLICANS		**HOUSE REPUBLICANS**	
Kennedy, Mark (MN)	$2,000	Capito, Shelley (WV)	$1,000
		Hastert, Dennis J. (IL)	$1,000
		Kline, John P (MN)	$1,000
		Weller, Jerry (IL)	$1,000

Corporate Foundations and Giving Programs

Ecolab Foundation

Contact: Kris Taylor

Ecolab Inc.

** continued from previous page*

Ecolab Center
370 N. Wabasha St.
St. Paul, MN 55102
Tel: (651) 293 - 2259
Fax: (651) 225 - 2092

Annual Grant Total: $1,000,000 - $2,000,000

Recent local recipients include: Business Economics Education Foundation (Minneapolis) and St. Paul Chamber Orchestra (St. Paul). Guidelines are available.

Geographic Preference: Area(s) in which the company operates
Primary Interests: Education

Public Affairs and Related Activities Personnel

At Headquarters

FORSYTHE, John G. "Jack"
Senior V. President, Tax and Public Affairs
jack.forsythe@ecolabl.com
Tel: (651) 293 - 2642
Fax: (651) 225 - 2092

LEWIS, Diana D.
V. President, Human Resources
diana.lewis@ecolab.com
Tel: (651) 293 - 2344
Fax: (651) 225 - 2092

MONAHAN, Michael J.
V. President, External Relations
michael.monahan@ecolab.com
Tel: (651) 293 - 2809
Fax: (651) 225 - 3123
Responsibilities include corporate contributions and investor relations.

MORELLI, Carla A.
Administrative Assistant
carla.morelli@ecolab.com
Tel: (651) 293 - 2148
Fax: (651) 225 - 3274
Responsibilities include government affairs.

PETERSON, Jeffrey K.
Director, Government Relations; and PAC Administrator
jeff.k.peterson@ecolab.com
Tel: (651) 293 - 2557
Fax: (651) 225 - 3274

TAYLOR, Kris
Director, Community Relations
Tel: (651) 293 - 2259
Fax: (651) 225 - 2092

WESTERHAUS, James
V. President, Government Relations
jim.westerhaus@ecolab.com
Tel: (651) 293 - 2183
Fax: (651) 225 - 3274

Eddie Bauer, Inc.

www.eddiebauer.com

President and Chief Exec. Officer
MANSSON, Fabian
Tel: (425) 755 - 6100
Fax: (425) 755 - 7696

Main Headquarters
Mailing: 15010 NE 36th St.
Redmond, WA 98052
Tel: (425) 755 - 6100
Fax: (425) 755 - 7696

Public Affairs and Related Activities Personnel

At Headquarters

BORRELLI, Elizabeth
Director, Public Affairs and Corporate Social Responsibility
Tel: (425) 755 - 6643
Fax: (425) 755 - 7696

Edison Internat'l

A generator and distributor of electric power anad an investor in infrastructure and energy assets includin renewable energy. Parent company of Southern California Edison (see separate listing).

www.edison.com
Annual Revenues: $10.2 billion

Chairman, President and Chief Exec. Officer
BRYSON, John E.
john.bryson@edisonintl.com
Tel: (626) 302 - 2222

Main Headquarters
Mailing: 2244 Walnut Grove Ave.
Rosemead, CA 91770
Tel: (626) 302 - 1212

Washington Office
Contact: Polly L. Gault
Mailing: 555 12th St. NW
Suite 640
Washington, DC 20004-2505
Tel: (202) 393 - 3075
Fax: (202) 393 - 1497

Political Action Committees

Edison Internat'l PAC
Contact: Paul E. Shay, Jr.
2244 Walnut Grove Ave.
Rosemead, CA 91770
Tel: (626) 302 - 1984
Fax: (626) 302 - 6315

Contributions to Candidates: $121,000 (01/05 - 09/05)
Democrats: $49,000; Republicans: $72,000.

Principal Recipients

SENATE DEMOCRATS

HOUSE DEMOCRATS

Matsui, Doris (CA)	$5,000

SENATE REPUBLICANS

Lugar, Richard G (IN)	$5,000
Allen, George (VA)	$2,000
Smith, Gordon (OR)	$2,000
Thomas, Craig (WY)	$2,000

HOUSE REPUBLICANS

Shadegg, John (AZ)	$6,000
McKeon, Howard (CA)	$5,000
Royce, Ed Mr (CA)	$5,000
Lungren, Daniel E (CA)	$4,500

Corporate Foundations and Giving Programs

Edison International Foundation/ Edison International Corporate Giving
Contact: Beverly P. Ryder
2244 Walnut Grove Ave.
Rosemead, CA 91770
Tel: (626) 302 - 2204
Fax: (626) 302 - 2240

Assets: $72,000 (2005)
Annual Grant Total: over $5,000,000

Geographic Preference: Area in which the company is headquartered; California
Primary Interests: Arts and Humanities; Community Development; Environment/Conservation; Higher Education

Public Affairs and Related Activities Personnel

At Headquarters

KELLEY, Kevin
Manager, Media Relations
kevin.kelley@edisonintl.com
Tel: (626) 302 - 1033

LEONI, Nanette
Manager, Investor Relations
nanette.leoni@edisonintl.com
Tel: (626) 302 - 3680

NEWTON, Jo Ann
V. President, Investor Relations
joann.newton@edisonintl.com
Tel: (626) 302 - 2515

PARSKY, Barbara J.
V. President, Corporate Communications
barbara.parsky@edisonintl.com
Tel: (626) 302 - 2204

RYDER, Beverly P.
V. President, Community Involvement and Secretary
beverly.ryder@sce.com
Tel: (626) 302 - 2204
Fax: (626) 302 - 2240

SHAY, Paul E., Jr.
PAC Treasurer
Tel: (626) 302 - 1984
Fax: (626) 302 - 6315

TOWNSHEND-ZELLNER, Heidi
Manager, Shareholder Services
heidi.townshend@edisonintl.com
Tel: (626) 302 - 1453

At Washington Office

GAULT, Polly L.
V. President, Public Affairs
Tel: (202) 393 - 3075
Fax: (202) 393 - 1497

SANTOS, Barbara J.
Government Relations Assistant
Tel: (202) 393 - 3075
Fax: (202) 393 - 1497

SHOTWELL, James P.
Director, Federal Regulatory Affairs
Tel: (202) 393 - 3075
Fax: (202) 393 - 1497

WEINSTEIN, Warren
Manager, Federal Affairs
Tel: (202) 393 - 3075
Fax: (202) 393 - 1497

EDS Corp.

An information technology services company.

www.eds.com
Annual Revenues: $21.543 billion

Chairman and Chief Exec. Officer
JORDAN, Michael H.
Tel: (972) 604 - 6000
Fax: (972) 605 - 6841

Main Headquarters
Mailing: 5400 Legacy Dr.
Plano, TX 75024-3199
Tel: (972) 605 - 6000
Fax: (972) 605 - 6841

Washington Office
Contact: William R. Sweeney, Jr.
Mailing: 1331 Pennsylvania Ave. NW
Suite 1300 North
Washington, DC 20004
Tel: (202) 637 - 6700
Fax: (202) 637 - 6759

Political Action Committees

EDS PAC
Contact: William R. Sweeney, Jr.
1331 Pennsylvania Ave. NW
Suite 1300 North
Washington, DC 20004
Tel: (202) 637 - 6751
Fax: (202) 637 - 4974

Contributions to Candidates: $33,500 (01/05 - 09/05)
Democrats: $12,500; Republicans: $21,000.

Principal Recipients

SENATE DEMOCRATS

Bingaman, Jeff (NM)	$1,000
Cardin, Benjamin (MD)	$1,000
Lieberman, Joe (CT)	$1,000

HOUSE DEMOCRATS

Murtha, John P Mr. (PA)	$2,500
Moran, James (VA)	$2,000
Skelton, Ike (MO)	$2,000

SENATE REPUBLICANS

Bennett, Robert F (UT)	$2,000
Ensign, John Eric (NV)	$2,000
Burns, Conrad (MT)	$1,000
Hutchison, Kay Bailey (TX)	$1,000
Kyl, Jon L (AZ)	$1,000

HOUSE REPUBLICANS

Johnson, Nancy (CT)	$2,000
McCrery, Jim (LA)	$2,000

EDS Corp.

• continued from previous page

Corporate Foundations and Giving Programs

EDS Corporate Foundation
Contact: Diane Spradlin
5400 Legacy Dr. — Tel: (972) 605 - 6000
Plano, TX 75024-3199 — Fax: (972) 605 - 6841

Annual Grant Total: $100,000 - $200,000
The company places emphasis on volunteers over dollars and sponsors several programs reflecting this, including: EDS Global Volunteer Day; EDS Education Outreach Program; EDS Loaned Executive Program.

Geographic Preference: International; National
Primary Interests: Agriculture; Education; Health and Human Services

Public Affairs and Related Activities Personnel

At Headquarters

BLOCKER, Lisa A. — Tel: (972) 605 - 6091
Exec. Director, State Government Affairs — Fax: (972) 605 - 6090
Mailstop: M/S H3-6F-47

HAMOOD, Al — Tel: (972) 605 - 6001
V. President, Investor Relations — Fax: (972) 605 - 6841

HEALY, Sean — Tel: (972) 605 - 8173
Director, Corporate Public Relations — Fax: (972) 605 - 6841
shealy@eds.com

MATTIA, Tom — Tel: (972) 604 - 6000
V. President, Global Corporate Communications — Fax: (972) 605 - 6841
tom.mattia@eds.com

SIVINSKI, Tina — Tel: (972) 605 - 6000
Exec. V. President, Human Resources — Fax: (972) 605 - 6841

SPRADLIN, Diane — Tel: (972) 605 - 6000
Exec. Director, Foundation — Fax: (972) 605 - 6841

THORNTON, Lora — Tel: (972) 605 - 6818
Manager, Global Community Affairs and Corporate Contributions — Fax: (972) 605 - 6841
lora.thornton@eds.com

At Washington Office

BANCROFT, Virginia D. "Gina" — Tel: (202) 637 - 6702
PAC Director; Director, Global Government Affairs — Fax: (202) 637 - 6759
gina.bancroft@eds.com
Registered Federal Lobbyist.

BROWN, Gwen — Tel: (202) 637 - 6715
Director, Healthcare Policy — Fax: (202) 637 - 6759
gwen.brown@eds.com
Registered Federal Lobbyist.

DOVE, Randolph V. — Tel: (202) 637 - 6728
Exec. Director, Government Relations — Fax: (202) 637 - 6759
randy.dove@eds.com
Registered Federal Lobbyist.

FRANZ, Liesyl — Tel: (202) 637 - 6722
Director, Financial Industry Policy — Fax: (202) 637 - 6759
liesyl.franz@eds.com

JAMESON, Booth — Tel: (202) 637 - 6741
Director, Global Government Affairs — Fax: (202) 637 - 6759
booth.jameson@eds.com
Registered Federal Lobbyist.

MYERS, Karen Magee — Tel: (202) 637 - 6720
Director, Tax and Treasury Policy — Fax: (202) 637 - 6759
karen.myers@eds.com
Registered Federal Lobbyist.

SWEENEY, William R., Jr. — Tel: (202) 637 - 6751
V. President, Global Government Affairs — Fax: (202) 637 - 4974
bill.sweeney@eds.com
Registered Federal Lobbyist.

WARD, Stephen D. — Tel: (202) 637 - 6709
Director, Global Government Affairs — Fax: (202) 637 - 6759
stephen.ward@eds.com
Registered Federal Lobbyist.

At Other Offices

ADAMI, Kenneth R. — Tel: (402) 812 - 2885
Regional Director, Government Affairs, Southeast — Fax: (402) 812 - 2956
3715 Northside Pkwy.
Bldg. 100, Suite 800
Atlanta, GA 30327
ken.adami@eds.com

KWAPIS, Jennifer — Tel: (248) 650 - 0390
Mid-Atlantic and Midwest Regional Director, State Government
700 Tower Dr.
Troy, MI 48098
jennifer.kwapis@eds.com

SCHACHER, Alden — Tel: (415) 912 - 5250
Regional Director, State Government Affairs, West — Fax: (415) 912 - 5399
101 California St.
10th Floor
San Francisco, CA 94111
alden.schacher@eds.com

Edwards and Sons, Inc., A.G.

See listing on page 176 under A G Edwards, Inc.

Edwards Lifesciences Corp.

A member of the Public Affairs Council. Designs and manufactures products for persons with heart disease.

www.edwards.com
Annual Revenues: $704 million

Chairman and Chief Exec. Officer — Tel: (949) 250 - 2500
MUSSALLEM, Michael A. — Fax: (949) 250 - 2525
TF: (800) 424 - 3278

Main Headquarters
Mailing: One Edwards Way — Tel: (949) 250 - 2500
Irvine, CA 92614-5688 — Fax: (949) 250 - 2525
TF: (800) 424 - 3278

Political Action Committees

Edwards Lifesciences PAC (EWPAC)
Contact: Neleen Eisinger
One Edwards Way — Tel: (949) 250 - 2500
Irvine, CA 92614-5688 — Fax: (949) 250 - 2525
TF: (800) 424 - 3278

Contributions to Candidates: $2,000 (01/05 - 09/05)
Republicans: $2,000.

Principal Recipients

SENATE REPUBLICANS		HOUSE REPUBLICANS
Enzi, Michael B (WY)	$1,000	
Hatch, Orrin (UT)	$1,000	

Public Affairs and Related Activities Personnel

At Headquarters

EISINGER, Neleen — Tel: (949) 250 - 2500
Treasurer, EWPAC — Fax: (949) 250 - 2525
TF: (800) 424 - 3278

ERICKSON, David — Tel: (949) 250 - 6826
V. President, Investor Relations — Fax: (949) 250 - 2248
TF: (800) 424 - 3278

GARVEY, Patricia L., Ph.D. — Tel: (949) 250 - 2500
Corporate V. President, Regulatory, Quality and Clinical Affairs — Fax: (949) 250 - 2525
TF: (800) 424 - 3278

JACKSON, Laura Min — Tel: (949) 250 - 2500 Ext: 6804
V. President, Global Communications — Fax: (949) 250 - 2525
laura_jackson@edwards.com — TF: (800) 424 - 3278

LIDEN, Barry — Tel: (949) 250 - 6881
Director, Global Communications — Fax: (949) 250 - 2733
TF: (800) 424 - 3278

REINDL, Robert C. — Tel: (949) 250 - 2500
V. President, Human Resources — Fax: (949) 250 - 2525
TF: (800) 424 - 3278

A. G. Edwards, Inc.

Financial services and investment trust, asset management, and insurance banking. It's primary subsidiary is the brokerage firm A.G. Edwards and Sons, Inc.

www.agedwards.com
Annual Revenues: $2.6 billion

Chairman and Chief Exec. Officer — Tel: (314) 955 - 3000
BAGBY, Robert L. — Fax: (314) 955 - 5913
TF: (877) 835 - 7877

Main Headquarters
Mailing: One N. Jefferson Ave. — Tel: (314) 955 - 3000
St. Louis, MO 63103 — Fax: (314) 955 - 2890
TF: (877) 835 - 7877

Washington Office
Mailing: 5301 Wisconsin Ave. NW — Tel: (202) 364 - 1600
Suite 400 — Fax: (202) 537 - 4876
Washington, DC 20015

Corporate Foundations and Giving Programs

A. G. Edwards & Sons Corporate Giving Program
Contact: Justin J. Gioia

A. G. Edwards, Inc.

** continued from previous page*

One N. Jefferson Ave.
St. Louis, MO 63103
Tel: (314) 955 - 2379
Fax: (314) 955 - 5913
TF: (877) 835 - 7877

Annual Grant Total: none reported

Primary Interests: Arts and Culture; Community Development; Financial Planning; Health and Human Services

Recent Recipients: American Red Cross; United Way

Public Affairs and Related Activities Personnel

At Headquarters

CONWAY, Elaine
V. President/Manager, Corporate Communications
Tel: (314) 955 - 3355
Fax: (314) 955 - 2890
TF: (877) 835 - 7877

GIOIA, Justin J.
Associate V. President and Director of Investor Relations
Tel: (314) 955 - 2379
Fax: (314) 955 - 5913
TF: (877) 835 - 7877

Responsibilities include corporate philanthropy.

UNDERWOOD, Brian C.
V. President, Director of Compliance
Tel: (314) 955 - 3711
Fax: (314) 955 - 4308
TF: (877) 835 - 7877

WELCH, Margaret G.
Director, Public Relations
Tel: (314) 955 - 5912
Fax: (314) 955 - 5547
TF: (877) 835 - 7877

At Washington Office

TART, Wallace L.
Manager, DC Office
Tel: (202) 364 - 1600
Fax: (202) 537 - 4876

EG&G, Inc.

See listing on page 378 under PerkinElmer, Inc.

El Paso Corp.

A transporter of natural gas. Acquired The Coastal Corp. in 2001 and Sonat, Inc. in 1999.

www.elpaso.com

Annual Revenues: $57.475 billion

Chairman of the Board
KUEHN, Ronald L.
Tel: (713) 420 - 2131
Fax: (713) 420 - 4993

President and Chief Exec. Officer
FASHEE, Douglas L.
Tel: (713) 420 - 2600
Fax: (713) 420 - 4993

Main Headquarters

Mailing: P.O. Box 2511
Houston, TX 77252-2511
Tel: (713) 420 - 2600
Fax: (713) 420 - 4993

Street: 1001 Louisiana St.
Houston, TX 77002

Washington Office

Mailing: 555 11th St. NW
Suite 750
Washington, DC 20004
Tel: (202) 637 - 3506
Fax: (202) 637 - 3504

Political Action Committees

El Paso Corp. Political Action Committee
P.O. Box 2511
Houston, TX 77252-2511
Tel: (713) 420 - 2600
Fax: (713) 420 - 4993

Contributions to Candidates: $22,000 (01/05 - 09/05)

Democrats: $5,000; Republicans: $17,000.

Principal Recipients

SENATE DEMOCRATS

Nelson, Benjamin (NE) $2,000
Bingaman, Jeff (NM) $1,000

SENATE REPUBLICANS

Kyl, Jon L (AZ) $5,000
Craig, Larry (ID) $1,000
Vitter, David (LA) $1,000

HOUSE DEMOCRATS

Green, Gene (TX) $1,000
Grijalva, Raul (AZ) $1,000

HOUSE REPUBLICANS

Renzi, Richard (AZ) $4,000
Blackburn, Marsha (TN) $1,000
Bonilla, Henry (TX) $1,000
Cannon, Christopher (UT) $1,000
Carter, John (TX) $1,000
Cubin, Barbara L (WY) $1,000
Linder, John (GA) $1,000

Corporate Foundations and Giving Programs

El Paso Corp. Foundation
P.O. Box 2511
Houston, TX 77252-2511
Tel: (713) 420 - 2600
Fax: (713) 420 - 4993

Assets: $20,852,761 (2001)

Annual Grant Total: over $5,000,000

Geographic Preference: Area(s) in which the company operates

Public Affairs and Related Activities Personnel

At Headquarters

BAERG, Bill
Manager, Investor Relations
Tel: (713) 420 - 2906
Fax: (713) 420 - 4993

BISHOP, Alan
Director, Shareholder Relations
alan.bishop@elpaso.com
Tel: (713) 420 - 5429
Fax: (713) 420 - 4099

CONNERY, Bruce L.
V. President, Investor and Public Relations
Tel: (713) 420 - 5855
Fax: (713) 420 - 4417

JASKOSKI, Peter J.
Director, Government Affairs
Tel: (713) 420 - 2600
Fax: (713) 420 - 4993

JONES, Chris
Manager, Investor Relations
Tel: (713) 420 - 4136
Fax: (713) 420 - 4417

MORITZ, Gloria
Coordinator, Community Relations
Tel: (713) 420 - 2600
Fax: (713) 420 - 4993

WHEATLEY, Richard
Manager, Media Relations
Tel: (713) 420 - 6828
Fax: (713) 420 - 4993

At Washington Office

BURPOE, Merryl
Director, International Government Affairs
Tel: (202) 637 - 3506
Fax: (202) 637 - 3504

El Paso Electric Co.

www.epelectric.com

Annual Revenues: $754.5 million

Chairman of the Board
EDWARDS, George W., Jr.
Tel: (915) 543 - 5711
Fax: (915) 521 - 4766
TF: (800) 351 - 1621

President and Chief Exec. Officer
HEDRICK, Gary R.
ghedrick@epelectric.com
Tel: (915) 543 - 5711
Fax: (915) 521 - 4766
TF: (800) 351 - 1621

Main Headquarters

Mailing: P.O. Box 982
El Paso, TX 79960
Tel: (915) 543 - 5711
Fax: (915) 521 - 4766
TF: (800) 351 - 1621

Street: 123 W. Mills
El Paso, TX 79901-1341

Political Action Committees

EPIC/El Paso Electric Company
Contact: Frank H. Vegil
P.O. Box 982
El Paso, TX 79960
Tel: (915) 543 - 5711
Fax: (915) 521 - 4766
TF: (800) 351 - 1621

Contributions to Candidates: none reported (01/05 - 09/05)

Public Affairs and Related Activities Personnel

At Headquarters

BUSSER, Steven P.
V. President, Regulatory Affairs and Treasurer
Tel: (915) 543 - 5711
Fax: (915) 521 - 4766
TF: (800) 351 - 1621

GAMEZ, Cynthia
Manager, Investor Relations
cgamez1@epelectric.com
Tel: (915) 543 - 2213
Fax: (915) 543 - 2299
TF: (800) 351 - 1621

QUINTANA, Henry, Jr.
Manager, Public Relations
hquintan@epelectric.com
Tel: (915) 543 - 5824
Fax: (915) 521 - 4766
TF: (800) 351 - 1621

RODRIGUEZ, Raymund
Governmental Affairs Representative
rrodrigu@epelectric.com
Tel: (915) 543 - 4156
Fax: (915) 543 - 2299
TF: (800) 351 - 1621

SOUZA, Teresa
News and Public Information Representative
Tel: (915) 543 - 5823
Fax: (915) 521 - 4766
TF: (800) 351 - 1621

VEGIL, Frank H.
PAC Treasurer
Tel: (915) 543 - 5711
Fax: (915) 521 - 4766
TF: (800) 351 - 1621

WILLIAMS, Rachelle
Investor Relations
rwilli5@epelectric.com
Tel: (915) 543 - 5711
Fax: (915) 521 - 4766
TF: (800) 351 - 1621

WILLIAMS KNOPP, Hellen
V. President, Public Affairs
hknopp@epelectric.com
Tel: (915) 543 - 5711
Fax: (915) 521 - 4766
TF: (800) 351 - 1621

El Paso Energy Corp.

See listing on page 177 under El Paso Corp.

Electrolux North America, Inc.

Formerly known as White Consolidated Industries, Inc. A diversified manufacturer of appliances for the home and outdoor power products for the lawn and garden. A subsidiary of Electrolux AB of Stockholm, Sweden.

www.electroluxusa.com

Main Headquarters

Mailing: P.O. Box 35920, Cleveland, OH 44135-0920 — Tel: (216) 898 - 1800; Fax: (216) 898 - 2393

Street: 20445 Emerald Pkwy. SW, Suite 250, Cleveland, OH 44135-0920

Public Affairs and Related Activities Personnel

At Headquarters

EDWARDS, Donna F.
Immigration/Legislative Specialist
Tel: (216) 898 - 2341
Fax: (216) 898 - 2366

MIX, Douglas
V. President, Regulatory Affairs
Tel: (216) 898 - 1800
Fax: (216) 898 - 2393

At Other Offices

EVANS, Anton N.
V. President, Communications
8252 Millhouse Ln.
Dublin, OH 43106
tony.evans@electrolux.com
Tel: (614) 761 - 2633
Fax: (614) 761 - 0689

Electronic Arts Inc.

Publishes software for entertainment purposes.

www.ea.com

Annual Revenues: $2.5 billion

Chairman and Chief Exec. Officer

PROBST, Lawrence F., III
Tel: (650) 628 - 1500
Fax: (650) 628 - 1415

Main Headquarters

Mailing: 209 Redwood Shores Pkwy., Redwood City, CA 94065-1175 — Tel: (650) 628 - 1500; Fax: (650) 628 - 1415

Public Affairs and Related Activities Personnel

At Headquarters

BROWN, Jeff
V. President, Corporate Communications
Tel: (650) 628 - 1500
Fax: (650) 628 - 1415

MULLER, Trudy
Senior Manager, Corporate Communications
Tel: (650) 628 - 1500
Fax: (650) 628 - 1415

NEWMAN, Neilly
Assistant V. President, Corporate Communications
Tel: (650) 628 - 1500
Fax: (650) 628 - 1415

RUEFF, J. Russell, Jr.
Exec. V. President, Human Resources
Tel: (650) 628 - 1500
Fax: (650) 628 - 1415

SANSOT, Karen
Director, Investor Relations
Tel: (650) 628 - 5597
Fax: (650) 628 - 1415

Electronic Data Systems Corp.

See listing on page 175 under EDS Corp.

EMC Corp.

A builder of information storage infrastructures.

www.emc.com

Chairman of the Board

RUETTGERS, Mike
Tel: (508) 435 - 1000
Fax: (508) 435 - 7954
TF: (800) 424 - 3622

President and Chief Exec. Officer

TUCCI, Joseph
Tel: (508) 435 - 1000
Fax: (508) 435 - 7954
TF: (800) 424 - 3622

Main Headquarters

Mailing: P.O. Box 9103, Hopkinton, MA 01748 — Tel: (508) 435 - 1000; Fax: (508) 497 - 6912; TF: (800) 424 - 3622

Street: 171 South St., Hopkinton, MA 01748

Washington Office

Mailing: 2011 Crystal Dr., Crystal Park 1, Suite 907, Arlington, VA 22202 — Tel: (703) 769 - 6203; Fax: (703) 892 - 0091

Political Action Committees

EMC Corp. Political Action Committee
Contact: Irina Simmons
P.O. Box 9103
Hopkinton, MA 01748
Tel: (508) 435 - 1000
Fax: (508) 435 - 7954
TF: (800) 424 - 3622

Contributions to Candidates: $26,000 (01/05 - 09/05)

Democrats: $8,500; Republicans: $17,500.

Principal Recipients

SENATE DEMOCRATS

Byrd, Robert C (WV)	$1,000

HOUSE DEMOCRATS

Clyburn, James (SC)	$2,000
Mollohan, Alan (WV)	$2,000
Moran, James (VA)	$2,000

SENATE REPUBLICANS

Allen, George (VA)	$1,000
Bond, Christopher (MO)	$1,000
Burns, Conrad (MT)	$1,000
Burr, Richard (NC)	$1,000
Chambliss, Saxby (GA)	$1,000
Ensign, John Eric (NV)	$1,000
Hutchison, Kay Bailey (TX)	$1,000

HOUSE REPUBLICANS

Bonilla, Henry (TX)	$2,000
Wicker, Roger (MS)	$2,000

Corporate Foundations and Giving Programs

EMC Corporate Giving Program
P.O. Box 9103
Hopkinton, MA 01748
Tel: (508) 435 - 1000
Fax: (508) 497 - 6912
TF: (800) 424 - 3622

Annual Grant Total: none reported

Geographic Preference: Area(s) in which employees live and work

Primary Interests: Community Development; K-12 Education; Math and Science; Minority Opportunities; Women

Recent Recipients: Boston Symphony Orchestra

Public Affairs and Related Activities Personnel

At Headquarters

DREYER, Jennifer
Manager, International Public Relations
dreyer_jennifer@emc.com
Tel: (508) 435 - 1000 Ext: 77238
Fax: (508) 497 - 6912
TF: (800) 424 - 3622

EDEN, Greg
Manager, Corporate Public Relations
eden_greg@emc.com
Tel: (508) 435 - 1000 Ext: 77195
Fax: (508) 435 - 7954
TF: (800) 424 - 3622

FREDERICKSON, Mark
V. President, Corporate Communications
Tel: (508) 435 - 1000 Ext: 77137
Fax: (508) 435 - 7954
TF: (800) 424 - 3622

GALLANT, Michael
Director, Public Relations
gallant_michael@emc.com
Tel: (508) 435 - 1000 Ext: 76357
Fax: (508) 435 - 7954
TF: (800) 424 - 3622

MOLLEN, John T. "Jack"
Senior V. President, Human Resources
Tel: (508) 435 - 1000
Fax: (508) 497 - 6912
TF: (800) 424 - 3622

PACE, Anne
Corporate Public Relations Manager
pace_anne@emc.com
Tel: (508) 435 - 1000 Ext: 77932
Fax: (508) 435 - 7954
TF: (800) 424 - 3622

SIMMONS, Irina
Senior V. President and PAC Treasurer
Tel: (508) 435 - 1000
Fax: (508) 435 - 7954
TF: (800) 424 - 3622

At Washington Office

HARTELL, Steve
Manager, Government Relations
Registered Federal Lobbyist.
Tel: (703) 892 - 0120
Fax: (703) 892 - 0091

LESSTRANG, David
Manager, Government Affairs
lesstrang_david@emc.com
Registered Federal Lobbyist.
Tel: (703) 769 - 6202
Fax: (703) 892 - 0091

METZ, Craig
Manager, Government Affairs
metz_craig@emc.com
Registered Federal Lobbyist.
Tel: (703) 769 - 6202
Fax: (703) 892 - 0091

SALISBURY, Keith
Director, Government Affairs
salisbury_keith@emc.com
Registered Federal Lobbyist.
Tel: (703) 769 - 6202
Fax: (703) 892 - 0091

EMCOR Group, Inc.

Specializes in mechanical and electrical construction, energy infrastucture and end-to-end facilities services.

www.emcorgroup.com

EMCOR Group, Inc.

* continued from previous page

Chairman and Chief Exec. Officer
MACINNIS, Frank — Tel: (203) 849 - 7800, Fax: (203) 849 - 7850
frank_macinnis@emcorgroup.com

Main Headquarters
Mailing: 301 Merritt Seven, Sixth Floor, Norwalk, CT 06851 — Tel: (203) 849 - 7800, Fax: (203) 849 - 7900, TF: (866) 890 - 7794

Public Affairs and Related Activities Personnel

At Headquarters

HEFFLER, Mava — Tel: (203) 849 - 7800, Fax: (203) 849 - 7870
V. President, Marketing and Communications

MATZ, R. Kevin — Tel: (203) 849 - 7800, Fax: (203) 849 - 7810
Senior V. President, Shared Services
kevin_matz@emcorgroup.com

NAMES, Christine — Tel: (203) 849 - 7800, Fax: (203) 849 - 7900
V. President, Human Resources

THRASHER, Rex C. — Tel: (203) 849 - 7800, Fax: (203) 849 - 7840
V. President, Risk Management
rex_thrasher@emcorgroup.com

Emerson

Formerly Emerson Electric Co. A manufacturer of electrical and electronic equipment.
www.gotoemerson.com

Chairman and Chief Exec. Officer
FARR, David N. — Tel: (314) 553 - 2000, Fax: (314) 553 - 3527

Main Headquarters
Mailing: P.O. Box 4100, St. Louis, MO 63136-8506 — Tel: (314) 553 - 2000, Fax: (314) 553 - 3527
Street: 8000 W. Florissant Ave., St. Louis, MO 63136-8506

Washington Office
Contact: Robert D. McDonald
Mailing: 700 13th St., N.W., Suite 700, Washington, DC 20005-3960 — Tel: (202) 508 - 6303, Fax: (202) 508 - 6305

Political Action Committees

Emerson Responsible Government Fund
Contact: Perry A. Roberts
P.O. Box 4100
St. Louis, MO 63136-8506 — Tel: (314) 553 - 3289, Fax: (314) 553 - 3414

Contributions to Candidates: $67,500 (01/05 - 09/05)
Democrats: $22,500; Republicans: $45,000.

Principal Recipients

SENATE DEMOCRATS		HOUSE DEMOCRATS	
Baucus, Max (MT)	$4,000	Jefferson, William (LA)	$3,000
Nelson, Benjamin (NE)	$3,000		
Lieberman, Joe (CT)	$2,500		

SENATE REPUBLICANS		HOUSE REPUBLICANS	
Talent, James (MO)	$9,000	Hastert, Dennis J. (IL)	$5,000
Dewine, Richard (OH)	$5,000	Blunt, Roy (MO)	$3,000

Corporate Foundations and Giving Programs

Emerson Charitable Trust
Contact: Robert Cox
P.O. Box 4100
St. Louis, MO 63136-8506 — Tel: (314) 553 - 2015, Fax: (314) 553 - 3527

Annual Grant Total: over $5,000,000
Geographic Preference: Area(s) in which the company operates; Arkansas; Illinois; Minnesota; Missouri; New Jersey; New York; Ohio
Primary Interests: Adult Education and Training; Engineering; Medicine and Health Care; Youth Services
Recent Recipients: United Way; University of Missouri

Public Affairs and Related Activities Personnel

At Headquarters

COX, Robert — Tel: (314) 553 - 2015, Fax: (314) 553 - 3527
Senior V. President
Mailstop: M/S 3722

FARMER, Jack — Tel: (314) 982 - 8630, Fax: (314) 982 - 9199
Media Relations Contact

HUTCHINSON, Phil — Tel: (314) 553 - 3420, Fax: (314) 553 - 3527
V. President, Human Resources
Mailstop: M/S 2278

POLZIN, Mark — Tel: (314) 982 - 1758, Fax: (314) 982 - 9100
Media Relations Contact

ROBERTS, Perry A. — Tel: (314) 553 - 3289, Fax: (314) 553 - 3414
V. President, Public Affairs
Mailstop: M/S 3289
perry.roberts@emrsn.com
Responsibilities include political action.

TUCKER, Chris — Tel: (314) 553 - 2197, Fax: (314) 553 - 1213
Director, Investor Relations
Mailstop: M/S 1068
Responsibilites include corporate communications.

At Washington Office

JACKSON, Lisa — Tel: (202) 508 - 6303, Fax: (202) 508 - 6305
Washington Representative

Registered Federal Lobbyist.

MCDONALD, Robert D. — Tel: (202) 508 - 6303, Fax: (202) 508 - 6305
V. President, Government Affairs
Registered Federal Lobbyist.

Emerson Electric Co.

See listing on page 179 under Emerson.

Emmis Communications Corp.

A media company including publishing, radio and t.v. broadcasting services.
www.emmis.com
Annual Revenues: $614.4 million

Chairman, President and Chief Exec. Officer
SMULYAN, Jeffrey H. — Tel: (317) 266 - 0100, Fax: (317) 631 - 3750

Main Headquarters
Mailing: 40 Monument Circle, Suite 700, Indianapolis, IN 46204 — Tel: (317) 266 - 0100, Fax: (317) 631 - 3750

Public Affairs and Related Activities Personnel

At Headquarters

HEALEY, Kate — Tel: (317) 684 - 6576, Fax: (317) 631 - 3750
Director, Investor Relations and Media Relations
kate@emmis.com

LEVITAN, Mickey — Tel: (317) 266 - 0100, Fax: (317) 631 - 3750
Senior V. President, Human Resources

LUND, Peter — Tel: (317) 266 - 0100, Fax: (317) 631 - 3750
Media Consultant

Empire Blue Cross and Blue Shield

www.empireblue.com
Annual Revenues: $5.8 billion

Chairman of the Board
MCGILLICUDDY, John — Tel: (212) 476 - 1000, Fax: (212) 476 - 1281

President and Chief Exec. Officer
STOCKER, Michael A., M.D. — Tel: (212) 476 - 1000, Fax: (212) 476 - 1281

Main Headquarters
Mailing: 11 W. 42nd St., New York, NY 10035 — Tel: (212) 476 - 1000, Fax: (212) 476 - 1281

Political Action Committees

WellChoice PAC
Contact: Deborah Loeb Bohren
11 W. 42nd St.
New York, NY 10035 — Tel: (212) 476 - 3552, Fax: (212) 476 - 1430

Contributions to Candidates: $2,000 (01/05 - 09/05)
Democrats: $2,000.

Principal Recipients

SENATE DEMOCRATS		HOUSE DEMOCRATS
Baucus, Max (MT)	$2,000	

Public Affairs and Related Activities Personnel

At Headquarters

BOHREN, Deborah Loeb — Tel: (212) 476 - 3552, Fax: (212) 476 - 1430
Senior V. President, Communications
Mailstop: 18th Floor
Responsibilities include investor relations.

EARLY, Karen — Tel: (212) 476 - 1000, Fax: (212) 476 - 1281
Assistant V. President, Communications

LAWRENCE, Robert W. — Tel: (212) 476 - 1000, Fax: (212) 476 - 1281
Senior V. President, Human Resources

Empire District Electric Co.

An electric utility serving S.W. Missouri, N.W. Arkansas, N.E. Oklahoma and S.E. Kansas.
www.empiredistrict.com

Chairman of the Board
MCKINNEY, Myron W. — Tel: (417) 625 - 5100, Fax: (417) 625 - 5155, TF: (800) 206 - 2300
mmckinney@empiredistrict.com

Empire District Electric Co.

** continued from previous page*

President and Chief Exec. Officer
GIPSON, Bill
bgipson@empiredistrict.com
Tel: (417) 625 - 5100
Fax: (417) 625 - 5155
TF: (800) 206 - 2300

Main Headquarters
Mailing: P.O. Box 127
Joplin, MO 64802-0127
Tel: (417) 625 - 5100
Fax: (417) 625 - 5155
TF: (800) 206 - 2300

Street: 602 Joplin St.
Joplin, MO 64802

Political Action Committees

Empire District Electric Co. PAC
Contact: David Martin
P.O. Box 127
Joplin, MO 64802-0127
Tel: (417) 625 - 6107
Fax: (417) 625 - 5155
TF: (800) 206 - 2300

Contributions to Candidates: $2,000 (01/05 - 09/05)
Republicans: $2,000.

Principal Recipients

SENATE REPUBLICANS		HOUSE REPUBLICANS
Talent, James (MO)	$2,000	

Public Affairs and Related Activities Personnel

At Headquarters

BASS, Amy
Director, Corporate Communications
abass@empiredistrict.com
Tel: (417) 625 - 5114
Fax: (417) 625 - 6198
TF: (800) 206 - 2300

GIBSON, David W.
V. President, Regulatory and General Services
Tel: (417) 625 - 5100
Fax: (417) 625 - 5155
TF: (800) 206 - 2300

MARTIN, David
Manager, Governmental Relations
dmartin@empiredistrict.com
Responsibilities include political action.
Tel: (417) 625 - 6107
Fax: (417) 625 - 5155
TF: (800) 206 - 2300

MAUS, Julie
Communications Specialist
jmaus@empiredistrict.com
Tel: (417) 625 - 5101
Fax: (417) 625 - 5155
TF: (800) 206 - 2300

WILLIAMS, Jay
PAC Treasurer
Tel: (417) 625 - 5100
Fax: (417) 625 - 5155
TF: (800) 206 - 2300

Empire HealthChoice, Inc.

See listing on page 179 under Empire Blue Cross and Blue Shield.

Employers Insurance Co. of Wausau

Formerly Wausau Insurance Company.
www.wausau.com

Main Headquarters
Mailing: P.O. Box 8017
Wausau, WI 54402-8017
Tel: (715) 845 - 5211
Fax: (715) 847 - 8740
TF: (800) 435 - 4401

Street: 2000 Westwood Dr.
Wausau, WI 54401-7881

Corporate Foundations and Giving Programs

Wausau Insurance Companies Corporate Contributions Program
Contact: Brad L. Zweck
P.O. Box 8017
Wausau, WI 54402-8017
Tel: (715) 842 - 6570
Fax: (715) 847 - 8740
TF: (800) 435 - 4401

Annual Grant Total: $750,000 - $1,000,000
Affiliated with Nationwide Insurance Enterprises.
Geographic Preference: Wisconsin
Primary Interests: Arts and Culture; Community Affairs; Education
Recent Recipients: American Players Theater; Salvation Army; United Way

Public Affairs and Related Activities Personnel

At Headquarters

ZWECK, Brad L.
Manager, Communications and Public Affairs
brad.zweck@wausau.com
Tel: (715) 842 - 6570
Fax: (715) 847 - 8740
TF: (800) 435 - 4401

Encyclopaedia Britannica, Inc.

www.britannica.com

Chairman of the Board
SAFRA, Jacob E.
Tel: (312) 347 - 7000
Fax: (312) 294 - 2158

Main Headquarters
Mailing: Britannica Centre
310 S. Michigan Ave.
Chicago, IL 60604
Tel: (312) 347 - 7000
Fax: (312) 294 - 2158

Corporate Foundations and Giving Programs

Encyclopaedia Britannica Corporate Contributions
Contact: Tom Panelas
Britannica Centre
310 S. Michigan Ave.
Chicago, IL 60604
Tel: (312) 347 - 7309
Fax: (312) 294 - 2158

Annual Grant Total: none reported

Public Affairs and Related Activities Personnel

At Headquarters

BOWE, William
V. President, Human Resources
Tel: (312) 347 - 7000
Fax: (312) 294 - 2158

PANELAS, Tom
Director, Public Relations
tpanelas@us.britannica.com
Tel: (312) 347 - 7309
Fax: (312) 294 - 2158

TOBACK, Andrea
Exec. Director, Human Resources and Benefits
Tel: (312) 347 - 7000
Fax: (312) 294 - 2158

Energen Corp.

A diversified energy holding company.
www.energen.com

Chairman and Chief Exec. Officer
WARREN, William Michael, Jr.
mwarren@energen.com
Tel: (205) 326 - 8166
Fax: (205) 322 - 6895
TF: (800) 654 - 3206

Main Headquarters
Mailing: 605 Richard Arrington Jr. Blvd. North
Birmingham, AL 35203-2707
Tel: (205) 326 - 2700
Fax: (205) 322 - 6895
TF: (800) 654 - 3206

Political Action Committees

Energen Corp. PAC
605 Richard Arrington Jr. Blvd. North
Birmingham, AL 35203-2707
Tel: (205) 326 - 2700
Fax: (205) 322 - 6895
TF: (800) 654 - 3206

Contributions to Candidates: $5,000 (01/05 - 09/05)
Democrats: $1,000; Republicans: $4,000.

Principal Recipients

SENATE DEMOCRATS		HOUSE DEMOCRATS	
		Davis, Artur (AL)	$1,000
SENATE REPUBLICANS		**HOUSE REPUBLICANS**	
Burns, Conrad (MT)	$2,000	Aderholt, Robert B (AL)	$1,000
		Rogers, Michael (AL)	$1,000

Corporate Foundations and Giving Programs

Energen Corp./Alabama Gas Corp. Contributions Program
Contact: Andre Taylor
605 Richard Arrington Jr. Blvd. North
Birmingham, AL 35203-2707
Tel: (205) 326 - 1613
Fax: (205) 714 - 5039
TF: (800) 654 - 3206

Annual Grant Total: $500,000 - $750,000
Geographic Preference: Area(s) in which the company operates
Primary Interests: Education; Health and Human Services
Recent Recipients: Salvation Army; Tuskegee University; United Negro College Fund; United Way; YWCA

Public Affairs and Related Activities Personnel

At Headquarters

CHAPMAN, Steven R.
V. President, Governmental Affairs
Tel: (205) 326 - 8181
Fax: (205) 322 - 6895
TF: (800) 654 - 3206

REYNOLDS, Dudley C.
PAC Treasurer
Tel: (205) 326 - 2700
Fax: (205) 322 - 6895
TF: (800) 654 - 3206

RYLAND, Julie S.
V. President, Investor Relations
Tel: (205) 326 - 8421
Fax: (205) 322 - 6895
TF: (800) 654 - 3206

SELF, W. David
V. President, Human Resources and Administration
Tel: (205) 326 - 8100
Fax: (205) 326 - 2704
TF: (800) 654 - 3206

STEWART, Amy Watson
V. President, Rates and Regulations
(Alabama Gas. Corp.)
Tel: (205) 326 - 8144
Fax: (205) 326 - 8140
TF: (800) 654 - 3206

TAYLOR, Andre
V. President, Communications
(Alabama Gas. Corp.)
Responsibilities include coporate philanthropy.
Tel: (205) 326 - 1613
Fax: (205) 714 - 5039
TF: (800) 654 - 3206

Energizer Holdings Inc.

A manufacturer of primary batteries and flashlights. The parent company of Schick-Wilkinson Sword, a manufacturer of wet shave products.

www.energizer.com

Chairman of the Board
STIRITZ, William
Tel: (314) 985 - 2000
Fax: (314) 982 - 2201
TF: (800) 383 - 7328

Chief Exec. Officer
KLEIN, Ward
Tel: (314) 985 - 2000
Fax: (314) 982 - 2201
TF: (800) 383 - 7328

Main Headquarters
Mailing: 533 Maryville University Dr.
St. Louis, MO 63141
Tel: (314) 985 - 2000
Fax: (314) 982 - 2201
TF: (800) 383 - 7328

Public Affairs and Related Activities Personnel

At Headquarters

BURWITZ, Jacqueline E.
V. President, Investor Relations
Tel: (314) 985 - 2169
Fax: (314) 985 - 2224
TF: (800) 383 - 7328

Energy East Corp.

A member of the Public Affairs Council. A regional energy services and delivery company. Subsidiaries include Central Maine Power Co., Connecticut Natural Gas Corp., New York State Electric & Gas Corp., Rochester Gas and Electric Corp., The Berkshire Gas Co., and The Southern Connecticut Gas Co.

www.energyeast.com

Main Headquarters
Mailing: P.O. Box 12904
Albany, NY 12212-2904
Tel: (518) 434 - 3049

Washington Office
Mailing: 601 13th St. NW
Suite 720 South
Washington, DC 20005
Tel: (202) 783 - 5521
Fax: (202) 783 - 5117

Political Action Committees

Connecticut Natural Gas Federal PAC
76 Meadows St.
East Hartford, CT 06108

Contributions to Candidates: none reported (01/05 - 09/05)

Energy East Corp. PAC
Contact: Paul T. Karakantas
89 East Ave.
Rochester, NY 14649

Contributions to Candidates: none reported (01/05 - 09/05)

New York State Electric and Gas Corp. Political Action Committee (NYSEGPAC)
P.O. Box 5224
Binghamton, NY 13902-5224

Contributions to Candidates: $4,250 (01/05 - 09/05)
Democrats: $1,000; Republicans: $3,250.

Principal Recipients

SENATE DEMOCRATS

HOUSE DEMOCRATS
Towns, Edolphus (NY) $1,000

SENATE REPUBLICANS
Allen, George (VA) $1,000

HOUSE REPUBLICANS
Sweeney, John E. (NY) $1,000
Upton, Fred (MI) $1,000

Public Affairs and Related Activities Personnel

At Headquarters

SPARKS-BEDDOE, Angela M.
V. President, Public Affairs
amsparks@energyeast.com
Responsibilities include government affairs.
Tel: (518) 434 - 6002

At Other Offices

BERGIN, Robert
Director, Public Affairs
(New York State Electric & Gas Corp. (NYSEG), Rochester Gas and Electric Corp. (RG&E))
89 East Ave.
Rochester, NY 14649-0001
robert_bergin@rge.com
Tel: (585) 771 - 2294

CARROLL, John
Manager, Corporate Communications
(Central Maine Power Co. (CMP))
83 Edison Dr.
Augusta, ME 04336
john.carroll@cmpco.com
Tel: (207) 629 - 1023

CASE, Kathy
V. President, Customer Services
(Central Maine Power Co. (CMP))
83 Edison Dr.
Augusta, ME 04336
kathleen.case@cmpco.com
Tel: (207) 626 - 9516

CHADWICK, Cindy
Manager, State Government Affairs
(New York State Electric & Gas Corp. (NYSEG))
P.O. Box 5224
Binghamton, NY 13902-5224
ctchadwick@nyseg.com
Tel: (607) 762 - 7310

DOBOS, John
Director, External Affairs
(Connecticut Natural Gas Corp. (CNG), Southern Connecticut Gas Co., The (SCG))
855 Main St.
Bridgeport, CT 06604-4918
jdobos@soconngas.com
Tel: (203) 382 - 8644

ELLIS, Clayton M.
Manager, Corporate Communications
(New York State Electric & Gas Corp. (NYSEG))
P.O. Box 5224
Binghamton, NY 13902-5224
cmellis@nyseg.com
Tel: (607) 762 - 7336
Fax: (607) 762 - 8595

FARRELL, Chris
Manager, Corporate Communications and Government Relations
(Berkshire Gas Co., The (Berkshire))
115 Cheshire Rd.
Pittsfield, MA 01201
cfarrell@berkshiregas.com
Tel: (413) 445 - 0312

KARAKANTAS, Paul T.
Treasurer, Energy East PAC
89 East Ave.
Rochester, NY 14649

EnergyNorth

See listing on page 279 under KeySpan Corp.

EnergyNorth Natural Gas

See listing on page 279 under KeySpan Corp.

Enesco Group, Inc.

www.enesco.com

Chairman of the Board
VERVILLE, Anne-Lee
Tel: (630) 875 - 5300
Ext: 5553
Fax: (630) 875 - 5858
TF: (800) 436 - 3726

Chief Exec. Officer
PASSMORE-MCLAUGHLIN, Cynthia
Tel: (630) 875 - 5300
Fax: (630) 875 - 5858
TF: (800) 436 - 3726

Main Headquarters
Mailing: 225 Windsor Dr.
Itasca, IL 60143
Tel: (630) 875 - 5300
Fax: (630) 875 - 5858
TF: (800) 436 - 3726

Corporate Foundations and Giving Programs

Enesco Corporate Contributions
225 Windsor Dr.
Itasca, IL 60143
Tel: (630) 875 - 5300
Fax: (630) 875 - 5858
TF: (800) 436 - 3726

Annual Grant Total: none reported
Geographic Preference: Area(s) in which the company operates; Chicago, IL
Primary Interests: Human Welfare; Persons with Disabilities; Women's Health
Recent Recipients: Easter Seal Soc.

Public Affairs and Related Activities Personnel

At Headquarters

SHAULTS, Donna
Director, Corporate Communications
Tel: (630) 875 - 5300
Ext: 5464
Fax: (630) 875 - 5858
TF: (800) 436 - 3726

Engelhard Corp.

A manufacturer of specialty chemical and engineered materials.

www.engelhard.com

Chairman and Chief Exec. Officer
PERRY, Barry W.
Tel: (732) 205 - 5000
Fax: (732) 632 - 9253
TF: (800) 631 - 9505

Main Headquarters
Mailing: 101 Wood Ave.
Iselin, NJ 08830
Tel: (732) 205 - 5000
Fax: (732) 321 - 1161
TF: (800) 631 - 9505

Corporate Foundations and Giving Programs

Engelhard Corporate Giving Program

Engelhard Corp.

* continued from previous page

101 Wood Ave.
Iselin, NJ 08830
Tel: (732) 205 - 5000
Fax: (732) 321 - 1161
TF: (800) 631 - 9505

Annual Grant Total: none reported
Geographic Preference: Area(s) in which the company operates
Primary Interests: Education; Engineering; Human Welfare; Medicine and Health Care; Technology

Public Affairs and Related Activities Personnel

At Headquarters

BELL, Garvin A., CFA
V. President, Inestor Relations
Tel: (732) 205 - 6106
Fax: (732) 321 - 5079
TF: (800) 631 - 9505

DRESNER, Mark
V. President, Corporate Communications
Tel: (732) 205 - 5000
Fax: (732) 632 - 9253
TF: (800) 631 - 9505

GALLAGHER, Donna
Corporate Communications Specialist
Tel: (732) 205 - 5000
Fax: (732) 632 - 9253
TF: (800) 631 - 9505

LOWAN, Ted
Director, Corporate Communications
Tel: (732) 205 - 6360
Fax: (732) 321 - 1161
TF: (800) 631 - 9505

Enova Corp.

See listing on page 432 under Sempra Energy.

Enron Capital & Trade Resources Co.

See listing on page 182 under Enron Corp.

Enron Corp.

An energy services company.
www.enron.com

Interim Chief Exec. Officer and Chief Restructuring Officer
COOPER, Stephen F.
Tel: (713) 853 - 6161

Main Headquarters
Mailing: 1221 Lamar
Suite 1600
Houston, TX 77010
Tel: (713) 853 - 6161

Political Action Committees

Enron Corp. PAC
Contact: Mark E. Lindsey
1221 Lamar
Suite 1600
Houston, TX 77010
Tel: (713) 853 - 6161

Contributions to Candidates: none reported (01/05 - 09/05)

Public Affairs and Related Activities Personnel

At Headquarters

HILTABRAND, Leslie
Public Relations Contact
Tel: (713) 853 - 5670

LINDSEY, Mark E.
PAC Treasurer
Tel: (713) 853 - 6161

Enron Energy Services, Inc.

See listing on page 182 under Enron Corp.

ENSCO Internat'l Inc.

An offshore oil and gas drilling contractor.
www.enscous.com

Chairman and Chief Exec. Officer
THORNE, Carl F.
Tel: (214) 397 - 3000
Fax: (214) 397 - 3379
TF: (800) 423 - 8006

Main Headquarters
Mailing: 500 N. Akard St.
Suite 4300
Dallas, TX 75201-3331
Tel: (214) 397 - 3000
Fax: (214) 397 - 3370
TF: (800) 423 - 8006

Public Affairs and Related Activities Personnel

At Headquarters

ANDERSON, Michelle A.
Investor Relations Advisor
manderson@enscous.com
Tel: (214) 397 - 3045
Fax: (214) 397 - 3370
TF: (800) 423 - 8006

LEBLANC, Richard A.
V. President, Investor Relations
rleblanc@enscous.com
Tel: (214) 397 - 3011
Fax: (214) 397 - 3370
TF: (800) 423 - 8006

MILLS, Charles A.
V. President, Human Resources and Security
Tel: (214) 397 - 3000
Fax: (214) 397 - 3376
TF: (800) 423 - 8006

Enterasys Networks

www.enterasys.com

Executive Chairman of the Board
O'BRIEN, William
Tel: (978) 684 - 1000
Fax: (978) 684 - 1658

Chief Exec. Officer
ASLETT, Mark
Tel: (978) 684 - 1000
Fax: (978) 684 - 1658

Main Headquarters
Mailing: 50 Minuteman Rd.
Andover, MA 01810
Tel: (978) 684 - 1000
Fax: (978) 684 - 1658

Public Affairs and Related Activities Personnel

At Headquarters

FLANAGAN, Kevin
Director, Corporate Communications
kflanaga@entersys.com
Tel: (978) 684 - 1473
Fax: (978) 684 - 1658

HANNAY, Lori
V. President, Human Resources
Tel: (978) 684 - 1000
Fax: (978) 684 - 1658

SHEPPARD, Kristen
V. President, Investor Relations and Corporate Affairs
ksheppar@enterasys.com
Tel: (978) 684 - 1000
Fax: (978) 684 - 1658

Entergy Arkansas, Inc.

A subsidiary of Entergy Corp. (see separate listing). More information about Entergy Arkansas can be found on the parent company's website at www.entergy.com.
www.entergy-arkansas.com

Chief Exec. Officer
MCDONALD, Hugh
Tel: (501) 377 - 4000
TF: (800) 377 - 4448

Main Headquarters
Mailing: 425 W. Capitol, 40th Floor
Little Rock, AR 72201
Tel: (501) 377 - 4000
TF: (800) 377 - 4448

Corporate Foundations and Giving Programs

Entergy Arkansas, Inc. Corporate Contributions Program
Contact: Marsha Udouj
425 W. Capitol, 40th Floor
Little Rock, AR 72201
Tel: (501) 377 - 3522
TF: (800) 377 - 4448

Annual Grant Total: $1,000,000 - $2,000,000
Geographic Preference: Arkansas
Primary Interests: Community Development; Higher Education; Social Services
Recent Recipients: American Red Cross; University of Arkansas

Public Affairs and Related Activities Personnel

At Headquarters

DAUGHERTY, Dan H.
Manager, Communications
Tel: (501) 377 - 4000
TF: (800) 377 - 4448

MEANS, Paul
Manager, State Government Affairs
pmeans@entergy.com
Tel: (501) 377 - 4000
TF: (800) 377 - 4448

STRICKLAND, Steve
V. President, Regulatory Affairs
Tel: (501) 377 - 4000
TF: (800) 377 - 4448

UDOUJ, Marsha
Corporate Contributions Coordinator
mudouj@entergy.com
Tel: (501) 377 - 3522
TF: (800) 377 - 4448

Entergy Corp.

A member of the Public Affairs Council. Electric utilities holding company; independent power producer.
www.entergy.com
Annual Revenues: $9.621 billion

Chairman of the Board
LUFT, Robert V.D. "Bob"
Tel: (504) 576 - 4000
Fax: (504) 576 - 4428

Chief Exec. Officer
LEONARD, J. Wayne
Tel: (504) 576 - 4000
Fax: (504) 576 - 4428

Main Headquarters
Mailing: P.O. Box 61000
New Orleans, LA 70161
Tel: (504) 576 - 4000
Fax: (504) 576 - 4428
Street: 639 Loyola Ave.
New Orleans, LA 70113

Washington Office
Contact: Jerald V. Halvorsen
Mailing: 101 Constitution Ave., NW
Suite 200 East
Washington, DC 20001
Tel: (202) 530 - 7300
Fax: (202) 530 - 7350

Political Action Committees

Entergy PAC (EnPAC)
Contact: Trevin Dalton
101 Constitution Ave., NW
Suite 200 East
Washington, DC 20001
Tel: (202) 530 - 7300
Fax: (202) 530 - 7350

Entergy Corp.

* continued from previous page

Contributions to Candidates: $130,277 (01/05 - 09/05)
Democrats: $54,777; Republicans: $74,500; Other: $1,000.

Principal Recipients

SENATE DEMOCRATS		HOUSE DEMOCRATS	
Carper, Thomas R (DE)	$3,580	Melancon, Charlie (LA)	$11,000
Kennedy, John Neely (LA)	$2,000		
Landrieu, Mary (LA)	$2,000		
Pryor, Mark (AR)	$1,352		
SENATE REPUBLICANS		**HOUSE REPUBLICANS**	
Burns, Conrad (MT)	$3,000	Vitter, David (LA)	$5,000
Lott, Trent (MS)	$2,000	Alexander, Rodney (LA)	$4,000
Thomas, Craig (WY)	$2,000	Baker, Hugh (LA)	$3,500
		Jindal, Bobby (LA)	$3,500

Corporate Foundations and Giving Programs

Entergy Corporate Giving Program
Contact: Patty Riddle-Barger
425 W. Capitol Ave.
P.O. Box 551
Little Rock, AR 72203

Annual Grant Total: none reported

Public Affairs and Related Activities Personnel

At Headquarters

GENO, Patricia — Tel: (504) 576 - 2364
Director, Employee Communications and Special Services — Fax: (504) 576 - 4428
pgeno@entergy.com

HEBERT, Curtis L. — Tel: (504) 576 - 4743
Exec. V. President, External Affairs — Fax: (504) 576 - 4428
cheber7@entergy.com

LAROSA, Paul — Tel: (504) 576 - 4878
Director, Investor Relations — Fax: (504) 576 - 4428
plarosa@entergy.com

MOROVICH, Nancy C. — Tel: (504) 576 - 5506
V. President, Investor Relations — Fax: (504) 576 - 4428
nmorovi@entergy.com

WIESE, Arthur E. F., Jr. — Tel: (504) 576 - 2547
V. President, Corporate Communications — Fax: (504) 576 - 4428
awiese@entergy.com

At Washington Office

DALTON, Trevin — Tel: (202) 530 - 7300
PAC Manager — Fax: (202) 530 - 7350

HALVORSEN, Jerald V. — Tel: (202) 530 - 7300
V. President, Federal Government Affairs — Fax: (202) 530 - 7350

PRIDE, Ann L. — Tel: (202) 530 - 7300
Director, Public Affairs Policy and Strategy — Fax: (202) 530 - 7350

At Other Offices

ALSTADT, Sandra R. — Tel: (501) 377 - 3547
Director, Utility Group Communications
425 W. Capitol Ave.
P.O. Box 551
Little Rock, AR 72203
salstad@entergy.com

ARNOLD, Kay Kelly — Tel: (501) 377 - 3553
V. President, System Governmental Affairs
425 W. Capitol Ave.
P.O. Box 551
Little Rock, AR 72203
karnold@entergy.com

DREHER, Murphy A. — Tel: (225) 381 - 5849
V. President, Government Affairs - Louisiana
446 North Blvd.
Baton Rouge, LA 70802
mdreher@entergy.com

FERGUSON, Judy J. — Tel: (601) 969 - 2327
Communications Specialist - Mississippi — Fax: (601) 969 - 2581
308 E. Pearl St.
Jackson, MS 39201
jfergu1@entergy.com

FOSTER, Kent — Tel: (501) 377 - 3525
V. President, System Regulatory Affairs and Affiliate Rule Compliance
425 W. Capitol Ave.
P.O. Box 551
Little Rock, AR 72203

RIDDLE-BARGER, Patty
Director, Corporate Contributions
425 W. Capitol Ave.
P.O. Box 551
Little Rock, AR 72203

Entergy Gulf States, Inc.

See listing on page 182 under Entergy Corp.

Entergy Mississippi

Formerly known as Mississippi Power and Light Co. An electric utility subsidiary of Entergy Corp. (see separate listing).
www.entergy-mississippi.com

President and Chief Exec. Officer — Tel: (601) 368 - 5000
SHANKS, Carolyn C. — Fax: (601) 964 - 2400
cshanks@entergy.com

Main Headquarters
Mailing: P.O. Box 1640, Jackson, MS 39215-1640 — Tel: (601) 368 - 5000; Fax: (601) 964 - 2400
Street: 308 E. Pearl St., Jackson, MS 39201

Public Affairs and Related Activities Personnel

At Headquarters

HERRINGTON, Checky — Tel: (601) 368 - 5000
Manager, Communications — Fax: (601) 964 - 2400

LESLEY, Robert — Tel: (601) 368 - 5000
Coordinator, Media Relations — Fax: (601) 964 - 2400
rlesley@entergy.com

MAYO, Will — Tel: (601) 368 - 5000
V. President, Government Affairs -- Mississippi — Fax: (601) 964 - 2400

PAIGE, Bennie F. — Tel: (601) 969 - 2455
Director, State Governmental Affairs — Fax: (601) 964 - 2400
bpaige@entergy.com

Entergy New Orleans

Formerly known as Louisiana Power & Light Co./New Orleans Public Service Inc. A subsidiary of Entergy Corp. (see separate listing).
www.entergy-neworleans.com

President and Chief Exec. Officer — Tel: (504) 576 - 4000
PACKER, Daniel F. — Fax: (504) 576 - 4001

Main Headquarters
Mailing: P.O. Box 61000, New Orleans, LA 70161 — Tel: (504) 576 - 4000; Fax: (504) 576 - 4001
Street: 639 Loyola Ave., New Orleans, LA 70113

Corporate Foundations and Giving Programs

Entergy New Orleans Corporate Giving Program
Contact: Donna Riddle-Barger
P.O. Box 61000 — Tel: (504) 576 - 4000
New Orleans, LA 70161 — Fax: (504) 576 - 4001

Annual Grant Total: none reported

Public Affairs and Related Activities Personnel

At Headquarters

GARIBALDI, Alvin — Tel: (504) 576 - 4000
Governmental Affairs Executive, Customer Service — Fax: (504) 576 - 4001

RIDDLE-BARGER, Donna — Tel: (504) 576 - 4000
Director, Corporate Contributions — Fax: (504) 576 - 4001

Entergy Services, Inc.

A subsidiary of Entergy Corp. (see separate listing).
www.entergy.com

Chairman and Chief Exec. Officer — Tel: (504) 576 - 4000
LEONARD, J. Wayne
jleonard@entergy.com

Main Headquarters
Mailing: P.O. Box 61000, New Orleans, LA 70161 — Tel: (504) 576 - 4000

Washington Office
Contact: Jerald V. Halvorsen
Mailing: 101 Constitution Ave. NW, Suite 200 East, Washington, DC 20001 — Tel: (202) 530 - 7300; Fax: (202) 530 - 7350

Corporate Foundations and Giving Programs

Entergy Services Corporate Contributions Program
P.O. Box 61000 — Tel: (504) 576 - 4000
New Orleans, LA 70161

Annual Grant Total: none reported

Public Affairs and Related Activities Personnel

At Washington Office

CARROLL, Kenneth — Tel: (202) 530 - 7300
Director, Tax and Environmental Legislative Policy (Middle South Utility System) — Fax: (202) 530 - 7350
Registered Federal Lobbyist.

Entergy Services, Inc.
** continued from previous page*

HALVORSEN, Jerald V. — Tel: (202) 530 - 7300
V. President, Federal Government Affairs — Fax: (202) 530 - 7350
Registered Federal Lobbyist.

PRIDE, Ann L. — Tel: (202) 530 - 7300
Director, Public Affairs Policy and Strategy — Fax: (202) 530 - 7350
apride@entergy.com
Registered Federal Lobbyist.

SIMMS, Kristine D. — Tel: (202) 530 - 7300
Director, Federal Government Affairs — Fax: (202) 530 - 7350
ksimms@entergy.com
Registered Federal Lobbyist.

Entergy Texas
An electric utility formerly known as Gulf States Utilities Co. A subsidiary of Entergy Corp. (see separate listing).
www.entergy-texas.com

President and Chief Exec. Officer — Tel: (409) 838 - 6631
DOMINO, Joe

Main Headquarters
Mailing: P.O. Box 2951 — Tel: (409) 838 - 6631
Beaumont, TX 77704

Public Affairs and Related Activities Personnel

At Headquarters

DERRICK, Debi — Tel: (409) 838 - 6631
Communications Specialist

ROGERS, Michael T. — Tel: (409) 838 - 6631
Communications Specialist

Enterprise Rent-A-Car Co.
A passenger car rental and leasing company.
www.enterprise.com

Chairman and Chief Exec. Officer — Tel: (314) 512 - 5000
TAYLOR, Andrew C. — Fax: (314) 512 - 4706

Main Headquarters
Mailing: 600 Corporate Park Dr. — Tel: (314) 512 - 5000
St. Louis, MO 63105 — Fax: (314) 512 - 5281

Political Action Committees

Enterprise Rent-A-Car Co. Political Action Committee
Contact: Raymond T. Wagner, Jr.
600 Corporate Park Dr. — Tel: (314) 512 - 2897
St. Louis, MO 63105 — Fax: (314) 512 - 4897

Contributions to Candidates: $83,850 (01/05 - 09/05)
Democrats: $26,850; Republicans: $57,000.

Principal Recipients

SENATE DEMOCRATS		HOUSE DEMOCRATS	
Nelson, Bill (FL)	$5,000	Holden, Timothy (PA)	$5,000
Lieberman, Joe (CT)	$3,500	Davis, Lincoln (TN)	$3,500
Carper, Thomas R (DE)	$2,500		
SENATE REPUBLICANS		**HOUSE REPUBLICANS**	
Burns, Conrad (MT)	$5,000	Barton, Joe L (TX)	$5,000
Inhofe, James M (OK)	$5,000	Hastert, Dennis J. (IL)	$5,000
Thomas, Craig (WY)	$5,000	Graves, Sam (MO)	$4,000
Talent, James (MO)	$4,000	Akin, William Todd (MO)	$3,500
Lugar, Richard G (IN)	$3,000	DeLay, Tom (TX)	$2,500
Stevens, Ted (AK)	$2,500	Young, Don E (AK)	$2,500

Corporate Foundations and Giving Programs

Enterprise Rent-A-Car Foundation
Contact: Jo Ann T. Kindle
600 Corporate Park Dr. — Tel: (314) 512 - 2754
St. Louis, MO 63105 — Fax: (314) 512 - 4706

Annual Grant Total: under $100,000
Organizations must have involvement by employees, their families, customers, or their families in order to be eligible to receive grants.
Geographic Preference: Area(s) in which the company operates
Primary Interests: Arts and Humanities; Education; Human Welfare; Urban Affairs
Recent Recipients: Children's Hospital; United Way

Public Affairs and Related Activities Personnel

At Headquarters

ADAMS, Edward — Tel: (314) 512 - 5000
Senior V. President, Human Resources — Fax: (314) 512 - 4706
eadams@erac.com

BROUGHTON, Lee — Tel: (314) 512 - 5000
Manager, Public Relations — Fax: (314) 512 - 5281

CONRAD, Christy — Tel: (314) 512 - 2706
Assistant V. President, Public Relations — Fax: (314) 512 - 4706
cconrad@erac.com

KINDLE, Jo Ann T. — Tel: (314) 512 - 2754
President, Enterprise Rent-A-Car Foundation — Fax: (314) 512 - 4706
jkindle@erac.com

LANGHORST, Rosemary — Tel: (314) 512 - 5000
Treasurer, Enterprise Rent-A-Car Co. PAC — Fax: (314) 512 - 4706
rlanghorst@erac.com

WAGNER, Raymond T., Jr. — Tel: (314) 512 - 2897
V. President, Governmental and Legislative Affairs — Fax: (314) 512 - 4897
rwagner@erac.com

Equifax Inc.
A supplier of information solutions for businesses.
www.equifax.com
Annual Revenues: $1.139 billion

Chairman and Chief Exec. Officer — Tel: (404) 885 - 8000
CHAPMAN, Thomas F. — Fax: (404) 885 - 8078

Main Headquarters
Mailing: 1550 Peachtree St., N.W. — Tel: (404) 885 - 8000
Atlanta, GA 30309 — Fax: (404) 885 - 8078

Political Action Committees

Equifax Inc. Political Action Committee
Contact: Kirby A. Thompson
1550 Peachtree St., N.W. — Tel: (404) 885 - 8360
Atlanta, GA 30309 — Fax: (404) 885 - 8215

Contributions to Candidates: $25,500 (01/05 - 09/05)
Democrats: $11,500; Republicans: $14,000.

Principal Recipients

SENATE DEMOCRATS		HOUSE DEMOCRATS	
Carper, Thomas R (DE)	$4,000	Hooley, Darlene (OR)	$2,000
		Moore, Dennis (KS)	$2,000
		Scott, David (GA)	$2,000
SENATE REPUBLICANS		**HOUSE REPUBLICANS**	
Santorum, Richard (PA)	$1,000	Price, Thomas (GA)	$3,000
Talent, James (MO)	$1,000	Bachus, Spencer (AL)	$2,000
		Kelly, Sue W (NY)	$2,000
		Royce, Ed Mr (CA)	$2,000
		Stearns, Clifford (FL)	$2,000

Corporate Foundations and Giving Programs

The Equifax Foundation, Inc.
Contact: Kirby A. Thompson
1550 Peachtree St., N.W. — Tel: (404) 885 - 8360
Atlanta, GA 30309 — Fax: (404) 885 - 8215

Assets: $2,400,000 (2001)
Annual Grant Total: $750,000 - $1,000,000
Recent recipients include consumer credit counseling and the Georgia Council on Economic Education.
Geographic Preference: Georgia; Atlanta, GA
Primary Interests: Education; Financial Planning

Public Affairs and Related Activities Personnel

At Headquarters

DODGE, Jeff — Tel: (404) 885 - 8804
V. President, Investor Relations — Fax: (404) 885 - 8078
jeff.dodge@equifax.com

RUBINGER, David — Tel: (404) 885 - 8555
V. President, Communications — Fax: (404) 885 - 8078
david.rubinger@equifax.com

THOMPSON, Kirby A. — Tel: (404) 885 - 8360
V. President, Legislative Affairs and Community Affairs — Fax: (404) 885 - 8215
kirby.thompson@equifax.com

Equitable Resources, Inc.
An integrated energy company.
www.eqt.com
Annual Revenues: $1.764 billion

Chairman, President and Chief Exec. Officer — Tel: (412) 553 - 5700
GERBER, Murry S. — Fax: (412) 553 - 5757

Main Headquarters
Mailing: One Oxford Center, Suite 3300 — Tel: (412) 553 - 5700
Pittsburgh, PA 15219 — Fax: (412) 553 - 5757

Political Action Committees

Equitable Resources Inc. Political Involvement Committee (EPIC)
Contact: Tobhiyah Williams
One Oxford Center, Suite 3300 — Tel: (412) 553 - 5700
Pittsburgh, PA 15219 — Fax: (412) 553 - 5757

Contributions to Candidates: none reported (01/05 - 09/05)

Equitable Resources, Inc.

* continued from previous page

Corporate Foundations and Giving Programs

Equitable Resources Foundation
Contact: Bruce Bickel
Two P & C Plaza — Tel: (412) 553 - 5700
620 Liberty Ave.
Pittsburgh, PA 15222

Annual Grant Total: none reported
Primary Interests: Children; Education; Housing
Recent Recipients: Meals on Wheels

Public Affairs and Related Activities Personnel

At Headquarters

PETRELLI, Charlene — Tel: (412) 553 - 5712
V. President, Human Resources — Fax: (412) 553 - 5732

THAMERT, Thomas E. — Tel: (412) 553 - 7712
Manager, Government Affairs — Fax: (412) 553 - 5757

WILLIAMS, Tobhiyah — Tel: (412) 553 - 5700
PAC Treasurer — Fax: (412) 553 - 5757

At Other Offices

BICKEL, Bruce — Tel: (412) 553 - 5700
Exec. Director, Foundation
Two P & C Plaza
620 Liberty Ave.
Pittsburgh, PA 15222

Equity Office Properties Trust

An owner and manager of office properties.
www.equityoffice.com
Annual Revenues: $3 billion

Chairman of the Board — Tel: (312) 466 - 3300
ZELL, Samuel — Fax: (312) 454 - 0332

President and Chief Exec. Officer — Tel: (312) 466 - 3300
KINCAID, Richard D. — Fax: (312) 454 - 0332

Main Headquarters
Mailing: Two N. Riverside Plaza — Tel: (312) 466 - 3300
Suite 2100 — Fax: (312) 454 - 0332
Chicago, IL 60606

Public Affairs and Related Activities Personnel

At Headquarters

CORONELLI, Elizabeth — Tel: (312) 466 - 3300
Senior V. President, Investor Relations — Fax: (312) 454 - 0332
Responsibilities include public relations.

HOLT, Terry — Tel: (312) 466 - 3102
V. President, Public Relations — Fax: (312) 559 - 3102
terry_holt@equityoffice.com

KREMA, Lawrence J. — Tel: (312) 466 - 3300
Senior V. President, Human Resources and Communications — Fax: (312) 454 - 0332
lawrence_krema@equityoffice.com

Equity Residential

An apartment owner.
www.equityapartments.com
Annual Revenues: $2 billion

Chairman of the Board — Tel: (312) 474 - 1300
ZELL, Samuel — Fax: (312) 454 - 8703

Chief Exec. Officer — Tel: (312) 474 - 1300
DUNCAN, Bruce W. — Fax: (312) 454 - 8703

Main Headquarters
Mailing: Two N. Riverside Plaza — Tel: (312) 474 - 1300
Suite 400 — Fax: (312) 454 - 8703
Chicago, IL 60606

Corporate Foundations and Giving Programs

Equity Residential Foundation
Contact: Marty McKenna
Two N. Riverside Plaza — Tel: (312) 928 - 1901
Suite 400 — Fax: (312) 454 - 0614
Chicago, IL 60606

Annual Grant Total: none reported
Geographic Preference: National

Public Affairs and Related Activities Personnel

At Headquarters

MCKENNA, Marty — Tel: (312) 928 - 1901
Assistant V. President, Investor Relations and Public Relations — Fax: (312) 454 - 0614
Responsibilities include corporate philanthropy.

SALOMON, Catherine — Tel: (312) 928 - 1282
Director, Corporate Human Resources — Fax: (312) 454 - 9588

Ericsson Inc.

Manufacturer of business communicators and telecommunications systems.
www.ericsson.com/us/

President and Chief Exec. Officer — Tel: (972) 583 - 0000
RUIZ, Angel — Fax: (972) 889 - 9846

Main Headquarters
Mailing: 6300 Legacy Dr. — Tel: (972) 583 - 0000
Plano, TX 75024 — Fax: (972) 889 - 9846

Washington Office
Contact: Barbara Baffer
Mailing: 1634 I St. NW, Suite 600 — Tel: (202) 783 - 2200
Washington, DC 20006-4083 — Fax: (202) 783 - 2206

Public Affairs and Related Activities Personnel

At Washington Office

BAFFER, Barbara — Tel: (202) 783 - 2200
Manager, Public Affairs and Regulation — Fax: (202) 783 - 2206
barbara.baffer@ericsson.com
Registered Federal Lobbyist.

At Other Offices

EGAN, Kathy — Tel: (212) 843 - 8422
V. President, Communications — Fax: (212) 213 - 0159
100 Park Ave., Suite 2705
New York, NY 10017
kathy.egan@ericsson.com

FRENCH, Michelle
Director, Media and Industry Analyst Relations
100 Park Ave., Suite 2705
New York, NY 10017
m.french@ericsson.com

MOZDINIEWICZ, Nathalie
Investor Relations Program Coordinator
100 Park Ave., Suite 2705
New York, NY 10017

SAPADIN, Glenn — Tel: (212) 685 - 4030
Manager, Investor Relations — Fax: (212) 213 - 0159
100 Park Ave., Suite 2705
New York, NY 10017

Erie Indeminity Co.

A multi-line insurance company.
www.erieinsurance.com
Annual Revenues: $3.44 billion

Chairman of the Board — Tel: (814) 870 - 2270
HIRT, F. William — Fax: (814) 870 - 3126

President and Chief Exec. Officer — Tel: (814) 870 - 2507
LUDROF, Jeffrey A. — Fax: (814) 870 - 3126

Main Headquarters
Mailing: 100 Erie Insurance Pl. — Tel: (814) 870 - 2000
Erie, PA 16530 — Fax: (814) 870 - 3126

Political Action Committees

Erie Indeminity Co. PAC-Federal
Contact: Jan R. Van Gorder
100 Erie Insurance Pl. — Tel: (814) 870 - 2000
Erie, PA 16530 — Fax: (814) 870 - 3126

Contributions to Candidates: none reported (01/05 - 09/05)

Corporate Foundations and Giving Programs

Erie Indeminity Co. Corporate Contributions Program
Contact: Michael J. Krahe, Ph.D.
100 Erie Insurance Pl. — Tel: (814) 870 - 2850
Erie, PA 16530 — Fax: (814) 870 - 2444

Annual Grant Total: none reported

Public Affairs and Related Activities Personnel

At Headquarters

DOMBROWSKI, Mark — Tel: (814) 870 - 2285
Supervisor, Public and Media Relations — Fax: (814) 870 - 3126
(Erie Insurance Group)
mark.dombrowski@erieinsurance.com

KRAHE, Michael J., Ph.D. — Tel: (814) 870 - 2850
Exec. V. President, Human Development and Leadership — Fax: (814) 870 - 2444

PHILLIPS, Karen Kraus — Tel: (814) 870 - 4665
Manager and V. President, Corporate Communications and Investor Relations — Fax: (814) 870 - 3126

VAN GORDER, Jan R. — Tel: (814) 870 - 2000
PAC Treasurer — Fax: (814) 870 - 3126

Ernst & Young LLP

A provider of assurance, tax, and transaction advisory services.
www.ey.com
Annual Revenues: $10 billion

Chairman and Chief Exec. Officer
TURLEY, James S. — Tel: (212) 773 - 3000 — Fax: (212) 773 - 6350
james.turley@ey.com

Main Headquarters
Mailing: Five Times Square
New York, NY 10036 — Tel: (212) 773 - 3000 — Fax: (212) 773 - 6350

Washington Office
Contact: Les Brorsen
Mailing: 1225 Connecticut Ave. NW
Washington, DC 20036 — Tel: (202) 327 - 6000

Political Action Committees

Ernst & Young Political Action Committee
Contact: Kathryn "K.C." Tominovich
1225 Connecticut Ave. NW
Washington, DC 20036

Contributions to Candidates: $336,257 (01/05 - 09/05)
Democrats: $73,251; Republicans: $261,506; Other: $1,500.

Principal Recipients

SENATE DEMOCRATS
Feinstein, Dianne (CA) $5,000
Ford, Harold E Jr (TN) $5,000
Conrad, Kent (ND) $4,200

HOUSE DEMOCRATS

SENATE REPUBLICANS
Allen, George (VA) $10,000
Kyl, Jon L (AZ) $10,000
Snowe, Olympia (ME) $8,500
Santorum, Richard (PA) $6,500
Harris, Katherine (FL) $5,000
Talent, James (MO) $3,253

HOUSE REPUBLICANS
Fitzpatrick, Michael (PA) $10,000
Gerlach, Jim (PA) $10,000
Northup, Anne M. (KY) $10,000
Oxley, Michael (OH) $10,000
Porter, Jon (NV) $10,000
Reichert, Dave (WA) $10,000
Renzi, Richard (AZ) $10,000
Simmons, Rob (CT) $10,000
Wilson, Heather (NM) $10,000

Corporate Foundations and Giving Programs

Ernst & Young Foundation
Contact: Ellen L. Glazerman
1285 Ave. of the Americas
New York, NY 10019 — Tel: (212) 773 - 5686

Annual Grant Total: $2,000,000 - $5,000,000
Geographic Preference: National
Primary Interests: Adult Education and Training

Public Affairs and Related Activities Personnel

At Headquarters

KERRIGAN, Kenneth — Tel: (212) 773 - 3000
Deputy Director, Public Relations — Fax: (212) 773 - 6350

PERKINS, Charlie — Tel: (212) 773 - 2418
Director, Public Relations — Fax: (212) 773 - 7982

SPEROS, James — Tel: (212) 773 - 3000
Director, Marketing Communications — Fax: (212) 773 - 6350
james.speros@ey.com

At Washington Office

BRORSEN, Les — Tel: (202) 327 - 6000
National Director, Political and Government Relations
les.brorsen@ey.com
Registered Federal Lobbyist.

PEARSON, Mary Frances — Tel: (202) 327 - 6000
Partner; National Director, Government Relations
maryfrances.pearson@ey.com
Registered Federal Lobbyist.

ROSENBLUM, Jay E. — Tel: (202) 327 - 6000
Director, Government Relations
jay.rosemblum@ey.com

TOMINOVICH, Kathryn "K.C."
Political and Legislative Director
kathryn.tominovich@ey.com
Registered Federal Lobbyist.

At Other Offices

GLAZERMAN, Ellen L. — Tel: (212) 773 - 5686
Contact, Ernst & Young Foundation
1285 Ave. of the Americas
New York, NY 10019
ellen.glazerman@ey.com

Essex Gas

See listing on page 279 under KeySpan Corp.

Estee Lauder Companies, Inc.

A manufacturer of cosmetics and fragrances.
www.elcompanies.com
Annual Revenues: $4.608 billion

Chairman of the Board
LAUDER, Leonard A. — Tel: (212) 572 - 4200 — Fax: (212) 572 - 6633

President and Chief Exec. Officer
LAUDER, William P. — Tel: (212) 572 - 4200 — Fax: (212) 572 - 6633

Main Headquarters
Mailing: 767 Fifth Ave.
New York, NY 10153-0023 — Tel: (212) 572 - 4200 — Fax: (212) 572 - 6633

Corporate Foundations and Giving Programs

Estee Lauder Corporate Giving
Contact: Deborah Krulewitch
767 Fifth Ave. — Tel: (212) 572 - 4200
New York, NY 10153-0023 — Fax: (212) 572 - 6633

Annual Grant Total: none reported

Public Affairs and Related Activities Personnel

At Headquarters

CAVANAUGH, Andrew J. — Tel: (212) 572 - 4200
Senior V. President, Global Human Resources — Fax: (212) 572 - 6633

D'ANDREA, Dennis — Tel: (212) 572 - 4200
V. President, Investor Relations — Fax: (212) 572 - 6633
ddandrea@estee.com

DIORIO, Marianne — Tel: (212) 572 - 4200
Senior V. President, Communications and Specialty Brands — Fax: (212) 572 - 6633
mdoria@estee.com

KRULEWITCH, Deborah — Tel: (212) 572 - 4200
Assistant to Chairman and V. President, Corporate Administration — Fax: (212) 572 - 6633
dkrulewitch@estee.com
Responsibilities include corporate philanthropy.

SUSMAN, Sally — Tel: (212) 572 - 4200
Senior V. President, Global Communications — Fax: (212) 572 - 6633
ssussman@estee.com

Ethan Allen Interiors Inc.

A holding company for household furnishings.
www.ethanallen.com
Annual Revenues: $892.3 million

Chairman, President and Chief Exec. Officer
KATHWARI, M. Farooq — Tel: (203) 743 - 8500 — Fax: (203) 743 - 8298

Main Headquarters
Mailing: Ethan Allen Dr.
P.O. Box 1966
Danbury, CT 06813-2966 — Tel: (203) 743 - 8000 — Fax: (203) 743 - 8298

Public Affairs and Related Activities Personnel

At Headquarters

COMO-PUSWICS, Sandy — Tel: (203) 743 - 8575
Public Realtions Specialist — Fax: (203) 743 - 8298

FARFUGLIA, Charles J. — Tel: (203) 743 - 8000
V. President, Human Resources — Fax: (203) 743 - 8298

LUPTON, Margaret "Peg" — Tel: (203) 743 - 8234
Director, Investor Relations; and Assistant Secretary — Fax: (203) 743 - 8298
plupton@ethanalleninc.com

Ethicon Inc.

See listing on page 270 under Johnson & Johnson.

Ethyl Corp.

See listing on page 347 under NewMarket Corp.

E*TRADE Financial Corp.

An online financial services holding company.
www.etrade.com
Annual Revenues: $866.7 million

Chief Exec. Officer
CAPLAN, Mitchell H. — Tel: (916) 636 - 2510

Main Headquarters
Mailing: 135 E. 57th St.
New York, NY 10022 — Tel: (916) 636 - 2510

Washington Office
Contact: Betsy Barclay

E*TRADE Financial Corp.

** continued from previous page*

Mailing: 1101 Pennsylvania Ave. NW, Sixth Floor, Washington, DC 20004 — Tel: (202) 756 - 7750; Fax: (202) 756 - 7545

Public Affairs and Related Activities Personnel

At Headquarters

DOTSON, Connie M.
Chief Communications Officer — Tel: (916) 636 - 2510

At Washington Office

BARCLAY, Betsy
Chief Government Affairs Officer — Tel: (202) 756 - 7750; Fax: (202) 756 - 7545
bbarclay@etrade.com
Registered Federal Lobbyist.

WADE, Tara
Legislative Policy Analyst — Tel: (202) 756 - 7750; Fax: (202) 756 - 7545
Registered Federal Lobbyist.

EVI, Inc.

See listing on page 514 under Weatherford Internat'l Ltd.

Excellus, Inc.

See listing on page 293 under The Lifetime Healthcare Companies.

Exellus Blue Cross Blue Shield

Formerly known as Blue Cross Blue Shield of Central New York. A health insurer providing managed care, point of service and traditional products. A subsidiary of The Lifetime Healthcare Companies (see separate listing).

excellusbcbs.com

Chairman of the Board
BELLARDINI, Mary Alice — Tel: (315) 448 - 3700

Chief Exec. Officer
HILL, Kevin N. — Tel: (585) 454 - 1700; Fax: (585) 238 - 4233

Main Headquarters
Mailing: 165 Court St., Rochester, NY 14647 — Tel: (585) 454 - 1700; Fax: (585) 238 - 4233

Public Affairs and Related Activities Personnel

At Headquarters

FLOOD, Jeff
V. President, External Relations, Utica Region — Tel: (315) 671 - 6400

MARTIN, Elizabeth
V. President, Communications, Central New York Region — Tel: (315) 671 - 6408; Fax: (315) 448 - 3939
emartin@bcbscny.org

Exelon Corp.

A member of the Public Affairs Council. A diversified energy company. The company has announced plans to merge with PSE&G (see separate listing). Completion of the merger is expected in the first or second quarter of 2006.

www.exeloncorp.com

Chairman and Chief Exec. Officer
ROWE, John W. — Tel: (312) 394 - 5725

Main Headquarters
Mailing: P.O. Box A-3005, Chicago, IL 60690-3005 — Tel: (312) 394 - 7398
Street: 10 S. Dearborn St., 37th Floor, Chicago, IL 60690

Washington Office
Contact: Elizabeth A. "Betsy" Moler
Mailing: 101 Constitution Ave., NW, Suite 400 East, Washington, DC 20001 — Tel: (202) 347 - 7500; Fax: (202) 347 - 7501

Political Action Committees

Exelon PAC
Contact: Ellie Shaw
101 Constitution Ave., NW
Suite 400 East
Washington, DC 20001 — Tel: (202) 347 - 7500; Fax: (202) 347 - 7501

Contributions to Candidates: $193,000 (01/05 - 09/05)
Democrats: $80,500; Republicans: $112,500.

Principal Recipients

SENATE DEMOCRATS

Lautenberg, Frank (NJ)	$15,000
Bingaman, Jeff (NM)	$5,000
Landrieu, Mary (LA)	$2,000
Nelson, Benjamin (NE)	$2,000
Pryor, Mark (AR)	$2,000
Salazar, Ken (CO)	$2,000

HOUSE DEMOCRATS

Boucher, Fredrick (VA)	$5,000
Emanuel, Rahm (IL)	$5,000
Pallone, Frank (NJ)	$5,000
Sires, Albio (NJ)	$5,000

SENATE REPUBLICANS

Santorum, Richard (PA)	$4,000
Allen, George (VA)	$3,000
Chafee, Lincoln (RI)	$2,000
Smith, Gordon (OR)	$2,000
Talent, James (MO)	$2,000
Thomas, Craig (WY)	$2,000

HOUSE REPUBLICANS

Biggert, Judy (IL)	$5,000
Ferguson, Mike (NJ)	$5,000
Fitzpatrick, Michael (PA)	$5,000
Gerlach, Jim (PA)	$5,000
Hastert, Dennis J. (IL)	$5,000
Kirk, Mark Steven (IL)	$5,000
Murphy, Tim (PA)	$5,000
Pearce, Steve (NM)	$5,000
Shimkus, John (IL)	$5,000
Weller, Jerry (IL)	$5,000
Wilson, Heather (NM)	$5,000

Corporate Foundations and Giving Programs

Exelon Corp. Contributions Program
P.O. Box A-3005
Chicago, IL 60690-3005 — Tel: (312) 394 - 7398

Annual Grant Total: none reported
Geographic Preference: Chicago, IL; Philadelphia, PA
Primary Interests: Arts and Culture; Community Affairs; Education; Health and Human Services

Public Affairs and Related Activities Personnel

At Headquarters

CLARK, Frank M.
Exec. V. President — Tel: (312) 394 - 7184
frank.clark@exeloncorp.com

KIRCHOFFNER, Don
V. President, Corporate Communications — Tel: (312) 394 - 3001; Fax: (312) 394 - 2995

At Washington Office

BROWN, David C.
V. President, Congressional Affairs — Tel: (202) 347 - 0808; Fax: (202) 347 - 7501
davidc.brown@exeloncorp.com
Registered Federal Lobbyist.

BROWN, R. Scott
V. President and Director, Policy Development — Tel: (202) 347 - 7500; Fax: (202) 347 - 7501

HILL, Karen
V. President and Director, Federal Regulatory Affairs — Tel: (202) 347 - 7500; Fax: (202) 347 - 7501

MOLER, Elizabeth A. "Betsy"
Exec. V. President, Government and Environmental Affairs and Public Policy — Tel: (202) 347 - 7500; Fax: (202) 347 - 7501
elizabeth.moler@exeloncorp.com
Registered Federal Lobbyist.

SHAW, Ellie
Manager, Public Affairs — Tel: (202) 347 - 7500; Fax: (202) 347 - 7501
ellie.shaw@exeloncorp.com

At Other Offices

DAVIS, Tabrina
Director, Communications (ComEd) — Tel: (312) 394 - 7919; Fax: (312) 394 - 8693
P.O. Box 805379
Chicago, IL 60680-5379
tabrina.davis@exeloncorp.com

FREEMAN, Jan H.
V. President, Public Affairs — Tel: (610) 765 - 6906; Fax: (610) 765 - 6902
300 Exelon Way
Kennett Square, PA 19348
jan.freeman@exeloncorp.com

WOODS, David W.
Senior V. President, Public Affairs — Tel: (610) 765 - 6900; Fax: (610) 765 - 6902
300 Exelon Way
Kennett Square, PA 19348
david.woods@exeloncorp.com
Responsibilities include government affairs.

Express Scripts, Inc.

A member of the Public Affairs Council. A specialty managed care and full-service pharmacy benefit management company.

www.express-scripts.com
Annual Revenues: $15.1 billion

Chairman of the Board
TOAN, Barrett A. — Tel: (314) 770 - 1666; Fax: (314) 702 - 7037; TF: (800) 332 - 5455

President and Chief Exec. Officer
PAZ, George — Tel: (314) 770 - 1666; Fax: (314) 702 - 7037; TF: (800) 332 - 5455

Main Headquarters
Mailing: 13900 Riverport Dr., Maryland Heights, MO 63043 — Tel: (314) 770 - 1666; Fax: (314) 702 - 7037; TF: (800) 332 - 5455

Express Scripts, Inc.

* continued from previous page

Washington Office
Mailing: 601 Pennsylvania Ave. NW, Washington, DC — Tel: (202) 756 - 7219 Fax: (202) 207 - 3623

Political Action Committees

Express Scripts, Inc. Political Fund
13900 Riverport Dr.
Maryland Heights, MN 63043 — Tel: (952) 837 - 5103 Fax: (952) 837 - 7103

Contributions to Candidates: $16,000 (01/05 - 09/05)
Democrats: $7,500; Republicans: $8,500.

Principal Recipients

SENATE DEMOCRATS
Clinton, Hillary Rodham (NY) $5,000
Bingaman, Jeff (NM) $2,500

HOUSE DEMOCRATS

SENATE REPUBLICANS
Santorum, Richard (PA) $1,500

HOUSE REPUBLICANS
Barton, Joe L (TX) $2,000
Hart, Melissa (PA) $2,000
Hulshof, Kenny (MO) $1,000
Northup, Anne M. (KY) $1,000
Shadegg, John (AZ) $1,000

Corporate Foundations and Giving Programs

Express Scripts Foundation
13900 Riverport Dr.
Maryland Heights, MO 63043 — Tel: (314) 770 - 1666 Fax: (314) 702 - 7037 TF: (800) 332 - 5455

Annual Grant Total: none reported

Public Affairs and Related Activities Personnel

At Headquarters

LITTLEJOHN, Steve
V. President, Public Relations
Mailstop: M/S STL2IN
slittlejohn@express-scripts.com — Tel: (314) 702 - 7556 Fax: (314) 702 - 7059

MYERS, David
V. President, Investor Relations — Tel: (314) 702 - 7173 Fax: (314) 702 - 7037

At Washington Office

ROSADO, Mary
V. President, Federal Government Affairs — Tel: (202) 756 - 7219 Fax: (202) 207 - 3623

At Other Offices

MACK, Michelle D.
Government Affairs Analyst
6625 W. 78th St.
Mailstop: M/S BL0220
Bloomington, MN 55439 — Tel: (952) 820 - 7000 Fax: (952) 837 - 7103

ROWAN, Vernon C.
V. President, Government Affairs
6625 W. 78th St.
Bloomington, MN 55439
rowenc@express-scripts.com — Tel: (952) 837 - 5136 Fax: (952) 837 - 7103

Extended Stay America, Inc.

A hotel chain owner/operator.
www.extstay.com

Chairman of the Board
HUIZENGA, H. Wayne — Tel: (864) 573 - 1600 Fax: (864) 573 - 1695

Chief Exec. Officer
JOHNSON, George D., Jr. — Tel: (864) 573 - 1600 Fax: (864) 573 - 1695

Main Headquarters
Mailing: 100 Dunbar St., Spartanburg, SC 29306 — Tel: (864) 573 - 1600 Fax: (864) 573 - 1695

Public Affairs and Related Activities Personnel

At Headquarters

DILDY, Marshall L.
V. President, Human Resources — Tel: (864) 573 - 1600 Fax: (864) 573 - 1695

GROVES, Tim
Media Relations — Tel: (864) 573 - 1600 Fax: (864) 573 - 1695

Exxon Chemical Co.

See listing on page 188 under Exxon Mobil Chemical Co.

Exxon Mobil Chemical Co.

www.exxonmobil.com/chemical
Annual Revenues: $20.310 billion

Main Headquarters
Mailing: 13501 Katy Fwy., Houston, TX 77079 — Tel: (281) 870 - 6000 Fax: (281) 870 - 6661

Public Affairs and Related Activities Personnel

At Headquarters

WETZ, Philip A.
Worldwide Manager, Public Affairs — Tel: (281) 870 - 6075 Fax: (281) 588 - 4772

Exxon Mobil Corp.

A member of the Public Affairs Council. A multi-national energy corporation, formed by the merger of Exxon Corp. and Mobil Corp. in 1999, involved in all phases of petroleum exploration, refining and marketing. Subsidiaries include ExxonMobil Chemical Co., and ExxonMobil Coal and Minerals Co.
www.exxonmobil.com
Annual Revenues: $204.5 billion

Chairman and Chief Exec. Officer
RAYMOND, Lee R. — Tel: (972) 444 - 1000 Fax: (972) 444 - 1350

Main Headquarters
Mailing: 5959 Las Colinas Blvd., Irving, TX 75039-2298 — Tel: (972) 444 - 1000 Fax: (972) 444 - 1350

Washington Office
Contact: R. D. "Dan" Nelson
Mailing: 2000 K St., NW, Suite 710, Washington, DC 20006 — Tel: (202) 862 - 0200 Fax: (202) 862 - 0267

Political Action Committees

Exxon Mobil Corp. Political Action Committee (EXPAC)
Contact: Larry D. Swales
5959 Las Colinas Blvd.
Irving, TX 75039-2298 — Tel: (972) 444 - 1000 Fax: (972) 444 - 1350

Contributions to Candidates: $162,600 (01/05 - 09/05)
Democrats: $14,850; Republicans: $147,750.

Principal Recipients

SENATE DEMOCRATS

HOUSE DEMOCRATS
Edwards, Chet (TX) $4,000

SENATE REPUBLICANS
Burns, Conrad (MT) $8,000
Allen, George (VA) $5,000
Chafee, Lincoln (RI) $3,000
Ensign, John Eric (NV) $3,000
Kyl, Jon L (AZ) $3,000
Vitter, David (LA) $2,500
Hutchison, Kay Bailey (TX) $2,250

HOUSE REPUBLICANS
Wilson, Heather (NM) $5,050
Barton, Joe L (TX) $5,000
Blunt, Roy (MO) $5,000
DeLay, Tom (TX) $5,000
Hastert, Dennis J. (IL) $5,000
Musgrave, Marilyn (CO) $5,000
Pombo, Richard (CA) $4,000
Hayes, Robert (NC) $3,500

ExxonMobil Corporation Political Action Committee(Exxonmobil Pac)
Contact: Dean Phillips
325 Pennsylvania Ave. SE
P.O. Box 280
Washington, DC 20003

Contributions to Candidates: none reported (01/05 - 09/05)

Corporate Foundations and Giving Programs

Exxon Mobil Foundation
Contact: Edward F. Ahnert
5959 Las Colinas Blvd.
Irving, TX 75039-2298 — Tel: (972) 444 - 1124 Fax: (972) 444 - 1405

Annual Grant Total: over $5,000,000
Geographic Preference: National
Primary Interests: Education; Engineering; Math and Science

Exxon Mobil Corp. Contributions Program
Contact: Edward F. Ahnert
5959 Las Colinas Blvd.
Irving, TX 75039-2298 — Tel: (972) 444 - 1124 Fax: (972) 444 - 1405

Annual Grant Total: over $5,000,000
Geographic Preference: Area(s) in which the company operates; National
Primary Interests: Arts and Culture; Community Affairs; Education; Environment/Conservation; Health and Human Services; Minority Opportunities

Public Affairs and Related Activities Personnel

At Headquarters

AHNERT, Edward F.
Manager, Contributions and President, ExxonMobil Foundation — Tel: (972) 444 - 1124 Fax: (972) 444 - 1405

Exxon Mobil Corp.

• continued from previous page

CAVANAUGH, L. J.
V. President, Human Resources
Tel: (972) 444 - 1000
Fax: (972) 444 - 1350

CIRIGLIANO, Tom J.
Manager, Media Relations
Tel: (972) 444 - 1109
Fax: (972) 444 - 1138

COHEN, Kenneth P.
V. President, Public Affairs
Tel: (972) 444 - 1000
Fax: (972) 444 - 1130

MCCARRON, Suzanne
Manager, Communications
Tel: (972) 444 - 1125
Fax: (972) 444 - 1139

RILEY, James R.
Operations Manager, Public Affairs
Mailstop: Suite 2380
Tel: (972) 444 - 1190
Fax: (972) 444 - 1168

SPROW, Frank B.
V. President, Safety, Health and Environment
Tel: (972) 444 - 1677
Fax: (972) 444 - 1350

SWALES, Larry D.
Issues Advisor, Public Affairs
Tel: (972) 444 - 1000
Fax: (972) 444 - 1350

WANG, Bill
Manager, Investor Relations
Tel: (972) 444 - 1000
Fax: (972) 444 - 1350

WARRELL, Andrew
Manager, Investor Relations
Tel: (972) 444 - 1000
Fax: (972) 444 - 1350

At Washington Office

BLOOM, Jon
Washington Representative, Government Agencies
Tel: (202) 862 - 0200
Fax: (202) 862 - 0267

BUCHHOLTZ, Walt F.
Senior Washington Representative, Environmental Issues
Registered Federal Lobbyist.
Tel: (202) 862 - 0200
Fax: (202) 862 - 0267

FRANCIS, Peter
Senior International Advisor, Europe, Eurasia, and the Caspian
Tel: (202) 862 - 0200
Fax: (202) 862 - 0267

HAINES, Robert W.
Deputy Manager, International Relations
Registered Federal Lobbyist.
Tel: (202) 862 - 0222
Fax: (202) 862 - 0267

JACKSON, Lorie D.
Washington Representative, Senate
Tel: (202) 862 - 0200
Fax: (202) 862 - 0267

LEWIS, Buford
Washington Representative - U.S. Senate
Tel: (202) 862 - 0200
Fax: (202) 862 - 0267

MEALS, Simeon
International Advisor, Africa
Tel: (202) 862 - 0200
Fax: (202) 862 - 0267

MITCHELL, Jeanne
Washington Representative, House of Representatives
Registered Federal Lobbyist.
Tel: (202) 862 - 0200
Fax: (202) 862 - 0269

NELSON, R. D. "Dan"
V. President, Washington Office
Registered Federal Lobbyist.
Tel: (202) 862 - 0200
Fax: (202) 862 - 0267

TACKETT, Bruce
Washington Representative, Government Agencies
Registered Federal Lobbyist.
Tel: (202) 862 - 0275
Fax: (202) 862 - 0267

ZANDONA, Oliver
International Advisor, Middle East
Tel: (202) 862 - 0200
Fax: (202) 862 - 0267

At Other Offices

PHILLIPS, Dean
Pac Treasurer
325 Pennsylvania Ave. SE
P.O. Box 280
Washington, DC 20003

Fairchild Semiconductor Internat'l, Inc.

www.fairchildsemi.com

Chairman of the Board
POND, Kirk P.
Tel: (207) 775 - 8100
Fax: (207) 761 - 6020
TF: (800) 341 - 0392

Chief Exec. Officer
THOMPSON, Martk S.
Tel: (207) 775 - 8100
Fax: (207) 761 - 6020
TF: (800) 341 - 0392

Main Headquarters
Mailing: 82 Running Hill Rd.
South Portland, ME 04106-6020
Tel: (207) 775 - 8100
Fax: (207) 761 - 6020
TF: (800) 341 - 0392

Public Affairs and Related Activities Personnel

At Headquarters

HARRISON, Fran
Director, Corporate Communications and Governmental Relations
Tel: (207) 775 - 8100
Fax: (207) 761 - 8161
TF: (800) 341 - 0392

JANSON, Dan
Senior Director, Investor Relations
Tel: (207) 775 - 8660
Fax: (207) 761 - 3415
TF: (800) 341 - 0392

LONDON, Kevin B.
Senior V. President, Human Resources
Tel: (207) 775 - 8100
Fax: (207) 761 - 6020
TF: (800) 341 - 0392

OLSON, Patty
Media Relations
Tel: (207) 775 - 8728
Fax: (207) 761 - 6020
TF: (800) 341 - 0392

Family Dollar Stores, Inc.

A discount store chain.
www.familydollar.com
Annual Revenues: $4.6 billion

Chairman and Chief Exec. Officer
LEVINE, Howard R.
hlevine@familydollar.com
Tel: (704) 847 - 6961
Fax: (704) 847 - 0189

Main Headquarters
Mailing: P.O. Box 1017
Charlotte, NC 28201-1017
Tel: (704) 847 - 6961
Fax: (704) 847 - 0189

Public Affairs and Related Activities Personnel

At Headquarters

MAHONEY, George R., Jr.
Director
gmahoney@familydollar.com
Responsibilities include investor relations and corporate communications.
Tel: (704) 814 - 3252
Fax: (704) 841 - 1401

MCPHERSON, Samuel N.
Senior V. President, Human Resources
smcpherson@familydollar.com
Tel: (704) 814 - 3518
Fax: (704) 847 - 0189

Fannie Mae

A member of the Public Affairs Council. Formerly Federal Nat'l Mortgage Ass'n, the company legally changed its name to Fannie Mae in 1997. A federally chartered private corporation that supplies home mortgage funds by purchasing mortgage loans from private lenders.
www.fanniemae.com
Annual Revenues: $50.803 billion

Chairman and Chief Exec. Officer
RAINES, Franklin D.
Tel: (202) 752 - 7000
Fax: (202) 752 - 6014

Main Headquarters
Mailing: 3900 Wisconsin Ave. NW
Washington, DC 20016
Tel: (202) 752 - 7000
Fax: (202) 752 - 6099

Political Action Committees

Federal National Mortgage Association Political Action Committee (Fannie Mae PAC)
Contact: Duane Duncan
3900 Wisconsin Ave. NW
Washington, DC 20016
Tel: (202) 752 - 7000
Fax: (202) 752 - 6014

Contributions to Candidates: $167,950 (01/05 - 09/05)
Democrats: $100,950; Republicans: $67,000.

Principal Recipients

SENATE DEMOCRATS		HOUSE DEMOCRATS	
Carper, Thomas R (DE)	$6,000	Pelosi, Nancy (CA)	$5,000
Conrad, Kent (ND)	$6,000	Waters, Maxine (CA)	$5,000
Durbin, Richard J (IL)	$3,500	Kanjorski, Paul (PA)	$3,500
Stabenow, Debbie (MI)	$3,500	Israel, Steve (NY)	$3,000
SENATE REPUBLICANS		**HOUSE REPUBLICANS**	
Harris, Katherine (FL)	$9,000	Cantor, Eric (VA)	$5,000
Bennett, Robert F (UT)	$5,000	Feeney, Tom (FL)	$5,000
Santorum, Richard (PA)	$3,000	Bachus, Spencer (AL)	$4,000
		McHenry, Patrick (NC)	$4,000
		Ney, Robert W (OH)	$3,000
		Renzi, Richard (AZ)	$3,000

Corporate Foundations and Giving Programs

Fannie Mae Foundation
Contact: Stacey Davis
4000 Wisconsin Ave. NW
North Tower, Suite One
Washington, DC 20016-2804
Tel: (202) 274 - 8000
Fax: (202) 274 - 8111

Annual Grant Total: over $5,000,000
Recent recipients include: Nat'l Rural Development and Finance Corp., Homesign, Marshall Heights Community Development Organization, Development Corp. of Columbia Heights.
Primary Interests: Community Development; Housing

Public Affairs and Related Activities Personnel

At Headquarters

BANKS, Pamela F.
V. President, Regulatory Compliance
pamela_f_banks@fanniemae.com
Tel: (202) 752 - 7000
Fax: (202) 752 - 6099

Fannie Mae

* continued from previous page

BOHLEY, David
Tel: (202) 752 - 7000
Fax: (202) 752 - 6099

BURTON, Raschelle
Director, Mission Communications
Tel: (202) 752 - 7000
Fax: (202) 752 - 7044

DALEY, William R.
V. President, Government and Industry Relations
Tel: (202) 752 - 7000
Fax: (202) 752 - 6099

DAUE, Janice
V. President, News and Public Affairs
Tel: (202) 752 - 2131
Fax: (202) 752 - 3808

DAVIS, Michele
V. President, Regulatory Policy
Tel: (202) 752 - 7000
Fax: (202) 752 - 6099

DONILON, Thomas
Exec. V. President, Law and Policy
Tel: (202) 752 - 7000
Fax: (202) 752 - 6099

DUNCAN, Duane
Senior V. President, Government and Industry Relations
Tel: (202) 752 - 7000
Fax: (202) 752 - 6014

FITZPATRICK, Jeanne
Director, Consumer Resources
Tel: (202) 752 - 5717
Fax: (202) 753 - 019

GATTEN, Nathan
V. President, Government and Industry Relations
Tel: (202) 752 - 7000
Fax: (202) 752 - 6099

GREENER, Charles V. "Chuck"
Senior V. President, Communications
Tel: (202) 752 - 7000
Fax: (202) 752 - 6099

HILL, Sandra
Tel: (202) 752 - 7000
Fax: (202) 752 - 6099

LEVIN, Robert
Exec. V. President, Housing and Community Development
Tel: (202) 752 - 7000
Fax: (202) 752 - 6099

LIU, Margaret C.
V. President, Government and Industry Relations
Tel: (202) 752 - 7000
Fax: (202) 752 - 6099

LOWREY, Carmen Guzman
Tel: (202) 752 - 7000
Fax: (202) 752 - 6099

MALONEY, Robert H.
V. President, Government and Industry Relations
robert_h_maloney@fanniemae.com
Tel: (202) 752 - 7958
Fax: (202) 752 - 6014

MAURANO, Richard "Rick" V.
Director, Government and Industry Relations
Tel: (202) 752 - 7000
Fax: (202) 752 - 6099

SMITH, Janis
Director, Financial Communications
Tel: (202) 752 - 6673
Fax: (202) 752 - 7044

SUAREZ, Aquiles
Tel: (202) 752 - 7000
Fax: (202) 752 - 6099

THOMPSON, Michael
Tel: (202) 752 - 7000
Fax: (202) 752 - 6099

VAN ETTEN, Laura
Director, Government and Industry Relations
Tel: (202) 752 - 1442
Fax: (202) 752 - 6099

At Other Offices

DAVIS, Stacey
President and Chief Exec. Officer, Fannie Mae Foundation
4000 Wisconsin Ave. NW
North Tower, Suite One
Washington, DC 20016-2804
Tel: (202) 274 - 8000
Fax: (202) 274 - 8111

Farmers Group, Inc.

A member of the Public Affairs Council. An insurance management company. A member of the Zurich Financial Services Group.

www.farmers.com

Chairman and Chief Exec. Officer
FEINSTEIN, Martin D.
Tel: (323) 932 - 3211
Fax: (323) 932 - 3101

Main Headquarters
Mailing: 4680 Wilshire Blvd.
Los Angeles, CA 90010
Tel: (323) 932 - 3200
Fax: (323) 932 - 3101

Washington Office
Contact: Eric Rizzo
Mailing: 1201 F St., NW
Washington, DC 20004
Tel: (202) 737 - 1445
Fax: (202) 737 - 1446

Political Action Committees

Farmers Group Inc. PAC
Contact: Mark Royer
4680 Wilshire Blvd.
Los Angeles, CA 90010
Tel: (323) 964 - 8020
Fax: (323) 964 - 8095

Contributions to Candidates: $27,500 (01/05 - 09/05)
Democrats: $3,000; Republicans: $24,500.

Principal Recipients

SENATE DEMOCRATS

HOUSE DEMOCRATS

Vargas, Juan (CA)	$1,000

SENATE REPUBLICANS

Allen, George (VA)	$1,000
Inhofe, James M (OK)	$1,000
Kennedy, Mark (MN)	$1,000
Kyl, Jon L (AZ)	$1,000
Santorum, Richard (PA)	$1,000
Sununu, John (NH)	$1,000

HOUSE REPUBLICANS

Blunt, Roy (MO)	$1,000
Campbell, John (CA)	$1,000
Dreier, David (CA)	$1,000
Hastert, Dennis J. (IL)	$1,000
Hensarling, Jeb (TX)	$1,000
Herger, Wally (CA)	$1,000
Latham, Thomas P (IA)	$1,000
Porter, Jon (NV)	$1,000
Rogers, Michael J (MI)	$1,000
Royce, Ed Mr (CA)	$1,000
Simpson, Michael (ID)	$1,000
Thomas, William M (CA)	$1,000

Corporate Foundations and Giving Programs

Farmers Group, Inc. Corporate Contributions Program
Contact: Luisa Acosta-Franco
4680 Wilshire Blvd.
Los Angeles, CA 90010
Tel: (323) 932 - 3200

Annual Grant Total: $2,000,000 - $5,000,000

Geographic Preference: Area(s) in which the company operates

Primary Interests: Arts and Culture; Civic and Public Affairs; Education; Health and Human Services; Youth Services

Recent Recipients: Boys and Girls Club; Junior Achievement; Los Angeles Children's Museum; Nat'l Safety Council

Public Affairs and Related Activities Personnel

At Headquarters

ACOSTA-FRANCO, Luisa
Manager, Community Relations
Tel: (323) 932 - 3200

BEYER, Jeffrey C.
Senior V. President and Chief Communications Officer
(Farmers Insurance Group of Companies)
Tel: (323) 932 - 3200
Fax: (323) 932 - 3101

ROYER, Mark
Director, Political Action and Administration
mark.royer@farmersinsurance.com
Tel: (323) 964 - 8020
Fax: (323) 964 - 8095

TASAKA, Diane
Director, Corporate Communications
Tel: (323) 932 - 3018

TOOHEY, Mark
Assistant V. President, Government Affairs
Tel: (323) 930 - 6397
Fax: (323) 964 - 8095

WILSON, Wayne
V. President, Legislative and Regulatory Affairs
(Farmers Insurance Group of Companies)
Tel: (323) 932 - 3177
Fax: (323) 964 - 8095

At Washington Office

RIZZO, Eric
Director, Federal Affairs
(Farmers Insurance Group of Companies)
Registered Federal Lobbyist.
Tel: (202) 737 - 1445

At Other Offices

BACON, Kevin
Legislative Representative
(Farmers Insurance Group of Companies)
2400 Farmers Dr.
Columbus, OH 43235
Tel: (614) 764 - 7266

BENKO, JoAnna
Legislative Representative
100 Farmers Circle
Austin, TX 78728
Tel: (512) 238 - 4349
Fax: (512) 238 - 4348

BENSCHNEIDER, Mike
Legislative Representative
7535 E. Hampden Ave.
Suite 310
Denver, CO 80231
Tel: (303) 283 - 6126
Fax: (303) 283 - 6117

COMPAN, Bob
Legislative Representative
4425 Spring Mountain Rd.
Suite 350
Las Vegas, NV 89102
Tel: (702) 826 - 8666

DECHER, Kim
Legislative Representative
5314 S. Yale Dr.
Tulsa, OK 74135
Tel: (918) 496 - 3244
Fax: (918) 496 - 3286

DOWNS, Joe
Legislative Representative
(Farmers Insurance Group of Companies)
225 Eastwood Dr.
Jefferson City, MO 65101
Tel: (573) 635 - 9611

Farmers Group, Inc.

* continued from previous page

GALBRAITH, Russ — Tel: (501) 227 - 0553
Legislative Representative
P.O. Box 8204
Little Rock, AR 72221-8204

GARAVAGLIA, Burt — Tel: (323) 930 - 4016, Fax: (323) 964 - 8095
Director, Government Affairs
4680 Wilshire Blvd.
Los Angeles, CA 90010

HAYDEN, Kerry — Tel: (480) 926 - 0891, Fax: (480) 926 - 8951
Legislative Representative
1365 S. Gilbert Rd.
Floor 1-A
Mesa, AZ 85204

KAPPLAHN, Mike — Tel: (253) 857 - 8801, Fax: (253) 857 - 8816
Legislative Representative
P.O. Box 1074
Gig Harbor, WA 98335

KISTLER, Brenda Peters — Tel: (217) 632 - 2691, Fax: (217) 632 - 2710
Government Affairs Advocate
RR 1, Box 88A
Tallula, IL 62688
brenda-kistler@worldnet.att.net

MARCHANT, Ross H. — Tel: (801) 272 - 8081
Legislative Representative
P.O. Box 17357
Salt Lake City, UT 84117

MILLER, Brian — Tel: (503) 888 - 7765
Legislative Representative
(Farmers Insurance Group of Companies)
P.O. Box 42308
Portland, OR 97242

SAUCIER, Christine — Tel: (317) 581 - 3400
Legislative Representative
9555 Delegates Row
Indianapolis, IN 46240

STRANSKY, Paul — Tel: (616) 956 - 4096
Director, Government Affairs
(Farmers Insurance Group of Companies)
5600 Beech Tree Ln.
Caledonia, MI 49316

WRIGHT, Lee E. — Tel: (913) 661 - 6300
Legislative Representative
(Farmers Insurance Group of Companies)
P.O. Box 2910
Shawnee Mission, KS 66201

Farmers Insurance Group of Companies

See listing on page 190 under Farmers Group, Inc.

Farmers Insurance of Columbus, Inc.

See listing on page 190 under Farmers Group, Inc.

Farmers Mutual Insurance Co. of Nebraska

See listing on page 190 under Farmers Group, Inc.

Fastenal Co.

Manufactures and distributes fasteners, industrial products and construction products.
www.fastenal.com

Founder and Chairman — Tel: (507) 454 - 5374, Fax: (507) 453 - 8049
KIERLIN, Robert A.

Chief Exec. Officer and President — Tel: (507) 454 - 5374, Fax: (507) 453 - 8049
OBERTON, Willard D.

Main Headquarters
Mailing: P.O. Box 978, Winona, MN 55987 — Tel: (507) 454 - 5374, Fax: (507) 453 - 8049
Street: 2001 Theurer Blvd., Winona, MN 55987-1500

Public Affairs and Related Activities Personnel

At Headquarters

SLAGGIE, Stephen M. — Tel: (507) 453 - 8212, Fax: (507) 453 - 8049
Secretary
smslaggi@fastenal.com
Responsibilities include corporate philanthropy and investor relations.

WISECUP, Reyne K. — Tel: (507) 453 - 8112, Fax: (507) 453 - 8049
V. President, Employee Development

Federal Home Loan Mortgage Corp.

See listing on page 204 under Freddie Mac.

Federal-Mogul Corp.

A global manufacturer of a broad range of precision parts primarily for automobiles, trucks, and farm and construction vehicles.
www.federal-mogul.com

Chairman and Chief Exec. Officer — Tel: (248) 354 - 7700, Fax: (248) 354 - 8950
ALAPONT, Jose M.

Main Headquarters
Mailing: 26555 Northwestern Hwy., Southfield, MI 48034 — Tel: (248) 354 - 7700, Fax: (248) 354 - 8950

Political Action Committees

Federal-Mogul Corp. Employees' Political Action Committee
Contact: Mark Seng
26555 Northwestern Hwy.
Southfield, MI 48034 — Tel: (248) 354 - 7700, Fax: (248) 354 - 8950

Contributions to Candidates: $1,000 (01/05 - 09/05)
Republicans: $1,000.

Principal Recipients

SENATE REPUBLICANS	HOUSE REPUBLICANS	
	Knollenberg, Joe (MI)	$1,000

Corporate Foundations and Giving Programs

Federal-Mogul Corporate Contributions Program
Contact: Richard P. Randazzo
26555 Northwestern Hwy.
Southfield, MI 48034 — Tel: (248) 354 - 4380, Fax: (248) 354 - 8950

Annual Grant Total: none reported

Public Affairs and Related Activities Personnel

At Headquarters

HALPIN, Janet — Tel: (248) 354 - 8847, Fax: (248) 354 - 8950
Director, Investor Relations
janet_halpin@fmo.com

RANDAZZO, Richard P. — Tel: (248) 354 - 4380, Fax: (248) 354 - 8950
Senior V. President, Human Resources
richard_randazzo@fmo.com
Responsibilities include corporate contributions.

REMBOULIS, Marie — Tel: (248) 354 - 9809, Fax: (248) 354 - 7060
V. President, Corporate Communications

SENG, Mark — Tel: (248) 354 - 7700, Fax: (248) 354 - 8950
PAC Treasurer

Federal Nat'l Mortgage Ass'n

See listing on page 189 under Fannie Mae.

Federal Signal Corp.

Manufacturer of safety, signaling and communications equipment.
www.federalsignal.com

Chairman of the Board — Tel: (630) 954 - 2000
JANNING, James C.

President and Chief Exec. Officer — Tel: (630) 954 - 2000
WELDING, Robert D.

Main Headquarters
Mailing: 1415 W. 22nd St., Suite 1100, Oak Brook, IL 60523 — Tel: (630) 954 - 2000

Public Affairs and Related Activities Personnel

At Headquarters

DICKENS, Kim L. — Tel: (630) 954 - 2000
V. President, Human Resources

KUSHNER, Stephanie K. — Tel: (630) 954 - 2020
V. President and Chief Financial Officer
Responsibilities include investor relations.

WITTIG, Paul — Tel: (630) 954 - 2030
Director, Rish Management, Trade and Finance

Federated Department Stores, Inc.

A member of the Public Affairs Council. Federated currently operates department stores nationally under the names of Macy's, Bon-Macy's, Burdines-Macy's, Rich's-Macy's, Lazarus-Macy's, Goldsmith's-Macy's, and Bloomingdale's (see separate listing). The company acquired The May Department Stores Co. in August of 2005.
www.federated-fds.com
Annual Revenues: $604 million

Chairman, President and Chief Exec. Officer — Tel: (513) 579 - 7000, Fax: (513) 579 - 7555, TF: (800) 261 - 5385
LUNDGREN, Terry

Main Headquarters
Mailing: Seven W. Seventh St., Cincinnati, OH 45202 — Tel: (513) 579 - 7000, Fax: (513) 579 - 7555, TF: (800) 261 - 5385

Federated Department Stores, Inc.

* continued from previous page

Political Action Committees

Federated Department Stores Inc. Political Action Committee
Contact: Joel Belsky
Seven W. Seventh St. — Tel: (513) 579 - 7000
Cincinnati, OH 45202 — Fax: (513) 579 - 7555
TF: (800) 261 - 5385

Contributions to Candidates: none reported (01/05 - 09/05)

Federated Retail Holdings Inc. PAC
Contact: Richard A. Cohen
611 Olive St. — Tel: (314) 342 - 6725
Suite 1730 — Fax: (314) 342 - 3066
St. Louis, MO 63101

Contributions to Candidates: $32,000 (01/05 - 09/05)
Democrats: $4,000; Republicans: $28,000.

Corporate Foundations and Giving Programs

Federated Department Stores Foundation
Contact: Dixie Barker
Seven W. Seventh St. — Tel: (513) 579 - 7569
Cincinnati, OH 45202 — Fax: (513) 579 - 7185
TF: (800) 261 - 5385

Assets: $17,576,870 (2001)
Annual Grant Total: over $5,000,000
Foundation and non-Foundation contributions totalled $15.4 million in 2001.
Geographic Preference: Area in which the company is headquartered; Area(s) in which the company operates
Primary Interests: AIDS/HIV; Community Development; Women
Recent Recipients: American Cancer Society; Children's Museum; Nat'l Ass'n for the Advancement of Colored People; Women's Crisis Center

Public Affairs and Related Activities Personnel

At Headquarters

BARKER, Dixie — Tel: (513) 579 - 7569
Manager, Corporate Contributions; and Foundation Administrator — Fax: (513) 579 - 7185; TF: (800) 261 - 5385

BELSKY, Joel — Tel: (513) 579 - 7000
Corporate Controller, Federated Department Stores Inc. Political Action Committee — Fax: (513) 579 - 7555; TF: (800) 261 - 5385

CLARK, David W. — Tel: (513) 579 - 7000
Senior V. President, Human Resources — Fax: (513) 579 - 7555; TF: (800) 261 - 5385

CODY, Thomas G. — Tel: (513) 579 - 7000
V. Chairman — Fax: (513) 579 - 7555; TF: (800) 261 - 5385
Responsibilities include legal, human resources, external affairs, and corporate philanthropy.

COGGAN, Jean Reisinger — Tel: (513) 579 - 7315
Director, Community Relations — Fax: (513) 579 - 7555; TF: (800) 261 - 5385

ROBINSON, Susan — Tel: (513) 579 - 7778
Operating V. President, Investor Relations — Fax: (513) 579 - 7393; TF: (800) 261 - 5385

SHAWMEKER, Mary Ann — Tel: (513) 579 - 7292
Operations V. President, Corporate Communications — Fax: (513) 579 - 7185; TF: (800) 261 - 5385

ZORN, Michael — Tel: (513) 579 - 7000
V. President, Employee Relations — Fax: (513) 579 - 7555; TF: (800) 261 - 5385

At Other Offices

COHEN, Richard A. — Tel: (314) 342 - 6725
V. President, Public Affairs and Senior Counsel — Fax: (314) 342 - 3066
611 Olive St.
Suite 1730
Mailstop: M/S 1750
St. Louis, MO 63101

GOLDBERG, Edward — Tel: (212) 494 - 5568
V. President, Government Affairs
(Macy's East)
151 West 34th St.
New York, NY 10001

MEUNIER, Louis — Tel: (415) 954 - 6406
Exec. V. President, External Affairs — Fax: (415) 984 - 7137
(Macy's West)
50 O'Farrell St.
San Francisco, CA 94108

FedEx Corp.

A member of the Public Affairs Council. FedEx Corp. is composed of five operating companies including FedEx Express, FedEx Ground, Fed Ex Freight (see separate listing), FedEx Trade Networks, and Fed Ex Custom Critical.
www.fedex.com
Annual Revenues: $20.607 billion

Chairman, President and Chief Exec. Officer — Tel: (901) 369 - 3600
SMITH, Frederick W. — TF: (800) 238 - 5355

Main Headquarters
Mailing: 942 S. Shady Grove Rd. — Tel: (901) 369 - 3600
Memphis, TN 38120 — TF: (800) 238 - 5355

Washington Office
Contact: Kathryn Rand
Mailing: 101 Constitution Ave., NW — Tel: (202) 218 - 3800
Suite 801 East
Washington, DC 20001

Political Action Committees

FedEx PAC
Contact: Kathryn Rand
101 Constitution Ave., NW — Tel: (202) 218 - 3800
Suite 801 East
Washington, DC 20001

Contributions to Candidates: $346,900 (01/05 - 09/05)
Democrats: $119,500; Republicans: $227,400.

Principal Recipients

SENATE DEMOCRATS		HOUSE DEMOCRATS	
Ford, Harold E Jr (TN)	$10,000	Thompson, Bennie (MS)	$8,000
Byrd, Robert C (WV)	$5,000		

SENATE REPUBLICANS		HOUSE REPUBLICANS	
Burns, Conrad (MT)	$7,000	Porter, Jon (NV)	$6,000
Thomas, Craig (WY)	$6,500	Wilson, Heather (NM)	$6,000
Ensign, John Eric (NV)	$5,000		
Enzi, Michael B (WY)	$5,000		
Kyl, Jon L (AZ)	$5,000		
Lott, Trent (MS)	$5,000		

Corporate Foundations and Giving Programs

Global FedEx Community Relations
Contact: Rose Flonorl
3610 Hacks Cross Rd. — Tel: (901) 434 - 7773
Memphis, TN 38125 — Fax: (901) 434 - 7882

Annual Grant Total: none reported
Guidelines available.
Primary Interests: Education; Health and Human Services; Social Services
Recent Recipients: American Red Cross; March of Dimes; United Way

Public Affairs and Related Activities Personnel

At Headquarters

CLIPPARD, J. H., Jr. — Tel: (901) 818 - 7468
Staff V. President, Investor Relations — TF: (800) 238 - 5355
jhclippard@fedex.com

GLENN, T. Michael — Tel: (901) 369 - 3600
Exec. V. President, Market Development and Corporate Communications — TF: (800) 238 - 5355

LIPTROT, Martin — Tel: (901) 369 - 3600
Managing Director, Global Communications — TF: (800) 238 - 5355

MARGARITIS, Bill — Tel: (901) 818 - 7090
Corporate V. President, Worldwide Corporate Communications and Investor Relations — TF: (800) 238 - 5355
wgmargaritis@fedex.com

MUNOZ, Sandra — Tel: (901) 434 - 7781
Government Affairs and International Media Relations Contact — TF: (800) 238 - 5355
smunoz@fedex.com

PARKER, Virginia M. — Tel: (901) 818 - 7443
Administrator, Government Affairs — Fax: (901) 818 - 7194; TF: (800) 238 - 5355

ROBERTSON, Pamela — Tel: (901) 434 - 7048
Community Relations Contact — TF: (800) 238 - 5355
pam.robertson@fedex.com

At Washington Office

ADAMS, Gina — Tel: (202) 218 - 3800
Corporate V. President, Government Affairs — Fax: (202) 218 - 3803
gfadams@fedex.com
Registered Federal Lobbyist.

DICKEY, Ann S. — Tel: (202) 218 - 3800
Registered Federal Lobbyist.

HUGHES, Gerald F. — Tel: (202) 218 - 3800
Registered Federal Lobbyist.

KRAUSE, Kristin — Tel: (202) 218 - 3800
Senior Communications Specialist — Fax: (202) 218 - 3803
kristin.krause@fedex.com

FedEx Corp.

* continued from previous page

MASTERSON, Ken — Tel: (202) 218 - 3800
Executive Vice President
Registered Federal Lobbyist.

O'KEEFE, Rush — Tel: (202) 218 - 3800
V. President, Regulatory
Registered Federal Lobbyist.

PRYOR, David, Jr. — Tel: (202) 218 - 3800
Senior Federal Affairs Representative
Registered Federal Lobbyist.

RAND, Kathryn — Tel: (202) 218 - 3800
Manager; PAC Treasurer
Registered Federal Lobbyist.

RODGERS, Richard F. — Tel: (202) 218 - 3800
Staff V. President, Government Affairs

At Other Offices

FLONORL, Rose — Tel: (901) 434 - 7773; Fax: (901) 434 - 7882
Manager, Global Community Relations
3610 Hacks Cross Rd.
Memphis, TN 38125

FedEx Freight

A less-than-truckload subsidiary of FedEx Corp. (see separate listing) that consists of FedEx Freight East (formerly known as American Freightways) and FedEx Freight West (formerly known as Viking Freight).

www.fedexfreight.fedex.com

Annual Revenues: $2 billion

President and Chief Exec. Officer — Tel: (901) 434 - 3122
DUNCAN, Douglas G.

Main Headquarters
Mailing: 1715 Aaron Brenner Dr. — Tel: (901) 434 - 3122
Renaissance Center, Suite 600
Memphis, TN 38120

Public Affairs and Related Activities Personnel

At Headquarters

PHILLIPS, Debra — Tel: (901) 434 - 3122; Fax: (901) 434 - 3155
Managing Director, Communications
debra.phillips@fedex.com

FedEx Kinko's Office and Print Services

Formerly known as Kinko's, Inc. A photocopying, duplicating and printing service company. The former Kinko's, Inc. was acquired by FedEx Corp. (see separate listing) in February, 2004.

www.fedexkinkos.com

President and Chief Exec. Officer — Tel: (214) 550 - 7000
KUSIN, Gary

Main Headquarters
Mailing: Three Galleria Tower — Tel: (214) 550 - 7000; TF: (800) 254 - 6567
13155 Noel Rd., Suite 1600
Dallas, TX 75240

Public Affairs and Related Activities Personnel

At Headquarters

FISHER, Charlie — Tel: (214) 550 - 7000; TF: (800) 254 - 6567
Senior V. President, Human Resources

ROGERO, Larry — Tel: (214) 550 - 7000
Director, Environmental Affairs

THILL, Maggie — Tel: (214) 550 - 7026; Fax: (214) 550 - 7217
Corporate Communications
maggie.thill@fedexkinkos.com

Feld Entertainment, Inc.

An amusement and recreation services company. Shows include Ringling Brothers & Barnum & Bailey Circus, Walt Disney on Ice, and Siegfried & Roy.

www.feldentertainment.com

Chairman and Chief Exec. Officer — Tel: (703) 448 - 4000; Fax: (703) 448 - 4091
FELD, Kenneth

Main Headquarters
Mailing: 8607 Westwood Center Dr. — Tel: (703) 448 - 4000; Fax: (703) 448 - 4100
Vienna, VA 22182

Public Affairs and Related Activities Personnel

At Headquarters

ALBERT, Thomas L. — Tel: (703) 448 - 4000; Fax: (703) 448 - 4100
V. President, Government Relations

FOLK, Cassie — Tel: (703) 448 - 4000; Fax: (703) 448 - 4100
Manager, Government Relations

MAYER, Jerome — Tel: (703) 448 - 4000; Fax: (703) 448 - 4100
Legislative Representative

PAK, Shannon — Tel: (703) 448 - 4000; Fax: (703) 448 - 4100
Contact, Public Relations

Fellowes Manufacturing Co.

Manufacturer of office equipment and computer accessories.

www.fellowes.com

Chairman and Chief Exec. Officer — Tel: (630) 893 - 1600
FELLOWES, James E.

Main Headquarters
Mailing: 1789 Norwood Ave. — Tel: (630) 893 - 1600; TF: (800) 955 - 0959
Itasca, IL 60143-1095

Public Affairs and Related Activities Personnel

At Headquarters

GARRARD, Julie — Tel: (630) 893 - 1600 Ext: 2563; Fax: (630) 893 - 1683; TF: (800) 955 - 0959
Corporate Marketing Manager
jgarrard@fellowes.com

Responsibilities include public relations.

Ferro Corp.

A manufacturer of specialty materials and chemicals.

www.ferro.com

Annual Revenues: $1.6 million

Chairman and Chief Exec. Officer — Tel: (216) 641 - 8580
ORTINO, Hector R.

Main Headquarters
Mailing: 1000 Lakeside Ave. — Tel: (216) 641 - 8580; Fax: (216) 875 - 6195
Cleveland, OH 44114-7000

Corporate Foundations and Giving Programs

Ferro Foundation
Contact: Don Katchman
1000 Lakeside Ave. — Tel: (216) 875 - 6241; Fax: (216) 875 - 7237
Cleveland, OH 44114-7000

Annual Grant Total: $400,000 - $500,000
Geographic Preference: Cleveland, OH
Primary Interests: Arts and Humanities; Civic and Public Affairs; Education; Health and Human Services
Recent Recipients: Nat'l Merit Scholarship; United Negro College Fund; United Way; YMCA

Public Affairs and Related Activities Personnel

At Headquarters

KATCHMAN, Don — Tel: (216) 875 - 6241; Fax: (216) 875 - 7237
V. President, Ferro Foundation; and Corporate Risk Manager
katchman@ferro.com

FHP Internat'l Corp.

See listing on page 369 under PacifiCare Health Systems, Inc.

Fidelity Investments

See listing on page 200 under FMR Corp.

Fidelity Nat'l Financial, Inc.

A title insurance underwriter and provider of selected financial services. Subsidiaries include Chicago Title, Ticor Title, Security Union Title, Fidelity Nat'l Title, and Alamo Title.

www.fnf.com

Chairman and Chief Exec. Officer — Tel: (904) 854 - 8100
FOLEY, William P., II

Main Headquarters
Mailing: 601 Riverside Ave. — Tel: (904) 854 - 8100; Fax: (904) 357 - 1007
Jacksonville, FL 32204

Political Action Committees

Fidelity Nat'l Financial Inc. PAC
Contact: Peter T. Sadowski
601 Riverside Ave. — Tel: (904) 854 - 8100
Jacksonville, FL 32204

Contributions to Candidates: $3,250 (01/05 - 09/05)
Republicans: $3,250.

Principal Recipients

SENATE REPUBLICANS		HOUSE REPUBLICANS	
Santorum, Richard (PA)	$1,000	Bachus, Spencer (AL)	$1,000
		Baker, Hugh (LA)	$1,000

Fidelity Nat'l Financial, Inc.

** continued from previous page*

Public Affairs and Related Activities Personnel

At Headquarters

MURPHY, Dan K. — Tel: (904) 854 - 8120
Senior V. President, Finance and Investor Relations — Fax: (904) 357 - 1023
dkmurphy@fnf.com
Responsibilities include media relations.

SADOWSKI, Peter T. — Tel: (904) 854 - 8100
Treasurer, Fidelity Nat'l Financial Inc. Political Action Committee
Mailstop: Suite 220
ptsadowski@fnf.com

Fiesta Mart Inc.

Retail supermarkets.
www.fiestamart.com

President and Chief Exec. Officer
KATOPODIS, Louis — Tel: (713) 869 - 5060; Fax: (713) 869 - 6197

Main Headquarters
Mailing: 5235 Katy Fwy.
Houston, TX 77007 — Tel: (713) 869 - 5060; Fax: (713) 869 - 6197

Corporate Foundations and Giving Programs

Fiesta Mart Inc. Giving Program
Contact: Juanita Elizondo
5235 Katy Fwy.
Houston, TX 77007 — Tel: (713) 869 - 5060 Ext: 3268; Fax: (713) 869 - 6197

Annual Grant Total: none reported

Public Affairs and Related Activities Personnel

At Headquarters

ELIZONDO, Juanita — Tel: (713) 869 - 5060 Ext: 3268
Contact, Fiesta Mart Inc. Giving Program — Fax: (713) 869 - 6197

MURPHY, Bernie — Tel: (713) 869 - 5060 Ext: 243
Director, Public Affairs — Fax: (713) 869 - 6197

PARRISH, Laura — Tel: (713) 869 - 5060
Human Resources Contact — Fax: (713) 869 - 6197

Fifth Third Bancorp.

A bank holding corporation. Acquired Old Kent Financial Corp. in October of 2001.
www.53.com

President and Chief Exec. Officer
SCHAEFER, George A., Jr. — Tel: (513) 579 - 5300; Fax: (513) 579 - 5226; TF: (800) 972 - 3030

Main Headquarters
Mailing: 38 Fountain Square
Cincinnati, OH 45263 — Tel: (513) 579 - 5300; Fax: (513) 579 - 5226; TF: (800) 972 - 3030

Political Action Committees

Fifth Third Bancorp PAC
Contact: Vernon Bailey
38 Fountain Square
Cincinnati, OH 45263 — Tel: (513) 579 - 5300; Fax: (513) 579 - 5226; TF: (800) 972 - 3030

Contributions to Candidates: $17,000 (01/05 - 09/05)
Republicans: $17,000.

Principal Recipients

SENATE REPUBLICANS

HOUSE REPUBLICANS

Dewine, R. Pat (OH)	$5,000
Pryce, Deborah (OH)	$3,500
Tiberi, Patrick (OH)	$3,000
Davis, Geoffrey (KY)	$2,500
Hobson, David (OH)	$1,500
Ney, Robert W (OH)	$1,500

Corporate Foundations and Giving Programs

Fifth Third Foundation
Contact: Heidi B. Jark
38 Fountain Square
Cincinnati, OH 45263 — Tel: (513) 579 - 5300; Fax: (513) 579 - 5226; TF: (800) 972 - 3030

Annual Grant Total: over $5,000,000
Geographic Preference: Area(s) in which the company operates; Florida; Indiana; Kentucky; Ohio; Tennessee; Pennsylvania; Michigan; Illinois; Missouri
Primary Interests: Arts and Culture; Higher Education; United Way Campaigns
Recent Recipients: Boy Scouts of America

Public Affairs and Related Activities Personnel

At Headquarters

BAILEY, Vernon — Tel: (513) 579 - 5300; Fax: (513) 579 - 5226; TF: (800) 972 - 3030
PAC Treasurer

DECOURAY, Debra — Tel: (513) 579 - 4153; Fax: (513) 534 - 6701; TF: (800) 972 - 3030
V. President, Corporate Communications

FINDLEY, Mary Sue — Tel: (513) 579 - 5300; Fax: (513) 579 - 5226; TF: (800) 972 - 3030
V. President, Human Resources

JARK, Heidi B. — Tel: (513) 579 - 5300; Fax: (513) 579 - 5226; TF: (800) 972 - 3030
Foundation Contact

JENNINGS, Roberta R. — Tel: (513) 579 - 4153; Fax: (513) 579 - 5226; TF: (800) 972 - 3030
V. President and Corporate Director

RUEBEL, Thomas J. — Tel: (513) 579 - 5300; Fax: (513) 579 - 5226; TF: (800) 972 - 3030
Director, Government Affairs

The First American Corp.

A provider of business information.
www.firstam.com
Annual Revenues: $4.7 billion

Chairman, President and Chief Exec. Officer
KENNEDY, Parker S. — Tel: (714) 800 - 3000; Fax: (714) 800 - 4790

Main Headquarters
Mailing: One First American Way
Santa Ana, CA 92707 — Tel: (714) 800 - 3000; Fax: (714) 800 - 4790

Political Action Committees

The First American Corp. PAC
Contact: Kenneth DeGiorgio
One First American Way
Santa Ana, CA 92707 — Tel: (714) 800 - 3000; Fax: (714) 800 - 4790

Contributions to Candidates: none reported (01/05 - 09/05)

Corporate Foundations and Giving Programs

First American Financial Foundation
Contact: Parker S. Kennedy
One First American Way
Santa Ana, CA 92707 — Tel: (714) 800 - 3000; Fax: (714) 800 - 4790

Assets: $213,991,000 (2002)
Annual Grant Total: $500,000 - $750,000
Geographic Preference: California
Primary Interests: Arts and Humanities; Education; Health and Human Services

Public Affairs and Related Activities Personnel

At Headquarters

BANDY, Jo Etta — Tel: (714) 800 - 3298
V. President, Corporate Communications — Fax: (714) 800 - 4790

DEGIORGIO, Kenneth — Tel: (714) 800 - 3000
Senior V. President and General Counsel; PAC Treasurer — Fax: (714) 800 - 4790

WARREN, Denise M. — Tel: (714) 800 - 3915
V. President and Director, Investor Relations — Fax: (714) 800 - 4790
dwarren@firstam.com

First Bank System, Inc.

See listing on page 497 under US Bancorp.

First Citizens BancShares

A bank holding company.
www.firstcitizens.com

Main Headquarters
Mailing: P.O. Box 27131
Raleigh, NC 27611 — Tel: (919) 716 - 7000; Fax: (919) 716 - 7074
Street: 3128 Smoketree Ct.
Raleigh, NC 27604

Political Action Committees

First Citizens BancShares Inc. Political Action Committee
Contact: Alex G. MacFadyen, Jr.
P.O. Box 27131
Raleigh, NC 27611 — Tel: (919) 716 - 3127; Fax: (919) 716 - 7074

Contributions to Candidates: $4,500 (01/05 - 09/05)

First Citizens BancShares

** continued from previous page*

Democrats: $2,000; Republicans: $2,500.

Principal Recipients

SENATE DEMOCRATS		HOUSE DEMOCRATS	
		Etheridge, Bob (NC)	$1,000
		McIntyre, Mike (NC)	$1,000
SENATE REPUBLICANS		**HOUSE REPUBLICANS**	
		Jones, Walter (NC)	$1,000
		Myrick, Sue (NC)	$1,000

Corporate Foundations and Giving Programs

First Citizens Bank Corporate Contributions
Contact: Barbara W. Thompson
P.O. Box 27131 Tel: (919) 716 - 2716
Raleigh, NC 27611 Fax: (919) 716 - 7074

Annual Grant Total: none reported
Geographic Preference: North Carolina; Virginia; West Virginia

Public Affairs and Related Activities Personnel

At Headquarters

HAGGERTY, Terry Tel: (919) 716 - 7459
Manager, Internal Communications Fax: (919) 716 - 7074

MACFADYEN, Alex G., Jr. Tel: (919) 716 - 3127
Group V. President and Director, Government Affairs (First Citizens Bank) Fax: (919) 716 - 7074

THOMPSON, Barbara W. Tel: (919) 716 - 2716
Senior V. President and Public Relations Manager Fax: (919) 716 - 7074
Responsibilities include corporate philanthropy.

First Citizens Bank

See listing on page 194 under First Citizens BancShares.

First Data

Provides credit, debit, smart card and stored-value card issuing and merchant transaction processing services; Internet commerce solutions; Western Union money transfers and money orders; and check processing and verification services. Acquired EuroProcessing Internat'l in 2005.

www.firstdata.com

Chairman and Chief Exec. Officer Tel: (303) 488 - 8000
FOTE, Charlie Fax: (303) 967 - 6705

Main Headquarters
Mailing: 6200 S. Quebec St. Tel: (303) 967 - 8000
Greenwood Village, CO 80111 Fax: (303) 967 - 6705

Political Action Committees

First Data Corp. Employees for Responsible Government
Contact: Joe Samuel
6200 S. Quebec St. Tel: (303) 967 - 7195
Greenwood Village, CO 80111 Fax: (303) 967 - 6705

Contributions to Candidates: $11,500 (01/05 - 09/05)
Democrats: $6,000; Republicans: $5,500.

Principal Recipients

SENATE DEMOCRATS		HOUSE DEMOCRATS	
Carper, Thomas R (DE)	$2,000	Salazar, John (CO)	$2,000
		Menendez, Robert (NJ)	$1,000
		Moore, Dennis (KS)	$1,000
SENATE REPUBLICANS		**HOUSE REPUBLICANS**	
Hatch, Orrin (UT)	$2,500	LaTourette, Steve (OH)	$1,000
Allen, George (VA)	$1,000	Reynolds, Thomas (NY)	$1,000

Corporate Foundations and Giving Programs

First Data Western Union Foundation
Contact: Luella Chavez D'Angelo
6200 S. Quebec St. Tel: (303) 967 - 6493
Greenwood Village, CO 80111 Fax: (303) 967 - 6705

Annual Grant Total: over $5,000,000
More information about the foundation can be found on the web at the following address: www.firstdatawesternunion.org.
Primary Interests: Disaster Relief; Education; Health and Human Services
Recent Recipients: Goodwill Industries; Habitat for Humanity; Int'l Fed. of Red Cross and Red Crescent Socs.

Public Affairs and Related Activities Personnel

At Headquarters

CHAYET, Victor Tel: (303) 967 - 8000
V. President, Corporate Communications Fax: (303) 889 - 6287

D'ANGELO, Luella Chavez Tel: (303) 967 - 6493
President, Foundation Fax: (303) 967 - 6705
Mailstop: Suite 370AU
luella.d'angelo@firstdatacorp.com

DALY, Tim Tel: (303) 967 - 5222
Senior V. President, Government Affairs Fax: (303) 967 - 6705

NIEHAUS, Fred Tel: (303) 967 - 8000
Senior V. President, Public Affairs Fax: (303) 967 - 6705

SAMUEL, Joe Tel: (303) 967 - 7195
V. President, Government Relations Fax: (303) 967 - 6705

WHEELER, Colin Tel: (303) 967 - 6553
V. President, Media Relations Fax: (303) 967 - 6705
colin.wheeler@firstdatacorp.com

First Hawaiian Bank

See listing on page 60 under BancWest Corp.

First Health

A member of the Public Affairs Council. A health care cost management company.
www.firsthealth.com
Annual Revenues: $890.9 million

President and Chief Exec. Officer Tel: (630) 737 - 7900
WRISTEN, Edward L. Fax: (630) 737 - 7856
TF: (800) 445 - 1425

Main Headquarters
Mailing: 3200 Highland Ave. Tel: (630) 737 - 7900
Downers Grove, IL 60515-1223 Fax: (630) 737 - 7856
TF: (800) 445 - 1425

Washington Office
Contact: Patricia A. Quealy
Mailing: 1133 21st St. NW Tel: (202) 872 - 0556
Suite 450 Fax: (202) 872 - 0908
Washington, DC 20036

Political Action Committees

First Health Group Corp. PAC (FHGPAC)
Contact: Joseph H. Whitters
3200 Highland Ave. Tel: (630) 737 - 7900
Downers Grove, IL 60515-1223 Fax: (630) 719 - 0093
TF: (800) 719 - 9701

Contributions to Candidates: $24,500 (01/05 - 09/05)
Democrats: $6,000; Republicans: $18,500.

Principal Recipients

SENATE DEMOCRATS		HOUSE DEMOCRATS	
Carper, Thomas R (DE)	$1,000	Hoyer, Steny (MD)	$2,000
Conrad, Kent (ND)	$1,000	Matheson, James (UT)	$1,000
Nelson, Benjamin (NE)	$1,000		
SENATE REPUBLICANS		**HOUSE REPUBLICANS**	
Kyl, Jon L (AZ)	$3,000	Hart, Melissa (PA)	$5,000
Santorum, Richard (PA)	$1,000	Weller, Jerry (IL)	$1,500
		Biggert, Judy (IL)	$1,000
		Boehner, John (OH)	$1,000
		Camp, David Lee (MI)	$1,000
		Deal, Nathan (GA)	$1,000
		English, Philip S (PA)	$1,000
		Hulshof, Kenny (MO)	$1,000
		Northup, Anne M. (KY)	$1,000
		Shadegg, John (AZ)	$1,000

Public Affairs and Related Activities Personnel

At Headquarters

GOSPO, Nancy Tel: (630) 737 - 8557
Director, Advertising and Public Relations Fax: (630) 737 - 7856
nancygospo@firsthealth.com TF: (800) 445 - 1425

HIRD, Andrea Tel: (630) 737 - 7900
Director, Communications Fax: (630) 737 - 7856
communications@firsthealth.com TF: (800) 445 - 1425

WHITTERS, Joseph H. Tel: (630) 737 - 7900
V. President, Finance and Chief Financial Officer Fax: (630) 719 - 0093
TF: (800) 719 - 9701
Responsibilities include political action and public affairs.

At Washington Office

DODSON, Melissa Tel: (202) 872 - 0556
Assistant V. President, Government Affairs Fax: (202) 872 - 0908
Registered Federal Lobbyist.

QUEALY, Patricia A. Tel: (202) 872 - 0556
V. President, Government Affairs Fax: (202) 872 - 0908
Registered Federal Lobbyist.

First Horizon Nat'l Corp.

Formerly known as First Tennessee Nat'l Corp. A financial services company.

www.ftb.com

Chairman, President and Chief Exec. Officer
GLASS, J. Kenneth — Tel: (901) 523 - 4444

Main Headquarters
Mailing: 165 Madison Ave.
Memphis, TN 38103
Tel: (901) 523 - 4444
Fax: (901) 523 - 4030

Political Action Committees

First Horizon Nat'l Corp. Federal PAC
Contact: J. Terrence Lee
165 Madison Ave.
Memphis, TN 38103
Tel: (901) 523 - 4380
Fax: (901) 523 - 4354

Contributions to Candidates: $500 (01/05 - 09/05)
Democrats: $500.

Principal Recipients

SENATE DEMOCRATS		HOUSE DEMOCRATS	
		Gordon, Barton (TN)	$500

Corporate Foundations and Giving Programs

First Horizon Nat'l Corp. Contributions Program
Contact: J. Terrence Lee
165 Madison Ave.
Memphis, TN 38103
Tel: (901) 523 - 4380
Fax: (901) 523 - 4354

Annual Grant Total: $1,000,000 - $2,000,000
All decisions are made by local bank presidents and in cities outside of Memphis. All requests should be directed to their attention. Contributions are made only in cities where the bank has locations. Most funds are committed to bank-initiated projects such as Lesson Line.
Geographic Preference: Area(s) in which the company operates

Public Affairs and Related Activities Personnel

At Headquarters

CHERRY, Kim
V. President, Corporate Communications
Tel: (901) 523 - 4726
Fax: (901) 523 - 4354

DAWSON, Walter
Senior Communications Specialist
Tel: (901) 523 - 4444

HILLIARD, Herb
Exec. V. President, Risk Management
Responsibilities include government relations.
Tel: (901) 523 - 4826
Fax: (901) 523 - 4934

LEE, J. Terrence
Senior V. President, Corporate Communications
Tel: (901) 523 - 4380
Fax: (901) 523 - 4354

First Midwest Bancorp, Inc.

A banking holding company.

www.firstmidwest.com

Chairman of the Board
O'MEARA, Robert P.
Tel: (630) 875 - 7450
Fax: (630) 875 - 7369

President and Chief Exec. Officer
O'MEARA, John M.
Tel: (630) 875 - 7201
Fax: (630) 875 - 7393

Main Headquarters
Mailing: One Pierce Place
Suite 1500
Itasca, IL 60143
Tel: (630) 875 - 7450
Fax: (630) 875 - 7369

Political Action Committees

First Midwest Bancorp, Inc. Government Affairs Fund
Contact: Mark M. Dietrich
One Pierce Place
Suite 1500
Itasca, IL 60143
Tel: (630) 875 - 7226
Fax: (630) 875 - 7388

Contributions to Candidates: $2,000 (01/05 - 09/05)
Republicans: $2,000.

Principal Recipients

SENATE REPUBLICANS		HOUSE REPUBLICANS	
		Bartels, Teresa (IL)	$2,000

Public Affairs and Related Activities Personnel

At Headquarters

DIETRICH, Mark M.
Exec. V. President and Chief Operating Officer; PAC Treasurer
Tel: (630) 875 - 7226
Fax: (630) 875 - 7388

SHAPIRO, Steven H.
Exec. V. President and Corporate Secretary
Responsibilities include investor and media relations.
Tel: (630) 875 - 7345
Fax: (630) 875 - 7360

First Tennessee Nat'l Corp.

See listing on page 196 under First Horizon Nat'l Corp.

FirstEnergy Corp.

A registered public utility holding company. FirstEnergy subsidiaries and affiliates are involved in the generation, transmission and distribution of electicity; and energy management and other energy-related services.

www.firstenergycorp.com
Annual Revenues: $12.3 billion

President and Chief Exec. Officer
ALEXANDER, Anthony
Fax: (330) 384 - 5791
TF: (800) 646 - 0400

Main Headquarters
Mailing: 76 S. Main St.
Akron, OH 44308-1890
Fax: (330) 384 - 5791
TF: (800) 646 - 0400

Washington Office
Mailing: 801 Pennsylvania Ave. NW
Suite 310
Washington, DC 20004
Tel: (202) 434 - 8150
Fax: (202) 434 - 8156

Political Action Committees

FE PAC
Contact: David C. Luff
76 S. Main St.
Akron, OH 44308-1890
Tel: (330) 384 - 5798
Fax: (330) 761 - 4204
TF: (800) 633 - 4766

Contributions to Candidates: $68,900 (01/05 - 09/05)
Democrats: $15,000; Republicans: $53,900.

Principal Recipients

SENATE DEMOCRATS		HOUSE DEMOCRATS	
		Menendez, Robert (NJ)	$5,000
SENATE REPUBLICANS		**HOUSE REPUBLICANS**	
Dewine, Richard (OH)	$4,000	Dewine, R. Pat (OH)	$5,000
Santorum, Richard (PA)	$3,900	Ferguson, Mike (NJ)	$5,000
		Ney, Robert W (OH)	$5,000
		LaTourette, Steve (OH)	$4,000
		Barton, Joe L (TX)	$3,500
		DeLay, Tom (TX)	$2,500
		Hart, Melissa (PA)	$2,500

Corporate Foundations and Giving Programs

FirstEnergy Foundation
Contact: Mary Beth Carroll
76 S. Main St.
Akron, OH 44308-1890
Tel: (330) 761 - 4112
Fax: (330) 834 - 8788
TF: (800) 633 - 4766

Annual Grant Total: none reported
Giving is limited to programs that benefit the customer and employee communities in the service area of FirstEnergy companies.
Geographic Preference: Area in which the company is headquartered; Area(s) in which the company operates
Primary Interests: Civic and Cultural Activities; Education; Health; Human Welfare

Public Affairs and Related Activities Personnel

At Headquarters

CARROLL, Mary Beth
V. President
Responsibilities include corporate philanthropy.
Tel: (330) 761 - 4112
Fax: (330) 834 - 8788
TF: (800) 633 - 4766

CAVALIER, Lynn M.
V. President, Human Resources
Tel: (330) 384 - 5626
Fax: (330) 384 - 5791
TF: (800) 646 - 0400

DINICOLA, Ralph J.
V. President, Communications
Tel: (330) 384 - 5939
Fax: (330) 384 - 4539
TF: (800) 633 - 4766

LUFF, David C.
V. President, State Government Affairs
Tel: (330) 384 - 5798
Fax: (330) 761 - 4204
TF: (800) 633 - 4766

POEPPELMEIER, David C.
Director, Employee Communications
Tel: (330) 384 - 5813
Fax: (330) 384 - 4539
TF: (800) 633 - 4766

STEEN, Daniel V.
V. President, Environmental
Tel: (330) 384 - 3704
Fax: (330) 384 - 5433
TF: (800) 633 - 4766

TUROSKY, Kurt
Director, Investor Relations
Tel: (330) 384 - 5500
Fax: (330) 384 - 5902

FirstEnergy Corp.
** continued from previous page*

WELSH, Thomas M. — Tel: (330) 384 - 5804
Senior V. President, External Affairs — Fax: (330) 384 - 4539; TF: (800) 633 - 4766

At Washington Office

BAILEY, Joel — Tel: (202) 434 - 8150
Director, Federal Governmental Affairs — Fax: (202) 434 - 8156
Registered Federal Lobbyist.

BRUBAKER, Joel — Tel: (202) 434 - 8150
Federal Affairs Representative — Fax: (202) 434 - 8156

LOVENG, Jeff — Tel: (202) 434 - 8150
Manager, Federal Government Affairs — Fax: (202) 434 - 8156
Registered Federal Lobbyist.

FirstMerit Corporation
A financial services holding company.
www.firstmerit.com

Chairman and Chief Exec. Officer
COCHRAN, John R. — Tel: (330) 384 - 7068; Fax: (330) 384 - 7008

Main Headquarters
Mailing: III Cascade Plaza, Akron, OH 44308-1103 — Tel: (330) 996 - 6300

Public Affairs and Related Activities Personnel

At Headquarters

SIRLOUIS, Jacque — Tel: (330) 846 - 8877
Director, Public Relations — Fax: (330) 384 - 7008

Fiserv, Inc.
Provides data processing and information management services and products to financial institutions.
www.fiserv.com

Chairman of the Board
DILLON, Donald F. — Tel: (262) 879 - 5000; TF: (800) 872 - 7882

President and Chief Exec. Officer
MUMA, Leslie M. — Tel: (262) 879 - 5000; TF: (800) 872 - 7882

Main Headquarters
Mailing: P.O. Box 979, Brookfield, WI 53008-0979 — Tel: (262) 879 - 5000; Fax: (262) 879 - 5013; TF: (800) 872 - 7882

Street: 255 Fiserv Dr., Brookfield, WI 53045

Public Affairs and Related Activities Personnel

At Headquarters

DOHERTY, Chuck — Tel: (262) 879 - 5966
Director, Corporate Public Relations — Fax: (262) 879 - 5013
chuck.doherty@fiserv.com — TF: (800) 872 - 7882

Fisher Scientific Internat'l Inc.
Fisher is a provider of products and services to the scientific community. Fisher facilitates discovery by supplying researchers and clinicians in labs around the world with the tools they need.
www.fisherscientific.com

Chairman and Chief Exec. Officer
MONTRONE, Paul M. — Tel: (603) 929 - 5911; Fax: (603) 929 - 2379

Main Headquarters
Mailing: Liberty Ln., Hampton, NH 03842 — Tel: (603) 926 - 5911; Fax: (603) 929 - 2379

Political Action Committees

Fisher Scientific Internat'l Inc. Employees' Committee For Sensible Government
Contact: Rick Jenkinson
Liberty Ln. — Tel: (603) 926 - 5911
Hampton, NH 03842 — Fax: (603) 929 - 2379

Contributions to Candidates: $2,500 (01/05 - 09/05)
Democrats: $2,500.

Principal Recipients

SENATE DEMOCRATS	HOUSE DEMOCRATS
Carper, Thomas R (DE) $2,500	

Public Affairs and Related Activities Personnel

At Headquarters

CLARK, Kevin P. — Tel: (603) 926 - 5911
PAC Treasurer — Fax: (603) 929 - 2379

JENKINSON, Rick — Tel: (603) 926 - 5911
V. President, Government Affairs and Public Relations — Fax: (603) 929 - 2379

MENTA, Chet — Tel: (603) 929 - 2381
V. President and Treasurer — Fax: (603) 929 - 2260
chet.menta@fishersci.com

OEI, Gia L. — Tel: (603) 929 - 2489
Director, Coporate Communications — Fax: (603) 929 - 2449
gia.oei@fishersci.com

Fleetwood Enterprises
A manufacturer of mobile homes and recreational vehicles.
www.fleetwood.com

Chairman of the Board
PITCHER, Thomas B. — Tel: (909) 351 - 3500; Fax: (909) 351 - 3931

President and Chief Exec. Officer
SMITH, Elden L. — Tel: (909) 351 - 3500; Fax: (909) 351 - 3931

Main Headquarters
Mailing: 3125 Myers St., Riverside, CA 92503 — Tel: (909) 351 - 3500; Fax: (909) 351 - 3931

Corporate Foundations and Giving Programs

Fleetwood Enterprises, Inc. Corporate Contributions Program
Contact: Lyle N. Larkin
3125 Myers St. — Tel: (909) 351 - 3535
Riverside, CA 92503 — Fax: (909) 351 - 3931

Annual Grant Total: none reported

Public Affairs and Related Activities Personnel

At Headquarters

LARKIN, Lyle N. — Tel: (909) 351 - 3535
V. President, Treasurer and Assistant Secretary — Fax: (909) 351 - 3931
Responsibilities include corporate philanthropy, communications, and investor relations.

MOORE, John R. — Tel: (909) 351 - 3500
V. President, Human Resources — Fax: (909) 351 - 3931

MUNSON, Kathy — Tel: (909) 351 - 3650
Director, Investor Relations — Fax: (909) 351 - 3931
kathy.munson@fleetwood.com

FlightSafety Internat'l
A provider of high technology aviation and marine training. A subsidiary of Berkshire Hathaway (see separate listing).
www.flightsafety.com

Main Headquarters
Mailing: Marine Air Terminal, LaGuardia Airport, Flushing, NY 11371 — Tel: (718) 565 - 4100; Fax: (718) 565 - 4174

Washington Office
Contact: John Marino
Mailing: 1235 S. Clark St., Suite 708, Arlington, VA 22202 — Tel: (703) 414 - 5500; Fax: (703) 414 - 5504

Public Affairs and Related Activities Personnel

At Headquarters

STOUT, Robert R. — Tel: (718) 565 - 4774
Corporate Director, Human Resources — Fax: (718) 565 - 4134

At Washington Office

MARINO, John — Tel: (703) 414 - 5501
V. President, Government Relations — Fax: (703) 414 - 5504
john.marino@flightsafety.com

MOSES, Glenn — Tel: (703) 414 - 5502
Director, Government Relations — Fax: (703) 414 - 5504
glenn.moses@flightsafety.com

Flint Hills Resources, LP
See listing on page 282 under Koch Industries, Inc.

Flint Ink Corp.
A manufacturer of printing inks, pigments and dispersions.
www.flintink.com
Annual Revenues: $1.47 billion

Chairman of the Board
FLINT, David B. — Tel: (734) 622 - 6000; Fax: (734) 622 - 6131

Chief Executive Officer
FRESCOLN, Leonard D. — Tel: (734) 622 - 6000; Fax: (734) 622 - 6131

Main Headquarters
Mailing: 4600 Arrowhead Dr., Ann Arbor, MI 48105 — Tel: (734) 622 - 6000; Fax: (734) 622 - 6131

Public Affairs and Related Activities Personnel

At Headquarters

CONRAD, Rita A. — Tel: (734) 622 - 6362
V. President, Corporate Communications — Fax: (734) 622 - 6131
rita.conrad@flintink.com

KING, Larry — Tel: (734) 622 - 6000
General Counsel — Fax: (734) 622 - 6141

Florida Power & Light Company
See listing on page 203 under FPL Group, Inc.

Florida Progress Corp.
See listing on page 395 under Progress Energy.

Florida Rock Industries, Inc.
A supplier of construction materials.
www.flarock.com

Chairman of the Board — Tel: (904) 355 - 1781
BAKER, Edward L. — Fax: (904) 355 - 0817

Chief Exec. Officer — Tel: (904) 355 - 1781
BAKER, John D., II — Fax: (904) 355 - 0817

Main Headquarters
Mailing: P.O. Box 4667 — Tel: (904) 355 - 1781
Jacksonville, FL 32201 — Fax: (904) 355 - 0817
Street: 155 E. 21st St.
Jacksonville, FL 32206

Political Action Committees

Florida Rock Good Government Committee
Contact: John D. Milton, Jr.
P.O. Box 4667 — Tel: (904) 355 - 1781
Jacksonville, FL 32201 — Fax: (904) 355 - 0817

Contributions to Candidates: $4,000 (01/05 - 09/05)
Republicans: $4,000.

Principal Recipients

SENATE REPUBLICANS		HOUSE REPUBLICANS	
		Crenshaw, Ander (FL)	$2,000
		Young, Don E (AK)	$2,000

Corporate Foundations and Giving Programs

Florida Rock Industries Foundation, Inc.
Contact: John D. Milton, Jr.
P.O. Box 4667 — Tel: (904) 355 - 1781
Jacksonville, FL 32201 — Fax: (904) 355 - 0817

Assets: $2,663,821 (2002)
Annual Grant Total: $300,000 - $400,000
Geographic Preference: Area in which the company is headquartered
Primary Interests: Arts and Humanities; Children; Health and Human Services; Higher Education

Public Affairs and Related Activities Personnel

At Headquarters

MILTON, John D., Jr. — Tel: (904) 355 - 1781
Exec. V. President, Treasurer and Chief Financial Officer — Fax: (904) 355 - 0817
Responsibilities include political action and corporate philanthropy.

Flowers Foods
Flowers Foods is a producer and marketer of packaged bakery foods for retail and foodservice customers. It operates more than 30 bakeries that produce a wide range of bakery products marketed regionally through an extensive direct-store-delivery network and nationwide through other delivery systems. Among the company's brands are Nature's Own, Cobblestone Mill, BlueBird, Mrs. Freshley's, and European Bakers.
www.flowersfoods.com

Chairman of the Board — Tel: (229) 226 - 9110
MCMULLIAN, Amos R. — Fax: (229) 225 - 3806

President and Chief Exec. Officer — Tel: (229) 226 - 9110
DEESE, George E. — Fax: (229) 225 - 3806

Main Headquarters
Mailing: 1919 Flowers Circle — Tel: (229) 226 - 9110
Thomasville, GA 31757 — Fax: (229) 225 - 3806

Corporate Foundations and Giving Programs

Flowers Corporate Contributions Program
Contact: Marta Jones Turner
1919 Flowers Circle — Tel: (229) 227 - 2317
Thomasville, GA 31757 — Fax: (229) 225 - 3806

Annual Grant Total: none reported

Public Affairs and Related Activities Personnel

At Headquarters

JONES TURNER, Marta — Tel: (229) 227 - 2317
Senior V. President, Corporate Relations — Fax: (229) 225 - 3806
Responsibilities include corporate philanthropy.

KRIER, Mary — Tel: (229) 227 - 2333
V. President, Communications — Fax: (229) 225 - 3806

Flowserve Corp.
A member of the Public Affairs Council. A manufacturer of pumps, valves, and seals. Formed by the merger of BW/IP and Durco (formerly Duriron Co., Inc.) in 1997.
www.flowserve.com

Interim Chief Executive Officer — Tel: (972) 443 - 6500
SHEEHAN, Kevin — Fax: (972) 443 - 6800

Main Headquarters
Mailing: 5215 N. O'Connor Blvd. — Tel: (972) 443 - 6500
Suite 2300 — Fax: (972) 443 - 6800
Irving, TX 75039

Washington Office
Mailing: 1200 G St. NW — Tel: (202) 434 - 8773
Suite 800
Washington, DC 20005

Public Affairs and Related Activities Personnel

At Headquarters

CONLEY, Micheal — Tel: (972) 443 - 6557
Director, Investor Relations — Fax: (972) 443 - 6800
mconley@flowserve.com

JACKO, John H., Jr. — Tel: (972) 443 - 6500
V. President, Marketing and Communications — Fax: (972) 443 - 6800

ROSENE, Lars — Tel: (972) 443 - 6500
Director, Public Affairs — Fax: (972) 443 - 6800
lrosene@flowserve.com

Fluke Corporation
A manufacturer of precision test and measurement tools. A wholly owned subsidiary of Danaher Corp. (see separate listing).
www.fluke.com

Main Headquarters
Mailing: P.O. Box 9090 — Tel: (425) 347 - 6100
Everett, WA 98206-9090 — Fax: (425) 446 - 5116
TF: (800) 44F - LUKE
Street: 6920 Seaway Blvd.
Everett, WA 98203

Public Affairs and Related Activities Personnel

At Headquarters

WILSON, Larry — Tel: (425) 446 - 5671
Manager, Public Relations — Fax: (425) 446 - 5116
Mailstop: 250E
larry.wilson@fluke.com

Fluor Corp.
A member of the Public Affairs Council. A global engineering, procurement and maintenance company.
www.fluor.com
Annual Revenues: $12 billion

Chairman and Chief Exec. Officer — Tel: (949) 349 - 2000
BOECKMANN, Alan L. — Fax: (949) 349 - 5981
alan.boeckmann@fluor.com

Main Headquarters
Mailing: One Enterprise Dr. — Tel: (949) 349 - 2000
Aliso Viejo, CA 92656-2606 — Fax: (949) 349 - 2585

Washington Office
Contact: David Marventano
Mailing: 403 E. Capitol St. SE — Tel: (202) 548 - 5800
Washington, DC 20003 — Fax: (202) 548 - 5810

Political Action Committees

Fluor Corp. Public Affairs Committee (FLUOR PAC)
Contact: David Marvin Yano
One Enterprise Dr. — Tel: (949) 349 - 7171
Aliso Viejo, CA 92656-2606 — Fax: (949) 349 - 5375

Contributions to Candidates: $98,000 (01/05 - 09/05)
Democrats: $16,000; Republicans: $82,000.

Principal Recipients

SENATE DEMOCRATS		HOUSE DEMOCRATS	
		Spratt, John (SC)	$6,000

SENATE REPUBLICANS		HOUSE REPUBLICANS	
Santorum, Richard (PA)	$5,000	Barrett, James (SC)	$10,000
Hatch, Orrin (UT)	$4,000	Kennedy, Mark (MN)	$9,000
Smith, Gordon (OR)	$2,500	Cantor, Eric (VA)	$5,000
		Dewine, R. Pat (OH)	$2,500
		Hastings, Doc (WA)	$2,500
		Inglis, Bob (SC)	$2,500
		Schmidt, Jeannette (OH)	$2,500

Corporate Foundations and Giving Programs

Fluor Foundation
Contact: J. Robert Fluor, II

Fluor Corp.

* continued from previous page

One Enterprise Dr.
Aliso Viejo, CA 92656-2606
Tel: (949) 349 - 7171
Fax: (949) 349 - 5375

Annual Grant Total: $2,000,000 - $5,000,000
Geographic Preference: Area(s) in which the company operates
Primary Interests: Education; Math and Science; Youth Services

Public Affairs and Related Activities Personnel

At Headquarters

FLUOR, J. Robert, II
V. President, Global Public Affairs
robert.fluor@fluor.com
Tel: (949) 349 - 7171
Fax: (949) 349 - 5375

GILBERT, H. Steven
Senior V. President, Human Resources and Administration
Tel: (949) 349 - 2000
Fax: (949) 349 - 2585

HOLLOWAY, Jerry
Director, Media Relations
jerry.holloway@fluor.com
Tel: (949) 349 - 7411
Fax: (949) 349 - 5981

LOCKWOOD, Ken
V. President, Investor Relations
Tel: (949) 349 - 3909
Fax: (949) 349 - 5375

TASHJIAN, Lee
V. President, Corporate Communications
Tel: (949) 349 - 2000
Fax: (949) 349 - 2585

YANO, David Marvin
PAC Contact
Tel: (949) 349 - 7171
Fax: (949) 349 - 5375

At Washington Office

BONNIN, Nydia
Director, Government Relations
Tel: (202) 548 - 5800
Fax: (202) 548 - 5810

HOLMES, Diane
Senior Washington Representative
diane.holmes@fluor.com
Registered Federal Lobbyist.
Tel: (202) 548 - 5800
Fax: (202) 548 - 5810

MARVENTANO, David
Senior V. President, Government Relations
Registered Federal Lobbyist.
Tel: (202) 548 - 5800
Fax: (202) 548 - 5810

VAUGHN, Philip
Senior Director, Government Relations
philip.vaughn@fluor.com
Registered Federal Lobbyist.
Tel: (202) 548 - 5800
Fax: (202) 548 - 5810

FLYi, Inc.

A regional airline. Formerly known as Atlantic Coast Airlines Holdings, Inc.
www.flyi.com
Annual Revenues: $761 million

Chairman and Chief Exec. Officer
SKEEN, Kerry B.
Tel: (703) 650 - 6000
Fax: (703) 650 - 6299

Main Headquarters
Mailing: 45200 Business Ct.
Suite 100
Dulles, VA 20166-6715
Tel: (703) 650 - 6000
Fax: (703) 650 - 6299

Public Affairs and Related Activities Personnel

At Headquarters

DELISI, Rick
Director, Corporate Communications
mediarelations@flyi.com
Tel: (703) 650 - 6019
Fax: (703) 650 - 6299

SHERMER, Angie M.
V. President, Employee Services
Tel: (703) 650 - 6000
Fax: (703) 650 - 6299

FMC Corp.

PUBLIC AFFAIRS COUNCIL

A member of the Public Affairs Council. International producer of chemicals for industry and agriculture. Spun off FMC Technologies (see separate listing) in December of 2001.
www.fmc.com
Annual Revenues: $2.05 billion

Chairman, President and Chief Exec. Officer
WALTER, William G.
Tel: (215) 299 - 6000

Main Headquarters
Mailing: 1735 Market St.
Philadelphia, PA 19103
Tel: (215) 299 - 6000
Fax: (215) 299 - 5998

Washington Office
Contact: Gerald R. Prout
Mailing: 1667 K St. NW
Suite 460
Washington, DC 20006
Tel: (202) 956 - 5200
Fax: (202) 956 - 5235

Political Action Committees

FMC Corp. Good Government Program
Contact: Gerald R. Prout
1667 K St. NW
Suite 460
Washington, DC 20006
Tel: (202) 956 - 5200
Fax: (202) 956 - 5235

Contributions to Candidates: $12,080 (01/05 - 09/05)
Democrats: $4,580; Republicans: $7,500.

Principal Recipients

SENATE DEMOCRATS		HOUSE DEMOCRATS	
Nelson, Bill (FL)	$1,000	Brown, Corrine (FL)	$1,000
		Cardin, Ben (MD)	$1,000
		Ruppersberger, Dutch (MD)	$1,000

SENATE REPUBLICANS		HOUSE REPUBLICANS	
Enzi, Michael B (WY)	$1,000	Cubin, Barbara L (WY)	$2,000
Thomas, Craig (WY)	$1,000	Hobson, David (OH)	$1,000
		Myrick, Sue (NC)	$1,000
		Simpson, Michael (ID)	$1,000

Corporate Foundations and Giving Programs

FMC Philanthropy.
Contact: Judy H. Smeltzer
1735 Market St.
Philadelphia, PA 19103
Tel: (215) 299 - 6710
Fax: (215) 299 - 6274

Annual Grant Total: none reported
The FMC program is structured to support the company's local operational sites. The company has an employee matching gifts program.
Geographic Preference: Area(s) in which the company operates
Primary Interests: Arts and Culture; Higher Education
Recent Recipients: Nat'l Merit Scholarship; United Way

Public Affairs and Related Activities Personnel

At Headquarters

ARNDT, Brennen
Director, Investor Relations
brennen_arndt@fmc.com
Tel: (215) 299 - 6000
Fax: (215) 299 - 6266

DAY, Kathy
Exec. Administrative Assistant
kathy_day@fmc.com
Responsibilities include corporate public affairs.
Tel: (215) 299 - 6000
Fax: (215) 299 - 6568

FITZWATER, James
Manager, Corporate Communications
james_fitzwater@fmc.com
Tel: (215) 299 - 6633
Fax: (215) 299 - 6568

GARRETT, Kenneth R.
V. President, Human Resources and Corporate Communications
Tel: (215) 299 - 6021
Fax: (215) 299 - 6568

SMELTZER, Judy H.
Director, State Government Relations
Tel: (215) 299 - 6710
Fax: (215) 299 - 6274

At Washington Office

DAVIS, Lizanne H.
Director, Government Affairs
Registered Federal Lobbyist.
Tel: (202) 956 - 5200
Fax: (202) 956 - 5235

PROUT, Gerald R.
V. President, Government and Public Affairs
jerry_prout@fmc.com
Registered Federal Lobbyist.
Tel: (202) 956 - 5200
Fax: (202) 956 - 5235

RIPPENGER, Patricia
Government Affairs Assistant
Registered Federal Lobbyist.
Tel: (202) 956 - 5200
Fax: (202) 956 - 5235

FMC Technologies, Inc.

Involved in the energy, food processing and air transportation idustries. Spun off from FMC Corp. (see separate listing) in December of 2001.
www.fmctechnologies.com

Chariman, President and Chief Exec. Officer
NETHERLAND, Joseph H.
Tel: (281) 591 - 4100
Fax: (281) 591 - 4102

Main Headquarters
Mailing: 1803 Gears Rd.
Houston, TX 60601
Tel: (281) 591 - 4000
Fax: (281) 591 - 4102

Political Action Committees

FMC Technologies Employee PAC
Contact: Jill Mitchell
1803 Gears Rd.
Houston, TX 60601
Tel: (281) 591 - 4166
Fax: (281) 591 - 4134

Contributions to Candidates: $5,000 (01/05 - 09/05)
Democrats: $2,000; Republicans: $3,000.

Principal Recipients

SENATE DEMOCRATS		HOUSE DEMOCRATS	
Nelson, Bill (FL)	$2,000		

SENATE REPUBLICANS		HOUSE REPUBLICANS	
		Keller, Richard (FL)	$2,000
		Poe, Ted (TX)	$1,000

FMC Technologies, Inc.

** continued from previous page*

Corporate Foundations and Giving Programs

FMC Technologies Corporate Contributions
Contact: Jill Mitchell
1803 Gears Rd. — Tel: (281) 591 - 4166
Houston, TX 60601 — Fax: (281) 591 - 4134

Annual Grant Total: none reported

Public Affairs and Related Activities Personnel

At Headquarters

BULLOCK, W. Bruce — Tel: (281) 591 - 4429
Director, Corporate Communications and Public Affairs — Fax: (281) 591 - 4134
bruce.bullock@fmcti.com

MITCHELL, Jill — Tel: (281) 591 - 4166
Supervisor, Communications Projects and Programs — Fax: (281) 591 - 4134
jille.mitchell@fmcti.com

MURRAY, Michael W. — Tel: (281) 591 - 4556
V. President, Human Resources — Fax: (281) 591 - 4102
michael.murray@fmcti.com

FMR Corp.

A member of the Public Affairs Council. The company is also known by the name Fidelity Investments.
www.fidelity.com
Annual Revenues: $8.9 billion

Chairman and Chief Exec. Officer — Tel: (617) 563 - 7000
JOHNSON, Edward C., III — Fax: (617) 476 - 6150

Main Headquarters
Mailing: 82 Devonshire St. — Tel: (617) 563 - 7000
Boston, MA 02109-3614 — Fax: (617) 476 - 6150

Political Action Committees

FMR Corp. PAC
Contact: Paul T. Ryan
82 Devonshire St. — Tel: (617) 563 - 7000
Boston, MA 02109-3614 — Fax: (617) 476 - 6150

Contributions to Candidates: $7,000 (01/05 - 09/05)
Democrats: $1,000; Republicans: $6,000.

FMR Corp. PAC--Federal
Contact: Paul T. Ryan
82 Devonshire St. — Tel: (617) 563 - 7000
Boston, MA 02109-3614 — Fax: (617) 476 - 6150

Contributions to Candidates: $84,000 (01/05 - 09/05)
Democrats: $35,000; Republicans: $49,000.

Principal Recipients

SENATE DEMOCRATS		HOUSE DEMOCRATS	
Nelson, Benjamin (NE)	$3,500	Crowley, Joseph (NY)	$5,000
		Langevin, James (RI)	$2,500
		Matheson, James (UT)	$2,500
		Menendez, Robert (NJ)	$2,500
SENATE REPUBLICANS		**HOUSE REPUBLICANS**	
Sununu, John (NH)	$5,000	Ney, Robert W (OH)	$4,500
Thomas, Craig (WY)	$5,000	Baker, Hugh (LA)	$3,500
Bennett, Robert F (UT)	$4,000	Bradley, Joseph (NH)	$3,500
		Cantor, Eric (VA)	$3,500
		Barton, Joe L (TX)	$2,500
		Thomas, William M (CA)	$2,500

Corporate Foundations and Giving Programs

Fidelity Foundation
Contact: Anne-Marie Soulliere
82 Devonshire St. — Tel: (617) 563 - 7000
Boston, MA 02109-3614 — Fax: (617) 476 - 6150

Annual Grant Total: over $5,000,000
Geographic Preference: Dallas, TX; Boston, MA; Cincinnati, OH; Covington, KY; Salt Lake City, UT
Primary Interests: Arts and Culture; Community Affairs; Social Services

Public Affairs and Related Activities Personnel

At Headquarters

CROWLEY, Anne — Tel: (617) 563 - 5800
Senior V. President, Media Relations and Public Affairs — Fax: (617) 476 - 6150

EIDSON, Tom — Tel: (617) 563 - 7000
Exec. V. President and Director, Corporate Affairs — Fax: (617) 476 - 6150

LACKEY, Dave — Tel: (617) 563 - 7000
Director, Public Relations — Fax: (617) 476 - 6150

LOPORCHIO, Vincent — Tel: (617) 563 - 5800
V. President, Media Relations — Fax: (617) 476 - 6150

RYAN, Paul T. — Tel: (617) 563 - 7000
PACs' Treasurer — Fax: (617) 476 - 6150

SOULLIERE, Anne-Marie — Tel: (617) 563 - 7000
Senior V. President, Foundation — Fax: (617) 476 - 6150

WEINSTEIN, David — Tel: (617) 563 - 7000
Chief Administrator — Fax: (617) 476 - 6150
Responsibilities include government relations.

Foamex Internat'l Inc.

Manufacturer of flexible polyurethane foam and foam products.
www.foamex.com

Chairman of the Board — Tel: (610) 859 - 3000
MABUS, Raymond E. — Fax: (610) 859 - 3035
TF: (800) 776 - 3626

President and Chief Exec. Officer — Tel: (610) 859 - 3000
CHORMAN, Thomas E. — Fax: (610) 859 - 3035

Main Headquarters
Mailing: 1000 Columbia Ave. — Tel: (610) 859 - 3000
Linwood, PA 19061-3998 — Fax: (610) 859 - 3035
TF: (800) 776 - 3626

Public Affairs and Related Activities Personnel

At Headquarters

PRUSKY, Andrew R. — Tel: (610) 859 - 3000
Assistant General Counsel — Fax: (610) 859 - 3035
TF: (800) 776 - 3626
Responsibilities include investor relations.

Food Lion LLC

A supermarket chain. A subsidiary of Delhaize America, the U.S. division of Brussels-based Delhaize Group.
www.foodlion.com

President and Chief Exec. Officer — Tel: (704) 633 - 8250
ANICETTI, Rick — Fax: (704) 633 - 8250

Main Headquarters
Mailing: P.O. Box 1330 — Tel: (704) 633 - 8250
Salisbury, NC 28145-1330 — Fax: (704) 633 - 8250
Street: 2110 Executive Dr.
Salisbury, NC 28145-1330

Political Action Committees

Food Lion Inc. Political Action Committee
Contact: Melinda Dabbs
P.O. Box 1330 — Tel: (704) 633 - 8250
Salisbury, NC 28145-1330 — Fax: (704) 633 - 8250

Contributions to Candidates: $4,000 (01/05 - 09/05)
Republicans: $4,000.

Principal Recipients

SENATE REPUBLICANS		HOUSE REPUBLICANS	
Allen, George (VA)	$1,000	Foxx, Virginia (NC)	$1,000
Chambliss, Saxby (GA)	$1,000		

Corporate Foundations and Giving Programs

Food Lion LLC Corporate Contributions Program
Contact: Kyna Foster
P.O. Box 1330 — Tel: (704) 633 - 8250
Salisbury, NC 28145-1330 — Fax: (704) 633 - 8250

Annual Grant Total: none reported

Public Affairs and Related Activities Personnel

At Headquarters

DABBS, Melinda — Tel: (704) 633 - 8250
PAC Treasurer — Fax: (704) 633 - 8250

FOSTER, Kyna — Tel: (704) 633 - 8250
Community Affairs Manager — Fax: (704) 633 - 8250

JOHNSON, Darrell — Tel: (704) 633 - 8250 Ext: 3064
Senior V. President, Human Resources — Fax: (704) 633 - 8250

KINZEY, Ruth — Tel: (704) 633 - 8250 Ext: 2892
Corporate Communications Director — Fax: (704) 633 - 8250

YOUNG, Teross — Tel: (704) 633 - 8250
Manager, Government Affairs — Fax: (704) 633 - 8250

Foodmaker, Inc.

See listing on page 266 under Jack in the Box Inc.

Footlocker Inc.

Formerly known as Venator Group. A major retail holding company.
www.footlocker-inc.com

Chairman, President and Chief Exec. Officer
SERRA, Matthew D. Tel: (212) 720 - 3700
mserra@footlocker-inc.com Fax: (212) 720 - 4397

Main Headquarters
Mailing: 112 W. 34th St. Tel: (212) 720 - 3700
New York, NY 10120 Fax: (212) 720 - 4397

Corporate Foundations and Giving Programs

Footlocker Foundation
Contact: Lori Ann Kober
112 W. 34th St. Tel: (212) 720 - 3700
New York, NY 10120 Fax: (212) 720 - 4397

Annual Grant Total: none reported

Public Affairs and Related Activities Personnel

At Headquarters

BROWN, Peter D. Tel: (212) 720 - 4254
V. President, Investor Relations Fax: (212) 720 - 4660
pbrown@footlocker-inc.com

KOBER, Lori Ann Tel: (212) 720 - 3700
V. President, Public Relations Fax: (212) 720 - 4397
lkober@footlocker-inc.com

PETRUCCI, Laurie J. Tel: (212) 720 - 3700
Senior V. President, Human Resources Fax: (212) 720 - 4397

Forbes, Inc.

Publisher of business and financial magazine.
www.forbes.com

Chairman of the Board Tel: (212) 620 - 2200
WEINBERGER, Caspar Fax: (212) 620 - 2245

Chief Exec. Officer Tel: (212) 620 - 2200
FORBES, Steve Fax: (212) 620 - 2245

Main Headquarters
Mailing: 60 Fifth Ave. Tel: (212) 620 - 2200
New York, NY 10010 Fax: (212) 620 - 2245

Corporate Foundations and Giving Programs

Forbes Foundation
Contact: Leonard H. Yablon
60 Fifth Ave. Tel: (212) 620 - 2200
New York, NY 10010 Fax: (212) 620 - 2245

Assets: $3,133,000 (2003)
Annual Grant Total: $1,000,000 - $2,000,000
Geographic Preference: New York City
Primary Interests: Arts and Humanities; Health and Human Services; Higher Education; Social Services
Recent Recipients: Susan G. Komen Breast Cancer Foundation; YMCA

Public Affairs and Related Activities Personnel

At Headquarters

BEGLEY FEUREY, Monie Tel: (212) 620 - 2200
Senior V. President, Corporate Communications Fax: (212) 620 - 2245

YABLON, Leonard H. Tel: (212) 620 - 2200
Secretary/Treasurer, Foundation Fax: (212) 620 - 2245

Ford Motor Co.

A member of the Public Affairs Council. The nation's second largest automobile manufacturer.
www.ford.com
Annual Revenues: $162.412 billion

Chairman and Chief Exec. Officer Tel: (313) 322 - 3000
FORD, William Clay, Jr. TF: (800) 555 - 5259

Main Headquarters
Mailing: One American Rd. Tel: (313) 322 - 3000
Dearborn, MI 48126 Fax: (313) 845 - 6073
TF: (800) 555 - 5259

Washington Office
Mailing: 1350 I St. NW Tel: (202) 962 - 5400
Suite 1000 Fax: (202) 336 - 7223
Washington, DC 20005

Corporate Foundations and Giving Programs

Ford Motor Co. Fund
Contact: Sandy Ulsh
One American Rd. Tel: (313) 845 - 8711
Dearborn, MI 48126 Fax: (313) 337 - 6680
TF: (800) 555 - 5259

Annual Grant Total: over $5,000,000
Geographic Preference: Area in which the company is headquartered; Area(s) in which the company operates; National; International
Primary Interests: Arts and Humanities; Civic and Public Affairs; Community Development; Education; Environment/Conservation; Health; Social Services
Recent Recipients: Detroit Symphony Orchestra; Michigan State University; United Way

Public Affairs and Related Activities Personnel

At Headquarters

BYERS, Raymond Tel: (313) 337 - 6180
Director, U.S., State and Local Government Relations Fax: (313) 323 - 2683
Mailstop: Room 338 TF: (800) 555 - 5259
rbyers@ford.com

CISCHKE, Susan M. Tel: (313) 248 - 2137
V. President, Environmental and Safety Engineering Fax: (313) 248 - 2171
scischke@ford.com TF: (800) 555 - 5259

GASPER, Barbara L. Tel: (313) 322 - 3000
V. President, Investor Relations TF: (800) 555 - 5259

HOLLERAN, Charles B. Tel: (313) 322 - 3000
V. President, Public Affairs; and Chief Communications Officer TF: (800) 555 - 5259
chollera@ford.com

KELLY, William P. Tel: (313) 323 - 9223
Director, International Governmental Affairs Fax: (313) 248 - 3514
TF: (800) 555 - 5259

LAYMON, Joe W. Tel: (313) 322 - 3000
Group V. President, Corporate Human Resources TF: (800) 555 - 5259

O'BRIEN, Timothy J. Tel: (313) 322 - 3000
V. President, Corporate Relations TF: (800) 555 - 5259

RAY, Glenn Tel: (313) 594 - 4410
Manager, Corporate Communications Fax: (313) 845 - 0570
gray2@ford.com TF: (800) 555 - 5259

ROMINE, Francine Tel: (313) 322 - 1185
Strategic Communications Manager, National Communications TF: (800) 555 - 5259
fromine@ford.com

ULSH, Sandy Tel: (313) 845 - 8711
President, Ford Fund Fax: (313) 337 - 6680
Mailstop: Room 335 TF: (800) 555 - 5259
sulsh@ford.com

WOOD, Paul Tel: (313) 621 - 2961
Manager, Public Affairs Fax: (313) 248 - 9204
Mailstop: M/S 8N/184 TF: (800) 555 - 5259
pwood@ford.com

At Washington Office

ARAPIS, Peter Tel: (202) 962 - 5400
Legislative Manager Fax: (202) 336 - 7223

BIEGUN, Stephen E. Tel: (202) 962 - 5400
V. President, International Government Affairs Fax: (202) 336 - 7223

BIGGS, Jennifer Tel: (202) 962 - 5363
Public Affairs Coordinator Fax: (202) 962 - 5417
jbiggs12@ford.com

BROUILLETTE, Dan R. Tel: (202) 962 - 5400
V. President, Washington Affairs Fax: (202) 336 - 7223
Registered Federal Lobbyist.

JOHNANNES, Mary P. Tel: (202) 962 - 5384
Legislative Manager, Financial Services Fax: (202) 336 - 7223
mjohnannes@ford.com
Registered Federal Lobbyist.

JONES, Alison Tel: (202) 962 - 5400
Legislative Manager Fax: (202) 336 - 7223

KIRKISH, Sara Tel: (202) 962 - 5379
Regulatory Manager, Safety and Energy Fax: (202) 336 - 7228
Registered Federal Lobbyist.

MAGLEBY, Curtis N. Tel: (202) 962 - 5367
Legislative Manager, Clean Air and Fuels Fax: (202) 336 - 7223
Registered Federal Lobbyist.

MORAN, Mike Tel: (202) 962 - 5416
Director, Washington Regional Officer Fax: (202) 962 - 5417
mmoran@ford.com

MORGAN, J. Railton Tel: (202) 962 - 5400
Legislative Manager; Energy, Environment, and Safety Fax: (202) 336 - 7223
Registered Federal Lobbyist.

MULLINS-GRISSOM, Janet Tel: (202) 962 - 5377
V. President, Washington Affairs Fax: (202) 962 - 5377
Registered Federal Lobbyist.

OJAKLI, Ziad S. Tel: (202) 962 - 5400
Group V. President, Corporate Affairs Fax: (202) 336 - 7223
Registered Federal Lobbyist.

REINHART, Tony Tel: (202) 962 - 5400
Legislative Manager Fax: (202) 336 - 7223

ROUSSEL, Jerry Tel: (202) 962 - 5386
Regulatory Manager, Environment Fax: (202) 336 - 7226
jroussel@ford.com
Registered Federal Lobbyist.

YOUNG, J. T. Tel: (202) 962 - 5400
Legislative Manager Fax: (202) 336 - 7223

Ford Motor Credit Co.

See listing on page 201 under Ford Motor Co.

Foremost Corp. of America

Specializes in mobile home, motor home, travel trailer, specialty dwelling, motorcycle, off-road vehicle, snowmobile, personal watercraft, and boat and collectible auto insurance. Also maintains a website at www.foremoststar.com.

www.foremost.com

Main Headquarters

Mailing: P.O. Box 2450
Grand Rapids, MI 49501
Tel: (616) 942 - 3000
Fax: (616) 956 - 2093
TF: (800) 527 - 3905

Street: 5600 Beech Tree Ln.
Caledonia, MI 49316

Public Affairs and Related Activities Personnel

At Headquarters

KALINKA, John T.
Assistant V. President, Corporate Communications
kalinka@foremost.com
Tel: (616) 942 - 3000
Fax: (616) 956 - 2093

WALKER, Ruth
Manager, Public Relations and Corporate Communications
walker@foremost.com
Tel: (616) 942 - 3000
Fax: (616) 956 - 2093

Forest City Enterprises, Inc.

A real estate development company.

www.fceinc.com

Co-Chairman of the Board
MILLER, Samuel H.
Tel: (216) 621 - 6060
Fax: (216) 263 - 4808

Co-Chairman of the Board
RATNER, Albert B.
Tel: (216) 621 - 6060
Fax: (216) 263 - 4808

President and Chief Exec. Officer
RATNER, Charles A.
Tel: (216) 621 - 6060
Fax: (216) 263 - 4808

Main Headquarters

Mailing: 1100 Terminal Tower
50 Public Square
Cleveland, OH 44113-2203
Tel: (216) 621 - 6060
Fax: (216) 263 - 4808

Corporate Foundations and Giving Programs

Forest City Enterprises Charitable Foundation
Contact: Allan C. Krulak
1100 Terminal Tower
50 Public Square
Cleveland, OH 44113-2203
Tel: (216) 621 - 6060
Fax: (216) 263 - 4808

Assets: $227,203,000 (2002)
Annual Grant Total: $2,000,000 - $5,000,000
Geographic Preference: Cleveland, OH; Area(s) in which the company operates; New York City
Primary Interests: Civil Rights; Economic Development; Education; Religion
Recent Recipients: American Red Cross; United Way

Public Affairs and Related Activities Personnel

At Headquarters

KMIECIK, Tom
Assistant Treasurer
tomkmiecik@forestcity.net
Responsibilities include investor relations.
Tel: (216) 416 - 3215
Fax: (216) 263 - 4808

KRULAK, Allan C.
V. President and Director, Community Affairs
Tel: (216) 621 - 6060
Fax: (216) 263 - 4808

MCCANN, Nancy
V. President, Marketing
nancymccann@forestcity.net
Responsibilities include media relations.
Tel: (216) 416 - 3004
Fax: (216) 263 - 4808

MONCHEIN, Minta A.
V. President and Director, Human Resources
Tel: (216) 621 - 6060
Fax: (216) 263 - 4808

TALTON, Jim
Exec. V. President, Human Resources
Tel: (216) 621 - 6060
Fax: (216) 263 - 4808

Forest Laboratories, Inc.

Develops, manufactures and distributes pharmaceutical products.

www.frx.com
Annual Revenues: $1.7 billion

Chairman and Chief Exec. Officer
SOLOMON, Howard
Tel: (212) 421 - 7850
Fax: (212) 750 - 9152
TF: (800) 947 - 5227

Main Headquarters

Mailing: 909 Third Ave.
New York, NY 10022
Tel: (212) 421 - 7850
Fax: (212) 750 - 9152
TF: (800) 947 - 5227

Corporate Foundations and Giving Programs

Forest Laboratories, Inc. Corporate Giving
909 Third Ave.
New York, NY 10022
Tel: (212) 421 - 7850
Fax: (212) 750 - 9152
TF: (800) 947 - 5227

Annual Grant Total: none reported

Public Affairs and Related Activities Personnel

At Headquarters

TRIANO, Charles E.
V. President, Investor Relations
Responsibilities also include corporate communications.
Tel: (212) 246 - 714
Fax: (212) 750 - 9152
TF: (800) 947 - 5227

Fortis, Inc.

See listing on page 50 under Assurant.

Fortune Brands, Inc.

An international consumer products company.

www.fortunebrands.com

Chairman and Chief Exec. Officer
WESLEY, Norman H.
Tel: (847) 484 - 4400

Main Headquarters

Mailing: 300 Tower Pkwy.
Lincolnshire, IL 60069
Tel: (847) 484 - 4400

Washington Office

Mailing: 1301 K St. NW
Suite 250 West Tower
Washington, DC 20005
Tel: (202) 962 - 0551
Fax: (202) 962 - 0561

Public Affairs and Related Activities Personnel

At Headquarters

DIAZ, Anthony J.
V. President, Investor Relations
tony_diaz@fortunebrands.com
Tel: (847) 484 - 4400
Fax: (847) 484 - 4497

HINE, C. Clarkson
V. President, Corporate Communications
clarkson_hine@fortunebrands.com
Tel: (847) 484 - 4400
Fax: (847) 484 - 4497

ROCHE, Mark A.
Senior V. President, General Counsel and Secretary
mark_roche@fortunebrands.com
Tel: (847) 484 - 4400
Fax: (847) 484 - 4490

At Washington Office

STANTON, Matt
Director, Government Affairs
(Jim Beam Brands Worldwide, Inc.)
Registered Federal Lobbyist.
Tel: (202) 962 - 0551
Fax: (202) 962 - 0561

Fossil Inc.

Manufactures and markets fashion accessories.

www.fossil.com

Chairman of the Board
KARTSOTIS, Tom
tkartsotis@fossil.com
Tel: (972) 234 - 2525
Fax: (972) 234 - 4669

President and Chief Exec. Officer
KARTSOTIS, Kosta N.
kkartsotis@fossil.com
Tel: (972) 234 - 2525
Fax: (972) 234 - 4669

Main Headquarters

Mailing: 2280 N. Greenville Ave.
Richardson, TX 75082
Tel: (972) 234 - 2525
Fax: (972) 234 - 4669

Public Affairs and Related Activities Personnel

At Headquarters

CARTER, Dean
V. President, Human Resources
dcarter@fossil.com
Tel: (972) 699 - 6949
Fax: (972) 699 - 6948

HALE, Timothy G.
Senior V. President and Image Director
thale@fossil.com
Tel: (972) 699 - 6807
Fax: (972) 234 - 4669

KOVAR, Mike L.
Senior V. President, Chief Financial Officer, and Treasurer
mkovar@fossil.com
Responsibilities include investor relations.
Tel: (972) 699 - 2229
Fax: (972) 498 - 9448

STEAD, Justin
V. President, National Sales Manager and Marketing
Responsibilities include corporate philanthropy.
Tel: (972) 234 - 2525
Fax: (972) 234 - 4669

L. B. Foster Co.

A manufacturer of pipe, rail and construction products.

www.lbfoster.com
Annual Revenues: $282 million

Chairman of the Board
FOSTER, Lee B., II
lfoster@lbfosterco.com
Tel: (412) 928 - 3417
Fax: (412) 928 - 7891
TF: (800) 255 - 4500

L. B. Foster Co.

* continued from previous page

President and Chief Exec. Officer
HASSELBUSCH, Stan L.
shasselbusch@lbfosterco.com
Tel: (412) 928 - 3417
Fax: (412) 928 - 7891
TF: (800) 255 - 4500

Main Headquarters
Mailing: 415 Holiday Dr.
Pittsburgh, PA 15220-2793
Tel: (412) 928 - 3417
Fax: (412) 928 - 7891
TF: (800) 255 - 4500

Corporate Foundations and Giving Programs

L. B. Foster Charitable Trust
Contact: Linda Moore
415 Holiday Dr.
Pittsburgh, PA 15220-2793
Tel: (412) 928 - 3417
Fax: (412) 928 - 7891
TF: (800) 255 - 4500

Annual Grant Total: under $100,000
Organizations not considered include: controversial organizations; universities; and organizations providing services to or sponsored by a singular religious or ethnic group. The Trust does not purchase advertising or tables. All recipients must be 501(c)(3) certified.
Geographic Preference: National
Primary Interests: Community Affairs; Minority Opportunities; Performing Arts; Persons with Disabilities; Women
Recent Recipients: American Red Cross; California Institute of Technology; Salvation Army; Students Against Destructive Decisions; United Way

Public Affairs and Related Activities Personnel

At Headquarters

HOWARD, Robert J.
V. President, Human Resources
rhoward@lbfosterco.com
Tel: (412) 928 - 3417
Fax: (412) 928 - 3422
TF: (800) 255 - 4500

MOORE, Linda
Contact, L.B. Foster Charitable Trust
lmoore@lbfosterco.com
Tel: (412) 928 - 3417
Fax: (412) 928 - 7891
TF: (800) 255 - 4500

Foster Wheeler Ltd.

A global company offering, through its subsidiaries, design, engineering, construction, manufacturing, project development and management, research, and plant operations.
www.fwc.com
Annual Revenues: $3.4 billion

Chairman and Chief Exec. Officer
MILCHOVICH, Raymond J.
Tel: (908) 730 - 4000
Fax: (908) 730 - 5315

Main Headquarters
Mailing: Perryville Corporate Park
Clinton, NJ 08809-4000
Tel: (908) 730 - 4000
Fax: (908) 730 - 5315

Political Action Committees

Foster Wheeler Corp. PAC
Contact: Mr. Thierry Desmaris
Perryville Corporate Park
Clinton, NJ 08809-4000
Tel: (908) 730 - 4000
Fax: (908) 730 - 5315

Contributions to Candidates: $1,000 (01/05 - 09/05)
Republicans: $1,000.

Principal Recipients

SENATE REPUBLICANS		HOUSE REPUBLICANS	
Hatch, Orrin (UT)	$1,000		

Public Affairs and Related Activities Personnel

At Headquarters

BINGERT, Maureen
Corporate Communications Contact
maureen_bingert@fwl.com
Tel: (908) 730 - 4444
Fax: (908) 730 - 5315

DESMARIS, Mr. Thierry
PAC Treasurer
Tel: (908) 730 - 4000
Fax: (908) 730 - 5315

Foundation Health Systems, Inc.

See listing on page 238 under Health Net, Inc.

FPL Group, Inc.

A member of the Public Affairs Council. The parent company of Florida Power & Light Company with other subsidiaries engaged in energy production.
www.fplgroup.com
Annual Revenues: $8.475 billion

FPL Group, Chairman, President and Chief Exec. Officer
HAY, Lewis, III
lew_hay@fpl.com
Tel: (561) 694 - 4705
Fax: (561) 694 - 4620

Main Headquarters
Mailing: P.O. Box 14000
Juno Beach, FL 33408-0420
Street: 700 Universe Blvd.
Juno Beach, FL 33408-2657
Tel: (561) 694 - 4000
Fax: (561) 694 - 4620

Washington Office
Contact: Michael M. Wilson
Mailing: 801 Pennsylvania Ave. NW
Suite 220
Washington, DC 20004-2604
Tel: (202) 347 - 7082
Fax: (202) 347 - 7076

Political Action Committees

FPL PAC
Contact: Thomas Grieser
P.O. Box 14000
Juno Beach, FL 33408-0420
Tel: (561) 694 - 4000
Fax: (561) 694 - 4620

Contributions to Candidates: $147,000 (01/05 - 09/05)
Democrats: $25,500; Republicans: $121,500.

Principal Recipients

SENATE DEMOCRATS		HOUSE DEMOCRATS	
Conrad, Kent (ND)	$6,000	Gonzalez, Charles A (TX)	$2,000
Carper, Thomas R (DE)	$5,000		
Salazar, Ken (CO)	$3,000		

SENATE REPUBLICANS		HOUSE REPUBLICANS	
Allen, George (VA)	$10,000	Latham, Thomas P (IA)	$6,000
Grassley, Charles (IA)	$6,000	Barton, Joe L (TX)	$5,000
Lott, Trent (MS)	$6,000	DeLay, Tom (TX)	$5,000
Smith, Gordon (OR)	$5,000	Hart, Melissa (PA)	$5,000
Sununu, John (NH)	$4,000	Hastert, Dennis J. (IL)	$5,000
Chafee, Lincoln (RI)	$3,000	Hensarling, Jeb (TX)	$3,500
Snowe, Olympia (ME)	$3,000	Shaw, Clay (FL)	$3,500
Talent, James (MO)	$3,000	Crenshaw, Ander (FL)	$2,500
Chambliss, Saxby (GA)	$2,500	Bilirakis, Gus (FL)	$2,000
Martinez, Mel (FL)	$2,500	Foley, Mark (FL)	$2,000
Thomas, Craig (WY)	$2,000	Hall, Ralph (TX)	$2,000
		McCrery, Jim (LA)	$2,000
		Shuster, William (PA)	$2,000
		Stearns, Clifford (FL)	$2,000
		Thomas, William M (CA)	$2,000

Corporate Foundations and Giving Programs

FPL Group Foundation
Contact: John L. Kitchens
P.O. Box 029100
Miami, FL 33102
Tel: (305) 552 - 4806
Fax: (305) 552 - 2144

Assets: $6,300,000 (2002)
Annual Grant Total: $1,000,000 - $2,000,000
Geographic Preference: Area(s) in which the company operates
Primary Interests: Community Development; Education; Environment/Conservation; Higher Education; Minority Opportunities; Senior Citizens
Recent Recipients: Nat'l Audubon Soc.; United Way

Public Affairs and Related Activities Personnel

At Headquarters

GRIESER, Thomas
PAC Treasurer
Tel: (561) 694 - 4000
Fax: (561) 694 - 4620

KELLEHER, Lawrence J.
V. President, Human Resources
Tel: (561) 694 - 4642
Fax: (561) 694 - 4620

KROMER, Mary Lou
V. President, Corporate Communications
(Florida Power & Light Company)
Tel: (561) 694 - 6464
Fax: (561) 694 - 4620

At Washington Office

CHAPEL, Christopher
Manager, Federal Governmental Affairs, Washington Office
christopher_chapel@fpl.com
(Florida Power & Light Company)
Registered Federal Lobbyist.
Tel: (202) 347 - 7082
Fax: (202) 347 - 7076

WILSON, Michael M.
V. President, Governmental Affairs
michael_m_wilson@fpl.com
(Florida Power & Light Company)
Registered Federal Lobbyist.
Tel: (202) 347 - 7082
Fax: (202) 347 - 7076

At Other Offices

HAMILTON, Paul W.
V. President, State Legislative Affairs
(Florida Power & Light Company)
215 S. Monroe St.
Suite 810
Tallahassee, FL 32301-1888
Tel: (850) 224 - 7517
Fax: (850) 224 - 7197

FPL Group, Inc.

** continued from previous page*

KITCHENS, John L.
Corporate Contributions Administrator
(Florida Power & Light Company)
P.O. Box 029100
Miami, FL 33102
john_kitchens@fpl.com
Tel: (305) 552 - 4806
Fax: (305) 552 - 2144

SCOTT, Kathy A.
Media Relations
P.O. Box 029100
Miami, FL 33102
kathy_scott@fpl.com
Tel: (305) 552 - 2368
Fax: (305) 552 - 2144

SWANK, William E.
Media Relations
(Florida Power & Light Company)
P.O. Box 029100
Miami, FL 33102
bill_swank@fpl.com
Tel: (305) 552 - 3231
Fax: (305) 552 - 2144

WALKER, William G., III
V. President, Regulatory Affairs
(Florida Power & Light Company)
215 S. Monroe St., Suite 810
Tallahassee, FL 32301
Tel: (850) 224 - 7517
Fax: (850) 224 - 7197

Franklin Resources, Inc.

See listing on page 204 under Franklin Templeton Investments.

Franklin Templeton Investments

A financial services holding company.

www.franklintempleton.com

Chairman of the Board
JOHNSON, Charles B.
Tel: (650) 312 - 3001
TF: (800) 342 - 5236

Co-Chief Exec. Officer
FLANAGAN, Martin L.
mflanagan@frk.com
Tel: (650) 312 - 5818
Fax: (650) 574 - 5012
TF: (800) 342 - 5236

President and Chief Exec. Officer
JOHNSON, Gregory E.
Tel: (650) 312 - 2000
Fax: (650) 312 - 5606
TF: (800) 632 - 2350

Main Headquarters

Mailing: One Franklin Pkwy.
San Mateo, CA 94403-1906
Tel: (650) 312 - 2000
Fax: (650) 312 - 5606
TF: (800) 632 - 2350

Public Affairs and Related Activities Personnel

At Headquarters

ALEXANDER, Penny S.
V. President, Human Resources - U.S.
psmith@frk.com
Tel: (650) 312 - 2000
TF: (800) 342 - 5236

GALLEGOS, Lisa
Manager, Corporate Communications
lgallegos@frk.com
Tel: (650) 312 - 3395
Fax: (650) 574 - 5012
TF: (800) 342 - 5236

GIBSON-BRADY, Holly E.
V. President, Corporate Communications
hgibson@frk.com
Tel: (650) 312 - 4701
Fax: (650) 574 - 5012
TF: (800) 342 - 5236

IKEDA, Donna
Senior V. President, Human Resources International
dikeda@frk.com
Tel: (650) 312 - 2000
Fax: (650) 312 - 3655
TF: (800) 342 - 5236

JOHNSTON, Stacey
Senior Coordinator, Public Relations
sjohnst@frk.com
Tel: (650) 525 - 7558
TF: (800) 342 - 5236

WALSH, Matt
Senior Coordinator, Public Relations
mwalsh1@frk.com
Tel: (650) 312 - 2245
TF: (800) 342 - 5236

Fred's Inc.

A dollar and drug store operator.

www.fredsinc.com

Annual Revenues: $911 million

Chief Exec. Officer
HAYES, Michael J.
Tel: (901) 365 - 8880
Fax: (901) 328 - 0354
TF: (800) 374 - 7417

Main Headquarters

Mailing: 4300 New Getwell Rd.
Memphis, TN 38118-6801
Tel: (901) 365 - 8880
Fax: (901) 328 - 0354
TF: (800) 374 - 7417

Corporate Foundations and Giving Programs

Fred's Corporate Contributions
Contact: Tommy Burkley
4300 New Getwell Rd.
Memphis, TN 38118-6801
Tel: (901) 365 - 8880
Fax: (901) 328 - 0354
TF: (800) 374 - 7417

Annual Grant Total: none reported

Geographic Preference: National

Primary Interests: Community Affairs

Recent Recipients: United Way

Public Affairs and Related Activities Personnel

At Headquarters

BURKLEY, Tommy
Contact, Fred's Corporate Contributions
Tel: (901) 365 - 8880
Fax: (901) 328 - 0354
TF: (800) 374 - 7417

SHORE, Jerry A.
Chief Financial Officer and Exec. V. President
Tel: (901) 365 - 3733
Ext: 2217
Fax: (901) 328 - 0354
TF: (800) 374 - 7417

Responsibilities include investor relations.

Freddie Mac

A publicly-chartered corporation which is a major issuer of mortgage-backed securities.

www.freddiemac.com

Annual Revenues: $4.9 billion

Chairman and Chief Exec. Officer
SYRON, Richard F.
Mailstop: M/S 431
Tel: (703) 903 - 3000
Fax: (703) 903 - 3495
TF: (800) 373 - 3343

Main Headquarters

Mailing: 8200 Jones Branch Dr.
McLean, VA 22102
Tel: (703) 903 - 2000
Fax: (703) 903 - 2447
TF: (800) 373 - 3343

Washington Office

Mailing: 401 Ninth St., NW
Suite 600
Washington, DC 20004
Tel: (202) 434 - 8600
Fax: (202) 434 - 8626

Political Action Committees

Federal Home Loan Mortgage Corp. Political Action Committee (FreddiePAC)
Contact: Robert Tsien
8200 Jones Branch Dr.
McLean, VA 22102
Tel: (703) 903 - 2000
Fax: (703) 903 - 2447
TF: (800) 373 - 3343

Contributions to Candidates: $102,000 (01/05 - 09/05)

Democrats: $51,000; Republicans: $51,000.

Principal Recipients

SENATE DEMOCRATS		HOUSE DEMOCRATS	
Carper, Thomas R (DE)	$6,000	Kanjorski, Paul (PA)	$3,000
Conrad, Kent (ND)	$4,000	Hoyer, Steny (MD)	$2,500
Johnson, Tim (SD)	$3,000	Frank, Barney (MA)	$2,000
Nelson, Benjamin (NE)	$3,000		
Stabenow, Debbie (MI)	$3,000		
Dorgan, Byron (ND)	$2,000		
Mikulski, Barbara (MD)	$2,000		

SENATE REPUBLICANS		HOUSE REPUBLICANS	
Bennett, Robert F (UT)	$5,000	Bachus, Spencer (AL)	$5,000
McConnell, Mitch (KY)	$5,000	DeLay, Tom (TX)	$5,000
Burns, Conrad (MT)	$4,500	Dreier, David (CA)	$5,000
Snowe, Olympia (ME)	$2,000	Ney, Robert W (OH)	$5,000
		Pryce, Deborah (OH)	$5,000
		Lewis, Jerry (CA)	$2,000

Corporate Foundations and Giving Programs

Freddie Mac Foundation
Contact: Maxine B. Baker

Freddie Mac

** continued from previous page*

8200 Jones Branch Dr.
McLean, VA 22102
Tel: (703) 918 - 8840
Fax: (703) 918 - 8895
TF: (800) 373 - 3343

Annual Grant Total: over $5,000,000

Sponsors the "Reach Out to a Child" campaign and promotes employee volunteerism.

Geographic Preference: Washington, DC metropolitan area (including Northern Virginia and Suburban Maryland)

Primary Interests: AIDS/HIV; Child Abuse and Neglect Prevention; Early Childhood Education; Education; Families

Recent Recipients: Nat'l Head Start Association; Parents Anonymous; Washington AIDS Partnership

Public Affairs and Related Activities Personnel

At Headquarters

BAKER, Maxine B.
V. President, Community Relations; and President and Chief Exec. Officer, Freddie Mac Foundation
Mailstop: A40
maxine_baker@freddiemac.com
Tel: (703) 918 - 8840
Fax: (703) 918 - 8895
TF: (800) 373 - 3343

BOYD, Ralph, Jr.
Exec. V. President, Community Relations
Tel: (703) 903 - 2000
Fax: (703) 903 - 2447
TF: (800) 373 - 3343

FITZPATRICK, Eileen B.
Senior Communications Specialist
Mailstop: M/S 409
eileen_fitzpatrick@freddiemac.com
Tel: (703) 903 - 2446
Fax: (703) 903 - 2447
TF: (800) 373 - 3343

FUENTES, Patricia
Manager, Public Relations
Tel: (703) 903 - 2000
Fax: (703) 903 - 2447
TF: (800) 373 - 3343

GERMAN, Brad
Manager, Public Relations
Mailstop: M/S 409
brad_german@freddiemac.com
Tel: (703) 903 - 2437
Fax: (703) 903 - 2447
TF: (800) 373 - 3343

MCHALE, Sharon
Director, Public Relations
sharon_mchale@freddiemac.com
Tel: (703) 903 - 2438
Fax: (703) 903 - 2447
TF: (800) 373 - 3343

PALOMBI, David R.
V. President, Corporate Communications and Marketing Department
Mailstop: M/S 407
david_palombi@freddiemac.com
Tel: (703) 903 - 2512
Fax: (703) 903 - 2447
TF: (800) 373 - 3343

TSIEN, Robert
PAC Contact
Tel: (703) 903 - 2000
Fax: (703) 903 - 2447
TF: (800) 373 - 3343

At Washington Office

FETTIG, Dwight
Director, Government Relations
Mailstop: M/S 600
Registered Federal Lobbyist.
Tel: (202) 434 - 8600
Fax: (202) 434 - 8626

FISCHER, Danna S.
Director, Government Relations
Mailstop: M/S 600
danna_fischer@freddiemac.com
Registered Federal Lobbyist.
Tel: (202) 434 - 8600
Fax: (202) 434 - 8626

FOX, Barbara
Director, Government Relations
Mailstop: M/S 600
barbara_fox@freddiemac.com
Registered Federal Lobbyist.
Tel: (202) 434 - 8618
Fax: (202) 434 - 8626

JOHNSON-OBEY, Kristen
Senior Director, Government Relations
Mailstop: M/S 600
Tel: (202) 434 - 8613
Fax: (202) 434 - 8626

LYNCH, David H.
Director, Government Relations
Tel: (202) 434 - 8609
Fax: (202) 434 - 8626

SMITH, Brian
Director, Government Relations
Mailstop: M/S 600
brian_smith@freddiemac.com
Tel: (202) 434 - 8637
Fax: (202) 434 - 8626

ZIMMER, Robert
V. President, Government Relations, House Relations
robert_zimmer@freddiemac.com
Tel: (202) 434 - 8639
Fax: (202) 434 - 8626

Freedom Communications Inc.

A newspaper and magazine publisher.

www.freedom.com

Chairman of the Board
BASSETT, Thomas W.
Tel: (949) 253 - 2300
Fax: (949) 474 - 7675

President and Chief Exec. Officer
BELL, Alan
Tel: (949) 553 - 9292
Fax: (949) 474 - 7675

Main Headquarters
Mailing: 17666 Fitch
Irvine, CA 92614
Tel: (949) 253 - 2300
Fax: (949) 474 - 7675

Public Affairs and Related Activities Personnel

At Headquarters

BRUSKIN, Marcy
V. President, Human Resources and Organizational Development
Tel: (949) 253 - 2300
Fax: (949) 474 - 7675

MICLOT, Stephanie
Director, Corporate Communications and Marketing
Tel: (949) 253 - 2339
Fax: (949) 474 - 7675

NORTON, JoAnne
V. President, Shareholder Relations
Tel: (949) 253 - 2300
Fax: (949) 474 - 7675

WALLACE, Richard K.
V. President, Corporate Affairs
Tel: (949) 553 - 9292
Fax: (949) 474 - 7675

Freeport-McMoRan Copper and Gold Inc.

A natural resource company formed by the merger of Freeport Minerals Co. and McMoRan Oil and Gas Co. Active in the mining of gold and copper.

www.fcx.com

Chairman of the Board
MOFFETT, James R.
Tel: (504) 582 - 4000
Fax: (504) 582 - 1847
TF: (800) 535 - 7094

President and Chief Exec. Officer
ADKERSON, Richard
Tel: (504) 582 - 4000
Fax: (504) 582 - 1847
TF: (800) 535 - 7094

Main Headquarters
Mailing: P.O. Box 51777
New Orleans, LA 70151
Tel: (504) 582 - 4000
Fax: (504) 582 - 1847
TF: (800) 535 - 7094

Street: 1615 Poydras St.
New Orleans, LA 70112

Political Action Committees

Freeport McMoRan Copper and Gold Inc. Citizenship Committee
Contact: Dean T. Falgoust
P.O. Box 51777
New Orleans, LA 70151
Tel: (504) 582 - 4000
Fax: (504) 582 - 1847
TF: (800) 535 - 7094

Contributions to Candidates: $16,000 (01/05 - 09/05)
Democrats: $8,000; Republicans: $8,000.

Principal Recipients

SENATE DEMOCRATS		HOUSE DEMOCRATS	
Landrieu, Mary (LA)	$3,000	Jefferson, William (LA)	$2,000
Nelson, Benjamin (NE)	$2,000		
Conrad, Kent (ND)	$1,000		

SENATE REPUBLICANS		HOUSE REPUBLICANS	
Thomas, Craig (WY)	$2,000	Burton, Danny (IN)	$2,000
Talent, James (MO)	$1,000	Alexander, Rodney (LA)	$1,000
		King, Steven (IA)	$1,000
		LaHood, Ray (IL)	$1,000

McMoran Exploration Co. Citizenship Committee
Contact: Jerene B. Guidry
P.O. Box 51777
New Orleans, LA 70151
Tel: (504) 582 - 4000
Fax: (504) 582 - 1847
TF: (800) 535 - 7094

Contributions to Candidates: $7,000 (01/05 - 09/05)
Democrats: $4,000; Republicans: $3,000.

Corporate Foundations and Giving Programs

Freeport-McMoRan Foundation
Contact: David Lowry, Ph.D.
P.O. Box 51777
New Orleans, LA 70151
Tel: (504) 582 - 1803
Fax: (504) 582 - 1847
TF: (800) 535 - 7094

Annual Grant Total: $1,000,000 - $2,000,000

Contributions totalled over $8 million; research grants exceeded $4 million.

Geographic Preference: Area(s) in which the company operates; Louisiana

Primary Interests: Arts and Humanities; Community Affairs; Higher Education

Recent Recipients: American Lung Ass'n; American Red Cross; Anti-Defamation League

Public Affairs and Related Activities Personnel

At Headquarters

COLLIER, William L.
V. President, Communications
william_collier@fmi.com
Tel: (504) 582 - 1750
Fax: (504) 582 - 1847
TF: (800) 535 - 7094

FALGOUST, Dean T.
PAC Treasurer, Freeport-McMoRan Copper and Gold Citizenship Committee
Tel: (504) 582 - 4000
Fax: (504) 582 - 1847
TF: (800) 535 - 7094

Freeport-McMoRan Copper and Gold Inc.

• continued from previous page

GUIDRY, Jerene B.
Assistant PAC Treasurer; and Projects Coordinator, Communications
Tel: (504) 582 - 4000
Fax: (504) 582 - 1847
TF: (800) 535 - 7094

JOINT, David
Manager, Investor Relations
Tel: (504) 582 - 4000
Fax: (504) 582 - 1847
TF: (800) 535 - 7094

KING, W. Russell
Senior V. President, International Relations and Federal Government Relations
Tel: (504) 582 - 4000
Fax: (504) 582 - 1847
TF: (800) 535 - 7094

LOWRY, David, Ph.D.
President and Exec. Director, Freeport-McMoRan Foundation
david_lowry@fmi.com
Tel: (504) 582 - 1803
Fax: (504) 582 - 1847
TF: (800) 535 - 7094

MILLER, D. James
V. President, Environmental Affairs and Safety
Tel: (504) 582 - 4239
Fax: (504) 582 - 1847
TF: (800) 535 - 7094

MILLER, Ralph R.
V. President, State Government Relations
ralph_miller@fmi.com
Tel: (504) 582 - 4711
Fax: (504) 582 - 1847
TF: (800) 535 - 7094

Freightliner LLC

Manufacturer of trucks. A subsidiary of DaimlerChrysler Corp. (see separate listing).

www.freightliner.com

President and Chief Exec. Officer
PATTERSON, Chris
Tel: (503) 745 - 8000
Fax: (503) 745 - 8921

Main Headquarters
Mailing: 4747 N. Channel Ave.
Portland, OR 97217
Tel: (503) 745 - 8000
Fax: (503) 745 - 8921

Corporate Foundations and Giving Programs

Freightliner Corporate Contributions
Contact: Jeffrey Fisher
4747 N. Channel Ave.
Portland, OR 97217
Tel: (503) 745 - 8000
Fax: (503) 745 - 5996

Annual Grant Total: none reported

Public Affairs and Related Activities Personnel

At Headquarters

BRANDT, Chris
Manager, Public Relations
chrisbrandt@freightliner.com
Tel: (503) 745 - 5471
Fax: (503) 745 - 5096

FISHER, Jeffrey
General Manager, Corporate Communications
jeffreyfisher@freightliner.com
Tel: (503) 745 - 8000
Fax: (503) 745 - 5996

Fremont General Corp.

A financial services holding company.

www.fremontgeneral.com

Chairman of the Board
MCINTYRE, James A.
jmcintyre@fmt.com
Tel: (310) 315 - 5500
Fax: (310) 315 - 5599

Chief Exec. Officer
RAMPINO, Louis J.
Tel: (310) 315 - 5500
Fax: (310) 315 - 5599

Main Headquarters
Mailing: 2020 Santa Monica Blvd., Suite 600
Santa Monica, CA 90404-2208
Tel: (310) 315 - 5500
Fax: (310) 315 - 5599

Public Affairs and Related Activities Personnel

At Headquarters

HAUGE, Marilyn I.
Assistant Secretary and Director, Corporate Compliance and Investor Relations
mhauge@fmt.com
Tel: (310) 315 - 5500
Fax: (310) 315 - 5599

LEE, Robin
Director, Human Resources
rlee@fmt.com
Tel: (310) 315 - 5500
Fax: (310) 315 - 5599

MAURY, Nicole F.
Director, Corporate Communications
nmaury@fmt.com
Tel: (310) 315 - 5508
Fax: (310) 315 - 5599

Friday's Hospitality Worldwide

See listing on page 103 under Carlson Companies.

Friendly Ice Cream Corp.

Acquired by Tennessee Restaurant Co.

www.friendlys.com
Annual Revenues: $561.9 billion

Chairman of the Board
SMITH, Donald N.
Tel: (413) 543 - 2400
Fax: (413) 543 - 9355
TF: (800) 966 - 9970

Chief Exec. Officer and President
CUTTER, John L.
Tel: (413) 543 - 2400
Fax: (413) 543 - 9355
TF: (800) 966 - 9970

Main Headquarters
Mailing: 1855 Boston Rd.
Wilbraham, MA 01095
Tel: (413) 543 - 2400
Fax: (413) 543 - 9366
TF: (800) 966 - 9970

Corporate Foundations and Giving Programs

Friendly Ice Cream Corp. Contributions Program
Contact: Maura C. Tobias
1855 Boston Rd.
Wilbraham, MA 01095
Tel: (413) 543 - 2400
Ext: 2814
Fax: (413) 543 - 3966
TF: (800) 966 - 9970

Annual Grant Total: none reported

Public Affairs and Related Activities Personnel

At Headquarters

BURNS, Debbie
Manager, Investment Relations
Tel: (413) 543 - 2400
Ext: 3317
Fax: (413) 543 - 9355
TF: (800) 966 - 9970

TOBIAS, Maura C.
Director, Corporate Public Affairs
Tel: (413) 543 - 2400
Ext: 2814
Fax: (413) 543 - 3966
TF: (800) 966 - 9970

ULRICH, Garrett J.
V. President, Human Resources
Tel: (413) 543 - 2400
Fax: (413) 543 - 9355
TF: (800) 966 - 9970

Frito-Lay, Inc.

A snack food producer. A separate operating division of PepsiCo, Inc. (see separate listing).

www.fritolay.com
Annual Revenues: $14.504 billion

Chairman and Chief Exec. Officer
ROSENFELD, Irene B.
Tel: (972) 334 - 7000
Fax: (972) 334 - 2019

Main Headquarters
Mailing: P.O. Box 660634
Dallas, TX 75266-0634
Street: 7701 Legacy Dr.
Plano, TX 75024-4099
Tel: (972) 334 - 7000
Fax: (972) 334 - 2019

Corporate Foundations and Giving Programs

Frito-Lay, Inc. Corporate Contributions Program
Contact: Kathy Cloud
P.O. Box 660634
Dallas, TX 75266-0634
Tel: (972) 334 - 2725
Fax: (972) 334 - 2045

Annual Grant Total: none reported
Geographic Preference: Texas

Public Affairs and Related Activities Personnel

At Headquarters

CLOUD, Kathy
Corporate Contributions Program Contact
Tel: (972) 334 - 2725
Fax: (972) 334 - 2045

MARKLEY, Lynn
Senior V. President, Public Relations
Tel: (972) 334 - 2404
Fax: (972) 334 - 2045

Frontier Airlines, Inc.

Provides budget airline services.

www.frontierairlines.com

Chairman of the Board
ADDOMS, Samuel D.
Tel: (720) 374 - 4200
Fax: (720) 374 - 4375
TF: (800) 265 - 5505

President and Chief Exec. Officer
POTTER, Jeff S.
jpotter@flyfrontier.com
Tel: (720) 374 - 4200
Fax: (720) 374 - 4375
TF: (800) 265 - 5505

Main Headquarters
Mailing: 7001 Tower Rd.
Denver, CO 80249-7312
Tel: (720) 374 - 4200
Fax: (720) 374 - 4375
TF: (800) 265 - 5505

Corporate Foundations and Giving Programs

Frontier Airlines Inc. Corporate Giving
Contact: Jennifer Hartman

Frontier Airlines, Inc.

* continued from previous page

7001 Tower Rd.
Denver, CO 80249-7312
Tel: (720) 374 - 4375
TF: (800) 265 - 5505

Annual Grant Total: none reported

Public Affairs and Related Activities Personnel

At Headquarters

HARTMAN, Jennifer
Community Relations Contact
Tel: (720) 374 - 4375
TF: (800) 265 - 5505

HODAS, Jo
Senior Manager, Corporate Communications
Tel: (720) 374 - 4504
Fax: (720) 374 - 4375
TF: (800) 265 - 5505

Frontier Oil Corp.

An oil refining and marketing company.
www.fronteroil.com

Chairman, President and Chief Exec. Officer
GIBBS, James R.
jgibbs@frontieroil.com
Tel: (713) 688 - 9600
Fax: (713) 688 - 0616

Main Headquarters
Mailing: 10000 Memorial Dr.
Suite 600
Houston, TX 77024-3341
Tel: (713) 688 - 9600
Fax: (713) 688 - 0616

Political Action Committees

Frontier PAC
Contact: J. Currie Bechtol
10000 Memorial Dr.
Suite 600
Houston, TX 77024-3341
Tel: (713) 688 - 9600
Fax: (713) 688 - 0616

Contributions to Candidates: none reported (01/05 - 09/05)

Public Affairs and Related Activities Personnel

At Headquarters

ARON, Doug S.
Director, Investor Relations
Tel: (713) 688 - 9600
Fax: (713) 688 - 0616

BECHTOL, J. Currie
Treasurer, Frontier PAC
cbechtol@frontieroil.com
Tel: (713) 688 - 9600
Fax: (713) 688 - 0616

At Other Offices

FAUDEL, Gerald B.
V. President, Corporate Relations
(Frontier Refining)
4610 S. Ulster St., Suite 200
Denver, CO 80237
gfaudel@frontieroil.com
Responsibilities include government relations.
Tel: (303) 714 - 0168
Fax: (303) 714 - 0130

Frontier Refining

See listing on page 207 under Frontier Oil Corp.

Frost Capital Group

See listing on page 207 under Frost Nat'l Bank.

Frost Nat'l Bank

A bank holding company. Also known as Cullen/Frost Bankers, Inc.
www.frostbank.com

Chairman and Chief Exec. Officer
EVANS, Richard W., Jr.
Tel: (210) 220 - 4393
Fax: (210) 220 - 4117

Main Headquarters
Mailing: P.O. Box 1600
San Antonio, TX 78296
Street: 100 W. Houston
San Antonio, TX 78205
Tel: (210) 220 - 4011

Corporate Foundations and Giving Programs

Frost Bank Corporate Contributions Program
Contact: Melissa Adams
P.O. Box 1600
San Antonio, TX 78296
Tel: (210) 220 - 4353
Fax: (210) 220 - 5144

Annual Grant Total: none reported
Geographic Preference: Texas
Primary Interests: Arts and Culture; Economic Development; Education; Health and Human Services; Youth Services

Public Affairs and Related Activities Personnel

At Headquarters

ADAMS, Melissa
Corporate Donations Officer
Tel: (210) 220 - 4353
Fax: (210) 220 - 5144

Fruit of the Loom, Inc.

See listing on page 71 under Berkshire Hathaway.

H. B. Fuller Co.

A manufacturer of adhesives, sealants, coatings, paints, and other specialty chemicals.
www.hbfuller.com

Chairman, President, and Chief Exec. Officer
STROUCKEN, Albert P. L.
Tel: (651) 236 - 5900
Fax: (651) 236 - 5165
TF: (800) 214 - 2523

Main Headquarters
Mailing: 1200 Willow Lake Blvd.
P.O. Box 64683
St. Paul, MN 55164-0683
Tel: (651) 236 - 5900
Fax: (651) 236 - 5165
TF: (800) 214 - 2523

Corporate Foundations and Giving Programs

H. B. Fuller Co. Foundation
Contact: Karen P. Muller
1200 Willow Lake Blvd.
P.O. Box 64683
St. Paul, MN 55164-0683
Tel: (651) 236 - 5207
Fax: (651) 236 - 5056
TF: (800) 214 - 2523

Annual Grant Total: $400,000 - $500,000
Grants are not made to individuals, religious or fraternal organizations, or political or lobbying groups.
Geographic Preference: Area(s) in which the company operates
Primary Interests: Arts and Culture; Environment/Conservation; Health and Human Services; Social Services
Recent Recipients: Minnesota Orchestra; Minnesota Private College Fund; University of Minnesota

Public Affairs and Related Activities Personnel

At Headquarters

DVORAK, Scott
Director, Investor Relations
scott.dvorak@hbfuller.com
Tel: (651) 236 - 5150
Fax: (651) 236 - 5165
TF: (800) 214 - 2523

GROFF, Keralyn
Director, Public Relations
Keralyn.Groff@hbfuller.com
Tel: (651) 236 - 5104
Fax: (651) 236 - 5056
TF: (800) 214 - 2523

MUELLER, Kathleen
Manager, Corporate Communications
kathy.mueller@hbfuller.com
Tel: (651) 236 - 5161
Fax: (651) 236 - 5165
TF: (800) 214 - 2523

MULLER, Karen P.
Exec. Director, Foundation
karen.muller@hbfuller.com
Tel: (651) 236 - 5207
Fax: (651) 236 - 5056
TF: (800) 214 - 2523

Furniture Brands Internat'l, Inc.

A manufacturer of furniture.
www.furniturebrands.com
Annual Revenues: $2.4 billion

Chairman and Chief Exec. Officer
HOLLIMAN, W. G. "Mickey"
Tel: (314) 863 - 1100
Fax: (314) 863 - 5306

Main Headquarters
Mailing: 101 S. Hanley Rd.
St. Louis, MO 63105-3493
Tel: (314) 863 - 1100
Fax: (314) 863 - 5306

Corporate Foundations and Giving Programs

Furniture Brands Internat'l Charitable Trust
Contact: Mike Loynd
101 S. Hanley Rd.
St. Louis, MO 63105-3493
Tel: (314) 863 - 1100
Fax: (314) 863 - 7047

Annual Grant Total: under $100,000
Geographic Preference: St. Louis, MO
Primary Interests: Arts and Culture; Community Affairs; Community Development; Higher Education

Public Affairs and Related Activities Personnel

At Headquarters

LOCKARD, Richard A.
Director, Employee Benefits and Risk Management
rlockard@furniturebrands.com
Tel: (314) 863 - 1100
Fax: (314) 863 - 5306

LOYND, Mike
Administrator, Charitable Trust
Tel: (314) 863 - 1100
Fax: (314) 863 - 7047

RICHMOND, Marty
Manager, Corporate Communications
mrichmond@furniturebrands.com
Tel: (314) 862 - 7133
Fax: (314) 863 - 7047

Arthur J. Gallagher & Co.

An insurance broker.
www.ajg.com
Annual Revenues: $1.1 billion

Chairman of the Board
GALLAGHER, Robert E.
Tel: (630) 773 - 3800
Fax: (630) 285 - 4000

Arthur J. Gallagher & Co.

** continued from previous page*

President and Chief Exec. Officer
GALLAGHER, J. Patrick, Jr. — Tel: (630) 773 - 3800, Fax: (630) 285 - 4000

Main Headquarters
Mailing: The Gallagher Center, Two Pierce Pl., Itasca, IL 60143-3141 — Tel: (630) 773 - 3800, Fax: (630) 285 - 4000

Corporate Foundations and Giving Programs

Arthur J. Gallagher Foundation
Contact: J. Patrick Gallagher, Jr.
The Gallagher Center, Two Pierce Pl., Itasca, IL 60143-3141 — Tel: (630) 773 - 3800, Fax: (630) 285 - 4000

Assets: $7,841,297 (2002)
Annual Grant Total: $100,000 - $200,000
Geographic Preference: Florida; Illinois
Primary Interests: Human Welfare; Persons with Disabilities; Religion
Recent Recipients: Michigan Technological University

Public Affairs and Related Activities Personnel

At Headquarters

AKIN, Marsha J.
Investor Relations Contact — Tel: (630) 773 - 3800, Fax: (630) 285 - 4000

Ernest and Julio Gallo Winery

www.gallo.com
Annual Revenues: $1.65 billion

Chairman of the Board
GALLO, Ernest — Tel: (209) 341 - 3111, Fax: (209) 341 - 8993

Chief Exec. Officer
GALLO, Joseph E. — Tel: (209) 341 - 3111, Fax: (209) 341 - 3569

Main Headquarters
Mailing: P.O. Box 1130, Modesto, CA 95353 — Tel: (209) 341 - 3111, Fax: (209) 341 - 3569
Street: 600 Yosemite Blvd., Modesto, CA 95354

Corporate Foundations and Giving Programs

Gallo Foundation
Contact: Ron Emerzian
P.O. Box 1130, Modesto, CA 95353 — Tel: (209) 341 - 3141, Fax: (209) 341 - 3208

Annual Grant Total: $750,000 - $1,000,000
Geographic Preference: National
Primary Interests: Medical Research; Minority Opportunities; Performing Arts; Persons with Disabilities; Religion
Recent Recipients: Nat'l Ass'n for the Advancement of Colored People; United Way

Public Affairs and Related Activities Personnel

At Headquarters

CHASE, Mike
V. President, Human Resources — Tel: (209) 341 - 4146, Fax: (209) 341 - 4559

EMERZIAN, Ron
V. President, Community Affairs, Gallo Foundation — Tel: (209) 341 - 3141, Fax: (209) 341 - 3208

MARTIN, Larry
V. President, Government Affairs — Tel: (209) 341 - 3016, Fax: (209) 341 - 3208

MCCLELLAND, Sue
V. President, Media — Tel: (209) 341 - 3188, Fax: (209) 341 - 8993

Gannett Co., Inc.

A diversified publishing and communications company.
www.gannett.com
Annual Revenues: $6.2 billion

Chairman of the Board
MCCORKINDALE, Douglas H. — Tel: (703) 854 - 6000, Ext: 6046, Fax: (703) 276 - 2046

President and Chief Exec. Officer
DUBOW, Craig A. — Tel: (703) 854 - 6000, Fax: (703) 276 - 2046

Main Headquarters
Mailing: 7950 Jones Branch Dr., McLean, VA 22107 — Tel: (703) 854 - 6000, Fax: (703) 276 - 2046

Corporate Foundations and Giving Programs

Gannett Foundation
Contact: Irma E. Simpson
7950 Jones Branch Dr., McLean, VA 22107 — Tel: (703) 854 - 6000, Ext: 6046, Fax: (703) 276 - 2046

Assets: $25,500,132 (2002)
Annual Grant Total: over $5,000,000
Donations totalled $8 million in 2000.
Geographic Preference: Area(s) in which the company operates
Primary Interests: Arts and Culture; Community Affairs; Economic Development; Education; Environment/Conservation; Social Services
Recent Recipients: Greater Shreveport Economic Development Foundation; Lowry Park Zoological Society of Tampa; North Coast Community Homes; Zacchaeus Soup Kitchen

Public Affairs and Related Activities Personnel

At Headquarters

BERRIOS, Jose A.
V. President, Human Resources and Diversity — Tel: (703) 854 - 6000, Fax: (703) 276 - 2046

CONNELL, Tara J.
V. President, Corporate Communications
tjconnel@gannett.com — Tel: (703) 854 - 6000, Fax: (703) 276 - 2046

FLEMING, David
Senior Legal Counsel
defleming@gannett.com — Tel: (703) 854 - 6000, Fax: (703) 276 - 2046

MARTORE, Gracia C.
Senior V. President and Chief Financial Officer
gmartore@gannett.com — Tel: (703) 854 - 6918, Fax: (703) 276 - 2046
Responsibilities include investor relations.

SIMPSON, Irma E.
Manager, Gannett Foundation — Tel: (703) 854 - 6000, Ext: 6046, Fax: (703) 276 - 2046

Gap Inc.

A clothing retail chain. Other divisions maintain websites at www.gapkids.com, www.babygap.com, www.bananarepublic.com, www.oldnavy.com, and www.gap.com.
www.gapinc.com
Annual Revenues: $13.848 billion

Chairman of the Board
FISHER, Robert J. — Tel: (650) 952 - 4400, Fax: (415) 427 - 2553, TF: (800) 333 - 7899

President and Chief Exec. Officer
PRESSLER, Paul S. — Tel: (650) 952 - 4400, Fax: (415) 427 - 2553, TF: (800) 333 - 7899

Main Headquarters
Mailing: Two Folsom St., San Francisco, CA 94105 — Tel: (650) 952 - 4400, Fax: (415) 427 - 2553, TF: (800) 333 - 7899

Political Action Committees

The Gap Inc. PAC
Contact: Tamsin S. Randlett
Two Folsom St., San Francisco, CA 94105 — Tel: (650) 952 - 4400, Fax: (415) 427 - 2553, TF: (800) 333 - 7899

Contributions to Candidates: $17,500 (01/05 - 09/05)
Democrats: $10,500; Republicans: $7,000.

Principal Recipients

SENATE DEMOCRATS

HOUSE DEMOCRATS
Rangel, Charles B (NY) $5,000
Cuellar, Henry (TX) $2,000

SENATE REPUBLICANS
Talent, James (MO) $2,000

HOUSE REPUBLICANS
Pryce, Deborah (OH) $2,000
Shaw, Clay (FL) $2,000

Corporate Foundations and Giving Programs

The Gap Foundation
Contact: Dotti Hatcher
Two Folsom St., San Francisco, CA 94105 — Tel: (650) 952 - 4400, Fax: (415) 427 - 2553, TF: (800) 333 - 7899

Annual Grant Total: $2,000,000 - $5,000,000
Geographic Preference: Chicago, IL; New York City; San Francisco Bay Area; Washington, DC
Primary Interests: AIDS/HIV; Arts and Culture; Children; Environment/Conservation; K-12 Education
Recent Recipients: Gay Men's Health Crisis; New York City Arts Connection; Omega Boys Club; Save San Francisco Bay Foundation; United Negro College Fund

Gap Inc.

** continued from previous page*

Public Affairs and Related Activities Personnel

At Headquarters

HATCHER, Dotti
Senior Director, Gap Inc. Community Relations
Tel: (650) 952 - 4400
Fax: (415) 427 - 2553
TF: (800) 333 - 7899

MARKS, Alan
V. President, Corporate Communications
Tel: (650) 952 - 4400
Fax: (415) 427 - 2553
TF: (800) 333 - 7899

RANDLETT, Tamsin S.
Senior Director, Government Affairs
Tel: (650) 952 - 4400
Fax: (415) 427 - 2553
TF: (800) 333 - 7899

Gartner, Inc.

Provides research and advisory services.

www.gartner.com
Annual Revenues: $893.8 million

Chairman of the Board
SMITH, James C.
Tel: (203) 964 - 0096
Fax: (203) 316 - 6488

Chief Exec. Officer
HALL, Gene
Tel: (203) 964 - 0096
Fax: (203) 316 - 6488

Main Headquarters
Mailing: 56 Top Gallant Rd.
Stamford, CT 06904
Tel: (203) 964 - 0096
Fax: (203) 316 - 6488

Public Affairs and Related Activities Personnel

At Headquarters

GARDNER, Colette
Senior V. President, Human Resources
colette.gardner@gartner.com
Tel: (203) 316 - 6994
Fax: (203) 316 - 6488

HAYES, Tom
Group V. President, Public Relations
tom.hayes@gartner.com
Tel: (203) 316 - 6835
Fax: (203) 316 - 6488

SCHWARTZ, Lew
Senior V. President and General Counsel
Responsibilities include public affairs.
Tel: (203) 316 - 6311
Fax: (203) 316 - 6488

Gates Rubber Co.

A diversified manufacturer of automotive and industrial rubber and fiber products, and automotive power transmission accessories. Also develops oil and gas properties. A wholly-owned subsidiary of Tomkins plc.

www.gates.com

Main Headquarters
Mailing: 1551 Wewatta St.
Denver, CO 80202-6173
Tel: (303) 744 - 1911
Fax: (303) 744 - 4443

Corporate Foundations and Giving Programs

Gates Corp. Giving Program
Contact: Marge Hoppe
1551 Wewatta St.
Denver, CO 80202-6173
Tel: (303) 744 - 1911
Fax: (303) 744 - 4443

Annual Grant Total: none reported

Public Affairs and Related Activities Personnel

At Headquarters

BELL, Richard
President
Tel: (303) 744 - 1911
Fax: (303) 744 - 4443

HOFFMAN, Gordon
Manager, Public Relations
ghoffman@gates.com
Tel: (303) 744 - 1911
Ext: 4595
Fax: (303) 744 - 4443

HOPPE, Marge
Contact, Gates Corporate Giving Program
Tel: (303) 744 - 1911
Fax: (303) 744 - 4443

Gateway, Inc.

Manufacturer and marketer of personal computers.

www.gateway.com

Chairman of the Board
SNYDER, Richard D.
Tel: (949) 471 - 7000
Fax: (949) 471 - 7041

President and Chief Exec. Officer
INOUYE, Wayne
Tel: (949) 471 - 7000
Fax: (949) 471 - 7041

Main Headquarters
Mailing: 7565 Irvine Center Dr.
Irvine, CA 92618
Tel: (949) 471 - 7000
Fax: (949) 471 - 7041

Washington Office
Contact: Donald W. McClellan, Jr.
Mailing: 707 D St. NW
Washington, DC 20004
Tel: (202) 737 - 2000

Political Action Committees

Gateway Good Government PAC
Contact: Donald W. McClellan, Jr.
707 D St. NW
Washington, DC 20004
Tel: (202) 737 - 2000
Fax: (202) 737 - 2688

Contributions to Candidates: $2,000 (01/05 - 09/05)
Democrats: $1,000; Republicans: $1,000.

Principal Recipients

SENATE DEMOCRATS
Feinstein, Dianne (CA) $1,000

HOUSE DEMOCRATS

SENATE REPUBLICANS

HOUSE REPUBLICANS
Barton, Joe L (TX) $1,000

Corporate Foundations and Giving Programs

Gateway Foundation
Contact: Glenn J. Anderson
7565 Irvine Center Dr.
Irvine, CA 92618
Tel: (949) 471 - 7000
Fax: (949) 471 - 7041

Assets: $2,487,464 (2001)
Annual Grant Total: $750,000 - $1,000,000

Public Affairs and Related Activities Personnel

At Headquarters

ANDERSON, Glenn J.
Foundation Director
Tel: (949) 471 - 7000
Fax: (949) 471 - 7041

NIENABER, Kelli
Manager, Government Relations
Tel: (949) 471 - 7000
Fax: (949) 471 - 7041

SHERBIN, Bob
Director, Corporate Communications
Tel: (949) 471 - 7000
Fax: (949) 471 - 7041

At Washington Office

MCCLELLAN, Donald W., Jr.
V. President, Government Relations
donald.mcclellan@gateway.com
Registered Federal Lobbyist.
Tel: (202) 737 - 2000
Fax: (202) 737 - 2688

At Other Offices

JOHNSON, Marlys
Manager, Investor Relations
610 Gateway Dr.
North Sioux City, SD 57049-2000
marlys.johnson@gateway.com
Tel: (800) 846 - 4503
Fax: (605) 232 - 2757

GATX Corp.

A finance and leasing company specializing in railcar, locomotive and aircraft operating leasing.

www.gatx.com
Annual Revenues: $1.489 billion

Chairman of the Board
ZECH, Ronald H.
Tel: (312) 621 - 6200
Fax: (312) 612 - 6648
TF: (800) 428 - 8161

President and Chief Executive Officer
KENNEY, Brian A.
Tel: (312) 621 - 6200
Fax: (312) 621 - 6648
TF: (800) 428 - 8161

Main Headquarters
Mailing: 500 W. Monroe St.
Chicago, IL 60661
Tel: (312) 621 - 6200
Fax: (312) 621 - 6648
TF: (800) 428 - 8161

Political Action Committees

GATX Corp. Good Government Program
Contact: William J. Hasek
500 W. Monroe St.
Chicago, IL 60661
Tel: (312) 621 - 6200
Fax: (312) 621 - 6648
TF: (800) 428 - 8161

Contributions to Candidates: $2,000 (01/05 - 09/05)
Democrats: $500; Republicans: $1,000; Other: $500.

Principal Recipients

SENATE REPUBLICANS

HOUSE REPUBLICANS
LaTourette, Steve (OH) $1,000

Corporate Foundations and Giving Programs

GATX Community Partnerships Program
Contact: Allison Dean

GATX Corp.

* continued from previous page

500 W. Monroe St. | Tel: (312) 621 - 4274
Chicago, IL 60661 | Fax: (312) 621 - 8062
TF: (800) 428 - 8161

Annual Grant Total: $2,000,000 - $5,000,000
Geographic Preference: Area(s) in which the company operates
Primary Interests: Education; Environment/Conservation; Families

Public Affairs and Related Activities Personnel

At Headquarters

DEAN, Allison — Tel: (312) 621 - 4274
Community Affairs Specialist — Fax: (312) 621 - 8062
TF: (800) 428 - 8161

DOMINGUEZ, Irma — Tel: (312) 621 - 8799
Investor Relations Coordinator — Fax: (312) 621 - 6648
ir@gatx.com — TF: (800) 428 - 8161

DUDDY, Gail L. — Tel: (312) 621 - 6220
Senior V. President, Human Resources — Fax: (312) 621 - 6637
TF: (800) 428 - 8161

HASEK, William J. — Tel: (312) 621 - 6200
PAC Treasurer — Fax: (312) 621 - 6648
TF: (800) 428 - 8161

JOHNSON, Rhonda S. — Tel: (312) 621 - 6200
Director, Inverstor Relations — Fax: (312) 621 - 6648
rhonda.johnson@gatx.com — TF: (800) 428 - 8161

Gaylord Entertainment Co.

A hospitality and entertainment company which owns and operates Gaylord Hotels branded properties. Entertainment brands include the Grand Ole Opry, Ryman Auditorium and General Jackson Showboat, among others. Other interests include two radio stations and the Nashville Predators.

www.gaylordentertainment.com
Annual Revenues: $400 million

Chairman, and Chief Exec. Officer — Tel: (615) 316 - 6000
REED, Colin V. — Fax: (615) 316 - 6060
creed@gaylordentertainment.com

Main Headquarters
Mailing: One Gaylord Dr. — Tel: (615) 316 - 6000
Nashville, TN 37214 — Fax: (615) 316 - 6555

Political Action Committees

Gaylord Entertainment Co. PAC
Contact: Rod Connor
One Gaylord Dr. — Tel: (615) 316 - 6000
Nashville, TN 37214 — Fax: (615) 316 - 6060

Contributions to Candidates: $8,500 (01/05 - 09/05)
Democrats: $1,000; Republicans: $7,500.

Principal Recipients

SENATE DEMOCRATS
Ford, Harold E Jr (TN) $1,000

HOUSE DEMOCRATS

SENATE REPUBLICANS
Corker Jr, Robert P (TN) $5,000

HOUSE REPUBLICANS
Blackburn, Marsha (TN) $2,500

Public Affairs and Related Activities Personnel

At Headquarters

BUCHANAN, Stephen — Tel: (615) 316 - 6000
Senior V. President, Media and Entertainment — Fax: (615) 316 - 6060

BUFFINGTON, Melissa — Tel: (615) 316 - 6000
Senior V. President, Human Resources and Communications — Fax: (615) 316 - 6060

CONNOR, Rod — Tel: (615) 316 - 6000
PAC Treasurer — Fax: (615) 316 - 6060

MORGAN, Jason — Tel: (615) 316 - 6561
V. President, Strategic Planning and Investor Relations — Fax: (615) 316 - 6751

ROSSITER, Greg — Tel: (615) 316 - 6000
V. President, Corporate Communications — Fax: (615) 316 - 6060
grossiter@gaylordentertainment.com

GBC

See listing on page 212 under General Binding Corp.

GE Consumer Products

See listing on page 213 under General Electric Co.

GEICO Corp.

An insurance and financial services subsidiary of Berkshire Hathaway Inc. (see separate listing).

www.geico.com
Annual Revenues: $6.06 billion

Chairman and Chief Exec. Officer — Tel: (301) 986 - 3000
NICELY, Olza M. — Fax: (301) 986 - 2888

Main Headquarters
Mailing: One GEICO Plaza — Tel: (301) 986 - 3000
Washington, DC 20076 — Fax: (301) 986 - 2888

Corporate Foundations and Giving Programs

GEICO Corporate Contributions Program
Contact: David L. Schindler
One GEICO Plaza — Tel: (301) 986 - 3000
Washington, DC 20076 — Fax: (301) 986 - 2068

Annual Grant Total: $2,000,000 - $5,000,000
Geographic Preference: Area(s) in which the company operates
Primary Interests: Community Affairs; Environment/Conservation; Safety; Social Services
Recent Recipients: American Red Cross; United Way

GEICO Philanthropic Foundation
Contact: Karen Watson
One GEICO Plaza — Tel: (301) 986 - 3000
Washington, DC 20076 — Ext: 2387
Fax: (301) 986 - 2068

Annual Grant Total: $1,000,000 - $2,000,000
Geographic Preference: Area(s) in which the company operates
Primary Interests: Children; Medical Research; Youth Services
Recent Recipients: American Lung Ass'n; United Way

Public Affairs and Related Activities Personnel

At Headquarters

MINSHALL, Janice — Tel: (301) 986 - 3000
Assistant V. President, Communications — Fax: (301) 986 - 2068

NAYDEN, Hank — Tel: (301) 986 - 3000
V. President and Legislative Counsel — Fax: (301) 986 - 2888

ROST, Rynthia M. — Tel: (301) 986 - 3839
V. President, Public Affairs — Fax: (301) 986 - 2888

SCHINDLER, David L. — Tel: (301) 986 - 3000
Senior V. President, Human Resources — Fax: (301) 986 - 2068
dschindler@geico.com

WATSON, Karen — Tel: (301) 986 - 3000
Administrator, GEICO Philanthropic Foundation — Ext: 2387
Fax: (301) 986 - 2068

GenAmerica Corp.

See listing on page 210 under GenAmerica Financial Corp.

GenAmerica Financial Corp.

Formerly GenAmerica Corp. A life and health insurance and related financial services company. A subsidiary of MetLife, Inc. (see separate listing).

www.genam.com

Main Headquarters
Mailing: 700 Market St. — Tel: (314) 843 - 8700
St. Louis, MO 63101 — Fax: (314) 444 - 0681

Corporate Foundations and Giving Programs

General American Life Insurance Co. Contributions Program
700 Market St. — Tel: (314) 843 - 8700
St. Louis, MO 63101 — Fax: (314) 444 - 0681

Annual Grant Total: $750,000 - $1,000,000
Geographic Preference: St. Louis, MO
Primary Interests: Education; Health; Medical Research
Recent Recipients: St. Louis University; United Way

Public Affairs and Related Activities Personnel

At Headquarters

LARANCE, Charles L. — Tel: (314) 843 - 8700
V. President, Corporate Relations — Fax: (314) 444 - 0681

MAYUGA, Ann Marie — Tel: (314) 843 - 8700
Media Contact — Fax: (314) 444 - 0681
ammayuga@genam.com

GenCorp

A technology-based company with strong interests in aerospace and defense, pharmaceutical fine chemicals, and real estate.

www.gencorp.com

Chairman, President, and Chief Exec. Officer — Tel: (916) 355 - 4000
HALL, Terry L. — Fax: (916) 351 - 8668

Main Headquarters
Mailing: P.O. Box 537012 — Tel: (916) 355 - 4000
Sacramento, CA 95853-7012 — Fax: (916) 351 - 8668
Street: Highway 50 and Aerojet Rd.
Rancho Cordova, CA 95670

Washington Office
Contact: Don Brownlee
Mailing: 1025 Connecticut Ave. NW, Suite 501 — Tel: (202) 828 - 6800
Washington, DC 20036 — Fax: (202) 828 - 6849

Political Action Committees

GenCorp Inc. PAC - GENPAC
Contact: Michael Velasquez
1025 Connecticut Ave. NW, Suite 501 — Tel: (202) 828 - 6830
Washington, DC 20036 — Fax: (202) 828 - 6849

GenCorp

** continued from previous page*

Contributions to Candidates: $23,400 (01/05 - 09/05)

Democrats: $9,500; Republicans: $13,900.

Principal Recipients

SENATE DEMOCRATS		HOUSE DEMOCRATS	
Kennedy, Ted (MA)	$2,500	Matsui, Doris (CA)	$2,000
Feinstein, Dianne (CA)	$1,000	Inslee, Jay (WA)	$1,000
Pryor, Mark (AR)	$1,000	Ross, Michael Avery (AR)	$1,000
		Udall, Mark (CO)	$1,000

SENATE REPUBLICANS		HOUSE REPUBLICANS	
Santorum, Richard (PA)	$1,000	Weldon, David (FL)	$3,000
		Lungren, Daniel E (CA)	$2,500
		Doolittle, John (CA)	$1,400
		Calvert, Ken (CA)	$1,000
		Dreier, David (CA)	$1,000
		Lewis, Jerry (CA)	$1,000
		Pearce, Steve (NM)	$1,000
		Wilson, Heather (NM)	$1,000
		Wolf, Frank R (VA)	$1,000

Corporate Foundations and Giving Programs

GenCorp Foundation
P.O. Box 537012
Sacramento, CA 95853-7012
Tel: (916) 355 - 4000
Fax: (916) 351 - 8668

Assets: $17,000,000 (2002)

Annual Grant Total: $2,000,000 - $5,000,000

The GenCorp Foundation supports the communities where its employees live, work, and volunteer.

Geographic Preference: Area(s) in which the company operates

Primary Interests: Arts and Humanities; Education; Health and Human Services

Recent Recipients: California State University, Sacramento; Nat'l Merit Scholarship

Public Affairs and Related Activities Personnel

At Headquarters

CUTLER, Linda
V. President, Corporate Communications
linda.cutler@gencorp.com
Tel: (916) 355 - 8650
Fax: (916) 351 - 8667

At Washington Office

BROWNLEE, Don
V. President, Washington Operations
Tel: (202) 828 - 6800
Fax: (202) 828 - 6849

VELASQUEZ, Michael
Director, Congressional Relations
michael.velasquez@aerojet.com
(Aerojet)
Tel: (202) 828 - 6830
Fax: (202) 828 - 6849

Genentech, Inc.

A member of the Public Affairs Council. A genetic engineering, drugs and health care company.

www.gene.com

Annual Revenues: $2.2 billion

Chairman and Chief Exec. Officer
LEVINSON, Arthur D.
alevinson@gene.com
Tel: (650) 225 - 1000
Fax: (650) 225 - 6000

Main Headquarters
Mailing: One DNA Way
San Francisco, CA 94080-4990
Tel: (650) 225 - 1000
Fax: (650) 225 - 6000

Washington Office
Contact: Walter K. Moore
Mailing: 808 17th St. NW
Suite 250
Washington, DC 20006
Tel: (202) 296 - 7272
Fax: (202) 296 - 7290

Political Action Committees

Genentech Inc. Political Action Committee (GenenPAC)
Contact: Leo Redmond
460 Point San Bruno Blvd.
San Francisco, CA 94080

Contributions to Candidates: $54,500 (01/05 - 09/05)

Democrats: $25,500; Republicans: $29,000.

Principal Recipients

SENATE DEMOCRATS		HOUSE DEMOCRATS	
Feinstein, Dianne (CA)	$6,000	Eshoo, Anna (CA)	$3,000
Lieberman, Joe (CT)	$5,000	Lantos, Tom (CA)	$2,500
Kennedy, Ted (MA)	$2,000		

SENATE REPUBLICANS		HOUSE REPUBLICANS	
Hatch, Orrin (UT)	$2,500	Deal, Nathan (GA)	$5,500
Ensign, John Eric (NV)	$2,000	Beauprez, Robert (CO)	$2,000
		Dreier, David (CA)	$2,000

Corporate Foundations and Giving Programs

Genentech Foundation for Biomedical Sciences
Contact: Leo Redmond
460 Point San Bruno Blvd.
San Francisco, CA 94080

Annual Grant Total: $750,000 - $1,000,000

Geographic Preference: California

Primary Interests: Education; Math and Science; Medical Research

Recent Recipients: San Francisco Unified School District; Save San Francisco Bay Foundation; University of California - San Francisco

Public Affairs and Related Activities Personnel

At Headquarters

CHARLESWORTH, Debra
Director, General Corporate Media, Corporate Issues, and Financial Media
Tel: (650) 225 - 1000
Fax: (650) 225 - 6000

GARNICK, Robert, Ph.D.
Senior V. President, Regulatory, Quality and Compliance
rgarnick@gene.com
Tel: (650) 225 - 1000
Fax: (650) 225 - 6000

LITTRELL, Kathee, Ph.D., R.N.
Director, Investor Relations
Tel: (650) 225 - 1034
Fax: (650) 225 - 6000

MURANO, Genesio, Ph.D.
V. President, Regulatory Affairs
Tel: (650) 225 - 1000
Fax: (650) 225 - 6000

SCHRICK, Diane
Manager, Investor Relations
Tel: (650) 225 - 1599
Fax: (650) 225 - 6000

STUTTS, Mary
Director, Corporate Relations
Tel: (650) 225 - 5759
Fax: (650) 225 - 6000

TEETER, Geoff
Director, Employee/Community Relations
Tel: (650) 225 - 8171
Fax: (650) 225 - 6000

At Washington Office

FARBSTEIN, Marcus
Federal Government Liaison
Tel: (202) 296 - 7272
Fax: (202) 296 - 7290

MOORE, Walter K.
V. President, Government Affairs
wmoore@gene.com
Registered Federal Lobbyist.
Tel: (202) 296 - 7272
Fax: (202) 296 - 7290

WAGNER, Heidi L.
Senior Director, Government Affairs
Registered Federal Lobbyist.
Tel: (202) 296 - 7272
Fax: (202) 296 - 7290

At Other Offices

REDMOND, Leo
PAC Treasurer; and Foundation Contact
460 Point San Bruno Blvd.
San Francisco, CA 94080

General American Corp.

See listing on page 210 under GenAmerica Financial Corp.

General Atomics

Nuclear energy and advanced technologies.

www.generalatomics.com

Chairman, Chief Exec. Officer
BLUE, James N.
Tel: (858) 455 - 3000
Fax: (858) 455 - 3621

Main Headquarters
Mailing: 3550 General Atomics Ct.
San Diego, CA 92121
Tel: (858) 455 - 3000
Fax: (858) 455 - 3621

Washington Office
Contact: Mark Haynes
Mailing: 1899 Pennsylvania Ave., NW
Suite 300
Washington, DC 20006
Tel: (202) 496 - 8200
Fax: (202) 659 - 1110

Political Action Committees

General Atomics PAC
Contact: Danielle Proctor
3550 General Atomics Ct.
San Diego, CA 92121
Tel: (858) 455 - 3000
Fax: (858) 455 - 3545

Contributions to Candidates: $121,000 (01/05 - 09/05)

General Atomics

• continued from previous page

Democrats: $41,500; Republicans: $79,500.

Principal Recipients

SENATE DEMOCRATS		HOUSE DEMOCRATS	
Kennedy, Ted (MA)	$2,000	Skelton, Ike (MO)	$10,000
		Murtha, John P Mr. (PA)	$5,000
		Visclosky, Peter (IN)	$5,000
		Filner, Bob (CA)	$4,500

SENATE REPUBLICANS		HOUSE REPUBLICANS	
Ensign, John Eric (NV)	$10,000	Hobson, David (OH)	$5,000
Burns, Conrad (MT)	$5,000	Knollenberg, Joe (MI)	$5,000
Allard, A Wayne (CO)	$3,000	Wicker, Roger (MS)	$5,000
		Cunningham, Duke (CA)	$4,500
		Hunter, Duncan (CA)	$4,000
		Calvert, Ken (CA)	$3,500

Public Affairs and Related Activities Personnel

At Headquarters

FOUQUET, Douglas M.
Coordinator, Community Public Relations
Tel: (858) 455 - 3000 Ext: 2173
Fax: (858) 455 - 3545

PROCTOR, Danielle
PAC Treasurer
Tel: (858) 455 - 3000
Fax: (858) 455 - 3545

At Washington Office

HAYNES, Mark
V. President, Washington Operations
haynes@ga.radix.net
Registered Federal Lobbyist.
Tel: (202) 496 - 8200
Fax: (202) 659 - 1110

HOPPER, Gary
V. President, Washington Operations
Registered Federal Lobbyist.
Tel: (202) 496 - 8200
Fax: (202) 659 - 1110

ROPER, Bart
V. President, Washington Operations
(General Atomics Aeronautical Systems, Inc.)
Registered Federal Lobbyist.
Tel: (202) 496 - 8200
Fax: (202) 659 - 1110

General Atomics Aeronautical Systems, Inc.

See listing on page 211 under General Atomics.

General Binding Corp.

Manufacturer of products that bind, laminate and display information.
www.gbc.com

Chairman and Chief Exec. Officer
MARTIN, Dennis
Tel: (847) 272 - 3700
Fax: (847) 272 - 3723

Main Headquarters
Mailing: One GBC Plaza
Northbrook, IL 60062
Tel: (847) 272 - 3700
Fax: (847) 272 - 1389

Public Affairs and Related Activities Personnel

At Headquarters

ANDREOLI, Cindy
Director, Marketing Communications
candreoli@gbc.com
Responsibilities include media relations.
Tel: (847) 272 - 3700
Fax: (847) 272 - 1389

GIULIANO, Tony
Treasurer and Director, Investor Relations
tgiuliano@gbc.com
Tel: (847) 291 - 5451
Fax: (847) 291 - 6371

ZUKOWSKI, Perry
V. President, Human Resources
pzukowski@gbc.com
Tel: (847) 291 - 5456
Fax: (847) 272 - 3723

General Cable Corp.

Develops, designs, manufactures, markets and distributes copper, aluminum and fiber optic wire and cable products.
www.generalcable.com
Annual Revenues: $1.5 billion

President and Chief Exec. Officer
KENNY, Gregory B.
Tel: (859) 572 - 8000
Fax: (859) 572 - 8458

Main Headquarters
Mailing: Four Tesseneer Dr.
Highland Heights, KY 41076
Tel: (859) 572 - 8000
Fax: (859) 572 - 8458

Public Affairs and Related Activities Personnel

At Headquarters

LAWSON, Lisa B.
V. President, Corporate Communications
Tel: (859) 572 - 8000
Fax: (859) 572 - 8458

MONTGOMERY, Paul
Director, Finance and Investor Relations
Tel: (859) 572 - 8684
Fax: (859) 572 - 8458

OLMSTED, Peter J.
Senior V. President, Human Resources
Tel: (859) 572 - 8000
Fax: (859) 572 - 8458

General Dynamics Corporation

Specializes in mission-critical information systems and technologies; land and expeditionary combat systems, armaments and munitions; shipbuilding and marine systems; and business aviation. The parent company of Gulfstream Aerospace Corp. (see separate listing).
www.generaldynamics.com
Annual Revenues: $19.2 billion

Chairman and Chief Exec. Officer
CHABRAJA, Nicholas D.
Tel: (703) 876 - 3000
Fax: (703) 876 - 3125

Main Headquarters
Mailing: 2941 Fairview Park Dr.
Falls Church, VA 22042-4513
Tel: (703) 876 - 3000
Fax: (703) 876 - 3125

Political Action Committees

General Dynamics Voluntary Political Contribution Plan
Contact: Diane L. Mossler
2941 Fairview Park Dr.
Falls Church, VA 22042-4513
Tel: (703) 876 - 3000
Fax: (703) 876 - 3125

Contributions to Candidates: $416,000 (01/05 - 09/05)
Democrats: $155,000; Republicans: $259,000; Other: $2,000.

Principal Recipients

SENATE DEMOCRATS		HOUSE DEMOCRATS	
Nelson, Bill (FL)	$9,750	Langevin, James (RI)	$10,000
Kennedy, Ted (MA)	$8,000	Murtha, John P Mr. (PA)	$10,000
		Skelton, Ike (MO)	$10,000
		Pastor, Edward (AZ)	$6,500
		Moran, James (VA)	$6,000
		Visclosky, Peter (IN)	$6,000

SENATE REPUBLICANS		HOUSE REPUBLICANS	
Talent, James (MO)	$10,000	Hayes, Robert (NC)	$10,000
Snowe, Olympia (ME)	$9,000	Hunter, Duncan (CA)	$7,000
Burns, Conrad (MT)	$8,000	Rehberg, Dennis (MT)	$7,000
		Simmons, Rob (CT)	$6,000

Corporate Foundations and Giving Programs

General Dynamics Corporate Giving Program
Contact: Kendell Pease
2941 Fairview Park Dr.
Falls Church, VA 22042-4513
Tel: (703) 876 - 3093
Fax: (703) 876 - 3555

Annual Grant Total: none reported

Public Affairs and Related Activities Personnel

At Headquarters

COLBURN, Cordis B. "Cork"
V. President, Government Relations
Tel: (703) 876 - 3034
Fax: (703) 876 - 3600

DOOLITTLE, Robert E.
Director, Public Affairs
Tel: (703) 876 - 3199
Fax: (703) 876 - 3186

GARDEPE, William M.
Staff V. President, Legislative Affairs
Tel: (703) 876 - 3494
Fax: (703) 876 - 3600

HUMPHREYS, Mary
Manager, Public Affairs
Tel: (703) 876 - 3389
Fax: (703) 876 - 3555

JOHNSON, Karl D.
Director, Public Affairs
Tel: (703) 876 - 3172
Fax: (703) 876 - 3555

LEWIS, Ray
Staff V. President, Investor Relations
Tel: (703) 876 - 3195
Fax: (703) 876 - 3186

MOSSLER, Diane L.
PAC Treasurer
Tel: (703) 876 - 3000
Fax: (703) 876 - 3125

OLIVER, Walter M.
V. President, Human Resources
Tel: (703) 876 - 3000
Fax: (703) 876 - 3125

PEASE, Kendell
V. President, Communications
Tel: (703) 876 - 3093
Fax: (703) 876 - 3555

RILEY, Carey J.
Staff V. President, Government Relations
Tel: (703) 876 - 3309
Fax: (703) 876 - 3600

RITTER, Douglas
Staff V. President, Government Relations
Tel: (703) 876 - 3254
Fax: (703) 876 - 3600

SAVNER, David
Senior V. President and General Counsel
Tel: (703) 876 - 3000
Fax: (703) 876 - 3125

TEMENAK, James M.
Staff V. President, Marine Systems
Tel: (703) 876 - 3000
Fax: (703) 876 - 3600

General Electric Co.

A diversified company with businesses in technology, services and manufacturing.
www.ge.com
Annual Revenues: $125.679 billion

Chairman and Chief Exec. Officer
IMMELT, Jeffrey R. — Tel: (203) 373 - 2211, Fax: (203) 373 - 3131
jeffrey.immelt@corporate.ge.com

Main Headquarters
Mailing: 3135 Easton Tpk.
Bldg. E2E
Fairfield, CT 06431
Tel: (203) 373 - 2211
Fax: (203) 373 - 3131

Washington Office
Contact: Nancy P. Dorn
Mailing: 1299 Pennsylvania Ave. NW
11th Floor West
Washington, DC 20004-2407
Tel: (202) 637 - 4000
Fax: (202) 637 - 4006

Political Action Committees

General Electric Co. Political Action Committee
Contact: Marie Talwar
1299 Pennsylvania Ave. NW
11th Floor West
Washington, DC 20004-2407
Tel: (202) 637 - 4000
Fax: (202) 637 - 4006

Contributions to Candidates: $426,150 (01/05 - 09/05)
Democrats: $145,150; Republicans: $281,000.

Principal Recipients

SENATE DEMOCRATS		HOUSE DEMOCRATS	
Byrd, Robert C (WV)	$3,500	Murtha, John P Mr. (PA)	$10,000
Kennedy, Ted (MA)	$3,500	Kanjorski, Paul (PA)	$5,000
Nelson, Benjamin (NE)	$3,500		
Bingaman, Jeff (NM)	$3,000		
Ford, Harold E Jr (TN)	$3,000		

SENATE REPUBLICANS		HOUSE REPUBLICANS	
Allen, George (VA)	$8,000	McCrery, Jim (LA)	$6,000
Burns, Conrad (MT)	$7,500	Blunt, Roy (MO)	$5,000
Smith, Gordon (OR)	$5,000	Capito, Shelley (WV)	$5,000
Snowe, Olympia (ME)	$4,000	Dewine, R. Pat (OH)	$5,000
Talent, James (MO)	$3,500	English, Philip S (PA)	$5,000
Chafee, Lincoln (RI)	$3,000	LaHood, Ray (IL)	$5,000
Thomas, Craig (WY)	$3,000	Myrick, Sue (NC)	$5,000
		Pickering, Chip (MS)	$5,000
		Rogers, Harold (KY)	$5,000
		Ryan, Paul D (WI)	$5,000

Corporate Foundations and Giving Programs

GE Fund
Contact: Robert Corcoran
3135 Easton Tpk.
Bldg. E2E
Fairfield, CT 06431
Tel: (203) 373 - 2211
Fax: (203) 373 - 3131

Annual Grant Total: over $5,000,000
Most proposals supported by the GE Fund are submitted upon invitation.
Geographic Preference: National; International
Primary Interests: Arts and Culture; Engineering; Higher Education; Math and Science
Recent Recipients: Jackie Robinson Foundation; Nat'l Action Council for Minorities in Engineering; United Way

Public Affairs and Related Activities Personnel

At Headquarters

CARY, William H. — Tel: (203) 373 - 2468, Fax: (203) 373 - 3131
V. President, Corporate Investor Communications

CONATY, William J. — Tel: (203) 373 - 2211, Fax: (203) 373 - 3131
Senior V. President, Corporate Human Resources

CORCORAN, Robert — Tel: (203) 373 - 2211, Fax: (203) 373 - 3131
President, GE Fund

HEINEMAN, Ben W., Jr. — Tel: (203) 373 - 2211, Fax: (203) 373 - 3131
Senior V. President, Law and Public Affairs

KLEIN, Jonathan — Tel: (203) 373 - 2241, Fax: (203) 373 - 3131
Corporate Communications Contact
jonathan.klein@ge.com

MORRIS, JoAnna H. — Tel: (203) 373 - 2211, Fax: (203) 373 - 3131
Director, Corporate Investor Communicatons

REINKE, Melissa — Tel: (203) 749 - 2227, Fax: (203) 373 - 3131
Manager, Corporate Relations

SHEFFER, Gary — Tel: (203) 373 - 2211, Fax: (203) 373 - 3131
Exec. Director, Communications and Public Affairs
gary.sheffer@ge.com

WARD, Nancy K. — Tel: (203) 921 - 2063, Fax: (203) 373 - 3131
Manager, Government Relations
nancy.ward@corporate.ge.com

At Washington Office

BOGGS, Larry A. — Tel: (202) 637 - 4000, Fax: (202) 637 - 4006
Counsel, Environmental Programs
larry.boggs@corporate.ge.com
Registered Federal Lobbyist.

BOYD, Robert — Tel: (202) 637 - 4000, Fax: (202) 637 - 4006
Registered Federal Lobbyist.

CABRAL, Victor G. — Tel: (202) 637 - 4000, Fax: (202) 637 - 4006
Registered Federal Lobbyist.

CLEMENTS, William "Bill" — Tel: (202) 637 - 4000, Fax: (202) 637 - 4300
Senior Manager, International Trade Regulation
Registered Federal Lobbyist.

COOPER, Thomas E. — Tel: (202) 637 - 4000, Fax: (202) 637 - 4006
V. President, Aerospace Technology
Registered Federal Lobbyist.

DORN, Nancy P. — Tel: (202) 637 - 4000, Fax: (202) 637 - 4006
V. President, Corporate Government Relations
Registered Federal Lobbyist.

FARRELL, Pamela — Tel: (202) 637 - 4000, Fax: (202) 637 - 4006
Technology, Research and Development
Registered Federal Lobbyist.

FRENKEL, Orit — Tel: (202) 637 - 4000, Fax: (202) 637 - 4006
Senior Manager, International Law and Policy
orit.frenkel@corporate.ge.com
Registered Federal Lobbyist.

FULTON, Kathryn — Tel: (202) 637 - 4222, Fax: (202) 637 - 4066
Manager, Government Relations
kathryn.fulton@corporate.ge.com
Registered Federal Lobbyist.

GADBAW, R. Michael — Tel: (202) 637 - 4000, Fax: (202) 637 - 4006
V. President and Senior Counsel, International Law and Policy
michael.gadbaw@corporate.ge.com
Registered Federal Lobbyist.

HOWLETT, Steven — Tel: (202) 637 - 4000, Fax: (202) 637 - 4006
Registered Federal Lobbyist.

MERBER, Selig S. — Tel: (202) 637 - 4116, Fax: (202) 637 - 4006
Counsel, International Trade Regulation
Registered Federal Lobbyist.

OKUN, B. Robert — Tel: (202) 637 - 4532, Fax: (202) 637 - 4006
V. President, NBC Universal Washington
Registered Federal Lobbyist.

PELLETIER, Eric — Tel: (202) 637 - 4000, Fax: (202) 637 - 4006
Senior Manager, Government Relations

POMEROY, Glenn — Tel: (202) 637 - 4000, Fax: (202) 637 - 4006
Registered Federal Lobbyist.

PROWITT, Peter D. — Tel: (202) 637 - 4000, Fax: (202) 637 - 4006
Manager, Federal Government Relations
peter.prowitt@corporate.ge.com
Registered Federal Lobbyist.

REECE, Gary — Tel: (202) 637 - 4000, Fax: (202) 637 - 4006
Registered Federal Lobbyist.

RICHARDS, Timothy J. — Tel: (202) 637 - 4000, Fax: (202) 637 - 4006
Senior Manager, International Trade and Investment
timothy.richards@corporate.ge.com
Registered Federal Lobbyist.

TALWAR, Marie — Tel: (202) 637 - 4000, Fax: (202) 637 - 4006
PAC Treasurer

THOMSON, Lynn Harding — Tel: (202) 637 - 4022, Fax: (202) 637 - 4006
Manager, Federal Government Relations
lynn.thomson@corporate.ge.com
Registered Federal Lobbyist.

WALLACE, Rob — Tel: (202) 637 - 4000, Fax: (202) 637 - 4006
Manager, Government and Industry Programs
rob.wallace@corporate.ge.com
Registered Federal Lobbyist.

At Other Offices

JONES, Earl F. — Tel: (502) 452 - 3164
Senior Counsel, Government Relations
(GE Consumer Products)
AP2-225
Louisville, KY 40225

General Growth Properties Inc.

A shopping mall owner, developer, and manager.
www.generalgrowth.com

Chairman of the Board
BUCKSBAUM, Matthew — Tel: (312) 960 - 5000 Fax: (312) 960 - 5475

Chief Exec. Officer
BUCKSBAUM, John — Tel: (312) 960 - 5000 Fax: (312) 960 - 5475

Main Headquarters
Mailing: 110 N. Wacker Dr.
Chicago, IL 60606-1511 — Tel: (312) 960 - 5000 Fax: (312) 960 - 5475

Political Action Committees

General Growth Properties Inc. PAC
Contact: Ronald Gern
110 N. Wacker Dr.
Chicago, IL 60606-1511 — Tel: (312) 960 - 5000 Fax: (312) 960 - 5475

Contributions to Candidates: none reported (01/05 - 09/05)

Public Affairs and Related Activities Personnel

At Headquarters

GERN, Ronald
Treasurer, General Growth Properties Inc. PAC — Tel: (312) 960 - 5000 Fax: (312) 960 - 5475

KEATING, David
Senior Manager, Media Relations — Tel: (312) 960 - 6325 Fax: (312) 960 - 5475

SPRECK, Nicole
Manager, Corporate Communications — Tel: (312) 960 - 6386 Fax: (312) 960 - 5475

General Mills

A member of the Public Affairs Council. Major business area is consumer foods.
www.generalmills.com
Annual Revenues: $12.5 billion

Chairman and Chief Exec. Officer
SANGER, Stephen W. — Tel: (763) 764 - 7600

Main Headquarters
Mailing: One General Mills Blvd.
Minneapolis, MN 55426 — Tel: (763) 764 - 7600 Fax: (763) 764 - 7384

Washington Office
Contact: Mary Catherine Toker
Mailing: 601 13th St. NW
Suite 510 South
Washington, DC 20005 — Tel: (202) 737 - 8200 Fax: (202) 638 - 4914

Political Action Committees

General Mills, Inc. Political Action Committee (GM PAC)
Contact: Lee A. Anderson
One General Mills Blvd.
Minneapolis, MN 55426 — Tel: (763) 764 - 2293 Fax: (763) 764 - 3734

Contributions to Candidates: $40,000 (01/05 - 09/05)
Democrats: $6,500; Republicans: $31,500; Other: $2,000.

Principal Recipients

SENATE REPUBLICANS		HOUSE REPUBLICANS	
Kennedy, Mark (MN)	$5,000	Bonilla, Henry (TX)	$3,000
Talent, James (MO)	$2,000	Kline, John P (MN)	$3,000
		Gutknecht, Gil (MN)	$2,000
		Wilson, Heather (NM)	$2,000

Corporate Foundations and Giving Programs

General Mills Foundation and Community Action
Contact: Ellen Goldberg Lugar
One General Mills Blvd.
Minneapolis, MN 55426 — Tel: (763) 764 - 7600 Fax: (763) 764 - 7384

Assets: $38,073,967 (2003)
Annual Grant Total: over $5,000,000
Geographic Preference: Minneapolis, MN; Area(s) in which the company operates
Primary Interests: Arts and Culture; Education; Families; Health; Nutrition
Recent Recipients: Boys and Girls Club; Junior Achievement; United Negro College Fund

Public Affairs and Related Activities Personnel

At Headquarters

ANDERSON, Lee A.
Manager, State Government Relations — Tel: (763) 764 - 2293 Fax: (763) 764 - 3734

FORSYTHE, Thomas M.
V. President, Corporate Communications — Tel: (763) 764 - 3103 Fax: (763) 764 - 3734

LUGAR, Ellen Goldberg
Exec. Director, General Mills Foundation — Tel: (763) 764 - 7600 Fax: (763) 764 - 7384

MARSHALL, Siri S.
Senior V. President, General Counsel, and Chief Governance and Compliance Officer — Tel: (763) 764 - 7600

PEEL, Michael A.
Senior V. President, Human Resources and Corporate Services — Tel: (763) 764 - 7600

SHEA, Christina S.
Senior V. President, External Relations and President, General Mills Foundation — Tel: (763) 764 - 3413

THORSGAARD, Marybeth
Director, Corporate Relations — Tel: (763) 764 - 6364 Fax: (763) 764 - 3734

WENKER, Kris
V. President, Investor Relations — Tel: (763) 764 - 2607

At Washington Office

SHAPIRO, Jeffrey Alan
Washington Representative
Registered Federal Lobbyist. — Tel: (202) 737 - 8200 Fax: (202) 638 - 4914

TOKER, Mary Catherine
V. President, Government Relations — Tel: (202) 737 - 8200 Fax: (202) 638 - 4914

Registered Federal Lobbyist.

General Motors Acceptance Corp. (GMAC)

A financial services company. Specializes in automotive finance, insurance, mortgages, and commercial finance. A subsidiary of General Motors Corp. (see separate listing).
www.gmacfs.com

Chairman of the Board
FELDSTEIN, Eric A. — Tel: (313) 556 - 5000 Fax: (313) 556 - 5108 TF: (800) 200 - 4622

President
MUIR, William F. — Tel: (313) 556 - 5000 Fax: (313) 556 - 5108 TF: (800) 200 - 4622

Main Headquarters
Mailing: 200 Renaissance Center
Detroit, MI 48265 — Tel: (313) 556 - 5000 Fax: (313) 556 - 5108 TF: (800) 200 - 4622

Washington Office
Contact: Michele Lieber
Mailing: 1660 L St. NW
Suite 400
Washington, DC 20036 — Tel: (202) 775 - 5027 Fax: (202) 775 - 5045

Corporate Foundations and Giving Programs

General Motors Acceptance Corp. (GMAC) Contributions Program
Contact: Joanne K. Krell
200 Renaissance Center
Detroit, MI 48265 — Tel: (313) 556 - 5000 Fax: (313) 556 - 5108 TF: (800) 200 - 4622

Annual Grant Total: none reported

Public Affairs and Related Activities Personnel

At Headquarters

KRELL, Joanne K.
Contact, Corporate Contributions — Tel: (313) 556 - 5000 Fax: (313) 556 - 5108 TF: (800) 200 - 4622

TOSCH, Gay G.
V. President, Human Resources — Tel: (313) 556 - 5000 Fax: (313) 556 - 5108 TF: (800) 200 - 4622

At Washington Office

LIEBER, Michele
Director, Legislative and Regulatory Affairs, Financial Services — Tel: (202) 775 - 5027 Fax: (202) 775 - 5044

At Other Offices

SIMONETTI, Ms. Toni
V. President, Communications and Public Policy
767 Fifth Ave.
New York, NY 10153 — Tel: (212) 418 - 6380

General Motors Corp.

A member of the Public Affairs Council. An automotive industry giant.
www.gmability.com
Annual Revenues: $185.5 billion

Chairman and Chief Exec. Officer
WAGONER, G. Richard, Jr. — Tel: (313) 556 - 5000 Fax: (248) 696 - 7300

Main Headquarters
Mailing: P.O. Box 300
Detroit, MI 48265-1000 — Tel: (313) 556 - 5000 Fax: (248) 696 - 7300
Street: 300 Renaissance Center
Detroit, MI 48265

Washington Office
Contact: Kenneth W. Cole
Mailing: 1660 L St. NW
Fourth Floor
Washington, DC 20036 — Tel: (202) 775 - 5027 Fax: (202) 775 - 5045

General Motors Corp.

* continued from previous page

Political Action Committees

GMPAC
Contact: J. Edward Berry
P.O. Box 300
Detroit, MI 48265-1000
Tel: (313) 556 - 5000
Fax: (248) 696 - 7300

Contributions to Candidates: $252,080 (01/05 - 09/05)

Democrats: $47,080; Republicans: $205,000.

Principal Recipients

SENATE DEMOCRATS		HOUSE DEMOCRATS	
Clinton, Hillary Rodham (NY)	$5,000	Matsui, Doris (CA)	$5,000
		Levin, Sander (MI)	$3,500
		Rangel, Charles B (NY)	$2,500

SENATE REPUBLICANS		HOUSE REPUBLICANS	
Allen, George (VA)	$10,000	Hoekstra, Peter (MI)	$10,000
Smith, Gordon (OR)	$10,000	Knollenberg, Joe (MI)	$8,500
Dewine, Richard (OH)	$9,000	Barton, Joe L (TX)	$5,500
Santorum, Richard (PA)	$7,000	Blunt, Roy (MO)	$5,000
Talent, James (MO)	$7,000	Hastert, Dennis J. (IL)	$5,000
Ensign, John Eric (NV)	$5,000	Oxley, Michael (OH)	$5,000
Kyl, Jon L (AZ)	$4,000	Thomas, William M (CA)	$5,000
Burr, Richard (NC)	$2,500	Camp, David Lee (MI)	$4,000
		Rogers, Michael J (MI)	$4,000
		Bass, Charles (NH)	$3,000
		Buyer, Steve (IN)	$3,000
		Cantor, Eric (VA)	$3,000
		Emerson, Jo Ann (MO)	$3,000
		Latham, Thomas P (IA)	$3,000
		Schwarz, John (MI)	$3,000
		Sherwood, Donald L (PA)	$3,000
		DeLay, Tom (TX)	$2,500
		Ney, Robert W (OH)	$2,500
		Pickering, Chip (MS)	$2,500

Corporate Foundations and Giving Programs

General Motors Cancer Research Foundation
Contact: Debbie I. Dingell
300 Renaissance Center
Detroit, MI 48265-3000
Tel: (313) 556 - 5000
Fax: (313) 665 - 0735

Annual Grant Total: none reported

Awards three annual prizes in the field of cancer research. Donations made through General Motors Foundation.

Primary Interests: Medical Research

General Motors Foundation
Contact: Lorna Utley
300 Renaissance Center
Detroit, MI 48265-3000
Tel: (313) 556 - 5000
Fax: (313) 665 - 0746

Annual Grant Total: over $5,000,000

Primary Interests: Engineering; Higher Education; Math and Science

Recent Recipients: American Indian Science and Engineering Society; Nat'l Action Council for Minorities in Engineering; Society of Hispanic Professional Engineers; Society of Women Engineers; United Negro College Fund

Public Affairs and Related Activities Personnel

At Headquarters

BARCLAY, Katy
V. President, Global Human Resources
Tel: (313) 556 - 5000
Fax: (248) 696 - 7300

BERRY, J. Edward
Director, State-Local Government Relations, Public Policy Center
Tel: (313) 556 - 5000
Fax: (248) 696 - 7300

DONOVAN, Edward J.
Director, Municipal Government Relations
Tel: (313) 556 - 5000
Fax: (248) 696 - 7300

GILLUM, Roderick D.
V. President, Corporate Responsibility and Diversity
Tel: (313) 556 - 5000
Fax: (248) 696 - 7300

GOTTSCHALK, Thomas A.
Exec. V. President, Law and Public Policy
Tel: (313) 556 - 5000
Fax: (248) 696 - 7300

KOWALSKI, Tom
V. President, Global Communications
Tel: (313) 556 - 5000
Fax: (248) 696 - 7300

KRELL, Joanne K.
Manager, Energy/Environment Communciations
joanne.k.krell@gm.com
Tel: (313) 665 - 2443
Fax: (248) 696 - 7300

LOWERY, Elizabeth A.
V. President, Environment and Energy
Tel: (313) 556 - 5000
Fax: (248) 696 - 7300

NEELY, Anthony
Manager, External Communications
anthony.neely@gm.com
Tel: (313) 665 - 9536
Fax: (248) 696 - 7300

WAUN DE RESTREPO, Susan
Staff Assistant, Stockholder Relations
susan.waun@gm.com
Tel: (313) 556 - 5000
Fax: (248) 696 - 7300

At Washington Office

BARNES, Victoria
Washington Representative, Government Relations
Tel: (202) 775 - 5027
Fax: (202) 775 - 5045

BAZEMORE, Melvin J.
Director External Affairs, Washington Office
Registered Federal Lobbyist.
Tel: (202) 775 - 5098
Fax: (202) 775 - 5024

COLE, Keith N.
Director, Legislative and Regulatory Affairs
Registered Federal Lobbyist.
Tel: (202) 775 - 5040
Fax: (202) 775 - 5024

COLE, Kenneth W.
V. President, Government Relations
Registered Federal Lobbyist.
Tel: (202) 775 - 5090
Fax: (202) 775 - 5023

GUARISCO, Annette J.
Deputy Director, Washington Office
Registered Federal Lobbyist.
Tel: (202) 775 - 5080
Fax: (202) 775 - 5045

HICKS, Carolyn
Manager, Legislative and Regulatory Affairs - Health
Tel: (202) 775 - 5027
Fax: (202) 775 - 5045

HIPPLER, Kimberly E.
Manager, Government Policy and Technology Communications
kimberly.hippler@gm.com
Tel: (202) 775 - 5015
Fax: (202) 775 - 5049

KEMMER, Mark L.
Director, Legislative and Regulatory Affairs/Energy
Registered Federal Lobbyist.
Tel: (202) 775 - 5066
Fax: (202) 775 - 5024

LIEBER, Michele
Director, Legislative and Regulatory Policy, Financial Services
Tel: (202) 775 - 5027
Fax: (202) 775 - 5045

O'TOOLE, Stephen E.
Director, Legislative and Regulatory Affairs/Safety
Registered Federal Lobbyist.
Tel: (202) 775 - 5056
Fax: (202) 775 - 5045

PREUSS, J. Christopher
Staff Director, Washington and Advanced Technology Communications
jchristopher.preuss@gm.com
Tel: (202) 775 - 5008
Fax: (202) 775 - 5045

ROOSA, Bryan R.
Director, State Government Relations
Registered Federal Lobbyist.
Tel: (202) 775 - 5086
Fax: (202) 775 - 5024

WASHBURN, Barbara J.
Director, Legislative and Regulatory Affairs/Tax
Registered Federal Lobbyist.
Tel: (202) 775 - 5026
Fax: (202) 775 - 5097

ZEBROSKI, Shirley
Director, Legislative and Regulatory Affairs
Registered Federal Lobbyist.
Tel: (202) 775 - 5082
Fax: (202) 775 - 5097

At Other Offices

BARTHMUSS, David K.
California Environment and Energy Communications Manager
515 Marin St.
Suite 216
Thousand Oaks, CA 91360
dave.barthmuss@gm.com
Tel: (805) 373 - 9572
Fax: (805) 373 - 9648

BUTTACAVOLI, Raymond D.
Regional Director, Sacramento
925 L St., Suite 1485
Sacramento, CA 95814
Tel: (916) 444 - 5788
Fax: (916) 443 - 2100

DINGELL, Debbie I.
V. Chairman, General Motors Foundation and Exec. Dir., Gov. and Community Affairs
300 Renaissance Center
Mailstop: M/C 482-C27-D21
Detroit, MI 48265-3000
Tel: (313) 556 - 5000
Fax: (313) 665 - 0735

LOGAN, James A.
Director, Washington Operations
(Allison Transmission Division)
601 Madison St.
Suite 200
Alexandria, VA 22314
Tel: (703) 549 - 9266
Fax: (703) 549 - 9268

SPROLES, Joseph D.
Regional Director, Lansing
508 Michigan National Tower
124 West Allegan
Lansing, MI 48933
Tel: (517) 377 - 6906
Fax: (517) 377 - 5369

General Motors Corp.

** continued from previous page*

SWENSON, Curtis A. — Tel: (708) 387 - 6264
Director, Marketing and ebusiness — Fax: (708) 387 - 3944
9301 W. 55th St.
LaGrange, IL 60525
curt.swenson@gm.com

TRICE, Patzetta M. — Tel: (317) 242 - 2615
Director, Communications and Public Affairs — Fax: (317) 242 - 0193
(Allison Transmission Division)
P.O. Box 894
Indianapolis, IN 46206
patzetta.trice@gm.com

UTLEY, Lorna — Tel: (313) 556 - 5000
President, General Motors Foundation — Fax: (313) 665 - 0746
300 Renaissance Center
Detroit, MI 48265-3000

WAKEFIELD, Tayce A. — Tel: (313) 665 - 5000
Exec. Director, Environment and Energy Public Policy Center — Fax: (313) 665 - 0746
300 Renaissance Center
Detroit, MI 48265-3000
tayce.wakefield@gm.com

WALLACE, Edward B., Jr. — Tel: (913) 573 - 3994
Regional Director, Midwest — Fax: (913) 573 - 3996
GM Fairfax Assembly
3201 Fairfax Trafficway
Kansas City, KS 66115-1307
edward.wallace@gm.com

WEVERSTAD, Alan R. — Tel: (313) 556 - 5000
Exec. Director, Environment and Energy Public Policy Center - Mobile — Fax: (313) 665 - 0746
300 Renaissance Center
Detroit, MI 48265-3000
alan.weverstad@gm.com

General Re Corp.

A major group of insurers and reinsurance companies. A subsidiary of Berkshire Hathaway (see separate listing).
www.gcre.com

Chairman and Chief Exec. Officer — Tel: (203) 328 - 5000
BRANDON, Joseph P. — Fax: (203) 328 - 6423; TF: (800) 431 - 9994

Main Headquarters
Mailing: Financial Center, 695 E. Main St., Stamford, CT 06901 — Tel: (203) 328 - 5000; Fax: (203) 328 - 6423; TF: (800) 431 - 9994

Corporate Foundations and Giving Programs

GeneralCologne Re Corporate Contributions Program
Contact: Richard W. Manz
Financial Center — Tel: (203) 328 - 5000 Ext: 5661
695 E. Main St.
Stamford, CT 06901 — Fax: (203) 328 - 6423; TF: (800) 431 - 9994

Annual Grant Total: $2,000,000 - $5,000,000
Geographic Preference: Area(s) in which the company operates; National
Primary Interests: Education; Health; Human Welfare; Safety

Public Affairs and Related Activities Personnel

At Headquarters

BELL, Sandra — Tel: (203) 328 - 5000 Ext: 5717
Senior V. President, Human Resources — Fax: (203) 328 - 6423; TF: (800) 431 - 9994

MANZ, Richard W. — Tel: (203) 328 - 5000 Ext: 5661
Contributions Contact — Fax: (203) 328 - 6423; TF: (800) 431 - 9994

General Semiconductor, Inc.

See listing on page 507 under Vishay Intertechnology, Inc.

GeneralCologne Re

See listing on page 216 under General Re Corp.

Genesco

www.genesco.com

Chairman of the Board, President and Chief Exec. Officer — Tel: (615) 367 - 7000
PENNINGTON, Hal N. — Fax: (615) 367 - 8278

Main Headquarters
Mailing: Genesco Park, Suite 490, P.O. Box 731, Nashville, TN 37202-0731 — Tel: (615) 367 - 7000; Fax: (615) 367 - 8278
Street: 1415 Murfreesboro Rd., Nashville, TN 37217-2829

Corporate Foundations and Giving Programs

Genesco Corporate Contributions
Contact: Claire S. McCall
Genesco Park, Suite 490 — Tel: (615) 367 - 8283
P.O. Box 731 — Fax: (615) 367 - 8278
Nashville, TN 37202-0731

Annual Grant Total: under $100,000
Primary Interests: Arts and Culture; Children; Education; Health; United Way Campaigns

Public Affairs and Related Activities Personnel

At Headquarters

CLINARD, John W. — Tel: (615) 367 - 7000
V. President, Administration and Human Resources — Fax: (615) 367 - 8278

MCCALL, Claire S. — Tel: (615) 367 - 8283
Director, Corporate Relations — Fax: (615) 367 - 8278
Responsibilities include corporate contributions.

Genesis HealthCare Corp.

Formerly known as HealthCare Corp. Specializes in geriatric healthcare services.
www.genesishcc.com

Chairman and Chief Exec. Officer — Tel: (610) 444 - 6350
HAGER, George V., Jr. — Fax: (610) 925 - 4000
info@genesishcc.com

Main Headquarters
Mailing: 101 E. State St., Kennett Square, PA 19348 — Tel: (610) 444 - 6350; Fax: (610) 925 - 4000

Political Action Committees

Genesis HealthCare PAC
Contact: Laurence F. Lane
101 E. State St. — Tel: (610) 444 - 8430
Kennett Square, PA 19348 — Fax: (610) 925 - 4242

Contributions to Candidates: $55,930 (01/05 - 09/05)
Democrats: $15,580; Republicans: $37,850; Other: $2,500.

Public Affairs and Related Activities Personnel

At Headquarters

LANE, Laurence F. — Tel: (610) 444 - 8430
V. President, Government Relations — Fax: (610) 925 - 4242
laurence.lane@genesishcc.com

MCKEOWN, James — Tel: (610) 444 - 6350
Chief Financial Officer — Fax: (610) 925 - 4000
info@genesishcc.com
Responsibilities include investor relations.

SALAMON, Lisa — Tel: (610) 444 - 8433
Director, Public Relations — Fax: (610) 925 - 4242
lisa.salamon@genesishcc.com

TABAK, James W. — Tel: (610) 444 - 6350
Senior V. President, Human Resources — Fax: (610) 925 - 4352
james.tabak@genesishcc.com

Genuine Parts Co.

A service company that distributes products.
www.genpt.com

Chief Exec. Officer — Tel: (770) 953 - 1700
GALLAGHER, Thomas C. — Fax: (770) 956 - 2211
tom_gallagher@genpt.com

Main Headquarters
Mailing: 2999 Circle 75 Pkwy., Atlanta, GA 30339 — Tel: (770) 953 - 1700; Fax: (770) 956 - 2211

Corporate Foundations and Giving Programs

Genuine Parts Co. Corporate Contributions Program
2999 Circle 75 Pkwy. — Tel: (770) 953 - 1700
Atlanta, GA 30339 — Fax: (770) 956 - 2211

Annual Grant Total: none reported

Public Affairs and Related Activities Personnel

At Headquarters

NIX, Jerry — Tel: (770) 953 - 1700
Executive V. President, Finance — Fax: (770) 956 - 2211
jerry_nix@genpt.com
Responsibilities include investor relations and corporate contributions and communications.

SPENCER, Gaylord — Tel: (770) 953 - 1700
V. President, Marketing Strategy — Fax: (770) 956 - 2211
gaylord_spencer@genpt.com
Responsibilities include corporate communications.

VAN STEDUM, Edward J. — Tel: (770) 953 - 1700
Senior V. President, Human Resources — Fax: (770) 956 - 2211
edward_vanstedum@genpt.com

YANCEY, Carol B. — Tel: (770) 953 - 1700
V. President and Corporate Secretary — Fax: (770) 956 - 2211
carol_yancey@genpt.com
Responsibilities include investor relations.

Genuity

See listing on page 291 under Level 3 Communications, Inc.

Genzyme Corp.

Provides services in the medical and technology areas.
www.genzyme.com
Annual Revenues: $1.224 billion

Chairman, President and Chief Exec. Officer
TERMEER, Henri A. — Tel: (617) 252 - 7500; Fax: (617) 252 - 7600

Main Headquarters
Mailing: 500 Kendall St., Cambridge, MA 02142 — Tel: (617) 252 - 7500; Fax: (617) 252 - 7600

Washington Office
Contact: Mary McGrane
Mailing: 1020 19th St., NW, Suite 550, Washington, DC 20036 — Tel: (202) 296 - 3280; Fax: (202) 296 - 3411

Political Action Committees

Genzyme Corp. PAC (Genz-PAC)
Contact: Michael S. Wyzga
1020 19th St., NW
Suite 550
Washington, DC 20036
Tel: (202) 296 - 3280; Fax: (202) 296 - 3411

Contributions to Candidates: $6,000 (01/05 - 09/05)
Democrats: $2,000; Republicans: $4,000.

Principal Recipients

SENATE DEMOCRATS
Kennedy, Ted (MA) $2,000

HOUSE DEMOCRATS

SENATE REPUBLICANS
Enzi, Michael B (WY) $1,000
Hatch, Orrin (UT) $1,000

HOUSE REPUBLICANS
Burgess, Michael (TX) $1,000
Ferguson, Mike (NJ) $1,000

Corporate Foundations and Giving Programs

Genzyme Charitable Foundation, Inc.
Contact: Henri A. Termeer
500 Kendall St.
Cambridge, MA 02142
Tel: (617) 252 - 7500; Fax: (617) 252 - 7600

Annual Grant Total: $2,000,000 - $5,000,000
Primary Interests: Medical Research

Public Affairs and Related Activities Personnel

At Headquarters

ARNSTEIN, Caren
V. President, Corporate Communications — Tel: (617) 252 - 7500; Fax: (617) 374 - 7368

CSIMMA, Zoltan
Senior V. President, Human Resources — Tel: (617) 252 - 7500; Fax: (617) 252 - 7600

CURLEY, Sally
V. President, Investor Relations — Tel: (617) 252 - 7500; Fax: (617) 252 - 7600

HILLBACK, Elliott D.
Senior V. President, Corporate Affairs — Tel: (617) 252 - 7500; Fax: (617) 374 - 7368

LAWTON, Alison
Senior V. President, Regulatory Affairs and Corporate Quality Systems — Tel: (617) 252 - 7500; Fax: (617) 374 - 7368

At Washington Office

FROCLICH, Sara
V. President, Government Relations — Tel: (202) 296 - 3280; Fax: (202) 296 - 3411
Registered Federal Lobbyist.

MCGRANE, Mary
Senior V. President — Tel: (202) 296 - 3280; Fax: (202) 296 - 3411
Registered Federal Lobbyist.

WYZGA, Michael S.
PAC Treasurer — Tel: (202) 296 - 3280; Fax: (202) 296 - 3411

Geon Co.

See listing on page 388 under PolyOne Corp.

Georgia Gulf Corp.

A manufacturer of chemicals.
www.ggc.com

Chairman, President and Chief Exec. Officer
SCHMITT, Edward A. — Tel: (770) 395 - 4500; Fax: (770) 395 - 4529

Main Headquarters
Mailing: 115 Perimeter Center Pl., Suite 460, Atlanta, GA 30346 — Tel: (770) 395 - 4500; Fax: (770) 395 - 4529

Corporate Foundations and Giving Programs

Georgia Gulf Corporate Contributions Program
Contact: James Worrell
115 Perimeter Center Pl.
Suite 460
Atlanta, GA 30346
Tel: (770) 395 - 4500; Fax: (770) 395 - 4529

Annual Grant Total: none reported
Emphasizes corporate and employee involvement.
Geographic Preference: National

Public Affairs and Related Activities Personnel

At Headquarters

MATTHEWS, Jim
V. President, Finance and Chief Financial Officer — Tel: (770) 395 - 4577; Fax: (770) 395 - 4529
Responsibilities include investor relations.

WORRELL, James
Director, Human Resources — Tel: (770) 395 - 4500; Fax: (770) 395 - 4529

Georgia-Pacific Corp.

A manufacturer of building products, pulp, paper and related chemicals. Acquired Fort James Corp. and Unisource Worldwide, Inc. in 2001.
www.gp.com
Annual Revenues: $19.656 billion

Chairman and Chief Exec. Officer
CORRELL, Alston D. "Pete", Jr. — Tel: (404) 652 - 5248; Fax: (404) 654 - 4789; TF: (800) 519 - 3111

Main Headquarters
Mailing: P.O. Box 105605, Atlanta, GA 30348 — Tel: (404) 652 - 4000; Fax: (404) 654 - 4789; TF: (800) 519 - 3111
Street: 133 Peachtree St. NE, Atlanta, GA 30303

Washington Office
Mailing: 1120 G St. NW, Suite 1050, Washington, DC 20005-3801 — Tel: (202) 347 - 4446; Fax: (202) 347 - 7058

Political Action Committees

G-P Employees Fund of Georgia-Pacific Corp.
Contact: Jackie D. Bell
1120 G St. NW
Suite 1050
Washington, DC 20005-3801
Tel: (202) 347 - 4446; Fax: (202) 347 - 7058

Contributions to Candidates: $84,250 (01/05 - 09/05)
Democrats: $26,250; Republicans: $58,000.

Principal Recipients

SENATE DEMOCRATS
Carper, Thomas R (DE) $3,500

HOUSE DEMOCRATS
Scott, David (GA) $5,000
Boyd, F Allen Jr (FL) $3,500
Ross, Michael Avery (AR) $3,500
Bishop, Sanford (GA) $2,500

SENATE REPUBLICANS
Allen, George (VA) $9,000
Thomas, Craig (WY) $2,500
Vitter, David (LA) $2,500
Talent, James (MO) $2,000

HOUSE REPUBLICANS
Gard, John G (WI) $5,000
Walden, Gregory (OR) $3,000
Young, Don E (AK) $3,000
Baker, Hugh (LA) $2,500
Rehberg, Dennis (MT) $2,500
Kingston, John (GA) $2,000
Pombo, Richard (CA) $2,000
Putnam, Adam (FL) $2,000

Corporate Foundations and Giving Programs

Georgia-Pacific Foundation
Contact: Curley Dossman
P.O. Box 105605
Atlanta, GA 30348
Tel: (404) 652 - 4182; Fax: (404) 654 - 4789; TF: (800) 519 - 3111

Annual Grant Total: $2,000,000 - $5,000,000
Geographic Preference: Area(s) in which the company operates
Primary Interests: Education; Environment/Conservation; Social Services
Recent Recipients: Boys and Girls Club; United Way; YMCA

Public Affairs and Related Activities Personnel

At Headquarters

BARNARD, Patricia A.
Exec. V. President, Human Resources — Tel: (404) 652 - 4000; Fax: (404) 654 - 4789; TF: (800) 519 - 3111

Georgia-Pacific Corp.

* continued from previous page

BOSTIC, James E., Jr.
Exec. V. President, Government Affairs and Governmental Environmental Affairs
Tel: (404) 652 - 4000
Fax: (404) 654 - 4789
TF: (800) 519 - 3111

DOSSMAN, Curley
Senior Director, Community Affairs and President, Georgia-Pacific Foundation
Tel: (404) 652 - 4182
Fax: (404) 654 - 4789
TF: (800) 519 - 3111

NOLLEN, Margaret R.
V. President, Investor Relations
Tel: (404) 652 - 4000
Fax: (404) 654 - 4789
TF: (800) 519 - 3111

THOMAS, Lee M.
President and Chief Operating Officer
Tel: (404) 652 - 4000
Fax: (404) 654 - 4789
TF: (800) 519 - 3111

WEIDMAN, Sheila
V. President, Corporate Communications and Corporate Marketing
Tel: (404) 652 - 4000
Fax: (404) 654 - 4789
TF: (800) 519 - 3111

At Washington Office

BELL, Jackie D.
V. President, Federal Government Affairs
Registered Federal Lobbyist.
Tel: (202) 347 - 4446
Fax: (202) 347 - 7058

KAUFMANN, Robert
Registered Federal Lobbyist.
Tel: (202) 347 - 4446
Fax: (202) 347 - 7058

MOORE, Susan F.
V. President, Environmental Affairs
Tel: (202) 347 - 4446
Fax: (202) 347 - 7058

At Other Offices

GUIDRY, George H., Jr.
Regional Manager, Government Affairs
One American Pl.
Suite 1840
Baton Rouge, LA 70825-2400
Tel: (225) 388 - 9061
Ext: 101
Fax: (225) 383 - 6218

HOOD, Charles H.
V. President, State Governmental Affairs
133 Peachtree St., N.E.
Atlanta, GA 30303
Tel: (404) 652 - 6483
Fax: (404) 584 - 1470

MCNAIR, Robert E., Jr.
Regional Manager, Government Affairs
1301 Gervais St., Suite 516
Columbia, SC 29201
Tel: (803) 254 - 7765

SATO, Peggy A.
Regional Manager, Government Affairs
528 Cottage St., N.E., Suite 1B
Salem, OR 97301
Tel: (503) 378 - 1576

TOMA, Al
Regional Manager, Government Affairs
1919 S. Broadway
Green Bay, WI 54304
Tel: (920) 438 - 2475

Georgia Power Co.

An electric utility subsidiary of Southern Co. (see separate listing).

www.southernco.com

President and Chief Exec. Officer
GARRETT, Michael D.
Tel: (404) 506 - 6526
Fax: (404) 506 - 3771

Main Headquarters
Mailing: 241 Ralph McGill Blvd. NE
Atlanta, GA 30308-3374
Tel: (404) 506 - 6526
Fax: (404) 506 - 3771

Washington Office
Contact: James M. McCool, Jr.
Mailing: 1130 Connecticut Ave. NW, Suite 830
Washington, DC 20036
Tel: (202) 261 - 5000
Fax: (202) 296 - 7937

Political Action Committees

Georgia Power Co. Federal PAC
Contact: Scott Orr
241 Ralph McGill Blvd. NE
Atlanta, GA 30308-3374
Tel: (404) 506 - 1366
Fax: (404) 506 - 3771

Contributions to Candidates: $49,500 (01/05 - 09/05)
Democrats: $16,500; Republicans: $33,000.

Principal Recipients

SENATE DEMOCRATS

HOUSE DEMOCRATS

Bishop, Sanford (GA)	$5,000
Scott, David (GA)	$5,000
Lewis, John (GA)	$3,000
Marshall, Jim (GA)	$2,500

SENATE REPUBLICANS

HOUSE REPUBLICANS

Westmoreland, Lynn (GA)	$8,000
Price, Thomas (GA)	$6,000
Kingston, John (GA)	$5,000
Norwood, Charles (GA)	$5,000
Gingrey, Phillip (GA)	$4,000
Linder, John (GA)	$4,000

Corporate Foundations and Giving Programs

Georgia Power Foundation, Inc.
Contact: Judy M. Anderson
241 Ralph McGill Blvd. NE
Atlanta, GA 30308-3374
Tel: (404) 526 - 7750
Fax: (404) 506 - 3771

Annual Grant Total: over $5,000,000
Geographic Preference: Area in which the company is headquartered; Georgia
Primary Interests: Civil Rights; Community Development; Higher Education; United Way Campaigns

Public Affairs and Related Activities Personnel

At Headquarters

ANDERSON, Judy M.
Senior V. President, Charitable Giving
Mailstop: BIN 10230
Responsibilities include corporate philanthropy.
Tel: (404) 526 - 7750
Fax: (404) 506 - 3771

ARCHER, William C.
Exec. V. President, External Affairs
Mailstop: Bin 10240
Tel: (404) 506 - 7930
Fax: (404) 506 - 3771

BARRS, Craig
V. President, Community and Economic Development
Tel: (404) 506 - 7740
Fax: (404) 506 - 3771

HOLCOMBE, Ed
V. President, Governmental and Regulatory Affairs
Mailstop: BIN 10230
Tel: (404) 506 - 6929
Fax: (404) 506 - 3771

HOLMES, Richard
Senior V. President, Employee and Corporate Relations
Tel: (404) 506 - 3701
Fax: (404) 506 - 3771

HULING, Charles H.
Director, Environmental Affairs
Tel: (404) 506 - 7716
Fax: (404) 506 - 3771

ORR, Scott
Federal Legislative Affairs Coordinator
Tel: (404) 506 - 1366
Fax: (404) 506 - 3771

At Washington Office

MCCOOL, James M., Jr.
Federal Legislative Affairs Director
Registered Federal Lobbyist.
Tel: (202) 261 - 5000
Fax: (202) 296 - 7937

Gerber Products Co.

A division of Novartis Consumer Health, Inc. A manufacturer of baby foods, clothing and nursery accessories.

www.gerber.com

Main Headquarters
Mailing: 200 Kimball Dr.
Parsippany, NJ 07054
Tel: (973) 503 - 8000
Fax: (973) 503 - 8400
TF: (800) 443 - 7237

Corporate Foundations and Giving Programs

The Gerber Foundation
Contact: Catherine A. Obits
447 W. 48th St.
Suite 153
Fremont, MI 49412
Tel: (231) 924 - 3175

Annual Grant Total: $2,000,000 - $5,000,000
Prefers to donate to 501(c)(3) organizations.
Geographic Preference: Area(s) in which the company operates; National; Area(s) in which employees live and work
Primary Interests: Children's Health; Education; Families; Scholarship Funds; Youth Services

Public Affairs and Related Activities Personnel

At Headquarters

BOYLAN, Terry
V. President, Communications
terry.boyland@ch.novartis.com
Tel: (973) 503 - 7801
Fax: (973) 503 - 8400
TF: (800) 443 - 7237

SCHMIDT, Kurt T.
President
Tel: (973) 503 - 8000
Fax: (973) 503 - 8400
TF: (800) 443 - 7237

At Other Offices

OBITS, Catherine A.
Program Manager, Gerber Foundation
447 W. 48th St.
Suite 153
Fremont, MI 49412
Tel: (231) 924 - 3175

Gerdau Ameristeel Corp.

Formerly known as AmeriSteel Corp. A steel company and producer of minimill steel. Serves customers in the eastern two-thirds of North America.

www.gerdauameristeel.com
Annual Revenues: $3.010 million

Chairman of the Board
JOHANNPETER, Jorge Gerard — Tel: (813) 286 - 8383 Fax: (813) 207 - 2251

President and Chief Exec. Officer
CASEY, Philip E. — Tel: (813) 286 - 8383 Fax: (813) 207 - 2251
pcasey@gerdauameristeel.com

Main Headquarters
Mailing: P.O. Box 31328
Tampa, FL 33631-3328 — Tel: (813) 286 - 8383 Fax: (813) 207 - 2251
Street: 4221 W. Boy Scout Blvd.
Suite 600
Tampa, FL 33607

Public Affairs and Related Activities Personnel

At Headquarters

ROGERS, James S. — Tel: (813) 286 - 8383 Fax: (813) 207 - 2251
V. President, Human Resources
jrogers@gerdauameristeel.com

SCARDOELLI, Harley — Tel: (813) 207 - 2372 Fax: (813) 207 - 2251
Investment Relations Contact
hscardoe@gerdauameristeel.com

SHELTON, Stephanie — Tel: (813) 207 - 2257 Fax: (813) 207 - 2280
Manager, Corporate Communications
sshelton@gerdauameristeel.com

Gevity HR, Inc.

Gevity is a provider of comprehensive human capital management solutions to small and medium-sized businesses in the U.S. The company provides employee recruitment and development assistance, payroll and benefits administration, workers' compensation insurance, health , welfare and retirement plans, and employment-related regulatory guidance.

www.gevityhr.com

Chairman and Chief Exec. Officer
VONK, Erik — Tel: (941) 741 - 4300 Fax: (941) 741 - 4333 TF: (800) 243 - 8489
erik.vonk@gevityhr.com

Main Headquarters
Mailing: 600 301 Blvd. West
Bradenton, FL 34205 — Tel: (941) 741 - 4300 Fax: (941) 744 - 8030 TF: (800) 243 - 8489

Public Affairs and Related Activities Personnel

At Headquarters

MEGELA, Anne-Marie — Tel: (941) 741 - 4672 Fax: (941) 744 - 8030 TF: (800) 243 - 8489
Senior Director, Investor Relations
annemarie.megela@gevityhr.com

Giant Food LLC

A supermarket chain retailer.

www.giantfood.com

Main Headquarters
Mailing: 6300 Sheriff Rd.
Landover, MD 20785 — Tel: (301) 341 - 4100 Fax: (301) 618 - 4967

Corporate Foundations and Giving Programs

Giant Food Foundation, Inc.
Contact: Barry F. Scher
6300 Sheriff Rd.
Landover, MD 20785 — Tel: (301) 341 - 4710 Fax: (301) 618 - 4967

Annual Grant Total: $400,000 - $500,000

Recent local recepients include: Corcoran Gallery of Art, NCI Foundation, and Maryland Therpeutic Riding.

Geographic Preference: Maryland; Delaware; Virginia; Washington, DC
Primary Interests: Community Affairs; Education; Hunger
Recent Recipients: Salvation Army

Public Affairs and Related Activities Personnel

At Headquarters

MATTHEWS, Odonna — Tel: (301) 341 - 4365 Fax: (301) 618 - 4968
V. President, Consumer Affairs

SCHER, Barry F. — Tel: (301) 341 - 4710 Fax: (301) 618 - 4967
V. President, Public Affairs
bscher@aholdusa.com

Giant Industries Arizona, Inc.

See listing on page 219 under Giant Industries, Inc.

Giant Industries, Inc.

Petroleum refining, and marketing; operator of gasoline service stations and food stores.

www.giant.com

Chairman and Chief Exec. Officer
HOLLINGER, Fred — Tel: (480) 585 - 8888 Fax: (480) 585 - 8893 TF: (800) 937 - 4937

Main Headquarters
Mailing: 23733 N. Scottsdale Rd.
Scottsdale, AZ 85255 — Tel: (480) 585 - 8888 Fax: (480) 585 - 8948 TF: (800) 937 - 4937

Public Affairs and Related Activities Personnel

At Headquarters

DOPP, Natalie — Tel: (480) 585 - 8888 Fax: (480) 585 - 8893 TF: (800) 937 - 4937
V. President, Human Resources
(Giant Industries Arizona, Inc.)

GOULD, S. Leland — Tel: (480) 585 - 8888 Fax: (480) 585 - 8893 TF: (800) 937 - 4937
Exec. V. President, Governmental Affairs and Real Estate
(Giant Industries Arizona, Inc.)

Gilbane Building Co.

www.gilbaneco.com

Chairman and Chief Exec. Officer
GILBANE, Thomas F., Jr. — Tel: (401) 456 - 5800 Fax: (401) 456 - 5404 TF: (800) 445 - 2263

Main Headquarters
Mailing: Seven Jackson Walkway
Providence, RI 02903 — Tel: (401) 456 - 5800 Fax: (401) 456 - 5404 TF: (800) 445 - 2263

Washington Office
Contact: William Choquette
Mailing: 4330 East-West Hwy.
Suite 314
Bethesda, MD 20814 — Tel: (301) 718 - 8860 Fax: (301) 718 - 8862

Corporate Foundations and Giving Programs

Gilbane Building Co. Corporate Giving Program
Contact: Wes Cotter
Seven Jackson Walkway
Providence, RI 02903 — Tel: (401) 456 - 5405 Fax: (401) 456 - 5930

Annual Grant Total: none reported
Program email address is giving@gilbane.com.

Public Affairs and Related Activities Personnel

At Headquarters

COTTER, Wes — Tel: (401) 456 - 5405 Fax: (401) 456 - 5930
Director, Corporate Communications
wcotter@gilbaneco.com
Responsibilities include government affairs and corporate contributions.

At Washington Office

CHOQUETTE, William — Tel: (301) 718 - 8860 Fax: (301) 718 - 8862
Senior V. President and Washington Contact
wchoquette@gilbaneco.com

The Gillette Company

A manufacturer of razors and blades, toiletries, writing instruments, small electrical appliances, batteries, electric shavers and oral care products. Subsidiaries include Duracell, Braun, Inc., and Oral-B Laboratories. In July of 2005, company shareholders approved a proposed merger with Procter & Gamble (see separate listing).

www.gillette.com
Annual Revenues: $8.961 billion

Chairman, President and Chief Exec. Officer
KILTS, James M. — Tel: (617) 421 - 7000 Fax: (617) 421 - 7123
james_kilts@gillette.com

Main Headquarters
Mailing: Prudential Tower Bldg.
Boston, MA 02199-8004 — Tel: (617) 421 - 7000 Fax: (617) 421 - 7123

Political Action Committees

The Gillette Co. Political Action Committee (Gillette Fed PAC)
Prudential Tower Bldg.
Boston, MA 02199-8004 — Tel: (617) 421 - 7000 Fax: (617) 421 - 7123

Contributions to Candidates: none reported (01/05 - 09/05)

Corporate Foundations and Giving Programs

Gillette Co. Charitable and Educational Foundation
Contact: Cathleen J. Chizauskas

The Gillette Company

** continued from previous page*

Prudential Tower Bldg.
Boston, MA 02199-8004
Tel: (617) 421 - 7000
Fax: (617) 421 - 7123

Annual Grant Total: over $5,000,000

Geographic Preference: Area(s) in which the company operates; Boston, MA
Primary Interests: Community Affairs; Housing; Literacy; Medicine and Health Care

Public Affairs and Related Activities Personnel

At Headquarters

CHIZAUSKAS, Cathleen J.
V. President, Civic Affairs
Tel: (617) 421 - 7000
Fax: (617) 421 - 7123

GAITLIN, John
PAC Treasurer
Tel: (617) 421 - 7000
Fax: (617) 421 - 7123

GUILLET, Edward E.
Senior V. President, Human Resources
ed_guillet@gillette.com
Tel: (617) 421 - 7000
Fax: (617) 421 - 7123

JAKUBIK, Chris
V. President, Corporate Public Relations
chris_jakubik@gillette.com
Tel: (617) 421 - 7000
Fax: (617) 421 - 7123

KRAUS, Eric A.
V. President, Corporate Communications
eric_kraus@gillette.com
Tel: (617) 421 - 7194
Fax: (617) 421 - 7123

MANFREDI, John F.
Senior V. President, Corporate Affairs
john_manfredi@gillette.com
Responsibilities include corporate communications and investor relations.
Tel: (617) 421 - 7000
Fax: (617) 421 - 7123

GlaxoSmithKline Research and Development

A researcher and manufacturer of prescription pharmaceuticals. Formed by the merger of Glaxo Wellcome Inc. and SmithKline Beecham.

www.gsk.com
Annual Revenues: $27 billion

Chairman of the Board
YAMADA, Tadataka
Tel: (919) 483 - 2100
Fax: (919) 549 - 7459

Chief Exec. Officer
GARNIER, Jean-Pierre
Tel: (919) 483 - 2100
Fax: (919) 315 - 6049

Main Headquarters
Mailing: P.O. Box 13398
Research Triangle Park, NC 27709
Street: Five Moore Dr.
Research Triangle Park, NC 27709
Tel: (919) 483 - 2100
Fax: (919) 549 - 7459

Washington Office
Contact: Janie Ann Kinney
Mailing: 1500 K St. NW
Suite 650
Washington, DC 20005
Tel: (202) 715 - 1000
Fax: (202) 715 - 1001

Political Action Committees

GlaxoSmithKline PAC
Contact: Gary J. Salamido
P.O. Box 13398
Research Triangle Park, NC 27709
Tel: (919) 363 - 7853
Fax: (919) 315 - 6049

Contributions to Candidates: $205,700 (01/05 - 09/05)
Democrats: $63,750; Republicans: $141,950.

Principal Recipients

SENATE DEMOCRATS		HOUSE DEMOCRATS	
Nelson, Benjamin (NE)	$3,750	Menendez, Robert (NJ)	$5,000
		Smith, Adam (WA)	$5,000
		Tauscher, Ellen O (CA)	$5,000

SENATE REPUBLICANS		HOUSE REPUBLICANS	
Kyl, Jon L (AZ)	$10,000	Hart, Melissa (PA)	$5,450
Talent, James (MO)	$10,000	Barton, Joe L (TX)	$5,000
Allen, George (VA)	$6,000	Bonilla, Henry (TX)	$5,000
Burns, Conrad (MT)	$5,000	DeLay, Tom (TX)	$5,000
Kennedy, Mark (MN)	$5,000	Johnson, Nancy (CT)	$5,000
Santorum, Richard (PA)	$4,500	Cantor, Eric (VA)	$3,000
Thomas, Craig (WY)	$4,000	Graves, Sam (MO)	$3,000
Ensign, John Eric (NV)	$3,000	Myrick, Sue (NC)	$3,000

Corporate Foundations and Giving Programs

GlaxoSmithKline Foundation
Contact: Marilyn Foote-Hudson
P.O. Box 13398
Research Triangle Park, NC 27709
Tel: (919) 483 - 2588
Fax: (919) 315 - 3015

Annual Grant Total: none reported

Public Affairs and Related Activities Personnel

At Headquarters

DEAN, Julie A.
Director, Exec. Communications
Tel: (919) 483 - 2839
Fax: (919) 483 - 0327

FOOTE-HUDSON, Marilyn
Director, GlaxoSmithKline Foundation
Tel: (919) 483 - 2588
Fax: (919) 315 - 3015

RHYNE, Mary Anne
Director, Media Relations
Tel: (919) 483 - 2839
Fax: (919) 549 - 7459

SALAMIDO, Gary J.
PAC Treasurer
Tel: (919) 363 - 7853
Fax: (919) 315 - 6049

SHORE, William A.
Director, Corporate Community Affairs
Tel: (919) 483 - 2719
Fax: (919) 483 - 8765

SLUDER, Rick
V. President, U.S. Pharmaceuticals Communications
Tel: (919) 483 - 2839
Fax: (919) 549 - 7459

YOUNGER, Jennie
Senior V. President, Corporate Communications and Community Partnerships
Tel: (919) 483 - 2100
Fax: (919) 315 - 6049

At Washington Office

KINNEY, Janie Ann
V. President, Federal Government Relations and Public Policy
Registered Federal Lobbyist.
Tel: (202) 715 - 1000
Fax: (202) 715 - 1001

MCLAIN, Patrick M.
Federal Government Relations
Registered Federal Lobbyist.
Tel: (202) 715 - 1000
Fax: (202) 715 - 1001

SCHUYLER, William J.
Director, Federal Government Relations
Registered Federal Lobbyist.
Tel: (202) 715 - 1000
Fax: (202) 715 - 1001

THEVENET, Philip M.
Federal Government Relations
Registered Federal Lobbyist.
Tel: (202) 715 - 1000
Fax: (202) 715 - 1001

WALSH, Sarah J.
Federal Government Relations
Registered Federal Lobbyist.
Tel: (202) 715 - 1000
Fax: (202) 715 - 1001

WILLIAMS, Kimberly A.
Federal Government Relations
Registered Federal Lobbyist.
Tel: (202) 715 - 1000
Fax: (202) 715 - 1001

YORK, Elizabeth
Federal Government Relations
Registered Federal Lobbyist.
Tel: (202) 715 - 1000
Fax: (202) 715 - 1001

At Other Offices

BLALACK, T. Gary
Exec. Manager, State Government Affairs
513 Cherrywood Point
Franklin, TN 37064
Tel: (615) 791 - 8438

BURRUS, Jan
State Government Affairs
227 N. Royal St.
Alexandria, VA 22314
Tel: (703) 684 - 3973

DALLAGO, Rochelle A.
Senior Manager, Professional and State Government Affairs
Seven Andreann Dr.
Annandale, NJ 08801
Tel: (908) 730 - 6335

LURIA, Robert S.
State Government Affairs
12 Spruce Run
East Greenbush, NY 12061-9611
Tel: (518) 477 - 2581

Global AgServices

See listing on page 152 under Deere & Company.

Global Crossing Ltd.

Telecommunications company.
www.globalcrossing.com

Chairman of the Board
VAN WACHEM, Lodewijk Christiaan
Tel: (973) 937 - 0100
Fax: (973) 360 - 0148
TF: (800) 336 - 7000

Chief Exec. Officer
LEGERE, John
Tel: (973) 937 - 0100
Fax: (973) 360 - 0148
TF: (800) 336 - 7000

Main Headquarters
Mailing: 200 Park Ave.
Suite 300
Florham Park, NJ 07932
Tel: (973) 937 - 0100
Fax: (973) 360 - 0148
TF: (800) 336 - 7000

Political Action Committees

Global Crossing Development Corp. PAC
Contact: Colleen C. McAndrews
1441 Fourth St.
Santa Monica, CA 90401
Tel: (310) 458 - 1405

Global Crossing Ltd.

* continued from previous page

Contributions to Candidates: none reported (01/05 - 09/05)

Public Affairs and Related Activities Personnel

At Headquarters

KOUROUPAS, Paul
V. President, and Senior Counsel (Regulatory Affairs)
Tel: (973) 937 - 0100
Fax: (973) 360 - 0148
TF: (800) 336 - 7000

KRESLER, Tisha
Media Relations Contact
Tel: (973) 937 - 0146
Fax: (973) 360 - 0148
TF: (800) 336 - 7000

PANG, Laurinda
V. President, Investor Relations
glbc@globalcrossing.com
Tel: (973) 937 - 0100
Fax: (973) 360 - 0148
TF: (800) 336 - 7000

SANTOS, Jerry
Senior V. President, Corporate Communications
jerry.santos@globalcrossing.com
Tel: (973) 937 - 0100
Fax: (973) 360 - 0148
TF: (800) 336 - 7000

YEAMANS, Becky
V. President, Media and Analysts Relations
becky.yeamans@globalcrossing.com
Tel: (973) 937 - 0155
Fax: (973) 360 - 0148
TF: (800) 336 - 7000

At Other Offices

MCANDREWS, Colleen C.
PAC Treasurer
1441 Fourth St.
Santa Monica, CA 90401
Tel: (310) 458 - 1405

Global Marine Inc.

See listing on page 221 under GlobalSantaFe Corp.

GlobalSantaFe Corp.

An international offshore drilling company formed by the merger of Global Marine Inc. and Santa Fe Internat'l Corp. in November 2001.
www.gsfdrill.com

Chairman of the Board
ROSE, Robert E.
rrose@gsfdrill.com
Tel: (281) 925 - 6000
Fax: (281) 925 - 6010

President and Chief Exec. Officer
MARSHALL, Jon A.
Tel: (281) 925 - 6000
Fax: (281) 925 - 6010

Main Headquarters
Mailing: P.O. Box 4577
Houston, TX 77210-4577
Street: 15375 Memorial Dr.
Houston, TX 77079-4101
Tel: (281) 925 - 6000
Fax: (281) 925 - 6010

Public Affairs and Related Activities Personnel

At Headquarters

HOFFMAN, Richard J.
V. President, Investor Relations
rhoffman@gsfdrill.com
Tel: (281) 925 - 6000
Fax: (281) 925 - 6010

RICHARD, Cheryl
Senior V. President, Human Resources
Tel: (281) 925 - 6000
Fax: (281) 925 - 6010

TUSHINGHAM, Julie
Manager, Media and Corporate Communications
julie.tushingham@gsfdrill.com
Tel: (281) 925 - 6443
Fax: (281) 925 - 6010

Globe Newspaper Co.

A publications company owned by The New York Times Co. (see separate listing).
www.bostonglobe.com

Main Headquarters
Mailing: 135 Morrissey Blvd.
Boston, MA 02107
Tel: (617) 929 - 2000
Fax: (617) 929 - 3220

Corporate Foundations and Giving Programs

Boston Globe Foundation
Contact: Suzanne W. Maas
135 Morrissey Blvd.
Boston, MA 02107
Tel: (617) 929 - 2041
Fax: (617) 929 - 2010

Annual Grant Total: $300,000 - $400,000
Preference is given to programs in Boston, Cambridge, Somerville and Chelsea, MA that serve youth (ages 0-22) who live in low-income neighborhoods. Contributions are only given to institutions and not individuals.
Geographic Preference: Massachusetts; Area(s) in which the company operates
Primary Interests: AIDS/HIV; Arts and Humanities; Education; Families; Literacy; Medicine and Health Care; Persons with Disabilities; Substance Abuse Prevention; Urban Affairs; Women's Health

Public Affairs and Related Activities Personnel

At Headquarters

GOULD, Harriet E.
V. President, Employee Relations
hgould@globe.com
Tel: (617) 929 - 2000
Fax: (617) 929 - 3220

MAAS, Suzanne W.
Exec. Director, Boston Globe Foundation
Tel: (617) 929 - 2041
Fax: (617) 929 - 2010

Gold Kist Inc.

The third largest poultry company in the U.S.
www.goldkist.com

Chief Exec. Officer
BEKKERS, John
john.bekkers@goldkist.com
Tel: (770) 393 - 5000
Fax: (770) 393 - 5347

Main Headquarters
Mailing: P.O. Box 2210
Atlanta, GA 30301-2210
Street: 244 Perimeter Center Pkwy., N.E.
Atlanta, GA 30346-2397
Tel: (770) 393 - 5000
Fax: (770) 393 - 5347

Political Action Committees

Gold Kist Political Action for Farmers Inc.
Contact: Wayne Lord
P.O. Box 2210
Atlanta, GA 30301-2210
Tel: (770) 393 - 5312
Fax: (770) 393 - 5347

Contributions to Candidates: $9,500 (01/05 - 09/05)
Democrats: $7,500; Republicans: $2,000.

Principal Recipients

SENATE DEMOCRATS

HOUSE DEMOCRATS
Etheridge, Bob (NC) $2,500
Marshall, Jim (GA) $2,500
Scott, David (GA) $2,500

SENATE REPUBLICANS

HOUSE REPUBLICANS
Goodlatte, Robert (VA) $1,000
Price, Thomas (GA) $1,000

Corporate Foundations and Giving Programs

Gold Kist Foundation, Inc.
Contact: Wayne Lord
P.O. Box 2210
Atlanta, GA 30301-2210
Tel: (770) 393 - 5312
Fax: (770) 393 - 5347

Annual Grant Total: none reported
Geographic Preference: Alabama; Florida; Georgia; North Carolina; South Carolina
Primary Interests: Agriculture; Community Development; Education

Public Affairs and Related Activities Personnel

At Headquarters

HARVILL, Karla
Manager, Public Relations
karla.harvill@goldkist.com
Tel: (770) 393 - 5091
Fax: (770) 393 - 5347

LORD, Wayne
V. President, Corporate Relations
wayne.lord@goldkist.com
Responsibilities include political action and corporate philanthropy.
Tel: (770) 393 - 5312
Fax: (770) 393 - 5347

MCDONALD, Harry T.
V. President, Human Resources
harry.mcdonald@goldkist.com
Tel: (770) 206 - 6918
Fax: (770) 393 - 5347

Golden Rule Insurance Co.

An insurance company.
www.goldenrule.com
Annual Revenues: $829 million

Chairman of the Board
ROONEY, Therese
Tel: (317) 943 - 8000
Fax: (618) 943 - 8031

President and Chief Exec. Officer
WHELAN, John
Tel: (317) 943 - 8000
Fax: (618) 943 - 8031

Main Headquarters
Mailing: 712 11th St
Lawrence, IL 62439
Tel: (317) 943 - 8000
Fax: (618) 943 - 8031

Washington Office
Contact: Brian McManus
Mailing: 1090 Vermont Ave. NW
Suite 1290
Washington, DC 20005
Tel: (202) 589 - 0088

Political Action Committees

Golden Rule Financial Corp. PAC
Contact: Patrick Carr
712 11th St
Lawrence, IL 62439
Tel: (317) 943 - 8000
Fax: (618) 943 - 8031

Contributions to Candidates: $8,000 (01/05 - 09/05)

Golden Rule Insurance Co.

* continued from previous page

Republicans: $8,000.

Principal Recipients

SENATE REPUBLICANS		HOUSE REPUBLICANS	
DeMint, James (SC)	$2,000	Hastert, Dennis J. (IL)	$1,000
		Johnson, Samuel (TX)	$1,000
		Kennedy, Mark (MN)	$1,000
		Pence, Mike (IN)	$1,000
		Renzi, Richard (AZ)	$1,000
		Sessions, Pete (TX)	$1,000

Public Affairs and Related Activities Personnel

At Headquarters

CARR, Patrick — Tel: (317) 943 - 8000
PAC Treasurer — Fax: (618) 943 - 8031

CHAPLIN, Neal E. — Tel: (317) 943 - 8000
Public Policy Specialist — Fax: (618) 943 - 8031

TOOMAN, Lee D., Jr. — Tel: (317) 943 - 8000
V. President, Government Relations — Fax: (618) 943 - 8031

At Washington Office

MCMANUS, Brian — Tel: (202) 589 - 0088
V. President, Federal Affairs
Registered Federal Lobbyist.

MILANO, Ann Marie — Tel: (202) 589 - 0400
Registered Federal Lobbyist.

ROONEY, Pat — Tel: (202) 589 - 0088
Registered Federal Lobbyist.

Golden West Financial Corp.

A savings and loan holding company.

www.gdw.com

Co-Chairman and Co-Chief Exec. Officer — Tel: (510) 446 - 3420
SANDLER, Herbert M. — Fax: (510) 446 - 4259

Co-Chairman and Co-Chief Exec. Officer — Tel: (510) 446 - 3420
SANDLER, Marion O. — Fax: (510) 446 - 4259

Main Headquarters
Mailing: 1901 Harrison St. — Tel: (510) 446 - 3420
Oakland, CA 94612 — Fax: (510) 446 - 4259

Corporate Foundations and Giving Programs

Golden West Financial Corp. Contributions Program
1901 Harrison St. — Tel: (510) 446 - 3420
Oakland, CA 94612 — Fax: (510) 446 - 4259

Annual Grant Total: none reported

Public Affairs and Related Activities Personnel

At Headquarters

NUNAN, William C. — Tel: (510) 446 - 3614
Group Senior V. President — Fax: (510) 446 - 4259

Goldman, Sachs and Co.

An investment banking and brokerage firm.

www.gs.com

Chairman and Chief Exec. Officer — Tel: (212) 902 - 1000
PAULSON, Henry M., Jr. — Fax: (212) 902 - 3000

Main Headquarters
Mailing: 85 Broad St. — Tel: (212) 902 - 1000
New York, NY 10004 — Fax: (212) 902 - 3000

Washington Office
Contact: Mark Patterson
Mailing: 101 Constitution Ave. NW — Tel: (202) 637 - 3700
Suite 1000 East — Fax: (202) 637 - 3773
Washington, DC 20001

Political Action Committees

Goldman Sachs Group Inc. PAC
Contact: Judah C. Sommer
101 Constitution Ave. NW — Tel: (202) 637 - 3700
Suite 1000 East — Fax: (202) 637 - 3773
Washington, DC 20001

Contributions to Candidates: $113,000 (01/05 - 09/05)

Democrats: $39,000; Republicans: $74,000.

Principal Recipients

SENATE DEMOCRATS		HOUSE DEMOCRATS	
Conrad, Kent (ND)	$6,000	Menendez, Robert (NJ)	$10,000
Nelson, Benjamin (NE)	$2,500	Emanuel, Rahm (IL)	$3,500
Stabenow, Debbie (MI)	$2,000	Dingell, John D (MI)	$2,500
		Scott, David (GA)	$2,500
		Engel, Eliot (NY)	$2,000
		Rangel, Charles B (NY)	$2,000

SENATE REPUBLICANS		HOUSE REPUBLICANS	
Bennett, Robert F (UT)	$5,000	Oxley, Michael (OH)	$10,000
Kyl, Jon L (AZ)	$2,000	Baker, Hugh (LA)	$5,000
Santorum, Richard (PA)	$2,000	McCrery, Jim (LA)	$5,000
Talent, James (MO)	$2,000	Renzi, Richard (AZ)	$3,000
		Blunt, Roy (MO)	$2,500
		Dreier, David (CA)	$2,500
		Hart, Melissa (PA)	$2,500
		Ney, Robert W (OH)	$2,500
		Boehlert, Sherwood (NY)	$2,000
		Fitzpatrick, Michael (PA)	$2,000
		Gerlach, Jim (PA)	$2,000
		Kuhl, John R Jr (NY)	$2,000
		McHenry, Patrick (NC)	$2,000
		McMorris, Cathy (WA)	$2,000
		Moran, Jerry (KS)	$2,000
		Pearce, Steve (NM)	$2,000
		Reynolds, Thomas (NY)	$2,000

Corporate Foundations and Giving Programs

Goldman Sachs Foundation
Contact: Stephanie Bell-Rose
375 Park Ave., Suite 1002 — Tel: (212) 902 - 5402
New York, NY 10152

Annual Grant Total: over $5,000,000

Provides grants and scholarship funds for the education of employee families. Matches the gifts of employees to educational institutions.

Geographic Preference: Canada; National

Primary Interests: Education; Scholarship Funds

Recent Recipients: Harvard University; United Negro College Fund

Public Affairs and Related Activities Personnel

At Headquarters

BLANKFEIN, LLoyd C. — Tel: (212) 902 - 1000
Managing Director and Chief Operating Officer, Media Relations — Fax: (212) 902 - 3000

At Washington Office

COSTELLO, Ann S. — Tel: (202) 637 - 3700
V. President — Fax: (202) 637 - 3773

DOSWELL, W. Carter — Tel: (202) 637 - 3700
V. President — Fax: (202) 637 - 3773

LAUDIEN, Lori E. — Tel: (202) 637 - 3700
V. President, Government Affairs — Fax: (202) 637 - 3773

PATTERSON, Mark — Tel: (202) 637 - 3700
V. President, Governmental Affairs — Fax: (202) 637 - 3773

SOMMER, Judah C. — Tel: (202) 637 - 3700
PAC Treasurer — Fax: (202) 637 - 3773

At Other Offices

BELL-ROSE, Stephanie — Tel: (212) 902 - 5402
President, Goldman Sachs Foundation
375 Park Ave., Suite 1002
New York, NY 10152

Golub Corp.

Grocery stores.

www.pricechopper.com

Chairman of the Board — Tel: (518) 355 - 5000
GOLUB, Lewis — Fax: (518) 379 - 3515

President and Chief Exec. Officer — Tel: (518) 355 - 5000
GOLUB, Neil M. — Fax: (518) 379 - 3515

Main Headquarters
Mailing: P.O. Box 1074 — Tel: (518) 355 - 5000
Schenectady, NY 12301 — Fax: (518) 379 - 3515
TF: (800) 666 - 7667

Street: 501 Duanesburg Rd.
Schenectady, NY 12306-1074

Golub Corp.

* continued from previous page

Corporate Foundations and Giving Programs

Golub Foundation
Contact: Nancy Huggins
P.O. Box 1074 — Tel: (518) 355 - 5000
Schenectady, NY 12301 — Fax: (518) 379 - 3515

Annual Grant Total: $400,000 - $500,000
Geographic Preference: New York
Primary Interests: Arts and Humanities; Civic and Public Affairs; Education; Health; Religion; Social Services
Recent Recipients: Arthritis Foundation; Junior Achievement; United Way

Public Affairs and Related Activities Personnel

At Headquarters

GOLUB, Mona — Tel: (518) 355 - 5000
Director, Public Relations and Consumer Services — Fax: (518) 379 - 3515

HUGGINS, Nancy — Tel: (518) 355 - 5000
Contact, Golub Foundation — Fax: (518) 379 - 3515

PAGE, Barbara — Tel: (518) 355 - 5000
Promotions and Special Events Manager — Fax: (518) 379 - 3515
Responsibilities include public relations.

Goodrich Co., B. F.

See listing on page 223 under Goodrich Corporation.

Goodrich Corp. - Aerostructures

Formerly called Rohr, Inc. A manufacturer of aircraft components and related products.
www.aerostructures.goodrich.com

Main Headquarters
Mailing: 850 Lagoon Dr. — Tel: (619) 691 - 4111
Chula Vista, CA 91910-2098 — Fax: (619) 691 - 2584

Corporate Foundations and Giving Programs

Goodrich Corp. -Aerostructures Will-Share Club
Contact: Pauline Box
850 Lagoon Dr. — Tel: (619) 691 - 4111
Chula Vista, CA 91910-2098 — Fax: (619) 691 - 2584

Annual Grant Total: $100,000 - $200,000

Public Affairs and Related Activities Personnel

At Headquarters

BOX, Pauline — Tel: (619) 691 - 4111
Contact, Will-Share Club — Fax: (619) 691 - 2584

HULEWICZ, Geoffrey M. — Tel: (619) 691 - 3635
Senior Employee Communications Specialist — Fax: (619) 691 - 2584

MCCLELLAND, Valorie A. — Tel: (619) 691 - 3688
Manager, Communications — Fax: (619) 691 - 2584

Goodrich Corporation

A member of the Public Affairs Council. A worldwide supplier of aerospace components, systems and services, as well as sealing and compressor systems and other engineered industrial products.
www.goodrich.com
Annual Revenues: $4.185 billion

Chairman, President and Chief Exec. Officer — Tel: (704) 423 - 7000
LARSEN, Marshall O. — Fax: (704) 423 - 7100

Main Headquarters
Mailing: Four Colesium Center — Tel: (704) 423 - 7000
2730 W. Tyvola Rd. — Fax: (704) 423 - 7100
Charlotte, NC 28217

Washington Office
Contact: Ms. Gerrie Bjornson
Mailing: 1100 Wilson Blvd. — Tel: (703) 558 - 8250
Suite 900 — Fax: (703) 558 - 8262
Arlington, VA 22209-2297

Political Action Committees

Goodrich PAC
Contact: Sally L. Geib
Four Colesium Center — Tel: (704) 423 - 7000
2730 W. Tyvola Rd. — Fax: (704) 423 - 7100
Charlotte, NC 28217

Contributions to Candidates: $21,000 (01/05 - 09/05)
Democrats: $9,500; Republicans: $11,500.

Principal Recipients

SENATE DEMOCRATS		HOUSE DEMOCRATS	
Leahy, Patrick (VT)	$1,000	Larson, John B (CT)	$2,000
Lieberman, Joe (CT)	$1,000	Murtha, John P Mr. (PA)	$1,500
		Dicks, Norm D (WA)	$1,000
		Filner, Bob (CA)	$1,000
		Skelton, Ike (MO)	$1,000
		Taylor, Gene Mr. (MS)	$1,000
SENATE REPUBLICANS		**HOUSE REPUBLICANS**	
Chambliss, Saxby (GA)	$1,000	Bonner, Josiah (AL)	$1,000
		Calvert, Ken (CA)	$1,000
		Cunningham, Duke (CA)	$1,000
		Hayes, Robert (NC)	$1,000
		Hobson, David (OH)	$1,000
		Hunter, Duncan (CA)	$1,000
		Kingston, John (GA)	$1,000
		Lewis, Jerry (CA)	$1,000
		Myrick, Sue (NC)	$1,000
		Wilson, Heather (NM)	$1,000

Corporate Foundations and Giving Programs

Goodrich Foundation
Contact: Natalie English
Four Colesium Center — Tel: (704) 423 - 7489
2730 W. Tyvola Rd.
Charlotte, NC 28217

Annual Grant Total: $2,000,000 - $5,000,000
Geographic Preference: Area(s) in which the company operates

Public Affairs and Related Activities Personnel

At Headquarters

BOTTLE, Lisa — Tel: (704) 423 - 7060
V. President, Corporate Communications — Fax: (704) 423 - 7127
lisa.bottle@goodrich.com

ENGLISH, Natalie — Tel: (704) 423 - 7489
Director, Community Relations
natalie.english@goodrich.com

GEIB, Sally L. — Tel: (704) 423 - 7000
V. President, Associate General Counsel and Secretary — Fax: (704) 423 - 7100
sally.geib@goodrich.com
Responsibilities include political action.

GIFFORD, Paul S. — Tel: (704) 423 - 5517
V. President, Investor Relations — Fax: (704) 423 - 5516
paul.gifford@goodrich.com

LINNERT, Terrence G. — Tel: (704) 423 - 7000
Exec. V. President, Administration and General Counsel — Fax: (704) 423 - 7100

WARNER, Gail K. — Tel: (704) 423 - 7048
Director, Media Relations — Fax: (704) 423 - 7127
gail.warner@goodrich.com

At Washington Office

BJORNSON, Ms. Gerrie — Tel: (703) 558 - 8250
V. President, Government Relations — Fax: (703) 558 - 8262
gerrie.bjornson@goodrich.com
Registered Federal Lobbyist.

The Goodyear Tire & Rubber Company

A manufacturer of tires, rubber and chemical products.
www.goodyear.com
Annual Revenues: $18 billion

Chairman of the Board, Chief Exec. Officer and President — Tel: (330) 796 - 2121
KEEGAN, Robert J. — Fax: (330) 796 - 2222

Main Headquarters
Mailing: 1144 E. Market St. — Tel: (330) 796 - 2121
Akron, OH 44316-0001 — Fax: (330) 796 - 2222

Washington Office
Contact: Isabel H. Jasinowski
Mailing: 1420 New York Ave. NW — Tel: (202) 682 - 9250
Suite 200 — Fax: (202) 682 - 1533
Washington, DC 20005

Political Action Committees

Goodyear Tire & Rubber Co. Good Government Fund
1144 E. Market St. — Tel: (330) 796 - 2121
Akron, OH 44316-0001 — Fax: (330) 796 - 2222

Contributions to Candidates: $30,000 (01/05 - 09/05)

The Goodyear Tire & Rubber Company

* continued from previous page

Democrats: $3,000; Republicans: $27,000.

Principal Recipients

SENATE DEMOCRATS		HOUSE DEMOCRATS	
		Ryan, Timothy (OH)	$2,000
SENATE REPUBLICANS		**HOUSE REPUBLICANS**	
Allen, George (VA)	$3,000	Hunter, Duncan (CA)	$2,000
Dewine, Richard (OH)	$3,000	Tiahrt, Todd W. (KS)	$2,000
Kyl, Jon L (AZ)	$2,000		
Talent, James (MO)	$2,000		

Corporate Foundations and Giving Programs

The Goodyear Tire & Rubber Co. Contributions Program
Contact: Faith Stewart
1144 E. Market St. — Tel: (330) 796 - 8928
Akron, OH 44316-0001 — Fax: (330) 796 - 2806

Annual Grant Total: $2,000,000 - $5,000,000
Geographic Preference: Area(s) in which the company operates
Primary Interests: Civic and Cultural Activities; Education; United Way Campaigns
Recent Recipients: Nat'l Urban League; Ohio Foundation of Independent Colleges

Public Affairs and Related Activities Personnel

At Headquarters

ARNOLD, Jennifer — Tel: (330) 796 - 2121
Manager, Global Airship Public Relations — Fax: (330) 796 - 8399
jennifer_arnold@goodyear.com

BREI, Amy — Tel: (330) 796 - 2121
Communications Manager, Tires, North America — Fax: (330) 796 - 1237

INGRAHAM, Tricia — Tel: (330) 796 - 8517
Manager, Business and Financial Communications — Fax: (330) 796 - 1817
tricia_ingraham@goodyear.com

PRICE, Keith J. — Tel: (330) 796 - 1863
Director, Corporate Communications Programs — Fax: (330) 796 - 1817
kprice@goodyear.com

SCHERER, Skip — Tel: (330) 796 - 1054
Manager, Communications, Engineered and Chemical Products — Fax: (330) 796 - 1817
wkscherer@goodyear.com

SINCLAIR, Charles L. — Tel: (330) 796 - 2154
Senior V. President, Global Communications — Fax: (330) 796 - 9112

STEWART, Faith — Tel: (330) 796 - 8928
Director, Community Involvement — Fax: (330) 796 - 2806

SWARTZ, Carole — Tel: (330) 796 - 2936
Manager, Racing Public Relations — Fax: (330) 796 - 1237
cswartz@goodyear.com

At Washington Office

BURTSCHI, Mark — Tel: (202) 682 - 9250
Director, Federal and State Affairs — Fax: (202) 682 - 1533

JASINOWSKI, Isabel H. — Tel: (202) 682 - 9250
V. President, Government Relations and Head of Washington, DC Office — Fax: (202) 682 - 1533
ihjasinowski@goodyear.com
Registered Federal Lobbyist.

At Other Offices

ANDREWS, Jo B. — Tel: (336) 495 - 2269
Communications Specialist
890 Pineview Rd.
Asheboro, NC 27203
jo_andrews@goodyear.com

CAGLE, Jimmy D. — Tel: (901) 885 - 1255
Manager, Public Relations — Fax: (901) 885 - 1379
P.O. Box 570
Union City, TN 38261
jimmy_cagle@goodyear.com

EVANS, Richard L. — Tel: (910) 630 - 5210
Manager, Public Affairs
(Kelly-Springfield Tire Co.)
6650 Ramsey St.
Fayetteville, NC 28311
richardevans@goodyear.com

HEARN, Gary — Tel: (405) 531 - 5842
Manager, Communications — Fax: (405) 531 - 5899
One Goodyear Blvd.
Lawton, OK 73505
gary.hearn@goodyear.com

Google Inc.

Provides internet search services.
www.google.com

Chairman and Chief Exec. Officer
SCHMIDT, Dr. Eric E. — Tel: (650) 623 - 4000 / Fax: (650) 618 - 1499

Main Headquarters
Mailing: 1600 Amphitheatre Pkwy. — Tel: (650) 623 - 4000
Mountain View, CA 94043 — Fax: (650) 618 - 1499

Public Affairs and Related Activities Personnel

At Headquarters

KRANE, David — Tel: (650) 623 - 4096
Corporate Public Relations Contact — Fax: (650) 618 - 1499
david@google.com

LANGDON, Steve — Tel: (650) 623 - 4950
Manager,Public Relations — Fax: (650) 618 - 1499
slangdon@google.com

MAYZEL, Michael — Tel: (650) 623 - 4000
Manager, Advertising — Fax: (650) 618 - 1499

Government Employees Insurance Co.

See listing on page 210 under GEICO Corp.

Goya Foods, Inc.

A wholesale food distributor.
www.goya.com

Main Headquarters
Mailing: 100 Seaview Dr. — Tel: (201) 348 - 4900
Secaucus, NJ 07096 — Fax: (201) 348 - 6609

Corporate Foundations and Giving Programs

Goya Foods Corporate Giving Program
Contact: Ralph Toro
100 Seaview Dr. — Tel: (201) 348 - 4900 Ext: 2238
Secaucus, NJ 07096 — Fax: (201) 348 - 6609

Annual Grant Total: none reported

Public Affairs and Related Activities Personnel

At Headquarters

TORO, Ralph — Tel: (201) 348 - 4900 Ext: 2238
Director, Public Relations — Fax: (201) 348 - 6609
rafael.toro@goya.com

UNANNE, Robert I. — Tel: (201) 348 - 4900
President — Fax: (201) 348 - 6609

W. R. Grace & Co.

A global supplier of catalysts and silica products, specialty construction chemicals and building materials, and container sealants and closure systems.
www.grace.com
Annual Revenues: $1.723 billion

Chairman of the Board
NORRIS, Paul J. — Tel: (410) 531 - 4000 / Fax: (410) 531 - 4367

President and Chief Exec. Officer
FESTA, Alfred E. — Tel: (410) 531 - 4000 / Fax: (410) 531 - 4367

Main Headquarters
Mailing: 7500 Grace Dr. — Tel: (410) 531 - 4000
Columbia, MD 21044 — Fax: (410) 531 - 4367

Corporate Foundations and Giving Programs

Grace Foundation Inc.
7500 Grace Dr. — Tel: (410) 531 - 4000
Columbia, MD 21044 — Fax: (410) 531 - 4367

Annual Grant Total: $2,000,000 - $5,000,000
Geographic Preference: Area(s) in which the company operates
Primary Interests: Community Affairs; Health; Higher Education; Youth Services
Recent Recipients: Alzheimer's Ass'n; Boys and Girls Club

Public Affairs and Related Activities Personnel

At Headquarters

CORCORAN, William M. — Tel: (410) 531 - 4203
V. President, Public and Regulatory Affairs

PIERGROSSI, Michael N. — Tel: (410) 531 - 4000
V. President, Leadership and Organization Development — Fax: (410) 531 - 4367
Responsibilities include human resources.

Graco Inc.

An international manufacturer and marketer of industrial fluid handling and spray finishing equipment and systems.

www.graco.com

Chairman of the Board
MITAU, Lee R.
Tel: (612) 623 - 6000
Fax: (612) 623 - 6777
TF: (800) 328 - 0211

Chief Exec. Officer and President
ROBERTS, David A.
Tel: (612) 623 - 6000
Fax: (612) 623 - 6944
TF: (800) 328 - 0211

Main Headquarters
Mailing: P.O. Box 1441
Minneapolis, MN 55440-1441
Tel: (612) 623 - 6000
Fax: (612) 623 - 6777
TF: (800) 328 - 0211

Street: 88 11th Ave., N.E.
Minneapolis, MN 55413

Corporate Foundations and Giving Programs

The Graco Foundation
Contact: Robert M. Mattison
P.O. Box 1441
Minneapolis, MN 55440-1441
Tel: (612) 623 - 6000
Fax: (612) 623 - 6944
TF: (800) 328 - 0211

Annual Grant Total: $1,000,000 - $2,000,000
Geographic Preference: Area in which the company is headquartered
Primary Interests: Education; Social Services
Recent Recipients: Girl Scouts of America; United Way

Public Affairs and Related Activities Personnel

At Headquarters

GALLIVAN, Karen
V. President, Human Resources
Tel: (612) 623 - 6000
Fax: (612) 623 - 6640
TF: (800) 328 - 0211

MATTISON, Robert M.
President, The Graco Foundation
Tel: (612) 623 - 6000
Fax: (612) 623 - 6944
TF: (800) 328 - 0211

SKAALRUD, Nancy
Secretary, The Graco Foundation
Tel: (612) 623 - 6684
Fax: (612) 623 - 6944
TF: (800) 328 - 0211

W. W. Grainger, Inc.

A leading distributor of maintenance, repair, and operating supplies and related information to the commercial, industrial, contractor and institutional markets in North America.

www.grainger.com

Chairman and Chief Exec. Officer
KEYSER, Richard L.
keyser.r@grainger.com
Tel: (847) 535 - 1000

Main Headquarters
Mailing: 100 Grainger Pkwy.
Lake Forest, IL 60045-5201
Tel: (847) 535 - 1000

Corporate Foundations and Giving Programs

W. W. Grainger, Inc. Corporate Contributions Program
Contact: Susan Kessler
100 Grainger Pkwy.
Lake Forest, IL 60045-5201
Tel: (847) 535 - 1543

Annual Grant Total: over $5,000,000
Donations total $11 million in cash and products.
Primary Interests: Disaster Relief; Vocational Training

Public Affairs and Related Activities Personnel

At Headquarters

CHAPMAN, William D.
Director, Investor Relations and External Communications
william.chapman@grainger.com
Tel: (847) 535 - 0881

COOK, Jeff
Corporate Communications
jeff.cook@grainger.com
Tel: (847) 535 - 0880

HOBOR, Nancy A.
Senior V. President, Communications and Investor Relations
nancy.hobor@grainger.com
Tel: (847) 535 - 0065
Fax: (847) 535 - 0878

KESSLER, Susan
Manager, Public Affairs
susie.kessler@grainger.com
Responsibilities include corporate philanthropy.
Tel: (847) 535 - 1543

PILON, Lawrence J.
Senior V. President, Human Resources
Tel: (847) 535 - 1000

TRATNIK, Janis
Director, Corporate Communications and Public Affairs
jan.tratnik@grainger.com
Tel: (847) 535 - 4339

Granite Construction Inc.

A heavy construction company. Builds roads, dams, bridges and other infrastructure related projects.

www.graniteconstruction.com

Chairman of the Board
WATTS, David H.
Tel: (831) 724 - 1011
Fax: (831) 722 - 9657
TF: (800) 482 - 1518

President and Chief Exec. Officer
DOREY, William G.
Tel: (831) 724 - 1011
Fax: (831) 722 - 9657
TF: (800) 482 - 1518

Main Headquarters
Mailing: P.O. Box 50085
Watsonville, CA 95077-5085
Tel: (831) 724 - 1011
Fax: (831) 722 - 9657
TF: (800) 482 - 1518

Street: 585 W. Beach St.
Watsonville, CA 95076

Political Action Committees

Granite Construction Inc. Employee PAC (Granite PAC)
Contact: Lisa Sprague
P.O. Box 50085
Watsonville, CA 95077-5085
Tel: (831) 724 - 1011
Fax: (831) 722 - 9657
TF: (800) 482 - 1518

Contributions to Candidates: $6,850 (01/05 - 09/05)
Democrats: $2,500; Republicans: $3,350; Other: $1,000.

Principal Recipients

SENATE DEMOCRATS

HOUSE DEMOCRATS
Filner, Bob (CA) $1,000

HOUSE OTHER
Oberstar, James L (MN) $1,000

SENATE REPUBLICANS

HOUSE REPUBLICANS
Issa, Darrell (CA) $1,000
Lungren, Daniel E (CA) $1,000

Corporate Foundations and Giving Programs

Granite Construction Inc. Corporate Contributions Program
Contact: Michael L. Thomas
P.O. Box 50085
Watsonville, CA 95077-5085
Tel: (831) 761 - 4709
Fax: (831) 722 - 9657
TF: (800) 482 - 1518

Annual Grant Total: none reported

Public Affairs and Related Activities Personnel

At Headquarters

EDMUNDS, Robin
Corporate Communications Contact
Tel: (831) 724 - 1011
Fax: (831) 722 - 9657
TF: (800) 482 - 1518

SPRAGUE, Lisa
PAC Treasurer
Tel: (831) 724 - 1011
Fax: (831) 722 - 9657
TF: (800) 482 - 1518

THOMAS, Michael L.
V. President, Human Resources
Responsibilities include corporate philanthropy.
Tel: (831) 761 - 4709
Fax: (831) 722 - 9657
TF: (800) 482 - 1518

UNDERDOWN, Jacqueline
Manager, Investor Relations
jaque.underdown@gcinc.com
Tel: (831) 761 - 4741
Fax: (831) 761 - 7871
TF: (800) 482 - 1518

Grant Thornton LLP

An accounting and tax consulting firm.

www.grantthornton.com

Chief Exec. Officer
NUSBAUM, Edward E.
edward.nusbaum@gt.com
Tel: (312) 856 - 0001
Fax: (312) 861 - 1340

Main Headquarters
Mailing: 175 W. Jackson Blvd.
20th Floor
Chicago, IL 60604
Tel: (312) 856 - 0200
Fax: (312) 602 - 8099

Public Affairs and Related Activities Personnel

At Headquarters

BARBARINO, Leslie
Director, Human Resources
Tel: (312) 856 - 0001
Fax: (312) 565 - 4719

VITA, John
National Director, Corporate Communications
john.vita@gt.com
Tel: (312) 602 - 8655
Fax: (312) 861 - 1340

Graybar Electric Co., Inc.

A wholesale distributor of electrical and communications/data products.

www.graybar.com

Graybar Electric Co., Inc.

* continued from previous page

Chairman, President and Chief Exec. Officer
REYNOLDS, Robert A., Jr.
Tel: (314) 512 - 9200
Fax: (314) 573 - 9455
TF: (800) 470 - 9227

Main Headquarters
Mailing: 34 N. Meramec Ave.
St. Louis, MO 63105
Tel: (314) 512 - 9200
Fax: (314) 573 - 9455
TF: (800) 470 - 9227

Corporate Foundations and Giving Programs

Graybar Foundation
Contact: Jack F. Van Pelt
34 N. Meramec Ave.
St. Louis, MO 63105
Tel: (314) 512 - 9200
Fax: (314) 573 - 9455
TF: (800) 470 - 9227

Annual Grant Total: none reported
Recent Recipients: United Way

Public Affairs and Related Activities Personnel

At Headquarters

HERREID, Beth S.
Director, Corporate Communications and Media Relations
Tel: (314) 512 - 9200
Fax: (314) 573 - 9455
TF: (800) 470 - 9227

OUCHI, Dawn
Manager, Public and Media Relations
Tel: (314) 512 - 9200
Fax: (314) 573 - 9455
TF: (800) 470 - 9227

VAN PELT, Jack F.
V. President, Human Resources
Tel: (314) 512 - 9200
Fax: (314) 573 - 9455
TF: (800) 470 - 9227

Great American Insurance Co.

See listing on page 31 under American Financial Group Inc.

The Great Atlantic and Pacific Tea Co.

A supermarket chain retailer.
www.aptea.com
Annual Revenues: $10.973 billion

Chairman of the Board
HAUB, Christian
Tel: (201) 571 - 4240
Fax: (201) 571 - 4445

President and Chief Exec. Officer
CLAUS, Eric
Tel: (201) 571 - 4240
Fax: (201) 571 - 8719

Main Headquarters
Mailing: Two Paragon Dr.
Montvale, NJ 07645
Tel: (201) 571 - 4240
Fax: (201) 571 - 8719

Corporate Foundations and Giving Programs

The Great Atlantic & Pacific Teac Co.
Two Paragon Dr.
Montvale, NJ 07645
Tel: (201) 571 - 4495
Fax: (201) 571 - 4034

Annual Grant Total: none reported

Public Affairs and Related Activities Personnel

At Headquarters

DESANTA, Richard P.
V. President, Corporate Affairs
Tel: (201) 571 - 4495
Fax: (201) 571 - 8719

MOSS, William
V. President and Treasurer
Responsibilities include investor relations.
Tel: (201) 571 - 4019
Fax: (201) 571 - 8719

RICHARDS, Allan
Senior V. President, Human Resources, Labor Relations and Legal Services
Tel: (201) 571 - 4240
Fax: (201) 571 - 8719

Great Lakes Bancorp FSB

See listing on page 465 under TCF Bank.

Great Lakes Chemical Corp.

See listing on page 114 under Chemtura.

Great Plains Energy, Inc.

An electric utility. Subsidiaries include Kansas City Power and Light Co. and KLT Inc.
www.greatplainsenergy.com

Chairman and Chief Exec. Officer
CHESSER, Michael C.
Tel: (816) 556 - 2200
Fax: (816) 556 - 2975

Main Headquarters
Mailing: P.O. Box 418679
Kansas City, MO 64141-9679
Tel: (816) 556 - 2200
Fax: (816) 556 - 2992

Washington Office
Contact: Mike Poling
Mailing: 701 Pennsylvania Ave. NW
Suite 300
Washington, DC 20004
Tel: (202) 742 - 4519
Fax: (202) 742 - 4644

Political Action Committees

KC Power PAC - Federal - Kansas City Power & Light Co.
Contact: G. Douglas Hewitt
P.O. Box 418679
Kansas City, MO 64141-9679
Tel: (816) 556 - 2200
Fax: (816) 556 - 2992

Contributions to Candidates: $17,250 (01/05 - 09/05)
Democrats: $3,250; Republicans: $14,000.

Principal Recipients

SENATE DEMOCRATS

HOUSE DEMOCRATS

Cleaver, Emanuel (MO)	$1,000
Moore, Dennis (KS)	$1,000
Skelton, Ike (MO)	$1,000

SENATE REPUBLICANS

Talent, James (MO)	$2,000
Inhofe, James M (OK)	$1,000
Roberts, Pat (KS)	$1,000

HOUSE REPUBLICANS

Graves, Sam (MO)	$2,000
Hastert, Dennis J. (IL)	$2,000
Barton, Joe L (TX)	$1,000
Hulshof, Kenny (MO)	$1,000
Moran, Jerry (KS)	$1,000
Ryun, Jim R (KS)	$1,000
Tiahrt, Todd W. (KS)	$1,000
Vitter, David (LA)	$1,000

Corporate Foundations and Giving Programs

Kansas City Power & Light Corporate Contributions Program
P.O. Box 418679
Kansas City, MO 64141-9679
Tel: (816) 556 - 2200
Fax: (816) 556 - 2992

Annual Grant Total: $750,000 - $1,000,000
Geographic Preference: Area in which the company is headquartered
Primary Interests: Community Affairs

Public Affairs and Related Activities Personnel

At Headquarters

CHRISTIAN, David C.
Manager, Governmental Affairs - Missouri
(Kansas City Power and Light Co.)
Tel: (816) 556 - 2977
Fax: (816) 556 - 2975

DEGGENDORFT, Michael
V. President, Public Affairs
Tel: (816) 556 - 2200
Fax: (816) 556 - 2975

GILES, Chris
V. President, Regulatory Affairs
Tel: (816) 556 - 2200
Fax: (816) 556 - 2975

HEWITT, G. Douglas
Pac Treasurer
Tel: (816) 556 - 2200
Fax: (816) 556 - 2992

KOBAYASHI, Todd
V. President, Strategy and Investor Relations
Tel: (816) 556 - 2904
Fax: (816) 556 - 2992

RIGGINS, William
V. President, Legal and Environmental Affairs
(Kansas City Power and Light Co.)
Tel: (816) 556 - 2200
Fax: (816) 556 - 2975

ROBINSON, Tom
Media Contact
Tel: (816) 556 - 2365
Fax: (816) 556 - 2222

At Washington Office

POLING, Mike
Manager, Federal Government Affairs
(Kansas City Power and Light Co.)
Tel: (202) 742 - 4519
Fax: (202) 742 - 4644

At Other Offices

MARULLO, Larry
Director, Government Affairs and Community Relations
(Kansas City Power and Light Co.)
1201 Walnut St.
Kansas City, MO 64106
Tel: (816) 556 - 2897
Fax: (816) 556 - 2995

Great River Energy

A member of the Public Affairs Council. An electric utility cooperative.
www.greatriverenergy.com

Chairman of the Board
HANSON, Henry A.
Tel: (763) 441 - 3121
Fax: (763) 241 - 2366

President and Chief Exec. Officer
VAN EPPES, Jim
Tel: (763) 441 - 3121
Fax: (763) 241 - 2366

Main Headquarters
Mailing: 17845 E. Hwy. 10
Elk River, MN 55330
Tel: (763) 441 - 3121
Fax: (763) 241 - 2366

Political Action Committees

Great River Energy Action Team
Contact: Bob Ambrose
17845 E. Hwy. 10
Elk River, MN 55330
Tel: (763) 441 - 3121
Fax: (763) 241 - 2366

Contributions to Candidates: $500 (01/05 - 09/05)

Great River Energy

* continued from previous page

Democrats: $500.

Principal Recipients

SENATE DEMOCRATS	HOUSE DEMOCRATS	
	Pomeroy, Earl (ND)	$500

Public Affairs and Related Activities Personnel

At Headquarters

AMBROSE, Bob — Tel: (763) 441 - 3121
Manager, Government Affairs; and PAC Treasurer — Fax: (763) 241 - 2366

LACANNE, Therese — Tel: (763) 241 - 2280
Media Contact — Fax: (763) 241 - 2366
tlacanne@grenergy.com

LANCASTER, Rick — Tel: (763) 241 - 2428
V. President, Public Affairs — Fax: (763) 241 - 6285

OLSEN, Kandace — Tel: (763) 241 - 2293
Manager, Communications — Fax: (763) 241 - 2366
kolsen@grenergy.com

ROTH, Mary Jo — Tel: (763) 441 - 3121
Manager, Environmental Services — Fax: (763) 241 - 2366

Green Bay Packaging Inc.

A manufacturer of corrugated boxes.
www.greenbaypackaging.com

Main Headquarters
Mailing: 1700 N. Webster Ct.
Green Bay, WI 54307-9017
Tel: (920) 433 - 5111
Fax: (920) 433 - 5471
TF: (800) 236 - 8400

Corporate Foundations and Giving Programs

George Kress Foundation
Contact: John Kress
1700 N. Webster Ct.
Green Bay, WI 54307-9017
Tel: (920) 433 - 5111
Fax: (920) 433 - 5471
TF: (800) 236 - 8400

Annual Grant Total: $1,000,000 - $2,000,000
Geographic Preference: Area in which the company is headquartered
Primary Interests: Children; Community Affairs; Education; Medicine and Health Care

Public Affairs and Related Activities Personnel

At Headquarters

DUFFY, Brian F. — Tel: (920) 433 - 5111
Corporate Environmental Co-Director — Fax: (920) 433 - 5471
TF: (800) 236 - 8400

DYBDAHL, Gordy — Tel: (920) 433 - 5111
Manager, Corporate Communications — Fax: (920) 433 - 5150
TF: (800) 236 - 8400

KRESS, John — Tel: (920) 433 - 5111
Secretary, George Kress Foundation — Fax: (920) 433 - 5471
TF: (800) 236 - 8400

KRESS, William F. — Tel: (920) 433 - 5111
President — Fax: (920) 433 - 5471
TF: (800) 236 - 8400

Greif Bros. Corp.

See listing on page 227 under Greif, Inc.

Greif, Inc.

Manufacturer of shipping and corrugated containers.
www.greif.com

Chairman and Chief Exec. Officer — Tel: (740) 549 - 6000
GASSER, Michael J. — Fax: (740) 549 - 6100

Main Headquarters
Mailing: 425 Winter Rd.
Delaware, OH 43015
Tel: (740) 549 - 6000
Fax: (740) 549 - 6100

Public Affairs and Related Activities Personnel

At Headquarters

ROANE, Michael L. — Tel: (740) 549 - 6000
Senior V. President, Human Resources and Communications — Fax: (740) 549 - 6100

STROHMAIER, Debra — Tel: (740) 549 - 6000
Director, Communications — Fax: (740) 549 - 6100
Responsibilities include government and investor relations.

Grey Global Group Inc.

www.grey.com

Chairman, Chief Exec. Officer and President — Tel: (212) 546 - 2000
MEYER, Edward H. — Fax: (212) 546 - 1495

Main Headquarters
Mailing: 777 Third Ave.
New York, NY 10017
Tel: (212) 546 - 2000
Fax: (212) 546 - 1495

Corporate Foundations and Giving Programs

Good Neighbor Foundation
Contact: Edward H. Meyer
777 Third Ave.
New York, NY 10017
Tel: (212) 546 - 2000
Fax: (212) 546 - 1495

Annual Grant Total: $750,000 - $1,000,000
Geographic Preference: California; New York
Primary Interests: AIDS/HIV; Arts and Humanities; Children; Education; Health and Human Services; Performing Arts

Public Affairs and Related Activities Personnel

At Headquarters

BROWN, Christine M. — Tel: (212) 546 - 2000
Senior V. President and Director, Corporate Communications — Fax: (212) 546 - 1495

SNEED, Jan — Tel: (212) 546 - 2000
Senior V. President, Corporate Affairs — Fax: (212) 546 - 1495
Responsibilities include corporate communications.

Greyhound Lines, Inc.

A commercial bus line and travel services company.
www.greyhound.com
Annual Revenues: $956.7 million

President and Chief Exec. Officer — Tel: (972) 789 - 7000
GORMAN, Stephen E. — Fax: (972) 789 - 7234

Main Headquarters
Mailing: P.O. Box 660606
M/S 490
Dallas, TX 75266-0606
Tel: (972) 789 - 7000
Fax: (972) 789 - 7234
Street: 15110 N. Dallas Pkwy.
Dallas, TX 75248

Washington Office
Contact: Ted Knappen
Mailing: 1101 14th St., NW
Washington, DC 20005
Tel: (202) 638 - 3490
Fax: (202) 638 - 3516

Political Action Committees

Greyhound Lines Political Action Committee
Contact: Richard Green
P.O. Box 660606
M/S 490
Dallas, TX 75266-0606
Tel: (972) 789 - 7000
Fax: (972) 789 - 7234

Contributions to Candidates: $11,000 (01/05 - 09/05)
Democrats: $7,000; Republicans: $4,000.

Principal Recipients

SENATE DEMOCRATS		HOUSE DEMOCRATS	
Baucus, Max (MT)	$1,000	Andrews, Robert (NJ)	$1,000
		Blumenauer, Earl (OR)	$1,000
		Cummings, Elijah (MD)	$1,000
		Defazio, Peter A (OR)	$1,000
		Johnson, Eddie (TX)	$1,000
		Olver, John (MA)	$1,000
SENATE REPUBLICANS		**HOUSE REPUBLICANS**	
		Emerson, Jo Ann (MO)	$1,000
		Petri, Thomas (WI)	$1,000
		Young, Don E (AK)	$1,000

Corporate Foundations and Giving Programs

Charitable Contributions
P.O. Box 660606
M/S 490
Dallas, TX 75266-0606
Tel: (972) 789 - 7000
Fax: (972) 789 - 7234

Annual Grant Total: none reported

Public Affairs and Related Activities Personnel

At Headquarters

CLARK, Harry A., Jr. — Tel: (972) 789 - 7000
V. President, Human Resources — Fax: (972) 789 - 7234

FOLMNSBEE, Anna — Tel: (972) 789 - 7206
Communications Specialist — Fax: (972) 789 - 7234
afolmns@greyhound.com

GREEN, Richard — Tel: (972) 789 - 7000
Assistant Treasurer — Fax: (972) 789 - 7234

PLASKETT, Kim — Tel: (972) 789 - 7204
Director, Corporate Commununications — Fax: (972) 789 - 7234
kplaske@greyhound.com

Greyhound Lines, Inc.

* continued from previous page

At Washington Office

KNAPPEN, Ted — Tel: (202) 638 - 3490
Consultant, Government Affairs — Fax: (202) 638 - 3516
tknappe@peyser.com

Griffon Corp.

Manufacturer of electronic communications systems and equipment.
www.griffoncorp.com

Chairman and Chief Exec. Officer — Tel: (516) 938 - 5544
BLAU, Harvey R. — Fax: (516) 938 - 5644

Main Headquarters
Mailing: 100 Jericho Quadrangle — Tel: (516) 938 - 5544
Jericho, NY 11753 — Fax: (516) 938 - 5644

Public Affairs and Related Activities Personnel

At Headquarters

MERCER, Howard — Tel: (516) 938 - 5544
Director, Public Relations — Fax: (516) 938 - 5644
Responsibilities also include investor relations.

Grolier Inc.

See listing on page 427 under Scholastic, Inc.

Group I Automotive, Inc.

Sells new and used cars and light trucks through its dealerships and Internet sites. Arranges related financing, vehicle services, and insurance contracts. Provides maintenance and repair services and sells replacement parts.
www.group1auto.com

Chairman of the Board — Tel: (713) 647 - 5700
ADAMS, John L. — Fax: (713) 647 - 5800

President and Chief Exec. Officer — Tel: (713) 647 - 5700
HESTERBERG, Earl J. — Fax: (713) 647 - 5800

Main Headquarters
Mailing: 950 Echo Lane, Suite 100 — Tel: (713) 647 - 5700
Houston, TX 77024 — Fax: (713) 647 - 5800

Political Action Committees

Group 1 Automotive Inc. PAC
Contact: Beth Sibley
950 Echo Lane, Suite 100 — Tel: (713) 647 - 5700
Houston, TX 77024 — Fax: (713) 647 - 5869

Contributions to Candidates: $1,000 (01/05 - 09/05)
Republicans: $1,000.

Principal Recipients

SENATE REPUBLICANS	HOUSE REPUBLICANS	
	DeLay, Tom (TX)	$1,000

Public Affairs and Related Activities Personnel

At Headquarters

RAY, Robert T. — Tel: (713) 647 - 5700
Senior V. President, Chief Financial Officer and Treasurer — Fax: (713) 647 - 5888
Responsibilities include investor relations.

SIBLEY, Beth — Tel: (713) 647 - 5700
PAC Treasurer — Fax: (713) 647 - 5869
bsibley@group1auto.com

GTECH Corp.

A gaming technology and systems provider.
www.gtech.com
Annual Revenues: $1.2 billion

Chairman of the Board — Tel: (401) 392 - 1000
DEWEY, Robert M., Jr. — Fax: (401) 392 - 1234

President and Chief Exec. Officer — Tel: (401) 392 - 1000
TURNER, W. Bruce — Fax: (401) 392 - 1234

Main Headquarters
Mailing: 55 Technology Way — Tel: (401) 392 - 1000
West Greenwich, RI 02817 — Fax: (401) 392 - 1234

Corporate Foundations and Giving Programs

GTECH Corporate Charitable Contributions
55 Technology Way — Tel: (401) 392 - 1000
West Greenwich, RI 02817 — Fax: (401) 392 - 1234

Annual Grant Total: none reported

Public Affairs and Related Activities Personnel

At Headquarters

NORTON, Mary — Tel: (401) 392 - 7603
Director, Investor Relations — Fax: (401) 392 - 0315
mary.norton@gtech.com

SWEITZER, Don R. — Tel: (401) 392 - 1000
Senior V. President, Global Business Development and Public Affairs — Fax: (401) 392 - 1234

VINCENT, Robert K. — Tel: (401) 392 - 7452
V. President, Corporate Communications — Fax: (401) 392 - 1234

Guardian Industries Corp.

www.guardian.com

President and Chief Exec. Officer — Tel: (248) 340 - 1800
DAVIDSON, William M. — Fax: (248) 340 - 2395

Main Headquarters
Mailing: 2300 Harmon Rd. — Tel: (248) 340 - 1800
Auburn Hills, MI 48326-1714 — Fax: (248) 340 - 9988

Political Action Committees

Guardian Industries Corp. Federal PAC
Contact: Peter Walters
2300 Harmon Rd. — Tel: (248) 340 - 1800
Auburn Hills, MI 48326-1714 — Fax: (248) 340 - 9988

Contributions to Candidates: $3,000 (01/05 - 09/05)
Democrats: $1,000; Republicans: $2,000.

Principal Recipients

SENATE DEMOCRATS	HOUSE DEMOCRATS	
	Levin, Sander (MI)	$1,000
SENATE REPUBLICANS	**HOUSE REPUBLICANS**	
	Boehlert, Sherwood (NY)	$2,000

Corporate Foundations and Giving Programs

Guardian Industries Educational Foundation
Contact: William M. Davidson
2300 Harmon Rd. — Tel: (248) 340 - 1800
Auburn Hills, MI 48326-1714 — Fax: (248) 340 - 2395

Annual Grant Total: $750,000 - $1,000,000

Public Affairs and Related Activities Personnel

At Headquarters

JOSEPH, Gayle — Tel: (248) 340 - 1800
Director, Communications — Fax: (248) 340 - 2395

WALTERS, Peter — Tel: (248) 340 - 1800
Group V. President; and PAC Treasurer — Fax: (248) 340 - 9988
Responsibilities include corporate public affairs.

Guardian Life Insurance Co. of America

www.glic.com

President and Chief Exec. Officer — Tel: (212) 598 - 8000
MANNING, Dennis J. — Fax: (212) 949 - 2170

Main Headquarters
Mailing: Seven Hanover Square — Tel: (212) 598 - 8000
M/S H-26-E — Fax: (212) 949 - 2170
New York, NY 10004-2616

Political Action Committees

Guardian Life Insurance Co. of America PAC
Contact: John R. Hurley
Seven Hanover Square — Tel: (212) 598 - 8000
M/S H-26-E — Fax: (212) 949 - 2170
New York, NY 10004-2616

Contributions to Candidates: $1,000 (01/05 - 09/05)
Republicans: $1,000.

Principal Recipients

SENATE REPUBLICANS	HOUSE REPUBLICANS	
	Kelly, Sue W (NY)	$1,000

Corporate Foundations and Giving Programs

Guardian Life Insurance Co. of America Contributions
Contact: Karen Olvany
Seven Hanover Square — Tel: (212) 598 - 8000
M/S H-26-E — Fax: (212) 949 - 2170
New York, NY 10004-2616

Annual Grant Total: $500,000 - $750,000
Geographic Preference: Area(s) in which the company operates; New York; Pennsylvania; Washington State; Wisconsin
Primary Interests: Education

Public Affairs and Related Activities Personnel

At Headquarters

HURLEY, John R. — Tel: (212) 598 - 8000
PAC Treasurer — Fax: (212) 949 - 2170

OLVANY, Karen — Tel: (212) 598 - 8000
Contributions Contact — Fax: (212) 949 - 2170

Guardian Life Insurance Co. of America

** continued from previous page*

RANTON, James D. — Tel: (212) 598 - 8000
Senior V. President, Human Resources — Fax: (212) 949 - 2170

SORELL, Thomas G., C.F.A. — Tel: (212) 598 - 8000
Exec. V. President and Chief Investment Officer — Fax: (212) 949 - 2170

TAGARIELLO, Alayna — Tel: (212) 598 - 8329
Media Contact — Fax: (212) 949 - 2170
alayna_tagariello@glic.com

Guidant Corp.

A member of the Public Affairs Council. Manufactures, develops and markets medical devices.
www.guidant.com

Chairman of the Board
CORNELIUS, James M. — Tel: (317) 971 - 2000; Fax: (317) 971 - 2040

President and Chief Exec. Officer
DOLLENS, Ronald W. — Tel: (317) 971 - 2000; Fax: (317) 971 - 2040

Main Headquarters
Mailing: 111 Monument Circle
29th Floor
Indianapolis, IN 46204-5129
Tel: (317) 971 - 2000; Fax: (317) 971 - 2040

Washington Office
Contact: Ann M. Gosier
Mailing: 1310 G St. NW
Suite 770
Washington, DC 20005
Tel: (202) 508 - 0800; Fax: (202) 508 - 0818

Political Action Committees

Guidant Corp. Political Action Committee
Contact: Ann M. Gosier
1310 G St. NW
Suite 770
Washington, DC 20005
Tel: (202) 508 - 0800; Fax: (202) 508 - 0818

Contributions to Candidates: $17,000 (01/05 - 09/05)
Democrats: $4,000; Republicans: $12,000; Other: $1,000.

Principal Recipients

SENATE DEMOCRATS

HOUSE DEMOCRATS
Eshoo, Anna (CA) $1,000
Honda, Mike (CA) $1,000
Lofgren, Zoe (CA) $1,000
Pomeroy, Earl (ND) $1,000

HOUSE OTHER
Pitts, Joseph R (PA) $1,000

SENATE REPUBLICANS
Hatch, Orrin (UT) $2,000
Santorum, Richard (PA) $2,000
Lugar, Richard G (IN) $1,000

HOUSE REPUBLICANS
Dreier, David (CA) $2,000
Bonilla, Henry (TX) $1,000
Ferguson, Mike (NJ) $1,000
Issa, Darrell (CA) $1,000
Johnson, Nancy (CT) $1,000
Ramstad, Jim (MN) $1,000

Corporate Foundations and Giving Programs

Guidant Foundation
Contact: Jim Baumgardt
111 Monument Circle
29th Floor
Indianapolis, IN 46204-5129
Tel: (317) 971 - 2000; Fax: (317) 971 - 2040

Annual Grant Total: over $5,000,000

Public Affairs and Related Activities Personnel

At Headquarters

BAUMGARDT, Jim — Tel: (317) 971 - 2000
President, Guidant Foundation — Fax: (317) 971 - 2040

MARCHETTI, Robert — Tel: (317) 971 - 2000
V. President, Human Resources — Fax: (317) 971 - 2040

RIETH, Andy — Tel: (317) 971 - 2061
Director, Investor Relations — Fax: (317) 971 - 2045
arieth@guidant.com

TRAGASH, Steven — Tel: (317) 971 - 2031
Director, Corporate Communications — Fax: (317) 971 - 2040
stragash@guidant.com

At Washington Office

CANTOR-WEINBERG, Julie — Tel: (202) 508 - 0800
Director, Government Affairs — Fax: (202) 508 - 0818

GOSIER, Ann M. — Tel: (202) 508 - 0800
V. President, Government Affairs — Fax: (202) 508 - 0818
Registered Federal Lobbyist.

Guilford Mills, Inc.

A manufacturer of textiles.
www.guilfordmills.com

President and Chief Exec. Officer
WHITE, Shannon — Tel: (336) 316 - 4000; Fax: (336) 316 - 4057

Main Headquarters
Mailing: 6001 W. Market St.
Greensboro, NC 27409
Tel: (336) 316 - 4000; Fax: (336) 316 - 4057

Corporate Foundations and Giving Programs

Guilford Mills Corporate Contributions Program
6001 W. Market St.
Greensboro, NC 27409
Tel: (336) 316 - 4000; Fax: (336) 316 - 4057

Annual Grant Total: none reported

Public Affairs and Related Activities Personnel

At Headquarters

NOVAK, Richard E. — Tel: (336) 316 - 4000
V. President, Human Resources — Fax: (336) 316 - 4057
rnovak@gfd.com
Responsibilities include communications.

Guinness/UDV

See listing on page 158 under Diageo North America.

Gulf Power Co.

An electric utility subsidiary of Southern Company (see separate listing).
www.gulfpower.com

President and Chief Exec. Officer
STORY, Susan N. — Tel: (850) 444 - 6111; Fax: (850) 444 - 6448; TF: (800) 225 - 5797

Main Headquarters
Mailing: One Energy Pl.
Pensacola, FL 32520
Tel: (850) 444 - 6111; Fax: (850) 444 - 6448; TF: (800) 225 - 5797

Political Action Committees

Responsible Government Committee of Gulf Employees Inc.
Contact: Ron Grissom
One Energy Pl.
Pensacola, FL 32520
Tel: (850) 444 - 6111; Fax: (850) 444 - 6448; TF: (800) 225 - 5797

Contributions to Candidates: $8,500 (01/05 - 09/05)
Democrats: $6,000; Republicans: $2,500.

Principal Recipients

SENATE DEMOCRATS

HOUSE DEMOCRATS
Boyd, F Allen Jr (FL) $4,500

SENATE REPUBLICANS

HOUSE REPUBLICANS
Miller, Jefferson (FL) $2,500

Corporate Foundations and Giving Programs

Gulf Power Foundation
Contact: Candace Klinglesmith
One Energy Pl.
Pensacola, FL 32520
Tel: (850) 444 - 6806; Fax: (850) 444 - 6448; TF: (800) 225 - 5797

Annual Grant Total: $100,000 - $200,000
Primary Interests: Arts and Humanities; Education; Social Services
Recent Recipients: American Red Cross

Public Affairs and Related Activities Personnel

At Headquarters

ERICKSON, Lynn — Tel: (850) 444 - 6249
Corporate Communications Supervisor — Fax: (850) 444 - 6448; TF: (800) 225 - 5797

GRISSOM, Ron — Tel: (850) 444 - 6111
PAC Treasurer — Fax: (850) 444 - 6448; TF: (800) 225 - 5797

HUTCHINSON, John L. — Tel: (850) 444 - 6750
Manager, Public Affairs — Fax: (850) 444 - 6448
jlhutchi@southernco.com — TF: (800) 225 - 5797

JACOB, Bernard — Tel: (850) 444 - 6111
V. President, External Affairs and Corporate Services — Fax: (850) 444 - 6448; TF: (800) 225 - 5797

KLINGLESMITH, Candace — Tel: (850) 444 - 6806
Corporate Services Specialist; and Foundation Contact — Fax: (850) 444 - 6448; TF: (800) 225 - 5797

Gulfstream Aerospace Corp.

A manufacturer of corporate/business and government service jet aircraft. A subsidiary of General Dynamics (see separate listing).

www.gulfstream.com
Annual Revenues: $3.289 billion

Main Headquarters

Mailing: P.O. Box 2206, Savannah, GA 31402-2206 — Tel: (912) 965 - 3000; Fax: (912) 965 - 3775
Street: 500 Gulfstream Rd., Savannah, GA 31407

Washington Office

Mailing: 1000 Wilson Blvd., Suite 2701, Arlington, VA 22209 — Tel: (703) 276 - 9500; Fax: (703) 276 - 9504

Political Action Committees

General Dynamic
2941 Fairview Park Drive
Suite 100
Falls Church, VA 22042

Contributions to Candidates: $416,000 (01/05 - 09/05)
Democrats: $155,000; Republicans: $259,000; Other: $2,000.

Principal Recipients

SENATE DEMOCRATS

HOUSE DEMOCRATS
Langevin, James (RI) $10,000
Murtha, John P Mr. (PA) $10,000
Skelton, Ike (MO) $10,000

SENATE REPUBLICANS
Talent, James (MO) $10,000

HOUSE REPUBLICANS
Hayes, Robert (NC) $10,000

Corporate Foundations and Giving Programs

Gulfstream Aerospace Corp. Contibutions Program
Contact: Greg Dziuban
P.O. Box 2206
Savannah, GA 31402-2206
Tel: (912) 965 - 7199
Fax: (912) 965 - 4466

Annual Grant Total: $500,000 - $750,000

Public Affairs and Related Activities Personnel

At Headquarters

BAUGNIET, Robert N.
Director, Corporate Communications
Mailstop: A-01
Tel: (912) 965 - 7372; Fax: (912) 965 - 4333

BERMAN, Ira
Senior V. President, Administration and General Counsel
Responsibilities include human resources.
Tel: (912) 965 - 3000; Fax: (912) 965 - 3775

DZIUBAN, Greg
Director, Employee Communications
Responsibilities include corporate philanthropy.
Tel: (912) 965 - 7199; Fax: (912) 965 - 4466

H & R Block, Inc.

A tax services company that also offers financial, mortgage and business products and services. H&R Block combines its national network of offices with a full range of do-it-yourself software and online tax solutions. The company combines its tax solutions with personalized financial advice about retirement savings, home ownership, and other opportunities to help clients.

www.hrblock.com
Annual Revenues: $3.318 billion

Chairman, President and Chief Exec. Officer
ERNST, Mark A.
mernst@hrblock.com
Tel: (816) 753 - 6900; Fax: (816) 753 - 5346; TF: (800) 829 - 7733

Main Headquarters

Mailing: 4400 Main St., Kansas City, MO 64111 — Tel: (816) 753 - 6900; Fax: (816) 753 - 5346; TF: (800) 829 - 7733

Washington Office

Contact: Robert A. Weinberger
Mailing: 700 13th St. NW, Suite 700, Washington, DC 20005-5922 — Tel: (202) 508 - 6363; Fax: (202) 508 - 6330

Political Action Committees

H&R Block Political Action Committee (BLOCKPAC)
Contact: Robert A. Weinberger
700 13th St. NW
Suite 700
Washington, DC 20005-5922
Tel: (202) 508 - 6364
Fax: (202) 508 - 6330

Contributions to Candidates: $30,500 (01/05 - 09/05)
Democrats: $18,500; Republicans: $12,000.

Principal Recipients

SENATE DEMOCRATS
Carper, Thomas R (DE) $2,000

HOUSE DEMOCRATS
Kanjorski, Paul (PA) $4,000
Levin, Sander (MI) $2,000

SENATE REPUBLICANS
Kyl, Jon L (AZ) $2,000

HOUSE REPUBLICANS
Hulshof, Kenny (MO) $3,000
Thomas, William M (CA) $2,000

Corporate Foundations and Giving Programs

The H&R Block Foundation
Contact: David Miles
4400 Main St.
Kansas City, MO 64111
Tel: (816) 932 - 4821
Fax: (816) 753 - 1585
TF: (800) 829 - 7733

Assets: $47,017,571 (2001)
Annual Grant Total: $1,000,000 - $2,000,000
Guidelines are available.
Geographic Preference: Area in which the company is headquartered
Primary Interests: Arts and Culture; Community Affairs; Education; Health and Human Services; United Way Campaigns; Youth Services
Recent Recipients: United Way; University of Missouri

Public Affairs and Related Activities Personnel

At Headquarters

ALLISON-PUTNAM, Andrea
Director, Community Relations
aputnam@hrblock.com
Tel: (816) 932 - 4895; Fax: (816) 932 - 8462; TF: (800) 829 - 7733

BARNETT, Mark
Director, Investor Relations
mbarnett@hrblock.com
Tel: (816) 701 - 4443; Fax: (816) 753 - 5346; TF: (800) 829 - 7733

LAMMARTINO, Nicholas
Director, Communications
Tel: (816) 753 - 6900; Fax: (816) 753 - 5346; TF: (800) 829 - 7733

MCDOUGALL, Linda M.
V. President, Corporate Communications
lmcdougall@hrblock.com
Tel: (816) 932 - 7542; Fax: (816) 753 - 8628; TF: (800) 829 - 7733

MILES, David
President, H&R Block Foundation
davmiles@hrblock.com
Tel: (816) 932 - 4821; Fax: (816) 753 - 1585; TF: (800) 829 - 7733

At Washington Office

BERESIK, Michael T.
Assistant V. President, Government Relations
Registered Federal Lobbyist.
Tel: (202) 508 - 6217; Fax: (202) 508 - 6330

WEINBERGER, Robert A.
V. President, Government Relations
rweinberger@hrblock.com
Registered Federal Lobbyist.
Tel: (202) 508 - 6364; Fax: (202) 508 - 6330

WILSON, Sarah
Legislative Assistant
Tel: (202) 508 - 6363; Fax: (202) 508 - 6330

Halliburton Company

An oil field services, engineering and construction firm.

www.halliburton.com
Annual Revenues: $12.939 billion

Main Headquarters

Mailing: Five Houston Center, 1401 McKinney, Suite 2400, Houston, TX 77010 — Tel: (713) 759 - 2600

Washington Office

Mailing: 1150 18th St. NW, Suite 200, Washington, DC 20036 — Tel: (202) 223 - 0820; Fax: (202) 223 - 2385

Corporate Foundations and Giving Programs

Halliburton Foundation, Inc.
Contact: Margaret E. Carriere
Five Houston Center
1401 McKinney, Suite 2400
Houston, TX 77010
Tel: (713) 759 - 2600

Assets: $12,000,000 (1999)
Annual Grant Total: $1,000,000 - $2,000,000
Geographic Preference: National; Texas
Primary Interests: Education
Recent Recipients: Oklahoma State University; Rice University; Texas A & M University

Public Affairs and Related Activities Personnel

At Headquarters

CARRIERE, Margaret E.
V. President and Secretary, Foundation
Tel: (713) 759 - 2600

Halliburton Company

* continued from previous page

MANN, Cathy — Tel: (713) 759 - 2605
Director, Public Relations
cathy.mann@halliburton.com

At Washington Office

JONES, Barbara — Tel: (202) 223 - 0820
Director, Government Affairs — Fax: (202) 223 - 2385
barbara.jones1@halliburton.com
Registered Federal Lobbyist.

At Other Offices

BRANCH, Zelma — Tel: (281) 988 - 2557
Manager, Public Relations - North America
10200 Bellaire Blvd.
Houston, TX 77020-5299
zelma.branch@halliburton.com

Hallmark Cards, Inc.

A member of the Public Affairs Council. A manufacturer and marketer of greeting cards and related personal expression products. Subsidiaries include Binney and Smith Inc. (see separate listing).

www.hallmark.com
Annual Revenues: $4.3 billion

Chairman of the Board — Tel: (816) 274 - 5111
HALL, Donald J., Sr. — Fax: (816) 274 - 5061

President and Chief Exec. Officer/Vice Chairman — Tel: (816) 274 - 5111
HALL, Donald J., Jr. — Fax: (816) 274 - 5061

Main Headquarters
Mailing: P.O. Box 419580 — Tel: (816) 274 - 5111
Kansas City, MO 64141-6580 — Fax: (816) 274 - 5061
TF: (800) 425 - 5627

Street: 2501 McGee St.
Kansas City, MO 64108

Political Action Committees

Hallmark Political Action Committee - Federal (HALLPAC-Federal)
Contact: Greg C. Swarens
P.O. Box 419580 — Tel: (816) 274 - 7457
Kansas City, MO 64141-6580 — Fax: (816) 274 - 5061

Contributions to Candidates: $1,580 (01/05 - 09/05)
Democrats: $1,580.

Principal Recipients

SENATE DEMOCRATS	HOUSE DEMOCRATS
	Cleaver, Emanuel (MO) $1,000

Corporate Foundations and Giving Programs

Hallmark Corporate Foundation
Contact: Karen Bartz
P.O. Box 419580 — Tel: (816) 274 - 8515
Kansas City, MO 64141-6580

Annual Grant Total: $2,000,000 - $5,000,000
Total annual giving exceeds $10,000,000. Guidelines are available.
Geographic Preference: Area in which the company is headquartered; Area(s) in which the company operates
Primary Interests: Arts and Humanities; Education; Social Services
Recent Recipients: United Way

Public Affairs and Related Activities Personnel

At Headquarters

BARTZ, Karen — Tel: (816) 274 - 8515
Manager, Community Development; and V. President, Foundation
kbartz1@hallmark.com

BUKATY, Molly — Tel: (816) 274 - 7611
Communications Manager — Fax: (816) 274 - 5061

CLARK, Jacqueline K. — Tel: (816) 274 - 8893
Manager, Public Affairs — Fax: (816) 274 - 5061
Mailstop: Mail #288
jclark7@hallmark.com

DOYAL, Stephen D. — Tel: (816) 274 - 4314
Senior V. President, Public Affairs and Communications — Fax: (816) 274 - 5061

GAFFEN, Eileen — Tel: (816) 274 - 4673
Manager, Public Relations — Fax: (816) 274 - 5061

KOIRTYOHANN, Barbara J. — Tel: (816) 274 - 5244
Director, Public Affairs — Fax: (816) 274 - 5061
Mailstop: Mail Drop 288
bkoirt2@hallmark.com

LAMPE, Anna Carol — Tel: (816) 274 - 3589
Research Project Leader — Fax: (816) 274 - 7397
Mailstop: M/S 203

MCCAFFREY, Diane — Tel: (816) 274 - 7926
Manager, Business Communications — Fax: (816) 274 - 5061

O'DELL, Julie — Tel: (816) 274 - 5961
Director, Public Relations — Fax: (816) 274 - 5061
jodell1@hallmark.com

OSKISON, Kathrine L. — Tel: (816) 274 - 3920
Public Relations Assistant — Fax: (816) 274 - 5061
TF: (800) 425 - 5627

RODENBOUGH, Dean T. — Tel: (816) 274 - 5111
Director, Corporate Communications — Fax: (816) 274 - 5061

SEIFERT, David P. — Tel: (816) 274 - 3761
Manager, Strategic Communications International — Fax: (816) 274 - 5061

SULLIVAN, Tonya — Tel: (816) 274 - 5220
Assistant, Public Affairs — Fax: (816) 274 - 5061

SWARENS, Greg C. — Tel: (816) 274 - 7457
Manager, Public Affairs — Fax: (816) 274 - 5061
Mailstop: MD 288

WINKER, Jeff — Tel: (816) 274 - 5111
Communications Strategist — Fax: (816) 274 - 5061

Hamilton Sundstrand

A global supplier of technologically advanced aerospace and industrial products. A subsidiary of United Technologies (see separate listing).

www.hamiltonsundstrand.com

Main Headquarters
Mailing: One Hamilton Rd. — Tel: (860) 654 - 6000
Windsor Locks, CT 06096-1010

Washington Office
Contact: Edward M. Bullard
Mailing: 1401 I St. NW — Tel: (202) 336 - 7468
Suite 600 — Fax: (202) 336 - 7518
Washington, DC 20005

Public Affairs and Related Activities Personnel

At Headquarters

HASHEM, Peg — Tel: (860) 654 - 3469
Manager, Public Relations — Fax: (860) 654 - 5060

At Washington Office

BULLARD, Edward M. — Tel: (202) 336 - 7468
Director, Washington Operations — Fax: (202) 336 - 7518
bullarde@corpdc.utc.com

Handleman Company

A category manager and distributor of music.

www.handleman.com
Annual Revenues: $1.2 billion

Chairman and Chief Exec. Officer — Tel: (248) 362 - 4400
STROME, Stephen — Fax: (248) 362 - 6409

Main Headquarters
Mailing: P.O. Box 7045 — Tel: (248) 362 - 4400
Troy, MI 48007-7045 — Fax: (248) 362 - 3615
Street: 500 Kirts Blvd.
Troy, MI 48084-4142

Public Affairs and Related Activities Personnel

At Headquarters

ALBRECHT, Mark — Tel: (248) 362 - 4400
Senior V. President, Human Resources — Ext: 608
Fax: (248) 362 - 6409

MIZE, Gregory — Tel: (248) 362 - 4400
V. President, Investor Relations — Ext: 211
Fax: (248) 362 - 0718
Responsibilities also include corporate communications.

Hanna Company, M. A.

See listing on page 388 under PolyOne Corp.

Hannaford Bros. Co.

An operator of supermarkets and retail drug stores. A wholly-owned subsidiary of Delhaize America, Inc.

www.hannaford.com

President and Chief Exec. Officer — Tel: (207) 883 - 2911
HODGE, Ronald — Fax: (207) 885 - 3165
rhodge@hannaford.com

Main Headquarters
Mailing: 145 Pleasant Hill Rd. — Tel: (207) 883 - 2911
Scarborough, ME 04074 — Fax: (207) 885 - 3165

Corporate Foundations and Giving Programs

Hannaford Charitable Foundation
Contact: Donna Boyce

Hannaford Bros. Co.

** continued from previous page*

145 Pleasant Hill Rd. Tel: (207) 883 - 2911
Scarborough, ME 04074 Fax: (207) 885 - 3165

Annual Grant Total: $1,000,000 - $2,000,000
Geographic Preference: Area(s) in which the company operates
Primary Interests: Arts and Culture; Education; Health and Human Services; Social Services
Recent Recipients: American Red Cross; Citizen's Scholarship Foundation of America; United Way; YMCA

Public Affairs and Related Activities Personnel

At Headquarters

BOYCE, Donna Tel: (207) 883 - 2911
Secretary, Hannaford Charitable Foundation Fax: (207) 885 - 3165
dboyce@hannaford.com

EPSTEIN, Karen Tel: (207) 883 - 2911
Manager, Public Relations Fax: (207) 885 - 3165

GREELEY, Marty Tel: (207) 883 - 2911
V. President, Government Relations Fax: (207) 885 - 3165

Hardee's Food Systems, Inc.

A system of company and franchise-owned quick-service restaurants. A wholly-owned subsidiary of CKE Restaurants, Inc.
www.hardees.com

Main Headquarters
Mailing: U.S. Bank Plaza Tel: (314) 259 - 6200
505 N. Seventh St. Ste 2000 Fax: (314) 621 - 1778
St. Louis, MO 63101

Corporate Foundations and Giving Programs

Hardee's Food Systems, Inc. Contributions/Sponsorships
Contact: Bev Pfeifer-Harms
U.S. Bank Plaza Tel: (314) 259 - 6315
505 N. Seventh St. Ste 2000 Fax: (314) 621 - 1778
St. Louis, MO 63101

Annual Grant Total: $500,000 - $750,000
Recent Recipients: Second Harvest

Public Affairs and Related Activities Personnel

At Headquarters

MOCHA, Jeff Tel: (314) 259 - 6200
Manager, Public Relations Fax: (314) 621 - 1778

PFEIFER-HARMS, Bev Tel: (314) 259 - 6315
Manager, Public Relations Fax: (314) 621 - 1778
Mailstop: Suite 3610
Responsibilities include corporate philanthropy.

John H. Harland Co.

A financial marketing services company that includes printed products, software, and data collection solutions.
www.harland.net

Chairman and Chief Exec. Officer
TUFF, Tim Tel: (770) 981 - 9460
ttuff@harland.net Fax: (770) 593 - 5367
TF: (800) 723 - 3690

Main Headquarters
Mailing: P.O. Box 105250 Tel: (770) 981 - 9460
Atlanta, GA 30348 Fax: (770) 593 - 5367
TF: (800) 723 - 3690

Street: 2939 Miller Rd.
Decatur, GA 30035

Public Affairs and Related Activities Personnel

At Headquarters

BATES, Arlene Tel: (770) 981 - 9460
Senior V. President, Human Resources Fax: (770) 593 - 5619
abates@harland.net TF: (800) 723 - 3690

BOND, Henry R. Tel: (770) 593 - 5697
V. President, Investor Relations; and Treasurer Fax: (770) 593 - 5367
hbond@harland.net TF: (800) 723 - 3690

PENSEC, John Tel: (770) 593 - 5443
Director, Corporate Communications and Community Relations Fax: (770) 593 - 5367
jpensec@harland.net TF: (800) 723 - 3690

Harley-Davidson Motor Company

A member of the Public Affairs Council. A manufacturer of motorcycles, recreational and commercial vehicles, parts and accessories.
www.harley-davidson.com

Chairman and Chief Exec. Officer
BLEUSTEIN, Jeffrey L. Tel: (414) 342 - 4680
Fax: (414) 343 - 8230

Main Headquarters
Mailing: 3700 W. Juneau Ave. Tel: (414) 342 - 4680
Milwaukee, WI 53208 Fax: (414) 343 - 8230

Political Action Committees

Harley-Davidson Motor Company PAC, Inc.
Contact: Timothy K. Hoelter
3700 W. Juneau Ave. Tel: (414) 342 - 4680
Milwaukee, WI 53208 Fax: (414) 343 - 8230

Contributions to Candidates: none reported (01/05 - 09/05)

Corporate Foundations and Giving Programs

Harley-Davidson Motor Company Foundation, Inc.
Contact: Mary Ann Martiny
3700 W. Juneau Ave. Tel: (414) 342 - 4680
Milwaukee, WI 53208 Fax: (414) 343 - 8230

Annual Grant Total: $2,000,000 - $5,000,000
Also sponsors a Volunteer Matching Hours Program which matches employee voluntary hours with monetary grants. The Program encourages volunteer work among employees, and enables them to help make choices about which charitable causes the company supports.
Geographic Preference: Area(s) in which the company operates
Primary Interests: Arts and Culture; Community Development; Education; Environment/Conservation; Medicine and Health Care
Recent Recipients: American Red Cross; Children's Hospital; United Way

Public Affairs and Related Activities Personnel

At Headquarters

CURTIN, Wayne Tel: (414) 342 - 4680
Director, Government Affairs Fax: (414) 343 - 8230
wayne.curtin@harley-davidson.com

DAVIDSON, Pat Tel: (414) 342 - 4680
Director, Investor Relations Fax: (414) 343 - 8230
pat.davidson@harley-davidson.com

HOELTER, Timothy K. Tel: (414) 342 - 4680
V. President, International Trade Regulatory Affairs; and PAC Treasurer Fax: (414) 343 - 8230

LAWLER, Kathleen A. Tel: (414) 342 - 4680
V. President, Communications Fax: (414) 343 - 8230
kathleen.lawler@harley-davidson.com

MARTINY, Mary Ann Tel: (414) 342 - 4680
Manager, Harley-Davidson Foundation Fax: (414) 343 - 8230

WALTON, Susan Tel: (414) 342 - 4680
Director, Corporate Communications Fax: (414) 343 - 8230

Harleysville Group

www.harleysvillegroup.com

Chairman of the Board
SCRANTON, William W., III Tel: (215) 256 - 5000
Fax: (215) 256 - 5799
TF: (800) 523 - 6344

Chief Exec. Officer
BROWNE, Michael L. Tel: (215) 256 - 5000
mbrowne@harleysvillegroup.com Fax: (215) 256 - 5799
TF: (800) 523 - 6344

Main Headquarters
Mailing: 355 Maple Ave. Tel: (215) 256 - 5000
Harleysville, PA 19438-2297 Fax: (215) 256 - 5799
TF: (800) 523 - 6344

Political Action Committees

Harleysville Insurance PAC (HIPAC)
Contact: Maria Kelly
355 Maple Ave. Tel: (215) 256 - 5022
Harleysville, PA 19438-2297 Fax: (215) 256 - 5799
TF: (800) 523 - 6344

Contributions to Candidates: $9,000 (01/05 - 09/05)
Republicans: $9,000.

Principal Recipients

SENATE REPUBLICANS

HOUSE REPUBLICANS
Gerlach, Jim (PA) $3,000
Sherwood, Donald L (PA) $3,000
Fitzpatrick, Michael (PA) $2,000

Corporate Foundations and Giving Programs

Harleysville Corporate Contributions Committee
Contact: Mark R. Cummins
355 Maple Ave. Tel: (215) 256 - 5025
Harleysville, PA 19438-2297 Fax: (215) 256 - 5601
TF: (800) 523 - 6344

Annual Grant Total: none reported

Public Affairs and Related Activities Personnel

At Headquarters

BUCKWALTER, Randy Tel: (215) 256 - 5288
Manager, Corporate Communications Fax: (215) 256 - 5799
rbuckwalter@harleysvillegroup.com TF: (800) 523 - 6344

Harleysville Group

** continued from previous page*

CUMMINS, Mark R.
Exec. V. President, Chief Investment Officer and Treasurer
mcummins@harleysvillegroup.com
Responsibilities include corporate philanthropy.
Tel: (215) 256 - 5025
Fax: (215) 256 - 5601
TF: (800) 523 - 6344

GAUGLER, Bonita
Director, Corporate Affairs and Assistant V. President
bgaugler@harleysvillegroup.com
Tel: (215) 256 - 5013
Fax: (215) 256 - 5008
TF: (800) 523 - 6344

KELLY, Maria
Government Affairs Counsel
Tel: (215) 256 - 5022
Fax: (215) 256 - 5799
TF: (800) 523 - 6344

MANERO, Linda
Manager, Marketing Communications
lmanero@harleysvillegroup.com
Tel: (215) 256 - 5061
Fax: (215) 256 - 5799
TF: (800) 523 - 6344

MCARDLE, Kevin J.
V. President, Communications
kmcardle@harleysvillegroup.com
Tel: (215) 256 - 5279
Fax: (215) 256 - 5799
TF: (800) 523 - 6344

STRAUSS, Catherine B.
Exec. V. President, Human Resources
cstrauss@harleysvillegroup.com
Tel: (215) 256 - 5000
Fax: (215) 256 - 5602
TF: (800) 523 - 6344

Harnischfeger Industries, Inc.

See listing on page 272 under Joy Global Inc.

Harrah's Entertainment, Inc.

PUBLIC AFFAIRS COUNCIL

A member of the Public Affairs Council. Operating companies include Harrah's Casinos, Rio All Suite Hotel & Casino, Showboat, and Harvey's Casinos. Merged with Caesars Entertainment, Inc. (see separate listing) in 2005.
www.harrahs.com

Chairman of the Board, President and Chief Exec. Officer
LOVEMAN, Gary
Tel: (702) 407 - 6000

Main Headquarters
Mailing: P.O. Box 98905
Las Vegas, NV 89193-8905
Tel: (702) 407 - 6000
Street: One Harrahs Ct.
Las Vegas, NV 89119-4312

Political Action Committees

Harrah's Entertainment, Inc. Employees' Political Action Committee
Contact: Courtney Sieluff
P.O. Box 98905
Las Vegas, NV 89193-8905
Tel: (702) 407 - 6000

Contributions to Candidates: $56,293 (01/05 - 09/05)
Democrats: $33,293; Republicans: $23,000.

Principal Recipients

SENATE DEMOCRATS		HOUSE DEMOCRATS	
Lautenberg, Frank (NJ)	$2,500	Berkley, Shelley (NV)	$5,000
		Hoyer, Steny (MD)	$5,000
		Menendez, Robert (NJ)	$5,000
		Sires, Albio (NJ)	$5,000
		Payne, Donald (NJ)	$3,000
		Thompson, Bennie (MS)	$2,793
Ensign, John Eric (NV)	$5,000	**HOUSE OTHER**	
Kean, Thomas (NJ)	$5,000	Lobiondo, Frank (NJ)	$5,000
		Porter, Jon (NV)	$5,000

Corporate Foundations and Giving Programs

Harrah's Entertainment Corporate Giving Program
Contact: Jan Jones
P.O. Box 98905
Las Vegas, NV 89193-8905
Tel: (702) 407 - 6387
Fax: (702) 407 - 6388

Annual Grant Total: none reported

Public Affairs and Related Activities Personnel

At Headquarters

ATWOOD, Charles L.
Senior V. President and Chief Financial Officer
catwood@harrahs.com
Responsibilities include investor relations.
Tel: (702) 407 - 6000
Fax: (702) 407 - 6311

BATJER, Marybel
V. President, Public Policy and Communications (Harrah's Operating Co., Inc.)
Tel: (702) 407 - 6000

JONES, Jan
Senior V. President, Communications and Government Relations
Tel: (702) 407 - 6387
Fax: (702) 407 - 6388

SIELUFF, Courtney
PAC Treasurer
Tel: (702) 407 - 6000

STROW, David
Assistant Director, Communications
dstrow@harrahs.com
Tel: (702) 407 - 6000
Fax: (702) 407 - 6530

At Other Offices

HESTERMANN, Dean
Government Relations
1023 Cherry Rd.
Memphis, TN 38117
dhesterman@harrahs.com
Tel: (901) 762 - 8787
Fax: (901) 762 - 8914

Harrah's Operating Co., Inc.

See listing on page 233 under Harrah's Entertainment, Inc.

Harris Bank

A subsidiary of Harris Bankcorp, Inc.
www.harrisbank.com

Chairman of the Board
GALLOWAY, David A.
Tel: (312) 461 - 2121
Fax: (312) 461 - 6640

President and Chief Exec. Officer
TECHAR, Frank J.
Tel: (312) 461 - 3500
Fax: (312) 461 - 6640

Main Headquarters
Mailing: 111 W. Monroe St.
Chicago, IL 60603-4095
Tel: (312) 461 - 2121
Fax: (312) 461 - 6640

Political Action Committees

Harris Government Affairs Fund
Contact: Paul Reagan
111 W. Monroe St.
Chicago, IL 60603-4095
Tel: (312) 461 - 3167

Contributions to Candidates: none reported (01/05 - 09/05)

Corporate Foundations and Giving Programs

Harris Bank Foundation
Contact: Mary Houpt
111 W. Monroe St.
Chicago, IL 60603-4095
Tel: (312) 461 - 6661
Fax: (312) 461 - 4702

Annual Grant Total: $2,000,000 - $5,000,000
The Foundation considers proposals from nonprofit, tax-exempt organizations, including United Way agencies, based on their merits. Giving is concentrated in the North Lawndale neighborhood of Chicago. Focuses on programs providing direct services in the primary interest areas listed.
Geographic Preference: Area in which the company is headquartered
Primary Interests: Education; Employment; Housing

Public Affairs and Related Activities Personnel

At Headquarters

COFFEY, Robin S.
Senior V. President
Responsibilities include community affairs.
Tel: (312) 461 - 2242
Fax: (312) 461 - 6114

HOUPT, Mary
V. President, Community Affairs
Responsibilities include corporate philanthropy.
Tel: (312) 461 - 6661
Fax: (312) 461 - 4702

LOWE, Michael B.
Executive V. President, Human Resources
Tel: (312) 461 - 2121
Fax: (312) 461 - 6640

MATTERN, John M.
V. President
Responsibilities include government relations.
Tel: (312) 461 - 3295
Fax: (312) 293 - 5811

PLEWS, Andy
V. President, Corporate Communications
Tel: (312) 461 - 6623
Fax: (312) 461 - 7869

REAGAN, Paul
Contact, Harris Government Affairs Fund
Tel: (312) 461 - 3167

TONGE, Charles R.
Exec. V. President, Community Banks
Tel: (312) 461 - 3911
Fax: (312) 461 - 5454

Harris Corp.

A communications equipment company.
www.harris.com

Chairman, President and Chief Exec. Officer
LANCE, Howard L.
Tel: (321) 727 - 9100
Fax: (321) 727 - 9646
TF: (800) 442 - 7747

Main Headquarters
Mailing: 1025 W. NASA Blvd.
Melbourne, FL 32919-0001
Tel: (321) 727 - 9100
Fax: (321) 727 - 9646
TF: (800) 442 - 7747

Washington Office
Contact: Raymon M. White, Jr.
Mailing: 1201 E. Abingdon Dr.
Suite 300
Alexandria, VA 22314
Tel: (703) 739 - 1946
Fax: (703) 739 - 2775

Political Action Committees

Harris Corp. Federal PAC
Contact: David S. Wasserman
1025 W. NASA Blvd.
Melbourne, FL 32919-0001
Tel: (321) 727 - 9194
Fax: (321) 727 - 9344
TF: (800) 442 - 7747

Harris Corp.

* continued from previous page

Contributions to Candidates: $48,000 (01/05 - 09/05)
Democrats: $1,000; Republicans: $47,000.

Principal Recipients

SENATE DEMOCRATS		HOUSE DEMOCRATS	
Nelson, Bill (FL)	$1,000		
SENATE REPUBLICANS		**HOUSE REPUBLICANS**	
Harris, Katherine (FL)	$5,000	Bonilla, Henry (TX)	$5,000
		Foley, Mark (FL)	$5,000
		Lewis, Jerry (CA)	$5,000
		Mica, John (FL)	$5,000
		Oxley, Michael (OH)	$5,000
		Reynolds, Thomas (NY)	$5,000
		Tiahrt, Todd W. (KS)	$5,000
		Weldon, David (FL)	$5,000

Corporate Foundations and Giving Programs

Harris Corp. Foundation
Contact: Nick E. Heldreth
1025 W. NASA Blvd. Tel: (321) 727 - 9314
Melbourne, FL 32919-0001 Fax: (321) 727 - 9344
TF: (800) 442 - 7747

Annual Grant Total: $750,000 - $1,000,000
Foundation giving is made through gift matching employee contributions to accredited colleges and universities that grant degrees, secondary schools that grant diplomas, and a limited number of local charitable, cultural and civic organizations that have been approved by the Board of Trustees.
Geographic Preference: Area(s) in which the company operates
Primary Interests: Higher Education
Recent Recipients: Florida State University; Georgia Tech.

Public Affairs and Related Activities Personnel

At Headquarters

HAUSMAN, Tom Tel: (321) 727 - 9131
Director, Media and Public Relations Fax: (321) 727 - 9646
thausm01@harris.com TF: (800) 442 - 7747

HELDRETH, Nick E. Tel: (321) 727 - 9314
V. President, Corporate Relations and Human Resources; Fax: (321) 727 - 9344
Secretary, Harris Corp. Foundation TF: (800) 442 - 7747

PADGETT, Pamela Tel: (321) 727 - 9383
V. President, Investor Relations Fax: (321) 727 - 9222
TF: (800) 442 - 7747

WASSERMAN, David S. Tel: (321) 727 - 9194
V. President and Treasurer; PAC Treasurer Fax: (321) 727 - 9344
dwasserman@harris.com TF: (800) 442 - 7747
Responsibilities include regulatory affairs.

At Washington Office

HALL, Joseph M. Tel: (703) 739 - 1937
V. President, Congressional Relations Fax: (703) 739 - 2775
jhall04@harris.com
Registered Federal Lobbyist.

HANNA, Tania Tel: (703) 739 - 1946
Director, Government Relations Fax: (703) 739 - 2775

POMEROY, Jill Tel: (703) 739 - 1946
Manager, Government Relations Fax: (703) 739 - 2775
jpomeroy@harris.com

WHITE, Raymon M., Jr. Tel: (703) 739 - 1937
V. President, Washington Operations Fax: (703) 739 - 2775
rwhite@harris.com
Registered Federal Lobbyist.

Harsco Corp.

A diversified industrial services and products company serving strategic worldwide industries, including steel, gas and energy, and infrastructure development.
www.harsco.com
Annual Revenues: $2.1 billion

Chairman, President and Chief Exec. Officer Tel: (717) 763 - 7064
HATHAWAY, Derek C. Fax: (717) 763 - 6424
dhathaway@harsco.com

Main Headquarters
Mailing: P.O. Box 8888 Tel: (717) 763 - 7064
Camp Hill, PA 17001-8888 Fax: (717) 763 - 6424
Street: 350 Poplar Church Rd.
Camp Hill, PA 17011

Political Action Committees

Harsco Corp. Political Action Committee (HARSCOPAC)
Contact: Stephen E. Barney
350 Popular Church Rd Tel: (717) 763 - 7064
Camp Hill, PA 17011 Fax: (717) 763 - 6424

Contributions to Candidates: $1,000 (01/05 - 09/05)
Republicans: $1,000.

Principal Recipients

SENATE REPUBLICANS		HOUSE REPUBLICANS
Santorum, Richard (PA)	$1,000	

Corporate Foundations and Giving Programs

Harsco Corporation Fund
Contact: Robert G. Yocum
P.O. Box 8888 Tel: (717) 763 - 7064
Camp Hill, PA 17001-8888 Fax: (717) 763 - 6424

Annual Grant Total: $1,000,000 - $2,000,000
Primary Interests: Education; Social Services
Recent Recipients: Nat'l Merit Scholarship; United Way

Public Affairs and Related Activities Personnel

At Headquarters

FAZZOLARI, Salvatore D. Tel: (717) 763 - 7064
Senior V. President and Treasurer Fax: (717) 763 - 6424

JULIAN, Ken D. Tel: (717) 763 - 7064
Director, Corporate Communications Fax: (717) 763 - 6402
kjulian@harsco.com

SWANGER, Russel S., Jr. Tel: (717) 763 - 7064
Senior Counsel and Director, Government Affairs Fax: (717) 763 - 6424

TRUETT, Eugene M. Tel: (717) 763 - 5677
Director, Investor Relations, Credit and Specialized Finance Fax: (717) 763 - 6402
etruett@harsco.com

YOCUM, Robert G. Tel: (717) 763 - 7064
Assistant Treasurer and Chairman, Harsco Corp. Fund Fax: (717) 763 - 6424
ryocum@harsco.com

At Other Offices

BARNEY, Stephen E. Tel: (717) 763 - 7064
Pac Treasurer Fax: (717) 763 - 6424
350 Popular Church Rd
Camp Hill, PA 17011

Harte-Hanks, Inc.

A nationwide communications company with subsidiaries involved in newspaper publishing, television, advertising publications and direct marketing.
www.harte-hanks.com

Chairman of the Board Tel: (210) 829 - 9000
FRANKLIN, Larry Fax: (210) 829 - 9403

President and Chief Exec. Officer Tel: (210) 829 - 9000
HOCHHAUSER, Richard M. Fax: (210) 829 - 9403

Main Headquarters
Mailing: P.O. Box 269 Tel: (210) 829 - 9000
San Antonio, TX 78291 Fax: (210) 829 - 9403
Street: Harte-Hanks Tower
200 Concord Plaza Dr., Suite 800
San Antonio, TX 78216

Corporate Foundations and Giving Programs

Harte-Hanks, Inc. Contributions
Contact: Larry Franklin
P.O. Box 269 Tel: (210) 829 - 9000
San Antonio, TX 78291 Fax: (210) 829 - 9403

Annual Grant Total: none reported

Harte-Hanks Media Development Foundation
Contact: Larry Franklin
P.O. Box 269 Tel: (210) 829 - 9000
San Antonio, TX 78291 Fax: (210) 829 - 9403

Annual Grant Total: under $100,000
Primary Interests: Civic and Public Affairs; Health; Religion; Social Services
Recent Recipients: American Press Institute; Big Brothers/Big Sisters

Public Affairs and Related Activities Personnel

At Headquarters

VAN PELT, Nessa Tel: (210) 829 - 9000
Administrative Assistant Fax: (210) 829 - 9403
Responsibilities include public affairs.

The Hartford Financial Services Group Inc.

A member of the Public Affairs Council. Formerly ITT Hartford Insurance Group. An insurance and financial services company.
www.thehartford.com

Chairman and Chief Exec. Officer Tel: (860) 547 - 5000
AYER, Ramani Fax: (860) 547 - 3799
rayer@thehartford.com

Main Headquarters
Mailing: Hartford Plaza Tel: (860) 547 - 5000
Hartford, CT 06115 Fax: (860) 547 - 3799

The Hartford Financial Services Group Inc.

* continued from previous page

Washington Office

Contact: Eric Thompson

Mailing: 1101 Connecticut Ave. NW, Suite 401, Washington, DC 20036 — Tel: (202) 296 - 7513, Fax: (202) 296 - 7514

Political Action Committees

Hartford Financial Services Group Inc. Advocates Fund
Contact: Robert Price
Hartford Plaza
Hartford, CT 06115 — Tel: (860) 547 - 5000, Fax: (860) 547 - 3799

Contributions to Candidates: $71,500 (01/05 - 09/05)
Democrats: $32,000; Republicans: $39,500.

Principal Recipients

SENATE DEMOCRATS

Lieberman, Joe (CT)	$9,000
Carper, Thomas R (DE)	$4,500
Nelson, Benjamin (NE)	$3,500
Conrad, Kent (ND)	$2,500

HOUSE DEMOCRATS

Larson, John B (CT)	$5,000

SENATE REPUBLICANS

Mcgavick, Michael Sean (WA)	$5,000
Kyl, Jon L (AZ)	$3,000
Santorum, Richard (PA)	$3,000
Talent, James (MO)	$2,000

HOUSE REPUBLICANS

Johnson, Nancy (CT)	$5,000
Shays, Christopher (CT)	$3,000
Baker, Hugh (LA)	$2,500
Cannon, Christopher (UT)	$2,000
Davis, Geoffrey (KY)	$2,000
Gerlach, Jim (PA)	$2,000
Price, Thomas (GA)	$2,000
Renzi, Richard (AZ)	$2,000

Corporate Foundations and Giving Programs

Hartford Financial Services Group Inc. Corporate Contributions
Contact: Lynda Godkin
Hartford Plaza
Hartford, CT 06115 — Tel: (860) 547 - 4993, Fax: (860) 547 - 6393

Annual Grant Total: $2,000,000 - $5,000,000
Geographic Preference: Area in which the company is headquartered; Area(s) in which the company operates

Public Affairs and Related Activities Personnel

At Headquarters

BENNETT, Naisha — Tel: (860) 547 - 8543, Fax: (860) 547 - 6393
State and Community Relations Coordinator

CLAPP, Carol — Tel: (860) 547 - 2944, Fax: (860) 547 - 6551
V. President, Government Affairs
Mailstop: HO-1-11
cclapp@thehartford.com

DE RAISMES, Ann M. — Tel: (860) 547 - 5000, Fax: (860) 547 - 3799
Exec. V. President, Human Resources

FREEDMAN, Joel — Tel: (860) 547 - 5480, Fax: (860) 547 - 6551
Senior V. President and Director, Government Affairs
Mailstop: HO-1-11
jfreedman@thehartford.com

GODKIN, Lynda — Tel: (860) 547 - 4993, Fax: (860) 547 - 6393
Senior V. President, State and Community Relations
Mailstop: T-12-56
lynda.godkin@thehartford.com
Responsibilities include corporate philanthropy.

KING, Joshua — Tel: (860) 547 - 2293, Fax: (860) 547 - 3799
V. President, Media Relations

PRICE, Robert — Tel: (860) 547 - 5000, Fax: (860) 547 - 3799
PAC Treasurer

WELSH, Walter — Tel: (860) 843 - 6453, Fax: (860) 843 - 6958
Senior V. President and Director, Government Affairs
walter.welsh@hartfordlife.com

YASS, Robert K. "Bob" — Tel: (860) 547 - 4963, Fax: (860) 547 - 6551
V. President, Government Affairs
Mailstop: HO 1-11
ryass@thehartford.com

At Washington Office

CAIN, David — Tel: (202) 296 - 7513, Fax: (202) 296 - 7514
Registered Federal Lobbyist.

DONOVAN, Laura — Tel: (202) 296 - 7513, Fax: (202) 296 - 7514
Director, Federal Affairs
laura.donovan@thehartford.com
Registered Federal Lobbyist.

RABITEAU, Marsha — Tel: (202) 296 - 7513, Fax: (202) 296 - 7514
Registered Federal Lobbyist.

THOMPSON, Eric — Tel: (202) 296 - 7513, Fax: (202) 296 - 7514
V. President, Federal Affairs
ethompson@thehartford.com
Registered Federal Lobbyist.

At Other Offices

FRY, Amy M. — Tel: (860) 843 - 8820, Fax: (860) 843 - 3390
V. President, Corporate Relations/Life
2000 Hopmeadow
Simsbury, CT 06079

Hartford Steam Boiler Inspection and Insurance Co.

A property and casualty insurance and engineering company. A wholly-owned subsidiary of American Internat'l Group (see separate listing).
www.hsb.com

President and Chief Exec. Officer — Tel: (860) 722 - 1866
BOOTH, Richard H.
richard_booth@hsb.com

Main Headquarters

Mailing: One State St., Hartford, CT 06103 — Tel: (860) 722 - 1866, Fax: (860) 722 - 5106

Corporate Foundations and Giving Programs

Hartford Steam Boiler Inspection & Insurance Co. Giving Program
One State St.
Hartford, CT 06103 — Tel: (860) 722 - 1866, Fax: (860) 722 - 5106

Annual Grant Total: $500,000 - $750,000
Employees' qualifying gifts up to $3,000 are matched dollar for dollar.
Geographic Preference: Area in which the company is headquartered
Primary Interests: Arts and Humanities; Education; Health

Public Affairs and Related Activities Personnel

At Headquarters

AHRENS, Susan W. — Tel: (860) 722 - 1866, Fax: (860) 722 - 5106
V. President, Human Resources

MILEWSKI, Dennis — Tel: (860) 722 - 5567
Manager, Media Relations
dennis_milewski@hsb.com

O'SHEA, Denis — Tel: (860) 722 - 5313, Fax: (860) 722 - 5106
V. President, Communications
denis_o'shea@hsb.com

Hartmarx

A manufacturer of men's and women's clothing.
www.hartmarx.com

Chairman and Chief Exec. Officer — Tel: (312) 372 - 5200, Fax: (312) 444 - 2710
PATEL, Hami B.

Main Headquarters

Mailing: 101 N. Wacker Dr., Chicago, IL 60606 — Tel: (312) 372 - 6300, Fax: (312) 444 - 2710

Political Action Committees

Hartmarx Corp. Government Relations Fund
101 N. Wacker Dr.
Chicago, IL 60606 — Tel: (312) 372 - 6300, Fax: (312) 444 - 2710

Contributions to Candidates: none reported (01/05 - 09/05)

Corporate Foundations and Giving Programs

Hartmarx Charitable Foundation
Contact: Kay C. Nalbach
101 N. Wacker Dr.
Chicago, IL 60606 — Tel: (312) 357 - 5331, Fax: (312) 444 - 2710

Annual Grant Total: $300,000 - $400,000
Geographic Preference: Area in which the company is headquartered; Area(s) in which the company operates
Primary Interests: Civic and Cultural Activities; Higher Education
Recent Recipients: Junior Achievement; Northwestern University

Public Affairs and Related Activities Personnel

At Headquarters

NALBACH, Kay C. — Tel: (312) 357 - 5331, Fax: (312) 444 - 2710
President, Hartmarx Charitable Foundation
knalbach@hartmarx.com

Hasbro Games

See listing on page 236 under Hasbro Inc.

Hasbro Inc.

A designer, manufacturer and marketer of games and toys ranging from traditional to high-tech. Brands include Playskool, Kenner, Tonka, Oddzon, Super Soaker, Milton Bradley, Parker Brothers, Tiger, Hasbro Interactive, Microporse, Galloob and Wizards of the Coast.

www.hasbro.com

Chairman of the Board
HASSENFELD, Alan G.
Tel: (401) 431 - 8697
Fax: (401) 431 - 8535

President and Chief Exec. Officer
VERRECCHIA, Alfred J.
Tel: (401) 431 - 8697
Fax: (401) 431 - 8535

Main Headquarters
Mailing: P.O. Box 1059
Pawtucket, RI 02862
Tel: (401) 431 - 8697
Fax: (401) 431 - 8535
Street: 1027 Newport Ave.
Pawtucket, RI 02862

Corporate Foundations and Giving Programs

Hasbro Children's Foundation
Contact: Jane S. Englebardt
P.O. Box 1059
Pawtucket, RI 02862
Tel: (401) 606 - 6226
Fax: (401) 431 - 8535

Annual Grant Total: $2,000,000 - $5,000,000
Geographic Preference: National
Primary Interests: Child Abuse and Neglect Prevention; Children's Health; Education; Youth Services
Recent Recipients: Children's Aid Society; Johns Hopkins Medical Center

Hasbro Charitable Trust
Contact: Karen M. Davis
P.O. Box 1059
Pawtucket, RI 02862
Tel: (401) 727 - 5429
Fax: (401) 431 - 8535

Annual Grant Total: $500,000 - $750,000
Geographic Preference: Area(s) in which the company operates; Rhode Island
Primary Interests: Education; Human Welfare
Recent Recipients: United Way

Public Affairs and Related Activities Personnel

At Headquarters

CARNIAUX, Robert
Senior V. President, Human Resources
Tel: (401) 727 - 5654
Fax: (401) 431 - 8535

CARVELLI, Gail
Manager, Media Relations
gcarvelli@hasbro.com
Tel: (401) 727 - 5318
Fax: (401) 431 - 8535

CHARNESS, Wayne S.
Senior V. President, Corporate Communications
wcharness@hasbro.com
Tel: (401) 727 - 5983
Fax: (401) 431 - 8535

DAVIS, Karen M.
Director, Hasbro Charitable Trust
kdavis@hasbro.com
Tel: (401) 727 - 5429
Fax: (401) 431 - 8535

DESIMONE, Audrey
Manager, Corporate Communications
adesimone@hasbro.com
Tel: (401) 727 - 5857
Fax: (401) 431 - 8535

ENGLEBARDT, Jane S.
Exec. Director, Hasbro Children's Foundation
Tel: (401) 606 - 6226
Fax: (401) 431 - 8535

SERBY, Gary
V. President, Public Relations
gserby@hasbro.com
Tel: (401) 727 - 5582
Fax: (401) 431 - 8535

WARREN, Karen A.
Senior V. President, Investor Relations
kwarren@hasbro.com
Tel: (401) 727 - 5401
Fax: (401) 431 - 8535

At Other Offices

MORRIS, Mark E.
Director, Public Relations
(Hasbro Games)
443 Shaker Rd.
East Longmeadow, MA 01028-3101
mmorris@hasbro.com
Tel: (413) 525 - 6411
Fax: (413) 525 - 4365

Hawaiian Electric Co., Inc.

See listing on page 236 under Hawaiian Electric Industries, Inc.

Hawaiian Electric Industries, Inc.

www.hei.com

Chairman, President and Chief Exec. Officer
CLARKE, Robert F.
Tel: (808) 543 - 5662
Fax: (808) 543 - 7966

Main Headquarters
Mailing: P.O. Box 730
Honolulu, HI 96808-0730
Tel: (808) 543 - 5662
Fax: (808) 543 - 7966
Street: 900 Richards St.
Honolulu, HI 96813

Corporate Foundations and Giving Programs

Hawaiian Electric Industries Charitable Foundation
Contact: Alan Yamamoto
P.O. Box 730
Honolulu, HI 96808-0730
Tel: (808) 543 - 5662
Fax: (808) 543 - 7966

Annual Grant Total: $1,000,000 - $2,000,000
Geographic Preference: Hawaii
Primary Interests: Community Development; Education; Environment/Conservation; Families; United Way Campaigns
Recent Recipients: American Cancer Society; Nature Conservancy

Public Affairs and Related Activities Personnel

At Headquarters

CHANG, Andy
V. President, Government Relations
Tel: (808) 543 - 5662
Fax: (808) 543 - 7966

HOLLINGER, Suzy A.P.
Manager, Investor Relations
shollinger@hei.com
Tel: (808) 543 - 7385
Fax: (808) 543 - 7966

YAMAMOTO, Alan
Director, Community Relations
atyamamoto@hei.com
Tel: (808) 543 - 5662
Fax: (808) 543 - 7966

At Other Offices

ALM, Robert
Senior V. President, Public Affairs
(Hawaiian Electric Co., Inc.)
P.O. Box 2750
Honolulu, HI 96840-0001
robert.alm@heco.com

UNEMORI, Lynne
Director, Corporate Communications
(Hawaiian Electric Co., Inc.)
P.O. Box 2750
Honolulu, HI 96840-0001
lynne.unemori@heco.com
Tel: (808) 543 - 7972
Fax: (808) 543 - 7790

Hawaiian Holdings, Inc.

www.hawaiianair.com

Chairman of the Board
HERSHFIELD, Lawrence S.
Tel: (808) 835 - 3700
Fax: (808) 835 - 6735

Chief Exec. Officer
DUNKERLEY, Mark
Tel: (808) 835 - 3700
Fax: (808) 835 - 3690

Main Headquarters
Mailing: P.O. Box 30008
Honolulu, HI 96820
Tel: (808) 835 - 3700
Fax: (808) 835 - 3690
Street: 3375 Koapaka St., Suite G350
Honolulu, HI 96819

Public Affairs and Related Activities Personnel

At Headquarters

JENSO, Randall L.
Treasurer and Secretary
Tel: (808) 835 - 3700
Fax: (808) 835 - 3690

NAKANELUA-RICHARDS, Debbie
Senior Manager, Government and Community Relations
Tel: (808) 835 - 3700
Fax: (808) 838 - 6746

WAGNER, Keoni
V. President, Corporate Communications
Tel: (808) 838 - 6778
Fax: (808) 840 - 8213

Haworth Inc.

A private manufacturer of office furniture.

www.haworth.com

Chairman of the Board
HAWORTH, Richard G.
Tel: (616) 393 - 1144
Fax: (616) 393 - 1570
TF: (800) 344 - 2600

President and Chief Exec. Officer
BIANCHI, Franco
Tel: (616) 393 - 3000
Fax: (616) 393 - 1570
TF: (800) 344 - 2600

Main Headquarters
Mailing: One Haworth Center
Holland, MI 49423
Tel: (616) 393 - 3000
Fax: (616) 393 - 1570
TF: (800) 344 - 2600

Corporate Foundations and Giving Programs

Haworth Corporate Contributions Program
Contact: Virginia Conklin
One Haworth Center
Holland, MI 49423
Tel: (616) 393 - 3551
Fax: (616) 393 - 1570
TF: (800) 344 - 2600

Annual Grant Total: none reported
Primary Interests: Education

Haworth Inc.

* continued from previous page

Public Affairs and Related Activities Personnel

At Headquarters

CONKLIN, Virginia
Exec. Assistant and Contributions Coordinator
Tel: (616) 393 - 3551
Fax: (616) 393 - 1570
TF: (800) 344 - 2600

MICKNA, Karl
Media Specialist
Tel: (616) 393 - 1865
Fax: (616) 393 - 1570
TF: (800) 344 - 2600

TEUTSCH, Nancy
V. President, Global Human Resources
Tel: (616) 393 - 1304
Fax: (616) 393 - 1570
TF: (800) 344 - 2600

WRAY, Susan
Manager, Public and Member Communications
Tel: (616) 393 - 1604
Fax: (616) 393 - 3138
TF: (800) 344 - 2600

Hayes Lemmerz Internat'l, Inc.

Designs, engineers and manufactures automotive parts.

www.hayes-lemmerz.com

Chairman, President, and Chief Exec. Officer
CLAWSON, Curtis J.
cclawson@hayes-lemmerz.com
Tel: (734) 737 - 5000
Fax: (734) 737 - 2198

Main Headquarters
Mailing: 15300 Centennial Dr.
Northville, MI 48168
Tel: (734) 737 - 5000
Fax: (734) 737 - 2198
TF: (800) 521 - 0515

Corporate Foundations and Giving Programs

Hayes Lemmerz Internat'l, Inc. Contributions
Contact: Marika Diamond
15300 Centennial Dr.
Northville, MI 48168
Tel: (734) 737 - 5162
Fax: (734) 737 - 2198

Annual Grant Total: none reported

Public Affairs and Related Activities Personnel

At Headquarters

DIAMOND, Marika
Director, Public Relations and Communications
Tel: (734) 737 - 5162
Fax: (734) 737 - 2198

Responsibilities include corporate philanthropy and investor relations.

HCA

A member of the Public Affairs Council. Owns and operates hospitals.

www.hcahealthcare.com

Chairman and Chief Exec. Officer
BOVENDER, Jack O.
Tel: (615) 344 - 9551
Fax: (615) 344 - 5722

Main Headquarters
Mailing: P.O. Box 550
Nashville, TN 37202
Street: One Park Plaza
Nashville, TN 37203
Tel: (615) 344 - 9551
Fax: (615) 344 - 5722

Political Action Committees

HCA Good Government Fund
Contact: David Anderson
P.O. Box 550
Nashville, TN 37202
Tel: (615) 344 - 9551
Fax: (615) 344 - 5722

Contributions to Candidates: $74,999 (01/05 - 09/05)
Democrats: $20,500; Republicans: $54,499.

Principal Recipients

SENATE DEMOCRATS		HOUSE DEMOCRATS	
Conrad, Kent (ND)	$4,000	Boyd, F Allen Jr (FL)	$2,500
Nelson, Benjamin (NE)	$4,000		
Bingaman, Jeff (NM)	$2,000		

SENATE REPUBLICANS		HOUSE REPUBLICANS	
Ensign, John Eric (NV)	$5,000	Norwood, Charles (GA)	$5,000
Snowe, Olympia (ME)	$4,000	Thomas, William M (CA)	$5,000
Burr, Richard (NC)	$2,500	Johnson, Nancy (CT)	$4,999
Hatch, Orrin (UT)	$2,500	Beauprez, Robert (CO)	$3,000
Vitter, David (LA)	$2,500	Gingrey, Phillip (GA)	$2,000
		Ryan, Paul D (WI)	$2,000
		Tiahrt, Todd W. (KS)	$2,000
		Wamp, Zach (TN)	$2,000

Corporate Foundations and Giving Programs

HCA Foundation
Contact: Lois Abrams
P.O. Box 550
Nashville, TN 37202
Tel: (615) 344 - 9551
Fax: (615) 344 - 5722

Annual Grant Total: over $5,000,000

Public Affairs and Related Activities Personnel

At Headquarters

ABRAMS, Lois
Administrative Coordinator, Foundation
Tel: (615) 344 - 9551
Fax: (615) 344 - 5722

ANDERSON, David
PAC Treasurer
Tel: (615) 344 - 9551
Fax: (615) 344 - 5722

BROOKS, Pat
Legislative Analyst
patricia.brooks@hcahealthcare.com
Tel: (615) 344 - 2527
Fax: (615) 344 - 1128

CRITCHLOW, David
Director, Government Relations
david.critchlow@hcahealthcare.com
Tel: (615) 344 - 2791
Fax: (615) 344 - 1128

GRAYSON, Jon
Director, Government Relations
jon.grayson@hcahealthcare.com
Tel: (615) 344 - 2709
Fax: (615) 344 - 1128

JOUSTRA, Jana
V. Preisdent, Communications
Tel: (615) 344 - 9551
Fax: (615) 344 - 5722

TUCKER, Debi
Manager, Government Relations
debi.tucker@hcahealthcare.com
Tel: (615) 963 - 3830
Fax: (615) 963 - 3841

At Other Offices

SHERRILL, Parker
Consultant, Government Relations
310 25th Ave. North, Suite 101
Nashville, TN 37203
parker.sherrill@hcahealthcare.com
Tel: (615) 320 - 9028
Fax: (615) 963 - 3841

TARDY, Warren
Consultant, Government Relations
310 25th Ave. North
Suite 101
Nashville, TN 37203
warren.tardy@hcahealthcare.com
Tel: (615) 320 - 8797
Fax: (615) 963 - 3841

Health Care and Retirement Corp. (HCR)

See listing on page 303 under Manor Care, Inc.

Health Care Service Corp.

Parent company of Blue Cross and Blue Shield of Illinois.

www.hcsc.net

President and Chief Exec. Officer
MCCASKEY, Raymond
mccaskeyr@bcbsil.com
Tel: (312) 653 - 6000
Fax: (312) 819 - 1220

Main Headquarters
Mailing: 300 E. Randolph St.
Chicago, IL 60601
Tel: (312) 653 - 6000
Fax: (312) 819 - 1220

Political Action Committees

Blue Cross and Blue Shield of Illinois PAC
Contact: Brian Van Vlierbergen
300 E. Randolph St.
Chicago, IL 60601
Tel: (312) 653 - 6000
Fax: (312) 819 - 1220

Contributions to Candidates: none reported (01/05 - 09/05)

Public Affairs and Related Activities Personnel

At Headquarters

KIECKHEFER, Robert
V. President, Public Affairs
Tel: (312) 653 - 6629
Fax: (312) 819 - 1220

O'CONNOR, Patrick
Senior V. President, Human Resources Business
Tel: (312) 653 - 6000
Fax: (312) 819 - 1220

VAN VLIERBERGEN, Brian
PAC Treasurer
(Blue Cross and Blue Shield of Illinois)
Tel: (312) 653 - 6000
Fax: (312) 819 - 1220

Health Management Associates, Inc.

Provides general acute care health services in rural communities.

www.hma-corp.com
Annual Revenues: $2.6 billion

Chairman of the Board
SCHOEN, William J.
Tel: (239) 598 - 3175
Fax: (239) 596 - 1426

Health Management Associates, Inc.

** continued from previous page*

President and Chief Exec. Officer
VUMBACCO, Joseph V. — Tel: (239) 597 - 7161; Fax: (239) 597 - 5794

Main Headquarters
Mailing: 5811 Pelican Bay Blvd., Suite 500, Naples, FL 34108-2710 — Tel: (239) 598 - 3131; Fax: (239) 598 - 2705

Public Affairs and Related Activities Personnel

At Headquarters

DROW, Frederick L. — Tel: (239) 598 - 3133; Fax: (239) 597 - 5794
Senior V. President, Human Resources

MERRIWETHER, John C. — Tel: (239) 598 - 3104; Fax: (239) 597 - 5794
V. President, Financial Relations
John.Merriwether@hma.com
Responsibilities include investor relations and corporate communications.

Health Net, Inc.

A member of the Public Affairs Council. Formerly Foundation Health Systems, Inc., the company is a national managed health care organization.
www.healthnet.com

Chairman of the Board
GREAVES, Roger F. — Tel: (818) 676 - 6000; Fax: (818) 676 - 8591; TF: (800) 291 - 6911

President and Chief Exec. Officer
GELLERT, Jay M. — Tel: (818) 676 - 6000; Fax: (818) 676 - 6616; TF: (800) 474 - 6676
jay.m.gellert@healthnet.com

Main Headquarters
Mailing: 21650 Oxnard St., Woodland Hills, CA 91367 — Tel: (818) 676 - 6000; Fax: (818) 676 - 8591; TF: (800) 291 - 6911

Washington Office
Mailing: 2107 Wilson Blvd., Arlington, VA 22201 — Tel: (571) 227 - 6561; Fax: (571) 227 - 6709

Political Action Committees

Health Net Inc. PAC
Contact: Adrienne B. Morrell
2107 Wilson Blvd.
Arlington, VA 22201 — Tel: (571) 227 - 6561; Fax: (571) 227 - 6709

Contributions to Candidates: $27,500 (01/05 - 09/05)
Democrats: $12,000; Republicans: $15,500.

Principal Recipients

SENATE DEMOCRATS		HOUSE DEMOCRATS	
Lieberman, Joe (CT)	$3,000	Murtha, John P Mr. (PA)	$2,500
Clinton, Hillary Rodham (NY)	$2,000	Moran, James (VA)	$2,000
Nelson, Benjamin (NE)	$1,000	Matsui, Doris (CA)	$1,000

SENATE REPUBLICANS		HOUSE REPUBLICANS	
Kyl, Jon L (AZ)	$1,000	Hastert, Dennis J. (IL)	$5,000
		Johnson, Nancy (CT)	$4,000
		Deal, Nathan (GA)	$1,500
		Ferguson, Mike (NJ)	$1,000
		Northup, Anne M. (KY)	$1,000
		Pryce, Deborah (OH)	$1,000
		Simmons, Rob (CT)	$1,000

Public Affairs and Related Activities Personnel

At Headquarters

OLSON, David W. — Tel: (818) 676 - 6978; Fax: (818) 676 - 8591; TF: (800) 474 - 6676
Senior V. President, Corporate Communications
david.w.olson@healthnet.com

At Washington Office

MORRELL, Adrienne B. — Tel: (571) 227 - 6561; Fax: (571) 227 - 6709
V. President, Government Relations; Contact Health Net Inc. PAC
adrienne.b.morrell@healthnet.com

HealthCare Corp.

See listing on page 216 under Genesis HealthCare Corp.

HealthNow New York Inc.

The parent company of Blue Cross and Blue Shield of Western New York and Blue Cross and Blue Shield of North Eastern New York.
www.healthnowny.com

President and Chief Exec. Officer
O'NEIL-WHITE, Alphonso — Tel: (716) 887 - 6900; Fax: (716) 887 - 8981; TF: (888) 249 - 2583

Main Headquarters
Mailing: 1901 Main St., Buffalo, NY 14208-0080 — Tel: (716) 887 - 6900; Fax: (716) 887 - 8981; TF: (888) 249 - 2583

Public Affairs and Related Activities Personnel

At Headquarters

INGALLS, Donald R. — Tel: (716) 887 - 6900; Fax: (716) 887 - 8981; TF: (888) 249 - 2583
V. President, Government Affairs and Community Relations

MERKELLIBERTORE, Karen — Tel: (716) 887 - 6900 Ext: 8811; Fax: (716) 887 - 8981; TF: (888) 249 - 2583
Media Relations Contact

VOLPE, Ralph — Tel: (716) 887 - 6900; Fax: (716) 887 - 8981; TF: (888) 249 - 2583
V. President, Human Resources and Administrative Services

HealthSouth Corp.

Medical rehabilitation services.
www.healthsouth.com
Annual Revenues: $4.38 billion

Chairman of the Board
MAY, Robert P. — Tel: (205) 967 - 7116; Fax: (205) 969 - 6889; TF: (888) 476 - 8849

Chief Exec. Officer and President
GRINNEY, Jay — Tel: (205) 967 - 7116; Fax: (205) 969 - 6889; TF: (888) 476 - 8849

Main Headquarters
Mailing: One Healthsouth Pkwy., Birmingham, AL 35243 — Tel: (205) 967 - 7116; Fax: (205) 969 - 6889; TF: (888) 476 - 8849

Public Affairs and Related Activities Personnel

At Headquarters

GILMORE, Kristi — Tel: (205) 967 - 7116; Fax: (205) 969 - 6889; TF: (888) 476 - 8849
V. President, Corporate Public Relations
kristi.gilmore@healthsouth.com

MARKUS, John — Tel: (205) 967 - 7116; Fax: (205) 969 - 6889; TF: (888) 476 - 8849
Exec. V. President and Chief Compliance Officer
Responsibilities include government affairs.

WADE, Dennis — Tel: (205) 967 - 7116; Fax: (205) 969 - 6889; TF: (888) 476 - 8849
Group V. President, Human Resources
dennis.wade@healthsouth.com

The Hearst Corp.

A publisher of newspapers, magazines and books. Also active in radio and TV broadcasting and news service.
www.hearst.com
Annual Revenues: $3.4 billion

Chairman of the Board
HEARST, George R., Jr. — Tel: (212) 649 - 2000; Fax: (212) 765 - 3528

President and Chief Exec. Officer
GANZI, Victor F. — Tel: (212) 649 - 2103; Fax: (212) 246 - 3630

Main Headquarters
Mailing: 959 Eighth Ave., New York, NY 10019 — Tel: (212) 649 - 2000; Fax: (212) 765 - 3528

Corporate Foundations and Giving Programs

Hearst Foundation
959 Eighth Ave.
New York, NY 10019 — Tel: (212) 649 - 2000; Fax: (212) 765 - 3528

Annual Grant Total: none reported

Public Affairs and Related Activities Personnel

At Headquarters

CAMPO, Thomas W. — Tel: (212) 887 - 6827; Fax: (212) 765 - 3528
Director, Investor Relations

DIEM, Ruth — Tel: (212) 649 - 2000; Fax: (212) 765 - 3528
Senior V. President, Human Resources

LUTHRINGER, Paul — Tel: (212) 649 - 2000; Fax: (212) 765 - 3528
Exec. Director, Corporate Communications

SHRIVER, Debra — Tel: (212) 649 - 2461; Fax: (212) 765 - 3528
V. President and Chief Communications Officer

HEB Grocery Co.

Owns and operates a chain of grocery stores.

www.heb.com

Chairman and Chief Exec. Officer
BUTT, Charles C. — Tel: (210) 938 - 8000; Fax: (210) 938 - 8169
butt.charles@heb.com

Main Headquarters
Mailing: 646 S. Main Ave., San Antonio, TX 78204 — Tel: (210) 938 - 8000; Fax: (210) 938 - 8169

Corporate Foundations and Giving Programs

HEB Grocery Co. Corporate Contributions Program
646 S. Main Ave.
San Antonio, TX 78204 — Tel: (210) 938 - 8000; Fax: (210) 938 - 8169

Annual Grant Total: none reported

Public Affairs and Related Activities Personnel

At Headquarters

FLORES, Greg — Tel: (210) 938 - 8075; Fax: (210) 938 - 8169
Director, Legislative Affairs
flores.greg@heb.com

HERRON, Winnell — Tel: (210) 938 - 8000; Fax: (210) 938 - 8169
Group V. President, Public Affairs and Diversity
herron.winnell@heb.com

Hecla Mining Co.

A non-ferrous metal mining company.

www.hecla-mining.com

Chairman of the Board
BROWN, Arthur — Tel: (208) 769 - 4100; Fax: (208) 769 - 4107

President and Chief Exec. Officer
BAKER, Phillips S., Jr. — Tel: (208) 769 - 4100; Fax: (208) 769 - 7612

Main Headquarters
Mailing: 6500 N. Mineral Dr., Suite 200, Coeur d'Alene, ID 83815-9408 — Tel: (208) 769 - 4100; Fax: (208) 769 - 4107

Political Action Committees

Hecla Mining Co. Political Action Fund
Contact: Lewis Walde
6500 N. Mineral Dr., Suite 200
Coeur d'Alene, ID 83815-9408 — Tel: (208) 769 - 4100; Fax: (208) 769 - 4107

Contributions to Candidates: $500 (01/05 - 09/05)
Republicans: $500.

Principal Recipients

SENATE REPUBLICANS		HOUSE REPUBLICANS	
		McMorris, Cathy (WA)	$500

Public Affairs and Related Activities Personnel

At Headquarters

BUCKHAM, Robert H. — Tel: (208) 769 - 4100; Fax: (208) 769 - 4107
Director, Human Resources

GLADER, Paul — Tel: (208) 769 - 4100; Fax: (208) 769 - 4122
Manager, Environmental Services

VELTKAMP, Vicki — Tel: (208) 769 - 4100; Fax: (208) 769 - 7612
V. President, Investor and Public Relations

WALDE, Lewis — Tel: (208) 769 - 4100; Fax: (208) 769 - 4107
PAC Contact

Heineken USA Inc.

A member of the Public Affairs Council. A U.S. importer of European beer. A subsidiary of Heineken N.V. of Amsterdam, The Netherlands.

www.heineken.com/usa

President and Chief Exec. Officer
VAN DER MINNE, Frans — Tel: (914) 681 - 4111; Fax: (914) 681 - 1900

Main Headquarters
Mailing: 360 Hamilton Ave., Suite 1103, White Plains, NY 10601-1841 — Tel: (914) 681 - 4100; Fax: (914) 681 - 1900

Washington Office
Mailing: 1001 G St. NW, Suite 700 East, Washington, DC 20001 — Tel: (202) 737 - 5090; Fax: (202) 737 - 5095

Political Action Committees

Heineken USA Inc. Good Government Fund
Contact: T. Daniel Tearno
360 Hamilton Ave., Suite 1103
White Plains, NY 10601-1841 — Tel: (914) 681 - 4113; Fax: (914) 989 - 1003

Contributions to Candidates: $6,000 (01/05 - 09/05)
Democrats: $5,000; Republicans: $1,000.

Principal Recipients

SENATE DEMOCRATS		HOUSE DEMOCRATS	
Clinton, Hillary Rodham (NY)	$1,000	Christensen, Donna M (VI)	$1,000
Lieberman, Joe (CT)	$1,000	Cummings, Elijah (MD)	$1,000
		Payne, Donald (NJ)	$1,000
SENATE REPUBLICANS		**HOUSE REPUBLICANS**	
		Reynolds, Thomas (NY)	$1,000

Public Affairs and Related Activities Personnel

At Headquarters

ANCRUM, Charles — Tel: (914) 681 - 4100; Fax: (914) 681 - 1879
Manager, Industry and Government Affairs/Northeast
cancrum@heinekenusa.com

BARRIOS, Sergio — Tel: (914) 681 - 4100; Fax: (914) 681 - 1900; TF: (800) 801 - 4966
Manager, Industry and Government Affairs/West and Central
sbarrios@heinekenusa.com

LUCAS, Jamie — Tel: (914) 681 - 4114; Fax: (914) 989 - 1003
Director, Corporate Communications
jlucas@heinekenusa.com

MCFADDEN, Ernest — Tel: (914) 286 - 4757; Fax: (914) 286 - 4727; TF: (800) 811 - 4966
Manager, Industry and Government Affairs/Southeast
emcfadden@heinekenusa.com

TEARNO, T. Daniel — Tel: (914) 681 - 4113; Fax: (914) 989 - 1003
V. President, Corporate Affairs and Chairman, Heineken USA Good Government Fund
Also serves as the Washington Representative.

At Washington Office

COSGROVE, Suzanne — Tel: (202) 737 - 5090; Fax: (202) 737 - 5095
Manager, Corporate Responsibility
scosgrove@heinekenusa.com

H. J. Heinz Co.

A major food company.

www.heinz.com

Annual Revenues: $9.431 billion

Chairman, President and Chief Exec. Officer
JOHNSON, William R. — Tel: (412) 456 - 5700; Fax: (412) 456 - 6128

Main Headquarters
Mailing: P.O. Box 57, Pittsburgh, PA 15230-0057 — Tel: (412) 456 - 5700; Fax: (412) 456 - 6128
Street: 600 Grant St., Pittsburgh, PA 15219

Political Action Committees

H. J. Heinz Co. Political Action Committee
Contact: Leonard A. Cullo
P.O. Box 57
Pittsburgh, PA 15230-0057 — Tel: (412) 456 - 5700; Fax: (412) 456 - 6128

Contributions to Candidates: $16,500 (01/05 - 09/05)
Democrats: $2,000; Republicans: $14,500.

Principal Recipients

SENATE DEMOCRATS		HOUSE DEMOCRATS	
		Dingell, John D (MI)	$1,000
		Tierney, John (MA)	$1,000
SENATE REPUBLICANS		**HOUSE REPUBLICANS**	
Kennedy, Mark (MN)	$2,500	Murphy, Tim (PA)	$1,500
Kyl, Jon L (AZ)	$2,000	Hart, Melissa (PA)	$1,000
Talent, James (MO)	$1,500	Hayes, Robert (NC)	$1,000
Santorum, Richard (PA)	$1,000	Kirk, Mark Steven (IL)	$1,000
		Latham, Thomas P (IA)	$1,000
		McHugh, John (NY)	$1,000
		Shaw, Clay (FL)	$1,000

Corporate Foundations and Giving Programs

H. J. Heinz Co. Foundation

H. J. Heinz Co.

* continued from previous page

P.O. Box 57 Tel: (412) 456 - 5700
Pittsburgh, PA 15230-0057 Fax: (412) 456 - 6128

Assets: $754,271 (2000)
Annual Grant Total: $1,000,000 - $2,000,000
Contributions totalled over $6 million in 2000.
Geographic Preference: Area(s) in which the company operates
Primary Interests: Arts and Culture; Civic and Public Affairs; Education; Health and Human Services
Recent Recipients: America's Second Harvest; Pennsylvania Ass'n of Regional Food Banks; Reading is Fundamental; United Way

Public Affairs and Related Activities Personnel

At Headquarters

CAPONI, Catherine A. Tel: (412) 456 - 5700
V. President, Government Affairs and Economic Development Fax: (412) 456 - 6128

CULLO, Leonard A. Tel: (412) 456 - 5700
PAC Treasurer Fax: (412) 456 - 6128

FOSTER, Debora S. Tel: (412) 456 - 5778
V. President, Corporate Communications Fax: (412) 456 - 7883

RUNKEL, Jack Tel: (412) 456 - 6034
V. President, Investor Relations; Chairman, H. J. Heinz Co. Foundation Fax: (412) 456 - 6128

SMYTH, D. Edward I. "Ted" Tel: (412) 456 - 5780
Chief Administrative Officer; and Senior V. President, Corporate and Government Affairs Fax: (412) 456 - 6025
ted.smyth@hjheinz.com

STULL, Gail B. Tel: (412) 456 - 5782
Manager, On-Line Media Fax: (412) 456 - 7883
gail.stull@hjheinz.com

TEETS, Robin Tel: (412) 456 - 3562
Senior Manager, Communications, Heinz North America Fax: (412) 456 - 5776
robin.teets@hjheinz.com

Henkel Corp.

A producer of industrial chemicals and adhesives. A wholly-owned subsidiary of Henkel KGAA of Dusseldorf, West Germany.
www.henkelcorp.com

Main Headquarters
Mailing: 2200 Renaissance Blvd., Suite 200 Tel: (610) 270 - 8100
Gulph Mills, PA 19406-2755 Fax: (610) 270 - 8104

Corporate Foundations and Giving Programs

Henkel Corporate Contributions
Contact: William Read
2200 Renaissance Blvd., Suite 200 Tel: (610) 270 - 8100
Gulph Mills, PA 19406-2755 Fax: (610) 270 - 8104

Annual Grant Total: none reported

Public Affairs and Related Activities Personnel

At Headquarters

BRUNO, Mike Tel: (610) 571 - 5141
Corporate Communications Contact Fax: (610) 270 - 8104
michael.brown@henkel.com

CARR, Mary Tel: (610) 270 - 8100
Environmental Manager, Regulatory Affairs Fax: (610) 270 - 8104

DILEO, Mary Tel: (610) 571 - 5252
Corporate Communications Contact Fax: (610) 270 - 8104
mary.dileo@henkel.com

READ, William Tel: (610) 270 - 8100
V. President, Human Resources Fax: (610) 270 - 8104

At Other Offices

JACOBUS, Pattie Tel: (860) 571 - 5100
V. President, Corporate Communications
1001 Trout Brook Crossing
Rocky Hill, CT 06067
patti.jacobus@henkel.com

Henkels & McCoy, Inc.

Engaged in construction and maintenance of communications and energy utility lines.
www.henkels.com

Chairman of the Board Tel: (215) 283 - 7600
HENKELS, Paul M. Fax: (215) 283 - 7659

President and Chief Exec. Officer Tel: (215) 283 - 7600
HENKELS, T. Roderick Fax: (215) 283 - 7659

Main Headquarters
Mailing: 985 Jolly Rd. Tel: (215) 283 - 7600
Blue Bell, PA 19422-0900 Fax: (215) 283 - 7659

Public Affairs and Related Activities Personnel

At Headquarters

DEMARA, Paul Tel: (215) 283 - 7578
Manager, Corporate Communications and Marketing Fax: (215) 283 - 7659
pdemara@henkels.com
Responsibilities include media relations.

DILLAHUNTY, James M. Tel: (909) 451 - 2500
V. President, International Fax: (909) 451 - 2590

Henry Schein, Inc.

Distributes products and services to office-based healthcare practitioners.
www.henryschein.com

Chairman and Chief Exec. Officer Tel: (631) 843 - 5500
BERGMAN, Stanley M. Fax: (631) 843 - 5975

Main Headquarters
Mailing: 135 Duryea Rd. Tel: (631) 843 - 5500
Melville, NY 11747 Fax: (631) 843 - 5975

Public Affairs and Related Activities Personnel

At Headquarters

PALADINO, Steven Tel: (631) 843 - 5500
Exec. V. President and Chief Financial Officer Fax: (631) 843 - 5979

VASSALLO, Susan Tel: (631) 843 - 5611
Director, Corporate Communications Fax: (631) 843 - 5562
susan.vassallo@henryschein.com

Hercules Incorporated

A member of the Public Affairs Council. A manufacturer of chemical specialty products.
www.herc.com
Annual Revenues: $1.8 billion

Chairman of the Board Tel: (302) 594 - 5000
WULFF, John K. Fax: (302) 594 - 5400

President and Chief Exec. Officer Tel: (302) 594 - 5000
ROGERSON, Craig A. Fax: (302) 594 - 5400

Main Headquarters
Mailing: 1313 N. Market St. Tel: (302) 594 - 5000
Wilmington, DE 19894-0001 Fax: (302) 594 - 5400

Public Affairs and Related Activities Personnel

At Headquarters

CARRINGTON, Edward V. Tel: (302) 594 - 5000
V. President, Human Resources Fax: (302) 594 - 5400
ecarrington@herc.com

RILEY, John S. Tel: (302) 594 - 6025
Director, Public Affairs Fax: (302) 594 - 6909
jriley@herc.com

SPIZZO, Allen A. Tel: (302) 594 - 6491
V. Presidentand Chief Financial Officer Fax: (302) 594 - 5400
aspizzo@herc.com
Responsibilities include investor relations.

Herman Miller Inc.

A manufacturer of office furniture for industry, laboratory, healthcare, and industrial and residential environments.
www.hermanmiller.com
Annual Revenues: $1.34 billion

Chairman of the Board Tel: (616) 654 - 3000
VOLKEMA, Michael A. Fax: (616) 654 - 5234
michael_volkema@hermanmiller.com

President and Chief Exec. Officer Tel: (616) 654 - 3000
WALKER, Brian C. Fax: (616) 654 - 3632

Main Headquarters
Mailing: P.O. Box 302 Tel: (616) 654 - 3000
Zeeland, MI 49464-0302 Fax: (616) 654 - 5234
TF: (888) 443 - 4357

Street: 855 E. Main Ave.
Zeeland, MI 49464-0302

Public Affairs and Related Activities Personnel

At Headquarters

LOCK, Andrew Tel: (616) 654 - 3000
Senior V. President, Human Resources Fax: (616) 654 - 5234

MURRAY, Paul Tel: (616) 654 - 3000
Manager, Environmental Affairs Fax: (616) 654 - 5234
paul_murray@hermanmiller.com

Herman Miller Inc.

* continued from previous page

NOWICKI, Joe — Tel: (616) 654 - 3000
V. President, Investor Relations — Fax: (616) 654 - 3632

SCHURMAN, Mark W. — Tel: (616) 654 - 5498
Director, Corporate External Communications — Fax: (616) 654 - 5234
mark_schurman@hermanmiller.com

The Hershey Company

A member of the Public Affairs Council. Formerly known as Hershey Foods Corp. A manufacturer of chocolate and confectionery products.

www.hersheys.com
Annual Revenues: $4.5 billion

Chairman, President and Chief Exec. Officer
LENNY, Richard H. — Tel: (717) 534 - 4200; Fax: (717) 534 - 7015

Main Headquarters
Mailing: 100 Crystal A Dr.
P.O. Box 810
Hershey, PA 17033
Tel: (717) 534 - 4200; Fax: (717) 534 - 7015

Washington Office
Contact: Ronald P. Graf
Mailing: 601 Pennsylvania Ave. NW
Suite 900, South Bldg.
Washington, DC 20004
Tel: (202) 434 - 8278; Fax: (202) 434 - 8258

Political Action Committees

The Hershey Company PAC
Contact: Ronald P. Graf
601 Pennsylvania Ave. NW
Suite 900, South Bldg.
Washington, DC 20004
Tel: (202) 434 - 8278; Fax: (202) 434 - 8258

Contributions to Candidates: $9,000 (01/05 - 09/05)
Democrats: $1,000; Republicans: $8,000.

Principal Recipients

SENATE DEMOCRATS		HOUSE DEMOCRATS	
Ford, Harold E Jr (TN)	$1,000		
SENATE REPUBLICANS		**HOUSE REPUBLICANS**	
Santorum, Richard (PA)	$2,000	Gerlach, Jim (PA)	$1,000
Allen, George (VA)	$1,000	Kirk, Mark Steven (IL)	$1,000
Lugar, Richard G (IN)	$1,000	Shaw, Clay (FL)	$1,000
		Walsh, James T (NY)	$1,000

Corporate Foundations and Giving Programs

Hershey Foods Corporate Contributions
Contact: John C. Long
100 Crystal A Dr.
P.O. Box 810
Hershey, PA 17033
Tel: (717) 534 - 3237; Fax: (717) 534 - 7015

Annual Grant Total: $2,000,000 - $5,000,000
Total grants, excluding food donations but including Hershey Youth Program, exceed $2,000,000. Local institutions outside of Hershey, Lebanon, and Harrisburg, PA, who are seeking grants should contact local management of the corporation's installations.
Geographic Preference: Area(s) in which the company operates; Pennsylvania
Primary Interests: Arts and Culture; Civic and Public Affairs; Community Affairs; Environment/Conservation; Health and Human Services; Higher Education

Public Affairs and Related Activities Personnel

At Headquarters

ARLINE, Marcella K. — Tel: (717) 534 - 4380
Senior V. President and Chief People Officer — Fax: (717) 534 - 7015
marline@hersheys.com

EDRIS, James A. — Tel: (717) 534 - 7556
V. President, Investor Relations — Fax: (717) 534 - 7015
jedris@hersheys.com

HOGARTH, Judy — Tel: (717) 534 - 7631
Public Relations Contact — Fax: (717) 534 - 7015

LONG, John C. — Tel: (717) 534 - 3237
V. President, Public Affairs — Fax: (717) 534 - 7015
jlong@hersheys.com

RUSSELL, Richard G. — Tel: (717) 534 - 7547
Director, State and Local Government Relations — Fax: (717) 534 - 7038
rickrussell@hersheys.com

At Washington Office

GRAF, Ronald P. — Tel: (202) 434 - 8278
Senior Director, Government Relations — Fax: (202) 434 - 8258
rgraf@hersheys.com
Registered Federal Lobbyist.

Hershey Foods Corp.

See listing on page 241 under The Hershey Company.

Hertz Corp.

A car, truck and equipment renting company.

www.hertz.com
Annual Revenues: $6.7 billion

Chairman and Chief Exec. Officer
KOCH, Craig R. — Tel: (201) 307 - 2600; Fax: (201) 307 - 2644

Main Headquarters
Mailing: 225 Brae Blvd.
Park Ridge, NJ 07656
Tel: (201) 307 - 2000; Fax: (201) 307 - 2644

Corporate Foundations and Giving Programs

Hertz Corp. Contributions Program
225 Brae Blvd.
Park Ridge, NJ 07656
Tel: (201) 307 - 3412; Fax: (201) 307 - 2856

Annual Grant Total: none reported

Public Affairs and Related Activities Personnel

At Headquarters

BROOME, Richard — Tel: (201) 307 - 2486
V. President, Corporate Affairs — Fax: (201) 307 - 2856

POLLACK, Irwin — Tel: (201) 307 - 2619
Senior V. President, Employee Relations — Fax: (201) 307 - 2644

Hewitt Associates Inc.

Global human resources outsourcing and consulting firm.

www.hewitt.com
Annual Revenues: $2 billion

Chief Exec. Officer and Chairman
GIFFORD, Dale — Tel: (847) 295 - 5000; Fax: (847) 295 - 7634

Main Headquarters
Mailing: 100 Half Day Rd.
Lincolnshire, IL 60069
Tel: (847) 295 - 5000; Fax: (847) 295 - 7634

Washington Office
Contact: Frank McArdle
Mailing: 2401 Pennsylvania Ave. NW
Suite 450
Washington, DC 20037
Tel: (202) 331 - 155

Public Affairs and Related Activities Personnel

At Headquarters

KING, Steven Dale — Tel: (847) 295 - 5000
Chief Human Resources Officer — Fax: (847) 295 - 7634

ZITLOW, Kelly — Tel: (847) 442 - 7662
Manager, Public Relations — Fax: (847) 295 - 7634
kelly.zitlow@hewitt.com

At Washington Office

MCARDLE, Frank — Tel: (202) 331 - 155
Washington Representative

Hewlett-Packard Co.

A member of the Public Affairs Council. Computing and imaging products and services. Merged with Compaq Computer Corp. in May of 2002.

www.hp.com
Annual Revenues: $44.246 billion

Chairman of the Board
DUNN, Patricia C. — Tel: (650) 857 - 1501; Fax: (650) 857 - 5518; TF: (800) 752 - 0900

President and Chief Exec. Officer
HURD, Michael V. — Tel: (650) 857 - 1501; Fax: (650) 857 - 5518; TF: (800) 752 - 0900

Main Headquarters
Mailing: 3000 Hanover St.
Palo Alto, CA 94304
Tel: (650) 857 - 1501; Fax: (650) 857 - 5518; TF: (800) 752 - 0900

Washington Office
Contact: John D. Hassell
Mailing: 1100 New York Ave. NW
Suite 600W
Washington, DC 20005
Tel: (202) 378 - 2500; Fax: (202) 378 - 2550

Political Action Committees

Hewlett-Packard Co. Political Action Committee
Contact: Ann O. Baskins
3000 Hanover St.
Palo Alto, CA 94304
Tel: (650) 857 - 3755; Fax: (650) 857 - 5518; TF: (800) 752 - 0900

Contributions to Candidates: $60,900 (01/05 - 09/05)

Hewlett-Packard Co.

* *continued from previous page*

Democrats: $20,500; Republicans: $40,400.

Principal Recipients

SENATE DEMOCRATS		HOUSE DEMOCRATS	
Feinstein, Dianne (CA)	$5,000		
Lieberman, Joe (CT)	$4,000		
SENATE REPUBLICANS		**HOUSE REPUBLICANS**	
Smith, Gordon (OR)	$8,500	DeLay, Tom (TX)	$5,000
Ensign, John Eric (NV)	$5,000	Brady, Kevin Patrick (TX)	$2,000
Allen, George (VA)	$3,500	Hastert, Dennis J. (IL)	$2,000
Burns, Conrad (MT)	$2,000	Lewis, Jerry (CA)	$2,000

Corporate Foundations and Giving Programs

Hewlett-Packard Co. Foundation
Contact: Bess Stephens
3000 Hanover St.
Palo Alto, CA 94304
Tel: (650) 857 - 2857
Fax: (650) 857 - 5518
TF: (800) 752 - 0900

Annual Grant Total: $500,000 - $750,000

50% of grants are education-related. The company also maintains a large contributions program in addition to the Foundation. Scholarship funds are not available. Guidelines are available.

Geographic Preference: Area(s) in which the company operates; National

Primary Interests: Education; Engineering; Math and Science

Hewlett-Packard Co. Corporate Contributions Program
Contact: Bess Stephens
3000 Hanover St.
Palo Alto, CA 94304
Tel: (650) 857 - 2857
Fax: (650) 857 - 5518
TF: (800) 752 - 0900

Annual Grant Total: over $5,000,000

Most of the company's giving is to higher education in the form of HP equipment for teaching laboratories in computer science, engineering, medicine and business. A major national focus is K-12 mathematics and science education in the areas of curriculum development and teacher training, and equipment support for national arts and environmental causes. Local organizations are supported through the company's United Way matching program and community contributions programs in areas where there is a significant employee presence.

Primary Interests: Higher Education; K-12 Education; Math and Science

Recent Recipients: United Way

Public Affairs and Related Activities Personnel

At Headquarters

BASKINS, Ann O.
Senior V. President, General Counsel and Secretary; PAC Treasurer
ann_baskins@hp.com
Responsibilities include regulatory affairs.
Tel: (650) 857 - 3755
Fax: (650) 857 - 5518
TF: (800) 752 - 0900

DUNN, Debra L.
Senior V. President, Corporate Affairs
Tel: (650) 857 - 1501
Fax: (650) 857 - 5518
TF: (800) 752 - 0900

FAZZINO, Gary P.
V. President, Government and Public Affairs
Mailstop: MS 1035
gary_fazzino@hp.com
Tel: (650) 857 - 4321
Fax: (650) 857 - 5518
TF: (800) 752 - 0900

PAVLOVICH, Steve
Director, Investor Relations
Tel: (650) 857 - 3950
Fax: (650) 857 - 5518
TF: (800) 752 - 0900

STEPHENS, Bess
V. President, Philanthropy and Education
bess_stephens@hp.com
Tel: (650) 857 - 2857
Fax: (650) 857 - 5518
TF: (800) 752 - 0900

VILLARINO, Jose
Shareholder Relations
jose_villarino@hp.com
Tel: (650) 857 - 4872
Fax: (650) 857 - 5518
TF: (800) 752 - 0900

WAYMAN, Robert P.
Chief Financial Officer
Tel: (650) 857 - 1501
Fax: (650) 857 - 5518
TF: (800) 752 - 0900

At Washington Office

ALBERT, Stacey Stern
Government Affairs Manager
stacey.albert@hp.com
Registered Federal Lobbyist.
Tel: (202) 378 - 2500
Fax: (202) 378 - 2550

BLAIR, Michele
Government Affairs Manager
michelle.blair@hp.com
Tel: (202) 378 - 2500
Fax: (202) 378 - 2550

COOPER, Scott
Manager, Technology Policy
scott_cooper2@hp.com
Registered Federal Lobbyist.
Tel: (202) 378 - 2500
Fax: (202) 378 - 2550

ESTRADA, Larry
Director, Government and Public Affairs
larry.estrada@hp.com
Registered Federal Lobbyist.
Tel: (202) 378 - 2500
Fax: (202) 378 - 2550

HASSELL, John D.
Director, Federal and State Government Affairs
john.hassell@hp.com
Registered Federal Lobbyist.
Tel: (202) 378 - 2500
Fax: (202) 378 - 2550

HUGHES, Kristin
Manager, Federal and International Public Policy
kristin_hughes@hp.com
Registered Federal Lobbyist.
Tel: (202) 378 - 2500
Fax: (202) 378 - 2550

ISAACS, David
Director, Government and Public Policy
david_isaacs@hp.com
Registered Federal Lobbyist.
Tel: (202) 378 - 2500
Fax: (202) 378 - 2550

MAXWELL, William A.
Director, International Development and Finance
wmaxwell@hp.com
Registered Federal Lobbyist.
Tel: (202) 378 - 2500
Fax: (202) 378 - 2550

At Other Offices

PLUMB, Priscilla
Director, Public Affairs
20555 State Hwy. # 249
Houston, TX 77070-2698
priscilla.plumb@hp.com
Tel: (281) 514 - 5160
Fax: (281) 518 - 7491

Hexcel Corp.

A producer of technologically sophisticated, advanced composite materials and reinforcement fabrics.

www.hexcel.com

Chairman, President and Chief Exec. Officer
BERGES, David E.
Tel: (203) 969 - 0666
Fax: (203) 358 - 3977

Main Headquarters
Mailing: 281 Tresser Blvd.
Two Stamford Plaza
Stamford, CT 06901-3238
Tel: (203) 969 - 0666
Fax: (203) 358 - 3977

Political Action Committees

Hexcel Corp. Political Action Committee
Contact: Michael MacIntyre
281 Tresser Blvd.
Two Stamford Plaza
Stamford, CT 06901-3238
Tel: (203) 969 - 0666
Fax: (203) 358 - 3977

Contributions to Candidates: $13,000 (01/05 - 09/05)

Democrats: $6,000; Republicans: $7,000.

Principal Recipients

SENATE DEMOCRATS		HOUSE DEMOCRATS	
		Larsen, Rick (WA)	$2,000
		Tauscher, Ellen O (CA)	$2,000
		Holden, Timothy (PA)	$1,000
		Smith, Adam (WA)	$1,000
SENATE REPUBLICANS		**HOUSE REPUBLICANS**	
Graham, Lindsey (SC)	$1,000	Everett, Terry (AL)	$2,000
		Hayworth, J D (AZ)	$1,000
		Hunter, Duncan (CA)	$1,000
		Norwood, Charles (GA)	$1,000
		Rogers, Michael J (MI)	$1,000

Corporate Foundations and Giving Programs

Hexcel Foundation
Contact: Stephen Forsyth
281 Tresser Blvd.
Two Stamford Plaza
Stamford, CT 06901-3238
Tel: (203) 969 - 0666
Fax: (203) 358 - 3977

Annual Grant Total: under $100,000

Geographic Preference: Area(s) in which the company operates

Primary Interests: Education; Engineering; Math and Science; Scholarship Funds; Technology

Public Affairs and Related Activities Personnel

At Headquarters

BACAL, Michael
Communications and Investor Relations Manager
michael.bacal@hexcel.com
Tel: (203) 969 - 0666
Ext: 426
Fax: (203) 358 - 3993

FORSYTH, Stephen
Exec. V. President and Chief Financial Officer
stephen.forsyth@hexcel.com
Responsibilities include corporate philanthropy.
Tel: (203) 969 - 0666
Fax: (203) 358 - 3977

MACINTYRE, Michael
PAC Treasurer
Tel: (203) 969 - 0666
Fax: (203) 358 - 3977

Hexion Specialty Chemicals, Inc.

A producer of thermoset resins and coatings for industrial markets. Formed by the merger of Borden Chemical, Inc., Resolution Performance Products LLC, and Resolution Specialty Materials LLC.

www.hexionchem.com

Annual Revenues: $4.1 billion

President and Chief Exec. Officer
MORRISON, Craig D. — Tel: (614) 225 - 4000

Main Headquarters

Mailing: 180 E. Broad St.
Columbus, OH 43215-3799 — Tel: (614) 225 - 4000

Public Affairs and Related Activities Personnel

At Headquarters

LOSCOCCO, Peter F. — Tel: (614) 225 - 4127
V. President, Public Affairs
peter.loscocco@hexionchem.com
Responsibilities include investor relations.

Hibernia Corp.

A member of the Public Affairs Council. Bank holding company. In March of 2005 the company announced plans to merge with Capital One Financial Corp. (see separate listing). Completion of the merger is expected in the final quarter of 2005.

www.hibernia.com

Annual Revenues: $1.1 billion

Chairman of the Board
CAMPBELL, E. R. — Tel: (504) 533 - 3333; Fax: (504) 533 - 2367; TF: (800) 562 - 9007
bcampbell@hibernia.com

President and Chief Exec. Officer
BOYDSTUN, J. Herbert — Tel: (504) 533 - 3902; Fax: (504) 533 - 2367; TF: (800) 562 - 9007
hboydstun@hibernia.com

Main Headquarters

Mailing: 5718 Westheimer St.
Houston, TX 77057 — Tel: (713) 789 - 7879; TF: (800) 562 - 9007

Political Action Committees

Hibernia People For Good Government Inc. - Federal

Contact: Anne Oestriecher

5718 Westheimer St.
Houston, TX 77057 — Tel: (713) 789 - 7879; TF: (800) 562 - 9007

Contributions to Candidates: $37,500 (01/05 - 09/05)

Democrats: $12,500; Republicans: $25,000.

Principal Recipients

SENATE DEMOCRATS
Landrieu, Mary (LA) $2,500

HOUSE DEMOCRATS
Gonzalez, Charles A (TX) $2,500
Green, Alexander (TX) $2,500
Jefferson, William (LA) $2,500
Melancon, Charlie (LA) $2,500

SENATE REPUBLICANS
Vitter, David (LA) $2,500

HOUSE REPUBLICANS
Alexander, Rodney (LA) $2,500
Baker, Hugh (LA) $2,500
Boustany, Jr, Charles (LA) $2,500
Brady, Kevin Patrick (TX) $2,500
Gohmert, Louis (TX) $2,500
Hensarling, Jeb (TX) $2,500
Jindal, Bobby (LA) $2,500
McCrery, Jim (LA) $2,500
Poe, Ted (TX) $2,500

Corporate Foundations and Giving Programs

Hibernia Corporate Contributions Program

Contact: James F. Lestelle

5718 Westheimer St.
Houston, TX 77057 — Tel: (504) 533 - 5482; Fax: (504) 533 - 5841; TF: (800) 562 - 9007

Annual Grant Total: $2,000,000 - $5,000,000

Geographic Preference: Louisiana; Texas

Primary Interests: Education

Public Affairs and Related Activities Personnel

At Headquarters

HOADLEY, Russell S. — Tel: (504) 533 - 2028; Fax: (504) 533 - 5841; TF: (800) 562 - 9007
Exec. V. President and Chief Public Affairs
(Hibernia Nat'l Bank)
rhoadley@hibernia.com

LESTELLE, James F. — Tel: (504) 533 - 5482; Fax: (504) 533 - 5841; TF: (800) 562 - 9007
Senior V. President, Corporate Communications
jlestelle@hibernia.com

OESTRIECHER, Anne — Tel: (713) 789 - 7879; TF: (800) 562 - 9007
Pac Treasurer

VOLTZ CARLSON, Trisha — Tel: (504) 533 - 2180; Fax: (504) 533 - 2367; TF: (800) 562 - 9007
Senior V. President, Investor Relations
tvoltz@hibernia.com

ZAINEY, Michael S. — Tel: (713) 789 - 7879; TF: (800) 562 - 9007
Exec. V. President, Human Resources

Hibernia Nat'l Bank

See listing on page 243 under Hibernia Corp.

Highmark Inc.

A member of the Public Affairs Council. Formed by the merger of Pennsylvania Blue Shield and Blue Cross of Western Pennsylvania.

www.highmark.com

Annual Revenues: $8.1 billion

Chief Exec. Officer and President
MELANI, Ken, M.D. — Tel: (412) 544 - 7245; Fax: (412) 544 - 8240

Main Headquarters

Mailing: 1800 Center St.
Camp Hill, PA 17089 — Tel: (717) 302 - 3978; Fax: (717) 302 - 3969

Washington Office

Contact: Greg Englert

Mailing: 600 Pennsylvania Ave. SE
Suite 220
Washington, DC 20003 — Tel: (202) 544 - 8814; Fax: (202) 544 - 8853

Political Action Committees

Highmark Health PAC

Contact: Jane Rodkey

1800 Center St.
Camp Hill, PA 17089 — Tel: (717) 302 - 3977; Fax: (717) 302 - 3969

Contributions to Candidates: $12,500 (01/05 - 09/05)

Democrats: $1,000; Republicans: $11,500.

Principal Recipients

SENATE DEMOCRATS

HOUSE DEMOCRATS
Doyle, Mike (PA) $1,000

SENATE REPUBLICANS

HOUSE REPUBLICANS
Fitzpatrick, Michael (PA) $2,000
Hart, Melissa (PA) $2,000
Murphy, Tim (PA) $2,000
English, Philip S (PA) $1,000
Gerlach, Jim (PA) $1,000
Johnson, Nancy (CT) $1,000
Peterson, John Mr. (PA) $1,000
Shuster, William (PA) $1,000

Public Affairs and Related Activities Personnel

At Headquarters

GALLAHER, Candy M. — Tel: (717) 302 - 3982; Fax: (717) 302 - 3980
Director, Regulatory Affairs

KETCHEN, Valerie C. — Tel: (717) 302 - 3974; Fax: (717) 302 - 3969
Senior Representative, Government Affairs
(Clarity Vision, Inc., United Concordia Cos., Inc., Highmark Life and Casualty Group, Inc.)

RODKEY, Jane — Tel: (717) 302 - 3977; Fax: (717) 302 - 3969
Government Affairs Coordinator

STUART, Alyson B. — Tel: (717) 302 - 3978; Fax: (717) 302 - 3969
Government Affairs, Exec. Secretary

Highmark Inc.

* continued from previous page

WARFEL, Michael G. — Tel: (717) 302 - 3979
V. President, Government Affairs — Fax: (717) 302 - 3969
(Clarity Vision, Inc., United Concordia Cos., Inc., Highmark Life and Casualty Group, Inc.)

At Washington Office

ENGLERT, Greg — Tel: (202) 544 - 8814
Senior Government Affairs Representative — Fax: (202) 544 - 8853
Registered Federal Lobbyist.

At Other Offices

MCDERMOTT, John — Tel: (412) 544 - 8247
V. President, Corporate Communications — Fax: (412) 544 - 5318
120 Fifth Ave. Pl.
Suite 2628
Pittsburgh, PA 15222

O'BRIEN, David — Tel: (412) 544 - 5250
Exec. V. President, Government Services — Fax: (412) 544 - 8054
120 Fifth Ave. Pl.
Suite 3124
Pittsburgh, PA 15222

SANDERS, Manda — Tel: (412) 544 - 8030
Government Affairs Representative — Fax: (412) 544 - 5318
(Clarity Vision, Inc., United Concordia Cos., Inc., Highmark Life and Casualty Group, Inc.)
120 Fifth Ave. Pl.
Suite 2628
Pittsburgh, PA 15222

WALTON, Aaron — Tel: (412) 544 - 5439
Senior V. President, Corporate Affairs — Fax: (412) 544 - 8054
120 Fifth Ave. Pl.
Suite 3110
Pittsburgh, PA 15222

WEINSTEIN, Michael — Tel: (412) 544 - 7903
Senior Media and Communications Consultant — Fax: (412) 544 - 5318
120 Fifth Ave. Pl.
Suite 1933
Pittsburgh, PA 15222

Highmark Life and Casualty Group, Inc.

See listing on page 243 under Highmark Inc.

Hillenbrand Industries, Inc.

A public holding company for three diversified businesses serving health care (patient care systems and specialty therapy beds); death care (protective metal and hardwood burial caskets, cremation products); and life insurance for pre-need funeral planning. Subsidiaries are: Batesville Casket Co.; Hill-Rom, Inc.; and Forethought Financial Services, Inc.
www.hillenbrand.com

Chairman of the Board — Tel: (812) 934 - 7000
HILLENBRAND, Ray J. — Fax: (812) 934 - 7371

Vice Chairman and Interim Chief Exec. Officer — Tel: (812) 934 - 7000
CLASSON, Rolf A. — Fax: (812) 934 - 7371

Main Headquarters
Mailing: 700 State Route 46 East — Tel: (812) 934 - 7000
Batesville, IN 47006-8835 — Fax: (812) 934 - 7371

Political Action Committees

Hillenbrand Industries PAC (HI PAC)
Contact: Tom Jeffers
700 State Route 46 East — Tel: (812) 934 - 7000
Batesville, IN 47006-8835 — Fax: (812) 934 - 7371

Contributions to Candidates: $2,000 (01/05 - 09/05)
Democrats: $1,000; Republicans: $1,000.

Principal Recipients

SENATE DEMOCRATS
Kennedy, Ted (MA) $1,000

HOUSE DEMOCRATS

SENATE REPUBLICANS

HOUSE REPUBLICANS
Northup, Anne M. (KY) $1,000

Public Affairs and Related Activities Personnel

At Headquarters

BONNEVIER, Bruce — Tel: (812) 934 - 7000
V. President, Human Resources — Fax: (812) 934 - 7371

JEFFERS, Tom — Tel: (812) 934 - 7000
Contact, HI PAC — Fax: (812) 934 - 7371

UTTERBACK, Rob — Tel: (812) 934 - 7359
Communications Coordinator — Fax: (812) 934 - 7371
rob_utterback@hillenbrand.com

WILSON, Wendy — Tel: (812) 934 - 7670
V. President, Investor Relations — Fax: (812) 934 - 7371

Hilton Hotels Corp.

Owner and operator of hotels.
www.hiltonworldwide.com
Annual Revenues: $3.4 billion

Co-Chairman and Chief Exec. Officer — Tel: (310) 278 - 4321
BOLLENBACH, Stephen F.

Co-Chairman of the Board — Tel: (310) 278 - 4321
HILTON, Barron

Main Headquarters
Mailing: 9336 Civic Center Dr. — Tel: (310) 278 - 4321
Beverly Hills, CA 90210 — Fax: (310) 205 - 7678

Corporate Foundations and Giving Programs

Hilton Hotels Corporate Gving Program
Contact: Kathy Shepard
9336 Civic Center Dr. — Tel: (310) 205 - 7676
Beverly Hills, CA 90210 — Fax: (310) 205 - 7678

Annual Grant Total: $2,000,000 - $5,000,000
Geographic Preference: California; Tennessee
Primary Interests: Children's Health; Community Affairs; Education; Health and Human Services; Higher Education; K-12 Education

Public Affairs and Related Activities Personnel

At Headquarters

GROSSMAN, Marc A. — Tel: (310) 205 - 4030
Senior V. President, Corporate Affairs — Fax: (310) 205 - 7686
marc_grossman@hilton.com
Responsibilities include investor relations.

HOLLIS, Candace — Tel: (310) 205 - 8640
Senior Manager, Corporate Communications — Fax: (310) 861 - 5958
candace_hollis@hilton.com

MCKENZIE-SWARTS, Molly — Tel: (310) 205 - 4084
Senior V. President, Human Resources and Administration
molly_mckenzie-swarts@hilton.com

SHAH, Atish — Tel: (310) 205 - 8664
V. President, Investor Relations
atish_shah@hilton.com

SHEPARD, Kathy — Tel: (310) 205 - 7676
V. President, Corporate Communications — Fax: (310) 205 - 7678
kathy_shepard@hilton.com
Responsibilities include corporate contributions and government affairs.

At Other Offices

MCKINNEY, Joyce E. — Tel: (901) 374 - 5000 Ext: 6309
Senior Manager, Corporate Communications — Fax: (901) 374 - 5935
755 Crossover Ln.
Memphis, TN 38117
joyce_mckinney@hilton.com

Hitachi America, Ltd.

A manufacturer of electronics and electronics components. A U.S. subsidiary of Hitachi, Ltd. of Tokyo, Japan.
www.hitachi.com

Chief Exec. Officer — Tel: (650) 589 - 8300
HISADA, Masao — Fax: (650) 244 - 7920 — TF: (800) 448 - 2244

Main Headquarters
Mailing: 2000 Sierra Point Pkwy. — Tel: (650) 589 - 8300
Brisbane, CA 94005 — Fax: (650) 244 - 7920 — TF: (800) 448 - 2244

Washington Office
Mailing: 1900 K St. NW — Tel: (202) 828 - 9272
Suite 800 — Fax: (202) 828 - 9277
Washington, DC 20006

Corporate Foundations and Giving Programs

The Hitachi Foundation
Contact: Barbara Dyer
1509 22nd St. NW — Tel: (202) 457 - 0588
Washington, DC 20037 — Fax: (202) 296 - 1098

Annual Grant Total: $2,000,000 - $5,000,000
The Foundation no longer accepts unsolicited proposals. It only accepts responses to requests for proposals (RFPs).
Geographic Preference: Continental United States
Primary Interests: Community Development; Education
Recent Recipients: Chesapeake Bay Foundation; Futures for Children; Jobs for the Future

Public Affairs and Related Activities Personnel

At Headquarters

CORBETT, Gerard F. — Tel: (650) 244 - 7900
V. President and General Manager, Branding and Corporate Communications Group — Fax: (650) 244 - 7919 — TF: (800) 448 - 2244
gerard.corbett@hal.hitachi.com

TAKAHASHI, Matt — Tel: (650) 244 - 7902
Assistant Manager, Investor and Public Relations — Fax: (650) 244 - 7920 — TF: (800) 448 - 2244
masahiro.takahashi@hal.hitachi.com

Hitachi America, Ltd.

* continued from previous page

At Washington Office

GREEN, Carl J. — Tel: (202) 828 - 9272
Deputy Senior Representative — Fax: (202) 828 - 9277
carl.green@hal.hitachi.com

HORI, Tetsuro — Tel: (202) 828 - 9272
Liaison Manager for International Relations — Fax: (202) 828 - 9277

JOYA, Munehiko — Tel: (202) 828 - 9272
Manager, Government and Public Affairs — Fax: (202) 828 - 9277

OHDE, Takashi — Tel: (202) 828 - 9272
Senior Representative — Fax: (202) 828 - 9277
Registered Federal Lobbyist.

At Other Offices

DYER, Barbara — Tel: (202) 457 - 0588
President and Chief Exec. Officer, The Hitachi Foundation — Fax: (202) 296 - 1098
1509 22nd St. NW
Washington, DC 20037

HLR Service Corp.

See listing on page 245 under Hoffmann-La Roche Inc (Roche).

HNI Corp.

Formerly known as HON Industries, Inc. A manufacturer of office furniture and products. Also manufactures gas- and wood-burning fireplaces.

www.honi.com

Chairman and Chief Exec. Officer
ASKREN, Stanley A. — Tel: (563) 264 - 7400 — Fax: (563) 264 - 7217

Main Headquarters
Mailing: P.O. Box 1109, Muscatine, IA 52761-0071 — Tel: (563) 264 - 7400 — Fax: (563) 264 - 7217
Street: 414 E. Third St., Muscatine, IA 52761-7109

Corporate Foundations and Giving Programs

HON Industries Charitable Foundation
Contact: Susan Cradick
P.O. Box 1109 — Tel: (563) 264 - 7400
Muscatine, IA 52761-0071 — Fax: (563) 264 - 7217

Annual Grant Total: $1,000,000 - $2,000,000
Geographic Preference: Iowa
Primary Interests: Civic and Public Affairs; Education; Social Services
Recent Recipients: Boy Scouts of America; Junior Achievement; United Way

Public Affairs and Related Activities Personnel

At Headquarters

CRADICK, Susan — Tel: (563) 264 - 7400
Secretary-Treasurer, HON Industries Charitable Foundation — Fax: (563) 264 - 7217

ELLSWORTH, Melinda C. — Tel: (563) 264 - 7406
V. President, Treasurer Investor Relations — Fax: (563) 264 - 7217
ellsworthm@honi.com

MEAD, Donald T. — Tel: (563) 264 - 7400
V. President, Member and Community Relations — Fax: (563) 264 - 7217

Hoffmann-La Roche Inc. (Roche)

A member of the Public Affairs Council. Hoffmann-La Roche Inc. (Roche) is the U.S. prescription drug unit of the Roche Group, a research-based health care enterprise. Roche discovers, develops, manufactures and markets numerous important prescription drugs that enhance people's health, well-being and quality of life. Among the company's areas of therapeutic interest are: dermatology; genitourinary disease; infectious diseases, including influenza; inflammation, including arthritis and osteoporosis; metabolic diseases, including obesity and diabetes; neurology; oncology; transplantation; vascular diseases; and virology, including HIV/AIDS and hepatitis C.

www.rocheusa.com

President and Chief Exec. Officer
ABERCROMBIE, George B. — Tel: (973) 235 - 5000 — Fax: (973) 235 - 7605

Main Headquarters
Mailing: 340 Kingsland St., Nutley, NJ 07110-1199 — Tel: (973) 235 - 5000 — Fax: (973) 235 - 7605

Washington Office
Contact: Michael J. Eging
Mailing: 1425 K St. NW, Suite 650, Washington, DC 20005 — Tel: (202) 408 - 0090 — Fax: (202) 408 - 1750

Political Action Committees

Hoffmann-La Roche Inc. Good Government Committee
Contact: David McDede
340 Kingsland St. — Tel: (973) 235 - 5000
Nutley, NJ 07110-1199 — Fax: (973) 235 - 7605

Contributions to Candidates: $49,700 (01/05 - 09/05)
Democrats: $10,500; Republicans: $39,200.

Principal Recipients

SENATE DEMOCRATS

SENATE REPUBLICANS
Graham, Lindsey (SC) $5,000

HOUSE DEMOCRATS
Pascrell, William (NJ) $5,000

HOUSE REPUBLICANS
Bonilla, Henry (TX) $5,000
Davis, Tom (VA) $5,000
Ferguson, Mike (NJ) $5,000
Frelinghuysen, Rod (NJ) $5,000
Deal, Nathan (GA) $3,000
Granger, Kay N (TX) $3,000

Corporate Foundations and Giving Programs

Roche Foundation
Contact: Vivian L. Beetle
340 Kingsland St. — Tel: (973) 562 - 2055
Nutley, NJ 07110-1199 — Fax: (973) 562 - 2999

Annual Grant Total: $200,000 - $300,000
Funding consideration will be given to domestic, charitable non-profit organziations serving commmunities where Roche has a significant presence and interest. Grants are limited to the U.S.A. and are focused on the areas listed in the primary interests.
Geographic Preference: Area in which the company is headquartered; Area(s) in which the company operates; National
Primary Interests: Education; Health; Math and Science
Recent Recipients: United Negro College Fund; University of Texas

Hoffmann-La Roche Corporate Giving Program
Contact: Vivian L. Beetle
340 Kingsland St. — Tel: (973) 562 - 2055
Nutley, NJ 07110-1199 — Fax: (973) 562 - 2999

Annual Grant Total: none reported
Funding consideration will be given to domestic, charitable non-profit organizations serving communities where Roche has a significant presence and interest. Roche supports innovative programs that address identified community needs and are closely aligned with the corporate goals. Specifically, the company's funding priorities are health promotion and health education initiatives (with an emphasis on Virology, including HIV/AIDS and hepatitis C; Infectious diseases, including influenza; Cardiology; Neurology; Oncology; Transplantation; Metabolic Diseases, including obesity and diabetes) and educational programs (especially K-12 science and mathematics) focusing on teacher enrichment.
Geographic Preference: Area in which the company is headquartered; Area(s) in which the company operates
Primary Interests: Health; K-12 Education; Math and Science; Medical Research

Public Affairs and Related Activities Personnel

At Headquarters

BEETLE, Vivian L. — Tel: (973) 562 - 2055
Director, Public Affairs/Community Affairs — Fax: (973) 562 - 2999
vivian_l.beetle@roche.com
Responsibilities include corporate philanthropy.

GLYNN, Carolyn R. — Tel: (973) 562 - 2213
V. President, Public Affairs — Fax: (973) 562 - 2205
Mailstop: #85, Fourth Fl.

GROSSMAN, Steven D. — Tel: (973) 235 - 5000
V. President, Human Resources — Fax: (973) 235 - 7605

HURLEY, Terence — Tel: (973) 562 - 2882
Director, Product Public Affairs - Metabolic Disease, Anti-infectives — Fax: (973) 562 - 5589
terence_j.hurley@roche.com

MCDEDE, David — Tel: (973) 235 - 5000
PAC Treasurer — Fax: (973) 235 - 7605

MINEHART, Paul — Tel: (973) 562 - 6595
Director, Corporate and Business Communications — Fax: (973) 562 - 2208
paul.minehart@roche.com

O'LEARY, Kevin — Tel: (973) 235 - 5000
V. President, Business Policy and State Government Affairs

ROSENSTOCK, Shelley — Tel: (973) 562 - 2373
Director, Product Public Affairs - Oncology and Dermatology — Fax: (973) 562 - 2333
shelley.rosenstock@roche.com

THOMAS, Gregory M. — Tel: (973) 562 - 2198
Director, State Government Affairs (HLR Service Corp.) — Fax: (973) 562 - 2666
greg.thomas@roche.com

VAN HOUTEN, Pamela — Tel: (973) 562 - 2231
Director, Product Public Relations - Virology, Primary Care
pamela.vanhoute@roche.com

Hoffmann-La Roche Inc. (Roche)

** continued from previous page*

VAN NESS, Heather — Tel: (973) 562 - 2203
Director, Product Public Relations - HIV, Transplant
heather.vanness@roche.com

WILSON, Darien E. — Tel: (973) 562 - 2232; Fax: (973) 562 - 2206
Director, Corporate and Business Communications
darien_e.wilson@roche.com

At Washington Office

EGING, Michael J. — Tel: (202) 408 - 0090; Fax: (202) 408 - 1750
Exec. Director, Public Policy and Federal Government Affairs
michael_j.eging@roche.com
Registered Federal Lobbyist.

MILLS, Kelli A. — Tel: (202) 408 - 0090; Fax: (202) 408 - 1750
Assistant Director, Federal Government Affairs
kelli.mills@roche.com
Registered Federal Lobbyist.

NICHOLS, David — Tel: (202) 408 - 0090; Fax: (202) 408 - 1750
Director, Federal Government Affairs
david.nichols@roche.com
Registered Federal Lobbyist.

SHAH, Nimish — Tel: (202) 408 - 0090; Fax: (202) 408 - 1750
Manager, Public Policy
nimish.shah@roche.com
Registered Federal Lobbyist.

At Other Offices

MLYNARCZYK, Mark — Tel: (312) 492 - 9691; Fax: (312) 492 - 9693
Manager, Regional Government Affairs
1658 N. Milwaukee
Mailstop: M/S PMB293
Chicago, IL 60647-5412
mark.mlynarczyk@roche.com

SCHMIEDT, Robert — Tel: (770) 591 - 4460; Fax: (770) 591 - 6747
Senior Regional Manager, State Government Affairs
(HLR Service Corp.)
3259 Eagle Watch Dr.
Woodstock, GA 30189
robert.schmiedt@roche.com

SETZEPFANDT, Scott, R.Ph. — Tel: (952) 469 - 5452; Fax: (952) 469 - 5453
Senior Regional Manager, State Government Affairs
(HLR Service Corp.)
10330 Upper 196th Way West
Lakeville, MN 55044

SHEW, Archie R. — Tel: (614) 523 - 3921; Fax: (614) 523 - 3941
Senior Regional Manager, State Government Affairs
(HLR Service Corp.)
956 Woodsedge Ln.
Westerville, OH 43081
archie.shew@roche.com

WRIGHT, Michael J. — Tel: (512) 343 - 2915; Fax: (512) 343 - 7811
Senior Regional Manager, State Government Affairs
(HLR Service Corp.)
5710 Painted Valley Dr.
Austin, TX 78759
michael.wright@roche.com

Holcim (US) Inc.

A member of the Public Affairs Council. Formerly known as Holnam Inc. A cement and mineral components supplier.
www.holcim.com/us
Annual Revenues: $1.1 billion

President and Chief Exec. Officer
DOLBERG, Patrick — Tel: (734) 529 - 2411; Fax: (734) 529 - 5268; TF: (800) 854 - 4656

Main Headquarters
Mailing: 6211 N. Ann Arbor Rd.
P.O. Box 122
Dundee, MI 48131
Tel: (734) 529 - 2411; Fax: (734) 529 - 5268; TF: (800) 854 - 4656

Political Action Committees

Holcim (US) Inc. PAC
Contact: Stephen C. Arthur
6211 N. Ann Arbor Rd.
P.O. Box 122
Dundee, MI 48131
Tel: (734) 529 - 2411; Fax: (734) 529 - 5268; TF: (800) 854 - 4656

Contributions to Candidates: $11,500 (01/05 - 09/05)
Democrats: $1,000; Republicans: $9,500; Other: $1,000.

Principal Recipients

SENATE DEMOCRATS

HOUSE DEMOCRATS
Dingell, John D (MI) $1,000

HOUSE OTHER
Oberstar, James L (MN) $1,000

SENATE REPUBLICANS
Talent, James (MO) $5,000
Chafee, Lincoln (RI) $1,000

HOUSE REPUBLICANS
Dent, Charles W (PA) $1,000
Emerson, Jo Ann (MO) $1,000
Hulshof, Kenny (MO) $1,000

Corporate Foundations and Giving Programs

Holcim (US) Inc. Corporate Contributions Program
Contact: Linda McCormick
6211 N. Ann Arbor Rd.
P.O. Box 122
Dundee, MI 48131
Tel: (734) 529 - 2411; Fax: (734) 529 - 5268; TF: (800) 854 - 4656

Annual Grant Total: none reported
No phone solicitations accepted.
Geographic Preference: Area(s) in which the company operates
Primary Interests: Civic and Cultural Activities; Education; Health
Recent Recipients: American Red Cross; Special Olympics; United Negro College Fund

Public Affairs and Related Activities Personnel

At Headquarters

ARTHUR, Stephen C. — Tel: (734) 529 - 2411; Fax: (734) 529 - 5268; TF: (800) 854 - 4656
Manager, Public Affairs
steve.arthur@holcim.com

CHIZMADIA, Thomas A. — Tel: (734) 529 - 2411; Fax: (734) 529 - 5268; TF: (800) 854 - 4656
V. President, Communications and Public Affairs
tom.chizmadia@holcim.com

MCCORMICK, Linda — Tel: (734) 529 - 2411; Fax: (734) 529 - 5268; TF: (800) 854 - 4656
Administrator, Public Affairs
linda.mccormick@holcim.com
Responsibilities include corporate philanthropy.

Holnam Inc.

See listing on page 246 under Holcim (US) Inc.

Home Box Office (HBO)

A home entertainment programming subsidiary of Time Warner Inc. (see separate listing).
www.hbo.com
Annual Revenues: $3.1 billion

Chairman and Chief Exec. Officer
ALBRECHT, Chris — Tel: (212) 512 - 1000; Fax: (212) 512 - 1182

Main Headquarters
Mailing: 1100 Ave. of the Americas
New York, NY 10036
Tel: (212) 512 - 1000; Fax: (212) 512 - 1182

Corporate Foundations and Giving Programs

Home Box Office Corporate Giving Program
Contact: Deborah Rudolph
1100 Ave. of the Americas
New York, NY 10036
Tel: (212) 512 - 5119; Fax: (212) 512 - 1182

Annual Grant Total: none reported

Public Affairs and Related Activities Personnel

At Headquarters

FISCHEL, Mr. Shelley D. — Tel: (212) 512 - 1000; Fax: (212) 512 - 1182
Exec. V. President, Human Resources and Administration
shelley.fischel@hbo.com

PLEPLER, Richard L. — Tel: (212) 512 - 1960; Fax: (212) 512 - 1182
Exec. V. President, Corporate Communications
richard.plepler@hbo.com

RUDOLPH, Deborah — Tel: (212) 512 - 5119; Fax: (212) 512 - 1182
Contact, Corporate Giving Program

SCHAFFER, Quentin M. — Tel: (212) 512 - 1329; Fax: (212) 512 - 1182
Senior V. President, Corporate Communications
quentin.schaffer@hbo.com

The Home Depot, Inc.

A member of the Public Affairs Council. A retailer of home improvement products and services.
www.homedepot.com

Chairman, President and Chief Exec. Officer
NARDELLI, Robert L. — Tel: (770) 433 - 8211; Fax: (770) 384 - 2356

Main Headquarters
Mailing: 2455 Paces Ferry Rd.
Atlanta, GA 30339-4024
Tel: (770) 433 - 8211; Fax: (770) 384 - 2356

Washington Office
Mailing: 101 Constitution Ave., NW
Suite 800 West
Washington, DC 20001
Tel: (202) 772 - 2497; Fax: (202) 772 - 2496

Political Action Committees

Home Depot Inc. Better Government Committee
Contact: Heather Kennedy

The Home Depot, Inc.

* continued from previous page

101 Constitution Ave., NW
Suite 800 West
Washington, DC 20001
Tel: (202) 772 - 2497
Fax: (202) 772 - 2496

Contributions to Candidates: $221,500 (01/05 - 09/05)
Democrats: $42,000; Republicans: $178,500; Other: $1,000.

Principal Recipients

SENATE DEMOCRATS		HOUSE DEMOCRATS	
Nelson, Benjamin (NE)	$4,000	Scott, David (GA)	$10,000
Carper, Thomas R (DE)	$3,000	Bishop, Sanford (GA)	$3,000

SENATE REPUBLICANS		HOUSE REPUBLICANS	
Smith, Gordon (OR)	$20,000	Westmoreland, Lynn (GA)	$8,000
Kennedy, Mark (MN)	$10,000	Blunt, Roy (MO)	$5,000
Lott, Trent (MS)	$7,000	Bonilla, Henry (TX)	$5,000
Talent, James (MO)	$6,500	Cubin, Barbara L (WY)	$5,000
Allen, George (VA)	$5,000	Diaz-Balart, Lincoln (FL)	$5,000
Burns, Conrad (MT)	$5,000	Gingrey, Phillip (GA)	$5,000
Ensign, John Eric (NV)	$5,000	Hastert, Dennis J. (IL)	$5,000
Kyl, Jon L (AZ)	$5,000	Price, Thomas (GA)	$5,000
Santorum, Richard (PA)	$4,000	Ryan, Paul D (WI)	$5,000
Thomas, Craig (WY)	$4,000	Norwood, Charles (GA)	$4,000
Dewine, Richard (OH)	$3,500	Northup, Anne M. (KY)	$3,500
		Pickering, Chip (MS)	$3,000

Corporate Foundations and Giving Programs

The Home Depot Foundation
2455 Paces Ferry Rd.
Atlanta, GA 30339-4024
Tel: (770) 433 - 8211
Fax: (770) 384 - 2356

Annual Grant Total: $1,000,000 - $2,000,000
Geographic Preference: Canada; National
Primary Interests: Disaster Relief; Environment/Conservation; Housing; Youth Services

Public Affairs and Related Activities Personnel

At Headquarters

DAYHOFF, Diane
V. President, Investor Relations
diane_dayhoff@homedepot.com
Tel: (770) 384 - 2666
Fax: (770) 384 - 2356

DONOVAN, Dennis
Exec. V. President, Human Resources
Tel: (770) 433 - 8211
Fax: (770) 384 - 2356

FOUGHNER, Beth
Manager, Government Relations
Tel: (770) 433 - 8211
Fax: (770) 384 - 2356

SHAW, Brad
Senior V. President, Communications and External Affairs
Tel: (770) 433 - 8211
Fax: (770) 384 - 2356

SHIELDS, Jerry
Senior Manager, Public Relations
Mailstop: \
jerry_shields@homedepot.com
Tel: (770) 384 - 2741
Fax: (770) 384 - 2685

At Washington Office

FLICK, Rebecca I.
Treasurer, Home Depot Inc. Better Government Committee
Tel: (202) 772 - 2497
Fax: (202) 772 - 2496

JACOBS, Bryan
Director, Government Relations
Registered Federal Lobbyist.
Tel: (202) 772 - 2497
Fax: (202) 772 - 2496

KENNEDY, Heather
PAC Contact
Tel: (202) 772 - 2497
Fax: (202) 772 - 2496

KNUTSON, Kent
V. President, Government Relations
kent_knutson@homedepot.com
Registered Federal Lobbyist.
Tel: (202) 772 - 2497
Fax: (202) 772 - 2496

Home Shopping Network

See listing on page 250 under HSN, Inc.

Home-O-Nize

See listing on page 245 under HNI Corp.

HON Industries, Inc.

See listing on page 245 under HNI Corp.

Honda Manufacturing of Alabama LLC

See listing on page 32 under American Honda Motor Co, Inc.

Honda North America, Inc.

See listing on page 32 under American Honda Motor Co, Inc.

Honda of America Manufacturing, Inc.

See listing on page 32 under American Honda Motor Co, Inc.

Honeywell Aerospace

See listing on page 247 under Honeywell Internat'l, Inc.

Honeywell Internat'l, Inc.

A diversified high technology company involved in energy and safety controls, defense and aerospace and specialized instrumentation industries. Merged with AlliedSignal in 1999 and that company adopted the Honeywell name. Acquired Pittway Corp. in 2000.
www.honeywell.com
Annual Revenues: $23.652 billion

Chairman and Chief Exec. Officer
COTE, David M.
Tel: (973) 455 - 2000
Fax: (973) 455 - 4807

Main Headquarters
Mailing: 101 Columbia Rd.
Morristown, NJ 07962-4658
Tel: (973) 455 - 2000
Fax: (973) 455 - 4807

Washington Office
Contact: Timothy Keating
Mailing: 1001 Pennsylvania Ave. NW
Suite 700 South
Washington, DC 20004
Tel: (202) 662 - 2650
Fax: (202) 662 - 2674

Political Action Committees

Honeywell Internat'l, Inc. PAC
Contact: Christine M. Ciccone
1001 Pennsylvania Ave. NW
Suite 700 South
Washington, DC 20004
Tel: (202) 662 - 2650
Fax: (202) 662 - 2674

Contributions to Candidates: $10,349 (01/05 - 09/05)
Democrats: $6,849; Republicans: $3,500.

Principal Recipients

SENATE DEMOCRATS		HOUSE DEMOCRATS	
Baucus, Max (MT)	$5,000		
Byrd, Robert C (WV)	$1,000		

SENATE REPUBLICANS		HOUSE REPUBLICANS	
Allen, George (VA)	$1,000	Dewine, R. Pat (OH)	$2,500

Corporate Foundations and Giving Programs

Honeywell Foundation
Contact: Paul A. Boudreau
101 Columbia Rd.
Morristown, NJ 07962-4658
Tel: (973) 455 - 2010
Fax: (973) 455 - 3632

Annual Grant Total: none reported
Support tends to be concentrated especially on nonprofit groups involving Honeywell employees. Guidelines are available. Total foundation and company giving in 1999 was approximately $13 million.
Geographic Preference: Area(s) in which the company operates
Primary Interests: Arts and Humanities; Community Affairs; Education
Recent Recipients: Earth Day; Minnesota Private College Fund; United Way; University of Minnesota; YWCA

Public Affairs and Related Activities Personnel

At Headquarters

BENNETT, Mike
Director, Internal Communications
Tel: (973) 455 - 2753
Fax: (973) 455 - 3881

BOUDREAU, Paul A.
V. President, Corporate Relations; Exec. Director, Honeywell Foundation
Tel: (973) 455 - 2010
Fax: (973) 455 - 3632

BUCKMASTER, Thomas
V. President, Corporate Communications
Tel: (973) 455 - 5323
Fax: (973) 455 - 3881

NOVIELLO, Nick
Director, Investor Relations
Tel: (973) 455 - 2222
Fax: (973) 455 - 4807

WEIDENKOPF, Thomas W.
Senior V. President, Human Resources and Communications
Tel: (973) 455 - 2000
Fax: (973) 455 - 4807

At Washington Office

CICCONE, Christine M.
V. President, Government Relations
Registered Federal Lobbyist.
Tel: (202) 662 - 2650
Fax: (202) 662 - 2674

GRIFFIN, Brian
Director, Government Relations
Tel: (202) 662 - 2650
Fax: (202) 662 - 2674

KEATING, Timothy
Senior V. President, Government Relations
Tel: (202) 662 - 2650
Fax: (202) 662 - 2674

O'HOLLAREN, Sean B.
Senior Director, Government Relations
Tel: (202) 662 - 2650
Fax: (202) 662 - 2674

SIMONETTI, Arthur J.
Manager, Trade Legislation and Regulation
Registered Federal Lobbyist.
Tel: (202) 662 - 2671
Fax: (202) 662 - 2674

Honeywell Internat'l, Inc.

** continued from previous page*

ZURAWSKI, Paul R. — Tel: (202) 662 - 2650
Director, Tax and Benefits Policy — Fax: (202) 662 - 2674
Registered Federal Lobbyist.

At Other Offices

BENJAMIN, Karin L. — Tel: (505) 828 - 5857
Associate Communications Representative — Fax: (505) 828 - 5500
9201 San Mateo Blvd. NE
Albuquerque, NM 87113-5857

BIRTCIL, Bill — Tel: (602) 365 - 3859
V. President, Communications
(Honeywell Aerospace)
1944 E. Sky Harbor Circle
Phoenix, AZ 85034

H. P. Hood Inc.

A dairy manufacturing company.
www.hphood.com

Chairman, President and Chief Exec. Officer — Tel: (617) 887 - 3000
KANEB, John A. — Fax: (617) 887 - 8484

Main Headquarters
Mailing: 90 Everett Ave. — Tel: (617) 887 - 3000
Chelsea, MA 02150-2301 — Fax: (617) 887 - 8484
TF: (800) 343 - 6592

Corporate Foundations and Giving Programs

H. P. Hood Community Relations
Contact: Lynne M. Bohan
90 Everett Ave. — Tel: (617) 887 - 3000
Chelsea, MA 02150-2301 — Fax: (617) 887 - 8484

Annual Grant Total: none reported
The company does not have a formal corporate giving program and gives only to pre-determined organizations in the New England area. Gifts are primarily in the form of in-kind donations. The company does not accept unsolicited requests for funding.

Public Affairs and Related Activities Personnel

At Headquarters

BOHAN, Lynne M. — Tel: (617) 887 - 3000
Director, Public Relations and Government Affairs — Fax: (617) 887 - 8484

Horace Mann Educators Corp.

An insurance holding company.
www.horacemann.com
Annual Revenues: $771 million

Chairman of the Board — Tel: (217) 789 - 2500
MELONE, Joseph J. — Fax: (217) 788 - 5161

President and Chief Exec. Officer — Tel: (217) 789 - 2500
LOWER, Louis G., II — Fax: (217) 788 - 5161

Main Headquarters
Mailing: One Horace Mann Plaza — Tel: (217) 789 - 2500
Springfield, IL 62715-0001 — Fax: (217) 788 - 5161

Public Affairs and Related Activities Personnel

At Headquarters

HALLMAN, Dwayne D. — Tel: (217) 788 - 5708
Senior V. President, Finance — Fax: (217) 788 - 5161
Responsibilities include investor relations.

RUFFATTO, Karen — Tel: (217) 788 - 5707
Investor Relations Administrator — Fax: (217) 788 - 5161

WAPPEL, Paul — Tel: (217) 789 - 2500
Assistant V. President, Corporate Communications and Public Relations — Fax: (217) 788 - 5161

Horizon Air Industries

See listing on page 15 under Alaska Air Group, Inc.

Horizon Blue Cross Blue Shield of New Jersey

A member of the Public Affairs Council. Formerly Blue Cross and Blue Shield of New Jersey.
www.horizonblue.com

Chairman of the Board — Tel: (973) 466 - 4000
GIBLIN, Vincent — Fax: (973) 466 - 7077

President and Chief Exec. Officer — Tel: (973) 466 - 4000
MARINO, William J. — Fax: (973) 466 - 7077
Mailstop: M/S PP-16A

Main Headquarters
Mailing: Three Penn Plaza East — Tel: (973) 466 - 4000
PP-15V — Fax: (973) 466 - 8762
Newark, NJ 07105-2200

Political Action Committees

BluePAC
Contact: Brian J. Litten
Three Penn Plaza East — Tel: (973) 466 - 8753
PP-15V — Fax: (973) 466 - 7077
Newark, NJ 07105-2200
Contributions to Candidates: none reported (01/05 - 09/05)

Corporate Foundations and Giving Programs

Horizon Foundation
Contact: Susan G. Austin
Three Penn Plaza East — Tel: (973) 466 - 8332
PP-15V — Fax: (973) 466 - 8762
Newark, NJ 07105-2200

Annual Grant Total: none reported

Public Affairs and Related Activities Personnel

At Headquarters

AUSTIN, Susan G. — Tel: (973) 466 - 8332
Contact Horizon Foundation — Fax: (973) 466 - 8762

DEDEO, Patrick — Tel: (973) 466 - 8754
Senior Manager, Government Affairs — Fax: (973) 466 - 7077

HYNCIK, Sarah — Tel: (973) 466 - 8546
Government Affairs Associate — Fax: (973) 466 - 7077
Mailstop: M/S PP-16H

LITTEN, Brian J. — Tel: (973) 466 - 8753
Director, Government Affairs — Fax: (973) 466 - 7077
Mailstop: M/S PP-16H
Responsibilities include political action.

RUBINO, Thomas — Tel: (973) 466 - 8755
Director, Public Affairs — Fax: (973) 466 - 8762
Thomas_Rubino@horizonblue.com

Hormel Foods Corp.

A member of the Public Affairs Council. A food processor.
www.hormel.com

Chairman and Chief Exec. Officer — Tel: (507) 437 - 5611
JOHNSON, Joel W.

Main Headquarters
Mailing: One Hormel Pl. — Tel: (507) 437 - 5611
Austin, MN 55912-3680

Political Action Committees

Hormel Foods Corp. PAC (Hormel PAC)
Contact: Michael J. McCoy
One Hormel Pl. — Tel: (507) 437 - 5611
Austin, MN 55912-3680 — Fax: (507) 437 - 5129
Contributions to Candidates: none reported (01/05 - 09/05)

Corporate Foundations and Giving Programs

Hormel Foods Corporate Contributions
Contact: Julie Craven
One Hormel Pl. — Tel: (507) 437 - 5345
Austin, MN 55912-3680 — Fax: (507) 434 - 6721

Annual Grant Total: none reported

Public Affairs and Related Activities Personnel

At Headquarters

BOIK, Dennis — Tel: (507) 437 - 5611
Manager, Environmental Affairs

CAVANAUGH, James W. — Tel: (507) 437 - 5611
Senior V. President, External Affairs, General Counsel and Corporate Secretary
Responsibilties include investor relations.

CRAVEN, Julie — Tel: (507) 437 - 5345
V. President, Corporate Communications — Fax: (507) 434 - 6721

JORGENSON, James A. — Tel: (507) 437 - 5611
Senior V. President, Human Resources

KROC, Rochelle — Tel: (507) 437 - 5611
Manager, Consumer Affairs

MCCOY, Michael J. — Tel: (507) 437 - 5611
Senior V. President and Chief Financial Officer — Fax: (507) 437 - 5129
Responsibilities include political action and investor relations.

D. R. Horton, Inc.

A home-builder.
www.drhorton.com
Annual Revenues: $8.73 billion

Chairman of the Board — Tel: (817) 390 - 8200
HORTON, Donald R. — Fax: (817) 390 - 1715
dhorton@drhorton.com

D. R. Horton, Inc.

* continued from previous page

V. Chairman, President and Chief Exec. Officer
TOMNITZ, Donald J. — Tel: (817) 390 - 8200, Fax: (817) 390 - 1715
dtomnitz@drhorton.com

Main Headquarters
Mailing: 301 Commerce St.
Suite 500
Fort Worth, TX 76006
Tel: (817) 390 - 8200, Fax: (817) 390 - 1715

Public Affairs and Related Activities Personnel

At Headquarters

BROOKS, Shannon M. — Tel: (817) 390 - 8200, Fax: (817) 390 - 1715
Communications Coordinator
smbrooks@drhorton.com

DWYER, Stacey H. — Tel: (817) 390 - 8200, Fax: (817) 390 - 1715
Exec. V. President, Investor Relations
sdwyer@drhorton.com
Responsibilities include corporate communications.

HUNTER-PERKINS, Paula — Tel: (817) 390 - 8200, Fax: (817) 390 - 1715
V. President and Director, Human Resources

Host Marriott Corp.

www.hostmarriott.com
Annual Revenues: $3.799 billion

Chairman of the Board
MARRIOTT, Richard — Tel: (240) 744 - 1000
richard.marriott@hostmarriott.com

Chief Exec. Officer and President
NASSETTA, Christopher J. — Tel: (240) 744 - 1000
christopher.nassetta@hostmarriott.com

Main Headquarters
Mailing: 6903 Rockledge Dr.
Suite 1500
Bethesda, MD 20817
Tel: (240) 744 - 1000, Fax: (240) 744 - 5125

Public Affairs and Related Activities Personnel

At Headquarters

ABDOO, Elizabeth A. — Tel: (240) 744 - 1000
Senior V. President, General Counsel and Corporate Secretary

LARSON, Greg — Tel: (240) 744 - 5800
Treasurer and Senior V. President, Investor Relations
greg.larson@hostmarriott.com

Houghton Mifflin Co.

A publishing company. Acquired in December, 2002, by a group of private investment firms, including, Thomas H. Lee Partners, Bain Capital and funds managed by The Blackstone Group.
www.hmco.com

President and Chief Exec. Officer
LUCKI, Anthony — Tel: (617) 351 - 5000, Fax: (617) 351 - 1100

Main Headquarters
Mailing: 222 Berkeley St.
Boston, MA 02116
Tel: (617) 351 - 5000, Fax: (617) 351 - 1100

Washington Office
Contact: Larry S. Snowhite
Mailing: 1156 15th St.
Suite 1005
Washington, DC 20005
Tel: (202) 467 - 5350

Corporate Foundations and Giving Programs

Houghton Mifflin Co. Contributions
Contact: Collin Earnst
222 Berkeley St.
Boston, MA 02116
Tel: (617) 351 - 5113, Fax: (617) 351 - 1100

Annual Grant Total: $500,000 - $750,000
Geographic Preference: Area(s) in which the company operates
Primary Interests: Arts and Culture; Civic and Public Affairs; Education; Environment/Conservation; Health and Human Services; Minority Opportunities; United Way Campaigns

Public Affairs and Related Activities Personnel

At Headquarters

ARNOLD, Siobhan — Tel: (617) 351 - 5000, Fax: (617) 351 - 1100
Manager, Public Relations
siobhan_arnold@hmco.com

DIMARCO, Maureen — Tel: (617) 351 - 5000, Fax: (617) 351 - 1100
Senior V. President, Educational and Governmental Affairs

EARNST, Collin — Tel: (617) 351 - 5113, Fax: (617) 351 - 1100
V. President, Corporate Communications
collin_earnst@hmco.com

HUGHES, Gerald — Tel: (617) 351 - 5000, Fax: (617) 351 - 1100
Senior V. President, Human Resources

At Washington Office

SNOWHITE, Larry S. — Tel: (202) 467 - 5350
V. President, Government Relations
Registered Federal Lobbyist.

Household Finance Corp.

See listing on page 249 under HSBC North America Holdings Inc.

Household Financial Group Ltd.

See listing on page 249 under HSBC North America Holdings Inc.

Household International, Inc.

See listing on page 249 under HSBC North America Holdings Inc.

Hovnanian Enterprises, Inc.

A residential builder.
www.khov.com
Annual Revenues: $2.55 billion

Chairman of the Board
HOVNANIAN, Kevork S. — Tel: (732) 747 - 7800, Fax: (732) 747 - 6835

President and Chief Exec. Officer
HOVNANIAN, Ara K. — Tel: (732) 747 - 7800, Fax: (732) 747 - 6835

Main Headquarters
Mailing: Ten Hwy. 35
Red Bank, NJ 07701-5902
Tel: (732) 747 - 7800, Fax: (732) 747 - 6835

Public Affairs and Related Activities Personnel

At Headquarters

FENICHEL, Doug — Tel: (732) 225 - 4001, Fax: (732) 747 - 6835
Director, Public Relations

HAKE, Kevin — Tel: (732) 747 - 7800, Fax: (732) 747 - 6835
Senior V. President, Finance and Treasurer
Responsibilities include investor relations.

O'KEEFE, Jeffrey — Tel: (732) 747 - 7800, Fax: (732) 747 - 6835
Director, Investor Relations

HSB Group

See listing on page 235 under Hartford Steam Boiler Inspection and Insurance Co.

HSBC North America Holdings Inc.

Formerly known as Household International, Inc. A provider of consumer finance and credit card products in the United States, Canada and the United Kingdom. A subsidiary of HSBC Holdings plc, headquartered in London, UK.
www.household.com

Chairman and Chief Exec. Officer
MEHTA, Siddarth N. — Tel: (847) 564 - 5000, Fax: (847) 805 - 7452

Main Headquarters
Mailing: 2700 Sanders Rd.
Prospect Heights, IL 60070
Tel: (847) 564 - 5000, Fax: (847) 805 - 7452

Washington Office
Contact: J. Denis O'Toole
Mailing: 1401 I St. NW
Suite 520
Washington, DC 20005
Tel: (202) 466 - 3561, Fax: (202) 466 - 3583

Political Action Committees

Household International, Inc. PAC
Contact: Janet G. St. Amand
1401 I St. NW
Suite 520
Washington, DC 20005
Tel: (202) 466 - 3561, Fax: (202) 466 - 3583

Contributions to Candidates: $187,736 (01/05 - 09/05)
Democrats: $81,450; Republicans: $106,286.

Principal Recipients

SENATE DEMOCRATS		HOUSE DEMOCRATS	
Ford, Harold E Jr (TN)	$10,000	Crowley, Joseph (NY)	$5,000
Carper, Thomas R (DE)	$5,450	Scott, David (GA)	$5,000
SENATE REPUBLICANS		**HOUSE REPUBLICANS**	
Smith, Gordon (OR)	$6,000	Bachus, Spencer (AL)	$5,000
Bennett, Robert F (UT)	$5,000	Kirk, Mark Steven (IL)	$5,000
Santorum, Richard (PA)	$5,000	Ney, Robert W (OH)	$5,000

Corporate Foundations and Giving Programs

Household International Contributions Program

HSBC North America Holdings Inc.

** continued from previous page*

2700 Sanders Rd.
Prospect Heights, IL 60070
Tel: (847) 564 - 5000
Fax: (847) 805 - 7452

Annual Grant Total: $2,000,000 - $5,000,000
Guidelines available.
Geographic Preference: Area(s) in which the company operates
Primary Interests: Community Affairs; Health; Human Welfare

Public Affairs and Related Activities Personnel

At Headquarters

MORRISON, Kathleen A.
Director, Public Relations
kamorrison@household.com
Tel: (847) 564 - 6111
Fax: (847) 205 - 7490

NICHOLSON, Thomas
Public Affairs
Tel: (847) 564 - 5000
Fax: (847) 805 - 7452

PIEPER, James
Manager, Public Affairs
Tel: (847) 564 - 5000
Fax: (847) 805 - 7452

At Washington Office

GANGEMI, Hilary A.
Coordinator, Legislative and Political Affairs
Tel: (202) 466 - 3561
Fax: (202) 466 - 3583

ISLER, Micaela
PAC Director
Tel: (202) 466 - 3561
Fax: (202) 466 - 3583

O'TOOLE, J. Denis
Senior V. President, Government Relations
(Household Financial Group Ltd.)
Registered Federal Lobbyist.
Tel: (202) 466 - 3561
Fax: (202) 466 - 3583

ST. AMAND, Janet G.
Director/Counsel, Federal Governmental Relations
Registered Federal Lobbyist.
Tel: (202) 466 - 3561
Fax: (202) 466 - 3583

STEWARD, William R.
Director, Governmental Relations
Tel: (202) 466 - 3561
Fax: (202) 466 - 3583

At Other Offices

CESPEDES, Larisa
Regional Director, State Government Relations
980 Ninth St.
Sacramento, CA 95814
Tel: (916) 443 - 8570
Fax: (916) 443 - 8205

EMERICK, David A.
Regional Director, Government Relations
10139 S. Mountain Maple Court
Highlands Ranch, CO 80126-5435
Tel: (303) 346 - 0655

EVELAND, Edward E.
Regional Director, State Government Relations
500 Water's Edge
Harrisburg, PA 19073
Tel: (610) 325 - 5560

HECKNER, Kedron L. "Larry"
Regional Director/Team Leader, State Government Relations
102 Balzac Court
Cary, NC 27511
Tel: (919) 468 - 0066

PUGLIESE, Ronald J.
Regional Director/Team Leader, State Government Relations
213 Millville Ave.
Naugatuck, CT 06770
Tel: (203) 720 - 1614

TAYLOR, Greg D.
Regional Director, State Government Relations
2208 Joyce Bridge Ct.
Chesterfield, MO 63017
Tel: (636) 530 - 6350

VAN DOORN, John E.
Regional Director, State Government Relations
1040 Baumock Burn Dr.
Worthington, OH 43235
Tel: (614) 888 - 8891

ZITO, Greg A.
Regional Director, State Government Relations
31 W. 271 Prairie Ln.
Wayne, IL 60184
Tel: (630) 584 - 1183

HSBC USA, Inc.

The holding company for HSBC Bank USA. Owned by HSBC Holdings plc of the United Kingdom.
www.banking.us.hsbc.com

President and Chief Exec. Officer
GLYNN, Martin J. G.
Tel: (212) 525 - 5000
TF: (800) 975 - 4722

Main Headquarters
Mailing: 452 Fifth Ave.
New York, NY 10018
Tel: (212) 525 - 5000
TF: (800) 975 - 4722

Corporate Foundations and Giving Programs

HSBC in the Community
Contact: Kristen Alvanson
452 Fifth Ave.
New York, NY 10018
Tel: (212) 525 - 8239
TF: (800) 975 - 4722

Annual Grant Total: none reported
Geographic Preference: Area(s) in which the company operates
Primary Interests: Education; Environment/Conservation
Recent Recipients: United Way

Public Affairs and Related Activities Personnel

At Headquarters

ALVANSON, Kristen
Contact, Corporate Giving
Mailstop: Seventh Fl.
Tel: (212) 525 - 8239
TF: (800) 975 - 4722

EBERSOLE, Jeanne
Exec. V. President, Human Resources
Tel: (212) 525 - 5000
TF: (800) 975 - 4722

STRYKER-LUFTIG, Linda
Exec. V. President, Group Public Affairs
Mailstop: Seventh Fl.
linda.stryker-luftig@us.hsbc.com
Tel: (212) 525 - 5000
TF: (800) 975 - 4722

At Other Offices

PLEHN, Pamela
V. President, Group Public Affairs Media Relations
One HSBC Center
Buffalo, NY 14203
pamela.plehn@us.hsbc.com
Tel: (716) 841 - 5003

RIZZO YOUNG, Kathleen
First V. President, Group Public Affairs Media Relations
One HSBC Center
Buffalo, NY 14203
kathleen.rizzo.young@us.hsbc.com
Tel: (716) 841 - 5003

HSN, Inc.

An operating unit of IAC/InterActive Corp (see separate listing).
www.hsn.com

Chief Exec. Officer
MCINERNEY, Thomas J.
Tel: (727) 872 - 1000
Fax: (727) 872 - 6615

Main Headquarters
Mailing: One HSN Dr.
St. Petersburg, FL 33729
Tel: (727) 872 - 1000
Fax: (727) 872 - 6615

Public Affairs and Related Activities Personnel

At Headquarters

GRINGERI, Darris
Director, Public Relations
gringerid@hsn.net
Tel: (727) 872 - 1000
Fax: (727) 872 - 7406

Hubbard Broadcasting, Inc.

Television and radio broadcasting company.

Main Headquarters
Mailing: 3415 University Ave.
St. Paul, MN 55114
Tel: (651) 646 - 5555
Fax: (651) 642 - 4103

Corporate Foundations and Giving Programs

The Hubbard Broadcasting Foundation
Contact: Kathryn Hubbard Rominski
3415 University Ave.
St. Paul, MN 55114
Tel: (651) 642 - 4305
Fax: (651) 642 - 4103

Annual Grant Total: $1,000,000 - $2,000,000
Geographic Preference: Area(s) in which the company operates; Florida; Minnesota; New Mexico; New York
Primary Interests: Arts and Humanities; Health; Higher Education; Youth Services
Recent Recipients: Junior Achievement

Public Affairs and Related Activities Personnel

At Headquarters

ROMINSKI, Kathryn Hubbard
Exec. Director, Hubbard Foundation
Tel: (651) 642 - 4305
Fax: (651) 642 - 4103

Hubbell Incorporated

A manufacturer of electrical and electronic products.
www.hubbell.com

Chairman, President and Chief Exec. Officer
POWERS, Timothy H.
Tel: (203) 799 - 4100
Fax: (203) 799 - 4223

Main Headquarters
Mailing: 584 Derby Milford Rd.
Orange, CT 06477
Tel: (203) 799 - 4100
Fax: (203) 799 - 4205

Corporate Foundations and Giving Programs

Harvey Hubbell Foundation
Contact: Timothy H. Powers

Hubbell Incorporated

* continued from previous page

584 Derby Milford Rd.
Orange, CT 06477
Tel: (203) 799 - 4100
Fax: (203) 799 - 4223

Annual Grant Total: $100,000 - $200,000

Geographic Preference: Area(s) in which the company operates
Primary Interests: Community Affairs; Community Development; Health; Higher Education
Recent Recipients: Nat'l Merit Scholarship

Public Affairs and Related Activities Personnel

At Headquarters

CONLIN, Thomas R.
V. President, Public Affairs
Responsibilities include investor relations.
Tel: (203) 799 - 4293
Fax: (203) 799 - 4223

Huffy Corp.

A seller of bicycles, juvenile products, basketball backboards and related equipment. Also conducts an assembly service business.

www.huffy.com

Chairman of the Board
SULLIVAN, Thomas C.
Tel: (937) 866 - 6251
Fax: (937) 865 - 5470

Chief Exec. Officer
MUSKOVICH, John A.
Tel: (937) 866 - 6251
Fax: (937) 865 - 5470

Main Headquarters
Mailing: 225 Byers Rd.
Miamisburg, OH 45342
Tel: (937) 866 - 6251
Fax: (937) 865 - 5470

Political Action Committees

Huffy PAC
Contact: Marla J. Evans
225 Byers Rd.
Miamisburg, OH 45342
Tel: (937) 866 - 6251
Fax: (937) 865 - 5470

Contributions to Candidates: $49 (01/05 - 09/05)
Republicans: $49.

Corporate Foundations and Giving Programs

The Huffy Foundation, Inc.
Contact: Pamela K. Booher
225 Byers Rd.
Miamisburg, OH 45342
Tel: (937) 866 - 6251
Fax: (937) 865 - 5484

Assets: $165,066 (2000)
Annual Grant Total: $100,000 - $200,000

Focuses on capital and special programs with the highest priority of need in the locality. Guidelines are available.
Geographic Preference: Area(s) in which the company operates
Primary Interests: Arts and Culture; Higher Education; Medicine and Health Care; United Way Campaigns
Recent Recipients: Nat'l Ass'n for the Advancement of Colored People; Planned Parenthood Federation of America; United Negro College Fund; United Way

Public Affairs and Related Activities Personnel

At Headquarters

BOOHER, Pamela K.
Secretary, Foundation
Tel: (937) 866 - 6251
Fax: (937) 865 - 5484

EVANS, Marla J.
PAC Treasurer
Tel: (937) 866 - 6251
Fax: (937) 865 - 5470

LIPTON, Steven D.
Chief Financial Officer
Tel: (937) 866 - 6251
Fax: (937) 865 - 5470

Hughes Electronics Corp.

See listing on page 159 under The DIRECTV Group, Inc.

Hughes Supply, Inc.

A distributor of electrical, plumbing and other building supplies.

www.hughessupply.com

Chairman of the Board
HUGHES, David H.
dhughes@hughessupply.com
Tel: (407) 841 - 4755
Fax: (407) 649 - 1670

Chief Exec. Officer
MORGAN, Thomas I.
Tel: (407) 841 - 4755
Fax: (407) 649 - 1670

Main Headquarters
Mailing: One Hughes Way
Orlando, FL 32805-2205
Tel: (407) 841 - 4755
Fax: (407) 872 - 1895

Corporate Foundations and Giving Programs

Hughes Supply Foundation
Contact: Monroe Harrison
One Hughes Way
Orlando, FL 32805-2205
Tel: (407) 841 - 4755
Fax: (407) 649 - 1670

Annual Grant Total: none reported

Public Affairs and Related Activities Personnel

At Headquarters

HARRISON, Monroe
Manager, Corporate Citizenship
Tel: (407) 841 - 4755
Fax: (407) 649 - 1670

Humana Health Plan, Inc.

See listing on page 251 under Humana Inc.

Humana Inc.

A health care insurance company.

www.humana.com
Annual Revenues: $10.076 billion

Chairman of the Board
JONES, David
djones@humana.com
Tel: (502) 580 - 1000
Fax: (502) 580 - 3677
TF: (800) 486 - 2620

President and Chief Exec. Officer
MCCALLISTER, Michael B.
mmccallister@humana.com
Tel: (502) 580 - 1000
Fax: (502) 580 - 3677
TF: (800) 486 - 2620

Main Headquarters
Mailing: P.O. Box 1438
Louisville, KY 40201-1438
Tel: (502) 580 - 1000
Fax: (502) 580 - 3677
TF: (800) 486 - 2620

Street: The Humana Building
500 W. Main St.
Louisville, KY 40202

Washington Office
Mailing: 1776 I St. NW
Suite 890
Washington, DC 20006
Tel: (202) 467 - 5821
Fax: (202) 467 - 5825

Political Action Committees

Humana Inc. Political Action Committee
Contact: Edward Kaleta
1776 I St. NW
Suite 890
Washington, DC 20006
Tel: (202) 467 - 5821
Fax: (202) 467 - 5825

Contributions to Candidates: $47,100 (01/05 - 09/05)
Democrats: $14,000; Republicans: $33,100.

Principal Recipients

SENATE DEMOCRATS		**HOUSE DEMOCRATS**	
Conrad, Kent (ND)	$2,000	Schultz, Debbie (FL)	$5,000
		Castor, Katherine (FL)	$2,500
		Rush, Bobby (IL)	$2,500
SENATE REPUBLICANS		**HOUSE REPUBLICANS**	
McConnell, Mitch (KY)	$2,500	Davis, Geoffrey (KY)	$5,000
		Lewis, Ron (KY)	$2,000
		Northup, Anne M. (KY)	$2,000
		Sodrel, Michael (IN)	$2,000

Corporate Foundations and Giving Programs

Humana Foundation
Contact: Virginia Kelly-Judd
P.O. Box 1438
Louisville, KY 40201-1438
Tel: (502) 580 - 3041
Fax: (502) 580 - 3677
TF: (800) 486 - 2620

Annual Grant Total: over $5,000,000

Geographic Preference: Area in which the company is headquartered
Primary Interests: Arts and Humanities; Civic and Public Affairs; Education; Environment/Conservation; Health; Social Services
Recent Recipients: American Red Cross; Boy Scouts of America; United Negro College Fund; United Way

Public Affairs and Related Activities Personnel

At Headquarters

BROWN, Richard A.
Corporate Director, Media Relations
dbrown4@humana.com
Tel: (502) 580 - 3683
Fax: (502) 580 - 3677
TF: (800) 486 - 2620

HATHCOCK, Bonnie
Senior V. President and Chief Human Resources Officer
bhathcock@humana.com
Tel: (502) 580 - 1000
Ext: 3575
Fax: (502) 580 - 3677
TF: (800) 486 - 2620

HIPWELL, Art
Senior V. President, Regulatory Affairs and General Counsel
ahipwell@humana.com
Tel: (502) 580 - 1000
Fax: (502) 580 - 3677
TF: (800) 486 - 2620

KELLY-JUDD, Virginia
Exec. Director, Humana Foundation
Tel: (502) 580 - 3041
Fax: (502) 580 - 3677
TF: (800) 486 - 2620

LENAHAN, Joan O.
Corporate Secretary
jlenahan@humana.com
Responsibilities include investor relations.
Tel: (502) 580 - 3778
Fax: (502) 580 - 3677
TF: (800) 486 - 2620

Humana Inc.

** continued from previous page*

MARGULIS, Heidi
Senior V. President, Government Relations
hmargulis@humana.com
Tel: (502) 580 - 1854
Fax: (502) 580 - 3677
TF: (800) 486 - 2620

NETHERY, Regina
V. President, Investor Relations
rnethery@humana.com
Tel: (502) 580 - 3644
Fax: (502) 580 - 3677
TF: (800) 486 - 2620

NOLAND, Thomas
Senior V. President, Corporate Communications
Tel: (502) 580 - 3674
Fax: (502) 580 - 3677
TF: (800) 486 - 2620

SELLERS, Mary
Manager, Media Relations
msellers1@humana.com
Tel: (502) 580 - 3689
Fax: (502) 580 - 3677
TF: (800) 486 - 2620

SHIELDS, R. Eugene
Senior V. President, Government Programs
Tel: (502) 580 - 1000
Fax: (502) 580 - 3677
TF: (800) 486 - 2620

At Washington Office

KALETA, Edward
Pac Treasurer
Tel: (202) 467 - 5821
Fax: (202) 467 - 5825

At Other Offices

LOTT, Cherie Nanette
Manager, Regulatory Legislation
115 Perimeter Center Place, N.E.
Suite 650
Atlanta, GA 30346
Tel: (770) 399 - 5916

SNYDER, Timothy C.
Director, Regional Legislative Affairs, Midwest Region
16 E. Broad St.
Suite 301
Columbus, OH 43215
Tel: (502) 580 - 3580

Hunt Oil Co.

A member of the Public Affairs Council. A petroleum exploration and production company.
www.huntoil.com

Chairman of the Board
JENNINGS, James B.
Tel: (214) 978 - 8000
Fax: (214) 978 - 8888

Chief Exec. Officer
HUNT, Ray L.
Tel: (214) 978 - 8000
Fax: (214) 978 - 8888

Main Headquarters
Mailing: 1445 Ross at Field
Suite 1400
Dallas, TX 75202-2785
Tel: (214) 978 - 8000
Fax: (214) 978 - 8888

Political Action Committees

Hunt Oil Co. Political Action Committee
Contact: Ben Golding
1445 Ross at Field
Suite 1400
Dallas, TX 75202-2785
Tel: (214) 978 - 8260
Fax: (214) 978 - 8888

Contributions to Candidates: $10,000 (01/05 - 09/05)
Republicans: $10,000.

Principal Recipients

SENATE REPUBLICANS		HOUSE REPUBLICANS	
Allen, George (VA)	$4,000	Bonilla, Henry (TX)	$1,000
Burns, Conrad (MT)	$2,500	Granger, Kay N (TX)	$1,000
Cornyn, John (TX)	$1,000		

Corporate Foundations and Giving Programs

Hunt Oil Co. Corporate Contributions
1445 Ross at Field
Suite 1400
Dallas, TX 75202-2785
Tel: (214) 978 - 8000
Fax: (214) 978 - 8888

Annual Grant Total: none reported

Public Affairs and Related Activities Personnel

At Headquarters

GOLDING, Ben
Treasurer, Hunt Oil Co. Political Action Committee
Tel: (214) 978 - 8260
Fax: (214) 978 - 8888

MARTIN, Alisa
Director, Corporate Communications
Tel: (214) 978 - 8060
Fax: (214) 978 - 8888

PHILLIPS, Jeanne
Public Affairs
Tel: (214) 978 - 8534
Fax: (214) 978 - 8888

WEAVER, Laura
V. President, Human Resources
Tel: (214) 978 - 8000
Fax: (214) 978 - 8888

J. B. Hunt Transport Services, Inc.

A transportation provider.
www.jbhunt.com

Chairman of the Board
GARRISON, Wayne
Tel: (479) 820 - 0000
Fax: (479) 820 - 8397
TF: (800) 643 - 3622

President and Chief Exec. Officer
THOMPSON, J. Kirk
kirk-thompson@jbhunt.com
Tel: (479) 820 - 8110
Fax: (479) 820 - 8397
TF: (800) 643 - 3622

Main Headquarters
Mailing: 615 J.B. Hunt Corporate Dr.
P.O. Box 130
Lowell, AR 72745
Tel: (479) 820 - 0000
Fax: (479) 820 - 8249
TF: (800) 643 - 3622

Corporate Foundations and Giving Programs

J. B. Hunt Transport Services Corporate Contributions Program
Contact: Amy Bain
615 J.B. Hunt Corporate Dr.
P.O. Box 130
Lowell, AR 72745
Tel: (479) 820 - 8111
Fax: (479) 820 - 8397
TF: (800) 643 - 3622

Annual Grant Total: none reported

Public Affairs and Related Activities Personnel

At Headquarters

BAIN, Amy
Exec. Assistant to the President and Chief Exec. Officer
Tel: (479) 820 - 8111
Fax: (479) 820 - 8397
TF: (800) 643 - 3622
Responsibilities include corporate contributions.

GREENWAY, Mark
V. President, Human Resources
Tel: (479) 820 - 8240
Fax: (479) 820 - 8397
TF: (800) 643 - 3622

WALTON, Jerry W.
Exec. V. President, Finance and Administration; and Chief Financial Officer
jerry-walton@jbhunt.com
Tel: (479) 820 - 8120
Fax: (479) 820 - 8397
TF: (800) 643 - 3622
Responsibilities include government affairs.

YOUNG, Lisa
Manager, Corporate Communications
lisa-young@jbhunt.com
Tel: (479) 820 - 0000
Fax: (479) 820 - 4241
TF: (800) 643 - 3622

Huntington Bancshares Inc.

A bank holding company.
www.huntington.com
Annual Revenues: $2.5 billion

Chairman and Chief Exec. Officer
HOAGLIN, Thomas E.
Tel: (614) 480 - 5533
Fax: (614) 480 - 4973

Main Headquarters
Mailing: 41 S. High St.
Columbus, OH 43287
Tel: (614) 480 - 8300
Fax: (614) 480 - 4973

Political Action Committees

Huntington Bancshares Inc. Political Action Committee (HBI-PAC)
Contact: Barbara Benham
41 S. High St.
Columbus, OH 43287
Tel: (614) 480 - 4718
Fax: (614) 480 - 4973

Contributions to Candidates: $39,600 (01/05 - 09/05)
Democrats: $4,000; Republicans: $35,600.

Principal Recipients

SENATE DEMOCRATS		HOUSE DEMOCRATS	
Stabenow, Debbie (MI)	$2,000		
SENATE REPUBLICANS		**HOUSE REPUBLICANS**	
Dewine, Richard (OH)	$9,000	Blasdel, Chuck (OH)	$5,000
		Pryce, Deborah (OH)	$5,000
		Ney, Robert W (OH)	$3,500
		Boehner, John (OH)	$3,000
		Hobson, David (OH)	$2,500
		Dewine, R. Pat (OH)	$2,000
		Schmidt, Jeannette (OH)	$2,000

Corporate Foundations and Giving Programs

Huntington Bancshares Corporate Giving Program
Contact: Elfi DiBella
41 S. High St.
Columbus, OH 43287
Tel: (614) 480 - 4483
Fax: (614) 480 - 4973

Annual Grant Total: none reported
The company encourages employees to participate in philanthropic efforts and takes volunteer activities into consideration during performance appraisals.
Geographic Preference: Area(s) in which the company operates; Indiana; Kentucky; Michigan; Ohio; West Virginia; Florida
Primary Interests: Children; Economic Development; Education; Health and Human Services

Public Affairs and Related Activities Personnel

At Headquarters

BENHAM, Barbara
Senior V. President and Director, Government Relations
Tel: (614) 480 - 4718
Fax: (614) 480 - 4973

Huntington Bancshares Inc.

** continued from previous page*

DIBELLA, Elfi — Tel: (614) 480 - 4483
Senior V. President, Community Affairs — Fax: (614) 480 - 4973
Responsibilities include corporate philanthropy.

FIELDS, Steven — Tel: (614) 480 - 3278
Corporate Affairs Specialist — Fax: (614) 480 - 4973

NEWMAN, Ron — Tel: (614) 480 - 8300
Media Contact — Fax: (614) 480 - 746
ron.newman@huntington.com

THOMPSON, Denise Love — Tel: (614) 480 - 8300
Treasurer, HBI-PAC — Fax: (614) 480 - 4723

Huntsman Corp.

A manufacturer of petrochemicals and plastics.
www.huntsman.com

Chairman of the Board
HUNTSMAN, Jon M. — Tel: (801) 584 - 5700; Fax: (801) 584 - 5781

President and Chief Exec. Officer
HUNTSMAN, Peter — Tel: (713) 235 - 6000
peter_huntsman@huntsman.com

Main Headquarters
Mailing: 500 Huntsman Way, Salt Lake City, UT 84108 — Tel: (801) 584 - 5700; Fax: (801) 584 - 5781

Washington Office
Contact: Don H. Olsen
Mailing: 1300 Wilson Blvd., Arlington, VA 22209 — Tel: (703) 741 - 5885; Fax: (703) 741 - 6081

Political Action Committees

Huntsman Corp. Political Action Committee
Contact: Don H. Olsen
10003 Woodloch Forest Dr.
The Woodlands, TX 77380 — Tel: (281) 719 - 4175

Contributions to Candidates: $6,000 (01/05 - 09/05)
Democrats: $4,000; Republicans: $2,000.

Principal Recipients

SENATE DEMOCRATS
Conrad, Kent (ND) $3,000
Bingaman, Jeff (NM) $1,000

HOUSE DEMOCRATS

SENATE REPUBLICANS

HOUSE REPUBLICANS
Barton, Joe L (TX) $2,000

Public Affairs and Related Activities Personnel

At Headquarters

HESKETT, John — Tel: (801) 584 - 5768
V. President, Corporate Development and Investor Relations — Fax: (801) 584 - 5781
john_heskett@huntsman.com

At Other Offices

KERN, Michael J. — Tel: (713) 235 - 6000
Senior V. President, Environmental, Health, and Safety
3040 Post Oak Blvd.
Houston, TX 77056
mike_kern@huntsman.com

OLSEN, Don H. — Tel: (281) 719 - 4175
Senior V. President, Public Affairs
10003 Woodloch Forest Dr.
The Woodlands, TX 77380
don_olsen@huntsman.com

Hy-Vee, Inc.

A food and drug retailer.
www.hy-vee.com

Chairman of the Board
PEARSON, Ronald D. — Tel: (515) 267 - 2800; Fax: (515) 267 - 2817

President, Chief Exec. Officer and Chief Operating Officer
JURGENS, Richard N. — Tel: (515) 267 - 2800; Fax: (515) 267 - 2817

Main Headquarters
Mailing: 5820 Westown Pkwy., West Des Moines, IA 50266-8223 — Tel: (515) 267 - 2800; Fax: (515) 267 - 2817

Political Action Committees

Hy-Vee Inc. Employees PAC
Contact: John Brummit
5820 Westown Pkwy.
West Des Moines, IA 50266-8223 — Tel: (515) 267 - 2800; Fax: (515) 267 - 2817

Contributions to Candidates: none reported (01/05 - 09/05)

Corporate Foundations and Giving Programs

Hy-Vee Food Stores Inc. Corporate Giving Program
Contact: Ruth Mitchell
5820 Westown Pkwy.
West Des Moines, IA 50266-8223 — Tel: (515) 267 - 2893; Fax: (515) 267 - 2362

Annual Grant Total: none reported

Public Affairs and Related Activities Personnel

At Headquarters

BRUMMIT, John — Tel: (515) 267 - 2800
PAC Treasurer — Fax: (515) 267 - 2817

KNAACK-ESBECK, Jane — Tel: (515) 267 - 2840
V. President, Human Resources — Fax: (515) 267 - 2817

MITCHELL, Ruth — Tel: (515) 267 - 2893
Assistant V. President, Communications — Fax: (515) 267 - 2362

VOGEL, Vern — Tel: (515) 267 - 2848
Assistant V. President, Risk Management — Fax: (515) 267 - 2817

Global Hyatt Corp.

Hotel holding company. Subsidiaries include Hyatt Hotels Corporation.
www.hyatt.com
Annual Revenues: $3.95 billion

Chairman and Chief Exec. Officer
PRITZKER, Thomas J. — Tel: (312) 750 - 1234; Fax: (312) 750 - 8550

Main Headquarters
Mailing: 71 S. wacker Dr, Chicago, IL 60606 — Tel: (312) 750 - 1234; Fax: (312) 750 - 8550

Public Affairs and Related Activities Personnel

At Headquarters

ARMON, Lori — Tel: (312) 750 - 8069
Director, Public Relations — Fax: (312) 750 - 8550
(Hyatt Hotels Corp.)
larmon@corphq.hyatt.com

MEYER, Katie — Tel: (312) 750 - 1234
V. President, Communications — Fax: (312) 750 - 8550

MIKULINA, David — Tel: (312) 750 - 8264
Assistant V. President, Risk Management — Fax: (312) 750 - 8550
dmikulin@corphq.hyatt.com

SELL, Angela — Tel: (312) 920 - 2325
Manager, Public Relations — Fax: (312) 750 - 8550
(Hyatt Hotels Corp.)
asell@corphq.hyatt.com

Hyatt Corporation

See listing on page 253 under Global Hyatt Corp.

Hyatt Hotels Corp.

See listing on page 253 under Global Hyatt Corp.

Hyundai Motor America

An automobile manufacturer. Parent company is Hyundai Motor Co. of Seoul, Korea.
www.hyundaiusa.com

President and Chief Exec. Officer
COSMAI, Robert F. — Tel: (714) 965 - 3000; Fax: (714) 965 - 3149

Main Headquarters
Mailing: P.O. Box 20850, Fountain Valley, CA 92728-0850 — Tel: (714) 965 - 3000; Fax: (714) 965 - 3149
Street: 10550 Talbert Ave., Fountain Valley, CA 92708

Washington Office
Contact: Margo Grimm Eule
Mailing: 1667 K St., NW, Suite 1210, Washington, DC 20006 — Tel: (202) 296 - 5550; Fax: (202) 296 - 6436

Corporate Foundations and Giving Programs

Hyundai Motor America Corporate Contributions Program
Contact: Chris L. Hosford
P.O. Box 20850 — Tel: (714) 965 - 3000
Fountain Valley, CA 92728-0850

Annual Grant Total: none reported
Primary Interests: Education

Public Affairs and Related Activities Personnel

At Headquarters

GRUBER, Andrea — Tel: (714) 965 - 3000
Contact, Hyundai Motor America Corporate Contributions Program — Fax: (714) 965 - 3837

HOSFORD, Chris L. — Tel: (714) 965 - 3000
V. President, Communications
chosford@hmausa.com

Hyundai Motor America

* continued from previous page

At Washington Office

EULE, Margo Grimm
Manager, Government Relations
mgeule@potomacnet.com
Tel: (202) 296 - 5550
Fax: (202) 296 - 6436

SHIN, Hyun Kyu "Frank"
Representative
hyunkyushin@hyundai-motor.co
Serves as the senior public affairs officer.
Tel: (202) 296 - 5550
Fax: (202) 296 - 6436

i2 Technologies, Inc.

An e-business software provider.
www.i2.com

Chairman of the Board
SIDHU, Sanjiv S.
Tel: (469) 357 - 1000
Fax: (469) 357 - 1798

Chief Exec. Officer and President
MCGRATH, Michael E.
Tel: (469) 357 - 1000
Fax: (469) 357 - 1798

Main Headquarters
Mailing: One i2 Pl.
11701 Luna Rd.
Dallas, TX 75234
Tel: (469) 357 - 1000
Fax: (469) 357 - 1798

Corporate Foundations and Giving Programs

The i2Foundation
Contact: Melis Jones
One i2 Pl.
11701 Luna Rd.
Dallas, TX 75234
Tel: (469) 357 - 1000
Fax: (469) 357 - 1798

Annual Grant Total: none reported
Primary Interests: Economic Development; Education; Environment/Conservation; Medicine and Health Care

Public Affairs and Related Activities Personnel

At Headquarters

ELKIN, Beth
Director, Public Relations
beth_elkin@i2.com
Tel: (469) 357 - 4225
Fax: (469) 357 - 3677

JONES, Melis
Foundation Contact
Tel: (469) 357 - 1000
Fax: (469) 357 - 1798

MONBERG, Kirsten
Senior Specialist, Public Relations
kirsten_monberg@i2.com
Tel: (469) 357 - 4966
Fax: (469) 357 - 3677

IAC/InterActiveCorp

A member of the Public Affairs Council. Formerly InterActiveCorp. Operates television and internet oriented businesses.
www.usainteractive.com

Chairman and Chief Exec. Officer
DILLER, Barry
Tel: (212) 314 - 7300
Fax: (212) 314 - 7309

Main Headquarters
Mailing: 152 W. 57th St.
42nd Floor
New York, NY 10019
Tel: (212) 314 - 7300
Fax: (212) 314 - 7309

Political Action Committees

InterActiveCorp PAC
Contact: Bret Myers
152 W. 57th St.
42nd Floor
New York, NY 10019
Tel: (212) 314 - 7300
Fax: (212) 314 - 7309

Contributions to Candidates: $3,000 (01/05 - 09/05)
Republicans: $3,000.

Principal Recipients

SENATE REPUBLICANS		HOUSE REPUBLICANS	
Dole, Elizabeth (NC)	$1,000	Bachus, Spencer (AL)	$1,000
		Sensenbrenner, Jim (WI)	$1,000

Public Affairs and Related Activities Personnel

At Headquarters

CLARK, Roger
V. President, Investor Relations and Finance
Tel: (212) 314 - 7300
Fax: (212) 314 - 7309

MYERS, Bret
PAC Treasurer
Tel: (212) 314 - 7300
Fax: (212) 314 - 7309

RIGGS, Andrea
Director, Corporate Communications
Tel: (212) 314 - 7280
Fax: (212) 314 - 7309

ROTH, Deborah
V. President, Corporate Communications
Tel: (212) 314 - 7254
Fax: (212) 314 - 7309

IBM

See listing on page 260 under Internat'l Business Machines Corp (IBM).

ICI American Holdings, Inc.

The U.S. subsidiary of Imperial Chemicals Industries PLC, London, England. Products include materials, polyester films, catalysts, paints, polyurethanes, explosives, acrylics, CFC replacements and titanium dioxide.
www.ici.com

Chairman of the Board
DANZEISEN, John
Tel: (908) 203 - 2800

Main Headquarters
Mailing: Ten Finderne Ave.
Bridgewater, NJ 08807
Tel: (908) 685 - 5000
Fax: (908) 685 - 5005

Corporate Foundations and Giving Programs

ICI Americas Corporate Contributions Program
Contact: Judith Kleemeier
Ten Finderne Ave.
Bridgewater, NJ 08807
Tel: (908) 203 - 2800
Fax: (908) 203 - 2918

Annual Grant Total: $300,000 - $400,000
Preference: grants made only to 501(c)(3) charities with emphasis on organizations in which company employees are active.
Geographic Preference: Delaware
Primary Interests: Civic and Cultural Activities; Education; Social Services
Recent Recipients: United Way

Public Affairs and Related Activities Personnel

At Headquarters

KLEEMEIER, Judith
Director, Human Resources
Responsibilities include corporate philanthropy.
Tel: (908) 203 - 2800
Fax: (908) 203 - 2918

IDACORP, Inc.

A holding company.
www.idacorpinc.com

Chairman of the Board
MILLER, Jon H.
Fax: (208) 388 - 6955

President and Chief Exec. Officer
PACKWOOD, Jan B.
jpackwood@idahopower.com
Tel: (208) 388 - 2200
Fax: (208) 388 - 6955

Main Headquarters
Mailing: P.O. Box 70
Boise, ID 83707
Street: 1221 W. Idaho St.
Boise, ID 83702-5627
Tel: (208) 388 - 2200
Fax: (208) 388 - 6955

Political Action Committees

IDA-PAC Political Action Committee
Contact: Fran Martin
P.O. Box 70
Boise, ID 83707
Tel: (208) 388 - 2530
Fax: (208) 388 - 6955

Contributions to Candidates: $3,000 (01/05 - 09/05)
Republicans: $3,000.

Corporate Foundations and Giving Programs

Corporate Contributions
Contact: Fran Martin
P.O. Box 70
Boise, ID 83707
Tel: (208) 388 - 2530
Fax: (208) 388 - 6955

Annual Grant Total: $500,000 - $750,000
Geographic Preference: Area(s) in which the company operates
Primary Interests: Arts and Culture; Community Affairs; Education; Health and Human Services

Public Affairs and Related Activities Personnel

At Headquarters

BEAMAN, Jeff
Corporate Communications
(Idaho Power Co.)
Tel: (208) 388 - 2200
Fax: (208) 388 - 6955

HAHN, Richard L.
Senior Legislative Affairs Representative
(Idaho Power Co.)
rhahn@idahopower.com
Tel: (208) 388 - 2513
Fax: (208) 388 - 6955

MARTIN, Fran
Contact, Corporate Contributions and Ida-PAC
(Idaho Power Co.)
fmartin@idahopower.com
Tel: (208) 388 - 2530
Fax: (208) 388 - 6955

MEYERS, David W.
General Manager, Relicensing and Environmental Affairs
(Idaho Power Co.)
Tel: (208) 383 - 2728
Fax: (208) 388 - 6955

PANTER, Gregory W.
V. President, Public Affairs
Tel: (208) 388 - 2200
Fax: (208) 388 - 6955

SPENCER, Lawrence F.
Director, Investor Relations
lspencer@idahopower.com
Tel: (208) 388 - 2664
Fax: (208) 388 - 6955
TF: (800) 635 - 5406

Idaho Power Co.

See listing on page 254 under IDACORP, Inc.

IES Industries, Inc.

See listing on page 21 under Alliant Energy Corp.

Ikon Office Solutions, Inc.

Formerly Alco Standard Corp. A diversified conglomerate involved in the distribution of paper and office products, metal products, and in the manufacture of aerospace components.
www.ikon.com

Chairman and Chief Exec. Officer
ESPE, Matthew J. — Tel: (610) 296 - 8000
mespe@ikon.com — Fax: (610) 408 - 7025 — TF: (888) 275 - 4566

Main Headquarters
Mailing: P.O. Box 834, Valley Forge, PA 19482-0834 — Tel: (610) 296 - 8000 — Fax: (610) 408 - 7025 — TF: (888) 275 - 4566
Street: 70 Valley Stream Pkwy., Malvern, PA 19355-0989

Corporate Foundations and Giving Programs
Ikon Office Solutions Foundation
Contact: Cathy Lewis
P.O. Box 834 — Tel: (610) 296 - 8000
Valley Forge, PA 19482-0834 — Fax: (610) 408 - 7025 — TF: (888) 275 - 4566

Annual Grant Total: $300,000 - $400,000
Geographic Preference: Area(s) in which the company operates
Primary Interests: Arts and Humanities; Civic and Public Affairs; Education; Health; Math and Science
Recent Recipients: Nat'l Merit Scholarship; Nature Conservancy; Salvation Army

Public Affairs and Related Activities Personnel

At Headquarters

HALPIN, Carol — Tel: (610) 296 - 8000
Contact, Ikon Office Solutions Foundations — Fax: (610) 408 - 7025
chalpin@ikon.com — TF: (888) 275 - 4566

LEWIS, Cathy — Tel: (610) 296 - 8000
Senior V. President, Marketing — Fax: (610) 408 - 7025
clewis@ikon.com — TF: (888) 275 - 4566
Responsibilities include corporate communications and contributions.

MAS, Russ — Tel: (610) 408 - 7220
Manager, Public Relations — Fax: (610) 408 - 7025
rmas@ikon.com — TF: (888) 275 - 4566

MURPHY, Dan — Tel: (610) 408 - 7196
Director, Investor Realtions — Fax: (610) 408 - 7025 — TF: (888) 275 - 4566

SEXTON, Beth R. — Tel: (610) 408 - 7224
Senior V. President, Human Resources — Fax: (610) 408 - 7025
bsexton@ikon.com — TF: (888) 275 - 4566

Illinois Bell Telephone

See listing on page 423 under SBC Illinois.

Illinois Central Corp.

See listing on page 99 under Canadian Nat'l / Illinois Central.

Illinois Power Co.

See listing on page 28 under Ameren Corp.

Illinois Tool Works Inc.

A diversified manufacturer of industrial components and systems.
www.itw.com
Annual Revenues: $9.5 billion

Chief Executive Officer
SPEER, David — Tel: (847) 724 - 7500 — Fax: (847) 657 - 4268

Main Headquarters
Mailing: 3600 W. Lake Ave., Glenview, IL 60025-5811 — Tel: (847) 724 - 7500 — Fax: (847) 657 - 4268

Political Action Committees
Illinois Tool Works For Better Government Committee
Contact: Michael J. Lynch
3600 W. Lake Ave. — Tel: (847) 657 - 4232
Glenview, IL 60025-5811 — Fax: (847) 657 - 7892

Contributions to Candidates: none reported (01/05 - 09/05)

Corporate Foundations and Giving Programs
Illinois Tool Works Foundation
Contact: Mary Ann Mallahan
3600 W. Lake Ave. — Tel: (847) 657 - 4092
Glenview, IL 60025-5811 — Fax: (847) 657 - 4505

Assets: $13,465,701 (1999)
Annual Grant Total: $2,000,000 - $5,000,000
Operates an employee matching gifts program which makes contributions in excess of $2.1 million.
Geographic Preference: Chicago, IL
Primary Interests: Arts and Culture; Education
Recent Recipients: Crusade of Mercy; Museum of Science and Industry; United Way

Public Affairs and Related Activities Personnel

At Headquarters

BROOKLIER, John L. — Tel: (847) 657 - 4104
V. President, Investor Relations — Fax: (847) 657 - 4268

CALLAHAN, Robert — Tel: (847) 657 - 4096
Senior V. President, Human Resources — Fax: (847) 657 - 4268

LYNCH, Michael J. — Tel: (847) 657 - 4232
V. President, Government Affairs; and PAC Treasurer — Fax: (847) 657 - 7892

MALLAHAN, Mary Ann — Tel: (847) 657 - 4092
Manager, Community Relations — Fax: (847) 657 - 4505

Illinova Corp.

See listing on page 171 under Dynegy, Inc.

Imation Corp.

A manufacturer of data storage and removable media products.
www.imation.com

Chairman and Chief Exec. Officer
HENDERSON, Bruce A. — Tel: (651) 704 - 4000 — Fax: (651) 704 - 4200 — TF: (888) 466 - 3456

Main Headquarters
Mailing: One Imation Place, Oakdale, MN 55128-3414 — Tel: (651) 704 - 4000 — Fax: (651) 704 - 4200 — TF: (888) 466 - 3456

Corporate Foundations and Giving Programs
Imation Corp. Corporate Contributions Program
Contact: Patricia Kovacs
One Imation Place — Tel: (651) 704 - 4762
Oakdale, MN 55128-3414 — Fax: (651) 704 - 4200

Annual Grant Total: none reported
Geographic Preference: Area(s) in which the company operates
Primary Interests: Arts and Culture; Education; Technology

Public Affairs and Related Activities Personnel

At Headquarters

ALLEN, Bradley D. — Tel: (651) 704 - 3475
V. President, Corporate Communications and Investor Relations — Fax: (651) 704 - 4200

CHASE, Jacqueline A. — Tel: (651) 704 - 3182
V. President, Human Resources — Fax: (651) 704 - 4200

FINZEN-LETTS, Jennifer — Tel: (651) 704 - 3558
Manger, Public Relations — Fax: (651) 704 - 4200 — TF: (888) 466 - 3456

KOVACS, Patricia — Tel: (651) 704 - 4762
Manager, Corporate Communications and Community Affairs — Fax: (651) 704 - 4200
Responsibilities include corporate contributions.

IMC Global Corp.

See listing on page 334 under Mosaic Co.

Imperial Sugar Co.

A domestic refiner and processor of refined sugar.
www.imperialsugar.com

President and Chief Exec. Officer
PEISER, Robert A. — Tel: (281) 491 - 9181 — Fax: (281) 490 - 9584 — TF: (800) 727 - 8427

Main Headquarters
Mailing: P.O. Box Nine, Sugar Land, TX 77487 — Tel: (281) 491 - 9181 — Fax: (281) 490 - 9879 — TF: (800) 727 - 8427
Street: 8016 Hwy. 90-A, Sugar Land, TX 77478

Corporate Foundations and Giving Programs
Imperial Sugar Co. Corporate Contributions Program
Contact: William F. Schwer
P.O. Box Nine — Tel: (281) 490 - 9795
Sugar Land, TX 77487 — Fax: (281) 490 - 9584

Annual Grant Total: none reported

Public Affairs and Related Activities Personnel

At Headquarters

HASTINGS, T. Kay — Tel: (281) 491 - 9181
Senior V. President, Human Resources — Fax: (281) 490 - 9584 — TF: (800) 727 - 8427
Responsibilities include investor and media relations.

SCHWER, William F. — Tel: (281) 490 - 9795
Senior V. President, Secretary and General Counsel — Fax: (281) 490 - 9584
Responsibilities include corporate communications and corporate philanthropy.

Imperial Sugar Co.

* continued from previous page

SWANK, Darrell
Exec. V. President and Chief Financial Officer
dswank@imperialsugar.com
Responsibilities include coporate communications.
Tel: (281) 491 - 9181
Fax: (281) 490 - 9584

TRICE, Fran
Manager, Investor Relations
ftrice@imperialsugar.com
Tel: (281) 491 - 9181
Fax: (281) 490 - 9584

IMS Health, Inc.

www.imshealth.com

Chairman of the Board
THOMAS, David M.
dthomas@imshealth.com
Tel: (203) 319 - 4700
Fax: (203) 319 - 4701

Chief Exec. Officer
CARLUCCI, David R.
Tel: (203) 319 - 4700
Fax: (203) 319 - 4701

Main Headquarters
Mailing: 1499 Post Rd.
Fairfield, CT 06824
Tel: (203) 319 - 4700
Fax: (203) 319 - 4701

Public Affairs and Related Activities Personnel

At Headquarters

DEMITO, Patti
V. President, Global Human Resources
Tel: (203) 319 - 4700
Fax: (203) 319 - 4701

HUGHES, Bill
V. President, Global Communications
Tel: (203) 319 - 4700
Fax: (203) 319 - 4701

LEPPETITO, Caroline
Director, Public Relations
Tel: (610) 834 - 5716

LONGWELL, Lance
Manager, Public Realtions
Tel: (203) 319 - 4700
Fax: (203) 319 - 4701

WALSH, Jack
V. President, Investor Relations
jwalsh@imshealth.com
Tel: (203) 319 - 4700
Fax: (203) 319 - 4701

Independence Air

See listing on page 199 under FLYi, Inc.

Independence Blue Cross (Pennsylvania)

Chairman of the Board
YOUNG, Robert H.
Tel: (215) 636 - 9559
Fax: (215) 241 - 0403
TF: (800) 555 - 1514

Chief Exec. Officer
FRICK, Joseph A.
Tel: (215) 636 - 9559
Fax: (215) 241 - 0403
TF: (800) 555 - 1514

Main Headquarters
Mailing: 1901 Market St.
38th Floor
Philadelphia, PA 19103-1480
Tel: (215) 636 - 9559
Fax: (215) 241 - 0403
TF: (800) 555 - 1514

Public Affairs and Related Activities Personnel

At Headquarters

CASHMAN, Christopher
Senior V. President, Corporate and Public Affairs
christopher.cashman@ibx.com
Tel: (215) 636 - 9559
Fax: (215) 241 - 0403
TF: (800) 555 - 1514

MARSHALL-BLAKE, Lorina L.
V. President, Government Relations
lorina.marshall@ibx.com
Tel: (215) 636 - 9559
Fax: (215) 241 - 0403
TF: (800) 555 - 1514

WEBER, Gregory M.
Communications Specialist
gregory.weber@ibx.com
Tel: (215) 636 - 9559
Fax: (215) 241 - 0403
TF: (800) 555 - 1514

WILLA, Elizabeth
V. President, Corporate and Public Affairs
Tel: (215) 636 - 9559
Fax: (215) 241 - 0403
TF: (800) 555 - 1514

At Other Offices

MCMILLEN, Mary Ellen
V. President, Legislative Policy
500 N. Third St., Suite 500
Harrisburg, PA 17101
maryellen.mcmillen@ibx.com
Tel: (717) 233 - 6464
Fax: (717) 233 - 6773

Indiana Energy, Inc.

See listing on page 501 under Vectren Corp.

Indiana Michigan Power Co.

See listing on page 30 under American Electric Power Co Inc.

Indiana Power and Light

See listing on page 264 under IPL (an AES Company).

Information Resources, Inc.

A software developer specializing in the collection of detailed market information on sales of consumer goods.
www.infores.com
Annual Revenues: $555 million

Chairman of the Board
WADHWANI, Romesh
Tel: (312) 726 - 1221
Fax: (312) 726 - 0360
TF: (800) 317 - 6245

President and Chief Exec. Officer
KLEIN, Scott W.
Tel: (312) 726 - 1221
Fax: (312) 726 - 0360
TF: (800) 317 - 6245

Main Headquarters
Mailing: 150 N. Clinton St.
Chicago, IL 60661
Tel: (312) 726 - 1221
Fax: (312) 726 - 0360
TF: (800) 317 - 6245

Public Affairs and Related Activities Personnel

At Headquarters

MCINDOE, John
Director, Public Relations
john.mcindow@infores.com
Tel: (312) 474 - 7862
Fax: (312) 474 - 2542
TF: (800) 317 - 6245

NEWMAN, Gary
Exec. V. President, Chief People Officer, Human Resources
Tel: (312) 726 - 1221
Fax: (312) 726 - 0360
TF: (800) 317 - 6245

VAN, Kristin
V. President, Corporate Communications
Tel: (312) 726 - 1221
Fax: (312) 726 - 0360
TF: (800) 317 - 6245

ING Americas

A member of the Public Affairs Council. A financial services provider. Subsidiaries include ING Equitable Life and ING Life of Georgia. Acquired ReliaStar Financial Corp., AETNA Financial Services and AETNA Internat'l in 2000.
www.ing.com

Main Headquarters
Mailing: 5780 Powers Ferry Rd. NW
Atlanta, GA 30327
Tel: (770) 980 - 5100
Fax: (770) 980 - 3301

Political Action Committees

ING America Insurance Holdings Inc. PAC
Contact: Kevin P. Brown
5780 Powers Ferry Rd. NW
Atlanta, GA 30327
Tel: (770) 980 - 5100
Fax: (770) 980 - 3301

Contributions to Candidates: $14,500 (01/05 - 09/05)
Democrats: $7,000; Republicans: $7,500.

Principal Recipients

SENATE DEMOCRATS		HOUSE DEMOCRATS	
Conrad, Kent (ND)	$2,000	Frank, Barney (MA)	$1,000
Carper, Thomas R (DE)	$1,000	Larson, John B (CT)	$1,000
Lieberman, Joe (CT)	$1,000	Pomeroy, Earl (ND)	$1,000
SENATE REPUBLICANS		**HOUSE REPUBLICANS**	
		Johnson, Nancy (CT)	$4,500
		Baker, Hugh (LA)	$1,000
		Boehner, John (OH)	$1,000
		Castle, Michael (DE)	$1,000

Corporate Foundations and Giving Programs

ING Foundation/Corp. Contributions
5780 Powers Ferry Rd. NW
Atlanta, GA 30327
Tel: (770) 980 - 5100
Fax: (770) 980 - 3301

Annual Grant Total: $2,000,000 - $5,000,000
Geographic Preference: Area in which the company is headquartered; Minnesota; New York; Virginia; Washington State
Primary Interests: Education; Youth Services
Recent Recipients: Junior Achievement

Public Affairs and Related Activities Personnel

At Headquarters

BROWN, Kevin P.
PAC Treasurer
Tel: (770) 980 - 5100
Fax: (770) 980 - 3301

WALDRON, Thomas R.
Exec. V. President, Human Resources, Communications and Administration
Tel: (770) 980 - 5100
Fax: (770) 980 - 3301

WINTON, Deborah
Tel: (770) 980 - 5100
Fax: (770) 980 - 3301

Ingles Markets, Inc.

A supermarket chain.
www.ingles-markets.com

Chairman and Chief Exec. Officer
INGLE, II, Robert P. — Tel: (828) 669 - 2941; Fax: (828) 669 - 3667
ringle@ingles-markets.com

Main Headquarters
Mailing: P.O. Box 6676, Asheville, NC 28816 — Tel: (828) 669 - 2941; Fax: (828) 669 - 3678
Street: 2913 US Hwy. 70 West, Black Mountain, NC 28711-9103

Public Affairs and Related Activities Personnel

At Headquarters

BANKS, Jerry — Tel: (828) 669 - 2941; Fax: (828) 669 - 3667
Director, Human Resources
jbanks@ingles-markets.com

BROOKS, Cynthia L. — Tel: (828) 669 - 2941; Fax: (828) 669 - 3667
V. President, Human Resources
cbrooks@ingles-markets.com

PRESNELL, Florie — Tel: (828) 669 - 2941; Fax: (828) 669 - 3678
Controller
Responsibilities include corporate communications and investor relations.

Ingram Micro, Inc.

Wholesale distributor of computer hardware, software, peripherals and accessories.
www.ingrammicro.com

Chairman of the Board
FOSTER, Kent B. — Tel: (714) 566 - 1000; Fax: (714) 566 - 7900
kent.foster@ingrammicro.com

Chief Exec. Officer
SPIERKEL, Gregory M.E. — Tel: (714) 566 - 1000; Fax: (714) 566 - 7900

Main Headquarters
Mailing: 1600 E. St. Andrews Pl., Santa Ana, CA 92705 — Tel: (714) 566 - 1000; Fax: (714) 566 - 7900

Public Affairs and Related Activities Personnel

At Headquarters

BAIER, Jennifer — Tel: (714) 382 - 2692; Fax: (714) 566 - 7900
Director, Public Relations
jennifer.baier@ingrammicro.com

CARLSON, Ria — Tel: (714) 566 - 1000; Fax: (714) 566 - 7900
V. President, Strategy and Communications and Investor Relations

MEOLI, Marie — Tel: (714) 382 - 2190; Fax: (714) 566 - 7900
Senior Manager, Public Relations
marie.meoli@ingrammicro.com

SAUER, Matthew A. — Tel: (714) 566 - 1000; Fax: (714) 566 - 7900
Senior V. President, Human Resources

Inland Materials Distribution Group, Inc.

See listing on page 417 under Ryerson Tull.

Inland Steel Industries

See listing on page 265 under Ispat Inland Inc.

Insight Enterprises, Inc.

A director marketing and advertising company.
www.insight.com

Chairman of the Board
CROWN, Timothy A. — Tel: (480) 902 - 1001; Fax: (480) 902 - 1157; TF: (800) 467 - 4448
tcrown@insight.com

Chief Exec. Officer
FENNESY, Timothy A. — Tel: (480) 902 - 1001; Fax: (480) 902 - 1157; TF: (800) 467 - 4448

Main Headquarters
Mailing: 6820 S. Harl Ave., Tempe, AZ 85283 — Tel: (480) 902 - 1001; Fax: (480) 902 - 1157; TF: (800) 467 - 4448

Public Affairs and Related Activities Personnel

At Headquarters

DUDLE, Nancy — Tel: (480) 902 - 1001; Fax: (480) 902 - 1157; TF: (800) 467 - 4448
Public Relations Specialist
ndudle@insight.com

Instinet Group Inc.

An electronic stock trading company. A subsidiary of London-based Reuters Group PLC.
www.instinet.com
Annual Revenues: $1.5 billion

Chairman of the Board
STRACHAN, Ian — Tel: (212) 310 - 9500; Fax: (646) 223 - 9054; TF: (800) 225 - 5008

Chief Exec. Officer
NICOLL, Edward J. — Tel: (212) 310 - 9500; Fax: (646) 223 - 9054; TF: (800) 225 - 5008

Main Headquarters
Mailing: Three Times Square, New York, NY 10036 — Tel: (212) 310 - 9500; Fax: (646) 223 - 9054; TF: (800) 225 - 5008

Washington Office
Contact: James Kaplan
Mailing: 1333 H St., NW, Suite 410, Washington, DC 20005 — Tel: (202) 898 - 8343

Political Action Committees

Instinet Corp. PAC
Contact: John F. Fay
1333 H St., NW
Suite 410
Washington, DC 20005 — Tel: (202) 898 - 8343

Contributions to Candidates: $18,992 (01/05 - 09/05)
Democrats: $6,000; Republicans: $12,992.

Principal Recipients

SENATE DEMOCRATS		HOUSE DEMOCRATS	
Feinstein, Dianne (CA)	$1,000	Sherman, Brad (CA)	$2,000
		Capuano, Michael E (MA)	$1,000
		Lynch, Stephen (MA)	$1,000
		Scott, David (GA)	$1,000

SENATE REPUBLICANS		HOUSE REPUBLICANS	
Sununu, John (NH)	$2,000	Baker, Hugh (LA)	$3,000
Crapo, Michael D (ID)	$1,000	Bachus, Spencer (AL)	$2,000
Shelby, Richard (AL)	$1,000	Biggert, Judy (IL)	$1,000
		Kelly, Sue W (NY)	$1,000
		Ryun, Jim R (KS)	$1,000

Public Affairs and Related Activities Personnel

At Headquarters

DOWD, Mark — Tel: (212) 310 - 9500; Fax: (646) 223 - 9054; TF: (800) 225 - 5008
Director, Public Relations

GOLDMAN, Andrew — Tel: (212) 231 - 5047; Fax: (646) 223 - 9054; TF: (800) 225 - 5008
Exec. V. President, Global Marketing and Communications

KAMPF, Lisa — Tel: (212) 231 - 5022; Fax: (646) 223 - 9054; TF: (800) 225 - 5008
Exec. V. President, Investor Relations
lisa.kampf@instinet.com

At Washington Office

FAY, John F. — Tel: (202) 898 - 8343
PAC Treasurer

KAPLAN, James — Tel: (202) 898 - 8343
V. President, Government Relations

Integon Corp.

See listing on page 214 under General Motors Corp.

Integra Bank N.A.

A bank holding company operating 78 banking centers in Illinois, Indiana, Kentucky, and Ohio.
www.integrabank.com

Chairman, President and Chief Exec. Officer
VEA, Michael T. — Tel: (812) 464 - 9800; Fax: (812) 464 - 9825; TF: (800) 467 - 1928

Main Headquarters
Mailing: P.O. Box 868, Evansville, IN 47705-0868 — Tel: (812) 464 - 9677; Fax: (812) 464 - 9825; TF: (800) 467 - 1928
Street: 21 S.E. Third St., Evansville, IN 47705

Political Action Committees

IBNK PAC
Contact: Dan Carwile
P.O. Box 868
Evansville, IN 47705-0868 — Tel: (812) 464 - 9800; Fax: (812) 464 - 9825; TF: (800) 467 - 1928

Integra Bank N.A.

* continued from previous page

Contributions to Candidates: none reported (01/05 - 09/05)

Public Affairs and Related Activities Personnel

At Headquarters

CARWILE, Dan
Exec. V. President; and PAC Treasurer
Tel: (812) 464 - 9800
Fax: (812) 464 - 9825
TF: (800) 467 - 1928

DUNN, Gretchen
Shareholder Relations Contact
Tel: (812) 464 - 9677
Fax: (812) 464 - 9825
TF: (800) 467 - 1928

PENCE, Greg
Media Relations Contact
Tel: (812) 464 - 9800
Fax: (812) 464 - 9825
TF: (800) 467 - 1928

STOKE, Sheila A.
Senior V. President and Controller
Tel: (812) 464 - 9677
Fax: (812) 464 - 9825
TF: (800) 467 - 1928

Integrated Device Technology, Inc.

A manufacturer of semiconductor solutions for communications companies.

www.idt.com

Annual Revenues: $3.8 billion

Chairman of the Board
TAN, Hock E.
Tel: (408) 284 - 8200

President and Chief Exec. Officer
LANG, Gregory S.
gregory.lang@idt.com
Tel: (408) 284 - 8200

Main Headquarters

Mailing: 6024 Silver Creek Valley Rd.
San Jose, CA 95138
Tel: (408) 284 - 8200

Public Affairs and Related Activities Personnel

At Headquarters

BOUREKAS, Phil
V. President, Worldwide Marketing and Corporate Public Relations Contact
phil.bourekas@idt.com
Tel: (408) 284 - 2749

Intel Corp.

A member of the Public Affairs Council. A manufacturer of semiconductors, computer components, modules and systems for the computer industry.

www.intel.com

Annual Revenues: $30.1 billion

Chairman of the Board
BARRETT, Craig R.
Tel: (408) 765 - 8080
Fax: (408) 765 - 9904
TF: (800) 628 - 8686

Main Headquarters

Mailing: 2200 Mission College Blvd.
Santa Clara, CA 95052-8119
Tel: (408) 765 - 8080
Fax: (408) 765 - 9904
TF: (800) 628 - 8686

Washington Office

Contact: Jeremy Bonfini

Mailing: 1634 I St. NW
Suite 300
Washington, DC 20006-4021
Tel: (202) 628 - 3838
Fax: (202) 628 - 2525

Political Action Committees

Intel PAC

Contact: Jeremy Bonfini

1634 I St. NW
Suite 300
Washington, DC 20006-4021
Tel: (202) 626 - 4393
Fax: (202) 628 - 2525

Contributions to Candidates: $82,499 (01/05 - 09/05)

Democrats: $12,500; Republicans: $69,999.

Principal Recipients

SENATE DEMOCRATS

HOUSE DEMOCRATS

Jefferson, William (LA)	$2,000
Matheson, James (UT)	$2,000
Smith, Adam (WA)	$2,000
Tanner, John S. (TN)	$2,000

SENATE REPUBLICANS

Burns, Conrad (MT)	$3,000
Thomas, Craig (WY)	$3,000
Allen, George (VA)	$2,000
Bennett, Robert F (UT)	$2,000
Hatch, Orrin (UT)	$2,000
Lott, Trent (MS)	$2,000
Talent, James (MO)	$2,000

HOUSE REPUBLICANS

Blunt, Roy (MO)	$5,000
Flake, Jeff (AZ)	$5,000
Issa, Darrell (CA)	$5,000
Johnson, Nancy (CT)	$5,000
Wilson, Heather (NM)	$5,000
Lungren, Daniel E (CA)	$4,999
Cantor, Eric (VA)	$2,500
Smith, Lamar (TX)	$2,500
Boehner, John (OH)	$2,000
Lewis, Jerry (CA)	$2,000

Corporate Foundations and Giving Programs

Intel Foundation

Contact: Wendy Hawkins

5300 NE Elam Young Pkwy.
Hillsboro, OR 97123-6497
Tel: (503) 456 - 1539
Fax: (503) 696 - 8179

Annual Grant Total: over $5,000,000

Geographic Preference: Arizona; California; New Mexico; Oregon

Primary Interests: Education; Engineering; Math and Science; Minority Opportunities; Technology; Women

Recent Recipients: Junior Achievement; Massachusetts Institute of Technology; Nat'l Ass'n for the Advancement of Colored People

Public Affairs and Related Activities Personnel

At Headquarters

KOON, Tracy
Manager, Corporate Affairs
Mailstop: RN5-56
Tracy.Koon@intel.com
Tel: (408) 765 - 5609
Fax: (408) 765 - 5101
TF: (800) 628 - 8686

LUSK, Doug
Director, Investor Relations
Tel: (408) 765 - 1679
Fax: (408) 765 - 1966
TF: (800) 628 - 8686

MCVICKER, Melissa
Co-Director, Worldwide Press Relations
Tel: (408) 765 - 8080
Fax: (408) 765 - 9904
TF: (800) 628 - 8686

MURRAY, Patricia
Senior V. President and Director, Human Resources
Tel: (408) 765 - 8080
Fax: (408) 765 - 9904
TF: (800) 628 - 8686

OTELLINI, Paul S.
Chief Exec. Officer
Tel: (408) 765 - 8080
Fax: (408) 765 - 9904
TF: (800) 628 - 8686

WALDROP, Tom
Co-Director, Worldwide Press Relations
tom.waldrop@intel.com
Tel: (408) 765 - 8478
Fax: (408) 765 - 6008
TF: (800) 628 - 8686

At Washington Office

BONFINI, Jeremy
Manager, Government Relations
jeremy.bonfini@intel.com
Tel: (202) 626 - 4393
Fax: (202) 628 - 2525

CARROLL, Melika
Manager, Trade Policy
Tel: (202) 626 - 4383
Fax: (202) 628 - 2525

COMER, Douglas B.
Director, Legal Affairs
Registered Federal Lobbyist.
Tel: (202) 628 - 3838
Fax: (202) 628 - 2525

GREESON, Jennifer
Tel: (202) 628 - 3838
Fax: (202) 628 - 2525

HARPER, Stephen F.
Director, Environmental Health and Safety
Registered Federal Lobbyist.
Tel: (202) 628 - 3838
Fax: (202) 628 - 2525

PITSCH, Peter K.
Director, Communications Policy
Tel: (202) 626 - 4383
Fax: (202) 628 - 2525

ROSE, David
Director, Export/Import/InfoSec Affairs
david.rose@intel.com
Registered Federal Lobbyist.
Tel: (202) 626 - 4390
Fax: (202) 628 - 2525

VERDERY, Jenifer
Manager, Human Resources Policy
Tel: (202) 626 - 4383
Fax: (202) 628 - 2525

At Other Offices

GRINDATTO, Jami
Manager, Public Affairs
4100 Sara Rd. SE
Rio Rancho, NM 87124
Tel: (505) 893 - 3750
Fax: (505) 893 - 3116

Intel Corp.

* continued from previous page

HALL, Richard C.
Manager, Government Affairs
1900 Prairie City Rd.
Folsom, CA 95630
richard.c.hall@intel.com
Tel: (916) 356 - 6122
Fax: (916) 356 - 8070

HAWKINS, Wendy
Intel Foundation Contact
5300 NE Elam Young Pkwy.
Hillsboro, OR 97123-6497
Tel: (503) 456 - 1539
Fax: (503) 696 - 8179

InterActiveCorp

See listing on page 254 under IAC/InterActiveCorp.

interBiz

See listing on page 133 under Computer Associates Internat'l, Inc.

Interco Incorporated

See listing on page 207 under Furniture Brands Internat'l, Inc.

InterContinental Hotels Group

Formerly known as Six Continents Hotels. A major lodging franchising and management company.
www.ichotelsgroup.com

Chairman of the Board
WEBSTER, David
Tel: (770) 604 - 2000

Chief Exec. Officer
COSSLET, Andy
Tel: (770) 604 - 2000

Main Headquarters
Mailing: Three Ravinia Dr., Suite 100
Atlanta, GA 30346
Tel: (770) 604 - 2000

Corporate Foundations and Giving Programs

InterContinental Hotels Group Corporate Contributions
Contact: Vicki Gordon
Three Ravinia Dr., Suite 100
Atlanta, GA 30346
Tel: (770) 604 - 2284
Fax: (770) 604 - 8588

Annual Grant Total: none reported
Geographic Preference: No geographical restrictions
Primary Interests: Children; Education; Environment/Conservation; Minority Opportunities
Recent Recipients: American Red Cross; Give Kids the World Foundation; U.S. Fund for UNICEF; United Way

Public Affairs and Related Activities Personnel

At Headquarters

BURTON, Bill
Director, Corporate Affairs
bill.burton@ichotelsgroup.com
Tel: (770) 604 - 8149
Fax: (770) 604 - 2008

GORDON, Vicki
Senior V. President, Corporate Affairs
Tel: (770) 604 - 2284
Fax: (770) 604 - 8588

GULLETT, Natasha
Senior Manager, Public Relations
natasha.gullett@ichotelsgroup.com
Tel: (770) 604 - 5597
Fax: (770) 604 - 2059

HERGERT, Carolyn
Director, Corporate Communications
carolyn.hegert@ichotelsgroup.com
Tel: (770) 604 - 8248
Fax: (770) 604 - 2059

OSBORNE, Virginia
Senior Manager, Public Relations
virginia.osborne@ichotelsgroup.com
Tel: (770) 604 - 2037
Fax: (770) 604 - 2059

SCHULWOLF, Francie
V. President, Corporate Communications
fschulwolf@ichotelsgroup.com
Tel: (770) 604 - 2906
Fax: (770) 604 - 2059

YUDIN, Stephanie
Senior Manager, Public Relations
stephanie.yudin@ichotelsgroup.com
Tel: (770) 604 - 5083
Fax: (770) 604 - 2059

Interface Inc.

A manufacturer of carpet tiles, broadloom carpet, and fabrics.
www.interfaceinc.com
Annual Revenues: $1.25 billion

President and Chief Exec. Officer
HENDRIX, Daniel T.
Tel: (770) 437 - 6840
Fax: (770) 437 - 6887

Main Headquarters
Mailing: 2859 Paces Ferry Rd., Suite 2000
Atlanta, GA 30339
Tel: (770) 437 - 6800
Fax: (770) 437 - 6809

Public Affairs and Related Activities Personnel

At Headquarters

LYNCH, Patrick C.
Chief Financial Officer
patrick.lynch@us.interfaceinc.com
Tel: (770) 437 - 6800
Fax: (770) 437 - 6809
Responsibilities include corporate communications, corporate philanthropy, and investor relations.

REYNOLDS, William G., Jr.
Manager, Human Resources
Tel: (770) 437 - 6880
Fax: (770) 319 - 0070

Intergraph Corp.

A manufacturer of interactive computer graphics systems.
www.intergraph.com

Chairman of the Board
MCDONALD, Sidney
Tel: (256) 730 - 2000
TF: (800) 345 - 4856

President and Chief Exec. Officer
WISE, R. Halsey
Tel: (256) 730 - 2000
TF: (800) 345 - 4856

Main Headquarters
Mailing: P.O. Box 240000
170 Graphics Dr.
Huntsville, AL 35758
Tel: (256) 730 - 2000
Fax: (256) 730 - 2048
TF: (800) 345 - 4856

Political Action Committees

Intergraph Corp. PAC
Contact: Edward A. Wilkinson, Jr.
1881 Campus Commons Dr.
Reston, VA 20191
Tel: (703) 264 - 5644

Contributions to Candidates: $21,000 (01/05 - 09/05)
Democrats: $8,000; Republicans: $13,000.

Principal Recipients

SENATE DEMOCRATS		HOUSE DEMOCRATS	
		Cramer, Bud (AL)	$7,000
		Gordon, Barton (TN)	$1,000
SENATE REPUBLICANS		**HOUSE REPUBLICANS**	
Chambliss, Saxby (GA)	$2,000	Kingston, John (GA)	$5,000
Burns, Conrad (MT)	$1,000	Aderholt, Robert B (AL)	$1,000
Isakson, John (GA)	$1,000	Everett, Terry (AL)	$1,000
Stevens, Ted (AK)	$1,000	Hunter, Duncan (CA)	$1,000

Corporate Foundations and Giving Programs

Intergraph Corporate Contributions Program
P.O. Box 240000
170 Graphics Dr.
Huntsville, AL 35758
Tel: (256) 730 - 2000
Fax: (256) 730 - 2048
TF: (800) 345 - 4856

Annual Grant Total: none reported

Public Affairs and Related Activities Personnel

At Headquarters

HOFFMAN, Ian
V. President, Marketing and Communications
ian.hoffman@intergraph.com
Tel: (256) 730 - 2604
Fax: (256) 730 - 2048
TF: (800) 345 - 4856

WROBEL, Gene
V. President and Treasurer
Tel: (256) 730 - 2000
TF: (800) 345 - 4856
Responsibilities include investor relations.

At Other Offices

WILKINSON, Edward A., Jr.
Treasurer, Intergraph Corp. PAC
1881 Campus Commons Dr.
Reston, VA 20191
ewilkinson@ingr.com
Tel: (703) 264 - 5644

Interim Services Inc.

See listing on page 450 under Spherion Corp.

Intermedia Communications Inc.

See listing on page 314 under MCI, Inc.

Intermet Corp.

An automotive manufacturing supplier.
www.intermet.com
Annual Revenues: $815 million

Chairman and Chief Executive Officer
RUFF, Gary F.
Tel: (248) 952 - 2500
Fax: (248) 952 - 2501

Main Headquarters
Mailing: 5445 Corporate Dr.
Suite 200
Troy, MI 48098-2683
Tel: (248) 952 - 2500
Fax: (248) 952 - 2501

Public Affairs and Related Activities Personnel

At Headquarters

KELLY, Mike
Director, Communications
mkelly@intermet.com
Tel: (248) 952 - 2546
Fax: (248) 952 - 2501

MILLS, Bytha
Vice President, Administration
bmills@intermet.com
Tel: (248) 952 - 2500
Fax: (248) 952 - 2501
Responsibilities include public affairs.

Intermountain Gas Co.

A natural gas service company.

Chairman of the Board
HOKIN, Richard — Tel: (208) 377 - 6840 Fax: (208) 377 - 6097

Main Headquarters
Mailing: P.O. Box 7608, Boise, ID 83707 — Tel: (208) 377 - 6840 Fax: (208) 377 - 6097
Street: 555 S. Cole Rd., Boise, ID 83709

Corporate Foundations and Giving Programs

Intermountain Gas Industries Corporate Giving Program
Contact: Diane Norris
P.O. Box 7608
Boise, ID 83707 — Tel: (208) 377 - 6840 Fax: (208) 377 - 6097

Annual Grant Total: none reported

Public Affairs and Related Activities Personnel

At Headquarters

GLYNN, William C. — Tel: (208) 377 - 6840 Fax: (208) 377 - 6097
President

HUNTINGTON, Michael E. — Tel: (208) 377 - 6840 Fax: (208) 377 - 6097
V. President, Marketing and External Affairs

NORRIS, Diane — Tel: (208) 377 - 6840 Fax: (208) 377 - 6097
Assistant to the President
Responsibilities include corporate philanthropy.

SIMMERMAN, Ed — Tel: (208) 377 - 6840 Fax: (208) 377 - 6097
Assistant Corporate Treasurer
Responsibilities include corporate philanthropy.

Internat'l Business Machines Corp. (IBM)

A member of the Public Affairs Council. A company that creates, develops and manufactures advanced information technologies, including computer systems, software, networking systems, storage devices and microelectronics. Acquired Rational Software Corp. in 2003.

www.ibm.com
Annual Revenues: $88 billion

Chairman, President and Chief Exec. Officer
PALMISANO, Samuel J. — Tel: (914) 499 - 1900 Fax: (914) 499 - 7382 TF: (800) 426 - 4968

Main Headquarters
Mailing: New Orchard Rd., Armonk, NY 10504 — Tel: (914) 499 - 1900 Fax: (914) 499 - 7382 TF: (800) 426 - 4968

Washington Office
Contact: Christopher G. Caine
Mailing: 1301 K St. NW, Suite 1200, Washington, DC 20005 — Tel: (202) 515 - 5000

Corporate Foundations and Giving Programs

IBM Corporate Support Programs
New Orchard Rd.
Armonk, NY 10504 — Tel: (914) 499 - 1900 Fax: (914) 499 - 7382 TF: (800) 426 - 4968

Annual Grant Total: over $5,000,000
Grants are not provided to individuals, political, labor, religious, or fraternal organizations or sports groups. (Guidelines are available.)
Geographic Preference: Area in which the company is headquartered; National; International
Primary Interests: Adult Education and Training; Environment/Conservation; K-12 Education

Public Affairs and Related Activities Personnel

At Washington Office

BARNES, David — Tel: (202) 515 - 5036 Fax: (202) 515 - 4943
Director, Human Resources and Policy Driven Growth

BRUNER, Cheryl — Tel: (202) 515 - 4031
Governmental Programs Executive

CAINE, Christopher G. — Tel: (202) 515 - 5000 Fax: (202) 515 - 5113
V. President, Governmental Programs
ccaine@us.ibm.com
Registered Federal Lobbyist.

COLOMBARO, Geri J. — Tel: (202) 515 - 5003 Fax: (202) 515 - 5055
Program Director, Human Resources
Registered Federal Lobbyist.

COMEDY, Yolanda — Tel: (202) 515 - 5513
Governmental Programs Executive

EVANS, Linda C. — Tel: (202) 515 - 5526 Fax: (202) 515 - 5078
Program Manager, Taxes and Finance
levans@us.ibm.com
Registered Federal Lobbyist.

HACKMAN, Timothy B. — Tel: (202) 515 - 5115 Fax: (202) 515 - 4943
Director, Public Affairs, Science and Technology
thackman@us.ibm.com
Registered Federal Lobbyist.

KINGSCOTT, Kathleen N. — Tel: (202) 515 - 5193 Fax: (202) 515 - 4943
Director, Public Policy Programs
Registered Federal Lobbyist.

MARIETTA, Sally Scott — Tel: (202) 515 - 5013
Corporate Community Relations Manager

MARKS, Debra — Tel: (202) 515 - 5184
Government Relations

MARSHO, Kim M. — Tel: (202) 515 - 4522
Program Manager, Market Access/Trade

MCCULLOCH, Ned — Tel: (202) 515 - 4019 Fax: (202) 515 - 5194
Governmental Programs Executive
nmcculloch@us.ibm.com

MUSTAIN, Christopher — Tel: (202) 515 - 5000
Governmental Programs Executive
Registered Federal Lobbyist.

PERRY, Edmund F. — Tel: (202) 515 - 5039 Fax: (202) 515 - 5906
Director, Political Programs
Registered Federal Lobbyist.

RAYMOND, Brian J. — Tel: (202) 515 - 5434 Fax: (202) 515 - 5906
Program Manager, Grassroots and Political Programs
braymond@us.ibm.com
Registered Federal Lobbyist.

REDIFER, Paul — Tel: (202) 515 - 5081
Regional Manager, Government Relations
rediferp@us.ibm.com

RHONE, Adrienne G. — Tel: (202) 515 - 5103 Fax: (202) 515 - 5906
Director, Government Relations
Registered Federal Lobbyist.

SHEEHY, Timothy J. — Tel: (202) 515 - 5077 Fax: (202) 515 - 5078
Director, Networked Economy
Registered Federal Lobbyist.

STEWART, Steve W. — Tel: (202) 515 - 5054 Fax: (202) 515 - 4943
Director, Market Access/Trade/Telecom
stewarts@us.ibm.com
Registered Federal Lobbyist.

TUTTLE, Susan C. — Tel: (202) 515 - 5503 Fax: (202) 515 - 5078
Program Manager, Public Affairs, Trade and Investment
stuttle@us.ibm.com
Registered Federal Lobbyist.

WADDELL, Greg — Tel: (202) 515 - 5446
Program Manager, Networked Society

WARNER, William H. — Tel: (202) 515 - 5000
Registered Federal Lobbyist.

WILLIAMS, Marcus P. — Tel: (202) 515 - 5522 Fax: (202) 515 - 5528
Counsel, Governmental Programs

ZIVANOVIC-SMITH, Maria — Tel: (202) 515 - 5109 Fax: (202) 515 - 4943
Senior Professional, Governmental Programs

At Other Offices

BALTA, Wayne S. — Tel: (914) 766 - 2720 Fax: (914) 766 - 2824
Director, Corporate Environmental Programs
Route 100
Somers, NY 10589

COFFEY, John — Tel: (781) 372 - 5848
Public Relations Manager
(Rational Software)
83 Hartwell Ave.
Lexington, MA 02421
jkcoffey@us.ibm.com

DURLING, Bill — Tel: (781) 372 - 5886
Director, Communications
(Rational Software)
83 Hartwell Ave.
Lexington, MA 02421
wdurling@us.ibm.com

STETSON, Karl — Tel: (425) 497 - 4065
Manager, Public Relations
(Rational Software)
8383 158th Ave. Northeast
Redmond, WA 98052
kstetson@us.ibm.com

Internat'l Data Group

A media, research, events, and information technology company.

www.idg.com

Founder and Chairman
MCGOVERN, Patrick J. — Tel: (617) 534 - 4200 Fax: (617) 423 - 0240
patrick_mcgovern@idg.com

Internat'l Data Group

* continued from previous page

Chief Exec. Officer
KENEALY, Pat — Tel: (617) 534 - 4200; Fax: (617) 423 - 0240

Main Headquarters
Mailing: One Exeter Plaza
15 Floor
Boston, MA 02116
Tel: (617) 534 - 4200; Fax: (617) 423 - 0240

Public Affairs and Related Activities Personnel

At Headquarters

HINDS, Susanna
Manager, Communications
susanna_hinds@idg.com
Tel: (617) 534 - 4200; Fax: (617) 423 - 0240

SHOLKIN, Howie
Director, Corporate Communications
howard_sholkin@idg.com
Tel: (617) 534 - 4200; Fax: (617) 423 - 0240

Internat'l Flavors and Fragrances

A creator and manufacturer of flavors, fragrances and aroma chemicals.
www.iff.com

Chairman and Chief Exec. Officer
GOLDSTEIN, Richard A. — Tel: (212) 765 - 5500; Fax: (212) 708 - 7132

Main Headquarters
Mailing: 521 W. 57th St.
New York, NY 10019
Tel: (212) 765 - 5500; Fax: (212) 708 - 7132

Corporate Foundations and Giving Programs

IFF Foundation
Contact: Douglas J. Wetmore
521 W. 57th St.
New York, NY 10019
Tel: (212) 708 - 7145; Fax: (212) 708 - 7132

Annual Grant Total: $400,000 - $500,000
Geographic Preference: New York City; New Jersey
Primary Interests: Arts and Culture; Education; Medical Research; Medicine and Health Care; Mental Health
Recent Recipients: Memorial Sloan-Kettering Hospital; New York Botanical Garden; New York City Ballet; United Way

Public Affairs and Related Activities Personnel

At Headquarters

HEASLIP, Steven J.
Senior V. President, Human Resources
Tel: (212) 765 - 5500; Fax: (212) 708 - 7132

MEANY, Dennis M.
Senior V. President, General Counsel and Secretary
Responsibilities include government relations.
Tel: (212) 708 - 7243; Fax: (212) 708 - 7191

WETMORE, Douglas J.
Senior V. President and Chief Financial Officer
Responsibilities include corporate philanthropy and investor relations.
Tel: (212) 708 - 7145; Fax: (212) 708 - 7132

Internat'l Game Technology

Designs, manufactures and markets gaming machines and systems products.
www.igt.com

Chairman and Chief Exec. Officer
MATTHEWS, T. J. — Tel: (775) 448 - 7777

Main Headquarters
Mailing: P.O. Box 10580
Reno, NV 89510-0580
Tel: (775) 448 - 7777
Street: 9295 Prototype Dr.
Reno, NV 89521

Political Action Committees

Internat'l Game Technology Political Action Committee
Contact: J. Kenneth Creighton
P.O. Box 10580
Reno, NV 89510-0580
Tel: (775) 448 - 7777

Contributions to Candidates: $6,000 (01/05 - 09/05)
Democrats: $2,000; Republicans: $4,000.

Principal Recipients

SENATE DEMOCRATS
Pallone, Frank (NJ) $1,000

SENATE REPUBLICANS
Burns, Conrad (MT) $1,000

HOUSE DEMOCRATS
Grijalva, Raul (AZ) $1,000

HOUSE REPUBLICANS
Calvert, Ken (CA) $1,000
Cole, Tom (OK) $1,000
Taylor, Charles H (NC) $1,000

Public Affairs and Related Activities Personnel

At Headquarters

CREIGHTON, J. Kenneth
Treasurer, Internat'l Game Technology Political Action Committee
Tel: (775) 448 - 7777

SORENSEN, Rick
Manager, Public Relations
Tel: (775) 448 - 7777; Fax: (775) 448 - 0960

At Other Offices

CHATIGNY, Michelle
V. President, Compliance
1085 Palms Airport Dr.
Las Vegas, NV 89119-3715
Responsibilities include regulatory affairs.
Tel: (702) 896 - 8500

Internat'l Harvester

See listing on page 342 under Navistar Internat'l Corp.

Internat'l Multifoods Corp.

See listing on page 442 under The J M Smucker Company.

Internat'l Paper

A manufacturer of paper, paperboard and packaging products, wood products, specialty products. Merged with Federal Paper Board Co. in 1996, Union Camp Corp in 1999, and Champion Internat'l Corp. in 2000.
www.internationalpaper.com
Annual Revenues: $26.363 billion

Chairman and Chief Exec. Officer
FARACI, John V. — Tel: (203) 541 - 8000; Fax: (203) 541 - 8200; TF: (800) 223 - 1268

Main Headquarters
Mailing: 400 Atlantic St.
Stamford, CT 06921
Tel: (203) 541 - 8000; Fax: (203) 541 - 8200; TF: (800) 223 - 1268

Washington Office
Mailing: 1101 Pennsylvania Ave. NW
Suite 200
Washington, DC 20004
Tel: (202) 628 - 1223; Fax: (202) 628 - 1368

Political Action Committees

Internat'l Paper Political Action Committee (IP PAC)
Contact: John C. Runyan
1101 Pennsylvania Ave. NW
Suite 200
Washington, DC 20004
Tel: (202) 628 - 1223 Ext: 30; Fax: (202) 628 - 1368

Contributions to Candidates: $94,499 (01/05 - 09/05)
Democrats: $17,000; Republicans: $77,499.

Principal Recipients

SENATE DEMOCRATS
Carper, Thomas R (DE) $3,500
Nelson, Benjamin (NE) $2,500
Baucus, Max (MT) $2,000

Allen, George (VA) $10,000
Talent, James (MO) $7,000
Burns, Conrad (MT) $5,000
Smith, Gordon (OR) $5,000
Ensign, John Eric (NV) $4,000
Kennedy, Mark (MN) $3,999
Kyl, Jon L (AZ) $3,000
Snowe, Olympia (ME) $3,000
Hatch, Orrin (UT) $2,000

HOUSE DEMOCRATS
Scott, David (GA) $5,000

HOUSE OTHER
Rogers, Michael (AL) $2,500
Sweeney, John E. (NY) $2,500
Pombo, Richard (CA) $2,000

Corporate Foundations and Giving Programs

Internat'l Paper Co. Foundation
Contact: Aleesa Blum
400 Atlantic St.
Stamford, CT 06921
Tel: (203) 541 - 8565; Fax: (203) 541 - 8268; TF: (800) 223 - 1268

Annual Grant Total: over $5,000,000
Emphasizes programs in IP communities and projects in which company employees play a significant volunteer role. Recent recipients include: Florida A&M University; Citizens Against Spouse Abuse; Coalition for Natural Resource Education; Louisiana Special Education Center. Guidelines are available.
Geographic Preference: Area(s) in which the company operates
Primary Interests: Arts and Culture; Community Affairs; Education; Health; Minority Opportunities

Public Affairs and Related Activities Personnel

At Headquarters

BARK, Kathleen
Communications
Tel: (203) 541 - 8418; Fax: (203) 541 - 8200; TF: (800) 223 - 1268

Internat'l Paper

* continued from previous page

BLUM, Aleesa
V. President, Communications; and President, Internat'l Paper Co. Foundation
aleesa.blum@ipaper.com
Tel: (203) 541 - 8565
Fax: (203) 541 - 8268
TF: (800) 223 - 1268

BOARDMAN, Jenny
Manager, Media Relations
Tel: (203) 541 - 8407
Fax: (203) 541 - 8200
TF: (800) 223 - 1268

CARTER, Jerome W.
Senior V. President, Human Resources
Tel: (203) 541 - 8653
Fax: (203) 541 - 8261
TF: (800) 223 - 1268

EPP, Phyllis M.
Exec. Director, IPCO Foundation
phyllis.epp@ipaper.com
Tel: (203) 541 - 8678
Fax: (203) 541 - 8309
TF: (800) 223 - 1268

JORLING, Thomas C.
V. President, Environmental Affairs
thomas.jorling@ipaper.com
Tel: (203) 541 - 8649
Fax: (203) 541 - 8257
TF: (800) 223 - 1268

THOMAS, W. Dennis
Senior V. President, Public Affairs and Communications
dennis.thomas@ipaper.com
Tel: (203) 541 - 8000
Fax: (203) 541 - 8200
TF: (800) 223 - 1268
Responsibilities include corporate contributions.

TUTUNDGY, Carol S.
V. President, Investor Relations
carol.tutundgy@ipaper.com
Tel: (203) 541 - 8000
Fax: (203) 541 - 8200
TF: (800) 223 - 1268

At Washington Office

GEHLHAART, Donna
Washington Representative
donna.gehlhaart@ipaper.com
Tel: (202) 628 - 1223 Ext: 20
Fax: (202) 628 - 1368
Registered Federal Lobbyist.

MANN, Mary M.
Washington Representative
mary.mann@ipaper.com
Tel: (202) 628 - 1223 Ext: 19
Fax: (202) 628 - 1368
Registered Federal Lobbyist.

MCGUIRE, Mark
V. President and Deputy General Counsel, Legal and External Affairs
Tel: (202) 628 - 1223
Fax: (202) 628 - 1368

NEALE, Karen
Washington Representative
karen.neale@ipaper.com
Tel: (202) 628 - 1223 Ext: 34
Fax: (202) 628 - 1368
Registered Federal Lobbyist.

RUNYAN, John C.
Washington Representative
john.runyan@ipaper.com
Tel: (202) 628 - 1223 Ext: 30
Fax: (202) 628 - 1368
Registered Federal Lobbyist.

WROBLESKI, Ann
V. President, Public Affairs
Tel: (202) 628 - 1223
Fax: (202) 628 - 1368

At Other Offices

CLARKIN, Stephen C.
Regional Public Affairs Manager
Nine Green St.
Augusta, ME 04330
Tel: (207) 621 - 4217

ORR, Deano
Regional Public Affairs Manager
Five W. Haggett St., Suite 914
Raleigh, NC 27601
deano.orr@ipaper.com
Tel: (919) 831 - 4764

PITTMAN, Lee
Manager, Public Affairs
501 Woodlane St., Suite 103
Little Rock, AR 72201
lee.pittman@ipaper.com
Tel: (501) 374 - 8927
Fax: (501) 374 - 7118

STEGEMANN, Robert S.
Manager, Public Affairs
99 Washington Ave., Suite 1950
Albany, NY 12207
robert.stegemann@ipaper.com
Tel: (518) 465 - 5600 Ext: 3103
Fax: (518) 465 - 5618

Internat'l Steel Group Inc.

Operates steel making facilities. Acquired the assets of Bethlehem Steel Corp. in May, 2003.
www.intlsteel.com

Chairman of the Board
ROSS, Wilbur L., Jr.
Fax: (330) 659 - 9135

Chief Exec. Officer and President
MOTT, Rodney B.
Fax: (330) 659 - 9135

Main Headquarters
Mailing: 3250 Interstate Dr.
Richfield, OH 44286
Fax: (330) 659 - 9135

Public Affairs and Related Activities Personnel

At Headquarters

DERRICO, Blaise
Manager, Investor Relations
bderrico@intlsteel.com
Tel: (330) 659 - 7430
Fax: (330) 659 - 9135

GLAZER, Charles T.
Manager, Communications and Public Relations
cglazer@intlsteel.com
Tel: (330) 659 - 9121
Fax: (330) 659 - 9135

Internat'l Textiles Group

Formed from the merger of Burlington Industries LLC and Cone Mills Corp. in the spring of 2004.
www.burlington.com

Chairman of the Board
ROSS, Wilbur L., Jr.
Tel: (336) 379 - 2000
Fax: (336) 379 - 4504

President and Chief Exec. Officer
GORGA, Joseph L.
Tel: (336) 379 - 2000
Fax: (336) 379 - 4504

Main Headquarters
Mailing: 804 Green Valley Rd.
Greensboro, NC 27408
Tel: (336) 379 - 2000
Fax: (336) 349 - 6287

Political Action Committees

Burlington Industries Good Government Committee
Contact: Faye Morton
804 Green Valley Rd.
Greensboro, NC 27408
Tel: (336) 379 - 2000
Fax: (336) 379 - 4504

Contributions to Candidates: none reported (01/05 - 09/05)

Cone Mills PAC
Contact: Neil W. Koonce
804 Green Valley Rd.
Greensboro, NC 27415

Contributions to Candidates: none reported (01/05 - 09/05)

Public Affairs and Related Activities Personnel

At Headquarters

GARREN, Robert "Bob"
V. President, Human Resources
Tel: (336) 379 - 2000
Fax: (336) 349 - 6287

MORTON, Faye
Treasurer, Burlington Industries Good Government Committee
Tel: (336) 379 - 2000
Fax: (336) 379 - 4504

SIDES, Delores
Director, Corporate Communications
Tel: (336) 379 - 2903
Fax: (336) 379 - 4504

At Other Offices

KOONCE, Neil W.
Treasurer, Cone Mills PAC
804 Green Valley Rd.
Greensboro, NC 27415

Internat'l Truck and Engine Corp.

A member of the Public Affairs Council. See listing on page 342 under Navistar Internat'l Corp.

The Interpublic Group of Companies

A marketing and communications company.
www.interpublic.com

Chairman of the Board and Chief Executive Officer
ROTH, Michael I.
Tel: (212) 704 - 1200

Main Headquarters
Mailing: 1114 Ave. of the Americas
New York, NY 10036
Tel: (212) 704 - 1200

Corporate Foundations and Giving Programs

Interpublic Group of Companies Corporate Contributions
1114 Ave. of the Americas
New York, NY 10036
Tel: (212) 704 - 1200

Annual Grant Total: none reported

Public Affairs and Related Activities Personnel

At Headquarters

KRAKOWSKY, Philippe
Senior V. President and Director, Corporate Communications
pkrakowsky@interpublic.com
Tel: (212) 704 - 1328

LESHNE, Jerry
V. President, Financial Planning and Analysis and Investor Relations
Tel: (212) 704 - 1439

SOMPOLSKI, Timothy A.
Exec. V. President and Chief Human Resources Officer
Tel: (212) 704 - 1200

Interstate Bakeries Corp.

A baker and distributor of fresh delivered bread and snack cakes in the U.S.
www.interstatebakeriescorp.com
Annual Revenues: $3.526 billion

Chairman of the Board
BENATAR, Leo
Tel: (816) 502 - 4000
Fax: (816) 502 - 4155

Interstate Bakeries Corp.

* continued from previous page

Chief Exec. Officer
ALVAREZ, II, Antonio C. — Tel: (816) 502 - 4000; Fax: (816) 502 - 4155

Main Headquarters
Mailing: 12 E. Armour Blvd.
Kansas City, MO 64111
Tel: (816) 502 - 4000; Fax: (816) 502 - 4155

Corporate Foundations and Giving Programs

Interstate Brands Foundation
Contact: Isabelle Ervin
12 E. Armour Blvd.
Kansas City, MO 64111
Tel: (816) 502 - 4000; Fax: (816) 502 - 4155

Annual Grant Total: none reported

Public Affairs and Related Activities Personnel

At Headquarters

ERVIN, Isabelle — Tel: (816) 502 - 4000; Fax: (816) 502 - 4155
Human Resources Associate
ervin_isabelle@interstatebrands.com
Responsibilities include corporate philanthropy.

GUENIN, Steve — Tel: (816) 502 - 4000; Fax: (816) 502 - 4155
Director, Environmental Affairs

THOMPSON, Linda L. — Tel: (816) 502 - 4230; Fax: (816) 502 - 4155
Director, Stockholder Relations and Assistant Corporate Secretary
thompson_linda@interstatebrands.com

YARICK, Paul E. — Tel: (816) 502 - 4164; Fax: (816) 502 - 4155
V. President and Treasurer
yarick_paul@interstatebrands.com
Responsibilities include corporate communications.

Intuit Inc.

A member of the Public Affairs Council. A developer and marketer of personal, small business, and tax preparation software. Products include Quicken, QuickBooks, and TurboTax.
www.intuit.com
Annual Revenues: $1.261 billion

Chairman of the Board
CAMPBELL, Willam V. — Tel: (650) 944 - 6000; Fax: (650) 944 - 3699

President and Chief Exec. Officer
BENNETT, Stephen M. — Tel: (650) 944 - 6000; Fax: (650) 944 - 3699

Main Headquarters
Mailing: 2632 Marine Way
Mountain View, CA 94043
Tel: (650) 944 - 6000; Fax: (650) 944 - 3699; TF: (800) 446 - 8848

Washington Office
Contact: Bernard F. McKay
Mailing: 601 Pennsylvania Ave. NW
North Bldg., Suite 200
Washington, DC 20004
Tel: (202) 484 - 1490

Political Action Committees

Intuit 21st Century Leadership Fund
Contact: Rina Heinze
2700 Coast Ave.
Mountain View, CA 94043
Tel: (650) 944 - 6000

Contributions to Candidates: $8,000 (01/05 - 09/05)
Republicans: $8,000.

Principal Recipients

SENATE REPUBLICANS		HOUSE REPUBLICANS	
Ensign, John Eric (NV)	$2,000	Cantor, Eric (VA)	$1,000
		Lewis, Jerry (CA)	$1,000
		Northup, Anne M. (KY)	$1,000
		Oxley, Michael (OH)	$1,000
		Sensenbrenner, Jim (WI)	$1,000

Public Affairs and Related Activities Personnel

At Headquarters

KOURAKOS, Jessica — Tel: (650) 944 - 6000; Fax: (650) 944 - 3699
V. President, Investor Relations

PFORZHEIMER, Harry — Tel: (650) 944 - 6000; Fax: (650) 944 - 3699
V. President, Communications

WHITELEY, Sherry — Tel: (650) 944 - 6000; Fax: (650) 944 - 3999
Senior V. President, Human Resources

At Washington Office

MCKAY, Bernard F. — Tel: (202) 484 - 1490
V. President, Government Affairs

At Other Offices

HEINZE, Rina — Tel: (650) 944 - 6000
PAC Treasurer
2700 Coast Ave.
Mountain View, CA 94043

Invacare Corp.

Manufactures home healthcare equipment.
www.invacare.com

Chairman and Chief Exec. Officer
MIXON, A Malachi, III — Tel: (440) 329 - 6000; Fax: (440) 366 - 9008; TF: (800) 333 - 6900

Main Headquarters
Mailing: One Invacare Way
Elyria, OH 44035
Tel: (440) 329 - 6000; Fax: (440) 366 - 9008; TF: (800) 333 - 6900

Washington Office
Contact: Cara C. Bachenheimer
Mailing: 600 Cameron St.
Suite 402
Alexandria, VA 22314
Tel: (440) 329 - 6226

Political Action Committees

Invacare Corp. Political Action Committee (Inva PAC)
Contact: Jerome E. Fox, Jr.
One Invacare Way
Elyria, OH 44035
Tel: (440) 329 - 6000; Fax: (440) 366 - 9008; TF: (800) 333 - 6900

Contributions to Candidates: $5,500 (01/05 - 09/05)
Democrats: $1,000; Republicans: $4,500.

Principal Recipients

SENATE DEMOCRATS		HOUSE DEMOCRATS	
		Tanner, John S. (TN)	$1,000
SENATE REPUBLICANS		**HOUSE REPUBLICANS**	
Crapo, Michael D (ID)	$1,000	Barton, Joe L (TX)	$2,000
		Dewine, R. Pat (OH)	$1,500

Corporate Foundations and Giving Programs

Invacare Foundation
Contact: Jerome E. Fox, Jr.
One Invacare Way
Elyria, OH 44035
Tel: (440) 329 - 6000; Fax: (440) 366 - 9008; TF: (800) 333 - 6900

Annual Grant Total: $100,000 - $200,000
Primary Interests: Civic and Public Affairs; Education; Health and Human Services; Social Services
Recent Recipients: Arthritis Foundation; Boy Scouts of America; Easter Seal Soc.; Nat'l MS Soc.

Public Affairs and Related Activities Personnel

At Headquarters

BROWNLEE, Jan — Tel: (440) 329 - 6000; Fax: (440) 366 - 9008; TF: (800) 333 - 6900
Director, Regulatory Affairs

DAVIE, Diane J. — Tel: (440) 329 - 6000; Fax: (440) 366 - 9008; TF: (800) 333 - 6900
Senior V. President, Human Resources
rgudbranson@invacare.com

ELDER, Susan — Tel: (440) 329 - 6000; Fax: (440) 329 - 6568; TF: (800) 333 - 6900
Director, Marketing Communications
susan.elder@invacare.com

FOX, Jerome E., Jr. — Tel: (440) 329 - 6000; Fax: (440) 366 - 9008; TF: (800) 333 - 6900
Treasurer, Inva PAC; Secretary-Treasurer, Foundation
jfox@invacare.com

GUDBRANSON, Robert K. — Tel: (440) 329 - 6001; Fax: (440) 366 - 9008; TF: (800) 333 - 6900
Director, Investor Relations

USAJ, Joseph — Tel: (440) 329 - 6000; Fax: (440) 366 - 9008; TF: (800) 333 - 6900
Senior V. President, Human Resources

At Washington Office

BACHENHEIMER, Cara C. — Tel: (440) 329 - 6226
V. President, Government Relations
cbachenheimer@invacare.com
Registered Federal Lobbyist.

GRAEFE, Fred — Tel: (440) 329 - 6226
Registered Federal Lobbyist.

Invensys Process Systems

See listing on page 264 under Invensys Systems, Inc.

Invensys Systems, Inc.

A manufacturer of process automation systems.

www.invensys.com

Chairman of the Board
JAY, Martin
Tel: (508) 549 - 2424
Fax: (508) 549 - 4999
TF: (866) 746 - 6477

Chief Executive
HENRIKSSON, Ulf
Tel: (508) 549 - 2424
Fax: (508) 549 - 4999
TF: (866) 746 - 6477

Main Headquarters
Mailing: 33 Commercial St.
Foxboro, MA 02035
Tel: (508) 549 - 2424
Fax: (508) 549 - 4999
TF: (866) 746 - 6477

Corporate Foundations and Giving Programs

Foxboro Corp. Contributions Program
33 Commercial St.
Foxboro, MA 02035
Tel: (508) 549 - 2424
Fax: (508) 549 - 4999
TF: (866) 746 - 6477

Annual Grant Total: none reported
Geographic Preference: Area(s) in which employees live and work; Massachusetts; Rhode Island; Texas
Primary Interests: Community Affairs; Education; Health; Youth Services

Public Affairs and Related Activities Personnel

At Headquarters

CONRAD, Craig
Director, Marketing and Communications
Tel: (508) 549 - 6250
Fax: (508) 549 - 4999
TF: (866) 746 - 6477

MARSHALL-HOWARTH, Rebecca
Manager, Marketing Communications
rebecca.marshall-howarth@invensys.com
Tel: (508) 549 - 2424
Fax: (508) 549 - 4999
TF: (866) 746 - 6477

MILLER, Paul
Manager, Public Relations
(Invensys Process Systems)
paul.miller@ivensys.com
Tel: (508) 549 - 6240
Fax: (508) 549 - 4834
TF: (866) 746 - 6477

PETERSON, Sheila
Manager, Community Relations (Public Affairs)
speterson@foxboro.com
Tel: (508) 549 - 3218
Fax: (508) 549 - 2626
TF: (866) 746 - 6477

SCARTH, Victoria
Senior V. President, Group Marketing and Communications
Tel: (508) 549 - 2424
Fax: (508) 549 - 4999
TF: (866) 746 - 6477

Invitrogen Corp.

A member of the Public Affairs Council. Acquired Dexter Corp. and its subsidiary, Life Technologies, Inc. in 2000.

www.invitrogen.com

Chairman and Chief Exec. Officer
LUCIER, Gergory T.
Tel: (760) 603 - 7200
Fax: (760) 602 - 6500
TF: (800) 955 - 6288

Main Headquarters
Mailing: P.O. Box 6482
1600 Faraday Ave.
Carlsbad, CA 92008
Tel: (760) 603 - 7200
Fax: (760) 602 - 6500
TF: (800) 955 - 6288

Washington Office
Contact: Janet Lynch Lambert
Mailing: 1455 Pennsylvania Ave. NW
Suite 100
Washington, DC 20004
Tel: (202) 756 - 0184

Political Action Committees

Invitrogen Corp. Employees Political Action Committee
Contact: David H. Smith
1455 Pennsylvania Ave. NW
Suite 100
Washington, DC 20004
Tel: (202) 756 - 0184

Contributions to Candidates: $3,000 (01/05 - 09/05)
Democrats: $1,000; Republicans: $2,000.

Principal Recipients

SENATE DEMOCRATS
Lieberman, Joe (CT) $1,000

HOUSE DEMOCRATS

SENATE REPUBLICANS

HOUSE REPUBLICANS
Issa, Darrell (CA) $1,000
Sensenbrenner, Jim (WI) $1,000

Public Affairs and Related Activities Personnel

At Headquarters

CASSONI, Mary
V. President, Corporate Communications
Tel: (760) 603 - 7200
Fax: (760) 602 - 6500
TF: (800) 955 - 6288

GEISSMAN, Greg
Manager, Public Relations
gergory.geissman@invitrogen.com
Tel: (760) 476 - 7032
Fax: (760) 602 - 6500
TF: (800) 955 - 6288

RODRIGUEZ, Joseph L.
Senior V. President, Human Resources
Tel: (760) 603 - 7200
Fax: (760) 602 - 6500
TF: (800) 955 - 6288

TAICH, Adam S.
V. President, Investor Relations
Tel: (760) 603 - 7200
Fax: (760) 602 - 6500
TF: (800) 955 - 6288

At Washington Office

LAMBERT, Janet Lynch
Director, Government Relations
Registered Federal Lobbyist.
Tel: (202) 756 - 0184

SMITH, David H.
PAC Treasurer
Tel: (202) 756 - 0184

Iomega Corp.

Manufactures high performance, removable media disk drives and sub-systems; computer peripherals.

www.iomega.com

Chairman of the Board
DAVID, Stephen N.
Tel: (858) 314 - 7000
Fax: (858) 314 - 7001

President and Chief Exec. Officer
HEID, Werner T.
heid@iomega.com
Tel: (858) 314 - 7000
Fax: (858) 314 - 7001

Main Headquarters
Mailing: 10955 Vista Sorrento Pkwy.
San Diego, CA 92130
Tel: (858) 314 - 7000
Fax: (858) 314 - 7001

Public Affairs and Related Activities Personnel

At Headquarters

AGUIRRE, Anna L.
V. President, Human Resources and Facilities
aguirre@iomega.com
Tel: (858) 314 - 7000
Fax: (858) 314 - 7001

KAMPFER, Tom
Exec. V. President, Business Solutions
Tel: (858) 314 - 7000
Fax: (858) 314 - 7001

ROMOSER, Chris
Director, Corporate Communications and Public Relations
romoser@iomega.com
Tel: (858) 314 - 7180
Fax: (858) 314 - 7001

Iowa-Ilinois Gas and Electric Co.

See listing on page 326 under MidAmerican Energy Holdings Co.

IPALCO Enterprises, Inc.

See listing on page 264 under IPL (an AES Company).

IPL (an AES Company)

Public utility holding company. Acquired by AES in 2001.

www.ipalco.com

Main Headquarters
Mailing: P.O. Box 1595
Indianapolis, IN 46206-1595
Tel: (317) 261 - 8261
Fax: (317) 630 - 5726
Street: One Monument Circle
Indianapolis, IN 46204

Public Affairs and Related Activities Personnel

At Headquarters

FENNIG, Greg
V. President, Public Affairs
Tel: (317) 261 - 8261
Fax: (317) 630 - 5726

LIVERS-POWERS, Crystal
Director, Media Relations
crystal.liverspowers@aes.com
Tel: (317) 261 - 8423
Fax: (317) 630 - 5726

MILLS, Fred
Director, Government Affairs
Tel: (317) 261 - 8261
Fax: (317) 630 - 5726

MURTLOW, Ann D.
Chairman and Chief Exec. Officer
Tel: (317) 261 - 8261
Fax: (317) 630 - 5726

The Irvine Company

A real estate investment and land development company.

www.irvinecompany.com

Chairman of the Board
BREN, Donald
Tel: (949) 720 - 2000
Fax: (949) 720 - 2501

Main Headquarters
Mailing: 550 Newport Center Dr.
Newport Beach, CA 92660
Tel: (949) 720 - 2000
Fax: (949) 720 - 2501

Political Action Committees

The Irvine Co. Employees' Political Action Committee
Contact: Tony Russo
550 Newport Center Dr.
Newport Beach, CA 92660
Tel: (949) 720 - 2471
Fax: (949) 720 - 2450

The Irvine Company

** continued from previous page*

Contributions to Candidates: $11,000 (01/05 - 09/05)
Republicans: $11,000.

Principal Recipients

SENATE REPUBLICANS		HOUSE REPUBLICANS	
Talent, James (MO)	$1,000	Royce, Ed Mr (CA)	$4,500
		Hobson, David (OH)	$2,500
		Calvert, Ken (CA)	$2,000
		Dreier, David (CA)	$1,000

Public Affairs and Related Activities Personnel

At Headquarters

RUSSO, Tony — Tel: (949) 720 - 2471
PAC Contact — Fax: (949) 720 - 2450

THOMAS, Larry — Tel: (949) 720 - 3232
Group Senior V. President, Corporate Communications — Fax: (949) 720 - 2501

YOUNG, Dan — Tel: (949) 720 - 2526
Exec. V. President, Entitlement and Public Affairs — Fax: (949) 720 - 2575

Ispat Inland Inc.

A member of the Public Affairs Council. Produces raw steel from iron ore and scrap to make flat-rolled and coated sheet for automobiles, appliances, office furniture, electric motors and other products. Also manufactures special-quality bar for a wide variety of end uses. A unit of Ispat Internat'l.

www.ispat.com

Chief Exec. Officer — Tel: (219) 399 - 1200
MUKHERJEE, Malay — Fax: (219) 399 - 5544

Main Headquarters
Mailing: 3210 Watling St. — Tel: (219) 399 - 1200
East Chicago, IN 46312 — Fax: (219) 399 - 5544

Political Action Committees

Ispat Inland Good Government Fund
Contact: Thomas A. McCue
3210 Watling St. — Tel: (219) 399 - 5166
East Chicago, IN 46312 — Fax: (219) 399 - 1898

Contributions to Candidates: $3,500 (01/05 - 09/05)
Democrats: $2,000; Republicans: $1,500.

Principal Recipients

SENATE DEMOCRATS	HOUSE DEMOCRATS	
	Mollohan, Alan (WV)	$1,000
SENATE REPUBLICANS	**HOUSE REPUBLICANS**	
	Capito, Shelley (WV)	$1,000

Public Affairs and Related Activities Personnel

At Headquarters

ALLEN, David — Tel: (219) 399 - 5430
Manager, Communications and Media Relations — Fax: (219) 399 - 7715
david.allen@ispat.com

EKAITIS, David M. — Tel: (219) 399 - 5379
Manager, Risk Management and Insurance — Fax: (219) 399 - 4448
david.ekaitis@ispat.com

FEKETE, John D. — Tel: (219) 399 - 4191
Director, Environmental Affairs — Fax: (219) 399 - 6039
john.fekete@ispat.com

MCCUE, Thomas A. — Tel: (219) 399 - 5166
Treasurer — Fax: (219) 399 - 1898
thomas.mccue@ispat.com
Responsibilities include political action.

NIELSEN, John A. — Tel: (219) 399 - 6631
Director, Government and Public Affairs — Fax: (219) 399 - 6637
john.nielsen@ispat.com

PFISTER, Barbara — Tel: (219) 399 - 7873
Legislative Assistant, Government and Public Affairs — Fax: (219) 399 - 6637
barbara.pfister@ispat.com

IT Group, Inc., The

See listing on page 435 under The Shaw Group Inc.

ITT Corp.

See listing on page 455 under Starwood Hotels and Resorts Worldwide, Inc.

ITT Hartford Insurance Group

See listing on page 234 under The Hartford Financial Services Group Inc.

ITT Industries

Automotive, defense, electronics and fluid technologies.

www.itt.com
Annual Revenues: $4.676 billion

Chairman and Chief Exec. Officer — Tel: (914) 641 - 2000
LORANGER, Steven R. — Fax: (914) 696 - 2950

Main Headquarters
Mailing: Four W. Red Oak Ln. — Tel: (914) 641 - 2000
White Plains, NY 10604 — Fax: (914) 696 - 2950

Washington Office
Contact: James Crumley
Mailing: 1650 Tysons Blvd. — Tel: (703) 790 - 6300
Suite 1700 — Fax: (703) 790 - 6365
McLean, VA 22201

Political Action Committees

ITT Industries Political Action Committee (INNPAC)
Contact: Catherine Lupinacci
Four W. Red Oak Ln. — Tel: (914) 641 - 2000
White Plains, NY 10604 — Fax: (914) 696 - 2950

Contributions to Candidates: $52,500 (01/05 - 09/05)
Democrats: $17,000; Republicans: $35,500.

Principal Recipients

SENATE DEMOCRATS		HOUSE DEMOCRATS	
Clinton, Hillary Rodham (NY)	$2,000	Visclosky, Peter (IN)	$5,000
		Moran, James (VA)	$3,500
		Murtha, John P Mr. (PA)	$2,500
		Rothman, Steven R (NJ)	$2,000
SENATE REPUBLICANS		**HOUSE REPUBLICANS**	
Allen, George (VA)	$3,000	Goodlatte, Robert (VA)	$2,500
Dewine, Richard (OH)	$2,000	Hoekstra, Peter (MI)	$2,500
Hatch, Orrin (UT)	$2,000	Hobson, David (OH)	$2,000
		Kuhl, John R Jr (NY)	$2,000
		Lewis, Jerry (CA)	$2,000
		Wilson, Heather (NM)	$2,000
		Wolf, Frank R (VA)	$2,000

Corporate Foundations and Giving Programs

ITT Industries Corporate Contributions Program
Contact: Thomas R. Martin
Four W. Red Oak Ln. — Tel: (914) 641 - 2157
White Plains, NY 10604 — Fax: (914) 696 - 2977

Annual Grant Total: none reported

Public Affairs and Related Activities Personnel

At Headquarters

CRUM, Scott A. — Tel: (914) 641 - 2000
Senior V. President and Director, Human Resources — Fax: (914) 696 - 2950

GLOVER, Tom — Tel: (914) 641 - 2160
Director, Public Relations — Fax: (914) 696 - 2977
tom.glover@itt.com

LUPINACCI, Catherine — Tel: (914) 641 - 2000
PAC Treasurer — Fax: (914) 696 - 2950

MARTIN, Thomas R. — Tel: (914) 641 - 2157
Senior V. President and Director, Corporate Relations — Fax: (914) 696 - 2977
tom.martin@itt.com
Responsibilities include corporate philanthropy, community relations and domestic government affairs.

POWERS, Robert — Tel: (914) 641 - 2030
V. President, Investor Relations — Fax: (914) 696 - 2960
robert.powers@itt.com

WRIGHT, Usha — Tel: (914) 641 - 2053
V. President, Associate General Counsel, and Director, Environment, Safety and Health — Fax: (914) 696 - 2950
usha.wright@itt.com

At Washington Office

CRUMLEY, James — Tel: (703) 790 - 6300
V. President, Government Relations — Fax: (703) 790 - 6365

ROGERS, Millie D. — Tel: (703) 790 - 6300
Director, Marketing Communications and Public Relations — Fax: (703) 790 - 6365
millie.rogers@itt.com

SYERS, Doc — Tel: (703) 790 - 6328
Director, Congressional Relations — Fax: (703) 790 - 6365

Registered Federal Lobbyist.

J & H - Marsh & McLennan

See listing on page 306 under Marsh Inc.

J. Crew Group, Inc.

An apparel retailer.

www.jcrew.com

Chairman and Chief Exec. Officer
DREXLER, Millard S. "Mickey" — Tel: (212) 209 - 8500 Fax: (212) 209 - 2666

Main Headquarters
Mailing: 770 Broadway, New York, NY 10003 — Tel: (212) 209 - 8500 Fax: (212) 209 - 2666

Public Affairs and Related Activities Personnel

At Headquarters

BRUNELL, Margaret
Director, Public Relations — Tel: (212) 209 - 8500 Fax: (212) 209 - 2666

J. Ray McDermott, SA

See listing on page 312 under McDermott Internat'l, Inc.

Jabil Circuit, Inc.

Designs and manufactures electronic circuit boards.

www.jabil.com

Chairman of the Board
MOREAN, William D. — Tel: (727) 577 - 9749 Fax: (727) 579 - 8529

President and Chief Exec. Officer
MAIN, Timothy L.
time_maine@jabil.com — Tel: (727) 577 - 9749 Fax: (727) 579 - 8529

Main Headquarters
Mailing: 10560 Dr. Martin Luther King Jr. St. North, St. Petersburg, FL 33716 — Tel: (727) 577 - 9749 Fax: (727) 579 - 8529

Public Affairs and Related Activities Personnel

At Headquarters

WALTERS, Beth A.
V. President, Communications and Investor Relations
beth_walters@jabil.com — Tel: (727) 803 - 3349 Fax: (727) 579 - 8529

Jack in the Box Inc.

A restaurant company.

www.jackinthebox.com

Annual Revenues: $2.3 billion

Chairman and Chief Exec. Officer
NUGENT, Robert J. — Tel: (858) 571 - 2121 Fax: (858) 571 - 2225

Main Headquarters
Mailing: 9330 Balboa Ave., San Diego, CA 92123-1516 — Tel: (858) 571 - 2121 Fax: (858) 571 - 2225

Corporate Foundations and Giving Programs

Jack in the Box Foundation
Contact: Kathy Kovacevich
9330 Balboa Ave.
San Diego, CA 92123-1516 — Tel: (858) 571 - 2544 Fax: (858) 571 - 4064

Annual Grant Total: none reported
Recent Recipients: Big Brothers/Big Sisters

Public Affairs and Related Activities Personnel

At Headquarters

BRIGANDI, Steve
Senior Public Affairs Exec. — Tel: (858) 571 - 2121 Fax: (858) 571 - 2225

CETTI, Carlo
Senior V. President, Human Resources and Strategic Planning — Tel: (858) 571 - 2414 Fax: (858) 571 - 2225

KOVACEVICH, Kathy
Contact, Jack in the Box Foundation — Tel: (858) 571 - 2544 Fax: (858) 571 - 4064

LUSCOMB, Brian
Div. V. President, Corporate Communications — Tel: (858) 571 - 2121 Fax: (858) 571 - 2225

REBEL, Jerry P.
Senior V. President and Chief Financial Officer — Tel: (858) 571 - 2121 Fax: (858) 571 - 2225
Responsibilities include investor relations.

Jackson Nat'l Life Insurance Co.

A life insurance company. A U.S. subsidiary of the United Kingdom's Prudential plc.

www.jnl.com

President and Chief Exec. Officer
MANNING, Clark P. — Tel: (517) 381 - 5500 Fax: (517) 706 - 5517 TF: (800) 644 - 4565

Main Headquarters
Mailing: One Corporate Way, Lansing, MI 48951 — Tel: (517) 381 - 5500 Fax: (517) 706 - 5517 TF: (800) 644 - 4565

Political Action Committees

Brooke Holdings Inc. and Jackson Nat'l Life Insurance Co. Separate Segregated Fund
Contact: Robert Fritts
One Corporate Way
Lansing, MI 48951 — Tel: (517) 381 - 5500 Fax: (517) 706 - 5517 TF: (800) 644 - 4565

Contributions to Candidates: $16,000 (01/05 - 09/05)
Democrats: $3,500; Republicans: $12,500.

Principal Recipients

SENATE DEMOCRATS
Baucus, Max (MT) $1,500
Carper, Thomas R (DE) $1,000
Stabenow, Debbie (MI) $1,000

HOUSE DEMOCRATS

SENATE REPUBLICANS
Santorum, Richard (PA) $1,500
Smith, Gordon (OR) $1,500

HOUSE REPUBLICANS
Camp, David Lee (MI) $2,500
Hulshof, Kenny (MO) $2,000
Johnson, Nancy (CT) $2,000
McCotter, Thaddeus (MI) $2,000
Knollenberg, Joe (MI) $1,000

Corporate Foundations and Giving Programs

Jackson Nat'l Life Insurance Foundation
One Corporate Way
Lansing, MI 48951 — Tel: (517) 381 - 5500 Fax: (517) 706 - 5517 TF: (800) 644 - 4565

Annual Grant Total: none reported

Public Affairs and Related Activities Personnel

At Headquarters

BROWN, John H.
V. President, Government Relations — Tel: (517) 381 - 5500 Fax: (517) 706 - 5517 TF: (800) 644 - 4565

FRITTS, Robert
PAC Treasurer — Tel: (517) 381 - 5500 Fax: (517) 706 - 5517 TF: (800) 644 - 4565

HRAPKIEWICZ, Steve
Senior V. President, Human Resources — Tel: (517) 381 - 5500 Fax: (517) 706 - 5517 TF: (800) 644 - 4565

PADOT, Tim
Director, Corporate Communications — Tel: (517) 702 - 2425 Fax: (517) 706 - 5517 TF: (800) 644 - 4565

Jacobs Engineering Group Inc.

An engineering and construction company.

www.jacobs.com

Chairman and Chief Exec. Officer
WATSON, Noel G. — Tel: (626) 578 - 6801 Fax: (626) 578 - 6875

Main Headquarters
Mailing: 1111 S. Arroyo Pkwy., P.O. Box 7084, Pasadena, CA 91105 — Tel: (626) 578 - 3500 Fax: (626) 578 - 6916

Washington Office
Contact: Nicholai Kolesnikoff
Mailing: 413 New Jersey Ave., SE, Washington, DC 20003 — Tel: (202) 543 - 3866 Fax: (202) 543 - 1680

Political Action Committees

JEG Good Government Fund
Contact: William C. Markley, III
1111 S. Arroyo Pkwy.
P.O. Box 7084
Pasadena, CA 91105 — Tel: (626) 578 - 6855 Fax: (626) 578 - 6837

Contributions to Candidates: $83,722 (01/05 - 09/05)
Democrats: $35,500; Republicans: $48,222.

Jacobs Engineering Group Inc.

* continued from previous page

Principal Recipients

SENATE DEMOCRATS		HOUSE DEMOCRATS	
Mikulski, Barbara (MD)	$5,000	Hoyer, Steny (MD)	$5,000
		Mollohan, Alan (WV)	$5,000
		Olver, John (MA)	$5,000
		Visclosky, Peter (IN)	$5,000
		Gordon, Barton (TN)	$2,500
		Skelton, Ike (MO)	$2,000

SENATE REPUBLICANS		HOUSE REPUBLICANS	
Allen, George (VA)	$9,000	Blunt, Roy (MO)	$5,000
Ensign, John Eric (NV)	$2,500	Young, Don E (AK)	$3,222
Martinez, Mel (FL)	$2,500	Davis, Tom (VA)	$2,500
Lott, Trent (MS)	$2,000	Hobson, David (OH)	$2,000
		Thomas, William M (CA)	$2,000
		Wamp, Zach (TN)	$2,000

Corporate Foundations and Giving Programs

Jacobs Engineering Foundation
Contact: John W. Prosser, Jr.
1111 S. Arroyo Pkwy. — Tel: (626) 578 - 6803
P.O. Box 7084 — Fax: (626) 578 - 6875
Pasadena, CA 91105

Annual Grant Total: $500,000 - $750,000
Also awards scholarships for eligible children of employees.
Geographic Preference: Area(s) in which the company operates
Primary Interests: K-12 Education; United Way Campaigns; Youth Services
Recent Recipients: Rice University

Public Affairs and Related Activities Personnel

At Headquarters

HOAG, Kim — Tel: (626) 578 - 6808
V. President, Federal Programs — Fax: (626) 578 - 6875

MARKLEY, William C., III — Tel: (626) 578 - 6855
V. President, Law; PAC Treasurer — Fax: (626) 578 - 6837

PROSSER, John W., Jr. — Tel: (626) 578 - 6803
Senior V. President, Finance and Administration — Fax: (626) 578 - 6875
Responsibilities include corporate philanthropy and investor relations.

At Washington Office

KOLESNIKOFF, Nicholai — Tel: (202) 543 - 1749
V. President, Government Relations — Fax: (202) 543 - 1680
Registered Federal Lobbyist.

SHEPARD, Stacey — Tel: (202) 543 - 3486
Director, Government Affairs — Fax: (202) 543 - 1680
Registered Federal Lobbyist.

Jacuzzi Brands, Inc.

A global manufacturer and distributor of bath and plumbing products.
www.jacuzzibrands.com

Chairman and Chief Exec. Officer — Tel: (561) 514 - 3838
CLARKE, David H. — Fax: (561) 514 - 3839

Main Headquarters
Mailing: 777 S. Flagler Dr. — Tel: (561) 514 - 3838
Suite 1100 West — Fax: (561) 514 - 3839
West Palm Beach, FL 33401

Public Affairs and Related Activities Personnel

At Headquarters

BURTON, Diana E. — Tel: (561) 514 - 3850
V. President, Investor Relations — Fax: (561) 514 - 3839
Responsibilities include corporate communications.

Jarden Corp.

Brands include Coleman, Mr. Coffee, and Sunbeam.
www.jarden.com
Annual Revenues: $838.6 million

Chairman and Chief Exec. Officer — Tel: (914) 967 - 9400
FRANKLIN, Martin E. — Fax: (914) 967 - 9405

Main Headquarters
Mailing: 555 Theodore Fremd Ave. — Tel: (914) 967 - 9400
Rye, NY 10580-1455 — Fax: (914) 967 - 9405

Public Affairs and Related Activities Personnel

At Headquarters

ASHKEN, Ian G. H. — Tel: (914) 967 - 9400
Chief Financial Office and Investor Relations Contact — Fax: (914) 967 - 9405

TOLBERT, J. David — Tel: (914) 967 - 9400
Senior V. President, Human Resources and Corporate Risk — Fax: (914) 967 - 9405

JDS Uniphase Corp.

Manufactures, designs and markets electrical machinery and components.
www.jdsu.com

Chairman of the Board — Tel: (408) 546 - 5000
KAPLAN, Martin A. — Fax: (408) 954 - 0760

Chief Exec. Officer — Tel: (408) 546 - 5000
KENNEDY, Kevin J. — Fax: (408) 546 - 4300

Main Headquarters
Mailing: 1768 Automation Pkwy. — Tel: (408) 546 - 5000
San Jose, CA 95131 — Fax: (408) 546 - 4300

Public Affairs and Related Activities Personnel

At Headquarters

CURTIS, Jayne — Tel: (408) 546 - 4714
Public Relations Contact — Fax: (408) 546 - 4300

ROSS, Jacquie — Tel: (408) 546 - 5000
Investor Relations Contact — Fax: (408) 546 - 4300

Jefferson-Pilot Corp.

A holding company with interests in insurance, radio and television. In October of 2005, the company announced plans to merge with Lincoln Nat'l Corp. (see separate listing under Lincoln Financial Group). Completion of the merger is expected in the first quarter of 2006.
www.jpfinancial.com

Chairman of the Board — Tel: (336) 691 - 3000
STONECIPHER, David A. — Fax: (336) 691 - 3938
david.stonecipher@jpfinancial.com

President and Chief Exec. Officer — Tel: (336) 691 - 3000
GLASS, Dennis R. — Fax: (336) 691 - 3938

Main Headquarters
Mailing: P.O. Box 21008 — Tel: (336) 691 - 3000
Greensboro, NC 27420 — Fax: (336) 691 - 3938
Street: 100 N. Greene St.
Greensboro, NC 27401

Political Action Committees

Jefferson-Pilot Corp. Fed. Good Government Committee
Contact: Frank A. Sutherland
P.O. Box 21008 — Tel: (336) 691 - 3469
Greensboro, NC 27420 — Fax: (336) 691 - 3938

Contributions to Candidates: $6,750 (01/05 - 09/05)
Democrats: $1,000; Republicans: $5,750.

Principal Recipients

SENATE DEMOCRATS		HOUSE DEMOCRATS	
Carper, Thomas R (DE)	$1,000		

SENATE REPUBLICANS		HOUSE REPUBLICANS	
Gregg, Judd (NH)	$1,000	Foxx, Virginia (NC)	$1,000
Hagel, Charles T (NE)	$1,000	Hayes, Robert (NC)	$1,000
		Jones, Walter (NC)	$1,000

Corporate Foundations and Giving Programs

Jefferson-Pilot Foundation
Contact: May Whittaker
P.O. Box 21008 — Tel: (336) 691 - 3039
Greensboro, NC 27420 — Fax: (336) 691 - 3311

Annual Grant Total: none reported
Geographic Preference: Area(s) in which the company operates
Primary Interests: Arts and Culture; Education; Health and Human Services

Public Affairs and Related Activities Personnel

At Headquarters

MASON, Paul — Tel: (336) 691 - 3313
V. President, Corporate Affairs — Fax: (336) 691 - 3311
paul.mason@jpfinancial.com

SUTHERLAND, Frank A. — Tel: (336) 691 - 3469
V. President, Legal — Fax: (336) 691 - 3938
(Jefferson-Pilot Life Insurance Co.)
Responsibilities include political action.

WHITTAKER, May — Tel: (336) 691 - 3039
Budget and Contributions Assistant — Fax: (336) 691 - 3311
may.whittaker@jpfinancial.com

Jefferson-Pilot Life Insurance Co.

See listing on page 267 under Jefferson-Pilot Corp.

JELD-WEN, Inc.

A wood-milling company.
www.jeld-wen.com

JELD-WEN, Inc.

* continued from previous page

Chairman of the Board
WENDT, Richard
Tel: (541) 882 - 3451
Fax: (541) 855 - 7454
TF: (800) 535 - 3936

Main Headquarters
Mailing: 401 Harbor Isles Blvd.
Klamath Falls, OR 97601
Tel: (541) 882 - 3451
Fax: (541) 855 - 7454
TF: (800) 535 - 3936

Corporate Foundations and Giving Programs

JELD-WEN Foundation
Contact: Roderick C. Wendt
401 Harbor Isles Blvd.
Klamath Falls, OR 97601
Tel: (541) 882 - 3451
Fax: (541) 855 - 7454
TF: (800) 535 - 3936

Annual Grant Total: over $5,000,000
Geographic Preference: Area in which the company is headquartered; Area(s) in which the company operates
Primary Interests: Children's Health; Families; Higher Education; Social Services; United Way Campaigns
Recent Recipients: Ronald McDonald House; United Way

Public Affairs and Related Activities Personnel

At Headquarters

CLINE, Teri
Manager, Marketing Communications
Tel: (541) 882 - 3451
Fax: (541) 855 - 7454
TF: (800) 535 - 3936

MEIHOFF, Darcie
Director, Public Affairs
Tel: (541) 882 - 3451
Fax: (541) 855 - 7454
TF: (800) 535 - 3936

WENDT, Roderick C.
President
Tel: (541) 882 - 3451
Fax: (541) 855 - 7454
TF: (800) 535 - 3936
Responsibilities include corporate philanthropy.

Jenny Craig, Inc.

A provider of weight management products and services.
www.jennycraig.com

Chairman of the Board
KREH, Kent
Tel: (760) 696 - 4000
Fax: (760) 696 - 4009
TF: (800) 597 - 5366

Vice Chairman and Chief Exec. Officer
LARCHET, Patricia A.
Tel: (760) 696 - 4000
Fax: (760) 696 - 4009
TF: (800) 597 - 5366

Main Headquarters
Mailing: 5770 Fleet St.
Carlsbad, CA 92008
Tel: (760) 696 - 4000
Fax: (760) 696 - 4009
TF: (800) 597 - 5366

Public Affairs and Related Activities Personnel

At Headquarters

BAADE, Roberta C., Ph.D.
V. President, Human Resources
Tel: (760) 696 - 4000
Fax: (760) 696 - 4009
TF: (800) 597 - 5366

MANGINELLI, Gail
Communications
gail@jennycraig.com
Tel: (760) 696 - 4000
Fax: (760) 696 - 4009
TF: (800) 597 - 5366

PHIFER, Cozette
Director, Public Relations
cphifer@jennycraig.com
Tel: (760) 696 - 4000
Fax: (760) 696 - 4009
TF: (800) 597 - 5366

Jeppesen

Formerly Jeppesen Sanderson. Provides aeronautical information services. A wholly owned subsidiary of The Boeing Co. (see separate listing).
www.jeppesen.com

Main Headquarters
Mailing: 55 Inverness Dr. East
Englewood, CO 80112-5498
Tel: (303) 799 - 9090
Fax: (303) 328 - 4153

Washington Office
Contact: David Goehler
Mailing: 515 Prince St.
Alexandria, VA 22314-3115
Tel: (703) 519 - 5295
Fax: (703) 519 - 5296

Corporate Foundations and Giving Programs

Jeppesen Corporate Contributions Program
Contact: Eric Anderson
55 Inverness Dr. East
Englewood, CO 80112-5498
Tel: (303) 328 - 4767
Fax: (303) 328 - 4130

Annual Grant Total: none reported

Public Affairs and Related Activities Personnel

At Headquarters

ANDERSON, Eric
Public Relations Specialist
eric.anderson@jeppesen.com
Tel: (303) 328 - 4767
Fax: (303) 328 - 4130

CUSTODIO, Dominic
V. President, Government and Military Services
Tel: (303) 799 - 9090
Fax: (303) 328 - 4153

DIFRAIA, Alice
Director, Human Resources
alice.difraia@jeppesen.com
Tel: (303) 799 - 9090
Fax: (303) 784 - 4121

At Washington Office

GOEHLER, David
Director, Washington Office
dave.goehler@jeppesen.com
Tel: (703) 519 - 5295
Fax: (703) 519 - 5296

Jeppesen Sanderson, Inc.

See listing on page 268 under Jeppesen.

Jiffy Lube Internat'l, Inc.

Franchised oil change and lubrication centers. A subsidary of Shell Oil Co. (see separate listing).
www.jiffylube.com

Main Headquarters
Mailing: P.O. Box 4427
Houston, TX 77210-4427
Street: 700 Milan St.
Houston, TX 77002
Tel: (713) 546 - 4100
Fax: (713) 546 - 4041

Corporate Foundations and Giving Programs

The Jimmy Fund
Contact: Karen Cummings
P.O. Box 4427
Houston, TX 77210-4427
Tel: (713) 546 - 4100
Fax: (713) 546 - 4041

Annual Grant Total: none reported
Geographic Preference: National
Primary Interests: Children's Health; Education; Environment/Conservation
Recent Recipients: Brain Injury Prevention Program; Buckle-Up America; Earth Day; Kids In Back; Recycles Day; Women's Advisory Board of the Nat'l Car Care Council

Public Affairs and Related Activities Personnel

At Headquarters

CUMMINGS, Karen
Contact, The Jimmy Fund
Tel: (713) 546 - 4100
Fax: (713) 546 - 4041

LANDERS, Cindy
Director, Alliance and Identity
Tel: (713) 546 - 6272
Fax: (713) 546 - 4041
Responsibilities include public relations.

Jim Beam Brands Worldwide, Inc.

See listing on page 202 under Fortune Brands, Inc.

JLG Industries, Inc.

A manufacturer of specialized hydraulic machinery.
www.jlg.com
Annual Revenues: $1.192 billion

Chairman, President and Chief Exec. Officer
LASKY, William M.
Tel: (717) 485 - 5161
Fax: (717) 485 - 6417
TF: (877) 534 - 5438

Main Headquarters
Mailing: One JLG Dr.
McConnellsburg, PA 17233-9533
Tel: (717) 485 - 5161
Fax: (717) 485 - 6417
TF: (877) 534 - 5438

Public Affairs and Related Activities Personnel

At Headquarters

CORONA, Lisa
Senior V. President, Human Resources
Tel: (717) 485 - 5161
Fax: (717) 485 - 6417
TF: (877) 534 - 5438

At Other Offices

ROWLAND, Juna
V. President, Corporate and Investor Relations
13224 Fountainhead Plaza
Hagerstown, MD 21742
ir@jlg.com
Tel: (240) 313 - 1816

JM Family Enterprises, Inc.

A member of the Public Affairs Council. A diversified automotive corporation whose principal businesses focus on vehicle distribution and processing, finance and warranty services, and insurance activities.
www.jmfamily.com

Chairman of the Board
MORAN, Patricia — Tel: (954) 429 - 2000 Fax: (954) 429 - 2300

President and Chief Exec. Officer
BROWN, Colin — Tel: (954) 429 - 2000 Fax: (954) 429 - 2300

Main Headquarters
Mailing: 100 Jim Moran Blvd.
Deerfield Beach, FL 33442 — Tel: (954) 429 - 2000 Fax: (954) 429 - 2300

Political Action Committees

JM Family Enterprises, Inc. PAC
Contact: Gary C. Thomas
100 Jim Moran Blvd.
Deerfield Beach, FL 33442 — Tel: (954) 429 - 2603 Fax: (954) 429 - 2300

Contributions to Candidates: $17,500 (01/05 - 09/05)
Democrats: $15,000; Republicans: $2,500.

Principal Recipients

SENATE DEMOCRATS		HOUSE DEMOCRATS	
Nelson, Bill (FL)	$10,000	Davis, Artur (AL)	$1,000
		Klein, Ron (FL)	$1,000
		Lewis, John (GA)	$1,000
		Wexler, Robert (FL)	$1,000
SENATE REPUBLICANS		**HOUSE REPUBLICANS**	
		Bachus, Spencer (AL)	$1,000
		Mack, Connie (FL)	$1,000

Corporate Foundations and Giving Programs

JM Family Enterprises Inc. Corporate Giving
Contact: Kim Bentley
100 Jim Moran Blvd.
Deerfield Beach, FL 33442 — Tel: (954) 418 - 5037 Fax: (954) 429 - 2300

Annual Grant Total: none reported
Geographic Preference: Area(s) in which the company operates
Primary Interests: Arts and Culture; Education; Youth Services

Public Affairs and Related Activities Personnel

At Headquarters

ALLISON, Jay
V. President, Government Relations — Tel: (954) 429 - 2000 Fax: (954) 429 - 2300

BENTLEY, Kim
Director, Charitable Giving — Tel: (954) 418 - 5037 Fax: (954) 429 - 2300

DONAGHUE, Chad
Media Contact
chad.donaghue@jmfamily.com — Tel: (954) 429 - 2349 Fax: (954) 429 - 2300

KITEI, Lisa
V. President, Corporate Communications — Tel: (954) 429 - 2000 Fax: (954) 429 - 2300

MORAN, Jan
V. President, Community Relations and Marine Departments — Tel: (954) 429 - 2000 Fax: (954) 429 - 2300

NEMEROFF, Anne-Beth
Director, Corporate Communications
anne-beth.nemeroff@jmfamily.com — Tel: (954) 429 - 2387 Fax: (954) 429 - 2300

THOMAS, Gary C.
Exec. V. President, Human Resources
gary.thomas@jmfamily.com — Tel: (954) 429 - 2603 Fax: (954) 429 - 2300

Jo-Ann Stores, Inc.

A chain of specialty craft anf fabric stores.
www.joann.com

Chairman, President and Chief Exec. Officer
ROSSKAMM, Alan — Tel: (330) 656 - 2600 Fax: (330) 463 - 6675

Main Headquarters
Mailing: 5555 Darrow Rd.
Hudson, OH 44236 — Tel: (330) 656 - 2600 Fax: (330) 463 - 6675

Corporate Foundations and Giving Programs

Jo-Ann Stores Corporate Giving
5555 Darrow Rd.
Hudson, OH 44236 — Tel: (330) 656 - 2600 Fax: (330) 463 - 6675

Annual Grant Total: none reported
Primary Interests: Education
Recent Recipients: United Way

Public Affairs and Related Activities Personnel

At Headquarters

CARNEY, Brian
Exec. V. President and Chief Financial Officer — Tel: (330) 463 - 3436 Fax: (330) 463 - 6675
Responsibilities include investor relations.

GENTILE-SACHS, Valerie
Exec. V. President and General Counsel — Tel: (330) 656 - 2600 Fax: (330) 463 - 6675

KLINE, Riddi
Public Relations Contact — Tel: (330) 463 - 6915 Fax: (330) 463 - 6675

ROSSKAMM, Betty
Senior V. President — Tel: (330) 656 - 2600 Fax: (330) 463 - 6675
Responsibilities include corporate philanthropy.

THOMPSON, Rosalind
Exec. V. President, Human Resources — Tel: (330) 463 - 3489 Fax: (330) 463 - 6675

TOMOFF, Donald
V. President, Finance — Tel: (330) 656 - 2600 Fax: (330) 463 - 6675
Responsibilities include investor and media relations.

John Hancock Financial Services

A provider of insurance, investment, and other financial services. A subsidiary of Manulife Financial Corp., based in Canada.
www.johnhancock.com

President and Chief Exec. Officer
DESPREZ, John D., III — Tel: (617) 572 - 6000

Main Headquarters
Mailing: P.O. Box 111
Boston, MA 02117 — Tel: (617) 572 - 6000
Street: 200 Clarendon St.
Boston, MA 02116

Political Action Committees

John Hancock Financial Services Inc. Federal Political Action Committee
Contact: Thomas E. Samoluk
P.O. Box 111
Boston, MA 02117 — Tel: (617) 572 - 1300 Fax: (617) 572 - 1545

Contributions to Candidates: $16,580 (01/05 - 09/05)
Democrats: $8,580; Republicans: $8,000.

Principal Recipients

SENATE DEMOCRATS		HOUSE DEMOCRATS	
Nelson, Benjamin (NE)	$1,000	Lynch, Stephen (MA)	$2,500
Stabenow, Debbie (MI)	$1,000	Neal, Richard E Mr. (MA)	$2,000
		Cardin, Ben (MD)	$1,000
SENATE REPUBLICANS		**HOUSE REPUBLICANS**	
Martinez, Mel (FL)	$1,000	Johnson, Nancy (CT)	$2,000
		Camp, David Lee (MI)	$1,000
		Cantor, Eric (VA)	$1,000
		Knollenberg, Joe (MI)	$1,000
		Ramstad, Jim (MN)	$1,000
		Weller, Jerry (IL)	$1,000

Corporate Foundations and Giving Programs

John Hancock Financial Services Contributions Program
Contact: Carol Fulp
P.O. Box 111
Boston, MA 02117 — Tel: (617) 572 - 0451 Fax: (617) 572 - 6290

Annual Grant Total: $2,000,000 - $5,000,000
Guidelines are available for Boston organizations.
Geographic Preference: Boston, MA
Primary Interests: Youth Services
Recent Recipients: Boston College; Boston Police Department; Children's Museum; Sport in Society

Public Affairs and Related Activities Personnel

At Headquarters

FULP, Carol
V. President, Community Relations
Mailstop: T-58 — Tel: (617) 572 - 0451 Fax: (617) 572 - 6290

SAMOLUK, Thomas E.
V. President, Government Relations — Tel: (617) 572 - 1300 Fax: (617) 572 - 1545

Johns Manville Corp.

A wholly-owned subsidiary of Berkshire Hathaway (see separate listing).
www.jm.com
Annual Revenues: $2 billion

Chairman, President and Chief Exec. Officer
HOCHHAUSER, Steven B. — Tel: (303) 978 - 2000 Fax: (303) 978 - 2318 TF: (800) 654 - 3103

Main Headquarters
Mailing: P.O. Box 5108
Denver, CO 80217-5108 — Tel: (303) 978 - 2000 Fax: (303) 978 - 2318 TF: (800) 654 - 3103
Street: 717 17th St.
Denver, CO 80202

Johns Manville Corp.

* continued from previous page

Corporate Foundations and Giving Programs

Johns Manvile Fund
Contact: M. K. Rhinehart
P.O. Box 5108
Denver, CO 80217-5108
Tel: (303) 978 - 2000
Fax: (303) 978 - 2318
TF: (800) 654 - 3103

Annual Grant Total: under $100,000
Primarily interested in organizations which employees are involved in as volunteers.
Geographic Preference: Area(s) in which the company operates

Public Affairs and Related Activities Personnel

At Headquarters

DUNBAR, Melody W.
Manager, Corporate Relations
dunbarm@jm.com
Tel: (303) 978 - 2350
Fax: (303) 978 - 2919
TF: (800) 654 - 3103

LOWE, D. Fred
V. President, Human Resources
Tel: (303) 978 - 2000
Fax: (303) 978 - 2318
TF: (800) 654 - 3103

RHINEHART, M. K.
President, Foundation
Tel: (303) 978 - 2000
Fax: (303) 978 - 2318
TF: (800) 654 - 3103

Johnson & Higgins

See listing on page 306 under Marsh Inc.

Johnson & Johnson

A member of the Public Affairs Council. A manufacturer of health care products.
www.jnj.com
Annual Revenues: $33.004 billion

Chairman and Chief Exec. Officer
WELDON, William C.
Tel: (732) 524 - 0400
Fax: (732) 524 - 5848
TF: (800) 635 - 6789

Main Headquarters
Mailing: One Johnson & Johnson Plaza
New Brunswick, NJ 08933-7204
Tel: (732) 524 - 0400
Fax: (732) 214 - 0334
TF: (800) 635 - 6789

Washington Office
Contact: Charles Nau
Mailing: 1350 I St. NW
Suite 1210
Washington, DC 20005-3305
Tel: (202) 408 - 9482
Fax: (202) 408 - 9490

Political Action Committees

Johnson & Johnson Employees' Good Government Fund
Contact: Richard W. Lloyd
One Johnson & Johnson Plaza
New Brunswick, NJ 08933-7204
Tel: (732) 524 - 3726
Fax: (732) 524 - 3005
TF: (800) 635 - 6789

Contributions to Candidates: $225,000 (01/05 - 09/05)
Democrats: $94,000; Republicans: $130,000; Other: $1,000.

Principal Recipients

SENATE DEMOCRATS		HOUSE DEMOCRATS	
Nelson, Benjamin (NE)	$9,000	Menendez, Robert (NJ)	$10,000
		Thompson, Mike (CA)	$7,000
		Bean, Melissa (IL)	$5,000
		Farr, Sam (CA)	$5,000
		Gordon, Barton (TN)	$5,000
		Honda, Mike (CA)	$5,000
		Jefferson, William (LA)	$5,000
SENATE REPUBLICANS		**HOUSE REPUBLICANS**	
Santorum, Richard (PA)	$5,000	Deal, Nathan (GA)	$8,000
		Ferguson, Mike (NJ)	$8,000
		Barton, Joe L (TX)	$7,500
		Thomas, William M (CA)	$7,500
		Crenshaw, Ander (FL)	$5,000
		Frelinghuysen, Rod (NJ)	$5,000
		Johnson, Nancy (CT)	$5,000
		Lungren, Daniel E (CA)	$5,000

Corporate Foundations and Giving Programs

Johnson & Johnson Family of Companies Contribution Fund
Contact: Russell C. Deyo
One Johnson & Johnson Plaza
New Brunswick, NJ 08933-7204
Tel: (732) 524 - 0400
Ext: 2440
Fax: (732) 214 - 0334
TF: (800) 635 - 6789

Annual Grant Total: over $5,000,000
Also supports the Johnson & Johnson Focused Giving Program, Johnson & Johnson Community Health Program, Johnson & Johnson Wharton Nurse Fellowship Program and the Johnson & Johnson LIVE FOR LIFE School Nurse Fellowship Program. Guidelines and annual report are available.
Geographic Preference: Area(s) in which the company operates; National; International
Primary Interests: Adult Education and Training; Families; Health

Public Affairs and Related Activities Personnel

At Headquarters

DEYO, Russell C.
V. President, General Counsel
rdeyo@corus.jnj.com
Tel: (732) 524 - 0400
Ext: 2440
Fax: (732) 214 - 0334
TF: (800) 635 - 6789

Responsibilities include corporate philanthropy.

GORDON, Tina
Exec. Director, Corporate Communications
tgordon@corus.jnj.com
Tel: (732) 524 - 3540
Fax: (732) 524 - 3564
TF: (800) 635 - 6789

GORRIE, Thomas M., Ph.D.
V. President, Government Affairs and Policy
Mailstop: WT701
Tel: (732) 524 - 6730
Fax: (732) 524 - 5310
TF: (800) 635 - 6789

JORDAN, Raymond
V. President, Corporate Communications
Tel: (732) 524 - 0400
Ext: 3535
Fax: (732) 524 - 3564
TF: (800) 635 - 6789

LLOYD, Richard W.
Executive Director, Government Affairs
rlloyd@corus.jnj.com
Tel: (732) 524 - 3726
Fax: (732) 524 - 3005
TF: (800) 635 - 6789

MAYS, Alfred
V. President, Corporate Contributions
amays@corus.jnj.com
Tel: (732) 524 - 3372
Fax: (732) 214 - 0334
TF: (800) 635 - 6789

MOLINO, Patricia
V. President, Corporate Communications
pmolino@corus.jnj.com
Tel: (908) 524 - 3373
Fax: (908) 524 - 3621
TF: (800) 635 - 6789

MONSEAU, Marc
Assistant Director, Corporate Communications
mmonseau@corus.jnj.com
Tel: (732) 524 - 1130
Fax: (732) 214 - 0334
TF: (800) 635 - 6789

ODENTHAL, Susan M.
V. President, Corporate Communications
sodente@corus.jnj.com
Tel: (732) 524 - 0400
Fax: (732) 214 - 0334
TF: (800) 635 - 6789

PAI CHIN, Vivian
Director, Environmental Regulatory Affairs
Tel: (732) 524 - 0400
Fax: (732) 214 - 0334
TF: (800) 635 - 6789

SHORT, Hellen F.
V. President, Investor Relations
Tel: (732) 524 - 6491
Fax: (732) 214 - 0334
TF: (800) 635 - 6789

SOSA, Jose F.
Director, External Affairs
jsosa@corus.jnj.com
Tel: (732) 524 - 3070
Fax: (732) 524 - 3005
TF: (800) 635 - 6789

WILLIAMS, Ather
V. President, Environmental Affairs
Tel: (732) 524 - 0400
Fax: (732) 214 - 0334
TF: (800) 635 - 6789

At Washington Office

ADAMS, Jane M.
Director, Federal Affairs
Tel: (202) 408 - 9482
Fax: (202) 408 - 9490

ALLEN, Jeremy W.
Director, Federal Affairs
Tel: (202) 408 - 9482
Fax: (202) 408 - 9490

BOHN, Donald W.
V. President, State Government Affairs
dbohn@corus.jnj.com
Registered Federal Lobbyist.
Tel: (202) 589 - 1016
Fax: (202) 589 - 1001

BURNS, Brian
Exec. Director, Federal Affairs
Registered Federal Lobbyist.
Tel: (202) 408 - 9482
Fax: (202) 408 - 9490

BUTO, Kathleen A.
V. President, Health Policy
Tel: (202) 589 - 1000
Fax: (202) 589 - 1001

DOOLEY, Cathleen M.
Exec. Director, Federal Affairs
Tel: (202) 589 - 1000
Ext: 1008
Fax: (202) 589 - 1001

Registered Federal Lobbyist.

JODREY, Darrel Cox
Executive Director, Federal Affairs
Mailstop: M/S 1006
Registered Federal Lobbyist.
Tel: (202) 589 - 1000
Fax: (202) 589 - 1001

Johnson & Johnson

** continued from previous page*

NAU, Charles — Tel: (202) 589 - 1000
Director, Federal Affairs — Fax: (202) 408 - 9490
Registered Federal Lobbyist.

REARDON, Susan — Tel: (202) 408 - 9482
Director, Federal Affairs — Fax: (202) 408 - 9490

SALMON, Shannon — Tel: (202) 589 - 1000
V. President, Federal Affairs — Fax: (202) 408 - 9490
ssalmon@corus.jnj.com
Registered Federal Lobbyist.

At Other Offices

BAHNSEN, Lynn B. — Tel: (706) 353 - 4434
Regional Director, Government Affairs
1440 Olympic Dr.
Athens, GA 30608-8001

CANNON, James F. — Tel: (570) 586 - 8127
Director, State Government Affairs — Fax: (570) 587 - 3340
P.O. Box 204
Clarks Summit, PA 18411
jcannon@corus.jnj.com

CECCHINI, Peter M. — Tel: (908) 218 - 2457
Project Manager, Regulatory Affairs — Fax: (908) 218 - 2813
(Ethicon Inc.)
U.S. Route 22
Somerville, NJ 08876

COELLN, Jacqueline — Tel: (908) 704 - 5829
Manager, Drug Regulatory Affairs — Fax: (908) 722 - 5867
U.S. Route 22
Somerville, NJ 08876

IRVING, George C. — Tel: (770) 664 - 7151
Director, State Government Affairs — Fax: (770) 751 - 7485
3110 Glenn Knolls Ct.
Alpharetta, GA 30022

QUINN, Margaret — Tel: (215) 273 - 7759
Manager, Government Affairs and Policy — Fax: (215) 273 - 4145
(McNeil Consumer & Specialty Pharmaceuticals)
7050 Camp Hill Rd.
Fort Washington, PA 19034

SHESTAK, David A. — Tel: (916) 443 - 2010
Director, State Government Affairs — Fax: (916) 446 - 6896
1201 K St., Suite 815
Sacramento, CA 95814
dshestak@corus.jnj.com

WALKER, Nancy — Tel: (908) 218 - 6636
V. President, Public Affairs — Fax: (908) 218 - 1416
(Ortho-McNeil Pharmaceutical, Inc.)
U.S. Route 202, P.O. Box 300
Raritan, NJ 08869-0602

Johnson and Son, Inc., S. C.

See listing on page 425 under SC Johnson.

Johnson Controls, Inc.

A leader in automotive sytems and facility management and control.

www.jci.com
Annual Revenues: $22.6 billion

Chairman and Chief Exec. Officer — Tel: (414) 524 - 1200
BARTH, John M. — Fax: (414) 524 - 2077

Main Headquarters
Mailing: 5757 N. Green Bay Ave. — Tel: (414) 524 - 1200
Milwaukee, WI 53201-0591 — Fax: (414) 524 - 2077

Washington Office
Contact: Mark F. Wagner
Mailing: 400 N. Capitol St. NW — Tel: (202) 393 - 3224
Suite 590 — Fax: (202) 393 - 7718
Washington, DC 20001

Political Action Committees

Johnson Controls Inc. Federal PAC
Contact: John P. Kennedy
5757 N. Green Bay Ave. — Tel: (414) 524 - 1200
Milwaukee, WI 53201-0591 — Fax: (414) 524 - 2077

Contributions to Candidates: $5,500 (01/05 - 09/05)
Democrats: $2,000; Republicans: $3,500.

Principal Recipients

SENATE DEMOCRATS
Conrad, Kent (ND) $1,000
Lieberman, Joe (CT) $1,000

HOUSE DEMOCRATS

SENATE REPUBLICANS

HOUSE REPUBLICANS
Davis, Tom (VA) $2,000
Hunter, Duncan (CA) $1,000

Corporate Foundations and Giving Programs

Johnson Controls Foundation
Contact: Kathy Szczupakiewicz
5757 N. Green Bay Ave. — Tel: (414) 524 - 1200
Milwaukee, WI 53201-0591 — Fax: (414) 524 - 2077

Annual Grant Total: $2,000,000 - $5,000,000
Guidelines are available. All proposals must include a copy of tax-exempt, nonprofit status. The company also maintains a matching gifts program.
Geographic Preference: National
Primary Interests: Arts and Culture; Civic and Cultural Activities; Higher Education; Social Services
Recent Recipients: Children's Hospital; United Performing Arts Fund; United Way

Public Affairs and Related Activities Personnel

At Headquarters

DAVIS, Susan F. — Tel: (414) 524 - 2253
V. President, Human Resources — Fax: (414) 524 - 2077
susan.davis@jci.com

GUMM, Arlene — Tel: (414) 524 - 2363
Corporate Administrator, Shareholder Relations — Fax: (414) 524 - 0118
arlene.gumm@jci.com

KENNEDY, John P. — Tel: (414) 524 - 1200
Senior V. President, Secretary and General Counsel; PAC Contact — Fax: (414) 524 - 2077

PONCZAK, Glen — Tel: (414) 524 - 2375
Director, External Communications — Fax: (414) 524 - 2077
glen.l.ponczak@jci.com

SZCZUPAKIEWICZ, Kathy — Tel: (414) 524 - 1200
Foundation Administrator, Johnson Controls Foundation — Fax: (414) 524 - 2077

ZUTZ, Denise M. — Tel: (414) 524 - 3155
V. President, Corporate Communications and Investor Relations — Fax: (414) 524 - 2077
denise.zutz@jci.com

At Washington Office

WAGNER, Mark F. — Tel: (202) 393 - 3224
Director, Government Affairs — Fax: (202) 393 - 7718
Registered Federal Lobbyist.

Jones Apparel Group

Manufacturer of men's and women's apparel. Brand names include Jones New York, Evan-Piccone, Nine West, Easy Spirit, Lauren by Ralph Lauren, Ralph by Ralph Lauren, and Enzo Angiolini, among others.

www.jny.com

Chairman of the Board and Director — Tel: (215) 785 - 4000
KIMMEL, Sydney — Fax: (215) 785 - 1228

President and Chief Exec. Officer — Tel: (215) 785 - 4000
BONEPARTH, Peter — Fax: (215) 785 - 1228

Main Headquarters
Mailing: 250 Rittenhouse Circle — Tel: (215) 785 - 4000
Bristol, PA 19007 — Fax: (215) 785 - 1228

Public Affairs and Related Activities Personnel

At Headquarters

BRITT, Anita — Tel: (215) 785 - 4000
Exec. V. President, Finance and Investor Relations — Fax: (215) 785 - 1795

TEJERO-DECOLLI, Aida — Tel: (215) 785 - 4000
Senior V. President, Human Resources — Fax: (215) 785 - 1795

Jones Intercable, Inc.

See listing on page 271 under Jones Internat'l, Ltd.

Jones Internat'l, Ltd.

The corporate parent of multiple subsidiaries in the Internet, e-commerce, software, education, entertainment, radio, and cable television programming industries.

www.jones.com

President and Chief Exec. Officer — Tel: (303) 792 - 3111
JONES, Glenn R. — Fax: (303) 792 - 8211

Main Headquarters
Mailing: 9697 E. Mineral Ave. — Tel: (303) 792 - 3111
Englewood, CO 80112 — Fax: (303) 784 - 8508

Political Action Committees

Jones International, Ltd. PAC
Contact: Stacey C. Slaughter
9697 E. Mineral Ave. — Tel: (303) 792 - 3111
Englewood, CO 80112 — Fax: (303) 784 - 8508

Contributions to Candidates: none reported (01/05 - 09/05)

Jones Internat'l, Ltd.

* continued from previous page

Public Affairs and Related Activities Personnel

At Headquarters

KETCHEL, Kim — Tel: (303) 792 - 3111
V. President, Marketing and Communications — Fax: (303) 784 - 8508

SLAUGHTER, Stacey C. — Tel: (303) 792 - 3111
Assistant Treasurer — Fax: (303) 784 - 8508

Jones Lang LaSalle Inc.

A corporate real estate and investment firm.
www.am.joneslanglasalle.com
Annual Revenues: $840 million

Chairman of the Board — Tel: (312) 782 - 5800
PENROSE, Sheila A. — Fax: (312) 782 - 4339

President and Chief Exec. Officer — Tel: (312) 782 - 5800
DYER, Colin — Fax: (312) 782 - 4339

Main Headquarters
Mailing: 200 E. Randolph St. — Tel: (312) 782 - 5800
Chicago, IL 60601-6436 — Fax: (312) 782 - 4339

Political Action Committees

Jones Lang LaSalle Americas Inc. PAC
Contact: Thomas Morande
200 E. Randolph St. — Tel: (312) 782 - 5800
Chicago, IL 60601-6436 — Fax: (312) 782 - 4339

Contributions to Candidates: none reported (01/05 - 09/05)

Public Affairs and Related Activities Personnel

At Headquarters

KANTRO, Ms. Gayle — Tel: (312) 782 - 5800
Director, Public Relations — Fax: (312) 782 - 4339

KELLY, Molly A. — Tel: (312) 782 - 5800
Chief Marketing and Communications Officer — Fax: (312) 782 - 4339

MORANDE, Thomas — Tel: (312) 782 - 5800
Treasurer, Jones Lang LaSalle Americas Inc. PAC — Fax: (312) 782 - 4339

RAZI, Nazneen — Tel: (312) 782 - 5800
Chief Human Resources Officer — Fax: (312) 782 - 4339

Jostens, Inc.

A subsidiary of Visant Holding Corp. A producer of class rings, yearbooks and other specialized products which recognize achievement and affiliation.
www.jostens.com
Annual Revenues: $780 million

Chief Exec. Officer — Tel: (952) 830 - 3300
BAILEY, Michael

Main Headquarters
Mailing: 5501 American Blvd. West — Tel: (952) 830 - 3300
Minneapolis, MN 55437 — Fax: (952) 830 - 3293

Corporate Foundations and Giving Programs

Jostens Foundation, The
5501 American Blvd. West — Tel: (952) 830 - 3300
Minneapolis, MN 55437 — Fax: (952) 830 - 3293

Annual Grant Total: $400,000 - $500,000
Primary Interests: Children; Youth Services

Public Affairs and Related Activities Personnel

At Headquarters

GOETZ, Julie — Tel: (952) 830 - 3332
Manager, Communications — Fax: (952) 830 - 3293
julie.goetz@jostens.com

KLIMEK, Mary — Tel: (952) 830 - 3235
Foundation Director

STOEBE, Rich — Tel: (952) 830 - 3300
Director, Communications — Fax: (952) 897 - 4116
richard.stoebe@jostens.com

Journal Communications, Inc.

A communications company involved in newspaper publishing, printing and radio and television broadcasting.
www.journalcommunications.com
Annual Revenues: $820.8 million

Chairman and Chief Exec. Officer — Tel: (414) 224 - 2000
SMITH, Steven J. — Fax: (414) 224 - 2469

Main Headquarters
Mailing: P.O. Box 661 — Tel: (414) 224 - 2616
Milwaukee, WI 53201-0661 — Fax: (414) 224 - 2469
Street: 333 W. State St.
Milwaukee, WI 53203

Corporate Foundations and Giving Programs

Journal Communications Corporate Giving Program
Contact: Robert M. Dye
P.O. Box 661 — Tel: (414) 224 - 2725
Milwaukee, WI 53201-0661 — Fax: (414) 224 - 2469

Annual Grant Total: none reported
Geographic Preference: Wisconsin
Primary Interests: Civic and Cultural Activities; Education; Social Services

Public Affairs and Related Activities Personnel

At Headquarters

DYE, Robert M. — Tel: (414) 224 - 2725
V. President, Corporate Affairs — Fax: (414) 224 - 2469
Responsibilities include corporate philanthropy.

HARMSEN, Dan — Tel: (414) 224 - 2099
V. President, Human Resources — Fax: (414) 224 - 2469

Joy Global Inc.

A holding company for two subsidiaries involved in the manufacture of surface mining and material handling equipment.
www.joyglobal.com

Chairman, President and Chief Exec. Officer — Tel: (414) 319 - 8500
HANSON, John Nils — Fax: (414) 319 - 8510

Main Headquarters
Mailing: P.O. Box 554 — Tel: (414) 319 - 8500
Milwaukee, WI 53201 — Fax: (414) 319 - 8510
Street: 100 E. Wisconsin Ave.
Suite 2780
Milwaukee, WI 53202

Political Action Committees

Joy Global Inc. Political Action Committee
Contact: Kenneth J. Stark
P.O. Box 554 — Tel: (414) 319 - 8500
Milwaukee, WI 53201 — Fax: (414) 319 - 8510

Contributions to Candidates: $6,750 (01/05 - 09/05)
Democrats: $2,000; Republicans: $4,750.

Principal Recipients

SENATE DEMOCRATS		HOUSE DEMOCRATS	
Lincoln, Blanche (AR)	$1,000	Boucher, Fredrick (VA)	$1,000
SENATE REPUBLICANS		**HOUSE REPUBLICANS**	
Santorum, Richard (PA)	$1,000	Peterson, John Mr. (PA)	$1,000

Corporate Foundations and Giving Programs

Joy Global Inc. Foundation
Contact: Sandra L. McKenzie
P.O. Box 554 — Tel: (414) 319 - 8500
Milwaukee, WI 53201 — Fax: (414) 319 - 8510

Annual Grant Total: $750,000 - $1,000,000
Geographic Preference: Area(s) in which the company operates
Primary Interests: Arts and Humanities; Community Affairs; Education; Health

Public Affairs and Related Activities Personnel

At Headquarters

CHOKEY, James A. — Tel: (414) 319 - 8500
Exec. V. President and General Counsel — Fax: (414) 319 - 8510

MCKENZIE, Sandra L. — Tel: (414) 319 - 8500
Contact, Joy Global Foundation — Fax: (414) 319 - 8510
Responsibilities include investor relations.

ROOF, Donald C. — Tel: (414) 319 - 8500
Exec. V. President and Chief Financial Officer — Fax: (414) 319 - 8510
Responsibilities include investor relations.

STARK, Kenneth J. — Tel: (414) 319 - 8500
PAC Contact — Fax: (414) 319 - 8510

WINKLEMAN, Dennis R. — Tel: (414) 319 - 8500
Exec. V. President, Human Resources — Fax: (414) 319 - 8510

Juniper Networks, Inc.

Provides IP infrastructure systems to ISPs.
www.juniper.net

Chairman and Chief Exec. Officer — Tel: (408) 745 - 2000
KRIENS, Scott
skriens@juniper.net

Main Headquarters
Mailing: 1194 N. Mathilda Ave. — Tel: (408) 745 - 2000
Sunnyvale, CA 94089-1206 — Fax: (408) 745 - 2100
TF: (888) 584 - 737

Corporate Foundations and Giving Programs

Juniper Networks Foundation Fund

Juniper Networks, Inc.

** continued from previous page*

1194 N. Mathilda Ave.
Sunnyvale, CA 94089-1206
Tel: (408) 745 - 2000
Fax: (408) 745 - 2100
TF: (888) 584 - 737

Annual Grant Total: $1,000,000 - $2,000,000

The company maintains a matching gifts program.

Geographic Preference: Area(s) in which the company operates

Primary Interests: Disaster Relief; Education; Technology; Vocational Training

Recent Recipients: Leukemia Society; Second Harvest

Public Affairs and Related Activities Personnel

At Headquarters

DURR, Kathy
Media Relations Contact
kdurr@juniper.net
Tel: (408) 745 - 5058
Fax: (408) 936 - 3033

FEIGIN, Randi P.
Director, Investor Relations
randi@juniper.net
Tel: (408) 745 - 2371
Fax: (408) 745 - 8921

LEVINE, Michelle
Senior Manager, Investor Relations
Tel: (408) 936 - 2775
Fax: (408) 745 - 2100

PHILPOTT, Fred
V. President, Human Resources
Tel: (408) 745 - 2000
Fax: (408) 745 - 2100
TF: (888) 584 - 737

Kaiser Aluminum & Chemical Corp.

A producer of bauxite, alumina, aluminum, and fabricated aluminum products.

www.kaiseral.com

Chairman of the Board
HAYMAKER, George T., Jr.
Tel: (949) 614 - 1740
Fax: (949) 614 - 1930

President and Chief Exec. Officer
HOCKEMA, Jack A.
Tel: (949) 614 - 1740
Fax: (949) 614 - 1930

Main Headquarters
Mailing: 27422 Portola Pkwy
Suite 350
Foothill Ranch, CA 92610-2831
Tel: (949) 614 - 1740
Fax: (949) 614 - 1930

Political Action Committees

Kaiser Aluminum & Chemical Corp. Political Action Committee
Contact: John M. Donnan
27422 Portola Pkwy
Suite 350
Foothill Ranch, CA 92610-2831
Tel: (949) 614 - 1740
Fax: (949) 614 - 1930

Contributions to Candidates: $2,000 (01/05 - 09/05)
Republicans: $2,000.

Principal Recipients

SENATE REPUBLICANS

HOUSE REPUBLICANS

Marchant, Kenny (TX)	$1,000
Royce, Ed Mr (CA)	$1,000

Corporate Foundations and Giving Programs

Kaiser Aluminum & Chemical Corporate Contributions Program
27422 Portola Pkwy
Suite 350
Foothill Ranch, CA 92610-2831
Tel: (949) 614 - 1740
Fax: (949) 614 - 1930

Annual Grant Total: none reported

Public Affairs and Related Activities Personnel

At Headquarters

DONNAN, John M.
Deputy General Counsel; PAC Treasurer
john.donnan@kaiseral.com
Tel: (949) 614 - 1740
Fax: (949) 614 - 1930

LAMB, W. Scott
V. President, Investor Relations and Corporate Communications
scott.lamb@kaiseral.com
Tel: (949) 614 - 1740
Fax: (949) 614 - 1930

Kaiser Aluminum Corp.

See listing on page 273 under Kaiser Aluminum & Chemical Corp.

Kaiser Foundation Health Plan of Georgia

See listing on page 273 under Kaiser Permanente.

Kaiser Foundation Health Plan, Inc.

See listing on page 273 under Kaiser Permanente.

Kaiser Foundation Health Plan, Inc.

See listing on page 273 under Kaiser Permanente.

Kaiser Permanente

A not-for-profit health maintenance organization.

www.kaiserpermanente.org.
Annual Revenues: $19.7 billion

Chairman and Chief Exec. Officer
HALVORSON, George
Tel: (510) 271 - 5910
Fax: (510) 271 - 6493

Main Headquarters
Mailing: Ordway Bldg.
One Kaiser Plaza
Oakland, CA 94612
Tel: (510) 271 - 5800
Fax: (510) 267 - 7524

Washington Office
Mailing: 1333 H St. NW
Suite 300 West
Washington, DC 20005
Tel: (202) 296 - 1314
Fax: (202) 296 - 4067

Corporate Foundations and Giving Programs

Kaiser Permanente Corporate Giving Program
Ordway Bldg.
One Kaiser Plaza
Oakland, CA 94612
Tel: (510) 271 - 5800
Fax: (510) 267 - 7524

Annual Grant Total: none reported

The company supports the Kaiser Permanente Cares For Kids program, which subsidizes health coverage for up to 50,000 children a year from low-income families.

Primary Interests: Children's Health

Public Affairs and Related Activities Personnel

At Headquarters

BARCO, Kathleen
Associate Media Director - Northern California Region
Tel: (510) 987 - 3900
Fax: (510) 873 - 5345

HAYON, Beverly
Director, National Media Relations
beverly.hayon@kp.org
Tel: (510) 271 - 5953
Fax: (510) 271 - 6493

MALASPINA, Rick
Media Director - Northern California Region
rick.malaspina@kp.org
Tel: (510) 987 - 3900
Fax: (510) 873 - 5345

RUBIO, Lea
Senior Media Representative - Northern California Region
Tel: (510) 987 - 3900
Fax: (510) 873 - 5345

ZATKIN, Steven R.
Senior V. President, Government Relations
Tel: (510) 271 - 2626
Fax: (510) 271 - 5917

At Washington Office

BURNETT, Laird
Vice President, Federal Government Relations
Tel: (202) 296 - 1314
Fax: (202) 296 - 4067

COLE, Steven R.
Director, Public Policy
Tel: (202) 296 - 1314
Fax: (202) 296 - 4067

FROH, Richard B.
V. President, Government Relations
Registered Federal Lobbyist.
Tel: (202) 296 - 1314
Fax: (202) 296 - 4067

At Other Offices

ANDERSON, Jim
Associate Media Director - Southern California Region
393 E. Walnut St.
Pasadena, CA 91188
Tel: (626) 405 - 5157
Fax: (626) 405 - 3176

BLACKBURN, Kathleen A.
V. President, Public Affairs - California Division
1950 Franklin St., Third Floor
Oakland, CA 94612
Tel: (510) 987 - 2703
Fax: (510) 873 - 5029

BYRNE, Mike
Media Representative - Southern California Region
393 E. Walnut St.
Pasadena, CA 91188
Tel: (626) 405 - 5528
Fax: (626) 405 - 3176

DENDLE, Phyllis J. Baumwell
Director, Government Affairs
1441 Kapiolani Blvd., 17th Floor
Honolulu, HI 96814-4407
Tel: (808) 983 - 4981

FLATT, Dennis O.
V. President and Legislative Representative
1215 K St.
Suite 2030
Sacramento, CA 95814
Tel: (916) 448 - 8866
Fax: (916) 973 - 6476

GERSBACH, Jim
Communications and Community Relations Contact-Northwest Region
500 N.E. Multnomah St.
Suite 100
Portland, OR 97232-2099
jim.n.gersbach@kp.org
Tel: (503) 813 - 4827
Fax: (503) 813 - 4235

GUINN, Vicki E.
Communications and External Affairs
500 N.E. Multnomah St.
Suite 100
Portland, OR 97232-2099
Tel: (503) 813 - 4823
Fax: (503) 813 - 4576

Kaiser Permanente

** continued from previous page*

HAWKINS, J. Michael
Senior Legislative Counsel
1201 K St., Suite 1850
Sacramento, CA 95814
Tel: (916) 448 - 6512
Fax: (916) 973 - 6476

LOVELAND, Darcy
Counsel, Government Relations
(Kaiser Foundation Health Plan, Inc.)
Three Rockledge Rd.
Laguna Beach, CA 92651
Tel: (949) 497 - 2907
Fax: (949) 497 - 2927

MCELROY, Jerel
Community and Government Relations Representative
10350 E. Dakota Ave.
Denver, CO 80231-1314
Tel: (303) 344 - 7245

MONTGOMERY, Jacque
Media Representative - Colorado Region
10350 E. Dakota Ave.
Denver, CO 80231-1314
jacque.montgomery@kp.org
Tel: (303) 344 - 7410

PABLO, Christopher G.
Director, Government and Community Affairs
1441 Kapiolani Blvd., 17th Floor
Honolulu, HI 96814-4407
Tel: (808) 983 - 4982

PERRY, Earnestine
Media Representative - Georgia Region
3495 Piedmont Rd. NE
Atlanta, GA 30305-1736
earnestine.perry@kp.org
Tel: (404) 364 - 4754

RUSSELL, Alison
Media Representative - Hawaii Region
1441 Kapiolani Blvd.
17th Floor
Honolulu, HI 96814-4407
alison.x.russell@kp.org
Tel: (808) 432 - 4983

SERRANO, Socorro L.
Senior Media Representative - Southern Califonia Region
393 E. Walnut St.
Pasadena, CA 91188
Tel: (626) 405 - 3004
Fax: (626) 405 - 3176

SIMON, Susan Whyte
Media Representative - MidAtlantic Region
2101 E. Jefferson St.
Rockville, MD 20852
susan.whyte.simon@kp.org
Tel: (301) 816 - 6264

THOMAS, Beverly
V. President, Communications and Public Affairs
3495 Piedmont Rd. NE
Atlanta, GA 30305-1736
Tel: (404) 364 - 4713
Fax: (404) 364 - 4794

WOODS, Mary
Corporate Communications
2101 E. Jefferson St.
Rockville, MD 20852
Tel: (301) 816 - 2424
Fax: (301) 816 - 7119

YANCEY, H. Evonne
Director, Government and Community Affairs
(Kaiser Foundation Health Plan of Georgia)
3495 Piedmont Rd., N.E.
Atlanta, GA 30305
Tel: (404) 364 - 7037
Fax: (404) 364 - 4792

Kaman Corp.

A diversified manufacturing and distribution company.
www.kaman.com

Chairman, President and Chief Exec. Officer
KUHN, Paul R.
Tel: (860) 243 - 7100
Fax: (860) 243 - 6101

Main Headquarters
Mailing: 1332 Blue Hills Ave.
P.O. Box 1
Bloomfield, CT 06002-0001
Street: 1332 Blue Hills Ave.
Bloomfield, CT 06002-0001
Tel: (860) 243 - 7100
Fax: (860) 243 - 6365

Political Action Committees

Kaman Corp. Good Government Fund
Contact: Russell H. Jones
1332 Blue Hills Ave.
P.O. Box 1
Bloomfield, CT 06002-0001
Tel: (860) 243 - 6307
Fax: (860) 243 - 6365

Contributions to Candidates: $6,500 (01/05 - 09/05)
Democrats: $2,000; Republicans: $4,500.

Principal Recipients

SENATE DEMOCRATS
Nelson, Bill (FL) $2,000

HOUSE DEMOCRATS

SENATE REPUBLICANS

HOUSE REPUBLICANS
Tiahrt, Todd W. (KS) $2,500
Weldon, Curt (PA) $2,000

Corporate Foundations and Giving Programs

Kaman Corp. Contributions Program
Contact: Russell H. Jones
1332 Blue Hills Ave.
P.O. Box 1
Bloomfield, CT 06002-0001
Tel: (860) 243 - 6307
Fax: (860) 243 - 6365

Annual Grant Total: $200,000 - $300,000
Geographic Preference: Area(s) in which employees live and work; Area(s) in which the company operates; Connecticut

Public Affairs and Related Activities Personnel

At Headquarters

JONES, Russell H.
Senior V. President, Chief Investment Officer and Treasurer
rhj-corp@kaman.com
Tel: (860) 243 - 6307
Fax: (860) 243 - 6365
Responsibilities include public relations and corporate contributions.

Kaneb Services, Inc.

See listing on page 527 under Xanser Corp.

Kansas City Life Insurance Co.

Kansas City Life Insurance Company markets individual life, annuity and group insurance products through approximately 2,700 general agents and agents located throughout the United States.
www.kclife.com
Annual Revenues: $502 million

Chairman, President and Chief Exec. Officer
BIXBY, R. Philip
Tel: (816) 753 - 7000
Fax: (816) 753 - 4902

Main Headquarters
Mailing: P.O. Box 219139
Kansas City, MO 64121-9139
Street: 3520 Broadway
Kansas City, MO 64111
Tel: (816) 753 - 7000
Fax: (816) 753 - 4902

Political Action Committees

Kansas City Life Insurance Co. Employees' PAC
Contact: Dallas A. Polen
P.O. Box 219139
Kansas City, MO 64121-9139
Tel: (816) 753 - 7000
Ext: 8713
Fax: (816) 753 - 4902

Contributions to Candidates: $500 (01/05 - 09/05)
Republicans: $500.

Principal Recipients

SENATE REPUBLICANS

HOUSE REPUBLICANS
Hulshof, Kenny (MO) $500

Corporate Foundations and Giving Programs

Kansas City Life Insurance Co. Corporate Contributions
Contact: Dallas A. Polen
P.O. Box 219139
Kansas City, MO 64121-9139
Tel: (816) 753 - 7000
Ext: 8713
Fax: (816) 753 - 4902

Annual Grant Total: none reported

Public Affairs and Related Activities Personnel

At Headquarters

POLEN, Dallas A.
Director, Governmental Affairs
Tel: (816) 753 - 7000
Ext: 8713
Fax: (816) 753 - 4902
Responsibilities include corporate philanthropy.

STRAUTMAN, Alex
Director, Communications and Public Information
Tel: (816) 753 - 7299
Ext: 8825
Fax: (816) 753 - 0138

Kansas City Power and Light Co.

A member of the Public Affairs Council. *See listing on page 226 under Great Plains Energy, Inc.*

Kansas City Southern

A holding company diversified into railroads and financial services.
www.kcsi.com

Chairman, President, and Chief Exec. Officer
HAVERTY, Michael R.
Tel: (816) 983 - 1303
Fax: (816) 983 - 1124
TF: (800) 468 - 6740

Main Headquarters
Mailing: 427 W. 12th St.
Kansas City, MO 64105
Tel: (816) 983 - 1303
Fax: (816) 983 - 1108
TF: (800) 468 - 6740

Political Action Committees

Kansas City Southern Employee PAC
Contact: Barbara Blevins
427 W. 12th St.
Kansas City, MO 64105
Tel: (816) 983 - 1303
Fax: (816) 983 - 1192
TF: (800) 468 - 6740

Kansas City Southern

** continued from previous page*

Contributions to Candidates: $23,000 (01/05 - 09/05)
Democrats: $1,000; Republicans: $22,000.

Principal Recipients

SENATE DEMOCRATS		HOUSE DEMOCRATS	
		Cleaver, Emanuel (MO)	$1,000
SENATE REPUBLICANS		**HOUSE REPUBLICANS**	
Lott, Trent (MS)	$10,000	Emerson, Jo Ann (MO)	$1,000
Roberts, Pat (KS)	$5,000		
Talent, James (MO)	$5,000		
Allen, George (VA)	$1,000		

Corporate Foundations and Giving Programs

Kansas City Southern Corporate Contributions
Contact: Warren K. Erdman
427 W. 12th St.
Kansas City, MO 64105
Tel: (816) 983 - 1454
Fax: (816) 983 - 1124
TF: (800) 282 - 8700

Annual Grant Total: none reported

Public Affairs and Related Activities Personnel

At Headquarters

BLEVINS, Barbara
Treasurer, Kansas City Southern Employee PAC
Tel: (816) 983 - 1303
Fax: (816) 983 - 1192
TF: (800) 468 - 6740

ERDMAN, Warren K.
V. President, Corporate Affairs
Tel: (816) 983 - 1454
Fax: (816) 983 - 1124
TF: (800) 282 - 8700
Responsibilities include government affairs.

GALLIGAN, William H.
Assistant V. President, Investor Relations
william.h.galligan@kcsr.com
Tel: (816) 983 - 1551
Fax: (816) 983 - 1640
TF: (800) 282 - 8700

KANE, Doniele
Director, Corporate Communications
doniele.c.kane@kcsr.com
Tel: (816) 983 - 1372
Fax: (816) 983 - 1124
TF: (800) 468 - 6740

Kansas City Southern Industries, Inc.

See listing on page 274 under Kansas City Southern.

Kaplan, Inc.

See listing on page 513 under The Washington Post Co.

Kaufman and Broad Home Corp.

See listing on page 275 under KB HOME.

KB HOME

Formerly Kaufman and Broad Home Corp. A homebuilder with communities in the Western United States.

www.kbhome.com

Chairman and Chief Exec. Officer
KARATZ, Bruce
bkaratz@kbhome.com
Tel: (310) 231 - 4000
Fax: (310) 231 - 4222

Main Headquarters
Mailing: 10990 Wilshire Blvd.
Seventh Floor
Los Angeles, CA 90024
Tel: (310) 231 - 4000
Fax: (310) 231 - 4222
TF: (888) 524 - 6637

Public Affairs and Related Activities Personnel

At Headquarters

GOTLIEB, Lawrence B.
V. President, Government and Public Affairs; and Associate Corporate Counsel
lgotlieb@kbhome.com
Tel: (310) 231 - 4000
Fax: (310) 231 - 4222

HALL, Derrick
V. President, Communications
pr@kbhome.com
Tel: (310) 231 - 4000
Fax: (310) 231 - 4222

MASUDA, Kelly
V. President and Investor Relations Contact
kmasuda@kbhome.com
Tel: (310) 231 - 4184
Fax: (310) 388 - 1470

RAY, Gary A.
Senior V. President, Human Resources
gray@kbhome.com
Tel: (310) 231 - 4000
Fax: (310) 231 - 4222

KBR, Inc.

See listing on page 275 under Kellogg Brown and Root.

Keane, Inc.

An information technology consulting company.

www.keane.com
Annual Revenues: $873 million

Chairman of the Board
KEANE, John F.
john_f_keane@keane.com
Tel: (617) 241 - 9200
Fax: (617) 241 - 8027

President and Chief Exec. Officer
KEANE, Brian T.
brian_t_keane@keane.com
Tel: (617) 241 - 9200
Fax: (617) 241 - 8027

Main Headquarters
Mailing: 100 City Square
Boston, MA 02129
Tel: (617) 241 - 9200
Fax: (617) 241 - 8027

Washington Office
Contact: Glenn Giles
Mailing: 1410 Spring Hill Rd., Suite 500
McLean, VA 22102
Tel: (703) 848 - 7200
Fax: (703) 848 - 7600

Political Action Committees

Keane, Inc. PAC
Contact: Robert L. Raasch
100 City Square
Boston, MA 02129
Tel: (617) 241 - 9200
Fax: (617) 241 - 8027

Contributions to Candidates: none reported (01/05 - 09/05)

Public Affairs and Related Activities Personnel

At Headquarters

CAMPANELLO, Russ
Senior V. President, Human Resources
Tel: (617) 241 - 9200
Fax: (617) 241 - 8027

KIDO, Veronica
Director, Marketing Communications
vkido@keane.com
Tel: (617) 241 - 9200
Ext: 1390
Fax: (617) 241 - 8027

RAASCH, Robert L.
Director, Government Affairs
(Keane Federal Systems, Inc.)
robert_l_raasch@keane.com
Tel: (617) 241 - 9200
Fax: (617) 241 - 8027

VALE, Larry M.
V. President, Investor Relations
larry_m_vale@keane.com
Tel: (617) 241 - 9200
Ext: 1290
Fax: (617) 241 - 8027

At Washington Office

GILES, Glenn
V. President
Tel: (703) 848 - 7200
Fax: (703) 848 - 7600

Kellogg Brown and Root

A subsidiary of Halliburton Co. (see separate listing). A technology-based engineering, procurement, construction, and maintenance contractor.

www.kbr.com

Main Headquarters
Mailing: 601 Jefferson St.
Houston, TX 77002
Tel: (713) 753 - 2000
Fax: (713) 753 - 5353

Washington Office
Mailing: 1150 18th St. NW, Suite 200
Washington, DC 20036
Tel: (202) 223 - 0820
Fax: (202) 223 - 2385

Corporate Foundations and Giving Programs

Kellogg Brown and Root Contributions
601 Jefferson St.
Houston, TX 77002
Tel: (713) 753 - 2000
Fax: (713) 753 - 5353

Annual Grant Total: none reported
Geographic Preference: Area in which the company is headquartered
Primary Interests: Arts and Humanities; Medicine and Health Care

Public Affairs and Related Activities Personnel

At Headquarters

LANE, Andrew
Chief Operating Officer
Tel: (713) 759 - 2600
Fax: (713) 753 - 5353

LESAR, David J.
Chairman and Chief Exec. Officer
Tel: (713) 753 - 2000
Fax: (713) 753 - 5353

MIRE, Evelyn M.
V. President, Investor Relations
Tel: (713) 753 - 2633
Fax: (713) 759 - 5353

MIRE, Weldon J.
V. President, Human Resources
Tel: (713) 753 - 2000
Fax: (713) 753 - 5353

At Washington Office

DELINE, Donald A.
V. President, Government Affairs
Tel: (202) 223 - 0820
Fax: (202) 223 - 2385

Kellogg Brown and Root

** continued from previous page*

At Other Offices

SIGALOS, George P.
Director, Government Relations
1550 Wilson Blvd.
Suite 200
Arlington, VA 22209
Tel: (703) 526 - 7500
Fax: (703) 526 - 7585

Kellogg Co.

A major food company. Acquired Keebler Co. in 2001.

www.kelloggs.com

Annual Revenues: $8.853 billion

Main Headquarters

Mailing: P.O. Box 3599
Battle Creek, MI 49016-3599
Tel: (269) 961 - 2000
Fax: (269) 961 - 2871
TF: (800) 962 - 1413

Street: One Kellogg Square
Battle Creek, MI 49016-3599

Washington Office

Mailing: 1725 I St. NW
Suite 300
Washington, DC 20006
Tel: (202) 349 - 3788
Fax: (202) 349 - 3789

Political Action Committees

Kellogg Better Government Committee
Contact: James Sholl
P.O. Box 3599
Battle Creek, MI 49016-3599
Tel: (269) 961 - 2000
Fax: (269) 961 - 2871
TF: (800) 535 - 5644

Contributions to Candidates: $24,500 (01/05 - 09/05)
Democrats: $12,000; Republicans: $12,500.

Principal Recipients

SENATE DEMOCRATS		HOUSE DEMOCRATS	
Ford, Harold E Jr (TN)	$2,000	Meek, Kendrick (FL)	$2,500
Nelson, Bill (FL)	$1,000	Thompson, Bennie (MS)	$1,500
Stabenow, Debbie (MI)	$1,000		
SENATE REPUBLICANS		**HOUSE REPUBLICANS**	
Talent, James (MO)	$1,500	Upton, Fred (MI)	$1,500
Chambliss, Saxby (GA)	$1,000		
Santorum, Richard (PA)	$1,000		

Corporate Foundations and Giving Programs

Kellogg Company Twenty-Five Year Employees Fund, Inc.
Contact: Timothy S. Knowlton
P.O. Box 3599
Battle Creek, MI 49016-3599
Tel: (269) 961 - 2837
Fax: (269) 961 - 6646
TF: (800) 535 - 5644

Assets: $40,000,000 (2001)
Annual Grant Total: $2,000,000 - $5,000,000
The Fund was established to provide assistance to impoverished employees with 25 years of service or more. Assistance to these individuals around the world constitutes the vast majority of expenditures.
Geographic Preference: International
Primary Interests: Human Welfare; Hunger

Kellogg Corporate Citizenship Fund
Contact: Timothy S. Knowlton
P.O. Box 3599
Battle Creek, MI 49016-3599
Tel: (269) 961 - 2837
Fax: (269) 961 - 6646
TF: (800) 535 - 5644

Assets: $14,000,000 (2001)
Annual Grant Total: over $5,000,000
Contributes to non-profit organizations exempt under section 501(c)3. Organizations seeking funding from the Kellogg Company should forward a copy of the organization's 501(c)3 IRS determination letter, state the amount requested, briefly explain the organization's activities and need, and provide a copy of their last two years' financial statements along with an operating budget, major funding sources and a list of current board members. Unsolicited requests are rarely funded.
Geographic Preference: Area(s) in which employees live and work; National
Primary Interests: Education

Public Affairs and Related Activities Personnel

At Headquarters

CERIOLI, Annunciata
V. President, Human Resources
Tel: (269) 961 - 2000
Fax: (269) 961 - 2871
TF: (800) 535 - 5644

CLARK, Dr. Celeste A.
Senior V. President, Corporate Affairs
Tel: (269) 961 - 3799
Fax: (269) 961 - 2871
TF: (800) 535 - 5644

ENOCHSON, Jenny
Public Relations Contact
jenny.enochson@kellogg.com
Tel: (269) 961 - 3799
Fax: (269) 961 - 2871
TF: (800) 535 - 5644

FRANKLIN, George A.
V. President, Worldwide Government Relations
george.franklin@kellogg.com
Tel: (269) 961 - 2820
Fax: (269) 961 - 6646
TF: (800) 535 - 5644

GOODE, Kimberly Crews
V. President, Worldwide Communications
Tel: (269) 961 - 2000
Fax: (269) 961 - 2871
TF: (800) 535 - 5644

JENNESS, James M.
Chairman abd Chief Exec. Officer
Tel: (269) 961 - 2000
Fax: (269) 961 - 2871
TF: (800) 962 - 1413

KNOWLTON, Timothy S.
V. President, Corporate Social Responsibility
Tel: (269) 961 - 2837
Fax: (269) 961 - 6646
TF: (800) 535 - 5644

RENWICK, John P., IV
V. President, Investor Relations and Corporate Planning
john.renwick@kellogg.com
Tel: (269) 961 - 6365
Fax: (269) 961 - 2871
TF: (800) 535 - 5644

SHOLL, James
Treasurer, Kellogg Better Government Committee
Tel: (269) 961 - 2000
Fax: (269) 961 - 2871
TF: (800) 535 - 5644

At Washington Office

MOORE, Tiffany M.
Associate Director, Government Relations
tiffany.moore@kellogg.com
Registered Federal Lobbyist.
Tel: (202) 349 - 3788
Fax: (202) 349 - 3789

Kellogg Co., M. W.

See listing on page 275 under Kellogg Brown and Root.

Kellwood Co.

A marketer of women's, men's and intimate apparel, soft goods and recreational camping products.

www.kellwood.com

Chairman of the Board
UPBIN, Hal J.
hju@kellwood.com
Tel: (314) 576 - 3100
Fax: (314) 576 - 3460

Main Headquarters

Mailing: 600 Kellwood Pkwy.
Chesterfield, MO 63017
Tel: (314) 576 - 3100
Fax: (314) 576 - 3460

Corporate Foundations and Giving Programs

Kellwood Corporate Giving
600 Kellwood Pkwy.
Chesterfield, MO 63017
Tel: (314) 576 - 3100
Fax: (314) 576 - 3460

Annual Grant Total: $200,000 - $300,000
Each division of the company approves and grants contributions in its own community.
Geographic Preference: Area(s) in which the company operates
Primary Interests: Civic and Public Affairs; Education; Health and Human Services
Recent Recipients: Nat'l Jewish & Research Medical Center; United Way

Public Affairs and Related Activities Personnel

At Headquarters

JOSEPH, Roger D.
V. President, Investor Relations and Treasurer
roger_joseph@kellwood.com
Tel: (314) 576 - 3437
Fax: (314) 576 - 3460

SKINNER, Robert, Jr.
President and Chief Exec. Officer
Tel: (314) 576 - 3100
Fax: (314) 576 - 3460

TAYLOR, Corina
Director, Corporate Communications
corina.taylor@kellwood.com
Tel: (314) 576 - 3391
Fax: (314) 576 - 3460

At Other Offices

WEAVER, Donna B.
V. President, Corporate Communications
120 W. 45th St.
Floor 27
New York, NY 10036
donna.weaver@kellwood.com
Tel: (212) 329 - 8072
Fax: (212) 329 - 8073

Kelly Services, Inc.

A member of the Public Affairs Council. A company which provides staffing services and human resources solutions to a broad spectrum of business customers.

www.kellyservices.com

Chairman and Chief Exec. Officer
ADDERLEY, Terence E.
Tel: (248) 362 - 4444
Fax: (248) 244 - 7572

Main Headquarters

Mailing: 999 W. Big Beaver Rd.
Troy, MI 48084-4782
Tel: (248) 362 - 4444
Fax: (248) 244 - 7572

Political Action Committees

Kelly Services Inc. Political Action Committee (KellyPAC)
Contact: James D. McIntire
999 W. Big Beaver Rd.
Troy, MI 48084-4782
Tel: (248) 244 - 5370
Fax: (248) 244 - 5497

Kelly Services, Inc.
** continued from previous page*

Contributions to Candidates: $1,000 (01/05 - 09/05)
Democrats: $1,000.

Principal Recipients

SENATE DEMOCRATS

HOUSE DEMOCRATS
Levin, Sander (MI) $1,000

Corporate Foundations and Giving Programs

Kelly Services Inc. Foundation
Contact: James D. McIntire
999 W. Big Beaver Rd. Tel: (248) 244 - 5370
Troy, MI 48084-4782 Fax: (248) 244 - 5497

Annual Grant Total: none reported

Public Affairs and Related Activities Personnel

At Headquarters

CAMDEN, Carl Tel: (248) 362 - 4444
President and Chief Operating Officer Fax: (248) 244 - 7572

DURIK, Michael Tel: (248) 244 - 4349
Exec. V. President and Chief Administrative Officer Fax: (248) 244 - 7572
michael_durik@kellyservices.com

GERBER, William K. Tel: (248) 362 - 4444
Exec. V. President and Chief Operating Officer Fax: (248) 244 - 7572

HAY, David Tel: (248) 362 - 4522
Senior Director, Government Affairs Fax: (248) 244 - 7572

MCINTIRE, James D. Tel: (248) 244 - 5370
V. President, Public Affairs Fax: (248) 244 - 5497
james_mcintire@kellyservices.com
Responsibilities include political action.

POLEHNA, James Tel: (248) 244 - 4586
Director, Investor Relations Fax: (248) 244 - 5515
james_polehna@kellyservices.com

WALKER, Renee Tel: (248) 362 - 4444
Manager, Public Relations Fax: (248) 244 - 7572
renee_walker@kellyservices.com

Kelly-Springfield Tire Co.
See listing on page 223 under The Goodyear Tire & Rubber Company.

KEMET Corp.
A manufacturer of solid tantalum and multilayer ceramic capacitors used in electronic equipment.
www.kemet.com

President and Chief Exec. Officer Tel: (864) 963 - 6300
LOOF, Per-Olef Fax: (864) 963 - 6322

Main Headquarters
Mailing: P.O. Box 5928 Tel: (864) 963 - 6300
Greenville, SC 29606 Fax: (864) 963 - 6322
Street: 2835 KEMET Way
Simpsonville, SC 29681

Public Affairs and Related Activities Personnel

At Headquarters

BRANDENBURG, Frank G. Tel: (864) 963 - 6300
Chairman of the Board Fax: (864) 963 - 6322

WARNER, John R. Tel: (864) 963 - 6640
V. President, Strategy and Communications Fax: (864) 963 - 6322
investorrelations@kamet.com

Kennametal Inc.
Markets, manufactures and distributes a broad range of tooling, engineered components and advanced materials.
www.kennametal.com
Annual Revenues: $2.5 billion

Chairman, President, and Chief Exec. Officer Tel: (724) 539 - 5000
TAMBAKERAS, Markos I. Fax: (724) 539 - 4710

Main Headquarters
Mailing: P.O. Box 231 Tel: (724) 539 - 5000
Latrobe, PA 15650 Fax: (724) 539 - 7835
Street: 1600 Technology Way
Latrobe, PA 15650

Political Action Committees

Kennametal Employees for Effective Government
Contact: Joy Chandler
P.O. Box 231 Tel: (724) 539 - 5000
Latrobe, PA 15650 Fax: (724) 539 - 4710

Contributions to Candidates: none reported (01/05 - 09/05)

Corporate Foundations and Giving Programs

Kennametal Foundation
P.O. Box 231 Tel: (724) 539 - 5000
Latrobe, PA 15650 Fax: (724) 539 - 7835

Annual Grant Total: none reported
Geographic Preference: National
Primary Interests: Community Affairs; Education

Public Affairs and Related Activities Personnel

At Headquarters

CHANDLER, Joy Tel: (724) 539 - 5000
Director, Corporate Relations Fax: (724) 539 - 4710

WALLING, Kevin R. Tel: (724) 539 - 5000
V. President and Chief Human Resources Officer Fax: (724) 539 - 4710

Kennecott Energy Co.
A subsidiary of Rio Tinto of Australia.
www.kenergy.com

President and Chief Exec. Officer Tel: (307) 687 - 6000
CLAYTON, Bret K. Fax: (307) 687 - 6015

Main Headquarters
Mailing: 505 Gillette Ave. Tel: (307) 687 - 6000
Gillette, WY 82717 Fax: (307) 687 - 6015

Washington Office
Contact: Michael Flannigan
Mailing: Kennecott US Borax Tel: (202) 393 - 0266
1325 Pennsylvania Ave. NW, Seventh Floor Fax: (202) 393 - 0232
Washington, DC 20004

Public Affairs and Related Activities Personnel

At Headquarters

BLAKE, Rick Tel: (307) 687 - 6000
V. President, Human Resources Fax: (307) 687 - 6015

At Washington Office

FLANNIGAN, Michael Tel: (202) 393 - 0266
V. President, Federal Government Affairs Fax: (202) 393 - 0232
Registered Federal Lobbyist.

Kennecott Land
www.kennecottland.com

Main Headquarters
Mailing: 5295 S. 300 West Tel: (801) 743 - 4624
Suite 475 Fax: (801) 743 - 4659
Murray, UT 84107

Washington Office
Contact: Michael Flannigan
Mailing: Kennecott US Borax Tel: (202) 393 - 0266
1325 Pennsylvania Ave. NW, Seventh Floor Fax: (202) 393 - 0232
Washington, DC 20004

Public Affairs and Related Activities Personnel

At Headquarters

UTLEY, Kort Tel: (801) 743 - 4624
Manager, Community Relations Fax: (801) 743 - 4659
kort.utley@kennecott.com

VARELA, Vicki Tel: (801) 743 - 4624
V. President, Public Policy Fax: (801) 743 - 4659
vicki.varela@kennecott.com

At Washington Office

FLANNIGAN, Michael Tel: (202) 393 - 0266
V. President, Federal Government Affairs Fax: (202) 393 - 0232
Registered Federal Lobbyist.

Kennecott US Borax
See listing on page 277 under Kennecott Utah Copper.

Kennecott Utah Copper
www.kennecott.com

President and Chief Exec. Officer Tel: (801) 569 - 6000
CHAMPION, William Fax: (801) 569 - 6045

Main Headquarters
Mailing: 8309 W. 3595 S Tel: (801) 569 - 6000
P.O. Box 6333 Fax: (801) 569 - 6045
Magna, UT 84044-6333
Street: 8362 W. 10200 S.
Bingham Canyon, UT 84006

Washington Office
Contact: Michael Flannigan
Mailing: Kennecott US Borax Tel: (202) 393 - 0266
1325 Pennsylvania Ave. NW, Seventh Floor Fax: (202) 393 - 0232
Washington, DC 20004

Kennecott Utah Copper

** continued from previous page*

Political Action Committees

Kennecott Holdings Corp. PAC
Contact: Tom Myatt
8309 W. 3595 S — Tel: (801) 569 - 6000
P.O. Box 6333 — Fax: (801) 569 - 6045
Magna, UT 84044-6333

Contributions to Candidates: $14,000 (01/05 - 09/05)
Democrats: $2,000; Republicans: $12,000.

Principal Recipients

SENATE DEMOCRATS		HOUSE DEMOCRATS	
Nelson, Benjamin (NE)	$1,000	Berkley, Shelley (NV)	$1,000
SENATE REPUBLICANS		**HOUSE REPUBLICANS**	
Thomas, Craig (WY)	$4,000	Cubin, Barbara L (WY)	$2,000
Burns, Conrad (MT)	$1,000	Pombo, Richard (CA)	$2,000
		Cannon, Christopher (UT)	$1,000
		Flake, Jeff (AZ)	$1,000
		Gibbons, James A (NV)	$1,000

Corporate Foundations and Giving Programs

Kennecott Utah Copper Visitors Center Charitable Foundation (aka Kennecott Charitable Foundation)
Contact: Louis J. Cononelos
8309 W. 3595 S — Tel: (801) 569 - 6000
P.O. Box 6333 — Fax: (801) 569 - 6045
Magna, UT 84044-6333

Annual Grant Total: $400,000 - $500,000
Contributes to charitable and non-profit organizations whose primary concern is providing for the needy.
Geographic Preference: Salt Lake City, UT
Primary Interests: Children; Human Welfare; Senior Citizens

Public Affairs and Related Activities Personnel

At Headquarters

CONONELOS, Louis J. — Tel: (801) 569 - 6000
Director, Government and Public Affairs — Fax: (801) 569 - 6045

MYATT, Tom — Tel: (801) 569 - 6000
Treasurer, Kennecott Holdings Corp. PAC — Fax: (801) 569 - 6045

At Washington Office

FLANNIGAN, Michael — Tel: (202) 393 - 0266
V. President, Federal Government Affairs — Fax: (202) 393 - 0232

Registered Federal Lobbyist.

Kentucky Utilities Company

A subsidiary of LG&E Energy Corp. (see separate listing).
www.lgeenergy.com

Chairman and Chief Exec. Officer — Tel: (859) 255 - 2100
STAFFIERI, Victor A. — Fax: (502) 627 - 3609
TF: (800) 331 - 7370

Main Headquarters
Mailing: One Quality St. — Tel: (859) 255 - 2100
Lexington, KY 40507 — Fax: (502) 627 - 3609
TF: (800) 331 - 7370

Public Affairs and Related Activities Personnel

At Headquarters

FELTHAM, Cliff — Tel: (859) 367 - 1105
Manager, Statewide Media Relations — Fax: (859) 367 - 1185

FREIBERT, David — Tel: (859) 367 - 1271
Director, External Affairs — Fax: (859) 367 - 1197

RHOADS, Jeff — Tel: (859) 367 - 5517
Communications Specialist — Fax: (859) 367 - 1185

Kerr-McGee Corp.

An energy and chemical company engaged in oil and gas exploration and production; and the production and marketing of titanium dioxide pigment. Acquired Oryx Energy Co. in 1999.
www.kerr-mcgee.com
Annual Revenues: $3.638 million

Chairman and Chief Exec. Officer — Tel: (405) 270 - 1313
CORBETT, Luke R. — Fax: (405) 270 - 3029
TF: (800) 786 - 2556

Main Headquarters
Mailing: Kerr-McGee Center, Box 25861 — Tel: (405) 270 - 1313
Oklahoma City, OK 73125 — Fax: (405) 270 - 3029
TF: (800) 786 - 2556

Street: 123 Robert S. Kerr Ave.
Oklahoma City, OK 73102

Washington Office
Contact: Peter M. Frank
Mailing: 1667 K St. NW — Tel: (202) 728 - 9600
Suite 250 — Fax: (202) 728 - 9587
Washington, DC 20006

Political Action Committees

Kerr-McGee Corp. PAC
Contact: Peter M. Frank
1667 K St. NW — Tel: (202) 728 - 9600
Suite 250 — Fax: (202) 728 - 9587
Washington, DC 20006

Contributions to Candidates: $22,500 (01/05 - 09/05)
Democrats: $6,000; Republicans: $16,500.

Principal Recipients

SENATE DEMOCRATS		HOUSE DEMOCRATS	
		Boren, David (OK)	$2,000
SENATE REPUBLICANS		**HOUSE REPUBLICANS**	
Burns, Conrad (MT)	$2,000	Barton, Joe L (TX)	$2,000
Smith, Gordon (OR)	$2,000	Sullivan, John (OK)	$2,000
Ensign, John Eric (NV)	$1,000		
Thomas, Craig (WY)	$1,000		

Corporate Foundations and Giving Programs

Kerr-McGee Corporate Contributions Program
Contact: Jon Trudgeon
Kerr-McGee Center, Box 25861 — Tel: (405) 270 - 1313
Oklahoma City, OK 73125 — Fax: (405) 270 - 3029
TF: (800) 786 - 2556

Annual Grant Total: $1,000,000 - $2,000,000
Geographic Preference: Area(s) in which the company operates; Oklahoma
Primary Interests: Civic and Cultural Activities; Health; Higher Education; Social Services

Public Affairs and Related Activities Personnel

At Headquarters

BUTERBAUGH, Richard — Tel: (405) 270 - 1313
V. President, Investor Relations — Fax: (405) 270 - 3029
TF: (800) 786 - 2556

CHRISTIANSEN, George — Tel: (405) 270 - 1313
V. President, Safety and Environmental Affairs — Fax: (405) 270 - 3029
TF: (800) 786 - 2556

RAGAN, Debbie — Tel: (405) 270 - 1313
Communications Specialist — Fax: (405) 270 - 3029
TF: (800) 786 - 2556

ROWTEN, Michael J. — Tel: (405) 270 - 3199
Director, Community Relations — Fax: (405) 270 - 3029
TF: (800) 786 - 2556

SCHRAMM, Deborah A. — Tel: (405) 270 - 2877
V. President, Corporate Communications — Fax: (405) 270 - 3029
TF: (800) 786 - 2556

TRUDGEON, Jon — Tel: (405) 270 - 1313
Administrator, Corporate Relations and Contributions — Fax: (405) 270 - 3029
TF: (800) 786 - 2556

VANLANDINGHAM, Mark D. — Tel: (405) 270 - 2028
Manager, State Relations — Fax: (405) 270 - 3029
TF: (800) 786 - 2556

At Washington Office

FRANK, Peter M. — Tel: (202) 728 - 9600
V. President, Public Affairs — Fax: (202) 728 - 9587
Registered Federal Lobbyist.

SMITH, Lem — Tel: (202) 728 - 9600
Director, Federal Relations — Fax: (202) 728 - 9587

KeyCorp

A bank holding company.
www.key.com
Annual Revenues: $91 billion

Chairman and Chief Exec. Officer — Tel: (216) 689 - 3000
MEYER, Henry, III — Fax: (216) 689 - 8710

Main Headquarters
Mailing: 127 Public Square — Tel: (216) 689 - 3000
Cleveland, OH 44114

Political Action Committees

KeyCorp Advocates Fund
127 Public Square — Tel: (216) 689 - 3000
Cleveland, OH 44114

Contributions to Candidates: $47,150 (01/05 - 09/05)

KeyCorp

** continued from previous page*

Democrats: $4,500; Republicans: $42,650.

Principal Recipients

SENATE DEMOCRATS		HOUSE DEMOCRATS	
Carper, Thomas R (DE)	$2,500		
SENATE REPUBLICANS		**HOUSE REPUBLICANS**	
Santorum, Richard (PA)	$2,500	Dewine, R. Pat (OH)	$5,000
Voinovich, George (OH)	$2,500	Ney, Robert W (OH)	$5,000
		Pryce, Deborah (OH)	$5,000
		Blasdel, Chuck (OH)	$2,500
		Price, Thomas (GA)	$2,000
		Renzi, Richard (AZ)	$2,000

Corporate Foundations and Giving Programs

KeyCorp Foundation
Contact: Margot James-Copeland
127 Public Square — Tel: (216) 689 - 4724
Cleveland, OH 44114 — Fax: (216) 689 - 3865

Annual Grant Total: none reported
Support is given to a selected group of organizations. Applications for other grants are not accepted.
Geographic Preference: Area(s) in which the company operates
Primary Interests: Economic Development

Public Affairs and Related Activities Personnel

At Headquarters

CADE, Erskine E. — Tel: (216) 689 - 4486
Senior V. President and Director, Government Relations — Fax: (216) 689 - 8710
erskine_cade@keybank.com

FELEPPELLE, Anne — Tel: (216) 689 - 4971
Senior V. President, Issues Manager — Fax: (216) 689 - 8710
Mailstop: OH-01-27-1710

JAMES-COPELAND, Margot — Tel: (216) 689 - 4724
Exec. V. President, Civic Affairs and Corporate Diversity; Chairman, KeyCorp Foundation — Fax: (216) 689 - 3865
margot_copeland@keybank.com

MONROE, Michael J. — Tel: (216) 689 - 3509
Exec. V. President, Public Affairs — Fax: (216) 689 - 0848
michael_monroe@keybank.com

KeySpan Corp.

A member of the Public Affairs Council. Comprised of core regulated natural gas and electric utilities and unregulated subsidiary companies and investments. Distributes natural gas under the KeySpan Energy Delivery name to customers in New York City, on Long Island, and in New England. Formed from the merger of Brooklyn Union and Long Island Lighting Co. in 1998. Acquired Eastern Enterprises and EnergyNorth in 2000. All former Eastern Enterprises and EnergyNorth utilities are now identified as KeySpan Energy Delivery.
www.keyspanenergy.com
Annual Revenues: $6.633 billion

Chairman and Chief Exec. Officer — Tel: (718) 403 - 2000
CATELL, Robert B. — Fax: (718) 488 - 1763

Main Headquarters
Mailing: One MetroTech Center — Tel: (718) 403 - 2000
Brooklyn, NY 11201 — Fax: (718) 488 - 1763

Political Action Committees

KeySpan Energy Political Action Committee (KEYPAC)
Contact: Edward Carr
175 E. Old Country Rd. — Tel: (516) 545 - 4405
Hicksville, NY 11801 — Fax: (516) 545 - 5064

Contributions to Candidates: $11,150 (01/05 - 09/05)
Democrats: $8,650; Republicans: $2,500.

Principal Recipients

SENATE DEMOCRATS		HOUSE DEMOCRATS	
Clinton, Hillary Rodham (NY)	$3,000	Bishop, Timothy (NY)	$1,500
		Capuano, Michael E (MA)	$1,000
		Israel, Steve (NY)	$1,000
		Towns, Edolphus (NY)	$1,000
SENATE REPUBLICANS		**HOUSE REPUBLICANS**	
		Reynolds, Thomas (NY)	$1,000
		Sweeney, John E. (NY)	$1,000

Corporate Foundations and Giving Programs

KeySpan Foundation
Contact: Robert G. Keller
175 E. Old Country Rd. — Tel: (516) 545 - 5147
Hicksville, NY 11801 — Fax: (516) 545 - 8193

Assets: $20,000,000 (1999)
Annual Grant Total: over $5,000,000
Geographic Preference: Area(s) in which the company operates; International
Primary Interests: Education; Environment/Conservation

Public Affairs and Related Activities Personnel

At Headquarters

ADAMO, Pam — Tel: (718) 403 - 2000
V. President, Public Affairs and Community Development — Fax: (718) 488 - 1763

BODANZA, Joseph F. — Tel: (718) 403 - 2000
Senior V. President, Regulatory Affairs and Chief Accounting Officer — Fax: (718) 488 - 1763

CARLSON, Susan E. — Tel: (718) 403 - 2000
Senior Analyst, Corporate Affairs-New England — Fax: (718) 488 - 1763

JANZEN, Margaret — Tel: (718) 403 - 8592
Investor Relations Contact — Fax: (718) 488 - 1763

KESSLER, Ellen — Tel: (718) 403 - 6977
Investor Relations Contact — Fax: (718) 488 - 1763

LASKARIS, George — Tel: (718) 403 - 2526
Director, Investor Relations — Fax: (718) 488 - 1763

MANNING, David J. — Tel: (718) 403 - 2000
Senior V. President, Corporate Affairs — Fax: (718) 488 - 1763
Responsibilities include corporate communications and community and government affairs.

TAUNTON, Michael J. — Tel: (718) 403 - 3265
V. President and Treasurer — Fax: (718) 488 - 1763
Responsibilities include investor relations.

TESORIERO, Jean — Tel: (718) 403 - 2000
Grant Analyst, KeySpan Foundation — Fax: (718) 488 - 1763

WEINSTEIN, Elaine — Tel: (718) 403 - 2000
Senior V. President, Human Resources and Chief Diversity Officer — Fax: (718) 488 - 1763

At Other Offices

CARDILLO, Mary — Tel: (516) 545 - 5507
Director, Public Affairs and Media Services — Fax: (516) 545 - 8193
175 E. Old Country Rd.
Hicksville, NY 11801

CARR, Edward — Tel: (516) 545 - 4405
Senior Analyst, Government Relations; and PAC Treasurer — Fax: (516) 545 - 5064
175 E. Old Country Rd.
Hicksville, NY 11801
ecarr@keyspanenergy.com

DEJESU, Thomas — Tel: (516) 545 - 4449
Director, Government and Regulatory Relations (KeySpan Services, Inc.)
175 E. Old Country Rd.
Hicksville, NY 11801

FISHER, Jody — Tel: (516) 545 - 5052
Manager, Media Relations, Brooklyn/Hicksville — Fax: (516) 545 - 8193
175 E. Old Country Rd.
Hicksville, NY 11801
jfisher@keyspanenergy.com

KELLER, Robert G. — Tel: (516) 545 - 5147
Exec. Director, KeySpan Foundation — Fax: (516) 545 - 8193
175 E. Old Country Rd.
Hicksville, NY 11801

KeySpan Services, Inc.

See listing on page 279 under KeySpan Corp.

KFC

See listing on page 530 under YUM! Brands, Inc.

Peter Kiewit Sons', Inc.

A commercial development and construction company.
www.kiewit.com

Chairman and Chief Exec. Officer — Tel: (402) 342 - 2052
STINSON, Kenneth E. — Fax: (402) 271 - 2939

Main Headquarters
Mailing: 1000 Kiewit Plaza — Tel: (402) 342 - 2052
Omaha, NE 68131 — Fax: (402) 271 - 2939

Corporate Foundations and Giving Programs

The Kiewit Companies Foundation
Contact: Michael L. Faust
1000 Kiewit Plaza — Tel: (402) 342 - 2052
Omaha, NE 68131 — Fax: (402) 271 - 2939

Annual Grant Total: over $5,000,000
Geographic Preference: Area in which the company is headquartered; Nebraska
Primary Interests: Arts and Humanities; Higher Education
Recent Recipients: University of Nebraska

Public Affairs and Related Activities Personnel

At Headquarters

CHAPMAN, J. Brad — Tel: (402) 342 - 2052
V. President, Human Resources — Fax: (402) 271 - 2939

Peter Kiewit Sons', Inc.

** continued from previous page*

FAUST, Michael L.
Assistant to the Chairman
Tel: (402) 342 - 2052
Fax: (402) 271 - 2939
Responsibilities include corporate philanthropy.

PFEFFER, Gerald S.
V. President, Marketing
Tel: (402) 342 - 2052
Fax: (402) 271 - 2939
Responsibilities include corporate communications.

Kimball International, Inc.

Manufacturer of office, lodging and home furniture, and a contract manufacturer of electronic assemblies and components.

www.kimball.com

Chairman of the Board
HABIG, Douglas
Tel: (812) 482 - 1600
Fax: (812) 482 - 8300
TF: (800) 482 - 1616

Chief Exec. Officer
THYEN, James C.
Tel: (812) 482 - 1600
Fax: (812) 482 - 8300
TF: (800) 482 - 1616

Main Headquarters
Mailing: 1600 Royal St.
Jasper, IN 47549-1001
Tel: (812) 482 - 1600
Fax: (812) 482 - 8300
TF: (800) 482 - 1616

Corporate Foundations and Giving Programs

The Kimball International-Habig Foundation, Inc.
Contact: Douglas Habig
1600 Royal St.
Jasper, IN 47549-1001
Tel: (812) 482 - 1600
Fax: (812) 482 - 8300
TF: (800) 482 - 1616

Annual Grant Total: $400,000 - $500,000
Geographic Preference: Area in which the company is headquartered; Area(s) in which the company operates
Primary Interests: Civic and Public Affairs; Community Development; Education; Health and Human Services

Public Affairs and Related Activities Personnel

At Headquarters

CATT, Randall L.
Exec. V. President, Human Resources
Tel: (812) 482 - 1600
Fax: (812) 482 - 8300
TF: (800) 482 - 1616

ECKERLE, Greg J.
Employee Communications Director
Tel: (812) 482 - 8474
Fax: (812) 482 - 8300
TF: (800) 482 - 1616

SERMERSHEIM, Ronald J.
V. President, Environmental Health and Safety
Tel: (812) 482 - 1600
Fax: (812) 482 - 8300
TF: (800) 482 - 1616

VAUGHT, Martin W.
Director, Public Relations
Tel: (812) 482 - 8255
Fax: (812) 482 - 8300
TF: (800) 482 - 1616

At Other Offices

MASTERSON, Keith
Environmental Manager
1600 Royal St.
Jasper, IN 47549
Tel: (812) 634 - 3234
Fax: (812) 634 - 3060

Kimberly-Clark Corp.

A diversified manufacturer of fiber-based products for personal care, health care and other diverse markets.

www.kimberly-clark.com

Annual Revenues: $14.524 billion

Chairman and Chief Exec. Officer
FALK, Thomas J.
Tel: (972) 281 - 1200
Fax: (972) 281 - 1490
TF: (800) 639 - 1352

Main Headquarters
Mailing: DWF Airport Station, P.O. Box 619100
Dallas, TX 75261-9100
Tel: (972) 281 - 1200
Fax: (972) 281 - 1490
TF: (800) 639 - 1352

Street: 351 Phelphs Dr.
Irving, TX 75038

Corporate Foundations and Giving Programs

Kimberly-Clark Foundation
Contact: Carolyn Mentesana
DWF Airport Station, P.O. Box 619100
Dallas, TX 75261-9100
Tel: (972) 281 - 1485
Fax: (972) 281 - 1490
TF: (800) 639 - 1352

Annual Grant Total: over $5,000,000
Geographic Preference: Area(s) in which the company operates
Primary Interests: Child Welfare; Education; Families
Recent Recipients: Boys and Girls Club; Partnership for a Drug-Free America; Ronald McDonald House

Public Affairs and Related Activities Personnel

At Headquarters

ALEXANDER, Paul J.
Manager, Investor Relations
palexand@kcc.com
Tel: (972) 281 - 1440
Fax: (972) 281 - 1490
TF: (800) 639 - 1352

BARRY, Tina S.
Senior V. President, Corporate Communications
tbarry@kcc.com
Tel: (972) 281 - 1484
Fax: (972) 281 - 1490
TF: (800) 639 - 1352

DICKSON, Dave
Corporate Communications Contact
ddickson@kcc.com
Tel: (972) 281 - 1481
Fax: (972) 281 - 1490
TF: (800) 639 - 1352

GOTTUNG, lizanne C.
Senior V. President, Human Resources
Tel: (972) 281 - 1200
Fax: (972) 281 - 1490
TF: (800) 639 - 1352

MASSETH, Michael D.
V. President, Investor Relations
mmasseth@kcc.com
Tel: (972) 281 - 1478
Fax: (972) 281 - 1490
TF: (800) 639 - 1352

MCCRAY, Ronald D.
Senior V. President, Law and Government Affairs
Tel: (972) 281 - 1215
Fax: (972) 281 - 1492
TF: (800) 639 - 1352

MENTESANA, Carolyn
V. President, Kimberly-Clark Foundation
Tel: (972) 281 - 1485
Fax: (972) 281 - 1490
TF: (800) 639 - 1352

SAYE-ARMIJO, Stephanie
Corporate Communications Contact
sarmijo@kcc.com
Tel: (972) 281 - 1443
Fax: (972) 281 - 1490
TF: (800) 639 - 1352

At Other Offices

HILL, B. Eugene, Jr.
Senior Director, Government Relations
1400 Holcomb Bridge Rd.
Roswell, GA 30076
Tel: (770) 587 - 8636
Fax: (770) 587 - 7199

SHAFFER, Fred
Senior Director, Government Relations
351 Phelps Dr.
Irving, TX 75038
fshaffer@kcc.com
Tel: (920) 721 - 3117

Kinder Morgan, Inc.

An energy company.

www.kindermorgan.com

Chairman, President and Chief Exec. Officer
KINDER, Richard D.
Tel: (713) 369 - 9000
Fax: (713) 369 - 9100
TF: (800) 324 - 2900

Main Headquarters
Mailing: 500 Dallas St., Suite 1000
Houston, TX 77002
Tel: (713) 369 - 9000
Fax: (713) 369 - 9100
TF: (800) 324 - 2900

Public Affairs and Related Activities Personnel

At Headquarters

ALLEN, Kimberly J.
V. President, Investor Relations and Treasurer
Tel: (713) 369 - 9000
Fax: (713) 369 - 9100
TF: (800) 324 - 2900

PIERCE, Larry
Director, Corporate Communications
Tel: (713) 369 - 9000
Fax: (713) 369 - 9100
TF: (800) 324 - 2900

STREET, James E.
V. President, Human Resources
Tel: (713) 369 - 9000
Fax: (713) 369 - 9100
TF: (800) 324 - 2900

At Other Offices

BULKLEY, Maureen
Coordinator, Community Relations
370 Van Gordon St.
Lakewood, CO 80228
Tel: (303) 763 - 3471
Responsibilities include corporate philanthropy.

KinderCare Learning Centers, Inc.

Provides early childhood education.

www.kindercare.com

KinderCare Learning Centers, Inc.

• continued from previous page

Chairman and Chief Exec. Officer
JOHNSON, David J. — Tel: (503) 872 - 1300 Fax: (503) 872 - 1349 TF: (800) 633 - 1488

Main Headquarters
Mailing: 650 N.E. Holladay, Suite 1400
Portland, OR 97232 — Tel: (503) 872 - 1300 Fax: (503) 872 - 1349 TF: (800) 633 - 1488

Public Affairs and Related Activities Personnel

At Headquarters

EILAND, Jill
Senior Director, Government Affairs and Public Relations — Tel: (503) 872 - 1519 Fax: (503) 872 - 1349 TF: (800) 633 - 1488

JACKSON, Dan
Exec. V. President and Chief Financial Officer — Tel: (503) 872 - 1300 Fax: (503) 872 - 1349 TF: (800) 633 - 1488
Responsibilities include investor relations.

Kindred Healthcare, Inc.

A long-term, acute health care provider.
www.kindredhealthcare.com

Chairman of the Board
KUNTZ, Edward L. — Tel: (502) 596 - 7300 Fax: (502) 596 - 4099

President and Chief Exec. Officer
DIAZ, Paul J. — Tel: (502) 596 - 7300 Fax: (502) 596 - 4099

Main Headquarters
Mailing: 680 S. Fourth Ave.
Louisville, KY 40202-2412 — Tel: (502) 596 - 7300 Fax: (502) 596 - 4170

Political Action Committees

Kindred Healthcare, Inc. PAC
Contact: Hank Robinson
680 S. Fourth Ave.
Louisville, KY 40202-2412 — Tel: (502) 596 - 7300 Fax: (502) 596 - 4099

Contributions to Candidates: $81,250 (01/05 - 09/05)
Democrats: $11,250; Republicans: $70,000.

Principal Recipients

SENATE REPUBLICANS		HOUSE REPUBLICANS	
McConnell, Mitch (KY)	$10,000	Thomas, William M (CA)	$6,000
Hatch, Orrin (UT)	$7,500	Hastert, Dennis J. (IL)	$5,000
Santorum, Richard (PA)	$6,500	Northup, Anne M. (KY)	$5,000
		Pryce, Deborah (OH)	$5,000

Corporate Foundations and Giving Programs

Kindred Foundation Inc.
Contact: Susan E. Moss
680 S. Fourth Ave.
Louisville, KY 40202-2412 — Tel: (502) 596 - 7296 Fax: (502) 596 - 4099

Assets: $383,682 (2002)
Annual Grant Total: under $100,000

Public Affairs and Related Activities Personnel

At Headquarters

ALTMAN, Bill M.
Senior V. President, Compliance and Government Programs — Tel: (502) 596 - 7161 Fax: (502) 596 - 4099

LECHLEITER, Richard A.
Senior V. President and Chief Financial Officer — Tel: (502) 596 - 7734 Fax: (502) 596 - 4063
rich_lechleiter@kindredhealthcare.com
Responsibilities include investor relations.

MOSS, Susan E.
V. President, Corporate Communications — Tel: (502) 596 - 7296 Fax: (502) 596 - 4099

ROBINSON, Hank
Treasurer, Kindred Healthcare, Inc. PAC — Tel: (502) 596 - 7300 Fax: (502) 596 - 4099

King Kullen Grocery Co.

A food store chain.
www.kingkullen.com

Chairman and Chief Exec. Officer
KENNEDY, Bernard — Tel: (516) 733 - 7100 Fax: (516) 827 - 6262
bkennedy@kingkullen.com

Main Headquarters
Mailing: 185 Central Ave.
Bethpage, NY 11714 — Tel: (516) 733 - 7100 Fax: (516) 827 - 6263

Corporate Foundations and Giving Programs

King Kullen Grocery Co., Inc. Corporate Giving Program
Contact: Thomas K. Cullen
185 Central Ave.
Bethpage, NY 11714 — Tel: (516) 733 - 7114 Fax: (516) 827 - 6263

Annual Grant Total: none reported

Public Affairs and Related Activities Personnel

At Headquarters

CULLEN, Thomas K.
V. President, Government, Industry and Public Relations — Tel: (516) 733 - 7114 Fax: (516) 827 - 6263
tcullen@kingkullen.com

King Pharmaceuticals, Inc.

Markets, develops, and distributes pharmaceutical products.
www.kingpharm.com

President and Chief Exec. Officer
MARKISON, Brian A. — Tel: (423) 989 - 8000 Fax: (423) 274 - 8677

Main Headquarters
Mailing: 501 Fifth St.
Bristol, TN 37620 — Tel: (423) 989 - 8000 Fax: (423) 274 - 8677

Corporate Foundations and Giving Programs

King Pharmaceuticals, Inc. Corporate Giving
Contact: Terry Eckley
501 Fifth St.
Bristol, TN 37620 — Tel: (423) 989 - 8000 Fax: (423) 274 - 8677

Annual Grant Total: none reported
Primary Interests: Arts and Culture; Community Development; Education; Health; Religion; Youth Services

Public Affairs and Related Activities Personnel

At Headquarters

ECKLEY, Terry
Senior Director, Public Relations — Tel: (423) 989 - 8000 Fax: (423) 274 - 8677

GREEN, James E.
Exec. V. President, Corporate Affairs — Tel: (423) 989 - 8125 Fax: (423) 274 - 8677

Kinko's, Inc.

See listing on page 193 under FedEx Kinko's Office and Print Services.

KLA-Tencor

Manufactures test equipment for computer chips.
www.kla-tencor.com
Annual Revenues: $1.6 billion

Chairman of the Board
LEVY, Kenneth — Tel: (408) 875 - 3000 Fax: (408) 875 - 4266

Chief Exec. Officer
SCHROEDER, Kenneth L. — Tel: (408) 875 - 3000 Fax: (408) 875 - 4266

Main Headquarters
Mailing: 160 Rio Robles
San Jose, CA 95134 — Tel: (408) 875 - 3000 Fax: (408) 875 - 4144

Public Affairs and Related Activities Personnel

At Headquarters

BEARE, Kern
V. President, Corporate Communications — Tel: (408) 875 - 7039 Fax: (408) 875 - 4144
kern.beare@kla-tencor.com

HUANG, Albert
Manager, Investor Relations — Tel: (408) 875 - 3000 Fax: (408) 875 - 4144
albert.huang@kla-tencor.com

SUBRAMANIAM, Uma
Senior MarCom Manager — Tel: (408) 875 - 5473 Fax: (408) 875 - 4144
uma.subramaniam@kla-tencor.com

KLT Inc.

See listing on page 226 under Great Plains Energy, Inc.

Kmart Holding Corp.

See listing on page 431 under Sears Holding Corp.

Knight Ridder

A publisher of a nationwide group of newspapers.
www.kri.com
Annual Revenues: $2.8 billion

Chairman and Chief Exec. Officer
RIDDER, P. Anthony — Tel: (408) 938 - 7700 Fax: (408) 938 - 7766

Main Headquarters
Mailing: 50 W. San Fernando St.
15th Floor
San Jose, CA 95113 — Tel: (408) 938 - 7700 Fax: (408) 938 - 7766

Corporate Foundations and Giving Programs

Knight-Ridder, Inc. Fund
Contact: Polk Laffoon, IV

Knight Ridder

* continued from previous page

50 W. San Fernando St. | Tel: (408) 938 - 7838
15th Floor | Fax: (408) 938 - 7766
San Jose, CA 95113

Annual Grant Total: $1,000,000 - $2,000,000
The fund does not accept unsolicited applications for grants.
Geographic Preference: San Jose, CA
Primary Interests: Journalism

Public Affairs and Related Activities Personnel

At Headquarters

LAFFOON, Polk, IV | Tel: (408) 938 - 7838
V. President, Corporate Relations | Fax: (408) 938 - 7766
Responsibilities include corporate contributions.

Koch Industries, Inc.

A member of the Public Affairs Council. Based in Wichita, Kansas, owns a diverse group of companies engaged in trading, investment and operations worldwide.
www.kochind.com

Chairman and Chief Exec. Officer
KOCH, Charles G. | Tel: (316) 828 - 5500 | Fax: (316) 828 - 5739

Main Headquarters
Mailing: 4111 E. 37th St., North, Wichita, KS 67220 | Tel: (316) 828 - 5500 | Fax: (316) 828 - 5739

Washington Office
Contact: Matt Schlapp
Mailing: 655 15th St. NW, Suite 445, Washington, DC 20005 | Tel: (202) 737 - 1977 | Fax: (202) 737 - 8111

Political Action Committees

Koch Industries Inc. PAC (KochPAC)
Contact: Lacye E. Tennille
655 15th St. NW | Tel: (202) 737 - 1977
Suite 445 | Fax: (202) 737 - 8111
Washington, DC 20005

Contributions to Candidates: $129,500 (01/05 - 09/05)
Democrats: $13,500; Republicans: $116,000.

Principal Recipients

SENATE REPUBLICANS		HOUSE REPUBLICANS	
Santorum, Richard (PA)	$7,000	Dreier, David (CA)	$10,000
Allen, George (VA)	$5,000	DeLay, Tom (TX)	$7,500
Talent, James (MO)	$5,000	Tiahrt, Todd W. (KS)	$5,500
Vitter, David (LA)	$5,000	Pearce, Steve (NM)	$5,000

Corporate Foundations and Giving Programs

Koch Industries Contributions Program
Contact: Susan Addington
4111 E. 37th St., North | Tel: (316) 828 - 5500
Wichita, KS 67220 | Fax: (316) 828 - 5739

Annual Grant Total: none reported
Primary Interests: Education; Youth Services
Recent Recipients: Big Brothers/Big Sisters; Boys and Girls Club; Junior Achievement; Salvation Army

Public Affairs and Related Activities Personnel

At Headquarters

ADDINGTON, Susan | Tel: (316) 828 - 5500
Contact, Koch Industries Contributions Program | Fax: (316) 828 - 5739
philanthropy@kochind.com

ALTIMARI, Kristin | Tel: (316) 828 - 1000
Director, Communication | Fax: (316) 828 - 1121
(INVISTA)

GIBBENS, Dale | Tel: (316) 828 - 5606
V. President, Human Resources | Fax: (316) 828 - 5739

HARWELL, Tom | Tel: (316) 828 - 7082
Director, Community Outreach | Fax: (316) 828 - 5739

JARVIS, Mary Beth | Tel: (316) 828 - 3756
Director, Communication | Fax: (316) 828 - 6997
jarvism@kochind.com

MORGAN, Michael K. | Tel: (316) 828 - 5274
Director, Government and Public Affairs | Fax: (316) 828 - 5739

PALAZZO, Marc | Tel: (316) 828 - 5500
Director, Public Affairs | Fax: (316) 828 - 5739

RAMSEYER, Roger | Tel: (316) 828 - 1525
Director, Public Affairs | Fax: (316) 828 - 1121
(INVISTA)

SEBITS, Trent | Tel: (316) 828 - 8896
Manager, Government and Public Affairs | Fax: (316) 828 - 5739

STAVINOHA, Katie | Tel: (316) 828 - 3621
Manager, Communication | Fax: (316) 828 - 5739

WRIGHT, Allen | Tel: (316) 828 - 8721
V. President, Public Affairs | Fax: (316) 828 - 4228
(Flint Hills Resources, LP)
allen.wright@fhr.com

At Washington Office

CLAY, Don R. | Tel: (202) 737 - 1977
Managing Director, Environmental and Regulatory Affairs | Fax: (202) 737 - 8111

FINK, Richard H. | Tel: (202) 737 - 1977
Exec. V. President, Government and Public Affairs | Fax: (202) 737 - 8111

HALL, Robert P., III | Tel: (202) 879 - 8515
Director, Government Affairs | Fax: (202) 737 - 8111
(INVISTA)
Registered Federal Lobbyist.

PYLE, Tom | Tel: (202) 737 - 1977
Director, Government Affairs | Fax: (202) 737 - 8111
Registered Federal Lobbyist.

SCHLAPP, Matt | Tel: (202) 737 - 1977
Exec. Director, Federal Affairs | Fax: (202) 737 - 8111

TENNILLE, Lacye E. | Tel: (202) 737 - 1977
Pac Treasurer | Fax: (202) 737 - 8111

At Other Offices

BROWN, Craig | Tel: (512) 476 - 4795
Director, Public Affairs-Southern Tier | Fax: (512) 477 - 3586
701 Brazos St., Suite 495
Austin, TX 78701

ELLENDER, Philip | Tel: (225) 767 - 4114
V. President, Public Affairs | Fax: (225) 767 - 4177
(INVISTA)
4332 Emory Ave.
Baton Rouge, LA 70808

OSWALD, J. William "Bill" | Tel: (512) 476 - 4795
Director, Government Affairs | Ext: 6722
701 Brazos St., Suite 495 | Fax: (512) 477 - 3586
Austin, TX 78701

Kohl's Corp.

A general merchandise retailer.
www.kohls.com

Chairman and Chief Exec. Officer
MONTGOMERY, Larry | Tel: (262) 703 - 7000 | Fax: (262) 703 - 6143

Main Headquarters
Mailing: N56 W17000 Ridgewood Dr., Menomonee Falls, WI 53051 | Tel: (262) 703 - 7000 | Fax: (262) 703 - 6143

Corporate Foundations and Giving Programs

Kohl's Cares for Kids
N56 W17000 Ridgewood Dr. | Tel: (262) 703 - 7000
Menomonee Falls, WI 53051 | Fax: (262) 703 - 6143

Annual Grant Total: none reported
Geographic Preference: Area(s) in which the company operates
Primary Interests: Children's Health; Education

Public Affairs and Related Activities Personnel

At Headquarters

MANN, Steve | Tel: (262) 703 - 6397
Coordinator, Public Relations | Fax: (262) 703 - 6143

MANSELL, Kevin B. | Tel: (262) 703 - 7000
President | Fax: (262) 703 - 6143

SANSOUCIE, Lori | Tel: (262) 703 - 6572
Manager, Public Relations | Fax: (262) 703 - 6501

SHAMION, Vicki | Tel: (262) 703 - 1464
Director, Public Relations | Fax: (262) 703 - 7115

Kohler Co.

A manufacturer of plumbing fixtures and other products for the home and consumer markets.
www.kohler.com

Chairman, President and Chief Exec. Officer
KOHLER, Herbert V., Jr. | Tel: (920) 457 - 4441
herbert.kohler@kohler.com | Fax: (920) 457 - 1271

Main Headquarters
Mailing: 444 Highland Dr., Kohler, WI 53044 | Tel: (920) 457 - 4441 | Fax: (920) 457 - 9064

Corporate Foundations and Giving Programs

Kohler Co. Corporate Giving Program
Contact: Lynn Kulow

Kohler Co.

* continued from previous page

444 Highland Dr. Tel: (920) 457 - 4441
Kohler, WI 53044 Fax: (920) 457 - 9064

Annual Grant Total: none reported
Geographic Preference: Wisconsin
Primary Interests: Arts and Humanities; Education; Health; Human Welfare

Public Affairs and Related Activities Personnel

At Headquarters

KOHLER, Laura — Tel: (920) 457 - 4441 Ext: 72607
Senior V. President, Human Resources
laura.kohler@kohler.com — Fax: (920) 459 - 1839

KULOW, Lynn — Tel: (920) 457 - 4441
Senior Communications Specialist - Corporate Giving and Civic Services — Fax: (920) 457 - 9064

STALL, Nancy — Tel: (920) 457 - 4441
Manager, Public Affairs — Fax: (920) 459 - 1623

WESTPHAL, Steven — Tel: (920) 457 - 4441 Ext: 74740
Attorney
steven.westphal@kohler.com — Fax: (920) 459 - 1583
Responsibilities include government affairs.

KPMG LLP

A member of the Public Affairs Council. An international accounting, tax and management consulting firm.
www.us.kpmg.com
Annual Revenues: $12.16 billion

Chairman and Chief Exec. Officer — Tel: (212) 872 - 7925
FLYNN, Timothy P. — Fax: (212) 758 - 9819

Main Headquarters
Mailing: Three Chestnut Ridge Rd. — Tel: (201) 307 - 7000
Montvale, NJ 07645-0435 — Fax: (201) 930 - 8617

Washington Office
Contact: Stephen E. Allis
Mailing: 2001 M St. NW — Tel: (202) 533 - 3000
Washington, DC 20036-3310 — Fax: (202) 533 - 8500

Political Action Committees

KPMG Partnerships/Principals and Employees PAC
Contact: Stephen E. Allis
2001 M St. NW — Tel: (202) 533 - 3126
Washington, DC 20036-3310 — Fax: (202) 533 - 8516

Contributions to Candidates: $172,694 (01/05 - 09/05)
Democrats: $41,500; Republicans: $131,194.

Principal Recipients

SENATE REPUBLICANS		HOUSE REPUBLICANS	
Bennett, Robert F (UT)	$5,000	Hensarling, Jeb (TX)	$10,000
Santorum, Richard (PA)	$4,000	Cantor, Eric (VA)	$6,000
Smith, Gordon (OR)	$3,500	Ney, Robert W (OH)	$5,000
		Fossella, Vito (NY)	$4,000
		Gerlach, Jim (PA)	$4,000
		McHenry, Patrick (NC)	$4,000
		Price, Thomas (GA)	$4,000
		Brown-Waite, Virginia (FL)	$3,500
		Dreier, David (CA)	$3,500

Corporate Foundations and Giving Programs

KPMG Foundation
Contact: Bernard J. Milano
Three Chestnut Ridge Rd. — Tel: (201) 505 - 3400
Montvale, NJ 07645-0435 — Fax: (201) 505 - 3404

Annual Grant Total: over $5,000,000
Guidelines are available.
Geographic Preference: No geographical restrictions
Primary Interests: Higher Education; Minority Opportunities
Recent Recipients: University of Texas; William and Mary

Public Affairs and Related Activities Personnel

At Headquarters

HAYAT, Suzanne — Tel: (212) 909 - 5000
Director, International Public Relations — Fax: (212) 909 - 5299

MILANO, Bernard J. — Tel: (201) 505 - 3400
President — Fax: (201) 505 - 3404
Responsibilities include corporate philanthropy.

At Washington Office

ALLIS, Stephen E. — Tel: (202) 533 - 3126
Partner-in-Charge of Government Affairs — Fax: (202) 533 - 8516
Registered Federal Lobbyist.

KANOY, Erin J. — Tel: (202) 533 - 5256
Senior Legislative Analyst, Government Affairs — Fax: (202) 533 - 8500
Registered Federal Lobbyist.

MCLUCAS, Scott — Tel: (202) 533 - 3000
Manager, Government Affairs — Fax: (202) 533 - 8500

Kraft Foods, Inc.

A subsidiary of Altria Group, Inc. (see separate listing). Acquired Nabisco in 2001.
www.kraft.com
Annual Revenues: $29.7 billion

Chairman of the Board — Tel: (847) 646 - 2000
CAMILLERI, Louis C. — Fax: (847) 646 - 6005

Chief Exec. Officer — Tel: (847) 646 - 2000
DEROMEDI, Roger K. — Fax: (847) 646 - 6005

Main Headquarters
Mailing: Three Lakes Dr. — Tel: (847) 646 - 2000
Northfield, IL 60093-2753 — Fax: (847) 646 - 6005

Washington Office
Mailing: 101 Constitution Ave. NW, Suite 400W — Tel: (202) 354 - 1500
Washington, DC 20001 — Fax: (202) 354 - 1505

Political Action Committees

Kraft Foods Global Inc. Political Action Committee (KF PAC)
Contact: Shaunise Washington
101 Constitution Ave. NW, Suite 400W — Tel: (202) 354 - 1500
Washington, DC 20001 — Fax: (202) 354 - 1505

Contributions to Candidates: none reported (01/05 - 09/05)

Corporate Foundations and Giving Programs

Kraft Foods Contributions
Contact: Amina Dickerson
Three Lakes Dr. — Tel: (847) 646 - 3332
Northfield, IL 60093-2753 — Fax: (847) 646 - 6005

Annual Grant Total: over $5,000,000
Formed in early 1990 by the merger of the Kraft Foundation and the General Foods Fund. Total annual giving is about $13 million.
Geographic Preference: Area(s) in which the company operates
Primary Interests: Arts and Culture; Domestic Violence; Hunger
Recent Recipients: America's Second Harvest; Art Institute of Chicago

Public Affairs and Related Activities Personnel

At Headquarters

CHARLES, Kris — Tel: (847) 646 - 6251
Director, Public Affairs — Fax: (847) 646 - 6005

DAIGLER, Nancy — Tel: (847) 646 - 4106
V. President, Corporate Affairs — Fax: (847) 646 - 6005

DICKERSON, Amina — Tel: (847) 646 - 3332
Director, Corporate Contributions — Fax: (847) 646 - 6005
adickerson@kraft.com

FAULK, Terry M. — Tel: (847) 646 - 2000
Exec. V. President, Human Resources — Fax: (847) 646 - 6005

GARZA, Patricia — Tel: (847) 646 - 3082
Manager, Corporate Contributions — Fax: (847) 646 - 6005
pgarza@kraft.com

HODEL, Joyce — Tel: (847) 646 - 6938
Senior Manager, Internal Communications — Fax: (847) 646 - 6005
jhodel@kraft.com

KNUTH, Kathy S. — Tel: (847) 646 - 2666
Senior Director, Corporate Affairs, North America Commercial — Fax: (847) 646 - 6005
kknuth@kraft.com

MAHERAS, John — Tel: (847) 646 - 2472
Government Affairs Liaison — Fax: (847) 646 - 6005

MUDD, Michael — Tel: (847) 646 - 2868
Exec. V. President, Global Corporate Affairs — Fax: (847) 646 - 6005

PERNU, Cathy — Tel: (847) 646 - 3946
Senior Manager, Corporate Communications — Fax: (847) 646 - 6005

SALETTA, Jill — Tel: (847) 646 - 5808
Senior Manager, Corporate Affairs — Fax: (847) 646 - 6005

SITKIEWICZ, Donna M. — Tel: (847) 646 - 5770
Director, Corporate Affairs — Fax: (847) 646 - 6005

At Washington Office

FOLKERTS, Brian — Tel: (202) 354 - 1598
Director, Federal Government Affairs — Fax: (202) 354 - 1506
Registered Federal Lobbyist.

NORRIS, Frances — Tel: (202) 354 - 1554
V. President, Federal Government Affairs - Food — Fax: (202) 354 - 1505
Registered Federal Lobbyist.

WASHINGTON, Shaunise — Tel: (202) 354 - 1500
Treasurer, Kraft Foods Global Inc. PAC — Fax: (202) 354 - 1505
shaunise.washington@altria.com

Kraft Foods, Inc.

** continued from previous page*

WESTFALL, Linda "Tuckie" — Tel: (202) 354 - 1500
Director, Federal Government Affairs — Fax: (202) 354 - 1505
Registered Federal Lobbyist.

Kraus-Anderson Communications Group

See listing on page 284 under Kraus-Anderson Cos Inc.

Kraus-Anderson Cos. Inc.

General contractor, construction management, real estate investment, management and related services, insurance agency, capital leasing and financing, and advertisement/communications services.

www.krausanderson.com

Chairman and Chief Exec. Officer
ENGELSMA, Bruce W. — Tel: (612) 332 - 7281; Fax: (612) 332 - 0217

Main Headquarters
Mailing: 525 S. Eighth St.
Minneapolis, MN 55404
Tel: (612) 332 - 7281; Fax: (612) 332 - 0217

Public Affairs and Related Activities Personnel

At Headquarters

LONDON, MaryAnne — Tel: (612) 332 - 7281; Fax: (612) 332 - 0217
Senior V. President, Public Relations
(Kraus-Anderson Communications Group)

The Kroger Co.

A supermarket chain and convenience store operator.

www.kroger.com
Annual Revenues: $51.8 billion

Chairman and Chief Exec. Officer
DILLON, David B. — Tel: (513) 762 - 4000; Fax: (513) 762 - 1295

Main Headquarters
Mailing: 1014 Vine St.
Cincinnati, OH 45202-1100
Tel: (513) 762 - 4000; Fax: (513) 762 - 1295

Political Action Committees

Kroger Political Action Committee (KroPAC)
Contact: Janet Ausdenmoore
1014 Vine St.
Cincinnati, OH 45202-1100
Tel: (513) 762 - 4939; Fax: (513) 762 - 1295

Contributions to Candidates: $9,000 (01/05 - 09/05)
Republicans: $9,000.

Principal Recipients

SENATE REPUBLICANS		HOUSE REPUBLICANS	
Dewine, Richard (OH)	$1,000	Thomas, William M (CA)	$5,000
		Boehner, John (OH)	$2,000
		Dewine, R. Pat (OH)	$1,000

Corporate Foundations and Giving Programs

Kroger Co. Foundation
Contact: Janet Ausdenmoore
1014 Vine St.
Cincinnati, OH 45202-1100
Tel: (513) 762 - 4939; Fax: (513) 762 - 1295

Annual Grant Total: $2,000,000 - $5,000,000
Provides grants to 501(c) (3) organizations.
Geographic Preference: Area(s) in which the company operates

Ralph's/Food for Less Foundation
Contact: Janet Ausdenmoore
1014 Vine St.
Cincinnati, OH 45202-1100
Tel: (513) 762 - 4939; Fax: (513) 762 - 1295

Annual Grant Total: none reported

Public Affairs and Related Activities Personnel

At Headquarters

AUSDENMOORE, Janet — Tel: (513) 762 - 4939; Fax: (513) 762 - 1295
Foundation Administrator
Ms. Ausdenmoore is also the Administrator of KroPAC.

AVERY, David — Tel: (513) 762 - 4270; Fax: (513) 762 - 4197
V. President, Human Resources

CALDWELL, Brian — Tel: (513) 762 - 4765; Fax: (513) 762 - 4818
Manager, Consumer Affairs

FIKE, Carin — Tel: (513) 762 - 4000; Fax: (513) 762 - 1295
Director, Investor Relations

MARMER, Ms. Lynn — Tel: (513) 762 - 4441; Fax: (513) 762 - 1295
Group V. President, Corporate Affairs

RHODES, Gary — Tel: (513) 762 - 1304; Fax: (513) 762 - 1295
Director, Corporate Communications

L-3 Communications Corp.

A merchant supplier to aerospace, military and commercial primes.

www.l-3com.com
Annual Revenues: $over 5 billion

Chairman and Chief Exec. Officer
LANZA, Frank C. — Tel: (212) 697 - 1111; Fax: (212) 867 - 5249; TF: (866) 463 - 6555

Main Headquarters
Mailing: 600 Third Ave
New York, NY 10016
Tel: (212) 697 - 1111; Fax: (212) 867 - 5249; TF: (866) 463 - 6555

Washington Office
Contact: Robert W. Riscassi
Mailing: 1215 S. Clark St.
Suite1205
Arlington, VA 22202
Tel: (703) 412 - 7190

Political Action Committees

L-3 Communications Corp. Political Action Committee
Contact: Stephen M. Souza
600 Third Ave
New York, NY 10016
Tel: (212) 697 - 1111; Fax: (212) 867 - 5249; TF: (866) 463 - 6555

Contributions to Candidates: $100,000 (01/05 - 09/05)
Democrats: $46,000; Republicans: $53,000; Other: $1,000.

Principal Recipients

SENATE DEMOCRATS		HOUSE DEMOCRATS	
Feinstein, Dianne (CA)	$2,500	Andrews, Robert (NJ)	$5,000
		Edwards, Chet (TX)	$5,000
		Israel, Steve (NY)	$5,000
		Murtha, John P Mr. (PA)	$5,000
		Sanchez, Loretta (CA)	$5,000
SENATE REPUBLICANS		**HOUSE REPUBLICANS**	
		Bonilla, Henry (TX)	$5,000
		Hunter, Duncan (CA)	$5,000
		Lobiondo, Frank (NJ)	$5,000

Public Affairs and Related Activities Personnel

At Headquarters

MANNE, Kenneth W. — Tel: (212) 697 - 1111; Fax: (212) 867 - 5249; TF: (866) 463 - 6555
V. President, Human Resources

SOUZA, Stephen M. — Tel: (212) 697 - 1111; Fax: (212) 867 - 5249; TF: (866) 463 - 6555
V. President and Treasurer, L-3 Communications Corp. PAC

SWAIN, Cynthia — Tel: (212) 697 - 1111; Fax: (212) 867 - 5249; TF: (866) 463 - 6555
V. President, Corporate Communications

At Washington Office

ADAMS, Jimmie V. — Tel: (703) 412 - 7190
V. President, Washington, DC Operations

RISCASSI, Robert W. — Tel: (703) 412 - 7190
V. President, Washington, DC Operations

WAHL, Fred — Tel: (703) 412 - 7190
V. President, Government Affairs

L-3 Communications Titan Group

Provides technology solutions to clients specializing in communications, information technology, and food pasteurization. Formerly The Titan Corp., the company was acquired by L-3 Communications in 2005.

www.titan.com

Chairman, President and Chief Exec. Officer
RAY, Gene W. — Tel: (858) 552 - 9500; Fax: (858) 552 - 9645
gray@titan.com

Main Headquarters
Mailing: 3033 Science Park Rd.
San Diego, CA 92121-1199
Tel: (858) 552 - 9500; Fax: (858) 552 - 9645

Washington Office
Contact: John H. Dressendorfer
Mailing: 400 Virginia Ave. SW
Suite C150
Washington, DC 20024-2714
Tel: (202) 488 - 9740; Fax: (202) 544 - 9071

Political Action Committees

The Titan Corp. Political Action Committee
Contact: John H. Dressendorfer
400 Virginia Ave. SW
Suite C150
Washington, DC 20024-2714
Tel: (202) 488 - 9740; Fax: (202) 544 - 9071

Contributions to Candidates: $66,150 (01/05 - 09/05)

L-3 Communications Titan Group

* continued from previous page

Democrats: $6,000; Republicans: $60,150.

Principal Recipients

SENATE DEMOCRATS		HOUSE DEMOCRATS	
		Dicks, Norm D (WA)	$5,000
SENATE REPUBLICANS		**HOUSE REPUBLICANS**	
Burns, Conrad (MT)	$2,000	Cunningham, Duke (CA)	$10,000
		Hunter, Duncan (CA)	$10,000
		Lewis, Jerry (CA)	$10,000
		Issa, Darrell (CA)	$5,000
		Weldon, David (FL)	$5,000
		Young, C. W. Bill (FL)	$5,000

Public Affairs and Related Activities Personnel

At Headquarters

WILLIAMS, Ralph "Wil" — Tel: (858) 552 - 9724
V. President, Corporate Communications — Fax: (858) 552 - 9477

At Washington Office

DRESSENDORFER, John H. — Tel: (202) 488 - 9740
V. President, Government Relations — Fax: (202) 544 - 9071
jdressendorfer@titan.com
Registered Federal Lobbyist.

L. L. Bean, Inc.

A member of the Public Affairs Council. A manufacturer and retailer of outdoor apparel and gear.
www.llbean.com
Annual Revenues: $1.2 billion

Chairman of the Board — Tel: (207) 865 - 4761
GORMAN, Leon A. — Fax: (207) 552 - 6821
TF: (800) 221 - 4221

Chief Exec. Officer — Tel: (207) 865 - 4761
MCCORMICK, Chris — Fax: (207) 552 - 6821
TF: (800) 221 - 4221

Main Headquarters
Mailing: One Casco St. — Tel: (207) 865 - 4761
Freeport, ME 04033 — Fax: (207) 552 - 6821
TF: (800) 221 - 4221

Corporate Foundations and Giving Programs

L. L. Bean Corporate Contributions
Contact: Janet Wyper
One Casco St. — Tel: (207) 552 - 6038
Freeport, ME 04033 — Fax: (207) 552 - 6821
TF: (800) 221 - 4221

Annual Grant Total: $1,000,000 - $2,000,000
Geographic Preference: Maine; National
Primary Interests: Arts and Culture; Education; Environment/Conservation; Health and Human Services

Public Affairs and Related Activities Personnel

At Headquarters

BEEM, Carolyn — Tel: (207) 552 - 6016
Manager, Environmental and Government Affairs — Fax: (207) 552 - 6821
TF: (800) 221 - 4221

DONALDSON, Rich — Tel: (207) 552 - 6022
Manager, Public Relations — Fax: (207) 552 - 6821
TF: (800) 221 - 4221

OLIVER, John V. — Tel: (207) 552 - 6006
V. President, Public Affairs — Fax: (207) 552 - 6821
TF: (800) 221 - 4221

WYPER, Janet — Tel: (207) 552 - 6038
Manager, Community Relations — Fax: (207) 552 - 6821
TF: (800) 221 - 4221

La Quinta Inns

A hotel chain.
www.laquinta.com
Annual Revenues: $651.4 million

Chairman and Chief Exec. Officer and Director — Tel: (214) 492 - 6600
CASH, Francis W. "Butch" — Fax: (214) 492 - 6616

Main Headquarters
Mailing: 909 Hidden Ridge, Suite 600 — Tel: (214) 492 - 6600
Irving, TX 75038 — Fax: (214) 492 - 6616

Corporate Foundations and Giving Programs

La Quinta Inns Corporate Giving Program
Contact: Teresa Ferguson
909 Hidden Ridge, Suite 600 — Tel: (214) 492 - 6937
Irving, TX 75038 — Fax: (214) 492 - 6616

Annual Grant Total: none reported

Public Affairs and Related Activities Personnel

At Headquarters

FERGUSON, Noel — Tel: (214) 492 - 6600
Senior V. President, Human Resources — Fax: (214) 492 - 6616

FERGUSON, Teresa — Tel: (214) 492 - 6937
Manager, Public Relations — Fax: (214) 492 - 6616
teresa.ferguson@laquinta.com

SEYER, Sheryl A. — Tel: (214) 492 - 6689
Manager, Investor Relations — Fax: (214) 596 - 6013
sheryl.seyer@laquinta.com

La-Z-Boy Incorporated

A manufacturer of furniture.
www.la-z-boy.com
Annual Revenues: $2 billion

Chairman of the Board — Tel: (734) 242 - 1444
NORTON, Patrick H. — Fax: (734) 457 - 4910

President and Chief Exec. Officer — Tel: (734) 242 - 1444
DARROW, Kurt L. — Fax: (734) 457 - 2005

Main Headquarters
Mailing: 1284 N. Telegraph Rd. — Tel: (734) 242 - 1444
Monroe, MI 48162 — Fax: (734) 457 - 2005

Corporate Foundations and Giving Programs

La-Z-Boy Foundation
Contact: Donald E. Blohm
1284 N. Telegraph Rd. — Tel: (734) 241 - 3680
Monroe, MI 48162 — Fax: (734) 457 - 2005

Assets: $20,800,000 (2003)
Annual Grant Total: $750,000 - $1,000,000
Geographic Preference: Area(s) in which the company operates
Primary Interests: Education; Health and Human Services; Social Services; Youth Services
Recent Recipients: American Red Cross; Salvation Army; United Way; YMCA

Public Affairs and Related Activities Personnel

At Headquarters

BLOHM, Donald E. — Tel: (734) 241 - 3680
Administrator, La-Z-Boy Foundation — Fax: (734) 457 - 2005

RINDSKOPF, Steven P. — Tel: (734) 241 - 2888
V. President, Human Resources — Fax: (734) 241 - 3452

STEGEMAN, Mark A. — Tel: (734) 242 - 4418
V. President and Treasurer — Fax: (734) 457 - 2005
Responsibilities include investor relations.

Labor Ready, Inc.

A member of the Public Affairs Council. A provider of temporary manual labor.
www.laborready.com
Annual Revenues: $1 billion

Chairman of the Board — Tel: (253) 383 - 9101
SULLIVAN, Robert J. — TF: (800) 610 - 8920

Chief Exec. Officer — Tel: (253) 383 - 9101
SAMBATARO, Joseph P., Jr. — TF: (800) 610 - 8920

Main Headquarters
Mailing: P.O. Box 2910 — Tel: (253) 383 - 9101
Tacoma, WA 98401-2910 — TF: (800) 610 - 8920

Political Action Committees

Labor Ready Inc. PAC
Contact: Joanna Monroe
P.O. Box 2910 — Tel: (253) 383 - 9101
Tacoma, WA 98401-2910 — TF: (800) 610 - 8920

Contributions to Candidates: $5,500 (01/05 - 09/05)
Democrats: $3,000; Republicans: $2,500.

Principal Recipients

SENATE DEMOCRATS		HOUSE DEMOCRATS	
Murray, Patty (WA)	$1,000	Dicks, Norm D (WA)	$1,000
		Hoyer, Steny (MD)	$1,000
SENATE REPUBLICANS		**HOUSE REPUBLICANS**	
Burns, Conrad (MT)	$1,500	McMorris, Cathy (WA)	$1,000

Corporate Foundations and Giving Programs

Community Involvement Fund
Contact: Tracy Peacock

Labor Ready, Inc.

** continued from previous page*

P.O. Box 2910 Tel: (253) 383 - 9101
Tacoma, WA 98401-2910 TF: (800) 610 - 8920

Annual Grant Total: none reported

Public Affairs and Related Activities Personnel

At Headquarters

BURKE, Stacey Tel: (253) 383 - 9101
Director, Corporate Communications TF: (800) 610 - 8920

COOPER, Steven C. Tel: (253) 383 - 9101
Chief Financial Officer TF: (800) 610 - 8920
Responsibilities include investor relations.

MONROE, Joanna Tel: (253) 383 - 9101
V. President, Legal and Governmental Affairs TF: (800) 610 - 8920

OTTO, Billie Tel: (253) 383 - 9101
V. President and Controller/Chief Information Officer TF: (800) 610 - 8920

PEACOCK, Tracy Tel: (253) 383 - 9101
Contact, Community Involvement Fund TF: (800) 610 - 8920

Laboratory Corp. of America Holdings

Operates nationwide laboratories that perform diagnostic tests for physicians, health care organizations, industrial companies, and other clinical laboratories.

www.labcorp.com
Annual Revenues: $2.9 billion

Chairman and Chief Exec. Officer
MACMAHON, Thomas P.

Main Headquarters
Mailing: 358 S. Main St. Tel: (336) 229 - 1127
Burlington, NC 27215 Fax: (336) 436 - 1205
TF: (800) 334 - 5261

Political Action Committees

Laboratory Corp. of America Holdings Political Participation Committee
Contact: Teresa Rigsbee
231 Maple Ave. Tel: (336) 584 - 5171
Burlington, NC 27215

Contributions to Candidates: $1,000 (01/05 - 09/05)
Republicans: $1,000.

Principal Recipients

SENATE REPUBLICANS

HOUSE REPUBLICANS
Johnson, Nancy (CT) $1,000

Corporate Foundations and Giving Programs

Laboratory Corp. of America Contributions
Contact: Teresa Mansfield
358 S. Main St. Tel: (336) 229 - 1127
Burlington, NC 27215 Fax: (336) 436 - 1205
TF: (800) 334 - 5261

Annual Grant Total: none reported
Geographic Preference: Alamance County, NC
Primary Interests: Arts and Culture; Education; Health; Human Welfare
Recent Recipients: American Cancer Society; Juvenile Diabetes Foundation; March of Dimes; United Way; YMCA

Public Affairs and Related Activities Personnel

At Headquarters

HAYES, Brad Tel: (336) 229 - 1127
Senior V. President, Investor Relations Fax: (336) 436 - 1205
TF: (800) 334 - 5261

MANSFIELD, Teresa Tel: (336) 229 - 1127
Community Affairs Contact Fax: (336) 436 - 1205
TF: (800) 334 - 5261
Responsibilities include corporate philanthropy.

At Other Offices

LITTLE, Brian K. Tel: (336) 436 - 5005
Manager, Corporate Communications
Corporate Communications Dept.
430 S. Spring St.
Burlington, NC 27215
media@labcorp.com

RIGSBEE, Teresa Tel: (336) 584 - 5171
PAC Treasurer
231 Maple Ave.
Burlington, NC 27215

SMITH, Bradford T.
Exec. V. President, Public Affairs, Law and Compliance
Corporate Communications Dept.
430 S. Spring St.
Mailstop: M/S 65050
Burlington, NC 27215

Laclede Gas Co.

See listing on page 286 under The Laclede Group.

The Laclede Group

Formerly known as Laclede Gas Co. A gas distribution company.

www.lacledegas.com
Annual Revenues: $1.002 billion

Chairman and Chief Exec. Officer Tel: (314) 342 - 0500
YAEGER, Douglas H. Fax: (314) 421 - 1979

Main Headquarters
Mailing: 720 Olive St. Tel: (314) 342 - 0500
St. Louis, MO 63101 Fax: (314) 421 - 1979

Corporate Foundations and Giving Programs

Laclede Gas Charitable Trust
Contact: Mary C. Kullman
720 Olive St. Tel: (314) 342 - 0531
St. Louis, MO 63101 Fax: (314) 421 - 1979

Annual Grant Total: none reported
Not accepting any new applications at the time this edition went to press.
Geographic Preference: Area(s) in which the company operates
Primary Interests: Civic and Cultural Activities; Community Development; Education; Youth Services
Recent Recipients: St. Louis Symphony; United Way

Public Affairs and Related Activities Personnel

At Headquarters

HARGRAVES, Richard N. Tel: (314) 342 - 0652
Director, Corporate Communications Fax: (314) 436 - 3166
Mailstop: Room 800

KULLMAN, Mary C. Tel: (314) 342 - 0531
Secretary and Associate General Counsel Fax: (314) 421 - 1979
Mailstop: Room 1527
Responsibilities include corporate philanthropy.

NEISES, Kenneth J. Tel: (314) 342 - 0601
Exec. V. President, Energy and Administration Services Fax: (314) 421 - 1979
Responsibilities include regulatory affairs.

SHERWIN, R. Lawrence Tel: (314) 342 - 0500
Assistant V. President, Regulatory Administration Fax: (314) 421 - 1979

Lafarge North America, Inc.

A cement and concrete manufacturing company.

www.lafargenorthamerica.com
Annual Revenues: $3.3 billion

Chairman of the Board Tel: (703) 480 - 3600
COLLOMB, Bertrand P. Fax: (703) 796 - 2214

President and Chief Exec. Officer Tel: (703) 480 - 3600
ROLLIER, Philippe R. Fax: (703) 796 - 2214

Main Headquarters
Mailing: 12950 Worldgate Dr. Tel: (703) 480 - 3600
Suite 600 Fax: (703) 796 - 2214
Herndon, VA 20170

Political Action Committees

Lafarge North America Inc. PAC
Contact: Jonathan S. Collard
12950 Worldgate Dr. Tel: (703) 480 - 3622
Suite 600 Fax: (703) 796 - 2219
Herndon, VA 20170

Contributions to Candidates: $8,000 (01/05 - 09/05)
Democrats: $4,000; Republicans: $4,000.

Principal Recipients

SENATE DEMOCRATS
Clinton, Hillary Rodham (NY) $1,000

HOUSE DEMOCRATS
Cleaver, Emanuel (MO) $1,000
Clyburn, James (SC) $1,000
Salazar, John (CO) $1,000

SENATE REPUBLICANS
Talent, James (MO) $2,000

HOUSE REPUBLICANS
Dent, Charles W (PA) $1,000
Wilson, Heather (NM) $1,000

Corporate Foundations and Giving Programs

Lafarge Corporate Giving Program
Contact: Jonathan S. Collard

Lafarge North America, Inc.

** continued from previous page*

12950 Worldgate Dr.
Suite 600
Herndon, VA 20170
Tel: (703) 480 - 3622
Fax: (703) 796 - 2219

Annual Grant Total: none reported

Geographic Preference: Washington, DC metropolitan area (including Northern Virginia and Suburban Maryland); National

Primary Interests: Arts and Humanities; Children; Environment/Conservation; Financially Disadvantaged

Public Affairs and Related Activities Personnel

At Headquarters

COLLARD, Jonathan S.
Director, Public and Government Affairs
jonathan.collard@lafarge-na.com
Tel: (703) 480 - 3622
Fax: (703) 796 - 2219

DISNEY, Peggy
Director, Media Relations
Tel: (703) 480 - 6623
Fax: (703) 796 - 2214

JACKSON, Jennifer
Coordinator, Public Affairs
jennifer.jackson@lafarge-na.com
Tel: (703) 480 - 3600
Fax: (703) 796 - 2214

NEALIS, Jim
Senior V. President, Human Resources
jim.nealis@lafargecorp.com
Tel: (703) 480 - 3600
Fax: (703) 796 - 2214

PESKE, Sherry E.
V. President, Corporate Communications and Public Affairs
sherry.peske@lafarge-na.com
Tel: (703) 480 - 3600
Fax: (703) 796 - 2214

WILLIAMS, Andrew
Manager, Internal and Online Communications
Tel: (703) 480 - 3600
Fax: (703) 796 - 2214

Lam Research Corp.

A supplier of wafer fabrication equipment and services to the world's semiconductor industry.

www.lamrc.com

Chairman of the Board
BAGLEY, James W.
Tel: (510) 572 - 0200
Fax: (510) 572 - 6454

President and Chief Exec. Officer
NEWBERRY, Steven
Tel: (510) 572 - 0200
Fax: (510) 572 - 2935

Main Headquarters
Mailing: 4650 Cushing Pkwy.
Fremont, CA 94538-6470
Tel: (510) 572 - 0200
Fax: (510) 572 - 2935

Corporate Foundations and Giving Programs

Lam Research Community Outreach Program
Contact: Julie Moore
4650 Cushing Pkwy.
Fremont, CA 94538-6470
Tel: (510) 572 - 0200
Fax: (510) 572 - 6454

Annual Grant Total: none reported

The company also has an employee matching gifts program.

Geographic Preference: Area(s) in which the company operates

Primary Interests: Education; Math and Science

Public Affairs and Related Activities Personnel

At Headquarters

BELA, Kathleen
Director, Investor Relations and Corporate Communications
kathleen.bela@lamrc.com
Tel: (510) 572 - 4566
Fax: (510) 572 - 2935

HICKMAN, Sue
Administrator, Investor Relations
sue.hickman@lamrc.com
Tel: (510) 572 - 5910
Fax: (510) 572 - 6454

LYNCH, Shawn
Manager, Corporate Relations
shawn.lynch@lamrc.com
Tel: (510) 572 - 1776
Fax: (510) 572 - 2935

MOORE, Julie
Corporate Contributions Contact
Tel: (510) 572 - 0200
Fax: (510) 572 - 6454

Lance, Inc.

A manufacturer of snacks and other packaged food products.

www.lancesnacks.com

Chairman of the Board
PREZZANO, Wilbur J.
Tel: (704) 554 - 1421
Fax: (704) 554 - 5562
TF: (800) 438 - 1880

President and Chief Exec. Officer
SINGER, David V.
Tel: (704) 554 - 1421
Fax: (704) 554 - 5562
TF: (800) 438 - 1880

Main Headquarters
Mailing: 8600 South Blvd.
Charlotte, NC 28273
Tel: (704) 554 - 1421
Fax: (704) 554 - 5562
TF: (800) 438 - 1880

Corporate Foundations and Giving Programs

Lance Foundation
Contact: Zean Jamison, Jr.
8600 South Blvd.
Charlotte, NC 28273
Tel: (704) 554 - 1421
Fax: (704) 554 - 5562
TF: (800) 438 - 1880

Annual Grant Total: $400,000 - $500,000

Geographic Preference: Area in which the company is headquartered

Primary Interests: Civic and Public Affairs; Higher Education; Youth Services

Recent Recipients: Independent College Fund; United Way

Public Affairs and Related Activities Personnel

At Headquarters

ALLEN, Russell G.
Director, Planning and Investor Relations
Tel: (704) 557 - 8219
Fax: (704) 554 - 5562
TF: (800) 438 - 1880

JAMISON, Zean, Jr.
Director, Foundation
Tel: (704) 554 - 1421
Fax: (704) 554 - 5562
TF: (800) 438 - 1880

LEAKE, Earl D.
V. President, Human Resources
Tel: (704) 554 - 1421
Fax: (704) 554 - 5562
TF: (800) 438 - 1880

Land O'Lakes, Inc.

PUBLIC AFFAIRS COUNCIL

A member of the Public Affairs Council. A farmer-owned food and agricultural cooperative that processes and markets dairy and other food products and distributes farm supplies and services.

www.landolakesinc.com

Annual Revenues: $5.973 billion

Chairman of the Board
KAPPELMAN, Pete
Tel: (651) 481 - 2222
Fax: (651) 481 - 2000
TF: (800) 328 - 4155

Chief Exec. Officer
GHERTY, James E.
jegherty@landolakes.com
Tel: (651) 481 - 2222
Fax: (651) 481 - 2000
TF: (800) 328 - 4155

Main Headquarters
Mailing: P.O. Box 64101
St. Paul, MN 55164-0101
Tel: (651) 481 - 2222
Fax: (651) 481 - 2000
TF: (800) 328 - 4155

Street: 4001 Lexington Ave., North
Arden Hills, MN 55126-2998

Political Action Committees

Land O'Lakes, Inc. Political Action Committee
Contact: Steven Krikava
P.O. Box 64101
St. Paul, MN 55164-0101
Tel: (651) 481 - 2222
Fax: (651) 481 - 2000
TF: (800) 328 - 4155

Contributions to Candidates: $68,000 (01/05 - 09/05)
Democrats: $27,500; Republicans: $35,500; Other: $5,000.

Principal Recipients

SENATE DEMOCRATS		**HOUSE DEMOCRATS**	
Feinstein, Dianne (CA)	$2,000	Obey, David R (WI)	$5,000
		HOUSE OTHER	
		Peterson, Collin (MN)	$5,000
SENATE REPUBLICANS		**HOUSE REPUBLICANS**	
		Nunes, Devin (CA)	$5,000

Corporate Foundations and Giving Programs

Land O'Lakes Foundation
Contact: Bonnie Bassett
P.O. Box 64101
St. Paul, MN 55164-0101
Tel: (651) 481 - 2222
Fax: (651) 481 - 2000
TF: (800) 328 - 4155

Assets: $3,000,000 (1999)
Annual Grant Total: $1,000,000 - $2,000,000

Geographic Preference: California; Maryland; Virginia; New Jersey; Ohio; Michigan; Indiana

Primary Interests: Civic and Public Affairs; Education; Hunger

Recent Recipients: Meals on Wheels; United Negro College Fund; United Way

Public Affairs and Related Activities Personnel

At Headquarters

BASSETT, Bonnie
Director, Community Relations and Exec. Director, Land O'Lakes Foundation
bbassett@landolakes.com
Tel: (651) 481 - 2222
Fax: (651) 481 - 2000
TF: (800) 328 - 4155

BOTHAM, Lydia
Director, Communications
lrbotham@landolakes.com
Tel: (651) 481 - 2222
Fax: (651) 481 - 2000
TF: (800) 328 - 4155

DEBEAU, Lee
Manager, Environmental Compliance
lsdebeau@landolakes.com
Tel: (651) 481 - 2222
Fax: (651) 481 - 2000
TF: (800) 328 - 4155

Land O'Lakes, Inc.

** continued from previous page*

GRABOW, Karen
V. President, Human Resources
kmgrabow@landolakes.com
Tel: (651) 481 - 2222
Fax: (651) 481 - 2000
TF: (800) 328 - 4155

KRIKAVA, Steven
Director, Government Relations
spkrikava@landolakes.com
Tel: (651) 481 - 2222
Fax: (651) 481 - 2000
TF: (800) 328 - 4155

SWOVERLAND, Gary
Director, Corporate Risk
gaswoverland@landolakes.com
Tel: (651) 481 - 2222
Fax: (651) 481 - 2000
TF: (800) 328 - 4155

LandAmerica Financial Group, Inc.

A real estate transaction services company.
www.landam.com
Annual Revenues: $2.58 billion

Chairman of the Board
FOSTER, Charles H., Jr.
Tel: (804) 267 - 8000
Fax: (804) 267 - 8836
TF: (800) 446 - 7086

President and Chief. Exec. Officer
CHANDLER, Theodore L., Jr.
Tel: (804) 267 - 8000
Fax: (804) 267 - 8836
TF: (800) 446 - 7086

Main Headquarters
Mailing: Gateway One
101 Gateway Centre Pkwy.
Richmond, VA 23235
Tel: (804) 267 - 8000
Fax: (804) 267 - 8836
TF: (800) 446 - 7086

Corporate Foundations and Giving Programs

LandAmerica Foundation
Contact: W. Riker Purcell
Gateway One
101 Gateway Centre Pkwy.
Richmond, VA 23235
Tel: (804) 267 - 8330
Fax: (804) 267 - 8836
TF: (800) 446 - 7086

Annual Grant Total: none reported
Maintains an employee matching gifts program
Geographic Preference: Area(s) in which the company operates

Public Affairs and Related Activities Personnel

At Headquarters

DORNEMAN, Ross W.
Exec. V. President, Human Resources
Tel: (804) 267 - 8000
Fax: (804) 267 - 8836
TF: (800) 446 - 7086

EVANS, George William
Exec. V. President and Chief Financial Officer
bevans@landam.com
Tel: (804) 267 - 8000
Fax: (804) 267 - 8836
TF: (800) 446 - 7086
Responsibilities include investor relations.

FARMER, H. Randolph
Senior V. President, Corporate Communications
Tel: (804) 267 - 8120
Fax: (804) 267 - 8836
TF: (800) 446 - 7086

KOLBE, Peter
V. President, Government Relations
Tel: (804) 267 - 8000
Fax: (804) 267 - 8836
TF: (800) 446 - 7086

PURCELL, W. Riker
Secretary, LandAmerica Foundation
Tel: (804) 267 - 8330
Fax: (804) 267 - 8836
TF: (800) 446 - 7086

Landmark Communications, Inc.

A company engaged in newspaper publishing, broadcasting and cable programming.
www.landmarkcom.com

Chairman and Chief Exec. Officer
BATTEN, Frank, Jr.
Tel: (757) 446 - 2010
Fax: (757) 446 - 2489

Main Headquarters
Mailing: P.O. Box 449
Norfolk, VA 23510-0449
Tel: (757) 446 - 2010
Fax: (757) 446 - 2489
Street: 150 W. Brambleton Ave.
Norfolk, VA 23510-2075

Corporate Foundations and Giving Programs

Landmark Communications Foundation
P.O. Box 449
Norfolk, VA 23510-0449
Tel: (757) 446 - 2010
Fax: (757) 446 - 2489

Assets: $50,000,000 (2003)
Annual Grant Total: $1,000,000 - $2,000,000
Giving figures for Landmark Communications, Inc. in 2000 were over $2.7 million.
Geographic Preference: Greensboro, NC; Las Vegas, NV; Nashville, TN; Norfolk, VA; Roanoke, VA
Primary Interests: Education; Human Welfare
Recent Recipients: Hampton Roads Business Consortium for Arts Support; United Way; Virginia Foundation of Independent Colleges

Public Affairs and Related Activities Personnel

At Headquarters

HILL, Charlie W.
Exec. V. President, Human Resources
Tel: (757) 446 - 2010
Fax: (757) 446 - 2489

Landstar System, Inc.

A non asset based transportation services company.
www.landstar.com

Chairman of the Board
CROWE, Jeffrey C.
jcrowe@landstar.com
Tel: (904) 398 - 9400
Fax: (904) 390 - 1325
TF: (800) 872 - 9400

President and Chief Exec. Officer
GERKENS, Henry H.
Tel: (904) 398 - 9400
Fax: (904) 390 - 1437
TF: (800) 872 - 9400

Main Headquarters
Mailing: 13410 Sutton Park Dr. South
Jacksonville, FL 32224
Tel: (904) 398 - 9400
Fax: (904) 390 - 1437
TF: (800) 872 - 9400

Corporate Foundations and Giving Programs

Landstar Scholarship Fund
Contact: Roberta Lee
13410 Sutton Park Dr. South
Jacksonville, FL 32224
Tel: (904) 398 - 9400
Fax: (904) 390 - 1437
TF: (800) 872 - 9400

Annual Grant Total: under $100,000

Public Affairs and Related Activities Personnel

At Headquarters

LEE, Roberta
Contact, Landstar Scholarship Fund
Tel: (904) 398 - 9400
Fax: (904) 390 - 1437
TF: (800) 872 - 9400

MELLION, Donna
V. President, Corporate Communications
dmellion@landstar.com
Tel: (904) 398 - 9400
Fax: (904) 390 - 1437
TF: (800) 872 - 9400

NORVE, Joan
V. President, Human Resources
jnorve@landstar.com
Tel: (904) 390 - 1516
Fax: (904) 390 - 1216
TF: (800) 872 - 9400

WHITCHER, Ginger
Manager, Corporate Communications
gwhitcher@landstar.com
Tel: (904) 398 - 9400
Fax: (904) 390 - 1437
TF: (800) 872 - 9400

LaSalle Bank N.A.

A commercial bank.
www.lasallebank.com
Annual Revenues: $4.02 billion

Chairman of the Board
KUIPER, Joost
Tel: (312) 904 - 2000
Fax: (312) 904 - 6521

President and Chief Exec. Officer
BOBINS, Norman R.
Tel: (312) 904 - 2000
Fax: (312) 904 - 6521

Main Headquarters
Mailing: 135 S. LaSalle St.
Chicago, IL 60603
Tel: (312) 904 - 2000
Fax: (312) 904 - 6521

Political Action Committees

LaSalle Bank Corp./Standard Federal Bank PAC
Contact: Katherine Thompson
135 S. LaSalle St.
Chicago, IL 60603
Tel: (312) 904 - 2000
Fax: (312) 904 - 6521

Contributions to Candidates: $26,500 (01/05 - 09/05)
Democrats: $12,500; Republicans: $14,000.

Principal Recipients

SENATE DEMOCRATS		HOUSE DEMOCRATS	
Carper, Thomas R (DE)	$1,000	Jackson, Jesse (IL)	$2,000
Durbin, Richard J (IL)	$1,000		
SENATE REPUBLICANS		**HOUSE REPUBLICANS**	
		Hastert, Dennis J. (IL)	$5,000

Corporate Foundations and Giving Programs

LaSalle Bank N.A. Corporate Contributions Program
135 S. LaSalle St.
Chicago, IL 60603
Tel: (312) 904 - 2000
Fax: (312) 904 - 6521

Annual Grant Total: none reported
Focus on organizations on whose boards bank employees serve.
Geographic Preference: Area in which the company is headquartered; Chicago, IL
Primary Interests: Arts and Culture; Community Development; Education; Health; Social Services

Public Affairs and Related Activities Personnel

At Headquarters

BALLAST, Brad
Contact, Corporate Contributions
Tel: (312) 904 - 2000
Fax: (312) 904 - 6521

LaSalle Bank N.A.

** continued from previous page*

LARAIA, Mary — Tel: (312) 904 - 6038
Group Senior V. President, Civic and Community Development — Fax: (312) 904 - 4050

PLATT, Shawn M. — Tel: (312) 904 - 7240
Director, Communications — Fax: (312) 904 - 6521
shawn.platt@abnamro.com

SCULLY, John — Tel: (312) 904 - 2000
Senior V. President, Human Resources — Fax: (312) 904 - 6521

THOMPSON, Katherine — Tel: (312) 904 - 2000
Pac Treasurer — Fax: (312) 904 - 6521

Laureate Education, Inc.

An international provider of higher education services with universities in over 12 countries.
www.laureate-inc.com
Annual Revenues: $604 million

Chairman and Chief Exec. Officer — Tel: (410) 843 - 8000
BECKER, Douglas L. — Fax: (410) 843 - 8065

Main Headquarters
Mailing: 1001 Fleet St.
Baltimore, MD 21202-4346
Tel: (410) 843 - 6100
Fax: (410) 843 - 8065
TF: (866) 452 - 8732

Corporate Foundations and Giving Programs

Sylvan/Laureate Foundation, Inc.
1001 Fleet St.
Baltimore, MD 21202-4346
Tel: (410) 843 - 6100
Fax: (410) 843 - 8065
TF: (866) 452 - 8732

Assets: $11,720,000 (2004)
Annual Grant Total: $750,000 - $1,000,000
Geographic Preference: Baltimore, MD; Maryland
Primary Interests: Arts and Humanities; Higher Education; K-12 Education; Medicine and Health Care; Recreation
Recent Recipients: Baltimore Zoo; United Way

Public Affairs and Related Activities Personnel

At Headquarters

SYMANOSKIE, Chris — Tel: (410) 843 - 6394
Director, Investor Relations and Corporate Communications — Fax: (410) 843 - 8065
chris.symanoskie@laureate-inc.com

Leap Wireless International, Inc.

A wireless communications carrier.
www.leapwireless.com
Annual Revenues: $751 million

Chairman of the Board — Tel: (858) 882 - 6000
RACHESKY, Mark H. — Fax: (858) 882 - 6010

Chief Exec. Officer — Tel: (858) 882 - 6000
HUTCHESON, Stewart — Fax: (858) 882 - 6010

Main Headquarters
Mailing: 10307 Pacific Center Ct.
San Diego, CA 92121
Tel: (858) 882 - 6000
Fax: (858) 882 - 6010

Public Affairs and Related Activities Personnel

At Headquarters

ITKIN, Laurie — Tel: (858) 882 - 6000
Director, Government Affairs — Fax: (858) 882 - 6010

SEINES, James — Tel: (858) 882 - 6000
Director, Public Affairs and Investor Relations — Fax: (858) 882 - 6030
jseines@leapwireless.com

STEPHENS, Leonard C. — Tel: (858) 882 - 6000
Senior V. President, Human Resources — Fax: (858) 882 - 6010

Lear Corporation

A manufacturer of automotive interiors.
www.lear.com
Annual Revenues: $15.7 billion

Chairman and Chief Exec. Officer — Tel: (248) 447 - 1500
ROSSITER, Robert E.

Main Headquarters
Mailing: 21557 Telegraph Rd.
Southfield, MI 48034
Tel: (248) 447 - 1500
Fax: (248) 447 - 1722

Political Action Committees

Lear Corp. PAC
Contact: Shari Burgess
21557 Telegraph Rd.
Southfield, MI 48034
Tel: (248) 447 - 1500
Fax: (248) 447 - 1722

Contributions to Candidates: $3,000 (01/05 - 09/05)
Democrats: $500; Republicans: $2,500.

Principal Recipients

SENATE DEMOCRATS
Obama, Barack (IL) $500

HOUSE DEMOCRATS

SENATE REPUBLICANS

HOUSE REPUBLICANS
Knollenberg, Joe (MI) $2,500

Corporate Foundations and Giving Programs

Lear Corp. Contributions
Contact: Valencia Y. Morris
21557 Telegraph Rd.
Southfield, MI 48034
Tel: (248) 447 - 5938
Fax: (248) 447 - 1722

Annual Grant Total: none reported

Public Affairs and Related Activities Personnel

At Headquarters

BURGESS, Shari — Tel: (248) 447 - 1500
PAC Treasurer — Fax: (248) 447 - 1722

JACKSON, Roger A. — Tel: (248) 447 - 1562
Senior V. President, Human Resources and Corporate Relations — Fax: (248) 447 - 1722
rjackson@lear.com

LUKIEWSKI, Carolyn — Tel: (248) 447 - 1684
Investor Relations Contact — Fax: (248) 447 - 1722
clukiewski@lear.com

MORRIS, Valencia Y. — Tel: (248) 447 - 5938
Manager, Community Relations — Fax: (248) 447 - 1722
vmorris@lear.com
Responsibilities include corporate philanthropy.

PUCHALSKY, Andrea — Tel: (248) 447 - 1651
Director, Corporate Communications — Fax: (248) 447 - 1722
apuchalsky@lear.com

STEPHENS, Melvin — Tel: (248) 447 - 1500
V. President, Investor Relations and Corporate Communications — Fax: (248) 447 - 1722

WAJSGRAS, David C. — Tel: (248) 447 - 1500
Senior V. President and Chief Financial Officer — Fax: (248) 447 - 1722
Responsibilities include investor relations.

Lee Enterprises

A newspaper publishing company. Acquired Pulitzer Inc. in June 2005.
www.leeenterprises.com

Chairman, President and Chief Exec. Officer — Tel: (563) 383 - 2100
JUNCK, Mary E.

Main Headquarters
Mailing: 201 N. Harrison St.
Davenport, IA 52801-1939
Tel: (563) 383 - 2100

Public Affairs and Related Activities Personnel

At Headquarters

HAYES, Daniel K. — Tel: (563) 383 - 2100
V. President, Communications

KURAITIS, Vytenis P. — Tel: (563) 383 - 2100
V. President, Human Resources

Leggett & Platt, Inc.

A member of the Public Affairs Council. A manufacturer of components for the home furnishings industry.
www.leggett.com

Chairman and Chief Exec. Officer — Tel: (417) 358 - 8131
WRIGHT, Felix E. — Fax: (417) 358 - 7155
felix.wright@leggett.com

Main Headquarters
Mailing: P.O. Box 757
Carthage, MO 64836-0757
Tel: (417) 358 - 8131
Fax: (417) 358 - 5840
Street: One Leggett Rd.
Carthage, MO 64836

Political Action Committees

Leggett and Platt Political Involvement Fund
Contact: Wendy Watson
P.O. Box 757
Carthage, MO 64836-0757
Tel: (417) 358 - 8131

Contributions to Candidates: $10,000 (01/05 - 09/05)
Republicans: $10,000.

Principal Recipients

SENATE REPUBLICANS

HOUSE REPUBLICANS
Blunt, Roy (MO) $5,000
Graves, Sam (MO) $5,000

Corporate Foundations and Giving Programs

Leggett and Platt Corporate Contributions
Contact: Sylvia Vance

Leggett & Platt, Inc.

* continued from previous page

P.O. Box 757 Tel: (417) 358 - 8131
Carthage, MO 64836-0757

Annual Grant Total: none reported

Public Affairs and Related Activities Personnel

At Headquarters

ANDERSON, C. Robert — Tel: (417) 358 - 8131; Fax: (417) 358 - 7155
Corporate Director, Environmental Affairs

BESHORE, Lance G., Ph.D. — Tel: (417) 358 - 8131; Fax: (417) 358 - 6045
V. President, Public Affairs and Government Relations
lance.beshore@leggett.com
Responsibilities include corporate philanthropy and political action.

DESONIER, David M. — Tel: (417) 358 - 8131 Ext: 2363; Fax: (417) 359 - 5114
V. President, Investor Relations
david.desonier@leggett.com

HALE, John A. — Tel: (417) 358 - 8131 Ext: 3000; Fax: (417) 358 - 5840
V. President, Human Resources
john.hale@leggett.com

MCCOY, Susan R. — Tel: (417) 358 - 8131
Director, Investor Relations

VANCE, Sylvia — Tel: (417) 358 - 8131
Contact, Leggett & Platt Corporate Contributions
svance@leggett.com

WATSON, Wendy — Tel: (417) 358 - 8131
Contact, Leggett and Platt Political Involvement Fund

Lehigh Cement Company

A manufacturer of cement and concrete products. A wholly-owned subsidiary of HeidelbergCement AG of Heidelberg, Germany.

www.lehighcement.com

Chief Exec. Officer — Tel: (610) 366 - 4600; Fax: (610) 366 - 4684; TF: (800) 523 - 5488
ERHARD, Helmut S.

Main Headquarters
Mailing: 7660 Imperial Way, Allentown, PA 18195-1040 — Tel: (610) 366 - 4600; Fax: (610) 366 - 4851; TF: (800) 523 - 5488

Public Affairs and Related Activities Personnel

At Headquarters

BACHMAN, Corliss — Tel: (610) 366 - 4600; Fax: (610) 366 - 4684; TF: (800) 523 - 5488
Coordinator, Communications
cbachman@lehighcement.com

MIKOLS, Elizabeth H. — Tel: (610) 366 - 4753; Fax: (610) 366 - 4684; TF: (800) 523 - 5488
Manager, Public Affairs
emikols@lehighcement.com

Lehigh Portland Cement Co.

See listing on page 290 under Lehigh Cement Company.

Lehman Brothers

A provider of diversified financial services, including investment banking, securities brokerage and advisory services. Acquired Neuberger Berman, Inc. in October, 2003.

www.lehman.com

Chairman and Chief Exec. Officer — Tel: (212) 526 - 7000
FULD, Richard S., Jr.

Main Headquarters
Mailing: 745 Seventh Ave., New York, NY 10019 — Tel: (212) 526 - 7000; Fax: (212) 526 - 8766; TF: (800) 666 - 2388

Washington Office
Contact: Judith A. Winchester
Mailing: 800 Connecticut Ave. NW, Suite 1200, Washington, DC 20006 — Tel: (202) 452 - 4700; Fax: (202) 452 - 4791

Political Action Committees

Action Fund of Lehman Brothers Holdings Inc.
Contact: Judith A. Winchester
800 Connecticut Ave. NW — Tel: (202) 452 - 4700; Fax: (202) 452 - 4791
Suite 1200
Washington, DC 20006

Contributions to Candidates: $43,500 (01/05 - 09/05)
Democrats: $20,500; Republicans: $23,000.

Principal Recipients

SENATE DEMOCRATS
Lieberman, Joe (CT) $7,500

SENATE REPUBLICANS
Hatch, Orrin (UT) $3,000
Santorum, Richard (PA) $2,500

HOUSE DEMOCRATS

HOUSE REPUBLICANS
Hastert, Dennis J. (IL) $5,000
Bachus, Spencer (AL) $2,500
Baker, Hugh (LA) $2,500
Ney, Robert W (OH) $2,500

Corporate Foundations and Giving Programs

Lehman Brothers Philanthropy
Contact: Francine Kittredge
745 Seventh Ave. — Tel: (212) 526 - 7000
New York, NY 10019

Annual Grant Total: none reported

Public Affairs and Related Activities Personnel

At Headquarters

COHEN, Kerrie — Tel: (212) 526 - 4092; Fax: (212) 526 - 8766
Media Contact

KITTREDGE, Francine — Tel: (212) 526 - 7000
Managing Director, Lehman Brothers Philanthropy

At Washington Office

WINCHESTER, Judith A. — Tel: (202) 452 - 4700; Fax: (202) 452 - 4791
Managing Director, Government Affairs
Registered Federal Lobbyist.

Leiner Health Products, Inc.

A manufacturer of nutritional supplements and personal hygiene products.

www.leiner.com

Chairman of the Board — Tel: (310) 835 - 8400; Fax: (310) 952 - 7760
BAIRD, Charles F.

Chief Exec. Officer — Tel: (310) 835 - 8400; Fax: (310) 952 - 7760
KAMINSKI, Robert M.

Main Headquarters
Mailing: 901 E. 233rd St., Carson, CA 90745-6204 — Tel: (310) 835 - 8400; Fax: (310) 952 - 7760

Washington Office
Contact: Crystal Wright
Mailing: 1355 Jefferson St. NW, Washington, DC 20011 — Tel: (202) 772 - 2039

Public Affairs and Related Activities Personnel

At Headquarters

REYNOLDS, Rob — Tel: (310) 952 - 1511; Fax: (310) 952 - 7760
Chief Financial Officer
Responsibilities include investor relations.

At Washington Office

WRIGHT, Crystal — Tel: (202) 291 - 8481
V. President, Public Relations

Lennar Corp.

A homebuilder with operations in Florida, California, Texas, Arizona, and Nevada. Subsidiaries include U.S. Home Corp. Acquired Patriot Homes of Baltimore, Maryland on January 17, 2002. Merged with Newhall Land and Farming Co. in 2004.

www.lennar.com

Chairman of the Board — Tel: (305) 559 - 4000; Fax: (305) 229 - 6453; TF: (800) 741 - 4663
STRUDLER, Robert J.

President and Chief Exec. Officer — Tel: (305) 559 - 4000; Fax: (305) 229 - 6453; TF: (800) 741 - 4663
MILLER, Stuart A.

Main Headquarters
Mailing: 700 N.W. 107th Ave., Miami, FL 33172 — Tel: (305) 559 - 4000; Fax: (305) 229 - 6453; TF: (800) 741 - 4663

Corporate Foundations and Giving Programs

Lennar Foundation
Contact: Marshall Ames
700 N.W. 107th Ave. — Tel: (305) 485 - 2092; Fax: (305) 229 - 6453; TF: (800) 741 - 4663
Miami, FL 33172

Annual Grant Total: none reported

Lennar Corp.

** continued from previous page*

Public Affairs and Related Activities Personnel

At Headquarters

AMES, Marshall — Tel: (305) 485 - 2092
V. President — Fax: (305) 229 - 6453
mames@lennar.com — TF: (800) 741 - 4663
Responsibilities include media and investor relations.

JOHNSON, Craig M. — Tel: (305) 559 - 4000
V. President, Community Development — Fax: (305) 229 - 6453
TF: (800) 741 - 4663

At Other Offices

HOWARD, Kay — Tel: (713) 877 - 2363
Director, Communications
10707 Clay Rd.
P.O. Box 2863
Houston, TX 77252

MATTHEWS, Frank — Tel: (713) 877 - 2348
Director, Human Resources
10707 Clay Rd.
P.O. Box 2863
Houston, TX 77252
frank.matthews@ushome.com

Lennox Internat'l

PUBLIC AFFAIRS COUNCIL

A member of the Public Affairs Council. Provides global solutions for the heating, ventilation, air conditioning, and refrigeration markets.
www.lennoxinternational.com
Annual Revenues: $3 billion

Chairman of the Board — Tel: (972) 497 - 5000
NORRIS, John W., Jr. — Fax: (972) 497 - 5299
john.norris@lennoxintl.com

Chief Exec. Officer — Tel: (972) 497 - 5000
SCHJERVEN, Robert E. — Fax: (972) 497 - 5299

Main Headquarters
Mailing: P.O. Box 799900 — Tel: (972) 497 - 5000
Dallas, TX 75379-9900 — Fax: (972) 497 - 5292
Street: 2140 Lake Park Blvd.
Richardson, TX 75080

Political Action Committees

Lennox Employee Advocacy Program (LEAP)
Contact: Kathy Minde
P.O. Box 799900 — Tel: (972) 497 - 5000
Dallas, TX 75379-9900 — Fax: (972) 497 - 5292

Contributions to Candidates: none reported (01/05 - 09/05)

Corporate Foundations and Giving Programs

Lennox Foundation
Contact: Sue Manno
P.O. Box 799900 — Tel: (972) 497 - 5094
Dallas, TX 75379-9900 — Fax: (972) 497 - 5299

Annual Grant Total: $400,000 - $500,000

Public Affairs and Related Activities Personnel

At Headquarters

GILLEY, Kyle — Tel: (972) 497 - 6218
Contact, Lennox Employee Advocacy Program — Fax: (972) 497 - 5268

LEWIS, David F. — Tel: (972) 497 - 5316
V. President, Government Affairs — Fax: (972) 497 - 5268

MANNO, Sue — Tel: (972) 497 - 5094
Foundation Contact — Fax: (972) 497 - 5299

MINDE, Kathy — Tel: (972) 497 - 5000
Treasurer, Lennox Employee Advocacy Program — Fax: (972) 497 - 5292

MOLTNER, Bill — Tel: (972) 497 - 6670
V. President, Investor Relations — Fax: (972) 497 - 5292
bill.moltner@lennoxintl.com

O'SHEA, Karen — Tel: (972) 497 - 5172
V. President, Communications and Public Relations — Fax: (972) 497 - 5292
karen.oshea@lennoxintl.com

YOHMAN, Mark — Tel: (972) 497 - 5069
Director, Environmental Affairs — Fax: (972) 497 - 5299
mark.yohman@lennoxintl.com

Leucadia Nat'l Corp.

A diversified insurance, financial services, real estate, manufacturing and banking and lending company.

Chairman of the Board — Tel: (212) 460 - 1900
CUMMING, Ian — Fax: (212) 598 - 4869

Main Headquarters
Mailing: 315 Park Ave. South — Tel: (212) 460 - 1900
New York, NY 10010 — Fax: (212) 598 - 4869

Corporate Foundations and Giving Programs

Leucadia Foundation
Contact: Laura Ulbrantt
315 Park Ave. South — Tel: (212) 460 - 1900
New York, NY 10010 — Fax: (212) 598 - 4869

Annual Grant Total: none reported

Public Affairs and Related Activities Personnel

At Headquarters

ULBRANTT, Laura — Tel: (212) 460 - 1900
Corporate Secretary — Fax: (212) 598 - 4869
Responsibilities include investor relations and corporate philanthropy.

Level 3 Communications, Inc.

A worldwide communications and information services company. Acquired Genuity in February, 2003.
www.level3.com

Chairman of the Board — Tel: (720) 888 - 1000
SCOTT, Walter, Jr. — Fax: (720) 888 - 5085

Chief Exec. Officer — Tel: (720) 888 - 1000
CROWE, James Q. — Fax: (720) 888 - 5085

Main Headquarters
Mailing: 1025 Eldorado Blvd. — Tel: (720) 888 - 1000
Broomfield, CO 80021 — Fax: (720) 888 - 5085

Political Action Committees

Level 3 Communications, Inc. PAC
Contact: James C. Pribyl
1025 Eldorado Blvd. — Tel: (720) 888 - 1000
Broomfield, CO 80021 — Fax: (720) 888 - 5085

Contributions to Candidates: $39,000 (01/05 - 09/05)
Democrats: $17,000; Republicans: $22,000.

Principal Recipients

SENATE DEMOCRATS		HOUSE DEMOCRATS	
Nelson, Benjamin (NE)	$5,000	Hoyer, Steny (MD)	$2,000
Nelson, Bill (FL)	$5,000	Boucher, Fredrick (VA)	$1,000
Lieberman, Joe (CT)	$2,000	Conyers, John Jr. (MI)	$1,000
		Delahunt, William (MA)	$1,000

SENATE REPUBLICANS		HOUSE REPUBLICANS	
Hagel, Charles T (NE)	$5,000	Davis, Tom (VA)	$2,500
Burns, Conrad (MT)	$3,000	Pickering, Chip (MS)	$2,500
Dewine, Richard (OH)	$2,000	Sensenbrenner, Jim (WI)	$2,500
Allen, George (VA)	$1,000	Terry, Lee (NE)	$1,500
Stevens, Ted (AK)	$1,000	Wilson, Heather (NM)	$1,000

Public Affairs and Related Activities Personnel

At Headquarters

ADAMS, Linda — Tel: (720) 888 - 1000
Group V. President, Human Resources — Fax: (720) 888 - 5085

CURLANDER, Sandra — Tel: (720) 888 - 2501
Manager, Investor Relations — Fax: (720) 888 - 5085

GREY, Robin — Tel: (720) 888 - 2518
Senior V. President, Investor Relations — Fax: (720) 888 - 5085
TF: (877) 585 - 8266

HOWELL, Joseph M., III — Tel: (720) 888 - 2517
Group V. President, Corporate Marketing — Fax: (720) 888 - 5085
Responsibilities include media relations.

LONNEGREN, Paul — Tel: (720) 888 - 6099
Director, Marketing Communications and Public Relations — Fax: (720) 888 - 5085

PRIBYL, James C. — Tel: (720) 888 - 1000
Director, Government Affairs; and PAC Treasurer — Fax: (720) 888 - 5085
james.pribyl@level3.com

ROBINSON, Heather — Tel: (720) 888 - 2097
Manager, Corporate Communications — Fax: (720) 888 - 5085

Levi Strauss and Co.

An apparel manufacturer.
www.levistrauss.com
Annual Revenues: $4.1 billion

Chairman of the Board — Tel: (415) 501 - 6000
HAAS, Robert D. — Fax: (415) 501 - 7112
TF: (800) 872 - 5384

Levi Strauss and Co.

** continued from previous page*

President and Chief Exec. Officer
MARINEAU, Philip A.
Tel: (415) 501 - 6000
Fax: (415) 501 - 7112
TF: (800) 872 - 5384

Main Headquarters
Mailing: 1155 Battery St.
San Francisco, CA 94111
Tel: (415) 501 - 6000
Fax: (415) 501 - 7112
TF: (800) 872 - 5384

Corporate Foundations and Giving Programs

Levi Strauss Foundation
Contact: Theresa Fay-Bustillos
1155 Battery St.
San Francisco, CA 94111
Tel: (415) 501 - 6000
Fax: (415) 501 - 7112
TF: (800) 872 - 5384

Annual Grant Total: over $5,000,000
Also sponsors Community Involvement Teams and Employee Matching Gifts Programs. Guidelines are available.
Geographic Preference: Area(s) in which the company operates
Primary Interests: AIDS/HIV; Economic Development; Education

Public Affairs and Related Activities Personnel

At Headquarters

BECKMAN, Jeff
Senior Manager, Worldwide and U.S. Communications
Tel: (415) 501 - 1698
Fax: (415) 501 - 7112
TF: (800) 872 - 5384

BURDEN, Stuart
Director, Community Affairs, U.S., Canada and Latin America
Tel: (415) 501 - 6000
Fax: (415) 501 - 7112
TF: (800) 872 - 5384

CARROLL, Kevin
Senior Manager, Branded Philanthropy and Employee Involvement
Tel: (415) 501 - 6000
Fax: (415) 501 - 7112
TF: (800) 872 - 5384

CHEW, Dan
V. President, U.S. and Worldwide Communications
Tel: (415) 501 - 1380
Fax: (415) 501 - 7112
TF: (800) 872 - 5384

FAY-BUSTILLOS, Theresa
Exec. Director, Levi Strauss Foundation
Tel: (415) 501 - 6000
Fax: (415) 501 - 7112
TF: (800) 872 - 5384

LEE, Daniel
Manager, Community Affairs and Corporate Affairs
Tel: (415) 501 - 6000
Fax: (415) 501 - 7112
TF: (800) 872 - 5384

PAULENICH, Fred
Senior V. President, Worldwide Human Resources
Tel: (415) 501 - 6000
Fax: (415) 501 - 7112
TF: (800) 872 - 5384

Lexmark Internat'l, Inc.

Holding company which manufactures, develops and sells laser, inkjet, dot matrix printers and associated consumable supplies
www.lexmark.com

Chairman and Chief Exec. Officer
CURLANDER, Paul J.
Tel: (859) 232 - 2000
Fax: (859) 232 - 7529
TF: (800) 539 - 6275

Main Headquarters
Mailing: 740 W. New Circle Rd.
Lexington, KY 40550
Tel: (859) 232 - 2000
Fax: (859) 232 - 2403
TF: (800) 539 - 6275

Corporate Foundations and Giving Programs

Lexmark Internat'l Group, Inc. Contributions
Contact: Laura Voss
740 W. New Circle Rd.
Lexington, KY 40550
Tel: (859) 232 - 7551
Fax: (859) 232 - 7529
TF: (800) 539 - 6275

Annual Grant Total: $1,000,000 - $2,000,000
The company also maintains an Employee Matching Gifts Program.
Recent Recipients: Habitat for Humanity; United Way; YMCA

Public Affairs and Related Activities Personnel

At Headquarters

FITZPATRICK, Tim
V. President, Corporate Communications
Tel: (859) 232 - 2000
Fax: (859) 232 - 2403
TF: (800) 539 - 6275

SISK, Mark D.
V. President, Investor Relations
sisk@lexmark.com
Tel: (859) 232 - 5934
Fax: (859) 232 - 7529
TF: (800) 539 - 6275

STROMQUIST, Jeri
V. President, Human Resources
Tel: (859) 232 - 2000
Fax: (859) 232 - 2403
TF: (800) 539 - 6275

VOSS, Laura
Director, Community Relations
lvoss@lexmark.com
Tel: (859) 232 - 7551
Fax: (859) 232 - 7529
TF: (800) 539 - 6275
Responsibilities include corporate philanthropy and government affairs.

LG&E Energy LLC

An electric utility and gas distribution company.
www.lgeenergy.com
Annual Revenues: $2.303 billion

Main Headquarters
Mailing: P.O. Box 32010
Louisville, KY 40232-2010
Tel: (502) 627 - 2000
Fax: (502) 217 - 2654
Street: 220 W. Main St.
Louisville, KY 40202

Political Action Committees

Federal Louisville Gas & Electric Co. Political Action Committee (FEDLOUPAC)
Contact: Bruce Raque
P.O. Box 32010
Louisville, KY 40232-2010
Tel: (502) 627 - 4846
Fax: (502) 217 - 2654

Contributions to Candidates: $4,000 (01/05 - 09/05)
Democrats: $1,000; Republicans: $3,000.

Principal Recipients

SENATE DEMOCRATS

HOUSE DEMOCRATS
Chandler, Ben (KY) $1,000

SENATE REPUBLICANS

HOUSE REPUBLICANS
Lewis, Ron (KY) $1,000
Northup, Anne M. (KY) $1,000
Whitfield, Ed (KY) $1,000

Corporate Foundations and Giving Programs

LG&E Energy Foundation
Contact: Shauna Damin
P.O. Box 32010
Louisville, KY 40232-2010
Tel: (502) 627 - 2363
Fax: (502) 217 - 2654

Annual Grant Total: $1,000,000 - $2,000,000
Primary Interests: Education

Public Affairs and Related Activities Personnel

At Headquarters

DAMIN, Shauna
Grants Administrator, LG&E Foundation
Tel: (502) 627 - 2363
Fax: (502) 217 - 2654

KEELING, Chip
V. President, U.S. Communications
chip.keeling@lgeenergy.com
Tel: (502) 627 - 2502

RAQUE, Bruce
Treasurer, FEDLOUPAC
bruce.raque@lgeenergy.com
Tel: (502) 627 - 4846
Fax: (502) 217 - 2654

SHOBE, Debbie
Associate Community Relations Specialist (Louisville Gas & Electric Co.)
debbie.shobe@lgeenergy.com
Tel: (502) 627 - 4793

SIEMENS, George R., Jr.
V. President, External Affairs
george.siemens@lgeenergy.com
Tel: (502) 627 - 2323
Fax: (502) 217 - 2654

Liberty Corp.

Operations include broadcasting.
www.libertycorp.com

Chairman and Chief Exec. Officer
HIPP, W. Hayne
Tel: (864) 241 - 5400
Fax: (864) 241 - 5401

Main Headquarters
Mailing: P.O. Box 502
Greenville, SC 29602
Tel: (864) 241 - 5400
Fax: (864) 241 - 5401
Street: 135 S. Main St.
Greenville, SC 29602

Political Action Committees

Liberty Corp. Federal PAC
Contact: Sandra L. Kirkus
P.O. Box 502
Greenville, SC 29602
Tel: (864) 241 - 5400
Fax: (864) 241 - 5401

Contributions to Candidates: $3,500 (01/05 - 09/05)
Republicans: $3,500.

Principal Recipients

SENATE REPUBLICANS
DeMint, James (SC) $1,000
Graham, Lindsey (SC) $1,000

HOUSE REPUBLICANS
Inglis, Bob (SC) $1,000

Corporate Foundations and Giving Programs

Liberty Corp. Foundation
Contact: Sophia G. Vergas

Liberty Corp.

* continued from previous page

P.O. Box 502
Greenville, SC 29602
Tel: (864) 241 - 5496
Fax: (864) 241 - 5401

Annual Grant Total: $300,000 - $400,000
Geographic Preference: South Carolina
Primary Interests: Higher Education; Youth Services
Recent Recipients: Nature Conservancy; YMCA

Public Affairs and Related Activities Personnel

At Headquarters

BUNTON, Mary Anne
V. President, Human Resources
Tel: (864) 241 - 5400
Fax: (864) 241 - 5401

KIRKUS, Sandra L.
Treasurer, Libety Corp. Federal PAC
Tel: (864) 241 - 5400
Fax: (864) 241 - 5401

VERGAS, Sophia G.
Secretary, Liberty Corp. Foundation
Tel: (864) 241 - 5496
Fax: (864) 241 - 5401

Liberty Media Corp.

A cable television programming producer and distributor.
www.libertymedia.com

Chairman and Chief Exec. Officer
MALONE, John C.
Tel: (720) 875 - 5400
Fax: (720) 875 - 5401

Main Headquarters
Mailing: 12300 Liberty Blvd.
Englewood, CO 80112
Tel: (720) 875 - 5400
Fax: (720) 875 - 5401

Public Affairs and Related Activities Personnel

At Headquarters

BENNETT, Robert R.
President
Tel: (720) 875 - 5400
Fax: (720) 875 - 5401

ERICKSON, Michael
V. President, Investor Relations and Media Relations
Tel: (875) 875 - 5400
Fax: (720) 875 - 5445

Liberty Mutual Insurance Co.

A member of the Public Affairs Council. Fire, marine and casualty insurance.
www.libertymutual.com

Chairman, President, and Chief Exec. Officer
KELLY, Edmund F.
Tel: (617) 357 - 9500
Fax: (617) 350 - 7648

Main Headquarters
Mailing: 175 Berkeley St.
Boston, MA 02116
Tel: (617) 357 - 9500
Fax: (617) 350 - 7648

Washington Office
Mailing: 1730 Rhode Island Ave. NW
Suite 406
Washington, DC 20036
Tel: (202) 775 - 0445
Fax: (202) 775 - 0874

Political Action Committees

Liberty Mutual Insurance Co. Political Action Committee
Contact: Laurence H.S. Yahia
175 Berkeley St.
Boston, MA 02116
Tel: (617) 357 - 9500
Fax: (617) 350 - 7648

Contributions to Candidates: $78,000 (01/05 - 09/05)
Democrats: $38,500; Republicans: $39,500.

Principal Recipients

SENATE DEMOCRATS

Kennedy, Ted (MA)	$5,000
Carper, Thomas R (DE)	$3,500
Nelson, Benjamin (NE)	$3,000

HOUSE DEMOCRATS

Lynch, Stephen (MA)	$2,500
Neal, Richard E Mr. (MA)	$2,500
Hoyer, Steny (MD)	$2,000
Matheson, James (UT)	$2,000
Moore, Dennis (KS)	$2,000

SENATE REPUBLICANS

Smith, Gordon (OR)	$3,000
Cornyn, John (TX)	$2,500

HOUSE REPUBLICANS

Baker, Hugh (LA)	$5,000
Bradley, Joseph (NH)	$3,500
Oxley, Michael (OH)	$3,000
DeLay, Tom (TX)	$2,500
Gerlach, Jim (PA)	$2,000
McHenry, Patrick (NC)	$2,000
Renzi, Richard (AZ)	$2,000

Corporate Foundations and Giving Programs

Liberty Mutual Group Contributions Program
Contact: Paul Mattera
175 Berkeley St.
Boston, MA 02116
Tel: (617) 574 - 5679
Fax: (617) 350 - 7648

Annual Grant Total: $2,000,000 - $5,000,000
Geographic Preference: Area in which the company is headquartered; National
Primary Interests: Economic Development; Education; Health; Persons with Disabilities; Safety; Youth Services
Recent Recipients: Howard University; Students Against Destructive Decisions

Public Affairs and Related Activities Personnel

At Headquarters

ANGEVINE, Richard
Senior Public Relations Specialist
richard.angevine@libertymutual.com
Tel: (617) 574 - 6638
Fax: (617) 350 - 7648

ARMSTRONG, Jack
Assistant V. President
Tel: (617) 357 - 9500
Fax: (617) 350 - 7648

COYLE, Matthew T.
V. President and Director, Investor Relations
Tel: (617) 654 - 3331
Fax: (617) 350 - 7648

CUSOLITO, John
V. President and Manager, External Relations
john.cusolito@libertymutual.com
Tel: (617) 574 - 5512
Fax: (617) 350 - 7648

GREENBERG, Glenn
Consultant, Public Relations
glenn.greenberg@libertymutual.com
Tel: (617) 574 - 5874
Fax: (617) 350 - 7648

KAUFMAN, Adrianne
Senior Public Relations Specialist
adrianne.kaufman@libertymutual.com
Tel: (617) 574 - 5983
Fax: (617) 350 - 7648

MATTERA, Paul
Senior V. President and Chief Public Affairs Officer
Mailstop: MS 07E
Tel: (617) 574 - 5679
Fax: (617) 350 - 7648

MCCARTHY, Kathleen
Public Affairs Associate
kathleen.mccarthy@libertymutual.com
Tel: (617) 654 - 3022
Fax: (617) 350 - 7648

MUELLER, Carl
Manager, Internal Communications
Tel: (617) 357 - 9500
Fax: (617) 350 - 7648

MURPHY, John P.
Legislative Counsel
Tel: (617) 357 - 9500
Fax: (617) 350 - 7648

SAYLES, Helen E. R.
Senior V. President, Human Resources and Administration
Tel: (617) 357 - 9500
Fax: (617) 350 - 7648

YAHIA, Laurence H.S.
Pac Treasurer
Tel: (617) 357 - 9500
Fax: (617) 350 - 7648

At Washington Office

BENNETT, Douglas F.
V. President, Federal Affairs
douglas.bennett@libertymutual.com
Tel: (202) 775 - 0445
Fax: (202) 775 - 0874

Liberty Northwest Insurance Corp.

See listing on page 293 under Liberty Mutual Insurance Co.

The Lifetime Healthcare Companies

Formerly known as Excellus, Inc.
www.excellusbcbs.com
Annual Revenues: $4 billion

Chairman of the Board
KURNATH, Joseph F., M.D.
Tel: (585) 454 - 1700
Fax: (585) 238 - 4233

Chief Exec. Officer
KLEIN, David H.
Tel: (585) 454 - 1700
Fax: (585) 238 - 4233

Main Headquarters
Mailing: 165 Court St.
Rochester, NY 14647
Tel: (585) 454 - 1700
Fax: (585) 238 - 4233

Public Affairs and Related Activities Personnel

At Headquarters

MACK, David J.
Senior V. President, Corporate Affairs
Tel: (585) 454 - 1700
Fax: (585) 238 - 4233

NANGREAVE, Richard
V. President, Human Resources
Tel: (585) 454 - 1700
Fax: (585) 238 - 4233

PUCHALSKI, Philip J.
Corporate V. President, Corporate Communications
Tel: (585) 238 - 4367
Fax: (585) 238 - 4233

REDMOND, James
Regional V. President, Communications
Tel: (585) 238 - 4579
Fax: (585) 238 - 4233

TAYLOR, Geoffrey E.
Senior V. President, Corporate Communications
Tel: (585) 454 - 1700
Fax: (585) 238 - 4233

Eli Lilly and Company

A global research-based pharmaceutical corporation that works with customers to ensure disease prevention, management and cure.
www.lilly.com
Annual Revenues: $11.542 billion

Chairman, President and Chief Exec. Officer
TAUREL, Sidney
Tel: (317) 276 - 2000
Fax: (317) 277 - 6579

Main Headquarters
Mailing: Lilly Corporate Center
Indianapolis, IN 46285
Tel: (317) 276 - 2000
Fax: (317) 277 - 6579
TF: (800) 545 - 5979

Eli Lilly and Company

** continued from previous page*

Washington Office

Contact: Joseph B. Kelley
Mailing: 555 12th St. NW
Suite 650
Washington, DC 20004-1205
Tel: (202) 393 - 7950
Fax: (202) 393 - 7960

Political Action Committees

Eli Lilly and Company PAC
Contact: James Davlin
Lilly Corporate Center
Indianapolis, IN 46285
Tel: (317) 276 - 2000
Fax: (317) 277 - 6579

Contributions to Candidates: $117,500 (01/05 - 09/05)
Democrats: $26,500; Republicans: $91,000.

Principal Recipients

SENATE DEMOCRATS
Ford, Harold E Jr (TN) $5,000

HOUSE DEMOCRATS

SENATE REPUBLICANS
Smith, Gordon (OR) $8,000
Kyl, Jon L (AZ) $5,000
Lugar, Richard G (IN) $5,000
Santorum, Richard (PA) $3,500

HOUSE REPUBLICANS
Johnson, Nancy (CT) $5,000
Barton, Joe L (TX) $3,500

Corporate Foundations and Giving Programs

Eli Lilly and Company Foundation
Contact: Thomas A. King
Lilly Corporate Center
Indianapolis, IN 46285
Tel: (317) 276 - 2000
Fax: (317) 277 - 6579

Annual Grant Total: over $5,000,000
Unsolicited requests are not accepted.
Geographic Preference: Area in which the company is headquartered
Primary Interests: Adult Education and Training; Arts and Humanities; Social Services
Recent Recipients: American Diabetes Ass'n; Nat'l Mental Health Ass'n; United Way

Public Affairs and Related Activities Personnel

At Headquarters

DAVLIN, James
PAC Treasurer
Tel: (317) 276 - 2000
Fax: (317) 277 - 6579

FRANSON, Timothy
V. President, Global Regulatory Affairs
Tel: (317) 276 - 2000
Fax: (317) 277 - 6579

FRISS, Karen
Director, Public Policy Planning and Development
Tel: (317) 276 - 2000
Fax: (317) 277 - 6579

KING, Thomas A.
Manager, Community Relations; President, Foundation
Tel: (317) 276 - 2000
Fax: (317) 277 - 6579

NOBLES, Anne
V. President, Corporate Affairs
Tel: (317) 276 - 2000
Fax: (317) 277 - 6579

SANTINI, Gino
Senior V. President, Corporate Strategy and Policy
Tel: (317) 276 - 2000
Fax: (317) 277 - 6579

SMITH, Robert
Director, Corporate Communications/Public Affairs
Tel: (317) 276 - 2000
Fax: (317) 277 - 6579

STEMME, Brian
Government Relations Associate
Tel: (317) 276 - 2000
Fax: (317) 277 - 6579

At Washington Office

ALVAREZ, Kira
Manager, International and Public Government Relations
Registered Federal Lobbyist.
Tel: (202) 393 - 7950
Fax: (202) 393 - 7960

BEAL, Chris
Manager, State Advocacy
Tel: (202) 393 - 7950
Fax: (202) 393 - 7960

BEAULIEU, Jennifer
Manager, Advocacy Relations
Tel: (202) 393 - 7950
Fax: (202) 393 - 7960

BONITT, John E.
Director, Federal Affairs
Registered Federal Lobbyist.
Tel: (202) 393 - 7950
Fax: (202) 393 - 7960

BRAYSHAW, Francis
Senior Government Affairs Associate
Registered Federal Lobbyist.
Tel: (202) 393 - 7950
Fax: (202) 393 - 7960

BRIGGS, Kern
Senior Associate, International and Public Government Relations
Tel: (202) 393 - 7950
Fax: (202) 393 - 7960

BURGESS, Chaka
Senior Associate, Federal Affairs
Registered Federal Lobbyist.
Tel: (202) 393 - 7950
Fax: (202) 393 - 7960

COOK, Harrison
Manager, International and Public Government Relations
Tel: (202) 393 - 7950
Fax: (202) 393 - 7960

FILIPPONE, Desiree
Manager, International and Public Government Relations
Registered Federal Lobbyist.
Tel: (202) 393 - 7950
Fax: (202) 393 - 7960

GUERRIERO, Chuck
Manager, Advocacy Relations
Tel: (202) 393 - 7950
Fax: (202) 393 - 7960

HUNTINGTON, Erin B.
Manager, International and Public Government Relations
Registered Federal Lobbyist.
Tel: (202) 393 - 7950
Fax: (202) 393 - 7960

KAROL, Kathryn Dickey
Director, International and Public Government Affairs
Registered Federal Lobbyist.
Tel: (202) 393 - 7950
Fax: (202) 393 - 7960

KELLEY, Joseph B.
V. President, Government Relations and Public Affairs
Tel: (202) 393 - 7950
Fax: (202) 393 - 7960

MIHALSKI, Edmund J.
Director, Federal Affairs
Registered Federal Lobbyist.
Tel: (202) 393 - 7950
Fax: (202) 393 - 7960

RUBIN, Elizabeth
Senior Associate, Advocacy Relations
Tel: (202) 393 - 7950
Fax: (202) 393 - 7960

SOTAK, Sonya D.
Manager, Government Affairs
Tel: (202) 393 - 7950
Fax: (202) 393 - 7960

WALLACE, Tom
Director, U.S. Advocacy
Tel: (202) 393 - 7950
Fax: (202) 393 - 7960

The Limited Brands

PUBLIC AFFAIRS COUNCIL

A member of the Public Affairs Council. An international specialty fashion retailer. Stores include Express, Victoria's Secret, and Bath and Body Works, among others.
www.limited.com

Chairman and Chief Exec. Officer
WEXNER, Leslie
Tel: (614) 415 - 7000
Fax: (614) 415 - 7079

Main Headquarters
Mailing: Three Limited Pkwy.
Columbus, OH 43230
Tel: (614) 415 - 7000
Fax: (614) 415 - 7079

Political Action Committees

Limited Brands Political Action Committee
Contact: Theodore Adams
Three Limited Pkwy.
Columbus, OH 43230
Tel: (614) 415 - 7078
Fax: (614) 415 - 7079

Contributions to Candidates: $86,500 (01/05 - 09/05)
Democrats: $23,500; Republicans: $63,000.

Principal Recipients

SENATE DEMOCRATS
Clinton, Hillary Rodham (NY) $10,000
Bayh, Evan (IN) $5,000

HOUSE DEMOCRATS
Boucher, Fredrick (VA) $5,000

SENATE REPUBLICANS
Hatch, Orrin (UT) $10,000
Dewine, Richard (OH) $7,500
Allen, George (VA) $5,000

HOUSE REPUBLICANS
Boehner, John (OH) $5,000
Goodlatte, Robert (VA) $5,000
Hobson, David (OH) $5,000
Pryce, Deborah (OH) $5,000
Tiberi, Patrick (OH) $5,000

Corporate Foundations and Giving Programs

The Limited Brands Corporate Contributions Program
Three Limited Pkwy.
Columbus, OH 43230
Tel: (614) 415 - 7000
Fax: (614) 415 - 7079

Annual Grant Total: over $5,000,000
Geographic Preference: Area in which the company is headquartered

Public Affairs and Related Activities Personnel

At Headquarters

ADAMS, Theodore
Director, Government Affairs
Responsibilities also include political action.
Tel: (614) 415 - 7078
Fax: (614) 415 - 7079

HEBRON, Anthony
V. President, External Communications
Tel: (614) 415 - 7072
Fax: (614) 415 - 1144

KATZENMEYER, Tom
V. President, Investor Relations
Tel: (614) 415 - 7000
Fax: (614) 415 - 7079

SCHMALTZ, Heather Dahlberg
Government Affairs Manager
Tel: (614) 415 - 7282
Fax: (614) 415 - 7080

Limited Inc., The

See listing on page 294 under The Limited Brands.

Limited, Too

See listing on page 477 under Too, Inc.

Lincoln Electric Holdings, Inc.

A manufacturer of arc welding and cutting products.
www.lincolnelectric.com
Annual Revenues: $1.04 million

Chairman and Chief Exec. Officer
STROPKI, John M., Jr. — Tel: (216) 481 - 8100; Fax: (216) 486 - 1751

Main Headquarters
Mailing: 22801 St. Clair Ave.
Cleveland, OH 44117-1199 — Tel: (216) 481 - 8100; Fax: (216) 486 - 1751

Corporate Foundations and Giving Programs

Lincoln Electric Foundation
Contact: Roy L. Morrow
22801 St. Clair Ave.
Cleveland, OH 44117-1199 — Tel: (216) 383 - 4893; Fax: (216) 383 - 8220

Annual Grant Total: $500,000 - $750,000
Geographic Preference: Ohio
Primary Interests: Health; Higher Education
Recent Recipients: Case Western Reserve University; Cleveland Clinic Foundation; United Way

Public Affairs and Related Activities Personnel

At Headquarters

FARRELL, Gretchen — Tel: (216) 481 - 8100; Fax: (216) 486 - 1751
V. President, Human Resources
gretchen_farrell@lincolnelectric.com

MORROW, Roy L. — Tel: (216) 383 - 4893; Fax: (216) 383 - 8220
Director, Corporate Relations
Roy_Morrow@lincolnelectric.com
Responsibilities include corporate philanthropy, public relations, and investor relations.

STUEBER, Frederick — Tel: (216) 481 - 8100; Fax: (216) 486 - 1751
Senior V. President, Secretary and General Counsel
Serves as the Senior Public Affairs Exec. at headquarters.

Lincoln Financial Group

A member of the Public Affairs Council. An insurance and financial services holding company. The company is also known by the name Lincoln Nat'l Corp. In October of 2005, the company announced plans to merge with Jefferson-Pilot Corp. (see separate listing). Completion of the merger is expected in the first quarter of 2006.
www.lfg.com

Chairman and Chief Exec. Officer
BOSCIA, Jon A. — Tel: (215) 448 - 1400; TF: (877) 275 - 5462

Main Headquarters
Mailing: Centre Square, West Tower
1500 Market St., Suite 3900
Philadelphia, PA 19102-2112 — Tel: (215) 448 - 1400; Fax: (215) 448 - 3962; TF: (877) 275 - 5462

Washington Office
Contact: James A. Morrill
Mailing: 1455 Pennsylvania Ave., N.W., Suite 1260
Washington, DC 20004 — Tel: (202) 783 - 0350; Fax: (202) 783 - 3332

Political Action Committees

Lincoln Nat'l Corp. Political Action Committee
Contact: Fred Crawford
1300 S. Clinton St.
Fort Wayne, IN 46801-8863

Contributions to Candidates: $47,500 (01/05 - 09/05)
Democrats: $16,000; Republicans: $31,500.

Principal Recipients

SENATE DEMOCRATS		HOUSE DEMOCRATS	
		Pomeroy, Earl (ND)	$2,000
SENATE REPUBLICANS		**HOUSE REPUBLICANS**	
Lugar, Richard G (IN)	$2,000	Thomas, William M (CA)	$2,500
Santorum, Richard (PA)	$2,000	Chocola, Christopher (IN)	$2,000
Snowe, Olympia (ME)	$2,000		

Corporate Foundations and Giving Programs

Lincoln Nat'l Foundation, Inc.
Centre Square, West Tower
1500 Market St., Suite 3900
Philadelphia, PA 19102-2112 — Tel: (215) 448 - 1400; Fax: (215) 448 - 3962; TF: (877) 275 - 5462

Annual Grant Total: over $5,000,000
Guidelines are available.
Geographic Preference: Area(s) in which the company operates; Portland, ME; Fort Wayne, IN; Schaumburg, IL; Syracuse, NY; Philadelphia, PA; Hartford, CT
Primary Interests: Arts and Culture; Education; Human Welfare
Recent Recipients: Big Brothers/Big Sisters; United Way; YMCA; YWCA

Public Affairs and Related Activities Personnel

At Headquarters

BROWN, Priscilla — Tel: (215) 448 - 1422; Fax: (215) 448 - 3962; TF: (877) 275 - 5462
V. President and Director, Investor Relations

FLEENER, Rob — Tel: (215) 448 - 1400; Fax: (215) 448 - 3962; TF: (877) 275 - 5462
Media Contact

MONGAN, Adrienne — Tel: (215) 448 - 1400; Fax: (215) 448 - 3962; TF: (877) 275 - 5462
Manager, Strategic Communications
amongan@lfg.com

SEGAL, Susan A. — Tel: (215) 448 - 1400; Fax: (215) 448 - 3962; TF: (877) 275 - 5462
Charitable Giving Contact (Philadelphia, PA)
sasegal@lfg.com

At Washington Office

MORRILL, James A. — Tel: (202) 783 - 0350; Fax: (202) 783 - 3332
V. President and Director, Federal Relations, Legislative and Regulatory Management
Registered Federal Lobbyist.

At Other Offices

CRAWFORD, Fred
PAC Treasurer
1300 S. Clinton St.
Fort Wayne, IN 46801-8863

CURRAN, Lisa M.
Charitable Giving Contact (Hartford, CT)
350 Church St.
Mailstop: M/S I1
Hartford, CT 06103-1106
lmcurran@lnc.com

FORKEL, Vicki — Tel: (847) 466 - 8585
Charitable Giving Contact (Schaumburg, IL)
P.O. Box 4011
Schaumburg, IL 60168-4011
vforkel@lnc.com

KEMMISH, Sandra — Tel: (260) 455 - 389
Charitable Giving Contact (Fort Wayne, IN)
1300 S. Clinton St.
Fort Wayne, IN 46801-8863
skemmish@lnc.com

RAHN, Stephen E. — Tel: (260) 455 - 3140
V. President and Associate General Director, State Relations
(Lincoln Nat'l Life Insurance Co., The)
1300 S. Clinton St.
Fort Wayne, IN 46801-8863

TIELINEN, Roberta — Tel: (207) 842 - 9461
Charitable Giving Contact (Portland, ME)
P.O. Box 9740
Portland, ME 04104-5001
rtielinen@lnc.com

Lincoln Nat'l Corp.

See listing on page 295 under Lincoln Financial Group.

Lincoln Nat'l Life Insurance Co., The

See listing on page 295 under Lincoln Financial Group.

Liquid Air Corp.

See listing on page 13 under Air Liquide America Corp.

Little Caesar Enterprises

Carryout and delivery pizza chain. A subsidiary of Ilitch Holdings, Inc.
www.littlecaesars.com

Chairman and Chief Exec. Officer
ILTCH, Michael — Tel: (313) 983 - 6000; Fax: (313) 983 - 6197

Main Headquarters
Mailing: Fox Office Center
2211 Woodward Ave.
Detroit, MI 48201-3400 — Tel: (313) 983 - 6000; Fax: (313) 983 - 6390

Public Affairs and Related Activities Personnel

At Headquarters

BURGESS, Laura — Tel: (313) 983 - 6000; Fax: (313) 983 - 6197
Coordinator, Corporate Communications and Public Affairs

NELSON, Joanie — Tel: (313) 983 - 6000; Fax: (313) 983 - 6390
V. President, Human Resources

SCRIVANO, David — Tel: (313) 983 - 6000; Fax: (313) 983 - 6390
President

Litton Industries, Inc.

See listing on page 353 under Northrop Grumman Corp.

Litton PRC Inc.

See listing on page 353 under Northrop Grumman Corp.

Liz Claiborne Inc.

A designer and marketer of fashion apparel and accessories.
www.lizclaiborne.com

Chairman and Chief Exec. Officer
CHARRON, Paul R. — Tel: (212) 354 - 4900 Fax: (212) 626 - 3416

Main Headquarters
Mailing: 1441 Broadway
New York, NY 10018 — Tel: (212) 354 - 4900 Fax: (212) 626 - 3416

Corporate Foundations and Giving Programs

Liz Claiborne Foundation
Contact: Melanie Lyons
1440 Broadway
New York, NY 10018 — Tel: (212) 626 - 5704 Fax: (212) 626 - 5304

Annual Grant Total: $1,000,000 - $2,000,000
Geographic Preference: New Jersey; New York City; Alabama; Massachusetts; Los Angeles, CA
Primary Interests: Child Abuse and Neglect Prevention; Economic Development; Women
Recent Recipients: Girls Incorporated; Montgomery AIDS Outreach; New Destiny Housing Corp.; Women at Risk

Public Affairs and Related Activities Personnel

At Headquarters

VILL, Robert J.
Treasurer and V. President, Investor Relations — Tel: (212) 354 - 4900 Fax: (212) 626 - 3416

At Other Offices

KARP, Roberta
Senior V. President, Corporate Affairs, and General Counsel
1441 Broadway
New York, NY 10018 — Tel: (212) 625 - 3408

LYONS, Melanie
Foundation Contact
1440 Broadway
New York, NY 10018 — Tel: (212) 626 - 5704 Fax: (212) 626 - 5304

RANDEL, Jane
V. President, Public Relations
1441 Broadway
New York, NY 10018 — Tel: (212) 625 - 3408 Fax: (212) 626 - 5813

STAMBAUGH, Dana
Media Contact
1441 Broadway
New York, NY 10018 — Tel: (212) 626 - 3491

Lockheed Martin Aeronautics Co.

A subsidiary of Lockheed Martin Corp. (see separate lising).
www.lmaeronautics.com

Main Headquarters
Mailing: P.O. Box 748
Fort Worth, TX 76101 — Tel: (817) 777 - 2000 Fax: (817) 777 - 2115

Corporate Foundations and Giving Programs

Lockheed Martin Aeronautics Community Relations Program
Contact: Norman B. Robbins
P.O. Box 748
Fort Worth, TX 76101 — Tel: (817) 777 - 8294 Fax: (817) 777 - 2115

Annual Grant Total: none reported
Geographic Preference: Area(s) in which the company operates
Primary Interests: Education; Engineering; Human Welfare; Hunger

Public Affairs and Related Activities Personnel

At Headquarters

FOX, Eric V.
Director, Government Relations
eric.v.fox@lmcoc.com — Tel: (817) 777 - 8585 Fax: (817) 777 - 2115

POLIDORE, Mary Jo
V. President, Communications
mary.jo.polidore@lmco.com — Tel: (817) 777 - 6736 Fax: (817) 777 - 2115

ROBBINS, Norman B.
Manager, Community Relations — Tel: (817) 777 - 8294 Fax: (817) 777 - 2115

STOUT, Joe W.
Director, Communications
joe.w.stout@lmco.com — Tel: (817) 763 - 4086 Fax: (817) 777 - 2115

At Other Offices

GRIZZLE, Sam
Director, Program Communications and Trade Relations
86 S. Cobb Dr.
Marietta, GA 30063-0226 — Tel: (770) 494 - 3211 Fax: (770) 494 - 0146

JOHNSTONE, Brian
Director, Public Affairs
86 S. Cobb Dr.
Marietta, GA 30063-0226
brian.johnstone@lmco.com — Tel: (770) 494 - 4124 Fax: (770) 494 - 0146

Lockheed Martin Corp.

A member of the Public Affairs Council. Formed in 1995 by the merger of Lockheed Corp. (Calabasas, CA) and Martin Marietta Corporation (Bethesda, MD).
www.lockheedmartin.com
Annual Revenues: $23.99 billion

President, Chief Exec. Officer, and Chairman of the Board
STEVENS, Robert J. — Tel: (301) 897 - 6000 Fax: (301) 897 - 6083

Main Headquarters
Mailing: 6801 Rockledge Dr.
Bethesda, MD 20817-1877 — Tel: (301) 897 - 6000 Fax: (301) 897 - 6083

Washington Office
Mailing: 1550 Crystal Dr.
Crystal Square 2, Suite 300
Arlington, VA 22202 — Tel: (703) 413 - 5601 Fax: (703) 413 - 5636

Political Action Committees

Lockheed Martin Employees Political Action Committee
Contact: Zach Sherman
1550 Crystal Dr.
Crystal Square 2, Suite 300
Arlington, VA 22202 — Tel: (703) 413 - 5915 Fax: (703) 413 - 5636

Contributions to Candidates: $380,560 (01/05 - 09/05)
Democrats: $151,810; Republicans: $220,750; Other: $8,000.

Principal Recipients

SENATE DEMOCRATS
Bingaman, Jeff (NM) $5,000
Clinton, Hillary Rodham (NY) $5,000
Conrad, Kent (ND) $5,000

HOUSE DEMOCRATS
Murtha, John P Mr. (PA) $10,000
Skelton, Ike (MO) $10,000
Thompson, Mike (CA) $10,000
Meek, Kendrick (FL) $5,778
Edwards, Chet (TX) $5,000
Harman, Jane (CA) $5,000
Visclosky, Peter (IN) $5,000

HOUSE OTHER
Peterson, Collin (MN) $5,000

SENATE REPUBLICANS
Lugar, Richard G (IN) $10,000
Hatch, Orrin (UT) $5,000
Kyl, Jon L (AZ) $5,000

HOUSE REPUBLICANS
Bonilla, Henry (TX) $10,000
Young, Don E (AK) $7,000
Burton, Danny (IN) $6,000
Gibbons, James A (NV) $6,000
Granger, Kay N (TX) $5,000
Hobson, David (OH) $5,000
Hoekstra, Peter (MI) $5,000
Sherwood, Donald L (PA) $5,000
Wilson, Heather (NM) $5,000
Cox, Christopher (CA) $2,000

Corporate Foundations and Giving Programs

Lockheed Martin Foundation
Contact: David E. Phillips
6801 Rockledge Dr.
Bethesda, MD 20817-1877 — Tel: (301) 897 - 6292 Fax: (301) 897 - 6252

Annual Grant Total: none reported

Public Affairs and Related Activities Personnel

At Headquarters

BOXX, Dennis R.
V. President, Corporate Communications — Tel: (301) 897 - 6543 Fax: (301) 897 - 6252

DISKON, Ken
Senior V. President, Human Resources — Tel: (301) 897 - 6950 Fax: (301) 897 - 6758

GABALY, Mike
Director, Investor Relations — Tel: (301) 897 - 6455 Fax: (301) 897 - 6919

JURKOWSKY, Tom
V. President, Media Relations — Tel: (301) 897 - 6352 Fax: (301) 897 - 6289

PHILLIPS, David E.
Manager, Lockheed Martin Foundation
david.phillips@lmco.com — Tel: (301) 897 - 6292 Fax: (301) 897 - 6252

RYAN, James R.
V. President, Investor Relations — Tel: (301) 897 - 6584 Fax: (301) 897 - 6919

RYMER, Gail
Director, Corporate Affairs — Tel: (301) 897 - 6293 Fax: (301) 897 - 6252
Responsibilities include corporate philanthropy.

Lockheed Martin Corp.

* continued from previous page

VASAN, Regina M. "Jenny"
V. President, Management Communications
Tel: (301) 897 - 6290
Fax: (301) 897 - 6252

WHITNEY, Lee
V. President, Strategy and Marketing Communications
Tel: (301) 897 - 6121
Fax: (301) 897 - 6289

At Washington Office

CHAUDET, Stephen E.
V. President, State and Local Government Affairs and PAC Treasurer
Tel: (703) 413 - 5996
Fax: (703) 413 - 5846

CORTESE, Steve
V. President, Policy and Budget
Tel: (703) 413 - 5681
Fax: (703) 413 - 5744

DAHLBERG, Gregory
V. President, Legislative Affairs
Tel: (703) 413 - 5632
Fax: (703) 413 - 5846

DESMOND, James M.
V. President, Energy Sector Legislation
Registered Federal Lobbyist.
Tel: (703) 413 - 5721
Fax: (703) 413 - 5846

DUNCAN, Lawrence, III
V. President, Congressional Relations, Trade and Regulatory Affairs
Tel: (703) 413 - 5855
Fax: (703) 413 - 5617

FORTIER, Alison
V. President, Space and Strategic Missile Legislative Affairs
Tel: (703) 413 - 5979
Fax: (703) 413 - 5617

HANSEN, William
V.P., Army Programs, Civil Agencies SI, & Tech. Serv.
Tel: (703) 413 - 5601
Fax: (703) 413 - 5636

HARVEY, Gerald
V. President, Legislative Affairs, Technology Services
Tel: (703) 413 - 5859
Fax: (703) 413 - 5749

HERMANDORFER, Wayne
Director, Aeronautical Legislative Affairs
wayne.hermandorfer@lmco.com
Registered Federal Lobbyist.
Tel: (703) 413 - 5777
Fax: (703) 413 - 5617

INGLEE, William
V. President, Legislative Affairs
Registered Federal Lobbyist.
Tel: (703) 413 - 5984
Fax: (703) 413 - 5617

KIRTMAN, Deanna M.
Director, Legislative Affairs, Navy Programs
Registered Federal Lobbyist.
Tel: (703) 413 - 5911
Fax: (703) 413 - 5888

MALONE, Harry
Director, Legislative Affairs, Army Programs
harry.malone@lmco.com
Registered Federal Lobbyist.
Tel: (703) 413 - 5753
Fax: (703) 413 - 5617

MARAGHY, Susan
V. President, Homeland Security and Information Technology
Tel: (703) 413 - 5601
Fax: (703) 413 - 5636

MAYNARD, Ray
Director, Legislative Affairs, Space Systems
Tel: (703) 413 - 5607
Fax: (703) 413 - 5636

MCCLEAN, Scott D.
Director, Aeronautical Legislative Affairs
scott.mcclean@lmco.com
Registered Federal Lobbyist.
Tel: (703) 413 - 5955
Fax: (703) 413 - 5617

MITCHELL, Mike
Tel: (703) 413 - 5601
Fax: (703) 413 - 5636

MUSARRA, Gerald
V. President, Trade and Regulatory Affairs
Tel: (703) 413 - 5791
Fax: (703) 413 - 5908

OVERSTREET, Jack C.
V. President, Aeronautical Legislative Affairs
Registered Federal Lobbyist.
Tel: (703) 413 - 5634
Fax: (703) 413 - 5737

ROBBINS, Michelle E.
Director, Space Legislative Affairs, NASA Programs
Registered Federal Lobbyist.
Tel: (703) 413 - 5612
Fax: (703) 413 - 5819

SAUER, Ann E.
V. President, Navy, Marine Corps, Coast Guard and Air Force, SI Programs
Tel: (703) 413 - 5601
Fax: (703) 413 - 5636

SCHLEGEL, Nancy
Director, International Relations and Trade
Tel: (703) 413 - 5680
Fax: (703) 413 - 5908

SHERMAN, Zach
Political Programs Manager, Lockheed Martin Employees Political Action Committee
Tel: (703) 413 - 5915
Fax: (703) 413 - 5636

WALTERS, Gregory
Tel: (703) 413 - 5601
Fax: (703) 413 - 5636

WILDFONG, John
V. President, Fixed Wing Aviation
Tel: (703) 413 - 5601
Fax: (703) 413 - 5636

Lockheed Martin Electronics & Missiles

See listing on page 296 under Lockheed Martin Corp.

Lockheed Martin Skunk Works

See listing on page 296 under Lockheed Martin Aeronautics Co.

Lockheed Martin Space Systems Company

A subsidiary of Lockheed Martin Corp. (see separate listing). More information about Lockheed Martin Space Systems Company can be found on their parent company's website: www.lockheedmartin.com.

Main Headquarters

Mailing: 1111 Lockheed Martin Way
Bldg. 157
Sunnyvale, CA 94089
Tel: (408) 742 - 4321
Fax: (408) 743 - 2239

Corporate Foundations and Giving Programs

Lockheed Martin Missiles and Space Corporate Contributions Program
Contact: Leslie Murdock
1111 Lockheed Martin Way
Bldg. 157
Sunnyvale, CA 94089
Tel: (408) 742 - 5605
Fax: (408) 743 - 2239

Annual Grant Total: none reported

Public Affairs and Related Activities Personnel

At Headquarters

MURDOCK, Leslie
Manager, Community Relations
Tel: (408) 742 - 5605
Fax: (408) 743 - 2239

WRATHER, Janet V.
V. President, Communications
janet.wrather@lmco.com
Tel: (408) 742 - 6688
Fax: (408) 743 - 2239

Loews Corporation

A diversified financial holding company involved in hotels, tobacco, insurance, watches and clocks, oil drilling fleets, and gas pipelines.

www.loews.com
Annual Revenues: $17.495 billion

Chairman of the Board
TISCH, Preston Robert
btisch@loews.com
Tel: (212) 521 - 2000
Fax: (212) 521 - 2416

President and Chief Exec. Officer
TISCH, James S.
Tel: (212) 521 - 2000
Fax: (212) 521 - 2416

Main Headquarters

Mailing: 667 Madison Ave.
New York, NY 10021-8087
Tel: (212) 521 - 2000
Fax: (212) 521 - 2525

Corporate Foundations and Giving Programs

Loews Foundation
Contact: Candace Leeds
667 Madison Ave.
New York, NY 10021-8087
Tel: (212) 521 - 2416
Fax: (212) 521 - 2860

Annual Grant Total: $2,000,000 - $5,000,000
The Foundation does not emphasize any particular field of interest.
Geographic Preference: No geographical restrictions
Recent Recipients: Gay Men's Health Crisis; Meals on Wheels; United Jewish Appeal

Public Affairs and Related Activities Personnel

At Headquarters

KAHN, Joshua E.
Manager, Investor Relations
jkahn@loews.com
Tel: (212) 521 - 2788
Fax: (212) 521 - 2714

KANDERS, Emily
Director, Public Relations
(Loews Hotels)
ekanders@loews.com
Tel: (212) 521 - 2833
Fax: (212) 521 - 2379

LEEDS, Candace
V. President, Public Affairs
(Loews Hotels)
cleeds@loews.com
Responsibilities include corporate communications and corporate philanthropy.
Tel: (212) 521 - 2416
Fax: (212) 521 - 2860

MOMEYER, Alan
V. President, Human Resources
amomeyer@loews.com
Tel: (212) 521 - 2500
Fax: (212) 521 - 2466

Loews Hotels

See listing on page 297 under Loews Corporation.

Lone Star Industries

See listing on page 96 under Buzzi Unicem USA.

Long Island Lighting Co.

See listing on page 279 under KeySpan Corp.

The Longaberger Co.

Manufactures and markets baskets, pottery and other crafts.

www.longaberger.com

The Longaberger Co.

* continued from previous page

President and Chief Exec. Officer
LONGABERGER, Tami — Tel: (740) 322 - 5000 Fax: (740) 322 - 5240
tlongaberger@longaberger.com

Main Headquarters
Mailing: 1500 E. Main St. Newark, OH 43055 — Tel: (740) 322 - 5000 Fax: (740) 322 - 5240

Corporate Foundations and Giving Programs

Longaberger Foundation
Contact: Rachel Longaberger
1500 E. Main St.
Newark, OH 43055 — Tel: (740) 322 - 5000 Fax: (740) 322 - 5240

Annual Grant Total: none reported

Public Affairs and Related Activities Personnel

At Headquarters

FOWLER, Bonny — Tel: (740) 322 - 5257 Fax: (740) 322 - 5240
Public Relations Representative
bfowler1@longaberger.com

LONGABERGER, Rachel — Tel: (740) 322 - 5000 Fax: (740) 322 - 5240
President, Longaberger Foundation
rlongaberger@longaberger.com

MACKEY, Rachel — Tel: (740) 322 - 5414 Fax: (740) 322 - 5240
Public Relations Representative
rmackey@longaberger.com

Longs Drug Stores Corp.

A retail drug store chain.
www.longs.com

Chairman, President and Chief Exec. Officer
BRYANT, Warren F. — Tel: (925) 937 - 1170 Fax: (925) 210 - 6886

Main Headquarters
Mailing: 141 N. Civic Dr. Walnut Creek, CA 94596 — Tel: (925) 937 - 1170 Fax: (925) 210 - 6886

Political Action Committees

Longs Drugs Good Government Committee
Contact: Steven F. McCann
141 N. Civic Dr.
Walnut Creek, CA 94596 — Tel: (925) 937 - 1170 Fax: (925) 210 - 6886

Contributions to Candidates: none reported (01/05 - 09/05)

Corporate Foundations and Giving Programs

Longs Drug Stores Community Service
Contact: Grover L. White
141 N. Civic Dr.
Walnut Creek, CA 94596 — Tel: (925) 937 - 1170 Fax: (925) 210 - 6886

Annual Grant Total: none reported
Primary Interests: Disaster Relief; Environment/Conservation; Health; Vaccinations

Public Affairs and Related Activities Personnel

At Headquarters

CHELEMEDOS, Roger — Tel: (925) 937 - 1170 Fax: (925) 210 - 6886
PAC Treasurer

MCCANN, Steven F. — Tel: (925) 937 - 1170 Fax: (925) 210 - 6886
Exec. V. President, Chief Financial Officer, and Treasurer

PROFFER, Phyllis J. — Tel: (925) 979 - 3979 Fax: (925) 210 - 6400
V. President, Investor Relations and Corporate Communications
pproffer@longs.com

WATT, Linda M. — Tel: (925) 937 - 1170 Fax: (925) 210 - 6886
Senior V. President, Human Resources
lwatt@longs.com

WHITE, Grover L. — Tel: (925) 937 - 1170 Fax: (925) 210 - 6886
Contact,Corporate Giving Program

Longview Fibre Co.

A forest and paper products company.
www.longviewfibre.com

Chairman, President and Chief Exec. Officer
WOLLENBERG, Richard H. — Tel: (360) 425 - 1550 Fax: (360) 575 - 5934

Main Headquarters
Mailing: P.O. Box 639 Longview, WA 98632 — Tel: (360) 425 - 1550 Fax: (360) 575 - 5934
Street: 300 Fibre Way Longview, WA 98632

Public Affairs and Related Activities Personnel

At Headquarters

ARKELL, Robert B. — Tel: (360) 425 - 1550 Ext: 5916 Fax: (360) 575 - 5934
Senior V. President, Industrial Relations and General Counsel

COPENHAGEN, Curt R. — Tel: (360) 425 - 1550 Ext: 5906 Fax: (360) 575 - 5934
Director, Public Affairs

Responsibilities include corporate communications, advertising, lobbying, and government affairs.

Loral Skynet

See listing on page 298 under Loral Space & Communications.

Loral Space & Communications

Formerly known as Loral Corp. A high-technology company that primarily concentrates in defense electronics, communications, and systems integration.
www.loral.com

Chairman and Chief Exec. Officer
SCHWARTZ, Bernard L. — Tel: (212) 697 - 1105 Fax: (212) 338 - 5662
bernard.schwartz@hq.loral.com

Main Headquarters
Mailing: 600 Third Ave. 36th Floor New York, NY 10016 — Tel: (212) 697 - 1105 Fax: (212) 338 - 5662

Washington Office
Contact: Steven H. Flajser
Mailing: 1421 S. Clark St. Suite 810 Arlington, VA 22202 — Tel: (703) 414 - 1040 Fax: (703) 416 - 5582

Political Action Committees

Loral Spacecom Civic Responsibility Fund
Contact: Steven H. Flajser
1421 S. Clark St.
Suite 810
Arlington, VA 22202 — Tel: (703) 414 - 1042 Fax: (703) 414 - 1071

Contributions to Candidates: $13,000 (01/05 - 09/05)
Democrats: $10,000; Republicans: $3,000.

Principal Recipients

SENATE DEMOCRATS		HOUSE DEMOCRATS	
Mikulski, Barbara (MD)	$1,000	Harman, Jane (CA)	$3,000
		Eshoo, Anna (CA)	$1,500
		Dicks, Norm D (WA)	$1,000
		Lantos, Tom (CA)	$1,000
		Mollohan, Alan (WV)	$1,000
SENATE REPUBLICANS		**HOUSE REPUBLICANS**	
Burns, Conrad (MT)	$1,000	Calvert, Ken (CA)	$1,000
		Weldon, David (FL)	$1,000

Corporate Foundations and Giving Programs

Loral Space & Communications Giving Program
Contact: Bernard L. Schwartz
600 Third Ave.
36th Floor
New York, NY 10016 — Tel: (212) 697 - 1105 Fax: (212) 338 - 5662

Annual Grant Total: none reported

Public Affairs and Related Activities Personnel

At Headquarters

CLONAN, Jeanette H. — Tel: (212) 697 - 1105 Fax: (212) 338 - 5662
V. President, Communications and Investor Relations

MCCARTHY, John — Tel: (212) 697 - 1105 Fax: (212) 338 - 5662
Director, Communications

At Washington Office

ATLAS, Laurence D. — Tel: (703) 414 - 1057 Fax: (703) 414 - 1079
V. President, Government Relations and Telecommunications
Registered Federal Lobbyist.

FLAJSER, Steven H. — Tel: (703) 414 - 1042 Fax: (703) 414 - 1071
V. President, Corporate Legislative Relations
Registered Federal Lobbyist.

At Other Offices

BERNSTEIN, Victor — Tel: (908) 470 - 2300 Fax: (908) 470 - 2452
V. President, Government Relations and Legal (Loral Skynet)
500 Hills Dr.
P.O. Box 752
Bedminster, NJ 07921

LORD Corporation

Designs, manufactures and markets devices and systems to manage mechanical motion and control noise and vibration; formulates, produces and sells general purpose and specialty adhesives and coatings; and develops products and systems utilizing magnetically responsive technologies.

www.lord.com
Annual Revenues: $500 million

Chairman of the Board
BUCKLER, Dr. Sheldon A. Tel: (919) 468 - 5979 Fax: (919) 469 - 5777

President and Chief Exec. Officer
MCNEEL, Richard L. Tel: (919) 468 - 5979 Fax: (919) 469 - 5777

Main Headquarters
Mailing: 111 Lord Dr.
Cary, NC 27511 Tel: (919) 468 - 5979 Fax: (919) 469 - 5777

Corporate Foundations and Giving Programs

Lord Corporate Contributions
Contact: Tina Sebastian
111 Lord Dr.
Cary, NC 27511 Tel: (919) 468 - 5979 Fax: (919) 469 - 5777

Annual Grant Total: none reported
Geographic Preference: Area in which the company is headquartered
Primary Interests: Education; Health

Public Affairs and Related Activities Personnel

At Headquarters

DE LEON, Jack
V. President, Marketing and Business Development Tel: (919) 468 - 5979 Fax: (919) 469 - 5777
Reponsibilities include external affairs.

SEBASTIAN, Tina
Manager, Employee Relations Tel: (919) 468 - 5979 Fax: (919) 469 - 5777
tina_sebastian@lord.com

Lorillard Tobacco Co.

A manufacturer and marketer of cigarettes. A subsidiary of Loews Corp. (see separate listing).
www.lorillard.net

Chairman and Chief Exec. Officer
ORLOWSKY, Martin L. Tel: (336) 335 - 7000 Fax: (336) 335 - 7550 TF: (888) 278 - 1133

Main Headquarters
Mailing: P.O. Box 10529
Greensboro, NC 27404-0529 Tel: (336) 335 - 7000 Fax: (336) 335 - 7550 TF: (888) 278 - 1133

Street: 714 Green Valley Rd.
Greensboro, NC 27408

Political Action Committees

Lorillard Tobacco Co. Public Affairs Committee
Contact: Michael L. Diamond
P.O. Box 10529
Greensboro, NC 27404-0529 Tel: (336) 335 - 7000 Fax: (336) 335 - 7550 TF: (888) 278 - 1133

Contributions to Candidates: $37,750 (01/05 - 09/05)
Democrats: $6,000; Republicans: $31,750.

Principal Recipients

SENATE DEMOCRATS
Nelson, Benjamin (NE) $2,000

HOUSE DEMOCRATS
McIntyre, Mike (NC) $2,000

SENATE REPUBLICANS
Allen, George (VA) $10,000
Dole, Elizabeth (NC) $10,000
Ensign, John Eric (NV) $2,000

HOUSE REPUBLICANS
Lewis, Ron (KY) $2,000

Public Affairs and Related Activities Personnel

At Headquarters

BRESSLER, Jordan
Manager, External Affairs Tel: (336) 335 - 7744 Fax: (336) 335 - 7550 TF: (888) 278 - 1133

DIAMOND, Michael L.
PAC Treasurer Tel: (336) 335 - 7000 Fax: (336) 335 - 7550 TF: (888) 278 - 1133

Louisiana Coca-Cola Bottling Co. Ltd.

See listing on page 128 under Coca-Cola Enterprises Inc.

Louisiana-Pacific Corporation

A member of the Public Affairs Council. A leading building products manufacturer with 30 mills across North America and one in Chile.
www.lpcorp.com
Annual Revenues: $2.359 billion

Chairman of the Board
COOK, E. Gary Tel: (615) 986 - 5600 Fax: (615) 986 - 5666 TF: (877) 744 - 5600

Chief Exec. Officer
FROST, Richard W.

Main Headquarters
Mailing: 414 Union St.
Suite 2000
Nashville, TN 37219 Tel: (615) 986 - 5600 Fax: (615) 986 - 5666 TF: (877) 744 - 5600

Political Action Committees

Louisiana-Pacific Corp. Federal PAC
Contact: Dave Crowe
414 Union St.
Suite 2000
Nashville, TN 37219 Tel: (615) 986 - -560 Fax: (615) 986 - -566 TF: (877) 744 - 5600

Contributions to Candidates: none reported (01/05 - 09/05)

Corporate Foundations and Giving Programs

Louisiana-Pacific Foundation
Contact: Eric Barnes
414 Union St.
Suite 2000
Nashville, TN 37219 Tel: (615) 986 - 5600 TF: (877) 744 - 5600

Annual Grant Total: none reported
Geographic Preference: Area(s) in which the company operates
Primary Interests: Education; Environment/Conservation; Housing
Recent Recipients: Habitat for Humanity; Junior Achievement; Nature Conservancy; Project Learning Tree

Public Affairs and Related Activities Personnel

At Headquarters

BARCKLEY, Becky
Investor Relations Contact Tel: (615) 986 - 5600

BARNES, Eric
Foundation Contact Tel: (615) 986 - 5600 TF: (877) 744 - 5600

COHN, Mary
Media Relations Contact Tel: (615) 986 - 5886
mary.cohn@lpcorp.com

CROWE, Dave
PAC Contact Tel: (615) 986 - -560 Fax: (615) 986 - -566 TF: (877) 744 - 5600

GALLAND, Brad
PAC Treasurer TF: (800) 547 - 6331

HARVEY, Dane
V. President, Environmental Affairs Tel: (615) 986 - 5600

KINNEY, Mike
Investor Relations Contact Tel: (615) 986 - 5600 TF: (877) 744 - 5600

Louisville Gas & Electric Co.

See listing on page 292 under LG&E Energy LLC.

Lowe's Companies, Inc.

A hardware and building materials specialty retailer.
www.lowes.com
Annual Revenues: $30.8 billion

Chairman and Chief Exec. Officer
NIBLOCK, Robert A. Tel: (704) 758 - 100 Fax: (336) 658 - 4766 TF: (800) 445 - 6937

Main Headquarters
Mailing: 1000 Lowes Blvd.
Moorsville, NC 28117 Tel: (704) 758 - 100 Fax: (336) 658 - 4766 TF: (800) 445 - 6937

Political Action Committees

Lowe's Companies, Inc. PAC (LOWPAC)
Contact: Marshall A. Croom
1000 Lowes Blvd.
Moorsville, NC 28117 Tel: (704) 758 - 100 Fax: (336) 658 - 4766 TF: (800) 445 - 6937

Contributions to Candidates: $1,000 (01/05 - 09/05)
Republicans: $1,000.

Principal Recipients

SENATE REPUBLICANS

HOUSE REPUBLICANS
Foxx, Virginia (NC) $1,000

Corporate Foundations and Giving Programs

Lowe's Charitable and Educational Foundation
Contact: Robert J. Egleston

Lowe's Companies, Inc.

** continued from previous page*

1000 Lowes Blvd.
Moorsville, NC 28117

Tel: (704) 758 - 100
Fax: (336) 658 - 4766
TF: (800) 445 - 6937

Assets: $750,000 (1999)

Annual Grant Total: $2,000,000 - $5,000,000

Primary Interests: Community Development; Education

Public Affairs and Related Activities Personnel

At Headquarters

AHEARN, Ms. Chris
Director, Public Relations
Mailstop: RPS-4
chris.b.ahearn@lowes.com
Tel: (704) 758 - 100
Fax: (336) 658 - 4766
TF: (800) 445 - 6937

CROOM, Marshall A.
PAC Treasurer
Tel: (704) 758 - 100
Fax: (336) 658 - 4766
TF: (800) 445 - 6937

EGLESTON, Robert J.
Community Relations Manager
robert.j.egleston@lowes.com
Tel: (704) 758 - 100
Fax: (336) 658 - 4766
TF: (800) 445 - 6937

GFELLER, Robert J., Jr.
Senior V. President, Marketing Communications and Advertising
robert.j.gfeller@lowes.com
Tel: (704) 758 - 100
Fax: (336) 658 - 4766
TF: (800) 445 - 6937

LSI Logic Corp.

www.lsilogic.com
Annual Revenues: $1.69 billion

Chairman of the Board
CORRIGAN, Wilfred J.
wcorrigan@lsil.com
Tel: (408) 433 - 8000
Fax: (408) 954 - 3220
TF: (866) 574 - 5741

Chief Exec. Officer
TALWALKAR, Abhijit Y.
Tel: (408) 433 - 8000
Fax: (408) 954 - 3220
TF: (866) 574 - 5741

Main Headquarters
Mailing: 1621 Barber Ln.
Milpitas, CA 95035
Tel: (408) 433 - 8000
Fax: (408) 954 - 3220
TF: (866) 574 - 5741

Corporate Foundations and Giving Programs

LSI Logic Community Contributions Program
Contact: Tara Yingst
1621 Barber Ln.
Milpitas, CA 95035
Tel: (408) 433 - 8000
Fax: (408) 954 - 3220
TF: (866) 574 - 5741

Annual Grant Total: none reported

Primary Interests: Education

Recent Recipients: Junior Achievement; Milpitas Unified School District; Poudre School District

Public Affairs and Related Activities Personnel

At Headquarters

BRETT, Kevin
Director, Corporate Public Relations
Mailstop: D-125
kbrett@lsil.com
Responsibilities also include government affairs.
Tel: (408) 433 - 8000
Fax: (408) 954 - 3220
TF: (866) 574 - 5741

GIBSON, Jon R.
V. President, Human Resources
Tel: (408) 433 - 8000
Fax: (408) 954 - 3220
TF: (866) 574 - 5741

MATLEY, Diana L.
V. President, Investor Relations
Tel: (408) 433 - 8000
Fax: (408) 954 - 3220
TF: (866) 574 - 5741

YINGST, Tara
Manager, Corporate and Employee Communications
Mailstop: D-125
tara@lsil.com
Tel: (408) 433 - 8000
Fax: (408) 954 - 3220
TF: (866) 574 - 5741

The Lubrizol Corp.

A fluid technology company.

www.lubrizol.com
Annual Revenues: $1.839 billion

Chairman, Chief Exec. Officer and President
HAMBRICK, James L.
Tel: (440) 943 - 4200
Fax: (440) 943 - 5337

Main Headquarters
Mailing: 29400 Lakeland Blvd.
Wickliffe, OH 44092-2298
Tel: (440) 943 - 4200
Fax: (440) 943 - 5337

Corporate Foundations and Giving Programs

The Lubrizol Foundation
29400 Lakeland Blvd.
Wickliffe, OH 44092-2298
Tel: (440) 943 - 4200
Fax: (440) 943 - 5337

Annual Grant Total: $2,000,000 - $5,000,000

No grants are made for religious or political purposes, and applications must be submitted in writing.

Geographic Preference: Area(s) in which the company operates; Cleveland, OH; Houston, TX

Primary Interests: Arts and Culture; Education; Health and Human Services; Youth Services

Public Affairs and Related Activities Personnel

At Headquarters

COWEN, David L.
Manager, Public Relations
Tel: (440) 943 - 4200
Fax: (440) 943 - 5337

KUCHLING, Ginny
Community Relations Specialist
Tel: (440) 347 - 1241
Fax: (440) 347 - 1858

Responsibilities include corporate philanthropy.

MEISTER, Mark W.
V. President, Human Resources
mwm@lubrizol.com
Tel: (440) 347 - 5641
Fax: (440) 347 - 1858

WANSTREET, Joanne
V. President, Global Communications
Responsibilities include investor relations.
Tel: (440) 347 - 5253

ZASTUDIL, Thomas M.
Manager, Human Resources
tmz@lubrizol.com
Tel: (440) 347 - 1741
Fax: (440) 347 - 5317

Lucent Technologies

PUBLIC AFFAIRS COUNCIL

A member of the Public Affairs Council. Provider of broadband and mobile internet infrastructure and software. A spin-off company of AT&T.

www.lucent.com
Annual Revenues: $21.294 billion

Chairman and Chief Exec. Officer
RUSSO, Patricia F.
Tel: (908) 582 - 8500
Fax: (908) 508 - 2576
TF: (888) 458 - 2368

Main Headquarters
Mailing: 600 Mountain Ave.
Murray Hill, NJ 07974-0636
Tel: (908) 582 - 8500
Fax: (908) 508 - 2576
TF: (888) 458 - 2368

Washington Office
Contact: Patricia A. Rimo
Mailing: 1100 New York Ave. NW
Washington, DC 20005
Tel: (202) 669 - 8368

Political Action Committees

Lucent Technologies Inc. Political Action Committee
Contact: Michael E. Tiddy
1100 New York Ave. NW
Washington, DC 20005
Tel: (202) 669 - 8368

Contributions to Candidates: $29,500 (01/05 - 09/05)

Democrats: $9,500; Republicans: $20,000.

Principal Recipients

SENATE DEMOCRATS

HOUSE DEMOCRATS
Menendez, Robert (NJ) $2,500

SENATE REPUBLICANS
Santorum, Richard (PA) $3,000

HOUSE REPUBLICANS
Frelinghuysen, Rod (NJ) $5,000
Ferguson, Mike (NJ) $3,000
Manzullo, Donald (IL) $3,000

Corporate Foundations and Giving Programs

Lucent Technologies Foundation
Contact: Chris Park
600 Mountain Ave.
Murray Hill, NJ 07974-0636
Tel: (908) 582 - 8500
Fax: (908) 508 - 2576
TF: (888) 458 - 2368

Annual Grant Total: none reported

Primary Interests: K-12 Education

Lucent Technologies Inc. Corporate Contributions Program
Contact: Beatrice M. Tassot
600 Mountain Ave.
Murray Hill, NJ 07974-0636
Tel: (908) 582 - 8500
Fax: (908) 508 - 2576
TF: (888) 458 - 2368

Annual Grant Total: none reported

Primary Interests: Community Affairs; Education

Lucent Technologies

** continued from previous page*

Public Affairs and Related Activities Personnel

At Headquarters

AMBRUS, Mary Lou
V. President, Public Relations
mambrus@lucent.com
Tel: (908) 582 - 8500
Fax: (908) 508 - 2576
TF: (888) 458 - 2368

KIMMET, Pamela
Senior V. President, Human Resources
Tel: (908) 582 - 8500
Fax: (908) 508 - 2576
TF: (888) 458 - 2368

PARK, Chris
President, Lucent Technologies Foundation
Tel: (908) 582 - 8500
Fax: (908) 508 - 2576
TF: (888) 458 - 2368

TASSOT, Beatrice M.
Director, Corporate Contributions
Mailstop: Room 6F418
bmtassot@lucent.com
Tel: (908) 582 - 8500
Fax: (908) 508 - 2576
TF: (888) 458 - 2368

At Washington Office

DONAHUE, Karen L.
Registered Federal Lobbyist.
Tel: (202) 669 - 8368

MATHIAS, Charles B.
Registered Federal Lobbyist.
Tel: (202) 669 - 8368

RIMO, Patricia A.
V. President, Global Government Affairs
primo@lucent.com
Registered Federal Lobbyist.
Tel: (202) 669 - 8368

TIDDY, Michael E.
Pac Treasurer
Registered Federal Lobbyist.
Tel: (202) 669 - 8368

Lykes Bros. Steamship Co.

See listing on page 301 under Lykes Lines Limited.

Lykes Lines Limited

Formerly known as Lykes Bros. Steamship Co. A subsidiary of CP Ships.
www.lykeslines.com

Main Headquarters
Mailing: 401 E. Jackson St., Suite 3300
Tampa, FL 33602
Tel: (813) 276 - 4600
Fax: (813) 315 - 5388
TF: (800) 242 - 7447

Political Action Committees

Lykes Bros. Inc. PAC
Contact: Michael L. Carrere
401 E. Jackson St., Suite 3300
Tampa, FL 33602
Tel: (813) 276 - 4600
Fax: (813) 315 - 5388
TF: (800) 242 - 7447

Contributions to Candidates: $1,500 (01/05 - 09/05)
Democrats: $1,500.

Principal Recipients

SENATE DEMOCRATS		HOUSE DEMOCRATS
Nelson, Bill (FL)	$1,500	

Public Affairs and Related Activities Personnel

At Headquarters

CARRERE, Michael L.
PAC Treasurer
Tel: (813) 276 - 4600
Fax: (813) 315 - 5388
TF: (800) 242 - 7447

VARGAS, Nelson
Manager, Public Relations and Advertising
Tel: (813) 276 - 4600
Fax: (813) 242 - 7447
TF: (800) 242 - 7447

Lyondell Chemical Co.

Formerly Lyondell Petrochemical Co. A producer of petrochemicals and refined petroleum products. Merged with Millennium Chemicals in 1997 and acquired ARCO Chemical Co. in 1998.
www.lyondell.com
Annual Revenues: $3.226 billion

Chairman of the Board
BUTLER, Dr. William T.
Tel: (713) 652 - 7200

President and Chief Exec. Officer
SMITH, Dan F.
Tel: (713) 652 - 7200

Main Headquarters
Mailing: One Houston Center
1221 McKinney Ave.
Houston, TX 77010
Tel: (713) 652 - 7200

Washington Office
Contact: Ms. Edlu J. Thom
Mailing: 1101 Pennsylvania Ave., NW
Suite 515
Washington, DC 20004
Tel: (202) 639 - 0750

Political Action Committees

Lyondell Chemical Co. Political Action Committee
Contact: Ms. Edlu J. Thom
1101 Pennsylvania Ave., NW
Suite 515
Washington, DC 20004
Tel: (202) 434 - 8938
Fax: (202) 434 - 4585

Contributions to Candidates: $29,000 (01/05 - 09/05)
Democrats: $7,000; Republicans: $21,000; Other: $1,000.

Principal Recipients

SENATE DEMOCRATS		HOUSE DEMOCRATS	
		Green, Gene (TX)	$5,000
		Edwards, Chet (TX)	$2,000
		HOUSE OTHER	
		Oberstar, James L (MN)	$1,000
SENATE REPUBLICANS		**HOUSE REPUBLICANS**	
Cornyn, John (TX)	$1,000	Barton, Joe L (TX)	$5,000
Martinez, Mel (FL)	$1,000	DeLay, Tom (TX)	$5,000
McConnell, Mitch (KY)	$1,000	McCrery, Jim (LA)	$2,000
Santorum, Richard (PA)	$1,000	Young, Don E (AK)	$2,000
		Bonilla, Henry (TX)	$1,000
		Boustany, Jr, Charles (LA)	$1,000
		Nussle, Jim (IA)	$1,000

Corporate Foundations and Giving Programs

Lyondell Corporate Giving Program
Contact: David A. Harpole
One Houston Center
1221 McKinney Ave.
Houston, TX 77010
Tel: (713) 652 - 4125
Fax: (713) 652 - 4151

Annual Grant Total: none reported

Public Affairs and Related Activities Personnel

At Headquarters

HARPOLE, David A.
Manager, Public Affairs
david.harpole@lyondell.com
Tel: (713) 652 - 4125
Fax: (713) 652 - 4151

HOLLINSHEAD, John
V. President, Human Resources
Tel: (713) 652 - 7200

PIKE, Doug
Director, Investor Relations
Tel: (713) 652 - 4590

STEBEL, Eric
Manager, Marketing Communications
eric.stebel@lyondell.com
Tel: (713) 309 - 3987

At Washington Office

HODGEN, Roy
Manager, Federal Government Affairs
Registered Federal Lobbyist.
Tel: (202) 434 - 8938
Fax: (202) 434 - 4585

TAYLOR, Kristina
Coordinator, Government Affairs
Tel: (202) 639 - 0750

THOM, Ms. Edlu J.
Director, Government Affairs; and PAC Treasurer
ejthom@cais.com
Registered Federal Lobbyist.
Tel: (202) 434 - 8938
Fax: (202) 434 - 4585

Lyondell Petrochemical Co.

See listing on page 301 under Lyondell Chemical Co.

Lyondell-Citgo Refining, Ltd.

See listing on page 301 under Lyondell Chemical Co.

M&T Bank Corporation

A commercial bank. Acquired Allfirst Financial, Inc. in April, 2003.
www.mandtbank.com

Chairman of the Board
WILMERS, Robert G.
Tel: (716) 842 - 5445
Fax: (716) 842 - 5839
TF: (800) 836 - 1500

President and Chief Exec. Officer
SADLER, Robert E., Jr.
Tel: (716) 842 - 5445
Fax: (716) 842 - 5839
TF: (800) 836 - 1500

Main Headquarters
Mailing: One M & T Plaza
Buffalo, NY 14203
Tel: (716) 842 - 5445
Fax: (716) 842 - 5839
TF: (800) 836 - 1500

Political Action Committees

Manufacturers and Traders Co. Political Action Committee
Contact: Marlene Tomaselli
One M & T Plaza
Buffalo, NY 14203
Tel: (716) 842 - 5445
Fax: (716) 842 - 5839
TF: (800) 836 - 1500

M&T Bank Corporation

** continued from previous page*

Contributions to Candidates: $5,000 (01/05 - 09/05)
Democrats: $2,000; Republicans: $3,000.

Principal Recipients

SENATE DEMOCRATS	HOUSE DEMOCRATS	
	Ruppersberger, Dutch (MD)	$1,500
SENATE REPUBLICANS	**HOUSE REPUBLICANS**	
	Kelly, Sue W (NY)	$1,000

Corporate Foundations and Giving Programs

M&T Charitable Foundation
Contact: Shelly Drake
One M & T Plaza — Tel: (716) 842 - 5445
Buffalo, NY 14203 — Fax: (716) 842 - 5839
TF: (800) 836 - 1500

Annual Grant Total: $1,000,000 - $2,000,000
Geographic Preference: Area(s) in which the company operates; New York; Pennsylvania; Maryland; West Virginia

Public Affairs and Related Activities Personnel

At Headquarters

DRAKE, Shelly — Tel: (716) 842 - 5445
Administrative V. President — Fax: (716) 842 - 5839
TF: (800) 836 - 1500
Responsibilities include corporate philanthropy.

KAZMIERCZAK, Theresa — Tel: (716) 842 - 5445
Manager, Corporate and Community Affairs — Fax: (716) 842 - 5839
TF: (800) 836 - 1500

TOMASELLI, Marlene — Tel: (716) 842 - 5445
Treasurer, Manufacturers and Traders Trust Co. PAC — Fax: (716) 842 - 5839
TF: (800) 836 - 1500

ZABEL, C. Michael — Tel: (716) 842 - 5445
V. President and Manager, Corporate Communications — Fax: (716) 842 - 5839
TF: (800) 836 - 1500

Mack Trucks, Inc.

A truck manufacturer. A subsidiary of Volvo Group North America, Inc. (see separate listing).
www.macktrucks.com

President and Chief Exec. Officer — Tel: (610) 709 - 3011
VIKNER, Paul L. — Fax: (610) 709 - 3308

Main Headquarters
Mailing: P.O. Box M — Tel: (610) 709 - 3011
Allentown, PA 18105-5000 — Fax: (610) 709 - 3308
Street: 2100 Mack Blvd.
Allentown, PA 18103

Public Affairs and Related Activities Personnel

At Headquarters

MARTIN, Robert J. — Tel: (610) 709 - 2670
Senior Manager, Communications — Fax: (610) 709 - 3308

MIES, John — Tel: (610) 709 - 3011
V. President, Communications — Fax: (610) 709 - 3308

Macy's East

See listing on page 191 under Federated Department Stores, Inc.

Macy's West

See listing on page 191 under Federated Department Stores, Inc.

Madison Gas and Electric Co.

A public utility.
www.mge.com

Chairman, President, and Chief Exec. Officer — Tel: (608) 252 - 7000
WOLTER, Gary J. — Fax: (608) 252 - 7098
TF: (800) 356 - 6423

Main Headquarters
Mailing: P.O. Box 1231 — Tel: (608) 252 - 7000
Madison, WI 53701-1231 — Fax: (608) 252 - 7098
TF: (800) 356 - 6423
Street: 133 S. Blair St.
Madison, WI 53701

Corporate Foundations and Giving Programs

Madison Gas and Electric Foundation
Contact: Lynn Hobbie
P.O. Box 1231 — Tel: (608) 252 - 7000
Madison, WI 53701-1231 — Fax: (608) 252 - 7098
TF: (800) 356 - 6423

Annual Grant Total: $100,000 - $200,000
Geographic Preference: Area(s) in which the company operates
Primary Interests: Arts and Humanities; Civic and Public Affairs; Education; Social Services
Recent Recipients: University of Wisconsin

Public Affairs and Related Activities Personnel

At Headquarters

HOBBIE, Lynn — Tel: (608) 252 - 7000
Senior V. President, Marketing — Fax: (608) 252 - 7098
lhobbie@mge.com — TF: (800) 356 - 6423
Responsibilities include corporate philanthropy.

KRAUS, Steve — Tel: (608) 252 - 7907
Manager, Media Relations — Fax: (608) 252 - 7098
skraus@mge.com — TF: (800) 356 - 6423

MOHRBACHER, James A. — Tel: (608) 252 - 7000
Manager, Government and Business Relations — Fax: (608) 252 - 7098
jmohrbacher@mge.com — TF: (800) 356 - 6423

RICCIARDI, Mike — Tel: (608) 252 - 7000
Director, Safety and Environmental Affairs — Fax: (608) 252 - 7098
TF: (800) 356 - 6423

Magellan Health Services, Inc.

A managed behavioral healthcare organization.
www.magellanhealth.com
Annual Revenues: $1.755 billion

Chairman and Chief Exec. Officer — Tel: (860) 507 - 1900
SHULMAN, Steven J. — Fax: (860) 507 - 1990
TF: (800) 410 - 8312

Main Headquarters
Mailing: 55 Nod Rd — Tel: (860) 507 - 1900
Avon, CT 06001 — Fax: (860) 507 - 1990
TF: (800) 410 - 8312

Political Action Committees

Magellan Health Services Employee Committee for Good Government
Contact: M. Robin Copeland
6950 Columbia Gateway Dr. — Tel: (410) 953 - 1000
Columbia, MD 21046 — Fax: (410) 953 - 5200

Contributions to Candidates: none reported (01/05 - 09/05)

Public Affairs and Related Activities Personnel

At Other Offices

BRUNNWORTH, Kristin L. — Tel: (410) 953 - 1000
Media Relations Specialist — Fax: (410) 953 - 5200
6950 Columbia Gateway Dr.
Columbia, MD 21046
klbrunnworth@magellanhealth.com

COONEY, Christopher W. — Tel: (410) 953 - 1000
Chief Branding and Communications Officer — Fax: (410) 953 - 5200
6950 Columbia Gateway Dr.
Columbia, MD 21046

COPELAND, M. Robin — Tel: (410) 953 - 1000
PAC Treasurer — Fax: (410) 953 - 5200
6950 Columbia Gateway Dr.
Columbia, MD 21046

LEWIS-CLAPPER, Caskie — Tel: (410) 953 - 1000
Chief Human Resources Officer — Fax: (410) 953 - 5200
6950 Columbia Gateway Dr.
Columbia, MD 21046

ROSE, Melissa L. — TF: (877) 645 - 6464
Senior V. President, Investor Relations
6950 Columbia Gateway Dr.
Columbia, MD 21046

SOMERS, Erin S. — Tel: (410) 953 - 1000
V. President, Public Relations and Communications — Fax: (410) 953 - 5200
6950 Columbia Gateway Dr.
Columbia, MD 21046
essomers@magellanhealth.com

Magnetek, Inc.

A manufacturer of electrical equipment. The administrative office (public relations, human resources and etc.) of MagneTek is located at the Nashville, Tennessee office listed below.
www.magnetek.com
Annual Revenues: $200 million

Chairman of the Board — Tel: (310) 208 - 1980
GALEF, Andrew A. — Fax: (310) 208 - 6133
agalef@magnetek.com

President and Chief Exec. Officer — Tel: (310) 208 - 1980
BORE, Thomas G. — Fax: (310) 208 - 6133

Main Headquarters
Mailing: 10900 Wilshire Blvd. — Tel: (310) 208 - 1980
Suite 850 — Fax: (310) 208 - 6133
Los Angeles, CA 90024

Corporate Foundations and Giving Programs

MagneTek, Inc. Corporate Contributions
Contact: Robert W. Murray

Magnetek, Inc.
** continued from previous page*

10900 Wilshire Blvd.
Suite 850
Los Angeles, CA 90024
Tel: (310) 208 - 1980
Fax: (310) 208 - 6133

Annual Grant Total: none reported

Public Affairs and Related Activities Personnel

At Headquarters

MURRAY, Robert W.
V. President, Communications and Public Relations
bmurray@magnetek.com
Tel: (310) 208 - 1980
Fax: (310) 208 - 6133

MAIR Holdings, Inc.
An airline company.

www.mesaba.com

Chairman of the Board
POHLAND, Carl R.
Tel: (612) 333 - 0021
Fax: (612) 337 - 0355

President and Chief Exec. Officer
FOLEY, Paul F.
foley_paul@mesaba.com
Tel: (612) 333 - 0021
Fax: (612) 337 - 0355

Main Headquarters
Mailing: Fifth St. Towers, Suite 1360
150 S. Fifth St.
Minneapolis, MN 55402
Tel: (612) 333 - 0021
Fax: (612) 337 - 0355

Public Affairs and Related Activities Personnel

At Headquarters

COSTELLO, Elizabeth
Manager, Internal Communication
Tel: (612) 333 - 5264
Fax: (612) 337 - 0355

GROEBE, Peggy
Director, Human Resources
(Mesaba Airlines)
groebe_peggy@mesaba.com
Tel: (612) 333 - 0021
Fax: (651) 367 - 5392

MAMSI
See listing on page 325 under Mid Atlantic Medical Services Inc.

Mandalay Resort Group
See listing on page 324 under MGM MIRAGE.

The Manitowoc Co., Inc.
Manufactures foodservice, cranes and marine products.

www.manitowoc.com
Annual Revenues: $1.4 billion

Chairman and Chief Exec. Officer
GROWCOCK, Terry D.
Tel: (920) 684 - 4410
Fax: (920) 652 - 9778

Main Headquarters
Mailing: P.O. Box 66
Manitowoc, WI 54221-0066
Tel: (920) 684 - 4410
Fax: (920) 652 - 9778
Street: 2400 S. 44th St.
Manitowoc, WI 54220

Washington Office
Contact: Al J. Bernard
Mailing: 80 M St. SE
Suite 410
Washington, DC 20003
Tel: (202) 867 - 3607

Political Action Committees

Manitowoc Co. PAC
Contact: Carl J. Laurino
P.O. Box 66
Manitowoc, WI 54221-0066
Tel: (920) 652 - 1720
Fax: (920) 652 - 9778

Contributions to Candidates: $16,000 (01/05 - 09/05)
Democrats: $3,000; Republicans: $12,000; Other: $1,000.

Principal Recipients

SENATE DEMOCRATS

HOUSE DEMOCRATS
Obey, David R (WI) $2,000

SENATE REPUBLICANS

HOUSE REPUBLICANS
Gard, John G (WI) $5,000
Shuster, William (PA) $2,000

Public Affairs and Related Activities Personnel

At Headquarters

KHAIL, Steve
Director, Investor Relations and Corporate Communications
Tel: (920) 652 - 1713
Fax: (920) 652 - 9778

LAURINO, Carl J.
Senior V. President and Chief Financial Officer; PAC Treasurer
Tel: (920) 652 - 1720
Fax: (920) 652 - 9778

MUSIAL, Thomas G.
Senior V. President, Human Resources and Administration
Tel: (920) 684 - 4410
Fax: (920) 652 - 9778

At Washington Office

BERNARD, Al J.
V. President, Government Relations
Registered Federal Lobbyist.
Tel: (202) 867 - 3607

Manning Selvage & Lee
See listing on page 95 under Leo Burnett Worldwide.

Manor Care, Inc.
An integrated health care provider. Operates nursing centers through its operating company, HCR Manor Care, under the names Heartland, ManorCare and Arden Courts.

www.hcr-manorcare.com
Annual Revenues: $2.694 billion

Chairman, President and Chief Exec. Officer
ORMOND, Paul A.
Tel: (419) 252 - 5535
Fax: (419) 252 - 5564

Main Headquarters
Mailing: 333 N. Summit St.
16th Floor.
Toledo, OH 43604-2617
Tel: (419) 252 - 5500
Fax: (419) 252 - 5554

Political Action Committees

HCR Manor Care PAC
Contact: Frank Jannazo
333 N. Summit St.
16th Floor.
Toledo, OH 43604-2617
Tel: (419) 252 - 5500
Fax: (419) 252 - 5554

Contributions to Candidates: $46,700 (01/05 - 09/05)
Democrats: $8,750; Republicans: $37,950.

Principal Recipients

SENATE DEMOCRATS
Conrad, Kent (ND) $4,250
Cardin, Benjamin (MD) $2,500
Mikulski, Barbara (MD) $2,000

HOUSE DEMOCRATS

SENATE REPUBLICANS
Santorum, Richard (PA) $5,000
Hatch, Orrin (UT) $4,500
Kyl, Jon L (AZ) $4,200
Snowe, Olympia (ME) $4,000
Dewine, Richard (OH) $3,000
Smith, Gordon (OR) $3,000

HOUSE REPUBLICANS
English, Philip S (PA) $2,500
Johnson, Nancy (CT) $2,500
Cantor, Eric (VA) $2,250
Gerlach, Jim (PA) $2,000

Corporate Foundations and Giving Programs

HCR Manor Care Foundation
Contact: Jennifer Steiner
333 N. Summit St.
16th Floor.
Toledo, OH 43604-2617
Tel: (419) 252 - 5989
Fax: (419) 252 - 5521

Assets: $4,200,000 (2001)
Annual Grant Total: $100,000 - $200,000
Geographic Preference: Arizona; California; Colorado; Delaware; Florida; Georgia; Illinois; Indiana; Iowa; Kansas; Maryland; Michigan; Missouri; Nevada; New Jersey; New Mexico; North Carolina; North Dakota; Ohio; Oklahoma; Pennsylvania; South Carolina; South Dakota; Texas; Utah; Virginia; Washington State; Wisconsin
Primary Interests: Medicine and Health Care; Senior Citizens

Public Affairs and Related Activities Personnel

At Headquarters

JANNAZO, Frank
PAC Treasurer
Tel: (419) 252 - 5500
Fax: (419) 252 - 5554

RUMP, Rick
Director, Corporate Communications
rrump@hcr-manorcare.com
Tel: (419) 252 - 5981
Fax: (419) 252 - 5596

STEINER, Jennifer
Exec. Director, HCR Manor Care Foundation
jsteiner@hcr-manorcare.com
Tel: (419) 252 - 5989
Fax: (419) 252 - 5521

Manpower Inc.
A provider of staffing and workforce management solutions.

www.manpower.com
Annual Revenues: $12 billion

Chairman and Chief Exec. Officer
JOERRES, Jeffrey A.
Tel: (414) 961 - 1000
Fax: (414) 961 - 7081

Main Headquarters
Mailing: 5301 N. Ironwood Rd.
Milwaukee, WI 53217
Tel: (414) 961 - 1000
Fax: (414) 961 - 7985

Manpower Inc.

** continued from previous page*

Corporate Foundations and Giving Programs

Manpower Foundation
Contact: Peggy Pischke
5301 N. Ironwood Rd. Tel: (414) 961 - 1000
Milwaukee, WI 53217 Fax: (414) 961 - 7985

Assets: $500,000 (2000)
Annual Grant Total: $200,000 - $300,000
Geographic Preference: National
Primary Interests: Arts and Culture; Education; Employment
Recent Recipients: Boys and Girls Club; Nat'l Ass'n for the Advancement of Colored People; United Performing Arts Fund; United Way; Urban League

Public Affairs and Related Activities Personnel

At Headquarters

GERSTENKORN, Margaret — Tel: (414) 906 - 6336
Director, Public Relations — Fax: (414) 961 - 7985

PISCHKE, Peggy — Tel: (414) 961 - 1000
Contact, Manpower Foundation — Fax: (414) 961 - 7985

SHILOBRIT, Tracy — Tel: (414) 906 - 6088
Director, Corporate and Global Communications — Fax: (414) 961 - 8780
tracy.shilobrit@manpower.com

Marathon Oil Corp.

Formerly known as USX Corp. The company changed its name after spinning off its subsidiary United States Steel Corp. (see separate listing) into its own separate company. Engaged in petroleum exploration, production, refining, marketing, transportation, and supply and research.
www.marathon.com

President and Chief Exec. Officer — Tel: (713) 629 - 6600
CAZALOTT, Clarence P., Jr. — Fax: (713) 296 - 3394

Main Headquarters
Mailing: 5555 San Felipe Rd. — Tel: (713) 629 - 6600
Houston, TX 77056 — Fax: (713) 296 - 2952

Washington Office
Contact: Patricia M. Richards
Mailing: 700 13th St., NW — Tel: (202) 654 - 4499
Suite 950 — Fax: (202) 654 - 4493
Washington, DC 20005

Political Action Committees

Marathon Oil Co. Employees PAC (MEPAC)
Contact: Joseph P. Horstman
539 S. Main St.
Room 2635
Findlay, OH 45840

Contributions to Candidates: $58,600 (01/05 - 09/05)
Democrats: $7,000; Republicans: $51,600.

Principal Recipients

SENATE DEMOCRATS		HOUSE DEMOCRATS	
		Cuellar, Henry (TX)	$3,000
SENATE REPUBLICANS		**HOUSE REPUBLICANS**	
Hutchison, Kay Bailey (TX)	$5,000	Cubin, Barbara L (WY)	$4,000
		DeLay, Tom (TX)	$2,500
Allen, George (VA)	$4,100	Rehberg, Dennis (MT)	$2,500
Vitter, David (LA)	$2,500		

Public Affairs and Related Activities Personnel

At Headquarters

CAMPBELL, Eileen M. — Tel: (713) 629 - 6600
V. President, Human Resources — Fax: (713) 296 - 2952

GUTIERREZ, Hugo — Tel: (713) 629 - 6600
Manager, State Government Affairs — Fax: (713) 296 - 2952

HOWARD, Jerry — Tel: (713) 629 - 6600
Senior V. President, Corporate Affairs — Fax: (713) 296 - 2952
Responsibilities include government affairs.

MATHENY, Kenneth L. — Tel: (713) 296 - 4114
V. President, Investor Relations and Public Affairs — Fax: (713) 296 - 2952
klmatheny@marathonoil.com

RICHARDSON, Susan — Tel: (713) 296 - 3915
External Affairs Coordinator — Fax: (713) 296 - 2952
slrichardson@marathonoil.com

SULLENBARGER, Daniel T. — Tel: (713) 629 - 6600
V. President, Health, Environment and Safety — Fax: (713) 296 - 2952

THIERWECHTER, Douglas E. — Tel: (713) 629 - 3918
Manager, State Government Affairs — Fax: (713) 296 - 3394
dethierwechter@marathonoil.com

THILL, Howard S. — Tel: (713) 629 - 4140
Manager, Investor Relations — Fax: (713) 296 - 2952
hjthill@marathonoil.com

TREVINO, J. Michael — Tel: (713) 629 - 6600
General Manager, Public Affairs — Fax: (713) 296 - 3394
mjtrevino@marathonoil.com

WEEDITZ, Paul — Tel: (713) 296 - 3910
Director, External Communications — Fax: (713) 296 - 2952
peweeditz@marathonoil.com

At Washington Office

BREIDENBACH, David — Tel: (202) 654 - 4499
Fax: (202) 654 - 4493

FREER, Paula D. — Tel: (202) 654 - 4499
Director, Federal Government Affairs — Fax: (202) 654 - 4493
pdfreer@marathonoil.com
Registered Federal Lobbyist.

GRAVES, Angelica — Tel: (202) 654 - 4499
Director, Public and State Government Affairs — Fax: (202) 654 - 4493

HARRIS, Marilyn A., Ph.D. — Tel: (202) 654 - 4480
V. President, Federal Government Affairs — Fax: (202) 654 - 4493
maharris@marathonoil.com
Registered Federal Lobbyist.

KIRKHAM, Brandan — Tel: (202) 654 - 4499
Representative, Federal Government Affairs — Fax: (202) 654 - 4493
Registered Federal Lobbyist.

RICHARDS, Patricia M. — Tel: (202) 654 - 4499
Director, Federal Government Affairs — Fax: (202) 654 - 4493
pmrichards@marathonoil.com
Registered Federal Lobbyist.

At Other Offices

HORSTMAN, Joseph P.
PAC Treasurer
539 S. Main St.
Room 2635
Findlay, OH 45840

Mariner Post-Acute Network, Inc.

See listing on page 422 under Sava Senior Care LLC.

Maritz Inc.

A provider of integrated performance improvement, incentive travel and consumer market research services.
www.maritz.com

Chairman and Chief Exec. Officer — Tel: (636) 827 - 4000
MARITZ, Steve — Fax: (636) 827 - 2089

Main Headquarters
Mailing: 1375 N. Highway Dr. — Tel: (636) 827 - 4000
Fenton, MO 63099

Corporate Foundations and Giving Programs

Maritz, Inc. Corporate Giving Program
Contact: Beth Rusert
1375 N. Highway Dr. — Tel: (636) 827 - 2949
Fenton, MO 63099 — Fax: (636) 827 - 8605

Annual Grant Total: none reported
Recent Recipients: Toys for Tots; United Way

Public Affairs and Related Activities Personnel

At Headquarters

LARSEN, Jennifer — Tel: (636) 827 - 1523
Director, Public Relations — Fax: (636) 827 - 8605
jennifer.larsen@maritz.com

MCGRATH, Con — Tel: (636) 827 - 4000
V. President, People and Organizational Development — Fax: (636) 827 - 2089

RUSERT, Beth — Tel: (636) 827 - 2949
V. President, Public Relations and Corporate Communications Communications — Fax: (636) 827 - 8605
beth.rusert@maritz.com

Mark IV Industries, Inc.

Manufacturer of engineered systems and components utilizing mechanical and fluid power transmission, fluid transfer, and power systems and components.
www.mark-iv.com
Annual Revenues: $1.2 billion

Chairman — Tel: (716) 689 - 4972
JOHANSSON, Kurt J. — Fax: (716) 568 - 6098

Chief Exec. Officer — Tel: (716) 689 - 4972
MONTAGUE, William P. — Fax: (716) 568 - 6098

Main Headquarters
Mailing: P.O. Box 810 — Tel: (716) 689 - 4972
Amherst, NY 14226 — Fax: (716) 568 - 6098
Street: One Towne Centre
501 John James Audubon Pkwy.
Amherst, NY 14228

Mark IV Industries, Inc.

** continued from previous page*

Corporate Foundations and Giving Programs

Mark IV Foundation
Contact: Joann Eckert
P.O. Box 810
Amherst, NY 14226
Tel: (716) 689 - 4980 Ext: 417
Fax: (716) 568 - 6098

Assets: $853,165,000 (2003)
Annual Grant Total: $100,000 - $200,000
Geographic Preference: Area in which the company is headquartered
Primary Interests: Children; Community Development; Education; Medicine and Health Care; Performing Arts; Religion
Recent Recipients: Junior Achievement; United Way

Public Affairs and Related Activities Personnel

At Headquarters

ACQUILINA, Michelle
Manager, Corporate Human Resources
Tel: (716) 689 - 4980 Ext: 323
Fax: (716) 568 - 6098

ECKERT, Joann
Contact, Mark IV Foundation
joann_eckert@mark-iv.com
Tel: (716) 689 - 4980 Ext: 417
Fax: (716) 568 - 6098

TIBOLLO, Colleen
Director, Corporate Communications
colleen_tibollo@mark-iv.com
Tel: (716) 689 - 4972
Fax: (716) 568 - 6098

The Marmon Group, Inc.

Provides consulting and adminstrative services to associations of manufacturing and service companies.
www.marmon.com
Annual Revenues: $6.3 billion

President and Chief Exec. Officer
NICHOLS, John D.
Tel: (312) 372 - 9500
Fax: (312) 845 - 5305

Main Headquarters
Mailing: 225 W. Washington St.
Chicago, IL 60606-3418
Tel: (312) 372 - 9500
Fax: (312) 845 - 5305

Public Affairs and Related Activities Personnel

At Headquarters

DEES, David
Director, Communications
Tel: (312) 845 - 5343
Fax: (312) 372 - 2808

Marriott Internat'l, Inc.

A worldwide hospitality company with over 2,600 lodging properties in the U.S. and 68 other countries and territories. The company operates and franchises hotels under the Marriott, JW Marriott, Ritz-Carlton, Renaissance, Residence Inn, Courtyard, TownePlace Suites, Fairfield Inn, SpringHill Suites, and Ramada International brand names. Marriott Internat'l also develops and operates vacation ownership resorts under the Marriott Vacation Club Internat'l, Horizons, The Ritz-Carlton Club and Marriott Grand Residence Club brands. The company operates Marriott Executive Apartments, provides furnished corporate housing through its Marriott ExecuSaty division, and operates conference centers.
www.marriott.com
Annual Revenues: $8.441 billion

Chairman and Chief Exec. Officer
MARRIOTT, J. W., Jr.
Tel: (301) 380 - 3000
Fax: (301) 380 - 8957

Main Headquarters
Mailing: One Marriott Dr.
Washington, DC 20058
Tel: (301) 380 - 3000
Fax: (301) 380 - 3969

Political Action Committees

Marriott Internat'l Political Action Committee
Contact: Thomas E. Ladd
One Marriott Dr.
Washington, DC 20058
Tel: (301) 380 - 1236
Fax: (301) 380 - 8957

Contributions to Candidates: $16,250 (01/05 - 09/05)
Democrats: $2,000; Republicans: $14,250.

Principal Recipients

SENATE DEMOCRATS

HOUSE DEMOCRATS
Lantos, Tom (CA) $1,000
Melancon, Charlie (LA) $1,000

SENATE REPUBLICANS
Hatch, Orrin (UT) $5,000

HOUSE REPUBLICANS
Lungren, Daniel E (CA) $5,000
Reynolds, Thomas (NY) $2,000
Goode, Virgil H. Jr. (VA) $1,000

Corporate Foundations and Giving Programs

Marriott Internat'l Corporate Contributions Program
Contact: Judi A. Hadfield
One Marriott Dr.
Washington, DC 20058
Tel: (301) 380 - 7430
Fax: (301) 380 - 2843

Annual Grant Total: none reported
Geographic Preference: Area(s) in which the company operates; Washington, DC; Bethesda, MD
Primary Interests: Civic and Public Affairs; Health and Human Services; Minority Opportunities; Persons with Disabilities; Urban Affairs

Marriott Foundation for People with Disabilities
Contact: Tad Asbury
One Marriott Dr.
Washington, DC 20058
Tel: (301) 380 - 7137
Fax: (301) 380 - 8957

Annual Grant Total: none reported

Public Affairs and Related Activities Personnel

At Headquarters

ASBURY, Tad
Director, Marriott Foundation for People with Disabilities
Tel: (301) 380 - 7137
Fax: (301) 380 - 8957

CARROLL, Matthew
Senior Manager, North American Communicatons
Tel: (301) 380 - 3000
Fax: (301) 380 - 8957

CHELSON, Debbie J.
Manager, Human Resources Internal Communications
Mailstop: Dept. 51/931.12
debbie.chelson@marriott.com
Tel: (301) 380 - 2291
Fax: (301) 380 - 5764

CONNER, Roger W.
V. President, North American Communications
roger.conner@marriott.com
Tel: (301) 380 - 5605
Fax: (301) 897 - 9014

FARRELL, June
V. President, International Communications
june.farrell@marriott.com
Tel: (301) 380 - 7796
Fax: (301) 380 - 4684

FROEHLICH, Melissa
Director, Legislative Affairs
Tel: (301) 380 - 3000
Fax: (301) 380 - 8957

HADFIELD, Judi A.
V. President, Community Relations and Corporate Projects
judi.hadfield@marriott.com
Tel: (301) 380 - 7430
Fax: (301) 380 - 2843

HAMPTON, Stephanie L.
Senior Director, Media Relations
stephanie.hampton@marriott.com
Tel: (301) 380 - 1217
Fax: (301) 897 - 9014

KEEGAN, Brendan M.
Exec. V. President, Human Resources
brendan.keegan@marriott.com
Tel: (301) 380 - 1010
Fax: (301) 380 - 4055

LADD, Thomas E.
Senior V. President, Government Affairs
thomas.ladd@marriott.com
Tel: (301) 380 - 1236
Fax: (301) 380 - 8957

LAMBOURNE, Gordon
V. President Brand Public Relations
gordon.lambourne@marriott.com
Tel: (301) 380 - 1368
Fax: (301) 897 - 9014

MARDER, Thomas O.
V. President, Corporate Relations
thomas.marder@marriott.com
Tel: (301) 380 - 2553
Fax: (301) 897 - 9014

PAUGH, Laura E.
Senior V. President, Investor Relations
laura.paugh@marriott.com
Tel: (301) 380 - 7418
Fax: (301) 380 - 5067

STERLING, Charlotte B.
Exec. V. President, Communications
charlotte.sterling@marriott.com
Tel: (301) 380 - 7406
Fax: (301) 897 - 9014

WEISZ, Terry M.
V. President, Internal Communications
Mailstop: Dept. 93527
terry.weisz@Marriott.com
Tel: (301) 380 - 1033
Fax: (301) 380 - 5764

Mars, Inc.

A snack food, main meal and pet food manufacturer.
www.mars.com
Annual Revenues: $14 billion

Chairman of the Board
MARS, John Franklyn
Tel: (703) 821 - 4900
Fax: (703) 448 - 9678

Main Headquarters
Mailing: 6885 Elm St.
McLean, VA 22101
Tel: (703) 821 - 4900
Fax: (703) 448 - 9678

Corporate Foundations and Giving Programs

Mars, Inc. Corporate Contributions Program
6885 Elm St.
McLean, VA 22101
Tel: (703) 821 - 4900
Fax: (703) 448 - 9678

Annual Grant Total: none reported

Public Affairs and Related Activities Personnel

At Headquarters

MICHAELS, Paul S.
President
Tel: (703) 821 - 4900
Fax: (703) 448 - 9678

Mars, Inc.

* continued from previous page

At Other Offices

MACHUT, Marlene — Tel: (908) 852 - 1000
Director, External Affairs
800 High St.
Hackettstown, NJ 07840

Marsh & McLennan Companies, Inc.

A global professional services firm with risk and insurance services, investment management, and consulting businesses.

www.mmc.com
Annual Revenues: $12 billion

Chairman and Chief Exec. Officer — Tel: (212) 345 - 5000
CHERKASKY, Michael G. — Fax: (212) 345 - 4808

Chairman of the Board — Tel: (212) 345 - 5000
ERUBURU, Robert F. — Fax: (212) 345 - 4808

Main Headquarters
Mailing: 1166 Ave. of The Americas — Tel: (212) 345 - 5000
New York, NY 10036-2774 — Fax: (212) 345 - 4808

Corporate Foundations and Giving Programs

Marsh & McLennan Companies, Inc. Corporate Contributions Program
Contact: Gloria Chin
1166 Ave. of The Americas — Tel: (212) 345 - 5645
New York, NY 10036-2774 — Fax: (212) 345 - 4838

Annual Grant Total: over $5,000,000
The company has no fixed priorities, but provides general support to a wide range of organizations that benefit large segments of the communities they serve. Guidelines are available.
Geographic Preference: National; Area(s) in which the company operates

Public Affairs and Related Activities Personnel

At Headquarters

BISCHOFF, J. Michael — Tel: (212) 345 - 5470
V. President, Corporate Development — Fax: (212) 345 - 5669
Responsibilities include investor relations.

CHIN, Gloria — Tel: (212) 345 - 5645
Corporate Contributions Administrator — Fax: (212) 345 - 4838
gloria.chin@mmc.com

PERLMUTTER, Barbara — Tel: (212) 345 - 5585
Senior V. President, Public Affairs — Fax: (212) 345 - 4838
barbara.perlmutter@mmc.com

Marsh Inc.

Global risk management and insurance brokerage consulting firm. Formerly known as Johnson & Higgins. A subsidiary of Marsh & McLennan Companies, Inc. (see separate listing).

www.marsh.com

Main Headquarters
Mailing: 1166 Ave. of the Americas — Tel: (212) 345 - 6000
New York, NY 10036 — Fax: (212) 345 - 2309

Public Affairs and Related Activities Personnel

At Headquarters

CHERKASKY, Michael G. — Tel: (212) 345 - 6000
Fax: (212) 345 - 2309

JONES, Christopher — Tel: (212) 345 - 3683
Assistant V. President, Media Relations — Fax: (212) 345 - 2309
christopher.r.jones@marsh.com

MODUGNO, Al — Tel: (212) 345 - 2448
Senior V. President, Media Relations — Fax: (212) 345 - 2309
alfred.j.modugno@marsh.com

WILLIAMSON, Anita — Tel: (212) 345 - 6000
Corporate Communications — Fax: (212) 345 - 2309

Marsh Supermarkets, Inc.

Operator of supermakets and convenience stores.

www.marsh.net

Chairman and Chief Exec. Officer — Tel: (317) 594 - 2100
MARSH, Don E. — Fax: (317) 594 - 2704

Main Headquarters
Mailing: 9800 Crosspoint Blvd. — Tel: (317) 594 - 2100
Indianapolis, IN 46256 — Fax: (317) 594 - 2704

Public Affairs and Related Activities Personnel

At Headquarters

ELBIN, John C. — Tel: (317) 594 - 2100
Chief Financial Officer — Fax: (317) 594 - 2704

MARSH, Jodi — Tel: (317) 594 - 2640
V. President, Community Relations — Fax: (317) 594 - 2705
Responsibilities include corporate philanthropy.

REDDEN, David M. — Tel: (317) 594 - 2101
Senior V. President, Human Resources — Fax: (317) 594 - 2704

Marshall & Ilsley Corp.

A diversified financial services company.

www.micorp.com

Chairman of the Board and Chief Exec. Officer — Tel: (414) 765 - 7700
KUESTER, Dennis J. — Fax: (414) 765 - 7899

Main Headquarters
Mailing: 770 N. Water St. — Tel: (414) 765 - 7700
Milwaukee, WI 53202 — Fax: (414) 765 - 7899

Political Action Committees

Marshall & Ilsley Corp. Political Action Committee Federal Account
Contact: Randy J. Erickson
770 N. Water St. — Tel: (414) 765 - 7700
Milwaukee, WI 53202 — Fax: (414) 765 - 7899

Contributions to Candidates: none reported (01/05 - 09/05)

Corporate Foundations and Giving Programs

Marshall & Ilsley Foundation
Contact: Meg Zentner
770 N. Water St. — Tel: (414) 765 - 7700
Milwaukee, WI 53202 — Fax: (414) 765 - 7899

Annual Grant Total: $2,000,000 - $5,000,000
Geographic Preference: Wisconsin; Milwaukee, WI
Primary Interests: Arts and Culture; Higher Education; Youth Services

Public Affairs and Related Activities Personnel

At Headquarters

BURMEISTER, Lisa — Tel: (414) 765 - 7801
Shareholder Relations Administrator — Fax: (414) 298 - 2921
Mailstop: 11th Floor

CADORIN, Patricia — Tel: (414) 765 - 7814
Senior V. President and Corporate Communications Director — Fax: (414) 298 - 2926
Mailstop: 11th Floor

ERICKSON, Randy J. — Tel: (414) 765 - 7700
PAC Treasurer — Fax: (414) 765 - 7899

LETKIEWICZ, James D. — Tel: (414) 765 - 7700
V. President, Human Resources — Fax: (414) 765 - 7899
Mailstop: Eighth Floor

RENARD, Paul — Tel: (414) 765 - 7700
Senior V. President, Corporate Human Resources — Fax: (414) 765 - 7899
Mailstop: Eighth Floor

ZENTNER, Meg — Tel: (414) 765 - 7700
Secretary, Marshall & Ilsley Foundation — Fax: (414) 765 - 7899
Mailstop: Sixth Floor

Martin Marietta Materials, Inc.

A producer of construction aggregates.

www.martinmarietta.com
Annual Revenues: $1.5 billion

Chairman, President and Chief Exec. Officer — Tel: (919) 781 - 4550
ZELNAK, Stephen P., Jr. — Fax: (919) 783 - 4695

Main Headquarters
Mailing: 2710 Wycliff Rd. — Tel: (919) 781 - 4550
Raleigh, NC 27607-3033 — Fax: (919) 783 - 4695

Public Affairs and Related Activities Personnel

At Headquarters

DIRISIO, Pamela — Tel: (919) 783 - 4562
Manager, Corporate Communications — Fax: (919) 783 - 4695

HENRY, Janice K. — Tel: (919) 781 - 4550
Senior V. President, Chief Financial Officer and Treasurer — Fax: (919) 783 - 4695
Responsibilities include investor relations.

STEWART, Jonathan T. — Tel: (919) 781 - 4550
Senior V. President, Human Resources — Fax: (919) 783 - 4695

Mary Kay Inc.

PAC PUBLIC AFFAIRS COUNCIL

A member of the Public Affairs Council. The holding company for Mary Kay Cosmetics, Inc.

www.marykay.com
Annual Revenues: $1.8 billion

Chairman and Chief Exec. Officer — Tel: (972) 687 - 6300
ROGERS, Richard R. — Fax: (972) 387 - 1611
rogersr@marykay.com — TF: (800) 627 - 9529

Main Headquarters
Mailing: P.O. Box 799045 — Tel: (972) 687 - 6300
Dallas, TX 75379-9045 — Fax: (972) 387 - 1611
TF: (800) 627 - 9529

Street: 16251 N. Dallas Pkwy.
Addison, TX 75001

Mary Kay Inc.

* continued from previous page

Corporate Foundations and Giving Programs

The Mary Kay Ash Charitable Foundation
Contact: Michael L. Lunceford
P.O. Box 799045 — Tel: (972) 687 - 6300
Dallas, TX 75379-9045 — Fax: (972) 387 - 1611
TF: (800) 627 - 9529

Annual Grant Total: none reported
Primary Interests: Domestic Violence; Medical Research; Women

Public Affairs and Related Activities Personnel

At Headquarters

CREWS, Anne C. — Tel: (972) 687 - 6300
V. President, Government Relations — Fax: (972) 387 - 1611
crewsa@marykay.com — TF: (800) 627 - 9529

LANCEFORD, Michael L. — Tel: (972) 687 - 5332
Manager, Media Relations — Fax: (972) 387 - 1611
TF: (800) 627 - 9529

LUNCEFORD, Michael L. — Tel: (972) 687 - 6300
Senior V. President, Government Relations — Fax: (972) 387 - 1611
luncefordm@marykay.com — TF: (800) 627 - 9529

ROBERTS, Leslie — Tel: (972) 687 - 6300
Fax: (972) 387 - 1611
TF: (800) 627 - 9529

Masco Corp.

A manufacturer of consumer and specialty products for the home and family.
www.masco.com
Annual Revenues: $12.1 billion

Chairman and Chief Exec. Officer
MANOOGIAN, Richard A. — Tel: (313) 274 - 7400 — Fax: (313) 792 - 6135

Main Headquarters
Mailing: 21001 Van Born Rd. — Tel: (313) 274 - 7400
Taylor, MI 48180 — Fax: (313) 792 - 6135

Political Action Committees

Masco Political Action Committee
Contact: Eugene A. Gargaro, Jr.
21001 Van Born Rd. — Tel: (313) 792 - 6261
Taylor, MI 48180 — Fax: (313) 792 - 6135

Contributions to Candidates: $500 (01/05 - 09/05)
Republicans: $500.

Principal Recipients

SENATE REPUBLICANS	HOUSE REPUBLICANS	
	Knollenberg, Joe (MI)	$500

Corporate Foundations and Giving Programs

Masco Corp. Charitable Trust
Contact: Melonie Colaianne
21001 Van Born Rd. — Tel: (313) 274 - 7400
Taylor, MI 48180 — Fax: (313) 792 - 6262

Annual Grant Total: none reported
Geographic Preference: National; Detroit, MI
Primary Interests: Arts and Culture; Higher Education; Medicine and Health Care; Youth Services
Recent Recipients: Boys and Girls Club; Detroit Institute of Arts; Harvard Medical School

Public Affairs and Related Activities Personnel

At Headquarters

BAUDER, Lillian — Tel: (313) 792 - 6970
V. President, Corporate Affairs and President, Masco Charitable Trust — Fax: (313) 792 - 6135

BRINGER, Maria — Tel: (313) 792 - 6653
V. President, Investor Relations — Fax: (313) 792 - 6135

COLAIANNE, Melonie — Tel: (313) 274 - 7400
Director, Corporate Affairs — Fax: (313) 792 - 6262

CULLEN, John M. — Tel: (313) 274 - 7400
Manager, Environmental Affairs — Fax: (313) 792 - 6935

FOLEY, Daniel R. — Tel: (313) 792 - 6691
V. President, Human Resources — Fax: (313) 792 - 6135

GARGARO, Eugene A., Jr. — Tel: (313) 792 - 6261
Vice President and Secretary; Treasurer, Masco Political Action Committee — Fax: (313) 792 - 6135

MODLIN, Kathleen — Tel: (313) 792 - 6382
Director, Corporate Communications — Fax: (313) 792 - 6666

ROTHWELL, Sharon — Tel: (313) 792 - 6028
V. President, Corporate Affairs — Fax: (313) 792 - 6135

VAN HISE, David W. — Tel: (313) 792 - 6961
V. President, International — Fax: (313) 792 - 6135

Masonite Corp.

See listing on page 307 under Masonite Internat'l Corp.

Masonite Internat'l Corp.

A manufacturer and merchandiser of doors. Based in Ontario.
www.masonite.com

Chairman of the Board, President and Chief Exec. Officer
ORSINO, Philip S. — Tel: (813) 877 - 2726 — Fax: (813) 739 - 0204

Main Headquarters
Mailing: One North Dale Mabry, Suite 950 — Tel: (813) 877 - 2726
Tampa, FL 33609 — Fax: (813) 739 - 0204

Public Affairs and Related Activities Personnel

At Headquarters

BRAVO, Mary Ann — Tel: (813) 877 - 2726
Marketing Manager — Fax: (813) 739 - 0204
Responsibilities include public affairs.

KOHNER, Phil — Tel: (813) 877 - 2726
Manager, Human Resources — Fax: (813) 739 - 0204

Massachusetts Mutual Life Insurance Co.

See listing on page 307 under MassMutual Financial Group.

Massey Energy Co.

A coal producer.
www.masseycoal.com
Annual Revenues: $1.6 billion

Chairman, President and Chief Exec. Officer
BLANKENSHIP, Don L. — Tel: (804) 788 - 1800 — Fax: (804) 788 - 1870

Main Headquarters
Mailing: Four N. Fourth St. — Tel: (804) 788 - 1800
Richmond, VA 23219-2230 — Fax: (804) 788 - 1870

Political Action Committees

A.T. Massey Coal Co. Inc. PAC
Contact: Nancy Cothran
Four N. Fourth St. — Tel: (804) 788 - 1800
Richmond, VA 23219-2230 — Fax: (804) 788 - 1870

Contributions to Candidates: none reported (01/05 - 09/05)

Corporate Foundations and Giving Programs

Massey Energy Community Support
Four N. Fourth St. — Tel: (804) 788 - 1800
Richmond, VA 23219-2230 — Fax: (804) 788 - 1870

Annual Grant Total: none reported
Primary Interests: Arts and Culture; Education; Historic Preservation

Public Affairs and Related Activities Personnel

At Headquarters

COTHRAN, Nancy — Tel: (804) 788 - 1800
PAC Treasurer — Fax: (804) 788 - 1870

KENNY, Katharine W. — Tel: (804) 788 - 1824
V. President, Investor Relations — Fax: (804) 788 - 1870
katharine.kenny@masseyenergyco.com

POMA, John M. — Tel: (804) 788 - 1800
V. President, Human Resources — Fax: (804) 788 - 1870

MassMutual Financial Group

A global, diversified financial services organization. The company also goes by the name Massachusetts Mutual Life Insurance Co.
www.massmutual.com
Annual Revenues: $15.98 billion

Chairman of the Board
BIRLE, James R. — Tel: (413) 744 - 8411 — Fax: (413) 744 - 6005 — TF: (800) 767 - 1000

President and Chief Exec. Officer
REESE, Stuart H. — Tel: (413) 744 - 8411 — Fax: (413) 744 - 6005 — TF: (800) 767 - 1000

Main Headquarters
Mailing: 1295 State St. — Tel: (413) 744 - 8411
Springfield, MA 01111-0001 — Fax: (413) 744 - 6005
TF: (800) 767 - 1000

Washington Office
Contact: Alison B. Weiss
Mailing: 601 Pennsylvania Ave., NW — Tel: (202) 737 - 0440
Suite 420, S. Bldg. — Fax: (202) 628 - 2313
Washington, DC 20004

Political Action Committees

Massachusetts Mutual Life Insurance Co. Political Action Committee
Contact: Bruce Frisbie
1295 State St. — Tel: (413) 744 - 2422
Springfield, MA 01111-0001 — Fax: (413) 744 - 6005
TF: (800) 767 - 1000

MassMutual Financial Group

* continued from previous page

Contributions to Candidates: $115,500 (01/05 - 09/05)
Democrats: $37,000; Republicans: $78,500.

Principal Recipients

SENATE DEMOCRATS		HOUSE DEMOCRATS	
Nelson, Benjamin (NE)	$3,000	Andrews, Robert (NJ)	$4,000
		Mcgovern, James (MA)	$3,000
SENATE REPUBLICANS		**HOUSE REPUBLICANS**	
		Boehner, John (OH)	$4,000
		Ryan, Paul D (WI)	$4,000
		Bachus, Spencer (AL)	$3,000
		Baker, Hugh (LA)	$3,000
		Dreier, David (CA)	$3,000
		Renzi, Richard (AZ)	$3,000
		Reynolds, Thomas (NY)	$3,000

Corporate Foundations and Giving Programs

Massachusetts Mutual Contributions Program
Contact: Ronald Copes
140 Garden St.
Hartford, CT 06154
Tel: (860) 987 - 3369
Fax: (860) 987 - 6532

Annual Grant Total: $2,000,000 - $5,000,000
The company also maintains a matching gifts program.
Geographic Preference: Hartford, CT; Springfield, MA
Primary Interests: Arts and Culture; Community Affairs; Education
Recent Recipients: United Way

MassMutual Foundation for Hartford, Inc.
Contact: Ronald Copes
140 Garden St.
Hartford, CT 06154
Tel: (860) 987 - 3369
Fax: (860) 987 - 6532

Annual Grant Total: over $5,000,000

Public Affairs and Related Activities Personnel

At Headquarters

COHEN, Kenneth S.
Senior V. President, Federal Government Relations and Deputy General Counsel
kcohen@massmutual.com
Tel: (413) 744 - 8411
Fax: (413) 744 - 6005
TF: (800) 767 - 1000

DI GIORGIO, Mark
Media Contact
Tel: (413) 744 - 7722
Fax: (413) 744 - 6005
TF: (800) 767 - 1000

FRISBIE, Bruce
Treasurer, Massachusetts Mutual Life Insurance Co. Political Action Committee
Tel: (413) 744 - 2422
Fax: (413) 744 - 6005
TF: (800) 767 - 1000

KOZLOWSKI, Elizabeth P.
Manager, Grassroots and Communications
Tel: (413) 744 - 5633
Fax: (413) 744 - 6005
TF: (800) 767 - 1000

LACEY, Jim
Assistant V. President, Media and Public Relations
Tel: (413) 744 - 2365
Fax: (413) 744 - 6005
TF: (800) 767 - 1000

At Washington Office

WEISS, Alison B.
Director, Government Relations
Registered Federal Lobbyist.
Tel: (202) 737 - 0440
Fax: (202) 628 - 2313

At Other Offices

COPES, Ronald
V. President, Community Relations
140 Garden St.
Hartford, CT 06154
Responsibilities include corporate philanthropy.
Tel: (860) 987 - 3369
Fax: (860) 987 - 6532

FYNTRILAKIS, Nicholas
Communications Consultant
140 Garden St.
Hartford, CT 06154
Tel: (860) 987 - 3283
Fax: (860) 987 - 6532

MasterCard Internat'l

A member of the Public Affairs Council. A global payments company.
www.mastercardinternational.com
Annual Revenues: $1.891 billion

Chairman
JAQUOTOT, Baldomero Falcones
Tel: (914) 249 - 2000
Fax: (914) 249 - 4206

President and Chief Exec. Officer
SELANDER, Robert W.
Tel: (914) 249 - 2000
Fax: (914) 249 - 4206

Main Headquarters
Mailing: 2000 Purchase St.
Purchase, NY 10577-2509
Tel: (914) 249 - 2000
Fax: (914) 249 - 4206

Washington Office
Contact: Joe Rubin
Mailing: 1401 I St. NW
Suite 240
Washington, DC 20005-2225
Tel: (202) 414 - 8000
Fax: (202) 414 - 8010

Political Action Committees

Mastercard Internat'l Employees PAC
Contact: Linda Kirkpatrick
2000 Purchase St.
Purchase, NY 10577-2509
Tel: (914) 249 - 2000
Fax: (914) 249 - 4206

Contributions to Candidates: $5,100 (01/05 - 09/05)
Republicans: $5,100.

Principal Recipients

SENATE REPUBLICANS		HOUSE REPUBLICANS
Allen, George (VA)	$2,100	
Bennett, Robert F (UT)	$2,000	
Talent, James (MO)	$1,000	

Corporate Foundations and Giving Programs

MasterCard Philanthropy Program
Contact: Diana McSweeney
2000 Purchase St.
Purchase, NY 10577-2509
Tel: (914) 249 - 6224
Fax: (914) 249 - 4206

Annual Grant Total: none reported
Primary Interests: Education

Public Affairs and Related Activities Personnel

At Headquarters

CLOUGH, Veronika
Director, Global Communications
Tel: (914) 249 - 3198
Fax: (914) 249 - 4206

GAMSIN, Sharon
V. President, Global Communications
sgamsin@mastercard.com
Tel: (914) 249 - 5622
Fax: (914) 249 - 4207

KIRKPATRICK, Linda
Treasurer, Mastercard Internat'l Employees PAC
Tel: (914) 249 - 2000
Fax: (914) 249 - 4206

MCSWEENEY, Diana
Contact, MasterCard Philanthropy Program
Tel: (914) 249 - 6224
Fax: (914) 249 - 4206

WATSON, Vicki
Cordinator, Global Communications
Tel: (914) 249 - 2000
Fax: (914) 249 - 4206

At Washington Office

RUBIN, Joe
V. President, Government Affairs
Tel: (202) 414 - 8000
Fax: (202) 414 - 8010

Matson Navigation Company, Inc.

An ocean freight shipping subsidiary of Alexander & Baldwin, Inc. (see separate listing).
www.matson.com

Chairman of the Board
STOCKHOLM, Charles M.
Tel: (510) 628 - 4000
Fax: (510) 628 - 7359

President and Chief Exec. Officer
ANDRASICK, James S.
Tel: (510) 628 - 4000
Fax: (510) 628 - 7359

Main Headquarters
Mailing: 555 12th St.
Eighth Floor
Oakland, CA 94607
Street: 333 Market St.
San Francisco, CA 94105
Tel: (510) 628 - 4000
Fax: (510) 628 - 7359

Washington Office
Contact: Philip M. Grill
Mailing: 1735 New York Ave., N.W.
Suite 500
Washington, DC 20006
Tel: (202) 662 - 8455
Fax: (202) 331 - 1024

Political Action Committees

Matson Navigation Co. Inc. Federal Election Committee
Contact: Tim H. Reid
555 12th St.
Eighth Floor
Oakland, CA 94607
Tel: (510) 628 - 4000
Fax: (510) 628 - 7359

Contributions to Candidates: $21,500 (01/05 - 09/05)
Democrats: $14,000; Republicans: $6,500; Other: $1,000.

Principal Recipients

SENATE DEMOCRATS		HOUSE DEMOCRATS	
Akaka, Daniel (HI)	$4,000	Abercrombie, Neil (HI)	$4,000
SENATE REPUBLICANS		**HOUSE REPUBLICANS**	
Stevens, Ted (AK)	$2,000		

Corporate Foundations and Giving Programs

Matson Navigation Co. Corporate Giving Program
Contact: Jeffrey S. Hull

Matson Navigation Company, Inc.

** continued from previous page*

555 12th St.
Eighth Floor
Oakland, CA 94607
Tel: (510) 628 - 4534
Fax: (510) 628 - 7359

Annual Grant Total: none reported

Public Affairs and Related Activities Personnel

At Headquarters

HULL, Jeffrey S.
Manager, Public Relations
jhull@matson.com
Tel: (510) 628 - 4534
Fax: (510) 628 - 7359

REID, Tim H.
PAC Treasurer
treid@matson.com
Tel: (510) 628 - 4000
Fax: (510) 628 - 7359

At Washington Office

GRILL, Philip M.
V. President, Government Relations
pgrill@mindspring.com
Registered Federal Lobbyist.
Tel: (202) 662 - 8455
Fax: (202) 331 - 1024

Matsushita Consumer Electronics Co.

See listing on page 309 under Matsushita Electric Corp of America.

Matsushita Electric Corp. of America

A subsidiary of Matsushita Electric Industrial Co., Ltd. of Osaka, Japan.
www.panasonic.com

Chairman and Chief Executive Officer
YAMADA, Yoshihiko
Tel: (201) 348 - 7000
Fax: (201) 392 - 6007
TF: (888) 275 - 2995

Main Headquarters
Mailing: One Panasonic Way
Secaucus, NJ 07094
Tel: (201) 348 - 7000
Fax: (201) 392 - 6007
TF: (888) 275 - 2995

Washington Office
Contact: Peter F. Fannon
Mailing: 1130 Connecticut Ave. NW
Suite 1100
Washington, DC 20036
Tel: (202) 912 - 3800

Corporate Foundations and Giving Programs

The Panasonic Foundation
Contact: Sophie Sa, Ph.D.
One Panasonic Way
Secaucus, NJ 07094
Tel: (201) 392 - 4132
Fax: (201) 392 - 6910
TF: (888) 275 - 2995

Annual Grant Total: $1,000,000 - $2,000,000
Established in 1984. Works in long-term partnership with a small number of public school districts to provide technical assistance to these districts and their schools or to bring about school-based, whole-school, systemic reform. Current partnerships are with San Diego (CA), Allentown (PA), Lancaster (PA), Cincinnati (OH), Minneapolis (MN), Broward County (FL), and the State Department of Education of New Mexico. Grants on related topics are made only at the initiation of the Foundation.

Panasonic Corporate Contributions Program
Contact: Sophie Sa, Ph.D.
One Panasonic Way
Secaucus, NJ 07094
Tel: (201) 392 - 4132
Fax: (201) 392 - 6910
TF: (888) 275 - 2995

Annual Grant Total: $2,000,000 - $5,000,000
Geographic Preference: Canada; National; Mexico; Puerto Rico
Primary Interests: Education; Health; Minority Opportunities
Recent Recipients: March of Dimes; Nat'l Urban League

Public Affairs and Related Activities Personnel

At Headquarters

CAMERLENGO, Justin L.
Director, Corporate Communications
Mailstop: Panazip 3C-7
Tel: (201) 348 - 7000
Fax: (201) 392 - 6910
TF: (888) 275 - 2995

PRITCHARD, Bill
Public Relations
pritchardw@us.panasonic.com
Tel: (201) 348 - 7182
Fax: (201) 392 - 6007
TF: (888) 275 - 2995

SA, Sophie, Ph.D.
Exec. Director, The Panasonic Foundation
Mailstop: Panazip 3G-7A
Tel: (201) 392 - 4132
Fax: (201) 392 - 6910
TF: (888) 275 - 2995

SAFER, Will
Public Relations
saferw@us.panasonic.com
Tel: (201) 392 - 6124
Fax: (201) 392 - 6007
TF: (888) 275 - 2995

At Washington Office

ALEXANDER, Mary K.
Group Manager, Government and Public Affairs
Registered Federal Lobbyist.
Tel: (202) 912 - 3800

FANNON, Peter F.
V. President, Technology Policy and Regulatory Affairs
Registered Federal Lobbyist.
Tel: (202) 912 - 3800

SCHOMBURG, Paul
Manager, Government and Public Affairs
Registered Federal Lobbyist.
Tel: (202) 912 - 3800

SHARP, Mark
General Manager, Corporate Environmental Department
Registered Federal Lobbyist.
Tel: (202) 912 - 3800

TANII, Akahiro
Senior Representative
(Matsushita Electrical Industrial Co.)
Registered Federal Lobbyist.
Tel: (202) 912 - 3800

Matsushita Electrical Industrial Co.

See listing on page 309 under Matsushita Electric Corp of America.

Mattel, Inc.

A member of the Public Affairs Council. A toy manufacturer.
www.mattel.com
Annual Revenues: $4.804 billion

Chairman and Chief Exec. Officer
ECKERT, Robert A.
Tel: (310) 252 - 2000
Fax: (310) 252 - 2179

Main Headquarters
Mailing: 333 Continental Blvd.
El Segundo, CA 90245-5012
Tel: (310) 252 - 2000
Fax: (310) 252 - 2180

Political Action Committees

Mattel Political Action Committee
Contact: Kevin M. Farr
333 Continental Blvd.
El Segundo, CA 90245-5012
Tel: (310) 252 - 2000
Fax: (310) 252 - 2180

Contributions to Candidates: none reported (01/05 - 09/05)

Corporate Foundations and Giving Programs

Mattel Children's Foundation
Contact: Kim Manos
333 Continental Blvd.
El Segundo, CA 90245-5012
Tel: (310) 252 - 2908
Fax: (310) 252 - 4443

Annual Grant Total: over $5,000,000
No unsolicited proposals and videos accepted. Electronic annual report accessible at www.mattel.com. Funds are committed through 2005.
Primary Interests: Children; Children's Health; Early Childhood Education; Families; Youth Services
Recent Recipients: Alliance for Technology Access; Mattel Children's Hospital at UCLA

Public Affairs and Related Activities Personnel

At Headquarters

BONGIOVANNI, Lisa Marie
V. President, Corporate Communications and Government Affairs
Tel: (310) 252 - 3524
Fax: (310) 252 - 4443

FARR, Kevin M.
Chief Financial Officer
Mailstop: MI-1417
Responsibilities include political action.
Tel: (310) 252 - 2000
Fax: (310) 252 - 2180

JACKSON, Joleen
Director, Investor Relations
Tel: (310) 252 - 2000
Fax: (310) 252 - 2180

KAYE, Alan
Senior V. President, Human Resources
Tel: (310) 252 - 2000
Fax: (310) 252 - 2180

MANOS, Kim
Administrator, Mattel Children's Foundation
Tel: (310) 252 - 2908
Fax: (310) 252 - 4443

MURAT, Corinne
Senor Manager, Government Affairs
Mailstop: M1-1418
corinne.murat@mattel.com
Tel: (310) 252 - 6628
Fax: (310) 252 - 4443

SALOP, Mike A.
V. President, Investor Relations
Tel: (310) 252 - 2000
Fax: (310) 252 - 2180

Maxim Integrated Products

Design, development, manufacturing and marketing of linear and mixed signal circuits.
www.maxim-ic.com
Annual Revenues: $1.439 billion

Chairman, President and Chief Exec. Officer
GIFFORD, John F.
jgifford@maxim-ic.com
Tel: (408) 737 - 7600
Fax: (408) 737 - 7194
TF: (800) 998 - 9872

Main Headquarters
Mailing: 120 San Gabriel Dr.
Sunnyvale, CA 94086
Tel: (408) 737 - 7600
Fax: (408) 737 - 7194
TF: (800) 998 - 9872

Public Affairs and Related Activities Personnel

At Headquarters

JASPER, Carl W.
V. President
Tel: (408) 737 - 7600
Fax: (408) 737 - 7194
TF: (800) 998 - 9872

MAXIMUS, Inc.

A provider of program management, information technology, and consulting services to state and local government health and human service agencies.

www.maximus.com

Chairman of the Board
POND, Peter B.
Tel: (703) 251 - 8500
Fax: (703) 251 - 8240
TF: (888) 368 - 2152

President and Chief Exec. Officer
DAVENPORT, Lynn P.
Tel: (703) 251 - 8500
Fax: (703) 251 - 8240
TF: (888) 368 - 2152

Main Headquarters
Mailing: 11419 Sunset Hills Rd.
Reston, VA 20190-5207
Tel: (703) 251 - 8500
Fax: (703) 251 - 8240
TF: (888) 368 - 2152

Political Action Committees

Maximus, Inc. Political Action Committee (MAXPAC)
Contact: Glenn Yanis
11419 Sunset Hills Rd.
Reston, VA 20190-5207
Tel: (703) 251 - 8500
Fax: (703) 251 - 8240
TF: (888) 368 - 2152

Contributions to Candidates: none reported (01/05 - 09/05)

Corporate Foundations and Giving Programs

Maximus Charitable Foundation
Contact: Louis E. Chappuie
11419 Sunset Hills Rd.
Reston, VA 20190-5207
Tel: (703) 251 - 8500
Fax: (703) 251 - 8240
TF: (888) 368 - 2152

Annual Grant Total: none reported
Primary Interests: Youth Services
Recent Recipients: Boys and Girls Club; Children's Advocacy Center; Jacob's Ladder

Public Affairs and Related Activities Personnel

At Headquarters

CHAPPUIE, Louis E.
President, Maximus Charitable Foundation
louischa@comcast.net
Tel: (703) 251 - 8500
Fax: (703) 251 - 8240
TF: (888) 368 - 2152

GRANT, Jeremy
V. President
Tel: (703) 251 - 8500
Fax: (703) 251 - 8240
TF: (888) 368 - 2152

MILES, Lisa
Director, Investor Relations
lisamiles@maximus.com
Tel: (703) 251 - 8500
Fax: (703) 251 - 8240
TF: (888) 368 - 2152

ROWLAND, Rachael
V. President, Public and Media Relations
rrowland@maximus.com
Tel: (703) 251 - 8500
Fax: (703) 251 - 8240
TF: (888) 368 - 2152

YANIS, Glenn
PAC Contact
Tel: (703) 251 - 8500
Fax: (703) 251 - 8240
TF: (888) 368 - 2152

Maxtor Corp.

A manufacturer of computer disk drives.

www.maxtor.com
Annual Revenues: $4.1 billion

Chairman and Chief Exec. Officer
PARK, Dr. Chong Sup
Tel: (408) 894 - 5000
Fax: (408) 952 - 3600
TF: (800) 262 - 9867

Main Headquarters
Mailing: 500 McCarthy Blvd.
Milpitas, CA 95035
Tel: (408) 894 - 5000
Fax: (408) 952 - 3600
TF: (800) 262 - 9867

Corporate Foundations and Giving Programs

Maxtor Corporate Contributions Program
Contact: Stephen DiFranco
500 McCarthy Blvd.
Milpitas, CA 95035
Tel: (408) 894 - 5000
Fax: (408) 952 - 3600
TF: (800) 262 - 9867

Annual Grant Total: none reported
Gives monetary and in-kind gifts to non-profit, community-oriented organizations.
Geographic Preference: Area(s) in which the company operates
Primary Interests: Civic and Cultural Activities; Education; Health and Human Services

Public Affairs and Related Activities Personnel

At Headquarters

BERNHEIMER, Alan
Public Relations Contact, North, Central and South America
alan_bernheimer@maxtor.com
Tel: (408) 894 - 5000
Fax: (408) 952 - 3600
TF: (800) 262 - 9867

DIFRANCO, Stephen
Corporate Contributions Contact
Tel: (408) 894 - 5000
Fax: (408) 952 - 3600
TF: (800) 262 - 9867

HARTIN, Erin
Manager, Public Relations
erin_hartin@maxtor.com
Tel: (408) 678 - 2022
Fax: (408) 952 - 3600
TF: (800) 262 - 9867

KIRTLAND, Jennifer
Senior Director, Investor Relations
investor_relations@maxtor.com
Tel: (408) 324 - 7056
Fax: (408) 952 - 3600
TF: (800) 262 - 9867

KLINESTIVER, John
Senior V. President, Human Resources
Tel: (408) 894 - 5000
Fax: (408) 952 - 3600
TF: (800) 262 - 9867

MAXXAM Inc.

A holding company that operates in the aluminum, forest products, real estate, and racing industries.

Chairman and Chief Exec. Officer
HURWITZ, Charles E.
Tel: (713) 975 - 7600
Fax: (713) 267 - 3701

Main Headquarters
Mailing: 1330 post Oak Blvd.
Suite 2000
Houston, TX 77056
Tel: (713) 975 - 7600
Fax: (713) 267 - 3701

Political Action Committees

MAXXAM Inc. Federal PAC
Contact: M. Emily Madison
1330 post Oak Blvd.
Suite 2000
Houston, TX 77056
Tel: (713) 975 - 7600
Fax: (713) 267 - 3701

Contributions to Candidates: $10,600 (01/05 - 09/05)
Democrats: $600; Republicans: $10,000.

Principal Recipients

SENATE REPUBLICANS

HOUSE REPUBLICANS
DeLay, Tom (TX) $10,000

Public Affairs and Related Activities Personnel

At Headquarters

MADISON, M. Emily
V. President, Finance
Tel: (713) 975 - 7600
Fax: (713) 267 - 3701

May Department Stores Co.

See listing on page 191 under Federated Department Stores, Inc.

Mayflower Transit

See listing on page 486 under UniGroup, Inc.

Maytag Corp.

A manufacturer of home and commercial appliances sold throughout North America and international markets. Brands include Maytag, Hoover, Jenn-Air, Amana, and Dixie-Narco.

www.maytagcorp.com
Annual Revenues: $4.7 billion

Chairman and Chief Exec. Officer
HAKE, Ralph F.
rhake@maytag.com
Tel: (641) 792 - 7000
Fax: (641) 787 - 8376

Main Headquarters
Mailing: P.O. Box 39
Newton, IA 50208-0039
Street: 403 W. Fourth St., North
Newton, IA 50208
Tel: (641) 792 - 7000
Fax: (641) 787 - 8376

Washington Office
Contact: David P. Steiner
Mailing: 701 Pennsylvania Ave. NW
Suite 750
Washington, DC 20004
Tel: (202) 639 - 9420
Fax: (202) 639 - 9421

Political Action Committees

Maytag Corp. Dependability Fund
Contact: Mark Ayers
P.O. Box 39
Newton, IA 50208-0039
Tel: (641) 792 - 7000
Fax: (641) 787 - 8376

Contributions to Candidates: $6,500 (01/05 - 09/05)
Democrats: $1,000; Republicans: $5,500.

Principal Recipients

SENATE DEMOCRATS

HOUSE DEMOCRATS
Scott, David (GA) $1,000

SENATE REPUBLICANS

HOUSE REPUBLICANS
Camp, David Lee (MI) $1,000
Johnson, Nancy (CT) $1,000
McCrery, Jim (LA) $1,000
Nussle, Jim (IA) $1,000
Shimkus, John (IL) $1,000

Maytag Corp.

** continued from previous page*

Corporate Foundations and Giving Programs

Maytag Corporation Foundation
Contact: Michele Walstrom
P.O. Box 39 Tel: (641) 792 - 7000
Newton, IA 50208-0039 Fax: (641) 787 - 8376

Annual Grant Total: $2,000,000 - $5,000,000
Geographic Preference: Area(s) in which the company operates; Illinois; Iowa; Ohio; Tennessee; South Carolina
Primary Interests: Arts and Humanities; Community Development; Scholarship Funds
Recent Recipients: Ohio Foundation of Independent Colleges; YMCA

Public Affairs and Related Activities Personnel

At Headquarters

AYERS, Mark Tel: (641) 792 - 7000
PAC Treasurer Fax: (641) 787 - 8376

KRIVORUCHKA, Mark Tel: (641) 792 - 7000
Senior V. President, Human Resources Fax: (641) 787 - 8376
mkrivo@maytag.com

LYNN, Karen J. Tel: (641) 792 - 7000
V. President, Corporate Communications Fax: (641) 787 - 8376

WALLS, Carol Tel: (641) 792 - 7000
Coordinator, Shareholder Relations Fax: (641) 787 - 8102
cwalls@maytag.com

WALSTROM, Michele Tel: (641) 792 - 7000
Manager, Community Relations and Foundation Fax: (641) 787 - 8376
mwalst@maytag.com

At Washington Office

HARMS, Luke Tel: (202) 639 - 9420
Government Affairs Representative Fax: (202) 639 - 9421
Registered Federal Lobbyist.

STEINER, David P. Tel: (202) 639 - 9420
V. President, Government Affairs Fax: (202) 639 - 9421
Registered Federal Lobbyist.

Mazda North American Operations

The American subsidiary of the Japanese motor vehicle manufacturer.
www.mazdausa.com

President and Chief Exec. Officer; Chairman, Mazda Foundation (USA) Inc. Tel: (949) 727 - 1990
O'SULLIVAN, James J. Fax: (949) 727 - 6101
TF: (800) 222 - 5500

Main Headquarters
Mailing: P.O. Box 19734 Tel: (949) 727 - 1990
Irvine, CA 92623-9734 Fax: (949) 727 - 6101
TF: (800) 222 - 5500

Street: 1155 Irvine Center Dr.
Irvine, CA 92623

Washington Office
Contact: Barbara Nocera
Mailing: 1025 Connecticut Ave., N.W., Suite 910 Tel: (202) 467 - 5088
Washington, DC 20036

Corporate Foundations and Giving Programs

Mazda Foundations (USA) Inc.
Contact: Barbara Nocera
1025 Connecticut Ave., N.W., Suite 910 Tel: (202) 467 - 5096
Washington, DC 20036

Annual Grant Total: $2,000,000 - $5,000,000
The company also sponsors a matching gifts program. Further information about the Mazda USA Foundation can be found on their website: www.mazdafoundation.org.
Geographic Preference: National
Primary Interests: Arts and Culture; Education; Literacy; Performing Arts; Social Services

Public Affairs and Related Activities Personnel

At Headquarters

AMESTOY, Jay Tel: (949) 727 - 1990
V. President, Public and Government Affairs Fax: (949) 727 - 6813
jamestoy@mazdausa.com TF: (800) 222 - 5500

At Washington Office

NOCERA, Barbara Tel: (202) 467 - 5096
Director, Government and Public Affairs
bnocera@mazdausa.com
Registered Federal Lobbyist.

PENDER, Annemarie Tel: (202) 467 - 5088
Government and East Coast Public Affairs Representative
apender@mazdausa.com
Registered Federal Lobbyist.

RYAN, Dan Tel: (202) 467 - 5088
Manager, Government and Safety Affairs
Registered Federal Lobbyist.

MBIA, Inc.

Parent company of MBIA, a provider of financial guarantee insurance.
www.mbia.com

Chairman of the Board Tel: (914) 273 - 4545
BROWN, Joseph W. Fax: (914) 765 - 3163
joseph.brown@mbia.com

Chief Exec. Officer Tel: (914) 273 - 4545
DUNTON, Gary C. Fax: (914) 765 - 3163
gary.dunton@mbia.com

Main Headquarters
Mailing: 113 King St. Tel: (914) 273 - 4545
Armonk, NY 10504 Fax: (914) 765 - 3163

Corporate Foundations and Giving Programs

MBIA Foundation
Contact: Sue Voltz
113 King St. Tel: (914) 273 - 4545
Armonk, NY 10504 Fax: (914) 765 - 3163

Annual Grant Total: $2,000,000 - $5,000,000

Public Affairs and Related Activities Personnel

At Headquarters

BALLINGER, Michael Tel: (914) 765 - 3893
Director, Corporate Communications Fax: (914) 765 - 3163
michael.ballinger@mbia.com

GEISINGER, Ethel Tel: (914) 273 - 4545
V. President, Government Relations Fax: (914) 765 - 3163
ethel.geisinger@mbia.com

JAMES, Elizabeth Tel: (914) 765 - 3889
V. President, Corporate Communications Fax: (914) 765 - 3898
elizabeth.james@mbia.com

VOLTZ, Sue Tel: (914) 273 - 4545
MBIA Foundation Contact Fax: (914) 765 - 3163

MBNA Corp.

PUBLIC AFFAIRS COUNCIL

A member of the Public Affairs Council. National commercial bank. In July 2005, the company announced plans to merge with Bank of America Corp. (see separate listing).
www.mbna.com
Annual Revenues: $10.145 billion

Chairman of the Board Fax: (302) 456 - 8541
LERNER, Randolph D. TF: (800) 441 - 7048

President and Chief Exec. Officer Fax: (302) 456 - 8541
HAMMONDS, Bruce L. TF: (800) 441 - 7048

Main Headquarters
Mailing: 1100 N. King St. Tel: (302) 453 - 9930
Wilmington, DE 19880-127 Fax: (302) 456 - 8541
TF: (800) 441 - 7048

Political Action Committees

MBNA Corp. Federal Political Committee
Contact: Louis J. Freeh
1100 N. King St. Tel: (302) 432 - 0956
Wilmington, DE 19880-127 Fax: (302) 432 - 0039
TF: (800) 441 - 7048

Contributions to Candidates: $150,489 (01/05 - 09/05)
Democrats: $32,515; Republicans: $117,974.

Principal Recipients

SENATE DEMOCRATS		HOUSE DEMOCRATS	
		Menendez, Robert (NJ)	$10,000
		Meeks, Gregory W (NY)	$3,500
SENATE REPUBLICANS		**HOUSE REPUBLICANS**	
Talent, James (MO)	$10,000	Bachus, Spencer (AL)	$7,000
Allen, George (VA)	$8,000	Castle, Michael (DE)	$6,000
Santorum, Richard (PA)	$8,000	Dewine, R. Pat (OH)	$5,000
Snowe, Olympia (ME)	$6,500	Hastert, Dennis J. (IL)	$5,000
Ensign, John Eric (NV)	$5,000	Oxley, Michael (OH)	$5,000
Hatch, Orrin (UT)	$4,000	Price, Thomas (GA)	$5,000
Lott, Trent (MS)	$4,000	McHenry, Patrick (NC)	$4,474
		Sensenbrenner, Jim (WI)	$3,500

Corporate Foundations and Giving Programs

MBNA Foundation
Contact: Michael Shriver

MBNA Corp.

* continued from previous page

1100 N. King St.
Wilmington, DE 19880-127
Tel: (302) 453 - 9930
Fax: (302) 456 - 8541
TF: (800) 441 - 7048

Annual Grant Total: none reported

More information is available from the foundation's website: www.mbnafoundation.org.

Primary Interests: Arts and Humanities; Community Affairs; Education

Public Affairs and Related Activities Personnel

At Headquarters

COLLINGWOOD, John
Exec. V. President and Dirctor of Government Affairs
Mailstop: 0127
john.collingwood@mbna.com
Tel: (302) 432 - 0956
Fax: (302) 432 - 0304
TF: (800) 441 - 7048

FREEH, Louis J.
PAC Treasurer
Mailstop: 0127
Tel: (302) 432 - 0956
Fax: (302) 432 - 0039
TF: (800) 441 - 7048

JAMISON, Wendy
First V. President, Government Affairs
Mailstop: 0127
wendy.jamison@mbna.com
Tel: (302) 432 - 0956
Fax: (302) 432 - 0039
TF: (800) 441 - 7048

MINOTT, Darrell
Exec. V. President, Federal Government Affairs
Mailstop: 0127
darrell.minott@mbna.com
Fax: (302) 432 - 0705
TF: (302) 432 - 0039

MURPHY, Edward H.
Director, Investor Relations
Tel: (302) 456 - 8541
Fax: (302) 456 - 8541
TF: (800) 441 - 7048

SHRIVER, Michael
Contact, MBNA Foundation
Tel: (302) 453 - 9930
Fax: (302) 456 - 8541
TF: (800) 441 - 7048

STANZ, Paul L.
First V. President, State Government Affairs
paul.stanz@mbna.com
Tel: (469) 201 - 5971
Fax: (469) 201 - 4108
TF: (800) 441 - 7048

McAfee, Inc.

Formerly Network Associates, Inc. Supplies network and systems security products and services.

www.mcafee.com

Chairman and Chief Exec. Officer
SAMENUK, George
gsamenuk@mcafee.com
Tel: (408) 346 - 5101
TF: (800) 338 - 8754

Main Headquarters
Mailing: 3965 Freedom Circle
Santa Clara, CA 95054
Tel: (408) 988 - 3832
Fax: (408) 970 - 9727
TF: (866) 817 - 8766

Washington Office
Contact: Douglas Sabo
Mailing: 1908 New Hampshire Ave., NW
Washington, DC 20009
Tel: (202) 462 - 1976

Corporate Foundations and Giving Programs

McAfee in the Community
Contact: Douglas Sabo
1908 New Hampshire Ave., NW
Washington, DC 20009
Tel: (202) 462 - 1976

Annual Grant Total: none reported

Public Affairs and Related Activities Personnel

At Headquarters

BLOUGH, Kelly
V. President, Corporate and Investor Relations
kblough@mcafee.com
Tel: (408) 346 - 3481
Fax: (408) 346 - 5411
TF: (800) 338 - 8754

LAUBER, Gwyn
Director, Investor Relations
gwyn_lauber@mcafee.com
Tel: (408) 346 - 5358
Fax: (408) 346 - 3459
TF: (800) 338 - 8754

At Washington Office

SABO, Douglas
Director, Government and Community Relations
dsabo@nai.com
Responsibilities include corporate philanthropy.
Tel: (202) 462 - 1976

McCormick & Company, Inc.

A member of the Public Affairs Council. A producer of spices, seasonings, flavorings and other specialty foods.

www.mccormick.com
Annual Revenues: $2.5 billion

Chairman, President, and Chief Exec. Officer
LAWLESS, Robert J.
Tel: (410) 771 - 7301
Fax: (410) 771 - 7462

Main Headquarters
Mailing: 18 Loveton Circle
Sparks, MD 21152-6000
Tel: (410) 771 - 7301
Fax: (410) 771 - 7462

Political Action Committees

McCormick & Company, Inc. Political Action Committee
Contact: Diane E. Grim
18 Loveton Circle
Sparks, MD 21152-6000
Tel: (410) 771 - 7301
Fax: (410) 527 - 8289

Contributions to Candidates: none reported (01/05 - 09/05)

Corporate Foundations and Giving Programs

McCormick and Co. Fund
Contact: Allen M. Barrett, Jr.
18 Loveton Circle
Sparks, MD 21152-6000
Tel: (410) 771 - 7310
Fax: (410) 527 - 8289

Annual Grant Total: $750,000 - $1,000,000

Geographic Preference: Area in which the company is headquartered; Area(s) in which the company operates

Primary Interests: Education; Social Services

Public Affairs and Related Activities Personnel

At Headquarters

BARRETT, Allen M., Jr.
V. President, Communications
Tel: (410) 771 - 7310
Fax: (410) 527 - 8289

Responsibilities include corporate philanthropy.

BROOKS, Joyce
Assistant Treasurer, Investor Relations and Financial Services
joyce_brooks@mccormick.com
Tel: (410) 771 - 7244
Fax: (410) 771 - 7462

GRIM, Diane E.
Treasurer, McCormick & Co., Inc. PAC
diane_grim@mccormick.com
Tel: (410) 771 - 7301
Fax: (410) 527 - 8289

HAYES, Rodney
Regulatory Specialist
rodney_hayes@mccormick.com
Tel: (410) 771 - 7301
Fax: (410) 771 - 7462

LYNN, James N.
Manager, Print Communications
jim_lynn@mccormick.com
Tel: (410) 771 - 7301
Fax: (410) 771 - 7462

WEATHERHOLTZ, Karen D.
Senior V. President, Human Resources
Tel: (410) 771 - 7193
Fax: (410) 771 - 7462

At Other Offices

LAYMAN, Nancy
Manager, Trade Communications
211 Schilling Circle
Hunt Valley, MD 21031
Tel: (410) 527 - 6278

McDermott Internat'l, Inc.

A worldwide energy services company. Its subsidiaries provide engineering, fabrication, installation, procurement, and project management for customers involved in the production of energy and in other industries.

www.mcdermott.com
Annual Revenues: $1.9 billion

Chairman and Chief Exec. Officer
WILKINSON, Bruce W.
Tel: (281) 870 - 4411
Fax: (281) 870 - 5045

Main Headquarters
Mailing: 757 N. Eldridge
Houston, TX 77079
Tel: (281) 870 - 5000
Fax: (281) 870 - 5045

Political Action Committees

Better Government Fund of McDermott Inc.
Contact: David S. Black
2016 Mount Athos Rd.
Lynchburg, VA 24504

Contributions to Candidates: $1,500 (01/05 - 09/05)

Republicans: $1,500.

Principal Recipients

SENATE REPUBLICANS	HOUSE REPUBLICANS	
	Jindal, Bobby (LA)	$1,500

BWX Technologies Political Action Committee
Contact: David S. Black
2016 Mount Athos Rd.
Lynchburg, VA 24504

Contributions to Candidates: $47,250 (01/05 - 09/05)

Democrats: $9,000; Republicans: $38,250.

Corporate Foundations and Giving Programs

McDermott Corp. Contributions Program
Contact: David S. Black

McDermott Internat'l, Inc.

* continued from previous page

2016 Mount Athos Rd.
Lynchburg, VA 24504

Annual Grant Total: $300,000 - $400,000
Geographic Preference: Area in which the company is headquartered; National
Primary Interests: Civic and Public Affairs; Higher Education

Public Affairs and Related Activities Personnel

At Headquarters

SANNINO, Louis J. — Tel: (281) 870 - 5011
Senior V. President, Human Resources and Corporate Compliance Officer — Fax: (281) 870 - 5045

SCIPPA, Raymond A. — Tel: (281) 870 - 5025
Director, Public Relations — Fax: (281) 870 - 5045
(J. Ray McDermott, SA)
rscippa@mcdermott.com

At Other Offices

BLACK, David S.
PACs and Corporate Contributions Contact
(BWX Technologies)
2016 Mount Athos Rd.
Lynchburg, VA 24504
dsblack@mcdermott.com

CARTER, Regina W. — Tel: (804) 522 - 5937
Director, Government and Public Relations
(BWX Technologies)
1570 Mt. Athos Rd.
Lynchburg, VA 24504
rwcarter@bwxt.com

ROUECHE, Jay — Tel: (281) 870 - 5011
Director, Investor Relations and Communications
757 N. Eldridge
Houston, TX 77079
jroueche@mcdermott.com

WILLIAMS, Lisa T. — Tel: (504) 631 - 8609
Public Relations Supervisor
(J. Ray McDermott, SA)
P.O. Box 188
Morgan City, LA 70381
ltwilliams@mcdermott.com

McDonald's Corp.

A member of the Public Affairs Council. A quick service restaurant chain.

www.mcdonalds.com
Annual Revenues: $14.87 billion

Chairman and Chief Exec. Officer — Tel: (630) 623 - 3000
SKINNER, James A. — Fax: (630) 623 - 5004

Main Headquarters
Mailing: One McDonald's Plaza — Tel: (630) 623 - 3000
Oak Brook, IL 60523 — Fax: (630) 623 - 5004

Washington Office
Contact: Bo Bryant
Mailing: 1200 17th St., NW — Tel: (202) 887 - 8900
Suite 603 — Fax: (202) 887 - 8907
Washington, DC 20036

Political Action Committees

McDonald's Corp. Political Action Committee
Contact: Robert Donovan
One McDonald's Plaza — Tel: (630) 623 - 6754
Oak Brook, IL 60523 — Fax: (630) 623 - 3057

Contributions to Candidates: $35,500 (01/05 - 09/05)
Democrats: $5,000; Republicans: $30,500.

Principal Recipients

SENATE DEMOCRATS		HOUSE DEMOCRATS	
Nelson, Benjamin (NE)	$2,000		
SENATE REPUBLICANS		**HOUSE REPUBLICANS**	
Hatch, Orrin (UT)	$5,000	Blunt, Roy (MO)	$5,000
		Hastert, Dennis J. (IL)	$5,000
		Cantor, Eric (VA)	$2,500

Corporate Foundations and Giving Programs

McDonald's Corp. Charitable Foundation
Contact: Kenneth L. Barun
One McDonald's Plaza — Tel: (630) 623 - 5505
Oak Brook, IL 60523 — Fax: (630) 623 - 7488

Assets: $198,050 (2002)
Annual Grant Total: $100,000 - $200,000
Geographic Preference: Area in which the company is headquartered; National
Primary Interests: Children; Education; Persons with Disabilities; Safety
Recent Recipients: Nat'l Urban League

Ronald McDonald Children's Charities
Contact: Kenneth L. Barun
One McDonald's Plaza — Tel: (630) 623 - 5505
Oak Brook, IL 60523 — Fax: (630) 623 - 7488

Assets: $415,000 (2001)
Annual Grant Total: $2,000,000 - $5,000,000
Geographic Preference: National
Primary Interests: Arts and Culture; Children; Education; Medicine and Health Care; Social Services
Recent Recipients: Futures for Children

Public Affairs and Related Activities Personnel

At Headquarters

BARUN, Kenneth L. — Tel: (630) 623 - 5505
President and Chief Exec. Officer, Ronald McDonald House Charities — Fax: (630) 623 - 7488

COFFING, Bridget — Tel: (630) 623 - 6263
Corporate V. President, Corporate Communications — Fax: (630) 623 - 8005
bridget.coffing@mcd.com

CONKLIN, Edward — Tel: (630) 623 - 5724
Senior Director, Government Relations — Fax: (630) 623 - 3057
ed.conklin@mcd.com

CRAWFORD, Dick — Tel: (630) 623 - 6754
Corporate V. President, Government Relations — Fax: (630) 623 - 3057
dick.crawford@mcd.com

DALY, Jack — Tel: (630) 623 - 6743
Senior V. President, Corporate Relations — Fax: (630) 623 - 8843
jack.daly@mcd.com

DONAHUE, Michael — Tel: (630) 623 - 7833
V. President, U.S. Communications — Fax: (630) 623 - 8005
michael.donahue@mcd.com

DONOVAN, Robert — Tel: (630) 623 - 6754
PAC Treasurer — Fax: (630) 623 - 3057

FLOERSCH, Rich — Tel: (630) 623 - 8650
Corporate Exec. V. President, Human Resource Management — Fax: (630) 623 - 5004
richard.floersch@mcd.com

LYNN, Jim — Tel: (630) 623 - 3387
V. President, Communication Services — Fax: (630) 623 - 4999
jim.lynn@mcd.com

RIKER, Walt — Tel: (630) 623 - 7318
Corp. V. President, Corporate Communications — Fax: (630) 623 - 8843
walt.riker@mcd.com

SHAW, Mary Kay — Tel: (630) 623 - 7559
V. President, Investor Relations and Financial Communications — Fax: (630) 623 - 5004

At Washington Office

ADAMS, Victoria — Tel: (202) 887 - 8900
Coordinator — Fax: (202) 887 - 8907

BRYANT, Bo — Tel: (202) 887 - 8900
Director, Federal Relations — Fax: (202) 887 - 8907

The McGraw-Hill Companies, Inc.

A global information services provider for the financial services, education, and business information markets. Brands include Standard & Poor's, BusinessWeek, and McGraw-Hill Education.

www.mcgraw-hill.com
Annual Revenues: $4.8 billion

Chairman, President and Chief Exec. Officer — Tel: (212) 512 - 2000
MCGRAW, Harold, III

Main Headquarters
Mailing: 1221 Ave. of the Americas — Tel: (212) 512 - 2000
New York, NY 10020-1095

Washington Office
Contact: Cynthia H. Braddon
Mailing: 1200 G St. NW — Tel: (202) 383 - 3700
Suite 900 — Fax: (202) 383 - 3718
Washington, DC 20005-3802

Corporate Foundations and Giving Programs

The McGraw-Hill Companies Corporate Contributions and Community Relations
1221 Ave. of the Americas — Tel: (212) 512 - 2000
New York, NY 10020-1095 — Fax: (212) 512 - 3116

Annual Grant Total: none reported
Geographic Preference: Area(s) in which the company operates
Primary Interests: Financial Planning

The McGraw-Hill Companies, Inc.

** continued from previous page*

* continued from previous page

Public Affairs and Related Activities Personnel

At Headquarters

DIPIAZZA, Tom — Tel: (212) 512 - 4145
Director, Corporate Communications — Fax: (212) 512 - 3514
Mailstop: 47th Floor
tom_dipiazza@mcgraw-hill.com

FLEMING, Betty A. — Tel: (212) 512 - 2453
Senior Manager, Internal Communications
Mailstop: 47th Floor
betty_fleming@mcgraw-hill.com

GABRIELE, Eileen — Tel: (212) 512 - 3852
V. President, Corporate Affairs — Fax: (212) 512 - 3611
Mailstop: 47th Floor
eileen_gabriele@mcgraw-hill.com

GOLDBERG, Glenn S. — Tel: (212) 512 - 3724
Senior V. President, Corporate Affairs and Assistant to the Chairman and Chief Exec. Officer — Fax: (212) 512 - 2048
Mailstop: 49th Floor
glenn_goldberg@mcgraw-hill.com

HABER, Louis — Tel: (212) 512 - 3203
Director, Issues Management — Fax: (212) 512 - 2703
Mailstop: 47th Floor
louis_haber@mcgraw-hill.com

HUGHES, Celeste — Tel: (212) 512 - 2192
Manager, Communications and Investor Relations — Fax: (212) 512 - 3840
Mailstop: 48th Floor
celeste_hughes@mcgraw-hill.com

MURPHY, David L. — Tel: (212) 512 - 2000
Exec. V. President, Human Resources

RAYMOND, Louise — Tel: (212) 512 - 2001
Director, Global Corporate Social Responsibility — Fax: (212) 512 - 3611
Mailstop: 47th Floor
louise_raymond@mcgraw-hill.com

RUBIN, Donald S. — Tel: (212) 512 - 4321
Senior V. President, Investor Relations — Fax: (212) 512 - 3840
Mailstop: 48th Floor
donald_rubin@mcgraw-hill.com

SKAFIDAS, Mary — Tel: (212) 512 - 2826
Manager, Corporate Communications — Fax: (212) 512 - 2703
Mailstop: 47th Floor
mary_skafidas@mcgraw-hill.com

WEISS, Steven H. — Tel: (212) 512 - 2247
V. President, Corporate Communications — Fax: (212) 512 - 2507
Mailstop: 47th Floor
weissh@mcgraw-hill.com

At Washington Office

BRADDON, Cynthia H. — Tel: (202) 383 - 3701
V. President, Government Affairs — Fax: (202) 383 - 3718
cindy_braddon@mcgraw-hill.com
Registered Federal Lobbyist.

DEGIUSTI, Paul — Tel: (202) 383 - 3702
Director, Government Affairs — Fax: (202) 383 - 3718
Registered Federal Lobbyist.

JORDAN, William — Tel: (202) 383 - 3705
Director, Government Affairs and Communications — Fax: (202) 383 - 3718
Registered Federal Lobbyist.

KEAN, Michael H. — Tel: (202) 383 - 3700
Fax: (202) 383 - 3718
Registered Federal Lobbyist.

PEDRI, Melissa — Tel: (202) 383 - 3700
Fax: (202) 383 - 3718
Registered Federal Lobbyist.

MCI, Inc.

A leading global communications provider, delivering communications connectivity to businesses, governments and consumers. The company plans to merge with Verizon Communications (see separate listing). Completion of the merger is expected in late 2005 or early 2006.

www.mci.com
Annual Revenues: $35.179 billion

Chairman of the Board — Tel: (703) 886 - 5600
KATZENBACH, Nicholas — TF: (877) MCI - 1000

President and Chief Exec. Officer — Tel: (703) 886 - 5600
CAPELLAS, Michael D. — TF: (877) MCI - 1000

Main Headquarters
Mailing: 22001 Loudoun County Pkwy.
Ashburn, VA 20147
Tel: (703) 886 - 5600
Fax: (212) 885 - 0570
TF: (877) MCI - 1000

Washington Office
Mailing: 1133 19th St. NW
Washington, DC 20036
Tel: (202) 887 - 3830
Fax: (202) 887 - 3123

Political Action Committees

MCI Employees PAC
Contact: Chris B. Mackay
1133 19th St. NW — Tel: (202) 887 - 3830
Washington, DC 20036 — Fax: (202) 887 - 3123

Contributions to Candidates: $96,500 (01/05 - 09/05)
Democrats: $36,000; Republicans: $60,500.

Principal Recipients

SENATE DEMOCRATS

HOUSE DEMOCRATS
Stupak, Bart (MI) $5,000
Markey, Edward (MA) $3,500

SENATE REPUBLICANS
Allen, George (VA) $5,500

HOUSE REPUBLICANS
Pickering, Chip (MS) $5,000
Davis, Tom (VA) $3,500

Public Affairs and Related Activities Personnel

At Headquarters

CASACCIA, Daniel — Tel: (703) 886 - 5600
Exec. V. President, Human Resources — TF: (877) MCI - 1000

KELLY, Anastasia D. — Tel: (703) 886 - 5600
General Counsel and Exec. V. President — TF: (877) MCI - 1000
Responsibilities include legal, regulatory and legislative affairs.

TRENT, Grace Chen — Tel: (703) 886 - 5600
Senior V. President, Communications and Chief of Staff — TF: (877) MCI - 1000

At Washington Office

CANTREL, Francis J., Jr. — Tel: (202) 887 - 3112
Director, Government Relations — Fax: (202) 887 - 3123
Registered Federal Lobbyist.

CLAFFEY, Terri G. — Tel: (202) 887 - 3830
Senior Policy Advisor, Government Relations — Fax: (202) 887 - 3123
Registered Federal Lobbyist.

COLLINS, J. Christian — Tel: (202) 887 - 3830
Fax: (202) 887 - 3123
Registered Federal Lobbyist.

HOGAN, Liz — Tel: (202) 887 - 3830
Senior Policy Advisor, Government Relations — Fax: (202) 887 - 3123
Registered Federal Lobbyist.

KOPPEL, Robert — Tel: (202) 887 - 3830
V. President, Regulatory — Fax: (202) 887 - 3123
Registered Federal Lobbyist.

LUGAR, Kelly — Tel: (202) 887 - 3830
Fax: (202) 887 - 3123
Registered Federal Lobbyist.

MACKAY, Chris B. — Tel: (202) 887 - 3830
PAC Treasurer — Fax: (202) 887 - 3123
Registered Federal Lobbyist.

MAIMAN, Seth E. — Tel: (202) 887 - 3830
Fax: (202) 887 - 3123
Registered Federal Lobbyist.

MANSOURKIA, Maggie — Tel: (202) 887 - 3830
Fax: (202) 887 - 3123
Registered Federal Lobbyist.

SACKS, Barbara — Tel: (202) 887 - 3830
Fax: (202) 887 - 3123
Registered Federal Lobbyist.

SARGIS, Donna — Tel: (202) 887 - 3830
Regulatory Affairs — Fax: (202) 887 - 3123

SCARDINO, Kim — Tel: (202) 736 - 6478
Director, Federal Regulatory Affairs — Fax: (202) 887 - 3123

WHITT, Richard S. — Tel: (202) 887 - 3845
Director, Internet Policy — Fax: (202) 887 - 3123

WRIGHT, Lori E. — Tel: (202) 887 - 3830
Manager, FCC Regulatory — Fax: (202) 887 - 3123

McKee Foods Corp.

Manufacturer of baked goods. Brands include Little Debbie and Sunbelt.

www.mckeefoods.com

Chief Exec. Officer — Tel: (423) 238 - 7111
MCKEE, Jack C. — Fax: (423) 238 - 7101

Main Headquarters
Mailing: P.O. Box 750
Collegedale, TN 37315-0750
Tel: (423) 238 - 7111
Fax: (423) 238 - 7101
Street: 10260 McKee Rd.
Collegedale, TN 37315

Corporate Foundations and Giving Programs

McKee Foods Corp. Corporate Contributions Program

McKee Foods Corp.

* continued from previous page

P.O. Box 750 — Tel: (423) 238 - 7111
Collegedale, TN 37315-0750 — Fax: (423) 238 - 7101

Annual Grant Total: none reported

Geographic Preference: Area in which the company is headquartered; Area(s) in which the company operates
Primary Interests: Education; Environment/Conservation

Public Affairs and Related Activities Personnel

At Headquarters

GARREN, Ruth — Tel: (423) 238 - 7111
Manager, Corporate Communications and Public Relations — Fax: (423) 238 - 7101

MCKEE, Mike — Tel: (423) 238 - 7111
President — Fax: (423) 238 - 7101

McKesson Corp.

A member of the Public Affairs Council. A health care supply and information management company.

www.mckesson.com
Annual Revenues: $42 billion

Chairman and Chief Exec. Officer — Tel: (415) 983 - 8300
HAMMERGREN, John H. — Fax: (415) 983 - 7160

Main Headquarters
Mailing: One Post St. — Tel: (415) 983 - 8300
San Francisco, CA 94104-5296 — Fax: (415) 983 - 7160

Political Action Committees

McKesson Corp. Employees Political Fund
Contact: David Schintzius
One Post St. — Tel: (415) 983 - 8300
San Francisco, CA 94104-5296 — Fax: (415) 983 - 7160

Contributions to Candidates: $27,000 (01/05 - 09/05)
Democrats: $7,000; Republicans: $20,000.

Principal Recipients

SENATE DEMOCRATS		HOUSE DEMOCRATS	
Nelson, Benjamin (NE)	$4,000		
SENATE REPUBLICANS		**HOUSE REPUBLICANS**	
Kyl, Jon L (AZ)	$3,000	Johnson, Nancy (CT)	$5,000
Talent, James (MO)	$3,000		

Corporate Foundations and Giving Programs

McKesson Foundation and Direct Giving Program
Contact: Marcia M. Argyris
One Post St. — Tel: (415) 983 - 8300
San Francisco, CA 94104-5296 — Fax: (415) 983 - 7160

Annual Grant Total: $2,000,000 - $5,000,000

Past recipients: Mission High School Health Center, Californians for Drug-Free Youth, Alameda County Food Bank, Young Audiences of the Bay Area, Coleman Advocates for Youth. Guidelines are available.

Geographic Preference: Area(s) in which the company operates; San Francisco Bay Area
Primary Interests: Arts and Culture; Children's Health; Emergency Services; K-12 Education; Youth Services

Public Affairs and Related Activities Personnel

At Headquarters

ARGYRIS, Marcia M. — Tel: (415) 983 - 8300
Foundation President — Fax: (415) 983 - 7160

BERKEY, Ann Richardson — Tel: (415) 983 - 8494
V. President, Public Affairs — Fax: (415) 983 - 7160
Mailstop: 32nd Floor
ann.berkey@mckesson.com

KIRINCIC, Paul E. — Tel: (415) 983 - 8300
Senior V. President, Human Resources — Fax: (415) 983 - 7160

KURTZ, Larry — Tel: (415) 983 - 8418
V. President, Investor Relations — Fax: (415) 983 - 7160
Mailstop: 31st Floor
larry.kurtz@mckesson.com

LARKIN, James — Tel: (415) 983 - 8300
Director, Corporate Communications — Fax: (415) 983 - 7160
james.larkin@mckesson.com

MCANDREWS, Brian — Tel: (415) 983 - 8656
Director, Corporate Affairs — Fax: (415) 983 - 7160
brian.mcandrews@mckesson.com

ROHRBACH, Kate — Tel: (415) 983 - 8300
V. President, Corporate Communications — Fax: (415) 983 - 7160
Mailstop: 32nd Floor
kate.rohrbach@mckesson.com

SCHINTZIUS, David — Tel: (415) 983 - 8300
PAC Treasurer — Fax: (415) 983 - 7160

McKesson HBOC, Inc.

See listing on page 315 under McKesson Corp.

McLane Company, Inc.

A member of the Public Affairs Council. A wholly-owned subsidiary of Berkshire Hathaway, Inc. (see separate listing). McLane Company, Inc. provides distribution services to customers throughout the U.S. The company delivers food and non-food products to the convenience stores, mass merchandise, quick service restaurants, drug store chains, and movie theater industries.

www.mclaneco.com
Annual Revenues: $23 billion

President and Chief Exec. Officer — Tel: (254) 771 - 7500
ROSIER, W. Grady — Fax: (254) 771 - 2284

Main Headquarters
Mailing: 4747 McLane Pkwy. — Tel: (254) 771 - 7500
Temple, TX 76504 — Fax: (254) 771 - 7244

Political Action Committees

McLane Company, Inc. Federal PAC (MAC-PAC-USA)
Contact: Kevin Koch
4747 McLane Pkwy. — Tel: (254) 771 - 7500
Temple, TX 76504 — Fax: (254) 771 - 7244

Contributions to Candidates: none reported (01/05 - 09/05)

Corporate Foundations and Giving Programs

McLane Community Affairs
4747 McLane Pkwy. — Tel: (254) 771 - 7500
Temple, TX 76504 — Fax: (254) 771 - 7244

Annual Grant Total: none reported

Recent Recipients: Children's Miracle Network; United Way

Public Affairs and Related Activities Personnel

At Headquarters

KOCH, Kevin — Tel: (254) 771 - 7500
Treasurer, McLane Company Inc. Federal PAC — Fax: (254) 771 - 7244

WHITE, Barney — Tel: (254) 771 - 7500
Senior Manager, Governmental Affairs and Corporate Communications — Fax: (254) 771 - 7486

McLeod USA Inc.

A telephone communications service provider

www.mcleodusa.com

Chairman and Chief Exec. Officer — Tel: (319) 364 - 0000
DAVIS, Chris A. — Fax: (800) 896 - 8330
TF: (800) 896 - 8330

Main Headquarters
Mailing: McLeod USA Technology Park — Tel: (319) 364 - 0000
6400 C St., SW — Fax: (319) 790 - 7767
Cedar Rapids, IA 52406 — TF: (800) 896 - 8330

Public Affairs and Related Activities Personnel

At Headquarters

LANGEL, Kurt O. — Tel: (319) 364 - 0000
V. President, Human Resources — Fax: (319) 790 - 7767
TF: (800) 896 - 8330

NEMITZ, Bryce E. — Tel: (319) 364 - 0000
V. President, Corporate Communications and Investor Relations — Fax: (319) 364 - 7800
TF: (800) 896 - 8330

THOMPSON, James E. — Tel: (319) 364 - 0000
Group V. President, General Counsel and Secretary — Fax: (319) 790 - 7767
TF: (800) 896 - 8330

Responsibilities include government and regulatory affairs.

TIEMANN, Bruce — Tel: (319) 364 - 0000
Manager, Corporate Communications — Fax: (319) 790 - 7767
TF: (800) 896 - 8330

MCN Corp.

See listing on page 167 under DTE Energy Co.

MCN Energy Group Inc.

See listing on page 167 under DTE Energy Co.

McNeil Consumer & Specialty Pharmaceuticals

See listing on page 270 under Johnson & Johnson.

MDU Resources Group, Inc.

A diversified natural resource enterprise.

www.mduresources.com

MDU Resources Group, Inc.

** continued from previous page*

Chairman and Chief Exec. Officer
WHITE, Martin A.
Tel: (701) 222 - 7900
Fax: (701) 222 - 7607
TF: (800) 437 - 8000

Main Headquarters
Mailing: P.O. Box 5650
Bismarck, ND 58506-5650
Tel: (701) 222 - 7900
Fax: (701) 222 - 7607
TF: (800) 437 - 8000

Street: 918 E. Divide Ave.
Bismarck, ND 58501

Political Action Committees

MDU Resources Group Good Government Fund
Contact: Rita O'Neill
P.O. Box 5650
Bismarck, ND 58506-5650
Tel: (701) 222 - 7834
Fax: (701) 222 - 7859
TF: (800) 437 - 8000

Contributions to Candidates: $4,000 (01/05 - 09/05)
Democrats: $1,000; Republicans: $3,000.

Principal Recipients

SENATE DEMOCRATS

HOUSE DEMOCRATS
Pomeroy, Earl (ND) $1,000

SENATE REPUBLICANS
Burns, Conrad (MT) $1,000
Talent, James (MO) $1,000

HOUSE REPUBLICANS
Rehberg, Dennis (MT) $1,000

Corporate Foundations and Giving Programs

MDU Resources Foundation
Contact: Robert E. Wood
P.O. Box 5650
Bismarck, ND 58506-5650
Tel: (701) 222 - 7828
Fax: (701) 222 - 7607
TF: (800) 437 - 8000

Annual Grant Total: under $100,000
Contributions are restricted to tax-exempt organizations.
Geographic Preference: Area(s) in which the company operates
Primary Interests: Arts and Culture; Civic and Public Affairs; Community Affairs; Education; Environment/Conservation; Health and Human Services

Public Affairs and Related Activities Personnel

At Headquarters

BOYD, Dennis W. E.
Senior Governmental Affairs Representative
dennis.boyd@mduresources.com
Tel: (701) 222 - 7829
Fax: (701) 222 - 7859
TF: (800) 437 - 8000

LUEDER, Laura
Senior Public Information Representative
laura.lueder@mduresources.com
Tel: (701) 222 - 7874
Fax: (701) 222 - 7865
TF: (800) 437 - 8000

O'NEILL, Rita
Contact, MDUResources Group Good Government Fund
rita.oneill@mduresources.com
Tel: (701) 222 - 7834
Fax: (701) 222 - 7859
TF: (800) 437 - 8000

REDDING, Cindy
V. President, Human Resources
cindy.redding@mduresources.com
Tel: (701) 222 - 7795
Fax: (701) 222 - 7867
TF: (800) 437 - 8000

ROBINSON, Warren L.
Exec. V. President and Chief Financial Officer
warren.robinson@mduresources.com
Responsibilities include investor relations.
Tel: (701) 222 - 7991
Fax: (701) 222 - 7607
TF: (800) 437 - 8000

SIMON, Geoff
Director, State Governmental Affairs
geoff.simon@mduresources.com
Tel: (701) 222 - 7830
Fax: (701) 222 - 7859
TF: (800) 437 - 8000

STILLWELL, Arlene
Investor Relations Specialist
arlene.stillwell@mduresources.com
Tel: (701) 222 - 7900
Fax: (701) 222 - 7801
TF: (800) 437 - 8000

WOOD, Robert E.
Senior V. President, Governmental and Public Affairs
robert.wood@mduresources.com
Tel: (701) 222 - 7828
Fax: (701) 222 - 7607
TF: (800) 437 - 8000

At Other Offices

REDDING, E. J.
Governmental Affairs Representative
704 Maynard Rd.
Helena, MT 59602
e.j.redding@mduresources.com
Tel: (406) 431 - 0962
Fax: (406) 458 - 6091

Mead Corp., The

See listing on page 316 under MeadWestvaco Corp.

Mead Johnson Nutritionals

See listing on page 90 under Bristol-Myers Squibb Co.

MeadWestvaco Corp.

A member of the Public Affairs Council. Formed from the merger between The Mead Corp. and Westvaco Corp. in January of 2002. A producer of packaging, coated and specialty papers, consumer and office products and specialty chemicals.
www.meadwestvaco.com

Chairman and Chief Exec. Officer
LUKE, John A., Jr.
jaluke@meadwestvaco.com
Tel: (203) 461 - 7400

Main Headquarters
Mailing: One High Ridge Park
Stamford, CT 06905-1322
Tel: (203) 461 - 7400

Washington Office
Contact: Alexander S. Stoddard
Mailing: 1401 I St. NW
Suite 345
Washington, DC 20005
Tel: (202) 289 - 0802

Political Action Committees

MeadWestvaco Political Action Committee
Contact: Alexander S. Stoddard
1401 I St. NW
Suite 345
Washington, DC 20005
Tel: (202) 289 - 0802
Fax: (202) 289 - 8815

Contributions to Candidates: none reported (01/05 - 09/05)

Corporate Foundations and Giving Programs

MeadWestvaco Corp. Foundation
Contact: Kathryn A. Strawn
Courthouse Plaza NE
Dayton, OH 45463
Tel: (937) 495 - 3031
Fax: (937) 495 - 4103

Annual Grant Total: none reported

Public Affairs and Related Activities Personnel

At Headquarters

MASSEE, Ned W.
V. President, Corporate Affairs
Tel: (203) 461 - 7577
Fax: (203) 461 - 7521

POMERLEAU, Mark F.
Director, Investor Relations
mfp@meadwestvaco.com
Tel: (203) 461 - 7616

At Washington Office

STODDARD, Alexander S.
Manager, Federal Relations
ahstodd@meadwestvaco.com
Responsibilities include political action.
Tel: (202) 289 - 0802
Fax: (202) 289 - 8815

At Other Offices

BURTON, Richard N.
V. President, Environmental Affairs, Safety and Health
Courthouse Plaza NE
Dayton, OH 45463
Tel: (937) 495 - 9275

OWEN, Allen E.
Manager, Regional State Government Relations
1000 Broad St.
Phenix City, AL 36867
aeo@meadwestvaco.com
Tel: (334) 448 - 6356
Fax: (334) 448 - 6508

SHERMAN, Roger L.
Public Affairs Forester
P.O. Box 577
Rupert, WI 25984
Tel: (304) 392 - 6373

STRAWN, Kathryn A.
Manager, Corporate Contributions
Courthouse Plaza NE
Dayton, OH 45463
kas@meadwestvaco.com
Tel: (937) 495 - 3031
Fax: (937) 495 - 4103

TWILLEY, Wm. Edward, Jr.
Manager, Regional State Government Relations
P.O. Box 118005
Charleston, SC 29423
Tel: (803) 745 - 3024

Medco Health Solutions, Inc.

Formerly Merck Medco Managed Care, L.L.C. Spun-off as a separate independent company from Merck & Co. (see separate listing) in August, 2003.
www.medco.com

Chairman, President and Chief Exec. Officer
SNOW, David B., Jr.
Tel: (201) 269 - 3400

Main Headquarters
Mailing: 100 Parsons Pond Dr.
Franklin Lakes, NJ 07417
Tel: (201) 269 - 3400

Washington Office
Contact: Peter Begans
Mailing: 601 Pennsylvania Ave. NW
Suite 700
Washington, DC 20004
Tel: (202) 639 - 1881

Medco Health Solutions, Inc.

** continued from previous page*

Political Action Committees

Medco Health PAC
Contact: Peter Begans
601 Pennsylvania Ave. NW — Tel: (202) 639 - 1881
Suite 700
Washington, DC 20004

Contributions to Candidates: $57,000 (01/05 - 09/05)
Democrats: $24,000; Republicans: $33,000.

Principal Recipients

SENATE DEMOCRATS		HOUSE DEMOCRATS	
Carper, Thomas R (DE)	$2,000	Menendez, Robert (NJ)	$5,000
Conrad, Kent (ND)	$2,000		
Kennedy, Ted (MA)	$2,000		
Lieberman, Joe (CT)	$2,000		
SENATE REPUBLICANS		**HOUSE REPUBLICANS**	
Kyl, Jon L (AZ)	$3,000	Saxton, H. J (NJ)	$2,000
Ensign, John Eric (NV)	$2,000		

Public Affairs and Related Activities Personnel

At Headquarters

CRAMER, Susan — Tel: (201) 269 - 6187
Senior Director, Investor Relations

PRINCIVALLE, Karin — Tel: (201) 269 - 3400
Senior V. President, Human Resources

SIMEK, Jeffrey — Tel: (201) 269 - 6400
V. President, Public Affairs

SMITH, Ann — Tel: (201) 269 - 5984
Director, Public Affairs

At Washington Office

BEGANS, Peter — Tel: (202) 639 - 1881
V. President, Federal Goverment Affairs
Registered Federal Lobbyist.
Responsibilities include political action.

FRIEDELL, Andrew — Tel: (202) 639 - 1881
Manager, Policy and Analysis
Registered Federal Lobbyist.

LEWIS, Hallie — Tel: (202) 639 - 1881
Manager, Government Affairs
Registered Federal Lobbyist.

Media General Inc.

A diversified communications company with major interests in daily newspapers, broadcast television stations, and interactive media.
www.mediageneral.com

Chairman of the Board
BRYAN, J. Stewart, III — Tel: (804) 649 - 6000; Fax: (804) 649 - 6865
sbryan@mediageneral.com

Chief Exec.Officer
NORTON, Marshall N. — Tel: (804) 649 - 6000; Fax: (804) 649 - 6865

Main Headquarters
Mailing: P.O. Box 85333, Richmond, VA 23293-0001 — Tel: (804) 649 - 6000; Fax: (804) 649 - 6865
Street: 333 E. Franklin St., Richmond, VA 23219-6100

Public Affairs and Related Activities Personnel

At Headquarters

KOZAKEWICZ, Raymond — Tel: (804) 649 - 6748; Fax: (804) 649 - 6865
Media Contact
kozakewicz@mediageneral.com

NABHAN, Lou Anne — Tel: (804) 649 - 6103; Fax: (804) 649 - 6865
V. President, Corporate Communications
lnabhan@mediageneral.com

Medical Mutual of Ohio

A health insurance company.
www.medmutual.com
Annual Revenues: $1.2 billion

Chairman and Chief Exec. Officer
CLAPP, Kent W. — Tel: (216) 687 - 7000; Fax: (216) 687 - 6164
kent.clapp@mmoh.com

Main Headquarters
Mailing: 2060 E. Ninth St., Cleveland, OH 44115 — Tel: (216) 687 - 7000; Fax: (216) 687 - 6164

Public Affairs and Related Activities Personnel

At Headquarters

BYERS, Ed — Tel: (216) 687 - 2685; Fax: (216) 687 - 6164
Media Relations Specialist

CHANEY, Jared — Tel: (216) 687 - 6177; Fax: (216) 687 - 6164
Chief Communications Officer
Jared.Chaney@mmoh.com

GIBBONS, Joseph F., Jr. — Tel: (216) 687 - 7656; Fax: (216) 687 - 2623
Director, Government Relations
joseph.gibbons@mmoh.com

OLSON, Don — Tel: (216) 687 - 2899; Fax: (216) 687 - 6164
Manager, Media Relations

MedImmune, Inc.

A biotechnology company. Develops and markets products for infectious diseases, immune regulation, and cancer.
www.medimmune.com

Chairman of the Board
HOCKMEYER, Wayne T., Ph.D — Tel: (301) 398 - 0000; Fax: (301) 398 - 9000; TF: (877) 633 - 4411

V. Chairman, President and Chief Exec. Officer
MOTT, David M. — Tel: (301) 398 - 0000; Fax: (301) 398 - 9000; TF: (877) 633 - 4411
mottd@medimmune.com

Main Headquarters
Mailing: One MedImmune Way, Gaithersburg, MD 20878 — Tel: (301) 398 - 0000; Fax: (301) 398 - 9000; TF: (877) 633 - 4411

Political Action Committees

MedImmune Inc. Employee Political Awareness Committee
Contact: Brian Rosen
One MedImmune Way — Tel: (301) 398 - 0000; Fax: (301) 398 - 9000; TF: (877) 633 - 4411
Gaithersburg, MD 20878

Contributions to Candidates: $6,000 (01/05 - 09/05)
Democrats: $1,000; Republicans: $5,000.

Principal Recipients

SENATE DEMOCRATS	HOUSE DEMOCRATS	
	Eshoo, Anna (CA)	$1,000
SENATE REPUBLICANS	**HOUSE REPUBLICANS**	
	Barton, Joe L (TX)	$2,000
	Blackburn, Marsha (TN)	$1,000
	Deal, Nathan (GA)	$1,000
	Ferguson, Mike (NJ)	$1,000

Corporate Foundations and Giving Programs

MedImmune Community Involvement
Contact: Toni Stiefel
One MedImmune Way — Tel: (301) 398 - 0000; Fax: (301) 398 - 9000; TF: (877) 633 - 4411
Gaithersburg, MD 20878

Annual Grant Total: none reported
Primary Interests: Children's Health; Medical Research

Public Affairs and Related Activities Personnel

At Headquarters

LACEY, Jamie — Tel: (301) 398 - 4035; Fax: (301) 398 - 9000; TF: (877) 633 - 4411
Director, Public Relations

LUPIEN, Pam — Tel: (301) 398 - 0000; Fax: (301) 398 - 9000; TF: (877) 633 - 4411
V. President, Human Resources

PETERS, Linda — Tel: (301) 398 - 0000; Fax: (301) 398 - 9000; TF: (877) 633 - 4411
Senior V. President, Regulatory Affairs

ROSEN, Brian — Tel: (301) 398 - 0000; Fax: (301) 398 - 9000; TF: (877) 633 - 4411
Treasurer, MedImmune Inc. Employee Political Awareness Committee

STIEFEL, Toni — Tel: (301) 398 - 0000; Fax: (301) 398 - 9000; TF: (877) 633 - 4411
Contact, Corporate Contributions

WEIMAN, Lori — Tel: (301) 398 - 0000; Fax: (301) 398 - 9000; TF: (877) 633 - 4411
V. President, Corporate Communications
weimanl@medimmune.com
Responsibilities include investor relations.

WISNIEWSKI, Anthony — Tel: (301) 398 - 0000; Fax: (301) 398 - 9000; TF: (877) 633 - 4411
Director, Public Policy
wisniewskia@medimmune.com

YORK, Caroline — Tel: (301) 398 - 0000; Fax: (301) 398 - 9000; TF: (877) 633 - 4411
V. President, Government Affairs
yorkc@medimmune.com

Medline Industries, Inc.

A manufacturer and distributor of medical and surgical supplies.

www.medline.com

Chief Exec. Officer
MILLS, Charles S.
Tel: (847) 949 - 5500
Fax: (800) 351 - 1512
TF: (800) 633 - 5463

Main Headquarters
Mailing: One Medline Place
Mundelein, IL 60060
Tel: (847) 949 - 5500
Fax: (800) 351 - 1512
TF: (800) 633 - 5463

Public Affairs and Related Activities Personnel

At Headquarters

MARKS, John
Director, Corporate Communications
jmarks@medline.com
Tel: (847) 949 - 5500
Fax: (800) 351 - 1512
TF: (800) 633 - 5463

MILLS, Andy
President
Tel: (847) 949 - 5500
Fax: (800) 351 - 1512
TF: (800) 633 - 5463

MedPointe Inc.

A specialty pharmaceuticals company. Formerly known as Carter-Wallace, Inc. Carter-Wallace's Consumer Products Businesses were were sold in 2001 to Church and Dwight Co. (see separate listing) and ArmKel. MedPointe retains and has expanded the pharmaceuticals business of the former Carter-Wallace, Inc.

www.medpointpharma.com
Annual Revenues: $200 million

Chairman and Chief Exec. Officer
WILD, Anthony H., PhD
awild@medpointepharma.com
Tel: (732) 564 - 2222
Fax: (732) 564 - 2223

Main Headquarters
Mailing: 265 Davidson Ave.
Suite 300
Somerset, NJ 08873-4120
Tel: (732) 564 - 2200
Fax: (732) 564 - 2223

Public Affairs and Related Activities Personnel

At Headquarters

HAWKINS, John T. W.
Exec. V. President, Corporate Development and External Affairs
(MedPointe Pharmaceuticals)
jhawkins@medpointepharma.com
Tel: (732) 564 - 2233
Fax: (732) 564 - 2223

RENTON, George
V. President, Human Resources
Tel: (732) 564 - 2200
Fax: (732) 564 - 2223

MedPointe Pharmaceuticals

See listing on page 318 under MedPointe Inc.

Medtronic, Inc.

A medical technology company specializing in implantable and invasive therapies.

www.medtronic.com
Annual Revenues: $5.552 billion

Chairman and Chief Exec. Officer
COLLINS, Arthur D.
Tel: (763) 514 - 4000
Fax: (763) 514 - 4879
TF: (800) 328 - 2518

Main Headquarters
Mailing: 710 Medtronic Pkwy.
Minneapolis, MN 55432-5604
Tel: (763) 514 - 4000
Fax: (763) 514 - 4879
TF: (800) 328 - 2518

Washington Office
Mailing: 1420 New York Ave. NW
Suite 600
Washington, DC 20005
Tel: (202) 393 - 6444
Fax: (202) 289 - 9222

Political Action Committees

Medtronic, Inc. Medical Technology Fund
Contact: Gary L. Ellis
1420 New York Ave. NW
Suite 600
Washington, DC 20005
Tel: (202) 393 - 6444
Fax: (202) 289 - 9222

Contributions to Candidates: $90,347 (01/05 - 09/05)
Democrats: $25,000; Republicans: $64,347; Other: $1,000.

Principal Recipients

SENATE DEMOCRATS
Ford, Harold E Jr (TN) $5,000

HOUSE DEMOCRATS

SENATE REPUBLICANS

HOUSE REPUBLICANS
Ramstad, Jim (MN) $10,000
DeLay, Tom (TX) $5,000
Hayworth, J D (AZ) $5,000

Corporate Foundations and Giving Programs

The Medtronic Foundation
710 Medtronic Pkwy.
Minneapolis, MN 55432-5604
Tel: (763) 514 - 4000
Fax: (763) 514 - 4879
TF: (800) 328 - 2518

Assets: $15,367,200 (2000)
Annual Grant Total: over $5,000,000
In all focus areas, priority is given to programs that benefit people who are socioeconomically disadvantaged. Donated $12,064,689 in 2000.
Geographic Preference: Area in which the company is headquartered; Area(s) in which the company operates
Primary Interests: Arts and Humanities; Community Affairs; Education; Financially Disadvantaged; Health and Human Services

Medtronic Corporate Giving Program
710 Medtronic Pkwy.
Minneapolis, MN 55432-5604
Tel: (763) 514 - 4000
Fax: (763) 514 - 4879
TF: (800) 328 - 2518

Annual Grant Total: none reported

Public Affairs and Related Activities Personnel

At Headquarters

CAMPBELL-LOTH, Chris
Senior Public Relations Manager
christine.campbell.loth@medtronic.com
Tel: (763) 505 - 2633
Fax: (763) 514 - 4879
TF: (800) 328 - 2518

FIOLA, Janet S.
Senior V. President, Human Resources
Tel: (763) 514 - 4000
Fax: (763) 514 - 4879
TF: (800) 328 - 2518

FORBIS, Jeanne
V. President, Public Relations
jeanne.forbis@medtronic.com
Responsibilities include corporate philanthropy.
Tel: (763) 505 - 2814
Fax: (763) 514 - 4879
TF: (800) 328 - 2518

HANVIK, Bob N.
Director, Global Public and Media Relations
robert.n.hanvik@medtronic.com
Tel: (763) 505 - 2635
Fax: (763) 514 - 4879
TF: (800) 328 - 2518

JANASZ, Kathleen
Manager, Public Relations
Tel: (763) 505 - 2634
Fax: (763) 514 - 4879
TF: (800) 328 - 2518

LIND, Valerie L.
Manager, Public Relations
valerie.l.lind@medtronic.com
Tel: (763) 505 - 2631
Fax: (763) 514 - 4879
TF: (800) 328 - 2518

PAPILLON, Scott
Senior Public Relations Manager
scott.papillon@medtronic.com
Tel: (763) 505 - 2632
Fax: (763) 514 - 4879
TF: (800) 328 - 2518

RICH, Carol
Manager, Communications
Tel: (763) 514 - 4000
Fax: (763) 514 - 4879
TF: (800) 328 - 2518

SCHERER, Rachel
Director, Investor Relations
Tel: (763) 505 - 2694
Fax: (763) 514 - 6272
TF: (800) 328 - 2518

At Washington Office

DARCY, Shannon
Registered Federal Lobbyist.
Tel: (202) 393 - 6444
Fax: (202) 289 - 9222

ELLIS, Gary L.
PAC Treasurer
Tel: (202) 393 - 6444
Fax: (202) 289 - 9222

SLONE, Peter B.
V. President, Government Affairs
Tel: (202) 393 - 6444
Fax: (202) 289 - 9222

Meijer, Inc.

A privately owned retail store chain.

www.meijer.com

Co-Chairman
MEIJER, Doug
Tel: (616) 453 - 6711
Fax: (616) 791 - 2886

Co-Chairman and Chief Exec. Officer
MEIJER, Hendrik G. "Hank"
Tel: (616) 453 - 6711
Fax: (616) 791 - 2886

Main Headquarters
Mailing: 2929 Walker Ave. NW
Grand Rapids, MI 49544-1307
Tel: (616) 453 - 6711
Fax: (616) 791 - 2572

Corporate Foundations and Giving Programs

Meijer Supermarkets, Inc. Corporate Contributions
2929 Walker Ave. NW
Grand Rapids, MI 49544-1307
Tel: (616) 453 - 6711
Fax: (616) 791 - 2572

Annual Grant Total: none reported
Primary Interests: Education
Recent Recipients: American Red Cross; Habitat for Humanity; March of Dimes; Salvation Army

Public Affairs and Related Activities Personnel

At Headquarters

ALIGHIRE, Wendy
Senior V. President, Human Resources
Tel: (616) 453 - 6711
Fax: (616) 791 - 2886

Mellon Financial Corp.

A financial services company.

www.mellon.com

Chairman and Chief Exec. Officer
MCGUINN, Martin G. Tel: (412) 234 - 5000 Fax: (412) 236 - 1662

Main Headquarters
Mailing: One Mellon Center, 500 Grant St., Pittsburgh, PA 15258-0001 Tel: (412) 234 - 5000 Fax: (412) 234 - 9495

Political Action Committees

Bipartisan PAC/Mellon Financial Corp. (BIPAC/MFC)
Contact: Richard Labuskes
One Mellon Center
500 Grant St.
Pittsburgh, PA 15258-0001
Tel: (412) 234 - 4948 Fax: (412) 236 - 5150

Contributions to Candidates: $45,500 (01/05 - 09/05)
Democrats: $15,500; Republicans: $30,000.

Principal Recipients

SENATE DEMOCRATS
Carper, Thomas R (DE) $5,000

HOUSE DEMOCRATS
Menendez, Robert (NJ) $3,500

SENATE REPUBLICANS
Santorum, Richard (PA) $5,000

HOUSE REPUBLICANS
Hart, Melissa (PA) $5,000
Murphy, Tim (PA) $5,000

Corporate Foundations and Giving Programs

Mellon Charitable Giving Program
Contact: James P. McDonald
One Mellon Center
500 Grant St.
Pittsburgh, PA 15258-0001
Tel: (412) 234 - 2732 Fax: (412) 234 - 0831

Annual Grant Total: over $5,000,000

For more information about the program, see Mellon's Report to the Community via the web at www.mellon.com.

Geographic Preference: Philadelphia, PA; Boston, MA; Pittsburgh, PA

Public Affairs and Related Activities Personnel

At Headquarters

BLEIER, Michael E.
General Counsel
Mailstop: Room 1915
bleier.me@mellon.com
Tel: (412) 234 - 1537 Fax: (412) 236 - 4814

DAY, Walter R., III
Senior V. President, Government Affairs and Community Investment
Mailstop: Room 2850
day.wr@mellon.com
Tel: (412) 234 - 5930 Fax: (412) 236 - 5150

GABBIANELLI, Rose
Senior V. President, Corporate Affairs
gabbianelli.r@mellon.com
Tel: (412) 234 - 4003 Fax: (412) 236 - 1662

GRUENDL, Ron
Manager, Media Relations
Mailstop: Room 1840
gruendl.rr@mellon.com
Tel: (412) 234 - 7157 Fax: (412) 236 - 1662

HERZ, Ken
First V. President and Director, Corporate Communications
Mailstop: Room 1840
herz.kb@mellon.com
Tel: (412) 234 - 0850 Fax: (412) 236 - 1662

LABUSKES, Richard
First V. President, Government Affairs
Mailstop: Room 2850
labuskes.r@mellon.com
Tel: (412) 234 - 4948 Fax: (412) 236 - 5150

LACKEY, Stephen
First V. President, Investor Relations
Mailstop: Room 0370
lackey.s@mellon.com
Tel: (412) 234 - 5601 Fax: (412) 236 - 5461

MCDONALD, James P.
First V. President and Director, Community Affairs
Mailstop: Room 1830
Tel: (412) 234 - 2732 Fax: (412) 234 - 0831

SOMMER, Ron
V. President, Media Relations
sommer.rw@mellon.com
Tel: (412) 236 - 0082 Fax: (412) 236 - 1662

Memphis Light, Gas and Water Division

A public utility company.

www.mlgw.com

Chairman of the Board
JALENAK, C.R., Jr. Tel: (901) 528 - 4011 Fax: (901) 528 - 4758

President and Chief Exec. Officer
LEE, Joseph, III Tel: (901) 528 - 4011

Main Headquarters
Mailing: P.O. Box 430, Memphis, TN 30103 Tel: (901) 528 - 4011 Fax: (901) 528 - 4758
Street: 220 S. Main St., Memphis, TN 38101

Corporate Foundations and Giving Programs

Memphis Light Gas & Water Division Corporate Giving Program
Contact: Glen Thomas
P.O. Box 430
Memphis, TN 30103
Tel: (901) 528 - 4557 Fax: (901) 528 - 4758

Annual Grant Total: none reported

Public Affairs and Related Activities Personnel

At Headquarters

BREWER, Peggy
Community Relations Officer
pbrewer@mlgw.org
Tel: (901) 528 - 4820 Fax: (901) 528 - 4086

DEATON, Kimberly A.
Senior Communications Specialist
kdeaton@mlgw.org
Tel: (901) 528 - 4557 Fax: (901) 528 - 4758

HEUBERGER, Mark
Manager, Corporate Communications
mheuberger@mlgw.org
Tel: (901) 528 - 4491 Fax: (901) 528 - 4086

RITCHIE, Nicole
Supervisor, Corporate Communications
nritchie@mlgw.org
Tel: (901) 528 - 4557 Fax: (901) 528 - 4758

THOMAS, Glen
Senior Communications Specialist
Tel: (901) 528 - 4557 Fax: (901) 528 - 4758

Men's Wearhouse, Inc.

A retailer of men's apparel.

www.menswearhouse.com

Chairman and Chief Exec. Officer
ZIMMER, George A. Tel: (713) 592 - 7200 Fax: (713) 664 - 1957 TF: (800) 776 - 7848

Main Headquarters
Mailing: 5803 Glenmont Dr., Houston, TX 77081-1701 Tel: (713) 592 - 7200 Fax: (713) 664 - 1957 TF: (800) 776 - 7848

Corporate Foundations and Giving Programs

Men's Wearhouse Corporate Giving
Contact: Cynthia James
40650 Encyclopedia Circle
Fremont, CA 94538-2453
Tel: (510) 723 - 8621

Annual Grant Total: none reported

Public Affairs and Related Activities Personnel

At Headquarters

PRUITT, Claudia
V. President and Assistant Treasurer
capruitt@tmw.com
Tel: (713) 592 - 7322 Fax: (713) 592 - 7075 TF: (800) 776 - 7848
Responsibilities include investor relations.

At Other Offices

JAMES, Cynthia
Director, Corporate Giving
40650 Encyclopedia Circle
Fremont, CA 94538-2453
cjames@tmw.com
Tel: (510) 723 - 8621

MILLER, Melissa
Public Relations Coordinator
731 Market St.
Suite 410
San Francisco, CA 94103
mmiller2@tmw.com
Tel: (510) 723 - 8402

Menasha Corporation

A private company engaged in packaging, forest products, printing and plastic products manufacture.

www.menasha.com

Chairman of the Board
SHEPHARD, Donald C. "Buzz" Tel: (920) 751 - 1000 Fax: (920) 951 - 1236 TF: (800) 558 - 5073

President and Chief Exec. Officer
HUGE, Arthur Tel: (920) 751 - 1000 Fax: (920) 951 - 1236 TF: (800) 558 - 5073

Main Headquarters
Mailing: 1645 Bergstrom Rd., Neenah, WI 54956 Tel: (920) 751 - 1000 Fax: (920) 951 - 1236 TF: (800) 558 - 5073

Menasha Corporation

• continued from previous page

Corporate Foundations and Giving Programs

Menasha Corporation Foundation
Contact: Steve Kromholz
1645 Bergstrom Rd.
Neenah, WI 54956
Tel: (920) 751 - 1000
Fax: (920) 951 - 1236
TF: (800) 558 - 5073

Annual Grant Total: over $5,000,000
Includes matching gift and employee scholarship programs.
Geographic Preference: Area(s) in which the company operates
Primary Interests: Civic and Cultural Activities; Environment/Conservation; Health
Recent Recipients: American Players Theater; United Way

Public Affairs and Related Activities Personnel

At Headquarters

JOHN, Mike
Director, Communications
Tel: (920) 751 - 1000
Fax: (920) 951 - 1236
TF: (800) 558 - 5073

KROMHOLZ, Steve
President, Menasha Corp. Foundation
Tel: (920) 751 - 1000
Fax: (920) 951 - 1236
TF: (800) 558 - 5073

Mentor Graphics Corp.

Markets and designs electronic software.
www.mentor.com
Annual Revenues: $600.4 million

Chairman and Chief Exec. Officer
RHINES, Walden C.
Tel: (503) 685 - 7000
Fax: (503) 685 - 7704
TF: (800) 547 - 3000

Main Headquarters
Mailing: 8005 SW Boeckman Rd.
Wilsonville, OR 97070-7777
Tel: (503) 685 - 7000
Fax: (503) 685 - 7704
TF: (800) 547 - 3000

Public Affairs and Related Activities Personnel

At Headquarters

GRAHAM, Suzanne
Media Contact
suzanne_graham@mentor.com
Tel: (503) 685 - 7789
Fax: (503) 685 - 7704
TF: (800) 547 - 3000

ROTTY, Sharron
V. President, Human Resources
Tel: (503) 685 - 7000
Fax: (503) 685 - 7704
TF: (800) 547 - 3000

SCHWARK, Ryerson
Director, Public Relations and Investor Relations
ry_schwark@mentor.com
Tel: (503) 685 - 1462
Fax: (503) 685 - 7704
TF: (800) 547 - 3000

WELDON, Dennis
V. President, Investor Relations
dennis-weldon@mentor.com
Tel: (503) 685 - 1462
Fax: (503) 685 - 7704
TF: (800) 547 - 3000

Mercantile Bankshares Corporation

A bank holding company.
www.mercantile.net
Annual Revenues: $15 billion

Chairman and Chief Exec. Officer
KELLY, Edward J., III
Tel: (410) 237 - 5900
Fax: (410) 237 - 5364

Main Headquarters
Mailing: P.O. Box 1477
Baltimore, MD 21203
Tel: (410) 237 - 5900
Fax: (410) 237 - 5364
Street: Two Hopkins Plaza
Baltimore, MD 21201

Political Action Committees

Mercantile Bankshares PAC (MBC PAC)
Contact: John Unger
P.O. Box 1477
Baltimore, MD 21203
Tel: (410) 237 - 5900
Fax: (410) 237 - 5437

Contributions to Candidates: $3,500 (01/05 - 09/05)
Democrats: $3,000; Republicans: $500.

Principal Recipients

SENATE DEMOCRATS		HOUSE DEMOCRATS	
Mikulski, Barbara (MD)	$1,000	Hoyer, Steny (MD)	$1,000
		Wynn, Albert (MD)	$1,000

Corporate Foundations and Giving Programs

Mercantile-Safe Deposit and Trust Co. Fund
Contact: Janice Davis
P.O. Box 1477
Baltimore, MD 21203
Tel: (410) 237 - 5971
Fax: (410) 237 - 5979

Annual Grant Total: none reported

Public Affairs and Related Activities Personnel

At Headquarters

BOROWY, David E.
Senior V. President
(Mercantile-Safe Deposit and Trust Co.)
Responsibilities include investor relations.
Tel: (410) 347 - 8361
Fax: (410) 347 - 8270

DAVIS, Janice
Senior V. President, Corporate Communications
(Mercantile-Safe Deposit and Trust Co.)
Tel: (410) 237 - 5971
Fax: (410) 237 - 5979

UNGER, John
Exec. V. President, General Counsel and Secretary
(Mercantile-Safe Deposit and Trust Co.)
Responsibilities include political action.
Tel: (410) 237 - 5900
Fax: (410) 237 - 5437

Mercantile-Safe Deposit and Trust Co.

See listing on page 320 under Mercantile Bankshares Corporation.

Mercedes-Benz USA, LLC

A wholly-owned subsidiary of DaimlerChrysler Corp. (see separate listing). Responsible for the sales and marketing of Mercedes-Benz passenger vehicles.
www.mbusa.com

President and Chief Exec. Officer
HALATA, Paul

Main Headquarters
Mailing: One Mercedes Dr.
Montvale, NJ 07645
Tel: (201) 573 - 0600
Fax: (201) 573 - 0117
TF: (800) 367 - 6372

Corporate Foundations and Giving Programs

Mercedes-Benz USA Corporate Giving Program
Contact: Lesia Koropey
One Mercedes Dr.
Montvale, NJ 07645
Tel: (201) 573 - 4709
Fax: (201) 573 - 4370
TF: (800) 367 - 6372

Annual Grant Total: none reported
Geographic Preference: Area in which the company is headquartered; National
Primary Interests: Education

Public Affairs and Related Activities Personnel

At Headquarters

BOLAND, Donna
Manager, Corporate Communications
bolandd@mbusa.com
Tel: (201) 573 - 6893
Fax: (201) 476 - 2875
TF: (800) 367 - 6372

DAWSON, Kass
Community and Social Affairs
Tel: (201) 573 - 0600
Fax: (201) 573 - 0117
TF: (800) 367 - 6372

KOROPEY, Lesia
Community and Social Affairs
Tel: (201) 573 - 4709
Fax: (201) 573 - 4370
TF: (800) 367 - 6372

Merck & Co., Inc.

A member of the Public Affairs Council. A pharmaceutical company. Spun-off Medco Health Solutions, Inc. (see separate listing) as a separate independent company in August, 2003.
www.merck.com
Annual Revenues: $22.9 billion

President and Chief Executive Officer
CLARK, Richard T.
Tel: (908) 423 - 1000
Fax: (908) 735 - 1181
TF: (800) 423 - 1000

Main Headquarters
Mailing: P.O. Box 100
Whitehouse Station, NJ 08889-0100
Tel: (908) 423 - 1000
Fax: (908) 735 - 1181
TF: (800) 423 - 1000
Street: One Merck Dr.
Whitehouse Station, NJ 08889-0100

Washington Office
Contact: Nancy M. Carlton
Mailing: 601 Pennsylvania Ave. NW
North Bldg. Suite 1200
Washington, DC 20004
Tel: (202) 638 - 4170
Fax: (202) 638 - 3670

Political Action Committees

Merck & Co., Inc. PAC (MERCK PAC)
Contact: Lana Garvin
601 Pennsylvania Ave. NW
North Bldg. Suite 1200
Washington, DC 20004
Tel: (202) 638 - 4170
Fax: (202) 638 - 3670

Contributions to Candidates: $121,441 (01/05 - 09/05)

Merck & Co., Inc.

* continued from previous page

Democrats: $28,401; Republicans: $93,040.

Principal Recipients

SENATE DEMOCRATS		HOUSE DEMOCRATS	
		Menendez, Robert (NJ)	$5,000
SENATE REPUBLICANS		**HOUSE REPUBLICANS**	
Santorum, Richard (PA)	$8,000	Ferguson, Mike (NJ)	$10,000
		Barton, Joe L (TX)	$5,000
		Bonilla, Henry (TX)	$5,000
		DeLay, Tom (TX)	$5,000
		Frelinghuysen, Rod (NJ)	$5,000
		Hastert, Dennis J. (IL)	$5,000
		Johnson, Nancy (CT)	$5,000

Corporate Foundations and Giving Programs

The Merck Co. Foundation
Contact: Brenda Colatrella
P.O. Box 100 — Tel: (908) 423 - 2042
Whitehouse Station, NJ 08889-0100 — Fax: (908) 423 - -198
TF: (800) 423 - 1000

Annual Grant Total: over $5,000,000

Expanding access to medicines, vaccines and quality healthcare; building capacity in the biomedical and health sciences; promoting environments that encourage innovation, economic growth and development ina fair ethical econtext; supporting communities where Merck has a majjor presence. www.merck.com/about/cr

Geographic Preference: Area(s) in which the company operates

Primary Interests: Arts and Culture; Civic and Cultural Activities; Community Affairs; Environment/Conservation; Health and Human Services; Medicine and Health Care

Merck Corporate Contributions Program
Contact: Brenda Colatrella
P.O. Box 100 — Tel: (908) 423 - 2042
Whitehouse Station, NJ 08889-0100 — Fax: (908) 423 - -198
TF: (800) 423 - 1000

Annual Grant Total: over $5,000,000

The company's total philanthropic contributions totaled over $979 million in 2004, including $58 million in cash contributions.

Primary Interests: Arts and Culture; Civic and Cultural Activities; Community Affairs; Environment/Conservation; Health and Human Services; Medicine and Health Care

Public Affairs and Related Activities Personnel

At Headquarters

AVEDON, Marcia, Ph.D. — Tel: (908) 423 - 5144
Senior V. President, Human Resources — Fax: (908) 735 - 1247
TF: (800) 423 - 1000

BELL, Graeme — Tel: (908) 423 - 4465
Senior Director, Investor Relations — Fax: (908) 735 - 1253
TF: (800) 423 - 1000

COLATRELLA, Brenda — Tel: (908) 423 - 2042
Contact, Foundation and Corporate Contributions Program — Fax: (908) 423 - -198
TF: (800) 423 - 1000

LESHER, Michelle — Tel: (908) 423 - 4111
Coordinator, Public Policy Research and Analysis — Fax: (908) 735 - 1181
TF: (800) 423 - 1000

LEWENT, Judy C. — Tel: (908) 423 - 5244
Exec. V. President, Chief Financial Officer; and President, Human Health Asia — Fax: (908) 735 - 1270
TF: (800) 423 - 1000
Responsibilities include investor relations.

LODER, Christopher — Tel: (908) 423 - 3786
Media Contact — Fax: (908) 735 - 1181
TF: (800) 423 - 1000

ROSE, Amy — Tel: (908) 423 - 6537
Media Contact — Fax: (908) 735 - 1181
TF: (800) 423 - 1000

SKIDMORE, Janet — Tel: (908) 423 - 3046
Media Contact — Fax: (908) 735 - 1181
TF: (800) 423 - 1000

WAINWRIGHT, Joan E. — Tel: (908) 423 - 5257
V. President, Public Affairs — Fax: (908) 735 - 1196
TF: (800) 423 - 1000

At Washington Office

BLATTER, Victoria — Tel: (202) 638 - 4170
Exec. Director, Federal Government Relations — Fax: (202) 638 - 3670
Registered Federal Lobbyist.

BOMBELLES, Thomas — Tel: (202) 638 - 4170
Director, International Government Relations — Fax: (202) 638 - 3670
Registered Federal Lobbyist.

CARLTON, Nancy M. — Tel: (202) 638 - 4170
V. President,Government Relations — Fax: (202) 638 - 3670
Registered Federal Lobbyist.

CHAN, Julie — Tel: (202) 638 - 4170
Coordinator, Pubic Policy — Fax: (202) 638 - 3670

GARVIN, Lana — Tel: (202) 638 - 4170
Treasurer, Merck and Co. Inc, PAC — Fax: (202) 638 - 3670

HORVATH, Jane — Tel: (202) 638 - 4170
Director, Public Policy — Fax: (202) 638 - 3670

MICHEL, Laurie L. — Tel: (202) 638 - 4170
Senior Director, Counsel, Federal Policy and Government Relations — Fax: (202) 638 - 3670
Registered Federal Lobbyist.

RAMPY, Stacey — Tel: (202) 638 - 4170
Director, Government Relations — Fax: (202) 638 - 3670
Registered Federal Lobbyist.

SPATZ, Ian D. — Tel: (202) 638 - 4170
V. President, Public Policy — Fax: (202) 638 - 3670
Registered Federal Lobbyist.

VAN PELT, Jason — Tel: (202) 638 - 4170
Director, Goverment Relations — Fax: (202) 638 - 3670
Registered Federal Lobbyist.

Merck Medco Managed Care, L.L.C.

See listing on page 316 under Medco Health Solutions, Inc.

Merck Vaccine Division

See listing on page 320 under Merck & Co, Inc.

Meredith Corp.

PUBLIC AFFAIRS COUNCIL

A member of the Public Affairs Council. Magazine and book publishing, television broadcasting, and integrated and strategic marketing.

www.meredith.com

Chairman and Chief Exec. Officer
KERR, William T. — Tel: (515) 284 - 3000
bkerr@mdp.com — Fax: (515) 284 - 3806

Main Headquarters
Mailing: 1716 Locust St. — Tel: (515) 284 - 3000
Des Moines, IA 50309-3023 — Fax: (515) 284 - 3806

Political Action Committees

Meredith Corp. Employees Fund for Better Government
Contact: Jerry L. Hadenfeldt
1716 Locust St. — Tel: (515) 284 - 2780
Des Moines, IA 50309-3023 — Fax: (515) 284 - 2511

Contributions to Candidates: $12,649 (01/05 - 09/05)

Democrats: $5,000; Republicans: $7,649.

Principal Recipients

SENATE DEMOCRATS		HOUSE DEMOCRATS	
Lieberman, Joe (CT)	$1,000	Boswell, Leonard (IA)	$1,000
		Davis, Danny K (IL)	$1,000
		Menendez, Robert (NJ)	$1,000
SENATE REPUBLICANS		**HOUSE REPUBLICANS**	
Ensign, John Eric (NV)	$2,000	Nussle, Jim (IA)	$4,649

Corporate Foundations and Giving Programs

Meredith Corporate Contributions Program
Contact: Arthur J. "Art" Slusark
1716 Locust St. — Tel: (515) 284 - 3404
Des Moines, IA 50309-3023 — Fax: (515) 284 - 2511

Annual Grant Total: $1,000,000 - $2,000,000

Geographic Preference: Iowa

Primary Interests: Arts and Culture; Education; Health and Human Services

The Meredith Foundation
Contact: Arthur J. "Art" Slusark
1716 Locust St. — Tel: (515) 284 - 3404
Des Moines, IA 50309-3023 — Fax: (515) 284 - 2511

Annual Grant Total: none reported

Public Affairs and Related Activities Personnel

At Headquarters

EGGERSS, Linda — Tel: (515) 284 - 3125
Manager, Corporate Communications — Fax: (515) 284 - 3806

FRAZIER, Mell Meredith — Tel: (515) 284 - 2656
Director, Corporate Planning; V. President, The Meredith Foundation — Fax: (515) 284 - 3153

HADENFELDT, Jerry L. — Tel: (515) 284 - 2780
Director, Government Relations — Fax: (515) 284 - 2511

Meredith Corp.

* continued from previous page

RUNDALL, Scott — Tel: (515) 284 - 2325
V. President, Human Resources — Fax: (515) 284 - 3806
scott.rundall@meredith.com

SLUSARK, Arthur J. "Art" — Tel: (515) 284 - 3404
V. President, Corporate Communications and Government Relations — Fax: (515) 284 - 2511
art.slusark@meredith.com

ZEISER, John S. — Tel: (515) 284 - 2780
V. President, Corporate Development — Fax: (515) 284 - 2511
john.zieser@meredith.com
Responsibilities include public affairs.

Merrill Lynch & Co., Inc.

The holding company of a diversified group of companies providing investment banking; securities, commodities and individual brokerage; and other financial services.

www.ml.com
Annual Revenues: $19.963 billion

Chairman, Chief Exec. Officer, and President — Tel: (212) 236 - 1000
O'NEAL, E. Stanley

Main Headquarters
Mailing: Four World Financial Center, 250 Vesey St., New York, NY 10080 — Tel: (212) 449 - 1000

Washington Office
Contact: Bruce E. Thompson, Jr.
Mailing: 1455 Pennsylvania Ave. NW, Suite 950, Washington, DC 20004-1087 — Tel: (202) 661 - 7100; Fax: (202) 661 - 7110

Political Action Committees

Merrill Lynch & Co., Inc. Political Action Committee
Contact: Janelle C. M. Thibau
1455 Pennsylvania Ave. NW — Tel: (202) 661 - 7100
Suite 950 — Fax: (202) 661 - 7110
Washington, DC 20004-1087

Contributions to Candidates: $39,500 (01/05 - 09/05)
Democrats: $19,500; Republicans: $20,000.

Principal Recipients

SENATE DEMOCRATS
Ford, Harold E Jr (TN) $3,000

HOUSE DEMOCRATS

SENATE REPUBLICANS

HOUSE REPUBLICANS
McHenry, Patrick (NC) $3,000

Corporate Foundations and Giving Programs

Merrill Lynch and Co. Foundation, Inc.
Contact: Eddy Bayardelle
Four World Financial Center — Tel: (212) 236 - 1000
250 Vesey St.
New York, NY 10080

Assets: $36,346,680 (2000)
Annual Grant Total: over $5,000,000
Foundation emphasis on higher education is supplemented by major program of Matching Gifts. Other programs include ScholarshipBuilder, Christmas Calls, Employee Community Involvement and Access to the Arts Programs. Guidelines are available. Annual giving by the Foundation and direct corporate contributions total over $16 million.
Geographic Preference: Area(s) in which the company operates; International
Primary Interests: Arts and Culture; Civic and Public Affairs; Health and Human Services; Higher Education
Recent Recipients: Massachusetts Institute of Technology

Public Affairs and Related Activities Personnel

At Headquarters

BAYARDELLE, Eddy — Tel: (212) 236 - 1000
Contact, Merrill Lynch and Co. Foundation
eddy_bayardelle@ml.com

BUM, Jonathan — Tel: (212) 449 - 1000
Director, Investor Relations
investor_relations@ml.com

KAHN, Claudia — Tel: (212) 449 - 1000
Senior V. President, Public Policy

KASSEL, Terry — Tel: (212) 236 - 1000
Senior V. President, Leadership and Development

O'LOONEY, Michael — Tel: (212) 449 - 1000
First V. President, Corporate Communications

WRIGHT, Jason — Tel: (212) 236 - 1000
Senior V. President, Communications and Public Affairs

At Washington Office

THIBAU, Janelle C. M. — Tel: (202) 661 - 7100
V. President, Government Relations — Fax: (202) 661 - 7110
janelle_thibau@ml.com
Registered Federal Lobbyist.

THOMPSON, Bruce E., Jr. — Tel: (202) 661 - 7100
First V. President and Director, Government Relations — Fax: (202) 661 - 7110
Responsibilities include political action.

Merrill Lynch Pierce Fenner & Smith Inc.

See listing on page 322 under Merrill Lynch & Co, Inc.

Mervyn's

A department store chain.
www.mervyns.com

Exec. Chairwoman — Tel: (510) 727 - 3000
CASTAGNA, Vanessa J. — Fax: (510) 727 - 2300

Main Headquarters
Mailing: 22301 Foothill Blvd., Hayward, CA 94541 — Tel: (510) 727 - 3000; Fax: (510) 727 - 2300

Corporate Foundations and Giving Programs

Mervyn's Corporate Contributions Program
Contact: Sue Rogers
22301 Foothill Blvd. — Tel: (510) 727 - 5669
Hayward, CA 94541 — Fax: (510) 727 - 2300

Annual Grant Total: $2,000,000 - $5,000,000
Geographic Preference: Area(s) in which the company operates
Primary Interests: Arts and Culture; Education; Families
Recent Recipients: Child Care Aware; Family-to Family; United Way

Public Affairs and Related Activities Personnel

At Headquarters

BOUDREAUX, Bernard — Tel: (510) 727 - 5681
Manager, Community Relations — Fax: (510) 727 - 2300
Mailstop: M/S 4790
Responsibilities include corporate philanthropy.

HOWARD, Amber — Tel: (510) 727 - 3000
Manager, Internal Communications — Fax: (510) 727 - 2300

ROGERS, Sue — Tel: (510) 727 - 5669
Grants Administrator — Fax: (510) 727 - 2300
Mailstop: M/S 4790

WINTER, Katie — Tel: (510) 727 - 2634
Senior Manager, Public Relations — Fax: (510) 727 - 2300
Mailstop: MS 4050

Mesaba Airlines

See listing on page 303 under MAIR Holdings, Inc.

Metaldyne Corp.

A provider of metal components. Formed from the combination Mascotech, Simpson Industries and GMTI.
www.metaldyne.com
Annual Revenues: $2 billion

Chairman, President and Chief Exec. Officer — Tel: (734) 207 - 6200
LEULIETTE, Timothy D. — Fax: (734) 207 - 6500

Main Headquarters
Mailing: 47659 Halyard Dr., Plymouth, MI 48170 — Tel: (734) 207 - 6200; Fax: (734) 207 - 6500

Public Affairs and Related Activities Personnel

At Headquarters

KOZAK, Tina — Tel: (734) 207 - 6713
Public Relations Specialist — Fax: (734) 207 - 6696
tinadoher@metaldyne.com

MORELAND, Myra — Tel: (734) 207 - 6762
V. President, Corporate Affairs — Fax: (734) 207 - 6500

MetLife, Inc.

www.metlife.com
Annual Revenues: $39.2 billion

Chairman and Chief Exec. Officer — Tel: (212) 578 - 2211
BENMOSCHE, Robert H. — TF: (800) 638 - 5433

Main Headquarters
Mailing: 200 Park Ave., New York, NY 10166 — Tel: (212) 578 - 2211; TF: (800) 638 - 5433

Washington Office
Contact: Kathleen Mellody
Mailing: 1620 L St. NW, Suite 800, Washington, DC 20036-5617 — Tel: (202) 659 - 3575; Fax: (202) 659 - 1026

Political Action Committees

MetLife, Inc. Employees Political Participation Fund
200 Park Ave. — Tel: (212) 578 - 2211
New York, NY 10166 — TF: (800) 638 - 5433

MetLife, Inc.

* continued from previous page

Contributions to Candidates: $156,500 (01/05 - 09/05)
Democrats: $77,500; Republicans: $79,000.

Principal Recipients

SENATE DEMOCRATS		HOUSE DEMOCRATS	
Feinstein, Dianne (CA)	$4,000	Pelosi, Nancy (CA)	$5,000
		Pomeroy, Earl (ND)	$5,000
		Rangel, Charles B (NY)	$5,000
		Kanjorski, Paul (PA)	$4,500
		Crowley, Joseph (NY)	$4,000
SENATE REPUBLICANS		**HOUSE REPUBLICANS**	
Snowe, Olympia (ME)	$4,000	Oxley, Michael (OH)	$5,000
Thomas, Craig (WY)	$4,000	Baker, Hugh (LA)	$4,000
		Beauprez, Robert (CO)	$4,000
		Boehner, John (OH)	$4,000
		Johnson, Nancy (CT)	$4,000
		Thomas, William M (CA)	$4,000

Corporate Foundations and Giving Programs

MetLife Foundation
Contact: Sybil Jacobson
One MetLife Plaza
Long Island City, NY 11101

Assets: $171,268,620 (2005)
Annual Grant Total: over $5,000,000
The Social Investment Program provides below-market rate loans to communities across the country. Donations totaled over 25 million in 2003.
Geographic Preference: Area(s) in which the company operates; National
Primary Interests: Arts and Culture; Civic and Public Affairs; Education; Health
Recent Recipients: Alzheimer's Ass'n; Boys and Girls Club; Nat'l AIDS Fund; Trust for Public Land, The

Metropolitan Life Insurance Co. Corporate Contributions Program
200 Park Ave. — Tel: (212) 578 - 2211
New York, NY 10166 — TF: (800) 638 - 5433

Annual Grant Total: $2,000,000 - $5,000,000
Contact the program at 212-578-2211.

Public Affairs and Related Activities Personnel

At Headquarters

CONSIDINE, Thomas — Tel: (212) 578 - 2901
V. President, Government and Industry Relations — TF: (800) 638 - 5433

MONFRIED, David M. — Tel: (212) 578 - 2211
Senior V. President, Corporate Communications — TF: (800) 638 - 5433

At Washington Office

CAREY, Kate H. — Tel: (202) 659 - 3575
V. President, Government and Industry Relations — Fax: (202) 659 - 1026
Registered Federal Lobbyist.

KAHN, Melissa — Tel: (202) 659 - 3575
V. President, Government and Industry Relations — Fax: (202) 659 - 1026

MELLODY, Kathleen — Tel: (202) 659 - 3575
Counsel, Government Relations — Fax: (202) 659 - 1026
kmellody@metlife.com
Registered Federal Lobbyist.

PASTRE, Peter — Tel: (202) 659 - 3575
V. President — Fax: (202) 659 - 1026
Registered Federal Lobbyist.

YU, Shannon — Tel: (202) 659 - 3575
Assistant V. President — Fax: (202) 659 - 1026

ZARCONE, Michael A. — Tel: (202) 659 - 3575
Senior V. President, Government and Industry Relations — Fax: (202) 659 - 1026
Registered Federal Lobbyist.

At Other Offices

CALAGNA, John
V. President, Public Relations
One MetLife Plaza
Long Island City, NY 11101

JACOBSON, Sybil
Contact, MetLife Foundation
One MetLife Plaza
Long Island City, NY 11101

Metro-Goldwyn-Mayer Inc.

Formerly MGM Entertainment, Inc. Motion picture and television production distribution.
www.mgm.com

Chairman and Chief Exec. Officer — Tel: (310) 449 - 3000
YEMENIDJIAN, Alex — Fax: (310) 449 - 8757
ayemenidjian@mgm.com

Main Headquarters
Mailing: 10250 Constellation Blvd. — Tel: (310) 449 - 3000
Los Angeles, CA 90067-6241 — Fax: (310) 449 - 8757

Political Action Committees

Metro-Goldwyn-Mayer Political Action Committee
Contact: Deborah J. Arvesen
10250 Constellation Blvd. — Tel: (310) 449 - 3000
Los Angeles, CA 90067-6241 — Fax: (310) 449 - 8757

Contributions to Candidates: $5,200 (01/05 - 09/05)
Democrats: $1,000; Republicans: $4,200.

Principal Recipients

SENATE DEMOCRATS		HOUSE DEMOCRATS	
Feinstein, Dianne (CA)	$1,000		
SENATE REPUBLICANS		**HOUSE REPUBLICANS**	
Smith, Gordon (OR)	$2,000	Dreier, David (CA)	$1,000
Graham, Lindsey (SC)	$1,200		

Public Affairs and Related Activities Personnel

At Headquarters

ARVESEN, Deborah J. — Tel: (310) 449 - 3000
PAC Treasurer — Fax: (310) 449 - 8757

FITZGERALD, Joseph M. — Tel: (310) 449 - 3660
Exec. V. President, Corporate Communications and Investor Relations — Fax: (310) 449 - 8757
jfitzgerald@mgm.com

JANJIGIAN, Janet — Tel: (310) 449 - 3660
Senior V. President, Corporate Communications — Fax: (310) 449 - 8757

RAKOW, Jay — Tel: (310) 449 - 3000
Senior Exec. V. President and General Counsel — Fax: (310) 449 - 8757
Responsibilities include public affairs.

SHAW, Steve — Tel: (310) 449 - 3000
Senior V. President, Human Resources — Fax: (310) 449 - 8757
sshaw@mgm.com

Metrocall Holdings Inc.

See listing on page 497 under USA Mobility, Inc.

Metropolitan Life Insurance Co.

See listing on page 322 under MetLife, Inc.

Fred Meyer Stores

A food, apparel and general merchandise retailer. A division of the Kroger Co. (see separate listing).
www.fredmeyerstores.com

Main Headquarters
Mailing: P.O. Box 42121 — Tel: (503) 232 - 8844
Portland, OR 97242 — Fax: (503) 797 - 5609
TF: (800) 858 - 9202
Ext: 5605
Ext: 5605

Street: 3800 S.E. 22nd Ave.
Portland, OR 97202

Corporate Foundations and Giving Programs

Fred Meyer Foundation, Corporate Donations
Contact: Glynda Brockhoff
P.O. Box 42121 — Tel: (503) 797 - 3213
Portland, OR 97242 — Fax: (503) 797 - 5609
TF: (800) 858 - 9202
Ext: 5605
Ext: 5605

Annual Grant Total: none reported
The foundation does not accept unsolicited requests or proposals. The corporate donations program requires completion of a donation request form which may be found at the customer service desk available in Fred Meyer Stores.
Geographic Preference: Alaska; Idaho; Oregon; Washington State
Primary Interests: Hunger; Youth Services

Public Affairs and Related Activities Personnel

At Headquarters

BROCKHOFF, Glynda — Tel: (503) 797 - 3213
Coordinator, Philanthropy — Fax: (503) 797 - 5609
TF: (800) 858 - 9202
Ext: 5605
Ext: 5605

MGE Energy, Inc

See listing on page 302 under Madison Gas and Electric Co.

MGIC

See listing on page 333 under Mortgage Guaranty Insurance Corp (MGIC).

MGM Entertainment, Inc.

See listing on page 323 under Metro-Goldwyn-Mayer Inc.

MGM MIRAGE

Acquired Mandalay Resort Group in 2005.

www.mgmmirage.com

Main Headquarters

Mailing: 3600 Las Vegas Blvd. S.
Las Vegas, NV 89109
Tel: (702) 693 - 7111
Fax: (702) 693 - 8626

Political Action Committees

MGM MIRAGE PAC
Contact: Steven S. Lucas
591 Redwood Hwy.
Building 4000
Mill Valley, CA 94941

Contributions to Candidates: $50,500 (01/05 - 09/05)
Democrats: $19,500; Republicans: $31,000.

Principal Recipients

SENATE DEMOCRATS		HOUSE DEMOCRATS	
		Berkley, Shelley (NV)	$10,000
SENATE REPUBLICANS		**HOUSE REPUBLICANS**	
Ensign, John Eric (NV)	$5,000	Pombo, Richard (CA)	$5,000
Hatch, Orrin (UT)	$5,000	Porter, Jon (NV)	$5,000
Smith, Gordon (OR)	$5,000		

Corporate Foundations and Giving Programs

The MGM MIRAGE Voice Foundation
Contact: Merlinda Gallegos
3600 Las Vegas Blvd. S.
Las Vegas, NV 89109
Tel: (702) 650 - 7415
Fax: (702) 650 - 7401

Annual Grant Total: none reported
Geographic Preference: Area(s) in which the company operates; Michigan; Mississippi; Nevada; New Jersey
Primary Interests: Children; Community Development; Education

Public Affairs and Related Activities Personnel

At Headquarters

GALLEGOS, Merlinda
Contact, The MGM MIRAGE Voice Foundation
Tel: (702) 650 - 7415
Fax: (702) 650 - 7401

At Other Offices

FELDMAN, Alan
Senior V. President, Public Affairs
3799 Las Vegas Blvd. South
Las Vegas, NV 89109
Tel: (702) 891 - 7147
Fax: (702) 891 - 3096

LUCAS, Steven S.
PAC Treasurer
591 Redwood Hwy.
Building 4000
Mill Valley, CA 94941

MATHUR, Punam N.
V. President, Community Affairs
3260 Industrial Rd.
Las Vegas, NV 89109
punam@mirage.com
Tel: (702) 650 - 7406
Fax: (702) 650 - 7401
Responsibilities include political action, corporate philanthropy, and government affairs.

Michaels Stores, Inc.

A retailer of arts, crafts, frames, and home decorations.

www.michaels.com

Annual Revenues: $2.531 billion

Chairman of the Board
WYLY, Charles J., Jr.
Tel: (972) 409 - 1300
Fax: (972) 409 - 1556

President and Chief Exec. Officer
ROULEAU, R. Michael
Tel: (972) 409 - 1300
Fax: (972) 409 - 1556

Main Headquarters

Mailing: 8000 Bent Branch Dr.
Irving, TX 75063
Tel: (972) 409 - 1300
Fax: (972) 409 - 1556
TF: (800) 642 - 4235

Corporate Foundations and Giving Programs

Michaels Stores, Inc. Corporate Contributions Program
8000 Bent Branch Dr.
Irving, TX 75063
Tel: (972) 409 - 1300
Fax: (972) 409 - 1556
TF: (800) 642 - 4235

Annual Grant Total: none reported

Public Affairs and Related Activities Personnel

At Headquarters

BEASLEY, Mark V.
V. President, General Counsel and Secretary
Tel: (972) 409 - 1655
Fax: (972) 409 - 1556
Responsibilities include government relations.

CLARY, Thomas J.
Manager, Investor Relations and Corporate Communications
Tel: (972) 409 - 1300
Fax: (972) 409 - 1556

ELLIOTT, Sue
Senior V. President, Human Resources
elliott@michaels.com
Tel: (972) 409 - 5200
Fax: (972) 409 - 1556

MichCon

See listing on page 167 under DTE Energy Co.

Michelin North America, Inc.

www.michelin.com

Chairman and President
MICALI, James
Tel: (864) 458 - 5000
Fax: (864) 458 - 6359
TF: (800) 847 - 3435

Main Headquarters

Mailing: P.O. Box 19001
Greenville, SC 29602
Tel: (864) 458 - 5000
Fax: (864) 458 - 6359
TF: (800) 847 - 3435

Street: One Parkway South
Greenville, SC 29615

Corporate Foundations and Giving Programs

Michelin North America Corporate Contributions Program
Contact: John Tully
P.O. Box 19001
Greenville, SC 29602
Tel: (864) 458 - 5000
Fax: (864) 458 - 6359
TF: (800) 847 - 3435

Annual Grant Total: none reported
Geographic Preference: Area(s) in which the company operates; Alabama; Indiana; North Carolina; Oklahoma; South Carolina
Primary Interests: Arts and Humanities; Education
Recent Recipients: Clemson University; Greenville Symphony

Public Affairs and Related Activities Personnel

At Headquarters

EVERED, Steve
Director, Government Affairs
Tel: (864) 458 - 5080
Fax: (864) 458 - 6359
TF: (800) 847 - 3435

FANNING, Michael I.
V. President, Corporate Affairs
Tel: (864) 458 - 5000
Fax: (864) 458 - 6359
TF: (800) 847 - 3435

TULLY, John
Director, Community Relations
Tel: (864) 458 - 5000
Fax: (864) 458 - 6359
TF: (800) 847 - 3435

Micron Technology, Inc.

A manufacturer of semiconductor memory products.

www.micron.com

Chairman, President, and Chief Exec. Officer
APPLETON, Steven R.
Tel: (208) 368 - 4000
Fax: (208) 368 - 2536

Main Headquarters

Mailing: 8000 S. Federal Way
Boise, ID 83707
Tel: (208) 368 - 4000
Fax: (208) 368 - 2536

Corporate Foundations and Giving Programs

Micron Foundation
8000 S. Federal Way
Boise, ID 83707
Tel: (208) 368 - 4000
Fax: (208) 368 - 2536

Annual Grant Total: $2,000,000 - $5,000,000
Geographic Preference: Area(s) in which employees live and work
Primary Interests: Community Development; Higher Education; K-12 Education

Public Affairs and Related Activities Personnel

At Headquarters

ARNOLD, JoAnne S.
V. President, Human Resources
Tel: (208) 368 - 4000
Fax: (208) 368 - 2536

BEDARD, Kipp A.
V. President, Investor Relations
Mailstop: M/S 407
kbedard@micron.com
Tel: (208) 368 - 4400
Fax: (208) 368 - 2536

FAYLOR, Kami
Corporate Contributions Contact - Community and K-12 Relations
Tel: (208) 363 - 3675
Fax: (208) 368 - 2536

KLEINER, Amy
Tel: (208) 368 - 4000
Fax: (208) 368 - 2536

KREIZENBECK, Jason B.
Manager, Government Affairs
Tel: (208) 368 - 4400
Fax: (208) 368 - 2536

Micron Technology, Inc.

* continued from previous page

LEWIS, Roderic W.
V. President, Legal Affairs/General Counsel, and Corporate Secretary
Responsibilities include investor relations.
Tel: (208) 368 - 4000
Fax: (208) 368 - 2536

LOCKHART, Stan
Tel: (208) 368 - 4000
Fax: (208) 368 - 2536

NASH, Julie
Manager, Strategic Communications
jnash@micron.com
Tel: (208) 368 - 4400
Fax: (208) 368 - 2536

PARKER, David T.
Director, Corporate Communications
Mailstop: M/S 407
dtparker@micron.com
Tel: (208) 368 - 4400
Fax: (208) 368 - 2536

POPPEN, Joel
Tel: (208) 368 - 4000
Fax: (208) 368 - 2536

SPANGLER, Dan
Corporate Contributions Contact - University Relations
Tel: (208) 363 - 3675
Fax: (208) 368 - 2536

Microsoft Corporation

A member of the Public Affairs Council. A producer of computer software for business and personal usage.
www.microsoft.com
Annual Revenues: $25.296 billion

Chairman of the Board and Chief Software Architect
GATES, William H., III
Tel: (425) 882 - 8080
Fax: (425) 936 - 7329

Chief Exec. Officer
BALLMER, Steven A.
Tel: (425) 882 - 8080
Fax: (425) 936 - 7329

Main Headquarters
Mailing: One Microsoft Way
Redmond, WA 98052-6399
Tel: (425) 882 - 8080
Fax: (425) 936 - 7329

Washington Office
Contact: Jack Krumholtz
Mailing: 1401 I St., NW
Suite 500
Washington, DC 20005
Tel: (202) 263 - 5900
Fax: (202) 263 - 5902

Political Action Committees

Microsoft Corp. Political Action Committee
Contact: Ed Ingle
1401 I St., NW
Suite 500
Washington, DC 20005
Tel: (202) 263 - 5900
Fax: (202) 263 - 5902

Contributions to Candidates: $184,000 (01/05 - 09/05)
Democrats: $77,500; Republicans: $106,500.

Principal Recipients

SENATE DEMOCRATS		HOUSE DEMOCRATS	
		Pelosi, Nancy (CA)	$5,000
SENATE REPUBLICANS		**HOUSE REPUBLICANS**	
Smith, Gordon (OR)	$10,000	DeLay, Tom (TX)	$5,000
Burns, Conrad (MT)	$6,000	Dreier, David (CA)	$5,000
Santorum, Richard (PA)	$5,000	Gibbons, James A (NV)	$5,000
		Reichert, Dave (WA)	$5,000
		Smith, Lamar (TX)	$5,000

Corporate Foundations and Giving Programs

Microsoft Community Affairs
Contact: Pamela Passman
One Microsoft Way
Redmond, WA 98052-6399
Tel: (425) 882 - 8080
Fax: (425) 936 - 7329

Annual Grant Total: over $5,000,000
The company donated more than $246 million in cash and software in 2003. The company also maintains an employee matching gifts program.
Geographic Preference: International
Primary Interests: Disaster Relief; Technology

Public Affairs and Related Activities Personnel

At Headquarters

ANDERSON, Curt
General Manager, Investor Relations
Tel: (425) 706 - 3703
Fax: (425) 936 - 7329

DIPIETRO, Ken
Corporate V. President, Human Resources
Tel: (425) 882 - 8080
Fax: (425) 936 - 7329

HUMPHRIES, Fred
Director, State Government Affairs
Tel: (425) 882 - 8080
Fax: (425) 936 - 7329

MACCAUL, Cathy
Manager, Communications
Tel: (425) 882 - 8080
Fax: (425) 936 - 7329

MURPHY, Barry
Senior Manager, State Government Affairs
Tel: (425) 882 - 8080
Fax: (425) 703 - 7329

MURRAY, Mark
Director, Corporate Public Relations
Tel: (425) 882 - 8080
Fax: (425) 936 - 7329

PASSMAN, Pamela
Acting Director, Community Affairs; and Head, Corporate Affairs
Tel: (425) 882 - 8080
Fax: (425) 936 - 7329

SMITH, Bradford L.
Senior V. President, Law and Corporate Affairs
Tel: (425) 882 - 8080
Fax: (425) 936 - 7329

At Washington Office

BOYD, Paula
Regulatory Counsel
Registered Federal Lobbyist.
Tel: (202) 263 - 5900
Fax: (202) 263 - 5902

BRADY, Betsy
Policy Counsel
Registered Federal Lobbyist.
Tel: (202) 263 - 5900
Fax: (202) 263 - 5902

BUCKNER, Marland
Manager, Federal Government Affairs
Registered Federal Lobbyist.
Tel: (202) 263 - 5900
Fax: (202) 263 - 5902

GAVIN, Anne
Manager, State Government Affairs - Northeast Region
Tel: (202) 263 - 5900
Fax: (202) 263 - 5902

GELMAN, Matt
Manager, Federal Government Affairs
Tel: (202) 263 - 5900
Fax: (202) 263 - 5902

GUIDERA, Bill
Federal Government Affairs Manager
Registered Federal Lobbyist.
Tel: (202) 263 - 5900
Fax: (202) 263 - 5902

HOUTON, Jamie
Manager, Federal Government Affairs
Registered Federal Lobbyist.
Tel: (202) 263 - 5900
Fax: (202) 263 - 5902

INGLE, Ed
Senior Director, Legislative Affairs
Registered Federal Lobbyist.
Tel: (202) 263 - 5900
Fax: (202) 263 - 5902

KRUMHOLTZ, Jack
Associate General Counsel and Director, Federal Affairs
Registered Federal Lobbyist.
Tel: (202) 263 - 5910
Fax: (202) 263 - 5902

MANN, Susan O.
Manager, Federal Affairs
Registered Federal Lobbyist.
Tel: (202) 263 - 5900
Fax: (202) 263 - 5902

OTTO, Lori
Manager, Federal Government Affairs
Registered Federal Lobbyist.
Tel: (202) 263 - 5900
Fax: (202) 263 - 5902

REITINGER, Phil
Senior Security Strategist
Tel: (202) 263 - 5900
Fax: (202) 263 - 5902

ROESSER, Tom
Director, Tax Affairs
Registered Federal Lobbyist.
Tel: (202) 263 - 5900
Fax: (202) 263 - 5902

RUBINSTEIN, Ira
Registered Federal Lobbyist.
Tel: (202) 263 - 5900
Fax: (202) 263 - 5902

SAMPLE, Bill
Registered Federal Lobbyist.
Tel: (202) 263 - 5900
Fax: (202) 263 - 5902

SAMPSON, John
Manager, Federal Government Affairs
Registered Federal Lobbyist.
Tel: (202) 263 - 5900
Fax: (202) 263 - 5902

TIPSON, Fred
Director, International Trade and Development and Senior Policy Counsel
Registered Federal Lobbyist.
Tel: (202) 263 - 5900
Fax: (202) 263 - 5902

TONES, Frank
Registered Federal Lobbyist.
Tel: (202) 263 - 5900
Fax: (202) 263 - 5902

TORRES, Frank
Registered Federal Lobbyist.
Tel: (202) 263 - 5900
Fax: (202) 263 - 5902

Mid Atlantic Medical Services Inc.

Offers managed health care coverage and products in Delaware, Maryland, North Carolina, Pennsylvania, Virginia, Washington, DC, and West Virginia. A wholly-owned subsidiary of UnitedHealth Group (see separate listing).
www.mamsi.com
Annual Revenues: $2.313 billion

Chairman of the Board
GROBAN, Mark D., M.D.
Tel: (301) 762 - 8205
Fax: (301) 838 - 5682

President and Chief Exec. Officer- Mid-Atlantic
BARBARA, Thomas P.
Tel: (301) 762 - 8205
Fax: (301) 838 - 5682

Main Headquarters
Mailing: Four Taft Ct.
Rockville, MD 20850
Tel: (301) 762 - 8205
Fax: (301) 838 - 5682

Corporate Foundations and Giving Programs

MAMSI Children's Foundation, Inc.
Contact: Barbara K. Smerko

Mid Atlantic Medical Services Inc.

* continued from previous page

Four Taft Ct.
Rockville, MD 20850
Tel: (301) 838 - 5613
Fax: (301) 545 - 5972

Annual Grant Total: none reported

Public Affairs and Related Activities Personnel

At Headquarters

FLEIG, John E., Jr.
Senior V. President, Regulatory Affairs
Tel: (301) 838 - 5653
Fax: (301) 545 - 5972

SAMMIS, Elizabeth
Senior V. President, Corporate Communications
bsammis@mamsi.com
Tel: (301) 838 - 5638
Fax: (301) 545 - 5972

SMERKO, Barbara K.
Exec. Director, MAMSI Children's Foundation, Inc.
Tel: (301) 838 - 5613
Fax: (301) 545 - 5972

MidAmerican Energy Holdings Co.

A member of the Public Affairs Council. An electric and gas services company. Formed by the merger of Midwest Resources, Inc. and Iowa-Illinois Gas and Electric Co.

www.midamerican.com

Chairman and Chief Exec. Officer
SOKOL, David L.
Tel: (515) 242 - 4300
Fax: (515) 242 - 4080
TF: (888) 427 - 5632

Main Headquarters
Mailing: 666 Grand Ave.
P.O. Box 657
Des Moines, IA 50303-0657
Tel: (515) 242 - 4300
Fax: (515) 242 - 4080
TF: (888) 427 - 5632

Washington Office
Contact: Jonathan M. Weisgall
Mailing: 1200 New Hampshire Ave. NW
Suite 300
Washington, DC 20036
Tel: (202) 828 - 1378
Fax: (202) 828 - 1380

Political Action Committees

Effective Government Committee
Contact: Steven R. Evans
666 Grand Ave.
P.O. Box 657
Des Moines, IA 50303-0657
Tel: (515) 281 - 2288
Fax: (515) 242 - 4080
TF: (888) 427 - 5632

Contributions to Candidates: none reported (01/05 - 09/05)

MidAmerican Energy Co. Executive PAC
Contact: Steven R. Evans
666 Grand Ave.
P.O. Box 657
Des Moines, IA 50303-0657
Tel: (515) 281 - 2288
Fax: (515) 242 - 4080
TF: (888) 427 - 5632

Contributions to Candidates: $20,000 (01/05 - 09/05)
Democrats: $3,000; Republicans: $17,000.

Principal Recipients

SENATE REPUBLICANS		HOUSE REPUBLICANS	
Thomas, Craig (WY)	$2,000	Fortenberry, Jeffrey (NE)	$4,000
		Barton, Joe L (TX)	$2,000

Corporate Foundations and Giving Programs

MidAmerican Energy Corporate Contributions
Contact: Keith Hartje
666 Grand Ave.
P.O. Box 657
Des Moines, IA 50303-0657
Tel: (515) 281 - 2575
Fax: (515) 242 - 4080
TF: (888) 427 - 5632

Annual Grant Total: none reported

MidAmerican Energy Foundation
Contact: Keith Hartje
666 Grand Ave.
P.O. Box 657
Des Moines, IA 50303-0657
Tel: (515) 281 - 2575
Fax: (515) 242 - 4080
TF: (888) 427 - 5632

Annual Grant Total: none reported

Public Affairs and Related Activities Personnel

At Headquarters

EVANS, Steven R.
Treasurer PACs
srevans@midamerican.com
Tel: (515) 281 - 2288
Fax: (515) 242 - 4080
TF: (888) 427 - 5632

GALE, Brent
V. President, Legislation and Regulation Affairs
Tel: (515) 242 - 4002
Fax: (515) 242 - 4080
TF: (888) 427 - 5632

GRABINSKI, Tim
Director, Communications Services
tdgrabinski@midamerican.com
Tel: (515) 281 - 2343
Fax: (515) 242 - 4236
TF: (888) 427 - 5632

HARTJE, Keith
Senior V. President, Corporate Communications
Tel: (515) 281 - 2575
Fax: (515) 242 - 4080
TF: (888) 427 - 5632

KUNERT, Kathryn
V. President, Community Relations and Legislative Projects
(MidAmerican Energy Co.)
Tel: (515) 281 - 2287
Fax: (515) 242 - 4398
TF: (888) 427 - 5632

URLIS, Allan
Director, Media Relations
agurlis@midamerican.com
Tel: (515) 281 - 2785
Fax: (515) 242 - 4236
TF: (888) 427 - 5632

At Washington Office

WEISGALL, Jonathan M.
V. President, Legislative Affairs
jmweisgall@midamerican.com
Tel: (202) 828 - 1378
Fax: (202) 828 - 1380

Middle South Utility System

See listing on page 183 under Entergy Services, Inc.

Midwest Resources, Inc.

See listing on page 326 under MidAmerican Energy Holdings Co.

Milacron Inc.

Formerly Cincinnati Milacron Inc. A manufacturer of plastics machinery and industrial fluids.

www.milacron.com
Annual Revenues: $774.2 million

Chairman, President and Chief Exec. Officer
BROWN, Ronald D.
Tel: (513) 487 - 5000
Fax: (513) 487 - 5057

Main Headquarters
Mailing: 2090 Florence Ave.
Cincinnati, OH 45206
Tel: (513) 487 - 5000
Fax: (513) 487 - 5057

Corporate Foundations and Giving Programs

Milacron Foundation
Contact: John C. Francy
2090 Florence Ave.
Cincinnati, OH 45206
Tel: (513) 487 - 5912
Fax: (513) 487 - 5586

Annual Grant Total: $500,000 - $750,000

Geographic Preference: Area(s) in which the company operates; Area in which the company is headquartered; Massachusetts; Ohio; South Carolina
Primary Interests: Community Affairs; Higher Education; Youth Services
Recent Recipients: YMCA

Public Affairs and Related Activities Personnel

At Headquarters

BAKER, M. Bradley
V. President, Human Resources
Tel: (513) 487 - 5000
Fax: (513) 487 - 5057

BEAUPRE, Albert
Director, Corporate Communications and Investor Relations
albert.beaupre@milacron.com
Tel: (513) 487 - 5918
Fax: (513) 487 - 5586

FRANCY, John C.
V. President and Treasurer; Secretary, Milacron Foundation
Tel: (513) 487 - 5912
Fax: (513) 487 - 5586

Millennium Pharmaceuticals, Inc.

www.mlnm.com
Annual Revenues: $448.2 million

President and Chief Exec. Officer
DUNSIRE, Deborah, M.D.
Tel: (617) 679 - 7000
Fax: (617) 374 - 7788
TF: (800) 390 - 5663

Main Headquarters
Mailing: 40 Landsdowne St.
Cambridge, MA 02139
Tel: (617) 679 - 7000
Fax: (617) 374 - 7788
TF: (800) 390 - 5663

Washington Office
Mailing: 1401 H St., NW
Suite 650
Washington, DC 20005
Tel: (202) 289 - 6598
Fax: (202) 289 - 7257

Political Action Committees

Millenium Pharmaceuticals PAC
Contact: Joel Goldberg
40 Landsdowne St.
Cambridge, MA 02139
Tel: (617) 679 - 7000
Fax: (617) 374 - 7788
TF: (800) 390 - 5663

Contributions to Candidates: $4,000 (01/05 - 09/05)
Democrats: $3,000; Republicans: $1,000.

Millennium Pharmaceuticals, Inc.

** continued from previous page*

Principal Recipients

SENATE DEMOCRATS	HOUSE DEMOCRATS	
	Capuano, Michael E (MA)	$2,000
	Price, David E (NC)	$1,000
SENATE REPUBLICANS	**HOUSE REPUBLICANS**	
	Issa, Darrell (CA)	$1,000

Public Affairs and Related Activities Personnel

At Headquarters

GOLDBERG, Joel
PAC Treasurer
Tel: (617) 679 - 7000
Fax: (617) 374 - 7788
TF: (800) 390 - 5663

HENNESSY, Kelly
Manager, Communications and Corporate Public Affairs
pr@mlnm.com
Tel: (617) 444 - 3221
Fax: (617) 374 - 7788
TF: (800) 390 - 5663

KELLY-DOBAY, Pamela
Administrative Coordinator, Global Corporate Affairs
Tel: (617) 679 - 7323
Fax: (617) 374 - 7788
TF: (800) 390 - 5663
Responsibilities include investor and media relations.

PIETRUSKO, Robert
V. President, Worldwide Regulatory Affairs
pietrusko@mpi.com
Tel: (617) 679 - 7000
Fax: (617) 374 - 7788
TF: (800) 390 - 5663
Responsibilities include government relations.

PINE, Linda K.
Senior V. President, Human Resources
pine@mpi.com
Tel: (617) 679 - 7000
Fax: (617) 374 - 7788
TF: (800) 390 - 5663

TARBOX, Amy
Associate, Global Corporate Affairs
info@mlmn.com
Tel: (617) 551 - 5879
Fax: (617) 374 - 7788
TF: (800) 390 - 5663

At Washington Office

MUNROE, J. Brian
V. President, Government Relations and Public Policy
Registered Federal Lobbyist.
Tel: (202) 289 - 6598
Fax: (202) 289 - 7257

Miller Brewing Co.

A member of the Public Affairs Council. Acquired in 2002 and a wholly-owned subsidiary of SABMiller plc of the United Kingdom. More information about Miller Brewing Co. is also available from the following website: www.millerlite.com.
www.millerbrewing.com
Annual Revenues: $4.244 billion

President and Chief Exec. Officer
ADAMI, Norman Joseph
Tel: (414) 931 - 2000
Fax: (414) 931 - 3735

Main Headquarters
Mailing: P.O. Box 482
Milwaukee, WI 53201-0482
Tel: (414) 931 - 2000
Fax: (414) 931 - 6352
Street: 3939 W. Highland Blvd.
Milwaukee, WI 53208

Washington Office
Contact: Timothy H. Scully, Jr.
Mailing: 655 15th St.NW
Washington, DC 20005
Tel: (202) 661 - 8631

Political Action Committees

Miller Brewing Co. PAC
P.O. Box 482
Milwaukee, WI 53201-0482
Tel: (414) 931 - 2000
Fax: (414) 931 - 6352

Contributions to Candidates: $34,000 (01/05 - 09/05)
Democrats: $7,000; Republicans: $27,000.

Principal Recipients

SENATE REPUBLICANS		HOUSE REPUBLICANS	
Allen, George (VA)	$2,500	Blunt, Roy (MO)	$2,500
Frist, William H (TN)	$2,500	Boehner, John (OH)	$2,500
McConnell, Mitch (KY)	$2,500	DeLay, Tom (TX)	$2,500
		Hastert, Dennis J. (IL)	$2,500

Corporate Foundations and Giving Programs

Miller Brewing Co. Corporate Giving Program
Contact: Kim Marotta
P.O. Box 482
Milwaukee, WI 53201-0482
Tel: (414) 931 - 2817
Fax: (414) 931 - 6352

Annual Grant Total: none reported
Geographic Preference: Area(s) in which the company operates; Area in which the company is headquartered
Primary Interests: Arts and Culture; Higher Education; Hunger; Nutrition

Public Affairs and Related Activities Personnel

At Headquarters

BUSSEN, Scott
Life Category Public Relations Manager
sbussen@mbco.com
Tel: (414) 931 - 3848
Fax: (414) 931 - 6352

HENNICK, Michael
Director, Marketing Communications
mhennick@mbco.com
Tel: (414) 931 - 4536
Fax: (414) 931 - 6352

KUBASA, Julie
Manager, Corporate Affairs
jkubasa@mbco.com
Tel: (414) 931 - 4208
Fax: (414) 931 - 6352

LUCAS, Paul
Director, State Government Affairs
Tel: (414) 931 - 3129
Fax: (414) 931 - 3183

MAROTTA, Kim
Contact, Miller Brewing Co. Corporate Giving Program
Tel: (414) 931 - 2817
Fax: (414) 931 - 6352

MOERKE, Audrey
Senior Communication Programs Producer
amoerke@mbco.com
Tel: (414) 931 - 3365
Fax: (414) 931 - 6352

PEACOCK, Robert B., Jr.
Manager, Employee Communications
Tel: (414) 931 - 3443
Fax: (414) 931 - 6352

RUANO, Jose
Manager, Corporate Relations
jruano@mbco.com
Tel: (414) 931 - 4568
Fax: (414) 931 - 6312

At Washington Office

SCULLY, Timothy H., Jr.
V. President, Government Affairs
Registered Federal Lobbyist.
Tel: (202) 661 - 8631

Milliken & Co.

A privately-held textile and chemical manufacturer.
www.milliken.com

Chairman and Chief Exec. Officer
MILLIKEN, Roger
Tel: (864) 503 - 2020
Fax: (864) 503 - 2100

Main Headquarters
Mailing: 920 Milliken Rd.
Spartanburg, SC 29304
Tel: (864) 503 - 2020
Fax: (864) 503 - 2100

Washington Office
Contact: John F. Nash, Jr.
Mailing: 910 16th St. NW
Suite 402
Washington, DC 20006
Tel: (202) 775 - 0084
Fax: (202) 775 - 0784

Corporate Foundations and Giving Programs

Milliken Foundation
920 Milliken Rd.
Spartanburg, SC 29304
Tel: (864) 503 - 2020
Fax: (864) 503 - 2100

Annual Grant Total: $1,000,000 - $2,000,000
Geographic Preference: Area(s) in which the company operates; National
Primary Interests: Higher Education; Persons with Disabilities; Youth Services
Recent Recipients: Junior Achievement; March of Dimes

Public Affairs and Related Activities Personnel

At Headquarters

DILLARD, J. Richard
Director, Public Affairs
Mailstop: M-285
richard_dillard@milliken.com
Tel: (864) 503 - 2546
Fax: (864) 503 - 2100

HODGE, Tommy
V. President, Human Resources
Tel: (864) 503 - 2020
Fax: (864) 503 - 2100

At Washington Office

DUTILH, Katherine M.
Legislative Assistant
kdutilh@millikendc.com
Registered Federal Lobbyist.
Tel: (202) 775 - 0084
Fax: (202) 775 - 0784

NASH, John F., Jr.
Washington Counsel
Registered Federal Lobbyist.
Tel: (202) 775 - 0084
Fax: (202) 775 - 0784

TANTILLO, Auggie
Registered Federal Lobbyist.
Tel: (202) 775 - 0084
Fax: (202) 775 - 0784

THAXTON, Alysia
Legislative Assistant
Tel: (202) 775 - 0084
Fax: (202) 775 - 0784

Millipore Corp.

International bioscience company that provides technologies, tools and services for the discovery, development and production of therapeutic drugs.
www.millipore.com

Millipore Corp.
** continued from previous page*

Chairman, Chief Exec. Officer and President
MADOUS, Martin
Tel: (978) 715 - 4321
Fax: (978) 715 - 1393
TF: (800) 645 - 5476

Main Headquarters
Mailing: 290 Concord Rd.
Billerica, MA 01821
Tel: (978) 715 - 4321
Fax: (978) 715 - 1393
TF: (800) 645 - 5476

Corporate Foundations and Giving Programs

The Millipore Foundation
Contact: Charleen Johnson
290 Concord Rd.
Billerica, MA 01821
Tel: (978) 715 - 1268
Fax: (978) 715 - 1385

Assets: $153,313 (2004)
Annual Grant Total: $1,000,000 - $2,000,000
Foundation's mission is to support Millipore's interest in scientific and technological advancement: to support specific public policy issues that affect Millipore's stockholders, employees and customers, to help improve the quality of life in Millipore's communities, and to assist and encourage Millipore employees in volunteer efforts.
Geographic Preference: Massachusetts; New Hampshire
Primary Interests: Math and Science; Technology
Recent Recipients: Boston Biomedical Research Institute; Citizen's Scholarship Foundation of America; City Year, Inc.; United Negro College Fund

Public Affairs and Related Activities Personnel

At Headquarters

ANDERSON, Thomas
V. President, Corporate Communications
thomas_anderson@millipore.com
Tel: (978) 715 - 1043
Fax: (978) 715 - 1380

BALY, Aline
Corporate Communications Coordinator
Tel: (978) 715 - 1051
Fax: (978) 715 - 1393
TF: (800) 645 - 5476

HELLIWELL, Geoffrey
Treasurer and Director, Investor Relations
geoffrey_helliwell@millipore.com
Tel: (978) 715 - 1041

JOHNSON, Charleen
Exec. Director, Millipore Foundation
Charleen_Johnson@millipore.com
Tel: (978) 715 - 1268
Fax: (978) 715 - 1385

Mindspeed Technologies, Inc.
A provider of semiconductor products and systems solutions for internet infrastructure.
www.mindspeed.com

Chairman of the Board
DEEKER, Dwight
Tel: (949) 579 - 3000
Fax: (949) 579 - 3200

Chief Exec. Officer and Director
HALIM, Raouf Y.
Tel: (949) 579 - 3000
Fax: (949) 579 - 3200

Main Headquarters
Mailing: 4000 MacArthur Blvd.
Newport Beach, CA 92660
Tel: (949) 579 - 3000
Fax: (949) 579 - 3200

Public Affairs and Related Activities Personnel

At Headquarters

STITES, Thomas A.
Senior V. President, Communications
thomas.stites@mindspeed.com
Tel: (949) 579 - 3650
Fax: (949) 579 - 3200

Mine Safety Appliances Co. (MSA)
A manufacturer of safety equipment.
www.msanet.com
Annual Revenues: $850 million

Chairman and Chief Exec. Officer
RYAN, John T., III
john.ryan@msanet.com
Tel: (412) 967 - 3000
Fax: (412) 967 - 3452
TF: (800) 672 - 2222

Main Headquarters
Mailing: P.O. Box 426
Pittsburgh, PA 15230
Tel: (412) 967 - 3000
Fax: (412) 967 - 3056
TF: (800) 672 - 2222

Street: 121 Gamma Dr.
Pittsburgh, PA 15238

Political Action Committees

Mine Safety Appliances Co. Political Action Committee
Contact: Dennis L. Zeitler
P.O. Box 426
Pittsburgh, PA 15230
Tel: (412) 967 - 3046
Fax: (412) 967 - 3367
TF: (800) 672 - 2222

Contributions to Candidates: $6,000 (01/05 - 09/05)
Democrats: $2,500; Republicans: $3,500.

Principal Recipients

SENATE DEMOCRATS

HOUSE DEMOCRATS
Murtha, John P Mr. (PA) $2,500

SENATE REPUBLICANS
Santorum, Richard (PA) $2,000

HOUSE REPUBLICANS
Murphy, Tim (PA) $1,000

Corporate Foundations and Giving Programs

Mine Safety Appliances Co. Charitable Foundation
Contact: Dennis L. Zeitler
P.O. Box 426
Pittsburgh, PA 15230
Tel: (412) 967 - 3046
Fax: (412) 967 - 3367
TF: (800) 672 - 2222

Annual Grant Total: $500,000 - $750,000
Geographic Preference: Area in which the company is headquartered; Area(s) in which the company operates
Primary Interests: Arts and Humanities; Economic Development; Education; Youth Services
Recent Recipients: United Way

Public Affairs and Related Activities Personnel

At Headquarters

BERGER, Lawrence M.
Director, Environmental Affairs
lawrence.berger@msanet.com
Tel: (412) 967 - 3528
Fax: (412) 967 - 3309
TF: (800) 672 - 2222

BERNER, William J.
Risk Manager
william.berner@msanet.com
Tel: (412) 967 - 3043
Fax: (412) 967 - 3087
TF: (800) 672 - 2222

DEASY, Mark C.
Director, Public Relations and Strategic Communications
mark.deasy@msanet.com
Tel: (412) 967 - 3357
Fax: (412) 967 - 3056
TF: (800) 672 - 2222

DEMARIA, Benedict
V. President, Human Resources and Corporate Communications
Tel: (412) 967 - 3109
Fax: (412) 967 - 3056
TF: (800) 672 - 2222

LAMBERT, William M.
Chairman, Mine Safety Appliances Co. PAC
Tel: (412) 967 - 3194
Fax: (412) 967 - 3477
TF: (800) 672 - 2222

ZEITLER, Dennis L.
V. President, CFO and Treasurer
dennis.zeitler@msanet.com
Responsibilities include political action and corporate philanthropy.
Tel: (412) 967 - 3046
Fax: (412) 967 - 3367
TF: (800) 672 - 2222

Minnesota Life Insurance Co.
www.minnesotamutual.com

Main Headquarters
Mailing: 400 Robert St. North
St. Paul, MN 55101
Tel: (651) 665 - 3500
Fax: (651) 665 - 4488

Political Action Committees

Minnesota Life PAC
Contact: Allen L. Peterson
400 Robert St. North
St. Paul, MN 55101
Tel: (651) 665 - 3500
Fax: (651) 665 - 4488

Contributions to Candidates: none reported (01/05 - 09/05)

Corporate Foundations and Giving Programs

Minnesota Mutual Foundation
Contact: Lori J. Koutsky
400 Robert St. North
St. Paul, MN 55101
Tel: (651) 665 - 3501
Fax: (651) 665 - 4488

Annual Grant Total: $2,000,000 - $5,000,000
Geographic Preference: Area in which the company is headquartered; Minnesota
Primary Interests: Adult Education and Training; Arts and Humanities; Health and Human Services; Higher Education; United Way Campaigns

Public Affairs and Related Activities Personnel

At Headquarters

CAMPBELL, Keith M.
V. President, Human Resources and Management Services
keith.campbell@minnesotamutual.com
Tel: (651) 665 - 3500
Fax: (651) 665 - 4128

HIER, Mark B.
Second V. President, Communications and Research
mark.hier@minnesotamutual.com
Tel: (651) 665 - 3672
Fax: (651) 665 - 4128

JENSEN, Margaret "Maggie"
Consultant, Media Relations
margaret.jensen@minnesotalife.com
Tel: (651) 665 - 7558
Fax: (651) 665 - 4128

KOUTSKY, Lori J.
Manager, Community Relations and Foundation
lori.koutsky@minnesotamutual.com
Tel: (651) 665 - 3501
Fax: (651) 665 - 4488

MICHEL, Geoffrey S.
Director, Government Affairs
geoffrey.michel@minnesotamutual.com
Tel: (651) 665 - 3500
Fax: (651) 665 - 3853

PETERSON, Allen L.
PAC Treasurer
Tel: (651) 665 - 3500
Fax: (651) 665 - 4488

WOLFF, Stephen
Director, Communications
stephen.wolff@minnesotamutual.com
Tel: (651) 665 - 3500
Fax: (651) 665 - 4128

Minnesota Mining and Manufacturing Co.
See listing on page 1 under 3M Company.

Minnesota Power

See listing on page 20 under ALLETE.

Mirant Corp.

An energy company.
www.mirant.com
Annual Revenues: $4.572 billion

Chairman of the Board
DAHLBERG, A. W. "Bill" — Tel: (678) 579 - 5000 Fax: (678) 579 - 5001

President and Chief Exec. Officer
FULLER, S. Marce
marce.fuller@mirant.com — Tel: (678) 579 - 5000 Fax: (678) 579 - 5001

Main Headquarters
Mailing: 1155 Perimeter Center West
Atlanta, GA 30338 — Tel: (678) 579 - 5000 Fax: (678) 579 - 5001

Washington Office
Contact: Katharine A. Fredriksen
Mailing: 601 13th St. NW
Suite 850N
Washington, DC 20005 — Tel: (202) 585 - 3800 Fax: (202) 585 - 3806

Political Action Committees

Mirant Corp. PAC
Contact: Greg Weber
1155 Perimeter Center West
Atlanta, GA 30338 — Tel: (678) 579 - 5000 Fax: (678) 579 - 5001

Contributions to Candidates: $11,000 (01/05 - 09/05)
Republicans: $11,000.

Principal Recipients

SENATE REPUBLICANS		HOUSE REPUBLICANS	
Allen, George (VA)	$2,500	Barton, Joe L (TX)	$2,500
Santorum, Richard (PA)	$2,500	DeLay, Tom (TX)	$2,500
		Fossella, Vito (NY)	$1,000

Public Affairs and Related Activities Personnel

At Headquarters

AVRAM, Lloyd
Director, Corporate Communications — Tel: (678) 579 - 7531 Fax: (678) 579 - 5001

THOMPSON, David
Manager, Media Relations and Corporate Communications — Tel: (678) 579 - 5298 Fax: (678) 579 - 5001

WARNOCK, Lloyd "Aldie"
Senior V. President, Governmental and Regulatory Affairs — Tel: (678) 579 - 5145 Fax: (678) 579 - 5001

WEBER, Greg
Treasurer, Mirant Corp. PAC — Tel: (678) 579 - 5000 Fax: (678) 579 - 5001

At Washington Office

FREDRIKSEN, Katharine A.
Director, Federal Affairs
kathy.fredriksen@mirant.com — Tel: (202) 585 - 3832 Fax: (202) 585 - 3806

Mississippi Chemical Corp.

See listing on page 469 under Terra Industries Inc.

Mississippi Power Co.

An electric utility subsidiary of Southern Co. (see separate listing).
www.southernco.com/site/mspower

President and Chief Exec. Officer
TOPAZI, Anthony — Tel: (228) 864 - 1211 Fax: (228) 865 - 5616

Main Headquarters
Mailing: P.O. Box 4079
Gulfport, MS 39502 — Tel: (228) 864 - 1211 Fax: (228) 865 - 5616
Street: 2992 W. Beach
Gulfport, MS 39502

Political Action Committees

Mississippi Power Co. Federal PAC (MS Power Co. Employees Committee for Responsible Federal Government)
Contact: Allison Herndon
30 Hwy. 90 East
Bay St. Louis, MS 39520 — Tel: (228) 466 - 4221 Fax: (228) 466 - 4214

Contributions to Candidates: $12,000 (01/05 - 09/05)
Democrats: $2,500; Republicans: $9,500.

Principal Recipients

SENATE DEMOCRATS		HOUSE DEMOCRATS	
		Taylor, Gene Mr. (MS)	$2,500
SENATE REPUBLICANS		**HOUSE REPUBLICANS**	
Lott, Trent (MS)	$5,000	Pickering, Chip (MS)	$2,500
		Wicker, Roger (MS)	$2,000

Corporate Foundations and Giving Programs

Mississippi Power Education Foundation
Contact: Domenica L. Plitt
P.O. Box 4079
Gulfport, MS 39502 — Tel: (228) 865 - 5904 Fax: (228) 865 - 5876

Assets: $6,000,000 (1999)
Annual Grant Total: under $100,000
Guidelines are available at www.mspower.com/mpfnd or upon request.
Geographic Preference: Mississippi; Area in which the company is headquartered
Primary Interests: K-12 Education

Public Affairs and Related Activities Personnel

At Headquarters

COX, Lofton
Manager, State Legislative Affairs — Tel: (228) 865 - 5611 Fax: (228) 865 - 5616

FAIRBANK, Robert E., Jr.
Manager, Governmental and Environmental Relations — Tel: (228) 865 - 5515 Fax: (228) 865 - 5616

KELLY, Rex E.
Director, Corporate Communications — Tel: (228) 865 - 5778 Fax: (228) 865 - 5771

KERLEY, Bobby
V. President, Customer Services and Marketing — Tel: (228) 864 - 1211 Fax: (228) 865 - 5616

MASON, Don E.
V. President, External Affairs and Corporate Services — Tel: (228) 865 - 5339 Fax: (228) 865 - 5616

PLITT, Domenica L.
Exec. Director, Mississippi Power Education Foundation — Tel: (228) 865 - 5904 Fax: (228) 865 - 5876

TAYLOR, Teresa H.
Supervisor, Employee Communications — Tel: (228) 865 - 5468 Fax: (228) 865 - 5771

THORNTON, Billy F., Jr.
Manager, Regulatory and Federal Legislative Affairs — Tel: (228) 865 - 5295 Fax: (228) 865 - 5616

At Other Offices

HERNDON, Allison
Treasurer, Mississippi Power Co. Federal PAC
30 Hwy. 90 East
Bay St. Louis, MS 39520 — Tel: (228) 466 - 4221 Fax: (228) 466 - 4214

Missouri Gas Energy

See listing on page 447 under Southern Union Company.

Mitchell Energy & Development Corp.

See listing on page 157 under Devon Energy Corp.

Mitsubishi Electric & Electronics USA

Mitsubishi Electric US represents roughly a dozen companies that market lines of consumer, commercial and industrial electronics products. These include semiconductor devices; high-definition televisions, DVD players and VCRs; stadium display screens; systems and components for automobile manufacturers, elevators and escalators; heating and air conditioning systems; factory automation equipment, power products, and other items. With nearly 6,000 people in 30 locations throughout North America, sales in fiscal year 2004 were approximately $2 billion.
www.mitsubishielectric.com

President and Chief Exec. Officer
TASAKI, Akira — Tel: (714) 220 - 2500 Fax: (714) 229 - 3898

Main Headquarters
Mailing: 5665 Plaza Drive
Cypress, CA 90630-0007 — Tel: (714) 220 - 2500 Fax: (714) 229 - 3898

Washington Office
Contact: Peter J. Salavantis
Mailing: 1560 Wilson Blvd.
Suite 1175
Arlington, VA 22209 — Tel: (703) 276 - 3519 Fax: (703) 276 - 8168

Corporate Foundations and Giving Programs

Mitsubishi Electric America Foundation
Contact: Rayna Aylward
1560 Wilson Blvd.
Suite 1175
Arlington, VA 22209 — Tel: (703) 276 - 8240 Fax: (703) 276 - 8260

Assets: $19,113,000 (2003)
Annual Grant Total: $500,000 - $750,000
The Foundation's primary mission is to assist young Americans with disabilities in leading fuller and more productive lives. While requests from all areas of the United States will be considered, priority will be given to communities where the company has locations.
Geographic Preference: Area(s) in which the company operates; National
Primary Interests: Children; Persons with Disabilities
Recent Recipients: Boys and Girls Club; Partners for Youth with Disabilities

Public Affairs and Related Activities Personnel

At Headquarters

BLANCHARD, Cayce
V. President, Corporate Communications
cayce.blanchard@meus.mea.com — Tel: (714) 229 - 3837 Fax: (714) 229 - 3854

Mitsubishi Electric & Electronics USA

** continued from previous page*

At Washington Office

AYLWARD, Rayna — Tel: (703) 276 - 8240
Exec. Director, Mitsubishi Electric America Foundation — Fax: (703) 276 - 8260
Mailstop: Suite 1150
rayna.aylward@meus.mea.com

SALAVANTIS, Peter J. — Tel: (703) 276 - 3519
V. President, Public Affairs — Fax: (703) 276 - 8168
Mailstop: Suite 1175
pater.salavantis@meus.mea.com

Mitsubishi International Corporation

Mitsubishi International Corporation, a wholly owned subsidiary of Mitsubishi Corporation., is a multi-industry trading and investment company with 12 locations across the United States. Leveraging a worldwide network of international trading partners, the trading company conducts transactions in a comprehensive range of businesses, including chemicals, information technology, energy, metals machinery and living essentials.

www.mitsubishicorp-us.com
Annual Revenues: $1.1 billion

President and Chief Exec. Officer — Tel: (212) 605 - 2000
SAKURAI, Motoatsu — Fax: (212) 605 - 2597
motoatsu.sakurai@mitsubishicorp.com

Main Headquarters
Mailing: 655 Third Ave. — Tel: (212) 605 - 2000
New York, NY 10017 — Fax: (212) 605 - 1908

Corporate Foundations and Giving Programs

MIC Foundation
Contact: Tracy L. Austin
655 Third Ave. — Tel: (212) 605 - 2000
New York, NY 10017 — Fax: (212) 605 - 1908

Annual Grant Total: $2,000,000 - $5,000,000
Geographic Preference: North America
Primary Interests: Arts and Culture; Education; Environment/Conservation; Human Welfare; Literacy
Recent Recipients: Nat'l Audubon Soc.; Nature Conservancy; New York Botanical Garden

Public Affairs and Related Activities Personnel

At Headquarters

AUSTIN, Tracy L. — Tel: (212) 605 - 2000
Exec. Director, MIC Foundation — Fax: (212) 605 - 1908

BRUMM, James E. — Tel: (212) 605 - 2000
Exec. V. President — Fax: (212) 605 - 1908

KEEGAN, Mark — Tel: (212) 605 - 2000
Manager, Corporate Communications — Fax: (212) 605 - 1908
mark.keegan@mitsubishicorp.com

Mitsubishi Motors North America, Inc.

www.mitsucars.com

President and Chief Exec. Officer — Tel: (714) 372 - 6000
GILLIGAN, Rich — Fax: (714) 373 - 1020

Main Headquarters
Mailing: P.O. Box 6014 — Tel: (714) 372 - 6000
Cypress, CA 90630-0014 — Fax: (714) 373 - 1020
Street: 6400 Katella Ave.
Cypress, CA 90630-0064

Washington Office
Contact: Anna-Maria Schneider
Mailing: 1560 Wilson Blvd. — Tel: (703) 525 - 4800
Suite 1200
Arlington, VA 22209

Public Affairs and Related Activities Personnel

At Headquarters

GUTTAS, Mike — Tel: (714) 372 - 6000
V. President, Human Resources — Fax: (714) 373 - 1020
(MMNA Manufacturing)

SHULTZ, Gary — Tel: (714) 372 - 6000
V. President, Legal and Government Affairs and General Counsel — Fax: (714) 373 - 1020
(MMNA Manufacturing)

At Washington Office

SCHNEIDER, Anna-Maria — Tel: (703) 525 - 4800
Exec. Director, Government Relations, U.S. Operations
aschneider@mmsa.com
Registered Federal Lobbyist.

Mitsui and Co. (U.S.A.), Inc.

The American subsidiary of a diversified Japanese trading company.

www.mitsui.com

President and Chief Exec. Officer — Tel: (212) 878 - 4000
YOSHIDA, Motokazu

Main Headquarters
Mailing: 200 Park Ave. — Tel: (212) 878 - 4000
New York, NY 10166

Washington Office
Contact: Shinya Hamano
Mailing: 750 17th St. NW — Tel: (202) 861 - 0660
Suite 400 — Fax: (202) 861 - 0437
Washington, DC 20006

Corporate Foundations and Giving Programs

Mitsui USA Foundation
Contact: Shinichi Hirabayashi
200 Park Ave. — Tel: (212) 878 - 4068
New York, NY 10166

Annual Grant Total: $300,000 - $400,000
Preference: generally limited to main operating programs that promote international understanding in fields of interest to the company such as global commerce. Mitsui is not able to accept unsolicited applications for funding because of the overwhelming demand for contributions.

Public Affairs and Related Activities Personnel

At Headquarters

GARLAND, Janet E. — Tel: (212) 878 - 4072
Program Administrator, Mitsui USA Foundation

HIRABAYASHI, Shinichi — Tel: (212) 878 - 4068
President, Mitsui USA Foundation

At Washington Office

BELL, William C. — Tel: (202) 861 - 0660
Director, International Projects — Fax: (202) 861 - 0437

BRUSER, Lawrence — Tel: (202) 861 - 0665
Deputy General Manager and Director, Government Affairs — Fax: (202) 861 - 0437

EPSTEIN, Christopher — Tel: (202) 861 - 0660
Director, Export Controls Compliance — Fax: (202) 861 - 0437

HAMANO, Shinya — Tel: (202) 861 - 0660
General Manager, Washington Office — Fax: (202) 861 - 0437
Responsibilities include government relations.

Modine Manufacturing Company

A manufacturer of heat-transfer equipment.

www.modine.com
Annual Revenues: $1.54 billion

President and Chief Exec. Officer — Tel: (262) 636 - 1200
RAYBURN, David B. — Fax: (262) 636 - 1424

Main Headquarters
Mailing: 1500 DeKoven Ave. — Tel: (262) 636 - 1200
Racine, WI 53403-2552 — Fax: (262) 636 - 1424

Corporate Foundations and Giving Programs

The Modine Manufacturing Co. Charity Foundation
Contact: Lori Stafford
1500 DeKoven Ave. — Tel: (262) 636 - 1001
Racine, WI 53403-2552 — Fax: (262) 636 - 1424

Annual Grant Total: none reported
Geographic Preference: Area(s) in which the company operates; Area in which the company is headquartered
Primary Interests: Arts and Culture; Civic and Public Affairs; Education; Health and Human Services; United Way Campaigns

Public Affairs and Related Activities Personnel

At Headquarters

FAHL, Gary A. — Tel: (262) 636 - 1200
V. President, Environmental Safety and Security — Fax: (262) 636 - 1424

HETRICK, Roger L. — Tel: (262) 636 - 1200
V. President, Human Resources — Fax: (262) 636 - 1424

PRICHARD, David A. — Tel: (262) 636 - 8434
Director, Investor Relations and Corporate Communications — Fax: (262) 636 - 1424
d.a.pritchard@na.modine.com

STAFFORD, Lori — Tel: (262) 636 - 1001
Manager, Corporate Communications — Fax: (262) 636 - 1424
l.stafford@na.modine.com

Mohawk Industries, Inc.

A manufacturer and marketer of carpets, washable accent and bath rugs.

www.mohawkind.com
Annual Revenues: $368.6 million

Chairman, President and Chief Exec. Officer — Tel: (706) 629 - 7721
LORBERBAUM, Jeffrey S. — Fax: (706) 629 - 3851
jeff_lorberbaum@mohawkind.com — TF: (800) 241 - 4494

Main Headquarters
Mailing: P.O. Box 12069 — Tel: (706) 629 - 7721
Calhoun, GA 30703 — Fax: (706) 629 - 3851
TF: (800) 241 - 4494
Street: 160 S. Industrial Blvd.
Calhoun, GA 30701

Mohawk Industries, Inc.
* continued from previous page

Corporate Foundations and Giving Programs

Mohawk Industries Corporate Contributions
Contact: Frank H. Boykin
P.O. Box 12069 — Tel: (706) 624 - 2247
Calhoun, GA 30703 — Fax: (706) 625 - 3851
TF: (800) 241 - 4494

Annual Grant Total: none reported

Public Affairs and Related Activities Personnel

At Headquarters

BOYKIN, Frank H. — Tel: (706) 624 - 2247
V. President, Finance and Chief Financial Officer — Fax: (706) 625 - 3851
frank_boykin@mohawkind.com — TF: (800) 241 - 4494
Responsibilities include corporate philanthropy and investor relations.

MELTON, Jerry L. — Tel: (706) 629 - 7721
V. President, Human Resources — Fax: (706) 629 - 3851
TF: (800) 241 - 4494
Responsibilities also include public relations and communicatons.

Molex Incorporated
A manufacturer of electronic, electrical, and fiber optic components.
www.molex.com
Annual Revenues: $2.247 billion

Co-Chairman of the Board — Tel: (630) 969 - 4550
KREHBIEL, Frederick A. — Fax: (630) 969 - 1352
TF: (800) 786 - 6539

Co-Chairman of the Board — Tel: (630) 969 - 4550
KREHBIEL, John H., Jr. — Fax: (630) 969 - 1352
TF: (800) 786 - 6539

V. Chairman and Chief Exec. Officer — Tel: (630) 969 - 4550
KING, J. Joseph — Fax: (630) 969 - 1352
TF: (800) 786 - 6539

Chief Exec. Officer — Tel: (630) 969 - 4550
SLARK, Martin P. — Fax: (630) 969 - 1352
TF: (800) 786 - 6539

Main Headquarters
Mailing: 2222 Wellington Ct. — Tel: (630) 969 - 4550
Lisle, IL 60532 — Fax: (630) 969 - 1352
TF: (800) 786 - 6539

Corporate Foundations and Giving Programs

Molex Incorporated Corporate Contributions Program
2222 Wellington Ct. — Tel: (630) 969 - 4550
Lisle, IL 60532 — Fax: (630) 969 - 1352
TF: (800) 786 - 6539

Annual Grant Total: none reported

Public Affairs and Related Activities Personnel

At Headquarters

ARMITAGE, Susan — Tel: (630) 527 - 4561
Manager, Communications and Public Relations — Fax: (630) 512 - 8627
sarmitage@molex.com — TF: (800) 786 - 6539

LEFORT, G. Neil — Tel: (630) 527 - 4344
V. President, Investor Relations — Fax: (630) 969 - 1352
nlefort@molex.com — TF: (800) 786 - 6539

LOCKHART, Sandie — Tel: (630) 969 - 4550
Contact, Molex Incorporated Corporate Contributions Program — Fax: (630) 969 - 1352
TF: (800) 786 - 6539

REGAS, Kathi M. — Tel: (630) 527 - 4593
V. President, Human Resources — Fax: (630) 969 - 1352
TF: (800) 786 - 6539

Monsanto Co.
Makes and markets high-value agricultural products. Spun off from Pharmacia Corp. in August of 2002.
www.monsanto.com
Annual Revenues: $4.673 billion

Chairman, President and Chief Exec. Officer — Tel: (314) 694 - 1000
GRANT, Hugh

Main Headquarters
Mailing: 800 N. Lindbergh Blvd. — Tel: (314) 694 - 1000
St. Louis, MO 63167

Washington Office
Contact: Michael Dykes
Mailing: 1300 I St. NW — Tel: (202) 783 - 2460
Suite 450 East — Fax: (202) 789 - 1819
Washington, DC 20005-7211

Political Action Committees

Monsanto Citizenship Fund
Contact: Linda Strachan
1300 I St. NW — Tel: (202) 783 - 2460
Suite 450 East — Fax: (202) 789 - 1819
Washington, DC 20005-7211

Contributions to Candidates: $36,500 (01/05 - 09/05)
Democrats: $3,000; Republicans: $33,500.

Principal Recipients

SENATE REPUBLICANS		HOUSE REPUBLICANS	
Talent, James (MO)	$10,000	Hastert, Dennis J. (IL)	$5,000
Lugar, Richard G (IN)	$4,000	Hulshof, Kenny (MO)	$3,000
		Goodlatte, Robert (VA)	$2,000
		Graves, Sam (MO)	$2,000

Corporate Foundations and Giving Programs

Monsanto Fund
Contact: Deborah Patterson
800 N. Lindbergh Blvd. — Tel: (314) 694 - 4596
St. Louis, MO 63167 — Fax: (314) 694 - 7658

Annual Grant Total: over $5,000,000
Corporation's combined annual donations exceed $27 million.
Geographic Preference: Area(s) in which the company operates
Primary Interests: Arts and Culture; Community Development; Environment/Conservation; Math and Science
Recent Recipients: Nat'l Urban League; St. Louis Symphony; United Way

Monsanto Co. Contributions
Contact: Deborah Patterson
800 N. Lindbergh Blvd. — Tel: (314) 694 - 4596
St. Louis, MO 63167 — Fax: (314) 694 - 7658

Annual Grant Total: $1,000,000 - $2,000,000
Also supports a direct giving fund.
Geographic Preference: Area(s) in which the company operates
Primary Interests: Community Development; Social Services

Public Affairs and Related Activities Personnel

At Headquarters

DINICOLA, Natalie L. — Tel: (314) 694 - 3195
Associate Director, Special Projects
natalie.l.dinicola@monsanto.com
Responsibilities include corporate government affairs.

FISHER, Lori — Tel: (314) 694 - 8535
Director, External Communications

FOSTER, Scarlett Lee — Tel: (314) 694 - 2883
Director, Investor Relations
slfost@monsanto.com

GLOVER, Jerry P. — Tel: (314) 694 - 3133
V. President, External Affairs — Fax: (314) 694 - 4228
Jerry.P.Glover@monsanto.com

PATTERSON, Deborah — Tel: (314) 694 - 4596
President and Chairman, Monsanto Fund — Fax: (314) 694 - 7658

PLESCIA, Frank — Tel: (314) 694 - 6096
Director, State and Local Government Affairs

At Washington Office

BANDLER, Donald — Tel: (202) 783 - 2460
Senior V. President, Government Affairs — Fax: (202) 789 - 1819

DYKES, Michael — Tel: (202) 783 - 2460
Director, International Government Affairs — Fax: (202) 789 - 1819

ENGELBERG, Steven — Tel: (202) 783 - 2460
Senior V. President, Global Affairs — Fax: (202) 789 - 1819

SCHNEIDER, Russell P. — Tel: (202) 783 - 2460
Director, Agricultural Regulation — Fax: (202) 789 - 1819
russell.p.schneider@monsanto.com
Registered Federal Lobbyist.

STRACHAN, Linda — Tel: (202) 783 - 2460
PAC Contact — Fax: (202) 789 - 1819

TRAVIS, Jim — Tel: (202) 783 - 2460
Director, Federal Government Affairs — Fax: (202) 789 - 1819

Monster Worldwide, Inc.
Formerly TMP Worldwide, Inc. An online recruitment company.
http://www.monsterworldwide.com/
Annual Revenues: $845.5 million

Chairman and Chief Exec. Officer — Tel: (212) 351 - 7000
MCKELVEY, Andrew J.
andrew.mckelvey@tmp.com

Main Headquarters
Mailing: 622 Third Ave. — Tel: (212) 351 - 7000
39th Floor — Fax: (646) 658 - 0541
New York, NY 10017

Monster Worldwide, Inc.

** continued from previous page*

Political Action Committees

Monster PAC
Contact: David Rosa
622 Third Ave. Tel: (212) 351 - 7067
39th Floor
New York, NY 10017

Contributions to Candidates: none reported (01/05 - 09/05)

Corporate Foundations and Giving Programs

Monster Worldwide Social Responsibility
622 Third Ave. Tel: (212) 351 - 7000
39th Floor Fax: (646) 658 - 0541
New York, NY 10017

Annual Grant Total: none reported
Primary Interests: Children; Disaster Relief; Education; Families; Health
Recent Recipients: American Cancer Society; American Red Cross; Big Brothers/Big Sisters; United Way

Public Affairs and Related Activities Personnel

At Headquarters

BOND, Philip — Tel: (212) 351 - 7000
Senior V. President, Government Relations — Fax: (646) 658 - 0541

ROSA, David — Tel: (212) 351 - 7067
Senior V. President and Global Brand Manager
david.rosa@tmp.com
Responsibilities include corporate communications and political action.

MONY Group, The

See listing on page 58 under AXA Financial, Inc.

Moody's Corp.

A source used for credit ratings.
www.moodys.com
Annual Revenues: $1.438 billion

Chairman and Chief Exec. Officer — Tel: (212) 553 - 0300
MCDANIEL, Raymond W., Jr. — Fax: (212) 553 - 4820

Main Headquarters
Mailing: 99 Church St. — Tel: (212) 553 - 0300
New York, NY 10007-2707 — Fax: (212) 553 - 4820

Corporate Foundations and Giving Programs

Moody's Foundation
Contact: Daisy Dominguez
99 Church St. — Tel: (212) 553 - 0300
New York, NY 10007-2707 — Fax: (212) 553 - 4820

Annual Grant Total: none reported
Geographic Preference: Area(s) in which employees live and work
Primary Interests: Arts and Culture; Civic and Cultural Activities; Education; Health and Human Services
Recent Recipients: New York University Medical Center

Public Affairs and Related Activities Personnel

At Headquarters

COURTIAN, Michael D. — Tel: (212) 553 - 7194
V. President, Investor Relations and Corporate Finance — Fax: (212) 553 - 4820
michael.courtian@moodys.com

DERING, Jeanne — Tel: (212) 553 - 0300
Exec. V. President, Global Regulatory Affairs and Compliance — Fax: (212) 553 - 4820

DOMINGUEZ, Daisy — Tel: (212) 553 - 0300
Manager, Community Programs — Fax: (212) 553 - 4820

ELLIOT, Jennifer — Tel: (212) 553 - 0300
V. President and Chief Human Resources Officer — Fax: (212) 553 - 4820

LASERSON, Frances G. — Tel: (212) 553 - 7758
Senior V. President, Corporate Communications — Fax: (212) 553 - 4820
fran.laserson@moodys.com

Moog Inc.

A manufacturer of precision controls for aerospace and other industrial uses.
www.moog.com
Annual Revenues: $704 million

Chairman and Chief Exec. Officer — Tel: (716) 652 - 2000
BRADY, Robert T. — Ext: 4853
robert.brady@moog.com — Fax: (716) 687 - 4457

Main Headquarters
Mailing: Seneca St. at Jamison Rd. — Tel: (716) 652 - 2000
East Aurora, NY 14052 — Fax: (716) 687 - 4457

Corporate Foundations and Giving Programs

Moog Inc. Corporate Giving Program
Seneca St. at Jamison Rd. — Tel: (716) 652 - 2000
East Aurora, NY 14052 — Fax: (716) 687 - 4457

Annual Grant Total: none reported

Public Affairs and Related Activities Personnel

At Headquarters

JOHNSON, Susan — Tel: (716) 687 - 4225
Manager, Shareholder Relations — Fax: (716) 687 - 4595
sjohnson@moog.com

KEEBLER, Jack — Tel: (716) 652 - 2000
Manager, Human Resources — Fax: (716) 687 - 4457
jack.keebler@moog.com

J. P. Morgan Chase & Co.

A member of the Public Affairs Council. Formed by the merger of Chase Manhattan Bank and J. P. Morgan & Co. Incorporated in 2000. Acquired Bank One Corp. in July, 2004. At the time this edition went to press, J. P. Morgan Chase & Co. and Bank One Corp. were in the process of merging operations. No further information was available at that time.
www.jpmorganchase.com

Chairman and Chief Exec. Officer — Tel: (212) 270 - 6000
HARRISON, William B., Jr. — Fax: (212) 270 - 1648
william.harrison@jpmorganchase.com

Main Headquarters
Mailing: 270 Park Ave. — Tel: (212) 270 - 6000
New York, NY 10017-2070 — Fax: (212) 270 - 1648

Washington Office
Contact: Stephen S. Ruhlen
Mailing: 800 Connecticut Ave. NW — Tel: (202) 533 - 2100
Suite 950
Washington, DC 20006

Political Action Committees

J. P. Morgan Chase & Co.
Contact: Bridget Lawless
230 Park Ave. — Tel: (212) 622 - 3306
New York, NY 10017

Contributions to Candidates: $153,354 (01/05 - 09/05)
Democrats: $62,054; Republicans: $91,300.

J. P. Morgan Chase & Co. Federal PAC
Contact: Bridget Lawless
230 Park Ave. — Tel: (212) 622 - 3306
New York, NY 10017

Contributions to Candidates: $2,000 (01/05 - 09/05)
Democrats: $2,000.

J. P. Morgan Chase & Co. State and Federal PAC
Contact: Bridget Lawless
230 Park Ave. — Tel: (212) 622 - 3306
New York, NY 10017

Contributions to Candidates: none reported (01/05 - 09/05)

Corporate Foundations and Giving Programs

J. P. Morgan Chase Foundation
Contact: Warren Chapman
One Bank One Plaza — Tel: (312) 732 - 4000
Chicago, IL 60670

Assets: $57,509,497 (2002)
Annual Grant Total: over $5,000,000
Geographic Preference: National
Primary Interests: Children; Community Development; Education; Religion; Urban Affairs

Public Affairs and Related Activities Personnel

At Headquarters

EVANGELISTI, Joe — Tel: (212) 270 - 6000
Managing Director, Media Relations — Fax: (212) 270 - 1648

FARRELL, John J. — Tel: (212) 270 - 6000
Director, Human Resources — Fax: (212) 270 - 1648
john.farrell@jpmorganchase.com

GOLDMAN, Rachel — Tel: (212) 270 - 9906
Senior V. President, Corporate Internal Communications — Fax: (212) 270 - 1648
Mailstop: 34th Floor
rachel.goldman@jpmorganchase.com

HILL, Frederick W. — Tel: (212) 270 - 6000
Exec. V. President; and Head, Marketing and Communications — Fax: (212) 270 - 1648

At Washington Office

LAWSON, David — Tel: (202) 533 - 2100
Managing Director

J. P. Morgan Chase & Co.

** continued from previous page*

RUHLEN, Stephen S. — Tel: (202) 533 - 2100
V. President and Director, Government Affairs

At Other Offices

BLOCK, Tom — Tel: (312) 732 - 4000
Senior V. President, Government Relations
One Bank One Plaza
Chicago, IL 60670

CHAPMAN, Warren — Tel: (312) 732 - 4000
First V. President; and President, Chase Foundation
One Bank One Plaza
Chicago, IL 60670

FINCH, Brian — Tel: (312) 732 - 4000
Corporate Relations Manager
One Bank One Plaza
Chicago, IL 60670

HOLEVAS, Christine — Tel: (312) 732 - 4000
First V. President, Internal Retail Communications
One Bank One Plaza
Chicago, IL 60670

KELLER, James A. — Tel: (202) 585 - 8930
Federal Government Relations Respresentative
401 Ninth St. NW
Suite 640
Washington, DC 20004

KELLY, Thomas A. — Tel: (312) 732 - 4000
Senior V. President, Regional and Retail Media Relations
One Bank One Plaza
Chicago, IL 60670

LAWLESS, Bridget — Tel: (212) 622 - 3306
J. P. Morgan Chase & Co. Federal and State PACs Treasurer
230 Park Ave.
New York, NY 10017
bridget.lawless@jpmorganchase.com

LAZIO, Rick — Tel: (312) 732 - 4000
Exec. V. President, Global Government Relations and Public Policy
One Bank One Plaza
Chicago, IL 60670

MCMULLEN, Melinda — Tel: (312) 732 - 4000
President, Communications for Regional and Retail
One Bank One Plaza
Chicago, IL 60670

ROSTOW, Victoria P. "Penny" — Tel: (202) 585 - 8930
Senior V. President and Director, Federal Government Relations
401 Ninth St. NW
Suite 640
Washington, DC 20004

STEWART, Barbara L. — Tel: (312) 732 - 4000
Senior V. President and Director, State and Local Government Relations
One Bank One Plaza
Chicago, IL 60670

Morgan Stanley

Formerly known as Morgan Stanley Dean Witter & Co. Formed from the merger of Morgan Stanley Group, Inc. and Dean Witter, Discover & Co.

www.morganstanley.com

Chairman and Chief Exec. Officer
MACK, John J. — Tel: (212) 761 - 4000; Fax: (212) 761 - 0086

Main Headquarters
Mailing: 1585 Broadway, New York, NY 10036 — Tel: (212) 761 - 4000; Fax: (212) 761 - 0086

Washington Office
Contact: Samuel J. Baptista
Mailing: 401 Ninth St., NW, Suite 650, Washington, DC 20004 — Tel: (202) 654 - 2000; Fax: (202) 654 - 2100

Political Action Committees

Morgan Stanley PAC
Contact: James A. Runde
1585 Broadway
New York, NY 10036 — Tel: (212) 761 - 8413; Fax: (212) 761 - 0086

Contributions to Candidates: $195,330 (01/05 - 09/05)
Democrats: $39,330; Republicans: $156,000.

Principal Recipients

SENATE REPUBLICANS		HOUSE REPUBLICANS	
Hatch, Orrin (UT)	$14,000	Royce, Ed Mr (CA)	$7,000
Sununu, John (NH)	$14,000	DeLay, Tom (TX)	$5,000
Burns, Conrad (MT)	$8,000	Ney, Robert W (OH)	$5,000
Smith, Gordon (OR)	$6,000	Oxley, Michael (OH)	$5,000
Ensign, John Eric (NV)	$5,500		
Santorum, Richard (PA)	$5,000		

Corporate Foundations and Giving Programs

Morgan Stanley Community Affairs
1601 Broadway
12th Floor
New York, NY 10019 — Tel: (212) 259 - 1235

Annual Grant Total: over $5,000,000
Contributed over $38 million in 2003. The company also maintains a matching gifts program.
Primary Interests: Arts and Culture; Diversity; Youth Services

Public Affairs and Related Activities Personnel

At Headquarters

ALTMAN, Emily — Tel: (212) 761 - 4000; Fax: (212) 761 - 0086
Exec. Director, International Government Relations

O'ROURKE, Raymond J. — Tel: (212) 761 - 4262; Fax: (212) 761 - 0086
Managing Director, Corporate Affairs
Responsibilities include media relations

PIKE, William — Tel: (212) 761 - 4000; Fax: (212) 761 - 0086
Managing Director, Finance and Investor Relations

RUNDE, James A. — Tel: (212) 761 - 8413; Fax: (212) 761 - 0086
PAC Treasurer

At Washington Office

BAPTISTA, Samuel J. — Tel: (202) 654 - 2000; Fax: (202) 654 - 2100
Managing Director, Governmental Affairs
sam.baptista@morganstanley.com
Registered Federal Lobbyist.

MESSINA, Raymond A. — Tel: (202) 654 - 2000; Fax: (202) 654 - 2100
Exec. Director, Government Affairs
Registered Federal Lobbyist.

PEARCE, David F. — Tel: (202) 654 - 2000; Fax: (202) 654 - 2100
Exec. Director, Government Affairs
Registered Federal Lobbyist.

STEIN, Michael J. — Tel: (202) 654 - 2000; Fax: (202) 654 - 2100
Exec.Director, Government Affairs
Registered Federal Lobbyist.

M. A. Mortenson Company

A general contractor providing total facility services.
www.mortenson.com

Chairman and Chief Exec. Officer
MORTENSON, M. A., Jr. — Tel: (763) 522 - 2100; Fax: (763) 287 - 5430

Main Headquarters
Mailing: P.O. Box 710, Minneapolis, MN 54400-0710 — Tel: (763) 522 - 2100; Fax: (763) 287 - 5430
Street: 700 Meadow Ln. North, Minneapolis, MN 55422

Corporate Foundations and Giving Programs

M.A. Mortenson Co. Corporate Giving Program
P.O. Box 710
Minneapolis, MN 54400-0710 — Tel: (763) 522 - 2100; Fax: (763) 287 - 5430

Annual Grant Total: none reported

Public Affairs and Related Activities Personnel

At Headquarters

HAAG, Dan — Tel: (763) 522 - 2100; Fax: (763) 287 - 5430
V. President, Human Resources

MORTENSON, Alice — Tel: (763) 522 - 2100; Fax: (763) 287 - 5430
Director, Community Relations

Mortgage Guaranty Insurance Corp. (MGIC)

A mortgage insurance company.
www.mgic.com
Annual Revenues: $329 million

President and Chief Exec. Officer
CULVER, Curt S. — Tel: (414) 347 - 6480; Fax: (414) 347 - 6696; TF: (800) 558 - 9900

Main Headquarters
Mailing: 270 E. Kilbourn, Milwaukee, WI 53202 — Tel: (414) 347 - 6480; Fax: (414) 347 - 6696; TF: (800) 558 - 9900

Mortgage Guaranty Insurance Corp. (MGIC)

** continued from previous page*

Corporate Foundations and Giving Programs

MGIC Corporate Contributions Program
Contact: Kurt Thomas
270 E. Kilbourn
Milwaukee, WI 53202
Tel: (414) 347 - 6480
Fax: (414) 347 - 6696
TF: (800) 558 - 9900

Annual Grant Total: $500,000 - $750,000
Geographic Preference: Area in which the company is headquartered

Public Affairs and Related Activities Personnel

At Headquarters

COOPER, Geoffry F.
Director, Public Policy and Corporate Relations
Tel: (414) 347 - 2681
Fax: (414) 347 - 6802
TF: (800) 558 - 9900

MONFRE, Katie
Director, Corporate Relations
Tel: (414) 347 - 6480
Fax: (414) 347 - 6696
TF: (800) 558 - 9900

THOMAS, Kurt
V. President
Tel: (414) 347 - 6480
Fax: (414) 347 - 6696
TF: (800) 558 - 9900
Responsibilities also include corporate philanthropy.

ZIMMERMAN, Michael J.
V. President, Investor Relations
mike_zimmerman@mgic.com
Tel: (414) 347 - 6596
Fax: (414) 347 - 6696
TF: (800) 558 - 9900

Morton Internat'l, Inc.

See listing on page 413 under Rohm and Haas Co.

Mosaic Co.

Formed from the merger of IMC Global Corp. and Cargill Crop Nutrition in 2004.
www.mosaicco.com
Annual Revenues: $2.1 billion

Chairman of the Board
LUMPKINS, Robert L.
Tel: (800) 918 - 8270
Fax: (952) 984 - 0032

President and Chief Exec. Officer
CORRIGAN, Frederic W.
Tel: (800) 918 - 8270
Fax: (952) 984 - 0032

Main Headquarters
Mailing: 12800 Whitewater Dr.
Minnetonka, MN 55343
Tel: (800) 918 - 8270
Fax: (952) 984 - 0032

Public Affairs and Related Activities Personnel

At Headquarters

HOADLEY, Douglas
Investor Relations Contact
Tel: (952) 984 - 0234
Fax: (952) 984 - 0032

THRASHER, Linda K.
V. President, Public Affairs
Tel: (952) 984 - 0350
Fax: (952) 984 - 0032

WESSLING, David W.
V. President, Human Resources
Tel: (800) 918 - 8270
Fax: (952) 984 - 0032

Motorola, Inc.

PUBLIC AFFAIRS COUNCIL
A member of the Public Affairs Council. A diversified manufacturer of electronic systems, communication equipment, information systems and components.
www.motorola.com
Annual Revenues: $30.004 billion

Chairman and Chief Exec. Officer
ZANDER, Edward J.
Tel: (847) 576 - 5000
Fax: (847) 576 - 5372
TF: (800) 262 - 8509

Main Headquarters
Mailing: 1303 E. Algonquin Rd.
Schaumburg, IL 60196
Tel: (847) 576 - 5000
Fax: (847) 576 - 5372
TF: (800) 262 - 8509

Washington Office
Mailing: 1350 I St. NW
Suite 400
Washington, DC 20005-3306
Tel: (202) 371 - 6900
Fax: (202) 842 - 3578

Political Action Committees

Motorola Inc. PAC
Contact: Bruce Forsberg
1350 I St. NW
Suite 400
Washington, DC 20005-3306
Tel: (202) 371 - 6900
Fax: (202) 842 - 3578

Contributions to Candidates: $84,000 (01/05 - 09/05)
Democrats: $12,500; Republicans: $71,500.

Principal Recipients

SENATE REPUBLICANS		HOUSE REPUBLICANS	
Burns, Conrad (MT)	$10,000	Blunt, Roy (MO)	$5,000
		Reynolds, Thomas (NY)	$5,000
		Rogers, Harold (KY)	$5,000
		Sweeney, John E. (NY)	$5,000

Corporate Foundations and Giving Programs

Motorola Foundation
Contact: Carol Swinney
1303 E. Algonquin Rd.
Schaumburg, IL 60196
Tel: (847) 576 - 6200
Fax: (847) 576 - 5611
TF: (800) 262 - 8509

Assets: $92,648,562 (2001)
Annual Grant Total: over $5,000,000
Guidelines are available.
Geographic Preference: International; National
Primary Interests: Engineering; Environment/Conservation; Higher Education; Math and Science; Technology
Recent Recipients: Massachusetts Institute of Technology; Nat'l Merit Scholarship

Public Affairs and Related Activities Personnel

At Headquarters

BUDDENDECK, Alan
Director, Communications and Public Affairs, Public Communications Sector
alan.buddendeck@motorola.com
Tel: (847) 523 - 0679
TF: (800) 262 - 8509

DAVIDSMEYER, Darcy E.
Director, State and Local Government Relations
Mailstop: Seventh Floor
Tel: (847) 576 - 7672
Fax: (847) 576 - 5611
TF: (800) 262 - 8509

DIMARIA, Valerie T.
V. President, Communications and Public Affairs
Tel: (847) 576 - 5000
Fax: (847) 576 - 5372
TF: (800) 262 - 8509

GAMS, Ed
Senior V. President and Director, Investor Relations
Tel: (847) 576 - 6873
Fax: (847) 576 - 5611
TF: (800) 262 - 8509

GIENKO, Glenn A.
Exec. V. President and Director, Human Resources
Tel: (847) 576 - 5260
Fax: (847) 538 - 5191
TF: (800) 262 - 8509

HENDRICKS, Steven
Director, Communications and Public Affairs, Global Telecom Solutions Sector
steven.hendricks@motorola.com
Tel: (847) 632 - 6537
Fax: (847) 435 - 8735
TF: (800) 262 - 8509

MADSEN, Jeffrey
Director, Communications and Public Affairs, Integrated Electronic Systems Sector
jeffrey.madsen@motorola.com
Tel: (847) 862 - 0035
Fax: (847) 341 - 4462
TF: (800) 262 - 8509

OLIS, Dennis
Director, Investor Relations
Tel: (847) 576 - 4995
Fax: (847) 576 - 5372
TF: (800) 262 - 8509

PARKE, Bill
Director, Financial Communication
william.parke@motorola.com
Tel: (847) 576 - 4525
Fax: (847) 576 - 4554
TF: (800) 262 - 8509

SWINNEY, Carol
Manager, Community Relations and Motorola Foundation
Tel: (847) 576 - 6200
Fax: (847) 576 - 5611
TF: (800) 262 - 8509

WEYRAUCH, Jennifer
Director, Corporate Communications
jennifer.weyrauch@motorola.com
Tel: (847) 435 - 5320
Fax: (847) 576 - 4554
TF: (800) 262 - 8509

At Washington Office

ANAYA, William B.
Senior Director, Legislative Affairs
Registered Federal Lobbyist.
Tel: (202) 371 - 6900
Fax: (202) 842 - 3578

BARTH, Richard C.
V. President and Director, Telecommunications Strategy and Regulation
Registered Federal Lobbyist.
Tel: (202) 371 - 6900
Fax: (202) 842 - 3578

BRECHER, Richard
Assistant Director, International Trade Relations
Registered Federal Lobbyist.
Tel: (202) 371 - 6900
Fax: (202) 842 - 3578

BROONER, Mary E.
Director, Telecommunications Strategy and Regulation
Registered Federal Lobbyist.
Tel: (202) 371 - 6900
Fax: (202) 842 - 3578

BULAWKA, Bohdan
Director, ITU Global Strategy
Registered Federal Lobbyist.
Tel: (202) 371 - 6900
Fax: (202) 842 - 3578

CHORLINS, Marjorie
Director, Customer Solutions and Global Strategy
Registered Federal Lobbyist.
Tel: (202) 371 - 6900
Fax: (202) 842 - 3578

DILAPI, Christine
Senior Staff Engineer, Spectrum and Standards
Tel: (202) 371 - 6900
Fax: (202) 842 - 3578

EGER, Charles
Director, Office of Driver Safety
Registered Federal Lobbyist.
Tel: (202) 371 - 6900
Fax: (202) 842 - 3578

FORSBERG, Bruce
PAC Treasurer
Tel: (202) 371 - 6900
Fax: (202) 842 - 3578

Motorola, Inc.

* continued from previous page

GOLDSTEIN, James
Director, Government Acquisition Policy
Registered Federal Lobbyist.
Tel: (202) 371 - 6900
Fax: (202) 842 - 3578

JOHNSON, Randy
Director, U.S. Human Resources and Legislative Affairs
Registered Federal Lobbyist.
Tel: (202) 371 - 6900
Fax: (202) 842 - 3578

KENNEDY, Michael D.
Senior V. President and Director, Global Government Relations Organization
Registered Federal Lobbyist.
Tel: (202) 371 - 6900
Fax: (202) 842 - 3578

KUBIK, Rob
Manager, Spectrum and Regulatory Policy
Registered Federal Lobbyist.
Tel: (202) 371 - 6900
Fax: (202) 842 - 3578

LAMBERGMAN, Barry
Director, Government Relations and Regulatory Affairs
Registered Federal Lobbyist.
Tel: (202) 371 - 6900
Fax: (202) 842 - 3578

LYONS, John F.
Director, Telecommunications Regulation
Registered Federal Lobbyist.
Tel: (202) 371 - 6900
Fax: (202) 842 - 3578

O'CONNOR, Teresa
Director, Global Regulatory Relations
Registered Federal Lobbyist.
Tel: (202) 371 - 6900
Fax: (202) 842 - 3578

PAPOVITCH, Dale
Director, International Regulatory Affairs
Tel: (202) 371 - 6900
Fax: (202) 842 - 3578

PICCOLO, Joann
Corporate V. President and Director, U.S. Government Relations
Registered Federal Lobbyist.
Tel: (202) 371 - 6942
Fax: (202) 842 - 3578

POLTRONIERI, Jeanine
Director, Telecom Strategy and Regulation
Registered Federal Lobbyist.
Tel: (202) 371 - 6900
Fax: (202) 842 - 3578

SHARKEY, Steve
Director, Spectrum and Standards Strategy
Registered Federal Lobbyist.
Tel: (202) 371 - 6900
Fax: (202) 842 - 3578

WELCH, John F.
V. President and Director, Global EME Government Relations
Registered Federal Lobbyist.
Tel: (202) 371 - 6900
Fax: (202) 842 - 3578

Mott's Inc.

A U.S. subsidiary of Cadbury Schweppes PLC of London, England, a beverage and food company.
www.motts.com

Main Headquarters
Mailing: 900 King St.
Rye Brook, NY 10573
Tel: (914) 612 - 4000
Fax: (914) 612 - 4100
TF: (800) 426 - 4891

Street: Six High Ridge Park
Stamford, CT 06905

Corporate Foundations and Giving Programs

Mott's Corporate Giving Program
900 King St.
Rye Brook, NY 10573
Tel: (914) 612 - 4000
Fax: (914) 612 - 4100
TF: (800) 426 - 4891

Annual Grant Total: $300,000 - $400,000
The company's giving program partners with Save the Children.
Primary Interests: Children; Nutrition

Public Affairs and Related Activities Personnel

At Headquarters

GOLDSTEIN, Lewis
Corporate Communications Contact
Tel: (914) 612 - 4000
Fax: (914) 612 - 4100
TF: (800) 426 - 4891

Mountain State Blue Cross Blue Shield

www.msbcbs.com

Main Headquarters
Mailing: P.O. Box 7026
Wheeling, WV 26003
Tel: (304) 424 - 7700
Fax: (304) 424 - 7704
TF: (800) 344 - 5514

Street: 700 Market Square
Parkersburg, WV 26101

Public Affairs and Related Activities Personnel

At Headquarters

CALLISON, Carl
Director, Communications and Corporate Planning
ccallison@msbcbs.com
Tel: (304) 347 - 7728
Fax: (304) 347 - 7728
TF: (800) 344 - 5514

EARLEY, J. Fred, II
Senior V. President, External Operations and General Counsel
fearley@msbcbs.com
Tel: (304) 424 - 7798
Fax: (304) 424 - 7704
TF: (800) 344 - 5564

MSA

See listing on page 328 under Mine Safety Appliances Co (MSA).

MSI Insurance

See listing on page 142 under Country Insurance and Financial Services.

MTV Networks

See listing on page 505 under Viacom Inc/CBS Corp.

Murphy Oil Corp.

A producer, refiner and marketer of oil and natural gas.
www.murphyoilcorp.com
Annual Revenues: $4.467 billion

Chairman of the Board
NOLAN, William C.
Tel: (870) 862 - 6411
Fax: (870) 864 - 6373

President and Chief Exec. Officer
DEMING, Claiborne P.
Tel: (870) 862 - 6411
Fax: (870) 864 - 6373

Main Headquarters
Mailing: P.O. Box 7000
El Dorado, AR 71731-7000
Tel: (870) 862 - 6411
Fax: (870) 864 - 6373

Street: 200 Peach St.
El Dorado, AR 71730-5836

Political Action Committees

Murphy Oil Corporation PAC
Contact: Kevin G. Fitzgerald
P.O. Box 7000
El Dorado, AR 71731-7000
Tel: (870) 864 - 6272
Fax: (870) 864 - 6371

Contributions to Candidates: none reported (01/05 - 09/05)

Corporate Foundations and Giving Programs

Murphy Oil Corporate Contributions
Contact: Allison Parker
P.O. Box 7000
El Dorado, AR 71731-7000
Tel: (870) 864 - 6385
Fax: (870) 864 - 6373

Annual Grant Total: $750,000 - $1,000,000
Geographic Preference: Southeastern United States; Midwest
Primary Interests: Community Affairs; Education; Social Services
Recent Recipients: United Way

Public Affairs and Related Activities Personnel

At Headquarters

FITZGERALD, Kevin G.
PAC Contact
Tel: (870) 864 - 6272
Fax: (870) 864 - 6371

PARKER, Allison
Manager, Community and Public Relations
aparker@murphyoilcorp.com
Tel: (870) 864 - 6385
Fax: (870) 864 - 6373

WEST, Mindy
Director, Investor Relations
mwest@murphyoilcorp.com
Tel: (870) 864 - 6315
Fax: (870) 864 - 6373

Mutual of America Life Insurance Co.

A life insurance, pension and employee benefits company.
www.mutualofamerica.com

Chairman of the Board, President, and Chief Exec. Officer
MORAN, Thomas J.
Tel: (212) 224 - 1600
Fax: (212) 224 - 2518

Main Headquarters
Mailing: 320 Park Ave.
New York, NY 10022
Tel: (212) 224 - 1600
Fax: (212) 224 - 2500

Washington Office
Contact: Sean Mannion
Mailing: One Research Court
Suite 350
Rockville, MD 20850-3221
Tel: (301) 977 - 6717
Fax: (301) 977 - 6907

Corporate Foundations and Giving Programs

Mutual of America Foundation
Contact: Thomas Gilliam
320 Park Ave.
New York, NY 10022
Tel: (212) 224 - 1147
Fax: (212) 224 - 2500

Annual Grant Total: none reported

Public Affairs and Related Activities Personnel

At Headquarters

ARAMONY, Diane
Exec. V. President and Corporate Secretary
Responsibilities include corporate philanthropy.
Tel: (212) 224 - 1532
Fax: (212) 224 - 2519

GILLIAM, Thomas
Contact, Mutual of America Foundation
Tel: (212) 224 - 1147
Fax: (212) 224 - 2500

Mutual of America Life Insurance Co.

* continued from previous page

MULLALLY, Kathleen — Tel: (212) 224 - 1643
V. President, Corporate Communications — Fax: (212) 224 - 2529

RUANE, Robert W. — Tel: (212) 224 - 1641
Senior V. President, Corporate Communications — Fax: (212) 224 - 2529

At Washington Office

MANNION, Sean — Tel: (301) 977 - 6717
V. President and Washington Contact — Fax: (301) 977 - 6907

Mutual of Omaha Insurance Co.

A member of the Public Affairs Council. An insurance company.
www.mutualofomaha.com
Annual Revenues: $3.7 billion

Chairman and Chief Exec. Officer — Tel: (402) 342 - 7600
NEARY, Daniel P. — Fax: (402) 351 - 2775

Main Headquarters
Mailing: Mutual of Omaha Plaza, Omaha, NE 68175-0001 — Tel: (402) 342 - 7600; Fax: (402) 351 - 2775

Washington Office
Contact: Melissa S. Rewinkel
Mailing: 1700 Pennsylvania Ave. NW, Suite 500, Washington, DC 20006-4771 — Tel: (202) 393 - 6200; Fax: (202) 639 - 8808

Political Action Committees

Mutual of Omaha Companies PAC (IMPAC)
Contact: Galen F. Ullstrom
Mutual of Omaha Plaza — Tel: (402) 351 - 5235
Omaha, NE 68175-0001 — Fax: (402) 351 - 5710

Contributions to Candidates: $50,500 (01/05 - 09/05)
Democrats: $18,500; Republicans: $32,000.

Principal Recipients

SENATE DEMOCRATS		HOUSE DEMOCRATS	
Conrad, Kent (ND)	$4,000	Pomeroy, Earl (ND)	$2,500
		Towns, Edolphus (NY)	$2,000
SENATE REPUBLICANS		**HOUSE REPUBLICANS**	
Ensign, John Eric (NV)	$3,500	Cantor, Eric (VA)	$3,000
Sununu, John (NH)	$2,000	Blunt, Roy (MO)	$2,500
		Deal, Nathan (GA)	$2,000
		Pickering, Chip (MS)	$2,000

Mutual of Omaha Cos. General Managers PAC (COMPAC)
Contact: Carl Scott
Mutual of Omaha Plaza — Tel: (402) 351 - 8208
Omaha, NE 68175-0001 — Fax: (402) 351 - 5710

Contributions to Candidates: $9,000 (01/05 - 09/05)
Democrats: $1,000; Republicans: $8,000.

Corporate Foundations and Giving Programs

Mutual of Omaha Foundation
Mutual of Omaha Plaza — Tel: (402) 351 - 5319
Omaha, NE 68175 — Fax: (402) 351 - 2651

Annual Grant Total: $2,000,000 - $5,000,000
The Foundation's geographic preference is primarily eastern Nebraska.
Geographic Preference: Nebraska; Area in which the company is headquartered
Primary Interests: Arts and Culture; Community Development; Education; Health

Public Affairs and Related Activities Personnel

At Headquarters

NOLAN, James P. — Tel: (402) 351 - 2944
First V. President, Corporate Communications — Fax: (402) 351 - 2407
jim.nolan@mutualofomaha.com

OLSON, Kathleen P. — Tel: (402) 351 - 2192
V. President, Communications and Public Relations — Fax: (402) 351 - 2407
kathy.olson@mutualofomaha.com

OWENS, Michelle L. — Tel: (402) 351 - 4610
First V. President, Legislative Issues Management — Fax: (402) 351 - 2775
michelle.owens@mutualofomaha.com

SCHOLTZ, Stacy A. — Tel: (402) 351 - 4310
Exec. V. President, Corporate Services — Fax: (402) 351 - 2651
stacy.scholtz@mutualofomaha.com

SCOTT, Carl — Tel: (402) 351 - 8208
Contact, Mutual of Omaha Cos. General Managers PAC — Fax: (402) 351 - 5710
carl.scott@mutualofomaha.com

ULLSTROM, Galen F. — Tel: (402) 351 - 5235
Senior V. President, State Government Relations — Fax: (402) 351 - 5710
galen.ullstrom@mutualofomaha.com

At Washington Office

REWINKEL, Melissa S. — Tel: (202) 393 - 6205
V. President, Government Affairs — Fax: (202) 639 - 8808
melissa.rewinkel@mutualofomaha.com
Registered Federal Lobbyist.

Myers Industries, Inc.

Manufacturer of polymer products; distributor of tire repair tools, equipment and suppliers.
www.myersind.com
Annual Revenues: $661.1 million

Chairman of the Board — Tel: (330) 253 - 5592
MYERS, Stephen E. — Fax: (330) 761 - 6156

Chief Exec. Officer — Tel: (330) 253 - 5592
ORR, John C. — Fax: (330) 761 - 6156

Main Headquarters
Mailing: 1293 S. Main St., Akron, OH 44301 — Tel: (330) 253 - 5592; Fax: (330) 761 - 6156

Public Affairs and Related Activities Personnel

At Headquarters

BARTON, Max R., II — Tel: (330) 253 - 5592
Communications Services and Investor Relations Manager — Fax: (330) 761 - 6111
Responsibilities include public relations.

DURINKSY, Stephen — Tel: (330) 253 - 5592
Director, Corporate Communications — Fax: (330) 761 - 6111

STODNICK, Gregory — Tel: (330) 253 - 5592
V. President, Finance and Chief Financial Officer — Fax: (330) 761 - 6156
Responsibilities include investor relations.

Mylan Laboratories Inc.

A member of the Public Affairs Council. A fully integrated pharmaceutical manufacturer.
www.mylan.com

Chairman of the Board — Tel: (724) 514 - 1800
PUSKAR, Milan

V. Chairman and Chief Exec. Officer — Tel: (724) 514 - 1800
COURY, Robert J.

Main Headquarters
Mailing: 1500 Corporate Dr., Suite 400, Canonsburg, PA 15317 — Tel: (724) 514 - 1800

Political Action Committees

Mylan Laboratories Inc. PAC (Mylan Labs PAC)
Contact: Bob Billings
1500 Corporate Dr. — Tel: (724) 514 - 1887
Suite 400 — Fax: (724) 514 - 1870
Canonsburg, PA 15317

Contributions to Candidates: $12,500 (01/05 - 09/05)
Democrats: $2,000; Republicans: $10,500.

Principal Recipients

SENATE DEMOCRATS		HOUSE DEMOCRATS	
Rockefeller, John (WV)	$2,000		
SENATE REPUBLICANS		**HOUSE REPUBLICANS**	
Santorum, Richard (PA)	$3,000	Emerson, Jo Ann (MO)	$2,000
		Hart, Melissa (PA)	$1,500
		Deal, Nathan (GA)	$1,000
		English, Philip S (PA)	$1,000
		Goodlatte, Robert (VA)	$1,000
		Hoekstra, Peter (MI)	$1,000

Corporate Foundations and Giving Programs

Mylan Charitable Foundation
Contact: Patricia A. Sunseri
1500 Corporate Dr. — Tel: (724) 514 - 1825
Suite 400
Canonsburg, PA 15317

Annual Grant Total: $1,000,000 - $2,000,000

Public Affairs and Related Activities Personnel

At Headquarters

BILLINGS, Bob — Tel: (724) 514 - 1887
PAC Contact — Fax: (724) 514 - 1870

FITZGERALD, Patrick — Tel: (724) 514 - 1800
V. President, Public Relations

HARTMAN KING, Kris — Tel: (724) 514 - 1800
Director, Investor Relations
kking@mylan.com

SUNSERI, Patricia A. — Tel: (724) 514 - 1825
Senior V. President
Responsibilities include corporate contributions.

N L Industries, Inc.

See listing on page 500 under Valhi, Inc.

Nabisco

See listing on page 283 under Kraft Foods, Inc.

Nabors Industries, Ltd.

An oil and gas drilling contract.

www.nabors.com

Annual Revenues: $2.225 billion

Chairman and Chief Exec. Officer
ISENBERG, Eugene M. — Tel: (281) 874 - 0035; Fax: (281) 872 - 5205
eisenberg@nabors.com

Main Headquarters
Mailing: 515 W. Greens Rd., Suite 1200, Houston, TX 77067-4525 — Tel: (281) 874 - 0035; Fax: (281) 872 - 5205

Public Affairs and Related Activities Personnel

At Headquarters

SMITH, Dennis A. — Tel: (281) 775 - 8038; Fax: (281) 872 - 5205
Director, Corporate Development
dsmith@nabors.com
Responsibilities include corporate communications and investor relations.

NACCO Industries

A holding company with operating subsidiaries in forklift truck and related service parts, coal mining, and small electrical appliances.

www.nacco.com

Chairman, President and Chief Exec. Officer
RANKIN, Alfred M., Jr. — Tel: (440) 449 - 9600; Fax: (440) 449 - 9607

Main Headquarters
Mailing: 5875 Landerbrook Dr., Suite 300, Cleveland, OH 44124-4017 — Tel: (440) 449 - 9600; Fax: (440) 449 - 9607

Corporate Foundations and Giving Programs

NACCO Industries Corporate Contributions Program
Contact: Charles Bittenbender
5875 Landerbrook Dr., Suite 300, Cleveland, OH 44124-4017 — Tel: (440) 449 - 9600; Fax: (440) 449 - 9607

Annual Grant Total: none reported

Public Affairs and Related Activities Personnel

At Headquarters

BITTENBENDER, Charles — Tel: (440) 449 - 9600; Fax: (440) 449 - 9607
V. President, General Counsel and Secretary
Responsibilities include corporate philanthropy.

KMETKO, Christy — Tel: (440) 449 - 9669; Fax: (440) 449 - 9607
Investor Relations and Media Contact
ir@naccoind.com

Nalco Chemical Co.

See listing on page 337 under Nalco Co.

Nalco Co.

Formerly known as Ondeo Nalco Co. A manufacturer of specialty chemicals for water treatment and industrial uses.

www.nalco.com

Annual Revenues: $3 billion

Chairman and Chief Exec. Officer
JOYCE, William H. — Tel: (630) 305 - 1000; Fax: (630) 305 - 2900

Main Headquarters
Mailing: 1601 W. Diehl Rd., Naperville, IL 60563-1198 — Tel: (630) 305 - 1000; Fax: (630) 305 - 2900

Political Action Committees

Nalco Co. Political Action Committee (NalcoPAC)
Contact: Michael R. Bushman
1601 W. Diehl Rd., Naperville, IL 60563-1198 — Tel: (630) 305 - 1025; Fax: (630) 305 - 1973

Contributions to Candidates: none reported (01/05 - 09/05)

Corporate Foundations and Giving Programs

Nalco Foundation
Contact: Laurie Marsh
1601 W. Diehl Rd., Naperville, IL 60563-1198 — Tel: (630) 305 - 1753; Fax: (630) 305 - 2893

Annual Grant Total: none reported
The Nalco Foundation dedicates itself to making a lasting and positive impact by concentrating its giving on specific areas, each with a distinct reason and purpose. The Foundation strives to continue to support programs where it is possible to effect the greatest positive change. The foundation is not currently accepting request for new funding.
Geographic Preference: Area(s) in which employees live and work

Public Affairs and Related Activities Personnel

At Headquarters

BUSHMAN, Michael R. — Tel: (630) 305 - 1025; Fax: (630) 305 - 1973
Division V. President, Communications and Investor Relations

HOCKMAN, Dr. Deborah C. — Tel: (630) 305 - 1000; Fax: (630) 305 - 2900
V. President, Safety, Health and Environment and Global Analytical Services

MARSH, Laurie — Tel: (630) 305 - 1753; Fax: (630) 305 - 2893
President, Nalco Foundation

PAJOR, Charlie — Tel: (630) 305 - 1556; Fax: (630) 305 - 1973
Senior Manager, Communications

SCHOEN, John — Tel: (630) 305 - 1147; Fax: (630) 305 - 1973
Manager, Communications

SZMURLO, F. L. — Tel: (630) 305 - 1000; Fax: (630) 305 - 2944
Director, Insurance and Risk Management

Nash Finch Company

A food wholesaler and retailer.

www.nashfinch.com

Chairman of the Board
GRAHAM, Allister P. — Tel: (952) 832 - 0534; Fax: (952) 844 - 1234

Chief Exec. Officer
MARSHALL, Ron — Tel: (952) 832 - 0534; Fax: (952) 844 - 1234
rmarshall@nashfinch.com

Main Headquarters
Mailing: 7600 France Ave. South, Edina, MN 55435 — Tel: (952) 832 - 0534; Fax: (952) 844 - 1234

Corporate Foundations and Giving Programs

NFC Foundation
Contact: Brian Numainville
7600 France Ave. South, Edina, MN 55435 — Tel: (952) 832 - 0534; Fax: (952) 844 - 1234

Annual Grant Total: none reported

Public Affairs and Related Activities Personnel

At Headquarters

EULBERG, Joseph R. — Tel: (952) 832 - 0534; Fax: (952) 844 - 1234
Senior V. President, Human Resources

NUMAINVILLE, Brian — Tel: (952) 832 - 0534; Fax: (952) 844 - 1234
Senior Director, Research and Public Relations
brian.numainville@nashfinch.com

STEWART, LeAnne M. — Tel: (952) 844 - 1060; Fax: (952) 844 - 1239
Senior V. President, Chief Financial Officer and Treasurer
lstewart@nashfinch.com
Responsibilities include investor relations.

Nat'l Broadcasting Co.

See listing on page 342 under NBC Universal.

Nat'l City Bancshares, Inc.

See listing on page 257 under Integra Bank NA.

Nat'l City Bank, Pennsylvania

See listing on page 337 under Nat'l City Corp.

Nat'l City Corp.

Bank holding company.

www.nationalcity.com

Annual Revenues: $10.559 billion

Chairman and Chief Exec. Officer
DABERKO, David A. — Tel: (216) 222 - 2000; TF: (800) 622 - 6736

Main Headquarters
Mailing: National City Center, 1900 E. Ninth St., Cleveland, OH 44114-3484 — Tel: (216) 222 - 2000; Fax: (216) 575 - 2353; TF: (800) 622 - 6736

Political Action Committees

Nat'l City Corp. PAC (NCC PAC)
Contact: Bruce A. McCrodden
National City Center, 1900 E. Ninth St., Cleveland, OH 44114-3484 — Tel: (216) 222 - 2994; Fax: (216) 222 - 2670; TF: (800) 622 - 6736

Nat'l City Corp.

** continued from previous page*

Contributions to Candidates: $38,100 (01/05 - 09/05)

Democrats: $2,000; Republicans: $36,100.

Principal Recipients

SENATE REPUBLICANS		HOUSE REPUBLICANS	
Santorum, Richard (PA)	$5,000	Oxley, Michael (OH)	$5,000
		Pryce, Deborah (OH)	$5,000
		LaTourette, Steve (OH)	$4,000
		Dewine, R. Pat (OH)	$3,600

Nat'l City Corp. Political Action Committee
Contact: Bruce A. McCrodden
National City Center
1900 E. Ninth St.
Cleveland, OH 44114-3484
Tel: (216) 222 - 2994
Fax: (216) 222 - 2670
TF: (800) 622 - 6736

Contributions to Candidates: none reported (01/05 - 09/05)

Corporate Foundations and Giving Programs

Nat'l City/Corporation Charitable Foundation
Contact: Joanne Clark
National City Center
1900 E. Ninth St.
Cleveland, OH 44114-3484
Tel: (216) 222 - 2995
Fax: (216) 222 - 2670
TF: (800) 622 - 6736

Assets: $69,000,0000

Annual Grant Total: over $5,000,000

Each bank receives and acts upon grant requests from qualified non-profit organizations located within its respective area. Annual contributions total $15 million.

Geographic Preference: Area(s) in which the company operates; Indiana; Kentucky; Illinois; Ohio; Pennsylvania; Michigan; Missouri

Primary Interests: Arts and Culture; Civic and Public Affairs; Education; Health and Human Services

Public Affairs and Related Activities Personnel

At Headquarters

CLARK, Joanne
Contact, Nat'l City/Corporation Charitable Foundation
Mailstop: M/S 01-2157
joanne.clark@nationalcity.com
Tel: (216) 222 - 2995
Fax: (216) 222 - 2670
TF: (800) 622 - 6736

COUTURE, Jon N.
Exec. V. President and Director, Corporate Human Resources
Tel: (216) 222 - 2000
Fax: (216) 575 - 2353
TF: (800) 622 - 6736

HAMMARLUND, Jennifer
V. President and Manager, Investor Relations
Tel: (216) 222 - 2000
Fax: (216) 575 - 2353
TF: (800) 622 - 6736

KEMPER, Christopher
Media Contact
christopher.kemper@nationalcity.com
Tel: (513) 455 - 9228
Fax: (226) 575 - 2353
TF: (800) 622 - 6736

Media contact for Greater Cincinnati, Northern Kentucky and Missouri.

MCCRODDEN, Bruce A.
Senior V. President, Corporate Public Affairs
Mailstop: M/S 01-2157
bruce.mccrodden@nationalcity.com
Tel: (216) 222 - 2994
Fax: (216) 222 - 2670
TF: (800) 622 - 6736

Responsibilities include political action.

WAGNER, Kelly J.
Media Contact
kelly.j.wagner@nationalcity.com
Tel: (216) 222 - 9514
Fax: (216) 222 - 4221
TF: (800) 622 - 6736

Media contact for Ohio only

At Other Offices

EILER, William S.
V. President, Media Relations
(Nat'l City Bank, Pennsylvania)
20 Stanwix St.
Pittsburgh, PA 15222-4802
william.eiler@nationalcity.com
Tel: (412) 644 - 8073
Fax: (412) 644 - 7723

Media contact for Michigan, Pennsylvania and Youngstown, Ohio.

LYTTLE, Mr. Kim E.
V. President, Public Affairs
(Nat'l City Bank, Pennsylvania)
20 Stanwix St.
Mailstop: 14th Floor
Pittsburgh, PA 15222-4802
Tel: (412) 644 - 7710
Fax: (412) 644 - 7723

MAY, Darwin
V. President, Community Relations
101 W. Washington
Indianapolis, IN 46255
Tel: (317) 267 - 7000
Fax: (317) 267 - 3957

WILSON, Terri G.
V. President - Media Relations Officer
101 S. Fifth St.
Louisville, KY 40202
terri.wilson@nationalcity.com
Tel: (502) 581 - 4073
Fax: (502) 581 - 7953

Media contact for Illinois, Indiana and Kentucky.

Nat'l Fuel Gas Co.

An integrated energy company.

www.nationalfuelgas.com

Chairman, President and Chief Exec. Officer
ACKERMAN, Philip C.
Tel: (716) 857 - 7000
Fax: (716) 857 - 7439
TF: (800) 365 - 3234

Main Headquarters
Mailing: 6363 Main St.
Williamsville, NY 14221
Tel: (716) 857 - 7000
Fax: (716) 857 - 7439
TF: (800) 365 - 3234

Political Action Committees

Nat'l Fuel Political Action Committee
Contact: Gloria Kordasiewicz
6363 Main St.
Williamsville, NY 14221
Tel: (716) 857 - 7705
Fax: (716) 857 - 7439
TF: (800) 365 - 3234

Contributions to Candidates: $9,000 (01/05 - 09/05)

Democrats: $2,000; Republicans: $7,000.

Principal Recipients

SENATE DEMOCRATS		HOUSE DEMOCRATS	
Bingaman, Jeff (NM)	$1,000	Higgins, Brian M. (NY)	$1,000
SENATE REPUBLICANS		**HOUSE REPUBLICANS**	
Santorum, Richard (PA)	$1,000	Peterson, John Mr. (PA)	$2,000
		English, Philip S (PA)	$1,000
		Murphy, Tim (PA)	$1,000
		Reynolds, Thomas (NY)	$1,000
		Shuster, William (PA)	$1,000

Corporate Foundations and Giving Programs

National Fuel Gas Company Foundation
Contact: Julie Coppola Cox
6363 Main St.
Williamsville, NY 14221
Tel: (716) 857 - 7079
Fax: (716) 857 - 7439
TF: (800) 365 - 3234

Annual Grant Total: none reported

Public Affairs and Related Activities Personnel

At Headquarters

COX, Julie Coppola
Senior Manager, Corporate Communications
coxj@natfuel.com
Tel: (716) 857 - 7079
Fax: (716) 857 - 7439
TF: (800) 365 - 3234

Responsibilities include corporate philanthropy.

KORDASIEWICZ, Gloria
Contact, Nat'l Fuel Political Action Committee
kordasiewiczg@natfuel.com
Tel: (716) 857 - 7705
Fax: (716) 857 - 7439
TF: (800) 365 - 3234

MORRISON, Gary L.
General Manager, Government Affairs
morrisong@natfuel.com
Tel: (716) 857 - 7179
Fax: (716) 857 - 7439
TF: (800) 365 - 3234

PAUL, Patricia J.
Manager, Government Affairs
paulp@natfuel.com
Tel: (716) 857 - 7780
Fax: (716) 857 - 7439
TF: (800) 365 - 3234

ROSE, Michael M.
Manager, Government Affairs
rosem@natfuel.com
Tel: (716) 857 - 7438
Fax: (716) 857 - 7439
TF: (800) 365 - 3234

SHORT, Joseph A.
Treasurer, Nat'l Fuel Political Action Committee
shortj@natfuel.com
Tel: (716) 857 - 7842
Fax: (716) 857 - 7439
TF: (800) 365 - 3234

SUTO, Margaret M.
Director, Investor Relations
sutom@natfuel.com
Tel: (716) 857 - 6987
Fax: (716) 857 - 7439
TF: (800) 365 - 3234

TANSKI, Ronald J.
Treasurer, Investor Relations Officer
Tel: (716) 857 - 6904
Fax: (716) 857 - 1856
TF: (800) 365 - 3234

At Other Offices

YOCHIM, Maryann C.
Manager, Government Affairs
1100 State St.
Erie, PA 16501
yochimm@natfuel.com
Tel: (814) 871 - 8231

Nat'l Geographic Soc.

Publishes books and magazines and produces television documentaries.

www.nationalgeographic.com

Annual Revenues: $500 million

Chairman, Board of Trustees
GROSVENOR, Gilbert
Tel: (202) 857 - 7000
Fax: (202) 828 - 6679
TF: (800) 647 - 5463

President and Chief Exec. Officer
FAHEY, John M., Jr.
Tel: (202) 857 - 7000
Fax: (202) 828 - 6679
TF: (800) 647 - 5463

Main Headquarters

Mailing: P.O. Box 98199
Washington, DC 20090-8199
Tel: (202) 857 - 7000
Fax: (202) 828 - 6679
TF: (800) 647 - 5463

Street: 1145 17th St. NW
Washington, DC 20036-4688

Corporate Foundations and Giving Programs

Nat'l Geographic Education Foundation
Contact: Barbara Chow
P.O. Box 98199
Washington, DC 20090-8199
Tel: (202) 857 - 7000
Fax: (202) 828 - 6679
TF: (800) 647 - 5463

Annual Grant Total: none reported

Primary Interests: Education; Geography Education

Public Affairs and Related Activities Personnel

At Headquarters

ADAMSON, Terrence
Exec. V. President
Tel: (202) 857 - 7000
Fax: (202) 828 - 6679
Responsibilities include government relations.

CHOW, Barbara
Contact, Nat'l Geographic Education Foundation
Tel: (202) 857 - 7000
Fax: (202) 828 - 6679
TF: (800) 647 - 5463

HUDSON, Betty
Senior V. President, Communications
Tel: (202) 857 - 7000
Fax: (202) 828 - 6679
TF: (800) 647 - 5463

MOFFET, Barbara S.
Director, Media Relations
bmoffett@ngs.org
Tel: (202) 857 - 7756
Fax: (202) 828 - 6679

SABLO, Thomas A. "Tony"
Senior V. President, Human Resources
Tel: (202) 857 - 7000
Fax: (202) 828 - 6679
TF: (800) 647 - 5463

SEITZ, Carol
Director, Media Relations
cseitz@ngs.org
Tel: (202) 857 - 6678
Fax: (202) 828 - 6679
TF: (800) 647 - 5463

Nat'l Grid USA

An electric utility holding company. A wholly-owned subsidiary of Nat'l Grid Transco Group of the United Kingdom. Acquired Eastern Utilities Associates and New England Electric System in 2000 and Niagara Mohawk Holdings Inc. in 2002.

www.nationalgridus.com

President and Chief Exec. Officer
JESANIS, Mike
Tel: (508) 389 - 2000
Fax: (508) 389 - 2605

Main Headquarters

Mailing: 25 Research Dr.
Westborough, MA 01582
Tel: (508) 389 - 2000
Fax: (508) 389 - 2605

Washington Office

Mailing: 633 Pennsylvania Ave. NW
Sixth Floor
Washington, DC 20004
Tel: (202) 783 - 7959

Political Action Committees

Nat'l Grid USA Political Action Committee
Contact: Mari-Louise Messuri
25 Research Dr.
Westborough, MA 01582
Tel: (508) 389 - 2000
Fax: (508) 389 - 2605

Contributions to Candidates: $21,000 (01/05 - 09/05)

Democrats: $8,500; Republicans: $12,500.

Principal Recipients

SENATE DEMOCRATS		HOUSE DEMOCRATS	
Clinton, Hillary Rodham (NY)	$2,000		
SENATE REPUBLICANS		**HOUSE REPUBLICANS**	
Burns, Conrad (MT)	$3,000	Barton, Joe L (TX)	$2,000

Corporate Foundations and Giving Programs

New England Electric System Matching Gifts Program
Contact: Victor Tremblay
25 Research Dr.
Westborough, MA 01582
Tel: (508) 389 - 3709
Fax: (508) 836 - 5487

Annual Grant Total: none reported

Geographic Preference: Area(s) in which the company operates; Massachusetts; New Hampshire; New York; Rhode Island

Primary Interests: Arts and Culture; Education; Environment/Conservation; Health; Youth Services

Public Affairs and Related Activities Personnel

At Headquarters

ATWOOD, Amy Tull
Media Contact
Tel: (508) 389 - 2627
Fax: (508) 389 - 3198

BARRY, Jackie
Media Contact
Tel: (508) 389 - 3298
Fax: (508) 389 - 3198

DREW, Deborah
Media Contact
Tel: (508) 389 - 3102
Fax: (508) 389 - 3198

MESSURI, Mari-Louise
Treasurer, National Grid USA PAC
Tel: (508) 389 - 2000
Fax: (508) 389 - 2605

PASTUSZEK, Lydia
Senior V. President, Human Resources
Tel: (508) 389 - 3600
Fax: (508) 366 - 5498

POWERS, Edward
Director, Corporate Communications
Tel: (508) 389 - 3568
Fax: (508) 389 - 3198

REILLY, Lawrence J.
Senior V. President, General Counsel, and Corporate Secretary
Tel: (508) 389 - 9000
Fax: (508) 389 - 2605
Responsibilities include legal and external affairs; federal affairs; and regulatory research.

TREMBLAY, Victor
Contact, Matching Gifts Program
Tel: (508) 389 - 3709
Fax: (508) 836 - 5487

At Washington Office

FLYNN, Peter
Tel: (202) 783 - 7959
Registered Federal Lobbyist.

LAUSTEN, Connie L.
Manager, Federal Regulatory Affairs
connie.lausten@us.ngrid.com
Tel: (202) 783 - 7959
Registered Federal Lobbyist.

National Gypsum Co.

An integrated, diversified manufacturer and supplier of products and services used worldwide in building and construction.

www.nationalgypsum.com

Chairman, President and Chief Exec. Officer
NELSON, Thomas C.
Tel: (704) 365 - 7300
Fax: (704) 329 - 6421

Main Headquarters

Mailing: 2001 Rexford Rd.
Charlotte, NC 28211
Tel: (704) 365 - 7300
Fax: (800) 329 - 6421

Public Affairs and Related Activities Personnel

At Headquarters

RADIGAN, Patrick
Director, Environmental Service
Tel: (704) 365 - 7300
Fax: (704) 365 - 7406

RODONO, Nick
V. President, Human Resources
Tel: (704) 365 - 7300
Fax: (704) 365 - 7218

SPURLOCK, Nancy H.
Director, Corporate Communications
nhspurlock@nationalgypsum.com
Tel: (704) 365 - 7556
Fax: (704) 329 - 6421

Nat'l Life Insurance Co.

Does business as National Life of Vermont.

www.nationallife.com

Annual Revenues: $1.295 billion

Chairman, President and Chief Exec. Officer
MACLEAY, Thomas H.
Tel: (802) 229 - 3333
Fax: (802) 229 - 9281
TF: (800) 732 - 8939

Main Headquarters

Mailing: One Nat'l Life Dr.
Montpelier, VT 05604
Tel: (802) 229 - 3333
Fax: (802) 229 - 9281
TF: (800) 732 - 8939

Corporate Foundations and Giving Programs

Nat'l Life Insurance Corporate Contributions Program
Contact: Martha Trombley Oakes

Nat'l Life Insurance Co.

** continued from previous page*

One Nat'l Life Dr.
Montpelier, VT 05604
Tel: (802) 229 - 7214
Fax: (802) 229 - 9281
TF: (800) 732 - 8939

Annual Grant Total: $200,000 - $300,000
Written guidelines are available.
Geographic Preference: Area in which the company is headquartered
Primary Interests: Arts and Humanities; Community Affairs; Health; Higher Education; Safety; Youth Services

Public Affairs and Related Activities Personnel

At Headquarters

TROMBLEY OAKES, Martha
Corporate Contributions Contact
Tel: (802) 229 - 7214
Fax: (802) 229 - 9281
TF: (800) 732 - 8939
Responsibilities include media relations.

VACHON, Brian
V. President, Communications
bvachon@nationallife.com
Tel: (802) 229 - 3333
Fax: (802) 229 - 9281
TF: (800) 732 - 8939

Nat'l Life of Vermont

See listing on page 339 under Nat'l Life Insurance Co.

Nat'l Oilwell, Inc.

An oil component manufacturer.
www.natoil.com
Annual Revenues: $1.5 billion

Chairman, President and Chief Exec. Officer
MILLER, Merrill A. "Pete", Jr.
Tel: (713) 346 - 7500
Fax: (713) 435 - 2195

Main Headquarters
Mailing: 10000 Richmond Ave.
Fourth Floor
Houston, TX 77042-4200
Tel: (713) 346 - 7500
Fax: (713) 435 - 2195

Public Affairs and Related Activities Personnel

At Headquarters

HARGETT, Katina
Assistant, Investor Relations
Tel: (713) 346 - 7766
Fax: (713) 435 - 2195

MATHER, M. Gay
Director, Communications
Tel: (713) 346 - 7775
Fax: (713) 435 - 2195
Responsibilities include investor relations.

NIBLING, Kenneth L.
V. President, Human Resources
Tel: (713) 346 - 7500
Fax: (713) 435 - 2195

Nat'l Presto Industries, Inc.

A manufacturer of appliances.
www.gopresto.com

Chairman, President and Chief Exec. Officer
COHEN, Maryjo
Tel: (715) 839 - 2121
Fax: (715) 839 - 2122

Main Headquarters
Mailing: 3925 N. Hastings Way
Eau Claire, WI 54703-3703
Tel: (715) 839 - 2121
Fax: (715) 839 - 2122

Corporate Foundations and Giving Programs

Presto Foundation
Contact: Norma Jaenke
3925 N. Hastings Way
Eau Claire, WI 54703-3703
Tel: (715) 839 - 2121
Fax: (715) 839 - 2122

Annual Grant Total: $500,000 - $750,000
Geographic Preference: Area in which the company is headquartered; Wisconsin
Primary Interests: Education; Health and Human Services; Social Services
Recent Recipients: American Cancer Society; Goodwill Industries; Nat'l MS Soc.

Public Affairs and Related Activities Personnel

At Headquarters

JAENKE, Norma
Exec. Director, Presto Foundation
Tel: (715) 839 - 2121
Fax: (715) 839 - 2122

Nat'l Public Radio

National membership organization of public radio stations. Produces and/or distributes news programming, including "All Things Considered" and "Morning Edition", cultural and dramatic programs, and programs for specialized audiences. Represents member stations before Congress, the Federal Communications Commission and the Administration.
www.npr.org

Chairman of the Board
EBY, Tim
Tel: (202) 513 - 2000
Fax: (202) 513 - 3329

President and Chief Exec. Officer
KLOSE, Kevin
kklose@npr.org
Tel: (202) 513 - 2000
Fax: (202) 513 - 3329

Main Headquarters
Mailing: 635 Massachusetts Ave. NW
Washington, DC 20001
Tel: (202) 513 - 2000
Fax: (202) 513 - 3329

Corporate Foundations and Giving Programs

NPR Foundation
Contact: Barbara Hall
635 Massachusetts Ave. NW
Washington, DC 20001
Tel: (202) 513 - 2073
Fax: (202) 513 - 3329

Annual Grant Total: none reported

Public Affairs and Related Activities Personnel

At Headquarters

CAMPBELL, Chad
Manager, Media Relations
Tel: (202) 513 - 2304
Fax: (202) 513 - 3329

HALL, Barbara
V. President, Development and Exec. Director, NPR Foundation
Tel: (202) 513 - 2073
Fax: (202) 513 - 3329

JACKSON, Kathleen
V. President, Human Resources
Tel: (202) 513 - 2000
Fax: (202) 513 - 3329

JACKSON, Neal
V. President, Legal Affairs, General Counsel and Secretary
Tel: (202) 513 - 2000
Fax: (202) 513 - 3329
Responsibilities include legislative affairs.

LEWIS, Greg
Legal Counsel
Tel: (202) 513 - 2000
Fax: (202) 513 - 3329

RIKSEN, Michael R.
V. President, Government Relations
mriksen@npr.org
Tel: (202) 513 - 2741
Fax: (202) 513 - 3329

SHERMAN, Rachel
Manager, Government Relations
Tel: (202) 513 - 2000
Fax: (202) 513 - 3329

SPORKIN, Andi
V. President, Communications
Tel: (202) 513 - 2000
Fax: (202) 513 - 3329

Nat'l Railroad Passenger Corp.

See listing on page 38 under Amtrak.

Nat'l Semiconductor Corp.

A manufacturer of high-performance semiconductor and board-level connectivity products.
www.national.com

Chairman, President and Chief Exec. Officer
HALLA, Brian L.
brian.halla@nsc.com
Tel: (408) 721 - 5000
Fax: (408) 739 - 9803

Main Headquarters
Mailing: P.O. Box 58090
Santa Clara, CA 95052-8090
Tel: (408) 721 - 5000
Fax: (408) 739 - 9803

Political Action Committees

Nat'l Semiconductor Corp. Employees PAC
Contact: Jeanette Morgan
P.O. Box 58090
Santa Clara, CA 95052-8090
Tel: (408) 721 - 7874
Fax: (408) 739 - 9803

Contributions to Candidates: $2,500 (01/05 - 09/05)
Republicans: $2,500.

Principal Recipients

SENATE REPUBLICANS		HOUSE REPUBLICANS
Snowe, Olympia (ME)	$2,500	

Corporate Foundations and Giving Programs

Nat'l Semiconductor Foundation
Contact: Joan Scott
P.O. Box 58090
Santa Clara, CA 95052-8090
Tel: (408) 721 - 5000
Fax: (408) 739 - 9803

Annual Grant Total: none reported
Primary Interests: Community Affairs; Higher Education; K-12 Education
Recent Recipients: University of California - Berkeley

Public Affairs and Related Activities Personnel

At Headquarters

BROZDA, Mike
Manager, Public Relations
Mailstop: M/S G1-124
mike.brozda@nsc.com
Tel: (408) 721 - 3628
Fax: (408) 721 - 3238

FOLTZ, James
Treasurer and Director, Financial Relations
Mailstop: M/S G2-397
james.foltz@nsc.com
Tel: (408) 721 - 5693
Fax: (408) 721 - 7254
Responsibilities include investor relations.

FRASER, Lori
Director, Employee Communications
lori.fraser@nsc.com
Tel: (408) 721 - 5000
Fax: (408) 739 - 9803

Nat'l Semiconductor Corp.

* continued from previous page

GIBSON, Phil — Tel: (408) 721 - 5000, Fax: (408) 739 - 9803
V. President, Corporate Marketing and Communications and Web Business
Mailstop: M/S G1-120
phil.gibson@nsc.com

JENKINS, LuAnn — Tel: (408) 721 - 5000, Fax: (408) 739 - 9803
Manager, Exec. Communications

MORGAN, Jeanette — Tel: (408) 721 - 7874, Fax: (408) 739 - 9803
Director, Worldwide Government Affairs
Mailstop: M/S G2-129
jeanette.morgan@nsc.com

SCOTT, Joan — Tel: (408) 721 - 5000, Fax: (408) 739 - 9803
Director, Community Relations and Nat'l Semiconductor Foundation
Mailstop: M/S G2-129
joan.p.scott@nsc.com

SEUTTER, Susan — Tel: (408) 721 - 5000, Fax: (408) 739 - 9803
Director, Corporate Environmental, Health and Safety
Mailstop: M/S W-105
susan.seutter@nsc.com

SWEENEY, Edward — Tel: (408) 721 - 6101, Fax: (408) 739 - 9803
Senior V. President, Worldwide Human Resources
Mailstop: M/S C1-128
eddie.sweeney@nsc.com

WEIR, Jeff — Tel: (408) 721 - 5199, Fax: (408) 739 - 9803
Director, Worldwide Public Relations
Mailstop: M/S G1-124
jeff.weir@nsc.com

Nat'l Starch and Chemical Co.

A manufacturer of specialty products, including adhesives, starches, resins and chemicals. A member of the ICI Group.
www.nationalstarch.com

Chairman and Chief Exec. Officer
POWELL, William H. — Tel: (908) 685 - 5000, Fax: (609) 409 - 5699, TF: (800) 797 - 4992

Main Headquarters
Mailing: Ten Finderne Ave.
Bridgewater, NJ 08807-3300
Tel: (908) 685 - 5000, Fax: (609) 409 - 5699, TF: (800) 797 - 4992

Corporate Foundations and Giving Programs

Nat'l Starch and Chemical Foundation, Inc.
Contact: Carmen Ortiz
Ten Finderne Ave.
Bridgewater, NJ 08807-3300
Tel: (908) 685 - 5000, Fax: (908) 685 - 5096, TF: (800) 797 - 4992

Annual Grant Total: $2,000,000 - $5,000,000
Geographic Preference: Area(s) in which the company operates; California; Illinois; Maine; New Jersey; North Carolina; Wisconsin
Primary Interests: Arts and Humanities; Education; Health and Human Services
Recent Recipients: Nat'l Merit Scholarship; United Way

Public Affairs and Related Activities Personnel

At Headquarters

MCCORMICK, Fione — Tel: (908) 685 - 5000, Fax: (609) 409 - 5699, TF: (800) 797 - 4992
Senior V. President, Human Resources

ORTIZ, Carmen — Tel: (908) 685 - 5000, Fax: (908) 685 - 5096, TF: (800) 797 - 4992
Foundation Financial Specialist
carmen.ortiz@nstarch.com

PROULX, Damian — Tel: (908) 685 - 5148, Fax: (609) 409 - 5699, TF: (800) 797 - 4992
Employee Communications Editor
damian.proulx@nstarch.com

TORBERT, Martin — Tel: (908) 685 - 5185, Fax: (908) 685 - 5096, TF: (800) 797 - 4992
Director, Marketing Communications and Public Relations
martin.torbert@nstarch.com

Nat'l Steel Corp.

See listing on page 491 under United States Steel Corporation.

Nationwide

PUBLIC AFFAIRS COUNCIL

A member of the Public Affairs Council. An insurance company. Acquired Provident Mutual Life Insurance Co. in October of 2002.
www.nationwide.com

Chief Exec. Officer
JURGENSEN, William G. — Tel: (614) 249 - 7111, Fax: (614) 249 - 3073

Main Headquarters
Mailing: One Nationwide Plaza
Columbus, OH 43215-2220
Tel: (614) 249 - 7111, Fax: (614) 249 - 3073

Washington Office
Contact: Jeffrey D. Rouch
Mailing: 1120 G St. NW
Suite 850
Washington, DC 20005
Tel: (202) 347 - 5910, Fax: (202) 347 - 5916

Political Action Committees

Nationwide Political Participation Committee
Contact: Carol Dove
One Nationwide Plaza
Columbus, OH 43215-2220
Tel: (614) 249 - 7111, Fax: (614) 249 - 3073

Contributions to Candidates: $68,325 (01/05 - 09/05)
Democrats: $12,000; Republicans: $56,325.

Principal Recipients

SENATE REPUBLICANS		HOUSE REPUBLICANS	
Dewine, Richard (OH)	$5,250	Ney, Robert W (OH)	$5,400
Smith, Gordon (OR)	$4,500	Oxley, Michael (OH)	$5,000
		Pryce, Deborah (OH)	$5,000
		Bachus, Spencer (AL)	$3,500

Corporate Foundations and Giving Programs

Nationwide Insurance Enterprise Foundation
Contact: Chad Jester
One Nationwide Plaza
Columbus, OH 43215-2220
Tel: (614) 249 - 7111, Fax: (614) 249 - 3073

Annual Grant Total: over $5,000,000
Guidelines and applications are available.
Geographic Preference: Area in which the company is headquartered
Primary Interests: Health and Human Services; Higher Education
Recent Recipients: Columbus Symphony Orchestra; Ohio State University; United Way

Public Affairs and Related Activities Personnel

At Headquarters

BARON, Kevin P. — Tel: (614) 249 - 6914, Fax: (614) 249 - 3073
Legislative Affairs Officer
Mailstop: M/S 1-27-09

BREITSTADT, Charles P. — Tel: (614) 249 - 4572, Fax: (614) 249 - 3073
Director, Government Affairs
Mailstop: M/S 1-27-08

DAVIDSON, Mark D. — Tel: (614) 249 - 4889, Fax: (614) 249 - 3073
Area Legislative Affairs Representative - West Virginia and Kentucky
Mailstop: M/S 1-27-09

DOVE, Carol — Tel: (614) 249 - 7111, Fax: (614) 249 - 3073
PAC Treasurer

DYER, Deering — Tel: (614) 249 - 9392, Fax: (614) 249 - 3073
Manager, Government Relations

HAVILAND, Bryan — Tel: (614) 249 - 7111, Fax: (614) 249 - 3073
Officer, Public Relations
havilab@nationwide.com

HOFFMAN, Shelly — Tel: (614) 677 - 3551, Fax: (614) 249 - 6794
Director, Corporate Public Relations
Mailstop: M/S 1-22-08
hoffmas2@nationwide.com

JESTER, Chad — Tel: (614) 249 - 7111, Fax: (614) 249 - 3073
V. President, Corporate Public Involvement

O'BRIEN, Kevin — Tel: (614) 677 - 5331, Fax: (614) 249 - 3073
V. President, Investor Relations
obrienk1@nationwide.com

SIMON, Jim — Tel: (614) 249 - 7111, Fax: (614) 249 - 3073
V. President, Corporate Communications

ZIMPHER, W. Craig — Tel: (614) 249 - 4795, Fax: (614) 249 - 3073
V. President, Government Relations

At Washington Office

ENGLISH, Steven — Tel: (202) 347 - 5910, Fax: (202) 347 - 5916
Government Affairs Representative

FLYNN, Bridget — Tel: (202) 347 - 5910, Fax: (202) 347 - 5916
Government Affairs Representative

ROUCH, Jeffrey D. — Tel: (202) 347 - 5910, Fax: (202) 347 - 5916
V. President, Federal Relations

At Other Offices

ALAN, Larry — Tel: (860) 256 - 2521
Director, Government Affairs
30 Waterside Dr.
Farmington, CT 06032

Nationwide

** continued from previous page*

BECK, Jim C. Tel: (770) 830 - 9203
Director, Government Relations (Alabama, Georgia, and S. Carolina) Fax: (770) 830 - 9084
315 Bankhead Highway
Suite D
Carrollton, GA 30117

HAMILTON, Jonna K. Tel: (512) 472 - 1361
Area Legislative Affairs Representative Fax: (512) 472 - 1304
701 Brazos
Suite 1500
Austin, TX 78701

KRISTIANSEN, Lars B. Tel: (410) 972 - 2803
Representative, Legislative Affairs Fax: (410) 972 - 2940
1997 Annapolis Exchange Pkwy.
Suite 410
Annapolis, MD 21401

MARTINEZ, Andrew G. Tel: (850) 222 - 6200
Representative, Area Legislative Affairs Fax: (850) 222 - 6205
111-B S. Monroe St.
Tallahassee, FL 32301-1583

MELCHIONNI, William, III Tel: (518) 455 - 8930
Area Representative, Legislative Affairs Fax: (518) 426 - 5891
125 State St.
Albany, NY 12207

SNADER, Kristofer Tel: (717) 657 - 6763
Area Legislative Affairs Representative Fax: (717) 657 - 6601
1000 Nationwide Dr.
Harrisburg, PA 17110-2655

VALAURI, Susan R. Tel: (919) 571 - 3747
Director, Government Relations - North Carolina Fax: (919) 571 - 3732
4401 Creedmoor Rd.
P.O. Box 25458
Raleigh, NC 27611-1003

Natural Gas Clearinghouse

See listing on page 171 under Dynegy, Inc.

Navistar Internat'l Corp.

A manufacturer of trucks and diesel engines.
www.navistar.com
Annual Revenues: $6.679 billion

Chairman, President and Chief Exec. Officer Tel: (630) 753 - 5000
USTIAN, Daniel C.

Main Headquarters
Mailing: P.O. Box 1488 Tel: (630) 753 - 5000
4201 Winfield Rd.
Warrenfield, IL 60555

Political Action Committees

Internat'l Truck and Engine Corp. Good Government Committee
Contact: Brian B. Whalen
P.O. Box 1488 Tel: (630) 753 - 2604
4201 Winfield Rd. Fax: (630) 753 - 2192
Warrenfield, IL 60555

Contributions to Candidates: $5,500 (01/05 - 09/05)
Democrats: $2,500; Republicans: $3,000.

Principal Recipients

SENATE DEMOCRATS

HOUSE DEMOCRATS
Murtha, John P Mr. (PA) $2,500

SENATE REPUBLICANS
Dewine, Richard (OH) $1,500

HOUSE REPUBLICANS
Johnson, Samuel (TX) $1,000

Corporate Foundations and Giving Programs

Navistar Foundation
Contact: Brian B. Whalen
P.O. Box 1488 Tel: (630) 753 - 2604
4201 Winfield Rd. Fax: (630) 753 - 2192
Warrenfield, IL 60555

Annual Grant Total: $200,000 - $300,000
Formerly the Internat'l Harvester Foundation.
Geographic Preference: Area in which the company is headquartered; Midwest
Primary Interests: Education; Health; Safety

Public Affairs and Related Activities Personnel

At Headquarters

CREED, Julie Tel: (630) 753 - 5000
Investor Relations Contact

ELLIOTT, Gregg W. Tel: (630) 753 - 2300
V. President, Corporate Human Resources and Administration
greg.elliott@nav-international.com

WHALEN, Brian B. Tel: (630) 753 - 2604
V. President, Public Affairs; President, Navistar Foundation Fax: (630) 753 - 2192
(Internat'l Truck and Engine Corp.)
brian.whalen@nav-international.com

WILEY, Roy Tel: (630) 753 - 2627
Media Relations Contact
roy.wiley@nav-international.com

Navistar Internat'l Transportation Corp.

See listing on page 342 under Navistar Internat'l Corp.

NBC

See listing on page 342 under NBC Universal.

NBC Universal

Formed from the merger of Nat'l Broadcasting Co. (NBC) and Vivendi Universal Entertainment in May of 2004.
www.nbcuni.com
Annual Revenues: $7.2 billion

Main Headquarters
Mailing: 100 Universal City Plaza Tel: (818) 777 - 9632
Universal City, CA 91608 Fax: (818) 866 - 3363

Washington Office
Contact: B. Robert Okun
Mailing: 1299 Pennsylvania Ave. NW Tel: (202) 898 - 6406
Suite 1100W Fax: (202) 637 - 4531
Washington, DC 20004

Public Affairs and Related Activities Personnel

At Headquarters

KAHRS, Kenneth L. Tel: (818) 777 - 1000
Exec. V. President, Human Resources Fax: (818) 866 - 3363

O'CONNOR, Ann M. Tel: (818) 777 - 9632
V. President, Governmental Relations Fax: (818) 866 - 3363

TERESZCUK, Alexis Tel: (818) 777 - 8053
Manager, Government Relations Fax: (818) 866 - 8053

At Washington Office

LABEAU, Bill Tel: (202) 898 - 6406
Senior Regulatory Counsel Fax: (202) 637 - 4531

OKUN, B. Robert Tel: (202) 637 - 4532
V. President, Government Relations Fax: (202) 637 - 4531
Registered Federal Lobbyist.

NCR Corporation

Provides relationship technology solutions to customers worldwide in the retail, financial, communications, manufacturing, travel and transportation, and insurance markets.
www.ncr.com
Annual Revenues: $5.917 billion

Chairman of the Board Tel: (937) 445 - 5000
RINGLER, James M. (Jim) Fax: (937) 445 - 1847

President and Chief Exec. Officer Tel: (937) 445 - 5000
NUTI, William R. (Bill) Fax: (937) 445 - 1847

Main Headquarters
Mailing: 1700 S. Patterson Blvd. Tel: (937) 445 - 5000
Dayton, OH 45479 Fax: (937) 445 - 1847
TF: (800) 225 - 5627

Washington Office
Mailing: 555 12th St. NW, Suite 610 Tel: (202) 347 - 6745
Washington, DC 20004 Fax: (202) 347 - 6884

Political Action Committees

NCR Corp. Citizenship Fund
Contact: Tim Day
555 12th St. NW, Suite 610 Tel: (202) 347 - 6745
Washington, DC 20004 Fax: (202) 347 - 6884

Contributions to Candidates: $46,994 (01/05 - 09/05)
Democrats: $5,500; Republicans: $41,494.

Principal Recipients

SENATE REPUBLICANS
Dewine, Richard (OH) $6,994

HOUSE REPUBLICANS
Oxley, Michael (OH) $10,000
Dewine, R. Pat (OH) $5,000

Corporate Foundations and Giving Programs

NCR Corp. Foundation

NCR Corporation

• continued from previous page

1700 S. Patterson Blvd.
Dayton, OH 45479
Tel: (937) 445 - 5000
Fax: (937) 445 - 1847
TF: (800) 225 - 5627

Assets: $3,400,000 (1999)
Annual Grant Total: $750,000 - $1,000,000

Recent recipients include: Dayton Art Institute, Schuster Center for the Performing Arts, Carillon Park, and the Montgomery County Historical Society.

Geographic Preference: Area(s) in which employees live and work

Primary Interests: Civic and Cultural Activities; Education

Public Affairs and Related Activities Personnel

At Headquarters

BIRD, Shelley
V. President, Public Relations
Mailstop: WHQ5
shelley.bird@ncr.com
Tel: (937) 445 - 4435
Fax: (937) 445 - 1890

BREWER, Janet
Director, Community Relations, V. President, NCR Foundation
Tel: (937) 445 - 5000
Fax: (937) 445 - 1847
TF: (800) 225 - 5627

HOURIGAN, John
Director, Corporate Media Relations
john.hourigan@ncr.com
Tel: (937) 445 - 2078
Fax: (937) 445 - 1847

SWEARINGEN, Gregg
V. President, Investor Relations
gregg.swearingen@ncr.com
Tel: (937) 445 - 4700
Fax: (937) 445 - 5541

WALLACE, Christine
Senior V. President, Human Resources
christine.wallace@ncr.com
Tel: (937) 445 - 5000
Fax: (937) 445 - 1847
TF: (800) 225 - 5627

At Washington Office

DAY, Tim
V. President, Government Affairs, PAC Treasurer
Tel: (202) 347 - 6745
Fax: (202) 347 - 6884

SERVIDEA, Philip D.
V. President, Government Affairs
philip.d.servidea@ncr.com
Registered Federal Lobbyist.
Tel: (202) 347 - 6745
Fax: (202) 347 - 6884

NEC USA, Inc.

A subsidiary of NEC Corp. of Tokyo, Japan.

www.necus.com

President and Chief Exec. Officer
OKUYAMA, Hirofumi
Tel: (631) 753 - 7000
Fax: (631) 753 - 7041

Main Headquarters
Mailing: Eight Corporate Center Dr.
Melville, NY 11747
Tel: (631) 753 - 7000
Fax: (631) 753 - 7041

Corporate Foundations and Giving Programs

NEC Foundation of America
Contact: Sylvia Clark
Eight Corporate Center Dr.
Melville, NY 11747
Tel: (631) 232 - 2212
Fax: (631) 753 - 7041

Annual Grant Total: over $5,000,000

Early recipients of grants include: American Association for the Advancement of Science, Volunteers for Medical Engineering, Recording for the Blind, Foundation for Technology Access.

Geographic Preference: National

Primary Interests: Education; Math and Science; Persons with Disabilities; Technology

Public Affairs and Related Activities Personnel

At Headquarters

CLARK, Sylvia
Exec. Director, NEC Foundation of America
Tel: (631) 232 - 2212
Fax: (631) 753 - 7041

COGSWELL-WOJTECKI, Lourdes
General Manager, Corporate Communications
lwojtecki@necusa.com
Tel: (631) 753 - 7045
Fax: (631) 753 - 7041

Nestle Purina PetCare Co.

Formed in 2001 by the merger of Nestle S.A.'s Friskies division and Ralston Purina Co.

www.purina.com

President and Chief Exec. Officer
MCGINNIS, W. Patrick
Tel: (314) 982 - 1000
Fax: (314) 982 - 2752

Main Headquarters
Mailing: Checkerboard Square
St. Louis, MO 63164
Tel: (314) 982 - 1000
Fax: (314) 982 - 2752

Washington Office
Mailing: 818 Connecticut Ave. NW
Suite 225
Washington, DC 20006
Tel: (202) 776 - 0388

Political Action Committees

Nestle Purina PetCare Political Election Team (NP-PET)
Contact: Michael Oliger
Checkerboard Square
St. Louis, MO 63164
Tel: (314) 982 - 1000
Fax: (314) 982 - 2752

Contributions to Candidates: $2,000 (01/05 - 09/05)
Republicans: $2,000.

Principal Recipients

SENATE REPUBLICANS		HOUSE REPUBLICANS
Talent, James (MO)	$2,000	

Corporate Foundations and Giving Programs

Nestle Purina PetCare Co. Community Affairs Charitable Giving
Contact: Kasey Bergh
Checkerboard Square
St. Louis, MO 63164
Tel: (314) 982 - 1000
Fax: (314) 982 - 2752

Annual Grant Total: $2,000,000 - $5,000,000

The company maintains the Nestle Purina PetCare Trust Fund as part of its giving program.

Geographic Preference: Area in which the company is headquartered; Area(s) in which the company operates; St. Louis metro area

Primary Interests: Child Welfare; Education; Health and Human Services

Recent Recipients: United Way

Public Affairs and Related Activities Personnel

At Headquarters

BERGH, Kasey
Manager, Community Affairs
Tel: (314) 982 - 1000
Fax: (314) 982 - 2752

OLIGER, Michael
PAC Treasurer
Tel: (314) 982 - 1000
Fax: (314) 982 - 2752

SCHOPP, Keith M.
V. President, Public Relations
kschopp@purina.com
Tel: (314) 982 - 2577
Fax: (314) 982 - 2752

WINTE, Jill
Director, Employee and Corporate Communications
jwinte@purina.com
Tel: (314) 982 - 2929
Fax: (314) 982 - 2752

At Washington Office

KOPPERUD, Steve
Contact, Government Affairs
Registered Federal Lobbyist.
Tel: (202) 776 - 0071

Nestle USA, Inc.

A subsidiary of Nestle S.A. of Switzerland.

www.nestleusa.com
Annual Revenues: $12 billion

Chairman and Chief Exec. Officer
WELLER, Joe
joe.weller@us.nestle.com
Tel: (818) 549 - 6000
Fax: (818) 549 - 6952
TF: (800) 225 - 2270

Main Headquarters
Mailing: 800 N. Brand Blvd.
Glendale, CA 91203
Tel: (818) 549 - 6000
Fax: (818) 549 - 6952
TF: (800) 225 - 2270

Washington Office
Contact: Louise Hilsen
Mailing: 1101 Pennsylvania Ave. NW
Suite 600
Washington, DC 20004
Tel: (202) 756 - 2299
Fax: (202) 756 - 7556

Political Action Committees

Nestle USA Inc. Political Action Committee
Contact: Denise O'Neal
30003 Bainbridge Rd.
Solon, OH 44139
Tel: (440) 498 - 7733

Contributions to Candidates: $10,000 (01/05 - 09/05)
Democrats: $5,000; Republicans: $5,000.

Principal Recipients

SENATE DEMOCRATS		HOUSE DEMOCRATS	
Bingaman, Jeff (NM)	$1,000	Davis, Danny K (IL)	$1,000
		Schiff, Adam (CA)	$1,000
		Solis, Hilda (CA)	$1,000
		Spratt, John (SC)	$1,000
SENATE REPUBLICANS		**HOUSE REPUBLICANS**	
McConnell, Mitch (KY)	$2,000	Blunt, Roy (MO)	$1,000
		Boehner, John (OH)	$1,000
		Cantor, Eric (VA)	$1,000

Corporate Foundations and Giving Programs

Nestle Corporate Giving

Nestle USA, Inc.

** continued from previous page*

800 N. Brand Blvd.
Glendale, CA 91203
Tel: (818) 549 - 6000
Fax: (818) 549 - 6952
TF: (800) 225 - 2270

Annual Grant Total: none reported
Primary Interests: Education; Literacy
Recent Recipients: Reading is Fundamental; Teach for America; United Negro College Fund

Public Affairs and Related Activities Personnel

At Headquarters

CONSTANT, Kimberly
Coordinator, Corporate and Brand Affairs
kimberly.constan@us.nestle.com
Tel: (818) 549 - 7131
Fax: (818) 549 - 5884
TF: (800) 225 - 2270

DELL'OMO, Molly S.
Director, Corporate and Brand Affairs
molly.dellomo@us.nestle.com
Tel: (818) 549 - 6136
Fax: (818) 549 - 5884
TF: (800) 225 - 2270

MACDONALD, Laurie
V. President, Corporate and Brand Affairs
laurie.macdonald@us.nestle.com
Tel: (818) 549 - 7131
Fax: (818) 549 - 5884
TF: (800) 225 - 2270

STEFL, Allan
Senior V. President, Communications
allan.stefl@us.nestle.com
Tel: (818) 549 - 6000
Fax: (818) 549 - 5884
TF: (800) 225 - 2270

At Washington Office

FOGARTY, Molly
Government Relations
Registered Federal Lobbyist.
Tel: (202) 756 - 2299
Fax: (202) 756 - 7556

HILSEN, Louise
V. President, Government Relations
louise.hilsen@us.nestle.com
Registered Federal Lobbyist.
Tel: (202) 756 - 2299
Fax: (202) 756 - 7556

At Other Offices

O'NEAL, Denise
Treasurer, Nestle USA PAC
30003 Bainbridge Rd.
Solon, OH 44139
Tel: (440) 498 - 7733

Network Appliance, Inc.

A provider of network appliances that enhance the storage, management, and access of data.
www.netapp.com

Chief Exec. Officer
WARMENHOVEN, Daniel J.
dwarmenhoven@netapp.com
Tel: (408) 822 - 6000
Fax: (408) 822 - 4501

Main Headquarters
Mailing: 495 E. Java Dr.
Sunnyvale, CA 94089
Tel: (408) 822 - 6000
Fax: (408) 822 - 4501

Public Affairs and Related Activities Personnel

At Headquarters

BROWN, Eric
Director, Worldwide Public Relations
ebrown@netapp.com
Tel: (408) 822 - 6000
Fax: (408) 822 - 4501

CALHOUN, Tara
Senior Director, Investor Relations
Tel: (408) 822 - 6000
Fax: (408) 822 - 4501

LE, Jaime Leigh
Senior Program Manager, Public Relations
jaime.le@netapp.com
Tel: (408) 822 - 3761
Fax: (408) 822 - 4501

MCDONALD, Gwen
Senior V. President, Human Resources
Tel: (408) 822 - 6000
Fax: (408) 822 - 4501

STEEL, Elisa
V. President, Corporate Communications
Tel: (408) 822 - 6000
Fax: (408) 822 - 4501

Network Associates, Inc.

See listing on page 312 under McAfee, Inc.

Neuberger Berman, Inc.

See listing on page 290 under Lehman Brothers.

Nevada Power Co.

An electric utility. A subsidiary of Sierra Pacific Resources (see separate listing).
www.nevadapower.com

Chairman, President and Chief Exec. Officer
HIGGINS, Walter M., III
Tel: (702) 367 - 5000
Fax: (702) 367 - 5092
TF: (800) 331 - 3103

Main Headquarters
Mailing: P.O. Box 98910
Las Vegas, NV 89151-0001
Tel: (702) 367 - 5000
Fax: (702) 367 - 5092
TF: (800) 331 - 3103

Street: 6226 W. Sahara Ave.
Las Vegas, NV 89151

Corporate Foundations and Giving Programs

Nevada Power Corporate Giving Program
Contact: Doretha Graham-Easler
P.O. Box 98910
Las Vegas, NV 89151-0001
Tel: (702) 367 - 5741
Fax: (702) 579 - 0801
TF: (800) 331 - 3103

Annual Grant Total: none reported
Primary Interests: Child Welfare; Education; Safety

Public Affairs and Related Activities Personnel

At Headquarters

BROOKS, Joanna
Executive, Government Affairs
Mailstop: M/S 29
jbrooks@nevp.com
Tel: (702) 367 - 5000
Fax: (702) 579 - 0658
TF: (800) 331 - 3103

GRAHAM-EASLER, Doretha
Manager, Community Relations
Tel: (702) 367 - 5741
Fax: (702) 579 - 0801
TF: (800) 331 - 3103

HEADEN, Sonya
Media Contact
Tel: (702) 367 - 5222
Fax: (702) 367 - 5092
TF: (800) 331 - 3103

PATINO, Edgar
Government Affairs
Tel: (702) 367 - 5747
Fax: (702) 367 - 5092
TF: (800) 331 - 3103

SHALMY, Donald L. "Pat"
President
Responsibilities include corporate philanthropy.
Tel: (702) 367 - 5000
Fax: (702) 367 - 5092
TF: (800) 331 - 3103

SMITH, Andrea
Director, Corporate Communications
Mailstop: M/S 15
asmith@nevp.com
Tel: (702) 367 - 5843
Fax: (702) 367 - 5092
TF: (800) 331 - 3103

STOKEY, Judy
Executive, Government Affairs
Mailstop: M/S 29
jstokey@nevp.com
Tel: (702) 367 - 5000
Fax: (702) 579 - 0608
TF: (800) 331 - 3103

At Other Offices

SIMS, Don
Manager, Shareholder Relations
P.O. Box 30150
Reno, NV 89520
Tel: (775) 834 - 3616

New Balance Athletic Shoe, Inc.

A manufacturer of athletic footwear and apparel.
www.newbalance.com

Chairman and Chief Exec. Officer
DAVIS, James S.
Tel: (617) 783 - 4000
Fax: (617) 783 - 5152
TF: (800) 343 - 1395

Main Headquarters
Mailing: Brighton Landing, 20 Guest St.
Boston, MA 02135-2088
Tel: (617) 783 - 4000
Fax: (617) 787 - 9355
TF: (800) 343 - 1395

Corporate Foundations and Giving Programs

New Balance Foundation
Brighton Landing, 20 Guest St.
Boston, MA 02135-2088
Tel: (617) 783 - 4000
Fax: (617) 787 - 9355
TF: (800) 343 - 1395

Annual Grant Total: none reported
Geographic Preference: Massachusetts; Maine

Public Affairs and Related Activities Personnel

At Headquarters

O'DONNELL, Carol
V. President, Human Resources
Tel: (617) 783 - 4000 Ext: 2351
Fax: (617) 783 - 5152
TF: (800) 343 - 1395

SHEPARD, Katherine L.
Senior Manager, Corporate Communications
Tel: (617) 783 - 4000 Ext: 2240
Fax: (617) 746 - 6240
TF: (800) 343 - 4648

VREELAND, Amy
Manager, Corporate Communications
amy.vreeland@newbalance.com
Tel: (617) 746 - 2214
Fax: (617) 787 - 9355
TF: (800) 343 - 1395

New Century Energies, Inc.

See listing on page 528 under Xcel Energy, Inc.

New England Electric System

See listing on page 339 under Nat'l Grid USA.

New Jersey Natural Gas Co.

See listing on page 345 under New Jersey Resources Corp.

New Jersey Resources Corp.

An energy services company. Subsidiaries include New Jersey Natural Gas Co., NJR Natural Energy Co., and commercial Realty & Resources Corp., among others.
www.njresources.com

Chairman and Chief Exec. Officer
DOWNES, Laurence M. — Tel: (732) 938 - 1480
lmdownes@njresources.com — Fax: (732) 938 - 3154

Main Headquarters
Mailing: P.O. Box 1468, Wall, NJ 07719 — Tel: (732) 938 - 1000; Fax: (732) 938 - 3154
Street: 1415 Wyckoff Rd., Wall, NJ 07719

Corporate Foundations and Giving Programs

New Jersey Natural Gas Co. Corporate Contributions
P.O. Box 1468 — Tel: (732) 938 - 1000
Wall, NJ 07719 — Fax: (732) 938 - 3154

Annual Grant Total: none reported
Primary Interests: Economic Development; Education; Youth Services

Public Affairs and Related Activities Personnel

At Headquarters

KINNEY, Michael — Tel: (732) 938 - 1031
Media Contact — Fax: (732) 938 - 3154

KOBERLE, Roseanne — Tel: (732) 938 - 1112
Manager, Corporate Communications — Fax: (732) 938 - 3154

PUMA, Dennis R. — Tel: (732) 938 - 1229
Manager, Treasury Services — Fax: (732) 938 - 3154
Responsibilities include investor relations.

At Other Offices

BOTTINO, Hugo C. — Tel: (732) 938 - 1091
V. President, Human Resources — Fax: (732) 938 - 2620
(New Jersey Natural Gas Co.)
P.O. Box 1464
Wall, NJ 07719
hcbottino@njresources.com

HAYES, Thomas F. — Tel: (732) 938 - 1000
Director, Consumer Community Relations — Fax: (732) 938 - 2620
(New Jersey Natural Gas Co.)
P.O. Box 1464
Wall, NJ 07719

MOSS, Kevin A. — Tel: (732) 938 - 1214
Senior V. President, Regulatory Affairs — Fax: (732) 938 - 2620
(New Jersey Natural Gas Co.)
P.O. Box 1464
Wall, NJ 07719

RYBKA, Stephen J. — Tel: (732) 938 - 1280
Manager, Public Affairs — Fax: (732) 938 - 2620
(New Jersey Natural Gas Co.)
P.O. Box 1464
Wall, NJ 07719

The New Piper Aircraft Inc.

A manufacturer of single and twin engine aircraft.
www.newpiper.com

President and Chief Exec. Officer
BASS, James K. — Tel: (772) 567 - 4361; Fax: (772) 978 - 6584

Main Headquarters
Mailing: 2926 Piper Dr., Vero Beach, FL 32960 — Tel: (772) 567 - 4361; Fax: (772) 978 - 6584

Corporate Foundations and Giving Programs

The New Piper Aircraft Corporate Contributions Program
Contact: Patricia Ollis
2926 Piper Dr. — Tel: (772) 567 - 4361
Vero Beach, FL 32960 — Fax: (772) 978 - 6584

Annual Grant Total: none reported

Public Affairs and Related Activities Personnel

At Headquarters

MILLER, Mark S. — Tel: (772) 299 - 2900
Director, Corporate Communications — Fax: (772) 978 - 5697
m.miller@newpiper.com

OLLIS, Patricia — Tel: (772) 567 - 4361
Exec. Assistant to the President — Fax: (772) 978 - 6584
p.ollis@newpiper.com
Responsibilities include corporate philanthropy.

New York Community Bancorp, Inc.

A bank holding company for New York Community Bank, a branch network operating through seven divisions: Queens Co. Savings Bank; Roslyn Savings Bank; Richmond Co. Savings Bank; Roosevelt Savings Bank; CFS Bank; First Savings Bank of New Jersey; and Ironbound Bank.
www.roslyn.com

Co-Chairman of the Board
MANCINO, Joseph L. — Tel: (516) 683 - 4100

Co-Chairman of the Board
MANZULLI, Michael F. — Tel: (516) 683 - 4100

President and Chief Exec. Officer
FICALORA, Joseph R. — Tel: (516) 683 - 4100

Main Headquarters
Mailing: 615 Merrick Ave., Westbury, NY 11590 — Tel: (516) 683 - 4100

Public Affairs and Related Activities Personnel

At Headquarters

ANGAROLA, Ilene A. — Tel: (516) 683 - 4420
First Senior V. President, Investor Relations

New York Life Insurance Co.

A member of the Public Affairs Council. A life insurance company.
www.newyorklife.com
Annual Revenues: $25 billion

Chairman, President and Chief Exec. Officer
STERNBERG, Seymour — Tel: (212) 576 - 7000; Fax: (212) 576 - 8145

Main Headquarters
Mailing: 51 Madison Ave., New York, NY 10010 — Tel: (212) 576 - 7000; Fax: (212) 576 - 8145

Washington Office
Contact: Ronald J. Lefrancois
Mailing: 1501 K St. NW, Suite 575, Washington, DC 20005 — Tel: (202) 654 - 2940

Political Action Committees

New York Life Insurance Co. Political Action Committee
Contact: Jon Paone
51 Madison Ave. — Tel: (212) 576 - 7842
New York, NY 10010 — Fax: (212) 576 - 8145

Contributions to Candidates: $157,500 (01/05 - 09/05)
Democrats: $77,500; Republicans: $80,000.

Principal Recipients

SENATE DEMOCRATS

HOUSE DEMOCRATS
- Pomeroy, Earl (ND) $10,000
- Becerra, Xavier (CA) $5,000
- Cardin, Ben (MD) $5,000
- Hoyer, Steny (MD) $5,000
- Rangel, Charles B (NY) $5,000

SENATE REPUBLICANS
- Snowe, Olympia (ME) $5,000

HOUSE REPUBLICANS
- Thomas, William M (CA) $10,000
- Johnson, Nancy (CT) $6,000
- Oxley, Michael (OH) $5,000
- Shays, Christopher (CT) $5,000

Corporate Foundations and Giving Programs

New York Life Foundation
Contact: Peter Bushyeager
51 Madison Ave. — Tel: (212) 576 - 7341
New York, NY 10010

Assets: $71,737 (2002)
Annual Grant Total: over $5,000,000
Grants totaled over $6 million in 2003.
Geographic Preference: New York City; Cleveland, OH; San Francisco Bay Area; Dallas, TX; Minneapolis, MN; Tampa, FL; Atlanta, GA
Primary Interests: Arts and Culture; Children; Civic and Public Affairs; Education
Recent Recipients: Big Brothers/Big Sisters; Boys and Girls Club; Reading is Fundamental

Public Affairs and Related Activities Personnel

At Headquarters

BUSHYEAGER, Peter — Tel: (212) 576 - 7341
V. President, Corporate Responsibility; and President, New York Life Foundation

DUPUY, Fielding — Tel: (212) 576 - 7000
Corporate V. President, Corporate Communications — Fax: (212) 576 - 8145
fielding_dupuy@newyorklife.com

FELS, Lisa — Tel: (212) 576 - 7937
Media Representative — Fax: (212) 576 - 8145
lisa_fels@newyorklife.com

MARCHON, Theresa M. — Tel: (212) 576 - 5624
Media Representative — Fax: (212) 576 - 8145
theresa_m_marchon@newyorklife.com

PAONE, Jon — Tel: (212) 576 - 7842
Corporate V. President, Governmental Affairs — Fax: (212) 576 - 8145
Responsibilities include political action.

New York Life Insurance Co.

** continued from previous page*

TOMALSKI, Sarah — Tel: (212) 576 - 5897
Media Representative — Fax: (212) 576 - 8145
sarah_tomalski@newyorklife.com

WERFELMAN, William H. — Tel: (212) 576 - 5385
First V. President, Media Relations — Fax: (212) 447 - 4273
william_werfelman@newyorklife.com

At Washington Office

COLGATE, Ms. Jessie M. — Tel: (202) 654 - 2941
Senior V. President, Governmental Affairs — Fax: (202) 654 - 2945
Registered Federal Lobbyist.

GRIFFIN, Leslie — Tel: (202) 654 - 2940
Registered Federal Lobbyist.

LEFRANCOIS, Ronald J. — Tel: (202) 654 - 2943
V. President, Governmental Affairs — Fax: (202) 654 - 2945
Registered Federal Lobbyist.

SANDER, Raymond J. — Tel: (202) 654 - 2950
Senior V. President, N.Y. Life International — Fax: (202) 654 - 2955
Registered Federal Lobbyist.

SHORTELL, Alan — Tel: (202) 654 - 2940
Registered Federal Lobbyist.

VAN MERKENSTEIJN, James — Tel: (202) 654 - 2940
Registered Federal Lobbyist.

New York State Electric & Gas Corp. (NYSEG)

See listing on page 181 under Energy East Corp.

New York Stock Exchange, Inc.

www.nyse.com
Annual Revenues: $884 million

Chairman of the Board — Tel: (212) 656 - 3000
CARTER, Marshall — Fax: (212) 656 - 2347

Chief Exec. Officer — Tel: (212) 656 - 3000
THAIN, John A. — Fax: (212) 656 - 2347

Main Headquarters
Mailing: 11 Wall St. — Tel: (212) 656 - 3000
New York, NY 10005 — Fax: (212) 656 - 2347

Washington Office
Mailing: 801 Pennsylvania Ave. NW — Tel: (202) 347 - 4300
Suite 630 — Fax: (202) 347 - 4370
Washington, DC 20004

Political Action Committees

New York Stock Exchange Inc. Employee Political Action Committee (NYSE PAC)
Contact: Ananias "Andy" Blocker
801 Pennsylvania Ave. NW — Tel: (202) 347 - 4300
Suite 630 — Fax: (202) 347 - 4370
Washington, DC 20004

Contributions to Candidates: $17,000 (01/05 - 09/05)
Democrats: $8,000; Republicans: $9,000.

Principal Recipients

SENATE DEMOCRATS	HOUSE DEMOCRATS	
	Hoyer, Steny (MD)	$5,000
SENATE REPUBLICANS	**HOUSE REPUBLICANS**	
	Ackerman, Richard (CA)	$2,000
	Fossella, Vito (NY)	$2,000
	Shays, Christopher (CT)	$2,000

New York Stock Exchange Inc. Member Political Action Committee
Contact: Ananias "Andy" Blocker
801 Pennsylvania Ave. NW — Tel: (202) 347 - 4300
Suite 630 — Fax: (202) 347 - 4370
Washington, DC 20004

Contributions to Candidates: $39,000 (01/05 - 09/05)
Democrats: $23,000; Republicans: $16,000.

Corporate Foundations and Giving Programs

New York Stock Exchange Foundation, Inc., The
11 Wall St. — Tel: (212) 656 - 3000
New York, NY 10005 — Fax: (212) 656 - 2347

Annual Grant Total: $500,000 - $750,000
Geographic Preference: New York City
Primary Interests: Arts and Culture; Community Development; Higher Education; Social Services
Recent Recipients: Lincoln Center for the Performing Arts; Metropolitan Museum of Art; United Way; YMCA

Public Affairs and Related Activities Personnel

At Headquarters

LOFTUS, Jo-Ann — Tel: (212) 656 - 3367
Manager, Public Affairs — Fax: (212) 656 - 5605
Mailstop: 6th Floor

SULLIVAN, Veronica — Tel: (212) 656 - 3000
Director, State and City Government Relations — Fax: (212) 656 - 2347

TUTWILER, Margaret — Tel: (212) 656 - 3000
Exec. V. President, Communications and Government Relations — Fax: (212) 656 - 2347

At Washington Office

BLOCKER, Ananias "Andy" — Tel: (202) 347 - 4300
Vice President, Government Relations — Fax: (202) 347 - 4370
ablocker@nyse.com

EDGAR, Kevin R. — Tel: (202) 347 - 4300
Special Counsel, Government Relations and Director, Public Affairs — Fax: (202) 347 - 4370
kedgar@nyse.com
Registered Federal Lobbyist.

RICH, Linda D. — Tel: (202) 347 - 4300
Senior V. President, Government Relations — Fax: (202) 347 - 4370
Registered Federal Lobbyist.

New York Times Co.

A newspaper publisher, TV and radio broadcaster, and electronic media company.
www.nytco.com
Annual Revenues: $3.016 billion

Chairman and Publisher — Tel: (212) 556 - 1234
SULZBERGER, Arthur O., Jr.

President and Chief Exec. Officer — Tel: (212) 556 - 1234
ROBINSON, Janet L.

Main Headquarters
Mailing: 229 W. 43rd St. — Tel: (212) 556 - 1234
New York, NY 10036

Corporate Foundations and Giving Programs

New York Times Co. Foundation
Contact: Jack Rosenthal
229 W. 43rd St. — Tel: (212) 556 - 1234
New York, NY 10036

Annual Grant Total: over $5,000,000
Guidelines are available. For more information see the foundation's website: www.nytco.com/foundation.
Geographic Preference: Area in which the company is headquartered; Area(s) in which the company operates
Primary Interests: Arts and Culture; Community Affairs; Education; Environment/Conservation; Journalism
Recent Recipients: American Symphony Orchestra; Nat'l Audubon Soc.; Teach for America

Public Affairs and Related Activities Personnel

At Headquarters

HICKS, Uchenna — Tel: (212) 556 - 1757
Project Coordinator, Community Affairs and Media Relations
hicksul@nytimes.com

MATHIS, Catherine J. — Tel: (212) 556 - 1981
V. President, Corporate Communications — Fax: (212) 556 - 7389
mathicj@nytimes.com
Responsibilities include investor relations.

MCNULTY, Diane — Tel: (212) 556 - 5244
Group Director, Community Affairs and Media Relations
mcnuldc@nytimes.com

PARK, Kathy — Tel: (212) 556 - 4059
Manager, Public Relations — Fax: (212) 556 - 7389
parkk@nytimes.com

PAULY, Jennifer — Tel: (212) 556 - 1718
Assistant Director, Community Affairs and Media Relations
paulyj@nytimes.com

ROSENTHAL, Jack — Tel: (212) 556 - 1234
President, New York Times Co. Foundation

SCHWARTZ, Paula — Tel: (212) 556 - 5224
Manager, Investor Relations and Online Communications

USNIK, Toby — Tel: (212) 556 - 4425
Director, Public Relations
usnikt@nytimes.com

Newell Rubbermaid Inc.

A global manufacturer and full-service marketer of branded consumer products and their commercial extensions, serving the needs of volume purchasers, including department stores, discount stores and warehouse clubs, as well as home centers, hardware stroes, commercial distributors, office superstores and contract stationers. Brands include Sharpie, Paper Mate, Parker, Waterman, Rubbermaid, Roughneck, Little Tikes, Goody, Graco, Irwin, Lenox, and Marathon.

www.newellrubbermaid.com
Annual Revenues: $7 billion

Chairman of the Board
MAROHN, William — Tel: (770) 407 - 3800

Chief Exec. Officer
GALLI, Joseph, Jr. — Tel: (770) 407 - 3805

Main Headquarters
Mailing: Ten B Glenlake Pkwy.
Suite 600
Alpharetta, GA 30328
Tel: (770) 407 - 3800
Fax: (770) 407 - 3970

Corporate Foundations and Giving Programs

Newell Rubbermaid Co. Corporate Contributions
Ten B Glenlake Pkwy.
Suite 600
Alpharetta, GA 30328
Tel: (770) 407 - 3800
Fax: (770) 407 - 3970

Annual Grant Total: none reported

Public Affairs and Related Activities Personnel

At Headquarters

HERRON, Jesse
V. President, Investor Relations
Tel: (770) 407 - 3800

MASTERN, Susan
Director, Public Relations
Tel: (770) 407 - 3817
Fax: (770) 407 - 3983

SWEET, James
V. President, Human Resources
Tel: (770) 407 - 3800

NewMarket Corp.

The parent company for Afton Chemical Corp. and Ethyl Corp. formed in June, 2004. Afton Chemical Corp. develops and manufactures petroleum additive. Ethyl Corp. manufactures diesel cetane improver and gasoline performance additives.

www.newmarket.com

Chairman of the Board
GOTTWALD, Bruce C.
Tel: (804) 788 - 5000
Fax: (804) 788 - 5688
TF: (800) 535 - 3030

President and Chief Exec. Officer
GOTTWALD, Thomas E.
Tel: (804) 788 - 5000
Fax: (804) 788 - 5688
TF: (800) 535 - 3030

Main Headquarters
Mailing: P.O. Box 2189
Richmond, VA 23218-2189
Tel: (804) 788 - 5000
Fax: (804) 788 - 5688
TF: (800) 535 - 3030

Street: 330 S. Fourth St.
Richmond, VA 23218-2189

Washington Office
Contact: Barbara A. Little
Mailing: 1155 15th St., N.W., Suite 611
Washington, DC 20005
Tel: (202) 223 - 4411
Fax: (202) 223 - 1849

Political Action Committees

Ethyl Corp. PAC
Contact: Bruce Hazelgrove
P.O. Box 2189
Richmond, VA 23218-2189
Tel: (804) 788 - 5000
Fax: (804) 788 - 5688
TF: (800) 535 - 3030

Contributions to Candidates: none reported (01/05 - 09/05)

Corporate Foundations and Giving Programs

NewMarket Services Contributions Program
Contact: Bruce Hazelgrove
P.O. Box 2189
Richmond, VA 23218-2189
Tel: (804) 788 - 5000
Fax: (804) 788 - 5688
TF: (800) 535 - 3030

Annual Grant Total: $1,000,000 - $2,000,000
Guidelines are available on their web site.
Geographic Preference: Area(s) in which the company operates
Primary Interests: Adult Education and Training; Arts and Culture; Community Affairs; Health; United Way Campaigns

Public Affairs and Related Activities Personnel

At Headquarters

HAZELGROVE, Bruce
Contact, NewMarket Services Contributions Program; and PAC Treasurer
Tel: (804) 788 - 5000
Fax: (804) 788 - 5688
TF: (800) 535 - 3030

At Washington Office

LITTLE, Barbara A.
V. President, Government Relations
Registered Federal Lobbyist.
Tel: (202) 223 - 4411
Fax: (202) 223 - 1849

Newmont Gold Co.

See listing on page 347 under Newmont Mining Corp.

Newmont Mining Corp.

An international gold mining company with operations on five continents.

www.newmont.com
Annual Revenues: $3.2 billion

Chairman and Chief Exec. Officer
MURDY, Wayne W.
Tel: (303) 863 - 7414
Fax: (303) 837 - 5837

Main Headquarters
Mailing: 1700 Lincoln St.
Denver, CO 80203
Tel: (303) 863 - 7414
Fax: (303) 837 - 5837

Washington Office
Mailing: 101 Constitution Ave. NW
Suite 800
Washington, DC 20001
Tel: (202) 822 - 6777
Fax: (202) 822 - 6677

Political Action Committees

Newmont Mining Corp. Political Action Committee
Contact: Mary Beth Donnelly
101 Constitution Ave. NW
Suite 800
Washington, DC 20001
Tel: (202) 822 - 6777
Fax: (202) 822 - 6677

Contributions to Candidates: $21,000 (01/05 - 09/05)
Democrats: $2,000; Republicans: $19,000.

Principal Recipients

SENATE REPUBLICANS
Ensign, John Eric (NV) $5,000

HOUSE REPUBLICANS
Gibbons, James A (NV) $5,000
Porter, Jon (NV) $5,000

Corporate Foundations and Giving Programs

Newmont Mining Community Investment Program
Contact: Michie Ogura-Huerta
1700 Lincoln St.
Denver, CO 80203
Tel: (303) 863 - 7414
Fax: (303) 837 - 5837

Annual Grant Total: $400,000 - $500,000
Geographic Preference: Western United States
Primary Interests: Child Welfare; Education; Environment/Conservation

Public Affairs and Related Activities Personnel

At Headquarters

ANDERSON, Chris
Group Exec., External Affairs and Social Responsibility
Tel: (303) 863 - 7414
Fax: (303) 837 - 5837

BAKER, David A.
V. President, Environmental Affairs
Tel: (303) 863 - 7414

BALL, Russell
Group Exec., Investor Relations
Tel: (303) 863 - 7414
Fax: (303) 837 - 5837

CAUDLE, Darla
V. President, Human Resources
Tel: (303) 863 - 7414
Fax: (303) 837 - 5837

ENGEL, Randy
Investor Relations
Tel: (303) 837 - 6033
Fax: (303) 837 - 5837

HOCK, Doug
Director, Public Affairs and Communications
Tel: (303) 837 - 5812
Fax: (303) 837 - 6034

OGURA-HUERTA, Michie
Administrator, Contributions
Tel: (303) 863 - 7414
Fax: (303) 837 - 5837

YANG, Wendy
Director, Investor Relations
wyang@corp.newmont.com
Tel: (303) 863 - 7414
Fax: (303) 837 - 5837

At Washington Office

DONNELLY, Mary Beth
Group Executive, Government Relations
Registered Federal Lobbyist.
Tel: (202) 822 - 6777
Fax: (202) 822 - 6677

Newport News Shipbuilding

See listing on page 354 under Northrop Grumman Newport News.

News Corporation Ltd.

A multi-media production and distribution company. Acquired the former Hughes Electronics Corp. (now known as The DIRECTV Group, Inc. see separate listing) in March, 2004.

www.newscorp.com

Chairman and Chief Exec. Officer
MURDOCH, K. Rupert — Tel: (212) 852 - 7000

Main Headquarters
Mailing: 1211 Ave. of the Americas
New York, NY 10036
Tel: (212) 852 - 7000

News Corporation Ltd.

* continued from previous page

Washington Office

Contact: Michael Regan, Jr.

Mailing: 444 N. Capitol St., N.W., Suite 740
Washington, DC 20001
Tel: (202) 824 - 6500
Fax: (202) 824 - 6510

Political Action Committees

News America-Fox Political Action Committee
Contact: Rick Lane
444 N. Capitol St., N.W., Suite 740
Washington, DC 20001
Tel: (202) 824 - 6500
Fax: (202) 824 - 6510

Contributions to Candidates: $89,000 (01/05 - 09/05)

Democrats: $22,000; Republicans: $67,000.

Principal Recipients

SENATE DEMOCRATS

HOUSE DEMOCRATS

Markey, Edward (MA)	$5,000
Matsui, Doris (CA)	$5,000
Towns, Edolphus (NY)	$2,000

SENATE REPUBLICANS

Burns, Conrad (MT)	$8,000
Allen, George (VA)	$7,000
Ensign, John Eric (NV)	$5,000
Martinez, Mel (FL)	$5,000
McConnell, Mitch (KY)	$5,000
Stevens, Ted (AK)	$5,000
Santorum, Richard (PA)	$3,000
Smith, Gordon (OR)	$2,500
Graham, Lindsey (SC)	$2,000

HOUSE REPUBLICANS

Dreier, David (CA)	$2,500
Goodlatte, Robert (VA)	$2,500
Sensenbrenner, Jim (WI)	$2,500
Cannon, Christopher (UT)	$2,000
Carter, John (TX)	$2,000
Sullivan, John (OK)	$2,000

Public Affairs and Related Activities Personnel

At Headquarters

BUTCHER, Andrew
V. President, Corporate Affairs and Communications
abutcher@newscorp.com
Tel: (212) 852 - 7070
Fax: (212) 852 - 7147

EASTMAN, Natasha
Corporate Affairs Administrator
Tel: (212) 852 - 7073
Fax: (212) 852 - 7147

FELENSTEIN, Craig
V. President, Investor Relations
cfelenstein@newscorp.com
Tel: (212) 852 - 7084
Fax: (212) 852 - 7145

GINSBERG, Gary
Exec. V. President, Investor Relations and Corporate Communications
gginsberg@newscorp.com
Tel: (212) 852 - 7000

MOORE, Ian
Exec. V. President, Human Resources
Tel: (212) 852 - 7000

NOLTE, Reed
Senior V. President, Investor Relations
rnolte@newscorp.com
Tel: (212) 852 - 7092
Fax: (212) 852 - 7145

At Washington Office

JACKSON, Paul A.
Director, Government Relations
Tel: (202) 824 - 6500
Fax: (202) 824 - 6510

LANE, Rick
V. President, Government Relations
rlane@newscorp.com
Registered Federal Lobbyist.
Tel: (202) 824 - 6500
Fax: (202) 824 - 6510

O'CONNELL, Maureen A.
V. President, Regulatory and Government Affairs
moconnell@newscorp.com
Registered Federal Lobbyist.
Tel: (202) 824 - 6503
Fax: (202) 824 - 6510

REGAN, Michael, Jr.
Senior V. President, Regulatory and Government Affairs
mregan@newscorp.com
Registered Federal Lobbyist.
Tel: (202) 824 - 6502
Fax: (202) 824 - 6510

RUSH, Jimmie
Manager, Government Relations
jrush@newscorp.com
Tel: (202) 824 - 6504
Fax: (202) 824 - 6510

Newsweek, Inc.

A magazine publisher.

www.newsweek.com

Chairman of the Board and Editor in Chief
SMITH, Richard M.
Tel: (212) 445 - 4000
Fax: (212) 445 - 4757
TF: (800) 631 - 1040

Main Headquarters

Mailing: 251 W. 57th St.
22nd Floor
New York, NY 10019
Tel: (212) 445 - 4000
Fax: (212) 445 - 4757
TF: (800) 631 - 1040

Corporate Foundations and Giving Programs

Newsweek, Inc. Corporate Giving Program
251 W. 57th St.
22nd Floor
New York, NY 10019
Tel: (212) 445 - 4000
Fax: (212) 445 - 4757
TF: (800) 631 - 1040

Annual Grant Total: none reported

Public Affairs and Related Activities Personnel

At Headquarters

BLOCK, Mark
Director, External Relations
Tel: (212) 445 - 4000
Fax: (212) 445 - 4757
TF: (800) 631 - 1040

WEINE, Ken
Director, Corporate Communications
Tel: (212) 445 - 4000
Fax: (212) 445 - 4757
TF: (800) 631 - 1040

Nextel

See listing on page 450 under Sprint Nextel.

NGC Corp.

See listing on page 171 under Dynegy, Inc.

Niagara Mohawk Holdings Inc.

See listing on page 339 under Nat'l Grid USA.

Nickelodeon/Nick at Nite

See listing on page 505 under Viacom Inc/CBS Corp.

NICOR Gas

See listing on page 348 under Nicor, Inc.

Nicor, Inc.

The company's principal subsidiaries are Nicor Gas, one of the nation's largest gas utilities, and Tropical Shipping, a containerized shipping business that operates between Florida and the Caribbean. Nicor also owns several energy-related subsidiaries.

www.nicor.com

Chairman of the Board
FISHER, Thomas L.
Tel: (630) 305 - 9500
Fax: (630) 357 - 7534
TF: (888) 642 - 6748

Chief Exec. Officer
STROBEL, Russ M.
Tel: (630) 305 - 9500
Fax: (630) 357 - 7534
TF: (888) 642 - 6748

Main Headquarters

Mailing: P.O. Box 3014
Naperville, IL 60566-7014
Tel: (630) 305 - 9500
Fax: (630) 357 - 7534
TF: (888) 642 - 6748

Street: 1844 Ferry Rd.
Naperville, IL 60563-9600

Political Action Committees

Nicor, Inc. PAC
Contact: D. Scott Lewis
P.O. Box 190
Aurora, IL 60507-0190
Tel: (630) 983 - 8676
Ext: 3147
Fax: (630) 548 - 3574

Contributions to Candidates: $8,000 (01/05 - 09/05)

Republicans: $8,000.

Principal Recipients

SENATE REPUBLICANS

HOUSE REPUBLICANS

Weller, Jerry (IL)	$5,000
Roskam, Peter (IL)	$2,000
Biggert, Judy (IL)	$1,000

Corporate Foundations and Giving Programs

Nicor Gas Community Relations
Contact: Craig Whyte
P.O. Box 190
Aurora, IL 60507-0190

Annual Grant Total: none reported

Geographic Preference: Area in which the company is headquartered; Area(s) in which employees live and work
Primary Interests: Arts and Culture; Education; Health and Human Services
Recent Recipients: March of Dimes; United Way

Nicor, Inc.

** continued from previous page*

Public Affairs and Related Activities Personnel

At Headquarters

BROWN, Julian
Contact, Nicor, Inc. Contributions Program
jbrown@nicor.com
Tel: (630) 305 - 9500 Ext: 2673
Fax: (630) 548 - 3574
TF: (888) 642 - 6748

COLALILLO, Claudia J.
Senior V. President, Human Resources and Corporate Communications
Tel: (630) 305 - 9500 Ext: 2759
Fax: (630) 983 - 6620
TF: (888) 642 - 6748

KNOX, Mark A.
Director, Investor Relations
mknox@nicor.com
Tel: (630) 305 - 9500 Ext: 2529
Fax: (630) 357 - 7534
TF: (888) 642 - 6748

MARTINEZ, Annette
Manager, Media Relations
amartinez@nicor.com
Tel: (630) 388 - 2781
Fax: (630) 357 - 7534
TF: (888) 642 - 6748

At Other Offices

BAILEY, Koby A.
Director, Regulatory Affairs
(NICOR Gas)
P.O. Box 190
Aurora, IL 60507-0190
kbailey@nicor.com
Tel: (630) 983 - 8676 Ext: 3527
Fax: (630) 548 - 3574

INGLE, Don
Director, Corporate Communications
(NICOR Gas)
P.O. Box 190
Aurora, IL 60507-0190
dingle@nicor.com
Tel: (630) 983 - 8676 Ext: 2939
Fax: (630) 983 - 9183

LEWIS, D. Scott
Assistant V. President, Government Relations
(NICOR Gas)
P.O. Box 190
Aurora, IL 60507-0190
slewis@nicor.com
Tel: (630) 983 - 8676 Ext: 3147
Fax: (630) 548 - 3574

WHYTE, Craig
Director, Community Relations
P.O. Box 190
Aurora, IL 60507-0190

Nike, Inc.

More information about Nike, Inc. can be found on the Internet at their following website address, www.nikebiz.com.

www.nikebiz.com

Annual Revenues: $9.489 billion

Chairman of the Board
KNIGHT, Philip H.
Tel: (503) 671 - 6453
Fax: (503) 671 - 6300

President and Chief Exec. Officer
PEREZ, William D. "Bill"
Tel: (503) 671 - 6453
Fax: (503) 671 - 6300

Main Headquarters
Mailing: One Bowerman Dr.
Beaverton, OR 97005
Tel: (503) 671 - 6453
Fax: (503) 671 - 6300

Washington Office
Contact: Brad G. Figel
Mailing: 507 Second St. NE
Washington, DC 20002
Tel: (202) 543 - 6453
Fax: (202) 544 - 6453

Political Action Committees

Nike Inc. Federal Political Action Committee (NIKE Federal PAC)
Contact: Dennis Peterson
One Bowerman Dr.
Beaverton, OR 97005
Tel: (503) 671 - 6453
Fax: (503) 671 - 6300

Contributions to Candidates: $20,500 (01/05 - 09/05)

Democrats: $9,000; Republicans: $11,500.

Principal Recipients

SENATE DEMOCRATS

HOUSE DEMOCRATS
Blumenauer, Earl (OR) $2,000
Jefferson, William (LA) $2,000

SENATE REPUBLICANS
Hatch, Orrin (UT) $2,000

HOUSE REPUBLICANS
Dreier, David (CA) $2,000
Walden, Gregory (OR) $2,000

Corporate Foundations and Giving Programs

Nike Foundation
Contact: Maria S. Eitel
One Bowerman Dr.
Beaverton, OR 97005
Tel: (503) 671 - 6453
Fax: (503) 671 - 6300

Annual Grant Total: over $5,000,000

Donates over $30 million in product and cash globally. Also sponsors the Nike GO program to get kids moving and means to do it.

Geographic Preference: Area(s) in which the company operates; New Hampshire; Oregon; Tennessee

Primary Interests: Recreation; Youth Services

Recent Recipients: Boys and Girls Club; Special Olympics

Public Affairs and Related Activities Personnel

At Headquarters

BUONOCORE, Fred J.
Manager, Investor Relations
Tel: (503) 671 - 6453
Fax: (503) 671 - 6300

CATLETT, Pamela M.
V. President, Investor Relations
Tel: (503) 671 - 6453
Fax: (503) 671 - 6300

COLEMAN, Wesely
V. President, Global Human Resources
Tel: (503) 671 - 6453
Fax: (503) 671 - 6300

EITEL, Maria S.
President, Nike Foundation
maria.eitel@nike.com
Tel: (503) 671 - 6453
Fax: (503) 671 - 6300

HA, Dr. Joseph M.
V. President, International Business and Government Relations
Tel: (503) 671 - 6453
Fax: (503) 671 - 6300

PETERSON, Dennis
Treasurer, Nike Inc. Federal PAC
Tel: (503) 671 - 6453
Fax: (503) 671 - 6300

POWELL, Nigel
Director, Corporate Communications
Tel: (503) 671 - 6453
Fax: (503) 671 - 6300

SPELTZ, Robert
Director, Global Community Affairs
robert.speltz@nike.com
Tel: (503) 671 - 6453
Fax: (503) 671 - 6300

WHITE, Molly
Director, U.S. Community Affairs
Tel: (503) 671 - 6453
Fax: (503) 671 - 6300

At Washington Office

FIGEL, Brad G.
Director, Governmental Affairs and International Trade Counsel
brad.figel@nike.com
Registered Federal Lobbyist.
Tel: (202) 543 - 6453
Fax: (202) 544 - 6453

PORTER, Orson C.
Registered Federal Lobbyist.
Tel: (202) 543 - 6453
Fax: (202) 544 - 6453

NiSource Inc.

A member of the Public Affairs Council. An energy holding company with operations in the natural gas and electric industries. Merged with Columbia Energy Group in 2000.

www.nisource.com

Annual Revenues: $6.247 billion

Chairman of the Board
NEALE, Gary L.
Tel: (219) 647 - 5990
Fax: (219) 647 - 6225
TF: (877) 647 - 5990

Chief Exec. Officer
SKAGGS, Robert C., Jr.
Tel: (219) 647 - 6200
Fax: (219) 647 - 6225
TF: (877) 647 - 5990

Main Headquarters
Mailing: 801 E. 86th Ave.
Merrillville, IN 46410
Tel: (219) 647 - 6200
Fax: (219) 647 - 6225
TF: (877) 647 - 5990

Washington Office
Mailing: Ten G St. NE, Suite 580
Washington, DC 20002
Tel: (202) 216 - 9760
Fax: (202) 216 - 9785

Political Action Committees

Columbia Gas of Ohio, Inc. PAC
200 Civic Center Dr.
Columbus, OH 43215
Tel: (614) 460 - 4207

Contributions to Candidates: none reported (01/05 - 09/05)

Columbia Gas Transmission Corp. PAC
1700 MacCorkle Ave., S.E.
Charleston, WV 25314

Contributions to Candidates: none reported (01/05 - 09/05)

NiSource Inc. PAC
Contact: Timothy J. Tokish, Jr.
200 Civic Center Dr.
Columbus, OH 43215
Tel: (614) 460 - 4207

Contributions to Candidates: $46,000 (01/05 - 09/05)

NiSource Inc.

* continued from previous page

Democrats: $9,500; Republicans: $36,500.

Principal Recipients

SENATE DEMOCRATS		HOUSE DEMOCRATS	
		Visclosky, Peter (IN)	$2,000
SENATE REPUBLICANS		**HOUSE REPUBLICANS**	
Allen, George (VA)	$2,000	Murphy, Tim (PA)	$3,000
Thomas, Craig (WY)	$2,000	Peterson, John Mr. (PA)	$2,000

Northern Indiana Public Service Co. PAC
200 Civic Center Dr. — Tel: (614) 460 - 4207
Columbus, OH 43215

Contributions to Candidates: none reported (01/05 - 09/05)

Corporate Foundations and Giving Programs

NiSource Charitable Foundation
801 E. 86th Ave. — Tel: (219) 647 - 6200
Merrillville, IN 46410 — Fax: (219) 647 - 6225
TF: (877) 647 - 5990

Annual Grant Total: $2,000,000 - $5,000,000
Geographic Preference: Area(s) in which the company operates
Primary Interests: Economic Development; Education; Environment/Conservation; Health and Human Services; Safety

Public Affairs and Related Activities Personnel

At Headquarters

ARREDONDO, Ramon — Tel: (219) 647 - 6237
Assistant to the Chairman and Director, Legislative Affairs — Fax: (219) 647 - 6240
rarredondo@nisource.com — TF: (877) 647 - 5990

MCKAY, Barbara S. — Tel: (219) 647 - 6200
V. President, Communictions — Fax: (219) 647 - 6225
TF: (877) 647 - 5990

SENCHAK, Dennis E. — Tel: (219) 647 - 6200
V. President, Investor Relations, Assistant Treasurer and Assistant Secretary — Fax: (219) 647 - 6225
TF: (877) 647 - 5990

ZIMMERMAN, S. LaNette — Tel: (219) 647 - 6200
Exec. V. President, Human Resources and Communications — Fax: (219) 647 - 6225
TF: (877) 647 - 5990

At Washington Office

SCZUDLO, Rebecca T. — Tel: (202) 216 - 9760
V. President, Federal Government Affairs — Fax: (202) 216 - 9785

(NiSource Corporate Services)

At Other Offices

BRACK, Karl — Tel: (304) 357 - 2396
V. President, Communications — Fax: (304) 357 - 2138
(Columbia Gas Transmission Corp.)
1700 MacCorkle Ave., S.E.
Charleston, WV 25314
kbrack@nisource.com

TOKISH, Timothy J., Jr. — Tel: (614) 460 - 4207
PAC Treasurer
200 Civic Center Dr.
Columbus, OH 43215

Nissan North America, Inc.

North American headquarters for Nissan's operations in the United States, Canada, and Mexico.
www.nissanusa.com

Chief Exec. Officer — Tel: (310) 771 - 3111
GHOSN, Carlos — Fax: (310) 516 - 7967

Main Headquarters
Mailing: P.O. Box 191 — Tel: (310) 771 - 3111
Gardena, CA 90248-0191 — Fax: (310) 516 - 7967
Street: 18501 S. Figueroa St.
Gardena, CA 90248-0191

Washington Office
Contact: John Schilling
Mailing: 196 Van Buren St., Suite 450 — Tel: (703) 456 - 2553
Herndon, VA 20170-5337 — Fax: (703) 456 - 2551

Corporate Foundations and Giving Programs

Nissan Foundation
Contact: Tiarzha Taylor
P.O. Box 191 — Tel: (310) 771 - 3330
Gardena, CA 90248-0191 — Fax: (310) 516 - 7967

Assets: $6,000,000 (2003)
Annual Grant Total: $200,000 - $300,000
Recent recipients include: Art Center College of Design, Autry National Center, Japanese American National Museum, Pierce College, Self Help Graphics, Ford Theatre Foundation, Museum of Tolerance, Pasadena City College, Public Corporation for the Arts, and The Accelerated School.
Geographic Preference: Area in which the company is headquartered; Area(s) in which employees live and work
Primary Interests: Automobile and Highway Safety; Minority Opportunities

Public Affairs and Related Activities Personnel

At Headquarters

HINES, Terri — Tel: (310) 771 - 3111
Senior Manager, Lifestyle and Corporate Communications — Fax: (310) 516 - 7967

LEGREVES, Frederique — Tel: (310) 771 - 3111
V. President, Corporate Communications — Fax: (310) 771 - 5656

PASCO, Gina — Tel: (310) 771 - 3111
Manager, Corporate Communications — Fax: (310) 516 - 7967

STANDISH, Fred — Tel: (310) 771 - 3111
Director, Corporate Communications — Fax: (310) 516 - 7967
(Nissan Technical Center North America)

TAYLOR, Tiarzha — Tel: (310) 771 - 3330
Manager, Corporate Relations — Fax: (310) 516 - 7967

At Washington Office

REID, Harland — Tel: (703) 456 - 2553
Senior Director, Government Affairs — Fax: (703) 456 - 2551
Registered Federal Lobbyist.

SCHILLING, John — Tel: (703) 456 - 2553
Manager, Corporate Communications — Fax: (703) 456 - 2551

Nissan Technical Center North America

See listing on page 350 under Nissan North America, Inc.

Noble Drilling Corp.

Drilling contractors serving the worldwide petroleum industry.
www.noblecorp.com

Chairman and Chief Exec. Officer — Tel: (281) 276 - 6100
DAY, James C. — Fax: (281) 491 - 2092

Main Headquarters
Mailing: 13135 S. Dairy Ashford — Tel: (281) 276 - 6100
Suite 800 — Fax: (281) 491 - 2092
Sugar Land, TX 77478

Public Affairs and Related Activities Personnel

At Headquarters

RYND, John T. — Tel: (281) 276 - 6100
V. President, Investor Relations — Fax: (281) 491 - 2092

Nomura Securities Internat'l, Inc.

A brokerage firm. A subsidiary of Nomura Holding America, Inc.
www.nomurany.com

President and Chief Exec. Officer — Tel: (212) 667 - 9300
KOGA, Nobuyuki — Fax: (212) 667 - 1058

Main Headquarters
Mailing: Two World Financial Center — Tel: (212) 667 - 9300
Building B — Fax: (212) 667 - 1058
New York, NY 10028-1198

Corporate Foundations and Giving Programs

Nomura Securities Internat'l, Inc. Corporate Contributions Program
Two World Financial Center — Tel: (212) 667 - 9300
Building B — Fax: (212) 667 - 1058
New York, NY 10028-1198

Annual Grant Total: none reported

Public Affairs and Related Activities Personnel

At Headquarters

RUNCK, Elise — Tel: (212) 667 - 9300
Director, Human Resources — Fax: (212) 667 - 1058

SPRINGER, Anna — Tel: (212) 667 - 9300
Director, Corporate Communications — Fax: (212) 667 - 1058

WATANABE, Kenichi — Tel: (212) 667 - 9300
Exec. V. President — Fax: (212) 667 - 1058
Responsibilities include investor relations.

Nordson Corp.

A manufacturer of industrial equipment for applying adhesives, sealants, and coatings.
www.nordson.com

Chairman and Chief Exec. Officer — Tel: (440) 892 - 1580
CAMPBELL, Edward P. — Fax: (440) 892 - 9507

Main Headquarters
Mailing: 28601 Clemens Rd. — Tel: (440) 892 - 1580
Westlake, OH 44145 — Fax: (440) 892 - 9507

Nordson Corp.

* continued from previous page

Corporate Foundations and Giving Programs

Nordson Corp. Foundation
Contact: Cecelia Render
28601 Clemens Rd. — Tel: (440) 892 - 1580
Westlake, OH 44145 — Fax: (440) 892 - 9507

Annual Grant Total: $2,000,000 - $5,000,000
Geographic Preference: California; Georgia; Ohio
Primary Interests: Arts and Culture; Education; Human Welfare
Recent Recipients: Cleveland Clinic Foundation; Habitat for Humanity; Ohio Foundation of Independent Colleges; Salvation Army; Wilberforce University

Public Affairs and Related Activities Personnel

At Headquarters

FIELDS, Bruce H. — Tel: (440) 892 - 1580
V. President, Human Resources — Fax: (440) 892 - 9507
bfields@nordson.com

JOHNSON, Derrick — Tel: (440) 892 - 1580
Director, Corporate Public Relations — Fax: (440) 892 - 9507

PRICE, Barbara T. — Tel: (440) 414 - 5344
Manager, Shareholder Services — Fax: (440) 892 - 9507
bprice@nordson.com

RENDER, Cecelia — Tel: (440) 892 - 1580
Acting Director, Nordson Corp. Foundation — Fax: (440) 892 - 9507

Nordstrom, Inc.

A fashion specialty retailer.
www.nordstrom.com
Annual Revenues: $7.1 billion

Chairman of the Board — Tel: (206) 628 - 2111
NORDSTROM, Bruce A. — Fax: (206) 628 - 1795
bruce.nordstrom@nordstrom.com

Main Headquarters
Mailing: 1617 Sixth Ave. — Tel: (206) 628 - 2111
Suite 700 — Fax: (206) 628 - 1795
Seattle, WA 98101

Public Affairs and Related Activities Personnel

At Headquarters

ANDERS, Deniz — Tel: (206) 373 - 3038
Director, Business Public Relations — Fax: (206) 373 - 3039
deniz.anders@nordstroms.com

SUNDAY, Delena M. — Tel: (206) 628 - 2111
Exec. V. President, Human Resources and Diversity Affairs — Fax: (206) 628 - 1795
delena.sunday@nordstrom.com

WHITE, Brooke — Tel: (206) 373 - 3030
V. President, Corporate Communications — Fax: (206) 373 - 3039
brooke.white@nordstrom.com

At Other Offices

ALLEN, Stephanie — Tel: (206) 303 - 3262
Director, Investor Relations — Fax: (206) 303 - 3009
1700 Seventh Ave.
Suite 1000
Seattle, WA 98101-4407
stephanie.allen@nordstroms.com

Norfolk Southern Corp.

A transportation holding company that operates a freight railroad company, Norfolk Southern Railway.
www.nscorp.com
Annual Revenues: $6.47 billion

Chairman, President and Chief Exec. Officer — Tel: (757) 629 - 2600
GOODE, David R. — Fax: (757) 629 - 2822

Main Headquarters
Mailing: Three Commercial Pl. — Tel: (757) 629 - 2600
Norfolk, VA 23510-2191 — Fax: (757) 629 - 2822

Washington Office
Contact: Bruno Maestri
Mailing: 1500 K St. NW — Tel: (202) 383 - 4166
Suite 375 — Fax: (202) 383 - 4018
Washington, DC 20005

Political Action Committees

Norfolk Southern Corp. Good Government Fund
Contact: Christopher R. Neikirk
Three Commercial Pl. — Tel: (757) 533 - 4960
Norfolk, VA 23510-2191 — Fax: (757) 629 - 2822

Contributions to Candidates: $165,800 (01/05 - 09/05)
Democrats: $49,760; Republicans: $114,040; Other: $2,000.

Principal Recipients

SENATE DEMOCRATS		HOUSE DEMOCRATS	
Carper, Thomas R (DE)	$3,260	Rahall, Nick J Ii (WV)	$5,000
Conrad, Kent (ND)	$2,000		
Nelson, Benjamin (NE)	$2,000		
Nelson, Bill (FL)	$2,000		
SENATE REPUBLICANS		**HOUSE REPUBLICANS**	
Allen, George (VA)	$6,700	Cantor, Eric (VA)	$6,000
Burns, Conrad (MT)	$4,000	Duncan, John (TN)	$5,000
Santorum, Richard (PA)	$3,000	Shuster, William (PA)	$5,000
Ensign, John Eric (NV)	$2,000		
Kyl, Jon L (AZ)	$2,000		

Corporate Foundations and Giving Programs

Norfolk Southern Foundation
Contact: Deborah Wyld
P.O. Box 3040 — Tel: (757) 629 - 2881
Norfolk, VA 23501 — Fax: (757) 629 - 2361

Annual Grant Total: none reported

Public Affairs and Related Activities Personnel

At Headquarters

BROWN, Frank S. — Tel: (757) 629 - 2714
Assistant V. President, Public Relations — Fax: (757) 629 - 2822

CHAPMAN, Robin C. — Tel: (757) 629 - 2713
Manager, Public Relations — Fax: (757) 629 - 2822

ENEDY, Allison M. — Tel: (757) 629 - 2708
Manager, Online Communications — Fax: (757) 629 - 2822

FORT, Robert C. — Tel: (757) 629 - 2710
V. President, Public Relations — Fax: (757) 629 - 2822

HARRIS, Richard W. — Tel: (757) 629 - 2718
Director, Corporate Communications — Fax: (757) 629 - 2822

HIXON, James A. — Tel: (757) 629 - 2600
Exec. V. President, Finance and Public Affairs — Fax: (757) 629 - 2822

MACMAHON, Mark R. — Tel: (757) 629 - 2615
V. President, Labor Relations — Fax: (757) 629 - 2822

MARILLEY, Leanne D. — Tel: (757) 629 - 2861
Director, Investor Relations

NEIKIRK, Christopher R. — Tel: (757) 533 - 4960
Contact, Norfolk Southern Corp. Good Government Fund — Fax: (757) 629 - 2822

TERPAY, Susan M. — Tel: (757) 823 - 5204
Director, Public Relations — Fax: (757) 629 - 2822

TYREE, Larry D. — Tel: (757) 533 - 4810
Assistant Corporate Secretary, Stockholder Records — Fax: (757) 533 - 4917
Responsibilities include investor relations.

WEHRMEISTER, Charles J. — Tel: (757) 629 - 2600
V. President, Safety and Environmental — Fax: (757) 629 - 2822

At Washington Office

ANTHONY, Steven J. — Tel: (202) 383 - 4432
Assistant V. President — Fax: (202) 383 - 4018
Registered Federal Lobbyist.

LEDOUX, Marque I. — Tel: (202) 383 - 4166
Assistant V. President, Public Affairs — Fax: (202) 383 - 4018

MAESTRI, Bruno — Tel: (202) 383 - 4425
V. President, Public Affairs — Fax: (202) 383 - 4018

WILSON, Darrell — Tel: (202) 383 - 4123
Director, Public Affairs — Fax: (202) 383 - 4018
darrell.wilson@nscorp.com

At Other Offices

HARRELL, Joel E., III — Tel: (404) 897 - 313
Resident V. President — Fax: (404) 527 - 2773
185 Spring St. SW
Atlanta, GA 30303-3703
Responsibilities include corporate government relations and lobbying.

HARRIS, W. S., III — Tel: (614) 460 - 3510
Resident V. President, Public Affairs — Fax: (614) 464 - 1466
65 E. State St., Suite 1000
Columbus, OH 43215

LEWIS, H. Craig — Tel: (215) 209 - 4284
V. President, Corporate Affairs — Fax: (215) 209 - 4286
2001 Market St., Suite 29
Philadelphia, PA 19103

Norfolk Southern Corp.

• continued from previous page

WINGO, William Bruce — Tel: (804) 649 - 2485
Resident V. President — Fax: (804) 649 - 3447
325 Old City Hall
1001 E. Broad St.
Richmond, VA 23219-1908
Responsibilities include corporate public and government affairs.

WYLD, Deborah — Tel: (757) 629 - 2881
Exec. Director, Norfolk Southern Foundation — Fax: (757) 629 - 2361
P.O. Box 3040
Norfolk, VA 23501

Nortek Inc.

A manufacturer of commercial and residential building products.
www.nortek-inc.com

Chairman and Chief Exec. Officer — Tel: (401) 751 - 1600
BREADY, Richard L. — Fax: (401) 751 - 4610

Main Headquarters
Mailing: 50 Kennedy Plaza — Tel: (401) 751 - 1600
Providence, RI 02903 — Fax: (401) 751 - 4610

Public Affairs and Related Activities Personnel

At Headquarters

COONEY, Edward J. — Tel: (401) 751 - 1600
V. President and Treasurer — Fax: (401) 751 - 4610
Responsibilities include corporate communications and investor relations.

WHITE, Jane C. — Tel: (401) 751 - 1600
Director, Human Resources/Administration — Fax: (401) 751 - 4610

Nortel Networks

A member of the Public Affairs Council. Delivers innovative technology solutions encompassing end to end broadband, VOIP, multimedia services and applications and wireless broadband to both service providers and enterprise customers.
www.nortel.com
Annual Revenues: $9.81 billion

Chairman of the Board — Tel: (202) 312 - 8060
PEARCE, Harry

Main Headquarters
Mailing: 101 Constitution Ave. NW — Tel: (202) 312 - 8060
Suite 325 East
Washington, DC 20001

Political Action Committees

Nortel Political Action Committee
Contact: Mary Jo Dorr
2325 Dulles Corner Blvd.
200 Athens Way
Herndon, VA 20171

Contributions to Candidates: $6,110 (01/05 - 09/05)
Democrats: $2,970; Republicans: $3,140.

Principal Recipients

SENATE DEMOCRATS		HOUSE DEMOCRATS	
Nelson, Bill (FL)	$1,648		
Conrad, Kent (ND)	$1,322		
SENATE REPUBLICANS		**HOUSE REPUBLICANS**	
Thomas, Craig (WY)	$1,000	Reynolds, Thomas (NY)	$1,000
		Weller, Jerry (IL)	$1,000

Corporate Foundations and Giving Programs

Nortel Lean IT
Contact: Julie Fletcher
101 Constitution Ave. NW — Tel: (202) 312 - 8060
Suite 325 East
Washington, DC 20001

Annual Grant Total: $2,000,000 - $5,000,000
More information about the corporate contributions programs is available on their website: www.nortel.com/corporate/community/citizenship/foundation.html.
Geographic Preference: California; Georgia; North Carolina; Tennessee; Texas
Primary Interests: Math and Science; Technology

Public Affairs and Related Activities Personnel

At Headquarters

CARTER-MAGUIRE, Melanie — Tel: (202) 312 - 8060
V. President, Global Government Relations-International
cmaguire@nortel.com

FARMER, Greg — Tel: (202) 312 - 8060
Senior V. President, Global Government and Community Relations
gfarmer@nortel.com

FLETCHER, Julie — Tel: (202) 312 - 8060
V. President, Community Relations

GORDON, Mary — Tel: (202) 312 - 8060
V. President, Global Government Relations-Congressional Affairs
mgordon@nortel.com

PHILLIPS, Susan A. — Tel: (202) 312 - 8060
V. President, Global Government Relations
aphillip@nortel.com

STRASSBURGER, Raymond — Tel: (202) 312 - 8060
Senior Washington Counsel
rlstrass@nortel.com

At Other Offices

DORR, Mary Jo
Treasurer, Nortel PAC
2325 Dulles Corner Blvd.
200 Athens Way
Herndon, VA 20171

North American Coal Co.

See listing on page 337 under NACCO Industries.

Northeast Utilities

A member of the Public Affairs Council. An electric utility holding company.
www.nu.com
Annual Revenues: $6.874 billion

Chairman, President and Chief Exec. Officer — Tel: (860) 665 - 5000
SHIVERY, Charles W. — Fax: (860) 665 - 3177
TF: (800) 286 - 2000

Main Headquarters
Mailing: P.O. Box 270 — Tel: (860) 665 - 5000
Hartford, CT 06141-0270 — Fax: (860) 665 - 3177
TF: (800) 286 - 2000

Street: 107 Selden St.
Berlin, CT 06037

Washington Office
Mailing: 601 Pennsylvania Ave. NW — Tel: (202) 508 - 5301
Suite 620 — Fax: (202) 508 - 5304
Washington, DC 20004

Political Action Committees

Northeast Utilities Employees' Political Action Committee - Federal
Contact: Judith M. Ostronic
601 Pennsylvania Ave. NW — Tel: (202) 508 - 5301
Suite 620 — Fax: (202) 508 - 5304
Washington, DC 20004

Contributions to Candidates: $19,500 (01/05 - 09/05)
Democrats: $6,000; Republicans: $13,500.

Principal Recipients

SENATE DEMOCRATS		HOUSE DEMOCRATS	
Conrad, Kent (ND)	$1,000	Green, Gene (TX)	$2,000
Salazar, Ken (CO)	$1,000	Strickland, Ted (OH)	$1,000
		Wynn, Albert (MD)	$1,000
SENATE REPUBLICANS		**HOUSE REPUBLICANS**	
Burr, Richard (NC)	$1,000	Fossella, Vito (NY)	$2,000
Santorum, Richard (PA)	$1,000	Pombo, Richard (CA)	$2,000
Smith, Gordon (OR)	$1,000	Shimkus, John (IL)	$2,000
Thomas, Craig (WY)	$1,000	Bass, Charles (NH)	$1,000
		Ferguson, Mike (NJ)	$1,000
		Upton, Fred (MI)	$1,000

Corporate Foundations and Giving Programs

Northeast Utilities Foundation
Contact: Theresa Hopkins Staten
P.O. Box 270 — Tel: (860) 721 - 4063
Hartford, CT 06141-0270 — Fax: (860) 721 - 4331
TF: (800) 286 - 2000

Annual Grant Total: $400,000 - $500,000
Geographic Preference: Area(s) in which the company operates
Primary Interests: Arts and Culture; Civic and Public Affairs; Energy Conservation; Environment/Conservation

Public Affairs and Related Activities Personnel

At Headquarters

DORSEY, Thomas — Tel: (860) 665 - 3590
Manager, Governmental Affairs — Fax: (860) 665 - 3177
TF: (800) 286 - 2000

KEATING, Mary Jo — Tel: (860) 665 - 5181
V. President, Corporate Communications — Fax: (860) 665 - 5262
(Northeast Utilities Service Co.) — TF: (800) 286 - 2000
Mailstop: M/S BMN 1
KeatiMJ@nu.com

Northeast Utilities
* continued from previous page

KOTKIN, Jeffrey R.
V. President, Investor Relations
(Northeast Utilities Service Co.)
Mailstop: M/S BMW 1
Tel: (860) 665 - 5154
Fax: (860) 665 - 5457
TF: (800) 286 - 2000

LAVECCHIA, Jean
V. President, Human Resources and Environmental Services
(Northeast Utilities Service Co.)
Tel: (860) 665 - 3560
Fax: (860) 665 - 5078
TF: (800) 286 - 2000

MCHALE, David R.
V. President and Treasurer
Tel: (860) 665 - 5601
Fax: (860) 665 - 3177
TF: (800) 286 - 2000

Responsibilities include investor relations.

MORTON, Margaret L.
V. President, Government Affairs
(Northeast Utilities Service Co.)
Mailstop: M/S BMW 2
MortoML@nu.com
Tel: (860) 665 - 5000
Fax: (860) 665 - 3177
TF: (800) 286 - 2000

STATEN, Theresa Hopkins
Chairman and President, Northeast Utilities Foundation
Mailstop: M/S NUE 2
hopkit@nu.com
Tel: (860) 721 - 4063
Fax: (860) 721 - 4331
TF: (800) 286 - 2000

THIBDAUE, Lisa J.
V. President, Rates, Regulatory Affairs, and Compliance
(Northeast Utilities Service Co.)
Tel: (860) 665 - 5883
Fax: (860) 665 - 4853
TF: (800) 286 - 2000

At Washington Office

OSTRONIC, Judith M.
PAC Treasurer
Tel: (202) 508 - 5301
Fax: (202) 508 - 5304

At Other Offices

SMITH, Robert J.
Director, State Governmental Affairs
20 Greenfield St.
Brockton, MA 02401
SmithRJ@nu.com
Tel: (617) 725 - 8801
Fax: (617) 725 - 1002

Northeast Utilities Service Co.
See listing on page 352 under Northeast Utilities.

Northern States Power Co.
See listing on page 528 under Xcel Energy, Inc.

Northern Telecom
See listing on page 352 under Nortel Networks.

Northern Trust Co.
A bank holding company.
www.northerntrust.com

Chairman, President and Chief Exec. Officer
OSBORN, William A.
Tel: (312) 630 - 6000
TF: (888) 289 - 6542

Main Headquarters
Mailing: 50 S. LaSalle St.
Chicago, IL 60675
Tel: (312) 630 - 6000
TF: (888) 289 - 6542

Political Action Committees

Northern Trust Co. Good Government Committee
Contact: Irwin A. Mendelssohn
50 S. LaSalle St.
Chicago, IL 60675
Tel: (312) 557 - 7218
TF: (888) 289 - 6542

Contributions to Candidates: $800 (01/05 - 09/05)
Democrats: $800.

Principal Recipients

SENATE DEMOCRATS	HOUSE DEMOCRATS	
	Jackson, Jesse (IL)	$500

Corporate Foundations and Giving Programs

Northern Trust Co. Charitable Trust and Corp. Contributions
50 S. LaSalle St.
Chicago, IL 60675
Tel: (312) 630 - 6000
TF: (888) 289 - 6542

Annual Grant Total: $2,000,000 - $5,000,000
Guidelines are available.
Geographic Preference: Chicago, IL
Primary Interests: Children; Persons with Disabilities; Women

Public Affairs and Related Activities Personnel

At Headquarters

FLEMING, Beverly
Senior V. President, Investor Relations
Tel: (312) 630 - 6000
TF: (888) 289 - 6542

JUREK, Richard
V. President, Public Relations
Tel: (312) 444 - 5218
TF: (888) 289 - 6542

LIVERETT, Deborah
Contact, Northern Trust Co. Charitable Trust and Corp. Contributions
Tel: (312) 630 - 0679
Fax: (312) 630 - 1809

MENDELSSOHN, Irwin A.
Treasurer, North Trust Co. Political Action Committee
Tel: (312) 557 - 7218
TF: (888) 289 - 6542

Northrop Grumman Corp.
A member of the Public Affairs Council. Northrop Grumman Corp. is a global aerospace and defense company providing services and solutions in defense and commercial electronics, systems integration, information technology and non-nuclear shipbuilding and systems. Northrop Grumman serves U.S. and international military, government and commercial customers. Acquired Logicon in 1997, Litton Industries, Avondale Industries and Newport News Shipbuilding in 2001, and TRW, Inc. in 2002.
www.northropgrumman.com
Annual Revenues: $13.558 billion

Chairman, President and Chief Exec. Officer
SUGAR, Ronald D.
Tel: (310) 553 - 6262
Fax: (310) 201 - 3023

Main Headquarters
Mailing: 1840 Century Park East
Los Angeles, CA 90067-2199
Tel: (310) 553 - 6262
Fax: (310) 201 - 3023

Washington Office
Contact: Robert W. Helm
Mailing: 1000 Wilson Blvd., Suite 2300
Arlington, VA 22209
Tel: (703) 875 - 8400

Political Action Committees

Employees of Northrop Grumman Corp. PAC (ENGPAC)
Contact: Marsha H. Kwalwasser
1840 Century Park East
Los Angeles, CA 90067-2199
Tel: (310) 201 - 3398
Fax: (310) 556 - 4595

Contributions to Candidates: $484,000 (01/05 - 09/05)
Democrats: $196,000; Republicans: $288,000.

Corporate Foundations and Giving Programs

Northrop Grumman Corp. Contributions Program
1840 Century Park East
Los Angeles, CA 90067-2199
Tel: (310) 553 - 6262
Fax: (310) 201 - 3023

Assets: $36,423,585 (2001)
Annual Grant Total: $1,000,000 - $2,000,000
Geographic Preference: Area(s) in which employees live and work
Primary Interests: Arts and Humanities; Education; Engineering; Technology

Public Affairs and Related Activities Personnel

At Headquarters

HATELEY, J. Michael
Corporate V. President and Chief Human Resources and Administrative Officer
hatelmi@mail.northgrum.com
Tel: (310) 201 - 3043
Fax: (310) 556 - 4519

HENSON, Tom
Manager, Media Relations
thomas.henson@ngc.com
Tel: (310) 201 - 3458
Fax: (310) 556 - 4561

KENT, J. Gaston, Jr.
V. President, Investor Relations
Tel: (310) 553 - 6262
Fax: (310) 201 - 3023

KWALWASSER, Marsha H.
Director, Government Relations
Tel: (310) 201 - 3398
Fax: (310) 556 - 4595

MCSWEENEY, Denny
Director, Investor Relations
Tel: (310) 229 - 1311
Fax: (310) 201 - 3023

MOORE, Frank
Director, Media Relations
f.moore@ngc.com
Tel: (310) 201 - 3335
Fax: (310) 556 - 4561

O'BRIEN, Roseanne
Corporate V. President, Communications
Tel: (310) 201 - 3333
Fax: (310) 201 - 3023

At Washington Office

AVETISSIAN, Vic
Registered Federal Lobbyist.
Tel: (703) 875 - 8400

BELOTE, Brandon R., III
Director, Corporate Public Affairs and International Communications
randy.belote@ngc.com
Tel: (703) 875 - 8525
Fax: (703) 243 - 3190

GIANNINI, Thomas
Registered Federal Lobbyist.
Tel: (703) 875 - 8400

GULMERT, Gustav
Manager, Corporate Public Affairs and International Communications
gus.gulmert@nge.com
Tel: (703) 875 - 8450
Fax: (703) 243 - 3190

HARPER, Diane
Manager, Legislative Affairs
Tel: (703) 875 - 8400
Fax: (703) 276 - 0711

Registered Federal Lobbyist.

HELM, Robert W.
Corporate V. President, Government Relations
Tel: (703) 875 - 8500
Fax: (703) 276 - 0711

Registered Federal Lobbyist.

KELLY, Maureen
Registered Federal Lobbyist.
Tel: (703) 875 - 8400

Northrop Grumman Corp.

* continued from previous page

LANGKNECHT, John M. — Tel: (703) 875 - 8400
Registered Federal Lobbyist.

MELTSNER, James R. — Tel: (703) 875 - 5846
Manager, Legislative Affairs — Fax: (703) 276 - 0711
jim.meltsner@ngc.com
Registered Federal Lobbyist.

OTT, Kathleen — Tel: (703) 525 - 6767
Manager, Legislative Affairs — Fax: (703) 276 - 0711

PERKINS, Peter — Tel: (703) 525 - 6767
Manager, Legislative Affairs — Fax: (703) 276 - 0711
Registered Federal Lobbyist.

SUTTON, Stephen L. — Tel: (703) 875 - 8400
Manager, Legislative Affairs — Fax: (703) 276 - 0711

Registered Federal Lobbyist.

TAPP, Jim — Tel: (703) 875 - 8400
Registered Federal Lobbyist.

WINCHALL, Steve — Tel: (703) 875 - 8400
Registered Federal Lobbyist.

WOODS, Jerry D. — Tel: (703) 875 - 8400
Manager, Legislative Affairs — Fax: (703) 276 - 0711

Registered Federal Lobbyist.

Northrop Grumman Newport News

Formerly known as Newport News Shipbuilding. A shipbuilding, design, and repair facility. A subsidiary of Northrop Grumman Corp. (see separate listing).
www.nn.northropgrumman.com

Main Headquarters
Mailing: 4101 Washington Ave. — Tel: (757) 380 - 2000
Newport News, VA 23607-2770 — Fax: (757) 380 - 3875

Political Action Committees

Newport News Shipbuilding Political Action Committee (SHIPPAC)
Contact: Vince Schoenig
4101 Washington Ave. — Tel: (757) 380 - 2000
Newport News, VA 23607-2770 — Fax: (757) 380 - 3875

Contributions to Candidates: none reported (01/05 - 09/05)

Corporate Foundations and Giving Programs

Northrop Grumman Newport News Shipbuilding Community Relations
Contact: Brenda Roth
4101 Washington Ave. — Tel: (757) 380 - 3011
Newport News, VA 23607-2770

Annual Grant Total: $1,000,000 - $2,000,000
Geographic Preference: Area(s) in which the company operates; Virginia
Primary Interests: Arts and Culture; Community Affairs; Education; Health and Human Services

Public Affairs and Related Activities Personnel

At Headquarters

DELLAPENTA, Jennifer — Tel: (757) 380 - 3558
Senior Communications Specialist — Fax: (757) 380 - 3867
jennifer.dellapenta@ngc.com

ERMATINGER, William R. — Tel: (757) 380 - 2000
V. President, Human Resources and Administration — Fax: (757) 380 - 3875

FULLER DICKSESKI, Ms. Jerri — Tel: (757) 380 - 2341
Director, Communications — Fax: (757) 380 - 3867

PETTERS, C. Michael — Tel: (757) 380 - 2000
V. President, Human Resources, Administration and Trades — Fax: (757) 380 - 3875

ROTH, Brenda — Tel: (757) 380 - 3011
Community Relations Representative
brenda.roth@ngc.com

SCHOENIG, Vince — Tel: (757) 380 - 2000
PAC Treasurer — Fax: (757) 380 - 3875

Northwest Airlines, Inc.

Holding company; air transportation.
www.nwa.com
Annual Revenues: $11.5 billion

Chairman of the Board
WILSON, Gary L. — Tel: (612) 726 - 2111; Fax: (612) 726 - 0776

Chief Exec. Officer
STEENLAND, Doug — Tel: (612) 726 - 2111; Fax: (612) 726 - 0776; TF: (800) 225 - 2525

Main Headquarters
Mailing: 2700 Lone Oak Pkwy. — Tel: (612) 726 - 2111
Eagan, MN 55121 — Fax: (612) 726 - 0776
TF: (800) 225 - 2525

Washington Office
Contact: Andrea Fischer Newman
Mailing: 901 15th St. NW — Tel: (202) 842 - 3193
Suite 310 — Fax: (202) 289 - 6834
Washington, DC 20005

Political Action Committees

Northwest Airlines PAC
Contact: Sally Veith
901 15th St. NW — Tel: (202) 842 - 3193
Suite 310 — Fax: (202) 289 - 6834
Washington, DC 20005

Contributions to Candidates: $67,250 (01/05 - 09/05)
Democrats: $24,500; Republicans: $40,000; Other: $2,750.

Principal Recipients

SENATE DEMOCRATS		HOUSE DEMOCRATS	
Conrad, Kent (ND)	$7,000	Kilpatrick, Carolyn (MI)	$2,000
Ford, Harold E Jr (TN)	$5,000		
Stabenow, Debbie (MI)	$2,000		
		HOUSE OTHER	
		Oberstar, James L (MN)	$2,750
SENATE REPUBLICANS		**HOUSE REPUBLICANS**	
Coleman, Norm (MN)	$5,000	Kennedy, Mark (MN)	$5,000
Lott, Trent (MS)	$5,000	Kline, John P (MN)	$2,500
Burns, Conrad (MT)	$3,000	Knollenberg, Joe (MI)	$2,500
Kennedy, Mark (MN)	$2,500	Cantor, Eric (VA)	$2,000

Corporate Foundations and Giving Programs

Northwest Airlines AirCares Program
2700 Lone Oak Pkwy. — Tel: (612) 726 - 7581
Eagan, MN 55121 — Fax: (612) 726 - 3942

Annual Grant Total: $2,000,000 - $5,000,000
The program can be reached via e-mail at: AirCares@nwa.com.
Geographic Preference: No geographical restrictions
Primary Interests: Arts and Humanities; Education; Health and Human Services
Recent Recipients: United Way

Public Affairs and Related Activities Personnel

At Headquarters

CASMEY, Kim — Tel: (612) 727 - 0899
Specialist, Sponsorships — Fax: (612) 726 - 0776
Mailstop: M/S A1310 — TF: (800) 225 - 2525
kim.casmey@nwa.com

DAVIDMAN, Jeff — Tel: (612) 726 - 2111
Director, State and Local Affairs — Fax: (612) 726 - 0776
jeff.davidman@nwa.com — TF: (800) 225 - 2525

EBENHOCH, Kurt — Tel: (612) 727 - 4629
Director, Media Relations — Fax: (612) 726 - 3942
Mailstop: M/S A1310

LINDER, Mary C. — Tel: (612) 726 - 2111
Senior V. President, Corporate and Brand Communications — Fax: (612) 726 - 3942
Mailstop: M/S A1300 — TF: (800) 225 - 2525

MELLON, Bill — Tel: (612) 726 - 2331
Managing Director, Corporate Communications — Fax: (612) 727 - 4408
Mailstop: M/S A1310

MOORE, John W. — Tel: (901) 922 - 0382
Managing Director, State and Local Affairs — Fax: (901) 922 - 0375
Mailstop: M/S MEM 1150
john.moore@nwa.com

SMITH, Jeffrey R. — Tel: (612) 726 - 2331
Director, Internal Communications — Fax: (612) 726 - 3942
Mailstop: M/S A1310

At Washington Office

NEWMAN, Andrea Fischer — Tel: (202) 842 - 3193
Senior V. President, Government Affairs — Fax: (202) 289 - 6834
Mailstop: M/S WAS 1150

ROSIA, Megan — Tel: (202) 842 - 3193
Managing Director, Government Affairs and Associate General Counsel — Fax: (202) 289 - 6834
Mailstop: M/S WAS 1150

SKWAREK, Daniel — Tel: (202) 842 - 3193
Director, International and Regulatory Affairs — Fax: (202) 289 - 6834
Mailstop: M/S WAS 1150

VEITH, Sally — Tel: (202) 842 - 3193
Director, Government Affairs — Fax: (202) 289 - 6834
Mailstop: M/S WAS 1150
Registered Federal Lobbyist.

Northwest Natural Gas Co.

See listing on page 358 under NW Natural.

NorthWestern Corp.

A provider of services and solutions in the energy sectors. Acquired Montana Power's electrical and natural gas distribution assets in February, 2002.

www.northwesternenergy.com
Annual Revenues: $2 billion

Chairman of the Board
DRAPER, Dr. E. Linn, Jr. — Tel: (605) 978 - 2908; Fax: (605) 978 - 2840

Chief Exec. Officer
HANSON, Michael J.
mike.hanson@northwestern.com — Tel: (605) 978 - 2908; Fax: (605) 978 - 2840

Main Headquarters
Mailing: 125 S. Dakota Ave.
Sioux Falls, SD 57104-6403 — Tel: (605) 978 - 2908; Fax: (605) 978 - 2840

Political Action Committees

Citizens for Responsible Government - Employees of the Montana Power Co.
P.O. Box 1574
Great Falls, MT 59403

Contributions to Candidates: none reported (01/05 - 09/05)

NorthWestern Public Service Co. PAC (NWPS Employees' PAC)
33 Third St., S.E.
Huron, SD 57350 — Tel: (605) 358 - 8270; Fax: (605) 353 - 8216

Contributions to Candidates: none reported (01/05 - 09/05)

Public Affairs and Related Activities Personnel

At Headquarters

SCHRUM, Roger P.
V. President, Human Resources and Communications
roger.schrum@northwestern.com — Tel: (605) 978 - 2848; Fax: (605) 978 - 2840
Responsibilities include investor relations.

At Other Offices

FITZPATRICK, John
Director, Community Relations
208 N. Montana Ave.
Helena, MT 59601
john.fitzpatrick@northwestern.com — Tel: (406) 449 - 9818; Fax: (406) 449 - 8331

LOTSBERG, Warren K.
Director, South Dakota Government Relations
600 Market St. West
Huron, SD 57350
warren.lotsberg@northwestern.com — Tel: (605) 353 - 8240; Fax: (605) 353 - 8286

Northwestern Mutual Financial Network

A member of the Public Affairs Council. A life insurance and financial services company.

www.northwesternmutual.com

President and Chief Exec. Officer
ZORE, Edward J. — Tel: (414) 271 - 1444; Fax: (414) 665 - 2463; TF: (800) 323 - 7033

Main Headquarters
Mailing: 720 E. Wisconsin Ave.
Milwaukee, WI 53202-4797 — Tel: (414) 271 - 1444; Fax: (414) 665 - 2463; TF: (800) 323 - 7033

Political Action Committees

Northwestern Mutual Life Insurance Co. Federal PAC
Contact: Tammy Roou
720 E. Wisconsin Ave.
Milwaukee, WI 53202-4797 — Tel: (414) 271 - 1444; Fax: (414) 665 - 2463; TF: (800) 323 - 7033

Contributions to Candidates: $69,500 (01/05 - 09/05)
Democrats: $22,000; Republicans: $47,500.

Principal Recipients

SENATE DEMOCRATS		HOUSE DEMOCRATS	
Nelson, Benjamin (NE)	$2,500	Pomeroy, Earl (ND)	$2,500
		Rangel, Charles B (NY)	$2,000

SENATE REPUBLICANS		HOUSE REPUBLICANS	
Smith, Gordon (OR)	$5,000	Oxley, Michael (OH)	$5,000
Snowe, Olympia (ME)	$4,000	Reynolds, Thomas (NY)	$2,500
Hatch, Orrin (UT)	$3,000	Ryan, Paul D (WI)	$2,500
Kyl, Jon L (AZ)	$3,000	Cantor, Eric (VA)	$2,000
Bennett, Robert F (UT)	$2,000	Castle, Michael (DE)	$2,000
Lott, Trent (MS)	$2,000		
Thomas, Craig (WY)	$2,000		

Corporate Foundations and Giving Programs

Northwestern Mutual Foundation
Contact: Gil Llanas
720 E. Wisconsin Ave.
Milwaukee, WI 53202-4797 — Tel: (414) 271 - 1444; Fax: (414) 665 - 2463; TF: (800) 323 - 7033

Assets: $130,000,000 (1999)
Annual Grant Total: over $5,000,000
Also maintains a matching gift plan for colleges, universities, and private secondary schools. Donations of $15,000,000 were made in 2000.
Geographic Preference: Wisconsin
Primary Interests: Arts and Culture; Education; Health and Human Services; Public Broadcasting

Public Affairs and Related Activities Personnel

At Headquarters

BATES, Douglas P. — Tel: (414) 271 - 1444; Fax: (414) 665 - 2463; TF: (800) 323 - 7033

LLANAS, Gil
Foundation Contact — Tel: (414) 271 - 1444; Fax: (414) 665 - 2463; TF: (800) 323 - 7033

LUCKOW, Ericka
Media Contact
erikaluckow@northwsternmutual.com — Tel: (414) 271 - 1444; Fax: (414) 665 - 2463; TF: (800) 323 - 7033

LUEGER, Susan A.
V. President, Human Resources — Tel: (414) 665 - 7197; Fax: (414) 665 - 2463; TF: (800) 323 - 7033

RADKE, Steven M. — Tel: (414) 271 - 1444; Fax: (414) 665 - 2463; TF: (800) 323 - 7033

ROOU, Tammy
PAC Treasurer — Tel: (414) 271 - 1444; Fax: (414) 665 - 2463; TF: (800) 323 - 7033

SCHLUTER, Kathleen H. — Tel: (414) 271 - 1444; Fax: (414) 665 - 2463; TF: (800) 323 - 7033

SWEET, Frederic H.
Senior V. President, Government Relations — Tel: (414) 271 - 1444; Fax: (414) 665 - 2463; TF: (800) 323 - 7033

TOWELL, Jean
Media Contact
jeantowell@northwesternmutual.com — Tel: (414) 271 - 1444; Fax: (414) 665 - 2463; TF: (800) 323 - 7033

WHITE, W. Ward
V. President, Corporate Relations — Tel: (414) 665 - 2075; Fax: (414) 665 - 2463; TF: (800) 323 - 7033

YOUNGMAN, Michael L.
V. President, Government Relations — Tel: (414) 665 - 1891; Fax: (414) 665 - 5756; TF: (800) 323 - 7033

NorthWestern Public Service

See listing on page 355 under NorthWestern Corp.

Norwest Corp.

See listing on page 516 under Wells Fargo & Co.

Novartis Corporation

A member of the Public Affairs Council. CIBA-GEIGY and Sandoz merged to form Novartis, a healthcare company.

www.novartis.com

Main Headquarters
Mailing: 608 Fifth Ave.
New York, NY 10020 — Tel: (212) 307 - 1122

Washington Office
Mailing: 701 Pennsylvania Ave. NW
Suite 725
Washington, DC 20004 — Tel: (202) 638 - 7429; Fax: (202) 628 - 4763

Political Action Committees

Novartis Corp. PAC (Novartis PAC)
Contact: Dan P. Casserly
701 Pennsylvania Ave. NW
Suite 725
Washington, DC 20004 — Tel: (202) 638 - 7429; Fax: (202) 628 - 4763

Contributions to Candidates: $99,247 (01/05 - 09/05)

Novartis Corporation

* continued from previous page

Democrats: $25,425; Republicans: $73,822.

Principal Recipients

SENATE DEMOCRATS		HOUSE DEMOCRATS	
Kennedy, Ted (MA)	$2,000	Menendez, Robert (NJ)	$5,000
SENATE REPUBLICANS		**HOUSE REPUBLICANS**	
Dewine, Richard (OH)	$3,500	Blunt, Roy (MO)	$5,000
Hatch, Orrin (UT)	$2,000	DeLay, Tom (TX)	$5,000
		Price, Thomas (GA)	$3,000
		Barton, Joe L (TX)	$2,500
		Bonilla, Henry (TX)	$2,500
		Deal, Nathan (GA)	$2,500
		Johnson, Nancy (CT)	$2,500
		Norwood, Charles (GA)	$2,500
		Thomas, William M (CA)	$2,500
		Frelinghuysen, Rod (NJ)	$2,000
		Hart, Melissa (PA)	$2,000
		Shimkus, John (IL)	$2,000

Corporate Foundations and Giving Programs

Novartis US Foundation
Contact: Cameron Scott
608 Fifth Ave.
New York, NY 10020
Tel: (212) 830 - 2431
Fax: (212) 246 - 0185

Annual Grant Total: none reported
Primary Interests: Education

Public Affairs and Related Activities Personnel

At Headquarters

JONES, Sheldon
V. President, Corporate Communications
sheldon.jones@group.novartis.com
Tel: (212) 830 - 2457
Fax: (212) 246 - 0185

SCOTT, Cameron
Foundation Contact
Tel: (212) 830 - 2431
Fax: (212) 246 - 0185

TAMIR, Ronen
V. President, Investor Relations
Tel: (212) 830 - 2433
Fax: (212) 830 - 2405

At Washington Office

BLANCHARD, Brenda
Vice President, Public Affairs
Tel: (202) 638 - 7429
Fax: (202) 628 - 4763

BUMBAUGH, Deborah M.
Director, Federal Government Relations
deborah.bumbaugh@group.novartis.com
Registered Federal Lobbyist.
Tel: (202) 638 - 7429
Fax: (202) 628 - 4763

CASSERLY, Dan P.
Director, Federal Government Relations
dan.casserly@group.novartis.com
Registered Federal Lobbyist.
Tel: (202) 638 - 7429
Fax: (202) 628 - 4763

DRAKE, David P.
Exec. Director, Federal Government Relations
david.drake@group.novartis.com
Registered Federal Lobbyist.
Tel: (202) 638 - 7429
Fax: (202) 628 - 4764

ELKIN, James R.
V. President, Federal Government Relations
Registered Federal Lobbyist.
Tel: (202) 638 - 7429
Fax: (202) 628 - 4763

GILES, Tom
Exec. Director, Federal Government Relations
Tel: (202) 638 - 7429
Fax: (202) 628 - 4763

HALLER, Sarah E.
Exec. Director, International and Public Affairs
tracy.haller@group.novartis.com
Registered Federal Lobbyist.
Tel: (202) 638 - 7429
Fax: (202) 628 - 4763

At Other Offices

BONER, Barbara
Associate Director, Government Affairs
(Novartis Pharmaceuticals Corp.)
5970 Rain Dance Trail
Littleton, CO 80125
Tel: (303) 948 - 7319
Fax: (303) 948 - 7325

BRASHEAR, Denise
Associate Director, Public Relations
(Novartis Pharmaceuticals Corp.)
One Health Plaza
East Hanover, NJ 07936
Tel: (862) 778 - 7336
Fax: (862) 644 - 8585

FRABLE, Anna
Exec. Director, Public Relations
(Novartis Pharmaceuticals Corp.)
One Health Plaza
East Hanover, NJ 07936
anna.frable@pharma.novartis.com
Tel: (862) 778 - 5388
Fax: (862) 644 - 8585

GRAHAM, Ron
Manager, Business Relations
(Novartis Pharmaceuticals Corp.)
1311 Granite Creek Dr.
Bluesprings, MO 64015
Tel: (816) 228 - 5741
Fax: (816) 224 - 0393

HUMPHREY, Megan
Associate Director, Public Relations
(Novartis Pharmaceuticals Corp.)
One Health Plaza
East Hanover, NJ 07936
Tel: (862) 778 - 6724
Fax: (862) 644 - 8585

JOHNSON-DAVIS, Sara L.
Associate Director, State Government Affairs
(Novartis Pharmaceuticals Corp.)
560 Bloomfield Ave.
Bloomfield, CT 06002
Tel: (860) 286 - 0042
Fax: (860) 286 - 8926

JONES, Tom
Exec. Director, Public Relations
(Novartis Pharmaceuticals Corp.)
One Health Plaza
East Hanover, NJ 07936
tom.jones@pharma.novartis.com
Tel: (862) 778 - 3772
Fax: (862) 644 - 8585

KING, Kate
Associate Director, Public Relations
(Novartis Pharmaceuticals Corp.)
One Health Plaza
East Hanover, NJ 07936
kate.king@pharma.novartis.com
Tel: (862) 778 - 5588
Fax: (862) 644 - 8585

KNAPP, Rick
Head, State Government Affairs and Health Policy
59 Route Ten
Mailstop: Bldg. 404/306
East Hanover, NJ 07936
Tel: (862) 778 - 8421

LANDY, Christine
Associate Director, Public Relations
(Novartis Pharmaceuticals Corp.)
One Health Plaza
East Hanover, NJ 07936
christine.landy@pharma.novartis.com
Tel: (862) 778 - 8026
Fax: (862) 644 - 8585

LAVERTY, Bob
V. President, Communications
(Novartis Pharmaceuticals Corp.)
One Health Plaza
East Hanover, NJ 07936
bob.laverty@pharma.novartis.com
Tel: (862) 778 - 3564
Fax: (862) 644 - 8585

LONG, Margaret
Director, Government Affairs
822 Salem Dr.
Ballston Spa, NY 12020
Tel: (518) 885 - 8415
Fax: (518) 884 - 8045

LOWREY, Lon
Director, Government Affairs
16606 Jamestown Forest Dr.
Florissant, MO 63034
Tel: (314) 355 - 9631
Fax: (314) 355 - 9635

MITCHELL, Steven A.
Associate Director, Government Affairs
(Novartis Pharmaceuticals Corp.)
3901 Elmswick Ct.
Apex, NC 27502
Tel: (919) 662 - 3889
Fax: (919) 662 - 3217

MORGAN, Gina
Exec. Director, Public Relations
(Novartis Pharmaceuticals Corp.)
One Health Plaza
East Hanover, NJ 07936
Tel: (862) 778 - 5567
Fax: (862) 644 - 8585

MORGAN, Jim
Senior Associate Director, Government Affairs
1121 L St., Suite 211
Sacramento, CA 95814
Tel: (916) 442 - 7288
Fax: (916) 442 - 7293

STECHER, Don
Manager, Government Affairs
(Novartis Pharmaceuticals Corp.)
3826 Rivers Edge Dr.
Lake Oswego, OR 97034
Tel: (503) 638 - 5101
Fax: (503) 638 - 5202

STONE, Gloria
Director, Global Public Relations
(Novartis Pharmaceuticals Corp.)
One Health Plaza
East Hanover, NJ 07936
Tel: (862) 778 - 5587
Fax: (862) 644 - 8585

TAYLOR, Norman
Associate Director, Government Affairs
2570 Hunter Green Ct. SE
Grand Rapids, MI 49546
Tel: (616) 954 - 1738
Fax: (616) 954 - 1879

URBAS, Carrie
Associate Director, Public Relations
(Novartis Pharmaceuticals Corp.)
One Health Plaza
East Hanover, NJ 07936
Tel: (862) 778 - 7062
Fax: (862) 644 - 8585

Novartis Pharmaceuticals Corp.

See listing on page 355 under Novartis Corporation.

Novell, Inc.

A manufacturer of computer software and hardware.

www.novell.com
Annual Revenues: $1.04 billion

Chairman and Chief Exec. Officer
MESSMAN, Jack L. — Tel: (781) 464 - 8000; Fax: (781) 464 - 8100; TF: (800) 861 - 7000

Main Headquarters
Mailing: 404 Wyman St.
Suite 500
Waltham, MA 02451 — Tel: (781) 464 - 8000; Fax: (781) 464 - 8100

Corporate Foundations and Giving Programs

Novell Corporate Giving Program
Contact: Cheryl Pagan
404 Wyman St.
Suite 500
Waltham, MA 02451 — Tel: (781) 464 - 8000; Fax: (781) 464 - 8100

Annual Grant Total: none reported

Public Affairs and Related Activities Personnel

At Headquarters

CAPONE, Kerry
Coordinator, Public Relations
kerry.capone@novell.com — Tel: (781) 464 - 8042; Fax: (781) 464 - 8100

FRIEDMAN, Alan J.
Senior V. President, People
alan.friedman@novell.com — Tel: (781) 464 - 8000; Fax: (781) 464 - 8100

PAGAN, Cheryl
Foundation Contact — Tel: (781) 464 - 8000; Fax: (781) 464 - 8100

SMITH, Bill
V. President, Investor Relations
wsmith@novell.com — Tel: (781) 464 - 8052; Fax: (781) 464 - 8100

At Other Offices

LOWRY, Bruce
Director, Global Public Relations
2211 N. First St.
San Jose, CA 95131
blowry@novell.com — Tel: (415) 383 - 8408

NSTAR

A public utility holding company.

www.nstaronline.com
Annual Revenues: $3.5 billion

Chairman, President and Chief Exec. Officer
MAY, Thomas J. — Tel: (617) 424 - 2000; Fax: (617) 424 - 2523

Main Headquarters
Mailing: One NSTAR Way
Westwood, MA 02090 — Tel: (617) 424 - 2000; Fax: (617) 424 - 2523

Political Action Committees

NSTAR Advocates of a Better Congress
Contact: Mark L. Reed
One NSTAR Way
Westwood, MA 02090 — Tel: (617) 424 - 2000; Fax: (617) 424 - 2736

Contributions to Candidates: $1,000 (01/05 - 09/05)
Democrats: $1,000.

Principal Recipients

SENATE DEMOCRATS

HOUSE DEMOCRATS
Lynch, Stephen (MA) $1,000

Corporate Foundations and Giving Programs

NSTAR Foundation
Contact: Ann Marie Walsh
One NSTAR Way
Westwood, MA 02090 — Tel: (617) 424 - 2000; Fax: (617) 424 - 2523

Annual Grant Total: none reported
Geographic Preference: Area(s) in which the company operates
Primary Interests: Economic Development; Youth Services

Public Affairs and Related Activities Personnel

At Headquarters

LEMBO, Philip J.
Assistant Treasurer, Corporate Finance and Investor Relations
philip_lembo@nstaronline.com — Tel: (617) 424 - 3562; Fax: (617) 424 - 4032

MANNING, Tim
Senior V. President, Human Resources — Tel: (617) 424 - 2000; Fax: (617) 424 - 2523

MCKENNA, Christina
Media Contact
christina_mckenna@nstaronline.com — Tel: (617) 424 - 2107; Fax: (617) 424 - 2523

NOLAN, Joseph R., Jr.
Senior V. President, Customer and Corporate Relations
Mailstop: M/S P1700
joseph_nolan@nstaronline.com — Tel: (617) 424 - 2446; Fax: (617) 424 - 2523

REED, Mark L.
Director, Public Affairs
mark_reed@nstaronline.com — Tel: (617) 424 - 2000; Fax: (617) 424 - 2736

WALSH, Ann Marie
NSTAR Foundation Contact — Tel: (617) 424 - 2000; Fax: (617) 424 - 2523

At Other Offices

GAVIN, John F.
Manager, Investor Relations
151 University Ave.
Westwood, MA 02090 — Tel: (781) 441 - 8338; Fax: (781) 441 - 8013

NORTON, Margaret
Director, Corporate Communications
800 Boylston St.
Boston, MA 02199-8003
margaret_norton@nstaronline.com — Tel: (617) 424 - 2490; Fax: (617) 424 - 2736

Nu Horizons Electronics Corp.

Manufactures and distributes electronic components.

www.nuhorizons.com

Chairman, President and Chief Exec. Officer
NADATA, Arthur
anadata@nuhorizons.com — Tel: (631) 396 - 5000; Fax: (631) 696 - 5050

Main Headquarters
Mailing: 70 Maxess Rd.
Melville, NY 11747 — Tel: (631) 396 - 5000; Fax: (631) 696 - 5050

Corporate Foundations and Giving Programs

Nu Horizons Corporate Giving
Contact: John Antonucci
70 Maxess Rd.
Melville, NY 11747 — Tel: (631) 396 - 5000 Ext: 304; Fax: (631) 696 - 5050

Annual Grant Total: none reported

Public Affairs and Related Activities Personnel

At Headquarters

ANTONUCCI, John
Controller
jantonucci@nuhorizons.com — Tel: (631) 396 - 5000 Ext: 304; Fax: (631) 696 - 5050
Responsibilities include corporate philanthropy.

DURANDO, Paul
V. President, Finance
pdurando@nuhorizons.com — Tel: (631) 396 - 5000 Ext: 300; Fax: (631) 696 - 5050
Responsibilities include investor relations.

GIVNER, Elaine
V. President, Human Resources and Training Development
egivner@nuhorizons.com — Tel: (631) 396 - 5000; Fax: (631) 696 - 5050

WISCHHUSEN, John
Director, Marketing Communications
jwischhusen@nuhorizons.com — Tel: (631) 396 - 5000 Ext: 125; Fax: (631) 396 - 7576

Nu Skin Enterprises

A distributor of cosmetics, vitamins, hair care products and personal care products.

www.nuskinenterprises.com
Annual Revenues: $1.14 billion

Chairman of the Board
RONEY, Blake M.
broney@nuskin.net — Tel: (801) 345 - 1000; Fax: (801) 345 - 1099

President and Chief Exec. Officer
HUNT, M. Truman — Tel: (801) 345 - 1000; Fax: (801) 345 - 2799

Main Headquarters
Mailing: One Nu Skin Plaza
75 W. Center St.
Provo, UT 84601 — Tel: (801) 345 - 1000; Fax: (801) 345 - 2799

Corporate Foundations and Giving Programs

Force for Good Foundation
Contact: John Petersen

Nu Skin Enterprises

* continued from previous page

One Nu Skin Plaza — Tel: (801) 345 - 2104
75 W. Center St. — Fax: (801) 345 - 2799
Provo, UT 84601

Annual Grant Total: none reported

More information about the foundation is available from their website: www.forceforgood.org.
Geographic Preference: International
Primary Interests: Child Welfare; Environment/Conservation

Public Affairs and Related Activities Personnel

At Headquarters

AVERETT, Claire H. — Tel: (801) 345 - 1000
V. President, Human Resources — Fax: (801) 345 - 2799

HARTVIGSEN, Rich M. — Tel: (801) 345 - 1000
V. President, Global Regulatory Affairs — Fax: (801) 345 - 2799

PETERSEN, John — Tel: (801) 345 - 2104
Director, Public Relations — Fax: (801) 345 - 2799
jpeterse@nuskin.com
Responsibilities include corporate contributions.

SCHNECK, Kara L. — Tel: (801) 345 - 2116
Senior Director, Global Public Relations — Fax: (801) 345 - 2199
kschneck@nuskin.net

Nucor Corp.

A steel product manufacturer. Acquired the assets of Birmingham Steel Corp. in December, 2002.
www.nucor.com
Annual Revenues: $4.139 billion

Chairman of the Board — Tel: (704) 366 - 7000
BROWNING, Peter C. — Fax: (704) 362 - 4208

V. Chairman, President and Chief Exec. Officer — Tel: (704) 366 - 7000
DIMICCO, Daniel R. — Fax: (704) 362 - 4208
ddimicco@nucor.com

Main Headquarters
Mailing: 2100 Rexford Rd. — Tel: (704) 366 - 7000
Charlotte, NC 28211 — Fax: (704) 362 - 4208

Political Action Committees

Nucor Corp. Political Action Committee
Contact: A. Rae Eagle
2100 Rexford Rd. — Tel: (704) 366 - 7000
Charlotte, NC 28211 — Fax: (704) 362 - 4208

Contributions to Candidates: $33,000 (01/05 - 09/05)
Democrats: $7,000; Republicans: $26,000.

Principal Recipients

SENATE DEMOCRATS		HOUSE DEMOCRATS	
Durbin, Richard J (IL)	$1,000	Berry, Marion (AR)	$1,000
Nelson, Benjamin (NE)	$1,000	Clyburn, James (SC)	$1,000
		Connealy, Matthew (NE)	$1,000
		Cramer, Bud (AL)	$1,000
		Spratt, John (SC)	$1,000

SENATE REPUBLICANS		HOUSE REPUBLICANS	
Hatch, Orrin (UT)	$5,000	Myrick, Sue (NC)	$3,500
Lott, Trent (MS)	$2,000	English, Philip S (PA)	$2,000
Santorum, Richard (PA)	$2,000	Bachus, Spencer (AL)	$1,000
Bennett, Robert F (UT)	$1,000	Brown, Henry (SC)	$1,000
Graham, Lindsey (SC)	$1,000	Buyer, Steve (IN)	$1,000
		Foxx, Virginia (NC)	$1,000
		Hayes, Robert (NC)	$1,000
		Kuhl, John R Jr (NY)	$1,000
		Regula, Ralph S (OH)	$1,000
		Wilson, Joe (SC)	$1,000

Corporate Foundations and Giving Programs

Nucor Corporation Corporate Contributions Program
Contact: James M. Coblin
2100 Rexford Rd. — Tel: (704) 366 - 7000
Charlotte, NC 28211 — Fax: (704) 362 - 4208

Annual Grant Total: none reported

Public Affairs and Related Activities Personnel

At Headquarters

COBLIN, James M. — Tel: (704) 366 - 7000
V. President, Human Resources — Fax: (704) 362 - 4208
jcoblin@nucor.com
Responsibilities include corporate philanthropy and communications.

EAGLE, A. Rae — Tel: (704) 366 - 7000
PAC Treasurer and Corporate Secretary — Fax: (704) 362 - 4208

NUI Corp.

See listing on page 12 under AGL Resources, Inc.

NVIDIA Corp.

Manufacturer of advanced computer graphics and software.
www.nvidia.com

Chief Exec. Officer, President and Co-Founder — Tel: (408) 486 - 2000
HUANG, Jen-Hsun — Fax: (408) 486 - 2200

Main Headquarters
Mailing: 2701 San Tomas Exwy. — Tel: (408) 486 - 2000
Santa Clara, CA 95050 — Fax: (408) 486 - 2200

Corporate Foundations and Giving Programs

Corporate Donations and Fundraising Program
2701 San Tomas Exwy. — Tel: (408) 486 - 2000
Santa Clara, CA 95050 — Fax: (408) 486 - 2200

Annual Grant Total: none reported

Primary Interests: Arts and Humanities; Historic Preservation
Recent Recipients: American Red Cross; Humane Soc. of the U.S., The; Second Harvest

Public Affairs and Related Activities Personnel

At Headquarters

COLE, Calisa — Tel: (408) 486 - 6263
Director, Corporate Communications — Fax: (408) 486 - 2200
ccole@nvidia.com

HARA, Michael — Tel: (408) 486 - 2511
V. President, Investor Relations and Communications — Fax: (408) 486 - 2200
mhara@nvidia.com

PEREZ, Derek — Tel: (408) 486 - 2512
Director, Public Relations — Fax: (408) 486 - 4512
dperez@nvidia.com

WINSTON, Michael — Tel: (408) 486 - 2000
V. President, Human Resources — Fax: (408) 486 - 2200

NVR, Inc.

Specializes in homebuilding and financial services.
www.nvrinc.com

Chairman of the Board — Tel: (703) 761 - 2000
SCHAR, Dwight C. — Fax: (703) 761 - 2030

Chief Exec. Officer — Tel: (703) 761 - 2000
SAVILLE, Paul C. — Fax: (703) 761 - 2030

Main Headquarters
Mailing: 7601 Lewinsville Rd., Suite 300 — Tel: (703) 761 - 2000
McLean, VA 22102 — Fax: (703) 761 - 2030

Public Affairs and Related Activities Personnel

At Headquarters

MALZAHN, Dan — Tel: (703) 761 - 2137
Investor Relations Contact — Fax: (703) 761 - 2030

PAUL, Robert — Tel: (703) 761 - 2251
Senior V. President, Human Resources — Fax: (703) 761 - 2030

NW Natural

A natural gas utility.
www.nwnatural.com

Chairman of the Board — Tel: (503) 226 - 4211
WOOLWORTH, Richard — Fax: (503) 721 - 2508

Chief Exec. Officer — Tel: (503) 226 - 4211
DODSON, Mark — Fax: (503) 220 - 2584

Main Headquarters
Mailing: 220 NW Second Ave. — Tel: (503) 226 - 4211
Portland, OR 97209-3991 — Fax: (503) 721 - 2508

Political Action Committees

NW Natural PAC
Contact: Gary Bauer
220 NW Second Ave. — Tel: (503) 220 - 2431
Portland, OR 97209-3991 — Fax: (503) 721 - 2508

Contributions to Candidates: $1,125 (01/05 - 09/05)
Democrats: $125; Republicans: $1,000.

Principal Recipients

SENATE REPUBLICANS		HOUSE REPUBLICANS
Smith, Gordon (OR)	$1,000	

Corporate Foundations and Giving Programs

NW Natural Philanthropy Program
Contact: Von Summers

NW Natural

* continued from previous page

220 NW Second Ave.
Portland, OR 97209-3991
Tel: (503) 226 - 4211
Ext: 2348
Fax: (503) 721 - 2508

Annual Grant Total: $750,000 - $1,000,000

In addition to their primary interests, focuses on three major areas: affordable housing, quality of education, and quality of life/protection of the environment.

Primary Interests: Civic and Cultural Activities; Economic Development; Education; Environment/Conservation; Health and Human Services

Public Affairs and Related Activities Personnel

At Headquarters

BAUER, Gary
Manager, Government Relations
Responsibilities include political action.
Tel: (503) 220 - 2431
Fax: (503) 721 - 2508

DOOLITTLE, Lee Ann
V. President, Human Resources and Administrative Services
lad@nwnatural.com
Tel: (503) 226 - 4211
Fax: (503) 721 - 2584

HART, Sandra
Director, Environmental Services
Tel: (503) 226 - 4211
Fax: (503) 721 - 2508

HESS, Robert S.
Director, Investor Relations
Tel: (503) 226 - 4211
Fax: (503) 721 - 2508

KANTOR, Gregg
Senior V. President, Public Affairs and Communication
Tel: (503) 220 - 2425
Fax: (503) 220 - 2584

SECHRIST, Steve
Senior Specialist, Public Relations
sms@nwnatural.com
Tel: (503) 226 - 4211
Ext: 3517
Fax: (503) 721 - 2508

SUMMERS, Von
Contact, NW Natural Philanthropy Program
Tel: (503) 226 - 4211
Ext: 2348
Fax: (503) 721 - 2508

Occidental Chemical Corp.

A subsidiary of the Occidental Petroleum Corp. (see separate listing). The Washington, DC government relations office operates under the name of Occidental Internat'l and is shared by Occidental Chemical and Occidental Petroleum. (See the Occidental Internat'l listing for more information on this company's federal government affairs activities and personnel.)

www.oxychem.com

Annual Revenues: $3.092 bilion

Main Headquarters

Mailing: 5005 LBJ Fwy.
Dallas, TX 75244
Tel: (972) 404 - 3800
Fax: (972) 404 - 3669
TF: (800) 578 - 8880

Washington Office

Mailing: 1717 Pennsylvania Ave. NW
Suite 400
Washington, DC 20006
Tel: (202) 857 - 3000
Fax: (202) 857 - 3014

Public Affairs and Related Activities Personnel

At Headquarters

DILLINGHAM, Deborah
Communications and Community Affairs
deborah_dillingham@oxy.com
Tel: (972) 404 - 3800
Fax: (972) 404 - 3906
TF: (800) 578 - 8880

DOUCET, Jodie
V. President, Human Resources
Tel: (972) 404 - 3800
Fax: (972) 404 - 3669
TF: (800) 578 - 8880

DYKERS, Bill
Director, Communications and Web Development
Tel: (972) 404 - 3800
Fax: (972) 404 - 3669
TF: (800) 578 - 8880

KEMP, Steve B.
V. President, Health Environment and Safety
Tel: (972) 404 - 3800
Fax: (972) 404 - 3669
TF: (800) 578 - 8880

STUART, John H.
V. President, Public and Government Affairs
john_stuart@oxy.com
Tel: (972) 404 - 3800
Fax: (972) 404 - 3669
TF: (800) 578 - 8880

At Washington Office

HASSETT, Jace
V. President, Government Affairs
Registered Federal Lobbyist.
Tel: (202) 857 - 3000
Fax: (202) 857 - 3014

At Other Offices

MOORE, Julie W.
Manager - Texas State Government Affairs
604 W. 14th St.
Austin, TX 78701
julie_moore@oxy.com
Tel: (512) 476 - 2245
Fax: (512) 473 - 8476

Occidental Internat'l

The Washington, DC-based government affairs office shared by Occidental Petroleum and Occidental Chemical. More information about Occidental Internat'l is available from the parent company's website: www.oxy.com.

Main Headquarters

Mailing: 1717 Pennsylvania Ave. NW
Suite 400
Washington, DC 20006
Tel: (202) 857 - 3000
Fax: (202) 857 - 3030

Public Affairs and Related Activities Personnel

At Headquarters

COLLINS, William A.
Director, Health, Environment and Safety, Regulatory Affairs
al_collins@oxy.com
Tel: (202) 857 - 3051
Fax: (202) 857 - 3070

DAVIS, Ian M.
V. President, International Affairs
ian_davis@oxy.com
Tel: (202) 857 - 3041
Fax: (202) 857 - 3014

FETAPUTTER, Christopher M.
Government Affairs Associate
Tel: (202) 857 - 3074
Fax: (202) 857 - 3030

HASSETT, Jace
V. President, Government Affairs-Chemicals
jace_hassett@oxy.com
Tel: (202) 857 - 3047
Fax: (202) 857 - 3070

MCGEE, Robert M.
Vice President
Tel: (202) 857 - 3000
Fax: (202) 857 - 3030

MCPHEE, Gerald T.
Senior V. President, Federal Relations
jerry_mcphee@oxy.com
Tel: (202) 857 - 3038
Fax: (202) 857 - 3014

Occidental Oil and Gas Corp.

See listing on page 359 under Occidental Petroleum Corp.

Occidental Petroleum Corp.

Occidental Petroleum Corp. is engaged primarily in oil and gas exploration, development, production and sales, both domestically and internationally. The company also conducts operations in chemicals and natural gas transmission. Occidental Petroleum and Occidental Chemical share a Washington, DC government relations office, which operates under the name of Occidental Internat'l (see separate listing).

www.oxy.com

Annual Revenues: $13.985 billion

Chairman and Chief Exec. Officer
IRANI, Dr. Ray R.
Tel: (310) 208 - 8800
Fax: (310) 443 - 6690

Main Headquarters

Mailing: 10889 Wilshire Blvd.
Los Angeles, CA 90024
Tel: (310) 208 - 8800
Fax: (310) 443 - 6690

Washington Office

Mailing: 1717 Pennsylvania Ave., N.W., Suite 400
Washington, DC 20006
Tel: (202) 857 - 3000
Fax: (202) 857 - 3030

Political Action Committees

Occidental Petroleum Corp. PAC
Contact: Samuel Dominick, Jr.
10889 Wilshire Blvd.
Los Angeles, CA 90024
Tel: (310) 208 - 8800
Fax: (310) 443 - 6690

Contributions to Candidates: $99,500 (01/05 - 09/05)

Democrats: $10,000; Republicans: $88,500; Other: $1,000.

Principal Recipients

SENATE DEMOCRATS

Carper, Thomas R (DE)	$2,000

SENATE REPUBLICANS

Vitter, David (LA)	$2,500
Burns, Conrad (MT)	$2,000
Domenici, Pete (NM)	$2,000
Kyl, Jon L (AZ)	$2,000
Talent, James (MO)	$2,000

HOUSE DEMOCRATS

Melancon, Charlie (LA)	$2,000

HOUSE REPUBLICANS

Barton, Joe L (TX)	$4,000
Thomas, William M (CA)	$4,000
Blunt, Roy (MO)	$2,500
DeLay, Tom (TX)	$2,500
Gibbons, James A (NV)	$2,000
LaTourette, Steve (OH)	$2,000
Marchant, Kenny (TX)	$2,000
Pearce, Steve (NM)	$2,000
Pombo, Richard (CA)	$2,000
Sessions, Pete (TX)	$2,000
Whitfield, Ed (KY)	$2,000

Corporate Foundations and Giving Programs

Occidental Petroleum Corp. Social Responsibility
Contact: Christel Pauli

Occidental Petroleum Corp.

* continued from previous page

10889 Wilshire Blvd.
Los Angeles, CA 90024
Tel: (310) 208 - 8800
Fax: (310) 443 - 6690

Annual Grant Total: $500,000 - $750,000
Geographic Preference: Area(s) in which the company operates
Primary Interests: Arts and Culture; Education

Public Affairs and Related Activities Personnel

At Headquarters

DOMINICK, Samuel, Jr.
PAC Treasurer
Tel: (310) 208 - 8800
Fax: (310) 443 - 6690

HALLOCK, Richard W.
Exec. V. President, Human Resources
Tel: (310) 443 - 6537
Fax: (310) 443 - 6690

MERIAGE, Lawrence P.
V. President, Corporate Communications and Public Affairs
(Occidental Oil and Gas Corp.)
Tel: (310) 443 - 6562
Fax: (310) 443 - 6246

PAULI, Christel
Assistant Secretary, Occidental Petroleum Corp. Social Responsibility
Tel: (310) 208 - 8800
Fax: (310) 443 - 6690

At Washington Office

MCGEE, Robert M.
President
Registered Federal Lobbyist.
Responsibilities include government affairs.
Tel: (202) 857 - 3011
Fax: (202) 857 - 3030

MCPHEE, Gerald T.
Senior V. President, Federal Relations
Tel: (202) 857 - 3000
Fax: (202) 857 - 3030

At Other Offices

HUFFMAN, Kenneth J.
V. President, Investor Relations
1230 Ave. of the Americas
New York, NY 10020
investorrelations_newyork@oxy.com
Tel: (212) 603 - 8111

Ocean Energy

See listing on page 157 under Devon Energy Corp.

Ocean Spray Cranberries, Inc.

A processor of fruit products.
www.oceanspray.com
Annual Revenues: $1.3 billion

Chairman of the Board
ROSBE, Robert L., Jr.
Tel: (508) 946 - 1000
Fax: (508) 946 - 7704
TF: (800) 662 - 3263

Chief Exec. Officer
PAPADELLIS, Randy C.
Tel: (508) 946 - 1000
Fax: (508) 946 - 7704
TF: (800) 662 - 3263

Main Headquarters
Mailing: One Ocean Spray Dr.
Lakeville-Middleboro, MA 02349
Tel: (508) 946 - 1000
Fax: (508) 946 - 7704
TF: (800) 662 - 3263

Political Action Committees

Ocean Spray Cranberries, Inc. PAC
Contact: Karen DiGloria
One Ocean Spray Dr.
Lakeville-Middleboro, MA 02349
Tel: (508) 946 - 1000
Fax: (508) 946 - 7704
TF: (800) 662 - 3263

Contributions to Candidates: $1,500 (01/05 - 09/05)
Democrats: $1,000; Republicans: $500.

Principal Recipients

SENATE DEMOCRATS
Kennedy, Ted (MA) $1,000

HOUSE DEMOCRATS

SENATE REPUBLICANS

HOUSE REPUBLICANS
Lewis, Jerry (CA) $500

Public Affairs and Related Activities Personnel

At Headquarters

DIGLORIA, Karen
PAC Treasurer
kdigloria@oceanspray.com
Tel: (508) 946 - 1000
Fax: (508) 946 - 7704
TF: (800) 662 - 3263

NEWCOMB, Sharon
Public Relations Specialist, Marketing Public Relations
snewcomb@oceanspray.com
Tel: (508) 946 - 7185
Fax: (508) 946 - 7704
TF: (800) 662 - 3263

PERRY, Denise
Corporate Communications Contact
dperry@oceanspray.com
Tel: (508) 946 - 7634
Fax: (508) 946 - 7704
TF: (800) 662 - 3263

PHILLIPS, Christopher R.
Manager, Corporate Communications and Public Affairs
cphillips@oceanspray.com
Tel: (508) 946 - 7318
Fax: (508) 947 - 9791
TF: (800) 662 - 3263

Office Depot, Inc.

A member of the Public Affairs Council. An office supply operator.
www.officedepot.com
Annual Revenues: $12.4 billion

Chairman and Chief Exec. Officer
ODLAND, Steve
Tel: (561) 438 - 4800
Fax: (561) 438 - 4400

Main Headquarters
Mailing: 2200 Old Germantown Rd.
Delray Beach, FL 33445
Tel: (561) 438 - 4800
Fax: (561) 438 - 4400

Corporate Foundations and Giving Programs

Office Depot Foundation
2200 Old Germantown Rd.
Delray Beach, FL 33445
Tel: (561) 438 - 4800
Fax: (561) 438 - 4400

Annual Grant Total: none reported
Recent Recipients: American Red Cross

Public Affairs and Related Activities Personnel

At Headquarters

KRAMER, Mindy
Manager, Public Relations
Tel: (561) 438 - 4800
Fax: (561) 438 - 4400

LEVINE, Brian
Director, Public Relations
Tel: (561) 438 - 2895
Fax: (561) 438 - 4400

SCRUGGS, Frank
Exec. V. President, Human Resources
Tel: (561) 438 - 4800
Fax: (561) 438 - 4400

THARPE, Ray
Director, Investor Relations
rthorpe@officedepot.com
Tel: (561) 438 - 4800
Fax: (561) 438 - 4400

OfficeMax, Inc.

See listing on page 85 under Boise Cascade Corp.

OGE Energy Corp.

The holding company for Oklahoma Gas and Electric Co. and Enogex, Inc.
www.oge.com
Annual Revenues: $3.023 billion

Chairman, Chief Exec. Officer and President
MOORE, Steve E.
Mailstop: M/C 1100
Tel: (405) 553 - 3203
Fax: (405) 553 - 3760

Main Headquarters
Mailing: P.O. Box 321
Oklahoma City, OK 73101-0321
Street: 321 N. Harvey
Oklahoma City, OK 73102
Tel: (405) 553 - 3000

Political Action Committees

O G and E Employees PAC
Contact: Paul Renfrow
P.O. Box 321
Oklahoma City, OK 73101-0321
Tel: (405) 553 - 3287
Fax: (405) 553 - 3760

Contributions to Candidates: none reported (01/05 - 09/05)

Public Affairs and Related Activities Personnel

At Headquarters

ALFORD, Brian
Manager, Corporate Communications and Community Relations
Mailstop: M/C 1200
Tel: (405) 553 - 3187
Fax: (405) 553 - 3290

CLEMENTS, Richard
Manager, Economic Development
Mailstop: M/C 206
Responsibilities include community affairs.
Tel: (405) 553 - 3974
Fax: (405) 553 - 3838

GOEBEL, Summer
Manager, Environment Health and Safety
Mailstop: M/C 506
Tel: (405) 553 - 3523

HENNESY, Dale
Director, Human Resources
Mailstop: M/C 1000
Tel: (405) 553 - 3484

KILBY, Don
Coordinator, Shareowner Relations
Tel: (405) 553 - 3211

KOENIG, Bob
Manager, Regulatory Affairs
Tel: (405) 553 - 3358

RENFROW, Paul
V. President, Public Affairs
Mailstop: M/C 1111
Tel: (405) 553 - 3287
Fax: (405) 553 - 3760

Oglethorpe Power Corp.

A generation cooperative.

www.opc.com

Chairman of the Board
DENHAM, Benny
Tel: (770) 270 - 7600
Fax: (770) 270 - 7872
TF: (800) 241 - 5374

President and Chief Exec. Officer
SMITH, Thomas A.
Tel: (770) 270 - 7600
Fax: (770) 270 - 7077
TF: (800) 241 - 5374

Main Headquarters
Mailing: P.O. Box 1349
Tucker, GA 30085-1349
Tel: (770) 270 - 7600
Fax: (770) 270 - 7872
TF: (800) 241 - 5374

Street: 2100 E. Exchange Pl.
Tucker, GA 30084

Public Affairs and Related Activities Personnel

At Headquarters

JONES, Greg
Director, Public Relations
Tel: (770) 270 - 7890
Fax: (770) 270 - 7080
TF: (800) 241 - 5374

REUSCH, Jami
V. President, Human Resources
Tel: (770) 270 - 7600
Fax: (770) 270 - 7872
TF: (800) 241 - 5374

STEELE, Robert
V. President, External Affairs
Tel: (770) 270 - 7600
Fax: (770) 270 - 7080
TF: (800) 241 - 5374

Responsibilities include regulatory affairs.

The Ohio Casualty Group

A property and casualty insurance company.

www.ocas.com

Chairman of the Board
PONTIUS, Stanley N.
stanley.pontius@ocas.com
Tel: (513) 603 - 2600
Fax: (513) 609 - 7900
TF: (800) 843 - 6446

President, Chief Exec. Officer
CARMICHAEL, Dan R.
dan.carmichael@ocas.com
Tel: (513) 603 - 2600
Fax: (513) 609 - 7900
TF: (800) 843 - 6446

Main Headquarters
Mailing: 9450 Seward Rd.
Fairfield, OH 45014
Tel: (513) 603 - 2600
Fax: (513) 609 - 7900
TF: (800) 843 - 6446

Corporate Foundations and Giving Programs

Ohio Casualty Corp. Contributions Program
Contact: Cindy L. Denney
9450 Seward Rd.
Fairfield, OH 45014
Tel: (513) 603 - 2074
Fax: (513) 609 - 7900
TF: (800) 843 - 6446

Annual Grant Total: none reported
The company is a long-time partner in the Adopt-A-School program.
Geographic Preference: Area(s) in which the company operates
Recent Recipients: Harvard Medical School; United Way

Public Affairs and Related Activities Personnel

At Headquarters

CRANE, Debra
Senior V. President, Corporate Public Affairs
debra.crane@ocas.com
Tel: (513) 603 - 2600
Fax: (513) 609 - 7900
TF: (800) 843 - 6446

DENNEY, Cindy L.
Assistant V. President, Corporate Communications
cindy.denney@ocas.com
Tel: (513) 603 - 2074
Fax: (513) 609 - 7900
TF: (800) 843 - 6446

MCDANIEL, Dennis E.
V. President, Strategic Planning and Investor Relations
dennis.mcdaniel@ocas.com
Tel: (513) 603 - 2197
Fax: (513) 609 - 7900
TF: (800) 843 - 6446

Oklahoma Natural Gas Co.

See listing on page 363 under ONEOK, Inc.

Olin Corp.

A manufacturer of chemicals, metals, sporting ammunition, electronic materials and services.

www.olin.com
Annual Revenues: $1.6 billion

Chairman, President and Chief Exec. Officer
RUPP, Joseph D.
Tel: (314) 480 - 1400

Main Headquarters
Mailing: 190 Carondelet Plaza
Suite 1530
Clayton, MO 63105-3443
Tel: (314) 480 - 1400

Political Action Committees

Olin Corp. Good Government Fund
Contact: Edward J. Krygier
501 Merritt Seven
Norwalk, CT 06856-4500
Tel: (203) 750 - 3000

Contributions to Candidates: $2,000 (01/05 - 09/05)
Democrats: $1,000; Republicans: $1,000.

Principal Recipients

SENATE DEMOCRATS
Reid, Harry (NV) $500

HOUSE DEMOCRATS
Costello, Jerry F (IL) $500

SENATE REPUBLICANS

HOUSE REPUBLICANS
Wicker, Roger (MS) $1,000

Corporate Foundations and Giving Programs

Olin Corp. Charitable Trust
190 Carondelet Plaza
Suite 1530
Clayton, MO 63105-3443
Tel: (314) 480 - 1400

Annual Grant Total: $2,000,000 - $5,000,000
Geographic Preference: National; Area(s) in which the company operates
Primary Interests: Arts and Culture; Community Affairs; Health and Human Services; Higher Education; Minority Opportunities; Technology; Youth Services
Recent Recipients: University of Missouri

Public Affairs and Related Activities Personnel

At Headquarters

KOSCHE, Peter C.
Senior V. President, Corporate Affairs
pckosche@corp.olin.com
Tel: (314) 480 - 1400

MCGOUGH, Dennis
V. President, Human Resources
Tel: (314) 480 - 1400

At Other Offices

KROMIDAS, Larry P.
Director, Investor and Media Relations
427 N. Shamrock
East Alton, IL 62024
Tel: (618) 258 - 3206

KRYGIER, Edward J.
Treasurer, Olin Corp. Good Government Fund
501 Merritt Seven
Norwalk, CT 06856-4500
ejkrygier@corp.olin.com
Tel: (203) 750 - 3000

OM Group, Inc.

A producer of specialty chemicals.

www.omgi.com
Annual Revenues: $4.9 billion

Chairman of the Board
SCAMINACE, Joseph M. "Joe"
Tel: (216) 781 - 0083
Fax: (216) 781 - 1502
TF: (800) 519 - 0083

Chief Exec. Officer
MOONEY, James P.
Tel: (216) 781 - 0083
Fax: (216) 781 - 1502
TF: (800) 519 - 0083

Main Headquarters
Mailing: 127 Public Square
1500 Key Tower
Cleveland, OH 44114-1221
Tel: (216) 781 - 0083
Fax: (216) 781 - 1502
TF: (800) 519 - 0083

Public Affairs and Related Activities Personnel

At Headquarters

GRIFFITH, Greg
Director, Investor Relations
Tel: (216) 263 - 7455
Fax: (216) 781 - 1502
TF: (800) 519 - 0083

Responsibilities include corporate communications.

Omaha World-Herald Co.

A diversified communications company.

www.omaha.com

Chairman and Chief Exec. Officer
GOTTSCHALK, John
Tel: (402) 444 - 1000
Fax: (402) 348 - 1828

Main Headquarters
Mailing: World-Herald Square
Omaha, NE 68102
Tel: (402) 444 - 1000
Fax: (402) 348 - 1828

Street: 1334 Dodge St.
Omaha, NE 68102

Corporate Foundations and Giving Programs

Omaha World-Herald Foundation
Contact: Donna Grimm

Omaha World-Herald Co.

• continued from previous page

World-Herald Square — Tel: (402) 444 - 1000
Omaha, NE 68102 — Fax: (402) 348 - 1828

Annual Grant Total: none reported
Geographic Preference: Iowa; Nebraska
Primary Interests: Arts and Humanities; Education; Historic Preservation; Social Services; Youth Services

Public Affairs and Related Activities Personnel

At Headquarters

GRIMM, Donna — Tel: (402) 444 - 1000
Administrator, Omaha World-Herald Foundation — Fax: (402) 348 - 1828
grimm@owh.com

LONG, Joel — Tel: (402) 444 - 1493
Director, Public Relations — Fax: (402) 348 - 1828

WALENZ, Nicole — Tel: (402) 444 - 1121
Coordinator, Public Relations — Fax: (402) 348 - 1828

Omega Protein Corporation

An international company primarily involved in marine protein products.
www.omegaproteininc.com

Chairman of the Board — Tel: (713) 623 - 0060
GLAZER, Avram A. — Fax: (713) 940 - 6122

President and Chief Exec. Officer — Tel: (713) 623 - 0060
VON ROSENBERG, Joseph L., III — Fax: (713) 940 - 6122

Main Headquarters
Mailing: 1717 St. James Pl., Suite 550 — Tel: (713) 623 - 0060
Houston, TX 77056 — Fax: (713) 940 - 6122

Political Action Committees

Omega Protein Inc. PAC (Omega-PAC)
Contact: Toby M. Gascon
251 Florida St.
Suite 407
Baton Rouge, LA 70801

Contributions to Candidates: $7,000 (01/05 - 09/05)
Democrats: $1,000; Republicans: $6,000.

Principal Recipients

SENATE DEMOCRATS

HOUSE DEMOCRATS
Melancon, Charlie (LA) $1,000

SENATE REPUBLICANS
Stevens, Ted (AK) $1,000

HOUSE REPUBLICANS
Bonilla, Henry (TX) $2,500
Drake, Thelma Day (VA) $2,500

Public Affairs and Related Activities Personnel

At Headquarters

STOCKTON, Robert — Tel: (713) 623 - 0060
Exec. V. President, Chief Financial Officer and Secretary — Fax: (713) 940 - 6122
Responsibilities include media relations.

At Other Offices

GASCON, Toby M.
Treasurer, Omega-PAC
251 Florida St.
Suite 407
Baton Rouge, LA 70801
Responsibilities include media relations

Omnicare, Inc.

Offers pharmacy and related consulting services to long-term care institutions.
www.omnicare.com

President and Chief Exec. Officer — Tel: (859) 392 - 3300
GEMUNDER, Joel F. — Fax: (859) 392 - 3333

Main Headquarters
Mailing: 1600 River Center II — Tel: (859) 392 - 3300
100 E. River Center Blvd. — Fax: (859) 392 - 3333
Covington, KY 41011

Political Action Committees

Omnicare Inc. PAC
Contact: Tom Marsh
1600 River Center II — Tel: (859) 392 - 3300
100 E. River Center Blvd. — Fax: (859) 392 - 3333
Covington, KY 41011

Contributions to Candidates: none reported (01/05 - 09/05)

Public Affairs and Related Activities Personnel

At Headquarters

HODGES, Cheryl D. — Tel: (859) 392 - 3331
Senior V. President, Secretary, Investor Relations — Fax: (859) 392 - 3333

MARSH, Tom — Tel: (859) 392 - 3300
PAC Treasurer — Fax: (859) 392 - 3333

ROBERTS, J. Michael — Tel: (859) 392 - 3300
V. President, Human Resources — Fax: (859) 392 - 3333

VORDENBAUMEN, Timothy L., Sr. — Tel: (859) 392 - 3300
V. President, Government Affairs — Fax: (859) 392 - 3333

Omnicom Group Inc.

A marketing communications holding company.
www.omnicomgroup.com

Chairman of the Board — Tel: (212) 415 - 3600
CRAWFORD, Bruce — Fax: (212) 415 - 3530

President and Chief Exec. Officer — Tel: (212) 415 - 3600
WREN, John D. — Fax: (212) 415 - 3530

Main Headquarters
Mailing: 437 Madison Ave. — Tel: (212) 415 - 3600
Ninth Floor — Fax: (212) 415 - 3530
New York, NY 10022

Public Affairs and Related Activities Personnel

At Headquarters

CARLEY, Vera — Tel: (212) 415 - 2110
Coordinator, Public Relations — Fax: (212) 415 - 3414
vera.carley@ddb.com

CHIOCCO, Leslie — Tel: (212) 415 - 3605
V. President, Human Resources — Fax: (212) 415 - 3530
leslie_chiocco@omnicom.com

SLOAN, Patricia — Tel: (212) 415 - 2109
Senior V. President and Corporate Director, Public Affairs — Fax: (212) 415 - 3414
pat.sloan@ddb.com

OMNOVA Solutions Inc.

A provider of coatings and specialty chemicals
www.omnova.com
Annual Revenues: $746 million

Chairman, President and Chief Exec. Officer — Tel: (330) 869 - 4200
MCMULLEN, Kevin M. — Fax: (330) 869 - 4288

Main Headquarters
Mailing: 175 Ghent Rd. — Tel: (330) 869 - 4200
Fairlawn, OH 44333-3330 — Fax: (330) 869 - 4288

Political Action Committees

OMNOVA Solutions Inc. PAC (OPAC)
Contact: Jodie L. Litz
175 Ghent Rd. — Tel: (330) 869 - 4200
Fairlawn, OH 44333-3330 — Fax: (330) 869 - 4288

Contributions to Candidates: none reported (01/05 - 09/05)

Corporate Foundations and Giving Programs

OMNOVA Solutions Foundation
Contact: Theresa Carter
175 Ghent Rd. — Tel: (330) 869 - 4200
Fairlawn, OH 44333-3330 — Fax: (330) 869 - 4288

Annual Grant Total: none reported
Geographic Preference: Area(s) in which the company operates
Primary Interests: Education

Public Affairs and Related Activities Personnel

At Headquarters

CARTER, Theresa — Tel: (330) 869 - 4200
Director, OMNOVA Solutions Foundation — Fax: (330) 869 - 4288

HICKS, Michael — Tel: (330) 869 - 4411
Senior V. President and Chief Financial Officer — Fax: (330) 869 - 4288
Responsibilities include investor relations.

LITZ, Jodie L. — Tel: (330) 869 - 4200
Treasurer, OMNOVA Solutions Inc. PAC — Fax: (330) 869 - 4288

NOAH, Sandi — Tel: (330) 869 - 4292
Director, Communications — Fax: (330) 869 - 4288

TROY, Gregory T. — Tel: (330) 869 - 4200
Senior V. President, Human Resources — Fax: (330) 869 - 4288

ON Semiconductor Corp.

www.onsemi.com

Chairman of the Board — Tel: (602) 244 - 6600
MCCRANIE, J. Daniel — Fax: (602) 244 - 4830

ON Semiconductor Corp.

* continued from previous page

President and Chief Exec. Officer
JACKSON, Keith — Tel: (602) 244 - 6600; Fax: (602) 244 - 4830

Main Headquarters
Mailing: 5005 E. McDowell Rd.
Phoenix, AZ 85008 — Tel: (602) 244 - 6600; Fax: (602) 244 - 4830

Public Affairs and Related Activities Personnel

At Headquarters

AYOTTE, Ross — Tel: (602) 244 - 5978; Fax: (602) 244 - 4830
Director, Marketing Communications
ross.ayotte@onsemi.com

RIZVI, Ken — Tel: (602) 244 - 6600; Fax: (602) 244 - 4830
Director, Investor Relations

SPITZA, Anne — Tel: (602) 244 - 6398; Fax: (602) 244 - 4830
Manager, Media Relations
anne.spitza@onsemi.com

TACKETT, Everett — Tel: (602) 244 - 4534; Fax: (602) 244 - 4830
Director, Internal Communications
everett.tackett@onsemi.com

Ondeo Nalco Co.

See listing on page 337 under Nalco Co.

OneBeacon Insurance

Formerly CGU Insurance Group, the company changed its name to OneBeacon Insurance when it was acquired by White Mountains Insurance Group of Hamilton, Bermuda in 2001.
www.onebeacon.com

President and Chief Exec. Officer
MILLER, T. Michael — Tel: (617) 725 - 6000

Main Headquarters
Mailing: One Beacon St.
Boston, MA 02108 — Tel: (617) 725 - 6000

Political Action Committees

OneBeacon PAC (Federal)
Contact: Richard C. Hirtle
One Beacon St.
Boston, MA 02108 — Tel: (617) 725 - 6000

Contributions to Candidates: $5,500 (01/05 - 09/05)
Democrats: $5,500.

Principal Recipients

SENATE DEMOCRATS	HOUSE DEMOCRATS
	Murphy, Christopher (CT)$5,000

Corporate Foundations and Giving Programs

OneBeacon Insurance Foundation
One Beacon St.
Boston, MA 02108 — Tel: (617) 725 - 6000

Annual Grant Total: $2,000,000 - $5,000,000

Public Affairs and Related Activities Personnel

At Headquarters

DUARTE, Carmen — Tel: (617) 725 - 6598; Fax: (617) 725 - 7357
V. President, Corporate Communications
cduarte@onebeacon.com

HIRTLE, Richard C. — Tel: (617) 725 - 6000
PAC Treasurer

Oneida Ltd.

A manufacturer and marketer of silver and stainless steel flatware and other tableware.
www.oneida.com
Annual Revenues: $453 million

Chairman, President and Chief Exec. Officer
KALLET, Peter J. — Tel: (315) 361 - 3000

Main Headquarters
Mailing: 163-181 Kenwood Ave.
Oneida, NY 13421 — Tel: (315) 361 - 3000

Political Action Committees

Oneida Ltd. PAC
Contact: Catherine H. Suttmeier
163-181 Kenwood Ave.
Oneida, NY 13421 — Tel: (315) 361 - 3000; Fax: (315) 361 - 3700

Contributions to Candidates: none reported (01/05 - 09/05)

Public Affairs and Related Activities Personnel

At Headquarters

ALLEN, Wilber — Tel: (315) 361 - 3000
Director, Human Resources

CHURCH, Andrew G. — Tel: (315) 361 - 3000
Chief Financial Officer
Responsibilities include investor relations.

GYMBURCH, David — Tel: (315) 361 - 3000; Fax: (315) 361 - 3655
Manager, Public Relations

SUTTMEIER, Catherine H. — Tel: (315) 361 - 3000; Fax: (315) 361 - 3700
Corporate V. President, General Counsel and Secretary
Responsibilities include political action.

ONEOK, Inc.

Parent company of Oklahoma Natural Gas Co. and Kansas Gas Service Co., natural gas utilities. Engaged also in oil and gas exploration, processing, storage, transmission and gas marketing.
www.oneok.com
Annual Revenues: $1.36 billion

Chairman, President and Chief Exec. Officer
KYLE, David L. — Tel: (918) 588 - 7930; Fax: (918) 588 - 7960
dkyle@oneok.com

Main Headquarters
Mailing: P.O. Box 871
Tulsa, OK 74102-0871 — Tel: (918) 588 - 7000; Fax: (918) 588 - 7960
Street: 100 W. Fifth St.
Tulsa, OK 74103

Washington Office
Contact: G. Frank West
Mailing: 406 First St. SE
Third Floor
Washington, DC 20003 — Tel: (202) 488 - 8562; Fax: (202) 488 - 3803

Political Action Committees

ONEOK Inc. Employee Political Action Committee
P.O. Box 871
Tulsa, OK 74102-0871 — Tel: (918) 588 - 7000; Fax: (918) 588 - 7960

Contributions to Candidates: $500 (01/05 - 09/05)
Democrats: $500.

Principal Recipients

SENATE DEMOCRATS	HOUSE DEMOCRATS	
	Boren, David (OK)	$500

Corporate Foundations and Giving Programs

ONEOK Community Investment Program
Contact: Ginny Creveling
P.O. Box 871
Tulsa, OK 74102-0871 — Tel: (918) 588 - 7474; Fax: (918) 588 - 7490

Annual Grant Total: none reported

Public Affairs and Related Activities Personnel

At Headquarters

CHANCELLOR, Andrea — Tel: (918) 588 - 7570; Fax: (918) 588 - 7490
Manager, Corporate Communications and Advertising
achancellor@oneok.com

CREVELING, Ginny — Tel: (918) 588 - 7474; Fax: (918) 588 - 7490
Exec. Director
gcreveling@oneok.com
Responsibilities include corporate philanthropy.

HUDSON, David — Tel: (918) 588 - 7000; Fax: (918) 588 - 7960
PAC Treasurer

ROTH, David E. — Tel: (918) 588 - 7924; Fax: (918) 588 - 7960
V. President, Human Resources
droth@oneok.com

WATSON, Weldon L. — Tel: (918) 588 - 7158; Fax: (918) 588 - 7971
V. President, Investor Relations and Communications
wwatson@oneok.com

At Washington Office

WEST, G. Frank — Tel: (202) 488 - 8562; Fax: (202) 488 - 3803
Manager, Governmental Affairs - Federal
fwest@oneok.com
Registered Federal Lobbyist.

At Other Offices

JOHNSON, Steven C. — Tel: (913) 319 - 8604; Fax: (913) 319 - 8606
Manager, Government Affairs -- Kansas
7421 W. 129th St., Suite 300
Overland Park, KS 66213
sjohnson@kgas.com

LUBER, Eldridge H. — Tel: (405) 551 - 6706; Fax: (405) 551 - 6801
Manager, Governmental Affairs - Oklahoma
P.O. Box 401
Oklahoma City, OK 73101-0401
eluber@oneok.com

SHERRY, Don E. — Tel: (405) 551 - 6738; Fax: (405) 551 - 6779
Manager, Communications
(Oklahoma Natural Gas Co.)
Box 401
Oklahoma City, OK 73101-0401
dsherry@oneok.com

Oracle Corporation

A member of the Public Affairs Council. A software provider. Acquired PeopleSoft in 2005.
www.oracle.com
Annual Revenues: $11 billion

Chairman of the Board
HENLEY, Jeff
Tel: (650) 506 - 7000
Fax: (650) 633 - 1269
TF: (800) 672 - 2531

Chief Exec. Officer
ELLISON, Lawrence J.
Tel: (650) 506 - 7000
Fax: (650) 506 - 7200
TF: (800) 672 - 2531

Main Headquarters
Mailing: 500 Oracle Pkwy.
Redwood Shores, CA 94065
Tel: (650) 506 - 7000
Fax: (650) 633 - 1269
TF: (800) 672 - 2531

Washington Office
Contact: Kate McGee
Mailing: 1015 15th St. NW
Suite 200
Washington, DC 20005-2605
Tel: (202) 835 - 7360
Fax: (202) 467 - 4250

Political Action Committees

Oracle Corp. Political Action Committee
Contact: Deborah Lange
1015 15th St. NW
Suite 200
Washington, DC 20005-2605
Tel: (202) 835 - 7360
Fax: (202) 467 - 4250

Contributions to Candidates: $18,500 (01/05 - 09/05)
Democrats: $4,000; Republicans: $14,500.

Principal Recipients

SENATE DEMOCRATS		HOUSE DEMOCRATS	
Feinstein, Dianne (CA)	$2,000		
Carper, Thomas R (DE)	$1,000		
Stabenow, Debbie (MI)	$1,000		

SENATE REPUBLICANS		HOUSE REPUBLICANS	
Burns, Conrad (MT)	$3,000	Davis, Tom (VA)	$1,000
Santorum, Richard (PA)	$2,500	Dewine, R. Pat (OH)	$1,000
Allen, George (VA)	$2,000	Dreier, David (CA)	$1,000
Dewine, Richard (OH)	$2,000		
Ensign, John Eric (NV)	$2,000		

Corporate Foundations and Giving Programs

Oracle Corporate Giving Program
Contact: Kimberly Pineda
500 Oracle Pkwy.
Redwood Shores, CA 94065
Tel: (650) 506 - 8831
Fax: (650) 506 - 7200
TF: (800) 672 - 2531

Annual Grant Total: over $5,000,000
Primary Interests: Animal Protection; Environment/Conservation; K-12 Education; Math and Science; Medical Research

Public Affairs and Related Activities Personnel

At Headquarters

CATZ, Safra
President
Tel: (650) 506 - 7000
Fax: (650) 633 - 1269
TF: (800) 672 - 2531

FITZGERALD, Joelle
Senior Director, Investor Relations
Tel: (650) 506 - 4073
Fax: (650) 506 - 7122
TF: (800) 672 - 2531

PINEDA, Kimberly
Corporate Community Relations Contact
kimberly.pineda@oracle.com
Tel: (650) 506 - 8831
Fax: (650) 506 - 7200
TF: (800) 672 - 2531

WYNNE, Bob
V. President, Corporate Communications
bob.wynne@oracle.com
Tel: (650) 506 - 5834
Fax: (650) 633 - 1269
TF: (800) 672 - 2531

At Washington Office

ALHADEFF, Joseph
V. President, Global Public Policy
joseph.alhadeff@oracle.com
Registered Federal Lobbyist.
Tel: (202) 721 - 4816
Fax: (202) 467 - 4250

DAVIDSON, Mary Ann
Chief Security Officer
Registered Federal Lobbyist.
Tel: (202) 835 - 7360
Fax: (202) 467 - 4250

GLUECK, Kenneth
V. President, Government Affairs
kenneth.glueck@oracle.com
Registered Federal Lobbyist.
Tel: (202) 721 - 4815
Fax: (202) 467 - 4250

HINZMAN, Josh
Director, Federal Affairs
Registered Federal Lobbyist.
Tel: (202) 835 - 7360
Fax: (202) 467 - 4250

HOAG, Rick
V. President, Tax Policy
Registered Federal Lobbyist.
Tel: (202) 835 - 7360
Fax: (202) 467 - 4250

HOFFMAN, Robert
Vice President, Congressional and Legislative Affairs
robert.hoffman@oracle.com
Registered Federal Lobbyist.
Tel: (202) 721 - 4814
Fax: (202) 467 - 4250

LANGE, Deborah
PAC Contact
Registered Federal Lobbyist.
Tel: (202) 835 - 7360
Fax: (202) 467 - 4250

MCGEE, Kate
V. President, Corporate Affairs
kate.mcgee@oracle.com
Registered Federal Lobbyist.
Tel: (202) 721 - 4813
Fax: (202) 467 - 4250

PAVLOVIC, Dejan
Director, Regulatory Affairs and Development
dejan.pavlovic@oracle.com
Registered Federal Lobbyist.
Tel: (202) 721 - 4809
Fax: (202) 467 - 4250

PRASAD, Sanjay
Chief Patent Counsel
Registered Federal Lobbyist.
Tel: (202) 835 - 7360
Fax: (202) 467 - 4250

Orange and Rockland Utilities, Inc.

A member of the Public Affairs Council. An electric and gas utility. A wholly owned subsidiary of Consolidated Edison Co. of New York (see separate listing).
www.oru.com
Annual Revenues: $736.3 million

President and Chief Exec. Officer
MCMAHON, John
Tel: (845) 352 - 6000
Fax: (845) 577 - 6913
TF: (877) 434 - 4100

Main Headquarters
Mailing: One Blue Hill Plaza
Pearl River, NY 10965
Tel: (845) 352 - 6000
Fax: (845) 577 - 6913
TF: (877) 434 - 4100

Corporate Foundations and Giving Programs

Orange and Rockland Utilities Neighbor Fund
Contact: Linda Feger
One Blue Hill Plaza
Pearl River, NY 10965
Tel: (845) 577 - 2545
Fax: (845) 577 - 6913
TF: (877) 434 - 4100

Annual Grant Total: under $100,000
The Fund operates on customer, employee and vendor contributions and O&R matching funds. Assists O&R customers who are unable to pay their fuel bills.
Primary Interests: Financially Disadvantaged

Orange and Rockland Community Investment Committee
Contact: Linda Feger
One Blue Hill Plaza
Pearl River, NY 10965
Tel: (845) 577 - 2545
Fax: (845) 577 - 6913
TF: (877) 434 - 4100

Annual Grant Total: under $100,000

Public Affairs and Related Activities Personnel

At Headquarters

BRIZZOLARA, Thomas L.
Manager, Community Relations
Tel: (845) 577 - 2654
Fax: (845) 577 - 6989

DONOVAN, Mike
Manager, Media Relations
mdonovan@oru.com
Tel: (845) 577 - 2430
Fax: (845) 577 - 6913

DRIER, Cecille C.
Manager, Consumer Publications
Tel: (845) 577 - 2409
Fax: (845) 577 - 6913

FEGER, Linda
Manager, Corporate Programs
Tel: (845) 577 - 2545
Fax: (845) 577 - 6913
TF: (877) 434 - 4100

FREEDMAN, Alan M.
Director, Public Affairs
(Rockland Electric Co.)
Mailstop: Lobby Level
Tel: (845) 577 - 2922
Fax: (845) 577 - 6913

ILLOBRE, Nick
Director, Human Resources
Tel: (845) 577 - 2752
Fax: (845) 577 - 2958

LOIS, James E.
Manager, Corporate Communications
jelois@oru.com
Tel: (845) 577 - 2941
Fax: (845) 577 - 6913

STRUCK, Richard M.
Director, Public Policy and Economic Development
Tel: (845) 577 - 2498
Fax: (845) 577 - 6913

Orbital Sciences Corp.

A manufacturer of low-cost space systems. Designs, manufactures, operates, and markets infrastructure systems, satellite access products, and satellite-provided services.
www.orbital.com
Annual Revenues: $415.2 million

Orbital Sciences Corp.

* continued from previous page

Chairman and Chief Exec. Officer
THOMPSON, David W. Tel: (703) 406 - 5000
thompson.david@orbital.com Fax: (703) 406 - 5572

Main Headquarters
Mailing: 21839 Atlantic Blvd. Tel: (703) 406 - 5000
Dulles, VA 20166 Fax: (703) 406 - 5572

Political Action Committees

Political Action Committee of Orbital Sciences Corp. (ORBPAC)
Contact: Marie L. Craft
21839 Atlantic Blvd. Tel: (703) 406 - 5000
Dulles, VA 20166 Fax: (703) 406 - 5572

Contributions to Candidates: $39,250 (01/05 - 09/05)
Democrats: $8,000; Republicans: $31,250.

Principal Recipients

SENATE DEMOCRATS		HOUSE DEMOCRATS	
Mikulski, Barbara (MD)	$2,000	Cramer, Bud (AL)	$2,000
		Moran, James (VA)	$2,000
SENATE REPUBLICANS		**HOUSE REPUBLICANS**	
Allen, George (VA)	$7,000	Weldon, David (FL)	$3,750
		Cantor, Eric (VA)	$3,500
		Wolf, Frank R (VA)	$3,500
		Davis, Jo Ann (VA)	$2,500
		Drake, Thelma Day (VA)	$2,500
		Calvert, Ken (CA)	$2,000

Public Affairs and Related Activities Personnel

At Headquarters

BENDER, Emily Tel: (703) 406 - 5000
V. President, Human Resources Fax: (703) 406 - 5572

CRAFT, Marie L. Tel: (703) 406 - 5000
PAC Treasurer Fax: (703) 406 - 5572
craft.marie@orbital.com

At Other Offices

BENESKI, Barron Tel: (703) 406 - 5528
V. President, Public Relations Fax: (703) 406 - 5572
21700 Atlantic Blvd.
Dulles, VA 20166
beneski.barron@orbital.com
Responsibilities include investor relations.

BITTERMAN, Mark E. Tel: (703) 406 - 5523
Senior V. President, Government Relations Fax: (703) 406 - 5572
21700 Atlantic Blvd.
Dulles, VA 20166
bitterman.mark@orbital.com

MORRIS, Ed Tel: (703) 406 - 5000
21700 Atlantic Blvd. Fax: (703) 406 - 5572
Dulles, VA 20166

Oregon Steel Mills Inc.

Produces steel products.
www.osm.com
Annual Revenues: $905 million

Chairman of the Board
SWINDELLS, William Tel: (503) 223 - 9228
Fax: (503) 240 - 5232
TF: (800) 831 - 2187

President and Chief Exec. Officer
DECLUSIN, James E. Tel: (503) 223 - 9228
Fax: (503) 240 - 5232
TF: (800) 831 - 2187

Main Headquarters
Mailing: 1000 SW Broadway Tel: (503) 223 - 9228
Suite 2200 Fax: (503) 240 - 5232
Portland, OR 97205 TF: (800) 831 - 2187

Public Affairs and Related Activities Personnel

At Headquarters

ADAMS, Ray Tel: (503) 223 - 9228
Chief Financial Officer Fax: (503) 240 - 5232
TF: (800) 831 - 2187
Responsibilities include corporate affairs.

Orlando Sentinel Communications

Publisher of the Orlando Sentinel newspaper.
www.orlandosentinel.com

Main Headquarters
Mailing: 633 N. Orange Ave. Tel: (407) 420 - 5000
Orlando, FL 32801-1349 Fax: (407) 420 - 5350

Corporate Foundations and Giving Programs

Orlando Sentinel Family Fund
Contact: Cindy Williams
633 N. Orange Ave. Tel: (407) 420 - 5591
Orlando, FL 32801-1349 Fax: (407) 420 - 6258

Annual Grant Total: $1,000,000 - $2,000,000
A fund of the Robert R. McCormick Tribune Foundation. Giving figures for 2004 were $2.6 million. Areas of preference in Florida: the counties of Orange, Lake, Osceola, Seminole, and West Volusia.
Geographic Preference: Florida
Primary Interests: Children; Families; Literacy; Senior Citizens

Public Affairs and Related Activities Personnel

At Headquarters

WILLIAMS, Cindy Tel: (407) 420 - 5591
Manager, Family Fund Fax: (407) 420 - 6258
Mailstop: MP307
cwilliams@orlandosentinel.com

Ortho-McNeil Pharmaceutical, Inc.

See listing on page 270 under Johnson & Johnson.

Oshkosh B'Gosh, Inc.

Infants and children's wear, accessories, and workwear for adults.
www.oshkoshbgosh.com

Chairman and Chief Exec. Officer
HYDE, Douglas W. Tel: (920) 231 - 8800
Fax: (920) 231 - 8621
TF: (800) 282 - 4674

Main Headquarters
Mailing: P.O. Box 300 Tel: (920) 231 - 8800
Oshkosh, WI 54903-0300 Fax: (920) 231 - 8621
TF: (800) 282 - 4674
Street: 112 Otter Ave.
Oshkosh, WI 54901

Corporate Foundations and Giving Programs

Oshkosh B'Gosh Corporate Contributions Program
Contact: William Wyman
P.O. Box 300 Tel: (920) 231 - 8800
Oshkosh, WI 54903-0300 Fax: (920) 231 - 8621
TF: (800) 282 - 4674

Annual Grant Total: $300,000 - $400,000
Dedicated to providing financial support to charitable organizations that focus on the education, health and general well-being of children in at risk environments.
Geographic Preference: Area(s) in which the company operates
Primary Interests: Children's Health; Education

Public Affairs and Related Activities Personnel

At Headquarters

CHRISTENSEN, Paul Tel: (920) 231 - 8800
V. President, Human Resources Fax: (920) 231 - 8621
TF: (800) 282 - 4674

HERMAN, Cindy Tel: (920) 231 - 8800
Corporate Director, Advertising, Public Relations and Promotions Fax: (920) 231 - 8621
TF: (800) 282 - 4674

LAVELL, Jennifer Tel: (920) 231 - 8800
Public Relations Specialist Fax: (920) 231 - 8621
TF: (800) 282 - 4674

WACHOLTZ, Margaret Tel: (920) 231 - 8800
Corporate Grants Contact Fax: (920) 231 - 8621
TF: (800) 282 - 4674

WYMAN, William Tel: (920) 231 - 8800
Corporate Contributions Contact Fax: (920) 231 - 8621
TF: (800) 282 - 4674

Oshkosh Truck Corp.

Designs, manufactures, and markets specialty, fire, emergency, and military trucks, concrete pavement, and refuse hauling markets.
www.oshkoshtruckcorporation.com
Annual Revenues: $2.26 billion

Chairman, President and Chief Exec. Officer
BOHN, Robert G. Tel: (920) 235 - 9150
Fax: (920) 233 - 9314

Main Headquarters
Mailing: P.O. Box 2566 Tel: (920) 235 - 9150
Oshkosh, WI 54903-2566 Fax: (920) 233 - 9314
Street: 2307 Oregon St.
Oshkosh, WI 54902

Washington Office
Contact: Jay Kimmitt
Mailing: 1300 N. 17th St. Tel: (703) 525 - 8400
Suite 1040 Fax: (703) 525 - 8408
Arlington, VA 22209

Oshkosh Truck Corp.

** continued from previous page*

Political Action Committees

Oshkosh Truck Corp. Employees PAC (OTCEPAC)
Contact: Dave Sagehorn
P.O. Box 2566 — Tel: (920) 235 - 9150
Oshkosh, WI 54903-2566 — Fax: (920) 233 - 9251

Contributions to Candidates: $14,500 (01/05 - 09/05)
Democrats: $2,000; Republicans: $12,500.

Principal Recipients

SENATE DEMOCRATS		HOUSE DEMOCRATS	
Leahy, Patrick (VT)	$1,000	Obey, David R (WI)	$1,000
SENATE REPUBLICANS		**HOUSE REPUBLICANS**	
Stevens, Ted (AK)	$4,500	Hobson, David (OH)	$2,000
Burns, Conrad (MT)	$3,500	Feeney, Tom (FL)	$1,500
		Petri, Thomas (WI)	$1,000

Public Affairs and Related Activities Personnel

At Headquarters

ROHRKASTE, Michael — Tel: (920) 235 - 9150
V. President, Human Resources — Fax: (920) 233 - 9268
mrohrkaste@oshtruck.com

SAGEHORN, Dave — Tel: (920) 235 - 9150
V. President, Business Development — Fax: (920) 233 - 9251
Responsibilities include political action.

SKYBA, Kirsten — Tel: (920) 233 - 9621
V. President, Marketing Communications — Fax: (920) 233 - 9251
kskyba@oshtruck.com

SZEWS, Charlie — Tel: (920) 235 - 9151 Ext: 2332
Exec. V. President and Chief Financial Officer — Fax: (920) 233 - 9251
Responsibilities include investor relations.

At Washington Office

KIMMITT, Jay — Tel: (703) 525 - 8400
Senior V. President, Government Operations — Fax: (703) 525 - 8408

Otter Tail Power Co.

An electric utility.
www.otpco.com
Annual Revenues: $654.1 million

Chairman of the Board
MACFARLANE, John C. — Tel: (218) 739 - 8200
jmacfarlane@otpco.com — Fax: (218) 739 - 8218
TF: (866) 410 - 8780

Main Headquarters
Mailing: P.O. Box 496 — Tel: (218) 739 - 8200
215 S. Cascade St. S. — Fax: (218) 739 - 8218
Fergus Falls, MN 56538-0496 — TF: (866) 410 - 8780

Political Action Committees

Otter Tail Power Co. Political Action Committee
Contact: Steven Schultz
315 Second St. SE
P.O. Box 2220
Jamestown, ND 58402

Contributions to Candidates: $500 (01/05 - 09/05)
Democrats: $500.

Principal Recipients

SENATE DEMOCRATS	HOUSE DEMOCRATS	
	Pomeroy, Earl (ND)	$500

Corporate Foundations and Giving Programs

Otter Tail Corporate Giving
P.O. Box 496 — Tel: (218) 739 - 8200
215 S. Cascade St. S. — Fax: (218) 739 - 8218
Fergus Falls, MN 56538-0496 — TF: (866) 410 - 8780

Annual Grant Total: none reported

Public Affairs and Related Activities Personnel

At Headquarters

KANGAS, Nancy — Tel: (218) 739 - 8200
Director, Human Resources, IT and Safety — Fax: (218) 739 - 8218
TF: (866) 410 - 8780

KLING, Cris — Tel: (218) 739 - 8297
Director, Public Relations — Fax: (218) 739 - 8762
ckling@otpco.com — TF: (866) 410 - 8780

At Other Offices

SCHULTZ, Steven
PAC Treasurer
315 Second St. SE
P.O. Box 2220
Jamestown, ND 58402

Outback Steakhouse, Inc.

A restaurant chain.
www.outback.com
Annual Revenues: $2.127 billion

Chairman and Chief Exec. Officer
SULLIVAN, Chris T. — Tel: (813) 282 - 1225
Fax: (813) 282 - 1209

Main Headquarters
Mailing: 2202 N. Westshore Blvd. — Tel: (813) 282 - 1225
Fifth Floor — Fax: (813) 282 - 2114
Tampa, FL 33607

Political Action Committees

Outback Steakhouse Political Action Committee
Contact: Matthew P. Halme
2202 N. Westshore Blvd. — Tel: (813) 282 - 1225
Fifth Floor — Fax: (813) 281 - 2114
Tampa, FL 33607

Contributions to Candidates: $172,000 (01/05 - 09/05)
Democrats: $15,000; Republicans: $157,000.

Principal Recipients

SENATE DEMOCRATS		HOUSE DEMOCRATS	
Carper, Thomas R (DE)	$5,000		
Ford, Harold E Jr (TN)	$5,000		
SENATE REPUBLICANS		**HOUSE REPUBLICANS**	
Allen, George (VA)	$10,000	Dent, Charles W (PA)	$10,000
Kyl, Jon L (AZ)	$10,000	Keller, Richard (FL)	$10,000
Talent, James (MO)	$10,000	Mack, Connie (FL)	$10,000
Hatch, Orrin (UT)	$5,000	McCrery, Jim (LA)	$10,000
McConnell, Mitch (KY)	$5,000	McHenry, Patrick (NC)	$10,000
		Young, Don E (AK)	$10,000

Public Affairs and Related Activities Personnel

At Headquarters

AMBERG, Stephanie — Tel: (813) 282 - 1225
Media Contact — Fax: (813) 282 - 1209
stephanie.amberg@outback.com

HALME, Matthew P. — Tel: (813) 282 - 1225
Director, Government Relations — Fax: (813) 281 - 2114
matthewhalme@outback.com

HATHCOAT, Lisa — Tel: (813) 282 - 1225
Manager, Investor Relations — Fax: (813) 282 - 1209

KADOW, Joseph J. — Tel: (813) 282 - 1225
Treasurer, Outback Steakhouse PAC — Fax: (813) 282 - 1209

Overseas Shipholding Group, Inc.

Owner and operator of tankers and bulk dry cargo ships.
www.osg.com

President and Chief Exec. Officer
ARNTZEN, Morten — Tel: (212) 953 - 4100
Fax: (212) 578 - 1832

Main Headquarters
Mailing: 511 Fifth Ave. — Tel: (212) 953 - 4100
New York, NY 10017 — Fax: (212) 578 - 1832

Political Action Committees

Overseas Shiphilding Group Inc. PAC
Contact: James I. Edelson
511 Fifth Ave. — Tel: (212) 953 - 4100
New York, NY 10017 — Fax: (212) 578 - 1832

Contributions to Candidates: none reported (01/05 - 09/05)

Corporate Foundations and Giving Programs

OSG Foundation
Contact: Jeanne Principe
511 Fifth Ave. — Tel: (212) 953 - 4100
New York, NY 10017 — Fax: (212) 578 - 1832

Annual Grant Total: $1,000,000 - $2,000,000

Recent recipients include: Carnegie Hall Society, Financial Accounting Foundation, New York Medical College, Mount Sinai Medical Center, Beth Israel Medical Center, American Friends of Israel Nat'l Museum of Science, Coalition for the Homeless.

Geographic Preference: New York City

Primary Interests: Education; Medical Research

Overseas Shipholding Group, Inc.

* continued from previous page

Public Affairs and Related Activities Personnel

At Headquarters

COWEN, Robert
Senior V. President
Responsibilities include corporate public affairs.
Tel: (212) 953 - 4100 Ext: 1870

EDELSON, James I.
Treasurer, Overseas Shipholding Group Inc. PAC
Tel: (212) 953 - 4100
Fax: (212) 578 - 1832

PRINCIPE, Jeanne
Foundation Contact
Tel: (212) 953 - 4100
Fax: (212) 578 - 1832

Owens & Minor, Inc.

A national wholesale distributor of surgical, medical and related supplies.
www.owens-minor.com
Annual Revenues: $3.8 billion

Chairman of the Board
MINOR, G. Gilmore, III
Tel: (804) 747 - 9794
Fax: (804) 270 - 7281

Chief Exec. Officer
SMITH, Craig R.
Tel: (804) 747 - 9794
Fax: (804) 270 - 7281

Main Headquarters
Mailing: P.O. Box 27626
Richmond, VA 23261-7626
Street: 4800 Cox Rd.
Glen Allen, VA 23060-6292
Tel: (804) 747 - 9794
Fax: (804) 270 - 7281

Corporate Foundations and Giving Programs

Owens & Minor Corporate Giving Program
Contact: Hugh F. Gouldthorpe, Jr.
P.O. Box 27626
Richmond, VA 23261-7626
Tel: (804) 747 - 9794
Fax: (804) 965 - 1907

Annual Grant Total: none reported
Geographic Preference: Richmond, VA
Primary Interests: Children

Public Affairs and Related Activities Personnel

At Headquarters

ALLCOTT, Trudi
Manager, Corporate Communications
Tel: (804) 935 - 4291
Fax: (804) 965 - 1907

DAVIS, Erika T.
Senior V. President, Human Resources
Tel: (804) 965 - 5895
Fax: (804) 270 - 7281

GOULDTHORPE, Hugh F., Jr.
V. President, Quality and Communications
Responsibilities include corporate philanthropy.
Tel: (804) 747 - 9794
Fax: (804) 965 - 1907

GRAVES, Chuck
Shareholder Services
Tel: (804) 488 - 8850
Fax: (804) 270 - 7281

VICK, Craig
Manager, Recruitment and Employee Relations
Tel: (804) 965 - 5889
Fax: (804) 762 - 8589

Owens Corning

A manufacturer of glass and composite materials.
www.owenscorning.com
Annual Revenues: $5 billion

Chairman, Senior V. President and Chief Financial Officer
THAMAN, Michael H.
mike.thaman@owenscorning.com
Tel: (419) 248 - 7098
Fax: (419) 248 - 6227
TF: (800) 438 - 7465

President and Chief Exec. Officer
BROWN, David T.
dave.t.brown@owenscorning.com
Tel: (419) 248 - 7206
Fax: (419) 248 - 6352
TF: (800) 438 - 7465

Main Headquarters
Mailing: One Owens Corning Pkwy.
Toledo, OH 43659
Tel: (419) 248 - 8000
Fax: (419) 248 - 6227
TF: (800) 438 - 7465

Washington Office
Mailing: 1401 K St. NW
Suite 702
Washington, DC 20005
Tel: (202) 216 - 1080
Fax: (202) 216 - 1081

Political Action Committees

Owens-Corning Better Government Fund
Contact: Victor DeFilippis
One Owens Corning Pkwy.
Toledo, OH 43659
Tel: (419) 248 - 8000
Fax: (419) 248 - 6227
TF: (800) 438 - 7465

Contributions to Candidates: $16,000 (01/05 - 09/05)
Democrats: $3,000; Republicans: $13,000.

Principal Recipients

SENATE DEMOCRATS		HOUSE DEMOCRATS	
Cardin, Benjamin (MD)	$1,000	Thompson, Mike (CA)	$2,000

SENATE REPUBLICANS		HOUSE REPUBLICANS	
Dewine, Richard (OH)	$5,000	Weller, Jerry (IL)	$5,000
Santorum, Richard (PA)	$2,000	Dewine, R. Pat (OH)	$1,000

Corporate Foundations and Giving Programs

Owens Corning Foundation, Inc.
Contact: Connie Krabill
One Owens Corning Pkwy.
Toledo, OH 43659
Tel: (419) 248 - 8000
Fax: (419) 248 - 6227
TF: (800) 438 - 7465

Annual Grant Total: $2,000,000 - $5,000,000
Geographic Preference: Area(s) in which the company operates
Primary Interests: Civic and Public Affairs; Financially Disadvantaged; Health and Human Services; Housing; K-12 Education
Recent Recipients: United Way

Public Affairs and Related Activities Personnel

At Headquarters

DEFILIPPIS, Victor
PAC Treasurer
Tel: (419) 248 - 8000
Fax: (419) 248 - 6227
TF: (800) 438 - 7465

DIMMER, Dave
Corporate Media Relations Leader
dave.dimmer@owenscorning.com
Tel: (419) 248 - 8421
Fax: (419) 248 - 6227
TF: (800) 438 - 7465

KRABILL, Connie
Foundation Contact
Tel: (419) 248 - 8000
Fax: (419) 248 - 6227
TF: (800) 438 - 7465

MITCHELL, Suzanne
Business Media Relations Senior Specialist
suzanne.mitchell@owenscorning.com
Tel: (419) 248 - 6255
Fax: (419) 248 - 6227
TF: (800) 438 - 7465

At Washington Office

LIBONATI, John J.
Vice President, Government and Public Affairs
john.libonati@owenscorning.com
Registered Federal Lobbyist.
Tel: (202) 216 - 1080

Owens-Illinois, Inc.

A manufacturer of glass and plastic packaging products.
www.o-i.com
Annual Revenues: $6 billion

Chairman, President and Chief Exec. Officer
MCCRACKEN, Steven R.
steven.mccracken@us.o-i.com
Tel: (419) 247 - 5000
Fax: (419) 247 - 2839

Main Headquarters
Mailing: One Seagate
Toledo, OH 43666
Tel: (419) 247 - 5000
Fax: (419) 247 - 2839

Washington Office
Mailing: 1155 21st St. NW
Suite 310
Washington, DC 20036
Tel: (202) 785 - 3559
Fax: (202) 785 - 8534

Political Action Committees

Owens-Illinois Employees Good Citizenship Fund
Contact: Jennifer Vancil
One Seagate
Toledo, OH 43666
Tel: (419) 247 - 5000
Fax: (419) 247 - 2839

Contributions to Candidates: $1,000 (01/05 - 09/05)
Republicans: $1,000.

Principal Recipients

SENATE REPUBLICANS		HOUSE REPUBLICANS	
		Dewine, R. Pat (OH)	$1,000

Corporate Foundations and Giving Programs

Owens-Illinois Corp. Charities Foundation
Contact: Cheryl A. Johnson
One Seagate
Toledo, OH 43666
Tel: (419) 247 - 1386
Fax: (419) 247 - 2839

Annual Grant Total: $1,000,000 - $2,000,000
Geographic Preference: Area(s) in which the company operates
Primary Interests: Arts and Culture; Civic and Cultural Activities; Health and Human Services; Minority Opportunities

Public Affairs and Related Activities Personnel

At Headquarters

JOHNSON, Cheryl A.
Contributions Administrator
cheryl.johnson@us.o-i.com
Tel: (419) 247 - 1386
Fax: (419) 247 - 2839

NEMIRE, Laura B.
Human Resources Specialist
laura.nemire@us.o-i.com
Tel: (419) 247 - 8053
Fax: (419) 247 - 2839

VANCIL, Jennifer
PAC Contact
jennifer.vancil@us.o-i.com
Responsibilities include government affairs.
Tel: (419) 247 - 5000
Fax: (419) 247 - 2839

Owens-Illinois, Inc.

• continued from previous page

WEBER, James F. — Tel: (419) 247 - 2700
Director, Investor Relations — Fax: (419) 247 - 1218
james.weber@us.o-i.com
Responsibilities include investor relations.

YODER, Kelly — Tel: (419) 247 - 5000
Corporate Communications Supervisor — Fax: (419) 247 - 2839
Mailstop: 27th Floor
kyoder@o-i.com

At Washington Office

STEEN, Daniel K. — Tel: (202) 785 - 3559
Director, Public Affairs — Fax: (202) 785 - 8534
daniel.steen@us.o-i.com
Registered Federal Lobbyist.

Oxford Health Plans Inc.

A managed health care organization.

www.oxfordhealth.com

Chairman of the Board — Tel: (203) 459 - 6000
THIRY, Kent J. — Fax: (203) 851 - 2464
TF: (800) 889 - 7658

President and Chief Exec. Officer — Tel: (203) 459 - 6000
BERG, Charles G. — Fax: (203) 459 - 6330
cberg@oxhp.cm — TF: (800) 889 - 7658

Main Headquarters

Mailing: 48 Monroe Tpk. — Tel: (203) 459 - 6000
Trumbull, CT 06611 — Fax: (203) 459 - 6464
TF: (800) 889 - 7658

Political Action Committees

Oxford Health Plans Inc. Committee for Quality Health Care
Contact: Robert Della Corte

48 Monroe Tpk. — Tel: (203) 459 - 6000
Trumbull, CT 06611 — Fax: (203) 851 - 2464
TF: (800) 889 - 7658

Contributions to Candidates: none reported (01/05 - 09/05)

Public Affairs and Related Activities Personnel

At Headquarters

DELLA CORTE, Robert — Tel: (203) 459 - 6000
PAC Treasurer — Fax: (203) 851 - 2464
TF: (800) 889 - 7658

MEYER, Timothy B. — Tel: (203) 459 - 7271
V. President, Government Relations — Fax: (203) 452 - 4610
tmeyer@oxfordhealth.com — TF: (800) 889 - 7658

RUDELL, Jeanne — Tel: (203) 459 - 6000
V. President, Human Resources — Fax: (203) 452 - 4884
jrudell@oxhp.com — TF: (800) 889 - 7658

SHEKHOAR, Alexander — Tel: (203) 459 - 6000
Fax: (203) 459 - 6464
TF: (800) 889 - 7658

SHYDLO, Maria Gordon — Tel: (203) 459 - 7674
Director, Public and Community Relations — Fax: (203) 452 - 4644
mshydlo@oxhp.com — TF: (800) 889 - 7658

TETREAULT, Kristin S. — Tel: (203) 459 - 6000
Director, Internal Communications — Fax: (203) 452 - 4884
ktetreau@oxhp.com — TF: (800) 889 - 7658

P&C Communications

See listing on page 118 under CIGNA Corp.

PACCAR Inc.

A collection of companies engaged in truck manufacturing, finance, and auto parts retail.

www.paccar.com

Annual Revenues: $6.089 billion

Chairman and Chief Exec. Officer — Tel: (425) 468 - 7400
PIGOTT, Mark C. — Fax: (425) 468 - 8216

Main Headquarters

Mailing: P.O. Box 1518 — Tel: (425) 468 - 7400
Bellevue, WA 98009 — Fax: (425) 468 - 8216

Street: 777 106th Ave. NE
Bellevue, WA 98004

Political Action Committees

PACCAR Employees Organized for Leadership and Education (People PAC)
Contact: Chris Wells

P.O. Box 1518 — Tel: (425) 468 - 7400
Bellevue, WA 98009 — Fax: (425) 468 - 8216

Contributions to Candidates: $6,500 (01/05 - 09/05)

Democrats: $500; Republicans: $6,000.

Principal Recipients

SENATE DEMOCRATS	HOUSE DEMOCRATS	
	Cooper, James (TN)	$500
SENATE REPUBLICANS	**HOUSE REPUBLICANS**	
	Reichert, Dave (WA)	$5,000
	McMorris, Cathy (WA)	$1,000

Corporate Foundations and Giving Programs

PACCAR Foundation
Contact: James J. Waggoner

P.O. Box 1518 — Tel: (425) 468 - 7400
Bellevue, WA 98009 — Fax: (425) 468 - 8216

Annual Grant Total: $2,000,000 - $5,000,000

Geographic Preference: Area(s) in which the company operates
Primary Interests: Arts and Culture; Education; Health; Social Services
Recent Recipients: United Way; University of Washington; YMCA

Public Affairs and Related Activities Personnel

At Headquarters

D'AMATO, Janice M. — Tel: (425) 468 - 7400
Corporate Attorney — Fax: (425) 468 - 8216
jdamato@paccar.com
Responsibilities include investor relations.

HIGHLAND, Nick — Tel: (425) 468 - 7400
Exec. Director, Corporate Human Resources — Fax: (425) 468 - 8216
nhighland@paccar.com

WAGGONER, James J. — Tel: (425) 468 - 7400
V. President and General Manager, PACCAR Foundation — Fax: (425) 468 - 8216

WELLS, Chris — Tel: (425) 468 - 7400
Treasurer, People PAC — Fax: (425) 468 - 8216

Pacific Century Financial Corp.

See listing on page 61 under Bank of Hawaii Corp.

Pacific Enterprises

See listing on page 432 under Sempra Energy.

Pacific Gas and Electric Co.

See listing on page 380 under PG & E Corp.

Pacific Life Insurance Co.

PUBLIC AFFAIRS COUNCIL

A member of the Public Affairs Council. Formerly known as Pacific Mutual Life Insurance Co. Became Pacific Life Insurance Co. in 1997.

www.PacificLife.com

Chairman and Chief Exec. Officer — Tel: (949) 219 - 3011
SUTTON, Thomas C. — Fax: (949) 219 - 5130
TF: (800) 800 - 7646

Main Headquarters

Mailing: P.O. Box 9000 — Tel: (949) 219 - 3011
Newport Beach, CA 92658-9030 — Fax: (949) 219 - 5130
TF: (800) 800 - 7646

Street: 700 Newport Center Dr.
Newport Beach, CA 92660-6397

Political Action Committees

Pacific Life Insurance Co. Political Action Committee
Contact: Robert G. Haskell

P.O. Box 9000 — Tel: (949) 219 - 3022
Newport Beach, CA 92658-9030 — Fax: (949) 219 - 5130
TF: (800) 800 - 7646

Contributions to Candidates: $77,250 (01/05 - 09/05)

Democrats: $41,000; Republicans: $36,250.

Pacific Life Insurance Co.

* continued from previous page

Principal Recipients

SENATE DEMOCRATS		HOUSE DEMOCRATS	
Carper, Thomas R (DE)	$5,000	Vargas, Juan (CA)	$5,000
Nelson, Benjamin (NE)	$5,000	Tubbs-Jones, Stephanie (OH)	$3,000
Feinstein, Dianne (CA)	$2,000	Becerra, Xavier (CA)	$2,000
Stabenow, Debbie (MI)	$2,000	Cardin, Ben (MD)	$2,000
		Matsui, Doris (CA)	$2,000
		Pomeroy, Earl (ND)	$2,000

SENATE REPUBLICANS		HOUSE REPUBLICANS	
Snowe, Olympia (ME)	$3,000	Dreier, David (CA)	$5,000
Crapo, Michael D (ID)	$2,000	Beauprez, Robert (CO)	$4,000
		Johnson, Nancy (CT)	$3,000
		Oxley, Michael (OH)	$3,000
		Royce, Ed Mr (CA)	$2,250
		Chocola, Christopher (IN)	$2,000
		Lewis, Jerry (CA)	$2,000

Corporate Foundations and Giving Programs

Pacific Life Foundation
Contact: Robert G. Haskell
P.O. Box 9000
Newport Beach, CA 92658-9030
Tel: (949) 219 - 3022
Fax: (949) 219 - 5130
TF: (800) 800 - 7646

Assets: $48,100,000 (2004)
Annual Grant Total: $2,000,000 - $5,000,000
Geographic Preference: Area(s) in which the company operates; California
Primary Interests: Arts and Culture; Community Affairs; Education; Environment/Conservation; Health and Human Services

Public Affairs and Related Activities Personnel

At Headquarters

BONNO, Anthony J.
Senior V. President, Human Resources
Tel: (949) 219 - 3011
Fax: (949) 219 - 5130
TF: (800) 800 - 7646

GOODMAN, Milda C.
Assistant V. President, Public Relations and Advertising
mgoodman@pacificlife.com
Tel: (949) 219 - 3469
Fax: (949) 219 - 7614
TF: (800) 800 - 7646

HARDWIG, Brenda
Community Relations Coordinator
Tel: (949) 219 - 3787
Fax: (949) 219 - 7614
TF: (800) 800 - 7646

HASKELL, Robert G.
Senior V. President, Public Affairs
Tel: (949) 219 - 3022
Fax: (949) 219 - 5130
TF: (800) 800 - 7646

Responsibilities include corporate philanthropy.

MAYS, Thomas
V. President, Government Relations
Tel: (949) 219 - 3639
Fax: (949) 219 - 7614
TF: (800) 800 - 7646

MYSZKA, Michele
Director, Community Relations
Tel: (949) 219 - 3214
Fax: (949) 219 - 7614
TF: (800) 800 - 7646

Pacific Mutual Life Insurance Co.

See listing on page 368 under Pacific Life Insurance Co.

Pacific Power & Light Co.

See listing on page 369 under PacifiCorp.

PacifiCare Health Systems, Inc.

A member of the Public Affairs Council. A healthcare services company. Merged with FHP Internat'l Corp.
www.pacificare.com

Chairman and Chief Exec. Officer
PHANSTIEL, Howard G.
Tel: (714) 227 - 3000
Fax: (714) 226 - 3653

Main Headquarters
Mailing: P.O. Box 6006
Cypress, CA 90630
Tel: (714) 227 - 3000
Fax: (714) 226 - 3653
Street: 5995 Plaza Dr.
Cypress, CA 90630

Political Action Committees

PacifiCare Health Systems Inc. Employees PAC
Contact: Leigh Volkland
P.O. Box 6006
Cypress, CA 90630
Tel: (714) 226 - 3211
Fax: (714) 226 - 3653

Contributions to Candidates: $82,200 (01/05 - 09/05)
Democrats: $34,600; Republicans: $47,600.

Principal Recipients

SENATE DEMOCRATS		HOUSE DEMOCRATS	
Feinstein, Dianne (CA)	$5,000	Wu, David Mr. (OR)	$9,000
Baucus, Max (MT)	$2,000	Waxman, Henry A. (CA)	$5,000
Kennedy, Ted (MA)	$2,000	Sanchez, Loretta (CA)	$2,100
Stabenow, Debbie (MI)	$2,000	Matsui, Doris (CA)	$2,000

SENATE REPUBLICANS		HOUSE REPUBLICANS	
Kyl, Jon L (AZ)	$4,000	Bonilla, Henry (TX)	$5,000
Talent, James (MO)	$2,000	Hastert, Dennis J. (IL)	$5,000
		Thomas, William M (CA)	$4,000
		Oxley, Michael (OH)	$3,000
		DeLay, Tom (TX)	$2,500
		McCrery, Jim (LA)	$2,500
		Johnson, Samuel (TX)	$2,100
		Beauprez, Robert (CO)	$2,000
		Dreier, David (CA)	$2,000
		Gohmert, Louis (TX)	$2,000
		Hall, Ralph (TX)	$2,000

Corporate Foundations and Giving Programs

PacifiCare Foundation
Contact: Riva Gebel
P.O. Box 6006
Cypress, CA 90630
Tel: (714) 825 - 5126
Fax: (714) 825 - 5028

Annual Grant Total: over $5,000,000
Geographic Preference: Arizona; California; Colorado; Guam; Nevada; Oklahoma; Oregon; Texas; Washington State
Primary Interests: Children; Education; Health and Human Services; Youth Services

Public Affairs and Related Activities Personnel

At Headquarters

BLACK, Carol
Senior V. President, Human Resources
carol.black@phs.com
Tel: (714) 226 - 3084
Fax: (714) 226 - 3653

GEBEL, Riva
Director, PacifiCare Health Systems Foundation
Mailstop: LCO1-322
riva.gebel@phs.com
Tel: (714) 825 - 5126
Fax: (714) 825 - 5028

KINCAID, Tracey
V. President, Corporate Communications
tracy.kincaid@phs.com
Tel: (714) 226 - 3084
Fax: (714) 226 - 3581

MARTIN, Jennifer
Manager, Public Policy
jennifer.martim@phs.com
Tel: (714) 226 - 2725
Fax: (714) 226 - 3653

MASON, Tyler
V. President, Public Relations
Mailstop: C420-583
tyler.mason@phs.com
Tel: (714) 226 - 3530
Fax: (714) 226 - 3018

NEWPORT, Janet G.
V. President, Public Policy
Mailstop: C420-536
janet.newport@phs.com
Tel: (714) 226 - 3707
Fax: (714) 226 - 3653

VOLKLAND, Leigh
Director, Government Relations
leigh.volkland@phs.com
Tel: (714) 226 - 3211
Fax: (714) 226 - 3653

WOOD, C. William
V. President, Community Relations; President, PacifiCare Foundation
Mailstop: LC05-322
bill.wood@phs.com
Tel: (714) 825 - 5125
Fax: (714) 825 - 5028

YARBROUGH, Dan
Director, Investor Relations
Mailstop: C120-533
dan.yarbrough@phs.com
Tel: (714) 226 - 3540
Fax: (714) 226 - 3581

At Other Offices

GUINN, Joe
V. President, Public Affairs
6200 Northwest Pkwy.
San Antonio, TX 78249
joe.guinn@phs.com
Tel: (210) 478 - 4500
Fax: (210) 478 - 4504

PacifiCorp

A diversified electric utility company providing service to customers in seven states under the names of Pacific Power and Utah Power Co. A subsidiary of ScottishPower plc.
www.pacificorp.com
Annual Revenues: $6 billion

PacifiCorp

* continued from previous page

President and Chief Exec. Officer
JOHANSEN, Judi
Tel: (503) 813 - 5000
Fax: (503) 813 - 7247
TF: (888) 221 - 7070

Main Headquarters
Mailing: 825 N.E. Multnomah
Suite 2000
Portland, OR 97232
Tel: (503) 813 - 5000
Fax: (503) 813 - 7247
TF: (888) 221 - 7070

Washington Office
Mailing: 555 11th St. NW
Sixth Floor
Washington, DC 20004
Tel: (202) 508 - 3490
Fax: (202) 639 - 9464

Political Action Committees

PacifiCorp PPM Energy PAC
Contact: Kevin A. Lynch
825 N.E. Multnomah
Suite 2000
Portland, OR 97232
Tel: (503) 813 - 5678
Fax: (503) 813 - 5272
TF: (888) 221 - 7070

Contributions to Candidates: $1,000 (01/05 - 09/05)
Republicans: $1,000.

Principal Recipients

SENATE REPUBLICANS
Smith, Gordon (OR) $1,000

HOUSE REPUBLICANS

Corporate Foundations and Giving Programs

PacifiCorp Foundation for Learning
Contact: Isaac Regenstreif
825 N.E. Multnomah
Suite 2000
Portland, OR 97232
Tel: (503) 813 - 7257
Fax: (503) 813 - 7249
TF: (888) 221 - 7070

Assets: $38,000,000 (2003)
Annual Grant Total: $2,000,000 - $5,000,000
Geographic Preference: California; Idaho; Oregon; Utah; Washington State; Wyoming; Area(s) in which the company operates
Primary Interests: Arts and Culture; Civic and Public Affairs; Education; Health and Human Services

Public Affairs and Related Activities Personnel

At Headquarters

BRADFORD, Pam
Foundation Grants Manager
pam.bradford@pacificorp.com
Tel: (503) 813 - 7219
Fax: (503) 813 - 7247
TF: (888) 221 - 7070

LYNCH, Kevin A.
V. President, Government Affairs
kevin.lynch@pacificorp.com
Tel: (503) 813 - 5678
Fax: (503) 813 - 5272
TF: (888) 221 - 7070

REGENSTREIF, Isaac
Exec. Director, PacifiCorp Foundation for Learning
isaac.regenstreif@pacificorp.com
Tel: (503) 813 - 7257
Fax: (503) 813 - 7249
TF: (888) 221 - 7070

SHERRARD, Rachel
V. President, External Communications
rachel.sherrard@pacificorp.com
Tel: (503) 813 - 5688
Fax: (503) 813 - 5378
TF: (888) 221 - 7070

At Washington Office

GLICK, Rich
Director, Government Affairs
rich.glick@pacificorp.com
Registered Federal Lobbyist.
Tel: (202) 508 - 3490
Fax: (202) 639 - 9464

At Other Offices

BOARDMAN, Kevin W.
Director, Government Affairs
(Utah Power Co.)
201 S. Main St.
23rd Floor
Salt Lake City, UT 84140
Tel: (801) 220 - 6818
Fax: (801) 220 - 3116

ESKELSEN, David
Public Relations Contact
201 S. Main St.
23rd Floor
Salt Lake City, UT 84140
Tel: (801) 220 - 2447

TARANTOLA, Bob
V. President, Wyoming
2840 E. Yellowstone Hwy.
Casper, WY 82602
robert.tarantola@pacificorp.com
Responsibilities include public affairs.
Tel: (307) 577 - 6901

Pactiv Corp.

A specialty packaging company. Manufactures, markets, and sells consumer products and food/foodservice packaging. Brand names include Hefty, Baggies, Hefty One-Zip, Kordite, and E-Z Foil.
www.pactiv.com
Annual Revenues: $2.812 billion

Chairman and Chief Exec. Officer
WAMBOLD, Richard L.
rwambold@pactiv.com
Tel: (847) 482 - 2000
TF: (888) 828 - 2850

Main Headquarters
Mailing: 1900 W. Field Ct.
Lake Forest, IL 60045
Tel: (847) 482 - 2000
TF: (888) 828 - 2850

Public Affairs and Related Activities Personnel

At Headquarters

FOSS, Lisa K.
V. President, Communications
lfoss@pactiv.com
Tel: (847) 482 - 2704
Fax: (847) 482 - 3360
TF: (888) 828 - 2850

HANNEMAN, Christine
Investor Relations Contact
channeman@pactiv.com
Tel: (847) 482 - 2429
Fax: (847) 482 - 3360
TF: (888) 828 - 2850

Pall Corp.

A manufacturer of filtration, separation and purification products and systems.
www.pall.com
Annual Revenues: $1.8 billion

Chairman and Chief Exec. Officer
KRASNOFF, Eric
eric_krasnoff@pall.com
Tel: (516) 484 - 5400
Fax: (516) 484 - 5228
TF: (800) 876 - 7255

Main Headquarters
Mailing: 25 Harbor Park Dr.
Port Washington, NY 11050
Tel: (516) 484 - 5400
Fax: (516) 484 - 3649
TF: (800) 876 - 7255

Public Affairs and Related Activities Personnel

At Headquarters

CONENELLO, Jim
Director, Corporate Communications
jim_conenello@pall.com
Tel: (516) 801 - 9200
Fax: (516) 484 - 3649
TF: (800) 876 - 7255

IANNUCCI, Patricia J.
V. President, Corporate Communications
pat_iannucci@pall.com
Tel: (516) 801 - 9100
Fax: (516) 484 - 3649
TF: (800) 876 - 7255

KATZ, Marcia
Director, Public Relations
marcia_katz@pall.com
Tel: (516) 801 - 9128
Fax: (516) 484 - 3649
TF: (800) 876 - 7255

palmOne, Inc.

Formerly known as Palm, Inc. Manufactures hand-held computer systems and smartphones. Spun-off PalmSource, Inc. (see separate listing) in October, 2003.
www.palmone.com

Chairman of the Board
BENHAMOU, Eric A.
Tel: (408) 503 - 7000
Fax: (408) 503 - 2750

Main Headquarters
Mailing: 400 N. McCarthy Blvd.
Milpitas, CA 95035
Tel: (408) 503 - 7000
Fax: (408) 503 - 2750

Public Affairs and Related Activities Personnel

At Headquarters

LORION, Mike
V. President, Education
Tel: (408) 503 - 7000
Fax: (408) 503 - 2750

MORALI, Philippe
Interim Chief Financial Officer
Responsibilities include investor relations.
Tel: (408) 503 - 7000
Fax: (408) 503 - 2750

SOMSAK, Marlene
V. President, Corporate Communications
Tel: (408) 503 - 7000
Fax: (408) 503 - 2750

PalmSource, Inc.

Manufacturers Palm OS, the operating system that powers 35 million wireless devices. Spun-off from Palm, Inc. in October, 2003.
www.palmsource.com

Chairman of the Board
BENHAMOU, Eric A.
Tel: (408) 400 - 3000
Fax: (408) 400 - 1500

President and Chief Exec. Officer
NAGEL, David
Tel: (408) 400 - 3000
Fax: (408) 400 - 1500

Main Headquarters
Mailing: 1240 Crossman Ave.
Sunnyvale, CA 94089-1116
Tel: (408) 400 - 3000
Fax: (408) 400 - 1500

PalmSource, Inc.

* continued from previous page

Public Affairs and Related Activities Personnel

At Headquarters

MEINTZER, Kip E. — Tel: (408) 400 - 1909
Director, Investor Relations — Fax: (408) 400 - 1580
kip.meintzer@palmsource.com

SPINDLER, Laurie — Tel: (408) 400 - 1924
Public Relations Specialist — Fax: (408) 400 - 1500
laurie.spindler@palmsource.com

YOCHUM, Doreen "Dory" — Tel: (408) 400 - 3000
Chief Administrative Officer and Secretary — Fax: (408) 400 - 1500
Responsibilities include human resources.

Pan American Life Insurance Co.

www.panamericanlife.com
Annual Revenues: $280.9 million

Chairman and Interim Chief Exec. Officer — Tel: (504) 566 - 1300
KELLY, John T. — TF: (877) 989 - 4550

Main Headquarters
Mailing: P.O. Box 60219 — Tel: (504) 566 - 1300
New Orleans, LA 70160 — TF: (877) 989 - 4550
Street: 601 Poydras St., Suite 1400
New Orleans, LA 70130

Corporate Foundations and Giving Programs

Pan American Life Insurance Co. Contributions
Contact: Melissa Ann Eugene
P.O. Box 60219 — Tel: (504) 566 - 3101
New Orleans, LA 70160 — Fax: (504) 566 - 3335

Annual Grant Total: none reported
Geographic Preference: Area in which the company is headquartered
Primary Interests: Health and Human Services

Public Affairs and Related Activities Personnel

At Headquarters

EUGENE, Melissa Ann — Tel: (504) 566 - 3101
Coordinator, Corporate Communications — Fax: (504) 566 - 3335

MAUNOIR, Peter F. — Tel: (504) 566 - 3774
Second V. President, Government Relations

SCHEXNAYDER, Todd G. — Tel: (504) 566 - 1300
Senior V. President, Human Resources and Corporate Services — TF: (877) 989 - 4550

STEEN, William — Tel: (504) 566 - 1300
Corporate Secretary and Senior V. President, Government Relations
wsteen@wewill4u.com

Panasonic

See listing on page 309 under Matsushita Electric Corp of America.

The Pantry, Inc.

Operator of convenience stores under several names, including Big K, Minimart, Quick Stop and others.
www.thepantry.com
Annual Revenues: $2.6 billion

President and Chief Exec. Officer — Tel: (919) 774 - 6700
SODINI, Peter J. — Fax: (919) 774 - 3329

Main Headquarters
Mailing: P.O. Box 1410 — Tel: (919) 774 - 6700
Sanford, NC 27330 — Fax: (919) 774 - 3329
Street: 1801 Douglas Dr.
Sanford, NC 27330

Public Affairs and Related Activities Personnel

At Headquarters

KELLY, Dan — Tel: (919) 774 - 6700
V. President, Chief Financial Officer and Secretary — Fax: (919) 774 - 3329
Responsibilities include media relations

WRIGHT, Belinda — Tel: (919) 774 - 6700
Investor Relations Contact — Fax: (919) 774 - 3329

Papa John's Internat'l Inc.

A pizza company.
www.papajohns.com
Annual Revenues: $946.2 million

Chairman and Chief Exec. Officer — Tel: (502) 261 - 7272
SCHNATTER, John H. — Fax: (502) 261 - 4315

Main Headquarters
Mailing: P.O. Box 99900 — Tel: (502) 261 - 7272
Louisville, KY 40269-0900 — Fax: (502) 261 - 4315
Street: 2002 Papa Johns Blvd.
Louisville, KY 40299-2367

Corporate Foundations and Giving Programs

Papa John's Corporate Giving Program
P.O. Box 99900 — Tel: (502) 261 - 7272
Louisville, KY 40269-0900 — Fax: (502) 261 - 4315

Annual Grant Total: none reported
Geographic Preference: Area(s) in which employees live and work; Area in which the company is headquartered

Public Affairs and Related Activities Personnel

At Headquarters

FLANERY, David — Tel: (502) 261 - 4753
Senior V. President, Finance, Chief Financial Officer and Treasurer — Fax: (502) 261 - 4315
Responsibilities include media and investor relations.

SHERMAN, Karen — Tel: (502) 261 - 4987
V. President, Communications — Fax: (502) 261 - 4315
karen_sherman@papajohns.com

Parametric Technology Corp.

See listing on page 398 under PTC.

Paramount Parks

See listing on page 505 under Viacom Inc/CBS Corp.

Paramount Pictures Corp.

See listing on page 505 under Viacom Inc/CBS Corp.

Parker Hannifin Corp.

A producer of motion-control components and systems for industrial, automotive, aerospace and commercial markets. Acquired Commercial Intertech Corp. in 2000.
www.parker.com

Chairman of the Board — Tel: (216) 896 - 3000
COLLINS, Duane — Fax: (216) 896 - 4000
dcollins@parker.com — TF: (800) 272 - 7537

President and Chief Exec. Officer — Tel: (216) 896 - 3000
WASHKEWICZ, Don — Fax: (216) 896 - 4000
TF: (800) 272 - 7537

Main Headquarters
Mailing: 6035 Parkland Blvd. — Tel: (216) 896 - 3000
Cleveland, OH 44124-4141 — Fax: (216) 896 - 4000
TF: (800) 272 - 7537

Corporate Foundations and Giving Programs

Parker Hannifin Foundation
Contact: Thomas A. Piraino, Jr.
6035 Parkland Blvd. — Tel: (216) 896 - 3000
Cleveland, OH 44124-4141 — Fax: (216) 896 - 4000
TF: (800) 272 - 7537

Annual Grant Total: $1,000,000 - $2,000,000
Geographic Preference: National
Primary Interests: Arts and Culture; Community Affairs; Economic Development; Higher Education; Medicine and Health Care; Scholarship Funds; Social Services
Recent Recipients: American Red Cross; Case Western Reserve University; Cleveland Orchestra; Nat'l Merit Scholarship; Purdue University; United Negro College Fund

Public Affairs and Related Activities Personnel

At Headquarters

CRUM, Lorrie P. — Tel: (216) 896 - 3000
V. President, Corporate Communications — Fax: (216) 896 - 4000
TF: (800) 272 - 7537

GAREY, Daniel T. — Tel: (216) 896 - 3000
V. President, Human Resources — Fax: (216) 896 - 4000
TF: (800) 272 - 7537

PIRAINO, Thomas A., Jr. — Tel: (216) 896 - 3000
V. President, Secretary and General Counsel; Secretary, Parker Hannifin Foundation — Fax: (216) 896 - 4000
TF: (800) 272 - 7537
Responsibilities include investor relations.

PISTELL, Timothy K. — Tel: (216) 896 - 3000
Treasurer — Fax: (216) 896 - 4000
TF: (800) 272 - 7537
Responsibilities include political action.

SEMIK, Chris — Tel: (216) 896 - 3000
Contact, Parker Hannifin Foundation — Fax: (216) 896 - 4000
csemik@parker.com — TF: (800) 272 - 7537

At Other Offices

FLOHR, Cheryl C. — Tel: (949) 833 - 3000
Manager, Community Services — Fax: (949) 851 - 3277
18321 Jamboree Rd.
Irvine, CA 92612-1073

Parsons Brinckerhoff

Engineering/planning consultants.
www.pbworld.com
Annual Revenues: $1.4 billion

Chairman and Chief Exec. Officer
O'NEILL, Thomas J. — Tel: (212) 465 - 5000 Fax: (212) 465 - 5096

Main Headquarters
Mailing: One Penn Plaza, Second Floor, New York, NY 10119 — Tel: (212) 465 - 5000 Fax: (212) 465 - 5477

Washington Office
Mailing: 1401 K St. NW, Suite 701, Washington, DC 20005 — Tel: (202) 783 - 0241 Fax: (202) 783 - 0229

Political Action Committees

Parsons Brinckerhoff Inc. PAC
Contact: Catherine Connor
1401 K St. NW
Suite 701
Washington, DC 20005 — Tel: (202) 783 - 0241 Fax: (202) 783 - 0229

Contributions to Candidates: $32,000 (01/05 - 09/05)
Democrats: $14,500; Republicans: $16,500; Other: $1,000.

Principal Recipients

SENATE DEMOCRATS		HOUSE DEMOCRATS	
Feinstein, Dianne (CA)	$1,000	Blumenauer, Earl (OR)	$2,000
		Kilpatrick, Carolyn (MI)	$2,000
SENATE REPUBLICANS		**HOUSE REPUBLICANS**	
Talent, James (MO)	$4,000	Knollenberg, Joe (MI)	$2,500
Vitter, David (LA)	$1,000	Dewine, R. Pat (OH)	$1,500
		Tiahrt, Todd W. (KS)	$1,500
		Young, Don E (AK)	$1,500

Public Affairs and Related Activities Personnel

At Headquarters

COOPER, Judy
Senior V. President
cooperj@pbworld.com — Tel: (212) 465 - 5332 Fax: (212) 465 - 5477
Serves as the main headquarters Senior Public Affairs Executive.

RYAN, John J.
Senior V. President/Director, Human Resources — Tel: (212) 465 - 5000 Fax: (212) 465 - 5096

At Washington Office

CONNOR, Catherine
Senior Vice President, Government Relations — Tel: (202) 783 - 0241 Fax: (202) 783 - 0229

Parsons Corp.

Provides technical and management solutions to federal, regional, and local government agencies as well as private industries worldwide.
www.parsons.com
Annual Revenues: $3.6 billion

Chairman and Chief Exec. Officer
MCNULTY, James F. — Tel: (626) 440 - 2000 Fax: (626) 440 - 2630

Main Headquarters
Mailing: 100 W. Walnut St., Pasadena, CA 91124 — Tel: (626) 440 - 2000 Fax: (626) 440 - 2630

Washington Office
Mailing: 1133 15th St. NW, Suite 800, Washington, DC 20005-2701 — Tel: (202) 775 - 3300 Fax: (202) 775 - 3422

Political Action Committees

Parsons Corp. PAC
Contact: Robert W. Jones
100 W. Walnut St.
Pasadena, CA 91124 — Tel: (626) 440 - 2000 Fax: (626) 440 - 2630

Contributions to Candidates: $126,500 (01/05 - 09/05)
Democrats: $59,500; Republicans: $61,000; Other: $6,000.

Principal Recipients

SENATE DEMOCRATS		HOUSE DEMOCRATS	
Reid, Harry (NV)	$4,000	Schiff, Adam (CA)	$10,000
Feinstein, Dianne (CA)	$3,500	Hoyer, Steny (MD)	$5,000
Nelson, Bill (FL)	$2,000		
		HOUSE OTHER	
		Oberstar, James L (MN)	$5,000
SENATE REPUBLICANS		**HOUSE REPUBLICANS**	
		Blunt, Roy (MO)	$5,000
		DeLay, Tom (TX)	$5,000
		Hastert, Dennis J. (IL)	$5,000
		Hunter, Duncan (CA)	$5,000
		Young, Don E (AK)	$5,000

Corporate Foundations and Giving Programs

Parsons Corporate Giving Program
Contact: Erin Kuhlman
100 W. Walnut St.
Pasadena, CA 91124 — Tel: (626) 440 - 4590 Fax: (626) 440 - 2630

Annual Grant Total: none reported

Public Affairs and Related Activities Personnel

At Headquarters

GOODRICH, David R.
V. President, Human Resources — Tel: (626) 440 - 2000 Fax: (626) 440 - 2630

JONES, Robert W.
PAC Treasurer — Tel: (626) 440 - 2000 Fax: (626) 440 - 2630

KUHLMAN, Erin
V. President, Corporate Relations
erin.kuhlman@parsons.com — Tel: (626) 440 - 4590 Fax: (626) 440 - 2630

At Washington Office

BONDS, Andrew
V. President, Government Relations
andrew.bonds@parsons.com — Tel: (202) 775 - 3300 Fax: (202) 775 - 3422

SHOCKLEY, Larry G.
V. President, Government Relations — Tel: (202) 775 - 3300 Fax: (202) 775 - 3422

THRASH, James E.
Senior V. President, Government Relations — Tel: (202) 775 - 3300 Fax: (202) 775 - 3422

Pathmark Stores Inc.

A supermarket retailer.
www.pathmark.com

Chairman of the Board
MOODY, James L., Jr. — Tel: (732) 499 - 3000 Fax: (732) 499 - 6872

Chief Exec. Officer
SCOTT, Eileen R. — Tel: (732) 499 - 3500 Fax: (732) 499 - 6872

Main Headquarters
Mailing: 200 Milik St., Carteret, NJ 07008-1194 — Tel: (732) 499 - 3000 Fax: (732) 499 - 6872

Corporate Foundations and Giving Programs

Pathmark Stores Inc. Corporate Giving
Contact: Richard Savner
200 Milik St.
Carteret, NJ 07008-1194 — Tel: (732) 499 - 4327 Fax: (732) 499 - 3072

Annual Grant Total: under $100,000
Geographic Preference: Area(s) in which the company operates; Delaware; New Jersey; New York; Pennsylvania
Primary Interests: Community Development; Education; Youth Services
Recent Recipients: March of Dimes; St. Jude's Children's Research Hospital

Public Affairs and Related Activities Personnel

At Headquarters

GUTMAN, Harvey M.
Senior V. President, Retail Development — Tel: (732) 499 - 4327 Fax: (732) 499 - 3100
Responsibilities include investor relations.

JOYCE, Robert
Exec. V. President, Human Resources — Tel: (732) 499 - 3500 Fax: (732) 499 - 6872

SAVNER, Richard
Director, Public Affairs — Tel: (732) 499 - 4327 Fax: (732) 499 - 3072
Responsibilities include corporate communications, government affairs, and corporate philanthropy.

Payless ShoeSource

Provider of family footwear.
www.paylessshoesource.com

Chairman and Chief Exec. Officer
DOUGLASS, Steven J. — Tel: (785) 233 - 5171 Fax: (785) 295 - 6866

Main Headquarters
Mailing: 3231 S.E. Sixth St., Topeka, KS 66607 — Tel: (785) 233 - 5171 Fax: (785) 295 - 6866

Political Action Committees

Payless Shoe Source Political Action Committee
Contact: Ullrich Porzig
3231 S.E. Sixth St.
Topeka, KS 66607 — Tel: (785) 233 - 5171 Fax: (785) 295 - 6866

Payless ShoeSource

** continued from previous page*

Contributions to Candidates: $1,500 (01/05 - 09/05)
Republicans: $1,500.

Principal Recipients

SENATE REPUBLICANS		HOUSE REPUBLICANS	
		Weller, Jerry (IL)	$1,000
		Shaw, Clay (FL)	$500

Corporate Foundations and Giving Programs

Payless ShoeSource Foundation
3231 S.E. Sixth St. — Tel: (785) 233 - 5171
Topeka, KS 66607 — Fax: (785) 295 - 6866

Annual Grant Total: none reported

Public Affairs and Related Activities Personnel

At Headquarters

PORZIG, Ullrich — Tel: (785) 233 - 5171
PAC Treasurer — Fax: (785) 295 - 6866

REID, Timothy J. — Tel: (785) 295 - 6695
Director, Corporate Communications and Investor Relations — Fax: (785) 295 - 6866

PC Connection, Inc.

A direct marketer of computer products and solutions.
www.pcconnection.com

Chairman, President and Chief Exec. Officer — Tel: (603) 683 - 2000
GALLUP, Patricia — Fax: (603) 683 - 2041
pgallup@pcconnection.com

Main Headquarters
Mailing: 730 Milford Rd. — Tel: (603) 683 - 2000
Route 101A — Fax: (603) 683 - 2041
Merrimack, NH 03054-4631

Corporate Foundations and Giving Programs

PC Connection, Inc. Corporate Contributions Program
730 Milford Rd. — Tel: (603) 683 - 2000
Route 101A — Fax: (603) 683 - 2041
Merrimack, NH 03054-4631

Annual Grant Total: none reported
Gives only to 501(c)(3) organizations. Call 1-603-683-2163 for copy of guidelines.
Geographic Preference: New Hampshire; Ohio
Primary Interests: Arts and Culture; Children; Economic Development; Education; Environment/Conservation

Public Affairs and Related Activities Personnel

At Headquarters

BALDRIDGE, Steve — Tel: (603) 683 - 2000
V. President, Finance and Corporate Controller — Fax: (603) 683 - 2041
Responsibilities include public affairs.

BEFFA-NEGRINI, David — Tel: (603) 683 - 2000
V. President, Corporate Communications — Fax: (603) 683 - 2041

GAVIN, Mark — Tel: (603) 683 - 2000
Senior V. President, Finance, Chief Financial Officer and Director, Investor Relations — Fax: (603) 683 - 2041
mgavin@pcconnection.com

MOUSSEAU, Brad — Tel: (603) 683 - 2000
V. President, Human Resources — Fax: (603) 683 - 5748
bmousseau@pcconnection.com

Peabody Energy

A coal company with operations in the United States and Australia. Formerly known as the Peabody Group.
www.peabodyenergy.com
Annual Revenues: $2.7 billion

Chairman and Chief Exec. Officer — Tel: (314) 342 - 3400
ENGELHARDT, Irl F. — Fax: (314) 342 - 7797
iengelhardt@peabodyenergy.com

Main Headquarters
Mailing: 701 Market St. — Tel: (314) 342 - 3400
St. Louis, MO 63101-1826 — Fax: (314) 342 - 7799

Political Action Committees

Peabody Energy Political Action Committee
Contact: Richard A. Navarre
701 Market St. — Tel: (314) 342 - 7708
St. Louis, MO 63101-1826 — Fax: (314) 342 - 7597

Contributions to Candidates: $48,500 (01/05 - 09/05)
Democrats: $11,000; Republicans: $37,500.

Principal Recipients

SENATE DEMOCRATS		HOUSE DEMOCRATS	
Byrd, Robert C (WV)	$2,000	Boucher, Fredrick (VA)	$2,000
Conrad, Kent (ND)	$2,000		

SENATE REPUBLICANS		HOUSE REPUBLICANS	
Martinez, Mel (FL)	$2,500	Blunt, Roy (MO)	$5,000
Talent, James (MO)	$2,500	Hastert, Dennis J. (IL)	$5,000
Thomas, Craig (WY)	$2,000	Cantor, Eric (VA)	$4,000
		Hulshof, Kenny (MO)	$3,000
		Pombo, Richard (CA)	$2,000
		Wilson, Heather (NM)	$2,000

Corporate Foundations and Giving Programs

Peabody Energy Contributions Program
Contact: Sharon D. Fiehler
701 Market St. — Tel: (314) 342 - 7755
St. Louis, MO 63101-1826 — Fax: (314) 342 - 3499

Annual Grant Total: none reported

Public Affairs and Related Activities Personnel

At Headquarters

FIEHLER, Sharon D. — Tel: (314) 342 - 7755
Exec. V. President, Human Resources and Administration — Fax: (314) 342 - 3499
sfiehler@peabodyenergy.com

MADER, Kelly F. — Tel: (314) 342 - 7564
V. President, State Government Affairs — Fax: (314) 342 - 7799

MORROW, Christina A. — Tel: (314) 342 - 7651
Director, Investor Relations and Assistant Treasurer — Fax: (314) 342 - 7799

NAVARRE, Richard A. — Tel: (314) 342 - 7708
Exec. V. President and Chief Financial Officer — Fax: (314) 342 - 7597
rnavarre@peabodyenergy.com
Responsibilities include public affairs.

PALMER, Frederick D. — Tel: (314) 342 - 7624
Exec. V. President, Government Affairs — Fax: (314) 342 - 7614
fpalmer@peabodyenergy.com
Responsibilities include corporate philanthropy.

SCOTT, Lars W. — Tel: (314) 342 - 7594
Director, Coal Technology Development — Fax: (314) 342 - 7799
lscott@peabodyenergy.com
Responsibilities include environmental affairs.

SUTTON, Beth — Tel: (505) 287 - 2636
Manager, Public Affairs — Fax: (505) 287 - 5516
bsutton@peabodyenergy.com

SVEC, Victor P. — Tel: (314) 342 - 7768
V. President, Public and Investor Relations — Fax: (314) 342 - 7799
vsvec@peabodyenergy.com

Peabody Holding Co., Inc.

See listing on page 373 under Peabody Energy.

PECO Energy Co.

See listing on page 187 under Exelon Corp.

Pegasus Communications Corp.

Provides digital services to rural areas.
www.pgtv.com
Annual Revenues: $901.8 million

Chairman and Chief Exec. Officer — Tel: (610) 934 - 7000
PAGON, Marshall W. — Fax: (610) 934 - 7054
TF: (888) 438 - 7488

Main Headquarters
Mailing: 225 City Line Ave. — Tel: (610) 934 - 7000
Suite 200 — Fax: (610) 934 - 7054
Bala Cynwyd, PA 19004 — TF: (888) 438 - 7488

Political Action Committees

Pegasus Communications Corp. PAC
Contact: Ted S. Lodge
225 City Line Ave. — Tel: (610) 934 - 7000
Suite 200 — Fax: (610) 934 - 7054
Bala Cynwyd, PA 19004 — TF: (888) 438 - 7488

Contributions to Candidates: none reported (01/05 - 09/05)

Public Affairs and Related Activities Personnel

At Headquarters

BLANK, Scott A. — Tel: (610) 934 - 7000
Senior V. President, Legal and Corporate Affairs; General Counsel and Secretary — Fax: (610) 934 - 7054
TF: (888) 438 - 7488

Pegasus Communications Corp.

* continued from previous page

CRATE, Cheryl
V. President, Corporate Communications and Government Relations
cheryl.crate@pgtv.com
Tel: (703) 892 - 4230
Fax: (610) 934 - 7054
TF: (888) 438 - 7488

HEISLER, Karen M.
Senior V. President, Human Resources and Administrative Services
Tel: (610) 934 - 7000
Fax: (610) 934 - 7054
TF: (888) 438 - 7488

LODGE, Ted S.
President and Chief Operating Officer
Tel: (610) 934 - 7000
Fax: (610) 934 - 7054
TF: (888) 438 - 7488

Responsibilities include political action.

SMITH, Andrew
Investor Relations Contact
andrew.smith@pgtv.com
Tel: (610) 934 - 7000
Fax: (610) 934 - 7054
TF: (888) 438 - 7488

Pella Corp.

A manufacturer of wood windows and glass doors.

www.pella.com

President and Chief Exec. Officer
HAUGHT, Mel
Tel: (641) 621 - 1000
Fax: (641) 628 - 6070

Main Headquarters
Mailing: 102 Main St.
Pella, IA 50219
Tel: (641) 621 - 1000
Fax: (641) 628 - 6070

Corporate Foundations and Giving Programs

Pella Rolscreen Foundation
Contact: Mary Van Zante
102 Main St.
Pella, IA 50219
Tel: (641) 621 - 6224
Fax: (641) 628 - 6070

Annual Grant Total: $1,000,000 - $2,000,000

Geographic Preference: Iowa

Primary Interests: Arts and Culture; Community Development; Economic Development; Education; Environment/Conservation; Social Services

Recent Recipients: Central College (Pella, IA); Pella Library (Pella, IA); Pella Opera House (Pella, IA)

Public Affairs and Related Activities Personnel

At Headquarters

HARKEMA, Kathy
Public Affairs Specialist
krafka-harkemakk@pella.com
Tel: (641) 621 - 6971
Fax: (641) 628 - 6070

LINN, Myron
Manager, Government Affairs
Tel: (641) 621 - 6045
Fax: (641) 628 - 6070

VAN ZANTE, Mary
Director, Pella Rolscreen Foundation
Tel: (641) 621 - 6224
Fax: (641) 628 - 6070

The Penn Mutual Life Insurance Co.

www.pennmutual.com

Chairman and Chief Exec. Officer
CHAPPELL, Robert E.
Tel: (215) 956 - 8000
TF: (800) 523 - 0650

Main Headquarters
Mailing: 600 Dresher Rd.
Horsham, PA 19044
Tel: (215) 956 - 8000
TF: (800) 523 - 0650

Political Action Committees

The Penn Mutual Political Action Committee
Contact: Steven M. Herzberg
530 Walnut St.
Philadelphia, PA 19172

Contributions to Candidates: none reported (01/05 - 09/05)

Corporate Foundations and Giving Programs

Penn Mutual Corporate Contributions Program
Contact: Donna Beath
600 Dresher Rd.
Horsham, PA 19044
Tel: (215) 956 - 8000
TF: (800) 523 - 0650

Annual Grant Total: none reported

Public Affairs and Related Activities Personnel

At Headquarters

BEATH, Donna
Exec. Secretary
Responsibilities include corporate philanthropy.
Tel: (215) 956 - 8000
TF: (800) 523 - 0650

BIONDOLILLO, Michael A., JD
Exec. V. President, Human Resources
Tel: (215) 956 - 8000
TF: (800) 523 - 0650

At Other Offices

HERZBERG, Steven M.
Treasurer, Penn Mutual Political Action Committee
530 Walnut St.
Philadelphia, PA 19172

Penn Nat'l Insurance

A member of the Public Affairs Council. A regional, mutual insurance company.

www.pennnationalinsurance.com

Chairman of the Board
RHODES, John H.
Tel: (717) 234 - 4941
Fax: (717) 255 - 6850
TF: (800) 388 - 4764

President and Chief Exec. Officer
ROWE, Dennis C.
Tel: (717) 234 - 4941
Fax: (717) 255 - 6850
TF: (800) 388 - 4764

Main Headquarters
Mailing: P.O. Box 2361
Harrisburg, PA 17105-2361
Tel: (717) 234 - 4941
Fax: (717) 255 - 6850
TF: (800) 388 - 4764

Street: Two N. Second St.
Harrisburg, PA 17101

Public Affairs and Related Activities Personnel

At Headquarters

MARKLEY, Christopher D.
V. President, Corporate Communications
Tel: (717) 234 - 4941
Ext: 6895
Fax: (717) 257 - 6911
TF: (800) 388 - 4764

The Penn Traffic Co.

A food distributor store chain.

www.penntraffic.com

Main Headquarters
Mailing: 1200 State Fair Blvd.
Syracuse, NY 13221-4737
Tel: (315) 453 - 8500

Corporate Foundations and Giving Programs

The Penn Traffic Corporate Contributions Program
Contact: Mary Anne Hankins
1200 State Fair Blvd.
Syracuse, NY 13221-4737
Tel: (315) 453 - 8619
Fax: (315) 453 - 8672

Annual Grant Total: none reported

Public Affairs and Related Activities Personnel

At Headquarters

BREGANDE, Don
V. President, Human Resources
dbregande@penntraffic.com
Tel: (315) 461 - 2535
Fax: (315) 461 - 2324

HANKINS, Mary Anne
Director, Consumer and Public Affairs
Responsibilities include corporate philanthropy.
Tel: (315) 453 - 8619
Fax: (315) 453 - 8672

MARTIN, Randy
V. President and Chief Administrative Officer
rmartin@penntraffic.com
Responsibilities include investor relations.
Tel: (315) 453 - 2423
Fax: (315) 461 - 2645

J. C. Penney Co., Inc.

A national department store also engaged in insurance and real estate operations.

www.jcpenney.com

Annual Revenues: $32.004 billion

Chairman and Chief Exec. Officer
ULLMAN, Myron E., III
Tel: (972) 431 - 1000
Fax: (972) 431 - 1362
TF: (800) 222 - 6161

Main Headquarters
Mailing: 6501 Legacy Dr.
Plano, TX 75024-3698
Tel: (972) 431 - 1000
Fax: (972) 431 - 1362
TF: (800) 222 - 6161

Political Action Committees

PenneyPAC
Contact: Brian H. Weight
6501 Legacy Dr.
Plano, TX 75024-3698
Tel: (972) 431 - 1000
Fax: (972) 431 - 1362
TF: (800) 222 - 6161

Contributions to Candidates: $35,300 (01/05 - 09/05)

J. C. Penney Co., Inc.

* continued from previous page

Democrats: $5,000; Republicans: $30,300.

Principal Recipients

SENATE DEMOCRATS		HOUSE DEMOCRATS	
Nelson, Benjamin (NE)	$2,000	Jefferson, William (LA)	$1,000
Cardin, Benjamin (MD)	$1,000		
SENATE REPUBLICANS		**HOUSE REPUBLICANS**	
Allen, George (VA)	$3,100	Pryce, Deborah (OH)	$2,000
Santorum, Richard (PA)	$2,500	Sensenbrenner, Jim (WI)	$2,000
Hutchison, Kay Bailey (TX)	$2,100	Johnson, Samuel (TX)	$1,100
Dewine, Richard (OH)	$2,000	Cannon, Christopher (UT)	$1,000
Lugar, Richard G (IN)	$2,000	Cantor, Eric (VA)	$1,000
Talent, James (MO)	$2,000	Jindal, Bobby (LA)	$1,000
Burns, Conrad (MT)	$1,000	Marchant, Kenny (TX)	$1,000
Kyl, Jon L (AZ)	$1,000	Myrick, Sue (NC)	$1,000
		Portman, Robert J (OH)	$1,000
		Sessions, Pete (TX)	$1,000
		Weller, Jerry (IL)	$1,000

Corporate Foundations and Giving Programs

J. C. Penney Corporate Contributions
6501 Legacy Dr.
Plano, TX 75024-3698
Tel: (972) 431 - 1000
Fax: (972) 431 - 1362
TF: (800) 222 - 6161

Annual Grant Total: over $5,000,000
60% local giving by stores, 40% national giving by headquarters.
Geographic Preference: Area in which the company is headquartered; National
Primary Interests: K-12 Education; United Way Campaigns
Recent Recipients: Junior Achievement; Nat'l 4-H Council; Nat'l Urban League

J. C. Penney Co. Fund
Contact: Jeannette Siegel
6501 Legacy Dr.
Plano, TX 75024-3698
Tel: (972) 431 - 1000
Fax: (972) 431 - 1362
TF: (800) 222 - 6161

Annual Grant Total: $750,000 - $1,000,000
Geographic Preference: Area in which the company is headquartered; Area(s) in which the company operates; National
Primary Interests: Civic and Public Affairs; Education; Social Services
Recent Recipients: Junior Achievement

Public Affairs and Related Activities Personnel

At Headquarters

DOUGLASS, Susan
Manager, Shareholder Relations
sdoug2@jcpenney.com
Tel: (972) 431 - 1859
Fax: (972) 431 - 1362
TF: (800) 222 - 6161

PHILLIPS, Paula
Senior Government Relations Coordinator
Tel: (972) 431 - 1250
Fax: (972) 431 - 1362
TF: (800) 222 - 6161

SEYMOUR TOWERY, Anne
V. President and Director, Company Communications
Tel: (972) 431 - 4147
Fax: (972) 431 - 1362
TF: (800) 222 - 6161

SIEGEL, Jeannette
V. President, Foundations
Tel: (972) 431 - 1000
Fax: (972) 431 - 1362
TF: (800) 222 - 6161

THEILLMAN, Michael
Executive V. President, Chief Human resources and Administrative Officer
Tel: (972) 431 - 1000
Fax: (972) 431 - 1362
TF: (800) 222 - 6161

WATKINS, Wynfred C.
Senior V. President and Director, Communications and Public Affairs
Tel: (972) 431 - 1972
Fax: (972) 431 - 1362
TF: (800) 222 - 6161

WEIGHT, Brian H.
PAC Treasurer
Tel: (972) 431 - 1000
Fax: (972) 431 - 1362
TF: (800) 222 - 6161

WESLOW, Norman J.
Senior Government Relations Counsel
nweslow@jcpenney.com
Tel: (972) 431 - 4147
Fax: (972) 431 - 1362
TF: (800) 222 - 6161

Penske Truck Leasing Co. LP

www.penske-truckleasing.com

Chairman and Chief Exec. Officer
PENSKE, Roger S.
Tel: (248) 648 - 2500
Fax: (248) 648 - 2005

Main Headquarters
Mailing: Route 10 - Green Hills
P.O. Box 563
Reading, PA 19603
Tel: (610) 775 - 6325

Political Action Committees

Penske Truck Leasing Co. LP PAC
Contact: James A. Rosen
Route 10 - Green Hills
P.O. Box 563
Reading, PA 19603
Tel: (610) 775 - 6325

Contributions to Candidates: $10,500 (01/05 - 09/05)
Democrats: $4,000; Republicans: $6,500.

Principal Recipients

SENATE DEMOCRATS	HOUSE DEMOCRATS	
	Holden, Timothy (PA)	$3,000
	Tauscher, Ellen O (CA)	$1,000
SENATE REPUBLICANS	**HOUSE REPUBLICANS**	
	Gerlach, Jim (PA)	$3,000
	Young, Don E (AK)	$2,500
	Pombo, Richard (CA)	$1,000

Public Affairs and Related Activities Personnel

At Headquarters

ROSEN, James A.
V. President, Government Relations
james.rosen@penske.com
Responsibilities include political action.
Tel: (610) 775 - 6325

Pentair, Inc.

A diversified manufacturer.
www.pentair.com

Chairman and Chief Exec. Officer
HOGAN, Randall J.
Tel: (763) 545 - 1730

Main Headquarters
Mailing: 5500 Wayzata Blvd.
Suite 800
Golden Valley, MN 55416-1259
Tel: (763) 545 - 1730

Corporate Foundations and Giving Programs

Pentair Foundation
Contact: Michelle Murphy
5500 Wayzata Blvd.
Suite 800
Golden Valley, MN 55416-1259
Tel: (763) 545 - 1730

Annual Grant Total: $1,000,000 - $2,000,000
Primary Interests: Arts and Humanities; Education; Health; Human Welfare

Public Affairs and Related Activities Personnel

At Headquarters

CAIN, Mark J.
Director, Corporate Communications and Public Affairs
Responsibilities include government affairs.
Tel: (763) 545 - 1730

CATHCART, Richard J.
President, Pentair Foundation
Tel: (763) 545 - 1730

HARRISON, David D.
Exec. V. President and Chief Financial Officer
Responsibilities include investor relations.
Tel: (763) 545 - 1730

KOURY, Frederick S.
Senior V. President, Human Resources
Tel: (763) 545 - 1730

MURPHY, Michelle
Manager, Pentair Foundation
Tel: (763) 545 - 1730

People's Bank

www.peoples.com

Chairman, Chief Exec. Officer and President
KLEIN, John
john.klein@peoples.com
Tel: (203) 338 - 7171

Main Headquarters
Mailing: Bridgeport Center
850 Main St.
Bridgeport, CT 06604-4913
Tel: (203) 338 - 7171

Political Action Committees

People's Bank Federal PAC
Bridgeport Center
850 Main St.
Bridgeport, CT 06604-4913
Tel: (203) 338 - 7171

Contributions to Candidates: none reported (01/05 - 09/05)

Corporate Foundations and Giving Programs

People's Bank Community Relations
Contact: Barbara P. Johnson

People's Bank

* continued from previous page

Bridgeport Center
850 Main St.
Bridgeport, CT 06604-4913 — Tel: (203) 338 - 7171

Annual Grant Total: none reported
Geographic Preference: Connecticut
Primary Interests: Education; Housing

Public Affairs and Related Activities Personnel

At Headquarters

CARLSON, Valerie — Tel: (203) 338 - 7171
V. President, Communications
valerie.carlson@peoples.com

JOHNSON, Barbara P. — Tel: (203) 338 - 7171
Senior V. President, Community Relations
barbara.johnson@peoples.com

Peoples Energy Corp.

A diversified energy company.
www.peoplesenergy.com
Annual Revenues: $2.26 billion

Chairman, and Chief Exec. Officer — Tel: (312) 240 - 4403
PATRICK, Thomas M. — Fax: (312) 240 - 4541
Mailstop: 24th Floor
t.patrick@pecorp.com

Main Headquarters
Mailing: 130 E. Randolph Dr. — Tel: (312) 240 - 4000
Chicago, IL 60601 — Fax: (312) 240 - 4082

Political Action Committees

Peoples Energy Corp. Federal PAC
130 E. Randolph Dr. — Tel: (312) 240 - 4000
Chicago, IL 60601 — Fax: (312) 240 - 4082

Contributions to Candidates: $6,500 (01/05 - 09/05)
Democrats: $3,500; Republicans: $3,000.

Peoples Energy Corp. PAC
Contact: Rodrigo Sierra
130 E. Randolph Dr. — Tel: (312) 240 - 4380
Chicago, IL 60601 — Fax: (312) 240 - 4389

Contributions to Candidates: none reported (01/05 - 09/05)

Corporate Foundations and Giving Programs

Peoples Energy Corp. Contributions Program
Contact: Richard B. Turner
130 E. Randolph Dr. — Tel: (312) 240 - 7516
Chicago, IL 60601 — Fax: (312) 240 - 4389

Annual Grant Total: $1,000,000 - $2,000,000
Geographic Preference: Area(s) in which the company operates; Chicago, IL; Illinois
Primary Interests: Community Development; Education; Environment/Conservation

Public Affairs and Related Activities Personnel

At Headquarters

CASTRO, Elizabeth — Tel: (312) 240 - 3661
Manager, Public/Community Relations — Fax: (312) 240 - 4389
Mailstop: 18th Floor
e.castro@pecorp.com

CHITI, Jim — Tel: (312) 240 - 4730
Manager, Investor Relations — Fax: (312) 240 - 4220
Mailstop: 24th Floor

FIORELLA, Salvatore — Tel: (312) 240 - 3977
Manager, State Regulatory Affairs — Fax: (312) 240 - 4542
Mailstop: 24th Floor
s.fiorella@pecorp.com

JONES, Adrienne — Tel: (312) 240 - 3750
Director, Government Relations — Fax: (312) 240 - 4389
Mailstop: 24th Floor
a.jones@pecorp.com

MATUSZAK, S. J. — Tel: (312) 240 - 4100
Director, Environmental Affairs — Fax: (312) 240 - 4082
Mailstop: 24th Floor

ROY, Alex D. — Tel: (312) 240 - 7800
Manager, Financial and Shareholder Services — Fax: (312) 240 - 4220
Mailstop: 24th Floor
a.roy@pecorp.com

SCHUITEMA, George — Tel: (312) 240 - 4544
Manager, Risk Management — Fax: (312) 240 - 4937
Mailstop: 24th Floor
g.schuitema@pecorp.com

SIERRA, Rodrigo — Tel: (312) 240 - 4380
V. President, Communications and Government Relations — Fax: (312) 240 - 4389
Mailstop: 18th Floor
r.sierra@pecorp.com

TURNER, Richard B. — Tel: (312) 240 - 7516
Manager, Corporate Contributions — Fax: (312) 240 - 4389
Mailstop: 18th Floor

PeopleSoft

See listing on page 364 under Oracle Corporation.

The Pep Boys-Manny, Moe & Jack

A provider of automotive parts, accessories and services
www.pepboys.com
Annual Revenues: $2.1 billion

Chairman and Chief Exec. Officer — Tel: (215) 430 - 9095
STEVENSON, Lawrence N. — Fax: (215) 430 - 9533

Main Headquarters
Mailing: 3111 W. Allegheny Ave. — Tel: (215) 430 - 9095
Philadelphia, PA 19132 — Fax: (215) 430 - 9533

Corporate Foundations and Giving Programs

Pep Boys Corporate Giving
Contact: Dee Dalton
3111 W. Allegheny Ave. — Tel: (215) 430 - 9204
Philadelphia, PA 19132 — Fax: (215) 229 - 1410

Annual Grant Total: none reported
Geographic Preference: Area(s) in which the company operates
Primary Interests: Education; Employment; Historic Preservation
Recent Recipients: Big Brothers/Big Sisters

Public Affairs and Related Activities Personnel

At Headquarters

DALTON, Dee — Tel: (215) 430 - 9204
Administrative Assistant to the President — Fax: (215) 229 - 1410
dee_dalton@pepboys.com
Responsibilities include corporate philanthropy.

FURTKEVIC, William — Tel: (215) 430 - 9676
Director, Marketing Communications — Fax: (215) 430 - 3660
bill_furtkevic@pepboys.com

PIETAK, Carole L. — Tel: (215) 430 - 9095
V. President, Human Resources — Fax: (215) 430 - 9533

YANOWITZ, Harry F. — Tel: (215) 430 - 9720
Senior V. President, Strategy and Business Development — Fax: (215) 430 - 9533
Responsibilities include investor relations.

Pepco Holdings, Inc.

A member of the Public Affairs Council. Pepco Holdings, Inc. is a diversified energy holding company with headquarters in Washington, DC. Its principal utilities, Pepco and Conectiv (see separate listing), deliver power to customers in the District of Columbia, Delaware, Maryland, New Jersey, and Virginia. Pepco Holdings, Inc. engages in regulated utility operations by delivering electricity and natural gas and provides competitive energy, energy products, and services to residential and commercial customers.
www.pepcoholdings.com
Annual Revenues: $2.503 billion

Chairman, President and Chief Executive Officer — Tel: (202) 872 - 2000
WRAASE, Dennis R.

Main Headquarters
Mailing: 701 Ninth St. NW — Tel: (202) 872 - 2000
Washington, DC 20068

Political Action Committees

PEPCO Holdings Inc. PEPCO-Conectiv PAC (PHI PAC)
Contact: James S. Potts
701 Ninth St. NW — Tel: (202) 872 - 2000
Washington, DC 20068

Contributions to Candidates: $19,130 (01/05 - 09/05)
Democrats: $12,130; Republicans: $7,000.

Principal Recipients

SENATE DEMOCRATS
Bingaman, Jeff (NM) $2,500
Carper, Thomas R (DE) $1,580
Mikulski, Barbara (MD) $1,000

HOUSE DEMOCRATS
Hoyer, Steny (MD) $1,050
Andrews, Robert (NJ) $1,000
Boucher, Fredrick (VA) $1,000
Cummings, Elijah (MD) $1,000
Norton, Eleanor Holmes (DC) $1,000
Towns, Edolphus (NY) $1,000
Wynn, Albert (MD) $1,000

SENATE REPUBLICANS
Santorum, Richard (PA) $2,500

HOUSE REPUBLICANS
Barton, Joe L (TX) $1,000
Castle, Michael (DE) $1,000
Gillmor, Paul E (OH) $1,000
Lobiondo, Frank (NJ) $1,000

Pepco Holdings, Inc.

** continued from previous page*

Corporate Foundations and Giving Programs

Pepco Corporate Contributions Program
Contact: Pamela Holman
701 Ninth St. NW — Tel: (202) 872 - 3488
Washington, DC 20068

Annual Grant Total: none reported

Geographic Preference: Washington, DC metropolitan area (including Northern Virginia and Suburban Maryland)

Primary Interests: Arts and Humanities; Community Affairs; Higher Education

Public Affairs and Related Activities Personnel

At Headquarters

BOURSCHEID, Ernest J. — Tel: (202) 872 - 2797
Manager, Investor Relations — Fax: (202) 331 - 6874
ejbourscheid@pepco.com

DOBKIN, Robert A. — Tel: (202) 872 - 2680
Principal Media Representative — Fax: (202) 331 - 4857
radobkin@pepco.com

DOVE, Nathaniel E. — Tel: (202) 872 - 2000
PAC Treasurer

DOWNS, Jill R. — Tel: (202) 872 - 3187
V. President, Corporate Communications

ELLIOT, Kate — Tel: (202) 872 - 2000
Senior Government Affairs Representative

HOLMAN, Pamela — Tel: (202) 872 - 3488
Coordinator, Contributions and Membership Committee

JARVIS, Debbi L. — Tel: (202) 872 - 2680
Manager, Media Relations — Fax: (202) 331 - 4857
dljarvis@pepco.com

PERRY, Beverly L. — Tel: (202) 872 - 2373
Senior V. President, Government Affairs and Public Policy
blperry@pepco.com

POTTS, James S. — Tel: (202) 872 - 2000
PAC Contact

TORGERSON, William T. — Tel: (202) 872 - 2000
Vice Chairman and General Counsel

Pepperidge Farm, Inc.

See listing on page 99 under Campbell Soup Co.

The Pepsi Bottling Group

A manufacturer, seller, and distributor of Pepsi-Cola beverages. Became an independent, publicly traded company in 1998.

www.pbg.com

Chairman and Chief Exec. Officer — Tel: (914) 767 - 6894
CAHILL, John T. — Fax: (914) 767 - 7761

Main Headquarters
Mailing: One Pepsi Way — Tel: (914) 767 - 6000
Somers, NY 10589-2201 — Fax: (914) 767 - 7761

Corporate Foundations and Giving Programs

Pepsi Bottling Group Foundation
Contact: Angela Buonocore
One Pepsi Way — Tel: (914) 767 - 7472
Somers, NY 10589-2201 — Fax: (914) 767 - 1264

Annual Grant Total: none reported

Public Affairs and Related Activities Personnel

At Headquarters

BERISFORD, John L. — Tel: (914) 767 - 6000
Senior V. President, Human Resources — Fax: (914) 767 - 7761

BUONOCORE, Angela — Tel: (914) 767 - 7472
V. President, Corporate Communications — Fax: (914) 767 - 1264
angela.buonocore@pepsi.com
Responsibilities include corporate philanthropy.

MCANDREW, Kelly — Tel: (914) 767 - 7690
Director, Public Relations — Fax: (914) 767 - 1264
kelly.mcandrew@pepsi.com

SETTINO, Mary Winn — Tel: (914) 767 - 7216
Director, Investor Relations — Fax: (914) 767 - 1813
marwinn.settino@pepsi.com

Pepsi-Cola North America

See listing on page 377 under PepsiCo, Inc.

PepsiAmericas, Inc.

Formerly operated under the name Whitman Corp. A holding company for Pepsi-Cola General Bottlers.

www.pepsiamericas.com
Annual Revenues: $3.17 billion

Chairman and Chief Exec. Officer — Tel: (847) 818 - 5000
POHLAD, Robert C. — Fax: (847) 847 - 6880
robert.pohlad@pepsiamericas.com

Main Headquarters
Mailing: 3501 Algonquin Rd. — Tel: (847) 818 - 5000
Rolling Meadows, IL 60008 — Fax: (847) 847 - 6880

Corporate Foundations and Giving Programs

PepsiAmericas Foundation
3501 Algonquin Rd. — Tel: (847) 818 - 5000
Rolling Meadows, IL 60008 — Fax: (847) 847 - 6880

Assets: $5,629,670 (1999)
Annual Grant Total: $400,000 - $500,000

Supports organizations and projects in which employees are personally involved.

Geographic Preference: Chicago, IL

Primary Interests: Education

Public Affairs and Related Activities Personnel

At Headquarters

YOUNG, Larry D. — Tel: (847) 818 - 5000
Exec. V. President, Corporate Affairs — Fax: (847) 847 - 6880

At Other Offices

GIESE, Jean — Tel: (612) 661 - 3718
Director, Investor and Shareholder Relations
4000 Dain Rauscher Plaza
60 S. Sixth St.
Minneapolis, MN 55402

PepsiCo, Inc.

PUBLIC AFFAIRS COUNCIL

A member of the Public Affairs Council. A major manufacturer of beverages, snack foods, and juices. The company acquired Quaker Oats Co. in 2001.

www.pepsico.com
Annual Revenues: $29 billion

Chairman and Chief Exec. Officer — Tel: (914) 253 - 2000
REINEMUND, Steven S — Fax: (914) 253 - 2070

Main Headquarters
Mailing: 700 Anderson Hill Rd. — Tel: (914) 253 - 2000
Purchase, NY 10577-1444 — Fax: (914) 253 - 2203

Washington Office
Mailing: 101 Constitution Ave. NW — Tel: (202) 742 - 4408
Suite 900 — Fax: (202) 742 - 4422
Washington, DC 20001

Political Action Committees

PepsiCo Concerned Citizens Fund
Contact: Galen J. Reser
101 Constitution Ave. NW — Tel: (202) 742 - 4408
Suite 900 — Fax: (202) 742 - 4422
Washington, DC 20001

Contributions to Candidates: $36,592 (01/05 - 09/05)
Democrats: $6,000; Republicans: $30,592.

Principal Recipients

SENATE DEMOCRATS		HOUSE DEMOCRATS	
Leahy, Patrick (VT)	$1,000	Clyburn, James (SC)	$1,000
Nelson, Benjamin (NE)	$1,000	Pastor, Edward (AZ)	$1,000
		Ruppersberger, Dutch (MD)	$1,000
		Skelton, Ike (MO)	$1,000

SENATE REPUBLICANS		HOUSE REPUBLICANS	
Santorum, Richard (PA)	$5,000	Bonilla, Henry (TX)	$5,000
Dewine, Richard (OH)	$3,000	Graves, Sam (MO)	$2,000
Bryant, Edward (TN)	$2,000	Kline, John P (MN)	$2,000
Coleman, Norm (MN)	$2,000	Dewine, R. Pat (OH)	$1,000
Kennedy, Mark (MN)	$2,000	Hobson, David (OH)	$1,000
McConnell, Mitch (KY)	$1,000	LaHood, Ray (IL)	$1,000
		Northup, Anne M. (KY)	$1,000
		Rogers, Michael J (MI)	$1,000
		Wilson, Heather (NM)	$1,000

Corporate Foundations and Giving Programs

PepsiCo Foundation
Contact: Jacqueline R. Millan

PepsiCo, Inc.

* continued from previous page

700 Anderson Hill Rd.
Purchase, NY 10577-1444
Tel: (914) 253 - 3153
Fax: (914) 253 - 3553

Annual Grant Total: over $5,000,000

The PepsiCo Foundation emphasizes the support of non-profit organizations where Purchase-based employees are personally involved as volunteers. Guidelines are available.

Public Affairs and Related Activities Personnel

At Headquarters

ANDREWS, David R.
Senior V. President, Government Affairs, General Counsel and Secretary
Tel: (914) 253 - 2300
Fax: (914) 249 - 8166

BRYANT, Daniel J.
V. President, Government Affairs
Tel: (914) 253 - 3600
Fax: (914) 253 - 3669

CARBONELL, Nestor
V. President, International Public Affairs
nestor.carbonell@pepsi.com
Tel: (914) 253 - 3900
Fax: (914) 249 - 8159

DECECCO, Dave
Public Relations
(Pepsi-Cola North America)
Tel: (914) 253 - 2655
Fax: (914) 249 - 8202

FINNERTY, Louise Hoppe
V. President, International Government Affairs
louise.finnerty@pepsi.com
Tel: (914) 253 - 3890
Fax: (914) 249 - 8159

GONZALES, David
V. President, Community Affairs
david.gonzales@pepsi.com
Tel: (914) 253 - 2000
Fax: (914) 253 - 2070

HASKIN, Greg
Manager, Government Affairs
(Pepsi-Cola North America)
greg.haskin@pepsi.com
Tel: (949) 643 - 5762
Fax: (949) 425 - 8220

JABBONSKY, Larry
Public Relations
(Pepsi-Cola North America)
larry.jabbonsky@pepsi.com
Tel: (914) 253 - 2647
Fax: (914) 249 - 8202

MACKENZIE, Tod J.
Senior V. President, Corporate Communications
tod.mackenzie@pepsi.com
Tel: (914) 253 - 2000

MADEIRA, Rebecca W.
Senior V. President, Public Affairs
(Pepsi-Cola North America)
rebecca.madeira@pepsi.com
Tel: (914) 253 - 2000
Fax: (914) 767 - 7214

MILLAN, Jacqueline R.
Director, Corporate Contributions
Tel: (914) 253 - 3153
Fax: (914) 253 - 3553

PALMER, Elaine
Director, External Affairs
elaine.palmer@pepsi.com
Tel: (914) 253 - 3122
Fax: (914) 253 - 2203

SWINK, Philip
V. President, Government Affairs
(Pepsi-Cola North America)
Tel: (914) 253 - 2613
Fax: (914) 249 - 8201

WILCOX, Peter G.
Manager, Government Affairs - East
(Pepsi-Cola North America)
peter.wilcox@pepsi.com
Tel: (914) 253 - 2609
Fax: (914) 253 - 8201

At Washington Office

AVERY, Elizabeth
V. President, International Government Relations
Tel: (202) 742 - 4408
Fax: (202) 742 - 4422

RESER, Galen J.
V. President, North America Government Affairs
galen.reser@pepsi.com
Registered Federal Lobbyist.
Tel: (202) 742 - 4408
Fax: (202) 742 - 4422

At Other Offices

LEZMAN, Steve
Director, Government Affairs
(Tropicana Products)
555W. Monroe St.
Chicago, IL 60661
Tel: (941) 742 - 2578
Fax: (941) 749 - 3966

Perdue Farms

A poultry producer and processor.

www.perdue.com

Annual Revenues: $2.7 billion

Chairman and Chief Exec. Officer
PERDUE, James A.
Tel: (410) 543 - 3000
Fax: (410) 543 - 3884

Main Headquarters
Mailing: P.O. Box 1537
Salisbury, MD 21802-1537
Tel: (410) 543 - 3000
Fax: (410) 543 - 3884
Street: Old Ocean City Rd.
Salisbury, MD 21802

Corporate Foundations and Giving Programs

Arthur W. Perdue Foundation
Contact: Howard Millard
P.O. Box 1537
Salisbury, MD 21802-1537
Tel: (410) 543 - 3000
Fax: (410) 543 - 3884

Annual Grant Total: none reported

Awards scholarships to children of Perdue associates.

Primary Interests: Education

Public Affairs and Related Activities Personnel

At Headquarters

CHERRIER, Tita
Director, Public Relations
tita.cherrier@perdue.com
Tel: (410) 860 - 4407
Fax: (410) 341 - 2509

MILLARD, Howard
Foundation Contact
howard.millard@perdue.com
Tel: (410) 543 - 3000
Fax: (410) 543 - 3884

WHALEY, Christine G.
chris.whaley@perdue.com
Tel: (410) 543 - 3000
Fax: (410) 543 - 3884

Performance Food Group Co.

A food service distributor.

www.pfgc.com

Chairman, President and Chief Exec. Officer
SLEDD, Robert C.
bsledd@pfgc.com
Tel: (804) 285 - 7340
Fax: (804) 484 - 7701

Main Headquarters
Mailing: P.O. Box 29269
Richmond, VA 23242-9269
Tel: (804) 484 - 7700
Fax: (804) 484 - 7701
Street: 12500 W. Creek Pkwy.
Richmond, VA 23238

Corporate Foundations and Giving Programs

Performance Food Group Co. Corporate Contributions Program
P.O. Box 29269
Richmond, VA 23242-9269
Tel: (804) 484 - 7700
Fax: (804) 484 - 7701

Annual Grant Total: none reported

Primary Interests: Arts and Culture; Community Affairs; Education; Environment/Conservation; Health; Youth Services

Recent Recipients: American Heart Ass'n; American Red Cross; Junior Achievement; March of Dimes; United Negro College Fund; United Way

Public Affairs and Related Activities Personnel

At Headquarters

COLLIER, Kevin
Director, Investor Relations
Tel: (804) 484 - 7700
Fax: (804) 484 - 7701

MOORE, Cheryl
Director, Corporate Communications
Tel: (804) 484 - 6273
Fax: (804) 484 - 7701

PerkinElmer, Inc.

A global technology company that supplies products and technical services to manufacturers and end-users in industrial and government markets. Formerly known as EG&G, Inc.

www.perkinelmer.com

Chairman, Chief Exec. Officer and President
SUMME, Gregory L.
Tel: (781) 237 - 5100
Fax: (781) 431 - 4255

Main Headquarters
Mailing: 45 William St., Third Floor
Wellesley Hills, MA 02481-4078
Tel: (781) 237 - 5100
Fax: (781) 431 - 4255

Corporate Foundations and Giving Programs

PerkinElmer Foundation
Contact: Patricia Cucinotta
45 William St., Third Floor
Wellesley Hills, MA 02481-4078
Tel: (781) 237 - 5100
Fax: (781) 431 - 4255

Annual Grant Total: $300,000 - $400,000

Geographic Preference: Area(s) in which the company operates

Primary Interests: Higher Education; Medicine and Health Care; Youth Services

Recent Recipients: Dana Farber Cancer Institute; Partnership for a Drug-Free America; United Way

Public Affairs and Related Activities Personnel

At Headquarters

CUCINOTTA, Patricia
Assistant to Chairman
Responsibilities include corporate philanthropy.
Tel: (781) 237 - 5100
Fax: (781) 431 - 4255

SUTHERBY, Dan
Investor and Media Relations Contact
Tel: (781) 431 - 4306
Fax: (781) 431 - 4255

WALSH, Richard F.
Senior V. President, Human Resources
Tel: (781) 431 - 4122
Fax: (781) 431 - 4255

Perot Systems Corp.

An information technology service provider.

www.perotsystems.com
Annual Revenues: $1.205 billion

Chairman of the Board
PEROT, H. Ross — Tel: (972) 577 - 0000

President and Chief Exec. Officer
PEROT, H. Ross, Jr. — Tel: (972) 577 - 0000

Main Headquarters
Mailing: 2300 W. Plano Pkwy.
Plano, TX 75075 — Tel: (972) 577 - 0000

Public Affairs and Related Activities Personnel

At Headquarters

LAKES, Sharon — Tel: (972) 577 - 6012
Manager, Media Relations (Healthcare)
sharon.lakes@ps.net

LYON, John — Tel: (972) 577 - 0000
Director, Investor Relations — Fax: (972) 577 - 6790
invest@ps.net

MCNAMARA, Joe — Tel: (972) 577 - 6165
Director, Communications
joe.mcnamara@ps.net

REEVES, Eddie — Tel: (972) 577 - 0000
V. President, Corporate Communications

Perrigo Co.

Produces over-the-counter pharmaceuticals and nutritional supplements for store brands.

www.perrigo.com
Annual Revenues: $826.3 million

Chairman, President and Chief Exec. Officer
GIBBONS, David T. — Tel: (269) 673 - 8451; Fax: (269) 673 - 9128

Main Headquarters
Mailing: 515 Eastern Ave.
Allegan, MI 49010-9070 — Tel: (269) 673 - 8451; Fax: (269) 673 - 9128

Public Affairs and Related Activities Personnel

At Headquarters

SCHENK, Ernest J. — Tel: (269) 673 - 9212
Manager, Investor Relations and Communications — Fax: (269) 673 - 9128
eschenk@perrigo.com

PETCO Animal Supplies, Inc.

Operates stores with pet-related products and services.

www.petco.com
Annual Revenues: $1.5 billion

Chairman of the Board
DEVINE, Brian K. — Tel: (858) 453 - 7845; Fax: (858) 677 - 3489

Chief Exec. Officer
MYERS, James M. — Tel: (858) 453 - 7845; Fax: (858) 677 - 3489

Main Headquarters
Mailing: 9125 Rehco Rd.
San Diego, CA 92121-2270 — Tel: (858) 453 - 7845; Fax: (858) 677 - 3489

Corporate Foundations and Giving Programs

PETCO Foundation
9125 Rehco Rd.
San Diego, CA 92121-2270 — Tel: (858) 453 - 7845; Fax: (858) 677 - 3489

Annual Grant Total: over $5,000,000
Geographic Preference: Area(s) in which the company operates; National
Primary Interests: Animal Protection
Recent Recipients: Humane Soc. of the U.S., The

Public Affairs and Related Activities Personnel

At Headquarters

KASSEBAUM, Jim — Tel: (858) 453 - 7845
V. President, Corporate Communications — Fax: (858) 677 - 3489

MITCHELL, Janet D. — Tel: (858) 453 - 7845
Senior V. President, Human Resources and Administration — Fax: (858) 677 - 3489

UNDERWOOD, Shawn — Tel: (858) 453 - 7845 Ext: 3571
Communications Representative
shawnu@petco.com — Fax: (858) 677 - 3489

PETsMART, Inc.

A retailer of pet food, pet supplies, and pet services.

www.petsmart.com
Annual Revenues: $2.501 billion

Chairman and Chief Exec. Officer
FRANCIS, Philip L. — Tel: (623) 580 - 6100; Fax: (623) 580 - 6508
pfrancis@ssg.petsmart.com

Main Headquarters
Mailing: 19601 N. 27th Ave.
Phoenix, AZ 85027 — Tel: (623) 580 - 6100; Fax: (623) 580 - 6508

Corporate Foundations and Giving Programs

PETsMart Charities
Contact: Joyce Briggs
19601 N. 27th Ave.
Phoenix, AZ 85027 — Tel: (623) 580 - 6100; Fax: (623) 580 - 6508

Annual Grant Total: none reported
Primary Interests: Animal Protection

Public Affairs and Related Activities Personnel

At Headquarters

ADAMS, Lynne — Tel: (623) 587 - 2104
V. President, Corporate Communications — Fax: (623) 580 - 6508
ladams@ssg.petsmart.com

BRIGGS, Joyce — Tel: (623) 580 - 6100
Director, PETsMart Charities — Fax: (623) 580 - 6508
jbriggs@ssg.petsmart.com

KULLMAN, Timothy E. — Tel: (623) 580 - 6100
Senior V. President and Chief Financial Officer — Fax: (623) 580 - 6508

Responsibilities include investor relations.

Pfizer Inc.

A diversified, research-based health care company with businesses in pharmaceuticals, hospital products, animal health, consumer products, speciality chemicals, and speciality minerals. Acquired Warner-Lambert in 2000 and Pharmacia Corp. in 2002.

www.pfizer.com
Annual Revenues: $32.4 billion

Chairman and Chief Exec. Officer
MCKINNELL, Henry A., Ph.D. — Tel: (212) 573 - 2323; Fax: (212) 573 - 1853

Main Headquarters
Mailing: 235 E. 42nd St.
New York, NY 10017-5755 — Tel: (212) 733 - 2323; Fax: (212) 573 - 1853

Washington Office
Contact: M. Kenneth Bowler, Ph.D.
Mailing: 325 Seventh St. NW
Suite 1200
Washington, DC 20004-1007 — Tel: (202) 783 - 7070; Fax: (202) 347 - 2044

Political Action Committees

Pfizer Inc. PAC
Contact: Richard A. Passov
235 E. 42nd St.
New York, NY 10017-5755 — Tel: (212) 573 - 2323; Fax: (212) 573 - 1853

Contributions to Candidates: $445,250 (01/05 - 09/05)
Democrats: $102,500; Republicans: $341,750; Other: $1,000.

Principal Recipients

SENATE DEMOCRATS
Clinton, Hillary Rodham (NY) $5,000
Ford, Harold E Jr (TN) $5,000

HOUSE DEMOCRATS
Menendez, Robert (NJ) $10,000

SENATE REPUBLICANS
Dole, Elizabeth (NC) $5,000
Hatch, Orrin (UT) $5,000

HOUSE REPUBLICANS
Chocola, Christopher (IN) $12,000
Fitzpatrick, Michael (PA) $10,000
Fossella, Vito (NY) $10,000
Gerlach, Jim (PA) $10,000
Shaw, Clay (FL) $10,000
Simmons, Rob (CT) $10,000

Corporate Foundations and Giving Programs

The Pfizer Foundation
Contact: Charles A. "Chuck" Hardwick
235 E. 42nd St.
New York, NY 10017-5755 — Tel: (212) 573 - 7833; Fax: (212) 808 - 8880

Annual Grant Total: $2,000,000 - $5,000,000
Funds are contributed directly through Pfizer, Inc. and through the company-supported Pfizer Foundation.
Geographic Preference: National; New York City
Primary Interests: Arts and Culture; Community Affairs; Education; Health

Pfizer Corporate Giving Program
Contact: Rick Luftglass

Pfizer Inc.

* continued from previous page

235 E. 42nd St. Tel: (212) 573 - 7491
New York, NY 10017-5755 Fax: (212) 573 - 2883

Annual Grant Total: none reported

In addition to Foundation grants, Pfizer makes significant donations directly to improve the educational, cultural, health and social conditions in communities where it has facilities. Includes gifts in kind, product donations, matching gift program, and employee volunteer program.

Geographic Preference: Area(s) in which the company operates

Primary Interests: Arts and Culture; Community Affairs; Education; Health

Public Affairs and Related Activities Personnel

At Headquarters

ALDRIDGE, Ron
Senior Director, Investor Relations
ron.aldridge@pfizer.com
Tel: (212) 573 - 3685
Fax: (212) 573 - 1853

BAGGER, Richard
Senior V. President, Government Relations and Public Affairs
Tel: (212) 573 - 2323
Fax: (212) 573 - 1853

GARDNER, James R., Ph.D.
V. President, Investor Relations
Tel: (212) 573 - 2668
Fax: (212) 808 - 8617

HARDWICK, Charles A. "Chuck"
Senior V. President, Worldwide Gov't Relations, Comm., Media Relations, and Public Policy ; Pres. and Exec. Director, The Pfizer Foundation
chardwick@pfizer.com
Tel: (212) 573 - 7833
Fax: (212) 808 - 8880

JACKSON, Yvonne
Senior V. President and Head, Human Resources
Tel: (212) 733 - 2323
Fax: (212) 573 - 1853

LUFF, Paula
Director, International Philanthropy Programs
paula.luff@pfizer.com
Tel: (212) 573 - 2932
Fax: (212) 573 - 2883

LUFTGLASS, Rick
Director, U.S. Philanthropy
rich.luftglass@pfizer.com
Tel: (212) 573 - 7491
Fax: (212) 573 - 2883

MALLETT, Robert L.
Senior V. President, Corporate Affairs
robert.mallett@pfizer.com
Tel: (212) 733 - 0922
Fax: (212) 573 - 2883

MCCORMICK, Andy
V. President, Media Relations
amccormick@pfizer.com
Tel: (212) 573 - 1226
Fax: (212) 808 - 8799

PASSOV, Richard A.
PAC Treasurer
Tel: (212) 573 - 2323
Fax: (212) 573 - 1853

At Washington Office

BENNETT, Catherine P.
V. President, Federal Tax and Trade Legislation
cbennett@pfizer.com
Registered Federal Lobbyist.
Tel: (202) 783 - 7070
Fax: (202) 347 - 2044

BOLICK, Gary M.
Director, Government Relations
Tel: (202) 783 - 7070
Fax: (202) 347 - 2044

BOWLER, M. Kenneth, Ph.D.
V. President, Federal Government Relations
Registered Federal Lobbyist.
Tel: (202) 783 - 7070
Fax: (202) 347 - 2044

FINKELNBURG, Marjorie
Director, Government Relations
Registered Federal Lobbyist.
Tel: (202) 783 - 7070
Fax: (202) 347 - 2044

JUDGE, Dolly
Senior Director, Federal Relations
Registered Federal Lobbyist.
Tel: (202) 783 - 7070
Fax: (202) 347 - 2044

LAMARCA, Louis
Director, Federal Relations
Registered Federal Lobbyist.
Tel: (202) 783 - 7070
Fax: (202) 347 - 2044

MCCARTHY, Justin J.
Director, Government Relations
Registered Federal Lobbyist.
Tel: (202) 783 - 7070
Fax: (202) 347 - 2044

PRINCIPI, Anthony J.
V. President, Government Relations
Tel: (202) 783 - 7070
Fax: (202) 347 - 2044

At Other Offices

ARDOIN, Kenneth A.
Director, Government Relations
(Pfizer Pharmaceuticals, Inc.)
Seven Village Circle, Suite 500
Westlake, TX 76262
kardoin@pfizer.com
Tel: (817) 491 - 8410

BEATY, Sandy
Director, Government Relations
3200 W. End Ave., Suite 500
Nashville, TN 37203
Tel: (615) 783 - 1740
Fax: (615) 783 - 1739

BISHOP-MURPHY, Melissa
State Government Relations Manager - Georgia and Alabama
400 Perimeter Center Terrace, Suite 700
Atlanta, GA 30346
mbishop-murphy@pfizer.com
Tel: (770) 551 - 5170

CORYELL, Kristine, M.D.
Director, Government Relations
425 N. Martingale Rd.
Suite 900
Schaumburg, IL 60173
kristine.coryell@pfizer.com
Tel: (847) 413 - 4520
Fax: (847) 413 - 4507

JANUSHKOWSKY, Vera
Director, Government Relations
1201 K St., Suite 1010
Sacramento, CA 95814
vjanushkowsky@pfizer.com
Tel: (916) 557 - 1177
Ext: 7504
Fax: (916) 557 - 1175

MARITATO, Anna Maria
Director, Government Relations
284 State St., Second Floor
Albany, NY 12210
amaritato@pfizer.com
Tel: (518) 463 - 9133

NICKLES, J. David
Senior Government Relations Manager--Florida
400 Perimeter Center Terrace, Suite 1000
Atlanta, GA 30346
david.nickles@pfizer.com
Tel: (770) 551 - 5174
Fax: (770) 804 - 1783

SMITH-CALLAHAN, Deborah Ann
Director, Government Relations
400 Perimeter Center Terrace, Suite 1000
Atlanta, GA 30346
dsmith-callahan@pfizer.com
Tel: (770) 551 - 5173
Fax: (770) 804 - 1783

Pfizer Pharmaceuticals, Inc.

See listing on page 379 under Pfizer Inc.

PG & E Corp.

PUBLIC AFFAIRS COUNCIL

A member of the Public Affairs Council. An electric and gas utility. Subsidiaries include Pacific Gas and Electric Co.

www.pge-corp.com
Annual Revenues: $22.959 billion

Chairman of the Board
DARBEE, Peter A.
Tel: (415) 267 - 7000
Fax: (415) 267 - 7252

President and Chief Exec. Officer
KING, Thomas B.
Tel: (415) 267 - 7000
Fax: (415) 267 - 7268

Main Headquarters
Mailing: One Market
Spear Tower, Suite 2400
San Francisco, CA 94105
Tel: (415) 267 - 7000
Fax: (415) 267 - 7268

Washington Office
Contact: Steven L. Kline
Mailing: 900 Seventh St. NW, Suite 950
Washington, DC 20001-3886
Tel: (202) 638 - 3500
Fax: (202) 638 - 3522

Political Action Committees

PG & E Corp. Employees Energy PAC
Contact: George Opacic
77 Beale St.
San Francisco, CA 94105
Tel: (415) 973 - 7000
Fax: (415) 972 - 5105

Contributions to Candidates: $65,680 (01/05 - 09/05)

Democrats: $36,680; Republicans: $29,000.

Principal Recipients

SENATE DEMOCRATS		HOUSE DEMOCRATS	
Bingaman, Jeff (NM)	$4,000	Matsui, Doris (CA)	$3,000
Carper, Thomas R (DE)	$3,080	Capps, Lois G (CA)	$2,500
Landrieu, Mary (LA)	$1,000	Pelosi, Nancy (CA)	$2,500
Nelson, Benjamin (NE)	$1,000		

SENATE REPUBLICANS		HOUSE REPUBLICANS	
Burns, Conrad (MT)	$2,000	Barton, Joe L (TX)	$2,500
Burr, Richard (NC)	$1,000	DeLay, Tom (TX)	$2,500
Chafee, Lincoln (RI)	$1,000	Pombo, Richard (CA)	$2,100
Inhofe, James M (OK)	$1,000	Dreier, David (CA)	$2,000
Smith, Gordon (OR)	$1,000	Issa, Darrell (CA)	$2,000
Thomas, Craig (WY)	$1,000		
Vitter, David (LA)	$1,000		

Corporate Foundations and Giving Programs

Pacific Gas and Electric Co. Corporate Contributions
Contact: Dan Quigley

PG & E Corp.

* continued from previous page

77 Beale St.
San Francisco, CA 94105
Tel: (415) 973 - 1636
Fax: (415) 973 - 8239

Annual Grant Total: over $5,000,000

Emphasis is on organizations that prepare individuals to become productive, working members of society and that provide a transition from dependency to self-sufficiency. Guidelines are available.

Geographic Preference: Area(s) in which the company operates; California
Primary Interests: Civic and Public Affairs; Education; Health; Social Services

Public Affairs and Related Activities Personnel

At Headquarters

BASGAL, Ophelia
V. President, Civic Partnership and Community Initiatives
(Pacific Gas and Electric Co.)
Tel: (415) 267 - 7000
Fax: (415) 267 - 7268

BRENNAN, Jean F.
Senior Director, Corporate Human Resources Planning and Development
Tel: (415) 817 - 8248
Fax: (415) 817 - 8245

CHENG, Linda
V. President and Corporate Secretary
Responsibilities include investor relations.
Tel: (415) 267 - 7017
Fax: (415) 267 - 7260

HAPNER, DeAnn
V. President, Federal Regulatory Policy and Rates
(Pacific Gas and Electric Co.)
Tel: (415) 267 - 7000
Fax: (415) 267 - 7268

HERTZOG, Brian
Director, Corporate Communications
Tel: (415) 267 - 7205
Fax: (415) 267 - 7262

MCFADDEN, Nancy
V. President, Governmental Relations
(Pacific Gas and Electric Co.)
Tel: (415) 267 - 7000
Fax: (415) 267 - 7268

RICHARD, Daniel D., Jr.
Senior V. President, Public Policy and Government Affairs
Tel: (415) 267 - 7130
Fax: (415) 267 - 7255

TOGNERI, Gabriel B.
V. President, Investor Relations
Tel: (415) 267 - 7100
Fax: (415) 267 - 7262

At Washington Office

CARTER, Rick A.
Director, Federal Governmental Relations
Registered Federal Lobbyist.
Tel: (202) 638 - 3500
Fax: (202) 638 - 3522

KLINE, Steven L.
V. President, Federal Governmental and Regulatory Relations
(Pacific Gas and Electric Co.)
Registered Federal Lobbyist.
Tel: (202) 638 - 3500
Fax: (202) 638 - 3522

SHELBY, Melanie M.
Manager, Federal Governmental Relations
Tel: (202) 638 - 3500
Fax: (202) 638 - 3522

TRAMUTO, James A.
V. President, Governmental Relations
Tel: (202) 638 - 3500
Fax: (202) 638 - 3522

At Other Offices

GULIASI, Les
Director, State Agency Relations
(Pacific Gas and Electric Co.)
77 Beale St.
Mailstop: MC B10C
San Francisco, CA 94105
Tel: (415) 973 - 7000

HARRIS, Robert L.
V. President, Environmental Affairs
(Pacific Gas and Electric Co.)
77 Beale St.
Mailstop: MC B32
San Francisco, CA 94105
Tel: (415) 973 - 3833
Fax: (415) 973 - 1359

JACKSON, Russell M.
Senior V. President, Human Resources
(Pacific Gas and Electric Co.)
77 Beale St.
San Francisco, CA 94105
Tel: (415) 267 - 7136
Fax: (415) 267 - 7258

OPACIC, George
Manager, Political Contributions
77 Beale St.
Mailstop: MC B29H
San Francisco, CA 94105
Tel: (415) 973 - 7000
Fax: (415) 972 - 5105

PULLING, Wendy
Director, Environmental Services
(Pacific Gas and Electric Co.)
77 Beale St.
Mailstop: MC B24A
San Francisco, CA 94105
Tel: (415) 973 - 7000
Fax: (415) 973 - 0230

QUIGLEY, Dan
Director, Corporate Contributions
(Pacific Gas and Electric Co.)
77 Beale St.
Mailstop: MC B32
San Francisco, CA 94105
Tel: (415) 973 - 1636
Fax: (415) 973 - 8239

REGAN, Frank J.
V. President, Governmental Relations
(Pacific Gas and Electric Co.)
77 Beale St.
Mailstop: MC B32
San Francisco, CA 94105
Tel: (415) 973 - 6587
Fax: (415) 972 - 5529

SIMI, Lawrence J.
Director, Regional Governmental Relations
(Pacific Gas and Electric Co.)
77 Beale St.
Mailstop: MC B29H
San Francisco, CA 94105
Tel: (415) 973 - 3032
Fax: (415) 973 - 1718

SMITH-JANIS, Megan
Director, Governmental Relations
77 Beale St.
San Francisco, CA 94105
Tel: (415) 973 - 8190
Fax: (415) 973 - 7666

STOCK, Bill
Manager, Regulatory Relations
(Pacific Gas and Electric Co.)
77 Beale St.
Mailstop: MC B10C
San Francisco, CA 94105
Tel: (415) 973 - 7000
Fax: (415) 973 - 7226

TOMCALA, Karen A.
V. President, Regulatory Relations
77 Beale St.
San Francisco, CA 94105
Tel: (415) 973 - 7000
Fax: (415) 972 - 5625

WALSH, Kimberly
V. President, Communications
(Pacific Gas and Electric Co.)
77 Beale St.
San Francisco, CA 94105
Tel: (415) 973 - 0015
Fax: (415) 973 - 0951

Pharmaceutical Product Development, Inc.

www.ppdi.com
Annual Revenues: $727 million

Chairman and Chief Exec. Officer
ESHELMAN, Fred N.
Tel: (910) 251 - 0081
Fax: (910) 762 - 5820

Main Headquarters
Mailing: 3151 S. 17th St.
Wilmington, NC 28412-6461
Tel: (910) 251 - 0081
Fax: (910) 762 - 5820

Public Affairs and Related Activities Personnel

At Other Offices

CAUDLE, Louise
Director, Corporate Communications
3900 Paramount Pkwy.
Morrisville, NC 27560
Tel: (919) 462 - 4467

KITTNER, Bert
Manager, Corporate Communications
3900 Paramount Pkwy.
Morrisville, NC 27560
bert.kittner@rtp.ppdi.com
Tel: (919) 462 - 5509
Fax: (919) 462 - 4274

ZELENIAK, Nancy
Head, Corporate Communications
3900 Paramount Pkwy.
Morrisville, NC 27560
Tel: (919) 462 - 4088

Phelps Dodge Corp.

A copper mining and manufacturing company. Acquired Cyprus Amax Minerals Co. in 2000.

www.phelpsdodge.com
Annual Revenues: $4.002 billion

Chairman and Chief Exec. Officer
WHISLER, J. Steven
Tel: (602) 366 - 8100
Fax: (602) 234 - 8337
TF: (800) 528 - 1182

Main Headquarters
Mailing: One N. Central Ave.
Phoenix, AZ 85004-3014
Tel: (602) 366 - 8100
Fax: (602) 234 - 8337
TF: (800) 528 - 1182

Washington Office
Contact: Linda D. Findlay
Mailing: 100 S. Royal St.
Suite Two
Alexandria, VA 22314-3349
Tel: (703) 299 - 4430

Political Action Committees

Phelps Dodge Employees Fund for Good Government
Contact: Kevin R. Kinsall
One N. Central Ave.
Phoenix, AZ 85004-3014
Tel: (602) 366 - 8100
Fax: (602) 234 - 8337
TF: (800) 528 - 1182

Contributions to Candidates: $52,500 (01/05 - 09/05)

Phelps Dodge Corp.

* continued from previous page

Democrats: $6,000; Republicans: $46,500.

Principal Recipients

SENATE DEMOCRATS		HOUSE DEMOCRATS	
Nelson, Benjamin (NE)	$1,000	Jefferson, William (LA)	$2,000
SENATE REPUBLICANS		**HOUSE REPUBLICANS**	
Kyl, Jon L (AZ)	$10,000	Renzi, Richard (AZ)	$5,000
Burns, Conrad (MT)	$2,000	Flake, Jeff (AZ)	$2,000
Hagel, Charles T (NE)	$1,500	Franks, Trent (AZ)	$2,000
Dewine, Richard (OH)	$1,000	Hayworth, J D (AZ)	$2,000
Kennedy, Mark (MN)	$1,000	Pearce, Steve (NM)	$2,000
Pearce, Steve (NM)	$1,000	Pombo, Richard (CA)	$2,000
Talent, James (MO)	$1,000	Shadegg, John (AZ)	$2,000
		Wilson, Heather (NM)	$2,000

Corporate Foundations and Giving Programs

Phelps Dodge Foundation
Contact: Tracy L. Bame
One N. Central Ave.
Phoenix, AZ 85004-3014
Tel: (602) 366 - 8018
Fax: (602) 234 - 8082
TF: (800) 528 - 1182

Annual Grant Total: $1,000,000 - $2,000,000

Geographic Preference: Area(s) in which the company operates; Area in which the company is headquartered
Primary Interests: Arts and Culture; Civic and Public Affairs; Community Development; Education; Environment/Conservation
Recent Recipients: University of Arizona

Public Affairs and Related Activities Personnel

At Headquarters

BAME, Tracy L.
Manager, Community Affairs
tbame@phelpsdodge.com
Tel: (602) 366 - 8018
Fax: (602) 234 - 8082
TF: (800) 528 - 1182
Responsibilities include corporate philanthropy.

KINSALL, Kevin R.
Director, State and Local Governmental Relations
kkinsall@phelpsdodge.com
Tel: (602) 366 - 8100
Fax: (602) 234 - 8337
TF: (800) 528 - 1182

PULATIE, David L.
Senior V. President, Human Resources
dpulatie@phelpsdodge.com
Tel: (602) 366 - 8100
Fax: (602) 234 - 8337
TF: (800) 528 - 1182

TELLE, Jim
Manager, Corporate Communications
jtelle@phelpsdodge.com
Tel: (602) 366 - 7963
Fax: (602) 234 - 8337
TF: (800) 528 - 1182

VAUGHN, Ken
Manager, Mining Communications
kvaughn@phelpsdodge.com
Tel: (602) 366 - 8318
Fax: (602) 234 - 8337
TF: (800) 528 - 1182

WHITE, Lynda
Manager, State and Local Government Relations
Tel: (602) 366 - 8100
Fax: (602) 234 - 8337
TF: (800) 528 - 1182

At Washington Office

FINDLAY, Linda D.
V. President, Government Relations
lfindlay@phelpsdodge.com
Tel: (703) 299 - 4430
Registered Federal Lobbyist.

Philadelphia Electric Co.

See listing on page 187 under Exelon Corp.

Philip Morris U.S.A.

A wholly-owned subsidiary of Altria Group, Inc. (see separate listing).

www.philipmorrisusa.com
Annual Revenues: $24.784 billion

Chairman, President and Chief Exec. Officer
SZYMANCZYK, Michael
Tel: (804) 274 - 2000
Fax: (804) 484 - 8231

Main Headquarters
Mailing: 6601 W. Broad St.
Richmond, VA 23230
Tel: (804) 274 - 2000
Fax: (804) 484 - 8231

Public Affairs and Related Activities Personnel

At Other Offices

HARWARD, Floyce M.
Community Affairs Specialist, Communications and Programs
2321 Concord Pkwy., South
P.O. Box 1098
Concord, NC 28026-1098
Tel: (704) 788 - 5133
Fax: (704) 788 - 5139

Philips Electronics North America

A diversified manufacturer of electrical and electronic components and equipment, consumer products and lighting.

www.usa.philips.com

President and Chief Exec. Officer
WESTERHOF, Rob
Tel: (212) 536 - 0500
Fax: (212) 536 - 0875

Main Headquarters
Mailing: 1251 Ave. of the Americas
20th Floor
New York, NY 10020
Tel: (212) 536 - 0500
Fax: (212) 536 - 0875

Washington Office
Contact: Thomas B. Patton
Mailing: 1300 I St. NW
Suite 1070 East
Washington, DC 20005
Tel: (202) 962 - 8550
Fax: (202) 962 - 8560

Political Action Committees

Philips Electronics North America Political Action Committee
Contact: Randall B. Moorhead
1300 I St. NW
Suite 1070 East
Washington, DC 20005
Tel: (202) 962 - 8550
Fax: (202) 962 - 8560

Contributions to Candidates: $22,500 (01/05 - 09/05)

Democrats: $4,000; Republicans: $18,000; Other: $500.

Principal Recipients

SENATE DEMOCRATS		HOUSE DEMOCRATS	
Clinton, Hillary Rodham (NY)	$1,000	Murtha, John P Mr. (PA)	$2,000
SENATE REPUBLICANS		**HOUSE REPUBLICANS**	
Kyl, Jon L (AZ)	$2,750	Gillmor, Paul E (OH)	$2,000
Allen, George (VA)	$2,000	Oxley, Michael (OH)	$2,000
Burns, Conrad (MT)	$1,000	Kelly, Sue W (NY)	$1,000
Dewine, Richard (OH)	$1,000		
Ensign, John Eric (NV)	$1,000		

Corporate Foundations and Giving Programs

North American Philips Giving Program
1251 Ave. of the Americas
20th Floor
New York, NY 10020
Tel: (212) 536 - 0500
Fax: (212) 536 - 0875

Annual Grant Total: $200,000 - $300,000

Public Affairs and Related Activities Personnel

At Washington Office

MOORHEAD, Randall B.
V. President, Government Affairs
Tel: (202) 962 - 8550
Fax: (202) 962 - 8560
Registered Federal Lobbyist.

PATTON, Thomas B.
V. President, Government Relations
tom.patton@phillips.com
Tel: (202) 962 - 8550
Fax: (202) 962 - 8560
Registered Federal Lobbyist.

SHEIRE, James B.
Manager, Legislative and Regulatory Affairs
Tel: (202) 962 - 8550
Fax: (202) 962 - 8560
Registered Federal Lobbyist.

SWEENEY, Laurel
Tel: (202) 962 - 8550
Fax: (202) 962 - 8560
Registered Federal Lobbyist.

WORK, Dale
Vice President, Technology Policy and Industry Affairs
Tel: (202) 962 - 8550
Fax: (202) 962 - 8560
Registered Federal Lobbyist.

Phillips-Van Heusen Corp.

A manufacturer and retailer of footwear and apparel.

www.pvh.com

Chairman and Chief Exec. Officer
KLATSKY, Bruce J.
Tel: (212) 381 - 3500
Fax: (212) 381 - 3959

Main Headquarters
Mailing: 200 Madison Ave.
New York, NY 10016
Tel: (212) 381 - 3500
Fax: (212) 381 - 3959

Corporate Foundations and Giving Programs

The PVH Foundation
Contact: Bruce J. Klatsky
200 Madison Ave.
New York, NY 10016
Tel: (212) 381 - 3500
Fax: (212) 381 - 3959

Annual Grant Total: none reported

Geographic Preference: Area(s) in which the company operates; National
Primary Interests: Arts and Culture; Education; Health and Human Services
Recent Recipients: Earthshare; United Way

Phillips-Van Heusen Corp.

** continued from previous page*

Public Affairs and Related Activities Personnel

At Headquarters

CHIRICO, Emanuel — Tel: (212) 381 - 3503
Exec. V. President and Chief Financial Officer — Fax: (212) 381 - 3959
Responsibilities include investor relations.

HOOTKIN, Pamela N. — Tel: (212) 381 - 3500
V. President, Treasurer and Investor Relations — Fax: (212) 381 - 3959

KOZEL, David F. — Tel: (212) 381 - 3500
V. President, Human Resources — Fax: (212) 381 - 3959

VERNON, Kim — Tel: (212) 381 - 3500
Senior V. President, Global Advertising and Communications (Calvin Klein) — Fax: (212) 381 - 3959

The Phoenix Companies, Inc.

A life insurance and investment management company.
www.phoenixwm.com

Chairman, President and Chief Exec. Officer — Tel: (860) 403 - 5967
YOUNG, Dona Davis — Fax: (860) 403 - 5755

Main Headquarters
Mailing: One American Row, Hartford, CT 06102 — Tel: (860) 403 - 5000 — Fax: (860) 403 - 5755

Political Action Committees

The Phoenix Companies PAC
Contact: Maura L. Melley
One American Row — Tel: (860) 403 - 5025
Hartford, CT 06102 — Fax: (860) 403 - 5755

Contributions to Candidates: $9,000 (01/05 - 09/05)
Democrats: $4,000; Republicans: $5,000.

Principal Recipients

SENATE DEMOCRATS		HOUSE DEMOCRATS	
Conrad, Kent (ND)	$1,000	Larson, John B (CT)	$1,000
Lieberman, Joe (CT)	$1,000	Neal, Richard E Mr. (MA)	$1,000
SENATE REPUBLICANS		**HOUSE REPUBLICANS**	
Hatch, Orrin (UT)	$1,000	Kelly, Sue W (NY)	$1,000
Martinez, Mel (FL)	$1,000	Pryce, Deborah (OH)	$1,000
Snowe, Olympia (ME)	$1,000		

Corporate Foundations and Giving Programs

Phoenix Foundation
Contact: Jane L. Driscoll
One American Row — Tel: (860) 403 - 5630
Hartford, CT 06102 — Fax: (860) 403 - 5755

Annual Grant Total: none reported
Geographic Preference: Albany, NY; Hartford, CT
Primary Interests: Community Affairs; Education

Public Affairs and Related Activities Personnel

At Headquarters

DRISCOLL, Jane L. — Tel: (860) 403 - 5630
Assistant V. President, Public Affairs — Fax: (860) 403 - 5755
jane.driscoll@phoenixwm.com
Responsibilities include corporate philanthropy.

FARLEY, Michele U. — Tel: (860) 403 - 5393
Senior V. President, Corporate Communications — Fax: (860) 403 - 7887
michele.farley@phoenixwm.com

MALLEY, Bonnie J. — Tel: (860) 403 - 5000
Senior V. President, Human Resources and Corporate Services — Fax: (860) 403 - 5755

MELLEY, Maura L. — Tel: (860) 403 - 5025
Senior Advisor, Public Affairs — Fax: (860) 403 - 5755
maura.melley@phoenixwm.com

Phoenix Home Life Mutual Insurance Co.

See listing on page 383 under The Phoenix Companies, Inc.

Piedmont Natural Gas Co.

A member of the Public Affairs Council. A natural gas distributor.
www.piedmontng.com

Chairman, President and Chief Exec. Officer — Tel: (704) 364 - 3120
SKAINS, Thomas E.

Main Headquarters
Mailing: P.O. Box 33068, Charlotte, NC 28233 — Tel: (704) 364 - 3120
Street: 1915 Rexford Rd., Charlotte, NC 28211

Political Action Committees

Piedmont Natural Gas Co. ENPAC
Contact: Donald F. Harrow
P.O. Box 33068 — Tel: (704) 731 - 4318
Charlotte, NC 28233 — Fax: (704) 365 - 8515

Contributions to Candidates: $2,000 (01/05 - 09/05)
Democrats: $1,000; Republicans: $1,000.

Principal Recipients

SENATE DEMOCRATS	HOUSE DEMOCRATS	
	McIntyre, Mike (NC)	$1,000
SENATE REPUBLICANS	**HOUSE REPUBLICANS**	
	Foxx, Virginia (NC)	$500
	Pombo, Richard (CA)	$500

Corporate Foundations and Giving Programs

Piedmont Natural Gas Corporate Giving Progam
Contact: Donald F. Harrow
P.O. Box 33068 — Tel: (704) 731 - 4318
Charlotte, NC 28233 — Fax: (704) 365 - 8515

Annual Grant Total: none reported
Geographic Preference: Area(s) in which employees live and work
Primary Interests: Arts and Culture; Civic and Public Affairs; Education; Environment/Conservation; Health and Human Services

Public Affairs and Related Activities Personnel

At Headquarters

HARROW, Donald F. — Tel: (704) 731 - 4318
V. President, Governmental Relations — Fax: (704) 365 - 8515
Serves as the senior public affairs executive at company headquarters.

LANIER, Hope — Tel: (704) 731 - 4308
Manager, Government Relations

LINVILLE, Richard A. — Tel: (704) 364 - 3120
V. President, Human Resources

POPE, Gail — Tel: (704) 731 - 4683
Community Relations Representative

THOMAS, Headen B. — Tel: (704) 731 - 4438
Director, Investor Relations — Fax: (704) 764 - 1395
headen.thomas@piedmontng.com

TRUSTY, David L. — Tel: (704) 364 - 3120
V. President, Corporate Communications

Pier 1 Imports

www.pier1.com
Annual Revenues: $1.86 billion

Chairman and Chief Exec. Officer — Tel: (817) 252 - 8000
GIROUARD, Marvin J.

Main Headquarters
Mailing: 100 Pier 1 Place, Fort Worth, TX 76102 — Tel: (817) 252 - 8000

Corporate Foundations and Giving Programs

Pier 1 Imports Corporate Contributions Program
Contact: Tasa Anderson
100 Pier 1 Place — Tel: (817) 252 - 8153
Fort Worth, TX 76102 — Fax: (817) 252 - 7229

Annual Grant Total: none reported
Geographic Preference: National; International; Area in which the company is headquartered
Primary Interests: Arts and Culture; Children; Community Affairs
Recent Recipients: Susan G. Komen Breast Cancer Foundation; U.S. Fund for UNICEF; United Way

Public Affairs and Related Activities Personnel

At Headquarters

ANDERSON, Tasa — Tel: (817) 252 - 8153
Manager, Community Relations — Fax: (817) 252 - 7229
Responsibilities include corporate philanthropy.

HUMENESKY, Greg — Tel: (817) 252 - 8000
Exec. V. President, Human Resources

LAWRENCE, J. Rodney — Tel: (817) 252 - 8000
Exec. V. President, Legal Affairs and Corporate Secretary; PAC Treasurer

TURNER, Charles H. "Cary" — Tel: (817) 252 - 8000
Exec. V. President, Chief Financial Officer and Treasurer
Responsibilities include investor relations.

Pilgrim's Pride Corp.

A chicken products producer.
www.pilgrimspride.com

Chairman of the Board — Tel: (903) 855 - 1000
PILGRIM, Lonnie "Bo" — TF: (800) 824 - 1159

Main Headquarters
Mailing: P.O. Box 93, Pittsburg, TX 75686 — Tel: (903) 855 - 1000 — TF: (800) 824 - 1159

Pilgrim's Pride Corp.

* continued from previous page

Corporate Foundations and Giving Programs

Pilgrim's Pride Corp. Corporate Giving Program
P.O. Box 93 — Tel: (903) 855 - 1000
Pittsburg, TX 75686 — TF: (800) 824 - 1159

Annual Grant Total: none reported

Public Affairs and Related Activities Personnel

At Headquarters

BROOKSHIRE, Jane — Tel: (903) 855 - 1000
Senior V. President, Human Resources — TF: (800) 824 - 1159
jbrookshire@pilgrimspride.com

COGDILL, Richard A. — Tel: (903) 855 - 1000
Exec. V. President, Chief Financial Officer, Treasurer and Secretary — TF: (800) 824 - 1159
Responsibilities include investor relations.

WOOD, Barry — Tel: (903) 855 - 1000
Director, Media Relations and Communications — TF: (800) 824 - 1159

Pilkington North America

Manufacturer of automotive and flat glass products.
www.pilkington.com

Chairman and Chief Exec. Officer — Tel: (419) 247 - 3731
ZITO, Pat — Fax: (419) 247 - 3821

Main Headquarters
Mailing: P.O. Box 799 — Tel: (419) 247 - 3731
Toledo, OH 43695 — Fax: (419) 247 - 3821

Corporate Foundations and Giving Programs

Pilkington Corporate Giving Program
Contact: Alan Graham
P.O. Box 799 — Tel: (419) 247 - 3731
Toledo, OH 43695 — Fax: (419) 247 - 3821

Annual Grant Total: none reported

Public Affairs and Related Activities Personnel

At Headquarters

BERG, Randy — Tel: (419) 247 - 3731
V. President, Human Resources — Fax: (419) 247 - 3821

GRAHAM, Alan — Tel: (419) 247 - 3731
V. President, Legal and Corporate Affairs — Fax: (419) 247 - 3821

Pillsbury Co., The

See listing on page 214 under General Mills.

Pinnacle Entertainment, Inc.

A gaming company.
www.pinnacle-entertainment-inc.com
Annual Revenues: $514 million

Chairman and Chief Exec. Officer — Tel: (702) 784 - 7777
LEE, Daniel R.

Main Headquarters
Mailing: 3800 Howard Hughes Prkwy. — Tel: (702) 784 - 7777
Las Vegas, NV 89109

Political Action Committees

Pinnacle Entertainment Inc. PAC
Contact: Christopher E. Skinnell
591 Redwood Hwy.
Bldg. 4000
Mill Valley, CA 94941

Contributions to Candidates: none reported (01/05 - 09/05)

Public Affairs and Related Activities Personnel

At Headquarters

BARICH, James W. — Tel: (702) 784 - 7777
Senior V. President, Public Affairs

PLANT, Christopher K. — Tel: (702) 784 - 7777
V. President, Investor Relations and Treasurer

TRUEBA, Humberto, Jr. — Tel: (702) 784 - 7777
Senior V. President, Human Resources

At Other Offices

SKINNELL, Christopher E.
Treasurer, Pinnacle Entertainment Inc. PAC
591 Redwood Hwy.
Bldg. 4000
Mill Valley, CA 94941

Pinnacle West Capital Corp.

A member of the Public Affairs Council. Delivers electricity and energy-related products and services. Also involved in real estate development.
www.pinnaclewest.com
Annual Revenues: $2.8 billion

Chairman and Chief Exec. Officer — Tel: (602) 250 - 1000 Ext: 2588
POST, William J. — Fax: (602) 250 - 3002
Mailstop: M/S 9036
william.post@pinnaclewest.com

Main Headquarters
Mailing: P.O. Box 53999 — Tel: (602) 250 - 1000
Phoenix, AZ 85072-3999 — Fax: (602) 250 - 3803
Street: 400 N. Fifth St.
Phoenix, AZ 85004

Washington Office
Contact: Robert S. Aiken
Mailing: 801 Pennsylvania Ave. NW — Tel: (202) 293 - 2655
Suite 214 — Fax: (202) 293 - 2666
Washington, DC 20004

Political Action Committees

Pinnacle West Capital Corp. PAC
Contact: Robert S. Aiken
801 Pennsylvania Ave. NW — Tel: (202) 293 - 2655
Suite 214 — Fax: (202) 293 - 2666
Washington, DC 20004

Contributions to Candidates: $50,000 (01/05 - 09/05)
Democrats: $4,500; Republicans: $45,500.

Principal Recipients

SENATE DEMOCRATS		HOUSE DEMOCRATS	
Bingaman, Jeff (NM)	$1,000	Pastor, Edward (AZ)	$2,000
Carper, Thomas R (DE)	$1,000		

SENATE REPUBLICANS		HOUSE REPUBLICANS	
Allen, George (VA)	$9,000	Shadegg, John (AZ)	$4,000
Smith, Gordon (OR)	$2,000	Flake, Jeff (AZ)	$3,000
Snowe, Olympia (ME)	$1,500	Shaw, Clay (FL)	$2,500
Alexander, Lamar (TN)	$1,000	Franks, Trent (AZ)	$2,000
Burr, Richard (NC)	$1,000	Hayworth, J D (AZ)	$2,000
Craig, Larry (ID)	$1,000	Renzi, Richard (AZ)	$2,000
Ensign, John Eric (NV)	$1,000	Wilson, Heather (NM)	$2,000
Lott, Trent (MS)	$1,000	Barton, Joe L (TX)	$1,000
Martinez, Mel (FL)	$1,000	Boehner, John (OH)	$1,000
Thomas, Craig (WY)	$1,000	Hall, Ralph (TX)	$1,000
		Issa, Darrell (CA)	$1,000
		Kolbe, James (AZ)	$1,000
		McSweeney, David (IL)	$1,000
		Oxley, Michael (OH)	$1,000
		Weller, Jerry (IL)	$1,000

Corporate Foundations and Giving Programs

Pinnacle West Contributions and Foundation
Contact: Sandie Jones
P.O. Box 53999 — Tel: (602) 250 - 2257
Phoenix, AZ 85072-3999

Annual Grant Total: $2,000,000 - $5,000,000
Geographic Preference: Arizona
Primary Interests: Arts and Culture; Education; Health and Human Services
Recent Recipients: American Cancer Society; Anti-Defamation League; Phoenix Symphony; United Way

Public Affairs and Related Activities Personnel

At Headquarters

BUNNELL, Alan — Tel: (602) 250 - 3376
Manager, External Communications and Media Relations — Fax: (602) 250 - 2430
Mailstop: M/S 8508
alan.bunnell@pinnaclewest.com

DAVIS, Scott — Tel: (602) 250 - 3225
Leader, Environmental Health and Safety Department — Fax: (602) 250 - 3872
Mailstop: M/S 8376
scott.davis@pinnaclewest.com

FOX, Edward Z. — Tel: (602) 250 - 2916
V. President, Communications, Environment and Safety — Fax: (605) 250 - 3002
Mailstop: M/S 9085
edward.fox@pinnaclewest.com

HICKMAN, Rebecca L. — Tel: (602) 250 - 5668
Director, Investor Relations — Fax: (602) 250 - 2789
Mailstop: M/S 9998
rebecca.hickman@pinnaclewest.com

Pinnacle West Capital Corp.

* *continued from previous page*

HOLMES, Janie — Tel: (602) 250 - 2896; Fax: (602) 250 - 2430
Leader, Internal Communications Department
(Arizona Public Service Co.)
Mailstop: M/S 8508
janie.holmes@aps.com

HUNTER, Yvonne — Tel: (602) 250 - 4520; Fax: (602) 250 - 3887
Senior Public Affairs Representative
Mailstop: M/S 9988
yvonne.hunter@pinnaclewest.com

JONES, Sandie — Tel: (602) 250 - 2257
Contributions Coordinator
Mailstop: M/S 8010
sandie.jones@pinnaclewest.com

KITCHEL, Gretchen S. — Tel: (602) 250 - 2832
Senior Public Affairs Representative
Mailstop: M/S 9988
gretchen.kitchel@pinnaclewest.com

MIKULA, Jim I. — Tel: (602) 250 - 2232
Consultant, Environment
Mailstop: M/S 8376
jim.mikula@pinnaclewest.com

MOSKOWITZ, Louise A. — Tel: (602) 250 - 2291; Fax: (602) 250 - 2419
Coordinator, Corporate Events (CR/ED Consultant)
Mailstop: M/S 8010
louise.moskowitz@pinnaclewest.com
Responsibilities include community affairs.

REYNOLDS, Paul — Tel: (602) 250 - 5656; Fax: (602) 250 - 2772
Director, Corporate Communications
Mailstop: M/S 8516
paul.reynolds@pinnaclewest.com

SAHLMAN, Rachel — Tel: (602) 250 - 2192
Leader, E-Business Communications
(Arizona Public Service Co.)
Mailstop: M/S 8585
rachel.sahlman@aps.com

SHULTZ, Martin L. — Tel: (602) 250 - 2866; Fax: (602) 250 - 3902
V. President, Government Affairs
martin.shultz@pinnaclewest.com

THOMPSON, Charles P. — Tel: (602) 250 - 2888; Fax: (602) 250 - 2113
Manager, Rural Community Development
(Arizona Public Service Co.)
Mailstop: M/S 8010
charles.thompson@aps.com

VAN NESS, Jana — Tel: (602) 250 - 2310; Fax: (602) 250 - 3399
State Regulatory Group Leader
Mailstop: M/S 9905
jana.vanness@aps.com

At Washington Office

AIKEN, Robert S. — Tel: (202) 293 - 2655; Fax: (202) 293 - 2666
V. President, Federal Affairs
Mailstop: M/S A112
robbie.aiken@pinnaclewest.com
Registered Federal Lobbyist.

At Other Offices

MCDONALD, James E. — Tel: (602) 250 - 3704
Nuclear Communications
(Arizona Public Service Co.)
P.O. Box 52034
Mailstop: M/S 7602
Phoenix, AZ 85072-2034
james.mcdonald@aps.com

Pioneer Hi-Bred Internat'l, Inc.

A producer of farm seeds.

www.pioneer.com
Annual Revenues: $2.3 billion

Main Headquarters

Mailing: P.O. Box 14453, Des Moines, IA 50306-3453 — Tel: (515) 248 - 4800; TF: (800) 247 - 6803
Street: 400 Locust St., Des Moines, IA 50309-2340

Washington Office

Contact: Julie Manes
Mailing: 601 Pennsylvania Ave. NW, North Bldg. Suite 325, Washington, DC 20004 — Tel: (202) 728 - 3613; Fax: (202) 728 - 3649

Corporate Foundations and Giving Programs

Pioneer Hi-Bred Internat'l Community Investment
Contact: Steve Schaaf
P.O. Box 14453
Des Moines, IA 50306-3453
Tel: (515) 248 - 4800; Fax: (515) 248 - 4842; TF: (800) 247 - 6803

Annual Grant Total: over $5,000,000
Geographic Preference: Area(s) in which employees live and work
Primary Interests: Agriculture; Environment/Conservation; Health and Human Services; Higher Education

Public Affairs and Related Activities Personnel

At Headquarters

DREYER, Courtney Chabot — Tel: (515) 248 - 4800; Fax: (515) 334 - 4663; TF: (800) 247 - 6803
Manager, Public Affairs
courtney.dreyer@pioneer.com

FLETCHER-HAYES, Desiree — Tel: (515) 248 - 4800; Fax: (515) 270 - 4112; TF: (800) 247 - 6803
Coordinator, Public Relations
desiree.fletcher-hayes@pioneer.com

KARR, Doyle — Tel: (515) 248 - 4800; Fax: (515) 270 - 4112; TF: (800) 247 - 6803
Diretor, Communications
doyle.karr@pioneer.com

SCHAAF, Steve — Tel: (515) 248 - 4800; Fax: (515) 248 - 4842; TF: (800) 247 - 6803
Program Manager, Community Investment

At Washington Office

MANES, Julie — Tel: (202) 728 - 3613; Fax: (202) 728 - 3649
Washington Representative
julie.manes@pioneer.com

At Other Offices

TOWNSEND, Dr. Rod — Tel: (515) 270 - 4146; Fax: (515) 334 - 4478
Director, Regulatory Science
7250 NW 62nd Ave.
Johnston, IA 50131
rod.townsend@pioneer.com

Pioneer Natural Resources Co.

Independent oil and gas exploration and production company operating in the U.S., Canada, Argentina, Equatorial Guinea, Gabon, S. Africa, and Tunisia.

www.pioneernrc.com
Annual Revenues: $1.312 million

Chairman, President and Chief Exec. Officer
SHEFFIELD, Scott D. — Tel: (972) 444 - 9001; Fax: (972) 969 - 3516

Main Headquarters

Mailing: 5205 N. O'Connor Blvd., Suite 900, Irving, TX 75039 — Tel: (972) 444 - 9001; Fax: (972) 969 - 3516

Public Affairs and Related Activities Personnel

At Headquarters

HOPKINS, Frank — Tel: (972) 444 - 9001; Fax: (972) 969 - 3516
V. President, Investor Relations

SPRATLEN, Susan A. — Tel: (972) 444 - 9001; Fax: (972) 969 - 3576
V. President, Investor Relations and Communications

WALLACE, Roger — Tel: (972) 444 - 9001; Fax: (972) 969 - 3516
V. President, Government Affairs

Pioneer-Standard Electronics, Inc.

See listing on page 11 under Agilysys, Inc.

Piper Aircraft Inc.

See listing on page 345 under The New Piper Aircraft Inc.

Pitney Bowes Inc.

A member of the Public Affairs Council. A mail and messaging management provider.

www.pitneybowes.com
Annual Revenues: $4 billion

Chairman and Chief Exec. Officer
CRITELLI, Michael J. — Tel: (203) 356 - 5000; Fax: (203) 351 - 6303

Main Headquarters

Mailing: World Headquarters, One Elmcroft Rd., Stamford, CT 06926-0700 — Tel: (203) 356 - 5000; Fax: (203) 351 - 6303

Washington Office

Contact: Ernesto J. Rojas
Mailing: 409 12th St., S.W., Suite 701, Washington, DC 20024-2191 — Tel: (202) 488 - 4464; Fax: (202) 488 - 4396

Political Action Committees

Pitney Bowes Inc. Connecticut PAC
Contact: Joseph M. Ercolano
World Headquarters
One Elmcroft Rd.
Stamford, CT 06926-0700
Tel: (203) 351 - 6263; Fax: (203) 961 - 0291

Pitney Bowes Inc.

* continued from previous page

Contributions to Candidates: none reported (01/05 - 09/05)

Pitney Bowes Inc. Political Action Committee
Contact: David T. Nassef
2151 Jamieson Ave. Tel: (703) 566 - 2307
Alexandria, VA 22314 Fax: (703) 566 - 2311

Contributions to Candidates: $27,080 (01/05 - 09/05)
Democrats: $13,580; Republicans: $13,500.

Principal Recipients

SENATE DEMOCRATS
Lieberman, Joe (CT) $5,000
Carper, Thomas R (DE) $3,580
Clinton, Hillary Rodham (NY) $1,000

SENATE REPUBLICANS

HOUSE DEMOCRATS
Hoyer, Steny (MD) $2,000
Kilpatrick, Carolyn (MI) $1,000
Norton, Eleanor Holmes (DC) $1,000

HOUSE REPUBLICANS
McHugh, John (NY) $5,000
Shays, Christopher (CT) $5,000
Miller, Candice S. (MI) $3,000

Corporate Foundations and Giving Programs

Pitney Bowes Corporate Giving Program
Contact: Polly O'Brien
World Headquarters Tel: (203) 351 - 6669
One Elmcroft Rd. Fax: (203) 351 - 6303
Stamford, CT 06926-0700

Annual Grant Total: $2,000,000 - $5,000,000
Geographic Preference: Area in which the company is headquartered; Area(s) in which the company operates
Primary Interests: Adult Education and Training; Community Development; Economic Development; Housing; Minority Opportunities; Youth Services

Public Affairs and Related Activities Personnel

At Headquarters

BRODER, Matt Tel: (203) 351 - 6347
V. President, External Communications Fax: (203) 351 - 6303
Mailstop: MSC 63-11
matthew.broder@pb.com

ERCOLANO, Joseph M. Tel: (203) 351 - 6263
Director, Government Affairs Fax: (203) 961 - 0291
Mailstop: 64-23
joseph.ercolano@pb.com
Responsibilities include political action.

FULGENZI, Marianne Tel: (203) 351 - 6974
Director, External Affairs Fax: (203) 351 - 6303
Mailstop: MSC 63-15
marianne.fulgenzi@pb.com

O'BRIEN, Polly Tel: (203) 351 - 6669
Director, Community Affairs Fax: (203) 351 - 6303
Mailstop: 63-15
polly.obrien@pb.com
Responsibilities include corporate philanthropy.

TORSONE, Johnna G. Tel: (203) 356 - 5000
Senior V. President and Chief Human Resources Officer Fax: (203) 351 - 6303

At Washington Office

LINNEHAN, Ann M. Tel: (202) 488 - 4464
Fax: (202) 488 - 4396
Registered Federal Lobbyist.

ROJAS, Ernesto J. Tel: (202) 488 - 4464
Director, Regulatory Affairs Fax: (202) 488 - 4396
ernie.rojas@pb.com

At Other Offices

NASSEF, David T. Tel: (703) 566 - 2307
V. President, Federal Relations Fax: (703) 566 - 2311
2151 Jamieson Ave.
Alexandria, VA 22314
dtnassef@aol.com

Pittway

See listing on page 247 under Honeywell Internat'l, Inc.

Pizza Hut, Inc.

See listing on page 530 under YUM! Brands, Inc.

Plains Resources Inc.

An energy company. Parent company of Plains All American Pipeline, L.P.
www.plainsresources.com
Annual Revenues: $8.384 billion

Chairman of the Board Tel: (832) 239 - 6000
FLORES, James C.

Chief Exec. Officer and President Tel: (832) 239 - 6000
RAYMOND, John T.

Main Headquarters
Mailing: 700 Milam St. Tel: (832) 239 - 6000
Suite 3100
Houston, TX 77002

Public Affairs and Related Activities Personnel

At Headquarters

HILL, E. Lynn Tel: (832) 239 - 6000
Chief Accounting Officer
Responsibilities include media and investor relations.

PETERS, Mary O. Tel: (832) 239 - 6000
V. President, Administration and Human Resources

Plantronics, Inc.

Manufactures telecommunications products and accessories.
www.plantronics.com

Chairman of the Board Tel: (831) 426 - 5858
TSEU, Marvin Fax: (831) 426 - 6098
TF: (800) 544 - 4660

President and Chief Exec. Officer Tel: (831) 426 - 5858
KANNAPPAN, S. Kenneth Ext: 7741
Fax: (831) 426 - 6098
TF: (800) 544 - 4660

Main Headquarters
Mailing: 345 Encinal St. Tel: (831) 426 - 5858
Santa Cruz, CA 95060 Fax: (831) 426 - 6098
TF: (800) 544 - 4660

Corporate Foundations and Giving Programs

Plantronics, Inc. Corporate Giving
Contact: Jennifer DeToy
345 Encinal St. Tel: (831) 426 - 5858
Santa Cruz, CA 95060 Ext: 7400
Fax: (831) 426 - 0136
TF: (800) 544 - 4660

Annual Grant Total: none reported

Public Affairs and Related Activities Personnel

At Headquarters

ALVARADO, Jon Tel: (831) 426 - 5858
Manager, Treasury and Investor Relations Ext: 4452
jon.alvarado@plantronics.com Fax: (831) 423 - 4314
TF: (800) 544 - 4660

DETOY, Jennifer Tel: (831) 426 - 5858
Manager, Community Relations Ext: 7400
jennifer.detoy@plantronics.com Fax: (831) 426 - 0136
TF: (800) 544 - 4660
Responsibilities include corporate philanthropy.

MURPHY, Julie Tel: (831) 426 - 5858
V. President, Human Resources Ext: 7864
julie.murphy@plantronics.com Fax: (831) 426 - 6098
TF: (800) 544 - 4660

Platinum Equity, LLC

A global investment firm specializing in merger and acquisition of mission-critical services and solutions businesses. Current portfolio includes 20 operating companies in Europe, North America and Asia.
www.peh.com
Annual Revenues: $6.5 billion

Chairman and Chief Exec. Officer Tel: (310) 712 - 1850
GORES, Tom T. Fax: (310) 712 - 1848

Main Headquarters
Mailing: 360 N. Crescent Dr., S. Bldg. Tel: (310) 712 - 1850
Beverly Hills, CA 90210 Fax: (310) 712 - 1848

Public Affairs and Related Activities Personnel

At Headquarters

BARNHILL, Mark Tel: (310) 712 - 1850
Senior V. President, Corporate Relations Fax: (310) 712 - 1848

Playboy Enterprises, Inc.

Playboy Enterprises is a brand-driven, international multimedia entertainment company that publishes editions of Playboy magazine; operates television networks and distributes programming via home video and DVD globally; licenses the Playboy and Rabbit Head trademarks for a range of consumer products and services; and operates playboy.com, a leading men's lifestyle and entertainment website.
www.playboyenterprises.com
Annual Revenues: $291.2 million

Playboy Enterprises, Inc.

** continued from previous page*

Chairman and Chief Exec. Officer
HEFNER, Christie — Tel: (312) 751 - 8000 Fax: (312) 337 - 0271

Main Headquarters
Mailing: 680 N. Lake Shore Dr.
Chicago, IL 60611 — Tel: (312) 751 - 8000 Fax: (312) 751 - 2818

Corporate Foundations and Giving Programs

Playboy Foundation
Contact: Cleo F. Wilson
680 N. Lake Shore Dr.
Chicago, IL 60611 — Tel: (312) 373 - 2435 Fax: (312) 266 - 8506

Annual Grant Total: $500,000 - $750,000
Maintains a web site at http://www.playboyenterprises.com/foundation.
Geographic Preference: Area(s) in which the company operates; Chicago, IL; New York City; Los Angeles, CA
Primary Interests: Civil Rights; Human Welfare
Recent Recipients: American Civil Liberties Union; People for the American Way

Public Affairs and Related Activities Personnel

At Headquarters

DEVINE, Carol A.
Senior V. President, Human Resources — Tel: (312) 373 - 2040 Fax: (312) 642 - 5592

LINDEMAN, Martha O.
Senior V. President, Corporate Communications and Investor Relations — Tel: (312) 373 - 2430 Fax: (312) 266 - 8506

WILSON, Cleo F.
V. President, Public Affairs; Exec. Director, Playboy Foundation
cleow@playboy.com — Tel: (312) 373 - 2435 Fax: (312) 266 - 8506

Plum Creek Timber Co. Inc.

www.plumcreek.com

Chairman of the Board
DAVIDSON, Ian — Tel: (206) 467 - 3600 Fax: (206) 467 - 3795

President and Chief Exec. Officer
HOLLEY, Rick — Tel: (206) 467 - 3600 Fax: (206) 467 - 3795

Main Headquarters
Mailing: 999 Third Ave.
Suite 4300
Seattle, WA 98104 — Tel: (206) 467 - 3600 Fax: (206) 467 - 3795

Political Action Committees

Plum Creek Timber Co. Good Government Fund
Contact: Kirsten Smith
999 Third Ave.
Suite 4300
Seattle, WA 98104 — Tel: (206) 467 - 3600 Fax: (206) 467 - 3795

Contributions to Candidates: $29,500 (01/05 - 09/05)
Democrats: $13,000; Republicans: $16,500.

Principal Recipients

SENATE DEMOCRATS		HOUSE DEMOCRATS	
Baucus, Max (MT)	$9,000	Ross, Michael Avery (AR)	$2,000
		Dicks, Norm D (WA)	$1,000
		Michaud, Michael (ME)	$1,000
SENATE REPUBLICANS		**HOUSE REPUBLICANS**	
Burns, Conrad (MT)	$4,500	Alexander, Rodney (LA)	$1,000
Lott, Trent (MS)	$2,000	Hastings, Doc (WA)	$1,000
Chambliss, Saxby (GA)	$1,000	Petri, Thomas (WI)	$1,000
DeMint, James (SC)	$1,000	Pombo, Richard (CA)	$1,000
Smith, Gordon (OR)	$1,000	Rehberg, Dennis (MT)	$1,000
Vitter, David (LA)	$1,000	Walden, Gregory (OR)	$1,000

Public Affairs and Related Activities Personnel

At Headquarters

CROWE, Barbara L.
V. President, Human Resources — Tel: (206) 467 - 3600 Fax: (206) 467 - 3795

DUKE, Susanna N.
Corporate Secretary and Director, Law — Tel: (206) 467 - 3600 Fax: (206) 467 - 3795

HOBBS, John
Director, Investor Relations — Tel: (206) 467 - 3600 Fax: (206) 467 - 3795

JIRSA, Robert J.
Director, Corporate Affairs — Tel: (206) 467 - 3600 Fax: (206) 467 - 3795
Responsibilities include political action.

SMITH, Kirsten
Corporate Affairs — Tel: (206) 467 - 3600 Fax: (206) 467 - 3795

PNC Financial Services Group

A bank holding company. Acquired Midlantic Corporation in 1995.
www.pnc.com
Annual Revenues: $5.4 billion

Chairman and Chief Exec. Officer
ROHR, James E. — Tel: (412) 762 - 2000

Main Headquarters
Mailing: 249 Fifth Ave.
Pittsburgh, PA 15222-2707 — Tel: (412) 762 - 2000

Political Action Committees

PNCBANKPAC - Bipartisan Voluntary Public Affairs Committee of PNC Bank National Association
Contact: Ronald E. Varmecky
249 Fifth Ave.
Pittsburgh, PA 15222-2707 — Tel: (412) 762 - 2000

Contributions to Candidates: $5,500 (01/05 - 09/05)
Democrats: $500; Republicans: $5,000.

Principal Recipients

SENATE DEMOCRATS		HOUSE DEMOCRATS	
		Holden, Timothy (PA)	$500
SENATE REPUBLICANS		**HOUSE REPUBLICANS**	
Santorum, Richard (PA)	$5,000		

Corporate Foundations and Giving Programs

PNC Foundation
Contact: Mia Hallett Bernard
Two PNC Plaza, 34th Floor
Pittsburgh, PA 15222 — Tel: (412) 762 - 7076

Annual Grant Total: over $5,000,000
Primary Interests: Arts and Culture; Community Affairs; Education; Health; Human Welfare

Public Affairs and Related Activities Personnel

At Headquarters

CALLIHAN, William H.
Senior V. President and Director, Investor Relations — Tel: (412) 762 - 8257

CAPRETTO, Patrick J.
V. President and Manager, Internal Communications — Tel: (412) 762 - 3096 Fax: (412) 762 - 3463

GOERKE, Brian E.
V. President and Manager, Public Relations
brian.goerke@pnc.com — Tel: (412) 762 - 4304 Fax: (412) 762 - 3463

LAMB, Thomas F., Jr.
Senior V. President, Government Affairs — Tel: (412) 762 - 7558 Fax: (412) 762 - 2784

LAUGHLIN, Andrea J.
V. President and District Manager, Corporate Relations — Tel: (412) 762 - 2728 Fax: (412) 762 - 3463

PETERMAN, Donna C.
Senior V. President and Director, Corporate Communications — Tel: (412) 762 - 2000

ROSNER, William E.
Chief Human Resources Officer — Tel: (412) 762 - 2000

TYSARCZYK, Michael
V. President, Corporate Communications
Mailstop: 28th Floor — Tel: (412) 762 - 8148 Fax: (412) 762 - 3463

VARMECKY, Ronald E.
PAC Treasurer — Tel: (412) 762 - 2000

At Other Offices

HALLETT BERNARD, Mia
V. President and Manager, PNC Foundation
Two PNC Plaza, 34th Floor
Pittsburgh, PA 15222 — Tel: (412) 762 - 7076

Pocahontas Land Corp.

See listing on page 351 under Norfolk Southern Corp.

Pogo Producing Co.

An oil and gas exploration company.
www.pogoproducing.com
Annual Revenues: $751.4 million

Chairman, President and Chief Exec. Officer
VAN WAGENEN, Paul G. — Tel: (713) 297 - 5000 Fax: (713) 297 - 5100

Main Headquarters
Mailing: P.O. Box 2504
Houston, TX 77252-2504 — Tel: (713) 297 - 5000 Fax: (713) 297 - 5100
Street: Five Greenway Plaza, Suite 2700
Houston, TX 77046

Corporate Foundations and Giving Programs

Pogo Producing Co. Corporate Contributions
Contact: Kay Tyner

Pogo Producing Co.

** continued from previous page*

P.O. Box 2504 — Tel: (713) 297 - 5000
Houston, TX 77252-2504 — Fax: (713) 297 - 5100

Annual Grant Total: none reported

Public Affairs and Related Activities Personnel

At Headquarters

JEANSONNE, Clay — Tel: (713) 297 - 5000
Director, Investor Relations — Fax: (713) 297 - 5100

TYNER, Kay — Tel: (713) 297 - 5000
Contact, Pogo Producing Co. Corporate Contributions — Fax: (713) 297 - 5100

Polaris Industries Inc.

Designs, manufactures, and markets snowmobiles, all-terrain vehicles, personal watercrafts, motorcycles, sport boats, and professional series workmobiles for recreational and utility use.

www.polarisindustries.com

Chairman of the Board — Tel: (763) 417 - 8650
PALEN, Gregory R. — Fax: (763) 542 - 0599

President and Chief Exec. Officer — Tel: (763) 417 - 8650
TILLER, Thomas C. — Fax: (763) 542 - 0599

Main Headquarters
Mailing: 2100 Hwy. 55 — Tel: (763) 417 - 8650
Medina, MN 55340 — Fax: (763) 542 - 0599

Political Action Committees

Polaris Industries Inc. Political Participation Program
Contact: Mary Zins
2100 Hwy. 55 — Tel: (763) 417 - 8650
Medina, MN 55340 — Fax: (763) 542 - 0599

Contributions to Candidates: none reported (01/05 - 09/05)

Corporate Foundations and Giving Programs

Polaris Foundation
2100 Hwy. 55 — Tel: (763) 417 - 8650
Medina, MN 55340 — Fax: (763) 542 - 0599

Annual Grant Total: none reported

Public Affairs and Related Activities Personnel

At Headquarters

BOURGEOIS, Pat — Tel: (763) 417 - 8650
Coordinator, Public Relations — Fax: (763) 542 - 0599

CORNESS, John B. — Tel: (763) 417 - 8650
V. President, Human Resources — Fax: (763) 542 - 0599
john.corness@polarisind.com

EDWARDS, Richard — Tel: (763) 513 - 3477
Director, Investor Relations — Fax: (763) 542 - 0599
richard.edwards@polarisind.com

KNUTSON, Marlys — Tel: (763) 417 - 8650
Manager, Corporate Communications — Fax: (763) 542 - 0599
marlys.knutson@polarisind.com

ZINS, Mary — Tel: (763) 417 - 8650
Treasurer, Polaris Industries Inc. Political Participation Program — Fax: (763) 542 - 0599

Polaroid Corp.

A manufacturer of photographic equipment and supplies.

www.polaroid.com

Chairman of the Board — Tel: (781) 386 - 2000
PETTERS, Thomas J.

President and Chief Exec. Officer — Tel: (781) 386 - 2000
POCOCK, J. Michael

Main Headquarters
Mailing: 1265 Main St. — Tel: (781) 386 - 2000
Bldg. W. Three
Waltham, MA 02451

Corporate Foundations and Giving Programs

Polaroid Fund
Contact: Corey Davis
75 Arlington St. — Tel: (617) 338 - 2521
Boston, MA 02116 — Fax: (617) 338 - 1606

Annual Grant Total: $1,000,000 - $2,000,000
Geographic Preference: Boston, MA
Primary Interests: Adult Education and Training; Literacy

Public Affairs and Related Activities Personnel

At Headquarters

COLCORD, Skip — Tel: (781) 386 - 6624
Director, Corporate Comunications
colcors@polariod.com

At Other Offices

DAVIS, Corey — Tel: (617) 338 - 2521
Grants Manager, Polaroid Fund — Fax: (617) 338 - 1606
75 Arlington St.
Boston, MA 02116
cld@tbf.org

R.L. Polk & Co.

An automotive information solutions provider.

www.polk.com
Annual Revenues: $220 million

Chairman and Chief Exec. Officer — Tel: (248) 728 - 7000
POLK, Stephen — Fax: (248) 728 - 7777

Main Headquarters
Mailing: 26955 Northwestern Hwy. — Tel: (248) 728 - 7000
Southfield, MI 48034 — Fax: (248) 728 - 7777

Public Affairs and Related Activities Personnel

At Headquarters

SOWTON, Tim — Tel: (248) 728 - 7000
Regional Director, Government Relations — Fax: (248) 728 - 7777

Polo Ralph Lauren

Designs, markets, and distributes clothing, fragrances, and home furnishings.

www.polo.com
Annual Revenues: $4.8 billion

Chairman and Chief Exec. Officer — Tel: (212) 318 - 7000
LAUREN, Ralph — Fax: (212) 888 - 5780

Main Headquarters
Mailing: 650 Madison Ave. — Tel: (212) 318 - 7000
New York, NY 10022 — Fax: (212) 888 - 5780
TF: (800) 377 - 7656

Corporate Foundations and Giving Programs

Polo/Ralph Lauren Corporate Giving Program
650 Madison Ave. — Tel: (212) 318 - 7000
New York, NY 10022 — Fax: (212) 888 - 5780
TF: (800) 377 - 7656

Annual Grant Total: none reported
Primary Interests: Medical Research

Public Affairs and Related Activities Personnel

At Headquarters

GILLEN, Denise — Tel: (212) 318 - 7516
Investor Relations Contact — Fax: (212) 888 - 5780
TF: (800) 377 - 7656

KOSH, Mitchell A. — Tel: (212) 318 - 7000
Senior V. President, Human Resources — Fax: (212) 888 - 5780

MOORE, Erin — Tel: (212) 318 - 7402
Media Contact — Fax: (212) 888 - 5780
TF: (800) 377 - 7656

MURRAY, Nancy — Tel: (212) 318 - 7862
V. President, Investor Relations — Fax: (212) 888 - 5780

PALEY, Liz — Tel: (212) 318 - 7000
V. President, Ralph Lauren Advertising — Fax: (212) 888 - 5780

PolyOne Corp.

Formed by the merger of Geon Co. and M. A. Hanna Company in 2000. Manufactures plastic compounds and distributes plastic resins and shapes.

www.polyone.com
Annual Revenues: $3 billion

Chairman of the Board — Tel: (440) 930 - 1000
PATIENT, William F. — Fax: (440) 930 - 1750

President and Chief Exec. Officer — Tel: (440) 930 - 1000
WALTERMIRE, Thomas — Fax: (440) 930 - 1750

Main Headquarters
Mailing: 33587 Walker Rd. — Tel: (440) 930 - 1000
Avon Lake, OH 44093-0175 — Fax: (440) 930 - 1750

Political Action Committees

PolyOne Corp. PAC
Contact: Woodrow W. Ban
33587 Walker Rd. — Tel: (440) 930 - 1000
Avon Lake, OH 44093-0175 — Fax: (440) 930 - 1750

Contributions to Candidates: none reported (01/05 - 09/05)

PolyOne Corp.

* continued from previous page

Public Affairs and Related Activities Personnel

At Headquarters

BAN, Woodrow W. — Tel: (440) 930 - 1000
PAC Contact — Fax: (440) 930 - 1750
woodrow.ban@polyone.com

COCCO, Dennis — Tel: (440) 930 - 1538
V. President, Investor Relations and Communications — Fax: (440) 930 - 1750
dennis.cocc@polyone.com

Pope & Talbot, Inc.

A producer of pulp and wood products.

www.poptal.com

Chairman, President and Chief Exec. Officer — Tel: (503) 228 - 9161
FLANNERY, Michael — Fax: (503) 220 - 2722

Main Headquarters

Mailing: P.O. Box 8171, Portland, OR 97207 — Tel: (503) 228 - 9161; Fax: (503) 220 - 2722
Street: 1500 S.W. First Ave., Suite 200, Portland, OR 97201

Public Affairs and Related Activities Personnel

At Headquarters

ATKINSON, Richard K. — Tel: (503) 228 - 9161
V. President and Chief Financial Officer — Fax: (503) 220 - 2722
Responsibilities include investor relations.

HARDMAN, Beth — Tel: (503) 228 - 9161
Director, Human Resources — Fax: (503) 220 - 2722

Popeyes Chicken & Biscuits

See listing on page 9 under AFC Enterprises.

Porsche Cars North America, Inc.

www.porsche.com

President and Chief Exec. Officer — Tel: (770) 290 - 3500
SCHWARZENBAUER, Peter — Fax: (770) 290 - 3700

Main Headquarters

Mailing: 980 Hammond Dr. NE, Suite 1000, Atlanta, GA 30328-5313 — Tel: (770) 290 - 3500; Fax: (770) 290 - 3700

Corporate Foundations and Giving Programs

Porsche Foundation
980 Hammond Dr. NE — Tel: (770) 290 - 3500
Suite 1000 — Fax: (770) 290 - 3700
Atlanta, GA 30328-5313

Annual Grant Total: $100,000 - $200,000
Primary Interests: Arts and Humanities; Education; Financially Disadvantaged
Recent Recipients: Ronald McDonald House

Public Affairs and Related Activities Personnel

At Headquarters

BRITTON, Patricia — Tel: (770) 290 - 3500
Legal Counsel — Ext: 3609
pbritton@porschecars.com — Fax: (770) 290 - 3714
Responsibilities include government affairs and regulatory affairs.

HARLING, Bernd — Tel: (770) 290 - 3500
General Manager, Public Relations — Fax: (770) 290 - 3700

SMITH, Eleanor — Tel: (770) 290 - 3626
Public Relations Specialist — Fax: (770) 290 - 3706
esmith@porschecars.com

Portland General Electric Co.

A member of the Public Affairs Council. An electric utility. A subsidiary of Enron Corp. (see separate listing).

www.portlandgeneral.com
Annual Revenues: $1.751 billion

President and Chief Exec. Officer — Tel: (503) 464 - 8000
FOWLER, Peggy — Fax: (503) 464 - 2354
peggy_fowler@pgn.com — TF: (800) 542 - 8818

Main Headquarters

Mailing: 121 SW Salmon St., Portland, OR 97204 — Tel: (503) 464 - 8000; Fax: (503) 464 - 2354; TF: (800) 542 - 8818

Political Action Committees

Portland General Electric Co. Bi-Partisan Committee for Effective Gov't - Federal
Contact: Sunny Radcliffe
121 SW Salmon St. — Tel: (503) 464 - 8000
Portland, OR 97204 — Fax: (503) 464 - 2354

Contributions to Candidates: $3,500 (01/05 - 09/05)
Democrats: $3,500.

Principal Recipients

SENATE DEMOCRATS		HOUSE DEMOCRATS	
Murray, Patty (WA)	$1,000	Hooley, Darlene (OR)	$1,000

Corporate Foundations and Giving Programs

Portland General Electric Corporate Contributions Program
Contact: Carole Morse
121 SW Salmon St. — Tel: (503) 464 - 8000
Portland, OR 97204 — Fax: (503) 464 - 2354

Annual Grant Total: $400,000 - $500,000
Geographic Preference: Area in which the company is headquartered; Oregon
Primary Interests: Arts and Culture; Education; Environment/Conservation; Families

Public Affairs and Related Activities Personnel

At Headquarters

ARNTSON, Kregg — Tel: (503) 464 - 7693
Media Relations Representative — Fax: (503) 464 - 2929
Mailstop: 1WTC-0302
kregg_arntson@pgn.com

BAKER, Gail — Tel: (503) 464 - 8693
Manager, Corporate Communications and Community Affairs — Fax: (503) 464 - 2929; TF: (800) 542 - 8818
Mailstop: 1WTZ0302
gail_baker@pgn.com

DILLIN, Carol A. — Tel: (503) 464 - 8000
V. President, Public Policy — Fax: (503) 464 - 2929
Mailstop: 1WTC-1706
carol_dillin@pgn.com

LEI, Dr. Wayne — Tel: (503) 464 - 8000
Director, Environmental Policy Programs — Fax: (503) 464 - 2354
Mailstop: 1WTC-0303
wayne_lei@pgn.com

MORSE, Carole — Tel: (503) 464 - 8000
Consultant, Corporate Contributions and Community Affairs — Fax: (503) 464 - 2354
Mailstop: 1WTC-0303
carole_morse@pgn.com

RADCLIFFE, Sunny — Tel: (503) 464 - 8000
PAC Treasurer; Public Affairs — Fax: (503) 464 - 2354
Mailstop: MTC-0301
sania_radcliffe@pgn.com

ROBERTSON, Dave — Tel: (503) 464 - 8000
Director, Government Policy — Fax: (503) 464 - 2354
dave_robertson@pgn.com

Potlatch Corp.

A member of the Public Affairs Council. A manufacturer of wood products.

www.potlatchcorp.com
Annual Revenues: $1.286 billion

Chairman and Chief Exec. Officer — Tel: (509) 835 - 1500
SIEGAL, L. Pendleton — Fax: (509) 835 - 1555

Main Headquarters

Mailing: 601 W. Riverside Ave., Suite 1100, Spokane, WA 99201 — Tel: (509) 835 - 1500; Fax: (509) 835 - 1555

Political Action Committees

Potlatch Employees' Political Fund
Contact: Gerald L. Zuehlke
601 W. Riverside Ave. — Tel: (509) 835 - 1550
Suite 1100 — Fax: (509) 835 - 1555
Spokane, WA 99201

Contributions to Candidates: $2,500 (01/05 - 09/05)
Democrats: $2,000; Republicans: $500.

Principal Recipients

SENATE DEMOCRATS	HOUSE DEMOCRATS
	Ross, Michael Avery (AR) $2,000

Corporate Foundations and Giving Programs

Potlatch Corporate Giving
601 W. Riverside Ave. — Tel: (509) 835 - 1500
Suite 1100 — Fax: (509) 835 - 1555
Spokane, WA 99201

Annual Grant Total: $500,000 - $750,000
Geographic Preference: Area(s) in which the company operates; Arkansas; Idaho; Minnesota
Primary Interests: Civic and Public Affairs; Education; Health and Human Services

Potlatch Foundation for Higher Education
Contact: Sharon Pegau

Potlatch Corp.

* continued from previous page

601 W. Riverside Ave.
Suite 1100
Spokane, WA 99201
Tel: (509) 835 - 1515
Fax: (509) 835 - 1555

Annual Grant Total: $400,000 - $500,000
Geographic Preference: Area(s) in which the company operates
Primary Interests: Scholarship Funds

Public Affairs and Related Activities Personnel

At Headquarters

PEGAU, Sharon
Contact, Potlatch Foundation for Higher Education
Tel: (509) 835 - 1515
Fax: (509) 835 - 1555

RYERSE, Malcolm A. "Mac"
Secretary
Responsibilities include shareholder relations.
Tel: (509) 835 - 1512
Fax: (509) 835 - 1566

SULLIVAN, Michael D.
Director, Corporate Communications
miked.sullivan@potlatchcorp.com
Tel: (509) 835 - 1516
Fax: (509) 835 - 1559

ZUEHLKE, Gerald L.
Chief Financial Officer
Responsibilities include investor relations.
Tel: (509) 835 - 1550
Fax: (509) 835 - 1555

At Other Offices

BENSON, Mark
Director, Public Affairs
P.O. Box 1388
Lewiston, ID 83501
mark.benson@potlatchcorp.com
Tel: (208) 799 - 1781
Fax: (208) 799 - 1918

STOCKER, Lisa
Director, Public Affairs
P.O. Box 390
Warren, AR 71671
Tel: (870) 226 - 1114
Fax: (870) 226 - 6367

Potomac Electric Power Co.

See listing on page 376 under Pepco Holdings, Inc.

PP&L Resources

See listing on page 390 under PPL Corp.

PPG Industries Inc.

A member of the Public Affairs Council. A manufacturer of coatings, glass, chemicals, and fiberglass.
www.ppg.com
Annual Revenues: $8.169 billion

Chairman and Chief Exec. Officer
BUNCH, Charles E.
Tel: (412) 434 - 3131
Fax: (412) 434 - 4666

Main Headquarters
Mailing: One PPG Pl.
Pittsburgh, PA 15272
Tel: (412) 434 - 3131
Fax: (412) 434 - 4666

Political Action Committees

PPG Better Government Team
Contact: Judith F. Maskrey
One PPG Pl.
Pittsburgh, PA 15272
Tel: (412) 434 - 2476
Fax: (412) 434 - 4666

Contributions to Candidates: $9,750 (01/05 - 09/05)
Democrats: $3,000; Republicans: $6,750.

Principal Recipients

SENATE DEMOCRATS

HOUSE DEMOCRATS
Visclosky, Peter (IN) $2,000
Doyle, Mike (PA) $1,000

SENATE REPUBLICANS
Santorum, Richard (PA) $2,000
Domenici, Pete (NM) $1,000

HOUSE REPUBLICANS
Hobson, David (OH) $2,000

Corporate Foundations and Giving Programs

PPG Industries Foundation
Contact: Lynne D. Schmidt
One PPG Pl.
Pittsburgh, PA 15272
Tel: (412) 434 - 4397
Fax: (412) 434 - 4666

Annual Grant Total: $2,000,000 - $5,000,000
Guidelines available upon written request.
Geographic Preference: Area(s) in which the company operates; National
Primary Interests: Civic and Cultural Activities; Education; Health and Human Services
Recent Recipients: Carnegie Mellon University; Nat'l Merit Scholarship; United Way

Public Affairs and Related Activities Personnel

At Headquarters

MAGUIRE, Andrew G.
General Manager, Marketing and Communications
amaguire@ppg.com
Tel: (412) 434 - 2316
Fax: (412) 434 - 4666

MASKREY, Judith F.
Director, Government Affairs
Tel: (412) 434 - 2476
Fax: (412) 434 - 4666

MORALES, Vincent
Director, Investor Relations
Tel: (412) 434 - 3740
Fax: (412) 434 - 4666

NORTON, Reginald J.
Global Director, Environment, Health and Safety
rnorton@ppg.com
Tel: (412) 434 - 2398

SCHMIDT, Lynne D.
V. President, Government and Community Affairs; Exec. Director, PPG Industries Foundation
Mailstop: 40 East
Tel: (412) 434 - 4397
Fax: (412) 434 - 4666

WISE, Charles W. "Bud"
V. President, Human Resources
Mailstop: 12 North
Tel: (412) 434 - 3715
Fax: (412) 434 - 4666

WORDEN, Jeff
Manager, Public Relations
Mailstop: 7 South
Tel: (412) 434 - 3046
Fax: (412) 434 - 4666

PPL Corp.

A member of the Public Affairs Council. A public electric utility.
www.pplweb.com
Annual Revenues: $5.6 billion

Chairman, President and Chief Exec. Officer
HECHT, William F.
Tel: (610) 774 - 5151
Fax: (610) 774 - 5281
TF: (800) 345 - 3085

Main Headquarters
Mailing: Two N. Ninth St.
Allentown, PA 18101-1179
Tel: (610) 774 - 5151
Fax: (610) 774 - 5281
TF: (800) 345 - 3085

Washington Office
Mailing: 1331 Pennsylvania Ave. NW
Suite 512
Washington, DC 20004
Tel: (202) 662 - 8750
Fax: (202) 662 - 8749

Political Action Committees

PPL People for Good Government
Contact: Joanne H. Raphael
Two N. Ninth St.
Allentown, PA 18101-1179
Tel: (610) 774 - 5372
Fax: (610) 774 - 4751
TF: (800) 345 - 3085

Contributions to Candidates: $39,500 (01/05 - 09/05)
Democrats: $13,500; Republicans: $25,000; Other: $1,000.

Principal Recipients

SENATE DEMOCRATS
Baucus, Max (MT) $3,000

HOUSE DEMOCRATS
Murtha, John P Mr. (PA) $2,500
Kanjorski, Paul (PA) $2,000
Michaud, Michael (ME) $2,000

SENATE REPUBLICANS
Burns, Conrad (MT) $2,000
Santorum, Richard (PA) $2,000

HOUSE REPUBLICANS
Dent, Charles W (PA) $4,000
Sherwood, Donald L (PA) $3,000
English, Philip S (PA) $2,000
Fitzpatrick, Michael (PA) $2,000
Rehberg, Dennis (MT) $2,000
Shuster, William (PA) $2,000

Corporate Foundations and Giving Programs

PPL Corporate Contributions
Contact: Robert P. Daday
Two N. Ninth St.
Allentown, PA 18101-1179
Tel: (610) 774 - 7511
Fax: (610) 774 - 5281
TF: (800) 345 - 3085

Annual Grant Total: none reported

Public Affairs and Related Activities Personnel

At Headquarters

AYLWARD, Claire M.
Manager, Investor Services
Mailstop: TW14
cmaylward@pplweb.com
Tel: (610) 774 - 5804
Fax: (610) 774 - 5281
TF: (800) 345 - 3085

BIGGAR, John R.
Exec. V. President and Chief Financial Officer
jrbiggar@pplweb.com
Responsibilities include investor relations.
Tel: (610) 774 - 5613
Fax: (610) 774 - 4198
TF: (800) 345 - 3085

DADAY, Robert P.
Special Assistant to the President - Community Affairs
rpdaday@pplweb.com
Tel: (610) 774 - 7511
Fax: (610) 774 - 5281
TF: (800) 345 - 3085

PPL Corp.

** continued from previous page*

GENECZKO, Robert M.
V. President, Customer Services
rmgeneczko@pplweb.com
Tel: (484) 634 - 3248
Fax: (610) 774 - 5281
TF: (800) 345 - 3085

MCCARTHY, Daniel J.
Director, Corporate Communications
djmccarthy@pplweb.com
Tel: (610) 774 - 5758
Fax: (610) 774 - 5281
TF: (800) 345 - 3085

PAUKOVITS, Timothy J.
Manager, Investor Relations
tjpaukovits@pplweb.com
Tel: (610) 774 - 4124
Fax: (610) 774 - 5106
TF: (800) 345 - 3085

RAPHAEL, Joanne H.
V. President, External Affairs
jhraphael@pplweb.com
Tel: (610) 774 - 5372
Fax: (610) 774 - 4751
TF: (800) 345 - 3085

SANTANASTO, James A.
Manager, Employee and Marketing Communications
jasantanasto@pplweb.com
Tel: (610) 774 - 5910
Fax: (610) 774 - 5281
TF: (800) 345 - 3085

WIRTH, Paul G.
Manager, Public Relations
pgwirth@pplweb.com
Tel: (610) 774 - 5562
Fax: (610) 774 - 5281
TF: (800) 345 - 3085

At Washington Office

EAKIN, Laura
Representative, Federal Government Relations
Tel: (202) 662 - 8750
Fax: (202) 662 - 8749

ERLACHER, Laura Eakin
Manager, Federal Government Relations
Registered Federal Lobbyist.
Tel: (202) 662 - 8750
Fax: (202) 662 - 8749

LOUDA, Dale
Manager, Federal Government Relations
Tel: (202) 662 - 8750
Fax: (202) 662 - 8749

PIDCOCK, Paulette C.
V. President, Federal Government Relations
Tel: (202) 662 - 8750
Fax: (202) 662 - 8749

PPL Energy Plus

See listing on page 390 under PPL Corp.

Pratt & Whitney

A manufacturer of aircraft engines.
www.pratt-whitney.com
Annual Revenues: $7.679 billion

Main Headquarters
Mailing: 400 Main St.
East Hartford, CT 06108
Tel: (860) 565 - 4321

Washington Office
Contact: Michael H. Summers
Mailing: 1401 I St. NW
Suite 600
Washington, DC 20005
Tel: (202) 336 - 7427

Corporate Foundations and Giving Programs

Pratt & Whitney Corporate Giving
400 Main St.
East Hartford, CT 06108
Tel: (860) 565 - 4321

Annual Grant Total: $2,000,000 - $5,000,000
Primary Interests: Arts and Humanities; Education; Environment/Conservation; Health and Human Services; Math and Science; Technology; Youth Services
Recent Recipients: United Way

Public Affairs and Related Activities Personnel

At Headquarters

BOWLER, J. Thomas
V. President, Human Resources and Organization
Tel: (860) 565 - 4321

DOYLE, Kevin
V. President, Environment, Health and Safety
Tel: (860) 565 - 4321

SULLIVAN, Mark P.
Director, Media Relations
Tel: (860) 565 - 9600
Fax: (860) 565 - 8896

TRON, Dionn M.
V. President, Communications
Tel: (860) 565 - 4321

At Washington Office

SUMMERS, Michael H.
Director, Washington Operations
Tel: (202) 336 - 7427

Praxair, Inc.

A member of the Public Affairs Council. A manufacturer of industrial gases, ceramic and metallic powders and coating materials.
www.praxair.com

Chairman, President and Chief Exec. Officer
REILLEY, Dennis H.
Tel: (203) 837 - 2000
Fax: (203) 837 - 2505
TF: (800) 772 - 9247

Main Headquarters
Mailing: 39 Old Ridgebury Rd.
Danbury, CT 06810-5113
Tel: (203) 837 - 2000
Fax: (203) 837 - 2505
TF: (800) 772 - 9247

Washington Office
Contact: Thomas D. Finnigan
Mailing: 1200 G St., NW
Suite 550
Washington, DC 20005
Tel: (202) 393 - 0962
Fax: (202) 347 - 1684

Political Action Committees

Praxair Inc. Political Action Committee
39 Old Ridgebury Rd.
Danbury, CT 06810-5113
Tel: (203) 837 - 2000
Fax: (203) 837 - 2505
TF: (800) 772 - 9247

Contributions to Candidates: $4,000 (01/05 - 09/05)
Democrats: $1,000; Republicans: $3,000.

Principal Recipients

SENATE DEMOCRATS

HOUSE DEMOCRATS
Ross, Michael Avery (AR) $1,000

SENATE REPUBLICANS

HOUSE REPUBLICANS
Chocola, Christopher (IN) $1,000
Dent, Charles W (PA) $1,000
Renzi, Richard (AZ) $1,000

Corporate Foundations and Giving Programs

Praxair Foundation
Contact: Nigel D. Muir
39 Old Ridgebury Rd.
Danbury, CT 06810-5113
Tel: (203) 837 - 2240
Fax: (203) 837 - 2555
TF: (800) 772 - 9247

Annual Grant Total: none reported
Geographic Preference: Area(s) in which the company operates; International
Primary Interests: Community Affairs; Engineering; Environment/Conservation; Higher Education; Minority Opportunities
Recent Recipients: United Way

Public Affairs and Related Activities Personnel

At Headquarters

GORE, Susan Szita
Associate Director, Communications
susan_szita-gore@praxair.com
Tel: (203) 837 - 2311
Fax: (203) 837 - 2454
TF: (800) 772 - 9247

HIRSCH, Elizabeth T.
Director, Investor Relations
liz_hirsch@praxair.com
Tel: (203) 837 - 2354
Fax: (203) 837 - 2505
TF: (800) 772 - 9247

LEE, Jonathan
Media Contact
jon_lee@praxair.com
Tel: (203) 837 - 2039
Fax: (203) 837 - 2505
TF: (800) 772 - 9247

MUIR, Nigel D.
V. President, Communications and Public Relations; President, Praxair Foundation Inc.
nigel_muir@praxair.com
Tel: (203) 837 - 2240
Fax: (203) 837 - 2555
TF: (800) 772 - 9247

SAVOIA, Sally A.
V. President, Human Resources
Tel: (203) 837 - 2000
Fax: (203) 837 - 2505
TF: (800) 772 - 9247

At Washington Office

FINNIGAN, Thomas D.
Director, Government Relations
tom_finnigan@praxair.com
Registered Federal Lobbyist.
Tel: (202) 393 - 0962
Fax: (202) 347 - 1684

Precision Castparts Corp.

A manufacturer of complex metal components and products.
www.precast.com
Annual Revenues: $2.919 billion

Chairman and Chief Exec. Officer
DONEGAN, Mark
Tel: (503) 417 - 4800
Fax: (503) 417 - 4817

Main Headquarters
Mailing: 4650 SW Macadam Ave.
Suite 440
Portland, OR 97239-4254
Tel: (503) 417 - 4800
Fax: (503) 417 - 4817

Public Affairs and Related Activities Personnel

At Headquarters

COOKE, Roger A.
V. President, Regulatory and Legal Affairs
Tel: (503) 417 - 4822
Fax: (503) 417 - 4817

WEBER, Dwight E.
Director, Communications
Responsibilities include shareholder relations.
Tel: (503) 417 - 4855
Fax: (503) 417 - 4817

Premcor Inc.

A petroleum refiner and marketer.

www.premcor.com

Chairman and Chief Exec. Officer
O'MALLEY, Thomas D. — Tel: (203) 698 - 7500; Fax: (203) 698 - 7925

Main Headquarters
Mailing: 1700 E. Putnam Ave.
Suite 400
Greenwich, CT 06370
Tel: (203) 698 - 7500; Fax: (203) 698 - 7925

Public Affairs and Related Activities Personnel

At Headquarters

CARNICELLI, Christine
Corporate Human Resources Contact
Tel: (203) 698 - 5649; Fax: (203) 698 - 7925

KILIC, Michelle
Manager, Investor Relations
Tel: (203) 698 - 5921; Fax: (203) 698 - 7925

OVELMAN, Karen
V. President, Investor Relations and External Reporting
Responsibilities also include media relations.
Tel: (203) 698 - 5669; Fax: (203) 698 - 7925

Premdor Inc.

See listing on page 307 under Masonite Internat'l Corp.

Premera Blue Cross

A member of the Public Affairs Council. Serves members throughout Washington and Alaska. Subsidiaries also serve members in Oregon, and Arizona.

www.premera.com

Chairman, President and Chief Exec. Officer
BARLOW, H. R. Brereton — Tel: (425) 670 - 5900; Fax: (425) 670 - 5635

Main Headquarters
Mailing: 7001 220th S.W.
Mountlake Terrace, WA 98043-2124
Tel: (425) 918 - 5900; Fax: (425) 918 - 5635; TF: (800) 422 - 0032

Public Affairs and Related Activities Personnel

At Headquarters

FORSLUND, Scott
Director, Communications
Mailstop: Bldg. 3 M/S 308
scott.forslund@premera.com
Tel: (425) 918 - 5090; Fax: (425) 918 - 5575; TF: (800) 422 - 0032

JARVIS, Chris
Manager, Communications
Mailstop: Bldg. 3 M/S 308
chris.jarvis@premera.com
Tel: (425) 918 - 3368; Fax: (425) 918 - 5575; TF: (800) 422 - 0032

MCRAE, Jack
Senior V. President, Legislative and Congressional Affairs
Mailstop: MS 355
jack.mcrae@premera.com
Tel: (425) 918 - 5757; Fax: (425) 918 - 5635

MILO, Yori
Exec. V. President, Chief Legal and Public Policy Officer
Tel: (425) 918 - 5900; Fax: (425) 918 - 5635; TF: (800) 422 - 0032

MOORE, Bill
Manager, Legislative Policy
Mailstop: MS 354
bill.moore@premera.com
Tel: (425) 918 - 4720

Premiere Global Services, Inc.

Formerly PTEK Holdings, Inc. Provides business communications services and business process solutions.

www.premiereglobal.com
Annual Revenues: $500 million

Chairman and Chief Exec. Officer
JONES, Boland T.
boland.jones@premiereglobal.com
Tel: (404) 262 - 8400

Main Headquarters
Mailing: The Lenox Bldg., Suite 700
3399 Peachtree Rd. NE
Atlanta, GA 30326
Tel: (404) 262 - 8400

Public Affairs and Related Activities Personnel

At Headquarters

O'BRIEN, Sean P.
Senior V. President, Strategic Planning and Investor Relations
sean.obrien@premiereglobal.com
Tel: (404) 262 - 8462; Fax: (866) 825 - 7082

SALISBURY, Randy
Exec. V. President and Chief Marketing Officer
randy.salisbury@premiereglobal.com
Reponsibilities include media relations.
Tel: (404) 262 - 8461

PRG-Schultz Internat'l, Inc.

Formerly The Profit Recovery Group Internat'l, Inc. Works to recover lost profits for businesses and government agencies.

www.prgx.com

Chairman and Chief Exec. Officer
COOK, John M.
john.cook@prgx.com
Tel: (770) 779 - 3900; Fax: (770) 779 - 3042

Main Headquarters
Mailing: 600 Galleria Pkwy.
Suite 100
Atlanta, GA 30339
Tel: (770) 779 - 3900; Fax: (770) 779 - 3133; TF: (800) 752 - 5894

Public Affairs and Related Activities Personnel

At Headquarters

MASTER-PARKER, Linda
Corporate Communications Contact
lindamaster-parker@prgx.com
Tel: (770) 779 - 3295; Fax: (770) 779 - 3133; TF: (800) 752 - 5894

NEFF, Marie A.
Exec. V. President, Human Resources
marie.neff@prgx.com
Tel: (770) 779 - 3900; Fax: (770) 779 - 3042

T. Rowe Price Associates

A financial investments firm.

www.troweprice.com

Chairman and President
ROCHE, George
groche@troweprice.com
Tel: (410) 345 - 2000; Fax: (410) 345 - 4661; TF: (800) 638 - 7890

Main Headquarters
Mailing: 100 E. Pratt St.
Baltimore, MD 21202
Tel: (410) 345 - 2000; Fax: (410) 345 - 4661; TF: (800) 638 - 7890

Corporate Foundations and Giving Programs

T. Rowe Price Associates Foundation, Inc.
Contact: Christine Stein
100 E. Pratt St.
Baltimore, MD 21202
Tel: (410) 345 - 2000 Ext: 3603; Fax: (410) 345 - 4661; TF: (800) 638 - 7890

Annual Grant Total: $2,000,000 - $5,000,000

Geographic Preference: Baltimore, MD
Primary Interests: Arts and Culture; Civic and Public Affairs; Community Affairs; Education; Social Services
Recent Recipients: Baltimore Museum of Art; Baltimore Zoo

Public Affairs and Related Activities Personnel

At Headquarters

NORWITZ, Steven E.
V. President, Public Relations
steve_norwitz@troweprice.com
Tel: (410) 345 - 2124; Fax: (410) 345 - 4661; TF: (800) 638 - 7890

STEIN, Christine
Program Officer, T. Rowe Price Associates Foundation
cstein@troweprice.com
Tel: (410) 345 - 2000 Ext: 3603; Fax: (410) 345 - 4661; TF: (800) 638 - 7890

PriceWaterhouseCoopers LLP

Formed by the merger of Price Waterhouse LLP and Coopers and Lybrand in 1998. A professional services organization.

www.pwcglobal.com
Annual Revenues: $24 billion

Chief Exec. Officer
DIPIAZZA, Samuel A., Jr. — Tel: (646) 471 - 4000; Fax: (646) 394 - 5355

Main Headquarters
Mailing: 1301 Ave. of the Americas
New York, NY 10019
Tel: (646) 471 - 4000; Fax: (646) 394 - 5355

Washington Office
Contact: Allen J. Weltmann
Mailing: 1900 K St. NW
Suite 900
Washington, DC 20006
Tel: (202) 822 - 4000; Fax: (202) 822 - 5640

Political Action Committees

Pricewaterhouse Coopers PAC
Contact: Allen J. Weltmann
1900 K St. NW
Suite 900
Washington, DC 20006
Tel: (202) 822 - 4222; Fax: (202) 822 - 5800

Contributions to Candidates: $166,911 (01/05 - 09/05)

PriceWaterhouseCoopers LLP

* continued from previous page

Democrats: $46,706; Republicans: $118,453; Other: $1,752.

Principal Recipients

SENATE DEMOCRATS		HOUSE DEMOCRATS	
Nelson, Benjamin (NE)	$3,500	Frank, Barney (MA)	$5,000
Conrad, Kent (ND)	$3,000	Towns, Edolphus (NY)	$2,000
SENATE REPUBLICANS		**HOUSE REPUBLICANS**	
Bennett, Robert F (UT)	$5,000	Davis, Tom (VA)	$7,453
Kyl, Jon L (AZ)	$3,500	Bachus, Spencer (AL)	$6,500
Chafee, Lincoln (RI)	$2,500	Baker, Hugh (LA)	$6,500
Ensign, John Eric (NV)	$2,500	Blunt, Roy (MO)	$5,000
		Ney, Robert W (OH)	$5,000
		Oxley, Michael (OH)	$5,000
		Pearce, Steve (NM)	$4,000
		McHenry, Patrick (NC)	$3,000
		Price, Thomas (GA)	$3,000
		Renzi, Richard (AZ)	$2,000
		Reynolds, Thomas (NY)	$2,000
		Tiberi, Patrick (OH)	$2,000

Corporate Foundations and Giving Programs

PricewaterhouseCoopers Foundation
1301 Ave. of the Americas
New York, NY 10019
Tel: (646) 471 - 4000
Fax: (646) 394 - 5355

Annual Grant Total: none reported
Geographic Preference: No geographical restrictions
Primary Interests: Adult Education and Training
Recent Recipients: Columbia University; University of Notre Dame

Public Affairs and Related Activities Personnel

At Headquarters

NESTOR, David L.
Head, Public Relations
david.nestor@us.pwc.com
Tel: (646) 471 - 4855
Fax: (646) 394 - 5355

SILVER, Steven G.
Corporate Public Relations Contact
steven.g.silber@us.pwc.com
Tel: (646) 471 - 4059
Fax: (646) 394 - 5355

At Washington Office

BELL, Beverly
Director, Government and Professional Activities
Registered Federal Lobbyist.
Tel: (202) 822 - 4000
Fax: (202) 822 - 5800

PAULL, Lindy
Registered Federal Lobbyist.
Tel: (202) 822 - 4000
Fax: (202) 822 - 5640

PENN, Oren
Registered Federal Lobbyist.
Tel: (202) 822 - 4000
Fax: (202) 822 - 5640

PETITO, Joseph P.
Partner, Professional and Regulatory Activities
Responsibilities include government affairs.
Tel: (202) 822 - 5812
Fax: (202) 822 - 5640

WELTMANN, Allen J.
Partner in Charge, Professional and Regulatory Activities
Registered Federal Lobbyist.
Responsibilities include government affairs.
Tel: (202) 822 - 4222
Fax: (202) 822 - 5800

Pride Internat'l, Inc.

An international oil and gas drilling contractor.
www.prideinternational.com
Annual Revenues: $1.5 billion

Chairman of the Board
MACAULAY, William E.
Tel: (713) 789 - 1400
Fax: (713) 789 - 1430

President and Chief Exec. Officer
BRAGG, Paul A.
Tel: (713) 789 - 1400
Fax: (713) 952 - 6916

Main Headquarters
Mailing: 5847 San Felipe, Suite 3300
Houston, TX 77057
Tel: (713) 789 - 1400
Fax: (713) 789 - 1430

Public Affairs and Related Activities Personnel

At Headquarters

BANE, Lonnie D.
V. President, Human Resources
Tel: (713) 789 - 1400
Fax: (713) 789 - 1430

EVANOFF, Nicholas J.
V. President, Corporate and Governmental Affairs
Tel: (713) 789 - 1400
Fax: (713) 952 - 6916

OLDHAM, Steven D.
V. President, Treasury and Investor Relations
soldham@prideinternational.com
Tel: (713) 789 - 1400
Fax: (713) 789 - 1430

PrimeCo Personal Communications

See listing on page 504 under Verizon Wireless.

Primedia Inc.

A diversified communications company.
www.primedia.com
Annual Revenues: $1.3 billion

Chairman of the Board
NELSON, Dean B.
Tel: (212) 745 - 0100
Fax: (212) 745 - 0121

President and Chief Exec. Officer
CONLIN, Kelly P.
Tel: (212) 745 - 0100
Fax: (212) 745 - 0121

Main Headquarters
Mailing: 745 Fifth Ave.
New York, NY 10151
Tel: (212) 745 - 0100
Fax: (212) 745 - 0121

Public Affairs and Related Activities Personnel

At Headquarters

ASHER, Allison R.
Manager, Corporate Communications
allison.asher@primedia.com
Tel: (212) 745 - 0535
Fax: (212) 745 - 0131

BALLABON, Jeff
Exec. V. President, Network Affairs
Tel: (212) 745 - 1283
Fax: (212) 745 - 0121

CHELL, Beverly C.
V. Chairman, General Counsel and Secretary
bchell@primedia.com
Responsibilities include government relations.
Tel: (212) 745 - 0101
Fax: (212) 745 - 0121

DISCEPOLO, Michaelanne C.
Exec. V. President, Human Resources
mdiscepolo@primedia.com
Tel: (212) 745 - 0115
Fax: (212) 745 - 0121

MAGRONE, James
Senior V. President, Investor Relations
Tel: (212) 745 - 0100
Fax: (212) 745 - 0121

Primerica Financial Services, Inc.

A financial services company. A subsidiary of Citigroup. (see separate listing).
www.primerica.com

Co-Chief Exec. Officer
ADDISON, John A.
Tel: (770) 381 - 1000
Fax: (770) 564 - 6161

Co-Chief Exec. Officer
WILLIAMS, D. Richard
Tel: (770) 381 - 1000
Fax: (770) 564 - 6161

Main Headquarters
Mailing: 3120 Breckinridge Blvd.
Duluth, GA 30099-0001
Tel: (770) 381 - 1000
Fax: (770) 564 - 6110

Corporate Foundations and Giving Programs

PFS Local Contributions Program/Citigroup Foundation
Contact: Anne Soutter
3120 Breckinridge Blvd.
Duluth, GA 30099-0001
Tel: (770) 381 - 1000
Fax: (770) 564 - 6110

Annual Grant Total: $750,000 - $1,000,000

Public Affairs and Related Activities Personnel

At Headquarters

FINE, Karen
Exec. V. President, Human Resources
Tel: (770) 381 - 1000
Fax: (770) 564 - 6110

KING, Barbara T.
Exec. V. President, Field Communications
Tel: (770) 381 - 1000
Fax: (770) 564 - 6110

SOUTTER, Anne
Contact, PFS Local Contributions Program
Tel: (770) 381 - 1000
Fax: (770) 564 - 6110

SUPIC, Mark L.
Senior V. President, Corporate Relations
Tel: (770) 564 - 6328
Fax: (770) 564 - 6110

The Principal Financial Group

PUBLIC AFFAIRS COUNCIL

A member of the Public Affairs Council. A diversified family of financial services organizations.
www.principal.com

Chairman, President and Chief Exec. Officer
GRISWELL, J. Barry
griswell.barry@principal.com
Tel: (515) 247 - 5111
Fax: (515) 246 - 5475
TF: (800) 986 - 3343

Main Headquarters
Mailing: 711 High St.
Des Moines, IA 50392-0150
Tel: (515) 247 - 5111
Fax: (515) 246 - 5475
TF: (800) 986 - 3343

Washington Office
Contact: Stuart J. Brahs
Mailing: 1350 I St., N.W., Suite 1030
Washington, DC 20005-3305
Tel: (202) 682 - 1280
Fax: (202) 682 - 1412

Political Action Committees

Principal Life Insurance Co. PAC
Contact: James Lang
711 High St.
Des Moines, IA 50392-0150
Tel: (515) 247 - 5111
Fax: (515) 246 - 5475
TF: (800) 986 - 3343

The Principal Financial Group

** continued from previous page*

Contributions to Candidates: $67,065 (01/05 - 09/05)
Democrats: $41,065; Republicans: $26,000.

Principal Recipients

SENATE DEMOCRATS		HOUSE DEMOCRATS	
Nelson, Benjamin (NE)	$4,000	Pomeroy, Earl (ND)	$3,065
Baucus, Max (MT)	$2,000	Boswell, Leonard (IA)	$2,000
Conrad, Kent (ND)	$2,000	Cardin, Ben (MD)	$2,000
		Israel, Steve (NY)	$2,000
		Meeks, Gregory W (NY)	$2,000
SENATE REPUBLICANS		**HOUSE REPUBLICANS**	
		Latham, Thomas P (IA)	$2,000

Corporate Foundations and Giving Programs

The Principal Group Foundation, Inc.
Contact: Libby Jacobs
711 High St.
Des Moines, IA 50392-0150
Tel: (515) 248 - 3641
Fax: (515) 246 - 5475
TF: (800) 986 - 3343

Annual Grant Total: over $5,000,000
Geographic Preference: Area(s) in which the company operates; National
Primary Interests: Civic and Cultural Activities; Education; Health and Human Services
Recent Recipients: Des Moines Civic Center; Drake University

Public Affairs and Related Activities Personnel

At Headquarters

CLARK-LEYDA, Rhonda
Corporate Relations Contact
clark-leyda.rhonda@principal.com
Tel: (515) 247 - 6634
Fax: (515) 246 - 5475
TF: (800) 986 - 3343

CRAWFORD, Jim
Director, Government Affairs and Political Advocacy
crawford.jim@principal.com
Tel: (515) 247 - 5480
Fax: (515) 248 - 8469
TF: (800) 986 - 3343

GRAF, Tom
Senior V. President, Investor Relations
Tel: (515) 235 - 5491
Fax: (515) 246 - 5475
TF: (800) 986 - 3343

HOUSER, Susan
Media Relations Contact
houser.susan@principal.com
Responsibilities include investor relations.
Tel: (515) 248 - 2268
Fax: (515) 246 - 5475
TF: (800) 986 - 3343

JACOBS, Libby
Assistant Director, Community Relations
jacobs.libby@principal.com
Tel: (515) 248 - 3641
Fax: (515) 246 - 5475
TF: (800) 986 - 3343

LANG, James
Treasurer, Principal Life Insurance Co. PAC
Tel: (515) 247 - 5111
Fax: (515) 246 - 5475
TF: (800) 986 - 3343

MARCHETTI, Tina
Media Relations Contact, Financial Communications
marchetti.tina@principal.com
Tel: (515) 248 - 0065
Fax: (515) 246 - 5475
TF: (800) 986 - 3343

PALMER, Susan
Director, Government Relations
Tel: (515) 247 - 5111
Fax: (515) 246 - 5475
TF: (800) 986 - 3343

PEDERSON, Merle
V. President, Government Relations
pederson.merle@principal.com
Tel: (515) 248 - 2186
TF: (800) 986 - 3343

QUINN, Eva S.
Second V. President, Corporate Relations
quinn.eva@principal.com
Tel: (515) 247 - 7468
TF: (800) 986 - 3343

SHELL, Terri
Media Relations Contact
shell.terri@principal.com
Tel: (515) 283 - 8858
Fax: (515) 246 - 5475
TF: (800) 986 - 3343

TEHEL, Megan
Community Involvement Contact
tehel.megan@principal.com
Tel: (515) 246 - 4907
Fax: (515) 246 - 5475
TF: (800) 986 - 3343

At Washington Office

BLUMER, Patti R.
Assistant Federal Legislative Director
blumer.patti@principal.com
Registered Federal Lobbyist.
Tel: (202) 682 - 1280
Fax: (202) 682 - 1412

BRAHS, Stuart J.
V. President, Federal Government Relations
brahs.stuart@principal.com
Registered Federal Lobbyist.
Tel: (202) 682 - 1280
Fax: (202) 682 - 1412

LAWSON, Richard C.
V. President, Federal Government Relations
Registered Federal Lobbyist.
Tel: (202) 682 - 1280
Fax: (202) 682 - 1412

RIDDLE, R. Lucia
V. President, Government Relations
riddle.lucia@principal.com
Registered Federal Lobbyist.
Tel: (202) 682 - 1280
Fax: (202) 682 - 1412

The Procter & Gamble Company

A member of the Public Affairs Council. A manufacturer and distributor of cleaning and other household products, soap, health care, beauty care, paper products, snacks, and beverages. Acquired Iams in 1999, Clairol, Inc. in late fall of 2001 and Well A in 2003. The company announced plans to acquire The Gillette Company. Completion of the merger is expected in the final quarter of 2005.

www.pg.com/news
Annual Revenues: $51.4 billion

Chairman, President and Chief Exec. Officer
LAFLEY, Alan G.
lafley.ag@pg.com
Tel: (513) 983 - 1100
Fax: (513) 983 - 9181

Main Headquarters
Mailing: P.O. Box 599
Cincinnati, OH 45201-0599
Tel: (513) 983 - 1100
Fax: (513) 983 - 9369
Street: One Procter & Gamble Plaza
Cincinnati, OH 45202-3315

Washington Office
Mailing: 701 Pennsylvania Ave. NW
Suite 520
Washington, DC 20004-2604
Tel: (202) 393 - 3400
Fax: (202) 393 - 4606

Political Action Committees

Procter & Gamble Good Government Committee
Contact: Jeffrey A. Lane
P.O. Box 599
Cincinnati, OH 45201-0599

Contributions to Candidates: $95,000 (01/05 - 09/05)
Democrats: $22,500; Republicans: $72,500.

Principal Recipients

SENATE DEMOCRATS		HOUSE DEMOCRATS	
Carper, Thomas R (DE)	$5,000	Boucher, Fredrick (VA)	$3,000
Kennedy, Ted (MA)	$3,500	Cuellar, Henry (TX)	$2,000
		Tanner, John S. (TN)	$2,000
SENATE REPUBLICANS		**HOUSE REPUBLICANS**	
Kyl, Jon L (AZ)	$5,000	Blunt, Roy (MO)	$5,000
Allen, George (VA)	$3,000	Hastert, Dennis J. (IL)	$5,000
Santorum, Richard (PA)	$2,000	Schmidt, Jeannette (OH)	$5,000
Snowe, Olympia (ME)	$2,000	Cantor, Eric (VA)	$4,500
		Pryce, Deborah (OH)	$3,500
		DeLay, Tom (TX)	$2,500
		McCrery, Jim (LA)	$2,500
		Brady, Kevin Patrick (TX)	$2,000
		Oxley, Michael (OH)	$2,000
		Shaw, Clay (FL)	$2,000
		Thomas, William M (CA)	$2,000

Corporate Foundations and Giving Programs

Procter & Gamble Fund
Contact: Gayle Nesselhoff
P.O. Box 599
Cincinnati, OH 45201-0599
Tel: (513) 945 - 8454
Fax: (513) 845 - 8979

Annual Grant Total: over $5,000,000
Total giving is over $16.3 million. The company also supports volunteer programs.
Geographic Preference: Area(s) in which the company operates
Primary Interests: Arts and Culture; Children; Civic and Public Affairs; Health and Human Services; Higher Education
Recent Recipients: American Red Cross; Cincinnati Institute of Fine Arts; United Negro College Fund; United Way

Public Affairs and Related Activities Personnel

At Headquarters

BOWMNA, Ellen, Phd
Director, External Relations/ Global Healthcare
Tel: (513) 983 - 1100
Fax: (513) 983 - 9369

HUGHES, Louise S.
Associate Director, Ohio Government Relations
hughes.ls@pg.com
Tel: (513) 983 - 6357

LANE, Jeffrey A.
V. President, State and Local Government Relations
lane.ja@pg.com

LOFTUS, Terry E.
Associate Director, External Relations/Corporate Communications
loftus.te@pg.com
Tel: (513) 983 - 9736
Fax: (513) 983 - 0669

MAYER, Vicky
Corporate Communications
Tel: (513) 983 - 1100
Fax: (513) 983 - 9369

The Procter & Gamble Company

* continued from previous page

NESSELHOFF, Gayle
Contact, Procter and Gamble Fund
Tel: (513) 945 - 8454
Fax: (513) 845 - 8979

OTTO, Charlotte R.
Global External Relations Officer
otto.cr@pg.com
Tel: (513) 983 - 1100
Fax: (513) 983 - 8240

SMITH, Karen A.
Associate Director, State and Local Government Relations
smith.ka@pg.com
Tel: (513) 983 - 1100

TIPPL, Thomas
Director, Investor Relations and Shareholder Services
Tel: (513) 983 - 1100
Fax: (513) 983 - 9369

At Washington Office

BREHM, Carolyn
V. President, National Government Relations
Tel: (202) 393 - 3400
Fax: (202) 393 - 4606

DONAHUE, Caitlin
Manager, External Relations
Tel: (202) 393 - 3400
Fax: (202) 393 - 4606
Registered Federal Lobbyist.

GENOVESI, Jacqueline
Legislative Assistant
Tel: (202) 393 - 3400
Fax: (202) 393 - 4606
Registered Federal Lobbyist.

MCCARTHY, James R.
Director, National Government Relations
mccarthy.jr@pg.com
Tel: (202) 393 - 3400
Fax: (202) 393 - 4606
Registered Federal Lobbyist.

MILLER, R. Scott
Director, National Government Relations
miller.rs@pg.com
Tel: (202) 393 - 3404
Fax: (202) 393 - 4606
Registered Federal Lobbyist.

Profit Recovery Group Internat'l, Inc.

See listing on page 392 under PRG-Schultz Internat'l, Inc.

Progress Energy

A member of the Public Affairs Council. Formed from Carolina Power and Light Co.'s acquisition of Florida Progress Corp. in November of 2000. A diversified holding company providing electricity, natural gas, energy services and broadband capacity. Subsidiaries include CP&L and Florida Power.

www.progress-energy.com

Annual Revenues: $8.462 billion

Chairman and Chief Exec. Officer
MCGEHEE, Robert
Tel: (919) 546 - 7371
Fax: (919) 546 - 7536

Main Headquarters

Mailing: P.O. Box 1551
Raleigh, NC 27602-1551
Street: 411 Fayetteville St.
Raleigh, NC 27602
Tel: (919) 546 - 6111
Fax: (919) 546 - 7536

Washington Office

Contact: David G. Roberts

Mailing: 801 Pennsylvania Ave. NW
North Bldg., Suite 250
Washington, DC 20004
Tel: (202) 783 - 5530
Fax: (202) 783 - 5569

Political Action Committees

Progress Energy Employees Federal PAC

Contact: Leslie Allen

P.O. Box 1551
Raleigh, NC 27602-1551
Tel: (919) 546 - 2917
Fax: (919) 546 - 3329

Contributions to Candidates: $94,250 (01/05 - 09/05)

Democrats: $22,000; Republicans: $72,250.

Principal Recipients

SENATE DEMOCRATS

HOUSE DEMOCRATS

Etheridge, Bob (NC)	$3,500
Spratt, John (SC)	$2,500
McIntyre, Mike (NC)	$2,000
Miller, Brad (NC)	$2,000

SENATE REPUBLICANS

Dole, Elizabeth (NC)	$2,000

HOUSE REPUBLICANS

Myrick, Sue (NC)	$5,000
Taylor, Charles H (NC)	$4,750
Norwood, Charles (GA)	$3,500
McHenry, Patrick (NC)	$3,000
Barton, Joe L (TX)	$2,500
Barrett, James (SC)	$2,000
Cantor, Eric (VA)	$2,000
Coble, John (NC)	$2,000
Diaz-Balart, Lincoln (FL)	$2,000
Foxx, Virginia (NC)	$2,000
Hastert, Dennis J. (IL)	$2,000
Murphy, Tim (PA)	$2,000
Stearns, Clifford (FL)	$2,000
Wilson, Joe (SC)	$2,000

Corporate Foundations and Giving Programs

CP&L, A Progress Energy Co., Corporate Giving Program
P.O. Box 1551
Raleigh, NC 27602-1551
Tel: (919) 546 - 6111
Fax: (919) 546 - 7536

Annual Grant Total: $1,000,000 - $2,000,000

Progress Energy Foundation (formerly the CP&L Foundation)
P.O. Box 1551
Raleigh, NC 27602-1551
Tel: (919) 546 - 6111
Fax: (919) 546 - 7536

Annual Grant Total: over $5,000,000

Grants are only made to 501(c)(3) organizations operating within the geographic preferences. Please note that the Progress Energy Foundation is funded on a yearly basis by the Progress Energy Board of Directors. All funds are expended by December 31 each year. This is not an endowed foundation.

Geographic Preference: Area(s) in which the company operates; Florida; North Carolina; South Carolina

Primary Interests: Economic Development; Education; Environment/Conservation

Florida Power, A Progress Energy Co., Corporate Giving Program
P.O. Box 1551
Raleigh, NC 27602-1551
Tel: (919) 546 - 6111
Fax: (919) 546 - 7536

Annual Grant Total: $2,000,000 - $5,000,000

Public Affairs and Related Activities Personnel

At Headquarters

ALLEN, Leslie
PAC Manager
Tel: (919) 546 - 2917
Fax: (919) 546 - 3329

JOHNSON, William D.
Group President
Mailstop: Peb 1212
Responsibilities include public affairs.
Tel: (919) 546 - 6463
Fax: (919) 546 - 5245

RIDEOUT, Dana
Secretary-Treasurer, Federal and State PACs
Tel: (919) 546 - 7984

TEMPLE, Nancy H.
V. President, Corporate Communications
Tel: (919) 546 - 4550
Fax: (919) 546 - 6615

UPCHURCH, Gene
V. President, State Public Affairs
Tel: (919) 546 - 3302
Fax: (919) 546 - 7536

At Washington Office

ROBERTS, David G.
Director, Public Affairs-Federal
Tel: (202) 783 - 5530
Fax: (202) 783 - 5569
Registered Federal Lobbyist.

At Other Offices

DOLAN, Vincent M.
V. President, Regulatory and Public Affairs - Florida
100 Central Ave.
St. Petersburg, FL 33701
Tel: (727) 820 - 5001

JOYNER, Michael
Manager, State Public Affairs -Florida
106 E. College Ave., Suite 800
Tallahassee, FL 32301

MCARTHUR, John R.
Senior V. President, Corporate Relations
(Progress Energy Service Co., LLC)
410 S. Wilmington St.
Mailstop: PEB 13
Raleigh, NC 27601-1551
Tel: (919) 546 - 4070
Fax: (919) 546 - 5474

MCCAIN, Jeanelle Medlin
Manager, Public Affairs - SC
1201 Main St.
Suite 1850
Columbia, SC 29201
Tel: (803) 252 - 6830
Fax: (803) 252 - 6269

Progress Energy Service Co., LLC

See listing on page 395 under Progress Energy.

The Progressive Corporation

A property and casualty insurance company.
www.progressive.com
Annual Revenues: $13 billion

Chairman of the Board
LEWIS, Peter B.
Tel: (440) 461 - 5000
Fax: (440) 446 - 7168
TF: (800) 876 - 6327

President and Chief Exec. Officer
RENWICK, Glenn M.
Tel: (440) 461 - 5000
Fax: (440) 446 - 7168
TF: (800) 876 - 6327

Main Headquarters
Mailing: 6300 Wilson Mills Rd.
Mayfield Village, OH 44143
Tel: (440) 461 - 5000
Fax: (440) 446 - 7168
TF: (800) 776 - 4737

Public Affairs and Related Activities Personnel

At Headquarters

GRIFFITH, Susan Patricia
Chief Human Resources Officer
Tel: (440) 461 - 5000
Fax: (440) 446 - 7168
TF: (800) 776 - 4737

KING, Thomas A.
V. President and Treasurer
Tel: (440) 461 - 5000
Fax: (440) 446 - 7168
TF: (800) 776 - 4737
Responsibilities include investor relations.

At Other Offices

KOLLEDA, Leslie
Manager, Public Relations
1481 S. Nova Rd.
Daytona Beach, FL 32114
Tel: (386) 947 - 5158
Fax: (386) 258 - 7939

Protective Life Corp.

An insurance holding company.
www.protective.com

Chairman, President, and Chief Exec. Officer
JOHNS, John D.
Tel: (205) 268 - 1000

Main Headquarters
Mailing: 2801 Hwy. 280 South
P.O. Box 2606
Birmingham, AL 35223
Tel: (205) 268 - 1000

Political Action Committees

Protective Life Corp. Federal PAC
2801 Hwy. 280 South
P.O. Box 2606
Birmingham, AL 35223
Tel: (205) 268 - 1000

Contributions to Candidates: $5,500 (01/05 - 09/05)
Democrats: $5,000; Republicans: $500.

Principal Recipients

SENATE DEMOCRATS
Carper, Thomas R (DE) $1,000
Nelson, Benjamin (NE) $1,000

HOUSE DEMOCRATS
Davis, Artur (AL) $2,000
Pomeroy, Earl (ND) $1,000

Corporate Foundations and Giving Programs

The Protective Life Foundation
2801 Hwy. 280 South
P.O. Box 2606
Birmingham, AL 35223
Tel: (205) 268 - 1000

Annual Grant Total: $200,000 - $300,000
Geographic Preference: Alabama
Primary Interests: Arts and Culture; Education; Youth Services
Recent Recipients: United Way

Public Affairs and Related Activities Personnel

At Headquarters

COOK, Sheri
V. President, Corporate Finance and Investor Relations
Tel: (205) 268 - 3773

HAMER, J. William, Jr.
Senior V. President and Chief Human Resources Officer
Tel: (205) 268 - 1000

LONG, Deborah J.
Senior V. President, Secretary and General Counsel
Tel: (205) 268 - 1000
Responsibilities include government relations.

The Providence Journal Co.

A newspaper publishing company.
www.projo.com

Chairman, Publisher and Chief Exec. Officer
SUTTON, Howard G.
Tel: (401) 277 - 7000
Fax: (401) 277 - 7461

Main Headquarters
Mailing: 75 Fountain St.
Providence, RI 02902-0050
Tel: (401) 277 - 7000
Fax: (401) 277 - 7461

Corporate Foundations and Giving Programs

Providence Journal Charitable Foundation
Contact: Howard G. Sutton
75 Fountain St.
Providence, RI 02902-0050
Tel: (401) 277 - 7000
Fax: (401) 277 - 7461

Annual Grant Total: $750,000 - $1,000,000
Geographic Preference: Area in which the company is headquartered
Primary Interests: Arts and Humanities; Children; Education; Environment/Conservation; Youth Services
Recent Recipients: Nat'l Audubon Soc.; United Way

Public Affairs and Related Activities Personnel

At Headquarters

MCDONOUGH, Thomas
Director, Human Resources
Tel: (401) 277 - 7000
Fax: (401) 277 - 7461

Provident Mutual Life Insurance Co.

See listing on page 341 under Nationwide.

Providian Financial Corp.

Offers banking and financial services.
www.providian.com
Annual Revenues: $5.53 billion

Chairman, President and Chief Exec. Officer
SAUNDERS, Joseph
Tel: (415) 543 - 0404
Fax: (415) 278 - 6028

Main Headquarters
Mailing: 201 Mission St.
San Francisco, CA 94105
Tel: (415) 543 - 0404
Fax: (415) 278 - 6028

Washington Office
Contact: Daniel J. McDermott
Mailing: 1050 Connecticut Ave. NW, Suite 1000
Washington, DC 20036
Tel: (202) 772 - 1101
Fax: (202) 772 - 3367

Political Action Committees

Providian Financial Corporation PAC
Contact: Daniel Sanford
201 Mission St.
San Francisco, CA 94105
Tel: (415) 543 - 0404
Fax: (415) 278 - 6028

Contributions to Candidates: $29,000 (01/05 - 09/05)
Democrats: $14,000; Republicans: $15,000.

Principal Recipients

SENATE DEMOCRATS
Ford, Harold E Jr (TN) $3,500

HOUSE DEMOCRATS

SENATE REPUBLICANS

HOUSE REPUBLICANS
Ney, Robert W (OH) $4,000
Dreier, David (CA) $3,000
Oxley, Michael (OH) $2,000

Corporate Foundations and Giving Programs

Providian Financial Corp. Corporate Giving Program
201 Mission St.
San Francisco, CA 94105
Tel: (415) 543 - 0404
Fax: (415) 278 - 6028

Annual Grant Total: over $5,000,000
Primary Interests: Children; Community Affairs; Economic Development; Education; Health and Human Services; Housing
Recent Recipients: Big Brothers/Big Sisters; Boys and Girls Club; Girls Incorporated; Habitat for Humanity; Junior Achievement; YMCA; YWCA

Public Affairs and Related Activities Personnel

At Headquarters

CARSKY, Jack
Senior V. President, Investor Relations
Tel: (415) 278 - 4977
Fax: (415) 278 - 6028

ELIAS, Alan
V. President, Corporate Communications
alan_elias@providian.com
Tel: (415) 543 - 0404
Fax: (415) 278 - 6028

HORNING, Bill
Investor Relations Contact
Tel: (415) 278 - 4602
Fax: (415) 278 - 6028

LEWEKE, Richard A.
V. Chairman and Chief Human Resources Officer
Tel: (415) 543 - 0404
Fax: (415) 278 - 6028

LEWIS, Chris
V. President, Corporate Affairs
chris_lewis@providian.com
Tel: (415) 543 - 0404
Fax: (415) 278 - 6028

Prudential Financial

** continued from previous page*

SANFORD, Daniel
Senior V. President; PAC Treasurer
Tel: (415) 543 - 0404
Fax: (415) 278 - 6028

At Washington Office

MCDERMOTT, Daniel J.
Senior V. President, Government Relations
Dan_McDermott@providian.com
Registered Federal Lobbyist.
Tel: (202) 772 - 1101
Fax: (202) 772 - 3367

Prudential Financial

A member of the Public Affairs Council. Prudential Financial companies serve individual and institutional customers worldwide and include The Prudential Insurance Company of America, one of the largest life insurance companies in the United States. Offers a variety of products and services, including life insurance, mutual funds, annuities pension and retirement-related services and administration, asset management, securities brokerage, banking and trust services, real estate brokerage franchises and relocation services.

www.prudential.com
Annual Revenues: $19.985 billion

Chairman, President and Chief Exec. Officer
RYAN, Arthur F.
Mailstop: Floor 24
Tel: (973) 802 - 6000
Fax: (973) 802 - 3128
TF: (800) THE - ROCK

Main Headquarters
Mailing: 751 Broad St.
Newark, NJ 07102-3777
Tel: (973) 802 - 6000
Fax: (973) 802 - 6825
TF: (800) THE - ROCK

Washington Office
Mailing: 1140 Connecticut Ave. NW
Suite 510
Washington, DC 20036
Tel: (202) 327 - 5240
Fax: (202) 327 - 5249

Political Action Committees

Prudential Financial Inc. PAC
Contact: Peter B. Sayre
751 Broad St.
Newark, NJ 07102-3777
Tel: (973) 802 - 6000
Fax: (973) 802 - 6303
TF: (800) THE - ROCK

Contributions to Candidates: $88,050 (01/05 - 09/05)
Democrats: $41,550; Republicans: $46,500.

Principal Recipients

SENATE DEMOCRATS		HOUSE DEMOCRATS	
Carper, Thomas R (DE)	$9,000	Cardin, Ben (MD)	$4,000
Clinton, Hillary Rodham (NY)	$5,000	Pomeroy, Earl (ND)	$2,000
		Rangel, Charles B (NY)	$2,000
Conrad, Kent (ND)	$3,000		
Bingaman, Jeff (NM)	$2,500		
Nelson, Benjamin (NE)	$2,000		
Stabenow, Debbie (MI)	$2,000		

SENATE REPUBLICANS		HOUSE REPUBLICANS	
Ensign, John Eric (NV)	$5,000	Oxley, Michael (OH)	$5,000
Santorum, Richard (PA)	$5,000	Johnson, Samuel (TX)	$4,000
Kyl, Jon L (AZ)	$3,000	Johnson, Nancy (CT)	$2,500
McConnell, Mitch (KY)	$2,500	Thomas, William M (CA)	$2,500
Smith, Gordon (OR)	$2,000	Pryce, Deborah (OH)	$2,000

Corporate Foundations and Giving Programs

The Prudential Foundation
751 Broad St.
Newark, NJ 07102-3777
Tel: (973) 802 - 6000
Fax: (973) 802 - 6825
TF: (800) THE - ROCK

Assets: $101,178,198 (2001)
Annual Grant Total: over $5,000,000
Provides direct corporate donations to organizations and programs in areas of major company operations which are pursuing innovative and catalytic approaches to major social problems. The Company encourages employee volunteerism through its Office of Volunteerism and recognizes employees with its Community Champions Program.
Geographic Preference: Area in which the company is headquartered; Area(s) in which the company operates; Los Angeles, CA; Minneapolis, MN; Philadelphia, PA; Jacksonville, FL; Newark, NJ
Primary Interests: AIDS/HIV; Children; Education; Employment; Housing; Vocational Training

Public Affairs and Related Activities Personnel

At Headquarters

CLYMER, Brian W.
V. President, Government Affairs
Mailstop: 14th Floor
brian.clymer@prudential.com
Tel: (973) 367 - 2510
Fax: (973) 367 - 7030
TF: (800) THE - ROCK

DEFILLIPPO, Bob
Chief Communications Officer
Mailstop: 12th Floor
Bob.DeFillippo@prudential.com
Tel: (973) 802 - 4149
Fax: (973) 802 - 9443
TF: (800) THE - ROCK

PAYNE, Christopher
Project Manager, Government Affairs
Tel: (973) 802 - 6000
Fax: (973) 802 - 3128
TF: (800) THE - ROCK

PICKEL, Bryan
Lobbyist
Tel: (973) 802 - 6000
Fax: (973) 802 - 3128
TF: (800) THE - ROCK

SAYRE, Peter B.
Treasurer, Prudential Financial Inc. PAC
Mailstop: Third Floor
peter.sayre@prudential.com
Tel: (973) 802 - 6000
Fax: (973) 802 - 6303
TF: (800) THE - ROCK

At Washington Office

BRUBAKER, Alan
V. President, Government Affairs
alan.brubaker@prudential.com
Registered Federal Lobbyist.
Tel: (202) 327 - 5240
Fax: (202) 327 - 5249

JACOBS, Lynn
V. President, Government Affairs
Registered Federal Lobbyist.
Tel: (202) 327 - 5240
Fax: (202) 327 - 5249

WACKERLE, Rex
V. President, Government Relations
rex.wackerle@prudential.com
Registered Federal Lobbyist.
Tel: (202) 327 - 5240
Fax: (202) 327 - 5249

At Other Offices

CHANDLER, Christopher L.
V. President, Government Affairs
1301 Pennsylvania St.
Suite 900
Denver, CO 80203
chris.chandler@prudential.com
Tel: (303) 861 - 8788
Fax: (303) 832 - 5697

HERRMANN, Arthur F.
V. President, Government Affairs
50 W. State St., Suite 1116
Trenton, NJ 08608
art.herrman@prudential.com
Tel: (609) 989 - 7070
Fax: (609) 989 - 7045

JENNINGS, Michael A.
V. President, Government Affairs
701 San Marco Blvd.
12th Floor
Jacksonville, FL 32207
mike.jennings@prudential.com
Tel: (904) 313 - 3269
Fax: (904) 313 - 7884

Prudential Insurance Co. of America

See listing on page 397 under Prudential Financial.

PSE&G

A member of the Public Affairs Council. An electric and gas utility subsidiary of the Public Service Enterprise Group. The company announced plans to merge with Exelon Corp. (see separate listing). Completion of the merger is expected in the first or second quarter of 2006.

www.pseg.com
Annual Revenues: $6.1 billion

Chairman, President and Chief Exec. Officer
FERLAND, E. James
Mailstop: M/S T4B
e.james.ferland@pseg.com
Tel: (973) 430 - 7000

Main Headquarters
Mailing: 80 Park Plaza
Newark, NJ 07102-0570
Tel: (973) 430 - 7000

Washington Office
Contact: Patricia L. Thompson
Mailing: One Massachusetts Ave. NW
Suite 360
Washington, DC 20001
Tel: (202) 408 - 0183
Fax: (202) 408 - 0214

Corporate Foundations and Giving Programs

Public Service Electric and Gas Co. Contributions Program
Contact: William J. Walsh, Jr.
80 Park Plaza
Newark, NJ 07102-0570
Tel: (973) 430 - 5763
Fax: (973) 297 - 1480

Annual Grant Total: $2,000,000 - $5,000,000
Geographic Preference: Area(s) in which the company operates
Primary Interests: Community Affairs; Environment/Conservation; Higher Education; Minority Opportunities; Social Services; Urban Affairs

Public Affairs and Related Activities Personnel

At Headquarters

BROWN, Neil
Manager, Governmental Affairs PSEG
Mailstop: M/S T24D
neil.brown@pseg.com
Tel: (973) 430 - 6017
Fax: (973) 623 - 8711

PSE&G

• continued from previous page

DESANTI, Frederick D.
V. President, State Government Affairs PSE&G
Mailstop: M/S T4A
frederick.desanti@pseg.com
Tel: (973) 430 - 6400
Fax: (973) 242 - 0741

DOW, Jo Ann
Manager, Community Affairs
Mailstop: M/S T10C
joann.dow@pseg.com
Tel: (973) 430 - 5861
Fax: (973) 297 - 1480

GUIDA, Arthur S.
Director, Regional Public Affairs PSE&G
Mailstop: M/S T10C
arthur.guida@pseg.com
Tel: (973) 430 - 7135
Fax: (973) 622 - 4261

LA BRUNA, Stanley
V. President, Environment, Health and Safety
Mailstop: M/S T17A
stanley.labruna@pseg.com
Tel: (973) 430 - 7380
Fax: (973) 623 - 7758

O'NEILL, Marion C.
Manager, Corporate Contributions
Mailstop: M/S T10C
marion.oneill@pseg.com
Tel: (973) 430 - 7842
Fax: (973) 297 - 1480

PEGO, Margaret
V. President, Human Resources
Mailstop: M/S T21A
margaret.pego@pseg.com
Tel: (973) 430 - 7243
Fax: (973) 642 - 1689

SMITH, J. Brian
Director, Investor Relations
Mailstop: M/S T6B
Tel: (973) 430 - 6564
Fax: (973) 624 - 7491

TUOSTO, Michael R.
General Manager, Public Affairs; Contact, Public Service Electric and Gas Co. PAC
Mailstop: M/S T-10
michael.tuosto@pseg.com
Tel: (973) 430 - 6414
Fax: (973) 623 - 8711

WALSH, William J., Jr.
Director, Corporate Responsibility
Mailstop: M/S T10C
william.walsh3@pseg.com
Tel: (973) 430 - 5763
Fax: (973) 297 - 1480

At Washington Office

LUDECKE, Kristin
Manager, Government and Public Affairs
Tel: (202) 408 - 0183
Fax: (202) 408 - 0214

THOMPSON, Patricia L.
General Manager, Federal Affairs
patricia.thompson@pseg.com
Registered Federal Lobbyist.
Tel: (202) 408 - 0183
Fax: (202) 408 - 0214

At Other Offices

DIRIENZO, Josie
Manager, State Governmental Affairs
170 W. State St.
Trenton, NJ 08608
Tel: (609) 656 - 2750
Fax: (609) 393 - 1681

PSI Energy, Inc.

See listing on page 119 under Cinergy Corp.

PSS World Medical, Inc.

A wholesale distributor of medical supplies, products, pharmaceuticals and equipment to office-based physicians and elder care providers.

www.pssd.com
Annual Revenues: $1.4 billion

Chairman of the Board
JOHNSON, Clark
Tel: (904) 332 - 3000

Chief Exec. Officer
SMITH, David A.
Tel: (904) 332 - 3000

Main Headquarters
Mailing: 4345 Southpoint Blvd.
Jacksonville, FL 32216
Tel: (904) 332 - 3000

Public Affairs and Related Activities Personnel

At Headquarters

ANTHONY, Jeff
Senior V. President, Corporate Development
Tel: (904) 332 - 3000

JENNINGS, Mary
V. President, Compliance and Tax
Tel: (904) 332 - 3000

WEINER, Robert
V. President, Investor Relations
Tel: (904) 332 - 3000

PTC

Makers of software for product development.

www.ptc.com
Annual Revenues: $940 million

Chairman of the Board
POSTERNEK, Noel G.
Tel: (781) 370 - 5000
Fax: (781) 370 - 6000
TF: (800) 782 - 3776

President and Chief Exec. Officer
HARRISON, C. Richard
Tel: (781) 370 - 5000
Fax: (781) 370 - 6000
TF: (800) 782 - 3776

Main Headquarters
Mailing: 140 Kendrick St.
Needham, MA 02494
Tel: (781) 370 - 5000
Fax: (781) 370 - 6000
TF: (800) 782 - 3776

Corporate Foundations and Giving Programs

PTC Partnership for Innovative Learning
Contact: John Stuart
140 Kendrick St.
Needham, MA 02494
Tel: (781) 370 - 5979
Fax: (781) 370 - 5536
TF: (800) 782 - 3776

Annual Grant Total: none reported
Primary Interests: Engineering; Higher Education
Recent Recipients: Georgia Tech.; Harvard Business School

Public Affairs and Related Activities Personnel

At Headquarters

COHEN, Barry
Exec. V. President, Marketing and Human Resources
Tel: (781) 370 - 5000
Fax: (781) 370 - 6000
TF: (800) 782 - 3776

MENDOLA, Meredith
V. President, Corporate Communications
mmendola@ptc.com
Responsibilities include investor relations.
Tel: (781) 370 - 6151
Fax: (781) 370 - 5225
TF: (800) 782 - 3776

STUART, John
Contact, PTC Partnership for Innovative Learning
Tel: (781) 370 - 5979
Fax: (781) 370 - 5536
TF: (800) 782 - 3776

PTEK Holdings, Inc.

See listing on page 392 under Premiere Global Services, Inc.

Public Service Co. of New Mexico

An electric and gas utility.

www.pnm.com

Chairman, President and Chief Exec. Officer
STERBA, Jeff
Tel: (505) 241 - 2700
Fax: (505) 241 - 2355
TF: (800) 545 - 4425

Main Headquarters
Mailing: Alvarado Square
Albuquerque, NM 87158
Tel: (505) 241 - 2700
Fax: (505) 241 - 2355
TF: (800) 545 - 4425

Political Action Committees

Responsible Citizens Federal Group
Alvarado Square
Albuquerque, NM 87158
Tel: (505) 241 - 2700
Fax: (505) 241 - 2355
TF: (800) 545 - 4425

Contributions to Candidates: $11,500 (01/05 - 09/05)
Republicans: $11,500.

Principal Recipients

SENATE REPUBLICANS		HOUSE REPUBLICANS	
Domenici, Pete (NM)	$5,000	Barton, Joe L (TX)	$2,500
Santorum, Richard (PA)	$1,000	Wilson, Heather (NM)	$2,000
		Shadegg, John (AZ)	$1,000

Corporate Foundations and Giving Programs

PNM Foundation, Inc.
Alvarado Square
Albuquerque, NM 87158
Tel: (505) 241 - 2700
Fax: (505) 241 - 2355
TF: (800) 545 - 4425

Annual Grant Total: $200,000 - $300,000
The foundation also sponsors an employee matching gift program.
Geographic Preference: Area(s) in which the company operates; New Mexico
Primary Interests: Children; Education; Health and Human Services; Minority Opportunities; Senior Citizens

Public Affairs and Related Activities Personnel

At Headquarters

C' DEBACA, Ernest T.
V. President Government Affairs
Mailstop: MS 1110
ecdeba@pnm.com
Tel: (505) 241 - 2806
Fax: (505) 241 - 4386
TF: (800) 545 - 4425

REAL, Bill
Senior V. President, Public Policy
Tel: (505) 241 - 2700
Fax: (505) 241 - 2355
TF: (800) 545 - 4425

Public Service Co. of New Mexico

** continued from previous page*

REISTER, Lisa
Exec. Director, Investor Relations
Tel: (505) 241 - 2787
Fax: (505) 241 - 2355
TF: (800) 545 - 4425

REUTER, Joanne
V. President, Regulatory Affairs
Tel: (505) 241 - 2700
Fax: (505) 241 - 2355
TF: (800) 545 - 4425

Public Service Co. of North Carolina

See listing on page 426 under SCANA Corp.

Public Service Electric & Gas Co.

See listing on page 397 under PSE&G.

Publix Super Markets, Inc.

A member of the Public Affairs Council. A grocery store chain.
www.publix.com
Annual Revenues: $18.6 billion

Chairman of the Board
JENKINS, Howard M.
howard.jenkins@publix.com
Tel: (863) 688 - 7407
Fax: (863) 284 - 5532

Chief Exec. Officer
JENKINS, Charlie, Jr.
charlie.jenkins@publix.com
Tel: (863) 688 - 7407
Ext: 52227
Fax: (863) 284 - 5532

Main Headquarters
Mailing: P.O. Box 407
Lakeland, FL 33802-0407
Street: 3300 Airport Rd.
Lakeland, FL 33815
Tel: (863) 688 - 1188
Fax: (863) 284 - 5532

Political Action Committees

Publix Super Markets, Inc. Associates PAC
Contact: S. Randy Roberts
P.O. Box 407
Lakeland, FL 33802-0407
Tel: (863) 688 - 7407
Ext: 58978
Fax: (863) 284 - 5532

Contributions to Candidates: $2,000 (01/05 - 09/05)
Democrats: $1,000; Republicans: $1,000.

Principal Recipients

SENATE DEMOCRATS
Ford, Harold E Jr (TN) $1,000

HOUSE DEMOCRATS

SENATE REPUBLICANS
Chambliss, Saxby (GA) $1,000

HOUSE REPUBLICANS

Corporate Foundations and Giving Programs

Publix Super Markets Charities
Contact: Carol J. Barnett
P.O. Box 407
Lakeland, FL 33802-0407
Tel: (863) 688 - 1188
Fax: (863) 284 - 5532

Annual Grant Total: none reported
Recent Recipients: Children's Miracle Network; March of Dimes; Special Olympics; United Way

Public Affairs and Related Activities Personnel

At Headquarters

BARNETT, Carol J.
Chair, Publix Super Markets Charities
Tel: (863) 688 - 1188
Fax: (863) 284 - 5532

BROUS, Maria
Director, Media and Community Relations
maria.brous@publix.com
Tel: (863) 688 - 7407
Ext: 55339
Fax: (863) 284 - 5532

HOLLIS, M. Clayton, Jr.
V. President, Public Affairs
clayton.hollis@publix.com
Tel: (863) 284 - 5586
Fax: (863) 284 - 5532

HRABUSA, John
Senior V. President
Tel: (863) 688 - 1188
Ext: 53281
Fax: (863) 616 - 5693
Responsibilities include human resources and public affairs.

MILLER, Sharon
Executive Director, Publix Super Markets Charities, Inc.
Tel: (863) 688 - 1188
Fax: (863) 616 - 5755

ROBERTS, S. Randy
Director, Government Relations
Tel: (863) 688 - 7407
Ext: 58978
Fax: (863) 284 - 5532

At Other Offices

HENDRICKS, Anne
Manager, Media and Community Relations
P.O. Box 699030
Miami, FL 33269-9030
anne.hendricks@publix.com
Tel: (305) 652 - 2411
Ext: 3816
Fax: (305) 770 - 3309

REID, Brenda
Manager, Community Affairs
2600 Delk Rd.
Marietta, GA 30067-6202
brenda.reid@publix.com
Tel: (770) 952 - 6601
Ext: 3649
Fax: (770) 618 - 2581

STEVENS, Dwaine
Manager, Media and Community Relations
P.O. Box 2226-F
Jacksonville, FL 32231-0084
dwaine.stevens@publix.com
Tel: (904) 693 - 6107
Fax: (904) 693 - 6111

Puget Sound Energy

A member of the Public Affairs Council. Puget Sound Power and Light Co. merged with Washington Energy Co. in 1997 and became Puget Sound Energy.
www.pse.com

Chairman of the Board
BEIGHLE, Douglas P.
Tel: (425) 452 - 1234
Fax: (425) 462 - 3301

Main Headquarters
Mailing: P.O. Box 97034
Bellevue, WA 98009-9734
Street: 10885 N.E. Fourth St.
Bellevue, WA 98004-5591
Tel: (425) 452 - 1234
Fax: (425) 462 - 3301

Political Action Committees

Puget Sound Energy, Inc. Good Government Committee-Federal
Contact: Dale Easley
P.O. Box 97034
Bellevue, WA 98009-9734
Tel: (425) 452 - 1234
Fax: (425) 462 - 3301

Contributions to Candidates: $12,841 (01/05 - 09/05)
Democrats: $8,041; Republicans: $4,800.

Principal Recipients

SENATE DEMOCRATS

HOUSE DEMOCRATS
Larsen, Rick (WA) $6,041
Dicks, Norm D (WA) $1,000
Smith, Adam (WA) $1,000

SENATE REPUBLICANS
Burns, Conrad (MT) $1,000

HOUSE REPUBLICANS
Reichert, Dave (WA) $1,300
Hastings, Doc (WA) $1,000
Young, Don E (AK) $1,000

Corporate Foundations and Giving Programs

Puget Sound Energy Contributions Program
P.O. Box 97034
Bellevue, WA 98009-9734
Tel: (425) 452 - 1234
Fax: (425) 462 - 3301

Annual Grant Total: $500,000 - $750,000
Guidelines are available.
Geographic Preference: Area(s) in which the company operates; Washington State
Primary Interests: Arts and Culture; Civic and Public Affairs; Education; Health and Human Services

Public Affairs and Related Activities Personnel

At Headquarters

BADER, Tim
Media Contact
Tel: (425) 452 - 1234
Fax: (425) 462 - 3301

BUSSEY, Phil
V. President, Regional and Public Affairs
Tel: (425) 452 - 1234
Fax: (425) 462 - 3301

CLEMENTS, Michelle
V. President, Human Resources and Labor Relations
Tel: (425) 452 - 1234
Fax: (425) 462 - 3301

EASLEY, Dale
PAC Treasurer
Tel: (425) 452 - 1234
Fax: (425) 462 - 3301

HARRIS, Kimberly
V. President, Governmental and Regulatory Affairs
Tel: (425) 452 - 1234
Fax: (425) 462 - 3301

ODELL, Nina
Director, Government and Community Affairs
Tel: (425) 462 - 3330
Fax: (425) 462 - 3301

RINGEL, Grant
Director, Corporate Communications
Tel: (425) 462 - 3181
Fax: (425) 462 - 3301

WAITE, Durga
Director, Investor Relations
Mailstop: PSE12
durga.waite@pse.com
Tel: (425) 462 - 3808
Fax: (425) 462 - 3300

At Other Offices

OXLEY, Terry
Director, Community Services
3130 S. 38th St.
Tacoma, WA 98409
Tel: (253) 476 - 6334
Fax: (253) 476 - 6415

TRACY, W. Michael
Director, State Government Relations
1501 S. Capitol Way, Suite 204
Olympia, WA 98501
Tel: (360) 943 - 9115
Fax: (360) 786 - 5925

Pulitzer Inc.

See listing on page 289 under Lee Enterprises.

Pulte Homes, Inc.

Formerly Pulte Corp. A homebuilder and related financial services company. Acquired Del E. Webb Corp. in 2001.

www.pulte.com

Chairman of the Board
PULTE, William
Tel: (248) 647 - 2750
Fax: (248) 433 - 4598
TF: (800) 777 - 8583

President and Chief Exec. Officer
DUGAS, Richard
Tel: (248) 647 - 2750
Fax: (248) 433 - 4598
TF: (800) 777 - 8583

Main Headquarters
Mailing: 100 Bloomfield Hills Pkwy., Suite 300
Bloomfield Hills, MI 48304-2946
Tel: (248) 647 - 2750
Fax: (248) 433 - 4598
TF: (800) 777 - 8583

Public Affairs and Related Activities Personnel

At Headquarters

MARYMEE, Mark
Public Relations Contact
Tel: (248) 433 - 4648
Fax: (248) 433 - 4598
TF: (800) 777 - 8583

ZEUMER, James P.
V. President, Investor and Corporate Communications
Tel: (248) 647 - 2750
Fax: (248) 433 - 4598
TF: (800) 777 - 8583

Quad/Graphics, Inc.

A printing company

www.qg.com

Chief Exec. Officer
QUADRACCI, Thomas
Tel: (414) 566 - 6000
TF: (888) 782 - 3226

Main Headquarters
Mailing: N63 W23075 State Hwy. 74
Sussex, WI 53089-2827
Tel: (414) 566 - 6000
TF: (888) 782 - 3226

Public Affairs and Related Activities Personnel

At Headquarters

ESTOCK, Tom
Coordinator, Environment
Tel: (414) 566 - 6000
TF: (888) 782 - 3226

HO, Claire
Manager, Communications
Tel: (414) 466 - 2955
TF: (888) 782 - 3226

Qualcomm Inc.

Develops, manufactures, distributes and operates communications systems.

www.qualcomm.com

Chairman of the Board
JACOBS, Irwin
Tel: (858) 587 - 1121
Fax: (858) 658 - 2100

Chief Exec. Officer
JACOBS, Paul
Tel: (858) 587 - 1121
Fax: (858) 658 - 2100

Main Headquarters
Mailing: 5775 Morehouse Dr.
San Diego, CA 92121-2779
Tel: (858) 587 - 1121
Fax: (858) 658 - 2100

Washington Office
Contact: Jonas Neihardt
Mailing: 2001 Pennsylvania Ave. NW
Suite 650
Washington, DC 20006
Tel: (202) 263 - 0000
Fax: (202) 263 - 0010

Political Action Committees

Qualcomm PAC
Contact: Karen Laake
2001 Pennsylvania Ave. NW
Suite 650
Washington, DC 20006
Tel: (202) 263 - 0000
Fax: (202) 263 - 0010

Contributions to Candidates: $40,500 (01/05 - 09/05)
Democrats: $5,000; Republicans: $35,500.

Principal Recipients

SENATE REPUBLICANS		HOUSE REPUBLICANS	
Ensign, John Eric (NV)	$3,000	Blunt, Roy (MO)	$5,000
Allen, George (VA)	$2,500	Goodlatte, Robert (VA)	$5,000
		Upton, Fred (MI)	$3,500
		Lewis, Jerry (CA)	$3,000
		Oxley, Michael (OH)	$3,000
		Rogers, Harold (KY)	$2,000
		Shimkus, John (IL)	$2,000

Corporate Foundations and Giving Programs

Qualcomm Corporate Giving
Contact: Allison Kelly
5775 Morehouse Dr.
San Diego, CA 92121-2779
Tel: (858) 587 - 1121
Fax: (858) 651 - 3255

Annual Grant Total: none reported
Qualcomm provides cash donations of one to two percent of pre-tax profits each year to the communities in the geographic preferences. In addition to cash donations, Qualcomm contributes to the community through donations of computers and electronic equipment, information technology consulting and services, and the time and talents of a diverse employee base.
Geographic Preference: Area in which the company is headquartered; Area(s) in which employees live and work
Primary Interests: Arts and Culture; Health and Human Services; Math and Science

Public Affairs and Related Activities Personnel

At Headquarters

ALESSIO, Keri
Corporate Public Relations
Tel: (858) 587 - 1121
Fax: (858) 658 - 2100

BOLD, William
V. President, Government Affairs
wbold@qualcomm.com
Tel: (858) 651 - 2086
Fax: (858) 651 - 2590

KELLY, Allison
Corporate Giving Contact
Tel: (858) 587 - 1121
Fax: (858) 651 - 3255

RODRIGUEZ, Monique
Government Relations
Tel: (858) 587 - 1121
Fax: (858) 658 - 2100

TRIMBLE, Christine
Senior Director, Corporate Public Relations and Communications
Tel: (858) 587 - 1121
Fax: (858) 658 - 2100

At Washington Office

LAAKE, Karen
PAC Contact
Tel: (202) 263 - 0000
Fax: (202) 263 - 0010

MURPHY, Sean
Director, International Trade and Technology Policy
Registered Federal Lobbyist.
Tel: (202) 263 - 0000
Fax: (202) 263 - 0010

NEIHARDT, Jonas
V. President, Government Relations
jonasn@qualcomm.com
Registered Federal Lobbyist.
Tel: (202) 263 - 0000
Fax: (202) 263 - 0010

TORNQUIST, Alice
Director, Government Affairs
Registered Federal Lobbyist.
Tel: (202) 263 - 0000
Fax: (202) 263 - 0010

Quanex Corp.

A producer of specialized metal products.

www.quanex.com

Chairman, President and Chief Exec. Officer
JEAN, Raymond A.
rjean@quanex.com
Tel: (713) 961 - 4600
Fax: (713) 439 - 1016
TF: (800) 231 - 8176

Main Headquarters
Mailing: 1900 W. Loop South
Suite 1500
Houston, TX 77027
Tel: (713) 961 - 4600
Fax: (713) 439 - 1016
TF: (800) 231 - 8176

Corporate Foundations and Giving Programs

Quanex Foundation
Contact: Sandy Hatcher
1900 W. Loop South
Suite 1500
Houston, TX 77027
Tel: (713) 961 - 4600
Fax: (713) 877 - 5333
TF: (800) 231 - 8176

Annual Grant Total: $200,000 - $300,000
Primary Interests: Civic and Public Affairs; Education; Social Services
Recent Recipients: Nat'l Merit Scholarship; United Way

Public Affairs and Related Activities Personnel

At Headquarters

CALVERT, Valerie
Manager, Investor Relations
vcalvert@quanex.com
Tel: (713) 877 - 5305
Fax: (713) 877 - 5333
TF: (800) 231 - 8176

GALOW, Geoffrey G.
V. President, Investor Relations
Tel: (713) 877 - 5327
Fax: (713) 877 - 5333
TF: (800) 231 - 8176

HATCHER, Sandy
Manager, Human Resources Services
shatcher@quanex.com
Responsibilities include corporate philanthropy.
Tel: (713) 961 - 4600
Fax: (713) 877 - 5333
TF: (800) 231 - 8176

Quantum Corporation

A diversified mass storage company.

www.quantum.com

Chairman and Chief Exec. Officer
BELLUZZO, Richard
Tel: (408) 894 - 4000
Fax: (408) 894 - 3218

Main Headquarters
Mailing: 501 Sycamore Dr.
Milpitas, CA 95035
Tel: (408) 894 - 4000
Fax: (408) 894 - 3218

Quantum Corporation

** continued from previous page*

Corporate Foundations and Giving Programs

Capacity for Caring
Contact: Brad Cohen
501 Sycamore Dr. Tel: (408) 944 - 4044
Milpitas, CA 95035 Fax: (408) 944 - 6542

Annual Grant Total: none reported

E-mail: quantum.caring@quantum.com.

Geographic Preference: Area(s) in which the company operates; California; Massachusetts; Colorado; International

Primary Interests: Arts and Culture; K-12 Education; Math and Science; Technology; Youth Services

Public Affairs and Related Activities Personnel

At Headquarters

BARRETT, Barbara Tel: (408) 894 - 4000
V. President, Human Resources Fax: (408) 894 - 3218

COHEN, Brad Tel: (408) 944 - 4044
Director, Corporate Communications Fax: (408) 944 - 6542
brad.cohen@quantum.com

EWBANK, Lisa L. Tel: (408) 894 - 4000
V. President, Finance and Investor Relations Fax: (408) 894 - 3218

Quest Diagnostics Inc.

A member of the Public Affairs Council. A provider of diagnostic testing, information, and services.

www.questdiagnostics.com

Chairman of the Board
FREEMAN, Kenneth W. Tel: (201) 393 - 5000
Fax: (201) 393 - 4755
TF: (800) 222 - 0446

President and Chief Exec. Officer
MOHAPATRA, Surya N. Tel: (201) 393 - 5000
Fax: (201) 393 - 4755
TF: (800) 222 - 0446

Main Headquarters
Mailing: One Malcolm Ave. Tel: (201) 393 - 5000
Teterboro, NJ 07608 Fax: (201) 393 - 4755
TF: (800) 222 - 0446

Washington Office
Mailing: 815 Connecticut Ave. NW Tel: (202) 263 - 6260
Suite 330 Fax: (202) 728 - 0338
Washington, DC 20006

Political Action Committees

Quest Diagnostics Inc. PAC (QUEST PAC)
Contact: Kristen Cusick
815 Connecticut Ave. NW Tel: (202) 263 - 6263
Suite 330 Fax: (202) 728 - 0338
Washington, DC 20006

Contributions to Candidates: $12,000 (01/05 - 09/05)

Democrats: $5,000; Republicans: $7,000.

Principal Recipients

SENATE DEMOCRATS
Clinton, Hillary Rodham (NY) $2,000

HOUSE DEMOCRATS
Capps, Lois G (CA) $1,000
Gonzalez, Charles A (TX) $1,000
Rothman, Steven R (NJ) $1,000

SENATE REPUBLICANS
Santorum, Richard (PA) $2,000
Kyl, Jon L (AZ) $1,000

HOUSE REPUBLICANS
Johnson, Nancy (CT) $3,000
Pickering, Chip (MS) $1,000

Public Affairs and Related Activities Personnel

At Headquarters

PARK, Laure Tel: (201) 393 - 5030
Corporate V. President, Investor Relations Fax: (201) 393 - 4755
TF: (800) 222 - 0446

SAMUELS, Gary Tel: (201) 393 - 8363
V. President, External Communications Fax: (201) 393 - 4755
media@questdiagnostics.com TF: (800) 222 - 0446

At Washington Office

COLLING, Terese Tel: (202) 263 - 6260
Fax: (202) 728 - 0338
Registered Federal Lobbyist.

CUSICK, Kristen Tel: (202) 263 - 6263
Director, Government Affairs Fax: (202) 728 - 0338
kristin.m.cusick@questdiagnostic.com
Registered Federal Lobbyist.
Responsibilities include political action.

SWIFT, Al Tel: (202) 263 - 6260
Fax: (202) 728 - 0338
Registered Federal Lobbyist.

Questar Corporation

An integrated natural gas company.

www.questar.com
Annual Revenues: $1.4 billion

Chairman, President, Chief Exec. Officer
RATTIE, Keith O. Tel: (801) 324 - 5132
Fax: (801) 324 - 5483

Main Headquarters
Mailing: P.O. Box 45433 Tel: (801) 324 - 5555
Salt Lake City, UT 84145-0433 Fax: (801) 324 - 5483
Street: 180 E. First South
Salt Lake City, UT 84111

Washington Office
Contact: Robert K. Weidner
Mailing: 1101 30th St. NW Tel: (202) 342 - 9240
Suite 200 Fax: (202) 293 - 3484
Washington, DC 20007

Political Action Committees

Questar Corp. Better Government Committee
Contact: Ruland J. Gill, Jr.
P.O. Box 45433 Tel: (801) 324 - 5212
Salt Lake City, UT 84145-0433 Fax: (801) 324 - 5483

Contributions to Candidates: $4,000 (01/05 - 09/05)

Republicans: $4,000.

Principal Recipients

SENATE REPUBLICANS
Bennett, Robert F (UT) $2,000
Thomas, Craig (WY) $1,000

HOUSE REPUBLICANS
Pombo, Richard (CA) $1,000

Corporate Foundations and Giving Programs

Questar Corporate Contributions Program
Contact: Janice W. Bates
P.O. Box 45433 Tel: (801) 324 - 5435
Salt Lake City, UT 84145-0433 Fax: (801) 324 - 5483

Annual Grant Total: $750,000 - $1,000,000

No support is given to religious or fraternal organizations.

Geographic Preference: Utah; Wyoming; Oklahoma

Primary Interests: Arts and Culture; Children; Education; Health and Human Services

Recent Recipients: United Way

Public Affairs and Related Activities Personnel

At Headquarters

BATES, Janice W. Tel: (801) 324 - 5435
Director, Community Affairs Fax: (801) 324 - 5483
Mailstop: MS: QB811
jan.bates@questar.com
Responsibilities also include corporate philanthropy.

BURNETT, R. Curtis Tel: (801) 324 - 5647
V. President, Public Affairs Fax: (801) 324 - 5483
curt.burnett@questar.com
Responsibilities also include investor relations.

CRAVEN, Martin H. Tel: (801) 324 - 5077
Treasurer and Director, Investor Relations Fax: (801) 324 - 5483
martin.craven@questar.com

GILL, Ruland J., Jr. Tel: (801) 324 - 5212
V. President, Government Relations Fax: (801) 324 - 5483
ruland.gill@questar.com

GOW, Roland Tel: (801) 324 - 5594
Manager, Environmental Affairs Fax: (801) 324 - 5131
roland.gow@questar.com

At Washington Office

WEIDNER, Robert K. Tel: (202) 342 - 9240
Senior DC Office Exec. Fax: (202) 293 - 3484

Quintiles Transnat'l Corp.

A provider of information, technology and services to the pharmaceutical and healthcare industries.

www.quintiles.com
Annual Revenues: $1.6 billion

Quintiles Transnat'l Corp.

* continued from previous page

Chairman and Chief Exec. Officer
GILLINGS, Dennis, Ph.D. — Tel: (919) 998 - 2000; Fax: (919) 998 - 2098

Main Headquarters
Mailing: P.O. Box 13979, Research Triangle Park, NC 27709-3979 — Tel: (919) 998 - 2000; Fax: (919) 998 - 2098
Street: Riverbirch Bldg., Suite 200, 4709 Creekstone Dr., Durham, NC 27703-8411

Public Affairs and Related Activities Personnel

At Headquarters

CONNORS, Greg — Tel: (919) 998 - 2300; Fax: (919) 998 - 2098
Senior V. President, Strategic Planning and Investor Relations
greg.connors@quintiles.com

GREBE, Pat — Tel: (919) 998 - 2000; Fax: (919) 998 - 2046
V. President, Corporate Communication
pat.grebe@quintiles.com

JOHNSON, Jay — Tel: (919) 998 - 2066; Fax: (919) 998 - 2098
Senior Director, Corporate Communication
jay.johnson@quintiles.com

MORTIMER, Michael — Tel: (919) 998 - 2000; Fax: (919) 998 - 2098
Senior V. President, Human Resources

Quixtar Inc.

See listing on page 24 under Alticor Inc.

Qwest Communications

Provider of broadband communications services.
www.qwest.com
Annual Revenues: $19.74 billion

Chairman and Chief Exec. Officer
NOTEBAERT, Richard C. — Tel: (303) 992 - 1414; Fax: (303) 296 - 4097; TF: (800) 899 - 7780

Main Headquarters
Mailing: 1801 California St., 50th Floor, Denver, CO 80202 — Tel: (303) 992 - 1400; Fax: (303) 992 - 1724; TF: (800) 899 - 7780

Washington Office
Contact: Gary R. Lytle
Mailing: 607 14th St. NW, Suite 950, Washington, DC 20005 — Tel: (202) 429 - 3100; Fax: (202) 293 - 0561

Political Action Committees

Qwest Communications International Inc. Political Action Committee
Contact: Michael Rubin
607 14th St. NW
Suite 950
Washington, DC 20005 — Tel: (202) 429 - 0303; Fax: (202) 293 - 0561

Contributions to Candidates: $220,265 (01/05 - 09/05)
Democrats: $38,350; Republicans: $180,915; Other: $1,000.

Principal Recipients

SENATE DEMOCRATS

Nelson, Benjamin (NE)	$6,100

SENATE REPUBLICANS

Smith, Gordon (OR)	$10,000
Kyl, Jon L (AZ)	$8,500
Allen, George (VA)	$4,500
Hagel, Charles T (NE)	$4,315
Burns, Conrad (MT)	$4,000
Bennett, Robert F (UT)	$2,000
Craig, Larry (ID)	$2,000
Hatch, Orrin (UT)	$2,000

HOUSE DEMOCRATS

HOUSE REPUBLICANS

Beauprez, Robert (CO)	$10,000
Kennedy, Mark (MN)	$10,000
McMorris, Cathy (WA)	$6,000
Bishop, Robert (UT)	$5,000
Cannon, Christopher (UT)	$5,000
Cantor, Eric (VA)	$5,000
Hastert, Dennis J. (IL)	$5,000
Musgrave, Marilyn (CO)	$5,000
Oxley, Michael (OH)	$5,000
Terry, Lee (NE)	$5,000
Whitfield, Ed (KY)	$5,000

Corporate Foundations and Giving Programs

Qwest Foundation
Contact: Carey Macdonald
1801 California St.
50th Floor
Denver, CO 80202 — Tel: (303) 896 - 5386; TF: (800) 899 - 7780

Annual Grant Total: none reported
The Foundation is primarily interested in technology workforce development.
Primary Interests: Economic Development; Employment; K-12 Education; Technology

Public Affairs and Related Activities Personnel

At Headquarters

COMFORT, Stephanie Georges — Tel: (303) 992 - 6389; Fax: (303) 992 - 1822; TF: (800) 899 - 7780
Senior V. President, Investor Relations

DAVIS, R. Steven — Tel: (303) 896 - 4200; Fax: (303) 291 - 1724; TF: (800) 899 - 7780
Senior V. President, Policy and Law and Deputy General Counsel
Responsibilities include government affairs.

GRONBACH, Tyler — Tel: (303) 992 - 2155; Fax: (303) 896 - 3489; TF: (800) 899 - 7780
V. President, Corporate Communications
tyler.gronbach@qwest.com

HAMMACK, Steve — Tel: (303) 896 - 3030; Fax: (303) 965 - 3050; TF: (800) 899 - 7780
Senior Director, Corporate Communications
steve.hammack@qwest.com

MACDONALD, Carey — Tel: (303) 896 - 5386; TF: (800) 899 - 7780
Contact, Qwest Foundation

SANFORD, Jill — Tel: (303) 992 - 1400; Fax: (303) 992 - 1724; TF: (800) 899 - 7780
Chief Human Resources Officer

WALKER, Joan H. — Tel: (303) 992 - 1412; Fax: (303) 992 - 1028; TF: (800) 899 - 7780
Senior V. President, Corporate Communications

At Washington Office

DUNKEL, Robert — Tel: (202) 429 - 0303; Fax: (202) 293 - 0561
Exec. Director, Congressional Affairs
Registered Federal Lobbyist.

FIELDS, Drew — Tel: (202) 429 - 0303; Fax: (202) 293 - 0561
Executive Director, Congressional Affairs
Registered Federal Lobbyist.

LYTLE, Gary R. — Tel: (202) 429 - 0303; Fax: (202) 293 - 0561
Senior V. President, Federal Relations
Registered Federal Lobbyist.

NEWMAN, Melissa — Tel: (202) 429 - 3100; Fax: (202) 293 - 0561
V. President, Federal Regulatory

O'CONNELL, Cronan — Tel: (202) 429 - 3100; Fax: (202) 293 - 0561
V. President, Federal Regulatory

RUBIN, Michael — Tel: (202) 429 - 0303; Fax: (202) 293 - 0561
Vice President, Congressional Affairs
Registered Federal Lobbyist.
Responsibilities also include political action.

R. J. Reynolds Tobacco Co.

See listing on page 410 under Reynolds American Inc.

Radian Group, Inc.

A credit enhancement provider. Also maintains a website at www.radianbiz.com.
www.radiangroupinc.com
Annual Revenues: $1.4 billion

Chief Exec. Officer
IBRAHIM, S.A. — Tel: (215) 564 - 6600

Main Headquarters
Mailing: 1601 Market St., 12th Floor, Philadelphia, PA 19103 — Tel: (215) 564 - 6600

Political Action Committees

Radian Group Employees PAC
Contact: C. Robert Quint
1601 Market St.
12th Floor
Philadelphia, PA 19103 — Tel: (215) 564 - 6600

Contributions to Candidates: none reported (01/05 - 09/05)

Corporate Foundations and Giving Programs

Radian Group Corporate Contributions
1601 Market St.
12th Floor
Philadelphia, PA 19103 — Tel: (215) 564 - 6600

Annual Grant Total: none reported
Geographic Preference: Area(s) in which employees live and work
Primary Interests: Community Development; Economic Development; Education; Environment/Conservation; Housing; Human Welfare

Public Affairs and Related Activities Personnel

At Headquarters

QUINT, C. Robert — Tel: (215) 564 - 6600
President and Chief Operating Officer; PAC Treasurer

Radian Group, Inc.

* continued from previous page

RILEY, Emily — Tel: (215) 231 - 1328
Public Relations
(Radian Guaranty)
emily.riley@radian.biz

ZEEHANDELAAR, Mona — Tel: (215) 231 - 1674
V. President, Investor Relations

Radian Guaranty

See listing on page 402 under Radian Group, Inc.

Radio Shack Corporation

A retail marketer of electronic products. Formerly known as Tandy Corporation.
www.radioshack.com
Annual Revenues: $4.776 billion

Chairman and Chief Exec. Officer
ROBERTS, Leonard H. — Tel: (817) 415 - 3011 / Fax: (817) 415 - 2335

Main Headquarters
Mailing: 100 Throckmorton St.
Suite 1800
Fort Worth, TX 76102
Tel: (817) 415 - 3011 / Fax: (817) 415 - 2335

Political Action Committees

RadioShack Government Action Fund
Contact: Arnold Grothues
100 Throckmorton St.
Suite 1800
Fort Worth, TX 76102
Tel: (817) 415 - 3011 / Fax: (817) 415 - 2335

Contributions to Candidates: $10,700 (01/05 - 09/05)
Democrats: $1,700; Republicans: $9,000.

Principal Recipients

SENATE DEMOCRATS		HOUSE DEMOCRATS	
Nelson, Benjamin (NE)	$1,200		
SENATE REPUBLICANS		**HOUSE REPUBLICANS**	
Cornyn, John (TX)	$2,000	Granger, Kay N (TX)	$2,000
Talent, James (MO)	$1,500	Pryce, Deborah (OH)	$1,200

Corporate Foundations and Giving Programs

Radio Shack Contributions Program
Contact: Chris Olivera
100 Throckmorton St.
Suite 1800
Fort Worth, TX 76102
Tel: (817) 415 - 3011 / Fax: (817) 415 - 2335

Annual Grant Total: none reported
Primary Interests: Arts and Culture; Education; Health and Human Services

Public Affairs and Related Activities Personnel

At Headquarters

GRANT, James — Tel: (817) 415 - 7833 / Fax: (817) 415 - 2335
Senior Director, Investor Relations
james.grant@radioshack.com

GROTHUES, Arnold — Tel: (817) 415 - 3011 / Fax: (817) 415 - 2335
V. President, Industry and Government Affairs
arnold.grothues@radioshack.com

HODGES, Charles — Tel: (817) 415 - 3300 / Fax: (817) 415 - 2335
Director, Media Relations
charles.hodges@radioshack.com

MOORE, Laura K. — Tel: (817) 415 - 3327 / Fax: (817) 415 - 2335
Senior V. President and Chief Communications Officer
laura.moore@radioshack.com

OLIVERA, Chris — Tel: (817) 415 - 3011 / Fax: (817) 415 - 2335
Contributions Program Contact

PLATANIA, Lynn M. — Tel: (817) 415 - 3011 / Fax: (817) 415 - 2335
Director, Community Relations
Mailstop: TC2-14
lynn.platania@radioshack.com
Responsibilities include corporate philanthropy.

Ralcorp Holdings, Inc.

www.ralcorp.com

Co-Chief Exec. Officer and President
HUNT, Kevin J. — Tel: (314) 877 - 7990 / Fax: (314) 877 - 7667

Co-Chief Exec. Officer and President
SKARIE, David P. — Tel: (314) 877 - 7711 / Fax: (314) 877 - 7663

Main Headquarters
Mailing: P.O. Box 618
St. Louis, MO 63188-0618
Tel: (314) 877 - 7000 / Fax: (314) 877 - 7663
Street: 800 Market St.
St. Louis, MO 63101

Corporate Foundations and Giving Programs

Ralcorp Holdings Corporate Contributions Program
Contact: Nancy Ledbetter
P.O. Box 618
St. Louis, MO 63188-0618
Tel: (314) 877 - 7854 / Fax: (314) 877 - 7667

Annual Grant Total: none reported

Public Affairs and Related Activities Personnel

At Headquarters

LEDBETTER, Nancy — Tel: (314) 877 - 7854 / Fax: (314) 877 - 7667
Contributions Contact

SHEAHAN, Laurie — Tel: (314) 877 - 7994 / Fax: (314) 877 - 7667
Investor and Public Relations Contact

Raley's

A retail supermarket operator.
www.raleys.com
Annual Revenues: $3 billion

Co-Chairman of the Board
TEEL, Jim — Tel: (916) 373 - 3333 / Fax: (916) 371 - 1323
jteel@raleys.com

Co-Chairman of the Board
TEEL, Joyce Raley — Tel: (916) 373 - 3333 / Fax: (916) 371 - 1323
jrteel@raleys.com

Main Headquarters
Mailing: 500 W. Capitol Ave.
West Sacramento, CA 95605
Tel: (916) 373 - 3333 / Fax: (916) 371 - 1323

Public Affairs and Related Activities Personnel

At Headquarters

MCGAGIN, Nancy — Tel: (916) 373 - 3333 / Fax: (916) 371 - 1323
Manager, Corporate Consumer Affairs
nmcgagin@raleys.com

ORTEGA, Jennifer — Tel: (916) 373 - 6019 / Fax: (916) 371 - 1323
Media Contact
jortega@raleys.com

SZCZESNY, Jeff — Tel: (916) 373 - 3333 / Fax: (916) 371 - 1323
Senior V. President, Human Resources

Ralphs Grocery Co.

A division of Kroger Co. (see separate listing).
www.ralphs.com

Main Headquarters
Mailing: P.O. Box 54143
Los Angeles, CA 90054
Tel: (310) 884 - 9000 / Fax: (310) 884 - 2600

Corporate Foundations and Giving Programs

The Ralphs/Food 4 Less Foundation
P.O. Box 54143
Los Angeles, CA 90054
Tel: (310) 884 - 6250 / Fax: (310) 884 - 2569

Annual Grant Total: none reported
Geographic Preference: California
Primary Interests: Disaster Relief; Education; Health; Hunger; Youth Services

Public Affairs and Related Activities Personnel

At Headquarters

GOLLEHER, Jan — Tel: (310) 884 - 6210 / Fax: (310) 884 - 2569
Director, Community Relations
jgolleher@ralphs.com

JANEWAY, Barbara — Tel: (310) 884 - 2993 / Fax: (310) 884 - 2632
Public Relations Coordinator
bjaneway@ralphs.com

O'NEIL, Terry M. — Tel: (310) 884 - 4680 / Fax: (310) 884 - 2632
Director, Public Relations
toneil@ralphs.com

Rand McNally

A private company with operations in map and reference book publishing; retail map and travel stores; and mileage and routing information for commercial trucking and shipping companies.
www.randmcnally.com

President and Chief Exec. Officer
APATOFF, Robert S. — Tel: (847) 329 - 8100 / Fax: (847) 673 - 0813

Main Headquarters
Mailing: P.O. Box 7600
Chicago, IL 60680-7600
Tel: (847) 329 - 8100 / Fax: (847) 673 - 0813
Street: 8255 N. Central Park
Skokie, IL 60076

Corporate Foundations and Giving Programs

Rand McNally Foundation

Rand McNally

* continued from previous page

P.O. Box 7600 — Tel: (847) 329 - 8100
Chicago, IL 60680 — Fax: (847) 673 - 0534

Annual Grant Total: none reported
Recent Recipients: Toys for Tots

Public Affairs and Related Activities Personnel

At Headquarters

ARNOLD, Tara — Tel: (847) 329 - 6850
tarnold@randmcnally.com — Fax: (847) 673 - 0813

Rational Software

See listing on page 260 under Internat'l Business Machines Corp (IBM).

Raymond James Financial, Inc.

Provides investment and financial planning services.

www.raymondjames.com

Chairman and Chief Exec. Officer — Tel: (727) 567 - 1000
JAMES, Thomas A.

Main Headquarters
Mailing: 880 Carillon Pkwy. — Tel: (727) 567 - 1000
St. Petersburg, FL 33716

Corporate Foundations and Giving Programs

Raymond James Corporate Giving
880 Carillon Pkwy. — Tel: (727) 567 - 1000
St. Petersburg, FL 33716

Annual Grant Total: none reported
Primary Interests: Arts and Culture

Public Affairs and Related Activities Personnel

At Headquarters

BEDFORD, Terence — Tel: (727) 567 - 1000
Senior V. President, International

SILVER, Lawrence A. — Tel: (727) 567 - 1000
Senior V. President, Investor Relations
Responsibilities include public relations.

Rayonier Inc.

A member of the Public Affairs Council. A global supplier of speciality pulps, timber and wood products. Owns, leases or controls over 2.2 million acres of timber in the U.S. and New Zealand. With customers in 50 countries, approximately 40 percent of its sales are to international markets.

www.rayonier.com
Annual Revenues: $1.165 billion

Chairman and Chief Exec. Officer — Tel: (904) 357 - 9100
NUTTER, W. L. — Fax: (904) 357 - 9101

Main Headquarters
Mailing: 50 N. Laura St., Suite 1900 — Tel: (904) 357 - 9100
Jacksonville, FL 32202-3638 — Fax: (904) 357 - 9101

Corporate Foundations and Giving Programs

Rayonier Foundation
Contact: Jay A. Fredericksen
50 N. Laura St., Suite 1900 — Tel: (904) 357 - 9100
Jacksonville, FL 32202-3638 — Fax: (904) 357 - 9101

Annual Grant Total: none reported
Geographic Preference: Area(s) in which the company operates
Primary Interests: Community Affairs; Education
Recent Recipients: United Way

Public Affairs and Related Activities Personnel

At Headquarters

BHANSALI, Parag P. — Tel: (904) 357 - 9100
V. President, Investor Relations — Fax: (904) 357 - 9101

FREDERICKSEN, Jay A. — Tel: (904) 357 - 9100
V. President, Corporate Relations — Fax: (904) 357 - 9101
jay.fredericksen@rayonier.com

PUGNETTI, Wendy J. — Tel: (904) 357 - 9181
Director, Corporate Relations — Fax: (904) 357 - 9918
wendy.pugnetti@rayonier.com

At Other Offices

BELL, Michael M. — Tel: (912) 588 - 8216
Manager, Corporate Relations
4474 Savannah Hwy.
Jesup, GA 31545
mike.bell@rayonier.com

PARROTT, Joseph R. — Tel: (404) 250 - 3599
Manager, Government Relations
5825 Glenridge Dr.
Bldg. Three, Suite 101
Atlanta, GA 30328
joe.parrott@rayonier.com

Raytheon Aircraft Company

A subsidiary of Raytheon Co. (see separate listing). Manufactures, markets and services aircraft for the business, military and regional airline markets.

www.raytheonaircraft.com
Annual Revenues: $2.572 billion

Chairman and Chief Exec. Officer — Tel: (316) 676 - 7111
SCHUSTER, James E. — Fax: (316) 676 - 8286

Main Headquarters
Mailing: P.O. Box 85 — Tel: (316) 676 - 7111
Wichita, KS 67201-0085 — Fax: (316) 676 - 8286
Street: 9709 E. Central
Wichita, KS 67206

Washington Office
Contact: John R. Barnes
Mailing: 1100 Wilson Blvd. — Tel: (703) 841 - 5723
Suite 1500 — Fax: (703) 841 - 5792
Arlington, VA 22209

Public Affairs and Related Activities Personnel

At Headquarters

BERGER, Jackie — Tel: (316) 676 - 7690
V. President, Communications and Public Affairs — Fax: (316) 676 - 8867
jackie_berger@rac.ray.com

JIWANLAL, Rich — Tel: (316) 676 - 7111
V. President, Human Resources — Fax: (316) 676 - 8286

At Washington Office

BARNES, John R. — Tel: (703) 841 - 5723
V. President, Congressional Relations — Fax: (703) 841 - 5792

Raytheon Co.

A global technology company providing products and services in the areas of commercial and defense electronics, engineering and construction, and business and special mission aircraft. Operates throughout the United States and serves customers in more than 80 countries around the world.

www.raytheon.com
Annual Revenues: $18.1 billion

Chairman and Chief Exec. Officer — Tel: (781) 522 - 3000
SWANSON, William H.

Main Headquarters
Mailing: 870 Winter St. — Tel: (781) 522 - 3000
Waltham, MA 02451

Washington Office
Mailing: 1100 Wilson Blvd. — Tel: (703) 841 - 5700
Suite 1500 — Fax: (703) 841 - 5792
Arlington, VA 22209

Political Action Committees

Raytheon Co. PAC
Contact: Tanya Y. Donalty
1100 Wilson Blvd. — Tel: (703) 841 - 5700
Suite 1500 — Fax: (703) 841 - 5792
Arlington, VA 22209

Contributions to Candidates: $306,122 (01/05 - 09/05)

Democrats: $139,750; Republicans: $164,372; Other: $2,000.

Principal Recipients

SENATE DEMOCRATS		HOUSE DEMOCRATS	
Feinstein, Dianne (CA)	$9,000	Harman, Jane (CA)	$10,000
Nelson, Bill (FL)	$7,000	Murtha, John P Mr. (PA)	$10,000
Kennedy, Ted (MA)	$6,500	Dicks, Norm D (WA)	$5,000
		Hoyer, Steny (MD)	$5,000
		Langevin, James (RI)	$5,000
		Reyes, Silvestre (TX)	$5,000
		Skelton, Ike (MO)	$5,000

SENATE REPUBLICANS		HOUSE REPUBLICANS	
Kyl, Jon L (AZ)	$5,000	Hoekstra, Peter (MI)	$6,472
Lott, Trent (MS)	$5,000	Beauprez, Robert (CO)	$5,000
McConnell, Mitch (KY)	$5,000	Bonilla, Henry (TX)	$5,000
Sessions, Jeff (AL)	$4,000	Bradley, Joseph (NH)	$5,000
		Tiahrt, Todd W. (KS)	$5,000

Corporate Foundations and Giving Programs

Raytheon Co. Corporate Giving
Contact: Carol Ramsey

Raytheon Co.

* continued from previous page

870 Winter St.
Waltham, MA 02451 — Tel: (781) 522 - 3000

Annual Grant Total: over $5,000,000

Geographic Preference: Area(s) in which the company operates
Primary Interests: Education; Environment/Conservation; Math and Science; Technology

Public Affairs and Related Activities Personnel

At Headquarters

AUSTIN, Dennis G. — Tel: (781) 522 - 3000
Director, State Government Relations
dennis_g_austin@raytheon.com

LOEWENBERG, Stephen M. — Tel: (781) 522 - 3000
PAC Treasurer

PEDEN, Keith — Tel: (781) 522 - 3000
Senior V. President, Human Resources
keith.peden@raytheon.com

RAMSEY, Carol — Tel: (781) 522 - 3000
Director, Corporate Contributions

SHEPARD, Krista — Tel: (781) 522 - 3000
Director, Communications
krista_shepard@raytheon.com

SINGER, Jim — Tel: (781) 522 - 5136
Manger, Investor Relations

SMITH, Greg — Tel: (781) 522 - 5141
V. President, Investor Relations

WICKMAN, Pamela A. — Tel: (781) 522 - 3000
Senior V. President, Corporate Affairs and Communications

At Washington Office

BARAGER, Douglas W. — Tel: (703) 841 - 5700; Fax: (703) 841 - 5792
Senior Manager, Government Relations
Registered Federal Lobbyist.

BARNES, John R. — Tel: (703) 841 - 5700; Fax: (703) 841 - 5792
V. President, Government Relations for Defense Programs
Registered Federal Lobbyist.

BAROZIE, Beth Ann — Tel: (703) 841 - 5700; Fax: (703) 841 - 5792
Manager, Government Relations
Registered Federal Lobbyist.

DONALTY, Tanya Y. — Tel: (703) 841 - 5700; Fax: (703) 841 - 5792
PAC Contact

HELLER, Lauren M. — Tel: (703) 841 - 5700; Fax: (703) 841 - 5792
Director, Government Relations
Registered Federal Lobbyist.

HUGHES, R. Douglas — Tel: (703) 841 - 5700; Fax: (703) 841 - 5792
Senior Director, Government Relations

LEE, William J. — Tel: (703) 841 - 5700; Fax: (703) 841 - 5792
Director, Government Relations
william_j_lee@raytheon.com
Registered Federal Lobbyist.

LOMBARDI, Christopher J. — Tel: (703) 841 - 5700; Fax: (703) 841 - 5792
Manager, Government Relations
Registered Federal Lobbyist.

LYNN, William J. — Tel: (703) 841 - 5700; Fax: (703) 841 - 5792
Senior V. President, Government Operations
Registered Federal Lobbyist.

MCCOLLUM, Lauren M. — Tel: (703) 841 - 5700; Fax: (703) 841 - 5792
Manager, Government Relations (Air Force Programs)
Registered Federal Lobbyist.

MCFARLAND, Richard P. — Tel: (703) 841 - 5700; Fax: (703) 841 - 5792
Director, Government Relations
Registered Federal Lobbyist.

NORTON, Nancy T. — Tel: (703) 841 - 5700; Fax: (703) 841 - 5792
Director, Government Relations
Registered Federal Lobbyist.

PLECS, Scott — Tel: (703) 841 - 5700; Fax: (703) 841 - 5792
Director, Government Relations
Registered Federal Lobbyist.

SCHNABEL, Andrew G. — Tel: (703) 841 - 5700; Fax: (703) 841 - 5792
Director, Government Relations
Registered Federal Lobbyist.

RBC Dain Rauscher Corp.

Provides brokerage and investment banking services. A subsidiary of Royal Bank of Canada.
www.rbcdain.com.com
Annual Revenues: $1.181 billion

President and Chief Exec. Officer
PETERS, Brian — Tel: (612) 371 - 7750; Fax: (612) 371 - 2960

Main Headquarters
Mailing: Dain Rauscher Plaza
60 S. Sixth St., 19th Floor
Minneapolis, MN 55402-4422 — Tel: (612) 371 - 7750; Fax: (612) 371 - 2960

Corporate Foundations and Giving Programs

RBC Dain Rauscher Foundation
Contact: Sherry Koster
Dain Rauscher Plaza
60 S. Sixth St., 19th Floor
Minneapolis, MN 55402-4422 — Tel: (612) 371 - 2765; Fax: (612) 371 - 7933

Annual Grant Total: $2,000,000 - $5,000,000

Geographic Preference: Area(s) in which the company operates
Primary Interests: Arts and Humanities; Human Welfare; K-12 Education
Recent Recipients: Habitat for Humanity; Junior Achievement; Junior League; Juvenile Diabetes Foundation; United Way

Public Affairs and Related Activities Personnel

At Headquarters

CALLAHAN, Dan — Tel: (612) 313 - 1234
Director, Public Relations
dan.callahan@rbcdain.com

ELLISON, Jennifer — Tel: (612) 371 - 2225; Fax: (612) 371 - 2960
Senior Media Relations Specialist
jennifer.ellison@rbcdain.com

GUCK, Susan — Tel: (612) 371 - 7750; Fax: (612) 371 - 2960
Director, Corporate Communications
susan.guck@rbcdain.com

HAPPEL, Branden — Tel: (612) 371 - 2239; Fax: (612) 371 - 2960
Senior Public Relations Specialist
branden.happel@rbcdain.com

KOSTER, Sherry — Tel: (612) 371 - 2765; Fax: (612) 371 - 7933
Program Manager, RBC Dain Rauscher Foundation
sherry.koster@rbcdain.com

At Other Offices

CLAXTON, John — Tel: (303) 595 - 1112; Fax: (303) 595 - 1160
Manager, Communications (Central Rocky Mountain)
1200 17th St.
Denver, CO 80202-5822

CORDIAK, Bob — Tel: (214) 989 - 1602; Fax: (214) 582 - 1619
Manager, Southwest Communications
City Place Center East, Suite 2400
2711 N. Haskell Ave.
Dallas, TX 75204

RASMUSSEN, B. J. — Tel: (206) 621 - 3211; Fax: (206) 621 - 3151
Manager, Western Communications
1201 Third Ave.
Seattle, WA 98101-3044

RC Cement

See listing on page 96 under Buzzi Unicem USA.

Reader's Digest Ass'n, Inc.

A publisher best known for its global "Reader's Digest" magazine, Select Editions, series books, and general books covering a wide variety of topics, recorded music, special interest magazines, audio books, and new media.
www.rd.com

Chairman and Chief Exec. Officer
RYDER, Thomas — Tel: (914) 238 - 1000; Fax: (914) 238 - 4559; TF: (800) 234 - 9000
thomas_ryder@rd.com

Main Headquarters
Mailing: Reader's Digest Rd.
Pleasantville, NY 10570-7000 — Tel: (914) 238 - 1000; Fax: (914) 238 - 4559; TF: (800) 234 - 9000

Washington Office
Mailing: 1730 Rhode Island Ave., N.W., Suite 212
Washington, DC 20036 — Tel: (202) 223 - 9520; Fax: (202) 466 - 4626

Corporate Foundations and Giving Programs

Reader's Digest Foundation
Reader's Digest Rd.
Pleasantville, NY 10570-7000 — Tel: (914) 238 - 1000; Fax: (914) 238 - 4559; TF: (800) 234 - 9000

Annual Grant Total: $2,000,000 - $5,000,000

Is interested in assisting sending employees' children to college. Employees and retirees are also encouraged to contribute to their communities through volunteerism and individual philanthropy.
Geographic Preference: Area(s) in which the company operates
Primary Interests: K-12 Education; Literacy; Scholarship Funds

Public Affairs and Related Activities Personnel

At Headquarters

ADLER, William K. — Tel: (914) 244 - 7585; TF: (800) 234 - 9000
Senior Director, Global Communications
william.adler@rd.com

Reader's Digest Ass'n, Inc.
** continued from previous page*

BROWN, Susan K. — Tel: (914) 244 - 7340
Director, Global Communications — Fax: (914) 244 - 5324
susan.brown@rd.com — TF: (800) 234 - 9000

CLARK, Richard E. — Tel: (914) 244 - 5425
V. President, Investor Relations and Global Communiations — Fax: (914) 238 - 6643
richard.clark@rd.com — TF: (800) 234 - 9000

HANONIK, Francoise — Tel: (914) 238 - 1000
Chief Human Resources Officer; V. President, Human Resources North America — Fax: (914) 238 - 4559
TF: (800) 234 - 9000

JIMENEZ, Carlos A. — Tel: (914) 244 - 5308
Associate Director, Investor Relations — Fax: (914) 238 - 4559
carlos.jimenez@rd.com — TF: (800) 234 - 9000

At Washington Office

BEAMAN, William — Tel: (202) 223 - 8025
Washington Bureau Chief — Fax: (202) 466 - 4626
Responsibilities include government affairs.

Recreational Equipment, Inc.
National retailer of outdoor apparel and recreational equipment.
www.rei.com

Chairman of the Board — Tel: (253) 395 - 3780
WALKER, Doug — Fax: (253) 395 - 4368
Board@rei.com

President and Chief Exec. Officer — Tel: (253) 395 - 3780
JEWELL, Sally — Fax: (253) 395 - 4368
sjewell@rei.com

Main Headquarters
Mailing: P.O. Box 1938, Sumner, WA 98390-0800 — Tel: (253) 395 - 3780; Fax: (253) 395 - 4368
Street: 6750 S. 228th, Kent, WA 98032

Corporate Foundations and Giving Programs

REI Foundation Memorial Fund
Contact: David Jayo
P.O. Box 1938 — Tel: (253) 395 - 5928
Sumner, WA 98390-0800 — Fax: (253) 395 - 8135

Annual Grant Total: none reported
Primary Interests: Environment/Conservation; Search/Rescue; Youth Services

Public Affairs and Related Activities Personnel

At Headquarters

COLLINS, Michael — Tel: (253) 395 - 5926
V. President, Public Affairs — Fax: (253) 395 - 8135
mcollin@rei.com

HURLOW, Randy — Tel: (253) 395 - 5877
Manager, Public Relations — Fax: (253) 395 - 8135
rhurlow@rei.com

JAYO, David — Tel: (253) 395 - 5928
Manager, Corporate Giving — Fax: (253) 395 - 8135
djayo@rei.com

Reebok Internat'l Ltd.
A worldwide designer, marketer, and distributor of sports, fitness, and casual footwear, apparel, and equipment.
www.reebok.com
Annual Revenues: $2.993 billion

Chairman and Chief Exec. Officer — Tel: (781) 401 - 5000
FIREMAN, Paul B. — Fax: (781) 401 - 4000

Main Headquarters
Mailing: 1895 J W Foster Blvd., Canton, MA 02021 — Tel: (781) 401 - 5000; Fax: (781) 401 - 4000

Washington Office
Mailing: 1201 Pennsylvania Ave. NW, Suite 315, Washington, DC 20004 — Tel: (202) 783 - 3333; Fax: (202) 783 - 4422

Political Action Committees

Reebok Internat'l, Ltd. PAC
Contact: Peter Friedmann
1201 Pennsylvania Ave. NW — Tel: (202) 783 - 3333
Suite 315 — Fax: (202) 783 - 4422
Washington, DC 20004

Contributions to Candidates: $6,000 (01/05 - 09/05)
Democrats: $5,000; Republicans: $1,000.

Principal Recipients

SENATE DEMOCRATS

HOUSE DEMOCRATS
Hooley, Darlene (OR) $4,000
Mcgovern, James (MA) $1,000

SENATE REPUBLICANS
Chafee, Lincoln (RI) $1,000

HOUSE REPUBLICANS

Corporate Foundations and Giving Programs

The Reebok Human Rights Foundation
Contact: Paul Foster
1895 J W Foster Blvd. — Tel: (781) 401 - 7396
Canton, MA 02021 — Fax: (781) 401 - 4806

Annual Grant Total: $1,000,000 - $2,000,000
Grants are also awarded to activists under the age of 30 who have made a contribution toward the struggle for human rights. Reebok does not accept unsolicited applications for grants.
Geographic Preference: Area in which the company is headquartered; Area(s) in which the company operates
Primary Interests: Health and Human Services
Recent Recipients: Nat'l Ass'n for the Advancement of Colored People

Public Affairs and Related Activities Personnel

At Headquarters

FOSTER, Paul — Tel: (781) 401 - 7396
V. President, Foundation and Trade Relations — Fax: (781) 401 - 4806
paul.foster@reebok.com

KAIGLER, Denise — Tel: (781) 401 - 7869
Corporate V. President, Global Communicaitons — Fax: (781) 401 - 4000
denise.kaigler@reebok.com

KERMAN, Neil — Tel: (781) 401 - 7152
V. President, Corporate Finance — Fax: (781) 401 - 4422
neil.kerman@reebok.com
Responsibilities include investor relations.

MYERS, Robert — Tel: (781) 401 - 5000
Senior V. President and Chief Human Resources Officer — Fax: (781) 401 - 4000

At Washington Office

FRIEDMANN, Peter — Tel: (202) 783 - 3333
Director, International Trade Policy and Government Affairs — Fax: (202) 783 - 4422

Regence BlueCross BlueShield of Oregon
Formerly known as Blue Cross and Blue Shield of Oregon. An affiliate of The Regence Group, a unique affiliation of Blue Cross and Blue Shield Plans in Oregon, Washington, Idaho and Utah.
www.or.regence.com

Chairman of the Board — Tel: (503) 225 - 5228
WOOLWORTH, Dick — Fax: (503) 225 - 5283
Mailstop: M/S E15A

President and Chief Exec. Officer — Tel: (503) 225 - 5336
MCMULLAN, J. Bart, M.D. — Fax: (503) 225 - 5283

Main Headquarters
Mailing: P.O. Box 1271, Portland, OR 97207-1271 — Tel: (503) 225 - 5336; Fax: (503) 225 - 5283
Street: 100 SW Market St., Portland, OR 97207-1271

Corporate Foundations and Giving Programs

Corporate Giving Program
Contact: Julia Sims
P.O. Box 1271 — Tel: (503) 273 - 4682
Portland, OR 97207-1271 — Fax: (503) 225 - 5283

Annual Grant Total: none reported
Geographic Preference: Oregon; Washington State
Primary Interests: Community Affairs; Health
Recent Recipients: American Red Cross; Ronald McDonald House

Public Affairs and Related Activities Personnel

At Headquarters

BECKER, Michael S. — Tel: (503) 225 - 5221
V. President, Public Policy and Community Affairs — Fax: (503) 225 - 5283

KENNEY, Ryan — Tel: (503) 225 - 5336
Director, Human Resources — Fax: (503) 225 - 5283

LALLY, Pamela K. — Tel: (503) 225 - 6982
Manager, Legislative Affairs — Fax: (503) 225 - 5283
Mailstop: MS E12A
pklally@regence.com

SIMS, Julia — Tel: (503) 273 - 4682
Community Relations Coordinator — Fax: (503) 225 - 5283
Mailstop: MSE7C

Regence BlueCross BlueShield of Utah
An affiliate of The Regence Group, a unique affiliation of Blue Cross and Blue Shield Plans in Oregon, Washington, Idaho and Utah.
www.ut.regence.com

Chairman of the Board — Tel: (801) 333 - 2000
PITCHER, Jed

President and Chief Exec. Officer — Tel: (801) 333 - 2100
IDESON, D. Scott

Main Headquarters
Mailing: P.O. Box 30270, Salt Lake City, UT 84130-0270 — Tel: (801) 333 - 2100
Street: 2890 E. Cottonwood Pkwy., Salt Lake City, UT 84121

Regence BlueCross BlueShield of Utah

** continued from previous page*

Political Action Committees

Regence BluePAC
Contact: Jennifer B. Cannady
P.O. Box 30270 — Tel: (801) 333 - 5671
Salt Lake City, UT 84130-0270

Contributions to Candidates: $8,250 (01/05 - 09/05)
Democrats: $1,000; Republicans: $7,250.

Principal Recipients

SENATE DEMOCRATS		HOUSE DEMOCRATS	
		Wu, David Mr. (OR)	$1,000
SENATE REPUBLICANS		**HOUSE REPUBLICANS**	
Hatch, Orrin (UT)	$2,500	Reichert, Dave (WA)	$2,500
		Bishop, Robert (UT)	$2,000

Corporate Foundations and Giving Programs

Regence BlueCross BlueShield Corporate Giving
Contact: Kathleen Murphy
P.O. Box 30270 — Tel: (801) 333 - 5756
Salt Lake City, UT 84130-0270

Annual Grant Total: none reported
The company also maintains the Caring Foundation for Children, which provides free dental care for children.
Primary Interests: Children; Health and Human Services; Youth Services
Recent Recipients: American Red Cross; Big Brothers/Big Sisters; Easter Seal Soc.; Junior Achievement; Ronald McDonald House

Caring Foundation for Children
Contact: Kathleen Pitcher
P.O. Box 30270 — Tel: (801) 333 - 2100
Salt Lake City, UT 84130-0270

Annual Grant Total: none reported
Primary Interests: Child Welfare; Children's Health

Public Affairs and Related Activities Personnel

At Headquarters

BISCHOFF, J. Kevin — Tel: (801) 333 - 5285; Fax: (801) 333 - 6563
V. President, Public and Corporate Affairs
kbischoff@regence.com

CANNADY, Jennifer B. — Tel: (801) 333 - 5671
Assistant V. President, Legislative and Regulatory Affairs
jcannada@regence.com
Responsibilities include political action.

MURPHY, Kathleen — Tel: (801) 333 - 5756
Assistant Director, Corporate Communications
kathleen.murphy@regence.com

PITCHER, Kathleen — Tel: (801) 333 - 2100
Exec. Director, Caring Foundation for Children

Regence BlueShield of Idaho

An affiliate of The Regence Group, a unique affiliation of Blue Cross and Blue Shield Plans in Oregon, Washington, Idaho and Utah.
www.id.regence.com

Chairman of the Board — Tel: (208) 798 - 2280; Fax: (208) 798 - 2087
CHARLTON, Greg

President and Chief Exec. Officer — Tel: (208) 746 - 2671; Fax: (208) 798 - 2087
STELLMON, John

Main Headquarters
Mailing: P.O. Box 1106, Lewiston, ID 83501 — Tel: (208) 746 - 2671; Fax: (208) 798 - 2087
Street: 1602 21st Ave., Lewiston, ID 83501

Political Action Committees

Regence BluePAC
Contact: Tim Olson
1211 W. Myrtle St. — Tel: (208) 336 - 2420
Boise, ID 83702 — Fax: (208) 333 - 7896

Contributions to Candidates: $8,250 (01/05 - 09/05)
Democrats: $1,000; Republicans: $7,250.

Principal Recipients

SENATE REPUBLICANS		HOUSE REPUBLICANS	
Hatch, Orrin (UT)	$2,500	Reichert, Dave (WA)	$2,500
		Bishop, Robert (UT)	$2,000

Corporate Foundations and Giving Programs

Team Regence
Contact: Samantha Skinner
P.O. Box 1106 — Tel: (208) 798 - 2247
Lewiston, ID 83501 — Fax: (208) 798 - 2087

Annual Grant Total: none reported
Geographic Preference: Idaho
Primary Interests: Community Affairs; Health

Public Affairs and Related Activities Personnel

At Headquarters

SKINNER, Samantha — Tel: (208) 798 - 2247; Fax: (208) 798 - 2087
Contact, Team Regence

TATKO, Mike — Tel: (208) 798 - 2221; Fax: (208) 798 - 2087
Strategic Communications
mtatko.id@regence.com

At Other Offices

BENJAMIN, Georganne — Tel: (208) 395 - 7723; Fax: (208) 333 - 7873
Assistant Director, Strategic Communications
1211 W. Myrtle St.
Mailstop: Suite 210
Boise, ID 83702
gbenjamin.id@regence.com

OLSON, Tim — Tel: (208) 336 - 2420; Fax: (208) 333 - 7896
V. President, Community and Public Affairs
1211 W. Myrtle St.
Boise, ID 83702
tolson.id@regence.com
Responsibilities include political action.

Regions Financial Corp.

A financial services company. Merged with Union Planters Corp. in 2004.
www.regions.com

Chairman and Chief Exec. Officer — Tel: (205) 326 - 7273; Fax: (205) 326 - 7818; TF: (800) 734 - 4667
JONES, Carl E., Jr.

Main Headquarters
Mailing: P.O. Box 10247, Birmingham, AL 35202 — Tel: (205) 326 - 7100; Fax: (205) 244 - 2897; TF: (800) 734 - 4667
Street: 417 N. 20th St., Birmingham, AL 35203

Political Action Committees

Regions Financial Corp. Political Action Committee
Contact: Chris Sawyer
P.O. Box 10247 — Tel: (205) 326 - 7100; Fax: (205) 244 - 2897; TF: (800) 734 - 4667
Birmingham, AL 35202

Contributions to Candidates: $24,500 (01/05 - 09/05)
Democrats: $5,000; Republicans: $19,500.

Principal Recipients

SENATE DEMOCRATS		HOUSE DEMOCRATS	
Ford, Harold E Jr (TN)	$5,000		
SENATE REPUBLICANS		**HOUSE REPUBLICANS**	
		Whitfield, Ed (KY)	$2,500
		Aderholt, Robert B (AL)	$2,000
		Baker, Hugh (LA)	$2,000
		Blackburn, Marsha (TN)	$2,000
		McHenry, Patrick (NC)	$2,000
		Price, Thomas (GA)	$2,000
		Rogers, Michael (AL)	$2,000

Corporate Foundations and Giving Programs

Regions Financial Corp. Contributions Program
P.O. Box 10247 — Tel: (205) 326 - 7100; Fax: (205) 244 - 2897; TF: (800) 734 - 4667
Birmingham, AL 35202

Annual Grant Total: none reported
Geographic Preference: Area(s) in which the company operates
Primary Interests: Children; Families
Recent Recipients: Habitat for Humanity

Public Affairs and Related Activities Personnel

At Headquarters

DANIEL, John M. — Tel: (205) 326 - 7100; Fax: (205) 244 - 2897; TF: (800) 734 - 4667
Director, Human Resources

ELLIS, Kristi Lamont — Tel: (205) 326 - 7179; Fax: (205) 326 - 7105; TF: (800) 734 - 4667
Senior V. President, Corporate Communications
kristi.ellis@regions.com

Regions Financial Corp.

** continued from previous page*

GOFORTH, Jenifer M.
Senior V. President and Director, Investor Relations
jenifer.goforth@regions.com
Tel: (205) 244 - 2823
Fax: (205) 326 - 7784
TF: (800) 734 - 4667

SAWYER, Chris
Treasurer, Regions Financial Corp. Political Action Committee
Tel: (205) 326 - 7100
Fax: (205) 244 - 2897
TF: (800) 734 - 4667

Regis Corporation

Owner, operator, and franchiser of hair and retail product salons in the United States, Canada, Puerto Rico, the United Kingdom, France, Italy, Spain, Germany, Belgium, Switzerland and Poland.

www.regiscorp.com
Annual Revenues: $1.9 billion

Chairman and Chief Exec. Officer
FINKELSTEIN, Paul D.
Tel: (952) 947 - 7777

Main Headquarters
Mailing: 7201 Metro Blvd.
Minneapolis, MN 55439
Tel: (952) 947 - 7777

Corporate Foundations and Giving Programs

Regis Foundation for Breast Cancer Research
Contact: Janis Chamoun
7201 Metro Blvd.
Minneapolis, MN 55439
Tel: (952) 947 - 7433
Fax: (952) 995 - 319

Annual Grant Total: $2,000,000 - $5,000,000
Dedicated to raising awareness and funds for breast cancer research.
Primary Interests: Medical Research
Recent Recipients: Canadian Breast Cancer Institute; Mayo Clinic; Public Broadcasting System; Susan G. Komen Breast Cancer Foundation; University of Minnesota

Public Affairs and Related Activities Personnel

At Headquarters

CHAMOUN, Janis
Director, Corporate Communications
janis.chamoun@regiscorp.com
Responsibilities include corporate philanthropy.
Tel: (952) 947 - 7433
Fax: (952) 995 - 319

RehabCare Group, Inc.

Provides physical rehabilitation services in hospitals, nursing homes and other long-term care facilities.

www.rehabcare.com
Annual Revenues: $539.3 million

Chairman of the Board
TRUSHEIM, H. Edwin
Tel: (314) 863 - 7422
Fax: (314) 863 - 0769
TF: (800) 677 - 1238

Chief Exec. Officer
SHORT, John H.
Tel: (314) 863 - 7422
Fax: (314) 863 - 0769
TF: (800) 677 - 1238

Main Headquarters
Mailing: 7733 Forsyth Blvd.
Suite 2300
St. Louis, MO 63105
Tel: (314) 863 - 7422
Fax: (314) 863 - 0769
TF: (800) 677 - 1238

Political Action Committees

RehabCare Group Inc. PAC
Contact: Mark Anthony Bogovich
7733 Forsyth Blvd.
Suite 2300
St. Louis, MO 63105
Tel: (314) 863 - 7422
Fax: (314) 863 - 0769
TF: (800) 677 - 1238

Contributions to Candidates: $1,000 (01/05 - 09/05)
Republicans: $1,000.

Principal Recipients

SENATE REPUBLICANS
Ensign, John Eric (NV) $1,000

HOUSE REPUBLICANS

Public Affairs and Related Activities Personnel

At Headquarters

BOGOVICH, Mark Anthony
Treasurer, RehabCare Group Inc. PAC
Tel: (314) 863 - 7422
Fax: (314) 863 - 0769
TF: (800) 677 - 1238

CAMMARATA, Betty D.
Director, Investor Relations
bdcammarata@rehabcare.com
Tel: (314) 659 - 2285
Fax: (314) 659 - 2221
TF: (800) 677 - 1238

MCWILLIAMS, John
Senior V. President and Chief Human Resources Officer
Tel: (314) 863 - 7422
Fax: (314) 863 - 0769
TF: (800) 677 - 1238

TOTARO, David J.
Senior V. President, Marketing and Communications
djtotaro@rehabcare.com
Tel: (314) 659 - 2115
Fax: (314) 863 - 0769
TF: (800) 677 - 1238

REI

See listing on page 406 under Recreational Equipment, Inc.

Reichhold, Inc.

A manufacturer of high-performance coating and composite resins. A subsidiary of Dainippon Ink & Chemicals of Japan. Formerly Reichhold Chemicals, Inc.

www.reichhold.com
Annual Revenues: $1.3 billion

Chairman of the Board
TSUNEKAWA, Yasuji
Tel: (919) 990 - 7500
Fax: (919) 990 - 7711
TF: (800) 448 - 3482

President and Chief Exec. Officer
GAITHER, John S.
Tel: (919) 990 - 7500
Fax: (919) 990 - 7711
TF: (800) 448 - 3482

Main Headquarters
Mailing: P.O. Box 13582
Research Triangle Park, NC 27709
Tel: (919) 990 - 7500
Fax: (919) 990 - 7711
TF: (800) 448 - 3482

Street: 2400 Ellis Rd.
Durham, NC 27703

Public Affairs and Related Activities Personnel

At Headquarters

BRIDGES, Phil
Manager, Corporate Communications
phil.bridges@reichhold.com
Tel: (919) 990 - 7952
Fax: (919) 990 - 7922
TF: (800) 448 - 3482

VAN LEEUWEN, Mitzi
Senior V. President, Corporate Services
mitzi.vanleeuwen@reichhold.com
Tel: (919) 990 - 7500
Fax: (919) 990 - 7711
TF: (800) 448 - 3482

Reilly Industries, Inc.

www.reillyind.com

Chairman of the Board
YOCUM, Robert H.
Tel: (317) 247 - 8141
Fax: (317) 248 - 6472

President and Chief Exec. Officer
MCNEELEY, Robert D.
Tel: (317) 247 - 8141
Fax: (317) 248 - 6472

Main Headquarters
Mailing: 300 N. Meridian St., Suite 1500
Indianapolis, IN 46204-1763
Tel: (317) 247 - 8141
Fax: (317) 248 - 6472

Corporate Foundations and Giving Programs

Reilly Foundation
Contact: Rand Brooks
300 N. Meridian St., Suite 1500
Indianapolis, IN 46204-1763
Tel: (317) 247 - 8141
Fax: (317) 248 - 6472

Annual Grant Total: $400,000 - $500,000
Recent recipient: Butler University, Indianapolis.
Geographic Preference: Area in which the company is headquartered
Primary Interests: Education

Public Affairs and Related Activities Personnel

At Headquarters

BROOKS, Rand
Contact, Reilly Foundation
rbrooks@reillyind.com
Tel: (317) 247 - 8141
Fax: (317) 248 - 6472

POLACK, Rob
Public Affairs
Tel: (317) 247 - 8141
Fax: (317) 248 - 6472

REID, Robin
Communications Specialist
rreid@reillyind.com
Tel: (317) 247 - 8141
Fax: (317) 248 - 6472

Reliance Steel & Aluminum Co.

Processes and distributes metals.

www.rsac.com

Non-Exec. Chairman of the Board
CRIDER, Joe D.
Tel: (213) 687 - 7700
Fax: (213) 687 - 8792

Chief Exec. Officer
HANNAH, David H.
dhannah@rsac.com
Tel: (213) 687 - 7700
Fax: (213) 687 - 8792

Main Headquarters
Mailing: 350 S. Grand Ave., Suite 5100
Los Angeles, CA 90071
Tel: (213) 687 - 7700
Fax: (213) 687 - 8792

Public Affairs and Related Activities Personnel

At Headquarters

FEAZLE, Kim P.
Investor Relations
kfeazle@rsac.com
Tel: (213) 576 - 2428
Fax: (713) 610 - 9964

NEWTON, Donna
V. President, Human Resources
dnewton@rsac.com
Tel: (213) 687 - 7700
Fax: (213) 687 - 8792

Reliant Resources

A diversified, international energy services company. Formed by the spin-off of unregulated businesses from Reliant Energy, Inc. Reliant Energy's regulated businesses were spun off into a separate company called CenterPoint Energy (see separate listing).

www.reliantresources.com

Chairman, President and Chief Exec. Officer
STAFF, Joel V.
Tel: (281) 866 - 1167
Fax: (713) 488 - 5925
TF: (866) 872 - 6656

Main Headquarters
Mailing: P.O. Box 2286
Houston, TX 77252-2286
Tel: (281) 866 - 1167
Fax: (713) 488 - 5925
TF: (866) 872 - 6656

Street: 1000 Main St.
Houston, TX 77002

Washington Office
Contact: C. H. "Bud" Albright, Jr.
Mailing: 801 Pennsylvania Ave. NW
Suite 620
Washington, DC 20004-2615
Tel: (202) 783 - 7220
Fax: (202) 783 - 8127

Political Action Committees

Reliant Energy Inc. PAC
Contact: Gene Fisseler
P.O. Box 148
Houston, TX 77001

Contributions to Candidates: $10,000 (01/05 - 09/05)
Democrats: $4,500; Republicans: $5,500.

Principal Recipients

SENATE DEMOCRATS
Bingaman, Jeff (NM) $2,500

HOUSE DEMOCRATS
Green, Gene (TX) $1,000

SENATE REPUBLICANS
Santorum, Richard (PA) $2,500

HOUSE REPUBLICANS
Barton, Joe L (TX) $2,000
Murphy, Tim (PA) $1,000

Corporate Foundations and Giving Programs

Reliant Resources Corporate Contributions Program
P.O. Box 2286
Houston, TX 77252-2286
Tel: (281) 866 - 1167
Fax: (713) 488 - 5925
TF: (866) 872 - 6656

Annual Grant Total: $1,000,000 - $2,000,000
Geographic Preference: Area in which the company is headquartered; Area(s) in which the company operates
Primary Interests: Arts and Culture; Community Affairs; Education; Youth Services
Recent Recipients: United Way

Public Affairs and Related Activities Personnel

At Headquarters

BARBER, Dennis
Director, Investor Relations
dbarber@reliant.com
Tel: (713) 497 - 3042
Fax: (713) 488 - 5925
TF: (866) 872 - 6656

HAMMOND, Pat
Manager, Media Relations
Tel: (713) 497 - 7723
Fax: (713) 488 - 5925
TF: (866) 872 - 6656

LANGDON, Jerry J.
Exec. V. President, Public and Regulatory Affairs
Tel: (281) 866 - 1167
Fax: (713) 488 - 5925
TF: (866) 872 - 6656

SLAVIN, Stephanie
Director, Investor Relations and Communications
sslavin@reliant.com
Tel: (713) 497 - 6983
Fax: (713) 488 - 5925
TF: (866) 872 - 6656

TAYLOR, Karen D.
Senior V. President, Human Resources and Administration
Tel: (281) 866 - 1167
Fax: (713) 488 - 5925
TF: (866) 872 - 6656

At Washington Office

ALBRIGHT, C. H. "Bud", Jr.
V. President, Federal Relations
Tel: (202) 467 - 5040
Fax: (202) 783 - 8127
Registered Federal Lobbyist.

LASS, Holly B.
Manager, Federal Relations
Registered Federal Lobbyist.
Tel: (202) 783 - 7220
Fax: (202) 783 - 8127

At Other Offices

FISSELER, Gene
Treasurer, Reliant Energy Inc. PAC
P.O. Box 148
Houston, TX 77001

Renal Care Group, Inc.

Operates kidney dialysis centers.

www.renalcaregroup.com
Annual Revenues: $1.1 billion

Chairman of the Board
JOHNSTON, William P.
Tel: (615) 345 - 5500
Fax: (615) 345 - 5505

President and Chief Exec. Officer
BRUKARDT, Gary
Tel: (615) 345 - 5500
Fax: (615) 345 - 5505

Main Headquarters
Mailing: 2525 West End Ave., Suite 600
Nashville, TN 37203
Tel: (615) 345 - 5500
Fax: (615) 345 - 5505

Political Action Committees

Renal Care Group PAC
Contact: Raymond H. Hakim, M.D., Ph.d.
2525 West End Ave., Suite 600
Nashville, TN 37203
Tel: (615) 345 - 5577
Fax: (615) 345 - 5505

Contributions to Candidates: $23,000 (01/05 - 09/05)
Democrats: $10,000; Republicans: $13,000.

Principal Recipients

SENATE DEMOCRATS
Wyden, Ronald Lee (OR) $4,000
Baucus, Max (MT) $3,000

HOUSE DEMOCRATS
Johnson, Paul W. (IA) $2,000

SENATE REPUBLICANS
Santorum, Richard (PA) $7,000

HOUSE REPUBLICANS
Camp, David Lee (MI) $2,000
English, Philip S (PA) $2,000
Hulshof, Kenny (MO) $2,000

Public Affairs and Related Activities Personnel

At Headquarters

ANDERSON, John L.
V. President, Human Resources
Tel: (615) 370 - 2740
Fax: (615) 370 - 2735

HAKIM, Raymond H., M.D., Ph.d.
PAC Contact
Tel: (615) 345 - 5577
Fax: (615) 345 - 5505

PROVEAUX, Terry
Director, Corporate Communications and Investor Relations
Tel: (615) 345 - 5577
Fax: (615) 345 - 5505

Rent-A-Center, Inc.

A chain of rent to own stores featuring furniture, appliances, and electronics.

www.rentacenter.com

Chairman and Chief Exec. Officer
SPEESE, Mark E.
mspeese@racenter.com
Tel: (972) 801 - 1199
Fax: (972) 943 - 0116
TF: (800) 275 - 2696

Main Headquarters
Mailing: 5700 Tennyson Pkwy., Third Floor
Plano, TX 75024
Tel: (972) 801 - 1100
Fax: (972) 943 - 0112
TF: (800) 275 - 2696

Corporate Foundations and Giving Programs

Rent-A-Center, Inc. Corporate Giving Program
5700 Tennyson Pkwy., Third Floor
Plano, TX 75024
Tel: (972) 801 - 1100
Fax: (972) 943 - 0112
TF: (800) 275 - 2696

Annual Grant Total: none reported
Geographic Preference: National
Primary Interests: Children; Families
Recent Recipients: Big Brothers/Big Sisters; Nat'l Center for Missing and Exploited Children

Public Affairs and Related Activities Personnel

At Headquarters

CARPENTER, David
V. President, Investor Relations
dcarpenter@racenter.com
Tel: (972) 801 - 1214
Fax: (972) 943 - 0113
TF: (800) 275 - 2696
Responsibilities also include investor relations.

WISDOM, Jennifer
V. President, Human Resources
Tel: (972) 801 - 1100
Fax: (972) 943 - 0112
TF: (800) 275 - 2696

Rent-Way, Inc.

An equipment rental and leasing company.

www.rentway.com

Chairman and Chief Exec. Officer
MORGENSTERN, William E.
wmorgenstern@rentway.com
Tel: (814) 455 - 5378
Fax: (814) 461 - 5400
TF: (800) 736 - 8929

Main Headquarters
Mailing: One Rentway Place
Erie, PA 16505
Tel: (814) 455 - 5378
Fax: (814) 461 - 5400
TF: (800) 736 - 8929

Corporate Foundations and Giving Programs

Rentway Community Involvement

Rent-Way, Inc.

** continued from previous page*

One Rentway Place
Erie, PA 16505
Tel: (814) 455 - 5378
Fax: (814) 461 - 5400
TF: (800) 736 - 8929

Annual Grant Total: none reported
Primary Interests: Medical Research; Social Services

Public Affairs and Related Activities Personnel

At Headquarters

PETERSON, Deborah S. — Tel: (814) 455 - 1511 Ext: 5225
Manager, Investor Relations — Fax: (814) 461 - 5837
dpeterson@rentway.com — TF: (800) 736 - 8929

ZWINGER, Robert — Tel: (814) 455 - 5378
V. President, Advertising and Marketing — Fax: (814) 461 - 5400
TF: (800) 736 - 8929
Responsibilities include media relations.

Republic Industries

See listing on page 55 under AutoNation, Inc.

Republic Services, Inc.

Specializes in solid waste management.
www.republicservices.com
Annual Revenues: $2.258 billion

Chairman and Chief Exec. Officer — Tel: (954) 769 - 2400
O'CONNOR, James E. — Fax: (954) 769 - 2664

Main Headquarters
Mailing: 110 S.E. Sixth St. — Tel: (954) 769 - 2400
28th Floor — Fax: (954) 769 - 2664
Fort Lauderdale, FL 33301

Public Affairs and Related Activities Personnel

At Headquarters

BAYLOR, Kenneth M. — Tel: (954) 769 - 2400
V. President, Employee and Labor Relations — Fax: (954) 769 - 2664

FLOWER, Will — Tel: (954) 769 - 6392
V. President, Communications — Fax: (954) 769 - 2664

LANG, Edward A., III — Tel: (954) 769 - 3591
V. President, Finance and Treasurer — Fax: (954) 769 - 6407
Responsibilities include shareholder relations.

NICHOLS, Craig J. — Tel: (954) 769 - 2400
V. President, Human Resources — Fax: (954) 769 - 2664

Retail Ventures, Inc.

Formerly known as Value City Department Stores, Inc.
www.retailventuresinc.com
Annual Revenues: $2.45 billion

Chairman of the Board
SCHOTTENSTEIN, Jay L.

President and Chief Exec. Officer — Tel: (617) 348 - 7000
WILANSKY, Heywood

Main Headquarters
Mailing: 3241 Westerville Rd. — Tel: (614) 471 - 4722
Columbus, OH 43224 — Fax: (614) 478 - 2253

Public Affairs and Related Activities Personnel

At Headquarters

MCGRADY, James — Tel: (614) 478 - 2208
Chief Financial Officer — Fax: (614) 473 - 2721
Responsibilities include corporate communications and investor relations.

NORDEN, Jed L. — Tel: (614) 237 - 7100
Exec. V. President, Human Resources — Fax: (614) 238 - 5774

Revlon, Inc.

A cosmetics and personal care manufacturer.
www.revlon.com
Annual Revenues: $1.322 billion

Chairman of the Board — Tel: (212) 572 - 5000
PERELMAN, Ronald O.

President and Chief Exec. Officer — Tel: (212) 527 - 4000
STAHL, Jack L.

Main Headquarters
Mailing: 237 Park Ave. — Tel: (212) 527 - 4000
New York, NY 10017

Corporate Foundations and Giving Programs

Revlon Foundation
237 Park Ave. — Tel: (212) 527 - 4000
New York, NY 10017

Annual Grant Total: $2,000,000 - $5,000,000
Geographic Preference: Area(s) in which the company operates; National
Primary Interests: Minority Opportunities; Women's Health
Recent Recipients: Breast Cancer Coalition

Public Affairs and Related Activities Personnel

At Headquarters

FISHER, Catherine — Tel: (212) 527 - 5727
Senior V. President, Corporate Communications
catherine.fisher@revlon.com

MASSIMO, Mary — Tel: (212) 527 - 4915
Exec. V. President, Human Resources

SCEPPAGUERCIO, Maria A. — Tel: (212) 527 - 5230
Senior V. President, Investor Relations

Reynolds American Inc.

Formerly known as R. J. Reynolds Tobacco Holdings, Inc. The name change resulted from the acquistion of Brown and Williamson Tobacco Corp.'s U.S. operations by subsidiary R. J. Reynolds Tobacco Co. in July, 2004. A consumer product company traded on the NYSE.
www.reynoldsamerican.com

Chairman, President and Chief Exec. Officer — Tel: (336) 741 - 5500
IVEY, Susan — Fax: (336) 741 - 5511

Main Headquarters
Mailing: P.O. Box 2990 — Tel: (336) 741 - 5500
Winston-Salem, NC 27102 — Fax: (336) 741 - 5511
Street: 401 N. Main St.
Winston-Salem, NC 27101

Washington Office
Contact: John H. Fish
Mailing: 1201 F St. NW — Tel: (202) 626 - 7200
Suite 1000 — Fax: (202) 626 - 7208
Washington, DC 20004

Political Action Committees

R. J. Reynolds Political Action Committee
Contact: Randolph C. Tompson
P.O. Box 718 — Tel: (336) 741 - 7287
Winston-Salem, NC 27102 — Fax: (336) 741 - 1205

Contributions to Candidates: $329,500 (01/05 - 09/05)
Democrats: $43,000; Republicans: $285,500; Other: $1,000.

Principal Recipients

SENATE REPUBLICANS		HOUSE REPUBLICANS	
Allen, George (VA)	$6,000	Bonilla, Henry (TX)	$10,000
Hatch, Orrin (UT)	$5,000	DeLay, Tom (TX)	$9,500
Santorum, Richard (PA)	$5,000	Foxx, Virginia (NC)	$8,000
Burns, Conrad (MT)	$3,000	Cantor, Eric (VA)	$6,000
DeMint, James (SC)	$3,000	McHenry, Patrick (NC)	$6,000
Ensign, John Eric (NV)	$3,000	Latham, Thomas P (IA)	$5,500
		Whitfield, Ed (KY)	$5,500

Corporate Foundations and Giving Programs

R. J. Reynolds Tobacco Co. Foundation
P.O. Box 2990 — Tel: (336) 741 - 5500
Winston-Salem, NC 27102 — Fax: (336) 741 - 5511

Annual Grant Total: $2,000,000 - $5,000,000

Public Affairs and Related Activities Personnel

At Headquarters

JOHNSTON, Ann A. — Tel: (336) 741 - 5000
Exec. V. President, Human Resources

PAYNE, Maura — Tel: (336) 741 - 5000
V. President, Communications — Fax: (336) 741 - 5607
paynem@rjrt.com

PAYNE, Tommy J. — Tel: (336) 741 - 5000
Exec. V. President, External Relations — Fax: (336) 741 - 7975

STAWSBURG, Steve — Tel: (336) 741 - 5500
Foundation Contact — Fax: (336) 741 - 5511

At Washington Office

FISH, John H. — Tel: (202) 626 - 7210
V. President, Federal Government Affairs — Fax: (202) 626 - 7208
fishj@rjrt.com
(R. J. Reynolds Tobacco Co.)
Registered Federal Lobbyist.

FOREMAN, Donald D. — Tel: (202) 626 - 7200
Director, Federal Government Affairs — Fax: (202) 626 - 7208
(R. J. Reynolds Tobacco Co.)

GOMEZ, Bert — Tel: (202) 626 - 7200
Manager, Federal Government Affairs — Fax: (202) 626 - 7208
(R. J. Reynolds Tobacco Co.)

Reynolds American Inc.

* continued from previous page

At Other Offices

HOWARD, David | Tel: (336) 741 - 3489
Public Relations Representative | Fax: (336) 741 - 7220
(R. J. Reynolds Tobacco Co.)
P.O. Box 2959
Winston-Salem, NC 27102

TOMPSON, Randolph C. | Tel: (336) 741 - 7287
Senior Director, Legislative Support | Fax: (336) 741 - 1205
P.O. Box 718
Winston-Salem, NC 27102
tompsor@rjrt.com

Reynolds and Reynolds Co.

A provider of information management systems and related professional services to the automotive retail industry.

www.reyrey.com
Annual Revenues: $1 billion

Chairman of the Board
ODEEN, Philip | Tel: (937) 485 - 2000 | Fax: (937) 485 - 8980

President and Chief Exec. Officer
O'NEILL, Finbarr | Tel: (937) 485 - 2000 | Fax: (937) 485 - 1800
finbarr_oneill@reyrey.com

Main Headquarters
Mailing: One Reynolds Way, Kettering, OH 45430 | Tel: (937) 485 - 2000 | Fax: (937) 485 - 8980

Corporate Foundations and Giving Programs

Reynolds and Reynolds Co. Foundation
Contact: Alice Davisson
One Reynolds Way | Tel: (937) 485 - 8138
Kettering, OH 45430 | Fax: (937) 485 - 0941

Annual Grant Total: $500,000 - $750,000

All foundation information is available at www.reyrey.com/our_companyprofile/in_the_community/index.asp

Geographic Preference: Arizona; Area in which the company is headquartered; Maryland; North Carolina; Oklahoma; Texas; Indiana; Ohio

Primary Interests: Arts and Culture; Economic Development; K-12 Education; United Way Campaigns

Public Affairs and Related Activities Personnel

At Headquarters

BAKER, Leighann | Tel: (937) 485 - 1266
V. President, Human Resources | Fax: (937) 485 - 0975
leighann_baker@reyrey.com

DAVISSON, Alice | Tel: (937) 485 - 8138
Administrator, Reynolds Family Company Foundation | Fax: (937) 485 - 0941
alice_davisson@reyrey.com

FEIGHERY, Mark | Tel: (937) 485 - 8107
Director, Public Relations and Marketing Communications | Fax: (937) 485 - 8980
mark_feighery@reyrey.com

GUTHRIE, Paul S. | Tel: (937) 485 - 8104
V. President, Corporate Communications | Fax: (937) 485 - 8980
paul_guthrie@reyrey.com

PONITZ, Cathy | Tel: (937) 485 - 8140
Director, Community Relations | Fax: (937) 485 - 0941
catherine_ponitz@reyrey.com

Reynolds Tobacco Holdings, Inc., R. J.

See listing on page 410 under Reynolds American Inc.

RF Micro Devices, Inc.

A supplier of radio frequency integrated circuits for cellular headsets, wireless local area networks, global positioning systems, wireless technology, low power wireless, wireless infrastructure, and Bluetooth applications.

www.rfmd.com

Chairman of the Board
PALADINO, Dr. Albert E. | Tel: (336) 664 - 1233 | Fax: (336) 931 - 7454

Chief Exec. Officer
BRUGGEWORTH, Robert A. | Tel: (336) 664 - 1233 | Fax: (336) 931 - 7454

Main Headquarters
Mailing: 7628 Thorndike Rd., Greensboro, NC 27409-9421 | Tel: (336) 664 - 1233 | Fax: (336) 931 - 7454

Corporate Foundations and Giving Programs

RF Micro Devices, Inc. Corporate Contributions Program
Contact: Ralph Knupp
7628 Thorndike Rd. | Tel: (336) 664 - 1233
Greensboro, NC 27409-9421 | Fax: (336) 931 - 7454

Annual Grant Total: none reported

Public Affairs and Related Activities Personnel

At Headquarters

DELIETO, Doug | Tel: (336) 664 - 1233
V. President, Investor Relations | Fax: (336) 931 - 7454
investor@rfmd.com

GRANT, Gary J. | Tel: (336) 664 - 1233
V. President, Quality | Fax: (336) 931 - 7454

KNUPP, Ralph | Tel: (336) 664 - 1233
V. President, Human Resources | Fax: (336) 931 - 7454
Responsibilities include corporate philanthropy.

NEAL, Jerry D. | Tel: (336) 664 - 1233
Exec. V. President, Marketing and Strategic Development | Fax: (336) 931 - 7454
Responsibilities include corporate communications.

RUDY, Suzanne B. | Tel: (336) 664 - 1233
V. President and Corporate Treasurer | Fax: (336) 931 - 7454
Responsibilities include government relations.

Rhodia, Inc.

Formerly a subsidiary of Rhone-Poulenc S.A., the company was spun off in 1999. Rhodia is a specialty chemicals company developing value-added products, services and solutions in the areas of cosmetics, clothing, food, health, the environment, and industry.

www.us.rhodia.com
Annual Revenues: $6.488 billion

Main Headquarters
Mailing: 259 Prospect Plains Rd., Cranbury, NJ 08512 | Tel: (609) 860 - 4000

Political Action Committees

Rhodia, Inc. PAC
Contact: Mark A. Dahlinger
259 Prospect Plains Rd. | Tel: (609) 860 - 4000
Cranbury, NJ 08512

Contributions to Candidates: none reported (01/05 - 09/05)

Public Affairs and Related Activities Personnel

At Headquarters

DAHLINGER, Mark A. | Tel: (609) 860 - 4000
Chief Financial Officer
Responsibilities include political action.

KLUCSIK, David | Tel: (609) 860 - 3616
Director, Communications | Fax: (609) 409 - 8652

Richfood Holdings, Inc.

See listing on page 462 under Supervalu Inc.

Ricoh Corp.

A manufacturer of office equipment and cameras.

www.ricoh-usa.com
Annual Revenues: $2.8 billion

Chairman and Chief Exec. Officer
ICHIOKA, Sam | Tel: (973) 882 - 2000 | Fax: (973) 808 - 7555

Main Headquarters
Mailing: Five Dedrick Pl., West Caldwell, NJ 07006-6398 | Tel: (973) 882 - 2000 | Fax: (973) 808 - 7555

Corporate Foundations and Giving Programs

Ricoh Corporate Giving Program
Contact: Russell Marchetta
Five Dedrick Pl. | Tel: (973) 882 - 2075
West Caldwell, NJ 07006-6398 | Fax: (973) 882 - 2506

Annual Grant Total: none reported

Public Affairs and Related Activities Personnel

At Headquarters

MARCHETTA, Russell | Tel: (973) 882 - 2075
Manager, Public Relations | Fax: (973) 882 - 2506
russell.marchetta@ricoh-usa.com
Responsibilities include corporate philanthropy.

PATSKY, Deborah | Tel: (973) 882 - 2000
V. President, Human Resources | Fax: (973) 808 - 7555

Rite Aid Corp.

A chain of drugstores.

www.riteaid.com
Annual Revenues: $15.171 billion

Chairman of the Board
MILLER, Robert G. | Tel: (717) 761 - 2633

Rite Aid Corp.

* continued from previous page

President and Chief Exec. Officer Tel: (717) 761 - 2633
SAMMONS, Mary

Main Headquarters
Mailing: P.O. Box 3165 Tel: (717) 761 - 2633
Harrisburg, PA 17105
Street: 30 Hunter Lane
Camp Hill, PA 17011-2404

Political Action Committees

Rite Aid PAC
Contact: James E. Krahulec
P.O. Box 3165 Tel: (717) 975 - 5710
Harrisburg, PA 17105 Fax: (717) 975 - 3760

Contributions to Candidates: $2,500 (01/05 - 09/05)
Republicans: $2,500.

Principal Recipients

SENATE REPUBLICANS	HOUSE REPUBLICANS	
	Deal, Nathan (GA)	$2,500

Corporate Foundations and Giving Programs

Rite Aid Corporate Contributions Program
Contact: Gayle Rife
P.O. Box 3165 Tel: (717) 972 - 3940
Harrisburg, PA 17105 Fax: (717) 731 - 4737

Annual Grant Total: none reported
Primary Interests: Drug Abuse Prevention; Health; Poison Prevention
Recent Recipients: Children's Miracle Network

Rite Aid Foundation
P.O. Box 3165 Tel: (717) 761 - 2633
Harrisburg, PA 17105

Annual Grant Total: none reported
Geographic Preference: Area(s) in which the company operates
Primary Interests: Families; Health; Women

Public Affairs and Related Activities Personnel

At Headquarters

COOK, Jody Tel: (717) 731 - 6566
Manager, Public Relations

HART, Janet Tel: (717) 975 - 5758
Manager, Government Affairs Fax: (717) 975 - 3760

KRAHULEC, James E. Tel: (717) 975 - 5710
V. President, Government and Trade Relations Fax: (717) 975 - 3760

MCCARTY, Todd Tel: (717) 761 - 2633
Senior V. President, Human Resources

RIFE, Gayle Tel: (717) 972 - 3940
Coordinator, Contributions Fax: (717) 731 - 4737

RUGEN, Karen Tel: (717) 730 - 7766
Senior V. President, Corporate Communications and Public Affairs Fax: (717) 731 - 4737

TWOMEY, Kevin Tel: (717) 761 - 2633
Senior V. President and Chief Financial Officer
Responsibilities include investor relations.

Robert Half International Inc.

A provider of specialized staffing services. Markets served include accounting, finance, administration, information technology, law, marketing, and web design.
www.rhi.com
Annual Revenues: $2.7 billion

Chairman and Chief Exec. Officer Tel: (650) 234 - 6000
MESSMER, Harold M., Jr. Fax: (650) 234 - 6999

Main Headquarters
Mailing: 2884 Sand Hill Rd. Tel: (650) 234 - 6000
Suite 200 Fax: (650) 234 - 6999
Menlo Park, CA 94025

Public Affairs and Related Activities Personnel

At Headquarters

STATEN, Reesa M. Tel: (650) 234 - 6242
V. President, Corporate Communications Fax: (650) 234 - 6998

WADDELL, M. Keith Tel: (650) 234 - 6000
V. Chairman and Chief Financial Officer Fax: (650) 234 - 6999
Responsibilities include investor relations.

C.H. Robinson Worldwide, Inc.

A global provider of transportation services and logistics solutions. Sources and distributes fresh produce and food ingredients.
www.chrobinson.com
Annual Revenues: $4.3 billion

Chairman of the Board Tel: (952) 937 - 8500
VERDOORN, D. R. "Sid" Fax: (952) 937 - 6740

Chief Exec. Officer Tel: (952) 937 - 8500
WEIHOFF, John P. Fax: (952) 937 - 6740

Main Headquarters
Mailing: 8100 Mitchell Rd. Tel: (952) 937 - 8500
Eden Prairie, MN 55344 Fax: (952) 937 - 6740

Public Affairs and Related Activities Personnel

At Headquarters

FREEMAN, Angie Tel: (952) 937 - 7847
Director, Investor Relations and Marketing Communications Fax: (952) 937 - 6740
angie.freeman@chrobinson.com

GILLUND, Laura Tel: (952) 937 - 8500
V. President, Human Resources Fax: (952) 937 - 6740

LINDBLOOM, Chad M. Tel: (952) 937 - 7779
V. President and Chief Financial Officer Fax: (952) 937 - 6740
Responsibilities include investor relations.

MULVEHILL, Joseph J. Tel: (952) 937 - 8500
V. President, International Fax: (952) 937 - 6740
mulvjoe@chrobinson.com

Rochester Gas and Electric Corp. (RG&E)

See listing on page 181 under Energy East Corp.

Rockland Electric Co.

See listing on page 364 under Orange and Rockland Utilities, Inc.

Rockwell Automation

A global provider of industrial automation power, control and information solutions. Also provides contact management technologies and applications. Spun off it's subsidiary Rockwell Collins (see separate listing) in 2001 and changed its name from Rockwell Internat'l Corp. to Rockwell Automation.
www.rockwellautomation.com

Chairman and Chief Exec. Officer Tel: (414) 382 - 2000
NOSBUSCH, Keith Fax: (414) 382 - 4444

Main Headquarters
Mailing: 1201 S. Second St. Tel: (414) 382 - 2000
Milwaukee, WI 43204-2496 Fax: (414) 382 - 4444

Washington Office
Mailing: Commonwealth Towers Tel: (703) 516 - 8224
1300 Wilson Blvd., Suite 200 Fax: (703) 516 - 8284
Arlington, VA 22209-2307

Corporate Foundations and Giving Programs

Rockwell Internat'l Corp. Trust
Contact: Eileen M. Walter
1201 S. Second St. Tel: (414) 382 - 1548
Milwaukee, WI 43204-2496 Fax: (414) 382 - 1442

Annual Grant Total: $2,000,000 - $5,000,000
Geographic Preference: Area(s) in which the company operates
Primary Interests: Arts and Humanities; Civic and Public Affairs; Education; Health and Human Services; Math and Science; Youth Services
Recent Recipients: Nat'l Merit Scholarship; United Performing Arts Fund; United Way

Public Affairs and Related Activities Personnel

At Headquarters

COHN, John D. Tel: (414) 382 - 2000
Senior V. President, Strategic Development and Communications Fax: (414) 382 - 4444

GONRING, Matthew P. Tel: (414) 382 - 5575
V. President, Global Marketing and Communications Fax: (414) 382 - 4444
mpgonring@corp.rockwell.com

HALL, Mary Jane Tel: (414) 382 - 2000
Senior V. President, Human Resources Fax: (414) 382 - 4444

WALTER, Eileen M. Tel: (414) 382 - 1548
Global Community Relations Fax: (414) 382 - 1442
Responsibilities include corporate philanthropy.

YOUNG, Mary Lou Tel: (414) 382 - 2000
Director, State and Community Relations Fax: (414) 382 - 4444

At Washington Office

COGDELL, Martha L. Tel: (703) 516 - 8227
Director, Federal and State Government Relations Fax: (703) 516 - 8295
mlcogdel@collins.rockwell.com
Registered Federal Lobbyist.

MCDONALD, Michael K. Tel: (703) 516 - 8230
mkmcdona@collins.rockwell.com Fax: (703) 516 - 8298
Registered Federal Lobbyist.

Rockwell Automation

* continued from previous page

SADLER, Linda C. — Tel: (703) 516 - 8228; Fax: (703) 516 - 8295
Registered Federal Lobbyist.

Rockwell Collins, Inc

A member of the Public Affairs Council. Spun off from Rockwell Internat'l Corp. (see Rockwell Automation) and became a separate company in 2001.
www.rockwellcollins.com
Annual Revenues: $2.874 billion

Chairman, President and Chief Exec. Officer
JONES, Clayton M. — Tel: (319) 295 - 1000; Fax: (319) 295 - 5429

Main Headquarters
Mailing: 400 Collins Rd. NE, Cedar Rapids, IA 52498 — Tel: (319) 295 - 1000; Fax: (319) 295 - 5429

Washington Office
Mailing: Commonwealth Towers, 1300 Wilson Blvd., Suite 200, Arlington, VA 22209-2307 — Tel: (703) 516 - 8220; Fax: (703) 516 - 8295

Political Action Committees

Rockwell Collins Inc. Good Government Committee
Contact: Timothy A. Peterson
Commonwealth Towers
1300 Wilson Blvd., Suite 200
Arlington, VA 22209-2307
Tel: (703) 516 - 8220; Fax: (703) 516 - 8295

Contributions to Candidates: $17,500 (01/05 - 09/05)
Democrats: $8,000; Republicans: $9,500.

Principal Recipients

SENATE DEMOCRATS

HOUSE DEMOCRATS
Boswell, Leonard (IA) $1,000
Honda, Mike (CA) $1,000
Skelton, Ike (MO) $1,000
Taylor, Gene Mr. (MS) $1,000

SENATE REPUBLICANS

HOUSE REPUBLICANS
Cunningham, Duke (CA) $1,000
Hunter, Duncan (CA) $1,000
Lewis, Jerry (CA) $1,000
Weldon, Curt (PA) $1,000

Corporate Foundations and Giving Programs

Rockwell Collins Charitable Corporation and Rockwell Collins Community Partnership Fund
Contact: Cindy Dietz
400 Collins Rd. NE
Cedar Rapids, IA 52498
Tel: (319) 295 - 7444; Fax: (319) 295 - 9374

Annual Grant Total: none reported
Primary Interests: Arts and Culture; Civic and Cultural Activities; Education; Youth Services

Public Affairs and Related Activities Personnel

At Headquarters

CROOKSHANK, Dan — Investor Relations Contact — Tel: (319) 295 - 7575; Fax: (319) 295 - 5429

DIETZ, Cindy — Manager, Community Relations — Tel: (319) 295 - 7444; Fax: (319) 295 - 9374

HOBSON, Tom — Manager, Government Relations — Tel: (319) 295 - 1000; Fax: (319) 295 - 5429

WELSH, Nancy K. — Media Relations Contact — nkwelsh@rockwellcollins.com — Tel: (319) 295 - 2123; Fax: (319) 295 - 5429

At Washington Office

COGDELL, Martha L. — Government Relations — Tel: (703) 516 - 8220; Fax: (703) 516 - 8295
Registered Federal Lobbyist.

GAISFORD, Lisa A. — Tel: (703) 516 - 8220; Fax: (703) 516 - 8295
Registered Federal Lobbyist.

GIFFT, John — Manager, Govermental and Regulatory Affairs — Tel: (703) 516 - 8220; Fax: (703) 516 - 8295

MCDONALD, Michael K. — V. President, Government Operations — mkmcdona@collins.rockwell.com — Tel: (703) 516 - 8220; Fax: (703) 516 - 8298
Registered Federal Lobbyist.

PETERSON, Timothy A. — Director, Congressional Relations-Government Programs — Tel: (703) 516 - 8220; Fax: (703) 516 - 8295
Registered Federal Lobbyist.

SADLER, Linda C. — Director, Governmental and Regulatory Affairs — lcsadler@collins.rockwell.com — Tel: (703) 516 - 8220; Fax: (703) 516 - 8295
Registered Federal Lobbyist.

Rohm and Haas Co.

A member of the Public Affairs Council. A manufacturer of specialty chemicals, plastics, electronic materials and salt. Acquired Morton Internat'l, Inc. in 1999.
www.rohmhaas.com

Chairman, Chief Exec. Officer, and President
GUPTA, Raj L. — Tel: (215) 592 - 3000; Fax: (215) 592 - 3377

Main Headquarters
Mailing: 100 Independence Mall West, Philadelphia, PA 19106-2399 — Tel: (215) 592 - 3000; Fax: (215) 592 - 3377
Street: Sixth and Market Sts., Philadelphia, PA 19106-2399

Washington Office
Contact: Geoffrey B. Hurwitz
Mailing: 1300 Wilson Blvd., Arlington, VA 22209 — Tel: (703) 741 - 5880; Fax: (703) 741 - 5884

Political Action Committees

Rohm and Haas Co. Employees Ass'n for Better Government
Contact: Colleen A. Johnson
100 Independence Mall West
Philadelphia, PA 19106-2399
Tel: (215) 592 - 3000; Fax: (215) 592 - 3377

Contributions to Candidates: $4,000 (01/05 - 09/05)
Democrats: $1,000; Republicans: $3,000.

Principal Recipients

SENATE DEMOCRATS

HOUSE DEMOCRATS
Andrews, Robert (NJ) $1,000

SENATE REPUBLICANS
Alexander, Lamar (TN) $1,000

HOUSE REPUBLICANS
Northup, Anne M. (KY) $1,000
Weller, Jerry (IL) $1,000

Corporate Foundations and Giving Programs

Rohm and Haas Corporate Social Investment
Contact: Alexandra Samuels
100 Independence Mall West
Philadelphia, PA 19106-2399
Tel: (215) 592 - 3644; Fax: (215) 592 - 6808

Annual Grant Total: $2,000,000 - $5,000,000
Prefers to support discreet programs and projects. Requests for grants must be made in writing. The company encourages employee involvement in community organizations and has a matching gifts program.
Geographic Preference: Area(s) in which the company operates; California; Connecticut; Delaware; Illinois; Kentucky; Massachusetts; North Carolina; Pennsylvania; Texas
Primary Interests: Arts and Culture; Community Affairs; Health and Human Services; Higher Education

Public Affairs and Related Activities Personnel

At Headquarters

BOCHANSKI, George V., Jr. — Manager, Internal Communications — Tel: (215) 592 - 3248; Fax: (215) 592 - 6808

HADDEN, Laura L. — Manager, Marketing Communications — Tel: (215) 592 - 3054; Fax: (215) 592 - 6808

JOHNSON, Colleen A. — PAC Treasurer — Tel: (215) 592 - 3000; Fax: (215) 592 - 3377

LEWIS, Philip G. — V. President and Director, Environmental Health and Safety — Tel: (215) 785 - 7421; Fax: (215) 592 - 3377

LONERGAN, Robert — V. President, General Counsel; Secretary — Tel: (215) 592 - 3000; Fax: (215) 592 - 3377
Responsibilities include regulatory and environmental affairs.

MCKEOGH, John F. — V. President, Public Affairs — Tel: (215) 592 - 2740; Fax: (215) 592 - 3738

MCPEAK, Brian — Director, Corporate Communications — Tel: (215) 592 - 2741; Fax: (215) 592 - 6808

O'BRIEN, Gary — Director, Investor Relations — Tel: (215) 592 - 3409; Fax: (215) 592 - 3377

SAMUELS, Alexandra — Manager, Rohm and Haas Corporate Social Investment — Tel: (215) 592 - 3644; Fax: (215) 592 - 6808

WILLIAMS, Richard — Manager, Financial Communications — Tel: (215) 592 - 2409; Fax: (215) 592 - 6808

WILMS, Anne M. — V. President, Chief Information Officer, and Director, Human Resources — Tel: (215) 592 - 3000; Fax: (215) 592 - 3377

At Washington Office

HURWITZ, Geoffrey B. — Director, Government Relations — Tel: (703) 741 - 5881; Fax: (703) 741 - 5884
Registered Federal Lobbyist.

Rohm and Haas Co.

** continued from previous page*

WILLIAMS, Robin L. — Tel: (703) 741 - 5880
Director, State Government Relations — Fax: (703) 741 - 5884
Registered Federal Lobbyist.

At Other Offices

BEERHALTER, Danielle — Tel: (215) 641 - 7876
Manager, Public Affairs
727 Norristown Rd.
Springhouse, PA 19477
dbeerhalter@rohmhaas.com

CLARK, Charles A. — Tel: (615) 521 - 8443
Human Resources Director
P.O. Box 591
Knoxville, TN 37919

HICKS, Daniel J. — Tel: (502) 448 - 5200
Manager, Public Affairs
(Rohm and Haas Kentucky Inc.)
P.O. Box 32260
Louisville, KY 40232

MILLER, Christine M. — Tel: (713) 476 - 8109
Manager, Public Affairs
(Rohm and Haas Texas Inc.)
P.O. Box 672
Deer Park, TX 77536

Rohm and Haas Kentucky Inc.

See listing on page 413 under Rohm and Haas Co.

Rohm and Haas Texas Inc.

See listing on page 413 under Rohm and Haas Co.

Rohr, Inc.

See listing on page 223 under Goodrich Corp - Aerostructures.

Rollins, Inc.

A service company engaged in pest control.
www.rollins.com
Annual Revenues: $652.3 million

Chairman of the Board — Tel: (404) 888 - 2000
ROLLINS, R. Randall

Chief Exec. Officer, President and Chief Operating Officer — Tel: (404) 888 - 2000
ROLLINS, Gary

Main Headquarters
Mailing: 2170 Piedmont Road, N.E. — Tel: (404) 888 - 2000
Atlanta, GA 30324

Political Action Committees

Orkin Exterminating Co., Inc. PAC
Contact: Tom Diederich
2170 Piedmont Road, N.E. — Tel: (404) 888 - 2874
Atlanta, GA 30324

Contributions to Candidates: $1,000 (01/05 - 09/05)
Republicans: $1,000.

Principal Recipients

SENATE REPUBLICANS		HOUSE REPUBLICANS	
		DeLay, Tom (TX)	$1,000

Corporate Foundations and Giving Programs

Rollins Corporate Giving Program
2170 Piedmont Road, N.E. — Tel: (404) 888 - 2000
Atlanta, GA 30324

Annual Grant Total: none reported

Public Affairs and Related Activities Personnel

At Headquarters

CRAFT, Martha — Tel: (404) 888 - 2000
Director, Public Relations

DIEDERICH, Tom — Tel: (404) 888 - 2874
V. President, Government Relations

Rolls-Royce North America Inc.

The American management company for Rolls-Royce assets in North America, with particular emphasis on gas turbine technology for aerospace, marine, and industrial applications
www.rolls-royce.com

President and Chief Exec. Officer — Tel: (703) 834 - 1700
GUYETTE, James M. — Fax: (703) 709 - 6086

Main Headquarters
Mailing: 14850 Conference Center Dr. — Tel: (703) 834 - 1700
Chantilly, VA 20151 — Fax: (703) 709 - 6087

Political Action Committees

Rolls-Royce North America PAC
Contact: Kenneth E. Patterson
14850 Conference Center Dr. — Tel: (703) 834 - 1700
Chantilly, VA 20151 — Fax: (703) 709 - 6086

Contributions to Candidates: $59,500 (01/05 - 09/05)
Democrats: $19,000; Republicans: $40,500.

Principal Recipients

SENATE DEMOCRATS		HOUSE DEMOCRATS	
Baucus, Max (MT)	$2,000	Visclosky, Peter (IN)	$3,000
		Mollohan, Alan (WV)	$2,000
		Skelton, Ike (MO)	$2,000
SENATE REPUBLICANS		**HOUSE REPUBLICANS**	
Burns, Conrad (MT)	$3,000	Hastert, Dennis J. (IL)	$5,000
Lott, Trent (MS)	$3,000	Hunter, Duncan (CA)	$3,000
Allen, George (VA)	$2,000	Blunt, Roy (MO)	$2,000

Corporate Foundations and Giving Programs

Rolls Royce Corporate Contributions Program
Contact: Kenneth E. Patterson
14850 Conference Center Dr. — Tel: (703) 834 - 1700
Chantilly, VA 20151 — Fax: (703) 709 - 6086

Annual Grant Total: none reported

Public Affairs and Related Activities Personnel

At Headquarters

BERGSMAN, Michael — Tel: (703) 834 - 1700
Fax: (703) 709 - 6087

GILL, James W. — Tel: (703) 834 - 1700
Exec. V. President, Human Resources — Fax: (703) 709 - 6087

LARSON, Erik — Tel: (703) 407 - 5720
Manager, Communications and Planning — Fax: (703) 621 - 9140

MCINERNEY, Anne — Tel: (703) 621 - 2871
Director, Legislative Affairs — Fax: (703) 709 - 6086
anne.mcinerney@rolls-royce.com

PATTERSON, Kenneth E. — Tel: (703) 834 - 1700
Corporate Financial Controller — Fax: (703) 709 - 6086
ken.patterson@rolls-royce.com
Responsibilities include corporate philanthropy.

PEASE, Edward A. — Tel: (703) 621 - 2797
Senior V. President, Government Relations — Fax: (703) 621 - 4989

WALTON, Mia K. — Tel: (703) 621 - 2709
V. President, Corporate Communications — Fax: (703) 709 - 6086
mia.walton@rolls-royce.com

Roseburg Forest Products Co.

www.rfpco.com

Chairman, President and Chief Exec. Officer — Tel: (541) 679 - 3311
FORD, Allyn — Fax: (541) 679 - 9543
TF: (800) 245 - 1115

Main Headquarters
Mailing: P.O. Box 1088 — Tel: (541) 679 - 3311
Roseburg, OR 97470-0252 — Fax: (541) 679 - 9543
TF: (800) 245 - 1115

Corporate Foundations and Giving Programs

Roseburg Forest Products Co. Contributions
P.O. Box 1088 — Tel: (541) 679 - 3311
Roseburg, OR 97470-0252 — Fax: (541) 679 - 9543
TF: (800) 245 - 1115

Annual Grant Total: $2,000,000 - $5,000,000
Recent recipients: Oregon Independent College Foundation, Linfield College, Community Cancer Foundation, Oregon Museum of Science and Industry
Geographic Preference: Area in which the company is headquartered; Area(s) in which the company operates; California; Oregon
Primary Interests: Education; Math and Science

Public Affairs and Related Activities Personnel

At Headquarters

KIMMEL, Max — Tel: (541) 679 - 3311
Manager, Environmental Affairs — Fax: (541) 679 - 9543
TF: (800) 245 - 1115

SNOW, Hank — Tel: (541) 679 - 3311
V. President, Human Resources — Fax: (541) 679 - 2646
TF: (800) 245 - 1115

Ross Environmental Services, Inc.

A privately-owned hazardous waste management company.
www.rossenvironmental.com

Chairman and Chief Exec. Officer — Tel: (440) 366 - 2000
CROMLING, Maureen M.
mcromling@rossenvironmental.com

Main Headquarters
Mailing: 150 Innovation Dr. — Tel: (440) 366 - 2000
Elyria, OH 44035

Ross Environmental Services, Inc.

* continued from previous page

Corporate Foundations and Giving Programs

Ross Foundation
Contact: Margaret Kelch
35716 Royalton Rd. — Tel: (440) 366 - 2000
Grafton, OH 44044 — Fax: (440) 748 - 2200

Assets: $13,000 (1999)
Annual Grant Total: under $100,000
Geographic Preference: Area(s) in which the company operates; Ohio
Primary Interests: K-12 Education

Public Affairs and Related Activities Personnel

At Headquarters

HARGATE, Arthur — Tel: (440) 366 - 2000
V. President, Finance and Administration
ahargate@rossenvironmental.com
Responsibilities include government affairs.

At Other Offices

KELCH, Margaret — Tel: (440) 366 - 2000
Manager, Community Relations — Fax: (440) 748 - 2200
35716 Royalton Rd.
Grafton, OH 44044
mkelch@rossenvironmental.com

Ross Products Division

See listing on page 3 under Abbott Laboratories.

Ross Stores, Inc.

A retailer of clothing, shoes, home accents, fragrances, and accessories.
www.rossstores.com

Chairman of the Board — Tel: (510) 505 - 4400
FERBER, Norman A. — TF: (800) 945 - 7677

V. Chairman and Chief Exec. Officer — Tel: (510) 505 - 4400
BALMUTH, Michael — TF: (800) 945 - 7677

Main Headquarters
Mailing: 4440 Rosewood Dr. — Tel: (510) 505 - 4400
Pleasanton, CA 94588 — TF: (800) 945 - 7677

Public Affairs and Related Activities Personnel

At Headquarters

ASKANAS, Mark S. — Tel: (510) 505 - 4400
Senior V. President, Human Resources and General Counsel — TF: (800) 945 - 7677

LOUGHNOT, Katie — Tel: (925) 965 - 4509
V. President, Investor and Media Relations — TF: (800) 945 - 7677
katie.loughnot@ros.com

Roto Rooter, Inc.

See listing on page 113 under The Chemed Corporation.

Rowan Companies, Inc.

A provider of oilwell drilling, aviation and manufacturing services primarily to the petroleum industry.
www.rowancompanies.com

V. Chairman and Chief Adminstrative Officer — Tel: (713) 621 - 7800
CROYLE, Robert — Fax: (713) 960 - 7560

Chairman, President and Chief Exec. Officer — Tel: (713) 621 - 7800
MCNEASE, D. F. — Fax: (713) 960 - 7560

Main Headquarters
Mailing: 2800 Post Oak Blvd., Suite 5450 — Tel: (713) 621 - 7800
Houston, TX 77056-6196 — Fax: (713) 960 - 7560

Corporate Foundations and Giving Programs

Rowan Companies Corporate Contributions Program
Contact: E. E. Thiele
2800 Post Oak Blvd., Suite 5450 — Tel: (713) 621 - 7800
Houston, TX 77056-6196 — Fax: (713) 960 - 7560

Annual Grant Total: none reported

Public Affairs and Related Activities Personnel

At Headquarters

BUVENS, John L. — Tel: (713) 621 - 7800
V. President, Legal — Fax: (713) 960 - 7560

PROVINE, William C. — Tel: (713) 960 - 7575
V. President, Investor Relations — Fax: (713) 960 - 7560

THIELE, E. E. — Tel: (713) 621 - 7800
Senior V. President, Finance, Administration and Treasurer — Fax: (713) 960 - 7560
Responsibilities include corporate philanthropy.

Royal & SunAlliance USA Inc.

An insurance holding company.
www.royalsunalliance-usa.com
Annual Revenues: $3.051 billion

President and Chief Exec. Officer — Tel: (704) 522 - 2000
TIGHE, John — Fax: (704) 522 - 2055

Main Headquarters
Mailing: P.O. Box 1000 — Tel: (704) 522 - 2000
Charlotte, NC 28201-1000 — Fax: (704) 522 - 2055
Street: 9300 Arrow Point Blvd.
Charlotte, NC 28273-8135

Political Action Committees

Royal Indemnity Co. Voluntary PAC
Contact: Jeff Klein
P.O. Box 1000 — Tel: (704) 522 - 2000
Charlotte, NC 28201-1000 — Fax: (704) 522 - 2055

Contributions to Candidates: none reported (01/05 - 09/05)

Corporate Foundations and Giving Programs

The Royal & SunAlliance Insurance Foundation, Inc.
Contact: Elizabeth J. McLaughlin
P.O. Box 1000 — Tel: (704) 522 - 3064
Charlotte, NC 28201-1000 — Fax: (704) 522 - 2055

Annual Grant Total: $100,000 - $200,000
Geographic Preference: Area(s) in which the company operates
Primary Interests: Arts and Culture; Education; Health and Human Services

Public Affairs and Related Activities Personnel

At Headquarters

DIXON, Bob — Tel: (704) 522 - 2000
Senior Human Resources Officer — Fax: (704) 522 - 2055

KLEIN, Jeff — Tel: (704) 522 - 2000
PAC Contact — Fax: (704) 522 - 2055

MCLAUGHLIN, Elizabeth J. — Tel: (704) 522 - 3064
V. President, Corporate Communications and Corporate Citizenship — Fax: (704) 522 - 2055

Royal Caribbean Internat'l

A passenger cruiseline.
www.royalcaribbean.com
Annual Revenues: $3.434 billion

Chairman and Chief Exec. Officer — Tel: (305) 539 - 6000
FAIN, Richard D. — Fax: (305) 375 - 0711

Main Headquarters
Mailing: 1050 Caribbean Way — Tel: (305) 539 - 6000
Miami, FL 33132-3203 — Fax: (305) 375 - 0711

Public Affairs and Related Activities Personnel

At Headquarters

MARTENSTEIN, Lynn — Tel: (305) 539 - 6000
V. President, Corporate Communications — Fax: (305) 375 - 0711

MATHEWS, Dan — Tel: (305) 539 - 6153
Manager, Investor Relations — Fax: (305) 539 - 0562

MURRILL, Tom — Tel: (305) 539 - 6000
Chief Officer, Human Resources — Fax: (305) 375 - 0711

Royster-Clark, Inc.

A fertilizer manufacturer.
www.roysterclark.com
Annual Revenues: $898.1 million

Chairman and Chief Exec. Officer — Tel: (212) 332 - 2965
JENKINS, Francis P. — Fax: (212) 332 - 2999
fjenkins@roysterclark.com

Main Headquarters
Mailing: 1251 Ave. of the Americas, Suite 900 — Tel: (212) 332 - 2965
New York, NY 10020 — Fax: (212) 332 - 2999

Public Affairs and Related Activities Personnel

At Other Offices

MURPHY, Paul M. — Tel: (757) 222 - 9513
Director, Public Relations
999 Waterside Dr.
Eighth Floor
Norfolk, VA 23510
pmmurphy@roysterclark.com

RPM Internat'l Inc.

An industrial coatings manufacturer.
www.rpminc.com
Annual Revenues: $2 billion

Chairman of the Board
SULLIVAN, Thomas C. — Tel: (330) 273 - 5090 Fax: (330) 225 - 8743

President and Chief Exec. Officer
SULLIVAN, Frank C. — Tel: (330) 273 - 5090 Fax: (330) 225 - 8743

Main Headquarters
Mailing: P.O. Box 777, Medina, OH 44258 — Tel: (330) 273 - 5090 Fax: (330) 225 - 8743
Street: 2628 Pearl Rd., Medina, OH 44258

Corporate Foundations and Giving Programs

RPM Internat'l Inc. Corporate Contributions Program
Contact: Randell McShepard
P.O. Box 777
Medina, OH 44258 — Tel: (330) 273 - 8857 Fax: (330) 225 - 8743

Annual Grant Total: none reported

Public Affairs and Related Activities Personnel

At Headquarters

FINN, Dennis F.
V. President, Environmental and Regulatory Affairs — Tel: (330) 273 - 8847 Fax: (330) 225 - 8743

HASMAN, Glenn R.
V. President, Finance and Communications — Tel: (330) 273 - 8820 Fax: (330) 225 - 8743
ghasman@rpminc.com
Responsibilities include investor relations.

MCSHEPARD, Randell
Contributions Contact — Tel: (330) 273 - 8857 Fax: (330) 225 - 8743

ROGERS, Kathie M.
Manager, Investor Relations — Tel: (330) 776 - 4488 Fax: (330) 220 - 8636

The RTM Restaurant Group

Operates restaurants under the Arby's Roast Beef and Mrs. Winners Chicken & Biscuits names.
www.rtminc.com
Annual Revenues: $857 million

Chairman of the Board
COOPER, Dennis — Tel: (404) 256 - 4900 Fax: (404) 256 - 7277

Chief Exec. Officer
UMPHENOUR, Russell, Jr. — Tel: (404) 256 - 4900 Fax: (404) 256 - 7277

Main Headquarters
Mailing: 5995 Barfield Rd., Atlanta, GA 30328 — Tel: (404) 256 - 4900 Fax: (404) 256 - 7277

Public Affairs and Related Activities Personnel

At Headquarters

GRAY, John
Senior V. President, Corporate Communications and Public Relations — Tel: (404) 256 - 4900 Fax: (404) 256 - 7277

STRAIT, Melissa
Senior V. President, Human Resources Training and Development — Tel: (404) 256 - 4900 Fax: (404) 256 - 7277

Ruddick Corp.

A holding company with operating subsidiaries active in supermarkets and industrial sewing thread. Two major wholly-owned subsidiaries include, Harris Teeter, Inc. and American & Efird, Inc.
www.ruddickcorp.com
Annual Revenues: $2.7 billion

Chairman of the Board
DICKSON, Alan T. — Tel: (704) 372 - 5404 Fax: (704) 372 - 6409

President and Chief Exec. Officer
DICKSON, Thomas W. — Tel: (704) 372 - 5404 Fax: (704) 372 - 6409

Main Headquarters
Mailing: 301 S. Tryon St., Suite 1800, Charlotte, NC 28202 — Tel: (704) 372 - 5404 Fax: (704) 372 - 6409

Public Affairs and Related Activities Personnel

At Headquarters

WOODLEF, John B.
V. President, Finance and Chief Financial Officer — Tel: (704) 372 - 5404 Fax: (704) 372 - 6409
Responsibilities include investor relations.

Rural Metro Corp.

Provides ambulance and emergency services throughout North and South America.
www.ruralmetro.com
Annual Revenues: $497 million

Chairman of the Board
CLEMENT, Cor J. — Tel: (480) 994 - 3886 Fax: (480) 606 - 3328 TF: (800) 421 - 5718

President and Chief Exec. Officer
BRUCKER, Jack E. — Tel: (480) 994 - 3886 Fax: (480) 606 - 3328 TF: (800) 421 - 5718

Main Headquarters
Mailing: P.O. Drawer F, Scottsdale, AZ 85252 — Tel: (480) 994 - 3886 Fax: (480) 606 - 3328 TF: (800) 421 - 5718
Street: 8401 E. Indian School Rd., Scottsdale, AZ 85251

Public Affairs and Related Activities Personnel

At Headquarters

MERRITT, Liz
Director, Public Relations — Tel: (480) 660 - 3337 Fax: (480) 606 - 3328 TF: (800) 421 - 5718

Russell Corp.

A designer, manufacturer and marketer of activewear, casualwear, athletic uniforms, and sports equipment.
www.russellcorp.com
Annual Revenues: $1.164 billion

Chairman and Chief Exec. Officer
WARD, John F. "Jack" — Tel: (678) 742 - 8000

Main Headquarters
Mailing: 3330 Cumberland Blvd., Suite 800, Atlanta, GA 30339 — Tel: (678) 742 - 8000

Political Action Committees

Russell Corp. PAC
Contact: Larry E. Workman
P.O. Box 272
Alexander City, AL 35011

Contributions to Candidates: $5,500 (01/05 - 09/05)
Democrats: $1,000; Republicans: $4,500.

Principal Recipients

SENATE DEMOCRATS
Nelson, Benjamin (NE) $1,000

HOUSE DEMOCRATS

SENATE REPUBLICANS
Isakson, John (GA) $1,000

HOUSE REPUBLICANS
Everett, Terry (AL) $1,500
Price, Thomas (GA) $1,000
Rogers, Michael (AL) $1,000

Corporate Foundations and Giving Programs

Russell Corp. Corporate Giving Program
Contact: Nancy N. Young
3330 Cumberland Blvd.
Suite 800
Atlanta, GA 30339 — Tel: (678) 742 - 8118 Fax: (678) 742 - 8514

Annual Grant Total: none reported

Public Affairs and Related Activities Personnel

At Headquarters

CHAMPION, Christopher M.
Associate Counsel and Director, Government Relations and Assistant Secretary — Tel: (678) 742 - 8000
championchris@russellcorp.com

FLOWERS, Edsel W.
Senior V. President, Human Resources — Tel: (678) 742 - 8000

HOLLIDAY, Roger
V. President, Investor Relations — Tel: (678) 742 - 8000
hollidayroger@russellcorp.com

YOUNG, Nancy N.
V. President, Communications and Community Relations — Tel: (678) 742 - 8118 Fax: (678) 742 - 8514
youngnancy@russellcorp.com

At Other Offices

WORKMAN, Larry E.
Treasurer, Russell Corp. PAC
P.O. Box 272
Alexander City, AL 35011

Ryder System, Inc.

Provides logistics and transportation services.
www.ryder.com
Annual Revenues: $5.006 billion

Chairman, President and Chief Exec. Officer
SWIENTON, Gregory T. — Tel: (305) 500 - 4440 Fax: (305) 500 - 4490
gregory_swienton@ryder.com

Main Headquarters
Mailing: 11690 Northwest 105 St., Miami, FL 33178 — Tel: (305) 500 - 3726 Fax: (305) 500 - 4129

Ryder System, Inc.

** continued from previous page*

Political Action Committees

Ryder Employees Political Action Committee
Contact: Kathleen S. Partridge
11690 Northwest 105 St. — Tel: (305) 500 - 3726
Miami, FL 33178 — Fax: (305) 500 - 4129

Contributions to Candidates: $12,000 (01/05 - 09/05)
Democrats: $6,000; Republicans: $6,000.

Principal Recipients

SENATE DEMOCRATS		HOUSE DEMOCRATS	
Baucus, Max (MT)	$5,000	Boucher, Fredrick (VA)	$1,000
SENATE REPUBLICANS		**HOUSE REPUBLICANS**	
		Graves, Sam (MO)	$5,000
		Hastert, Dennis J. (IL)	$1,000

Corporate Foundations and Giving Programs

Ryder System Charitable Foundation, Inc.
11690 Northwest 105 St. — Tel: (305) 500 - 3726
Miami, FL 33178 — Fax: (305) 500 - 4129

Annual Grant Total: $200,000 - $300,000
Annual grant total in 2002 was over $1 million.
Geographic Preference: Area in which the company is headquartered; Area(s) in which the company operates
Primary Interests: Civic and Cultural Activities; Education; Health and Human Services

Public Affairs and Related Activities Personnel

At Headquarters

BRUCE, David — Tel: (305) 500 - 4999
Group Director, Corporate Communications — Fax: (305) 500 - 3203
david_bruce@ryder.com

BRUMFIELD, Lisa — Tel: (305) 500 - 3668
Senior Manager, Corporate Communications
lisa_brumfield@ryder.com

PARTRIDGE, Kathleen S. — Tel: (305) 500 - 3726
Treasurer, Ryder Employees PAC — Fax: (305) 500 - 4129

Ryerson Tull

A distributor and processor of metals and industrial plastics. Formerly Inland Materials Distribution Group, Inc.
www.ryersontull.com
Annual Revenues: $2.096 billion

Chairman, President and Chief Exec. Officer — Tel: (773) 762 - 2121
NOVICH, Neil S. — Fax: (773) 762 - 3311
neil.novich@ryersontull.com

Main Headquarters
Mailing: 2621 W. 15th Place — Tel: (773) 762 - 2121
Chicago, IL 60608 — Fax: (773) 762 - 3311

Public Affairs and Related Activities Personnel

At Headquarters

KORDA, William — Tel: (773) 788 - 3358
V. President, Human Resources — Fax: (773) 762 - 2194
william.korda@ryersontull.com

ROGERS, Terence R. — Tel: (773) 762 - 2153
V. President, Finance; and Treasurer — Ext: 3720
terence.rogers@ryersontull.com — Fax: (773) 762 - 3311
Responsibilities include investor relations

The Ryland Group, Inc.

A home building and mortgage finance company.
www.ryland.com
Annual Revenues: $3.4 billion

Chairman, President and Chief Exec. Officer — Tel: (818) 223 - 7500
DREIER, R. Chad — Fax: (818) 223 - 7667
cdreier@ryland.com — TF: (800) 267 - 0998

Main Headquarters
Mailing: 24025 Park Sorrento — Tel: (818) 223 - 7500
Suite 400 — Fax: (818) 223 - 7667
Calabasas, CA 91302 — TF: (800) 267 - 0998

Corporate Foundations and Giving Programs

The Ryland Group Corporate Contributions Program
Contact: Maurice M. Simpkins
6011 University Blvd. — Tel: (410) 712 - 7012
Suite 260
Ellicott City, MD 21043

Annual Grant Total: $1,000,000 - $2,000,000
Gives annually about 2% of pre-tax earnings.
Geographic Preference: Area(s) in which the company operates
Primary Interests: Domestic Violence; Health; Hunger; Senior Citizens; Substance Abuse Prevention

Public Affairs and Related Activities Personnel

At Headquarters

CUNNION, Robert J., III — Tel: (818) 223 - 7500
Senior V. President, Human Resources — Fax: (818) 223 - 7667
rcunnion@ryland.com — TF: (800) 267 - 0998

ELDER, Eric — Tel: (818) 223 - 7500
Senior V. President, Marketing and Communications — Fax: (818) 223 - 7667
TF: (800) 267 - 0998

JONES, Marya — Tel: (818) 223 - 7591
Director, Communications — Fax: (818) 223 - 7667
TF: (800) 267 - 0998

LOWE, Cathey S. — Tel: (818) 223 - 7530
Senior V. President, Finance — Fax: (818) 223 - 7667
clowe@ryland.com — TF: (800) 267 - 0998
Responsibilities include investor relations.

NANDA, Jyoti — Tel: (818) 223 - 7615
Manager, Communications — Fax: (818) 223 - 7667
jnanda@ryland.com — TF: (800) 267 - 0998

At Other Offices

SIMPKINS, Maurice M. — Tel: (410) 712 - 7012
V. President, Public Affairs
6011 University Blvd.
Suite 260
Ellicott City, MD 21043
msimpkins@ryland.com

Sabre Holdings Corp.

An information technology provider for the travel industry. Subsidiaries include Travelocity.com Inc.
www.sabre-holdings.com
Annual Revenues: $2.056 billion

Chairman, President and Chief Exec. Officer — Tel: (682) 605 - 1000
GILLILAND, Sam — Fax: (682) 264 - 9000

Main Headquarters
Mailing: 3150 Sabre Dr. — Tel: (682) 605 - 1000
Southlake, TX 76092 — Fax: (682) 264 - 9000

Washington Office
Mailing: 1101 17th St. NW — Tel: (202) 467 - 8208
Suite 602 — Fax: (202) 467 - 8204
Washington, DC 20036

Political Action Committees

Sabre Political Action Committee
Contact: Bruce J. Charendoff
1101 17th St. NW — Tel: (202) 467 - 8201
Suite 602 — Fax: (202) 467 - 8204
Washington, DC 20036

Contributions to Candidates: $25,750 (01/05 - 09/05)
Democrats: $13,250; Republicans: $11,500; Other: $1,000.

Principal Recipients

SENATE DEMOCRATS		HOUSE DEMOCRATS	
Carper, Thomas R (DE)	$1,000	Menendez, Robert (NJ)	$2,000
Nelson, Benjamin (NE)	$1,000	Bean, Melissa (IL)	$1,000
Nelson, Bill (FL)	$1,000	Boswell, Leonard (IA)	$1,000
Pryor, Mark (AR)	$1,000	Edwards, Chet (TX)	$1,000
		Lofgren, Zoe (CA)	$1,000
		Matheson, James (UT)	$1,000
		Salazar, John (CO)	$1,000
		HOUSE OTHER	
		Oberstar, James L (MN)	$1,000
SENATE REPUBLICANS		**HOUSE REPUBLICANS**	
Allen, George (VA)	$4,000	Burgess, Michael (TX)	$2,500
Chafee, Lincoln (RI)	$1,000	Boozman, John (AR)	$1,000
Lott, Trent (MS)	$1,000	Emerson, Jo Ann (MO)	$1,000
		Pearce, Steve (NM)	$1,000

Public Affairs and Related Activities Personnel

At Headquarters

BERMAN, Michael — Tel: (682) 605 - 2397
V. President, Corporate Media Relations — Fax: (682) 264 - 0502
michael.berman@sabre-holdings.com

Sabre Holdings Corp.

* continued from previous page

BLACKMON, Kimberly — Tel: (682) 605 - 3286
Corporate Media Relations — Fax: (682) 264 - 9000
kimberly.blackmon@sabre-holdings.com

DORMAN, Dawn — Tel: (682) 605 - 2246
Senior Manager, Media Relations — Fax: (682) 264 - 0502
(Sabre Travel Network)
dawn.dorman@sabre-holdings.com

FUGATE, Karen — Tel: (682) 605 - 2343
V. President, Investor Relations — Fax: (682) 264 - 8343
karen.fugate@sabre-holdings.com

HAEFNER, Michael — Tel: (682) 605 - 7031
Senior V. President, Human Resources — Fax: (682) 264 - 7029

HAYDEN, Kathryn — Tel: (682) 605 - 2252
Senior Manager, Public Relations — Fax: (682) 264 - 0502
(Sabre Airline Solutions)
kathryn.hayden@sabre-holdings.com

NESTER, Chris — Tel: (682) 605 - 1000
Manager, Investor Relations — Fax: (682) 264 - 9000

PRICE, Leslie A. — Tel: (682) 605 - 2267
Senior V. President, Corporate Communications — Fax: (682) 264 - 8267
leslie.price@sabre-holdings.com

WILLIAMS, Nanci — Tel: (682) 605 - 2271
Senior Manager, Media Relations — Fax: (682) 264 - 0502
(Sabre Travel Network)
nanci.williams@sabre-holdings.com

At Washington Office

CHARENDOFF, Bruce J. — Tel: (202) 467 - 8201
Senior V. President, Government Affairs — Fax: (202) 467 - 8204
bruce.charendoff@sabre-holdings.com
Registered Federal Lobbyist.

GOODELL, Jeffrey — Tel: (202) 467 - 8208
V. President, Government Affairs — Fax: (202) 467 - 8204
Registered Federal Lobbyist.

At Other Offices

COMEAUX, Al — Tel: (817) 785 - 8107
V. President, Public Relations — Fax: (817) 785 - 8003
(Travelocity.com Inc.)
15100 Trinity Blvd.
Forth Worth, TX 76155
al.comeaux@travelocity.com

SAFECO Corp.

An insurance, financial services and real estate development company.
www.safeco.com
Annual Revenues: $7.065 billion

Chairman, President, and Chief Exec. Officer — Tel: (206) 545 - 5000
MCGAVICK, Mike

Main Headquarters
Mailing: SAFECO Plaza, Seattle, WA 98185 — Tel: (206) 545 - 5000
Street: 4333 Brooklyn Ave. NE, Seattle, WA 28185

Political Action Committees

SAFECO-PAC
Contact: Neal Fuller
SAFECO Plaza — Tel: (206) 545 - 5537
Seattle, WA 98185

Contributions to Candidates: $2,000 (01/05 - 09/05)
Democrats: $1,000; Republicans: $1,000.

Principal Recipients

SENATE DEMOCRATS

HOUSE DEMOCRATS
Vargas, Juan (CA) $1,000

SENATE REPUBLICANS
Burns, Conrad (MT) $1,000

HOUSE REPUBLICANS

Corporate Foundations and Giving Programs

SAFECO Corp. Contributions Committee
Contact: Rose Lincoln
SAFECO Plaza — Tel: (206) 545 - 5000
Seattle, WA 98185

Annual Grant Total: over $5,000,000
Geographic Preference: Area(s) in which the company operates; California; Illinois; Colorado; Georgia; Missouri; Ohio; Oregon; Tennessee; Texas; Washington State; Connecticut; Florida; Indiana; New York; Virginia
Primary Interests: Civic and Cultural Activities
Recent Recipients: Alzheimer's Ass'n; Nat'l Child Safety Council

Public Affairs and Related Activities Personnel

At Headquarters

FULLER, Neal — Tel: (206) 545 - 5537
Contact, Investor Relations and SAFECO-PAC

HOLLIE, Paul — Tel: (206) 545 - 3048
Media Relations Contact

LINCOLN, Rose — Tel: (206) 545 - 5000
Manager, Corporate Contributions

MORAN, Jim — Tel: (206) 545 - 5291
Representative, Community Relations

MYSLIWY, Allie — Tel: (206) 545 - 5000
Exec. V. President, Human Resources

Safeguard Scientifics, Inc.

An information technology holding company that identifies, develops, and operates emerging infrastructure technology companies. Focuses on three sectors: software, communications, and eServices.
www.safeguard.com
Annual Revenues: $1.685 billion

Chairman of the Board — Tel: (610) 293 - 0600
KEITH, Robert E. — Fax: (610) 293 - 0601; TF: (888) 733 - 1200

President and Chief Exec. Officer — Tel: (610) 293 - 0600
BONI, Peter J. — Fax: (610) 293 - 0601; TF: (888) 733 - 1200

Main Headquarters
Mailing: 800 The Safeguard Bldg., 435 Devon Park Dr., Wayne, PA 19087-1945 — Tel: (610) 293 - 0600; Fax: (610) 293 - 0601; TF: (888) 733 - 1200

Corporate Foundations and Giving Programs

Safeguard Scientifics Foundation
800 The Safeguard Bldg. — Tel: (610) 293 - 0600
435 Devon Park Dr. — Fax: (610) 293 - 0601
Wayne, PA 19087-1945 — TF: (888) 733 - 1200

Annual Grant Total: $1,000,000 - $2,000,000
Gives to preselected organizations only.
Primary Interests: Arts and Humanities; Civic and Public Affairs; Education; Health
Recent Recipients: American Red Cross; Habitat for Humanity; Juvenile Diabetes Foundation

Public Affairs and Related Activities Personnel

At Headquarters

DUSOSSOIT, Janine — Tel: (610) 293 - 0600
V. President, Investor Relations — Fax: (610) 293 - 0601; TF: (888) 733 - 1200
Responsibilities include media relations.

Safety-Kleen Systems, Inc.

A provider of parts washers, environmental services, and hazardous waste management services.
www.safety-kleen.com
Annual Revenues: $1.515 billion

Chairman of the Board — Tel: (972) 265 - 2000
HADDOCK, Ron — TF: (800) 669 - 5740

Chief Exec. Officer — Tel: (972) 265 - 2000
FLORJANCIC, Frederick J. — TF: (800) 669 - 5740

Main Headquarters
Mailing: 5400 Legacy Dr., Cluster II, Bldg. 3, Plano, TX 75024 — Tel: (972) 265 - 2000; TF: (800) 669 - 5740

Political Action Committees

Safety-Kleen PAC
Contact: Catherine Shipp
5400 Legacy Dr., Cluster II, Bldg. 3 — Tel: (972) 265 - 2000
Plano, TX 75024 — TF: (800) 669 - 5740

Contributions to Candidates: none reported (01/05 - 09/05)

Public Affairs and Related Activities Personnel

At Headquarters

KYTE, John — Tel: (972) 265 - 2030
Director, Corporate Communications and Government Relations — TF: (800) 669 - 5740
john_kyte@was.bm.com

SHIPP, Catherine — Tel: (972) 265 - 2000
PAC Treasurer — TF: (800) 669 - 5740

WILLIAMS, C. Michael — Tel: (972) 265 - 2000
Senior V. President, Human Resources — TF: (800) 669 - 5740

Safeway Inc.

PUBLIC AFFAIRS COUNCIL
A member of the Public Affairs Council. A multi-regional supermarket retail chain.
www.safeway.com
Annual Revenues: $34.301 billion

Safeway Inc.

* continued from previous page

Chairman, President and Chief Exec. Officer Tel: (925) 467 - 3000
BURD, Steven A.

Main Headquarters
Mailing: P.O. Box 99, Pleasanton, CA 94566-0009 Tel: (925) 467 - 3000
Street: 5918 Stoneridge Mall Rd., Pleasanton, CA 94588-3229

Political Action Committees

Safeway Inc. PAC
Contact: Dominick Giaraldi
P.O. Box 99 Tel: (925) 467 - 3000
Pleasanton, CA 94566-0009

Contributions to Candidates: $68,000 (01/05 - 09/05)
Democrats: $21,500; Republicans: $46,500.

Principal Recipients

SENATE DEMOCRATS		HOUSE DEMOCRATS	
Feinstein, Dianne (CA)	$5,000	Case, Edward (HI)	$2,000
Carper, Thomas R (DE)	$3,500	Salazar, John (CO)	$2,000
Mikulski, Barbara (MD)	$2,000		
SENATE REPUBLICANS		**HOUSE REPUBLICANS**	
Allen, George (VA)	$10,000	Thomas, William M (CA)	$5,000
Santorum, Richard (PA)	$5,000	Goodlatte, Robert (VA)	$3,500
Talent, James (MO)	$5,000	McMorris, Cathy (WA)	$3,500
Chambliss, Saxby (GA)	$2,000	Pearce, Steve (NM)	$2,000
		Renzi, Richard (AZ)	$2,000
		Sessions, Pete (TX)	$2,000

Corporate Foundations and Giving Programs

The Safeway Foundation
Contact: Barbara Koon
P.O. Box 99 Tel: (925) 467 - 3135
Pleasanton, CA 94566-0009

Annual Grant Total: over $5,000,000
Donations are primarily made at the store level.
Geographic Preference: Middle Atlantic States; Western United States; Area(s) in which the company operates
Primary Interests: Education; Health and Human Services; Hunger
Recent Recipients: Easter Seal Soc.

Public Affairs and Related Activities Personnel

At Headquarters

BOWLBY, David Tel: (925) 467 - 3000
V. President, Corporate Strategic Government Alliances

CONWAY, Thomas J. Tel: (925) 467 - 3273
V. President, Communications Fax: (925) 467 - 3323

DOWLING, Brian G. Tel: (925) 467 - 3787
V. President, Public Affairs Fax: (925) 467 - 3323

GIARALDI, Dominick Tel: (925) 467 - 3000
PAC Treasurer

HERGLOTZ, Kevin Tel: (925) 467 - 3000
V. President, Government Relations and Legislative Affairs

KOON, Barbara Tel: (925) 467 - 3135
Coordinator, Safeway Foundation

MASSINGILL, Teena Tel: (925) 467 - 3361
Northern California Public Affairs

MAYES, Jonathan O. Tel: (925) 467 - 3070
V. President, Government Relations Fax: (925) 467 - 3323

PLAISANCE, Melissa C. Tel: (925) 467 - 3000
Senior V. President, Finance and Investor Relations

RENDA, Larree M. Tel: (925) 467 - 3000
Exec. V. President, Retail Operations, Human Resources, Public Affairs, Labor and Government Relations, Reengineering and Communications

At Other Offices

FLANAGAN, Bridget A. Tel: (503) 657 - 6287
Director, Public Affairs
16300 S.E. Evelyn St.
Clackamas, OR 97015

LUGINBILL, Kerry Tel: (480) 929 - 8014
Director, Public Affairs Fax: (480) 894 - 4176
2750 S. Priest Dr.
Tempe, AZ 85282

MYERS, Cherie
Director, Public Affairs
1121 124th NE
Bellevue, WA 98005

STROH, Jeff
Director, Public Affairs
6900 S. Yosemite
Englewood, CO 80112-1412

TEN EYCK, Greg Tel: (301) 918 - 6500
Director, Public Affairs
4551 Forbes Blvd.
Lanham, MD 20706
greg.teneyck@safeway.com

SAIC

See listing on page 429 under Science Applications Internat'l Corp.

Saint-Gobain Corp.

Provides services involving the following materials: building materials, glass containers, glass, ceramics, abrasives, reinforcements and plastics. Subsidiaries include CertainTeed Corp.

www.saint-gobain.com
Annual Revenues: $6 billion

Chief Exec. Officer Tel: (610) 341 - 7000
PHELIZON, Jean-Francois Fax: (610) 341 - 7777

Main Headquarters
Mailing: P.O. Box 860, Valley Forge, PA 19482 Tel: (610) 341 - 7000 Fax: (610) 341 - 7777
Street: 750 E. Swedesford Rd., Valley Forge, PA 19482

Corporate Foundations and Giving Programs

Saint-Gobain Corp. Foundation
P.O. Box 860 Tel: (610) 341 - 7000
Valley Forge, PA 19482 Fax: (610) 341 - 7777

Annual Grant Total: none reported
Supports 501(c)(3) organizations.
Primary Interests: Arts and Culture; Education; Medicine and Health Care

Public Affairs and Related Activities Personnel

At Headquarters

SEIBERLICH, William C. Tel: (610) 341 - 7187
Manager, Communications Fax: (610) 341 - 7777

SMITH, Jim Tel: (610) 341 - 7000
Director, Environmental Affairs Fax: (610) 341 - 7777

WACKERMAN, Dorothy C. Tel: (610) 341 - 7000
V. President, Communications Fax: (610) 341 - 7777

Saks, Inc.

Operates as Saks Department Store Group under the names Parisian, Proffitt's, McRae's, Younkers, Herberger's, Carson Pirie Scott, Bergner's, Boston Store, and Club Libby Lu. Also operates Saks Fifth Avenue Enterprises, which consists of Saks Fifth Avenue and Saks Off 5th stores.

www.saksincorporated.com
Annual Revenues: $6.071 billion

Chairman and Chief Exec. Officer Tel: (205) 940 - 4000
MARTIN, R. Brad
brad_martin@saksinc.com

Main Headquarters
Mailing: 750 Lakeshore Pkwy., Birmingham, AL 35211 Tel: (205) 940 - 4000

Political Action Committees

Saks Inc. Fund for Retail Growth
Contact: James H. Scully
750 Lakeshore Pkwy. Tel: (205) 940 - 4000
Birmingham, AL 35211

Contributions to Candidates: none reported (01/05 - 09/05)

Corporate Foundations and Giving Programs

Saks Incorporated Giving Program
750 Lakeshore Pkwy. Tel: (205) 940 - 4000
Birmingham, AL 35211

Annual Grant Total: none reported
Primary Interests: Community Development; Education; Environment/Conservation; Medical Research
Recent Recipients: United Way

Public Affairs and Related Activities Personnel

At Headquarters

MARTIN, Jeffrey C. Tel: (205) 940 - 4000
Senior V. President, Compliance and Government Affairs

SCULLY, James H. Tel: (205) 940 - 4000
PAC Treasurer

Saks, Inc.

** continued from previous page*

At Other Offices

BENTLEY, Julia A. — Tel: (865) 981 - 6243
Senior V. President, Investor Relations and Communications — Fax: (865) 981 - 6325
115 N. Calderwood
P.O. Box 9388
Alcoa, TN 37701
julia_bentley@saksinc.com

Sallie Mae (USA Education)

See listing on page 440 under SLM Corp.

Salton, Inc.

Manufactures and distributes electronic household appliances.

www.saltoninc.com

Annual Revenues: $922.5 million

Chairman and Secretary
SABIN, David C. — Tel: (847) 803 - 4600; Fax: (847) 803 - 5629; TF: (800) 272 - 5629

Chief Exec. Officer
DREIMANN, Leonard — Tel: (847) 803 - 4600; Fax: (847) 803 - 5629; TF: (800) 272 - 5629

Main Headquarters
Mailing: 1955 Field Ct.
Lake Forest, IL 60045 — Tel: (847) 803 - 4600; Fax: (847) 803 - 5629; TF: (800) 272 - 5629

Public Affairs and Related Activities Personnel

At Headquarters

MULDER, David M. — Tel: (847) 803 - 4600
Exec. V. President, Chief Administrative Officer, and Senior Financial Officer — Fax: (847) 803 - 5629; TF: (800) 272 - 5629
Responsibilities include investor relations.

San Diego Gas and Electric Co.

An electric and gas utility. A subsidiary of Sempra Energy Corp. (see separate listing).

www.sdge.com

Main Headquarters
Mailing: 8326 Century Park
San Diego, CA 92123 — Tel: (619) 696 - 2000; Fax: (619) 696 - 1868

Corporate Foundations and Giving Programs

San Diego Gas and Electric Co. Corporate Contributions
8326 Century Park — Tel: (619) 696 - 2000
San Diego, CA 92123 — Fax: (619) 696 - 1868

Annual Grant Total: $1,000,000 - $2,000,000

Geographic Preference: Area(s) in which the company operates

Primary Interests: Arts and Culture; Community Affairs; Education; Health and Human Services; Substance Abuse Prevention

Public Affairs and Related Activities Personnel

At Headquarters

CARTMILL, Molly — Tel: (619) 696 - 2000
Director, Corporate Relations — Fax: (619) 696 - 1814

KYD, Margot A. — Tel: (619) 696 - 2000
Senior V. President and Chief Administrative Officer, Human Resources — Fax: (619) 696 - 1814

LORENZ, Lad — Tel: (619) 696 - 2000
V. President, Regulatory Affairs — Fax: (619) 696 - 1868

MCDONALD, Sammantha — Tel: (619) 696 - 2000
Manager, Corporate Community Relations — Fax: (619) 696 - 1868
smcdonald@semprautilities.com

REED, William L. — Tel: (858) 650 - 4093
Senior V. President, Regulatory Affairs and Strategic Planning — Fax: (858) 650 - 6145
wreed@semprautilities.com

SCHAVIEN, Lee — Tel: (619) 696 - 2000
V. President, Regulatory Affairs — Fax: (619) 696 - 1868

SCHOTT, Buzz — Tel: (619) 696 - 2000
Director, Regional Public Affairs — Fax: (619) 696 - 1868

VAN HERIK, Ed — Tel: (619) 696 - 2000
Manager, Communications — Fax: (619) 696 - 1868

Sanmina-SCI Corp.

An electronics contract manufacturer. Formed from the merger between Sanmina Corp. and SCI Systems, Inc. in December of 2001.

www.sanmina.com

Chairman and Chief Exec. Officer
SOLA, Jure — Tel: (408) 964 - 3500; Fax: (408) 964 - 3636
jure.sola@sanmina-sci.com

Main Headquarters
Mailing: 2700 N. First St.
San Jose, CA 95134 — Tel: (408) 964 - 3500; Fax: (408) 964 - 3636

Political Action Committees

SCI Systems Political Action Committee
Contact: Robert G. Sibold, Jr.
2700 N. First St. — Tel: (408) 964 - 3500
San Jose, CA 95134 — Fax: (408) 964 - 3636

Contributions to Candidates: none reported (01/05 - 09/05)

Public Affairs and Related Activities Personnel

At Headquarters

BOMBINO, Paige — Tel: (408) 964 - 3610
Investor Relations — Fax: (408) 964 - 3636
paige.bombino@sanmina-sci.com

RENZULLI, Carmine — Tel: (408) 964 - 3500
Senior V. President, Global Human Resources — Fax: (408) 964 - 3636

SIBOLD, Robert G., Jr. — Tel: (408) 964 - 3500
Treasurer, SCI Systems PAC — Fax: (408) 964 - 3636

WHITE, David — Tel: (408) 964 - 3500
Exec. V. President and Chief Financial Officer — Fax: (408) 964 - 3636
Responsibilities include investor relations.

Sanofi Pasteur, Inc.

A vaccine producer. Formerly Aventis Pasteur. A subsidiary of Sanofi-Aventis of France.

www.sanofipasteur.us

Annual Revenues: $2.215 billion

Main Headquarters
Mailing: Discovery Dr.
Swiftwater, PA 18370 — Tel: (570) 839 - 7187; Fax: (570) 839 - 7235

Washington Office
Mailing: 801 Pennsylvania Ave. NW — Tel: (202) 898 - 3192
Suite 725 — Fax: (202) 371 - 1107
Washington, DC 20004

Political Action Committees

Sanofi Pasteur Inc. PAC
Contact: Frank Epifano
Discovery Dr. — Tel: (570) 839 - 7187
Swiftwater, PA 18370 — Fax: (570) 839 - 7235

Contributions to Candidates: $42,500 (01/05 - 09/05)
Democrats: $15,500; Republicans: $27,000.

Principal Recipients

SENATE DEMOCRATS		HOUSE DEMOCRATS	
Kennedy, Ted (MA)	$4,000	Honda, Mike (CA)	$2,500
Bingaman, Jeff (NM)	$1,000	Gonzalez, Charles A (TX)	$1,500
Nelson, Benjamin (NE)	$1,000	Dingell, John D (MI)	$1,000
Pryor, Mark (AR)	$1,000	Jefferson, William (LA)	$1,000
		Roybal-Allard, Lucille (CA)	$1,000
		Solis, Hilda (CA)	$1,000

SENATE REPUBLICANS		HOUSE REPUBLICANS	
Santorum, Richard (PA)	$2,500	Bonilla, Henry (TX)	$5,000
Dole, Elizabeth (NC)	$2,000	Ferguson, Mike (NJ)	$3,500
Dewine, Richard (OH)	$1,000	Deal, Nathan (GA)	$2,000
Hatch, Orrin (UT)	$1,000	Beauprez, Robert (CO)	$1,000
		Blackburn, Marsha (TN)	$1,000
		Fitzpatrick, Michael (PA)	$1,000
		Gerlach, Jim (PA)	$1,000
		Hart, Melissa (PA)	$1,000
		Pickering, Chip (MS)	$1,000
		Sensenbrenner, Jim (WI)	$1,000
		Shays, Christopher (CT)	$1,000
		Shuster, William (PA)	$1,000
		Simpson, Michael (ID)	$1,000

Public Affairs and Related Activities Personnel

At Headquarters

EPIFANO, Frank — Tel: (570) 839 - 7187
PAC Treasurer — Fax: (570) 839 - 7235

LAVENDA, Len — Tel: (570) 839 - 4446
U.S. Media Relations — Fax: (570) 839 - 5415
len.lavenda@sanofipasteur.com

Sanofi Pasteur, Inc.

** continued from previous page*

SCHINDLER, Ellyn
U.S. Media Relations
ellyn.schindler@sanofipasteur.com
Tel: (570) 895 - 2689
Fax: (570) 839 - 7235

WATERS, Beth
Senior V. President, Communications
Tel: (570) 839 - 7187
Fax: (570) 839 - 7235

At Washington Office

CALLINICOS, Sean
Director, Federal Government Affairs
Registered Federal Lobbyist.
Tel: (202) 898 - 3192
Fax: (202) 371 - 1107

WILKINSON, Andrea
Registered Federal Lobbyist.
Tel: (202) 898 - 3192
Fax: (202) 371 - 1107

Sanofi-Aventis Inc.

A pharmaceutical manufacturer. A subsidiary of Sanofi-Aventis of France.
www.sanofi-aventis.com
Annual Revenues: $15 billion

President and Chief Exec. Officer
ROTHWELL, Tim
Tel: (908) 243 - 6000
Fax: (908) 231 - 3614
TF: (800) 981 - 2491

Main Headquarters
Mailing: 300 Somerset Corporate Blvd.
Bridgewater, NJ 08807-2854
Tel: (908) 243 - 6000
Fax: (908) 231 - 3614
TF: (800) 981 - 2491

Washington Office
Contact: Eddie D. Evans
Mailing: 801 Pennsylvania Ave. NW
Suite 725
Washington, DC 20004
Tel: (202) 628 - 0500
Fax: (202) 682 - 0538

Political Action Committees

Sanofi-Aventis Group Employees PAC
Contact: Timothy Clark
801 Pennsylvania Ave. NW
Suite 725
Washington, DC 20004
Tel: (202) 628 - 0500
Fax: (202) 682 - 0538

Contributions to Candidates: $5,000 (01/05 - 09/05)
Democrats: $1,000; Republicans: $4,000.

Principal Recipients

SENATE DEMOCRATS

SENATE REPUBLICANS

HOUSE DEMOCRATS

Degette, Diana L (CO)	$1,000

HOUSE REPUBLICANS

Deal, Nathan (GA)	$1,000
Ferguson, Mike (NJ)	$1,000
Hart, Melissa (PA)	$1,000
Saxton, H. J (NJ)	$1,000

Public Affairs and Related Activities Personnel

At Headquarters

GREEN, Marc
Media Relations Contact
Tel: (212) 551 - 4000

KENNEDY, Lisa
Product and Scientific Communications
Tel: (908) 243 - 6361
Fax: (908) 231 - 3614
TF: (800) 981 - 2491

LILLBACK, David
V. President, Human Resources
Tel: (908) 243 - 6000
Fax: (908) 231 - 3614
TF: (800) 981 - 2491

REAVIS, Kirk
V. President, Industrial Relations
Tel: (908) 243 - 6000
Fax: (908) 231 - 3614
TF: (800) 981 - 2491

ROUSE, Charles F., III
V. President, Communications and Corporate Affairs
Mailstop: M/S SC3-835A
charles.rouse@sanofi-aventis.com
Tel: (908) 243 - 6050
Fax: (908) 231 - 3614
TF: (800) 981 - 2491

At Washington Office

CLARK, Timothy
PAC Treasurer
Tel: (202) 628 - 0500
Fax: (202) 682 - 0538

EVANS, Eddie D.
V. President, Federal Government Affairs
eddie.evans@sanofi-aventis.com
Registered Federal Lobbyist.
Tel: (202) 628 - 0500
Fax: (202) 682 - 0538

HODGE, Richard
Senior Manager, Federal Relations and Public Policy
richard.hodge@sanofi-aventis.com
Registered Federal Lobbyist.
Responsibilities include political action.
Tel: (202) 628 - 0500
Fax: (202) 682 - 0538

TAYLOR, Ann
Director, Health Policy and Pharmaceutical Programs
ann.taylor@sanofi-aventis.com
Registered Federal Lobbyist.
Tel: (202) 628 - 0500
Fax: (202) 682 - 0538

WISE COOK, Judith
Director, Health Policy and Biotechnology Programs
judy.cook@sanofi-aventis.com
Registered Federal Lobbyist.
Tel: (202) 883 - 3184
Fax: (202) 682 - 0538

Santa Fe Internat'l Corp.

See listing on page 221 under GlobalSantaFe Corp.

Santa Fe Snyder Corp.

See listing on page 157 under Devon Energy Corp.

Sara Lee Corp.

A global manufacturer comprised of three business segments: Food and Beverage; Intimates and Underwear; and Household Products. Major brands include Sara Lee, Douwe Egberts, Hillshire Farm, Kiwi, Hanes, Playtex, and Bali. In 2001, The Earthgrains Co. merged with Sara Lee Bakery to become Sara Lee Bakery Group, a division of Sara Lee Corp.
www.saralee.com
Annual Revenues: $17.6 billion

Chairman, President and Chief Exec. Officer
MCMILLAN, C. Steven
Tel: (312) 726 - 2600
Fax: (312) 726 - 3712
TF: (800) 727 - 2533

Main Headquarters
Mailing: Three First National Plaza
70 W. Madison St.
Chicago, IL 60602-4260
Tel: (312) 726 - 2600
Fax: (312) 726 - 3712
TF: (800) 727 - 2533

Corporate Foundations and Giving Programs

Sara Lee Foundation
Contact: Robin S. Tryloff
Three First National Plaza
70 W. Madison St.
Chicago, IL 60602-4260
Tel: (312) 558 - 8448
Fax: (312) 419 - 3192
TF: (800) 727 - 2533

Annual Grant Total: over $5,000,000
Guidelines are available. In addition to the Foundation's programs, the operating companies and divisions of the Corporation administer direct giving programs based on the needs of the communities where they operate. These include cash donations, in-kind gifts and employee work for community-based organizations.
Geographic Preference: Area in which the company is headquartered
Primary Interests: Arts and Culture; Social Services

Public Affairs and Related Activities Personnel

At Headquarters

BERGMAN, Janet E.
V. President, Investor Relations and Corporate Affairs
Tel: (312) 558 - 8651
TF: (800) 727 - 2533

KETAY, Julie
Exec. Director, Corporate Media Relations
Tel: (312) 558 - 8727
Fax: (312) 558 - 8653
TF: (800) 727 - 2533

PULLEY, Cassandra M.
V. President, Public Responsibility
Tel: (312) 726 - 2600
Fax: (312) 726 - 3712
TF: (800) 727 - 2533

TRYLOFF, Robin S.
Director, Community Relations and Exec. Director, Sara Lee Foundation
Tel: (312) 558 - 8448
Fax: (312) 419 - 3192
TF: (800) 727 - 2533

WHITE, J. Randall
V. President, Public Affairs
Tel: (312) 726 - 2600
Fax: (312) 726 - 3712
TF: (800) 727 - 2533

At Other Offices

CARTER, Peggy
V. President, Corporate Affairs
(Sara Lee Branded Apparel)
1000 E. Hanes Mill Rd.
Winston-Salem, NC 27105
peggy.carter@slkp.com
Tel: (336) 519 - 7563
Fax: (336) 519 - 7555

COOK, James J.
V. President, International Trade
(Sara Lee Knit Products)
1000 E. Hanes Mill Rd.
Winston-Salem, NC 27105

HALL, Matthew T.
V. President, Public Relations
(Sara Lee Bakery Group)
8400 Maryland Ave.
Clayton, MO 63105
Tel: (314) 259 - 7223
Fax: (314) 259 - 7036
TF: (800) 449 - 4284

TAYLOR, Goldie
Director, Communications and Public Relations
(Sara Lee Foods)
10151 Carver Rd.
Cincinnati, OH 45242
Tel: (513) 936 - 2001
Fax: (513) 936 - 2020

SAS Institute, Inc.

A software research and development company.
www.sas.com
Annual Revenues: $1.18 billion

Chairman and Chief Exec. Officer
GOODNIGHT, Dr. James H. — Tel: (919) 677 - 8000; Fax: (919) 677 - 4444
jim.goodnight@sas.com

Main Headquarters
Mailing: SAS Campus Dr.
Cary, NC 27513-2414 — Tel: (919) 677 - 8000; Fax: (919) 677 - 4444

Corporate Foundations and Giving Programs

SAS Institute Community Relations
SAS Campus Dr.
Cary, NC 27513-2414 — Tel: (919) 677 - 8000; Fax: (919) 677 - 4444

Annual Grant Total: none reported
Primary Interests: K-12 Education; Technology

Public Affairs and Related Activities Personnel

At Headquarters

DORNAN, John — Tel: (919) 531 - 5234; Fax: (919) 677 - 4444
Manager, Corporate Public Relations
john.dornan@sas.com

MEEK, Pamela — Tel: (919) 531 - 7883; Fax: (919) 677 - 4444
Director, Global Public Relations
pamela.meek@sas.com

MUSACCHIA, Mary U. — Tel: (919) 677 - 8000; Fax: (919) 677 - 4444
Counsel to the President/Chief Exec. Officer, Government Affairs
mary.musacchia@sas.com

TINDAL, Mike — Tel: (919) 531 - 0789; Fax: (919) 677 - 4444
Senior Director, Global Corporate Communications
mike.tindal@sas.com

Sava Senior Care LLC

Formerly Mariner Post-Acute Network, Inc. Operates long-term care and nursing home facilities.
www.marinerhealthcare.com

Chief Exec. Officer
OGLESBY, Tony E. — Tel: (678) 443 - 7000; Fax: (678) 393 - 8054; TF: (800) 929 - 4762

Main Headquarters
Mailing: One Ravinia Dr.
Suite 1500
Atlanta, GA 30346 — Tel: (678) 443 - 7000; Fax: (678) 393 - 8054; TF: (800) 929 - 4762

Political Action Committees

Mariner Health Care Federal Political Action Committee
Contact: Cynthia Rifkin
One Ravinia Dr.
Suite 1500
Atlanta, GA 30346 — Tel: (678) 443 - 7000; Fax: (678) 393 - 8054; TF: (800) 929 - 4762

Contributions to Candidates: $1,000 (01/05 - 09/05)
Democrats: $1,000.

Principal Recipients

SENATE DEMOCRATS		HOUSE DEMOCRATS	
		Cuellar, Henry (TX)	$500
		Edwards, Chet (TX)	$500

Public Affairs and Related Activities Personnel

At Headquarters

GENTRY, Boyd P. — Tel: (678) 443 - 6872; Fax: (678) 443 - 6874
Senior V. President, Investor Relations and Treasurer
bgentry@marinerhealthcare.com

RIFKIN, Cynthia — Tel: (678) 443 - 7000; Fax: (678) 393 - 8054; TF: (800) 929 - 4762
Pac Treasurer

Save Mart Supermarkets

Chairman and Chief Exec. Officer
PICCININI, Robert M. — Tel: (209) 574 - 6210; Fax: (209) 577 - 3845

Main Headquarters
Mailing: P.O. Box 4278
Modesto, CA 95352 — Tel: (209) 577 - 1600; Fax: (209) 577 - 3845

Public Affairs and Related Activities Personnel

At Headquarters

SANBORN, Sally — Tel: (209) 574 - 6226; Fax: (209) 577 - 3845
Director, Marketing
ssanborn@savemart.com
Responsibilities include corporate communications and government affairs.

SIVEIRA, Mike — Tel: (209) 577 - 6303; Fax: (209) 577 - 3857
V. President, Human Resources and Law
mike@savemartcorp.com
Responsibilities also include government relations.

SPENGLER, Bob — Tel: (209) 577 - 1600; Fax: (209) 577 - 3845
President and Chief Operating Officer

Savin Corp.

A distributor of black and white photocopiers, facsimile machines, supplies, and color digital imaging systems.
www.savin.com

Main Headquarters
Mailing: P.O. Box 10270
Stamford, CT 06904-2270 — Tel: (203) 967 - 5000; Fax: (203) 967 - 5014; TF: (800) 234 - 1900

Street: 333 Ludlow St.
Stamford, CT 06902

Corporate Foundations and Giving Programs

Savin Corporate Giving Program
P.O. Box 10270
Stamford, CT 06904-2270 — Tel: (203) 967 - 5000; Fax: (203) 967 - 5014; TF: (800) 234 - 1900

Annual Grant Total: none reported

Public Affairs and Related Activities Personnel

At Headquarters

STIX, Louise A. — Tel: (203) 967 - 5194; Fax: (203) 967 - 5229
Senior Manager, Advertising, Branding and Communications

SBC Communications Inc.

The parent corporation of Southwestern Bell Telephone Co. Acquired Pacific Telesis in 1997 and SBC Ameritech in October of 1999. The company has announced plans to acquire AT&T (see separate listing). Completion of the merger is expected in the first half of 2006.
www.sbc.com
Annual Revenues: $41 billion

Chairman and Chief Exec. Officer
WHITACRE, Edward E., Jr. — Tel: (210) 821 - 4105; Fax: (210) 351 - 2198; TF: (800) 351 - 7221

Main Headquarters
Mailing: P.O. Box 2933
San Antonio, TX 78299-2933 — Tel: (210) 821 - 4105; TF: (800) 351 - 7221
Street: 175 E. Houston
San Antonio, TX 78205-2233

Washington Office
Mailing: 1401 I St. NW
Suite 1100
Washington, DC 20005 — Tel: (202) 326 - 8800; Fax: (202) 408 - 4796

Political Action Committees

SBC Communications Inc. Employee Federal PAC
Contact: Jonathan P. Klug
P.O. Box 2933
San Antonio, TX 78299-2933 — Tel: (210) 821 - 4105; TF: (800) 351 - 7221

Contributions to Candidates: $568,300 (01/05 - 09/05)
Democrats: $184,000; Republicans: $384,300.

Principal Recipients

SENATE DEMOCRATS		HOUSE DEMOCRATS	
Nelson, Benjamin (NE)	$8,000		
Byrd, Robert C (WV)	$5,000		
Lautenberg, Frank (NJ)	$5,000		
SENATE REPUBLICANS		**HOUSE REPUBLICANS**	
Talent, James (MO)	$7,000	Bonilla, Henry (TX)	$10,000
Ensign, John Eric (NV)	$5,000	Sodrel, Michael (IN)	$8,000

Corporate Foundations and Giving Programs

SBC Foundation
P.O. Box 2933
San Antonio, TX 78299-2933 — Tel: (210) 821 - 4105; TF: (800) 351 - 7221

Annual Grant Total: none reported
Primary Interests: Economic Development; Education; Technology

Public Affairs and Related Activities Personnel

At Headquarters

COFFEY, Mike — Tel: (210) 821 - 4105; Fax: (210) 351 - 2198; TF: (800) 351 - 7221
Exec. Director, Investor Relations
mike.coffey@sbc.com

JENNINGS, Karen E. — Tel: (210) 821 - 4105; Fax: (210) 351 - 2198; TF: (800) 351 - 7221
Senior Exec. V. President, Human Resources and Communications

KLUG, Jonathan P. — Tel: (210) 821 - 4105; TF: (800) 351 - 7221
Treasurer, SBC Communications Inc. Employee Federal PAC

SBC Communications Inc.

** continued from previous page*

MANCINI, Paul
V. President, External Affairs
Tel: (210) 821 - 4105
TF: (800) 351 - 7221

MILLER, Forrest E.
Group President, External Affairs and Planning
Tel: (210) 821 - 4105
TF: (800) 351 - 7221

SOLOMON, Larry
Press Contact, Corporate/Financial Issues
lary.solomon@sbc.com
Tel: (210) 351 - 3990
TF: (800) 351 - 7221

At Washington Office

ATTWOOD, Dorothy
Senior Vice President, Federal Regulatory Strategy
Tel: (202) 326 - 8836
Fax: (202) 289 - 3699

BALMORIS, Mike
Press Contact, Federal Regulatory/Legislation
michael.balmoris@sbc.com
Tel: (202) 326 - 8800
Fax: (202) 408 - 4796

BANKS, Katreice
Exec. Director, Federal Relations
Registered Federal Lobbyist.
Tel: (202) 326 - 8800
Fax: (202) 408 - 4796

BYRD, Bruce R.
V. President and General Counsel, Washington
bruce.byrd@sbc.com
Registered Federal Lobbyist.
Tel: (202) 236 - 8868
Fax: (202) 408 - 4796

DONOHO, Wendy L.
Exec. Director, Federal Relations
Registered Federal Lobbyist.
Tel: (202) 326 - 8814
Fax: (202) 408 - 8717

HOGAN, Gerald F.
Exec. Director, Federal Relations
Registered Federal Lobbyist.
Tel: (202) 326 - 8815
Fax: (202) 408 - 4797

HUTCHISON, Barry
Exec. Director, Federal Relations
Registered Federal Lobbyist.
Tel: (202) 326 - 8836
Fax: (202) 289 - 3699

KAVANAUGH, Kathleen
Associate Director
Tel: (202) 326 - 8836
Fax: (202) 289 - 3699

KENNEDY, Sean
Exec. Director, Federal Relations
Tel: (202) 326 - 8913
Fax: (202) 289 - 3699

MCDOWELL, Marian E.
Exec. Director, Federal Relations
Registered Federal Lobbyist.
Tel: (202) 326 - 8861
Fax: (202) 408 - 7817

MCGIVERN, Timothy
Exec. Director, Federal Relations
Registered Federal Lobbyist.
Tel: (202) 326 - 8877
Fax: (202) 408 - 4796

MCKONE, Timothy P.
V. President, Federal Relations
Registered Federal Lobbyist.
Tel: (202) 326 - 8820
Fax: (202) 408 - 4808

SMITH, James C.
Senior V. President, FCC
Tel: (202) 326 - 8800
Fax: (202) 408 - 4796

SMITH, Rodney A.
Exec. Director, Federal Relations
Registered Federal Lobbyist.
Tel: (202) 326 - 8818
Fax: (202) 408 - 4796

At Other Offices

BAILEY, Clark T., II
Manager, External Affairs
800 N. Harvey
Room 399
Oklahoma City, OK 73102
Tel: (405) 291 - 5855
Fax: (405) 236 - 7340

BROWN, Larry Robert
Area Manager, External Affairs
800 N. Harvey
Oklahoma City, OK 73102
Tel: (405) 377 - 4944

CHAMBERS, Michael G.
Regional Director, External Affairs
(Southwestern Bell Telephone Co.)
320 N. Tenth St.
Room 412
St. Joseph, MO 64501
Tel: (816) 271 - 2459

HUNTER, Thom
Area Manager, Corporate Communications
(Southwestern Bell Telephone Co.)
800 N. Harvey, Room 399
Oklahoma City, OK 73102
Tel: (405) 291 - 6078
Fax: (405) 278 - 4628

MILLER, David N.
Exec. Director, External Affairs
(SBC Pacific Bell)
2700 Watt Ave.
P.O. Box 15038
Sacramento, CA 95851
Tel: (916) 972 - 4545
Fax: (916) 979 - 1388

SBC Illinois

An operating company of SBC Communications, Inc. (see separate listing).
www.sbc.com

Main Headquarters

Mailing: 225 W. Randolph St.
Chicago, IL 60606
Tel: (312) 727 - 4000
TF: (800) 327 - 9346

Political Action Committees

SBC Illinois PAC
Contact: Stephen F. Selcke
225 W. Randolph St.
Chicago, IL 60606
Tel: (312) 220 - 8717
Fax: (312) 727 - 3722
TF: (800) 327 - 9346

Contributions to Candidates: none reported (01/05 - 09/05)

Corporate Foundations and Giving Programs

SBC Illinois Corporate Giving Program
Contact: Rick Erickson
225 W. Randolph St.
Chicago, IL 60606
Tel: (312) 727 - 2080
Fax: (312) 727 - 3722
TF: (800) 327 - 9346

Annual Grant Total: over $5,000,000
Geographic Preference: Illinois
Primary Interests: Arts and Culture; Civic and Public Affairs; Economic Development; Education; Health and Human Services; Technology

Public Affairs and Related Activities Personnel

At Headquarters

ALBA, Miguel
Area Manager, External Affairs
Mailstop: 27 C
Tel: (312) 727 - 1344
Fax: (312) 727 - 3722
TF: (800) 327 - 9346

BALARK, Sam
Area Manager, External Affairs
Mailstop: 27 C
Tel: (312) 727 - 7572
Fax: (312) 727 - 3722
TF: (800) 327 - 9346

BLAKEMAN, Marc D.
Regional V. President, External Affairs
Mailstop: 27 B
Tel: (312) 727 - 4221
Fax: (312) 727 - 3722
TF: (800) 327 - 9346

ERICKSON, Rick
Contact, Corporate Giving Program
Mailstop: 27 B
Tel: (312) 727 - 2080
Fax: (312) 727 - 3722
TF: (800) 327 - 9346

GAINER, Bill
Director, Government Relations
Mailstop: 27 B
Tel: (312) 727 - 7569
Fax: (312) 727 - 3722
TF: (800) 327 - 9346

HIGHTMAN, Carrie
President
Mailstop: 27 B
Serves as the company's senior public affairs executive at the headquarters.
Tel: (312) 727 - 4000
TF: (800) 327 - 9346

LIETEAU, Michael P.
Director, Government Relations
Mailstop: 27 B
Tel: (312) 727 - 6105
Fax: (312) 727 - 3722
TF: (800) 327 - 9346

MITCHELL, Eileen
Senior V. President
Mailstop: 27 B
Tel: (312) 220 - 2377
Fax: (312) 727 - 3722
TF: (800) 327 - 9346

REGAN, Mary Pat
V. President, Regulatory Affairs
Mailstop: 27 B
Tel: (312) 220 - 2345
Fax: (312) 727 - 3722
TF: (800) 327 - 9346

SELCKE, Stephen F.
V. President, External Affairs
Mailstop: 27 B
Responsibilities include political action.
Tel: (312) 220 - 8717
Fax: (312) 727 - 3722
TF: (800) 327 - 9346

At Other Offices

BRUGGEMAN, Valerie
Area Manager, External Affairs
225 W. Wesley Ave.
Wheaton, IL 60187
Tel: (630) 462 - 6030
Fax: (630) 462 - 6024

CONSTANTINO, Nancy L.
Director, Government Relations
555 E. Cook St.
Mailstop: Floor 1E
Springfield, IL 62721
Tel: (217) 789 - 5390
Fax: (217) 789 - 5223

JENSEN, Brad
Area Manager, External Affairs
211 N. Church St., Floor 3
Rockford, IL 61108
Tel: (815) 987 - 3697
Fax: (815) 987 - 3420

MCCALL-LINK, Susan
Area Manager, External Affairs
Ten N. Martin Luther King Jr. Ave, Floor One
Waukegan, IL 60085
Tel: (847) 244 - 9977
Fax: (847) 336 - 5808

MYTYCH, Jerome
Area Manager, External Affairs
2004 Miner St.
Des Plaines, IL 60016
Tel: (847) 759 - 5261
Fax: (847) 759 - 5263

SBC Illinois

** continued from previous page*

PAULEY, Dennis
Area Manager, External Affairs
635 18th St.
Rock Island, IL 61201
Tel: (309) 788 - 7312
Fax: (309) 793 - 5410

QUINN, John
Area Manager, External Affairs
65 W. Webster St.
Joliet, IL 60432
Tel: (815) 727 - 0424
Fax: (815) 727 - 0426

STRAHL, David
Area Manager, External Affairs
2000 SBC Center Dr.
4B03B
Hoffman Estates, IL 60196
Tel: (847) 248 - 8616
Fax: (847) 248 - 2277

SBC Indiana

An operating company of SBC Communications (see separate listing).

www.sbc.com

Main Headquarters

Mailing: 220 N. Meridian St.
Indianapolis, IN 46204
Tel: (317) 265 - 2266
Fax: (317) 265 - 4354
TF: (800) 257 - 0902

Corporate Foundations and Giving Programs

SBC Indiana Corporate Giving Program
Contact: Duane Hazelbaker
220 N. Meridian St.
Indianapolis, IN 46204
Tel: (317) 265 - 5266
Fax: (317) 265 - 3995
TF: (800) 257 - 0902

Annual Grant Total: none reported

Public Affairs and Related Activities Personnel

At Headquarters

HAZELBAKER, Duane
Director, Corporate Affairs
Tel: (317) 265 - 5266
Fax: (317) 265 - 3995
TF: (800) 257 - 0902

MARKER, Mike
Media Relations Contact
Tel: (317) 265 - 4020
TF: (800) 257 - 0902

POWELL, Stephen
Director, External Affairs - City Government
Tel: (317) 265 - 5965
Fax: (317) 265 - 3995
TF: (800) 257 - 0902

ROGERS, Steve
Director, Government Affairs
Tel: (317) 265 - 3903
Fax: (317) 265 - 4354
TF: (800) 257 - 0902

SOARDS, Bill
Director, Government Affairs
Tel: (317) 265 - 2707
Fax: (317) 265 - 4354
TF: (800) 257 - 0902

SBC Michigan

An operating company of SBC Communications (see separate listing). More information about the company is available through a link from the parent company's website: www.sbc.com.

www.sbc.com

Main Headquarters

Mailing: 444 Michigan Ave.
Detroit, MI 48226
Tel: (517) 334 - 3400
TF: (800) 257 - 0902

Corporate Foundations and Giving Programs

SBC Ameritech Michigan Corporate Contributions Program
Contact: Lisa Hamway
444 Michigan Ave.
Detroit, MI 48226
Tel: (517) 334 - 3400
TF: (800) 257 - 0902

Annual Grant Total: $2,000,000 - $5,000,000

Geographic Preference: Michigan

Primary Interests: Economic Development; Education

Recent Recipients: Nat'l Ass'n for the Advancement of Colored People; United Way; University of Michigan; Urban League

Public Affairs and Related Activities Personnel

At Headquarters

BURKE, Donna
V. President, External Affairs
Mailstop: Room 1700
Tel: (313) 223 - 6688
Fax: (313) 223 - 9008
TF: (800) 257 - 0902

HAMWAY, Lisa
Director, Corporate Contributions and External Affairs
Mailstop: Room 1700
Tel: (517) 334 - 3400
TF: (800) 257 - 0902

At Other Offices

BALASIA, Steve
V. President, Government Affairs
201 N. Washington Square, Suite 920
Lansing, MI 48933
Tel: (517) 334 - 3404
Fax: (517) 334 - 3429

BALBIERZ, Steve
Manager, External Affairs
3255 U.S. 41 West
Marquette, MI 49855
Tel: (906) 225 - 6700
Fax: (906) 225 - 0599

NORMAN, Brian
Manager, External Affairs
502 Beach St., Room 119C
Flint, MI 48502
Tel: (810) 768 - 0394
Fax: (810) 768 - 0386

ROEHR, Mary
Manager, External Affairs
201 N. Washington Square, Suite 920
Lansing, MI 48933
Tel: (517) 334 - 3412
Fax: (517) 334 - 3429

SCHWARTZ, John
Manager, External Affairs
114 N. Division, Room G2
Grand Rapids, MI 49503
Tel: (616) 732 - 1966
Fax: (616) 776 - 6595

WEATHERS, Frank
Director, External Affairs
304 S. Jackson, Third Floor
Jackson, MI 49201
Tel: (517) 780 - 3846
Fax: (517) 780 - 3847

WEBB, Diane
Manager, External Affairs
4000 Allen Rd., Room 201
Allen Park, MI 48101
Tel: (734) 266 - 4208
Fax: (734) 523 - 2589

SBC Ohio

Formerly Ohio Bell Telephone Co. An operating company of SBC Communications (see separate listing).

www.sbc.com

Main Headquarters

Mailing: 45 Erieview Plaza
Cleveland, OH 44114
Tel: (216) 822 - 9700

Political Action Committees

SBC Ohio State PAC
Contact: Christie Angel
150 E. Gay St.
Columbus, OH 43215
Tel: (614) 223 - 6226
Fax: (614) 223 - 6296

Contributions to Candidates: none reported (01/05 - 09/05)

Corporate Foundations and Giving Programs

SBC Ohio Corporate Contributions Program
45 Erieview Plaza
Cleveland, OH 44114
Tel: (216) 822 - 4445

Annual Grant Total: $2,000,000 - $5,000,000

The foundation is specifically interested in the use of technology to aid education and workforce development.

Geographic Preference: Ohio; Area(s) in which the company operates

Primary Interests: Education; Technology

Public Affairs and Related Activities Personnel

At Headquarters

BENNETT, Douglas E.
Director, External Affairs
Mailstop: Room 1500
douglas.e.bennett@sbc.com
Tel: (216) 822 - 5100
Fax: (216) 822 - 1791

DUNN, Denis
Director, External Affairs
Mailstop: Room 1500
Tel: (216) 822 - 2937
Fax: (216) 822 - 1791

LYNCH, Kevin
Director, External Affairs
Mailstop: Room 1500
kl1652@sbc.com
Tel: (216) 822 - 7283
Fax: (216) 822 - 1791

REYNOLDS, Rob
Senior Director, External Affairs
Mailstop: Room 1600
rob.x.reynolds@sbc.com
Tel: (216) 822 - 1178
Fax: (216) 822 - 8220

At Other Offices

ANGEL, Christie
Director, Government Affairs
150 E. Gay St.
Mailstop: Room 4A
Columbus, OH 43215
Tel: (614) 223 - 6226
Fax: (614) 223 - 6296

BLAZER, J. Robert
V. President, State Government Relations
150 E. Gay St., Suite 4A
Columbus, OH 43215
bob.blazer@sbc.com
Tel: (614) 223 - 7311
Fax: (614) 223 - 4017

SBC Ohio

** continued from previous page*

GILLISPIE, Toni Perry — Tel: (937) 227 - 7578
Director, External Affairs — Fax: (937) 227 - 4099
300 W. First St.
Dayton, OH 45402
latonia.s.perry@sbc.com

HELLMANN, Dennis — Tel: (419) 245 - 7112
Director, External Affairs — Fax: (419) 245 - 7240
130 N. Erie St.
Room 114
Toledo, OH 43624
dennis.j.hellmann@sbc.com

KANDEL, David L. — Tel: (614) 223 - 5652
Director, External Affairs — Fax: (614) 223 - 6296
150 E. Gay St.
Room 4-A
Columbus, OH 43215
david.l.kandel@sbc.com

KEHOE, Michael E. — Tel: (614) 223 - 8236
V. President, External Affairs — Fax: (614) 223 - 6296
150 E. Gay St., Room 4A
Columbus, OH 43215
michael.kehoe@sbc.com

KRISTAN, Stephen M. — Tel: (330) 797 - 2750
Director, External Affairs — Fax: (330) 797 - 2753
2933 Salt Springs Rd.
Youngstown, OH 44509
stephen.m.kristan@sbc.com

SMITH, B. J. — Tel: (740) 454 - 3471
Director, External Affairs — Fax: (740) 454 - 3478
3935 Northpointe Dr.
Zanesville, OH 43701
bj.smith@sbc.com

WEIRTZ, Paul — Tel: (614) 223 - 4145
Senior Director, Government Affairs — Fax: (614) 223 - 4017
150 E. Gay St.
Mailstop: Suite 4A
Columbus, OH 43215

WILLIAMS, Margaret — Tel: (330) 384 - 3281
Director, External Affairs
50 W. Bowary
Room 457
Akro, OH 44308
margaret.williams@sbc.com

SBC Pacific Bell

See listing on page 422 under SBC Communications Inc.

SBC SNET

A subsidiary of SBC Communications (see separate listing). Formerly known as Southern New England Telephone Co.
www.sbc.com

President and Chief Exec. Officer — Tel: (203) 771 - 5200
MACAUDA, Michele — Fax: (203) 497 - 9184

Main Headquarters
Mailing: 310 Orange St. — Tel: (203) 771 - 5200
New Haven, CT 06510 — Fax: (203) 497 - 9184

Corporate Foundations and Giving Programs

SNET Corporate Contributions Program
Contact: Toni Boulay
310 Orange St. — Tel: (203) 771 - 4607
New Haven, CT 06510 — Fax: (203) 497 - 9184

Annual Grant Total: $1,000,000 - $2,000,000
Recent recipients: SeniorNet Learning Centers, Computers For Kids.
Geographic Preference: Connecticut
Primary Interests: Economic Development; Education

Public Affairs and Related Activities Personnel

At Headquarters

BOULAY, Toni — Tel: (203) 771 - 4607
Contact, Corporate Contributions Program — Fax: (203) 497 - 9184

CARLOW, Ramona — Tel: (203) 771 - 5748
Exec. Director, Regulatory Affairs

EMRA, John — Tel: (203) 771 - 5200
Exec. Director, External Affairs — Fax: (203) 497 - 9184

LEVY, Beverly — Tel: (203) 771 - 4474
Company Spokesperson, Media and External Affairs

At Other Offices

MACINTOSH, Wendy W. — Tel: (860) 947 - 7033
Director, Legislative Affairs
111 Trumbull St.
Hartford, CT 06103

SBC Wisconsin

Formerly Wisconsin Bell Telephone Co. An operating company of SBC Communications (see separate listing).
www.sbc.com

Main Headquarters
Mailing: 722 N. Broadway — TF: (800) 257 - 0902
18th Floor
Milwaukee, WI 53202

Corporate Foundations and Giving Programs

SBC Wisconsin Corporate Contributions Program
722 N. Broadway — TF: (800) 257 - 0902
18th Floor
Milwaukee, WI 53202

Annual Grant Total: $2,000,000 - $5,000,000
Geographic Preference: Wisconsin
Primary Interests: Economic Development; Education
Recent Recipients: Junior Achievement; United Performing Arts Fund

Public Affairs and Related Activities Personnel

At Headquarters

MAURER, James — TF: (800) 257 - 0902
V. President
Responsibilities include public affairs.

WETTSTAEDT, Lisa — Tel: (414) 270 - 5915
Manager, External Affairs — Fax: (414) 28- - 5909
TF: (800) 257 - 0902

SC Johnson

A manufacturer of consumer household cleaning, personal care, air care, insect control and home storage products.
www.scjohnson.com
Annual Revenues: $6.5 billion

Chairman and Chief Exec. Officer — Tel: (262) 260 - 2000
JOHNSON, Dr. H. Fisk — Fax: (262) 260 - 6004

Main Headquarters
Mailing: 1525 Howe St. — Tel: (262) 260 - 2000
Racine, WI 53403 — Fax: (262) 260 - 6004

Washington Office
Contact: Nancy R. Levenson
Mailing: 1133 Connecticut Ave. NW — Tel: (202) 331 - 1186
Suite 650 — Fax: (202) 659 - 2338
Washington, DC 20036

Political Action Committees

S C Johnson & Son Inc. Political Action Committee (SCJPAC)
Contact: Nancy R. Levenson
1133 Connecticut Ave. NW — Tel: (202) 331 - 1186
Suite 650 — Fax: (202) 659 - 2338
Washington, DC 20036

Contributions to Candidates: $10,000 (01/05 - 09/05)
Democrats: $1,000; Republicans: $9,000.

Principal Recipients

SENATE DEMOCRATS		HOUSE DEMOCRATS	
		Matsui, Doris (CA)	$1,000
SENATE REPUBLICANS		**HOUSE REPUBLICANS**	
Inhofe, James M (OK)	$5,000	Hastert, Dennis J. (IL)	$1,000
Allen, George (VA)	$1,000	Shadegg, John (AZ)	$1,000
Talent, James (MO)	$1,000		

Corporate Foundations and Giving Programs

SC Johnson Fund, Inc
Contact: Diana Farris
1525 Howe St. — Tel: (262) 260 - 2119
Racine, WI 53403 — Fax: (262) 260 - 2652

Annual Grant Total: none reported

Public Affairs and Related Activities Personnel

At Headquarters

ANDEREGG, Gregory L. — Tel: (262) 260 - 2156
Program Manager, Education and Youth — Fax: (262) 260 - 6189

ANDERSON, Brian — Tel: (262) 260 - 5262
Program Manager, Community Development — Fax: (262) 260 - 2652

BREWER, F. H. "Chip", III — Tel: (262) 260 - 2493
Director, Government Relations Worldwide — Fax: (262) 260 - 2944

FARRIS, Diana — Tel: (262) 260 - 2119
Manager, Administration and Volunteerism — Fax: (262) 260 - 2652

HUTTERLY, Jane M. — Tel: (262) 260 - 2000
Exec. V. President, Worldwide Corporate and Environmental Affairs — Fax: (262) 260 - 6004

SC Johnson

* continued from previous page

KOSTERMAN, Gayle P. — Tel: (262) 260 - 2000
Exec. V. President, Worldwide Human Resources — Fax: (262) 260 - 6004

REIGLE, Thomas — Tel: (262) 260 - 4440
Director, Community Leadership — Fax: (262) 260 - 2652

SEMRAU, Kelly M. — Tel: (262) 260 - 2000
V. President, Global Public Affairs and Communication — Fax: (262) 260 - 6004

At Washington Office

LEVENSON, Nancy R. — Tel: (202) 331 - 1186
Director, U.S. Federal Government Relations — Fax: (202) 659 - 2338
Registered Federal Lobbyist.

SCANA Corp.

The holding company for South Carolina Electric & Gas Co.
www.scana.com
Annual Revenues: $2.954 billion

Chairman, President, and Chief Exec. Officer — Tel: (803) 748 - 3000
TIMMERMAN, William B. — Fax: (803) 217 - 8825

Main Headquarters
Mailing: 1426 Main St. — Tel: (803) 748 - 3000
Columbia, SC 29218 — Fax: (803) 217 - 8825

Political Action Committees

SCANA Corp. Federal PAC
Contact: Mark R. Cannon
1426 Main St. — Tel: (803) 748 - 3000
Columbia, SC 29218 — Fax: (803) 217 - 8825

Contributions to Candidates: $15,250 (01/05 - 09/05)
Democrats: $2,000; Republicans: $13,250.

Principal Recipients

SENATE DEMOCRATS		HOUSE DEMOCRATS	
		Clyburn, James (SC)	$1,500
SENATE REPUBLICANS		**HOUSE REPUBLICANS**	
DeMint, James (SC)	$3,000	Barrett, James (SC)	$2,500
Chambliss, Saxby (GA)	$1,000	Brown, Henry (SC)	$1,000
Graham, Lindsey (SC)	$1,000	Rogers, Harold (KY)	$1,000
Santorum, Richard (PA)	$1,000	Taylor, Charles H (NC)	$1,000

Corporate Foundations and Giving Programs

SCANA Corporate Contributions Program
Contact: Jo Ann Butler
1426 Main St. — Tel: (803) 217 - 9394
Columbia, SC 29218

Annual Grant Total: none reported
Primary Interests: Education

Public Affairs and Related Activities Personnel

At Headquarters

BOOMHOWER, Eric — Tel: (803) 217 - 7701
Manager, Public Affairs — Fax: (803) 217 - 8825
eboomhower@scana.com

BOUKNIGHT, Joseph — Tel: (803) 748 - 3000
Senior V. President, Human Resources — Fax: (803) 217 - 8825

BROWN, Mary Green — Tel: (803) 217 - 8833
Public Affairs Coordinator — Fax: (803) 217 - 8825
Mailstop: Fifth Floor
mbrown@scana.com

BURWELL, James D. — Tel: (803) 748 - 3000
Director, Federal Affairs

BUTLER, Jo Ann — Tel: (803) 217 - 9394
Coordinator, Community Services and Corporate Affairs Manager
jbutler@scana.com

CANNON, Mark R. — Tel: (803) 748 - 3000
PAC Treasurer — Fax: (803) 217 - 8825

DUNCAN, Brian K. — Tel: (803) 217 - 9501
Public Affairs Coordinator
bduncan@scana.com

GRIFFIN, Therese — Tel: (803) 217 - 7240
Manager, Corporate Communications
(South Carolina Electric and Gas Co.)
tgriffin@scana.com

LOVE, Cathy B. — Tel: (803) 217 - 7777
General Manager, Public Affairs
clove@scana.com

MCFADDEN, Charles B. — Tel: (803) 217 - 9247
Senior V. President, Governmental Affairs and Economic Development
cmcfadden@scana.com

MONTGOMERY, Robin — Tel: (803) 576 - 8649
Manager, Public Affairs — Fax: (803) 217 - 8825
rmontgomery@scana.com

WINN, H. John, III — Tel: (803) 217 - 9240
Manager, Investor Relations and Shareholder Services — Fax: (803) 217 - 8825
jwinn@scana.com

At Other Offices

MCAULAY, William A. — Tel: (919) 836 - 2327
Director, Legislative and Regulatory Relations — Fax: (919) 836 - 2343
(Public Service Co. of North Carolina)
P.O. Box 1349
Raleigh, NC 27602-1349

ROBERTS-SMITH, Jodie — Tel: (704) 834 - 6427
Public Affairs Coordinator
(Public Service Co. of North Carolina)
P.O. Box 1398
Gastonia, NC 28053-1398
jroberts-smith@scana.com

TOWNSEND, Angie D. — Tel: (919) 836 - 2321
Communications Specialist — Fax: (919) 836 - 2343
(Public Service Co. of North Carolina)
P.O. Box 1349
Raleigh, NC 27602-1349
adtownsend@scana.com

Schering Berlin, Inc.

See listing on page 72 under Berlex, Inc.

Schering-Plough Corporation

A global science-based health care company with prescription, consumer and animal health products.
www.schering-plough.com
Annual Revenues: $8.3 billion

Chairman and Chief Exec. Officer — Tel: (908) 298 - 7340
HASSAN, Fred

Main Headquarters
Mailing: 2000 Galloping Hill Rd. — Tel: (908) 298 - 4000
Kenilworth, NJ 07033

Washington Office
Contact: Robert W. Lively
Mailing: 1130 Connecticut Ave. NW — Tel: (202) 463 - 7372
Suite 500 — Fax: (202) 463 - 8809
Washington, DC 20036

Political Action Committees

Schering-Plough Corp. Better Government Fund
Contact: Paul C. Ehrlich
1130 Connecticut Ave. NW — Tel: (202) 463 - 7372
Suite 500 — Fax: (202) 463 - 8809
Washington, DC 20036

Contributions to Candidates: $40,500 (01/05 - 09/05)
Democrats: $12,000; Republicans: $28,500.

Principal Recipients

SENATE DEMOCRATS		HOUSE DEMOCRATS	
Nelson, Benjamin (NE)	$5,000	Menendez, Robert (NJ)	$5,000
SENATE REPUBLICANS		**HOUSE REPUBLICANS**	
Santorum, Richard (PA)	$5,000	Ferguson, Mike (NJ)	$5,000
		Oxley, Michael (OH)	$5,000
		Bonilla, Henry (TX)	$2,500
		Carter, John (TX)	$2,000
		Duncan, John (TN)	$2,000

Corporate Foundations and Giving Programs

Schering-Plough Foundation
Contact: Christine Fahey
2000 Galloping Hill Rd. — Tel: (908) 298 - 7232
Kenilworth, NJ 07033 — Fax: (908) 298 - 7349

Assets: $10,307,660 (2004)
Annual Grant Total: $2,000,000 - $5,000,000
Giving totals $2.6 million.
Geographic Preference: Area(s) in which the company operates
Primary Interests: Community Affairs; Education; Health and Human Services
Recent Recipients: Boys and Girls Club; Kean University; Overlook Hospital; Susan G. Komen Breast Cancer Foundation; Thurgood Marshall Scholarship Fund; United Negro College Fund; YMCA

Schering-Plough Corporate Contributions Program
Contact: Christine Fahey

Schering-Plough Corporation

* continued from previous page

2000 Galloping Hill Rd.
Kenilworth, NJ 07033
Tel: (908) 298 - 7232
Fax: (908) 298 - 7349

Annual Grant Total: $100,000 - $200,000

Giving through the Foundation is complemented by a direct corporate giving program which focuses on support for community-based, non-profit organizations in the areas of the primary interests shown. Giving totals $4.5 million.

Primary Interests: Community Affairs; Community Development; Education; Health
Recent Recipients: Independent College Fund; Kean University; United Way

Public Affairs and Related Activities Personnel

At Headquarters

BOWLES, Richard, III, Ph.D.
Senior V. President, Global Quality Operations
Tel: (908) 298 - 5245
Fax: (908) 298 - 4673

CARDILLO, Linda A.
Group V. President, Human Resources and Global Prescription Business
Tel: (908) 298 - 5772
Fax: (908) 298 - 5242

CHEELEY, C. Ron
Senior V. President, Global Human Resources
Tel: (908) 298 - 7430

CONSALVO, Robert
Director, Global Product Communications and Advocacy Development
Tel: (908) 298 - 7409
Fax: (908) 298 - 7653

FAHEY, Christine
Senior Contributions Administration; and V. President, Schering-Plough Foundation
Tel: (908) 298 - 7232
Fax: (908) 298 - 7349

FARAJI, Mary-Frances
V. President, Global Product Communications and Advocacy Development
Tel: (908) 298 - 7109

FERRY, Erica
Senior Director, Community Affairs
Tel: (908) 298 - 7371

FOX, Denise
Manager, Global Product Communications and Advocacy Development
Tel: (908) 298 - 7616

GALPIN, Stephen K., Jr.
Staff V. President, Corporate Communications
Tel: (908) 298 - 7415
Fax: (908) 298 - 7653

HIGGINS, Grainne
Exec. Director, Global Human Resources
Tel: (908) 298 - 4000

KELLY, Alex
V. President, Investor Relations
Tel: (908) 298 - 7450

KOESTLER, Thomas P., Ph.D.
Exec. V. President, Global Regulatory Affairs and Global Project Management
Tel: (908) 740 - 2204

LUX, Julie
Director, Global Product Communications and Advocacy Development
Tel: (908) 298 - 4774

STARKEY, Joseph P.
Exec. Director, Public Affairs; and President, Schering-Plough Foundation
Tel: (908) 298 - 7418
Fax: (908) 298 - 7349

SUZUKI, Cynthia
Director, Government Affairs
Tel: (908) 298 - 4000

VILA, Aracelia
V. President, Public Affairs and Global Marketing
Tel: (908) 298 - 4035

WINTON, Jeffrey A.
Group V. President, Global Communications
Tel: (908) 298 - 7662

YANCOSEK, Rosemarie
Exec. Director, Global Communications
Tel: (908) 298 - 7476

At Washington Office

ATKINS, G. Lawrence
Senior Director, Public Health Policy and Reimbursement
Tel: (202) 463 - 7372

EHRLICH, Paul C.
Manager, Legislative Affairs
Registered Federal Lobbyist.
Tel: (202) 463 - 7372
Fax: (202) 463 - 8809

LIVELY, Robert W.
Staff V. President, Federal Government Affairs
Registered Federal Lobbyist.
Tel: (202) 463 - 7372
Fax: (202) 463 - 8809

At Other Offices

GIAMFORTONE, Joseph Edward
Senior Government Affairs Manager
418 Plantain Terrace
Peachtree City, GA 30269
Tel: (770) 486 - 0584

MOFFITT, Gus
V. President, Global Safety and Environmental Affairs
1095 Morris Ave.
Union, NJ 07083

SIGMON, Scott
Government Affairs Executive
8846 Walter Ct. SW
Olympia, WA 98512
Tel: (360) 943 - 3466

TALLEY, Drew J.
Staff V. President, Risk Management and Insurance
One Giralda Farms
Madison, NJ 07940
Tel: (973) 822 - 7390
Fax: (973) 822 - 7048

Schlumberger Limited

A global technology services company consisting of two business segments. Schlumberger Oilfield Services is a provider of technology services and solutions to the international petroleum industry. SchlumbergerSema is an IT services company.

www.slb.com
Annual Revenues: $9.6 billion

President and Chief Operating Officer; Chairman and Chief Exec. Officer
GOULD, Andrew
Tel: (212) 350 - 9400
Fax: (212) 350 - 9564

Main Headquarters
Mailing: 153 E. 53rd St., 57th Floor
New York, NY 10022-4624
Tel: (212) 350 - 9400
Fax: (212) 350 - 9564

Corporate Foundations and Giving Programs

Schlumberger Foundation
Contact: Johana Dunlop
153 E. 53rd St., 57th Floor
New York, NY 10022-4624
Tel: (212) 350 - 9455
Fax: (212) 350 - 9564

Annual Grant Total: $750,000 - $1,000,000
Primary Interests: Education; Math and Science; Technology
Recent Recipients: University of Texas

Public Affairs and Related Activities Personnel

At Headquarters

DUNLOP, Johana
Manager, Schlumberger Foundation
Tel: (212) 350 - 9455
Fax: (212) 350 - 9564

LOUREIRO, Paulo
Manager, Investor Relations
Tel: (212) 350 - 9400
Fax: (212) 350 - 9564

PFERDEHIRT, Dough
V. President, Communications and Investor Relations
Tel: (212) 350 - 9400
Fax: (212) 350 - 9564

At Other Offices

SILINSKY-KEPHART, Linda
Manager, Public Affairs
225 Schlumberger Dr.
Sugarland, TX 77478
Tel: (281) 285 - 4270

Schnuck Markets, Inc.

A grocery store chain.

www.schnucks.com
Annual Revenues: $2.107 billion

Chairman and Chief Exec. Officer
SCHNUCK, Craig D.
Tel: (314) 994 - 9900
Fax: (314) 994 - 4465

Main Headquarters
Mailing: 11420 Lackland Rd.
St. Louis, MO 63146-6928
Tel: (314) 994 - 9900
Fax: (314) 994 - 4465

Public Affairs and Related Activities Personnel

At Headquarters

JONES, William H.
V. President, Human Resources
Tel: (314) 994 - 9900

SCHNUCK, Todd
Corporate V. President and Chief Financial Officer
Responsibilities include investor relations.
Tel: (314) 944 - 9900

TAYLOR, Joan
Director, Consumer Relations
jtaylor@schnucks.com
Tel: (314) 944 - 9900

WILLIS, Lori
Director, Communications
lwillis@schnucks.com
Tel: (314) 994 - 4602

Scholastic, Inc.

A publisher of magazines, books, computer software and video materials for children. Acquired Grolier Inc. in 2001.

www.scholastic.com
Annual Revenues: $2.2 billion

Chairman and Chief Exec. Officer
ROBINSON, Richard
rrobinson@scholastic.com
Tel: (212) 343 - 6100
Fax: (212) 343 - 6736

Main Headquarters
Mailing: 557 Broadway
New York, NY 10012
Tel: (212) 343 - 6100
Fax: (212) 343 - 6736

Corporate Foundations and Giving Programs

Scholastic Book Grants Program
Contact: Karen Proctor

Scholastic, Inc.

* continued from previous page

557 Broadway
New York, NY 10012
Tel: (212) 343 - 6157

Annual Grant Total: none reported
The program provides in-kind giving only.
Primary Interests: Education; Literacy
Recent Recipients: Reading is Fundamental

Public Affairs and Related Activities Personnel

At Headquarters

FLEISHMAN, Ernest B.
Senior V. President, Education/Corporate Relations
efleishman@scholastic.com
Tel: (212) 343 - 6100
Fax: (212) 343 - 6802

GOOD, Ms. Kyle
V. President, Corporate Communications and Media Relations
Tel: (212) 343 - 6100
Fax: (212) 343 - 6736

HOLLAND, Larry V.
Senior V. President, Corporate Human Resources and Employee Services
lholland@scholastic.com
Tel: (212) 343 - 6100
Fax: (212) 343 - 4876

PROCTOR, Karen
V. President, Community Affairs and Government Relations
kproctor@scholastic.com
Responsibilities include corporate philanthropy.
Tel: (212) 343 - 6157

Schreiber Foods, Inc.

A food processor.
www.sficorp.com
Annual Revenues: $1.45 billion

Main Headquarters
Mailing: P.O. Box 19010
Green Bay, WI 54307-9010
Tel: (920) 437 - 7601
Fax: (920) 437 - 1617
Street: 425 Pine St.
Green Bay, WI 54301-5179

Corporate Foundations and Giving Programs

Schreiber Foods, Inc. Corporate Giving Program
P.O. Box 19010
Green Bay, WI 54307-9010
Tel: (920) 437 - 7601
Fax: (920) 437 - 1617

Annual Grant Total: none reported
Primary Interests: Education

Public Affairs and Related Activities Personnel

At Headquarters

VAN DYK, Deborah
V. President, Industry and Regulatory Affairs
Tel: (920) 437 - 7601
Fax: (920) 437 - 1617

The Charles Schwab Corp.

A financial and brokerage services company.
www.schwab.com
Annual Revenues: $5.281 billion

Chairman and Chief Exec. Officer
SCHWAB, Charles R.
charles.schwab@schwab.com
Tel: (415) 627 - 7000
TF: (800) 435 - 4000

Main Headquarters
Mailing: 101 Montgomery St.
San Francisco, CA 94104
Tel: (415) 627 - 7000
TF: (800) 435 - 4000

Washington Office
Contact: Geoffrey Gradler
Mailing: 555 12th St., NW
Suite 740 North
Washington, DC 20004
Tel: (202) 638 - 3750

Political Action Committees

Charles Schwab Corp. Political Action Committee
Contact: Pamela Brewster
101 Montgomery St.
San Francisco, CA 94104
Tel: (415) 636 - 5021
Fax: (415) 636 - 5305
TF: (800) 435 - 4000

Contributions to Candidates: $16,000 (01/05 - 09/05)
Democrats: $10,000; Republicans: $6,000.

Principal Recipients

SENATE DEMOCRATS

Carper, Thomas R (DE)	$2,000
Feinstein, Dianne (CA)	$2,000
Cardin, Benjamin (MD)	$1,000

HOUSE DEMOCRATS

Frank, Barney (MA)	$2,000
Hooley, Darlene (OR)	$1,000
Moore, Dennis (KS)	$1,000
Sherman, Brad (CA)	$1,000

SENATE REPUBLICANS

Allen, George (VA)	$2,000
Ensign, John Eric (NV)	$1,500
Santorum, Richard (PA)	$1,500

HOUSE REPUBLICANS

Castle, Michael (DE)	$1,000

Corporate Foundations and Giving Programs

Schwab Fund for Charitable Giving
Contact: Elinore Robey
101 Montgomery St.
San Francisco, CA 94104
Tel: (877) 408 - 5438
Fax: (415) 636 - 3262

Annual Grant Total: $2,000,000 - $5,000,000
Charles Schwab & Co., Inc. provides cash and in-kind contributions to qualifying nonprofit organizations and institutions. Through the Corporate Foundation, Employee Matching Gift Program, and employee volunteer program, the company supports services and programs that improve and enhance the quality of life in the communities in which it operates.
Geographic Preference: Area(s) in which employees live and work
Primary Interests: Arts and Culture; Health and Human Services

Public Affairs and Related Activities Personnel

At Headquarters

ASERON, Alma
Traffic Coordinator, Corporate Public Relations
Tel: (415) 636 - 9748
Fax: (415) 636 - 5970
TF: (800) 435 - 4000

BREWSTER, Pamela
V. President, Government Affairs
Tel: (415) 636 - 5021
Fax: (415) 636 - 5305
TF: (800) 435 - 4000

FOWLER, Richard G.
Senior V. President, Investor Relations
Tel: (415) 636 - 9869
TF: (800) 435 - 4000

GABLE, Greg
Senior V. President, Corporate Public Relations
greg.gable@schwab.com
Tel: (415) 636 - 5454
Fax: (415) 636 - 5970
TF: (800) 435 - 4000

HIER-KING, Jan
Exec. V. President, Human Resources
Tel: (415) 627 - 7000
TF: (800) 435 - 4000

ROBEY, Elinore
Contact, Charles Schwab Corp. Foundation
Tel: (877) 408 - 5438
Fax: (415) 636 - 3262

WRIGHT-VIOLICH, Kimberly
President, Schwab Fund for Charitable Giving
Tel: (415) 627 - 7000
TF: (800) 435 - 4000

At Washington Office

GRADLER, Geoffrey
Senior V. President and Head, Government Affairs
geof.gradler@schwab.com
Registered Federal Lobbyist.
Tel: (202) 638 - 3752

POLLEY, Greg
Registered Federal Lobbyist.
Tel: (202) 638 - 3750

QUISH, Kimberly M.
V. President, Government Affairs
Registered Federal Lobbyist.
Tel: (202) 638 - 3757
Fax: (202) 638 - 3823

SCHAFFER, Laurie
Registered Federal Lobbyist.
Tel: (202) 638 - 3750

TOWNSEND, Michael T.
V. President, Public Policy
michael.townsend@schwab.com
Registered Federal Lobbyist.
Tel: (202) 638 - 3755
Fax: (202) 638 - 3823

The Schwan Food Co.

Formerly known as Schwan's Sales Enterprises Inc. A food processor.
www.theschwanfoodcompany.com

Chairman of the Board
SCHWAN, Alfred
Tel: (507) 532 - 3274
Fax: (507) 537 - 8224
TF: (800) 533 - 5290

President and Chief Exec. Officer
PIPPIN, M. Lenny
Tel: (507) 532 - 3274
Fax: (507) 537 - 8224
TF: (800) 533 - 5290

Main Headquarters
Mailing: 115 W. College Dr.
Marshall, MN 56258
Tel: (507) 532 - 3274
Fax: (507) 537 - 8224
TF: (800) 533 - 5290

Political Action Committees

Schwan Food Co. PAC
Contact: Gordon Crow
115 W. College Dr.
Marshall, MN 56258
Tel: (507) 532 - 3274
Fax: (507) 537 - 8224
TF: (800) 533 - 5290

Contributions to Candidates: $5,000 (01/05 - 09/05)
Republicans: $4,000; Other: $1,000.

The Schwan Food Co.

* continued from previous page

Principal Recipients

SENATE REPUBLICANS		HOUSE OTHER	
		Peterson, Collin (MN)	$1,000
		HOUSE REPUBLICANS	
Santorum, Richard (PA)	$1,000	Bonilla, Henry (TX)	$1,000
		Goodlatte, Robert (VA)	$1,000
		Neugebauer, Randy (TX)	$1,000

Public Affairs and Related Activities Personnel

At Headquarters

CROW, Gordon
Director, Government and Community Affairs
Tel: (507) 532 - 3274
Fax: (507) 537 - 8224
TF: (800) 533 - 5290

KNIK, Bernadette
Senior V. President, Human Resources
Tel: (507) 532 - 3274
Fax: (507) 537 - 8224
TF: (800) 533 - 5290

MILLER, Howard
V. President, Corporate Relations
Tel: (507) 532 - 8700
Fax: (507) 537 - 8794
TF: (800) 533 - 5290

Schwan's Sales Enterprises Inc.

See listing on page 428 under The Schwan Food Co.

Science Applications Internat'l Corp.

An employee-owned provider of high tech products and services. Also involved in research and development.

www.saic.com
Annual Revenues: $5.902 billion

Chairman, President and Chief Exec. Officer
DAHLBERG, Ken C.
Tel: (858) 826 - 6000
Fax: (858) 826 - 6634

Main Headquarters
Mailing: 10260 Campus Point Dr.
San Diego, CA 92121
Tel: (858) 826 - 6000
Fax: (858) 826 - 6634

Washington Office
Contact: R.A. Rosenberg
Mailing: 1919 Pennsylvania Ave. NW
Suite 650
Washington, DC 20006
Tel: (202) 530 - 8900
Fax: (202) 530 - 5641

Political Action Committees

Science Applications Internat'l Corp Voluntary PAC
Contact: Stephen P. Fisher
10260 Campus Point Dr.
San Diego, CA 92121
Tel: (858) 826 - 6000
Fax: (858) 826 - 6634

Contributions to Candidates: $150,500 (01/05 - 09/05)
Democrats: $68,000; Republicans: $82,500.

Principal Recipients

SENATE DEMOCRATS		HOUSE DEMOCRATS	
		Harman, Jane (CA)	$10,000
		Murtha, John P Mr. (PA)	$10,000
		Moran, James (VA)	$7,000
		Dicks, Norm D (WA)	$5,000
		Visclosky, Peter (IN)	$5,000
SENATE REPUBLICANS		**HOUSE REPUBLICANS**	
Allen, George (VA)	$6,000	Hunter, Duncan (CA)	$6,000
Burns, Conrad (MT)	$4,000	Lewis, Jerry (CA)	$5,000
Hatch, Orrin (UT)	$2,000		
Stevens, Ted (AK)	$2,000		

Corporate Foundations and Giving Programs

Science Applications Internat'l Corp. Giving Program
Contact: Sally Rob
1710 SAIC Dr.
McLean, VA 22102
Tel: (703) 676 - 4343
Fax: (703) 676 - 7732

Annual Grant Total: none reported

Public Affairs and Related Activities Personnel

At Headquarters

FISHER, Stephen P.
PAC Contact
Tel: (858) 826 - 6000
Fax: (858) 826 - 6634

PUNARO, Arnold L.
Exec. V. President, Government Affairs and Communications
Tel: (858) 826 - 6000
Fax: (858) 826 - 6634

ROCKWOOD, Stephen D.
Director, Employee Relations
Tel: (858) 826 - 6000
Fax: (858) 826 - 6634

ZOLLARS, Ron
Director, Public Affairs
zollarsr@saic.com
Tel: (858) 826 - 7896
Fax: (858) 826 - 6634

At Washington Office

KILLEEN, John J. "Jay"
Senior V. President, Government Affairs
killeenj@saic.com
Registered Federal Lobbyist.
Tel: (202) 530 - 8905
Fax: (202) 530 - 5641

At Other Offices

ADAMS, Jared
Media Relations
1701 SAIC Dr.
McLean, VA 22102
adamsjared@saic.com
Tel: (703) 676 - 4343

ROB, Sally
Contact, Corporate Giving Program
1710 SAIC Dr.
McLean, VA 22102
sally.d.rob@saic.com
Tel: (703) 676 - 4343
Fax: (703) 676 - 7732

ROSENBERG, R.A.
Exec. V. President, Washington Operations
1710 SAIC Dr.
McLean, VA 22102
rosenbergr@saic.com
Tel: (703) 676 - 4343
Fax: (703) 676 - 7732

WILLIAMS, Alison
Director, Public Affairs
1701 SAIC Dr.
McLean, VA 22102
Tel: (703) 676 - 6762

Scientific-Atlanta, Inc.

A supplier of transmission networks for cable TV systems, digital set-tops, cable modems and support services.

www.scientificatlanta.com
Annual Revenues: $1.45 billion

Chairman, President and Chief Exec. Officer
MCDONALD, James F.
Tel: (770) 236 - 5000
Fax: (770) 236 - 4775
TF: (800) 236 - 5000

Main Headquarters
Mailing: 5030 Sugarloaf Pkwy.
Lawrenceville, GA 30042-2869
Tel: (770) 236 - 5000
Fax: (770) 236 - 4775
TF: (800) 236 - 5000

Political Action Committees

Scientific-Atlanta Political Action Committee
Contact: Kenneth M. Massaroni
5030 Sugarloaf Pkwy.
Lawrenceville, GA 30042-2869
Tel: (770) 236 - 5000
Fax: (770) 236 - 4775
TF: (800) 236 - 5000

Contributions to Candidates: none reported (01/05 - 09/05)

Corporate Foundations and Giving Programs

Scientific-Atlanta Corporate Contributions
Contact: William McCargo
5030 Sugarloaf Pkwy.
Lawrenceville, GA 30042-2869
Tel: (770) 236 - 4607
Fax: (770) 236 - 4751
TF: (800) 236 - 5000

Annual Grant Total: $750,000 - $1,000,000
The company does not accept unsolicited applications for contributions.
Geographic Preference: Georgia
Primary Interests: Education; Health and Human Services
Recent Recipients: American Cancer Society; Juvenile Diabetes Foundation

Public Affairs and Related Activities Personnel

At Headquarters

BALLARD, Peggy
V. President, Strategic Communications
peggy.ballard@sciatl.com
Tel: (770) 236 - 7871
Fax: (770) 236 - 2291
TF: (800) 236 - 5000

KOENIG, Brian C.
Senior V. President, Human Resources
brian.koenig@sciatl.com
Tel: (770) 236 - 5000
Fax: (770) 236 - 4775
TF: (800) 236 - 5000

MALLARD, Daren
Manager, Investor Relations
daren.mallard@sciatl.com
Tel: (770) 236 - 4770
Fax: (770) 236 - 4775
TF: (800) 236 - 5000

MASSARONI, Kenneth M.
Treasurer, Scientific-Atlantic PAC
Tel: (770) 236 - 5000
Fax: (770) 236 - 4775
TF: (800) 236 - 5000

MCCARGO, William
Director, Community Affairs
Responsibilities include corporate philanthropy.
Tel: (770) 236 - 4607
Fax: (770) 236 - 4751
TF: (800) 236 - 5000

Scientific-Atlanta, Inc.

* continued from previous page

ROBEY, Tom — Tel: (770) 236 - 4608
V. President, Investor Relations — Fax: (770) 236 - 4775
tom.robey@sciatl.com — TF: (800) 236 - 5000

STUTZENSTEIN, Sara — Tel: (770) 236 - 2181
Manager, Public Relations — Fax: (770) 236 - 3088
sara.stutzenstein@sciatl.com — TF: (800) 236 - 5000

The Scotts Company

A lawn and garden care products manufacturer. Formerly O. M. Scott and Sons.
www.scotts.com
Annual Revenues: $1.76 billion

Chairman, President and Chief Exec. Officer
HAGEDORN, Jim — Tel: (937) 644 - 0011
jim.hagedorn@scottsco.com — Fax: (937) 644 - 7184
TF: (800) 543 - 8873

Main Headquarters
Mailing: 14111 Scottslawn Rd.
Marysville, OH 43041
Tel: (937) 644 - 0011
Fax: (937) 644 - 7184
TF: (800) 543 - 8873

Corporate Foundations and Giving Programs

Give Back to Grow Program
14111 Scottslawn Rd.
Marysville, OH 43041
Tel: (937) 644 - 0011
Fax: (937) 644 - 7184
TF: (800) 543 - 8873

Annual Grant Total: none reported
Geographic Preference: International
Primary Interests: Children; Education; Environment/Conservation; Families; Social Services

Public Affairs and Related Activities Personnel

At Headquarters

KING, Jim — Tel: (937) 578 - 5622
Senior Director, Investor Relations and Corporate Communications — Fax: (937) 644 - 7184
jim.king@scottsco.com — TF: (800) 543 - 8873

LOKE, Su — Tel: (937) 578 - 5169
Manager, Public Relations — Fax: (937) 644 - 7184
su.lok@scotts.com — TF: (800) 543 - 8873

STUMP, Denise S. — Tel: (937) 644 - 0011
Exec. V. President, Global Human Resources — Fax: (937) 644 - 7184
TF: (800) 543 - 8873

The Scoular Co.

A grain marketing and trading company.
www.scoular.com
Annual Revenues: $2.1 billion

Chairman of the Board
FAITH, Marshall E. — Tel: (402) 342 - 3500
mfaith@scoular.com — Fax: (402) 342 - 5568
TF: (800) 488 - 3500

President and Chief Exec. Officer
LINVILLE, Randal L. — Tel: (913) 338 - 1474
rlinville@scoular.com — Fax: (913) 338 - 2999

Main Headquarters
Mailing: The Scoular Bldg.
2027 Dodge St.
Omaha, NE 68102
Tel: (402) 342 - 3500
Fax: (402) 342 - 5568
TF: (800) 488 - 3500

Political Action Committees

Scoular Co. Fund for Effective Government
Contact: Roger Lee Barber
The Scoular Bldg.
2027 Dodge St.
Omaha, NE 68102
Tel: (402) 342 - 3500
Fax: (402) 342 - 5568
TF: (800) 488 - 3500

Contributions to Candidates: $500 (01/05 - 09/05)
Republicans: $500.

Principal Recipients

SENATE REPUBLICANS		HOUSE REPUBLICANS
Chambliss, Saxby (GA)	$500	

Public Affairs and Related Activities Personnel

At Headquarters

BARBER, Roger Lee — Tel: (402) 342 - 3500
Chief Financial Officer, Treasurer, Scoular Co. Fund for Effective Government — Fax: (402) 342 - 5568
rbarber@scoular.com — TF: (800) 488 - 3500

JACKSON, Eric — Tel: (402) 342 - 3500
Senior V. President and Media Contact — Fax: (402) 342 - 5568
ejackson@scoular.com — TF: (800) 488 - 3500

SCP Pool Corp.

A wholesale swimming pool supply distributor.
www.scppool.com

Chairman of the Board
SEXTON, Wilson B. — Tel: (985) 892 - 5521
Fax: (985) 892 - 1657

President and Chief Exec. Officer
PEREZ DE LA MESA, Manuel J. — Tel: (985) 892 - 5521
Fax: (985) 892 - 1657

Main Headquarters
Mailing: 109 Northpark Blvd.
Covington, LA 70433-5001
Tel: (985) 892 - 5521
Fax: (985) 892 - 1657

Corporate Foundations and Giving Programs

SCP Pool Corp. Corporate Contributions Program
109 Northpark Blvd.
Covington, LA 70433-5001
Tel: (985) 892 - 5521
Fax: (985) 892 - 1657

Annual Grant Total: none reported

Public Affairs and Related Activities Personnel

At Headquarters

HUBBARD, Craig K. — Tel: (985) 801 - 5117
Treasurer and Secretary — Ext: 5117
craig.hubbard@scppool.com — Fax: (985) 809 - 1045
Responsibilities include investor relations.

E. W. Scripps Co.

A communications conglomerate whose operations include newspaper publishing, television broadcasting, and television programming franchises.
www.scripps.com
Annual Revenues: $1.535 billion

Chairman of the Board
BURLEIGH, William R. — Tel: (513) 977 - 3000
Fax: (513) 977 - 3721

President and Chief Exec. Officer
LOWE, Kenneth W. — Tel: (513) 977 - 3000
lowe@scripps.com — Fax: (513) 977 - 3721

Main Headquarters
Mailing: 312 Walnut St.
2800 Scripps Center
Cincinnati, OH 45202
Tel: (513) 977 - 3000
Fax: (513) 977 - 3721

Corporate Foundations and Giving Programs

Scripps Howard Foundation
Contact: Judith G. Clabes
312 Walnut St.
2800 Scripps Center
Cincinnati, OH 45202
Tel: (513) 977 - 3048
Fax: (513) 977 - 3721

Annual Grant Total: $2,000,000 - $5,000,000
Awards scholarships to print and broadcast journalism students; provides assistance to organizations working to improve journalism education; gives annual competitive journalism awards and cash prizes in 14 categories. Web site: http://www.scripps.com/foundation
Geographic Preference: Area(s) in which the company operates; National
Primary Interests: Arts and Culture; Civic and Public Affairs; Education; Journalism

Public Affairs and Related Activities Personnel

At Headquarters

CLABES, Judith G. — Tel: (513) 977 - 3048
President and Chief Exec. Officer, Scripps Howard Foundation — Fax: (513) 977 - 3721
clabes@scripps.com

EBEL, Gregory — Tel: (513) 977 - 3813
V. President, Human Resources — Fax: (513) 977 - 3721
ebel@scripps.com

STAUTBERG, Timothy E. — Tel: (513) 977 - 3826
V. President, Communications and Investor Relations — Fax: (513) 977 - 3721
stautberg@scripps.com

Seaboard Corporation

A food distributor.
www.seaboardcorp.com
Annual Revenues: $1.829 billion

Chairman, President and Chief Exec. Officer
BRESKY, H. Harry — Tel: (913) 676 - 8800
Fax: (913) 676 - 8872

Main Headquarters
Mailing: 9000 W. 67th St.
Shawnee Mission, KS 66202
Tel: (913) 676 - 8800
Fax: (913) 676 - 8872

Washington Office
Contact: Ralph L. Moss
Mailing: 818 Connecticut Ave., Suite 801
Washington, DC 20006
Tel: (202) 955 - 6111
Fax: (202) 955 - 6118

Political Action Committees

Seaboard Corp. Political Action Committee
Contact: David M. Dannov
9000 W. 67th St.
Shawnee Mission, KS 66202
Tel: (913) 676 - 8800
Fax: (913) 676 - 8872

Seaboard Corporation

** continued from previous page*

Contributions to Candidates: $10,850 (01/05 - 09/05)

Democrats: $3,850; Republicans: $7,000.

Principal Recipients

SENATE DEMOCRATS		HOUSE DEMOCRATS	
		Payne, Donald (NJ)	$1,850
		Cleaver, Emanuel (MO)	$1,000
		Rangel, Charles B (NY)	$1,000
SENATE REPUBLICANS		**HOUSE REPUBLICANS**	
Coburn, Thomas (OK)	$1,000	Lucas, Frank D (OK)	$1,500
Inhofe, James M (OK)	$1,000	Burton, Danny (IN)	$1,000
Lugar, Richard G (IN)	$1,000	Pombo, Richard (CA)	$1,000

Corporate Foundations and Giving Programs

Seaboard Corporate Contributions Program
Contact: John A. Virgo
9000 W. 67th St. — Tel: (913) 676 - 8800
Shawnee Mission, KS 66202 — Fax: (913) 676 - 8872

Annual Grant Total: none reported

Public Affairs and Related Activities Personnel

At Headquarters

DANNOV, David M. — Tel: (913) 676 - 8800
PAC Treasurer — Fax: (913) 676 - 8872

HOSKINS, Adriana — Tel: (913) 676 - 8800
Manager, Treasury — Fax: (913) 676 - 8976
adriana_hoskins@seaboardcorp.com
Responsibilities include investor relations.

VIRGO, John A. — Tel: (913) 676 - 8800
V. President, Corporate Controller and Chief Accounting Officer — Fax: (913) 676 - 8872
john_virgo@seaboardcorp.com
Responsibilities include corporate philanthropy.

At Washington Office

FLORIO, Michael G. — Tel: (202) 955 - 6111
Government Affairs Assistant — Fax: (202) 955 - 6118
Registered Federal Lobbyist.

MOSS, Ralph L. — Tel: (202) 452 - 7960
V. President, Government Affairs — Fax: (202) 452 - 7942
ralph_moss@seaboardcorp.com
Registered Federal Lobbyist.

Seagate Technology

A manufacturer of data storage products.

www.seagate.com
Annual Revenues: $6.486 billion

Chairman of the Board — Tel: (831) 438 - 6550
LUCZO, Stephen J. — Fax: (831) 438 - 0558

Chief Exec. Officer — Tel: (831) 438 - 6550
WATKINS, William — Fax: (831) 438 - 0558

Main Headquarters

Mailing: P.O. Box 66360 — Tel: (831) 438 - 6550
Scotts Valley, CA 95067-0360 — Fax: (831) 438 - 0558
Street: 920 Disc Dr.
Scotts Valley, CA 95066

Corporate Foundations and Giving Programs

Seagate Technology Corporate Contributions Program
Contact: Gina Katz
P.O. Box 66360 — Tel: (831) 439 - 2691
Scotts Valley, CA 95067-0360 — Fax: (831) 438 - 4127

Annual Grant Total: none reported

Public Affairs and Related Activities Personnel

At Headquarters

COOPER, Rod — Tel: (831) 438 - 6550
Senior Director, Investor Relations — Fax: (831) 438 - 0558

HANLON, Karen — Tel: (831) 439 - 2485
Senior V. President, Worldwide Human Resources — Fax: (831) 438 - 0558
karen.hanlon@seagate.com

KATZ, Gina — Tel: (831) 439 - 2691
Manager, Corporate Communications — Fax: (831) 438 - 4127
gina.katz@seagate.com
Responsibilities include corporate philanthropy.

MONROY, Woody — Tel: (831) 439 - 2838
Exec. Director, Corporate Communications — Fax: (831) 438 - 4127
woody_monroy@seagate.com

STILL, Julie A. — Tel: (831) 439 - 2276
V. President, Corporate Communications — Fax: (831) 438 - 4127
julie_still@seagate.com

Sealaska Corp.

A holding company. Principal business concerns are timber, minerals, telecommunications, entertainment, and portfolio management.

www.sealaska.com

Chairman of the Board — Tel: (907) 586 - 1512
KOOKESH, Albert M. — Fax: (907) 586 - 2304

President and Chief Exec. Officer — Tel: (907) 586 - 1512
MCNEIL, Chris E., Jr. — Fax: (907) 586 - 2304

Main Headquarters

Mailing: One Sealaska Plaza, Suite 400 — Tel: (907) 586 - 1512
Juneau, AK 99801-1276 — Fax: (907) 586 - 2304

Public Affairs and Related Activities Personnel

At Headquarters

ANTIOQUIA, Todd P. — Tel: (907) 586 - 1512
Director, Corporate Communications — Fax: (907) 586 - 2304

SOUTHERLAND, Kenneth L. — Tel: (907) 586 - 1512
Manager, Human Resources — Fax: (907) 586 - 2304

Sealed Air Corp.

PUBLIC AFFAIRS COUNCIL

A member of the Public Affairs Council. A manufacturer of packaging materials and systems.

www.sealedaircorp.com
Annual Revenues: $3.5 billion

President and Chief Exec. Officer — Tel: (201) 791 - 7600
HICKEY, William V. — Fax: (201) 703 - 4205

Main Headquarters

Mailing: Park 80 East — Tel: (201) 791 - 7600
Saddle Brook, NJ 07663-5291 — Fax: (201) 703 - 4205

Public Affairs and Related Activities Personnel

At Headquarters

BURRELL, Eric D. — Tel: (201) 791 - 7600
Director, Corporate Communications and Investor Relations — Fax: (201) 703 - 4205

COVENTRY, Mary A. — Tel: (201) 791 - 7600
V. President, Communications and Government Relations — Fax: (201) 703 - 4205

Sears Holding Corp.

Formed in 2005 by the merger of Sears, Roebuck and Co. and Kmart Holding Corp. Brands and labels include Kenmore, Craftsman, DieHard, Lands' End, Jaclyn Smith, Joe Boxer, Apostrophe, Covington, and Martha Stewart Everyday.

www.searsholdings.com
Annual Revenues: $41.078 billion

Chairman of the Board — Tel: (847) 286 - 2500
LAMPERT, Edward S. — Fax: (847) 286 - 7881
TF: (800) 732 - 7780

V. Chairman and Chief Exec. Officer — Tel: (847) 286 - 2500
LACY, Alan J. — Fax: (847) 286 - 7881
TF: (800) 732 - 7780

Main Headquarters

Mailing: 3333 Beverly Rd. — Tel: (847) 286 - 2500
Hoffman Estates, IL 60179-0001 — Fax: (847) 286 - 7881
TF: (800) 732 - 7780

Washington Office

Mailing: 1725 I St. NW — Tel: (202) 349 - 3797
Suite 300 — Fax: (202) 348 - 3788
Washington, DC 20006

Political Action Committees

Sears Political Action Committee
Contact: Heidi Rudolph
3333 Beverly Rd. — Tel: (847) 286 - 2500
Hoffman Estates, IL 60179-0001 — Fax: (847) 286 - 7881
TF: (800) 732 - 7780

Contributions to Candidates: $77,500 (01/05 - 09/05)

Sears Holding Corp.

* continued from previous page

Democrats: $21,000; Republicans: $56,500.

Principal Recipients

SENATE DEMOCRATS		HOUSE DEMOCRATS	
Baucus, Max (MT)	$5,000	Emanuel, Rahm (IL)	$5,000
Nelson, Benjamin (NE)	$4,000		
Bingaman, Jeff (NM)	$2,000		
Carper, Thomas R (DE)	$2,000		

SENATE REPUBLICANS		HOUSE REPUBLICANS	
Dewine, Richard (OH)	$5,000	Hastert, Dennis J. (IL)	$5,000
Hatch, Orrin (UT)	$3,000	Kirk, Mark Steven (IL)	$5,000
Kyl, Jon L (AZ)	$2,000	LaHood, Ray (IL)	$5,000
Lugar, Richard G (IN)	$2,000	Musgrave, Marilyn (CO)	$5,000
Talent, James (MO)	$2,000	Sensenbrenner, Jim (WI)	$4,000
		Manzullo, Donald (IL)	$2,500
		Cannon, Christopher (UT)	$2,000
		Pryce, Deborah (OH)	$2,000
		Shimkus, John (IL)	$2,000

Corporate Foundations and Giving Programs

The Sears Foundation
Contact: Susan Duchak
3333 Beverly Rd. — Tel: (847) 286 - 2500
Hoffman Estates, IL 60179-0001 — Fax: (847) 286 - 5918
TF: (800) 732 - 7780

Assets: $2,800,000 (1999)
Annual Grant Total: $750,000 - $1,000,000
Geographic Preference: National
Primary Interests: Civic and Cultural Activities; Families; Women

Sears Contributions
Contact: Cheryl Ann Lambert
3333 Beverly Rd. — Tel: (847) 286 - 4714
Hoffman Estates, IL 60179-0001 — Fax: (847) 286 - 7881
TF: (800) 732 - 7780

Annual Grant Total: over $5,000,000
Focuses on not-for-profit organizations that support the Sears American Dream Campaign, the company's $100 million community commitment to help millions of Americans become home owners and outfit and maintain homes and families. Contributions are made to national and Chicago-area not-for-profit organizations with priority given to programs that support the Sears American Dream Campaign, offer unique and innovative services to a large, diverse population, serve families in communities where Sears has a significant presence, and engage a large number of Sears employees and retirees in community service. Complete funding guidelines and program information can be found at www.sears.com/community.
Geographic Preference: Area in which the company is headquartered; National
Primary Interests: Families; Housing
Recent Recipients: Enterprise Foundation; Local Initiative Support Corp. (LISC); NeighborWorks; United Way

Public Affairs and Related Activities Personnel

At Headquarters

BRATHWAITE, Chris — Tel: (847) 286 - 4681
Director, Media Relations — Fax: (847) 286 - 8351
TF: (800) 732 - 7780

DUCHAK, Susan — Tel: (847) 286 - 2500
Contact, Sears Roebuck Foundation and Contributions — Fax: (847) 286 - 5918
Mailstop: BC-110A — TF: (800) 732 - 7780

LAMBERT, Cheryl Ann — Tel: (847) 286 - 4714
Contact Contributions — Fax: (847) 286 - 7881
clambe4@sears.com — TF: (800) 732 - 7780

MCDOUGAL, Ted — Tel: (847) 286 - 2500
V. President, Public Relations — Fax: (847) 286 - 7881
TF: (800) 732 - 7780

RUDOLPH, Heidi — Tel: (847) 286 - 2500
Treasurer, Sears Holdings Corp. PAC — Fax: (847) 286 - 7881
Mailstop: BC-113A — TF: (800) 732 - 7780

SCIBARRAS, Don — Tel: (847) 286 - 0324
Government Affairs — Fax: (847) 286 - 7881
TF: (800) 732 - 7780

Sears, Roebuck and Co.

See listing on page 431 under Sears Holding Corp.

Security Benefit Life Insurance Co.

www.securitybenefit.com

Chairman of the Board
FRICKE, Howard R. — Tel: (785) 438 - 3000; TF: (800) 888 - 2461

President and Chief Exec. Officer
ROBBINS, Kris — Tel: (785) 438 - 3000; TF: (800) 888 - 2461

Main Headquarters
Mailing: One Security Benefit Pl. — Tel: (785) 438 - 3000
Topeka, KS 66636-0001 — TF: (800) 888 - 2461

Political Action Committees

Security Benefit Group Inc. Federal PAC
Contact: Natalie Haag
One Security Benefit Pl. — Tel: (785) 438 - 3000
Topeka, KS 66636-0001 — TF: (800) 888 - 2461

Contributions to Candidates: none reported (01/05 - 09/05)

Corporate Foundations and Giving Programs

Security Benefit Life Insurance Co. Charitable Trust
Contact: Mal Robinson
One Security Benefit Pl. — Tel: (785) 438 - 3000
Topeka, KS 66636-0001 — TF: (800) 888 - 2461

Annual Grant Total: $200,000 - $300,000
Foundation donations take the form of employee matching gifts.
Geographic Preference: Area in which the company is headquartered
Primary Interests: Arts and Culture; Education; Medicine and Health Care; Social Services
Recent Recipients: American Red Cross; Friends of the Zoo; United Way

Public Affairs and Related Activities Personnel

At Headquarters

COLE, Michel — Tel: (785) 438 - 3396
V. President, Corporate Communications — TF: (800) 888 - 2461
michel.cole@securitybenefit.com

HAAG, Natalie — Tel: (785) 438 - 3000
PAC Contact — TF: (800) 888 - 2461

ROBINSON, Mal — Tel: (785) 438 - 3000
Contact, Security Benefit Life Insurance Co. Charitable Trust — TF: (800) 888 - 2461

SEMCO ENERGY, Inc.

A diversified energy and infrastructure company distributing natural gas to customers in Michigan and Alaska.

www.semcoenergy.com
Annual Revenues: $445 million

Chairman of the Board
ALBERTINE, John M. — Tel: (248) 702 - 6000; Fax: (248) 702 - 6300

President and Chief Exec. Officer
SCHREIBER, George A., Jr. — Tel: (248) 702 - 6000; Fax: (248) 702 - 6300

Main Headquarters
Mailing: PO Box 5004 — Tel: (248) 702 - 6000
Port Huron, MI 48060 — Fax: (248) 702 - 6300

Corporate Foundations and Giving Programs

Semco Energy Corporate Contributions
PO Box 5004 — Tel: (248) 702 - 6000
Port Huron, MI 48060 — Fax: (248) 702 - 6300

Annual Grant Total: none reported

Public Affairs and Related Activities Personnel

At Headquarters

CONNELLY, Thomas — Tel: (248) 702 - 6240
Director, Investor Relations — Fax: (248) 702 - 6300

At Other Offices

LUBBERS, Tim — Tel: (810) 987 - 7900
Director, Marketing and Corporate Communications — Fax: (810) 989 - 4098
405 Water St.
P.O. Box 5026
Port Huron, MI 48061-5026

TYCOCKI, Elaine S. — Tel: (517) 482 - 8026
Director, Government Affairs — Fax: (517) 482 - 8064
216 N. Chestnut St.
Lansing, MI 48933-1021

Sempra Energy

A member of the Public Affairs Council. Formed from the merger of Enova Corp. and Pacific Enterprises.

www.sempra.com
Annual Revenues: $9.4 billion

Chairman and Chief Exec. Officer
BAUM, Stephen L.

Main Headquarters
Mailing: 101 Ash St. — Tel: (619) 696 - 2000
San Diego, CA 92101-3017 — TF: (877) 736 - 7721

Sempra Energy

** continued from previous page*

Washington Office

Mailing: 1399 New York Ave. NW
Suite 350
Washington, DC 20005
Tel: (202) 662 - 1700
Fax: (202) 293 - 2887

Political Action Committees

Sempra Energy Employee PAC
Contact: Linda L. Keene
101 Ash St.
San Diego, CA 92101-3017
Tel: (619) 696 - 2063
Fax: (619) 696 - 4838
TF: (877) 736 - 7721

Contributions to Candidates: $39,500 (01/05 - 09/05)
Democrats: $19,500; Republicans: $20,000.

Principal Recipients

SENATE DEMOCRATS
Bingaman, Jeff (NM) $4,500
Conrad, Kent (ND) $3,500

HOUSE DEMOCRATS
Roybal-Allard, Lucille (CA)Roybal-Allard, Lucille (CA) $2,500

SENATE REPUBLICANS
Allen, George (VA) $2,500
Santorum, Richard (PA) $2,500

HOUSE REPUBLICANS
Pombo, Richard (CA) $4,500
Vitter, David (LA) $2,500
Radanovich, George (CA) $2,000

Corporate Foundations and Giving Programs

Sempra Energy Contributions
Contact: Molly Cartmill
101 Ash St.
San Diego, CA 92101-3017
Tel: (619) 696 - 4299
Fax: (619) 696 - 1868
TF: (877) 736 - 7721

Annual Grant Total: over $5,000,000
Contributions totalled 9.8 million in 2004.
Geographic Preference: North America; South America; Central United States
Primary Interests: Arts and Culture; Community Affairs; Economic Development; Education; Environment/Conservation; Health and Human Services

Public Affairs and Related Activities Personnel

At Headquarters

ANDREWA, Jennifer
Manager, Public Relations
Mailstop: hq15a
jandrews@sempra.com
Tel: (619) 696 - 4457
Fax: (619) 696 - 4379
TF: (877) 736 - 7721

ARRIOLA, Dennis V.
V. President, Investor Relations and Corporate Communications
Tel: (619) 696 - 2000
Fax: (619) 696 - 1868
TF: (877) 736 - 7721

BRILL, Tom
Assistant General Counsel
Mailstop: HQ13A
tbrill@sempra.com
Tel: (619) 696 - 4265
Fax: (619) 696 - 4266
TF: (877) 736 - 7721

CARTMILL, Molly
Director, Corporate Community Relations and Corporate Events
Mailstop: HQ15E
mcartmill@sempra.com
Tel: (619) 696 - 4299
Fax: (619) 696 - 1868
TF: (877) 736 - 7721

FARMER, Laura
Director, Communications and Advertising
Mailstop: HQ15A
lfarmer@sempra.com
Tel: (619) 696 - 4415
Fax: (619) 696 - 4379
TF: (877) 736 - 7721

HAARER, Mark
Manager, Governent Affairs
Mailstop: hq08d
mhaarer@sempra.com
Tel: (619) 696 - 2035
Fax: (619) 696 - 4379
TF: (877) 736 - 7721

KEENE, Linda L.
Treasurer, Sempra Energy Employee PAC and Legal Support Supervisor
Tel: (619) 696 - 2063
Fax: (619) 696 - 4838
TF: (877) 736 - 7721

KEITH, Erbin
V. President, Global Regulatory Affairs and Administration
Mailstop: hq17
ekeith@sempra.com
Tel: (619) 696 - 4676
Fax: (619) 696 - 4656
TF: (877) 736 - 7721

KLINE, Douglas E.
Director, Public Relations
Mailstop: HQ15A
dkline@sempra.com
Tel: (619) 696 - 4866
Fax: (619) 696 - 4379
TF: (877) 736 - 7721

LARSON, Art
Manager, Public Relations
Mailstop: hq15a
alarson@sempra.com
Tel: (619) 696 - 4307
Fax: (619) 696 - 4379
TF: (877) 736 - 7721

LAVIN, Cathy
Program Administrator, Corporate Community Relations
Mailstop: Hq. 15E
Tel: (619) 696 - 2069
Fax: (619) 696 - 1868
TF: (877) 736 - 7721

MCNAMARA, Will
Manager, Legislative Policy and Analysis
Mailstop: hq13f
wmcnamara@sempra.com
Tel: (619) 696 - 2006
Fax: (619) 696 - 4266
TF: (877) 736 - 7721

MURRAY, Mike
Director, Legislative Policy and Analysis
Mailstop: hq13f
mmurray@sempra.com
Tel: (619) 696 - 2320
Fax: (619) 696 - 4266
TF: (877) 736 - 7721

NELSON, W. Mark
Director, Governmental Affairs
Mailstop: hq08d
wmnelson@sempraglobal.com
Tel: (619) 696 - 2060
Fax: (619) 696 - 2500
TF: (877) 736 - 7721

PRASSER, Kelly
Manager, Community Relations and Events
Mailstop: HQ15G
kprasser@sempra.com
Tel: (619) 696 - 4230
Fax: (619) 696 - 2500
TF: (877) 736 - 7721

SAYLES, Thomas S.
V. President, Governmental and Community Affairs
Mailstop: HQ18
tsayles@sempra.com
Tel: (619) 696 - 4614
Fax: (619) 696 - 9202
TF: (877) 736 - 7721

VILLEGOS, Pedro
Government Affairs Manager
Mailstop: hqu8d
pvillegos@sempra.com
Tel: (619) 696 - 4016
Fax: (619) 696 - 2500
TF: (877) 736 - 7721

ZOBEL, Bill
Environmental Legislative Manager
Mailstop: hq13f
Tel: (619) 696 - 2512
Fax: (619) 696 - 4266
TF: (877) 736 - 7721

At Washington Office

LANSINGER, William C., Jr.
Director, FERC Relations
Registered Federal Lobbyist.
Tel: (202) 662 - 1700
Fax: (202) 293 - 2887

WILLIAMS, George P.
Manager, Governmental Affairs
gwilliams@sempra.com
Registered Federal Lobbyist.
Tel: (202) 662 - 1701
Fax: (202) 293 - 2887

At Other Offices

HOWELL, Cynthia
Manager, Governmental Affairs- State Agency Affairs
925 L St., Suite 650
Sacramento, CA 95814
crhowell@sempra.com
Tel: (916) 492 - 4243
Fax: (916) 443 - 2994

MCINTYRE, Carolyn
Regional V. President, State Government Affairs
925 L St., Suite 650
Sacramento, CA 95814
cmcintyre@sempra.com
Tel: (916) 492 - 4245
Fax: (916) 443 - 2994

OROZCO, Bernie
Manager, Governmental Affairs- State Agency Affairs
925 L St.
Suite 650
Sacramento, CA 95814
borozco@sempra.com
Tel: (916) 492 - 4244

SCHOTT, Laurence F.
V. President, Regional Public Affairs
8330 Century Park Ct.
San Diego, CA 92123
San Diego Gas and Electric
Tel: (858) 654 - 6305
Fax: (858) 654 - 6301
TF: (877) 736 - 7729

Sensient Technology Corp.

An ingredient manufacturer. Formerly known as Universal Foods Corp.
www.sensient-tech.com
Annual Revenues: $939.9 million

Chairman, President and Chief Exec. Officer
MANNING, Kenneth P.
kenneth.manning@sensient-tech.com
Tel: (414) 271 - 6755
Fax: (414) 347 - 3785

Main Headquarters

Mailing: 777 E. Wisconsin Ave., 11th Floor
Milwaukee, WI 53202-5304
Tel: (414) 271 - 6755
Fax: (414) 347 - 3785
TF: (800) 558 - 9892

Corporate Foundations and Giving Programs

Sensient Technologies Foundation, Inc.
Contact: Doug Arnold
777 E. Wisconsin Ave., 11th Floor
Milwaukee, WI 53202-5304
Tel: (414) 271 - 6755
Fax: (414) 347 - 3785

Annual Grant Total: $750,000 - $1,000,000
Has a matching gifts program.
Geographic Preference: Area(s) in which the company operates; California; Illinois; Indiana; Maryland; Michigan; Missouri; Wisconsin; National
Primary Interests: Health; Higher Education
Recent Recipients: Boys and Girls Club; United Performing Arts Fund; United Way; University of Wisconsin

Public Affairs and Related Activities Personnel

At Headquarters

ARNOLD, Doug
Contact, Corporate Philanthropy
Tel: (414) 271 - 6755
Fax: (414) 347 - 3785

Sensient Technology Corp.

* continued from previous page

ROLFS, Stephen J. Tel: (414) 347 - 3743
V. President, Controller and Chief Accounting Officer Fax: (414) 347 - 3785
stephen.rolfs@sensient-tech.com
Responsibilities include investor relations.

Sensormatic Electronics Corp.

See listing on page 483 under Tyco Internat'l (US), Inc.

Sentinel Communications

See listing on page 365 under Orlando Sentinel Communications.

Sentry Insurance

A mutual insurance company.
www.sentryinsurance.com
Annual Revenues: $1.88 billion

Chairman and Chief Exec. Officer
SCHUH, Dale R. Tel: (715) 346 - 6000 Fax: (715) 346 - 6346

Main Headquarters
Mailing: 1800 N. Point Dr. Stevens Point, WI 54481 Tel: (715) 346 - 6000 Fax: (715) 346 - 6346

Corporate Foundations and Giving Programs

Sentry Foundation
Contact: Peg Sullivan
1800 N. Point Dr.
Stevens Point, WI 54481 Tel: (715) 346 - 6000 Fax: (715) 346 - 6346

Annual Grant Total: $400,000 - $500,000
Geographic Preference: Wisconsin
Primary Interests: Education

Public Affairs and Related Activities Personnel

At Headquarters

LEE, Misha Tel: (715) 346 - 6000
Manager, Government Relations Fax: (715) 346 - 6346

O'REILLY, Bill Tel: (715) 346 - 6000
V. President, General Counsel, and Corporate Secretary Fax: (715) 346 - 6346
Responsibilities include public affairs.

OLSON, Don D. Tel: (715) 346 - 6000
V. President, Human Resources Fax: (715) 346 - 6346

SULLIVAN, Peg Tel: (715) 346 - 6000
Exec. Director, Sentry Foundation Fax: (715) 346 - 6346

WELLER, Mary Tel: (715) 346 - 6000
Director, Advertising and Promotions Fax: (715) 346 - 6363
Responsibilities include public affairs.

Sequa Corp.

A manufacturer and remanufacturer of jet engine components and a producer of automotive products, industrial machinery, and specialty chemicals. Subsidiaries include Atlantic Research Corp. and Chromalloy Gas Turbine Corp.
www.sequa.com
Annual Revenues: $1.864 billion

Exec. Chairman
ALEXANDER, Norman E. Tel: (212) 986 - 5500 Fax: (212) 370 - 1969

V. Chairman and Chief Exec. Officer
WEINSTEIN, Dr. Martin Tel: (212) 986 - 5500 Fax: (212) 370 - 1969

Main Headquarters
Mailing: 200 Park Ave. New York, NY 10166 Tel: (212) 986 - 5500 Fax: (212) 370 - 1969

Corporate Foundations and Giving Programs

Sequa Corporate Contributions Program
200 Park Ave.
New York, NY 10166 Tel: (212) 986 - 5500 Fax: (212) 370 - 1969

Annual Grant Total: none reported

Public Affairs and Related Activities Personnel

At Headquarters

KYRIAKOU, Linda G. Tel: (212) 986 - 5500 Ext: 5253
V. President, Corporate Communications
linda_kyriakou@sequa.com Fax: (212) 370 - 1969
Responsibilities include investor relations.

Service Corp. Internat'l

Operator of funeral homes and cemeteries.
www.sci-corp.com

Chairman and Chief Exec. Officer
WALTRIP, Robert L. Tel: (713) 522 - 5141 Fax: (713) 525 - 2800

Main Headquarters
Mailing: 1929 Allen Pkwy. Houston, TX 77019 Tel: (713) 522 - 5141 Fax: (713) 525 - 2800

Political Action Committees

Service Corp. Internat'l PAC (SRV/PAC)
Contact: Caressa F. Hughes
1929 Allen Pkwy.
Houston, TX 77019 Tel: (713) 525 - 5230 Fax: (713) 525 - 7674

Contributions to Candidates: $2,000 (01/05 - 09/05)
Republicans: $2,000.

Principal Recipients

SENATE REPUBLICANS

HOUSE REPUBLICANS

Barton, Joe L (TX)	$1,000
Poe, Ted (TX)	$1,000

Corporate Foundations and Giving Programs

Service Corp. Corporate Giving Program
1929 Allen Pkwy.
Houston, TX 77019 Tel: (713) 522 - 5141 Fax: (713) 525 - 2800

Annual Grant Total: none reported

Public Affairs and Related Activities Personnel

At Headquarters

HEMEYER, Terry Tel: (713) 525 - 5497
Managing Director, Corporate Communications Fax: (713) 525 - 2800
terry.hemeyer@sci-us.com

HUGHES, Caressa F. Tel: (713) 525 - 5230
Managing Director, Governmental Affairs Fax: (713) 525 - 7674
caressa.hughes@sci-us.com

JONES, Jane D. Tel: (713) 522 - 5141
V. President, Human Resources Fax: (713) 525 - 2800

TANZBERGER, Eric D. Tel: (713) 522 - 5141
V. President and Corporate Controller Fax: (713) 525 - 2800
Responsibilities include investor relations.

YOUNG, Debbie Tel: (713) 525 - 9088
Director, Investor Relations Fax: (713) 525 - 2800
debbie.young@sci-us.com

The ServiceMaster Co.

Provides lawn care and landscape maintenance; termite and pest control; plumbing, heating and air conditioning maintenance and repair; appliance maintenance and repair; cleaning and furniture maintenance; and home warranties. Serves residential consumers and serves commercial and international markets
www.servicemaster.com
Annual Revenues: $3.589 billion

Chairman and Chief Exec. Officer
WARD, Jonathan P. Tel: (630) 663 - 2000 Fax: (630) 663 - 2001
jonathan.ward@servicemaster.com

Main Headquarters
Mailing: 3250 Lacey Rd., Suite 600 Downers Grove, IL 60515 Tel: (630) 663 - 2000 Fax: (630) 663 - 2001

Corporate Foundations and Giving Programs

ServiceMaster Foundation
3250 Lacey Rd., Suite 600
Downers Grove, IL 60515 Tel: (630) 663 - 2000 Fax: (630) 663 - 2001

Annual Grant Total: none reported

Public Affairs and Related Activities Personnel

At Headquarters

BONO, Steven Tel: (630) 663 - 2150
Senior V. President, Corporate Communications Fax: (630) 663 - 2001
steven.bond@servicemaster.com

BYOTS, Bruce J. Tel: (630) 663 - 2906
V. President, Investor Relations Fax: (630) 663 - 2001
bruce.byots@servicemaster.com

GOETTEL, Lisa Tel: (901) 681 - 1852
Senior V. President, Human Resources Fax: (901) 766 - 1107
lisa.gottel@servicemaster.com

RICHARDSON, Kevin C. Tel: (630) 663 - 2025
Senior V. President, Government Affairs Fax: (630) 663 - 2023
kevin.richardson@servicemaster.com

Sesame Workshop

Develops educational content for various forms of media and outreach. Founded in 1968 as the Children's Television Workshop.
www.sesameworkshop.org
Annual Revenues: $83.6 million

Chairman of the Board
MAI, Vincent A. Tel: (212) 595 - 3456 Fax: (212) 875 - 6088

Sesame Workshop

** continued from previous page*

President and Chief Exec. Officer
KNELL, Gary E. — Tel: (212) 595 - 3456; Fax: (212) 875 - 6088

Main Headquarters
Mailing: One Lincoln Plaza, New York, NY 10023 — Tel: (212) 595 - 3456; Fax: (212) 875 - 6088

Public Affairs and Related Activities Personnel

At Headquarters

WESTIN, Sherrie Rollins
Exec. V. President, Corporate Affairs, Education and Development — Tel: (212) 595 - 3456; Fax: (212) 875 - 6088

SGI

www.sgi.com
Annual Revenues: $842 million

Chairman and Chief Exec. Officer
BISHOP, Robert R. — Tel: (650) 933 - 1132; Fax: (650) 933 - 0316

Main Headquarters
Mailing: 1500 Crittenden Lane, Mountain View, CA 94043 — Tel: (650) 960 - 1980; Fax: (650) 933 - 0316

Washington Office
Contact: William Bartolone
Mailing: SGI Federal, 12200-G Plum Orchid Dr., Silver Spring, MD 20904 — Tel: (703) 578 - 3556; Fax: (703) 578 - 0272

Corporate Foundations and Giving Programs

SGI Corporate Giving Program
Contact: Christopher Bargeron
1500 Crittenden Lane
Mountain View, CA 94043 — Tel: (650) 960 - 1980

Annual Grant Total: none reported
Main focus of corporate giving is to provide programs and partnerships that benefit the community and our employees.
Geographic Preference: California; Wisconsin; Minnesota
Primary Interests: Education; Health and Human Services; Minority Opportunities

Public Affairs and Related Activities Personnel

At Headquarters

BABBITT, Ginny
Product Public Relations Contact — Tel: (650) 933 - 4519; Fax: (650) 933 - 0283

BARGERON, Christopher
Community Relations — Tel: (650) 960 - 1980

COLEMAN, Marty
Press Relations Contact
prdept@sgi.com — Tel: (650) 933 - 8119; Fax: (650) 933 - 0591

PISTACCHIO, Lisa
Corporate Public Relations Contact — Tel: (650) 933 - 5683; Fax: (650) 933 - 0283

At Washington Office

BARTOLONE, William
Director, Government Affairs
billb@sgi.com
Registered Federal Lobbyist. — Tel: (703) 578 - 3556; Fax: (703) 578 - 0272

Shaklee Corp.

A manufacturer of nutritional, personal care and household products.
www.shaklee.com

Chairman and Chief Exec. Officer
BARNETT, Roger — Tel: (925) 924 - 2000; Fax: (925) 924 - 2862

Main Headquarters
Mailing: 4747 Willow Rd., Pleasanton, CA 94588 — Tel: (925) 924 - 2000; Fax: (925) 924 - 2862

Corporate Foundations and Giving Programs

Shaklee Corporation Contributions Program
4747 Willow Rd.
Pleasanton, CA 94588 — Tel: (925) 924 - 2000; Fax: (925) 924 - 2862

Annual Grant Total: $400,000 - $500,000
Also sponsors Shaklee Scholarships and a "2 for 1" Matching Gift Program to foster employee support. Guidelines are available. Annual total given above is of cash only; it does not include value of donated products.
Geographic Preference: California; Oklahoma
Primary Interests: Health

Shaklee CARES
4747 Willow Rd.
Pleasanton, CA 94588 — Tel: (925) 924 - 2000; Fax: (925) 924 - 2862

Annual Grant Total: $2,000,000 - $5,000,000
Primary Interests: Disaster Relief

Public Affairs and Related Activities Personnel

At Headquarters

THOMPSON, Jenifer
Manager, Corporate Relations
jthompson@shaklee.com — Tel: (925) 924 - 2004; Fax: (925) 924 - 2280

Sharp Electronics Corp.

American subsidiary of the Japanese electronics manufacturer.
www.sharp-usa.com
Annual Revenues: $3.2 billion

Chairman and Chief Exec. Officer
FUJIMOTO, Toshihiko — Tel: (201) 529 - 8200; Fax: (201) 529 - 8819

Main Headquarters
Mailing: One Sharp Plaza, Mahwah, NJ 07430-2135 — Tel: (201) 529 - 8200; Fax: (201) 529 - 8819

Corporate Foundations and Giving Programs

Sharp Electronics Corporate Giving Program
One Sharp Plaza
Mahwah, NJ 07430-2135 — Tel: (201) 529 - 8200; Fax: (201) 529 - 8819

Annual Grant Total: none reported
Primary Interests: AIDS/HIV; Health and Human Services; Medical Research; Medicine and Health Care
Recent Recipients: Toys for Tots

Public Affairs and Related Activities Personnel

The Shaw Group Inc.

Provider of complete piping systems and comprehensive engineering, procurement and construction services. Subsidiaries include Stone & Webster, Inc. (see separate listing).
www.shawgrp.com
Annual Revenues: $762 million

Chairman, President and Chief Exec. Officer
BERNHARD, James M., Jr.
james.bernhard@shawgrp.com — Tel: (225) 932 - 2500; Fax: (225) 932 - 2661; TF: (800) 747 - 3322

Main Headquarters
Mailing: 4171 Essen Lane, Baton Rouge, LA 70809 — Tel: (225) 932 - 2500; Fax: (225) 932 - 2661; TF: (800) 747 - 3322

Washington Office
Mailing: 1717 Pennsylvania Ave. NW, Suite 900, Washington, DC 20006 — Tel: (202) 261 - 1900; Fax: (202) 261 - 1948

Public Affairs and Related Activities Personnel

At Headquarters

SAMMONS, Christopher D.
V. President, Investor Relations and Corporate Communications — Tel: (225) 932 - 2546; Fax: (225) 932 - 2661; TF: (800) 747 - 3322

At Washington Office

MARLO, Stephen M.
V. President, Government Affairs
stephen.marlo@shawgrp.com
Registered Federal Lobbyist. — Tel: (202) 261 - 1900; Fax: (202) 261 - 1948

Shaw Industries

A subsidiary of Berkshire Hathaway (see separate listing). A manufacturer of carpets, laminate, and area rugs.
www.shawinc.com
Annual Revenues: $4.334 billion

Chairman and Chief Exec. Officer
SHAW, Robert E. — Tel: (706) 278 - 3812; Fax: (706) 275 - 1719

Main Headquarters
Mailing: P.O. Drawer 2128, Dalton, GA 30722-2128 — Tel: (706) 278 - 3812; Fax: (706) 275 - 1719

Corporate Foundations and Giving Programs

Shaw Industries Corporate Contributions Program
Contact: Gerald Embry
P.O. Drawer 2128
Dalton, GA 30722-2128 — Tel: (706) 278 - 3812; Fax: (706) 275 - 1719

Annual Grant Total: none reported

Public Affairs and Related Activities Personnel

At Headquarters

BEVIL, C.K. "Buddy", Jr.
Director, Marketing Communications — Tel: (706) 278 - 3812; Fax: (706) 275 - 1719

EMBRY, Gerald
V. President, Administration
Responsibilities include corporate philanthropy. — Tel: (706) 278 - 3812; Fax: (706) 275 - 1719

SANDLIN, Scott
V. President, Marketing and Communications — Tel: (706) 278 - 3812; Fax: (706) 275 - 1719

Shaw Industries

** continued from previous page*

SHAW, Julius — Tel: (706) 278 - 3812
Exec. V. President — Fax: (706) 275 - 1719
Responsibilities include external communications.

Shaw's Supermarkets, Inc.

Operates a chain of supermarkets. A subsidiary of J. Sainsbury PLC of London, England.
www.shaws.com
Annual Revenues: $4.4 billion

President and Chief Exec. Officer
DIFELICE, Nicola — Tel: (508) 313 - 4000 — Fax: (508) 313 - 3112

Main Headquarters
Mailing: 750 W. Center St., West Bridgewater, MA 02379 — Tel: (508) 313 - 4000 — Fax: (508) 313 - 3112

Corporate Foundations and Giving Programs

Shaw's Supermarkets Community Commitment
750 W. Center St.
West Bridgewater, MA 02379 — Tel: (508) 313 - 4000 — Fax: (508) 313 - 3112

Annual Grant Total: none reported
Geographic Preference: Area(s) in which the company operates
Recent Recipients: America's Second Harvest; United Way

Public Affairs and Related Activities Personnel

At Headquarters

DONILON, Terrence — Tel: (508) 313 - 3318
Media Contact — Fax: (508) 313 - 3112

Sheetz, Inc.

Operator of convenience store chain.
www.sheetz.com
Annual Revenues: $1.92 billion

Chairman of the Board
SHEETZ, Stephen G. — Tel: (814) 946 - 3611 — Fax: (814) 946 - 4375 — TF: (800) 487 - 5444

President and Chief Exec. Officer
SHEETZ, Stanton R. — Tel: (814) 946 - 3611 — Fax: (814) 946 - 4375 — TF: (800) 487 - 5444

Main Headquarters
Mailing: 5700 Sixth Ave., Altoona, PA 16602 — Tel: (814) 946 - 3611 — Fax: (814) 946 - 4375 — TF: (800) 487 - 5444

Political Action Committees

SheetzPAC
Contact: Stanton R. Sheetz
5700 Sixth Ave.
Altoona, PA 16602 — Tel: (814) 946 - 3611 — Fax: (814) 946 - 4375 — TF: (800) 487 - 5444

Contributions to Candidates: $1,000 (01/05 - 09/05)
Republicans: $1,000.

Principal Recipients

SENATE REPUBLICANS		HOUSE REPUBLICANS	
Santorum, Richard (PA)	$1,000		

Corporate Foundations and Giving Programs

Sheetz, Inc. Corporate Giving Program
5700 Sixth Ave.
Altoona, PA 16602 — Tel: (814) 946 - 3611 — Fax: (814) 946 - 4375 — TF: (800) 487 - 5444

Annual Grant Total: none reported
Recent Recipients: Salvation Army; Special Olympics

Public Affairs and Related Activities Personnel

At Headquarters

FREEMAN, Phil — Tel: (814) 946 - 3611
V. President, Human Resources — Fax: (814) 946 - 4375 — TF: (800) 487 - 5444

Shell Chemical Co.

See listing on page 436 under Shell Oil Co.

Shell Noreast Co.

See listing on page 436 under Shell Oil Co.

Shell Oil Co.

A major producer, refiner and marketer of petroleum products and chemicals. Affiliated with the Royal Dutch/Shell Group of companies. Acquired Pennzoil-Quaker State Co. in October of 2002.
www.shell.com

Chairman of the Board
VAN DER VEER, Jeroen — Tel: (713) 241 - 6161 — Fax: (713) 241 - 4044

Main Headquarters
Mailing: P.O. Box 2463, Houston, TX 77252-2463 — Tel: (713) 241 - 6161 — Fax: (713) 241 - 4044
Street: One Shell Plaza, 910 Louisiana St., Houston, TX 77002

Washington Office
Contact: Brian P. Malnak
Mailing: 1401 I St. NW, Suite 1030, Washington, DC 20005 — Tel: (202) 466 - 1405 — Fax: (202) 466 - 1498

Political Action Committees

Shell Oil Co. Employees' Political Awareness Committee
Contact: Susan D. Sherman
P.O. Box 2463
Houston, TX 77252-2463 — Tel: (713) 241 - 6161 — Fax: (713) 241 - 4044

Contributions to Candidates: $14,000 (01/05 - 09/05)
Democrats: $2,000; Republicans: $12,000.

Principal Recipients

SENATE DEMOCRATS		HOUSE DEMOCRATS	
Landrieu, Mary (LA)	$1,000	Green, Gene (TX)	$1,000
SENATE REPUBLICANS		**HOUSE REPUBLICANS**	
Allen, George (VA)	$2,000	Barton, Joe L (TX)	$3,000
Hutchison, Kay Bailey (TX)		Capito, Shelley (WV)	$1,000
	$2,000	Taylor, Charles H (NC)	$1,000
Burns, Conrad (MT)	$1,000		
Lugar, Richard G (IN)	$1,000		
Thomas, Craig (WY)	$1,000		

Public Affairs and Related Activities Personnel

At Headquarters

DECYK, Roxanne — Tel: (713) 241 - 0780
Senior V. President, Corporate Affairs and Human Resources — Fax: (713) 241 - 1681

KNISELY, Anne — Tel: (713) 241 - 6161
Manager, Media Relations — Fax: (713) 241 - 6988

MORLEY, Patricia — Tel: (713) 241 - 0494
Manager, Corporate Communications — Fax: (713) 241 - 6988

SHERMAN, Susan D. — Tel: (713) 241 - 6161
PAC Treasurer — Fax: (713) 241 - 4044

At Washington Office

GLENN, Sara — Tel: (202) 466 - 1400
Washington Counsel — Fax: (202) 466 - 1498
sara.glenn@shell.com
Registered Federal Lobbyist.

MALNAK, Brian P. — Tel: (202) 466 - 1405
V. President, Government Affairs — Fax: (202) 466 - 1498

MYRES, Albert H. — Tel: (202) 466 - 1474
Senior Advisor — Fax: (202) 466 - 1498
albert.myres@shell.com
(Shell Chemical Co.)
Registered Federal Lobbyist.

RICH, James E., Jr. — Tel: (202) 466 - 1425
Senior Washington Counsel — Fax: (202) 466 - 1498
james.rich@shell.com
Registered Federal Lobbyist.

WELCH, Nicholas — Tel: (202) 466 - 1416
Advisor, International Relations — Fax: (202) 466 - 1498
nicholas.welch@shell.com

Shell Western E & P, Inc.

See listing on page 436 under Shell Oil Co.

Sherwin-Williams Co.

A manufacturer of paints, varnishes and related products. Distributes these products through more than 2,000 company-owned stores.
www.sherwin-williams.com
Annual Revenues: $5.066 billion

Chairman and Chief Exec. Officer
CONNOR, Christopher M. — Tel: (216) 566 - 2000 — Fax: (216) 566 - 3312

Main Headquarters
Mailing: 101 Prospect Ave. NW, Cleveland, OH 44115 — Tel: (216) 566 - 2000 — Fax: (216) 566 - 2947

Sherwin-Williams Co.

* continued from previous page

Corporate Foundations and Giving Programs

Sherwin-Williams Foundation
Contact: Barbara L. Gadosik
101 Prospect Ave. NW — Tel: (216) 566 - 2511
Cleveland, OH 44115 — Fax: (216) 566 - 3312

Annual Grant Total: $750,000 - $1,000,000
Interested in programs which (1) produce a mutual benefit for the company and the recipient; (2) assist community organizations to keep control of their activities and (3) help the company take its proper role in industry, citizenship and leadership.
Geographic Preference: Area(s) in which the company operates
Primary Interests: Civic and Cultural Activities; Education; Health and Human Services
Recent Recipients: Future Farmers of America; Junior Achievement; United Negro College Fund; United Way

Public Affairs and Related Activities Personnel

At Headquarters

GADOSIK, Barbara L. — Tel: (216) 566 - 2511
Director, Corporate Contributions — Fax: (216) 566 - 3312

HOPKINS, Thomas E. — Tel: (216) 566 - 2071
Senior V. President, Human Resources — Fax: (216) 566 - 3312

IVY, Conway G. — Tel: (216) 566 - 2140
Senior V. President, Corporate Planning and Development — Fax: (216) 566 - 2947
Responsibilities include corporate communications and public relations and development.

WELLS, Robert J. — Tel: (216) 566 - 2244
V. President, Corporate Planning and Communications — Fax: (216) 566 - 3312

Shopko Stores, Inc.

A chain of discount stores.
www.shopko.com
Annual Revenues: $3.252 billion

Main Headquarters
Mailing: 700 Pilgrim Way — Tel: (920) 429 - 2211
Green Bay, WI 54304 — Fax: (920) 429 - 5328

Corporate Foundations and Giving Programs

Shopko Contributions
700 Pilgrim Way — Tel: (920) 429 - 2211
Green Bay, WI 54304 — Fax: (920) 429 - 5328

Assets: $4,000,000 (1999)
Annual Grant Total: none reported
Geographic Preference: Area(s) in which the company operates
Primary Interests: Arts and Culture; Education; Families; Persons with Disabilities
Recent Recipients: Special Olympics; United Way

Public Affairs and Related Activities Personnel

At Headquarters

ANDREWS, Steven R. — Tel: (920) 429 - 2211
V. President, Human Resources — Fax: (920) 429 - 5328

VIGELAND, John — Tel: (920) 429 - 4132
Director, Corporate Communications — Fax: (920) 429 - 5328

Showtime Networks Inc.

See listing on page 505 under Viacom Inc/CBS Corp.

Siebel Systems, Inc.

Developer of computer software.
www.siebel.com
Annual Revenues: $1.635 billion

Chairman of the Board
SIEBEL, Thomas M. — Tel: (650) 295 - 5000
tsiebel@siebel.com — Fax: (650) 295 - 5111 — TF: (800) 356 - 3321

Chief Exec. Officer
SHAHEEN, George T. — Tel: (650) 295 - 5000 — Fax: (650) 295 - 5111 — TF: (800) 356 - 3321

Main Headquarters
Mailing: 2207 Bridgepoint Pkwy. — Tel: (650) 295 - 5000
San Mateo, CA 94404 — Fax: (650) 295 - 5111 — TF: (800) 356 - 3321

Washington Office
Mailing: 1776 I St. NW — Tel: (202) 756 - 1400
Suite 900 — Fax: (202) 756 - 1414
Washington, DC 20006

Political Action Committees

Siebel Systems, Inc. EGovernment PAC
Contact: Kenneth A. Goldman
2207 Bridgepoint Pkwy. — Tel: (650) 295 - 5000
San Mateo, CA 94404 — Fax: (650) 295 - 5111 — TF: (800) 356 - 3321

Contributions to Candidates: $75,500 (01/05 - 09/05)
Democrats: $2,500; Republicans: $73,000.

Principal Recipients

SENATE DEMOCRATS

HOUSE DEMOCRATS
Lofgren, Zoe (CA) $2,500

SENATE REPUBLICANS
Burns, Conrad (MT) $10,000
Allen, George (VA) $5,000
Collins, Susan M (ME) $5,000
Ensign, John Eric (NV) $3,000

HOUSE REPUBLICANS
Cunningham, Duke (CA) $10,000
Blunt, Roy (MO) $5,000
Davis, Tom (VA) $5,000
Dreier, David (CA) $5,000
Hunter, Duncan (CA) $5,000
Nunes, Devin (CA) $5,000
Hayworth, J D (AZ) $2,500
Jindal, Bobby (LA) $2,500
Lewis, Jerry (CA) $2,500
Weldon, Curt (PA) $2,500
Weller, Jerry (IL) $2,500
Wilson, Heather (NM) $2,500

Public Affairs and Related Activities Personnel

At Headquarters

GOLDMAN, Kenneth A. — Tel: (650) 295 - 5000
Senior V. President, Finance and Adminstration and Chief Financial Officer — Fax: (650) 295 - 5111 — TF: (800) 356 - 3321
kgoldman@siebel.com
Responsibilities include investor relations.

HANSON, Mark D. — Tel: (650) 295 - 5000
Senior V. President, Coporate Development and Investor Relations — Fax: (650) 295 - 5111 — TF: (800) 356 - 3321

TOLEDANO, Gabrielle — Tel: (650) 295 - 5000
V. President, Human Resources — Fax: (650) 295 - 5111 — TF: (800) 356 - 3321

At Washington Office

GANN, Tom — Tel: (703) 796 - 9429
Vice President and General Manager, Public Sector and Homeland Security — Fax: (703) 796 - 7227
tgann@siebel.com
Responsibilities include government relations.

HOOLEY, Jim — Tel: (202) 756 - 1413
Exec. Director, U.S. Government Affairs — Fax: (202) 756 - 1414
jhooley@siebel.com
Registered Federal Lobbyist.

Siemens Corp.

A member of the Public Affairs Council. The holding company for the shares of Siemens companies in the U.S. Provides coordination, corporate services and support to Siemens operating companies.
www.usa.siemens.com
Annual Revenues: $20.677 billion

Chief Exec.Officer
NOLAN, George C. — Tel: (212) 258 - 4000 — Fax: (212) 767 - 0580 — TF: (800) 743 - 6367

Main Headquarters
Mailing: 153 E. 53rd St. — Tel: (212) 258 - 4000
56th Floor — Fax: (212) 767 - 0580
New York, NY 10022-4611 — TF: (800) 743 - 6367

Washington Office
Contact: Gregg Ward
Mailing: 701 Pennsylvania Ave. NW — Tel: (202) 434 - 4800
Suite 720 — Fax: (202) 347 - 4015
Washington, DC 20004

Political Action Committees

Siemens Corp. PAC
Contact: Gregg Ward
701 Pennsylvania Ave. NW — Tel: (202) 434 - 4800
Suite 720 — Fax: (202) 347 - 4015
Washington, DC 20004

Contributions to Candidates: $127,499 (01/05 - 09/05)
Democrats: $36,500; Republicans: $86,000; Other: $4,999.

Siemens Corp.

* continued from previous page

Principal Recipients

SENATE DEMOCRATS		HOUSE DEMOCRATS	
Kennedy, Ted (MA)	$5,000	Lofgren, Zoe (CA)	$3,500
Nelson, Bill (FL)	$3,000		
Bingaman, Jeff (NM)	$2,000		
		HOUSE OTHER	
		Pitts, Joseph R (PA)	$4,999
SENATE REPUBLICANS		**HOUSE REPUBLICANS**	
Dewine, Richard (OH)	$5,000	Myrick, Sue (NC)	$5,000
Allen, George (VA)	$4,000	Gerlach, Jim (PA)	$4,500
Ensign, John Eric (NV)	$3,000	Pickering, Chip (MS)	$4,500
Hatch, Orrin (UT)	$3,000	Cantor, Eric (VA)	$3,500
Burns, Conrad (MT)	$2,000	Upton, Fred (MI)	$3,500

Corporate Foundations and Giving Programs

The Siemens Foundation
Contact: Veronica Angeles
170 Wood Ave. South
Iselin, NJ 08830
Tel: (877) 822 - 5233
Fax: (732) 603 - 5890

Annual Grant Total: none reported
Maintains a web site at http://www.siemens-foundation.org.

Public Affairs and Related Activities Personnel

At Headquarters

BERGEN, Jack D.
Senior V. President, Corporate Affairs and Marketing
Tel: (212) 258 - 4000
Fax: (212) 767 - 0580
TF: (800) 743 - 6367

DAVIS, Paula
Director, Public Relations
paula.davis@siemens.com
Tel: (212) 258 - 4260
Fax: (212) 767 - 0580
TF: (800) 743 - 6367

PANIGEL, Michael
Senior V. President, Human Resources
Tel: (212) 258 - 4000
Fax: (212) 767 - 0580
TF: (800) 743 - 6367

At Washington Office

HENRY, Marion
Tel: (202) 434 - 4800
Fax: (202) 347 - 4015
Registered Federal Lobbyist.

KERR, Eleanor
Director, Legislative Affairs -- Healthcare Appropriations
eleanor.kerr@sc.siemens.com
Registered Federal Lobbyist.
Tel: (202) 434 - 4800
Fax: (202) 347 - 4015

MIKEL, John
Director, Legislative Affairs
Registered Federal Lobbyist.
Tel: (202) 434 - 4800
Fax: (202) 347 - 4015

PHILLIPS, Tom
Tel: (202) 434 - 4800
Fax: (202) 347 - 4015
Registered Federal Lobbyist.

WARD, Gregg
Senior V. President, Government Affairs
gregg.ward@siemens.com
Tel: (202) 434 - 4800
Fax: (202) 347 - 4015

At Other Offices

ANGELES, Veronica
Program Director
170 Wood Ave. South
Iselin, NJ 08830
Tel: (877) 822 - 5233
Fax: (732) 603 - 5890

Sierra Health Services, Inc.

A member of the Public Affairs Council. Offers managed care benefit plans for individuals, employers, and government programs.
www.sierrahealth.com
Annual Revenues: $1.278 billion

Chairman and Chief Exec. Officer
MARLON, Anthony M., M.D.
Tel: (702) 242 - 7000
Fax: (702) 242 - 1531

Main Headquarters
Mailing: P.O. Box 15645
Las Vegas, NV 89114-5645
Tel: (702) 242 - 7000
Fax: (702) 242 - 1531
Street: 2724 N. Tenaya Way
Las Vegas, NV 89128-0424

Political Action Committees

Sierra Health Services Political Action Committee (SHSPAC)
Contact: Marie H. Soldo
P.O. Box 15645
Las Vegas, NV 89114-5645
Tel: (702) 242 - 7000
Fax: (702) 242 - 1531

Contributions to Candidates: $22,575 (01/05 - 09/05)
Democrats: $3,000; Republicans: $19,575.

Principal Recipients

SENATE REPUBLICANS		HOUSE REPUBLICANS	
Kyl, Jon L (AZ)	$4,000	Porter, Jon (NV)	$5,075
Ensign, John Eric (NV)	$2,000	Johnson, Nancy (CT)	$3,000
		Heller, Dean (NV)	$2,500
		Johnson, Samuel (TX)	$2,000

Public Affairs and Related Activities Personnel

At Headquarters

KRUGER, Dan
V. President, Human Resources
Tel: (702) 242 - 7000
Fax: (702) 242 - 1531

O'NEILL, Peter
V. President, Public and Investor Relations
Tel: (702) 242 - 7000
Fax: (702) 242 - 1531

SOLDO, Marie H.
Exec. V. President, Government Affairs and Special Projects
Responsibilities include political action.
Tel: (702) 242 - 7000
Fax: (702) 242 - 1531

Sierra Pacific Power Co.

See listing on page 438 under Sierra Pacific Resources.

Sierra Pacific Resources

A member of the Public Affairs Council. An electric, gas and water utility. Subsidiaries include Nevada Power Co. (see separate listing) and Sierra Pacific Power Co.
www.sierrapacific.com
Annual Revenues: $2.991 billion

Chairman, President and Chief Exec. Officer
HIGGINS, Walter M., III
Tel: (702) 367 - 5600
TF: (800) 962 - 0399

Main Headquarters
Mailing: P.O. Box 10100
Reno, NV 89520-0026
Tel: (775) 834 - 4444
Fax: (775) 834 - 4202
TF: (800) 962 - 0399
Street: 6100 Neil Rd.
Reno, NV 89502

Corporate Foundations and Giving Programs

Sierra Pacific Resources Foundation for Charitable Contributions
Contact: Karen Foster
P.O. Box 10100
Reno, NV 89520-0026
Tel: (775) 834 - 5741
Fax: (775) 834 - 4339
TF: (800) 962 - 0399

Annual Grant Total: none reported
Geographic Preference: Area(s) in which the company operates; California; Nevada

Public Affairs and Related Activities Personnel

At Headquarters

FOSTER, Karen
Manager, Community Relations
(Sierra Pacific Power Co.)
karenfoster@sppc.com
Tel: (775) 834 - 5741
Fax: (775) 834 - 4339
TF: (800) 962 - 0399

LANGLEY, Kelly
Investor Relations Contact
Tel: (775) 834 - 5723
Fax: (775) 834 - 5462
TF: (800) 962 - 0399

Sigma-Aldrich Corp.

Manufactures biochemicals and organic chemical products used in scientific and genomic research, biotechnology, pharmaceutical development, disease diagnosis and high technology manufacturing.
www.sigma-aldrich.com
Annual Revenues: $1.409 billion

Chairman, President, and Chief Exec. Officer
HARVEY, David R.
dharvey@sial.com
Tel: (314) 771 - 5765
Fax: (800) 325 - 5052
TF: (800) 325 - 3010

Main Headquarters
Mailing: 3050 Spruce St.
St. Louis, MO 63103
Tel: (314) 771 - 5765
Fax: (800) 325 - 5052
TF: (800) 325 - 3010

Corporate Foundations and Giving Programs

Sigma-Aldrich Foundation
Contact: Kirk A. Richter
3050 Spruce St.
St. Louis, MO 63103
Tel: (314) 286 - 8004
Fax: (314) 286 - 7874
TF: (800) 325 - 3010

Annual Grant Total: none reported

Public Affairs and Related Activities Personnel

At Headquarters

RICHTER, Kirk A.
Treasurer
Tel: (314) 286 - 8004
Fax: (314) 286 - 7874
TF: (800) 325 - 3010
Responsibilities include corporate philanthropy and investor relations.

Silicon Graphics, Inc.

See listing on page 435 under SGI.

Simon & Schuster Inc.

See listing on page 505 under Viacom Inc/CBS Corp.

Simon Property Group

A self-administered/self-managed real estate investment trust.
www.simon.com
Annual Revenues: $2.44 billion

Co-Chairman of the Board
SIMON, Herbert — Tel: (317) 636 - 1600 Fax: (317) 263 - 2318

Co-Chairman of the Board
SIMON, Melvin — Tel: (317) 636 - 1600 Fax: (317) 263 - 2318

Chief Exec. Officer
SIMON, David — Tel: (317) 636 - 1600 Fax: (317) 263 - 2318

Main Headquarters
Mailing: P.O. Box 7033
Indianapolis, IN 46207 — Tel: (317) 636 - 1600 Fax: (317) 263 - 2318 TF: (800) 509 - 3676
Street: 115 W. Washington St.
Indianapolis, IN 46204

Corporate Foundations and Giving Programs

Simon Youth Foundation
Contact: Richard Markoff, Ph.D.
P.O. Box 7033
Indianapolis, IN 46207 — Tel: (317) 263 - 2361 Fax: (317) 263 - 2318

Annual Grant Total: none reported
Primary Interests: Education; Youth Services

Public Affairs and Related Activities Personnel

At Headquarters

DORAN, Shelly J.
V. President, Investor Relations
sdoran@simon.com — Tel: (317) 685 - 7330 Fax: (317) 263 - 2318

MARKOFF, Richard, Ph.D.
Exec. Director, Simon Youth Foundation
rmarkoff@simon.com — Tel: (317) 263 - 2361 Fax: (317) 263 - 2318

MCCARTY, Michael P.
Senior V. President, Research and Corporate Communications
mimccarty@simon.com — Tel: (317) 263 - 2925 Fax: (317) 263 - 2318

MORRIS, Les
Manager, Corporate Public Affairs — Tel: (317) 263 - 7711 Fax: (317) 263 - 2318

SCOTT, Billie
Director, Public Relations
bscott@simon.com — Tel: (317) 263 - 7148 Fax: (317) 263 - 2318

J. R. Simplot Co.

An agribusiness company with operations in food processing, farming, cattle feeding, fertilizer manufacturing, and turf products.
www.simplot.com
Annual Revenues: $3 billion

Chairman of the Board
SIMPLOT, Scott R. — Tel: (208) 336 - 2110 Fax: (208) 389 - 7515

President and Chief Exec. Officer
HLOBIK, Lawrence S.
lhlobik@simplot.com — Tel: (208) 336 - 2110 Fax: (208) 389 - 7515

Main Headquarters
Mailing: P.O. Box 27
Boise, ID 83707 — Tel: (208) 336 - 2110 Fax: (208) 389 - 7515
Street: One Capital Center
999 Main St.
Boise, ID 83702

Political Action Committees

J. R. Simplot Co. Political Action Committee (SIM-PAC)
Contact: Mark A. Dunn
P.O. Box 27
Boise, ID 83707 — Tel: (208) 389 - 7377 Fax: (208) 389 - 7433

Contributions to Candidates: $7,000 (01/05 - 09/05)
Republicans: $7,000.

Principal Recipients

SENATE REPUBLICANS
Smith, Gordon (OR) $5,000

HOUSE REPUBLICANS
Pombo, Richard (CA) $1,000
Walden, Gregory (OR) $1,000

Corporate Foundations and Giving Programs

J. R. Simplot Co. Corporate Contributions Program
Contact: Fred Zerza
P.O. Box 27
Boise, ID 83707 — Tel: (208) 389 - 7337 Fax: (208) 389 - 7433

Annual Grant Total: none reported

Public Affairs and Related Activities Personnel

At Headquarters

DUNN, Mark A.
V. President, Government Affairs
madunn@simplot.com — Tel: (208) 389 - 7377 Fax: (208) 389 - 7433
Responsibilities include political action.

ZERZA, Fred
V. President, Public and Government Relations
fzerza@simplot.com — Tel: (208) 389 - 7337 Fax: (208) 389 - 7433
Responsibilities include corporate philanthropy.

Simpson Investment Co.

A holding company for a forest products firm.
www.simpson.com
Annual Revenues: $800 million

Chairman and Chief Exec. Officer
MOSELEY, Colin — Tel: (253) 779 - 6400 Fax: (253) 280 - 9000

Main Headquarters
Mailing: 917 E. 11th St.
Tacoma, WA 98421 — Tel: (253) 779 - 6400 Fax: (253) 280 - 9000

Political Action Committees

Simpson Investment Co. PAC
Contact: Joseph R. Breed
917 E. 11th St.
Tacoma, WA 98421 — Tel: (253) 779 - 6400 Fax: (253) 280 - 9000

Contributions to Candidates: $2,000 (01/05 - 09/05)
Democrats: $1,000; Republicans: $1,000.

Principal Recipients

SENATE DEMOCRATS

HOUSE DEMOCRATS
Smith, Adam (WA) $1,000

SENATE REPUBLICANS

HOUSE REPUBLICANS
Knollenberg, Joe (MI) $1,000

Corporate Foundations and Giving Programs

Simpson Fund
917 E. 11th St.
Tacoma, WA 98421 — Tel: (253) 779 - 6400 Fax: (253) 280 - 9000

Annual Grant Total: none reported

Public Affairs and Related Activities Personnel

At Headquarters

BREED, Joseph R.
PAC Treasurer
Mailstop: # 2800 — Tel: (253) 779 - 6400 Fax: (253) 280 - 9000

HOLLAND, Beverly J.
Manager, Public Affairs
bhollan@simpson.com — Tel: (253) 779 - 6400 Fax: (253) 280 - 9000

Sinclair Oil Corp.

A privately-held company.
www.sinclairoil.com
Annual Revenues: $2.3 billion

Chief Exec. Officer
HOLDING, R. Earl — Tel: (801) 524 - 2700 Fax: (801) 524 - 2848

Main Headquarters
Mailing: P.O. Box 30825
Salt Lake City, UT 84130-0825 — Tel: (801) 524 - 2700 Fax: (801) 524 - 2880
Street: 550 E. South Temple
Salt Lake City, UT 84130-0825

Public Affairs and Related Activities Personnel

At Headquarters

ENSIGN, Clinton W.
V. President, Government Relations — Tel: (801) 524 - 2767 Fax: (801) 524 - 2848

HARDY, Lowell
Director, Human Resources — Tel: (801) 524 - 2700 Fax: (801) 526 - 3000

SIRVA, Inc.

A global relocation and moving services business. Brands include Allied Van Lines, NorthAmerican Van Lines, Global Van Lines, and SIRVA Relocation.
www.sirva.com

SIRVA, Inc.
** continued from previous page*

President and Chief Exec. Officer
KELLEY, Brian P. — Tel: (630) 570 - 3000 Fax: (630) 570 - 3606

Main Headquarters
Mailing: 700 Oakmont Lane
Westmont, IL 60559 — Tel: (630) 570 - 3000 Fax: (630) 570 - 3606

Public Affairs and Related Activities Personnel

At Headquarters

SCHORR, Todd W.
Senior V. President, Human Resources — Tel: (630) 570 - 3000 Fax: (630) 570 - 3606

TRAINOR, Jim
V. President, Corporate Communications — Tel: (630) 570 - 4828 Fax: (630) 570 - 3606

WOHLT, Judith A.
Manager, Corporate Communications — Tel: (630) 570 - 3000 Fax: (630) 570 - 3606

Six Flags, Inc.
A theme park company.
www.sixflags.com
Annual Revenues: $1 billion

Chairman and Chief Exec. Officer
BURKE, Kieran E. — Tel: (405) 475 - 2500 Fax: (405) 475 - 2558

Main Headquarters
Mailing: 11501 Northeast Exwy.
Oklahoma City, OK 73131-6499 — Tel: (405) 475 - 2500 Fax: (405) 475 - 2555

Public Affairs and Related Activities Personnel

At Headquarters

NAUSER, Debbie
V. President, Public Relations — Tel: (405) 475 - 2500 Fax: (405) 475 - 2558

SALEMI, Hank
Senior V. President, Marketing — Tel: (405) 475 - 2500 Fax: (405) 475 - 2558
Responsibilities include public relations.

Skechers U.S.A., Inc.
Designs, develops, and markets branded lifestyle footwear for men, women, and children.
www.skx.com
Annual Revenues: $943.6 million

Chairman and Chief Exec. Officer
GREENBERG, Robert — Tel: (310) 318 - 3100

Main Headquarters
Mailing: 228 Manhattan Beach Blvd.
Manhattan Beach, CA 90266 — Tel: (310) 318 - 3100 Fax: (310) 318 - 5019

Public Affairs and Related Activities Personnel

At Headquarters

CLAY, Jennifer
Press Contact — Tel: (310) 798 - 9662 Fax: (310) 318 - 5019

WEINBERG, David — Tel: (310) 318 - 3100
Exec. V. President and Chief Financial Officer
Responsibilities include investor relations.

SKF USA, Inc.
A manufacturer of anti-friction bearings products. A subsidiary of the Swedish firm Aktiebologet SKF.
www.skfusa.com

Chairman of the Board
SCHARP, Anders — Tel: (610) 630 - 2800 Fax: (610) 630 - 2801
anders.scharp@skf.com

President and Chief Exec. Officer
JOHNSTONE, Tom — Tel: (610) 630 - 2800 Fax: (610) 630 - 2801

Main Headquarters
Mailing: 1111 Adams Ave.
Norristown, PA 19403-2403 — Tel: (610) 630 - 2800 Fax: (610) 630 - 2801

Corporate Foundations and Giving Programs

SKF U.S.A. Corporate Giving Fund
1111 Adams Ave.
Norristown, PA 19403-2403 — Tel: (610) 630 - 2800 Fax: (610) 630 - 2801

Annual Grant Total: none reported

Public Affairs and Related Activities Personnel

At Headquarters

MCGLOCKLIN, Bill
Director, Environmental Affairs — Tel: (610) 630 - 2800 Fax: (610) 630 - 2801
bill.mcglocklin@skf.com

SORTINO, Gus C.
Director, Communications — Tel: (610) 630 - 2800 Fax: (610) 630 - 2801
gus.c.sortino@skf.com

SLM Corp.
A member of the Public Affairs Council. Formerly known as Sallie Mae (USA Education). Provides funds for educational loans.
www.salliemae.com
Annual Revenues: $3.978 billion

Chairman of the Board
LORD, Albert L. — Tel: (703) 810 - 3000 Fax: (703) 810 - 7053

Vice Chairman and Chief Exec. Officer
FITZPATRICK, Thomas J. — Tel: (703) 810 - 3000 Fax: (703) 810 - 7053

Main Headquarters
Mailing: 12061 Bluemont Way
Reston, VA 20190 — Tel: (703) 810 - 3000 Fax: (703) 810 - 7053

Washington Office
Contact: Rose DiNapoli
Mailing: 901 E St. NW
Fourth Floor
Washington, DC 20004-2037 — Tel: (202) 969 - 8000 Fax: (202) 969 - 8031

Political Action Committees

Sallie Mae Inc. Political Action Committee (Sallie Mae PAC)
12061 Bluemont Way
Reston, VA 20190 — Tel: (703) 810 - 3000 Fax: (703) 810 - 7053

Contributions to Candidates: $83,000 (01/05 - 09/05)
Democrats: $26,000; Republicans: $57,000.

Principal Recipients

SENATE DEMOCRATS
Conrad, Kent (ND) $2,000

HOUSE DEMOCRATS
Andrews, Robert (NJ) $5,000
Gordon, Barton (TN) $5,000
Hoyer, Steny (MD) $2,000

SENATE REPUBLICANS
Kyl, Jon L (AZ) $3,000
Ensign, John Eric (NV) $2,000

HOUSE REPUBLICANS
Hastert, Dennis J. (IL) $5,000
McKeon, Howard (CA) $5,000
McMorris, Cathy (WA) $5,000
Wolf, Frank R (VA) $5,000
Kuhl, John R Jr (NY) $3,500
Boehner, John (OH) $2,500
DeLay, Tom (TX) $2,500
Burton, Danny (IN) $2,000
Musgrave, Marilyn (CO) $2,000

Corporate Foundations and Giving Programs

Sallie Mae Fund
Contact: Hugh Rosen
12061 Bluemont Way
Reston, VA 20190 — Tel: (703) 984 - 6227 Fax: (703) 810 - 7053

Annual Grant Total: over $5,000,000
Annual giving exceeds $12 million.
Geographic Preference: Area(s) in which the company operates
Primary Interests: Higher Education

Public Affairs and Related Activities Personnel

At Headquarters

COLLIGAN, Charles A.
PAC Treasurer — Tel: (703) 810 - 3000 Fax: (703) 810 - 7053

DE LASKI, Kathleen
Senior V. President and Chief Communications Officer — Tel: (703) 810 - 3000 Fax: (703) 810 - 7053

HEINZ, Jeffrey R.
Assistant V. President, Investor Relations — Tel: (703) 810 - 7743 Fax: (703) 810 - 7053

JOYCE, Tom
V. President, Corporate Communications — Tel: (703) 984 - 5610 Fax: (703) 810 - 7053
tom.joyce@slma.com

ROSEN, Hugh
Press Contact, Sallie Mae Fund — Tel: (703) 984 - 6227 Fax: (703) 810 - 7053
hugh.rosen@slma.com

STOHLER, Thom
Press Contact, Government Relations and Policy — Tel: (703) 984 - 5586 Fax: (703) 810 - 7053
thom.stohler@slma.com

At Washington Office

BUCHANAN, Scott — Tel: (202) 969 - 8000 Fax: (202) 969 - 8031
Registered Federal Lobbyist.

DAVIS, Sara P.
Director, Government Relations — Tel: (202) 969 - 8020 Fax: (202) 969 - 8030
Registered Federal Lobbyist.

DINAPOLI, Rose
V. President, Government and Industry Relations — Tel: (202) 969 - 8020 Fax: (202) 969 - 8031
rose.dinapoli@slma.com
Registered Federal Lobbyist.

SLM Corp.

** continued from previous page*

DUCICH, Sarah
Director, Government and Industry Relations
Registered Federal Lobbyist.
Tel: (202) 969 - 8020
Fax: (202) 969 - 8031

HEYMAN, Steve
Registered Federal Lobbyist.
Tel: (202) 969 - 8000
Fax: (202) 969 - 8031

STEVENS, Jonathan
Registered Federal Lobbyist.
Tel: (202) 969 - 8000
Fax: (202) 969 - 8031

A. O. Smith Corp.

A manufacturer of electric motors and water heating equipment.
www.aosmith.com
Annual Revenues: $1.15 billion

Chairman and Chief Exec. Officer
O'TOOLE, Robert J.
Tel: (414) 359 - 4000
Fax: (414) 359 - 4064

Main Headquarters
Mailing: 11270 W. Park Place
Milwaukee, WI 53224-9510
Tel: (414) 359 - 4000
Fax: (414) 359 - 4064

Political Action Committees

A. O. Smith Corp. Political Action Committee (AOSPAC)
Contact: Patricia K. Ackerman
Box 23966
Milwaukee, WI 53224-9505
Tel: (414) 359 - 4129
Fax: (414) 359 - 4064

Contributions to Candidates: none reported (01/05 - 09/05)

Corporate Foundations and Giving Programs

A. O. Smith Foundation
Contact: Edward J. O'Connor
11270 W. Park Place
Milwaukee, WI 53224-9510
Tel: (414) 359 - 4101
Fax: (414) 359 - 4198

Annual Grant Total: $1,000,000 - $2,000,000
Also sponsors an employee matching gift program. Guidelines are available.
Geographic Preference: Area(s) in which the company operates; Illinois; Kentucky; North Carolina; Ohio; South Carolina; Tennessee; Washington State; Wisconsin
Primary Interests: Civic and Cultural Activities; Education; Health and Human Services
Recent Recipients: United Performing Arts Fund; United Way

Public Affairs and Related Activities Personnel

At Headquarters

LUBY, Ellen
Manager, Human Resources
Tel: (414) 359 - 4128
Fax: (414) 359 - 4198

O'CONNOR, Edward J.
Foundation Contact
Responsibilities also include corporate philanthropy.
Tel: (414) 359 - 4101
Fax: (414) 359 - 4198

PETRACRA, Mark
V. President, Human Resources and Public Affairs
Tel: (414) 359 - 4000
Fax: (414) 359 - 4064

PIRKEY, Herbert L.
Director, Safety, Health and Environment
Tel: (414) 359 - 4126
Fax: (414) 359 - 4064

SMITH, Roger S.
Manager, Corporate Advertising and Public Affairs
Responsibilities include government affairs.
Tel: (414) 359 - 4129
Fax: (414) 359 - 4064

WATSON, Craig
Director, Investor Relations
cwatson@aosmith.com
Tel: (414) 359 - 4009
Fax: (414) 359 - 4198

WRIGHT, Charles S.
Manager, Corporate Communications
Tel: (414) 359 - 4104
Fax: (414) 359 - 4064

At Other Offices

ACKERMAN, Patricia K.
Treasurer, A. O. Smith Corp. Political Action Committee
Box 23966
Milwaukee, WI 53224-9505
Tel: (414) 359 - 4129
Fax: (414) 359 - 4064

Smith Internat'l, Inc.

A supplier of products and services to the oil and gas exploration and production industry.
www.smith.com
Annual Revenues: $3.17 billion

Chairman and Chief Exec. Officer
ROCK, Doug
Tel: (281) 443 - 3370
TF: (800) 877 - 6484

Main Headquarters
Mailing: P.O. Box 60068
Houston, TX 77205-0068
Street: 16740 Hardy St
Houston, TX 77205
Tel: (281) 443 - 3370
TF: (800) 877 - 6484

Corporate Foundations and Giving Programs

Smith Internat'l, Inc. Corporate Giving Program
Contact: Neal S. Sutton
P.O. Box 60068
Houston, TX 77205-0068
Tel: (281) 443 - 3370
TF: (800) 877 - 6484

Annual Grant Total: none reported

Public Affairs and Related Activities Personnel

At Headquarters

DORMAN, Margaret K.
Senior V. President and Chief Financial Officer
mdorman@smith.com
Responsibilities include investor relations.
Tel: (281) 443 - 3370
TF: (800) 877 - 6484

SUTTON, Neal S.
Senior V. President, Administration, General Counsel and Secretary
nsutton@smith.com
Responsibilities include corporate philanthropy.
Tel: (281) 443 - 3370
TF: (800) 877 - 6484

Smithfield Foods, Inc.

A meat packing company.
www.smithfieldfoods.com
Annual Revenues: $9.267 billion

Chairman and Chief Exec. Officer
LUTER, Joseph W., III
Tel: (757) 365 - 3000
Fax: (757) 365 - 3017
TF: (888) 366 - 6767

Main Headquarters
Mailing: 200 Commerce St.
Smithfield, VA 23430
Tel: (757) 365 - 3000
Fax: (757) 365 - 3017
TF: (888) 366 - 6767

Washington Office
Mailing: 1050 Connecticut Ave. NW
Suite 1200
Washington, DC 20036
Tel: (202) 857 - 2411
Fax: (202) 857 - 1737

Political Action Committees

Smithfield Foods Inc. Political Action Committee (HamPAC)
Contact: Jerry H. Goodwin
1050 Connecticut Ave. NW
Suite 1200
Washington, DC 20036
Tel: (202) 857 - 2411
Fax: (202) 857 - 1737

Contributions to Candidates: $29,500 (01/05 - 09/05)
Democrats: $3,000; Republicans: $26,500.

Principal Recipients

SENATE DEMOCRATS

HOUSE DEMOCRATS

Boucher, Fredrick (VA)	$1,000
Evans, Lane (IL)	$1,000
McIntyre, Mike (NC)	$1,000

SENATE REPUBLICANS

Chambliss, Saxby (GA)	$3,500
Alexander, Lamar (TN)	$1,000
Santorum, Richard (PA)	$1,000
Talent, James (MO)	$1,000

HOUSE REPUBLICANS

Dewine, R. Pat (OH)	$5,000
Hastert, Dennis J. (IL)	$5,000
Davis, Jo Ann (VA)	$2,000
Bonilla, Henry (TX)	$1,000
Burton, Danny (IN)	$1,000
Cantor, Eric (VA)	$1,000
Gillmor, Paul E (OH)	$1,000
Goodlatte, Robert (VA)	$1,000
Graves, Sam (MO)	$1,000
Gutknecht, Gil (MN)	$1,000
Moran, Jerry (KS)	$1,000

Public Affairs and Related Activities Personnel

At Headquarters

TREACY, Dennis H.
V. President, Environmental and Government Affairs
Tel: (757) 365 - 3000
Fax: (757) 365 - 3017
TF: (888) 366 - 6767

At Washington Office

GOODWIN, Jerry H.
PAC Contact
Tel: (202) 857 - 2411
Fax: (202) 857 - 1737

At Other Offices

HOSTETTER, Jerry
V. President, Investor Relations and Corporate Communications
499 Park Ave.
New York, NY 10022
Responsibilities also include government relations.
Tel: (212) 758 - 8568
Fax: (212) 758 - 8421

The J. M. Smucker Company

A producer of jams and jellies, ice cream toppings, peanut butters, shortening, oils, health and natural foods and beverages. Acquired Internat'l Multifoods Corp. in June, 2004.

www.smuckers.com

Annual Revenues: $1.311 billion

Chairman and Co-Chief Exec. Officer
SMUCKER, Timothy P.
Tel: (330) 682 - 3000
Fax: (330) 684 - 6410
TF: (888) 550 - 9555

President, Co-Chief Exec. Officer and Chief Financial Officer
SMUCKER, Richard K.
Tel: (330) 682 - 3000
Fax: (330) 684 - 6410
TF: (888) 550 - 9555

Main Headquarters

Mailing: Strawberry Lane
Orrville, OH 44667-0280
Tel: (330) 682 - 3000
Fax: (330) 684 - 6410
TF: (888) 550 - 9555

Street: Strawberry Lane
Orrville, OH 44667

Corporate Foundations and Giving Programs

The J.M. Smucker Company
Contact: Maribeth Badertscher
Strawberry Lane
Orrville, OH 44667-0280
Tel: (330) 682 - 3000
Fax: (330) 684 - 6410
TF: (888) 550 - 9555

Annual Grant Total: $500,000 - $750,000
Geographic Preference: Area(s) in which the company operates
Primary Interests: Education; Youth Services
Recent Recipients: Boys and Girls Club; Junior Achievement; YMCA

Public Affairs and Related Activities Personnel

At Headquarters

BADERTSCHER, Maribeth
Manager, Community Initiatives
Tel: (330) 682 - 3000
Fax: (330) 684 - 6410
TF: (888) 550 - 9555

Responsibilities include corporate philanthropy.

DEMPSEY, Brenda
Director, Corporate Communications
Tel: (330) 682 - 3000
Fax: (330) 684 - 6410
TF: (888) 550 - 9555

ELLIS, Robert E.
V. President, Human Resources
Tel: (330) 682 - 3000
Fax: (330) 684 - 6410
TF: (888) 550 - 9555

Smurfit-Stone Container

Formed by the merger of Jefferson Smurfit Corp. and Stone Container Corp. Producer of containerboard, kraft paper, paper sacks and bags, multiwall shipping sacks, newsprint, groundwood paper and wood products.

www.smurfit-stone.com

Annual Revenues: $7.483 billion

Chairman and Chief Exec. Officer
MOORE, Patrick J.
Tel: (312) 346 - 6600
Fax: (312) 580 - 4919

Main Headquarters

Mailing: 150 N. Michigan Ave.
Suite 1700
Chicago, IL 60601-7568
Tel: (312) 346 - 6600
Fax: (312) 580 - 4919

Political Action Committees

Smurfit-Stone Container Corp. PAC
Contact: Charles A. Hinrichs
150 N. Michigan Ave.
Suite 1700
Chicago, IL 60601-7568
Tel: (312) 346 - 6600
Fax: (312) 580 - 4919

Contributions to Candidates: $10,550 (01/05 - 09/05)
Democrats: $2,000; Republicans: $8,550.

Principal Recipients

SENATE DEMOCRATS
Carper, Thomas R (DE) $1,000
Kennedy, John Neely (LA) $1,000

HOUSE DEMOCRATS

SENATE REPUBLICANS
Talent, James (MO) $2,550
Vitter, David (LA) $2,000
Burns, Conrad (MT) $1,000

HOUSE REPUBLICANS
Boehner, John (OH) $1,000
Hastert, Dennis J. (IL) $1,000
Hulshof, Kenny (MO) $1,000

Corporate Foundations and Giving Programs

Stone Foundation
150 N. Michigan Ave.
Suite 1700
Chicago, IL 60601-7568
Tel: (312) 346 - 6600
Fax: (312) 580 - 4919

Annual Grant Total: $750,000 - $1,000,000
Geographic Preference: Illinois
Primary Interests: Higher Education; Social Services
Recent Recipients: United Way

Public Affairs and Related Activities Personnel

At Headquarters

BARTON, Curtis A.
V. President, Environmental Affairs
Tel: (312) 346 - 6600
Fax: (312) 580 - 4919

HACKNEY, Ronald D.
Senior V. President, Human Resources
Tel: (312) 346 - 6600
Fax: (312) 580 - 4919

HINRICHS, Charles A.
Senior V. President and Chief Financial Officer
Tel: (312) 346 - 6600
Fax: (312) 580 - 4919
Responsibilities include political action.

MCKENNA, Tim
Senior V. President, Investor Relations and Communications
Tel: (312) 580 - 4637
Fax: (312) 580 - 4919

At Other Offices

BRADFORD, James E.
Manager, Government Affairs
Mill St.
Hodge, LA 71247
Tel: (318) 259 - 5358

HAUDRICH, John
Investor Relations Contact
8182 Maryland Ave.
Clayton, MO 63105
Tel: (314) 746 - 1266

LANGE, Tom
Director, Public Relations
8182 Maryland Ave.
Clayton, MO 63105
Tel: (314) 746 - 1236
Fax: (314) 746 - 1437

Snap-on Incorporated

A global developer, manufacturer and marketer of tool equipment and service solutions for professional tool users.

www.snapon.com

Annual Revenues: $212 billion

Chairman, President and Chief Exec. Officer
ELLIOTT, Dale F.
dale.elliott@snapon.com
Tel: (414) 656 - 5200
Fax: (414) 656 - 5577

Main Headquarters

Mailing: P.O. Box 1430
Kenosha, WI 53141-1430
Tel: (262) 656 - 5200
Fax: (262) 656 - 5577

Street: 10801 Corporate Dr.
Pleasant Prairie, WI 53158

Public Affairs and Related Activities Personnel

At Headquarters

BRADY, Sharon M.
V. President and Chief Human Resources Officer
Tel: (414) 656 - 5315
Fax: (414) 656 - 5577

MARRINAN, Susan F.
V. President, Secretary and General Counsel
susan.marrinan@snapon.com
Tel: (414) 656 - 5550
Fax: (414) 656 - 5577
Responsibilities include government affairs.

PFUND, William H.
V. President, Investor Relations
Tel: (414) 656 - 6488
Fax: (414) 656 - 5577

SECOR, Richard M.
Director, Corporate Communications
richard.secor@snapon.com
Tel: (414) 656 - 5561
Fax: (414) 656 - 5577

Snapple

See listing on page 97 under Cadbury Schweppes Americas Beverages.

SNET

See listing on page 425 under SBC SNET.

Solectron Corp.

Provides electronic manufacturing services.

www.solectron.com

Annual Revenues: $12.276 billion

President and Chief Exec. Officer
CANNON, Michael R.
Tel: (408) 957 - 8500
Fax: (408) 957 - 2855

Main Headquarters

Mailing: 847 Gibraltar Dr.
Milpitas, CA 95035
Tel: (408) 957 - 8500

Corporate Foundations and Giving Programs

Solectron Corp. Giving Program

Solectron Corp.

* continued from previous page

847 Gibraltar Dr.
Milpitas, CA 95035 — Tel: (408) 957 - 8500

Annual Grant Total: none reported

Primary Interests: Arts and Culture; Community Affairs; Education; Health and Human Services
Recent Recipients: American Cancer Society; Habitat for Humanity; Junior Achievement; March of Dimes; Salvation Army; Special Olympics

Public Affairs and Related Activities Personnel

At Headquarters

DAVIDSON, Anne — Tel: (408) 586 - 4232
Mailstop: Bldg. 5 — Fax: (408) 956 - 7699

GUARDINO, Leslee — Tel: (408) 586 - 4232
Senior Director, Government and Community Relations — Fax: (408) 956 - 7699
Mailstop: Bldg. 5
lesleecoleman@ca.slr.com

HAYES, Perry G. — Tel: (408) 957 - 8500
Treasurer and V. President, Investor Relations

HINES, Gregory — Tel: (408) 586 - 4232
Mailstop: Bldg. 5 — Fax: (408) 956 - 7699

O'CONNOR, Kevin — Tel: (408) 957 - 8500
Exec. V. President, Human Resources

WHALEN, Kevin — Tel: (408) 956 - 6854
V. President, Corporate Communications — Fax: (408) 956 - 6075
kevinwhalen@ca.slr.com

Solutia Inc.

An applied chemistry company.
www.solutia.com
Annual Revenues: $2.241 billion

President and Chief Exec. Officer
QUINN, Jeffry N. — Tel: (314) 674 - 1000; Fax: (314) 674 - 1585

Main Headquarters
Mailing: P.O. Box 66760, St. Louis, MO 63166-6760 — Tel: (314) 674 - 1000; Fax: (314) 674 - 1585
Street: 575 Maryville Center Dr., St. Louis, MO 63141

Washington Office
Contact: Greg Wilson
Mailing: 1776 I St. NW, Suite 1030, Washington, DC 20006 — Tel: (202) 822 - 1690; Fax: (202) 822 - 1693

Political Action Committees

Solutia Inc. Citizenship Fund
Contact: Alan G. Faust
P.O. Box 66760
St. Louis, MO 63166-6760 — Tel: (314) 674 - 1000; Fax: (314) 674 - 1585

Contributions to Candidates: $3,750 (01/05 - 09/05)
Democrats: $1,000; Republicans: $2,750.

Principal Recipients

SENATE DEMOCRATS

HOUSE DEMOCRATS
Costello, Jerry F (IL) $1,000

SENATE REPUBLICANS
Talent, James (MO) $2,500

HOUSE REPUBLICANS

Corporate Foundations and Giving Programs

Solutia Fund
P.O. Box 66760
St. Louis, MO 63166-6760 — Tel: (314) 674 - 1000; Fax: (314) 674 - 1585

Annual Grant Total: none reported

Public Affairs and Related Activities Personnel

At Headquarters

BERRA, Paul J. — Tel: (314) 674 - 5325
Assistant General Counsel and Director, Government Affairs — Fax: (314) 674 - 1585
pjberr@solutia.com

BEVINGTON, Susan — Tel: (314) 674 - 1000
V. President, Human Resources — Fax: (314) 674 - 1585

FAUST, Alan G. — Tel: (314) 674 - 1000
Treasurer, Solutia Inc. Citizenship Fund — Fax: (314) 674 - 1585

LIVINGSTON, Liesl — Tel: (314) 674 - 7777
Director, Investor Relations — Fax: (314) 674 - 2899
lmlivi@solutia.com

At Washington Office

WILSON, Greg — Tel: (202) 822 - 1690, Ext: 12
Director, Federal Affairs — Fax: (202) 822 - 1693

Registered Federal Lobbyist.

Sonic Automotive, Inc.

A retailer of new and used cars. Also offers parts and services, financing, and insurance.
www.sonicautomotive.com
Annual Revenues: $7.071 billion

Chairman and Chief Exec. Officer
SMITH, O. Bruton — Tel: (704) 566 - 2400; Fax: (704) 536 - 4668

Main Headquarters
Mailing: 6415 Idlewild Rd., Suite 109, Charlotte, NC 28212 — Tel: (704) 566 - 2400; Fax: (704) 536 - 4668

Political Action Committees

Sonic Automotive Inc. Federal PAC
Contact: E. Lee Wyatt, Jr.
6415 Idlewild Rd., Suite 109
Charlotte, NC 28212 — Tel: (704) 566 - 2400; Fax: (704) 536 - 4668

Contributions to Candidates: none reported (01/05 - 09/05)

Sonic Automotive Inc. State PAC
Contact: E. Lee Wyatt, Jr.
6415 Idlewild Rd., Suite 109
Charlotte, NC 28212 — Tel: (704) 566 - 2400; Fax: (704) 536 - 4668

Contributions to Candidates: none reported (01/05 - 09/05)

Public Affairs and Related Activities Personnel

At Headquarters

STEERS, Bill — Tel: (704) 566 - 2400
Manager, Media Relations — Fax: (704) 536 - 4668

WALL, Rhonda — Tel: (704) 566 - 2400
Divisional Human Resources Manager, Northern Region — Fax: (704) 536 - 4668
rhonda.wall@sonicautomotive.com

WYATT, E. Lee, Jr. — Tel: (704) 566 - 2400
Treasurer, Sonic Automotive Inc. Federal PAC and Sonic Automotive Inc. State PAC — Fax: (704) 536 - 4668

At Other Offices

ATENHAN, J. Todd — Fax: (770) 425 - 7740
Manager, Investor Relations — TF: (888) 766 - 4218
210 Interstate N. Pkwy., Suite 700
Atlanta, GA 30339
todd.atenhan@sonicautomotive.com

Sonoco Products Co.

A manufacturer of packaging products and provider of packaging services.
www.sonoco.com
Annual Revenues: $3.2 billion

Chairman of the Board, President and Chief Exec. Officer
DELOACH, Harris E., Jr. — Tel: (843) 383 - 7000; Fax: (843) 383 - 7478

Main Headquarters
Mailing: P.O. Box 160, Hartsville, SC 29551-0160 — Tel: (843) 383 - 7000; Fax: (843) 383 - 7478
Street: N. Second St., Hartsville, SC 29550-3305

Corporate Foundations and Giving Programs

Sonoco Foundation
Contact: Joyce S. Beasley
P.O. Box 160
Hartsville, SC 29551-0160 — Tel: (843) 383 - 7851, Ext: 7851; Fax: (843) 383 - 7008

Annual Grant Total: none reported
Primarily concerned with education in the South Carolina area.
Geographic Preference: Area(s) in which the company operates; South Carolina
Primary Interests: Education

Public Affairs and Related Activities Personnel

At Headquarters

BEASLEY, Joyce S. — Tel: (843) 383 - 7851, Ext: 7851
Manager, Financial Communications and Community Relations — Fax: (843) 383 - 7008
Mailstop: A09
joyce.beasley@sonoco.com
Responsibilities also include corporate philanthropy.

CECIL, Allan V. — Tel: (843) 383 - 7524
V. President, Investor Relations and Corporate Affairs — Fax: (843) 383 - 7478
allan.cecil@sonoco.com

Sony Corp. of America

Sony Corp. of America, based in New York City, is the U.S. subsidiary of Sony Corp., headquartered in Tokyo. A manufacturer of audio, video, communications and information technology products for the consumer and professional markets. Sony's principal U.S. businesses include Sony Electronics Inc., Sony Pictures Entertainment, Sony BMG Music Entertainment Inc., and Sony Computer Entertainment America Inc.

www.sony.com
Annual Revenues: $20.4 billion

Chairman and Chief Exec. Officer
STRINGER, Howard — Tel: (212) 833 - 6800; Fax: (212) 833 - 6932

Main Headquarters
Mailing: 550 Madison Ave.
New York, NY 10022-3211
Tel: (212) 833 - 6800
TF: (800) 618 - 4550

Washington Office
Contact: Joel Wiginton
Mailing: 1667 K St. NW
Suite 200
Washington, DC 20006
Tel: (202) 429 - 3652

Political Action Committees

Sony Pictures Entertainment Inc. Political Action Committee
Contact: Hope Boonshaft
10202 W. Washington Blvd.
Culver City, CA 90232
Tel: (310) 244 - 6660
Fax: (310) 244 - 2467

Contributions to Candidates: $91,500 (01/05 - 09/05)
Democrats: $39,500; Republicans: $52,000.

Principal Recipients

SENATE DEMOCRATS
Feinstein, Dianne (CA) $3,500
Nelson, Benjamin (NE) $2,000

SENATE REPUBLICANS
Stevens, Ted (AK) $8,000
Santorum, Richard (PA) $3,000

HOUSE DEMOCRATS
Hoyer, Steny (MD) $2,500
Harman, Jane (CA) $2,000

HOUSE REPUBLICANS
Hastert, Dennis J. (IL) $5,000
Pence, Mike (IN) $3,000
Dreier, David (CA) $2,500
Goodlatte, Robert (VA) $2,500
Sensenbrenner, Jim (WI) $2,500
Cannon, Christopher (UT) $2,000

Corporate Foundations and Giving Programs

Sony USA Foundation, Inc.
Contact: Ann L. Morfogen
550 Madison Ave.
New York, NY 10022-3211
Tel: (212) 833 - 6873
Fax: (212) 833 - 6862

Annual Grant Total: none reported
Grants awarded in the U.S. through major Sony subsidiaries and business groups. Funds for education and cultural programs are awarded nationally and locally. For more information, please go to www.sony.com/SCA/philanthropy.shtml.
Geographic Preference: Area in which the company is headquartered; Area(s) in which the company operates; National
Primary Interests: Civic and Cultural Activities; Education

Public Affairs and Related Activities Personnel

At Headquarters

BEY, Isisara
V. President, Corporate Affairs
(Sony BMG Music Entertainment, Inc.)
isisara_bey@sonymusic.com
Tel: (212) 833 - 7912
Fax: (212) 833 - 7917

KELSO, Karen
Senior Director, Public Affairs
karen_kelso@sonyusa.com
Tel: (212) 833 - 6033
Fax: (212) 833 - 6997

MORFOGEN, Ann L.
Senior V. President, Communications and Public Affairs; President, Sony USA Foundation
ann_morfogen@sonyusa.com
Tel: (212) 833 - 6873
Fax: (212) 833 - 6862

TYRRELL, Thomas
Exec. V. President, External and Governmental Affairs
(Sony BMG Music Entertainment, Inc.)
thomas_tyrrell@sonymusic.com
Tel: (212) 833 - 7907
Fax: (212) 833 - 7888

At Washington Office

GODFREY, John
(Sony Electronics Inc.)
Registered Federal Lobbyist.
Tel: (202) 429 - 3652

TELLALIAN, Christina
Senior Manager, Public and Government Affairs
christina.tellalian@am.sony.com
(Sony Electronics Inc.)
Registered Federal Lobbyist.
Tel: (202) 429 - 3652
Fax: (202) 429 - 3663

WIGINTON, Joel
V. President and Senior Counsel, Government Affairs
joel.wiginton@am.sony.com
(Sony Electronics Inc.)
Registered Federal Lobbyist.
Tel: (202) 429 - 3652
Fax: (202) 429 - 3663

At Other Offices

BOONSHAFT, Hope
Exec. V. President, External Affairs
(Sony Pictures Entertainment)
10202 W. Washington Blvd.
Mailstop: Thalberg 2514
Culver City, CA 90232
hope_boonshaft@spe.sony.com
Tel: (310) 244 - 6660
Fax: (310) 244 - 2467

CLANCY, Rick
Senior V. President, Corporate Communications
(Sony Electronics Inc.)
16530 Via Esprillo
San Diego, CA 92127
rick.clancy@am.sony.com
Tel: (858) 842 - 3020
Fax: (858) 842 - 8186

TICK, Susan
Senior V. President, Corporate Communications
(Sony Pictures Entertainment)
10202 W. Washington Blvd.
Mailstop: Thalberg 1131
Culver City, CA 90232
susan_tick@spe.sony.com
Tel: (310) 244 - 6660
Fax: (310) 244 - 0177

WALLACE, Edward
Senior Manager, Community Affairs
(Sony Electronics Inc.)
16530 Via Esprillo
San Diego, CA 92127
ed.wallace@am.sony.com

Sony Electronics Inc.

See listing on page 444 under Sony Corp of America.

Sony Pictures Entertainment

See listing on page 444 under Sony Corp of America.

Sotheby's Holdings, Inc.

An auctioneer of fine art and jewelry.

www.sothebys.com
Annual Revenues: $336.2 million

Chairman of the Board
WEITMAN, Warren, Jr. — Tel: (212) 606 - 7000; Fax: (212) 606 - 7107

President and Chief Exec. Officer
RUPRECHT, William — Tel: (212) 606 - 7000; Fax: (212) 606 - 7107

Main Headquarters
Mailing: 1334 York Ave.
New York, NY 10021
Tel: (212) 606 - 7000
Fax: (212) 606 - 7107

Public Affairs and Related Activities Personnel

At Headquarters

ALEXANDER, Susan
Senior V. President, Worldwide Human Resources
susan.alexander@sothebys.com
Tel: (212) 606 - 7202
Fax: (212) 606 - 7107

BREWER, Victoria
Senior Manager, Investor Relations
victoria.brewer@sothebys.com
Tel: (212) 508 - 8070
Fax: (212) 508 - 8072

PHILLIPS, Diana
Senior V. President, Corporate Affairs
diana.phillips@sothebys.com
Tel: (212) 606 - 7176
Fax: (212) 606 - 7107

South Carolina Electric and Gas Co.

See listing on page 426 under SCANA Corp.

South Jersey Gas Co.

Provides natural gas utility service to residential, commercial and industrial customers within the seven southern counties of New Jersey.

www.sjindustries.com

Chief Exec. Officer
GRAHAM, Edward J. — Tel: (609) 561 - 9000; Fax: (609) 561 - 8225

Main Headquarters
Mailing: One S. Jersey Plaza
Folsom, NJ 08037
Tel: (609) 561 - 9000
Fax: (609) 561 - 8225

Corporate Foundations and Giving Programs

South Jersey Gas Co. Corporate Giving Program
Contact: Joanne M. Brigandi

South Jersey Gas Co.

** continued from previous page*

One S. Jersey Plaza
Folsom, NJ 08037
Tel: (609) 561 - 9000
Ext: 4240
Fax: (609) 561 - 6955

Annual Grant Total: $100,000 - $200,000
Geographic Preference: New Jersey
Recent Recipients: United Way

Public Affairs and Related Activities Personnel

At Headquarters

BRIGANDI, Joanne M.
Director, Corporate Communications
Tel: (609) 561 - 9000
Ext: 4240
Fax: (609) 561 - 6955

LAMB, Michele
Communications Specialist
Tel: (609) 561 - 9000
Ext: 4171
Fax: (609) 561 - 8225

NICKELS, Janet
Sr. Vice President, Corporate Comm. and Admin. Services
Tel: (609) 561 - 9000
Fax: (609) 561 - 8225

NIXON, Michael
Supervisor, Corporate Communications
Tel: (609) 561 - 9000
Ext: 4464
Fax: (609) 561 - 8225

Southern Bell Telephone Co.

See listing on page 422 under SBC Communications Inc.

Southern California Edison, an Edison Internat'l Co.

A member of the Public Affairs Council. An electric utility.
www.sce.com
Annual Revenues: $8.126 billion

Chairman of the Board
BRYSON, John E.
brysonje@sce.com
Tel: (626) 302 - 2265
Fax: (626) 302 - 2993

Chief Exec. Officer
FOHRER, Alan J.
fohreraj@sce.com
Tel: (626) 302 - 1379
Fax: (626) 302 - 4737

Main Headquarters
Mailing: 2244 Walnut Grove Ave.
Rosemead, CA 91770
Tel: (626) 302 - 1212

Washington Office
Contact: Polly L. Gault
Mailing: 555 12th St. NW
Suite 640
Washington, DC 20004-1200
Tel: (202) 393 - 3075
Fax: (202) 393 - 1497

Corporate Foundations and Giving Programs

Southern California Edison Co. Contributions Program
Contact: Lucia Galindo
2244 Walnut Grove Ave.
Rosemead, CA 91770
Tel: (626) 302 - 2313
Fax: (626) 302 - 8114

Annual Grant Total: over $5,000,000
The company also makes in-kind donations, in addition to monetary support.
Geographic Preference: California; Area(s) in which the company operates
Primary Interests: Civic and Public Affairs; Economic Development; Education; Minority Opportunities; Social Services; Women

Public Affairs and Related Activities Personnel

At Headquarters

FOSTER, Robert G.
President
fosterrg@sce.com
Tel: (626) 302 - 9210
Fax: (626) 302 - 9213
Responsibilities include regulatory affairs, public affairs, and communications.

GALINDO, Lucia
Manager, Community Involvement
galindle@sce.com
Tel: (626) 302 - 2313
Fax: (626) 302 - 8114

HANSEN, Steven M.
Communications Specialist
hansensm@sce.com
Tel: (626) 302 - 7969
Fax: (626) 302 - 8066

HERTEL, Michael M.
Director, Environmental Affairs
hertelmm@sce.com
Tel: (626) 302 - 9456
Fax: (626) 302 - 9730

KLEIN, Paul N.
Manager, Corporate Communications
kleinpn@sce.com
Tel: (626) 302 - 7935
Fax: (626) 302 - 8066

MIDDELBURG, Suzanne J.
Manager, Consumer Affairs
middelsj@sce.com
Tel: (626) 302 - 2433
Fax: (626) 302 - 8003

MUNIZ-BANDONI, Katharyn O.
Employee Contributions Chair
munizbko@sce.com
Tel: (626) 302 - 3503
Fax: (626) 302 - 3007

PARSKY, Barbara J.
V. President, Corporate Communications
parskybj@sce.com
Tel: (626) 302 - 2257
Fax: (626) 302 - 3330

PATMOR, Roxanne I.
Manager, Strategic Communications
patmorri@sce.com
Tel: (626) 302 - 7982
Fax: (626) 302 - 6262

ROUNDS, Becky
Manager, Corporate Communications
roundsra@sce.com
Tel: (626) 302 - 7953
Fax: (626) 302 - 8066

SHAY, Paul E., Jr.
Director, Corporate Public Affairs
shaype@sce.com
Tel: (626) 302 - 1984
Fax: (626) 302 - 6315

SULLIVAN, Steve R.
Regional V. President
sullivsr@sce.com
Tel: (626) 302 - 1951
Fax: (626) 302 - 1959
Serves as the company's senior public affairs official.

At Washington Office

GAULT, Polly L.
Regional V. President, Washington D.C.
gaultpl@sce.com
Tel: (202) 393 - 3075
Fax: (202) 393 - 1497

SANTOS, Barbara J.
Government Relations Assistant
santosbj@sce.com
Tel: (202) 393 - 3075
Fax: (202) 393 - 1497

At Other Offices

FOSTER, Bruce C.
V. President, San Francisco Region
601 Van Ness Ave., Suite 2040
San Francisco, CA 94102
fosterbc@sce.com
Tel: (415) 775 - 1856
Fax: (415) 474 - 3080
Responsibilities include government relations.

HACKNEY, Catherine
Manager, Public Affairs - Sacramento
1201 K St., Suite 1810
Sacramento, CA 95814
hacknece@sce.com
Tel: (916) 441 - 3966
Fax: (916) 441 - 4047

HUGHES, John P.
Manager, Regulatory Affairs
601 Van Ness Ave., Suite 2040
San Francisco, CA 94102
hughesjp@sce.com
Tel: (415) 775 - 1856
Fax: (415) 474 - 3080

ROSS, Tommy
V. President, Public Affairs - Sacramento Region
1201 K St., Suite 1810
Sacramento, CA 95814
rosst@sce.com
Tel: (916) 441 - 3966
Fax: (916) 441 - 4047

SCHOONYAN, Gary L.
Director, Regulatory Policy and Affairs
601 Van Ness Ave., Suite 2040
San Francisco, CA 94102
schoongl@sce.com
Tel: (415) 775 - 1856
Fax: (415) 474 - 3080

ZAMORANO, Manuel
Corporate Representative
1201 K St., Suite 1810
Sacramento, CA 95814
zamoram@sce.com
Tel: (916) 441 - 3966
Fax: (916) 441 - 4047

Southern California Gas Co.

A gas utility subsidiary of Sempra Energy (see separate listing).
www.socalgas.com

Chairman and Chief Exec. Officer
GUILES, Edwin A.
Tel: (213) 244 - 1200
Fax: (213) 244 - 8292

Main Headquarters
Mailing: P.O. Box 513249
Los Angeles, CA 90051-1249
Street: 555 W. Fifth St.
Los Angeles, CA 90013
Tel: (213) 244 - 1200
Fax: (213) 244 - 8292

Washington Office
Contact: George P. Williams
Mailing: 1001 G St. NW
Sixth Floor East
Washington, DC 20001-4545
Tel: (202) 662 - 1700
Fax: (202) 293 - 2887

Political Action Committees

Southern California Gas Co. Political Action Committee
Contact: Michael De La Torre
P.O. Box 513249
Los Angeles, CA 90051-1249
Tel: (213) 244 - 2545
Fax: (213) 244 - 4997

Contributions to Candidates: $39,500 (01/05 - 09/05)
Democrats: $19,500; Republicans: $20,000.

Principal Recipients

SENATE DEMOCRATS
Bingaman, Jeff (NM) $4,500
Conrad, Kent (ND) $3,500

HOUSE DEMOCRATS
Roybal-Allard, Lucille (CA) $2,500

SENATE REPUBLICANS
Allen, George (VA) $2,500
Santorum, Richard (PA) $2,500

HOUSE REPUBLICANS
Pombo, Richard (CA) $4,500
Vitter, David (LA) $2,500
Radanovich, George (CA) $2,000

Southern California Gas Co.

** continued from previous page*

Corporate Foundations and Giving Programs

The Gas Co. Charitable Contributions Program
Contact: Carolyn R. Williams
P.O. Box 513249 — Tel: (213) 244 - 2555
Los Angeles, CA 90051-1249 — Fax: (213) 244 - 8254

Annual Grant Total: $2,000,000 - $5,000,000
Geographic Preference: Area(s) in which the company operates
Primary Interests: Community Affairs; Economic Development; Environment/Conservation

Public Affairs and Related Activities Personnel

At Headquarters

DE LA TORRE, Michael — Tel: (213) 244 - 2545
Governmental Affairs Manager, L.A. City and County — Fax: (213) 244 - 4997

KASPER-GWYN, Laurie — Tel: (213) 244 - 2580
Manager, Policy and Strategy — Fax: (213) 244 - 4997

LOPEZ-BAFFO, Minnie — Tel: (213) 244 - 2523
Project Manager, Regional Affairs — Fax: (213) 244 - 4997

WILLIAMS, Carolyn R. — Tel: (213) 244 - 2555
Manager, Community Relations — Fax: (213) 244 - 8254
crwilliams@semprautilities.com

At Washington Office

WILLIAMS, George P. — Tel: (202) 662 - 1701
Director, Federal Governmental Affairs — Fax: (202) 293 - 2887
gwilliams@sempra.com
Registered Federal Lobbyist.

Southern Company

A member of the Public Affairs Council. An electric utility holding company. Subsidiaries include Alabama Power Co., Georgia Power Co., Gulf Power Co., Mississippi Power Co. and the Southern Nuclear Operating Co., each of which is listed separately in this directory, as well as Savannah Electric & Power Co, and Southern Energy Inc.

www.southernco.com
Annual Revenues: $10.155 billion

Chairman, President and Chief Exec. Officer — Tel: (404) 506 - 5000
RATCLIFFE, David M.

Main Headquarters
Mailing: 270 Peachtree St. NW — Tel: (404) 506 - 5000
Atlanta, GA 30303

Washington Office
Contact: Joseph A. "Buzz" Miller
Mailing: 601 Pennsylvania Ave. NW — Tel: (202) 261 - 5000
Suite 800 — Fax: (202) 296 - 7937
Washington, DC 20004

Political Action Committees

Southern Company Employees PAC
Contact: James A. Mason, Jr.
241 Ralph McGill Blvd. — Tel: (404) 506 - 7750
Atlanta, GA 30308

Contributions to Candidates: $63,500 (01/05 - 09/05)
Democrats: $13,000; Republicans: $50,500.

Principal Recipients

SENATE DEMOCRATS		HOUSE DEMOCRATS	
Nelson, Benjamin (NE)	$3,000		
Conrad, Kent (ND)	$2,000		
SENATE REPUBLICANS		**HOUSE REPUBLICANS**	
Allen, George (VA)	$8,000	Blunt, Roy (MO)	$2,500
Burns, Conrad (MT)	$6,000	DeLay, Tom (TX)	$2,500
Vitter, David (LA)	$5,000	Latham, Thomas P (IA)	$2,500
Smith, Gordon (OR)	$3,500	Vitter, David (LA)	$2,500
Talent, James (MO)	$3,000	Blackburn, Marsha (TN)	$2,000
Thomas, Craig (WY)	$2,000	Whitfield, Ed (KY)	$2,000

Corporate Foundations and Giving Programs

Southern Co. Services, Inc. Corporate Giving Program
Contact: Judy M. Anderson
241 Ralph McGill Blvd. — Tel: (404) 506 - 7750
Atlanta, GA 30308 — Fax: (404) 506 - 7752

Annual Grant Total: none reported

Public Affairs and Related Activities Personnel

At Headquarters

ALTMAN, David R. — Tel: (404) 506 - 0650
V. President, Corporate Communications and Advertising — Fax: (404) 506 - 0662
Mailstop: Bin 908A

EVANS, Dwight H. — Tel: (404) 506 - 5000
Exec. V. President, External Affairs

GOODMAN, Charles H. — Tel: (404) 257 - 6325
Senior V. President, Research and Environmental Affairs — Fax: (404) 506 - 0662

KUNDERT, Glen A. — Tel: (404) 506 - 5135
Director, Investor Relations

LINDEMANN, Ellen — Tel: (404) 506 - 5000
Senior V. President, Human Resources

RICE, Marc — Tel: (404) 506 - 5333
Media Relations

TERRELL, Todd A. — Tel: (404) 506 - 0566
Director, Corporate Communications — Fax: (404) 506 - 0584
Mailstop: Bin 908A

At Washington Office

EDELSTON, Bruce H. — Tel: (202) 261 - 5000
Fax: (202) 296 - 7937
Registered Federal Lobbyist.

HARRY, L. Ray — Tel: (202) 261 - 5000
Director, Environmental Issues — Fax: (202) 296 - 7937
Registered Federal Lobbyist.

LAWRENCE, H. Adam — Tel: (202) 261 - 5000
Director, Federal Legislative Affairs — Fax: (202) 296 - 7937
halawrence@southernco.com
Registered Federal Lobbyist.

MCCOOL, James M., Jr. — Tel: (202) 775 - 0944
Director, Government Affairs — Fax: (202) 296 - 7937

MILLER, Joseph A. "Buzz" — Tel: (202) 261 - 5000
V. President, Governmental Relations — Fax: (202) 296 - 7937
Registered Federal Lobbyist.

MOOR, Karl P. — Tel: (202) 261 - 5000
Fax: (202) 296 - 7937
Registered Federal Lobbyist.

PEMBERTON, John L. — Tel: (202) 261 - 5000
Director, Federal Affairs — Fax: (202) 296 - 7937
Registered Federal Lobbyist.

RIITH, Michael J. — Tel: (202) 261 - 5000
Manager, Federal Legislative Affairs — Fax: (202) 296 - 7937
Registered Federal Lobbyist.

WOLAK, Jeanne B. — Tel: (202) 261 - 5000
Director, Federal Legislative Affairs — Fax: (202) 296 - 7937
Registered Federal Lobbyist.

YELVERTON, Todd W. — Tel: (202) 261 - 5000
Director, Federal Regulatory Affairs — Fax: (202) 296 - 7937
Registered Federal Lobbyist.

At Other Offices

ANDERSON, Judy M. — Tel: (404) 506 - 7750
Senior V. President, Charitable Giving — Fax: (404) 506 - 7752
241 Ralph McGill Blvd.
Mailstop: BIN 10230
Atlanta, GA 30308

MASON, James A., Jr. — Tel: (404) 506 - 7750
Contact, Southern Company Employees PAC
241 Ralph McGill Blvd.
Atlanta, GA 30308

Southern Connecticut Gas Co., The (SCG)

See listing on page 181 under Energy East Corp.

Southern Indiana Gas and Electric Co.

See listing on page 501 under Vectren Corp.

Southern New England Telecommunications Corp.

See listing on page 425 under SBC SNET.

Southern Nuclear Operating Co.

A subsidiary of Southern Company (see separate listing). The company may be reached on the Internet through its parent company's web site at: www.southernco.com.

Chairman of the Board — Tel: (205) 992 - 5752
HAIRSTON, W. G. (George), III — Fax: (205) 992 - 5363

President and Chief Exec. Officer — Tel: (205) 992 - 5752
BEASLEY, James B., Jr. — Fax: (205) 992 - 5363

Main Headquarters
Mailing: P.O. Box 1295 — Tel: (205) 992 - 5752
Birmingham, AL 35201 — Fax: (205) 992 - 5363
Street: 40 Inverness Center Pkwy.
Birmingham, AL 35242

Political Action Committees

Southern Nuclear Operating Inc. PAC
Contact: David J. Handly
P.O. Box 1295 — Tel: (205) 992 - 5752
Birmingham, AL 35201 — Fax: (205) 992 - 5363

Southern Nuclear Operating Co.

* continued from previous page

Contributions to Candidates: $18,000 (01/05 - 09/05)
Democrats: $3,000; Republicans: $15,000.

Principal Recipients

SENATE DEMOCRATS		HOUSE DEMOCRATS	
		Towns, Edolphus (NY)	$2,000
		Ross, Michael Avery (AR)	$1,000
SENATE REPUBLICANS		**HOUSE REPUBLICANS**	
Smith, Gordon (OR)	$1,500	Vitter, David (LA)	$2,500
Allen, George (VA)	$1,000	Cubin, Barbara L (WY)	$2,000
Graham, Lindsey (SC)	$1,000	Shadegg, John (AZ)	$2,000
Kennedy, Mark (MN)	$1,000	Knollenberg, Joe (MI)	$1,000
Santorum, Richard (PA)	$1,000	McCrery, Jim (LA)	$1,000
Talent, James (MO)	$1,000		

Public Affairs and Related Activities Personnel

At Headquarters

HANDLY, David J.
Treasurer, Southern Nuclear Operating Inc. PAC
Tel: (205) 992 - 5752
Fax: (205) 992 - 5363

HIGGINBOTTOM, Q. Steve
Manager, Corporate Communications
qshiggin@southernco.com
Tel: (205) 992 - 5752
Fax: (205) 992 - 5363

PHILLIPS, Carrie
Manager, Government Relations
Tel: (205) 992 - 5168
Fax: (205) 992 - 6165

WALLER, Regina T.
Communications Specialist
rtwaller@southernco.com
Tel: (205) 992 - 5752
Fax: (205) 992 - 5363

Southern States Cooperative

A farmer-owned cooperative.
www.southernstates.com
Annual Revenues: $1.3 billion

Chairman of the Board
WARD, Wilbur
Tel: (804) 281 - 1000
Fax: (804) 281 - 1119

President and Chief Exec. Officer
SCRIBNER, Thomas R.
tom.scribner@sscoop.com
Tel: (804) 281 - 1000
Fax: (804) 281 - 1119

Main Headquarters
Mailing: P.O. Box 26234
Richmond, VA 23260-6234
Tel: (804) 281 - 1000
Fax: (804) 281 - 1119
Street: 6606 W. Broad St.
Richmond, VA 23230-1717

Public Affairs and Related Activities Personnel

At Headquarters

ERICKSON, James R.
Director, Corporate Communications, Member Relations and Public Affairs
jim.erickson@sscoop.com
Tel: (804) 281 - 1392
Fax: (804) 281 - 1119

SCHEXNAYDER, Alexandra
Manager, Corporate Communications
alexandra.schexnayder@sscoop.com
Tel: (804) 281 - 1368
Fax: (804) 281 - 1119

WALKER, Jerry
V. President, Human Resources
jerry.walker@sscoop.com
Tel: (804) 281 - 1000
Fax: (804) 281 - 1119

Southern Union Company

A natural gas distribution, pipeline transmisson and storage company.
www.southernunionco.com
Annual Revenues: $1.8 billion

Chairman and Chief Exec. Officer
LINDEMANN, George L.

Main Headquarters
Mailing: 417Lackawanna Ave.
Scranton, PA 18503

Political Action Committees

New England Gas Co. PAC
Contact: David L. Black
100 Weybosset St.
Providence, RI 02903
Tel: (401) 272 - 5040
Fax: (401) 273 - 4243

Contributions to Candidates: $1,000 (01/05 - 09/05)
Republicans: $1,000.

Principal Recipients

SENATE REPUBLICANS		HOUSE REPUBLICANS	
		Emerson, Jo Ann (MO)	$1,000

Public Affairs and Related Activities Personnel

At Headquarters

MARSHALL, Richard N.
V. President and Treasurer
Responsibilities include investor relations.

WALSH, John F.
Director, Investor Relations

At Other Offices

ALBANESE, Marisa
Manager, Community Relations
(New England Gas Co.)
100 Weybosset St.
Providence, RI 02903
malbanese@negasco.com
Tel: (401) 272 - 5040
Ext: 2062
Fax: (401) 273 - 4243

BARNETT, John P.
Director, External Affairs
544 Westheimer Rd.
Houston, TX 77056
Tel: (713) 989 - 7556

BLACK, David L.
Treasurer, New England Gas Co. PAC
(New England Gas Co.)
100 Weybosset St.
Providence, RI 02903
Tel: (401) 272 - 5040
Fax: (401) 273 - 4243

LEVETZOW, Pam
Director, Public Affairs
3520 Broadway
Kansas City, MO 64111
Tel: (816) 360 - 5753

MEDICI, Christopher J.
Director, Communications
(New England Gas Co.)
100 Weybosset St.
Providence, RI 02903
cmedici@negasco.com
Tel: (401) 574 - 2068
Fax: (401) 273 - 4243

SNIDER, Paul
Public Affairs Specialist
(Missouri Gas Energy)
3420 Broadway
Kansas City, MO 64111-2404
Fax: (816) 360 - 5541

STAFFORD, Sherri
Corporate Affairs Representative
544 Westheimer Rd.
Houston, TX 77056
Tel: (713) 989 - 7652

TAYLOR, Gina A.
Director, Internal Affairs
544 Westheimer Rd.
Houston, TX 77056
Tel: (713) 989 - 7557

Southern Wine & Spirits of America

Wholesale distributor of wine and distilled beverages.
www.southernwineca.com
Annual Revenues: $3.75 billion

Chairman and Chief Exec. Officer
CHAPLIN, Harvey
Tel: (305) 625 - 4171
Fax: (305) 625 - 2790

Main Headquarters
Mailing: 1600 N.W. 163rd St.
Miami, FL 33169
Tel: (305) 625 - 4171
Fax: (305) 625 - 2790

Political Action Committees

Southern Wine & Spirits PAC
Contact: Steven Becker
1600 N.W. 163rd St.
Miami, FL 33169
Tel: (305) 625 - 4171
Fax: (305) 625 - 2790

Contributions to Candidates: $21,500 (01/05 - 09/05)
Democrats: $11,000; Republicans: $10,500.

Principal Recipients

SENATE DEMOCRATS		HOUSE DEMOCRATS	
Nelson, Bill (FL)	$2,000	Abercrombie, Neil (HI)	$5,000
		Meek, Kendrick (FL)	$2,000
		Obey, David R (WI)	$2,000
SENATE REPUBLICANS		**HOUSE REPUBLICANS**	
		Ros-Lehtinen, Ileana (FL)	$5,000
		Shaw, Clay (FL)	$2,500
		Miller, Gary (CA)	$2,000

Public Affairs and Related Activities Personnel

At Headquarters

BECKER, Steven
Treasurer, Southern Wine & Spirits PAC
Tel: (305) 625 - 4171
Fax: (305) 625 - 2790

KRAUSS, Mark
National Director, Human Resources
Tel: (305) 625 - 4171
Fax: (305) 625 - 2790

Southland Corp., The

See listing on page 2 under 7-Eleven, Inc.

SouthTrust Corp.

See listing on page 509 under Wachovia Corp.

Southwest Airlines Co.

A shorthaul, low-fare passenger air carrier.
www.southwest.com
Annual Revenues: $5.555 billion

Chairman of the Board
KELLEHER, Herbert D. — Tel: (214) 792 - 4000; TF: (800) 435 - 9792

V. Chairman and Chief Exec. Officer
KELLY, Gary C. — Tel: (214) 792 - 4000; TF: (800) 435 - 9792

Main Headquarters
Mailing: P.O. Box 36611, Dallas, TX 75235-1611 — Tel: (214) 792 - 4000; TF: (800) 435 - 9792
Street: 2702 Love Field Dr., Dallas, TX 75235

Washington Office
Contact: Tom Chapman
Mailing: 1901 L St. NW, Suite 640, Washington, DC 20036 — Tel: (202) 263 - 6283; Fax: (202) 263 - 6291

Political Action Committees

Southwest Airlines Co. Freedom Fund
Contact: Jose L. Sanchez
1155 Westmoreland, Suite 234
El Paso, TX 79925 — Tel: (915) 771 - 8856

Contributions to Candidates: $36,000 (01/05 - 09/05)
Democrats: $9,500; Republicans: $26,500.

Principal Recipients

SENATE DEMOCRATS		HOUSE DEMOCRATS	
Cardin, Benjamin (MD)	$2,500		
SENATE REPUBLICANS		**HOUSE REPUBLICANS**	
Kyl, Jon L (AZ)	$5,000	DeLay, Tom (TX)	$4,000
Burns, Conrad (MT)	$2,500	Duncan, John (TN)	$2,000
Ensign, John Eric (NV)	$2,500	Knollenberg, Joe (MI)	$2,000
		Rogers, Harold (KY)	$2,000

Corporate Foundations and Giving Programs

Southwest Airlines Civic and Charitable Contributions
Contact: Tracie Martin
P.O. Box 36611
Dallas, TX 75235-1611 — Tel: (214) 792 - 4103

Annual Grant Total: none reported
Geographic Preference: National
Primary Interests: Civic and Public Affairs

Public Affairs and Related Activities Personnel

At Headquarters

EICHINGER, Whitney
Regional Manager, Public Relations
Mailstop: HDQ-1PR — Tel: (214) 792 - 6604; Fax: (214) 792 - 4200; TF: (800) 435 - 9792

GOODMAN, Susan
Director, Legislative Awareness Department
Mailstop: HDQ-KA — Tel: (214) 792 - 7944; Fax: (214) 792 - 6703

HARDAGE, Ginger C.
Senior V. President, Corporate Communications — Tel: (214) 792 - 4524

KING, Brandy
Regional Manager, Public Relations — Tel: (214) 792 - 5138; Fax: (214) 792 - 4200

MARTIN, Tracie
Manager, Civic and Charitable Contributions — Tel: (214) 792 - 4103

MONTAGUE, Tonda A.
Director, Employee Communications — Tel: (214) 792 - 4362

RICKS, Ron
Senior V. President, Law, Airports and Public Affairs — Tel: (214) 792 - 4174

RUPPEL, Jim
V. President, Customer Relations and Rapid Rewards — Tel: (214) 792 - 4000; Fax: (214) 792 - 5099

RUTHERFORD, Linda
Director, Public Relations — Tel: (214) 792 - 4625

STEWART, Edward L.
Senior Director, Public Relations — Tel: (214) 792 - 4187

At Washington Office

CHAPMAN, Tom
Legislative Counsel — Tel: (202) 263 - 6282; Fax: (202) 263 - 6291

At Other Offices

SANCHEZ, Jose L.
Director, Governmental Affairs
1155 Westmoreland, Suite 234
El Paso, TX 79925 — Tel: (915) 771 - 8856

Southwest Gas Corp.

A natural gas distributor.
www.swgas.com
Annual Revenues: $1.397 billion

Chairman of the Board
HARTLEY, Thomas Y. — Tel: (702) 876 - 7247; Fax: (702) 364 - 3444

Chief Exec. Officer
SHAW, Jeffrey W. — Tel: (702) 876 - 7011; Fax: (702) 364 - 3444

Main Headquarters
Mailing: P.O. Box 98510, Las Vegas, NV 89193-8510 — Tel: (702) 876 - 7011; Fax: (702) 364 - 3045
Street: 5241 Spring Mountain Rd., Las Vegas, NV 89150

Political Action Committees

Southwest Gas Corp. Political Action Committee
Contact: Debra Jacobson
P.O. Box 98510
Las Vegas, NV 89193-8510 — Tel: (702) 876 - 7163; Fax: (702) 873 - 3820

Contributions to Candidates: $17,275 (01/05 - 09/05)
Democrats: $2,000; Republicans: $15,275.

Principal Recipients

SENATE DEMOCRATS		HOUSE DEMOCRATS	
		Berkley, Shelley (NV)	$1,500
SENATE REPUBLICANS		**HOUSE REPUBLICANS**	
Kyl, Jon L (AZ)	$4,500	Hayworth, J D (AZ)	$3,000
Ensign, John Eric (NV)	$1,500	Kolbe, James (AZ)	$2,000
		Gibbons, James A (NV)	$1,500
		Porter, Jon (NV)	$1,500
		Renzi, Richard (AZ)	$1,000

Corporate Foundations and Giving Programs

Southwest Gas Corp. Foundation
Contact: Suzanne Farinas
P.O. Box 98510
Las Vegas, NV 89193-8510 — Tel: (702) 876 - 7247; Fax: (702) 364 - 3444

Assets: $379,003 (2003)
Annual Grant Total: $400,000 - $500,000
Contributions limited to non-profit organizations.
Geographic Preference: Area(s) in which the company operates; Arizona; California; Nevada
Primary Interests: Arts and Culture; Education; Environment/Conservation; Health and Human Services; Youth Services
Recent Recipients: American Heart Ass'n; United Way; University of Nevada

Public Affairs and Related Activities Personnel

At Headquarters

BLOCKEY, Joanna L.
Communications Representative — Tel: (702) 876 - 7368; Fax: (702) 220 - 4736

CLAYTON, Robyn
Manager, Community Relations — Tel: (702) 364 - 3297; Fax: (702) 220 - 4736
Responsibilities include corporate communications.

COVER, Fred W.
V. President, Human Resources — Tel: (702) 876 - 7210; Fax: (702) 367 - 3304

FARINAS, Suzanne
Assistant to the Chief Exec. Officer — Tel: (702) 876 - 7247; Fax: (702) 364 - 3444
Responsibilities include corporate philanthropy.

HOBBS, Laura E.
Director, Human Resources — Tel: (702) 364 - 3534; Fax: (702) 367 - 3304

JACOBSON, Debra
Senior Manager, State Regulatory Affairs — Tel: (702) 876 - 7163; Fax: (702) 873 - 3820
Responsibilities include political action.

MESSINA, Cynthia
Administrator, Communications — Tel: (702) 876 - 7011; Fax: (702) 220 - 4736

At Other Offices

HOWELL, Adrienne
Administrator, Consumer Affairs
P.O. Box 52075
Phoenix, AZ 85072-2075 — Tel: (602) 395 - 4045

LORETO, Marty
Administrator, Consumer Affairs
P.O. Box 26500
Tucson, AZ 85726-6500 — Tel: (520) 794 - 6416

Southwest Gas Corp.

** continued from previous page*

O'NEAL, Al
Administrator, Consumer Affairs
P.O. Box 98512
Las Vegas, NV 89193-8512
Tel: (702) 365 - 2076

SENSEMAN, Kathryn
Government Affairs Specialist
P.O. Box 52075
Phoenix, AZ 85072
Tel: (602) 395 - 4045

TAYLOR, Penny R.
Specialist, Government Relations
P.O. Box 52075
Phoenix, AZ 85072-2075
Tel: (602) 395 - 4085

Southwestern Bell Messaging Services

See listing on page 422 under SBC Communications Inc.

Southwestern Bell Mobile Systems

See listing on page 422 under SBC Communications Inc.

Southwestern Bell Telephone Co.

See listing on page 422 under SBC Communications Inc.

Southwestern Energy Co.

Natural gas exploration, production, transmission, marketing and distribution.
www.swn.com
Annual Revenues: $344.9 million

Chairman, President and Chief Exec. Officer
KORELL, Harold M.
Tel: (281) 618 - 4700
Fax: (281) 618 - 4820

Main Headquarters
Mailing: 2350 N. Sam Houston Pkwy. East
Suite 300
Houston, TX 77032
Tel: (281) 618 - 4700
Fax: (281) 618 - 4820

Political Action Committees

Southwestern Energy Co. PAC
Contact: Melissa D. McCarty
2350 N. Sam Houston Pkwy. East
Suite 300
Houston, TX 77032
Tel: (281) 618 - 4700
Fax: (281) 618 - 4820

Contributions to Candidates: $2,000 (01/05 - 09/05)
Democrats: $1,000; Republicans: $1,000.

Principal Recipients

SENATE DEMOCRATS
Bingaman, Jeff (NM) $1,000

HOUSE DEMOCRATS

SENATE REPUBLICANS

HOUSE REPUBLICANS
Cubin, Barbara L (WY) $1,000

Public Affairs and Related Activities Personnel

At Headquarters

KERLEY, Greg D.
Exec. V. President and Chief Financial Officer
Responsibilities include investor relations.
Tel: (281) 618 - 4700
Fax: (281) 618 - 4820

MCCARTY, Melissa D.
Treasurer, Southwestern Energy Co. PAC
Tel: (281) 618 - 4700
Fax: (281) 618 - 4820

SYLVESTER, Brad
Investor Relations Coordinator
Tel: (281) 618 - 4700
Fax: (281) 618 - 4820

At Other Offices

LIDELL, Steve
Manager, Environmental Affairs
P.O. Box 1408
Fayetteville, AR 72702-1408

Southwire Co.

A producer of electrical wire and cable.
www.mysouthwire.com
Annual Revenues: $1.7 billion

President and Chief Exec. Officer
THORN, Stu
Tel: (770) 832 - 4242
Fax: (770) 832 - 4584
TF: (800) 444 - 1700

Main Headquarters
Mailing: P.O. Box 1000
Carrollton, GA 30119
Tel: (770) 832 - 4242
Fax: (770) 832 - 4584
TF: (800) 444 - 1700

Street: One Southwire Dr.
Carrollton, GA 30119

Corporate Foundations and Giving Programs

Southwire Co. Community Relations
P.O. Box 1000
Carrollton, GA 30119
Tel: (770) 832 - 4242
Fax: (770) 832 - 4584
TF: (800) 444 - 1700

Annual Grant Total: none reported
Geographic Preference: Area(s) in which the company operates
Primary Interests: Education; Environment/Conservation; Families; Health and Human Services; Youth Services

Public Affairs and Related Activities Personnel

At Headquarters

LEFTWICH, Gary
Senior Communications Specialist
gary_leftwich@southwire.com
Responsibilities include corporate philanthropy.
Tel: (770) 832 - 4884
Fax: (770) 832 - 4584
TF: (800) 444 - 1700

WIGGINS, Michael
V. President, Human Resources
Tel: (770) 832 - 4242
Ext: 4963
Fax: (770) 832 - 4584
TF: (800) 444 - 1700

Sovereign Bancorp, Inc.

A financial services company.
www.sovereignbank.com
Annual Revenues: $2.492 billion

Chairman and Chief Exec. Officer
SIDHU, Jay
Tel: (610) 320 - 8400
Fax: (610) 320 - 8448

Main Headquarters
Mailing: P.O. Box 12646
Reading, PA 19612
TF: (877) 768 - 2265
Street: 1130 Berkshire Blvd.
Wyomissing, PA 19610

Corporate Foundations and Giving Programs

Sovereign Bank Foundation
P.O. Box 12646
Reading, PA 19612
TF: (877) 768 - 2265

Annual Grant Total: $750,000 - $1,000,000
Geographic Preference: Area(s) in which the company operates
Primary Interests: Arts and Humanities; Community Development; Education
Recent Recipients: Habitat for Humanity

Public Affairs and Related Activities Personnel

At Headquarters

BROWN, Carl
Manager, Public Relations
cbrown6@sovereignbank.com
Tel: (610) 378 - 6162
Fax: (610) 320 - 8448

EHST, Dick
Exec. V. President and Managing Director, Corporate Communications
dehst@sovereignbank.com
Tel: (610) 378 - 6158
Fax: (610) 320 - 8448

SHULTZ, Ed
Vice President and Director, Public Relations
eshultz1@sovereignbank.com
Tel: (610) 378 - 6159
Fax: (610) 378 - 6155

Spartan Stores Inc.

Merchandiser of food and non-food products.
www.spartanstores.com
Annual Revenues: $2.148 bilion

Chairman, President and Chief Exec. Officer
STURKEN, Craig C.
Tel: (616) 878 - 2000
Fax: (616) 878 - 2775

Main Headquarters
Mailing: P.O. Box 8700
Grand Rapids, MI 49518
Tel: (616) 878 - 2000
Fax: (616) 878 - 2775
Street: 850 76th St., S.W.
Grand Rapids, MI 49518

Corporate Foundations and Giving Programs

Spartan Stores Community Affairs
Contact: Terry Blanding
P.O. Box 8700
Grand Rapids, MI 49518
Tel: (616) 878 - 8447
Fax: (616) 878 - 2900

Annual Grant Total: none reported

Public Affairs and Related Activities Personnel

At Headquarters

BLANDING, Terry
Donations/Community Affairs
terry_blanding@spartanstores.com
Tel: (616) 878 - 8447
Fax: (616) 878 - 2900

DECHOW, Mary Jane Fair
Director, Government Relations
mary_dechow@spartanstores.com
Tel: (616) 878 - 2469
Fax: (616) 878 - 8242

ERIKS, Mark
V. President, Human Resources
mark_eriks@spartanstores.com
Tel: (616) 878 - 2000
Fax: (616) 878 - 2775

Spartan Stores Inc.

** continued from previous page*

KIRKBRIDE, Jean — Tel: (616) 878 - 8319
Exec. Assistant — Fax: (616) 878 - 2775
jean_kirkbride@spartanstores.com
Responsibilities include investor relations.

NORCROSS, Jeanne — Tel: (616) 878 - 2830
Director, Public Relations — Fax: (616) 878 - 2775
jeanne_norcross@spartanstores.com

Sparton Corp.

Designer and manufacturer of technical products for commercial, governmental, industrial and telecommunications customers worldwide.
www.sparton.com
Annual Revenues: $149.7 million

President and Chief Exec. Officer — Tel: (517) 787 - 8600
HOCKENBROCHT, David W. — Fax: (517) 787 - 1822
dhockenbrocht@sparton.com — TF: (800) 248 - 9579

Main Headquarters
Mailing: 2400 E. Ganson — Tel: (517) 787 - 8600
Jackson, MI 49202 — Fax: (517) 787 - 1822
TF: (800) 248 - 9579

Corporate Foundations and Giving Programs

Sparton Corp. Giving Program
Contact: David W. Hockenbrocht
2400 E. Ganson — Tel: (517) 787 - 8600
Jackson, MI 49202 — Fax: (517) 787 - 1822
TF: (800) 248 - 9579

Annual Grant Total: none reported

Public Affairs and Related Activities Personnel

At Headquarters

ALDRICH, Rhonda — Tel: (517) 787 - 8600
Director, Corporate Communications and Marketing Information — Fax: (517) 787 - 1822
raldrich@sparton.com — TF: (800) 248 - 9579

Spherion Corp.

A human capital management organization.
www.spherion.com
Annual Revenues: $2.116 billion

President and Chief Operating Officer — Tel: (954) 308 - 7600
KRAUSE, Roy G. — Fax: (954) 938 - 7790

Main Headquarters
Mailing: 2050 Spectrum Blvd. — Tel: (954) 308 - 7600
Fort Lauderdale, FL 33309 — Fax: (954) 938 - 7790

Public Affairs and Related Activities Personnel

At Headquarters

LAMAND, Richard A. — Tel: (954) 308 - 7600
Senior V. President and Chief Human Resources Officer — Fax: (954) 938 - 7790

MILLER, Teri L. — Tel: (954) 308 - 7600
Director, Strategic Analysis — Fax: (954) 351 - 8117
terilmiller@sherion.com
Responsibilities include shareholder relations.

PALERMO, Liza Fiore — Tel: (954) 308 - 7600
V. President, Corporate Communications — Fax: (954) 938 - 7790
lizapalermo@spherion.com

The Sports Authority, Inc.

A sporting goods store operator.
www.thesportsauthority.com
Annual Revenues: $1.5 billion

Chairman, President and Chief Exec. Officer — Tel: (303) 200 - 5050
MORTON, John Douglas — Fax: (303) 863 - 2240

Main Headquarters
Mailing: 1050 W. Hampden Ave. — Tel: (303) 200 - 5050
Englewood, CO 80110 — Fax: (303) 863 - 2240

Corporate Foundations and Giving Programs

The Sports Authority Corporate Contributions Program
Contact: Rachel Johnson
1050 W. Hampden Ave. — Tel: (303) 200 - 5050
Englewood, CO 80110 — Fax: (303) 863 - 2240

Annual Grant Total: none reported
Recent Recipients: Boys and Girls Club

Public Affairs and Related Activities Personnel

At Headquarters

HENDRICKSON, Thomas T. — Tel: (303) 200 - 5050
V. Chairman, Chief Accounting Officer, Chief Financial Officer and Treasurer — Fax: (303) 863 - 2240
Responsibilities include investor relations.

JOHNSON, Rachel — Tel: (303) 200 - 5050
Administrative Assistant, Advertising — Fax: (303) 863 - 2240
rachel_vargas@sportsauthority.com
Responsibilities include corporate philanthropy.

Sprectrum Brands

Battery and lighting product manufacturer and marketer.
www.rayovac.com
Annual Revenues: $573 million

Chairman and Chief Exec. Officer — Tel: (770) 829 - 6200
JONES, David A.

Main Headquarters
Mailing: Six Concourse Pkwy. — Tel: (770) 829 - 6200
Suite 3300
Atlanta, GA 30328

Public Affairs and Related Activities Personnel

At Headquarters

O'DONNELL, Nancy — Tel: (770) 289 - 6208
V. President, Investor Relations

At Other Offices

DAGGETT, John — Tel: (608) 275 - 4912
Director, Corporate Communications — Fax: (608) 275 - 4967
601 Rayovac Dr.
Madison, WI 53711-2460

MASTERS, Janet — Tel: (608) 275 - 4967
Director, Corporate Communications — Fax: (608) 275 - 4967
601 Rayovac Dr.
Madison, WI 53711-2460
janet.masters@spectrumbrands.com

Springs Industries, Inc.

A manufacturer of finished fabrics and home furnishings.
www.springs.com
Annual Revenues: $2.1 billion

Chairman and Chief Exec. Officer — Tel: (803) 547 - 1500
BOWLES, Ms. Crandall
crandall.bowles@springs.com

Main Headquarters
Mailing: P.O. Box 70 — Tel: (803) 547 - 1500
Fort Mill, SC 29716 — Fax: (803) 547 - 1636
Street: 205 N. White St.
Fort Mill, SC 29715

Political Action Committees

Springs Industries, Inc. PAC (SPRINGSPAC)
205 N. White St. — Tel: (803) 547 - 3738
Fort Mill, SC 29715

Contributions to Candidates: none reported (01/05 - 09/05)

Corporate Foundations and Giving Programs

Springs Industries Corporate Giving Program
Contact: Ted S. Matthews
P.O. Box 70 — Tel: (803) 547 - 1500
Fort Mill, SC 29716 — Fax: (803) 547 - 1636

Annual Grant Total: $750,000 - $1,000,000
Geographic Preference: Area(s) in which the company operates; Alabama; California; Georgia; North Carolina; Pennsylvania; South Carolina; Tennessee; Wisconsin; New York; Mississippi; Mexico; Canada; Oklahoma
Primary Interests: Arts and Culture; Education; Medicine and Health Care

Public Affairs and Related Activities Personnel

At Headquarters

COLEMAN, Gracie P. — Tel: (803) 547 - 1500
Senior V. President, Human Resources
gracie.coleman@springs.com

KUTCHER, Kenneth — Tel: (803) 547 - 1500
Exec. V. President and Chief Financial Officer

MATTHEWS, Ted S. — Tel: (803) 547 - 1500
V. President, Corporate Communications — Fax: (803) 547 - 1636
ted.matthews@springs.com
Responsibilities also include corporate philanthropy.

Sprint Nextel

PUBLIC AFFAIRS COUNCIL

A member of the Public Affairs Council. A global communications company formed by the 2005 merger of Sprint Communications Corp. and Nextel Communications Inc.
www.sprint.com
Annual Revenues: $26.071 billion

Exec. Chairman — Tel: (703) 433 - 4000
DONAHUE, Timothy M.

President and Chief Exec. Officer — Tel: (703) 433 - 4000
FORSEE, Gary D.

Main Headquarters
Mailing: 2001 Edmund Halley Dr. — Tel: (703) 433 - 4000
Reston, VA 20191

Sprint Nextel

** continued from previous page*

Washington Office

Contact: Vonya B. McCann

Mailing: 401 Ninth St. NW
Suite 400
Washington, DC 20004

Tel: (202) 585 - 1900
Fax: (202) 585 - 1899

Political Action Committees

Sprint Corp. PAC
Contact: Sarah Brown
6450 Sprint Pkwy.
Overland Park, KS 66251

Contributions to Candidates: $185,500 (01/05 - 09/05)

Democrats: $61,000; Republicans: $124,500.

Principal Recipients

SENATE DEMOCRATS		HOUSE DEMOCRATS	
Reid, Harry (NV)	$3,000	Cleaver, Emanuel (MO)	$3,000
Clinton, Hillary Rodham (NY)	$2,500	Wynn, Albert (MD)	$3,000
		Conyers, John Jr. (MI)	$2,000
Conrad, Kent (ND)	$2,500	Eshoo, Anna (CA)	$2,000
Dorgan, Byron (ND)	$2,000	Markey, Edward (MA)	$2,000
Inouye, Daniel K (HI)	$2,000	Moore, Dennis (KS)	$2,000
Nelson, Bill (FL)	$2,000	Stupak, Bart (MI)	$2,000
SENATE REPUBLICANS		**HOUSE REPUBLICANS**	
Ensign, John Eric (NV)	$8,000	Blunt, Roy (MO)	$5,000
Burns, Conrad (MT)	$7,000	Hastert, Dennis J. (IL)	$5,000
Talent, James (MO)	$7,000	Pickering, Chip (MS)	$4,000
Allen, George (VA)	$5,500	Upton, Fred (MI)	$4,000
Smith, Gordon (OR)	$4,000	Davis, Tom (VA)	$3,000
Dole, Elizabeth (NC)	$2,000	DeLay, Tom (TX)	$3,000
Stevens, Ted (AK)	$2,000	Rogers, Michael J (MI)	$3,000
		Cannon, Christopher (UT)	$2,500
		Dewine, R. Pat (OH)	$2,000
		Dreier, David (CA)	$2,000
		Fossella, Vito (NY)	$2,000
		Graves, Sam (MO)	$2,000
		Keller, Richard (FL)	$2,000
		Moran, Jerry (KS)	$2,000
		Pryce, Deborah (OH)	$2,000
		Ryan, Paul D (WI)	$2,000
		Ryun, Jim R (KS)	$2,000
		Shimkus, John (IL)	$2,000
		Stearns, Clifford (FL)	$2,000
		Terry, Lee (NE)	$2,000
		Thomas, William M (CA)	$2,000
		Tiahrt, Todd W. (KS)	$2,000
		Wilson, Heather (NM)	$2,000

Sprint Nextel Corp. Mid-Atlantic Region Telecom PAC
Contact: Lawrence K. Mathiot
150 Fayetteville St. Mall
Suite 2810
Raleigh, NC 27601

Contributions to Candidates: none reported (01/05 - 09/05)

Sprint Nextel Corp. Nextel Political Action Committee
Contact: Lonnie Taylor
2001 Edmund Halley Dr.
Reston, VA 20191
Tel: (703) 433 - 4000

Contributions to Candidates: $29,000 (01/05 - 09/05)

Democrats: $8,500; Republicans: $20,500.

Corporate Foundations and Giving Programs

Sprint Foundation
2001 Edmund Halley Dr.
Reston, VA 20191
Tel: (703) 433 - 4000

Annual Grant Total: over $5,000,000

Preference given to groups in Kansas City, Atlanta, Dallas and Washington, DC. Recent recipients: Kansas Internat'l Museum, State Ballet of Missouri, Woodruff Arts Center (Atlanta), Nat'l Conference of Christians and Jews, Spoleto Festival, Lyric Opera of Kansas City, Heart of America Shakespeare Festival.

Geographic Preference: Area(s) in which the company operates

Primary Interests: Arts and Culture; Civic and Public Affairs; Community Affairs; Education

Public Affairs and Related Activities Personnel

At Headquarters

CARLSON, Jared — Tel: (703) 433 - 4000

COX, Bruce — Tel: (703) 433 - 4000

DAY, Chris — Tel: (703) 433 - 4000

DOHERTY, Christopher — Tel: (703) 433 - 4656
V. President, Internal Communications

FAWKES, Kurt — Tel: (703) 433 - 4000
V. President, Investor Relations
kurt.fawkes@mail.sprint.com

GOLDSTEIN, Jim — Tel: (703) 433 - 4000

HANBURY, Trey — Tel: (703) 433 - 4000

HOLLOWAY, Laura — Tel: (703) 433 - 4000

KISSINGER, Jim — Tel: (703) 433 - 4000
Senior V. President, Human Resources

KLEIN, Alex — Tel: (703) 433 - 4000

KREVOR, Lawrence R. — Tel: (703) 433 - 4000
V. President, Government Affairs

MUHLBERG, Judith A. — Tel: (703) 433 - 4000
Senior V. President, Corporate Communications

MURPHY, Thomas E. — Tel: (703) 433 - 4000
Senior V. President, Corporate Communications and Brand Management

NAKAMURA, Kent — Tel: (703) 433 - 4000

ROBERTS, Denton C. — Tel: (703) 433 - 4000
V. President and Chief State External Affairs Officer

STEARN, Geoffrey — Tel: (703) 433 - 4000

SWEERS, Nick — Tel: (703) 433 - 4000
National Media Contact
nicholas.sweers@sprint.com

TAYLOR, Lonnie — Tel: (703) 433 - 4000
V. President, State and Federal Relations

WHITE, Bill — Tel: (703) 433 - 4000
V. President, Corporate Communications
bill.white@mail.sprint.com

At Washington Office

BARLOON, William J. — Tel: (202) 585 - 1928; Fax: (202) 585 - 1899
Senior Director, Government Affairs
Registered Federal Lobbyist.

FOOSANER, Robert S. — Tel: (202) 585 - 1900; Fax: (202) 585 - 1899
Senior V. President, Government Affairs and Chief Regulatory Officer
Registered Federal Lobbyist.

JUHNKE, Richard — Tel: (202) 585 - 1912; Fax: (202) 585 - 1899
V. President, Federal Regulatory -- LDD

KILGORE, Gregory — Tel: (202) 585 - 1930; Fax: (202) 585 - 1899
Director, Government Affairs
Registered Federal Lobbyist.

MCCANN, Vonya B. — Tel: (202) 585 - 1902; Fax: (202) 585 - 1899
Senior V. President, External Affairs

O'NEILL, William S. — Tel: (202) 585 - 1933; Fax: (202) 585 - 1899
Director, Government Affairs
Registered Federal Lobbyist.

At Other Offices

BROWN, Sarah
Treasurer, Sprint Corp. PAC
6450 Sprint Pkwy.
Mailstop: KSOPHN02122A454
Overland Park, KS 66251

HICKCOX, Charlotte
Treasurer, Sprint/United Telephone Co. of Ohio Political Leadership Program PAC
50 W. Broad St.
Suite 3600
Columbus, OH 43215

HORNER, Leigh — Tel: (919) 465 - 3712
Director, Public Affairs
434 Fayetteville St. Mall
Suite 1610
Raleigh, NC 27601

MATHIOT, Lawrence K.
Treasurer, Sprint Nextel Corp. Mid-Atlantic Region Telecom PAC
150 Fayetteville St. Mall
Suite 2810
Raleigh, NC 27601

SPX Corp.

A manufacturer and marketer of speciality service tools and original equipment components for the global motor vehicle industry. Acquired General Signal Corp. in 1998 and United Dominion Industries Ltd. in 2001.

www.spx.com
Annual Revenues: $5.08 billion

SPX Corp.

• continued from previous page

Chairman, President and Chief Exec. Officer Tel: (704) 752 - 4400
BLYSTONE, John B.

Main Headquarters
Mailing: 13515 Ballantyne Corp. Pl. Tel: (704) 752 - 4400
Charlotte, NC 28277

Corporate Foundations and Giving Programs

SPX Foundation
Contact: Tina L. Betlejewski
13515 Ballantyne Corp. Pl. Tel: (704) 752 - 4454
Charlotte, NC 28277

Annual Grant Total: $200,000 - $300,000
Geographic Preference: Area(s) in which the company operates
Primary Interests: Arts and Culture; Education

Public Affairs and Related Activities Personnel

At Headquarters

BETLEJEWSKI, Tina L. Tel: (704) 752 - 4454
Manager, Communications
tina.betlejewski@spx.com
Responsibilities also include corporate philanthropy.

FOREMAN, Robert B. Tel: (704) 752 - 4400
V. President, Human Resources

Square D/Schneider Electric

A subsidiary of Schneider Electric of Paris, France. Manufactures electrical equipment and electronic products and components.
www.squared.com

President and Chief Exec. Officer Tel: (847) 397 - 2600
PETRATIS, David D. Fax: (847) 925 - 7500

Main Headquarters
Mailing: 1415 Roselle Rd. Tel: (847) 397 - 2600
Palatine, IL 60067 Fax: (847) 925 - 7500

Public Affairs and Related Activities Personnel

At Headquarters

FIORANI, R. P. Tel: (847) 397 - 2600
V. President, Communications Fax: (847) 925 - 7271

GANN, Peggy Tel: (847) 397 - 2600
V. President, Human Resources and Administration Fax: (847) 925 - 7500

SRI International

A multi-disciplinary research and consulting company.
www.sri.com
Annual Revenues: $164 million

Chairman of the Board Tel: (650) 859 - 2000
ARMACOST, Samuel Fax: (650) 326 - 5512

President and Chief Exec. Officer Tel: (650) 859 - 2000
CARLSON, Curtis R. Fax: (650) 326 - 5512

Main Headquarters
Mailing: 333 Ravenswood Ave. Tel: (650) 859 - 2000
Menlo Park, CA 94025-3493 Fax: (650) 326 - 5512

Washington Office
Mailing: 1100 Wilson Blvd. Tel: (703) 524 - 2053
Suite 2800 Fax: (703) 247 - 8569
Arlington, VA 22209-2268

Political Action Committees

Sarnoff Corp. PAC, The
Contact: James S. Crofton
201 Washington Rd.
Princeton, NJ 08540

Contributions to Candidates: $6,200 (01/05 - 09/05)
Democrats: $4,100; Republicans: $2,100.

Principal Recipients

SENATE DEMOCRATS		HOUSE DEMOCRATS	
		Rothman, Steven R (NJ)	$2,100
		Andrews, Robert (NJ)	$2,000
SENATE REPUBLICANS		**HOUSE REPUBLICANS**	
		Ferguson, Mike (NJ)	$2,100

Public Affairs and Related Activities Personnel

At Headquarters

HARMAN, Philip Tel: (650) 859 - 2000
Director, Congressional Relations Fax: (650) 326 - 5512

RESNICK, Alice R. Tel: (650) 859 - 2000
V. President, Corporate and Marketing Communications Fax: (650) 326 - 5512
inquiry.line@sri.com

At Other Offices

CROFTON, James S.
PAC Treasurer
201 Washington Rd.
Princeton, NJ 08540

St. Jude Medical, Inc.

A member of the Public Affairs Council. A medical device developer and manufacturer.
www.sjm.com
Annual Revenues: $2.3 billion

Chairman, President, and Chief Exec. Officer Tel: (651) 483 - 2000
STARKS, Daniel J. Fax: (651) 766 - 3045

Main Headquarters
Mailing: One Lillehei Plaza Tel: (651) 483 - 2000
St. Paul, MN 55117-9983 Fax: (651) 766 - 3045

Corporate Foundations and Giving Programs

St. Jude Medical Foundation
Contact: David C. Fetah
One Lillehei Plaza Tel: (651) 481 - 7615
St. Paul, MN 55117-9983 Fax: (651) 481 - 7707

Annual Grant Total: none reported

Public Affairs and Related Activities Personnel

At Headquarters

CRAIG, Angela Tel: (651) 483 - 2000
V. President, Corporate Communications Fax: (651) 766 - 3045

FETAH, David C. Tel: (651) 481 - 7615
Contact, Corporate Giving Program Fax: (651) 481 - 7707

MERRIAM, Laura Tel: (651) 766 - 3029
Director, Investor Relations Fax: (651) 766 - 3045
lmerriam@sjm.com

St. Paul Travelers Cos., Inc.

Formed from the merger of Travelers Property Casualty Corp. and The St. Paul Cos. in April of 2004. A provider of insurance products and services for commercial markets and for auto and homeowners insurance for consumers.
www.stpaultravelers.com

Chairman of the Board Tel: (860) 954 - 3273
LIPP, Robert I. Fax: (860) 954 - 1161

President and Chief Exec. Officer Tel: (651) 310 - 7911
FISHMAN, Jay S.

Main Headquarters
Mailing: 385 Washington St. Tel: (651) 310 - 7911
St. Paul, MN 55102

Washington Office
Mailing: 1331 F St. NW Tel: (202) 628 - 1176
Suite 975 Fax: (202) 628 - 1656
Washington, DC 20005

Political Action Committees

St. Paul Travelers Cos., Inc. Political Action Committee (STA PAC)
Contact: Katie Chipps
One Tower Sq. Tel: (860) 277 - 8208
Hartford, CT 06183 Fax: (860) 277 - 4836

Contributions to Candidates: $97,819 (01/05 - 09/05)
Democrats: $24,819; Republicans: $73,000.

Principal Recipients

SENATE DEMOCRATS		HOUSE DEMOCRATS	
Lieberman, Joe (CT)	$7,819	Larson, John B (CT)	$8,500
SENATE REPUBLICANS		**HOUSE REPUBLICANS**	
Kennedy, Mark (MN)	$8,000	McHenry, Patrick (NC)	$3,000
Talent, James (MO)	$4,000	Shays, Christopher (CT)	$3,000
Santorum, Richard (PA)	$3,000	Simmons, Rob (CT)	$3,000
Allen, George (VA)	$2,500	Cantor, Eric (VA)	$2,500
		Johnson, Nancy (CT)	$2,500
		Kelly, Sue W (NY)	$2,500
		Davis, Geoffrey (KY)	$2,000
		Feeney, Tom (FL)	$2,000
		Fitzpatrick, Michael (PA)	$2,000
		Gerlach, Jim (PA)	$2,000
		Kennedy, Mark (MN)	$2,000
		Price, Thomas (GA)	$2,000
		Renzi, Richard (AZ)	$2,000

St. Paul Travelers Cos., Inc. Volunteers for Good Government
Contact: Gohn Mangino

St. Paul Travelers Cos., Inc.

** continued from previous page*

385 Washington St.
St. Paul, MN 55102
Tel: (860) 277 - 0406

Contributions to Candidates: none reported (01/05 - 09/05)

Corporate Foundations and Giving Programs

St. Paul Travelers Cos., Inc. Foundation
Contact: Mary E. Pickard
385 Washington St.
St. Paul, MN 55102
Tel: (651) 310 - 7359
Fax: (651) 310 - 2327

Annual Grant Total: none reported

St. Pauls Travelers Connecticut Foundation
Contact: Marlene Ibsen
One Tower Sq.
Hartford, CT 06183
Tel: (860) 277 - 9039
Fax: (860) 954 - 8497

Annual Grant Total: none reported

Public Affairs and Related Activities Personnel

At Headquarters

BOYD, Shane
Chief Communications Officer
Tel: (651) 310 - 3846
Fax: (651) 310 - 3660

MANGINO, Gohn
PAC Treasurer
Tel: (860) 277 - 0406

PICKARD, Mary E.
President, St. Paul Travelers Cos., Inc. Foundation and V. President Community Affairs
Tel: (651) 310 - 7359
Fax: (651) 310 - 2327

TURNER, Beverly
V. President, Specialty Commercial Government Relations
Tel: (651) 310 - 5890
Fax: (651) 310 - 6306

At Other Offices

ALLEGUE, Raul
V. President, Commercial Lines, Government Relations
One Tower Sq.
Hartford, CT 06183
Tel: (860) 277 - 4738
Fax: (860) 277 - 4563

CAMPBELL, Timothy R.
Senior V. President, Government Relations
One Tower Sq.
Hartford, CT 06183
Tel: (860) 954 - 3716
Fax: (860) 277 - 4836

CHIPPS, Katie
Director, Political Affairs
One Tower Sq.
Hartford, CT 06183
Tel: (860) 277 - 8208
Fax: (860) 277 - 4836

FRITTER, Lynne E.
Counsel, Personal Lines, Government Relations
One Tower Sq.
Hartford, CT 06183
Tel: (860) 277 - 5476
Fax: (860) 277 - 2808

IBSEN, Marlene
President, St. Paul's Travelers Connecticut Foundation
One Tower Sq.
Hartford, CT 06183
Tel: (860) 277 - 9039
Fax: (860) 954 - 8497

LARKIN, Courtney
Counsel, Personal Lines, Government Relations
One Tower Sq.
Hartford, CT 06183
Tel: (860) 654 - 7869
Fax: (860) 277 - 2808

MILETTI, John D.
V. President, Personal Lines, Government Relations
One Tower Sq.
Hartford, CT 06183
Tel: (860) 277 - 0459
Fax: (860) 277 - 2808

STEBBINS, Michele
Second V. President, Commercial Lines Government Relations
One Tower Sq.
Hartford, CT 06183
Tel: (860) 277 - 2894
Fax: (860) 277 - 4563

Stage Stores, Inc.

www.stagestoresinc.com
Annual Revenues: $875.6 million

Chairman, President and Chief Exec. Officer
SCARBOROUGH, Jim
jscarborough@stagestoresinc.com
Tel: (713) 667 - 5601
Fax: (713) 295 - 5486
TF: (800) 324 - 3244

Main Headquarters
Mailing: P.O. Box 35167
Houston, TX 77235
Tel: (713) 667 - 5601
Fax: (713) 295 - 5486
TF: (800) 324 - 3244

Street: 10201 Main St.
Houston, TX 77025

Corporate Foundations and Giving Programs

Stages Stores, Inc. Community Involvement
Contact: Cindy Kothmann
P.O. Box 35167
Houston, TX 77235
Tel: (713) 667 - 5601
Fax: (713) 295 - 5486
TF: (800) 324 - 3244

Annual Grant Total: none reported

Public Affairs and Related Activities Personnel

At Headquarters

ARONSON, Bob
V. President, Investor Relations
baronson@stagestoresinc.com
Tel: (713) 667 - 5601
Fax: (713) 295 - 5486
TF: (800) 324 - 3244

KOTHMANN, Cindy
Community Relations Contact
ckothmann@stagestores.com
Tel: (713) 667 - 5601
Fax: (713) 295 - 5486
TF: (800) 324 - 3244

LUCAS, Ron
Exec. V. President, Human Resources
rlucas@stagestoresinc.com
Tel: (713) 667 - 5601
Fax: (713) 295 - 5486
TF: (800) 324 - 3244

Standard Commercial Corp.

See listing on page 20 under Alliance One Internat'l Inc.

Standard Federal Bank

www.standardfederalbank.com
Annual Revenues: $2.537.4 billion

Chairman, President, and Chief Exec. Officer
HEITMANN, Scott K.
Tel: (248) 643 - 9600
Fax: (248) 637 - 2749
TF: (800) 643 - 9600

Main Headquarters
Mailing: 2600 W. Big Beaver Rd.
Troy, MI 48084
Tel: (248) 643 - 9600
Fax: (248) 637 - 2749
TF: (800) 643 - 9600

Corporate Foundations and Giving Programs

Standard Federal Bank Corporate Giving Program
Contact: Mary M. Fowlie
2600 W. Big Beaver Rd.
Troy, MI 48084
Tel: (248) 643 - 9600
Fax: (248) 637 - 5016
TF: (800) 643 - 9600

Annual Grant Total: none reported
Primary Interests: Community Development; Education; Health and Human Services

Public Affairs and Related Activities Personnel

At Headquarters

DARMANIN, Robert T.
Director, Corporate Relations
robert.darmanin@abnamro.com
Tel: (248) 637 - 2521
Fax: (248) 637 - 2749
TF: (800) 643 - 9600

FOWLIE, Mary M.
Group Senior V. President, Regulatory Affairs and Compliance
Tel: (248) 643 - 9600
Fax: (248) 637 - 5016
TF: (800) 643 - 9600

Standard Insurance Co.

A subsidiary of StanCorp. Financial Group, Inc.
www.standard.com

Chairman, President and Chief Exec. Officer
PARSONS, Eric E.
Tel: (503) 321 - 7000
Fax: (503) 321 - 7935

Main Headquarters
Mailing: P.O. Box 711
Portland, OR 97207
Tel: (503) 321 - 7000
Fax: (503) 321 - 6776
Street: 1100 S. W. Sixth Ave.
Portland, OR 97204

Political Action Committees

Standard Insurance Co. Political Action Committee (StanPac)
Contact: Justin Delaney
P.O. Box 711
Portland, OR 97207
Tel: (503) 321 - 8541
Fax: (503) 478 - 5243

Contributions to Candidates: none reported (01/05 - 09/05)

Public Affairs and Related Activities Personnel

At Headquarters

DELANEY, Justin
Contact, Standard Insurance Co. PAC
Tel: (503) 321 - 8541
Fax: (503) 478 - 5243

HIGGS, Kira
Assistant V. President, Public Affairs and Communications
Mailstop: P2A
Tel: (503) 321 - 6418
Fax: (503) 321 - 6776

Standard Pacific Corp.

A residential construction company.
www.standardpacifichomes.com

Standard Pacific Corp.

** continued from previous page*

Chairman and Chief Exec. Officer
SCARBOROUGH, Stephen J. Tel: (949) 789 - 1600 Fax: (949) 789 - 1609

Main Headquarters
Mailing: 15326 Alton Pkwy. Irvine, CA 92618 Tel: (949) 789 - 1600 Fax: (949) 789 - 1609

Public Affairs and Related Activities Personnel

At Headquarters

BEAUFORD, Shiree
Contact, Investor Relations
Tel: (949) 789 - 1600 Fax: (949) 789 - 1609

PARNES, Andrew H.
Exec. V. President, Finance/Chief Financial Officer
Tel: (949) 789 - 1600 Fax: (949) 789 - 1609

Standard Register Co.

A producer of business forms, document management equipment and systems.
www.standardregister.com
Annual Revenues: $1.028 billion

Chairman of the Board
GRANZOW, Paul H. Tel: (937) 221 - 1000 Fax: (937) 221 - 1239 TF: (800) 755 - 6405

Chief Exec. Officer
REDIKER, Dennis L. Tel: (937) 221 - 1000 Fax: (937) 221 - 1239 TF: (800) 755 - 6405

Main Headquarters
Mailing: P.O. Box 1167 Dayton, OH 45401-1167 Tel: (937) 221 - 1000 Fax: (937) 221 - 1239 TF: (800) 755 - 6405

Street: 600 Albany St. Dayton, OH 45408-1442

Corporate Foundations and Giving Programs

The Sherman-Standard Register Foundation
Contact: Barbara Widera
P.O. Box 1167
Dayton, OH 45401-1167
Tel: (937) 221 - 1000 Fax: (937) 221 - 1239 TF: (800) 755 - 6405

Annual Grant Total: $100,000 - $200,000
Geographic Preference: Ohio
Primary Interests: Arts and Culture; Civic and Public Affairs; Health; Higher Education; Youth Services

Public Affairs and Related Activities Personnel

At Headquarters

BROWN, Craig
Chief Financial Officer
Tel: (937) 221 - 1000 Fax: (937) 221 - 1239 TF: (800) 755 - 6405
Responsibilities include public affairs.

CESTELLI, Robert J.
Associate V. President, Investor Relations
robert.cestelli@standardregister.com
Tel: (937) 221 - 1304 Fax: (937) 221 - 1205 TF: (800) 755 - 6405

MCEWAN, Julie
Manager, Public Relations
julie.mcewan@standardregister.com
Tel: (937) 221 - 1825 Fax: (937) 221 - 1486 TF: (800) 755 - 6405

MORGAN, Joseph P.
V. President and Chief Technology Officer
joe.morgan@standardregister.com
Responsibilities include public affairs.
Tel: (937) 913 - 6377 Fax: (937) 221 - 1239 TF: (800) 755 - 6405

WIDERA, Barbara
Contact, The Sherman-Standard Register Foundation
barbara.widera@standardregister.com
Tel: (937) 221 - 1000 Fax: (937) 221 - 1239 TF: (800) 755 - 6405

Stanford Research Institute

See listing on page 452 under SRI International.

Stanhome Inc.

See listing on page 181 under Enesco Group, Inc.

The Stanley Works

A worldwide manufacturer and marketer of tools, hardware and door systems for home improvement, consumer, industrial and professional use.
www.stanleyworks.com
Annual Revenues: $2.593 billion

Chairman and Chief Exec. Officer
LUNDGREN, John F. Tel: (860) 225 - 5111 Fax: (860) 827 - 3937

Main Headquarters
Mailing: 1000 Stanley Dr. New Britain, CT 06053 Tel: (860) 225 - 5111 Fax: (860) 827 - 3937

Political Action Committees

Stanley Works PAC
Contact: Don Allan
1000 Stanley Dr.
New Britain, CT 06053
Tel: (860) 225 - 5111 Fax: (860) 827 - 3937

Contributions to Candidates: none reported (01/05 - 09/05)

Corporate Foundations and Giving Programs

Stanley Works Corporate Contributions
1000 Stanley Dr.
New Britain, CT 06053
Tel: (860) 225 - 5111 Fax: (860) 827 - 3937

Annual Grant Total: $1,000,000 - $2,000,000
Geographic Preference: Area(s) in which the company operates; Connecticut; Georgia; Michigan; North Carolina; South Carolina; Rhode Island
Primary Interests: Arts and Culture; Community Affairs; Health; Housing
Recent Recipients: Junior Achievement; United Way

Public Affairs and Related Activities Personnel

At Headquarters

ALLAN, Don
V. President and Corporate Conroller
Responsibilities include political action.
Tel: (860) 225 - 5111 Fax: (860) 827 - 3937

GOULD, Gerard J.
V. President, Investor Relations
ggould@stanleyworks.com
Tel: (860) 827 - 3833 Fax: (860) 827 - 3895

MATHIEU, Mark J.
V. President, Human Resources
mmathieu@stanleyworks.com
Tel: (860) 827 - 3818 Fax: (860) 827 - 3809

Staples, Inc.

A retailer of office products.
www.staples.com
Annual Revenues: $14.4 billion

Chief Exec. Officer and Chairman of the Board
SARGENT, Ronald L.
ron.sargent@staples.com
Tel: (508) 253 - 5000 Ext: 37510

Main Headquarters
Mailing: 500 Staples Dr. Framingham, MA 01702 Tel: (508) 253 - 5000

Corporate Foundations and Giving Programs

Staples Foundation for Learning
500 Staples Dr.
Framingham, MA 01702
Tel: (508) 253 - 5000

Annual Grant Total: none reported
Primary Interests: Education

Public Affairs and Related Activities Personnel

At Headquarters

CAPELLI, Paul
V. President, Public Relations
paul.capelli@staples.com
Tel: (508) 253 - 5000 Ext: 38530

HOYT, Susan S.
Exec. V. President, Human Resources
susan.hoyt@staples.com
Tel: (508) 253 - 7234 Ext: 37231 Fax: (508) 253 - 8955

LEFEBVRE, Laurel
V. President, Investor Relations
laurel.lefebvre@staples.com
Tel: (508) 253 - 5000 Ext: 34080 Fax: (508) 253 - 8955

MAHONEY, John J.
Exec. V. President, Chief Administrative Officer and Chief Financial Officer
john.mahoney@staples.com
Responsibilities include government affairs.
Tel: (508) 253 - 8969 Ext: 37298 Fax: (508) 253 - 8955

Star Tribune

www.startribune.com
Annual Revenues: $359.1 million

Main Headquarters
Mailing: 425 Portland Ave. Minneapolis, MN 55415 Tel: (612) 673 - 4000 TF: (800) 829 - 8742

Corporate Foundations and Giving Programs

Star Tribune Foundation
Contact: Ms. Sam Fleitman
425 Portland Ave.
Minneapolis, MN 55415
Tel: (612) 673 - 7051 Fax: (612) 673 - 7847 TF: (800) 829 - 8742

Annual Grant Total: $2,000,000 - $5,000,000
Priority lies with organizations and programs that enable people to move from dependency to self-reliance; the cultural community, with emphasis on preeminent institutions and on writing-related programs; and programs that strengthen the place of media in society.
Geographic Preference: Area in which the company is headquartered; Minnesota
Primary Interests: Financially Disadvantaged; Journalism
Recent Recipients: Minnesota Orchestra; United Way; University of Minnesota

Star Tribune

** continued from previous page*

Public Affairs and Related Activities Personnel

At Headquarters

FLEITMAN, Ms. Sam
Coordinator, Star Tribune Foundation
Tel: (612) 673 - 7051
Fax: (612) 673 - 7847
TF: (800) 829 - 8742

NELSON, Sally
Director, Communications and Community Affairs
Tel: (612) 673 - 7771
Fax: (612) 673 - 4835
TF: (800) 829 - 8742

TAYLOR, Ben
Senior V. President, Communications
Tel: (612) 673 - 7457
Fax: (612) 673 - 4835
TF: (800) 829 - 8742

Starbucks Corp.

A member of the Public Affairs Council. Owner and operator of specialty coffee shops and distributor of coffee and novelty items.
www.starbucks.com
Annual Revenues: $2.649 billion

Chairman and Chief Global Strategist
SCHULTZ, Howard
Tel: (206) 447 - 1575
Fax: (206) 682 - 9051

President and Chief Exec. Officer
SMITH, Orin C.
Tel: (206) 447 - 1575
Fax: (206) 682 - 9051

Main Headquarters
Mailing: P.O. Box 34067
Seattle, WA 98124-1067
Tel: (206) 447 - 1575
Fax: (206) 682 - 9051
Street: 2401 Utah Ave. South
Suite 800
Seattle, WA 98134

Corporate Foundations and Giving Programs

Starbucks Foundation
P.O. Box 34067
Seattle, WA 98124-1067
Tel: (206) 447 - 1575
Fax: (206) 682 - 9051

Annual Grant Total: none reported
Primary Interests: Literacy

Public Affairs and Related Activities Personnel

At Headquarters

HERNDON, Wanda
Senior V. President, Worldwide Communications and Public Affairs
Mailstop: S-CM1
Tel: (206) 447 - 1575
Ext: 88191
Fax: (206) 447 - 9866

MORAN, Tracy
Director, Investor Relations
Tel: (206) 318 - 7806
Fax: (206) 318 - 0635

SPRAUVE, Anthony
V. President, Worldwide Public Affairs
Tel: (206) 447 - 1575
Fax: (206) 682 - 9051

WALSH, Jennifer
Public Relations Specialist
Tel: (206) 447 - 1575
Fax: (206) 682 - 9051

Starwood Hotels and Resorts Worldwide, Inc.

Investment trust. Acquired ITT Corp. in 1998.
www.starwoodhotels.com
Annual Revenues: $4.659 billion

Exec. Chairman and Chief Design Officer
STERNLICHT, Barry S.
barry.sternlicht@starwoodhotels.com
Tel: (914) 640 - 8200
Fax: (914) 640 - 8310
TF: (877) 443 - 4585

Chief Exec. Officer
HEYER, Steven J.
Tel: (914) 640 - 8200
Fax: (914) 640 - 8310
TF: (877) 443 - 4585

Main Headquarters
Mailing: 1111 Westchester Ave.
White Plains, NY 10604
Tel: (914) 640 - 8100
Fax: (914) 640 - 8310
TF: (877) 443 - 4585

Political Action Committees

Starwood Hotels and Resorts Worldwide Inc. PAC (Starwood PAC)
1111 Westchester Ave.
White Plains, NY 10604
Tel: (914) 640 - 8100
Fax: (914) 640 - 8310
TF: (877) 443 - 4585

Contributions to Candidates: none reported (01/05 - 09/05)

Corporate Foundations and Giving Programs

Starwood Community Relations
Contact: Beth Shanholtz
1111 Westchester Ave.
White Plains, NY 10604
Tel: (914) 640 - 8112
Fax: (914) 640 - 8310
TF: (877) 443 - 4585

Annual Grant Total: none reported
Primary Interests: Children
Recent Recipients: Habitat for Humanity; Junior Achievement; Juvenile Diabetes Foundation

Public Affairs and Related Activities Personnel

At Headquarters

GIBSON, F. Daniel
Senior V. President, Corporate Affairs
Tel: (914) 640 - 8175
Fax: (914) 640 - 8310
TF: (877) 443 - 4585
Responsibilities include investor relations.

KAVANAGH, K. C.
V. President, Public Relations, Cross Branded Programs/Lead National Publicist
kc.kavanagh@starwoodhotels.com
Tel: (914) 640 - 8339
Fax: (914) 640 - 8310
TF: (877) 443 - 4585

NORTON, David K.
Exec. V. President, Human Resources
david.norton@starwoodhotels.com
Tel: (914) 640 - 5253
Fax: (914) 640 - 8310
TF: (877) 443 - 4585

SHANHOLTZ, Beth
Executive, Starwood Foundation
beth.shanholtz@starwoodhotels.com
Tel: (914) 640 - 8112
Fax: (914) 640 - 8310
TF: (877) 443 - 4585

SIEGEL, Kenneth S.
Exec. V. President, General Counsel and Secretary
kenneth.siegel@starwoodhotels.com
Tel: (914) 640 - 8200
Fax: (914) 640 - 8310
TF: (877) 443 - 4585
Responsibilities include government affairs.

At Other Offices

ARNELL, Robyn
PAC Treasurer
2231 Camelback Rd.
Suite 400
Phoenix, AZ 85016

State Farm Insurance Cos.

A member of the Public Affairs Council. An insurance company.
www.statefarm.com
Annual Revenues: $46.7 billion

Chairman and Chief Exec. Officer
RUST, Edward B., Jr.
Tel: (309) 766 - 2871

Main Headquarters
Mailing: One State Farm Plaza
Bloomington, IL 61710-0001
Tel: (309) 766 - 2311

Washington Office
Contact: Art Ruiz
Mailing: 1900 M St. NW
Suite 730
Washington, DC 20036
Tel: (202) 263 - 4400
Fax: (202) 263 - 4435

Corporate Foundations and Giving Programs

State Farm Companies Foundation
Contact: Lori Manning
One State Farm Plaza
Bloomington, IL 61710-0001
Tel: (309) 766 - 9739

Annual Grant Total: over $5,000,000
Geographic Preference: Area in which the company is headquartered
Primary Interests: Higher Education; Medicine and Health Care; Youth Services
Recent Recipients: Nat'l Merit Scholarship; St. Joseph Medical Center; Students Against Destructive Decisions

Public Affairs and Related Activities Personnel

At Headquarters

ADAMS, Clayton
V. President, Communication Alliances
Mailstop: M/S B-4
Tel: (309) 766 - 3164
Fax: (309) 766 - 0860

CALLIS, Kevin
Assistant V. President, External Communications
Mailstop: M/S B-4
Tel: (309) 766 - 2621
Fax: (309) 766 - 0860

CLAPPER, Kellie
Director, Public Affairs
Mailstop: M/S B-4
Tel: (309) 766 - 8865
Fax: (309) 766 - 0860

ECHOLS, Margaret A.
V. President, Corporate Communications and External Relations
Mailstop: M/S B-4
Tel: (309) 766 - 6688
Fax: (309) 766 - 0860

LYONS, Kelly
Director, Public Affairs
(State Farm Mutual Automobile Insurance Co.)
Tel: (309) 766 - 1115

MANNING, Lori
Director, Public Affairs; Contact, State Farm Companies Foundation
Tel: (309) 766 - 9739

ROSENSTOCK, John
Director, Public Affairs
Mailstop: (B-4)
Tel: (309) 766 - 3379

ROSS-RINGER, Cindy
Director, Public Affairs
Mailstop: (B-4)
Tel: (309) 763 - 5906
Fax: (309) 766 - 2670

State Farm Insurance Cos.

* continued from previous page

SUPPLE, Phil — Tel: (309) 766 - 9921
Director, Public Affairs

WALLACE, Brad — Tel: (309) 766 - 9273
Public Affairs Consultant
Mailstop: M/S (B-4)

WALLER, Tony — Tel: (309) 766 - 9765
Public Affairs Consultant
Mailstop: M/S B-4

WHEELER, Deb L. — Tel: (309) 766 - 9580
Public Affairs Consultant

At Washington Office

DILLARD, Regina K. — Tel: (202) 263 - 4400
Counsel — Fax: (202) 263 - 4435
Registered Federal Lobbyist.

MANESS, Alan D. — Tel: (202) 263 - 4400
Associate General Counsel — Fax: (202) 263 - 4435
Registered Federal Lobbyist.

RUIZ, Art — Tel: (202) 263 - 4400
Director, Federal Affairs — Fax: (202) 263 - 4435

At Other Offices

ADAMS, M. Richard — Tel: (301) 620 - 6640
Manager, Public Affairs — Fax: (301) 620 - 6645
One State Farm Dr.
Frederick, MD 21701-9332

BRANDAU, Herman — Tel: (309) 662 - 0066
Associate
2216 Woodfield Rd.
Bloomington, IL 61704

BRANDT, Mark — Tel: (480) 293 - 6011
Manager, Public Affairs — Fax: (602) 784 - 3950
2700 S. Sunland Dr.
Tempe, AZ 85282-3387

HARBERT, Sophie — Tel: (512) 918 - 5887
Assistant Manager, Public Affairs Communications
8900 Amberglen Blvd.
Austin, TX 78729-1110

IRVIN, Carolin — Tel: (610) 358 - 8320
Manager, Public Affairs — Fax: (610) 358 - 7698
One State Farm Dr.
Concordville, PA 19339

LARE, James J. — Tel: (610) 358 - 7009
Director, Government Relations — Fax: (610) 358 - 7698
One State Farm Dr.
Concordville, PA 19339-0001

LOWENTHAL, Rob — Tel: (678) 455 - 2320
Manager, Public Affairs
3325 Paddocks Pkwy.
Suite 100
Suwanee, Ga 30024-6060

MCCONKEY, Judy — Tel: (740) 364 - 5400
Assistant Manager, Public Affairs — Fax: (740) 364 - 5410
1440 Granville Rd.
Newark, OH 43055-1519

MILLER, Alan D. — Tel: (970) 351 - 5350
Assistant Manager, Public Affairs — Fax: (970) 351 - 5424
1555 Promontery Circle
Greeley, CO 80638-0001

NEILS, Michelle — Tel: (610) 361 - 4115
Manager, Government Affairs
225 Wilmington
Suite 500
Chadds Ford, PA 19317-9039

OZANNE, Colleen K. — Tel: (402) 327 - 5677
Public Affairs Specialist
P.O. Box 82542
Lincoln, NE 68501

PICKAR, Joy Keyser — Tel: (970) 395 - 5150
Assistant Manager, Public Affairs
(State Farm Mutual Automobile Insurance Co.)
1555 Promontery Circle
Greeley, CO 80638-0001

SIROLA, Bill — Tel: (916) 321 - 6927
Manager, Public Affairs — Fax: (916) 321 - 6902
1201 K St., Suite 920
Greater California-Corporate Law West
Sacramento, CA 95814

SMITH, Brenda — Tel: (661) 663 - 2771
Manager, Public Affairs - California — Fax: (661) 663 - 2799
900 Old River Rd.
Bakersfield, CA 93311-6000

State Farm Mutual Automobile Insurance Co.

See listing on page 455 under State Farm Insurance Cos.

State Street Corp.

www.statestreet.com
Annual Revenues: $5.395 billion

Chairman and Chief Exec. Officer — Tel: (617) 786 - 3000
LOGUE, Ronald E. — Fax: (617) 664 - 4999

Main Headquarters
Mailing: 225 Franklin St. — Tel: (617) 786 - 3000
Boston, MA 02110 — Fax: (617) 664 - 4999

Political Action Committees

State Street Bank and Trust Co. Voluntary Political Action Committee
Contact: George A. Russell, Jr.
225 Franklin St. — Tel: (617) 664 - 3866
Boston, MA 02110 — Fax: (617) 451 - 6315

Contributions to Candidates: $2,000 (01/05 - 09/05)
Democrats: $1,000; Republicans: $1,000.

Principal Recipients

SENATE DEMOCRATS	HOUSE DEMOCRATS
	Neal, Richard E Mr. (MA) $1,000
SENATE REPUBLICANS	**HOUSE REPUBLICANS**
	Ney, Robert W (OH) $1,000

Corporate Foundations and Giving Programs

State Street Global Philanthropy Program
Contact: George A. Bowman, Jr.
225 Franklin St. — Tel: (617) 664 - 3381
Boston, MA 02110 — Fax: (617) 451 - 6315

Annual Grant Total: over $5,000,000
Donations totaled over $9.3 million in 2004. Guidelines are available.
Geographic Preference: Area(s) in which the company operates
Primary Interests: Arts and Culture; Community Development; Disaster Relief; Education; Employment; Health and Human Services; Youth Services

Public Affairs and Related Activities Personnel

At Headquarters

BARRY, Joseph J. — Tel: (617) 664 - 1254
V. President, Industry Affairs — Fax: (617) 664 - 4999
jjbarry@statestreet.com

BOWMAN, George A., Jr. — Tel: (617) 664 - 3381
V. President, Community Affairs — Fax: (617) 451 - 6315
gabowman@statestreet.com

MACDONALD, Kelley S. — Tel: (617) 786 - 3000
Senior V. President, Investor Relations — Fax: (617) 664 - 4999

O'LEARY, David — Tel: (617) 786 - 3000
Exec. V. President, Global Human Resources — Fax: (617) 664 - 4999

RUSSELL, George A., Jr. — Tel: (617) 664 - 3866
Exec. V. President, Community Affairs — Fax: (617) 451 - 6315
garussell@statestreet.com

Steelcase Inc.

A Fortune 500 designer and manufacturer of architecture, furniture and technology for the office.
www.steelcase.com
Annual Revenues: $2.586 billion

President, Chief Exec. Officer and Director — Tel: (616) 247 - 2710
HACKETT, James P. — Fax: (616) 473 - 2200

Main Headquarters
Mailing: P.O. Box 1967 — Tel: (616) 247 - 2710
Grand Rapids, MI 49501-1967 — Fax: (616) 473 - 2200
Street: 901 44th St. SE
Grand Rapids, MI 49508

Corporate Foundations and Giving Programs

Steelcase Foundation
Contact: Susan Broman
P.O. Box 1967 — Tel: (616) 246 - 4695
Grand Rapids, MI 49501-1967 — Fax: (616) 475 - 2200

Assets: $124,948,460 (2000)
Annual Grant Total: over $5,000,000
Geographic Preference: Area(s) in which the company operates; Alabama; California; Michigan; North Carolina; Indiana; Canada; Mexico
Primary Interests: Arts and Culture; Community Development; Diversity; Education; Environment/Conservation; Health and Human Services
Recent Recipients: United Way; YMCA

Steelcase Inc.

* continued from previous page

Public Affairs and Related Activities Personnel

At Headquarters

BECKER, Richard
Manager, Corporate Relations
Mailstop: CH5W
rbecker@steelcase.com
Tel: (616) 246 - 9332
Fax: (616) 475 - 2599

BROMAN, Susan
Exec. Director, Steelcase Foundation
Mailstop: CH4E
sbroman@steelcase.com
Tel: (616) 246 - 4695
Fax: (616) 475 - 2200

GEBBEN, Phyllis
Coordinator, Steelcase Foundation Donations
Mailstop: CH4E
pgebben@steelcase.com
Tel: (616) 246 - 9860
Fax: (616) 475 - 2200

HICKEY, Nancy W.
Senior V. President, Global Human Resources; and Chief Administrative Officer
Mailstop: CH4E
nhickey@steelcase.com
Tel: (616) 248 - 7292
Fax: (616) 248 - 7400

RINARD, David
Director, Corporate Environmental Quality
Mailstop: PS
drinard@steelcase.com
Tel: (616) 247 - 2996
Fax: (616) 246 - 9191

Stephens Inc.

An investment banking firm.

www.stephens.com

Chairman, President, and Chief Exec. Officer
STEPHENS, Warren A.
Tel: (501) 377 - 2000
Fax: (501) 377 - 2666
TF: (800) 643 - 9691

Main Headquarters
Mailing: 111 Center St.
Little Rock, AR 72201
Tel: (501) 377 - 2000
Fax: (501) 377 - 2666
TF: (800) 643 - 9691

Political Action Committees

Stephens Inc. Federal Political Action Committee
Contact: Robert L. Schulte
111 Center St.
Little Rock, AR 72201
Tel: (501) 377 - 2000
Fax: (501) 377 - 2666
TF: (800) 643 - 9691

Contributions to Candidates: $14,500 (01/05 - 09/05)
Democrats: $14,500.

Principal Recipients

SENATE DEMOCRATS		HOUSE DEMOCRATS	
Baucus, Max (MT)	$10,000	Berry, Marion (AR)	$2,500
Carper, Thomas R (DE)	$2,000		

Public Affairs and Related Activities Personnel

At Headquarters

GRAY, Ellen
Senior V. President, Human Resources
Tel: (501) 377 - 2000
Fax: (501) 377 - 2666
TF: (800) 643 - 9691

SCHULTE, Robert L.
PAC Treasurer
Tel: (501) 377 - 2000
Fax: (501) 377 - 2666
TF: (800) 643 - 9691

THOMAS, Frank
V. President, Media and Government Relations
Tel: (501) 377 - 2000
Fax: (501) 377 - 3453
TF: (800) 643 - 9691

STERIS Corp.

Provides infection prevention, contamination prevention, and microbial reduction products and services.

www.steris.com
Annual Revenues: $1 billion

Chairman of the Board
ROBERTSON, Jerry E.
Tel: (440) 354 - 2600
Fax: (440) 639 - 4450
TF: (800) 548 - 4873

President and Chief Exec. Officer
VINNEY, Les C.
Tel: (440) 354 - 2600
Fax: (440) 639 - 4450
TF: (800) 548 - 4873

Main Headquarters
Mailing: 5960 Heisley Rd.
Mentor, OH 44060-1834
Tel: (440) 354 - 2600
Fax: (440) 639 - 4450
TF: (800) 548 - 4873

Political Action Committees

STERIS Corp. Good Government Fund (STERISPAC)
Contact: William L. Aamoth
5960 Heisley Rd.
Mentor, OH 44060-1834
Tel: (440) 354 - 2600
Fax: (440) 639 - 4450
TF: (800) 548 - 4873

Contributions to Candidates: $16,550 (01/05 - 09/05)
Republicans: $16,550.

Principal Recipients

SENATE REPUBLICANS		HOUSE REPUBLICANS	
Dewine, Richard (OH)	$5,500	Dewine, R. Pat (OH)	$1,000
Voinovich, George (OH)	$2,500	Hobson, David (OH)	$1,000
Chambliss, Saxby (GA)	$2,000	Kingston, John (GA)	$1,000
Shelby, Richard (AL)	$1,000		
Stevens, Ted (AK)	$1,000		
Talent, James (MO)	$1,000		

Public Affairs and Related Activities Personnel

At Headquarters

AAMOTH, William L.
V. President and Corporate Treasurer
Tel: (440) 354 - 2600
Fax: (440) 639 - 4450
TF: (800) 548 - 4873

GORMLEY, Aidan
Senior Director, Corporate Communications and Investor Relations
aidan_gormley@steris.com
Tel: (440) 392 - 7607
Fax: (440) 639 - 4450
TF: (800) 548 - 4873

Sterling Chemicals, Inc.

Manufactures commodity petrochemicals.

www.sterlingchemicals.com
Annual Revenues: $590 million

Chief Exec. Officer and President
CRUMP, Rick
Tel: (713) 650 - 3700
Fax: (713) 654 - 9552

Main Headquarters
Mailing: 333 Clay St.
Suite 3600
Houston, TX 70002-4109
Tel: (713) 650 - 3700
Fax: (713) 654 - 9552

Public Affairs and Related Activities Personnel

At Headquarters

VANDERHAVEN, Paul
Senior V. President, Finance and Chief Financial Officer
Tel: (713) 650 - 3700
Fax: (713) 654 - 9552

Stewart & Stevenson Services, Inc.

A manufacturer and distributor of industrial and energy-related equipment.

www.ssss.com
Annual Revenues: $1.145 billion

Chairman of the Board
WOLF, Howard
Tel: (713) 868 - 7614
Fax: (713) 426 - 1331

President and Chief Exec. Officer
LUKENS, Max L.
m.lukens@ssss.com
Tel: (713) 868 - 7605
Fax: (713) 426 - 1331

Main Headquarters
Mailing: P.O. Box 1637
Houston, TX 77251-1637
Street: 2707 N. Loop West
Houston, TX 77008
Tel: (713) 868 - 7700
Fax: (713) 868 - 7692

Washington Office
Contact: William Chadbourne
Mailing: 1729 King. St.
Suite 300
Alexandria, VA 22314
Tel: (703) 836 - 0697
Fax: (703) 836 - 6878

Political Action Committees

Stewart & Stevenson Services Inc. Good Government Committee
P.O. Box 1637
Houston, TX 77251-1637
Tel: (713) 868 - 7700
Fax: (713) 868 - 7692

Contributions to Candidates: $12,500 (01/05 - 09/05)
Democrats: $2,500; Republicans: $10,000.

Principal Recipients

SENATE DEMOCRATS		HOUSE DEMOCRATS	
		Edwards, Chet (TX)	$1,500
		Moran, James (VA)	$1,000

Stewart & Stevenson Services, Inc.

** continued from previous page*

SENATE REPUBLICANS
Hutchison, Kay Bailey (TX) $2,000

HOUSE REPUBLICANS
Brady, Kevin Patrick (TX) $2,000
McCaul, Michael (TX) $2,000
Bonilla, Henry (TX) $1,000
Carter, John (TX) $1,000
Conaway, K Michael (TX) $1,000
Hunter, Duncan (CA) $1,000

Public Affairs and Related Activities Personnel

At Washington Office

CHADBOURNE, William
V. President, Marketing and Government Affairs
Tel: (703) 836 - 0697
Fax: (703) 836 - 6879

Stewart Enterprises, Inc.

Provides funeral home and cemetery services.
www.stewartenterprises.com
Annual Revenues: $3.2 billion

President and Chief Exec. Officer
BUDDE, Kenneth
Tel: (504) 837 - 5880
Fax: (504) 849 - 2307
TF: (800) 535 - 6017

Chairman of the Board
ROWE, William E.
Tel: (504) 837 - 5880
Fax: (504) 849 - 2307
TF: (800) 535 - 6017

Main Headquarters
Mailing: P.O. Box 19925
Metairie, LA 70179-0925
Tel: (504) 837 - 5880
Fax: (504) 849 - 2307
TF: (800) 535 - 6017

Street: 110 Veterans Blvd.
New Orleans, LA 70005

Public Affairs and Related Activities Personnel

At Headquarters

DE LAUREAL, Martin
V. President, Investor Relations
Tel: (504) 837 - 5880
Fax: (504) 849 - 2307
TF: (800) 535 - 6017

LOCANTRO, Karen
Manager, External Communications
Tel: (504) 837 - 5880
Fax: (504) 849 - 2307
TF: (800) 535 - 6017

Stone & Webster Engineering

See listing on page 458 under Stone & Webster, Inc.

Stone & Webster, Inc.

A subsidiary of The Shaw Group, Inc. (see separate listing).
www.shawgrp.com/stonewebster/index.cfm

President and Chief Exec. Officer
BARFIELD, T. A., Jr.
Tel: (225) 932 - 2500
Fax: (225) 932 - 2657

Main Headquarters
Mailing: 4171 Essen Lane
Baton Rouge, LA 70809
Tel: (225) 932 - 2500
Fax: (225) 932 - 2657

Washington Office
Contact: Stephen M. Marlo
Mailing: 1717 Pennsylvania Ave. NW
Suite 900
Washington, DC 20006
Tel: (202) 261 - 1900
Fax: (202) 261 - 1948

Political Action Committees

Shaw Group Inc. / Stone & Webster Inc. Political Action Committee
Contact: Stephen M. Marlo
1717 Pennsylvania Ave. NW
Suite 900
Washington, DC 20006
Tel: (202) 261 - 1909
Fax: (202) 261 - 1949

Contributions to Candidates: $51,500 (01/05 - 09/05)
Democrats: $20,500; Republicans: $31,000.

Principal Recipients

SENATE DEMOCRATS
Kennedy, Ted (MA) $5,000
Bingaman, Jeff (NM) $3,000

HOUSE DEMOCRATS
Melancon, Charlie (LA) $5,000
Jefferson, William (LA) $2,500

SENATE REPUBLICANS
Stevens, Ted (AK) $2,000

HOUSE REPUBLICANS
Alexander, Rodney (LA) $5,000
Jindal, Bobby (LA) $5,000
Baker, Hugh (LA) $2,500
Barton, Joe L (TX) $2,000
Murphy, Tim (PA) $2,000
Wilson, Joe (SC) $2,000

Corporate Foundations and Giving Programs

Stone & Webster Corporate Contributions Program
4171 Essen Lane
Baton Rouge, LA 70809
Tel: (225) 932 - 2500
Fax: (225) 932 - 2657

Annual Grant Total: none reported

Public Affairs and Related Activities Personnel

At Washington Office

MARLO, Stephen M.
Manager, Washington Operations
(Stone & Webster Engineering)
Registered Federal Lobbyist.
Tel: (202) 261 - 1909
Fax: (202) 261 - 1949

The Stop & Shop Supermarket Co.

www.stopandshop.com
Annual Revenues: $35 billion

President and Chief Exec. Officer
SMITH, Mark
Tel: (781) 380 - 8000
Fax: (781) 770 - 6416
TF: (800) 767 - 7772

Main Headquarters
Mailing: P.O. Box 55888
Boston, MA 02205-5888
Tel: (781) 380 - 8000
Fax: (781) 770 - 6416
TF: (800) 767 - 7772

Street: 1385 Hancock St.
Quincy, MA 02169

Corporate Foundations and Giving Programs

Stop & Shop Family Foundation
P.O. Box 55888
Boston, MA 02205-5888
Tel: (781) 380 - 8000
Fax: (781) 770 - 6416
TF: (800) 767 - 7772

Annual Grant Total: none reported
Geographic Preference: Area(s) in which the company operates
Primary Interests: Children; Education

Public Affairs and Related Activities Personnel

At Headquarters

CHACE-MARINO, Elizabeth
Director, Government Affairs
Tel: (781) 380 - 8000
Fax: (781) 770 - 6416
TF: (800) 767 - 7772

MCGURL, Maureen K.
Exec. V. President, Human Resources and Support Services
Tel: (781) 380 - 8000
Fax: (781) 770 - 6416
TF: (800) 767 - 7772

WEINER, Faith
Senior Director, Government and Public Affairs
Tel: (781) 380 - 8000
Fax: (781) 770 - 6416
TF: (800) 767 - 7772

Stora Enso North America

A paper manufacturer.
www.storaenso.com/na
Annual Revenues: $2 billion

Main Headquarters
Mailing: P.O. Box 8050
Wisconsin Rapids, WI 54495-8050
Tel: (715) 422 - 3111
Fax: (715) 422 - 3469
Street: 231 First Ave., North
Wisconsin Rapids, WI 54495-8050

Public Affairs and Related Activities Personnel

At Headquarters

AUSTIN, Jesse J.
Manager, Communications
Tel: (715) 422 - 1573
Fax: (715) 422 - 3882

DAVIS, Carol R.
Director, Employee Communications
Tel: (715) 422 - 3878

DEBYL, Mary M.
Manager, Communications
Tel: (715) 422 - 3996

LAATSCH, Tim
Senior V. President, Communications
Tel: (715) 422 - 4023
Fax: (715) 422 - 3882

StorageTek

A member of the Public Affairs Council. An information storage equipment manufacturer. Acquired by Sun Microsystems (see separate listing) in August of 2005. Further details were unavailable at the time the 2006 edition went to press. Please contact the individuals below for further information.
www.storagetek.com
Annual Revenues: $2.2 billion

Main Headquarters
Mailing: One StorageTek Dr.
Louisville, CO 80028-4377
Tel: (303) 673 - 5151

Political Action Committees

Storage Technology Corp. Political Action Committee
Contact: Annette Bendickson
One StorageTek Dr.
Louisville, CO 80028-4377
Tel: (303) 673 - 5151

StorageTek

** continued from previous page*

Contributions to Candidates: $2,000 (01/05 - 09/05)
Republicans: $2,000.

Principal Recipients

SENATE REPUBLICANS		HOUSE REPUBLICANS	
Allard, A Wayne (CO)	$1,000	Beauprez, Robert (CO)	$1,000

Corporate Foundations and Giving Programs

StorageTek Foundation
One StorageTek Dr. — Tel: (303) 673 - 5151
Louisville, CO 80028-4377

Annual Grant Total: $500,000 - $750,000
Geographic Preference: Colorado
Primary Interests: Arts and Culture; Education; Health and Human Services
Recent Recipients: Special Olympics; United Way

Public Affairs and Related Activities Personnel

At Headquarters

BENDICKSON, Annette — Tel: (303) 673 - 5151
PAC Treasurer

DRAGO, Chris — Tel: (303) 661 - 2262
Press Contact, Global Media and Analyst Relations
chris_drago@storagetek.com

FUENTES, Joseph J. — Tel: (303) 661 - 2523
Press Contact, Community Issues
joe_fuentes@storagetek.com

STORY, Jeremy — Tel: (303) 661 - 6169
Press Contact, Corporate and Legal Issues
jeremy_story@storagetek.com

The Stride Rite Corp.

A footwear manufacturer and retailer.
www.strideri te.com
Annual Revenues: $532 million

Chairman and Chief Exec. Officer — Tel: (617) 824 - 6000
CHAMBERLAIN, David M.
david_chamberlain@striderite.com

Main Headquarters
Mailing: 191 Spring St. — Tel: (617) 824 - 6000
Lexington, MA 02421-9191

Corporate Foundations and Giving Programs

Stride Rite Philanthropic Foundation
191 Spring St. — Tel: (617) 824 - 6000
Lexington, MA 02421-9191

Annual Grant Total: none reported
Geographic Preference: Boston, MA; Cambridge, MA
Primary Interests: Children's Health; Youth Services
Recent Recipients: United Way

Public Affairs and Related Activities Personnel

At Headquarters

CARUSO, Frank A. — Tel: (617) 824 - 6611
Chief Financial Officer and Investor Relations Contact
frank_caruso@striderite.com

Stryker Corp.

Manufactures and distributes surgical and medical products.
www.strykercorp.com
Annual Revenues: $3.012 billion

Chairman and Chief Exec. Officer — Tel: (616) 385 - 2600; Fax: (616) 385 - 1062
BROWN, John W.

Main Headquarters
Mailing: 2725 Fairfield Rd. — Tel: (616) 385 - 2600
Kalamazoo, MI 49002 — Fax: (616) 385 - 1062

Public Affairs and Related Activities Personnel

At Headquarters

ANDERSON, J. Patrick — Tel: (616) 385 - 2600
V. President, Strategy and Communications — Fax: (616) 385 - 1062

BERGY, Dean H. — Tel: (616) 385 - 2600
V. President, Chief Financial Officer, and Secretary — Fax: (616) 385 - 1062
Responsibilities include investor relations.

HOFF, Jud — Tel: (616) 385 - 2600
V. President, Regulatory Affairs and Quality Assurance — Fax: (616) 385 - 1062

RUDE, Michael W. — Tel: (616) 385 - 2600
V. President, Human Resources — Fax: (616) 385 - 1062

Student Loan Marketing Ass'n

See listing on page 440 under SLM Corp.

Subaru of America, Inc.

A wholly-owned subsidiary of Fuji Heavy Industries, Ltd, which serves as a marketer of vehicles, parts and accessories in the U.S.
www.subaru.com

Chairman, President, and Chief Exec. Officer — Tel: (856) 488 - 8500
ISHIGAMI, Kunio — Fax: (856) 488 - 0485
kishigami@subaru.com

Main Headquarters
Mailing: P.O. Box 6000 — Tel: (856) 488 - 8500
Cherry Hill, NJ 08034-6000 — Fax: (856) 488 - 0485

Corporate Foundations and Giving Programs

Subaru of America Foundation
P.O. Box 6000 — Tel: (856) 488 - 8500
Cherry Hill, NJ 08034-6000 — Fax: (856) 488 - 0485

Annual Grant Total: $200,000 - $300,000

Public Affairs and Related Activities Personnel

At Headquarters

CAPELL, Sandra E. — Tel: (856) 488 - 8500
Manager, Community Services — Fax: (856) 488 - 0485
scapell@subaru.com

DALTON, Dan — Tel: (856) 488 - 8500
V. President, Human Resources — Fax: (856) 488 - 0485
ddalton@subaru.com

INFANTE, Dominick — Tel: (856) 488 - 8500
Manager, Product Public Relations — Fax: (856) 488 - 0485

PLANTE, Gerald — Tel: (856) 488 - 8500
General Manager, Governmental Affairs — Fax: (856) 488 - 0485
gplante@subaru.com

WHELAN, Mike — Tel: (856) 488 - 8500
National Manager, Corporate Communications — Fax: (856) 488 - 0485

Sun Co., Inc.

See listing on page 461 under Sunoco, Inc.

Sun Healthcare Group, Inc.

A healthcare provider. Sun's inpatient services subsidiaries, including SunBridge Healthcare Corp., operate skilled nursing, long-term care and assisted living facilities. Other Sun affiliates provide rehabilitation therapy, home healthcare, medical staffing and other services.
www.sunh.com
Annual Revenues: $1.9 billion

Chairman and Chief Exec. Officer — Tel: (949) 255 - 7100; Fax: (949) 255 - 7054; TF: (800) 509 - 4340
MATROS, Richard K.

Main Headquarters
Mailing: 18831 Von Karman, Suite 400 — Tel: (949) 255 - 7100
Irvine, CA 92612 — Fax: (949) 255 - 7054; TF: (800) 509 - 4340

Political Action Committees

Sun HealthCare PAC
Contact: David W. Mason
101 Sun Ave. NE — Fax: (505) 468 - 4023
Albuquerque, NM 87109

Contributions to Candidates: $18,250 (01/05 - 09/05)
Democrats: $2,500; Republicans: $15,750.

Principal Recipients

SENATE DEMOCRATS		HOUSE DEMOCRATS	
Conrad, Kent (ND)	$2,500		
SENATE REPUBLICANS		**HOUSE REPUBLICANS**	
Snowe, Olympia (ME)	$2,250	Thomas, William M (CA)	$2,000
Hatch, Orrin (UT)	$2,000	English, Philip S (PA)	$1,500
Santorum, Richard (PA)	$2,000	Johnson, Nancy (CT)	$1,500
Kyl, Jon L (AZ)	$1,750	Cantor, Eric (VA)	$1,000
Smith, Gordon (OR)	$1,750		

Public Affairs and Related Activities Personnel

At Headquarters

FISHER, Heidi J. — Tel: (949) 255 - 7100
Senior V. President, Human Resources — Fax: (949) 255 - 7054
heidi.fisher@sunh.com — TF: (800) 509 - 4340

KERN, Ms. Terri — Tel: (949) 255 - 7100
Senior V. President, Communications and Business Develoment — Fax: (949) 255 - 7054
terri.kern@sunh.com — TF: (800) 509 - 4340

At Other Offices

MASON, David W. — Fax: (505) 468 - 4023
PAC Contact
101 Sun Ave. NE
Albuquerque, NM 87109

Sun Life Financial

A financial services company. A subsidiary of Sun Life Financial Services of Canada Inc.

www.sunlife-usa.com

Annual Revenues: $14.678 billion

Chairman of the Board
STINSON, William W.
Tel: (781) 237 - 6030
Fax: (781) 304 - 5383
TF: (800) 225 - 3950

Chief Exec. Officer
STEWART, Donald A.
donald_stewart@sunlife.com
Tel: (781) 237 - 6030
Fax: (781) 304 - 5383
TF: (800) 225 - 3950

Main Headquarters
Mailing: One Sun Life Executive Park
Wellesley Hills, MA 02481
Tel: (781) 237 - 6030
Fax: (781) 304 - 5383
TF: (800) 225 - 3950

Corporate Foundations and Giving Programs

Sun Life Financial Community Relations Program
One Sun Life Executive Park
Wellesley Hills, MA 02481
Tel: (781) 237 - 6030
Fax: (781) 304 - 5383
TF: (800) 225 - 3950

Annual Grant Total: none reported

Primary Interests: Arts and Culture; Education; Health and Human Services

Public Affairs and Related Activities Personnel

At Headquarters

HARKINS, Katharin R.
V. President, Public Relations and Communications
Tel: (781) 237 - 6030
Fax: (781) 304 - 5383
TF: (800) 225 - 3950

LANDIS, Jeff
Manager, Community and Creative Services
Mailstop: SC 2132
Jeff_Landis@sunlife.com
Tel: (781) 446 - 1955
Fax: (781) 304 - 5383
TF: (800) 225 - 3950

LAPHAM, Elise
Communications Officer
elise_lapham@sunlife.com
Tel: (781) 237 - 6030
Fax: (781) 304 - 5383
TF: (800) 225 - 3950

LEDUC, Michael R.
V. President, Industry and Government Affairs
Tel: (781) 237 - 6030
Fax: (781) 304 - 5383
TF: (800) 225 - 3950

MCLAREN, K. Louise
V. President, Human Resources
Tel: (781) 237 - 6030
Fax: (781) 304 - 5383
TF: (800) 225 - 3950

REID, Thomas G.
V. President, Investor Relations
Tel: (781) 237 - 6030
Fax: (781) 304 - 5383
TF: (800) 225 - 3950

Sun Microsystems, Inc.

A provider of industrial-strength hardware, software and services. Acquired StorageTek (see separate listing) in August of 2005. Further information was unavailable at the time the 2006 edition went to press.

www.sun.com

Annual Revenues: $11.185 billion

Chairman and Chief Exec. Officer
MCNEALY, Scott
scott.mcnealy@sun.com
Tel: (650) 786 - 8843
TF: (800) 555 - 9786

Main Headquarters
Mailing: 4150 Network Circle
Santa Clara, CA 95054
Tel: (650) 960 - 1300
TF: (800) 555 - 9786

Washington Office
Contact: Christopher Hankin
Mailing: 1300 I St. NW
Suite 420 East
Washington, DC 20005
Tel: (202) 326 - 7520
Fax: (202) 326 - 7525

Political Action Committees

Sun Microsystems Inc. Political Action Committees
Contact: Kirk Alan Pessner
20 Park Rd., Suite E
Burlingame, CA 94010
Tel: (650) 401 - 8735
Fax: (650) 401 - 8739

Contributions to Candidates: $26,500 (01/05 - 09/05)

Democrats: $11,400; Republicans: $15,100.

Principal Recipients

SENATE DEMOCRATS

HOUSE DEMOCRATS

Lofgren, Zoe (CA)	$2,400
Eshoo, Anna (CA)	$2,000
Thompson, Mike (CA)	$2,000
Boucher, Fredrick (VA)	$1,000
McIntyre, Mike (NC)	$1,000
Menendez, Robert (NJ)	$1,000
Smith, Adam (WA)	$1,000

SENATE REPUBLICANS

Allen, George (VA)	$3,600
Ensign, John Eric (NV)	$2,000
Burns, Conrad (MT)	$1,000

HOUSE REPUBLICANS

Dreier, David (CA)	$5,000
Baker, Hugh (LA)	$1,500
Goodlatte, Robert (VA)	$1,000
Reynolds, Thomas (NY)	$1,000

Corporate Foundations and Giving Programs

Sun Microsystems Foundation, Inc.
4150 Network Circle
Santa Clara, CA 95054
Tel: (650) 960 - 1300
TF: (800) 555 - 9786

Annual Grant Total: $1,000,000 - $2,000,000

Recent recipients: San Jose Discovery Museum, Community Foundation, Santa Clara County Office, Center for Training, San Mateo County of Education, Charities Aid Foundation, and Acre Family Day Care.

Geographic Preference: Area(s) in which the company operates; California; Massachusetts; International

Primary Interests: Education; Employment; Small Business Development

Public Affairs and Related Activities Personnel

At Headquarters

BEVERIDGE, Crawford
Exec. V. President and Chief Human Resources Officer
Mailstop: UMPK10241
crawford.beveridge@sun.com
Tel: (650) 786 - 8857
Fax: (650) 856 - 2114
TF: (800) 555 - 9786

COLE, Ms. Piper
V. President, Global Government and Community Affairs
Mailstop: UMPK15225
piper.cole@sun.com
Tel: (650) 786 - 5267
Fax: (650) 786 - 0835
TF: (800) 555 - 9786

VAN DEN HOOGEN, Ingrid
V. President, Global Communications
Tel: (650) 960 - 1300
TF: (800) 555 - 9786

At Washington Office

HANKIN, Christopher
Director, U.S. Federal Policy
Mailstop: WAS02
christopher.hankin@sun.com
Tel: (202) 326 - 7520
Fax: (202) 326 - 7525

SACHS, Lowell
Manager, Government Affairs
Mailstop: WAS02
lowell.sachs@sun.com
Registered Federal Lobbyist.
Tel: (202) 326 - 7520
Fax: (202) 326 - 7525

At Other Offices

PESSNER, Kirk Alan
PAC Treasurer
20 Park Rd., Suite E
Burlingame, CA 94010
kirk.pessner@sun.com
Tel: (650) 401 - 8735
Fax: (650) 401 - 8739

SunAmerica Inc.

See listing on page 13 under AIG SunAmerica Inc.

SunGard Data Systems, Inc.

Offers integrated IT services and eProcessing for financial services.

www.sungard.com

Annual Revenues: $2.53 billion

Chairman of the Board
MANN, James L.
james.mann@sungard.com
Tel: (484) 582 - 5506
Fax: (484) 225 - 1120

President and Chief Exec. Officer
CONDE, Cristobal I.
Tel: (484) 582 - 5506
Fax: (484) 225 - 1120

Main Headquarters
Mailing: 680 E. Swedesford Rd.
Wayne, PA 19087
Tel: (484) 582 - 5506
Fax: (484) 225 - 1120

Public Affairs and Related Activities Personnel

At Headquarters

BLOCK, Kris
Investor Relations Specialist
kris.block@sungard.com
Tel: (484) 582 - 5505
Fax: (484) 225 - 1120

HOPKINS, Madeline
V. President, Investor Relations
madeline.hopkins@sungard.com
Tel: (484) 582 - 5506
Fax: (484) 225 - 1120

JEFFERS, Paul
V. President, Human Resources
paul.jeffers@sungard.com
Tel: (484) 582 - 5506
Fax: (484) 225 - 1120

ROBINS, Brian
Press Contact
Tel: (484) 582 - 5468
Fax: (484) 225 - 1120

Sunkist Growers

www.sunkist.com

Annual Revenues: $975 million

Sunkist Growers

** continued from previous page*

Chairman of the Board
KRAUSE, David W.
Tel: (818) 986 - 4800
Fax: (818) 379 - 7381

Main Headquarters
Mailing: P.O. Box 7888
Van Nuys, CA 91409-7888
Tel: (818) 986 - 4800
Fax: (818) 379 - 7511
Street: 14130 Riverside Dr.
Sherman Oaks, CA 91423

Political Action Committees

Sunkist Growers, Inc. PAC
Contact: Michael J. Wootton
P.O. Box 7888
Van Nuys, CA 91409-7888
Tel: (818) 986 - 4800
Fax: (818) 379 - 7511

Contributions to Candidates: $12,750 (01/05 - 09/05)
Democrats: $4,500; Republicans: $7,250; Other: $1,000.

Principal Recipients

SENATE DEMOCRATS

HOUSE DEMOCRATS

Capps, Lois G (CA)	$1,000
Costa, Jim (CA)	$1,000
Harman, Jane (CA)	$1,000
Matsui, Doris (CA)	$1,000

HOUSE OTHER

Peterson, Collin (MN)	$1,000

SENATE REPUBLICANS

HOUSE REPUBLICANS

Bonilla, Henry (TX)	$1,000
Goodlatte, Robert (VA)	$1,000
Herger, Wally (CA)	$1,000
Lewis, Jerry (CA)	$1,000
Lungren, Daniel E (CA)	$1,000
Nunes, Devin (CA)	$1,000
Pombo, Richard (CA)	$1,000

Corporate Foundations and Giving Programs

A. W. Bodine-Sunkist Memorial Scholarship
Contact: Claire H. Smith
P.O. Box 7888
Van Nuys, CA 91409-7888
Tel: (818) 379 - 7455
Fax: (818) 379 - 7141

Annual Grant Total: under $100,000
Supports scholarships for needy students with a connection to agriculture in California and Arizona.
Geographic Preference: Arizona; California

Public Affairs and Related Activities Personnel

At Headquarters

SMITH, Claire H.
Director, Corporate Communications
csmith@sunistgrowers.com
Tel: (818) 379 - 7455
Fax: (818) 379 - 7141

WOOTTON, Michael J.
V. President, Corporate Relations/Counsel
mwootton@sunkistgrowers.com
Tel: (818) 986 - 4800
Fax: (818) 379 - 7511

Sunoco, Inc.

A member of the Public Affairs Council. A major refiner and marketer of petroleum and chemical products, coke.
www.sunocoinc.com
Annual Revenues: $12.322 billion

Chairman, Chief Exec. Officer and President
DROSDICK, John G.
Tel: (215) 977 - 3000
Fax: (215) 977 - 3409

Main Headquarters
Mailing: Ten Penn Center
1801 Market St.
Philadelphia, PA 19103-1699
Tel: (215) 977 - 3000
Fax: (215) 977 - 3409

Washington Office
Contact: Albert B. Knoll
Mailing: 1130 Connecticut Ave. NW
Suite 710
Washington, DC 20036
Tel: (202) 628 - 1010
Fax: (202) 628 - 1041

Political Action Committees

SunPAC
Contact: Katria N. Kowal
Ten Penn Center
1801 Market St.
Philadelphia, PA 19103-1699
Tel: (215) 977 - 3000
Fax: (215) 977 - 3409

Contributions to Candidates: $42,500 (01/05 - 09/05)
Democrats: $12,000; Republicans: $30,500.

Principal Recipients

SENATE DEMOCRATS

HOUSE DEMOCRATS

Murtha, John P Mr. (PA)	$4,500
Dingell, John D (MI)	$2,500
Doyle, Mike (PA)	$2,000

SENATE REPUBLICANS

Dewine, Richard (OH)	$5,000
Burns, Conrad (MT)	$3,000

HOUSE REPUBLICANS

DeLay, Tom (TX)	$5,000
Hart, Melissa (PA)	$5,000
Murphy, Tim (PA)	$3,000
Barton, Joe L (TX)	$2,500
Fitzpatrick, Michael (PA)	$2,000

Corporate Foundations and Giving Programs

Sunoco, Inc. Corporate Contributions Program
Ten Penn Center
1801 Market St.
Philadelphia, PA 19103-1699
Tel: (215) 977 - 3000
Fax: (215) 977 - 3409

Annual Grant Total: none reported
Geographic Preference: Area(s) in which the company operates
Primary Interests: Arts and Culture; Community Affairs; Economic Development; Education; Health and Human Services

Public Affairs and Related Activities Personnel

At Headquarters

DAVIS, Gerald T.
Manager, Media and Public Relations
Tel: (215) 977 - 6298
Fax: (215) 977 - 3409

DELANEY, Terrence P.
V. President, Investor Relations and Planning
Tel: (215) 977 - 6106
Fax: (215) 977 - 3409

KOWAL, Katria N.
PAC Treasurer
Tel: (215) 977 - 3000
Fax: (215) 977 - 3409

NAKU, Rolf D.
Senior V. President, Human Resouces and Public Affairs
Tel: (215) 977 - 3000
Fax: (215) 977 - 3409

At Washington Office

KNOLL, Albert B.
Director, Federal Government Relations
abknoll@sunocoinc.com
Registered Federal Lobbyist.
Tel: (202) 628 - 1010
Fax: (202) 628 - 1041

At Other Offices

PETERS, Jeffrey R.
Director, Government Affairs and Media Relations
Cranberry Court, Suite 101
212 N. Third St.
Harrisburg, PA 17101
Tel: (717) 232 - 5634
Fax: (717) 232 - 0691

Sunrise Assisted Living, Inc.

A provider of assisted living for seniors.
www.sunriseassistedliving.com
Annual Revenues: $505.9 million

Founder, Chairman, and Chief Exec. Officer
KLAASSEN, Paul J.
Tel: (703) 273 - 7500
Fax: (703) 744 - 1601
TF: (888) 434 - 4648

Main Headquarters
Mailing: 7902 Westpark Dr.
McLean, VA 22102
Tel: (703) 273 - 7500
Fax: (703) 744 - 1601
TF: (888) 434 - 4648

Corporate Foundations and Giving Programs

Sunrise Assisted Living Foundation, Inc.
Contact: Teresa M. Klaassen
7902 Westpark Dr.
McLean, VA 22102
Tel: (703) 273 - 7500
Fax: (703) 744 - 1601
TF: (888) 434 - 4648

Annual Grant Total: none reported

Public Affairs and Related Activities Personnel

At Headquarters

EVERS, Sarah
V. President, Communications
Tel: (703) 744 - 1620
Fax: (703) 744 - 1601
TF: (888) 434 - 4648

JASNOFF, Jeffrey M.
Senior V. President, Human Resources
Tel: (703) 273 - 7500
Fax: (703) 744 - 1601
TF: (888) 434 - 4648

KLAASSEN, Teresa M.
Secretary, Sunrise Assisted Living Foundation, Inc.
Tel: (703) 273 - 7500
Fax: (703) 744 - 1601
TF: (888) 434 - 4648

SunTrust Banks, Inc.

A commercial banking organization operating through an extensive distribution network in Alabama, Florida, Georgia, Maryland, Tennessee, Virginia and the District of Columbia. It also serves markets nationally.

www.suntrust.com
Annual Revenues: $5.4 billion

Chairman and Chief Exec. Officer
HUMANN, L. Phillip — Tel: (404) 588 - 7711 — Fax: (404) 581 - 1664
phil.humann@suntrust.com

Main Headquarters
Mailing: P.O. Box 4410, Atlanta, GA 30302 — Tel: (404) 588 - 7711 — Fax: (404) 581 - 1664
Street: 303 Peachtree St., Atlanta, GA 30309

Political Action Committees

SunTrust Bank Good Government Group--Florida
Contact: Linda T. Brinkley
215 S. Monroe St., Suite 125 — Tel: (850) 222 - 2231
Tallahassee, FL 32301

Contributions to Candidates: $13,000 (01/05 - 09/05)
Democrats: $3,000; Republicans: $10,000.

SunTrust Bank Good Government Group--Mid Atlantic
Contact: Brenda L. Skidmore
919 E. Main St. — Tel: (804) 782 - 5000
Richmond, VA 23219 — Fax: (804) 782 - 7064

Contributions to Candidates: $8,500 (01/05 - 09/05)
Democrats: $1,000; Republicans: $7,500.

SunTrust Bank Good Government Group-Georgia
Contact: Chris Byers
P.O. Box 4655 — Tel: (404) 588 - 7711
Atlanta, GA 30302 — Fax: (404) 581 - 1664

Contributions to Candidates: $3,500 (01/05 - 09/05)
Democrats: $500; Republicans: $3,000.

Principal Recipients

SENATE REPUBLICANS		HOUSE REPUBLICANS	
Chambliss, Saxby (GA)	$1,000	Price, Thomas (GA)	$1,000
Isakson, John (GA)	$1,000		

Suntrust Bank PAC
Contact: Brenda L. Skidmore
919 E. Main St. — Tel: (804) 782 - 5000
Richmond, VA 23219 — Fax: (804) 782 - 7064

Contributions to Candidates: $6,000 (01/05 - 09/05)
Democrats: $1,000; Republicans: $5,000.

SunTrust Banks of Tennessee Inc. Good Government Fund
P.O. Box 305110
8th Fl., Suntrust Center
Nashville, TN 37230

Contributions to Candidates: $1,500 (01/05 - 09/05)
Republicans: $1,500.

Principal Recipients

SENATE REPUBLICANS		HOUSE REPUBLICANS	
Corker Jr, Robert P (TN)	$1,000	Wamp, Zach (TN)	$500

Public Affairs and Related Activities Personnel

At Headquarters

MCCAY, Mike — Tel: (404) 588 - 7230
Media Relations Officer — Fax: (404) 581 - 1664
michael.mccay@suntrust.com

STEELE, Mary — Tel: (404) 588 - 7711
Director, Human Resources — Fax: (404) 581 - 1664

At Other Offices

BRINKLEY, Linda T. — Tel: (850) 222 - 2231
PAC Contact, SunTrust Good Government Group--Florida
215 S. Monroe St., Suite 125
Tallahassee, FL 32301

BYERS, Chris — Tel: (404) 588 - 7711
Treasurer, SunTrust Good Government Fund--Georgia — Fax: (404) 581 - 1664
P.O. Box 4655
Mailstop: MC 221
Atlanta, GA 30302

KOLING, Barry R. — Tel: (804) 782 - 5000
First V. President and Director, Corporate Communications — Fax: (804) 782 - 7064
919 E. Main St.
Richmond, VA 23219
barry.koling@suntrust.com

SKIDMORE, Brenda L. — Tel: (804) 782 - 5000
Senior V. President, Government Relations — Fax: (804) 782 - 7064
919 E. Main St.
Richmond, VA 23219
brenda.skidmore@suntrust.com

Supervalu Inc.

A food distribution and retailing company.

www.supervalu.com
Annual Revenues: $19.16 billion

Chairman, President and Chief Exec. Officer
NODDLE, Jeff — Tel: (952) 828 - 4000 — Fax: (952) 828 - 8998

Main Headquarters
Mailing: P.O. Box 990, Minneapolis, MN 55440 — Tel: (952) 828 - 4000 — Fax: (952) 828 - 8998
Street: 11840 Valley View Rd., Eden Prairie, MN 55344

Corporate Foundations and Giving Programs

Supervalu Inc. Foundation
Contact: Terry Polk
P.O. Box 990 — Tel: (952) 828 - 4000
Minneapolis, MN 55440 — Fax: (952) 828 - 8998

Annual Grant Total: $750,000 - $1,000,000
Primary Interests: Arts and Culture; Higher Education; Hunger; Social Services
Recent Recipients: United Way

Public Affairs and Related Activities Personnel

At Headquarters

POLK, Terry — Tel: (952) 828 - 4000
Contact, Supervalu Foundation — Fax: (952) 828 - 8998

SCHARTON, Yolanda M. — Tel: (952) 828 - 4000
V. President, Investor Relations and Corporate Communications — Fax: (952) 828 - 8998

TORTELLI, Ronald C. — Tel: (952) 828 - 4201
Senior V. President, Human Resources — Fax: (952) 828 - 8998

Swedish Match North America Inc.

A tobacco company. Formerly the Pinkerton Group, Inc., the company adopted its new name in 1997.

www.smna.com

Main Headquarters
Mailing: P.O. Box 13297, Richmond, VA 23225 — Tel: (804) 302 - 1700 — Fax: (804) 302 - 1760
Street: 7300 Beaufont Springs Dr., Richmond, VA 23225

Political Action Committees

Swedish Match PAC
Contact: Wanda T. Blake
P.O. Box 13297 — Tel: (804) 302 - 1700
Richmond, VA 23225 — Fax: (804) 302 - 1760

Contributions to Candidates: $7,128 (01/05 - 09/05)
Democrats: $500; Republicans: $6,628.

Principal Recipients

SENATE REPUBLICANS		HOUSE REPUBLICANS	
Allen, George (VA)	$1,000	Cantor, Eric (VA)	$2,000
		Lewis, Ron (KY)	$2,000
		Everett, Terry (AL)	$1,000

Corporate Foundations and Giving Programs

Swedish Match Corporate Giving Program
P.O. Box 13297 — Tel: (804) 302 - 1700
Richmond, VA 23225 — Fax: (804) 302 - 1760

Annual Grant Total: none reported

Public Affairs and Related Activities Personnel

At Headquarters

BLAKE, Wanda T. — Tel: (804) 302 - 1700
PAC Treasurer — Fax: (804) 302 - 1760

STALNAKER, Buddy — Tel: (804) 302 - 1700
V. President, Human Resources and Administration — Fax: (804) 302 - 1760

Swiss Re America Corp.

A reinsurance company.

www.swissre.com

Swiss Re America Corp.

* *continued from previous page*

Chief Exec. Officer, Americas Division
BEERLI, Mr. Andreas
andreas_beerli@swissre.com
Tel: (914) 828 - 8000
Fax: (914) 828 - 7000
TF: (888) 794 - 7773

Main Headquarters
Mailing: 175 King St.
Armonk, NY 10504
Tel: (914) 828 - 8000
Fax: (914) 828 - 7000
TF: (888) 794 - 7773

Public Affairs and Related Activities Personnel

At Headquarters

MCNAMARA, Michael D.
Corporate Communications Contact
Tel: (212) 317 - 5663

SIMON, Cosette R.
Senior V. President
Tel: (914) 828 - 8000
Fax: (914) 828 - 7000
TF: (888) 794 - 7773

VOGEL, Gloria
Investor Relations Contact
Tel: (914) 828 - 8078
Fax: (914) 828 - 7000
TF: (888) 794 - 7773

Sybase, Inc.

A data applications development company.
www.sybase.com
Annual Revenues: $829.9 million

Chairman, President and Chief Exec. Officer
CHEN, John S.
john.chen@sybase.com
Tel: (925) 236 - 5000

Main Headquarters
Mailing: 1 Sybase Dr.
Dublin, CA 94568
Tel: (925) 236 - 5000

Public Affairs and Related Activities Personnel

At Headquarters

CONNOLLY, Julie
Contact, Product, Partner and Customer Public Relations
julie.connolly@sybase.com
Tel: (925) 236 - 8696

FARRIS, Lynne
Investor Relations Contact
Tel: (925) 236 - 8797
Fax: (925) 236 - 6164

FRONSKE, Joan
Community Relations and International Public Relations Liaison
joan.fronske@sybase.com
Tel: (925) 236 - 4893

HEARST, Edward
Government Affairs
Tel: (925) 236 - 7515

NAKAJIMA, Leslie M.
Contact, Corporate and International Public Relations
leslien@sybase.com
Tel: (925) 236 - 8650

PETERSON, Heather
Corporate and International Public Relations Contact
heather.peterson@sybase.com
Tel: (925) 236 - 6517

WHITE-IVY, Nita C.
V. President, Human Resources
nita.white-ivey@sybase.com
Tel: (925) 236 - 5000

Sykes Enterprises, Inc.

A provider of outsourced customer care management solutions. Offers technical support, customer service, consulting, staffing, training and development, and fulfillment services.
www.sykes.com
Annual Revenues: $452.7 million

Chairman of the Board
WHITING, Paul L.
Tel: (813) 274 - 1000
Fax: (813) 273 - 0148

President and Chief Exec. Officer
SYKES, Charles E.
Tel: (813) 274 - 1000
Fax: (813) 273 - 0148

Main Headquarters
Mailing: 400 N. Ashley Dr.
Tampa, FL 33602
Tel: (813) 274 - 1000
Fax: (813) 273 - 0148

Public Affairs and Related Activities Personnel

At Headquarters

BURNETT, Andrea
Manager, Media and Public Relations
andrea.burnett@sykes.com
Tel: (813) 233 - 2132
Fax: (813) 273 - 0148

JENSEN, Conway W.
V. President, Public Relations and Corporate Administration
conway.jensen@sykes.com
Tel: (813) 274 - 1000
Fax: (813) 273 - 0148

KUMAR, Subhaash
Senior Director, Investor Relations
Tel: (813) 274 - 1000
Fax: (813) 273 - 0148

NELSON, Jenna R.
Group Executive and Senior V. President, Human Resources and Administration
jenna.nelson@sykes.com
Tel: (813) 274 - 1000
Fax: (813) 273 - 0148

Sylvan Learning Systems

See listing on page 289 under Laureate Education, Inc.

Symantec Corp.

A member of the Public Affairs Council. An Internet security technology company. Provides virus protection, intrusion prevention, Internet content and e-mail filtering, and other security services.
www.symantec.com
Annual Revenues: $1.4 billion

Chairman and Chief Exec. Officer
THOMPSON, John W.
jthompson@symantec.com
Tel: (408) 517 - 8000
Fax: (408) 517 - 8186

Main Headquarters
Mailing: 20330 Stevens Creek Blvd.
Cupertino, CA 95014-2132
Tel: (408) 517 - 8000
Fax: (408) 517 - 8186

Corporate Foundations and Giving Programs

The Symantec Corporate Giving Program
20330 Stevens Creek Blvd.
Cupertino, CA 95014-2132
Tel: (408) 517 - 8000
Fax: (408) 517 - 8186

Annual Grant Total: none reported
E-mail inquiries to corpgiving@symantec.com.
Geographic Preference: Area(s) in which the company operates
Primary Interests: Education

Public Affairs and Related Activities Personnel

At Headquarters

CORCOS, Helyn
V. President, Investor Relations
hcorcos@symantec.com
Tel: (408) 517 - 8324
Fax: (408) 517 - 8186

FRISCHMANN, Donald E.
Senior V. President, Communications and Brand Management
Responsibilities include investor relations.
Tel: (408) 517 - 7983
Fax: (408) 517 - 7801

GENNARELLI, David
Director, Investor Relations
david_gennarelli@symantec.com
Tel: (408) 517 - 5272
Fax: (408) 517 - 8186

HALDEMAN, Genevieve L.
Director, Corporate Public Relations
glhaldeman@symantec.com
Tel: (408) 517 - 7642
Fax: (408) 517 - 8152

JONES, Tiffany
Tel: (408) 517 - 8000
Fax: (408) 517 - 8186

LEWIS, Maris
Manager, Investor Relations
marisa_lewis@symantec.com
Tel: (408) 517 - 8239
Fax: (408) 517 - 8186

RAK, Adam
Director, Government Relations
Tel: (408) 517 - 8231
Fax: (408) 517 - 8186

RANNINGER, Rebecca A.
Senior V. President, Human Resources
branninger@symantec.com
Tel: (408) 517 - 8280
Fax: (408) 517 - 8186

Symbol Technologies, Inc.

Manufacturers laser scanners and mobile computers.
www.symbol.com
Annual Revenues: $1.32 billion

Chairman of the Board
CHRENC, Robert J.
Tel: (631) 738 - 2400
Fax: (631) 738 - 5990
TF: (800) 722 - 6234

Interim President and Chief Exec. Officer
IANNUZI, Salvatore
Tel: (631) 738 - 2400
Fax: (631) 738 - 5990
TF: (800) 722 - 6234

Main Headquarters
Mailing: One Symbol Plaza
Holtsville, NY 11742-1300
Tel: (631) 738 - 2400
Fax: (631) 738 - 5990
TF: (800) 722 - 6234

Corporate Foundations and Giving Programs

Symbol Technologies, Inc. Community Affairs
One Symbol Plaza
Holtsville, NY 11742-1300
Tel: (631) 738 - 2400
Fax: (631) 738 - 5990
TF: (800) 722 - 6234

Annual Grant Total: none reported
Primary Interests: Arts and Culture; Children; Education; Housing; Hunger
Recent Recipients: Family Service League; Institute for Student Achievement; Staller Center for the Arts

Symbol Technologies, Inc.

** continued from previous page*

Public Affairs and Related Activities Personnel

At Headquarters

ABELSON, Bill — Tel: (631) 738 - 4751
Media Contact — Fax: (631) 738 - 5990
abelsonb@symbol.com — TF: (800) 722 - 6234

DEMAYO, Carole — Tel: (631) 738 - 2400
Senior V. President, Global Human Resources — Fax: (631) 738 - 5990
TF: (800) 722 - 6234

TULLY, Nancy — Tel: (631) 738 - 5050
V. President, Corporate Communications — Fax: (631) 738 - 4645
tullyn@symbol.com — TF: (800) 722 - 6234
Responsibilities include investor relations.

Synovus Financial Corp.

A multi-financial services company.
www.synovus.com
Annual Revenues: $2.067 billion

Chairman of the Board — Tel: (706) 649 - 2267
YANCEY, James D. — Fax: (706) 641 - 6555

Chief Exec. Officer — Tel: (706) 649 - 2311
BLANCHARD, James H. — Fax: (706) 641 - 6555

Main Headquarters
Mailing: P.O. Box 120 — Tel: (706) 649 - 2267
Columbus, GA 31902-0120 — Fax: (706) 641 - 6555
Street: 901 Front Ave., Suite 301
Columbus, GA 31901

Political Action Committees

Synovus Financial Corp. Committee for Good Leadership
Contact: Katherine Ray
P.O. Box 120 — Tel: (706) 649 - 2267
Columbus, GA 31902-0120 — Fax: (706) 641 - 6555

Contributions to Candidates: $500 (01/05 - 09/05)
Democrats: $250; Republicans: $250.

Principal Recipients

SENATE DEMOCRATS	HOUSE DEMOCRATS	
	Davis, Artur (AL)	$250
SENATE REPUBLICANS	**HOUSE REPUBLICANS**	
	Bachus, Spencer (AL)	$250

Synovus Financial Corp. Fund for Effective Leadership
Contact: G. Sanders Griffith, III
P.O. Box 120 — Tel: (706) 649 - 2311
Columbus, GA 31902-0120 — Fax: (706) 641 - 6555

Contributions to Candidates: $8,500 (01/05 - 09/05)
Democrats: $4,500; Republicans: $4,000.

Principal Recipients

SENATE DEMOCRATS	HOUSE DEMOCRATS	
	Bishop, Sanford (GA)	$3,500
	Lewis, John (GA)	$1,000
SENATE REPUBLICANS	**HOUSE REPUBLICANS**	
	Westmoreland, Lynn (GA)	$3,000
	Price, Thomas (GA)	$1,000

Corporate Foundations and Giving Programs

Synovus Financial Corp./Synovus Foundation
Contact: Calvin Smyre
P.O. Box 120 — Tel: (706) 649 - 2243
Columbus, GA 31902-0120 — Fax: (706) 641 - 6555

Annual Grant Total: none reported
Geographic Preference: Area in which the company is headquartered
Primary Interests: Arts and Culture; Education; Health and Human Services
Recent Recipients: American Heart Ass'n; Ronald McDonald House; United Negro College Fund; United Way; YMCA

Public Affairs and Related Activities Personnel

At Headquarters

DAVIS, Aimee — Tel: (706) 644 - 0528
Manager, Media Relations — Fax: (706) 641 - 6555
aimeedavis@sfcts.com

DOWE, Alison — Tel: (706) 642 - 3781
Director, Communications — Fax: (706) 641 - 6555
adowe@sfcts.com

GRIFFITH, G. Sanders, III — Tel: (706) 649 - 2311
Senior Exec. V. President, General Counsel and Secretary — Fax: (706) 641 - 6555
Responsibilities include governmental and regulatory affairs and strategic planning.

RAY, Katherine — Tel: (706) 649 - 2267
Contact, Synovus Financial Corp. Committee for Good Leadership — Fax: (706) 641 - 6555

REYNOLDS, Patrick A. — Tel: (706) 649 - 5216
Senior V. President and Director, Investor Relations — Fax: (706) 644 - 8065
SNVIR@synovus.com

SMYRE, Calvin — Tel: (706) 649 - 2243
Exec. V. President, Corporate Affairs — Fax: (706) 641 - 6555

WILLOUGHBY, Jeannine — Tel: (706) 649 - 5850
Senior Communications Specialist — Fax: (706) 641 - 6555
jwilloug@synovusservicecorp.com

Sysco Corp.

A wholesale food distributor.
www.sysco.com
Annual Revenues: $26.140 billion

Chairman and Chief Exec. Officer — Tel: (281) 584 - 1390
SCHNIEDERS, Richard J. — Fax: (281) 584 - 2721

Main Headquarters
Mailing: 1390 Enclave Pkwy. — Tel: (281) 584 - 1390
Houston, TX 77077-2099 — Fax: (281) 584 - 2721

Political Action Committees

Sysco Corp. Good Government Political Action Committee (Sysco PAC)
Contact: Michael C. Nichols
1390 Enclave Pkwy. — Tel: (281) 584 - 1390
Houston, TX 77077-2099 — Fax: (281) 584 - 2721

Contributions to Candidates: $4,000 (01/05 - 09/05)
Democrats: $2,000; Republicans: $2,000.

Principal Recipients

SENATE DEMOCRATS		HOUSE DEMOCRATS	
		Menendez, Robert (NJ)	$2,000
SENATE REPUBLICANS		**HOUSE REPUBLICANS**	
Isakson, John (GA)	$1,000	Bonilla, Henry (TX)	$1,000

Corporate Foundations and Giving Programs

Sysco Corporate Contributions
1390 Enclave Pkwy. — Tel: (281) 584 - 1390
Houston, TX 77077-2099 — Fax: (281) 584 - 2721

Annual Grant Total: none reported

Public Affairs and Related Activities Personnel

At Headquarters

KELSO, Alan W. — Tel: (281) 584 - 1759
Assistant V. President, Safety and Labor Relations — Fax: (281) 584 - 2721

NICHOLS, Michael C. — Tel: (281) 584 - 1390
V. President, General Counsel, Corp. Secretary; and PAC Treasurer — Fax: (281) 584 - 2721

PALIZZA, John M. — Tel: (281) 584 - 1390
Assistant Treasurer — Fax: (281) 584 - 2721
Responsibilities include investor relations.

SPIGELMYER, Toni R. — Tel: (281) 554 - 1458
Media Contact — Fax: (281) 584 - 2721

WATSON, Craig G. — Tel: (281) 584 - 1390
V. President, Quality Assurance — Fax: (281) 584 - 2721

Systemax Inc.

A marketer of PC hardware and computer products.
www.systemax.com
Annual Revenues: $1.55 billion

Chairman and Chief Exec. Officer — Tel: (516) 608 - 7000
LEEDS, Richard — Fax: (516) 625 - 0038
service@globalindustrial.com

Main Headquarters
Mailing: 11 Harbor Park Dr. — Tel: (516) 625 - 4300
Port Washington, NY 11050 — Fax: (516) 625 - 4072

Public Affairs and Related Activities Personnel

At Headquarters

FLAMMER, Maureen — Tel: (516) 608 - 7000
Manager, Human Resources — Fax: (516) 625 - 0038

GOLDSHEIN, Steven M. — Tel: (516) 608 - 7000
Investor Relations Contact — Fax: (516) 625 - 4072

Taco Bell Corp.

See listing on page 530 under YUM! Brands, Inc.

Take-Two Interactive Software, Inc.

Develops and distributes interactive computer games.
www.take2games.com

Take-Two Interactive Software, Inc.

** continued from previous page*

Chairman and Chief Exec. Officer Tel: (646) 536 - 2842
ROEDEL, Richard

Main Headquarters
Mailing: 622 Broadway, New York, NY 10012 — Tel: (646) 536 - 2842

Public Affairs and Related Activities Personnel

At Headquarters

ANKNER, James — Tel: (646) 536 - 3006
Investor Relations and Media Relations

Talley Defense Systems Inc.

See listing on page 103 under Carpenter Technology Corp.

Target Corp.

A member of the Public Affairs Council. Specializes in large store general merchandise formats, including discount stores. The company operates 1,330 stores in 47 states.
www.target.com
Annual Revenues: $46.839 billion

Chairman and Chief Exec. Officer Tel: (612) 304 - 6073
ULRICH, Robert J.

Main Headquarters
Mailing: 1000 Nicollet Mall, Minneapolis, MN 55403 — Tel: (612) 304 - 6073

Political Action Committees

Target Citizen's Federal Forum
Contact: Nathan Keller Garvis
1000 Nicollet Mall
Minneapolis, MN 55403 — Tel: (612) 304 - 6073

Contributions to Candidates: $63,570 (01/05 - 09/05)
Democrats: $17,570; Republicans: $45,000; Other: $1,000.

Principal Recipients

SENATE DEMOCRATS		HOUSE DEMOCRATS	
Nelson, Benjamin (NE)	$3,070	Thompson, Mike (CA)	$5,000
Conrad, Kent (ND)	$2,000	Jefferson, William (LA)	$2,500
SENATE REPUBLICANS		**HOUSE REPUBLICANS**	
Talent, James (MO)	$5,000	Blunt, Roy (MO)	$10,000
		Kennedy, Mark (MN)	$10,000
		Dreier, David (CA)	$5,000
		Hastert, Dennis J. (IL)	$5,000
		Royce, Ed Mr (CA)	$2,000

Corporate Foundations and Giving Programs

Target Foundation and Community Relations
Contact: Laysha Ward
1000 Nicollet Mall
Minneapolis, MN 55403 — Tel: (612) 304 - 6073

Annual Grant Total: over $5,000,000
Contributions total $107 million. Guidelines are available.
Geographic Preference: Area(s) in which the company operates
Primary Interests: Arts and Culture; Education; Social Services

Public Affairs and Related Activities Personnel

At Headquarters

BROOKTER, Carolyn — Tel: (612) 304 - 6073
Director, Corporate Communications (Target Stores)
media.relations@target.com

GARVIS, Nathan Keller — Tel: (612) 304 - 6073
V. President, Government Affairs

KAHN, Susan — Tel: (612) 304 - 6073
V. President, Investor Relations
investor.relations@target.com

WARD, Laysha — Tel: (612) 304 - 6073
V. President, Community Relations
community.relations@target.com

Target Stores

See listing on page 465 under Target Corp.

Tasty Baking Co.

www.tastykake.com
Annual Revenues: $255 million

Chairman of the Board Tel: (215) 221 - 8500; Fax: (215) 228 - 3970; TF: (800) 248 - 2789
KSANSNAK, James

President and Chief Exec. Officer Tel: (215) 221 - 8500 Ext: 8696; Fax: (215) 228 - 3970; TF: (800) 248 - 2789
PIZZI, Charles P.

Main Headquarters
Mailing: 2801 Hunting Park Ave., Philadelphia, PA 19129 — Tel: (215) 221 - 8500; Fax: (215) 228 - 3970; TF: (800) 248 - 2789

Corporate Foundations and Giving Programs

Tasty Baking Foundation
Contact: Marie Mann
2801 Hunting Park Ave.
Philadelphia, PA 19129 — Tel: (215) 221 - 8500 Ext: 8573; Fax: (215) 228 - 3970; TF: (800) 248 - 2789

Annual Grant Total: under $100,000
Geographic Preference: Philadelphia, PA
Primary Interests: Arts and Culture; Economic Development; Education; Health

Public Affairs and Related Activities Personnel

At Headquarters

BORNEMAN, Mary C. — Tel: (215) 221 - 8537; Fax: (215) 228 - 3970; TF: (800) 248 - 2789
Manager, Investor Relations
mary.borneman@tastykake.com

MANN, Marie — Tel: (215) 221 - 8500 Ext: 8573; Fax: (215) 228 - 3970; TF: (800) 248 - 2789
Contact, Tasty Baking Foundation

O'TOOLE, Nancy — Tel: (215) 221 - 8500 Ext: 8593; Fax: (215) 228 - 3288; TF: (800) 248 - 2789
V. President, Human Resources
nancy.otoole@tastykake.com

TBS

See listing on page 482 under Turner Broadcasting System, Inc.

TCF Bank

A national bank and financial services supplier. Formerly Great Lakes Nat'l Bank. A subsidiary of TCF Financial Corp. (see separate listing).
www.tcfbank.com

Main Headquarters
Mailing: 401 E. Liberty, Ann Arbor, MI 48104-2298 — Tel: (734) 769 - 8300; Fax: (734) 930 - 6750

Corporate Foundations and Giving Programs

TCF Bank Corporate Giving Program
Contact: Donald Hawkins
401 E. Liberty
Ann Arbor, MI 48104-2298 — Tel: (734) 669 - 5084; Fax: (734) 930 - 6750

Annual Grant Total: none reported
Primary Interests: Arts and Culture; Community Development; Education; Health and Human Services

Public Affairs and Related Activities Personnel

At Headquarters

ELKINS, Gilda — Tel: (734) 930 - 6011; Fax: (734) 930 - 6721
Community Development, Home Improvement Lender

HAWKINS, Donald — Tel: (734) 669 - 5084; Fax: (734) 930 - 6750
Senior V. President, Community Affairs

TCF Financial Corp.

www.tcfexpress.com
Annual Revenues: $1.152 billion

Chairman and Chief Exec. Officer Tel: (952) 475 - 7904; Fax: (952) 475 - 7975
COOPER, William A.

Main Headquarters
Mailing: 200 Lake St. E., Wayzata, MN 55391 — Tel: (612) 661 - 6500

Political Action Committees

TCF PAC
Contact: Douglas L. Young
200 Lake St. E.
Wayzata, MN 55391 — Tel: (952) 475 - 7064; Fax: (952) 475 - 7969

Contributions to Candidates: $16,000 (01/05 - 09/05)

TCF Financial Corp.

** continued from previous page*

Democrats: $1,000; Republicans: $15,000.

Principal Recipients

SENATE REPUBLICANS	HOUSE REPUBLICANS	
	Kennedy, Mark (MN)	$10,000
	Krinkie, Philip B (MN)	$3,000
	Yecke, Cheri (MN)	$2,000

Corporate Foundations and Giving Programs

TCF Foundation
Contact: Jason Korstange
200 Lake St. E. — Tel: (952) 745 - 2755
Wayzata, MN 55391 — Fax: (952) 745 - 2775

Annual Grant Total: $1,000,000 - $2,000,000
Geographic Preference: Minnesota
Primary Interests: Community Development; Education; Health and Human Services
Recent Recipients: Easter Seal Soc.

Public Affairs and Related Activities Personnel

At Headquarters

KORSTANGE, Jason — Tel: (952) 745 - 2755
President, TCF Foundation — Fax: (952) 745 - 2775
Responsibilities include corporate communications.

YOUNG, Douglas L. — Tel: (952) 475 - 7064
Compliance Officer, Legal Department — Fax: (952) 475 - 7969
Responsibilities include political action.

Tech Data Corp.

A wholesale distributor of computer-related equipment.
www.techdata.com
Annual Revenues: $17.4 billion

Chairman and Chief Exec. Officer
RAYMUND, Steven A. — Tel: (727) 539 - 7429
steve.raymund@techdata.com — Fax: (727) 538 - 5866 — TF: (800) 237 - 8931

Main Headquarters
Mailing: 5350 Tech Data Dr.
Clearwater, FL 33760
Tel: (727) 539 - 7429
Fax: (727) 538 - 5866
TF: (800) 237 - 8931

Corporate Foundations and Giving Programs

Tech Data Corporate Contributions Program
Contact: Gayle McAlexander
5350 Tech Data Dr. — Tel: (727) 539 - 7429 Ext: 85013
Clearwater, FL 33760 — TF: (800) 237 - 8931

Annual Grant Total: none reported

Public Affairs and Related Activities Personnel

At Headquarters

ANDERSON, Danyle — Tel: (727) 539 - 7429
Director, Investor Relations — TF: (800) 237 - 8931
danyle.anderson@techdata.com

BOHANAN, Lynette — Tel: (727) 539 - 7429 Ext: 86270
Manager, Corporate Communications
Mailstop: MS A3-10 — Fax: (727) 571 - 9140
lynette.bohanan@techdata.com — TF: (800) 237 - 8931

HAMILTON, Lawrence W. — Tel: (727) 539 - 7429 Ext: 77013
Senior V. President, Human Resources
lawrence.hamilton@techdata.com — TF: (800) 237 - 8931

LE FEBVRE, Jarred — Tel: (727) 539 - 7429
Communications Specialist — Fax: (727) 538 - 5866
jarred.lefebvre@techdata.com — TF: (800) 237 - 8931

MCALEXANDER, Gayle — Tel: (727) 539 - 7429 Ext: 85013
Coordinator, Human Resources
Mailstop: MS D1-10 — TF: (800) 237 - 8931
gayle.mcalexander@techdata.com
Responsibilities include corporate contributions.

MILLER, Chuck — Tel: (727) 571 - 9305
Director, Corporate Communications — Fax: (727) 571 - 9140
chuck.miller@techdata.com — TF: (800) 237 - 8931

TECO Energy, Inc./Tampa Electric Co.

TECO Energy, Inc. is an energy-related holding company with five core businesses, including two regulated utilities.
www.tecoenergy.net
Annual Revenues: $2.649 billion

Chairman and Chief Exec. Officer
HUDSON, Sherrill W. — Tel: (813) 228 - 4111 — Fax: (813) 228 - 4811

Main Headquarters
Mailing: TECO Plaza
702 N. Franklin St.
Tampa, FL 33602
Tel: (813) 228 - 4111
Fax: (813) 228 - 4811

Washington Office
Contact: Janet L. Sena
Mailing: 1301 Pennsylvania Ave. NW
Suite 1030
Washington, DC 20004
Tel: (202) 824 - 0411
Fax: (202) 824 - 0651

Political Action Committees

TECO Energy Inc. Employees' PAC
Contact: Chrys A. Remmers
TECO Plaza — Tel: (813) 228 - 4111
702 N. Franklin St. — Fax: (813) 228 - 4811
Tampa, FL 33602

Contributions to Candidates: $16,500 (01/05 - 09/05)
Democrats: $4,000; Republicans: $12,500.

Principal Recipients

SENATE DEMOCRATS		HOUSE DEMOCRATS	
Bingaman, Jeff (NM)	$2,000	Boucher, Fredrick (VA)	$1,000
		Jefferson, William (LA)	$1,000

SENATE REPUBLICANS		HOUSE REPUBLICANS	
Hatch, Orrin (UT)	$2,000	Shaw, Clay (FL)	$3,500
Allen, George (VA)	$1,000	Bilirakis, Michael (FL)	$1,000
Burns, Conrad (MT)	$1,000	Murphy, Tim (PA)	$1,000
Lott, Trent (MS)	$1,000	Shimkus, John (IL)	$1,000
		Stearns, Clifford (FL)	$1,000

Corporate Foundations and Giving Programs

TECO Energy Inc. Contributions Program
Contact: Jack Amor
TECO Plaza — Tel: (813) 228 - 4111
702 N. Franklin St. — Fax: (813) 228 - 4811
Tampa, FL 33602

Annual Grant Total: none reported
Geographic Preference: Area(s) in which the company operates
Primary Interests: Arts and Culture; Community Development; Education; Health and Human Services

Public Affairs and Related Activities Personnel

At Headquarters

AMOR, Jack — Tel: (813) 228 - 4111
Director, Community Affairs — Fax: (813) 228 - 4811

BANNISTER, Ross — Tel: (813) 228 - 4111
Media Contact — Fax: (813) 228 - 4811

BROWN, Deirdre A. — Tel: (813) 228 - 4111
V. President, Regulatory Affairs — Fax: (813) 228 - 4811

CHILDRESS, Clinton E. — Tel: (813) 228 - 4111
Senior V. President, Corporate Services — Fax: (813) 228 - 4811

DUDA, Laura — Tel: (813) 228 - 4111
Director, Communications — Fax: (813) 228 - 4811
lpduda@tecoenergy.com

KANE, Mark M. — Tel: (813) 228 - 4111
Director, Investor Relations — Fax: (813) 228 - 4262
mmkane@tecoenergy.com

REMMERS, Chrys A. — Tel: (813) 228 - 4111
PAC Treasurer — Fax: (813) 228 - 4811

At Washington Office

HIRST, Fritz — Tel: (202) 824 - 0414
Director, Federal Relations — Fax: (202) 824 - 0651
fhirst@tecoenergy.com
Registered Federal Lobbyist.

SENA, Janet L. — Tel: (202) 824 - 0411
V. President, Federal Affairs — Fax: (202) 824 - 0651
jlsena@tecoenergy.com
Registered Federal Lobbyist.

At Other Offices

HINSON, Chuck
V. President, State Governmental Affairs
101 N. Monroe St.
Suite 1060
Tallahassee, FL 32301

Tektronix, Inc.

A manufacturer of electronic test and measurement, computer graphics and professional broadcast equipment.
www.tek.com
Annual Revenues: $1.235 billion

Tektronix, Inc.

* continued from previous page

Chairman, President and Chief Exec. Officer
WILLS, Richard H. — Tel: (503) 627 - 7111
richard.wills@tek.com — Fax: (503) 567 - 3449 — TF: (800) 835 - 9433

Main Headquarters
Mailing: P.O. Box 500, Beaverton, OR 97077 — Tel: (503) 627 - 7111 — Fax: (503) 567 - 3449 — TF: (800) 835 - 9433

Street: 14200 S.W. Karl Braun Dr., Beaverton, OR 97077

Corporate Foundations and Giving Programs

Tektronix Foundation
Contact: Karen Montague
P.O. Box 500 — Tel: (503) 627 - 7111
Beaverton, OR 97077 — Fax: (503) 567 - 3449 — TF: (800) 835 - 9433

Annual Grant Total: $1,000,000 - $2,000,000
Geographic Preference: Oregon
Primary Interests: Arts and Culture; Education; Social Services
Recent Recipients: United Way

Public Affairs and Related Activities Personnel

At Headquarters

GOFF, Alisha — Tel: (503) 627 - 7075
Manager, Corporate Communications — Fax: (503) 567 - 3449
alisha.goff@tektronix.com — TF: (800) 835 - 9433

KIRBY, Sue — Tel: (503) 627 - 7111
V. President, Human Resources — Fax: (503) 567 - 3449 — TF: (800) 835 - 9433

MONTAGUE, Karen — Tel: (503) 627 - 7111
Contact, Tektronix Foundation — Fax: (503) 567 - 3449 — TF: (800) 835 - 9433

SMITH, Brian — Tel: (503) 627 - 7111
Manager, Investor Relations — Fax: (503) 567 - 3449 — TF: (800) 835 - 9433

Telcordia Technologies, Inc.

A provider of operations support systems, network software and consulting and engineering services to the telecommunications industry. Formerly known as Bellcore. A subsidiary of Science Applications Internat'l Corp. (see separate listing).
www.telcordia.com
Annual Revenues: $1.084 billion

Chief Exec. Officer
CARROLL, Daniel J., Jr. — Tel: (732) 699 - 2000

Main Headquarters
Mailing: One Telecordia Dr., Piscataway, NJ 08854-4157 — Tel: (732) 699 - 2000

Washington Office
Mailing: 2020 K St. NW, Washington, DC 20037 — Tel: (202) 530 - 8910 — Fax: (202) 530 - 5641

Corporate Foundations and Giving Programs

Telecordia Corporate Giving
One Telecordia Dr. — Tel: (732) 699 - 2000
Piscataway, NJ 08854-4157

Annual Grant Total: $500,000 - $750,000
Primary Interests: Arts and Culture; Community Affairs; Education; Health and Human Services
Recent Recipients: Nat'l Merit Scholarship; United Way

Public Affairs and Related Activities Personnel

At Headquarters

HENDERSON, Michael J. — Tel: (732) 699 - 2000
President, Global Communication Solutions

ODDY, Sharon — Tel: (732) 699 - 4203
Senior Specialist, Communications
oddys@telcordia.com

VILLA, Linda D. — Tel: (732) 699 - 2000
Corporate V. President, Human Resources

At Other Offices

LAZER, Bob — Tel: (732) 699 - 5955
Contact, Telecordia Corporate Giving — Fax: (732) 336 - 3433
45 Knightsbridge Rd.
Piscataway, NJ 08854

Teleflex Inc.

A diversified designer, manufacturer, and distributor of engineered products and services for the automotive, marine, industrial, medical and aerospace markets.
www.teleflex.com
Annual Revenues: $2.076 billion

Chairman of the Board
BLACK, Lennox K. — Tel: (610) 948 - 5100 — Fax: (610) 948 - 0811

President and Chief Exec. Officer
BLACK, Jeffrey P. — Tel: (610) 948 - 5100 — Fax: (610) 948 - 0811

Main Headquarters
Mailing: 155 S. Limerick Rd., Limerick, PA 19468 — Tel: (610) 948 - 5100 — Fax: (610) 948 - 0811

Corporate Foundations and Giving Programs

Teleflex Foundation
Contact: Thelma Fretz
155 S. Limerick Rd. — Tel: (610) 948 - 5100
Limerick, PA 19468 — Fax: (610) 948 - 2859

Annual Grant Total: none reported
Geographic Preference: Area(s) in which the company operates
Primary Interests: Education; Health

Public Affairs and Related Activities Personnel

At Headquarters

FRETZ, Thelma — Tel: (610) 948 - 5100
Contact, Teleflex Foundation — Fax: (610) 948 - 2859
foundation@teleflex.com

MCDOWELL, Julie — Tel: (610) 948 - 5100
V. President, Corporate Communications — Fax: (610) 948 - 0811

PILCICKI, Mary — Tel: (610) 948 - 2850
Project Manager — Fax: (610) 948 - 1055
mpilcicki@teleflex.com

SALINAS, Susan — Tel: (610) 948 - 5100
Director, Safety and Environmental Affairs — Fax: (610) 948 - 0811

Telephone and Data Systems, Inc.

A provider of telecommunications services.
www.teldta.com
Annual Revenues: $2.3 billion

Chairman of the Board
CARLSON, Walter C.D. — Tel: (312) 630 - 1900 — Fax: (312) 630 - 1908

President and Chief Exec. Officer
CARLSON, LeRoy T., Jr. — Tel: (312) 630 - 1900 — Fax: (312) 630 - 1908

Main Headquarters
Mailing: 30 N. LaSalle St., Suite 4000, Chicago, IL 60602-2507 — Tel: (312) 630 - 1900 — Fax: (312) 630 - 1908

Public Affairs and Related Activities Personnel

At Headquarters

HERBERT, C. Theodore — Tel: (312) 630 - 1900
V. President, Human Resources — Fax: (312) 630 - 1908
ted.herbert@teldta.com

MATHEWS, Julie — Tel: (312) 592 - 5341
Manager, Investor Relations — Fax: (312) 630 - 1908
julie.mathews@teldta.com

STEINKRAUSS, Mark A. — Tel: (312) 592 - 5384
V. President, Corporate Relations — Fax: (312) 630 - 1908
mark.steinkrauss@teldta.com

TeleTech Holdings, Inc.

www.teletech.com
Annual Revenues: $992 billion

Chairman and Chief Exec. Officer
TUCHMAN, Kenneth — Tel: (303) 397 - 8100
ken.tuchman@teletech.com — Fax: (303) 397 - 8199 — TF: (800) 835 - 3832

Main Headquarters
Mailing: 9197 S. Peoria St., Englewood, CO 80112-5833 — Tel: (303) 397 - 8100 — Fax: (303) 397 - 8199 — TF: (800) 835 - 3832

Corporate Foundations and Giving Programs

Teletech Community Relations Program
9197 S. Peoria St. — Tel: (303) 397 - 8100
Englewood, CO 80112-5833 — Fax: (303) 397 - 8199 — TF: (800) 835 - 3832

Annual Grant Total: none reported
Primary Interests: Education; Vocational Training

Public Affairs and Related Activities Personnel

At Headquarters

BREEN, Karen — Tel: (303) 397 - 8592
Contact, Investor Relations — Fax: (303) 397 - 8199 — TF: (800) 835 - 3832

TeleTech Holdings, Inc.

** continued from previous page*

CAMPBELL, Dan — Tel: (303) 397 - 8634
Director, Investor Relations — Fax: (303) 397 - 8199
dan.campbell@teletech.com — TF: (800) 835 - 3832
Responsibilities also include corporate communications.

KOEHLER, Susan — Tel: (303) 397 - 8313
Media Relations — Fax: (303) 397 - 8199
TF: (800) 835 - 3832

SIMON, John R. — Tel: (303) 397 - 8100
Senior V. President, Human Resources — Fax: (303) 397 - 8199
john.simon@teletech.com — TF: (800) 835 - 3832

Tellabs

Acquired Advanced Fibre Communications, Inc.
www.tellabs.com

Chairman of the Board — Tel: (630) 798 - 8800
BIRCK, Michael J. — Fax: (630) 852 - 7346

President and Chief Exec. Officer — Tel: (630) 798 - 8800
PRABHU, Krish A. — Fax: (630) 798 - 2000

Main Headquarters
Mailing: One Tellabs Center — Tel: (630) 798 - 8800
1415 W. Diehl Rd. — Fax: (630) 798 - 2000
Naperville, IL 60563 — TF: (888) 290 - 8377

Corporate Foundations and Giving Programs

Tellabs Foundation
Contact: Meredith Hilt
One Tellabs Center — Tel: (630) 798 - 2506
1415 W. Diehl Rd. — Fax: (630) 798 - 4778
Naperville, IL 60563

Assets: $27,612,576 (2004)
Annual Grant Total: $1,000,000 - $2,000,000
Geographic Preference: Area(s) in which employees live and work
Primary Interests: Education; Environment/Conservation; Health and Human Services
Recent Recipients: American Cancer Society; Nature Conservancy; United Negro College Fund

Public Affairs and Related Activities Personnel

At Headquarters

HILT, Meredith — Tel: (630) 798 - 2506
Exec. Director, Tellabs Foundation — Fax: (630) 798 - 4778
Mailstop: MS 10
meredith.hilt@tellabs.com

NIKITAS, Ariana — Tel: (630) 798 - 2532
Manager, Public Relations — Fax: (630) 798 - 2000
ariana.nikitas@tellabs.com

SCOTTINO, Tom — Tel: (630) 798 - 3602
Manager, Investor Relations — Fax: (630) 798 - 3333
tom.scottino@tellabs.com

STENITZER, George — Tel: (630) 798 - 3800
V. President, Corporate Communications — Fax: (630) 798 - 4776
george.stenitzer@tellabs.com

Temple-Inland Inc.

A manufacturer of corrugated packaging and building products, with a diversified financial services operation.
www.templeinland.com
Annual Revenues: $5 billion

Chairman and Chief Exec. Officer — Tel: (512) 434 - 5800
JASTROW, Kenneth M., II

Main Headquarters
Mailing: P.O. Box 40 — Tel: (512) 434 - 5800
Austin, TX 78767

Political Action Committees

Committee for Responsible Government of Temple-Inland Inc.
Contact: Thomas Todd Morgan
P.O. Box 40 — Tel: (512) 615 - 1108
Austin, TX 78767

Contributions to Candidates: $22,000 (01/05 - 09/05)
Democrats: $3,000; Republicans: $19,000.

Principal Recipients

SENATE REPUBLICANS		HOUSE REPUBLICANS	
Cornyn, John (TX)	$2,500	DeLay, Tom (TX)	$2,500
		Sessions, Pete (TX)	$2,500
		Smith, Lamar (TX)	$2,500
		McCrery, Jim (LA)	$2,000

Corporate Foundations and Giving Programs

Temple-Inland Foundation
Contact: Evonne Nerren
P.O. Box 40 — Tel: (936) 829 - 1721
Austin, TX 78767

Annual Grant Total: $2,000,000 - $5,000,000
Geographic Preference: Area(s) in which the company operates
Primary Interests: Education; Health; Youth Services
Recent Recipients: Boys and Girls Club; Ronald McDonald House; Salvation Army; United Way

Public Affairs and Related Activities Personnel

At Headquarters

BENNETT, Richard A. "Tony" — Tel: (512) 615 - 1108
V. President, Government Affairs — Fax: (512) 615 - 1561
tonybennett@templeinland.com

MORGAN, Thomas Todd — Tel: (512) 615 - 1108
PAC Treasurer

NERREN, Evonne — Tel: (936) 829 - 1721
Secretary - Treasurer, Temple-Inland Foundation

NINES, Chris — Tel: (512) 434 - 5587
Director, Investor Relations — Fax: (512) 434 - 3750
chrisnines@templeinland.com
Responsibilities include corporate communications.

REISENWEBER, Richard L. — Tel: (512) 434 - 5800
V. President, Environmental Affairs

Tenet Healthcare Corp.

An owner and operator of acute care hospitals.
www.tenethealth.com
Annual Revenues: $13 billion

Chairman of the Board — Tel: (805) 563 - 7000
KANGAS, Edward A. — Fax: (805) 563 - 7070

President and Chief Exec. Officer — Tel: (805) 563 - 7000
FETTER, Trevor — Fax: (805) 563 - 7070

Main Headquarters
Mailing: P.O. Box 31907 — Tel: (805) 563 - 7000
Santa Barbara, CA 93130 — Fax: (805) 563 - 7070
Street: 3820 State St.
Santa Barbara, CA 93105

Political Action Committees

Tenet Healthcare Corp. PAC
Contact: Todd Plott
13737 Noel Rd.
Dallas, TX 75240

Contributions to Candidates: $15,500 (01/05 - 09/05)
Democrats: $6,000; Republicans: $9,500.

Principal Recipients

SENATE DEMOCRATS		HOUSE DEMOCRATS	
Nelson, Benjamin (NE)	$3,000		
Conrad, Kent (ND)	$2,000		
SENATE REPUBLICANS		**HOUSE REPUBLICANS**	
Hatch, Orrin (UT)	$5,000	Deal, Nathan (GA)	$2,000
Kyl, Jon L (AZ)	$1,000	Ryan, Paul D (WI)	$1,000

Corporate Foundations and Giving Programs

Tenet Healthcare Foundation
Contact: Kathy Charnonneau
P.O. Box 31907 — Tel: (805) 563 - 7000
Santa Barbara, CA 93130 — Fax: (805) 563 - 7070

Assets: $10,800,000 (2003)
Annual Grant Total: under $100,000
National funding for specific healthcare initiatives; regional and local giving recommended by Tenet facilities; specific employee giving programs.
Geographic Preference: Area(s) in which the company operates
Primary Interests: Arts and Humanities; Community Affairs; Education; Health

Public Affairs and Related Activities Personnel

At Headquarters

ANDERSON, Harry — Tel: (805) 563 - 6816
V. President, Corporate Communications — Fax: (805) 563 - 7180
harry.anderson@tenethealth.com

BLANCO, Janelle — Tel: (818) 952 - 2015
V. President, Government Relations — Fax: (818) 952 - 2404
janelle.blanco@tenethealth.com

CAMPANINI, Steve — Tel: (805) 563 - 6838
Director, Media Relations and Corporate Communications — Fax: (805) 563 - 6871
steven.campanini@tenethealth.com

CHARNONNEAU, Kathy — Tel: (805) 563 - 7000
Grants Administrator — Fax: (805) 563 - 7070

HOPKINS, Gary — Tel: (805) 563 - 7000
Senior Director, Corporate Communciations — Ext: 6885
gary.hopkins@tenethealth.com — Fax: (805) 563 - 6840

Tenet Healthcare Corp.

** continued from previous page*

MARTINEAU PLANKENTON, Maria — Tel: (805) 563 - 7000
Exec. Director, Foundation — Fax: (805) 563 - 7070

RICE, Thomas — Tel: (805) 563 - 6883
Senior V. President, Investor Relations — Fax: (805) 563 - 6877
thomas.rice@tenethealth.com

WILLETT, Mark — Tel: (805) 563 - 6863
V. President, Government Programs — Fax: (805) 682 - 5462

At Other Offices

ARMIN, Craig — Tel: (310) 966 - 3034
Senior V. President, Government Programs — Fax: (310) 966 - 3141
11620 Wilshire Blvd.
Suite 1100
Los Angeles, CA 90025
craig.armin@tenethealth.com

BOSCH, Joe — Tel: (469) 893 - 6170
Senior V. President, Human Resources — Fax: (469) 893 - 8170
13737 Noel Rd.
Dallas, TX 75240

HUSKEY, Teresa — Tel: (469) 893 - 2293
Senior Director, Government Relations — Fax: (469) 893 - 8637
13737 Noel Rd.
Dallas, TX 75240
teresa.huskey@tenethealth.com

PLOTT, Todd
PAC Treasurer
13737 Noel Rd.
Dallas, TX 75240

Tenneco Automotive

One of the world's largest designers, manufacturers and marketers of emission control and risk control products and systems for the automotive original equipment market and aftermarket.

www.tenneco-automotive.com
Annual Revenues: $3.5 billion

Chairman and Chief Exec. Officer — Tel: (847) 482 - 5080
FRISSORA, Mark P. — Fax: (847) 482 - 5049
mark.frissora@tenneco-automotive.com

Main Headquarters
Mailing: 500 N. Field Dr. — Tel: (847) 482 - 5000
Lake Forest, IL 60045 — Fax: (847) 482 - 5049

Corporate Foundations and Giving Programs

Tenneco Automotive Corporate Giving Program
Contact: Jane Ostrander
500 N. Field Dr. — Tel: (847) 482 - 5607
Lake Forest, IL 60045 — Fax: (847) 482 - 5049

Annual Grant Total: none reported

Public Affairs and Related Activities Personnel

At Headquarters

HUNZIKER, Leslie — Tel: (847) 482 - 5042
Director, Investor Relations — Fax: (847) 482 - 5049
leslie.hunziker@tenneco-automotive.com

OSTRANDER, Jane — Tel: (847) 482 - 5607
Director, Corporate Communications — Fax: (847) 482 - 5049
jane.ostrander@tenneco-automotive.com

SPANGLER, James K. — Tel: (847) 482 - 5810
V. President, Global Communications — Fax: (847) 482 - 5049
james.spangler@tenneco-automotive.com

Teradyne, Inc.

A manufacturer of electronic test systems.

www.teradyne.com
Annual Revenues: $1.222 billion

Chairman of the Board — Tel: (617) 482 - 2700
CHAMILLARD, George W. — Fax: (617) 422 - 2910

President and Chief Exec. Officer — Tel: (617) 482 - 2700
BRADLEY, Michael A. — Fax: (617) 422 - 2910

Main Headquarters
Mailing: 321 Harrison Ave. — Tel: (617) 482 - 2700
Boston, MA 02118-2238 — Fax: (617) 422 - 2910

Corporate Foundations and Giving Programs

Teradyne, Inc. Corporate Contributions
Contact: Thomas B. Newman, Jr.
321 Harrison Ave. — Tel: (617) 482 - 2425
Boston, MA 02118-2238 — Fax: (617) 422 - 2910

Annual Grant Total: none reported

Public Affairs and Related Activities Personnel

At Headquarters

NEWMAN, Thomas B., Jr. — Tel: (617) 482 - 2425
V. President, Corporate Relations — Fax: (617) 422 - 2910
Responsibilities include investor relations.

At Other Offices

GABERT, Charla — Tel: (978) 370 - 6225
Manager, Worldwide Marketing and Communications
600 Riverpark Dr.
N. Reading, MA 01864

Terex Corp.

Terex Corp. is a diversified global manufacturer based in Westport, CT. Terex is involved in a broad range of construction, infrastructure, recycling and mining-related capital equipment.

www.terex.com
Annual Revenues: $3.9 billion

Chairman and Chief Exec. Officer — Tel: (203) 222 - 5902
DEFEO, Ronald M. — Fax: (203) 226 - 2303

Main Headquarters
Mailing: 500 Post Rd. East — Tel: (203) 222 - 7170
Suite 320 — Fax: (203) 222 - 7976
Westport, CT 06880

Political Action Committees

Terex Corp. Political Action Committee
Contact: Eric Cohen
500 Post Rd. East — Tel: (203) 222 - 5950
Suite 320 — Fax: (203) 227 - 1647
Westport, CT 06880

Contributions to Candidates: none reported (01/05 - 09/05)

Public Affairs and Related Activities Personnel

At Headquarters

BARR, Kevin — Tel: (203) 222 - 5905
V. President, Human Resources — Fax: (203) 226 - 2303

COHEN, Eric — Tel: (203) 222 - 5950
PAC Contact — Fax: (203) 227 - 1647

GAAL, Elizabeth K. — Tel: (203) 222 - 5942
Investor Relations Associate — Fax: (203) 222 - 0130

GELSTON, Tom — Tel: (203) 222 - 5943
Director, Investor Relations and Corporate Communications — Fax: (203) 222 - 0130

Terra Industries Inc.

A marketer and producer of nitrogen fertilizer and methanol. Acquired Mississippi Chemical Corp. in 2005.

www.terraindustries.com
Annual Revenues: $1 billion

Chairman of the Board
SLACK, Henry R.

President and Chief Exec. Officer — Tel: (712) 277 - 1340
BENNETT, Michael L. — Fax: (712) 277 - 7383
mbennett@terraindustries.com

Main Headquarters
Mailing: P.O. Box 6000 — Tel: (712) 277 - 1340
Sioux City, IA 51102-6000 — Fax: (712) 277 - 7383
Street: Terra Centre
600 Fourth St.
Sioux City, IA 51101

Political Action Committees

Terra Industries Inc. Political Action Committee
Contact: Vaughn M. Klopfenstein
P.O. Box 6000 — Tel: (712) 277 - 1340
Sioux City, IA 51102-6000 — Fax: (712) 277 - 7383

Contributions to Candidates: none reported (01/05 - 09/05)

Corporate Foundations and Giving Programs

Terra Industries Corporate Contributions Program
Contact: W. Mark Rosenbury
P.O. Box 6000 — Tel: (712) 279 - 8756
Sioux City, IA 51102-6000 — Fax: (712) 294 - 1130

Annual Grant Total: none reported

Public Affairs and Related Activities Personnel

At Headquarters

KLOPFENSTEIN, Vaughn M. — Tel: (712) 277 - 1340
Treasurer, Terra Industries Inc. PAC — Fax: (712) 277 - 7383

MATHERS, Kim — Tel: (712) 233 - 6411
Manager, Communications — Fax: (712) 277 - 7383
kmathers@terraindustries.com

ROSENBURY, W. Mark — Tel: (712) 279 - 8756
Senior V. President and Chief Administrative Officer — Fax: (712) 294 - 1130
mrosenbury@terraindustries.com
Responsibilities include corporate communications and investor relations.

Tesoro Alaska Co.

See listing on page 470 under Tesoro Petroleum Corp.

Tesoro Petroleum Corp.

A member of the Public Affairs Council. A natural resource company engaged in the refining and marketing of petroleum products and the wholesale marketing of fuel and lubricants.

www.tesoropetroleum.com
Annual Revenues: $7.12 billion

Chairman, President, and Chief Exec. Officer
SMITH, Bruce A. — Tel: (210) 283 - 2001; Fax: (210) 283 - 2003; TF: (800) 837 - 8768

Main Headquarters
Mailing: 300 Concord Plaza Dr., San Antonio, TX 78216 — Tel: (210) 828 - 8484; Fax: (210) 283 - 2003; TF: (800) 837 - 8768

Political Action Committees

Tesoro Hawaii PAC
Contact: Dan Riley
3450 S. 344th Way
Suite 201
Auburn, WA 98001 — Tel: (253) 896 - 7300

Contributions to Candidates: none reported (01/05 - 09/05)

Tesoro Petroleum Corp. Political Action Committee
Contact: Gene Burden
300 Concord Plaza Dr.
San Antonio, TX 78216 — Tel: (210) 283 - 2001; Fax: (210) 283 - 2003; TF: (800) 837 - 8768

Contributions to Candidates: $5,500 (01/05 - 09/05)
Democrats: $4,000; Republicans: $1,500.

Principal Recipients

SENATE DEMOCRATS

HOUSE DEMOCRATS
Larsen, Rick (WA) $2,000
Gonzalez, Charles A (TX) $1,000
Miller, George (CA) $1,000

SENATE REPUBLICANS

HOUSE REPUBLICANS
Brady, Kevin Patrick (TX) $1,000

Corporate Foundations and Giving Programs

Tesoro Petroleum Corp. Corporate Contributions Program
Contact: Tara Ford Payne
300 Concord Plaza Dr.
San Antonio, TX 78216 — Tel: (210) 283 - 2676; Fax: (210) 283 - 2003; TF: (800) 837 - 8768

Annual Grant Total: $1,000,000 - $2,000,000

Public Affairs and Related Activities Personnel

At Headquarters

BURDEN, Gene
Senior V. President, External Affairs
gburden@tesoropetroleum.com
Oversees all Government Affairs.
Tel: (210) 283 - 2001; Fax: (210) 283 - 2003; TF: (800) 837 - 8768

DUBOIS, A. Pierre
Manager, Investor Relations
Tel: (210) 828 - 8484; Fax: (210) 283 - 2003; TF: (800) 837 - 8768

LERETTE, Susan
V. President, Human Resources
Tel: (210) 283 - 2001; Fax: (210) 283 - 2003; TF: (800) 837 - 8768

PAYNE, Tara Ford
Director, Public Relations and Corporate Communications
tford@tesoropetroleum.com
Tel: (210) 283 - 2676; Fax: (210) 283 - 2003; TF: (800) 837 - 8768

ROBERTSON, John
Director, Investor Relations
jrobertson@@tesoropetroleum.com
Tel: (210) 283 - 2001; Fax: (210) 283 - 2003; TF: (800) 837 - 8768

SIMPSON, Sarah S.
V. President, Corporate Communications
Tel: (210) 828 - 8484; Fax: (210) 283 - 2003; TF: (800) 837 - 8768

At Other Offices

RILEY, Dan
Manager, Government Affairs
3450 S. 344th Way
Suite 201
Auburn, WA 98001
Tel: (253) 896 - 7300

Tetra Tech, Inc.

Provides consulting, engineering and technical services.

www.tetratech.com
Annual Revenues: $740.7 million

Chairman and Chief Exec. Officer
HWANG, Dr. Li-San — Tel: (626) 351 - 4664; Fax: (626) 351 - 5291

Main Headquarters
Mailing: 3475 East Foothill Blvd., Pasadena, CA 91107 — Tel: (626) 351 - 4664; Fax: (626) 351 - 5291

Public Affairs and Related Activities Personnel

At Headquarters

BIEBER, Michael A.
V. President, Investor Relations
Tel: (626) 351 - 4664; Fax: (626) 351 - 5291

BUSH, Michael C.
Exec. V. President, Communications
Tel: (626) 351 - 4664; Fax: (626) 351 - 5291

Texas Eastern Products Pipeline Company, LLC (TEPPCO)

A limited partnership providing pipeline transportation of refined petroleum products, liquefied petroleum gases, crude oil and natural gas liquids.

www.teppco.com
Annual Revenues: $4.25 billion

Chairman of the Board
CUNNINGHAM, Dr. Ralph S. — Tel: (713) 759 - 3636; Fax: (713) 759 - 3957; TF: (800) 877 - 3636

President and Chief Exec. Officer
PEARL, Barry — Tel: (713) 759 - 3636; Fax: (713) 759 - 3957; TF: (800) 877 - 3636

Main Headquarters
Mailing: P.O. Box 2521, Houston, TX 77252-2521 — Tel: (713) 759 - 3636; Fax: (713) 759 - 3957; TF: (800) 877 - 3636
Street: 2929 Allen Pkwy., Houston, TX 77019

Public Affairs and Related Activities Personnel

At Headquarters

CARROLL, Barbara
V. President, Environment, Health, and Safety
Tel: (713) 759 - 3636; Fax: (713) 759 - 3957; TF: (800) 877 - 3636

NIKOLIS, William G.
Director, Government and Public Affairs
wnikolis@teppco.com
Tel: (713) 759 - 3636; Fax: (713) 759 - 3645; TF: (800) 877 - 3636

PETERS, Brenda J.
Director, Investor Relations
bpeters@teppco.com
Tel: (713) 759 - 3954; Fax: (713) 759 - 3957; TF: (800) 877 - 3636

SAUVE, Kathleen A.
Director, Public and Media Relations
kasauve@teppco.com
Tel: (713) 759 - 3635; Fax: (713) 759 - 3957; TF: (800) 877 - 3636

Texas Industries, Inc.

A producer of steel and construction materials, including cement, aggregates and concrete. Also involved in the real estate industry.

www.txi.com
Annual Revenues: $1.673 billion

Chairman of the Board
ROGERS, Robert D. — Tel: (972) 647 - 6700; Fax: (972) 647 - 3878

President and Chief Exec. Officer
BREKHUS, Mel G.
mbrekhus@txi.com
Tel: (972) 647 - 6700; Fax: (972) 647 - 3878

Main Headquarters
Mailing: 1341 W. Mockingbird Ln., Dallas, TX 75247 — Tel: (972) 647 - 6700; Fax: (972) 647 - 3878

Political Action Committees

Texas Industries, Inc. Political Action Committee
Contact: Julia P. Fuller
1341 W. Mockingbird Ln.
Dallas, TX 75247 — Tel: (972) 647 - 6700; Fax: (972) 647 - 3878

Contributions to Candidates: $14,000 (01/05 - 09/05)
Republicans: $14,000.

Principal Recipients

SENATE REPUBLICANS
Allen, George (VA) $4,000
Hatch, Orrin (UT) $2,000

HOUSE REPUBLICANS
Barton, Joe L (TX) $5,000
Sessions, Pete (TX) $2,000
Carter, John (TX) $1,000

Corporate Foundations and Giving Programs

Texas Industries Corporate Contributions Program
Contact: D. Randall Jones

Texas Industries, Inc.

• continued from previous page

1341 W. Mockingbird Ln.
Dallas, TX 75247
Tel: (972) 647 - 6701
Fax: (972) 647 - 3355

Annual Grant Total: none reported

Public Affairs and Related Activities Personnel

At Headquarters

DURBIN, William J.
V. President, Human Resources
bdurbin@txi.com
Tel: (972) 647 - 6700
Fax: (972) 647 - 3878

ENGLISH, Linda K.
Administrator, Investor and Shareholder Relations
lenglish@txi.com
Tel: (972) 647 - 6732
Fax: (972) 647 - 3776

FACIANE, E. Leo
V. President, Environmental Affairs
lfaciane@txi.com
Tel: (972) 647 - 6700
Fax: (972) 647 - 3878

FULLER, Julia P.
Assistant Treasurer, Texas Industries Inc. Political Action Committee
jfuller@txi.com
Tel: (972) 647 - 6700
Fax: (972) 647 - 3878

JONES, D. Randall
V. President, Corporate Communications and Government Affairs
rjones@txi.com
Tel: (972) 647 - 6701
Fax: (972) 647 - 3355

Texas Instruments Incorporated

A member of the Public Affairs Council. Provides DSP and Analog technologies to meet customers' real world signal processing requirements. In addition to Semiconductor, the company's businesses include Sensors & Controls, and Educational & Productivity Solutions. Maintains manufacturing, design or sales operations in more than 25 countries.

www.ti.com
Annual Revenues: $9.88 billion

Chairman of the Board
ENGIBOUS, Thomas J.
Tel: (214) 995 - 2011
Fax: (214) 995 - 5150
TF: (800) 336 - 5236

President and Chief Exec. Officer
TEMPLETON, Richard K.
Tel: (214) 995 - 2011
Fax: (214) 995 - 5150
TF: (800) 336 - 5236

Main Headquarters
Mailing: P.O. Box 660199
Dallas, TX 75266-0199
Tel: (214) 995 - 2011
Fax: (214) 995 - 5150
TF: (800) 336 - 5236

Street: 12500 TI Blvd.
Dallas, TX 75243

Washington Office
Contact: John K. Boidock
Mailing: 1455 Pennsylvania Ave. NW
Suite 375
Washington, DC 20004
Tel: (202) 628 - 3133
Fax: (202) 628 - 2980

Political Action Committees

Constructive Citizenship Program of Texas Instruments
Contact: Ms. Gray Mayes
P.O. Box 660199
Dallas, TX 75266-0199
Tel: (214) 480 - 6870
Fax: (214) 480 - 6820
TF: (800) 336 - 5236

Contributions to Candidates: $20,000 (01/05 - 09/05)
Democrats: $2,500; Republicans: $17,500.

Principal Recipients

SENATE DEMOCRATS
Carper, Thomas R (DE) $1,000

SENATE REPUBLICANS
Cornyn, John (TX) $1,500
Kyl, Jon L (AZ) $1,000

HOUSE DEMOCRATS
Gonzalez, Charles A (TX)$1,000

HOUSE REPUBLICANS
DeLay, Tom (TX) $2,000
Sessions, Pete (TX) $1,500
Burgess, Michael (TX) $1,000
Carter, John (TX) $1,000
Dreier, David (CA) $1,000
Johnson, Nancy (CT) $1,000
Johnson, Samuel (TX) $1,000
Lewis, Jerry (CA) $1,000
Marchant, Kenny (TX) $1,000
McCaul, Michael (TX) $1,000
Regula, Ralph S (OH) $1,000
Sweeney, John E. (NY) $1,000
Thomas, William M (CA) $1,000

Corporate Foundations and Giving Programs

Texas Instruments Foundation
Contact: Jack E. Swindle
P.O. Box 660199
Dallas, TX 75266-0199
Tel: (214) 480 - 3221
Fax: (214) 480 - 6820
TF: (800) 336 - 5236

Assets: $18,300,000 (2003)
Annual Grant Total: over $5,000,000
Guidelines are available on the web at: www.ti.com/tifoundation. Donations total over $7 million.
Geographic Preference: National
Primary Interests: Arts and Culture; Education; United Way Campaigns
Recent Recipients: Head Start; United Way

Public Affairs and Related Activities Personnel

At Headquarters

BORDERS, Gerald
Director, Community Relations
Mailstop: M/S 8656
g-borders@ti.com
Tel: (214) 480 - 6890
Fax: (214) 480 - 6820
TF: (800) 336 - 5236

CUNNINGHAM, Trisha
Director, Company Communications
Mailstop: M/S 8726
t-cunningham@ti.com
Tel: (214) 480 - 6417
Fax: (214) 480 - 6881
TF: (800) 336 - 5236

LEVEN, Stephen H.
Senior V. President, Human Resources
Mailstop: M/S 8658
s-leven@ti.com
Tel: (214) 480 - 4700
Fax: (214) 480 - 1977
TF: (800) 336 - 5236

MAYES, Ms. Gray
Director, Public Affairs and Manager, State and Community Affairs
Mailstop: M/S 8656
gmayes@ti.com
Responsibilities include political action.
Tel: (214) 480 - 6870
Fax: (214) 480 - 6820
TF: (800) 336 - 5236

POMYKAL, Elizabeth Ann
Director, Public Affairs and Contributions Manager
Mailstop: MS 8656
annpomykal@ti.com
Tel: (214) 480 - 6873
Fax: (214) 480 - 6820
TF: (800) 336 - 5236

SWINDLE, Jack E.
President, Texas Instruments Foundation
Mailstop: M/S 8656
tifoundation@ti.com
Tel: (214) 480 - 3221
Fax: (214) 480 - 6820
TF: (800) 336 - 5236

WEST, Teresa Lynne
Senior V. President and Manager, Communications and Investor Relations
Mailstop: MS 8657
t-west@ti.com
Tel: (214) 480 - 5030
Fax: (214) 480 - 5025
TF: (800) 336 - 5236

At Washington Office

BOIDOCK, John K.
V. President, Government Relations
Mailstop: MS 4072
jboidock@ti.com
Registered Federal Lobbyist.
Tel: (202) 628 - 3133
Fax: (202) 628 - 2980

COLLINS, Paula
Director, Government Relations (Human Relations and Education)
Mailstop: MS 4072
pcollins@ti.com
Registered Federal Lobbyist.
Tel: (202) 628 - 3133
Fax: (202) 628 - 2980

JOHNSON, Cynthia K.
Director, Government Relations-International Trade
Mailstop: MS 4072
ckjohnson@ti.com
Registered Federal Lobbyist.
Tel: (202) 628 - 3133
Fax: (202) 628 - 2980

LARSON, Daniel M.
Director, Government and Media Relations
Mailstop: MS 4072
danlarson@ti.com
Registered Federal Lobbyist.
Tel: (202) 628 - 3133
Fax: (202) 628 - 2980

Texas Utilities Co.

See listing on page 482 under TXU.

Textron Inc.

A member of the Public Affairs Council. A multi-industry company with operations in aircraft, automotive, industrial and finance markets. Bell Helicopter Textron and The Cessna Aircraft Co. (see separate listings) are both divisions of the company.

www.textron.com
Annual Revenues: $13 billion

Chairman, President and Chief Exec. Officer
CAMPBELL, Lewis B.
Tel: (401) 421 - 2800
Fax: (401) 421 - 2878

Main Headquarters
Mailing: 40 Westminster St.
Providence, RI 02903-2525
Tel: (401) 421 - 2800
Fax: (401) 421 - 2878

Textron Inc.

* continued from previous page

Washington Office

Contact: Mary L. Howell

Mailing: 1101 Pennsylvania Ave. NW
Suite 400
Washington, DC 20004-2504
Tel: (202) 637 - 3800
Fax: (202) 637 - 3860

Political Action Committees

Textron Inc. Political Action Committee
Contact: Michael Harrington
40 Westminster St.
Providence, RI 02903-2525
Tel: (401) 421 - 2800
Fax: (401) 457 - 3598

Contributions to Candidates: $186,000 (01/05 - 09/05)

Democrats: $58,500; Republicans: $127,500.

Principal Recipients

SENATE DEMOCRATS		HOUSE DEMOCRATS	
Kennedy, Ted (MA)	$5,000	Murtha, John P Mr. (PA)	$15,000
		Visclosky, Peter (IN)	$5,000
SENATE REPUBLICANS		**HOUSE REPUBLICANS**	
Allen, George (VA)	$9,000	Granger, Kay N (TX)	$15,000
Chafee, Lincoln (RI)	$5,000	Bonilla, Henry (TX)	$10,000
Hutchison, Kay Bailey (TX)		Tiahrt, Todd W. (KS)	$10,000
	$5,000	Burgess, Michael (TX)	$5,000
Burns, Conrad (MT)	$3,000	Wicker, Roger (MS)	$5,000
Lott, Trent (MS)	$2,000		
Lugar, Richard G (IN)	$2,000		

Corporate Foundations and Giving Programs

Textron Charitable Trust
Contact: Cate Roberts
40 Westminster St.
Providence, RI 02903-2525
Tel: (401) 457 - 3172
Fax: (401) 457 - 3598

Annual Grant Total: over $5,000,000

Guidelines are available.

Geographic Preference: Area in which the company is headquartered; Area(s) in which the company operates

Primary Interests: Education; Environment/Conservation; Medicine and Health Care; Minority Opportunities; Women; Youth Services

Recent Recipients: Nature Conservancy; United Way

Public Affairs and Related Activities Personnel

At Headquarters

BUTLER, John D.
Exec. V. President, Administration and Chief Human Resources Officer
Tel: (401) 421 - 2800
Fax: (401) 421 - 2878

GORDON, Karen
Manager, Corporate Communications and Media Relations
kgordon@textron.com
Tel: (401) 457 - 2362
Fax: (401) 457 - 3598

HARRINGTON, Michael
Treasurer, Textron Inc. Political Action Committee
Tel: (401) 421 - 2800
Fax: (401) 457 - 3598

ROBERTS, Cate
Director, Community Affairs
Tel: (401) 457 - 3172
Fax: (401) 457 - 3598

TARDANICO, Susan
Exec. Director, Corporate Communications
stardanico@textron.com
Tel: (401) 457 - 2354
Fax: (401) 457 - 3598

WILBURNE, Douglas R.
V. President, Communications and Investor Relations
Tel: (401) 457 - 3606
Fax: (401) 457 - 3598

At Washington Office

AUGONE, Barbara
Executive Director, Public Affairs
Tel: (202) 637 - 3800
Fax: (202) 637 - 3860

FERNANDEZ, Manuel
Registered Federal Lobbyist.
Tel: (202) 637 - 3800
Fax: (202) 637 - 3860

HOWELL, Mary L.
Exec. V. President, Government, International Investor Relations, and Corporate Communications
Registered Federal Lobbyist.
Tel: (202) 637 - 3802
Fax: (202) 637 - 3860

HUTCHESON, Randy
Registered Federal Lobbyist.
Tel: (202) 637 - 3800
Fax: (202) 637 - 3860

KRAMUNE, Bruce
Registered Federal Lobbyist.
Tel: (202) 637 - 3800
Fax: (202) 637 - 3860

ROWLAND, Robert O.
V. President, Government Affairs
Registered Federal Lobbyist.
Tel: (202) 637 - 3800
Fax: (202) 637 - 3862

STEWART, Marise R.
Director, Government Affairs
Registered Federal Lobbyist.
Tel: (202) 637 - 3818
Fax: (202) 637 - 3863

THOMAS, Gordon M.
Director, Government Affairs
gthomas@dc.textron.com
Registered Federal Lobbyist.
Tel: (202) 637 - 3821
Fax: (202) 637 - 3863

WHITEHURST, Calvert S.
Manager, Public Affairs
Registered Federal Lobbyist.
Tel: (202) 637 - 3833
Fax: (202) 637 - 3863

Thermo Electron Corp.

Develops, manufactures and markets environmental and analytical instruments, laboratory equipment, software and services for life science customers. Also provides process instruments to industry.

www.thermo.com
Annual Revenues: $2.3 billion

President and Chief Exec. Officer
DEKKERS, Marijn E.
Tel: (781) 622 - 1000
Fax: (781) 622 - 1207

Main Headquarters

Mailing: 81 Wyman St.
Waltham, MA 02454-9046
Tel: (781) 622 - 1000
Fax: (781) 622 - 1207

Corporate Foundations and Giving Programs

Thermo Electron Foundation
81 Wyman St.
Waltham, MA 02454-9046
Tel: (781) 622 - 1000
Fax: (781) 622 - 1207

Annual Grant Total: none reported

Geographic Preference: Area in which the company is headquartered

Primary Interests: Arts and Humanities; Civic and Public Affairs; Education; Health

Public Affairs and Related Activities Personnel

At Headquarters

APICEMO, Ken
V. President, Investor Relations and Treasurer
Tel: (781) 622 - 1000
Fax: (781) 622 - 1207

GORSKI, Lori
Manager, Public Relations
lori.gorski@thermo.com
Tel: (781) 622 - 1242
Fax: (781) 622 - 1207

SHEEHAN, Stephen G.
V. President, Human Resources
stephen.sheehan@thermo.com
Tel: (781) 622 - 1000
Fax: (781) 622 - 1207

Thomas & Betts Corp.

A producer of connectors and components for worldwide electrical, communications, and utility markets.

www.tnb.com
Annual Revenues: $1.346 billion

Chairman of the Board
DUNNIGAN, T. Kevin
Tel: (901) 252 - 5000

Chief Exec. Officer
PILEGGI, Dominic J.
Tel: (901) 252 - 5000

Main Headquarters

Mailing: 8155 T & B Blvd.
Memphis, TN 38125
Tel: (901) 252 - 5000

Public Affairs and Related Activities Personnel

At Headquarters

BERGERON, Patricia A.
V. President, Investor and Corporate Relations
Mailstop: 4A-31
tricia_bergeron@tnb.com
Tel: (901) 252 - 8266
Fax: (901) 252 - 1306

WEIDERHOLT, James R.
V. President, Communications
Tel: (901) 252 - 5000

Thomas Industries Inc.

A manufacturer of pumps and compressors.

www.thomasind.com
Annual Revenues: $240.6 million

Chairman, President and Chief Exec. Officer
BROWN, Timothy C.
llyons@thomasind.com
Tel: (502) 893 - 4612
Fax: (502) 895 - 6618
TF: (800) 626 - 2847

Main Headquarters

Mailing: 4360 Brownsboro Rd.
Suite 300
Louisville, KY 40207
Tel: (502) 893 - 4600
Fax: (502) 895 - 6618
TF: (800) 626 - 2847

Corporate Foundations and Giving Programs

Thomas Industries Corporate Contributions Program
Contact: Phillip J. Stuecker

Thomas Industries Inc.

** continued from previous page*

4360 Brownsboro Rd.
Suite 300
Louisville, KY 40207
Tel: (502) 893 - 4600
Fax: (502) 895 - 6618
TF: (800) 626 - 2847

Annual Grant Total: none reported

Public Affairs and Related Activities Personnel

At Headquarters

LYONS, Laurie S.
V. President, Corporate Communications
llyons@thomasind.com
Tel: (502) 893 - 4600
Fax: (502) 895 - 6618
TF: (800) 626 - 2847

STUECKER, Phillip J.
V. President; Chief Financial Officer and Secretary
pstuecker@thomasind.com
Tel: (502) 893 - 4600
Fax: (502) 895 - 6618
TF: (800) 626 - 2847
Responsibilities include corporate philanthropy.

J. Walter Thompson Co.

An advertising, marketing and communications company.

www.jwtworld.com
Annual Revenues: $996.9 million

Chairman and Chief Exec. Officer
JEFFREY, Bob
Tel: (212) 210 - 7000
Fax: (212) 210 - 7770

Main Headquarters
Mailing: 466 Lexington Ave.
New York, NY 10017
Tel: (212) 210 - 7000
Fax: (212) 210 - 7770

Corporate Foundations and Giving Programs

J. Walter Thompson Co. Fund
466 Lexington Ave.
New York, NY 10017
Tel: (212) 210 - 7000
Fax: (212) 210 - 7770

Annual Grant Total: $1,000,000 - $2,000,000
The Fund concentrates on education through employee matching gifts. Direct corporate contributions go to various organizations generally for client-related causes.
Geographic Preference: National
Primary Interests: Arts and Culture; Education; United Way Campaigns
Recent Recipients: Nat'l Merit Scholarship; United Way

Public Affairs and Related Activities Personnel

At Headquarters

JOHNSON, Erin
Director, Corporate Communications
erin.johnson@jwt.com
Tel: (212) 210 - 7243
Fax: (212) 210 - 7770

The Thomson Corporation

A global integrated information solutions provider to business and professional customers.

www.thomson.com
Annual Revenues: $7.8 billion

Chairman of the Board
THOMSON, David K. R.
Tel: (203) 539 - 8000
Fax: (203) 539 - 7734
TF: (800) 969 - 9974

President and Chief Exec. Officer
HARRINGTON, Richard J.
Tel: (203) 539 - 8000
Fax: (203) 539 - 7734
TF: (800) 969 - 9974

Main Headquarters
Mailing: Metro Center
One Station Pl.
Stamford, CT 06902
Tel: (203) 539 - 8000
Fax: (203) 539 - 7734
TF: (800) 969 - 9974

Corporate Foundations and Giving Programs

Giving Advantage
Contact: Laura Jachino
Metro Center
One Station Pl.
Stamford, CT 06902
Tel: (203) 539 - 8000
Fax: (203) 539 - 7734
TF: (800) 969 - 9974

Annual Grant Total: none reported
Geographic Preference: Connecticut; New York City; London, UK; Toronto, Canada
Primary Interests: Adult Education and Training; Literacy
Recent Recipients: YMCA

Public Affairs and Related Activities Personnel

At Headquarters

BECKER, Joshua
Director, Investor Relations
Tel: (203) 539 - 8000
Fax: (203) 539 - 7734
TF: (800) 969 - 9974

BOGGARD, Robert B.
Exec. V. President, Human Resources
Tel: (203) 539 - 8000
Fax: (203) 539 - 7734
TF: (800) 969 - 9974

GOLDEN, Frank
V. President, Investor Relations
frank.golden@thomson.com
Tel: (203) 539 - 8470
Fax: (203) 539 - 7709
TF: (800) 969 - 9974

JACHINO, Laura
Manager, Corporate Giving
Tel: (203) 539 - 8000
Fax: (203) 539 - 7734
TF: (800) 969 - 9974

LOYD, Janey
V. President, Corporate Communications
janey.loyd@thomson.com
Tel: (203) 539 - 8000
Fax: (203) 539 - 7734
TF: (800) 969 - 9974

MARTIN, Brian T.
Senior V. President, Corporate Affairs
Tel: (203) 539 - 8000
Fax: (203) 539 - 7734
TF: (800) 969 - 9974

STEWART, Jason
V. President, Media Relations
jason.stewart@thomson.com
Tel: (203) 539 - 8339
Fax: (203) 539 - 7734
TF: (800) 969 - 9974

Thomson West

PUBLIC AFFAIRS COUNCIL

A member of the Public Affairs Council. A provider of e-information and solutions to the U.S. legal market. A division of The Thomson Corporation (see separate listing).

www.west.thomson.com

Main Headquarters
Mailing: 610 Opperman Dr.
Eagan, MN 55123-1340
Tel: (651) 687 - 7000
Fax: (651) 687 - 7302
TF: (800) 328 - 9352

Corporate Foundations and Giving Programs

Thomson West Contributions Program
610 Opperman Dr.
Eagan, MN 55123-1340
Tel: (651) 687 - 7000
Fax: (651) 687 - 7302
TF: (800) 328 - 9352

Annual Grant Total: none reported

Public Affairs and Related Activities Personnel

At Headquarters

CHRISTENSEN, Kyle
Corporate Communications
kyle.christensen@thomson.com
Tel: (651) 687 - 7082
Fax: (651) 687 - 5388
TF: (800) 328 - 9352

MORAN, Tom
Senior V. President, Human Resources
thomas.moran@thomson.com
Tel: (651) 687 - 7000
Fax: (651) 687 - 7302
TF: (800) 328 - 9352

SHAUGHNESSY, John
Corporate Communications
john.shaughnessy@thomson.com
Tel: (651) 687 - 4749
Fax: (651) 687 - 5388
TF: (800) 328 - 9352

WARWICK, Peter
President and Chief Exec. Officer
Tel: (651) 687 - 7000
Fax: (651) 687 - 7302
TF: (800) 328 - 9352

Thrifty Inc.

See listing on page 161 under Dollar Thrifty Automotive Group, Inc.

Thrivent Financial for Lutherans

PUBLIC AFFAIRS COUNCIL

A member of the Public Affairs Council. A fraternal benefit society formed from the merger of Aid Association for Lutherans and Lutheran Brotherhood.

www.thrivent.com
Annual Revenues: $5.6 billion

Chairman, President and Chief Exec. Officer
NICHOLSON, Bruce J.
bruce.nicholson@thrivent.com
Tel: (612) 340 - 7000
Fax: (612) 340 - 7373

Main Headquarters
Mailing: 625 Fourth Ave. South
Minneapolis, MN 55415
Tel: (612) 340 - 7000
Fax: (612) 340 - 7373

Political Action Committees

Thrivent Financial for Lutherans-Employee PAC
Contact: Marsha J. Mahan
625 Fourth Ave. South
Minneapolis, MN 55415
Tel: (612) 340 - 7000
Fax: (612) 340 - 7373

Contributions to Candidates: $3,500 (01/05 - 09/05)
Democrats: $1,500; Republicans: $2,000.

Principal Recipients

SENATE DEMOCRATS
Baucus, Max (MT) $1,000

HOUSE DEMOCRATS

SENATE REPUBLICANS

HOUSE REPUBLICANS
Ramstad, Jim (MN) $1,000

Corporate Foundations and Giving Programs

Thrivent Financial for Lutherans Foundation
Contact: Tim Yagow

Thrivent Financial for Lutherans

* continued from previous page

625 Fourth Ave. South — Tel: (612) 340 - 5821
Minneapolis, MN 55415 — Fax: (612) 340 - 7373

Annual Grant Total: over $5,000,000
Primarily supports protestant agencies and churches.
Geographic Preference: National
Primary Interests: Religion

Public Affairs and Related Activities Personnel

At Headquarters

HALEY, Mariellen — Tel: (612) 340 - 8352
Media Relations Administrator — Fax: (612) 340 - 7373
mariellen.haley@thrivent.com

KELASH, Paul — Tel: (612) 340 - 4274
Director, Media Relations — Fax: (612) 340 - 4070
paul.kelash@thrivent.com

MAHAN, Marsha J. — Tel: (612) 340 - 7000
PAC Treasurer — Fax: (612) 340 - 7373
marsha.mahan@thrivent.com

MARTIN, Jennifer H., PhD — Tel: (612) 340 - 7000
Senior V. President, Human Resources — Fax: (612) 340 - 7373

RUSTAD, Dave — Tel: (612) 340 - 7037
Senior Media Relations Specialist — Fax: (612) 340 - 7373
dave.rustad@thrivent.com

UHRICH, Marie A. — Tel: (612) 340 - 7000
Senior V. President, Communications — Fax: (612) 340 - 7373

YAGOW, Tim — Tel: (612) 340 - 5821
Foundation Contact — Fax: (612) 340 - 7373

Thyssenkrupp Budd Company

Formerly known as The Budd Company. A Thyssenkrupp Automotive company. Manufactures automotive equipment.
www.thyssenkruppbudd.com
Annual Revenues: $2.8 billion

Chairman of the Board — Tel: (248) 643 - 3500
MOERSDORF, Wolfram — Fax: (248) 643 - 3687

President and Chief Exec. Officer — Tel: (248) 643 - 3500
ZAPS, Dietrich — Fax: (248) 643 - 3687

Main Headquarters
Mailing: P.O. Box 2601 — Tel: (248) 643 - 3500
Troy, MI 48007-2601 — Fax: (248) 643 - 3687
Street: 3155 W. Big Beaver Rd.
Troy, MI 48007

Public Affairs and Related Activities Personnel

At Headquarters

FLANCBAUM, Paul — Tel: (248) 643 - 3644
Manager, Corporate Communications — Fax: (248) 643 - 3687

HUSSEY, Terry A. — Tel: (248) 643 - 3500
V. President, Human Resources — Fax: (248) 643 - 3687

PAYNE, Charles — Tel: (248) 643 - 3500
Corporate Manager, Environmental Affairs — Fax: (248) 643 - 3687

TIAA/CREF

A nationwide financial services organization whose full name is Teachers Insurance and Annuity Association-College Retirement Equities Fund.
www.tiaa-cref.org
Annual Revenues: $19 billion

Chairman, President, and Chief Exec. Officer — Tel: (212) 490 - 9000
ALLISON, Herbert M., Jr. — Fax: (212) 916 - 4840

Main Headquarters
Mailing: 730 Third Ave. — Tel: (212) 490 - 9000
New York, NY 10017-3206 — Fax: (212) 916 - 5952

Washington Office
Contact: Milly C. Stanges
Mailing: 1101 Pennsylvania Ave., NW — Tel: (202) 637 - 8925
Suite 800 — Fax: (202) 637 - 8930
Washington, DC 20004

Public Affairs and Related Activities Personnel

At Headquarters

BREWSTER, Lemuel — Tel: (212) 916 - 5717
Media Contact — Fax: (212) 916 - 5952
lbrewster@tiaa-cref.org

COHEN GLASS, Stephanie — Tel: (212) 916 - 4993
Director, Corporate Media Relations — Fax: (212) 916 - 5952
scohenglass@tiaa-cref.org

CONNOR, Patrick — Tel: (212) 916 - 5769
Media Contact — Fax: (212) 916 - 5952
pconnor@tiaa-cref.org

GOLDSTEIN, I. Steven — Tel: (212) 490 - 9000
Exec. V. President, Public Affairs — Fax: (212) 916 - 4840
sgoldstein@tiaa-cref.org

GOLDSTEIN, L. Steven — Tel: (212) 490 - 9000
Exec. V. President, Public Affairs — Fax: (212) 916 - 5952

O'BRIEN, Dermot J. — Tel: (212) 490 - 9000
Exec. V. President, Human Resources — Fax: (212) 916 - 5952

WEINER, Glen — Tel: (212) 490 - 9000
Media Contact — Ext: 5986
gweiner@tiaa-cref.org — Fax: (212) 916 - 5952

At Washington Office

STANGES, Milly C. — Tel: (202) 637 - 8925
V. President, Federal Relations — Fax: (202) 637 - 8930
mstanges@tiaa-cref.org

Tidewater Inc.

Owns and operates the world's largest fleet of marine vessels serving the international offshore energy industry. Also owns and operates a shipyard in southern Louisiana.
www.tdw.com
Annual Revenues: $635 million

Chairman, President, and Chief Exec. Officer — Tel: (504) 568 - 1010
TAYLOR, Dean E. — Fax: (504) 566 - 4580

Main Headquarters
Mailing: 601 Poydras St. — Tel: (504) 568 - 1010
Suite 1900 — Fax: (504) 566 - 4580
New Orleans, LA 70130

Political Action Committees

Tidewater Inc. Political Action Committee (TIDEPAC)
Contact: Earl F. Dobson
601 Poydras St. — Tel: (504) 568 - 1010
Suite 1900 — Fax: (504) 566 - 4580
New Orleans, LA 70130

Contributions to Candidates: $3,000 (01/05 - 09/05)
Democrats: $1,000; Republicans: $2,000.

Principal Recipients

SENATE DEMOCRATS
Landrieu, Mary (LA) $1,000

HOUSE DEMOCRATS

SENATE REPUBLICANS

HOUSE REPUBLICANS
Hunter, Duncan (CA) $1,000
Young, Don E (AK) $1,000

Public Affairs and Related Activities Personnel

At Headquarters

DOBSON, Earl F. — Tel: (504) 568 - 1010
PAC Treasurer — Fax: (504) 566 - 4580

HADEED, Rebecca — Tel: (504) 568 - 1010
Manager, Public Affairs and Corporate Communications — Fax: (504) 566 - 4580
rhadeed@tdw.com

Tiffany & Co.

A retailer of fine jewelry, timepieces, china, crystal, sterling silver, leather goods, fragrances, stationery, and accessories.
www.tiffany.com
Annual Revenues: $1.706 billion

Chairman, President and Chief Exec. Officer — Tel: (212) 755 - 8000
KOWALSKI, Michael J. — Fax: (212) 230 - 6734

Main Headquarters
Mailing: 727 Fifth Ave. — Tel: (212) 755 - 8000
New York, NY 10022 — Fax: (212) 230 - 6734

Corporate Foundations and Giving Programs

Tiffany & Co. Corporate Contributions Program
Contact: Fernanda M. Kellogg
727 Fifth Ave. — Tel: (212) 230 - 5343
New York, NY 10022 — Fax: (212) 230 - 6734

Annual Grant Total: $1,000,000 - $2,000,000
Recent Recipients: Metropolitan Museum of Art; Wildlife Conservation Soc., The

Public Affairs and Related Activities Personnel

At Headquarters

DORSEY, Patrick B. — Tel: (212) 230 - 5320
Senior V. President, General Counsel and Secretary — Fax: (212) 230 - 6734
Responsibilities include government affairs.

KELLOGG, Fernanda M. — Tel: (212) 230 - 5343
Senior V. President, Public Relations — Fax: (212) 230 - 6734

At Other Offices

AARON, Mark L. — Tel: (212) 230 - 5301
V. President, Investor Relations
600 Madison Ave.
New York, NY 10021
maaron@tiffany.com

The Timberland Co.

Manufacturer of footwear and apparel.
www.timberland.com
Annual Revenues: $1.3 billion

Chairman of the Board
SWARTZ, Sidney W. — Tel: (603) 772 - 9500 Fax: (603) 773 - 1251

President and Chief Exec. Officer
SWARTZ, Jeffrey B. — Tel: (603) 772 - 9500 Fax: (603) 773 - 1251

Main Headquarters
Mailing: 200 Domain Dr.
Stratham, NH 03885 — Tel: (603) 772 - 9500 Fax: (603) 773 - 1251

Corporate Foundations and Giving Programs

Timberland Co. Path of Service Program
200 Domain Dr.
Stratham, NH 03885 — Tel: (603) 772 - 9500 Fax: (603) 773 - 1251

Annual Grant Total: $1,000,000 - $2,000,000
Primary Interests: Civic and Cultural Activities; Economic Development; Environment/Conservation; Hunger

Public Affairs and Related Activities Personnel

At Headquarters

GIAMPA, Robin
Manager, Corporate Communications — Tel: (603) 773 - 1174 Fax: (603) 773 - 1251

JOHNSON, Bruce C.
Senior V. President, Human Resources — Tel: (603) 772 - 9500 Fax: (603) 773 - 1251

Time Warner Cable

See listing on page 475 under Time Warner Inc.

Time Warner Communications

See listing on page 475 under Time Warner Inc.

Time Warner Inc.

Formerly known as AOL Time Warner Inc. A media and communications company, whose business includes interactive services, cable systems, publishing, music, TV networks and filmed entertainment. Time Warner businesses include: America Online, Time Warner Cable, Home Box Office (see separate listing) and more.
www.timewarner.com
Annual Revenues: $38.23 billion

Chairman and Chief Exec. Officer
PARSONS, Richard D. — Tel: (212) 484 - 8000 Fax: (212) 489 - 6183

Main Headquarters
Mailing: One Time Warner Center
New York, NY 10019 — Tel: (212) 484 - 8000 Fax: (212) 489 - 6183

Washington Office
Contact: Susan Brophy
Mailing: 800 Connecticut Ave. NW
Suite 800
Washington, DC 20006 — Tel: (202) 457 - 8582 Fax: (202) 457 - 8861

Political Action Committees

Time Warner PAC
Contact: Lisa Nelson
800 Connecticut Ave. NW
Suite 800
Washington, DC 20006 — Tel: (202) 457 - 8582 Fax: (202) 457 - 8861

Contributions to Candidates: $119,500 (01/05 - 09/05)
Democrats: $50,000; Republicans: $69,500.

Principal Recipients

SENATE DEMOCRATS
Kennedy, Ted (MA) $5,000
Conrad, Kent (ND) $3,000
Lieberman, Joe (CT) $3,000
Nelson, Benjamin (NE) $2,000
Reid, Harry (NV) $2,000

HOUSE DEMOCRATS
Waxman, Henry A. (CA) $5,000
Towns, Edolphus (NY) $3,000
Lewis, John (GA) $2,000
Menendez, Robert (NJ) $2,000
Schiff, Adam (CA) $2,000
Tauscher, Ellen O (CA) $2,000

SENATE REPUBLICANS
Stevens, Ted (AK) $8,000
Smith, Gordon (OR) $5,000
Graham, Lindsey (SC) $4,000
Santorum, Richard (PA) $4,000
Allen, George (VA) $3,000

HOUSE REPUBLICANS
DeLay, Tom (TX) $5,000
Hastert, Dennis J. (IL) $5,000
Sensenbrenner, Jim (WI) $3,500
Dreier, David (CA) $2,500
Goodlatte, Robert (VA) $2,500
Cannon, Christopher (UT) $2,000
Cantor, Eric (VA) $2,000

Time Warner Telecom Inc. Political Action Committee
Contact: Mark Peters
10475 Park Meadows Dr.
Littleton, CO 80124

Contributions to Candidates: $17,000 (01/05 - 09/05)
Democrats: $7,000; Republicans: $10,000.

Principal Recipients

SENATE DEMOCRATS
Pryor, Mark (AR) $2,500
Nelson, Benjamin (NE) $1,500

HOUSE DEMOCRATS
Conyers, John Jr. (MI) $1,000
Markey, Edward (MA) $1,000

SENATE REPUBLICANS
Ensign, John Eric (NV) $2,000
Stevens, Ted (AK) $2,000
Snowe, Olympia (ME) $1,000

HOUSE REPUBLICANS
Pickering, Chip (MS) $2,500
Marchant, Kenny (TX) $2,000

Corporate Foundations and Giving Programs

Time Warner Foundation
One Time Warner Center
New York, NY 10019 — Tel: (212) 484 - 8000 Fax: (212) 489 - 6183

Annual Grant Total: none reported
Primary Interests: Arts and Culture; Education; Youth Services

Time Warner Cable Community Involvement
290 Harbor Dr.
Stamford, CT 06902 — Tel: (203) 328 - 0600 Fax: (203) 328 - 0690

Annual Grant Total: $2,000,000 - $5,000,000
Primary Interests: Education

Public Affairs and Related Activities Personnel

At Headquarters

ADLER, Edward I.
Exec. V. President, Corporate Communications — Tel: (212) 484 - 6630

CARBONELL, Mia
Director, Corporate Communications — Tel: (212) 484 - 6684 Fax: (212) 489 - 6183

MARTIN, John K.
V. President, Investor Relations — Tel: (212) 484 - 8000 Fax: (212) 489 - 6183

WALLACE, Tricia Primrose
V. President, Corporate Communications — Tel: (212) 484 - 7450 Fax: (212) 489 - 6183

At Washington Office

AN, Edward
Director, Domestic Policy — Tel: (202) 457 - 8582 Fax: (202) 457 - 8861
Registered Federal Lobbyist.

BENTLEY, Shawn
V. President, Domestic Policy — Tel: (202) 457 - 8582 Fax: (202) 457 - 8861
Registered Federal Lobbyist.

BROPHY, Susan
Senior V. President, Domestic Policy — Tel: (202) 457 - 8582 Fax: (202) 457 - 8861
Registered Federal Lobbyist.

JACOBSEN, Jennifer
Director, Domestic Public Policy — Tel: (202) 457 - 8582 Fax: (202) 457 - 8861
Registered Federal Lobbyist.

KIMMITT, Robert M.
Exec. V. President, Global Public Policy — Tel: (202) 457 - 8582 Fax: (202) 457 - 8861
robert.kimmett@timewarner.com
Registered Federal Lobbyist.

LANE, Laura — Tel: (202) 457 - 8582 Fax: (202) 457 - 8861
Registered Federal Lobbyist.

LESSER, Jill A.
Senior Policy Advisor — Tel: (202) 457 - 8582 Fax: (202) 457 - 8861
Registered Federal Lobbyist.

NELSON, Lisa
V. President, External Relations — Tel: (202) 457 - 8582 Fax: (202) 457 - 8861
Registered Federal Lobbyist.

PERLMUTTER, Shira — Tel: (202) 457 - 8582 Fax: (202) 457 - 8861
Registered Federal Lobbyist.

RUSSINOFF, Paul
Director, State Policy — Tel: (202) 457 - 8582 Fax: (202) 457 - 8861

Time Warner Inc.
** continued from previous page*

TEPLITZ, Steven N. — Tel: (202) 457 - 8582
V. President and Associate General Counsel — Fax: (202) 457 - 8861
Registered Federal Lobbyist.

At Other Offices

BLOSS-BAUM, Linda — Tel: (202) 354 - 8248
V. President, Public Policy and Government Relations
(Warner Music Group Inc.)
607 14th St. NW
Suite 500
Washington, DC 20005
linda.bloss-baum@wmg.com

BUCKLEY, John
Exec. V. President, Corporate Communications
(America Online, Inc.)
22000 AOL Way
Dulles, VA 20166-9302

FLEISHMAN, Susan — Tel: (818) 954 - 6000
Exec. V. President, Corporate Communications
(Warner Brothers Entertainment)
4000 Warner Blvd.
Burbank, CA 91522

PETERS, Mark
Treasurer, Time Warner Telecom Inc. PAC
10475 Park Meadows Dr.
Littleton, CO 80124

ROWE, Scott — Tel: (818) 954 - 5806
V. President, Corporate Communications
(Warner Brothers Entertainment)
4000 Warner Blvd.
Burbank, CA 91522
scott.rowe@warnerbros.com

YAEGER, Lynn — Tel: (203) 328 - 0600
Exec. V. President, Corporate Affairs — Fax: (203) 328 - 0690
(Time Warner Cable)
290 Harbor Dr.
Stamford, CT 06902

The Timken Co.
A member of the Public Affairs Council. A manufacturer of anti-friction bearings and quality alloy steel products. Acquired Torrington Co. in February, 2003.
www.timken.com
Annual Revenues: $1.392 billion
Annual Revenues: $4.5 billioon

Chairman of the Board — Tel: (330) 438 - 3000
TIMKEN, W. R. "Tim", Jr. — Fax: (330) 471 - 4041
Mailstop: GME-15 — TF: (800) 223 - 1954

President and Chief Exec. Officer — Tel: (330) 438 - 3000
GRIFFITH, James W. — Fax: (330) 471 - 4041
Mailstop: GNE-17 — TF: (800) 223 - 1954
james.griffith@timken.com

Main Headquarters
Mailing: 1835 Dueber Ave. SW — Tel: (330) 438 - 3000
Canton, OH 44706 — Fax: (330) 471 - 3810
TF: (800) 223 - 1954

Political Action Committees

The Timken Co. Good Government Fund
Contact: Robert J. Lapp
1835 Dueber Ave. SW — Tel: (330) 471 - 4275
Canton, OH 44706 — Fax: (330) 471 - 3541
TF: (800) 223 - 1954

Contributions to Candidates: $10,000 (01/05 - 09/05)
Democrats: $1,000; Republicans: $9,000.

Principal Recipients

SENATE DEMOCRATS

HOUSE DEMOCRATS
Spratt, John (SC) $1,000

SENATE REPUBLICANS
Allen, George (VA) $5,000

HOUSE REPUBLICANS
Barrett, James (SC) $1,000
English, Philip S (PA) $1,000
Goode, Virgil H. Jr. (VA) $1,000
Myrick, Sue (NC) $1,000

Corporate Foundations and Giving Programs

Timken Foundation of Canton
Contact: Nancy Knudsen
1835 Dueber Ave. SW — Tel: (330) 438 - 3000
Canton, OH 44706 — Fax: (330) 471 - 3810
TF: (800) 223 - 1954

Annual Grant Total: $2,000,000 - $5,000,000
Geographic Preference: Area(s) in which the company operates; International; National
Primary Interests: Economic Development; Youth Services
Recent Recipients: Case Western Reserve University

Timken Co. Educational Fund
Contact: Debbie Rankine
1835 Dueber Ave. SW — Tel: (330) 438 - 3000
Canton, OH 44706 — Fax: (330) 471 - 6633
TF: (800) 223 - 1954

Assets: $1,574,856 (2002)
Annual Grant Total: $500,000 - $750,000
Geographic Preference: Ohio; Pennsylvania
Primary Interests: Scholarship Funds

Public Affairs and Related Activities Personnel

At Headquarters

BOWLER, Denise — Tel: (330) 471 - 3485
Manager, Public Relations — Fax: (330) 471 - 4118
Mailstop: GNW-37 — TF: (800) 223 - 1954
denise.bowler@timken.com

GRISCHOW, Patricia A. — Tel: (330) 471 - 4255
Senior Government Affairs Specialist — Fax: (330) 471 - 3541
Mailstop: GNE 01 — TF: (800) 223 - 1954
pat.grischow@timken.com

KNUDSEN, Nancy — Tel: (330) 438 - 3000
Program Director, Timken Foundation of Canton — Fax: (330) 471 - 3810
TF: (800) 223 - 1954

LAPP, Robert J. — Tel: (330) 471 - 4275
V. President, Government Affairs — Fax: (330) 471 - 3541
Mailstop: GNE-01 — TF: (800) 223 - 1954
robert_lapp@timken.com

MILLER, Debra L. — Tel: (330) 438 - 3000
Senior V. President, Communications and Community Affairs — Fax: (330) 471 - 4041
Mailstop: GNE-20 — TF: (800) 223 - 1954
deb.miller@timken.com

RANKINE, Debbie — Tel: (330) 438 - 3000
Contact, Timken Co. Educational Fund — Fax: (330) 471 - 6633
Mailstop: BLC-24 — TF: (800) 223 - 1954
debbie.rankine@timken.com

THARP, Christina — Tel: (330) 471 - 3294
Manager, Marketing Communications — Fax: (330) 471 - 7032
Mailstop: GNW-37 — TF: (800) 223 - 1954
christina.tharp@timken.com

TSCHIEGG, Steven D. — Tel: (330) 471 - 7446
Manager, Investor Relations — Fax: (330) 471 - 2797
Mailstop: GNE-26 — TF: (800) 223 - 1954
steve.tschiegg@timken.com

WALKER, Donald L. — Tel: (330) 438 - 3000
Senior V. President, Human Resources and Organizational Advancement — Fax: (330) 471 - 4041
Mailstop: GNE-17 — TF: (800) 223 - 1954
donald.l.walker@timken.com

Titan Corp.
See listing on page 284 under L-3 Communications Titan Group.

The TJX Companies, Inc.
An off-price retailer of apparel.
www.tjx.com
Annual Revenues: $11.98 billion

Chairman and Chief Exec. Officer — Tel: (508) 390 - 1000
CAMMARATA, Bernard — Fax: (508) 390 - 2091

Main Headquarters
Mailing: 770 Cochituate Rd. — Tel: (508) 390 - 1000
Framingham, MA 01701 — Fax: (508) 390 - 2091

Corporate Foundations and Giving Programs

TJX Foundation, Inc.
Contact: Christine Strickland
770 Cochituate Rd. — Tel: (508) 390 - 3199
Framingham, MA 01701 — Fax: (508) 390 - 2091

Annual Grant Total: none reported
Primary Interests: Children; Disaster Relief; Domestic Violence; Education; Families; Social Services
Recent Recipients: American Red Cross; Boys and Girls Club; Juvenile Diabetes Foundation

Public Affairs and Related Activities Personnel

At Headquarters

LANG, Sherry — Tel: (508) 390 - 2323
V. President, Investor and Public Relations — Fax: (508) 390 - 2091

NELSON, Virginia — Tel: (508) 390 - 1000
Assistant V. President, Community Relations — Ext: 2467

STRICKLAND, Christine — Tel: (508) 390 - 3199
Manager, TJX Foundation — Fax: (508) 390 - 2091

TMP Worldwide, Inc.
See listing on page 331 under Monster Worldwide, Inc.

Togo's

See listing on page 169 under Dunkin' Brands.

Toll Brothers, Inc.

A luxury home builder.
www.tollbrothers.com
Annual Revenues: $2.315 billion

Chairman and Chief Exec. Officer
TOLL, Robert I. — Tel: (215) 938 - 8000; Fax: (215) 938 - 8019
rtoll@tollbrothersinc.com

Main Headquarters
Mailing: 3103 Philmont Ave., Huntingdon Valley, PA 19006 — Tel: (215) 938 - 8000; Fax: (215) 938 - 8019

Washington Office
Mailing: 21630 Ridgetop Circle, Suite 130, Dulles, VA 20166 — Tel: (703) 433 - 6200

Corporate Foundations and Giving Programs

Toll Brothers Corporate Contributions Program
3103 Philmont Ave.
Huntingdon Valley, PA 19006 — Tel: (215) 938 - 8000; Fax: (215) 938 - 8019

Annual Grant Total: none reported

Public Affairs and Related Activities Personnel

At Headquarters

COOPER, Frederick N.
Investor Relations Contact — Tel: (215) 938 - 8312; Fax: (215) 938 - 8019
fcooper@tollbrothersinc.com

DOWNS, Jonathan C.
V. President, Human Resources — Tel: (215) 938 - 8000; Fax: (215) 938 - 8019
jdowns@tollbrothersinc.com

SICREE, Joseph R.
V. President, Chief Accounting Officer and Director, Investor Relations — Tel: (215) 938 - 8045; Fax: (215) 938 - 8010
jsicree@tollbrothersinc.com

At Washington Office

DESPAIN, Cory
V. President, Operations — Tel: (703) 433 - 6200
Responsibilities include government affairs.

Too, Inc.

A subsidiary of The Limited Brands (see separate listing). Operates under the name Limited, Too.
www.tooinc.com
Annual Revenues: $647.5 million

Chairman, President and Chief Exec. Officer
RAYDEN, Michael W. — Tel: (614) 775 - 3500, Ext: 3510; Fax: (614) 479 - 3619
mrayden@limitedtoo.com

Main Headquarters
Mailing: 3885 Morse Rd., Columbus, OH 43219 — Tel: (614) 775 - 3500; Fax: (614) 479 - 3619

Public Affairs and Related Activities Personnel

At Headquarters

ATKINSON, Robert C.
Director, Investor Relations — Tel: (614) 775 - 3739; Fax: (614) 479 - 3720
batkinson@limitedtoo.com
Responsibilities include media relations.

SYKES, Ronald
Senior V. President, Human Resources — Tel: (614) 775 - 3500, Ext: 3810; Fax: (614) 479 - 3619
rsykes@limitedtoo.com
Responsibilities also include corporate philanthropy.

Tops Markets LLC

A food retail chain.
www.topsmarkets.com

President and Chief Exec. Officer
SCHIANO, Anthony — Tel: (716) 635 - 5000; Fax: (716) 633 - 0898; TF: (800) 522 - 2522

Main Headquarters
Mailing: 6363 Main St., Williamsville, NY 14221 — Tel: (716) 635 - 5000; Fax: (716) 633 - 0898; TF: (800) 522 - 2522

Corporate Foundations and Giving Programs

Tops Markets Corporate Contributions
6363 Main St.
Williamsville, NY 14221 — Tel: (716) 635 - 5000; Fax: (716) 633 - 0898; TF: (800) 522 - 2522

Annual Grant Total: none reported
Geographic Preference: New York; Ohio; Pennsylvania
Primary Interests: Early Childhood Education; Hunger

Public Affairs and Related Activities Personnel

At Headquarters

BUSSENGER, John
Exec. V. President, Human Resources — Tel: (716) 635 - 5000; Fax: (716) 633 - 0898; TF: (800) 522 - 2522

HOPKINS, Denny
V. President, Advertising and Public Relations — Tel: (716) 635 - 5000; Fax: (716) 633 - 0898; TF: (800) 522 - 2522

MINEO, John
V. President, General Counsel and Corporate Secretary — Tel: (716) 635 - 5000; Fax: (716) 633 - 0898; TF: (800) 522 - 2522
Responsibilities include government relations.

ZAKOWICZ, Stefanie
Director, Public Relations — Tel: (716) 635 - 5885; Fax: (716) 633 - 0898; TF: (800) 522 - 2522

Torchmark Corp.

An insurance and financial services holding company.
www.torchmarkcorp.com
Annual Revenues: $2.738 billion

Chairman and Chief Exec. Officer
HUDSON, C. B. — Tel: (205) 325 - 4200; Fax: (205) 325 - 4198

Chief Exec. Officer
MCANDREW, Mark S. — Tel: (205) 325 - 4200; Fax: (205) 325 - 4198

Main Headquarters
Mailing: P.O. Box 2612, Birmingham, AL 35202 — Tel: (205) 325 - 4200; Fax: (205) 325 - 4198
Street: 2001 Third Ave. South, Birmingham, AL 35233

Political Action Committees

Torchmark Corp. Political Action Committee (Torch-PAC)
Contact: Stephen W. Still
P.O. Box 2612
Birmingham, AL 35202 — Tel: (205) 325 - 4200; Fax: (205) 325 - 4198

Contributions to Candidates: $6,000 (01/05 - 09/05)
Republicans: $6,000.

Principal Recipients

SENATE REPUBLICANS		HOUSE REPUBLICANS	
DeMint, James (SC)	$1,000	Aderholt, Robert B (AL)	$1,000
		Everett, Terry (AL)	$1,000
		Johnson, Nancy (CT)	$1,000
		Ramstad, Jim (MN)	$1,000
		Rogers, Michael (AL)	$1,000

Corporate Foundations and Giving Programs

Torchmark Corporate Contributions Program
Contact: Carol A. McCoy
P.O. Box 2612
Birmingham, AL 35202 — Tel: (205) 325 - 4200; Fax: (205) 325 - 4198

Annual Grant Total: $750,000 - $1,000,000
Geographic Preference: Area in which the company is headquartered; Alabama
Primary Interests: Higher Education; Medicine and Health Care

Public Affairs and Related Activities Personnel

At Headquarters

MCCOY, Carol A.
V. President, Associate General Counsel and Secretary — Tel: (205) 325 - 4200; Fax: (205) 325 - 4198

STILL, Stephen W.
Treasurer, Torchmark Corp. PAC — Tel: (205) 325 - 4200; Fax: (205) 325 - 4198

At Other Offices

LANE, Joyce L.
V. President, Investor Relations — Tel: (972) 569 - 3627; Fax: (972) 569 - 3696
P.O. Box 8080
McKinney, TX 75070
jlane@torchmarkco.com

The Toro Co.

An independent manufacturer and marketer of outdoor maintenance and irrigation equipment.
www.thetorocompany.com
Annual Revenues: $1.399 billion

Chairman of the Board
MELROSE, Kendrick B. — Tel: (952) 888 - 8801; Fax: (952) 887 - 7961

President and Chief Exec. Officer
HOFFMAN, Michael J. — Tel: (952) 888 - 8801; Fax: (952) 887 - 7961

Main Headquarters
Mailing: 8111 Lyndale Ave. South, Bloomington, MN 55420-1196 — Tel: (952) 888 - 8801; Fax: (952) 887 - 7961

The Toro Co.

* continued from previous page

Corporate Foundations and Giving Programs

The Toro Foundation
8111 Lyndale Ave. South — Tel: (952) 888 - 8801
Bloomington, MN 55420-1196 — Fax: (952) 887 - 7961

Annual Grant Total: $500,000 - $750,000

Public Affairs and Related Activities Personnel

At Headquarters

KOTKE, Connie — Tel: (952) 887 - 8984
Media Relations Contact — Fax: (952) 887 - 7961
pr@toro.com

WATSON, Ellen — Tel: (952) 888 - 8801
Foundation Coordinator — Fax: (952) 887 - 7961

WOLFE, Stephen P. — Tel: (952) 888 - 8801
V. President, Finance, Chief Financial Officer and Treasurer — Fax: (952) 887 - 7961
Responsibilities include investor relations.

WRIGHT, John — Tel: (952) 887 - 8865
Director, Investor Relations — Fax: (952) 887 - 7961

Total Petrochemicals USA, Inc.

Formerly ATOFINA Petrochemicals, Inc. A subsidiary of Total S.A.
Annual Revenues: $5.3 billion

Main Headquarters
Mailing: 15710 John F. Kennedy Blvd. — Tel: (281) 227 - 5000
Houston, TX 77032 — Fax: (281) 227 - 5455

Political Action Committees

Total Petrochemicals USA, Inc. Employee PAC
Contact: Cliff McFarland
15710 John F. Kennedy Blvd. — Tel: (281) 227 - 5000
Houston, TX 77032 — Fax: (281) 227 - 5455

Contributions to Candidates: $2,000 (01/05 - 09/05)
Republicans: $1,000; Other: $1,000.

Principal Recipients

HOUSE OTHER
Oberstar, James L (MN) $1,000

SENATE REPUBLICANS

HOUSE REPUBLICANS
Barton, Joe L (TX) $1,000

Corporate Foundations and Giving Programs

Total Petrochemicals Foundation
Contact: Rick Charter
15710 John F. Kennedy Blvd. — Tel: (281) 227 - 5000
Houston, TX 77032 — Fax: (281) 227 - 5455

Annual Grant Total: $100,000 - $200,000
Geographic Preference: Area(s) in which the company operates
Primary Interests: Arts and Culture; Higher Education; Medicine and Health Care; Social Services

Public Affairs and Related Activities Personnel

At Headquarters

CHARTER, Rick — Tel: (281) 227 - 5000
Chairman, Total Petrochemicals Foundation — Fax: (281) 227 - 5455

GRACE, Karyn — Tel: (281) 227 - 5466
Manager, Public Affairs and Corporate Communications — Fax: (281) 227 - 5455
karyn.grace@total.com

HAGAR, Rick — Tel: (281) 227 - 5432
Public Affairs Advisor — Fax: (281) 227 - 5466
rick.hagar@total.com

MCFARLAND, Cliff — Tel: (281) 227 - 5000
PAC Treasurer — Fax: (281) 227 - 5455

Tower Automotive, Inc.

Manufacturer of auto parts.
www.towerautomotive.com
Annual Revenues: $2.754 billion

Chairman of the Board — Tel: (248) 675 - 6000
JOHNSON, S. A. "Tony" — Fax: (248) 675 - 6200

President and Chief Exec. Officer — Tel: (248) 675 - 6000
LIGOCKI, Kathleen — Fax: (248) 675 - 6200

Main Headquarters
Mailing: 27175 Haggerty Rd. — Tel: (248) 675 - 6000
Novi, MI 48377 — Fax: (248) 675 - 6200

Public Affairs and Related Activities Personnel

At Headquarters

KERSTIN, Jeff — Tel: (248) 675 - 6000
Manager, Investor Relations — Fax: (248) 675 - 6200

NEWSOME, Susan — Tel: (248) 675 - 6000
Leader, Human Resources — Fax: (248) 675 - 6200

WENZL, Sharon — Tel: (248) 675 - 6000
Manager, Marketing and Public Relations — Fax: (248) 675 - 6200

Towers Perrin

A management, human resource and administration consulting firm.
www.towers.com
Annual Revenues: $1.441 billion

Chairman and Chief Exec. Officer — Tel: (203) 326 - 5400
MACTAS, Mark — Fax: (203) 326 - 5499
mactasm@towers.com

Main Headquarters
Mailing: One Stamford Plaza — Tel: (203) 326 - 5400
263 Tresser Blvd. — Fax: (203) 326 - 5499
Stamford, CT 06901

Public Affairs and Related Activities Personnel

At Headquarters

BODNAR, Anne Donovan — Tel: (203) 326 - 5400
Managing Director, Human Resources — Fax: (203) 326 - 5499
bodnara@towers.com

At Other Offices

CONWAY, Joseph — Tel: (914) 745 - 4175
Director, Media Relations — Fax: (914) 745 - 4180
100 Summit Lake Dr.
Valhalla, NY 10595
conwayj@towers.com

YOUNG, Kevin — Tel: (215) 246 - 6120
General Counsel — Fax: (215) 246 - 4463
Center Square
1500 Market St.
Philadelphia, PA 19102
Responsibilities include government affairs.

Toyota Motor Manufacturing North America

See listing on page 478 under Toyota Motor North America, Inc.

Toyota Motor North America, Inc.

A member of the Public Affairs Council. The American production, sales and service research and finance affiliates of the major Japanese automobile and truck manufacturer.
www.toyota.com
Annual Revenues: $128.9 billion

President and Chief Exec. Officer — Tel: (212) 223 - 0303
OTAKA, Hideaki (Harry) — Fax: (212) 750 - 3564

Main Headquarters
Mailing: Nine W. 57th St. — Tel: (212) 223 - 0303
Suite 4900 — Fax: (212) 750 - 3564
New York, NY 10019

Washington Office
Mailing: 1850 M St. NW — Tel: (202) 775 - 1700
Suite 600 — Fax: (202) 822 - 0928
Washington, DC 20036

Corporate Foundations and Giving Programs

Toyota Motor Sales, U.S.A. Corporate Giving Program
Contact: Tracy Underwood
19001 S. Western Ave. — Tel: (310) 468 - 5278
Torrance, CA 90509 — Fax: (310) 468 - 7809

Annual Grant Total: $750,000 - $1,000,000
Geographic Preference: California
Primary Interests: Arts and Culture; Health; Senior Citizens; Social Services; Youth Services
Recent Recipients: American Red Cross; Urban League

Toyota USA Foundation
Contact: Jennifer Rochkind
Nine W. 57th St. — Tel: (212) 223 - 0303
Suite 4900 — Fax: (212) 750 - 3564
New York, NY 10019

Annual Grant Total: $1,000,000 - $2,000,000
Established in 1987. Recent recipients: Learning Through Art (New York, NY), Los Angeles Educational Partnership, Louisiana Tech University, Massachusetts Pre-Engineering Program, Bay Area Video Coalition, Madison Children's Museum (Wisconsin), Pacific Science Center (Seattle), Challenger Learning Center at California State (Carson, CA), and Miami Museum of Science.
Geographic Preference: National
Primary Interests: K-12 Education; Math and Science

Toyota Motor Manufacturing North America Corporate Giving Program
Contact: Helen Donaldson
25 Atlantic Ave. — Tel: (859) 746 - 4000
Erlanger, KY 41018

Annual Grant Total: none reported

Toyota Motor North America, Inc.

** continued from previous page*

Public Affairs and Related Activities Personnel

At Headquarters

PINEDA, Patricia — Tel: (212) 223 - 0303
Group V. President, Corporate Communications and General Counsel — Fax: (212) 750 - 3564

ROCHKIND, Jennifer — Tel: (212) 223 - 0303
Contact, Toyota USA Foundation — Fax: (212) 750 - 3564

At Washington Office

CHIAPPETTA, Robert — Tel: (202) 775 - 1700
Government Affairs Representatives — Fax: (202) 822 - 0928
Registered Federal Lobbyist.

COHEN, Alan — Tel: (202) 775 - 1700
Fax: (202) 822 - 0928
Registered Federal Lobbyist.

COOPER, Josephine S. — Tel: (202) 775 - 1700
V. President, Government and Industry Affairs — Fax: (202) 822 - 0928
Registered Federal Lobbyist.

ING, Charles E. — Tel: (202) 775 - 1700
Director, Government Affairs — Fax: (202) 822 - 0928
Registered Federal Lobbyist.

QUIST, Earl C. — Tel: (202) 775 - 1700
Director, Industry Affairs — Fax: (202) 822 - 0928
Registered Federal Lobbyist.

VENNETT, David J. — Tel: (202) 775 - 1700
National Manager, Government Affairs and Special Projects — Fax: (202) 822 - 0928

VOSS, Martha — Tel: (202) 775 - 1700
Manager, Public Affairs and Issues Communications — Fax: (202) 822 - 0928

At Other Offices

DOMINICIS, Xavier — Tel: (310) 468 - 5089
National Manager, Media Relations
(Toyota Motor Sales - USA)
19001 S. Western Ave.
Torrance, CA 90509

DONALDSON, Helen — Tel: (859) 746 - 4000
Contact, Toyota Motor Manufacturing North America Giving Program
25 Atlantic Ave.
Erlanger, KY 41018

KINNAW, Kevin J. — Tel: (310) 468 - 3938
Manager, National State Government Affairs — Fax: (310) 468 - 7808
(Toyota Motor Sales - USA)
19001 S. Western Ave.
Mailstop: M/S A107
Torrance, CA 90509

KIRKPATRICK, Ron — Tel: (310) 468 - 7802
National Manager, Internal Communications — Fax: (310) 468 - 7800
19001 S. Western Ave.
Torrance, CA 90509

MILLER, Irving — Tel: (310) 468 - 5030
Group V. President, Corporate Communications — Fax: (310) 468 - 7809
(Toyota Motor Sales - USA)
19001 S. Western Ave.
Torrance, CA 90509

SIEGER, Daniel — Tel: (859) 372 - 3871
Manager, Media Relations — Fax: (859) 746 - 4569
(Toyota Motor Manufacturing North America)
25 Atlantic Ave.
Erlanger, KY 41018

UNDERWOOD, Tracy — Tel: (310) 468 - 5278
Contact, Toyota Motor Sales, U.S.A. Corporate Giving Program and Toyota USA Foundation — Fax: (310) 468 - 7809
(Toyota Motor Sales - USA)
19001 S. Western Ave.
Torrance, CA 90509

Toyota Motor Sales - USA

See listing on page 478 under Toyota Motor North America, Inc.

Toys "R" Us, Inc.

A chain of toy retail stores.

www.toysrus.com
Annual Revenues: $13 billion

Interim Chief Exec. Officer — Tel: (973) 617 - 3500
MARKEE, Richard L.

Main Headquarters
Mailing: One Geoffrey Way, Wayne, NJ 07470-2030 — Tel: (973) 617 - 3500

Corporate Foundations and Giving Programs

Children's Fund, Inc.
One Geoffrey Way
Wayne, NJ 07470-2030 — Tel: (973) 617 - 3500

Annual Grant Total: $2,000,000 - $5,000,000
Geographic Preference: National
Primary Interests: Children's Health; Social Services
Recent Recipients: Children's Miracle Network; Juvenile Diabetes Foundation; Make-A-Wish Foundation; Special Olympics

Public Affairs and Related Activities Personnel

At Headquarters

DERBY, Deborah M. — Tel: (973) 617 - 3500
Exec. V. President, Human Resources

KAY, Christopher K. — Tel: (973) 617 - 3500
Exec. V. President, Operations, General Counsel and Corporate Secretary
Responsibilities include corporate communications and corporate philanthropy.

MCLAUGHLIN, Susan — Tel: (973) 617 - 5900
Manager, Public Relations

MORAN, Ursula H. — Tel: (973) 617 - 5756
V. President, Investor Relations

Transamerica Corp.

See listing on page 8 under AEGON USA, Inc.

TransMontaigne, Inc.

Transports, stores and markets refined petroleum products and crude oil.

www.transmontaigne.com
Annual Revenues: $8.3 billion

Chairman of the Board — Tel: (303) 626 - 8200
DIETLER, Cortlandt S. — Fax: (303) 626 - 8228
cdietler@transmontaigne.com

V. Chairman, President and Chief Exec. Officer — Tel: (303) 626 - 8200
ANDERSON, Donald H. — Fax: (303) 626 - 8228
danderson@transmontaigne.com

Main Headquarters — Tel: (303) 626 - 8200; Fax: (303) 626 - 8228
Mailing: P.O. Box 5660, Denver, CO 80217
Street: 1670 Broadway, Suite 3100, Denver, CO 80202

Public Affairs and Related Activities Personnel

At Headquarters

KINARD, Judy — Tel: (303) 626 - 8213
Director, Corporate Communications — Fax: (303) 626 - 8228
jkinard@transmontaigne.com

LASRSON, Randall J. — Tel: (303) 626 - 8200
Exec. V. President and Chief Financial Officer — Fax: (303) 626 - 8228
rlarson@transmontaigne.com
Responsibilities include investor relations.

Transocean Inc.

Formerly known as Transocean Sedco Forex Inc. The world's largest offshore drilling contractor, Transocean specializes in deepwater and harsh environment drilling.

www.deepwater.com
Annual Revenues: $2.67 billion

Chairman of the Board — Tel: (713) 232 - 7500
TALBERT, J. Michael — Fax: (713) 232 - 7031

President and Chief Exec. Officer — Tel: (713) 232 - 7500
LONG, Robert L. — Fax: (713) 232 - 7031

Main Headquarters — Tel: (713) 232 - 7500; Fax: (713) 232 - 7031
Mailing: P.O. Box 2765, Houston, TX 77255-2765
Street: Four Greenway Plaza, Houston, TX 77046

Public Affairs and Related Activities Personnel

At Headquarters

CANTWELL, Guy A. — Tel: (713) 232 - 7647
Manager, Corporate Communications — Fax: (713) 232 - 7034

CHASTAIN, Jeffrey L. — Tel: (713) 232 - 7551
V. President, Investor Relations and Corporate Communications — Fax: (713) 232 - 7031

JURAN, Tim — Tel: (713) 232 - 7500
V. President, Human Resources — Fax: (713) 232 - 7031

NEWMAN, Steven L. — Tel: (713) 232 - 7500
V. President, Human Resources — Fax: (713) 232 - 7031

Transocean Sedco Forex Inc.

See listing on page 479 under Transocean Inc.

TravelCenters of America, Inc.

www.tatravelcenters.com
Annual Revenues: $2.7 billion

Chairman of the Board
KUHN, Edward P.
Tel: (440) 808 - 9100
Fax: (440) 808 - 4458
TF: (800) 961 - 2961

Chief Exec. Officer
DOANE, Tim
Tel: (440) 808 - 9100
Fax: (440) 808 - 4458
TF: (800) 961 - 2961

Main Headquarters
Mailing: 24601 Center Ridge Rd.
Suite 200
Westlake, OH 44145-5639
Tel: (440) 808 - 9100
Fax: (440) 808 - 4458
TF: (800) 961 - 2961

Public Affairs and Related Activities Personnel

At Headquarters

LIUTKUS, Tom
Director, Advertising and Public Relations
liutkus.tom@tatravelcenters.com
Tel: (440) 808 - 7364
Fax: (440) 808 - 4458
TF: (800) 961 - 2961

Travelocity.com Inc.

See listing on page 417 under Sabre Holdings Corp.

Tredegar Corp.

Manufactures plastic films and non-ferrous metal extrusions.
www.tredegar.com
Annual Revenues: $749.2 million

Chairman of the Board
GOTTWALD, John D.
Tel: (804) 330 - 1000
Fax: (804) 330 - 1177

President and Chief Exec. Officer
SCHER, Norman A.
Tel: (804) 330 - 1000
Fax: (804) 330 - 1177

Main Headquarters
Mailing: 1100 Boulders Pkwy.
Richmond, VA 23225-4035
Tel: (804) 330 - 1000
Fax: (804) 330 - 1177

Public Affairs and Related Activities Personnel

At Headquarters

CUMMINGS, Tammy H.
V. President, Human Resources
Tel: (804) 330 - 1000
Fax: (804) 330 - 1177

CUNNINGHAM, Edward A.
V. President, Corporate Communications and Investor Relations
Tel: (804) 330 - 1000
Fax: (804) 330 - 1177

Triad Hospitals, Inc.

Owns and manages hospitals and ambulatory surgery centers in small cities and selected high growth markets.
www.triadhospitals.com
Annual Revenues: $1.3 billion

Chairman and Chief Exec. Officer
SHELTON, James D.
Tel: (214) 473 - 7000

Main Headquarters
Mailing: 5800 Tennyson Pkwy.
Plano, TX 75024
Tel: (214) 473 - 7000

Political Action Committees

Triad Hospitals, Inc. Good Government Fund
Contact: Patricia G. Ball
5800 Tennyson Pkwy.
Plano, TX 75024
Tel: (214) 473 - 7000
Ext: 3752

Contributions to Candidates: $17,750 (01/05 - 09/05)
Democrats: $9,000; Republicans: $8,750.

Principal Recipients

SENATE DEMOCRATS
Conrad, Kent (ND) $5,000

HOUSE DEMOCRATS
Cramer, Bud (AL) $2,000

SENATE REPUBLICANS

HOUSE REPUBLICANS
Barton, Joe L (TX) $5,000
Ryan, Paul D (WI) $2,000

Public Affairs and Related Activities Personnel

At Headquarters

BALDWIN, Laura
Director, Finance and Investor Relations
Tel: (214) 473 - 7000
Ext: 3969

BALL, Patricia G.
V. President, Marketing and Public Affairs
Tel: (214) 473 - 7000
Ext: 3752

FRAZIER, Thomas H.
Senior V. President, Administration
Responsibilities include human resources and public affairs.
Tel: (214) 473 - 7000
Ext: 3735

THOMASON, Rick
V. President, Human Resouces
Tel: (214) 473 - 7000

Triarc Companies, Inc.

The franchisor of Arby's restaurant system and owner of approximately 235 Arby's restaurants in the U.S.
www.triarc.com

Chairman and Chief Exec. Officer
PELTZ, Nelson
Tel: (212) 451 - 3000
Fax: (212) 451 - 3134

Main Headquarters
Mailing: 280 Park Ave.
New York, NY 10017
Tel: (212) 451 - 3000
Fax: (212) 451 - 3134

Corporate Foundations and Giving Programs

Arby's Foundation
Contact: Candace Hawkins
1000 Corporate Dr.
Fort Lauderdale, FL 33334
Tel: (954) 351 - 5100
Fax: (954) 351 - 5390

Annual Grant Total: none reported
Primary Interests: Education; Youth Services
Recent Recipients: Big Brothers/Big Sisters; Boys and Girls Club

Public Affairs and Related Activities Personnel

At Headquarters

TARBELL, Anne A.
Senior V. President, Corporate Communications and Investor Relations
atarbell@triarc.com
Tel: (212) 451 - 3030
Fax: (212) 451 - 3134

At Other Offices

HAWKINS, Candace
Foundation Contact
(Arby's, Inc.)
1000 Corporate Dr.
Fort Lauderdale, FL 33334
Tel: (954) 351 - 5100
Fax: (954) 351 - 5390

Tribune Broadcasting Co.

See listing on page 480 under Tribune Co.

Tribune Co.

A leading media company with operations in television and radio broadcasting, publishing, and interactive ventures. Acquired the Times Mirror Co. in 2000.
www.tribune.com
Annual Revenues: $5.6 billion

Chairman, President and Chief Exec. Officer
FITZSIMONS, Dennis J.
Tel: (312) 222 - 9100
Fax: (312) 222 - 1573

Main Headquarters
Mailing: 435 N. Michigan Ave.
Chicago, IL 60611
Tel: (312) 222 - 9100
Fax: (312) 222 - 1573

Washington Office
Contact: Shaun M. Sheehan
Mailing: 1501 K St. NW
Suite 550
Washington, DC 20005
Tel: (202) 775 - 7750
Fax: (202) 223 - 3844

Corporate Foundations and Giving Programs

McCormick Tribune Foundation
Contact: Vicky Dinges
435 N. Michigan Ave.
Chicago, IL 60611
Tel: (312) 222 - 3512
Fax: (312) 222 - 3523

Assets: $1,500,000,000 (2004)
Annual Grant Total: over $5,000,000
Grants totalled $109 million in 2004.
Geographic Preference: National
Primary Interests: Children; Education; Health; Housing; Hunger; Journalism

Public Affairs and Related Activities Personnel

At Headquarters

DINGES, Vicky
V. President, External Affairs
Tel: (312) 222 - 3512
Fax: (312) 222 - 3523

HOWELL, Steve
V. President, Safety and Security Services
showell@tribune.com
Tel: (312) 222 - 5650
Fax: (312) 222 - 1573

LEWIN, Luis E.
Senior V. President, Human Resources
llewin@tribune.com
Tel: (312) 222 - 4581
Fax: (312) 222 - 1573

MUSIL, Ruthellyn
Senior V. President, Corporate Relations
rmusil@tribune.com
Responsibilities include investor relations.
Tel: (312) 222 - 3787
Fax: (312) 222 - 1573

REITER, Jeff
Director, Corporate Communications
jreiter@tribune.com
Tel: (312) 222 - 3303
Fax: (312) 222 - 1573

Tribune Co.

** continued from previous page*

SCHEID, Jay — Tel: (312) 222 - 4567
Director, Environmental Safety and Risk Management
jscheid@tribune.com

WEITMAN, Gary — Tel: (312) 222 - 3394, Fax: (312) 222 - 1573
V. President, Communications
gweitman@tribune.com

At Washington Office

SHEEHAN, Shaun M. — Tel: (202) 775 - 7750, Fax: (202) 223 - 3844
V. President, Washington Affairs
ssheehan@tribune.com
(Tribune Broadcasting Co.)
Registered Federal Lobbyist.

Trinity Industries, Inc.

A manufacturer of transportation, construction, and industrial products.
www.trin.net
Annual Revenues: $1.487 billion

Chairman, President and Chief Exec. Officer
WALLACE, Timothy R. — Tel: (214) 631 - 4420, Fax: (214) 689 - 0501
timothy.wallace@trin.net

Main Headquarters
Mailing: 2525 Stemmons Fwy.
Dallas, TX 75207-2401 — Tel: (214) 631 - 4420, Fax: (214) 689 - 0501

Political Action Committees

Trinity Industries Employee PAC (SF) Inc.
Contact: Mike Mason
2525 Stemmons Fwy.
Dallas, TX 75207-2401 — Tel: (214) 631 - 4420, Fax: (214) 689 - 0501

Contributions to Candidates: $10,600 (01/05 - 09/05)
Democrats: $2,500; Republicans: $8,100.

Principal Recipients

SENATE DEMOCRATS	HOUSE DEMOCRATS	
	Edwards, Chet (TX)	$2,500
SENATE REPUBLICANS	**HOUSE REPUBLICANS**	
	Johnson, Samuel (TX)	$2,100
	DeLay, Tom (TX)	$2,000

Public Affairs and Related Activities Personnel

At Headquarters

CUNNINGHAM, Jack — Tel: (214) 631 - 4420, Fax: (214) 689 - 0501
V. President, Human Resources
jack.cunningham@trin.net

MASON, Mike — Tel: (214) 631 - 4420, Fax: (214) 689 - 0501
PAC Treasurer
mike.mason@trin.net

SHOOP, Neil — Tel: (214) 631 - 4420, Fax: (214) 689 - 0501
Director, Investor Relations
neil.shoop@trin.net

At Other Offices

SICKELS, Linda S. — Tel: (512) 478 - 4844
V. President, Government Relations
316 W. 12th St.
Suite 102
Austin, TX 78701
linda.sickels@trin.net

Triple Canopy, Inc.

A security solutions company.
www.triplecanopy.com

Main Headquarters
Mailing: 2250 Corporate Park Dr.
Suite 300
Herndon, VA 20171-4835 — Tel: (703) 673 - 5000, Fax: (703) 673 - 5001

Public Affairs and Related Activities Personnel

At Headquarters

MAYO, Joseph — Tel: (703) 673 - 5000, Fax: (703) 673 - 5001
Director, Public Affairs

PTAK, Alan C. — Tel: (703) 673 - 5000, Fax: (703) 673 - 5001
V. President, Government Relations

Tropicana Products

See listing on page 377 under PepsiCo, Inc.

Truckstops of America

See listing on page 480 under TravelCenters of America, Inc.

True Value Company

Formerly TruServ Corp. A hardware retailer.
www.truevaluecompany.com

Chairman of the Board
ABLEIDINGER, Bryan — Tel: (773) 695 - 5000

President and Chief Exec. Officer
HEIDEMANN, Lyle — Tel: (773) 695 - 5000

Main Headquarters
Mailing: 8600 W. Bryn Mawr Ave.
Chicago, IL 60631-3505 — Tel: (773) 695 - 5000

Public Affairs and Related Activities Personnel

At Headquarters

MYSEL, Amy — Tel: (773) 695 - 5000
Senior V. President, Human Resources and Communications

Trump Hotels and Casino Resorts, Inc.

Real estate holding company.
www.trumponline.com
Annual Revenues: $1.23 billion

Chairman, President, and Chief Exec. Officer
TRUMP, Donald J. — Tel: (212) 832 - 2000, Fax: (212) 935 - 0141

Main Headquarters
Mailing: 725 Fifth Ave.
18th Floor
New York, NY 10022 — Tel: (212) 891 - 1500, Fax: (212) 935 - 0141

Public Affairs and Related Activities Personnel

At Headquarters

FUSCO, Joseph A. — Tel: (212) 891 - 1500, Fax: (212) 935 - 0141
Exec. V. President, Government Relations and Regulatory Affairs

TruServ Corp.

See listing on page 481 under True Value Company.

Trustmark Nat'l Bank

PUBLIC AFFAIRS COUNCIL

www.trustmark.com
Annual Revenues: $547.8 million

Chairman and Chief Exec. Officer
HICKSON, Richard G. — Tel: (601) 208 - 5111

Main Headquarters
Mailing: P.O. Box 291
Jackson, MS 39205-0291 — Tel: (601) 208 - 5111
Street: 248 E. Capitol St.
Jackson, MS 39201

Corporate Foundations and Giving Programs

Trustmark Nat'l Bank Corporate Contributions
Contact: R. Gray Wiggers, Jr.
P.O. Box 291
Jackson, MS 39205-0291 — Tel: (601) 208 - 5111

Annual Grant Total: none reported
Geographic Preference: Area(s) in which the company operates; Mississippi
Primary Interests: Arts and Culture; Community Development; Economic Development; Education; Health; Human Welfare
Recent Recipients: American Cancer Society; Make-A-Wish Foundation

Public Affairs and Related Activities Personnel

At Headquarters

WIGGERS, R. Gray, Jr. — Tel: (601) 208 - 5111
Senior V. President, Public Affairs
Responsibilities include corporate philanthropy.

TRW Automotive

An automotive supplier. The Blackstone Group L.P., located in New York, New York, owns an 80% stake in the company and Northrop Grumman Corp. (see separate listing) owns a 20% stake.
www.trwauto.com

President and Chief Exec. Officer
PLANT, John C. — Tel: (734) 855 - 2600, Fax: (734) 855 - 2473

Main Headquarters
Mailing: 12025 Tech Center Dr.
Livonia, MI 48150 — Tel: (734) 855 - 2600, Fax: (734) 855 - 5702

Washington Office
Contact: Kevin McMahon
Mailing: 1100 Wilson Blvd.
Suite 1225
Arlington, VA 22209 — Tel: (703) 224 - 0931

Political Action Committees

TRW Acquisition Corp. Good Government Fund
Contact: Kevin McMahon
1100 Wilson Blvd.
Suite 1225
Arlington, VA 22209 — Tel: (703) 224 - 0931

TRW Automotive

** continued from previous page*

Contributions to Candidates: $2,000 (01/05 - 09/05)
Republicans: $2,000.

Principal Recipients

SENATE REPUBLICANS	HOUSE REPUBLICANS	
	Knollenberg, Joe (MI)	$1,000
	Rogers, Michael J (MI)	$1,000

Public Affairs and Related Activities Personnel

At Headquarters

FORD, Manley — Tel: (734) 855 - 2616
Director, Public Relations and Communications — Fax: (734) 855 - 2696
manley.l.ford@trw.com

WILKERSON, John — Tel: (734) 855 - 3864
Senior Manager, Communications - North America — Fax: (734) 855 - 2450
john.wilkerson@trw.com

At Washington Office

MCMAHON, Kevin — Tel: (703) 224 - 0931
V. President, Government Relations
Registered Federal Lobbyist.
Responsiblities include political action and government affairs.

TRW, Inc.

See listing on page 353 under Northrop Grumman Corp.

TU Electric

See listing on page 482 under TXU.

Tupperware Corp.

Direct seller of storage and serving containers and toys.
www.tupperware.com
Annual Revenues: $1.114 billion

Chairman and Chief Exec. Officer — Tel: (407) 826 - 5050
GOINGS, E. V. "Rick" — Fax: (407) 826 - 4525
TF: (800) 366 - 3800

Main Headquarters
Mailing: P.O. Box 2353 — Tel: (407) 826 - 5050
Orlando, FL 32802-2353 — Fax: (407) 826 - 4525
TF: (800) 366 - 3800

Street: 14901 S. Orange Blossom Trail
Orlando, FL 32837

Political Action Committees

Tupperware PAC
P.O. Box 2353 — Tel: (407) 826 - 5050
Orlando, FL 32802-2353 — Fax: (407) 826 - 4525
TF: (800) 366 - 3800

Contributions to Candidates: none reported (01/05 - 09/05)

Corporate Foundations and Giving Programs

Tupperware Children's Foundation
Contact: Mark W. Shamley
P.O. Box 2353 — Tel: (407) 826 - 8755
Orlando, FL 32802-2353 — Fax: (407) 826 - 4525

Annual Grant Total: none reported

Public Affairs and Related Activities Personnel

At Headquarters

GARCIA, Lillian D. — Tel: (407) 826 - 8224
Senior V. President, Human Resources-Worldwide — Fax: (407) 826 - 4525
lilliangarcia@tupperware.com — TF: (800) 366 - 3800

GARRARD, Jane — Tel: (407) 826 - 8266
V. President, Investor and Media Relations — Fax: (407) 826 - 4510
finrel@tupperware.com — TF: (800) 366 - 3800

SHAMLEY, Mark W. — Tel: (407) 826 - 8755
Director, Global Corporate Citizenship — Fax: (407) 826 - 4525
markshamley@tupperware.com

Turner Broadcasting System, Inc.

A leading global media company and subsidiary of Time Warner Inc. (see separate listing), which includes 12 U.S. and international television networks, movie and animation studios, and professional sports franchises.
www.turner.com
Annual Revenues: $7.655 billion

Chairman and Chief Exec. Officer — Tel: (404) 827 - 1700
KENT, Philip I. — Fax: (404) 827 - 2024

Main Headquarters
Mailing: P.O. Box 105366 — Tel: (404) 827 - 1700
One CNN Center — Fax: (404) 827 - 2024
Atlanta, GA 30348-5366

Street: One CNN Center
Atlanta, GA 30303

Corporate Foundations and Giving Programs

Turner Broadcasting Corporate Contributions
101 Marietta St. — Tel: (404) 878 - 1073
15th Floor
Atlanta, GA 30303

Annual Grant Total: none reported
Geographic Preference: Atlanta, GA
Primary Interests: Arts and Culture; Education; Environment/Conservation

Public Affairs and Related Activities Personnel

At Headquarters

CHASTAIN, Judy — Tel: (404) 827 - 1700
Senior V. President, Media Services — Fax: (404) 827 - 2024
judy.chastain@turner.com

CHRISTY, Kristina — Tel: (404) 878 - 1073
Manager, Corporate Contributions — Fax: (404) 827 - 6575
krsitina.koldoff@turner.com

FEAZELL, Donna — Tel: (404) 827 - 3835
Community Relations — Fax: (404) 827 - 2024
(Atlanta Hawks)

HICKMAN, Terri — Tel: (404) 827 - 3149
Director, Community Relations — Fax: (404) 827 - 2024
(Atlanta Thrashers)

HOLLAND, Betsy — Tel: (404) 827 - 1170
Manager, Community Relations — Fax: (404) 827 - 2437
betsy.humphries@turner.com

REGAL, Kelly — Tel: (404) 827 - 1700
Exec. V. President, Human Resources and Corporate Communications — Fax: (404) 827 - 2024

The Turner Corp.

A commercial, industrial, institutional and multi-unit residential construction company.
www.turnerconstruction.com
Annual Revenues: $6.06 billion

Chairman and Chief Exec. Officer — Tel: (212) 229 - 6000
LEPPERT, Thomas C. — Fax: (212) 229 - 6390

Main Headquarters
Mailing: 375 Hudson St. — Tel: (212) 229 - 6000
New York, NY 10014 — Fax: (212) 229 - 6390

Public Affairs and Related Activities Personnel

At Headquarters

ECKHART, Shannon B. — Tel: (212) 229 - 6084
Public Relations Associate — Fax: (212) 229 - 6390
seckhart@tcco.com

KUFLICK, Terry — Tel: (212) 229 - 6379
Director, Public Relations — Fax: (212) 229 - 6390
tkuflik@tcco.com

SLEEMAN, Donald G. — Tel: (212) 229 - 6000
Exec. V. President and Chief Financial Officer — Fax: (212) 229 - 6390
dsleeman@tcco.com
Responsibilities include investor relations.

TXU

A member of the Public Affairs Council. A provider of integrated energy solutions.
www.txucorp.com
Annual Revenues: $10 billion

Chairman, President and Chief Exec. Officer — Tel: (214) 812 - 4447
WILDER, C. John

Main Headquarters
Mailing: P.O. Box 227097 — Tel: (214) 812 - 4600
Dallas, TX 75222-7097
Street: Energy Plaza
1601 Bryan St.
Dallas, TX 75201-3411

Washington Office
Mailing: 601 Pennsylvania Ave. NW — Tel: (202) 628 - 2747
South Bldg., Suite 850 — Fax: (202) 628 - 1007
Washington, DC 20004

Political Action Committees

Electrical Delivery PAC of TXU Corp.
Contact: Tammy Porter
500 N. Akard St. — Tel: (214) 812 - 4600
Suite 12-045
Dallas, TX 75201

Contributions to Candidates: $60,008 (01/05 - 09/05)

TXU

* continued from previous page

Democrats: $10,008; Republicans: $50,000.

Principal Recipients

SENATE DEMOCRATS		HOUSE DEMOCRATS	
		Ortiz, Solomon (TX)	$2,500
		Edwards, Chet (TX)	$2,000

SENATE REPUBLICANS		HOUSE REPUBLICANS	
		Barton, Joe L (TX)	$7,000
		Bonilla, Henry (TX)	$5,000
		Burgess, Michael (TX)	$5,000
		DeLay, Tom (TX)	$5,000
		Gohmert, Louis (TX)	$4,000
		Conaway, K Michael (TX)	$3,000
		Poe, Ted (TX)	$3,000
		Sessions, Pete (TX)	$3,000
		Blunt, Roy (MO)	$2,000
		Brady, Kevin Patrick (TX)	$2,000
		Hall, Ralph (TX)	$2,000
		Marchant, Kenny (TX)	$2,000
		Neugebauer, Randy (TX)	$2,000

Power and Energy PAC of TXU Corp.
Contact: Jacob Gonzales
1717 Main St.
Dallas, TX 75201

Contributions to Candidates: $47,500 (01/05 - 09/05)
Democrats: $15,500; Republicans: $32,000.

Principal Recipients

SENATE DEMOCRATS		HOUSE DEMOCRATS	
		Green, Gene (TX)	$3,500
		Edwards, Chet (TX)	$2,000
		Gonzalez, Charles A (TX)	$2,000
		Reyes, Silvestre (TX)	$2,000

SENATE REPUBLICANS		HOUSE REPUBLICANS	
Thomas, Craig (WY)	$3,000	Carter, John (TX)	$4,000
		Barton, Joe L (TX)	$3,000
		McCaul, Michael (TX)	$3,000
		Granger, Kay N (TX)	$2,500
		Hall, Ralph (TX)	$2,000
		Pombo, Richard (CA)	$2,000

TXU Corp. Political Action Committee
Contact: Jeff Westerheide
P.O. Box 227097 — Tel: (214) 812 - 4600
Dallas, TX 75222-7097

Contributions to Candidates: $23,000 (01/05 - 09/05)
Democrats: $3,500; Republicans: $19,500.

Corporate Foundations and Giving Programs

TXU Contributions Program
P.O. Box 227097 — Tel: (214) 812 - 4600
Dallas, TX 75222-7097

Annual Grant Total: $750,000 - $1,000,000
Geographic Preference: Area(s) in which the company operates; Texas

Public Affairs and Related Activities Personnel

At Headquarters

ATTERIDGE, Susan — Tel: (214) 812 - 8822
Senior V. President and Chief Communications Officer
susan.atteridge@txu.com

HARRISON, Jackie — Tel: (214) 812 - 4715; Fax: (214) 812 - 7077
Manager, Shareholder Services
jackie.harrison@txu.com

HOGAN, Timothy R. — Tel: (214) 875 - 9275
Director, Investor Relations
thogan@txu.com

JORDAN, Walt — Tel: (214) 812 - 2660; Fax: (214) 812 - 3455
Director, Policy Campaign
Mailstop: Suite 37-024

ROSE, Tom — Tel: (214) 812 - 3247; Fax: (214) 812 - 3455
Director, Public Policy
Mailstop: Suite 37-054
tom.rose@txu.com

SCHEIN, Chris — Tel: (214) 812 - 5338; Fax: (214) 812 - 3176
Director, Media and Public Relations

SEIDLITS, Curtis — Tel: (214) 812 - 4600; Fax: (214) 812 - 4758
Senior V. President, Governmental Advocacy
cseidlits@txu.com

WESTERHEIDE, Jeff — Tel: (214) 812 - 4600
Treasurer, TXU Corp. PAC

YANAWAY, Diane — Tel: (214) 812 - 4905; Fax: (214) 812 - 4974
Director, Public Advocacy
dyanawa1@txu.com

At Washington Office

LYNCH, David — Tel: (202) 628 - 2748; Fax: (202) 628 - 1007
Director, Federal Advocacy
dlynch1@txu.com

MCNEILL, Laura — Tel: (202) 628 - 2749; Fax: (202) 628 - 1007
Manager, Federal Advocacy

At Other Offices

GONZALES, Jacob
Treasurer, Power and Energy PAC of TXU Corp.
1717 Main St.
Dallas, TX 75201

PORTER, Tammy — Tel: (214) 812 - 4600
Treasurer, Electrical Delivery PAC of TXU Corp.
500 N. Akard St.
Suite 12-045
Dallas, TX 75201

Tyco Capital

See listing on page 121 under The CIT Group, Inc.

Tyco Electronics Corp.

A manufacturer of electronic and fiber-optic connectors and interconnection systems components. A subsidiary of Tyco Internat'l (U.S.) (see separate listing).
www.tycoelectronics.com

Main Headquarters
Mailing: P.O. Box 3608, Harrisburg, PA 17105-3608 — Tel: (717) 564 - 0100; Fax: (717) 592 - 4022
Street: 2901 Fulling Mill Rd., Middletown, PA 17057

Corporate Foundations and Giving Programs

Tyco Electronics Foundation
Contact: Mary Rakoczy
P.O. Box 3608 — Tel: (717) 592 - 4869; Fax: (717) 592 - 4022
Harrisburg, PA 17105-3608

Assets: $15,400,000 (2004)
Annual Grant Total: $1,000,000 - $2,000,000
Formerly the AMP Foundation. Preference: emphasis given to programs that address a business or community concern of Tyco Electronics and communities where the company has a significant employee presence.
Geographic Preference: Area(s) in which the company operates
Primary Interests: Children; Education; Math and Science
Recent Recipients: Massachusetts Institute of Technology; Pennsylvania State University

Public Affairs and Related Activities Personnel

At Headquarters

RAKOCZY, Mary — Tel: (717) 592 - 4869; Fax: (717) 592 - 4022
Contact, Tyco Electronics Foundation
Mailstop: MS 140-10
mjrakoczy@tycoelectronic.com

Tyco Healthcare Group

See listing on page 483 under Tyco Internat'l (US), Inc.

Tyco Internat'l (U.S.), Inc.

PUBLIC AFFAIRS COUNCIL

A member of the Public Affairs Council. Formerly known as Tyco Laboratories, Inc. A manufacturer of fire protection and flow control products, packaging materials and electrical and electronic components. Acquired Sensormatic Electronics Corp. in 2001.
www.tyco.com
Annual Revenues: $34.037 billion

Chairman and Chief Exec. Officer
BREEN, Edward D. — Tel: (609) 720 - 4200; Fax: (609) 720 - 4208

Main Headquarters
Mailing: Nine Roszel Rd., Princeton, NJ 08540 — Tel: (609) 720 - 4200; Fax: (609) 720 - 4208

Washington Office
Mailing: 122 C St. NW, Suite 520, Washington, DC 20001 — Tel: (202) 393 - 5100; Fax: (202) 393 - 5110

Corporate Foundations and Giving Programs

Tyco Internat'l Corporate Giving Fund

Tyco Internat'l (U.S.), Inc.

** continued from previous page*

Nine Roszel Rd.
Princeton, NJ 08540
Tel: (609) 720 - 4200
Fax: (609) 720 - 4208

Annual Grant Total: none reported

Public Affairs and Related Activities Personnel

At Headquarters

ARDITTE, Ed
Senior V. President, Investor Relations
Tel: (609) 720 - 4621
Fax: (609) 720 - 4208

POLK, David
Media Contact
dpolk@tyco.com
Tel: (609) 720 - 4387
Fax: (609) 720 - 4208

SIEGEL, Laurie
Senior V. President, Human Resources
Tel: (609) 720 - 4200
Fax: (609) 720 - 4208

WOODRUFF, Sheri L.
Media Contact
Tel: (609) 720 - 4399
Fax: (609) 720 - 4208

YOUNG, Charles
Senior V. President, Corporate Marketing and Communications
Responsibilities include corporate philanthropy and community relations.
Tel: (609) 720 - 4200
Fax: (609) 720 - 4208

At Washington Office

BUNNING, Susan
Manager, Public Affairs
(Tyco Healthcare Group)
Registered Federal Lobbyist.
Tel: (202) 393 - 5100
Fax: (202) 393 - 5110

HARSANYI, Dr. Fruzsina M.
V. President, Public Affairs
Registered Federal Lobbyist.
Tel: (202) 393 - 5100
Fax: (202) 393 - 5110

JONES, Art
Registered Federal Lobbyist.
Tel: (202) 393 - 5100
Fax: (202) 393 - 5110

POLGAR, Thomas C.
Senior V. President, Public Affairs
Tel: (202) 393 - 5100
Fax: (202) 393 - 5110

Tyco Laboratories

See listing on page 483 under Tyco Internat'l (US), Inc.

Tyson Foods, Inc.

A processor of chicken, beef, and pork and a manufacturer of flour and corn tortilla products.

www.tyson.com
Annual Revenues: $24.5 billion

Chairman and Chief Exec. Officer
TYSON, John H.
john.tyson@tyson.com
Tel: (479) 290 - 4000
Fax: (479) 290 - 7849
TF: (800) 643 - 3410

Main Headquarters
Mailing: P.O. Box 2020
Springdale, AR 72765-2020
Tel: (479) 290 - 4000
TF: (800) 424 - 4253
Street: 2210 W. Oaklawn Dr.
Springdale, AR 72762-6999

Washington Office
Contact: Sara J. Lilygren
Mailing: 601 Pennsylvania Ave., NW
Suite 750 South
Washington, DC 20004
Tel: (202) 393 - 3921
Fax: (202) 393 - 3922

Political Action Committees

Tyson Foods Inc. Political Action Committee (TYPAC)
Contact: Chris Alsip
P.O. Box 2020
Springdale, AR 72765-2020
Tel: (479) 290 - 4000
Fax: (479) 290 - 7984
TF: (800) 643 - 3410

Contributions to Candidates: $34,885 (01/05 - 09/05)
Democrats: $13,385; Republicans: $21,500.

Principal Recipients

SENATE DEMOCRATS		HOUSE DEMOCRATS	
		Berry, Marion (AR)	$4,385
		Thompson, Bennie (MS)	$2,000
SENATE REPUBLICANS		**HOUSE REPUBLICANS**	
Talent, James (MO)	$3,000	Blunt, Roy (MO)	$2,000
Santorum, Richard (PA)	$2,500	Bonilla, Henry (TX)	$2,000
		Boozman, John (AR)	$2,000
		King, Steven (IA)	$2,000

Corporate Foundations and Giving Programs

Tyson Foods Foundation
Contact: Annetta Young
P.O. Box 2020
Springdale, AR 72765-2020
Tel: (479) 290 - 4000
Fax: (479) 290 - 7984
TF: (800) 424 - 4253

Assets: $995,028 (2003)
Annual Grant Total: $1,000,000 - $2,000,000

Sponsors the Tyson Foundation 2/4 Year Scholarship Program for students majoring in certain areas of Business, Agriculture, Engineering, Computer Science, or Nursing. Sponsors only children of team members.

Geographic Preference: Area(s) in which the company operates; Arkansas; Georgia; Illinois; Iowa; Mississippi; Missouri; North Carolina; Oklahoma; Pennsylvania; Tennessee; Texas; Virginia; Alabama

Primary Interests: Community Affairs; Education; Social Services

Public Affairs and Related Activities Personnel

At Headquarters

ALSIP, Chris
Treasurer, Tyson Foods Inc. PAC
chris.alsip@tyson.com
Tel: (479) 290 - 4000
Fax: (479) 290 - 7984
TF: (800) 643 - 3410

BARBER, Willie
Consumer Relations Manager
willie.barber@tyson.com
Tel: (479) 290 - 4000
Fax: (479) 290 - 7930
TF: (800) 643 - 3410

GOTTSPONER, Louis C., Jr.
Assistant Secretary and Director, Investor Relations
louis.gottsponer@tyson.com
Tel: (479) 290 - 4826
Fax: (479) 290 - 4061
TF: (800) 643 - 3410

KIMBRO, Kenneth J.
Senior V. President, Human Resources
ken.kimbro@tyson.com
Tel: (479) 290 - 4000
TF: (800) 424 - 4253

LAWSON, Libby
V. President, Public and Community Relations
libby.lawson@tyson.com
Tel: (479) 290 - 3486
Fax: (479) 290 - 7984
TF: (800) 424 - 4253

MICKELSON, Gary R.
Director, Corporate Media Relations
gary.mickelson@tyson.com
Tel: (479) 290 - 4000
Fax: (479) 290 - 7984
TF: (800) 424 - 4253

MOHNEY, Mike
Director, Internal Communications
mike.mohney@tyson.com
Tel: (479) 290 - 4000
Fax: (479) 290 - 7984
TF: (800) 643 - 3410

NICHOLSON, Ed
Director, Corporate Community Relations
ed.nicholson@tyson.com
Tel: (479) 290 - 4591
Fax: (479) 290 - 7984
TF: (800) 643 - 3410

SCHAFFER, Archie, III
Senior V. President, External Relations
archie.schffer@tyson.com
Responsibilities include corporate contributions.
Tel: (479) 290 - 7232
Fax: (479) 290 - 7984
TF: (800) 643 - 3410

YOUNG, Annetta
Administrator, Corporate Giving
annetta.young@tyson.com
Tel: (479) 290 - 4000
Fax: (479) 290 - 7984
TF: (800) 424 - 4253

At Washington Office

LILYGREN, Sara J.
Director, Federal Government Affairs
sara.lilygren@tyson.com
Tel: (202) 393 - 3921
Fax: (202) 393 - 3922

VENEGAS, Nora H.
Manager, Federal Government Relations
Tel: (202) 393 - 3921
Fax: (202) 393 - 3922

U-Haul Internat'l, Inc.

See listing on page 28 under AMERCO.

U.S. Bancorp Piper Jaffray Inc.

www.piperjaffray.com
Annual Revenues: $831 million

Chairman of the Board
DUFF, Andrew S.
Tel: (612) 303 - 6000

Main Headquarters
Mailing: 800 Nicollet Mall
Suite 800
Minneapolis, MN 55402
Tel: (612) 303 - 6000

Corporate Foundations and Giving Programs

U.S. Bancorp Piper Jaffray Inc. Corporate Contributions Program
800 Nicollet Mall
Suite 800
Minneapolis, MN 55402
Tel: (612) 303 - 6000

Annual Grant Total: none reported

Public Affairs and Related Activities Personnel

At Headquarters

BEATTY, Susan
V. President, Communications
Tel: (612) 303 - 6000

U.S. Bancorp Piper Jaffray Inc.

* continued from previous page

CLAYTON, Pamela L. — Tel: (612) 303 - 6000
Head of Human Resources

KEWITSCH, Kris — Tel: (612) 303 - 6000
Manager, Community Relations
Mailstop: JI3S25
kristin.k.kewitsch@pjc.com

OLSON-GOUDE, Jennifer A. — Tel: (612) 303 - 6277
Director, Communications and Investor Relations
jennifer.a.olson-goude@pjc.com

At Other Offices

FREEMAN, Erin K. — Tel: (415) 277 - 1595
Director, Public Relations
353 Sacramento St.
Suite 1600
San Francisco, CA 94111

WADE, Dana H.
V. President, Public Affairs and Media Relations
345 California St.
Suite 2200
San Francisco, CA 94104
dana.h.wade@pjc.com

U.S. Borax Inc.

www.borax.com

Main Headquarters
Mailing: 26877 Tourney Rd. — Tel: (661) 287 - 5400
Valencia, CA 91355 — Fax: (661) 287 - 5495

Public Affairs and Related Activities Personnel

At Headquarters

KEEFE, Susan — Tel: (661) 287 - 5484
Manager, Global Public Affairs — Fax: (661) 287 - 5495
susan.keefe@borax.com

SAPERSTEIN, Steve — Tel: (661) 287 - 5400
Chief Human Resources Officer — Fax: (661) 287 - 5495
steve.saperstein@borax.com

U.S. Foodservice

Distributes food and related products to restaurants.
www.usfoodservice.com
Annual Revenues: $17 billion

Chief Exec. Officer — Tel: (410) 312 - 7100
BENJAMIN, Lawrence S. — Fax: (410) 312 - 7167

Main Headquarters
Mailing: 9755 Patuxent Woods Dr. — Tel: (410) 312 - 7100
Columbia, MD 21046 — Fax: (410) 312 - 7167

Public Affairs and Related Activities Personnel

At Headquarters

RILEY, Dawn — Tel: (410) 312 - 7100
Public Relations Contact — Fax: (410) 312 - 7167

U.S. Trust Corp.

A wealth management company that provides investment management, fiduciary planning, and private banking services to affluent individuals, families, and institutions. A subsidiary of The Charles Schwab Corp. (see separate listing).
www.ustrust.com

Chairman and Chief Exec. Officer — Tel: (212) 852 - 1000
SCATURRO, Peter K. — Fax: (212) 852 - 1140

Main Headquarters
Mailing: 114 W. 47th St. — Tel: (212) 852 - 1000
New York, NY 10036 — Fax: (212) 852 - 1140

Washington Office
Mailing: 600 14th St. NW — Tel: (202) 585 - 4100
Suite 400
Washington, DC 20005

Corporate Foundations and Giving Programs

U.S. Trust Corp. Foundation
Contact: Carol A. Strickland
114 W. 47th St. — Tel: (212) 852 - 1400
New York, NY 10036 — Fax: (212) 852 - 1341

Annual Grant Total: none reported
Email address is foundation@ustrust.com. Giving is concentrated in, but not exclusive to, New York City.
Geographic Preference: New York City
Primary Interests: Arts and Culture; Civic and Cultural Activities; Community Affairs; Housing; Social Services; Urban Affairs

Public Affairs and Related Activities Personnel

At Headquarters

KELLOGG, Allison Cooke — Tel: (212) 852 - 1127
Senior V. President, Public Relations — Fax: (212) 852 - 1140

STRICKLAND, Carol A. — Tel: (212) 852 - 1400
Managing Director, Corporate Secretary — Fax: (212) 852 - 1341
Responsibilities include corporate philanthropy.

At Washington Office

SMITH, Leslie — Tel: (202) 585 - 4100
Managing Director, Washington Office

UBS Financial Services Inc.

Formerly UBS PaineWebber Inc.
www.ubs.com

Main Headquarters
Mailing: 1285 Ave. of the Americas — Tel: (212) 713 - 2000
New York, NY 10019-6028 — Fax: (212) 713 - 1087

Washington Office
Contact: John Savercool
Mailing: 1501 K St. NW — Tel: (202) 585 - 4000
Suite 1100
Washington, DC 20005

Political Action Committees

UBS Americas Fund for Better Government
Contact: Per Dyrvik
1285 Ave. of the Americas — Tel: (212) 713 - 2000
New York, NY 10019-6028 — Fax: (212) 713 - 1087

Contributions to Candidates: $284,500 (01/05 - 09/05)
Democrats: $106,500; Republicans: $178,000.

Principal Recipients

SENATE DEMOCRATS		HOUSE DEMOCRATS	
Baucus, Max (MT)	$10,000	Cardin, Ben (MD)	$10,000
Carper, Thomas R (DE)	$10,000	Moore, Dennis (KS)	$10,000
Lieberman, Joe (CT)	$10,000		

SENATE REPUBLICANS		HOUSE REPUBLICANS	
Allen, George (VA)	$9,000	Baker, Hugh (LA)	$10,000
Kyl, Jon L (AZ)	$8,000	Sessions, Pete (TX)	$10,000
Bennett, Robert F (UT)	$5,000	Shays, Christopher (CT)	$10,000
Santorum, Richard (PA)	$5,000	Hensarling, Jeb (TX)	$6,000

Corporate Foundations and Giving Programs

UBS Giving Program
1285 Ave. of the Americas — Tel: (212) 713 - 2000
New York, NY 10019-6028 — Fax: (212) 713 - 1087

Annual Grant Total: none reported
Primary Interests: Education

Public Affairs and Related Activities Personnel

At Headquarters

ARENA, Mark — Tel: (212) 713 - 2027
Managing Director, Corporate Communications — Fax: (212) 713 - 1087

DYRVIK, Per — Tel: (212) 713 - 2000
Treasurer, UBS Americas Fund for Better Government — Fax: (212) 713 - 1087

KAGEL, Kris — Tel: (212) 713 - 8703
Contact, Community Affairs — Fax: (212) 713 - 1087

At Washington Office

COLE, Jason — Tel: (202) 585 - 4000
Associate Director, Federal Affairs Manager, UBS Americas
Registered Federal Lobbyist.

SAVERCOOL, John — Tel: (202) 585 - 4000
Exec. Director and Senior Lobbyist, UBS Americas
Registered Federal Lobbyist.

UBS PaineWebber Inc.

See listing on page 485 under UBS Financial Services Inc.

UGI Corp.

Retail distributor of propane and natural gas and electricity.
www.ugicorp.com
Annual Revenues: $2.21 billion

Chairman and Chief Exec. Officer — Tel: (610) 337 - 1000
GREENBERG, Lon R. — Fax: (610) 992 - 3254
greenbergl@ugicorp.com

Main Headquarters
Mailing: P.O. Box 858 — Tel: (610) 337 - 1000
Valley Forge, PA 19482 — Fax: (610) 992 - 3259
Street: 460 N. Gulph Rd.
King of Prussia, PA 19406

Political Action Committees

UGI Corp. Political Action Committee (UGI/PAC)

UGI Corp.

** continued from previous page*

P.O. Box 858
Valley Forge, PA 19482
Tel: (610) 337 - 1000
Fax: (610) 992 - 3259

Contributions to Candidates: none reported (01/05 - 09/05)

Public Affairs and Related Activities Personnel

At Headquarters

BLAKE, Brenda
Media/Investor Relations Coordinator
blakeb@ugicorp.com
Tel: (610) 337 - 1000 Ext: 3202
Fax: (610) 992 - 3259

MCCOWN, Lynn
V. President, Human Resources
Tel: (610) 337 - 1000
Fax: (610) 992 - 3259

At Other Offices

WHITMOYER, Heidi A. F.
PAC Treasurer
P.O. Box 13009
Reading, PA 19612

UMB Financial Corp.

A financial holding company.

www.umb.com
Annual Revenues: $606.9 million

Chairman and Chief Exec. Officer
KEMPER, J. Mariner
Tel: (816) 860 - 7000
Fax: (816) 860 - 5675

Main Headquarters
Mailing: P.O. Box 419226
Kansas City, MO 64141-6226
Tel: (816) 860 - 7000
Fax: (816) 860 - 5675
Street: 1010 Grand Blvd.
Kansas City, MO 64106

Corporate Foundations and Giving Programs

UMB Financial Corp. Corporate Contributions Program
Contact: Jan Leonard
P.O. Box 419226
Kansas City, MO 64141-6226
Tel: (816) 860 - 7000
Fax: (816) 860 - 5675

Annual Grant Total: none reported

Public Affairs and Related Activities Personnel

At Headquarters

LEONARD, Jan
Managing Director, Charitable Trust
Responsibilites include corporate philanthropy.
Tel: (816) 860 - 7000
Fax: (816) 860 - 5675

MILLER, Heather K.
Senior V. President, Marketing Communications
Tel: (816) 860 - 7000
Fax: (816) 860 - 5675

UNC Inc.

See listing on page 213 under General Electric Co.

Unicom Corp.

See listing on page 187 under Exelon Corp.

Unifi, Inc.

A manufacturer of yarns by texturing of synthetic filament polyester and nylon fibers and the spinning of cotton and cotton blend fibers.

www.unifi-inc.com
Annual Revenues: $849.1 million

Chairman, President and Chief Exec. Officer
PARKE, Brian R.
Tel: (336) 294 - 4410
Fax: (336) 294 - 5422

Main Headquarters
Mailing: P.O. Box 19109
Greensboro, NC 27419-9109
Tel: (336) 294 - 4410
Fax: (336) 294 - 5422
Street: 7201 W. Friendly Ave.
Greensboro, NC 27410

Public Affairs and Related Activities Personnel

At Headquarters

JOHNSON, Jane L.
Director, Governmental Affairs
Tel: (336) 294 - 4410
Fax: (336) 294 - 5422

LOWE, William M., Jr.
Chief Operating Officer and Chief Financial Officer
Responsibilities include investor relations.
Tel: (336) 316 - 5664
Fax: (336) 294 - 5422

Unified Western Grocers, Inc.

A food products distributor.

www.uwgrocers.com
Annual Revenues: $2.8 billion

President and Chief Exec. Officer
PLAMANN, Alfred A.
Tel: (323) 264 - 5200 Ext: 4268
Fax: (323) 265 - 4261

Main Headquarters
Mailing: 5200 Sheila St.
Commerce, CA 90040
Tel: (323) 264 - 5200
Fax: (323) 265 - 4261

Corporate Foundations and Giving Programs

Unified Western Grocers Corporate Contributions Program
5200 Sheila St.
Commerce, CA 90040
Tel: (323) 264 - 5200
Fax: (323) 265 - 4261

Annual Grant Total: none reported

Public Affairs and Related Activities Personnel

At Headquarters

GILPIN, Don
V. President, Human Resources
Tel: (323) 264 - 5200 Ext: 8643
Fax: (323) 265 - 4261

SCHAFFNER, Tom
Contact Communications
Tel: (323) 264 - 5200 Ext: 4150
Fax: (323) 265 - 4261

UniGroup, Inc.

A household goods transportation company.

www.unigroupinc.com
Annual Revenues: $1.89 billion

Chairman and Chief Exec. Officer
STADLER, Gerry
Tel: (636) 326 - 3100
Fax: (636) 326 - 1106

Main Headquarters
Mailing: One United Dr.
Fenton, MO 63026
Tel: (636) 326 - 3100
Fax: (636) 326 - 1106

Political Action Committees

UniGroup Inc. Political Action Committee (UPAC)
Contact: Jan Robey Alonzo
One United Dr.
Fenton, MO 63026
Tel: (636) 326 - 3100
Fax: (636) 326 - 1106

Contributions to Candidates: $4,000 (01/05 - 09/05)
Republicans: $4,000.

Principal Recipients

SENATE REPUBLICANS		HOUSE REPUBLICANS
Talent, James (MO)	$4,000	

Public Affairs and Related Activities Personnel

At Headquarters

ALONZO, Jan Robey
Treasurer, UniGroup Inc. PAC
Tel: (636) 326 - 3100
Fax: (636) 326 - 1106

BONHAM, Jennifer
Media Relations
(Mayflower Transit)
jennifer_bonham@mayflower.com
Tel: (636) 349 - 2508
Fax: (636) 326 - 1106

Unilever Home & Personal Care - North America

Formed from the merger of Helene Curtis Industries, Chesebrough-Pond's USA, and Lever Brothers. Develops, manufactures, and markets home and personal care products. A subsidiary of Unilever PLC, the British-based parent company of Unilever. Products/brands include: All, Wisk, Surf, Dove, Mentadent, Degree, Pond's, Lever 2000, Suave, and Finesse.

www.unilever.com

Chairman of the Board
FITZGERALD, Niall
Tel: (203) 661 - 2000
Fax: (203) 625 - 2370
TF: (800) 366 - 4011

Main Headquarters
Mailing: 33 Benedict Pl.
Greenwich, CT 06830
Tel: (203) 661 - 2000
Fax: (203) 625 - 2370
TF: (800) 366 - 4011

Washington Office
Contact: David Vernon Lustig
Mailing: 816 Connecticut Ave. NW
Suite 700
Washington, DC 20006
Tel: (202) 828 - 1010
Fax: (202) 828 - 4550

Corporate Foundations and Giving Programs

Unilever Home & Personal Care - North America Corporate Giving Program
Contact: Stacie Nevadomski
33 Benedict Pl.
Greenwich, CT 06830
Tel: (203) 625 - 1101
Fax: (203) 625 - 2142
TF: (800) 366 - 4011

Annual Grant Total: none reported

Unilever Home & Personal Care - North America

* continued from previous page

Public Affairs and Related Activities Personnel

At Headquarters

NEVADOMSKI, Stacie
Director, Corporate Affairs
Tel: (203) 625 - 1101
Fax: (203) 625 - 2142
TF: (800) 366 - 4011

Responsibilities include corporate philanthropy.

YEATMAN, C. Perry
V. President, Corporate Affairs
Tel: (203) 661 - 2000
Fax: (203) 625 - 2370
TF: (800) 366 - 4011

At Washington Office

LUSTIG, David Vernon
Director, Government Relations
Tel: (202) 828 - 1010 Ext: 1
Fax: (202) 828 - 4550

Unilever United States, Inc.

A member of the Public Affairs Council. A subsidiary of Unilever N.V., Rotterdam, The Netherlands and Unilever PLC, London, England. Acquired Bestfoods in 2000.

www.unilever.com
Annual Revenues: $47 billion

Main Headquarters

Mailing: Lever House, 390 Park Ave.
New York, NY 10022-4698
Tel: (212) 888 - 1260
Fax: (212) 906 - 4666

Washington Office

Contact: David Vernon Lustig
Mailing: 816 Connecticut Ave. NW
Seventh Floor
Washington, DC 20006-2705
Tel: (202) 828 - 1010
Fax: (202) 828 - 4550

Corporate Foundations and Giving Programs

Unilever United States Foundation, Inc.
Contact: Paul W. Wood
Lever House, 390 Park Ave.
New York, NY 10022-4698
Tel: (212) 888 - 1260
Fax: (212) 688 - 3411

Annual Grant Total: over $5,000,000
Geographic Preference: Area(s) in which the company operates
Primary Interests: Arts and Culture; Civic and Public Affairs; Environment/Conservation; Health and Human Services; Nutrition; Women's Health

Public Affairs and Related Activities Personnel

At Headquarters

GOLDFARB, Nancy L.
Director, Public Relations
nancy.goldfarb@unilever.com
Tel: (212) 888 - 1260
Fax: (212) 906 - 4666

HERNANDEZ, Mary A.
Public Affairs Coordinator
mary.hernandez@unilever.com
Tel: (212) 888 - 1260
Fax: (212) 906 - 4666

WOOD, Paul W.
V. President, Corporate Affairs
paul.wood@unilever.com
Tel: (212) 888 - 1260
Fax: (212) 688 - 3411

At Washington Office

BECK, Lauren E.
Manager, Government Relations
lauren.beck@unilever.com
Registered Federal Lobbyist.
Tel: (202) 828 - 1010
Fax: (202) 828 - 4550

LANGAN, Thomas P.
Manager, Government Affairs
Registered Federal Lobbyist.
Tel: (202) 828 - 1010
Fax: (202) 828 - 4550

LUSTIG, David Vernon
Director, Government Relations
david.lustig@unilever.com
Registered Federal Lobbyist.
Tel: (202) 828 - 1010
Fax: (202) 828 - 4550

Union Bank of California

www.uboc.com
Annual Revenues: $2.3 billion

Chairman of the Board
SHIMURA, Tetsuo
Tel: (415) 765 - 0400
Fax: (415) 765 - 3257

President and Chief Exec. Officer
MORIMURA, Takashi
Tel: (415) 765 - 0400
Fax: (415) 765 - 3257

Main Headquarters

Mailing: 400 California St.
San Francisco, CA 94104
Tel: (415) 765 - 0400
Fax: (415) 765 - 3257

Political Action Committees

UnionBanCal Corp. Political Action Committee
Contact: Daniel Brigham
400 California St.
San Francisco, CA 94104
Tel: (415) 765 - 2761
Fax: (415) 765 - 2841

Contributions to Candidates: $5,650 (01/05 - 09/05)
Democrats: $5,650.

Principal Recipients

SENATE DEMOCRATS		HOUSE DEMOCRATS	
Feinstein, Dianne (CA)	$2,000	Vargas, Juan (CA)	$3,000

Corporate Foundations and Giving Programs

Union Bank of California Foundation
Contact: Carl Ballton
445 S. Figueroa St.
Los Angeles, CA 90071-1655
Tel: (213) 236 - 4140
Fax: (213) 236 - 6982

Annual Grant Total: over $5,000,000
Donations total over $10 million.
Geographic Preference: California; Oregon; Washington State
Primary Interests: Economic Development; Education; Health and Human Services; Housing
Recent Recipients: Habitat for Humanity; Urban League

Public Affairs and Related Activities Personnel

At Headquarters

BRIGHAM, Daniel
V. President, Government Affairs
daniel.brigham@uboc.com
Tel: (415) 765 - 2761
Fax: (415) 765 - 2841

FEARER, Paul F.
Exec. V. President and Director, Human Resources
Tel: (415) 765 - 0400
Fax: (415) 765 - 3257

JOHNSON, Stephen L.
Senior V. President and Director, Public Relations and Government Affairs
Mailstop: 17th Floor
stephen.johnson@uboc.com
Tel: (415) 765 - 3252
Fax: (415) 765 - 3257

MADDEN, Kathryn
Manager, Media Relations and Vice President, Public Relations
Tel: (415) 765 - 0400
Fax: (415) 765 - 3257

At Other Offices

BALLTON, Carl
President, Union Bank of California Foundation
445 S. Figueroa St.
Los Angeles, CA 90071-1655
carl.ballton@uboc.com
Tel: (213) 236 - 4140
Fax: (213) 236 - 6982

CURRAN, Joanne
Senior V. President, External Communications
445 S. Figueroa St.
Los Angeles, CA 90071
Joanne.Curran@uboc.com
Tel: (213) 236 - 5017
Fax: (213) 236 - 4147

WOODSON-BRYANT, Sharon
V. President, Corporate Communications
445 S. Figueroa St.
Los Angeles, CA 90071
sharonw.bryant@uboc.com
Tel: (213) 236 - 4145
Fax: (213) 236 - 4147

Union Pacific Corp.

A member of the Public Affairs Council. A holding company for subsidiaries engaged in railroad and other transportation.

www.up.com
Annual Revenues: $11.973 billion

Chairman, President and Chief Exec. Officer
DAVIDSON, Richard K.
Tel: (402) 544 - 5000

Main Headquarters

Mailing: 1400 Douglas St.
Omaha, NE 68179
Tel: (402) 544 - 5000

Washington Office

Contact: Mary E. McAuliffe
Mailing: 600 13th St. NW
Suite 340 West
Washington, DC 20005
Tel: (202) 662 - 0100
Fax: (202) 662 - 0199

Political Action Committees

Union Pacific Corp. Fund for Effective Government
Contact: Katherine W. Maness
600 13th St. NW
Suite 340 West
Washington, DC 20005
Tel: (202) 662 - 0140
Fax: (202) 662 - 0199

Contributions to Candidates: $357,768 (01/05 - 09/05)

Union Pacific Corp.

* continued from previous page

Democrats: $63,500; Republicans: $292,268; Other: $2,000.

Principal Recipients

SENATE DEMOCRATS		HOUSE DEMOCRATS	
		Matsui, Doris (CA)	$5,000
SENATE REPUBLICANS		**HOUSE REPUBLICANS**	
Talent, James (MO)	$10,000	Young, Don E (AK)	$7,000
Ensign, John Eric (NV)	$9,000	LaTourette, Steve (OH)	$6,000
Hatch, Orrin (UT)	$6,000	Latham, Thomas P (IA)	$5,500
Kennedy, Mark (MN)	$5,000	Bishop, Robert (UT)	$5,000
Kyl, Jon L (AZ)	$5,000	Blunt, Roy (MO)	$5,000
Thomas, Craig (WY)	$5,000	Bonilla, Henry (TX)	$5,000
		Cantor, Eric (VA)	$5,000
		Cubin, Barbara L (WY)	$5,000
		Dewine, R. Pat (OH)	$5,000
		Graves, Sam (MO)	$5,000
		Hastert, Dennis J. (IL)	$5,000
		Shuster, William (PA)	$5,000
		Terry, Lee (NE)	$5,000
		Walden, Gregory (OR)	$5,000
		Whitfield, Ed (KY)	$5,000

Corporate Foundations and Giving Programs

Union Pacific Foundation
Contact: Bob Turner
1400 Douglas St.
Omaha, NE 68179 — Tel: (402) 544 - 5255

Annual Grant Total: over $5,000,000

No grants are made to national health, political, religious or veterans' organizations; nor to individuals, social clubs, fraternal organizations, special events and publications. Guidelines and application form are available.

Geographic Preference: Area(s) in which the company operates; Western United States
Primary Interests: Arts and Culture; Higher Education; Social Services
Recent Recipients: Boy Scouts of America; United Way

Public Affairs and Related Activities Personnel

At Headquarters

BATEMAN, Joseph R., Jr. — Tel: (402) 544 - 3878
Senior Assistant V. President, Government Affairs

BROMLEY, John E. — Tel: (402) 544 - 3320
Director, Media Relations

DAVIS, Mark W. — Tel: (402) 544 - 5459
Regional Director, Public Relations

HERWEG, Darlynn — Tel: (402) 544 - 5034
Director, Contributions

JONES, Mary S. — Tel: (402) 544 - 6111
V. President and Treasurer
Responsibilities include investor relations.

SCHAEFER, Barbara W. — Tel: (402) 544 - 5747
Senior V. President, Human Resources

TURNER, Bob — Tel: (402) 544 - 5255
President, Union Pacific Foundation; and Senior V. President, Corporate Relations

At Washington Office

ANDRES, Susan Auther — Tel: (202) 662 - 0120; Fax: (202) 662 - 0199
Director, Washington Affairs - Transportation
Registered Federal Lobbyist.

BOLIN, Printz — Tel: (202) 662 - 0104; Fax: (202) 662 - 0199
Director, Washington Affairs, Tax and Environment
Registered Federal Lobbyist.

MANESS, Katherine W. — Tel: (202) 662 - 0140; Fax: (202) 662 - 0199
Director, Political Affairs
Registered Federal Lobbyist.

MCAULIFFE, Mary E. — Tel: (202) 662 - 0100; Fax: (202) 662 - 0199
V. President, External Relations
Registered Federal Lobbyist.

ROCK, Michael A. — Tel: (202) 662 - 0130; Fax: (202) 662 - 0199
Assistant V. President, External Affairs
Registered Federal Lobbyist.

At Other Offices

HARTMAN, Richard M. — Tel: (307) 778 - 3359; Fax: (307) 778 - 3385
Special Representative - Cheyenne
(Union Pacific Railroad Co.)
2424 Pioneer Ave., Suite 301
Cheyenne, WY 82001

PAYETTE, Michael W. — Tel: (312) 853 - 8402; Fax: (312) 853 - 8420
Government Affairs
101 N. Wacker Dr., Suite 1910
Chicago, IL 60606

RYAN, Mary E. "Beth"
Legislative Representative
103 The Mayfair, 625 S. 14th St.
Lincoln, NE 68508

ZAPLER, Thomas A. — Tel: (312) 853 - 8402; Fax: (312) 853 - 8420
Government Affairs
101 N. Wacker Dr., Suite 1910
Chicago, IL 60606

Union Pacific Railroad Co.

See listing on page 487 under Union Pacific Corp.

UniSource Energy Corp.

An electric utility holding company. Subsidiaries include Tucson Electric Power Co. and Millennium Energy Holdings, Inc.

www.unisourceenergy.com

Chairman, President, and Chief Exec. Officer — Tel: (520) 884 - 3623; TF: (800) 328 - 8853
PIGNATELLI, James S.
jpignatelli@tep.com

Main Headquarters
Mailing: P.O. Box 711
Tucson, AZ 85702 — Fax: (520) 884 - 3606; TF: (800) 328 - 8853

Political Action Committees

Unisource Energy Political Action Committee
P.O. Box 711
Tucson, AZ 85702 — Fax: (520) 884 - 3606; TF: (800) 328 - 8853

Contributions to Candidates: $1,000 (01/05 - 09/05)
Republicans: $1,000.

Principal Recipients

SENATE REPUBLICANS		HOUSE REPUBLICANS
Kyl, Jon L (AZ)	$1,000	

Corporate Foundations and Giving Programs

Tuscon Electric Power Co. Corporate Giving Program
Contact: Sharon B. Foltz
P.O. Box 711
Tucson, AZ 85702 — Tel: (520) 884 - 3740; Fax: (520) 884 - 3606; TF: (800) 328 - 8853

Annual Grant Total: none reported
Geographic Preference: Pima, AZ
Primary Interests: Education; Social Services; Youth Services

Public Affairs and Related Activities Personnel

At Headquarters

FOLTZ, Sharon B. — Tel: (520) 884 - 3740; Fax: (520) 884 - 3606; TF: (800) 328 - 8853
Director, Community Relations
Mailstop: UE 102
sfoltz@tep.com

LYNN, Steve — Tel: (520) 884 - 3629; Fax: (520) 884 - 3606; TF: (800) 328 - 8853
Senior V. President, Communications and Government Relations
slynn@tep.com

SMITH, Joe — Tel: (520) 884 - 3650; Fax: (520) 884 - 3606; TF: (800) 328 - 8853
Director, Investor Relations
josmith@uns.com

Unisys Corp.

A member of the Public Affairs Council. An information technology solutions provider.

www.unisys.com
Annual Revenues: $6.018 billion

Chairman of the Board — Tel: (215) 986 - 4011; Fax: (215) 986 - 6850
WEINBACH, Lawrence A.
lawrence.weinbach@unisys.com

President and Chief Exec. Officer — Tel: (215) 986 - 4011; Fax: (215) 986 - 6850
MCGRATH, Joseph W.

Main Headquarters
Mailing: Unisys Way
Blue Bell, PA 19424 — Tel: (215) 986 - 4011; Fax: (215) 986 - 6850

Washington Office
Contact: Dan Hoydysh
Mailing: 11720 Plaza America Dr.
Tower 3
Reston, VA 20190 — Tel: (703) 439 - 5000; Fax: (703) 439 - 5172

Political Action Committees

Unisys Corp. Employees PAC
Contact: Kim Dortone
Unisys Way
Blue Bell, PA 19424 — Tel: (215) 986 - 4011; Fax: (215) 986 - 6850

Contributions to Candidates: $27,000 (01/05 - 09/05)

Unisys Corp.

** continued from previous page*

Democrats: $11,500; Republicans: $15,500.

Principal Recipients

SENATE DEMOCRATS
Reid, Harry (NV) $2,000

SENATE REPUBLICANS

HOUSE DEMOCRATS
Schwartz, Allyson (PA) $2,000

HOUSE REPUBLICANS
Hastert, Dennis J. (IL) $5,000
Davis, Tom (VA) $3,000
Simmons, Rob (CT) $2,500

Corporate Foundations and Giving Programs

Unisys Corporate Contributions Program
Unisys Way
Blue Bell, PA 19424
Tel: (215) 986 - 4011
Fax: (215) 986 - 6850

Annual Grant Total: none reported
Geographic Preference: Area(s) in which the company operates
Primary Interests: Literacy; Math and Science; Technology

Public Affairs and Related Activities Personnel

At Headquarters

BRADFORD, Patricia A.
Senior V. President, Worldwide Human Resources
Tel: (215) 986 - 4011
Fax: (215) 986 - 6850

DORTONE, Kim
PAC Treasurer
Tel: (215) 986 - 4011
Fax: (215) 986 - 6850

DOUGLASS, Elizabeth
V. President, Corporate Media Relations
elizabeth.douglass@unisys.com
Tel: (215) 986 - 6583
Fax: (215) 986 - 6850

KERR, James B.
Director, Investor Relations
Mailstop: M/S A2-17
james.kerr@unn.unisys.com
Tel: (215) 986 - 5795
Ext: 4386
Fax: (215) 986 - 2312

MCHALE, Jack F.
Corporate V. President, Investor Relations
jack.mchale@unisys.com
Tel: (215) 986 - 6999
Fax: (215) 986 - 2312

At Washington Office

HOYDYSH, Dan
Director, Washington Office
dan.hoydysh@unisys.com
Registered Federal Lobbyist.
Tel: (703) 439 - 5000
Fax: (703) 439 - 5172

United Airlines

A commercial air carrier.
www.united.com
Annual Revenues: $16.138 billion

Chairman, President and Chief Exec. Officer
TILTON, Glenn F.
Tel: (847) 700 - 4000
Fax: (847) 700 - 4899

Main Headquarters
Mailing: P.O. Box 66100
Chicago, IL 60666
Tel: (847) 700 - 4000
Fax: (847) 700 - 4899
Street: 1200 E. Algonquin Rd.
Elk Grove Village, IL 60007-0100

Washington Office
Contact: Mark R. Anderson
Mailing: 1025 Connecticut Ave. NW
Suite 1210
Washington, DC 20036
Tel: (202) 296 - 2337
Fax: (202) 296 - 2873

Political Action Committees

United Airlines PAC
Contact: Kathryn Mikells
P.O. Box 66100
Chicago, IL 60666
Tel: (847) 700 - 4000
Fax: (847) 700 - 4899

Contributions to Candidates: $12,000 (01/05 - 09/05)
Democrats: $2,000; Republicans: $10,000.

Principal Recipients

SENATE DEMOCRATS
Kennedy, Ted (MA) $2,000

SENATE REPUBLICANS
Dewine, Richard (OH) $5,000

HOUSE DEMOCRATS

HOUSE REPUBLICANS
Knollenberg, Joe (MI) $2,000
Davis, Tom (VA) $1,500
Reynolds, Thomas (NY) $1,500

Corporate Foundations and Giving Programs

United Airlines Foundation
P.O. Box 66100
Chicago, IL 60666
Tel: (847) 700 - 4000
Fax: (847) 700 - 4899

Annual Grant Total: $2,000,000 - $5,000,000
In addition to aiding organizations in areas where large numbers of employees are concentrated, the Foundation conducts an annual Employee United Way Campaign and assists children of employees through National Merit Scholarships. E-mail address for the Foundation is uafoundation@UAL.com. Guidelines are available.
Geographic Preference: Area(s) in which the company operates
Primary Interests: Arts and Culture; Education; Health; Math and Science; Minority Opportunities
Recent Recipients: Habitat for Humanity; I Have A Dream Foundation; Nat'l Merit Scholarship; United Way

Public Affairs and Related Activities Personnel

At Headquarters

CHIU, Sandra L.
Director, International Affairs
sandra.chiu@ual.com
Tel: (847) 700 - 3956
Fax: (847) 700 - 5931

FRENCH, Barry
V. President, Corporate Communications
Tel: (847) 700 - 4000
Fax: (847) 700 - 4899

KAIN, Peter B.
Vice President, Labor Relations
Tel: (847) 700 - 4000
Fax: (847) 700 - 4899

KRAKOWSKI, Capt. Henry P.
Vice President, Corporate Safety and Quality Assurance
Tel: (847) 700 - 4000
Fax: (847) 700 - 4899

MIKELLS, Kathryn
PAC Treasurer
Tel: (847) 700 - 4000
Fax: (847) 700 - 4899

MOORE, Rosemary
Senior Vice President, Corporate and Gov. Affairs
Tel: (847) 700 - 4000
Fax: (847) 700 - 4899

ROCH, Elizabeth
Director, Communications Services
elizabeth.a.roch@ual.com
Tel: (847) 700 - 6564
Fax: (847) 700 - 4081

TOVELLO, Pam
Worldwide Communications
pam.tovello@ual.com
Tel: (847) 700 - 4000
Fax: (847) 700 - 4899

WHITAKER, Michael G.
V. President, International and Regulatory Affairs
michael.whitaker@ual.com
Tel: (847) 700 - 3955
Fax: (847) 700 - 4165

At Washington Office

ANDERSON, Mark R.
V. President, Governmental Affairs
mark.anderson@ual.com
Registered Federal Lobbyist.
Tel: (202) 296 - 1950
Fax: (202) 296 - 2873

GLASGOW, Karin
Manager, Government Affairs
karin.glasgow@united.com
Tel: (202) 296 - 1712
Fax: (202) 296 - 2873

MORRISEY, Stephen
Senior Director, Governmental Affairs
Registered Federal Lobbyist.
Tel: (202) 296 - 2733
Fax: (202) 296 - 2873

United Auto Group, Inc.

An automobile and truck dealership operator.
www.unitedauto.com
Annual Revenues: $7 billion

Chairman and Chief Exec. Officer
PENSKE, Roger S.
Tel: (248) 648 - 2500
Fax: (248) 648 - 2525

Main Headquarters
Mailing: 2555 Telegraph Rd.
Bloomfield Hills, MI 48302-0954
Tel: (248) 648 - 2500
Fax: (248) 648 - 2525

Public Affairs and Related Activities Personnel

At Headquarters

HARTZ, Phillip M.
Senior V. President, Manufacturer Relations and Corporate Communications
Tel: (248) 648 - 2500
Fax: (248) 648 - 2525

PORDON, Anthony R.
V. President, Investor Relations
tony.pordon@unitedauto.com
Tel: (248) 648 - 2500
Fax: (248) 648 - 2600

VERMILLION, Nancy
Specialist, Corporate Communications
nvermillion@unitedauto.com
Tel: (248) 648 - 2500
Fax: (248) 648 - 2525

United Concordia Cos., Inc.

See listing on page 243 under Highmark Inc.

United HealthCare Corp.

See listing on page 494 under UnitedHealth Group.

The United Illuminating Company

An electric utility and energy services company.
www.uinet.com

The United Illuminating Company

** continued from previous page*

Chairman and Chief Exec. Officer
WOODSON, Nathaniel — Tel: (203) 499 - 2000
nathaniel.woodson@uinet.com — Fax: (203) 499 - 3626
TF: (800) 722 - 5584

Main Headquarters
Mailing: P.O. Box 1564, New Haven, CT 06506-0901 — Tel: (203) 499 - 2000; Fax: (203) 499 - 3626; TF: (800) 722 - 5584
Street: 157 Church St., New Haven, CT 06510

Political Action Committees

Electric Employees Committee of The United Illuminating Co.
Contact: David K. Ricciardi
P.O. Box 1564 — Tel: (203) 499 - 2000
New Haven, CT 06506-0901 — Fax: (203) 499 - 3626
TF: (800) 722 - 5584

Contributions to Candidates: none reported (01/05 - 09/05)

Corporate Foundations and Giving Programs

United Illuminating Community Affairs
P.O. Box 1564 — Tel: (203) 499 - 2000
New Haven, CT 06506-0901 — Fax: (203) 499 - 3626
TF: (800) 722 - 5584

Annual Grant Total: none reported
Primary Interests: Arts and Culture; Environment/Conservation; Health and Human Services

Public Affairs and Related Activities Personnel

At Headquarters

ALLEN, Susan E. — Tel: (203) 499 - 2409
V. President, Investor Relations; Corporate Secretary and Assistant Treasurer — Fax: (203) 499 - 3626
susan.allen@uinet.com — TF: (800) 722 - 5584

HRABCHAK, Dennis — Tel: (203) 499 - 2000
V. President, Corporate Affairs — Fax: (203) 499 - 3626
TF: (800) 722 - 5584

MOORE, Kevin — Tel: (203) 499 - 2000
Director, Communications — Fax: (203) 499 - 3626
TF: (800) 722 - 5584

MULLEN, Susan — Tel: (203) 499 - 2000
Senior Human Resources Exec. — Fax: (203) 499 - 3626
TF: (800) 722 - 5584

RICCIARDI, David K. — Tel: (203) 499 - 2000
Treasurer, Electric Employees Committee of The United Illuminating Co. — Fax: (203) 499 - 3626
TF: (800) 722 - 5584

VAZQUEZ, Carlos M. — Tel: (203) 499 - 2825
Director,Government Affairs — Fax: (203) 499 - 3626
carlos.vazquez@uinet.com — TF: (800) 722 - 5584

United Parcel Service (UPS)

PUBLIC AFFAIRS COUNCIL

A member of the Public Affairs Council. A provider of air and ground express package delivery services in the U.S. and over 220 countries worldwide.
www.ups.com
Annual Revenues: $30.6 billion

Chairman and Chief Exec. Officer
ESKEW, Michael L. — Tel: (404) 828 - 7223
mleskew@ups.com — Fax: (404) 828 - 6619

Main Headquarters
Mailing: 55 Glenlake Pkwy. NE, Atlanta, GA 30328 — Tel: (404) 828 - 6000; Fax: (404) 828 - 6619

Washington Office
Contact: Arnold F. Wellman, Jr.
Mailing: 316 Pennsylvania Ave. SE, Suite 300, Washington, DC 20003 — Tel: (202) 675 - 4220; Fax: (202) 675 - 4230

Political Action Committees

UPSPAC
Contact: Royal Roth
316 Pennsylvania Ave. SE — Tel: (202) 675 - 4220
Suite 300 — Fax: (202) 675 - 4230
Washington, DC 20003

Contributions to Candidates: $685,674 (01/05 - 09/05)
Democrats: $184,399; Republicans: $498,775; Other: $2,500.

Principal Recipients

SENATE DEMOCRATS

HOUSE DEMOCRATS

Edwards, Chet (TX)	$10,000

SENATE REPUBLICANS

Harris, Katherine (FL)	$10,000
Santorum, Richard (PA)	$9,499
Burns, Conrad (MT)	$8,000
Kyl, Jon L (AZ)	$7,000
Thomas, Craig (WY)	$7,000
Talent, James (MO)	$5,500

HOUSE REPUBLICANS

Boehner, John (OH)	$10,000
Brown-Waite, Virginia (FL)	$10,000
Kennedy, Mark (MN)	$10,000
Northup, Anne M. (KY)	$10,000
Sweeney, John E. (NY)	$10,000

Corporate Foundations and Giving Programs

The UPS Foundation
Contact: Ms. Evern Cooper
55 Glenlake Pkwy. NE — Tel: (404) 828 - 6251
Atlanta, GA 30328 — Fax: (404) 828 - 7435

Annual Grant Total: over $5,000,000
Geographic Preference: National
Primary Interests: Economic Development; Health and Human Services; Higher Education; Hunger; Literacy; Minority Opportunities; Persons with Disabilities
Recent Recipients: American Foundation for the Blind; Boys and Girls Club

Public Affairs and Related Activities Personnel

At Headquarters

COOPER, Ms. Evern — Tel: (404) 828 - 6251
Exec. Director, UPS Foundation — Fax: (404) 828 - 7435
ecooper@ups.com

FINLEY, Teresa — Tel: (404) 828 - 7359
V. President, Investor Relations
tfinley@ups.com

HINDS, Clifford L. — Tel: (404) 828 - 6000
PAC Treasurer — Fax: (404) 828 - 6619

PERRY, Bill — Tel: (404) 828 - 4184
Manager, Communications — Fax: (404) 828 - 6971
bperry@ups.com

SOUPATA, Lea — Tel: (404) 828 - 6000
Senior V. President, Human Resources — Fax: (404) 828 - 6619
lsoupata@ups.com

STERNAD, Kenneth B. — Tel: (404) 828 - 7123
V. President, Public Relations — Fax: (404) 828 - 6593
ksternad@ups.com

At Washington Office

ALAGNA, Mark — Tel: (202) 675 - 4220
Manager, Public Affairs — Fax: (202) 675 - 4230

AMEND, Betty — Tel: (202) 675 - 4220
Manager, Public Affairs — Fax: (202) 675 - 4230

BERGMAN, Bob — Tel: (202) 675 - 3354
V. President, Public Affairs — Fax: (202) 675 - 4230
bbergman@ups.com
Registered Federal Lobbyist.

BOLGER, David A. — Tel: (202) 675 - 4220
Manager, Public Relations — Fax: (202) 675 - 4230

BONILLA, Sheryl W. — Tel: (202) 675 - 4220
Manager, Public Affairs — Fax: (202) 675 - 4230
sshelby@ups.com
Registered Federal Lobbyist.

DUBOIS, Marcel — Tel: (202) 675 - 4237
V. President, Public Affairs — Fax: (202) 675 - 4230
marceldubois@ups.com
Registered Federal Lobbyist.

FRANCESCONI, Michael — Tel: (202) 675 - 4220
Manager, Public Affairs — Fax: (202) 675 - 4230

JACKSON, Selina — Tel: (202) 675 - 4220
Manager, Public Affairs — Fax: (202) 675 - 4230

JENSEN, Thomas F. — Tel: (202) 675 - 4220
Manager, Public Affairs — Fax: (202) 675 - 4230
tjensen@ups.com
Registered Federal Lobbyist.

LEWIS, Nicholas — Tel: (202) 675 - 4222
Manager, Public Affairs — Fax: (202) 675 - 4230
nlewis@ups.com
Registered Federal Lobbyist.

ROTH, Royal — Tel: (202) 675 - 4220
PAC Contact — Fax: (202) 675 - 4230

THOMAS, Pat — Tel: (202) 675 - 4220
Manager, Public Affairs — Fax: (202) 675 - 4230

United Parcel Service (UPS)

* continued from previous page

WELLMAN, Arnold F., Jr. — Tel: (202) 675 - 4251
Corporate V. President, Domestic and International Public Affairs — Fax: (202) 675 - 3384
awellman@ups.com
Registered Federal Lobbyist.

At Other Offices

LUCIEN, Arthur — Tel: (212) 631 - 6565
Manager, Public Affairs
643 W. 43rd St., Eighth Floor
New York, NY 10036
alucien@ups.com

MACRAE, Bruce — Tel: (949) 452 - 2082
Manager, Public Affairs — Fax: (949) 452 - 2040
25201 Paseo de Alicia
Suite 200
Laguna Hills, CA 12653
bmacrae@ups.com

NELSON, Tim — Tel: (610) 595 - 7079
Manager, Public Affairs — Fax: (610) 595 - 7002
Two International Plaza, Suite 240
Philadelphia, PA 19113

SMITH, Dan — Tel: (972) 788 - 7707
Manager, Public Affairs — Fax: (972) 788 - 7795
6400 Seven States Blvd.
San Antonio, TX 78244

SNYDER, Bob — Tel: (770) 417 - 2104
Manager, Public Affairs
5335 Triangle Pkwy.
Suite 500
Norcross, GA 30092-2556

United Refining Co.

www.urc.com

Chairman and Chief Exec. Officer — Tel: (814) 723 - 1500
CATSIMATIDIS, John A. — Fax: (814) 726 - 4602

Main Headquarters
Mailing: P.O. Box 780, Warren, PA 16365 — Tel: (814) 723 - 1500; Fax: (814) 726 - 4602
Street: 15 Bradley St., Warren, PA 16365

Political Action Committees

United Refining Co. PAC
Contact: Dennis E. Bee, Jr.
P.O. Box 780 — Tel: (814) 723 - 1500
Warren, PA 16365 — Fax: (814) 726 - 4602

Contributions to Candidates: none reported (01/05 - 09/05)

Corporate Foundations and Giving Programs

United Refining Corporate Contributions Program
Contact: Larry Loughlin
P.O. Box 780 — Tel: (814) 723 - 1500
Warren, PA 16365 — Fax: (814) 726 - 4602

Annual Grant Total: none reported

Public Affairs and Related Activities Personnel

At Headquarters

BEE, Dennis E., Jr. — Tel: (814) 723 - 1500
Treasurer, United Refining Co. PAC — Fax: (814) 726 - 4602
Responsibilities include investor relations.

LOUGHLIN, Larry — Tel: (814) 723 - 1500
V. President, Human Resources — Fax: (814) 726 - 4602

United Services Automobile Ass'n (USAA)

PUBLIC AFFAIRS COUNCIL

A member of the Public Affairs Council. An insurance and diversified financial services association.

www.usaa.com
Annual Revenues: $9.22 billion

Chairman, President and Chief Exec. Officer — Tel: (210) 456 - 1800
DAVIS, Robert G. — Fax: (210) 498 - 9940

Main Headquarters
Mailing: 9800 Fredericksburg Rd., San Antonio, TX 78288-0122 — Tel: (210) 456 - 1800; Fax: (210) 498 - 9940

Washington Office
Contact: Christopher C. Seeger
Mailing: 1455 F St. NW, Suite 420, Washington, DC 20004 — Tel: (202) 628 - 6442; Fax: (202) 628 - 6537

Political Action Committees

United Services Automobile Ass'n Group PAC (USAA Group PAC)
Contact: Jose Robles, Jr
9800 Fredericksburg Rd. — Tel: (210) 456 - 1800
San Antonio, TX 78288-0122 — Fax: (210) 498 - 9940

Contributions to Candidates: $167,250 (01/05 - 09/05)
Democrats: $32,000; Republicans: $135,250.

Principal Recipients

SENATE DEMOCRATS		HOUSE DEMOCRATS	
Lieberman, Joe (CT)	$2,000	Cuellar, Henry (TX)	$5,000
Nelson, Benjamin (NE)	$2,000	Gonzalez, Charles A (TX)	$5,000
SENATE REPUBLICANS		**HOUSE REPUBLICANS**	
Talent, James (MO)	$7,000	Bonilla, Henry (TX)	$5,000
Ensign, John Eric (NV)	$5,000	DeLay, Tom (TX)	$5,000
Santorum, Richard (PA)	$5,000	Drake, Thelma Day (VA)	$5,000
Allen, George (VA)	$3,500	Pearce, Steve (NM)	$5,000
Sununu, John (NH)	$2,000	Smith, Lamar (TX)	$5,000
		Wilson, Heather (NM)	$5,000

Corporate Foundations and Giving Programs

USAA Educational Foundation
9800 Fredericksburg Rd. — Tel: (210) 456 - 1800
San Antonio, TX 78288-0122 — Fax: (210) 498 - 9940

Annual Grant Total: none reported
Primary Interests: Children; Education

Public Affairs and Related Activities Personnel

At Headquarters

BERRY, Paul — Tel: (210) 498 - 1562
Public Affairs Representative — Fax: (210) 498 - 8754
Mailstop: D-3-E

CONKLYN, Elizabel D. — Tel: (210) 456 - 1800
Exec. V. President, Human Resources — Fax: (210) 498 - 9940

GENTRY, Barbara — Tel: (210) 498 - 1225
Senior V. President, Community Affairs — Fax: (210) 498 - 8216

ROBLES, Jose, Jr — Tel: (210) 456 - 1800
Exec. V. President, Chief Financial Officer and Corporate Treasurer — Fax: (210) 498 - 9940
Responsibilities include political action.

SNOWDEN, David — Tel: (210) 456 - 1800
Exec. Director, Property and Casualty Communications — Fax: (210) 498 - 9940
Mailstop: D-3-E

STRONG, Wendi I. — Tel: (210) 456 - 1800
Exec. V. President, Corporate Communications — Fax: (210) 498 - 9940

At Washington Office

CALLANAN, Susan W. — Tel: (202) 628 - 6442
Assistant V. President, Federal Legislative Affairs — Fax: (202) 628 - 6537
Registered Federal Lobbyist.

PERROS, Georgette — Tel: (202) 628 - 6442; Fax: (202) 628 - 6537
Registered Federal Lobbyist.

SEEGER, Christopher C. — Tel: (202) 528 - 6442
Senior V. President, Federal Government Relations — Fax: (202) 628 - 6537
chris.seeger@usaa.com
Registered Federal Lobbyist.

U.S. Can Corp.

www.uscanco.com
Annual Revenues: $772 million

Chief Exec. Officer — Tel: (630) 678 - 8000
MENGEL, Phillip — Fax: (630) 678 - 8131

Main Headquarters
Mailing: 700 E. Butterfield Rd., Suite 250, Lombard, IL 60148 — Tel: (630) 678 - 8000; Fax: (630) 678 - 8131

Public Affairs and Related Activities Personnel

At Headquarters

AKINS, Jim — Tel: (630) 678 - 8000
Senior V. President, Human Resources — Fax: (630) 678 - 8131

PASCHAL, Annelle — Tel: (630) 678 - 8022
Director, Corporate Professional Relations — Fax: (630) 678 - 8131
Responsibilities include corporate communications.

United States Steel Corporation

Spun off from USX Corp. in 2001 to form its own independent company. A manufacturer of steel products and coke and taconite pellets with operations in the U.S. and Central Europe. Acquired the integrated steelmaking assets of Nat'l Steel Corp. in May, 2003.

www.ussteel.com
Annual Revenues: $41.1 billion

Chairman of the Board — Tel: (412) 433 - 1101
USHER, Thomas J.

United States Steel Corporation

** continued from previous page*

President and Chief Exec. Officer Tel: (412) 433 - 1121
SURMA, John P., Jr.

Main Headquarters
Mailing: 600 Grant St. Tel: (412) 433 - 1121
Pittsburgh, PA 15219-2800

Washington Office
Contact: Terrence D. Straub
Mailing: 1101 Pennsylvania Ave. NW Tel: (202) 783 - 6333
Suite 510 Fax: (202) 783 - 6309
Washington, DC 20004

Political Action Committees

United States Steel Corp. PAC
Contact: Mindy Fleishman
600 Grant St. Tel: (412) 433 - 1121
Pittsburgh, PA 15219-2800

Contributions to Candidates: $74,707 (01/05 - 09/05)
Democrats: $30,500; Republicans: $44,207.

Principal Recipients

SENATE DEMOCRATS		HOUSE DEMOCRATS	
Byrd, Robert C (WV)	$2,000	Cardin, Ben (MD)	$8,000
Clinton, Hillary Rodham (NY)	$2,000	Murtha, John P Mr. (PA)	$5,000
		Costello, Jerry F (IL)	$2,000
		Dingell, John D (MI)	$2,000

SENATE REPUBLICANS		HOUSE REPUBLICANS	
Santorum, Richard (PA)	$9,000	Ney, Robert W (OH)	$3,000
Dewine, Richard (OH)	$4,000	Murphy, Tim (PA)	$2,500
Hatch, Orrin (UT)	$2,000	Boehner, John (OH)	$2,000
		Fitzpatrick, Michael (PA)	$2,000
		Tiberi, Patrick (OH)	$2,000

Corporate Foundations and Giving Programs

United States Steel Foundation, Inc.
Contact: Susan M. Kapusta
600 Grant St. Tel: (412) 433 - 1121
Pittsburgh, PA 15219-2800

Annual Grant Total: $750,000 - $1,000,000
Geographic Preference: Area(s) in which the company operates; National
Primary Interests: Civic and Cultural Activities; Education; Health and Human Services; Math and Science
Recent Recipients: Carnegie Mellon University; YWCA

Public Affairs and Related Activities Personnel

At Headquarters

ARMSTRONG, D. John Tel: (412) 433 - 6792
Manager, Public Affairs Fax: (412) 433 - 6847
Mailstop: Room 685

FLEISHMAN, Mindy Tel: (412) 433 - 1121
Treasurer, United States Steel Corp. PAC

GARRAUX, James D. Tel: (412) 433 - 1121
V. President, Labor Relations

HARPER, Nick Tel: (412) 433 - 1184
Manager, Investor Relations Fax: (412) 433 - 1167

KAPUSTA, Susan M. Tel: (412) 433 - 1121
General Manager, United States Steel Foundation, Inc.

RICE, Charles L. Tel: (412) 433 - 1121
General Manager, Public Affairs

STERLING, Thomas W. Tel: (412) 433 - 1121
Senior V. President, Human Resources and Business Services

TODD, Stephen K. Tel: (412) 433 - 1121
V. President, Law and Environmental Affairs

VARGO, Carlee J. Tel: (412) 433 - 6777
Public Affairs Representative Fax: (412) 433 - 6847
Mailstop: Room 685

At Washington Office

SALMON, Scott R. Tel: (202) 783 - 6797
Managing Director, Government Affairs--Europe Fax: (202) 783 - 6309
Registered Federal Lobbyist.

SNEERINGER, Thomas M. Tel: (202) 783 - 6333
Director, Governmental Affairs Fax: (202) 783 - 6309
Registered Federal Lobbyist.

STRAUB, Terrence D. Tel: (202) 783 - 6331
Senior V. President, Public Policy and Governmental Affairs Fax: (202) 783 - 6309
Registered Federal Lobbyist.

United States Sugar Corp.

A sugar cane and citrus grower and processor and a sugar refiner.
www.ussugar.com

President and Chief Exec. Officer Tel: (863) 983 - 8121
DOLSON, Robert Fax: (863) 983 - 9827

Main Headquarters
Mailing: 111 Ponce de Leon Ave. Tel: (863) 983 - 8121
Clewiston, FL 33440 Fax: (863) 983 - 9827

Political Action Committees

United States Sugar Employee Stock Ownership Plan Political Action Committee
Contact: Sherry Bell
111 Ponce de Leon Ave. Tel: (863) 983 - 8121
Clewiston, FL 33440 Fax: (863) 983 - 9827

Contributions to Candidates: $14,500 (01/05 - 09/05)
Democrats: $11,500; Republicans: $3,000.

Principal Recipients

SENATE DEMOCRATS		HOUSE DEMOCRATS	
Nelson, Benjamin (NE)	$2,500	Marshall, Jim (GA)	$2,000
Ford, Harold E Jr (TN)	$1,000	Bishop, Sanford (GA)	$1,000
		Kaptur, Marcy (OH)	$1,000
		Klein, Ron (FL)	$1,000
		Meek, Carrie (FL)	$1,000
		Schultz, Debbie (FL)	$1,000
		Wexler, Robert (FL)	$1,000

SENATE REPUBLICANS		HOUSE REPUBLICANS	
Burns, Conrad (MT)	$1,000	Bilirakis, Michael (FL)	$1,000
		Hastert, Dennis J. (IL)	$1,000

Corporate Foundations and Giving Programs

United States Sugar Corp. Charitable Trust
Contact: Robert E. Coker
111 Ponce de Leon Ave. Tel: (863) 902 - 2461
Clewiston, FL 33440 Fax: (863) 983 - 9827

Annual Grant Total: $400,000 - $500,000
Geographic Preference: Florida
Primary Interests: Health; Higher Education; Social Services
Recent Recipients: Boy Scouts of America

Public Affairs and Related Activities Personnel

At Headquarters

BELL, Sherry Tel: (863) 983 - 8121
PAC Contact Fax: (863) 983 - 9827

COKER, Robert E. Tel: (863) 902 - 2461
Senior V. President, Public Affairs Fax: (863) 983 - 9827

SANCHEZ, Judy Tel: (863) 983 - 8121
Director, Corporate Communications Fax: (863) 983 - 9827

United Stationers Inc.

A business products distributor.
www.unitedstationers.com

Chairman of the Board Tel: (847) 699 - 5000
HEGI, Frederick B., Jr. Fax: (847) 699 - 8046

President and Chief Exec. Officer Tel: (847) 699 - 5000
GOCHNAUER, Richard W. Fax: (847) 699 - 8046

Main Headquarters
Mailing: 2200 E. Golf Rd. Tel: (847) 699 - 5000
Des Plaines, IL 60016-1267 Fax: (847) 699 - 8046

Public Affairs and Related Activities Personnel

At Headquarters

DISCLAFANI, Mary Tel: (847) 669 - 5000
Investor Relations Contact Ext: 2772
mdisclafani@ussco.com Fax: (847) 699 - 8046

DVORAK, Kathleen S. Tel: (847) 699 - 4723
Senior V. President and Chief Financial Officer Fax: (847) 699 - 4716
Responsibilities include investor relations and corporate communications.

SLOAN, John Tel: (847) 699 - 5000
Senior V. President, Human Resources Fax: (847) 699 - 8046

United Technologies Corp.

A broad-based designer and manufacturer of high technology products, the best known of which include Pratt & Whitney aircraft engines, Sikorsky helicoptors, Otis elevators, Norden radar systems, environmental controls and space suits and automotive components and systems. Important products for the U.S. space program are produced by Space Transportation Systems and other units of UTC's Aerospace and Defense Group.
www.utc.com
Annual Revenues: $31 billion

United Technologies Corp.

* continued from previous page

Chairman and Chief Exec. Officer
DAVID, George
Tel: (860) 728 - 7000
Fax: (860) 728 - 6494

Main Headquarters
Mailing: United Technologies Bldg.
One Financial Plaza
Hartford, CT 06101
Tel: (860) 728 - 7000
Fax: (860) 728 - 6494

Washington Office
Contact: Ruth R. Harkin
Mailing: 1401 I St. NW
Suite 600
Washington, DC 20005
Tel: (202) 336 - 7400
Fax: (202) 336 - 7515

Political Action Committees

United Technologies Corp. PAC
Contact: John Humphries
1401 I St. NW
Suite 600
Washington, DC 20005
Tel: (202) 336 - 7400
Fax: (202) 336 - 7515

Contributions to Candidates: $169,000 (01/05 - 09/05)
Democrats: $54,500; Republicans: $113,500; Other: $1,000.

Principal Recipients

SENATE DEMOCRATS		HOUSE DEMOCRATS	
Lieberman, Joe (CT)	$6,000	DeLauro, Rosa (CT)	$5,000
Nelson, Bill (FL)	$4,500	Murtha, John P Mr. (PA)	$5,000
Akaka, Daniel (HI)	$2,000		
Ford, Harold E Jr (TN)	$2,000		

SENATE REPUBLICANS		HOUSE REPUBLICANS	
Snowe, Olympia (ME)	$5,000	Bonilla, Henry (TX)	$5,000
Burns, Conrad (MT)	$2,000	Everett, Terry (AL)	$5,000
Dewine, Richard (OH)	$2,000	Hunter, Duncan (CA)	$5,000
Lott, Trent (MS)	$2,000	Lewis, Jerry (CA)	$5,000
Talent, James (MO)	$2,000	Manzullo, Donald (IL)	$5,000

Corporate Foundations and Giving Programs

United Technologies Corp. Contributions Program
Contact: Krista Pilot
United Technologies Bldg.
One Financial Plaza
Hartford, CT 06101
Tel: (860) 728 - 7000
Fax: (860) 728 - 6494

Annual Grant Total: over $5,000,000
Annually gives over $14 million. The company also maintains an employee matching gifts program.
Geographic Preference: Area(s) in which the company operates; National
Primary Interests: Arts and Culture; Community Affairs; Education; Health and Human Services

Public Affairs and Related Activities Personnel

At Headquarters

BENNETT, Richard
V. President, Environment, Health and Safety
Tel: (860) 728 - 7000
Fax: (860) 728 - 6494

BUCKNALL, William L., Jr.
Senior V. President, Human Resources
Tel: (860) 728 - 7000
Fax: (860) 728 - 6494

JAMISON, George H., III
V. President, Communications
Tel: (860) 728 - 7000
Fax: (860) 728 - 6494

LEARY, John P.
V. President, Employee Relations
Tel: (860) 728 - 7000
Fax: (860) 728 - 6494

LINTNER, Nancy L.
V. President, Communications
Tel: (860) 728 - 7000
Fax: (860) 728 - 6494

MURPHY, Peter
Director, Worldwide Public Relations
Tel: (860) 728 - 7977
Fax: (860) 728 - 6255

PILOT, Krista
Director, Corporate Giving and Community Relations
Tel: (860) 728 - 7000
Fax: (860) 728 - 6494

At Washington Office

BAYER, Judith
Director, Environmental Government Affairs
bayerj@corpdc.utc.com
Registered Federal Lobbyist.
Tel: (202) 336 - 7400
Fax: (202) 336 - 7529

BECKER, Darby M. R.
Manager and Counsel, Government Relations and PAC Treasurer
Registered Federal Lobbyist.
Tel: (202) 336 - 7400
Fax: (202) 336 - 7515

BULLARD, Ed
Registered Federal Lobbyist.
Tel: (202) 336 - 7400
Fax: (202) 336 - 7515

CANEVARI, Holly
Congressional Relations Representative
Registered Federal Lobbyist.
Tel: (202) 336 - 7400
Fax: (202) 336 - 7515

FAUSER, Krissi Kearns
Strategic Planning and Defense Policy Advisor
Registered Federal Lobbyist.
Tel: (202) 336 - 7400
Fax: (202) 336 - 7515

GRANDJEAN, Sherry
Congressional Relations Representative
Registered Federal Lobbyist.
Tel: (202) 336 - 7400
Fax: (202) 336 - 7515

HARKIN, Ruth R.
Senior V. President, International Affairs and Government Relations
Tel: (202) 336 - 7463
Fax: (202) 336 - 7515

HELLIER, Richard G.
Registered Federal Lobbyist.
Tel: (202) 336 - 7400
Fax: (202) 336 - 7515

HUMPHRIES, John
PAC Treasurer
Tel: (202) 336 - 7400
Fax: (202) 336 - 7515

HUMPHRIES, John M.
V. President, Government Relations and PAC Chair
jack.humphries@utc.com
Registered Federal Lobbyist.
Tel: (202) 336 - 7474
Fax: (202) 336 - 7515

JORDAN, Peter
Registered Federal Lobbyist.
Tel: (202) 336 - 7400
Fax: (202) 336 - 7515

KAUFMAN, Lisi
Senior V. President, Government and International Affairs
Tel: (202) 336 - 7400
Fax: (202) 336 - 7515

KOPECKY, John J., Sr.
Registered Federal Lobbyist.
Tel: (202) 336 - 7400
Fax: (202) 336 - 7515

MANKE, Dave
Interim Sr. V. President, Gov. Rels. and Int'l Affairs
Tel: (202) 336 - 7400
Fax: (202) 336 - 7515

MARKS, Jeffrey
Manager and Counsel, Environment and Energy
Tel: (202) 336 - 7400
Fax: (202) 336 - 7515

PEACE, Chris
Congressional Relations Representative
Registered Federal Lobbyist.
Tel: (202) 336 - 7400
Fax: (202) 336 - 7515

PREISS, Jeremy
Chief International Trade Counsel
Registered Federal Lobbyist.
Tel: (202) 336 - 7400
Fax: (202) 336 - 7515

SELIGMAN, Scott D.
Director, Public Relations
Tel: (202) 336 - 7400
Fax: (202) 336 - 7530

SMITH, Keith
Senior Manager, International Trade and Tax Policy
Registered Federal Lobbyist.
Tel: (202) 336 - 7400
Fax: (202) 336 - 7515

WALSH, Susan M.
Registered Federal Lobbyist.
Tel: (202) 336 - 7400
Fax: (202) 336 - 7515

United Water Resources

A water utility.
www.unitedwater.com
Annual Revenues: $500 million

Chairman of the Board
BARR, Edward E.
Tel: (201) 767 - 9300
Fax: (201) 767 - 2892
TF: (800) 230 - 2685

V. Chairman and Chief Exec. Officer
HARDING, Anthony J.
Tel: (201) 767 - 9300
Fax: (201) 767 - 2892
TF: (800) 230 - 2685

Main Headquarters
Mailing: 200 Old Hook Rd.
Harrington Park, NJ 07640
Tel: (201) 767 - 9300
Fax: (201) 767 - 2892
TF: (800) 230 - 2685

Public Affairs and Related Activities Personnel

At Headquarters

HENNING, Richard
Assistant V. President, Communications
rich.henning@unitedwater.com
Tel: (201) 767 - 2869
Fax: (201) 767 - 2892
TF: (800) 230 - 2685

RIZZI, Deborah
Director, Corporate Communications
deborah.rizzi@unitedwater.com
Tel: (201) 767 - 2867
Fax: (201) 767 - 2892
TF: (800) 230 - 2685

WALL, Charles T.
Senior V. President, Human Resources
Tel: (201) 767 - 9300
Fax: (201) 767 - 2892
TF: (800) 230 - 2685

UnitedGlobalCom, Inc.

A broadband communications provider.

www.lgi.com

Annual Revenues: $2.6 billion

Main Headquarters

Mailing: 4643 S. Ulster St.
Suite 1300
Denver, CO 80237-2868
Tel: (303) 220 - 6600
Fax: (303) 220 - 6601

Public Affairs and Related Activities Personnel

At Headquarters

ABBOTT, Richard S. L.
Investor Relations - Denver
Tel: (303) 220 - 6600
Fax: (303) 220 - 6601

NOYES, Chris
Investor Relations- Denver
Tel: (303) 220 - 6693
Fax: (303) 220 - 6662

UnitedHealth Group

PUBLIC AFFAIRS COUNCIL

A member of the Public Affairs Council. Health care management and evaluation services. Formerly United HealthCare Corp. Acquired Mid Atlantic Medical Services Inc. (MAMSI) (see separate listing) in February, 2004.

www.unitedhealthgroup.com

Annual Revenues: $25.02 billion

Chairman and Chief Exec. Officer
MCGUIRE, William W.
Tel: (952) 936 - 1300
Fax: (952) 936 - 0044
TF: (800) 328 - 5979

Main Headquarters

Mailing: 9900 Bren Rd. East
Minneapolis, MN 55343
Tel: (952) 936 - 1300
Fax: (952) 936 - 0044
TF: (800) 328 - 5979

Washington Office

Contact: Elise A. Gemeinhardt

Mailing: 1225 New York Ave. NW
Suite 475
Washington, DC 20005
Tel: (202) 371 - 1303
Fax: (202) 371 - 5569

Political Action Committees

UnitedHealth Group PAC
Contact: Patrick Erlandson
9900 Bren Rd. East
Minneapolis, MN 55343
Tel: (952) 936 - 1300
Fax: (952) 936 - 0044
TF: (800) 328 - 5979

Contributions to Candidates: $76,500 (01/05 - 09/05)

Democrats: $31,000; Republicans: $43,500; Other: $2,000.

Principal Recipients

SENATE DEMOCRATS

Carper, Thomas R (DE)	$3,000
Clinton, Hillary Rodham (NY)	$2,000
Conrad, Kent (ND)	$2,000
Kennedy, Ted (MA)	$2,000
Lieberman, Joe (CT)	$2,000
Nelson, Benjamin (NE)	$2,000

HOUSE DEMOCRATS

Cardin, Ben (MD)	$2,000
Israel, Steve (NY)	$2,000
Pomeroy, Earl (ND)	$2,000
Rush, Bobby (IL)	$2,000
Skelton, Ike (MO)	$2,000
Towns, Edolphus (NY)	$2,000

HOUSE OTHER

Peterson, Collin (MN)	$2,000

SENATE REPUBLICANS

Harris, Katherine (FL)	$2,500
Allen, George (VA)	$2,000
Kyl, Jon L (AZ)	$2,000
Santorum, Richard (PA)	$2,000

HOUSE REPUBLICANS

Boehner, John (OH)	$2,000
Buyer, Steve (IN)	$2,000
Deal, Nathan (GA)	$2,000
Ferguson, Mike (NJ)	$2,000
Gutknecht, Gil (MN)	$2,000
Hart, Melissa (PA)	$2,000
Hayworth, J D (AZ)	$2,000
Hulshof, Kenny (MO)	$2,000
Northup, Anne M. (KY)	$2,000
Ramstad, Jim (MN)	$2,000
Reynolds, Thomas (NY)	$2,000
Rogers, Michael J (MI)	$2,000
Ryan, Paul D (WI)	$2,000

Corporate Foundations and Giving Programs

UnitedHealth Foundation
Contact: Susan Hayes
9900 Bren Rd. East
Minneapolis, MN 55343
Tel: (952) 936 - 1300
Fax: (952) 936 - 0044
TF: (800) 328 - 5979

Annual Grant Total: $500,000 - $750,000

Primary Interests: Medicine and Health Care

Recent Recipients: United Way; University of Minnesota

Public Affairs and Related Activities Personnel

At Headquarters

ERLANDSON, Patrick
PAC Treasurer
Tel: (952) 936 - 1300
Fax: (952) 936 - 0044
TF: (800) 328 - 5979

HAYES, Susan
Associate Director, Foundation
Tel: (952) 936 - 1300
Fax: (952) 936 - 0044
TF: (800) 328 - 5979

LINDSAY, Mark
Director, Public Communications and Strategy
Tel: (952) 992 - 4297
Fax: (952) 936 - 0044
TF: (800) 328 - 5979

PENSHORN, John S.
Senior V. President
Tel: (952) 936 - 7214
Fax: (952) 936 - 0044
TF: (800) 328 - 5979

Responsibilities include investor relations.

At Washington Office

GEMEINHARDT, Elise A.
V. President, Federal Affairs
Registered Federal Lobbyist.
Tel: (202) 371 - 1303
Fax: (202) 371 - 5569

HOFFMEIER, Donna
V. President, Government Affairs and Strategic Policy
Registered Federal Lobbyist.
Tel: (202) 371 - 1303
Fax: (202) 371 - 5569

Univar USA, Inc.

A chemical distribution company. Spun off from Royal Vopak and now operates as a unit of Univar N.V.

www.univarusa.com

Annual Revenues: $2.35 billion

Chairman and Chief Exec. Officer
PRUITT, Gary E.
Tel: (425) 889 - 3400
Fax: (425) 889 - 4100

Main Headquarters

Mailing: P.O. Box 34325
Seattle, WA 98124-1325
Tel: (425) 889 - 3400
Fax: (425) 889 - 4100

Street: 6100 Carillon Point
Kirkland, WA 98033

Public Affairs and Related Activities Personnel

At Headquarters

RIZK, Mo
Manager, Regulatory Affairs
Tel: (425) 889 - 3400
Fax: (425) 889 - 4100

SLOATE, Gregg
Director, Investor Relations
gregg.sloate@univarcorp.com
Tel: (425) 638 - 4911
Fax: (425) 638 - 4953

WEBER-MILLSTEIN, Karen
Manager, Corporate Communications
Tel: (425) 889 - 3475
Fax: (425) 889 - 4138

Universal Corp.

The holding company for leaf tobacco processors and other agri-products.

www.universalcorp.com

Annual Revenues: $3.3 billion

Chairman, President and Chief Exec. Officer
KING, Allen B.
Tel: (804) 359 - 9311
Fax: (804) 254 - 3584

Main Headquarters

Mailing: P.O. Box 25099
Richmond, VA 23260
Tel: (804) 359 - 9311
Fax: (804) 254 - 3584

Street: 1501 N. Hamilton St.
Richmond, VA 23230

Political Action Committees

Universal Leaf Tobacco Co. Inc. Political Action Committee
P.O. Box 25099
Richmond, VA 23260
Tel: (804) 359 - 9311
Fax: (804) 254 - 3584

Contributions to Candidates: $5,750 (01/05 - 09/05)

Democrats: $1,500; Republicans: $4,250.

Principal Recipients

SENATE DEMOCRATS

HOUSE DEMOCRATS

Etheridge, Bob (NC)	$1,000

SENATE REPUBLICANS

Allen, George (VA)	$1,500

HOUSE REPUBLICANS

Cantor, Eric (VA)	$1,250

Corporate Foundations and Giving Programs

Universal Leaf Tobacco Foundation
Contact: Julian Keevil

Universal Corp.

* continued from previous page

P.O. Box 25099
Richmond, VA 23260
Tel: (804) 359 - 9311
Fax: (804) 254 - 3541

Annual Grant Total: none reported

Public Affairs and Related Activities Personnel

At Headquarters

KEEVIL, Julian
V. President; and Foundation Contact (Universal Leaf Tobacco Co., Inc.)
Tel: (804) 359 - 9311
Fax: (804) 254 - 3541

STARKEY, James H., III
V. President, External Affairs
Tel: (804) 359 - 9311 Ext: 724

WHELAN, Karen M. L.
V. President and Treasurer
Responsibilities include investor relations.
Tel: (804) 359 - 9311

Universal Forest Products, Inc.

A manufacturer of lumber products.
www.ufpi.com
Annual Revenues: $1.64 billion

Chairman of the Board
SECCHIA, Peter F.
psecchia@ufpi.com
Tel: (616) 364 - 6161
Fax: (616) 364 - 5558

V. Chairman and Chief Exec. Officer
CURRIE, William G.
wcurrie@ufpi.com
Tel: (616) 364 - 6161
Fax: (616) 364 - 5558

Main Headquarters
Mailing: 2801 E. Beltline NE
Grand Rapids, MI 49525
Tel: (616) 364 - 6161
Fax: (616) 364 - 5558

Corporate Foundations and Giving Programs

Universal Forest Products, Inc. Corporate Contributions Program
Contact: Peter F. Secchia
2801 E. Beltline NE
Grand Rapids, MI 49525
Tel: (616) 364 - 6161
Fax: (616) 364 - 5558

Annual Grant Total: none reported

Public Affairs and Related Activities Personnel

At Headquarters

AFENDOULIS, Lynn
Director, Public Affairs
lafendoulis@ufpi.com
Responsibilities include corporate philanthropy.
Tel: (616) 364 - 6161
Fax: (616) 364 - 5558

DEREMO, Mark
Director, Marketing Communications
maderemo@ufpi.com
Tel: (616) 364 - 6161
Fax: (616) 364 - 5558

Universal Health Services, Inc.

A hospital management company.
www.uhsinc.com
Annual Revenues: $3.94 billion

Chairman and Chief Exec. Officer
MILLER, Alan B.
Tel: (610) 768 - 3300
Fax: (610) 768 - 3312

Main Headquarters
Mailing: P.O. Box 61558
King of Prussia, PA 19406-0958
Tel: (610) 768 - 3300
Fax: (610) 768 - 3312
Street: 367 S. Gulph Rd.
King of Prussia, PA 19406

Political Action Committees

Universal Health Services Inc. Employees' Good Government Fund
Contact: Cheryl K. Ramagano
P.O. Box 61558
King of Prussia, PA 19406-0958
Tel: (610) 768 - 3402
Fax: (610) 382 - 4407

Contributions to Candidates: $10,500 (01/05 - 09/05)
Democrats: $6,500; Republicans: $4,000.

Principal Recipients

SENATE DEMOCRATS		HOUSE DEMOCRATS	
Conrad, Kent (ND)	$4,000		
Baucus, Max (MT)	$2,500		
SENATE REPUBLICANS		**HOUSE REPUBLICANS**	
Hatch, Orrin (UT)	$2,000	Ryan, Paul D (WI)	$1,000
Cornyn, John (TX)	$1,000		

Public Affairs and Related Activities Personnel

At Headquarters

FILTON, Steve
Chief Financial Officer
Responsibilities include investor relations.
Tel: (610) 768 - 3300
Fax: (610) 768 - 3312

RAMAGANO, Cheryl K.
Treasurer and PAC Contact
Responsibilities include shareholder relations.
Tel: (610) 768 - 3402
Fax: (610) 382 - 4407

Universal Leaf Tobacco Co., Inc.

See listing on page 494 under Universal Corp.

Universal Music Group

A subsidiary of Vivendi Universal (see separate listing).
www.umusic.com

Chairman and Chief Exec. Officer
MORRIS, Doug
Tel: (212) 841 - 8000

Main Headquarters
Mailing: 1755 Broadway
New York, NY 10019
Tel: (212) 841 - 8000

Public Affairs and Related Activities Personnel

At Headquarters

LOFRUMENTO, Peter
Senior V. President, Corporate Communications
Tel: (212) 841 - 8000

Universal Underwriters Insurance Co.

See listing on page 190 under Farmers Group, Inc.

UNOCAL Corp.

PUBLIC AFFAIRS COUNCIL

A member of the Public Affairs Council. An energy resource and project development company.
www.unocal.com
Annual Revenues: $6.664 billion

Chairman and Chief Exec. Officer
WILLIAMSON, Charles R.
cwilliamson@unocal.com
Tel: (310) 726 - 7600

Main Headquarters
Mailing: 2141 Rosecrans Ave., Suite 4000
El Segundo, CA 90245
Tel: (310) 726 - 7600

Washington Office
Mailing: 1150 Connecticut Ave. NW
Suite 1025
Washington, DC 20036
Tel: (202) 367 - 2760
Fax: (202) 367 - 2790

Political Action Committees

Union Oil (UNOCAL) Political Awareness Fund
Contact: J. William Ichord
1150 Connecticut Ave. NW
Suite 1025
Washington, DC 20036
Tel: (202) 367 - 2773
Fax: (202) 367 - 2790

Contributions to Candidates: $1,000 (01/05 - 09/05)
Republicans: $1,000.

Principal Recipients

SENATE REPUBLICANS		HOUSE REPUBLICANS
Thomas, Craig (WY)	$1,000	

Corporate Foundations and Giving Programs

UNOCAL Foundation
Contact: Laurie Regelbrugge
1150 Connecticut Ave. NW
Suite 1025
Washington, DC 20036
Tel: (202) 367 - 2760
Fax: (202) 367 - 2790

Annual Grant Total: $2,000,000 - $5,000,000
Geographic Preference: National
Primary Interests: Arts and Culture; Higher Education; Math and Science; Persons with Disabilities; Youth Services

Public Affairs and Related Activities Personnel

At Headquarters

LANE, Barry
Manager, Public Relations
blane@unocal.com
Tel: (310) 726 - 7731

THACHER, Michael W.
General Manager, Public Relations and Communications
mthacher@unocal.com
Tel: (310) 726 - 7734

WRIGHT, Robert E.
V. President, Investor Relations
Tel: (310) 726 - 7665
Fax: (310) 726 - 7818

At Washington Office

HUDSON, Laura C.
Government Relations Specialist, International and Federal Affairs
lhudson@unocal.com
Registered Federal Lobbyist.
Tel: (202) 367 - 2760
Fax: (202) 367 - 2790

HUGER, Gregory F.
Director, Corporate Responsibility
ghuger@unocal.com
Tel: (202) 367 - 2760
Fax: (202) 367 - 2790

UNOCAL Corp.

* *continued from previous page*

ICHORD, J. William — Tel: (202) 367 - 2773
V. President, Government and International Relations — Fax: (202) 367 - 2790
wichord@unocal.com
Registered Federal Lobbyist.

REGELBRUGGE, Laurie — Tel: (202) 367 - 2760
Manager, UNOCAL Foundation — Fax: (202) 367 - 2790
lregelbrugge@unocal.com

At Other Offices

SAUER, Nancy L. — Tel: (281) 287 - 5826
State Government Relations Director — Fax: (281) 287 - 5162
14141 Southwest Fwy.
Sugar Land, TX 77478-3435
nsauer@unocal.com

UNOVA, Inc.

An industrial technologies company offering integrated system solutions. Serves the automotive, aerospace, and heavy equipment industries.
www.unova.com
Annual Revenues: $1.12 billion

Chairman, President and Chief Exec. Officer — Tel: (425) 265 - 2400
BRADY, Larry D. — Fax: (425) 265 - 2425
lbrady@unova.com

Main Headquarters
Mailing: 6001 36th Ave. West — Tel: (425) 265 - 2400
Everett, WA 98203-9280 — Fax: (425) 265 - 2425

Corporate Foundations and Giving Programs

UNOVA Foundation
6001 36th Ave. West — Tel: (425) 265 - 2400
Everett, WA 98203-9280 — Fax: (425) 265 - 2425

Annual Grant Total: none reported

Public Affairs and Related Activities Personnel

At Headquarters

MCCARTY, Kevin Patrick — Tel: (425) 265 - 2490
Director, Corporate Public Relations and Investor Relations — Fax: (425) 356 - 3549

TAYLOR, Sue — Tel: (425) 265 - 2400
Chief Information Officer and V. President, Human Resources — Fax: (425) 265 - 2425

UnumProvident Corp.

A member of the Public Affairs Council. A group of insurance companies. Formed by the merger of UNUM Corp. and Provident Companies, Inc. Also headquartered in Chattanooga, TN.
www.unumprovident.com
Annual Revenues: $10.465 billion

Chairman of the Board — Tel: (207) 575 - 2211
POLLARD, C. William

President and Chief Exec. Officer — Tel: (423) 294 - 6866
WATJEN, Thomas R. — Fax: (423) 294 - 3194
twatjen@unumprovident.com

Main Headquarters
Mailing: 2211 Congress St. — Tel: (207) 575 - 2211
Portland, ME 04122-0545

Washington Office
Contact: Sandy Cook
Mailing: 601 Pennsylvania Ave. NW — Tel: (202) 434 - 8190
South Bldg. Suite 900 — Fax: (202) 347 - 1909
Washington, DC 20004

Political Action Committees

UnumProvident Political Action Committee
Contact: Donna T. Mundy
2211 Congress St. — Tel: (207) 575 - 4354
Portland, ME 04122-0545 — Fax: (207) 575 - 4304

Contributions to Candidates: $4,500 (01/05 - 09/05)
Democrats: $1,000; Republicans: $3,500.

Principal Recipients

SENATE DEMOCRATS

HOUSE DEMOCRATS
Vargas, Juan (CA) $1,000

SENATE REPUBLICANS
Talent, James (MO) $1,000

HOUSE REPUBLICANS
McCrery, Jim (LA) $1,500
Johnson, Samuel (TX) $1,000

Corporate Foundations and Giving Programs

UnumProvident Foundation
Contact: Thomas A. H. White
One Fountain Square — Tel: (423) 294 - 8996
Chattanooga, TN 37402 — Fax: (423) 294 - 3962

Annual Grant Total: $2,000,000 - $5,000,000
Geographic Preference: Area(s) in which the company operates; Maine; Massachusetts; Tennessee; South Carolina
Primary Interests: Education; Persons with Disabilities

Public Affairs and Related Activities Personnel

At Headquarters

BEVERIDGE, Bonnie A. — Tel: (207) 575 - 4310
Legislative Systems Coordinator — Fax: (207) 575 - 4304
Mailstop: M/S B159
bbeveridge@unumprovident.com

BRENERMAN, David H. — Tel: (207) 575 - 4311
Assistant V. President, Government Relations — Fax: (207) 575 - 4304
Mailstop: M/S B159
dbrenerman@unumprovident.com

DAVIS, J. Michael — Tel: (207) 575 - 4326
V. President, State Relations — Fax: (207) 575 - 4304
Mailstop: M/S B159
jmichaeldavis@unumprovident.com

FAVINGER, Laura L. — Tel: (207) 575 - 4303
Assistant V. President, Government Relations — Fax: (207) 575 - 4304
Mailstop: M/S B159
lfavinger@unumprovident.com

MUNDY, Donna T. — Tel: (207) 575 - 4354
Senior V. President, Government Relations — Fax: (207) 575 - 4304
Mailstop: M/S B128
dmundy@unumprovident.com

At Washington Office

COOK, Sandy — Tel: (202) 434 - 8190
V. President, Government Relations — Fax: (202) 347 - 1909
awcook@unumprovident.com
Registered Federal Lobbyist.

At Other Offices

HARDIN, Henry T., III — Tel: (423) 294 - 1810
Senior Counsel
One Fountain Square
Chattanooga, TN 37402
hhardiniii@unumprovident.com
Responsibilities include TN political action.

WHITE, Thomas A. H. — Tel: (423) 294 - 8996
V. President, Corporate Relations — Fax: (423) 294 - 3962
One Fountain Square
Chattanooga, TN 37402
tawhite@unumprovident.com

UPN

See listing on page 505 under Viacom Inc/CBS Corp.

UPS

See listing on page 490 under United Parcel Service (UPS).

URS Corp.

Provides planning and design and construction services.
www.urscorp.com
Annual Revenues: $3.186 billion

Chairman, President and Chief Exec. Officer — Tel: (415) 774 - 2700
KOFFEL, Martin M. — Fax: (415) 398 - 1904

Main Headquarters
Mailing: 600 Montgomery St. — Tel: (415) 774 - 2700
26th Floor — Fax: (415) 398 - 1905
San Francisco, CA 94111-2728

Public Affairs and Related Activities Personnel

At Headquarters

NELSON, David — Tel: (415) 774 - 2700
Investor Relations Contact — Fax: (415) 398 - 1905

At Other Offices

KILGANNON, Susan B. — Tel: (212) 330 - 1998
V. President, Communications — Fax: (212) 947 - 6975
One Penn Plaza
New York, NY 10119

LILLARD, Judith — Tel: (212) 736 - 4444
Corporate Communications Contact — Fax: (212) 947 - 6975
One Penn Plaza
New York, NY 10119

US Airways Group, Inc.

A commercial air carrier. Acquired America West Airlines in 2005.
www.usairways.com
Annual Revenues: $6 billion

Chairman of the Board — Tel: (703) 872 - 7000
BRONNER, Dr. David G. — Fax: (703) 872 - 7093

President and Chief Exec. Officer — Tel: (703) 872 - 7000
LAKEFIELD, Bruce R. — Fax: (703) 872 - 7093

Main Headquarters
Mailing: 2345 Crystal Dr. — Tel: (703) 872 - 7000
Arlington, VA 22227 — Fax: (703) 872 - 5134

US Airways Group, Inc.

* continued from previous page

Political Action Committees

US Airways Political Action Committee
2345 Crystal Dr. Tel: (703) 872 - 7000
Arlington, VA 22227 Fax: (703) 872 - 5134

Contributions to Candidates: $4,000 (01/05 - 09/05)
Democrats: $2,000; Republicans: $2,000.

Principal Recipients

SENATE DEMOCRATS

HOUSE DEMOCRATS
Menendez, Robert (NJ) $1,000
Thompson, Bennie (MS) $1,000

SENATE REPUBLICANS
Santorum, Richard (PA) $2,000

HOUSE REPUBLICANS

Corporate Foundations and Giving Programs

US Airways Group Corporate Contributions
Contact: Deborah Thompson
2345 Crystal Dr. Tel: (703) 872 - 5100
Arlington, VA 22227 Fax: (703) 872 - 5134

Annual Grant Total: none reported
Gives specifically in the Philadelphia and Pittsburgh areas in Pennsylvania and in the Charlotte area in North Carolina.
Geographic Preference: North Carolina; Pennsylvania; Washington, DC
Primary Interests: Arts and Culture; Civic and Public Affairs; Community Affairs; Education; Environment/Conservation; Health and Human Services

Public Affairs and Related Activities Personnel

At Headquarters

CASTELVETER, David A. Tel: (703) 872 - 5100
Managing Director, Corporate Communications Fax: (703) 872 - 5134
david_castelveter@usairways.com

KUDWA, Amy Tel: (703) 872 - 5182
Manager, Public Relations Fax: (703) 872 - 5104
akudwa@usairways.com

LANIER, Elizabeth K. Tel: (703) 872 - 7000
Exec. V. President, Corporate Affairs; General Counsel Fax: (703) 872 - 5208
liz_lanier@usairways.com

MURRAY, Rosemary G. Tel: (703) 872 - 5140
V. President, Government Affairs Fax: (703) 872 - 5109
rosemary_murray@usairways.com

THOMPSON, Deborah Tel: (703) 872 - 5100
Corporate Contributions Contact Fax: (703) 872 - 5134

U.S. Bancorp

A member of the Public Affairs Council. A bank holding company. Merged with Firstar Corp. in 2001.
www.usbank.com
Annual Revenues: $14.7 billion

Main Headquarters
Mailing: 800 Nicollet Mall Tel: (651) 466 - 3000
Minneapolis, MN 55402

Political Action Committees

U.S. Bancorp Political Participation Program
Contact: Jim T. Nikolai
800 Nicollet Mall Tel: (612) 303 - 7860
Minneapolis, MN 55402 Fax: (612) 303 - 0788

Contributions to Candidates: $77,300 (01/05 - 09/05)
Democrats: $17,000; Republicans: $60,300.

Principal Recipients

SENATE DEMOCRATS
Carper, Thomas R (DE) $5,000
Nelson, Benjamin (NE) $2,000

HOUSE DEMOCRATS
Moore, Dennis (KS) $2,000

SENATE REPUBLICANS
Kennedy, Mark (MN) $10,000
Santorum, Richard (PA) $5,000
Talent, James (MO) $5,000
McConnell, Mitch (KY) $4,500

HOUSE REPUBLICANS
Dewine, R. Pat (OH) $5,000
Hastert, Dennis J. (IL) $5,000
Akin, William Todd (MO) $4,000
Manzullo, Donald (IL) $2,500
Emerson, Jo Ann (MO) $2,100
Pryce, Deborah (OH) $2,000
Ryun, Jim R (KS) $2,000
Schmidt, Jeannette (OH) $2,000
Tiberi, Patrick (OH) $2,000

Corporate Foundations and Giving Programs

U.S. Bancorp Foundation
Contact: Teresa B. Bonner
800 Nicollet Mall Tel: (612) 303 - 0742
Minneapolis, MN 55402 Fax: (612) 303 - 0787

Annual Grant Total: over $5,000,000
Contributed over $20 million in 2004. The company also maintains an employee matching gifts program and a five star volunteer awards program.
Primary Interests: Arts and Culture; Economic Development; Education; Financially Disadvantaged; Housing
Recent Recipients: United Way

Public Affairs and Related Activities Personnel

At Headquarters

BONNER, Teresa B. Tel: (612) 303 - 0742
Contact, Corporate Philanthropy and Community Relations Fax: (612) 303 - 0787
Mailstop: BCMNH23K

BURKE, Deborah M. Tel: (612) 303 - 0746
Manager, Government Relations

CARLSON, Jennie P. Tel: (651) 466 - 3000
Exec. V. President, Human Resources
Mailstop: BCMNH147A

CHAREST, Teri L. Tel: (612) 303 - 0732
Assistant V. President, Media Relations Fax: (612) 303 - 0735
Mailstop: BCMNH23K
teri.charest@usbank.com

DALE, Steve W. Tel: (612) 303 - 0784
Senior V. President, Media Relations Fax: (612) 303 - 0735
Mailstop: BCMNH23K
steve.dale@usbank.com

FRANTTI, Amy B. Tel: (612) 303 - 0733
Assistant V. President, Media Relations Fax: (612) 303 - 0735
Mailstop: BCMNH23K
amy.frantti@usbank.com

KAUFMAN, Andrea J. Tel: (612) 303 - 7824
Treasurer, U.S. Bancorp Political Participation Program Fax: (612) 303 - 7884
Mailstop: BCMNH210

MURPHY, Judith T. Tel: (612) 303 - 0783
V. President, Investor Relations Fax: (612) 303 - 0782
Mailstop: BCMNH23K
judith.murphy@usbank.com

NIKOLAI, Jim T. Tel: (612) 303 - 7860
PAC Contact Fax: (612) 303 - 0788

US Filter Indianapolis Water LLC

See listing on page 501 under Veolia Water Indianapolis, LLC.

USA Mobility, Inc.

Formed by the merger of Metrocall Holdings Inc. and Arch Wireless Inc. A provider of wireless solutions.
www.usamobility.com

Chairman of the Board Tel: (703) 660 - 6677
YUDKOFF, Royce R. Fax: (703) 768 - 9622

President and Chief Exec. Officer Tel: (703) 660 - 6677
KELLY, Vincent D. Fax: (703) 768 - 9622

Main Headquarters
Mailing: 6677 Richmond Hwy. Tel: (703) 660 - 6677
Alexandria, VA 22306 Fax: (703) 768 - 9622

Public Affairs and Related Activities Personnel

At Other Offices

LOUGEE, Robert W., Jr. Tel: (508) 870 - 6771
Contact, Public Relations and Investor Relations Fax: (508) 366 - 8966
1800 W. Park Dr.
Suite 250
Westborough, MA 01581-3989
bob.lougee@usamobility.com

USAA

See listing on page 491 under United Services Automobile Ass'n (USAA).

USEC Inc.

A global energy company. Supplies enriched uranium fuel to commercial nuclear power plants.
www.usec.com
Annual Revenues: $707.8 million

Chairman, President and Chief Exec. Officer Tel: (301) 564 - 3200
MELLOR, James R. Fax: (301) 564 - 3201
mellorjr@usec.com

Main Headquarters
Mailing: Two Democracy Center Tel: (301) 564 - 3200
6903 Rockledge Dr. Fax: (301) 564 - 3201
Bethesda, MD 20817-1818

Political Action Committees

USEC Inc. PAC
Contact: Ellen Wolf

USEC Inc.

** continued from previous page*

Two Democracy Center
6903 Rockledge Dr.
Bethesda, MD 20817-1818
Tel: (301) 564 - 3200
Fax: (301) 564 - 3201

Contributions to Candidates: $22,500 (01/05 - 09/05)
Democrats: $3,000; Republicans: $19,500.

Principal Recipients

SENATE REPUBLICANS		HOUSE REPUBLICANS	
McConnell, Mitch (KY)	$2,000	Whitfield, Ed (KY)	$3,000
		Schmidt, Jeannette (OH)	$2,500
		Dewine, R. Pat (OH)	$2,000
		Hobson, David (OH)	$2,000

Public Affairs and Related Activities Personnel

At Headquarters

FERGUSON, Sydney M.
Tel: (301) 564 - 3200
Fax: (301) 564 - 3201

GREEN, Ron
Tel: (301) 564 - 3200
Fax: (301) 564 - 3201

MAJOR-SOSIAS, Mari Angeles
Manager, Investor Relations
Tel: (301) 564 - 3200
Fax: (301) 564 - 3201

NEUMANN, E. John
V. President, Government Relations
Tel: (301) 564 - 3200
Fax: (301) 564 - 3201

SAZAWAL, Vijay
Tel: (301) 564 - 3200
Fax: (301) 564 - 3201

SCOTT, Dennis
Tel: (301) 564 - 3200
Fax: (301) 564 - 3201

STUCKLE, Elizabeth
Director, Corporate Communications
stucklee@usec.com
Tel: (301) 564 - 3200
Fax: (301) 564 - 3201

WARD, Caleb
Government Relations Associate
Tel: (301) 564 - 3200
Fax: (301) 564 - 3201

WINGFIELD, Steven
Director, Investor Relations
wingfieldd@usec.com
Tel: (301) 564 - 3200
Fax: (301) 564 - 3201

WOLF, Ellen
Pac Treasurer
Tel: (301) 564 - 3200
Fax: (301) 564 - 3201

WRIGHT, W. Lance
V. President, Human Resources and Administration
Tel: (301) 564 - 3200
Fax: (301) 564 - 3201

USG Corp.

A producer of gypsum, wallboard, ceiling tile and other building materials.
www.usg.com
Annual Revenues: $4.5 billion

Chairman and Chief Exec. Officer
FOOTE, William C.
Tel: (312) 606 - 4000
Fax: (312) 606 - 5598

Main Headquarters
Mailing: P.O. Box 6721
Chicago, IL 60680-6721
Tel: (312) 606 - 4000
Fax: (312) 606 - 5598
Street: 125 S. Franklin St.
Chicago, IL 60606-4678

Corporate Foundations and Giving Programs

USG Foundation
Contact: Peter K. Maitland
P.O. Box 6721
Chicago, IL 60680-6721
Tel: (312) 606 - 4024
Fax: (312) 606 - 3872

Annual Grant Total: $300,000 - $400,000
Guidelines are available.
Geographic Preference: National; Area(s) in which the company operates; International
Primary Interests: Arts and Culture; Education; Medicine and Health Care
Recent Recipients: Nat'l Merit Scholarship; United Way

Public Affairs and Related Activities Personnel

At Headquarters

BELL, Robert
Director, Government Affairs
rbell@usg.com
Tel: (312) 606 - 3992
Fax: (312) 606 - 4802

BENCOMO, James
Director, Investor Relations and Pension
jbencomo@usg.com
Tel: (312) 606 - 3839
Fax: (312) 606 - 5725

COOK, Brian J.
Senior V. President, Human Resources
bcook@usg.com
Tel: (312) 606 - 3997
Fax: (312) 606 - 5646

KAMINSKY, Marci N.
Senior V. President, Communications
mkaminsky@usg.com
Tel: (312) 606 - 4124
Fax: (312) 606 - 5301

MAITLAND, Peter K.
V. President, Compensation, Benefits, and Administration
pmaitland@usg.com
Responsibilities include corporate philanthropy.
Tel: (312) 606 - 4024
Fax: (312) 606 - 3872

WILLIAMS, Robert E.
Director, Corporate Communications
rewilliams@usg.com
Tel: (312) 606 - 4356
Fax: (312) 606 - 5301

WONNELL, David
Director, Environment and Manufacturing Services
dgwonnel@usg.com
Tel: (312) 606 - 4016
Fax: (312) 606 - 4484

UST Inc.

A member of the Public Affairs Council. A holding company for its principal subsidiaries: U.S. Smokeless Tobacco Company and International Wine and Spirits, Ltd. U.S.
www.ustinc.com
Annual Revenues: $1.68 billion

Chairman, President and Chief Exec. Officer
GIERER, Vincent A., Jr.
Tel: (203) 661 - 1100
Fax: (203) 863 - 7250

Main Headquarters
Mailing: 100 W. Putnam Ave.
Greenwich, CT 06830
Tel: (203) 661 - 1100
Fax: (203) 863 - 7250

Washington Office
Contact: Todd A. Walker
Mailing: 655 15th St., NW
Suite 410
Washington, DC 20005
Tel: (202) 638 - 6890
Fax: (202) 220 - 3619

Political Action Committees

UST Executives Administrators and Managers Political Action Committee (USTeamPAC)
Contact: Todd A. Walker
655 15th St., NW
Suite 410
Washington, DC 20005
Tel: (202) 638 - 6890
Fax: (202) 220 - 3619

Contributions to Candidates: $102,500 (01/05 - 09/05)
Democrats: $16,000; Republicans: $86,500.

Principal Recipients

SENATE DEMOCRATS		HOUSE DEMOCRATS	
Nelson, Benjamin (NE)	$2,000	Boyd, F Allen Jr (FL)	$2,500
		Davis, Lincoln (TN)	$2,000
		McIntyre, Mike (NC)	$2,000

SENATE REPUBLICANS		HOUSE REPUBLICANS	
Burns, Conrad (MT)	$6,000	DeLay, Tom (TX)	$5,000
Allen, George (VA)	$5,000	Norwood, Charles (GA)	$3,500
Vitter, David (LA)	$5,000	Simpson, Michael (ID)	$3,500
Ensign, John Eric (NV)	$3,000	Lewis, Ron (KY)	$3,000
Bryant, Edward (TN)	$2,500	Blackburn, Marsha (TN)	$2,500
Chambliss, Saxby (GA)	$2,500	Buyer, Steve (IN)	$2,500
Graham, Lindsey (SC)	$2,500	Hayes, Robert (NC)	$2,500
Hatch, Orrin (UT)	$2,000	Whitfield, Ed (KY)	$2,500
Santorum, Richard (PA)	$2,000	Cubin, Barbara L (WY)	$2,000
		Everett, Terry (AL)	$2,000
		Stearns, Clifford (FL)	$2,000

Corporate Foundations and Giving Programs

UST Corporate Contributions Committee
Contact: Scot B. Weicker
100 W. Putnam Ave.
Greenwich, CT 06830
Tel: (203) 622 - 3282
Fax: (203) 863 - 7259

Annual Grant Total: $2,000,000 - $5,000,000
Primary Interests: Arts and Culture, Education, Human Services
Geographic Preference: Area in which the company is headquartered; Area(s) in which the company operates
Primary Interests: Arts and Culture; Education
Recent Recipients: American Red Cross; Literacy Volunteers of America; United Way

Public Affairs and Related Activities Personnel

At Headquarters

BALDWIN, W. Preston, III
V. President, State Government Relations
Tel: (203) 622 - 3364
Fax: (203) 622 - 3315

BAZINET, Michael G.
Director, Corporate Communications and Public Affairs
Tel: (203) 622 - 3529
Fax: (203) 863 - 7228

BOLGER, Thomas J.
Director, State Government Relations-East
Tel: (203) 622 - 3216
Fax: (203) 863 - 7240

COLLINS, Sean M.
Regional Manager, State Government Relations/Northeast
Tel: (203) 622 - 3497
Fax: (203) 863 - 7240

KOHLBERGER, Richard A.
Senior V. President, Human Resources and Corporate Administration, General Counsel and Corporate Secretary
Tel: (203) 622 - 3674
Fax: (203) 863 - 7250

UST Inc.

** continued from previous page*

KRATOVIL, Edward D.
Senior V. President, Worldwide Government Relations
Tel: (203) 622 - 3667
Fax: (203) 622 - 3315

ROZELLE, Mark A.
V. President, Investor Relations and Corporate Communications
Tel: (203) 622 - 3520
Fax: (203) 622 - 3561

WEICKER, Scot B.
Director, Corporate Contributions and Events
Tel: (203) 622 - 3282
Fax: (203) 863 - 7259

At Washington Office

MITCHELL, Michael
Tel: (202) 638 - 6890
Fax: (202) 220 - 3619

STANTON, Shanti
Tel: (202) 638 - 6890
Fax: (202) 220 - 3619

VERHEIJ, Richard H.
Tel: (202) 638 - 6890
Fax: (202) 220 - 3619
Registered Federal Lobbyist.

VERSAGGI, John D.
Tel: (202) 638 - 6890
Fax: (202) 220 - 3619
Registered Federal Lobbyist.

WALKER, Todd A.
V. President, Federal Government Relations
(UST Public Affairs Inc. (USTPA))
Registered Federal Lobbyist.
Tel: (202) 638 - 6890
Fax: (202) 220 - 3619

At Other Offices

DONALDSON, R. Eric
Regional Manager, State Government Relations/Southwest
7801 Mesquite Bend Dr., Suite 101
Irving, TX 75063
Tel: (214) 296 - 6113
Fax: (214) 296 - 6112

FOTJIK, Brian J.
Regional Manager, State Government Relations/Great Lakes
2640 White Oak Circle, Suite E
Aurora, IL 60504
Tel: (630) 692 - 6060
Fax: (630) 692 - 6062

FUCHS, Daniel
Regional Manager, State Government Relations/Rocky Mountain
1301 Pennsylvania
Suite 900
Denver, CO 80203
Tel: (303) 831 - 6268
Fax: (303) 831 - 9214

PAULSON, Kerry L.
Director, State Government Relations/West
2640 White Oak Circle
Suite E
Aurora, IL 60504
Tel: (630) 692 - 6060
Fax: (630) 692 - 6062

SANDERS, Joshua
Regional Manager, State Government Relations/Mid-Atlantic
2436 Pennsylvania Ave.
Suite 4
Weirton, WV 26062
Tel: (304) 723 - 1016
Fax: (304) 723 - 4377

VAN NIEUWBURG, Eric M.
Regional Manager, State Government Relations/Pacific
3164 Gold Camp Dr.
Suite B-230
Rancho Cordova, CA 95670
Tel: (916) 631 - 0282
Fax: (916) 853 - 9067

Utah Power Co.

See listing on page 369 under PacifiCorp.

UtiliCorp United Inc.

See listing on page 45 under Aquila, Inc.

Valassis Communications, Inc.

A provider of marketing products and services.

www.valassis.com

Annual Revenues: $916.5 million

Chairman, President and Chief Exec. Officer
SCHULTZ, Alan F.
schultza@valassis.com
Tel: (734) 591 - 3000
Ext: 17326
Fax: (734) 591 - 4503
TF: (800) 437 - 0479

Main Headquarters
Mailing: 19975 Victor Pkwy.
Livonia, MI 48152-7001
Tel: (734) 591 - 3000
Fax: (734) 591 - 4994
TF: (800) 437 - 0479

Corporate Foundations and Giving Programs

Valassis Communications, Inc. Giving Committee
19975 Victor Pkwy.
Livonia, MI 48152-7001
Tel: (734) 591 - 3000
Fax: (734) 591 - 4994
TF: (800) 437 - 0479

Annual Grant Total: under $100,000
Focuses on organizations concerned with multiple schlerosis.
Geographic Preference: Kansas; North Carolina; Massachusetts; California; Michigan
Recent Recipients: Alzheimer's Ass'n; American Diabetes Ass'n

Public Affairs and Related Activities Personnel

At Headquarters

HOFFMAN, Barry
Exec. V. President and General Counsel
hoffman@valassis.com
Tel: (734) 591 - 3000
Ext: 16386
Fax: (734) 591 - 4503
TF: (800) 437 - 0479
Serves as the company's senior public affairs officer.

HYDE, Marcia
V. President, Human Resources and Communications Center
hydem@valassis.com
Tel: (734) 591 - 3000
Ext: 16343
Fax: (734) 591 - 4503
TF: (800) 437 - 0479

LAUDERBACK, Sherry
Director, Investor Relations and Communications Center
lauderbacks@valassis.com
Tel: (734) 591 - 7374
Ext: 17374
Fax: (734) 591 - 4503
TF: (800) 437 - 0479

MCANUFF, Stacie
Communications Center Supervisor
mcanuffs@valassis.com
Tel: (734) 591 - 7375
Ext: 17375
Fax: (734) 591 - 4503
TF: (800) 437 - 0479

OLIVERIO, Tamara
Public Relations Specialist
oliverit@valassis.com
Tel: (734) 591 - 3000
Ext: 14955
Fax: (734) 591 - 4503
TF: (800) 437 - 0479

Valero Energy Corp.

A leading independent refining and marketing company. A producer of environmentally clean products such as reformulated gasoline, CARB Phase II gasoline, low-sulfur diesel, and oxygenates. Acquired Ultramar Diamond Shamrock Corp. in Januaury of 2002.

www.valero.com

Chairman and Chief Exec. Officer
GREEHEY, William E.
Tel: (210) 345 - 2000
Fax: (210) 345 - 2646
TF: (800) 531 - 7911

Main Headquarters
Mailing: P.O. Box 500
San Antonio, TX 78249-112
Tel: (210) 345 - 2000
Fax: (210) 345 - 2646
TF: (800) 531 - 7911

Street: One Valero Pl.
San Antonio, TX 78212-3186

Washington Office
Mailing: 601 Pennsylvania Ave. NW
Suite 900, South Bldg.
Washington, DC 20004
Tel: (202) 434 - 8927

Political Action Committees

Valero Energy Corp. Political Action Committee
Contact: Jim Greenwood
P.O. Box 500
San Antonio, TX 78249-112
Tel: (210) 345 - 2016
Fax: (210) 345 - 2646
TF: (800) 531 - 7911

Contributions to Candidates: $140,500 (01/05 - 09/05)
Democrats: $17,500; Republicans: $123,000.

Principal Recipients

SENATE DEMOCRATS

HOUSE DEMOCRATS
Edwards, Chet (TX) $5,000
Gonzalez, Charles A (TX) $5,000

SENATE REPUBLICANS
Santorum, Richard (PA) $8,500
Ensign, John Eric (NV) $5,000
Hutchison, Kay Bailey (TX) $5,000
DeMint, James (SC) $3,500
Kyl, Jon L (AZ) $3,000

HOUSE REPUBLICANS
Bonilla, Henry (TX) $10,000
Cole, Tom (OK) $10,000
Sessions, Pete (TX) $7,500
Wilson, Heather (NM) $7,500
DeLay, Tom (TX) $5,000
Hastert, Dennis J. (IL) $5,000
McCaul, Michael (TX) $5,000
Smith, Lamar (TX) $5,000

Corporate Foundations and Giving Programs

Valero Energy Corporate Contributions
Contact: Mary Rose Brown

Valero Energy Corp.

** continued from previous page*

P.O. Box 500 — Tel: (210) 345 - 2314
San Antonio, TX 78249-112 — Fax: (210) 345 - 2646
TF: (800) 531 - 7911

Annual Grant Total: none reported
Recent Recipients: United Way

Public Affairs and Related Activities Personnel

At Headquarters

BROWN, Mary Rose — Tel: (210) 345 - 2314
V. President, Corporate Communications — Fax: (210) 345 - 2646
brownmr@valero.com — TF: (800) 531 - 7911

FISHER, Eric — Tel: (210) 345 - 3896
V. President, Investor Relations — Fax: (210) 345 - 2646
TF: (800) 531 - 7911

GREENWOOD, Jim — Tel: (210) 345 - 2016
V. President, Government Affairs — Fax: (210) 345 - 2646
jim.greenwood@valero.com — TF: (800) 531 - 7911

KLUMPYAN, Julie K. — Tel: (210) 345 - 2435
Manager, Government Affairs — Fax: (210) 345 - 2646
TF: (800) 531 - 7911

RENFRO, Norman L. — Tel: (210) 345 - 2069
V. President, Health, Safety and Environmental — Fax: (210) 345 - 2646
renfron@valero.com — TF: (800) 531 - 7911

TITZMAN, Donna — Tel: (210) 345 - 2000
Treasurer, Valero Energy Corp. Political Action Committee — Fax: (210) 345 - 2646
titzmand@valero.com

At Washington Office

FELNER, Craig — Tel: (202) 434 - 8927
Director, Federal Governmental Affairs
Registered Federal Lobbyist.

Valhi, Inc.

A holding company. Interests include chemical manufacturing; fast food, hardware, and forest products.
Annual Revenues: $1.079 billion

Chairman of the Board — Tel: (972) 233 - 1700
SIMMONS, Harold C. — Fax: (972) 448 - 1445

President and Chief Exec. Officer — Tel: (972) 233 - 1700
WATSON, Steven L. — Fax: (972) 448 - 1445

Main Headquarters
Mailing: Three Lincoln Center — Tel: (972) 233 - 1700
5430 LBJ Fwy., Suite 1700 — Fax: (972) 448 - 1445
Dallas, TX 75240-2697

Political Action Committees

NL Industries PAC
Contact: John Sy. Wrba
Three Lincoln Center — Tel: (972) 233 - 1700
5430 LBJ Fwy., Suite 1700 — Fax: (972) 448 - 1445
Dallas, TX 75240-2697

Contributions to Candidates: none reported (01/05 - 09/05)

Public Affairs and Related Activities Personnel

At Headquarters

BROWNLEE, Kathy — Tel: (972) 233 - 1700
Director, Personnel — Fax: (972) 448 - 1445

LOUIS, Andrew R. — Tel: (972) 450 - 4243
Secretary — Fax: (972) 448 - 1445
Responsibilities include investor relations.

SY. WRBA, John — Tel: (972) 233 - 1700
PAC Treasurer — Fax: (972) 448 - 1445

At Other Offices

OTTOSEN, Karl J. — Tel: (703) 978 - 8038
V. President, Government Affairs — Fax: (703) 978 - 8039
(N L Industries, Inc.)
6916 Wolf Run Shoals
Fairfax Station, VA 22309

Valmont Industries, Inc.

A manufacturer of poles, towers and structures for the lighting, communication and utility markets. Also engaged in the production of mechanized agricultural irrigation equipment and a wide variety of fabricated products for commercial and industrial applications, and supplies galvanizing and powder coatings services.
www.valmont.com
Annual Revenues: $854.9 million

Chairman and Chief Exec. Officer — Tel: (402) 963 - 1000
BAY, Mogens C. — Fax: (402) 963 - 1095

Main Headquarters
Mailing: One Valmont Plaza — Tel: (402) 963 - 1000
Omaha, NE 68154-5215 — Fax: (402) 963 - 1095

Political Action Committees

Valmont Industries Political Action Committee
Contact: Mark C. Jaksich
One Valmont Plaza — Tel: (402) 963 - 1000
Omaha, NE 68154-5215 — Fax: (402) 963 - 1095

Contributions to Candidates: none reported (01/05 - 09/05)

Corporate Foundations and Giving Programs

Valmont Industries Corporate Contributions Program
Contact: Edward Burchfield
One Valmont Plaza — Tel: (402) 963 - 1050
Omaha, NE 68154-5215 — Fax: (402) 963 - 1095

Annual Grant Total: none reported

Valmont Foundation
Contact: Edward Burchfield
One Valmont Plaza — Tel: (402) 963 - 1050
Omaha, NE 68154-5215 — Fax: (402) 963 - 1095

Annual Grant Total: none reported
Geographic Preference: Nebraska

Public Affairs and Related Activities Personnel

At Headquarters

ASHFORD, Ann F. — Tel: (402) 963 - 1000
V. President, Human Resources — Fax: (402) 963 - 1095

BURCHFIELD, Edward — Tel: (402) 963 - 1050
Director, Corporate Relations and Administration — Fax: (402) 963 - 1095
elb2@valmont.com

JAKSICH, Mark C. — Tel: (402) 963 - 1000
Treasurer, Valmont Industries PAC — Fax: (402) 963 - 1095

LAUDIN, Jeff — Tel: (402) 963 - 1158
Manager, Investor Relations — Fax: (402) 963 - 1197
jsl1@valmont.com

TAYLOR, Bill — Tel: (402) 359 - 2201
Director, Environmental Affairs — Fax: (402) 359 - 2848
wrt@valmont.com

Valspar Corp.

A manufacturer of paints, coatings and chemicals.
www.valspar.com
Annual Revenues: $2.13 billion

Chairman of the Board — Tel: (612) 332 - 7371
MCBURNEY, Thomas R. — Fax: (612) 375 - 7723

President and Chief Exec. Officer — Tel: (612) 332 - 7371
MANSFIELD, William L. — Fax: (612) 375 - 7723

Main Headquarters
Mailing: 1101 Third St. South — Tel: (612) 332 - 7371
Minneapolis, MN 55415 — Fax: (612) 375 - 7723

Corporate Foundations and Giving Programs

Valspar Foundation
Contact: Gwen Liefeld
4900 IDS Center — Tel: (612) 337 - 5903
80 S. Eighth St. — Fax: (612) 337 - 5904
Minneapolis, MN 55402

Annual Grant Total: none reported

Public Affairs and Related Activities Personnel

At Headquarters

ENGH, Rolph — Tel: (612) 375 - 7705
Exec. V. President, General Counsel and Secretary — Fax: (612) 375 - 7313
rengh@valspar.com
Responsibilities include government affairs.

GARDNER, Gary E. — Tel: (612) 375 - 7737
V. President, Human Resources and Public Relations — Fax: (612) 375 - 7723
ggardner@valspar.com

WALKER, Lori A. — Tel: (612) 332 - 7371
V. President, Treasurer and Controller — Fax: (612) 375 - 7723

WEISS, Deborah H. — Tel: (612) 375 - 7302
Director, Public Relations — Fax: (612) 375 - 7723
dweiss@valspar.com

At Other Offices

LIEFELD, Gwen — Tel: (612) 337 - 5903
Manager, Valspar Foundation — Fax: (612) 337 - 5904
4900 IDS Center
80 S. Eighth St.
Minneapolis, MN 55402

Value City Department Stores, Inc.

See listing on page 410 under Retail Ventures, Inc.

Van Waters & Rogers Inc.

See listing on page 494 under Univar USA, Inc.

Varian Medical Systems, Inc.

Designs and manufactures medical equipment systems and software for the treatment of cancer.

www.varian.com

Annual Revenues: $1 billion

Chairman, President and Chief Exec. Officer
LEVY, Richard M. — Tel: (650) 493 - 4000; Fax: (650) 842 - 5196

Main Headquarters
Mailing: 3100 Hansen Way, Palo Alto, CA 94304-1030 — Tel: (650) 493 - 4000; Fax: (650) 842 - 5196

Public Affairs and Related Activities Personnel

At Headquarters

GINSBERG, Meryl
Manager, Public Relations
meryl.ginsberg@varian.com
Tel: (650) 424 - 6444; Fax: (650) 842 - 5196

SIAS, Spencer
Director, Corporate Communications and Investor Relations
spencer.sias@varian.com
Tel: (650) 424 - 5782; Fax: (650) 842 - 5196

Vectren Corp.

A provider of energy and related applied technology solutions. Formed from the merger of Indiana Energy, Inc. and SIGCORP in 2000.

www.vectren.com

Annual Revenues: $1.8 billion

Chairman, President and Chief Exec. Officer
ELLERBROOK, Niel C. — Tel: (812) 491 - 4000; Fax: (812) 491 - 4078; TF: (800) 227 - 1376

Main Headquarters
Mailing: 211 Riverside Dr., Evansville, IN 47708-1251 — Tel: (812) 491 - 4000; Fax: (812) 491 - 4078; TF: (800) 227 - 1376

Political Action Committees

Vectren Corp. Employees Federal PAC
Contact: Leslie Blenner
20 NW Ninth St.
Evansville, IN 47741

Contributions to Candidates: $8,600 (01/05 - 09/05)
Republicans: $8,600.

Principal Recipients

SENATE REPUBLICANS		HOUSE REPUBLICANS	
Dewine, Richard (OH)	$2,500	Boehner, John (OH)	$2,500
		Hobson, David (OH)	$2,100
		Burton, Danny (IN)	$1,000

Corporate Foundations and Giving Programs

Vectren Foundation
Contact: Mark Miller
211 Riverside Dr.
Evansville, IN 47708-1251
Tel: (812) 491 - 4000; Fax: (812) 491 - 4078; TF: (800) 227 - 1376

Annual Grant Total: none reported
Primary Interests: Arts and Culture; Civic and Cultural Activities; Education; Health and Human Services

Public Affairs and Related Activities Personnel

At Headquarters

LYNCH, Richard G.
Senior V. President, Human Resources and Administration
Tel: (812) 491 - 4000; Fax: (812) 491 - 4078; TF: (800) 227 - 1376

MILLER, Mark
Foundation Contact
mmiller@vectren.com
Tel: (812) 491 - 4000; Fax: (812) 491 - 4078; TF: (800) 227 - 1376

PETITT, Douglas
V. President, Government Affairs
Tel: (812) 491 - 4000; Fax: (812) 491 - 4078; TF: (800) 227 - 1376

SCHEIN, Steve M.
V. President, Investor Relations
sschein@vectren.com
Tel: (812) 491 - 4000; Fax: (812) 491 - 4078; TF: (800) 227 - 1376

WHITESIDE, Jeffrey W.
V. President, Corporate Communications and Public Affairs
Tel: (812) 491 - 4000; Fax: (812) 491 - 4078; TF: (800) 227 - 1376

At Other Offices

BLENNER, Leslie
Treasurer, Vectren Corp. Employees Federal PAC
20 NW Ninth St.
Evansville, IN 47741

Velsicol Chemical Corp.

A privately held chemical manufacturing corporation.

www.velsicol.com

Chairman, President and Chief Exec. Officer
SIGEL, Arthur R. — Tel: (847) 298 - 9000; Fax: (847) 298 - 9018; TF: (800) 826 - 4449

Main Headquarters
Mailing: 10400 W. Higgins, Suite 600, Rosemont, IL 60018 — Tel: (847) 298 - 9000; Fax: (847) 298 - 9018; TF: (800) 826 - 4449

Public Affairs and Related Activities Personnel

At Headquarters

HANSON, Charles R.
V. President, Environmental Health and Safety
Tel: (847) 298 - 9000; Fax: (847) 298 - 9018; TF: (800) 826 - 4449

JENNINGS, Donna N.
V. President, Human Resources and Communications
Tel: (847) 298 - 9000 Ext: 3474; Fax: (847) 298 - 9018; TF: (800) 826 - 4449

Vencor, Inc.

See listing on page 281 under Kindred Healthcare, Inc.

Veolia Water Indianapolis, LLC

Formerly US Filter. A water utility.

ww.indianapoliswater.com

Main Headquarters
Mailing: P.O. Box 1220, Indianapolis, IN 46206 — Tel: (317) 639 - 1431; Fax: (317) 263 - 6414
Street: 1220 Waterway Blvd., Indianapolis, IN 46202

Public Affairs and Related Activities Personnel

At Headquarters

GILES, Charlene
Director, Human Resources
charlene.giles@veoliawaterna.com
Tel: (317) 639 - 1431; Fax: (317) 263 - 6414

HEWITT, Timothy M.
President and Operations Manager
Tel: (317) 639 - 1431; Fax: (317) 263 - 6414

MOSBY-WILLIAMS, Carolyn
V. President, Communications and Community Relations
carolyn.mosby-williams@veoliawaterna.com
Tel: (317) 639 - 1431; Fax: (317) 263 - 6414

Veridian Corp.

See listing on page 212 under General Dynamics Corporation.

VeriSign, Inc.

Provides services for internet and telecommunications networks.

www.verisign.com

Annual Revenues: $1.222 billion

Chairman and Chief Exec. Officer
SCLAVOS, Stratton D. — Tel: (650) 961 - 7500; Fax: (650) 961 - 7300

Main Headquarters
Mailing: 487 E. Middlefield Rd., Mountain View, CA 94043-4047 — Tel: (650) 961 - 7500; Fax: (650) 961 - 7300

Washington Office
Contact: Tom Galvin
Mailing: 1666 K St., NW, Suite 410, Washington, DC 20006 — Tel: (202) 973 - 6600; Fax: (202) 466 - 9103

Political Action Committees

VeriSign, Inc. PAC
Contact: Shane Tews
1666 K St., NW
Suite 410
Washington, DC 20006
Tel: (202) 973 - 6603; Fax: (202) 466 - 9103

Contributions to Candidates: $13,000 (01/05 - 09/05)
Democrats: $2,000; Republicans: $11,000.

VeriSign, Inc.

* continued from previous page

Principal Recipients

SENATE DEMOCRATS		HOUSE DEMOCRATS	
		Eshoo, Anna (CA)	$1,000
		Porter, Jon (TX)	$1,000
SENATE REPUBLICANS		**HOUSE REPUBLICANS**	
Burns, Conrad (MT)	$5,000	Ferguson, Mike (NJ)	$1,000
Allen, George (VA)	$2,500	Pickering, Chip (MS)	$1,000
Ensign, John Eric (NV)	$1,000		

Public Affairs and Related Activities Personnel

At Headquarters

O'SHAUGHNESSY, Brian — Tel: (650) 961 - 7500
Director, Public Affairs — Fax: (650) 961 - 7300

At Washington Office

ALSENBERG, Michael — Tel: (202) 973 - 6611
Director, Government Affairs — Fax: (202) 466 - 9103

CUTE, Brian — Tel: (202) 973 - 6615
Director, Government Relations — Fax: (202) 466 - 9103

GALVIN, Tom — Tel: (202) 973 - 6610
V. President, Government Relations — Fax: (202) 466 - 9103

TEWS, Shane — Tel: (202) 973 - 6603
Director, Government Relations; and PAC Director — Fax: (202) 466 - 9103

Verizon Communications Inc.

A member of the Public Affairs Council. A national-global voice/data/wireless/information services provider formed from the merger of GTE Corp. and Bell Atlantic Corp. The company plans to merge with MCI (see separate listing). Completion of the merger is expected in late 2005 or early 2006.

www.verizon.com
Annual Revenues: $67.190 billion

Chairman and Chief Exec. Officer
SEIDENBERG, Ivan G. — Tel: (212) 395 - 2121; TF: (800) 621 - 9900
ivan.seidenberg@verizon.com

Main Headquarters
Mailing: 1095 Ave. of the Americas
New York, NY 10036
Tel: (212) 395 - 2121
Fax: (212) 869 - 3265
TF: (800) 621 - 9900

Washington Office
Contact: Hon. Thomas J. Tauke
Mailing: 1300 I St. NW
Suite 400 West
Washington, DC 20005
Tel: (202) 515 - 2400

Political Action Committees

Verizon Communications Inc. Good Government Club
Contact: Kevin McLernon
1300 I St. NW
Suite 400 West
Washington, DC 20005
Tel: (202) 515 - 2400

Contributions to Candidates: $305,300 (01/05 - 09/05)
Democrats: $102,500; Republicans: $202,800.

Principal Recipients

SENATE DEMOCRATS		HOUSE DEMOCRATS	
Kennedy, Ted (MA)	$3,500	Engel, Eliot (NY)	$9,000
Nelson, Bill (FL)	$3,500	Matsui, Robert (CA)	$7,000
		Menendez, Robert (NJ)	$5,000
SENATE REPUBLICANS		**HOUSE REPUBLICANS**	
Stevens, Ted (AK)	$6,500	Bachus, Spencer (AL)	$5,000
Hatch, Orrin (UT)	$5,000	Blunt, Roy (MO)	$5,000
Snowe, Olympia (ME)	$5,000	Bono, Mary (CA)	$5,000
Allen, George (VA)	$4,000	Cantor, Eric (VA)	$5,000
Burns, Conrad (MT)	$3,500	Dewine, R. Pat (OH)	$5,000
		Terry, Lee (NE)	$5,000

Corporate Foundations and Giving Programs

Verizon Foundation
Contact: Patrick R. Gaston
1095 Ave. of the Americas
New York, NY 10036
Tel: (212) 395 - 2121
Fax: (212) 840 - 6988
TF: (800) 621 - 9900

Annual Grant Total: over $5,000,000
Maintains a web site at www.verizonfoundation.com.
Primary Interests: Community Affairs; Economic Development; Education; Literacy; Persons with Disabilities

Public Affairs and Related Activities Personnel

At Headquarters

BARTLETT, Thomas A. — Tel: (212) 395 - 1842
Senior V. President, Investor Relations — TF: (800) 621 - 9900
thomas.a.bartlett@verizon.com

DEVARD, Jerri — Tel: (212) 395 - 2121
Senior V. President, Brand Management and Marketing Communications — TF: (800) 621 - 9900

GASTON, Patrick R. — Tel: (212) 395 - 2121
President, Verizon Foundation — Fax: (212) 840 - 6988
patrick.g.gaston@verizon.com — TF: (800) 621 - 9900

HAYES, Susan — Tel: (212) 395 - 2121
Director, Public Affairs Programs — TF: (800) 621 - 9900

REED, Marc C. — Tel: (212) 395 - 2121
Exec. V. President, Human Resources — TF: (800) 621 - 9900

THONIS, Peter — Tel: (212) 395 - 2355
Senior V. President, Public Affairs — Fax: (212) 730 - 0901
peter.thonis@verizon.com — TF: (800) 621 - 9900

VARETTONI, Robert A. — Tel: (212) 395 - 7726
Exec. Director, Financial Media Relations — TF: (800) 621 - 9900
robert.a.varettoni@verizon.com

At Washington Office

BARR, William P. — Tel: (202) 515 - 2400
Exec. V. President and General Counsel

CZWARTACKI, John — Tel: (202) 515 - 2400
Exec. Director, External Communications

DAVIDSON, Peter — Tel: (202) 515 - 2400
Senior V. President, Federal Government Relations; and Deputy General Counsel — Fax: (202) 336 - 7920
Registered Federal Lobbyist.

DILLOW, Frank W. — Tel: (202) 515 - 2400
V. President, Federal Legislative Relations and Deputy General Counsel
Registered Federal Lobbyist.

EVE, Eric — Tel: (202) 515 - 2400
V. President, Federal Government Relations
eric.eve@verizon.com
Registered Federal Lobbyist.

FISH, David — Tel: (202) 515 - 2400
Director, Media Relations

FLANNERY, John — Tel: (202) 515 - 2400
Registered Federal Lobbyist.

FULTON, B. Keith — Tel: (202) 515 - 2400
V. President, Strategic Alliances

GONZALEZ, Emilio — Tel: (202) 515 - 2400
Director, Public Policy and Strategic Outreach

HOEWING, C. Lincoln "Link" — Tel: (202) 515 - 2420
Assistant V. President, Internet and Technology Policy — Fax: (202) 336 - 7923

MCLERNON, Kevin — Tel: (202) 515 - 2400
Exec. Director, Political Operations

MEKELBURG, Andrew — Tel: (202) 515 - 2400
Assistant V. President, Federal Government Relations
Registered Federal Lobbyist.

MOTT, Roger — Tel: (202) 515 - 2400
V. President, Federal Government Relations
Registered Federal Lobbyist.

MULLET, Mark S. — Tel: (202) 515 - 2553
V. President, Federal Government Relations
mark.s.mullet@verizon.com
Registered Federal Lobbyist.

SENN, W. Edward — Tel: (202) 515 - 2400
V. President, Government Affairs - House
Registered Federal Lobbyist.

TAUKE, Hon. Thomas J. — Tel: (202) 515 - 2400
Exec. V. President, Public Affairs and Communications — Fax: (202) 336 - 7921
thomas.j.tauke@verizon.com
Registered Federal Lobbyist.

WHITE, Walter — Tel: (202) 515 - 2400
V. President, State and Local Government

YOUNG, Edward D., III — Tel: (202) 515 - 2400
Senior V. President, Federal Government Relations
edward.d.young@verizon.com

ZANOWIC, Kathleen — Tel: (202) 515 - 2400
Assistant V. President, Federal Government Relations
Registered Federal Lobbyist.

Verizon Communications Inc.

* continued from previous page

At Other Offices

BRETON, Daniel B. — Tel: (207) 797 - 1188; Fax: (207) 797 - 1392
Director, Public Affairs Programs
One Davis Farm Rd.
Portland, ME 04103
daniel.b.breton@verizon.com

DUDLEY, Andrea — Tel: (617) 743 - 0551; Fax: (617) 743 - 8886
Director, Public Affairs Programs
185 Franklin St.
Mailstop: Room 1800
Boston, MA 02110
andrea.dudley@verizon.com

HOEY, John P. — Tel: (617) 743 - 4760
Director, Northeast Bureau Media Relations
185 Franklin St.
Boston, MA 02110
john.p.hoey@verizon.com

KULA, William R. — Tel: (972) 718 - 6924
Director, Western Bureau Media Relations
600 Hidden Ridge
Irving, TX 75015-2092

MENDEZ, Ivette — Tel: (973) 649 - 4834; TF: (800) 621 - 9900
Director, International Media Relations
540 Broad St.
18th Floor
Newark, NJ 07102
ivette.mendez@verizon.com

MITCHELL, Harry J. — Tel: (304) 344 - 7562
Director, Mid-Atlantic Bureau Media Relations
1500 MacCorckle Ave., S.E.
Charleston, WV 25314
harry.j.mitchell@verizon.com

PIERCE, Darryl — Tel: (603) 226 - 1550; Fax: (603) 225 - 9861
Director, Public Affairs Programs
Four Park St.
Concord, NH 03301

RABE, Eric W. — Tel: (215) 963 - 6531
V. President, Telecom Media Relations
1717 Arch St.
Philadelphia, PA 19103

STADLER, John W. — Tel: (804) 772 - 1534; Fax: (804) 772 - 1539
Director, Government Relations
600 E. Main St.
Richmond, VA 23219

STEIN, Mary — Tel: (972) 453 - 7016; Fax: (972) 453 - 7413
Director, Public Affairs Programs
(Verizon Information Services Inc.)
P.O. Box 619810
DFW Airport, TX 76261

Verizon Delaware Inc.

An operating subsidiary of Verizon Communications Inc. (see separate listing).
www.verizon.com

Main Headquarters
Mailing: 901 N. Tatnall St., Second Floor, Wilmington, DE 19801 — Tel: (302) 571 - 1571; Fax: (302) 576 - 1132

Corporate Foundations and Giving Programs

Verizon Foundation
Contact: Kay Fowler-McFadden
901 N. Tatnall St., Second Floor
Wilmington, DE 19801 — Tel: (302) 571 - 1571; Fax: (302) 777 - 0491

Annual Grant Total: $200,000 - $300,000
Requests for grants are accepted from 501(c)(3) organizations. Guidelines are available at the foundation's web site: www.verizonfoundation.com.
Geographic Preference: Delaware
Primary Interests: K-12 Education; Math and Science; Technology

Public Affairs and Related Activities Personnel

At Headquarters

ALLEN, William R. — Tel: (302) 571 - 1571; Fax: (302) 576 - 1132
President

EDWARDS, Ellsworth — Tel: (302) 571 - 1571; Fax: (302) 576 - 1132
Manager, Media Relations

FOWLER-MCFADDEN, Kay — Tel: (302) 571 - 1571; Fax: (302) 777 - 0491
Director, External Affairs and Community Relations

METZ, Bonnie — Tel: (302) 571 - 1571; Fax: (302) 576 - 1132
Chief Lobbyist, State Affairs

Verizon Information Services Inc.

See listing on page 502 under Verizon Communications Inc.

Verizon Maryland Inc.

An operating company of Verizon Communications Inc. (see separate listing).
www.verizon.com

Main Headquarters
Mailing: One E. Pratt St., Baltimore, MD 21202 — TF: (800) 621 - 9900

Public Affairs and Related Activities Personnel

At Headquarters

BUTTA, Susan — Tel: (410) 393 - 7450; Fax: (410) 393 - 4756; TF: (800) 621 - 9900
V. President, Public Affairs
Mailstop: M/S 8N
susan.butta@verizon.com

GILBERT, John R. — Tel: (410) 393 - 4178; Fax: (410) 234 - 0320; TF: (800) 621 - 9900
V. President, Regulatory Affairs/Issues Analysis
Mailstop: M/S 8E
john.r.gilbert@verizon.com

At Other Offices

WOOD, Paul G. — Tel: (410) 269 - 6653; Fax: (410) 269 - 5719
V. President, Government Affairs
12 West St.
Mailstop: M/S 8N
Annapolis, MD 21401
paul.g.wood@verizon.com

Verizon New Jersey, Inc.

PUBLIC AFFAIRS COUNCIL

A member of the Public Affairs Council. An operating company of Verizon Communications Inc. (see separate listing).
www.verizon.com/nj

Main Headquarters
Mailing: 540 Broad St., Newark, NJ 07101 — Tel: (973) 649 - 9900; Fax: (973) 481 - 2660

Corporate Foundations and Giving Programs

Verizon New Jersey, Inc. Corporate Contributions
Contact: Peter A. Ventimiglia, Ph.D.
540 Broad St.
Newark, NJ 07101 — Tel: (973) 649 - 9900; Fax: (973) 643 - 5106

Annual Grant Total: $1,000,000 - $2,000,000
Geographic Preference: New Jersey
Primary Interests: Arts and Culture; Education; Medicine and Health Care; Social Services

Public Affairs and Related Activities Personnel

At Headquarters

KAINE, Mike — Tel: (973) 649 - 9900; Fax: (973) 643 - 5106
Manager, Communications

SCALERA, Ciro — Tel: (973) 649 - 3186; Fax: (973) 624 - 7410
Director, Public Affairs

VENTIMIGLIA, Peter A., Ph.D. — Tel: (973) 649 - 9900; Fax: (973) 643 - 5106
V. President, External Affairs/Statewide Community Relations
Responsibilities include corporate philanthropy.

YOUNG, Rich — Tel: (973) 649 - 9900; Fax: (973) 643 - 5106
Manager, Media Relations

At Other Offices

DOTTO, Ellen M. — Tel: (609) 989 - 9961; Fax: (609) 989 - 8305
V. President, State Government Affairs
172 W. State St.
Trenton, NJ 08608
ellen.m.dotto@verizon.com

MANNION, Eileen — Tel: (609) 989 - 9906; Fax: (609) 599 - 2189
Director, State Government Affairs
172 W. State St.
Trenton, NJ 08608

MCCURVILL, John
Director, State Government Affairs
172 W. State St.
Trenton, NJ 08608

Verizon Pennsylvania Inc.

A telephone operating company of Verizon Communications Inc. (see separate listing).
www.verizon.com

President and Chief Exec. Officer — Tel: (215) 466 - 9900
O'ROURKE, James V., Sr.

Main Headquarters
Mailing: 1717 Arch St., 17th Floor, Philadelphia, PA 19103 — Tel: (215) 466 - 9900

Corporate Foundations and Giving Programs

Verizon Pennsylvania Contributions Program
Contact: Denise Loughlin

Verizon Pennsylvania Inc.

** continued from previous page*

1717 Arch St., 17th Floor — Tel: (215) 466 - 3351
Philadelphia, PA 19103 — Fax: (215) 466 - 5931

Annual Grant Total: $2,000,000 - $5,000,000
Geographic Preference: Pennsylvania
Primary Interests: Economic Development; Education; Medicine and Health Care

Public Affairs and Related Activities Personnel

At Headquarters

LOUGHLIN, Denise — Tel: (215) 466 - 3351
Director, External Affairs — Fax: (215) 466 - 5931
denise.g.loughlin@verizon.com

REAVY, Dan — Tel: (215) 362 - 1900
Director, External Affairs — Fax: (215) 466 - 5931
daniel.j.reavy@verizon.com

REED, Jim — Tel: (215) 466 - 4838
Director, External Affairs — Fax: (215) 466 - 5931
james.a.reed@verizon.com

At Other Offices

CARNAHAN, William B. — Tel: (412) 497 - 7001
V. President, External Affairs
31 S. Mercer St.
Newcastle, PA 16101

HENDRICKS, Dave — Tel: (717) 777 - 4183
Director, External Affairs
Strawberry Square, Fourth Floor
Harrisburg, PA 17101
david.r.hendricks@verizon.com

KEMERER, Russ — Tel: (412) 633 - 3248
Director, External Relations
201 Stanwix St.
Second Floor
Pittsburgh, PA 15222

Verizon Washington D.C. Inc.

An operating company of Verizon Communications Inc. (see separate listing).
www.verizon.com

Main Headquarters
Mailing: 1710 H St. NW — Tel: (202) 392 - 9900
Tenth Floor — Fax: (202) 546 - 5111
Washington, DC 20006

Public Affairs and Related Activities Personnel

At Headquarters

AMBROSE, J. Henry "Hank" — Tel: (202) 392 - 9900
V. President, Regulatory Matters — Fax: (202) 546 - 5111

ARNETTE, Sandra — Tel: (202) 392 - 1021
Media Relations — Fax: (202) 546 - 5111

HILL, David Anthony — Tel: (202) 392 - 9900
V. President and General Counsel — Fax: (202) 546 - 5111
Reponsibilities include regulatory affairs.

Verizon West Virginia Inc.

An operating company of Verizon Communications Inc. (see separate listing).
www.verizon.com

Main Headquarters
Mailing: 1500 MacCorkle Ave. SE — Tel: (304) 343 - 9911
Charleston, WV 25314 — Fax: (304) 344 - 6397

Corporate Foundations and Giving Programs

Verizon West Virginia Contributions Program
1500 MacCorkle Ave. SE — Tel: (304) 343 - 9911
Charleston, WV 25314 — Fax: (304) 344 - 6397

Annual Grant Total: none reported
Geographic Preference: West Virginia
Primary Interests: Arts and Culture; Economic Development; Education; Technology

Public Affairs and Related Activities Personnel

At Headquarters

BECK, George H. — Tel: (304) 353 - 5574
Manager, Strategic Initiatives and External Affairs
george.h.beck@verizon.com

BUCKLEY, Kathy L. — Tel: (304) 344 - 7084
Director, Regulatory Matters
kathy.l.buckley@verizon.com

CIPOLETTI, Sam E. — Tel: (304) 344 - 7216
Manager, Government Relations and External Affairs - Huntington and Weeling
samuel.cipoletti.jr@verizon.com

GOLDEN, John E. — Tel: (304) 344 - 7223
Manager, External Affairs
john.e.golden@verizon.com

LONG, Joe B. — Tel: (304) 344 - 7267
Manager, Corporate Communications and External Affairs — Fax: (304) 344 - 6397
joseph.b.long@verizon.com

Verizon Wireless

A coast-to-coast wireless provider.
www.verizonwireless.com
Annual Revenues: $22.5 billion

Chairman, President and Chief Exec. Officer — Tel: (212) 395 - 2121
STRIGL, Dennis F. — Fax: (212) 869 - 3265

Main Headquarters
Mailing: 1095 Ave. of the Americas — Tel: (212) 395 - 2121
New York, NY 10036 — Fax: (212) 869 - 3265

Washington Office
Contact: Paul Nash
Mailing: 1300 I St. NW — Tel: (202) 589 - 3781
Suite 400 West — Fax: (202) 589 - 3750
Washington, DC 20005

Political Action Committees

Verizon Wireless/Verizon Communications Inc. Political Action Committee
Contact: Paul D'Auria
1095 Ave. of the Americas — Tel: (212) 395 - 2121
New York, NY 10036 — Fax: (212) 869 - 3265

Contributions to Candidates: $46,000 (01/05 - 09/05)
Democrats: $16,500; Republicans: $29,500.

Principal Recipients

SENATE DEMOCRATS		HOUSE DEMOCRATS	
Byrd, Robert C (WV)	$5,000	Clyburn, James (SC)	$2,500
		Watt, Melvin (NC)	$2,000
SENATE REPUBLICANS		**HOUSE REPUBLICANS**	
Snowe, Olympia (ME)	$10,000	Pickering, Chip (MS)	$2,000
Burns, Conrad (MT)	$3,500		
Santorum, Richard (PA)	$2,000		

Corporate Foundations and Giving Programs

Verizon Wireless Corporate Contributions
1095 Ave. of the Americas — Tel: (212) 395 - 2121
New York, NY 10036 — Fax: (212) 869 - 3265

Annual Grant Total: none reported

Public Affairs and Related Activities Personnel

At Headquarters

D'AURIA, Paul — Tel: (212) 395 - 2121
PAC Treasurer — Fax: (212) 869 - 3265

DELEHANTY, Martha — Tel: (212) 395 - 2121
V. President, Human Resources — Fax: (212) 869 - 3265

GERACE, James J. — Tel: (212) 395 - 2121
V. President, Corporate Communications — Fax: (212) 869 - 3265
james.gerace@verizonwireless.com

NELSON, Jeffrey — Tel: (212) 395 - 2121
Exec. Director, Media Relations and Public Policy — Fax: (212) 869 - 3265
jeffrey.nelson@verizonwireless.com

ZIPPERSTEIN, Steve — Tel: (212) 395 - 2121
V. President, Legal and External Affairs — Fax: (212) 869 - 3265
Responsibilities include regulatory affairs and public policy matters.

At Washington Office

AZARE, Monica — Tel: (202) 589 - 3781
Director, House Relations — Fax: (202) 589 - 3750
Registered Federal Lobbyist.

BRITTINGHAM, Donald — Tel: (202) 589 - 3781
Fax: (202) 589 - 3750
Registered Federal Lobbyist.

CANNING, Annabelle — Tel: (202) 589 - 3781
Fax: (202) 589 - 3750
Registered Federal Lobbyist.

NASH, Paul — Tel: (202) 515 - 2400
Director, Federal Relations
Registered Federal Lobbyist.

WOOLLEY, Howard — Tel: (202) 589 - 3740
V. President, Federal Relations
howard.woolley@verizonwireless.com
Registered Federal Lobbyist.

V. F. Corporation

A clothing manufacturer.

www.vfc.com

Annual Revenues: $5.08 billion

Chairman, President, and Chief Exec. Officer
MCDONALD, Mackey J.
mackey_mcdonald@vfc.com
Tel: (336) 424 - 6000
Fax: (336) 424 - 7631

Main Headquarters

Mailing: P.O. Box 21488
Greensboro, NC 27420-1488
Tel: (336) 424 - 6000
Fax: (336) 424 - 7631

Street: 105 Corporate Center Blvd.
Greensboro, NC 27408

Corporate Foundations and Giving Programs

V. F. Corp. Giving Program

Contact: Susan L. Williams

P.O. Box 21488
Greensboro, NC 27420-1488
Tel: (336) 424 - 6000
Fax: (336) 424 - 7631

Annual Grant Total: none reported

Public Affairs and Related Activities Personnel

At Headquarters

BERNER, Jocelyn
Media Contact
jocelyn_berner@vfc.com
Tel: (336) 424 - 7806
Fax: (336) 424 - 7631

CUMMINGS, Candace S.
V. President, Administration, General Counsel and Secretary
candace_cummings@vfc.com
Responsibilities include investor relations.
Tel: (336) 424 - 6000
Fax: (336) 424 - 7631

KNOEBEL, Cindy
V. President, Financial and Corporate Communications
cindy_knoebel@vfc.com
Responsibilities include investor relations.
Tel: (336) 424 - 6189
Fax: (336) 424 - 7631

QUICK, Kate
Specialist, Human Resources
kate_quick@vfc.com
Responsibilities include corporate contributions.
Tel: (336) 424 - 7747
Fax: (336) 424 - 7631

WILLIAMS, Susan L.
V. President, Human Resources
susan_williams@vfc.com
Tel: (336) 424 - 6000
Fax: (336) 424 - 7631

VH-I

See listing on page 505 under Viacom Inc/CBS Corp.

Viacom Inc./CBS Corp.

A holding company for television and motion picture companies, television and radio stations, amusement parks, and movie theater operators. A global media company with positions in broadcast and cable television, radio, outdoor advertising and online. Creates, promotes and distributes entertainment, news, sports, music and comedy. The company has announced plans to split into two independent companies in the first quarter of 2006: Viacom Inc., which will include the MTV Network, BET, Paramount Pictures, Paramount Home Entertainment and Famous Music; and CBS Corporation, which will include CBS and UPN broadcast networks, Viacom Television Stations Group, Infinity Broadcasting, Viacom Outdoor, the CBS, Paramount and King World television production and syndication operations, Showtime, Simon & Schuster, and Paramount Parks.

www.viacom.com

Annual Revenues: $23.223 billion

Chairman and Chief Exec. Officer
REDSTONE, Sumner
Tel: (212) 258 - 6000

Main Headquarters

Mailing: 1515 Broadway
New York, NY 10036
Tel: (212) 258 - 6000

Washington Office

Mailing: 1501 M St. NW
Suite 1100
Washington, DC 20005
Tel: (202) 785 - 7300
Fax: (202) 785 - 6360

Political Action Committees

Viacom International Inc. PAC Corp.

Contact: Anne C. Lucey

1501 M St. NW
Suite 1100
Washington, DC 20005
Tel: (202) 785 - 7300
Fax: (202) 785 - 6360

Contributions to Candidates: $79,500 (01/05 - 09/05)

Democrats: $16,000; Republicans: $63,500.

Principal Recipients

SENATE DEMOCRATS

Clinton, Hillary Rodham (NY)	$2,000
Nelson, Benjamin (NE)	$2,000

HOUSE DEMOCRATS

SENATE REPUBLICANS

Stevens, Ted (AK)	$6,500
Smith, Gordon (OR)	$5,000
Allen, George (VA)	$3,000
Martinez, Mel (FL)	$2,000
Santorum, Richard (PA)	$2,000

HOUSE REPUBLICANS

Hastert, Dennis J. (IL)	$5,000
Sensenbrenner, Jim (WI)	$4,500
Stearns, Clifford (FL)	$3,000
DeLay, Tom (TX)	$2,500
Dreier, David (CA)	$2,500
Goodlatte, Robert (VA)	$2,500
Smith, Lamar (TX)	$2,500
Pickering, Chip (MS)	$2,000
Reynolds, Thomas (NY)	$2,000

Corporate Foundations and Giving Programs

Viacom Inc. Contributions Program

Contact: Karen Zatorski

1515 Broadway
New York, NY 10036
Tel: (212) 258 - 6369
Fax: (212) 258 - 6464

Annual Grant Total: none reported

Public Affairs and Related Activities Personnel

At Headquarters

FOLTA, Carl D.
Exec V. President, Corporate Relations
Mailstop: 52nd Floor
Tel: (212) 258 - 6352
Fax: (212) 846 - 1727

IOACHIM, Jackie
V. President, Consumer Public Relations- Movies (Showtime Networks Inc.)
Tel: (212) 708 - 1600

MARTINSEN, Dan
Senior V. President, Communications (Nickelodeon/Nick at Nite)
Tel: (212) 258 - 6000
Ext: 8116
Fax: (212) 258 - 1773

NELSON, Laura
Senior V. President, Corporate Communications (VH-1)
Mailstop: 20th Floor
Tel: (212) 846 - 7920
Fax: (212) 258 - 7705

O'BRIEN, Rosemary
V. President, Communications (Nickelodeon/Nick at Nite)
Tel: (212) 258 - 6000
Fax: (212) 258 - 7705

ROBINSON, Carole
Exec. V. President, Press Relations (MTV Networks)
Tel: (212) 258 - 6000
Ext: 8760
Fax: (212) 258 - 8100

SHEA, Martin M.
Exec. V. President, Investor Relations
Tel: (212) 846 - 6515
Fax: (212) 258 - 1705

WARD, Paul
Senior V. President, Communications (Nickelodeon/Nick at Nite)
Tel: (212) 258 - 7704
Fax: (212) 258 - 7705

ZATORSKI, Karen
V. President, Corporate Relations
Tel: (212) 258 - 6369
Fax: (212) 258 - 6464

At Washington Office

BROWN, Josh
Director, Government Relations
Registered Federal Lobbyist.
Tel: (202) 785 - 7300
Fax: (202) 785 - 6360

FRANKS, Martin D.
Exec. V. President, Policy and Government Relations, CBS Corp.
Tel: (202) 785 - 7300
Fax: (202) 785 - 6360

FRESE, Elizabeth Norris
Office Manager, Government Affairs
Tel: (202) 785 - 7300
Fax: (202) 785 - 6360

LEA, DeDe
Senior V. President, Government Relations, Viacom Inc.
Tel: (202) 785 - 7300
Fax: (202) 785 - 6360

LUCEY, Anne C.
Senior V. President, Regulatory Policy, CBS Corp.
Registered Federal Lobbyist.
Tel: (202) 785 - 7300
Fax: (202) 785 - 6360

MACKINNON, Gail G.
Senior V. President, Washington, CBS Corp.
Registered Federal Lobbyist.
Tel: (202) 785 - 7300
Fax: (202) 785 - 6360

SONNICHSEN, Ethan A.
Legislative Assistant
Tel: (202) 785 - 7300
Fax: (202) 785 - 6360

Viacom Inc./CBS Corp.

• continued from previous page

SUTPHEN, David — Tel: (202) 785 - 7300
V. President, Government Affairs — Fax: (202) 785 - 6360

At Other Offices

BOWEN, Jama — Tel: (615) 457 - 8581
Director, Communications — Fax: (615) 457 - 8581
(Country Music Television)
2806 Opryland Dr.
Nashville, TN 37214

HILL, Janet — Tel: (310) 752 - 8073
Head, West Cost Communications
(MTV Networks)
2600 Colorado Ave.
Santa Monica, CA 90404

KELLY, Kimberly A. — Tel: (202) 608 - 2000
Counsel, Government Affairs and Affiliate Regulations — Fax: (202) 608 - 2595
(BET)
One BET Plaza
1900 W Pl. NE
Washington, DC 20018
kimberly.kelly@bet.net

LEWELLEN, Michael — Tel: (202) 608 - 2003
V. President, Communications — Fax: (202) 608 - 2518
(BET)
One BET Plaza
1235 W Pl., N.E.
Washington, DC 20018

LOWRY, Joanna — Tel: (310) 575 - 7080
Senior V. President, Media Relations — Fax: (310) 575 - 7280
(UPN)
11800 Wilshire Blvd.
Los Angeles, CA 90025

MANDT, David — Tel: (704) 587 - 9051
Director, Marketing/Communications
(Paramount Parks)
8720 Red Oak Blvd.
Suite 315
Charlotte, NC 28217

MOONVES, Leslie — Tel: (323) 575 - 2345
Chairman, President and Chief Exec. Officer
(CBS Television)
7800 Beverly Blvd.
Los Angeles, CA 90036

ROTHBERG, Adam — Tel: (212) 698 - 1132
V. President, Communications — Fax: (212) 698 - 7297
(Simon & Schuster Inc.)
1230 Ave. of the Americas
New York, NY 20020

WENTWORTH, John A. — Tel: (323) 956 - 5394
Exec. V. President, Media Relations
5555 Melrose Ave.
Los Angeles, CA 90038

Viad Corp

A convention and event services company.

www.viad.com
Annual Revenues: $785.7 million

Chairman, President and Chief Exec. Officer — Tel: (602) 207 - 4000
BOHANNON, Robert H.
rbohannon@viad.com

Main Headquarters
Mailing: 1850 N. Central Ave. — Tel: (602) 207 - 4000
Suite 800 — Fax: (602) 207 - 5900
Phoenix, AZ 85004-4545

Political Action Committees

Viad Good Government Project
Contact: Steven J. Twist
1850 N. Central Ave. — Tel: (602) 207 - 2940
Suite 800
Phoenix, AZ 85004-4545

Contributions to Candidates: $275 (01/05 - 09/05)
Republicans: $275.

Principal Recipients

SENATE REPUBLICANS		HOUSE REPUBLICANS	
		Shadegg, John (AZ)	$275

Corporate Foundations and Giving Programs

Viad Fund
Contact: Angela Phoenix
1850 N. Central Ave. — Tel: (602) 207 - 5608
Suite 800 — Fax: (602) 207 - 5900
Phoenix, AZ 85004-4545

Annual Grant Total: none reported

Recent local recipients include: Boys and Girls Clubs of Metropolitan Phoenix, Chicanos por la Causa, St. Mary's Food Bank, Salvation Army, St. Vincent de Paul, the Phoenix Urban League, and the Arizona Heart Foundation.

Geographic Preference: Arizona

Primary Interests: Arts and Culture; Civic and Public Affairs; Community Affairs; Education; Health; Minority Opportunities

Recent Recipients: Boys and Girls Club; Spelman College

Public Affairs and Related Activities Personnel

At Headquarters

LONG, Carrie — Tel: (602) 207 - 4000
Director, Investor Relations — Ext: 2681
clong@viad.com

PEARL, Suzanne — Tel: (602) 207 - 2817
V. President, Human Resources — Fax: (602) 207 - 5455
spearl@viad.com

PHOENIX, Angela — Tel: (602) 207 - 5608
Manager, Corporate Communications — Fax: (602) 207 - 5900
aphoenix@viad.com

TWIST, Steven J. — Tel: (602) 207 - 2940
Assistant General Counsel
stwist@viad.com
Responsibilities include political action.

Viking Freight

See listing on page 193 under FedEx Freight.

Virginia Power

See listing on page 162 under Dominion Resources, Inc.

Visa U.S.A. Inc.

A member of the Public Affairs Council. A payment card and financial services company. VISA USA Inc. is the U.S. subsidiary of Visa Internat'l.

www.visa.com
Annual Revenues: $3 billion

Chairman of the Board — Tel: (650) 432 - 3200
PHILLIPS, G. Patrick — Fax: (650) 432 - 3631

Chief Exec. Officer — Tel: (650) 432 - 3200
COGHLAN, John P. — Fax: (650) 432 - 3631

Main Headquarters
Mailing: 900 Metro Center Blvd. — Tel: (650) 432 - 3200
Foster City, CA 94404-2172 — Fax: (650) 432 - 3631

Washington Office
Contact: W. Lamar Smith
Mailing: 1300 Connecticut Ave. NW — Tel: (202) 296 - 9230
Suite 900 — Fax: (202) 862 - 5498
Washington, DC 20036

Political Action Committees

VISA USA Political Action Committee
Contact: Mark MacCarthy
1300 Connecticut Ave. NW — Tel: (202) 296 - 9230
Suite 900 — Fax: (202) 862 - 5498
Washington, DC 20036

Contributions to Candidates: $8,000 (01/05 - 09/05)
Republicans: $8,000.

Principal Recipients

SENATE REPUBLICANS		HOUSE REPUBLICANS
Dewine, Richard (OH)	$3,500	
Hatch, Orrin (UT)	$2,500	
Allen, George (VA)	$2,000	

Public Affairs and Related Activities Personnel

At Headquarters

BAPTIE, Colin — Tel: (650) 432 - 4631
Media Contact — Fax: (650) 432 - 3631

HEINONEN, Cheryl — Tel: (650) 432 - 4671
Media Contact — Fax: (650) 432 - 3631

MICHELMAN, Douglas — Tel: (650) 432 - 3200
Exec. V. President, Corporate Relations — Fax: (650) 432 - 3631

At Washington Office

BENTZ, Rhonda — Tel: (202) 296 - 9230
Director, Public Affairs — Fax: (202) 862 - 5498
rbentz@visa.com
Registered Federal Lobbyist.

Visa U.S.A. Inc.

** continued from previous page*

KABEISEMAN, Margaret M. — Tel: (202) 296 - 9230
Legislative Manager — Fax: (202) 862 - 5498
mmuskett@visa.com
Registered Federal Lobbyist.

MACCARTHY, Mark — Tel: (202) 296 - 9230
Contact, VISA USA Political Action Committee — Fax: (202) 862 - 5498
mmaccarthy@visa.com
Registered Federal Lobbyist.

SMITH, W. Lamar — Tel: (202) 296 - 9230
Senior V. President, Government Relations — Fax: (202) 862 - 5498
lsmith@visa.com
Registered Federal Lobbyist.

Vishay Intertechnology, Inc.

A manufacturer of discrete semiconductors and passive electronic components.
www.vishay.com

Chairman and Chief Business Development Officer — Tel: (610) 644 - 1300
ZANDMAN, Felix — Fax: (610) 296 - 0657
felix.zandman@vishay.com

President and Chief Exec. Officer — Tel: (610) 644 - 1300
PAUL, Gerald — Fax: (610) 889 - 9349

Main Headquarters
Mailing: 63 Lincoln Hwy. — Tel: (610) 644 - 1300
Malvern, PA 19355-2120 — Fax: (610) 296 - 0657

Corporate Foundations and Giving Programs

Vishay Intertechnology Corporate Giving
Contact: William J. Spires
63 Lincoln Hwy. — Tel: (610) 251 - 5255
Malvern, PA 19355-2120 — Fax: (610) 296 - 0657

Annual Grant Total: none reported

Public Affairs and Related Activities Personnel

At Headquarters

FREECE, Robert A. — Tel: (610) 251 - 5252
Exec. V. President — Fax: (610) 889 - 9349
bob.freece@vishay.com
Responsibilities include investor relations.

POST, Andrew — Tel: (610) 251 - 5287
Manager, Global Communications — Fax: (610) 889 - 9349
andrew.post@vishay.com

SPIRES, William J. — Tel: (610) 251 - 5255
Senior V. President and Secretary — Fax: (610) 296 - 0657
william.spires@vishay.com
Responsibilities include corporate contributions.

TATE, Brenda K. — Tel: (610) 644 - 1300
Corporate Investor Relations Contact — Fax: (610) 889 - 9349
brenda.tate@vishay.com

Visteon Corp.

PUBLIC AFFAIRS COUNCIL

A member of the Public Affairs Council. An automotive components manufacturer.
www.visteon.com

Chairman, President and Chief Exec. Officer — Tel: (313) 755 - 2800
JOHNSTON, Michael F. — TF: (800) VIS - TEON

Main Headquarters
Mailing: One Village Dr. — Tel: (313) 755 - 2800
Van Buren Township, MI 48111 — Fax: (313) 755 - 7983
TF: (800) VIS - TEON

Corporate Foundations and Giving Programs

Visteon Corp. Corporate Contributions Program
One Village Dr. — Tel: (313) 755 - 2800
Van Buren Township, MI 48111 — Fax: (313) 755 - 7983
TF: (800) VIS - TEON

Annual Grant Total: none reported

Public Affairs and Related Activities Personnel

At Headquarters

BILICKI, Liane — Tel: (313) 755 - 2916
Manager, Corporate Communications — Fax: (313) 722 - 1658
lbilicki@visteon.com — TF: (800) VIS - TEON

COLLINS, Chris — Tel: (313) 755 - 2800
Manager, Investor and Shareholder Relations — TF: (800) VIS - TEON
ccolli16@visteon.com

FIEBIG, Derek A. — Tel: (313) 755 - 0635
Assistant Treasurer, Investor Relations — Fax: (313) 755 - 7983
dfiebig@visteon.com — TF: (800) VIS - TEON

FISHER, Jim — Tel: (313) 755 - 0635
Director, Corporate Communications — Fax: (313) 722 - 1658
jfishe89@visteon.com — TF: (800) VIS - TEON

HALLUMS, Tammera — Tel: (313) 755 - 0998
Manager, U.S. Employee Communications — Fax: (313) 557 - 983
thallums@visteon.com — TF: (800) VIS - TEON

MARCIN, Robert H. — Tel: (313) 755 - 2800
Senior V. President, Corporate Relations — TF: (800) VIS - TEON

WELCH, Kimberly A. — Tel: (313) 755 - 3537
V. President, Corporate Communications — Fax: (313) 722 - 1658
kwelch5@visteon.com — TF: (800) VIS - TEON

VITAS Healthcare Corporation

www.vitas.com

Chairman of the Board — Tel: (305) 374 - 4143
MCNAMARA, Kevin J.

Chief Exec. Officer — Tel: (305) 374 - 4143
O'TOOLE, Timothy
tim.otoole@vitas.com

Main Headquarters
Mailing: 100 S. Biscayne Blvd., Suite 1500 — Tel: (305) 374 - 4143
Miami, FL 33131

Washington Office
Contact: Timothy O'Toole
Mailing: 555 13th St. NW — Tel: (202) 637 - 7228
Suite 3 - East — Fax: (202) 637 - 8715
Washington, DC 20004

Corporate Foundations and Giving Programs

Foundation for End-of-Life Care and VITAS Hospice Charitable Fund
100 S. Biscayne Blvd., Suite 1500 — Tel: (305) 374 - 4143
Miami, FL 33131

Annual Grant Total: none reported

Public Affairs and Related Activities Personnel

At Headquarters

BAILEY, Mark — Tel: (305) 374 - 4143
Senior Director, Community and Public Affairs — Fax: (305) 350 - 6970
mark.bailey@vitas.com

At Washington Office

HOWE, Deirdre — Tel: (202) 637 - 7228
Exec. V. President — Fax: (202) 637 - 8715
deirdre.howe@vitas.com

MCMASTER, Helen — Tel: (202) 637 - 7228
Corporate Administrator — Fax: (202) 637 - 8715
helen.mcmaster@vitas.com

At Other Offices

MEIER, Cherry — Tel: (512) 252 - 2843
Senior Director, Public Affairs — Fax: (512) 252 - 2847
13309 Chasewood Cove
Austin, TX 78727
cherry.meier@vitas.com

SWIGER, Holly — Tel: (951) 791 - 8623
Senior Director, Public Affairs — Fax: (951) 203 - 9600
41625 Thornton Ave.
Hemet, CA 92544
holly.swiger@vitas.com

Vivendi Universal

Entertainment operations in recorded music, films, theme parks and retail stores. Subsidiaries include Vivendi Universal Games (see separate listing) and Universal Music Group (see separate listing). Also owns a minority share in NBC Universal (see separate listing).
www.vivendiuniversal.com
Annual Revenues: $61 billion

Chairman and Chief Exec. Officer — Tel: (212) 572 - 7000
LEVY, Jean-Bernard

Main Headquarters
Mailing: 800 Third Ave., Fourth Floor — Tel: (212) 572 - 7000
New York, NY 10022

Public Affairs and Related Activities Personnel

At Headquarters

LEMARCHAND-WOOD, Flavie — Tel: (212) 572 - 1118
Director, Corporate Communications

Vivendi Universal Entertainment

See listing on page 342 under NBC Universal.

Vivendi Universal Games

A subsidiary of Vivendi Universal (see separate listing).
www.vugames.com
Annual Revenues: $647.9 million

Vivendi Universal Games

* continued from previous page

Chief Exec. Officer
HACK, Bruce
Tel: (310) 431 - 4000
Fax: (310) 342 - 0533

Main Headquarters
Mailing: 6060 Center Dr., Fifth Floor
Los Angeles, CA 90045
Tel: (310) 431 - 4000
Fax: (310) 342 - 0533

Public Affairs and Related Activities Personnel

At Headquarters

HOLLINGSHEAD, Leslie
V. President, Corporate Communications
Tel: (310) 431 - 4533
Fax: (310) 342 - 0533

Volkswagen of America, Inc.

The American subsidiary of the German automobile manufacturer.
www.vw.com

President and Chief Exec. Officer
WITTER, Frank
Tel: (248) 754 - 5000
Fax: (248) 754 - 4930

Main Headquarters
Mailing: 3800 Hamlin Rd.
Auburn Hills, MI 48326
Tel: (248) 754 - 5000
Fax: (248) 754 - 4930

Washington Office
Contact: David Geanacopoulos
Mailing: 1300 Pennsylvania Ave. NW
Suite 860
Washington, DC 20004
Tel: (202) 842 - 5800
Fax: (202) 842 - 8612

Public Affairs and Related Activities Personnel

At Headquarters

KEYES, Steve
Director, Corporate Communications
Tel: (248) 754 - 5054
Fax: (248) 754 - 4930

At Washington Office

BROWN, Louis J.
Government Technical Affairs Manager
Tel: (202) 842 - 5800
Fax: (202) 842 - 8612

GEANACOPOULOS, David
Director, Industry-Government Relations
Registered Federal Lobbyist.
Tel: (202) 842 - 5800
Fax: (202) 842 - 8612

SMITH, S. Marijke
Government Relations Assistant
Tel: (202) 842 - 5800
Fax: (202) 842 - 8612

Volt Information Sciences, Inc.

Provides services in the staffing services and the telecommunications and information solutions marketplaces.
www.volt.com
Annual Revenues: $1.5 billion

Chairman, President, and Chief Exec. Officer
SHAW, William
wshaw@volt.com
Tel: (212) 704 - 2400
Fax: (212) 704 - 2411
TF: (800) 533 - 2401

Main Headquarters
Mailing: 560 Lexington Ave.
15th Floor
New York, NY 10022
Tel: (212) 704 - 2400
Fax: (212) 704 - 2417
TF: (800) 533 - 2401

Public Affairs and Related Activities Personnel

At Headquarters

KOCHMAN, Ron
V. President, Investor Relations and Corporate Communicatons
rkochman@volt.com
Tel: (212) 704 - 2490
Fax: (212) 704 - 2424
TF: (800) 533 - 2401

ROSS, Louise
V. President, Human Resources
lross@volt.com
Tel: (212) 704 - 2458
Fax: (212) 704 - 2424
TF: (800) 533 - 2401

WITT, Warren
Director, Risk Management
wwitt@volt.com
Tel: (212) 704 - 2400
Fax: (212) 704 - 2417
TF: (800) 533 - 2401

At Other Offices

RUFE, Ellen
Director, Marketing Communications
6130 Stoneridge Mall Rd., Suite 150
Pleasanton, CA 94588
erufe@volt.com
Tel: (925) 463 - 2871
Fax: (925) 463 - 2807

Volvo Group North America, Inc.

North American arm of AB Volvo, Swedish manufacturer of commercial vehicles. Subsidiaries include Mack Trucks Inc. (see separate listing).
www.volvo.com

Main Headquarters
Mailing: 570 Lexington Ave.
20th Floor
New York, NY 10022
Tel: (212) 418 - 7400

Washington Office
Contact: Geoff Merrill
Mailing: 1201 Pennsylvania Ave. NW
Suite 300
Washington, DC 20004
Tel: (202) 661 - 4770
Fax: (202) 661 - 4771

Public Affairs and Related Activities Personnel

At Headquarters

HARTWELL, John
Director, Investor Relations, North America
john.hartwell@volvo.com
Tel: (212) 418 - 7432

At Washington Office

MERRILL, Geoff
V. President, Government Relations and Public Affairs
geoff.merrill@volvo.com
Registered Federal Lobbyist.
Tel: (202) 661 - 4770
Fax: (202) 661 - 4771

PETERSEN, LeeAnn M.
Manager, Government Relations and Public Affairs
leeann.peterson@volvo.com
Registered Federal Lobbyist.
Tel: (202) 661 - 4770
Fax: (202) 661 - 4771

Vons

A supermarket chain. A division of Safeway, Inc. (see separate listing).
www.vons.com

President and Chief Exec. Officer
KELLER, Thomas C.
Tel: (626) 821 - 7000
Fax: (626) 821 - 7933

Main Headquarters
Mailing: P.O. Box 513338
Los Angeles, CA 90051-1338
Tel: (626) 821 - 7000
Fax: (626) 821 - 7933
Street: 618 S. Michillinda Ave.
Arcadia, CA 91007

Corporate Foundations and Giving Programs

The Vons Companies Corporate Contributions Program
Contact: Carol Egenias
P.O. Box 513338
Los Angeles, CA 90051-1338
Tel: (626) 821 - 7560

Annual Grant Total: none reported

Public Affairs and Related Activities Personnel

At Headquarters

CALDERON, Sandra
Director, Public Affairs
Tel: (626) 821 - 7291

CONRAD, Deborah L.
Director, Human Resources
Tel: (626) 821 - 7000
Fax: (626) 821 - 7933

EGENIAS, Carol
Donations Contact
Tel: (626) 821 - 7560

Vopak USA, Inc.

See listing on page 494 under Univar USA, Inc.

Vulcan Materials Co.

A member of the Public Affairs Council. A producer of construction aggregates and industrial chemicals.
www.vulcanmaterials.com
Annual Revenues: $3.02 billion

Chairman and Chief Exec. Officer
JAMES, Donald M.
Tel: (205) 298 - 3000
Fax: (205) 298 - 2960

Main Headquarters
Mailing: P.O. Box 385014
Birmingham, AL 35238-5014
Tel: (205) 298 - 3000
Fax: (205) 298 - 2960
Street: 1200 Urban Center Dr.
Birmingham, AL 35242

Political Action Committees

Vulcan Materials Co. Political Action Committee
Contact: Mary S. Russom
P.O. Box 385014
Birmingham, AL 35238-5014
Tel: (205) 298 - 3229
Fax: (205) 298 - 2960

Contributions to Candidates: $23,000 (01/05 - 09/05)
Democrats: $5,000; Republicans: $18,000.

Corporate Foundations and Giving Programs

Vulcan Materials Co. Foundation
Contact: Mary S. Russom

Vulcan Materials Co.

** continued from previous page*

P.O. Box 385014 Tel: (205) 298 - 3229
Birmingham, AL 35238-5014 Fax: (205) 298 - 2960

Assets: $4,000,000 (2003)
Annual Grant Total: $2,000,000 - $5,000,000
Geographic Preference: Area(s) in which the company operates
Primary Interests: Education; Environment/Conservation
Recent Recipients: United Negro College Fund

Public Affairs and Related Activities Personnel

At Headquarters

BUMPERS, Bennie W. Tel: (205) 298 - 3000
Director, Corporate Risk Fax: (205) 298 - 2960
bumpersb@vmcmail.com

DONALDSON, David A. Tel: (205) 298 - 3021
Director, Community Relations Fax: (205) 298 - 2960
donaldsond@vmcmail.com
Serves as the Senior Public Affairs Executive at company headquarters.

ENGLISH, John E. Tel: (205) 298 - 3189
Manager, Public Affairs Fax: (205) 298 - 3246
englishj@vmcmail.com

HOUSTON, J. Wayne Tel: (205) 298 - 3171
V. President, Human Resources Fax: (205) 298 - 2960
houstonw@vmcmail.com

PRINTZ, Peter Tel: (205) 298 - 3000
V. President, Safety, Health, and Environment Fax: (205) 298 - 2960
printzp@vmcmail.com

RUSSOM, Mary S. Tel: (205) 298 - 3229
Manager, Community Programs Fax: (205) 298 - 2960
russomm@vmcmail.com

At Other Offices

CARROLL, Thomas E. Tel: (336) 744 - 2032
Manager, Business and Government Relations Fax: (336) 744 - 0145
P.O. Box 4239
Winston-Salem, NC 27115
carrollt@vmcmail.com

FLEMING, J. F. Tel: (770) 458 - 4481
Manager, Human Resources and Government Affairs Fax: (770) 452 - 9505
P.O. Box 80730
Atlanta, GA 30366-0730
flemingj@vmcmail.com

SPITLER, Todd M. Tel: (323) 474 - 3208
Manager, Community Outreach Fax: (323) 258 - 3289
P.O. Box 2950
Los Angeles, CA 90051
spitlert@vmcmail.com

Wabtec Corp.

See listing on page 519 under Westinghouse Air Brake Technologies Corp.

Wachovia Corp.

A member of the Public Affairs Council. A bank holding company. Acquired SouthTrust Corp. in November of 2004.

www.wachovia.com
Annual Revenues: $22.396 billion

Chairman, President and Chief Exec. Officer Tel: (704) 374 - 6565
THOMPSON, G. Kennedy Fax: (704) 374 - 3425
Mailstop: NC 0005 TF: (800) 275 - 3862
ken.thompson@wachovia.com

Main Headquarters
Mailing: 301 S. College St., Suite 4000 Tel: (704) 374 - 6565
One Wachovia Center Fax: (704) 374 - 3425
Charlotte, NC 28288-0370 TF: (800) 275 - 3862

Political Action Committees

Wachovia Corp. Employees Good Government Fund I
301 S. College St., Suite 4000 Tel: (704) 374 - 6565
One Wachovia Center Fax: (704) 374 - 3425
Charlotte, NC 28288-0370 TF: (800) 275 - 3862

Contributions to Candidates: $135,500 (01/05 - 09/05)
Democrats: $22,000; Republicans: $113,500.

Principal Recipients

SENATE DEMOCRATS

Ford, Harold E Jr (TN)	$5,000
Conrad, Kent (ND)	$3,500

HOUSE DEMOCRATS

SENATE REPUBLICANS

Allen, George (VA)	$10,000
McConnell, Mitch (KY)	$5,000
Santorum, Richard (PA)	$2,500

HOUSE REPUBLICANS

Dreier, David (CA)	$10,000
Bachus, Spencer (AL)	$8,000
Cantor, Eric (VA)	$5,500
McHenry, Patrick (NC)	$5,500
Hensarling, Jeb (TX)	$5,000
Kennedy, Mark (MN)	$5,000
Myrick, Sue (NC)	$5,000
Ney, Robert W (OH)	$4,500

Corporate Foundations and Giving Programs

Wachovia Foundation
Contact: Denise McGregor Armbrister
123 Broad St. Tel: (215) 670 - 4310
Third Floor Fax: (215) 670 - 4313
Philadelphia, PA 19109

Annual Grant Total: over $5,000,000
Any organization requesting a contribution must submit a written proposal outlining the overall project and how the funds will be applied. Certification of IRS tax status must accompany the proposal.
Geographic Preference: Florida; Georgia; North Carolina; South Carolina; Virginia; Area(s) in which the company operates
Primary Interests: Arts and Culture; Community Affairs; Economic Development; Education; Health and Human Services; Housing; Youth Services

Wachovia Regional Foundation
Contact: Denise McGregor Armbrister
123 Broad St. Tel: (215) 670 - 4310
Third Floor Fax: (215) 670 - 4313
Philadelphia, PA 19109

Annual Grant Total: none reported
Geographic Preference: New Jersey; Pennsylvania; Delaware
Primary Interests: Community Development; Economic Development

Public Affairs and Related Activities Personnel

At Headquarters

ESHET, Mary Tel: (704) 374 - 6565
Senior V. President and Manager, Corporate Media Relations Fax: (704) 374 - 3425
Mailstop: NC 0570 TF: (800) 275 - 3862
mary.eshet@wachovia.com

JEFFRIES, Russ E., Jr. Tel: (704) 374 - 3488
PAC Contact Fax: (704) 374 - 7021
TF: (800) 275 - 3862

LEHMAN, Alice L. Tel: (704) 374 - 6565
Senior V. President and Managing Director, Investor Relations Fax: (704) 374 - 3425
Mailstop: NC 0206 TF: (800) 275 - 3862
alice.lehman@wachovia.com

MACKIN, Ginny Tel: (704) 374 - 6565
Senior V. President and Director, Corporate Communications Fax: (704) 374 - 3425
Mailstop: NC 0570 TF: (800) 275 - 3862
ginny.mackin@wachovia.com

MCFAYDEN, Shannon Tel: (704) 374 - 6565
Head of Human Resources and Corporate Relations Fax: (704) 374 - 3425
TF: (800) 275 - 3862

PRICE, Walter Tel: (704) 374 - 6565
Fax: (704) 374 - 3425
TF: (800) 275 - 3862

At Other Offices

ARMBRISTER, Denise McGregor Tel: (215) 670 - 4310
Senior V. President and Exec. Director, Wachovia Regional Foundation Fax: (215) 670 - 4313
123 Broad St.
Third Floor
Philadelphia, PA 19109

The Wackenhut Corporation

A diversified business services company providing security services, investigations, facility management and staffing/temp services.

www.wackenhut.com
Annual Revenues: $2.5 billion

Chairman and Chief Exec. Officer Tel: (561) 622 - 5656
SANDERS, Gary A. Fax: (561) 691 - 6738
TF: (800) 922 - 6488

Main Headquarters
Mailing: 4200 Wackenhut Dr. Tel: (561) 622 - 5656
Palm Beach Gardens, FL 33410-4243 Fax: (561) 691 - 6738
TF: (800) 922 - 6488

The Wackenhut Corporation

** continued from previous page*

Political Action Committees

Wackenhut Corp. Political Action Committee (WAC-PAC)
Contact: Jeff Cappalletti
4200 Wackenhut Dr.
Palm Beach Gardens, FL 33410-4243
Tel: (561) 622 - 5656
Fax: (561) 691 - 6738
TF: (800) 922 - 6488

Contributions to Candidates: $1,000 (01/05 - 09/05)
Republicans: $1,000.

Principal Recipients

SENATE REPUBLICANS	HOUSE REPUBLICANS	
	Barton, Joe L (TX)	$1,000

Wackenhut Corrections Corp. PAC
4200 Wackenhut Dr.
Palm Beach Gardens, FL 33410-4243
Tel: (561) 622 - 5656
Fax: (561) 691 - 6738
TF: (800) 922 - 6488

Contributions to Candidates: $47,000 (01/05 - 09/05)
Democrats: $13,000; Republicans: $34,000.

Principal Recipients

SENATE DEMOCRATS	HOUSE DEMOCRATS	
	Edwards, Chet (TX)	$2,500
	Towns, Edolphus (NY)	$2,000

SENATE REPUBLICANS	HOUSE REPUBLICANS	
	Bonilla, Henry (TX)	$10,000
	Rogers, Harold (KY)	$10,000
	Wolf, Frank R (VA)	$5,000

Public Affairs and Related Activities Personnel

At Headquarters

CAPPALLETTI, Jeff
Treasurer, Wac-PAC
Tel: (561) 622 - 5656
Fax: (561) 691 - 6738
TF: (800) 922 - 6488

NUSBAUM, Sandra
Senior V. President, Human Resources
snusbaum@wackenhut.com
Tel: (561) 622 - 5656
Fax: (561) 691 - 6738
TF: (800) 922 - 6488

SHAPIRO, Marc
V. President, Strategic Partnerships
Tel: (561) 622 - 5656
Fax: (561) 691 - 6738
TF: (800) 922 - 6488

Responsibilities include investor relations.

Wal-Mart Stores

A discount retail store chain.
www.walmartstores.com
Annual Revenues: $244.5 billion

Chairman of the Board
WALTON, S. Robson
Mailstop: M/S 0105
Tel: (479) 273 - 4000
Fax: (479) 273 - 4053

President and Chief Exec. Officer
SCOTT, H. Lee
Mailstop: M/S 0105
Tel: (479) 273 - 4000
Fax: (479) 273 - 4053

Main Headquarters
Mailing: 702 SW Eighth St.
Bentonville, AR 72716
Tel: (479) 273 - 4000
Fax: (479) 273 - 4053

Washington Office
Contact: Normand G. Lezy
Mailing: 575 Seventh St. NW
Terrell Bldg.
Washington, DC 20004
Tel: (202) 737 - 5523
Fax: (202) 737 - 6069

Political Action Committees

Wal-Mart Stores, Inc. PAC for Responsible Government
Contact: Jay Allen
702 SW Eighth St.
Bentonville, AR 72716
Tel: (479) 273 - 4786
Fax: (479) 277 - 2473

Contributions to Candidates: $285,050 (01/05 - 09/05)
Democrats: $81,550; Republicans: $202,500; Other: $1,000.

Principal Recipients

SENATE DEMOCRATS		HOUSE DEMOCRATS	
Clinton, Hillary Rodham (NY)	$5,000	Jefferson, William (LA)	$5,000
		Menendez, Robert (NJ)	$5,000
Ford, Harold E Jr (TN)	$5,000	Scott, David (GA)	$5,000

SENATE REPUBLICANS		HOUSE REPUBLICANS	
Allen, George (VA)	$10,000	Young, Don E (AK)	$7,500
Talent, James (MO)	$5,000	Boustany, Jr, Charles (LA)	$5,000
Kyl, Jon L (AZ)	$3,000	Capito, Shelley (WV)	$5,000
		Chocola, Christopher (IN)	$5,000
		Dreier, David (CA)	$5,000
		Duncan, John (TN)	$5,000
		Fitzpatrick, Michael (PA)	$5,000
		Fortenberry, Jeffrey (NE)	$5,000
		Fossella, Vito (NY)	$5,000
		Gerlach, Jim (PA)	$5,000
		Goodlatte, Robert (VA)	$5,000
		Hayes, Robert (NC)	$5,000
		Kuhl, John R Jr (NY)	$5,000
		Musgrave, Marilyn (CO)	$5,000
		Northup, Anne M. (KY)	$5,000
		Porter, Jon (NV)	$5,000
		Reichert, Dave (WA)	$5,000
		Renzi, Richard (AZ)	$5,000
		Rogers, Michael (AL)	$5,000
		Shaw, Clay (FL)	$5,000
		Shays, Christopher (CT)	$5,000
		Simmons, Rob (CT)	$5,000
		Sodrel, Michael (IN)	$5,000
		Wilson, Heather (NM)	$5,000

Corporate Foundations and Giving Programs

Wal-Mart Foundation
Contact: Betsy Reithemeyer
702 SW Eighth St.
Bentonville, AR 72716
Tel: (479) 277 - 0357
Fax: (479) 273 - 6850

Annual Grant Total: over $5,000,000
Primary interests: local fund raising projects.
Geographic Preference: Area(s) in which the company operates
Recent Recipients: Children's Miracle Network; United Negro College Fund; United Way

Public Affairs and Related Activities Personnel

At Headquarters

ALLEN, Jay
Senior V. President, Corporate Relations
Mailstop: M/S 0150
Tel: (479) 273 - 4786
Fax: (479) 277 - 2473
Responsibilities include corporate communications, political action and government affairs.

BRACY, Ray
V. President, International Corporate Affairs
Mailstop: M/S 0130
Tel: (479) 277 - 0934
Fax: (479) 273 - 4053

FITZSIMMONS, Joseph J. "Jay"
Senior V. President, Finance and Treasurer
Tel: (479) 273 - 6445
Fax: (479) 273 - 4053
Responsibilities include investor relations.

HYDE, Thomas D.
Exec. V. President, Legal and Corporate Affairs and Secretary
Tel: (479) 273 - 4000
Fax: (479) 273 - 4053

MCADAM, Robert "Bob"
V. President, State and Local Government Affairs
Mailstop: M/S 0150
Tel: (479) 277 - 0284
Fax: (479) 277 - 2473

PETERSON, Coleman
Exec. V. President, Human Resources
Mailstop: M/S 0200
Tel: (479) 273 - 4000
Fax: (479) 273 - 4053

REITHEMEYER, Betsy
Director, Wal-Mart Foundation
Mailstop: M/S 0150
Tel: (479) 277 - 0357
Fax: (479) 273 - 6850

WHITCOMB, Gus
Media Relations Contact
Tel: (479) 273 - 4314
Fax: (479) 273 - 4053

WILLIAMS, Mona
V. President, Corporate Communications
Mailstop: M/S 0150
Tel: (479) 273 - 4314
Fax: (479) 273 - 4053

At Washington Office

BAILEY, James R. "Tres"
Tel: (202) 737 - 5523
Fax: (202) 737 - 6069

GARZA, Belinda
Office Manager, National Government Relations
Tel: (202) 737 - 5523
Fax: (202) 737 - 6069
Registered Federal Lobbyist.

HOFMANN, Angie M.
Director, International Trade
Tel: (202) 737 - 5523
Fax: (202) 737 - 6069
Registered Federal Lobbyist.

Wal-Mart Stores

** continued from previous page*

LEZY, Normand G. — Tel: (202) 737 - 5523
V. President, National Government Relations — Fax: (202) 737 - 6069
nlezy@wal-mart.com
Registered Federal Lobbyist.

SMALLING, Laurie — Tel: (202) 737 - 5523
Manager, Corporate Affairs — Fax: (202) 737 - 6069
Registered Federal Lobbyist.

WINBORN, Erik — Tel: (202) 737 - 5523
Director, National Government Relations — Fax: (202) 737 - 6069
Registered Federal Lobbyist.

WOODARD, Kimberly — Tel: (202) 737 - 5523
Director, National Government Relations — Fax: (202) 737 - 6069
Registered Federal Lobbyist.

Walgreen Co.

PUBLIC AFFAIRS COUNCIL

A member of the Public Affairs Council. A retail drug store chain.
www.walgreens.com
Annual Revenues: $28.68 billion

Chairman and Chief Exec. Officer
BERNAUER, David W. — Tel: (847) 914 - 2500
dave.bernauer@walgreens.com — Fax: (847) 914 - 3652

Main Headquarters
Mailing: 200 Wilmot Rd.
Deerfield, IL 60015-4616 — Tel: (847) 914 - 2500

Political Action Committees

Walgreen Co. PAC
Contact: Bryan Schnieder
104 Wilmot Rd. — Tel: (847) 315 - 4440
mail stop 1444 — Fax: (847) 315 - 4660
Deerfield, IL 60015

Contributions to Candidates: $24,000 (01/05 - 09/05)
Democrats: $11,500; Republicans: $12,500.

Principal Recipients

SENATE DEMOCRATS		HOUSE DEMOCRATS	
Nelson, Benjamin (NE)	$2,000	Schakowsky, Janice (IL)	$4,000
		Davis, Danny K (IL)	$1,500

SENATE REPUBLICANS		HOUSE REPUBLICANS	
Vitter, David (LA)	$2,000	Hastert, Dennis J. (IL)	$5,000
		Deal, Nathan (GA)	$2,500

Corporate Foundations and Giving Programs

Walgreen Corporate Contributions Program
Contact: John F. Gremer
104 Wilmot Rd. — Tel: (847) 315 - 2856
mail stop 1444 — Fax: (847) 315 - 4417
Deerfield, IL 60015

Annual Grant Total: $2,000,000 - $5,000,000
Focuses primarily on single-disease agencies and one-on-one tutorial programs in inner cities.

Public Affairs and Related Activities Personnel

At Headquarters

GLEESON, John — Tel: (847) 914 - 2500
Corporate V. President and Treasurer — Fax: (847) 914 - 3417
Responsibilities include investor relations.

GREEN, Dana I. — Tel: (847) 914 - 3010
General Counsel — Fax: (847) 914 - 3962
dana.green@walgreens.com

HANS, Rick J. — Tel: (847) 914 - 2385
Assistant Treasurer and Director, Finance — Fax: (847) 914 - 2678
rick.hans@walgreens.com
Responsibilities include investor relations.

MEYER, Laurie L. — Tel: (847) 914 - 2920
Divisional V. President, Corporate Communications — Fax: (847) 914 - 3086
laurie.meyer@walgreens.com

POLZIN, Michael — Tel: (847) 914 - 2925
Manager, External Communications — Fax: (847) 914 - 3086
Mailstop: M/S #2166
michael.polzin@walgreens.com

At Other Offices

CRANE, Ruth
Manager, Charitable Giving
104 Wilmot Rd.
mail stop 1444
Deerfield, IL 60015

GREMER, John F. — Tel: (847) 315 - 2856
Foundation Contact — Fax: (847) 315 - 4417
104 Wilmot Rd.
mail stop 1444
Deerfield, IL 60015

SCHNIEDER, Bryan — Tel: (847) 315 - 4440
PAC Contact — Fax: (847) 315 - 4660
104 Wilmot Rd.
mail stop 1444
Deerfield, IL 60015

Walter Industries, Inc.

Homebuilding and financing, natural resources, building materials and industrial products.
www.walterind.com
Annual Revenues: $1.9 billion

Chairman, President, and Chief Exec. Officer
DEFOSSET, Don — Tel: (813) 871 - 4811
ddefosset@walterind.com — Fax: (813) 871 - 4420

Main Headquarters
Mailing: 4211 W. Boyscout Blvd. — Tel: (813) 871 - 4811
Tampa, FL 33607 — Fax: (813) 871 - 4399

Political Action Committees

Walter Industries Inc. PAC (WaltPAC)
Contact: Cynthia B. Eisch
4211 W. Boyscout Blvd. — Tel: (813) 871 - 4811
Tampa, FL 33607 — Fax: (813) 871 - 4420

Contributions to Candidates: $4,000 (01/05 - 09/05)
Republicans: $4,000.

Principal Recipients

SENATE REPUBLICANS	HOUSE REPUBLICANS	
	Young, Don E (AK)	$4,000

Corporate Foundations and Giving Programs

The Walter Foundation
4211 W. Boyscout Blvd. — Tel: (813) 871 - 4811
Tampa, FL 33607 — Fax: (813) 871 - 4399

Annual Grant Total: $300,000 - $400,000
Geographic Preference: Area(s) in which the company operates; Florida
Primary Interests: Arts and Culture; Civic and Public Affairs; Higher Education; Social Services
Recent Recipients: Boys and Girls Club; Junior Achievement; YMCA

Public Affairs and Related Activities Personnel

At Headquarters

EISCH, Cynthia B. — Tel: (813) 871 - 4811
Treasurer, Walter Industries Inc. PAC — Fax: (813) 871 - 4420

MONAHAN, Michael — Tel: (813) 871 - 4132
Director, Corporate Communications — Fax: (813) 871 - 4399

TROY, Joe — Tel: (813) 871 - 4404
Senior V. President, Financial Services — Fax: (813) 871 - 4420
Responsibilities include investor relations.

WILLIAMS, Larry — Tel: (813) 871 - 4811
Senior V. President, Human Resources — Fax: (813) 871 - 4399

At Other Offices

CROWE, Robert T. — Tel: (205) 254 - 7254
V. President, Public Affairs — Fax: (205) 254 - 7150
3300 First Ave. North
P.O. Box 10406
Birmingham, AL 35202

Responsibilities include government affairs.

Warner Brothers Entertainment

See listing on page 475 under Time Warner Inc.

Warner Music Group Inc.

See listing on page 475 under Time Warner Inc.

Washington Gas

PUBLIC AFFAIRS COUNCIL

A member of the Public Affairs Council. A natural gas utility.
www.washgas.com
Annual Revenues: $1.58 billion

Chairman and Chief Exec. Officer
DEGRAFFENREIDT, James H., Jr. — Tel: (703) 750 - 2000 / Fax: (703) 750 - 4574

Main Headquarters
Mailing: 101 Constitution Ave. NW — Tel: (703) 750 - 2000
Washington, DC 20080 — Fax: (703) 750 - 4574

Political Action Committees

Washington Gas Light Co. Federal Political Action Committee
Contact: Doreen C. Hope
101 Constitution Ave. NW — Tel: (703) 750 - 2000
Washington, DC 20080 — Fax: (703) 750 - 4574

Washington Gas

** continued from previous page*

Contributions to Candidates: $9,000 (01/05 - 09/05)

Democrats: $8,000; Republicans: $1,000.

Principal Recipients

Bingaman, Jeff (NM)	$1,000	**HOUSE OTHER**	
Byrd, Robert C (WV)	$1,000	Norton, Eleanor Holmes (DC)	$2,000
		Hoyer, Steny (MD)	$1,500
		Wynn, Albert (MD)	$1,500
		Moran, James (VA)	$1,000
SENATE REPUBLICANS		**HOUSE REPUBLICANS**	
Allen, George (VA)	$1,000		

Corporate Foundations and Giving Programs

Washington Gas Corporate Giving Program
Contact: Steven Jumper
101 Constitution Ave. NW — Tel: (703) 750 - 2000
Washington, DC 20080 — Fax: (703) 750 - 4574

Annual Grant Total: none reported

Primary Interests: Education; Environment/Conservation; Health

Public Affairs and Related Activities Personnel

At Headquarters

BATTLE, Lynn — Tel: (703) 750 - 2000
Public Affairs Specialist — Fax: (703) 750 - 4574
lbattle@washgas.com

CHAPMAN, Adrian P. — Tel: (703) 750 - 2000
V. President, Regulatory Affairs and Energy Acquisition — Fax: (703) 750 - 4574
achapman@washgas.com

HOPE, Doreen C. — Tel: (703) 750 - 2000
Director, Federal Affairs — Fax: (703) 750 - 4574
dhope@washgas.com

JUMPER, Steven — Tel: (703) 750 - 2000
Director, DC and Maryland Public Affairs — Fax: (703) 750 - 4574
sjumper@washgas.com
Responsibilities include corporate contributions.

SARGEANT, Timothy J. — Tel: (703) 750 - 2000
Media Spokesperson — Fax: (703) 750 - 4574
tsargeant@washgas.com

SIMS, Roberta W. — Tel: (703) 750 - 2000
V. President, Corporate Relations — Fax: (703) 750 - 4574
rsims@washgas.com

At Other Offices

WILLIAMS, Alexia — Tel: (703) 750 - 5637
Virginia Public Affairs Contact
6801 Industrial Rd.
Springfield, VA 22151

Washington Group Internat'l

A member of the Public Affairs Council. An engineering construction company operating worldwide.

www.wgint.com
Annual Revenues: $3 billion

Chairman of the Board — Tel: (208) 386 - 5000
WASHINGTON, Dennis R. — Fax: (208) 386 - 7186

President and Chief Exec. Officer — Tel: (208) 386 - 5000
HANKS, Stephen G. — Fax: (208) 386 - 7186

Main Headquarters

Mailing: P.O. Box 73 — Tel: (208) 386 - 5000
Boise, ID 83729 — Fax: (208) 386 - 7186

Street: Morrison Knudsen Plaza
720 Park Blvd.
Boise, ID 83712

Washington Office

Contact: Cynthia M. Stinger
Mailing: 2345 Crystal Dr. — Tel: (703) 236 - 2700
Suite 708 — Fax: (703) 236 - 1931
Arlington, VA 22202

Political Action Committees

Washington Group Internat'l Inc. Political Action Committee
P.O. Box 73 — Tel: (208) 386 - 5000
Boise, ID 83729 — Fax: (208) 386 - 7186

Contributions to Candidates: $204,012 (01/05 - 09/05)

Democrats: $70,500; Republicans: $132,512; Other: $1,000.

Principal Recipients

SENATE DEMOCRATS		**HOUSE DEMOCRATS**	
		Menendez, Robert (NJ)	$15,000
		Murtha, John P Mr. (PA)	$7,500
		Clyburn, James (SC)	$5,000
SENATE REPUBLICANS		**HOUSE REPUBLICANS**	
Burns, Conrad (MT)	$12,000	Barrett, James (SC)	$7,177
Allen, George (VA)	$9,000	Hastings, Doc (WA)	$5,000
DeMint, James (SC)	$4,999	Norwood, Charles (GA)	$5,000
Graham, Lindsey (SC)	$4,000	Wilson, Joe (SC)	$5,000
Santorum, Richard (PA)	$4,000		
Craig, Larry (ID)	$3,000		
Ensign, John Eric (NV)	$3,000		

Corporate Foundations and Giving Programs

Washington Group Internat'l Inc. Foundation
Contact: Marlene Puckett
P.O. Box 73 — Tel: (208) 386 - 5201
Boise, ID 83729 — Fax: (208) 386 - 6166

Annual Grant Total: $300,000 - $400,000

Makes grants directly to needy individuals for basic necessities excluding business or education-related needs. Occasionally grants funds to 501(c)(3) organizations working in the primary interests areas.

Primary Interests: Arts and Culture; Community Affairs; Education; Health and Human Services; Human Welfare

Public Affairs and Related Activities Personnel

At Headquarters

HUNT, Rod — Tel: (208) 386 - 5254
Director, Corporate Communications — Fax: (208) 386 - 5065
rod.hunt@wgint.com

MYERS, Larry L. — Tel: (208) 386 - 5000
Senior V. President, Human Resources — Fax: (208) 386 - 7186

PUCKETT, Marlene — Tel: (208) 386 - 5201
Administrator, Director, and Secretary, Washington Internat'l Group Inc. Foundation — Fax: (208) 386 - 6166
marlene.puckett@wgint.com

SPIEGELBERG, Laurie A. — Tel: (208) 386 - 5255
V. President, Communications — Fax: (208) 386 - 7186

At Washington Office

CAVEY, Brian — Tel: (703) 236 - 2756
Director, Government Affairs — Fax: (703) 236 - 1931

DUVALL, Suzanne — Tel: (703) 236 - 2700
Fax: (703) 236 - 1931
Registered Federal Lobbyist.

ROTHROCK-HARKE, Jill — Tel: (703) 236 - 2751
Manager, Government Affairs — Fax: (703) 236 - 1931
Registered Federal Lobbyist.

STINGER, Cynthia M. — Tel: (703) 236 - 2740
V. President, Government Affairs — Fax: (703) 236 - 1930
cynthia.stinger@wgint.com
Registered Federal Lobbyist.

Washington Mutual Bank

See listing on page 512 under Washington Mutual, Inc.

Washington Mutual, Inc.

A member of the Public Affairs Council. A financial services company. Acquired Dime Bancorp, Inc. in January of 2002.

www.wamu.com
Annual Revenues: $19 billion

Chairman, President and Chief Exec. Officer — Tel: (206) 461 - 2000
KILLINGER, Kerry — Fax: (206) 554 - 4807
kerry.killinger@wamu.net — TF: (800) 756 - 8000

Main Headquarters

Mailing: P.O. Box 834 — Tel: (206) 461 - 2000
Seattle, WA 98101 — Fax: (206) 554 - 4807
TF: (800) 756 - 8000

Street: 1201 Third Ave.
Seattle, WA 98101

Political Action Committees

Washington Mutual PAC
Contact: Randy Churchill
1215 Fourth Ave.
Suite 1620
Seattle, WA 28181

Contributions to Candidates: $120,100 (01/05 - 09/05)

Washington Mutual, Inc.

** continued from previous page*

Democrats: $53,000; Republicans: $67,100.

Principal Recipients

SENATE DEMOCRATS		HOUSE DEMOCRATS	
Murray, Patty (WA)	$2,500	Crowley, Joseph (NY)	$4,000
Conrad, Kent (ND)	$2,000	Menendez, Robert (NJ)	$3,500
Feinstein, Dianne (CA)	$2,000		
Stabenow, Debbie (MI)	$2,000		
SENATE REPUBLICANS		**HOUSE REPUBLICANS**	
Bennett, Robert F (UT)	$5,000	Ney, Robert W (OH)	$5,000
Allen, George (VA)	$2,500	Royce, Ed Mr (CA)	$5,000
Martinez, Mel (FL)	$2,500	McMorris, Cathy (WA)	$4,500
Kyl, Jon L (AZ)	$2,000	Bachus, Spencer (AL)	$4,000

Corporate Foundations and Giving Programs

Washington Mutual Foundation
Contact: Cheryl Di Re
P.O. Box 834
Seattle, WA 98101
Tel: (206) 461 - 3465
Fax: (206) 554 - 4807
TF: (800) 756 - 8000

Annual Grant Total: $1,000,000 - $2,000,000
Geographic Preference: Area(s) in which the company operates; California; Florida; Idaho; Oregon; Texas; Utah; Washington State; Arizona; Georgia; New York; New Jersey; Nevada
Primary Interests: Education; Housing

Public Affairs and Related Activities Personnel

At Headquarters

DAVID, Daryl D.
Exec. V. President, Human Resources
daryl.david@wamu.net
Tel: (206) 461 - 8890
Fax: (206) 554 - 4807
TF: (800) 756 - 8000

DAVIS, J. Bradley
Exec. V. President, Chief Communications and Marketing Officer
Tel: (206) 461 - 2000
Fax: (206) 554 - 4807
TF: (800) 756 - 8000

DI RE, Cheryl
First V. President and Manager, Community Affairs
Mailstop: WMT 1213
Tel: (206) 461 - 3465
Fax: (206) 554 - 4807
TF: (800) 756 - 8000
Responsibilities include corporate philanthropy.

EHRLICH, Bill
Exec. V. President, Strategic Communications
Tel: (206) 461 - 2000
Fax: (206) 554 - 4807
TF: (800) 756 - 8000

GASPARD, M. Scott
Senior V. President, Government and Industry Relations
Tel: (206) 461 - 2000
Fax: (206) 554 - 4807
TF: (800) 756 - 8000

HUTCHINSON, Libby
First V. President and Manager, Corporate Public Relations
Mailstop: WMT 0735
libby.hutchinson@wamu.net
Tel: (206) 461 - 2484
Fax: (206) 554 - 4807
TF: (800) 756 - 8000

KUHLMANN, David
Corporate Public Relations
david.kuhlman@wamu.net
Tel: (206) 377 - 4072
Fax: (206) 554 - 4807
TF: (800) 756 - 8000

PARKER, Gary
Tel: (206) 461 - 2000
Fax: (206) 554 - 4807
TF: (800) 756 - 8000

PORTER, J. Benson
Senior V. President, Community and External Affairs
(Washington Mutual Bank)
Mailstop: WMT 1706
benson.porter@wamu.net
Tel: (206) 461 - 8854
Fax: (206) 554 - 4807
TF: (800) 756 - 8000

RODRIGUEZ, Adrian
Manager, Corporate Public Relations
adrian.rodriguez@wamu.net
Tel: (206) 377 - 3268
Fax: (206) 554 - 4807
TF: (800) 756 - 8000

WATSON, Allison
Tel: (206) 461 - 2000
Fax: (206) 554 - 4807
TF: (800) 756 - 8000

At Other Offices

CHURCHILL, Randy
PAC Treasurer
1215 Fourth Ave.
Suite 1620
Seattle, WA 28181

The Washington Post Co.

A diversified media and education company whose principal operations include television broadcasting, newspaper publishing, cable television, magazine publishing, education, and career services.

www.washpostco.com
Annual Revenues: $2.417 billion

Chairman and Chief Exec. Officer
GRAHAM, Donald E.
Tel: (202) 334 - 6000
Fax: (202) 334 - 4536

Main Headquarters
Mailing: 1150 15th St. NW
Washington, DC 20071
Tel: (202) 334 - 6000
Fax: (202) 334 - 4536

Corporate Foundations and Giving Programs

The Washington Post Co. Contributions
Contact: Rima Calderon
1150 15th St. NW
Washington, DC 20071
Tel: (202) 334 - 6617
Fax: (202) 334 - 4536

Annual Grant Total: $2,000,000 - $5,000,000
Grant total includes the company's matching gifts program. All subsidiaries of the Washington Post Co. participate in the Contributions Program.
Geographic Preference: Area in which the company is headquartered
Primary Interests: Civic and Cultural Activities; Early Childhood Education; Literacy; Youth Services

The Washington Post Newspaper Giving Program
Contact: Eric Grant
1150 15th St. NW
Washington, DC 20071
Tel: (202) 334 - 6466
Fax: (202) 334 - 5609

Annual Grant Total: none reported
Primary Interests: Civic and Public Affairs; Community Affairs; Education

Public Affairs and Related Activities Personnel

At Headquarters

BRYANT, Candice
Contact, The Philip L. Graham Fund
Tel: (202) 334 - 5104
Fax: (202) 334 - 4536

BUTLER, Patrick
V. President, Government Affairs
butlerp@washpost.com
Tel: (202) 334 - 6635
Fax: (202) 334 - 6664

CALDERON, Rima
Director, Corporate Communications
calderonr@washpost.com
Tel: (202) 334 - 6617
Fax: (202) 334 - 4536
Responsibilities include corporate philanthropy.

CAMPOVERDE, Rebecca O.
Director, Public Affairs
(Kaplan, Inc.)
Mailstop: Sixth Floor
Tel: (202) 334 - 6684
Fax: (202) 334 - 4536

GRANT, Eric
Director, Public Relations and Contributions
Tel: (202) 334 - 6466
Fax: (202) 334 - 5609

MELAMED, Carol
V. President, Government Relations
Tel: (202) 334 - 6000

MORSE, John B., Jr.
Chief Financial Officer and V. President, Finance
morsej@washpost.com
Tel: (202) 334 - 6662
Fax: (202) 334 - 1031
Responsibilities include investor relations.

RICHARDS, Shawna
Coordinator, Corporate Affairs
richardss@washpost.com
Tel: (202) 334 - 6632
Fax: (202) 334 - 4536

Waste Management of Louisiana, Inc.

See listing on page 513 under Waste Management, Inc.

Waste Management of Texas, Inc.

See listing on page 513 under Waste Management, Inc.

Waste Management, Inc.

An international environmental services and waste management company.

www.wm.com
Annual Revenues: $11.322 billion

Chairman of the Board
MYERS, A. Maurice
Tel: (713) 512 - 6200
Fax: (713) 512 - 6299

Chief Exec. Officer
STEINER, David P.
Tel: (713) 512 - 6200
Fax: (713) 512 - 6299

Main Headquarters
Mailing: 1001 Fannin St., Suite 4000
Houston, TX 77002
Tel: (713) 512 - 6200
Fax: (713) 512 - 6299

Washington Office
Mailing: 601 Pennsylvania Ave. NW
North Bldg. Suite 300
Washington, DC 20004
Tel: (202) 628 - 3500
Fax: (202) 628 - 0400

Political Action Committees

Waste Management Inc. Employees Better Government Fund
Contact: Kimberley A. Engle
601 Pennsylvania Ave. NW
North Bldg. Suite 300
Washington, DC 20004
Tel: (202) 628 - 3500
Fax: (202) 628 - 0400

Waste Management, Inc.

* continued from previous page

Contributions to Candidates: $46,000 (01/05 - 09/05)

Democrats: $12,000; Republicans: $34,000.

Principal Recipients

SENATE DEMOCRATS		HOUSE DEMOCRATS	
Baucus, Max (MT)	$5,000	Boucher, Fredrick (VA)	$2,500
		Lee, Sheila Jackson (TX)	$2,500
		Ross, Michael Avery (AR)	$2,000
SENATE REPUBLICANS		**HOUSE REPUBLICANS**	
Hutchison, Kay Bailey (TX)	$5,000	Camp, David Lee (MI)	$5,000
		Fossella, Vito (NY)	$5,000
Smith, Gordon (OR)	$5,000	Reynolds, Thomas (NY)	$5,000
Santorum, Richard (PA)	$2,500	Bass, Charles (NH)	$2,500

Corporate Foundations and Giving Programs

Waste Management Corporate Giving Program
1001 Fannin St., Suite 4000
Houston, TX 77002
Tel: (713) 512 - 6200
Fax: (713) 512 - 6299

Annual Grant Total: none reported

Public Affairs and Related Activities Personnel

At Headquarters

BROWN, Marilyn
Contributions Contact
Tel: (713) 512 - 6200
Fax: (713) 512 - 6299

CALDWELL, Barry H.
Senior V. President, Government Affairs and Corporate Communications
bcaldwell@wm.com
Tel: (713) 512 - 6200
Fax: (713) 512 - 6299

RICE, Cherie C.
V. President, Investor Relations
crice@wm.com
Tel: (713) 512 - 6574
Fax: (713) 512 - 6299

At Washington Office

BRIGGUM, Sue M.
Director, Environmental Affairs
sbriggum@wm.com
Tel: (202) 628 - 3500
Fax: (202) 628 - 0400

EISENBUD, Robert
Director, Legislative Affairs
beisenbudwm.com
Registered Federal Lobbyist.
Tel: (202) 628 - 3500
Fax: (202) 628 - 0400

ENGLE, Kimberley A.
Manager, Government Affairs
kengle@wm.com
Tel: (202) 628 - 3500
Fax: (202) 628 - 0400

KARDELL, Lisa R.
Manager, Federal and State Government Affairs
lkardell@wm.com
Tel: (202) 628 - 3500
Fax: (202) 628 - 0400

SKERNOLIS, Edmund J.
Director, Government Affairs
eskernolis@wm.com
Tel: (202) 628 - 3500
Fax: (202) 628 - 0400

Waters Corp.

Develops instruments for scientific testing purposes.

www.waters.com
Annual Revenues: $890 million

Chairman, President and Chief Exec. Officer
BERTHIAUME, Douglas A.
Tel: (508) 478 - 2000
Fax: (508) 872 - 1990
TF: (800) 252 - 4752

Main Headquarters
Mailing: 34 Maple St.
Milford, MA 01757
Tel: (508) 478 - 2000
Fax: (508) 872 - 1990
TF: (800) 252 - 4752

Public Affairs and Related Activities Personnel

At Headquarters

CASSIS, Eugene G.
V. President, Investor Relations
Gene_Cassis@waters.com
Tel: (508) 478 - 2349
Fax: (508) 872 - 1990
TF: (800) 252 - 4752

MAZER, Brian K.
Seniot V. President, Human Resources, Investor Relations
Tel: (508) 478 - 2000
Fax: (508) 872 - 1990
TF: (800) 252 - 4752

MURPHY, Brian J.
Manager, Corporate Communications
brian_j_murphy@waters.com
Tel: (508) 478 - 2614
Fax: (508) 872 - 1990
TF: (800) 252 - 4752

Wausau Insurance Companies

See listing on page 180 under Employers Insurance Co of Wausau.

Wawa, Inc.

Operates a chain of convenience stores.

www.wawa.com
Annual Revenues: $2 billion

Chairman of the Board
WOOD, Richard D., Jr.
Tel: (610) 358 - 8000
Fax: (610) 358 - 8878
TF: (800) 283 - 9292

Chief Exec. Officer
STOECKEL, Howard B.
Tel: (610) 358 - 8000
Fax: (610) 358 - 8878
TF: (800) 283 - 9292

Main Headquarters
Mailing: 260 Baltimore Pike
Wawa, PA 19063
Tel: (610) 358 - 8000
Fax: (610) 358 - 8878
TF: (800) 283 - 9292

Political Action Committees

Wawa Inc. Political Action Committee
423 W. Sixth Ave.
Parkesburg, PA 19365

Contributions to Candidates: none reported (01/05 - 09/05)

Corporate Foundations and Giving Programs

Wawa Inc. Corporate Charities Program
Contact: Lori A. Bruce
260 Baltimore Pike
Wawa, PA 19063
Tel: (610) 358 - 8039
Fax: (610) 358 - 8878
TF: (800) 283 - 9292

Annual Grant Total: none reported
Geographic Preference: Area(s) in which employees live and work
Primary Interests: AIDS/HIV; Children's Health; Domestic Violence; Hunger

Public Affairs and Related Activities Personnel

At Headquarters

BRUCE, Lori A.
Chairperson, Wawa Inc. Corporate Charities Committee
lori.a.bruce@wawa.com
Tel: (610) 358 - 8039
Fax: (610) 358 - 8878
TF: (800) 283 - 9292

DIMEGLIO, John
Treasurer, Wawa Inc. Political Action Committee
Tel: (610) 358 - 8000
Fax: (610) 358 - 8878
TF: (800) 283 - 9292

We Energies

PUBLIC AFFAIRS COUNCIL

A member of the Public Affairs Council. A natural gas distribution utility. A subsidiary of Wisconsin Energy Corp. (see separate listing).

www.we-energies.com

Chairman and Chief Exec. Officer
KLAPPA, Gale E.
Tel: (414) 221 - 4525
Fax: (414) 221 - 4519

Main Headquarters
Mailing: 231 W. Michigan
Milwaukee, WI 53203
Tel: (414) 221 - 2345
Fax: (414) 221 - 3814

Washington Office
Mailing: 122 C St. NW
Suite 840
Washington, DC 20001
Tel: (202) 662 - 4340
Fax: (202) 662 - 4359

Corporate Foundations and Giving Programs

Wisconsin Energy Corporation Foundation
231 W. Michigan
Milwaukee, WI 53203
Tel: (414) 221 - 2345
Fax: (414) 221 - 3814

Annual Grant Total: none reported

Public Affairs and Related Activities Personnel

At Headquarters

CIESLAK, Richard
Manager, External Communications
richard.cieslak@we-energies.com
Tel: (414) 221 - 4510
Fax: (414) 221 - 2821

HENDERSON, Colleen
Manager of Strategic Planning and Investor Relations
colleen.henderson@we-energies.com
Tel: (414) 221 - 3152
Fax: (414) 221 - 2594

KUNICKI, Walter
V. President, Customer Relations
Mailstop: P446
walter.kunicki@we-energies.com
Tel: (414) 221 - 3414
Fax: (414) 221 - 4655

MARTIN, Beth
Communications Specialist
Tel: (414) 221 - 3687
Fax: (414) 221 - 2821

SIAS, Thelma
V. President, Local Affairs
thelma.sias@we-energies.com
Tel: (414) 221 - 3651
Fax: (414) 221 - 3853

Weatherford Internat'l Ltd.

Offers oil and gas field exploration services, machinery and equipment.

www.weatherford.com
Annual Revenues: $2.3 billion

Weatherford Internat'l Ltd.

* continued from previous page

Chairman and Chief Exec. Officer
DUROC-DANNER, Bernard J.
Tel: (713) 693 - 4000
Fax: (713) 693 - 4323
TF: (800) 257 - 3826

Main Headquarters
Mailing: 515 Post Oak Blvd., Suite 600
Houston, TX 77027-3415
Tel: (713) 693 - 4000
Fax: (713) 693 - 4323
TF: (800) 257 - 3826

Public Affairs and Related Activities Personnel

At Headquarters

NICHOLSON, Jon R.
Senior V. President, Human Resources
Tel: (713) 693 - 4194
Fax: (713) 693 - 4323
TF: (800) 257 - 3826

WebMD Corp.

www.webmd.com
Annual Revenues: $925.96 million

President and Chief Exec. Officer
GATTINELLA, Wayne T.
Tel: (201) 703 - 3400
Fax: (201) 703 - 3401

Main Headquarters
Mailing: 669 River Dr.
Elmwood Park, NJ 07407
Tel: (201) 703 - 3400
Fax: (201) 703 - 3401

Public Affairs and Related Activities Personnel

At Headquarters

FISHER, Risa
V. President, Investor Relations
rfisher@webmd.net
Tel: (201) 703 - 3415
Fax: (201) 703 - 3401

At Other Offices

MEYER, Jennifer
V. President, Communications
224 W. 30th St.
New York, NY 10001
jmeyer@webmd.net
Tel: (212) 624 - 3912
Fax: (212) 624 - 3881

Webster Financial Corp.

A bank holding company.
www.websterbank.com
Annual Revenues: $877.6 million

Chairman and Chief Exec. Officer
SMITH, James C.
jsmith@websterbank.com
Tel: (800) 325 - 2424

Main Headquarters
Mailing: Webster Plaza
145 Bank St.
Waterbury, CT 06702
Tel: (203) 578 - 2476
Fax: (203) 573 - 8680
TF: (800) 325 - 2424

Political Action Committees

Webster Bank PAC - Federal
Webster Plaza
145 Bank St.
Waterbury, CT 06702
Tel: (203) 578 - 2476
Fax: (203) 573 - 8680
TF: (800) 325 - 2424

Contributions to Candidates: none reported (01/05 - 09/05)

Corporate Foundations and Giving Programs

Webster Financial Corp. Corporate Contributions Program
Contact: Jill Bradley
Webster Plaza
145 Bank St.
Waterbury, CT 06702
Tel: (203) 578 - 2396
Fax: (203) 578 - 2507

Annual Grant Total: none reported
Primary Interests: Economic Development; Health and Human Services; Housing; Hunger

Public Affairs and Related Activities Personnel

At Headquarters

BRADLEY, Jill
V. President, Community Affairs
Mailstop: MO 210
jabradley@websterbank.com
Tel: (203) 578 - 2396
Fax: (203) 578 - 2507

BROWN, Jeffrey N.
Exec. V. President, Marketing and Communications
Mailstop: MO 210
jbrown@websterbank.com
Tel: (203) 578 - 2566
Fax: (203) 755 - 5539

FINLEY, Clark
Assistnat V. President, Public Affairs
cfinley@websterbank.com
Tel: (203) 578 - 2287
Fax: (203) 573 - 8680
TF: (800) 325 - 2424

MANGAN, Terrence K.
Senior V. President, Investor Relations
Mailstop: MO 315
tmangan@websterbank.com
Tel: (203) 578 - 2318
TF: (800) 325 - 2424

MURPHY, Patrick T.
Exec. V. President, Human Resources
Mailstop: MO 405
ptmurphy@websterbank.com
Tel: (203) 578 - 2273
Fax: (203) 755 - 5539

Weight Watchers Internat'l

Weight loss/management company.
www.weightwatchers.com
Annual Revenues: $623.9 million

Main Headquarters
Mailing: 175 Crossways Park West
Woodbury, NY 11797
Tel: (516) 390 - 1400
Fax: (516) 390 - 1302

Corporate Foundations and Giving Programs

Weight Watchers Foundation
175 Crossways Park West
Woodbury, NY 11797
Tel: (516) 390 - 1400
Fax: (516) 390 - 1302

Annual Grant Total: none reported

Public Affairs and Related Activities Personnel

At Headquarters

DEBBANE, Raymond
Chairman of the Board
Tel: (516) 390 - 1400
Fax: (516) 390 - 1302

FONTANA, Donna
V. President, Public Relations
Tel: (516) 390 - 1452
Fax: (516) 390 - 1390

HUETT, Linda
President and Chief Exec. Officer
Tel: (516) 390 - 1400
Fax: (516) 390 - 1302

Weis Markets, Inc.

A supermarket chain.
www.weismarkets.com
Annual Revenues: $2.01 billion

Chairman of the Board
WEIS, Robert F.
Tel: (570) 286 - 4571
Fax: (570) 286 - 3286

President and Chief Exec. Officer
RICH, Norman S.
Tel: (570) 286 - 4571
Fax: (570) 286 - 3286

Main Headquarters
Mailing: P.O. Box 471
Sunbury, PA 17801
Tel: (570) 286 - 4571
Fax: (570) 286 - 3286
Street: 1000 S. Second St.
Sunbury, PA 17801

Public Affairs and Related Activities Personnel

At Headquarters

CURTIN, Dennis V.
Director, Public Relations
Tel: (570) 286 - 4571
Fax: (570) 286 - 3286

MILLS, William R.
Senior V. President, Finance; and Treasurer
Responsibilities include shareholder relations.
Tel: (570) 286 - 3229
Fax: (570) 286 - 3625

SCHMEIDER, Robert
Director, Quality Control
Tel: (570) 286 - 4571
Fax: (570) 286 - 3286

Welch's

A manufacturer and marketer of grape juices, jellies and concentrates. A subsidiary of the Nat'l Grape Co-op Ass'n.
www.welchs.com
Annual Revenues: $649.6 million

Chairman of the Board
GRAHAM, Rudolph H.
Tel: (978) 371 - 1000
Fax: (978) 371 - 3860

President and Chief Exec. Officer
DILLON, Daniel P.
Tel: (978) 371 - 1000
Fax: (978) 371 - 3860

Main Headquarters
Mailing: Three Concord Farms
575 Virginia Rd.
Concord, MA 01742
Tel: (978) 371 - 1000
Fax: (978) 371 - 3879

Corporate Foundations and Giving Programs

Welch Foods Contributions Program
Three Concord Farms
575 Virginia Rd.
Concord, MA 01742
Tel: (978) 371 - 1000
Fax: (978) 371 - 3879

Annual Grant Total: none reported

Public Affairs and Related Activities Personnel

At Headquarters

CALLAHAN, James M.
Director, Corporate Communications
Tel: (978) 371 - 1000
Fax: (978) 371 - 3860

Wellmark, Inc.

www.wellmark.com

Chairman and Chief Exec. Officer
FORSYTH, John D. Tel: (515) 245 - 4548
forsythjd@wellmark.com Fax: (515) 245 - 5090

Main Headquarters
Mailing: 636 Grand Ave.
Des Moines, IA 50309
Tel: (515) 245 - 4500
Fax: (515) 245 - 5090
TF: (800) 362 - 1697

Political Action Committees

Wellmark Inc. PAC
Contact: Frank J. Stork
636 Grand Ave.
Des Moines, IA 50309
Tel: (515) 248 - 5388
Fax: (515) 245 - 5090
TF: (800) 362 - 1697

Contributions to Candidates: $3,000 (01/05 - 09/05)
Democrats: $2,000; Republicans: $1,000.

Principal Recipients

SENATE DEMOCRATS		HOUSE DEMOCRATS	
Johnson, Tim (SD)	$1,000	Herseth, Stephanie (SD)	$1,000
SENATE REPUBLICANS		**HOUSE REPUBLICANS**	
		Latham, Thomas P (IA)	$1,000

Corporate Foundations and Giving Programs

The Wellmark Foundation
636 Grand Ave.
Des Moines, IA 50309
Tel: (515) 245 - 4500
Fax: (515) 245 - 5090
TF: (800) 362 - 1697

Annual Grant Total: none reported
Geographic Preference: Iowa; South Dakota
Primary Interests: Community Affairs; Health

Public Affairs and Related Activities Personnel

At Headquarters

GOLD, Clifford D. Tel: (515) 245 - 4842
Group V. President, Marketing and External Relations Fax: (515) 245 - 5090
goldcd@wellmark.com

GRIFFIN, Janet Tel: (515) 248 - 5388
V. President, Public Policy and Government Relations Fax: (515) 245 - 5090
griffinj@wellmark.com

JACKSON, Laura J. Tel: (515) 235 - 4473
Senior V. President, Human Resources Fax: (515) 248 - 5528
jacksonlj@wellmark.com

MCNEILL, Dana W. Tel: (515) 235 - 4178
V. President, Corporate and Marketing Communications Fax: (515) 248 - 5382
mcneilldw@wellmark.com

STORK, Frank J. Tel: (515) 248 - 5388
Treasurer, Wellmark Inc. PAC Fax: (515) 245 - 5090
storkfj@wellmark.com TF: (800) 362 - 1697

Wellpoint Health Networks Inc.

See listing on page 516 under Wellpoint, Inc.

Wellpoint, Inc.

PUBLIC AFFAIRS COUNCIL

A member of the Public Affairs Council. A healthcare company. Formerly Anthem, Inc. Anthem, Inc. acquired Wellpoint Health Networks Inc. in 2004.
www.wellpoint.com
Annual Revenues: $40 billion

Chairman of the Board Tel: (317) 532 - 6000
SCHAEFFER, Leonard D.

President and Chief Exec. Officer Tel: (317) 532 - 6000
GLASSCOCK, Larry C.

Main Headquarters
Mailing: 120 Monument Circle
Indianapolis, IN 46204
Tel: (317) 532 - 6000

Washington Office
Mailing: 655 15th St. NW
Suite 425
Washington, DC 20005
Tel: (202) 628 - 7840
Fax: (202) 638 - 1096

Political Action Committees

Wellpoint, Inc. (WELLPAC)
Contact: Tracy Winn
120 Monument Circle
Indianapolis, IN 46204
Tel: (317) 488 - 6134

Contributions to Candidates: $120,280 (01/05 - 09/05)
Democrats: $19,080; Republicans: $101,200.

Principal Recipients

SENATE DEMOCRATS		HOUSE DEMOCRATS	
Conrad, Kent (ND)	$2,000	Pomeroy, Earl (ND)	$5,000
Lieberman, Joe (CT)	$2,000	Boucher, Fredrick (VA)	$2,000

SENATE REPUBLICANS		HOUSE REPUBLICANS	
Smith, Gordon (OR)	$7,000	Blunt, Roy (MO)	$5,000
Allen, George (VA)	$6,000	Deal, Nathan (GA)	$5,000
Lugar, Richard G (IN)	$5,500	Dreier, David (CA)	$5,000
Collins, Susan M (ME)	$5,000	Johnson, Nancy (CT)	$5,000
Hatch, Orrin (UT)	$5,000	Hulshof, Kenny (MO)	$3,625
McConnell, Mitch (KY)	$5,000	Gard, John G (WI)	$2,500
Lott, Trent (MS)	$3,000	Buyer, Steve (IN)	$2,000
Ensign, John Eric (NV)	$2,000	Northup, Anne M. (KY)	$2,000
Santorum, Richard (PA)	$2,000	Price, Thomas (GA)	$2,000

Corporate Foundations and Giving Programs

Anthem Blue Cross and Blue Shield Foundation
Contact: Vicki Perkins
120 Monument Circle
Indianapolis, IN 46204
Tel: (317) 488 - 6216

Assets: $26,285,123 (2001)
Annual Grant Total: $1,000,000 - $2,000,000
Gives to non-profit health access organizations working to improve the accessibility and affordability of healthcare.

Wellpoint, Inc. Charitable Contributions Program
Contact: Susan Nagy
One Wellpoint Way
Thousand Oak, CA 91362-5035
Tel: (805) 557 - 6788
Fax: (805) 557 - 6831

Assets: $130,000,000 (2004)
Annual Grant Total: over $5,000,000
Gives to non-profit health access organizations working to improve the accessibility and affordability of healthcare.

Public Affairs and Related Activities Personnel

At Headquarters

DAVIS, Deborah Tel: (317) 488 - 6350
Director, Media Relations

DURLE, Tami Tel: (317) 488 - 6390
V. President, Investor Relations

MAGINN, Marjorie Tel: (317) 488 - 6032
V. President, Industry and Political Affairs

MCMURTRY, Dana Tel: (317) 532 - 6000
V. President, Health Policy and Analysis
dana.mcmurtry@wellpoint.com

MORRISON, Andrew F. Tel: (317) 488 - 6296
Senior V. President, Public Affairs Fax: (317) 488 - 6896
Mailstop: IN 13A-312
andrew.morrison@wellpoint.com

PERKINS, Vicki Tel: (317) 488 - 6216
Exec. Director, Anthem Blue Cross and Blue Shield Foundation

WEST, Edward Tel: (317) 488 - 6100
Senior V. President, Corporate Communications
ed.west@wellpoint.com

WINN, Tracy Tel: (317) 488 - 6134
PAC Contact

At Washington Office

MACARTHUR, Kip Tel: (202) 628 - 7840
Director, Legislative Affairs Fax: (202) 638 - 1096

STEFFL, Jerry Tel: (202) 628 - 7840
Director, Legislative Affairs Fax: (202) 638 - 1096

At Other Offices

NAGY, Susan Tel: (805) 557 - 6788
Contact, Wellpoint, Inc. Corporate Contributions Program Fax: (805) 557 - 6831
One Wellpoint Way
Thousand Oak, CA 91362-5035

Wells Fargo & Co.

PUBLIC AFFAIRS COUNCIL

A member of the Public Affairs Council. A bank holding company. The company merged with Norwest Corp. in 1999 and with First Security Bank of Idaho, N.A. in 2000.
www.wellsfargo.com
Annual Revenues: $26.891 billion

Chairman, President and Chief Exec. Officer Tel: (415) 396 - 6408
KOVACEVICH, Richard M. TF: (800) 411 - 4932

Main Headquarters
Mailing: 420 Montgomery St.
San Francisco, CA 94104
Tel: (415) 396 - 6408
TF: (800) 411 - 4932

Political Action Committees

Wells Fargo Employee PAC
Contact: Anita B. Eoloff
Wells Fargo Center
Sixth & Marquette
Minneapolis, MN 55479
Tel: (612) 667 - 9917
Fax: (612) 667 - 9403

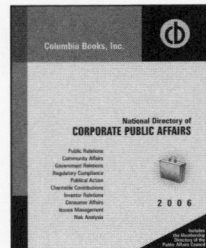

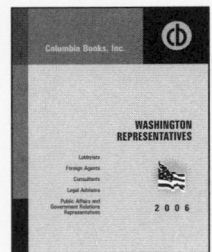

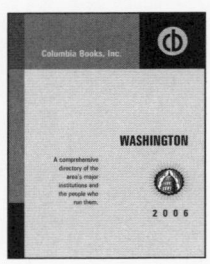

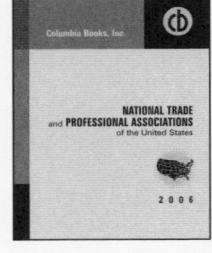

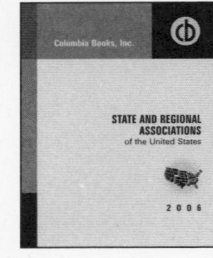

Wells Fargo & Co.

* continued from previous page

Contributions to Candidates: $140,000 (01/05 - 09/05)

Democrats: $63,500; Republicans: $73,000; Other: $3,500.

Principal Recipients

SENATE DEMOCRATS		HOUSE DEMOCRATS	
Byrd, Robert C (WV)	$10,000	Crowley, Joseph (NY)	$5,000
Feinstein, Dianne (CA)	$7,500	Pelosi, Nancy (CA)	$5,000
Conrad, Kent (ND)	$5,000		
Nelson, Benjamin (NE)	$5,000		
Stabenow, Debbie (MI)	$3,000		
SENATE REPUBLICANS		**HOUSE REPUBLICANS**	
Santorum, Richard (PA)	$5,000	Ney, Robert W (OH)	$6,000
Allen, George (VA)	$2,500	Royce, Ed Mr (CA)	$5,000
Lugar, Richard G (IN)	$2,000	Thomas, William M (CA)	$5,000
		Bachus, Spencer (AL)	$4,000

Corporate Foundations and Giving Programs

Wells Fargo Bank and Wells Fargo Foundation
Contact: Pam Erwin
550 California St.
San Francisco, CA 94104
Tel: (415) 396 - 3247
Fax: (415) 975 - 6260

Annual Grant Total: over $5,000,000

The company is also quite active in community outreach, sponsoring a social service leave program to permit employees to work as volunteers in community services agencies while retaining company salary and benefits. Employees may also participate in an organized volunteer network which encourages volunteer efforts by matching employees' skills to community non-profit needs. Foundation giving is supplemented by substantial direct corporate contributions.

Geographic Preference: California

Primary Interests: Economic Development; Housing; K-12 Education

Recent Recipients: Accelerated School (Los Angeles); Local Initiative Support Corp. (LISC)

Wells Fargo Foundation Minnesota
Contact: Carolyn Roby
Wells Fargo Center
Sixth & Marquette
Minneapolis, MN 55479
Tel: (612) 667 - 7860
Fax: (612) 667 - 8283

Annual Grant Total: none reported

Public Affairs and Related Activities Personnel

At Headquarters

HAEG, Lawrence P.
Exec. V. President and Director, Corporate Communications
Mailstop: M/S A0163-029
Tel: (415) 396 - 3070
TF: (800) 411 - 4932

HANLON, Tim
V. President, Wells Fargo Foundation and Manager, Community Support Programs
Mailstop: M/S A0112-073
Tel: (415) 396 - 3567
TF: (800) 411 - 4932

MODJTABAI, Avid
Exec. V. President, Human Resources
Tel: (415) 396 - 3612
TF: (800) 411 - 4932

STRICKLAND, Robert S.
Manager, Investor Relations
Mailstop: M/S A0163-024
Tel: (415) 396 - 0523
TF: (800) 411 - 4932

At Other Offices

BRIGHTBILL, Peter
Director, State Government Relations
633 Folsom St.
Seventh Floor
Mailstop: M/S A0149-072
San Francisco, CA 94107
Tel: (415) 396 - 6319
Fax: (415) 546 - 0829

DE LA VEGA, Robert
Director, State Government Relations
Wells Fargo Center
Sixth & Marquette
Mailstop: M/S N9305-171
Minneapolis, MN 55479
Tel: (612) 667 - 5051
Fax: (612) 667 - 9403

EOLOFF, Anita B.
Director, Federal Government Relations and PAC Treasurer
Wells Fargo Center
Sixth & Marquette
Mailstop: M/S N9305-171
Minneapolis, MN 55479
Tel: (612) 667 - 9917
Fax: (612) 667 - 9403

ERWIN, Pam
Contact, Wells Fargo Bank and Wells Fargo Foundation
550 California St.
Mailstop: M/S A0112-073
San Francisco, CA 94104
Tel: (415) 396 - 3247
Fax: (415) 975 - 6260

EVANS, John R.
Director, State Government Relations
Wells Fargo Center
Sixth & Marquette
Mailstop: M/S N9305-171
Minneapolis, MN 55479
Tel: (612) 667 - 9193
Fax: (612) 667 - 9403

LILLY, Diane P.
Senior V. President and Manager, Government Relations
Wells Fargo Center
Sixth & Marquette
Mailstop: M/S N9305-171
Minneapolis, MN 55479
Tel: (612) 667 - 8308
Fax: (612) 667 - 9403

MCINNIS, Ellen
Director, Local and Minnesota Government Relations
Wells Fargo Center
Sixth & Marquette
Mailstop: M/S N9305-171
Minneapolis, MN 55479
Tel: (612) 667 - 7618
Fax: (612) 667 - 9403

ROBY, Carolyn
V. President, Wells Fargo Foundation Minnesota
Wells Fargo Center
Sixth & Marquette
Minneapolis, MN 55479
Tel: (612) 667 - 7860
Fax: (612) 667 - 8283

Wendy's Internat'l, Inc.

PUBLIC AFFAIRS COUNCIL

A member of the Public Affairs Council. A quick service restaurant chain.
www.wendys.com

Chairman and Chief Exec. Officer
SCHUESSLER, John T. "Jack"
jack_schuessler@wendys.com
Tel: (614) 764 - 3100
Fax: (614) 764 - 3459

Main Headquarters
Mailing: P.O. Box 256
Dublin, OH 43017
Street: One Dave Thomas Blvd.
Dublin, OH 43017
Tel: (614) 764 - 3100
Fax: (614) 764 - 3330

Political Action Committees

Wendy's Internat'l Inc. Political Action Committee
P.O. Box 256
Dublin, OH 43017
Tel: (614) 764 - 3100
Fax: (614) 764 - 3330

Contributions to Candidates: $15,500 (01/05 - 09/05)

Democrats: $1,500; Republicans: $14,000.

Principal Recipients

SENATE DEMOCRATS		HOUSE DEMOCRATS	
		Boren, David (OK)	$1,500
SENATE REPUBLICANS		**HOUSE REPUBLICANS**	
Allen, George (VA)	$5,000	Dewine, R. Pat (OH)	$3,000
Hatch, Orrin (UT)	$5,000		
Smith, Gordon (OR)	$1,000		

Corporate Foundations and Giving Programs

Wendy's Internat'l, Inc. Corporate Giving Program
P.O. Box 256
Dublin, OH 43017
Tel: (614) 764 - 3100
Fax: (614) 764 - 3330

Annual Grant Total: none reported

Dave Thomas Foundation for Adoption
Contact: Rita Soronen
P.O. Box 256
Dublin, OH 43017
Tel: (614) 764 - 8482
Fax: (614) 766 - 3871

Annual Grant Total: $1,000,000 - $2,000,000

Recent Recipients: Nat'l Adoption Center; Nat'l Council of Juvenile and Family Court Judges; North American Council on Adoptable Children

Public Affairs and Related Activities Personnel

At Headquarters

BARKER, John D.
Senior V. President, Investor Relations and Financial Communications
john_barker@wendys.com
Tel: (614) 764 - 3044
Fax: (614) 766 - 3775

CAVA, Jeffrey M.
Exec. V. President, Human Resources
Tel: (614) 764 - 3100
Fax: (614) 764 - 3459

GORDON, Marsha L.
Investor and Shareholder Relations Specialist
Tel: (614) 764 - 3109
Fax: (614) 764 - 3775

LYNCH, Dennis L.
Senior V. President, Communications
Tel: (614) 764 - 3553
Fax: (614) 764 - 3459

MUNGER, Kitty
Manager, Communications
kitty_munger@wendys.com
Tel: (614) 764 - 3241
Ext: 3241
Fax: (614) 764 - 6707

POPLAR, David D.
Director, Investor Relations
Tel: (614) 764 - 3100
Fax: (614) 764 - 7335

SORONEN, Rita
Exec. Director, Dave Thomas Foundation for Adoption
rita_soronen@wendys.com
Tel: (614) 764 - 8482
Fax: (614) 766 - 3871

Werner Enterprises, Inc.

A provider of transportation services.
www.werner.com
Annual Revenues: $1.3 billion

Chairman and Chief Exec. Officer
WERNER, Clarence L.
Tel: (402) 895 - 6640
Fax: (402) 894 - 3990
TF: (800) 228 - 2240

Main Headquarters
Mailing: P.O. Box 37308
Omaha, NE 68137
Tel: (402) 895 - 6640
Fax: (402) 894 - 3927
TF: (800) 228 - 2240

Street: 14507 Frontier Rd.
Omaha, NE 68138

Political Action Committees

Werner Enterprises, Inc. PAC
Contact: Robert E. Synowicki
P.O. Box 37308
Omaha, NE 68137
Tel: (402) 895 - 6640
Fax: (402) 894 - 3990
TF: (800) 228 - 2240

Contributions to Candidates: $500 (01/05 - 09/05)
Republicans: $500.

Principal Recipients

SENATE REPUBLICANS

HOUSE REPUBLICANS
Terry, Lee (NE) $500

Public Affairs and Related Activities Personnel

At Headquarters

SYNOWICKI, Robert E.
Exec. V. President
Tel: (402) 895 - 6640
Fax: (402) 894 - 3990
TF: (800) 228 - 2240

Responsibilities include political action.

WESCO Internat'l, Inc.

www.wescodist.com

Chairman, President and Chief Exec. Officer
HALEY, Roy W.
rhaley@wescodist.com
Tel: (412) 454 - 2200
Fax: (412) 454 - 2505

Main Headquarters
Mailing: 225 W. Station Square Dr.
suite 700
Pittsburgh, PA 15219
Tel: (412) 454 - 2200
Fax: (412) 454 - 2505

Public Affairs and Related Activities Personnel

At Headquarters

BRAILER, Daniel A.
Director, Investor Relations and Treasurer
Tel: (412) 454 - 2200
Fax: (412) 454 - 2505

DZIEWICZ, Michael S.
Director, Human Resources
mdziewicz@wescodist.com
Tel: (412) 454 - 2382
Fax: (412) 454 - 2505

West Group

See listing on page 473 under Thomson West.

West Pharmaceutical Services

A manufacturer of specialized packaging for the pharmaceutical and medical device industries.
www.westpharma.com
Annual Revenues: $419.7 million

Chairman, President, and Chief Exec. Officer
MOREL, Donald E., Jr.
Tel: (610) 594 - 2900
Fax: (610) 594 - 3000
TF: (800) 345 - 9800

Main Headquarters
Mailing: 101 Gordon Dr.
Lionville, PA 19341
Tel: (610) 594 - 2900
Fax: (610) 594 - 3000
TF: (800) 345 - 9800

Corporate Foundations and Giving Programs

Herman O. West Foundation
Contact: Maureen Goebel
101 Gordon Dr.
Lionville, PA 19341
Tel: (610) 594 - 2900
Fax: (610) 594 - 3000
TF: (800) 345 - 9800

Annual Grant Total: $300,000 - $400,000
Primary interest: non-profit organizations.
Geographic Preference: Area(s) in which the company operates; Florida; Nebraska; New Jersey; North Carolina; Pennsylvania
Primary Interests: Arts and Culture; Civic and Public Affairs; Health
Recent Recipients: YMCA

Public Affairs and Related Activities Personnel

At Headquarters

ANDERSON, Michael A.
V. President and Treasurer
Tel: (610) 594 - 2900
Fax: (610) 594 - 3000
TF: (800) 345 - 9800

Responsibilities include investor relations.

GOEBEL, Maureen
Administrator, Herman O. West Foundation
Tel: (610) 594 - 2900
Fax: (610) 594 - 3000
TF: (800) 345 - 9800

LUZZI, Richard D.
V. President, Human Resources
Tel: (610) 594 - 2900
Fax: (610) 594 - 3000
TF: (800) 345 - 9800

Westar Energy, Inc.

Formed by the 1992 merger of Kansas Power & Light with Kansas Gas & Electric, doing business as KPL, KGE.
www.wr.com
Annual Revenues: $6.5 billion

President and Chief Exec. Officer
HAINES, James S., Jr.
Tel: (785) 575 - 6300
Fax: (785) 575 - 8182

Main Headquarters
Mailing: P.O. Box 889
Topeka, KS 66601-0889
Tel: (785) 575 - 6300
Fax: (785) 575 - 1796
Street: 818 S. Kansas Ave.
Topeka, KS 66612-1217

Political Action Committees

Westar Energy Employees PAC
Contact: Jeffrey L. Martin
818 S. Kansas Ave.
Topeka, KS 66601
Tel: (785) 575 - 6300
Fax: (785) 575 - 1796

Contributions to Candidates: $500 (01/05 - 09/05)
Republicans: $500.

Principal Recipients

SENATE REPUBLICANS

HOUSE REPUBLICANS
Tiahrt, Todd W. (KS) $500

Corporate Foundations and Giving Programs

Westar Energy Foundation
Contact: Cynthia McCarvel
P.O. Box 889
Topeka, KS 66601-0889
Tel: (785) 575 - 1544
Fax: (785) 575 - 6399

Annual Grant Total: none reported
Geographic Preference: Area(s) in which the company operates

Public Affairs and Related Activities Personnel

At Headquarters

BURNS, Bruce
Director, Investor Relations
burns@wr.ocm
Tel: (785) 575 - 8227
Fax: (785) 575 - 1796

CHANDLER, Charles Q., IV
Chairman of the Board
Tel: (785) 575 - 6300
Fax: (785) 575 - 8182

HARRISON, Kelly B.
V. President, Regulatory
Tel: (785) 575 - 1636
Fax: (785) 575 - 6427

LUDWIG, Jim
V. President, Public Affairs
Tel: (785) 575 - 6300
Fax: (785) 575 - 8182

MCCARVEL, Cynthia
Contact, Westar Energy Foundation
Tel: (785) 575 - 1544
Fax: (785) 575 - 6399

At Other Offices

MARTIN, Jeffrey L.
PAC Treasurer
818 S. Kansas Ave.
Topeka, KS 66601
Tel: (785) 575 - 6300
Fax: (785) 575 - 1796

Western and Southern Life Insurance Co.

www.westernsouthernlife.com

Chairman, President, and Chief Exec.Officer
BARRETT, John
Tel: (513) 629 - 1905
Fax: (513) 629 - 1081
TF: (800) 936 - 1212

Main Headquarters
Mailing: 400 Broadway
Cincinnati, OH 45202
Tel: (513) 629 - 1800
Fax: (513) 629 - 1220
TF: (800) 936 - 1212

Political Action Committees

Western and Southern Life Insurance Co. PAC
Contact: Edward J. Babbitt
400 Broadway
Cincinnati, OH 45202
Tel: (513) 629 - 1464
Fax: (513) 629 - 1050
TF: (800) 936 - 1212

Contributions to Candidates: $1,500 (01/05 - 09/05)
Republicans: $1,500.

Principal Recipients

SENATE REPUBLICANS

HOUSE REPUBLICANS
Dewine, R. Pat (OH) $1,000

Western and Southern Life Insurance Co.

• continued from previous page

Corporate Foundations and Giving Programs

Western-Southern Foundation, Inc.
Contact: Richard Taulbee
400 Broadway
Cincinnati, OH 45202
Tel: (513) 629 - 1905
Fax: (513) 629 - 1220
TF: (800) 936 - 1212

Annual Grant Total: $750,000 - $1,000,000
Geographic Preference: Ohio
Primary Interests: Arts and Culture; Civic and Public Affairs; Education; Medicine and Health Care; Social Services; United Way Campaigns
Recent Recipients: Cincinnati Museum of Art; United Way

Public Affairs and Related Activities Personnel

At Headquarters

BABBITT, Edward J.
V. President, Government Relations and Senior Counsel
Tel: (513) 629 - 1464
Fax: (513) 629 - 1050
TF: (800) 936 - 1212

BROWN, Herbert R.
Senior V. President, Public Relations and Corporate Communications
Tel: (513) 629 - 1136
Fax: (513) 629 - 1308
TF: (800) 936 - 1212

HAYES, Noreen J.
Senior V. President, Human Resources
Tel: (513) 629 - 1905
Fax: (513) 629 - 1050
TF: (800) 936 - 1212

MARQUES, Jose
Manager, Media Relations
Tel: (513) 629 - 1448
Fax: (513) 629 - 1220
TF: (800) 936 - 1212

TAULBEE, Richard
Contact, Corporate Giving
Tel: (513) 629 - 1905
Fax: (513) 629 - 1220
TF: (800) 936 - 1212

Western Digital Corp.

Designs and manufactures hard drives.
www.wdc.com
Annual Revenues: $2.719 billion

Chairman and Chief Exec. Officer
MASSENGILL, Matthew E.
Tel: (949) 672 - 7000
Fax: (949) 672 - 5408

Main Headquarters
Mailing: 20511 Lake Forest Dr.
Lake Forest, CA 92630-7741
Tel: (949) 672 - 7000
Fax: (949) 672 - 5408

Corporate Foundations and Giving Programs

Western Digital Community Relations
20511 Lake Forest Dr.
Lake Forest, CA 92630-7741
Tel: (949) 672 - 7000
Fax: (949) 672 - 5408

Annual Grant Total: none reported
Primary Interests: Arts and Culture; Civic and Public Affairs; Education; Health and Human Services

Public Affairs and Related Activities Personnel

At Headquarters

GRIFFITHS, Constance A.
Senior Press Relations Specialist
constance.griffiths@wdc.com
Tel: (949) 672 - 7891
Fax: (949) 672 - 5408

SAFFELL, Michelle A.
Coordinator, Investor Relations
michelle.a.saffell@wdc.com
Tel: (949) 672 - 7908
Fax: (949) 672 - 5408

SCOTT, Cathy N.
V. President, Marketing Communications
Tel: (949) 672 - 7000
Fax: (949) 672 - 5408

SHATTUCK, Steve
Director, Public Relations
steve.shattuck@wdc.com
Tel: (949) 672 - 7817
Fax: (949) 672 - 5408

Western Gas Resources, Inc.

A natural gas processing and transmission company.
www.westerngas.com
Annual Revenues: $2.5 billion

Chairman of the Board
SENTY, James A.
Tel: (303) 452 - 5603
Fax: (303) 457 - 8482
TF: (800) 933 - 5603

President and Chief Exec. Officer
DEA, Peter A.
Tel: (303) 452 - 5603
Fax: (303) 457 - 8482
TF: (800) 933 - 5603

Main Headquarters
Mailing: 1099 18th St.
Suite 1200
Denver, CO 80202
Tel: (303) 452 - 5603
Fax: (303) 457 - 8482
TF: (800) 933 - 5603

Corporate Foundations and Giving Programs

Western Gas Resources, Inc. Corporate Giving
Contact: Teresa Perry
1099 18th St.
Suite 1200
Denver, CO 80202
Tel: (303) 252 - 6087
Fax: (303) 457 - 8482
TF: (800) 933 - 5603

Annual Grant Total: none reported

Public Affairs and Related Activities Personnel

At Headquarters

EVERSMAN, Janet
Manager, Human Resources
jebersma@westerngas.com
Tel: (303) 452 - 5603
Fax: (303) 457 - 8482
TF: (800) 933 - 5603

MUTCH, Krista
Manager, Government Relations
kmutch@westerngas.com
Tel: (303) 252 - 6094
Fax: (303) 457 - 8482
TF: (800) 933 - 5603

PERRY, Teresa
Director, Corporate Communications and Services
tmassaro@westerngas.com
Responsibilities also include corporate philanthropy.
Tel: (303) 252 - 6087
Fax: (303) 457 - 8482
TF: (800) 933 - 5603

WIRTH, Ronald O.
Director, Investor Relations
rwirth@westerngas.com
Tel: (303) 252 - 6090
Fax: (303) 457 - 8482
TF: (800) 933 - 5603

Westinghouse Air Brake Technologies Corp.

Formerly Wabtec Corp. Provides goods and services for the transportation industry, including the railroad industry.
www.wabtec.com
Annual Revenues: $696.2 million

Chairman, President and Chief Exec. Officer
KASSLING, William E.
Tel: (412) 825 - 1000
Fax: (412) 825 - 1019

Main Headquarters
Mailing: 1001 Air Brake Ave.
Wilmerding, PA 15148-1036
Tel: (412) 825 - 1000
Fax: (412) 825 - 1091

Political Action Committees

Wabtec Corp. PAC (WABTEC PAC)
Contact: James E. McClaine
1001 Air Brake Ave.
Wilmerding, PA 15148-1036
Tel: (412) 825 - 1000
Fax: (412) 825 - 1019

Contributions to Candidates: none reported (01/05 - 09/05)

Public Affairs and Related Activities Personnel

At Headquarters

LEPRI, Sandy
Manager, Public Relations
Tel: (412) 825 - 1000
Fax: (412) 825 - 1019

MCCLAINE, James E.
V. President, Railroad Sevice; Treasurer, Wabtec Corp. PAC
Tel: (412) 825 - 1000
Fax: (412) 825 - 1019

WAHLSTROM, Scott E.
V. President, Human Resources
Tel: (412) 825 - 1000
Fax: (412) 825 - 1091

WESLEY, Timothy R.
V. President, Investor Relations and Corporate Communications
Tel: (412) 825 - 1543
Fax: (412) 825 - 1789

Westinghouse Electric Company LLC

A major supplier of technology-based products and services for the commercial nuclear power industry worldwide. Westinghouse Electric Company LLC is a BNFL Group company.
www.westinghousenuclear.com

President and Chief Exec. Officer
TRITCH, Stephen R.
Tel: (412) 374 - 4111

Main Headquarters
Mailing: P.O. Box 355
Pittsburgh, PA 15230-0355
Tel: (412) 374 - 4111
Street: 4350 Northern Pike
Monroeville, PA 15146-2886

Washington Office
Contact: Robert R. Zoglman
Mailing: 900 19th St. NW
Suite 350
Washington, DC 20006
Tel: (202) 945 - 6401
Fax: (202) 945 - 6404

Political Action Committees

Westinghouse Electric Co. PAC
Contact: Robert R. Zoglman
900 19th St. NW
Suite 350
Washington, DC 20006
Tel: (202) 945 - 6405
Fax: (202) 945 - 6404

Contributions to Candidates: $8,000 (01/05 - 09/05)
Democrats: $2,000; Republicans: $6,000.

Westinghouse Electric Company LLC

** continued from previous page*

Principal Recipients

SENATE DEMOCRATS		HOUSE DEMOCRATS	
		Doyle, Mike (PA)	$2,000
SENATE REPUBLICANS		**HOUSE REPUBLICANS**	
Santorum, Richard (PA)	$2,000	Murphy, Tim (PA)	$2,000
Inhofe, James M (OK)	$1,000	Hobson, David (OH)	$1,000

Public Affairs and Related Activities Personnel

At Headquarters

GILBERT, H. Vaughn — Tel: (412) 374 - 3896
Manager, Public Relations — Fax: (412) 374 - 3272
gilberthv@westinghouse.com

GRECO, Anthony D. — Tel: (412) 374 - 4111
Senior V. President, Human Resources and Corporate Relations

REID, Lynnann — Tel: (412) 374 - 6824
Manager, Employee Communications and Community Relations — Fax: (412) 374 - 3272
reid1ls@westinghouse.com

SHAW, Scott — Tel: (412) 374 - 6737
Communications Specialist — Fax: (412) 374 - 3244
shawsa@westinghouse.com

At Washington Office

ZOGLMAN, Robert R. — Tel: (202) 945 - 6405
V. President, Government and International Affairs — Fax: (202) 945 - 6404
Registered Federal Lobbyist.

Westmoreland Coal Co.

A coal mining and energy company.

www.westmorelandcoal.com

Annual Revenues: $315.7 million

Chairman, President, and Chief Exec. Officer — Tel: (719) 442 - 2600
SEGLEM, Christopher K. — Fax: (719) 448 - 5824

Main Headquarters

Mailing: Two N. Cascade Ave. — Tel: (719) 442 - 2600
14th Floor — Fax: (719) 448 - 5824
Colorado Springs, CO 80903

Corporate Foundations and Giving Programs

Westmoreland Coal Co./Penn Virginia Corp. Foundation

Two N. Cascade Ave. — Tel: (719) 442 - 2600
14th Floor — Fax: (719) 448 - 5824
Colorado Springs, CO 80903

Annual Grant Total: under $100,000
Geographic Preference: Area(s) in which the company operates
Primary Interests: Scholarship Funds

Public Affairs and Related Activities Personnel

At Headquarters

JONES, Diane S. — Tel: (719) 448 - 5814
V. President, Corporate Relations — Fax: (719) 448 - 5824
diane.jones@westmoreland.com

WestPoint Stevens Inc.

A manufacturer of textiles for the apparel, household furnishings and industrial markets.

www.westpointstevens.com

Annual Revenues: $1.81 billion

President and Chief Exec. Officer — Tel: (706) 645 - 4000
FONTENOT, M. L. — Fax: (706) 645 - 4121

Main Headquarters

Mailing: 507 W. Tenth St. — Tel: (706) 645 - 4000
West Point, GA 31833 — Fax: (706) 645 - 4121

Corporate Foundations and Giving Programs

WestPoint Stevens Foundation

507 W. Tenth St. — Tel: (706) 645 - 4000
West Point, GA 31833 — Fax: (706) 645 - 4121

Annual Grant Total: $500,000 - $750,000
A small foundation with limited purposes.
Geographic Preference: Area(s) in which the company operates
Recent Recipients: Boy Scouts of America; Georgia Tech.

Public Affairs and Related Activities Personnel

At Headquarters

CAUBLE, Toni M. — Tel: (706) 645 - 4879
V. President, Corporate Communications — Fax: (706) 645 - 4121
cauble.toni@wpstv.com

At Other Offices

MILLER, Lorraine D. — Tel: (404) 378 - 0491
Senior V. President, Finance and External Communications
Prominence in Buckhead, 3475 Piedmont Rd. North East
Suite 1420
Atlanta, GA 30305
miller.lorraine@wpstv.com
Responsibilities include investor relations.

Westvaco Corp.

See listing on page 316 under MeadWestvaco Corp.

Weyerhaeuser Co.

A member of the Public Affairs Council. A major producer of forest products. Acquired Willamette Industries Inc. in June of 2002.

www.weyerhaeuser.com

Annual Revenues: $19.873 billion

Chairman, President, and Chief Exec. Officer — Tel: (253) 924 - 3456
ROGEL, Steven R. — Fax: (253) 924 - 3685
TF: (800) 525 - 5440

Main Headquarters

Mailing: P.O. Box 9777 — Tel: (253) 924 - 2345
Federal Way, WA 98063-9777 — Fax: (253) 924 - 285
TF: (800) 525 - 5440

Street: 33663 Weyerhaeuser Way South
Federal Way, WA 98003

Washington Office

Mailing: 1100 Connecticut Ave. NW — Tel: (202) 293 - 7222
Suite 530 — Fax: (202) 293 - 2955
Washington, DC 20036

Political Action Committees

Weyerhaeuser Co. Special Shareholders Political Action Committee
Contact: John Driscoll
2100 First Nat'l Bank Bldg. — Tel: (651) 228 - 0935
St. Paul, MN 55101 — Fax: (651) 228 - 0776

Contributions to Candidates: none reported (01/05 - 09/05)

Weyerhaeuser Political Action Committee
Contact: Annis Upshur
1100 Connecticut Ave. NW — Tel: (202) 293 - 7222
Suite 530 — Fax: (202) 293 - 2955
Washington, DC 20036

Contributions to Candidates: $80,000 (01/05 - 09/05)
Democrats: $10,000; Republicans: $70,000.

Principal Recipients

SENATE DEMOCRATS		HOUSE DEMOCRATS	
		Larsen, Rick (WA)	$3,000
		Dicks, Norm D (WA)	$2,000
		Filner, Bob (CA)	$2,000
SENATE REPUBLICANS		**HOUSE REPUBLICANS**	
Smith, Gordon (OR)	$4,000	McMorris, Cathy (WA)	$5,000
Santorum, Richard (PA)	$3,000	Miller, Gary (CA)	$5,000
Allen, George (VA)	$2,000	Reichert, Dave (WA)	$5,000
Burns, Conrad (MT)	$2,000	Walden, Gregory (OR)	$5,000
Thomas, Craig (WY)	$2,000	Hunter, Duncan (CA)	$4,000
		Vitter, David (LA)	$2,500
		Cunningham, Duke (CA)	$2,000
		Hastings, Doc (WA)	$2,000
		McCrery, Jim (LA)	$2,000
		Peterson, John Mr. (PA)	$2,000
		Pombo, Richard (CA)	$2,000
		Rehberg, Dennis (MT)	$2,000

Corporate Foundations and Giving Programs

Weyerhaeuser Co. Foundation

Weyerhaeuser Co.

** continued from previous page*

P.O. Box 9777
Federal Way, WA 98063-9777
Tel: (253) 924 - 2345
Fax: (253) 924 - 285
TF: (800) 525 - 5440

Annual Grant Total: over $5,000,000
Geographic Preference: Area(s) in which the company operates
Primary Interests: Community Affairs; Education; Social Services
Recent Recipients: Nature Conservancy; Project Learning Tree

Public Affairs and Related Activities Personnel

At Headquarters

AGNEW, Ms. Creigh H.
V. President, Government Affairs and Corporate Contributions
Mailstop: M/S CH 1M31
Tel: (253) 924 - 3770
Fax: (253) 924 - 4652
TF: (800) 525 - 5440

BARNUM, Paul
Director, Corporate Public Relations
Mailstop: M/S EC2-2D7
paul.barnum@weyerhaeuser.com
Tel: (253) 924 - 3920
Fax: (253) 924 - 5921
TF: (800) 525 - 5440

CROSSMAN, Elizabeth A.
Director, Corporate Contributions
Mailstop: M/S EC2-28A
Tel: (253) 924 - 3169
Fax: (253) 924 - 3658
TF: (800) 525 - 5440

KENDALL, Sara
V. President, Office of the Environment
Mailstop: M/S EC2-2C1
sara.kendall@weyerhaeuser.com
Tel: (253) 924 - 3290
Fax: (253) 924 - 2013
TF: (800) 525 - 5440

LARSEN, David
V. President, Corporate Communications
Tel: (253) 924 - 3456
Fax: (253) 924 - 3685
TF: (800) 525 - 5440

MCAULEY, Kathryn F.
V. President, Investor Relations
Mailstop: M/S CH1C32
kathy.mcauley@weyerhaeuser.com
Tel: (253) 924 - 2058
Fax: (253) 924 - 3870
TF: (800) 525 - 5440

TAGGART, Richard
Exec. V. President and Chief Financial Officer
Mailstop: M/S CH1C32
Tel: (253) 924 - 3892
Fax: (253) 924 - 3543
TF: (800) 525 - 5440

YUCKERT, Gregory H.
V. President, Labor Relations
greg.yuckert@weyerhaeuser.com
Tel: (253) 924 - 3770
Fax: (253) 924 - 3685
TF: (800) 525 - 5440

At Washington Office

BIGGS BROCK, Heidi
V. President, Federal and International Affairs
Registered Federal Lobbyist.
Tel: (202) 293 - 7222
Fax: (202) 293 - 2955

BISHOP, Cherae
Manager, Government Affairs
Tel: (202) 293 - 7222
Fax: (202) 293 - 2955

SCHAFFER, Amy E.
Manager, Federal Regulatory Affairs
Registered Federal Lobbyist.
Tel: (202) 293 - 7222
Fax: (202) 293 - 2955

UPSHUR, Annis
Treasurer, Weyerhaeuser Co. PAC
Mailstop: M/S CH1M31
annis.upshur@weyerhaeuser.com
Tel: (202) 293 - 7222
Fax: (202) 293 - 2955

At Other Offices

BECKETT, Bruce K.
Director, Government Affairs - Washington State
1501 S. Capitol Way, Suite 301
Olympia, WA 98507
bruce.beckett@weyerhaeuser.com
Tel: (360) 943 - 5350

COOK, C. Michelle
Government Affairs Manager - North Carolina Region
Rexwoods IV, Suite 311
Raleigh, NC 27607-7509
michelle.cook@weyerhaeuser.com
Tel: (919) 786 - 2417
Fax: (919) 510 - 9341

DRISCOLL, John
Contact, Weyerhaeuser Co. Special Shareholders Political Action Committee
2100 First Nat'l Bank Bldg.
St. Paul, MN 55101
Tel: (651) 228 - 0935
Fax: (651) 228 - 0776

HARRIS, Rullie
Manager, Government Affairs - Georgia
1412 Eatonton
Madison, GA 31068
rullie.harris@weyerhaeuser.com
Tel: (706) 342 - 3306
Fax: (706) 343 - 1895

MILLER, Gregory A.
Manager, Government Affairs (Oregon)
698 12th St., S.E., Suite 220
Salem, OR 97301
Tel: (503) 588 - 0311

ROBINETTE, Lee
Communications Director, Southern Region
P.O. Box 1060
Hot Springs, AR 71902-1060
Tel: (501) 624 - 8138

Wheeling-Pittsburgh Steel Corp.

A manufacturer of steel and steel products.
www.wpsc.com

Chairman and Chief Exec. Officer
BRADLEY, James G.
Tel: (304) 234 - 2400
Fax: (304) 234 - 2261

Main Headquarters
Mailing: 1134 Market St.
Wheeling, WV 26003
Tel: (304) 234 - 2400
Fax: (304) 234 - 2261

Political Action Committees

Wheeling-Pittsburgh Steel PAC
Contact: Dan Keaton
1134 Market St.
Wheeling, WV 26003
Tel: (304) 234 - 2400
Fax: (304) 234 - 2261

Contributions to Candidates: $6,000 (01/05 - 09/05)
Democrats: $5,000; Republicans: $1,000.

Principal Recipients

SENATE DEMOCRATS
Byrd, Robert C (WV) $5,000

HOUSE DEMOCRATS

SENATE REPUBLICANS
Santorum, Richard (PA) $1,000

HOUSE REPUBLICANS

Public Affairs and Related Activities Personnel

At Headquarters

KEATON, Dan
V. President, Human Resources
Responsibilities include political action.
Tel: (304) 234 - 2400
Fax: (304) 234 - 2261

KOSOWSKI, James "Jim"
PAC Contact
Tel: (304) 234 - 2440
Fax: (304) 234 - 2442

Whirlpool Corp.

PUBLIC AFFAIRS COUNCIL

A member of the Public Affairs Council. A manufacturer and marketer of major household appliances.
www.whirlpool.com
Annual Revenues: $10.343 billion

Chairman and Chief Exec. Officer
FETTIG, Jeff M.
Tel: (269) 923 - 5000
Fax: (269) 923 - 5443

Main Headquarters
Mailing: Administrative Center
2000 N. M-63
Benton Harbor, MI 49022-2692
Tel: (269) 923 - 5000
Fax: (269) 923 - 5443

Political Action Committees

Whirlpool Corp. PAC
Contact: Thomas F. Catania, Jr.
Administrative Center
2000 N. M-63
Benton Harbor, MI 49022-2692
Tel: (269) 923 - 4648
Fax: (269) 923 - 4652

Contributions to Candidates: $5,445 (01/05 - 09/05)
Democrats: $2,000; Republicans: $3,445.

Principal Recipients

SENATE DEMOCRATS
Pryor, Mark (AR) $1,000

HOUSE DEMOCRATS
Jefferson, William (LA) $1,000

SENATE REPUBLICANS
Lott, Trent (MS) $1,000

HOUSE REPUBLICANS
Camp, David Lee (MI) $2,445

Corporate Foundations and Giving Programs

Whirlpool Foundation
Contact: Barbara Hall
Administrative Center
2000 N. M-63
Benton Harbor, MI 49022-2692
Tel: (269) 923 - 5000
Fax: (269) 923 - 5443

Annual Grant Total: over $5,000,000
The Foundation also sponsors an employee matching gifts program. Website is www.whirlpoolcorp.com/whr/foundation/index.html.
Geographic Preference: Area(s) in which the company operates
Primary Interests: Arts and Culture; Civic and Public Affairs; Families; Health and Human Services; Higher Education; Historic Preservation
Recent Recipients: Junior Achievement; Local Initiative Support Corp. (LISC); United Way

Public Affairs and Related Activities Personnel

At Headquarters

BINKLEY, David A.
Senior V. President, Global Human Resources
Tel: (269) 923 - 5000
Fax: (269) 923 - 5443

CATANIA, Thomas F., Jr.
V. President, Government Relations
Mailstop: M/S MD 3005
thomas_f_catania@email.whirlpool.com
Tel: (269) 923 - 4648
Fax: (269) 923 - 4652

DUTHIE, Steve J.
Manager, Media Relations
steve_j_duthie@email.whirlpool.com
Tel: (269) 923 - 3373
Fax: (269) 923 - 5443

Whirlpool Corp.

** continued from previous page*

HALL, Barbara
Contact, Whirlpool Foundation
Tel: (269) 923 - 5000
Fax: (269) 923 - 5443

HOPP, Daniel F.
Senior V. President, Corporate Affairs and General Counsel
daniel_f_hopp@email.whirlpool.com
Tel: (269) 923 - 5000
Fax: (269) 923 - 5443

KLINE, Thomas E.
Director, External Communications
thomas_e_kline@email.whirlpool.com
Tel: (269) 923 - 3738
Fax: (269) 923 - 5443

NOEL, Jeff
V. President, Communications and Public Affairs
Tel: (269) 923 - 5000
Fax: (269) 923 - 5443

VENTURELLI, Larry
Director, Investor Relations
Tel: (269) 923 - 5000
Fax: (269) 923 - 5443

WEST, Heather O.
Tel: (269) 923 - 5000
Fax: (269) 923 - 5443

Whitman Corp.

See listing on page 377 under PepsiAmericas, Inc.

Whole Foods Market, Inc.

A retailer of natural and organic foods.
www.wholefoodsmarket.com
Annual Revenues: $2.7 billion

Chairman and Chief Exec. Officer
MACKEY, John P.
Tel: (512) 477 - 4455
Fax: (512) 477 - 1069

Main Headquarters
Mailing: 550 Bowie St.
Austin, TX 78703
Tel: (512) 477 - 4455
Fax: (512) 477 - 1069

Corporate Foundations and Giving Programs

Whole Foods Market, Inc. Corporate Contributions Program
550 Bowie St.
Austin, TX 78703
Tel: (512) 477 - 4455
Fax: (512) 477 - 1069

Annual Grant Total: $2,000,000 - $5,000,000
Geographic Preference: Area(s) in which the company operates
Primary Interests: Environment/Conservation; Health and Human Services

Public Affairs and Related Activities Personnel

At Headquarters

BRADLEY, Cindy
V. President, Human Resources
Tel: (512) 477 - 4455
Fax: (512) 322 - 9873

HOFENSPERGER, Amy
Manager, National Public Relations
Tel: (512) 542 - 0380
Fax: (512) 477 - 1069

LOWERY, Kate
National Director, Public Relations
Tel: (512) 477 - 4455

MCCANN, Cynthia M.
V. President, Investor Relations
Tel: (512) 477 - 4455
Fax: (512) 477 - 1069

WITTENBERG, Margaret
V. President, Marketing and Public Affairs
Tel: (512) 477 - 4455
Fax: (512) 477 - 1069

Wild Oats Markets, Inc.

Owns and operates a chain of natural food supermarkets.
www.wildoats.com
Annual Revenues: $919.1 million

Chairman of the Board
MILLER, Robert A.
Tel: (303) 440 - 5220
Fax: (303) 928 - 0022
TF: (800) 494 - 9453

President and Chief Exec. Officer
ODAK, Perry D.
Tel: (303) 440 - 5220
Fax: (303) 928 - 0022
TF: (800) 494 - 9453

Main Headquarters
Mailing: 3375 Mitchell Lane
Boulder, CO 80301
Tel: (303) 440 - 5220
Fax: (303) 928 - 0012
TF: (800) 494 - 9453

Corporate Foundations and Giving Programs

Wild Oats Giving Program
3375 Mitchell Lane
Boulder, CO 80301
Tel: (303) 440 - 5220
Fax: (303) 928 - 0012
TF: (800) 494 - 9453

Annual Grant Total: none reported
Primary Interests: Agriculture; Animal Protection; Education; Environment/Conservation; Health and Human Services; International Affairs

Public Affairs and Related Activities Personnel

At Headquarters

TUITELE, Sonja
Director, Corporate Communications
Tel: (303) 440 - 5220
Fax: (303) 928 - 0022
TF: (800) 494 - 9453

WILLIAMS, Peter
V. President, Human Resources
Tel: (303) 440 - 5220
Fax: (303) 928 - 0022
TF: (800) 494 - 9453

John Wiley & Sons, Inc.

A book publisher.
www.wiley.com
Annual Revenues: $923 million

Chairman of the Board
WILEY, Peter B.
Mailstop: M/S 7-02
Tel: (201) 748 - 6000
Fax: (201) 748 - 6008

President and Chief Exec. Officer
PESCE, William J.
Mailstop: M/S 7-02
Tel: (201) 748 - 6000
Fax: (201) 748 - 6008

Main Headquarters
Mailing: 111 River St.
Hoboken, NJ 07030-5774
Tel: (201) 748 - 6000
Fax: (201) 748 - 6008
TF: (800) 225 - 5945

Corporate Foundations and Giving Programs

Wiley Corporate Giving
Contact: Deborah E. Wiley
111 River St.
Hoboken, NJ 07030-5774
Tel: (201) 748 - 6000
Fax: (201) 748 - 6008

Annual Grant Total: none reported
The company also maintains an employee matching gift program and a ServiceMatch Program, through which the company recognizes employee volunteerism by making a monetary donation to eligible organizations at which the employee volunteers.
Geographic Preference: New York City; New Jersey
Primary Interests: Civic and Cultural Activities; Education
Recent Recipients: New York City Ballet; New York Public Library; September 11th Fund

Public Affairs and Related Activities Personnel

At Headquarters

ARLINGTON, William J.
Senior V. President, Human Resources
Mailstop: M/S 3-02
Tel: (201) 748 - 6000
Fax: (201) 748 - 6008

WILEY, Deborah E.
Senior V. President, Corporate Communications
Mailstop: M/S 7-01
Tel: (201) 748 - 6000
Fax: (201) 748 - 6008

Williams

A gas pipeline, energy services and communications company.
www.williams.com

Chairman and Chief Exec. Officer
MALCOLM, Steven J.
Tel: (918) 573 - 2000
TF: (800) 945 - 5426

Main Headquarters
Mailing: One Williams Center
Tulsa, OK 74172
Tel: (918) 573 - 2000
TF: (800) 945 - 5426

Washington Office
Contact: Deborah B. Lawrence
Mailing: 1627 I St. NW
Suite 900
Washington, DC 20006
Tel: (202) 833 - 8994
Fax: (202) 835 - 0707

Political Action Committees

Williams Companies Political Action Committee
Contact: Deborah B. Lawrence
1627 I St. NW
Suite 900
Washington, DC 20006
Tel: (202) 833 - 8994
Fax: (202) 835 - 0707

Contributions to Candidates: $43,500 (01/05 - 09/05)
Democrats: $6,000; Republicans: $37,500.

Principal Recipients

SENATE DEMOCRATS

HOUSE DEMOCRATS
Matheson, James (UT) $2,000

SENATE REPUBLICANS
Allen, George (VA) $3,500
Santorum, Richard (PA) $2,500
Thomas, Craig (WY) $2,000

HOUSE REPUBLICANS
Pombo, Richard (CA) $4,000
Barton, Joe L (TX) $3,000
Sullivan, John (OK) $3,000
Pearce, Steve (NM) $2,000
Myrick, Sue (NC) $1,500

Corporate Foundations and Giving Programs

The Williams Companies Foundation

Williams

** continued from previous page*

One Williams Center — Tel: (918) 573 - 2000
Tulsa, OK 74172 — TF: (800) 945 - 5426

Annual Grant Total: over $5,000,000
Geographic Preference: Area(s) in which employees live and work; Area(s) in which the company operates
Primary Interests: Civic and Cultural Activities; Community Development; Environment/Conservation; Higher Education
Recent Recipients: United Way

Williams Gas Pipelines-Transco
2800 Post Oak Blvd. — Tel: (713) 215 - 2000
Box 1396 — Fax: (713) 215 - 4154
Houston, TX 77056

Annual Grant Total: none reported
Geographic Preference: Area in which the company is headquartered; Area(s) in which the company operates
Primary Interests: Civic and Cultural Activities; Education; United Way Campaigns

Public Affairs and Related Activities Personnel

At Headquarters

CAMPBELL, Travis — Tel: (918) 573 - 2944
Investor Relations and Corporate Communications — TF: (800) 945 - 5426

CHURCH, Brad — Tel: (918) 573 - 3679
Media Relations Contact — TF: (800) 945 - 5426

HENDERSON, Jay — Tel: (918) 573 - 2000
V. President, Investor Relations — TF: (800) 945 - 5426
jay.henderson@williams.com

MALONE STANCAVAGE, Kerry L. — Tel: (918) 573 - 2110
Director, Corporate Communications — Fax: (918) 573 - 6714
Mailstop: 47th Floor — TF: (800) 945 - 5426
kerry.malone@williams.com

SWAN, Kelly — Tel: (918) 573 - 6932
Manager, Public Relations — TF: (800) 945 - 5426

At Washington Office

EMLING, Gretchen — Tel: (202) 833 - 8994
Manager, Government Relations — Fax: (202) 835 - 0707
Registered Federal Lobbyist.

JACKSON, Glenn F. — Tel: (202) 833 - 8994
Director, Government Affairs — Fax: (202) 835 - 0707
glenn.jackson@williams.com
Registered Federal Lobbyist.

LAWRENCE, Deborah B. — Tel: (202) 833 - 8994
V. President, Government Affairs — Fax: (202) 835 - 0707
deborah.lawrence@williams.com

At Other Offices

DRAPER, Delbert M. — Tel: (801) 583 - 8800
Manager, Western Region State Government Affairs — Fax: (801) 584 - 6483
(Williams Gas Pipelines-West)
295 Tipito Way
Salt Lake City, UT 84158

STOCKTON, Chris — Tel: (713) 215 - 2010
Coordinator, External Communications — Fax: (713) 215 - 4154
(Williams Gas Pipelines-Transco)
2800 Post Oak Blvd.
Box 1396
Houston, TX 77056

Williams Gas Pipelines-Transco

See listing on page 522 under Williams.

Williams Gas Pipelines-West

See listing on page 522 under Williams.

Williams-Sonoma, Inc.

A retailer of home furnishings.
www.williams-sonomainc.com
Annual Revenues: $2.087 billion

Chairman of the Board — Tel: (415) 421 - 7900
LESTER, W. Howard — Fax: (415) 616 - 8463

Chief Exec. Officer — Tel: (415) 421 - 7900
MUELLER, Edward A. — Fax: (415) 616 - 8463

Main Headquarters
Mailing: 3250 Van Ness Ave. — Tel: (415) 421 - 7900
San Francisco, CA 94109 — Fax: (415) 616 - 8359

Public Affairs and Related Activities Personnel

At Headquarters

NELSON, Steven C. — Tel: (415) 616 - 8754
Director, Investor Relations — Fax: (415) 616 - 8463

SELLMAN, Patricia — Tel: (415) 733 - 3168
V. President, Public Relations — Fax: (415) 616 - 8463

Wilmington Trust Co.

www.wilmingtontrust.com
Annual Revenues: $655 million

Chairman and Chief Exec. Officer — Tel: (302) 651 - 1000
CECALA, Ted T. — Fax: (302) 651 - 8937
TF: (800) 441 - 7120

Main Headquarters
Mailing: 1100 N. Market St. — Tel: (302) 651 - 1000
Wilmington, DE 19890 — Fax: (302) 651 - 8937
TF: (800) 441 - 7120

Political Action Committees

Wilmington Trust Co. PAC
Contact: Carl Hostetter
1100 N. Market St. — Tel: (302) 651 - 1000
Wilmington, DE 19890 — Fax: (302) 651 - 8937
TF: (800) 441 - 7120

Contributions to Candidates: $1,500 (01/05 - 09/05)
Republicans: $1,500.

Principal Recipients

SENATE REPUBLICANS

HOUSE REPUBLICANS
Castle, Michael (DE) $1,000

Corporate Foundations and Giving Programs

Wilmington Trust Corporate Contributions Program
1100 N. Market St. — Tel: (302) 651 - 1000
Wilmington, DE 19890 — Fax: (302) 651 - 8937
TF: (800) 441 - 7120

Annual Grant Total: $1,000,000 - $2,000,000
Geographic Preference: Delaware
Primary Interests: Arts and Culture; Social Services; Youth Services

Public Affairs and Related Activities Personnel

At Headquarters

BENINTENDE, Bill — Tel: (302) 651 - 8268
Director, Media Relations — Fax: (302) 651 - 8937
TF: (800) 441 - 7120

HOSTETTER, Carl — Tel: (302) 651 - 1000
PAC Contact — Fax: (302) 651 - 8937
TF: (800) 441 - 7120

ROBERTS, Ellen J. — Tel: (302) 651 - 8069
V. President, Investor Relations — Fax: (302) 651 - 8937
eroberts@wilmingtontrust.com — TF: (800) 441 - 7120

Winn-Dixie Stores

A supermarket chain.
www.winn-dixie.com
Annual Revenues: $12.903 billion

Chairman of the Board — Tel: (904) 783 - 5000
SKELTON, H. Jay — Fax: (904) 783 - 5294

President and Chief Exec Officer — Tel: (904) 783 - 5000
LYNCH, Peter L. — Fax: (904) 783 - 5294

Main Headquarters
Mailing: P.O. Box B — Tel: (904) 783 - 5000
Jacksonville, FL 32203-0297 — Fax: (904) 783 - 5294
Street: 5050 Edgewood Ct.
Jacksonville, FL 32254-3669

Political Action Committees

WIN-PAC of Winn-Dixie Stores, Inc.
Contact: Jeffrey Gleason
P.O. Box B — Tel: (904) 783 - 5000
Jacksonville, FL 32203-0297 — Fax: (904) 783 - 5294

Contributions to Candidates: $5,000 (01/05 - 09/05)
Democrats: $1,000; Republicans: $3,000; Other: $1,000.

Principal Recipients

SENATE DEMOCRATS

HOUSE DEMOCRATS
Boyd, F Allen Jr (FL) $1,000

HOUSE OTHER
Peterson, Collin (MN) $1,000

SENATE REPUBLICANS
Allen, George (VA) $1,000
Chambliss, Saxby (GA) $1,000

HOUSE REPUBLICANS
Shaw, Clay (FL) $1,000

Winn-Dixie Stores

** continued from previous page*

Corporate Foundations and Giving Programs

Winn-Dixie Stores Foundation
P.O. Box B — Tel: (904) 783 - 5000
Jacksonville, FL 32203-0297 — Fax: (904) 783 - 5294

Annual Grant Total: over $5,000,000
Most giving takes the form of employee matching gifts program.
Geographic Preference: Area(s) in which the company operates; Southern United States
Primary Interests: Education; Environment/Conservation; Health; Social Services; United Way Campaigns; Youth Services
Recent Recipients: American Red Cross; Junior Achievement; United Way; YMCA; YWCA

Public Affairs and Related Activities Personnel

At Headquarters

GLEASON, Jeffrey — Tel: (904) 783 - 5000
PAC Treasurer — Fax: (904) 783 - 5294

HUTTON, Randall L. — Tel: (904) 783 - 5408
V. President/Director, Government Relations — Fax: (904) 783 - 5294
randyhutton@winndixie.com

LUSSIER, Kathy — Tel: (904) 370 - 6025
Senior Director, Communications — Fax: (904) 783 - 5294
kathylussier@winn-dixie.com

NUSSBAUM, Bennett L. — Tel: (904) 370 - 6655
Senior V. President and Chief Financial Officer — Fax: (904) 783 - 5294
bennettnussbaum@winn-dixie.com
Responsibilities include investor relations.

Winnebago Industries, Inc.

A manufacturer of motor homes.
www.winnebagoind.com
Annual Revenues: $1.1 billion

Chairman and Chief Exec. Officer — Tel: (641) 585 - 3535
HERTZKE, Bruce D. — Fax: (641) 585 - 6966

Main Headquarters
Mailing: P.O. Box 152 — Tel: (641) 585 - 3535
Forest City, IA 50436-0152 — Fax: (641) 585 - 6966
Street: 605 W. Crystal Lake Rd.
Forest City, IA 50436

Corporate Foundations and Giving Programs

Winnebago Industries Foundation
Contact: Elsie Felland
P.O. Box 152 — Tel: (641) 585 - 3535
Forest City, IA 50436-0152 — Fax: (641) 585 - 6966

Annual Grant Total: under $100,000
Geographic Preference: Iowa; Area in which the company is headquartered
Primary Interests: Health; Higher Education; Recreation

Public Affairs and Related Activities Personnel

At Headquarters

BEEBE, Raymond M. — Tel: (641) 585 - 3535
V. President, General Counsel and Secretary — Fax: (641) 585 - 6966
Responsibilities include public affairs.

DAVIS, Sheila M. — Tel: (641) 585 - 6803
Public Relations/Investor Relations Manager — Fax: (641) 585 - 6966
sdavis@winnebagoind.com

FELLAND, Elsie — Tel: (641) 585 - 3535
Secretary, Winnebago Industries Foundation — Fax: (641) 585 - 6966

Wisconsin Energy Corp.

An electric, natural gas and steam utility.
www.we-energies.com
Annual Revenues: $3.929 billion

Chairman, President and Chief Exec. Officer — Tel: (414) 221 - 4525
KLAPPA, Gale E. — Fax: (414) 221 - 3814
gale.klappa@we-energies.com

Main Headquarters
Mailing: 231 W. Michigan St. — Tel: (414) 221 - 2345
Milwaukee, WI 53201 — Fax: (414) 221 - 3814

Washington Office
Mailing: 122 C St. NW — Tel: (202) 622 - 4340
Suite 840 — Fax: (202) 622 - 4359
Washington, DC 20001

Political Action Committees

Wisconsin Energy Corp. Political Action Committee
Contact: Judy Job
231 W. Michigan St. — Tel: (414) 221 - 2348
Milwaukee, WI 53201 — Fax: (414) 221 - 3814

Contributions to Candidates: $9,000 (01/05 - 09/05)
Democrats: $3,000; Republicans: $6,000.

Principal Recipients

SENATE DEMOCRATS

HOUSE DEMOCRATS

Boucher, Fredrick (VA)	$1,000
Kind, Ron (WI)	$1,000
Stupak, Bart (MI)	$1,000

SENATE REPUBLICANS

HOUSE REPUBLICANS

Schultz, Dale W (WI)	$2,000
Barton, Joe L (TX)	$1,000
Petri, Thomas (WI)	$1,000
Sensenbrenner, Jim (WI)	$1,000
Shimkus, John (IL)	$1,000

Corporate Foundations and Giving Programs

Wisconsin Energy Corp. Foundation
Contact: Patti McNew
231 W. Michigan St. — Tel: (414) 221 - 2107
Milwaukee, WI 53201 — Fax: (414) 221 - 2412

Annual Grant Total: $2,000,000 - $5,000,000
Geographic Preference: Michigan; Wisconsin
Primary Interests: Arts and Culture; Community Affairs; Education; Health; Youth Services
Recent Recipients: Boys and Girls Club; United Performing Arts Fund; YMCA

Public Affairs and Related Activities Personnel

At Headquarters

CIESLAK, Richard — Tel: (414) 221 - 4510
Manager, Media Relations — Fax: (414) 221 - 2824
Mailstop: P478
richard.cieslak@we-energies.com

HAUBRICH, Joel — Tel: (414) 221 - 4102
Manager, State Government Affairs — Fax: (414) 221 - 3814
Mailstop: P346
joel.haubrich@we-energies.com

JOB, Judy — Tel: (414) 221 - 2348
PAC Administrator — Fax: (414) 221 - 3814
Mailstop: P346
judy.job@@we-energies.com

MCKINNEY, Mr. Kris A. — Tel: (414) 221 - 2157
Manager, Environmental Strategy — Fax: (414) 221 - 2169
Mailstop: A231
kris.mckinney@we-energies.com

MCNEW, Patti — Tel: (414) 221 - 2107
Administrator, Wisconsin Energy Corp. Foundation — Fax: (414) 221 - 2412
patti.mcnew@we-energies.com

MCNULTY, Barry J. — Tel: (414) 221 - 2235
Director, PTF Public Affairs — Fax: (414) 221 - 2395
Mailstop: P346
barry.mcnulty@we-energies.com

SIAS, Thelma — Tel: (414) 221 - 3651
V. President, Local Affairs — Fax: (414) 221 - 3853
Mailstop: P421
thelma.sias@we-energies.com

WHITE, Richard J. — Tel: (414) 221 - 2555
V. President, Communications — Fax: (414) 221 - 2310
Mailstop: P453
rick.white@we-energies.com

ZINTEK, Arthur — Tel: (414) 221 - 3149
V. President, Human Resources — Fax: (414) 221 - 4608
Mailstop: P456
arthur.zintek@we-energies.com

At Washington Office

DE MASTERS, Darnell — Tel: (202) 622 - 4340
Assistant V. President, Federal Policy — Fax: (202) 622 - 4359
darnell.demasters@we-energies.com
Registered Federal Lobbyist.

At Other Offices

MILLER, Rodney K. — Tel: (906) 779 - 2478
Principal Representative, State Relations - Michigan — Fax: (906) 779 - 2488
1401 S. Carpenter Ave.
Iron Mountain, MI 49801
rod.miller@we-energies.com

Wisconsin Public Service Corp.

An electric and gas utility. A subsidiary of WPS Resources Corp. (see separate listing).
www.wpsc.wpsr.com

Wisconsin Public Service Corp.

** continued from previous page*

Chairman and Chief Exec. Officer
WEYERS, Larry L. — Tel: (920) 433 - 1334
Mailstop: M/S G6 — Fax: (920) 433 - 1693
lweyers@wpsr.com — TF: (800) 450 - 7260

Main Headquarters
Mailing: P.O. Box 19001, Green Bay, WI 54307-9001 — Fax: (920) 433 - 1693; TF: (800) 450 - 7260
Street: 700 N. Adams St., Green Bay, WI 54307

Political Action Committees

Wisconsin Public Service Corp. Responsible Government Committee
Contact: Thomas P. Meinz
P.O Box 19002 — Tel: (920) 433 - 1293
Green Bay, WI 54307-9002 — Fax: (920) 433 - 5741

Contributions to Candidates: $1,000 (01/05 - 09/05)
Republicans: $1,000.

Principal Recipients

SENATE REPUBLICANS	HOUSE REPUBLICANS	
	Gard, John G (WI)	$500
	Petri, Thomas (WI)	$500

Corporate Foundations and Giving Programs

Wisconsin Public Service Foundation
Contact: Kathy Hartman
P.O. Box 19001 — Tel: (920) 433 - 1248
Green Bay, WI 54307-9001 — Fax: (920) 433 - 1693
TF: (800) 450 - 7260

Annual Grant Total: $1,000,000 - $2,000,000
Written guidelines available upon request.
Geographic Preference: Area(s) in which the company operates; Michigan; Wisconsin
Primary Interests: Community Affairs; Environment/Conservation; Higher Education; Medicine and Health Care
Recent Recipients: American Red Cross; Boys and Girls Club; United Way; YMCA; YWCA

Public Affairs and Related Activities Personnel

At Headquarters

ANTONNEAU, Ron — Tel: (920) 443 - 4965
Director, Governmental Affairs — Fax: (920) 433 - 5741
Mailstop: M/S A2 — TF: (800) 450 - 7260
rantonn@wpsr.com

HARTMAN, Kathy — Tel: (920) 433 - 1248
Foundation Contact — Fax: (920) 433 - 1693
khartma@wpsc.com — TF: (800) 450 - 7260

LEMKE, Karmen — Tel: (920) 433 - 1433
Leader, Community Relations — Fax: (920) 433 - 1693
Mailstop: M/S A2 — TF: (800) 450 - 7260
klemke@wpsc.com

STEFFEN, Todd — Tel: (920) 433 - 1617
Director, Corporate Communications — Fax: (920) 433 - 5741
Mailstop: M/S A2 — TF: (800) 450 - 7260
tsteffe@wpsr.com

At Other Offices

KLEIN, Mary — Tel: (920) 433 - 5522
Foundation Contact — Fax: (920) 433 - 5741
P.O Box 19002
Green Bay, WI 54307-9002
mklein@wpsr.com

MEINZ, Thomas P. — Tel: (920) 433 - 1293
Exec. V. President, Public Affairs; PAC Treasurer — Fax: (920) 433 - 5741
P.O Box 19002
Green Bay, WI 54307-9002
tmeinz@wpsr.com

WJ Communications

A wireless communications and electronics manufacturer.
www.wj.com
Annual Revenues: $40.2 million

Chairman of the Board
PAINE, W. Dexter, III — Tel: (408) 577 - 6200
dexter.paine@wj.com — Fax: (408) 577 - 6620

President and Chief Exec. Officer
DIAMOND, Bruce W. — Tel: (408) 577 - 6200; Fax: (408) 577 - 6620

Main Headquarters
Mailing: 401 River Oaks Pkwy., San Jose, CA 95134 — Tel: (408) 577 - 6200; Fax: (408) 577 - 6620

Corporate Foundations and Giving Programs

WJ Communications Corporate Contributions Program
401 River Oaks Pkwy. — Tel: (408) 577 - 6200
San Jose, CA 95134 — Fax: (408) 577 - 6620

Annual Grant Total: none reported

Public Affairs and Related Activities Personnel

At Headquarters

MCLEAN, Leah — Tel: (408) 577 - 6200
Media Relations — Fax: (408) 577 - 6620
leah.mclean@wj.com

Wolverine World Wide, Inc.

A shoe manufacturer.
www.wolverineworldwide.com
Annual Revenues: $991 million

President, Chief Exec. Officer and Chairman of the Board
O'DONOVAN, Timothy J. — Tel: (616) 866 - 5500; Fax: (616) 866 - 0257

Main Headquarters
Mailing: 9341 Courtland Dr. NE, Rockford, MI 49351 — Tel: (616) 866 - 5500; Fax: (616) 866 - 0257

Corporate Foundations and Giving Programs

Wolverine World Wide Foundation
Contact: Christi Cowdin
9341 Courtland Dr. NE — Tel: (616) 866 - 6222
Rockford, MI 49351 — Fax: (616) 866 - 0257

Annual Grant Total: $500,000 - $750,000
Primary Interests: Civic and Cultural Activities; Community Affairs; Education; Health; Social Services

Public Affairs and Related Activities Personnel

At Headquarters

COWDIN, Christi — Tel: (616) 866 - 6222
Director, Investor Relations and Communications — Fax: (616) 866 - 0257

GULIS, Stephen L., Jr. — Tel: (616) 866 - 5570
Exec. V. President and Chief Financial Officer — Fax: (616) 866 - 0257
Responsibilities include investor relations.

LA BARGE, Susan — Tel: (616) 866 - 5500
Foundation Contact — Fax: (616) 866 - 0257
Mailstop: hb211

World Kitchen, Inc.

www.worldkitchen.com

Chairman of the Board
PEETS, Terry R. — Tel: (703) 456 - 4700; Fax: (607) 377 - 8962; TF: (800) 999 - 3436

President and Chief Exec. Officer
SHARMAN, James A. — Tel: (703) 456 - 4700; Fax: (607) 377 - 8962; TF: (800) 999 - 3436

Main Headquarters
Mailing: 11911 Freedom Dr., Suite 600, Reston, VA 20190 — Tel: (703) 456 - 4700; Fax: (607) 377 - 8962; TF: (800) 999 - 3436

Public Affairs and Related Activities Personnel

At Headquarters

JOHNSON, Hope — Tel: (607) 377 - 5258
Media Relations — Fax: (607) 377 - 8962
johnsonhe@worldkitchen.com — TF: (800) 999 - 3436

Worldcom, Inc.

See listing on page 314 under MCI, Inc.

Worthington Industries

A steel processor and manufacturer of metals related products.
www.worthingtonindustries.com

Chairman and Chief Exec. Officer
MCCONNELL, John P. — Tel: (614) 438 - 3210; Fax: (614) 438 - 3136

Main Headquarters
Mailing: 200 Old Wilson Bridge Rd., Columbus, OH 43085 — Tel: (614) 438 - 3210; Fax: (614) 840 - 4150

Political Action Committees

Worthington Industries PAC
200 Old Wilson Bridge Rd. — Tel: (614) 438 - 3210
Columbus, OH 43085 — Fax: (614) 840 - 4150

Contributions to Candidates: $2,500 (01/05 - 09/05)
Republicans: $2,500.

Principal Recipients

SENATE REPUBLICANS	HOUSE REPUBLICANS	
	Tiberi, Patrick (OH)	$1,500
	Boehner, John (OH)	$1,000

Worthington Industries

** continued from previous page*

Corporate Foundations and Giving Programs

Worthington Industries Corporate Contributions
Contact: Cathy Lyttle
200 Old Wilson Bridge Rd. Tel: (614) 438 - 3077
Columbus, OH 43085 Fax: (614) 840 - 4150

Annual Grant Total: none reported
Geographic Preference: Area(s) in which the company operates; Ohio
Primary Interests: Education; Health and Human Services
Recent Recipients: Children's Hospital

Public Affairs and Related Activities Personnel

At Headquarters

GOUSSETIS, Harry A. Tel: (614) 438 - 3210
V. President, Human Resources Fax: (614) 438 - 3136

LYTTLE, Cathy Tel: (614) 438 - 3077
V. President, Corporate Communications Fax: (614) 840 - 4150
cmlyttle@worthingtonindustries.com

SANDERS, Allison Tel: (614) 438 - 3133
Manager, Investor Relations Fax: (614) 438 - 3136

STANFORD, Janna Tel: (614) 840 - 3498
PAC Contact Fax: (614) 840 - 4150

WPS Resources Corp.

An energy holding company.
www.wpsr.com
Annual Revenues: $4.4 billion

Chairman, President and Chief Exec. Officer Tel: (920) 433 - 4901
WEYERS, Larry L. Fax: (920) 433 - 1526
lweyers@wpsr.com

Main Headquarters
Mailing: 700 N. Adams St. Tel: (920) 433 - 4901
Green Bay, WI 54301 Fax: (920) 433 - 1526

Political Action Committees

WP Resources Corporate Responsibility Government Committee
Contact: Thomas P. Meinz
700 N. Adams St. Tel: (920) 433 - 4901
Green Bay, WI 54301 Fax: (920) 433 - 1526

Contributions to Candidates: $1,000 (01/05 - 09/05)
Republicans: $1,000.

Principal Recipients

SENATE REPUBLICANS		HOUSE REPUBLICANS	
		Gard, John G (WI)	$500
		Petri, Thomas (WI)	$500

Corporate Foundations and Giving Programs

WPS Foundation, Inc.
Contact: P. J. Reinhard
700 N. Adams St. Tel: (920) 433 - 4901
Green Bay, WI 54301 Fax: (920) 433 - 1526

Annual Grant Total: $750,000 - $1,000,000
Geographic Preference: Michigan; Wisconsin
Primary Interests: Arts and Humanities; Education; Environment/Conservation; Health and Human Services; Historic Preservation; Performing Arts

Public Affairs and Related Activities Personnel

At Headquarters

MEINZ, Thomas P. Tel: (920) 433 - 4901
Senior V. President, Public Affairs Fax: (920) 433 - 1526
tmeinz@wpsr.com
Responsibilities include government affairs.

REINHARD, P. J. Tel: (920) 433 - 4901
Foundation Contact Fax: (920) 433 - 1526

TREML, Bernard J. Tel: (920) 433 - 4901
V. President, Human Resources Fax: (920) 433 - 1526
btreml@wpsr.com

Wm. Wrigley Jr. Co.

A chewing gum and confectionery manufacturer and marketer.
www.wrigley.com
Annual Revenues: $3.6 billion

Chairman, President and Chief Exec. Officer Tel: (312) 644 - 2121
WRIGLEY, William, Jr. Ext: 4132
Fax: (312) 644 - 0015

Main Headquarters
Mailing: 410 N. Michigan Ave. Tel: (312) 644 - 2121
Chicago, IL 60611 Fax: (312) 644 - 0015

Corporate Foundations and Giving Programs

Wm. Wrigley Jr. Co. Foundation
Contact: Christopher J. Perille
410 N. Michigan Ave. Tel: (312) 645 - 4077
Chicago, IL 60611 Fax: (312) 644 - 0015

Annual Grant Total: $2,000,000 - $5,000,000
Primary Interests: Education; Youth Services

Public Affairs and Related Activities Personnel

At Headquarters

BENEFIELD, Aronda Tel: (312) 645 - 4073
Administrator, Consumer Relations and Public Affairs Ext: 4073
abenefield@wrigley.com Fax: (312) 644 - 0015

HENDERSON, Susan Tel: (312) 644 - 2121
V. President, Corporate Communications Fax: (312) 644 - 0015

MCGRAIL, Kelly Tel: (312) 645 - 4754
Director, Investor and Public Relations Fax: (312) 644 - 0015
kmcgrail@wrigley.com

PERILLE, Christopher J. Tel: (312) 645 - 4077
Senior Director, Corporate Communications Fax: (312) 644 - 0015
cperille@wrigley.com
Responsibilities include government affairs.

Wyeth

A member of the Public Affairs Council. Formerly known as American Home Products Corp. Wyeth is a research driven pharmaceutical and health care products company. The company is involved in the discovery, development, manufacturing, and marketing of pharmaceuticals, vaccines, biotechnology products and nonprescription medicines that improve the quality of life for people worldwide.
www.wyeth.com
Annual Revenues: $17.4 billion

Chairman, President and Chief Exec. Officer Tel: (973) 660 - 5000
ESSNER, Robert Fax: (973) 660 - 5771

Main Headquarters
Mailing: Five Giralda Farms Tel: (973) 660 - 5000
Madison, NJ 07940 Fax: (973) 660 - 5771

Washington Office
Contact: Leo C. Jardot
Mailing: 1667 K St. NW Tel: (202) 659 - 8320
Suite 1270 Fax: (202) 659 - 2158
Washington, DC 20036

Political Action Committees

Wyeth Good Government Fund
Contact: Leo C. Jardot
1667 K St. NW Tel: (202) 659 - 8320
Suite 1270 Fax: (202) 659 - 2158
Washington, DC 20036

Contributions to Candidates: $72,500 (01/05 - 09/05)
Democrats: $22,000; Republicans: $49,500; Other: $1,000.

Principal Recipients

SENATE DEMOCRATS		HOUSE DEMOCRATS	
Nelson, Benjamin (NE)	$3,500	Menendez, Robert (NJ)	$2,500
Carper, Thomas R (DE)	$2,500		
Lieberman, Joe (CT)	$2,500		

SENATE REPUBLICANS		HOUSE REPUBLICANS	
Santorum, Richard (PA)	$5,000	Bonilla, Henry (TX)	$2,500
Allen, George (VA)	$2,500	Cantor, Eric (VA)	$2,500
Cochran, Thad (MS)	$2,500	DeLay, Tom (TX)	$2,500
Dewine, Richard (OH)	$2,500	Latham, Thomas P (IA)	$2,500
Hatch, Orrin (UT)	$2,500	Deal, Nathan (GA)	$2,000
Enzi, Michael B (WY)	$1,500	Pickering, Chip (MS)	$2,000
		Sensenbrenner, Jim (WI)	$2,000

Corporate Foundations and Giving Programs

Wyeth Corporate Contributions Program
Contact: Marilyn Phillips
600 Third Ave. Tel: (212) 878 - 5007
28th Fl. Fax: (212) 878 - 5079
New York, NY 10017-4085

Annual Grant Total: none reported
Geographic Preference: New Jersey; New York
Primary Interests: Health and Human Services

Public Affairs and Related Activities Personnel

At Headquarters

FADEM, Bruce Tel: (973) 660 - 5980
V. President, Corporate Information Services and Chief Information Officer Fax: (973) 660 - 7167

Responsibilities include corporate communications.

Wyeth

** continued from previous page*

LEWIN, Rene R. — Tel: (973) 660 - 5258
Senior V. President, Human Resources — Fax: (973) 660 - 5771

PLUES, Patrick — Tel: (484) 865 - -516
Contact, Wyeth Good Government Fund — Fax: (484) 865 - 6420

PRINCE, Sharon — Tel: (973) 660 - 5034
Assistant V. President, Corporate Communications
princes@wyeth.com

RHUDY, Marily — Tel: (973) 660 - 5141
Senior V. President, Public Affairs — Fax: (973) 660 - 7322
rhudym@wyeth.com

STOLTENBERG, Jessica — Tel: (973) 660 - 5000
V. President, Corporate Communications — Fax: (973) 660 - 6900
stoltj@wyeth.com

SULLIVAN, Francis — Tel: (973) 660 - 6923
Director, Public Affairs — Fax: (973) 660 - 5771
(Wyeth Consumer Healthcare)

TASHER, Steven A. — Tel: (973) 660 - 5210
V. President, Environmental Affairs, Facilities Operations and Associate General Counsel — Fax: (973) 660 - 5771

TESKA, Liz — Tel: (973) 660 - 5000
Corporate Public Affairs — Fax: (973) 660 - 5771

VICTORIA, Justin R. — Tel: (973) 660 - 5340
V. President, Investor Relations — Fax: (973) 660 - 5771
victorj@wyeth.com

WATKINS, James P. "Jim" — Tel: (973) 660 - 5027
Director, State Government Affairs
watkinj@wyeth.com
Responsibilities include political action.

At Washington Office

JARDOT, Leo C. — Tel: (202) 659 - 8320
V. President, Government Relations — Fax: (202) 659 - 2158
jardotl@wyeth.com
Registered Federal Lobbyist.

KAYE, Bronwen A. — Tel: (202) 659 - 8320
Senior Director, Government Relations — Fax: (202) 659 - 2158
kayeb@wyeth.com
Registered Federal Lobbyist.

RABINOWITZ, Julie M. — Tel: (202) 659 - 8320
Senior Director and Counsel, Government Relations — Fax: (202) 659 - 2158
Registered Federal Lobbyist.

At Other Offices

PHILLIPS, Marilyn — Tel: (212) 878 - 5007
Director, Corporate Contributions — Fax: (212) 878 - 5079
600 Third Ave.
28th Fl.
New York, NY 10017-4085

Wyeth Consumer Healthcare

See listing on page 526 under Wyeth.

Wyeth Pharmaceuticals

Formerly known as Wyeth-Ayerst Laboratories. A pharmaceutical manufacturing subsidiary of Wyeth (see separate listing).
www.wyeth.com
Annual Revenues: $14 billion

Main Headquarters

Mailing: 500 Arcola Rd. — Tel: (484) 865 - 5000
Collegeville, PA 19426

Washington Office

Contact: Leo C. Jardot
Mailing: 1667 K St. NW — Tel: (202) 659 - 8320
Suite 1270 — Fax: (202) 659 - 2158
Washington, DC 20006

Public Affairs and Related Activities Personnel

At Headquarters

BURLINGTON, Bruce — Tel: (484) 865 - 5000
Exec. V. President, Regulatory, Compliance and Global Safety

DE VANE, Natalie — Tel: (484) 865 - 5000
Senior Director, Public Relations
devanen@wyeth.com

PETKUS, Douglas — Tel: (484) 865 - 5000
V. President, Global Public Relations
petkusd@wyeth.com

At Washington Office

JARDOT, Leo C. — Tel: (202) 659 - 8320
V. President, Government Relations — Fax: (202) 659 - 2158

At Other Offices

HOKE, John Greg — Tel: (281) 359 - 2905
Associate Director, State Government Affairs
1342 Trailwood Village Dr.
Kingwood, TX 77339
hokeg@wyeth.com

ISERMAN, Katrina M. — Tel: (617) 266 - 3112
Associate Director, State Government Affairs
280 Beacon St.
Boston, MA 02116
isermank@wyeth.com

IVERSON, Betty — Tel: (303) 909 - 0304
Associate Director, State Government Affairs
3100 S. Sheridan
IC-339
Denver, CO 80227
iversonb@wyeth.com

KULESHER, Kate M. — Tel: (402) 420 - 2445
Associate Director, State Government Affairs — Fax: (402) 420 - 2737
7430 Birch Creek Pl.
Lincoln, NE 68516
kuleshk@wyeth.com

MAJESKIE, Dennis — Tel: (507) 344 - 4393
Director State Government Affairs — Fax: (507) 344 - 4394
180 Jo Ray Ct.
Mankato, MN 56001
majeskd@wyeth.com

MIDDLETON, John J. — Tel: (856) 802 - 0074
Director, State Government Affairs
Five Jillian Way
Mt. Laurel, NJ 08054
middletj@wyeth.com

MOODY, Dave — Tel: (414) 352 - 1016
Director, State Government Affairs
310 E. Daphne Rd.
Fox Point, WI 53217
moodyd2@wyeth.com

RHUDY, Marily — Tel: (973) 660 - 5141
V. President, Public Affairs
Five Giralda Farms
Madison, NJ 07940
rhudym@wyeth.com

SIMONS, Ann — Tel: (360) 789 - 7699
Director, State Government Affairs
1106 Villanova St. NE
Olympia, WA 98516
simonsa@wyeth.com

SUTTER, Thomas — Tel: (850) 385 - 8877
Associate Director, State Government Affairs
2937 Tipperary Dr.
Tallahassee, FL 32309
suttert@wyeth.com

THOMAS, Sandi — Tel: (678) 355 - 5642
Director, State Government Affairs
1825 Barrett Lakes Blvd. NW
Suite 400
Kennesaw, GA 30144
thomass@wyeth.com

WARREN, Gregory A. — Tel: (740) 927 - 3521
Director, State Government Affairs — Fax: (740) 927 - 3591
13858 Bainwick Dr. NW
Pickerington, OH 43147
warreng@wyeth.com

WATKINS, James P. "Jim" — Tel: (973) 660 - 5027
Associate Director, State Government Affairs
Five Giralda Farms
Madison, NJ 07940
watkinj@wyeth.com

WOOD, Tom — Tel: (916) 491 - 4051
Associate Director, State Government Relations
1127 11th St., Suite 747B
Sacramento, CA 95814
woodt@wyeth.com

Wyeth-Ayerst Laboratories

See listing on page 527 under Wyeth Pharmaceuticals.

Wyndham Internat'l

See listing on page 108 under Cendant Corp.

Xanser Corp.

Formerly Kaneb Services, Inc. Provides technology-based and technical services worldwide.
www.xanser.com
Annual Revenues: $131.4 million

Xanser Corp.

** continued from previous page*

Chairman and Chief Exec. Officer
BARNES, John R.
Tel: (972) 699 - 4000
Fax: (972) 699 - 4025

Main Headquarters
Mailing: P.O. Box 650283
Dallas, TX 75265-0283
Tel: (972) 699 - 4000
Fax: (972) 699 - 4025
Street: 2435 N. Central Exwy.
Suite 700
Richardson, TX 75080

Corporate Foundations and Giving Programs

Xanser Corp. Corporate Contributions Program
Contact: William H. Kettler, Jr.
P.O. Box 650283
Dallas, TX 75265-0283
Tel: (972) 699 - 4000
Fax: (972) 699 - 4025

Annual Grant Total: under $100,000
Geographic Preference: Area in which the company is headquartered; Southwestern United States

Public Affairs and Related Activities Personnel

At Headquarters

KETTLER, William H., Jr.
V. President, Human Resources
Tel: (972) 699 - 4000
Fax: (972) 699 - 4025

ROSE, Michael L.
President and Chief Operating Officer
Tel: (972) 699 - 4000
Fax: (972) 699 - 4025

TURNER, Sheila
Investor Relations
Tel: (972) 699 - 4000
Fax: (972) 699 - 4025

WADSWORTH, Howard C.
Senior V. President, Chief Financial Officer, Treasurer and Secretary
investor@kaneb.com
Responsibilities include corporate communications and investor relations.
Tel: (972) 699 - 4055
Fax: (972) 699 - 3524

Xcel Energy, Inc.

A member of the Public Affairs Council. An electric and natural gas utility company.
www.xcelenergy.com
Annual Revenues: $14.811 billion

Chairman of the Board
BRUNETTI, Wayne H.
Tel: (612) 330 - 5500
Fax: (612) 330 - 6947

Chief Exec. Officer
KELLY, Richard C.
Tel: (612) 330 - 5500
Fax: (612) 330 - 6947
TF: (800) 328 - 8226

Main Headquarters
Mailing: 414 Nicollet Mall
Minneapolis, MN 55401-1927
Tel: (612) 330 - 5500
Fax: (612) 330 - 6947
TF: (800) 328 - 8226

Washington Office
Contact: John A. O'Donnell
Mailing: 801 Pennsylvania Ave. NW
Suite 212
Washington, DC 20004
Tel: (202) 783 - 5505
Fax: (202) 783 - 6873

Political Action Committees

NRG Energy Inc. PAC
Contact: Timothy Wegmann
901 Marquette Ave., # 2300
Minneapolis, MN 55402

Contributions to Candidates: $4,000 (01/05 - 09/05)
Democrats: $1,000; Republicans: $3,000.

Principal Recipients

SENATE DEMOCRATS		HOUSE DEMOCRATS	
Lieberman, Joe (CT)	$1,000		
SENATE REPUBLICANS		**HOUSE REPUBLICANS**	
Cochran, Thad (MS)	$2,000	Pickering, Chip (MS)	$1,000

Xcel Energy Employee PAC (XPAC)
Contact: Karen Hyde
1225 17th St.
Denver, CO 80202
Tel: (303) 571 - 7511
Fax: (303) 294 - 8120

Contributions to Candidates: $48,600 (01/05 - 09/05)
Democrats: $13,000; Republicans: $35,500; Other: $100.

Principal Recipients

SENATE DEMOCRATS		HOUSE DEMOCRATS	
Salazar, Ken (CO)	$2,000	Towns, Edolphus (NY)	$2,000
SENATE REPUBLICANS		**HOUSE REPUBLICANS**	
Kennedy, Mark (MN)	$5,000	Kennedy, Mark (MN)	$2,000
Coleman, Norm (MN)	$3,000	Musgrave, Marilyn (CO)	$2,000
Domenici, Pete (NM)	$2,000	Ramstad, Jim (MN)	$2,000
Thomas, Craig (WY)	$2,000		

Corporate Foundations and Giving Programs

Xcel Energy Foundation
Contact: John Pacheco
414 Nicollet Mall
Minneapolis, MN 55401-1927
Tel: (612) 330 - 5500
Fax: (612) 330 - 6947
TF: (800) 328 - 8226

Annual Grant Total: $2,000,000 - $5,000,000
Geographic Preference: Area(s) in which the company operates
Primary Interests: Arts and Culture; Community Affairs; Education
Recent Recipients: Catholic Charities; Greater Minneapolis Metropolitan Housing Corp.; Junior Achievement; Salvation Army; United Way

Public Affairs and Related Activities Personnel

At Headquarters

KOLKMANN, Richard J.
Managing Director, Investor Relations
dick.kolkmann@xcelenergy.com
Tel: (612) 215 - 4559

PACHECO, John
Director, Xcel Energy Foundation
Tel: (612) 330 - 5500
Fax: (612) 330 - 6947
TF: (800) 328 - 8226

RHOADS, James D.
Contributions Specialist, Xcel Energy Foundation
Tel: (612) 330 - 5500
Fax: (612) 330 - 6947
TF: (800) 328 - 8226

SPARBY, David M.
V. President, Regulatory and Government Affairs
Tel: (612) 330 - 7752

WILLIS, Elizabeth "Beth"
V. President, Corporate Communications
Tel: (612) 215 - 5320

At Washington Office

O'DONNELL, John A.
Director, Federal Public Affairs
john.a.odonnell@xcelenergy.com
Registered Federal Lobbyist.
Tel: (202) 783 - 5505
Fax: (202) 783 - 6873

At Other Offices

HYDE, Karen
Xcel Energy Employee PAC (XPAC)
1225 17th St.
Denver, CO 80202
Tel: (303) 571 - 7511
Fax: (303) 294 - 8120

PALMER, Roy
Interim Director, State Government Affairs
1225 17th St.
Denver, CO 80202
Tel: (303) 294 - 2808
Fax: (303) 294 - 8120

ROALSTAD, Steve
Director, Media Relations
1225 17th St.
Denver, CO 80202
steve.roalstad@xcelenergy.com
Tel: (303) 294 - 2000
Fax: (303) 294 - 8120

WEGMANN, Timothy
Treasurer, NRG Energy Inc. PAC
901 Marquette Ave., # 2300
Minneapolis, MN 55402

WEST, Pete
Director, Community Services
1225 17th St.
Denver, CO 80202
Tel: (303) 571 - 7511
Fax: (303) 294 - 8120

Xerox Corp.

A provider of document solutions, services and systems -- including color and black-and-white printers, digital presses, multifunction devices and digital copiers -- designed for offices and production-printing environments. Xerox also offers associated supplies, software and support.
www.xerox.com
Annual Revenues: $15.7 billion

Chairman and Chief Exec. Officer
MULCAHY, Anne M.
Tel: (203) 968 - 3000
TF: (800) 275 - 9376

Main Headquarters
Mailing: 800 Long Ridge Rd.
Stamford, CT 06904
Tel: (203) 968 - 3000
TF: (800) 275 - 9376

Washington Office
Contact: J. Michael Farren
Mailing: 1401 H St. NW
Suite 200
Washington, DC 20005
Tel: (202) 414 - 1200
Fax: (202) 414 - 1217

Political Action Committees

Xerox Corp. Political Action Committee (XPAC)
Contact: J. Michael Farren
1401 H St. NW
Suite 200
Washington, DC 20005
Tel: (202) 414 - 1285
Fax: (202) 789 - 1336

Contributions to Candidates: $7,000 (01/05 - 09/05)
Democrats: $6,000; Republicans: $1,000.

Xerox Corp.

* continued from previous page

Principal Recipients

SENATE DEMOCRATS		HOUSE DEMOCRATS	
Lieberman, Joe (CT)	$5,000	Slaughter, Louise M (NY)	$1,000
SENATE REPUBLICANS		**HOUSE REPUBLICANS**	
		Boehner, John (OH)	$1,000

Corporate Foundations and Giving Programs

Xerox Foundation
Contact: Joseph M. Cahalan
800 Long Ridge Rd.
Stamford, CT 06904
Tel: (203) 968 - 3333
Fax: (203) 968 - 4312
TF: (800) 275 - 9376

Annual Grant Total: over $5,000,000
Contributed $12 million in 2005.
Geographic Preference: Area(s) in which the company operates; National
Primary Interests: Civic and Cultural Activities; Community Affairs; Education; Math and Science; Technology

Public Affairs and Related Activities Personnel

At Headquarters

CAHALAN, Joseph M.
V. President, Xerox Foundation
Mailstop: STHQ-3-3-E
joseph.cahalan@xerox.com
Responsibilities include corporate philanthropy.
Tel: (203) 968 - 3333
Fax: (203) 968 - 4312
TF: (800) 275 - 9376

CARONE, Christa
V. President, Corporate Public Relations and Communications
christa.carone@xerox.com
Tel: (203) 968 - 3000
TF: (800) 275 - 9376

WIESE, Nancy
V. President, Corporate Advertising/Branding/Sponsorships
Mailstop: M/S STHQ
nancy.wiese@xerox.com
Tel: (203) 968 - 3374

At Washington Office

CAHN, Michele L.
Manager, Domestic Government Policy
Registered Federal Lobbyist.
Tel: (202) 414 - 1288
Fax: (202) 414 - 1217

FARREN, J. Michael
Corporate V. President, External Affairs
Registered Federal Lobbyist.
Responsibilities include government affairs.
Tel: (202) 414 - 1285
Fax: (202) 789 - 1336

KLEIN, Kenneth H.
Director, International External Affairs
Registered Federal Lobbyist.
Tel: (202) 414 - 1287
Fax: (202) 414 - 1217

At Other Offices

CHOQUETTE, Kara
Manager, Corporate Public Relations
4600 S. Ulster
Suite 1000
Denver, CO 80237
kara.choquette@xerox.com
Tel: (303) 796 - 6420

GALA, Ed
V. President, Products/Solutions/Services Public Relations
100 S. Clinton Ave.
Mailstop: M/S XRX2-004
Rochester, NY 14644
ed.gala@xerox.com
Tel: (585) 423 - 5230
Fax: (585) 423 - 4272

Xilinx, Inc.

A maker of integrated circuits and software.
www.xilinx.com
Annual Revenues: $1.156 billion

Chairman, President and Chief Exec. Officer
ROELANDTS, Willem P.
Tel: (408) 559 - 7778
Fax: (408) 559 - 7114
TF: (800) 836 - 4002

Main Headquarters
Mailing: 2100 Logic Dr.
San Jose, CA 95124-3400
Tel: (408) 559 - 7778
Fax: (408) 559 - 7114
TF: (800) 836 - 4002

Corporate Foundations and Giving Programs

Xilinx Charitable Giving
2100 Logic Dr.
San Jose, CA 95124-3400
Tel: (408) 559 - 7778
Fax: (408) 559 - 7114
TF: (800) 836 - 4002

Annual Grant Total: none reported
Primary Interests: Arts and Culture; Community Affairs; Education; Health; Social Services

Public Affairs and Related Activities Personnel

At Headquarters

GIANELLI, Silvia
Manager, Worldwide Corporate Public Relations
silvia.gianelli@xilinx.com
Tel: (408) 626 - 4328
Fax: (408) 317 - 4926
TF: (800) 836 - 4002

LEWIS, Scott
Director, Corporate Communications
scottl@xilinx.com
Tel: (408) 879 - 4556
Fax: (408) 371 - 4926
TF: (800) 836 - 4002

OWEN, Lori
Investor Relations Analyst
lori.owen@xilinx.com
Tel: (408) 559 - 7778
Fax: (408) 559 - 7114
TF: (800) 836 - 4002

QUILLARD, Maria
Manager, Investor Relations
maria.quillard@xilinx.com
Tel: (408) 879 - 4988
Fax: (408) 559 - 7114
TF: (800) 836 - 4002

WASHINGTON, Lisa
Director, WW Public Relations
lisa.washington@xilinx.com
Tel: (408) 626 - 6272

WYNN, Peg
V. President, Worldwide Human Resources
peg.wynn@xilinx.com
Tel: (408) 559 - 7778
Ext: 5031
Fax: (408) 559 - 7114
TF: (800) 836 - 4002

XO Communications, Inc.

Provides communications services.
www.xo.com
Annual Revenues: $1.3 billion

Chairman of the Board
ICAHN, Charles
Tel: (703) 547 - 2000
Fax: (703) 547 - 2881

Chief Exec. Officer
GRIVNER, Carl J.
Tel: (703) 547 - 2000
Fax: (703) 547 - 2881

Main Headquarters
Mailing: 11111 Sunset Hills Dr.
Reston, VA 20190-5339
Tel: (703) 547 - 2000
Fax: (703) 547 - 2881

Political Action Committees

XO Communications Inc. PAC (XO PAC)
Contact: Laura Iniss
11111 Sunset Hills Dr.
Reston, VA 20190-5339
Tel: (703) 547 - 2000
Fax: (703) 547 - 2881

Contributions to Candidates: $3,000 (01/05 - 09/05)
Republicans: $3,000.

Principal Recipients

SENATE REPUBLICANS		HOUSE REPUBLICANS	
Allen, George (VA)	$1,000	Blackburn, Marsha (TN)	$1,000
		Sensenbrenner, Jim (WI)	$1,000

Public Affairs and Related Activities Personnel

At Headquarters

BURKE, Terri
V. President, Human Resources
Tel: (703) 547 - 2000
Fax: (703) 547 - 2881

BURNETT GOLD, Heather
Senior V. President, Government Relations
Tel: (703) 547 - 2000
Fax: (703) 547 - 2881

COUSER, Chad
Manager, Public Relations
Tel: (703) 547 - 2000
Fax: (703) 547 - 2881

INISS, Laura
Financial Analyst and PAC Treasurer
Tel: (703) 547 - 2000
Fax: (703) 547 - 2881

SCOTT, Ron
Senior V. President, XO Communications
Tel: (703) 547 - 2000
Fax: (703) 547 - 2881

Yahoo! Inc.

An internet communications company.
www.yahoo.com
Annual Revenues: $717.4 million

Chairman and Chief Exec. Officer
SEMEL, Terry
terry@yahoo-inc.com
Tel: (408) 731 - 3300
Fax: (408) 616 - 3301

Main Headquarters
Mailing: 701 First Ave.
Sunnyvale, CA 94089
Tel: (408) 731 - 3300
Fax: (408) 616 - 3301

Washington Office
Contact: John Scheibel
Mailing: 2000 Pennsylvania Ave. NW
Suite 4200
Washington, DC 20006
Tel: (202) 887 - 6932
Fax: (202) 887 - 6933

Political Action Committees

Yahoo! Inc. Political Action Committee
Contact: John Scheibel
2000 Pennsylvania Ave. NW
Suite 4200
Washington, DC 20006
Tel: (202) 887 - 6932
Fax: (202) 887 - 6933

Yahoo! Inc.

* continued from previous page

Contributions to Candidates: $50,500 (01/05 - 09/05)
Democrats: $16,500; Republicans: $34,000.

Principal Recipients

SENATE DEMOCRATS		HOUSE DEMOCRATS	
Nelson, Benjamin (NE)	$2,000	Menendez, Robert (NJ)	$2,000
		Boucher, Fredrick (VA)	$1,500

SENATE REPUBLICANS		HOUSE REPUBLICANS	
Allen, George (VA)	$3,500	Myrick, Sue (NC)	$3,000
Burns, Conrad (MT)	$3,000	Blunt, Roy (MO)	$2,000
Brownback, Sam (KS)	$2,000	Cannon, Christopher (UT)	$2,000
Coleman, Norm (MN)	$2,000		
Sununu, John (NH)	$2,000		
Ensign, John Eric (NV)	$1,500		

Public Affairs and Related Activities Personnel

At Headquarters

CASTRO, Christine — Tel: (408) 731 - 3300
Senior V. President and Chief Communications Officer — Fax: (408) 616 - 3301

HOLLERBACH, Paul — Tel: (408) 349 - 3598
V. President, Investor Relations — Fax: (408) 616 - 3301
paulh@yahoo-inc.com

SARTAIN, Libby — Tel: (408) 731 - 3300
Senior V. President, Human Resources — Fax: (408) 616 - 3301

At Washington Office

BANKER, Elizabeth — Tel: (202) 887 - 6932
Associate General Counsel — Fax: (202) 887 - 6933

DUNLAP, Leslie — Tel: (202) 887 - 6932
Director, Federal Relations — Fax: (202) 887 - 6933
Registered Federal Lobbyist.

HEIBERG, Danielle Dowling — Tel: (202) 887 - 6932
Manager, Legislative Affairs — Fax: (202) 887 - 6933

SCHEIBEL, John — Tel: (202) 887 - 6932
V. President, Public Policy — Fax: (202) 887 - 6933
scheibel@yahoo-inc.com
Registered Federal Lobbyist.
Responsibilities also include political action.

Yellow Roadway Corporation

A member of the Public Affairs Council. Formed from the merger of Yellow Corp. and Roadway Corp. in December, 2003.
www.yellowroadway.com

Chairman, President and Chief Exec. Officer — Tel: (913) 696 - 6100 Ext: 6110
ZOLLARS, William D. — Fax: (913) 696 - 6116

Main Headquarters
Mailing: 10990 Roe Ave. — Tel: (913) 696 - 6100
Overland Park, KS 66211 — Fax: (913) 696 - 6116

Political Action Committees

Yellow Roadway Corporation PAC
Contact: Mike Kelley
10990 Roe Ave. — Tel: (913) 696 - 6121
Overland Park, KS 66211 — Fax: (913) 323 - 9710

Contributions to Candidates: $10,000 (01/05 - 09/05)
Republicans: $10,000.

Principal Recipients

SENATE REPUBLICANS		HOUSE REPUBLICANS	
Allen, George (VA)	$1,000	Kline, John P (MN)	$2,500
Burns, Conrad (MT)	$1,000	Tiberi, Patrick (OH)	$2,500
Stevens, Ted (AK)	$1,000	Hulshof, Kenny (MO)	$1,000
		Johnson, Samuel (TX)	$1,000

Corporate Foundations and Giving Programs

Yellow Roadway Corporation
Contact: Mike Kelley
10990 Roe Ave. — Tel: (913) 696 - 6121
Overland Park, KS 66211 — Fax: (913) 323 - 9710

Annual Grant Total: none reported

Public Affairs and Related Activities Personnel

At Headquarters

GAINES, Phil J. — Tel: (913) 696 - 6100
Senior V. President, Investor Relations, Government Relations and Corporate Development — Fax: (913) 696 - 6116
phil.gaines@yellowroadway.com

KELLEY, Mike — Tel: (913) 696 - 6121
V. President, Government Relations — Fax: (913) 323 - 9710

REID, Gregory A. — Tel: (913) 696 - 6100 Ext: 6193
Senior V. President and Chief Marketing Officer — Fax: (913) 696 - 6128

YAMASAKI, Steven T. — Tel: (913) 696 - 6100
Senior V. President, Human Resources — Fax: (913) 696 - 6116

York Internat'l Corp.

An air conditioning, heating, ventilating and refrigeration company.
www.york.com
Annual Revenues: $4.51 billion

Chief Exec. Officer — Tel: (717) 771 - 7890
MYERS, C. David — Fax: (717) 771 - 6473

Main Headquarters
Mailing: 631 S. Richland Ave. — Tel: (717) 771 - 7890
York, PA 17403 — Fax: (717) 771 - 7381

Corporate Foundations and Giving Programs

York Internat'l Corporate Contributions Program
Contact: Beverly Scott
631 S. Richland Ave. — Tel: (717) 771 - 7000
York, PA 17403 — Fax: (717) 771 - 7252

Annual Grant Total: none reported

Public Affairs and Related Activities Personnel

At Headquarters

GARD, Jeff — Tel: (717) 771 - 7890
Corporate V. President, Human Resources — Fax: (717) 771 - 7381
jeff.gard@york.com

MARSTELLER, Helen — Tel: (717) 771 - 7890
V. President, Investor Relations — Fax: (717) 771 - 7381

SCOTT, Beverly — Tel: (717) 771 - 7000
Contact, Corporate Giving — Fax: (717) 771 - 7252

Yukon Pacific Corp.

See listing on page 146 under CSX Corp.

YUM! Brands, Inc.

Formerly known as Tricon Global Restaurants, Inc. The parent company of Pizza Hut, Inc., KFC, and Taco Bell, Inc.
www.yum.com
Annual Revenues: $6.953 billion

Chairman and Chief Exec. Officer — Tel: (502) 874 - 8300
NOVAK, David C.

Main Headquarters
Mailing: P.O. Box 32070 — Tel: (502) 874 - 8300
Louisville, KY 40232
Street: 1441 Gardiner Lane
Louisville, KY 40213

Political Action Committees

YUM-Brands Inc. Good Government Fund
Contact: William J. Ehrig
P.O. Box 32070 — Tel: (502) 874 - 8049
Louisville, KY 40232

Contributions to Candidates: $18,500 (01/05 - 09/05)
Democrats: $2,000; Republicans: $16,500.

Principal Recipients

SENATE DEMOCRATS		HOUSE DEMOCRATS	
		Chandler, Ben (KY)	$2,000

SENATE REPUBLICANS		HOUSE REPUBLICANS	
Santorum, Richard (PA)	$2,500	Blunt, Roy (MO)	$5,000
		Lewis, Ron (KY)	$3,000
		Northup, Anne M. (KY)	$2,000

Corporate Foundations and Giving Programs

YUM! Brands Corporate Contributions Program
P.O. Box 32070 — Tel: (502) 874 - 8300
Louisville, KY 40232

Annual Grant Total: none reported

Colonel's Kids Charity
1900 Colonel Sanders Lane
Louisville, KY 40213

Annual Grant Total: none reported
Primary Interests: Child Welfare

Public Affairs and Related Activities Personnel

At Headquarters

BLUM, Jonathan D. — Tel: (502) 874 - 8300
Senior V. President, Public Affairs — Fax: (502) 874 - 8324

YUM! Brands, Inc.

* continued from previous page

EHRIG, William J. — Tel: (502) 874 - 8049
Senior Director, Government Affairs

JERZYK, Tim — Tel: (502) 874 - 8300
V. President, Investor Relations

NGHE, Quan V. — Tel: (502) 874 - 8300
Director, Investor Relations

RIENDEAU, Brian — Tel: (502) 874 - 8434; Fax: (502) 456 - 8662
V. President, Government Affairs
brian.riendeau@yum.com

SHERWOOD, Amy — Tel: (502) 874 - 8200; Fax: (502) 874 - 8324
V. President, Public Relations and Consumer Affairs

WARSCHAUER, Bonnie — Tel: (502) 874 - 8300
Director, Public Relations
(KFC)

At Other Offices

GANNON, Laurie — Tel: (949) 863 - 4500
Manager, Public Relations
(Taco Bell Corp.)
17901 Von Karman Ave.
Irvine, CA 92614

SULLIVAN, Patty — Tel: (972) 338 - 7700; Fax: (972) 338 - 6869
Public Relations Contact
(Pizza Hut, Inc.)
14841 Dallas Pkwy.
Dallas, TX 75254
patty.sullivan@pizzahut.com

Zachry Construction Corporation

PUBLIC AFFAIRS COUNCIL

A member of the Public Affairs Council. Provides services including construction, project development, construction management and industrial maintenance. In addition, several Zachry affiliates and subsidiaries are engaged in other industries, such as oil and gas exploration, real estate development, and manufacturing and distributing aggregate products.

www.zachry.com
Annual Revenues: $1.94 billion

Chairman of the Board
ZACHRY, H. B., Jr. — Tel: (210) 475 - 8000; Fax: (210) 475 - 8060
zachryhb@zachry.com

Chief Exec. Officer
ZACHRY, John B. — Tel: (210) 475 - 8000; Fax: (210) 475 - 8060

Main Headquarters
Mailing: P.O. Box 240130
San Antonio, TX 78224-0130 — Tel: (210) 475 - 8000; Fax: (210) 475 - 8060
Street: 527 Logwood
San Antonio, TX 78221

Political Action Committees

ZACOPAC
Contact: Joe J. Lozano
P.O. Box 240130 — Tel: (210) 475 - 8000 Ext: 8019
San Antonio, TX 78224-0130 — Fax: (210) 475 - 8602

Contributions to Candidates: $8,500 (01/05 - 09/05)
Democrats: $5,000; Republicans: $3,500.

Principal Recipients

SENATE DEMOCRATS	HOUSE DEMOCRATS	
	Cuellar, Henry (TX)	$2,500
	Gonzalez, Charles A (TX)	$2,500

SENATE REPUBLICANS		HOUSE REPUBLICANS	
Hutchison, Kay Bailey (TX)	$2,500	Gohmert, Louis (TX)	$1,000

Corporate Foundations and Giving Programs

ZCC Corporate Contributions
P.O. Box 240130 — Tel: (210) 475 - 8000
San Antonio, TX 78224-0130 — Fax: (210) 475 - 8060

Annual Grant Total: $2,000,000 - $5,000,000
Geographic Preference: Area(s) in which the company operates
Primary Interests: Early Childhood Education; Social Services; United Way Campaigns

Public Affairs and Related Activities Personnel

At Headquarters

GREEN, Cathy Obriotti — Tel: (210) 475 - 8000; Fax: (210) 475 - 8060
V. President, Community Relations

HOECH, Stephen L. — Tel: (210) 475 - 8000; Fax: (210) 475 - 8060
V. President, Employee Relations

LOZANO, Joe J. — Tel: (210) 475 - 8000 Ext: 8019; Fax: (210) 475 - 8602
Senior V. President/Controller
Responsibilities include political action.

At Other Offices

HOLDEN, LuAnn — Tel: (210) 258 - 2664; Fax: (210) 258 - 2699
Manager, Public Affairs
310 S. St. Mary's
Suite 2400
San Antonio, TX 78205
holdenl@zachry.com

WADDY, Victoria J. — Tel: (210) 258 - 2662; Fax: (210) 258 - 2688
Director, Public Affairs
310 S. St. Mary's
Suite 2400
San Antonio, TX 78205
waddyvj@zachry.com

Zale Corp.

A retailer of fine jewelry.
www.zalecorp.com
Annual Revenues: $2.19 billion

Chairman of the Board
MARCUS, Richard C. — Tel: (972) 580 - 4000; Fax: (972) 580 - 5523

President and Chief Exec. Officer
FORTE, Mary L. — Tel: (972) 580 - 4000; Fax: (972) 580 - 5523

Main Headquarters
Mailing: 901 W. Walnut Hill Ln.
Irving, TX 75038-1003 — Tel: (972) 580 - 4000; Fax: (972) 580 - 5523

Corporate Foundations and Giving Programs

Zale Corp. Contributions Program
901 W. Walnut Hill Ln. — Tel: (972) 580 - 4000
Irving, TX 75038-1003 — Fax: (972) 580 - 5523

Annual Grant Total: $100,000 - $200,000
Geographic Preference: Texas
Primary Interests: Civic and Public Affairs; Education; Health and Human Services
Recent Recipients: Make-A-Wish Foundation; United Way

Public Affairs and Related Activities Personnel

At Headquarters

STEINBLITZ, David H. — Tel: (972) 580 - 4000; Fax: (972) 580 - 5523
V. President and Treasurer
Responsibilities include investor and media relations.

Zebra Technologies Corp.

Manufactures bar-code label printers and supplies.
www.zebra.com
Annual Revenues: $475.6 million

Chairman and Chief Exec. Officer
KAPLAN, Edward L. — Tel: (847) 634 - 6700; Fax: (847) 913 - 8766; TF: (800) 423 - 0422
ekaplan@zebra.com

Main Headquarters
Mailing: 333 Corporate Woods Pkwy.
Vernon Hills, IL 60061-3109 — Tel: (847) 634 - 6700; Fax: (847) 913 - 8766; TF: (800) 423 - 0422

Public Affairs and Related Activities Personnel

At Headquarters

BEYER, Leslie — Tel: (847) 793 - 2652; Fax: (847) 913 - 8766; TF: (800) 423 - 0422
Director, Public Relations
lbeyer@zebra.com

FOX, Douglas A. — Tel: (847) 793 - 6735; Fax: (847) 821 - 2545; TF: (800) 423 - 0422
Director, Investor Relations
dfox@zebra.com

SAKS, Larry — Tel: (847) 793 - 6909; Fax: (847) 913 - 8766; TF: (800) 423 - 0422
Director, Human Resources
lsaks@zebra.com

Zenith Electronics Corp.

Marketer of digital consumer electronics products.
www.zenith.com
Annual Revenues: $559.4 million

President and Chief Exec. Officer
AHN, Michael K. — Tel: (847) 391 - 7000; Fax: (847) 391 - 8177

Main Headquarters
Mailing: 2000 Millbrook Dr.
Lincolnshire, IL 60069 — Tel: (847) 391 - 7000; Fax: (847) 391 - 8177

Public Affairs and Related Activities Personnel

At Headquarters

TAYLOR, John I. — Tel: (847) 391 - 8181; Fax: (847) 391 - 8177
V. President, Public Affairs and Communications
john.taylor@zenith.com

Zimmer Holdings, Inc.

Manufactures orthopaedic products.
www.zimmer.com
Annual Revenues: $1.9 billion

Chairman, President and Chief Exec. Officer
ELLIOTT, J. Raymond — Tel: (574) 267 - 6131; Fax: (574) 372 - 4988; TF: (800) 613 - 6131

Main Headquarters
Mailing: P.O. Box 708
Warsaw, IN 46581-0708 — Tel: (574) 267 - 6131; Fax: (574) 372 - 4988; TF: (800) 613 - 6131

Street: 345 E. Main St.
Warsaw, IN 46580-2746

Corporate Foundations and Giving Programs

Zimmer Holdings, Inc. Corporate Giving Program
P.O. Box 708
Warsaw, IN 46581-0708 — Tel: (574) 267 - 6131; Fax: (574) 372 - 4988; TF: (800) 613 - 6131

Annual Grant Total: none reported
Primary Interests: Civic and Cultural Activities; Education

Public Affairs and Related Activities Personnel

At Headquarters

BISHOP, Brad
Director, Public Affairs — Tel: (574) 372 - 4291; Fax: (574) 372 - 4988; TF: (800) 613 - 6131

DVORAK, David
Senior V. President, Corporate Affairs and General Counsel — Tel: (574) 267 - 6131; Fax: (574) 372 - 4988; TF: (800) 613 - 6131

OSTERMANN, Marc
Manager, Investor Relations — Tel: (574) 267 - 6131; Fax: (574) 372 - 4988; TF: (800) 613 - 6131

SIMPSON, James P.
V. President, Quality Regulatory and Government Affairs — Tel: (574) 267 - 6131; Fax: (574) 372 - 4988; TF: (800) 613 - 6131

Zions Bancorporation

A bank holding company.
www.zionsbancorporation.com
Annual Revenues: $1.8 billion

Chairman, President and Chief Exec. Officer
SIMMONS, Harris H. — Tel: (801) 524 - 4730

Main Headquarters
Mailing: Kennecott Bldg.
One S. Main St., Suite 1380
Salt Lake City, UT 84111 — Tel: (801) 524 - 4730

Political Action Committees

Zions Bancorporation PAC
Contact: John Richards
255 N. Admiral Byrd Rd.
Salt Lake City, UT 84116

Contributions to Candidates: $750 (01/05 - 09/05)
Republicans: $750.

Principal Recipients

SENATE REPUBLICANS		HOUSE REPUBLICANS
Hatch, Orrin (UT)	$750	

Corporate Foundations and Giving Programs

Zions Bancorporation Foundation
Kennecott Bldg.
One S. Main St., Suite 1380
Salt Lake City, UT 84111 — Tel: (801) 524 - 4730

Annual Grant Total: none reported

Public Affairs and Related Activities Personnel

At Headquarters

HINCKLEY, Clark B.
Senior V. President, Investor Relations
Mailstop: M/S KC11 066
chinckley@zionsbank.com — Tel: (801) 524 - 4787

At Other Offices

RICHARDS, John
Treasurer, Zions Bancorporation PAC
255 N. Admiral Byrd Rd.
Salt Lake City, UT 84116

WALL, Merrill S.
Senior V. President, Human Resources
11622 El Camino Real
Mailstop: M/S SBTR 0837
San Diego, CA 92130

2006 National Directory of Corporate Public Affairs

The People

This alphabetical listing comprises a current and comprehensive index of leaders of the corporate public affairs profession in the United States. Regardless of the specific titles they bear or the organizational element in which they work, the individuals listed in this section are persons identified as engaged in one or more of their companies' principal public affairs programs — corporate communications and public information, government relations and political action, lobbying, and corporate philanthropy. Company Chairmen and Chief Executive Officers have also been included in this edition.

AAMOTH, William L.
5960 Heisley Rd.
Mentor, OH 44060-1834
Tel: (440) 354 - 2600
Fax:(440) 639 - 4450
TF: (800) 548 - 4873

Serves As:
- V. President and Corporate Treasurer, STERIS Corp.

AARON, Mark L.
600 Madison Ave.
New York, NY 10021
maaron@tiffany.com
Tel: (212) 230 - 5301

Serves As:
- V. President, Investor Relations, Tiffany & Co.

ABATEMARCO, Michael
383 Madison Ave.
New York, NY 10179
Tel: (212) 272 - 2000
Fax:(212) 272 - 5143
TF: (800) 417 - 2327

Serves As:
- PAC Treasurer, Bear, Stearns and Co. Inc.

ABBOTT, Jr., Herschel L.
1133 21st St. NW
Suite 900
Washington, DC 20036
herschel.abbott@bellsouth.com
Tel: (202) 463 - 4104
Fax:(202) 463 - 4141

Registered Federal Lobbyist.
Serves As:
- V. President, Governmental Affairs, BellSouth Corp.

ABBOTT, Richard S. L.
4643 S. Ulster St.
Suite 1300
Denver, CO 80237-2868
Tel: (303) 220 - 6600
Fax:(303) 220 - 6601

Serves As:
- Investor Relations - Denver, UnitedGlobalCom, Inc.

ABDOO, Elizabeth A.
6903 Rockledge Dr.
Suite 1500
Bethesda, MD 20817
Tel: (240) 744 - 1000

Serves As:
- Senior V. President, General Counsel and Corporate Secretary, Host Marriott Corp.

ABELE, John E.
One Boston Scientific Pl.
Natick, MA 01760-1537
Tel: (508) 650 - 8000
Fax:(508) 647 - 2200

Serves As:
- Chairman of the Board, Boston Scientific Corp.

ABELSON, Bill
One Symbol Plaza
Holtsville, NY 11742-1300
abelsonb@symbol.com
Tel: (631) 738 - 4751
Fax:(631) 738 - 5990
TF: (800) 722 - 6234

Serves As:
- Media Contact, Symbol Technologies, Inc.

ABERCROMBIE, George B.
340 Kingsland St.
Nutley, NJ 07110-1199
Tel: (973) 235 - 5000
Fax:(973) 235 - 7605

Serves As:
- President and Chief Exec. Officer, Hoffmann-La Roche Inc. (Roche)

ABERDEEN, Jeffery D.
P.O. Box 419248
Kansas City, MO 64141-6248
jeff.aberdeen@commercebank.com
Tel: (816) 234 - 2081
TF: (800) 892 - 7100

Serves As:
- Controller, Commerce Bancshares Inc.

Responsibilities include investor relations.

ABLEIDINGER, Bryan
8600 W. Bryn Mawr Ave.
Chicago, IL 60631-3505
Tel: (773) 695 - 5000

Serves As:
- Chairman of the Board, True Value Company

ABRAHAM, Aji
P.O. Box 772531
Harrisburg, PA 17177-2531
Tel: (717) 541 - 6134
Fax:(717) 541 - 6072

Serves As:
- Director, Government Liaison, Capital BlueCross (Pennsylvania)

ABRAMOWICZ, Daniel A.
One Crown Way
Philadelphia, PA 19154-4599
Tel: (215) 698 - 5100
Fax:(215) 698 - 5201

Serves As:
- Exec. V. President, Corporate Technologies and Regulatory Affairs, Crown Holdings, Inc.

ABRAMS, Lois
P.O. Box 550
Nashville, TN 37202
Tel: (615) 344 - 9551
Fax:(615) 344 - 5722

Serves As:
- Administrative Coordinator, Foundation, HCA

ABREU, Rafael Gomez
P.O. Box 4689
Houston, TX 77210
Tel: (832) 486 - 4000
Fax:(832) 486 - 1814

Serves As:
- V. President, Strategic Shareholder Relations, Government and Public Affairs, CITGO Petroleum Corporation

ACKERMAN, F. Duane
1155 Peachtree St. NE
Atlanta, GA 30309-3610
Tel: (404) 249 - 2000
Fax:(404) 249 - 3839

Serves As:
- Chairman and Chief Exec. Officer, BellSouth Corp.

ACKERMAN, Patricia K.
Box 23966
Milwaukee, WI 53224-9505
Tel: (414) 359 - 4129
Fax:(414) 359 - 4064

Serves As:
- Treasurer, A. O. Smith Corp. Political Action Committee, A. O. Smith Corp.

ACKERMAN, Philip C.
6363 Main St.
Williamsville, NY 14221
Tel: (716) 857 - 7000
Fax:(716) 857 - 7439
TF: (800) 365 - 3234

Serves As:
• Chairman, President and Chief Exec. Officer, Nat'l Fuel Gas Co.

ACKERMAN, Stephanie
Two Waterfront Plaza
Suite 500
Honolulu, HI 96813
sackerman@alohaairlines.com
Tel: (808) 836 - 4172
Fax:(808) 836 - 0303

Serves As:
• Senior V. President, Public Relations and Government Affairs, Aloha Airlines, Inc.

ACOSTA, Juan M.
1127 11th St., Suite 242
Sacramento, CA 95814-3883
juan.acosta@bnsf.com
Tel: (916) 448 - 4086
Fax:(916) 448 - 8937

Serves As:
• Director, Government Affairs, Burlington Northern Santa Fe Corporation

ACOSTA-FRANCO, Luisa
4680 Wilshire Blvd.
Los Angeles, CA 90010
Tel: (323) 932 - 3200

Serves As:
• Manager, Community Relations, Farmers Group, Inc.

ACQUILINA, Michelle
P.O. Box 810
Amherst, NY 14226
Tel: (716) 689 - 4980
Ext: 323
Fax:(716) 568 - 6098

Serves As:
• Manager, Corporate Human Resources, Mark IV Industries, Inc.

ADACHI, Yoroku
One Canon Plaza
Lake Success, NY 11042-1198
Tel: (516) 328 - 5000
Fax:(516) 328 - 5069

Serves As:
• President and Chief Exec. Officer, Canon U.S.A., Inc.

ADAMI, Kenneth R.
3715 Northside Pkwy.
Bldg. 100, Suite 800
Atlanta, GA 30327
ken.adami@eds.com
Tel: (402) 812 - 2885
Fax:(402) 812 - 2956

Serves As:
• Regional Director, Government Affairs, Southeast, EDS Corp.

ADAMI, Norman Joseph
P.O. Box 482
Milwaukee, WI 53201-0482
Tel: (414) 931 - 2000
Fax:(414) 931 - 3735

Serves As:
• President and Chief Exec. Officer, Miller Brewing Co.

ADAMO, Pam
One MetroTech Center
Brooklyn, NY 11201
Tel: (718) 403 - 2000
Fax:(718) 488 - 1763

Serves As:
• V. President, Public Affairs and Community Development, KeySpan Corp.

ADAMS, Clayton
One State Farm Plaza
M/S B-4
Bloomington, IL 61710-0001
Tel: (309) 766 - 3164
Fax:(309) 766 - 0860

Serves As:
• V. President, Communication Alliances, State Farm Insurance Cos.

ADAMS, Edward
600 Corporate Park Dr.
St. Louis, MO 63105
eadams@erac.com
Tel: (314) 512 - 5000
Fax:(314) 512 - 4706

Serves As:
• Senior V. President, Human Resources, Enterprise Rent-A-Car Co.

ADAMS, Gina
101 Constitution Ave., NW
Suite 801 East
Washington, DC 20001
gfadams@fedex.com
Tel: (202) 218 - 3800
Fax:(202) 218 - 3803

Registered Federal Lobbyist.
Serves As:
• Corporate V. President, Government Affairs, FedEx Corp.

ADAMS, Jane M.
1350 I St. NW
Suite 1210
Washington, DC 20005-3305
Tel: (202) 408 - 9482
Fax:(202) 408 - 9490

Serves As:
• Director, Federal Affairs, Johnson & Johnson

ADAMS, Jared
1701 SAIC Dr.
McLean, VA 22102
adamsjared@saic.com
Tel: (703) 676 - 4343

Serves As:
• Media Relations, Science Applications Internat'l Corp.

ADAMS, Jimmie V.
1215 S. Clark St.
Suite1205
Arlington, VA 22202
Tel: (703) 412 - 7190

Serves As:
• V. President, Washington, DC Operations, L-3 Communications Corp.

ADAMS, John L.
950 Echo Lane, Suite 100
Houston, TX 77024
Tel: (713) 647 - 5700
Fax:(713) 647 - 5800

Serves As:
• Chairman of the Board, Group 1 Automotive, Inc.

ADAMS, Linda
1025 Eldorado Blvd.
Broomfield, CO 80021
Tel: (720) 888 - 1000
Fax:(720) 888 - 5085

Serves As:
• Group V. President, Human Resources, Level 3 Communications, Inc.

ADAMS, Louis
6820 LBJ Fwy.
Dallas, TX 75240
louis.adams@brinker.com
Tel: (972) 770 - 4967

Serves As:
• Director, Public Relations, Brinker Internat'l, Inc.

ADAMS, Lynne
19601 N. 27th Ave.
Phoenix, AZ 85027
ladams@ssg.petsmart.com
Tel: (623) 587 - 2104
Fax:(623) 580 - 6508

Serves As:
• V. President, Corporate Communications, PETsMART, Inc.

ADAMS, M. Richard
One State Farm Dr.
Frederick, MD 21701-9332
Tel: (301) 620 - 6640
Fax:(301) 620 - 6645

Serves As:
• Manager, Public Affairs, State Farm Insurance Cos.

ADAMS, Melissa
P.O. Box 1600
San Antonio, TX 78296
Tel: (210) 220 - 4353
Fax:(210) 220 - 5144

Serves As:
• Corporate Donations Officer, Frost Nat'l Bank

ADAMS, Ray
1000 SW Broadway
Suite 2200
Portland, OR 97205
Tel: (503) 223 - 9228
Fax:(503) 240 - 5232
TF: (800) 831 - 2187

Serves As:
• Chief Financial Officer, Oregon Steel Mills Inc.
Responsibilities include corporate affairs.

ADAMS, Susie C.
P.O. Box 1244
M/S EC12X
Charlotte, NC 28201-1244
sadams@duke-energy.com
Tel: (704) 382 - 8978
Fax:(704) 382 - 4629

Serves As:
• V. President, Public Affairs/Duke Power, Duke Energy Corp.

ADAMS, Theodore
Three Limited Pkwy.
Columbus, OH 43230
Tel: (614) 415 - 7078
Fax:(614) 415 - 7079

Serves As:
• Director, Government Affairs, The Limited Brands
Responsibilities also include political action.

ADAMS, Victoria
1200 17th St., NW
Suite 603
Washington, DC 20036
Tel: (202) 887 - 8900
Fax:(202) 887 - 8907

Serves As:
• Coordinator, McDonald's Corp.

ADAMSON, Terrence
P.O. Box 98199
Washington, DC 20090-8199
Tel: (202) 857 - 7000
Fax:(202) 828 - 6679

Serves As:
• Exec. V. President, Nat'l Geographic Soc.
Responsibilities include government relations.

ADCOCK, Bradley T.
P.O. Box 2291
Durham, NC 27702-2291
brad.adcock@bcbsnc.com
Tel: (919) 765 - 4119
Fax:(919) 765 - 4837

Serves As:
• V. President, Government Affairs, Blue Cross and Blue Shield of North Carolina
Responsibilities include political action.

ADDERLEY, Terence E.
999 W. Big Beaver Rd.
Troy, MI 48084-4782
Tel: (248) 362 - 4444
Fax:(248) 244 - 7572

Serves As:
• Chairman and Chief Exec. Officer, Kelly Services, Inc.

ADDINGTON, Susan
4111 E. 37th St., North
Wichita, KS 67220
philanthropy@kochind.com
Tel: (316) 828 - 5500
Fax:(316) 828 - 5739

Serves As:
• Contact, Koch Industries Contributions Program, Koch Industries, Inc.

ADDISON, John A.
3120 Breckinridge Blvd.
Duluth, GA 30099-0001
Tel: (770) 381 - 1000
Fax:(770) 564 - 6161

Serves As:
• Co-Chief Exec. Officer, Primerica Financial Services, Inc.

ADDOMS, Samuel D.
7001 Tower Rd.
Denver, CO 80249-7312
Tel: (720) 374 - 4200
Fax:(720) 374 - 4375
TF: (800) 265 - 5505

Serves As:
• Chairman of the Board, Frontier Airlines, Inc.

ADELMAN, Dean
10 Burton Hills Blvd.
Nashville, TN 37215
dean.adelman@correctionscorp.com
Tel: (615) 263 - 3017
Fax:(615) 263 - 3140
TF: (800) 624 - 2931

Serves As:
• V. President, Human Resources, Corrections Corp. of America

ADERS, Robert O.
101 Wolf Dr.
Thorofare, NJ 08086
Tel: (856) 848 - 1800
Fax:(856) 848 - 0937
TF: (800) 257 - 5540

Serves As:
• Chairman of the Board, Checkpoint Systems, Inc.

ADKERSON, Richard
P.O. Box 51777
New Orleans, LA 70151
Tel: (504) 582 - 4000
Fax:(504) 582 - 1847
TF: (800) 535 - 7094

Serves As:
• President and Chief Exec. Officer, Freeport-McMoRan Copper and Gold Inc.

ADLER, Edward I.
One Time Warner Center
New York, NY 10019
Tel: (212) 484 - 6630

Serves As:
• Exec. V. President, Corporate Communications, Time Warner Inc.

ADLER, William K.
Reader's Digest Rd.
Pleasantville, NY 10570-7000
william.adler@rd.com
Tel: (914) 244 - 7585
TF: (800) 234 - 9000

Serves As:
• Senior Director, Global Communications, Reader's Digest Ass'n, Inc.

AESCHBACH, Joni
P.O. Box 77007
Madison, WI 53707-1007
joniaeschbach@alliantenergy.com
Tel: (608) 458 - 3407
Fax:(608) 458 - 3321

Serves As:
• Manager, Shareowner Services, Alliant Energy Corp.

AFABLE, Mark
6000 American Pkwy.
Madison, WI 53783
mafable@amfam.com
Tel: (608) 249 - 2111
Fax:(608) 245 - 8619

Serves As:
• V. President, Government Affairs and Compliance, American Family Insurance Group
Responsibilities include political action.

AFENDOULIS, Lynn
2801 E. Beltline NE
Grand Rapids, MI 49525
lafendoulis@ufpi.com
Tel: (616) 364 - 6161
Fax:(616) 364 - 5558

Serves As:
• Director, Public Affairs, Universal Forest Products, Inc.
Responsibilities include corporate philanthropy.

AGNEW, Ms. Creigh H.
P.O. Box 9777
M/S CH 1M31
Federal Way, WA 98063-9777
Tel: (253) 924 - 3770
Fax:(253) 924 - 4652
TF: (800) 525 - 5440

Serves As:
• V. President, Government Affairs and Corporate Contributions, Weyerhaeuser Co.

AGUIRRE, Anna L.
10955 Vista Sorrento Pkwy.
San Diego, CA 92130
aguirre@iomega.com
Tel: (858) 314 - 7000
Fax:(858) 314 - 7001

Serves As:
• V. President, Human Resources and Facilities, Iomega Corp.

AGUIRRE, Fernando
250 E. Fifth St.
Cincinnati, OH 45202
Tel: (513) 784 - 8000
Fax:(513) 784 - 8030

Serves As:
• Chairman, President and Chief Exec. Officer, Chiquita Brands Internat'l, Inc.

AHEARN, Ms. Chris
1000 Lowes Blvd.
RPS-4
Moorsville, NC 28117
chris.b.ahearn@lowes.com
Tel: (704) 758 - 100
Fax:(336) 658 - 4766
TF: (800) 445 - 6937

Serves As:
• Director, Public Relations, Lowe's Companies, Inc.

AHLSTROM, Lee
717 Texas Ave.
Suite 2100
Houston, TX 77002-2712
Tel: (713) 624 - 9548
Fax:(713) 624 - 9645

Serves As:
• Director, Investor Relations, Burlington Resources Inc.

AHN, Michael K.
2000 Millbrook Dr.
Lincolnshire, IL 60069
Tel: (847) 391 - 7000
Fax:(847) 391 - 8177

Serves As:
• President and Chief Exec. Officer, Zenith Electronics Corp.

AHNERT, Edward F.
5959 Las Colinas Blvd.
Irving, TX 75039-2298
Tel: (972) 444 - 1124
Fax:(972) 444 - 1405

Serves As:
• Manager, Contributions and President, ExxonMobil Foundation, Exxon Mobil Corp.

AHRENS, Susan W.
One State St.
Hartford, CT 06103
Tel: (860) 722 - 1866
Fax:(860) 722 - 5106

Serves As:
• V. President, Human Resources, Hartford Steam Boiler Inspection and Insurance Co.

AIGOTTI, Diane M.
200 E.Randolph St.
Chicago, IL 60601
Tel: (312) 381 - 1000
Fax:(312) 381 - 0240

Serves As:
• Senior V. President and Treasurer; PAC Treasurer, Aon Corp.

AIKEN, Robert S.
801 Pennsylvania Ave. NW
Suite 214
M/S A112
Washington, DC 20004
robbie.aiken@pinnaclewest.com
Tel: (202) 293 - 2655
Fax:(202) 293 - 2666

Registered Federal Lobbyist.
Serves As:
• V. President, Federal Affairs, Pinnacle West Capital Corp.

AKIN, Marsha J.
The Gallagher Center
Two Pierce Pl.
Itasca, IL 60143-3141
Tel: (630) 773 - 3800
Fax:(630) 285 - 4000

Serves As:
• Investor Relations Contact, Arthur J. Gallagher & Co.

AKINS, Jim
700 E. Butterfield Rd.
Suite 250
Lombard, IL 60148
Tel: (630) 678 - 8000
Fax:(630) 678 - 8131

Serves As:
• Senior V. President, Human Resources, U.S. Can Corp.

ALAGNA, Mark
316 Pennsylvania Ave. SE
Suite 300
Washington, DC 20003
Tel: (202) 675 - 4220
Fax:(202) 675 - 4230

Serves As:
• Manager, Public Affairs, United Parcel Service (UPS)

ALAN, Larry
30 Waterside Dr.
Farmington, CT 06032
Tel: (860) 256 - 2521

Serves As:
- Director, Government Affairs, Nationwide

ALAPONT, Jose M.
26555 Northwestern Hwy.
Southfield, MI 48034
Tel: (248) 354 - 7700
Fax:(248) 354 - 8950

Serves As:
- Chairman and Chief Exec. Officer, Federal-Mogul Corp.

ALBA, Miguel
225 W. Randolph St.
27 C
Chicago, IL 60606
Tel: (312) 727 - 1344
Fax:(312) 727 - 3722
TF: (800) 327 - 9346

Serves As:
- Area Manager, External Affairs, SBC Illinois

ALBANESE, Marisa
100 Weybosset St.
Providence, RI 02903
malbanese@negasco.com
Tel: (401) 272 - 5040
Ext: 2062
Fax:(401) 273 - 4243

Serves As:
- Manager, Community Relations, (New England Gas Co.), Southern Union Company

ALBERT, Debbie
The ARAMARK Tower
1101 Market St.
Philadelphia, PA 19107
albert_debbie@aramark.com
Tel: (215) 238 - 3614
Fax:(215) 415 - 8511
TF: (800) 999 - 8989

Serves As:
- Senior Communications Director, ARAMARK

ALBERT, Stacey Stern
1100 New York Ave. NW
Suite 600W
Washington, DC 20005
stacey.albert@hp.com
Tel: (202) 378 - 2500
Fax:(202) 378 - 2550

Registered Federal Lobbyist.
Serves As:
- Government Affairs Manager, Hewlett-Packard Co.

ALBERT, Thomas L.
8607 Westwood Center Dr.
Vienna, VA 22182
Tel: (703) 448 - 4000
Fax:(703) 448 - 4100

Registered Federal Lobbyist.
Serves As:
- V. President, Government Relations, Feld Entertainment, Inc.

ALBERTINE, John M.
PO Box 5004
Port Huron, MI 48060
Tel: (248) 702 - 6000
Fax:(248) 702 - 6300

Serves As:
- Chairman of the Board, SEMCO ENERGY, Inc.

ALBRECHT, Chris
1100 Ave. of the Americas
New York, NY 10036
Tel: (212) 512 - 1000
Fax:(212) 512 - 1182

Serves As:
- Chairman and Chief Exec. Officer, Home Box Office (HBO)

ALBRECHT, Mark
P.O. Box 7045
Troy, MI 48007-7045
Tel: (248) 362 - 4400
Ext: 608
Fax:(248) 362 - 6409

Serves As:
- Senior V. President, Human Resources, Handleman Company

ALBRIGHT, Jr., C. H. "Bud"
801 Pennsylvania Ave. NW
Suite 620
Washington, DC 20004-2615
Tel: (202) 467 - 5040
Fax:(202) 783 - 8127

Registered Federal Lobbyist.
Serves As:
- V. President, Federal Relations, Reliant Resources

ALDEN, Linda
P.O. Box 50
Boise, ID 83728-0001
Tel: (208) 384 - 7037
Fax:(208) 384 - 7224

Serves As:
- Communications Manager - Boise Paper, Boise Cascade Corp.

ALDRICH, Rhonda
2400 E. Ganson
Jackson, MI 49202
raldrich@sparton.com
Tel: (517) 787 - 8600
Fax:(517) 787 - 1822
TF: (800) 248 - 9579

Serves As:
- Director, Corporate Communications and Marketing Information, Sparton Corp.

ALDRIDGE, Ron
235 E. 42nd St.
New York, NY 10017-5755
ron.aldridge@pfizer.com
Tel: (212) 573 - 3685
Fax:(212) 573 - 1853

Serves As:
- Senior Director, Investor Relations, Pfizer Inc.

ALESIO, Steven W.
103 JFK Pkwy.
Short Hills, NJ 07078
Tel: (973) 921 - 5500

Serves As:
- Chairman and Chief Exec. Officer, The Dun & Bradstreet Corp.

ALESSIO, Keri
5775 Morehouse Dr.
San Diego, CA 92121-2779
Tel: (858) 587 - 1121
Fax:(858) 658 - 2100

Serves As:
- Corporate Public Relations, Qualcomm Inc.

ALEXANDER, Anthony
76 S. Main St.
Akron, OH 44308-1890
Fax:(330) 384 - 5791
TF: (800) 646 - 0400

Serves As:
- President and Chief Exec. Officer, FirstEnergy Corp.

ALEXANDER, Bart
P.O. Box 4030
M/S NH250
Golden, CO 80401-0030
Tel: (303) 277 - 6401
Fax:(303) 277 - 5723

Serves As:
- Director, Corporate Responsibility, Coors Brewing Co.

ALEXANDER, Jimmy
2200 Kensington Ct.
Oak Brook, IL 60523-2100
Tel: (630) 990 - 6620
Fax:(630) 990 - 1742

Serves As:
- V. President, Human Resources, Ace Hardware Corp.

ALEXANDER, Kobi
170 Crossways Park Dr.
Woodbury, NY 11797
kobi_alexander@comverse.com
Tel: (516) 677 - 7200
Fax:(516) 677 - 7355

Serves As:
- Chairman and Chief Exec. Officer, Comverse Technology, Inc.

ALEXANDER, Mary K.
1130 Connecticut Ave. NW
Suite 1100
Washington, DC 20036
Tel: (202) 912 - 3800

Registered Federal Lobbyist.
Serves As:
- Group Manager, Government and Public Affairs, Matsushita Electric Corp. of America

ALEXANDER, Nancy
P.O. Box 1400
Rapid City, SD 57709-1400
Tel: (605) 721 - 1700

Serves As:
- Director, Human Resources, Black Hills Corp.

ALEXANDER, Norman E.
200 Park Ave.
New York, NY 10166
Tel: (212) 986 - 5500
Fax:(212) 370 - 1969

Serves As:
- Exec. Chairman, Sequa Corp.

ALEXANDER, Paul J.
DWF Airport Station, P.O. Box 619100
Dallas, TX 75261-9100
palexand@kcc.com
Tel: (972) 281 - 1440
Fax:(972) 281 - 1490
TF: (800) 639 - 1352

Serves As:
- Manager, Investor Relations, Kimberly-Clark Corp.

ALEXANDER, Penny S.
One Franklin Pkwy.
San Mateo, CA 94403-1906
psmith@frk.com
Tel: (650) 312 - 2000
TF: (800) 342 - 5236

Serves As:
- V. President, Human Resources - U.S., Franklin Templeton Investments

ALEXANDER, Stuart
P.O. Box 64235
St. Paul, MN 55164-0235
stu.alexander@deluxe.com
Tel: (651) 483 - 7358
Fax:(651) 481 - 4477

Serves As:
- V. President, Investor Relations and Public Affairs; President, Deluxe Corp. Foundation, Deluxe Corp.

ALEXANDER, Susan
1334 York Ave.
New York, NY 10021
susan.alexander@sothebys.com
Tel: (212) 606 - 7202
Fax:(212) 606 - 7107

Serves As:
- Senior V. President, Worldwide Human Resources, Sotheby's Holdings, Inc.

ALFARO, Charles
389 Interpace
Parsippany, NJ 07054
charles.alfaro@am.csplc.com
Tel: (973) 909 - 2585

Serves As:
- V. President, Corporate Communications, Cadbury Schweppes Americas Beverages

ALFORD, Brian
P.O. Box 321
M/C 1200
Oklahoma City, OK 73101-0321
Tel: (405) 553 - 3187
Fax:(405) 553 - 3290

Serves As:
- Manager, Corporate Communications and Community Relations, OGE Energy Corp.

ALFORD, Chip
100 NE Adams St.
Peoria, IL 61629-1465
Tel: (309) 675 - 1464
Fax:(309) 675 - 6155

Serves As:
- Coordinator, Corporate Communications, Caterpillar Inc.

ALHADEFF, Joseph
1015 15th St. NW
Suite 200
Washington, DC 20005-2605
joseph.alhadeff@oracle.com
Tel: (202) 721 - 4816
Fax:(202) 467 - 4250

Registered Federal Lobbyist.
Serves As:
- V. President, Global Public Policy, Oracle Corporation

ALIGHIRE, Wendy
2929 Walker Ave. NW
Grand Rapids, MI 49544-1307
Tel: (616) 453 - 6711
Fax:(616) 791 - 2886

Serves As:
- Senior V. President, Human Resources, Meijer, Inc.

ALLAN, Don
1000 Stanley Dr.
New Britain, CT 06053
Tel: (860) 225 - 5111
Fax:(860) 827 - 3937

Serves As:
- V. President and Corporate Conroller, The Stanley Works

Responsibilities include political action.

ALLCOTT, Trudi
P.O. Box 27626
Richmond, VA 23261-7626
Tel: (804) 935 - 4291
Fax:(804) 965 - 1907

Serves As:
- Manager, Corporate Communications, Owens & Minor, Inc.

ALLEGUE, Raul
One Tower Sq.
Hartford, CT 06183
Tel: (860) 277 - 4738
Fax:(860) 277 - 4563

Serves As:
- V. President, Commercial Lines, Government Relations, St. Paul Travelers Cos., Inc.

ALLEN, Amy
801 Cherry St.
Suite 3900
Fort Worth, TX 76102-6803
amy.allen@americredit.com
Tel: (817) 302 - 7423
Fax:(817) 302 - 7479
TF: (800) 644 - 2297

Serves As:
- Manager, Public Relations, AmeriCredit Corp.

ALLEN, Bradley D.
One Imation Place
Oakdale, MN 55128-3414
Tel: (651) 704 - 3475
Fax:(651) 704 - 4200

Serves As:
- V. President, Corporate Communications and Investor Relations, Imation Corp.

ALLEN, David
3210 Watling St.
East Chicago, IN 46312
david.allen@ispat.com
Tel: (219) 399 - 5430
Fax:(219) 399 - 7715

Serves As:
- Manager, Communications and Media Relations, Ispat Inland Inc.

ALLEN, David
2901 Via Fortuna
Austin, TX 78746
Tel: (512) 851 - 4000
TF: (800) 888 - 5016

Serves As:
- V. President, Investor Relations; and Treasurer, Cirrus Logic, Inc.

ALLEN, James R.
3240 Hillview Ave.
Palo Alto, CA 94304
allen.jim@cnf.com
Tel: (650) 813 - 5335
Fax:(650) 813 - 0158

Registered Federal Lobbyist.
Serves As:
- V. President, Public Affairs and Corporate Communications, CNF Inc.

Responsibilities include government affairs.

ALLEN, Jane
P.O. Box 9300
MS 5
Minneapolis, MN 55440-9300
jane_allen@cargill.com
Tel: (952) 742 - 7110

Serves As:
- Treasurer, Cargill Inc. Political Action Committee, Cargill, Incorporated

ALLEN, Jay
702 SW Eighth St.
M/S 0150
Bentonville, AR 72716
Tel: (479) 273 - 4786
Fax:(479) 277 - 2473

Serves As:
- Senior V. President, Corporate Relations, Wal-Mart Stores

Responsibilities include corporate communications, political action and government affairs.

ALLEN, Jeremy W.
1350 I St. NW
Suite 1210
Washington, DC 20005-3305
Tel: (202) 408 - 9482
Fax:(202) 408 - 9490

Serves As:
- Director, Federal Affairs, Johnson & Johnson

ALLEN, Kimberly J.
500 Dallas St., Suite 1000
Houston, TX 77002
Tel: (713) 369 - 9000
Fax:(713) 369 - 9100
TF: (800) 324 - 2900

Serves As:
- V. President, Investor Relations and Treasurer, Kinder Morgan, Inc.

ALLEN, Larry W.
7201 Hamilton Blvd.
Allentown, PA 18195-1501
allenlw@airproducts.com
Tel: (610) 481 - 6289
Fax:(610) 841 - 5900

Serves As:
- V. President, Environment, Health, Safety and Quality, Air Products and Chemicals, Inc.

ALLEN, Leslie
P.O. Box 1551
Raleigh, NC 27602-1551
Tel: (919) 546 - 2917
Fax:(919) 546 - 3329

Serves As:
- PAC Manager, Progress Energy

ALLEN, Paul G.
12405 Powerscourt Dr.
St. Louis, MO 63131
pallen@chartercom.com
Tel: (314) 965 - 0555
Fax:(314) 965 - 5761

Serves As:
- Chairman of the Board, Charter Communications, Inc.

ALLEN, Paul J.
750 E. Pratt St.
18th Floor
Baltimore, MD 21202
paul.j.allen@constellation.com
Tel: (410) 783 - 3024
Fax:(410) 783 - 3029
TF: (888) 460 - 2002

Serves As:
- Senior V. President, Corporate Affairs, Constellation Energy

ALLEN, Russell G.
8600 South Blvd.
Charlotte, NC 28273
Tel: (704) 557 - 8219
Fax:(704) 554 - 5562
TF: (800) 438 - 1880

Serves As:
- Director, Planning and Investor Relations, Lance, Inc.

ALLEN, Scott
4000 MacArthur Blvd.
Newport Beach, CA 92660
Tel: (949) 483 - 4600

Serves As:
- Senior V. President, Communications, Conexant Systems, Inc.

ALLEN, Sharon L.
1633 Broadway
New York, NY 10019
Tel: (212) 489 - 1600
Fax:(212) 489 - 1687

Serves As:
- Chairman of the Board, Deloitte & Touche LLP

ALLEN, Stephanie
1700 Seventh Ave. Tel: (206) 303 - 3262
Suite 1000 Fax:(206) 303 - 3009
Seattle, WA 98101-4407
stephanie.allen@nordstroms.com

Serves As:
- Director, Investor Relations, Nordstrom, Inc.

ALLEN, Susan E.
P.O. Box 1564 Tel: (203) 499 - 2409
New Haven, CT 06506-0901 Fax:(203) 499 - 3626
susan.allen@uinet.com TF: (800) 722 - 5584

Serves As:
- V. President, Investor Relations; Corporate Secretary and Assistant Treasurer, The United Illuminating Company

ALLEN, Wilber
163-181 Kenwood Ave. Tel: (315) 361 - 3000
Oneida, NY 13421

Serves As:
- Director, Human Resources, Oneida Ltd.

ALLEN, William R.
901 N. Tatnall St., Second Floor Tel: (302) 571 - 1571
Wilmington, DE 19801 Fax:(302) 576 - 1132

Serves As:
- President, Verizon Delaware Inc.

ALLENDER, Patrick W.
2099 Pennsylvania Ave. NW Tel: (202) 828 - 0850
Washington, DC 20006 Fax:(202) 828 - 0860

Serves As:
- Exec. V. President, Chief Financial Officer , Secretary; and President, Foundation, Danaher Corp.

ALLEY, III, John M.
1133 S.W. Topeka Blvd. Tel: (785) 291 - 8700
Topeka, KS 66629 Fax:(785) 291 - 8216

Serves As:
- Chariman of the Board, Blue Cross and Blue Shield of Kansas, Inc.

ALLIS, Stephen E.
2001 M St. NW Tel: (202) 533 - 3126
Washington, DC 20036-3310 Fax:(202) 533 - 8516

Registered Federal Lobbyist.
Serves As:
- Partner-in-Charge of Government Affairs, KPMG LLP

ALLISON, Jr., Herbert M.
730 Third Ave. Tel: (212) 490 - 9000
New York, NY 10017-3206 Fax:(212) 916 - 4840

Serves As:
- Chairman, President, and Chief Exec. Officer, TIAA/CREF

ALLISON, Jay
100 Jim Moran Blvd. Tel: (954) 429 - 2000
Deerfield Beach, FL 33442 Fax:(954) 429 - 2300

Serves As:
- V. President, Government Relations, JM Family Enterprises, Inc.

ALLISON, IV, John A.
200 W. Second St. Tel: (336) 733 - 2000
Winston-Salem, NC 27101

Serves As:
- Chairman and Chief Exec. Officer, BB&T Corp.

ALLISON, Jr., Robert J.
1201 Lake Robbins Dr. Tel: (832) 636 - 1000
The Woodlands, TX 77380
robert_allison@anadarko.com

Serves As:
- Chairman of the Board, Anadarko Petroleum Corp.

ALLISON-PUTNAM, Andrea
4400 Main St. Tel: (816) 932 - 4895
Kansas City, MO 64111 Fax:(816) 932 - 8462
aputnam@hrblock.com TF: (800) 829 - 7733

Serves As:
- Director, Community Relations, H & R Block, Inc.

ALLRED, Glenda
Colonial Financial Center Tel: (334) 240 - 5000
One Commerce St. TF: (800) 285 - 5886
Montgomery, AL 36104

Serves As:
- Investor Relations, The Colonial Bancgroup, Inc.

ALM, John R.
P.O. Box 723040 Tel: (770) 989 - 3000
Atlanta, GA 31139-0040 Fax:(770) 989 - 3363

Serves As:
- President and Chief Exec. Officer, Coca-Cola Enterprises Inc.

ALM, Robert
P.O. Box 2750
Honolulu, HI 96840-0001
robert.alm@heco.com

Serves As:
- Senior V. President, Public Affairs, (Hawaiian Electric Co., Inc.), Hawaiian Electric Industries, Inc.

ALONZO, Jan Robey
One United Dr. Tel: (636) 326 - 3100
Fenton, MO 63026 Fax:(636) 326 - 1106

Serves As:
- Treasurer, UniGroup Inc. PAC, UniGroup, Inc.

ALPHIN, Steele
Bank of America Corporate Center Tel: (704) 386 - 4343
100 N. Tryon St. Fax:(704) 386 - 6699
Charlotte, NC 28255-0001
steele.alphin@bankofamerica.com

Serves As:
- Global Personnel Executive, Bank of America Corp.

ALSENBERG, Michael
1666 K St., NW Tel: (202) 973 - 6611
Suite 410 Fax:(202) 466 - 9103
Washington, DC 20006

Serves As:
- Director, Government Affairs, VeriSign, Inc.

ALSIP, Chris
P.O. Box 2020 Tel: (479) 290 - 4000
Springdale, AR 72765-2020 Fax:(479) 290 - 7984
chris.alsip@tyson.com TF: (800) 643 - 3410

Serves As:
- Treasurer, Tyson Foods Inc. PAC, Tyson Foods, Inc.

ALSTADT, Sandra R.
425 W. Capitol Ave. Tel: (501) 377 - 3547
P.O. Box 551
Little Rock, AR 72203
salstad@entergy.com

Serves As:
- Director, Utility Group Communications, Entergy Corp.

ALTER, Dennis
P.O. Box 844 Tel: (215) 657 - 4000
Spring House, PA 19477-0844 Fax:(215) 444 - 5101

Serves As:
- Chairman and Chief Exec. Officer, Advanta Corp.

ALTIMARI, Kristin
4111 E. 37th St., North Tel: (316) 828 - 1000
Wichita, KS 67220 Fax:(316) 828 - 1121

Serves As:
- Director, Communication, (INVISTA), Koch Industries, Inc.

ALTMAN, Bill M.
680 S. Fourth Ave. Tel: (502) 596 - 7161
Louisville, KY 40202-2412 Fax:(502) 596 - 4099

Registered Federal Lobbyist.
Serves As:
- Senior V. President, Compliance and Government Programs, Kindred Healthcare, Inc.

ALTMAN, David R.
270 Peachtree St. NW Tel: (404) 506 - 0650
Bin 908A Fax:(404) 506 - 0662
Atlanta, GA 30303

Serves As:
- V. President, Corporate Communications and Advertising, Southern Company

ALTMAN, Emily
1585 Broadway Tel: (212) 761 - 4000
New York, NY 10036 Fax:(212) 761 - 0086

Registered Federal Lobbyist.
Serves As:
- Exec. Director, International Government Relations, Morgan Stanley

ALVANSON, Kristen
452 Fifth Ave. Tel: (212) 525 - 8239
Seventh Fl. TF: (800) 975 - 4722
New York, NY 10018

Serves As:
- Contact, Corporate Giving, HSBC USA, Inc.

ALVARADO, Jon
345 Encinal St.
Santa Cruz, CA 95060
jon.alvarado@plantronics.com
Tel: (831) 426 - 5858
Ext: 4452
Fax:(831) 423 - 4314
TF: (800) 544 - 4660

Serves As:
- Manager, Treasury and Investor Relations, Plantronics, Inc.

ALVAREZ, Amy
1120 20th St. NW
Suite 1000
Washington, DC 20036-3406
Tel: (202) 457 - 3810
Fax:(202) 457 - 2008

Registered Federal Lobbyist.
Serves As:
- V. President, Federal Regulatory Affairs, AT&T

ALVAREZ, Kira
555 12th St. NW
Suite 650
Washington, DC 20004-1205
Tel: (202) 393 - 7950
Fax:(202) 393 - 7960

Registered Federal Lobbyist.
Serves As:
- Manager, International and Public Government Relations, Eli Lilly and Company

ALVAREZ, II, Antonio C.
12 E. Armour Blvd.
Kansas City, MO 64111
Tel: (816) 502 - 4000
Fax:(816) 502 - 4155

Serves As:
- Chief Exec. Officer, Interstate Bakeries Corp.

ALZIARI, Lucien
1345 Ave. of the Americas
New York, NY 10020
Tel: (212) 282 - 7000
Fax:(212) 282 - 6220

Serves As:
- Senior V. President, Human Resources, Avon Products, Inc.

AMANN, R. Scott
1333 West Loop South
Suite 1700
Houston, TX 77027
Tel: (713) 513 - 3344
Fax:(713) 513 - 3456

Serves As:
- V. President, Investor Relations, Cooper Cameron Corp.

Responsibilities also include corporate communications.

AMARAL, Celeste
343 State St.
Rochester, NY 14650-0516
Tel: (585) 724 - 4000
Fax:(585) 724 - 1724

Serves As:
- Treasurer, Eastman Kodak Co. Employee PAC, Eastman Kodak Company

AMBERG, Stephanie
2202 N. Westshore Blvd.
Fifth Floor
Tampa, FL 33607
stephanie.amberg@outback.com
Tel: (813) 282 - 1225
Fax:(813) 282 - 1209

Serves As:
- Media Contact, Outback Steakhouse, Inc.

AMBROSE, Bob
17845 E. Hwy. 10
Elk River, MN 55330
Tel: (763) 441 - 3121
Fax:(763) 241 - 2366

Serves As:
- Manager, Government Affairs; and PAC Treasurer, Great River Energy

AMBROSE, J. Henry "Hank"
1710 H St. NW
Tenth Floor
Washington, DC 20006
Tel: (202) 392 - 9900
Fax:(202) 546 - 5111

Serves As:
- V. President, Regulatory Matters, Verizon Washington D.C. Inc.

AMBRUS, Mary Lou
600 Mountain Ave.
Murray Hill, NJ 07974-0636
mambrus@lucent.com
Tel: (908) 582 - 8500
Fax:(908) 508 - 2576
TF: (888) 458 - 2368

Serves As:
- V. President, Public Relations, Lucent Technologies

AMEND, Betty
316 Pennsylvania Ave. SE
Suite 300
Washington, DC 20003
Tel: (202) 675 - 4220
Fax:(202) 675 - 4230

Serves As:
- Manager, Public Affairs, United Parcel Service (UPS)

AMES, Marshall
700 N.W. 107th Ave.
Miami, FL 33172
mames@lennar.com
Tel: (305) 485 - 2092
Fax:(305) 229 - 6453
TF: (800) 741 - 4663

Serves As:
- V. President, Lennar Corp.

Responsibilities include media and investor relations.

AMESTOY, Jay
P.O. Box 19734
Irvine, CA 92623-9734
jamestoy@mazdausa.com
Tel: (949) 727 - 1990
Fax:(949) 727 - 6813
TF: (800) 222 - 5500

Serves As:
- V. President, Public and Government Affairs, Mazda North American Operations

AMOR, Jack
TECO Plaza
702 N. Franklin St.
Tampa, FL 33602
Tel: (813) 228 - 4111
Fax:(813) 228 - 4811

Serves As:
- Director, Community Affairs, TECO Energy, Inc./Tampa Electric Co.

AMOS, Daniel P.
1932 Wynnton Rd.
Columbus, GA 31999
Tel: (706) 323 - 3431
Fax:(706) 660 - 7333
TF: (800) 992 - 3522

Serves As:
- Chairman and Chief Exec. Officer, AFLAC Incorporated

AN, Edward
800 Connecticut Ave. NW
Suite 800
Washington, DC 20006
Tel: (202) 457 - 8582
Fax:(202) 457 - 8861

Registered Federal Lobbyist.
Serves As:
- Director, Domestic Policy, Time Warner Inc.

ANAYA, William B.
1350 I St. NW
Suite 400
Washington, DC 20005-3306
Tel: (202) 371 - 6900
Fax:(202) 842 - 3578

Registered Federal Lobbyist.
Serves As:
- Senior Director, Legislative Affairs, Motorola, Inc.

ANCRUM, Charles
360 Hamilton Ave., Suite 1103
White Plains, NY 10601-1841
cancrum@heinekenusa.com
Tel: (914) 681 - 4100
Fax:(914) 681 - 1879

Serves As:
- Manager, Industry and Government Affairs/Northeast, Heineken USA Inc.

ANDEREGG, Gregory L.
1525 Howe St.
Racine, WI 53403
Tel: (262) 260 - 2156
Fax:(262) 260 - 6189

Serves As:
- Program Manager, Education and Youth, SC Johnson

ANDERS, Deniz
1617 Sixth Ave.
Suite 700
Seattle, WA 98101
deniz.anders@nordstroms.com
Tel: (206) 373 - 3038
Fax:(206) 373 - 3039

Serves As:
- Director, Business Public Relations, Nordstrom, Inc.

ANDERSEN, David C.
12405 Powerscourt Dr.
St. Louis, MO 63131
dandersen@chartercom.com
Tel: (314) 543 - 2213
Fax:(314) 965 - 8793

Serves As:
- Senior V. President, Communications, Charter Communications, Inc.

Responsibilities include political action.

ANDERSEN, Kathy
P.O. Box 619616
MD 5575
Dallas-Fort Worth Airport, TX 75261
kathy.andersen@aa.com
Tel: (817) 967 - 3545
Fax:(817) 967 - 9784

Serves As:
- Administrator, AMR/American Airlines Foundation, AMR Corp.

ANDERSON, Allen J.
P.O. Box 64089
St. Paul, MN 55164-0089
al.anderson@chsinc.com
Tel: (651) 355 - 6000
Fax:(651) 355 - 6432
TF: (800) 232 - 3639

Serves As:
- V. President, Governmental Affairs, CHS Inc.

ANDERSON, Bob
523 Third Ave.
International Falls, MN 56649-2387
Tel: (218) 285 - 5312
Fax:(218) 285 - 5528

Serves As:
• Public Affairs Manager - Boise Paper, Boise Cascade Corp.

ANDERSON, Bradbury H.
7601 Penn Ave. South
Richfield, MN 55423
brad.anderson@bestbuy.com
Tel: (612) 291 - 1000
Fax:(612) 292 - 2195

Serves As:
• V. Chairman and Chief Exec. Officer, Best Buy Co., Inc.

ANDERSON, Brenda G.
555 12th St. NW
Suite 620 North
Washington, DC 20004
bfleming@ashland.com
Tel: (202) 223 - 8290
Fax:(202) 293 - 2913

Registered Federal Lobbyist.
Serves As:
• Representative, Federal Government Relations, Ashland Inc.

ANDERSON, Brian
1525 Howe St.
Racine, WI 53403
Tel: (262) 260 - 5262
Fax:(262) 260 - 2652

Serves As:
• Program Manager, Community Development, SC Johnson

ANDERSON, Bryan D.
800 Connecticut Ave. NW
Suite 711
Washington, DC 20006
banderson@na.ko.com
Tel: (202) 973 - 2663
Fax:(202) 466 - 2262

Registered Federal Lobbyist.
Serves As:
• Assistant V. President, Government Relations, The Coca-Cola Co.

ANDERSON, C. Robert
P.O. Box 757
Carthage, MO 64836-0757
Tel: (417) 358 - 8131
Fax:(417) 358 - 7155

Serves As:
• Corporate Director, Environmental Affairs, Leggett & Platt, Inc.

ANDERSON, Chris
1700 Lincoln St.
Denver, CO 80203
Tel: (303) 863 - 7414
Fax:(303) 837 - 5837

Serves As:
• Group Exec., External Affairs and Social Responsibility, Newmont Mining Corp.

ANDERSON, Curt
One Microsoft Way
Redmond, WA 98052-6399
Tel: (425) 706 - 3703
Fax:(425) 936 - 7329

Serves As:
• General Manager, Investor Relations, Microsoft Corporation

ANDERSON, Danyle
5350 Tech Data Dr.
Clearwater, FL 33760
danyle.anderson@techdata.com
Tel: (727) 539 - 7429
TF: (800) 237 - 8931

Serves As:
• Director, Investor Relations, Tech Data Corp.

ANDERSON, David
23 Hunter Run Blvd.
Cohoes, NY 12047
david.anderson@az.com
Tel: (518) 785 - 4589
Fax:(518) 785 - 0883
TF: (877) 893 - 0390
Ext: 41877

Serves As:
• Director, State Government Affairs, AstraZeneca Pharmaceuticals

ANDERSON, David
P.O. Box 550
Nashville, TN 37202
Tel: (615) 344 - 9551
Fax:(615) 344 - 5722

Serves As:
• PAC Treasurer, HCA

ANDERSON, Dick
1000 Alfred Nobel Dr.
Hercules, CA 94547-1811
Tel: (510) 724 - 7000
Fax:(510) 741 - 5817
TF: (800) 424 - 6723

Serves As:
• Director, Human Resources, Bio-Rad Laboratories, Inc.

ANDERSON, Donald H.
P.O. Box 5660
Denver, CO 80217
danderson@transmontaigne.com
Tel: (303) 626 - 8200
Fax:(303) 626 - 8228

Serves As:
• V. Chairman, President and Chief Exec. Officer, TransMontaigne, Inc.

ANDERSON, Eric
55 Inverness Dr. East
Englewood, CO 80112-5498
eric.anderson@jeppesen.com
Tel: (303) 328 - 4767
Fax:(303) 328 - 4130

Serves As:
• Public Relations Specialist, Jeppesen

ANDERSON, Glenn J.
7565 Irvine Center Dr.
Irvine, CA 92618
Tel: (949) 471 - 7000
Fax:(949) 471 - 7041

Serves As:
• Foundation Director, Gateway, Inc.

ANDERSON, Harry
P.O. Box 31907
Santa Barbara, CA 93130
harry.anderson@tenethealth.com
Tel: (805) 563 - 6816
Fax:(805) 563 - 7180

Serves As:
• V. President, Corporate Communications, Tenet Healthcare Corp.

ANDERSON, Hayes
P.O. Box 5204
Norwalk, CT 06856-5204
Tel: (203) 229 - 2900
Fax:(203) 229 - 3213
TF: (877) 275 - 6973

Serves As:
• V. President, Human Resources, Arch Chemicals, Inc.

ANDERSON, J. Patrick
2725 Fairfield Rd.
Kalamazoo, MI 49002
Tel: (616) 385 - 2600
Fax:(616) 385 - 1062

Serves As:
• V. President, Strategy and Communications, Stryker Corp.

ANDERSON, Jennifer A.
P.O. Box 64235
St. Paul, MN 55164-0235
jenny.anderson@deluxe.com
Tel: (651) 483 - 7842
Fax:(651) 481 - 4477

Serves As:
• Director, Foundations, Deluxe Corp.

ANDERSON, Jim
393 E. Walnut St.
Pasadena, CA 91188
Tel: (626) 405 - 5157
Fax:(626) 405 - 3176

Serves As:
• Associate Media Director - Southern California Region, Kaiser Permanente

ANDERSON, John L.
2525 West End Ave., Suite 600
Nashville, TN 37203
Tel: (615) 370 - 2740
Fax:(615) 370 - 2735

Serves As:
• V. President, Human Resources, Renal Care Group, Inc.

ANDERSON, John T.
1301 Pennsylvania Ave. NW
Suite 1030
Washington, DC 20004
john.t.anderson@delphi.com
Tel: (202) 824 - 0401
Fax:(202) 628 - 5815

Registered Federal Lobbyist.
Serves As:
• Director, Corporate Affairs, Delphi Corp.

ANDERSON, Judy M.
241 Ralph McGill Blvd. NE
BIN 10230
Atlanta, GA 30308-3374
Tel: (404) 526 - 7750
Fax:(404) 506 - 3771

Serves As:
• Senior V. President, Charitable Giving, Georgia Power Co.
• Senior V. President, Charitable Giving, Southern Company

ANDERSON, Karen
1101 Pennsylvania Ave. NW
Suite 1000
Washington, DC 20004
andersonk@citigroup.com
Tel: (202) 879 - 6871
Fax:(202) 783 - 4460

Serves As:
• V. President, Deputy Director - State and Local Government Relations, Citigroup, Inc.

ANDERSON, Kristin
35 W. Wacker Dr.
Chicago, IL 60601
Tel: (312) 220 - 5959
Fax:(312) 220 - 3299

Serves As:
• Senior V. President and Director, Community Affairs, Leo Burnett Worldwide

ANDERSON, Lee A.
One General Mills Blvd.
Minneapolis, MN 55426
Tel: (763) 764 - 2293
Fax:(763) 764 - 3734

Serves As:
• Manager, State Government Relations, General Mills

ANDERSON, Mark R.
1025 Connecticut Ave. NW
Suite 1210
Washington, DC 20036
mark.anderson@ual.com
Tel: (202) 296 - 1950
Fax:(202) 296 - 2873

Registered Federal Lobbyist.
Serves As:
• V. President, Governmental Affairs, United Airlines

ANDERSON, Michael A.
101 Gordon Dr.
Lionville, PA 19341
Tel: (610) 594 - 2900
Fax:(610) 594 - 3000
TF: (800) 345 - 9800

Serves As:
• V. President and Treasurer, West Pharmaceutical Services
Responsibilities include investor relations.

ANDERSON, Michael D.
P.O. Box 2181
320 W. Capitol
Little Rock, AR 72203-2181
Tel: (501) 378 - 2220

Serves As:
• Governmental Relations Representative, Arkansas Blue Cross and Blue Shield

ANDERSON, Michael J.
P.O. Box 119
Maumee, OH 43537
Tel: (419) 893 - 5050
Fax:(419) 891 - 6670

Serves As:
• President and Chief Exec. Officer, The Andersons, Inc.

ANDERSON, Michelle A.
500 N. Akard St.
Suite 4300
Dallas, TX 75201-3331
manderson@enscous.com
Tel: (214) 397 - 3045
Fax:(214) 397 - 3370
TF: (800) 423 - 8006

Serves As:
• Investor Relations Advisor, ENSCO Internat'l Inc.

ANDERSON, Nicole
1201 Winterson Rd.
Linthicum, MD 21090
Tel: (410) 694 - 5786
Fax:(410) 865 - 8929

Serves As:
• Public Relations Contact, CIENA Corp.

ANDERSON, Paul M.
P.O. Box 1244
M/S EC3XB
Charlotte, NC 28201-1244
pmanderson@duke-energy.com
Tel: (704) 382 - 3525
Fax:(704) 382 - 3588

Serves As:
• Chairman and Chief Exec. Officer, Duke Energy Corp.

ANDERSON, Richard P.
P.O. Box 119
Maumee, OH 43537
Tel: (419) 893 - 5050
Fax:(419) 891 - 6670

Serves As:
• Chairman of the Board, The Andersons, Inc.

ANDERSON, Sam
P.O. Box 1411
Tyler, TX 75710-1411
samanderson@brookshires.com
Tel: (903) 534 - 3112
Fax:(903) 534 - 2198

Serves As:
• Director, Public Relations, Brookshire Grocery Co.

ANDERSON, Tasa
100 Pier 1 Place
Fort Worth, TX 76102
Tel: (817) 252 - 8153
Fax:(817) 252 - 7229

Serves As:
• Manager, Community Relations, Pier 1 Imports
Responsibilities include corporate philanthropy.

ANDERSON, Thomas
290 Concord Rd.
Billerica, MA 01821
thomas_anderson@millipore.com
Tel: (978) 715 - 1043
Fax:(978) 715 - 1380

Serves As:
• V. President, Corporate Communications, Millipore Corp.

ANDERSON, Thomas H.
P.O. Box 119
Maumee, OH 43537
Tel: (419) 891 - 6405
Fax:(419) 891 - 6695

Serves As:
• Chairman, Anderson Foundation, The Andersons, Inc.

ANDRASICK, James S.
555 12th St.
Eighth Floor
Oakland, CA 94607
Tel: (510) 628 - 4000
Fax:(510) 628 - 7359

Serves As:
• President and Chief Exec. Officer, Matson Navigation Company, Inc.

ANDREAS, G. Allen
P.O. Box 1470
Decatur, IL 62525
Tel: (217) 424 - 5200
Fax:(217) 424 - 5839

Serves As:
• Chairman and Chief Executive, Archer Daniels Midland Co. (ADM)

ANDREOLI, Cindy
One GBC Plaza
Northbrook, IL 60062
candreoli@gbc.com
Tel: (847) 272 - 3700
Fax:(847) 272 - 1389

Serves As:
• Director, Marketing Communications, General Binding Corp.
Responsibilities include media relations.

ANDRES, Susan Auther
600 13th St. NW
Suite 340 West
Washington, DC 20005
Tel: (202) 662 - 0120
Fax:(202) 662 - 0199

Registered Federal Lobbyist.
Serves As:
• Director, Washington Affairs - Transportation, Union Pacific Corp.

ANDREW, T. Peter
P.O. Box 57013
Irvine, CA 92619-7013
andrewtp@broadcom.com
Tel: (949) 926 - 5663
Fax:(949) 450 - 8710

Serves As:
• Senior Director, Investor Relations, Broadcom Corp.

ANDREWA, Jennifer
101 Ash St.
hq15a
San Diego, CA 92101-3017
jandrews@sempra.com
Tel: (619) 696 - 4457
Fax:(619) 696 - 4379
TF: (877) 736 - 7721

Serves As:
• Manager, Public Relations, Sempra Energy

ANDREWS, David R.
700 Anderson Hill Rd.
Purchase, NY 10577-1444
Tel: (914) 253 - 2300
Fax:(914) 249 - 8166

Serves As:
• Senior V. President, Government Affairs, General Counsel and Secretary, PepsiCo, Inc.

ANDREWS, Jo B.
890 Pineview Rd.
Asheboro, NC 27203
jo_andrews@goodyear.com
Tel: (336) 495 - 2269

Serves As:
• Communications Specialist, The Goodyear Tire & Rubber Company

ANDREWS, Michael A.
2711 N. Haskell Ave.
Dallas, TX 75204
Tel: (214) 828 - 7011
Fax:(214) 828 - 7090

Registered Federal Lobbyist.
Serves As:
• Representative, 7-Eleven, Inc.

ANDREWS, Michael P.
1101 Pennsylvania Ave. NW
Suite 1000
Washington, DC 20004
andrewsm@citigroup.com
Tel: (202) 879 - 6810
Fax:(202) 783 - 4460

Registered Federal Lobbyist.
Serves As:
• V. President and Director, International Business Affairs, Citigroup, Inc.

ANDREWS, Steven R.
700 Pilgrim Way
Green Bay, WI 54304
Tel: (920) 429 - 2211
Fax:(920) 429 - 5328

Serves As:
• V. President, Human Resources, Shopko Stores, Inc.

ANDREWS, Todd G.
One CVS Dr.
Woonsocket, RI 02895
tgandrews@cvs.com
Tel: (401) 770 - 5717
Fax:(401) 762 - 9227

Serves As:
• Director, Corporate Communications, CVS

ANDREWS, William F.
10 Burton Hills Blvd.
Nashville, TN 37215
Tel: (615) 263 - 3000
Fax:(615) 263 - 3140
TF: (800) 624 - 2931

Serves As:
• Chairman of the Board, Corrections Corp. of America

ANDRIANO, Nicole
200 Carillon Pkwy.
St. Petersburg, FL 33716
nicole.andriso@catalinamarketing.com
Tel: (727) 579 - 5000
Fax:(727) 556 - 2700

Serves As:
- Manager, Public Relations, Catalina Marketing Corp.

ANGAROLA, Ilene A.
615 Merrick Ave.
Westbury, NY 11590
Tel: (516) 683 - 4420

Serves As:
- First Senior V. President, Investor Relations, New York Community Bancorp, Inc.

ANGEL, Christie
150 E. Gay St.
Room 4A
Columbus, OH 43215
Tel: (614) 223 - 6226
Fax:(614) 223 - 6296

Serves As:
- Director, Government Affairs, SBC Ohio

ANGELES, Veronica
170 Wood Ave. South
Iselin, NJ 08830
Tel: (877) 822 - 5233
Fax:(732) 603 - 5890

Serves As:
- Program Director, Siemens Corp.

ANGELINI, Michael P.
440 Lincoln St.
Worcester, MA 01653
Tel: (508) 855 - 1000

Serves As:
- Chairman of the Board, Allmerica Property & Casualty Companies, Inc.

ANGELLO, Matthew J.
P.O. Box 3001
Lancaster, PA 17604-3001
Tel: (717) 397 - 0611

Serves As:
- Senior V. President, Human Resources, (Armstrong World Industries), Armstrong Holdings, Inc.

ANGELSON, Mark A.
111 S. Wacker Dr.
Chicago, IL 60606
Tel: (312) 326 - 8000
Fax:(312) 326 - 8494

Serves As:
- Chief Exec. Officer, R R Donnelley

ANGEVINE, Richard
175 Berkeley St.
Boston, MA 02116
richard.angevine@libertymutual.com
Tel: (617) 574 - 6638
Fax:(617) 350 - 7648

Serves As:
- Senior Public Relations Specialist, Liberty Mutual Insurance Co.

ANICETTI, Rick
P.O. Box 1330
Salisbury, NC 28145-1330
Tel: (704) 633 - 8250
Fax:(704) 633 - 8250

Serves As:
- President and Chief Exec. Officer, Food Lion LLC

ANIXTER, Benjamin M.
One AMD Pl.
P.O. Box 3453
Sunnyvale, CA 94088
Tel: (408) 749 - 4000
Fax:(408) 749 - 3127
TF: (800) 538 - 8450

Serves As:
- V. President, External Affairs, Advanced Micro Devices, Inc.

ANKNER, James
622 Broadway
New York, NY 10012
Tel: (646) 536 - 3006

Serves As:
- Investor Relations and Media Relations, Take-Two Interactive Software, Inc.

ANSLEY, Robert
1755 S. Clark St.
Suite 1100
Arlington, VA 22202
Tel: (703) 416 - 8000
Fax:(703) 416 - 8010

Serves As:
- V. President, Congressional Affairs, DRS Technologies, Inc.

ANTHONY, Jeff
4345 Southpoint Blvd.
Jacksonville, FL 32216
Tel: (904) 332 - 3000

Serves As:
- Senior V. President, Corporate Development, PSS World Medical, Inc.

ANTHONY, Scott
P.O. Box 723040
Atlanta, GA 31139-0040
Tel: (770) 989 - 3105
Fax:(770) 989 - 3788

Serves As:
- V. President, Investor Relations, Coca-Cola Enterprises Inc.

ANTHONY, Steven J.
1500 K St. NW
Suite 375
Washington, DC 20005
Tel: (202) 383 - 4432
Fax:(202) 383 - 4018

Registered Federal Lobbyist.
Serves As:
- Assistant V. President, Norfolk Southern Corp.

ANTIOQUIA, Todd P.
One Sealaska Plaza, Suite 400
Juneau, AK 99801-1276
Tel: (907) 586 - 1512
Fax:(907) 586 - 2304

Serves As:
- Director, Corporate Communications, Sealaska Corp.

ANTONIUS, Kurt
1919 Torrance Blvd.
M/S 100-3C-2A
Torrance, CA 90501-2746
kurt_antonius@ahm.honda.com
Tel: (310) 783 - 3170
Fax:(310) 783 - 3622

Serves As:
- Assistant V. President, Public Relations, American Honda Motor Co., Inc.

ANTONNEAU, Ron
P.O. Box 19001
M/S A2
Green Bay, WI 54307-9001
rantonn@wpsr.com
Tel: (920) 443 - 4965
Fax:(920) 433 - 5741
TF: (800) 450 - 7260

Serves As:
- Director, Governmental Affairs, Wisconsin Public Service Corp.

ANTONUCCI, John
70 Maxess Rd.
Melville, NY 11747
jantonucci@nuhorizons.com
Tel: (631) 396 - 5000
Ext: 304
Fax:(631) 696 - 5050

Serves As:
- Controller, Nu Horizons Electronics Corp.

Responsibilities include corporate philanthropy.

APATOFF, Robert S.
P.O. Box 7600
Chicago, IL 60680-7600
Tel: (847) 329 - 8100
Fax:(847) 673 - 0813

Serves As:
- President and Chief Exec. Officer, Rand McNally

Responsibilities include corporate philanthropy. Serves as principal contact for the Rand McNally Foundation.

APICEMO, Ken
81 Wyman St.
Waltham, MA 02454-9046
Tel: (781) 622 - 1000
Fax:(781) 622 - 1207

Serves As:
- V. President, Investor Relations and Treasurer, Thermo Electron Corp.

APPLETON, Steven R.
8000 S. Federal Way
Boise, ID 83707
Tel: (208) 368 - 4000
Fax:(208) 368 - 2536

Registered Federal Lobbyist.
Serves As:
- Chairman, President, and Chief Exec. Officer, Micron Technology, Inc.

ARAMONY, Diane
320 Park Ave.
New York, NY 10022
Tel: (212) 224 - 1532
Fax:(212) 224 - 2519

Serves As:
- Exec. V. President and Corporate Secretary, Mutual of America Life Insurance Co.

Responsibilities include corporate philanthropy.

ARAPIS, Peter
1350 I St. NW
Suite 1000
Washington, DC 20005
Tel: (202) 962 - 5400
Fax:(202) 336 - 7223

Serves As:
- Legislative Manager, Ford Motor Co.

ARCHER, William C.
241 Ralph McGill Blvd. NE
Bin 10240
Atlanta, GA 30308-3374
Tel: (404) 506 - 7930
Fax:(404) 506 - 3771

Serves As:
- Exec. V. President, External Affairs, Georgia Power Co.

ARCHIBALD, Nolan D.
701 E. Joppa Rd.
Towson, MD 21286
nolan.archibald@bdk.com
Tel: (410) 716 - 3900
Fax:(410) 716 - 2933

Serves As:
- Chairman, President, and Chief Exec. Officer, The Black & Decker Corp.

ARDITTE, Ed
Nine Roszel Rd.
Princeton, NJ 08540
Tel: (609) 720 - 4621
Fax:(609) 720 - 4208

Serves As:
- Senior V. President, Investor Relations, Tyco Internat'l (U.S.), Inc.

ARDOIN, Kenneth A.
Seven Village Circle, Suite 500
Westlake, TX 76262
kardoin@pfizer.com
Tel: (817) 491 - 8410

Serves As:
- Director, Government Relations, (Pfizer Pharmaceuticals, Inc.), Pfizer Inc.

ARENA, Mark
1285 Ave. of the Americas
New York, NY 10019-6028
Tel: (212) 713 - 2027
Fax:(212) 713 - 1087

Serves As:
- Managing Director, Corporate Communications, UBS Financial Services Inc.

ARENDS, Herman J.
6101 Anacapri Blvd.
Lansing, MI 48917
Tel: (517) 323 - 1200
Fax:(517) 323 - 8796

Serves As:
- Chairman of the Board, Auto-Owners Insurance Group

ARGENTO, Lisa
55 Water St.
49th Floor
New York, NY 10041-0099
largento@dtcc.com
Tel: (212) 855 - 5302
Fax:(212) 785 - 9681

Serves As:
- Director, Corporate Communications, The Depository Trust & Clearing Corp.

ARGYRIS, Marcia M.
One Post St.
San Francisco, CA 94104-5296
Tel: (415) 983 - 8300
Fax:(415) 983 - 7160

Serves As:
- Foundation President, McKesson Corp.

ARISON, Micky
Carnival Pl.
3655 N.W. 87th Ave.
Miami, FL 33178-2428
marison@carnival.com
Tel: (305) 599 - 2600
Fax:(305) 406 - 4700

Serves As:
- Chairman and Chief Exec. Officer, Carnival Corp.

ARKELL, Robert B.
P.O. Box 639
Longview, WA 98632
Tel: (360) 425 - 1550
Ext: 5916
Fax:(360) 575 - 5934

Serves As:
- Senior V. President, Industrial Relations and General Counsel, Longview Fibre Co.

ARKY, M. Elizabeth
800 Connecticut Ave. NW
Suite 600
Washington, DC 20006
m.elizabeth.arky@accenture.com
Tel: (202) 533 - 1100
Fax:(202) 533 - 1111

Registered Federal Lobbyist.
Serves As:
- Director, Government Relations, Accenture

ARLINE, Marcella K.
100 Crystal A Dr.
P.O. Box 810
Hershey, PA 17033
marline@hersheys.com
Tel: (717) 534 - 4380
Fax:(717) 534 - 7015

Serves As:
- Senior V. President and Chief People Officer, The Hershey Company

ARLINGTON, William J.
111 River St.
M/S 3-02
Hoboken, NJ 07030-5774
Tel: (201) 748 - 6000
Fax:(201) 748 - 6008

Serves As:
- Senior V. President, Human Resources, John Wiley & Sons, Inc.

ARMACOST, Samuel
333 Ravenswood Ave.
Menlo Park, CA 94025-3493
Tel: (650) 859 - 2000
Fax:(650) 326 - 5512

Serves As:
- Chairman of the Board, SRI International

ARMBRISTER, Denise McGregor
123 Broad St.
Third Floor
Philadelphia, PA 19109
Tel: (215) 670 - 4310
Fax:(215) 670 - 4313

Serves As:
- Senior V. President and Exec. Director, Wachovia Regional Foundation, Wachovia Corp.

ARMIN, Craig
11620 Wilshire Blvd.
Suite 1100
Los Angeles, CA 90025
craig.armin@tenethealth.com
Tel: (310) 966 - 3034
Fax:(310) 966 - 3141

Serves As:
- Senior V. President, Government Programs, Tenet Healthcare Corp.

ARMITAGE, Susan
2222 Wellington Ct.
Lisle, IL 60532
sarmitage@molex.com
Tel: (630) 527 - 4561
Fax:(630) 512 - 8627
TF: (800) 786 - 6539

Serves As:
- Manager, Communications and Public Relations, Molex Incorporated

ARMON, Lori
71 S. wacker Dr
Chicago, IL 60606
larmon@corphq.hyatt.com
Tel: (312) 750 - 8069
Fax:(312) 750 - 8550

Serves As:
- Director, Public Relations, (Hyatt Hotels Corp.), Global Hyatt Corp.

ARMSTRONG, Andre
9191 S. Jamaica St.
Englewood, CO 80112
andre.armstrong@ch2m.com
Tel: (303) 286 - 2425
Fax:(720) 286 - 9250

Serves As:
- Media Relations Contact, CH2M Hill Companies, Inc.

ARMSTRONG, D. John
600 Grant St.
Room 685
Pittsburgh, PA 15219-2800
Tel: (412) 433 - 6792
Fax:(412) 433 - 6847

Serves As:
- Manager, Public Affairs, United States Steel Corporation

ARMSTRONG, Eric
851 W. Cypress Creek Rd.
Fort Lauderdale, FL 33309
eric.armstrong@citrix.com
Tel: (954) 267 - 2977
Fax:(954) 267 - 2525
TF: (800) 424 - 8749

Serves As:
- Director, Public and Analyst Relations, Citrix Systems, Inc.

ARMSTRONG, Jack
175 Berkeley St.
Boston, MA 02116
Tel: (617) 357 - 9500
Fax:(617) 350 - 7648

Registered Federal Lobbyist.
Serves As:
- Assistant V. President, Liberty Mutual Insurance Co.

ARMSTRONG, Jr., Phil M.
1100 CommScope Pl. SE
Hickory, NC 28603
parmstro@commscope.com
Tel: (828) 323 - 4848
Fax:(828) 323 - 4849

Serves As:
- V. President, Investor Relations and Corporate Communications, CommScope

ARNALL, Maurice
P.O. Box 13287
Kansas City, MO 64199-3287
maurice.arnall@aquila.com
Tel: (816) 737 - 7751
Fax:(816) 743 - 3751

Serves As:
- Director, Regulatory Services - Analytical Support, Aquila, Inc.

ARNDT, Brennen
1735 Market St.
Philadelphia, PA 19103
brennen_arndt@fmc.com
Tel: (215) 299 - 6000
Fax:(215) 299 - 6266

Serves As:
- Director, Investor Relations, FMC Corp.

ARNELL, Robyn
2231 Camelback Rd.
Suite 400
Phoenix, AZ 85016

Serves As:
- PAC Treasurer, Starwood Hotels and Resorts Worldwide, Inc.

ARNETT, Bradley C.
P.O. Box 960
Cincinnati, OH 45201-0960
bradley.arnett@cinergy.com
Tel: (513) 287 - 3024

Serves As:
- Managing Director, Investor Relations and Assistant Treasurer, Cinergy Corp.

ARNETTE, Sandra
1710 H St. NW
Tenth Floor
Washington, DC 20006
Tel: (202) 392 - 1021
Fax:(202) 546 - 5111

Serves As:
- Media Relations, Verizon Washington D.C. Inc.

ARNOLD, Doug
777 E. Wisconsin Ave., 11th Floor
Milwaukee, WI 53202-5304
Tel: (414) 271 - 6755
Fax:(414) 347 - 3785

Serves As:
- Contact, Corporate Philanthropy, Sensient Technology Corp.

ARNOLD, Jennifer
1144 E. Market St.
Akron, OH 44316-0001
jennifer_arnold@goodyear.com
Tel: (330) 796 - 2121
Fax:(330) 796 - 8399

Serves As:
- Manager, Global Airship Public Relations, The Goodyear Tire & Rubber Company

ARNOLD, JoAnne S.
8000 S. Federal Way
Boise, ID 83707
Tel: (208) 368 - 4000
Fax:(208) 368 - 2536

Serves As:
- V. President, Human Resources, Micron Technology, Inc.

ARNOLD, Kay Kelly
425 W. Capitol Ave.
P.O. Box 551
Little Rock, AR 72203
karnold@entergy.com
Tel: (501) 377 - 3553

Serves As:
- V. President, System Governmental Affairs, Entergy Corp.

ARNOLD, Siobhan
222 Berkeley St.
Boston, MA 02116
siobhan_arnold@hmco.com
Tel: (617) 351 - 5000
Fax:(617) 351 - 1100

Serves As:
- Manager, Public Relations, Houghton Mifflin Co.

ARNOLD, Tara
P.O. Box 7600
Chicago, IL 60680-7600
tarnold@randmcnally.com
Tel: (847) 329 - 6850
Fax:(847) 673 - 0813

Serves As:
- Representative, Rand McNally

ARNSTEIN, Caren
500 Kendall St.
Cambridge, MA 02142
Tel: (617) 252 - 7500
Fax:(617) 374 - 7368

Serves As:
- V. President, Corporate Communications, Genzyme Corp.

ARNTSON, Kregg
121 SW Salmon St.
1WTC-0302
Portland, OR 97204
kregg_arntson@pgn.com
Tel: (503) 464 - 7693
Fax:(503) 464 - 2929

Serves As:
- Media Relations Representative, Portland General Electric Co.

ARNTZEN, Morten
511 Fifth Ave.
New York, NY 10017
Tel: (212) 953 - 4100
Fax:(212) 578 - 1832

Serves As:
- President and Chief Exec. Officer, Overseas Shipholding Group, Inc.

ARON, Doug S.
10000 Memorial Dr.
Suite 600
Houston, TX 77024-3341
Tel: (713) 688 - 9600
Fax:(713) 688 - 0616

Serves As:
- Director, Investor Relations, Frontier Oil Corp.

ARONSON, Bob
P.O. Box 35167
Houston, TX 77235
baronson@stagestoresinc.com
Tel: (713) 667 - 5601
Fax:(713) 295 - 5486
TF: (800) 324 - 3244

Serves As:
- V. President, Investor Relations, Stage Stores, Inc.

ARPEY, Gerard J.
P.O. Box 619616
Dallas-Fort Worth Airport, TX 75261
Tel: (817) 963 - 1234
Fax:(817) 967 - 2523

Serves As:
- Chairman, President and Chief Exec. Officer, AMR Corp.

ARREDONDO, Ramon
801 E. 86th Ave.
Merrillville, IN 46410
rarredondo@nisource.com
Tel: (219) 647 - 6237
Fax:(219) 647 - 6240
TF: (877) 647 - 5990

Serves As:
- Assistant to the Chairman and Director, Legislative Affairs, NiSource Inc.

ARRINGTON, John R.
P.O. Box 489
Bristol, CT 06011-0489
Tel: (860) 583 - 7070
Fax:(860) 589 - 3507

Serves As:
- Senior V. President, Human Resources, Barnes Group Inc.

ARRIOLA, Dennis V.
101 Ash St.
San Diego, CA 92101-3017
Tel: (619) 696 - 2000
Fax:(619) 696 - 1868
TF: (877) 736 - 7721

Serves As:
- V. President, Investor Relations and Corporate Communications, Sempra Energy

ARSENAULT, Helen
P.O. Box 75000
mc 3015
Detroit, MI 48275
Tel: (313) 222 - 2840
Fax:(313) 965 - 4648
TF: (800) 521 - 1190

Serves As:
- First V. President, Investor Relations, Comerica Incorporated

ARTHUR, Stephen C.
6211 N. Ann Arbor Rd.
P.O. Box 122
Dundee, MI 48131
steve.arthur@holcim.com
Tel: (734) 529 - 2411
Fax:(734) 529 - 5268
TF: (800) 854 - 4656

Registered Federal Lobbyist.
Serves As:
- Manager, Public Affairs, Holcim (US) Inc.

ARVESEN, Deborah J.
10250 Constellation Blvd.
Los Angeles, CA 90067-6241
Tel: (310) 449 - 3000
Fax:(310) 449 - 8757

Serves As:
- PAC Treasurer, Metro-Goldwyn-Mayer Inc.

ASBURY, Tad
One Marriott Dr.
Washington, DC 20058
Tel: (301) 380 - 7137
Fax:(301) 380 - 8957

Serves As:
- Director, Marriott Foundation for People with Disabilities, Marriott Internat'l, Inc.

ASERON, Alma
101 Montgomery St.
San Francisco, CA 94104
Tel: (415) 636 - 9748
Fax:(415) 636 - 5970
TF: (800) 435 - 4000

Serves As:
- Traffic Coordinator, Corporate Public Relations, The Charles Schwab Corp.

ASHER, Allison R.
745 Fifth Ave.
New York, NY 10151
allison.asher@primedia.com
Tel: (212) 745 - 0535
Fax:(212) 745 - 0131

Serves As:
- Manager, Corporate Communications, Primedia Inc.

ASHER, John
700 Central Ave.
Louisville, KY 40208
Tel: (502) 636 - 4400
Fax:(502) 636 - 4430
TF: (800) 283 - 3729

Serves As:
- V. President, Racing Communications, Churchill Downs, Inc.

ASHFORD, Ann F.
One Valmont Plaza
Omaha, NE 68154-5215
Tel: (402) 963 - 1000
Fax:(402) 963 - 1095

Serves As:
- V. President, Human Resources, Valmont Industries, Inc.

ASHKEN, Ian G. H.
555 Theodore Fremd Ave.
Rye, NY 10580-1455
Tel: (914) 967 - 9400
Fax:(914) 967 - 9405

Serves As:
- Chief Financial Office and Investor Relations Contact, Jarden Corp.

ASK, Tanya
P.O. Box 4309
Helena, MT 59604-4309
Tel: (406) 444 - 8975
Fax:(406) 447 - 8607
TF: (800) 447 - 7828

Serves As:
- Senior V. President, Government and Public Affairs, Blue Cross and Blue Shield of Montana

ASKANAS, Mark S.
4440 Rosewood Dr.
Pleasanton, CA 94588
Tel: (510) 505 - 4400
TF: (800) 945 - 7677

Serves As:
- Senior V. President, Human Resources and General Counsel, Ross Stores, Inc.

ASKREN, Stanley A.
P.O. Box 1109
Muscatine, IA 52761-0071
Tel: (563) 264 - 7400
Fax:(563) 264 - 7217

Serves As:
- Chairman and Chief Exec. Officer, HNI Corp.

ASLETT, Mark
50 Minuteman Rd.
Andover, MA 01810
Tel: (978) 684 - 1000
Fax:(978) 684 - 1658

Serves As:
- Chief Exec. Officer, Enterasys Networks

ASMAN, Laura Brightwell
P.O. Box 723040
Atlanta, GA 31139-0040
Tel: (770) 989 - 3023
Fax:(770) 989 - 3790

Serves As:
- Corporate Director, Public Affairs, Coca-Cola Enterprises Inc.

ASPAN, Rick
10500 W. 153rd St.
Orland Park, IL 60462
rick.aspan@andrew.com
Tel: (708) 349 - 5166
Fax:(708) 349 - 5444

Serves As:
- Director, Public Relations, Andrew Corp.

ASPLUNDH, Christopher
708 Blair Mill Rd.
Willow Grove, PA 19090
Tel: (215) 784 - 4200
Fax:(215) 784 - 4493

Serves As:
- Chairman and Chief Exec. Officer, Asplundh Tree Expert Co.

ASTON, Jr., Verlon R.
P.O. Box 650205
Dallas, TX 75265-0205
Tel: (972) 934 - 9227
Fax:(972) 855 - 3030
TF: (800) 382 - 8667

Serves As:
- V. President, Governmental and Public Affairs, Atmos Energy Corp.

ATENHAN, J. Todd
210 Interstate N. Pkwy., Suite 700
Atlanta, GA 30339
todd.atenhan@sonicautomotive.com
Fax:(770) 425 - 7740
TF: (888) 766 - 4218

Serves As:
- Manager, Investor Relations, Sonic Automotive, Inc.

ATKINS, Debbie
203 E. Main St.
Spartanburg, SC 29319-0001
Tel: (864) 597 - 8361
Fax:(864) 597 - 7538

Serves As:
- Director, Public Relations, Denny's Corp.

ATKINS, G. Lawrence
1130 Connecticut Ave. NW
Suite 500
Washington, DC 20036
Tel: (202) 463 - 7372

Serves As:
- Senior Director, Public Health Policy and Reimbursement, Schering-Plough Corporation

ATKINS, Trina
123 S. Front St.
Memphis, TN 38103
Tel: (901) 495 - 6500
Fax:(901) 495 - 8300

Serves As:
- Manager, Communications, AutoZone, Inc.

ATKINSON, Richard K.
P.O. Box 8171
Portland, OR 97207
Tel: (503) 228 - 9161
Fax:(503) 220 - 2722

Serves As:
- V. President and Chief Financial Officer, Pope & Talbot, Inc.

Responsibilities include investor relations.

ATKINSON, Robert C.
3885 Morse Rd.
Columbus, OH 43219
batkinson@limitedtoo.com
Tel: (614) 775 - 3739
Fax:(614) 479 - 3720

Serves As:
- Director, Investor Relations, Too, Inc.

Responsibilities include media relations.

ATLAS, Laurence D.
1421 S. Clark St.
Suite 810
Arlington, VA 22202
Tel: (703) 414 - 1057
Fax:(703) 414 - 1079

Registered Federal Lobbyist.
Serves As:
- V. President, Government Relations and Telecommunications, Loral Space & Communications

ATORCHA, L. Nicole
555 13th St. NW
Suite 600 West
Washington, DC 20004
nickiea@amgen.com
Tel: (202) 585 - 9610

Registered Federal Lobbyist.
Serves As:
- Manager, Federal Government Affairs, Amgen Inc.

ATTERIDGE, Susan
P.O. Box 227097
Dallas, TX 75222-7097
susan.atteridge@txu.com
Tel: (214) 812 - 8822

Serves As:
- Senior V. President and Chief Communications Officer, TXU

ATTWOOD, Dorothy
1401 I St. NW
Suite 1100
Washington, DC 20005
Tel: (202) 326 - 8836
Fax:(202) 289 - 3699

Serves As:
- Senior Vice President, Federal Regulatory Strategy, SBC Communications Inc.

ATWELL, Robert
1755 S. Clark St.
Suite 1100
Arlington, VA 22202
atwell@drs-esg.com
Tel: (703) 416 - 8000
Fax:(703) 416 - 8010

Serves As:
- V. President, Army Programs, DRS Technologies, Inc.

ATWOOD, Amy Tull
25 Research Dr.
Westborough, MA 01582
Tel: (508) 389 - 2627
Fax:(508) 389 - 3198

Serves As:
- Media Contact, Nat'l Grid USA

ATWOOD, Charles L.
P.O. Box 98905
Las Vegas, NV 89193-8905
catwood@harrahs.com
Tel: (702) 407 - 6000
Fax:(702) 407 - 6311

Serves As:
- Senior V. President and Chief Financial Officer, Harrah's Entertainment, Inc.

Responsibilities include investor relations.

AUGONE, Barbara
1101 Pennsylvania Ave. NW
Suite 400
Washington, DC 20004-2504
Tel: (202) 637 - 3800
Fax:(202) 637 - 3860

Serves As:
- Executive Director, Public Affairs, Textron Inc.

AUMILLER, Wendy L.
P.O. Box 960
Cincinnati, OH 45201-0960
Tel: (513) 421 - 9500

Serves As:
- PAC Treasurer, Cinergy Corp.

AUSDENMOORE, Janet
1014 Vine St.
Cincinnati, OH 45202-1100
Tel: (513) 762 - 4939
Fax:(513) 762 - 1295

Serves As:
- Foundation Administrator, The Kroger Co.

Ms. Ausdenmoore is also the Administrator of KroPAC.

AUSTELL, Theodore "Ted"
1200 Wilson Blvd.
Arlington, VA 22209-2305
Tel: (703) 465 - 3876
Fax:(703) 465 - 3018

Serves As:
- V. President, International Policy, The Boeing Co.

AUSTENFELD, Steve
P.O. Box 24305
Oakland, CA 94623-1305
Tel: (510) 271 - 2270
Fax:(510) 208 - 1546

Serves As:
- V. President, Investor Relations, The Clorox Co.

AUSTIN, Dennis G.
870 Winter St.
Waltham, MA 02451
dennis_g_austin@raytheon.com
Tel: (781) 522 - 3000

Serves As:
- Director, State Government Relations, Raytheon Co.

AUSTIN, Jesse J.
P.O. Box 8050
Wisconsin Rapids, WI 54495-8050
Tel: (715) 422 - 1573
Fax:(715) 422 - 3882

Serves As:
- Manager, Communications, Stora Enso North America

AUSTIN, Susan
50606 AXP Financial Center
Minneapolis, MN 55474
susan.2.austin@ameriprise.com
Tel: (612) 671 - 1359
Fax:(612) 671 - 5112
TF: (800) 328 - 8300

Serves As:
- Manager, Public Affairs and Communications, Ameriprise Financial Services Inc.

AUSTIN, Susan G.
Three Penn Plaza East
PP-15V
Newark, NJ 07105-2200
Tel: (973) 466 - 8332
Fax:(973) 466 - 8762

Serves As:
- Contact Horizon Foundation, Horizon Blue Cross Blue Shield of New Jersey

AUSTIN, Tracy L.
655 Third Ave.
New York, NY 10017
Tel: (212) 605 - 2000
Fax:(212) 605 - 1908

Serves As:
- Exec. Director, MIC Foundation, Mitsubishi International Corporation

AUSURA, Maureen K.
P.O. Box 1470
Decatur, IL 62525
Tel: (217) 424 - 5200
Fax:(217) 424 - 5839

Serves As:
- V. President, Human Resources, Archer Daniels Midland Co. (ADM)

AVEDON, Ph.D., Marcia
P.O. Box 100
Whitehouse Station, NJ 08889-0100
Tel: (908) 423 - 5144
Fax:(908) 735 - 1247
TF: (800) 423 - 1000

Serves As:
- Senior V. President, Human Resources, Merck & Co., Inc.

AVERETT, Claire H.
One Nu Skin Plaza
75 W. Center St.
Provo, UT 84601
Tel: (801) 345 - 1000
Fax:(801) 345 - 2799

Serves As:
- V. President, Human Resources, Nu Skin Enterprises

AVERY, David
1014 Vine St.
Cincinnati, OH 45202-1100
Tel: (513) 762 - 4270
Fax:(513) 762 - 4197

Serves As:
- V. President, Human Resources, The Kroger Co.

AVERY, David
One Allied Dr.
Little Rock, AR 72202
david.avery@alltel.com
Tel: (501) 905 - 5876
Fax:(501) 905 - 6018

Serves As:
- Staff Manager, Corporate Communications, ALLTEL

AVERY, Elizabeth
101 Constitution Ave. NW
Suite 900
Washington, DC 20001
Tel: (202) 742 - 4408
Fax:(202) 742 - 4422

Serves As:
- V. President, International Government Relations, PepsiCo, Inc.

AVETISSIAN, Vic
1000 Wilson Blvd., Suite 2300
Arlington, VA 22209
Tel: (703) 875 - 8400

Registered Federal Lobbyist.
Serves As:
- Representative, Northrop Grumman Corp.

AVRAM, Lloyd
1155 Perimeter Center West
Atlanta, GA 30338
Tel: (678) 579 - 7531
Fax:(678) 579 - 5001

Serves As:
- Director, Corporate Communications, Mirant Corp.

AXELROD, Beth
2145 Hamilton Ave.
San Jose, CA 95125
Tel: (408) 558 - 7400
Fax:(408) 558 - 7401
TF: (800) 322 - 9266

Serves As:
- Senior V. President, Human Resources, eBay, Inc.

AYER, Ramani
Hartford Plaza
Hartford, CT 06115
rayer@thehartford.com
Tel: (860) 547 - 5000
Fax:(860) 547 - 3799

Serves As:
- Chairman and Chief Exec. Officer, The Hartford Financial Services Group Inc.

AYER, William S.
P.O. Box 68900
Seattle, WA 98168-0947
Tel: (206) 433 - 3200
Fax:(206) 431 - 5558

Serves As:
- Chairman, President and Chief Exec. Officer, Alaska Air Group, Inc.

AYERS, Mark
P.O. Box 39
Newton, IA 50208-0039
Tel: (641) 792 - 7000
Fax:(641) 787 - 8376

Serves As:
- PAC Treasurer, Maytag Corp.

AYLWARD, Claire M.
Two N. Ninth St.
TW14
Allentown, PA 18101-1179
cmaylward@pplweb.com
Tel: (610) 774 - 5804
Fax:(610) 774 - 5281
TF: (800) 345 - 3085

Serves As:
- Manager, Investor Services, PPL Corp.

AYLWARD, Rayna
1560 Wilson Blvd.
Suite 1175
Suite 1150
Arlington, VA 22209
rayna.aylward@meus.mea.com
Tel: (703) 276 - 8240
Fax:(703) 276 - 8260

Serves As:
- Exec. Director, Mitsubishi Electric America Foundation, Mitsubishi Electric & Electronics USA

AYOTTE, Ross
5005 E. McDowell Rd.
Phoenix, AZ 85008
ross.ayotte@onsemi.com
Tel: (602) 244 - 5978
Fax:(602) 244 - 4830

Serves As:
- Director, Marketing Communications, ON Semiconductor Corp.

AZAR, Barbara
3401 N.W. 63rd St
Oklahoma City, Ok 73116
bazar@bcbsok.com
Tel: (405) 841 - 9597
Fax:(405) 841 - 9663

Serves As:
- Public Affairs, BlueCross BlueShield of Oklahoma

AZARE, Monica
1300 I St. NW
Suite 400 West
Washington, DC 20005
Tel: (202) 589 - 3781
Fax:(202) 589 - 3750

Registered Federal Lobbyist.
Serves As:
- Director, House Relations, Verizon Wireless

BAAB, Carl F.
P.O. Box 26666
Richmond, VA 23261-6666
Carl_Baab@dom.com
Tel: (804) 771 - 4557

Serves As:
- Director, Media Relations and Internet Communications, Dominion Resources, Inc.

BAADE, Ph.D., Roberta C.
5770 Fleet St.
Carlsbad, CA 92008
Tel: (760) 696 - 4000
Fax:(760) 696 - 4009
TF: (800) 597 - 5366

Serves As:
- V. President, Human Resources, Jenny Craig, Inc.

BABB, Henry C.
2201 Miller Rd.
Wilson, NC 27893
Tel: (252) 237 - 1106
Fax:(252) 237 - 0018

Serves As:
- Senior V. President, Chief Legal Officer and Secretary, Alliance One Internat'l Inc.

Responsibilities include public affairs and media relations.

BABB, Jr., Ralph W.
P.O. Box 75000
Detroit, MI 48275
Tel: (313) 222 - 6918
Fax:(313) 964 - 0638
TF: (800) 521 - 1190

Serves As:
- Chairman, President and Chief Exec. Officer, Comerica Incorporated

BABBITT, Edward J.
400 Broadway
Cincinnati, OH 45202
Tel: (513) 629 - 1464
Fax:(513) 629 - 1050
TF: (800) 936 - 1212

Serves As:
- V. President, Government Relations and Senior Counsel, Western and Southern Life Insurance Co.

BABBITT, Ginny
1500 Crittenden Lane
Mountain View, CA 94043
Tel: (650) 933 - 4519
Fax:(650) 933 - 0283

Serves As:
• Product Public Relations Contact, SGI

BABINGTON, Catherine V.
100 Abbott Park Rd.
Dept. 383, AP6D
Abbott Park, IL 60064-3500
Tel: (847) 937 - 3931

Serves As:
• V. President, Public Affairs, Abbott Laboratories

BABYAK, Gregory R.
1399 New York Ave. NW
11th Floor
Washington, DC 20005-4711
Tel: (202) 624 - 1952
Fax:(202) 624 - 1300

Registered Federal Lobbyist.
Serves As:
• Counsel, Bloomberg L.P.

BACAL, Michael
281 Tresser Blvd.
Two Stamford Plaza
Stamford, CT 06901-3238
michael.bacal@hexcel.com
Tel: (203) 969 - 0666
Ext: 426
Fax:(203) 358 - 3993

Serves As:
• Communications and Investor Relations Manager, Hexcel Corp.

BACHELLER, Burt P.
1200 Wilson Blvd.
Arlington, VA 22209-2305
Tel: (703) 465 - 3500

Serves As:
• Director, International Programs, The Boeing Co.

BACHENHEIMER, Cara C.
600 Cameron St.
Suite 402
Alexandria, VA 22314
cbachenheimer@invacare.com
Tel: (440) 329 - 6226

Registered Federal Lobbyist.
Serves As:
• V. President, Government Relations, Invacare Corp.

BACHMAN, Corliss
7660 Imperial Way
Allentown, PA 18195-1040
cbachman@lehighcement.com
Tel: (610) 366 - 4600
Fax:(610) 366 - 4684
TF: (800) 523 - 5488

Serves As:
• Coordinator, Communications, Lehigh Cement Company

BACON, Kevin
2400 Farmers Dr.
Columbus, OH 43235
Tel: (614) 764 - 7266

Serves As:
• Legislative Representative, (Farmers Insurance Group of Companies), Farmers Group, Inc.

BADER, Tim
P.O. Box 97034
Bellevue, WA 98009-9734
Tel: (425) 452 - 1234
Fax:(425) 462 - 3301

Serves As:
• Media Contact, Puget Sound Energy

BADERTSCHER, Maribeth
Strawberry Lane
Orrville, OH 44667-0280
Tel: (330) 682 - 3000
Fax:(330) 684 - 6410
TF: (888) 550 - 9555

Serves As:
• Manager, Community Initiatives, The J. M. Smucker Company
Responsibilities include corporate philanthropy.

BAERG, Bill
P.O. Box 2511
Houston, TX 77252-2511
Tel: (713) 420 - 2906
Fax:(713) 420 - 4993

Serves As:
• Manager, Investor Relations, El Paso Corp.

BAEZ, Diana
Three World Financial Center
200 Vesey St.
New York, NY 10285
Tel: (212) 640 - 2000

Serves As:
• Coordinator, Corporate and Financial Public Relations, American Express Co.

BAFFER, Barbara
1634 I St. NW, Suite 600
Washington, DC 20006-4083
barbara.baffer@ericsson.com
Tel: (202) 783 - 2200
Fax:(202) 783 - 2206

Registered Federal Lobbyist.
Serves As:
• Manager, Public Affairs and Regulation, Ericsson Inc.

BAGBY, Robert L.
One N. Jefferson Ave.
St. Louis, MO 63103
Tel: (314) 955 - 3000
Fax:(314) 955 - 5913
TF: (877) 835 - 7877

Serves As:
• Chairman and Chief Exec. Officer, A. G. Edwards, Inc.

BAGGER, Richard
235 E. 42nd St.
New York, NY 10017-5755
Tel: (212) 573 - 2323
Fax:(212) 573 - 1853

Registered Federal Lobbyist.
Serves As:
• Senior V. President, Government Relations and Public Affairs, Pfizer Inc.

BAGGS, David
500 Water St.
C110
Jacksonville, FL 32203
david_baggs@csx.com
Tel: (904) 359 - 4812
Fax:(904) 359 - 1899

Serves As:
• Assistant V. President, Treasury and Investor Relations, CSX Corp.

BAGLEY, James W.
4650 Cushing Pkwy.
Fremont, CA 94538-6470
Tel: (510) 572 - 0200
Fax:(510) 572 - 6454

Serves As:
• Chairman of the Board, Lam Research Corp.

BAGLEY, John F. "Jack"
901 D St. SW
Suite 900
Washington, DC 20024
Tel: (202) 479 - 0500
Fax:(202) 646 - 5271

Registered Federal Lobbyist.
Serves As:
• V. President, External Relations, Battelle

BAGLIEN, Brent A.
1627 I St. NW, Suite 950
Washington, DC 20006
Tel: (202) 223 - 5115
Fax:(202) 223 - 5118

Registered Federal Lobbyist.
Serves As:
• V. President, Government Affairs, ConAgra Foods, Inc.

BAHNSEN, Lynn B.
1440 Olympic Dr.
Athens, GA 30608-8001
Tel: (706) 353 - 4434

Serves As:
• Regional Director, Government Affairs, Johnson & Johnson

BAIER, Jennifer
1600 E. St. Andrews Pl.
Santa Ana, CA 92705
jennifer.baier@ingrammicro.com
Tel: (714) 382 - 2692
Fax:(714) 566 - 7900

Serves As:
• Director, Public Relations, Ingram Micro, Inc.

BAILEY, Antoinette
World Headquarters
100 N. Riverside
Chicago, IL 60606-1596
Tel: (312) 544 - 2000
Fax:(312) 544 - 2304

Serves As:
• V. President, Community and Education Relations, The Boeing Co.

BAILEY, Cindy
P.O. Box 196612
Anchorage, AK 99519-6612
Tel: (907) 564 - 5537
Fax:(907) 564 - 4124

Serves As:
• Associate Director, Local Government Affairs, (BP Exploration - Alaska, Inc.), BP

BAILEY, II, Clark T.
800 N. Harvey
Room 399
Oklahoma City, OK 73102
Tel: (405) 291 - 5855
Fax:(405) 236 - 7340

Serves As:
• Manager, External Affairs, SBC Communications Inc.

BAILEY, Donna
607 E. Adams St.
Springfield, IL 62739
Tel: (217) 535 - 5025
Fax:(217) 535 - 5095

Serves As:
• Legislative and Community Relations Supervisor, Contact, Ameren Federal Political Action Committee, Ameren Corp.

BAILEY, Gerald E.
One Carrier Pl.
Farmington, CT 06034-4015
gerald.bailey@carrier.utc.com
Tel: (860) 674 - 3398
Fax:(860) 674 - 3193

Serves As:
• V. President, Environmental Health and Safety, Carrier Corp.

BAILEY, James R. "Tres"
575 Seventh St. NW
Terrell Bldg.
Washington, DC 20004
Tel: (202) 737 - 5523
Fax:(202) 737 - 6069

Serves As:
- Representative, Wal-Mart Stores

BAILEY, Joel
801 Pennsylvania Ave. NW
Suite 310
Washington, DC 20004
Tel: (202) 434 - 8150
Fax:(202) 434 - 8156

Registered Federal Lobbyist.
Serves As:
- Director, Federal Governmental Affairs, FirstEnergy Corp.

BAILEY, Joette
P.O. Box 5000
Broomfield, CO 80038-5000
jbailey@ball.com
Tel: (303) 469 - 5511
Fax:(303) 460 - 5256

Serves As:
- Director, Environmental Services, Ball Corp.

BAILEY, Koby A.
P.O. Box 190
Aurora, IL 60507-0190
kbailey@nicor.com
Tel: (630) 983 - 8676
Ext: 3527
Fax:(630) 548 - 3574

Serves As:
- Director, Regulatory Affairs, (NICOR Gas), Nicor, Inc.

BAILEY, Mark
100 S. Biscayne Blvd., Suite 1500
Miami, FL 33131
mark.bailey@vitas.com
Tel: (305) 374 - 4143
Fax:(305) 350 - 6970

Serves As:
- Senior Director, Community and Public Affairs, VITAS Healthcare Corporation

BAILEY, Michael
5501 American Blvd. West
Minneapolis, MN 55437
Tel: (952) 830 - 3300

Serves As:
- Chief Exec. Officer, Jostens, Inc.

BAILEY, S. Graham
1133 S.W. Topeka Blvd.
MS 510
Topeka, KS 66629
graham.bailey@bcbsks.com
Tel: (785) 291 - 8846
Fax:(785) 291 - 7664

Serves As:
- V. President, Corporate Communications and Public Relations, Blue Cross and Blue Shield of Kansas, Inc.

BAILEY, Vernon
38 Fountain Square
Cincinnati, OH 45263
Tel: (513) 579 - 5300
Fax:(513) 579 - 5226
TF: (800) 972 - 3030

Serves As:
- PAC Treasurer, Fifth Third Bancorp.

BAILY, Dori Sera
5929 College Ave.
Oakland, CA 94618
dsbaily@dreyers.com
Tel: (510) 601 - 4241
Fax:(510) 601 - 4400

Serves As:
- Director, Corporate Communications, Dreyer's Grand Ice Cream Holdings, Inc.

BAIN, Amy
615 J.B. Hunt Corporate Dr.
P.O. Box 130
Lowell, AR 72745
Tel: (479) 820 - 8111
Fax:(479) 820 - 8397
TF: (800) 643 - 3622

Serves As:
- Exec. Assistant to the President and Chief Exec. Officer, J. B. Hunt Transport Services, Inc.

Responsibilities include corporate contributions.

BAIN, Mark
7575 Fulton St. East
M/S 49-2N
Ada, MI 49355-0001
Tel: (616) 787 - 8636
Fax:(616) 787 - 5669

Serves As:
- V. President, Corporate Communications, Alticor Inc.

BAIRD, Charles F.
901 E. 233rd St.
Carson, CA 90745-6204
Tel: (310) 835 - 8400
Fax:(310) 952 - 7760

Serves As:
- Chairman of the Board, Leiner Health Products, Inc.

BAIRD, Patrick S.
1111 N. Charles St.
Baltimore, MD 21201
Tel: (410) 576 - 4501
Fax:(410) 374 - 8685

Serves As:
- President and Chief Exec. Officer, AEGON USA, Inc.

BAJENSKI, Richard J.
P.O. Box 4446
Houston, TX 77210-4446
bajenski@cooperindustries.com
Tel: (713) 209 - 8610
Fax:(713) 209 - 8981

Serves As:
- V. President, Investor Relations and Public Affairs, Cooper Industries

BAKER, David A.
1700 Lincoln St.
Denver, CO 80203
Tel: (303) 863 - 7414

Serves As:
- V. President, Environmental Affairs, Newmont Mining Corp.

BAKER, Dennis W.
One Salem Lake Dr.
Long Grove, IL 60047
dbaker@cfindustries.com
Tel: (847) 438 - 9500
Fax:(847) 438 - 0211

Serves As:
- Treasurer and Contact, C F Industries, Inc. PAC, C F Industries, Inc.

BAKER, Douglas
Ecolab Center
370 N. Wabasha St.
St. Paul, MN 55102
Tel: (651) 293 - 2233
Fax:(651) 225 - 2092

Serves As:
- Chief Exec. Officer, Ecolab Inc.

BAKER, Edward L.
P.O. Box 4667
Jacksonville, FL 32201
Tel: (904) 355 - 1781
Fax:(904) 355 - 0817

Serves As:
- Chairman of the Board, Florida Rock Industries, Inc.

BAKER, Eileen
103 JFK Pkwy.
Short Hills, NJ 07078
bakere@dnb.com
Tel: (973) 921 - 5500

Serves As:
- Manager, The Dun & Bradstreet Corp. Foundation, The Dun & Bradstreet Corp.

BAKER, Gail
121 SW Salmon St.
1WTZ0302
Portland, OR 97204
gail_baker@pgn.com
Tel: (503) 464 - 8693
Fax:(503) 464 - 2929
TF: (800) 542 - 8818

Serves As:
- Manager, Corporate Communications and Community Affairs, Portland General Electric Co.

BAKER, II, John D.
P.O. Box 4667
Jacksonville, FL 32201
Tel: (904) 355 - 1781
Fax:(904) 355 - 0817

Serves As:
- Chief Exec. Officer, Florida Rock Industries, Inc.

BAKER, Kate
P.O. Box 13466
Phoenix, AZ 85002-3466
Tel: (602) 864 - 4616
Fax:(602) 864 - 4242
TF: (800) 232 - 2345

Serves As:
- Contact, Healthy Government Committee, Blue Cross and Blue Shield of Arizona

BAKER, Leighann
One Reynolds Way
Kettering, OH 45430
leighann_baker@reyrey.com
Tel: (937) 485 - 1266
Fax:(937) 485 - 0975

Serves As:
- V. President, Human Resources, Reynolds and Reynolds Co.

BAKER, Lisa
19 N. Main St.
Wilkes-Barre, PA 18711-0302
lisa.baker@bcnepa.com
Tel: (570) 200 - 6305
Fax:(570) 200 - 6699

Serves As:
- Exec. Director, Foundation for Funding Community-Based Health Initiatives, Blue Cross of Northeastern Pennsylvania

BAKER, M. Bradley
2090 Florence Ave.
Cincinnati, OH 45206
Tel: (513) 487 - 5000
Fax:(513) 487 - 5057

Serves As:
- V. President, Human Resources, Milacron Inc.

BAKER, Maxine B.
8200 Jones Branch Dr.
A40
McLean, VA 22102
maxine_baker@freddiemac.com
Tel: (703) 918 - 8840
Fax:(703) 918 - 8895
TF: (800) 373 - 3343

Serves As:
- V. President, Community Relations; and President and Chief Exec. Officer, Freddie Mac Foundation, Freddie Mac

BAKER, Patricia A.
Avid Technology Park
One Park West
Tewksbury, MA 01876
Tel: (978) 640 - 6789
Fax:(978) 640 - 1366

Serves As:
- V. President, Human Resources, Avid Technology, Inc.

BAKER, Paul D.
170 Crossways Park Dr.
Woodbury, NY 11797
paul_baker@comverse.com
Tel: (516) 677 - 7226
Fax:(516) 677 - 7323

Serves As:
- V. President, Corporate Marketing and Communications, Comverse Technology, Inc.

Responsibilities also include investor relations.

BAKER, Jr., Phillips S.
6500 N. Mineral Dr., Suite 200
Coeur d'Alene, ID 83815-9408
Tel: (208) 769 - 4100
Fax:(208) 769 - 7612

Serves As:
- President and Chief Exec. Officer, Hecla Mining Co.

BAKER, Steve
P.O. Box 1624
Alpharetta, GA 30009-9934
Fax:(678) 762 - 2315
TF: (800) 275 - 3004

Serves As:
- Manager, Media and Marketing, Colonial Pipeline Co.

BAKO, Jennifer
5995 Mayfair Rd.
P.O. Box 3077
North Canton, OH 44720-8077
Tel: (330) 490 - 4000
Fax:(330) 490 - 3794

Serves As:
- Senior Specialist, Investor Relations and Communications, Diebold, Inc.

BALARK, Sam
225 W. Randolph St.
27 C
Chicago, IL 60606
Tel: (312) 727 - 7572
Fax:(312) 727 - 3722
TF: (800) 327 - 9346

Serves As:
- Area Manager, External Affairs, SBC Illinois

BALASIA, Steve
201 N. Washington Square, Suite 920
Lansing, MI 48933
Tel: (517) 334 - 3404
Fax:(517) 334 - 3429

Serves As:
- V. President, Government Affairs, SBC Michigan

BALBIERZ, Steve
3255 U.S. 41 West
Marquette, MI 49855
Tel: (906) 225 - 6700
Fax:(906) 225 - 0599

Serves As:
- Manager, External Affairs, SBC Michigan

BALDERSON, James C.
5100 E. Virginia Beach Blvd.
Norfolk, VA 23502

Serves As:
- Treasurer, Virginia Natural Gas Committee for Effective Government, AGL Resources, Inc.

BALDINO, Jr., Ph.D., Frank
41 Moores Rd.
Frazer, PA 19355
Tel: (610) 344 - 0200
Fax:(610) 344 - 6590

Serves As:
- Chairman and Chief Exec. Officer, Cephalon, Inc.

BALDONADO, Andrew
15800 Roscoe Blvd.
Van Nuys, CA 91406-1379
Tel: (818) 908 - 5507
Fax:(818) 908 - 5695

Serves As:
- Region V. President, Government Affairs, Anheuser-Busch Cos., Inc.

BALDRIDGE, Steve
730 Milford Rd.
Route 101A
Merrimack, NH 03054-4631
Tel: (603) 683 - 2000
Fax:(603) 683 - 2041

Serves As:
- V. President, Finance and Corporate Controller, PC Connection, Inc.

Responsibilities include public affairs.

BALDWIN, Laura
5800 Tennyson Pkwy.
Plano, TX 75024
Tel: (214) 473 - 7000
Ext: 3969

Serves As:
- Director, Finance and Investor Relations, Triad Hospitals, Inc.

BALDWIN, Patricia
3030 LBJ Frwy.
Suite 700
Dallas, TX 75234
Tel: (972) 243 - 6191
Fax:(972) 888 - 7555

Serves As:
- V. President, Corporate Communications, ClubCorp Internat'l Inc.

BALDWIN, III, W. Preston
100 W. Putnam Ave.
Greenwich, CT 06830
Tel: (203) 622 - 3364
Fax:(203) 622 - 3315

Serves As:
- V. President, State Government Relations, UST Inc.

BALES, Thom
100 Phoenix Dr.
Ann Arbor, MI 48108
Tel: (734) 477 - 1100
Fax:(734) 477 - 1517

Serves As:
- Administrator, Borders Group Foundation, Borders Group, Inc.

BALL, Mary
5159 Federal Blvd.
San Diego, CA 92105
mary.ball@cox.com
Tel: (619) 266 - 5203
Fax:(619) 266 - 5555

Serves As:
- V. President, Government and Community Relations, Cox Enterprises, Inc.

BALL, Patricia G.
5800 Tennyson Pkwy.
Plano, TX 75024
Tel: (214) 473 - 7000
Ext: 3752

Serves As:
- V. President, Marketing and Public Affairs, Triad Hospitals, Inc.

BALL, Russell
1700 Lincoln St.
Denver, CO 80203
Tel: (303) 863 - 7414
Fax:(303) 837 - 5837

Serves As:
- Group Exec., Investor Relations, Newmont Mining Corp.

BALLABON, Jeff
745 Fifth Ave.
New York, NY 10151
Tel: (212) 745 - 1283
Fax:(212) 745 - 0121

Registered Federal Lobbyist.
Serves As:
- Exec. V. President, Network Affairs, Primedia Inc.

BALLARD, Peggy
5030 Sugarloaf Pkwy.
Lawrenceville, GA 30042-2869
peggy.ballard@sciatl.com
Tel: (770) 236 - 7871
Fax:(770) 236 - 2291
TF: (800) 236 - 5000

Serves As:
- V. President, Strategic Communications, Scientific-Atlanta, Inc.

BALLAST, Brad
135 S. LaSalle St.
Chicago, IL 60603
Tel: (312) 904 - 2000
Fax:(312) 904 - 6521

Serves As:
- Contact, Corporate Contributions, LaSalle Bank N.A.

BALLINGER, Michael
113 King St.
Armonk, NY 10504
michael.ballinger@mbia.com
Tel: (914) 765 - 3893
Fax:(914) 765 - 3163

Serves As:
- Director, Corporate Communications, MBIA, Inc.

BALLMER, Steven A.
One Microsoft Way
Redmond, WA 98052-6399
Tel: (425) 882 - 8080
Fax:(425) 936 - 7329

Serves As:
- Chief Exec. Officer, Microsoft Corporation

BALLOU, Roger H.
1717 Arch St.
35th Floor
Philadelphia, PA 19103-2768
Tel: (215) 569 - 2200
Fax:(215) 569 - 1452

Serves As:
- President and Chief Exec. Officer, CDI Corp.

BALLTON, Carl
445 S. Figueroa St.
Los Angeles, CA 90071-1655
carl.ballton@uboc.com
Tel: (213) 236 - 4140
Fax:(213) 236 - 6982

Serves As:
- President, Union Bank of California Foundation, Union Bank of California

BALMORIS, Mike
1401 I St. NW
Suite 1100
Washington, DC 20005
michael.balmoris@sbc.com
Tel: (202) 326 - 8800
Fax:(202) 408 - 4796

Serves As:
• Press Contact, Federal Regulatory/Legislation, SBC Communications Inc.

BALMUTH, Michael
4440 Rosewood Dr.
Pleasanton, CA 94588
Tel: (510) 505 - 4400
TF: (800) 945 - 7677

Serves As:
• V. Chairman and Chief Exec. Officer, Ross Stores, Inc.

BALTA, Wayne S.
Route 100
Somers, NY 10589
Tel: (914) 766 - 2720
Fax:(914) 766 - 2824

Serves As:
• Director, Corporate Environmental Programs, Internat'l Business Machines Corp. (IBM)

BALY, Aline
290 Concord Rd.
Billerica, MA 01821
Tel: (978) 715 - 1051
Fax:(978) 715 - 1393
TF: (800) 645 - 5476

Serves As:
• Corporate Communications Coordinator, Millipore Corp.

BAME, Tracy L.
One N. Central Ave.
Phoenix, AZ 85004-3014
tbame@phelpsdodge.com
Tel: (602) 366 - 8018
Fax:(602) 234 - 8082
TF: (800) 528 - 1182

Serves As:
• Manager, Community Affairs, Phelps Dodge Corp.
Responsibilities include corporate philanthropy.

BAN, Woodrow W.
33587 Walker Rd.
Avon Lake, OH 44093-0175
woodrow.ban@polyone.com
Tel: (440) 930 - 1000
Fax:(440) 930 - 1750

Serves As:
• PAC Contact, PolyOne Corp.

BANCROFT, Virginia D. "Gina"
1331 Pennsylvania Ave. NW
Suite 1300 North
Washington, DC 20004
gina.bancroft@eds.com
Tel: (202) 637 - 6702
Fax:(202) 637 - 6759

Registered Federal Lobbyist.
Serves As:
• PAC Director; Director, Global Government Affairs, EDS Corp.

BANDLER, Donald
1300 I St. NW
Suite 450 East
Washington, DC 20005-7211
Tel: (202) 783 - 2460
Fax:(202) 789 - 1819

Serves As:
• Senior V. President, Government Affairs, Monsanto Co.

BANDY, Jo Etta
One First American Way
Santa Ana, CA 92707
Tel: (714) 800 - 3298
Fax:(714) 800 - 4790

Serves As:
• V. President, Corporate Communications, The First American Corp.

BANE, Lonnie D.
5847 San Felipe, Suite 3300
Houston, TX 77057
Tel: (713) 789 - 1400
Fax:(713) 789 - 1430

Serves As:
• V. President, Human Resources, Pride Internat'l, Inc.

BANKER, Elizabeth
2000 Pennsylvania Ave. NW
Suite 4200
Washington, DC 20006
Tel: (202) 887 - 6932
Fax:(202) 887 - 6933

Serves As:
• Associate General Counsel, Yahoo! Inc.

BANKS, Jerry
P.O. Box 6676
Asheville, NC 28816
jbanks@ingles-markets.com
Tel: (828) 669 - 2941
Fax:(828) 669 - 3667

Serves As:
• Director, Human Resources, Ingles Markets, Inc.

BANKS, John H.
Four Irving Pl.
New York, NY 10003
Tel: (212) 460 - 2706
Fax:(212) 460 - 3730

Serves As:
• V. President, Government Relations, Consolidated Edison Co. of New York, Inc.

BANKS, Jonathan
1133 21st St. NW
Suite 900
Washington, DC 20036
jonathan.banks@bellsouth.com
Tel: (202) 463 - 4182
Fax:(202) 463 - 4141

Serves As:
• V. President, Exec. and Regulatory Affairs - BellSouth D.C., BellSouth Corp.

BANKS, Katreice
1401 I St. NW
Suite 1100
Washington, DC 20005
Tel: (202) 326 - 8800
Fax:(202) 408 - 4796

Registered Federal Lobbyist.
Serves As:
• Exec. Director, Federal Relations, SBC Communications Inc.

BANKS, M.D., Mark W.
3535 Blue Cross Rd.
Eagan, MN 55122--115
Tel: (651) 662 - 8000
TF: (800) 382 - 2000

Serves As:
• President and Chief Exec. Officer, Blue Cross and Blue Shield of Minnesota

BANKS, Pamela F.
3900 Wisconsin Ave. NW
Washington, DC 20016
pamela_f_banks@fanniemae.com
Tel: (202) 752 - 7000
Fax:(202) 752 - 6099

Serves As:
• V. President, Regulatory Compliance, Fannie Mae

BANKS, Sylvia
1007 Market St.
D-11046
Wilmington, DE 19898
Tel: (302) 773 - 2731
Fax:(302) 773 - 2919
TF: (800) 441 - 7515

Serves As:
• Team Leader, Corporate Contributions and Community Affairs, DuPont

BANMILLER, David A.
Two Waterfront Plaza
Suite 500
Honolulu, HI 96813
Tel: (808) 539 - 5909
Fax:(808) 836 - 0303

Serves As:
• President and Chief Exec. Officer, Aloha Airlines, Inc.

BANNISTER, Ross
TECO Plaza
702 N. Franklin St.
Tampa, FL 33602
Tel: (813) 228 - 4111
Fax:(813) 228 - 4811

Serves As:
• Media Contact, TECO Energy, Inc./Tampa Electric Co.

BANTHAM, Jim W.
P.O. Box 660237
Dallas, TX 75266-0237
banthamj@citi.com
Tel: (972) 652 - 4626

Serves As:
• V. President, Central Region - State and Local Government Relations, Citigroup, Inc.

BANWART, Sidney C.
100 NE Adams St.
Peoria, IL 61629-1465
Tel: (309) 675 - 5222
Fax:(309) 675 - 5330

Serves As:
• V. President, Human Services Division, Caterpillar Inc.

BAPTIE, Colin
900 Metro Center Blvd.
Foster City, CA 94404-2172
Tel: (650) 432 - 4631
Fax:(650) 432 - 3631

Serves As:
• Media Contact, Visa U.S.A. Inc.

BAPTIE, Ms. Tillie J.
500 S. Buena Vista St.
Burbank, CA 91521
tillie.baptie@corp.disney.com
Tel: (818) 560 - 5025
Fax:(818) 560 - 1930

Serves As:
• V. President, Corporate Relations, The Walt Disney Company

BAPTISTA, Samuel J.
401 Ninth St., NW, Suite 650
Washington, DC 20004
sam.baptista@morganstanley.com
Tel: (202) 654 - 2000
Fax:(202) 654 - 2100

Registered Federal Lobbyist.
Serves As:
• Managing Director, Governmental Affairs, Morgan Stanley

BARAGER, Douglas W.
1100 Wilson Blvd.
Suite 1500
Arlington, VA 22209
Tel: (703) 841 - 5700
Fax:(703) 841 - 5792

Registered Federal Lobbyist.
Serves As:
- Senior Manager, Government Relations, Raytheon Co.

BARANSKI, Susan Castiglione
P.O. Box 1624
Alpharetta, GA 30009-9934
Tel: (678) 762 - 2211
Fax:(678) 762 - 2883
TF: (800) 275 - 3004

Serves As:
- Senior Manager, Corporate and Public Affairs, Colonial Pipeline Co.

BARBARA, Thomas P.
Four Taft Ct.
Rockville, MD 20850
Tel: (301) 762 - 8205
Fax:(301) 838 - 5682

Serves As:
- President and Chief Exec. Officer- Mid-Atlantic, Mid Atlantic Medical Services Inc.

BARBARINO, Leslie
175 W. Jackson Blvd.
20th Floor
Chicago, IL 60604
Tel: (312) 856 - 0001
Fax:(312) 565 - 4719

Serves As:
- Director, Human Resources, Grant Thornton LLP

BARBER, Dennis
P.O. Box 2286
Houston, TX 77252-2286
dbarber@reliant.com
Tel: (713) 497 - 3042
Fax:(713) 488 - 5925
TF: (866) 872 - 6656

Serves As:
- Director, Investor Relations, Reliant Resources

BARBER, Roger Lee
The Scoular Bldg.
2027 Dodge St.
Omaha, NE 68102
rbarber@scoular.com
Tel: (402) 342 - 3500
Fax:(402) 342 - 5568
TF: (800) 488 - 3500

Serves As:
- Chief Financial Officer, Treasurer, Scoular Co. Fund for Effective Government, The Scoular Co.

BARBER, Willie
P.O. Box 2020
Springdale, AR 72765-2020
willie.barber@tyson.com
Tel: (479) 290 - 4000
Fax:(479) 290 - 7930
TF: (800) 643 - 3410

Serves As:
- Consumer Relations Manager, Tyson Foods, Inc.

BARCKLEY, Becky
414 Union St.
Suite 2000
Nashville, TN 37219
Tel: (615) 986 - 5600

Serves As:
- Investor Relations Contact, Louisiana-Pacific Corporation

BARCLAY, Betsy
1101 Pennsylvania Ave. NW
Sixth Floor
Washington, DC 20004
bbarclay@etrade.com
Tel: (202) 756 - 7750
Fax:(202) 756 - 7545

Registered Federal Lobbyist.
Serves As:
- Chief Government Affairs Officer, E*TRADE Financial Corp.

BARCLAY, Katy
P.O. Box 300
Detroit, MI 48265-1000
Tel: (313) 556 - 5000
Fax:(248) 696 - 7300

Serves As:
- V. President, Global Human Resources, General Motors Corp.

BARCO, Kathleen
Ordway Bldg.
One Kaiser Plaza
Oakland, CA 94612
Tel: (510) 987 - 3900
Fax:(510) 873 - 5345

Serves As:
- Associate Media Director - Northern California Region, Kaiser Permanente

BAREKSTEN, James
P.O. Box 64089
St. Paul, MN 55164-0089
Tel: (651) 355 - 6000
Fax:(651) 355 - 6432
TF: (800) 232 - 3639

Serves As:
- PAC Treasurer, CHS Inc.

BARFIELD, Jr., T. A.
4171 Essen Lane
Baton Rouge, LA 70809
Tel: (225) 932 - 2500
Fax:(225) 932 - 2657

Serves As:
- President and Chief Exec. Officer, Stone & Webster, Inc.

BARGERON, Christopher
1500 Crittenden Lane
Mountain View, CA 94043
Tel: (650) 960 - 1980

Serves As:
- Community Relations, SGI

BARICH, James W.
3800 Howard Hughes Prkwy.
Las Vegas, NV 89109
Tel: (702) 784 - 7777

Serves As:
- Senior V. President, Public Affairs, Pinnacle Entertainment, Inc.

BARK, Kathleen
400 Atlantic St.
Stamford, CT 06921
Tel: (203) 541 - 8418
Fax:(203) 541 - 8200
TF: (800) 223 - 1268

Serves As:
- Communications, Internat'l Paper

BARKER, Dixie
Seven W. Seventh St.
Cincinnati, OH 45202
Tel: (513) 579 - 7569
Fax:(513) 579 - 7185
TF: (800) 261 - 5385

Serves As:
- Manager, Corporate Contributions; and Foundation Administrator, Federated Department Stores, Inc.

BARKER, John D.
P.O. Box 256
Dublin, OH 43017
john_barker@wendys.com
Tel: (614) 764 - 3044
Fax:(614) 766 - 3775

Serves As:
- Senior V. President, Investor Relations and Financial Communications, Wendy's Internat'l, Inc.

BARLOON, William J.
401 Ninth St. NW
Suite 400
Washington, DC 20004
Tel: (202) 585 - 1928
Fax:(202) 585 - 1899

Registered Federal Lobbyist.
Serves As:
- Senior Director, Government Affairs, Sprint Nextel

BARLOW, H. R. Brereton
7001 220th S.W.
Mountlake Terrace, WA 98043-2124
Tel: (425) 670 - 5900
Fax:(425) 670 - 5635

Serves As:
- Chairman, President and Chief Exec. Officer, Premera Blue Cross

BARNARD, Patricia A.
P.O. Box 105605
Atlanta, GA 30348
Tel: (404) 652 - 4000
Fax:(404) 654 - 4789
TF: (800) 519 - 3111

Serves As:
- Exec. V. President, Human Resources, Georgia-Pacific Corp.

BARNES, David
1301 K St. NW
Suite 1200
Washington, DC 20005
Tel: (202) 515 - 5036
Fax:(202) 515 - 4943

Serves As:
- Director, Human Resources and Policy Driven Growth, Internat'l Business Machines Corp. (IBM)

BARNES, Eric
414 Union St.
Suite 2000
Nashville, TN 37219
Tel: (615) 986 - 5600
TF: (877) 744 - 5600

Serves As:
- Foundation Contact, Louisiana-Pacific Corporation

BARNES, Jesse
6565 N. MacArthur Blvd.
Suite 800
Irving, TX 75039
jbarnes@commercialmetals.com
Tel: (214) 689 - 4300
Fax:(214) 689 - 5886

Serves As:
- Manager, Human Resources, Commercial Metals Co.

BARNES, John R.
P.O. Box 650283
Dallas, TX 75265-0283
Tel: (972) 699 - 4000
Fax:(972) 699 - 4025

Serves As:
- Chairman and Chief Exec. Officer, Xanser Corp.

BARNES, John R.
1100 Wilson Blvd.
Suite 1500
Arlington, VA 22209
Tel: (703) 841 - 5700
Fax:(703) 841 - 5792
Registered Federal Lobbyist.
Serves As:
- V. President, Government Relations for Defense Programs, Raytheon Co.
- V. President, Congressional Relations, Raytheon Aircraft Company

BARNES, Rudy
901 D St. SW
Suite 900
Washington, DC 20024
Tel: (202) 646 - 5255
Fax:(202) 646 - 5271
Registered Federal Lobbyist.
Serves As:
- Director, Government Relations for Dept. of Energy Programs, Battelle

BARNES, Thomas O.
P.O. Box 489
Bristol, CT 06011-0489
Tel: (860) 583 - 7070
Fax:(860) 589 - 3507
Serves As:
- Chairman of the Board, Barnes Group Inc.

BARNES, Victoria
1660 L St. NW
Fourth Floor
Washington, DC 20036
Tel: (202) 775 - 5027
Fax:(202) 775 - 5045
Serves As:
- Washington Representative, Government Relations, General Motors Corp.

BARNETT, Carol J.
P.O. Box 407
Lakeland, FL 33802-0407
Tel: (863) 688 - 1188
Fax:(863) 284 - 5532
Serves As:
- Chair, Publix Super Markets Charities, Publix Super Markets, Inc.

BARNETT, John P.
544 Westheimer Rd.
Houston, TX 77056
Tel: (713) 989 - 7556
Serves As:
- Director, External Affairs, Southern Union Company

BARNETT, Mark
4400 Main St.
Kansas City, MO 64111
mbarnett@hrblock.com
Tel: (816) 701 - 4443
Fax:(816) 753 - 5346
TF: (800) 829 - 7733
Serves As:
- Director, Investor Relations, H & R Block, Inc.

BARNETT, Roger
4747 Willow Rd.
Pleasanton, CA 94588
Tel: (925) 924 - 2000
Fax:(925) 924 - 2862
Serves As:
- Chairman and Chief Exec. Officer, Shaklee Corp.

BARNEY, Stephen E.
350 Popular Church Rd
Camp Hill, PA 17011
Tel: (717) 763 - 7064
Fax:(717) 763 - 6424
Serves As:
- Pac Treasurer, Harsco Corp.

BARNHILL, Mark
360 N. Crescent Dr., S. Bldg.
Beverly Hills, CA 90210
Tel: (310) 712 - 1850
Fax:(310) 712 - 1848
Serves As:
- Senior V. President, Corporate Relations, Platinum Equity, LLC

BARNUM, Paul
P.O. Box 9777
M/S EC2-2D7
Federal Way, WA 98063-9777
paul.barnum@weyerhaeuser.com
Tel: (253) 924 - 3920
Fax:(253) 924 - 5921
TF: (800) 525 - 5440
Serves As:
- Director, Corporate Public Relations, Weyerhaeuser Co.

BARON, Kevin P.
One Nationwide Plaza
M/S 1-27-09
Columbus, OH 43215-2220
Tel: (614) 249 - 6914
Fax:(614) 249 - 3073
Serves As:
- Legislative Affairs Officer, Nationwide

BARONE, Gloria
Two Liberty Pl.
1601 Chestnut St.
Philadelphia, PA 19192-1553
gloria.barone@cigna.com
Tel: (215) 761 - 4758
Serves As:
- Director, CIGNA Group Insurance Communications, CIGNA Corp.

BAROZIE, Beth Ann
1100 Wilson Blvd.
Suite 1500
Arlington, VA 22209
Tel: (703) 841 - 5700
Fax:(703) 841 - 5792
Registered Federal Lobbyist.
Serves As:
- Manager, Government Relations, Raytheon Co.

BARR, Edward E.
200 Old Hook Rd.
Harrington Park, NJ 07640
Tel: (201) 767 - 9300
Fax:(201) 767 - 2892
TF: (800) 230 - 2685
Serves As:
- Chairman of the Board, United Water Resources

BARR, Kevin
500 Post Rd. East
Suite 320
Westport, CT 06880
Tel: (203) 222 - 5905
Fax:(203) 226 - 2303
Serves As:
- V. President, Human Resources, Terex Corp.

BARR, William P.
1300 I St. NW
Suite 400 West
Washington, DC 20005
Tel: (202) 515 - 2400
Serves As:
- Exec. V. President and General Counsel, Verizon Communications Inc.

BARRAZA, Richard D.
50 W. San Fernando St.
San Jose, CA 95113
rickb@calpine.com
Tel: (408) 792 - 1125
Fax:(408) 294 - 2877
TF: (800) 359 - 5115
Serves As:
- Senior V. President, Investor Relations, Calpine Corp.

BARRETT, Jr., Allen M.
18 Loveton Circle
Sparks, MD 21152-6000
Tel: (410) 771 - 7310
Fax:(410) 527 - 8289
Serves As:
- V. President, Communications, McCormick & Company, Inc.

Responsibilities include corporate philanthropy.

BARRETT, Barbara
501 Sycamore Dr.
Milpitas, CA 95035
Tel: (408) 894 - 4000
Fax:(408) 894 - 3218
Serves As:
- V. President, Human Resources, Quantum Corporation

BARRETT, Craig R.
2200 Mission College Blvd.
Santa Clara, CA 95052-8119
Tel: (408) 765 - 8080
Fax:(408) 765 - 9904
TF: (800) 628 - 8686
Serves As:
- Chairman of the Board, Intel Corp.

BARRETT, John
400 Broadway
Cincinnati, OH 45202
Tel: (513) 629 - 1905
Fax:(513) 629 - 1081
TF: (800) 936 - 1212
Serves As:
- Chairman, President, and Chief Exec.Officer, Western and Southern Life Insurance Co.

BARRETT, Nancy E.
2145 Hamilton Ave.
San Jose, CA 95125
Tel: (408) 558 - 7400
Fax:(408) 558 - 7401
TF: (800) 322 - 9266
Serves As:
- V. President, Human Resources, eBay, Inc.

BARRIOS, Sergio
360 Hamilton Ave., Suite 1103
White Plains, NY 10601-1841
sbarrios@heinekenusa.com
Tel: (914) 681 - 4100
Fax:(914) 681 - 1900
TF: (800) 801 - 4966
Serves As:
- Manager, Industry and Government Affairs/West and Central, Heineken USA Inc.

BARRON, David M.
1133 21st St. NW
Suite 900
Washington, DC 20036
david.barron@bellsouth.com
Tel: (202) 463 - 4100
Fax:(202) 463 - 4141
Registered Federal Lobbyist.
Serves As:
- Assistant V. President, Federal Relations/National Security, BellSouth Corp.

BARROW, Craig S.
1776 I St. NW
Suite 1050
Washington, DC 20006
Tel: (202) 429 - 3400
Fax:(202) 429 - 3467

Registered Federal Lobbyist.
Serves As:
- Director, Science Policy, The Dow Chemical Company

BARROWS, John
Six Sylvan Way
Parsippany, NJ 07054
john.barrows@cendant.com
Tel: (973) 496 - 7865
Fax:(973) 496 - 3585

Serves As:
- V. President, Corporate Communications and Public Affairs, (Cendant Car Rental Group), Cendant Corp.

BARRS, Craig
241 Ralph McGill Blvd. NE
Atlanta, GA 30308-3374
Tel: (404) 506 - 7740
Fax:(404) 506 - 3771

Serves As:
- V. President, Community and Economic Development, Georgia Power Co.

BARRY, Albert P.
1235 S. Clark St.
Suite 1100
Arlington, VA 22202
Barry@aaicorp.com
Tel: (703) 412 - 4170
Fax:(703) 416 - 4820

Registered Federal Lobbyist.
Serves As:
- V. President, Washington Operations, AAI Corp.

BARRY, Brian R.
730 Central Ave.
Murray Hill, NJ 07974
Tel: (908) 277 - 8000
Fax:(908) 277 - 8078
TF: (800) 367 - 2273

Serves As:
- V. President, Regulatory and Clinical Affairs, C. R. Bard, Inc.

BARRY, Gery J.
P.O. Box 98029
Baton Rouge, LA 70898-9029
Tel: (225) 295 - 3307
Fax:(225) 295 - 2054
TF: (800) 599 - 2583

Serves As:
- President and Chief Exec. Officer, Blue Cross and Blue Shield of Louisiana

BARRY, Jackie
25 Research Dr.
Westborough, MA 01582
Tel: (508) 389 - 3298
Fax:(508) 389 - 3198

Serves As:
- Media Contact, Nat'l Grid USA

BARRY, Joseph J.
225 Franklin St.
Boston, MA 02110
jjbarry@statestreet.com
Tel: (617) 664 - 1254
Fax:(617) 664 - 4999

Registered Federal Lobbyist.
Serves As:
- V. President, Industry Affairs, State Street Corp.

BARRY, Lisa B.
1401 I St. NW
Suite 1200
Washington, DC 20005-2225
Tel: (202) 408 - 5800
Fax:(202) 408 - 5845

Registered Federal Lobbyist.
Serves As:
- V. President and General Manager, Government Affairs, Chevron Corp.

BARRY, Paul E.
1331 Pennsylvania Ave. NW
Suite 550 South
Washington, DC 20004
Tel: (202) 637 - 8020
Fax:(202) 637 - 8028

Registered Federal Lobbyist.
Serves As:
- Director, International Health Policy, Boston Scientific Corp.

BARRY, Robert
222 W. Adams
Suite 1500
Chicago, IL 60606
Tel: (312) 230 - 2560
Fax:(312) 230 - 8835

Serves As:
- State Director, Government Affairs, AT&T

BARRY, Susan
P.O. Box 3727
Spokane, WA 99220-3727
Tel: (509) 489 - 0500
Fax:(509) 495 - 8725
TF: (800) 727 - 9170

Serves As:
- PAC Treasurer, Avista Corp.

BARRY, Tina S.
DWF Airport Station, P.O. Box 619100
Dallas, TX 75261-9100
tbarry@kcc.com
Tel: (972) 281 - 1484
Fax:(972) 281 - 1490
TF: (800) 639 - 1352

Serves As:
- Senior V. President, Corporate Communications, Kimberly-Clark Corp.

BARTH, John M.
5757 N. Green Bay Ave.
Milwaukee, WI 53201-0591
Tel: (414) 524 - 1200
Fax:(414) 524 - 2077

Serves As:
- Chairman and Chief Exec. Officer, Johnson Controls, Inc.

BARTH, Richard C.
1350 I St. NW
Suite 400
Washington, DC 20005-3306
Tel: (202) 371 - 6900
Fax:(202) 842 - 3578

Registered Federal Lobbyist.
Serves As:
- V. President and Director, Telecommunications Strategy and Regulation, Motorola, Inc.

BARTHMUSS, David K.
515 Marin St.
Suite 216
Thousand Oaks, CA 91360
dave.barthmuss@gm.com
Tel: (805) 373 - 9572
Fax:(805) 373 - 9648

Serves As:
- California Environment and Energy Communications Manager, General Motors Corp.

BARTLETT, David
601 Pennsylvania Ave. NW
Suite 720
Washington, DC 20004
Tel: (202) 783 - 3970
Fax:(202) 783 - 3982

Registered Federal Lobbyist.
Serves As:
- Assistant V. President, Federal Regulatory Affairs, ALLTEL

BARTLETT, James
717 Texas Ave.
Suite 2100
Houston, TX 77002-2712
Tel: (713) 624 - 9354
Fax:(713) 624 - 9645

Serves As:
- Director, Corporate Communications, Burlington Resources Inc.

BARTLETT, Thomas A.
1095 Ave. of the Americas
New York, NY 10036
thomas.a.bartlett@verizon.com
Tel: (212) 395 - 1842
TF: (800) 621 - 9900

Serves As:
- Senior V. President, Investor Relations, Verizon Communications Inc.

BARTLING, James W.
730 N. Ridgeview
Olathe, KS 66061
James.Bartling@atmosenergy.com
Tel: (913) 764 - 0531
Ext: 225
Fax:(913) 764 - 1610

Serves As:
- Manager, Public Affairs - Kansas Division, Atmos Energy Corp.

BARTOLONE, William
SGI Federal
12200-G Plum Orchid Dr.
Silver Spring, MD 20904
billb@sgi.com
Tel: (703) 578 - 3556
Fax:(703) 578 - 0272

Registered Federal Lobbyist.
Serves As:
- Director, Government Affairs, SGI

BARTON, Curtis A.
150 N. Michigan Ave.
Suite 1700
Chicago, IL 60601-7568
Tel: (312) 346 - 6600
Fax:(312) 580 - 4919

Serves As:
- V. President, Environmental Affairs, Smurfit-Stone Container

BARTON, II, Max R.
1293 S. Main St.
Akron, OH 44301
Tel: (330) 253 - 5592
Fax:(330) 761 - 6111

Serves As:
- Communications Services and Investor Relations Manager, Myers Industries, Inc.

Responsibilities include public relations.

BARTZ, Carol
111 McInnis Pkwy.
San Rafael, CA 94903
Tel: (415) 507 - 5000
Fax:(415) 507 - 5100

Serves As:
- Chairman, President and Chief Exec. Officer, Autodesk Inc.

BARTZ, Karen
P.O. Box 419580
Kansas City, MO 64141-6580
kbartz1@hallmark.com
Tel: (816) 274 - 8515

Serves As:
- Manager, Community Development; and V. President, Foundation, Hallmark Cards, Inc.

BARUCH, Alexander
P.O. Box 4844
Syracuse, NY 13221-4844
Tel: (315) 433 - 0100
Fax:(315) 433 - 2345
TF: (800) 654 - 8838

Serves As:
- PAC Treasurer, Dairylea Cooperative Inc.

BARUN, Kenneth L.
One McDonald's Plaza
Oak Brook, IL 60523
Tel: (630) 623 - 5505
Fax:(630) 623 - 7488

Serves As:
- President and Chief Exec. Officer, Ronald McDonald House Charities, McDonald's Corp.

BASGAL, Ophelia
One Market
Spear Tower, Suite 2400
San Francisco, CA 94105
Tel: (415) 267 - 7000
Fax:(415) 267 - 7268

Serves As:
- V. President, Civic Partnership and Community Initiatives, (Pacific Gas and Electric Co.), PG & E Corp.

BASKINS, Ann O.
3000 Hanover St.
Palo Alto, CA 94304
ann_baskins@hp.com
Tel: (650) 857 - 3755
Fax:(650) 857 - 5518
TF: (800) 752 - 0900

Serves As:
- Senior V. President, General Counsel and Secretary; PAC Treasurer, Hewlett-Packard Co.

Responsibilities include regulatory affairs.

BASQUIN, Ashley
700 13th St. NW
Suite 220
Washington, DC 20005
ashley.basquin@bnsf.com
Tel: (202) 347 - 8662
Fax:(202) 347 - 8675

Registered Federal Lobbyist.
Serves As:
- Director, Government Affairs, Burlington Northern Santa Fe Corporation

BASS, Amy
P.O. Box 127
Joplin, MO 64802-0127
abass@empiredistrict.com
Tel: (417) 625 - 5114
Fax:(417) 625 - 6198
TF: (800) 206 - 2300

Serves As:
- Director, Corporate Communications, Empire District Electric Co.

BASS, James K.
2926 Piper Dr.
Vero Beach, FL 32960
Tel: (772) 567 - 4361
Fax:(772) 978 - 6584

Serves As:
- President and Chief Exec. Officer, The New Piper Aircraft Inc.

BASSETT, Bonnie
P.O. Box 64101
St. Paul, MN 55164-0101
bbassett@landolakes.com
Tel: (651) 481 - 2222
Fax:(651) 481 - 2000
TF: (800) 328 - 4155

Serves As:
- Director, Community Relations and Exec. Director, Land O'Lakes Foundation, Land O'Lakes, Inc.

BASSETT, Charles
P.O. Box 13466
Phoenix, AZ 85002-3466
Tel: (602) 864 - 4350
Fax:(602) 864 - 4242
TF: (800) 232 - 2345

Serves As:
- Director, Government Relations, Blue Cross and Blue Shield of Arizona

BASSETT, Harry
260 Interstate N. Circle NW
Atlanta, GA 30339
harry_bassett@assurant.com
Tel: (770) 763 - 1000
Fax:(770) 859 - 4403

Registered Federal Lobbyist.
Serves As:
- Senior V. President, Government Relations, (Assurant Solutions), Assurant

BASSETT, Thomas W.
17666 Fitch
Irvine, CA 92614
Tel: (949) 253 - 2300
Fax:(949) 474 - 7675

Serves As:
- Chairman of the Board, Freedom Communications Inc.

BASSLER, Thomas B.
P.O. Box 7408
Boise, ID 83707
tbassler@bcidaho.com
Tel: (208) 331 - 7385
Fax:(208) 331 - 7320

Serves As:
- General Counsel, Senior V. President, Legal Services and Government Affairs, Blue Cross of Idaho

BATEMAN, Jr., Joseph R.
1400 Douglas St.
Omaha, NE 68179
Tel: (402) 544 - 3878

Registered Federal Lobbyist.
Serves As:
- Senior Assistant V. President, Government Affairs, Union Pacific Corp.

BATES, Arlene
P.O. Box 105250
Atlanta, GA 30348
abates@harland.net
Tel: (770) 981 - 9460
Fax:(770) 593 - 5619
TF: (800) 723 - 3690

Serves As:
- Senior V. President, Human Resources, John H. Harland Co.

BATES, Douglas P.
720 E. Wisconsin Ave.
Milwaukee, WI 53202-4797
Tel: (414) 271 - 1444
Fax:(414) 665 - 2463
TF: (800) 323 - 7033

Registered Federal Lobbyist.
Serves As:
- Representative, Northwestern Mutual Financial Network

BATES, Janice W.
P.O. Box 45433
MS: QB811
Salt Lake City, UT 84145-0433
jan.bates@questar.com
Tel: (801) 324 - 5435
Fax:(801) 324 - 5483

Serves As:
- Director, Community Affairs, Questar Corporation

Responsibilities also include corporate philanthropy.

BATES, Joan
One Tower Ln.
Suite 1000
Oakbrook Terrace, IL 60181-4624
Tel: (630) 571 - 7700
Fax:(630) 571 - 0317
TF: (800) 225 - 8000

Serves As:
- Director, Investor Relations, DeVry Inc.

BATES, Richard M.
1150 17th St. NW
Suite 400
Washington, DC 20036
Tel: (202) 222 - 4700

Registered Federal Lobbyist.
Serves As:
- V. President, Government Relations, The Walt Disney Company

BATES, William B.
4500 Main St.
Kansas City, MO 64111
wbb@americancentury.com
Tel: (816) 340 - 4066
Fax:(816) 344 - 4816
TF: (800) 345 - 2021

Registered Federal Lobbyist.
Serves As:
- V. President, Government Affairs, American Century Cos., Inc.

Responsibilities include political action.

BATJER, Marybel
P.O. Box 98905
Las Vegas, NV 89193-8905
Tel: (702) 407 - 6000

Serves As:
- V. President, Public Policy and Communications, (Harrah's Operating Co., Inc.), Harrah's Entertainment, Inc.

BATSON, Bryan
P.O. Box 4569
Atlanta, GA 30302-4569
Tel: (404) 584 - 4000
Fax:(404) 584 - 3479

Serves As:
- Senior V. President, External Affairs, AGL Resources, Inc.

BATTCHER, Jeff
1155 Peachtree St. NE
19G03 Campanile
Atlanta, GA 30309-3610
jeff.battcher@bellsouth.com
Tel: (404) 249 - 2793
Fax:(404) 249 - 3839

Serves As:
- Director, Senior Corporate Media Relations, BellSouth Corp.

BATTEN, Jr., Frank
P.O. Box 449
Norfolk, VA 23510-0449
Tel: (757) 446 - 2010
Fax:(757) 446 - 2489

Serves As:
- Chairman and Chief Exec. Officer, Landmark Communications, Inc.

BATTLE, Lynn
101 Constitution Ave. NW
Washington, DC 20080
lbattle@washgas.com
Tel: (703) 750 - 2000
Fax:(703) 750 - 4574

Serves As:
• Public Affairs Specialist, Washington Gas

BATTON, Anne
2000 Post Oak Blvd., Suite 100
Houston, TX 77056-4400
anne.batton@apachecorp.com
Tel: (713) 296 - 6253
Fax:(713) 296 - 6480
TF: (800) 874 - 3262

Serves As:
• Manager, e-Commerce, Apache Corp.

BAUCUS, Claudia
5725 Delphi Dr.
Troy, MI 48098-2815
claudia.baucus@delphi.com
Tel: (248) 813 - 2942
Fax:(248) 813 - 2670

Serves As:
• Manager, Financial Communications, Delphi Corp.

BAUDER, Lillian
21001 Van Born Rd.
Taylor, MI 48180
Tel: (313) 792 - 6970
Fax:(313) 792 - 6135

Serves As:
• V. President, Corporate Affairs and President, Masco Charitable Trust, Masco Corp.

BAUER, Debbie A.
7201 Hamilton Blvd.
Allentown, PA 18195-1501
bauerd@airproducts.com
Tel: (610) 481 - 8061
Fax:(610) 841 - 5900

Serves As:
• Coordinator, Communications, Air Products and Chemicals, Inc.

BAUER, Gary
220 NW Second Ave.
Portland, OR 97209-3991
Tel: (503) 220 - 2431
Fax:(503) 721 - 2508

Serves As:
• Manager, Government Relations, NW Natural
Responsibilities include political action.

BAUER, James A.
3871 Lakefield Dr.
Suwanee, GA 30024
jim.bauer@arrisi.com
Tel: (770) 622 - 8400
Fax:(847) 615 - 8924

Serves As:
• Investor Relations Contact, ARRIS Group, Inc.

BAUERLEIN, Robert D.
1200 Wilson Blvd.
Arlington, VA 22209-2305
Tel: (703) 465 - 3505
Fax:(703) 465 - 3041

Serves As:
• V. President, International Operations, The Boeing Co.

BAUGNIET, Robert N.
P.O. Box 2206
A-01
Savannah, GA 31402-2206
Tel: (912) 965 - 7372
Fax:(912) 965 - 4333

Serves As:
• Director, Corporate Communications, Gulfstream Aerospace Corp.

BAUM, Stephen L.
101 Ash St.
San Diego, CA 92101-3017

Serves As:
• Chairman and Chief Exec. Officer, Sempra Energy

BAUMGARDNER, Vicki L.
700 Central Ave.
Louisville, KY 40208
Tel: (502) 636 - 4400
Fax:(502) 636 - 4430
TF: (800) 283 - 3729

Serves As:
• PAC Treasurer; and Foundation Treasurer, Churchill Downs, Inc.

BAUMGARDT, Jim
111 Monument Circle
29th Floor
Indianapolis, IN 46204-5129
Tel: (317) 971 - 2000
Fax:(317) 971 - 2040

Serves As:
• President, Guidant Foundation, Guidant Corp.

BAUSEWINE, George W.
P.O. Box 5000
Pineville, LA 71361-5000
george.bausewine@cleco.com
Tel: (318) 484 - 7400
Fax:(318) 484 - 7465

Serves As:
• V. President, Regulatory Affairs and Rates, Cleco Corp.

BAXTER, Marguerite D.
1300 I St. NW
Suite 1090
Washington, DC 20005
Tel: (202) 962 - 8640
Fax:(202) 289 - 6819

Registered Federal Lobbyist.
Serves As:
• V. President, Government Relations, Chiron Corp.

BAY, Mogens C.
One Valmont Plaza
Omaha, NE 68154-5215
Tel: (402) 963 - 1000
Fax:(402) 963 - 1095

Serves As:
• Chairman and Chief Exec. Officer, Valmont Industries, Inc.

BAYARDELLE, Eddy
Four World Financial Center
250 Vesey St.
New York, NY 10080
eddy_bayardelle@ml.com
Tel: (212) 236 - 1000

Serves As:
• Contact, Merrill Lynch and Co. Foundation, Merrill Lynch & Co., Inc.

BAYER, Judith
1401 I St. NW
Suite 600
Washington, DC 20005
bayerj@corpdc.utc.com
Tel: (202) 336 - 7400
Fax:(202) 336 - 7529

Registered Federal Lobbyist.
Serves As:
• Director, Environmental Government Affairs, United Technologies Corp.

BAYLOR, Kenneth M.
110 S.E. Sixth St.
28th Floor
Fort Lauderdale, FL 33301
Tel: (954) 769 - 2400
Fax:(954) 769 - 2664

Serves As:
• V. President, Employee and Labor Relations, Republic Services, Inc.

BAZEMORE, Melvin J.
1660 L St. NW
Fourth Floor
Washington, DC 20036
Tel: (202) 775 - 5098
Fax:(202) 775 - 5024

Registered Federal Lobbyist.
Serves As:
• Director External Affairs, Washington Office, General Motors Corp.

BAZINET, Michael G.
100 W. Putnam Ave.
Greenwich, CT 06830
Tel: (203) 622 - 3529
Fax:(203) 863 - 7228

Serves As:
• Director, Corporate Communications and Public Affairs, UST Inc.

BEAL, Chris
555 12th St. NW
Suite 650
Washington, DC 20004-1205
Tel: (202) 393 - 7950
Fax:(202) 393 - 7960

Serves As:
• Manager, State Advocacy, Eli Lilly and Company

BEAMAN, Jeff
P.O. Box 70
Boise, ID 83707
Tel: (208) 388 - 2200
Fax:(208) 388 - 6955

Serves As:
• Corporate Communications, (Idaho Power Co.), IDACORP, Inc.

BEAMAN, William
1730 Rhode Island Ave., N.W., Suite 212
Washington, DC 20036
Tel: (202) 223 - 8025
Fax:(202) 466 - 4626

Serves As:
• Washington Bureau Chief, Reader's Digest Ass'n, Inc.
Responsibilities include government affairs.

BEAR, Peter D.
3M Center
Bldg. 225-15-15
St. Paul, MN 55144-1000
Tel: (651) 733 - 3374
Fax:(651) 737 - 2901

Serves As:
• Manager, International Government Affairs and Government Markets, 3M Company

BEAR, Stephen E.
345 Park Ave.
New York, NY 10154-0037
steve.bear@bms.com
Tel: (212) 546 - 4000
Fax:(212) 546 - 4020

Serves As:
• Senior V. President, Human Resources, Bristol-Myers Squibb Co.

BEARD, Ronald S.
2180 Rutherford Rd.
Carlsbad, CA 92008-7328
Tel: (760) 931 - 1771
Fax:(760) 930 - 5015
TF: (800) 228 - 2767

Serves As:
- Chairman of the Board, Callaway Golf Co.

BEARE, Kern
160 Rio Robles
San Jose, CA 95134
kern.beare@kla-tencor.com
Tel: (408) 875 - 7039
Fax:(408) 875 - 4144

Serves As:
- V. President, Corporate Communications, KLA-Tencor

BEASLEY, Jr., James B.
P.O. Box 1295
Birmingham, AL 35201
Tel: (205) 992 - 5752
Fax:(205) 992 - 5363

Serves As:
- President and Chief Exec. Officer, Southern Nuclear Operating Co.

BEASLEY, Joyce S.
P.O. Box 160
A09
Hartsville, SC 29551-0160
joyce.beasley@sonoco.com
Tel: (843) 383 - 7851
Ext: 7851
Fax:(843) 383 - 7008

Serves As:
- Manager, Financial Communications and Community Relations, Sonoco Products Co.

Responsibilities also include corporate philanthropy.

BEASLEY, Mark V.
8000 Bent Branch Dr.
Irving, TX 75063
Tel: (972) 409 - 1655
Fax:(972) 409 - 1556

Serves As:
- V. President, General Counsel and Secretary, Michaels Stores, Inc.

Responsibilities include government relations.

BEATH, Donna
600 Dresher Rd.
Horsham, PA 19044
Tel: (215) 956 - 8000
TF: (800) 523 - 0650

Serves As:
- Exec. Secretary, The Penn Mutual Life Insurance Co.

Responsibilities include corporate philanthropy.

BEATRICE, Michael G.
100 Abbott Park Rd.
Abbott Park, IL 60064-3500
Tel: (847) 937 - 6100

Serves As:
- V. President, Corporate Regulatory and Quality Science, Abbott Laboratories

BEATTY, Susan
800 Nicollet Mall
Suite 800
Minneapolis, MN 55402
Tel: (612) 303 - 6000

Serves As:
- V. President, Communications, U.S. Bancorp Piper Jaffray Inc.

BEATY, Sandy
3200 W. End Ave., Suite 500
Nashville, TN 37203
Tel: (615) 783 - 1740
Fax:(615) 783 - 1739

Serves As:
- Director, Government Relations, Pfizer Inc.

BEAUCHAMP, Robert E.
2101 City West Blvd.
Houston, TX 77042-2827
bob_beauchamp@bmc.com
Tel: (713) 918 - 8800
Fax:(713) 918 - 8000
TF: (800) 841 - 2031

Serves As:
- President and Chief Exec. Officer, BMC Software

BEAUDET, Victor
1345 Ave. of the Americas
New York, NY 10020
Tel: (212) 282 - 5344
Fax:(212) 282 - 6220

Serves As:
- Exec. Director, Financial Communications and Corporate Communications, Avon Products, Inc.

BEAUFORD, Shiree
15326 Alton Pkwy.
Irvine, CA 92618
Tel: (949) 789 - 1600
Fax:(949) 789 - 1609

Serves As:
- Contact, Investor Relations, Standard Pacific Corp.

BEAULIEU, Jennifer
555 12th St. NW
Suite 650
Washington, DC 20004-1205
Tel: (202) 393 - 7950
Fax:(202) 393 - 7960

Serves As:
- Manager, Advocacy Relations, Eli Lilly and Company

BEAUPRE, Albert
2090 Florence Ave.
Cincinnati, OH 45206
albert.beaupre@milacron.com
Tel: (513) 487 - 5918
Fax:(513) 487 - 5586

Serves As:
- Director, Corporate Communications and Investor Relations, Milacron Inc.

BEAURIVAGE, Ane G.
One Learjet Way
Wichita, KS 67209
Tel: (316) 946 - 2000
Fax:(316) 946 - 2220

Serves As:
- Treasurer, Learjet Inc. PAC, Bombardier

BECHTEL, Riley P.
50 Beale St.
San Francisco, CA 94105-1895
Tel: (415) 768 - 1234
Fax:(415) 768 - 9038

Serves As:
- Chairman and Chief Exec. Officer, Bechtel Group, Inc.

BECHTOL, J. Currie
10000 Memorial Dr.
Suite 600
Houston, TX 77024-3341
cbechtol@frontieroil.com
Tel: (713) 688 - 9600
Fax:(713) 688 - 0616

Serves As:
- Treasurer, Frontier PAC, Frontier Oil Corp.

BECK, George H.
1500 MacCorkle Ave. SE
Charleston, WV 25314
george.h.beck@verizon.com
Tel: (304) 353 - 5574

Serves As:
- Manager, Strategic Initiatives and External Affairs, Verizon West Virginia Inc.

BECK, Jim C.
315 Bankhead Highway
Suite D
Carrollton, GA 30117
Tel: (770) 830 - 9203
Fax:(770) 830 - 9084

Serves As:
- Director, Government Relations (Alabama, Georgia, and S. Carolina), Nationwide

BECK, Lauren E.
816 Connecticut Ave. NW
Seventh Floor
Washington, DC 20006-2705
lauren.beck@unilever.com
Tel: (202) 828 - 1010
Fax:(202) 828 - 4550

Registered Federal Lobbyist.
Serves As:
- Manager, Government Relations, Unilever United States, Inc.

BECK, Toni
P.O. Box 1642
Houston, TX 77251-1642
Tel: (713) 627 - 5720

Serves As:
- V. President, Public Affairs, DEGT, Duke Energy Corp.

BECKER, Alton W.
P.O. Box 619616
Dallas-Fort Worth Airport, TX 75261
al.becker@aa.com
Tel: (817) 967 - 1577
Fax:(817) 967 - 3816

Serves As:
- Managing Director, Corporate Communications, AMR Corp.

BECKER, Darby M. R.
1401 I St. NW
Suite 600
Washington, DC 20005
Tel: (202) 336 - 7400
Fax:(202) 336 - 7515

Registered Federal Lobbyist.
Serves As:
- Manager and Counsel, Government Relations and PAC Treasurer, United Technologies Corp.

BECKER, Douglas L.
1001 Fleet St.
Baltimore, MD 21202-4346
Tel: (410) 843 - 8000
Fax:(410) 843 - 8065

Serves As:
- Chairman and Chief Exec. Officer, Laureate Education, Inc.

BECKER, Jan
111 McInnis Pkwy.
San Rafael, CA 94903
Tel: (415) 507 - 5000
Fax:(415) 507 - 5100

Serves As:
- V. President, Human Resources, Autodesk Inc.

BECKER, Joshua
Metro Center
One Station Pl.
Stamford, CT 06902
Tel: (203) 539 - 8000
Fax:(203) 539 - 7734
TF: (800) 969 - 9974

Serves As:
- Director, Investor Relations, The Thomson Corporation

BECKER, Kay
1110 American Parkway NE
Allentown, PA 18109-3229
kabecker@agere.com
Tel: (610) 712 - 3689
Fax:(610) 712 - 4106

Serves As:
• Media Relations Contact, Agere Systems Inc.

BECKER, Linda M.
1401 H St. NW
Suite 700
Washington, DC 20005
Tel: (202) 414 - 6757
Fax:(202) 414 - 6741

Registered Federal Lobbyist.
Serves As:
• Senior Manager, Public Policy and Communications, DaimlerChrysler Corp.

BECKER, Michael S.
P.O. Box 1271
Portland, OR 97207-1271
Tel: (503) 225 - 5221
Fax:(503) 225 - 5283

Registered Federal Lobbyist.
Serves As:
• V. President, Public Policy and Community Affairs, Regence BlueCross BlueShield of Oregon

BECKER, Richard
P.O. Box 1967
CH5W
Grand Rapids, MI 49501-1967
rbecker@steelcase.com
Tel: (616) 246 - 9332
Fax:(616) 475 - 2599

Serves As:
• Manager, Corporate Relations, Steelcase Inc.

BECKER, Steven
1600 N.W. 163rd St.
Miami, FL 33169
Tel: (305) 625 - 4171
Fax:(305) 625 - 2790

Serves As:
• Treasurer, Southern Wine & Spirits PAC, Southern Wine & Spirits of America

BECKERT, John A.
3030 LBJ Frwy.
Suite 700
Dallas, TX 75234
Tel: (972) 243 - 6191
Fax:(972) 888 - 7555

Serves As:
• President and Chief Exec. Officer, ClubCorp Internat'l Inc.

BECKETT, Bruce K.
1501 S. Capitol Way, Suite 301
Olympia, WA 98507
bruce.beckett@weyerhaeuser.com
Tel: (360) 943 - 5350

Serves As:
• Director, Government Affairs - Washington State, Weyerhaeuser Co.

BECKHARDT, Stacey
41 Moores Rd.
Frazer, PA 19355
sbeckhar@cephalon.com
Tel: (610) 738 - 6198
Fax:(610) 344 - 0981

Serves As:
• Senior Manager, Public Relations, Cephalon, Inc.

BECKMAN, Jeff
1155 Battery St.
San Francisco, CA 94111
Tel: (415) 501 - 1698
Fax:(415) 501 - 7112
TF: (800) 872 - 5384

Serves As:
• Senior Manager, Worldwide and U.S. Communications, Levi Strauss and Co.

BECTON, Barry
1301 K St. NW
Suite 1000 East Tower
Washington, DC 20005
Tel: (202) 715 - 1111
Fax:(202) 715 - 1114

Serves As:
• Foundation Contact, Diageo North America

BEDARD, Kipp A.
8000 S. Federal Way
M/S 407
Boise, ID 83707
kbedard@micron.com
Tel: (208) 368 - 4400
Fax:(208) 368 - 2536

Serves As:
• V. President, Investor Relations, Micron Technology, Inc.

BEDDOW, Thomas F.
1425 K St. NW
Suite 300
Washington, DC 20005
tfbeddow@mmm.com
Tel: (202) 414 - 3000
Fax:(202) 414 - 3037

Registered Federal Lobbyist.
Serves As:
• Staff V. President, Corporate Public Affairs, 3M Company

BEDFORD, Terence
880 Carillon Pkwy.
St. Petersburg, FL 33716
Tel: (727) 567 - 1000

Serves As:
• Senior V. President, International, Raymond James Financial, Inc.

BEE, Jr., Dennis E.
P.O. Box 780
Warren, PA 16365
Tel: (814) 723 - 1500
Fax:(814) 726 - 4602

Serves As:
• Treasurer, United Refining Co. PAC, United Refining Co.
Responsibilities include investor relations.

BEEBE, Raymond M.
P.O. Box 152
Forest City, IA 50436-0152
Tel: (641) 585 - 3535
Fax:(641) 585 - 6966

Serves As:
• V. President, General Counsel and Secretary, Winnebago Industries, Inc.
Responsibilities include public affairs.

BEEBER, Ronald
5725 Delphi Dr.
483-400-501
Troy, MI 48098-2815
Tel: (248) 813 - 2595
Fax:(248) 813 - 3253

Serves As:
• Corporate Director, Government and Community Relations, Delphi Corp.

BEEM, Carolyn
One Casco St.
Freeport, ME 04033
Tel: (207) 552 - 6016
Fax:(207) 552 - 6821
TF: (800) 221 - 4221

Serves As:
• Manager, Environmental and Government Affairs, L. L. Bean, Inc.

BEERHALTER, Danielle
727 Norristown Rd.
Springhouse, PA 19477
dbeerhalter@rohmhaas.com
Tel: (215) 641 - 7876

Serves As:
• Manager, Public Affairs, Rohm and Haas Co.

BEERLI, Mr. Andreas
175 King St.
Armonk, NY 10504
andreas_beerli@swissre.com
Tel: (914) 828 - 8000
Fax:(914) 828 - 7000
TF: (888) 794 - 7773

Serves As:
• Chief Exec. Officer, Americas Division, Swiss Re America Corp.

BEETLE, Vivian L.
340 Kingsland St.
Nutley, NJ 07110-1199
vivian_l.beetle@roche.com
Tel: (973) 562 - 2055
Fax:(973) 562 - 2999

Serves As:
• Director, Public Affairs/Community Affairs, Hoffmann-La Roche Inc. (Roche)
Responsibilities include corporate philanthropy.

BEFFA-NEGRINI, David
730 Milford Rd.
Route 101A
Merrimack, NH 03054-4631
Tel: (603) 683 - 2000
Fax:(603) 683 - 2041

Serves As:
• V. President, Corporate Communications, PC Connection, Inc.

BEGANS, Peter
601 Pennsylvania Ave. NW
Suite 700
Washington, DC 20004
Tel: (202) 639 - 1881

Registered Federal Lobbyist.
Serves As:
• V. President, Federal Goverment Affairs, Medco Health Solutions, Inc.
Responsibilities include political action.

BEGLEY FEUREY, Monie
60 Fifth Ave.
New York, NY 10010
Tel: (212) 620 - 2200
Fax:(212) 620 - 2245

Serves As:
• Senior V. President, Corporate Communications, Forbes, Inc.

BEHAN, William M.
1808 I St. NW
Eighth Floor
Washington, DC 20006
behanwilliamm@johndeere.com
Tel: (202) 223 - 4817
Fax:(202) 296 - 0011

Registered Federal Lobbyist.
Serves As:
• Director, Agricutural Affairs, Deere & Company

BEHRNS, Eric
1400 I St. NW
Suite 540
Washington, DC 20005
Tel: (202) 638 - 4434

Registered Federal Lobbyist.
Serves As:
- Representative, Applied Materials, Inc.

BEIDEMAN, Paul S.
1200 Hansen Rd.
Green Bay, WI 54304
Tel: (920) 491 - 7000
Fax:(920) 491 - 7090
TF: (800) 236 - 2722

Serves As:
- President and Chief Exec. Officer, Associated Banc-Corp.

BEIER, David W.
555 13th St. NW
Suite 600 West
Washington, DC 20004
Tel: (202) 585 - 9610

Registered Federal Lobbyist.
Serves As:
- Senior V. President, Global Government Affairs, Amgen Inc.

BEIGHLE, Douglas P.
P.O. Box 97034
Bellevue, WA 98009-9734
Tel: (425) 452 - 1234
Fax:(425) 462 - 3301

Serves As:
- Chairman of the Board, Puget Sound Energy

BEINECKE, Frederick W.
200 Carillon Pkwy.
St. Petersburg, FL 33716
Tel: (727) 579 - 5000
Fax:(727) 556 - 2700

Serves As:
- Chairman of the Board, Catalina Marketing Corp.

BEKKERS, John
P.O. Box 2210
Atlanta, GA 30301-2210
john.bekkers@goldkist.com
Tel: (770) 393 - 5000
Fax:(770) 393 - 5347

Serves As:
- Chief Exec. Officer, Gold Kist Inc.

BELA, Kathleen
4650 Cushing Pkwy.
Fremont, CA 94538-6470
kathleen.bela@lamrc.com
Tel: (510) 572 - 4566
Fax:(510) 572 - 2935

Serves As:
- Director, Investor Relations and Corporate Communications, Lam Research Corp.

BELATTI, Frank J.
555 Glenridge Connector NE
Suite 300
Atlanta, GA 30342
fbelatti@afce.com
Tel: (404) 459 - 4450

Serves As:
- Chairman and Chief Exec. Officer, AFC Enterprises

BELDA, Alain J. P.
201 Isabella St.
Pittsburgh, PA 15212-5858
alain.belda@alcoa.com
Tel: (412) 553 - 4545
Fax:(412) 553 - 4498

Serves As:
- Chairman and Chief Exec. Officer, Alcoa Inc.

BELK, Jr., Thomas M.
2801 W. Tyvola Rd.
Charlotte, NC 28217-4500
Tel: (704) 357 - 1064
Fax:(704) 357 - 1876

Serves As:
- Chairman and Chief Exec. Officer, Belk, Inc.

BELL, Alan
17666 Fitch
Irvine, CA 92614
Tel: (949) 553 - 9292
Fax:(949) 474 - 7675

Serves As:
- President and Chief Exec. Officer, Freedom Communications Inc.

BELL, Beverly
1900 K St. NW
Suite 900
Washington, DC 20006
Tel: (202) 822 - 4000
Fax:(202) 822 - 5800

Registered Federal Lobbyist.
Serves As:
- Director, Government and Professional Activities, PriceWaterhouseCoopers LLP

BELL, CFA, Garvin A.
101 Wood Ave.
Iselin, NJ 08830
Tel: (732) 205 - 6106
Fax:(732) 321 - 5079
TF: (800) 631 - 9505

Serves As:
- V. President, Inestor Relations, Engelhard Corp.

BELL, Graeme
P.O. Box 100
Whitehouse Station, NJ 08889-0100
Tel: (908) 423 - 4465
Fax:(908) 735 - 1253
TF: (800) 423 - 1000

Serves As:
- Senior Director, Investor Relations, Merck & Co., Inc.

BELL, Jackie D.
1120 G St. NW
Suite 1050
Washington, DC 20005-3801
Tel: (202) 347 - 4446
Fax:(202) 347 - 7058

Registered Federal Lobbyist.
Serves As:
- V. President, Federal Government Affairs, Georgia-Pacific Corp.

BELL, James A.
World Headquarters
100 N. Riverside
Chicago, IL 60606-1596
Tel: (312) 544 - 2000
Fax:(312) 544 - 2082

Serves As:
- Interim President and Chief Exec. Officer, The Boeing Co.
Also serves as the Chief Financial Officer

BELL, Jim
2000 Market St.
Philadelphia, PA 19103-9000
Tel: (215) 419 - 5293
Fax:(215) 419 - 7591
TF: (800) 225 - 7788

Serves As:
- Senior Communications Manager, ATOFINA Chemicals, Inc.

BELL, Melanie
920 Main St.
Kansas City, MO 64105-2017
mbell@amctheatres.com
Tel: (816) 480 - 2560
Fax:(816) 480 - 4617

Serves As:
- Director, Corporate Communications, AMC Entertainment Inc.

BELL, Michael M.
4474 Savannah Hwy.
Jesup, GA 31545
mike.bell@rayonier.com
Tel: (912) 588 - 8216

Serves As:
- Manager, Corporate Relations, Rayonier Inc.

BELL, Richard
1551 Wewatta St.
Denver, CO 80202-6173
Tel: (303) 744 - 1911
Fax:(303) 744 - 4443

Serves As:
- President, Gates Rubber Co.

BELL, Robert
P.O. Box 6721
Chicago, IL 60680-6721
rbell@usg.com
Tel: (312) 606 - 3992
Fax:(312) 606 - 4802

Serves As:
- Director, Government Affairs, USG Corp.

BELL, Sandra
Financial Center
695 E. Main St.
Stamford, CT 06901
Tel: (203) 328 - 5000
Ext: 5717
Fax:(203) 328 - 6423
TF: (800) 431 - 9994

Serves As:
- Senior V. President, Human Resources, General Re Corp.

BELL, Sherry
111 Ponce de Leon Ave.
Clewiston, FL 33440
Tel: (863) 983 - 8121
Fax:(863) 983 - 9827

Serves As:
- PAC Contact, United States Sugar Corp.

BELL, W. Donald
1941 Ringwood Ave.
San Jose, CA 95131-1721
Tel: (408) 451 - 9400
Fax:(408) 451 - 1632

Serves As:
- Chairman, President and Chief Exec. Officer, Bell Microproducts, Inc.

BELL, William C.
750 17th St. NW
Suite 400
Washington, DC 20006
Tel: (202) 861 - 0660
Fax:(202) 861 - 0437

Serves As:
- Director, International Projects, Mitsui and Co. (U.S.A.), Inc.

BELL-ROSE, Stephanie
375 Park Ave., Suite 1002
New York, NY 10152
Tel: (212) 902 - 5402

Serves As:
- President, Goldman Sachs Foundation, Goldman, Sachs and Co.

BELLARDINI, Mary Alice
165 Court St.
Rochester, NY 14647
Tel: (315) 448 - 3700

Serves As:
- Chairman of the Board, Exellus Blue Cross Blue Shield

BELLUZZO, Richard
501 Sycamore Dr.
Milpitas, CA 95035
Tel: (408) 894 - 4000
Fax:(408) 894 - 3218

Serves As:
- Chairman and Chief Exec. Officer, Quantum Corporation

BELOTE, III, Brandon R.
1000 Wilson Blvd., Suite 2300
Arlington, VA 22209
randy.belote@ngc.com
Tel: (703) 875 - 8525
Fax:(703) 243 - 3190

Serves As:
- Director, Corporate Public Affairs and International Communications, Northrop Grumman Corp.

BELSKY, Joel
Seven W. Seventh St.
Cincinnati, OH 45202
Tel: (513) 579 - 7000
Fax:(513) 579 - 7555
TF: (800) 261 - 5385

Serves As:
- Corporate Controller, Federated Department Stores Inc. Political Action Committee, Federated Department Stores, Inc.

BEN-HAIM, Laurie
1285 Ave. of the Americas
New York, NY 10019-6095
laurie.ben-haim@bbdo.com
Tel: (212) 459 - 5000
Fax:(212) 459 - 6645

Serves As:
- Press Relations, BBDO New York

BENARD, Michael
343 State St.
Rochester, NY 14650-0516
Tel: (585) 724 - 4000
Fax:(585) 724 - 4854

Serves As:
- V. President, Communications and Public Affairs, Eastman Kodak Company

BENATAR, Leo
12 E. Armour Blvd.
Kansas City, MO 64111
Tel: (816) 502 - 4000
Fax:(816) 502 - 4155

Serves As:
- Chairman of the Board, Interstate Bakeries Corp.

BENAVIDEZ, Troy
501 Laguna Blvd. SW
Alburquerque, NM 87104
troy.benavidez@astrazeneca.com
Tel: (505) 246 - 2030
Fax:(505) 246 - 8788
TF: (800) 822 - 9209
Ext: 60031

Serves As:
- Manager, State Government Affairs, AstraZeneca Pharmaceuticals

BENCOMO, James
P.O. Box 6721
Chicago, IL 60680-6721
jbencomo@usg.com
Tel: (312) 606 - 3839
Fax:(312) 606 - 5725

Serves As:
- Director, Investor Relations and Pension, USG Corp.

BENDER, Emily
21839 Atlantic Blvd.
Dulles, VA 20166
Tel: (703) 406 - 5000
Fax:(703) 406 - 5572

Serves As:
- V. President, Human Resources, Orbital Sciences Corp.

BENDER, Jeannine M.
41 Moores Rd.
Frazer, PA 19355
jbender@cephalon.com
Tel: (610) 344 - 6527
Fax:(610) 344 - 6590

Registered Federal Lobbyist.
Serves As:
- Director, Government Relations, Cephalon, Inc.

BENDER, Jeffrey M.
2000 Post Oak Blvd., Suite 100
Houston, TX 77056-4400
jeffrey.bender@apachecorp.com
Tel: (713) 296 - 6159
Fax:(713) 296 - 6480
TF: (800) 874 - 3262

Serves As:
- V. President, Human Resources, Apache Corp.

BENDICKSON, Annette
One StorageTek Dr.
Louisville, CO 80028-4377
Tel: (303) 673 - 5151

Serves As:
- PAC Treasurer, StorageTek

BENECKE, Mary Lou
P.O. Box 994
C1252
Midland, MI 48686-0994
Tel: (989) 496 - 8689
Fax:(989) 496 - 8240

Serves As:
- Manager, Media Relations, Dow Corning Corp.

BENEFIELD, Aronda
410 N. Michigan Ave.
Chicago, IL 60611
abenefield@wrigley.com
Tel: (312) 645 - 4073
Ext: 4073
Fax:(312) 644 - 0015

Serves As:
- Administrator, Consumer Relations and Public Affairs, Wm. Wrigley Jr. Co.

BENESKI, Barron
21700 Atlantic Blvd.
Dulles, VA 20166
beneski.barron@orbital.com
Tel: (703) 406 - 5528
Fax:(703) 406 - 5572

Serves As:
- V. President, Public Relations, Orbital Sciences Corp.

Responsibilities include investor relations.

BENHAM, Barbara
41 S. High St.
Columbus, OH 43287
Tel: (614) 480 - 4718
Fax:(614) 480 - 4973

Registered Federal Lobbyist.
Serves As:
- Senior V. President and Director, Government Relations, Huntington Bancshares Inc.

BENHAMOU, Eric A.
350 Campus Dr.
Marlborough, MA 01752-3064
Tel: (508) 323 - 5000
Fax:(508) 323 - 1111

Serves As:
- Chairman of the Board, 3Com Corp.
- Chairman of the Board, Cypress Semiconductor Corp.
- Chairman of the Board, palmOne, Inc.
- Chairman of the Board, PalmSource, Inc.

BENINTENDE, Bill
1100 N. Market St.
Wilmington, DE 19890
Tel: (302) 651 - 8268
Fax:(302) 651 - 8937
TF: (800) 441 - 7120

Serves As:
- Director, Media Relations, Wilmington Trust Co.

BENJAMIN, Georganne
1211 W. Myrtle St.
Suite 210
Boise, ID 83702
gbenjamin.id@regence.com
Tel: (208) 395 - 7723
Fax:(208) 333 - 7873

Serves As:
- Assistant Director, Strategic Communications, Regence BlueShield of Idaho

BENJAMIN, Karin L.
9201 San Mateo Blvd. NE
Albuquerque, NM 87113-5857
Tel: (505) 828 - 5857
Fax:(505) 828 - 5500

Serves As:
- Associate Communications Representative, Honeywell Internat'l, Inc.

BENJAMIN, Lawrence S.
9755 Patuxent Woods Dr.
Columbia, MD 21046
Tel: (410) 312 - 7100
Fax:(410) 312 - 7167

Serves As:
- Chief Exec. Officer, U.S. Foodservice

BENJAMIN, Timothy
P.O. Box 20670
Rochester, NY 14602-0670
tbenjamin@birdseyefoods.com
Tel: (585) 383 - 1850
Fax:(585) 383 - 1281
TF: (800) 999 - 5044

Serves As:
- PAC Contact, Birds Eye Foods

BENKO, JoAnna
100 Farmers Circle
Austin, TX 78728
Tel: (512) 238 - 4349
Fax:(512) 238 - 4348

Serves As:
- Legislative Representative, Farmers Group, Inc.

BENMOSCHE, Robert H.
200 Park Ave.
New York, NY 10166
Tel: (212) 578 - 2211
TF: (800) 638 - 5433

Serves As:
- Chairman and Chief Exec. Officer, MetLife, Inc.

BENNETT, Catherine P.

325 Seventh St. NW
Suite 1200
Washington, DC 20004-1007
cbennett@pfizer.com
Tel: (202) 783 - 7070
Fax:(202) 347 - 2044

Registered Federal Lobbyist.
Serves As:
- V. President, Federal Tax and Trade Legislation, Pfizer Inc.

BENNETT, Douglas E.

45 Erieview Plaza
Room 1500
Cleveland, OH 44114
douglas.e.bennett@sbc.com
Tel: (216) 822 - 5100
Fax:(216) 822 - 1791

Serves As:
- Director, External Affairs, SBC Ohio

BENNETT, Douglas F.

1730 Rhode Island Ave. NW
Suite 406
Washington, DC 20036
douglas.bennett@libertymutual.com
Tel: (202) 775 - 0445
Fax:(202) 775 - 0874

Serves As:
- V. President, Federal Affairs, Liberty Mutual Insurance Co.

BENNETT, Edith

2148 E. Orangeview Ln.
Orange, CA 92857

Serves As:
- Contact, Allergan Inc. Political Action Committee, Allergan Inc.

BENNETT, Michael L.

P.O. Box 6000
Sioux City, IA 51102-6000
mbennett@terraindustries.com
Tel: (712) 277 - 1340
Fax:(712) 277 - 7383

Serves As:
- President and Chief Exec. Officer, Terra Industries Inc.

BENNETT, Mike

101 Columbia Rd.
Morristown, NJ 07962-4658
Tel: (973) 455 - 2753
Fax:(973) 455 - 3881

Serves As:
- Director, Internal Communications, Honeywell Internat'l, Inc.

BENNETT, Naisha

Hartford Plaza
Hartford, CT 06115
Tel: (860) 547 - 8543
Fax:(860) 547 - 6393

Serves As:
- State and Community Relations Coordinator, The Hartford Financial Services Group Inc.

BENNETT, Richard

United Technologies Bldg.
One Financial Plaza
Hartford, CT 06101
Tel: (860) 728 - 7000
Fax:(860) 728 - 6494

Serves As:
- V. President, Environment, Health and Safety, United Technologies Corp.

BENNETT, Richard A. "Tony"

P.O. Box 40
Austin, TX 78767
tonybennett@templeinland.com
Tel: (512) 615 - 1108
Fax:(512) 615 - 1561

Serves As:
- V. President, Government Affairs, Temple-Inland Inc.

BENNETT, Robert R.

12300 Liberty Blvd.
Englewood, CO 80112
Tel: (720) 875 - 5400
Fax:(720) 875 - 5401

Serves As:
- President, Liberty Media Corp.

BENNETT, Stephen M.

2632 Marine Way
Mountain View, CA 94043
Tel: (650) 944 - 6000
Fax:(650) 944 - 3699

Serves As:
- President and Chief Exec. Officer, Intuit Inc.

BENNETT, Vickie

6710 Hartford Ave.
Lubbock, TX 79413
vickie.bennett@cox.com
Tel: (806) 771 - 6221

Serves As:
- Manager, Community Relations, (Cox Communications, Inc.), Cox Enterprises, Inc.

BENSCHNEIDER, Mike

7535 E. Hampden Ave.
Suite 310
Denver, CO 80231
Tel: (303) 283 - 6126
Fax:(303) 283 - 6117

Serves As:
- Legislative Representative, Farmers Group, Inc.

BENSON, Jo-Dee

2901 Via Fortuna
Austin, TX 78746
Tel: (512) 851 - 4653
TF: (800) 888 - 5016

Serves As:
- V. President, Integrated Communications, Cirrus Logic, Inc.

BENSON, Mark

P.O. Box 1388
Lewiston, ID 83501
mark.benson@potlatchcorp.com
Tel: (208) 799 - 1781
Fax:(208) 799 - 1918

Serves As:
- Director, Public Affairs, Potlatch Corp.

BENTAS, Lilly

777 Dedham St.
Canton, MA 02021
Tel: (781) 828 - 4900
Ext: 3385
Fax:(781) 828 - 5246
TF: (800) 225 - 9702

Serves As:
- Chairman and Chief Exec. Officer, Cumberland Farms, Inc.

BENTKOWSKI, Gayle V.

17800 Royalton Rd.
Cleveland, OH 44136-5149
gmvixler@ceresgp.com
Tel: (440) 572 - 8848
Fax:(440) 878 - 2959
TF: (800) 643 - 2474

Serves As:
- Senior V. President, Corporate Communications, Ceres Group, Inc.

Responsibilities include investor relations.

BENTLEY, Julia A.

115 N. Calderwood
P.O. Box 9388
Alcoa, TN 37701
julia_bentley@saksinc.com
Tel: (865) 981 - 6243
Fax:(865) 981 - 6325

Serves As:
- Senior V. President, Investor Relations and Communications, Saks, Inc.

BENTLEY, Kim

100 Jim Moran Blvd.
Deerfield Beach, FL 33442
Tel: (954) 418 - 5037
Fax:(954) 429 - 2300

Serves As:
- Director, Charitable Giving, JM Family Enterprises, Inc.

BENTLEY, Shawn

800 Connecticut Ave. NW
Suite 800
Washington, DC 20006
Tel: (202) 457 - 8582
Fax:(202) 457 - 8861

Registered Federal Lobbyist.
Serves As:
- V. President, Domestic Policy, Time Warner Inc.

BENTZ, Rhonda

1300 Connecticut Ave. NW
Suite 900
Washington, DC 20036
rbentz@visa.com
Tel: (202) 296 - 9230
Fax:(202) 862 - 5498

Registered Federal Lobbyist.
Serves As:
- Director, Public Affairs, Visa U.S.A. Inc.

BERESIK, Michael T.

700 13th St. NW
Suite 700
Washington, DC 20005-5922
Tel: (202) 508 - 6217
Fax:(202) 508 - 6330

Registered Federal Lobbyist.
Serves As:
- Assistant V. President, Government Relations, H & R Block, Inc.

BERG, Charles G.

48 Monroe Tpk.
Trumbull, CT 06611
cberg@oxhp.cm
Tel: (203) 459 - 6000
Fax:(203) 459 - 6330
TF: (800) 889 - 7658

Serves As:
- President and Chief Exec. Officer, Oxford Health Plans Inc.

BERG, Randy

P.O. Box 799
Toledo, OH 43695
Tel: (419) 247 - 3731
Fax:(419) 247 - 3821

Serves As:
- V. President, Human Resources, Pilkington North America

BERG, Susan

1000 Alfred Nobel Dr.
Hercules, CA 94547-1811
susan_berg@bio-rad.com
Tel: (510) 741 - 6063
Fax:(510) 741 - 5817
TF: (800) 424 - 6723

Serves As:
- Corporate Communications Manager, Bio-Rad Laboratories, Inc.

BERGEN, Jack D.
153 E. 53rd St.
56th Floor
New York, NY 10022-4611
Tel: (212) 258 - 4000
Fax:(212) 767 - 0580
TF: (800) 743 - 6367

Serves As:
- Senior V. President, Corporate Affairs and Marketing, Siemens Corp.

BERGER, Jackie
P.O. Box 85
Wichita, KS 67201-0085
jackie_berger@rac.ray.com
Tel: (316) 676 - 7690
Fax:(316) 676 - 8867

Serves As:
- V. President, Communications and Public Affairs, Raytheon Aircraft Company

BERGER, Lawrence M.
P.O. Box 426
Pittsburgh, PA 15230
lawrence.berger@msanet.com
Tel: (412) 967 - 3528
Fax:(412) 967 - 3309
TF: (800) 672 - 2222

Serves As:
- Director, Environmental Affairs, Mine Safety Appliances Co. (MSA)

BERGERON, Patricia A.
8155 T & B Blvd.
4A-31
Memphis, TN 38125
tricia_bergeron@tnb.com
Tel: (901) 252 - 8266
Fax:(901) 252 - 1306

Serves As:
- V. President, Investor and Corporate Relations, Thomas & Betts Corp.

BERGES, David E.
281 Tresser Blvd.
Two Stamford Plaza
Stamford, CT 06901-3238
Tel: (203) 969 - 0666
Fax:(203) 358 - 3977

Serves As:
- Chairman, President and Chief Exec. Officer, Hexcel Corp.

BERGH, Kasey
Checkerboard Square
St. Louis, MO 63164
Tel: (314) 982 - 1000
Fax:(314) 982 - 2752

Serves As:
- Manager, Community Affairs, Nestle Purina PetCare Co.

BERGIN, Robert
89 East Ave.
Rochester, NY 14649-0001
robert_bergin@rge.com
Tel: (585) 771 - 2294

Serves As:
- Director, Public Affairs, (New York State Electric & Gas Corp. (NYSEG), Rochester Gas and Electric Corp. (RG&E)), Energy East Corp.

BERGMAN, Adam
5673 Airport Rd.
Roanoke, VA 24012
Tel: (540) 362 - 4911

Serves As:
- V. President, Investor and Media Relations, Advance Auto Parts, Inc.

BERGMAN, Bob
316 Pennsylvania Ave. SE
Suite 300
Washington, DC 20003
bbergman@ups.com
Tel: (202) 675 - 3354
Fax:(202) 675 - 4230

Registered Federal Lobbyist.
Serves As:
- V. President, Public Affairs, United Parcel Service (UPS)

BERGMAN, Janet E.
Three First National Plaza
70 W. Madison St.
Chicago, IL 60602-4260
Tel: (312) 558 - 8651
TF: (800) 727 - 2533

Serves As:
- V. President, Investor Relations and Corporate Affairs, Sara Lee Corp.

BERGMAN, Stanley M.
135 Duryea Rd.
Melville, NY 11747
Tel: (631) 843 - 5500
Fax:(631) 843 - 5975

Serves As:
- Chairman and Chief Exec. Officer, Henry Schein, Inc.

BERGQUIST, Renee
250 E. Parkcenter Blvd.
Boise, ID 83706
Tel: (208) 395 - 6200
Fax:(208) 395 - 6631

Serves As:
- PAC Contact, Albertson's, Inc.

BERGREN, Byron L.
P.O. Box 2821
York, PA 17405-2821
Tel: (717) 757 - 7660
Fax:(717) 751 - 3196

Serves As:
- President and Chief Exec. Officer, The Bon Ton Stores, Inc.

BERGSMAN, Michael
14850 Conference Center Dr.
Chantilly, VA 20151
Tel: (703) 834 - 1700
Fax:(703) 709 - 6087

Registered Federal Lobbyist.
Serves As:
- Representative, Rolls-Royce North America Inc.

BERGY, Dean H.
2725 Fairfield Rd.
Kalamazoo, MI 49002
Tel: (616) 385 - 2600
Fax:(616) 385 - 1062

Serves As:
- V. President, Chief Financial Officer, and Secretary, Stryker Corp.

Responsibilities include investor relations.

BERISFORD, John L.
One Pepsi Way
Somers, NY 10589-2201
Tel: (914) 767 - 6000
Fax:(914) 767 - 7761

Serves As:
- Senior V. President, Human Resources, The Pepsi Bottling Group

BERKE, Lisa
1133 S.W. Topeka Blvd.
Topeka, KS 66629
lisa.berke@bcbsks.com
Tel: (785) 291 - 8860
Fax:(785) 291 - 8216

Serves As:
- PAC Treasurer, Blue Cross and Blue Shield of Kansas, Inc.

BERKE, Richard
One ADP Blvd.
Roseland, NJ 07068-1728
richard_burke@adp.com
Tel: (973) 994 - 5000
Fax:(973) 974 - 3302
TF: (800) 225 - 5237

Serves As:
- V. President, Human Resources, Automatic Data Processing, Inc.

BERKEY, Ann Richardson
One Post St.
32nd Floor
San Francisco, CA 94104-5296
ann.berkey@mckesson.com
Tel: (415) 983 - 8494
Fax:(415) 983 - 7160

Registered Federal Lobbyist.
Serves As:
- V. President, Public Affairs, McKesson Corp.

BERLIN, Michael
100 Brodhead Rd.
Suite 230
Bethlehem, PA 18017
Tel: (610) 866 - 4400
Fax:(610) 866 - 9430

Serves As:
- Senior V President, Marketing/Promotions and Governement Affairs, Buzzi Unicem USA

BERMAN, Ira
P.O. Box 2206
Savannah, GA 31402-2206
Tel: (912) 965 - 3000
Fax:(912) 965 - 3775

Serves As:
- Senior V. President, Administration and General Counsel, Gulfstream Aerospace Corp.

Responsibilities include human resources.

BERMAN, Michael
3150 Sabre Dr.
Southlake, TX 76092
michael.berman@sabre-holdings.com
Tel: (682) 605 - 2397
Fax:(682) 264 - 0502

Serves As:
- V. President, Corporate Media Relations, Sabre Holdings Corp.

BERMAN, Richard K.
One Becton Dr.
Franklin Lakes, NJ 07417-1880
richard_berman@bd.com
Tel: (201) 847 - 6800
Fax:(201) 847 - 6475

Serves As:
- PAC Treasurer, Becton, Dickinson and Co.

BERN, Dorrit J.
450 Winks Ln.
Bensalem, PA 19020
Tel: (215) 245 - 9100
Fax:(215) 638 - 6759

Serves As:
- Chairman, President and Chief Exec. Officer, Charming Shoppes, Inc.

BERNADINE, Thomas
35 W. Wacker Dr.
Chicago, IL 60601
Tel: (312) 220 - 5959
Fax:(312) 220 - 3299

Serves As:
- Chairman and Chief Exec. Officer, Leo Burnett Worldwide

BERNARD, Al J.
80 M St. SE
Suite 410
Washington, DC 20003
Tel: (202) 867 - 3607

Registered Federal Lobbyist.
Serves As:
• V. President, Government Relations, The Manitowoc Co., Inc.

BERNAUER, David W.
200 Wilmot Rd.
Deerfield, IL 60015-4616
dave.bernauer@walgreens.com
Tel: (847) 914 - 2500
Fax:(847) 914 - 3652

Serves As:
• Chairman and Chief Exec. Officer, Walgreen Co.

BERNER, Jocelyn
P.O. Box 21488
Greensboro, NC 27420-1488
jocelyn_berner@vfc.com
Tel: (336) 424 - 7806
Fax:(336) 424 - 7631

Serves As:
• Media Contact, V. F. Corporation

BERNER, William J.
P.O. Box 426
Pittsburgh, PA 15230
william.berner@msanet.com
Tel: (412) 967 - 3043
Fax:(412) 967 - 3087
TF: (800) 672 - 2222

Serves As:
• Risk Manager, Mine Safety Appliances Co. (MSA)

BERNHARD, Jr., James M.
4171 Essen Lane
Baton Rouge, LA 70809
james.bernhard@shawgrp.com
Tel: (225) 932 - 2500
Fax:(225) 932 - 2661
TF: (800) 747 - 3322

Serves As:
• Chairman, President and Chief Exec. Officer, The Shaw Group Inc.

BERNHEIMER, Alan
500 McCarthy Blvd.
Milpitas, CA 95035
alan_bernheimer@maxtor.com
Tel: (408) 894 - 5000
Fax:(408) 952 - 3600
TF: (800) 262 - 9867

Serves As:
• Public Relations Contact, North, Central and South America, Maxtor Corp.

BERNICK, Carol L.
2525 Armitage Ave.
Melrose Park, IL 60160
Tel: (708) 450 - 3000
Fax:(708) 450 - 3435

Serves As:
• Chairman of the Board, Alberto-Culver Co.

BERNICK, Howard B.
2525 Armitage Ave.
Melrose Park, IL 60160
hbernick@alberto.com
Tel: (708) 450 - 3000
Fax:(708) 450 - 3435

Serves As:
• President and Chief Exec. Officer, Alberto-Culver Co.

BERNSTEIN, Victor
500 Hills Dr.
P.O. Box 752
Bedminster, NJ 07921
Tel: (908) 470 - 2300
Fax:(908) 470 - 2452

Serves As:
• V. President, Government Relations and Legal, (Loral Skynet), Loral Space & Communications

BERRA, Paul J.
P.O. Box 66760
St. Louis, MO 63166-6760
pjberr@solutia.com
Tel: (314) 674 - 5325
Fax:(314) 674 - 1585

Serves As:
• Assistant General Counsel and Director, Government Affairs, Solutia Inc.

BERRIOS, Jose A.
7950 Jones Branch Dr.
McLean, VA 22107
Tel: (703) 854 - 6000
Fax:(703) 276 - 2046

Serves As:
• V. President, Human Resources and Diversity, Gannett Co., Inc.

BERRY, J. Edward
P.O. Box 300
Detroit, MI 48265-1000
Tel: (313) 556 - 5000
Fax:(248) 696 - 7300

Registered Federal Lobbyist.
Serves As:
• Director, State-Local Government Relations, Public Policy Center, General Motors Corp.

BERRY, Mark
505 King Ave.
Columbus, OH 43201-2693
berrym@battelle.org
Tel: (614) 424 - 5544
Fax:(614) 424 - 3260
TF: (800) 201 - 2011

Serves As:
• Manager, Media Relations, Battelle

BERRY, Paul
9800 Fredericksburg Rd.
D-3-E
San Antonio, TX 78288-0122
Tel: (210) 498 - 1562
Fax:(210) 498 - 8754

Serves As:
• Public Affairs Representative, United Services Automobile Ass'n (USAA)

BERSCHAUER, Dr. Friedrich
Two T.W. Alexander Dr.
P.O. Box 12
Research Triangle Park, NC 27009
Tel: (919) 549 - 2000

Serves As:
• Chairman of the Board, Bayer CropScience

BERTHIAUME, Douglas A.
34 Maple St.
Milford, MA 01757
Tel: (508) 478 - 2000
Fax:(508) 872 - 1990
TF: (800) 252 - 4752

Serves As:
• Chairman, President and Chief Exec. Officer, Waters Corp.

BERTHIAUME, Joanne
The Mountain
Framingham, MA 01701-9168
Tel: (508) 766 - 7882
Fax:(508) 766 - 7543

Serves As:
• Media Contact, Bose Corp.

BERTMAN, Michael
1301 K St. NW
Suite 1000 East Tower
Washington, DC 20005
Tel: (202) 715 - 1115
Fax:(202) 715 - 1114

Registered Federal Lobbyist.
Serves As:
• Director, Federal Affairs, Diageo North America

BERTRAND, Frederic H.
77 Grove St.
Rutland, VT 05701
Tel: (802) 773 - 2711
Fax:(802) 747 - 2199
TF: (800) 649 - 2877

Serves As:
• Chairman of the Board, Central Vermont Public Service Corp.

BESHORE, Ph.D., Lance G.
P.O. Box 757
Carthage, MO 64836-0757
lance.beshore@leggett.com
Tel: (417) 358 - 8131
Fax:(417) 358 - 6045

Serves As:
• V. President, Public Affairs and Government Relations, Leggett & Platt, Inc.
Responsibilities include corporate philanthropy and political action.

BESSANT, Jr., Thomas
Cash America Bldg.
1600 W. Seventh St.
Fort Worth, TX 76102-2599
Tel: (817) 335 - 1100
Fax:(817) 570 - 1645

Serves As:
• Media Contact, Cash America Internat'l, Inc.

BEST, Becky E.
645 W. Grand River
Howell, MI 48843

Serves As:
• Manager, Corporate Community Relations, (Citizens Insurance Co.), Allmerica Property & Casualty Companies, Inc.

BEST, Lawrence C.
One Boston Scientific Pl.
Natick, MA 01760-1537
bestl@bsci.com
Tel: (508) 650 - 8000
Fax:(508) 647 - 2200

Serves As:
• Senior V. President and Chief Financial Officer; PAC Treasurer, Boston Scientific Corp.

BEST, Robert W.
P.O. Box 650205
Dallas, TX 75265-0205
robert.best@atmosenergy.com
Tel: (972) 934 - 9227
Fax:(972) 855 - 3030
TF: (800) 382 - 8667

Serves As:
• Chairman, President and Chief Exec. Officer, Atmos Energy Corp.

BETLEJEWSKI, Tina L.
13515 Ballantyne Corp. Pl.
Charlotte, NC 28277
tina.betlejewski@spx.com
Tel: (704) 752 - 4454

Serves As:
• Manager, Communications, SPX Corp.
Responsibilities also include corporate philanthropy.

BETTY, Charles Garry
1375 Peachtree St.
Atlanta, GA 30309
Tel: (404) 815 - 0770
Fax:(404) 815 - 8805

Serves As:
• President and Chief Exec. Officer, Earthlink, Inc.

BETZ, Dennis M.
1155 Peachtree St. NE
1917 Campanile
Atlanta, GA 30309-3610
dennis.betz@bellsouth.com
Tel: (404) 249 - 3170
Fax:(404) 249 - 0149

Serves As:
- Assistant V. President, Media Relations, BellSouth Corp.

BEVERIDGE, Bonnie A.
2211 Congress St.
M/S B159
Portland, ME 04122-0545
bbeveridge@unumprovident.com
Tel: (207) 575 - 4310
Fax:(207) 575 - 4304

Serves As:
- Legislative Systems Coordinator, UnumProvident Corp.

BEVERIDGE, Crawford
4150 Network Circle
UMPK10241
Santa Clara, CA 95054
crawford.beveridge@sun.com
Tel: (650) 786 - 8857
Fax:(650) 856 - 2114
TF: (800) 555 - 9786

Serves As:
- Exec. V. President and Chief Human Resources Officer, Sun Microsystems, Inc.

BEVIL, Jr., C.K. "Buddy"
P.O. Drawer 2128
Dalton, GA 30722-2128
Tel: (706) 278 - 3812
Fax:(706) 275 - 1719

Serves As:
- Director, Marketing Communications, Shaw Industries

BEVINGTON, Susan
P.O. Box 66760
St. Louis, MO 63166-6760
Tel: (314) 674 - 1000
Fax:(314) 674 - 1585

Serves As:
- V. President, Human Resources, Solutia Inc.

BEY, Isisara
550 Madison Ave.
New York, NY 10022-3211
isisara_bey@sonymusic.com
Tel: (212) 833 - 7912
Fax:(212) 833 - 7917

Serves As:
- V. President, Corporate Affairs, (Sony BMG Music Entertainment, Inc.), Sony Corp. of America

BEYER, Jeffrey C.
4680 Wilshire Blvd.
Los Angeles, CA 90010
Tel: (323) 932 - 3200
Fax:(323) 932 - 3101

Serves As:
- Senior V. President and Chief Communications Officer, (Farmers Insurance Group of Companies), Farmers Group, Inc.

BEYER, Leslie
333 Corporate Woods Pkwy.
Vernon Hills, IL 60061-3109
lbeyer@zebra.com
Tel: (847) 793 - 2652
Fax:(847) 913 - 8766
TF: (800) 423 - 0422

Serves As:
- Director, Public Relations, Zebra Technologies Corp.

BEZOS, Jeffrey P.
P.O. Box 81226
Seattle, WA 98108-1226
Tel: (206) 266 - 1000
Fax:(206) 266 - 1821

Serves As:
- Chairman, President and Chief Exec. Officer, Amazon.com, Inc.

BHANSALI, Parag P.
50 N. Laura St., Suite 1900
Jacksonville, FL 32202-3638
Tel: (904) 357 - 9100
Fax:(904) 357 - 9101

Serves As:
- V. President, Investor Relations, Rayonier Inc.

BIAGIO, Jan
P.O. Box 3001
Lancaster, PA 17604-3001
Tel: (717) 397 - 2416

Serves As:
- Foundation Coordinator, Armstrong Holdings, Inc.

BIANCHI, Franco
One Haworth Center
Holland, MI 49423
Tel: (616) 393 - 3000
Fax:(616) 393 - 1570
TF: (800) 344 - 2600

Serves As:
- President and Chief Exec. Officer, Haworth Inc.

BICH, Bruno
500 Bic Dr.
Milford, CT 06460
Tel: (203) 783 - 2000
Fax:(203) 783 - 2081

Serves As:
- Chairman and Chief Exec. Officer, BIC Corp.

BICKEL, Bruce
Two P & C Plaza
620 Liberty Ave.
Pittsburgh, PA 15222
Tel: (412) 553 - 5700

Serves As:
- Exec. Director, Foundation, Equitable Resources, Inc.

BIEBER, Michael A.
3475 East Foothill Blvd.
Pasadena, CA 91107
Tel: (626) 351 - 4664
Fax:(626) 351 - 5291

Serves As:
- V. President, Investor Relations, Tetra Tech, Inc.

BIEBUYCK, Beatrice
1331 Pennsylvania Ave. NW
Suite 550 South
Washington, DC 20004
Tel: (202) 637 - 8020
Fax:(202) 637 - 8028

Registered Federal Lobbyist.
Serves As:
- Representative, Boston Scientific Corp.

BIEGUN, Stephen E.
1350 I St. NW
Suite 1000
Washington, DC 20005
Tel: (202) 962 - 5400
Fax:(202) 336 - 7223

Serves As:
- V. President, International Government Affairs, Ford Motor Co.

BIGGAR, John R.
Two N. Ninth St.
Allentown, PA 18101-1179
jrbiggar@pplweb.com
Tel: (610) 774 - 5613
Fax:(610) 774 - 4198
TF: (800) 345 - 3085

Serves As:
- Exec. V. President and Chief Financial Officer, PPL Corp.

Responsibilities include investor relations.

BIGGS, Jennifer
1350 I St. NW
Suite 1000
Washington, DC 20005
jbiggs12@ford.com
Tel: (202) 962 - 5363
Fax:(202) 962 - 5417

Serves As:
- Public Affairs Coordinator, Ford Motor Co.

BIGGS, Robert D.
1065 Woodman Dr.
Dayton, OH 45432
Tel: (937) 224 - 6000
Fax:(937) 259 - 7813

Serves As:
- Chairman of the Board, DPL Inc.

BIGGS BROCK, Heidi
1100 Connecticut Ave. NW
Suite 530
Washington, DC 20036
Tel: (202) 293 - 7222
Fax:(202) 293 - 2955

Registered Federal Lobbyist.
Serves As:
- V. President, Federal and International Affairs, Weyerhaeuser Co.

BILEK, Edward J.
P.O. Box 10566
Birmingham, AL 35296
ed.bilek@compassbnk.com
Tel: (205) 297 - 3331
Fax:(205) 297 - 4239
TF: (800) 239 - 2265

Serves As:
- Director, Investor Relations, Compass Bancshares, Inc.

BILICKI, Liane
One Village Dr.
Van Buren Township, MI 48111
lbilicki@visteon.com
Tel: (313) 755 - 2916
Fax:(313) 722 - 1658
TF: (800) VIS - TEON

Serves As:
- Manager, Corporate Communications, Visteon Corp.

BILLINGS, Bob
1500 Corporate Dr.
Suite 400
Canonsburg, PA 15317
Tel: (724) 514 - 1887
Fax:(724) 514 - 1870

Serves As:
- PAC Contact, Mylan Laboratories Inc.

BINDER, Robert
180 S. Clinton Ave.
Rochester, NY 14646-0500

Serves As:
- PAC Treasurer, Citizens Communications Co.

BINGERT, Maureen
Perryville Corporate Park
Clinton, NJ 08809-4000
maureen_bingert@fwl.com
Tel: (908) 730 - 4444
Fax:(908) 730 - 5315

Serves As:
- Corporate Communications Contact, Foster Wheeler Ltd.

BINKLEY, David A.
Administrative Center
2000 N. M-63
Benton Harbor, MI 49022-2692
Tel: (269) 923 - 5000
Fax:(269) 923 - 5443

Serves As:
- Senior V. President, Global Human Resources, Whirlpool Corp.

BINKOWSKI, Beverly
3401 N.W. 63rd St.
Oklahoma City, OK 73116
bbinkowski@bcbsok.com
Tel: (405) 841 - 9597
Fax:(405) 841 - 9663

Serves As:
- Public Affairs, BlueCross BlueShield of Oklahoma

BIONDOLILLO, JD, Michael A.
600 Dresher Rd.
Horsham, PA 19044
Tel: (215) 956 - 8000
TF: (800) 523 - 0650

Serves As:
- Exec. V. President, Human Resources, The Penn Mutual Life Insurance Co.

BIRCK, Michael J.
One Tellabs Center
1415 W. Diehl Rd.
Naperville, IL 60563
Tel: (630) 798 - 8800
Fax:(630) 852 - 7346

Serves As:
- Chairman of the Board, Tellabs

BIRD, Shelley
1700 S. Patterson Blvd.
WHQ5
Dayton, OH 45479
shelley.bird@ncr.com
Tel: (937) 445 - 4435
Fax:(937) 445 - 1890

Serves As:
- V. President, Public Relations, NCR Corporation

BIRD YEATER, Pamela
1540 Genesee St.
Kansas City, MO 64102
Tel: (816) 968 - 3000
Fax:(816) 968 - 3720

Serves As:
- Foundation Administrator, Butler Manufacturing Co.

BIRDSEYE, Wally
5251 DTC Pkwy.
Suite 1400
Greenwood Village, CO 80111-2742
Tel: (303) 220 - 0100
Fax:(303) 220 - 7100
TF: (800) 242 - 3799

Serves As:
- President, Federal Solutions, CIBER, Inc.

BIRLE, James R.
1295 State St.
Springfield, MA 01111-0001
Tel: (413) 744 - 8411
Fax:(413) 744 - 6005
TF: (800) 767 - 1000

Serves As:
- Chairman of the Board, MassMutual Financial Group

BIRNS, Ira
50 Marcus Dr.
Melville, NY 11747
Tel: (631) 847 - 2000

Serves As:
- V. President and Treasurer, Arrow Electronics, Inc.

BIRTCIL, Bill
1944 E. Sky Harbor Circle
Phoenix, AZ 85034
Tel: (602) 365 - 3859

Serves As:
- V. President, Communications, (Honeywell Aerospace), Honeywell Internat'l, Inc.

BISCHOFF, J. Kevin
P.O. Box 30270
Salt Lake City, UT 84130-0270
kbischoff@regence.com
Tel: (801) 333 - 5285
Fax:(801) 333 - 6563

Serves As:
- V. President, Public and Corporate Affairs, Regence BlueCross BlueShield of Utah

BISCHOFF, J. Michael
1166 Ave. of The Americas
New York, NY 10036-2774
Tel: (212) 345 - 5470
Fax:(212) 345 - 5669

Serves As:
- V. President, Corporate Development, Marsh & McLennan Companies, Inc.

Responsibilities include investor relations.

BISHOP, Alan
P.O. Box 2511
Houston, TX 77252-2511
alan.bishop@elpaso.com
Tel: (713) 420 - 5429
Fax:(713) 420 - 4099

Serves As:
- Director, Shareholder Relations, El Paso Corp.

BISHOP, Brad
P.O. Box 708
Warsaw, IN 46581-0708
Tel: (574) 372 - 4291
Fax:(574) 372 - 4988
TF: (800) 613 - 6131

Serves As:
- Director, Public Affairs, Zimmer Holdings, Inc.

BISHOP, Cherae
1100 Connecticut Ave. NW
Suite 530
Washington, DC 20036
Tel: (202) 293 - 7222
Fax:(202) 293 - 2955

Serves As:
- Manager, Government Affairs, Weyerhaeuser Co.

BISHOP, Laura
7601 Penn Ave. South
Richfield, MN 55423
laura.bishop@bestbuy.com
Tel: (612) 291 - 1000
Fax:(612) 292 - 4001

Serves As:
- Director, Government Relations, Best Buy Co., Inc.

BISHOP, Robert R.
1500 Crittenden Lane
Mountain View, CA 94043
Tel: (650) 933 - 1132
Fax:(650) 933 - 0316

Serves As:
- Chairman and Chief Exec. Officer, SGI

BISHOP, Russell E.
370 17th St., Suite 900
Denver, CO 80202
rbishop@duke-energy.com
Tel: (303) 605 - 1765
Fax:(303) 893 - 2613

Serves As:
- V. President, Governmental Affairs, Duke Energy Corp.

BISHOP-MURPHY, Melissa
400 Perimeter Center Terrace, Suite 700
Atlanta, GA 30346
mbishop-murphy@pfizer.com
Tel: (770) 551 - 5170

Serves As:
- State Government Relations Manager - Georgia and Alabama, Pfizer Inc.

BISSETT, William J.
40 Fountain Plaza
Buffalo, NY 14202
Tel: (716) 858 - 5000
Fax:(716) 858 - 5479

Serves As:
- V. President, External Affairs, Delaware North Companies

BITTENBENDER, Charles
5875 Landerbrook Dr.
Suite 300
Cleveland, OH 44124-4017
Tel: (440) 449 - 9600
Fax:(440) 449 - 9607

Serves As:
- V. President, General Counsel and Secretary, NACCO Industries

Responsibilities include corporate philanthropy.

BITTERMAN, Mark E.
21700 Atlantic Blvd.
Dulles, VA 20166
bitterman.mark@orbital.com
Tel: (703) 406 - 5523
Fax:(703) 406 - 5572

Registered Federal Lobbyist.
Serves As:
- Senior V. President, Government Relations, Orbital Sciences Corp.

BITTO, Ron
3900 Essex Ln., Suite 1200
Houston, TX 77027-5177
Tel: (713) 439 - 8391
Fax:(713) 439 - 8280

Serves As:
- Director, Communications, Baker Hughes Inc.

BIXBY, R. Philip
P.O. Box 219139
Kansas City, MO 64121-9139
Tel: (816) 753 - 7000
Fax:(816) 753 - 4902

Serves As:
- Chairman, President and Chief Exec. Officer, Kansas City Life Insurance Co.

BJORNSON, Ms. Gerrie
1100 Wilson Blvd.
Suite 900
Arlington, VA 22209-2297
gerrie.bjornson@goodrich.com
Tel: (703) 558 - 8250
Fax:(703) 558 - 8262

Registered Federal Lobbyist.
Serves As:
- V. President, Government Relations, Goodrich Corporation

BLACK, Carol
P.O. Box 6006
Cypress, CA 90630
carol.black@phs.com
Tel: (714) 226 - 3084
Fax:(714) 226 - 3653

Serves As:
- Senior V. President, Human Resources, PacifiCare Health Systems, Inc.

BLACK, David L.
100 Weybosset St.
Providence, RI 02903
Tel: (401) 272 - 5040
Fax:(401) 273 - 4243

Serves As:
- Treasurer, New England Gas Co. PAC, (New England Gas Co.), Southern Union Company

BLACK, David S.
2016 Mount Athos Rd.
Lynchburg, VA 24504
dsblack@mcdermott.com

Serves As:
- PACs and Corporate Contributions Contact, (BWX Technologies), McDermott Internat'l, Inc.
- PAC Treasurer, The Babcock & Wilcox Company

BLACK, Jeffrey P.
155 S. Limerick Rd.
Limerick, PA 19468
Tel: (610) 948 - 5100
Fax:(610) 948 - 0811

Serves As:
- President and Chief Exec. Officer, Teleflex Inc.

BLACK, Keith
P.O. Box 960
M/S 28AT
Cincinnati, OH 45201-0960
Tel: (513) 287 - 3704
Fax:(513) 287 - 2513

Serves As:
- General Manager, State Government Affairs, Cinergy Corp.

BLACK, Lennox K.
155 S. Limerick Rd.
Limerick, PA 19468
Tel: (610) 948 - 5100
Fax:(610) 948 - 0811

Serves As:
- Chairman of the Board, Teleflex Inc.

BLACK, Ruth
P.O. Box 196660
Anchorage, AK 99519-6660
Tel: (907) 787 - 8700
Fax:(907) 834 - 7585

Serves As:
- Manager, Valdez Communications, Alyeska Pipeline Service Co.

BLACKBURN, John D.
P.O. Box 2020
Bloomington, IL 61701-2020

Serves As:
- Chief Exec. Officer, Country Insurance and Financial Services

BLACKBURN, Kathleen A.
1950 Franklin St., Third Floor
Oakland, CA 94612
Tel: (510) 987 - 2703
Fax:(510) 873 - 5029

Serves As:
- V. President, Public Affairs - California Division, Kaiser Permanente

BLACKBURN, II, Kenneth E.
333 Commerce St., Suite 2102
Nashville, TN 37201-3300
kenny.blackburn@bellsouth.com

Serves As:
- Assistant V. President, External Affairs, BellSouth Corp.

BLACKMON, Kimberly
3150 Sabre Dr.
Southlake, TX 76092
kimberly.blackmon@sabre-holdings.com
Tel: (682) 605 - 3286
Fax:(682) 264 - 9000

Serves As:
- Corporate Media Relations, Sabre Holdings Corp.

BLAIR, Michele
1100 New York Ave. NW
Suite 600W
Washington, DC 20005
michelle.blair@hp.com
Tel: (202) 378 - 2500
Fax:(202) 378 - 2550

Serves As:
- Government Affairs Manager, Hewlett-Packard Co.

BLAKE, Brenda
P.O. Box 858
Valley Forge, PA 19482
blakeb@ugicorp.com
Tel: (610) 337 - 1000
Ext: 3202
Fax:(610) 992 - 3259

Serves As:
- Media/Investor Relations Coordinator, UGI Corp.

BLAKE, Rick
505 Gillette Ave.
Gillette, WY 82717
Tel: (307) 687 - 6000
Fax:(307) 687 - 6015

Serves As:
- V. President, Human Resources, Kennecott Energy Co.

BLAKE, Wanda T.
P.O. Box 13297
Richmond, VA 23225
Tel: (804) 302 - 1700
Fax:(804) 302 - 1760

Serves As:
- PAC Treasurer, Swedish Match North America Inc.

BLAKEMAN, Marc D.
225 W. Randolph St.
27 B
Chicago, IL 60606
Tel: (312) 727 - 4221
Fax:(312) 727 - 3722
TF: (800) 327 - 9346

Serves As:
- Regional V. President, External Affairs, SBC Illinois

BLALACK, T. Gary
513 Cherrywood Point
Franklin, TN 37064
Tel: (615) 791 - 8438

Serves As:
- Exec. Manager, State Government Affairs, GlaxoSmithKline Research and Development

BLANCHARD, Brenda
701 Pennsylvania Ave. NW
Suite 725
Washington, DC 20004
Tel: (202) 638 - 7429
Fax:(202) 628 - 4763

Serves As:
- Vice President, Public Affairs, Novartis Corporation

BLANCHARD, Cayce
5665 Plaza Drive
Cypress, CA 90630-0007
cayce.blanchard@meus.mea.com
Tel: (714) 229 - 3837
Fax:(714) 229 - 3854

Serves As:
- V. President, Corporate Communications, Mitsubishi Electric & Electronics USA

BLANCHARD, James H.
P.O. Box 120
Columbus, GA 31902-0120
Tel: (706) 649 - 2311
Fax:(706) 641 - 6555

Serves As:
- Chief Exec. Officer, Synovus Financial Corp.

BLANCHARD, John A.
P.O. Box 1101
Minneapolis, MN 55440-1101
Tel: (952) 938 - 8080
Fax:(952) 917 - 1717

Serves As:
- Chairman of the Board, ADC

BLANCHARD, Judith A.
1401 I St. NW
Suite 1200
Washington, DC 20005-2225
Tel: (202) 408 - 5800
Fax:(202) 408 - 5845

Registered Federal Lobbyist.
Serves As:
- Manager, Federal Relations, Chevron Corp.

BLANCO, Janelle
P.O. Box 31907
Santa Barbara, CA 93130
janelle.blanco@tenethealth.com
Tel: (818) 952 - 2015
Fax:(818) 952 - 2404

Serves As:
- V. President, Government Relations, Tenet Healthcare Corp.

BLANDING, Terry
P.O. Box 8700
Grand Rapids, MI 49518
terry_blanding@spartanstores.com
Tel: (616) 878 - 8447
Fax:(616) 878 - 2900

Serves As:
- Donations/Community Affairs, Spartan Stores Inc.

BLANK, Scott A.
225 City Line Ave.
Suite 200
Bala Cynwyd, PA 19004
Tel: (610) 934 - 7000
Fax:(610) 934 - 7054
TF: (888) 438 - 7488

Serves As:
- Senior V. President, Legal and Corporate Affairs; General Counsel and Secretary, Pegasus Communications Corp.

BLANK, Tony
1331 Pennsylvania Ave. NW
Suite 550 South
Washington, DC 20004
Tel: (202) 637 - 8020
Fax:(202) 637 - 8028

Registered Federal Lobbyist.
Serves As:
- Representative, Boston Scientific Corp.

BLANKENSHIP, Don L.
Four N. Fourth St.
Richmond, VA 23219-2230
Tel: (804) 788 - 1800
Fax:(804) 788 - 1870

Serves As:
- Chairman, President and Chief Exec. Officer, Massey Energy Co.

BLANKFEIN, LLoyd C.
85 Broad St.
New York, NY 10004
Tel: (212) 902 - 1000
Fax:(212) 902 - 3000

Serves As:
- Managing Director and Chief Operating Officer, Media Relations, Goldman, Sachs and Co.

BLANNING, Bill
P.O. Box 57013
Irvine, CA 92619-7013
blanning@broadcom.com
Tel: (949) 926 - 5555
Fax:(949) 450 - 0754

Serves As:
- V. President, Corporate Communications, Broadcom Corp.

BLATTER, Victoria
601 Pennsylvania Ave. NW
North Bldg. Suite 1200
Washington, DC 20004
Tel: (202) 638 - 4170
Fax:(202) 638 - 3670

Registered Federal Lobbyist.
Serves As:
- Exec. Director, Federal Government Relations, Merck & Co., Inc.

BLAU, Harvey R.
100 Jericho Quadrangle
Jericho, NY 11753
Tel: (516) 938 - 5544
Fax:(516) 938 - 5644

Serves As:
- Chairman and Chief Exec. Officer, Griffon Corp.

BLAZER, J. Robert
150 E. Gay St., Suite 4A
Columbus, OH 43215
bob.blazer@sbc.com
Tel: (614) 223 - 7311
Fax:(614) 223 - 4017

Serves As:
- V. President, State Government Relations, SBC Ohio

BLEDSOE, Steven R.
One Pershing Square
2301 Main St.
Kansas City, MO 64108
Tel: (816) 395 - 2086
Fax:(816) 395 - 2379

Serves As:
- V. President, Government Affairs, Blue Cross and Blue Shield of Kansas City

Responsibilities include political action.

BLEDSOE, Tracy
P.O. Box 511
Kingsport, TN 37662-5075
tracyb@eastman.com
Tel: (423) 224 - 0498
Fax:(423) 229 - 1004
TF: (800) 327 - 8626

Serves As:
- Communications Representative, Eastman Chemical Co.

BLEIER, Michael E.
One Mellon Center
500 Grant St.
Room 1915
Pittsburgh, PA 15258-0001
bleier.me@mellon.com
Tel: (412) 234 - 1537
Fax:(412) 236 - 4814

Serves As:
- General Counsel, Mellon Financial Corp.

BLENNER, Leslie
20 NW Ninth St.
Evansville, IN 47741

Serves As:
- Treasurer, Vectren Corp. Employees Federal PAC, Vectren Corp.

BLEUSTEIN, Jeffrey L.
3700 W. Juneau Ave.
Milwaukee, WI 53208
Tel: (414) 342 - 4680
Fax:(414) 343 - 8230

Serves As:
- Chairman and Chief Exec. Officer, Harley-Davidson Motor Company

BLEVINS, Barbara
427 W. 12th St.
Kansas City, MO 64105
Tel: (816) 983 - 1303
Fax:(816) 983 - 1192
TF: (800) 468 - 6740

Serves As:
- Treasurer, Kansas City Southern Employee PAC, Kansas City Southern

BLEVINS, Jennifer C.
1290 Ave. of the Americas
New York, NY 10104
Tel: (212) 554 - 1234
TF: (888) AXA - INFO

Serves As:
- Exec. V. President, Human Resources, AXA Financial, Inc.

BLINDE, Loral
9955 Airtran Blvd.
Orlando, FL 32827-5330
Tel: (407) 251 - 5600
Fax:(407) 251 - 5727

Serves As:
- V. President, Human Resources, AirTran Airways

BLISSIT, Doug
P.O. Box 20706
Atlanta, GA 30320-6001
Tel: (404) 715 - 2455
Fax:(404) 715 - 4779

Serves As:
- V. President, Public Affairs, Delta Air Lines, Inc.

BLOCK, Bill
Bandag Center
2905 N. Hwy. 61
Muscatine, IA 52761-5886
Tel: (563) 262 - 1400
Fax:(563) 262 - 1263

Serves As:
- Director, Corporate Communications, Bandag, Inc.

BLOCK, Kris
680 E. Swedesford Rd.
Wayne, PA 19087
kris.block@sungard.com
Tel: (484) 582 - 5505
Fax:(484) 225 - 1120

Serves As:
- Investor Relations Specialist, SunGard Data Systems, Inc.

BLOCK, Mark
251 W. 57th St.
22nd Floor
New York, NY 10019
Tel: (212) 445 - 4000
Fax:(212) 445 - 4757
TF: (800) 631 - 1040

Serves As:
- Director, External Relations, Newsweek, Inc.

BLOCK, Tom
One Bank One Plaza
Chicago, IL 60670
Tel: (312) 732 - 4000

Serves As:
- Senior V. President, Government Relations, J. P. Morgan Chase & Co.

BLOCKER, Ananias "Andy"
801 Pennsylvania Ave. NW
Suite 630
Washington, DC 20004
ablocker@nyse.com
Tel: (202) 347 - 4300
Fax:(202) 347 - 4370

Serves As:
- Vice President, Government Relations, New York Stock Exchange, Inc.

BLOCKER, Lisa A.
5400 Legacy Dr.
M/S H3-6F-47
Plano, TX 75024-3199
Tel: (972) 605 - 6091
Fax:(972) 605 - 6090

Serves As:
- Exec. Director, State Government Affairs, EDS Corp.

BLOCKEY, Joanna L.
P.O. Box 98510
Las Vegas, NV 89193-8510
Tel: (702) 876 - 7368
Fax:(702) 220 - 4736

Serves As:
- Communications Representative, Southwest Gas Corp.

BLOEMENDAAL, Dirk C.
7575 Fulton St. East
M/S 78-2G
Ada, MI 49355-0001
Tel: (616) 787 - 7560
Fax:(616) 787 - 5624

Serves As:
- Senior Corporate Counsel, North American Government Affairs, Alticor Inc.

BLOHM, Donald E.
1284 N. Telegraph Rd.
Monroe, MI 48162
Tel: (734) 241 - 3680
Fax:(734) 457 - 2005

Serves As:
- Administrator, La-Z-Boy Foundation, La-Z-Boy Incorporated

BLOODWORTH, Carolyn A.
One Energy Plaza
Jackson, MI 49201
cbloodworth@cmsenergy.com
Tel: (517) 788 - 0432
Fax:(517) 788 - 2281

Serves As:
- Director, Corporate Giving, CMS Energy Corp.

BLOOM, Cyndi
3402 E. University Dr.
Phoenix, AZ 85034
Tel: (602) 794 - 9604
Fax:(602) 794 - 9601

Serves As:
- Manager, Marketing Communications, Eagle-Picher Industries, Inc.

BLOOM, Elliot
Nine W. 57th St.
37th Floor
New York, NY 10019
elliot.bloom@cendant.com
Tel: (973) 496 - 8414

Serves As:
- Senior V. President, Corporate Communications, Cendant Corp.

BLOOM, Jon
2000 K St., NW
Suite 710
Washington, DC 20006
Tel: (202) 862 - 0200
Fax:(202) 862 - 0267

Serves As:
- Washington Representative, Government Agencies, Exxon Mobil Corp.

BLOOM-BAGLIN, Rachel
P.O. Box 15437
A1C-320
Wilmington, DE 19850-5437
rachel.bloom-baglin@astrazeneca.com
Tel: (302) 886 - 7858
Fax:(302) 886 - 5973
TF: (800) 456 - 3669

Serves As:
- Exec. Director, Corporate External Communications, AstraZeneca Pharmaceuticals

BLOSS-BAUM, Linda
607 14th St. NW
Suite 500
Washington, DC 20005
linda.bloss-baum@wmg.com
Tel: (202) 354 - 8248

Registered Federal Lobbyist.
Serves As:
- V. President, Public Policy and Government Relations, (Warner Music Group Inc.), Time Warner Inc.

BLOUGH, Kelly
3965 Freedom Circle
Santa Clara, CA 95054
kblough@mcafee.com
Tel: (408) 346 - 3481
Fax:(408) 346 - 5411
TF: (800) 338 - 8754

Serves As:
- V. President, Corporate and Investor Relations, McAfee, Inc.

BLUE, James N.
3550 General Atomics Ct.
San Diego, CA 92121
Tel: (858) 455 - 3000
Fax:(858) 455 - 3621

Serves As:
- Chairman, Chief Exec. Officer, General Atomics

BLUE, Robert M.
P.O. Box 26532
Richmond, VA 23261
Tel: (804) 771 - 4517
Fax:(804) 771 - 3643

Serves As:
- Managing Director, State Affairs and Corporate Public Policy, Dominion Resources, Inc.

BLUM, Aleesa
400 Atlantic St.
Stamford, CT 06921
aleesa.blum@ipaper.com
Tel: (203) 541 - 8565
Fax:(203) 541 - 8268
TF: (800) 223 - 1268

Serves As:
- V. President, Communications; and President, Internat'l Paper Co. Foundation, Internat'l Paper

BLUM, Jonathan D.
P.O. Box 32070
Louisville, KY 40232
Tel: (502) 874 - 8300
Fax:(502) 874 - 8324

Serves As:
- Senior V. President, Public Affairs, YUM! Brands, Inc.

BLUM, Steven
15501 N. Dial Blvd.
M/S 2125
Scottsdale, AZ 85260
blum@dialcorp.com
Tel: (480) 754 - 3425

Serves As:
- Senior V. President, Investor Relations, The Dial Corporation

BLUMER, Patti R.
1350 I St., N.W., Suite 1030
Washington, DC 20005-3305
blumer.patti@principal.com
Tel: (202) 682 - 1280
Fax:(202) 682 - 1412

Registered Federal Lobbyist.
Serves As:
- Assistant Federal Legislative Director, The Principal Financial Group

BLUNT, Abigail
101 Constitution Ave. NW
Suite 400 West
Washington, DC 20001
Tel: (202) 354 - 1500
Fax:(202) 354 - 1505

Serves As:
- Director, Government Affairs- Food, Altria Group, Inc.

BLYSTONE, John B.
13515 Ballantyne Corp. Pl.
Charlotte, NC 28277
Tel: (704) 752 - 4400

Serves As:
- Chairman, President and Chief Exec. Officer, SPX Corp.

BOALS, Richard L.
P.O. Box 13466
Phoenix, AZ 85002-3466
Tel: (602) 864 - 4400
Fax:(602) 864 - 4242
TF: (800) 232 - 2345

Serves As:
- President and Chief Exec. Officer, Blue Cross and Blue Shield of Arizona

BOARD, Virginia M.
P.O. Box 26666
Richmond, VA 23261-6666
Virginia_Board@dom.com
Tel: (804) 771 - 4491

Serves As:
- Director, Community Affairs, Dominion Resources, Inc.

BOARDMAN, Jenny
400 Atlantic St.
Stamford, CT 06921
Tel: (203) 541 - 8407
Fax:(203) 541 - 8200
TF: (800) 223 - 1268

Serves As:
- Manager, Media Relations, Internat'l Paper

BOARDMAN, Kevin W.
201 S. Main St.
23rd Floor
Salt Lake City, UT 84140
Tel: (801) 220 - 6818
Fax:(801) 220 - 3116

Serves As:
- Director, Government Affairs, (Utah Power Co.), PacifiCorp

BOBINS, Norman R.
135 S. LaSalle St.
Chicago, IL 60603
Tel: (312) 904 - 2000
Fax:(312) 904 - 6521

Serves As:
- President and Chief Exec. Officer, LaSalle Bank N.A.

BOCHANSKI, Jr., George V.
100 Independence Mall West
Philadelphia, PA 19106-2399
Tel: (215) 592 - 3248
Fax:(215) 592 - 6808

Serves As:
- Manager, Internal Communications, Rohm and Haas Co.

BODAKEN, Bruce G.
50 Beale St.
San Francisco, CA 94105-1808
Tel: (415) 229 - 5000
Fax:(415) 229 - 5070
TF: (800) 200 - 3242

Serves As:
- Chairman, President and Chief Exec. Officer, Blue Shield of California

BODANZA, Joseph F.
One MetroTech Center
Brooklyn, NY 11201
Tel: (718) 403 - 2000
Fax:(718) 488 - 1763

Serves As:
- Senior V. President, Regulatory Affairs and Chief Accounting Officer, KeySpan Corp.

BODKIN, Dave
5725 Delphi Dr.
Troy, MI 48098-2815
david.g.bodkin@delphi.com
Tel: (248) 813 - 2532
Fax:(248) 813 - 2670

Serves As:
- Director, Media Relations, Delphi Corp.

BODNAR, M.D., Andrew G.
345 Park Ave.
New York, NY 10154-0037
Tel: (212) 546 - 4000
Fax:(212) 546 - 4020

Serves As:
- Senior V. President, Strategy, Medical and External Affairs, Bristol-Myers Squibb Co.

BODNAR, Anne Donovan
One Stamford Plaza
263 Tresser Blvd.
Stamford, CT 06901
bodnara@towers.com
Tel: (203) 326 - 5400
Fax:(203) 326 - 5499

Serves As:
- Managing Director, Human Resources, Towers Perrin

BOECKMANN, Alan L.
One Enterprise Dr.
Aliso Viejo, CA 92656-2606
alan.boeckmann@fluor.com
Tel: (949) 349 - 2000
Fax:(949) 349 - 5981

Serves As:
- Chairman and Chief Exec. Officer, Fluor Corp.

BOEHM, Mary
1155 Peachtree St. NE
7H08 Campanile
Atlanta, GA 30309-3610
mary.boehm@bellsouth.com
Tel: (404) 249 - 2329
Fax:(404) 249 - 2071

Serves As:
- President, BellSouth Foundation, BellSouth Corp.

BOGAN, Thomas S.
851 W. Cypress Creek Rd.
Fort Lauderdale, FL 33309
Tel: (954) 267 - 3000
Fax:(954) 267 - 9319
TF: (800) 424 - 8749

Serves As:
- Chairman of the Board, Citrix Systems, Inc.

BOGGARD, Robert B.
Metro Center
One Station Pl.
Stamford, CT 06902
Tel: (203) 539 - 8000
Fax:(203) 539 - 7734
TF: (800) 969 - 9974

Serves As:
- Exec. V. President, Human Resources, The Thomson Corporation

BOGGS, Casey
One SunAmerica Center
Los Angeles, CA 90067-6022
Tel: (310) 772 - 6775
TF: (800) 871 - 2000

Serves As:
- Director, Public Relations, AIG SunAmerica Inc.

BOGGS, Larry A.
1299 Pennsylvania Ave. NW
11th Floor West
Washington, DC 20004-2407
larry.boggs@corporate.ge.com
Tel: (202) 637 - 4000
Fax:(202) 637 - 4006

Registered Federal Lobbyist.
Serves As:
- Counsel, Environmental Programs, General Electric Co.

BOGOVICH, Mark Anthony
7733 Forsyth Blvd.
Suite 2300
St. Louis, MO 63105
Tel: (314) 863 - 7422
Fax:(314) 863 - 0769
TF: (800) 677 - 1238

Serves As:
- Treasurer, RehabCare Group Inc. PAC, RehabCare Group, Inc.

BOHABOY, Scott A.
111 S. Wacker Dr.
Chicago, IL 60606
scott.a.bohaboy@rrd.com
Tel: (312) 326 - 7730
Fax:(312) 326 - 7748

Serves As:
- V. President, Investor Relations, R R Donnelley

BOHAN, Lynne M.
90 Everett Ave.
Chelsea, MA 02150-2301
Tel: (617) 887 - 3000
Fax:(617) 887 - 8484

Serves As:
- Director, Public Relations and Government Affairs, H. P. Hood Inc.

BOHANAN, Lynette
5350 Tech Data Dr.
MS A3-10
Clearwater, FL 33760
lynette.bohanan@techdata.com
Tel: (727) 539 - 7429
Ext: 86270
Fax:(727) 571 - 9140
TF: (800) 237 - 8931

Serves As:
- Manager, Corporate Communications, Tech Data Corp.

BOHANNON, Robert H.
1850 N. Central Ave.
Suite 800
Phoenix, AZ 85004-4545
rbohannon@viad.com
Tel: (602) 207 - 4000

Serves As:
- Chairman, President and Chief Exec. Officer, Viad Corp

BOHLEY, David
3900 Wisconsin Ave. NW
Washington, DC 20016
Tel: (202) 752 - 7000
Fax:(202) 752 - 6099

Registered Federal Lobbyist.
Serves As:
- Representative, Fannie Mae

BOHLING, B. J.
1185 Ave. of the Americas
New York, NY 10036
Tel: (212) 536 - 8147
Fax:(212) 536 - 8318

Serves As:
- Senior V. President, Human Resources, Amerada Hess Corp.

BOHN, Donald W.
1350 I St. NW
Suite 1210
Washington, DC 20005-3305
dbohn@corus.jnj.com
Tel: (202) 589 - 1016
Fax:(202) 589 - 1001

Registered Federal Lobbyist.
Serves As:
- V. President, State Government Affairs, Johnson & Johnson

BOHN, Robert G.
P.O. Box 2566
Oshkosh, WI 54903-2566
Tel: (920) 235 - 9150
Fax:(920) 233 - 9314

Serves As:
- Chairman, President and Chief Exec. Officer, Oshkosh Truck Corp.

BOHREN, Deborah Loeb
11 W. 42nd St.
18th Floor
New York, NY 10035
Tel: (212) 476 - 3552
Fax:(212) 476 - 1430

Serves As:
- Senior V. President, Communications, Empire Blue Cross and Blue Shield

Responsibilities include investor relations.

BOIDOCK, John K.
1455 Pennsylvania Ave. NW
Suite 375
MS 4072
Washington, DC 20004
jboidock@ti.com
Tel: (202) 628 - 3133
Fax:(202) 628 - 2980

Registered Federal Lobbyist.
Serves As:
- V. President, Government Relations, Texas Instruments Incorporated

BOIK, Dennis
One Hormel Pl.
Austin, MN 55912-3680
Tel: (507) 437 - 5611

Serves As:
- Manager, Environmental Affairs, Hormel Foods Corp.

BOLAND, Donna
One Mercedes Dr.
Montvale, NJ 07645
bolandd@mbusa.com
Tel: (201) 573 - 6893
Fax:(201) 476 - 2875
TF: (800) 367 - 6372

Serves As:
- Manager, Corporate Communications, Mercedes-Benz USA, LLC

BOLAND, Mary Kathryn "Kati"
7575 Fulton St. East
M/S 49-2N
Ada, MI 49355-0001
Tel: (616) 787 - 6972
Fax:(616) 787 - 4764

Serves As:
- Supervisor, External Affairs, Alticor Inc.

BOLD, William
5775 Morehouse Dr.
San Diego, CA 92121-2779
wbold@qualcomm.com
Tel: (858) 651 - 2086
Fax:(858) 651 - 2590

Serves As:
- V. President, Government Affairs, Qualcomm Inc.

BOLENS, Barbara G.
P.O. Box 571
Milwaukee, WI 53201-0571
Tel: (414) 358 - 6600
Fax:(800) 292 - 2289

Serves As:
- V. President, Treasurer and Director, Investor Relations, Brady Corp.

BOLES, Donna M.
One Becton Dr.
Franklin Lakes, NJ 07417-1880
Tel: (201) 847 - 6800
Fax:(201) 847 - 6475

Serves As:
- V. President, Human Resources, Becton, Dickinson and Co.

BOLGER, David A.
316 Pennsylvania Ave. SE
Suite 300
Washington, DC 20003
Tel: (202) 675 - 4220
Fax:(202) 675 - 4230

Serves As:
- Manager, Public Relations, United Parcel Service (UPS)

BOLGER, Thomas J.
100 W. Putnam Ave.
Greenwich, CT 06830
Tel: (203) 622 - 3216
Fax:(203) 863 - 7240

Serves As:
- Director, State Government Relations-East, UST Inc.

BOLICK, Gary M.
325 Seventh St. NW
Suite 1200
Washington, DC 20004-1007
Tel: (202) 783 - 7070
Fax:(202) 347 - 2044

Serves As:
- Director, Government Relations, Pfizer Inc.

BOLIN, Printz
600 13th St. NW
Suite 340 West
Washington, DC 20005
Tel: (202) 662 - 0104
Fax:(202) 662 - 0199

Registered Federal Lobbyist.
Serves As:
- Director, Washington Affairs, Tax and Environment, Union Pacific Corp.

BOLLENBACH, Stephen F.
9336 Civic Center Dr.
Beverly Hills, CA 90210
Tel: (310) 278 - 4321

Serves As:
• Co-Chairman and Chief Exec. Officer, Hilton Hotels Corp.

BOLTON, Roger
151 Farmington Ave.
Hartford, CT 06156
Tel: (860) 273 - 1704
Fax:(860) 273 - 1624

Serves As:
• Senior V. President, Communications, Aetna Inc.

BOMBELLES, Thomas
601 Pennsylvania Ave. NW
North Bldg. Suite 1200
Washington, DC 20004
Tel: (202) 638 - 4170
Fax:(202) 638 - 3670

Registered Federal Lobbyist.
Serves As:
• Director, International Government Relations, Merck & Co., Inc.

BOMBINO, Paige
2700 N. First St.
San Jose, CA 95134
paige.bombino@sanmina-sci.com
Tel: (408) 964 - 3610
Fax:(408) 964 - 3636

Serves As:
• Investor Relations, Sanmina-SCI Corp.

BONANNO, Kathy
P.O. Box 619616
Dallas-Fort Worth Airport, TX 75261
Tel: (817) 963 - 1234
Fax:(817) 967 - 2523

Serves As:
• Director, Investor Relations, AMR Corp.

BOND, Henry R.
P.O. Box 105250
Atlanta, GA 30348
hbond@harland.net
Tel: (770) 593 - 5697
Fax:(770) 593 - 5367
TF: (800) 723 - 3690

Serves As:
• V. President, Investor Relations; and Treasurer, John H. Harland Co.

BOND, Jeff
777 Scuddersmill Rd.
Plainsboro, NJ 08536
Tel: (609) 897 - 3850

Serves As:
• V. President, State Government Affairs, Bristol-Myers Squibb Co.

BOND, Philip
622 Third Ave.
39th Floor
New York, NY 10017
Tel: (212) 351 - 7000
Fax:(646) 658 - 0541

Serves As:
• Senior V. President, Government Relations, Monster Worldwide, Inc.

BOND, Ritchie L.
512 Bridge St.
Danville, VA 24541
Tel: (434) 791 - 6952
Fax:(434) 791 - 0415

Serves As:
• Senior V. President and Treasurer, Alliance One Internat'l Inc.
Responsibilities include investor and media relations.

BONDS, Andrew
1133 15th St. NW
Suite 800
Washington, DC 20005-2701
andrew.bonds@parsons.com
Tel: (202) 775 - 3300
Fax:(202) 775 - 3422

Serves As:
• V. President, Government Relations, Parsons Corp.

BONDS, Mike
P.O. Box 4607
Houston, TX 77210-4607
Tel: (713) 324 - 5000

Serves As:
• Senior V. President, Human Resources and Labor Relations, Continental Airlines

BONEPARTH, Peter
250 Rittenhouse Circle
Bristol, PA 19007
Tel: (215) 785 - 4000
Fax:(215) 785 - 1228

Serves As:
• President and Chief Exec. Officer, Jones Apparel Group

BONER, Barbara
5970 Rain Dance Trail
Littleton, CO 80125
Tel: (303) 948 - 7319
Fax:(303) 948 - 7325

Serves As:
• Associate Director, Government Affairs, (Novartis Pharmaceuticals Corp.), Novartis Corporation

BONFINI, Jeremy
1634 I St. NW
Suite 300
Washington, DC 20006-4021
jeremy.bonfini@intel.com
Tel: (202) 626 - 4393
Fax:(202) 628 - 2525

Serves As:
• Manager, Government Relations, Intel Corp.

BONGIOVANNI, Lisa Marie
333 Continental Blvd.
El Segundo, CA 90245-5012
Tel: (310) 252 - 3524
Fax:(310) 252 - 4443

Serves As:
• V. President, Corporate Communications and Government Affairs, Mattel, Inc.

BONHAM, Jennifer
One United Dr.
Fenton, MO 63026
jennifer_bonham@mayflower.com
Tel: (636) 349 - 2508
Fax:(636) 326 - 1106

Serves As:
• Media Relations, (Mayflower Transit), UniGroup, Inc.

BONI, Peter J.
800 The Safeguard Bldg.
435 Devon Park Dr.
Wayne, PA 19087-1945
Tel: (610) 293 - 0600
Fax:(610) 293 - 0601
TF: (888) 733 - 1200

Serves As:
• President and Chief Exec. Officer, Safeguard Scientifics, Inc.

BONILLA, Sheryl W.
316 Pennsylvania Ave. SE
Suite 300
Washington, DC 20003
sshelby@ups.com
Tel: (202) 675 - 4220
Fax:(202) 675 - 4230

Registered Federal Lobbyist.
Serves As:
• Manager, Public Affairs, United Parcel Service (UPS)

BONITT, John E.
555 12th St. NW
Suite 650
Washington, DC 20004-1205
Tel: (202) 393 - 7950
Fax:(202) 393 - 7960

Registered Federal Lobbyist.
Serves As:
• Director, Federal Affairs, Eli Lilly and Company

BONNER, Dave
4000 House Ave.
Cheyenne, WY 82000-1
Tel: (307) 634 - 1393
Fax:(307) 638 - 5742
TF: (800) 442 - 2376

Serves As:
• Chairman of the Board, Blue Cross and Blue Shield of Wyoming

BONNER, Teresa B.
800 Nicollet Mall
BCMNH23K
Minneapolis, MN 55402
Tel: (612) 303 - 0742
Fax:(612) 303 - 0787

Serves As:
• Contact, Corporate Philanthropy and Community Relations, U.S. Bancorp

BONNETT, Madelyn C.
P.O. Box 1943
Birmingham, AL 35201-1943
Tel: (205) 991 - 6600
Fax:(205) 995 - 1517

Serves As:
• Assistant General Manager, Corporate Communications, EBSCO Industries, Inc.

BONNEVIER, Bruce
700 State Route 46 East
Batesville, IN 47006-8835
Tel: (812) 934 - 7000
Fax:(812) 934 - 7371

Serves As:
• V. President, Human Resources, Hillenbrand Industries, Inc.

BONNIN, Nydia
403 E. Capitol St. SE
Washington, DC 20003
Tel: (202) 548 - 5800
Fax:(202) 548 - 5810

Serves As:
• Director, Government Relations, Fluor Corp.

BONNO, Anthony J.
P.O. Box 9000
Newport Beach, CA 92658-9030
Tel: (949) 219 - 3011
Fax:(949) 219 - 5130
TF: (800) 800 - 7646

Serves As:
• Senior V. President, Human Resources, Pacific Life Insurance Co.

BONO, Steven
3250 Lacey Rd., Suite 600
Downers Grove, IL 60515
steven.bond@servicemaster.com
Tel: (630) 663 - 2150
Fax:(630) 663 - 2001

Registered Federal Lobbyist.
Serves As:
• Senior V. President, Corporate Communications, The ServiceMaster Co.

BOOHER, Pamela K.
225 Byers Rd.
Miamisburg, OH 45342
Tel: (937) 866 - 6251
Fax:(937) 865 - 5484

Serves As:
- Secretary, Foundation, Huffy Corp.

BOOMHOWER, Eric
1426 Main St.
Columbia, SC 29218
eboomhower@scana.com
Tel: (803) 217 - 7701
Fax:(803) 217 - 8825

Serves As:
- Manager, Public Affairs, SCANA Corp.

BOONSHAFT, Hope
10202 W. Washington Blvd.
Thalberg 2514
Culver City, CA 90232
hope_boonshaft@spe.sony.com
Tel: (310) 244 - 6660
Fax:(310) 244 - 2467

Serves As:
- Exec. V. President, External Affairs, (Sony Pictures Entertainment), Sony Corp. of America

BOOTH, Richard H.
One State St.
Hartford, CT 06103
richard_booth@hsb.com
Tel: (860) 722 - 1866

Serves As:
- President and Chief Exec. Officer, Hartford Steam Boiler Inspection and Insurance Co.

BOOZER, Lyndon K.
1133 21st St. NW
Suite 900
Washington, DC 20036
lyndon.boozer@bellsouth.com
Tel: (202) 463 - 4100
Fax:(202) 463 - 4196

Registered Federal Lobbyist.
Serves As:
- Assistant V. President, Federal Relations, BellSouth Corp.

BORDERS, Gerald
P.O. Box 660199
M/S 8656
Dallas, TX 75266-0199
g-borders@ti.com
Tel: (214) 480 - 6890
Fax:(214) 480 - 6820
TF: (800) 336 - 5236

Serves As:
- Director, Community Relations, Texas Instruments Incorporated

BORE, Thomas G.
10900 Wilshire Blvd.
Suite 850
Los Angeles, CA 90024
Tel: (310) 208 - 1980
Fax:(310) 208 - 6133

Serves As:
- President and Chief Exec. Officer, Magnetek, Inc.

BOREL, Jam
1007 Market St.
Wilmington, DE 19898
Tel: (302) 774 - 1000
Fax:(302) 773 - 2919
TF: (800) 441 - 7515

Serves As:
- Senior V. President, Human Resources, DuPont

BORMAN, Mark P.
P.O. Box 1101
Minneapolis, MN 55440-1101
mark.borman@adc.com
Tel: (952) 917 - 0590
Fax:(952) 946 - 2147

Serves As:
- V. President, Investor Relations, ADC

BORNEMAN, Mary C.
2801 Hunting Park Ave.
Philadelphia, PA 19129
mary.borneman@tastykake.com
Tel: (215) 221 - 8537
Fax:(215) 228 - 3970
TF: (800) 248 - 2789

Serves As:
- Manager, Investor Relations, Tasty Baking Co.

BORON, Andrew
CNA Center
333 S. Wabash Ave.
Chicago, IL 60685
Tel: (312) 822 - 1739
Fax:(312) 822 - 1186

Serves As:
- Director, State Government Relations, CNA Financial Corp.

BOROWY, David E.
P.O. Box 1477
Baltimore, MD 21203
Tel: (410) 347 - 8361
Fax:(410) 347 - 8270

Serves As:
- Senior V. President, (Mercantile-Safe Deposit and Trust Co.), Mercantile Bankshares Corporation

Responsibilities include investor relations.

BORRELLI, Alice
1120 20th St. NW
Suite 1000
Washington, DC 20036-3406
aborrelli@att.com
Tel: (202) 457 - 3810
Fax:(202) 457 - 2267

Registered Federal Lobbyist.
Serves As:
- V. President, Congressional Relations, AT&T

BORRELLI, Elizabeth
15010 NE 36th St.
Redmond, WA 98052
Tel: (425) 755 - 6643
Fax:(425) 755 - 7696

Serves As:
- Director, Public Affairs and Corporate Social Responsibility, Eddie Bauer, Inc.

BOSCH, Joe
13737 Noel Rd.
Dallas, TX 75240
Tel: (469) 893 - 6170
Fax:(469) 893 - 8170

Serves As:
- Senior V. President, Human Resources, Tenet Healthcare Corp.

BOSCIA, Jon A.
Centre Square, West Tower
1500 Market St., Suite 3900
Philadelphia, PA 19102-2112
Tel: (215) 448 - 1400
TF: (877) 275 - 5462

Serves As:
- Chairman and Chief Exec. Officer, Lincoln Financial Group

BOSE, Amar G.
The Mountain
Framingham, MA 01701-9168
amar_bose@bose.com
Tel: (508) 879 - 7330
Fax:(508) 766 - 7543

Serves As:
- Chairman and Chief Exec. Officer, Bose Corp.

BOSSHART, Amy
2000 Market St.
Philadelphia, PA 19103-9000
Tel: (215) 419 - 7230
Fax:(215) 419 - 7591
TF: (800) 225 - 7788

Serves As:
- Manager Employee Communications/Communications Manager, ATOFINA Chemicals, Inc.

BOSTIC, Jr., James E.
P.O. Box 105605
Atlanta, GA 30348
Tel: (404) 652 - 4000
Fax:(404) 654 - 4789
TF: (800) 519 - 3111

Serves As:
- Exec. V. President, Government Affairs and Governmental Environmental Affairs, Georgia-Pacific Corp.

BOTHAM, Lydia
P.O. Box 64101
St. Paul, MN 55164-0101
lrbotham@landolakes.com
Tel: (651) 481 - 2222
Fax:(651) 481 - 2000
TF: (800) 328 - 4155

Serves As:
- Director, Communications, Land O'Lakes, Inc.

BOTTINO, Hugo C.
P.O. Box 1464
Wall, NJ 07719
hcbottino@njresources.com
Tel: (732) 938 - 1091
Fax:(732) 938 - 2620

Serves As:
- V. President, Human Resources, (New Jersey Natural Gas Co.), New Jersey Resources Corp.

BOTTLE, Lisa
Four Colesium Center
2730 W. Tyvola Rd.
Charlotte, NC 28217
lisa.bottle@goodrich.com
Tel: (704) 423 - 7060
Fax:(704) 423 - 7127

Serves As:
- V. President, Corporate Communications, Goodrich Corporation

BOTZ, Jan
P.O. Box 994
C01306
Midland, MI 48686-0994
jan.botz@dowcorning.com
Tel: (989) 496 - 6470
Fax:(989) 496 - 8240

Serves As:
- Exec. Director, Communications, Dow Corning Corp.

BOUDREAU, Paul A.
101 Columbia Rd.
Morristown, NJ 07962-4658
Tel: (973) 455 - 2010
Fax:(973) 455 - 3632

Serves As:
- V. President, Corporate Relations; Exec. Director, Honeywell Foundation, Honeywell Internat'l, Inc.

BOUDREAUX, Bernard
22301 Foothill Blvd.
M/S 4790
Hayward, CA 94541
Tel: (510) 727 - 5681
Fax:(510) 727 - 2300

Serves As:
- Manager, Community Relations, Mervyn's

Responsibilities include corporate philanthropy.

BOUGHMAN, Melany
20 N. Broadway, Suite 1500
Oklahoma City, OK 73102
Tel: (405) 552 - 4578
Fax:(405) 552 - 4667

Serves As:
- Investor Relations Analyst, Devon Energy Corp.

BOUGHNER, Derry
1101 15th St. NW
Suite 1000
Washington, DC 20005
Tel: (202) 530 - 8160
Fax:(202) 530 - 8180

Registered Federal Lobbyist.
Serves As:
- Representative, Cargill, Incorporated

BOUKNIGHT, Joseph
1426 Main St.
Columbia, SC 29218
Tel: (803) 748 - 3000
Fax:(803) 217 - 8825

Serves As:
- Senior V. President, Human Resources, SCANA Corp.

BOULAY, Toni
310 Orange St.
New Haven, CT 06510
Tel: (203) 771 - 4607
Fax:(203) 497 - 9184

Serves As:
- Contact, Corporate Contributions Program, SBC SNET

BOULDIN, Ken
444 N. Capitol St. NW
Suite 545
Washington, DC 20001
Tel: (202) 347 - 8717

Registered Federal Lobbyist.
Serves As:
- Representative, Corrections Corp. of America

BOUREKAS, Phil
6024 Silver Creek Valley Rd.
San Jose, CA 95138
phil.bourekas@idt.com
Tel: (408) 284 - 2749

Serves As:
- V. President, Worldwide Marketing and Corporate Public Relations Contact, Integrated Device Technology, Inc.

BOURGEOIS, Pat
2100 Hwy. 55
Medina, MN 55340
Tel: (763) 417 - 8650
Fax:(763) 542 - 0599

Serves As:
- Coordinator, Public Relations, Polaris Industries Inc.

BOURNE, Frances
60 Massachusetts Ave. NE
Washington, DC 20002
Tel: (202) 906 - 3000
Fax:(202) 906 - 3865

Serves As:
- Director, Intergovernmental Relations, Amtrak

BOURNS, Gordon L.
1200 Columbia Ave.
Riverside, CA 92507-2114
Tel: (909) 781 - 5690
Fax:(909) 781 - 5273

Serves As:
- Chairman and Chief Exec. Officer, Bourns, Inc.

Responsibilities include serving as President of the Bourns Foundation.

BOUROGIANNIS, Angela
P.O. Box 15437
M/S FOC 3C/W
Wilmington, DE 19850-5437
Tel: (302) 886 - 7855
Fax:(302) 886 - 3029
TF: (800) 456 - 3669

Serves As:
- Manager, Corporate and Community Affairs, AstraZeneca Pharmaceuticals

BOURSCHEID, Ernest J.
701 Ninth St. NW
Washington, DC 20068
ejbourscheid@pepco.com
Tel: (202) 872 - 2797
Fax:(202) 331 - 6874

Serves As:
- Manager, Investor Relations, Pepco Holdings, Inc.

BOVENDER, Jack O.
P.O. Box 550
Nashville, TN 37202
Tel: (615) 344 - 9551
Fax:(615) 344 - 5722

Serves As:
- Chairman and Chief Exec. Officer, HCA

BOWCOCK, Jennifer
5565 Glenridge Connector
Atlanta, GA 30342
jennifer.bowcock@cingular.com
Tel: (404) 236 - 6319
Fax:(866) 236 - 6323
TF: (800) 331 - 0500

Serves As:
- Director, Public Relations, Cingular Wireless

BOWE, William
Britannica Centre
310 S. Michigan Ave.
Chicago, IL 60604
Tel: (312) 347 - 7000
Fax:(312) 294 - 2158

Serves As:
- V. President, Human Resources, Encyclopaedia Britannica, Inc.

BOWEN, Jama
2806 Opryland Dr.
Nashville, TN 37214
Tel: (615) 457 - 8581
Fax:(615) 457 - 8581

Serves As:
- Director, Communications, (Country Music Television), Viacom Inc./CBS Corp.

BOWERS, Willard L.
P.O. Box 2641
Birmingham, AL 35291
Tel: (205) 257 - 1000
Fax:(205) 257 - 1860

Serves As:
- V. President, Environmental Affairs, Alabama Power Co.

BOWERS, William L.
6568 Oasis Dr.
Loveland, OH 45140
william.bowers2@astrazeneca.com
Tel: (513) 583 - 0264
Fax:(513) 583 - 1481
TF: (800) 822 - 9209
Ext: 60779

Serves As:
- Regional Director, State Government Affairs, AstraZeneca Pharmaceuticals

BOWLBY, David
P.O. Box 99
Pleasanton, CA 94566-0009
Tel: (925) 467 - 3000

Serves As:
- V. President, Corporate Strategic Government Alliances, Safeway Inc.

BOWLDEN, Taylor R.
1425 K St. NW
Suite 300
Washington, DC 20005
Tel: (202) 414 - 3000
Fax:(202) 414 - 3037

Registered Federal Lobbyist.
Serves As:
- Manager, Federal Government Affairs, Traffic Control Materials Division, 3M Company

BOWLER, Denise
1835 Dueber Ave. SW
GNW-37
Canton, OH 44706
denise.bowler@timken.com
Tel: (330) 471 - 3485
Fax:(330) 471 - 4118
TF: (800) 223 - 1954

Serves As:
- Manager, Public Relations, The Timken Co.

BOWLER, J. Thomas
400 Main St.
East Hartford, CT 06108
Tel: (860) 565 - 4321

Serves As:
- V. President, Human Resources and Organization, Pratt & Whitney

BOWLER, Ph.D., M. Kenneth
325 Seventh St. NW
Suite 1200
Washington, DC 20004-1007
Tel: (202) 783 - 7070
Fax:(202) 347 - 2044

Registered Federal Lobbyist.
Serves As:
- V. President, Federal Government Relations, Pfizer Inc.

BOWLER, Tom
1201 M St. SE
Suite 100
Washington, DC 20003
Tel: (202) 454 - 2900
Fax:(202) 454 - 2901

Serves As:
- V. President, Programs and Strategic Planning, Bath Iron Works Corp.

BOWLES, Ms. Crandall
P.O. Box 70
Fort Mill, SC 29716
crandall.bowles@springs.com
Tel: (803) 547 - 1500

Serves As:
- Chairman and Chief Exec. Officer, Springs Industries, Inc.

BOWLES, III, Ph.D., Richard
2000 Galloping Hill Rd.
Kenilworth, NJ 07033
Tel: (908) 298 - 5245
Fax:(908) 298 - 4673

Serves As:
- Senior V. President, Global Quality Operations, Schering-Plough Corporation

BOWLING, Dan
P.O. Box 723040 Tel: (770) 989 - 3000
Atlanta, GA 31139-0040 Fax:(770) 989 - 3781

Serves As:
- Senior V. President, Human Resources, Coca-Cola Enterprises Inc.

BOWMAN, Jr., George A.
225 Franklin St. Tel: (617) 664 - 3381
Boston, MA 02110 Fax:(617) 451 - 6315
gabowman@statestreet.com

Serves As:
- V. President, Community Affairs, State Street Corp.

BOWMAN, John
One AAR Pl. Tel: (630) 227 - 2145
1100 N. Wood Dale Rd. Fax:(630) 227 - 2019
Wood Dale, IL 60191

Serves As:
- Investor Relations Contact, AAR Corp.

BOWMAN, Karen Rhodes
5301 S. Superstition Mountain Dr. Tel: (480) 288 - 6907
Gield Canyon, AZ 85218 Fax:(480) 288 - 6909
karen.bowman@astrazeneca.com TF: (800) 822 - 9209
Ext: 60839

Serves As:
- Director, State Government Affairs (Western Region), AstraZeneca Pharmaceuticals

BOWMAN, Mike
1755 S. Clark St. Tel: (703) 416 - 8000
Suite 1100 Fax:(703) 416 - 8010
Arlington, VA 22202
bowman@drs-esg.com

Serves As:
- Executive V. President, Washington Operations, DRS Technologies, Inc.

BOWMAN, Paul
3050 Bowers Ave. Tel: (408) 563 - 1698
P.O. Box 58039 Fax:(408) 748 - 9943
Santa Clara, CA 95054-3299

Serves As:
- Managing Director, Investor Relations, Applied Materials, Inc.

BOWMAN, Roberta B.
P.O. Box 1244 Tel: (704) 382 - 8347
M/S PB040 Fax:(704) 382 - 3800
Charlotte, NC 28201-1244
rbowman@duke-energy.com

Serves As:
- V. President, External Relations, Duke Energy Corp.

BOWMAN, Roy
1667 K St. NW Tel: (202) 331 - 1424
Suite 400 Fax:(202) 775 - 8427
Washington, DC 20006
roy_bowman@apl.com

Registered Federal Lobbyist.
Serves As:
- V. President, Government Affairs, APL Americas

BOWMAN, Susan
350 Campus Dr. Tel: (508) 323 - 5000
Marlborough, MA 01752-3064 Fax:(508) 323 - 1111

Serves As:
- Senior V. President, Human Resources, 3Com Corp.

BOWMNA, Phd, Ellen
P.O. Box 599 Tel: (513) 983 - 1100
Cincinnati, OH 45201-0599 Fax:(513) 983 - 9369

Serves As:
- Director, External Relations/ Global Healthcare, The Procter & Gamble Company

BOWSER, Tom
One Pershing Square Tel: (816) 395 - 2222
2301 Main St.
Kansas City, MO 64108

Serves As:
- President and Chief Exec. Officer, Blue Cross and Blue Shield of Kansas City

BOX, Pauline
850 Lagoon Dr. Tel: (619) 691 - 4111
Chula Vista, CA 91910-2098 Fax:(619) 691 - 2584

Serves As:
- Contact, Will-Share Club, Goodrich Corp. - Aerostructures

BOXX, Dennis R.
6801 Rockledge Dr. Tel: (301) 897 - 6543
Bethesda, MD 20817-1877 Fax:(301) 897 - 6252

Serves As:
- V. President, Corporate Communications, Lockheed Martin Corp.

BOYANOVSKY, Harold
100 S. Saunders Rd. Tel: (847) 735 - 9200
Lake Forest, IL 60045

Serves As:
- President and Chief Exec. Officer, Case New Holland Inc.

BOYCE, Donna
145 Pleasant Hill Rd. Tel: (207) 883 - 2911
Scarborough, ME 04074 Fax:(207) 885 - 3165
dboyce@hannaford.com

Serves As:
- Secretary, Hannaford Charitable Foundation, Hannaford Bros. Co.

BOYCE, Paula
P.O. Box 3170 Tel: (808) 538 - 4945
Honolulu, HI 96802-3170

Serves As:
- Foundation Contact, Bank of Hawaii Corp.

BOYD, Dennis W. E.
P.O. Box 5650 Tel: (701) 222 - 7829
Bismarck, ND 58506-5650 Fax:(701) 222 - 7859
dennis.boyd@mduresources.com TF: (800) 437 - 8000

Serves As:
- Senior Governmental Affairs Representative, MDU Resources Group, Inc.

BOYD, James R.
One CityPlace Dr. Tel: (314) 994 - 2700
Suite 300 Fax:(314) 994 - 2719
St. Louis, MO 63141

Serves As:
- Chairman of the Board, Arch Coal, Inc.

BOYD, Janet C.
1776 I St. NW Tel: (202) 429 - 3400
Suite 1050 Fax:(202) 429 - 3467
Washington, DC 20006

Registered Federal Lobbyist.
Serves As:
- Director, Government Relations-Tax and Benefits, The Dow Chemical Company

BOYD, Jennifer
P.O. Box 10048 Tel: (479) 785 - 8892
Fort Smith, AR 72917 Fax:(479) 785 - 8992

Serves As:
- Public Relations/Corporate Communications Contact, Arkansas Best Corporation

BOYD, Norm
4205 River Green Pkwy. Tel: (770) 813 - 6144
Duluth, GA 30096-2568 Fax:(770) 813 - 6118

Serves As:
- Senior V. President, Human Resources, AGCO Corp.

BOYD, Paula
1401 I St., NW Tel: (202) 263 - 5900
Suite 500 Fax:(202) 263 - 5902
Washington, DC 20005

Registered Federal Lobbyist.
Serves As:
- Regulatory Counsel, Microsoft Corporation

BOYD, Jr., Ralph
8200 Jones Branch Dr. Tel: (703) 903 - 2000
McLean, VA 22102 Fax:(703) 903 - 2447
TF: (800) 373 - 3343

Serves As:
- Exec. V. President, Community Relations, Freddie Mac

BOYD, Rex Neil
P.O. Box 2641 Tel: (205) 257 - 2596
Birmingham, AL 35291 Fax:(205) 257 - 2622

Serves As:
- Manager, Governmental Projects - Government Relations, Alabama Power Co.

BOYD, Robert
1299 Pennsylvania Ave. NW Tel: (202) 637 - 4000
11th Floor West Fax:(202) 637 - 4006
Washington, DC 20004-2407

Registered Federal Lobbyist.
Serves As:
- Representative, General Electric Co.

BOYD, Shane
385 Washington St.
St. Paul, MN 55102
Tel: (651) 310 - 3846
Fax:(651) 310 - 3660

Serves As:
- Chief Communications Officer, St. Paul Travelers Cos., Inc.

BOYD, William S.
2950 Industrial Rd.
Las Vegas, NV 89109-1100
Tel: (702) 792 - 7200
Fax:(702) 792 - 7266
TF: (800) 695 - 2455

Serves As:
- Chairman and Chief Exec. Officer, Boyd Gaming Corp.

BOYDSTUN, J. Herbert
5718 Westheimer St.
Houston, TX 77057
hboydstun@hibernia.com
Tel: (504) 533 - 3902
Fax:(504) 533 - 2367
TF: (800) 562 - 9007

Serves As:
- President and Chief Exec. Officer, Hibernia Corp.

BOYKIN, Clete
601 Pennsylvania Ave. NW
North Bldg., Suite 325
Washington, DC 20004
Tel: (202) 728 - 3645
Fax:(202) 728 - 3649

Registered Federal Lobbyist.
Serves As:
- Senior Manager, Government Affairs, DuPont

BOYKIN, Frank H.
P.O. Box 12069
Calhoun, GA 30703
frank_boykin@mohawkind.com
Tel: (706) 624 - 2247
Fax:(706) 625 - 3851
TF: (800) 241 - 4494

Serves As:
- V. President, Finance and Chief Financial Officer, Mohawk Industries, Inc.

Responsibilities include corporate philanthropy and investor relations.

BOYLAN, Terry
200 Kimball Dr.
Parsippany, NJ 07054
terry.boyland@ch.novartis.com
Tel: (973) 503 - 7801
Fax:(973) 503 - 8400
TF: (800) 443 - 7237

Serves As:
- V. President, Communications, Gerber Products Co.

BOZE, Buck
P.O. Box 4030
M/S NH420
Golden, CO 80401-0030
Tel: (303) 277 - 5953
Fax:(303) 277 - 6132

Serves As:
- Manager, Corporate Contributions, Coors Brewing Co.

BOZZONE, Robert P.
411 Seventh Ave.
Pittsburgh, PA 15219
Tel: (412) 393 - 6000
Fax:(412) 393 - 6448

Serves As:
- Chairman of the Board, Duquesne Light Holdings

BRACK, Karl
1700 MacCorkle Ave., S.E.
Charleston, WV 25314
kbrack@nisource.com
Tel: (304) 357 - 2396
Fax:(304) 357 - 2138

Serves As:
- V. President, Communications, (Columbia Gas Transmission Corp.), NiSource Inc.

BRACY, Ray
702 SW Eighth St.
M/S 0130
Bentonville, AR 72716
Tel: (479) 277 - 0934
Fax:(479) 273 - 4053

Serves As:
- V. President, International Corporate Affairs, Wal-Mart Stores

BRADDON, Cynthia H.
1200 G St. NW
Suite 900
Washington, DC 20005-3802
cindy_braddon@mcgraw-hill.com
Tel: (202) 383 - 3701
Fax:(202) 383 - 3718

Registered Federal Lobbyist.
Serves As:
- V. President, Government Affairs, The McGraw-Hill Companies, Inc.

BRADFORD, James E.
Mill St.
Hodge, LA 71247
Tel: (318) 259 - 5358

Serves As:
- Manager, Government Affairs, Smurfit-Stone Container

BRADFORD, Pam
825 N.E. Multnomah
Suite 2000
Portland, OR 97232
pam.bradford@pacificorp.com
Tel: (503) 813 - 7219
Fax:(503) 813 - 7247
TF: (888) 221 - 7070

Serves As:
- Foundation Grants Manager, PacifiCorp

BRADFORD, Patricia A.
Unisys Way
Blue Bell, PA 19424
Tel: (215) 986 - 4011
Fax:(215) 986 - 6850

Serves As:
- Senior V. President, Worldwide Human Resources, Unisys Corp.

BRADLEY, Cindy
550 Bowie St.
Austin, TX 78703
Tel: (512) 477 - 4455
Fax:(512) 322 - 9873

Serves As:
- V. President, Human Resources, Whole Foods Market, Inc.

BRADLEY, Clara
P.O. Box 2197
Houston, TX 77252-2197
Tel: (281) 293 - 1000

Serves As:
- Manager, Community Relations, ConocoPhillips

BRADLEY, James G.
1134 Market St.
Wheeling, WV 26003
Tel: (304) 234 - 2400
Fax:(304) 234 - 2261

Serves As:
- Chairman and Chief Exec. Officer, Wheeling-Pittsburgh Steel Corp.

BRADLEY, Jill
Webster Plaza
145 Bank St.
MO 210
Waterbury, CT 06702
jabradley@websterbank.com
Tel: (203) 578 - 2396
Fax:(203) 578 - 2507

Serves As:
- V. President, Community Affairs, Webster Financial Corp.

BRADLEY, Michael A.
321 Harrison Ave.
Boston, MA 02118-2238
Tel: (617) 482 - 2700
Fax:(617) 422 - 2910

Serves As:
- President and Chief Exec. Officer, Teradyne, Inc.

BRADLEY, Rickford D.
5565 Glenridge Connector
Atlanta, GA 30342
Tel: (404) 236 - 6000
Fax:(866) 246 - 4852
TF: (800) 331 - 0500

Serves As:
- Exec. V. President, Human Resources, Cingular Wireless

BRADY, Betsy
1401 I St., NW
Suite 500
Washington, DC 20005
Tel: (202) 263 - 5900
Fax:(202) 263 - 5902

Registered Federal Lobbyist.
Serves As:
- Policy Counsel, Microsoft Corporation

BRADY, Bill
P.O. Box 5625
MS25
Minneapolis, MN 55440-5625
bill_brady@cargill.com
Tel: (952) 742 - 6608
Fax:(952) 742 - 6208

Serves As:
- Public Affairs Counselor, Cargill, Incorporated

BRADY, Larry D.
6001 36th Ave. West
Everett, WA 98203-9280
lbrady@unova.com
Tel: (425) 265 - 2400
Fax:(425) 265 - 2425

Serves As:
- Chairman, President and Chief Exec. Officer, UNOVA, Inc.

BRADY, Robert T.
Seneca St. at Jamison Rd.
East Aurora, NY 14052
robert.brady@moog.com
Tel: (716) 652 - 2000
Ext: 4853
Fax:(716) 687 - 4457

Serves As:
- Chairman and Chief Exec. Officer, Moog Inc.

BRADY, Sharon M.
P.O. Box 1430
Kenosha, WI 53141-1430
Tel: (414) 656 - 5315
Fax:(414) 656 - 5577

Serves As:
- V. President and Chief Human Resources Officer, Snap-on Incorporated

BRAGG, Paul A.
5847 San Felipe, Suite 3300 Tel: (713) 789 - 1400
Houston, TX 77057 Fax:(713) 952 - 6916
Serves As:
- President and Chief Exec. Officer, Pride Internat'l, Inc.

BRAHS, Stuart J.
1350 I St., N.W., Suite 1030 Tel: (202) 682 - 1280
Washington, DC 20005-3305 Fax:(202) 682 - 1412
brahs.stuart@principal.com
Registered Federal Lobbyist.
Serves As:
- V. President, Federal Government Relations, The Principal Financial Group

BRAILER, Daniel A.
225 W. Station Square Dr. Tel: (412) 454 - 2200
suite 700 Fax:(412) 454 - 2505
Pittsburgh, PA 15219
Serves As:
- Director, Investor Relations and Treasurer, WESCO Internat'l, Inc.

BRAMSTEDT, Susan
4750 International Airport Rd. Tel: (907) 266 - 7230
Anchorage, AK 99502 Fax:(907) 266 - 7229
susan.bramstedt@alaskaair.com
Serves As:
- Director, Public Affairs-Alaska, (Alaska Airlines, Inc.), Alaska Air Group, Inc.

BRANCH, Zelma
10200 Bellaire Blvd. Tel: (281) 988 - 2557
Houston, TX 77020-5299
zelma.branch@halliburton.com
Serves As:
- Manager, Public Relations - North America, Halliburton Company

BRANDAU, Herman
2216 Woodfield Rd. Tel: (309) 662 - 0066
Bloomington, IL 61704
Registered Federal Lobbyist.
Serves As:
- Associate, State Farm Insurance Cos.

BRANDENBURG, Frank G.
P.O. Box 5928 Tel: (864) 963 - 6300
Greenville, SC 29606 Fax:(864) 963 - 6322
Serves As:
- Chairman of the Board, KEMET Corp.

BRANDLIN, Laura
P.O. Box 57013 Tel: (949) 450 - 8700
Irvine, CA 92619-7013 Fax:(949) 450 - 8710
lbrandlin@broadcom.com
Serves As:
- Director, Marketing Communications, Broadcom Corp.

BRANDON, David A.
P.O. Box 997 Tel: (734) 930 - 3030
Ann Arbor, MI 48106-0997 Fax:(734) 930 - 4346
brandod@dominos.com
Serves As:
- Chairman and Chief Exec. Officer, Domino's Pizza, LLC

BRANDON, Joseph P.
Financial Center Tel: (203) 328 - 5000
695 E. Main St. Fax:(203) 328 - 6423
Stamford, CT 06901 TF: (800) 431 - 9994
Serves As:
- Chairman and Chief Exec. Officer, General Re Corp.

BRANDON, Rhonda S.
P.O. Box 1624 Fax:(678) 762 - 2883
Alpharetta, GA 30009-9934 TF: (800) 275 - 3004
Serves As:
- V. President, Human Resources, Colonial Pipeline Co.

BRANDT, Chris
4747 N. Channel Ave. Tel: (503) 745 - 5471
Portland, OR 97217 Fax:(503) 745 - 5096
chrisbrandt@freightliner.com
Serves As:
- Manager, Public Relations, Freightliner LLC

BRANDT, Mark
2700 S. Sunland Dr. Tel: (480) 293 - 6011
Tempe, AZ 85282-3387 Fax:(602) 784 - 3950
Serves As:
- Manager, Public Affairs, State Farm Insurance Cos.

BRANICK, Robert C.
555 11th St. NW Tel: (202) 393 - 2426
Suite 525 Fax:(202) 783 - 8410
Washington, DC 20004
Serves As:
- Director, Federal Affairs, CH2M Hill Companies, Inc.

BRANSON, Jr., Milton R.
750 E. Pratt St. Tel: (410) 783 - 5201
5th Floor Fax:(410) 230 - 4703
Baltimore, MD 21202 TF: (888) 460 - 2002
milton.r.branson@constellation.com
Serves As:
- Senior Government Relations Representative, Constellation Energy

BRASH, Steven L.
P.O. Box 960 Tel: (513) 287 - 2226
Cincinnati, OH 45201-0960 Fax:(513) 651 - 9196
Serves As:
- Manager, External Communications, Cinergy Corp.

BRASHEAR, Denise
One Health Plaza Tel: (862) 778 - 7336
East Hanover, NJ 07936 Fax:(862) 644 - 8585
Serves As:
- Associate Director, Public Relations, (Novartis Pharmaceuticals Corp.), Novartis Corporation

BRATHWAITE, Chris
3333 Beverly Rd. Tel: (847) 286 - 4681
Hoffman Estates, IL 60179-0001 Fax:(847) 286 - 8351
TF: (800) 732 - 7780
Serves As:
- Director, Media Relations, Sears Holding Corp.

BRAUNER, Susan
P.O. Box 1768 Tel: (916) 446 - 8354
Sacramento, CA 95812-1768 Fax:(916) 325 - 2880
sbrauner@bdgrowers.com
Serves As:
- Director, Communications, Blue Diamond Growers
Responsibilities include political action.

BRAVO, Mary Ann
One North Dale Mabry, Suite 950 Tel: (813) 877 - 2726
Tampa, FL 33609 Fax:(813) 739 - 0204
Serves As:
- Marketing Manager, Masonite Internat'l Corp.
Responsibilities include public affairs.

BRAYSHAW, Francis
555 12th St. NW Tel: (202) 393 - 7950
Suite 650 Fax:(202) 393 - 7960
Washington, DC 20004-1205
Registered Federal Lobbyist.
Serves As:
- Senior Government Affairs Associate, Eli Lilly and Company

BRAZELL, Wes
6201 South Fwy. Tel: (817) 293 - 0450
Fort Worth, TX 76134 Fax:(817) 551 - 4615
Serves As:
- Director, Investor Relations, Alcon Inc.

BREADY, Richard L.
50 Kennedy Plaza Tel: (401) 751 - 1600
Providence, RI 02903 Fax:(401) 751 - 4610
Serves As:
- Chairman and Chief Exec. Officer, Nortek Inc.

BREAULT, Sandra
One Mercer Rd. Tel: (508) 651 - 7400
Natick, MA 01760 Fax:(508) 651 - 6167
TF: (800) 257 - 2582
Serves As:
- Public Relations and Corporate Communications Contact, BJ's Wholesale Club, Inc.

BRECHER, Richard
1350 I St. NW Tel: (202) 371 - 6900
Suite 400 Fax:(202) 842 - 3578
Washington, DC 20005-3306
Registered Federal Lobbyist.
Serves As:
- Assistant Director, International Trade Relations, Motorola, Inc.

BRECHT MARR, Linda
P.O. Box 844 Tel: (215) 444 - 5073
Spring House, PA 19477-0844 Fax:(215) 444 - 5075
lbrechtmarr@advanta.com
Serves As:
- Director, Sponsorships, Advanta Corp.

BREED, John S.
P.O. Box 4446
Houston, TX 77210-4446
breed@cooperindustries.com
Tel: (713) 209 - 8835
Fax:(713) 209 - 8982

Serves As:
• Director, Media and Government Relations, Cooper Industries

BREED, Joseph R.
917 E. 11th St.
2800
Tacoma, WA 98421
Tel: (253) 779 - 6400
Fax:(253) 280 - 9000

Serves As:
• PAC Treasurer, Simpson Investment Co.

BREEN, Edward D.
Nine Roszel Rd.
Princeton, NJ 08540
Tel: (609) 720 - 4200
Fax:(609) 720 - 4208

Serves As:
• Chairman and Chief Exec. Officer, Tyco Internat'l (U.S.), Inc.

BREEN, Karen
9197 S. Peoria St.
Englewood, CO 80112-5833
Tel: (303) 397 - 8592
Fax:(303) 397 - 8199
TF: (800) 835 - 3832

Serves As:
• Contact, Investor Relations, TeleTech Holdings, Inc.

BREGANDE, Don
1200 State Fair Blvd.
Syracuse, NY 13221-4737
dbregande@penntraffic.com
Tel: (315) 461 - 2535
Fax:(315) 461 - 2324

Serves As:
• V. President, Human Resources, The Penn Traffic Co.

BREHM, Carolyn
701 Pennsylvania Ave. NW
Suite 520
Washington, DC 20004-2604
Tel: (202) 393 - 3400
Fax:(202) 393 - 4606

Serves As:
• V. President, National Government Relations, The Procter & Gamble Company

BREI, Amy
1144 E. Market St.
Akron, OH 44316-0001
Tel: (330) 796 - 2121
Fax:(330) 796 - 1237

Serves As:
• Communications Manager, Tires, North America, The Goodyear Tire & Rubber Company

BREIDENBACH, David
700 13th St., NW
Suite 950
Washington, DC 20005
Tel: (202) 654 - 4499
Fax:(202) 654 - 4493

Serves As:
• Representative, Marathon Oil Corp.

BREITSTADT, Charles P.
One Nationwide Plaza
M/S 1-27-08
Columbus, OH 43215-2220
Tel: (614) 249 - 4572
Fax:(614) 249 - 3073

Serves As:
• Director, Government Affairs, Nationwide

BREKHUS, Mel G.
1341 W. Mockingbird Ln.
Dallas, TX 75247
mbrekhus@txi.com
Tel: (972) 647 - 6700
Fax:(972) 647 - 3878

Serves As:
• President and Chief Exec. Officer, Texas Industries, Inc.

BREN, Donald
550 Newport Center Dr.
Newport Beach, CA 92660
Tel: (949) 720 - 2000
Fax:(949) 720 - 2501

Serves As:
• Chairman of the Board, The Irvine Company

BRENERMAN, David H.
2211 Congress St.
M/S B159
Portland, ME 04122-0545
dbrenerman@unumprovident.com
Tel: (207) 575 - 4311
Fax:(207) 575 - 4304

Serves As:
• Assistant V. President, Government Relations, UnumProvident Corp.

BRENN, James E.
P.O. Box 702
Milwaukee, WI 53201-0702
Tel: (414) 259 - 5333
Fax:(414) 479 - 1245

Serves As:
• Senior V. President and Chief Financial Officer, Briggs and Stratton Corp.
Responsibilities include investor relations.

BRENNAN, David R.
P.O. Box 15437
A2C
Wilmington, DE 19850-5437
davidms.brennan@astrazeneca.com
Tel: (302) 886 - 3000
Fax:(302) 886 - 1889
TF: (800) 456 - 3669

Serves As:
• President and Chief Exec. Officer, AstraZeneca Pharmaceuticals

BRENNAN, Jean F.
One Market
Spear Tower, Suite 2400
San Francisco, CA 94105
Tel: (415) 817 - 8248
Fax:(415) 817 - 8245

Serves As:
• Senior Director, Corporate Human Resources Planning and Development, PG & E Corp.

BRENNEMAN, Greg
5505 Blue Lagoon Dr.
Miami, FL 33126
Tel: (305) 378 - 3000
Fax:(305) 378 - 7910

Serves As:
• Chairman and Chief Exec. Officer, Burger King Corporation

BRENT, Richard
818 Connecticut Ave. NW
Suite 600
Washington, DC 20006-2702
Tel: (202) 466 - 0655
Fax:(202) 466 - 0684

Registered Federal Lobbyist.
Serves As:
• Washington Manager, Solar, Caterpillar Inc.

BRESEE, Elizabeth
1680 Capital One Dr.
12th Floor
McLean, VA 22102
Tel: (703) 875 - 1000

Registered Federal Lobbyist.
Serves As:
• Representative, Capital One Financial Corp.

BRESKY, H. Harry
9000 W. 67th St.
Shawnee Mission, KS 66202
Tel: (913) 676 - 8800
Fax:(913) 676 - 8872

Serves As:
• Chairman, President and Chief Exec. Officer, Seaboard Corporation

BRESLIN, Danielle
P.O. Box 2291
Durham, NC 27702-2291
danielle.breslin@bcbsnc.com
Tel: (919) 765 - 4114
Fax:(919) 765 - 4837

Serves As:
• Manager, BCBSNC Foundation, Blue Cross and Blue Shield of North Carolina

BRESNICK, G. I.
1185 Ave. of the Americas
New York, NY 10036
Tel: (212) 997 - 8500
Fax:(212) 536 - 8390

Serves As:
• V. President, Health, Safety and Environment, Amerada Hess Corp.

BRESS, Joseph M.
60 Massachusetts Ave. NE
Washington, DC 20002
Tel: (202) 906 - 3000
Fax:(202) 906 - 3865

Serves As:
• V. President, Labor Relations, Amtrak

BRESSLER, Jordan
P.O. Box 10529
Greensboro, NC 27404-0529
Tel: (336) 335 - 7744
Fax:(336) 335 - 7550
TF: (888) 278 - 1133

Serves As:
• Manager, External Affairs, Lorillard Tobacco Co.

BRETON, Daniel B.
One Davis Farm Rd.
Portland, ME 04103
daniel.b.breton@verizon.com
Tel: (207) 797 - 1188
Fax:(207) 797 - 1392

Serves As:
• Director, Public Affairs Programs, Verizon Communications Inc.

BRETT, Kevin
1621 Barber Ln.
D-125
Milpitas, CA 95035
kbrett@lsil.com
Tel: (408) 433 - 8000
Fax:(408) 954 - 3220
TF: (866) 574 - 5741

Serves As:
• Director, Corporate Public Relations, LSI Logic Corp.
Responsibilities also include government affairs.

BREVARD, Mary E.
3850 Hamlin Rd. Tel: (248) 754 - 9200
Auburn Hills, MI 48326
Serves As:
• V. President, Investor Relations and Communications, BorgWarner Inc.
Responsibilities include corporate contributions and government affairs.

BREWER, III, F. H. "Chip"
1525 Howe St. Tel: (262) 260 - 2493
Racine, WI 53403 Fax:(262) 260 - 2944
Serves As:
• Director, Government Relations Worldwide, SC Johnson

BREWER, Janet
1700 S. Patterson Blvd. Tel: (937) 445 - 5000
Dayton, OH 45479 Fax:(937) 445 - 1847
TF: (800) 225 - 5627
Serves As:
• Director, Community Relations, V. President, NCR Foundation, NCR Corporation

BREWER, Peggy
P.O. Box 430 Tel: (901) 528 - 4820
Memphis, TN 30103 Fax:(901) 528 - 4086
pbrewer@mlgw.org
Serves As:
• Community Relations Officer, Memphis Light, Gas and Water Division

BREWER, Victoria
1334 York Ave. Tel: (212) 508 - 8070
New York, NY 10021 Fax:(212) 508 - 8072
victoria.brewer@sothebys.com
Serves As:
• Senior Manager, Investor Relations, Sotheby's Holdings, Inc.

BREWIS, Sue
P.O. Box 10566 Tel: (205) 297 - 5738
Birmingham, AL 35296 Fax:(205) 297 - 5030
sue.brewis@compassbnk.com TF: (800) 239 - 2265
Serves As:
• Treasurer, Compass Bancshares PAC, Compass Bancshares, Inc.

BREWSTER, Joe
320 Racetrack Rd., N.W. Tel: (850) 314 - 8101
Ft. Walton Beach, FL 32549
joe.brewster@cox.com
Serves As:
• Director, Community Affairs, (Cox Communications, Inc.), Cox Enterprises, Inc.

BREWSTER, Lemuel
730 Third Ave. Tel: (212) 916 - 5717
New York, NY 10017-3206 Fax:(212) 916 - 5952
lbrewster@tiaa-cref.org
Serves As:
• Media Contact, TIAA/CREF

BREWSTER, Pamela
101 Montgomery St. Tel: (415) 636 - 5021
San Francisco, CA 94104 Fax:(415) 636 - 5305
TF: (800) 435 - 4000
Serves As:
• V. President, Government Affairs, The Charles Schwab Corp.

BRIAN, Mike
110 E. Wayne St. Tel: (260) 425 - 2137
Fort Wayne, IN 46802
Serves As:
• Public Affairs Contact, (Indiana Michigan Power Co.), American Electric Power Co. Inc.

BRIDGE, Mr. Tracy B.
800 LaSalle Ave. Tel: (612) 372 - 4664
Minneapolis, MN 55402-2006 Fax:(612) 321 - 5137
Serves As:
• Director, Government and Public Relations, (CenterPoint Energy Minnegasco), CenterPoint Energy

BRIDGES, Mike
1200 Columbia Ave. Tel: (909) 781 - 5397
Riverside, CA 92507-2114 Fax:(909) 781 - 5122
mike_bridges@bourns.com
Serves As:
• Manager, Marketing Services, Bourns, Inc.
Responsibilities include public relations.

BRIDGES, Phil
P.O. Box 13582 Tel: (919) 990 - 7952
Research Triangle Park, NC 27709 Fax:(919) 990 - 7922
phil.bridges@reichhold.com TF: (800) 448 - 3482
Serves As:
• Manager, Corporate Communications, Reichhold, Inc.

BRIDGES, Russell B.
6801 River Place Blvd. Tel: (512) 984 - 6561
A130-5N-07 Fax:(512) 984 - 3556
Austin, TX 78726-9000
Serves As:
• State Government Affairs Manager, 3M Company

BRIEN, Michael P.
1776 I St. NW Tel: (202) 457 - 6573
Suite 1000 Fax:(202) 457 - 6597
Washington, DC 20006-3707
brienmp@bp.com
Registered Federal Lobbyist.
Serves As:
• Chief of Staff, U.S. Government and Public Affairs, BP

BRIGANDI, Joanne M.
One S. Jersey Plaza Tel: (609) 561 - 9000
Folsom, NJ 08037 Ext: 4240
Fax:(609) 561 - 6955
Serves As:
• Director, Corporate Communications, South Jersey Gas Co.

BRIGANDI, Steve
9330 Balboa Ave. Tel: (858) 571 - 2121
San Diego, CA 92123-1516 Fax:(858) 571 - 2225
Serves As:
• Senior Public Affairs Exec., Jack in the Box Inc.

BRIGGS, Daniel J.
90 Park Ave. Tel: (212) 907 - 6134
Tenth Floor Fax:(212) 907 - 6001
New York, NY 10016-1301
daniel.briggs@bisys.com
Serves As:
• V. President, Finance and Investor Relations, The BISYS Group, Inc.
Responsibilities include media relations.

BRIGGS, Joyce
19601 N. 27th Ave. Tel: (623) 580 - 6100
Phoenix, AZ 85027 Fax:(623) 580 - 6508
jbriggs@ssg.petsmart.com
Serves As:
• Director, PETsMart Charities, PETsMART, Inc.

BRIGGS, Kendice
P.O. Box 6000 Tel: (949) 854 - 3100
Newport Beach, CA 92658-6000 Fax:(949) 854 - 4979
Serves As:
• Senior V. President and Director, Human Resources, Downey Savings and Loan Ass'n, F.A.

BRIGGS, Kern
555 12th St. NW Tel: (202) 393 - 7950
Suite 650 Fax:(202) 393 - 7960
Washington, DC 20004-1205
Serves As:
• Senior Associate, International and Public Government Relations, Eli Lilly and Company

BRIGGUM, Sue M.
601 Pennsylvania Ave. NW Tel: (202) 628 - 3500
North Bldg. Suite 300 Fax:(202) 628 - 0400
Washington, DC 20004
sbriggum@wm.com
Serves As:
• Director, Environmental Affairs, Waste Management, Inc.

BRIGHAM, Daniel
400 California St. Tel: (415) 765 - 2761
San Francisco, CA 94104 Fax:(415) 765 - 2841
daniel.brigham@uboc.com
Serves As:
• V. President, Government Affairs, Union Bank of California

BRIGHTBILL, Peter
633 Folsom St. Tel: (415) 396 - 6319
Seventh Floor Fax:(415) 546 - 0829
M/S A0149-072
San Francisco, CA 94107
Serves As:
• Director, State Government Relations, Wells Fargo & Co.

BRILL, Linda F.
P.O. Box 92957 Tel: (310) 336 - 1192
M1-447 Fax:(310) 336 - 8249
Los Angeles, CA 90009-2957
linda.f.brill@aero.org
Serves As:
• Principal Director, Corporate Communications, The Aerospace Corp.

BRILL, Tom
101 Ash St.
HQ13A
San Diego, CA 92101-3017
tbrill@sempra.com
Tel: (619) 696 - 4265
Fax:(619) 696 - 4266
TF: (877) 736 - 7721

Serves As:
- Assistant General Counsel, Sempra Energy

BRILLHART, Ember A.
1001 G St., NW
Suite 950
Washington, DC 20001
ember_brillhart@hma.honda.com
Tel: (202) 661 - 4400
Fax:(202) 661 - 4459

Serves As:
- Senior Legislative Coordinator, (Honda North America, Inc.), American Honda Motor Co., Inc.

BRINGER, Maria
21001 Van Born Rd.
Taylor, MI 48180
Tel: (313) 792 - 6653
Fax:(313) 792 - 6135

Serves As:
- V. President, Investor Relations, Masco Corp.

BRINKLEY, Linda T.
215 S. Monroe St., Suite 125
Tallahassee, FL 32301
Tel: (850) 222 - 2231

Serves As:
- PAC Contact, SunTrust Good Government Group--Florida, SunTrust Banks, Inc.

BRINKLEY, Teresa
P.O. Box 511
Kingsport, TN 37662-5075
Tel: (423) 229 - 6811
Fax:(423) 229 - 1008
TF: (800) 327 - 8626

Serves As:
- Advanced Community Relations Representative, Eastman Chemical Co.

BRINZO, John S.
1100 Superior Ave.
Cleveland, OH 44114-2589
jsbrinzo@cleveland-cliffs.com
Tel: (216) 694 - 5700
Fax:(216) 694 - 4880

Serves As:
- Chairman, President and Chief Exec. Officer, Cleveland-Cliffs Inc

BRITT, Anita
250 Rittenhouse Circle
Bristol, PA 19007
Tel: (215) 785 - 4000
Fax:(215) 785 - 1795

Serves As:
- Exec. V. President, Finance and Investor Relations, Jones Apparel Group

BRITTINGHAM, Donald
1300 I St. NW
Suite 400 West
Washington, DC 20005
Tel: (202) 589 - 3781
Fax:(202) 589 - 3750

Registered Federal Lobbyist.
Serves As:
- Representative, Verizon Wireless

BRITTO, Karen
601 Pennsylvania Ave. NW
Suite 350, North Bldg.
Washington, DC 20004-3613
brittok@dteenergy.com
Tel: (202) 347 - 8420
Fax:(202) 347 - 8423

Registered Federal Lobbyist.
Serves As:
- Manager, Federal Affairs, DTE Energy Co.

BRITTON, Patricia
980 Hammond Dr. NE
Suite 1000
Atlanta, GA 30328-5313
pbritton@porschecars.com
Tel: (770) 290 - 3500
Ext: 3609
Fax:(770) 290 - 3714

Serves As:
- Legal Counsel, Porsche Cars North America, Inc.

Responsibilities include government affairs and regulatory affairs.

BRIZZOLARA, Thomas L.
One Blue Hill Plaza
Pearl River, NY 10965
Tel: (845) 577 - 2654
Fax:(845) 577 - 6989

Serves As:
- Manager, Community Relations, Orange and Rockland Utilities, Inc.

BROAD, Eli
One SunAmerica Center
Los Angeles, CA 90067-6022
Tel: (310) 772 - 6000
TF: (800) 871 - 2000

Serves As:
- Chairman of the Board, AIG SunAmerica Inc.

BROCCOLINO, Livio
10455 Mill Run Circle
Owings Mills, MD 21117
Tel: (410) 581 - 3000
Fax:(410) 998 - 5133

Serves As:
- Deputy General Counsel, CareFirst BlueCross and BlueShield

Responsibilities include political action.

BROCK, Jr., Macon F.
500 Volvo Pkwy.
Chesapeake, VA 23320
Tel: (757) 321 - 5000
Fax:(757) 321 - 5292

Serves As:
- Chairman of the Board, Dollar Tree Stores, Inc.

BROCKELMAN, Amy
14 Cambridge Center
Cambridge, MA 02142
Tel: (617) 914 - 6524
Fax:(617) 679 - 2617

Serves As:
- Senior Manager, Public Affairs, Biogen Idec Inc.

BROCKHOFF, Glynda
P.O. Box 42121
Portland, OR 97242
Tel: (503) 797 - 3213
Fax:(503) 797 - 5609
TF: (800) 858 - 9202
Ext: 5605

Serves As:
- Coordinator, Philanthropy, Fred Meyer Stores

BRODER, Matt
World Headquarters
One Elmcroft Rd.
MSC 63-11
Stamford, CT 06926-0700
matthew.broder@pb.com
Tel: (203) 351 - 6347
Fax:(203) 351 - 6303

Serves As:
- V. President, External Communications, Pitney Bowes Inc.

BROGDON, Jessica
One Allied Dr.
Little Rock, AR 72202
Tel: (501) 905 - 8000
Fax:(501) 905 - 6018

Serves As:
- Contact, Corporate Contributions, ALLTEL

BROKAW, Steven E.
199 Benson Rd.
Middlebury, VT 06749
Tel: (203) 573 - 2000
Fax:(203) 573 - 3711

Serves As:
- PAC Treasurer, Chemtura

BROMAN, Susan
P.O. Box 1967
CH4E
Grand Rapids, MI 49501-1967
sbroman@steelcase.com
Tel: (616) 246 - 4695
Fax:(616) 475 - 2200

Serves As:
- Exec. Director, Steelcase Foundation, Steelcase Inc.

BROMLEY, John E.
1400 Douglas St.
Omaha, NE 68179
Tel: (402) 544 - 3320

Serves As:
- Director, Media Relations, Union Pacific Corp.

BRONNER, Dr. David G.
2345 Crystal Dr.
Arlington, VA 22227
Tel: (703) 872 - 7000
Fax:(703) 872 - 7093

Serves As:
- Chairman of the Board, US Airways Group, Inc.

BROOKE, Jr., F. Dixon
P.O. Box 1943
Birmingham, AL 35201-1943
dbrooke@ebsco.com
Tel: (205) 991 - 6600
Fax:(205) 995 - 1517

Serves As:
- Chief Exec. Officer, EBSCO Industries, Inc.

BROOKLIER, John L.
3600 W. Lake Ave.
Glenview, IL 60025-5811
Tel: (847) 657 - 4104
Fax:(847) 657 - 4268

Serves As:
- V. President, Investor Relations, Illinois Tool Works Inc.

BROOKS, Cynthia L.
P.O. Box 6676
Asheville, NC 28816
cbrooks@ingles-markets.com
Tel: (828) 669 - 2941
Fax:(828) 669 - 3667

Serves As:
- V. President, Human Resources, Ingles Markets, Inc.

BROOKS, Douglas
6820 LBJ Fwy.
Dallas, TX 75240
Tel: (972) 980 - 9917

Serves As:
- Chairman and Chief Exec. Officer, Brinker Internat'l, Inc.

BROOKS, Joanna
P.O. Box 98910
M/S 29
Las Vegas, NV 89151-0001
jbrooks@nevp.com
Tel: (702) 367 - 5000
Fax:(702) 579 - 0658
TF: (800) 331 - 3103

Serves As:
- Executive, Government Affairs, Nevada Power Co.

BROOKS, Joyce
18 Loveton Circle
Sparks, MD 21152-6000
joyce_brooks@mccormick.com
Tel: (410) 771 - 7244
Fax:(410) 771 - 7462

Serves As:
- Assistant Treasurer, Investor Relations and Financial Services, McCormick & Company, Inc.

BROOKS, Oakley
1808 I St. NW, Suite 400
Washington, DC 20006
Tel: (202) 414 - 8989
Fax:(202) 789 - 0076

Serves As:
- V. President, Government Affairs, Bombardier

BROOKS, Pat
P.O. Box 550
Nashville, TN 37202
patricia.brooks@hcahealthcare.com
Tel: (615) 344 - 2527
Fax:(615) 344 - 1128

Serves As:
- Legislative Analyst, HCA

BROOKS, Rand
300 N. Meridian St., Suite 1500
Indianapolis, IN 46204-1763
rbrooks@reillyind.com
Tel: (317) 247 - 8141
Fax:(317) 248 - 6472

Serves As:
- Contact, Reilly Foundation, Reilly Industries, Inc.

BROOKS, Roger K.
699 Walnut St.
Des Moines, IA 50309
Tel: (515) 362 - 3600

Serves As:
- Chairman and Chief Exec. Officer, AmerUs Group

BROOKS, Shannon M.
301 Commerce St.
Suite 500
Fort Worth, TX 76006
smbrooks@drhorton.com
Tel: (817) 390 - 8200
Fax:(817) 390 - 1715

Serves As:
- Communications Coordinator, D. R. Horton, Inc.

BROOKSHIRE, Jane
P.O. Box 93
Pittsburg, TX 75686
jbrookshire@pilgrimspride.com
Tel: (903) 855 - 1000
TF: (800) 824 - 1159

Serves As:
- Senior V. President, Human Resources, Pilgrim's Pride Corp.

BROOKSHIRE, Tim
P.O. Box 1411
Tyler, TX 75710-1411
timbrookshire@brookshires.com
Tel: (903) 534 - 3000
Fax:(903) 534 - 2198

Serves As:
- President, Human Resources and Financial Group, Brookshire Grocery Co.

BROOKTER, Carolyn
1000 Nicollet Mall
Minneapolis, MN 55403
media.relations@target.com
Tel: (612) 304 - 6073

Serves As:
- Director, Corporate Communications, (Target Stores), Target Corp.

BROOME, Richard
225 Brae Blvd.
Park Ridge, NJ 07656
Tel: (201) 307 - 2486
Fax:(201) 307 - 2856

Serves As:
- V. President, Corporate Affairs, Hertz Corp.

BROONER, Mary E.
1350 I St. NW
Suite 400
Washington, DC 20005-3306
Tel: (202) 371 - 6900
Fax:(202) 842 - 3578

Registered Federal Lobbyist.
Serves As:
- Director, Telecommunications Strategy and Regulation, Motorola, Inc.

BROPHY, Susan
800 Connecticut Ave. NW
Suite 800
Washington, DC 20006
Tel: (202) 457 - 8582
Fax:(202) 457 - 8861

Registered Federal Lobbyist.
Serves As:
- Senior V. President, Domestic Policy, Time Warner Inc.

BRORSEN, Les
1225 Connecticut Ave. NW
Washington, DC 20036
les.brorsen@ey.com
Tel: (202) 327 - 6000

Registered Federal Lobbyist.
Serves As:
- National Director, Political and Government Relations, Ernst & Young LLP

BROTMAN, Jeffrey H.
999 Lake Dr.
Issaquah, WA 98027
Tel: (425) 313 - 8100
Fax:(425) 313 - 6593

Serves As:
- Chairman of the Board, Costco Wholesale Corp.

BROTZ, Melissa
100 Abbott Park Rd.
Abbott Park, IL 60064-3500
Tel: (847) 935 - 3456

Serves As:
- Divisional V. President, External Communications, Abbott Laboratories

BROUGHTON, Lee
600 Corporate Park Dr.
St. Louis, MO 63105
Tel: (314) 512 - 5000
Fax:(314) 512 - 5281

Serves As:
- Manager, Public Relations, Enterprise Rent-A-Car Co.

BROUILLETTE, Dan R.
1350 I St. NW
Suite 1000
Washington, DC 20005
Tel: (202) 962 - 5400
Fax:(202) 336 - 7223

Registered Federal Lobbyist.
Serves As:
- V. President, Washington Affairs, Ford Motor Co.

BROUS, Maria
P.O. Box 407
Lakeland, FL 33802-0407
maria.brous@publix.com
Tel: (863) 688 - 7407
Ext: 55339
Fax:(863) 284 - 5532

Serves As:
- Director, Media and Community Relations, Publix Super Markets, Inc.

BROUSSARD, Susan
P.O. Box 5000
Pineville, LA 71361-5000
Tel: (318) 484 - 7773
Fax:(318) 484 - 7465

Serves As:
- Manager, Corporate and Strategic Communications, Cleco Corp.

BROWN, Arthur
6500 N. Mineral Dr., Suite 200
Coeur d'Alene, ID 83815-9408
Tel: (208) 769 - 4100
Fax:(208) 769 - 4107

Serves As:
- Chairman of the Board, Hecla Mining Co.

BROWN, Carl
P.O. Box 12646
Reading, PA 19612
cbrown6@sovereignbank.com
Tel: (610) 378 - 6162
Fax:(610) 320 - 8448

Serves As:
- Manager, Public Relations, Sovereign Bancorp, Inc.

BROWN, Carolyn
122 Fifth Ave.
New York, NY 10011
cbrown@bn.com
Tel: (212) 633 - 4062
Fax:(212) 807 - 6033

Serves As:
- Director, Corporate Communications, Barnes & Noble, Inc.

BROWN, Christine M.
777 Third Ave.
New York, NY 10017
Tel: (212) 546 - 2000
Fax:(212) 546 - 1495

Serves As:
- Senior V. President and Director, Corporate Communications, Grey Global Group Inc.

BROWN, Colin
100 Jim Moran Blvd.
Deerfield Beach, FL 33442
Tel: (954) 429 - 2000
Fax:(954) 429 - 2300

Serves As:
- President and Chief Exec. Officer, JM Family Enterprises, Inc.

BROWN, Craig
701 Brazos St., Suite 495
Austin, TX 78701
Tel: (512) 476 - 4795
Fax:(512) 477 - 3586

Serves As:
- Director, Public Affairs-Southern Tier, Koch Industries, Inc.

BROWN, Craig
1121 L St., Suite 310
Sacramento, CA 95814-0000
Tel: (916) 552 - 5830
Fax:(916) 443 - 7577

Serves As:
- Principal, Robinson & Associates, Inc.
- Chief Financial Officer, Standard Register Co.

Responsibilities include public affairs.

BROWN, David C.
101 Constitution Ave., NW
Suite 400 East
Washington, DC 20001
davidc.brown@exeloncorp.com
Tel: (202) 347 - 0808
Fax:(202) 347 - 7501

Registered Federal Lobbyist.
Serves As:
- V. President, Congressional Affairs, Exelon Corp.

BROWN, David T.
One Owens Corning Pkwy.
Toledo, OH 43659
dave.t.brown@owenscorning.com
Tel: (419) 248 - 7206
Fax:(419) 248 - 6352
TF: (800) 438 - 7465

Serves As:
- President and Chief Exec. Officer, Owens Corning

BROWN, Deirdre A.
TECO Plaza
702 N. Franklin St.
Tampa, FL 33602
Tel: (813) 228 - 4111
Fax:(813) 228 - 4811

Serves As:
- V. President, Regulatory Affairs, TECO Energy, Inc./Tampa Electric Co.

BROWN, Eric
495 E. Java Dr.
Sunnyvale, CA 94089
ebrown@netapp.com
Tel: (408) 822 - 6000
Fax:(408) 822 - 4501

Serves As:
- Director, Worldwide Public Relations, Network Appliance, Inc.

BROWN, Frank S.
Three Commercial Pl.
Norfolk, VA 23510-2191
Tel: (757) 629 - 2714
Fax:(757) 629 - 2822

Serves As:
- Assistant V. President, Public Relations, Norfolk Southern Corp.

BROWN, Gwen
1331 Pennsylvania Ave. NW
Suite 1300 North
Washington, DC 20004
gwen.brown@eds.com
Tel: (202) 637 - 6715
Fax:(202) 637 - 6759

Registered Federal Lobbyist.
Serves As:
- Director, Healthcare Policy, EDS Corp.

BROWN, Herbert R.
400 Broadway
Cincinnati, OH 45202
Tel: (513) 629 - 1136
Fax:(513) 629 - 1308
TF: (800) 936 - 1212

Serves As:
- Senior V. President, Public Relations and Corporate Communications, Western and Southern Life Insurance Co.

BROWN, J. Hyatt
220 S. Ridgewood Ave.
Daytona Beach, FL 32114
Tel: (386) 252 - 9601
TF: (800) 877 - 2769

Serves As:
- Chairman and Chief Exec. Officer, Brown & Brown, Inc.

BROWN, James M.
450 Riverchase Pkwy. East
Birmingham, AL 35244
Tel: (205) 220 - 2100
Fax:(205) 220 - 4841

Serves As:
- Senior V. President, Caring Foundation, Blue Cross and Blue Shield of Alabama

BROWN, Jeff
209 Redwood Shores Pkwy.
Redwood City, CA 94065-1175
Tel: (650) 628 - 1500
Fax:(650) 628 - 1415

Serves As:
- V. President, Corporate Communications, Electronic Arts Inc.

BROWN, Jeffrey N.
Webster Plaza
145 Bank St.
MO 210
Waterbury, CT 06702
jbrown@websterbank.com
Tel: (203) 578 - 2566
Fax:(203) 755 - 5539

Serves As:
- Exec. V. President, Marketing and Communications, Webster Financial Corp.

BROWN, JoBeth
One Busch Pl.
St. Louis, MO 63118-1852
Tel: (314) 577 - 3314
Fax:(314) 577 - 3251

Serves As:
- V. President; Corporate Secretary and; Chair, Contributions Committee, Anheuser-Busch Cos., Inc.

BROWN, Jody
1100 N. Glebe Rd.
Arlington, VA 22201-4798
jbrown@caci.com
Tel: (703) 841 - 7801
Fax:(703) 841 - 7882

Serves As:
- Exec. V. President, Public Relations, CACI Internat'l Inc.

BROWN, John H.
One Corporate Way
Lansing, MI 48951
Tel: (517) 381 - 5500
Fax:(517) 706 - 5517
TF: (800) 644 - 4565

Serves As:
- V. President, Government Relations, Jackson Nat'l Life Insurance Co.

BROWN, John W.
2725 Fairfield Rd.
Kalamazoo, MI 49002
Tel: (616) 385 - 2600
Fax:(616) 385 - 1062

Serves As:
- Chairman and Chief Exec. Officer, Stryker Corp.

BROWN, Joseph W.
113 King St.
Armonk, NY 10504
joseph.brown@mbia.com
Tel: (914) 273 - 4545
Fax:(914) 765 - 3163

Serves As:
- Chairman of the Board, MBIA, Inc.

BROWN, Josh
1501 M St. NW
Suite 1100
Washington, DC 20005
Tel: (202) 785 - 7300
Fax:(202) 785 - 6360

Registered Federal Lobbyist.
Serves As:
- Director, Government Relations, Viacom Inc./CBS Corp.

BROWN, Julian
P.O. Box 3014
Naperville, IL 60566-7014
jbrown@nicor.com
Tel: (630) 305 - 9500
Ext: 2673
Fax:(630) 548 - 3574
TF: (888) 642 - 6748

Serves As:
- Contact, Nicor, Inc. Contributions Program, Nicor, Inc.

BROWN, Kevin P.
5780 Powers Ferry Rd. NW
Atlanta, GA 30327
Tel: (770) 980 - 5100
Fax:(770) 980 - 3301

Serves As:
- PAC Treasurer, ING Americas

BROWN, Larry Robert
800 N. Harvey
Oklahoma City, OK 73102
Tel: (405) 377 - 4944

Serves As:
- Area Manager, External Affairs, SBC Communications Inc.

BROWN, Louis J.
1300 Pennsylvania Ave. NW
Suite 860
Washington, DC 20004
Tel: (202) 842 - 5800
Fax:(202) 842 - 8612

Serves As:
- Government Technical Affairs Manager, Volkswagen of America, Inc.

BROWN, Marilyn
1001 Fannin St., Suite 4000
Houston, TX 77002
Tel: (713) 512 - 6200
Fax:(713) 512 - 6299

Serves As:
- Contributions Contact, Waste Management, Inc.

BROWN, Mary Green
1426 Main St.
Fifth Floor
Columbia, SC 29218
mbrown@scana.com
Tel: (803) 217 - 8833
Fax:(803) 217 - 8825

Serves As:
- Public Affairs Coordinator, SCANA Corp.

BROWN, Mary Rose
P.O. Box 500
San Antonio, TX 78249-112
brownmr@valero.com
Tel: (210) 345 - 2314
Fax:(210) 345 - 2646
TF: (800) 531 - 7911

Serves As:
- V. President, Corporate Communications, Valero Energy Corp.

BROWN, Neil
80 Park Plaza
M/S T24D
Newark, NJ 07102-0570
neil.brown@pseg.com
Tel: (973) 430 - 6017
Fax:(973) 623 - 8711

Serves As:
- Manager, Governmental Affairs PSEG, PSE&G

BROWN, II, Owsley
850 Dixie Hwy.
Louisville, KY 40210
owsley_brown@b-f.com
Tel: (502) 585 - 1100
Fax:(502) 774 - 6633

Serves As:
- Chairman of the Board, Brown-Forman Corp.

BROWN, Patricia J.
P.O. Box 550
Findlay, OH 45839-0550
pjbrown@coopertire.com
Tel: (419) 424 - 4370

Serves As:
- V. President, Global Branding and Communications, Cooper Tire & Rubber Company

BROWN, Peter C.
920 Main St.
Kansas City, MO 64105-2017
Tel: (816) 221 - 4000
Fax:(816) 480 - 4617

Serves As:
- Chairman, President and Chief Exec. Officer, AMC Entertainment Inc.

BROWN, Peter D.
112 W. 34th St.
New York, NY 10120
pbrown@footlocker-inc.com
Tel: (212) 720 - 4254
Fax:(212) 720 - 4660

Serves As:
- V. President, Investor Relations, Footlocker Inc.

BROWN, Priscilla
Centre Square, West Tower
1500 Market St., Suite 3900
Philadelphia, PA 19102-2112
Tel: (215) 448 - 1422
Fax:(215) 448 - 3962
TF: (877) 275 - 5462

Serves As:
- V. President and Director, Investor Relations, Lincoln Financial Group

BROWN, R. Scott
101 Constitution Ave., NW
Suite 400 East
Washington, DC 20001
Tel: (202) 347 - 7500
Fax:(202) 347 - 7501

Serves As:
- V. President and Director, Policy Development, Exelon Corp.

BROWN, Richard A.
P.O. Box 1438
Louisville, KY 40201-1438
dbrown4@humana.com
Tel: (502) 580 - 3683
Fax:(502) 580 - 3677
TF: (800) 486 - 2620

Serves As:
- Corporate Director, Media Relations, Humana Inc.

BROWN, Ronald D.
2090 Florence Ave.
Cincinnati, OH 45206
Tel: (513) 487 - 5000
Fax:(513) 487 - 5057

Serves As:
- Chairman, President and Chief Exec. Officer, Milacron Inc.

BROWN, Sarah
6450 Sprint Pkwy.
KSOPHN02122A454
Overland Park, KS 66251

Serves As:
- Treasurer, Sprint Corp. PAC, Sprint Nextel

BROWN, Sharon Shiroma
P.O. Box 3200
Honolulu, HI 96847
Tel: (808) 525 - 7777
Fax:(808) 557 - 086

Serves As:
- President, First Hawaiian Foundation, (First Hawaiian Bank), BancWest Corp.

BROWN, Susan K.
Reader's Digest Rd.
Pleasantville, NY 10570-7000
susan.brown@rd.com
Tel: (914) 244 - 7340
Fax:(914) 244 - 5324
TF: (800) 234 - 9000

Serves As:
- Director, Global Communications, Reader's Digest Ass'n, Inc.

BROWN, Tim
P.O. Box 9239
79NC62
Newark, DE 19714-9239
tim.brown@conectiv.com
Tel: (302) 283 - 5803
TF: (800) 266 - 3284

Serves As:
- Director, Corporate Communications, Conectiv

BROWN, Timothy C.
4360 Brownsboro Rd.
Suite 300
Louisville, KY 40207
llyons@thomasind.com
Tel: (502) 893 - 4612
Fax:(502) 895 - 6618
TF: (800) 626 - 2847

Serves As:
- Chairman, President and Chief Exec. Officer, Thomas Industries Inc.

BROWNE, John
200 E. Randolph
Chicago, IL 60601
Tel: (312) 856 - 6111
Fax:(312) 856 - 2460

Serves As:
- Group Chief Executive, BP

BROWNE, Mary Jo
4500 Main St.
Kansas City, MO 64111
Tel: (816) 531 - 5575
Fax:(816) 340 - 7962
TF: (800) 345 - 2021

Serves As:
- Contact, American Century Co. Foundation, American Century Cos., Inc.

BROWNE, Michael L.
355 Maple Ave.
Harleysville, PA 19438-2297
mbrowne@harleysvillegroup.com
Tel: (215) 256 - 5000
Fax:(215) 256 - 5799
TF: (800) 523 - 6344

Serves As:
- Chief Exec. Officer, Harleysville Group

BROWNELL, Paul
1225 I St. NW
Suite 920
Washington, DC 20005
Tel: (202) 408 - 5538
Fax:(202) 408 - 7664

Registered Federal Lobbyist.
Serves As:
- Manager, Federal Government Relations, Dell Inc.

BROWNING, Peter C.
2100 Rexford Rd.
Charlotte, NC 28211
Tel: (704) 366 - 7000
Fax:(704) 362 - 4208

Serves As:
- Chairman of the Board, Nucor Corp.

BROWNLEE, Don
1025 Connecticut Ave. NW, Suite 501
Washington, DC 20036
Tel: (202) 828 - 6800
Fax:(202) 828 - 6849

Serves As:
- V. President, Washington Operations, GenCorp

BROWNLEE, Jan
One Invacare Way
Elyria, OH 44035
Tel: (440) 329 - 6000
Fax:(440) 366 - 9008
TF: (800) 333 - 6900

Serves As:
- Director, Regulatory Affairs, Invacare Corp.

BROWNLEE, John T.
800 Connecticut Ave. NW
Suite 711
Washington, DC 20006
jbrownlee@na.ko.com
Tel: (202) 973 - 2667
Fax:(202) 466 - 2262

Registered Federal Lobbyist.
Serves As:
- Manager, Government Relations, The Coca-Cola Co.

BROWNLEE, Kathy
Three Lincoln Center
5430 LBJ Fwy., Suite 1700
Dallas, TX 75240-2697
Tel: (972) 233 - 1700
Fax:(972) 448 - 1445

Serves As:
- Director, Personnel, Valhi, Inc.

BROZDA, Mike
P.O. Box 58090
M/S G1-124
Santa Clara, CA 95052-8090
mike.brozda@nsc.com
Tel: (408) 721 - 3628
Fax:(408) 721 - 3238

Serves As:
- Manager, Public Relations, Nat'l Semiconductor Corp.

BRUBAKER, Alan
1140 Connecticut Ave. NW
Suite 510
Washington, DC 20036
alan.brubaker@prudential.com
Tel: (202) 327 - 5240
Fax:(202) 327 - 5249

Registered Federal Lobbyist.
Serves As:
- V. President, Government Affairs, Prudential Financial

BRUBAKER, Joel
801 Pennsylvania Ave. NW
Suite 310
Washington, DC 20004
Tel: (202) 434 - 8150
Fax:(202) 434 - 8156

Serves As:
- Federal Affairs Representative, FirstEnergy Corp.

BRUCE, David
11690 Northwest 105 St.
Miami, FL 33178
david_bruce@ryder.com
Tel: (305) 500 - 4999
Fax:(305) 500 - 3203

Serves As:
- Group Director, Corporate Communications, Ryder System, Inc.

BRUCE, Lori A.
260 Baltimore Pike
Wawa, PA 19063
lori.a.bruce@wawa.com
Tel: (610) 358 - 8039
Fax:(610) 358 - 8878
TF: (800) 283 - 9292

Serves As:
- Chairperson, Wawa Inc. Corporate Charities Committee, Wawa, Inc.

BRUCE, Penny
170 W. Tasman Dr.
San Jose, CA 95134-1706
pebruce@cisco.com
Tel: (408) 853 - 9188
Fax:(408) 526 - 4100
TF: (800) 553 - 6387

Serves As:
- Media Contact, Public Affairs, Cisco Systems, Inc.

BRUCKER, Jack E.
P.O. Drawer F
Scottsdale, AZ 85252
Tel: (480) 994 - 3886
Fax:(480) 606 - 3328
TF: (800) 421 - 5718

Serves As:
- President and Chief Exec. Officer, Rural Metro Corp.

BRUGGEMAN, Valerie
225 W. Wesley Ave.
Wheaton, IL 60187
Tel: (630) 462 - 6030
Fax:(630) 462 - 6024

Serves As:
- Area Manager, External Affairs, SBC Illinois

BRUGGEWORTH, Robert A.
7628 Thorndike Rd.
Greensboro, NC 27409-9421
Tel: (336) 664 - 1233
Fax:(336) 931 - 7454

Serves As:
- Chief Exec. Officer, RF Micro Devices, Inc.

BRUKARDT, Gary
2525 West End Ave., Suite 600
Nashville, TN 37203
Tel: (615) 345 - 5500
Fax:(615) 345 - 5505

Serves As:
- President and Chief Exec. Officer, Renal Care Group, Inc.

BRUMFIELD, Lisa
11690 Northwest 105 St.
Miami, FL 33178
lisa_brumfield@ryder.com
Tel: (305) 500 - 3668

Serves As:
- Senior Manager, Corporate Communications, Ryder System, Inc.

BRUMM, James E.
655 Third Ave.
New York, NY 10017
Tel: (212) 605 - 2000
Fax:(212) 605 - 1908

Serves As:
- Exec. V. President, Mitsubishi International Corporation

BRUMMIT, John
5820 Westown Pkwy.
West Des Moines, IA 50266-8223
Tel: (515) 267 - 2800
Fax:(515) 267 - 2817

Serves As:
- PAC Treasurer, Hy-Vee, Inc.

BRUNDAGE, Jeffrey J.
P.O. Box 619616
Dallas-Fort Worth Airport, TX 75261
Tel: (817) 963 - 1234
Fax:(817) 967 - 2523

Serves As:
- Senior V. President, Human Resources, (American Airlines, Inc.), AMR Corp.

BRUNELL, Margaret
770 Broadway
New York, NY 10003
Tel: (212) 209 - 8500
Fax:(212) 209 - 2666

Serves As:
- Director, Public Relations, J. Crew Group, Inc.

BRUNER, Cheryl
1301 K St. NW
Suite 1200
Washington, DC 20005
Tel: (202) 515 - 4031

Serves As:
- Governmental Programs Executive, Internat'l Business Machines Corp. (IBM)

BRUNET, Pam M.
P.O. Box 4755, Bldg. 22
Syracuse, NY 13221-4755
pam.brunet@bms.com
Tel: (315) 432 - 2709

Serves As:
- Manager, Community Affairs, Bristol-Myers Squibb Co.

BRUNETTI, Wayne H.
414 Nicollet Mall
Minneapolis, MN 55401-1927
Tel: (612) 330 - 5500
Fax:(612) 330 - 6947

Serves As:
- Chairman of the Board, Xcel Energy, Inc.

BRUNGESS, Barbara A.
1300 Morris Dr.
Suite 100
Chesterbrook, PA 19087-5594
bbrungess@amerisourcebergen.com
Tel: (610) 727 - 7199
Fax:(610) 727 - 3603
TF: (800) 829 - 3132

Serves As:
- Manager, Corporate and Investor Relations, AmeriSource Bergen Corp.

BRUNICK, David
5619 DTC Pkwy.
Greenwood, CO 80111
Tel: (303) 268 - 6300
TF: (877) 496 - 6704

Serves As:
- Senior V. President, Human Resources, Adelphia Communications Corp.

BRUNNER, John
300 Chestnut Ridge Rd
Woodcliff Lake, NJ 07677
Tel: (201) 307 - 4000
Fax:(201) 573 - 8416

Serves As:
- Manager, Human Resources, BMW (U.S.) Holding Corp.

BRUNNWORTH, Kristin L.
6950 Columbia Gateway Dr.
Columbia, MD 21046
klbrunnworth@magellanhealth.com
Tel: (410) 953 - 1000
Fax:(410) 953 - 5200

Serves As:
- Media Relations Specialist, Magellan Health Services, Inc.

BRUNO, Mike
2200 Renaissance Blvd., Suite 200
Gulph Mills, PA 19406-2755
michael.brown@henkel.com
Tel: (610) 571 - 5141
Fax:(610) 270 - 8104

Serves As:
- Corporate Communications Contact, Henkel Corp.

BRUSE, J. Charles
1615 L St. NW
Suite 650
Washington, DC 20036
cbruse@allstate.com
Tel: (202) 626 - 8240

Registered Federal Lobbyist.
Serves As:
- V. President and Assistant General Counsel, Allstate Insurance Co.

BRUSER, Lawrence
750 17th St. NW
Suite 400
Washington, DC 20006
Tel: (202) 861 - 0665
Fax:(202) 861 - 0437

Serves As:
- Deputy General Manager and Director, Government Affairs, Mitsui and Co. (U.S.A.), Inc.

BRUSKIN, Marcy
17666 Fitch
Irvine, CA 92614
Tel: (949) 253 - 2300
Fax:(949) 474 - 7675

Serves As:
- V. President, Human Resources and Organizational Development, Freedom Communications Inc.

BRUTTON, Mary Beth
1133 S.W. Topeka Blvd.
MS 548
Topeka, KS 66629
Tel: (785) 291 - 8869
Fax:(785) 291 - 7664

Serves As:
- Public Information Coordinator, Blue Cross and Blue Shield of Kansas, Inc.

BRYAN, Catherine
100 Abbott Park Rd.
Abbott Park, IL 60064-3500
Tel: (847) 936 - 6722

Serves As:
- Director, External Communications, Abbott Laboratories

BRYAN, III, J. Stewart
P.O. Box 85333
Richmond, VA 23293-0001
sbryan@mediageneral.com
Tel: (804) 649 - 6000
Fax:(804) 649 - 6865

Serves As:
- Chairman of the Board, Media General Inc.

BRYANT, Bo
1200 17th St., NW
Suite 603
Washington, DC 20036
Tel: (202) 887 - 8900
Fax:(202) 887 - 8907

Serves As:
- Director, Federal Relations, McDonald's Corp.

BRYANT, Candice
1150 15th St. NW
Washington, DC 20071
Tel: (202) 334 - 5104
Fax:(202) 334 - 4536

Serves As:
- Contact, The Philip L. Graham Fund, The Washington Post Co.

BRYANT, Daniel J.
700 Anderson Hill Rd.
Purchase, NY 10577-1444
Tel: (914) 253 - 3600
Fax:(914) 253 - 3669

Serves As:
- V. President, Government Affairs, PepsiCo, Inc.

BRYANT, Dawn
7601 Penn Ave. South
Richfield, MN 55423
dawn.bryant@bestbuy.com
Tel: (612) 292 - 4000
Fax:(612) 292 - 4001

Serves As:
- Senior Corporate Public Relations Specialist, Best Buy Co., Inc.

BRYANT, Julie
1400 B Plaza Office Bldg.
Bartlesville, OK 74004

Serves As:
- Treasurer, ConocoPhillips Spirit PAC, ConocoPhillips

BRYANT, Warren F.
141 N. Civic Dr.
Walnut Creek, CA 94596
Tel: (925) 937 - 1170
Fax:(925) 210 - 6886

Serves As:
- Chairman, President and Chief Exec. Officer, Longs Drug Stores Corp.

BRYSON, John E.
2244 Walnut Grove Ave.
Rosemead, CA 91770
brysonje@sce.com
Tel: (626) 302 - 2265
Fax:(626) 302 - 2993

Serves As:
- Chairman of the Board, Southern California Edison, an Edison Internat'l Co.
- Chairman, President and Chief Exec. Officer, Edison Internat'l

BUBENHOFER, Rick
850 Dixie Hwy.
Louisville, KY 40210
Tel: (502) 585 - 1100
Fax:(502) 774 - 6633

Serves As:
- Assistant V. President and Director, Public Relations, Brown-Forman Corp.

BUCHANAN, Scott
901 E St. NW
Fourth Floor
Washington, DC 20004-2037
Tel: (202) 969 - 8000
Fax:(202) 969 - 8031

Registered Federal Lobbyist.
Serves As:
- Representative, SLM Corp.

BUCHANAN, Stephen
One Gaylord Dr.
Nashville, TN 37214
Tel: (615) 316 - 6000
Fax:(615) 316 - 6060

Serves As:
- Senior V. President, Media and Entertainment, Gaylord Entertainment Co.

BUCHHOLTZ, Walt F.
2000 K St., NW
Suite 710
Washington, DC 20006
Tel: (202) 862 - 0200
Fax:(202) 862 - 0267

Registered Federal Lobbyist.
Serves As:
- Senior Washington Representative, Environmental Issues, Exxon Mobil Corp.

BUCKHAM, Robert H.
6500 N. Mineral Dr., Suite 200
Coeur d'Alene, ID 83815-9408
Tel: (208) 769 - 4100
Fax:(208) 769 - 4107

Serves As:
- Director, Human Resources, Hecla Mining Co.

BUCKLER, Dr. Sheldon A.
111 Lord Dr.
Cary, NC 27511
Tel: (919) 468 - 5979
Fax:(919) 469 - 5777

Serves As:
- Chairman of the Board, LORD Corporation

BUCKLEY, George W.
One N. Field Ct.
Lake Forest, IL 60045-4811
george.buckley@brunswick.com
Tel: (847) 735 - 4700
Fax:(847) 735 - 4765

Serves As:
- Chairman and Chief Exec. Officer, Brunswick Corp.

BUCKLEY, Jerry D.
One Campbell Pl.
Camden, NJ 08103-1701
jerry_buckley@campbellsoup.com
Tel: (856) 342 - 6007
Fax:(856) 342 - 6314
TF: (800) 257 - 8443

Serves As:
- Senior V. President, Public Affairs; and Chairman, Campbell Soup Foundation, Campbell Soup Co.

BUCKLEY, John
22000 AOL Way
Dulles, VA 20166-9302

Serves As:
- Exec. V. President, Corporate Communications, (America Online, Inc.), Time Warner Inc.

BUCKLEY, Kathy L.
1500 MacCorkle Ave. SE
Charleston, WV 25314
kathy.l.buckley@verizon.com
Tel: (304) 344 - 7084

Serves As:
- Director, Regulatory Matters, Verizon West Virginia Inc.

BUCKLEY, Michael F.
440 Lincoln St.
Worcester, MA 01653
mibuckley@allmerica.com
Tel: (508) 855 - 3099
Fax:(508) 855 - 3675

Serves As:
- Director, Public Information, Allmerica Property & Casualty Companies, Inc.

BUCKLEY, Richard
701 Pennsylvania Ave. NW
Suite 500
Washington, DC 20004
Tel: (202) 350 - 5571
Fax:(202) 350 - 5510

Registered Federal Lobbyist.
Serves As:
- V. President, Federal Government Affairs, AstraZeneca Pharmaceuticals

BUCKMASTER, Thomas
101 Columbia Rd.
Morristown, NJ 07962-4658
Tel: (973) 455 - 5323
Fax:(973) 455 - 3881

Serves As:
- V. President, Corporate Communications, Honeywell Internat'l, Inc.

BUCKNALL, Jr., William L.
United Technologies Bldg.
One Financial Plaza
Hartford, CT 06101
Tel: (860) 728 - 7000
Fax:(860) 728 - 6494

Serves As:
- Senior V. President, Human Resources, United Technologies Corp.

BUCKNER, Marland
1401 I St., NW
Suite 500
Washington, DC 20005
Tel: (202) 263 - 5900
Fax:(202) 263 - 5902

Registered Federal Lobbyist.
Serves As:
- Manager, Federal Government Affairs, Microsoft Corporation

BUCKSBAUM, John
110 N. Wacker Dr.
Chicago, IL 60606-1511
Tel: (312) 960 - 5000
Fax:(312) 960 - 5475

Serves As:
- Chief Exec. Officer, General Growth Properties Inc.

BUCKSBAUM, Matthew
110 N. Wacker Dr.
Chicago, IL 60606-1511
Tel: (312) 960 - 5000
Fax:(312) 960 - 5475

Serves As:
- Chairman of the Board, General Growth Properties Inc.

BUCKWALTER, Randy

355 Maple Ave.
Harleysville, PA 19438-2297
rbuckwalter@harleysvillegroup.com
Tel: (215) 256 - 5288
Fax:(215) 256 - 5799
TF: (800) 523 - 6344

Serves As:
• Manager, Corporate Communications, Harleysville Group

BUDDE, Kenneth

P.O. Box 19925
Metairie, LA 70179-0925
Tel: (504) 837 - 5880
Fax:(504) 849 - 2307
TF: (800) 535 - 6017

Serves As:
• President and Chief Exec. Officer, Stewart Enterprises, Inc.

BUDDENDECK, Alan

1303 E. Algonquin Rd.
Schaumburg, IL 60196
alan.buddendeck@motorola.com
Tel: (847) 523 - 0679
TF: (800) 262 - 8509

Serves As:
• Director, Communications and Public Affairs, Public Communications Sector, Motorola, Inc.

BUECHEL, Kathleen W.

201 Isabella St.
Pittsburgh, PA 15212-5858
kathleen.buechel@alcoa.com
Tel: (412) 553 - 2348

Serves As:
• President and Treasurer, Alcoa Foundation, Alcoa Inc.

BUELL, L. Dick

200 Carillon Pkwy.
St. Petersburg, FL 33716
Tel: (727) 579 - 5000
Fax:(727) 556 - 2700

Serves As:
• Chief Exec. Officer, Catalina Marketing Corp.

BUFFETT, Warren E.

1440 Kiewit Plaza
Omaha, NE 68131
Tel: (402) 346 - 1400
Fax:(402) 346 - 3375

Serves As:
• Chairman and Chief Exec. Officer, Berkshire Hathaway

BUFFINGTON, Melissa

One Gaylord Dr.
Nashville, TN 37214
Tel: (615) 316 - 6000
Fax:(615) 316 - 6060

Serves As:
• Senior V. President, Human Resources and Communications, Gaylord Entertainment Co.

BUGEL, James

1818 N St. NW
Suite 800
Washington, DC 20036
Tel: (202) 419 - 3000
Ext: 3004
Fax:(202) 419 - 3030

Registered Federal Lobbyist.
Serves As:
• Exec. Director, External Affairs, Cingular Wireless

BUKATY, Molly

P.O. Box 419580
Kansas City, MO 64141-6580
Tel: (816) 274 - 7611
Fax:(816) 274 - 5061

Serves As:
• Communications Manager, Hallmark Cards, Inc.

BUKLAD, Barbara Ann

100 Campus Dr.
Florham Park, NJ 07932
Tel: (973) 245 - 6000
Fax:(973) 245 - 6002

Registered Federal Lobbyist.
Serves As:
• Representative, BASF Corporation

BULAWKA, Bohdan

1350 I St. NW
Suite 400
Washington, DC 20005-3306
Tel: (202) 371 - 6900
Fax:(202) 842 - 3578

Registered Federal Lobbyist.
Serves As:
• Director, ITU Global Strategy, Motorola, Inc.

BULKLEY, Maureen

370 Van Gordon St.
Lakewood, CO 80228
Tel: (303) 763 - 3471

Serves As:
• Coordinator, Community Relations, Kinder Morgan, Inc.
Responsibilities include corporate philanthropy.

BULL, Julie

P.O. Box 486
Little Rock, AR 72203
investor.relations@dillards.com
Tel: (501) 376 - 5965
Fax:(501) 376 - 5885
TF: (800) 643 - 8274

Serves As:
• Director, Investor Relations, Dillard's Inc.

BULLARD, Ed

1401 I St. NW
Suite 600
Washington, DC 20005
Tel: (202) 336 - 7400
Fax:(202) 336 - 7515

Registered Federal Lobbyist.
Serves As:
• Representative, United Technologies Corp.

BULLARD, Edward M.

1401 I St. NW
Suite 600
Washington, DC 20005
bullarde@corpdc.utc.com
Tel: (202) 336 - 7468
Fax:(202) 336 - 7518

Serves As:
• Director, Washington Operations, Hamilton Sundstrand

BULLOCK, W. Bruce

1803 Gears Rd.
Houston, TX 60601
bruce.bullock@fmcti.com
Tel: (281) 591 - 4429
Fax:(281) 591 - 4134

Serves As:
• Director, Corporate Communications and Public Affairs, FMC Technologies, Inc.

BUM, Jonathan

Four World Financial Center
250 Vesey St.
New York, NY 10080
investor_relations@ml.com
Tel: (212) 449 - 1000

Serves As:
• Director, Investor Relations, Merrill Lynch & Co., Inc.

BUMBAUGH, Deborah M.

701 Pennsylvania Ave. NW
Suite 725
Washington, DC 20004
deborah.bumbaugh@group.novartis.com
Tel: (202) 638 - 7429
Fax:(202) 628 - 4763

Registered Federal Lobbyist.
Serves As:
• Director, Federal Government Relations, Novartis Corporation

BUMPERS, Bennie W.

P.O. Box 385014
Birmingham, AL 35238-5014
bumpersb@vmcmail.com
Tel: (205) 298 - 3000
Fax:(205) 298 - 2960

Serves As:
• Director, Corporate Risk, Vulcan Materials Co.

BUNCH, Charles E.

One PPG Pl.
Pittsburgh, PA 15272
Tel: (412) 434 - 3131
Fax:(412) 434 - 4666

Serves As:
• Chairman and Chief Exec. Officer, PPG Industries Inc.

BUNNELL, Alan

P.O. Box 53999
M/S 8508
Phoenix, AZ 85072-3999
alan.bunnell@pinnaclewest.com
Tel: (602) 250 - 3376
Fax:(602) 250 - 2430

Serves As:
• Manager, External Communications and Media Relations, Pinnacle West Capital Corp.

BUNNING, Susan

122 C St. NW
Suite 520
Washington, DC 20001
Tel: (202) 393 - 5100
Fax:(202) 393 - 5110

Registered Federal Lobbyist.
Serves As:
• Manager, Public Affairs, (Tyco Healthcare Group), Tyco Internat'l (U.S.), Inc.

BUNTON, Karen

50 W. San Fernando St.
San Jose, CA 95113
investor-relations@calpine.com
Tel: (408) 792 - 1121
Fax:(408) 297 - 9688
TF: (800) 359 - 5115

Serves As:
• Investor Relations Contact, Calpine Corp.

BUNTON, Mary Anne

P.O. Box 502
Greenville, SC 29602
Tel: (864) 241 - 5400
Fax:(864) 241 - 5401

Serves As:
• V. President, Human Resources, Liberty Corp.

BUONOCORE, Angela

One Pepsi Way
Somers, NY 10589-2201
angela.buonocore@pepsi.com
Tel: (914) 767 - 7472
Fax:(914) 767 - 1264

Serves As:
• V. President, Corporate Communications, The Pepsi Bottling Group
Responsibilities include corporate philanthropy.

BUONOCORE, Fred J.
One Bowerman Dr. Tel: (503) 671 - 6453
Beaverton, OR 97005 Fax:(503) 671 - 6300

Serves As:
- Manager, Investor Relations, Nike, Inc.

BURCHFIELD, Edward
One Valmont Plaza Tel: (402) 963 - 1050
Omaha, NE 68154-5215 Fax:(402) 963 - 1095
elb2@valmont.com

Serves As:
- Director, Corporate Relations and Administration, Valmont Industries, Inc.

BURCKY, Claude
1399 New York Ave. NW Tel: (202) 378 - 2020
Suite 200 Fax:(202) 783 - 6631
Washington, DC 20005

Serves As:
- Divisional V. President, Global Government Affairs and Policy, Abbott Laboratories

BURD, Loretta
P.O. Box 391 Tel: (608) 238 - 5851
Madison, WI 53701 Fax:(608) 238 - 0830
TF: (800) 356 - 2644

Serves As:
- Chairman of the Board, CUNA Mutual Group

BURD, Steven A.
P.O. Box 99 Tel: (925) 467 - 3000
Pleasanton, CA 94566-0009

Serves As:
- Chairman, President and Chief Exec. Officer, Safeway Inc.

BURDEN, Gene
300 Concord Plaza Dr. Tel: (210) 283 - 2001
San Antonio, TX 78216 Fax:(210) 283 - 2003
gburden@tesoropetroleum.com TF: (800) 837 - 8768

Serves As:
- Senior V. President, External Affairs, Tesoro Petroleum Corp.

Oversees all Government Affairs.

BURDEN, Stuart
1155 Battery St. Tel: (415) 501 - 6000
San Francisco, CA 94111 Fax:(415) 501 - 7112
TF: (800) 872 - 5384

Serves As:
- Director, Community Affairs, U.S., Canada and Latin America, Levi Strauss and Co.

BURGESON, Christine McCarlie
1101 Pennsylvania Ave. NW Tel: (202) 879 - 6871
Suite 1000 Fax:(202) 783 - 4460
Washington, DC 20004

Registered Federal Lobbyist.
Serves As:
- V. President, Federal Government Affairs, Citigroup, Inc.

BURGESS, Chaka
555 12th St. NW Tel: (202) 393 - 7950
Suite 650 Fax:(202) 393 - 7960
Washington, DC 20004-1205

Registered Federal Lobbyist.
Serves As:
- Senior Associate, Federal Affairs, Eli Lilly and Company

BURGESS, Laura
Fox Office Center Tel: (313) 983 - 6000
2211 Woodward Ave. Fax:(313) 983 - 6197
Detroit, MI 48201-3400

Serves As:
- Coordinator, Corporate Communications and Public Affairs, Little Caesar Enterprises

BURGESS, Shari
21557 Telegraph Rd. Tel: (248) 447 - 1500
Southfield, MI 48034 Fax:(248) 447 - 1722

Serves As:
- PAC Treasurer, Lear Corporation

BURIGATTO, Carla
P.O. Box 15437 Tel: (302) 886 - 5953
Wilmington, DE 19850-5437 Fax:(302) 886 - 2972
TF: (800) 456 - 3669

Serves As:
- Director, Media Relations, AstraZeneca Pharmaceuticals

BURKE, Deborah M.
800 Nicollet Mall Tel: (612) 303 - 0746
Minneapolis, MN 55402

Serves As:
- Manager, Government Relations, U.S. Bancorp

BURKE, Donna
444 Michigan Ave. Tel: (313) 223 - 6688
Room 1700 Fax:(313) 223 - 9008
Detroit, MI 48226 TF: (800) 257 - 0902

Serves As:
- V. President, External Affairs, SBC Michigan

BURKE, Kevin
Four Irving Pl. Tel: (212) 460 - 4600
New York, NY 10003 Fax:(212) 477 - 2536

Serves As:
- President and Chief Exec. Officer, Consolidated Edison Co. of New York, Inc.

BURKE, Kieran E.
11501 Northeast Exwy. Tel: (405) 475 - 2500
Oklahoma City, OK 73131-6499 Fax:(405) 475 - 2558

Serves As:
- Chairman and Chief Exec. Officer, Six Flags, Inc.

BURKE, Stacey
P.O. Box 2910 Tel: (253) 383 - 9101
Tacoma, WA 98401-2910 TF: (800) 610 - 8920

Serves As:
- Director, Corporate Communications, Labor Ready, Inc.

BURKE, Terri
11111 Sunset Hills Dr. Tel: (703) 547 - 2000
Reston, VA 20190-5339 Fax:(703) 547 - 2881

Serves As:
- V. President, Human Resources, XO Communications, Inc.

BURKE, William F.
37 N. Valley Rd., Bldg. Four Tel: (610) 647 - 2121
P.O. Box 1764 Fax:(610) 323 - 9337
Paoli, PA 19301 TF: (800) 473 - 1286
bill.burke@ametek.com

Serves As:
- V. President, Investor and Corporate Relations, Ametek, Inc.

BURKLEY, Tommy
4300 New Getwell Rd. Tel: (901) 365 - 8880
Memphis, TN 38118-6801 Fax:(901) 328 - 0354
TF: (800) 374 - 7417

Serves As:
- Contact, Fred's Corporate Contributions, Fred's Inc.

BURLEIGH, William R.
312 Walnut St. Tel: (513) 977 - 3000
2800 Scripps Center Fax:(513) 977 - 3721
Cincinnati, OH 45202

Serves As:
- Chairman of the Board, E. W. Scripps Co.

BURLESON, Ron
5565 Glenridge Connector Tel: (404) 236 - 6000
Atlanta, GA 30342 Fax:(866) 236 - 6015
TF: (800) 331 - 0500

Serves As:
- V. President, State Relations, Regulatory and Legal, Cingular Wireless

BURLINGTON, Bruce
500 Arcola Rd. Tel: (484) 865 - 5000
Collegeville, PA 19426

Serves As:
- Exec. V. President, Regulatory, Compliance and Global Safety, Wyeth Pharmaceuticals

BURMEISTER, Lisa
770 N. Water St. Tel: (414) 765 - 7801
11th Floor Fax:(414) 298 - 2921
Milwaukee, WI 53202

Serves As:
- Shareholder Relations Administrator, Marshall & Ilsley Corp.

BURNES, Kennett F.
Two Seaport Ln. Tel: (617) 345 - 0100
Suite 1300 Fax:(617) 342 - 6103
Boston, MA 02210-2019

Serves As:
- Chairman, President and Chief Exec. Officer, Cabot Corp.

BURNETT, Andrea
400 N. Ashley Dr. Tel: (813) 233 - 2132
Tampa, FL 33602 Fax:(813) 273 - 0148
andrea.burnett@sykes.com

Serves As:
- Manager, Media and Public Relations, Sykes Enterprises, Inc.

BURNETT, Laird
1333 H St. NW
Suite 300 West
Washington, DC 20005
Tel: (202) 296 - 1314
Fax:(202) 296 - 4067

Serves As:
- Vice President, Federal Government Relations, Kaiser Permanente

BURNETT, Michael S.
15880 N. Greenway-Hayden Loop
Suite 100
Scottsdale, AZ 85260
Tel: (480) 627 - 2785
Fax:(480) 627 - 2701

Serves As:
- V. President, Investor Relations and Corporate Communications, Allied Waste Industries, Inc.

BURNETT, R. Curtis
P.O. Box 45433
Salt Lake City, UT 84145-0433
curt.burnett@questar.com
Tel: (801) 324 - 5647
Fax:(801) 324 - 5483

Serves As:
- V. President, Public Affairs, Questar Corporation

Responsibilities also include investor relations.

BURNETT GOLD, Heather
11111 Sunset Hills Dr.
Reston, VA 20190-5339
Tel: (703) 547 - 2000
Fax:(703) 547 - 2881

Serves As:
- Senior V. President, Government Relations, XO Communications, Inc.

BURNS, Brian
1350 I St. NW
Suite 1210
Washington, DC 20005-3305
Tel: (202) 408 - 9482
Fax:(202) 408 - 9490

Registered Federal Lobbyist.
Serves As:
- Exec. Director, Federal Affairs, Johnson & Johnson

BURNS, Bruce
P.O. Box 889
Topeka, KS 66601-0889
burns@wr.ocm
Tel: (785) 575 - 8227
Fax:(785) 575 - 1796

Serves As:
- Director, Investor Relations, Westar Energy, Inc.

BURNS, Debbie
1855 Boston Rd.
Wilbraham, MA 01095
Tel: (413) 543 - 2400
Ext: 3317
Fax:(413) 543 - 9355
TF: (800) 966 - 9970

Serves As:
- Manager, Investment Relations, Friendly Ice Cream Corp.

BURNS, Dona Harrington
P.O. Box 1624
Alpharetta, GA 30009-9934
Fax:(678) 762 - 2315
TF: (800) 275 - 3004

Serves As:
- Manager, Corporate Communications, Colonial Pipeline Co.

BURNS, Ed
5251 DTC Pkwy.
Suite 1400
Greenwood Village, CO 80111-2742
Tel: (303) 220 - 0100
Fax:(303) 220 - 7100
TF: (800) 242 - 3799

Serves As:
- President, State Government Solutions, CIBER, Inc.

BURNS, Michael J.
Box 1000
Toledo, OH 43697-1000
Tel: (419) 535 - 4500
Fax:(419) 535 - 4756

Serves As:
- Chairman, Chief Exec. Officer and President, Dana Corp.

BURNS, Mike
P.O. Box 5000
Pineville, LA 71361-5000
Tel: (318) 484 - 7663
Fax:(318) 484 - 7465

Serves As:
- Investor Relations Contact, Cleco Corp.

BURNS, Stephanie A.
P.O. Box 994
C01301
Midland, MI 48686-0994
Tel: (989) 496 - 4000
Fax:(989) 496 - 8240

Serves As:
- Chairman and Chief Exec. Officer, Dow Corning Corp.

BURNS, W. Craig
101 Wolf Dr.
Thorofare, NJ 08086
craig.burns@checkpt.com
Tel: (856) 384 - 3174
Fax:(856) 848 - 2042
TF: (800) 257 - 5540

Serves As:
- Chief Financial Officer, Exec. V. President and Treasurer, Checkpoint Systems, Inc.

Responsibilities include investor relations.

BURPOE, Merryl
555 11th St. NW
Suite 750
Washington, DC 20004
Tel: (202) 637 - 3506
Fax:(202) 637 - 3504

Serves As:
- Director, International Government Affairs, El Paso Corp.

BURR, Kevin
345 Park Ave.
M/S WT-18
San Jose, CA 95110-2704
Tel: (408) 536 - 6000
Fax:(408) 537 - 6000

Serves As:
- V. President, Corporate Communications, Adobe Systems Inc.

BURRELL, Eric D.
Park 80 East
Saddle Brook, NJ 07663-5291
Tel: (201) 791 - 7600
Fax:(201) 703 - 4205

Serves As:
- Director, Corporate Communications and Investor Relations, Sealed Air Corp.

BURRUS, Jan
227 N. Royal St.
Alexandria, VA 22314
Tel: (703) 684 - 3973

Serves As:
- State Government Affairs, GlaxoSmithKline Research and Development

BURTON, Bill
Three Ravinia Dr., Suite 100
Atlanta, GA 30346
bill.burton@ichotelsgroup.com
Tel: (770) 604 - 8149
Fax:(770) 604 - 2008

Serves As:
- Director, Corporate Affairs, InterContinental Hotels Group

BURTON, Diana E.
777 S. Flagler Dr.
Suite 1100 West
West Palm Beach, FL 33401
Tel: (561) 514 - 3850
Fax:(561) 514 - 3839

Serves As:
- V. President, Investor Relations, Jacuzzi Brands, Inc.

Responsibilities include corporate communications.

BURTON, Raschelle
3900 Wisconsin Ave. NW
Washington, DC 20016
Tel: (202) 752 - 7000
Fax:(202) 752 - 7044

Serves As:
- Director, Mission Communications, Fannie Mae

BURTON, Richard N.
Courthouse Plaza NE
Dayton, OH 45463
Tel: (937) 495 - 9275

Serves As:
- V. President, Environmental Affairs, Safety and Health, MeadWestvaco Corp.

BURTON, Terry C.
40 Fountain Plaza
Buffalo, NY 14202
Tel: (716) 858 - 5000
Fax:(716) 858 - 5125

Serves As:
- PAC Treasurer, Delaware North Companies

BURTON, Tom
P.O. Box 391
Madison, WI 53701
tom.burton@cunamutual.com
Tel: (608) 231 - 7272
Fax:(608) 236 - 7272
TF: (800) 356 - 2644

Serves As:
- Senior Manager, Editorial, CUNA Mutual Group

BURTSCHI, Mark
1420 New York Ave. NW
Suite 200
Washington, DC 20005
Tel: (202) 682 - 9250
Fax:(202) 682 - 1533

Serves As:
- Director, Federal and State Affairs, The Goodyear Tire & Rubber Company

BURWELL, James D.
1426 Main St.
Columbia, SC 29218
Tel: (803) 748 - 3000

Registered Federal Lobbyist.
Serves As:
- Director, Federal Affairs, SCANA Corp.

BURWITZ, Jacqueline E.
533 Maryville University Dr.
St. Louis, MO 63141
Tel: (314) 985 - 2169
Fax:(314) 985 - 2224
TF: (800) 383 - 7328

Serves As:
- V. President, Investor Relations, Energizer Holdings Inc.

BUSCH, III, August A.
One Busch Pl.
St. Louis, MO 63118-1852
Tel: (314) 577 - 2000
Fax:(314) 577 - 2900

Serves As:
- Chairman of the Board, Anheuser-Busch Cos., Inc.

BUSCH, Susan
7601 Penn Ave. South
Richfield, MN 55423
susan.busch@bestbuy.com
Tel: (612) 292 - 4000
Fax:(612) 292 - 4001

Serves As:
• Director, Corporate Public Relations, Best Buy Co., Inc.

BUSH, Lucille
One CVS Dr.
Woonsocket, RI 02895
Tel: (401) 765 - 1500
Fax:(401) 769 - 4488

Serves As:
• Director, Community Relations, CVS

BUSH, Michael C.
3475 East Foothill Blvd.
Pasadena, CA 91107
Tel: (626) 351 - 4664
Fax:(626) 351 - 5291

Serves As:
• Exec. V. President, Communications, Tetra Tech, Inc.

BUSH, W. Paul
P.O. Box 5204
Norwalk, CT 06856-5204
Tel: (203) 229 - 2900
Fax:(203) 229 - 3213
TF: (877) 275 - 6973

Serves As:
• PAC Treasurer, Arch Chemicals, Inc.

BUSHMAN, Michael R.
1601 W. Diehl Rd.
Naperville, IL 60563-1198
Tel: (630) 305 - 1025
Fax:(630) 305 - 1973

Registered Federal Lobbyist.
Serves As:
• Division V. President, Communications and Investor Relations, Nalco Co.

BUSHYEAGER, Peter
51 Madison Ave.
New York, NY 10010
Tel: (212) 576 - 7341

Serves As:
• V. President, Corporate Responsibility; and President, New York Life Foundation, New York Life Insurance Co.

BUSSEN, Scott
P.O. Box 482
Milwaukee, WI 53201-0482
sbussen@mbco.com
Tel: (414) 931 - 3848
Fax:(414) 931 - 6352

Serves As:
• Life Category Public Relations Manager, Miller Brewing Co.

BUSSENGER, John
6363 Main St.
Williamsville, NY 14221
Tel: (716) 635 - 5000
Fax:(716) 633 - 0898
TF: (800) 522 - 2522

Serves As:
• Exec. V. President, Human Resources, Tops Markets LLC

BUSSER, Steven P.
P.O. Box 982
El Paso, TX 79960
Tel: (915) 543 - 5711
Fax:(915) 521 - 4766
TF: (800) 351 - 1621

Serves As:
• V. President, Regulatory Affairs and Treasurer, El Paso Electric Co.

BUSSEY, Phil
P.O. Box 97034
Bellevue, WA 98009-9734
Tel: (425) 452 - 1234
Fax:(425) 462 - 3301

Serves As:
• V. President, Regional and Public Affairs, Puget Sound Energy

BUTCHER, Andrew
1211 Ave. of the Americas
New York, NY 10036
abutcher@newscorp.com
Tel: (212) 852 - 7070
Fax:(212) 852 - 7147

Serves As:
• V. President, Corporate Affairs and Communications, News Corporation Ltd.

BUTCHKO, Janet
Ten Westport Rd.
Wilton, CT 06897
Tel: (203) 761 - 3474

Serves As:
• Manager, Academic Development, Deloitte & Touche LLP
Responsibilities include corporate philanthropy.

BUTERA, Joseph
P.O. Box 772531
Harrisburg, PA 17177-2531
Tel: (717) 541 - 6139
Fax:(717) 541 - 6696

Serves As:
• Media Relations Specialist, Capital BlueCross (Pennsylvania)

BUTERBAUGH, Richard
Kerr-McGee Center, Box 25861
Oklahoma City, OK 73125
Tel: (405) 270 - 1313
Fax:(405) 270 - 3029
TF: (800) 786 - 2556

Serves As:
• V. President, Investor Relations, Kerr-McGee Corp.

BUTKUS, Al
P.O. Box 13287
Kansas City, MO 64199-3287
al.butkus@aquila.com
Tel: (816) 467 - 3616
Fax:(816) 467 - 3005

Serves As:
• V. President, Corporate Communications, Aquila, Inc.

BUTLER, Gale M.
AutoNation Tower
110 SE Sixth St.
20th Floor
Fort Lauderdale, FL 33301
butlerg@AutoNation.com
Tel: (954) 769 - 7209
Fax:(954) 769 - 6494

Serves As:
• V. President, Corporate Affairs, AutoNation, Inc.

BUTLER, Jo Ann
1426 Main St.
Columbia, SC 29218
jbutler@scana.com
Tel: (803) 217 - 9394

Serves As:
• Coordinator, Community Services and Corporate Affairs Manager, SCANA Corp.

BUTLER, John D.
40 Westminster St.
Providence, RI 02903-2525
Tel: (401) 421 - 2800
Fax:(401) 421 - 2878

Serves As:
• Exec. V. President, Administration and Chief Human Resources Officer, Textron Inc.

BUTLER, Kevin M.
5725 Delphi Dr.
M/S 483-400-606
Troy, MI 48098-2815
Tel: (248) 813 - 2000
Fax:(248) 813 - 2523

Serves As:
• V. President, Human Resources Management, Delphi Corp.

BUTLER, Patrick
1150 15th St. NW
Washington, DC 20071
butlerp@washpost.com
Tel: (202) 334 - 6635
Fax:(202) 334 - 6664

Serves As:
• V. President, Government Affairs, The Washington Post Co.

BUTLER, Dr. William T.
One Houston Center
1221 McKinney Ave.
Houston, TX 77010
Tel: (713) 652 - 7200

Serves As:
• Chairman of the Board, Lyondell Chemical Co.

BUTO, Kathleen A.
1350 I St. NW
Suite 1210
Washington, DC 20005-3305
Tel: (202) 589 - 1000
Fax:(202) 589 - 1001

Serves As:
• V. President, Health Policy, Johnson & Johnson

BUTT, Charles C.
646 S. Main Ave.
San Antonio, TX 78204
butt.charles@heb.com
Tel: (210) 938 - 8000
Fax:(210) 938 - 8169

Serves As:
• Chairman and Chief Exec. Officer, HEB Grocery Co.

BUTTA, Susan
One E. Pratt St.
M/S 8N
Baltimore, MD 21202
susan.butta@verizon.com
Tel: (410) 393 - 7450
Fax:(410) 393 - 4756
TF: (800) 621 - 9900

Serves As:
• V. President, Public Affairs, Verizon Maryland Inc.

BUTTACAVOLI, Raymond D.
925 L St., Suite 1485
Sacramento, CA 95814
Tel: (916) 444 - 5788
Fax:(916) 443 - 2100

Serves As:
• Regional Director, Sacramento, General Motors Corp.

BUVENS, John L.
2800 Post Oak Blvd., Suite 5450
Houston, TX 77056-6196
Tel: (713) 621 - 7800
Fax:(713) 960 - 7560

Serves As:
• V. President, Legal, Rowan Companies, Inc.

BUZZANCA, Frank N.
P.O. Box 1849
Bartow, FL 33831
Tel: (941) 533 - 0926

Serves As:
- V. President, Environmental, Health, Safety and Engineering, C F Industries, Inc.

BYER, David
One Infinite Loop
Cupertino, CA 95014
Tel: (408) 996 - 1010
Fax:(408) 996 - 0275

Registered Federal Lobbyist.
Serves As:
- Representative, Apple Computer, Inc.

BYERS, Chris
P.O. Box 4655
MC 221
Atlanta, GA 30302
Tel: (404) 588 - 7711
Fax:(404) 581 - 1664

Serves As:
- Treasurer, SunTrust Good Government Fund--Georgia, SunTrust Banks, Inc.

BYERS, Ed
2060 E. Ninth St.
Cleveland, OH 44115
Tel: (216) 687 - 2685
Fax:(216) 687 - 6164

Serves As:
- Media Relations Specialist, Medical Mutual of Ohio

BYERS, Raymond
One American Rd.
Room 338
Dearborn, MI 48126
rbyers@ford.com
Tel: (313) 337 - 6180
Fax:(313) 323 - 2683
TF: (800) 555 - 5259

Serves As:
- Director, U.S., State and Local Government Relations, Ford Motor Co.

BYFORD, David
1000 Louisiana St.
Suite 5800
Houston, TX 77002-5050
david.byford@dynegy.com
Tel: (713) 507 - 6400
Fax:(713) 507 - 3871

Serves As:
- Director, Public Relations, Dynegy, Inc.

Responsibilities include corporate philanthropy

BYOTS, Bruce J.
3250 Lacey Rd., Suite 600
Downers Grove, IL 60515
bruce.byots@servicemaster.com
Tel: (630) 663 - 2906
Fax:(630) 663 - 2001

Serves As:
- V. President, Investor Relations, The ServiceMaster Co.

BYRD, Bruce R.
1401 I St. NW
Suite 1100
Washington, DC 20005
bruce.byrd@sbc.com
Tel: (202) 236 - 8868
Fax:(202) 408 - 4796

Registered Federal Lobbyist.
Serves As:
- V. President and General Counsel, Washington, SBC Communications Inc.

BYRNE, Mr. Dana W.
1100 Superior Ave.
Cleveland, OH 44114-2589
dwbyrne@cleveland-cliffs.com
Tel: (216) 694 - 5700
Fax:(216) 694 - 5537

Registered Federal Lobbyist.
Serves As:
- V. President, Public Affairs, Cleveland-Cliffs Inc

Responsibilities include political action.

BYRNE, Karina
200 Park Ave.
New York, NY 10166
karina.byrne@barcap.com
Tel: (212) 412 - 7561

Serves As:
- Corporate Communications Contact, Barclays Capital

BYRNE, Mike
393 E. Walnut St.
Pasadena, CA 91188
Tel: (626) 405 - 5528
Fax:(626) 405 - 3176

Serves As:
- Media Representative - Southern California Region, Kaiser Permanente

BYRNES, Jim
One AT&T Way
Bedminster, NJ 07921-0752
jbyrnes@att.com
Tel: (908) 234 - 8754

Serves As:
- Corporate Media Relations Contact, AT&T

C' DEBACA, Ernest T.
Alvarado Square
MS 1110
Albuquerque, NM 87158
ecdeba@pnm.com
Tel: (505) 241 - 2806
Fax:(505) 241 - 4386
TF: (800) 545 - 4425

Serves As:
- V. President Government Affairs, Public Service Co. of New Mexico

CABRAL, Victor G.
1299 Pennsylvania Ave. NW
11th Floor West
Washington, DC 20004-2407
Tel: (202) 637 - 4000
Fax:(202) 637 - 4006

Registered Federal Lobbyist.
Serves As:
- Representative, General Electric Co.

CADE, Erskine E.
127 Public Square
Cleveland, OH 44114
erskine_cade@keybank.com
Tel: (216) 689 - 4486
Fax:(216) 689 - 8710

Serves As:
- Senior V. President and Director, Government Relations, KeyCorp

CADORIN, Patricia
770 N. Water St.
11th Floor
Milwaukee, WI 53202
Tel: (414) 765 - 7814
Fax:(414) 298 - 2926

Serves As:
- Senior V. President and Corporate Communications Director, Marshall & Ilsley Corp.

CAFFEY, Bill
P.O. Box 1624
Alpharetta, GA 30009-9934
Tel: (678) 762 - 2211
Fax:(678) 762 - 2883
TF: (800) 275 - 3004

Serves As:
- Chairman of the Board, Colonial Pipeline Co.

CAGLE, Ph.D., Gerald D.
6201 South Fwy.
Fort Worth, TX 76134
Tel: (817) 293 - 0450
Fax:(817) 551 - 4615

Serves As:
- Senior V. President, Research and Development, Alcon Inc.

Responsibilities include regulatory affairs.

CAGLE, Jimmy D.
P.O. Box 570
Union City, TN 38261
jimmy_cagle@goodyear.com
Tel: (901) 885 - 1255
Fax:(901) 885 - 1379

Serves As:
- Manager, Public Relations, The Goodyear Tire & Rubber Company

CAHALAN, Joseph M.
800 Long Ridge Rd.
STHQ-3-3-E
Stamford, CT 06904
joseph.cahalan@xerox.com
Tel: (203) 968 - 3333
Fax:(203) 968 - 4312
TF: (800) 275 - 9376

Serves As:
- V. President, Xerox Foundation, Xerox Corp.

Responsibilities include corporate philanthropy.

CAHILL, John T.
One Pepsi Way
Somers, NY 10589-2201
Tel: (914) 767 - 6894
Fax:(914) 767 - 7761

Serves As:
- Chairman and Chief Exec. Officer, The Pepsi Bottling Group

CAHN, Michele L.
1401 H St. NW
Suite 200
Washington, DC 20005
Tel: (202) 414 - 1288
Fax:(202) 414 - 1217

Registered Federal Lobbyist.
Serves As:
- Manager, Domestic Government Policy, Xerox Corp.

CAIN, David
1101 Connecticut Ave. NW
Suite 401
Washington, DC 20036
Tel: (202) 296 - 7513
Fax:(202) 296 - 7514

Registered Federal Lobbyist.
Serves As:
- Representative, The Hartford Financial Services Group Inc.

CAIN, Mark J.
5500 Wayzata Blvd.
Suite 800
Golden Valley, MN 55416-1259
Tel: (763) 545 - 1730

Serves As:
- Director, Corporate Communications and Public Affairs, Pentair, Inc.

Responsibilities include government affairs.

CAINE, Christopher G.
1301 K St. NW
Suite 1200
Washington, DC 20005
ccaine@us.ibm.com
Tel: (202) 515 - 5000
Fax:(202) 515 - 5113

Registered Federal Lobbyist.
Serves As:
- V. President, Governmental Programs, Internat'l Business Machines Corp. (IBM)

CAINS, Larry
One Chase Manhattan Plaza
41st Floor
New York, NY 10005
larry.cains@assurant.com
Tel: (212) 859 - -704
Fax:(212) 859 - 7010

Serves As:
- Senior V. President, Investor Relations, Assurant

CALABRO, Jack L.
One Tower Ln.
Suite 1000
Oakbrook Terrace, IL 60181-4624
Tel: (630) 571 - 7700
Fax:(630) 571 - 0317
TF: (800) 225 - 8000

Serves As:
- V. President, Human Resources, DeVry Inc.

CALADO, Miguel
2515 McKinney Ave., Suite 1200
Dallas, TX 75201
Tel: (214) 303 - 3400
Fax:(214) 303 - 3499

Serves As:
- Exec. V. President and President, International, Dean Foods Company

CALAGNA, John
One MetLife Plaza
Long Island City, NY 11101

Serves As:
- V. President, Public Relations, MetLife, Inc.

CALDERON, Rima
1150 15th St. NW
Washington, DC 20071
calderonr@washpost.com
Tel: (202) 334 - 6617
Fax:(202) 334 - 4536

Serves As:
- Director, Corporate Communications, The Washington Post Co.

Responsibilities include corporate philanthropy.

CALDERON, Sandra
P.O. Box 513338
Los Angeles, CA 90051-1338
Tel: (626) 821 - 7291

Serves As:
- Director, Public Affairs, Vons

CALDWELL, Barry H.
1001 Fannin St., Suite 4000
Houston, TX 77002
bcaldwell@wm.com
Tel: (713) 512 - 6200
Fax:(713) 512 - 6299

Serves As:
- Senior V. President, Government Affairs and Corporate Communications, Waste Management, Inc.

CALDWELL, Brian
1014 Vine St.
Cincinnati, OH 45202-1100
Tel: (513) 762 - 4765
Fax:(513) 762 - 4818

Serves As:
- Manager, Consumer Affairs, The Kroger Co.

CALHOUN, Essie L.
343 State St.
Rochester, NY 14650-0516
Tel: (585) 724 - 1980
Fax:(585) 724 - 1376

Serves As:
- Director, Community Relations and Contributions, Eastman Kodak Company

CALHOUN, Tara
495 E. Java Dr.
Sunnyvale, CA 94089
Tel: (408) 822 - 6000
Fax:(408) 822 - 4501

Serves As:
- Senior Director, Investor Relations, Network Appliance, Inc.

CALI, Leonard J.
1120 20th St. NW
Suite 1000
Washington, DC 20036-3406
lcali@att.com
Tel: (202) 457 - 2120
Fax:(202) 457 - 2545

Registered Federal Lobbyist.
Serves As:
- V. President - Law and Director, Federal Government Affairs, AT&T

CALIFF, Lee H.
1909 K St. NW
Suite 750
Washington, DC 20006-1171
lee.califf@alcoa.com
Tel: (202) 956 - 5306
Fax:(202) 956 - 5305

Registered Federal Lobbyist.
Serves As:
- Director, Government Affairs, Alcoa Inc.

CALIO, Nicholas E.
1101 Pennsylvania Ave. NW
Suite 1000
Washington, DC 20004
Tel: (202) 879 - 6871
Fax:(202) 783 - 4460

Registered Federal Lobbyist.
Serves As:
- Senior V. President, Global Government Affairs, Citigroup, Inc.

CALL, Laurel
One Chase Manhattan Plaza
41st Floor
New York, NY 10005
Tel: (212) 859 - 7000
Fax:(212) 859 - 7010

Registered Federal Lobbyist.
Serves As:
- Representative, Assurant

CALLAHAN, Dan
Dain Rauscher Plaza
60 S. Sixth St., 19th Floor
Minneapolis, MN 55402-4422
dan.callahan@rbcdain.com
Tel: (612) 313 - 1234

Serves As:
- Director, Public Relations, RBC Dain Rauscher Corp.

CALLAHAN, James M.
Three Concord Farms
575 Virginia Rd.
Concord, MA 01742
Tel: (978) 371 - 1000
Fax:(978) 371 - 3860

Serves As:
- Director, Corporate Communications, Welch's

CALLAHAN, Kathleen B.
3773 Howard Hughes Pkwy.
Suite 490
Las Vegas, NV 89109-0949
kathy.callahan@ameristar.com
Tel: (702) 567 - 7053
Fax:(702) 369 - 8860

Serves As:
- Director, Communications, Ameristar Casinos, Inc.

CALLAHAN, Patrick
1101 Pennsylvania Ave. NW
Suite 1000
Washington, DC 20004
callahanp@citi.com
Tel: (202) 879 - 6871
Fax:(202) 783 - 4460

Serves As:
- Chief of Staff, State and Local Government, Citigroup, Inc.

CALLAHAN, Robert
3600 W. Lake Ave.
Glenview, IL 60025-5811
Tel: (847) 657 - 4096
Fax:(847) 657 - 4268

Serves As:
- Senior V. President, Human Resources, Illinois Tool Works Inc.

CALLANAN, Susan W.
1455 F St. NW
Suite 420
Washington, DC 20004
Tel: (202) 628 - 6442
Fax:(202) 628 - 6537

Registered Federal Lobbyist.
Serves As:
- Assistant V. President, Federal Legislative Affairs, United Services Automobile Ass'n (USAA)

CALLIHAN, William H.
249 Fifth Ave.
Pittsburgh, PA 15222-2707
Tel: (412) 762 - 8257

Serves As:
- Senior V. President and Director, Investor Relations, PNC Financial Services Group

CALLINICOS, Sean
801 Pennsylvania Ave. NW
Suite 725
Washington, DC 20004
Tel: (202) 898 - 3192
Fax:(202) 371 - 1107

Registered Federal Lobbyist.
Serves As:
- Director, Federal Government Affairs, Sanofi Pasteur, Inc.

CALLIS, Kevin
One State Farm Plaza
M/S B-4
Bloomington, IL 61710-0001
Tel: (309) 766 - 2621
Fax:(309) 766 - 0860

Serves As:
- Assistant V. President, External Communications, State Farm Insurance Cos.

CALLISON, Carl
P.O. Box 7026
Wheeling, WV 26003
ccallison@msbcbs.com
Tel: (304) 347 - 7728
Fax:(304) 347 - 7728
TF: (800) 344 - 5514

Serves As:
- Director, Communications and Corporate Planning, Mountain State Blue Cross Blue Shield

CALPIN, Patrick
1001 G St., NW
Suite 950
Washington, DC 20001
patrick_calpin@hna.honda.com
Tel: (202) 661 - 4400
Fax:(202) 661 - 4459

Registered Federal Lobbyist.
Serves As:
- Analyst, Government Relations, (Honda North America, Inc.), American Honda Motor Co., Inc.

CALVERT, Barbara
1399 New York Ave. NW
Suite 200
Washington, DC 20005
Tel: (202) 378 - 2020
Fax:(202) 783 - 6631

Serves As:
- Director, Medical Products Reimbursement, Abbott Laboratories

CALVERT, Valerie
1900 W. Loop South
Suite 1500
Houston, TX 77027
vcalvert@quanex.com
Tel: (713) 877 - 5305
Fax:(713) 877 - 5333
TF: (800) 231 - 8176

Serves As:
- Manager, Investor Relations, Quanex Corp.

CAMARATA, Mary
691 S. Milpitas Blvd.
Milpitas, CA 95035-5473
mary_camarata@adeptec.com
Tel: (408) 957 - 1630
Fax:(408) 262 - 2533

Serves As:
- Director, Corporate Communications, Adaptec, Inc.

CAMDEN, Carl
999 W. Big Beaver Rd.
Troy, MI 48084-4782
Tel: (248) 362 - 4444
Fax:(248) 244 - 7572

Serves As:
- President and Chief Operating Officer, Kelly Services, Inc.

CAMERLENGO, Justin L.
One Panasonic Way
Panazip 3C-7
Secaucus, NJ 07094
Tel: (201) 348 - 7000
Fax:(201) 392 - 6910
TF: (888) 275 - 2995

Serves As:
- Director, Corporate Communications, Matsushita Electric Corp. of America

CAMERLO, Tom
P.O. Box 909700
Kansas City, MO 64190-9700
jcamerlo@dfamilk.com
Tel: (816) 801 - 6455
Fax:(816) 801 - 6590

Serves As:
- Chairman of the Board, Dairy Farmers of America, Inc.

CAMERON, Patricia M.
P.O. Box 4065
Monroe, LA 71211-4065
patricia.cameron@centurytel.com
Tel: (318) 388 - 9674
Fax:(318) 340 - 5520

Serves As:
- V. President, Corporate Communications, CenturyTel, Inc.

CAMILLERI, Louis C.
120 Park Ave.
New York, NY 10017
Tel: (917) 663 - 2121
Fax:(917) 663 - 2167

Serves As:
- Chairman and Chief Exec. Officer, Altria Group, Inc.
- Chairman of the Board, Kraft Foods, Inc.

CAMMARATA, Bernard
770 Cochituate Rd.
Framingham, MA 01701
Tel: (508) 390 - 1000
Fax:(508) 390 - 2091

Serves As:
- Chairman and Chief Exec. Officer, The TJX Companies, Inc.

CAMMARATA, Betty D.
7733 Forsyth Blvd.
Suite 2300
St. Louis, MO 63105
bdcammarata@rehabcare.com
Tel: (314) 659 - 2285
Fax:(314) 659 - 2221
TF: (800) 677 - 1238

Serves As:
- Director, Investor Relations, RehabCare Group, Inc.

CAMPANELLO, Russ
100 City Square
Boston, MA 02129
Tel: (617) 241 - 9200
Fax:(617) 241 - 8027

Serves As:
- Senior V. President, Human Resources, Keane, Inc.

CAMPANINI, Steve
P.O. Box 31907
Santa Barbara, CA 93130
steven.campanini@tenethealth.com
Tel: (805) 563 - 6838
Fax:(805) 563 - 6871

Serves As:
- Director, Media Relations and Corporate Communications, Tenet Healthcare Corp.

CAMPBELL, Brian
123 S. Front St.
Memphis, TN 38103
brian.campbell@autozone.com
Tel: (901) 495 - 7005
Fax:(901) 495 - 8300

Serves As:
- Investor Relations Contact, AutoZone, Inc.

CAMPBELL, C. Thomas
1776 I St. NW
Suite 1050
Washington, DC 20006
tcampbell@dow.com
Tel: (202) 429 - 3438
Fax:(202) 429 - 3467

Registered Federal Lobbyist.
Serves As:
- Manager, Federal Government Relations, Dow AgroSciences LLC

CAMPBELL, Chad
635 Massachusetts Ave. NW
Washington, DC 20001
Tel: (202) 513 - 2304
Fax:(202) 513 - 3329

Serves As:
- Manager, Media Relations, Nat'l Public Radio

CAMPBELL, Dan
9197 S. Peoria St.
Englewood, CO 80112-5833
dan.campbell@teletech.com
Tel: (303) 397 - 8634
Fax:(303) 397 - 8199
TF: (800) 835 - 3832

Serves As:
- Director, Investor Relations, TeleTech Holdings, Inc.

Responsibilities also include corporate communications.

CAMPBELL, E. R.
5718 Westheimer St.
Houston, TX 77057
bcampbell@hibernia.com
Tel: (504) 533 - 3333
Fax:(504) 533 - 2367
TF: (800) 562 - 9007

Serves As:
- Chairman of the Board, Hibernia Corp.

CAMPBELL, Edward P.
28601 Clemens Rd.
Westlake, OH 44145
Tel: (440) 892 - 1580
Fax:(440) 892 - 9507

Serves As:
- Chairman and Chief Exec. Officer, Nordson Corp.

CAMPBELL, Eileen M.
5555 San Felipe Rd.
Houston, TX 77056
Tel: (713) 629 - 6600
Fax:(713) 296 - 2952

Serves As:
- V. President, Human Resources, Marathon Oil Corp.

CAMPBELL, Jeffrey
601 Pennsylvania Ave. NW
Suite 520, N. Bldg.
Washington, DC 20004
Tel: (202) 661 - 4000
Fax:(202) 661 - 4041

Registered Federal Lobbyist.
Serves As:
- Director, Technology Policy, Cisco Systems, Inc.

CAMPBELL, John
P.O. Box 2047
Omaha, NE 68103-2047
Tel: (402) 496 - 5546
Fax:(402) 498 - 2215

Serves As:
- V. President, Government Relations and Industrial Products, AG Processing Inc

CAMPBELL, John D.
2200 Clarendon Blvd., Suite 1202
Arlington, VA 22201
Tel: (703) 284 - 5400
Fax:(703) 284 - 5449

Registered Federal Lobbyist.
Serves As:
- Manager, Legislative Affairs, Ball Corp.

CAMPBELL, John P.
1301 Pennsylvania Ave. NW
Suite 1030
Washington, DC 20004
Tel: (202) 824 - 0404
Fax:(202) 347 - 0132

Registered Federal Lobbyist.
Serves As:
- Representative, Allegheny Energy Inc.

CAMPBELL, Keith M.
400 Robert St. North
St. Paul, MN 55101
keith.campbell@minnesotamutual.com
Tel: (651) 665 - 3500
Fax:(651) 665 - 4128

Serves As:
- V. President, Human Resources and Management Services, Minnesota Life Insurance Co.

CAMPBELL, Leah
2902 Enterprise Dr.
Anderson, IN 46013
Tel: (765) 778 - 6848
Fax:(765) 778 - 6404
TF: (800) 372 - 5131

Serves As:
- Manager, Public Relations, Delco Remy Internat'l Inc.

CAMPBELL, Lewis B.
40 Westminster St.
Providence, RI 02903-2525
Tel: (401) 421 - 2800
Fax:(401) 421 - 2878

Serves As:
- Chairman, President and Chief Exec. Officer, Textron Inc.

CAMPBELL, Michael E.
P.O. Box 5204
Norwalk, CT 06856-5204
Tel: (203) 229 - 2900
Fax:(203) 229 - 3213
TF: (877) 275 - 6973

Serves As:
- Chairman, President and Chief Exec. Officer, Arch Chemicals, Inc.

CAMPBELL, Sabrina V.
801 Pennsylvania Ave. NW
Suite 320
Washington, DC 20004
Tel: (202) 628 - 1645
Fax:(202) 628 - 4276

Registered Federal Lobbyist.
Serves As:
- Director, Federal Agency Relations, American Electric Power Co. Inc.

CAMPBELL, Timothy R.
One Tower Sq.
Hartford, CT 06183
Tel: (860) 954 - 3716
Fax:(860) 277 - 4836

Serves As:
- Senior V. President, Government Relations, St. Paul Travelers Cos., Inc.

CAMPBELL, Travis
One Williams Center
Tulsa, OK 74172
Tel: (918) 573 - 2944
TF: (800) 945 - 5426

Serves As:
- Investor Relations and Corporate Communications, Williams

CAMPBELL, Willam V.
2632 Marine Way
Mountain View, CA 94043
Tel: (650) 944 - 6000
Fax:(650) 944 - 3699

Serves As:
- Chairman of the Board, Intuit Inc.

CAMPBELL, William B.
One Infinite Loop
Cupertino, CA 95014
Tel: (408) 996 - 1010
Fax:(408) 996 - 0275

Serves As:
- Chairman of the Board, Apple Computer, Inc.

CAMPBELL-LOTH, Chris
710 Medtronic Pkwy.
Minneapolis, MN 55432-5604
christine.campbell.loth@medtronic.com
Tel: (763) 505 - 2633
Fax:(763) 514 - 4879
TF: (800) 328 - 2518

Serves As:
- Senior Public Relations Manager, Medtronic, Inc.

CAMPION, Heather P.
One Citizens Plaza
Providence, RI 02903
Tel: (401) 456 - 7000
Fax:(401) 456 - 7819

Serves As:
- Group Exec. V. President, Corporate Affairs, Citizens Financial Group, Inc.

CAMPO, Thomas W.
959 Eighth Ave.
New York, NY 10019
Tel: (212) 887 - 6827
Fax:(212) 765 - 3528

Serves As:
- Director, Investor Relations, The Hearst Corp.

CAMPOVERDE, Rebecca O.
1150 15th St. NW
Sixth Floor
Washington, DC 20071
Tel: (202) 334 - 6684
Fax:(202) 334 - 4536

Registered Federal Lobbyist.
Serves As:
- Director, Public Affairs, (Kaplan, Inc.), The Washington Post Co.

CAMUSO, G. Craig
1590 Marietta Blvd.
Atlanta, GA 30318-3699
Tel: (404) 350 - 5227
Fax:(404) 350 - 5131

Serves As:
- Regional V. President, State Relations-Georgia, CSX Corp.

CANCELMI, Louis G.
P.O. Box 68900
Seattle, WA 98168-0947
Tel: (206) 433 - 5170
Fax:(206) 431 - 5558

Serves As:
- Staff V. President, Corporate Communications, (Alaska Airlines, Inc.), Alaska Air Group, Inc.

CANEVARI, Holly
1401 I St. NW
Suite 600
Washington, DC 20005
Tel: (202) 336 - 7400
Fax:(202) 336 - 7515

Registered Federal Lobbyist.
Serves As:
- Congressional Relations Representative, United Technologies Corp.

CANNADY, Jennifer B.
P.O. Box 30270
Salt Lake City, UT 84130-0270
jcannada@regence.com
Tel: (801) 333 - 5671

Registered Federal Lobbyist.
Serves As:
- Assistant V. President, Legislative and Regulatory Affairs, Regence BlueCross BlueShield of Utah

Responsibilities include political action.

CANNING, Annabelle
1300 I St. NW
Suite 400 West
Washington, DC 20005
Tel: (202) 589 - 3781
Fax:(202) 589 - 3750

Registered Federal Lobbyist.
Serves As:
- Representative, Verizon Wireless

CANNON, Ben
1776 I St. NW
Suite 1000
Washington, DC 20006-3707
Tel: (202) 785 - 4888
Ext: 6595
Fax:(202) 457 - 6597

Serves As:
- Director, Government Affairs, BP

CANNON, Jr., David C.
1301 Pennsylvania Ave. NW
Suite 1030
Washington, DC 20004
Tel: (202) 824 - 0404
Fax:(202) 347 - 0132

Registered Federal Lobbyist.
Serves As:
- Representative, Allegheny Energy Inc.

CANNON, James F.
P.O. Box 204
Clarks Summit, PA 18411
jcannon@corus.jnj.com
Tel: (570) 586 - 8127
Fax:(570) 587 - 3340

Serves As:
- Director, State Government Affairs, Johnson & Johnson

CANNON, III, John
One Liberty Pl.
1650 Market St.
Philadelphia, PA 19192
Tel: (215) 761 - 1000

Serves As:
- Senior V. President, Public Affairs; and Associate General Counsel, CIGNA Corp.

CANNON, Marc
AutoNation Tower
110 SE Sixth St.
20th Floor
Fort Lauderdale, FL 33301
cannonm@autonation.com
Tel: (954) 769 - 7208
Fax:(954) 679 - 6398

Serves As:
- V. President, Corporate Communications, AutoNation, Inc.

CANNON, Mark R.
1426 Main St.
Columbia, SC 29218
Tel: (803) 748 - 3000
Fax:(803) 217 - 8825

Serves As:
- PAC Treasurer, SCANA Corp.

CANNON, Michael R.
847 Gibraltar Dr.
Milpitas, CA 95035
Tel: (408) 957 - 8500
Fax:(408) 957 - 2855

Serves As:
- President and Chief Exec. Officer, Solectron Corp.

CANNON, W. Steven
9950 Mayland Dr.
Richmond, VA 23233
steve_cannon@circuitcity.com
Tel: (804) 527 - 4014
Fax:(804) 527 - 4164

Registered Federal Lobbyist.
Serves As:
- Senior V. President and General Counsel, Circuit City Stores, Inc.

CANTER, Stephen E.
200 Park Ave.
New York, NY 10166
Tel: (212) 922 - 6360
Fax:(212) 922 - 6585

Serves As:
- Chairman and Chief Exec. Officer, The Dreyfus Corp.

CANTERBURY, Norman
P.O. Box 2181
320 W. Capitol
Little Rock, AR 72203-2181
Tel: (501) 378 - 2000

Serves As:
- Director, Managed Pharmacy Program, Arkansas Blue Cross and Blue Shield

Responsibilities include lobbying.

CANTOR-WEINBERG, Julie
1310 G St. NW
Suite 770
Washington, DC 20005
Tel: (202) 508 - 0800
Fax:(202) 508 - 0818

Serves As:
- Director, Government Affairs, Guidant Corp.

CANTREL, Jr., Francis J.
1133 19th St. NW
Washington, DC 20036
Tel: (202) 887 - 3112
Fax:(202) 887 - 3123

Registered Federal Lobbyist.
Serves As:
- Director, Government Relations, MCI, Inc.

CANTRELL, Dean
P.O. Box 3005
Columbus, IN 47202-3005
Tel: (812) 377 - 0162
Fax:(812) 377 - 3334

Serves As:
- Director, Investor Relations, Cummins, Inc.

CANTWELL, Guy A.
P.O. Box 2765
Houston, TX 77255-2765
Tel: (713) 232 - 7647
Fax:(713) 232 - 7034

Serves As:
- Manager, Corporate Communications, Transocean Inc.

CAPELL, Sandra E.
P.O. Box 6000
Cherry Hill, NJ 08034-6000
scapell@subaru.com
Tel: (856) 488 - 8500
Fax:(856) 488 - 0485

Serves As:
- Manager, Community Services, Subaru of America, Inc.

CAPELLAS, Michael D.
22001 Loudoun County Pkwy.
Ashburn, VA 20147
Tel: (703) 886 - 5600
TF: (877) MCI - 1000

Serves As:
- President and Chief Exec. Officer, MCI, Inc.

CAPELLI, Paul
500 Staples Dr.
Framingham, MA 01702
paul.capelli@staples.com
Tel: (508) 253 - 5000
Ext: 38530

Serves As:
- V. President, Public Relations, Staples, Inc.

CAPLAN, Mitchell H.
135 E. 57th St.
New York, NY 10022
Tel: (916) 636 - 2510

Serves As:
- Chief Exec. Officer, E*TRADE Financial Corp.

CAPO, Joseph E.
P.O. Box 35985
Tulsa, OK 74153-0985
Tel: (918) 660 - 7700
Fax:(918) 669 - 2934

Serves As:
- Chairman of the Board, Dollar Thrifty Automotive Group, Inc.

CAPONE, Kerry
404 Wyman St.
Suite 500
Waltham, MA 02451
kerry.capone@novell.com
Tel: (781) 464 - 8042
Fax:(781) 464 - 8100

Serves As:
- Coordinator, Public Relations, Novell, Inc.

CAPONI, Catherine A.
P.O. Box 57
Pittsburgh, PA 15230-0057
Tel: (412) 456 - 5700
Fax:(412) 456 - 6128

Serves As:
- V. President, Government Affairs and Economic Development, H. J. Heinz Co.

CAPPALLETTI, Jeff
4200 Wackenhut Dr.
Palm Beach Gardens, FL 33410-4243
Tel: (561) 622 - 5656
Fax:(561) 691 - 6738
TF: (800) 922 - 6488

Serves As:
- Treasurer, Wac-PAC, The Wackenhut Corporation

CAPPELLO, Christine
120 Park Ave.
New York, NY 10017
Tel: (917) 663 - 4000
Fax:(914) 272 - 0349

Serves As:
- Manager, Employee Giving, Altria Group, Inc.

CAPPS, Thos. E.
P.O. Box 26532
Richmond, VA 23261
Tel: (804) 819 - 2000
Fax:(804) 819 - 2233

Serves As:
- Chairman, President and Chief Exec. Officer, Dominion Resources, Inc.

CAPRETTO, Patrick J.
249 Fifth Ave.
Pittsburgh, PA 15222-2707
Tel: (412) 762 - 3096
Fax:(412) 762 - 3463

Serves As:
- V. President and Manager, Internal Communications, PNC Financial Services Group

CAPTAIN, Lorie
1007 Market St.
Wilmington, DE 19898
Tel: (302) 774 - 1000
Fax:(302) 773 - 2919
TF: (800) 441 - 7515

Serves As:
- Manager, Public Affairs and Human Resources Communications, DuPont

CAPUTO, Robin
5251 DTC Pkwy.
Suite 1400
Greenwood Village, CO 80111-2742
Tel: (303) 220 - 0100
Fax:(303) 220 - 7100
TF: (800) 242 - 3799

Serves As:
- V. President, Marketing and Public Relations, CIBER, Inc.

CARAHER, Kelly
200 N. Milwaukee Ave.
Vernon Hills, IL 60061
Tel: (847) 968 - 0729
Fax:(847) 465 - 3444
TF: (800) 800 - 4239

Serves As:
- Public Relations Coordinator, CDW Corp.

CARBONELL, III, Joaquin R.
5565 Glenridge Connector
2094 W
Atlanta, GA 30342
joaquin.carbonell@cingular.com
Tel: (404) 236 - 6000
Ext: 6141
Fax:(404) 236 - 6145
TF: (800) 331 - 0500

Serves As:
- Senior V. President and General Counsel, Regulatory and Legal, Cingular Wireless

Responsibilities include federal and state legislative affairs.

CARBONELL, Mia
One Time Warner Center
New York, NY 10019
Tel: (212) 484 - 6684
Fax:(212) 489 - 6183

Serves As:
- Director, Corporate Communications, Time Warner Inc.

CARBONELL, Nestor
700 Anderson Hill Rd.
Purchase, NY 10577-1444
nestor.carbonell@pepsi.com
Tel: (914) 253 - 3900
Fax:(914) 249 - 8159

Serves As:
- V. President, International Public Affairs, PepsiCo, Inc.

CARDILLO, Linda A.
2000 Galloping Hill Rd.
Kenilworth, NJ 07033
Tel: (908) 298 - 5772
Fax:(908) 298 - 5242

Serves As:
- Group V. President, Human Resources and Global Prescription Business, Schering-Plough Corporation

CARDILLO, Mary
175 E. Old Country Rd. Tel: (516) 545 - 5507
Hicksville, NY 11801 Fax:(516) 545 - 8193

Serves As:
• Director, Public Affairs and Media Services, KeySpan Corp.

CAREY, Chase
P.O. Box 956 Tel: (310) 964 - 0700
El Segundo, CA 90245-0956 Fax:(310) 647 - 6212

Serves As:
• President and Chief Exec. Officer, The DIRECTV Group, Inc.

CAREY, Christopher J.
City National Center Tel: (310) 888 - 6777
400 N. Roxbury Dr. TF: (800) 773 - 7100
Beverly Hills, CA 90210
chris.carey@cnb.com

Serves As:
• Exec. V. President and Chief Financial Officer, (City Nat'l Bank), City Nat'l Corp.
Responsibilities include investor relations.

CAREY, Kate H.
1620 L St. NW Tel: (202) 659 - 3575
Suite 800 Fax:(202) 659 - 1026
Washington, DC 20036-5617

Registered Federal Lobbyist.
Serves As:
• V. President, Government and Industry Relations, MetLife, Inc.

CAREY, Kathryn
1919 Torrance Blvd. Tel: (310) 783 - 2000
Torrance, CA 90501-2746 Fax:(310) 783 - 3900
kathryn_carey@ahm.honda.com

Serves As:
• Foundation Manager, American Honda Motor Co., Inc.

CAREY, Kevin P.
55 Water St. Tel: (212) 855 - 3230
49th Floor
New York, NY 10041-0099
kcarey@dtcc.com

Serves As:
• Chief Administrative Officer, The Depository Trust & Clearing Corp.

CARLEY, Vera
437 Madison Ave. Tel: (212) 415 - 2110
Ninth Floor Fax:(212) 415 - 3414
New York, NY 10022
vera.carley@ddb.com

Serves As:
• Coordinator, Public Relations, Omnicom Group Inc.

CARLIN, J. David
607 14th St. NW Tel: (202) 354 - 8220
Suite 500 Fax:(202) 354 - 8201
Washington, DC 20005

Serves As:
• Representative, Bridgestone Americas Holding, Inc.

CARLISLE, Corey C.
1717 Pennsylvania Ave. NW Tel: (202) 974 - 1100
Suite 700 Fax:(202) 974 - 1128
Washington, DC 20006

Registered Federal Lobbyist.
Serves As:
• Representative, Countrywide Home Loans Inc.

CARLOW, Ramona
310 Orange St. Tel: (203) 771 - 5748
New Haven, CT 06510

Serves As:
• Exec. Director, Regulatory Affairs, SBC SNET

CARLSON, Curtis R.
333 Ravenswood Ave. Tel: (650) 859 - 2000
Menlo Park, CA 94025-3493 Fax:(650) 326 - 5512

Serves As:
• President and Chief Exec. Officer, SRI International

CARLSON, Gwen
4000 MacArthur Blvd. Tel: (949) 483 - 7363
Newport Beach, CA 92660

Serves As:
• Media Relations Contact, Conexant Systems, Inc.

CARLSON, Jared
2001 Edmund Halley Dr. Tel: (703) 433 - 4000
Reston, VA 20191

Registered Federal Lobbyist.
Serves As:
• Representative, Sprint Nextel

CARLSON, Jennie P.
800 Nicollet Mall Tel: (651) 466 - 3000
BCMNH147A
Minneapolis, MN 55402

Serves As:
• Exec. V. President, Human Resources, U.S. Bancorp

CARLSON, Jr., LeRoy T.
30 N. LaSalle St. Tel: (312) 630 - 1900
Suite 4000 Fax:(312) 630 - 1908
Chicago, IL 60602-2507

Serves As:
• President and Chief Exec. Officer, Telephone and Data Systems, Inc.

CARLSON, Ria
1600 E. St. Andrews Pl. Tel: (714) 566 - 1000
Santa Ana, CA 92705 Fax:(714) 566 - 7900

Serves As:
• V. President, Strategy and Communications and Investor Relations, Ingram Micro, Inc.

CARLSON, Susan E.
One MetroTech Center Tel: (718) 403 - 2000
Brooklyn, NY 11201 Fax:(718) 488 - 1763

Serves As:
• Senior Analyst, Corporate Affairs-New England, KeySpan Corp.

CARLSON, Valerie
Bridgeport Center Tel: (203) 338 - 7171
850 Main St.
Bridgeport, CT 06604-4913
valerie.carlson@peoples.com

Serves As:
• V. President, Communications, People's Bank

CARLSON, Walter C.D.
30 N. LaSalle St. Tel: (312) 630 - 1900
Suite 4000 Fax:(312) 630 - 1908
Chicago, IL 60602-2507

Serves As:
• Chairman of the Board, Telephone and Data Systems, Inc.

CARLSON NELSON, Marilyn
P.O. Box 59159 Tel: (763) 212 - 5000
Minneapolis, MN 55459-8212 Fax:(763) 212 - 2219

Serves As:
• Chairman and Chief Exec. Officer, Carlson Companies

CARLTON, Marianne
50 Marcus Dr. Tel: (631) 847 - 2000
Melville, NY 11747

Serves As:
• Director, Internal Communications and Charitable Giving, Arrow Electronics, Inc.

CARLTON, Nancy M.
601 Pennsylvania Ave. NW Tel: (202) 638 - 4170
North Bldg. Suite 1200 Fax:(202) 638 - 3670
Washington, DC 20004

Registered Federal Lobbyist.
Serves As:
• V. President,Government Relations, Merck & Co., Inc.

CARLUCCI, David R.
1499 Post Rd. Tel: (203) 319 - 4700
Fairfield, CT 06824 Fax:(203) 319 - 4701

Serves As:
• Chief Exec. Officer, IMS Health, Inc.

CARMICHAEL, Dan R.
9450 Seward Rd. Tel: (513) 603 - 2600
Fairfield, OH 45014 Fax:(513) 609 - 7900
dan.carmichael@ocas.com TF: (800) 843 - 6446

Serves As:
• President, Chief Exec. Officer, The Ohio Casualty Group

CARNAHAN, William B.
31 S. Mercer St. Tel: (412) 497 - 7001
Newcastle, PA 16101

Serves As:
• V. President, External Affairs, Verizon Pennsylvania Inc.

CARNEY, Brian
5555 Darrow Rd. Tel: (330) 463 - 3436
Hudson, OH 44236 Fax:(330) 463 - 6675

Serves As:
• Exec. V. President and Chief Financial Officer, Jo-Ann Stores, Inc.
Responsibilities include investor relations.

CARNIAUX, Robert
P.O. Box 1059
Pawtucket, RI 02862
Tel: (401) 727 - 5654
Fax:(401) 431 - 8535

Serves As:
- Senior V. President, Human Resources, Hasbro Inc.

CARNICELLI, Christine
1700 E. Putnam Ave.
Suite 400
Greenwich, CT 06370
Tel: (203) 698 - 5649
Fax:(203) 698 - 7925

Serves As:
- Corporate Human Resources Contact, Premcor Inc.

CARONE, Christa
800 Long Ridge Rd.
Stamford, CT 06904
christa.carone@xerox.com
Tel: (203) 968 - 3000
TF: (800) 275 - 9376

Serves As:
- V. President, Corporate Public Relations and Communications, Xerox Corp.

CAROZZA, Michael C.
655 15th St. NW
Suite 300
Washington, DC 20005
michael.carozza@bms.com
Tel: (202) 783 - 8659
Fax:(202) 783 - 2308

Registered Federal Lobbyist.
Serves As:
- V. President, Federal Government Affairs, Bristol-Myers Squibb Co.

CARP, Daniel A.
343 State St.
Rochester, NY 14650-0516
Tel: (585) 724 - 4000
Fax:(585) 724 - 1724

Serves As:
- Chairman of the Board, Eastman Kodak Company

CARPENTER, David
5700 Tennyson Pkwy., Third Floor
Plano, TX 75024
dcarpenter@racenter.com
Tel: (972) 801 - 1214
Fax:(972) 943 - 0113
TF: (800) 275 - 2696

Serves As:
- V. President, Investor Relations, Rent-A-Center, Inc.
Responsibilities also include investor relations.

CARPENTER, Edmund M.
P.O. Box 489
Bristol, CT 06011-0489
Tel: (860) 583 - 7070
Fax:(860) 589 - 3507

Serves As:
- President and Chief Exec. Officer, Barnes Group Inc.

CARPENTER, John A.
P.O. Box 619616
MD 5575
Dallas-Fort Worth Airport, TX 75261
Tel: (817) 967 - 1575
Fax:(817) 967 - 1477

Serves As:
- V. President, Corporate Affairs, (American Airlines, Inc.), AMR Corp.

CARPENTER, Jr., Jot D.
1120 20th St. NW
Suite 1000
Washington, DC 20036-3406
jdcjr@att.com
Tel: (202) 457 - 3810
Fax:(202) 457 - 2267

Registered Federal Lobbyist.
Serves As:
- V. President, Congressional Affairs, AT&T

CARPENTER, Patrick S.
17876 St. Clair Ave.
Cleveland, OH 44110
Tel: (216) 383 - 6835
Fax:(216) 383 - 4091
TF: (800) 321 - 2076

Serves As:
- Press Contact, Brush Engineered Materials Inc.

CARPENTER, Robert R.
1331 Pennsylvania Ave. NW
Suite 600
Washington, DC 20004-1790
RRCarpenter@celanese.com
Tel: (703) 637 - 3469
Fax:(972) 443 - 8685

Registered Federal Lobbyist.
Serves As:
- Director, State and Governmental Affairs, Celanese

CARR, Edward
175 E. Old Country Rd.
Hicksville, NY 11801
ecarr@keyspanenergy.com
Tel: (516) 545 - 4405
Fax:(516) 545 - 5064

Serves As:
- Senior Analyst, Government Relations; and PAC Treasurer, KeySpan Corp.

CARR, Mary
2200 Renaissance Blvd., Suite 200
Gulph Mills, PA 19406-2755
Tel: (610) 270 - 8100
Fax:(610) 270 - 8104

Serves As:
- Environmental Manager, Regulatory Affairs, Henkel Corp.

CARR, Patrick
712 11th St
Lawrence, IL 62439
Tel: (317) 943 - 8000
Fax:(618) 943 - 8031

Serves As:
- PAC Treasurer, Golden Rule Insurance Co.

CARR, Thomas A.
1850 K St. NW
Suite 500
Washington, DC 20006-2213
Tel: (202) 729 - 1700
Fax:(202) 729 - 1150
TF: (800) 417 - 2277

Serves As:
- Chairman and Chief Exec. Officer, CarrAmerica Realty Corp.

CARRERE, Michael L.
401 E. Jackson St., Suite 3300
Tampa, FL 33602
Tel: (813) 276 - 4600
Fax:(813) 315 - 5388
TF: (800) 242 - 7447

Serves As:
- PAC Treasurer, Lykes Lines Limited

CARRIERE, Margaret E.
Five Houston Center
1401 McKinney, Suite 2400
Houston, TX 77010
Tel: (713) 759 - 2600

Serves As:
- V. President and Secretary, Foundation, Halliburton Company

CARRINGTON, Edward V.
1313 N. Market St.
Wilmington, DE 19894-0001
ecarrington@herc.com
Tel: (302) 594 - 5000
Fax:(302) 594 - 5400

Serves As:
- V. President, Human Resources, Hercules Incorporated

CARROLL, Barbara
P.O. Box 2521
Houston, TX 77252-2521
Tel: (713) 759 - 3636
Fax:(713) 759 - 3957
TF: (800) 877 - 3636

Serves As:
- V. President, Environment, Health, and Safety, Texas Eastern Products Pipeline Company, LLC (TEPPCO)

CARROLL, Jr., Daniel J.
One Telecordia Dr.
Piscataway, NJ 08854-4157
Tel: (732) 699 - 2000

Serves As:
- Chief Exec. Officer, Telcordia Technologies, Inc.

CARROLL, J. Martin
900 Ridgebury Rd.
P.O. Box 368
Ridgefield, CT 06877
Tel: (203) 798 - 9988
Fax:(203) 791 - 6234

Serves As:
- Chief Exec. Officer, Boehringer Ingelheim Corp.

CARROLL, James M.
800 Connecticut Ave. NW
Suite 600
Washington, DC 20006
james.m.carroll@accenture.com
Tel: (202) 533 - 1174
Fax:(202) 533 - 1111

Registered Federal Lobbyist.
Serves As:
- Associate Partner, Government Relations, Accenture
Responsibilities also include political action.

CARROLL, John
83 Edison Dr.
Augusta, ME 04336
john.carroll@cmpco.com
Tel: (207) 629 - 1023

Serves As:
- Manager, Corporate Communications, (Central Maine Power Co. (CMP)), Energy East Corp.

CARROLL, Kenneth
101 Constitution Ave. NW
Suite 200 East
Washington, DC 20001
Tel: (202) 530 - 7300
Fax:(202) 530 - 7350

Registered Federal Lobbyist.
Serves As:
- Director, Tax and Environmental Legislative Policy, (Middle South Utility System), Entergy Services, Inc.

CARROLL, Kevin
1155 Battery St.
San Francisco, CA 94111
Tel: (415) 501 - 6000
Fax:(415) 501 - 7112
TF: (800) 872 - 5384

Serves As:
- Senior Manager, Branded Philanthropy and Employee Involvement, Levi Strauss and Co.

CARROLL, Mary Beth
76 S. Main St.
Akron, OH 44308-1890
Tel: (330) 761 - 4112
Fax:(330) 834 - 8788
TF: (800) 633 - 4766

Serves As:
- V. President, FirstEnergy Corp.

Responsibilities include corporate philanthropy.

CARROLL, Matthew
One Marriott Dr.
Washington, DC 20058
Tel: (301) 380 - 3000
Fax:(301) 380 - 8957

Serves As:
- Senior Manager, North American Communicatons, Marriott Internat'l, Inc.

CARROLL, Melika
1634 I St. NW
Suite 300
Washington, DC 20006-4021
Tel: (202) 626 - 4383
Fax:(202) 628 - 2525

Serves As:
- Manager, Trade Policy, Intel Corp.

CARROLL, Milton
1111 Louisiana St.
Houston, TX 77002
Tel: (713) 207 - 1111

Serves As:
- Chairman of the Board, CenterPoint Energy

CARROLL, Penny D.
305 Hartman Dr.
Lebanon, TN 37088
Tel: (615) 443 - 9807
Fax:(615) 443 - 9511

Serves As:
- Foundation Director, CBRL Group Foundation, CBRL Group, Inc.

CARROLL, Thomas E.
P.O. Box 4239
Winston-Salem, NC 27115
carrollt@vmcmail.com
Tel: (336) 744 - 2032
Fax:(336) 744 - 0145

Serves As:
- Manager, Business and Government Relations, Vulcan Materials Co.

CARSDALE, Robert J.
90 Park Ave.
Tenth Floor
New York, NY 10016-1301
Tel: (212) 907 - 6000
Fax:(212) 907 - 6014

Serves As:
- Chairman of the Board, The BISYS Group, Inc.

CARSKY, Jack
201 Mission St.
San Francisco, CA 94105
Tel: (415) 278 - 4977
Fax:(415) 278 - 6028

Serves As:
- Senior V. President, Investor Relations, Providian Financial Corp.

CARTER, David W.
151 Farmington Ave.
Hartford, CT 06156
carterdw@aetna.com
Tel: (860) 273 - 3658
TF: (800) 872 - 3862

Serves As:
- V. President, Public Relations, Aetna Inc.

CARTER, Dean
2280 N. Greenville Ave.
Richardson, TX 75082
dcarter@fossil.com
Tel: (972) 699 - 6949
Fax:(972) 699 - 6948

Serves As:
- V. President, Human Resources, Fossil Inc.

CARTER, Jerome W.
400 Atlantic St.
Stamford, CT 06921
Tel: (203) 541 - 8653
Fax:(203) 541 - 8261
TF: (800) 223 - 1268

Serves As:
- Senior V. President, Human Resources, Internat'l Paper

CARTER, Marshall
11 Wall St.
New York, NY 10005
Tel: (212) 656 - 3000
Fax:(212) 656 - 2347

Serves As:
- Chairman of the Board, New York Stock Exchange, Inc.

CARTER, Peggy
1000 E. Hanes Mill Rd.
Winston-Salem, NC 27105
peggy.carter@slkp.com
Tel: (336) 519 - 7563
Fax:(336) 519 - 7555

Serves As:
- V. President, Corporate Affairs, (Sara Lee Branded Apparel), Sara Lee Corp.

CARTER, Regina W.
1570 Mt. Athos Rd.
Lynchburg, VA 24504
rwcarter@bwxt.com
Tel: (804) 522 - 5937

Serves As:
- Director, Government and Public Relations, (BWX Technologies), McDermott Internat'l, Inc.

CARTER, Rick A.
900 Seventh St. NW, Suite 950
Washington, DC 20001-3886
Tel: (202) 638 - 3500
Fax:(202) 638 - 3522

Registered Federal Lobbyist.
Serves As:
- Director, Federal Governmental Relations, PG & E Corp.

CARTER, Theresa
175 Ghent Rd.
Fairlawn, OH 44333-3330
Tel: (330) 869 - 4200
Fax:(330) 869 - 4288

Serves As:
- Director, OMNOVA Solutions Foundation, OMNOVA Solutions Inc.

CARTER-MAGUIRE, Melanie
101 Constitution Ave. NW
Suite 325 East
Washington, DC 20001
cmaguire@nortel.com
Tel: (202) 312 - 8060

Serves As:
- V. President, Global Government Relations-International, Nortel Networks

CARTMILL, Molly
101 Ash St.
HQ15E
San Diego, CA 92101-3017
mcartmill@sempra.com
Tel: (619) 696 - 4299
Fax:(619) 696 - 1868
TF: (877) 736 - 7721

Serves As:
- Director, Corporate Community Relations and Corporate Events, Sempra Energy
- Director, Corporate Relations, San Diego Gas and Electric Co.

CARTWRIGHT, Peter
50 W. San Fernando St.
San Jose, CA 95113
petec@calpine.com
Tel: (408) 995 - 5115
Fax:(408) 297 - 9688
TF: (800) 359 - 5115

Serves As:
- Chairman, President and Chief Exec. Officer, Calpine Corp.

CARUSO, Frank A.
191 Spring St.
Lexington, MA 02421-9191
frank_caruso@striderite.com
Tel: (617) 824 - 6611

Serves As:
- Chief Financial Officer and Investor Relations Contact, The Stride Rite Corp.

CARVELLI, Gail
P.O. Box 1059
Pawtucket, RI 02862
gcarvelli@hasbro.com
Tel: (401) 727 - 5318
Fax:(401) 431 - 8535

Serves As:
- Manager, Media Relations, Hasbro Inc.

CARVER, Martin
Bandag Center
2905 N. Hwy. 61
Muscatine, IA 52761-5886
Tel: (563) 262 - 1400
Fax:(563) 262 - 1263

Serves As:
- Chairman and Chief Exec. Officer, Bandag, Inc.

CARWILE, Dan
P.O. Box 868
Evansville, IN 47705-0868
Tel: (812) 464 - 9800
Fax:(812) 464 - 9825
TF: (800) 467 - 1928

Serves As:
- Exec. V. President; and PAC Treasurer, Integra Bank N.A.

CARY, William H.
3135 Easton Tpk.
Bldg. E2E
Fairfield, CT 06431
Tel: (203) 373 - 2468
Fax:(203) 373 - 3131

Serves As:
- V. President, Corporate Investor Communications, General Electric Co.

CASACCIA, Daniel
22001 Loudoun County Pkwy.
Ashburn, VA 20147
Tel: (703) 886 - 5600
TF: (877) MCI - 1000

Serves As:
• Exec. V. President, Human Resources, MCI, Inc.

CASE, Gregory C.
200 E.Randolph St.
Chicago, IL 60601
Tel: (312) 381 - 1000
Fax:(312) 381 - 0240

Serves As:
• President and Chief Exec. Officer, Aon Corp.

CASE, Kathy
83 Edison Dr.
Augusta, ME 04336
kathleen.case@cmpco.com
Tel: (207) 626 - 9516

Serves As:
• V. President, Customer Services, (Central Maine Power Co. (CMP)), Energy East Corp.

CASELLINI, John P.
500 Water St.
Jacksonville, FL 32203
john_casellini@csx.com
Tel: (904) 359 - 3200

Serves As:
• V. President, State Relations, CSX Corp.

CASEY, Philip E.
P.O. Box 31328
Tampa, FL 33631-3328
pcasey@gerdauameristeel.com
Tel: (813) 286 - 8383
Fax:(813) 207 - 2251

Serves As:
• President and Chief Exec. Officer, Gerdau Ameristeel Corp.

CASH, Francis W. "Butch"
909 Hidden Ridge, Suite 600
Irving, TX 75038
Tel: (214) 492 - 6600
Fax:(214) 492 - 6616

Serves As:
• Chairman and Chief Exec. Officer and Director, La Quinta Inns

CASHMAN, Christopher
1901 Market St.
38th Floor
Philadelphia, PA 19103-1480
christopher.cashman@ibx.com
Tel: (215) 636 - 9559
Fax:(215) 241 - 0403
TF: (800) 555 - 1514

Serves As:
• Senior V. President, Corporate and Public Affairs, Independence Blue Cross (Pennsylvania)

CASMEY, Kim
2700 Lone Oak Pkwy.
M/S A1310
Eagan, MN 55121
kim.casmey@nwa.com
Tel: (612) 727 - 0899
Fax:(612) 726 - 0776
TF: (800) 225 - 2525

Serves As:
• Specialist, Sponsorships, Northwest Airlines, Inc.

CASPER, Bradley A.
15501 N. Dial Blvd.
Scottsdale, AZ 85260
Tel: (480) 754 - 3425
Fax:(480) 754 - 1098

Serves As:
• Chairman and Chief Exec. Officer, The Dial Corporation

CASSAGNE, Gil M.
P.O. Box 869077
Plano, TX 75086-9077
Tel: (972) 673 - 7000
Fax:(972) 673 - 7980
TF: (800) 696 - 5891

Serves As:
• President and Chief Exec. Officer, Cadbury Schweppes Americas Beverages

CASSERLY, Dan P.
701 Pennsylvania Ave. NW
Suite 725
Washington, DC 20004
dan.casserly@group.novartis.com
Tel: (202) 638 - 7429
Fax:(202) 628 - 4763

Registered Federal Lobbyist.
Serves As:
• Director, Federal Government Relations, Novartis Corporation

CASSIDY, John F.
P.O. Box 2301
Cincinnati, OH 45201-2301
Tel: (513) 397 - 9900
Fax:(513) 723 - 9815

Serves As:
• President and Chief Exec. Officer, Cincinnati Bell Inc.

CASSIS, Eugene G.
34 Maple St.
Milford, MA 01757
Gene_Cassis@waters.com
Tel: (508) 478 - 2349
Fax:(508) 872 - 1990
TF: (800) 252 - 4752

Serves As:
• V. President, Investor Relations, Waters Corp.

CASSONI, Mary
P.O. Box 6482
1600 Faraday Ave.
Carlsbad, CA 92008
Tel: (760) 603 - 7200
Fax:(760) 602 - 6500
TF: (800) 955 - 6288

Serves As:
• V. President, Corporate Communications, Invitrogen Corp.

CASTAGNA, Vanessa J.
22301 Foothill Blvd.
Hayward, CA 94541
Tel: (510) 727 - 3000
Fax:(510) 727 - 2300

Serves As:
• Exec. Chairwoman, Mervyn's

CASTANIA, Jennifer
4000 E. Union Pacific Ave.
City of Commerce, CA 90023
jenniferc@99only.com
Tel: (323) 980 - 8145
Fax:(323) 980 - 8160

Serves As:
• V. President, Human Resources, 99 Cents Only Stores

CASTELLANO, Joseph P.
One Busch Pl.
St. Louis, MO 63118-1852
Tel: (314) 577 - 2000
Fax:(314) 577 - 2900

Serves As:
• V. President, Corporate Human Resources, Anheuser-Busch Cos., Inc.

CASTELLANO, Laura
1345 Ave. of the Americas
New York, NY 10020
Tel: (212) 282 - 5345
Fax:(212) 282 - 6220

Serves As:
• Corporate Social Responsibility Contact, Avon Products, Inc.

CASTELVETER, David A.
2345 Crystal Dr.
Arlington, VA 22227
david_castelveter@usairways.com
Tel: (703) 872 - 5100
Fax:(703) 872 - 5134

Serves As:
• Managing Director, Corporate Communications, US Airways Group, Inc.

CASTRO, Christine
701 First Ave.
Sunnyvale, CA 94089
Tel: (408) 731 - 3300
Fax:(408) 616 - 3301

Serves As:
• Senior V. President and Chief Communications Officer, Yahoo! Inc.

CASTRO, Elizabeth
130 E. Randolph Dr.
18th Floor
Chicago, IL 60601
e.castro@pecorp.com
Tel: (312) 240 - 3661
Fax:(312) 240 - 4389

Serves As:
• Manager, Public/Community Relations, Peoples Energy Corp.

CATANIA, Jr., Thomas F.
Administrative Center
2000 N. M-63
M/S MD 3005
Benton Harbor, MI 49022-2692
thomas_f_catania@email.whirlpool.com
Tel: (269) 923 - 4648
Fax:(269) 923 - 4652

Registered Federal Lobbyist.
Serves As:
• V. President, Government Relations, Whirlpool Corp.

CATELL, Robert B.
One MetroTech Center
Brooklyn, NY 11201
Tel: (718) 403 - 2000
Fax:(718) 488 - 1763

Serves As:
• Chairman and Chief Exec. Officer, KeySpan Corp.

CATHCART, Richard J.
5500 Wayzata Blvd.
Suite 800
Golden Valley, MN 55416-1259
Tel: (763) 545 - 1730

Serves As:
• President, Pentair Foundation, Pentair, Inc.

CATLETT, Pamela M.
One Bowerman Dr.
Beaverton, OR 97005
Tel: (503) 671 - 6453
Fax:(503) 671 - 6300

Serves As:
• V. President, Investor Relations, Nike, Inc.

CATSIMATIDIS, John A.
P.O. Box 780
Warren, PA 16365
Tel: (814) 723 - 1500
Fax:(814) 726 - 4602

Serves As:
• Chairman and Chief Exec. Officer, United Refining Co.

CATT, Randall L.
1600 Royal St.
Jasper, IN 47549-1001
Tel: (812) 482 - 1600
Fax:(812) 482 - 8300
TF: (800) 482 - 1616

Serves As:
• Exec. V. President, Human Resources, Kimball International, Inc.

CATZ, Safra
500 Oracle Pkwy.
Redwood Shores, CA 94065
Tel: (650) 506 - 7000
Fax:(650) 633 - 1269
TF: (800) 672 - 2531

Registered Federal Lobbyist.
Serves As:
• President, Oracle Corporation

CAUBLE, Toni M.
507 W. Tenth St.
West Point, GA 31833
cauble.toni@wpstv.com
Tel: (706) 645 - 4879
Fax:(706) 645 - 4121

Serves As:
• V. President, Corporate Communications, WestPoint Stevens Inc.

CAUDLE, Darla
1700 Lincoln St.
Denver, CO 80203
Tel: (303) 863 - 7414
Fax:(303) 837 - 5837

Serves As:
• V. President, Human Resources, Newmont Mining Corp.

CAUDLE, Louise
3900 Paramount Pkwy.
Morrisville, NC 27560
Tel: (919) 462 - 4467

Serves As:
• Director, Corporate Communications, Pharmaceutical Product Development, Inc.

CAULK, Stece
9601 S. Meridian Blvd.
Englewood, CO 80112
Tel: (303) 723 - 1000
Fax:(303) 723 - 1399

Serves As:
• Director, Public Relations and Investor Relations, EchoStar Communications Corp.

CAUSEY, Jr., J. P.
1021 E. Cary St.
Richmond, VA 23217
Tel: (804) 697 - 1166
Fax:(804) 697 - 1199

Serves As:
• President, Chesapeake Corp. Foundation, Chesapeake Corp.

CAVA, Jeffrey M.
P.O. Box 256
Dublin, OH 43017
Tel: (614) 764 - 3100
Fax:(614) 764 - 3459

Serves As:
• Exec. V. President, Human Resources, Wendy's Internat'l, Inc.

CAVALIER, Lynn M.
76 S. Main St.
Akron, OH 44308-1890
Tel: (330) 384 - 5626
Fax:(330) 384 - 5791
TF: (800) 646 - 0400

Serves As:
• V. President, Human Resources, FirstEnergy Corp.

CAVANAUGH, Andrew J.
767 Fifth Ave.
New York, NY 10153-0023
Tel: (212) 572 - 4200
Fax:(212) 572 - 6633

Serves As:
• Senior V. President, Global Human Resources, Estee Lauder Companies, Inc.

CAVANAUGH, James W.
One Hormel Pl.
Austin, MN 55912-3680
Tel: (507) 437 - 5611

Serves As:
• Senior V. President, External Affairs, General Counsel and Corporate Secretary, Hormel Foods Corp.
Responsibilties include investor relations.

CAVANAUGH, L. J.
5959 Las Colinas Blvd.
Irving, TX 75039-2298
Tel: (972) 444 - 1000
Fax:(972) 444 - 1350

Serves As:
• V. President, Human Resources, Exxon Mobil Corp.

CAVEY, Brian
2345 Crystal Dr.
Suite 708
Arlington, VA 22202
Tel: (703) 236 - 2756
Fax:(703) 236 - 1931

Serves As:
• Director, Government Affairs, Washington Group Internat'l

CAYNE, James E.
383 Madison Ave.
New York, NY 10179
Tel: (212) 272 - 2000
Fax:(212) 272 - 5143
TF: (800) 417 - 2327

Serves As:
• Chairman and Chief Exec. Officer, Bear, Stearns and Co. Inc.

CAZALOTT, Jr., Clarence P.
5555 San Felipe Rd.
Houston, TX 77056
Tel: (713) 629 - 6600
Fax:(713) 296 - 3394

Serves As:
• President and Chief Exec. Officer, Marathon Oil Corp.

CECALA, Ted T.
1100 N. Market St.
Wilmington, DE 19890
Tel: (302) 651 - 1000
Fax:(302) 651 - 8937
TF: (800) 441 - 7120

Serves As:
• Chairman and Chief Exec. Officer, Wilmington Trust Co.

CECCHINI, Peter M.
U.S. Route 22
Somerville, NJ 08876
Tel: (908) 218 - 2457
Fax:(908) 218 - 2813

Serves As:
• Project Manager, Regulatory Affairs, (Ethicon Inc.), Johnson & Johnson

CECIL, Allan V.
P.O. Box 160
Hartsville, SC 29551-0160
allan.cecil@sonoco.com
Tel: (843) 383 - 7524
Fax:(843) 383 - 7478

Serves As:
• V. President, Investor Relations and Corporate Affairs, Sonoco Products Co.

CELANDER, Jeananne
699 Walnut St.
Suite 2000
Des Moines, IA 50309
Tel: (515) 362 - 3600

Serves As:
• Director, Corporate Relations and Assistant Corporate Secretary, AmerUs Group

CELONA, David
155 E. Broad St.
21st Floor
Columbus, OH 43215
Tel: (614) 221 - 7551
Fax:(614) 221 - 7556

Serves As:
• Manager, Government Affairs - Ohio, Cinergy Corp.

CERIOLI, Annunciata
P.O. Box 3599
Battle Creek, MI 49016-3599
Tel: (269) 961 - 2000
Fax:(269) 961 - 2871
TF: (800) 535 - 5644

Serves As:
• V. President, Human Resources, Kellogg Co.

CESARE, Denise S.
19 N. Main St.
Wilkes-Barre, PA 18711-0302
denise.cesare@bcnepa.com
Tel: (570) 200 - 6300

Serves As:
• President and Chief Exec. Officer, Blue Cross of Northeastern Pennsylvania

CESPEDES, Larisa
980 Ninth St.
Sacramento, CA 95814
Tel: (916) 443 - 8570
Fax:(916) 443 - 8205

Serves As:
• Regional Director, State Government Relations, HSBC North America Holdings Inc.

CESTELLI, Robert J.
P.O. Box 1167
Dayton, OH 45401-1167
robert.cestelli@standardregister.com
Tel: (937) 221 - 1304
Fax:(937) 221 - 1205
TF: (800) 755 - 6405

Serves As:
• Associate V. President, Investor Relations, Standard Register Co.

CETTI, Carlo
9330 Balboa Ave.
San Diego, CA 92123-1516
Tel: (858) 571 - 2414
Fax:(858) 571 - 2225

Serves As:
• Senior V. President, Human Resources and Strategic Planning, Jack in the Box Inc.

CHABRAJA, Nicholas D.
2941 Fairview Park Dr.
Falls Church, VA 22042-4513
Tel: (703) 876 - 3000
Fax:(703) 876 - 3125

Serves As:
• Chairman and Chief Exec. Officer, General Dynamics Corporation

CHABRIS, Margaret A.
2711 N. Haskell Ave.
Dallas, TX 75204
Tel: (214) 828 - 7345
Fax:(214) 828 - 7090

Serves As:
- Director, 7-Eleven Public Relations, 7-Eleven, Inc.

CHACE-MARINO, Elizabeth
P.O. Box 55888
Boston, MA 02205-5888
Tel: (781) 380 - 8000
Fax:(781) 770 - 6416
TF: (800) 767 - 7772

Serves As:
- Director, Government Affairs, The Stop & Shop Supermarket Co.

CHADBOURNE, William
1729 King. St.
Suite 300
Alexandria, VA 22314
Tel: (703) 836 - 0697
Fax:(703) 836 - 6879

Serves As:
- V. President, Marketing and Government Affairs, Stewart & Stevenson Services, Inc.

CHADWICK, Cindy
P.O. Box 5224
Binghamton, NY 13902-5224
ctchadwick@nyseg.com
Tel: (607) 762 - 7310

Serves As:
- Manager, State Government Affairs, (New York State Electric & Gas Corp. (NYSEG)), Energy East Corp.

CHAMBERLAIN, David M.
191 Spring St.
Lexington, MA 02421-9191
david_chamberlain@striderite.com
Tel: (617) 824 - 6000

Serves As:
- Chairman and Chief Exec. Officer, The Stride Rite Corp.

CHAMBERS, Caroline
P.O. Box 75000
mc 3390
Detroit, MI 48275
Tel: (313) 222 - 3571
Fax:(313) 222 - 5555
TF: (800) 521 - 1190

Serves As:
- Corporate Contributions Manager, Exec. Admin., Comerica Incorporated

CHAMBERS, John T.
170 W. Tasman Dr.
San Jose, CA 95134-1706
Tel: (408) 526 - 4000
Fax:(408) 526 - 4100
TF: (800) 553 - 6387

Serves As:
- President and Chief Exec. Officer, Cisco Systems, Inc.

CHAMBERS, Michael G.
320 N. Tenth St.
Room 412
St. Joseph, MO 64501
Tel: (816) 271 - 2459

Serves As:
- Regional Director, External Affairs, (Southwestern Bell Telephone Co.), SBC Communications Inc.

CHAMBLISS, Jr., C. Saxby "Bo"
701 Pennsylvania Ave. NW
Plaza Suit O1
Washington, DC 20004
Tel: (202) 638 - 3838
Fax:(202) 638 - 5799

Serves As:
- Associate Director, Government Relations, Chicago Mercantile Exchange Inc.

CHAMILLARD, George W.
321 Harrison Ave.
Boston, MA 02118-2238
Tel: (617) 482 - 2700
Fax:(617) 422 - 2910

Serves As:
- Chairman of the Board, Teradyne, Inc.

CHAMOUN, Janis
7201 Metro Blvd.
Minneapolis, MN 55439
janis.chamoun@regiscorp.com
Tel: (952) 947 - 7433
Fax:(952) 995 - 319

Serves As:
- Director, Corporate Communications, Regis Corporation

Responsibilities include corporate philanthropy.

CHAMPION, Christopher M.
3330 Cumberland Blvd.
Suite 800
Atlanta, GA 30339
championchris@russellcorp.com
Tel: (678) 742 - 8000

Serves As:
- Associate Counsel and Director, Government Relations and Assistant Secretary, Russell Corp.

CHAMPION, William
8309 W. 3595 S
P.O. Box 6333
Magna, UT 84044-6333
Tel: (801) 569 - 6000
Fax:(801) 569 - 6045

Serves As:
- President and Chief Exec. Officer, Kennecott Utah Copper

CHAN, Julie
601 Pennsylvania Ave. NW
North Bldg. Suite 1200
Washington, DC 20004
Tel: (202) 638 - 4170
Fax:(202) 638 - 3670

Serves As:
- Coordinator, Pubic Policy, Merck & Co., Inc.

CHANCELLOR, Andrea
P.O. Box 871
Tulsa, OK 74102-0871
achancellor@oneok.com
Tel: (918) 588 - 7570
Fax:(918) 588 - 7490

Serves As:
- Manager, Corporate Communications and Advertising, ONEOK, Inc.

CHANDLER, IV, Charles Q.
P.O. Box 889
Topeka, KS 66601-0889
Tel: (785) 575 - 6300
Fax:(785) 575 - 8182

Serves As:
- Chairman of the Board, Westar Energy, Inc.

CHANDLER, Christopher L.
1301 Pennsylvania St.
Suite 900
Denver, CO 80203
chris.chandler@prudential.com
Tel: (303) 861 - 8788
Fax:(303) 832 - 5697

Serves As:
- V. President, Government Affairs, Prudential Financial

CHANDLER, Joe
2180 Lake Blvd.
Suite 11C18
Atlanta, GA 30319
joe.chandler@bellsouth.net
Tel: (404) 829 - 8700

Serves As:
- Director, Media Relations, BellSouth Corp.

CHANDLER, Joy
P.O. Box 231
Latrobe, PA 15650
Tel: (724) 539 - 5000
Fax:(724) 539 - 4710

Serves As:
- Director, Corporate Relations, Kennametal Inc.

CHANDLER, Jr., Theodore L.
Gateway One
101 Gateway Centre Pkwy.
Richmond, VA 23235
Tel: (804) 267 - 8000
Fax:(804) 267 - 8836
TF: (800) 446 - 7086

Serves As:
- President and Chief. Exec. Officer, LandAmerica Financial Group, Inc.

CHANEY, Jared
2060 E. Ninth St.
Cleveland, OH 44115
Jared.Chaney@mmoh.com
Tel: (216) 687 - 6177
Fax:(216) 687 - 6164

Serves As:
- Chief Communications Officer, Medical Mutual of Ohio

CHANG, Andy
P.O. Box 730
Honolulu, HI 96808-0730
Tel: (808) 543 - 5662
Fax:(808) 543 - 7966

Serves As:
- V. President, Government Relations, Hawaiian Electric Industries, Inc.

CHAPEL, Christopher
801 Pennsylvania Ave. NW
Suite 220
Washington, DC 20004-2604
christopher_chapel@fpl.com
Tel: (202) 347 - 7082
Fax:(202) 347 - 7076

Registered Federal Lobbyist.
Serves As:
- Manager, Federal Governmental Affairs, Washington Office, (Florida Power & Light Company), FPL Group, Inc.

CHAPLIN, Harvey
1600 N.W. 163rd St.
Miami, FL 33169
Tel: (305) 625 - 4171
Fax:(305) 625 - 2790

Serves As:
- Chairman and Chief Exec. Officer, Southern Wine & Spirits of America

CHAPLIN, Neal E.
712 11th St
Lawrence, IL 62439
Tel: (317) 943 - 8000
Fax:(618) 943 - 8031

Serves As:
- Public Policy Specialist, Golden Rule Insurance Co.

CHAPMAN, Adrian P.
101 Constitution Ave. NW
Washington, DC 20080
achapman@washgas.com
Tel: (703) 750 - 2000
Fax:(703) 750 - 4574

Serves As:
- V. President, Regulatory Affairs and Energy Acquisition, Washington Gas

CHAPMAN, Barry
P.O. Box 740031
Louisville, KY 40201-7431
bchapman@louisvil.gannett.com
Tel: (502) 582 - 4225
TF: (800) 765 - 4011

Serves As:
- V. President, Human Resources, The Courier-Journal

CHAPMAN, J. Brad
1000 Kiewit Plaza
Omaha, NE 68131
Tel: (402) 342 - 2052
Fax:(402) 271 - 2939

Serves As:
- V. President, Human Resources, Peter Kiewit Sons', Inc.

CHAPMAN, Kelly G.
444 N. Capitol St. NW
Suite 729
Washington, DC 20001
kelly_chapman@dom.com
Tel: (202) 585 - 4211
Fax:(202) 737 - 3874

Registered Federal Lobbyist.
Serves As:
- Manager, Federal Policy, Dominion Resources, Inc.

CHAPMAN, Robin C.
Three Commercial Pl.
Norfolk, VA 23510-2191
Tel: (757) 629 - 2713
Fax:(757) 629 - 2822

Serves As:
- Manager, Public Relations, Norfolk Southern Corp.

CHAPMAN, Steven R.
605 Richard Arrington Jr. Blvd. North
Birmingham, AL 35203-2707
Tel: (205) 326 - 8181
Fax:(205) 322 - 6895
TF: (800) 654 - 3206

Serves As:
- V. President, Governmental Affairs, Energen Corp.

CHAPMAN, Thomas F.
1550 Peachtree St., N.W.
Atlanta, GA 30309
Tel: (404) 885 - 8000
Fax:(404) 885 - 8078

Serves As:
- Chairman and Chief Exec. Officer, Equifax Inc.

CHAPMAN, Tom
1901 L St. NW
Suite 640
Washington, DC 20036
Tel: (202) 263 - 6282
Fax:(202) 263 - 6291

Serves As:
- Legislative Counsel, Southwest Airlines Co.

CHAPMAN, Warren
One Bank One Plaza
Chicago, IL 60670
Tel: (312) 732 - 4000

Serves As:
- First V. President; and President, Chase Foundation, J. P. Morgan Chase & Co.

CHAPMAN, William D.
100 Grainger Pkwy.
Lake Forest, IL 60045-5201
william.chapman@grainger.com
Tel: (847) 535 - 0881

Serves As:
- Director, Investor Relations and External Communications, W. W. Grainger, Inc.

CHAPPELL, Robert E.
600 Dresher Rd.
Horsham, PA 19044
Tel: (215) 956 - 8000
TF: (800) 523 - 0650

Serves As:
- Chairman and Chief Exec. Officer, The Penn Mutual Life Insurance Co.

CHAPPUIE, Louis E.
11419 Sunset Hills Rd.
Reston, VA 20190-5207
louischa@comcast.net
Tel: (703) 251 - 8500
Fax:(703) 251 - 8240
TF: (888) 368 - 2152

Serves As:
- President, Maximus Charitable Foundation, MAXIMUS, Inc.

CHARENDOFF, Bruce J.
1101 17th St. NW
Suite 602
Washington, DC 20036
bruce.charendoff@sabre-holdings.com
Tel: (202) 467 - 8201
Fax:(202) 467 - 8204

Registered Federal Lobbyist.
Serves As:
- Senior V. President, Government Affairs, Sabre Holdings Corp.

CHAREST, Teri L.
800 Nicollet Mall
BCMNH23K
Minneapolis, MN 55402
teri.charest@usbank.com
Tel: (612) 303 - 0732
Fax:(612) 303 - 0735

Serves As:
- Assistant V. President, Media Relations, U.S. Bancorp

CHARLES, Kris
Three Lakes Dr.
Northfield, IL 60093-2753
Tel: (847) 646 - 6251
Fax:(847) 646 - 6005

Serves As:
- Director, Public Affairs, Kraft Foods, Inc.

CHARLESWORTH, Debra
One DNA Way
San Francisco, CA 94080-4990
Tel: (650) 225 - 1000
Fax:(650) 225 - 6000

Serves As:
- Director, General Corporate Media, Corporate Issues, and Financial Media, Genentech, Inc.

CHARLTON, Greg
P.O. Box 1106
Lewiston, ID 83501
Tel: (208) 798 - 2280
Fax:(208) 798 - 2087

Serves As:
- Chairman of the Board, Regence BlueShield of Idaho

CHARNESS, Wayne S.
P.O. Box 1059
Pawtucket, RI 02862
wcharness@hasbro.com
Tel: (401) 727 - 5983
Fax:(401) 431 - 8535

Serves As:
- Senior V. President, Corporate Communications, Hasbro Inc.

CHARNONNEAU, Kathy
P.O. Box 31907
Santa Barbara, CA 93130
Tel: (805) 563 - 7000
Fax:(805) 563 - 7070

Serves As:
- Grants Administrator, Tenet Healthcare Corp.

CHARRON, Paul R.
1441 Broadway
New York, NY 10018
Tel: (212) 354 - 4900
Fax:(212) 626 - 3416

Serves As:
- Chairman and Chief Exec. Officer, Liz Claiborne Inc.

CHARTER, Rick
15710 John F. Kennedy Blvd.
Houston, TX 77032
Tel: (281) 227 - 5000
Fax:(281) 227 - 5455

Serves As:
- Chairman, Total Petrochemicals Foundation, Total Petrochemicals USA, Inc.

CHASE, Jacqueline A.
One Imation Place
Oakdale, MN 55128-3414
Tel: (651) 704 - 3182
Fax:(651) 704 - 4200

Serves As:
- V. President, Human Resources, Imation Corp.

CHASE, Mike
P.O. Box 1130
Modesto, CA 95353
Tel: (209) 341 - 4146
Fax:(209) 341 - 4559

Serves As:
- V. President, Human Resources, Ernest and Julio Gallo Winery

CHASTAIN, Jeffrey L.
P.O. Box 2765
Houston, TX 77255-2765
Tel: (713) 232 - 7551
Fax:(713) 232 - 7031

Serves As:
- V. President, Investor Relations and Corporate Communications, Transocean Inc.

CHASTAIN, Judy
P.O. Box 105366
One CNN Center
Atlanta, GA 30348-5366
judy.chastain@turner.com
Tel: (404) 827 - 1700
Fax:(404) 827 - 2024

Serves As:
- Senior V. President, Media Services, Turner Broadcasting System, Inc.

CHATIGNY, Michelle
1085 Palms Airport Dr.
Las Vegas, NV 89119-3715
Tel: (702) 896 - 8500

Serves As:
- V. President, Compliance, Internat'l Game Technology

Responsibilities include regulatory affairs.

CHAUDET, Stephen E.
1550 Crystal Dr.
Crystal Square 2, Suite 300
Arlington, VA 22202
Tel: (703) 413 - 5996
Fax:(703) 413 - 5846

Serves As:
- V. President, State and Local Government Affairs and PAC Treasurer, Lockheed Martin Corp.

CHAVILLE, Bobbi
The ARAMARK Tower
1101 Market St.
Philadelphia, PA 19107
Tel: (215) 238 - 3726
Fax:(215) 238 - 3333
TF: (800) 999 - 8989

Serves As:
- Associate V. President, Investor Relations, ARAMARK

CHAYET, Victor
6200 S. Quebec St.
Greenwood Village, CO 80111
Tel: (303) 967 - 8000
Fax:(303) 889 - 6287

Serves As:
- V. President, Corporate Communications, First Data

CHEELEY, C. Ron
2000 Galloping Hill Rd.
Kenilworth, NJ 07033
Tel: (908) 298 - 7430

Serves As:
- Senior V. President, Global Human Resources, Schering-Plough Corporation

CHEETHAM, J. Randolph
935 Seventh Ave.
Huntington, WV 25701
Tel: (304) 522 - 5146
Fax:(304) 522 - 5714

Serves As:
- Regional V. President, State Relations - West Virginia, CSX Corp.

CHELEMEDOS, Roger
141 N. Civic Dr.
Walnut Creek, CA 94596
Tel: (925) 937 - 1170
Fax:(925) 210 - 6886

Serves As:
- PAC Treasurer, Longs Drug Stores Corp.

CHELL, Beverly C.
745 Fifth Ave.
New York, NY 10151
bchell@primedia.com
Tel: (212) 745 - 0101
Fax:(212) 745 - 0121

Serves As:
- V. Chairman, General Counsel and Secretary, Primedia Inc.

Responsibilities include government relations.

CHELSON, Debbie J.
One Marriott Dr.
Dept. 51/931.12
Washington, DC 20058
debbie.chelson@marriott.com
Tel: (301) 380 - 2291
Fax:(301) 380 - 5764

Serves As:
- Manager, Human Resources Internal Communications, Marriott Internat'l, Inc.

CHEN, John S.
1 Sybase Dr.
Dublin, CA 94568
john.chen@sybase.com
Tel: (925) 236 - 5000

Serves As:
- Chairman, President and Chief Exec. Officer, Sybase, Inc.

CHEN, Kenneth
555 13th St. NW
Suite 600 West
Washington, DC 20004
Tel: (202) 585 - 9610

Serves As:
- Director, Advocacy and Allied Development, Amgen Inc.

CHEN, Dr. Pehong
585 Broadway
Redwood City, CA 94063
pehong.chen@broadvision.com
Tel: (650) 542 - 5100
Fax:(650) 542 - 5900

Serves As:
- Chairman, President and Chief Exec. Officer, BroadVision, Inc.

CHENAULT, Kenneth I.
Three World Financial Center
200 Vesey St.
New York, NY 10285
Tel: (212) 640 - 2000

Serves As:
- Chairman and Chief Exec. Officer, American Express Co.

CHENEY, Gregory S.
Crystal Gateway 3, 1215 S. Clark St.
Suite 1510
Arlington, VA 22202
Tel: (703) 412 - 5977
Fax:(703) 412 - 5970

Registered Federal Lobbyist.
Serves As:
- Representative, Alliant Techsystems

CHENG, Linda
One Market
Spear Tower, Suite 2400
San Francisco, CA 94105
Tel: (415) 267 - 7017
Fax:(415) 267 - 7260

Serves As:
- V. President and Corporate Secretary, PG & E Corp.

Responsibilities include investor relations.

CHENG, Peter
345 Park Ave.
New York, NY 10154-0037
Tel: (212) 546 - 4000
Fax:(212) 546 - 4020

Serves As:
- PAC Treasurer, Bristol-Myers Squibb Co.

CHENGALUR, Soma
1250 H St. NW
Suite 800
Washington, DC 20005
Tel: (202) 857 - 3400
Fax:(202) 857 - 3401

Serves As:
- Director, Health, Safety and Environmental Policy, Eastman Kodak Company

CHERKASKY, Michael G.
1166 Ave. of The Americas
New York, NY 10036-2774
Tel: (212) 345 - 5000
Fax:(212) 345 - 4808

Serves As:
- Chairman and Chief Exec. Officer, Marsh & McLennan Companies, Inc.
- Representative, Marsh Inc.

CHERNY, Margaret
Two T.W. Alexander Dr.
P.O. Box 12
Research Triangle Park, NC 27009
Tel: (919) 549 - 2000

Serves As:
- V. President, Government Relations and Communications, Bayer CropScience

CHERRIER, Tita
P.O. Box 1537
Salisbury, MD 21802-1537
tita.cherrier@perdue.com
Tel: (410) 860 - 4407
Fax:(410) 341 - 2509

Serves As:
- Director, Public Relations, Perdue Farms

CHERRY, Jan E.
101 Constitution Ave., NW
Suite 980 East
Washington, DC 20001
jan.e.cherry@constellation.com
Tel: (202) 942 - 9840
Fax:(202) 942 - 9847
TF: (888) 460 - 2002

Serves As:
- Legislative Administrator, Constellation Energy

CHERRY, Kim
165 Madison Ave.
Memphis, TN 38103
Tel: (901) 523 - 4726
Fax:(901) 523 - 4354

Serves As:
- V. President, Corporate Communications, First Horizon Nat'l Corp.

CHESSER, Michael C.
P.O. Box 418679
Kansas City, MO 64141-9679
Tel: (816) 556 - 2200
Fax:(816) 556 - 2975

Serves As:
- Chairman and Chief Exec. Officer, Great Plains Energy, Inc.

CHETTLE, J. Anne
1331 Pennsylvania Ave. NW
Suite 560
Washington, DC 20004
Tel: (202) 783 - 8124
Fax:(202) 783 - 5929

Registered Federal Lobbyist.
Serves As:
- Director, Federal Affairs, CSX Corp.

Responsibilities include political action.

CHEW, Dan
1155 Battery St.
San Francisco, CA 94111
Tel: (415) 501 - 1380
Fax:(415) 501 - 7112
TF: (800) 872 - 5384

Serves As:
- V. President, U.S. and Worldwide Communications, Levi Strauss and Co.

CHIAPPETTA, Robert
1850 M St. NW
Suite 600
Washington, DC 20036
Tel: (202) 775 - 1700
Fax:(202) 822 - 0928

Registered Federal Lobbyist.
Serves As:
- Government Affairs Representatives, Toyota Motor North America, Inc.

CHICKERING, Louise
10 Burton Hills Blvd.
Nashville, TN 37215
louise.chickering@correctionscorp.com
Tel: (615) 263 - 3106
Fax:(615) 263 - 3140
TF: (800) 624 - 2931

Serves As:
- V. President, Marketing and Communications, Corrections Corp. of America

CHIEGER, Kathryn J.
One N. Field Ct.
Lake Forest, IL 60045-4811
kathryn.chieger@brunswick.com
Tel: (847) 735 - 4612
Fax:(847) 735 - 4750

Serves As:
- V. President, Corporate and Investor Relations, Brunswick Corp.

CHILDRESS, Clinton E.
TECO Plaza
702 N. Franklin St.
Tampa, FL 33602
Tel: (813) 228 - 4111
Fax:(813) 228 - 4811

Serves As:
- Senior V. President, Corporate Services, TECO Energy, Inc./Tampa Electric Co.

CHILDRESS, Mr. Jan
Four Irving Pl.
New York, NY 10003
Tel: (212) 460 - 6611
Fax:(212) 677 - 0734

Serves As:
- Investor Relations Contact, Consolidated Edison Co. of New York, Inc.

CHILDRESS, Mike
P.O. Box 7444
Longview, TX 75607-7444
Tel: (903) 237 - 5082
Fax:(903) 237 - 5704

Serves As:
- Manager, Communication and Public Affairs (Texas), Eastman Chemical Co.

CHIN, Gloria
1166 Ave. of The Americas
New York, NY 10036-2774
gloria.chin@mmc.com
Tel: (212) 345 - 5645
Fax:(212) 345 - 4838

Serves As:
- Corporate Contributions Administrator, Marsh & McLennan Companies, Inc.

CHIN, James
1399 New York Ave. NW
Suite 900
Washington, DC 20005
Tel: (202) 585 - 5800
Fax:(202) 585 - 5820

Registered Federal Lobbyist.
Serves As:
- Representative, American Internat'l Group, Inc.

CHING, Han H.
Two Waterfront Plaza
Suite 500
Honolulu, HI 96813
Tel: (808) 539 - 5909

Serves As:
- Chairman of the Board, Aloha Airlines, Inc.

CHING, Meredith J.
P.O. Box 3440
Honolulu, HI 96801-3440
mching@abinc.com
Tel: (808) 525 - 6611
Fax:(808) 525 - 6677

Serves As:
- V. President, Government and Community Relations, Alexander & Baldwin, Inc.

CHIOCCO, Leslie
437 Madison Ave.
Ninth Floor
New York, NY 10022
leslie_chiocco@omnicom.com
Tel: (212) 415 - 3605
Fax:(212) 415 - 3530

Serves As:
- V. President, Human Resources, Omnicom Group Inc.

CHIPMAN, Patti
708 Blair Mill Rd.
Willow Grove, PA 19090
pchip@asplundh.com
Tel: (215) 784 - 4214
Fax:(215) 784 - 4405
TF: (800) 248 - TREE

Serves As:
- Manager, Corporate Communications, Asplundh Tree Expert Co.

CHIPPS, Katie
One Tower Sq.
Hartford, CT 06183
Tel: (860) 277 - 8208
Fax:(860) 277 - 4836

Serves As:
- Director, Political Affairs, St. Paul Travelers Cos., Inc.

CHIRICO, Emanuel
200 Madison Ave.
New York, NY 10016
Tel: (212) 381 - 3503
Fax:(212) 381 - 3959

Serves As:
- Exec. V. President and Chief Financial Officer, Phillips-Van Heusen Corp.

Responsibilities include investor relations.

CHIRONNA, John G.
501 Merritt Seven
Norwalk, CT 06851
john.g.chironna@us.abb.com
Tel: (203) 750 - 7743
Fax:(203) 750 - 2262
TF: (800) 626 - 4999

Serves As:
- Director, Investor Relations, ABB Inc.

CHITI, Jim
130 E. Randolph Dr.
24th Floor
Chicago, IL 60601
Tel: (312) 240 - 4730
Fax:(312) 240 - 4220

Serves As:
- Manager, Investor Relations, Peoples Energy Corp.

CHIU, Sandra L.
P.O. Box 66100
Chicago, IL 60666
sandra.chiu@ual.com
Tel: (847) 700 - 3956
Fax:(847) 700 - 5931

Serves As:
- Director, International Affairs, United Airlines

CHIZAUSKAS, Cathleen J.
Prudential Tower Bldg.
Boston, MA 02199-8004
Tel: (617) 421 - 7000
Fax:(617) 421 - 7123

Serves As:
- V. President, Civic Affairs, The Gillette Company

CHIZEN, Bruce
345 Park Ave.
San Jose, CA 95110-2704
Tel: (408) 536 - 6000
Fax:(408) 537 - 6000

Serves As:
- President and Chief Exec. Officer, Adobe Systems Inc.

CHIZMADIA, Thomas A.
6211 N. Ann Arbor Rd.
P.O. Box 122
Dundee, MI 48131
tom.chizmadia@holcim.com
Tel: (734) 529 - 2411
Fax:(734) 529 - 5268
TF: (800) 854 - 4656

Registered Federal Lobbyist.
Serves As:
- V. President, Communications and Public Affairs, Holcim (US) Inc.

CHOATE, Chris A.
801 Cherry St.
Suite 3900
Fort Worth, TX 76102-6803
Tel: (817) 302 - 7000
Fax:(817) 302 - 7479
TF: (800) 644 - 2297

Serves As:
- Chief Financial Officer, Chief Legal Officer, and PAC Treasurer, AmeriCredit Corp.

CHOKEY, James A.
P.O. Box 554
Milwaukee, WI 53201
Tel: (414) 319 - 8500
Fax:(414) 319 - 8510

Serves As:
- Exec. V. President and General Counsel, Joy Global Inc.

CHOQUETTE, Kara
4600 S. Ulster
Suite 1000
Denver, CO 80237
kara.choquette@xerox.com
Tel: (303) 796 - 6420

Serves As:
- Manager, Corporate Public Relations, Xerox Corp.

CHOQUETTE, William
4330 East-West Hwy.
Suite 314
Bethesda, MD 20814
wchoquette@gilbaneco.com
Tel: (301) 718 - 8860
Fax:(301) 718 - 8862

Serves As:
- Senior V. President and Washington Contact, Gilbane Building Co.

CHORLINS, Marjorie
1350 I St. NW
Suite 400
Washington, DC 20005-3306
Tel: (202) 371 - 6900
Fax:(202) 842 - 3578

Registered Federal Lobbyist.
Serves As:
- Director, Customer Solutions and Global Strategy, Motorola, Inc.

CHORMAN, Thomas E.
1000 Columbia Ave.
Linwood, PA 19061-3998
Tel: (610) 859 - 3000
Fax:(610) 859 - 3035

Serves As:
- President and Chief Exec. Officer, Foamex Internat'l Inc.

CHOW, Barbara
P.O. Box 98199
Washington, DC 20090-8199
Tel: (202) 857 - 7000
Fax:(202) 828 - 6679
TF: (800) 647 - 5463

Serves As:
- Contact, Nat'l Geographic Education Foundation, Nat'l Geographic Soc.

CHRENC, Robert J.
One Symbol Plaza
Holtsville, NY 11742-1300
Tel: (631) 738 - 2400
Fax:(631) 738 - 5990
TF: (800) 722 - 6234

Serves As:
- Chairman of the Board, Symbol Technologies, Inc.

CHRIST, Richard
P.O. Box 126
Hunt Valley, MD 21030-0126
christ@aaicorp.com
Tel: (410) 628 - 3406
Fax:(410) 628 - 8740
TF: (800) 626 - 6283

Serves As:
- Treasurer, AAI Corp. Political Action Committee, AAI Corp.

CHRISTAL, Nancy R.
670 White Plains Rd.
Suite 210
Scarsdale, NY 10583
nrchristal@cvs.com
Tel: (914) 722 - 4704
Fax:(914) 722 - 0847

Serves As:
- V. President, Investor Relations, CVS

CHRISTENSEN, Kyle
610 Opperman Dr.
Eagan, MN 55123-1340
kyle.christensen@thomson.com
Tel: (651) 687 - 7082
Fax:(651) 687 - 5388
TF: (800) 328 - 9352

Serves As:
- Corporate Communications, Thomson West

CHRISTENSEN, Paul
P.O. Box 300
Oshkosh, WI 54903-0300
Tel: (920) 231 - 8800
Fax:(920) 231 - 8621
TF: (800) 282 - 4674

Serves As:
- V. President, Human Resources, Oshkosh B'Gosh, Inc.

CHRISTENSON, Arne L.
801 Pennsylvania Ave. NW
Suite 650
Washington, DC 20004
Tel: (202) 624 - 0761
Fax:(202) 624 - 0775

Registered Federal Lobbyist.
Serves As:
- Senior V. President, Government Affairs, American Express Co.

CHRISTIAN, David C.
P.O. Box 418679
Kansas City, MO 64141-9679
Tel: (816) 556 - 2977
Fax:(816) 556 - 2975

Serves As:
- Manager, Governmental Affairs - Missouri, (Kansas City Power and Light Co.), Great Plains Energy, Inc.

CHRISTIANSEN, David
P.O. Box 14662
Reading, PA 19612-4662
Tel: (610) 208 - 2000
Fax:(610) 208 - 3716

Serves As:
- PAC Treasurer, Carpenter Technology Corp.

CHRISTIANSEN, George
Kerr-McGee Center, Box 25861
Oklahoma City, OK 73125
Tel: (405) 270 - 1313
Fax:(405) 270 - 3029
TF: (800) 786 - 2556

Serves As:
- V. President, Safety and Environmental Affairs, Kerr-McGee Corp.

CHRISTIE, Blair
170 W. Tasman Dr.
San Jose, CA 95134-1706
Tel: (408) 526 - 4000
Fax:(408) 526 - 4100
TF: (800) 553 - 6387

Serves As:
- Director, Investor Relations, Cisco Systems, Inc.

CHRISTIE, Robert
P.O. Box 300
Princeton, NJ 08543
Tel: (609) 520 - 5143
Fax:(609) 520 - 5180

Serves As:
- Director, Corporate Communications, Dow Jones and Co.

CHRISTOPHER, Tom
4800 Hampden Ln.
Suite 1100
Bethesda, MD 20814
Tel: (301) 841 - 1600
Fax:(301) 841 - 1611

Serves As:
- Co-Chief Exec. Officer, AREVA Enterprises, Inc.

CHRISTY, Kristina
P.O. Box 105366
One CNN Center
Atlanta, GA 30348-5366
krsitina.koldoff@turner.com
Tel: (404) 878 - 1073
Fax:(404) 827 - 6575

Serves As:
- Manager, Corporate Contributions, Turner Broadcasting System, Inc.

CHU, Chinh E.
1601 W. LBJ Fwy.
Dallas, TX 75234
Tel: (972) 443 - 4000

Serves As:
- Chairman of the Board, Celanese

CHUANG, Alfred S.
2315 N. First St.
San Jose, CA 95131
alfred.chuang@bea.com
Tel: (408) 570 - 8000
Fax:(408) 570 - 8901

Serves As:
- Chairman and Chief Exec. Officer, BEA Systems, Inc.
Also is the founder of the company

CHUNG, Mary
86 Trinity Pl.
New York, NY 10006
mary.chung@amex.com
Tel: (212) 306 - 1641
Fax:(212) 306 - 1152

Serves As:
- Media Contact, American Stock Exchange

CHURCH, Andrew G.
163-181 Kenwood Ave.
Oneida, NY 13421
Tel: (315) 361 - 3000

Serves As:
- Chief Financial Officer, Oneida Ltd.
Responsibilities include investor relations.

CHURCH, Brad
One Williams Center
Tulsa, OK 74172
Tel: (918) 573 - 3679
TF: (800) 945 - 5426

Serves As:
- Media Relations Contact, Williams

CHURCHILL, Randy
1215 Fourth Ave.
Suite 1620
Seattle, WA 28181

Serves As:
- PAC Treasurer, Washington Mutual, Inc.

CHVALA, Vicki
6000 American Pkwy.
Madison, WI 53783
vchvala@amfam.com
Tel: (608) 249 - 2111
Fax:(608) 243 - 4928

Serves As:
- V. President, Human Resources, American Family Insurance Group

CICCONE, Christine M.
1001 Pennsylvania Ave. NW
Suite 700 South
Washington, DC 20004
Tel: (202) 662 - 2650
Fax:(202) 662 - 2674

Registered Federal Lobbyist.
Serves As:
- V. President, Government Relations, Honeywell Internat'l, Inc.

CICCONE, Stephen J.
1250 H St. NW
Suite 800
Washington, DC 20005
stephen.ciccone@kodak.com
Tel: (202) 857 - 3400
Fax:(202) 857 - 3401

Serves As:
- Director and V. President, Public Affairs, Eastman Kodak Company

CICCONI, James W.
1120 20th St. NW
Suite 1000
Washington, DC 20036-3406
jcicconi@att.com
Tel: (202) 457 - 3810
Fax:(202) 457 - 2244

Registered Federal Lobbyist.
Serves As:
- General Counsel and Exec. V. President, Law and Government Affairs, AT&T

CIESLAK, Richard
231 W. Michigan St.
P478
Milwaukee, WI 53201
richard.cieslak@we-energies.com
Tel: (414) 221 - 4510
Fax:(414) 221 - 2824

Serves As:
- Manager, Media Relations, Wisconsin Energy Corp.
- Manager, External Communications, We Energies

CIMINO, William P.
9950 Mayland Dr.
Richmond, VA 23233
Tel: (804) 418 - 8163
Fax:(804) 527 - 4164

Serves As:
- Director, Corporate Communications, Circuit City Stores, Inc.
Responsibilities include political action.

CINOTTI, Carolyn
The Mountain
Framingham, MA 01701-9168
Tel: (508) 879 - 7330
Fax:(508) 766 - 7543

Serves As:
- Director, Public Relations, Bose Corp.

CIPOLETTI, Sam E.
1500 MacCorkle Ave. SE
Charleston, WV 25314
samuel.cipoletti.jr@verizon.com
Tel: (304) 344 - 7216

Serves As:
- Manager, Government Relations and External Affairs - Huntington and Weeling, Verizon West Virginia Inc.

CIPPOLLONE, Tom
P.O. Box 593330
Orlando, FL 32859
tcippollone@darden.com
Tel: (407) 245 - 4969
Fax:(407) 245 - 6678

Serves As:
- Director, Risk Management, Darden Restaurants, Inc.

CIRIGLIANO, Tom J.
5959 Las Colinas Blvd.
Irving, TX 75039-2298
Tel: (972) 444 - 1109
Fax:(972) 444 - 1138

Serves As:
- Manager, Media Relations, Exxon Mobil Corp.

CIRILLO, Alex
3M Center
St. Paul, MN 55144-1000
Tel: (651) 733 - 1110
Fax:(651) 733 - 9973

Serves As:
- Staff V. President, Community Affairs and Workforce Diversity, 3M Company

CISCHKE, Susan M.
One American Rd.
Dearborn, MI 48126
scischke@ford.com
Tel: (313) 248 - 2137
Fax:(313) 248 - 2171
TF: (800) 555 - 5259

Serves As:
- V. President, Environmental and Safety Engineering, Ford Motor Co.

CLABES, Judith G.
312 Walnut St.
2800 Scripps Center
Cincinnati, OH 45202
clabes@scripps.com
Tel: (513) 977 - 3048
Fax:(513) 977 - 3721

Serves As:
- President and Chief Exec. Officer, Scripps Howard Foundation, E. W. Scripps Co.

CLADOUHOS, Sherry L.
P.O. Box 4309
Helena, MT 59604-4309
Tel: (406) 444 - 8200
Fax:(406) 447 - 3454
TF: (800) 447 - 7828

Serves As:
- President and Chief Exec. Officer, Blue Cross and Blue Shield of Montana

CLAFFEY, Terri G.
1133 19th St. NW
Washington, DC 20036
Tel: (202) 887 - 3830
Fax:(202) 887 - 3123

Registered Federal Lobbyist.
Serves As:
- Senior Policy Advisor, Government Relations, MCI, Inc.

CLAFLIN, Bruce
350 Campus Dr.
Marlborough, MA 01752-3064
Tel: (508) 323 - 5000
Fax:(508) 323 - 1111

Serves As:
- President and Chief Exec. Officer, 3Com Corp.

CLANCY, Rick
16530 Via Esprillo
San Diego, CA 92127
rick.clancy@am.sony.com
Tel: (858) 842 - 3020
Fax:(858) 842 - 8186

Serves As:
- Senior V. President, Corporate Communications, (Sony Electronics Inc.), Sony Corp. of America

CLANCY, Rob
One Allied Dr.
Little Rock, AR 72202
rob.clancy@alltel.com
Tel: (501) 905 - 8991

Serves As:
- V. President, Investor Relations, ALLTEL

CLAPP, Carol
Hartford Plaza
HO-1-11
Hartford, CT 06115
cclapp@thehartford.com
Tel: (860) 547 - 2944
Fax:(860) 547 - 6551

Serves As:
- V. President, Government Affairs, The Hartford Financial Services Group Inc.

CLAPP, Kent W.
2060 E. Ninth St.
Cleveland, OH 44115
kent.clapp@mmoh.com
Tel: (216) 687 - 7000
Fax:(216) 687 - 6164

Serves As:
- Chairman and Chief Exec. Officer, Medical Mutual of Ohio

CLAPPER, Kellie
One State Farm Plaza
M/S B-4
Bloomington, IL 61710-0001
Tel: (309) 766 - 8865
Fax:(309) 766 - 0860

Serves As:
- Director, Public Affairs, State Farm Insurance Cos.

CLARK, Dr. Celeste A.
P.O. Box 3599
Battle Creek, MI 49016-3599
Tel: (269) 961 - 3799
Fax:(269) 961 - 2871
TF: (800) 535 - 5644

Serves As:
- Senior V. President, Corporate Affairs, Kellogg Co.

CLARK, Charles A.
P.O. Box 591
Knoxville, TN 37919
Tel: (615) 521 - 8443

Serves As:
- Human Resources Director, Rohm and Haas Co.

CLARK, David W.
Seven W. Seventh St.
Cincinnati, OH 45202
Tel: (513) 579 - 7000
Fax:(513) 579 - 7555
TF: (800) 261 - 5385

Serves As:
- Senior V. President, Human Resources, Federated Department Stores, Inc.

CLARK, Frank M.
P.O. Box A-3005
Chicago, IL 60690-3005
frank.clark@exeloncorp.com
Tel: (312) 394 - 7184

Serves As:
- Exec. V. President, Exelon Corp.

CLARK, Jr., Harry A.
P.O. Box 660606
M/S 490
Dallas, TX 75266-0606
Tel: (972) 789 - 7000
Fax:(972) 789 - 7234

Serves As:
- V. President, Human Resources, Greyhound Lines, Inc.

CLARK, Jacqueline K.
P.O. Box 419580
Mail #288
Kansas City, MO 64141-6580
jclark7@hallmark.com
Tel: (816) 274 - 8893
Fax:(816) 274 - 5061

Serves As:
- Manager, Public Affairs, Hallmark Cards, Inc.

CLARK, Joanne
National City Center
1900 E. Ninth St.
M/S 01-2157
Cleveland, OH 44114-3484
joanne.clark@nationalcity.com
Tel: (216) 222 - 2995
Fax:(216) 222 - 2670
TF: (800) 622 - 6736

Serves As:
- Contact, Nat'l City/Corporation Charitable Foundation, Nat'l City Corp.

CLARK, Kevin P.
Liberty Ln.
Hampton, NH 03842
Tel: (603) 926 - 5911
Fax:(603) 929 - 2379

Serves As:
- PAC Treasurer, Fisher Scientific Internat'l Inc.

CLARK, Leslie
1540 Genesee St.
Kansas City, MO 64102
Tel: (816) 968 - 3525
Fax:(816) 968 - 6503

Serves As:
- Manager, Marketing Communications, Butler Manufacturing Co.

CLARK, Mechelle
1932 Wynnton Rd.
Columbus, GA 31999
meclark@aflac.com
Tel: (706) 243 - 8004
Fax:(706) 660 - 7333
TF: (800) 992 - 3522

Serves As:
- Media Contact, AFLAC Incorporated

CLARK, Neala
P.O. Box 13287
Kansas City, MO 64199-3287
neala.clark@aquila.com
Tel: (816) 467 - 3562
Fax:(816) 467 - 3435

Serves As:
- Director, Investor Relations, Aquila, Inc.

CLARK, Richard E.
Reader's Digest Rd.
Pleasantville, NY 10570-7000
richard.clark@rd.com
Tel: (914) 244 - 5425
Fax:(914) 238 - 6643
TF: (800) 234 - 9000

Serves As:
- V. President, Investor Relations and Global Communiations, Reader's Digest Ass'n, Inc.

CLARK, Richard T.
P.O. Box 100
Whitehouse Station, NJ 08889-0100
Tel: (908) 423 - 1000
Fax:(908) 735 - 1181
TF: (800) 423 - 1000

Serves As:
- President and Chief Executive Officer, Merck & Co., Inc.

CLARK, Roger
152 W. 57th St.
42nd Floor
New York, NY 10019
Tel: (212) 314 - 7300
Fax:(212) 314 - 7309

Serves As:
- V. President, Investor Relations and Finance, IAC/InterActiveCorp

CLARK, Sylvia
Eight Corporate Center Dr.
Melville, NY 11747
Tel: (631) 232 - 2212
Fax:(631) 753 - 7041

Serves As:
- Exec. Director, NEC Foundation of America, NEC USA, Inc.

CLARK, Timothy
801 Pennsylvania Ave. NW
Suite 725
Washington, DC 20004
Tel: (202) 628 - 0500
Fax:(202) 682 - 0538

Serves As:
- PAC Treasurer, Sanofi-Aventis Inc.

CLARK-LEYDA, Rhonda
711 High St.
Des Moines, IA 50392-0150
clark-leyda.rhonda@principal.com
Tel: (515) 247 - 6634
Fax:(515) 246 - 5475
TF: (800) 986 - 3343

Serves As:
- Corporate Relations Contact, The Principal Financial Group

CLARKE, David H.
777 S. Flagler Dr.
Suite 1100 West
West Palm Beach, FL 33401
Tel: (561) 514 - 3838
Fax:(561) 514 - 3839

Serves As:
- Chairman and Chief Exec. Officer, Jacuzzi Brands, Inc.

CLARKE, Lanae
701 Pennsylvania Ave. NW
Plaza Suit O1
Washington, DC 20004
Tel: (202) 638 - 3838
Fax:(202) 638 - 5799

Serves As:
- Manager, Government Relations, Chicago Mercantile Exchange Inc.

CLARKE, Robert F.
P.O. Box 730
Honolulu, HI 96808-0730
Tel: (808) 543 - 5662
Fax:(808) 543 - 7966

Serves As:
- Chairman, President and Chief Exec. Officer, Hawaiian Electric Industries, Inc.

CLARKE, Victoria "Tori"
2001 Pennsylvania Ave. NW
Suite 500
Washington, DC 20006
Tel: (202) 379 - 7100
Fax:(202) 466 - 7718

Serves As:
- Senior Advisor, Communications and Government Affairs, Comcast Corporation

CLARKIN, Stephen C.
Nine Green St.
Augusta, ME 04330
Tel: (207) 621 - 4217

Serves As:
- Regional Public Affairs Manager, Internat'l Paper

CLARY, Thomas J.
8000 Bent Branch Dr.
Irving, TX 75063
Tel: (972) 409 - 1300
Fax:(972) 409 - 1556

Serves As:
- Manager, Investor Relations and Corporate Communications, Michaels Stores, Inc.

CLASSON, Rolf A.
700 State Route 46 East
Batesville, IN 47006-8835
Tel: (812) 934 - 7000
Fax:(812) 934 - 7371

Serves As:
- Vice Chairman and Interim Chief Exec. Officer, Hillenbrand Industries, Inc.

CLAUNCH, Charles K.
P.O. Box 1244
M/S PB05D
Charlotte, NC 28201-1244
cclaunch@duke-energy.com
Tel: (704) 373 - 6622
Fax:(704) 382 - 3588

Serves As:
- Regional Director, State Government Affairs-South Carolina, Duke Energy Corp.

CLAUS, Eric
Two Paragon Dr.
Montvale, NJ 07645
Tel: (201) 571 - 4240
Fax:(201) 571 - 8719

Serves As:
- President and Chief Exec. Officer, The Great Atlantic and Pacific Tea Co.

CLAWSON, Curtis J.
15300 Centennial Dr.
Northville, MI 48168
cclawson@hayes-lemmerz.com
Tel: (734) 737 - 5000
Fax:(734) 737 - 2198

Serves As:
- Chairman, President, and Chief Exec. Officer, Hayes Lemmerz Internat'l, Inc.

CLAXTON, John
1200 17th St.
Denver, CO 80202-5822
Tel: (303) 595 - 1112
Fax:(303) 595 - 1160

Serves As:
- Manager, Communications (Central Rocky Mountain), RBC Dain Rauscher Corp.

CLAY, Don R.
655 15th St. NW
Suite 445
Washington, DC 20005
Tel: (202) 737 - 1977
Fax:(202) 737 - 8111

Serves As:
- Managing Director, Environmental and Regulatory Affairs, Koch Industries, Inc.

CLAY, Jennifer
228 Manhattan Beach Blvd.
Manhattan Beach, CA 90266
Tel: (310) 798 - 9662
Fax:(310) 318 - 5019

Serves As:
- Press Contact, Skechers U.S.A., Inc.

CLAYTON, Bret K.
505 Gillette Ave.
Gillette, WY 82717
Tel: (307) 687 - 6000
Fax:(307) 687 - 6015

Serves As:
- President and Chief Exec. Officer, Kennecott Energy Co.

CLAYTON, J. Kerry
One Chase Manhattan Plaza
41st Floor
New York, NY 10005
Tel: (212) 859 - 7000
Fax:(212) 859 - 7010

Serves As:
- President, Chief Exec. Officer and Director, Assurant

CLAYTON, Pamela L.
800 Nicollet Mall
Suite 800
Minneapolis, MN 55402
Tel: (612) 303 - 6000

Serves As:
- Head of Human Resources, U.S. Bancorp Piper Jaffray Inc.

CLAYTON, Robyn
P.O. Box 98510
Las Vegas, NV 89193-8510
Tel: (702) 364 - 3297
Fax:(702) 220 - 4736

Serves As:
- Manager, Community Relations, Southwest Gas Corp.

Responsibilities include corporate communications.

CLEARY, Michael B.
101 Madison St.
P.O. Box 780
Jefferson City, MO 65102
Tel: (573) 681 - 7137
Fax:(573) 681 - 7296

Serves As:
- Supervisor, Corporate Communications, Ameren Corp.

CLEMENS, Lisa
P.O. Box 5625
MS25
Minneapolis, MN 55440-5625
Tel: (952) 742 - 6405
Fax:(952) 742 - 6208

Serves As:
- Public Affairs Counselor, Cargill, Incorporated

CLEMENT, Cor J.
P.O. Drawer F
Scottsdale, AZ 85252
Tel: (480) 994 - 3886
Fax:(480) 606 - 3328
TF: (800) 421 - 5718

Serves As:
- Chairman of the Board, Rural Metro Corp.

CLEMENTS, Michelle
P.O. Box 97034 Tel: (425) 452 - 1234
Bellevue, WA 98009-9734 Fax:(425) 462 - 3301

Serves As:
• V. President, Human Resources and Labor Relations, Puget Sound Energy

CLEMENTS, Richard
P.O. Box 321 Tel: (405) 553 - 3974
M/C 206 Fax:(405) 553 - 3838
Oklahoma City, OK 73101-0321

Serves As:
• Manager, Economic Development, OGE Energy Corp.
Responsibilities include community affairs.

CLEMENTS, William "Bill"
1299 Pennsylvania Ave. NW Tel: (202) 637 - 4000
11th Floor West Fax:(202) 637 - 4300
Washington, DC 20004-2407

Registered Federal Lobbyist.
Serves As:
• Senior Manager, International Trade Regulation, General Electric Co.

CLENDENIN, Michael
Four Irving Pl. Tel: (212) 460 - 4111
New York, NY 10003 Fax:(212) 477 - 2536

Serves As:
• Director, Media Relations, Consolidated Edison Co. of New York, Inc.

CLIFFORD, Patricia A.
103 JFK Pkwy. Tel: (973) 921 - 5500
Short Hills, NJ 07078
cliffordp@dnb.com

Serves As:
• V. President, Human Resources, The Dun & Bradstreet Corp.
Responsibilities include corporate communications.

CLINARD, John W.
Genesco Park, Suite 490 Tel: (615) 367 - 7000
P.O. Box 731 Fax:(615) 367 - 8278
Nashville, TN 37202-0731

Serves As:
• V. President, Administration and Human Resources, Genesco

CLINE, Teri
401 Harbor Isles Blvd. Tel: (541) 882 - 3451
Klamath Falls, OR 97601 Fax:(541) 855 - 7454
TF: (800) 535 - 3936

Serves As:
• Manager, Marketing Communications, JELD-WEN, Inc.

CLINTON, James W.
12800 W. Little York
Houston, TX 77041

Serves As:
• PAC Treasurer, Air Liquide America Corp.

CLIPPARD, Jr., J. H.
942 S. Shady Grove Rd. Tel: (901) 818 - 7468
Memphis, TN 38120 TF: (800) 238 - 5355
jhclippard@fedex.com

Serves As:
• Staff V. President, Investor Relations, FedEx Corp.

CLOCK, Jeffrey A.
284 South Ave. Tel: (845) 452 - 5534
Poughkeepsie, NY 12601-4879 Fax:(845) 486 - 5465
TF: (800) 527 - 2714

Serves As:
• Director, Environmental Affairs, CH Energy Group, Inc.

CLONAN, Jeanette H.
600 Third Ave. Tel: (212) 697 - 1105
36th Floor Fax:(212) 338 - 5662
New York, NY 10016

Serves As:
• V. President, Communications and Investor Relations, Loral Space & Communications

CLOONAN, Edward T.
70 Pine St. Tel: (212) 770 - 7887
New York, NY 10270 Fax:(212) 770 - 6786

Registered Federal Lobbyist.
Serves As:
• V. President, Corporate Affairs, American Internat'l Group, Inc.

CLOSE, Carol
I-20 at Alpine Rd. Tel: (803) 264 - 3451
AX-215 Fax:(803) 264 - 0204
Columbia, SC 29219-0001 TF: (800) 288 - 2227
carol.close@bcbssc.com Ext: 43451

Serves As:
• Manager, Public Affairs, BlueCross BlueShield of South Carolina

CLOUD, Kathy
P.O. Box 660634 Tel: (972) 334 - 2725
Dallas, TX 75266-0634 Fax:(972) 334 - 2045

Serves As:
• Corporate Contributions Program Contact, Frito-Lay, Inc.

CLOUGH, Veronika
2000 Purchase St. Tel: (914) 249 - 3198
Purchase, NY 10577-2509 Fax:(914) 249 - 4206

Serves As:
• Director, Global Communications, MasterCard Internat'l

CLYMER, Brian W.
751 Broad St. Tel: (973) 367 - 2510
14th Floor Fax:(973) 367 - 7030
Newark, NJ 07102-3777 TF: (800) THE - ROCK
brian.clymer@prudential.com

Serves As:
• V. President, Government Affairs, Prudential Financial

COATES, Pam
411 Seventh Ave. Tel: (412) 393 - 6000
Pittsburgh, PA 15219 Fax:(412) 393 - 6448
pcoates@dqe.com

Serves As:
• Manager, Community Relations, Duquesne Light Holdings

COBB, Roger A.
17641 S. Ashland Ave.
P.O. Box 5025
Homewood, IL 60430

Serves As:
• PAC Treasurer, Canadian Nat'l / Illinois Central

COBLIN, James M.
2100 Rexford Rd. Tel: (704) 366 - 7000
Charlotte, NC 28211 Fax:(704) 362 - 4208
jcoblin@nucor.com

Serves As:
• V. President, Human Resources, Nucor Corp.
Responsibilities include corporate philanthropy and communications.

COCCO, Dennis
33587 Walker Rd. Tel: (440) 930 - 1538
Avon Lake, OH 44093-0175 Fax:(440) 930 - 1750
dennis.cocc@polyone.com

Serves As:
• V. President, Investor Relations and Communications, PolyOne Corp.

COCHRAN, John R.
III Cascade Plaza Tel: (330) 384 - 7068
Akron, OH 44308-1103 Fax:(330) 384 - 7008

Serves As:
• Chairman and Chief Exec. Officer, FirstMerit Corporation

CODY, Douglas
P.O. Box 59159 Tel: (763) 212 - 2488
Minneapolis, MN 55459-8212 Fax:(763) 212 - 2219
drcody@carlson.com

Serves As:
• V. President, Exec. Communications, Carlson Companies

CODY, Thomas G.
Seven W. Seventh St. Tel: (513) 579 - 7000
Cincinnati, OH 45202 Fax:(513) 579 - 7555
TF: (800) 261 - 5385

Serves As:
• V. Chairman, Federated Department Stores, Inc.
Responsibilities include legal, human resources, external affairs, and corporate philanthropy.

COELLN, Jacqueline
U.S. Route 22 Tel: (908) 704 - 5829
Somerville, NJ 08876 Fax:(908) 722 - 5867

Serves As:
• Manager, Drug Regulatory Affairs, Johnson & Johnson

COFFEY, Debora
1345 Ave. of the Americas Tel: (212) 282 - 5660
New York, NY 10020 Fax:(212) 282 - 6220

Serves As:
• V. President, Public Relations and Promotions, Avon Products, Inc.

COFFEY, John
83 Hartwell Ave. Tel: (781) 372 - 5848
Lexington, MA 02421
jkcoffey@us.ibm.com

Serves As:
• Public Relations Manager, (Rational Software), Internat'l Business Machines Corp. (IBM)

COFFEY, Mike
P.O. Box 2933
San Antonio, TX 78299-2933
mike.coffey@sbc.com
Tel: (210) 821 - 4105
Fax:(210) 351 - 2198
TF: (800) 351 - 7221

Serves As:
- Exec. Director, Investor Relations, SBC Communications Inc.

COFFEY, Robin S.
111 W. Monroe St.
Chicago, IL 60603-4095
Tel: (312) 461 - 2242
Fax:(312) 461 - 6114

Serves As:
- Senior V. President, Harris Bank

Responsibilities include community affairs.

COFFING, Bridget
One McDonald's Plaza
Oak Brook, IL 60523
bridget.coffing@mcd.com
Tel: (630) 623 - 6263
Fax:(630) 623 - 8005

Serves As:
- Corporate V. President, Corporate Communications, McDonald's Corp.

COGDELL, Martha L.
Commonwealth Towers
1300 Wilson Blvd., Suite 200
Arlington, VA 22209-2307
mlcogdel@collins.rockwell.com
Tel: (703) 516 - 8227
Fax:(703) 516 - 8295

Registered Federal Lobbyist.
Serves As:
- Director, Federal and State Government Relations, Rockwell Automation
- Government Relations, Rockwell Collins, Inc

COGDILL, Richard A.
P.O. Box 93
Pittsburg, TX 75686
Tel: (903) 855 - 1000
TF: (800) 824 - 1159

Serves As:
- Exec. V. President, Chief Financial Officer, Treasurer and Secretary, Pilgrim's Pride Corp.

Responsibilities include investor relations.

COGGAN, Jean Reisinger
Seven W. Seventh St.
Cincinnati, OH 45202
Tel: (513) 579 - 7315
Fax:(513) 579 - 7555
TF: (800) 261 - 5385

Serves As:
- Director, Community Relations, Federated Department Stores, Inc.

COGHLAN, John P.
900 Metro Center Blvd.
Foster City, CA 94404-2172
Tel: (650) 432 - 3200
Fax:(650) 432 - 3631

Serves As:
- Chief Exec. Officer, Visa U.S.A. Inc.

COGSWELL-WOJTECKI, Lourdes
Eight Corporate Center Dr.
Melville, NY 11747
lwojtecki@necusa.com
Tel: (631) 753 - 7045
Fax:(631) 753 - 7041

Serves As:
- General Manager, Corporate Communications, NEC USA, Inc.

COHAGEN, Dean
P.O. Box 2486
Birmingham, AL 35201-2486
Tel: (205) 940 - 9400
Fax:(205) 912 - 4628

Serves As:
- Chief Exec. Officer, Bruno's Inc.

COHEN, Alan
1850 M St. NW
Suite 600
Washington, DC 20036
Tel: (202) 775 - 1700
Fax:(202) 822 - 0928

Registered Federal Lobbyist.
Serves As:
- Representative, Toyota Motor North America, Inc.

COHEN, Barry
140 Kendrick St.
Needham, MA 02494
Tel: (781) 370 - 5000
Fax:(781) 370 - 6000
TF: (800) 782 - 3776

Serves As:
- Exec. V. President, Marketing and Human Resources, PTC

COHEN, Brad
501 Sycamore Dr.
Milpitas, CA 95035
brad.cohen@quantum.com
Tel: (408) 944 - 4044
Fax:(408) 944 - 6542

Serves As:
- Director, Corporate Communications, Quantum Corporation

COHEN, David L.
1500 Market St.
Philadelphia, PA 19102
david_cohen@comcast.com
Tel: (215) 981 - 7585
Fax:(215) 981 - 7790

Registered Federal Lobbyist.
Serves As:
- Exec. V. President, Comcast Corporation

COHEN, Ed
1001 G St., NW
Suite 950
Washington, DC 20001
Tel: (202) 661 - 4400
Fax:(202) 661 - 4459

Registered Federal Lobbyist.
Serves As:
- V. President, Government and Industry Relations, American Honda Motor Co., Inc.

COHEN, Eric
500 Post Rd. East
Suite 320
Westport, CT 06880
Tel: (203) 222 - 5950
Fax:(203) 227 - 1647

Serves As:
- PAC Contact, Terex Corp.

COHEN, Kenneth P.
5959 Las Colinas Blvd.
Irving, TX 75039-2298
Tel: (972) 444 - 1000
Fax:(972) 444 - 1130

Serves As:
- V. President, Public Affairs, Exxon Mobil Corp.

COHEN, Kenneth S.
1295 State St.
Springfield, MA 01111-0001
kcohen@massmutual.com
Tel: (413) 744 - 8411
Fax:(413) 744 - 6005
TF: (800) 767 - 1000

Registered Federal Lobbyist.
Serves As:
- Senior V. President, Federal Government Relations and Deputy General Counsel, MassMutual Financial Group

COHEN, Kerrie
745 Seventh Ave.
New York, NY 10019
Tel: (212) 526 - 4092
Fax:(212) 526 - 8766

Serves As:
- Media Contact, Lehman Brothers

COHEN, Maryjo
3925 N. Hastings Way
Eau Claire, WI 54703-3703
Tel: (715) 839 - 2121
Fax:(715) 839 - 2122

Serves As:
- Chairman, President and Chief Exec. Officer, Nat'l Presto Industries, Inc.

COHEN, Peter
400 W. 31st St.
PSCC Bldg. 5 North
New York, NY 10001
Tel: (212) 630 - 6373

Serves As:
- Director, Government Affairs - Northeast, (AMTRAK Northeast), Amtrak

COHEN, Richard A.
611 Olive St.
Suite 1730
M/S 1750
St. Louis, MO 63101
Tel: (314) 342 - 6725
Fax:(314) 342 - 3066

Serves As:
- V. President, Public Affairs and Senior Counsel, Federated Department Stores, Inc.

COHEN, Rochelle
1818 N St. NW
Suite 800
Washington, DC 20036
rochelle.cohen@cingular.com
Tel: (202) 419 - 3007
Fax:(202) 419 - 3030

Serves As:
- Senior Director, Media Relations, Cingular Wireless

COHEN GLASS, Stephanie
730 Third Ave.
New York, NY 10017-3206
scohenglass@tiaa-cref.org
Tel: (212) 916 - 4993
Fax:(212) 916 - 5952

Serves As:
- Director, Corporate Media Relations, TIAA/CREF

COHN, Amy
6205 Peachtree Dunwoody Rd.
Atlanta, GA 30328
amy.cohn@cox.com
Tel: (678) 645 - 0000

Serves As:
- Exec. Director, Public Affairs, (Cox Communications, Inc.), Cox Enterprises, Inc.

COHN, John D.
1201 S. Second St.
Milwaukee, WI 43204-2496
Tel: (414) 382 - 2000
Fax:(414) 382 - 4444

Serves As:
- Senior V. President, Strategic Development and Communications, Rockwell Automation

COHN, Mary
414 Union St.
Suite 2000
Nashville, TN 37219
mary.cohn@lpcorp.com
Tel: (615) 986 - 5886

Serves As:
- Media Relations Contact, Louisiana-Pacific Corporation

COKER, Robert E.
111 Ponce de Leon Ave.
Clewiston, FL 33440
Tel: (863) 902 - 2461
Fax:(863) 983 - 9827

Serves As:
- Senior V. President, Public Affairs, United States Sugar Corp.

COLAIANNE, Melonie
21001 Van Born Rd.
Taylor, MI 48180
Tel: (313) 274 - 7400
Fax:(313) 792 - 6262

Serves As:
- Director, Corporate Affairs, Masco Corp.

COLALILLO, Claudia J.
P.O. Box 3014
Naperville, IL 60566-7014
Tel: (630) 305 - 9500
Ext: 2759
Fax:(630) 983 - 6620
TF: (888) 642 - 6748

Serves As:
- Senior V. President, Human Resources and Corporate Communications, Nicor, Inc.

COLATRELLA, Brenda
P.O. Box 100
Whitehouse Station, NJ 08889-0100
Tel: (908) 423 - 2042
Fax:(908) 423 - -198
TF: (800) 423 - 1000

Serves As:
- Contact, Foundation and Corporate Contributions Program, Merck & Co., Inc.

COLBURN, Cordis B. "Cork"
2941 Fairview Park Dr.
Falls Church, VA 22042-4513
Tel: (703) 876 - 3034
Fax:(703) 876 - 3600

Registered Federal Lobbyist.
Serves As:
- V. President, Government Relations, General Dynamics Corporation

COLBY, Ansley
1000 Alderman Dr.
Suite 71-E
Alpharetta, GA 30005-4101
Tel: (770) 752 - 6000
Fax:(770) 752 - 6005

Serves As:
- V. President, ChoicePoint Cares, ChoicePoint Inc.

COLCORD, Skip
1265 Main St.
Bldg. W. Three
Waltham, MA 02451
colcors@polariod.com
Tel: (781) 386 - 6624

Serves As:
- Director, Corporate Comunications, Polaroid Corp.

COLE, Calisa
2701 San Tomas Exwy.
Santa Clara, CA 95050
ccole@nvidia.com
Tel: (408) 486 - 6263
Fax:(408) 486 - 2200

Serves As:
- Director, Corporate Communications, NVIDIA Corp.

COLE, Charlene
P.O. Box 75000
mc 3352
Detroit, MI 48275
Tel: (313) 222 - 3882
Fax:(313) 222 - 8720
TF: (800) 521 - 1190

Serves As:
- Educational Relations Officer, Civic Affairs, Comerica Incorporated

COLE, Jason
1501 K St. NW
Suite 1100
Washington, DC 20005
Tel: (202) 585 - 4000

Registered Federal Lobbyist.
Serves As:
- Associate Director, Federal Affairs Manager, UBS Americas, UBS Financial Services Inc.

COLE, Joe C.
2390 E. Camelback Rd.
Suite 400
Phoenix, AZ 85016-3452
joecole@aztar.com
Tel: (602) 381 - 4100
Fax:(602) 381 - 4107

Serves As:
- V. President, Corporate Communications, Aztar Corp.

COLE, Keith N.
1660 L St. NW
Fourth Floor
Washington, DC 20036
Tel: (202) 775 - 5040
Fax:(202) 775 - 5024

Registered Federal Lobbyist.
Serves As:
- Director, Legislative and Regulatory Affairs, General Motors Corp.

COLE, Kenneth W.
1660 L St. NW
Fourth Floor
Washington, DC 20036
Tel: (202) 775 - 5090
Fax:(202) 775 - 5023

Registered Federal Lobbyist.
Serves As:
- V. President, Government Relations, General Motors Corp.

COLE, Martin L.
1345 Ave. of the Americas
New York, NY 10105
Tel: (917) 452 - 4400
Fax:(917) 527 - 9915

Serves As:
- Group Chief Exec., Government, Accenture

COLE, Michel
One Security Benefit Pl.
Topeka, KS 66636-0001
michel.cole@securitybenefit.com
Tel: (785) 438 - 3396
TF: (800) 888 - 2461

Serves As:
- V. President, Corporate Communications, Security Benefit Life Insurance Co.

COLE, Ms. Piper
4150 Network Circle
UMPK15225
Santa Clara, CA 95054
piper.cole@sun.com
Tel: (650) 786 - 5267
Fax:(650) 786 - 0835
TF: (800) 555 - 9786

Serves As:
- V. President, Global Government and Community Affairs, Sun Microsystems, Inc.

COLE, Steven R.
1333 H St. NW
Suite 300 West
Washington, DC 20005
Tel: (202) 296 - 1314
Fax:(202) 296 - 4067

Serves As:
- Director, Public Policy, Kaiser Permanente

COLEGROVE, Dan
101 Constitution Ave. NW
Suite 400 West
Washington, DC 20001
dan.colegrove@altria.com
Tel: (202) 354 - 1500
Fax:(202) 354 - 1505

Serves As:
- District Director, (Altria Corporate Services, Inc.), Altria Group, Inc.

COLEMAN, Charles E.
150 N. Orange Grove Blvd.
Pasadena, CA 91103
charles.coleman@averydennison.com
Tel: (626) 304 - 2014
Fax:(626) 577 - 9587

Serves As:
- Director, Media Relations and Financial Communications, Avery Dennison Corp.

COLEMAN, E. Thomas
601 13th St. NW
Suite 200 North
Washington, DC 20005
colemae@basf.com
Tel: (202) 682 - 9462
Fax:(202) 682 - 9459

Registered Federal Lobbyist.
Serves As:
- V. President, Government Relations, BASF Corporation

COLEMAN, Gracie P.
P.O. Box 70
Fort Mill, SC 29716
gracie.coleman@springs.com
Tel: (803) 547 - 1500

Serves As:
- Senior V. President, Human Resources, Springs Industries, Inc.

COLEMAN, John
1200 K St., NW
Washington, DC 20005
Tel: (202) 414 - 3720
Fax:(202) 289 - 8274

Serves As:
- PAC Treasurer, Affiliated Computer Services, Inc. (ACS)

COLEMAN, Marty
1500 Crittenden Lane
Mountain View, CA 94043
prdept@sgi.com
Tel: (650) 933 - 8119
Fax:(650) 933 - 0591

Serves As:
• Press Relations Contact, SGI

COLEMAN, Wesely
One Bowerman Dr.
Beaverton, OR 97005
Tel: (503) 671 - 6453
Fax:(503) 671 - 6300

Serves As:
• V. President, Global Human Resources, Nike, Inc.

COLGATE, Ms. Jessie M.
1501 K St. NW
Suite 575
Washington, DC 20005
Tel: (202) 654 - 2941
Fax:(202) 654 - 2945

Registered Federal Lobbyist.
Serves As:
• Senior V. President, Governmental Affairs, New York Life Insurance Co.

COLIN, Mark
3M Center
St. Paul, MN 55144-1000
Tel: (651) 733 - 1110
Fax:(651) 733 - 9973

Serves As:
• Director, Investor Relations, 3M Company

COLL, Linda
Carnival Pl.
3655 N.W. 87th Ave.
Miami, FL 33178-2428
lcoll@carnival.com
Tel: (305) 599 - 2600
Ext: 10113
Fax:(305) 406 - 8630

Serves As:
• Director, Carnival Foundation, (Carnival Cruise Lines), Carnival Corp.

COLLAMORE, Thomas J.
120 Park Ave.
17th Floor
New York, NY 10017
Tel: (917) 663 - 3924
Fax:(917) 663 - 5464

Serves As:
• V. President, Public Affairs, Altria Group, Inc.

COLLARD, Jonathan S.
12950 Worldgate Dr.
Suite 600
Herndon, VA 20170
jonathan.collard@lafarge-na.com
Tel: (703) 480 - 3622
Fax:(703) 796 - 2219

Serves As:
• Director, Public and Government Affairs, Lafarge North America, Inc.

COLLIER, Kevin
P.O. Box 29269
Richmond, VA 23242-9269
Tel: (804) 484 - 7700
Fax:(804) 484 - 7701

Serves As:
• Director, Investor Relations, Performance Food Group Co.

COLLIER, William L.
P.O. Box 51777
New Orleans, LA 70151
william_collier@fmi.com
Tel: (504) 582 - 1750
Fax:(504) 582 - 1847
TF: (800) 535 - 7094

Serves As:
• V. President, Communications, Freeport-McMoRan Copper and Gold Inc.

COLLIGAN, Charles A.
12061 Bluemont Way
Reston, VA 20190
Tel: (703) 810 - 3000
Fax:(703) 810 - 7053

Serves As:
• PAC Treasurer, SLM Corp.

COLLING, Terese
815 Connecticut Ave. NW
Suite 330
Washington, DC 20006
Tel: (202) 263 - 6260
Fax:(202) 728 - 0338

Registered Federal Lobbyist.
Serves As:
• Representative, Quest Diagnostics Inc.

COLLINGWOOD, John
1100 N. King St.
0127
Wilmington, DE 19880-127
john.collingwood@mbna.com
Tel: (302) 432 - 0956
Fax:(302) 432 - 0304
TF: (800) 441 - 7048

Registered Federal Lobbyist.
Serves As:
• Exec. V. President and Dirctor of Government Affairs, MBNA Corp.

COLLINS, Arthur D.
710 Medtronic Pkwy.
Minneapolis, MN 55432-5604
Tel: (763) 514 - 4000
Fax:(763) 514 - 4879
TF: (800) 328 - 2518

Serves As:
• Chairman and Chief Exec. Officer, Medtronic, Inc.

COLLINS, Chris
One Village Dr.
Van Buren Township, MI 48111
ccolli16@visteon.com
Tel: (313) 755 - 2800
TF: (800) VIS - TEON

Serves As:
• Manager, Investor and Shareholder Relations, Visteon Corp.

COLLINS, Dan F.
One Riverfront Plaza
Corning, NY 14831-0001
collinsdf@corning.com
Tel: (607) 974 - 4197
Fax:(607) 974 - 8509

Serves As:
• V. President, Corporate Communications, Corning Incorporated

COLLINS, Duane
6035 Parkland Blvd.
Cleveland, OH 44124-4141
dcollins@parker.com
Tel: (216) 896 - 3000
Fax:(216) 896 - 4000
TF: (800) 272 - 7537

Serves As:
• Chairman of the Board, Parker Hannifin Corp.

COLLINS, J. Christian
1133 19th St. NW
Washington, DC 20036
Tel: (202) 887 - 3830
Fax:(202) 887 - 3123

Registered Federal Lobbyist.
Serves As:
• Representative, MCI, Inc.

COLLINS, James H.
One John Deere Pl.
Moline, IL 61265-8098
Tel: (309) 765 - 4311
Fax:(309) 765 - 9855

Serves As:
• Director, Community Relations and President, John Deere Foundation, Deere & Company

COLLINS, Michael
P.O. Box 1938
Sumner, WA 98390-0800
mcollin@rei.com
Tel: (253) 395 - 5926
Fax:(253) 395 - 8135

Serves As:
• V. President, Public Affairs, Recreational Equipment, Inc.

COLLINS, Paula
1455 Pennsylvania Ave. NW
Suite 375
MS 4072
Washington, DC 20004
pcollins@ti.com
Tel: (202) 628 - 3133
Fax:(202) 628 - 2980

Registered Federal Lobbyist.
Serves As:
• Director, Government Relations (Human Relations and Education), Texas Instruments Incorporated

COLLINS, Sean M.
100 W. Putnam Ave.
Greenwich, CT 06830
Tel: (203) 622 - 3497
Fax:(203) 863 - 7240

Serves As:
• Regional Manager, State Government Relations/Northeast, UST Inc.

COLLINS, William A.
1717 Pennsylvania Ave. NW
Suite 400
Washington, DC 20006
al_collins@oxy.com
Tel: (202) 857 - 3051
Fax:(202) 857 - 3070

Registered Federal Lobbyist.
Serves As:
• Director, Health, Environment and Safety, Regulatory Affairs, Occidental Internat'l

COLLOMB, Bertrand P.
12950 Worldgate Dr.
Suite 600
Herndon, VA 20170
Tel: (703) 480 - 3600
Fax:(703) 796 - 2214

Serves As:
• Chairman of the Board, Lafarge North America, Inc.

COLOMBARO, Geri J.
1301 K St. NW
Suite 1200
Washington, DC 20005
Tel: (202) 515 - 5003
Fax:(202) 515 - 5055

Registered Federal Lobbyist.
Serves As:
• Program Director, Human Resources, Internat'l Business Machines Corp. (IBM)

COLTHARP, James R.
2001 Pennsylvania Ave. NW
Suite 500
Washington, DC 20006
jim_coltharp@comcast.com
Tel: (202) 379 - 7100
Fax:(202) 466 - 7718

Registered Federal Lobbyist.
Serves As:
• Chief Policy Advisor, FCC and Regulatory, Comcast Corporation

COLWELL, Christopher S.
P.O. Box 2301 Tel: (513) 397 - 7540
M/S 102-890 Fax:(513) 723 - 9815
Cincinnati, OH 45201-2301
chris.colwell@cinbell.com

Registered Federal Lobbyist.
Serves As:
- V. President, Government Relations, Cincinnati Bell Inc.

COLWELL, Neil V.
802 W. Bannock Tel: (208) 343 - 3821
Suite 306 Fax:(208) 385 - 7328
Boise, ID 83702
ncolwell1@mindspring.com

Serves As:
- Director, State Government Relations-ID and MT, Avista Corp.

COMBE, Gloria
601 Pennsylvania Ave. NW, Suite 500 Tel: (202) 347 - 7196
Washington, DC 20004 Fax:(202) 347 - 8237
gloria.combe@cn.ca

Registered Federal Lobbyist.
Serves As:
- Washington Representative, Canadian Nat'l / Illinois Central

COMEAUX, Al
15100 Trinity Blvd. Tel: (817) 785 - 8107
Forth Worth, TX 76155 Fax:(817) 785 - 8003
al.comeaux@travelocity.com

Serves As:
- V. President, Public Relations, (Travelocity.com Inc.), Sabre Holdings Corp.

COMEDY, Yolanda
1301 K St. NW Tel: (202) 515 - 5513
Suite 1200
Washington, DC 20005

Serves As:
- Governmental Programs Executive, Internat'l Business Machines Corp. (IBM)

COMER, Douglas B.
1634 I St. NW Tel: (202) 628 - 3838
Suite 300 Fax:(202) 628 - 2525
Washington, DC 20006-4021

Registered Federal Lobbyist.
Serves As:
- Director, Legal Affairs, Intel Corp.

COMFORT, Stephanie Georges
1801 California St. Tel: (303) 992 - 6389
50th Floor Fax:(303) 992 - 1822
Denver, CO 80202 TF: (800) 899 - 7780

Serves As:
- Senior V. President, Investor Relations, Qwest Communications

COMO-PUSWICS, Sandy
Ethan Allen Dr. Tel: (203) 743 - 8575
P.O. Box 1966 Fax:(203) 743 - 8298
Danbury, CT 06813-2966

Serves As:
- Public Realtions Specialist, Ethan Allen Interiors Inc.

COMPAN, Bob
4425 Spring Mountain Rd. Tel: (702) 826 - 8666
Suite 350
Las Vegas, NV 89102

Serves As:
- Legislative Representative, Farmers Group, Inc.

CONANT, Douglas R.
One Campbell Pl. Tel: (856) 342 - 4800
Camden, NJ 08103-1701 Fax:(856) 342 - 3878
douglas_conant@campbellsoup.com TF: (800) 257 - 8443

Serves As:
- President and Chief Exec. Officer, Campbell Soup Co.

CONATY, William J.
3135 Easton Tpk. Tel: (203) 373 - 2211
Bldg. E2E Fax:(203) 373 - 3131
Fairfield, CT 06431

Serves As:
- Senior V. President, Corporate Human Resources, General Electric Co.

CONDE, Cristobal I.
680 E. Swedesford Rd. Tel: (484) 582 - 5506
Wayne, PA 19087 Fax:(484) 225 - 1120

Serves As:
- President and Chief Exec. Officer, SunGard Data Systems, Inc.

CONDIT, David
1120 20th St. NW Tel: (202) 457 - 3810
Suite 1000 Fax:(202) 457 - 2008
Washington, DC 20036-3406
dcondit@att.com

Serves As:
- V. President, Law and State Government Affairs, AT&T

CONDON, Leonard W.
101 Constitution Ave. NW Tel: (202) 354 - 1500
Suite 400 West Fax:(202) 354 - 1505
Washington, DC 20001
len.condon@altria.com

Serves As:
- Director, International Business Relations, Altria Group, Inc.

CONDRON, Christopher M. "Kip"
1290 Ave. of the Americas Tel: (212) 314 - 3788
New York, NY 10104 TF: (888) AXA - INFO
christopher.condron@axa-financial.com

Serves As:
- President and Chief Exec. Officer, AXA Financial, Inc.

CONENELLO, Jim
25 Harbor Park Dr. Tel: (516) 801 - 9200
Port Washington, NY 11050 Fax:(516) 484 - 3649
jim_conenello@pall.com TF: (800) 876 - 7255

Serves As:
- Director, Corporate Communications, Pall Corp.

CONIFF, Bill
P.O. Box 68900 Tel: (206) 431 - 4626
Seattle, WA 98168-0947 Fax:(206) 431 - 5558

Serves As:
- Director, Corporate Communications, (Horizon Air Industries), Alaska Air Group, Inc.

CONKLIN, Edward
One McDonald's Plaza Tel: (630) 623 - 5724
Oak Brook, IL 60523 Fax:(630) 623 - 3057
ed.conklin@mcd.com

Serves As:
- Senior Director, Government Relations, McDonald's Corp.

CONKLIN, Virginia
One Haworth Center Tel: (616) 393 - 3551
Holland, MI 49423 Fax:(616) 393 - 1570
TF: (800) 344 - 2600

Serves As:
- Exec. Assistant and Contributions Coordinator, Haworth Inc.

CONKLYN, Elizabel D.
9800 Fredericksburg Rd. Tel: (210) 456 - 1800
San Antonio, TX 78288-0122 Fax:(210) 498 - 9940

Serves As:
- Exec. V. President, Human Resources, United Services Automobile Ass'n (USAA)

CONLEY, Micheal
5215 N. O'Connor Blvd. Tel: (972) 443 - 6557
Suite 2300 Fax:(972) 443 - 6800
Irving, TX 75039
mconley@flowserve.com

Serves As:
- Director, Investor Relations, Flowserve Corp.

CONLEY, Terence P.
One Campus Dr. Tel: (973) 428 - 9700
Parsippany, NJ 07054

Serves As:
- Exec. V. President, Human Resources and Corporate Services, Cendant Corp.

CONLIN, Kelly P.
745 Fifth Ave. Tel: (212) 745 - 0100
New York, NY 10151 Fax:(212) 745 - 0121

Serves As:
- President and Chief Exec. Officer, Primedia Inc.

CONLIN, Thomas R.
584 Derby Milford Rd. Tel: (203) 799 - 4293
Orange, CT 06477 Fax:(203) 799 - 4223

Serves As:
- V. President, Public Affairs, Hubbell Incorporated

Responsibilities include investor relations.

CONNELL, Tara J.
7950 Jones Branch Dr. Tel: (703) 854 - 6000
McLean, VA 22107 Fax:(703) 276 - 2046
tjconnel@gannett.com

Serves As:
- V. President, Corporate Communications, Gannett Co., Inc.

CONNELLY, Jeannie
1401 H St. NW
Suite 510
Washington, DC 20005
jconnelly@calpine.com
Tel: (202) 589 - 0909

Registered Federal Lobbyist.
Serves As:
• V. President, Government Affairs, Calpine Corp.

CONNELLY, Thomas
PO Box 5004
Port Huron, MI 48060
Tel: (248) 702 - 6240
Fax:(248) 702 - 6300

Serves As:
• Director, Investor Relations, SEMCO ENERGY, Inc.

CONNER, Roger W.
One Marriott Dr.
Washington, DC 20058
roger.conner@marriott.com
Tel: (301) 380 - 5605
Fax:(301) 897 - 9014

Serves As:
• V. President, North American Communications, Marriott Internat'l, Inc.

CONNERY, Bruce L.
P.O. Box 2511
Houston, TX 77252-2511
Tel: (713) 420 - 5855
Fax:(713) 420 - 4417

Serves As:
• V. President, Investor and Public Relations, El Paso Corp.

CONNOLLY, Julie
1 Sybase Dr.
Dublin, CA 94568
julie.connolly@sybase.com
Tel: (925) 236 - 8696

Serves As:
• Contact, Product, Partner and Customer Public Relations, Sybase, Inc.

CONNOLLY, Steven
50606 AXP Financial Center
Minneapolis, MN 55474
steven.x.connolly@ameriprise.com
Tel: (612) 671 - 4146
Fax:(612) 671 - 5112
TF: (800) 328 - 8300

Serves As:
• Manager, Public Affairs and Communications, Ameriprise Financial Services Inc.

CONNOR, Catherine
1401 K St. NW
Suite 701
Washington, DC 20005
Tel: (202) 783 - 0241
Fax:(202) 783 - 0229

Serves As:
• Senior Vice President, Government Relations, Parsons Brinckerhoff

CONNOR, Christopher M.
101 Prospect Ave. NW
Cleveland, OH 44115
Tel: (216) 566 - 2000
Fax:(216) 566 - 3312

Serves As:
• Chairman and Chief Exec. Officer, Sherwin-Williams Co.

CONNOR, Patrick
730 Third Ave.
New York, NY 10017-3206
pconnor@tiaa-cref.org
Tel: (212) 916 - 5769
Fax:(212) 916 - 5952

Serves As:
• Media Contact, TIAA/CREF

CONNOR, Rod
One Gaylord Dr.
Nashville, TN 37214
Tel: (615) 316 - 6000
Fax:(615) 316 - 6060

Serves As:
• PAC Treasurer, Gaylord Entertainment Co.

CONNORS, Greg
P.O. Box 13979
Research Triangle Park, NC 27709-3979
greg.connors@quintiles.com
Tel: (919) 998 - 2300
Fax:(919) 998 - 2098

Serves As:
• Senior V. President, Strategic Planning and Investor Relations, Quintiles Transnat'l Corp.

CONNORTON, Jennifer
111 Eighth Ave.
Tenth Floor
New York, NY 10011
Tel: (212) 381 - 5183
Fax:(212) 287 - 1203

Serves As:
• Director, Public Relations, DoubleClick, Inc.

CONONELOS, Louis J.
8309 W. 3595 S
P.O. Box 6333
Magna, UT 84044-6333
Tel: (801) 569 - 6000
Fax:(801) 569 - 6045

Serves As:
• Director, Government and Public Affairs, Kennecott Utah Copper

CONRAD, Christy
600 Corporate Park Dr.
St. Louis, MO 63105
cconrad@erac.com
Tel: (314) 512 - 2706
Fax:(314) 512 - 4706

Serves As:
• Assistant V. President, Public Relations, Enterprise Rent-A-Car Co.

CONRAD, Craig
33 Commercial St.
Foxboro, MA 02035
Tel: (508) 549 - 6250
Fax:(508) 549 - 4999
TF: (866) 746 - 6477

Serves As:
• Director, Marketing and Communications, Invensys Systems, Inc.

CONRAD, Deborah L.
P.O. Box 513338
Los Angeles, CA 90051-1338
Tel: (626) 821 - 7000
Fax:(626) 821 - 7933

Serves As:
• Director, Human Resources, Vons

CONRAD, Rita A.
4600 Arrowhead Dr.
Ann Arbor, MI 48105
rita.conrad@flintink.com
Tel: (734) 622 - 6362
Fax:(734) 622 - 6131

Serves As:
• V. President, Corporate Communications, Flint Ink Corp.

CONSALVO, Robert
2000 Galloping Hill Rd.
Kenilworth, NJ 07033
Tel: (908) 298 - 7409
Fax:(908) 298 - 7653

Serves As:
• Director, Global Product Communications and Advocacy Development, Schering-Plough Corporation

CONSIDINE, Jill M.
55 Water St.
49th Floor
New York, NY 10041-0099
Tel: (212) 855 - 1000

Serves As:
• Chairman and Chief Exec. Officer, The Depository Trust & Clearing Corp.

CONSIDINE, Thomas
200 Park Ave.
New York, NY 10166
Tel: (212) 578 - 2901
TF: (800) 638 - 5433

Serves As:
• V. President, Government and Industry Relations, MetLife, Inc.

CONSLATO, Carol
118-29 Queens Blvd.
Forrest Hills, NY 11375
Tel: (718) 275 - 5657
Fax:(718) 575 - 3769

Serves As:
• Director, Public Affairs (Queens), Consolidated Edison Co. of New York, Inc.

CONSTANT, Kimberly
800 N. Brand Blvd.
Glendale, CA 91203
kimberly.constan@us.nestle.com
Tel: (818) 549 - 7131
Fax:(818) 549 - 5884
TF: (800) 225 - 2270

Serves As:
• Coordinator, Corporate and Brand Affairs, Nestle USA, Inc.

CONSTANTINE, Timothy J.
P.O. Box 1991
One Brandywine Gateway
Wilmington, DE 19899-1991
Tel: (302) 421 - 3000
Fax:(302) 421 - 2592

Serves As:
• President, Blue Cross and Blue Shield of Delaware

CONSTANTINO, Nancy L.
555 E. Cook St.
Floor 1E
Springfield, IL 62721
Tel: (217) 789 - 5390
Fax:(217) 789 - 5223

Serves As:
• Director, Government Relations, SBC Illinois

CONTI, Carl J.
691 S. Milpitas Blvd.
Milpitas, CA 95035-5473
Tel: (408) 945 - 8600
Fax:(408) 262 - 2533

Serves As:
• Chairman of the Board, Adaptec, Inc.

CONTINI, Anita F.
1211 Avenue of the Americas
New York, NY 10036
Tel: (212) 536 - 1390
Fax:(212) 536 - 1912

Serves As:
• Senior V. President and Director, Public and Corporate Affairs, The CIT Group, Inc.

CONWAY, Daniel J.
One Massachusetts Ave. NW
Suite 350
Washington, DC 20001
dconway@chubb.com
Tel: (202) 408 - 8123
Ext: 112
Fax:(202) 296 - 7683

Registered Federal Lobbyist.
Serves As:
• Senior V. President, External Affairs, The Chubb Corp.

CONWAY, Elaine
One N. Jefferson Ave.
St. Louis, MO 63103
Tel: (314) 955 - 3355
Fax:(314) 955 - 2890
TF: (877) 835 - 7877

Serves As:
• V. President/Manager, Corporate Communications, A. G. Edwards, Inc.

CONWAY, John W.
One Crown Way
Philadelphia, PA 19154-4599
jconway@crowncork.com
Tel: (215) 698 - 5170
Fax:(215) 698 - 5201

Serves As:
• Chairman, President and Chief Exec. Officer, Crown Holdings, Inc.
Responsibilities include corporate contributions.

CONWAY, Joseph
100 Summit Lake Dr.
Valhalla, NY 10595
conwayj@towers.com
Tel: (914) 745 - 4175
Fax:(914) 745 - 4180

Serves As:
• Director, Media Relations, Towers Perrin

CONWAY, Mike
1101 Pennsylvania Ave. NW
Suite 1000
Washington, DC 20004
Tel: (202) 879 - 6871
Fax:(202) 783 - 4460

Registered Federal Lobbyist.
Serves As:
• Treasurer, Citigroup Federal PAC, Citigroup, Inc.

CONWAY, Thomas J.
P.O. Box 99
Pleasanton, CA 94566-0009
Tel: (925) 467 - 3273
Fax:(925) 467 - 3323

Serves As:
• V. President, Communications, Safeway Inc.

COOK, Brian J.
P.O. Box 6721
Chicago, IL 60680-6721
bcook@usg.com
Tel: (312) 606 - 3997
Fax:(312) 606 - 5646

Serves As:
• Senior V. President, Human Resources, USG Corp.

COOK, C. Michelle
Rexwoods IV, Suite 311
Raleigh, NC 27607-7509
michelle.cook@weyerhaeuser.com
Tel: (919) 786 - 2417
Fax:(919) 510 - 9341

Serves As:
• Government Affairs Manager - North Carolina Region, Weyerhaeuser Co.

COOK, E. Gary
414 Union St.
Suite 2000
Nashville, TN 37219
Tel: (615) 986 - 5600
Fax:(615) 986 - 5666
TF: (877) 744 - 5600

Serves As:
• Chairman of the Board, Louisiana-Pacific Corporation

COOK, Harrison
555 12th St. NW
Suite 650
Washington, DC 20004-1205
Tel: (202) 393 - 7950
Fax:(202) 393 - 7960

Serves As:
• Manager, International and Public Government Relations, Eli Lilly and Company

COOK, James J.
1000 E. Hanes Mill Rd.
Winston-Salem, NC 27105

Serves As:
• V. President, International Trade, (Sara Lee Knit Products), Sara Lee Corp.

COOK, Jeff
100 Grainger Pkwy.
Lake Forest, IL 60045-5201
jeff.cook@grainger.com
Tel: (847) 535 - 0880

Serves As:
• Corporate Communications, W. W. Grainger, Inc.

COOK, Jill
P.O. Box 3005
Columbus, IN 47202-3005
Tel: (812) 377 - 5000
Fax:(812) 377 - 3334

Serves As:
• V. President, Human Resources, Cummins, Inc.

COOK, Jody
P.O. Box 3165
Harrisburg, PA 17105
Tel: (717) 731 - 6566

Serves As:
• Manager, Public Relations, Rite Aid Corp.

COOK, John M.
600 Galleria Pkwy.
Suite 100
Atlanta, GA 30339
john.cook@prgx.com
Tel: (770) 779 - 3900
Fax:(770) 779 - 3042

Serves As:
• Chairman and Chief Exec. Officer, PRG-Schultz Internat'l, Inc.

COOK, Mark
602 W. Ionia
Lansing, MI 48933
mcook@bcbsm.com
Tel: (517) 371 - 7908
Fax:(517) 371 - 7979

Serves As:
• Director, State Government Relations, Blue Cross Blue Shield of Michigan

COOK, Maura Rhea
1000 Chrysler Dr.
CIMS 485-10-95
Auburn Hills, MI 48326-2766
Tel: (248) 512 - 3348
Fax:(248) 512 - 3919
TF: (800) 992 - 1997

Serves As:
• Senior Manager, International Affairs and Public Policy, DaimlerChrysler Corp.

COOK, Sandy
601 Pennsylvania Ave. NW
South Bldg. Suite 900
Washington, DC 20004
awcook@unumprovident.com
Tel: (202) 434 - 8190
Fax:(202) 347 - 1909

Registered Federal Lobbyist.
Serves As:
• V. President, Government Relations, UnumProvident Corp.

COOK, Sheri
2801 Hwy. 280 South
P.O. Box 2606
Birmingham, AL 35223
Tel: (205) 268 - 3773

Serves As:
• V. President, Corporate Finance and Investor Relations, Protective Life Corp.

COOK, Susan J.
Eaton Center
1111 Superior Ave.
Cleveland, OH 44114-2584
susancook@eaton.com
Tel: (216) 523 - 4651
Fax:(216) 523 - 4787

Serves As:
• V. President, Human Resources, Eaton Corp.

COOK, William
P.O. Box 1299
Minneapolis, MN 55440-1299
Tel: (952) 887 - 3131
Fax:(952) 887 - 3155
TF: (800) 887 - 3131

Serves As:
• President and Chief Exec. Officer, Donaldson Company, Inc.

COOKE, Roger A.
4650 SW Macadam Ave.
Suite 440
Portland, OR 97239-4254
Tel: (503) 417 - 4822
Fax:(503) 417 - 4817

Serves As:
• V. President, Regulatory and Legal Affairs, Precision Castparts Corp.

COOLICK, Gayle M.
450 Winks Ln.
Bensalem, PA 19020
Tel: (215) 638 - 6955
Fax:(215) 638 - 6759

Serves As:
• Director, Investor Relations, Charming Shoppes, Inc.

COON, James W.
1200 Wilson Blvd.
Arlington, VA 22209-2305
Tel: (703) 465 - 3264
Fax:(703) 465 - 3004

Registered Federal Lobbyist.
Serves As:
• Director, Legislative Affairs, The Boeing Co.

COONEY, Christopher W.
6950 Columbia Gateway Dr.
Columbia, MD 21046
Tel: (410) 953 - 1000
Fax:(410) 953 - 5200

Serves As:
• Chief Branding and Communications Officer, Magellan Health Services, Inc.

COONEY, Edward J.
50 Kennedy Plaza
Providence, RI 02903
Tel: (401) 751 - 1600
Fax:(401) 751 - 4610

Serves As:
- V. President and Treasurer, Nortek Inc.

Responsibilities include corporate communications and investor relations.

COONS, Robert C.
P.O. Box 4442
Houston, TX 77210-4442
rcoons@bjservices.com
Tel: (713) 895 - 5873
Fax:(713) 895 - 5851

Serves As:
- Director, Corporate Communications, BJ Services Co.

COOPER, Dennis
5995 Barfield Rd.
Atlanta, GA 30328
Tel: (404) 256 - 4900
Fax:(404) 256 - 7277

Serves As:
- Chairman of the Board, The RTM Restaurant Group

COOPER, Ms. Evern
55 Glenlake Pkwy. NE
Atlanta, GA 30328
ecooper@ups.com
Tel: (404) 828 - 6251
Fax:(404) 828 - 7435

Serves As:
- Exec. Director, UPS Foundation, United Parcel Service (UPS)

COOPER, Frederick N.
3103 Philmont Ave.
Huntingdon Valley, PA 19006
fcooper@tollbrothersinc.com
Tel: (215) 938 - 8312
Fax:(215) 938 - 8019

Serves As:
- Investor Relations Contact, Toll Brothers, Inc.

COOPER, Geoffry F.
270 E. Kilbourn
Milwaukee, WI 53202
Tel: (414) 347 - 2681
Fax:(414) 347 - 6802
TF: (800) 558 - 9900

Serves As:
- Director, Public Policy and Corporate Relations, Mortgage Guaranty Insurance Corp. (MGIC)

COOPER, Josephine S.
1850 M St. NW
Suite 600
Washington, DC 20036
Tel: (202) 775 - 1700
Fax:(202) 822 - 0928

Registered Federal Lobbyist.
Serves As:
- V. President, Government and Industry Affairs, Toyota Motor North America, Inc.

COOPER, Judy
One Penn Plaza
Second Floor
New York, NY 10119
cooperj@pbworld.com
Tel: (212) 465 - 5332
Fax:(212) 465 - 5477

Serves As:
- Senior V. President, Parsons Brinckerhoff

Serves as the main headquarters Senior Public Affairs Executive.

COOPER, Margaret
1201 Lake Robbins Dr.
The Woodlands, TX 77380
margaret_cooper@anadarko.com
Tel: (832) 636 - 8355

Serves As:
- Senior Community and Public Affairs Coordinator, Anadarko Petroleum Corp.

Responsibilities include corporate philanthropy and media relations.

COOPER, Muriel
999 Lake Dr.
Issaquah, WA 98027
Tel: (425) 313 - 8100
Fax:(425) 313 - 6593

Serves As:
- Contact, Community Relations and Administration, Costco Wholesale Corp.

COOPER, Richard F.
P.O. Box 10048
Fort Smith, AR 72917
Tel: (479) 785 - 6130
Fax:(479) 785 - 6124

Serves As:
- V. President, Administration; Treasurer, Arkansas Best Corp. PAC, Arkansas Best Corporation

COOPER, Robin
P.O. Box 5000
Pineville, LA 71361-5000
Tel: (318) 484 - 7400
Fax:(318) 484 - 7465

Serves As:
- Advertising, Corporate Contributions Contact, Cleco Corp.

COOPER, Rod
P.O. Box 66360
Scotts Valley, CA 95067-0360
Tel: (831) 438 - 6550
Fax:(831) 438 - 0558

Serves As:
- Senior Director, Investor Relations, Seagate Technology

COOPER, Scott
1100 New York Ave. NW
Suite 600W
Washington, DC 20005
scott_cooper2@hp.com
Tel: (202) 378 - 2500
Fax:(202) 378 - 2550

Registered Federal Lobbyist.
Serves As:
- Manager, Technology Policy, Hewlett-Packard Co.

COOPER, Stephen F.
1221 Lamar
Suite 1600
Houston, TX 77010
Tel: (713) 853 - 6161

Serves As:
- Interim Chief Exec. Officer and Chief Restructuring Officer, Enron Corp.

COOPER, Steven C.
P.O. Box 2910
Tacoma, WA 98401-2910
Tel: (253) 383 - 9101
TF: (800) 610 - 8920

Serves As:
- Chief Financial Officer, Labor Ready, Inc.

Responsibilities include investor relations.

COOPER, Thomas E.
1299 Pennsylvania Ave. NW
11th Floor West
Washington, DC 20004-2407
Tel: (202) 637 - 4000
Fax:(202) 637 - 4006

Registered Federal Lobbyist.
Serves As:
- V. President, Aerospace Technology, General Electric Co.

COOPER, William A.
200 Lake St. E.
Wayzata, MN 55391
Tel: (952) 475 - 7904
Fax:(952) 475 - 7975

Serves As:
- Chairman and Chief Exec. Officer, TCF Financial Corp.

COORS, Peter H.
P.O. Box 4030
M/S NH300
Golden, CO 80401-0030
Tel: (303) 277 - 2410
Fax:(303) 277 - 6517

Serves As:
- Chairman of the Board, Coors Brewing Co.

COOVERT, Crystal
200 Carillon Pkwy.
St. Petersburg, FL 33716
Tel: (727) 579 - 5452
Fax:(727) 556 - 2700

Serves As:
- Exec. Director, Communications, Catalina Marketing Corp.

COPELAND, M. Robin
6950 Columbia Gateway Dr.
Columbia, MD 21046
Tel: (410) 953 - 1000
Fax:(410) 953 - 5200

Serves As:
- PAC Treasurer, Magellan Health Services, Inc.

COPENHAGEN, Curt R.
P.O. Box 639
Longview, WA 98632
Tel: (360) 425 - 1550
Ext: 5906
Fax:(360) 575 - 5934

Serves As:
- Director, Public Affairs, Longview Fibre Co.

Responsibilities include corporate communications, advertising, lobbying, and government affairs.

COPES, Ronald
140 Garden St.
Hartford, CT 06154
Tel: (860) 987 - 3369
Fax:(860) 987 - 6532

Serves As:
- V. President, Community Relations, MassMutual Financial Group

Responsibilities include corporate philanthropy.

COPLEY, David C.
P.O. Box 1530
La Jolla, CA 92038-1530
Tel: (858) 454 - 0411

Serves As:
- Chairman, President, and Chief Exec. Officer, The Copley Press, Inc.

COPPOLA, Michael N.
5673 Airport Rd.
Roanoke, VA 24012
Tel: (540) 362 - 4911

Serves As:
- President and Chief Exec. Officer, Advance Auto Parts, Inc.

CORALLO, Terry
One ADP Blvd. Tel: (973) 974 - 7640
Roseland, NJ 07068-1728 TF: (800) 225 - 5237
terrym_corallo@adp.com

Serves As:
- Director, Public Relations and Advertising, Automatic Data Processing, Inc.

CORBETT, Gerard F.
2000 Sierra Point Pkwy. Tel: (650) 244 - 7900
Brisbane, CA 94005 Fax:(650) 244 - 7919
gerard.corbett@hal.hitachi.com TF: (800) 448 - 2244

Serves As:
- V. President and General Manager, Branding and Corporate Communications Group, Hitachi America, Ltd.

CORBETT, Luke R.
Kerr-McGee Center, Box 25861 Tel: (405) 270 - 1313
Oklahoma City, OK 73125 Fax:(405) 270 - 3029
TF: (800) 786 - 2556

Serves As:
- Chairman and Chief Exec. Officer, Kerr-McGee Corp.

CORBIN, Larry C.
3776 S. High St. Tel: (614) 491 - 2225
Columbus, OH 43207-0863 Fax:(614) 492 - 4949
TF: (800) 272 - 7675

Serves As:
- President and Chief Exec. Officer, Bob Evans Farms, Inc.

CORCORAN, Robert
3135 Easton Tpk. Tel: (203) 373 - 2211
Bldg. E2E Fax:(203) 373 - 3131
Fairfield, CT 06431

Serves As:
- President, GE Fund, General Electric Co.

CORCORAN, William M.
7500 Grace Dr. Tel: (410) 531 - 4203
Columbia, MD 21044

Registered Federal Lobbyist.
Serves As:
- V. President, Public and Regulatory Affairs, W. R. Grace & Co.

CORCOS, Helyn
20330 Stevens Creek Blvd. Tel: (408) 517 - 8324
Cupertino, CA 95014-2132 Fax:(408) 517 - 8186
hcorcos@symantec.com

Serves As:
- V. President, Investor Relations, Symantec Corp.

CORDIAK, Bob
City Place Center East, Suite 2400 Tel: (214) 989 - 1602
2711 N. Haskell Ave. Fax:(214) 582 - 1619
Dallas, TX 75204

Serves As:
- Manager, Southwest Communications, RBC Dain Rauscher Corp.

CORNELIUS, James M.
111 Monument Circle Tel: (317) 971 - 2000
29th Floor Fax:(317) 971 - 2040
Indianapolis, IN 46204-5129

Serves As:
- Chairman of the Board, Guidant Corp.

CORNER, Greg
44 S. Washington St. Tel: (419) 629 - 2311
New Bremen, OH 45869 Fax:(419) 629 - 3796

Serves As:
- Manager, Marketing and Communications, Crown Equipment Corp.

CORNESS, John B.
2100 Hwy. 55 Tel: (763) 417 - 8650
Medina, MN 55340 Fax:(763) 542 - 0599
john.corness@polarisind.com

Serves As:
- V. President, Human Resources, Polaris Industries Inc.

CORONA, Lisa
One JLG Dr. Tel: (717) 485 - 5161
McConnellsburg, PA 17233-9533 Fax:(717) 485 - 6417
TF: (877) 534 - 5438

Serves As:
- Senior V. President, Human Resources, JLG Industries, Inc.

CORONA, Sharon
P.O. Box 126 Tel: (410) 666 - 1400
Hunt Valley, MD 21030-0126 Fax:(410) 628 - 3199
corona@aaicorp.com TF: (800) 626 - 2616

Serves As:
- Manager, Corporate Communications, AAI Corp.

CORONADO, Troup
1133 21st St. NW Tel: (202) 463 - 4100
Suite 900 Fax:(202) 463 - 4141
Washington, DC 20036

Registered Federal Lobbyist.
Serves As:
- Representative, BellSouth Corp.

CORONELLI, Elizabeth
Two N. Riverside Plaza Tel: (312) 466 - 3300
Suite 2100 Fax:(312) 454 - 0332
Chicago, IL 60606

Serves As:
- Senior V. President, Investor Relations, Equity Office Properties Trust

Responsibilities include public relations.

CORRELL, Jr., Alston D. "Pete"
P.O. Box 105605 Tel: (404) 652 - 5248
Atlanta, GA 30348 Fax:(404) 654 - 4789
TF: (800) 519 - 3111

Serves As:
- Chairman and Chief Exec. Officer, Georgia-Pacific Corp.

CORRIGAN, Frederic W.
12800 Whitewater Dr. Tel: (800) 918 - 8270
Minnetonka, MN 55343 Fax:(952) 984 - 0032

Serves As:
- President and Chief Exec. Officer, Mosaic Co.

CORRIGAN, Richard L.
555 11th St. NW Tel: (202) 393 - 2426
Suite 525 Fax:(202) 783 - 8410
Washington, DC 20004
rcorriga@ch2m.com

Serves As:
- Senior V. President, Governmental Affairs, CH2M Hill Companies, Inc.

CORRIGAN, Wilfred J.
1621 Barber Ln. Tel: (408) 433 - 8000
Milpitas, CA 95035 Fax:(408) 954 - 3220
wcorrigan@lsil.com TF: (866) 574 - 5741

Serves As:
- Chairman of the Board, LSI Logic Corp.

CORTESE, Steve
1550 Crystal Dr. Tel: (703) 413 - 5681
Crystal Square 2, Suite 300 Fax:(703) 413 - 5744
Arlington, VA 22202

Serves As:
- V. President, Policy and Budget, Lockheed Martin Corp.

CORYELL, M.D., Kristine
425 N. Martingale Rd. Tel: (847) 413 - 4520
Suite 900 Fax:(847) 413 - 4507
Schaumburg, IL 60173
kristine.coryell@pfizer.com

Serves As:
- Director, Government Relations, Pfizer Inc.

COSGROVE, Suzanne
1001 G St. NW Tel: (202) 737 - 5090
Suite 700 East Fax:(202) 737 - 5095
Washington, DC 20001
scosgrove@heinekenusa.com

Serves As:
- Manager, Corporate Responsibility, Heineken USA Inc.

COSMAI, Robert F.
P.O. Box 20850 Tel: (714) 965 - 3000
Fountain Valley, CA 92728-0850 Fax:(714) 965 - 3149

Serves As:
- President and Chief Exec. Officer, Hyundai Motor America

COSSLET, Andy
Three Ravinia Dr., Suite 100 Tel: (770) 604 - 2000
Atlanta, GA 30346

Serves As:
- Chief Exec. Officer, InterContinental Hotels Group

COST, Tim
The ARAMARK Tower Tel: (215) 238 - 7101
1101 Market St. Fax:(215) 238 - 3333
Philadelphia, PA 19107 TF: (800) 999 - 8989

Serves As:
- Exec. V. President, Corporate Affairs, ARAMARK

COSTELLO, Ann S.
101 Constitution Ave. NW Tel: (202) 637 - 3700
Suite 1000 East Fax:(202) 637 - 3773
Washington, DC 20001

Serves As:
- V. President, Goldman, Sachs and Co.

COSTELLO, Elizabeth
Fifth St. Towers, Suite 1360
150 S. Fifth St.
Minneapolis, MN 55402
Tel: (612) 333 - 5264
Fax:(612) 337 - 0355

Serves As:
• Manager, Internal Communication, MAIR Holdings, Inc.

COSTELLO, Lawrence B.
One Centennial Ave.
PO Box 6820
Piscataway, NJ 08854
Tel: (732) 980 - 3000
Fax:(732) 980 - 3335

Serves As:
• Senior V. President, Human Resources, American Standard Companies Inc.

COSTELLO, Steve
77 Grove St.
Rutland, VT 05701
scostel@cvps.com
Tel: (802) 747 - 5427
Fax:(802) 747 - 2199
TF: (800) 649 - 2877

Serves As:
• Director, Public Affairs, Central Vermont Public Service Corp.

COSTON, Sandra
4800 Deerwood Campus Pkwy.
Jacksonville, FL 32246-8273
Tel: (904) 791 - 6111
Fax:(904) 905 - 4486
TF: (800) 477 - 3736

Registered Federal Lobbyist.
Serves As:
• Representative, Blue Cross and Blue Shield of Florida

COTE, David M.
101 Columbia Rd.
Morristown, NJ 07962-4658
Tel: (973) 455 - 2000
Fax:(973) 455 - 4807

Serves As:
• Chairman and Chief Exec. Officer, Honeywell Internat'l, Inc.

COTHRAN, Nancy
Four N. Fourth St.
Richmond, VA 23219-2230
Tel: (804) 788 - 1800
Fax:(804) 788 - 1870

Serves As:
• PAC Treasurer, Massey Energy Co.

COTICCHIA, Michael L.
One Applied Plaza
Cleveland, OH 44115
mcoticchia@applied.com
Tel: (216) 426 - 4511
Ext: 4511
Fax:(216) 426 - 4844
TF: (877) 279 - 2799

Serves As:
• V. President, Human Resources and Administration, Applied Industrial Technologies

COTTAM, Barbara S.
One Citizens Plaza
Providence, RI 02903
Tel: (401) 456 - 7000
Fax:(401) 456 - 7644

Serves As:
• Senior V. President; and Director, Corporate Communications, Citizens Financial Group, Inc.

COTTER, Wes
Seven Jackson Walkway
Providence, RI 02903
wcotter@gilbaneco.com
Tel: (401) 456 - 5405
Fax:(401) 456 - 5930

Serves As:
• Director, Corporate Communications, Gilbane Building Co.
Responsibilities include government affairs and corporate contributions.

COTTON, Bruce
305 Hartman Dr.
Lebanon, TN 37088
Tel: (615) 444 - 5533
Fax:(615) 443 - 9511

Serves As:
• V. President, Government Relations, CBRL Group, Inc.

COTTON, Katie
One Infinite Loop
Cupertino, CA 95014
katiec@apple.com
Tel: (408) 972 - 7269
Fax:(408) 996 - 0275

Serves As:
• V. President, Worldwide Corporate Communications, Apple Computer, Inc.

COURTIAN, Michael D.
99 Church St.
New York, NY 10007-2707
michael.courtian@moodys.com
Tel: (212) 553 - 7194
Fax:(212) 553 - 4820

Serves As:
• V. President, Investor Relations and Corporate Finance, Moody's Corp.

COURY, Robert J.
1500 Corporate Dr.
Suite 400
Canonsburg, PA 15317
Tel: (724) 514 - 1800

Serves As:
• V. Chairman and Chief Exec. Officer, Mylan Laboratories Inc.

COUSER, Chad
11111 Sunset Hills Dr.
Reston, VA 20190-5339
Tel: (703) 547 - 2000
Fax:(703) 547 - 2881

Serves As:
• Manager, Public Relations, XO Communications, Inc.

COUTURE, Jon N.
National City Center
1900 E. Ninth St.
Cleveland, OH 44114-3484
Tel: (216) 222 - 2000
Fax:(216) 575 - 2353
TF: (800) 622 - 6736

Serves As:
• Exec. V. President and Director, Corporate Human Resources, Nat'l City Corp.

COVENTRY, Mary A.
Park 80 East
Saddle Brook, NJ 07663-5291
Tel: (201) 791 - 7600
Fax:(201) 703 - 4205

Serves As:
• V. President, Communications and Government Relations, Sealed Air Corp.

COVER, Fred W.
P.O. Box 98510
Las Vegas, NV 89193-8510
Tel: (702) 876 - 7210
Fax:(702) 367 - 3304

Serves As:
• V. President, Human Resources, Southwest Gas Corp.

COVEY, Jock
50 Beale St.
San Francisco, CA 94105-1895
Tel: (415) 768 - 1234
Fax:(415) 768 - 0263

Serves As:
• Manager, Corporate Affairs, Bechtel Group, Inc.

COWAN, Otis
P.O. Box 66149
MC100
St. Louis, MO 63166-6149
Tel: (314) 554 - 4740
Fax:(314) 554 - 2888
TF: (800) 552 - 7583

Serves As:
• Manager, Community Relations, Ameren Corp.

COWDIN, Christi
9341 Courtland Dr. NE
Rockford, MI 49351
Tel: (616) 866 - 6222
Fax:(616) 866 - 0257

Serves As:
• Director, Investor Relations and Communications, Wolverine World Wide, Inc.

COWEN, David L.
29400 Lakeland Blvd.
Wickliffe, OH 44092-2298
Tel: (440) 943 - 4200
Fax:(440) 943 - 5337

Serves As:
• Manager, Public Relations, The Lubrizol Corp.

COWEN, Robert
511 Fifth Ave.
New York, NY 10017
Tel: (212) 953 - 4100
Ext: 1870

Serves As:
• Senior V. President, Overseas Shipholding Group, Inc.
Responsibilities include corporate public affairs.

COX, Bruce
2001 Edmund Halley Dr.
Reston, VA 20191
Tel: (703) 433 - 4000

Registered Federal Lobbyist.
Serves As:
• Representative, Sprint Nextel

COX, Julie Coppola
6363 Main St.
Williamsville, NY 14221
coxj@natfuel.com
Tel: (716) 857 - 7079
Fax:(716) 857 - 7439
TF: (800) 365 - 3234

Serves As:
• Senior Manager, Corporate Communications, Nat'l Fuel Gas Co.
Responsibilities include corporate philanthropy.

COX, Kay
6201 South Fwy.
Fort Worth, TX 76134
Tel: (817) 293 - 0450
Fax:(817) 551 - 4615

Serves As:
• V. President, Human Resources, Alcon Inc.

COX, Lofton
P.O. Box 4079
Gulfport, MS 39502
Tel: (228) 865 - 5611
Fax:(228) 865 - 5616

Serves As:
• Manager, State Legislative Affairs, Mississippi Power Co.

COX, Mike
P.O. Box 482
Fort Worth, TX 76101
mcox@bellhelicopter.textron.com
Tel: (817) 280 - 8416
Fax:(817) 280 - 2321

Serves As:
• Manager, Advertising and Media Relations, Bell Helicopter Textron

COX, Rebecca G.
1350 I St. NW
Suite 1250
Washington, DC 20005
rcox01@coair.com
Tel: (202) 715 - 5433
Fax:(202) 289 - 1546

Registered Federal Lobbyist.
Serves As:
- Senior V. President, Government Affairs, Continental Airlines

COX, Robert
P.O. Box 4100
M/S 3722
St. Louis, MO 63136-8506
Tel: (314) 553 - 2015
Fax:(314) 553 - 3527

Serves As:
- Senior V. President, Emerson

COYLE, Matthew T.
175 Berkeley St.
Boston, MA 02116
Tel: (617) 654 - 3331
Fax:(617) 350 - 7648

Serves As:
- V. President and Director, Investor Relations, Liberty Mutual Insurance Co.

CRACCHIOLO, James C.
50606 AXP Financial Center
Minneapolis, MN 55474
Tel: (612) 671 - 3131
Fax:(612) 671 - 2741
TF: (800) 328 - 8300

Serves As:
- Chairman and Chief Exec. Officer, Ameriprise Financial Services Inc.

CRADICK, Susan
P.O. Box 1109
Muscatine, IA 52761-0071
Tel: (563) 264 - 7400
Fax:(563) 264 - 7217

Serves As:
- Secretary-Treasurer, HON Industries Charitable Foundation, HNI Corp.

CRAFT, Marie L.
21839 Atlantic Blvd.
Dulles, VA 20166
craft.marie@orbital.com
Tel: (703) 406 - 5000
Fax:(703) 406 - 5572

Serves As:
- PAC Treasurer, Orbital Sciences Corp.

CRAFT, Martha
2170 Piedmont Road, N.E.
Atlanta, GA 30324
Tel: (404) 888 - 2000

Serves As:
- Director, Public Relations, Rollins, Inc.

CRAFT, Ralph
900 Ridgebury Rd.
P.O. Box 368
Ridgefield, CT 06877
Tel: (203) 798 - 9988
Fax:(203) 791 - 6234

Serves As:
- President, Foundation, Boehringer Ingelheim Corp.

CRAGIN, Maureen P.
1200 Wilson Blvd.
Arlington, VA 22209-2305
Tel: (703) 465 - 3252
Fax:(703) 465 - 3032

Serves As:
- V. President, Communications, The Boeing Co.

CRAHAN, Pat
2727 N. Central Ave.
P.O. Box 21502
Phoenix, AZ 85004
Tel: (602) 263 - 6804
Fax:(602) 263 - 6889

Serves As:
- Director, Government Relations, (U-Haul Internat'l, Inc.), AMERCO

CRAIG, Angela
One Lillehei Plaza
St. Paul, MN 55117-9983
Tel: (651) 483 - 2000
Fax:(651) 766 - 3045

Serves As:
- V. President, Corporate Communications, St. Jude Medical, Inc.

CRAIGIE, James R.
469 N. Harrison St.
Princeton, NJ 08543-5297
Tel: (609) 683 - 5900
Fax:(609) 497 - 7269

Serves As:
- President and Chief Exec. Officer, Church & Dwight Co., Inc.

CRAMER, Jeffrey R.
15378 Ave. of Science
San Diego, CA 92128
Tel: (858) 716 - 3400
Fax:(858) 716 - 3775
TF: (800) 350 - 3044

Serves As:
- President and Chief Exec. Officer, Anacomp, Inc.

CRAMER, Susan
100 Parsons Pond Dr.
Franklin Lakes, NJ 07417
Tel: (201) 269 - 6187

Serves As:
- Senior Director, Investor Relations, Medco Health Solutions, Inc.

CRANE, Debra
9450 Seward Rd.
Fairfield, OH 45014
debra.crane@ocas.com
Tel: (513) 603 - 2600
Fax:(513) 609 - 7900
TF: (800) 843 - 6446

Serves As:
- Senior V. President, Corporate Public Affairs, The Ohio Casualty Group

CRANE, Ruth
104 Wilmot Rd.
mail stop 1444
Deerfield, IL 60015

Serves As:
- Manager, Charitable Giving, Walgreen Co.

CRATE, Cheryl
225 City Line Ave.
Suite 200
Bala Cynwyd, PA 19004
cheryl.crate@pgtv.com
Tel: (703) 892 - 4230
Fax:(610) 934 - 7054
TF: (888) 438 - 7488

Serves As:
- V. President, Corporate Communications and Government Relations, Pegasus Communications Corp.

CRAVEN, Julie
One Hormel Pl.
Austin, MN 55912-3680
Tel: (507) 437 - 5345
Fax:(507) 434 - 6721

Serves As:
- V. President, Corporate Communications, Hormel Foods Corp.

CRAVEN, Martin H.
P.O. Box 45433
Salt Lake City, UT 84145-0433
martin.craven@questar.com
Tel: (801) 324 - 5077
Fax:(801) 324 - 5483

Serves As:
- Treasurer and Director, Investor Relations, Questar Corporation

CRAVEN, William
1401 H St. NW
Suite 700
Washington, DC 20005
Tel: (202) 414 - 6711
Fax:(202) 414 - 6738

Registered Federal Lobbyist.
Serves As:
- Program Management Specialist, DaimlerChrysler Corp.

CRAWFORD, Bruce
437 Madison Ave.
Ninth Floor
New York, NY 10022
Tel: (212) 415 - 3600
Fax:(212) 415 - 3530

Serves As:
- Chairman of the Board, Omnicom Group Inc.

CRAWFORD, Derek L.
Three Lakes Dr. West
Northfield, IL 60093
Tel: (847) 646 - 0534
Fax:(847) 646 - 0979

Serves As:
- Regional Director, State Government Affairs, (Altria Corporate Services, Inc.), Altria Group, Inc.

CRAWFORD, Dick
One McDonald's Plaza
Oak Brook, IL 60523
dick.crawford@mcd.com
Tel: (630) 623 - 6754
Fax:(630) 623 - 3057

Serves As:
- Corporate V. President, Government Relations, McDonald's Corp.

CRAWFORD, E. Mac
211 Commerce St.
Suite 800
Nashville, TN 37201
Tel: (615) 743 - 6600

Serves As:
- Chairman, Chief Exec. Officer, and President, Caremark Rx, Inc.

CRAWFORD, Fred
1300 S. Clinton St.
Fort Wayne, IN 46801-8863

Serves As:
- PAC Treasurer, Lincoln Financial Group

CRAWFORD, Jane C.
2000 Market St.
Philadelphia, PA 19103-9000
Tel: (215) 419 - 7614
Fax:(215) 419 - 5229
TF: (800) 225 - 7788

Serves As:
- Chief Public Affairs Officer and President, Arkema Inc. Foundation, ATOFINA Chemicals, Inc.

CRAWFORD, Jim
711 High St.
Des Moines, IA 50392-0150
crawford.jim@principal.com
Tel: (515) 247 - 5480
Fax:(515) 248 - 8469
TF: (800) 986 - 3343

Serves As:
- Director, Government Affairs and Political Advocacy, The Principal Financial Group

CRAWFORD, Richard C.
801 Pennsylvania Ave. NW
Suite 252 North Bldg.
RR 896
Washington, DC 20004-2604
Tel: (202) 737 - 4444
Fax:(202) 737 - 0951

Registered Federal Lobbyist.
Serves As:
- Director, Federal Government Affairs, Coors Brewing Co.

CRAWFORD, Rollin H.
710 E. 24th St.
Minneapolis, MN 55404
Tel: (612) 775 - 5000

Serves As:
- Chairman of the Board, Allina Hospitals and Clinics

CREED, Julie
P.O. Box 1488
4201 Winfield Rd.
Warrenfield, IL 60555
Tel: (630) 753 - 5000

Serves As:
- Investor Relations Contact, Navistar Internat'l Corp.

CREIGHTON, J. Kenneth
P.O. Box 10580
Reno, NV 89510-0580
Tel: (775) 448 - 7777

Serves As:
- Treasurer, Internat'l Game Technology Political Action Committee, Internat'l Game Technology

CRESSY, Bryan C.
7701 Forsyth Blvd.
Suite 800
St. Louis, MO 63105-1861
Tel: (314) 854 - 8000
Fax:(314) 854 - 8001

Serves As:
- Chairman of the Board, Belden CDT Inc.

CREVELING, Ginny
P.O. Box 871
Tulsa, OK 74102-0871
gcreveling@oneok.com
Tel: (918) 588 - 7474
Fax:(918) 588 - 7490

Serves As:
- Exec. Director, ONEOK, Inc.

Responsibilities include corporate philanthropy.

CREVISTON, Sarah
One Baxter Pkwy.
Deerfield, IL 60015-4633
sarah_creviston@baxter.com
Tel: (847) 948 - 4278
Fax:(847) 948 - 2896

Serves As:
- V. President, Government Affairs, Baxter Internat'l Inc.

CREW, Douglas P.
100 NE Adams St.
Peoria, IL 61629-1465
crew_douglas_p@cat.com
Tel: (309) 675 - 5248
Fax:(309) 675 - 5815

Registered Federal Lobbyist.
Serves As:
- Manager, Governmental Affairs, Caterpillar Inc.

CREWS, Anne C.
P.O. Box 799045
Dallas, TX 75379-9045
crewsa@marykay.com
Tel: (972) 687 - 6300
Fax:(972) 387 - 1611
TF: (800) 627 - 9529

Registered Federal Lobbyist.
Serves As:
- V. President, Government Relations, Mary Kay Inc.

CRIDER, Joe D.
350 S. Grand Ave., Suite 5100
Los Angeles, CA 90071
Tel: (213) 687 - 7700
Fax:(213) 687 - 8792

Serves As:
- Non-Exec. Chairman of the Board, Reliance Steel & Aluminum Co.

CRILLY, Tim J.
4000 House Ave.
Cheyenne, WY 82000-1
tim.crilly@bcbswy.com
Tel: (307) 634 - 1393
Fax:(307) 638 - 6927

Serves As:
- President and Chief Exec. Officer, Blue Cross and Blue Shield of Wyoming

CRISSEY, Lara
900 Ridgebury Rd.
P.O. Box 368
Ridgefield, CT 06877
lcrissey@rdg.boehringer-ingelheim.com
Tel: (203) 798 - 4740
Fax:(203) 791 - 6234

Serves As:
- Media Contact, Boehringer Ingelheim Corp.

CRITCHLOW, David
P.O. Box 550
Nashville, TN 37202
david.critchlow@hcahealthcare.com
Tel: (615) 344 - 2791
Fax:(615) 344 - 1128

Serves As:
- Director, Government Relations, HCA

CRITELLI, Michael J.
World Headquarters
One Elmcroft Rd.
Stamford, CT 06926-0700
Tel: (203) 356 - 5000
Fax:(203) 351 - 6303

Serves As:
- Chairman and Chief Exec. Officer, Pitney Bowes Inc.

CROCKER, Michael
1755 S. Clark St.
Suite 1100
Arlington, VA 22202
mdcrocker@drs-esg.com
Tel: (703) 416 - 8000
Fax:(703) 416 - 8010

Serves As:
- V. President, Navy Programs, DRS Technologies, Inc.

CROCKETT, Joan M.
2775 Sanders Rd.
Northbrook, IL 60062-6127
jcrockett@allstate.com
Tel: (847) 402 - 5000
Fax:(847) 402 - 5448
TF: (800) 574 - 3553

Serves As:
- Senior V. President, Human Resources, Allstate Insurance Co.

CROFTON, James S.
201 Washington Rd.
Princeton, NJ 08540

Serves As:
- PAC Treasurer, SRI International

CROMACK, Dan
P.O. Box 4567
Houston, TX 77210

Serves As:
- PAC Treasurer, CenterPoint Energy

CROMLING, Maureen M.
150 Innovation Dr.
Elyria, OH 44035
mcromling@rossenvironmental.com
Tel: (440) 366 - 2000

Serves As:
- Chairman and Chief Exec. Officer, Ross Environmental Services, Inc.

CRONSON, Joan
P.O. Box 59159
Minneapolis, MN 55459-8212
jcronson@carlson.com
Tel: (763) 212 - 1418
Fax:(763) 212 - 3400

Serves As:
- Director, Public Relations (Hospitality Group), Carlson Companies

CROOKSHANK, Dan
400 Collins Rd. NE
Cedar Rapids, IA 52498
Tel: (319) 295 - 7575
Fax:(319) 295 - 5429

Serves As:
- Investor Relations Contact, Rockwell Collins, Inc

CROOM, Marshall A.
1000 Lowes Blvd.
Moorsville, NC 28117
Tel: (704) 758 - 100
Fax:(336) 658 - 4766
TF: (800) 445 - 6937

Serves As:
- PAC Treasurer, Lowe's Companies, Inc.

CROSSMAN, Elizabeth A.
P.O. Box 9777
M/S EC2-28A
Federal Way, WA 98063-9777
Tel: (253) 924 - 3169
Fax:(253) 924 - 3658
TF: (800) 525 - 5440

Serves As:
- Director, Corporate Contributions, Weyerhaeuser Co.

CROUCH, David B.
1100 Superior Ave.
Cleveland, OH 44114-2589
dbcrouch@cleveland-cliffs.com
Tel: (216) 694 - 5700
Fax:(216) 694 - 4880

Serves As:
- Director, Environmental Affairs, Cleveland-Cliffs Inc

CROW, Debbie
P.O. Box 550 Tel: (419) 427 - 4857
Findlay, OH 45839-0550 Fax:(419) 427 - 4719

Serves As:
- Manager, Internal Communications, Cooper Tire & Rubber Company

CROW, Gordon
115 W. College Dr. Tel: (507) 532 - 3274
Marshall, MN 56258 Fax:(507) 537 - 8224
TF: (800) 533 - 5290

Serves As:
- Director, Government and Community Affairs, The Schwan Food Co.

CROWDERS, Chuck E.
490 L'Enfant Plaza SW Tel: (202) 378 - 2374
Suite 511 Fax:(202) 220 - 7093
Washington, DC 20024
crowders@avaya.com

Registered Federal Lobbyist.
Serves As:
- V. President and Head, Government Affairs, Avaya Inc.

CROWE, Barbara L.
999 Third Ave. Tel: (206) 467 - 3600
Suite 4300 Fax:(206) 467 - 3795
Seattle, WA 98104

Serves As:
- V. President, Human Resources, Plum Creek Timber Co. Inc.

CROWE, Dave
414 Union St. Tel: (615) 986 - -560
Suite 2000 Fax:(615) 986 - -566
Nashville, TN 37219 TF: (877) 744 - 5600

Serves As:
- PAC Contact, Louisiana-Pacific Corporation

CROWE, James Q.
1025 Eldorado Blvd. Tel: (720) 888 - 1000
Broomfield, CO 80021 Fax:(720) 888 - 5085

Serves As:
- Chief Exec. Officer, Level 3 Communications, Inc.

CROWE, Jeffrey C.
13410 Sutton Park Dr. South Tel: (904) 398 - 9400
Jacksonville, FL 32224 Fax:(904) 390 - 1325
jcrowe@landstar.com TF: (800) 872 - 9400

Serves As:
- Chairman of the Board, Landstar System, Inc.

CROWE, Robert T.
3300 First Ave. North Tel: (205) 254 - 7254
P.O. Box 10406 Fax:(205) 254 - 7150
Birmingham, AL 35202

Serves As:
- V. President, Public Affairs, Walter Industries, Inc.

Responsibilities include government affairs.

CROWELL, Robert I.
P.O. Box 2900 Tel: (808) 538 - 4636
Honolulu, HI 96846 Fax:(808) 538 - 1788
TF: (888) 643 - 3888

Serves As:
- Treasurer, Pacific Century Financial Corp. Special Political Education Committee, Bank of Hawaii Corp.

CROWLEY, Anne
82 Devonshire St. Tel: (617) 563 - 5800
Boston, MA 02109-3614 Fax:(617) 476 - 6150

Serves As:
- Senior V. President, Media Relations and Public Affairs, FMR Corp.

CROWLEY, Jr., Thomas B.
155 Grand Ave. Tel: (510) 251 - 7500
Oakland, CA 94612 Fax:(510) 251 - 7788

Serves As:
- Chairman, President and Chief Exec. Officer, Crowley Maritime Corp.

CROWN, Timothy A.
6820 S. Harl Ave. Tel: (480) 902 - 1001
Tempe, AZ 85283 Fax:(480) 902 - 1157
tcrown@insight.com TF: (800) 467 - 4448

Serves As:
- Chairman of the Board, Insight Enterprises, Inc.

CROYLE, Robert
2800 Post Oak Blvd., Suite 5450 Tel: (713) 621 - 7800
Houston, TX 77056-6196 Fax:(713) 960 - 7560

Serves As:
- V. Chairman and Chief Adminstrative Officer, Rowan Companies, Inc.

Responsibilities include corporate public affairs.

CRUICKSHANK, John
350 N. Orleans Tel: (312) 321 - 3000
Chicago, IL 60654

Serves As:
- Chief Exec. Officer, Chicago Sun-Times

CRUM, Lorrie P.
6035 Parkland Blvd. Tel: (216) 896 - 3000
Cleveland, OH 44124-4141 Fax:(216) 896 - 4000
TF: (800) 272 - 7537

Serves As:
- V. President, Corporate Communications, Parker Hannifin Corp.

CRUM, Scott A.
Four W. Red Oak Ln. Tel: (914) 641 - 2000
White Plains, NY 10604 Fax:(914) 696 - 2950

Serves As:
- Senior V. President and Director, Human Resources, ITT Industries

CRUMLEY, James
1650 Tysons Blvd. Tel: (703) 790 - 6300
Suite 1700 Fax:(703) 790 - 6365
McLean, VA 22201

Serves As:
- V. President, Government Relations, ITT Industries

CRUMP, Rick
333 Clay St. Tel: (713) 650 - 3700
Suite 3600 Fax:(713) 654 - 9552
Houston, TX 70002-4109

Serves As:
- Chief Exec. Officer and President, Sterling Chemicals, Inc.

CRUZ, Thomas A.
201 E. Fourth St. Tel: (513) 723 - 7000
Cincinnati, OH 45202 Fax:(513) 451 - 8624
tom.cruz@convergys.com TF: (800) 344 - 3000

Serves As:
- Senior V. President, Human Resources and Administration, Convergys Corp.

CSASZAR, Bernice
535 Marriott Dr. Tel: (615) 937 - 0088
Nashville, TN 37214-8900 Fax:(615) 937 - 1414

Serves As:
- Administrator, Bridgetone/Firestone Trust Fund, Bridgestone Americas Holding, Inc.

CSIMMA, Zoltan
500 Kendall St. Tel: (617) 252 - 7500
Cambridge, MA 02142 Fax:(617) 252 - 7600

Serves As:
- Senior V. President, Human Resources, Genzyme Corp.

CUBE, Antonio
530 Water St. Tel: (510) 238 - 4360
Fifth Floor
Oakland, CA 94607

Serves As:
- Director, Government Affairs - West, (AMTRAK West), Amtrak

CUCINOTTA, Patricia
45 William St., Third Floor Tel: (781) 237 - 5100
Wellesley Hills, MA 02481-4078 Fax:(781) 431 - 4255

Serves As:
- Assistant to Chairman, PerkinElmer, Inc.

Responsibilities include corporate philanthropy.

CULLEN, John M.
21001 Van Born Rd. Tel: (313) 274 - 7400
Taylor, MI 48180 Fax:(313) 792 - 6935

Serves As:
- Manager, Environmental Affairs, Masco Corp.

CULLEN, Thomas K.
185 Central Ave. Tel: (516) 733 - 7114
Bethpage, NY 11714 Fax:(516) 827 - 6263
tcullen@kingkullen.com

Serves As:
- V. President, Government, Industry and Public Relations, King Kullen Grocery Co.

CULLERS, Jeanne
1601 W. LBJ Fwy. Tel: (972) 443 - 4847
Dallas, TX 75234 Fax:(972) 443 - 8519

Serves As:
- Media Contact, Celanese

CULLO, Leonard A.
P.O. Box 57 Tel: (412) 456 - 5700
Pittsburgh, PA 15230-0057 Fax:(412) 456 - 6128

Serves As:
- PAC Treasurer, H. J. Heinz Co.

CULP, Jr., H. Lawrence
2099 Pennsylvania Ave. NW Tel: (202) 828 - 0850
Washington, DC 20006 Fax:(202) 828 - 0860

Serves As:
- President and Chief Exec. Officer, Danaher Corp.

CULVER, Curt S.
270 E. Kilbourn Tel: (414) 347 - 6480
Milwaukee, WI 53202 Fax:(414) 347 - 6696
TF: (800) 558 - 9900

Serves As:
- President and Chief Exec. Officer, Mortgage Guaranty Insurance Corp. (MGIC)

CUMMING, Ian
315 Park Ave. South Tel: (212) 460 - 1900
New York, NY 10010 Fax:(212) 598 - 4869

Serves As:
- Chairman of the Board, Leucadia Nat'l Corp.

CUMMINGS, Candace S.
P.O. Box 21488 Tel: (336) 424 - 6000
Greensboro, NC 27420-1488 Fax:(336) 424 - 7631
candace_cummings@vfc.com

Serves As:
- V. President, Administration, General Counsel and Secretary, V. F. Corporation
Responsibilities include investor relations.

CUMMINGS, Karen
P.O. Box 4427 Tel: (713) 546 - 4100
Houston, TX 77210-4427 Fax:(713) 546 - 4041

Serves As:
- Contact, The Jimmy Fund, Jiffy Lube Internat'l, Inc.

CUMMINGS, Tammy H.
1100 Boulders Pkwy. Tel: (804) 330 - 1000
Richmond, VA 23225-4035 Fax:(804) 330 - 1177

Serves As:
- V. President, Human Resources, Tredegar Corp.

CUMMINS, James L.
905 West Blvd., North Tel: (574) 293 - 7511
Elkhart, IN 46514 Ext: 278
jcummins@ctscorp.com Fax:(574) 293 - 6146

Serves As:
- Trustee, CTS Corp. Foundation, CTS Corp.

CUMMINS, Lin M.
2135 W. Maple Rd. Tel: (248) 435 - 7112
Troy, MI 48084 Fax:(248) 435 - 1393
linda.cummins@arvinmeritor.com TF: (800) 535 - 5560

Serves As:
- Senior V. President, Communications, ArvinMeritor

CUMMINS, Mark R.
355 Maple Ave. Tel: (215) 256 - 5025
Harleysville, PA 19438-2297 Fax:(215) 256 - 5601
mcummins@harleysvillegroup.com TF: (800) 523 - 6344

Serves As:
- Exec. V. President, Chief Investment Officer and Treasurer, Harleysville Group
Responsibilities include corporate philanthropy.

CUNNINGHAM, Bryan
601 Pennsylvania Ave. NW Tel: (202) 661 - 4000
Suite 520, N. Bldg. Fax:(202) 661 - 4041
Washington, DC 20004

Registered Federal Lobbyist.
Serves As:
- Representative, Cisco Systems, Inc.

CUNNINGHAM, C. Baker
7701 Forsyth Blvd. Tel: (314) 854 - 8000
Suite 800 Fax:(314) 854 - 8001
St. Louis, MO 63105-1861

Serves As:
- President and Chief Exec. Officer, Belden CDT Inc.

CUNNINGHAM, Edward A.
1100 Boulders Pkwy. Tel: (804) 330 - 1000
Richmond, VA 23225-4035 Fax:(804) 330 - 1177

Serves As:
- V. President, Corporate Communications and Investor Relations, Tredegar Corp.

CUNNINGHAM, Jack
2525 Stemmons Fwy. Tel: (214) 631 - 4420
Dallas, TX 75207-2401 Fax:(214) 689 - 0501
jack.cunningham@trin.net

Serves As:
- V. President, Human Resources, Trinity Industries, Inc.

CUNNINGHAM, Larry
800/850 Ridgeview Dr. Tel: (610) 651 - 6000
Horsham, PA 19044 Fax:(610) 651 - 6100

Serves As:
- V. President, Human Resources, Centocor, Inc.

CUNNINGHAM, Dr. Ralph S.
P.O. Box 2521 Tel: (713) 759 - 3636
Houston, TX 77252-2521 Fax:(713) 759 - 3957
TF: (800) 877 - 3636

Serves As:
- Chairman of the Board,
Texas Eastern Products Pipeline Company, LLC (TEPPCO)

CUNNINGHAM, Scott
4300 Wilson Blvd. Tel: (703) 682 - 6336
11th Floor Fax:(703) 528 - 4510
Arlington, VA 22203

Serves As:
- V. President, Investor Relations, The AES Corp.

CUNNINGHAM, Trisha
P.O. Box 660199 Tel: (214) 480 - 6417
M/S 8726 Fax:(214) 480 - 6881
Dallas, TX 75266-0199 TF: (800) 336 - 5236
t-cunningham@ti.com

Serves As:
- Director, Company Communications, Texas Instruments Incorporated

CUNNION, III, Robert J.
24025 Park Sorrento Tel: (818) 223 - 7500
Suite 400 Fax:(818) 223 - 7667
Calabasas, CA 91302 TF: (800) 267 - 0998
rcunnion@ryland.com

Serves As:
- Senior V. President, Human Resources, The Ryland Group, Inc.

CUPP, Garland
2101 City West Blvd. Tel: (713) 918 - 8800
Houston, TX 77042-2827 Fax:(713) 918 - 8000
garland_cupp@bmc.com TF: (800) 841 - 2031

Serves As:
- Chairman of the Board, BMC Software

CURLANDER, Paul J.
740 W. New Circle Rd. Tel: (859) 232 - 2000
Lexington, KY 40550 Fax:(859) 232 - 7529
TF: (800) 539 - 6275

Serves As:
- Chairman and Chief Exec. Officer, Lexmark Internat'l, Inc.

CURLANDER, Sandra
1025 Eldorado Blvd. Tel: (720) 888 - 2501
Broomfield, CO 80021 Fax:(720) 888 - 5085

Serves As:
- Manager, Investor Relations, Level 3 Communications, Inc.

CURLER, Jeffrey H.
222 S. Ninth St. Tel: (612) 376 - 3000
Suite 2300 Fax:(612) 376 - 3150
Minneapolis, MN 55402-4099

Serves As:
- President, Chief Exec. Officer, and Chairman of the Board, Bemis Company, Inc.

CURLEY, Jay
401 Park Dr. Tel: (617) 246 - 5000
Boston, MA 02215 TF: (800) 325 - 2583

Serves As:
- Director, Government, Public and Regulatory Affairs,
Blue Cross and Blue Shield of Massachusetts

CURLEY, Sally
500 Kendall St. Tel: (617) 252 - 7500
Cambridge, MA 02142 Fax:(617) 252 - 7600

Serves As:
- V. President, Investor Relations, Genzyme Corp.

CURLEY, Tom
450 W. 33rd St.
New York, NY 10001
Tel: (212) 621 - 1500
Fax:(212) 621 - 5447

Serves As:
- President and Chief Exec. Officer, Associated Press

CURRAN, Christopher
P.O. Box 844
Spring House, PA 19477-0844
ccurran@advanta.com
Tel: (215) 657 - 4000
Fax:(215) 444 - 5101

Serves As:
- V. President, Investor Relations, Advanta Corp.

CURRAN, Joanne
445 S. Figueroa St.
Los Angeles, CA 90071
Joanne.Curran@uboc.com
Tel: (213) 236 - 5017
Fax:(213) 236 - 4147

Serves As:
- Senior V. President, External Communications, Union Bank of California

CURRAN, Lisa M.
350 Church St.
M/S 11
Hartford, CT 06103-1106
lmcurran@lnc.com

Serves As:
- Charitable Giving Contact (Hartford, CT), Lincoln Financial Group

CURRIE, Rodger
555 13th St. NW
Suite 600 West
Washington, DC 20004
Tel: (202) 585 - 9610

Registered Federal Lobbyist.
Serves As:
- V. President, Federal Government Affairs, Amgen Inc.

Responsibilities include political action.

CURRIE, William G.
2801 E. Beltline NE
Grand Rapids, MI 49525
wcurrie@ufpi.com
Tel: (616) 364 - 6161
Fax:(616) 364 - 5558

Serves As:
- V. Chairman and Chief Exec. Officer, Universal Forest Products, Inc.

CURTIN, Dennis V.
P.O. Box 471
Sunbury, PA 17801
Tel: (570) 286 - 4571
Fax:(570) 286 - 3286

Serves As:
- Director, Public Relations, Weis Markets, Inc.

CURTIN, Wayne
3700 W. Juneau Ave.
Milwaukee, WI 53208
wayne.curtin@harley-davidson.com
Tel: (414) 342 - 4680
Fax:(414) 343 - 8230

Serves As:
- Director, Government Affairs, Harley-Davidson Motor Company

CURTIS, Carol A.
P.O. Box 901-435
Kansas City, MO 64190
carol.curtis2@astrazeneca.com
Tel: (816) 436 - 5152
Fax:(816) 436 - 8385
TF: (800) 822 - 9209
Ext: 60077

Serves As:
- Director, State Government Affairs, AstraZeneca Pharmaceuticals

CURTIS, Jayne
1768 Automation Pkwy.
San Jose, CA 95131
Tel: (408) 546 - 4714
Fax:(408) 546 - 4300

Serves As:
- Public Relations Contact, JDS Uniphase Corp.

CURWIN, Ron
650 Liberty Ave.
Union, NJ 07083
Tel: (908) 688 - 0888
Ext: 4550
Fax:(908) 688 - 6483

Serves As:
- Chief Financial Officer and Investor Relations Contact, Bed Bath & Beyond Inc.

CUSICK, Kristen
815 Connecticut Ave. NW
Suite 330
Washington, DC 20006
kristin.m.cusick@questdiagnostic.com
Tel: (202) 263 - 6263
Fax:(202) 728 - 0338

Registered Federal Lobbyist.
Serves As:
- Director, Government Affairs, Quest Diagnostics Inc.

Responsibilities include political action.

CUSICK, Mary L.
3776 S. High St.
Columbus, OH 43207-0863
Tel: (614) 492 - 4920
Fax:(614) 492 - 4934
TF: (800) 272 - 7675

Serves As:
- Senior V. President, Investor Relations and Corporate Communications, Bob Evans Farms, Inc.

CUSOLITO, John
175 Berkeley St.
Boston, MA 02116
john.cusolito@libertymutual.com
Tel: (617) 574 - 5512
Fax:(617) 350 - 7648

Serves As:
- V. President and Manager, External Relations, Liberty Mutual Insurance Co.

CUSTODIO, Dominic
55 Inverness Dr. East
Englewood, CO 80112-5498
Tel: (303) 799 - 9090
Fax:(303) 328 - 4153

Serves As:
- V. President, Government and Military Services, Jeppesen

CUTE, Brian
1666 K St., NW
Suite 410
Washington, DC 20006
Tel: (202) 973 - 6615
Fax:(202) 466 - 9103

Serves As:
- Director, Government Relations, VeriSign, Inc.

CUTLER, Alexander M. "Sandy"
Eaton Center
1111 Superior Ave.
Cleveland, OH 44114-2584
Tel: (216) 523 - 4092
Fax:(216) 523 - 4787

Serves As:
- Chairman and Chief Exec. Officer, Eaton Corp.

CUTLER, Linda
P.O. Box 537012
Sacramento, CA 95853-7012
linda.cutler@gencorp.com
Tel: (916) 355 - 8650
Fax:(916) 351 - 8667

Serves As:
- V. President, Corporate Communications, GenCorp

CUTTER, John L.
1855 Boston Rd.
Wilbraham, MA 01095
Tel: (413) 543 - 2400
Fax:(413) 543 - 9355
TF: (800) 966 - 9970

Serves As:
- Chief Exec. Officer and President, Friendly Ice Cream Corp.

CYNKAR, Amy
One Baxter Pkwy.
Deerfield, IL 60015-4633
Tel: (847) 948 - 5166
Fax:(847) 948 - 2016

Serves As:
- Senior Communications Associate, External Communications, Baxter Internat'l Inc.

CZUDAK, Bob
370 Woodcliff Dr.
Suite 300
Fairport, NY 14450
bob.czudak@cbrands.com
Tel: (585) 218 - 3668
TF: (888) 724 - 2169

Serves As:
- Director, Investor Relations, Constellation Brands, Inc.

CZWARTACKI, John
1300 I St. NW
Suite 400 West
Washington, DC 20005
Tel: (202) 515 - 2400

Serves As:
- Exec. Director, External Communications, Verizon Communications Inc.

D'AMATO, Janice M.
P.O. Box 1518
Bellevue, WA 98009
jdamato@paccar.com
Tel: (425) 468 - 7400
Fax:(425) 468 - 8216

Serves As:
- Corporate Attorney, PACCAR Inc.

Responsibilities include investor relations.

D'AMOUR, Donald H.
P.O. Box 7840
Springfield, MA 01102
ddamour@bigy.com
Tel: (413) 784 - 0600
Fax:(413) 732 - 7350

Serves As:
- Chairman and Chief Exec. Officer, Big Y Foods Inc.

D'AMOUR-DALEY, Claire M.
P.O. Box 7840
Springfield, MA 01102
Tel: (413) 784 - 0600
Fax:(413) 732 - 7350

Serves As:
• V. President, Corporate Communications, Big Y Foods Inc.

D'ANDREA, Dennis
767 Fifth Ave.
New York, NY 10153-0023
ddandrea@estee.com
Tel: (212) 572 - 4200
Fax:(212) 572 - 6633

Serves As:
• V. President, Investor Relations, Estee Lauder Companies, Inc.

D'ANGELO, Luella Chavez
6200 S. Quebec St.
Suite 370AU
Greenwood Village, CO 80111
luella.d'angelo@firstdatacorp.com
Tel: (303) 967 - 6493
Fax:(303) 967 - 6705

Serves As:
• President, Foundation, First Data

D'AURIA, Paul
1095 Ave. of the Americas
New York, NY 10036
Tel: (212) 395 - 2121
Fax:(212) 869 - 3265

Serves As:
• PAC Treasurer, Verizon Wireless

D'AVERSA, Angela
3850 Hamlin Rd.
Auburn Hills, MI 48326
Tel: (248) 754 - 9200

Serves As:
• Acting V. President, Human Resources, BorgWarner Inc.

DAANE, John P.
101 Innovation Dr.
San Jose, CA 95134-1941
Tel: (408) 544 - 7000
Fax:(408) 544 - 7740

Serves As:
• Chairman, President and Chief Exec. Officer, Altera Corp.

DABAH, Ezra
915 Secaucus Rd.
Secaucus, NJ 07094
edabah@childrensplace.com
Tel: (201) 558 - 2400
Fax:(201) 558 - 2837
TF: (800) 527 - 5355

Serves As:
• Chairman and Chief Exec. Officer, The Children's Place Retail Stores, Inc.

DABBS, Melinda
P.O. Box 1330
Salisbury, NC 28145-1330
Tel: (704) 633 - 8250
Fax:(704) 633 - 8250

Serves As:
• PAC Treasurer, Food Lion LLC

DABERKO, David A.
National City Center
1900 E. Ninth St.
Cleveland, OH 44114-3484
Tel: (216) 222 - 2000
TF: (800) 622 - 6736

Serves As:
• Chairman and Chief Exec. Officer, Nat'l City Corp.

DADAY, Robert P.
Two N. Ninth St.
Allentown, PA 18101-1179
rpdaday@pplweb.com
Tel: (610) 774 - 7511
Fax:(610) 774 - 5281
TF: (800) 345 - 3085

Serves As:
• Special Assistant to the President - Community Affairs, PPL Corp.

DAGGETT, John
601 Rayovac Dr.
Madison, WI 53711-2460
Tel: (608) 275 - 4912
Fax:(608) 275 - 4967

Serves As:
• Director, Corporate Communications, Sprectrum Brands

DAGIAN, Glenn A.
1005 Congress Ave., Suite 830
Austin, TX 78701
Tel: (512) 477 - 3901

Serves As:
• Senior Government Affairs Representative, BP

DAHLBERG, A. W. "Bill"
1155 Perimeter Center West
Atlanta, GA 30338
Tel: (678) 579 - 5000
Fax:(678) 579 - 5001

Serves As:
• Chairman of the Board, Mirant Corp.

DAHLBERG, Gregory
1550 Crystal Dr.
Crystal Square 2, Suite 300
Arlington, VA 22202
Tel: (703) 413 - 5632
Fax:(703) 413 - 5846

Serves As:
• V. President, Legislative Affairs, Lockheed Martin Corp.

DAHLBERG, Ken C.
10260 Campus Point Dr.
San Diego, CA 92121
Tel: (858) 826 - 6000
Fax:(858) 826 - 6634

Serves As:
• Chairman, President and Chief Exec. Officer, Science Applications Internat'l Corp.

DAHLINGER, Mark A.
259 Prospect Plains Rd.
Cranbury, NJ 08512
Tel: (609) 860 - 4000

Serves As:
• Chief Financial Officer, Rhodia, Inc.
Responsibilities include political action.

DAI-MCGAUGHY, Claire
840 Gessner
Suite 1400
Houston, TX 77024
Tel: (713) 650 - 6200
Fax:(713) 653 - 6815

Serves As:
• Treasurer, Cemex Inc. Employees Political Action Committee, Cemex USA

DAIGLER, Nancy
Three Lakes Dr.
Northfield, IL 60093-2753
Tel: (847) 646 - 4106
Fax:(847) 646 - 6005

Serves As:
• V. President, Corporate Affairs, Kraft Foods, Inc.

DAIL, Betsy
15101 N. Scottsdale Rd.
Suite 5033
Scottsdale, AZ 85254
Tel: (480) 754 - 6172

Serves As:
• Director, Regulatory and Product Safety, The Dial Corporation

DALE, Steve W.
800 Nicollet Mall
BCMNH23K
Minneapolis, MN 55402
steve.dale@usbank.com
Tel: (612) 303 - 0784
Fax:(612) 303 - 0735

Serves As:
• Senior V. President, Media Relations, U.S. Bancorp

DALEY, Candice
P.O. Box 5625
MS25
Minneapolis, MN 55440-5625
Tel: (952) 742 - 6193
Fax:(952) 742 - 6208

Serves As:
• Public Affairs Counselor, Cargill, Incorporated

DALEY, William R.
3900 Wisconsin Ave. NW
Washington, DC 20016
Tel: (202) 752 - 7000
Fax:(202) 752 - 6099

Registered Federal Lobbyist.
Serves As:
• V. President, Government and Industry Relations, Fannie Mae

DALHOFF, Steven
1000 Louisiana St.
Suite 5800
Houston, TX 77002-5050
Tel: (713) 507 - 6400
Fax:(713) 507 - 3871

Serves As:
• Treasurer, Dynegy Inc. PAC, Dynegy, Inc.

DALLAGO, Rochelle A.
Seven Andreann Dr.
Annandale, NJ 08801
Tel: (908) 730 - 6335

Serves As:
• Senior Manager, Professional and State Government Affairs, GlaxoSmithKline Research and Development

DALTON, Dan
P.O. Box 6000
Cherry Hill, NJ 08034-6000
ddalton@subaru.com
Tel: (856) 488 - 8500
Fax:(856) 488 - 0485

Serves As:
• V. President, Human Resources, Subaru of America, Inc.

DALTON, Dee
3111 W. Allegheny Ave.
Philadelphia, PA 19132
dee_dalton@pepboys.com
Tel: (215) 430 - 9204
Fax:(215) 229 - 1410

Serves As:
• Administrative Assistant to the President, The Pep Boys-Manny, Moe & Jack
Responsibilities include corporate philanthropy.

DALTON, Trevin
101 Constitution Ave., NW
Suite 200 East
Washington, DC 20001
Tel: (202) 530 - 7300
Fax:(202) 530 - 7350

Serves As:
• PAC Manager, Entergy Corp.

DALY, Jack
One McDonald's Plaza
Oak Brook, IL 60523
jack.daly@mcd.com
Tel: (630) 623 - 6743
Fax:(630) 623 - 8843

Serves As:
- Senior V. President, Corporate Relations, McDonald's Corp.

DALY, Tim
6200 S. Quebec St.
Greenwood Village, CO 80111
Tel: (303) 967 - 5222
Fax:(303) 967 - 6705

Serves As:
- Senior V. President, Government Affairs, First Data

DAMIN, Shauna
P.O. Box 32010
Louisville, KY 40232-2010
Tel: (502) 627 - 2363
Fax:(502) 217 - 2654

Serves As:
- Grants Administrator, LG&E Foundation, LG&E Energy LLC

DAMONTI, John
345 Park Ave.
New York, NY 10154-0037
john.damonti@bms.com
Tel: (212) 546 - 4566
Fax:(212) 546 - 4020

Serves As:
- President, Bristol-Myers Squibb Foundation, Bristol-Myers Squibb Co.

DAN, Michael T.
P.O. Box 18100
Richmond, VA 23226-8100
Tel: (804) 289 - 9600
Fax:(804) 289 - 9770

Serves As:
- Chairman, President and Chief Exec. Officer, The Brink's Co.

DANIEL, John M.
P.O. Box 10247
Birmingham, AL 35202
Tel: (205) 326 - 7100
Fax:(205) 244 - 2897
TF: (800) 734 - 4667

Serves As:
- Director, Human Resources, Regions Financial Corp.

DANNOV, David M.
9000 W. 67th St.
Shawnee Mission, KS 66202
Tel: (913) 676 - 8800
Fax:(913) 676 - 8872

Serves As:
- PAC Treasurer, Seaboard Corporation

DANZEISEN, John
Ten Finderne Ave.
Bridgewater, NJ 08807
Tel: (908) 203 - 2800

Serves As:
- Chairman of the Board, ICI American Holdings, Inc.

DARBEE, Peter A.
One Market
Spear Tower, Suite 2400
San Francisco, CA 94105
Tel: (415) 267 - 7000
Fax:(415) 267 - 7252

Serves As:
- Chairman of the Board, PG & E Corp.

DARCY, Shannon
1420 New York Ave. NW
Suite 600
Washington, DC 20005
Tel: (202) 393 - 6444
Fax:(202) 289 - 9222

Registered Federal Lobbyist.
Serves As:
- Representative, Medtronic, Inc.

DARMAN, Richard G.
4300 Wilson Blvd.
11th Floor
Arlington, VA 22203
Tel: (202) 347 - 2626
Fax:(202) 347 - 1818

Serves As:
- Chairman of the Board, The AES Corp.

DARMANIN, Robert T.
2600 W. Big Beaver Rd.
Troy, MI 48084
robert.darmanin@abnamro.com
Tel: (248) 637 - 2521
Fax:(248) 637 - 2749
TF: (800) 643 - 9600

Serves As:
- Director, Corporate Relations, Standard Federal Bank

DARNOLD, Richard Alan
2950 Industrial Rd.
Las Vegas, NV 89109-1100
Tel: (702) 792 - 7200
Fax:(702) 792 - 7266
TF: (800) 695 - 2455

Serves As:
- PAC Treasurer, Boyd Gaming Corp.

DARROW, Kurt L.
1284 N. Telegraph Rd.
Monroe, MI 48162
Tel: (734) 242 - 1444
Fax:(734) 457 - 2005

Serves As:
- President and Chief Exec. Officer, La-Z-Boy Incorporated

DATTILO, Thomas
P.O. Box 550
Findlay, OH 45839-0550
Tel: (419) 423 - 1321
Fax:(419) 424 - 4108

Serves As:
- Chairman and Chief Exec. Officer, Cooper Tire & Rubber Company

DAUCH, Richard E.
One Dauch Dr.
Detroit, MI 48211
Tel: (313) 974 - 2000
Fax:(313) 758 - 3929

Serves As:
- Co-Founder, Chairman and Chief Exec. Officer, American Axle and Manufacturing, Inc.

DAUE, Janice
3900 Wisconsin Ave. NW
Washington, DC 20016
Tel: (202) 752 - 2131
Fax:(202) 752 - 3808

Serves As:
- V. President, News and Public Affairs, Fannie Mae

DAUGHERTY, Dan H.
425 W. Capitol, 40th Floor
Little Rock, AR 72201
Tel: (501) 377 - 4000
TF: (800) 377 - 4448

Serves As:
- Manager, Communications, Entergy Arkansas, Inc.

DAUGHERTY, Jack R.
Cash America Bldg.
1600 W. Seventh St.
Fort Worth, TX 76102-2599
jdaugherty@casham.com
Tel: (817) 335 - 1100
Fax:(817) 570 - 1645

Serves As:
- Chairman of the Board, Cash America Internat'l, Inc.

DAVENPORT, Lynn P.
11419 Sunset Hills Rd.
Reston, VA 20190-5207
Tel: (703) 251 - 8500
Fax:(703) 251 - 8240
TF: (888) 368 - 2152

Serves As:
- President and Chief Exec. Officer, MAXIMUS, Inc.

DAVID, Daryl D.
P.O. Box 834
Seattle, WA 98101
daryl.david@wamu.net
Tel: (206) 461 - 8890
Fax:(206) 554 - 4807
TF: (800) 756 - 8000

Serves As:
- Exec. V. President, Human Resources, Washington Mutual, Inc.

DAVID, George
United Technologies Bldg.
One Financial Plaza
Hartford, CT 06101
Tel: (860) 728 - 7000
Fax:(860) 728 - 6494

Serves As:
- Chairman and Chief Exec. Officer, United Technologies Corp.

DAVID, Javier
86 Trinity Pl.
New York, NY 10006
Tel: (212) 306 - 1440
Fax:(212) 306 - 1152

Serves As:
- Media Contact, American Stock Exchange

DAVID, Stephen N.
10955 Vista Sorrento Pkwy.
San Diego, CA 92130
Tel: (858) 314 - 7000
Fax:(858) 314 - 7001

Serves As:
- Chairman of the Board, Iomega Corp.

DAVIDMAN, Jeff
2700 Lone Oak Pkwy.
Eagan, MN 55121
jeff.davidman@nwa.com
Tel: (612) 726 - 2111
Fax:(612) 726 - 0776
TF: (800) 225 - 2525

Serves As:
- Director, State and Local Affairs, Northwest Airlines, Inc.

DAVIDSMEYER, Darcy E.
1303 E. Algonquin Rd.
Seventh Floor
Schaumburg, IL 60196
Tel: (847) 576 - 7672
Fax:(847) 576 - 5611
TF: (800) 262 - 8509

Serves As:
- Director, State and Local Government Relations, Motorola, Inc.

DAVIDSON, Anne
847 Gibraltar Dr.
Bldg. 5
Milpitas, CA 95035
Tel: (408) 586 - 4232
Fax:(408) 956 - 7699

Registered Federal Lobbyist.
Serves As:
• Representative, Solectron Corp.

DAVIDSON, Carole
2711 N. Haskell Ave.
Dallas, TX 75204
cdavid01@7-11.com
Tel: (214) 828 - 7021
Fax:(214) 828 - 7090

Serves As:
• V. President, Investor Relations, 7-Eleven, Inc.

DAVIDSON, Cary
520 S. Grand Ave.
Suite 700
Los Angeles, CA 90071

Serves As:
• PAC Treasurer, The DIRECTV Group, Inc.

DAVIDSON, Ian
999 Third Ave.
Suite 4300
Seattle, WA 98104
Tel: (206) 467 - 3600
Fax:(206) 467 - 3795

Serves As:
• Chairman of the Board, Plum Creek Timber Co. Inc.

DAVIDSON, Mark D.
One Nationwide Plaza
M/S 1-27-09
Columbus, OH 43215-2220
Tel: (614) 249 - 4889
Fax:(614) 249 - 3073

Serves As:
• Area Legislative Affairs Representative - West Virginia and Kentucky, Nationwide

DAVIDSON, Mary Ann
1015 15th St. NW
Suite 200
Washington, DC 20005-2605
Tel: (202) 835 - 7360
Fax:(202) 467 - 4250

Registered Federal Lobbyist.
Serves As:
• Chief Security Officer, Oracle Corporation

DAVIDSON, Pat
3700 W. Juneau Ave.
Milwaukee, WI 53208
pat.davidson@harley-davidson.com
Tel: (414) 342 - 4680
Fax:(414) 343 - 8230

Serves As:
• Director, Investor Relations, Harley-Davidson Motor Company

DAVIDSON, Peter
1300 I St. NW
Suite 400 West
Washington, DC 20005
Tel: (202) 515 - 2400
Fax:(202) 336 - 7920

Registered Federal Lobbyist.
Serves As:
• Senior V. President, Federal Government Relations; and Deputy General Counsel, Verizon Communications Inc.

DAVIDSON, Richard K.
1400 Douglas St.
Omaha, NE 68179
Tel: (402) 544 - 5000

Serves As:
• Chairman, President and Chief Exec. Officer, Union Pacific Corp.

DAVIDSON, Wesley C.
2525 Armitage Ave.
Melrose Park, IL 60160
wdavidson@alberto.com
Tel: (708) 450 - 3145
Fax:(708) 450 - 3435

Serves As:
• V. President, Corporate Development and Investor Relations, Alberto-Culver Co.

DAVIDSON, William M.
2300 Harmon Rd.
Auburn Hills, MI 48326-1714
Tel: (248) 340 - 1800
Fax:(248) 340 - 2395

Serves As:
• President and Chief Exec. Officer, Guardian Industries Corp.

DAVIE, Diane J.
One Invacare Way
Elyria, OH 44035
rgudbranson@invacare.com
Tel: (440) 329 - 6000
Fax:(440) 366 - 9008
TF: (800) 333 - 6900

Serves As:
• Senior V. President, Human Resources, Invacare Corp.

DAVIES, II, Robert A.
469 N. Harrison St.
Princeton, NJ 08543-5297
Tel: (609) 683 - 5900
Fax:(609) 497 - 7177

Serves As:
• Chairman of the Board, Church & Dwight Co., Inc.

DAVIS, Aaron L.
132 Fairgrounds Rd.
West Kingston, RI 02892
Tel: (401) 789 - 5735
Fax:(401) 789 - 3710
TF: (800) 788 - 2208

Serves As:
• V. President, Marketing Communications, American Power Conversion Corp.
Responsibilities include media relations.

DAVIS, Aimee
P.O. Box 120
Columbus, GA 31902-0120
aimeedavis@sfcts.com
Tel: (706) 644 - 0528
Fax:(706) 641 - 6555

Serves As:
• Manager, Media Relations, Synovus Financial Corp.

DAVIS, Bradley T.
P.O. Box 2047
Omaha, NE 68103-2047
Tel: (402) 496 - 7809
Fax:(402) 498 - 2215
TF: (800) 247 - 1345

Serves As:
• Chairman of the Board, AG Processing Inc

DAVIS, Carol R.
P.O. Box 8050
Wisconsin Rapids, WI 54495-8050
Tel: (715) 422 - 3878

Serves As:
• Director, Employee Communications, Stora Enso North America

DAVIS, Jr., Chester "Chip"
P.O. Box 15437
Wilmington, DE 19850-5437
chip.davis@astrazeneca.com
Tel: (302) 886 - 5650
Fax:(302) 886 - 5015
TF: (800) 456 - 3669

Registered Federal Lobbyist.
Serves As:
• V. President, Government Affairs, AstraZeneca Pharmaceuticals

DAVIS, Chris A.
McLeod USA Technology Park
6400 C St., SW
Cedar Rapids, IA 52406
Tel: (319) 364 - 0000
Fax:(800) 896 - 8330
TF: (800) 896 - 8330

Serves As:
• Chairman and Chief Exec. Officer, McLeod USA Inc.

DAVIS, Corey
75 Arlington St.
Boston, MA 02116
cld@tbf.org
Tel: (617) 338 - 2521
Fax:(617) 338 - 1606

Serves As:
• Grants Manager, Polaroid Fund, Polaroid Corp.

DAVIS, Craig A.
2511 Garden Rd.
Monterey, CA 93940-5330
Tel: (831) 642 - 9300
Fax:(831) 642 - 9399
TF: (888) 642 - 9300

Serves As:
• Chairman and Chief Exec. Officer, Century Aluminum Co.

DAVIS, David W.
1000 Alderman Dr.
Alpharetta, GA 30005-4101
Tel: (770) 752 - 6000
Fax:(770) 752 - 5939

Serves As:
• Corporate Secretary; and V. President, Government Affairs, ChoicePoint Inc.

DAVIS, Deborah
120 Monument Circle
Indianapolis, IN 46204
Tel: (317) 488 - 6350

Serves As:
• Director, Media Relations, Wellpoint, Inc.

DAVIS, Erika T.
P.O. Box 27626
Richmond, VA 23261-7626
Tel: (804) 965 - 5895
Fax:(804) 270 - 7281

Serves As:
• Senior V. President, Human Resources, Owens & Minor, Inc.

DAVIS, Jr., Erroll B.
P.O. Box 77007
Madison, WI 53707-1007
Tel: (608) 458 - 3311
Fax:(608) 458 - 3397

Serves As:
• Chairman of the Board, Alliant Energy Corp.

DAVIS, Gerald T.
Ten Penn Center
1801 Market St.
Philadelphia, PA 19103-1699
Tel: (215) 977 - 6298
Fax:(215) 977 - 3409

Serves As:
• Manager, Media and Public Relations, Sunoco, Inc.

DAVIS, Heather
CNA Center
333 S. Wabash Ave.
Chicago, IL 60685
Tel: (312) 822 - 1740
Fax:(312) 822 - 1186

Serves As:
- Senior V. President, Government Relations, CNA Financial Corp.

DAVIS, Ian M.
1717 Pennsylvania Ave. NW
Suite 400
Washington, DC 20006
ian_davis@oxy.com
Tel: (202) 857 - 3041
Fax:(202) 857 - 3014

Registered Federal Lobbyist.
Serves As:
- V. President, International Affairs, Occidental Internat'l

DAVIS, J. Bradley
P.O. Box 834
Seattle, WA 98101
Tel: (206) 461 - 2000
Fax:(206) 554 - 4807
TF: (800) 756 - 8000

Serves As:
- Exec. V. President, Chief Communications and Marketing Officer, Washington Mutual, Inc.

DAVIS, J. Michael
2211 Congress St.
M/S B159
Portland, ME 04122-0545
jmichaeldavis@unumprovident.com
Tel: (207) 575 - 4326
Fax:(207) 575 - 4304

Serves As:
- V. President, State Relations, UnumProvident Corp.

DAVIS, James
19 N. Main St.
Wilkes-Barre, PA 18711-0302
Tel: (570) 200 - 6300

Serves As:
- State Government Affairs Representative, Blue Cross of Northeastern Pennsylvania

DAVIS, James S.
Brighton Landing, 20 Guest St.
Boston, MA 02135-2088
Tel: (617) 783 - 4000
Fax:(617) 783 - 5152
TF: (800) 343 - 1395

Serves As:
- Chairman and Chief Exec. Officer, New Balance Athletic Shoe, Inc.

DAVIS, Jan L.
1815 Capitol Ave.
Omaha, NE 68102
jan.davis@aquila.com
Tel: (402) 221 - 2234
Fax:(402) 221 - 2601

Serves As:
- Director, Community Services, Aquila, Inc.

DAVIS, Janice
P.O. Box 1477
Baltimore, MD 21203
Tel: (410) 237 - 5971
Fax:(410) 237 - 5979

Serves As:
- Senior V. President, Corporate Communications, (Mercantile-Safe Deposit and Trust Co.), Mercantile Bankshares Corporation

DAVIS, Julie K.
305 Hartman Dr.
Lebanon, TN 37088
Tel: (615) 443 - 9266
Fax:(615) 443 - 9322

Serves As:
- Director, Corporate Communications, (Cracker Barrel Old Country Store, Inc.), CBRL Group, Inc.

DAVIS, Karen M.
P.O. Box 1059
Pawtucket, RI 02862
kdavis@hasbro.com
Tel: (401) 727 - 5429
Fax:(401) 431 - 8535

Serves As:
- Director, Hasbro Charitable Trust, Hasbro Inc.

DAVIS, Kristin
One Amgen Center Dr.
Thousand Oaks, CA 91320-1799
Tel: (805) 447 - 1000
Fax:(805) 447 - 1010

Serves As:
- Media Relations Contact, Amgen Inc.

DAVIS, Lizanne H.
1667 K St. NW
Suite 460
Washington, DC 20006
Tel: (202) 956 - 5200
Fax:(202) 956 - 5235

Registered Federal Lobbyist.
Serves As:
- Director, Government Affairs, FMC Corp.

DAVIS, Mark W.
1400 Douglas St.
Omaha, NE 68179
Tel: (402) 544 - 5459

Serves As:
- Regional Director, Public Relations, Union Pacific Corp.

DAVIS, Michele
3900 Wisconsin Ave. NW
Washington, DC 20016
Tel: (202) 752 - 7000
Fax:(202) 752 - 6099

Serves As:
- V. President, Regulatory Policy, Fannie Mae

DAVIS, Mike
19 N. Main St.
Wilkes-Barre, PA 18711-0302
Tel: (570) 200 - 6300

Serves As:
- Director, External Affairs, Blue Cross of Northeastern Pennsylvania

DAVIS, Nancy J.
1155 Peachtree St. NE
14K10 Campanile
Atlanta, GA 30309-3610
nancy.davis@bellsouth.com
Tel: (404) 249 - 3491
Fax:(404) 249 - 3839

Serves As:
- V. President, Investor Relations, BellSouth Corp.

DAVIS, Patricia
6705 Rockledge Dr.
Suite 100
Bethesda, MD 20817
Tel: (301) 581 - 0600
Fax:(301) 493 - 0705

Serves As:
- Chief Human Resources Officer, Coventry Health Care

DAVIS, Paula
153 E. 53rd St.
56th Floor
New York, NY 10022-4611
paula.davis@siemens.com
Tel: (212) 258 - 4260
Fax:(212) 767 - 0580
TF: (800) 743 - 6367

Serves As:
- Director, Public Relations, Siemens Corp.

DAVIS, R. Matthew
2030 Dow Center
Midland, MI 48674-0001
rmdavis@dow.com
Tel: (989) 636 - 1000
Fax:(989) 638 - 2359

Serves As:
- Public Affairs Director, Plastics, The Dow Chemical Company

DAVIS, R. Steven
1801 California St.
50th Floor
Denver, CO 80202
Tel: (303) 896 - 4200
Fax:(303) 291 - 1724
TF: (800) 899 - 7780

Serves As:
- Senior V. President, Policy and Law and Deputy General Counsel, Qwest Communications

Responsibilities include government affairs.

DAVIS, Robert G.
9800 Fredericksburg Rd.
San Antonio, TX 78288-0122
Tel: (210) 456 - 1800
Fax:(210) 498 - 9940

Serves As:
- Chairman, President and Chief Exec. Officer, United Services Automobile Ass'n (USAA)

DAVIS, Sara P.
901 E St. NW
Fourth Floor
Washington, DC 20004-2037
Tel: (202) 969 - 8020
Fax:(202) 969 - 8030

Registered Federal Lobbyist.
Serves As:
- Director, Government Relations, SLM Corp.

DAVIS, Scott
P.O. Box 53999
M/S 8376
Phoenix, AZ 85072-3999
scott.davis@pinnaclewest.com
Tel: (602) 250 - 3225
Fax:(602) 250 - 3872

Serves As:
- Leader, Environmental Health and Safety Department, Pinnacle West Capital Corp.

DAVIS, Sheila M.
P.O. Box 152
Forest City, IA 50436-0152
sdavis@winnebagoind.com
Tel: (641) 585 - 6803
Fax:(641) 585 - 6966

Serves As:
- Public Relations/Investor Relations Manager, Winnebago Industries, Inc.

DAVIS, Stacey
4000 Wisconsin Ave. NW
North Tower, Suite One
Washington, DC 20016-2804
Tel: (202) 274 - 8000
Fax:(202) 274 - 8111

Serves As:
- President and Chief Exec. Officer, Fannie Mae Foundation, Fannie Mae

DAVIS, Susan F.
5757 N. Green Bay Ave.
Milwaukee, WI 53201-0591
susan.davis@jci.com
Tel: (414) 524 - 2253
Fax:(414) 524 - 2077

Serves As:
- V. President, Human Resources, Johnson Controls, Inc.

DAVIS, Tabrina
P.O. Box 805379
Chicago, IL 60680-5379
tabrina.davis@exeloncorp.com
Tel: (312) 394 - 7919
Fax:(312) 394 - 8693

Serves As:
- Director, Communications, (ComEd), Exelon Corp.

DAVIS, III, Thomas
One Mercer Rd.
Natick, MA 01760
Tel: (508) 651 - 7400
Fax:(508) 651 - 6167
TF: (800) 257 - 2582

Serves As:
- Senior V. President and Director, Human Resources, BJ's Wholesale Club, Inc.

DAVIS, Tony
P.O. Box 4065
Monroe, LA 71211-4065
tony.davis@centurytel.com
Fax:(318) 388 - 9064
TF: (800) 833 - 1188

Serves As:
- V. President, Investor Relations, CenturyTel, Inc.

DAVIS, W. Derek
2208 S. Hamilton St.
Dalton, GA 30721
Tel: (706) 876 - 5804
Fax:(706) 876 - 5898
TF: (866) 606 - 7475

Serves As:
- V. President, Human Resources, The Dixie Group, Inc.

DAVISSON, Alice
One Reynolds Way
Kettering, OH 45430
alice_davisson@reyrey.com
Tel: (937) 485 - 8138
Fax:(937) 485 - 0941

Serves As:
- Administrator, Reynolds Family Company Foundation, Reynolds and Reynolds Co.

DAVLIN, James
Lilly Corporate Center
Indianapolis, IN 46285
Tel: (317) 276 - 2000
Fax:(317) 277 - 6579

Serves As:
- PAC Treasurer, Eli Lilly and Company

DAWSON, Kass
One Mercedes Dr.
Montvale, NJ 07645
Tel: (201) 573 - 0600
Fax:(201) 573 - 0117
TF: (800) 367 - 6372

Serves As:
- Community and Social Affairs, Mercedes-Benz USA, LLC

DAWSON, Walter
165 Madison Ave.
Memphis, TN 38103
Tel: (901) 523 - 4444

Serves As:
- Senior Communications Specialist, First Horizon Nat'l Corp.

DAY, Brenda T.
1401 H St. NW
Suite 700
Washington, DC 20005
Tel: (202) 414 - 6714
Fax:(202) 414 - 6743

Registered Federal Lobbyist.
Serves As:
- Director, Congressional Affairs, DaimlerChrysler Corp.

DAY, Chris
2001 Edmund Halley Dr.
Reston, VA 20191
Tel: (703) 433 - 4000

Registered Federal Lobbyist.
Serves As:
- Representative, Sprint Nextel

DAY, James C.
13135 S. Dairy Ashford
Suite 800
Sugar Land, TX 77478
Tel: (281) 276 - 6100
Fax:(281) 491 - 2092

Serves As:
- Chairman and Chief Exec. Officer, Noble Drilling Corp.

DAY, Kathy
1735 Market St.
Philadelphia, PA 19103
kathy_day@fmc.com
Tel: (215) 299 - 6000
Fax:(215) 299 - 6568

Serves As:
- Exec. Administrative Assistant, FMC Corp.

Responsibilities include corporate public affairs.

DAY, Tim
555 12th St. NW, Suite 610
Washington, DC 20004
Tel: (202) 347 - 6745
Fax:(202) 347 - 6884

Serves As:
- V. President, Government Affairs, PAC Treasurer, NCR Corporation

DAY, III, Walter R.
One Mellon Center
500 Grant St.
Room 2850
Pittsburgh, PA 15258-0001
day.wr@mellon.com
Tel: (412) 234 - 5930
Fax:(412) 236 - 5150

Registered Federal Lobbyist.
Serves As:
- Senior V. President, Government Affairs and Community Investment, Mellon Financial Corp.

DAYHOFF, Diane
2455 Paces Ferry Rd.
Atlanta, GA 30339-4024
diane_dayhoff@homedepot.com
Tel: (770) 384 - 2666
Fax:(770) 384 - 2356

Serves As:
- V. President, Investor Relations, The Home Depot, Inc.

DCAMP, Kate
170 W. Tasman Dr.
San Jose, CA 95134-1706
kdcamp@cisco.com
Tel: (408) 527 - 9530
Fax:(408) 526 - 4100
TF: (800) 553 - 6387

Serves As:
- Senior V. President, Human Resources, Cisco Systems, Inc.

DE CASTRIES, Henri
1290 Ave. of the Americas
New York, NY 10104
Tel: (212) 554 - 1234
TF: (888) AXA - INFO

Serves As:
- Chairman of the Board, AXA Financial, Inc.

DE CERVENS, Jeanne
1111 N. Charles St.
Baltimore, MD 21201
jdecervens@aegonusa.com
Tel: (410) 576 - 4529
Fax:(410) 374 - 8621

Serves As:
- Assistant General Counsel and Director, Government Relations, AEGON USA, Inc.

DE LA TORRE, Michael
P.O. Box 513249
Los Angeles, CA 90051-1249
Tel: (213) 244 - 2545
Fax:(213) 244 - 4997

Serves As:
- Governmental Affairs Manager, L.A. City and County, Southern California Gas Co.

DE LA VEGA, Robert
Wells Fargo Center
Sixth & Marquette
M/S N9305-171
Minneapolis, MN 55479
Tel: (612) 667 - 5051
Fax:(612) 667 - 9403

Serves As:
- Director, State Government Relations, Wells Fargo & Co.

DE LASKI, Kathleen
12061 Bluemont Way
Reston, VA 20190
Tel: (703) 810 - 3000
Fax:(703) 810 - 7053

Serves As:
- Senior V. President and Chief Communications Officer, SLM Corp.

DE LAUREAL, Martin
P.O. Box 19925
Metairie, LA 70179-0925
Tel: (504) 837 - 5880
Fax:(504) 849 - 2307
TF: (800) 535 - 6017

Serves As:
- V. President, Investor Relations, Stewart Enterprises, Inc.

DE LEON, Jack
111 Lord Dr.
Cary, NC 27511
Tel: (919) 468 - 5979
Fax:(919) 469 - 5777

Serves As:
- V. President, Marketing and Business Development, LORD Corporation

Reponsibilities include external affairs.

DE LEON, Rudy F.
1200 Wilson Blvd. Tel: (703) 465 - 3500
Arlington, VA 22209-2305
Registered Federal Lobbyist.
Serves As:
• Senior V. President, Washington DC Operations, The Boeing Co.

DE MASTERS, Darnell
122 C St. NW Tel: (202) 622 - 4340
Suite 840 Fax:(202) 622 - 4359
Washington, DC 20001
darnell.demasters@we-energies.com
Registered Federal Lobbyist.
Serves As:
• Assistant V. President, Federal Policy, Wisconsin Energy Corp.

DE RAISMES, Ann M.
Hartford Plaza Tel: (860) 547 - 5000
Hartford, CT 06115 Fax:(860) 547 - 3799
Serves As:
• Exec. V. President, Human Resources, The Hartford Financial Services Group Inc.

DE SOLLER, Marty Z.
29947 Avenida De Las Banderas Tel: (949) 546 - 2596
Rancho Santa Margarita, CA 92688
marty.zajic@cox.com
Serves As:
• V. President, Public Relations, Cox Enterprises, Inc.

DE STACY HARRISON, Patricia
401 Ninth St. NW Tel: (202) 879 - 9600
Washington, DC 20004-2129 Fax:(202) 879 - 9700
Serves As:
• President and Chief Exec. Officer, Corporation for Public Broadcasting

DE VANE, Natalie
500 Arcola Rd. Tel: (484) 865 - 5000
Collegeville, PA 19426
devanen@wyeth.com
Serves As:
• Senior Director, Public Relations, Wyeth Pharmaceuticals

DEA, Peter A.
1099 18th St. Tel: (303) 452 - 5603
Suite 1200 Fax:(303) 457 - 8482
Denver, CO 80202 TF: (800) 933 - 5603
Serves As:
• President and Chief Exec. Officer, Western Gas Resources, Inc.

DEAN, Allison
500 W. Monroe St. Tel: (312) 621 - 4274
Chicago, IL 60661 Fax:(312) 621 - 8062
TF: (800) 428 - 8161
Serves As:
• Community Affairs Specialist, GATX Corp.

DEAN, C. Fletcher
P.O. Box 511 Tel: (423) 229 - 3880
Kingsport, TN 37662-5075 Fax:(423) 229 - 1008
TF: (800) 327 - 8626
Serves As:
• Principal Communications Representative, Eastman Chemical Co.

DEAN, Julie A.
P.O. Box 13398 Tel: (919) 483 - 2839
Research Triangle Park, NC 27709 Fax:(919) 483 - 0327
Serves As:
• Director, Exec. Communications, GlaxoSmithKline Research and Development

DEANNA, Jennifer
601 Pennsylvania Ave. NW Tel: (202) 347 - 8420
Suite 350, North Bldg. Fax:(202) 347 - 8423
Washington, DC 20004-3613
deanna@dteenergy.com
Registered Federal Lobbyist.
Serves As:
• Legislative Assistant, (Detroit Edison), DTE Energy Co.

DEANS, Lawrence
1000 Beverly Way Tel: (479) 201 - 2000
Fort Smith, AR 72919-5273 Fax:(479) 201 - 1101
Serves As:
• Senior V. President, Human Resources, Beverly Enterprises, Inc.

DEASON, Darwin
2828 N. Haskell Ave. Tel: (214) 841 - 6111
Dallas, TX 75204
darwin.deason@acs-inc.com
Serves As:
• Chairman of the Board, Affiliated Computer Services, Inc. (ACS)

DEASY, Mark C.
P.O. Box 426 Tel: (412) 967 - 3357
Pittsburgh, PA 15230 Fax:(412) 967 - 3056
mark.deasy@msanet.com TF: (800) 672 - 2222
Serves As:
• Director, Public Relations and Strategic Communications, Mine Safety Appliances Co. (MSA)

DEATON, Chad C.
3900 Essex Ln., Suite 1200 Tel: (713) 439 - 8600
Houston, TX 77027-5177 Fax:(713) 439 - 8699
Serves As:
• Chairman and Chief Exec. Officer, Baker Hughes Inc.

DEATON, Kimberly A.
P.O. Box 430 Tel: (901) 528 - 4557
Memphis, TN 30103 Fax:(901) 528 - 4758
kdeaton@mlgw.org
Serves As:
• Senior Communications Specialist, Memphis Light, Gas and Water Division

DEBBANE, Raymond
175 Crossways Park West Tel: (516) 390 - 1400
Woodbury, NY 11797 Fax:(516) 390 - 1302
Serves As:
• Chairman of the Board, Weight Watchers Internat'l

DEBEAU, Lee
P.O. Box 64101 Tel: (651) 481 - 2222
St. Paul, MN 55164-0101 Fax:(651) 481 - 2000
lsdebeau@landolakes.com TF: (800) 328 - 4155
Serves As:
• Manager, Environmental Compliance, Land O'Lakes, Inc.

DEBLASI, Ugo
301 Merritt Seven Tel: (203) 840 - 2000
P.O. Box 5435 TF: (800) 761 - 5381
Norwalk, CT 06856-5435
Serves As:
• Exec. Director, Applera Charitable Foundation, Applera Corp.

DEBOER, Anne M.
P.O. Box 994 Tel: (989) 496 - 4000
Midland, MI 48686-0994 Fax:(989) 496 - 8240
anne.deboer@dowcorning.com
Serves As:
• Exec. Director, Foundation, Dow Corning Corp.

DEBRECENY, Peter
2775 Sanders Rd. Tel: (847) 402 - 3111
Northbrook, IL 60062-6127 Fax:(847) 326 - 7519
pdebreceny@allstate.com TF: (800) 574 - 3553
Serves As:
• V. President, Corporate Relations, Allstate Insurance Co.

DEBUCK, Donald
2100 E. Grand Ave. Tel: (310) 615 - 0311
El Segundo, CA 90245
Serves As:
• PAC Treasurer, Computer Sciences Corp.

DEBYL, Mary M.
P.O. Box 8050 Tel: (715) 422 - 3996
Wisconsin Rapids, WI 54495-8050
Serves As:
• Manager, Communications, Stora Enso North America

DECECCO, Dave
700 Anderson Hill Rd. Tel: (914) 253 - 2655
Purchase, NY 10577-1444 Fax:(914) 249 - 8202
Serves As:
• Public Relations, (Pepsi-Cola North America), PepsiCo, Inc.

DECHANTAL, RoJean
130 Royall St. Tel: (781) 737 - 5200
Canton, MA 02021 Fax:(781) 986 - 6987
Serves As:
• People Services Officer, Dunkin' Brands

DECHER, Kim
5314 S. Yale Dr. Tel: (918) 496 - 3244
Tulsa, OK 74135 Fax:(918) 496 - 3286
Serves As:
• Legislative Representative, Farmers Group, Inc.

DECHERD, Robert W.
P.O. Box 655237 Tel: (214) 977 - 6606
Dallas, TX 75265-5237 Fax:(214) 977 - 6603
Serves As:
• Chairman, President, and Chief Exec. Officer, Belo Corp.

DECHOW, Mary Jane Fair
P.O. Box 8700
Grand Rapids, MI 49518
mary_dechow@spartanstores.com
Tel: (616) 878 - 2469
Fax:(616) 878 - 8242

Serves As:
- Director, Government Relations, Spartan Stores Inc.

DECKER, Dwight W.
4000 MacArthur Blvd.
Newport Beach, CA 92660
Tel: (949) 483 - 4600

Serves As:
- Chairman and Chief Exec. Officer, Conexant Systems, Inc.

DECLUSIN, James E.
1000 SW Broadway
Suite 2200
Portland, OR 97205
Tel: (503) 223 - 9228
Fax:(503) 240 - 5232
TF: (800) 831 - 2187

Serves As:
- President and Chief Exec. Officer, Oregon Steel Mills Inc.

DECOURAY, Debra
38 Fountain Square
Cincinnati, OH 45263
Tel: (513) 579 - 4153
Fax:(513) 534 - 6701
TF: (800) 972 - 3030

Serves As:
- V. President, Corporate Communications, Fifth Third Bancorp.

DECROSTA, John
1667 K St. NW
Suite 400
Washington, DC 20006
Tel: (202) 331 - 1424
Fax:(202) 775 - 8427

Serves As:
- Director, Legislative Affairs, APL Americas

DECYK, Roxanne
P.O. Box 2463
Houston, TX 77252-2463
Tel: (713) 241 - 0780
Fax:(713) 241 - 1681

Serves As:
- Senior V. President, Corporate Affairs and Human Resources, Shell Oil Co.

DEDEO, Patrick
Three Penn Plaza East
PP-15V
Newark, NJ 07105-2200
Tel: (973) 466 - 8754
Fax:(973) 466 - 7077

Serves As:
- Senior Manager, Government Affairs, Horizon Blue Cross Blue Shield of New Jersey

DEDMAN, Jr., Robert H.
3030 LBJ Frwy.
Suite 700
Dallas, TX 75234
Tel: (972) 243 - 6191
Fax:(972) 888 - 7555

Serves As:
- Chairman of the Board, ClubCorp Internat'l Inc.

DEEGAN, Colleen A.
1015 15th St. NW
Suite 700
Washington, DC 20005-2605
Tel: (202) 828 - 5200
Fax:(202) 785 - 2645

Registered Federal Lobbyist.
Serves As:
- Manager, Government Programs, (Bechtel National, Inc.), Bechtel Group, Inc.

DEEHAN, William J.
77 Grove St.
Rutland, VT 05701
Tel: (800) 649 - 2877
Fax:(802) 747 - 2199
TF: (800) 649 - 2877

Serves As:
- V. President, Power Planning and Regulatory Affairs, Central Vermont Public Service Corp.

DEEKER, Dwight
4000 MacArthur Blvd.
Newport Beach, CA 92660
Tel: (949) 579 - 3000
Fax:(949) 579 - 3200

Serves As:
- Chairman of the Board, Mindspeed Technologies, Inc.

DEES, David
225 W. Washington St.
Chicago, IL 60606-3418
Tel: (312) 845 - 5343
Fax:(312) 372 - 2808

Serves As:
- Director, Communications, The Marmon Group, Inc.

DEESE, George E.
1919 Flowers Circle
Thomasville, GA 31757
Tel: (229) 226 - 9110
Fax:(229) 225 - 3806

Serves As:
- President and Chief Exec. Officer, Flowers Foods

DEFEO, Ronald M.
500 Post Rd. East
Suite 320
Westport, CT 06880
Tel: (203) 222 - 5902
Fax:(203) 226 - 2303

Serves As:
- Chairman and Chief Exec. Officer, Terex Corp.

DEFILIPPIS, Victor
One Owens Corning Pkwy.
Toledo, OH 43659
Tel: (419) 248 - 8000
Fax:(419) 248 - 6227
TF: (800) 438 - 7465

Serves As:
- PAC Treasurer, Owens Corning

DEFILLIPPO, Bob
751 Broad St.
12th Floor
Newark, NJ 07102-3777
Bob.DeFillippo@prudential.com
Tel: (973) 802 - 4149
Fax:(973) 802 - 9443
TF: (800) THE - ROCK

Serves As:
- Chief Communications Officer, Prudential Financial

DEFOE, Donald H.
600 S. Second St., Suite 101
Springfield, IL 62704
Tel: (217) 753 - 8050
Fax:(217) 753 - 3618

Serves As:
- Manager, State Governmental Affairs, Caterpillar Inc.

DEFOSSET, Don
4211 W. Boyscout Blvd.
Tampa, FL 33607
ddefosset@walterind.com
Tel: (813) 871 - 4811
Fax:(813) 871 - 4420

Serves As:
- Chairman, President, and Chief Exec. Officer, Walter Industries, Inc.

DEGGENDORFT, Michael
P.O. Box 418679
Kansas City, MO 64141-9679
Tel: (816) 556 - 2200
Fax:(816) 556 - 2975

Serves As:
- V. President, Public Affairs, Great Plains Energy, Inc.

DEGIORGIO, Kenneth
One First American Way
Santa Ana, CA 92707
Tel: (714) 800 - 3000
Fax:(714) 800 - 4790

Serves As:
- Senior V. President and General Counsel; PAC Treasurer, The First American Corp.

DEGIUSTI, Paul
1200 G St. NW
Suite 900
Washington, DC 20005-3802
Tel: (202) 383 - 3702
Fax:(202) 383 - 3718

Registered Federal Lobbyist.
Serves As:
- Director, Government Affairs, The McGraw-Hill Companies, Inc.

DEGRAFFENREIDT, Jr., James H.
101 Constitution Ave. NW
Washington, DC 20080
Tel: (703) 750 - 2000
Fax:(703) 750 - 4574

Serves As:
- Chairman and Chief Exec. Officer, Washington Gas

DEITCH, Penny
One Campus Martius
Detroit, MI 48226
Tel: (313) 227 - 7883
Fax:(313) 227 - 7555
TF: (800) 292 - 7432

Serves As:
- Contact, Diversity and Community Relations, Compuware Corp.

DEJESU, Thomas
175 E. Old Country Rd.
Hicksville, NY 11801
Tel: (516) 545 - 4449

Serves As:
- Director, Government and Regulatory Relations, (KeySpan Services, Inc.), KeySpan Corp.

DEKKERS, Marijn E.
81 Wyman St.
Waltham, MA 02454-9046
Tel: (781) 622 - 1000
Fax:(781) 622 - 1207

Serves As:
- President and Chief Exec. Officer, Thermo Electron Corp.

DEL REGNO, Nancy
P.O. Box 655237
Dallas, TX 75265-5237
ndelregno@belo.com
Tel: (214) 977 - 6606
Fax:(214) 977 - 7051

Serves As:
- Manager, Corporate Communications and Investor Relations, Belo Corp.

DELANEY, Justin
P.O. Box 711
Portland, OR 97207
Tel: (503) 321 - 8541
Fax:(503) 478 - 5243

Serves As:
• Contact, Standard Insurance Co. PAC, Standard Insurance Co.

DELANEY, Katy
505 King Ave.
Columbus, OH 43201-2693
delaneyk@battelle.org
Tel: (410) 306 - 8638

Serves As:
• Manager, National Media Relations, Battelle

DELANEY, Keenan
2828 N. Haskell Ave.
Dallas, TX 75204
Tel: (214) 841 - 6111

Serves As:
• V. President, Public Affairs, Affiliated Computer Services, Inc. (ACS)

DELANEY, Terrence P.
Ten Penn Center
1801 Market St.
Philadelphia, PA 19103-1699
Tel: (215) 977 - 6106
Fax:(215) 977 - 3409

Serves As:
• V. President, Investor Relations and Planning, Sunoco, Inc.

DELCASINO, Michael
1120 20th St. NW
Suite 1000
Washington, DC 20036-3406
Tel: (202) 457 - 3810
Fax:(202) 457 - 2008

Serves As:
• V. President, Federal Regulatory Affairs, AT&T

DELEHANTY, Martha
1095 Ave. of the Americas
New York, NY 10036
Tel: (212) 395 - 2121
Fax:(212) 869 - 3265

Serves As:
• V. President, Human Resources, Verizon Wireless

DELEON, Martin
P.O. Box 4607
Houston, TX 77210-4607
martin.deleon@coair.com
Tel: (713) 324 - 5000
Fax:(713) 324 - 2087

Serves As:
• Manager, Public Relations, Continental Airlines

DELIETO, Doug
7628 Thorndike Rd.
Greensboro, NC 27409-9421
investor@rfmd.com
Tel: (336) 664 - 1233
Fax:(336) 931 - 7454

Serves As:
• V. President, Investor Relations, RF Micro Devices, Inc.

DELINE, Donald A.
1150 18th St. NW, Suite 200
Washington, DC 20036
Tel: (202) 223 - 0820
Fax:(202) 223 - 2385

Serves As:
• V. President, Government Affairs, Kellogg Brown and Root

DELISI, Rick
45200 Business Ct.
Suite 100
Dulles, VA 20166-6715
mediarelations@flyi.com
Tel: (703) 650 - 6019
Fax:(703) 650 - 6299

Serves As:
• Director, Corporate Communications, FLYi, Inc.

DELL, Michael S.
One Dell Way
Round Rock, TX 78682
Tel: (512) 338 - 4400
Fax:(512) 728 - 3653
TF: (800) 289 - 3355

Serves As:
• Chairman of the Board, Dell Inc.

DELL'OMO, Molly S.
800 N. Brand Blvd.
Glendale, CA 91203
molly.dellomo@us.nestle.com
Tel: (818) 549 - 6136
Fax:(818) 549 - 5884
TF: (800) 225 - 2270

Serves As:
• Director, Corporate and Brand Affairs, Nestle USA, Inc.

DELLA CORTE, Robert
48 Monroe Tpk.
Trumbull, CT 06611
Tel: (203) 459 - 6000
Fax:(203) 851 - 2464
TF: (800) 889 - 7658

Serves As:
• PAC Treasurer, Oxford Health Plans Inc.

DELLAMARIA, Matt
475 W. Terra Cotta Ave.
Suite E
Crystal Lake, IL 60014-9695
Tel: (815) 477 - 0424
Fax:(815) 477 - 0481

Serves As:
• Director, Corporate Communications, AptarGroup, Inc.

DELLAPENTA, Jennifer
4101 Washington Ave.
Newport News, VA 23607-2770
jennifer.dellapenta@ngc.com
Tel: (757) 380 - 3558
Fax:(757) 380 - 3867

Serves As:
• Senior Communications Specialist, Northrop Grumman Newport News

DELLINGER, Kent
1001 G St., NW
Suite 950
Washington, DC 20001
kent_dellinger@hna.honda.com
Tel: (202) 661 - 4400
Fax:(202) 661 - 4459

Serves As:
• Manager, Government Relations, (Honda North America, Inc.), American Honda Motor Co., Inc.

DELLY, Gayla J.
3000 Technology Dr.
Angleton, TX 77515
gayla.delly@bench.com
Tel: (979) 849 - 6550
Ext: 1304
Fax:(979) 848 - 5270

Serves As:
• Exec. V. President, Chief Financial Officer and Treasurer, Benchmark Electronics
Responsibilities include investor relations.

DELOACH, Jr., Harris E.
P.O. Box 160
Hartsville, SC 29551-0160
Tel: (843) 383 - 7000
Fax:(843) 383 - 7478

Serves As:
• Chairman of the Board, President and Chief Exec. Officer, Sonoco Products Co.

DEMARA, Paul
985 Jolly Rd.
Blue Bell, PA 19422-0900
pdemara@henkels.com
Tel: (215) 283 - 7578
Fax:(215) 283 - 7659

Serves As:
• Manager, Corporate Communications and Marketing, Henkels & McCoy, Inc.
Responsibilities include media relations.

DEMARIA, Benedict
P.O. Box 426
Pittsburgh, PA 15230
Tel: (412) 967 - 3109
Fax:(412) 967 - 3056
TF: (800) 672 - 2222

Serves As:
• V. President, Human Resources and Corporate Communications, Mine Safety Appliances Co. (MSA)

DEMAYO, Carole
One Symbol Plaza
Holtsville, NY 11742-1300
Tel: (631) 738 - 2400
Fax:(631) 738 - 5990
TF: (800) 722 - 6234

Serves As:
• Senior V. President, Global Human Resources, Symbol Technologies, Inc.

DEMBECK, Allison L.
1300 I St. NW
Suite 420 East
Washington, DC 20005
Tel: (202) 789 - 6524
Fax:(202) 789 - 6593
Registered Federal Lobbyist.
Serves As:
• Manager, Government Relations, Ceridian Corp.

DEMERS, Cynthia A.
15501 N. Dial Blvd.
Suite 2160
Scottsdale, AZ 85260
demers@dialcorp.com
Tel: (480) 754 - 4090
Fax:(480) 754 - 8003

Serves As:
• V. President, Corporate and Government Affairs, The Dial Corporation
Responsibilities include corporate philanthropy.

DEMING, Claiborne P.
P.O. Box 7000
El Dorado, AR 71731-7000
Tel: (870) 862 - 6411
Fax:(870) 864 - 6373

Serves As:
• President and Chief Exec. Officer, Murphy Oil Corp.

DEMING, John L.
1825 I St., N.W., Suite 400
Washington, DC 20006
john.deming@cibasc.com
Tel: (202) 857 - 5200
Fax:(202) 857 - 5219
Registered Federal Lobbyist.
Serves As:
• V. President, Government Relations, Ciba Specialty Chemicals

DEMITO, Patti
1499 Post Rd.
Fairfield, CT 06824
Tel: (203) 319 - 4700
Fax:(203) 319 - 4701

Serves As:
- V. President, Global Human Resources, IMS Health, Inc.

DEMLER, Karin
10 Burton Hills Blvd.
Nashville, TN 37215
karin.demler@correctionscorp.com
Tel: (615) 263 - 3005
Fax:(615) 263 - 3140
TF: (800) 624 - 2931

Serves As:
- Director, Investor Relations, Corrections Corp. of America

DEMO, Murray
345 Park Ave.
San Jose, CA 95110-2704
Tel: (408) 536 - 6000
Fax:(408) 537 - 6000

Serves As:
- Senior V. President and Chief Financial Officer, Adobe Systems Inc.

Responsibilities include investor relations.

DEMOULAS, T. A.
286 Chelmsford St.
Chelmsford, MA 01824
Tel: (978) 851 - 8000
Fax:(978) 851 - 3942

Serves As:
- Foundation Contact, Demoulas Market Basket

DEMPSEY, Brenda
Strawberry Lane
Orrville, OH 44667-0280
Tel: (330) 682 - 3000
Fax:(330) 684 - 6410
TF: (888) 550 - 9555

Serves As:
- Director, Corporate Communications, The J. M. Smucker Company

DEMPSEY, Mary E.
47 State Circle, Suite 403
Annapolis, MD 21401
mary.e.dempsey@constellation.com
Tel: (410) 269 - 5283
Fax:(410) 269 - 5288
TF: (888) 460 - 2002

Serves As:
- Manager, Public Affairs, Constellation Energy

DEMPSEY, Maureen
200 Park Ave.
New York, NY 10166
dempsey.m@dreyfus.com
Tel: (212) 922 - 6648
Fax:(212) 922 - 6585

Serves As:
- Communications Specialist, The Dreyfus Corp.

DENDLE, Phyllis J. Baumwell
1441 Kapiolani Blvd., 17th Floor
Honolulu, HI 96814-4407
Tel: (808) 983 - 4981

Serves As:
- Director, Government Affairs, Kaiser Permanente

DENHAM, Benny
P.O. Box 1349
Tucker, GA 30085-1349
Tel: (770) 270 - 7600
Fax:(770) 270 - 7872
TF: (800) 241 - 5374

Serves As:
- Chairman of the Board, Oglethorpe Power Corp.

DENHAM, Robert
127 W. Webster St.
Whiteville, NC 28472
Tel: (910) 914 - 9073

Serves As:
- Senior V. President, Public Relations, BB&T Corp.

DENNEY, Cindy L.
9450 Seward Rd.
Fairfield, OH 45014
cindy.denney@ocas.com
Tel: (513) 603 - 2074
Fax:(513) 609 - 7900
TF: (800) 843 - 6446

Serves As:
- Assistant V. President, Corporate Communications, The Ohio Casualty Group

DENTON, Lawrence A.
2791 Research Dr.
Rochester Hills, MI 48309-3575
Tel: (248) 299 - 7500
Fax:(248) 299 - 7501

Serves As:
- President and Chief Exec. Officer, Dura Automotive Systems, Inc.

DEOL, Jasprit
1250 H St. NW
Suite 800
Washington, DC 20005
jasprit.deol@kodak.com
Tel: (202) 857 - 3400
Fax:(202) 857 - 3401

Serves As:
- Director, Technology Policy, Eastman Kodak Company

DERBY, Deborah M.
One Geoffrey Way
Wayne, NJ 07470-2030
Tel: (973) 617 - 3500

Serves As:
- Exec. V. President, Human Resources, Toys "R" Us, Inc.

DEREMO, Mark
2801 E. Beltline NE
Grand Rapids, MI 49525
maderemo@ufpi.com
Tel: (616) 364 - 6161
Fax:(616) 364 - 5558

Serves As:
- Director, Marketing Communications, Universal Forest Products, Inc.

DERGE, M. Jennie
800 Connecticut Ave. NW
Suite 600
Washington, DC 20006
Tel: (202) 533 - 1100
Fax:(202) 533 - 1134

Registered Federal Lobbyist.
Serves As:
- Representative, Accenture

DERING, Jeanne
99 Church St.
New York, NY 10007-2707
Tel: (212) 553 - 0300
Fax:(212) 553 - 4820

Serves As:
- Exec. V. President, Global Regulatory Affairs and Compliance, Moody's Corp.

DERN, John
World Headquarters
100 N. Riverside
Chicago, IL 60606-1596
Tel: (312) 544 - 2002
Fax:(312) 544 - 2082

Serves As:
- V. President, Media Relations, The Boeing Co.

DEROMEDI, Roger K.
Three Lakes Dr.
Northfield, IL 60093-2753
Tel: (847) 646 - 2000
Fax:(847) 646 - 6005

Serves As:
- Chief Exec. Officer, Kraft Foods, Inc.

DERRICK, Debi
P.O. Box 2951
Beaumont, TX 77704
Tel: (409) 838 - 6631

Serves As:
- Communications Specialist, Entergy Texas

DERRICO, Blaise
3250 Interstate Dr.
Richfield, OH 44286
bderrico@intlsteel.com
Tel: (330) 659 - 7430
Fax:(330) 659 - 9135

Serves As:
- Manager, Investor Relations, Internat'l Steel Group Inc.

DES CHAMPS, Steve
6601 Bermuda Rd.
Las Vegas, NV 89119-3605
Tel: (702) 270 - 7600
Fax:(702) 270 - 7679

Serves As:
- Senior V. President and Chief Financial Officer, Alliance Gaming Corp.

Responsibilities include investor and media relations.

DESABATO, Anthony A.
450 Winks Ln.
Bensalem, PA 19020
Tel: (215) 638 - 6636
Fax:(215) 638 - 6759

Serves As:
- Exec. V. President, Corporate and Labor Relations, Charming Shoppes, Inc.

DESANCTIS, Ellen R.
717 Texas Ave.
Suite 2100
Houston, TX 77002-2712
edesanctis@br-inc.com
Tel: (713) 624 - 9256
Fax:(713) 624 - 9645
TF: (800) 262 - 3456

Serves As:
- V. President, Investor Relations and Corporate Communications, Burlington Resources Inc.

DESANTA, Richard P.
Two Paragon Dr.
Montvale, NJ 07645
Tel: (201) 571 - 4495
Fax:(201) 571 - 8719

Serves As:
- V. President, Corporate Affairs, The Great Atlantic and Pacific Tea Co.

DESANTI, Frederick D.
80 Park Plaza
M/S T4A
Newark, NJ 07102-0570
frederick.desanti@pseg.com
Tel: (973) 430 - 6400
Fax:(973) 242 - 0741

Serves As:
- V. President, State Government Affairs PSE&G, PSE&G

DESCHENES, Elise
701 Pennsylvania Ave. NW
Suite 500
Washington, DC 20004
elise.deschenes@astrazeneca.com
Tel: (202) 350 - 5572
Fax:(202) 350 - 5510

Registered Federal Lobbyist.
Serves As:
- Senior Manager, Federal Government Affairs, AstraZeneca Pharmaceuticals

DESETA, Anne
601 13th St. NW
Suite 200 North
Washington, DC 20005
desetaa@basf-corp.com
Tel: (202) 414 - 6340
Fax:(202) 682 - 9459

Registered Federal Lobbyist.
Serves As:
- Manager, Grassroots Program, BASF Corporation

DESIMONE, Audrey
P.O. Box 1059
Pawtucket, RI 02862
adesimone@hasbro.com
Tel: (401) 727 - 5857
Fax:(401) 431 - 8535

Serves As:
- Manager, Corporate Communications, Hasbro Inc.

DESIMONE, Jim
P.O. Box 593330
Orlando, FL 32859
Tel: (407) 245 - 4567
Fax:(407) 245 - 4462

Serves As:
- V. President, Media and Communications, Darden Restaurants, Inc.

DESMARIS, Mr. Thierry
Perryville Corporate Park
Clinton, NJ 08809-4000
Tel: (908) 730 - 4000
Fax:(908) 730 - 5315

Serves As:
- PAC Treasurer, Foster Wheeler Ltd.

DESMOND, Carrie E.
901 D St. SW
Suite 900
Washington, DC 20024
Tel: (202) 646 - 5255
Fax:(202) 646 - 5271

Registered Federal Lobbyist.
Serves As:
- Assistant Director, Congressional Affairs, Battelle

DESMOND, James M.
1550 Crystal Dr.
Crystal Square 2, Suite 300
Arlington, VA 22202
Tel: (703) 413 - 5721
Fax:(703) 413 - 5846

Registered Federal Lobbyist.
Serves As:
- V. President, Energy Sector Legislation, Lockheed Martin Corp.

DESONIER, David M.
P.O. Box 757
Carthage, MO 64836-0757
david.desonier@leggett.com
Tel: (417) 358 - 8131
Ext: 2363
Fax:(417) 359 - 5114

Serves As:
- V. President, Investor Relations, Leggett & Platt, Inc.

DESPAIN, Cory
21630 Ridgetop Circle
Suite 130
Dulles, VA 20166
Tel: (703) 433 - 6200

Serves As:
- V. President, Operations, Toll Brothers, Inc.
Responsibilities include government affairs.

DESPREZ, III, John D.
P.O. Box 111
Boston, MA 02117
Tel: (617) 572 - 6000

Serves As:
- President and Chief Exec. Officer, John Hancock Financial Services

DETLEFTS, Suzanne
1000 Alderman Dr.
Alpharetta, GA 30005-4101
Tel: (770) 752 - 6000
Fax:(770) 752 - 5939

Serves As:
- Chief People Officer, ChoicePoint Inc.

DETMER, Kyra L.
1399 New York Ave. NW
Suite 900
Washington, DC 20005
Tel: (202) 585 - 5800
Fax:(202) 585 - 5820

Registered Federal Lobbyist.
Serves As:
- Director, Federal Government Affairs, American Internat'l Group, Inc.

DETOY, Jennifer
345 Encinal St.
Santa Cruz, CA 95060
jennifer.detoy@plantronics.com
Tel: (831) 426 - 5858
Ext: 7400
Fax:(831) 426 - 0136
TF: (800) 544 - 4660

Serves As:
- Manager, Community Relations, Plantronics, Inc.
Responsibilities include corporate philanthropy.

DETRICK, Edwin J.
One Liberty Pl.
1650 Market St.
Philadelphia, PA 19192
edwin.detrick@cigna.com
Tel: (215) 761 - 1414

Serves As:
- V. President, Investor Relations, CIGNA Corp.

DEUTERMAN, Pamela
840 First St. NE
Washington, DC 20002
Tel: (202) 479 - 8000
Fax:(202) 479 - 8323

Serves As:
- V. President, Federal Programs, CareFirst BlueCross and BlueShield

DEUTSCH, Ben
P.O. Box 1734
Atlanta, GA 30301
Tel: (404) 676 - 2121
Fax:(404) 676 - 6428

Serves As:
- Director, Financial Communications, The Coca-Cola Co.

DEVARD, Jerri
1095 Ave. of the Americas
New York, NY 10036
Tel: (212) 395 - 2121
TF: (800) 621 - 9900

Serves As:
- Senior V. President, Brand Management and Marketing Communications, Verizon Communications Inc.

DEVINE, Brian K.
9125 Rehco Rd.
San Diego, CA 92121-2270
Tel: (858) 453 - 7845
Fax:(858) 677 - 3489

Serves As:
- Chairman of the Board, PETCO Animal Supplies, Inc.

DEVINE, Carol A.
680 N. Lake Shore Dr.
Chicago, IL 60611
Tel: (312) 373 - 2040
Fax:(312) 642 - 5592

Serves As:
- Senior V. President, Human Resources, Playboy Enterprises, Inc.

DEVINE, William H.
1121 L St., Suite 801
Sacramento, CA 95814
bdevine@att.com
Tel: (916) 448 - 2853
Fax:(916) 443 - 6021

Serves As:
- State Director, Government Affairs, AT&T

DEVOS, Doug
7575 Fulton St. East
Ada, MI 49355-0001
Tel: (616) 787 - 6000
Fax:(616) 787 - 6177

Serves As:
- President, Alticor Inc.

DEVROY, Neil J.
P.O. Box 199000
Dallas, TX 75219-9000
ndevroy@centex.com
Tel: (214) 981 - 6154
Fax:(214) 981 - 6859

Serves As:
- V. President, Corporate Communications and Public Affairs, Centex Corporation

DEWALT, Michael
100 NE Adams St.
Peoria, IL 61629-1465
Tel: (309) 675 - 1000
Fax:(309) 675 - 6155

Serves As:
- Director, Investor Relations, Caterpillar Inc.

DEWEY, Jr., Robert M.
55 Technology Way
West Greenwich, RI 02817
Tel: (401) 392 - 1000
Fax:(401) 392 - 1234

Serves As:
- Chairman of the Board, GTECH Corp.

DEYO, Russell C.
One Johnson & Johnson Plaza
New Brunswick, NJ 08933-7204
rdeyo@corus.jnj.com
Tel: (732) 524 - 0400
Ext: 2440
Fax:(732) 214 - 0334
TF: (800) 635 - 6789

Serves As:
- V. President, General Counsel, Johnson & Johnson
Responsibilities include corporate philanthropy.

DEYOUNG, Caitlin
801 Cherry St.
Suite 3900
Fort Worth, TX 76102-6803
Tel: (817) 302 - 7394
Fax:(817) 302 - 7479
TF: (800) 644 - 2297

Serves As:
• V. President, Investor Relations, AmeriCredit Corp.

DEYOUNG, Patty
P.O. Box 593330
Orlando, FL 32859
pdeyoung@darden.com
Tel: (407) 245 - 5213
Fax:(407) 245 - 4310

Serves As:
• Representative, Foundation/Community Affairs, Darden Restaurants, Inc.

DI GIORGIO, Mark
1295 State St.
Springfield, MA 01111-0001
Tel: (413) 744 - 7722
Fax:(413) 744 - 6005
TF: (800) 767 - 1000

Serves As:
• Media Contact, MassMutual Financial Group

DI RE, Cheryl
P.O. Box 834
WMT 1213
Seattle, WA 98101
Tel: (206) 461 - 3465
Fax:(206) 554 - 4807
TF: (800) 756 - 8000

Serves As:
• First V. President and Manager, Community Affairs, Washington Mutual, Inc.
Responsibilities include corporate philanthropy.

DIAMOND, Bruce W.
401 River Oaks Pkwy.
San Jose, CA 95134
Tel: (408) 577 - 6200
Fax:(408) 577 - 6620

Serves As:
• President and Chief Exec. Officer, WJ Communications

DIAMOND, Henry A.
Nine W. 57th St.
37th Floor
New York, NY 10019
Tel: (212) 413 - 1920

Serves As:
• V. President, Investor Relations, Cendant Corp.

DIAMOND, Marika
15300 Centennial Dr.
Northville, MI 48168
Tel: (734) 737 - 5162
Fax:(734) 737 - 2198

Serves As:
• Director, Public Relations and Communications, Hayes Lemmerz Internat'l, Inc.
Responsibilities include corporate philanthropy and investor relations.

DIAMOND, Michael L.
P.O. Box 10529
Greensboro, NC 27404-0529
Tel: (336) 335 - 7000
Fax:(336) 335 - 7550
TF: (888) 278 - 1133

Serves As:
• PAC Treasurer, Lorillard Tobacco Co.

DIAZ, Anthony J.
300 Tower Pkwy.
Lincolnshire, IL 60069
tony_diaz@fortunebrands.com
Tel: (847) 484 - 4400
Fax:(847) 484 - 4497

Serves As:
• V. President, Investor Relations, Fortune Brands, Inc.

DIAZ, Paul J.
680 S. Fourth Ave.
Louisville, KY 40202-2412
Tel: (502) 596 - 7300
Fax:(502) 596 - 4099

Serves As:
• President and Chief Exec. Officer, Kindred Healthcare, Inc.

DIBELLA, Elfi
41 S. High St.
Columbus, OH 43287
Tel: (614) 480 - 4483
Fax:(614) 480 - 4973

Serves As:
• Senior V. President, Community Affairs, Huntington Bancshares Inc.
Responsibilities include corporate philanthropy.

DICAMILLO, LaDonna V.
3770 E. 26th St.
Los Angeles, CA 90023-4506
ladonna.dicamillo@bnsf.com
Tel: (323) 267 - 4041
Fax:(909) 946 - 0490

Serves As:
• Director, Government Affairs, Burlington Northern Santa Fe Corporation

DICK, Erin
P.O. Box 482
Fort Worth, TX 76101
edick@bellhelicopter.textron.com
Tel: (817) 280 - 8416
Fax:(817) 280 - 2321

Serves As:
• Press Contact, Bell Helicopter Textron

DICKE, II, James F.
44 S. Washington St.
New Bremen, OH 45869
Tel: (419) 629 - 2311
Fax:(419) 629 - 3796

Serves As:
• Chairman and Chief Exec. Officer, Crown Equipment Corp.

DICKENS, Kim L.
1415 W. 22nd St.
Suite 1100
Oak Brook, IL 60523
Tel: (630) 954 - 2000

Serves As:
• V. President, Human Resources, Federal Signal Corp.

DICKERSON, Amina
Three Lakes Dr.
Northfield, IL 60093-2753
adickerson@kraft.com
Tel: (847) 646 - 3332
Fax:(847) 646 - 6005

Serves As:
• Director, Corporate Contributions, Kraft Foods, Inc.

DICKERSON, Mike
2100 E. Grand Ave.
El Segundo, CA 90245
mdickers@csc.com
Tel: (310) 615 - 1647
Fax:(310) 615 - 1699

Serves As:
• Director, Corporate Communications, Computer Sciences Corp.

DICKEY, Ann S.
101 Constitution Ave., NW
Suite 801 East
Washington, DC 20001
Tel: (202) 218 - 3800

Registered Federal Lobbyist.
Serves As:
• Representative, FedEx Corp.

DICKEY, Ayla
4615 E. Elwood St.
Phoenix, AZ 85040-1958
ayla.dickey@apollogrp.edu
Tel: (480) 966 - 5394
Ext: 2952
Fax:(480) 379 - 3503
TF: (800) 990 - APOL

Serves As:
• Associate V. President, Public Relations, Apollo Group, Inc.

DICKOFF, Gil
100 First Stamford Pl.
Stamford, CT 06902
gdickoff@craneco.com
Tel: (203) 363 - 7277
Fax:(203) 363 - 7295

Serves As:
• Treasurer, Crane Foundation, Crane Co.

DICKSON, Alan T.
301 S. Tryon St., Suite 1800
Charlotte, NC 28202
Tel: (704) 372 - 5404
Fax:(704) 372 - 6409

Serves As:
• Chairman of the Board, Ruddick Corp.

DICKSON, Dave
DWF Airport Station, P.O. Box 619100
Dallas, TX 75261-9100
ddickson@kcc.com
Tel: (972) 281 - 1481
Fax:(972) 281 - 1490
TF: (800) 639 - 1352

Serves As:
• Corporate Communications Contact, Kimberly-Clark Corp.

DICKSON, John T.
1110 American Parkway NE
Allentown, PA 18109-3229
Tel: (610) 712 - 4323
Fax:(610) 712 - 4106

Serves As:
• President and Chief Exec. Officer, Agere Systems Inc.

DICKSON, Thomas W.
301 S. Tryon St., Suite 1800
Charlotte, NC 28202
Tel: (704) 372 - 5404
Fax:(704) 372 - 6409

Serves As:
• President and Chief Exec. Officer, Ruddick Corp.

DIEDERICH, Tom
2170 Piedmont Road, N.E.
Atlanta, GA 30324
Tel: (404) 888 - 2874

Serves As:
• V. President, Government Relations, Rollins, Inc.

DIEM, Ruth
959 Eighth Ave.
New York, NY 10019
Tel: (212) 649 - 2000
Fax:(212) 765 - 3528

Serves As:
• Senior V. President, Human Resources, The Hearst Corp.

DIETLER, Cortlandt S.
P.O. Box 5660
Denver, CO 80217
cdietler@transmontaigne.com
Tel: (303) 626 - 8200
Fax:(303) 626 - 8228

Serves As:
- Chairman of the Board, TransMontaigne, Inc.

DIETRICH, Mark M.
One Pierce Place
Suite 1500
Itasca, IL 60143
Tel: (630) 875 - 7226
Fax:(630) 875 - 7388

Serves As:
- Exec. V. President and Chief Operating Officer; PAC Treasurer, First Midwest Bancorp, Inc.

DIETZ, Cindy
400 Collins Rd. NE
Cedar Rapids, IA 52498
Tel: (319) 295 - 7444
Fax:(319) 295 - 9374

Serves As:
- Manager, Community Relations, Rockwell Collins, Inc

DIETZ, Katherine M.
One Riverfront Plaza
Corning, NY 14831-0001
dietzkm@corning.com
Tel: (607) 974 - 8217
Fax:(607) 974 - 8551

Serves As:
- V. President, Investor Relations, Corning Incorporated

DIFELICE, Nicola
750 W. Center St.
West Bridgewater, MA 02379
Tel: (508) 313 - 4000
Fax:(508) 313 - 3112

Serves As:
- President and Chief Exec. Officer, Shaw's Supermarkets, Inc.

DIFRAIA, Alice
55 Inverness Dr. East
Englewood, CO 80112-5498
alice.difraia@jeppesen.com
Tel: (303) 799 - 9090
Fax:(303) 784 - 4121

Serves As:
- Director, Human Resources, Jeppesen

DIFRANCO, Stephen
500 McCarthy Blvd.
Milpitas, CA 95035
Tel: (408) 894 - 5000
Fax:(408) 952 - 3600
TF: (800) 262 - 9867

Serves As:
- Corporate Contributions Contact, Maxtor Corp.

DIGLORIA, Karen
One Ocean Spray Dr.
Lakeville-Middleboro, MA 02349
kdigloria@oceanspray.com
Tel: (508) 946 - 1000
Fax:(508) 946 - 7704
TF: (800) 662 - 3263

Serves As:
- PAC Treasurer, Ocean Spray Cranberries, Inc.

DILAPI, Christine
1350 I St. NW
Suite 400
Washington, DC 20005-3306
Tel: (202) 371 - 6900
Fax:(202) 842 - 3578

Serves As:
- Senior Staff Engineer, Spectrum and Standards, Motorola, Inc.

DILDINE, Steven M.
2511 Garden Rd.
Monterey, CA 93940-5330
mdildine@centuryca.com
Tel: (831) 642 - 9364
Fax:(831) 642 - 9328
TF: (888) 642 - 9300

Serves As:
- Director, Corporate Communications, Century Aluminum Co.

Responsibilities include investor relations.

DILDY, Marshall L.
100 Dunbar St.
Spartanburg, SC 29306
Tel: (864) 573 - 1600
Fax:(864) 573 - 1695

Serves As:
- V. President, Human Resources, Extended Stay America, Inc.

DILEO, Mary
2200 Renaissance Blvd., Suite 200
Gulph Mills, PA 19406-2755
mary.dileo@henkel.com
Tel: (610) 571 - 5252
Fax:(610) 270 - 8104

Serves As:
- Corporate Communications Contact, Henkel Corp.

DILL, Julie
P.O. Box 1244
EC3XK
Charlotte, NC 28201-1244
jadill@duke-energy.com
Tel: (704) 382 - 4332
Fax:(704) 382 - 3588

Serves As:
- V. President, Investor Relations, Duke Energy Corp.

DILLAHUNTY, James M.
985 Jolly Rd.
Blue Bell, PA 19422-0900
Tel: (909) 451 - 2500
Fax:(909) 451 - 2590

Serves As:
- V. President, International, Henkels & McCoy, Inc.

DILLARD, J. Richard
920 Milliken Rd.
M-285
Spartanburg, SC 29304
richard_dillard@milliken.com
Tel: (864) 503 - 2546
Fax:(864) 503 - 2100

Serves As:
- Director, Public Affairs, Milliken & Co.

DILLARD, Jack K.
1005 Congress Ave.
Suite 850
Austin, TX 78702
Tel: (512) 478 - 3394
Fax:(512) 478 - 0647

Serves As:
- Regional Director, State Government Affairs (IX), (Altria Corporate Services, Inc.), Altria Group, Inc.

DILLARD, Regina K.
1900 M St. NW
Suite 730
Washington, DC 20036
Tel: (202) 263 - 4400
Fax:(202) 263 - 4435

Registered Federal Lobbyist.
Serves As:
- Counsel, State Farm Insurance Cos.

DILLARD, II, William T.
P.O. Box 486
Little Rock, AR 72203
Tel: (501) 376 - 5200
Fax:(501) 376 - 5885
TF: (800) 643 - 8274

Serves As:
- Chairman and Chief Exec. Officer, Dillard's Inc.

DILLER, Barry
152 W. 57th St.
42nd Floor
New York, NY 10019
Tel: (212) 314 - 7300
Fax:(212) 314 - 7309

Serves As:
- Chairman and Chief Exec. Officer, IAC/InterActiveCorp

DILLIN, Carol A.
121 SW Salmon St.
1WTC-1706
Portland, OR 97204
carol_dillin@pgn.com
Tel: (503) 464 - 8000
Fax:(503) 464 - 2929

Serves As:
- V. President, Public Policy, Portland General Electric Co.

DILLINGHAM, Deborah
5005 LBJ Fwy.
Dallas, TX 75244
deborah_dillingham@oxy.com
Tel: (972) 404 - 3800
Fax:(972) 404 - 3906
TF: (800) 578 - 8880

Serves As:
- Communications and Community Affairs, Occidental Chemical Corp.

DILLON, Daniel P.
Three Concord Farms
575 Virginia Rd.
Concord, MA 01742
Tel: (978) 371 - 1000
Fax:(978) 371 - 3860

Serves As:
- President and Chief Exec. Officer, Welch's

DILLON, David B.
1014 Vine St.
Cincinnati, OH 45202-1100
Tel: (513) 762 - 4000
Fax:(513) 762 - 1295

Serves As:
- Chairman and Chief Exec. Officer, The Kroger Co.

DILLON, Donald F.
P.O. Box 979
Brookfield, WI 53008-0979
Tel: (262) 879 - 5000
TF: (800) 872 - 7882

Serves As:
- Chairman of the Board, Fiserv, Inc.

DILLOW, Frank W.
1300 I St. NW
Suite 400 West
Washington, DC 20005
Tel: (202) 515 - 2400

Registered Federal Lobbyist.
Serves As:
- V. President, Federal Legislative Relations and Deputy General Counsel, Verizon Communications Inc.

DIMAIO, Mark A.
19 Lonacre Ct.
Hockessin, DE 19707
mark.dimaio2@astrazeneca.com
Tel: (302) 234 - 3179
Fax:(302) 234 - 3159
TF: (800) 822 - 9209
Ext: 60068

Serves As:
- Director, State Government Affairs, AstraZeneca Pharmaceuticals

DIMARCO, Maureen
222 Berkeley St.
Boston, MA 02116
Tel: (617) 351 - 5000
Fax:(617) 351 - 1100

Serves As:
- Senior V. President, Educational and Governmental Affairs, Houghton Mifflin Co.

DIMARIA, Valerie T.
1303 E. Algonquin Rd.
Schaumburg, IL 60196
Tel: (847) 576 - 5000
Fax:(847) 576 - 5372
TF: (800) 262 - 8509

Serves As:
- V. President, Communications and Public Affairs, Motorola, Inc.

DIMARZO, Maryanne
211 Mount Airy Rd.
Basking Ridge, NJ 07920
mdimarzo@avaya.com
Tel: (908) 953 - 6000
Fax:(908) 953 - 7609

Serves As:
- Senior V. President, Human Resources, Avaya Inc.

DIMASI, Steven
101 Constitution Ave. NW
Suite 800
Washington, DC 20001
Tel: (202) 742 - 4270
Fax:(202) 742 - 4271

Registered Federal Lobbyist.
Serves As:
- Senior Director, Government Relations, Cendant Corp.

DIMEGLIO, John
260 Baltimore Pike
Wawa, PA 19063
Tel: (610) 358 - 8000
Fax:(610) 358 - 8878
TF: (800) 283 - 9292

Serves As:
- Treasurer, Wawa Inc. Political Action Committee, Wawa, Inc.

DIMICCO, Daniel R.
2100 Rexford Rd.
Charlotte, NC 28211
ddimicco@nucor.com
Tel: (704) 366 - 7000
Fax:(704) 362 - 4208

Serves As:
- V. Chairman, President and Chief Exec. Officer, Nucor Corp.

DIMMER, Dave
One Owens Corning Pkwy.
Toledo, OH 43659
dave.dimmer@owenscorning.com
Tel: (419) 248 - 8421
Fax:(419) 248 - 6227
TF: (800) 438 - 7465

Serves As:
- Corporate Media Relations Leader, Owens Corning

DIMON, Wanda
P.O. Box 1943
Birmingham, AL 35201-1943
Tel: (205) 991 - 6600
Fax:(205) 995 - 1517

Serves As:
- Contact, EBSCO Industries, Inc. Corporate Giving Program, EBSCO Industries, Inc.

DIMOPOULOS, Jr., Linda
P.O. Box 593330
Orlando, FL 32859
Tel: (407) 245 - 4000

Serves As:
- Exec. V. President and Chief Financial Officer, Darden Restaurants, Inc.

Responsibilities include investor relations.

DINAPOLI, Rose
901 E St. NW
Fourth Floor
Washington, DC 20004-2037
rose.dinapoli@slma.com
Tel: (202) 969 - 8020
Fax:(202) 969 - 8031

Registered Federal Lobbyist.
Serves As:
- V. President, Government and Industry Relations, SLM Corp.

DINGELL, Debbie I.
300 Renaissance Center
M/C 482-C27-D21
Detroit, MI 48265-3000
Tel: (313) 556 - 5000
Fax:(313) 665 - 0735

Serves As:
- V. Chairman, General Motors Foundation and Exec. Dir., Gov. and Community Affairs, General Motors Corp.

DINGES, Brian
4101 Winfield Rd.
Warrenville, IL 60555
Tel: (630) 821 - 3174

Serves As:
- Contact, BP Foundation, Inc, BP

DINGES, Vicky
435 N. Michigan Ave.
Chicago, IL 60611
Tel: (312) 222 - 3512
Fax:(312) 222 - 3523

Serves As:
- V. President, External Affairs, Tribune Co.

DINICOLA, Natalie L.
800 N. Lindbergh Blvd.
St. Louis, MO 63167
natalie.l.dinicola@monsanto.com
Tel: (314) 694 - 3195

Serves As:
- Associate Director, Special Projects, Monsanto Co.

Responsibilities include corporate government affairs.

DINICOLA, Ralph J.
76 S. Main St.
Akron, OH 44308-1890
Tel: (330) 384 - 5939
Fax:(330) 384 - 4539
TF: (800) 633 - 4766

Serves As:
- V. President, Communications, FirstEnergy Corp.

DIORIO, Marianne
767 Fifth Ave.
New York, NY 10153-0023
mdoria@estee.com
Tel: (212) 572 - 4200
Fax:(212) 572 - 6633

Serves As:
- Senior V. President, Communications and Specialty Brands, Estee Lauder Companies, Inc.

DIPIAZZA, Jr., Samuel A.
1301 Ave. of the Americas
New York, NY 10019
Tel: (646) 471 - 4000
Fax:(646) 394 - 5355

Serves As:
- Chief Exec. Officer, PriceWaterhouseCoopers LLP

DIPIAZZA, Tom
1221 Ave. of the Americas
47th Floor
New York, NY 10020-1095
tom_dipiazza@mcgraw-hill.com
Tel: (212) 512 - 4145
Fax:(212) 512 - 3514

Serves As:
- Director, Corporate Communications, The McGraw-Hill Companies, Inc.

DIPIETRO, Ken
One Microsoft Way
Redmond, WA 98052-6399
Tel: (425) 882 - 8080
Fax:(425) 936 - 7329

Serves As:
- Corporate V. President, Human Resources, Microsoft Corporation

DIRAIMO, Carol
4551 W. 107th St.
Overland Park, KS 66207-4037
ca.diraimo@applebees.com
Tel: (913) 967 - 4109
Fax:(913) 341 - 1694

Serves As:
- V. President, Investor Relations, Applebee's Internat'l, Inc.

DIRIENZO, Josie
170 W. State St.
Trenton, NJ 08608
Tel: (609) 656 - 2750
Fax:(609) 393 - 1681

Serves As:
- Manager, State Governmental Affairs, PSE&G

DIRISIO, Pamela
2710 Wycliff Rd.
Raleigh, NC 27607-3033
Tel: (919) 783 - 4562
Fax:(919) 783 - 4695

Serves As:
- Manager, Corporate Communications, Martin Marietta Materials, Inc.

DISABATO, Michelle
120 Park Ave.
New York, NY 10017
Tel: (917) 663 - 3346
Fax:(917) 663 - 5431

Serves As:
- Manager, Planning and Analysis, Altria Group, Inc.

DISCEPOLO, Michaelanne C.
745 Fifth Ave.
New York, NY 10151
mdiscepolo@primedia.com
Tel: (212) 745 - 0115
Fax:(212) 745 - 0121

Serves As:
- Exec. V. President, Human Resources, Primedia Inc.

DISCLAFANI, Mary
2200 E. Golf Rd.
Des Plaines, IL 60016-1267
mdisclafani@ussco.com
Tel: (847) 669 - 5000
Ext: 2772
Fax:(847) 699 - 8046

Serves As:
- Investor Relations Contact, United Stationers Inc.

DISKON, Ken
6801 Rockledge Dr.
Bethesda, MD 20817-1877
Tel: (301) 897 - 6950
Fax:(301) 897 - 6758

Serves As:
- Senior V. President, Human Resources, Lockheed Martin Corp.

DISNEY, Peggy
12950 Worldgate Dr.
Suite 600
Herndon, VA 20170
Tel: (703) 480 - 6623
Fax:(703) 796 - 2214

Serves As:
- Director, Media Relations, Lafarge North America, Inc.

DISTURCO, Jean M.
Three High Ridge Park
Stamford, CT 06905
Tel: (203) 614 - 5600
Fax:(203) 614 - 4602

Serves As:
- Senior V. President, Human Resources, Citizens Communications Co.

DIXON, Bob
P.O. Box 1000
Charlotte, NC 28201-1000
Tel: (704) 522 - 2000
Fax:(704) 522 - 2055

Serves As:
- Senior Human Resources Officer, Royal & SunAlliance USA Inc.

DIXON, Diane B.
150 N. Orange Grove Blvd.
Pasadena, CA 91103
diane.dixon@averydennison.com
Tel: (626) 304 - 2118
Fax:(626) 792 - 7312

Serves As:
- Senior V. President, Worldwide Communications and Advertising, Avery Dennison Corp.

DLUGOLENSKI, Mary Lou
One Targeting Centre
Windsor, CT 06095
mldlugol@advoc.com
Tel: (860) 285 - 6197
Fax:(860) 285 - 1567
TF: (800) 559 - 2386

Serves As:
- Director, Communications, Advo Inc.

DOANE, Allen
P.O. Box 3440
Honolulu, HI 96801-3440
Tel: (808) 525 - 6611
Fax:(808) 525 - 6652

Serves As:
- President and Chief Exec. Officer, Alexander & Baldwin, Inc.

DOANE, Tim
24601 Center Ridge Rd.
Suite 200
Westlake, OH 44145-5639
Tel: (440) 808 - 9100
Fax:(440) 808 - 4458
TF: (800) 961 - 2961

Serves As:
- Chief Exec. Officer, TravelCenters of America, Inc.

DOBKIN, Robert A.
701 Ninth St. NW
Washington, DC 20068
radobkin@pepco.com
Tel: (202) 872 - 2680
Fax:(202) 331 - 4857

Serves As:
- Principal Media Representative, Pepco Holdings, Inc.

DOBOS, John
855 Main St.
Bridgeport, CT 06604-4918
jdobos@soconngas.com
Tel: (203) 382 - 8644

Serves As:
- Director, External Affairs, (Connecticut Natural Gas Corp. (CNG), Southern Connecticut Gas Co., The (SCG)), Energy East Corp.

DOBSON, Earl F.
601 Poydras St.
Suite 1900
New Orleans, LA 70130
Tel: (504) 568 - 1010
Fax:(504) 566 - 4580

Serves As:
- PAC Treasurer, Tidewater Inc.

DOCKSAI, Ph.D., Ronald F.
1275 Pennsylvania Ave. NW
Suite 801
Washington, DC 20004-2404
Tel: (202) 737 - 8900
Fax:(202) 737 - 8909

Registered Federal Lobbyist.
Serves As:
- V. President, Federal Government Relations, Bayer Corporation

DODD, Alan
19001 Crescent Springs Dr.
Kingwood, TX 77339-3802
alan_dodd@administaff.com
Tel: (281) 348 - 3105
Fax:(281) 348 - 2849
TF: (800) 237 - 3170

Serves As:
- Director, Corporate Communications, Administaff, Inc.

DODGE, Jeff
1550 Peachtree St., N.W.
Atlanta, GA 30309
jeff.dodge@equifax.com
Tel: (404) 885 - 8804
Fax:(404) 885 - 8078

Serves As:
- V. President, Investor Relations, Equifax Inc.

DODS, Jr., Walter A.
P.O. Box 3200
Honolulu, HI 96847
Tel: (808) 525 - 7000
Fax:(808) 557 - 086

Serves As:
- Chairman of the Board, BancWest Corp.

DODSON, Mark
220 NW Second Ave.
Portland, OR 97209-3991
Tel: (503) 226 - 4211
Fax:(503) 220 - 2584

Serves As:
- Chief Exec. Officer, NW Natural

DODSON, Melissa
1133 21st St. NW
Suite 450
Washington, DC 20036
Tel: (202) 872 - 0556
Fax:(202) 872 - 0908

Registered Federal Lobbyist.
Serves As:
- Assistant V. President, Government Affairs, First Health

DOGGETT, William B. "Barry"
Eaton Center
1111 Superior Ave.
Cleveland, OH 44114-2584
Tel: (216) 523 - 4664
Fax:(216) 479 - 7013

Serves As:
- V. President, Public and Community Affairs, Eaton Corp.

DOHERTY, Christopher
2001 Edmund Halley Dr.
Reston, VA 20191
Tel: (703) 433 - 4656

Serves As:
- V. President, Internal Communications, Sprint Nextel

DOHERTY, Chuck
P.O. Box 979
Brookfield, WI 53008-0979
chuck.doherty@fiserv.com
Tel: (262) 879 - 5966
Fax:(262) 879 - 5013
TF: (800) 872 - 7882

Serves As:
- Director, Corporate Public Relations, Fiserv, Inc.

DOHERTY, Frances P.
10455 Mill Run Circle
Owings Mills, MD 21117
Tel: (410) 998 - 5496
Fax:(410) 998 - 4500

Serves As:
- V. President, Government Affairs, CareFirst BlueCross and BlueShield

DOHNALEK, David
World Headquarters
100 N. Riverside
Chicago, IL 60606-1596
investor.relations@boeing.com
Tel: (312) 544 - 2000
Fax:(312) 544 - 2099

Serves As:
- V. President, Investor Relations, The Boeing Co.

DOLAN, Charles F.
1111 Stewart Ave.
Bethpage, NY 11714-3581
Tel: (516) 803 - 2300
Fax:(516) 803 - 1186

Serves As:
- Chairman of the Board, Cablevision Systems Corp.

DOLAN, James L.
1111 Stewart Ave.
Bethpage, NY 11714-3581
Tel: (516) 803 - 2300
Fax:(516) 803 - 1186

Serves As:
- President and Chief Exec. Officer, Cablevision Systems Corp.

DOLAN, Peter R.
345 Park Ave.
New York, NY 10154-0037
peter.dolan@bms.com
Tel: (212) 546 - 4000
Fax:(212) 546 - 4020

Serves As:
- Chairman and Chief Exec. Officer, Bristol-Myers Squibb Co.

DOLAN, Vincent M.
100 Central Ave.
St. Petersburg, FL 33701
Tel: (727) 820 - 5001

Serves As:
• V. President, Regulatory and Public Affairs - Florida, Progress Energy

DOLBERG, Patrick
6211 N. Ann Arbor Rd.
P.O. Box 122
Dundee, MI 48131
Tel: (734) 529 - 2411
Fax:(734) 529 - 5268
TF: (800) 854 - 4656

Serves As:
• President and Chief Exec. Officer, Holcim (US) Inc.

DOLCH, Gary
7000 Cardinal Pl.
Dublin, OH 43017
Tel: (614) 757 - 5000
Fax:(614) 757 - 6000
TF: (800) 234 - 8701

Serves As:
• Exec. V. President, Quality and Regulatory Affairs, Cardinal Health Inc.

DOLE, Gregory S.
1200 Wilson Blvd.
Arlington, VA 22209-2305
Tel: (703) 465 - 3619
Fax:(703) 465 - 3009

Serves As:
• Director, Commercial Trade Policy, The Boeing Co.

DOLLENS, Ronald W.
111 Monument Circle
29th Floor
Indianapolis, IN 46204-5129
Tel: (317) 971 - 2000
Fax:(317) 971 - 2040

Serves As:
• President and Chief Exec. Officer, Guidant Corp.

DOLLINGER, Lisa
200 E. Basse Rd.
San Antonio, TX 78209
lisadollinger@clearchannel.com
Tel: (210) 822 - 2828
Fax:(210) 822 - 2299

Serves As:
• Senior V. President and Chief Communications Officer, Clear Channel Communications

DOLSON, Robert
111 Ponce de Leon Ave.
Clewiston, FL 33440
Tel: (863) 983 - 8121
Fax:(863) 983 - 9827

Serves As:
• President and Chief Exec. Officer, United States Sugar Corp.

DOMBROWSKI, Mark
100 Erie Insurance Pl.
Erie, PA 16530
mark.dombrowski@erieinsurance.com
Tel: (814) 870 - 2285
Fax:(814) 870 - 3126

Serves As:
• Supervisor, Public and Media Relations, (Erie Insurance Group), Erie Indeminity Co.

DOMINGUEZ, Daisy
99 Church St.
New York, NY 10007-2707
Tel: (212) 553 - 0300
Fax:(212) 553 - 4820

Serves As:
• Manager, Community Programs, Moody's Corp.

DOMINGUEZ, Irma
500 W. Monroe St.
Chicago, IL 60661
ir@gatx.com
Tel: (312) 621 - 8799
Fax:(312) 621 - 6648
TF: (800) 428 - 8161

Serves As:
• Investor Relations Coordinator, GATX Corp.

DOMINGUEZ, Victor
970 W. 190th St.
Suite 100
Torrance, CA 90502
victor.dominguez@cbre.com
Tel: (310) 354 - 5064
Fax:(310) 380 - 5896

Serves As:
• Managing Director, Corporate Communications, CB Richard Ellis Services, Inc.

DOMINICIS, Xavier
19001 S. Western Ave.
Torrance, CA 90509
Tel: (310) 468 - 5089

Serves As:
• National Manager, Media Relations, (Toyota Motor Sales - USA), Toyota Motor North America, Inc.

DOMINICK, Jr., Samuel
10889 Wilshire Blvd.
Los Angeles, CA 90024
Tel: (310) 208 - 8800
Fax:(310) 443 - 6690

Serves As:
• PAC Treasurer, Occidental Petroleum Corp.

DOMINO, Joe
P.O. Box 2951
Beaumont, TX 77704
Tel: (409) 838 - 6631

Serves As:
• President and Chief Exec. Officer, Entergy Texas

DONAGHUE, Chad
100 Jim Moran Blvd.
Deerfield Beach, FL 33442
chad.donaghue@jmfamily.com
Tel: (954) 429 - 2349
Fax:(954) 429 - 2300

Serves As:
• Media Contact, JM Family Enterprises, Inc.

DONAHUE, Caitlin
701 Pennsylvania Ave. NW
Suite 520
Washington, DC 20004-2604
Tel: (202) 393 - 3400
Fax:(202) 393 - 4606

Registered Federal Lobbyist.
Serves As:
• Manager, External Relations, The Procter & Gamble Company

DONAHUE, Karen L.
1100 New York Ave. NW
Washington, DC 20005
Tel: (202) 669 - 8368

Registered Federal Lobbyist.
Serves As:
• Representative, Lucent Technologies

DONAHUE, Michael
One McDonald's Plaza
Oak Brook, IL 60523
michael.donahue@mcd.com
Tel: (630) 623 - 7833
Fax:(630) 623 - 8005

Serves As:
• V. President, U.S. Communications, McDonald's Corp.

DONAHUE, Timothy J.
One Crown Way
Philadelphia, PA 19154-4599
tdonahue@crowncork.com
Tel: (215) 698 - 5351
Fax:(215) 698 - 5201

Serves As:
• Senior V. President, Finance, Crown Holdings, Inc.
Responsibilities include investor relations.

DONAHUE, Timothy M.
2001 Edmund Halley Dr.
Reston, VA 20191
Tel: (703) 433 - 4000

Serves As:
• Exec. Chairman, Sprint Nextel

DONALDSON, David A.
P.O. Box 385014
Birmingham, AL 35238-5014
donaldsond@vmcmail.com
Tel: (205) 298 - 3021
Fax:(205) 298 - 2960

Serves As:
• Director, Community Relations, Vulcan Materials Co.
Serves as the Senior Public Affairs Executive at company headquarters.

DONALDSON, Helen
25 Atlantic Ave.
Erlanger, KY 41018
Tel: (859) 746 - 4000

Serves As:
• Contact, Toyota Motor Manufacturing North America Giving Program, Toyota Motor North America, Inc.

DONALDSON, R. Eric
7801 Mesquite Bend Dr., Suite 101
Irving, TX 75063
Tel: (214) 296 - 6113
Fax:(214) 296 - 6112

Serves As:
• Regional Manager, State Government Relations/Southwest, UST Inc.

DONALDSON, Rich
One Casco St.
Freeport, ME 04033
Tel: (207) 552 - 6022
Fax:(207) 552 - 6821
TF: (800) 221 - 4221

Serves As:
• Manager, Public Relations, L. L. Bean, Inc.

DONALTY, Tanya Y.
1100 Wilson Blvd.
Suite 1500
Arlington, VA 22209
Tel: (703) 841 - 5700
Fax:(703) 841 - 5792

Serves As:
• PAC Contact, Raytheon Co.

DONEGAN, Mark
4650 SW Macadam Ave.
Suite 440
Portland, OR 97239-4254
Tel: (503) 417 - 4800
Fax:(503) 417 - 4817

Serves As:
• Chairman and Chief Exec. Officer, Precision Castparts Corp.

DONILON, Terrence
750 W. Center St.
West Bridgewater, MA 02379
Tel: (508) 313 - 3318
Fax:(508) 313 - 3112

Serves As:
• Media Contact, Shaw's Supermarkets, Inc.

DONILON, Thomas
3900 Wisconsin Ave. NW
Washington, DC 20016
Tel: (202) 752 - 7000
Fax:(202) 752 - 6099

Registered Federal Lobbyist.
Serves As:
• Exec. V. President, Law and Policy, Fannie Mae

DONINI, Marilynn J.
120 Park Ave.
17th Floor
New York, NY 10017
Tel: (917) 663 - 4171
Fax:(917) 663 - 5874

Serves As:
• Manager, Contributions Program, (Altria Corporate Services, Inc.), Altria Group, Inc.

DONNAN, John M.
27422 Portola Pkwy
Suite 350
Foothill Ranch, CA 92610-2831
john.donnan@kaiseral.com
Tel: (949) 614 - 1740
Fax:(949) 614 - 1930

Serves As:
• Deputy General Counsel; PAC Treasurer, Kaiser Aluminum & Chemical Corp.

DONNELLY, Mary Beth
101 Constitution Ave. NW
Suite 800
Washington, DC 20001
Tel: (202) 822 - 6777
Fax:(202) 822 - 6677

Registered Federal Lobbyist.
Serves As:
• Group Executive, Government Relations, Newmont Mining Corp.

DONOHO, Wendy L.
1401 I St. NW
Suite 1100
Washington, DC 20005
Tel: (202) 326 - 8814
Fax:(202) 408 - 8717

Registered Federal Lobbyist.
Serves As:
• Exec. Director, Federal Relations, SBC Communications Inc.

DONOHUE, Craig S.
20 S. Wacker Dr.
Chicago, IL 60606-7499
Tel: (312) 930 - 1000

Serves As:
• Chief Exec. Officer, Chicago Mercantile Exchange Inc.

DONOHUE, Mark
P.O. Box 300
Princeton, NJ 08543
mark.donohue@dowjones.com
Tel: (609) 520 - 5660

Serves As:
• Director, Investor Relations, Dow Jones and Co.

DONOVAN, Jr., Daniel E.
Dominion CNG Tower
625 Liberty Ave.
Pittsburgh, PA 15222-3199
Daniel_E_Donovan@dom.com
Tel: (412) 690 - 1370
Fax:(412) 690 - 1020

Serves As:
• Manager Media Relations (Gas), Dominion Resources, Inc.

DONOVAN, Dennis
2455 Paces Ferry Rd.
Atlanta, GA 30339-4024
Tel: (770) 433 - 8211
Fax:(770) 384 - 2356

Serves As:
• Exec. V. President, Human Resources, The Home Depot, Inc.

DONOVAN, Edward J.
P.O. Box 300
Detroit, MI 48265-1000
Tel: (313) 556 - 5000
Fax:(248) 696 - 7300

Registered Federal Lobbyist.
Serves As:
• Director, Municipal Government Relations, General Motors Corp.

DONOVAN, Laura
1101 Connecticut Ave. NW
Suite 401
Washington, DC 20036
laura.donovan@thehartford.com
Tel: (202) 296 - 7513
Fax:(202) 296 - 7514

Registered Federal Lobbyist.
Serves As:
• Director, Federal Affairs, The Hartford Financial Services Group Inc.

DONOVAN, Mike
One Blue Hill Plaza
Pearl River, NY 10965
mdonovan@oru.com
Tel: (845) 577 - 2430
Fax:(845) 577 - 6913

Serves As:
• Manager, Media Relations, Orange and Rockland Utilities, Inc.

DONOVAN, Paul
One Boston Scientific Pl.
Natick, MA 01760-1537
Tel: (508) 650 - 8541
Fax:(508) 647 - 2200

Serves As:
• Senior V. President, Corporate Communications, Boston Scientific Corp.

DONOVAN, Robert
One McDonald's Plaza
Oak Brook, IL 60523
Tel: (630) 623 - 6754
Fax:(630) 623 - 3057

Serves As:
• PAC Treasurer, McDonald's Corp.

DOOLEY, Cathleen M.
1350 I St. NW
Suite 1210
Washington, DC 20005-3305
Tel: (202) 589 - 1000
Ext: 1008
Fax:(202) 589 - 1001

Registered Federal Lobbyist.
Serves As:
• Exec. Director, Federal Affairs, Johnson & Johnson

DOOLITTLE, Lee Ann
220 NW Second Ave.
Portland, OR 97209-3991
lad@nwnatural.com
Tel: (503) 226 - 4211
Fax:(503) 721 - 2584

Serves As:
• V. President, Human Resources and Administrative Services, NW Natural

DOOLITTLE, Robert E.
2941 Fairview Park Dr.
Falls Church, VA 22042-4513
Tel: (703) 876 - 3199
Fax:(703) 876 - 3186

Serves As:
• Director, Public Affairs, General Dynamics Corporation

DOOLITTLE, Thomas M.
100 NE Adams St.
Peoria, IL 61629-1465
Tel: (309) 675 - 6058
Fax:(309) 675 - 5815

Serves As:
• Manager, Corporate Communications, Caterpillar Inc.

DOONER, Marlene S.
1500 Market St.
Philadelphia, PA 19102
marlene_dooner@comcast.com
Tel: (215) 981 - 7392
Fax:(215) 981 - 7790

Serves As:
• V. President, Investor Relations, Comcast Corporation

DOPP, Natalie
23733 N. Scottsdale Rd.
Scottsdale, AZ 85255
Tel: (480) 585 - 8888
Fax:(480) 585 - 8893
TF: (800) 937 - 4937

Serves As:
• V. President, Human Resources, (Giant Industries Arizona, Inc.), Giant Industries, Inc.

DORAN, Shelly J.
P.O. Box 7033
Indianapolis, IN 46207
sdoran@simon.com
Tel: (317) 685 - 7330
Fax:(317) 263 - 2318

Serves As:
• V. President, Investor Relations, Simon Property Group

DOREY, William G.
P.O. Box 50085
Watsonville, CA 95077-5085
Tel: (831) 724 - 1011
Fax:(831) 722 - 9657
TF: (800) 482 - 1518

Serves As:
• President and Chief Exec. Officer, Granite Construction Inc.

DORMAN, David W.
One AT&T Way
Bedminster, NJ 07921-0752
Tel: (908) 234 - 3020

Serves As:
• Chairman and Chief Exec. Officer, AT&T

DORMAN, Dawn
3150 Sabre Dr.
Southlake, TX 76092
dawn.dorman@sabre-holdings.com
Tel: (682) 605 - 2246
Fax:(682) 264 - 0502

Serves As:
• Senior Manager, Media Relations, (Sabre Travel Network), Sabre Holdings Corp.

DORMAN, Devon C.
One Righter Pkwy., Second Floor
Brandywine Corporate Center
Wilmington, DE 19803
ddorman@advanta.com
Tel: (302) 529 - 6565

Serves As:
• PAC Administrator, Advanta Corp.

DORMAN, Larry
2180 Rutherford Rd.
Carlsbad, CA 92008-7328
Tel: (760) 931 - 1771
Fax:(760) 804 - 4154
TF: (800) 228 - 2767

Serves As:
• Senior V. President, Global Press and Public Relations, Callaway Golf Co.

DORMAN, Margaret K.
P.O. Box 60068
Houston, TX 77205-0068
mdorman@smith.com
Tel: (281) 443 - 3370
TF: (800) 877 - 6484

Serves As:
• Senior V. President and Chief Financial Officer, Smith Internat'l, Inc.
Responsibilities include investor relations.

DORN, Nancy P.
1299 Pennsylvania Ave. NW
11th Floor West
Washington, DC 20004-2407
Tel: (202) 637 - 4000
Fax:(202) 637 - 4006

Registered Federal Lobbyist.
Serves As:
• V. President, Corporate Government Relations, General Electric Co.

DORNAN, Beth A.
7575 Fulton St. East
M/S SC-2P
Ada, MI 49355-0001
Tel: (616) 787 - 6445
Fax:(616) 787 - 7102

Serves As:
• Director, Quixtar Communications, (Quixtar Inc.), Alticor Inc.

DORNAN, John
SAS Campus Dr.
Cary, NC 27513-2414
john.dornan@sas.com
Tel: (919) 531 - 5234
Fax:(919) 677 - 4444

Serves As:
• Manager, Corporate Public Relations, SAS Institute, Inc.

DORNEMAN, Ross W.
Gateway One
101 Gateway Centre Pkwy.
Richmond, VA 23235
Tel: (804) 267 - 8000
Fax:(804) 267 - 8836
TF: (800) 446 - 7086

Serves As:
• Exec. V. President, Human Resources, LandAmerica Financial Group, Inc.

DORR, Mary Jo
2325 Dulles Corner Blvd.
200 Athens Way
Herndon, VA 20171

Serves As:
• Treasurer, Nortel PAC, Nortel Networks

DORSEY, Patrick B.
727 Fifth Ave.
New York, NY 10022
Tel: (212) 230 - 5320
Fax:(212) 230 - 6734

Serves As:
• Senior V. President, General Counsel and Secretary, Tiffany & Co.
Responsibilities include government affairs.

DORSEY, Thomas
P.O. Box 270
Hartford, CT 06141-0270
Tel: (860) 665 - 3590
Fax:(860) 665 - 3177
TF: (800) 286 - 2000

Serves As:
• Manager, Governmental Affairs, Northeast Utilities

DORTONE, Kim
Unisys Way
Blue Bell, PA 19424
Tel: (215) 986 - 4011
Fax:(215) 986 - 6850

Serves As:
• PAC Treasurer, Unisys Corp.

DOSSMAN, Curley
P.O. Box 105605
Atlanta, GA 30348
Tel: (404) 652 - 4182
Fax:(404) 654 - 4789
TF: (800) 519 - 3111

Serves As:
• Senior Director, Community Affairs and President, Georgia-Pacific Foundation, Georgia-Pacific Corp.

DOSWELL, W. Carter
101 Constitution Ave. NW
Suite 1000 East
Washington, DC 20001
Tel: (202) 637 - 3700
Fax:(202) 637 - 3773

Serves As:
• V. President, Goldman, Sachs and Co.

DOTSON, Connie M.
135 E. 57th St.
New York, NY 10022
Tel: (916) 636 - 2510

Serves As:
• Chief Communications Officer, E*TRADE Financial Corp.

DOTTO, Ellen M.
172 W. State St.
Trenton, NJ 08608
ellen.m.dotto@verizon.com
Tel: (609) 989 - 9961
Fax:(609) 989 - 8305

Serves As:
• V. President, State Government Affairs, Verizon New Jersey, Inc.

DOUCET, Jodie
5005 LBJ Fwy.
Dallas, TX 75244
Tel: (972) 404 - 3800
Fax:(972) 404 - 3669
TF: (800) 578 - 8880

Serves As:
• V. President, Human Resources, Occidental Chemical Corp.

DOUGAN, Brady W.
11 Madison Ave.
New York, NY 10010-3629
brady.dougan@csfb.com
Tel: (212) 325 - 2000
Fax:(212) 538 - 4633

Serves As:
• Chief Exec. Officer, Credit Suisse First Boston

DOUGET, Susan E.
P.O. Box 4442
Houston, TX 77210-4442
Tel: (713) 462 - 4239
Fax:(713) 895 - 5897

Serves As:
• Director, Human Resources, BJ Services Co.
Responsibilities include corporate philanthropy.

DOUGLASS, Elizabeth
Unisys Way
Blue Bell, PA 19424
elizabeth.douglass@unisys.com
Tel: (215) 986 - 6583
Fax:(215) 986 - 6850

Serves As:
• V. President, Corporate Media Relations, Unisys Corp.

DOUGLASS, J. Lee
P.O. Box 2181
320 W. Capitol
Little Rock, AR 72203-2181
Tel: (501) 378 - 2000

Serves As:
• Senior V. President, Law and Government Relations, Arkansas Blue Cross and Blue Shield

DOUGLASS, Steven J.
3231 S.E. Sixth St.
Topeka, KS 66607
Tel: (785) 233 - 5171
Fax:(785) 295 - 6866

Serves As:
• Chairman and Chief Exec. Officer, Payless ShoeSource

DOUGLASS, Susan
6501 Legacy Dr.
Plano, TX 75024-3698
sdoug2@jcpenney.com
Tel: (972) 431 - 1859
Fax:(972) 431 - 1362
TF: (800) 222 - 6161

Serves As:
• Manager, Shareholder Relations, J. C. Penney Co., Inc.

DOVE, Carol
One Nationwide Plaza
Columbus, OH 43215-2220
Tel: (614) 249 - 7111
Fax:(614) 249 - 3073

Serves As:
• PAC Treasurer, Nationwide

DOVE, Nathaniel E.
701 Ninth St. NW
Washington, DC 20068
Tel: (202) 872 - 2000

Serves As:
• PAC Treasurer, Pepco Holdings, Inc.

DOVE, Randolph V.
1331 Pennsylvania Ave. NW
Suite 1300 North
Washington, DC 20004
randy.dove@eds.com
Tel: (202) 637 - 6728
Fax:(202) 637 - 6759

Registered Federal Lobbyist.
Serves As:
• Exec. Director, Government Relations, EDS Corp.

DOW, Jo Ann
80 Park Plaza
M/S T10C
Newark, NJ 07102-0570
joann.dow@pseg.com
Tel: (973) 430 - 5861
Fax:(973) 297 - 1480

Serves As:
- Manager, Community Affairs, PSE&G

DOW, Troy
1150 17th St. NW
Suite 400
Washington, DC 20036
Tel: (202) 222 - 4700
Fax:(202) 222 - 4799

Registered Federal Lobbyist.
Serves As:
- Representative, The Walt Disney Company

DOWD, Mark
Three Times Square
New York, NY 10036
Tel: (212) 310 - 9500
Fax:(646) 223 - 9054
TF: (800) 225 - 5008

Serves As:
- Director, Public Relations, Instinet Group Inc.

DOWDELL, Jr., Rodger B.
132 Fairgrounds Rd.
West Kingston, RI 02892
Tel: (401) 789 - 5735
Fax:(401) 789 - 3710
TF: (800) 788 - 2208

Serves As:
- Chairman, President and Chief Exec. Officer, American Power Conversion Corp.

DOWE, Alison
P.O. Box 120
Columbus, GA 31902-0120
adowe@sfcts.com
Tel: (706) 642 - 3781
Fax:(706) 641 - 6555

Serves As:
- Director, Communications, Synovus Financial Corp.

DOWE, Tammy
P.O. Box 4689
Houston, TX 77210
Tel: (832) 486 - 4000
Fax:(832) 486 - 1814

Serves As:
- Manager, Corporate Legislative Issues, CITGO Petroleum Corporation

DOWLING, Brian G.
P.O. Box 99
Pleasanton, CA 94566-0009
Tel: (925) 467 - 3787
Fax:(925) 467 - 3323

Serves As:
- V. President, Public Affairs, Safeway Inc.

DOWLING, Jeannine
Six Landmark Sq.
Stamford, CT 06901
Tel: (203) 359 - 7100

Serves As:
- V. President, Corporate Communications and External Affairs, Diageo North America

DOWLING, S. Colin
1101 Pennsylvania Ave. NW
Suite 1000
Washington, DC 20004
dowlingc@citigroup.com
Tel: (202) 879 - 6871
Fax:(202) 783 - 4460

Serves As:
- Senior V. President and Director, State and Local Government Relations, Citigroup, Inc.

DOWLING, Steve
One Infinite Loop
Cupertino, CA 95014
dowling@apple.com
Tel: (408) 974 - 1896
Fax:(408) 996 - 0275

Serves As:
- Senior Manager, Corporate Media Relations, Apple Computer, Inc.

DOWNES, Laurence M.
P.O. Box 1468
Wall, NJ 07719
lmdownes@njresources.com
Tel: (732) 938 - 1480
Fax:(732) 938 - 3154

Serves As:
- Chairman and Chief Exec. Officer, New Jersey Resources Corp.

DOWNEY, Bruce L.
400 Chesnut Ridge Rd.
Woodcliff Lake, NJ 07677
bdowney@barrlabs.com
Tel: (201) 930 - 3300
Fax:(201) 930 - 3330
TF: (800) 222 - 0190

Serves As:
- Chairman and Chief Exec. Officer, (Barr Laboratories, Inc.), Barr Pharmaceuticals, Inc.

DOWNS, Jill R.
701 Ninth St. NW
Washington, DC 20068
Tel: (202) 872 - 3187

Serves As:
- V. President, Corporate Communications, Pepco Holdings, Inc.

DOWNS, Joe
225 Eastwood Dr.
Jefferson City, MO 65101
Tel: (573) 635 - 9611

Serves As:
- Legislative Representative, (Farmers Insurance Group of Companies), Farmers Group, Inc.

DOWNS, Jr., John H.
P.O. Box 723040
Atlanta, GA 31139-0040
Tel: (770) 989 - 3775
Fax:(770) 989 - 3781

Serves As:
- Senior V. President, Public Affairs and Communications, Coca-Cola Enterprises Inc.

Responsibilities include government relations.

DOWNS, Jonathan C.
3103 Philmont Ave.
Huntingdon Valley, PA 19006
jdowns@tollbrothersinc.com
Tel: (215) 938 - 8000
Fax:(215) 938 - 8019

Serves As:
- V. President, Human Resources, Toll Brothers, Inc.

DOYAL, Stephen D.
P.O. Box 419580
Kansas City, MO 64141-6580
Tel: (816) 274 - 4314
Fax:(816) 274 - 5061

Serves As:
- Senior V. President, Public Affairs and Communications, Hallmark Cards, Inc.

DOYLE, Chris
4500 Main St.
Kansas City, MO 64111
Tel: (816) 531 - 5575
TF: (800) 345 - 2021

Serves As:
- V. President, Public Relations, American Century Cos., Inc.

DOYLE, Karen
2775 Sanders Rd.
Northbrook, IL 60062-6127
Tel: (847) 402 - 5000
Fax:(847) 326 - 7519
TF: (800) 574 - 3553

Serves As:
- National Media Contact, Allstate Insurance Co.

DOYLE, Kevin
400 Main St.
East Hartford, CT 06108
Tel: (860) 565 - 4321

Serves As:
- V. President, Environment, Health and Safety, Pratt & Whitney

DOYLE, Kevin J.
One State St. Plaza
New York, NY 10004
kdoyle@ambac.com
Tel: (212) 208 - 3283
Fax:(212) 208 - 3558
TF: (800) 221 - 1854

Serves As:
- Senior V. President, General Counsel and Internal Audit, Ambac Financial Group, Inc.

Responsibilities include government relations.

DRAGICS, David L.
1100 N. Glebe Rd.
Arlington, VA 22201-4798
ddragics@caci.com
Tel: (703) 841 - 7835
Fax:(703) 841 - 7882

Serves As:
- V. President, Investor Relations, CACI Internat'l Inc.

DRAGO, Chris
One StorageTek Dr.
Louisville, CO 80028-4377
chris_drago@storagetek.com
Tel: (303) 661 - 2262

Serves As:
- Press Contact, Global Media and Analyst Relations, StorageTek

DRAKE, David P.
701 Pennsylvania Ave. NW
Suite 725
Washington, DC 20004
david.drake@group.novartis.com
Tel: (202) 638 - 7429
Fax:(202) 628 - 4764

Registered Federal Lobbyist.
Serves As:
- Exec. Director, Federal Government Relations, Novartis Corporation

DRAKE, Michele
P.O. Box 10395
Palo Alto, CA 94303-0395
michele_drake@agilent.com
Tel: (650) 752 - 5296
Fax:(650) 752 - 5633

Serves As:
- Manager, Public Relations, Agilent Technologies, Inc.

DRAKE, Shelly
One M & T Plaza
Buffalo, NY 14203
Tel: (716) 842 - 5445
Fax:(716) 842 - 5839
TF: (800) 836 - 1500

Serves As:
- Administrative V. President, M&T Bank Corporation

Responsibilities include corporate philanthropy.

DRAKE, Thomas G.
12780 Levan Rd.
Livonia, MI 48150
Tel: (734) 464 - 4948

Serves As:
- Regional V. President, State Relations - Michigan/Indiana, CSX Corp.

DRAPER, Delbert M.
295 Tipito Way
Salt Lake City, UT 84158
Tel: (801) 583 - 8800
Fax:(801) 584 - 6483

Serves As:
- Manager, Western Region State Government Affairs, (Williams Gas Pipelines-West), Williams

DRAPER, Jr., Dr. E. Linn
125 S. Dakota Ave.
Sioux Falls, SD 57104-6403
Tel: (605) 978 - 2908
Fax:(605) 978 - 2840

Serves As:
- Chairman of the Board, NorthWestern Corp.

DRAYNA, Jonathan E.
1200 Hansen Rd.
Green Bay, WI 54304
jon.drayna@associatedbank.com
Tel: (920) 491 - 7006
Fax:(920) 491 - 7010
TF: (800) 236 - 2722

Serves As:
- Director, Corporate Communications, Associated Banc-Corp.

DREHER, Murphy A.
446 North Blvd.
Baton Rouge, LA 70802
mdreher@entergy.com
Tel: (225) 381 - 5849

Serves As:
- V. President, Government Affairs - Louisiana, Entergy Corp.

DREIER, R. Chad
24025 Park Sorrento
Suite 400
Calabasas, CA 91302
cdreier@ryland.com
Tel: (818) 223 - 7500
Fax:(818) 223 - 7667
TF: (800) 267 - 0998

Serves As:
- Chairman, President and Chief Exec. Officer, The Ryland Group, Inc.

DREIMANN, Leonard
1955 Field Ct.
Lake Forest, IL 60045
Tel: (847) 803 - 4600
Fax:(847) 803 - 5629
TF: (800) 272 - 5629

Serves As:
- Chief Exec. Officer, Salton, Inc.

DRENDEL, Frank M.
1100 CommScope Pl. SE
Hickory, NC 28603
frendel@commscope.com
Tel: (828) 324 - 2200

Serves As:
- Chairman and Chief Exec. Officer, CommScope

DRESNER, Mark
101 Wood Ave.
Iselin, NJ 08830
Tel: (732) 205 - 5000
Fax:(732) 632 - 9253
TF: (800) 631 - 9505

Serves As:
- V. President, Corporate Communications, Engelhard Corp.

DRESSENDORFER, John H.
400 Virginia Ave. SW
Suite C150
Washington, DC 20024-2714
jdressendorfer@titan.com
Tel: (202) 488 - 9740
Fax:(202) 544 - 9071

Registered Federal Lobbyist.
Serves As:
- V. President, Government Relations, L-3 Communications Titan Group

DREW, Deborah
25 Research Dr.
Westborough, MA 01582
Tel: (508) 389 - 3102
Fax:(508) 389 - 3198

Serves As:
- Media Contact, Nat'l Grid USA

DREXLER, Millard S. "Mickey"
770 Broadway
New York, NY 10003
Tel: (212) 209 - 8500
Fax:(212) 209 - 2666

Serves As:
- Chairman and Chief Exec. Officer, J. Crew Group, Inc.

DREYER, Courtney Chabot
P.O. Box 14453
Des Moines, IA 50306-3453
courtney.dreyer@pioneer.com
Tel: (515) 248 - 4800
Fax:(515) 334 - 4663
TF: (800) 247 - 6803

Serves As:
- Manager, Public Affairs, Pioneer Hi-Bred Internat'l, Inc.

DREYER, Jennifer
P.O. Box 9103
Hopkinton, MA 01748
dreyer_jennifer@emc.com
Tel: (508) 435 - 1000
Ext: 77238
Fax:(508) 497 - 6912
TF: (800) 424 - 3622

Serves As:
- Manager, International Public Relations, EMC Corp.

DREYFUS, Andrew
401 Park Dr.
Boston, MA 02215
andrew.dreyfus@bcbsmafoundation.org
Tel: (617) 246 - 5000
TF: (800) 325 - 2583

Serves As:
- President, Blue Cross and Blue Shield of Massachusetts Foundation, Blue Cross and Blue Shield of Massachusetts

DRIER, Cecille C.
One Blue Hill Plaza
Pearl River, NY 10965
Tel: (845) 577 - 2409
Fax:(845) 577 - 6913

Serves As:
- Manager, Consumer Publications, Orange and Rockland Utilities, Inc.

DRILLOCK, David M.
Five Garret Mountain Plaza
West Paterson, NJ 07424
Tel: (973) 357 - 3249
Fax:(973) 357 - 3088
TF: (800) 652 - 6013

Serves As:
- V. President, Investor Relations and Controller, Cytec Industries Inc.

DRISCOLL, Jane L.
One American Row
Hartford, CT 06102
jane.driscoll@phoenixwm.com
Tel: (860) 403 - 5630
Fax:(860) 403 - 5755

Serves As:
- Assistant V. President, Public Affairs, The Phoenix Companies, Inc.

Responsibilities include corporate philanthropy.

DRISCOLL, Jennifer
7601 Penn Ave. South
Richfield, MN 55423
jennifer.driscoll@bestbuy.com
Tel: (612) 291 - 1000
Fax:(612) 292 - 4001

Serves As:
- V. President, Investor Relations, Best Buy Co., Inc.

DRISCOLL, John
2100 First Nat'l Bank Bldg.
St. Paul, MN 55101
Tel: (651) 228 - 0935
Fax:(651) 228 - 0776

Serves As:
- Contact, Weyerhaeuser Co. Special Shareholders Political Action Committee, Weyerhaeuser Co.

DRISCOLL, Meghan
401 Park Dr.
Boston, MA 02215
Tel: (617) 246 - 5000
TF: (800) 325 - 2583

Serves As:
- Treasurer, Fed CarePAC, Blue Cross and Blue Shield of Massachusetts

DROSDICK, John G.
Ten Penn Center
1801 Market St.
Philadelphia, PA 19103-1699
Tel: (215) 977 - 3000
Fax:(215) 977 - 3409

Serves As:
- Chairman, Chief Exec. Officer and President, Sunoco, Inc.

DROW, Frederick L.
5811 Pelican Bay Blvd., Suite 500
Naples, FL 34108-2710
Tel: (239) 598 - 3133
Fax:(239) 597 - 5794

Serves As:
- Senior V. President, Human Resources, Health Management Associates, Inc.

DRUMMOND, Garry
P.O. Box 10246
Birmingham, AL 35202
Tel: (205) 945 - 6300
Fax:(205) 945 - 6521

Serves As:
- Chairman and Chief Exec. Officer, Drummond Co., Inc.

DUARTE, Carmen
One Beacon St.
Boston, MA 02108
cduarte@onebeacon.com
Tel: (617) 725 - 6598
Fax:(617) 725 - 7357

Serves As:
- V. President, Corporate Communications, OneBeacon Insurance

DUBOIS, A. Pierre
300 Concord Plaza Dr.
San Antonio, TX 78216
Tel: (210) 828 - 8484
Fax:(210) 283 - 2003
TF: (800) 837 - 8768

Serves As:
• Manager, Investor Relations, Tesoro Petroleum Corp.

DUBOIS, Marcel
316 Pennsylvania Ave. SE
Suite 300
Washington, DC 20003
marceldubois@ups.com
Tel: (202) 675 - 4237
Fax:(202) 675 - 4230

Registered Federal Lobbyist.
Serves As:
• V. President, Public Affairs, United Parcel Service (UPS)

DUBOW, Craig A.
7950 Jones Branch Dr.
McLean, VA 22107
Tel: (703) 854 - 6000
Fax:(703) 276 - 2046

Serves As:
• President and Chief Exec. Officer, Gannett Co., Inc.

DUBOW, Lawrence J.
4955 Orange Dr.
Davie, FL 33314
Tel: (954) 584 - 0300
Fax:(954) 382 - 7729
TF: (800) 621 - 7143

Serves As:
• Chairman of the Board, Andrx Corp.

DUCHAK, Susan
3333 Beverly Rd.
BC-110A
Hoffman Estates, IL 60179-0001
Tel: (847) 286 - 2500
Fax:(847) 286 - 5918
TF: (800) 732 - 7780

Serves As:
• Contact, Sears Roebuck Foundation and Contributions, Sears Holding Corp.

DUCHOSSOIS, Craig J.
845 Larch Ave.
Elmhurst, IL 60126
cjd@duch.com
Tel: (630) 279 - 3600
Fax:(630) 530 - 6057
TF: (800) 282 - 6225

Serves As:
• President and Chief Exec. Officer, Duchossois Industries, Inc.
Responsibilities include corporate philanthropy.

DUCHOSSOIS, Kimberly T.
845 Larch Ave.
Elmhurst, IL 60126
Tel: (630) 279 - 3600
Fax:(630) 530 - 6057
TF: (800) 282 - 6225

Serves As:
• President, Duchossois Family Foundation, Duchossois Industries, Inc.

DUCHOSSOIS, Richard L.
845 Larch Ave.
Elmhurst, IL 60126
Tel: (630) 279 - 3600
Fax:(630) 530 - 6091
TF: (800) 282 - 6225

Serves As:
• Chairman of the Board, Duchossois Industries, Inc.

DUCICH, Sarah
901 E St. NW
Fourth Floor
Washington, DC 20004-2037
Tel: (202) 969 - 8020
Fax:(202) 969 - 8031

Registered Federal Lobbyist.
Serves As:
• Director, Government and Industry Relations, SLM Corp.

DUDA, Laura
TECO Plaza
702 N. Franklin St.
Tampa, FL 33602
lpduda@tecoenergy.com
Tel: (813) 228 - 4111
Fax:(813) 228 - 4811

Serves As:
• Director, Communications, TECO Energy, Inc./Tampa Electric Co.

DUDAS, Jim
2775 Sanders Rd.
Northbrook, IL 60062-6127
Tel: (847) 402 - 5000
Fax:(847) 326 - 7519
TF: (800) 574 - 3553

Serves As:
• National Media Contact, Allstate Insurance Co.

DUDDY, Gail L.
500 W. Monroe St.
Chicago, IL 60661
Tel: (312) 621 - 6220
Fax:(312) 621 - 6637
TF: (800) 428 - 8161

Serves As:
• Senior V. President, Human Resources, GATX Corp.

DUDEK, Patricia
350 N. Orleans
Chicago, IL 60654
pdudek@suntimes.com
Tel: (312) 321 - 3000

Serves As:
• Foundation President, Chicago Sun-Times
Responsibilities include community affairs.

DUDLE, Nancy
6820 S. Harl Ave.
Tempe, AZ 85283
ndudle@insight.com
Tel: (480) 902 - 1001
Fax:(480) 902 - 1157
TF: (800) 467 - 4448

Serves As:
• Public Relations Specialist, Insight Enterprises, Inc.

DUDLEY, Andrea
185 Franklin St.
Room 1800
Boston, MA 02110
andrea.dudley@verizon.com
Tel: (617) 743 - 0551
Fax:(617) 743 - 8886

Serves As:
• Director, Public Affairs Programs, Verizon Communications Inc.

DUDLEY, Scott W.
P.O. Box 18100
Richmond, VA 23226-8100
sdudley@brinkscompany.com
Tel: (804) 289 - 9708
Fax:(804) 289 - 9770

Serves As:
• Director, Investor Relations, The Brink's Co.
Responsibilities include media relations.

DUFF, Andrew S.
800 Nicollet Mall
Suite 800
Minneapolis, MN 55402
Tel: (612) 303 - 6000

Serves As:
• Chairman of the Board, U.S. Bancorp Piper Jaffray Inc.

DUFFY, Brian F.
1700 N. Webster Ct.
Green Bay, WI 54307-9017
Tel: (920) 433 - 5111
Fax:(920) 433 - 5471
TF: (800) 236 - 8400

Serves As:
• Corporate Environmental Co-Director, Green Bay Packaging Inc.

DUFFY, Terrence A.
20 S. Wacker Dr.
Chicago, IL 60606-7499
Tel: (312) 930 - 1000

Serves As:
• Chairman of the Board, Chicago Mercantile Exchange Inc.

DUFOUR, Pierre
2700 Post Oak Blvd.
Suite 1800
Houston, TX 77056
Tel: (713) 624 - 8000
Fax:(713) 624 - 8085

Serves As:
• President and Chief Exec. Officer, Air Liquide America Corp.

DUGAS, Richard
100 Bloomfield Hills Pkwy., Suite 300
Bloomfield Hills, MI 48304-2946
Tel: (248) 647 - 2750
Fax:(248) 433 - 4598
TF: (800) 777 - 8583

Serves As:
• President and Chief Exec. Officer, Pulte Homes, Inc.

DUKE, Susanna N.
999 Third Ave.
Suite 4300
Seattle, WA 98104
Tel: (206) 467 - 3600
Fax:(206) 467 - 3795

Serves As:
• Corporate Secretary and Director, Law, Plum Creek Timber Co. Inc.

DULONG, Suzanne
1201 Winterson Rd.
Linthicum, MD 21090
ir@ciena.com
Tel: (410) 694 - 5700
Fax:(410) 694 - 5750

Serves As:
• Chief Communications Officer, CIENA Corp.

DUNBAR, Melody W.
P.O. Box 5108
Denver, CO 80217-5108
dunbarm@jm.com
Tel: (303) 978 - 2350
Fax:(303) 978 - 2919
TF: (800) 654 - 3103

Serves As:
• Manager, Corporate Relations, Johns Manville Corp.

DUNCAN, Brian K.
1426 Main St.
Columbia, SC 29218
bduncan@scana.com
Tel: (803) 217 - 9501

Serves As:
• Public Affairs Coordinator, SCANA Corp.

DUNCAN, Bruce W.
Two N. Riverside Plaza
Suite 400
Chicago, IL 60606
Tel: (312) 474 - 1300
Fax:(312) 454 - 8703

Serves As:
- Chief Exec. Officer, Equity Residential

DUNCAN, Connie
3050 Bowers Ave.
P.O. Box 58039
Santa Clara, CA 95054-3299
connie_duncan@appliedmaterials.com
Tel: (408) 563 - 6209
Fax:(408) 986 - 2855

Serves As:
- Manager, Product Public Relations, Applied Materials, Inc.

DUNCAN, Don
1776 I St. NW
Suite 700
Washington, DC 20006
drdunca@ppco.com
Tel: (202) 833 - 0907
Fax:(202) 785 - 0639

Registered Federal Lobbyist.
Serves As:
- V. President, Federal and International Affairs, ConocoPhillips

DUNCAN, Douglas G.
1715 Aaron Brenner Dr.
Renaissance Center, Suite 600
Memphis, TN 38120
Tel: (901) 434 - 3122

Serves As:
- President and Chief Exec. Officer, FedEx Freight

DUNCAN, Drue
101 Madison St.
P.O. Box 780
Jefferson City, MO 65102
Tel: (573) 681 - 7124
Fax:(573) 681 - 7296

Serves As:
- Manager, Legislative Affairs, (AmerenUE), Ameren Corp.

DUNCAN, Duane
3900 Wisconsin Ave. NW
Washington, DC 20016
Tel: (202) 752 - 7000
Fax:(202) 752 - 6014

Registered Federal Lobbyist.
Serves As:
- Senior V. President, Government and Industry Relations, Fannie Mae

DUNCAN, III, Lawrence
1550 Crystal Dr.
Crystal Square 2, Suite 300
Arlington, VA 22202
Tel: (703) 413 - 5855
Fax:(703) 413 - 5617

Serves As:
- V. President, Congressional Relations, Trade and Regulatory Affairs, Lockheed Martin Corp.

DUNKEL, Robert
607 14th St. NW
Suite 950
Washington, DC 20005
Tel: (202) 429 - 0303
Fax:(202) 293 - 0561

Registered Federal Lobbyist.
Serves As:
- Exec. Director, Congressional Affairs, Qwest Communications

DUNKERLEY, Mark
P.O. Box 30008
Honolulu, HI 96820
Tel: (808) 835 - 3700
Fax:(808) 835 - 3690

Serves As:
- Chief Exec. Officer, Hawaiian Holdings, Inc.

DUNLAP, Leslie
2000 Pennsylvania Ave. NW
Suite 4200
Washington, DC 20006
Tel: (202) 887 - 6932
Fax:(202) 887 - 6933

Registered Federal Lobbyist.
Serves As:
- Director, Federal Relations, Yahoo! Inc.

DUNLEAVY, Michael F.
One Crown Way
Philadelphia, PA 19154-4599
mdunleavy@crowncork.com
Tel: (215) 698 - 5351
Fax:(215) 698 - 5201

Serves As:
- V. President, Corporate Affairs and Public Relations/PAC Treasurer, Crown Holdings, Inc.

DUNLOP, Johana
153 E. 53rd St., 57th Floor
New York, NY 10022-4624
Tel: (212) 350 - 9455
Fax:(212) 350 - 9564

Serves As:
- Manager, Schlumberger Foundation, Schlumberger Limited

DUNN, Debra L.
3000 Hanover St.
Palo Alto, CA 94304
Tel: (650) 857 - 1501
Fax:(650) 857 - 5518
TF: (800) 752 - 0900

Serves As:
- Senior V. President, Corporate Affairs, Hewlett-Packard Co.

DUNN, Denis
45 Erieview Plaza
Room 1500
Cleveland, OH 44114
Tel: (216) 822 - 2937
Fax:(216) 822 - 1791

Serves As:
- Director, External Affairs, SBC Ohio

DUNN, Gretchen
P.O. Box 868
Evansville, IN 47705-0868
Tel: (812) 464 - 9677
Fax:(812) 464 - 9825
TF: (800) 467 - 1928

Serves As:
- Shareholder Relations Contact, Integra Bank N.A.

DUNN, Loretta L.
1200 Wilson Blvd.
Arlington, VA 22209-2305
Tel: (703) 465 - 3282
Fax:(703) 465 - 3341

Registered Federal Lobbyist.
Serves As:
- V. President, Satellite Systems, Boeing Satellite Systems, Inc., The Boeing Co.

DUNN, Mark A.
P.O. Box 27
Boise, ID 83707
madunn@simplot.com
Tel: (208) 389 - 7377
Fax:(208) 389 - 7433

Serves As:
- V. President, Government Affairs, J. R. Simplot Co.
Responsibilities include political action.

DUNN, Norma F.
P.O. Box 13287
Kansas City, MO 64199-3287
norma.dunn@aquila.com
Tel: (816) 467 - 3143
Fax:(816) 467 - 9143

Serves As:
- Senior V. President, Corporate Communications, Aquila, Inc.

DUNN, Patricia C.
3000 Hanover St.
Palo Alto, CA 94304
Tel: (650) 857 - 1501
Fax:(650) 857 - 5518
TF: (800) 752 - 0900

Serves As:
- Chairman of the Board, Hewlett-Packard Co.

DUNN, Robert
2515 McKinney Ave., Suite 1200
Dallas, TX 75201
Tel: (214) 303 - 3400
Fax:(214) 303 - 3499

Serves As:
- Senior V. President, Human Resources, Dean Foods Company

DUNNELL, Mary Ann
199 Benson Rd.
Middlebury, VT 06749
Tel: (203) 573 - 3034
Fax:(203) 573 - 3711

Serves As:
- Media Contact, Chemtura

DUNNEWALD, David A.
P.O. Box 4030
M/S NH370
Golden, CO 80401-0030
Tel: (303) 277 - 5308
Fax:(303) 277 - 7666

Serves As:
- Director, Investor Relations, Coors Brewing Co.

DUNNIGAN, T. Kevin
8155 T & B Blvd.
Memphis, TN 38125
Tel: (901) 252 - 5000

Serves As:
- Chairman of the Board, Thomas & Betts Corp.

DUNSIRE, M.D., Deborah
40 Landsdowne St.
Cambridge, MA 02139
Tel: (617) 679 - 7000
Fax:(617) 374 - 7788
TF: (800) 390 - 5663

Serves As:
- President and Chief Exec. Officer, Millennium Pharmaceuticals, Inc.

DUNTON, Gary C.
113 King St.
Armonk, NY 10504
gary.dunton@mbia.com
Tel: (914) 273 - 4545
Fax:(914) 765 - 3163

Serves As:
- Chief Exec. Officer, MBIA, Inc.

DUPUY, Fielding
51 Madison Ave. Tel: (212) 576 - 7000
New York, NY 10010 Fax:(212) 576 - 8145
fielding_dupuy@newyorklife.com

Serves As:
- Corporate V. President, Corporate Communications, New York Life Insurance Co.

DURANDO, Paul
70 Maxess Rd. Tel: (631) 396 - 5000
Melville, NY 11747 Ext: 300
pdurando@nuhorizons.com Fax:(631) 696 - 5050

Serves As:
- V. President, Finance, Nu Horizons Electronics Corp.

Responsibilities include investor relations.

DURBIN, William J.
1341 W. Mockingbird Ln. Tel: (972) 647 - 6700
Dallas, TX 75247 Fax:(972) 647 - 3878
bdurbin@txi.com

Serves As:
- V. President, Human Resources, Texas Industries, Inc.

DURIK, Michael
999 W. Big Beaver Rd. Tel: (248) 244 - 4349
Troy, MI 48084-4782 Fax:(248) 244 - 7572
michael_durik@kellyservices.com

Serves As:
- Exec. V. President and Chief Administrative Officer, Kelly Services, Inc.

DURINKSY, Stephen
1293 S. Main St. Tel: (330) 253 - 5592
Akron, OH 44301 Fax:(330) 761 - 6111

Serves As:
- Director, Corporate Communications, Myers Industries, Inc.

DURLE, Tami
120 Monument Circle Tel: (317) 488 - 6390
Indianapolis, IN 46204

Serves As:
- V. President, Investor Relations, Wellpoint, Inc.

DURLING, Bill
83 Hartwell Ave. Tel: (781) 372 - 5886
Lexington, MA 02421
wdurling@us.ibm.com

Serves As:
- Director, Communications, (Rational Software), Internat'l Business Machines Corp. (IBM)

DUROC-DANNER, Bernard J.
515 Post Oak Blvd., Suite 600 Tel: (713) 693 - 4000
Houston, TX 77027-3415 Fax:(713) 693 - 4323
TF: (800) 257 - 3826

Serves As:
- Chairman and Chief Exec. Officer, Weatherford Internat'l Ltd.

DURR, Kathy
1194 N. Mathilda Ave. Tel: (408) 745 - 5058
Sunnyvale, CA 94089-1206 Fax:(408) 936 - 3033
kdurr@juniper.net

Serves As:
- Media Relations Contact, Juniper Networks, Inc.

DURST, Sherri
2711 N. Haskell Ave. Tel: (214) 828 - 7011
Dallas, TX 75204 Fax:(214) 828 - 7090

Serves As:
- PAC Treasurer, 7-Eleven, Inc.

DUSOSSOIT, Janine
800 The Safeguard Bldg. Tel: (610) 293 - 0600
435 Devon Park Dr. Fax:(610) 293 - 0601
Wayne, PA 19087-1945 TF: (888) 733 - 1200

Serves As:
- V. President, Investor Relations, Safeguard Scientifics, Inc.

Responsibilities include media relations.

DUTHIE, Steve J.
Administrative Center Tel: (269) 923 - 3373
2000 N. M-63 Fax:(269) 923 - 5443
Benton Harbor, MI 49022-2692
steve_j_duthie@email.whirlpool.com

Serves As:
- Manager, Media Relations, Whirlpool Corp.

DUTILH, Katherine M.
910 16th St. NW Tel: (202) 775 - 0084
Suite 402 Fax:(202) 775 - 0784
Washington, DC 20006
kdutilh@millikendc.com

Registered Federal Lobbyist.
Serves As:
- Legislative Assistant, Milliken & Co.

DUVAL, Daniel
50 Marcus Dr. Tel: (631) 847 - 2000
Melville, NY 11747

Serves As:
- Chairman of the Board, Arrow Electronics, Inc.

DUVALL, C. J.
One Allied Dr. Tel: (501) 905 - 8000
Little Rock, AR 72202

Serves As:
- Senior V. President, Human Resources, ALLTEL

DUVALL, Carol
6201 South Fwy. Tel: (817) 293 - 0450
Fort Worth, TX 76134 Fax:(817) 551 - 4615

Serves As:
- PAC Treasurer, (Alcon Laboratories, Inc.), Alcon Inc.

DUVALL, Suzanne
2345 Crystal Dr. Tel: (703) 236 - 2700
Suite 708 Fax:(703) 236 - 1931
Arlington, VA 22202

Registered Federal Lobbyist.
Serves As:
- Representative, Washington Group Internat'l

DUXBURY, Peggy
1401 H St. NW Tel: (202) 589 - 0909
Suite 510 Fax:(202) 589 - 0922
Washington, DC 20005

Registered Federal Lobbyist.
Serves As:
- Representative, Calpine Corp.

DVORAK, David
P.O. Box 708 Tel: (574) 267 - 6131
Warsaw, IN 46581-0708 Fax:(574) 372 - 4988
TF: (800) 613 - 6131

Serves As:
- Senior V. President, Corporate Affairs and General Counsel, Zimmer Holdings, Inc.

DVORAK, Kathleen S.
2200 E. Golf Rd. Tel: (847) 699 - 4723
Des Plaines, IL 60016-1267 Fax:(847) 699 - 4716

Serves As:
- Senior V. President and Chief Financial Officer, United Stationers Inc.

Responsibilities include investor relations and corporate communications.

DVORAK, Scott
1200 Willow Lake Blvd. Tel: (651) 236 - 5150
P.O. Box 64683 Fax:(651) 236 - 5165
St. Paul, MN 55164-0683 TF: (800) 214 - 2523
scott.dvorak@hbfuller.com

Serves As:
- Director, Investor Relations, H. B. Fuller Co.

DWORKIN, Peter
850 Lincoln Center Dr. Tel: (650) 554 - 2479
Foster City, CA 94404-1128 Fax:(650) 554 - 2810
dworkipg@appliedbiosystems.com

Serves As:
- V. President, Investor Relations and Corporate Communications, Applera Corp.

DWORKIN, Philippa M.
370 Woodcliff Dr. Tel: (585) 218 - 3733
Suite 300 TF: (888) 724 - 2169
Fairport, NY 14450
philippa.dworkin@cbrands.com

Serves As:
- Senior V. President, Corporate Communications, Constellation Brands, Inc.

DWYER, Joseph P.
708 Blair Mill Rd. Tel: (215) 784 - 4200
Willow Grove, PA 19090 Fax:(215) 784 - 4493

Serves As:
- Secretary-Treasurer, Asplundh Tree Expert Co.

Responsibilities include political action.

DWYER, Kate
City National Center
400 N. Roxbury Dr.
Beverly Hills, CA 90210
TF: (800) 773 - 7100

Serves As:
• Exec. V. President, Human Resources, City Nat'l Corp.

DWYER, Stacey H.
301 Commerce St.
Suite 500
Fort Worth, TX 76006
sdwyer@drhorton.com
Tel: (817) 390 - 8200
Fax:(817) 390 - 1715

Serves As:
• Exec. V. President, Investor Relations, D. R. Horton, Inc.
Responsibilities include corporate communications.

DYBDAHL, Gordy
1700 N. Webster Ct.
Green Bay, WI 54307-9017
Tel: (920) 433 - 5111
Fax:(920) 433 - 5150
TF: (800) 236 - 8400

Serves As:
• Manager, Corporate Communications, Green Bay Packaging Inc.

DYE, Molly
4205 River Green Pkwy.
Duluth, GA 30096-2568
Tel: (770) 813 - 6044
Fax:(770) 813 - 6118

Serves As:
• V. President, Corporate Relations, AGCO Corp.

DYE, Robert J.
2000 Post Oak Blvd., Suite 100
Houston, TX 77056-4400
Tel: (713) 296 - 6662
Fax:(713) 296 - 6480
TF: (800) 874 - 3262

Serves As:
• V. President, Investor Relations, Apache Corp.

DYE, Robert M.
P.O. Box 661
Milwaukee, WI 53201-0661
Tel: (414) 224 - 2725
Fax:(414) 224 - 2469

Serves As:
• V. President, Corporate Affairs, Journal Communications, Inc.
Responsibilities include corporate philanthropy.

DYER, Barbara
1509 22nd St. NW
Washington, DC 20037
Tel: (202) 457 - 0588
Fax:(202) 296 - 1098

Serves As:
• President and Chief Exec. Officer, The Hitachi Foundation, Hitachi America, Ltd.

DYER, Colin
200 E. Randolph St.
Chicago, IL 60601-6436
Tel: (312) 782 - 5800
Fax:(312) 782 - 4339

Serves As:
• President and Chief Exec. Officer, Jones Lang LaSalle Inc.

DYER, Deering
One Nationwide Plaza
Columbus, OH 43215-2220
Tel: (614) 249 - 9392
Fax:(614) 249 - 3073

Serves As:
• Manager, Government Relations, Nationwide

DYER-BRUGGEMAN, Dianne
P.O. Box 57013
Irvine, CA 92619-7013
Tel: (949) 450 - 8700
Fax:(949) 450 - 8710

Serves As:
• V. President, Human Resources, Broadcom Corp.

DYKERS, Bill
5005 LBJ Fwy.
Dallas, TX 75244
Tel: (972) 404 - 3800
Fax:(972) 404 - 3669
TF: (800) 578 - 8880

Serves As:
• Director, Communications and Web Development, Occidental Chemical Corp.

DYKES, Michael
1300 I St. NW
Suite 450 East
Washington, DC 20005-7211
Tel: (202) 783 - 2460
Fax:(202) 789 - 1819

Serves As:
• Director, International Government Affairs, Monsanto Co.

DYRDAHL, Melissa
345 Park Ave.
San Jose, CA 95110-2704
Tel: (408) 536 - 6000
Fax:(408) 537 - 6000

Serves As:
• Senior V. President, Corporate Marketing and Communications, Adobe Systems Inc.

DYRVIK, Per
1285 Ave. of the Americas
New York, NY 10019-6028
Tel: (212) 713 - 2000
Fax:(212) 713 - 1087

Serves As:
• Treasurer, UBS Americas Fund for Better Government, UBS Financial Services Inc.

DYSON, Caryn L.
800 Connecticut Ave. NW
Suite 600
Washington, DC 20006
Tel: (202) 533 - 1100
Fax:(202) 533 - 1134

Registered Federal Lobbyist.
Serves As:
• Representative, Accenture

DZIEWICZ, Michael S.
225 W. Station Square Dr.
suite 700
Pittsburgh, PA 15219
mdziewicz@wescodist.com
Tel: (412) 454 - 2382
Fax:(412) 454 - 2505

Serves As:
• Director, Human Resources, WESCO Internat'l, Inc.

DZIUBAN, Greg
P.O. Box 2206
Savannah, GA 31402-2206
Tel: (912) 965 - 7199
Fax:(912) 965 - 4466

Serves As:
• Director, Employee Communications, Gulfstream Aerospace Corp.
Responsibilities include corporate philanthropy.

EAGLE, A. Rae
2100 Rexford Rd.
Charlotte, NC 28211
Tel: (704) 366 - 7000
Fax:(704) 362 - 4208

Serves As:
• PAC Treasurer and Corporate Secretary, Nucor Corp.

EAKIN, Laura
1331 Pennsylvania Ave. NW
Suite 512
Washington, DC 20004
Tel: (202) 662 - 8750
Fax:(202) 662 - 8749

Serves As:
• Representative, Federal Government Relations, PPL Corp.

EARLEY, Jr., Anthony F.
2000 Second Ave.
Detroit, MI 48226
Tel: (313) 235 - 8000

Serves As:
• Chairman and Chief Exec. Officer, DTE Energy Co.

EARLEY, II, J. Fred
P.O. Box 7026
Wheeling, WV 26003
fearley@msbcbs.com
Tel: (304) 424 - 7798
Fax:(304) 424 - 7704
TF: (800) 344 - 5564

Serves As:
• Senior V. President, External Operations and General Counsel, Mountain State Blue Cross Blue Shield

EARLY, Karen
11 W. 42nd St.
New York, NY 10035
Tel: (212) 476 - 1000
Fax:(212) 476 - 1281

Serves As:
• Assistant V. President, Communications, Empire Blue Cross and Blue Shield

EARNHARDT, John
170 W. Tasman Dr.
San Jose, CA 95134-1706
john.earnhardt@cisco.com
Tel: (408) 527 - 2180
Fax:(408) 526 - 4100
TF: (800) 553 - 6387

Serves As:
• Manager, Communications, Cisco Systems, Inc.

EARNST, Collin
222 Berkeley St.
Boston, MA 02116
collin_earnst@hmco.com
Tel: (617) 351 - 5113
Fax:(617) 351 - 1100

Serves As:
• V. President, Corporate Communications, Houghton Mifflin Co.

EASLEY, Dale
P.O. Box 97034
Bellevue, WA 98009-9734
Tel: (425) 452 - 1234
Fax:(425) 462 - 3301

Serves As:
• PAC Treasurer, Puget Sound Energy

EAST, Ellen M.
6205 Peachtree Dunwoody Rd.
Atlanta, GA 30328
ellen.east@cox.com
Tel: (678) 645 - 0000

Serves As:
• V. President, Corporate Communications and Public Affairs, (Cox Communications, Inc.), Cox Enterprises, Inc.

EASTERLING-CHARLES, Deborah
4800 Deerwood Campus Pkwy.
DCC3-4
Jacksonville, FL 32246-8273
Tel: (904) 905 - 6647
Fax:(904) 905 - 4486
TF: (800) 477 - 3736

Serves As:
- Government Relations Representative, Blue Cross and Blue Shield of Florida

EASTMAN, Natasha
1211 Ave. of the Americas
New York, NY 10036
Tel: (212) 852 - 7073
Fax:(212) 852 - 7147

Serves As:
- Corporate Affairs Administrator, News Corporation Ltd.

EATON, Ken
P.O. Box 486
Little Rock, AR 72203
Tel: (501) 376 - 5200
Fax:(501) 376 - 5885
TF: (800) 643 - 8274

Serves As:
- V. President, Advertising, Dillard's Inc.

Responsibilities include corporate philanthropy.

EBEL, Gregory
312 Walnut St.
2800 Scripps Center
Cincinnati, OH 45202
ebel@scripps.com
Tel: (513) 977 - 3813
Fax:(513) 977 - 3721

Serves As:
- V. President, Human Resources, E. W. Scripps Co.

EBEL, Gregory L.
P.O. Box 1244
M/S PB03E
Charlotte, NC 28201-1244
glebel@duke-energy.com
Tel: (704) 382 - 8118
Fax:(704) 382 - 0084

Serves As:
- V. President, Investor and Shareholder Relations, Duke Energy Corp.

EBENHOCH, Kurt
2700 Lone Oak Pkwy.
M/S A1310
Eagan, MN 55121
Tel: (612) 727 - 4629
Fax:(612) 726 - 3942

Serves As:
- Director, Media Relations, Northwest Airlines, Inc.

EBERSOLE, Jeanne
452 Fifth Ave.
New York, NY 10018
Tel: (212) 525 - 5000
TF: (800) 975 - 4722

Serves As:
- Exec. V. President, Human Resources, HSBC USA, Inc.

EBNER, John A.
One Allied Dr.
Little Rock, AR 72202
Tel: (501) 905 - 8000
Fax:(501) 905 - 6018

Serves As:
- PAC Treasurer, ALLTEL

EBY, Tim
635 Massachusetts Ave. NW
Washington, DC 20001
Tel: (202) 513 - 2000
Fax:(202) 513 - 3329

Serves As:
- Chairman of the Board, Nat'l Public Radio

ECCLESTON, Barry
198 Van Buren St.
Suite 300
Herndon, VA 20170
Tel: (703) 834 - 3400
Fax:(703) 834 - 3567

Serves As:
- President and Chief Exec. Officer, Airbus North America Holdings, Inc.

ECHOLS, Margaret A.
One State Farm Plaza
M/S B-4
Bloomington, IL 61710-0001
Tel: (309) 766 - 6688
Fax:(309) 766 - 0860

Registered Federal Lobbyist.
Serves As:
- V. President, Corporate Communications and External Relations, State Farm Insurance Cos.

ECHOLS, Matthew T.
P.O. Box 1734
USA 644
Atlanta, GA 30301
mechols@na.ko.com
Tel: (404) 676 - 2251
Fax:(404) 676 - 6792

Serves As:
- Director, State Government Relations, The Coca-Cola Co.

ECKARD, J. Michael
1301 Pennsylvania Ave. NW
Suite 1030
Washington, DC 20004
jeckard@alleghenyenergy.com
Tel: (202) 824 - 0404
Fax:(202) 347 - 0132

Registered Federal Lobbyist.
Serves As:
- Director, Federal Government Affairs, Allegheny Energy Inc.

ECKERLE, Greg J.
1600 Royal St.
Jasper, IN 47549-1001
Tel: (812) 482 - 8474
Fax:(812) 482 - 8300
TF: (800) 482 - 1616

Serves As:
- Employee Communications Director, Kimball International, Inc.

ECKERT, Joann
P.O. Box 810
Amherst, NY 14226
joann_eckert@mark-iv.com
Tel: (716) 689 - 4980
Ext: 417
Fax:(716) 568 - 6098

Serves As:
- Contact, Mark IV Foundation, Mark IV Industries, Inc.

ECKERT, Robert A.
333 Continental Blvd.
El Segundo, CA 90245-5012
Tel: (310) 252 - 2000
Fax:(310) 252 - 2179

Serves As:
- Chairman and Chief Exec. Officer, Mattel, Inc.

ECKHART, Shannon B.
375 Hudson St.
New York, NY 10014
seckhart@tcco.com
Tel: (212) 229 - 6084
Fax:(212) 229 - 6390

Serves As:
- Public Relations Associate, The Turner Corp.

ECKLEY, Terry
501 Fifth St.
Bristol, TN 37620
Tel: (423) 989 - 8000
Fax:(423) 274 - 8677

Serves As:
- Senior Director, Public Relations, King Pharmaceuticals, Inc.

EDDY, Julie
3753 Ivy Green Trail
Tallahassee, FL 32311
julie.eddy@astrazeneca.com
Tel: (850) 219 - 9011
Fax:(850) 219 - 9013
TF: (800) 822 - 9209
Ext: 60201

Serves As:
- Director, State Government Affairs, AstraZeneca Pharmaceuticals

EDELSON, Howard J.
One Energy Plaza
Jackson, MI 49201
hjedelso@cmsenergy.com
Tel: (517) 788 - 0091
Fax:(517) 788 - 1315

Registered Federal Lobbyist.
Serves As:
- Director, Political Affairs, CMS Energy Corp.

EDELSON, James I.
511 Fifth Ave.
New York, NY 10017
Tel: (212) 953 - 4100
Fax:(212) 578 - 1832

Serves As:
- Treasurer, Overseas Shipholding Group Inc. PAC, Overseas Shipholding Group, Inc.

EDELSTON, Bruce H.
601 Pennsylvania Ave. NW
Suite 800
Washington, DC 20004
Tel: (202) 261 - 5000
Fax:(202) 296 - 7937

Registered Federal Lobbyist.
Serves As:
- Representative, Southern Company

EDEN, Greg
P.O. Box 9103
Hopkinton, MA 01748
eden_greg@emc.com
Tel: (508) 435 - 1000
Ext: 77195
Fax:(508) 435 - 7954
TF: (800) 424 - 3622

Serves As:
- Manager, Corporate Public Relations, EMC Corp.

EDGAR, Kevin R.
801 Pennsylvania Ave. NW
Suite 630
Washington, DC 20004
kedgar@nyse.com
Tel: (202) 347 - 4300
Fax:(202) 347 - 4370

Registered Federal Lobbyist.
Serves As:
- Special Counsel, Government Relations and Director, Public Affairs, New York Stock Exchange, Inc.

EDMUNDS, Robin
P.O. Box 50085
Watsonville, CA 95077-5085
Tel: (831) 724 - 1011
Fax:(831) 722 - 9657
TF: (800) 482 - 1518

Serves As:
- Corporate Communications Contact, Granite Construction Inc.

EDRIS, James A.
100 Crystal A Dr.
P.O. Box 810
Hershey, PA 17033
jedris@hersheys.com
Tel: (717) 534 - 7556
Fax:(717) 534 - 7015

Serves As:
- V. President, Investor Relations, The Hershey Company

EDWARDS, Alan
1717 E. Interstate Ave.
Bismarck, ND 58503
Tel: (701) 223 - 0441
Fax:(701) 224 - 5336

Serves As:
- V. President, External Relations and Communications, Basin Electric Power Cooperative

EDWARDS, Donna F.
P.O. Box 35920
Cleveland, OH 44135-0920
Tel: (216) 898 - 2341
Fax:(216) 898 - 2366

Registered Federal Lobbyist.
Serves As:
- Immigration/Legislative Specialist, Electrolux North America, Inc.

EDWARDS, Ellsworth
901 N. Tatnall St., Second Floor
Wilmington, DE 19801
Tel: (302) 571 - 1571
Fax:(302) 576 - 1132

Serves As:
- Manager, Media Relations, Verizon Delaware Inc.

EDWARDS, Jr., George W.
P.O. Box 982
El Paso, TX 79960
Tel: (915) 543 - 5711
Fax:(915) 521 - 4766
TF: (800) 351 - 1621

Serves As:
- Chairman of the Board, El Paso Electric Co.

EDWARDS, Richard
2100 Hwy. 55
Medina, MN 55340
richard.edwards@polarisind.com
Tel: (763) 513 - 3477
Fax:(763) 542 - 0599

Serves As:
- Director, Investor Relations, Polaris Industries Inc.

EDWARDS, Warren
2828 N. Haskell Ave.
Dallas, TX 75204
Tel: (214) 841 - 6111

Serves As:
- Exec. V. President and Chief Financial Officer, Affiliated Computer Services, Inc. (ACS)
Responsibilities include investor relations.

EDWARDS, Winona
6201 South Fwy.
Fort Worth, TX 76134
Tel: (817) 293 - 0450
Fax:(817) 568 - 7000

Serves As:
- President, Alcon Foundation, Alcon Inc.

EDWARDSON, Bryan B.
1101 15th St. NW
Suite 1000
Washington, DC 20005
bryan_edwardson@cargill.com
Tel: (202) 530 - 8160
Fax:(202) 530 - 8180

Registered Federal Lobbyist.
Serves As:
- Director, Public Policy, Cargill, Incorporated

EDWARDSON, John A.
200 N. Milwaukee Ave.
Vernon Hills, IL 60061
Tel: (847) 465 - 6000
Fax:(847) 465 - 3444

Serves As:
- Chairman and Chief Exec. Officer, CDW Corp.

EGAN, Kathy
100 Park Ave., Suite 2705
New York, NY 10017
kathy.egan@ericsson.com
Tel: (212) 843 - 8422
Fax:(212) 213 - 0159

Serves As:
- V. President, Communications, Ericsson Inc.

EGENIAS, Carol
P.O. Box 513338
Los Angeles, CA 90051-1338
Tel: (626) 821 - 7560

Serves As:
- Donations Contact, Vons

EGER, Charles
1350 I St. NW
Suite 400
Washington, DC 20005-3306
Tel: (202) 371 - 6900
Fax:(202) 842 - 3578

Registered Federal Lobbyist.
Serves As:
- Director, Office of Driver Safety, Motorola, Inc.

EGGERSS, Linda
1716 Locust St.
Des Moines, IA 50309-3023
Tel: (515) 284 - 3125
Fax:(515) 284 - 3806

Serves As:
- Manager, Corporate Communications, Meredith Corp.

EGGL, Mike
1717 E. Interstate Ave.
Bismarck, ND 58503
meggl@bepc.com
Tel: (701) 223 - 0441
Fax:(701) 224 - 5336

Serves As:
- V. President, Government Relations, Basin Electric Power Cooperative

EGING, Michael J.
1425 K St. NW
Suite 650
Washington, DC 20005
michael_j.eging@roche.com
Tel: (202) 408 - 0090
Fax:(202) 408 - 1750

Registered Federal Lobbyist.
Serves As:
- Exec. Director, Public Policy and Federal Government Affairs, Hoffmann-La Roche Inc. (Roche)

EGLESTON, Robert J.
1000 Lowes Blvd.
Moorsville, NC 28117
robert.j.egleston@lowes.com
Tel: (704) 758 - 100
Fax:(336) 658 - 4766
TF: (800) 445 - 6937

Serves As:
- Community Relations Manager, Lowe's Companies, Inc.

EHLERT, Carolyn J.
One John Deere Pl.
Moline, IL 61265-8098
Tel: (309) 765 - 4954
Fax:(309) 765 - 5183

Serves As:
- Director, Public Affairs Policy and Program Support, Deere & Company

EHRIG, William J.
P.O. Box 32070
Louisville, KY 40232
Tel: (502) 874 - 8049

Registered Federal Lobbyist.
Serves As:
- Senior Director, Government Affairs, YUM! Brands, Inc.

EHRLICH, Bill
P.O. Box 834
Seattle, WA 98101
Tel: (206) 461 - 2000
Fax:(206) 554 - 4807
TF: (800) 756 - 8000

Serves As:
- Exec. V. President, Strategic Communications, Washington Mutual, Inc.

EHRLICH, Paul C.
1130 Connecticut Ave. NW
Suite 500
Washington, DC 20036
Tel: (202) 463 - 7372
Fax:(202) 463 - 8809

Registered Federal Lobbyist.
Serves As:
- Manager, Legislative Affairs, Schering-Plough Corporation

EHST, Dick
P.O. Box 12646
Reading, PA 19612
dehst@sovereignbank.com
Tel: (610) 378 - 6158
Fax:(610) 320 - 8448

Serves As:
- Exec. V. President and Managing Director, Corporate Communications, Sovereign Bancorp, Inc.

EHUDIN, Marc L.
1235 S. Clark St.
Suite 1100
Arlington, VA 22202
ehudin@aaicorp.com
Tel: (703) 412 - 4170
Fax:(703) 416 - 4820

Registered Federal Lobbyist.
Serves As:
- Director, Legislative Affairs, AAI Corp.

EICH, Jack
P.O. Box 391
Madison, WI 53701
jack.eich@cunamutual.com
Tel: (608) 232 - 6539
Fax:(608) 236 - 8685
TF: (800) 356 - 2644

Serves As:
- Manager, Media Relations, CUNA Mutual Group

EICHINGER, Whitney
P.O. Box 36611 Tel: (214) 792 - 6604
HDQ-1PR Fax:(214) 792 - 4200
Dallas, TX 75235-1611 TF: (800) 435 - 9792

Serves As:
- Regional Manager, Public Relations, Southwest Airlines Co.

EICHNER, Ira A.
One AAR Pl. Tel: (630) 227 - 2000
1100 N. Wood Dale Rd. Fax:(630) 227 - 2019
Wood Dale, IL 60191

Serves As:
- Chairman of the Board, AAR Corp.

EIDMAN, Diane
120 Park Ave. Tel: (917) 663 - 2845
New York, NY 10017 Fax:(917) 663 - 5874

Serves As:
- Director, Corporate Contributions, Altria Group, Inc.

EIDS, Susan
P.O. Box 956 Tel: (310) 964 - 0700
El Segundo, CA 90245-0956 Fax:(310) 647 - 6212

Registered Federal Lobbyist.
Serves As:
- Representative, The DIRECTV Group, Inc.

EIDSON, Tom
82 Devonshire St. Tel: (617) 563 - 7000
Boston, MA 02109-3614 Fax:(617) 476 - 6150

Serves As:
- Exec. V. President and Director, Corporate Affairs, FMR Corp.

EILAND, Jill
650 N.E. Holladay, Suite 1400 Tel: (503) 872 - 1519
Portland, OR 97232 Fax:(503) 872 - 1349
TF: (800) 633 - 1488

Serves As:
- Senior Director, Government Affairs and Public Relations, KinderCare Learning Centers, Inc.

EILER, William S.
20 Stanwix St. Tel: (412) 644 - 8073
Pittsburgh, PA 15222-4802 Fax:(412) 644 - 7723
william.eiler@nationalcity.com

Serves As:
- V. President, Media Relations, (Nat'l City Bank, Pennsylvania), Nat'l City Corp.

Media contact for Michigan, Pennsylvania and Youngstown, Ohio.

EINCK, Stacy
100 Fourth Ave. North Tel: (651) 264 - 5150
Bayport, MN 55003-1096

Serves As:
- Manager, Public Affairs, Andersen Corp.

EIREF, Zvi
469 N. Harrison St. Tel: (609) 279 - 7666
Princeton, NJ 08543-5297 Fax:(609) 497 - 7269

Serves As:
- Media and Investor Relations Contact, Church & Dwight Co., Inc.

EISCH, Cynthia B.
4211 W. Boyscout Blvd. Tel: (813) 871 - 4811
Tampa, FL 33607 Fax:(813) 871 - 4420

Serves As:
- Treasurer, Walter Industries Inc. PAC, Walter Industries, Inc.

EISELE, Mark O.
One Applied Plaza Tel: (216) 426 - 4000
Cleveland, OH 44115 Fax:(216) 426 - 4804
TF: (877) 279 - 2799

Serves As:
- V. President, Chief Financial Officer and Treasurer, Applied Industrial Technologies

Responsibilities include investor relations.

EISENBERG, Warren
650 Liberty Ave. Tel: (908) 688 - 0888
Union, NJ 07083 Ext: 4500
Fax:(908) 688 - 6483

Serves As:
- Co-Chairman of the Board, Bed Bath & Beyond Inc.

EISENBUD, Robert
601 Pennsylvania Ave. NW Tel: (202) 628 - 3500
North Bldg. Suite 300 Fax:(202) 628 - 0400
Washington, DC 20004
beisenbudwm.com

Registered Federal Lobbyist.
Serves As:
- Director, Legislative Affairs, Waste Management, Inc.

EISINGER, Neleen
One Edwards Way Tel: (949) 250 - 2500
Irvine, CA 92614-5688 Fax:(949) 250 - 2525
TF: (800) 424 - 3278

Serves As:
- Treasurer, EWPAC, Edwards Lifesciences Corp.

EISNER, Michael D.
500 S. Buena Vista St. Tel: (818) 560 - 6180
Burbank, CA 91521 Fax:(818) 560 - 1930
michael.eisner@corp.disney.com

Serves As:
- Chief Exec. Officer, The Walt Disney Company

EITEL, Maria S.
One Bowerman Dr. Tel: (503) 671 - 6453
Beaverton, OR 97005 Fax:(503) 671 - 6300
maria.eitel@nike.com

Serves As:
- President, Nike Foundation, Nike, Inc.

EKAITIS, David M.
3210 Watling St. Tel: (219) 399 - 5379
East Chicago, IN 46312 Fax:(219) 399 - 4448
david.ekaitis@ispat.com

Serves As:
- Manager, Risk Management and Insurance, Ispat Inland Inc.

ELBIN, John C.
9800 Crosspoint Blvd. Tel: (317) 594 - 2100
Indianapolis, IN 46256 Fax:(317) 594 - 2704

Serves As:
- Chief Financial Officer, Marsh Supermarkets, Inc.

ELDER, Eric
24025 Park Sorrento Tel: (818) 223 - 7500
Suite 400 Fax:(818) 223 - 7667
Calabasas, CA 91302 TF: (800) 267 - 0998

Serves As:
- Senior V. President, Marketing and Communications, The Ryland Group, Inc.

ELDER, Susan
One Invacare Way Tel: (440) 329 - 6000
Elyria, OH 44035 Fax:(440) 329 - 6568
susan.elder@invacare.com TF: (800) 333 - 6900

Serves As:
- Director, Marketing Communications, Invacare Corp.

ELDER, Timothy L.
100 NE Adams St. Tel: (309) 675 - 4872
Peoria, IL 61629-1465 Fax:(309) 675 - 5815

Serves As:
- Director, Corporate Public Affairs, Caterpillar Inc.

ELDRIDGE, Earle
1401 H St. NW Tel: (202) 414 - 6700
Suite 700 Fax:(202) 414 - 6716
Washington, DC 20005

Serves As:
- Senior Manager, Washington Public Affairs, DaimlerChrysler Corp.

ELIAS, Alan
201 Mission St. Tel: (415) 543 - 0404
San Francisco, CA 94105 Fax:(415) 278 - 6028
alan_elias@providian.com

Serves As:
- V. President, Corporate Communications, Providian Financial Corp.

ELICKER, John
345 Park Ave. Tel: (212) 546 - 3775
New York, NY 10154-0037 Fax:(212) 546 - 4020
john.elicker@bms.com

Serves As:
- V. President, Investor Relations, Bristol-Myers Squibb Co.

ELISE, Lori
P.O. Box 1590 Tel: (214) 443 - 5500
Dallas, TX 75221-1590 Fax:(214) 443 - 5622

Serves As:
- Director, Corporate Communications, Austin Industries

ELIZONDO, Juanita
5235 Katy Fwy. Tel: (713) 869 - 5060
Houston, TX 77007 Ext: 3268
Fax:(713) 869 - 6197

Serves As:
- Contact, Fiesta Mart Inc. Giving Program, Fiesta Mart Inc.

ELKIN, Beth
One i2 Pl.
11701 Luna Rd.
Dallas, TX 75234
beth_elkin@i2.com
Tel: (469) 357 - 4225
Fax:(469) 357 - 3677

Serves As:
- Director, Public Relations, i2 Technologies, Inc.

ELKIN, James R.
701 Pennsylvania Ave. NW
Suite 725
Washington, DC 20004
Tel: (202) 638 - 7429
Fax:(202) 628 - 4763

Registered Federal Lobbyist.
Serves As:
- V. President, Federal Government Relations, Novartis Corporation

ELKIN, Lisa
One Campus Martius
Detroit, MI 48226
lisa.elkin@compuware.com
Tel: (313) 227 - 7345
Fax:(313) 227 - 7555
TF: (800) 292 - 7432

Serves As:
- V. President, Corporate Communications and Investor Relations, Compuware Corp.

ELKINS, Gilda
401 E. Liberty
Ann Arbor, MI 48104-2298
Tel: (734) 930 - 6011
Fax:(734) 930 - 6721

Serves As:
- Community Development, Home Improvement Lender, TCF Bank

ELLENDER, Philip
4332 Emory Ave.
Baton Rouge, LA 70808
Tel: (225) 767 - 4114
Fax:(225) 767 - 4177

Serves As:
- V. President, Public Affairs, (INVISTA), Koch Industries, Inc.

ELLER, Timothy
P.O. Box 199000
Dallas, TX 75219-9000
Tel: (214) 981 - 5000
Fax:(214) 981 - 6859

Serves As:
- Chairman and Chief Exec. Officer, Centex Corporation

ELLERBROOK, Niel C.
211 Riverside Dr.
Evansville, IN 47708-1251
Tel: (812) 491 - 4000
Fax:(812) 491 - 4078
TF: (800) 227 - 1376

Serves As:
- Chairman, President and Chief Exec. Officer, Vectren Corp.

ELLIOT, Jennifer
99 Church St.
New York, NY 10007-2707
Tel: (212) 553 - 0300
Fax:(212) 553 - 4820

Serves As:
- V. President and Chief Human Resources Officer, Moody's Corp.

ELLIOT, Kate
701 Ninth St. NW
Washington, DC 20068
Tel: (202) 872 - 2000

Registered Federal Lobbyist.
Serves As:
- Senior Government Affairs Representative, Pepco Holdings, Inc.

ELLIOTT, Dale F.
P.O. Box 1430
Kenosha, WI 53141-1430
dale.elliott@snapon.com
Tel: (414) 656 - 5200
Fax:(414) 656 - 5577

Serves As:
- Chairman, President and Chief Exec. Officer, Snap-on Incorporated

ELLIOTT, David A.
1609 Biddle Ave.
W. Administration Bldg. 1-114
Wyandotte, MI 48192
elliotd1@basf-corp.com
Tel: (734) 324 - 6148
Fax:(734) 324 - 6549

Serves As:
- Manager, Communications NAFTA II (Coatings, Polymers and Fine Chemicals), BASF Corporation

ELLIOTT, Gregg W.
P.O. Box 1488
4201 Winfield Rd.
Warrenfield, IL 60555
greg.elliott@nav-international.com
Tel: (630) 753 - 2300

Serves As:
- V. President, Corporate Human Resources and Administration, Navistar Internat'l Corp.

ELLIOTT, J. Raymond
P.O. Box 708
Warsaw, IN 46581-0708
Tel: (574) 267 - 6131
Fax:(574) 372 - 4988
TF: (800) 613 - 6131

Serves As:
- Chairman, President and Chief Exec. Officer, Zimmer Holdings, Inc.

ELLIOTT, Jeffrey
999 Lake Dr.
Issaquah, WA 98027
Tel: (425) 313 - 8264
Fax:(425) 313 - 6430

Serves As:
- Director, Financial Planning and Investor Relations, Costco Wholesale Corp.

ELLIOTT, Robert A.
Eaton Center
1111 Superior Ave.
Cleveland, OH 44114-2584
Tel: (216) 523 - 5000
Fax:(216) 523 - 4787

Serves As:
- PAC Treasurer, Eaton Corp.

ELLIOTT, Sue
8000 Bent Branch Dr.
Irving, TX 75063
elliott@michaels.com
Tel: (972) 409 - 5200
Fax:(972) 409 - 1556

Serves As:
- Senior V. President, Human Resources, Michaels Stores, Inc.

ELLIS, Andrew K.
1200 Wilson Blvd.
Arlington, VA 22209-2305
Tel: (703) 465 - 3405
Fax:(703) 465 - 3985

Serves As:
- V. President, Integrated Defense Systems, The Boeing Co.

ELLIS, Clayton M.
P.O. Box 5224
Binghamton, NY 13902-5224
cmellis@nyseg.com
Tel: (607) 762 - 7336
Fax:(607) 762 - 8595

Serves As:
- Manager, Corporate Communications, (New York State Electric & Gas Corp. (NYSEG)), Energy East Corp.

ELLIS, Gary L.
1420 New York Ave. NW
Suite 600
Washington, DC 20005
Tel: (202) 393 - 6444
Fax:(202) 289 - 9222

Serves As:
- PAC Treasurer, Medtronic, Inc.

ELLIS, Kristi Lamont
P.O. Box 10247
Birmingham, AL 35202
kristi.ellis@regions.com
Tel: (205) 326 - 7179
Fax:(205) 326 - 7105
TF: (800) 734 - 4667

Serves As:
- Senior V. President, Corporate Communications, Regions Financial Corp.

ELLIS, Martin
6065 Parkland Blvd.
Cleveland, OH 44124
martin.ellis@agilysys.com
Tel: (440) 720 - 8682
Fax:(440) 720 - 8677
TF: (800) 422 - 2400

Serves As:
- Exec. V. President, Treasurer, and Chief Financial Officer, Agilysys, Inc.

ELLIS, Robert E.
Strawberry Lane
Orrville, OH 44667-0280
Tel: (330) 682 - 3000
Fax:(330) 684 - 6410
TF: (888) 550 - 9555

Serves As:
- V. President, Human Resources, The J. M. Smucker Company

ELLISON, Alice
One Pershing Square
2301 Main St.
Kansas City, MO 64108
Tel: (816) 395 - 2222

Serves As:
- V. President, Community Relations, Blue Cross and Blue Shield of Kansas City

ELLISON, Jennifer
Dain Rauscher Plaza
60 S. Sixth St., 19th Floor
Minneapolis, MN 55402-4422
jennifer.ellison@rbcdain.com
Tel: (612) 371 - 2225
Fax:(612) 371 - 2960

Serves As:
- Senior Media Relations Specialist, RBC Dain Rauscher Corp.

ELLISON, Laurie
4551 W. 107th St.
Overland Park, KS 66207-4037
laurie.ellison@applebees.com
Tel: (913) 967 - 2718
Fax:(913) 341 - 1694

Serves As:
- Exec. Director, Corporate Communications, Applebee's Internat'l, Inc.

ELLISON, Lawrence J.
500 Oracle Pkwy.
Redwood Shores, CA 94065
Tel: (650) 506 - 7000
Fax:(650) 506 - 7200
TF: (800) 672 - 2531

Serves As:
• Chief Exec. Officer, Oracle Corporation

ELLSWORTH, Melinda C.
P.O. Box 1109
Muscatine, IA 52761-0071
ellsworthm@honi.com
Tel: (563) 264 - 7406
Fax:(563) 264 - 7217

Serves As:
• V. President, Treasurer Investor Relations, HNI Corp.

ELVOVE, Roy
1285 Ave. of the Americas
New York, NY 10019-6095
Tel: (212) 459 - 5797
Fax:(212) 459 - 6645

Serves As:
• Exec. V. President, Director of Corp. Communications, BBDO New York

ELWELL, Dan
1101 17th St. NW
Suite 600
Washington, DC 20036
Tel: (202) 496 - 5654
Fax:(202) 496 - 5660

Registered Federal Lobbyist.
Serves As:
• Managing Director, International and Government Affairs, (American Airlines, Inc.), AMR Corp.

ELY, Gary
P.O. Box 3727
MSC-12
Spokane, WA 99220-3727
gary.ely@avistacorp.com
Tel: (509) 489 - 0500
Fax:(509) 495 - 8725

Serves As:
• Chairman, President and Chief Exec. Officer, Avista Corp.

ELY, James S.
P.O. Box 6675
Radnor, PA 19087-8675
jim.ely@airgas.com
Tel: (610) 902 - 6010
Fax:(610) 687 - 1052
TF: (800) 255 - 2165

Serves As:
• V. President, Communications, Airgas, Inc.

EMBRY, Gerald
P.O. Drawer 2128
Dalton, GA 30722-2128
Tel: (706) 278 - 3812
Fax:(706) 275 - 1719

Serves As:
• V. President, Administration, Shaw Industries
Responsibilities include corporate philanthropy.

EMERICK, David A.
10139 S. Mountain Maple Court
Highlands Ranch, CO 80126-5435
Tel: (303) 346 - 0655

Serves As:
• Regional Director, Government Relations, HSBC North America Holdings Inc.

EMERSON, Frances B.
One John Deere Pl.
Moline, IL 61265-8098
Tel: (309) 765 - 4634
Fax:(309) 765 - 5772

Serves As:
• V. President, Corporate Communications and Chairman, John Deere Foundation, Deere & Company

EMERY, David R.
P.O. Box 1400
Rapid City, SD 57709-1400
demery@bh-corp.com
Tel: (605) 721 - 1700
Fax:(605) 721 - 2599

Serves As:
• Chief Exec. Officer and President, Black Hills Corp.

EMERZIAN, Ron
P.O. Box 1130
Modesto, CA 95353
Tel: (209) 341 - 3141
Fax:(209) 341 - 3208

Serves As:
• V. President, Community Affairs, Gallo Foundation, Ernest and Julio Gallo Winery

EMKES, Mark A.
535 Marriott Dr.
Nashville, TN 37214-8900
Tel: (615) 937 - 0088
Fax:(615) 937 - 3612

Serves As:
• Chairman and Chief Exec. Officer, Bridgestone Americas Holding, Inc.

EMLING, Gretchen
1627 I St. NW
Suite 900
Washington, DC 20006
Tel: (202) 833 - 8994
Fax:(202) 835 - 0707

Registered Federal Lobbyist.
Serves As:
• Manager, Government Relations, Williams

EMPSON, Jon R.
1815 Capitol Ave.
Omaha, NE 68102
jon.empson@aquila.com
Tel: (402) 221 - 2375
Fax:(402) 221 - 2501

Serves As:
• Senior V. President, Regulated Operations, Aquila, Inc.

EMRA, John
310 Orange St.
New Haven, CT 06510
Tel: (203) 771 - 5200
Fax:(203) 497 - 9184

Serves As:
• Exec. Director, External Affairs, SBC SNET

ENDRES, Jr., Arthur P.
700 13th St. NW
Suite 220
Washington, DC 20005
skip.endres@bnsf.com
Tel: (202) 347 - 8662
Fax:(202) 347 - 8675

Registered Federal Lobbyist.
Serves As:
• V. President, Government Affairs, Burlington Northern Santa Fe Corporation

ENEDY, Allison M.
Three Commercial Pl.
Norfolk, VA 23510-2191
Tel: (757) 629 - 2708
Fax:(757) 629 - 2822

Serves As:
• Manager, Online Communications, Norfolk Southern Corp.

ENGEL, Brian E.
20 N. Broadway, Suite 1500
Oklahoma City, OK 73102
brian.engel@dvn.com
Tel: (405) 228 - 7750
Fax:(405) 552 - 7818

Serves As:
• Public Affairs Manager, Devon Energy Corp.

ENGEL, Randy
1700 Lincoln St.
Denver, CO 80203
Tel: (303) 837 - 6033
Fax:(303) 837 - 5837

Serves As:
• Investor Relations, Newmont Mining Corp.

ENGELBERG, Steven
1300 I St. NW
Suite 450 East
Washington, DC 20005-7211
Tel: (202) 783 - 2460
Fax:(202) 789 - 1819

Serves As:
• Senior V. President, Global Affairs, Monsanto Co.

ENGELBRET, Karen
5050 Lincoln Dr.
Edina, MN 55436
karen.engelbret@atk.com
Tel: (952) 351 - 2778
Fax:(952) 351 - 3009

Serves As:
• Foundation Contact, Alliant Techsystems

ENGELHARDT, Irl F.
701 Market St.
St. Louis, MO 63101-1826
iengelhardt@peabodyenergy.com
Tel: (314) 342 - 3400
Fax:(314) 342 - 7797

Serves As:
• Chairman and Chief Exec. Officer, Peabody Energy

ENGELHARDT, Michael
8201 Greensboro Dr., Suite 1000
McLean, VA 22102
mengelha@adobe.com
Tel: (703) 883 - 2831

Registered Federal Lobbyist.
Serves As:
• Senior Director, Public Policy, Adobe Systems Inc.

ENGELSMA, Bruce W.
525 S. Eighth St.
Minneapolis, MN 55404
Tel: (612) 332 - 7281
Fax:(612) 332 - 0217

Serves As:
• Chairman and Chief Exec. Officer, Kraus-Anderson Cos. Inc.

ENGH, Rolph
1101 Third St. South
Minneapolis, MN 55415
rengh@valspar.com
Tel: (612) 375 - 7705
Fax:(612) 375 - 7313

Serves As:
• Exec. V. President, General Counsel and Secretary, Valspar Corp.
Responsibilities include government affairs.

ENGIBOUS, Thomas J.
P.O. Box 660199
Dallas, TX 75266-0199
Tel: (214) 995 - 2011
Fax:(214) 995 - 5150
TF: (800) 336 - 5236

Serves As:
• Chairman of the Board, Texas Instruments Incorporated

ENGLE, Kimberley A.
601 Pennsylvania Ave. NW
North Bldg. Suite 300
Washington, DC 20004
kengle@wm.com
Tel: (202) 628 - 3500
Fax:(202) 628 - 0400

Serves As:
- Manager, Government Affairs, Waste Management, Inc.

ENGLEBARDT, Jane S.
P.O. Box 1059
Pawtucket, RI 02862
Tel: (401) 606 - 6226
Fax:(401) 431 - 8535

Serves As:
- Exec. Director, Hasbro Children's Foundation, Hasbro Inc.

ENGLERT, Greg
600 Pennsylvania Ave. SE
Suite 220
Washington, DC 20003
Tel: (202) 544 - 8814
Fax:(202) 544 - 8853

Registered Federal Lobbyist.
Serves As:
- Senior Government Affairs Representative, Highmark Inc.

ENGLES, Gregg L.
2515 McKinney Ave., Suite 1200
Dallas, TX 75201
Tel: (214) 303 - 3400
Fax:(214) 303 - 3499

Serves As:
- Chairman and Chief Exec. Officer, Dean Foods Company

ENGLISH, John E.
P.O. Box 385014
Birmingham, AL 35238-5014
englishj@vmcmail.com
Tel: (205) 298 - 3189
Fax:(205) 298 - 3246

Serves As:
- Manager, Public Affairs, Vulcan Materials Co.

ENGLISH, Linda K.
1341 W. Mockingbird Ln.
Dallas, TX 75247
lenglish@txi.com
Tel: (972) 647 - 6732
Fax:(972) 647 - 3776

Serves As:
- Administrator, Investor and Shareholder Relations, Texas Industries, Inc.

ENGLISH, Natalie
Four Colesium Center
2730 W. Tyvola Rd.
Charlotte, NC 28217
natalie.english@goodrich.com
Tel: (704) 423 - 7489

Serves As:
- Director, Community Relations, Goodrich Corporation

ENGLISH, Roderick
2902 Enterprise Dr.
Anderson, IN 46013
Tel: (765) 778 - 6499
Fax:(765) 778 - 6404
TF: (800) 372 - 5131

Serves As:
- Senior V. President, Human Resources, Delco Remy Internat'l Inc.

ENGLISH, Steven
1120 G St. NW
Suite 850
Washington, DC 20005
Tel: (202) 347 - 5910
Fax:(202) 347 - 5916

Serves As:
- Government Affairs Representative, Nationwide

ENOCHSON, Jenny
P.O. Box 3599
Battle Creek, MI 49016-3599
jenny.enochson@kellogg.com
Tel: (269) 961 - 3799
Fax:(269) 961 - 2871
TF: (800) 535 - 5644

Serves As:
- Public Relations Contact, Kellogg Co.

ENSIGN, Clinton W.
P.O. Box 30825
Salt Lake City, UT 84130-0825
Tel: (801) 524 - 2767
Fax:(801) 524 - 2848

Registered Federal Lobbyist.
Serves As:
- V. President, Government Relations, Sinclair Oil Corp.

ENTREKIN, David
151 Farmington Ave.
MS RW3H
Hartford, CT 06156
entrekind@aetna.com
Tel: (860) 273 - 7830
Fax:(860) 273 - 3971
TF: (800) 872 - 3862

Serves As:
- V. President, Investor Relations, Aetna Inc.

EOLOFF, Anita B.
Wells Fargo Center
Sixth & Marquette
M/S N9305-171
Minneapolis, MN 55479
Tel: (612) 667 - 9917
Fax:(612) 667 - 9403

Serves As:
- Director, Federal Government Relations and PAC Treasurer, Wells Fargo & Co.

EPIFANO, Frank
Discovery Dr.
Swiftwater, PA 18370
Tel: (570) 839 - 7187
Fax:(570) 839 - 7235

Serves As:
- PAC Treasurer, Sanofi Pasteur, Inc.

EPP, Phyllis M.
400 Atlantic St.
Stamford, CT 06921
phyllis.epp@ipaper.com
Tel: (203) 541 - 8678
Fax:(203) 541 - 8309
TF: (800) 223 - 1268

Serves As:
- Exec. Director, IPCO Foundation, Internat'l Paper

EPPEL, W.G.
One Salem Lake Dr.
Long Grove, IL 60047
weppel@cfindustries.com
Tel: (847) 438 - 9500
Ext: 3232
Fax:(847) 438 - 0211

Serves As:
- V. President, Human Resources, C F Industries, Inc.

EPPINGER, Frederick H.
440 Lincoln St.
Worcester, MA 01653
Tel: (508) 855 - 1000

Serves As:
- President and Chief Exec. Officer, Allmerica Property & Casualty Companies, Inc.

EPPLER, David M.
P.O. Box 5000
Pineville, LA 71361-5000
Tel: (318) 484 - 7400
Fax:(318) 484 - 7465

Serves As:
- President and Chief Exec. Officer, Cleco Corp.

EPSTEIN, Christopher
750 17th St. NW
Suite 400
Washington, DC 20006
Tel: (202) 861 - 0660
Fax:(202) 861 - 0437

Serves As:
- Director, Export Controls Compliance, Mitsui and Co. (U.S.A.), Inc.

EPSTEIN, Debra
One Canon Plaza
Lake Success, NY 11042-1198
Tel: (516) 488 - 6700
Fax:(516) 328 - 5069

Serves As:
- V. President and General Manager, Corporate Communications, Canon U.S.A., Inc.

Responsibilities include investor relations and corporate philanthropy.

EPSTEIN, Jan
2775 Sanders Rd.
Northbrook, IL 60062-6127
jepstein@allstate.com
Tel: (847) 402 - 2794
TF: (800) 574 - 3553

Serves As:
- Exec. Director, Allstate Foundation, Allstate Insurance Co.

EPSTEIN, Karen
145 Pleasant Hill Rd.
Scarborough, ME 04074
Tel: (207) 883 - 2911
Fax:(207) 885 - 3165

Serves As:
- Manager, Public Relations, Hannaford Bros. Co.

EPSTEIN, Tom
50 Beale St.
San Francisco, CA 94105-1808
Tel: (415) 229 - 5110
Fax:(415) 229 - 5070
TF: (800) 200 - 3242

Serves As:
- V. President, Public Affairs, Blue Shield of California

ERCOLANO, Joseph M.
World Headquarters
One Elmcroft Rd.
64-23
Stamford, CT 06926-0700
joseph.ercolano@pb.com
Tel: (203) 351 - 6263
Fax:(203) 961 - 0291

Serves As:
- Director, Government Affairs, Pitney Bowes Inc.

Responsibilities include political action.

ERDMAN, Warren K.
427 W. 12th St.
Kansas City, MO 64105
Tel: (816) 983 - 1454
Fax:(816) 983 - 1124
TF: (800) 282 - 8700

Registered Federal Lobbyist.
Serves As:
- V. President, Corporate Affairs, Kansas City Southern

Responsibilities include government affairs.

ERGEN, Charles W.
9601 S. Meridian Blvd.
Englewood, CO 80112
Tel: (303) 723 - 1000
Fax:(303) 723 - 1399

Serves As:
- Chairman and Chief Exec. Officer, EchoStar Communications Corp.

ERHARD, Helmut S.
7660 Imperial Way
Allentown, PA 18195-1040
Tel: (610) 366 - 4600
Fax:(610) 366 - 4684
TF: (800) 523 - 5488

Serves As:
- Chief Exec. Officer, Lehigh Cement Company

ERICKSON, David
One Edwards Way
Irvine, CA 92614-5688
Tel: (949) 250 - 6826
Fax:(949) 250 - 2248
TF: (800) 424 - 3278

Serves As:
- V. President, Investor Relations, Edwards Lifesciences Corp.

ERICKSON, James R.
P.O. Box 26234
Richmond, VA 23260-6234
jim.erickson@sscoop.com
Tel: (804) 281 - 1392
Fax:(804) 281 - 1119

Serves As:
- Director, Corporate Communications, Member Relations and Public Affairs, Southern States Cooperative

ERICKSON, Kelly Carper
750 W. John Carpenter Fwy.
Irving, TX 75039
Tel: (469) 524 - 7304

Serves As:
- V. President, External Communications, Caremark Rx, Inc.

ERICKSON, Lynn
One Energy Pl.
Pensacola, FL 32520
Tel: (850) 444 - 6249
Fax:(850) 444 - 6448
TF: (800) 225 - 5797

Serves As:
- Corporate Communications Supervisor, Gulf Power Co.

ERICKSON, Michael
12300 Liberty Blvd.
Englewood, CO 80112
Tel: (875) 875 - 5400
Fax:(720) 875 - 5445

Serves As:
- V. President, Investor Relations and Media Relations, Liberty Media Corp.

ERICKSON, Paula K.
2200 Kensington Ct.
Oak Brook, IL 60523-2100
erickson@acehardware.com
Tel: (630) 990 - 6920
Fax:(630) 990 - 3145

Serves As:
- Manager, Corporate Communications and Public Relations, Ace Hardware Corp.

Responsibilities include corporate philanthropy.

ERICKSON, Randy J.
770 N. Water St.
Milwaukee, WI 53202
Tel: (414) 765 - 7700
Fax:(414) 765 - 7899

Serves As:
- PAC Treasurer, Marshall & Ilsley Corp.

ERICKSON, Rick
225 W. Randolph St.
27 B
Chicago, IL 60606
Tel: (312) 727 - 2080
Fax:(312) 727 - 3722
TF: (800) 327 - 9346

Serves As:
- Contact, Corporate Giving Program, SBC Illinois

ERICKSON, Thomas J.
750 First St. NE
suite 1070
Washington, DC 20002
terickson@bunge.com
Tel: (202) 216 - 1780

Registered Federal Lobbyist.
Serves As:
- V. President, Government and Industry Affairs, Bunge Ltd.

ERIKS, Mark
P.O. Box 8700
Grand Rapids, MI 49518
mark_eriks@spartanstores.com
Tel: (616) 878 - 2000
Fax:(616) 878 - 2775

Serves As:
- V. President, Human Resources, Spartan Stores Inc.

ERIKSON, Sheldon R.
1333 West Loop South
Suite 1700
Houston, TX 77027
Tel: (713) 513 - 3312
Fax:(713) 513 - 3456

Serves As:
- Chairman, President and Chief Exec. Officer, Cooper Cameron Corp.

Responsibilities include corporate philanthropy.

ERKANAT, Judy
2655 Seely Ave.
Bldg. 8
San Jose, CA 95134
jerkanat@cadence.com
Tel: (408) 894 - 2302
Fax:(408) 944 - 0747

Serves As:
- Senior Public Relations Manager, Cadence Design Systems, Inc.

ERLACHER, Laura Eakin
1331 Pennsylvania Ave. NW
Suite 512
Washington, DC 20004
Tel: (202) 662 - 8750
Fax:(202) 662 - 8749

Registered Federal Lobbyist.
Serves As:
- Manager, Federal Government Relations, PPL Corp.

ERLANDSON, Patrick
9900 Bren Rd. East
Minneapolis, MN 55343
Tel: (952) 936 - 1300
Fax:(952) 936 - 0044
TF: (800) 328 - 5979

Serves As:
- PAC Treasurer, UnitedHealth Group

ERMATINGER, William R.
4101 Washington Ave.
Newport News, VA 23607-2770
Tel: (757) 380 - 2000
Fax:(757) 380 - 3875

Serves As:
- V. President, Human Resources and Administration, Northrop Grumman Newport News

ERNST, Mark A.
4400 Main St.
Kansas City, MO 64111
mernst@hrblock.com
Tel: (816) 753 - 6900
Fax:(816) 753 - 5346
TF: (800) 829 - 7733

Serves As:
- Chairman, President and Chief Exec. Officer, H & R Block, Inc.

ERUBURU, Robert F.
1166 Ave. of The Americas
New York, NY 10036-2774
Tel: (212) 345 - 5000
Fax:(212) 345 - 4808

Serves As:
- Chairman of the Board, Marsh & McLennan Companies, Inc.

ERVIN, Isabelle
12 E. Armour Blvd.
Kansas City, MO 64111
ervin_isabelle@interstatebrands.com
Tel: (816) 502 - 4000
Fax:(816) 502 - 4155

Serves As:
- Human Resources Associate, Interstate Bakeries Corp.

Responsibilities include corporate philanthropy.

ERWIN, Pam
550 California St.
M/S A0112-073
San Francisco, CA 94104
Tel: (415) 396 - 3247
Fax:(415) 975 - 6260

Serves As:
- Contact, Wells Fargo Bank and Wells Fargo Foundation, Wells Fargo & Co.

ESHELMAN, Fred N.
3151 S. 17th St.
Wilmington, NC 28412-6461
Tel: (910) 251 - 0081
Fax:(910) 762 - 5820

Serves As:
- Chairman and Chief Exec. Officer, Pharmaceutical Product Development, Inc.

ESHET, Mary
301 S. College St., Suite 4000
One Wachovia Center
NC 0570
Charlotte, NC 28288-0370
mary.eshet@wachovia.com
Tel: (704) 374 - 6565
Fax:(704) 374 - 3425
TF: (800) 275 - 3862

Serves As:
- Senior V. President and Manager, Corporate Media Relations, Wachovia Corp.

ESKELSEN, David
201 S. Main St.
23rd Floor
Salt Lake City, UT 84140
Tel: (801) 220 - 2447

Serves As:
• Public Relations Contact, PacifiCorp

ESKEW, Michael L.
55 Glenlake Pkwy. NE
Atlanta, GA 30328
mleskew@ups.com
Tel: (404) 828 - 7223
Fax:(404) 828 - 6619

Serves As:
• Chairman and Chief Exec. Officer, United Parcel Service (UPS)

ESLER, Susan B.
P.O. Box 391
Covington, KY 41012-0391
Tel: (859) 815 - 3333
Fax:(859) 815 - 4795

Serves As:
• V. President, Human Resources, Ashland Inc.

ESPE, Matthew J.
P.O. Box 834
Valley Forge, PA 19482-0834
mespe@ikon.com
Tel: (610) 296 - 8000
Fax:(610) 408 - 7025
TF: (888) 275 - 4566

Serves As:
• Chairman and Chief Exec. Officer, Ikon Office Solutions, Inc.

ESPOSITO, Anne
701 Pennsylvania Ave. NW
Suite 500
Washington, DC 20004
Tel: (202) 350 - 5571
Fax:(202) 350 - 5510

Serves As:
• Director, Federal Government Affairs, AstraZeneca Pharmaceuticals

ESPOSITO, Phylis M.
4211 S. 102nd St.
Omaha, NE 68127-1031
Tel: (402) 597 - 5658
Fax:(402) 597 - 7789
TF: (800) 237 - 8692

Serves As:
• Chief Stategy Officer, Ameritrade Holding Corp.

ESSNER, Robert
Five Giralda Farms
Madison, NJ 07940
Tel: (973) 660 - 5000
Fax:(973) 660 - 5771

Serves As:
• Chairman, President and Chief Exec. Officer, Wyeth

ESTOCK, Larry
450 Riverchase Pkwy. East
Birmingham, AL 35244
Tel: (205) 220 - 2100
Fax:(205) 220 - 4841

Serves As:
• Communications Coordinator, Blue Cross and Blue Shield of Alabama

ESTOCK, Tom
N63 W23075 State Hwy. 74
Sussex, WI 53089-2827
Tel: (414) 566 - 6000
TF: (888) 782 - 3226

Serves As:
• Coordinator, Environment, Quad/Graphics, Inc.

ESTRADA, Larry
1100 New York Ave. NW
Suite 600W
Washington, DC 20005
larry.estrada@hp.com
Tel: (202) 378 - 2500
Fax:(202) 378 - 2550

Registered Federal Lobbyist.
Serves As:
• Director, Government and Public Affairs, Hewlett-Packard Co.

ESTRADA, Ramiro G.
6001 Bollinger Canyon Rd.
San Ramon, CA 94583
Tel: (925) 842 - 1000

Serves As:
• Treasurer, Chevron PAC, Chevron Corp.

ETHERLY, Curtis
9770 Patuxent Woods Dr.
Columbia, MD 21046
Tel: (410) 290 - 3024

Serves As:
• V. President, Public Affairs, Coca-Cola Enterprises Inc.

EUGENE, Melissa Ann
P.O. Box 60219
New Orleans, LA 70160
Tel: (504) 566 - 3101
Fax:(504) 566 - 3335

Serves As:
• Coordinator, Corporate Communications, Pan American Life Insurance Co.

EULBERG, Joseph R.
7600 France Ave. South
Edina, MN 55435
Tel: (952) 832 - 0534
Fax:(952) 844 - 1234

Serves As:
• Senior V. President, Human Resources, Nash Finch Company

EULE, Margo Grimm
1667 K St., NW
Suite 1210
Washington, DC 20006
mgeule@potomacnet.com
Tel: (202) 296 - 5550
Fax:(202) 296 - 6436

Serves As:
• Manager, Government Relations, Hyundai Motor America

EVANGELISTI, Joe
270 Park Ave.
New York, NY 10017-2070
Tel: (212) 270 - 6000
Fax:(212) 270 - 1648

Serves As:
• Managing Director, Media Relations, J. P. Morgan Chase & Co.

EVANOFF, Nicholas J.
5847 San Felipe, Suite 3300
Houston, TX 77057
Tel: (713) 789 - 1400
Fax:(713) 952 - 6916

Serves As:
• V. President, Corporate and Governmental Affairs, Pride Internat'l, Inc.

EVANS, Anton N.
8252 Millhouse Ln.
Dublin, OH 43106
tony.evans@electrolux.com
Tel: (614) 761 - 2633
Fax:(614) 761 - 0689

Serves As:
• V. President, Communications, Electrolux North America, Inc.

EVANS, Dwayne
305 Hartman Dr.
Lebanon, TN 37088
Tel: (615) 444 - 5533
Fax:(615) 443 - 9511

Serves As:
• PAC Treasurer, CBRL Group, Inc.

EVANS, Dwight H.
270 Peachtree St. NW
Atlanta, GA 30303
Tel: (404) 506 - 5000

Serves As:
• Exec. V. President, External Affairs, Southern Company

EVANS, Eddie D.
801 Pennsylvania Ave. NW
Suite 725
Washington, DC 20004
eddie.evans@sanofi-aventis.com
Tel: (202) 628 - 0500
Fax:(202) 682 - 0538

Registered Federal Lobbyist.
Serves As:
• V. President, Federal Government Affairs, Sanofi-Aventis Inc.

EVANS, Edward A.
15880 N. Greenway-Hayden Loop
Suite 100
Scottsdale, AZ 85260
Tel: (480) 627 - 2700
Fax:(480) 627 - 2701

Serves As:
• Exec. V. President, Human Resources and Organizational Development, Allied Waste Industries, Inc.

EVANS, George William
Gateway One
101 Gateway Centre Pkwy.
Richmond, VA 23235
bevans@landam.com
Tel: (804) 267 - 8000
Fax:(804) 267 - 8836
TF: (800) 446 - 7086

Serves As:
• Exec. V. President and Chief Financial Officer, LandAmerica Financial Group, Inc.
Responsibilities include investor relations.

EVANS, James D.
AutoNation Tower
110 SE Sixth St.
Fort Lauderdale, FL 33301
evansj@autonation.com
Tel: (954) 769 - 7200
Fax:(954) 769 - 6494

Serves As:
• Senior V. President, Industry Relations, AutoNation, Inc.

EVANS, John R.
Wells Fargo Center
Sixth & Marquette
M/S N9305-171
Minneapolis, MN 55479
Tel: (612) 667 - 9193
Fax:(612) 667 - 9403

Serves As:
• Director, State Government Relations, Wells Fargo & Co.

EVANS, Linda C.
1301 K St. NW
Suite 1200
Washington, DC 20005
levans@us.ibm.com
Tel: (202) 515 - 5526
Fax:(202) 515 - 5078

Registered Federal Lobbyist.
Serves As:
- Program Manager, Taxes and Finance, Internat'l Business Machines Corp. (IBM)

EVANS, Linden
P.O. Box 1400
Rapid City, SD 57709-1400
Tel: (605) 721 - 1700
Fax:(605) 721 - 2599

Serves As:
- President and Chief Operating Officer, Retail Business Segment, Black Hills Corp.

EVANS, Marla J.
225 Byers Rd.
Miamisburg, OH 45342
Tel: (937) 866 - 6251
Fax:(937) 865 - 5470

Serves As:
- PAC Treasurer, Huffy Corp.

EVANS, Richard L.
6650 Ramsey St.
Fayetteville, NC 28311
richardevans@goodyear.com
Tel: (910) 630 - 5210

Serves As:
- Manager, Public Affairs, (Kelly-Springfield Tire Co.), The Goodyear Tire & Rubber Company

EVANS, Jr., Richard W.
P.O. Box 1600
San Antonio, TX 78296
Tel: (210) 220 - 4393
Fax:(210) 220 - 4117

Serves As:
- Chairman and Chief Exec. Officer, Frost Nat'l Bank

EVANS, Robert S.
100 First Stamford Pl.
Stamford, CT 06902
Tel: (203) 363 - 7300
Fax:(203) 363 - 7295

Serves As:
- Chairman of the Board, Crane Co.

EVANS, Steven R.
666 Grand Ave.
P.O. Box 657
Des Moines, IA 50303-0657
srevans@midamerican.com
Tel: (515) 281 - 2288
Fax:(515) 242 - 4080
TF: (888) 427 - 5632

Serves As:
- Treasurer PACs, MidAmerican Energy Holdings Co.

EVANSON, Paul J.
800 Cabin Hill Dr.
Greensburg, PA 15601
Tel: (724) 837 - 3000

Registered Federal Lobbyist.
Serves As:
- Chairman, President and Chief Exec. Officer, Allegheny Energy Inc.

EVE, Eric
1300 I St. NW
Suite 400 West
Washington, DC 20005
eric.eve@verizon.com
Tel: (202) 515 - 2400

Registered Federal Lobbyist.
Serves As:
- V. President, Federal Government Relations, Verizon Communications Inc.

EVELAND, Edward E.
500 Water's Edge
Harrisburg, PA 19073
Tel: (610) 325 - 5560

Serves As:
- Regional Director, State Government Relations, HSBC North America Holdings Inc.

EVERED, Steve
P.O. Box 19001
Greenville, SC 29602
Tel: (864) 458 - 5080
Fax:(864) 458 - 6359
TF: (800) 847 - 3435

Registered Federal Lobbyist.
Serves As:
- Director, Government Affairs, Michelin North America, Inc.

EVERETT, Brenda
One Dell Way
Round Rock, TX 78682
Tel: (512) 728 - 7800
Fax:(512) 728 - 3653
TF: (800) 289 - 3355

Serves As:
- Investor Relations Contact, Dell Inc.

EVERETT, George T.
P.O. Box 1244
M/S EC12H
Charlotte, NC 28201-1244
gteverett@duke-energy.com
Tel: (704) 373 - 4363
Fax:(704) 373 - 5393

Serves As:
- V. President, Environment and Public Policy/Duke Power, Duke Energy Corp.

EVERS, Sarah
7902 Westpark Dr.
McLean, VA 22102
Tel: (703) 744 - 1620
Fax:(703) 744 - 1601
TF: (888) 434 - 4648

Serves As:
- V. President, Communications, Sunrise Assisted Living, Inc.

EVERSMAN, Janet
1099 18th St.
Suite 1200
Denver, CO 80202
jebersma@westerngas.com
Tel: (303) 452 - 5603
Fax:(303) 457 - 8482
TF: (800) 933 - 5603

Serves As:
- Manager, Human Resources, Western Gas Resources, Inc.

EWBANK, Lisa L.
501 Sycamore Dr.
Milpitas, CA 95035
Tel: (408) 894 - 4000
Fax:(408) 894 - 3218

Serves As:
- V. President, Finance and Investor Relations, Quantum Corporation

EYNON, Edward T.
26950 Agoura Rd.
Calabasas Hills, CA 91301-5335
Tel: (818) 871 - 3000
Fax:(818) 871 - 3100

Serves As:
- Senior V. President, Human Resources, Cheesecake Factory Inc.

FACIANE, E. Leo
1341 W. Mockingbird Ln.
Dallas, TX 75247
lfaciane@txi.com
Tel: (972) 647 - 6700
Fax:(972) 647 - 3878

Serves As:
- V. President, Environmental Affairs, Texas Industries, Inc.

FADEM, Bruce
Five Giralda Farms
Madison, NJ 07940
Tel: (973) 660 - 5980
Fax:(973) 660 - 7167

Serves As:
- V. President, Corporate Information Services and Chief Information Officer, Wyeth

Responsibilities include corporate communications.

FAFORD, Mark E.
P.O. Box 5204
Norwalk, CT 06856-5204
mefaford@archchemicals.com
Tel: (203) 229 - 2654
Fax:(203) 229 - 3507
TF: (877) 275 - 6973

Serves As:
- Director, Investor Relations and Communications, Arch Chemicals, Inc.

FAGAN, Elizabeth A. "Beth"
P.O. Box 29
St. Louis, MO 63166-0029
bfagan@brownshoe.com
Tel: (314) 854 - 4093
Fax:(314) 854 - 4091

Serves As:
- V. President, Public Affairs, Brown Shoe Co., Inc.

FAGAN, Mary Frances
Box 66065, O'Hare Airport
Chicago, IL 60666
mary.frances.fagan@aa.com
Tel: (773) 686 - 5614

Serves As:
- Manager, Corporate Communications, (American Airlines, Inc.), AMR Corp.

FAGER, Dan L.
1401 I St. NW
Suite 1200
Washington, DC 20005-2225
Tel: (202) 408 - 5800
Fax:(202) 408 - 5845

Registered Federal Lobbyist.
Serves As:
- Manager, Federal Relations, Chevron Corp.

FAHEY, Christine
2000 Galloping Hill Rd.
Kenilworth, NJ 07033
Tel: (908) 298 - 7232
Fax:(908) 298 - 7349

Serves As:
- Senior Contributions Administration; and V. President, Schering-Plough Foundation, Schering-Plough Corporation

FAHEY, Jr., John M.
P.O. Box 98199
Washington, DC 20090-8199
Tel: (202) 857 - 7000
Fax:(202) 828 - 6679
TF: (800) 647 - 5463

Serves As:
- President and Chief Exec. Officer, Nat'l Geographic Soc.

FAHL, Gary A.
1500 DeKoven Ave.
Racine, WI 53403-2552
Tel: (262) 636 - 1200
Fax:(262) 636 - 1424

Serves As:
- V. President, Environmental Safety and Security, Modine Manufacturing Company

FAHNHORST, Kathy
3311 E. Old Shakopee Rd.
Minneapolis, MN 55425-1640
kathleen.p.fahnhorst@ceridian.com
Tel: (952) 853 - 3457
Fax:(952) 853 - 5082

Serves As:
- Manager, Employee/Community Affairs, Ceridian Corp.

FAHRENTHOLD, Brian C.
P.O. Box 1642
Houston, TX 77251-1642
bcfahren@duke-energy.com
Tel: (713) 627 - 4814
Fax:(713) 989 - 3076

Serves As:
- Regional Director, State Governmental Affairs, Duke Energy Corp.

FAIN, Richard D.
1050 Caribbean Way
Miami, FL 33132-3203
Tel: (305) 539 - 6000
Fax:(305) 375 - 0711

Serves As:
- Chairman and Chief Exec. Officer, Royal Caribbean Internat'l

FAIRBANK, Richard D.
1680 Capital One Dr.
12th Floor
McLean, VA 22102
Tel: (703) 875 - 1000

Serves As:
- Chairman and Chief Exec. Officer, Capital One Financial Corp.

FAIRBANK, Jr., Robert E.
P.O. Box 4079
Gulfport, MS 39502
Tel: (228) 865 - 5515
Fax:(228) 865 - 5616

Serves As:
- Manager, Governmental and Environmental Relations, Mississippi Power Co.

FAISON, Ralph E.
10500 W. 153rd St.
Orland Park, IL 60462
Tel: (708) 349 - 3300
Fax:(708) 349 - 5444

Serves As:
- President and Chief Exec. Officer, Andrew Corp.

FAITH, Marshall E.
The Scoular Bldg.
2027 Dodge St.
Omaha, NE 68102
mfaith@scoular.com
Tel: (402) 342 - 3500
Fax:(402) 342 - 5568
TF: (800) 488 - 3500

Serves As:
- Chairman of the Board, The Scoular Co.

FALCONA, Samuel
P.O. Box 2197
MA3158
Houston, TX 77252-2197
sfalco@ppco.com
Tel: (281) 293 - 5966
Fax:(281) 293 - 2152

Serves As:
- V. President, Corporate Communications, ConocoPhillips

FALGOUST, Dean T.
P.O. Box 51777
New Orleans, LA 70151
Tel: (504) 582 - 4000
Fax:(504) 582 - 1847
TF: (800) 535 - 7094

Serves As:
- PAC Treasurer, Freeport-McMoRan Copper and Gold Citizenship Committee, Freeport-McMoRan Copper and Gold Inc.

FALK, Thomas J.
DWF Airport Station, P.O. Box 619100
Dallas, TX 75261-9100
Tel: (972) 281 - 1200
Fax:(972) 281 - 1490
TF: (800) 639 - 1352

Serves As:
- Chairman and Chief Exec. Officer, Kimberly-Clark Corp.

FALLAT, Dale W.
P.O. Box 119
Maumee, OH 43537
dale_fallat@andersoninc.com
Tel: (419) 891 - 6474
Fax:(419) 891 - 6695

Serves As:
- V. President, Corporate Services, The Andersons, Inc.

Responsibilities include corporate contributions.

FALLATI, Donald
3191 Broadbridge Ave.
Stratford, CT 06614-2559
dfal@dictaphone.com
Tel: (203) 381 - 7218

Serves As:
- Executive V. President, Marketing and Strategic Planning, Dictaphone Corp.

Responsibilities include media relations.

FALLON, Willard G.
1200 Wilson Blvd.
Arlington, VA 22209-2305
Tel: (703) 465 - 3500

Registered Federal Lobbyist.
Serves As:
- Representative, The Boeing Co.

FALLOW, Kerianne
250 E. Parkcenter Blvd.
Boise, ID 83706
Tel: (208) 395 - 6200
Fax:(208) 395 - 6631
TF: (877) 932 - 7948

Serves As:
- Corporate Director, Government Relations, Albertson's, Inc.

FANNING, Michael I.
P.O. Box 19001
Greenville, SC 29602
Tel: (864) 458 - 5000
Fax:(864) 458 - 6359
TF: (800) 847 - 3435

Registered Federal Lobbyist.
Serves As:
- V. President, Corporate Affairs, Michelin North America, Inc.

FANNING, Sean
2211 S. 47th St.
Phoenix, AZ 85034
sean.fanning@avnet.com
Tel: (480) 643 - 7824

Serves As:
- Senior V. President, Global Communications, (Avnet Electronics Marketing), Avnet Inc.

FANNON, Peter F.
1130 Connecticut Ave. NW
Suite 1100
Washington, DC 20036
Tel: (202) 912 - 3800

Registered Federal Lobbyist.
Serves As:
- V. President, Technology Policy and Regulatory Affairs, Matsushita Electric Corp. of America

FANSHAW, Lee
6000 American Pkwy.
Madison, WI 53783
lfanshaw@amfam.com
Tel: (608) 249 - 2111
Fax:(608) 245 - 8619

Serves As:
- Counsel, Government Affairs, American Family Insurance Group

FARACI, John V.
400 Atlantic St.
Stamford, CT 06921
Tel: (203) 541 - 8000
Fax:(203) 541 - 8200
TF: (800) 223 - 1268

Serves As:
- Chairman and Chief Exec. Officer, Internat'l Paper

FARAJI, Mary-Frances
2000 Galloping Hill Rd.
Kenilworth, NJ 07033
Tel: (908) 298 - 7109

Serves As:
- V. President, Global Product Communications and Advocacy Development, Schering-Plough Corporation

FARBSTEIN, Marcus
808 17th St. NW
Suite 250
Washington, DC 20006
Tel: (202) 296 - 7272
Fax:(202) 296 - 7290

Serves As:
- Federal Government Liaison, Genentech, Inc.

FARFUGLIA, Charles J.
Ethan Allen Dr.
P.O. Box 1966
Danbury, CT 06813-2966
Tel: (203) 743 - 8000
Fax:(203) 743 - 8298

Serves As:
- V. President, Human Resources, Ethan Allen Interiors Inc.

FARINAS, Suzanne
P.O. Box 98510
Las Vegas, NV 89193-8510
Tel: (702) 876 - 7247
Fax:(702) 364 - 3444

Serves As:
- Assistant to the Chief Exec. Officer, Southwest Gas Corp.

Responsibilities include corporate philanthropy.

FARLEY, Michele U.
One American Row
Hartford, CT 06102
michele.farley@phoenixwm.com
Tel: (860) 403 - 5393
Fax:(860) 403 - 7887

Serves As:
- Senior V. President, Corporate Communications, The Phoenix Companies, Inc.

FARMER, Greg
101 Constitution Ave. NW
Suite 325 East
Washington, DC 20001
gfarmer@nortel.com
Tel: (202) 312 - 8060

Registered Federal Lobbyist.
Serves As:
- Senior V. President, Global Government and Community Relations, Nortel Networks

FARMER, H. Randolph
Gateway One
101 Gateway Centre Pkwy.
Richmond, VA 23235
Tel: (804) 267 - 8120
Fax:(804) 267 - 8836
TF: (800) 446 - 7086

Serves As:
- Senior V. President, Corporate Communications, LandAmerica Financial Group, Inc.

FARMER, Jack
P.O. Box 4100
St. Louis, MO 63136-8506
Tel: (314) 982 - 8630
Fax:(314) 982 - 9199

Serves As:
- Media Relations Contact, Emerson

FARMER, Jeremy G. O.
200 E.Randolph St.
Chicago, IL 60601
Tel: (312) 381 - 1000
Fax:(312) 381 - 0240

Serves As:
- Senior V. President, Human Resources, Aon Corp.

FARMER, Laura
101 Ash St.
HQ15A
San Diego, CA 92101-3017
lfarmer@sempra.com
Tel: (619) 696 - 4415
Fax:(619) 696 - 4379
TF: (877) 736 - 7721

Serves As:
- Director, Communications and Advertising, Sempra Energy

FARNAN, Lisa
50 Beale St.
San Francisco, CA 94105-1808
Tel: (415) 229 - 5000
Fax:(415) 229 - 5070
TF: (800) 200 - 3242

Serves As:
- V. President, Provider Relations and Network Development, Blue Shield of California

FARR, David N.
P.O. Box 4100
St. Louis, MO 63136-8506
Tel: (314) 553 - 2000
Fax:(314) 553 - 3527

Serves As:
- Chairman and Chief Exec. Officer, Emerson

FARR, Kevin M.
333 Continental Blvd.
MI-1417
El Segundo, CA 90245-5012
Tel: (310) 252 - 2000
Fax:(310) 252 - 2180

Serves As:
- Chief Financial Officer, Mattel, Inc.

Responsibilities include political action.

FARRELL, Chris
115 Cheshire Rd.
Pittsfield, MA 01201
cfarrell@berkshiregas.com
Tel: (413) 445 - 0312

Serves As:
- Manager, Corporate Communications and Government Relations, (Berkshire Gas Co., The (Berkshire)), Energy East Corp.

FARRELL, Gretchen
22801 St. Clair Ave.
Cleveland, OH 44117-1199
gretchen_farrell@lincolnelectric.com
Tel: (216) 481 - 8100
Fax:(216) 486 - 1751

Serves As:
- V. President, Human Resources, Lincoln Electric Holdings, Inc.

FARRELL, John J.
270 Park Ave.
New York, NY 10017-2070
john.farrell@jpmorganchase.com
Tel: (212) 270 - 6000
Fax:(212) 270 - 1648

Serves As:
- Director, Human Resources, J. P. Morgan Chase & Co.

FARRELL, June
One Marriott Dr.
Washington, DC 20058
june.farrell@marriott.com
Tel: (301) 380 - 7796
Fax:(301) 380 - 4684

Serves As:
- V. President, International Communications, Marriott Internat'l, Inc.

FARRELL, Pamela
1299 Pennsylvania Ave. NW
11th Floor West
Washington, DC 20004-2407
Tel: (202) 637 - 4000
Fax:(202) 637 - 4006

Registered Federal Lobbyist.
Serves As:
- Technology, Research and Development, General Electric Co.

FARREN, J. Michael
1401 H St. NW
Suite 200
Washington, DC 20005
Tel: (202) 414 - 1285
Fax:(202) 789 - 1336

Registered Federal Lobbyist.
Serves As:
- Corporate V. President, External Affairs, Xerox Corp.

Responsibilities include government affairs.

FARRINGTON, Jennifer
One Becton Dr.
Franklin Lakes, NJ 07417-1880
jennifer_farrington@bd.com
Tel: (201) 847 - 7065
Fax:(201) 847 - 5305

Serves As:
- Manager, Community Relations, Becton, Dickinson and Co.

FARRIS, Diana
1525 Howe St.
Racine, WI 53403
Tel: (262) 260 - 2119
Fax:(262) 260 - 2652

Serves As:
- Manager, Administration and Volunteerism, SC Johnson

FARRIS, G. Steven
2000 Post Oak Blvd., Suite 100
Houston, TX 77056-4400
Tel: (713) 296 - 6000
Fax:(713) 296 - 6480
TF: (800) 874 - 3262

Serves As:
- President and Chief Exec. Officer, Apache Corp.

Also serves as the Chied Operating Officer.

FARRIS, Lynne
1 Sybase Dr.
Dublin, CA 94568
Tel: (925) 236 - 8797
Fax:(925) 236 - 6164

Serves As:
- Investor Relations Contact, Sybase, Inc.

FASHEE, Douglas L.
P.O. Box 2511
Houston, TX 77252-2511
Tel: (713) 420 - 2600
Fax:(713) 420 - 4993

Serves As:
- President and Chief Exec. Officer, El Paso Corp.

FAST, Eric C.
100 First Stamford Pl.
Stamford, CT 06902
Tel: (203) 363 - 7300
Fax:(203) 363 - 7295

Serves As:
- President and Chief Exec. Officer, Crane Co.

FAUDEL, Gerald B.
4610 S. Ulster St., Suite 200
Denver, CO 80237
gfaudel@frontieroil.com
Tel: (303) 714 - 0168
Fax:(303) 714 - 0130

Serves As:
- V. President, Corporate Relations, (Frontier Refining), Frontier Oil Corp.

Responsibilities include government relations.

FAULK, Terry M.
Three Lakes Dr.
Northfield, IL 60093-2753
Tel: (847) 646 - 2000
Fax:(847) 646 - 6005

Serves As:
- Exec. V. President, Human Resources, Kraft Foods, Inc.

FAULKNER, John W.
One Campbell Pl.
Camden, NJ 08103-1701
john_w_faulkner@campbellsoup.com
Tel: (856) 342 - 3738
Fax:(856) 541 - 8185
TF: (800) 257 - 8443

Serves As:
- Director, Brand Communications, Campbell Soup Co.

FAULKNER, Kevin
2315 N. First St.
San Jose, CA 95131
kevin.faulkner@bea.com
Tel: (408) 570 - 8000
Fax:(408) 570 - 8901

Serves As:
- V. President, Investor Relations, BEA Systems, Inc.

FAUSER, Krissi Kearns
1401 I St. NW
Suite 600
Washington, DC 20005
Tel: (202) 336 - 7400
Fax:(202) 336 - 7515

Registered Federal Lobbyist.
Serves As:
• Strategic Planning and Defense Policy Advisor, United Technologies Corp.

FAUST, Alan G.
P.O. Box 66760
St. Louis, MO 63166-6760
Tel: (314) 674 - 1000
Fax:(314) 674 - 1585

Serves As:
• Treasurer, Solutia Inc. Citizenship Fund, Solutia Inc.

FAUST, Michael L.
1000 Kiewit Plaza
Omaha, NE 68131
Tel: (402) 342 - 2052
Fax:(402) 271 - 2939

Serves As:
• Assistant to the Chairman, Peter Kiewit Sons', Inc.
Responsibilities include corporate philanthropy.

FAVINGER, Laura L.
2211 Congress St.
M/S B159
Portland, ME 04122-0545
lfavinger@unumprovident.com
Tel: (207) 575 - 4303
Fax:(207) 575 - 4304

Serves As:
• Assistant V. President, Government Relations, UnumProvident Corp.

FAWKES, Kurt
2001 Edmund Halley Dr.
Reston, VA 20191
kurt.fawkes@mail.sprint.com
Tel: (703) 433 - 4000

Serves As:
• V. President, Investor Relations, Sprint Nextel

FAY, Elizabeth
1101 15th St. NW
Suite 1000
Washington, DC 20005
Tel: (202) 530 - 8160
Fax:(202) 530 - 8180

Registered Federal Lobbyist.
Serves As:
• Director, Public Policy, Cargill, Incorporated

FAY, John F.
1333 H St., NW
Suite 410
Washington, DC 20005
Tel: (202) 898 - 8343

Serves As:
• PAC Treasurer, Instinet Group Inc.

FAY-BUSTILLOS, Theresa
1155 Battery St.
San Francisco, CA 94111
Tel: (415) 501 - 6000
Fax:(415) 501 - 7112
TF: (800) 872 - 5384

Serves As:
• Exec. Director, Levi Strauss Foundation, Levi Strauss and Co.

FAYLOR, Kami
8000 S. Federal Way
Boise, ID 83707
Tel: (208) 363 - 3675
Fax:(208) 368 - 2536

Serves As:
• Corporate Contributions Contact - Community and K-12 Relations, Micron Technology, Inc.

FAZZINO, Gary P.
3000 Hanover St.
MS 1035
Palo Alto, CA 94304
gary_fazzino@hp.com
Tel: (650) 857 - 4321
Fax:(650) 857 - 5518
TF: (800) 752 - 0900

Registered Federal Lobbyist.
Serves As:
• V. President, Government and Public Affairs, Hewlett-Packard Co.

FAZZOLARI, Salvatore D.
P.O. Box 8888
Camp Hill, PA 17001-8888
Tel: (717) 763 - 7064
Fax:(717) 763 - 6424

Serves As:
• Senior V. President and Treasurer, Harsco Corp.

FEALY, Robert L.
845 Larch Ave.
Elmhurst, IL 60126
rfealy@duch.com
Tel: (630) 279 - 3600
Fax:(630) 993 - 8644
TF: (800) 282 - 6225

Serves As:
• Treasurer, Duchossois Industries Inc. Political Action Committee, Duchossois Industries, Inc.

FEARER, Paul F.
400 California St.
San Francisco, CA 94104
Tel: (415) 765 - 0400
Fax:(415) 765 - 3257

Serves As:
• Exec. V. President and Director, Human Resources, Union Bank of California

FEAZELL, Donna
P.O. Box 105366
One CNN Center
Atlanta, GA 30348-5366
Tel: (404) 827 - 3835
Fax:(404) 827 - 2024

Serves As:
• Community Relations, (Atlanta Hawks), Turner Broadcasting System, Inc.

FEAZLE, Kim P.
350 S. Grand Ave., Suite 5100
Los Angeles, CA 90071
kfeazle@rsac.com
Tel: (213) 576 - 2428
Fax:(713) 610 - 9964

Serves As:
• Investor Relations, Reliance Steel & Aluminum Co.

FEEHAN, Daniel R.
Cash America Bldg.
1600 W. Seventh St.
Fort Worth, TX 76102-2599
dfeehan@casham.com
Tel: (817) 335 - 1100
Fax:(817) 570 - 1645

Serves As:
• President and Chief Exec. Officer, Cash America Internat'l, Inc.

FEGER, Linda
One Blue Hill Plaza
Pearl River, NY 10965
Tel: (845) 577 - 2545
Fax:(845) 577 - 6913
TF: (877) 434 - 4100

Serves As:
• Manager, Corporate Programs, Orange and Rockland Utilities, Inc.

FEIDER, David
P.O. Box 5625
MS25
Minneapolis, MN 55440-5625
david_feider@cargill.com
Tel: (952) 742 - 6910
Fax:(952) 742 - 6208

Serves As:
• Public Affairs Counselor, Cargill, Incorporated

FEIGHERY, Mark
One Reynolds Way
Kettering, OH 45430
mark_feighery@reyrey.com
Tel: (937) 485 - 8107
Fax:(937) 485 - 8980

Serves As:
• Director, Public Relations and Marketing Communications, Reynolds and Reynolds Co.

FEIGIN, Randi P.
1194 N. Mathilda Ave.
Sunnyvale, CA 94089-1206
randi@juniper.net
Tel: (408) 745 - 2371
Fax:(408) 745 - 8921

Serves As:
• Director, Investor Relations, Juniper Networks, Inc.

FEIKENS, Beth
3850 Hamlin Rd.
Auburn Hills, MI 48326
Tel: (248) 754 - 0883

Serves As:
• Manager, Corporate Communications, BorgWarner Inc.

FEINSTEIN, Leonard
650 Liberty Ave.
Union, NJ 07083
Tel: (908) 688 - 0888
Fax:(908) 688 - 6483

Serves As:
• Co-Chairman of the Board, Bed Bath & Beyond Inc.

FEINSTEIN, Martin D.
4680 Wilshire Blvd.
Los Angeles, CA 90010
Tel: (323) 932 - 3211
Fax:(323) 932 - 3101

Serves As:
• Chairman and Chief Exec. Officer, Farmers Group, Inc.

FEKETE, John D.
3210 Watling St.
East Chicago, IN 46312
john.fekete@ispat.com
Tel: (219) 399 - 4191
Fax:(219) 399 - 6039

Serves As:
• Director, Environmental Affairs, Ispat Inland Inc.

FELD, Kenneth
8607 Westwood Center Dr.
Vienna, VA 22182
Tel: (703) 448 - 4000
Fax:(703) 448 - 4091

Serves As:
• Chairman and Chief Exec. Officer, Feld Entertainment, Inc.

FELDMAN, Alan
3799 Las Vegas Blvd. South
Las Vegas, NV 89109
Tel: (702) 891 - 7147
Fax:(702) 891 - 3096

Serves As:
• Senior V. President, Public Affairs, MGM MIRAGE

FELDMAN, Sheila B.
One CityPlace Dr.
Suite 300
St. Louis, MO 63141
Tel: (314) 994 - 2700
Fax:(314) 994 - 2719

Serves As:
• V. President, Human Resources, Arch Coal, Inc.

FELDSTEIN, Eric A.
200 Renaissance Center
Detroit, MI 48265
Tel: (313) 556 - 5000
Fax:(313) 556 - 5108
TF: (800) 200 - 4622

Serves As:
• Chairman of the Board, General Motors Acceptance Corp. (GMAC)

FELENSTEIN, Craig
1211 Ave. of the Americas
New York, NY 10036
cfelenstein@newscorp.com
Tel: (212) 852 - 7084
Fax:(212) 852 - 7145

Serves As:
• V. President, Investor Relations, News Corporation Ltd.

FELEPPELLE, Anne
127 Public Square
OH-01-27-1710
Cleveland, OH 44114
Tel: (216) 689 - 4971
Fax:(216) 689 - 8710

Serves As:
• Senior V. President, Issues Manager, KeyCorp

FELLAND, Elsie
P.O. Box 152
Forest City, IA 50436-0152
Tel: (641) 585 - 3535
Fax:(641) 585 - 6966

Serves As:
• Secretary, Winnebago Industries Foundation, Winnebago Industries, Inc.

FELLOWES, James E.
1789 Norwood Ave.
Itasca, IL 60143-1095
Tel: (630) 893 - 1600

Serves As:
• Chairman and Chief Exec. Officer, Fellowes Manufacturing Co.

FELLOWS, George
2180 Rutherford Rd.
Carlsbad, CA 92008-7328
Tel: (760) 931 - 1771
Fax:(760) 930 - 5015
TF: (800) 228 - 2767

Serves As:
• President and Chief Exec. Officer, Callaway Golf Co.

FELNER, Craig
601 Pennsylvania Ave. NW
Suite 900, South Bldg.
Washington, DC 20004
Tel: (202) 434 - 8927

Registered Federal Lobbyist.
Serves As:
• Director, Federal Governmental Affairs, Valero Energy Corp.

FELRICE, Barry
1401 H St. NW
Suite 700
Washington, DC 20005
Tel: (202) 414 - 6730
Fax:(202) 414 - 6738

Registered Federal Lobbyist.
Serves As:
• Director, Regulatory Affairs, DaimlerChrysler Corp.

FELS, Lisa
51 Madison Ave.
New York, NY 10010
lisa_fels@newyorklife.com
Tel: (212) 576 - 7937
Fax:(212) 576 - 8145

Serves As:
• Media Representative, New York Life Insurance Co.

FELTES, Karen S.
P.O. Box 3727
Spokane, WA 99220-3727
Tel: (509) 489 - 0500
Fax:(509) 495 - 8725
TF: (800) 727 - 9170

Serves As:
• V. President, Human Resources and Corporate Secretary, Avista Corp.

FELTHAM, Cliff
One Quality St.
Lexington, KY 40507
Tel: (859) 367 - 1105
Fax:(859) 367 - 1185

Serves As:
• Manager, Statewide Media Relations, Kentucky Utilities Company

FENDLEY, Stanley G.
1350 I St. NW
Suite 500
Washington, DC 20005-3305
fendleysg@corning.com
Tel: (202) 682 - 3133
Fax:(202) 682 - 3130

Registered Federal Lobbyist.
Serves As:
• Director, Legislative and Regulatory Affairs, Corning Incorporated

FENICHEL, Doug
Ten Hwy. 35
Red Bank, NJ 07701-5902
Tel: (732) 225 - 4001
Fax:(732) 747 - 6835

Serves As:
• Director, Public Relations, Hovnanian Enterprises, Inc.

FENIMORE, Jamie
3240 Hillview Ave.
Palo Alto, CA 94304
Tel: (650) 494 - 2900
Fax:(650) 813 - 0158

Serves As:
• Public Relations Contact, CNF Inc.

FENNESY, Timothy A.
6820 S. Harl Ave.
Tempe, AZ 85283
Tel: (480) 902 - 1001
Fax:(480) 902 - 1157
TF: (800) 467 - 4448

Serves As:
• Chief Exec. Officer, Insight Enterprises, Inc.

FENNIG, Greg
P.O. Box 1595
Indianapolis, IN 46206-1595
Tel: (317) 261 - 8261
Fax:(317) 630 - 5726

Serves As:
• V. President, Public Affairs, IPL (an AES Company)

FENTON, Geoffrey D.
1430 Waukegan Rd.
McGaw Park, IL 60085
Tel: (847) 578 - 4432
Fax:(847) 578 - 4438

Serves As:
• V. President, Communications,
(Cardinal Health Medical Products and Services), Cardinal Health Inc.

FERBER, Norman A.
4440 Rosewood Dr.
Pleasanton, CA 94588
Tel: (510) 505 - 4400
TF: (800) 945 - 7677

Serves As:
• Chairman of the Board, Ross Stores, Inc.

FERDINANDI, Michael
One CVS Dr.
Woonsocket, RI 02895
Tel: (401) 765 - 1500
Fax:(401) 769 - 4488

Serves As:
• Senior V. President, Human Resources and Corporate Communications, CVS

FERGUSON, J. Brian
P.O. Box 511
Kingsport, TN 37662-5075
ferguson@eastman.com
Tel: (423) 229 - 5901
Fax:(423) 224 - 0323
TF: (800) 327 - 8626

Serves As:
• Chairman and Chief Exec. Officer, Eastman Chemical Co.

FERGUSON, J. Bruce
86 Trinity Pl.
New York, NY 10006
Tel: (212) 306 - 1403
Fax:(212) 306 - 1152

Serves As:
• Associate General Counsel, American Stock Exchange
Responsibilities include political action.

FERGUSON, John D.
10 Burton Hills Blvd.
Nashville, TN 37215
john.ferguson@correctionscorp.com
Tel: (615) 263 - 3000
Fax:(615) 263 - 3140
TF: (800) 624 - 2931

Serves As:
• President and Chief Exec. Officer, Corrections Corp. of America

FERGUSON, Judy J.
308 E. Pearl St.
Jackson, MS 39201
jfergu1@entergy.com
Tel: (601) 969 - 2327
Fax:(601) 969 - 2581

Serves As:
• Communications Specialist - Mississippi, Entergy Corp.

FERGUSON, Noel
909 Hidden Ridge, Suite 600
Irving, TX 75038
Tel: (214) 492 - 6600
Fax:(214) 492 - 6616

Serves As:
• Senior V. President, Human Resources, La Quinta Inns

FERGUSON, Sydney M.
Two Democracy Center
6903 Rockledge Dr.
Bethesda, MD 20817-1818
Tel: (301) 564 - 3200
Fax:(301) 564 - 3201

Registered Federal Lobbyist.
Serves As:
- Representative, USEC Inc.

FERGUSON, Teresa
909 Hidden Ridge, Suite 600
Irving, TX 75038
teresa.ferguson@laquinta.com
Tel: (214) 492 - 6937
Fax:(214) 492 - 6616

Serves As:
- Manager, Public Relations, La Quinta Inns

FERLAND, E. James
80 Park Plaza
M/S T4B
Newark, NJ 07102-0570
e.james.ferland@pseg.com
Tel: (973) 430 - 7000

Serves As:
- Chairman, President and Chief Exec. Officer, PSE&G

FERNANDEZ, Manuel
1101 Pennsylvania Ave. NW
Suite 400
Washington, DC 20004-2504
Tel: (202) 637 - 3800
Fax:(202) 637 - 3860

Registered Federal Lobbyist.
Serves As:
- Representative, Textron Inc.

FERNANDEZ, Michael
One ConAgra Dr.
Omaha, NE 68102-5001
Tel: (402) 595 - 4000

Serves As:
- Senior V. President, Corporate Affairs; and Chief Communications Officer, ConAgra Foods, Inc.

FERRANDO, Jon
AutoNation Tower
110 SE Sixth St.
Fort Lauderdale, FL 33301
ferrandoj@autonation.com
Tel: (954) 769 - 7200
Fax:(954) 769 - 6494

Serves As:
- Chief Counsel, AutoNation, Inc.

Responsibilities include corporate public affairs.

FERRARA, Jr., Albert
703 Curtis St.
Middletown, OH 45043
Tel: (513) 425 - 5000
Fax:(513) 425 - 2676
TF: (800) 331 - 5050

Serves As:
- V. President, Finance, Chief Financial Officer and PAC Treasurer, AK Steel Corp.

Responsibilities include investor relations.

FERRARA, Gerald P.
1601 W. LBJ Fwy.
Dallas, TX 75234
gpferrara@celanese.com
Tel: (972) 443 - 3848
Fax:(972) 443 - 8476

Registered Federal Lobbyist.
Serves As:
- V. President, Governmental Affairs, Celanese

FERREL, Celia Clinch
13220 California St.
Omaha, NE 68154
Tel: (402) 514 - 5306
Fax:(402) 514 - 5486
TF: (800) 228 - 5023

Serves As:
- Manager, Public Relations, Commercial Federal Corp.

FERRY, Erica
2000 Galloping Hill Rd.
Kenilworth, NJ 07033
Tel: (908) 298 - 7371

Serves As:
- Senior Director, Community Affairs, Schering-Plough Corporation

FERRY, Holly
1401 H St. NW
Suite 700
Washington, DC 20005
Tel: (202) 414 - 6713
Fax:(202) 414 - 6743

Registered Federal Lobbyist.
Serves As:
- Grassroots Program Manager, DaimlerChrysler Corp.

FESTA, Alfred E.
7500 Grace Dr.
Columbia, MD 21044
Tel: (410) 531 - 4000
Fax:(410) 531 - 4367

Serves As:
- President and Chief Exec. Officer, W. R. Grace & Co.

FETAH, David C.
One Lillehei Plaza
St. Paul, MN 55117-9983
Tel: (651) 481 - 7615
Fax:(651) 481 - 7707

Serves As:
- Contact, Corporate Giving Program, St. Jude Medical, Inc.

FETAPUTTER, Christopher M.
1717 Pennsylvania Ave. NW
Suite 400
Washington, DC 20006
Tel: (202) 857 - 3074
Fax:(202) 857 - 3030

Serves As:
- Government Affairs Associate, Occidental Internat'l

FETTER, Trevor
P.O. Box 31907
Santa Barbara, CA 93130
Tel: (805) 563 - 7000
Fax:(805) 563 - 7070

Serves As:
- President and Chief Exec. Officer, Tenet Healthcare Corp.

FETTIG, Dwight
401 Ninth St., NW
Suite 600
M/S 600
Washington, DC 20004
Tel: (202) 434 - 8600
Fax:(202) 434 - 8626

Registered Federal Lobbyist.
Serves As:
- Director, Government Relations, Freddie Mac

FETTIG, Jeff M.
Administrative Center
2000 N. M-63
Benton Harbor, MI 49022-2692
Tel: (269) 923 - 5000
Fax:(269) 923 - 5443

Serves As:
- Chairman and Chief Exec. Officer, Whirlpool Corp.

FICALORA, Joseph R.
615 Merrick Ave.
Westbury, NY 11590
Tel: (516) 683 - 4100

Serves As:
- President and Chief Exec. Officer, New York Community Bancorp, Inc.

FICK, Irene T.
P.O. Box 15437
FOC 3C/W
Wilmington, DE 19850-5437
irene.fick@astrazeneca.com
Tel: (302) 886 - 3278
Fax:(302) 886 - 3029
TF: (800) 456 - 3669

Serves As:
- Senior Manager, Corporate and Community Affairs, AstraZeneca Pharmaceuticals

FIEBIG, Derek A.
One Village Dr.
Van Buren Township, MI 48111
dfiebig@visteon.com
Tel: (313) 755 - 0635
Fax:(313) 755 - 7983
TF: (800) VIS - TEON

Serves As:
- Assistant Treasurer, Investor Relations, Visteon Corp.

FIEHLER, Sharon D.
701 Market St.
St. Louis, MO 63101-1826
sfiehler@peabodyenergy.com
Tel: (314) 342 - 7755
Fax:(314) 342 - 3499

Serves As:
- Exec. V. President, Human Resources and Administration, Peabody Energy

FIELDS, Bruce H.
28601 Clemens Rd.
Westlake, OH 44145
bfields@nordson.com
Tel: (440) 892 - 1580
Fax:(440) 892 - 9507

Serves As:
- V. President, Human Resources, Nordson Corp.

FIELDS, Drew
607 14th St. NW
Suite 950
Washington, DC 20005
Tel: (202) 429 - 0303
Fax:(202) 293 - 0561

Registered Federal Lobbyist.
Serves As:
- Executive Director, Congressional Affairs, Qwest Communications

FIELDS, Michael D.
P.O. Box 419248
Kansas City, MO 64141-6248
Tel: (816) 234 - 2000
TF: (800) 892 - 7100

Serves As:
- President, Foundation, Commerce Bancshares Inc.

FIELDS, Steven
41 S. High St.
Columbus, OH 43287
Tel: (614) 480 - 3278
Fax:(614) 480 - 4973

Serves As:
- Corporate Affairs Specialist, Huntington Bancshares Inc.

FIENBERG, Bruce
101 Innovation Dr. Tel: (408) 544 - 6397
San Jose, CA 95134-1941 Fax:(408) 544 - 7740

Serves As:
- Senior Manager, Public Relations, Altera Corp.

FIGEL, Brad G.
507 Second St. NE Tel: (202) 543 - 6453
Washington, DC 20002 Fax:(202) 544 - 6453
brad.figel@nike.com

Registered Federal Lobbyist.
Serves As:
- Director, Governmental Affairs and International Trade Counsel, Nike, Inc.

FIKE, Carin
1014 Vine St. Tel: (513) 762 - 4000
Cincinnati, OH 45202-1100 Fax:(513) 762 - 1295

Serves As:
- Director, Investor Relations, The Kroger Co.

FILIPPONE, Desiree
555 12th St. NW Tel: (202) 393 - 7950
Suite 650 Fax:(202) 393 - 7960
Washington, DC 20004-1205

Registered Federal Lobbyist.
Serves As:
- Manager, International and Public Government Relations, Eli Lilly and Company

FILTON, Steve
P.O. Box 61558 Tel: (610) 768 - 3300
King of Prussia, PA 19406-0958 Fax:(610) 768 - 3312

Serves As:
- Chief Financial Officer, Universal Health Services, Inc.

Responsibilities include investor relations.

FINCH, Brian
One Bank One Plaza Tel: (312) 732 - 4000
Chicago, IL 60670

Serves As:
- Corporate Relations Manager, J. P. Morgan Chase & Co.

FINDLAY, Linda D.
100 S. Royal St. Tel: (703) 299 - 4430
Suite Two
Alexandria, VA 22314-3349
lfindlay@phelpsdodge.com

Registered Federal Lobbyist.
Serves As:
- V. President, Government Relations, Phelps Dodge Corp.

FINDLEY, Mary Sue
38 Fountain Square Tel: (513) 579 - 5300
Cincinnati, OH 45263 Fax:(513) 579 - 5226
TF: (800) 972 - 3030

Serves As:
- V. President, Human Resources, Fifth Third Bancorp.

FINE, Karen
3120 Breckinridge Blvd. Tel: (770) 381 - 1000
Duluth, GA 30099-0001 Fax:(770) 564 - 6110

Serves As:
- Exec. V. President, Human Resources, Primerica Financial Services, Inc.

FINK, Richard H.
655 15th St. NW Tel: (202) 737 - 1977
Suite 445 Fax:(202) 737 - 8111
Washington, DC 20005

Serves As:
- Exec. V. President, Government and Public Affairs, Koch Industries, Inc.

FINKELNBURG, Marjorie
325 Seventh St. NW Tel: (202) 783 - 7070
Suite 1200 Fax:(202) 347 - 2044
Washington, DC 20004-1007

Registered Federal Lobbyist.
Serves As:
- Director, Government Relations, Pfizer Inc.

FINKELSTEIN, Paul D.
7201 Metro Blvd. Tel: (952) 947 - 7777
Minneapolis, MN 55439

Serves As:
- Chairman and Chief Exec. Officer, Regis Corporation

FINKLE, James P.
370 Woodcliff Dr. Tel: (585) 218 - 3600
Suite 300 Fax:(585) 218 - 2155
Fairport, NY 14450 TF: (888) 724 - 2169
james.finkle@cbrands.com

Serves As:
- Senior V. President, External Affairs, Constellation Brands, Inc.

Responsibilities include government relations and political action.

FINLEY, Clark
Webster Plaza Tel: (203) 578 - 2287
145 Bank St. Fax:(203) 573 - 8680
Waterbury, CT 06702 TF: (800) 325 - 2424
cfinley@websterbank.com

Serves As:
- Assistnat V. President, Public Affairs, Webster Financial Corp.

FINLEY, Teresa
55 Glenlake Pkwy. NE Tel: (404) 828 - 7359
Atlanta, GA 30328
tfinley@ups.com

Serves As:
- V. President, Investor Relations, United Parcel Service (UPS)

FINN, Dennis F.
P.O. Box 777 Tel: (330) 273 - 8847
Medina, OH 44258 Fax:(330) 225 - 8743

Serves As:
- V. President, Environmental and Regulatory Affairs, RPM Internat'l Inc.

FINNEGAN, John D.
P.O. Box 1615 Tel: (908) 903 - 2000
Warren, NJ 07061-1615 Fax:(908) 903 - 2027

Serves As:
- Chaiman, President and Chief Exec. Officer, The Chubb Corp.

FINNERTY, Elizabeth
65 E. State St. Tel: (614) 228 - 7959
Columbus, OH 43215 Fax:(614) 228 - 7965
bfinnerty@att.com

Serves As:
- State Director, Government Affairs, AT&T

FINNERTY, Louise Hoppe
700 Anderson Hill Rd. Tel: (914) 253 - 3890
Purchase, NY 10577-1444 Fax:(914) 249 - 8159
louise.finnerty@pepsi.com

Registered Federal Lobbyist.
Serves As:
- V. President, International Government Affairs, PepsiCo, Inc.

FINNIGAN, Thomas D.
1200 G St., NW Tel: (202) 393 - 0962
Suite 550 Fax:(202) 347 - 1684
Washington, DC 20005
tom_finnigan@praxair.com

Registered Federal Lobbyist.
Serves As:
- Director, Government Relations, Praxair, Inc.

FINZEN-LETTS, Jennifer
One Imation Place Tel: (651) 704 - 3558
Oakdale, MN 55128-3414 Fax:(651) 704 - 4200
TF: (888) 466 - 3456

Serves As:
- Manger, Public Relations, Imation Corp.

FIOLA, Janet S.
710 Medtronic Pkwy. Tel: (763) 514 - 4000
Minneapolis, MN 55432-5604 Fax:(763) 514 - 4879
TF: (800) 328 - 2518

Serves As:
- Senior V. President, Human Resources, Medtronic, Inc.

FIORANI, R. P.
1415 Roselle Rd. Tel: (847) 397 - 2600
Palatine, IL 60067 Fax:(847) 925 - 7271

Serves As:
- V. President, Communications, Square D/Schneider Electric

FIORELLA, Salvatore
130 E. Randolph Dr. Tel: (312) 240 - 3977
24th Floor Fax:(312) 240 - 4542
Chicago, IL 60601
s.fiorella@pecorp.com

Serves As:
- Manager, State Regulatory Affairs, Peoples Energy Corp.

FIREMAN, Paul B.
1895 J W Foster Blvd.
Canton, MA 02021
Tel: (781) 401 - 5000
Fax:(781) 401 - 4000

Serves As:
- Chairman and Chief Exec. Officer, Reebok Internat'l Ltd.

FISCHEL, Mr. Shelley D.
1100 Ave. of the Americas
New York, NY 10036
shelley.fischel@hbo.com
Tel: (212) 512 - 1000
Fax:(212) 512 - 1182

Serves As:
- Exec. V. President, Human Resources and Administration, Home Box Office (HBO)

FISCHER, Danna S.
401 Ninth St., NW
Suite 600
M/S 600
Washington, DC 20004
danna_fischer@freddiemac.com
Tel: (202) 434 - 8600
Fax:(202) 434 - 8626

Registered Federal Lobbyist.
Serves As:
- Director, Government Relations, Freddie Mac

FISH, David
1300 I St. NW
Suite 400 West
Washington, DC 20005
Tel: (202) 515 - 2400

Serves As:
- Director, Media Relations, Verizon Communications Inc.

FISH, John H.
1201 F St. NW
Suite 1000
Washington, DC 20004
fishj@rjrt.com
Tel: (202) 626 - 7210
Fax:(202) 626 - 7208

Registered Federal Lobbyist.
Serves As:
- V. President, Federal Government Affairs, (R. J. Reynolds Tobacco Co.), Reynolds American Inc.

FISH, Lawrence K.
One Citizens Plaza
Providence, RI 02903
Tel: (401) 456 - 7000
Fax:(401) 456 - 7819

Serves As:
- Chairman, President and Chief Exec. Officer, Citizens Financial Group, Inc.

FISHER, Catherine
237 Park Ave.
New York, NY 10017
catherine.fisher@revlon.com
Tel: (212) 527 - 5727

Serves As:
- Senior V. President, Corporate Communications, Revlon, Inc.

FISHER, Charlie
Three Galleria Tower
13155 Noel Rd., Suite 1600
Dallas, TX 75240
Tel: (214) 550 - 7000
TF: (800) 254 - 6567

Serves As:
- Senior V. President, Human Resources, FedEx Kinko's Office and Print Services

FISHER, Eric
P.O. Box 500
San Antonio, TX 78249-112
Tel: (210) 345 - 3896
Fax:(210) 345 - 2646
TF: (800) 531 - 7911

Serves As:
- V. President, Investor Relations, Valero Energy Corp.

FISHER, Heidi J.
18831 Von Karman, Suite 400
Irvine, CA 92612
heidi.fisher@sunh.com
Tel: (949) 255 - 7100
Fax:(949) 255 - 7054
TF: (800) 509 - 4340

Serves As:
- Senior V. President, Human Resources, Sun Healthcare Group, Inc.

FISHER, Jeanne
1300 Morris Dr.
Suite 100
Chesterbrook, PA 19087-5594
Tel: (610) 727 - 7000
Fax:(610) 727 - 3600
TF: (800) 829 - 3132

Serves As:
- Senior V. President, Human Resources, AmeriSource Bergen Corp.

FISHER, Jeffrey
4747 N. Channel Ave.
Portland, OR 97217
jeffreyfisher@freightliner.com
Tel: (503) 745 - 8000
Fax:(503) 745 - 5996

Serves As:
- General Manager, Corporate Communications, Freightliner LLC

FISHER, Jim
One Village Dr.
Van Buren Township, MI 48111
jfishe89@visteon.com
Tel: (313) 755 - 0635
Fax:(313) 722 - 1658
TF: (800) VIS - TEON

Serves As:
- Director, Corporate Communications, Visteon Corp.

FISHER, Jody
175 E. Old Country Rd.
Hicksville, NY 11801
jfisher@keyspanenergy.com
Tel: (516) 545 - 5052
Fax:(516) 545 - 8193

Serves As:
- Manager, Media Relations, Brooklyn/Hicksville, KeySpan Corp.

FISHER, Kevin
1101 17th St. NW
Suite 600
Washington, DC 20036
Tel: (202) 496 - 5654
Fax:(202) 496 - 5660

Registered Federal Lobbyist.
Serves As:
- Legislative Coordinator, (American Airlines, Inc.), AMR Corp.

FISHER, Linda
1007 Market St.
Wilmington, DE 19898
Tel: (302) 774 - 4060
Fax:(302) 773 - 2919
TF: (800) 441 - 7515

Serves As:
- V. President, Safety, Health and Environment, DuPont

FISHER, Lori
800 N. Lindbergh Blvd.
St. Louis, MO 63167
Tel: (314) 694 - 8535

Serves As:
- Director, External Communications, Monsanto Co.

FISHER, R. Bruce
One Centennial Ave.
PO Box 6820
Piscataway, NJ 08854
bfisher@americanstandard.com
Tel: (732) 980 - 6095
Fax:(732) 980 - 3335

Serves As:
- V. President, Strategic Planning and Investor Relations, American Standard Companies Inc.

FISHER, Randall D.
5619 DTC Pkwy.
Greenwood, CO 80111
Tel: (303) 268 - 6300
TF: (877) 496 - 6704

Serves As:
- Treasurer, Adelphia Communications Corp. PAC, Adelphia Communications Corp.

FISHER, Risa
669 River Dr.
Elmwood Park, NJ 07407
rfisher@webmd.net
Tel: (201) 703 - 3415
Fax:(201) 703 - 3401

Serves As:
- V. President, Investor Relations, WebMD Corp.

FISHER, Robert
1401 I St., NW
Suite 401
Washington, DC 20005
robertfisher@clearchannel.com
Tel: (202) 289 - 3230
Fax:(202) 289 - 0050

Registered Federal Lobbyist.
Serves As:
- Director, Government Affairs, Clear Channel Communications

FISHER, Robert J.
Two Folsom St.
San Francisco, CA 94105
Tel: (650) 952 - 4400
Fax:(415) 427 - 2553
TF: (800) 333 - 7899

Serves As:
- Chairman of the Board, Gap Inc.

FISHER, Scott S.
400 Technecenter Dr.
Suite 302
Milford, OH 45150
Tel: (800) 554 - 9406
Fax:(513) 831 - 7219

Serves As:
- Regional Director, State Government Affairs, (Altria Corporate Services, Inc.), Altria Group, Inc.

FISHER, Stephen P.
10260 Campus Point Dr.
San Diego, CA 92121
Tel: (858) 826 - 6000
Fax:(858) 826 - 6634

Serves As:
- PAC Contact, Science Applications Internat'l Corp.

FISHER, Thomas L.
P.O. Box 3014
Naperville, IL 60566-7014
Tel: (630) 305 - 9500
Fax:(630) 357 - 7534
TF: (888) 642 - 6748

Serves As:
- Chairman of the Board, Nicor, Inc.

FISHMAN, Jay S.
385 Washington St.
St. Paul, MN 55102
Tel: (651) 310 - 7911

Serves As:
- President and Chief Exec. Officer, St. Paul Travelers Cos., Inc.

FISHMAN, Jerald G.
One Technology Way
P.O. Box 9106
Norwood, MA 02062-9106
Tel: (781) 329 - 4700
Fax:(781) 326 - 8703
TF: (800) 262 - 5643

Serves As:
- President and Chief Exec. Officer, Analog Devices, Inc.

FISHMAN, Steven S.
300 Phillipi Rd.
Columbus, OH 43228-5311
Tel: (614) 278 - 6800
Fax:(614) 278 - 6676

Serves As:
- Chairman and Chief Exec. Officer, Big Lots Inc.

FISSELER, Gene
P.O. Box 148
Houston, TX 77001

Serves As:
- Treasurer, Reliant Energy Inc. PAC, Reliant Resources

FISTER, Michael J.
2655 Seely Ave.
San Jose, CA 95134
Tel: (408) 943 - 1234
Fax:(408) 943 - 0513
TF: (800) 862 - 4522

Serves As:
- President and Chief Exec. Officer, Cadence Design Systems, Inc.

FITCH, Robert J.
1300 N. 17th St.
Suite 1400
Arlington, VA 22209
Tel: (703) 907 - 8200
Fax:(703) 907 - 8300

Serves As:
- Senior V. President, Government Relations and Marketing, BAE Systems North America

FITZGERALD, Doug
111 S. Wacker Dr.
Chicago, IL 60606
doug.fizgerald@rrd.com
Tel: (630) 322 - 6830

Serves As:
- Senior V. President, Marketing and Communications, R R Donnelley

Responsibilities include media relations.

FITZGERALD, Joelle
500 Oracle Pkwy.
Redwood Shores, CA 94065
Tel: (650) 506 - 4073
Fax:(650) 506 - 7122
TF: (800) 672 - 2531

Serves As:
- Senior Director, Investor Relations, Oracle Corporation

FITZGERALD, Joseph M.
10250 Constellation Blvd.
Los Angeles, CA 90067-6241
jfitzgerald@mgm.com
Tel: (310) 449 - 3660
Fax:(310) 449 - 8757

Serves As:
- Exec. V. President, Corporate Communications and Investor Relations, Metro-Goldwyn-Mayer Inc.

FITZGERALD, Kevin G.
P.O. Box 7000
El Dorado, AR 71731-7000
Tel: (870) 864 - 6272
Fax:(870) 864 - 6371

Serves As:
- PAC Contact, Murphy Oil Corp.

FITZGERALD, Niall
33 Benedict Pl.
Greenwich, CT 06830
Tel: (203) 661 - 2000
Fax:(203) 625 - 2370
TF: (800) 366 - 4011

Serves As:
- Chairman of the Board, Unilever Home & Personal Care - North America

FITZGERALD, Patrick
1500 Corporate Dr.
Suite 400
Canonsburg, PA 15317
Tel: (724) 514 - 1800

Serves As:
- V. President, Public Relations, Mylan Laboratories Inc.

FITZGERALD, William A.
13220 California St.
Omaha, NE 68154
Tel: (402) 554 - 9200
Fax:(402) 514 - 5486
TF: (800) 228 - 5023

Serves As:
- Chairman and Chief Exec. Officer, Commercial Federal Corp.

FITZGIBBONS, Dennis B.
1401 H St. NW
Suite 700
Washington, DC 20005
Tel: (202) 414 - 6764
Fax:(202) 414 - 6741

Registered Federal Lobbyist.

Serves As:
- Director, Public Policy, DaimlerChrysler Corp.

FITZHENRY, Jack R.
101 Innovation Dr.
San Jose, CA 95134-1941
Tel: (408) 544 - 7000
Fax:(408) 544 - 7740

Serves As:
- V. President, Human Resources, Altera Corp.

FITZPATRICK, Barclay
P.O. Box 772531
Harrisburg, PA 17177-2531
Tel: (717) 541 - 7752
Fax:(717) 651 - 8424

Serves As:
- V. President, Corporate Communications, Capital BlueCross (Pennsylvania)

FITZPATRICK, Eileen B.
8200 Jones Branch Dr.
M/S 409
McLean, VA 22102
eileen_fitzpatrick@freddiemac.com
Tel: (703) 903 - 2446
Fax:(703) 903 - 2447
TF: (800) 373 - 3343

Serves As:
- Senior Communications Specialist, Freddie Mac

FITZPATRICK, Jeanne
3900 Wisconsin Ave. NW
Washington, DC 20016
Tel: (202) 752 - 5717
Fax:(202) 753 - 019

Serves As:
- Director, Consumer Resources, Fannie Mae

FITZPATRICK, John
208 N. Montana Ave.
Helena, MT 59601
john.fitzpatrick@northwestern.com
Tel: (406) 449 - 9818
Fax:(406) 449 - 8331

Serves As:
- Director, Community Relations, NorthWestern Corp.

FITZPATRICK, Thomas J.
12061 Bluemont Way
Reston, VA 20190
Tel: (703) 810 - 3000
Fax:(703) 810 - 7053

Serves As:
- Vice Chairman and Chief Exec. Officer, SLM Corp.

FITZPATRICK, Tim
740 W. New Circle Rd.
Lexington, KY 40550
Tel: (859) 232 - 2000
Fax:(859) 232 - 2403
TF: (800) 539 - 6275

Serves As:
- V. President, Corporate Communications, Lexmark Internat'l, Inc.

FITZPATRICK, Tim
1500 Market St.
Philadelphia, PA 19102
Tel: (215) 981 - 8515
Fax:(215) 981 - 7790

Serves As:
- Director, Corporate Communications, Comcast Corporation

FITZSIMMONS, Ellen M.
500 Water St.
Jacksonville, FL 32203
Tel: (904) 359 - 3200

Serves As:
- Senior V. President, Law and Public Affairs, CSX Corp.

FITZSIMMONS, Joseph J. "Jay"
702 SW Eighth St.
Bentonville, AR 72716
Tel: (479) 273 - 6445
Fax:(479) 273 - 4053

Serves As:
- Senior V. President, Finance and Treasurer, Wal-Mart Stores

Responsibilities include investor relations.

FITZSIMONS, Dennis J.
435 N. Michigan Ave.
Chicago, IL 60611
Tel: (312) 222 - 9100
Fax:(312) 222 - 1573

Serves As:
- Chairman, President and Chief Exec. Officer, Tribune Co.

FITZWATER, James
1735 Market St.
Philadelphia, PA 19103
james_fitzwater@fmc.com
Tel: (215) 299 - 6633
Fax:(215) 299 - 6568

Serves As:
- Manager, Corporate Communications, FMC Corp.

FLACHBART, Ray
P.O. Box 7408
Boise, ID 83707
rflachbart@bcidaho.com
Tel: (208) 345 - 4550
Fax:(208) 331 - 7311

Serves As:
- President and Chief Exec. Officer, Blue Cross of Idaho

FLACHMAN, Jennifer
2727 N. Central Ave.
P.O. Box 21502
Phoenix, AZ 85004
Tel: (602) 263 - 6568
Fax:(602) 263 - 6772

Serves As:
- Director, Investor Relations, AMERCO

FLAHARTY, Gary R.
3900 Essex Ln., Suite 1200
Houston, TX 77027-5177
gary.flaharty@bakerhughes.com
Tel: (713) 439 - 8039
Fax:(713) 439 - 8472

Serves As:
- Director, Investor Relations, Baker Hughes Inc.

FLAJSER, Steven H.
1421 S. Clark St.
Suite 810
Arlington, VA 22202
Tel: (703) 414 - 1042
Fax:(703) 414 - 1071

Registered Federal Lobbyist.
Serves As:
- V. President, Corporate Legislative Relations, Loral Space & Communications

FLAMMER, Maureen
11 Harbor Park Dr.
Port Washington, NY 11050
Tel: (516) 608 - 7000
Fax:(516) 625 - 0038

Serves As:
- Manager, Human Resources, Systemax Inc.

FLANAGAN, Bridget A.
16300 S.E. Evelyn St.
Clackamas, OR 97015
Tel: (503) 657 - 6287

Serves As:
- Director, Public Affairs, Safeway Inc.

FLANAGAN, Kevin
50 Minuteman Rd.
Andover, MA 01810
kflanaga@entersys.com
Tel: (978) 684 - 1473
Fax:(978) 684 - 1658

Serves As:
- Director, Corporate Communications, Enterasys Networks

FLANAGAN, Martin L.
One Franklin Pkwy.
San Mateo, CA 94403-1906
mflanagan@frk.com
Tel: (650) 312 - 5818
Fax:(650) 574 - 5012
TF: (800) 342 - 5236

Serves As:
- Co-Chief Exec. Officer, Franklin Templeton Investments

FLANCBAUM, Paul
P.O. Box 2601
Troy, MI 48007-2601
Tel: (248) 643 - 3644
Fax:(248) 643 - 3687

Serves As:
- Manager, Corporate Communications, Thyssenkrupp Budd Company

FLANERY, David
P.O. Box 99900
Louisville, KY 40269-0900
Tel: (502) 261 - 4753
Fax:(502) 261 - 4315

Serves As:
- Senior V. President, Finance, Chief Financial Officer and Treasurer, Papa John's Internat'l Inc.

Responsibilities include media and investor relations.

FLANNERY, John
1300 I St. NW
Suite 400 West
Washington, DC 20005
Tel: (202) 515 - 2400

Registered Federal Lobbyist.
Serves As:
- Representative, Verizon Communications Inc.

FLANNERY, Michael
P.O. Box 8171
Portland, OR 97207
Tel: (503) 228 - 9161
Fax:(503) 220 - 2722

Serves As:
- Chairman, President and Chief Exec. Officer, Pope & Talbot, Inc.

FLANNIGAN, Michael
Kennecott US Borax
1325 Pennsylvania Ave. NW, Seventh Floor
Washington, DC 20004
Tel: (202) 393 - 0266
Fax:(202) 393 - 0232

Registered Federal Lobbyist.
Serves As:
- V. President, Federal Government Affairs, Kennecott Utah Copper
- V. President, Federal Government Affairs, Kennecott Energy Co.
- V. President, Federal Government Affairs, Kennecott Land

FLATT, Dennis O.
1215 K St.
Suite 2030
Sacramento, CA 95814
Tel: (916) 448 - 8866
Fax:(916) 973 - 6476

Serves As:
- V. President and Legislative Representative, Kaiser Permanente

FLEENER, Rob
Centre Square, West Tower
1500 Market St., Suite 3900
Philadelphia, PA 19102-2112
Tel: (215) 448 - 1400
Fax:(215) 448 - 3962
TF: (877) 275 - 5462

Serves As:
- Media Contact, Lincoln Financial Group

FLEIG, Jr., John E.
Four Taft Ct.
Rockville, MD 20850
Tel: (301) 838 - 5653
Fax:(301) 545 - 5972

Serves As:
- Senior V. President, Regulatory Affairs, Mid Atlantic Medical Services Inc.

FLEISHMAN, Ernest B.
557 Broadway
New York, NY 10012
efleishman@scholastic.com
Tel: (212) 343 - 6100
Fax:(212) 343 - 6802

Serves As:
- Senior V. President, Education/Corporate Relations, Scholastic, Inc.

FLEISHMAN, Mindy
600 Grant St.
Pittsburgh, PA 15219-2800
Tel: (412) 433 - 1121

Serves As:
- Treasurer, United States Steel Corp. PAC, United States Steel Corporation

FLEISHMAN, Susan
4000 Warner Blvd.
Burbank, CA 91522
Tel: (818) 954 - 6000

Serves As:
- Exec. V. President, Corporate Communications, (Warner Brothers Entertainment), Time Warner Inc.

FLEITMAN, Ms. Sam
425 Portland Ave.
Minneapolis, MN 55415
Tel: (612) 673 - 7051
Fax:(612) 673 - 7847
TF: (800) 829 - 8742

Serves As:
- Coordinator, Star Tribune Foundation, Star Tribune

FLEMING, Betty A.
1221 Ave. of the Americas
47th Floor
New York, NY 10020-1095
betty_fleming@mcgraw-hill.com
Tel: (212) 512 - 2453

Serves As:
- Senior Manager, Internal Communications, The McGraw-Hill Companies, Inc.

FLEMING, Beverly
50 S. LaSalle St.
Chicago, IL 60675
Tel: (312) 630 - 6000
TF: (888) 289 - 6542

Serves As:
- Senior V. President, Investor Relations, Northern Trust Co.

FLEMING, David
7950 Jones Branch Dr.
McLean, VA 22107
defleming@gannett.com
Tel: (703) 854 - 6000
Fax:(703) 276 - 2046

Registered Federal Lobbyist.
Serves As:
- Senior Legal Counsel, Gannett Co., Inc.

FLEMING, J. F.
P.O. Box 80730
Atlanta, GA 30366-0730
flemingj@vmcmail.com
Tel: (770) 458 - 4481
Fax:(770) 452 - 9505

Serves As:
- Manager, Human Resources and Government Affairs, Vulcan Materials Co.

FLEMING, Mark A.
P.O. Box 8003
Menasha, WI 54952-8003
Tel: (920) 751 - 7713
Fax:(920) 751 - 7790

Serves As:
- Director, Investor and Corporate Communications, Banta Corp.

FLETCHER, Julie
101 Constitution Ave. NW
Suite 325 East
Washington, DC 20001
Tel: (202) 312 - 8060

Serves As:
• V. President, Community Relations, Nortel Networks

FLETCHER, Kristin
35 W. Wacker Dr.
Chicago, IL 60601
kristin.fletcher@chi.leoburnett.com
Tel: (312) 220 - 4795
Fax:(312) 220 - 3299

Serves As:
• Manager, Corporate Communications, Leo Burnett Worldwide

FLETCHER-HAYES, Desiree
P.O. Box 14453
Des Moines, IA 50306-3453
desiree.fletcher-hayes@pioneer.com
Tel: (515) 248 - 4800
Fax:(515) 270 - 4112
TF: (800) 247 - 6803

Serves As:
• Coordinator, Public Relations, Pioneer Hi-Bred Internat'l, Inc.

FLICK, Donald
343 State St.
Rochester, NY 14650-0516
donald.flick@kodak.com
Tel: (585) 724 - 4683
Fax:(585) 724 - 1089

Serves As:
• Director, Investor Relations, Eastman Kodak Company

FLICK, Rebecca I.
101 Constitution Ave., NW
Suite 800 West
Washington, DC 20001
Tel: (202) 772 - 2497
Fax:(202) 772 - 2496

Serves As:
• Treasurer, Home Depot Inc. Better Government Committee, The Home Depot, Inc.

FLIGGE, Lori
P.O. Box 5625
MS25
Minneapolis, MN 55440-5625
Tel: (952) 742 - 2275
Fax:(952) 742 - 6208

Serves As:
• Public Affairs Counselor, Cargill, Incorporated

FLINT, David B.
4600 Arrowhead Dr.
Ann Arbor, MI 48105
Tel: (734) 622 - 6000
Fax:(734) 622 - 6131

Serves As:
• Chairman of the Board, Flint Ink Corp.

FLIPPIN, Mark
One Moody Plaza
Galveston, TX 77550-7999
mark.flippin@anico.com
Tel: (409) 766 - 6537
Fax:(409) 766 - 6663
TF: (800) 899 - 6502

Serves As:
• Secretary, American Nat'l Insurance Co.
Responsibilities include political action.

FLIPPIN, Stephen R.
1331 Pennsylvania Ave. NW
Suite 560
Washington, DC 20004
Tel: (202) 783 - 8124
Fax:(202) 783 - 5929

Registered Federal Lobbyist.
Serves As:
• Director, Government Relations, CSX Corp.

FLOERSCH, Rich
One McDonald's Plaza
Oak Brook, IL 60523
richard.floersch@mcd.com
Tel: (630) 623 - 8650
Fax:(630) 623 - 5004

Serves As:
• Corporate Exec. V. President, Human Resource Management, McDonald's Corp.

FLOHR, Cheryl C.
18321 Jamboree Rd.
Irvine, CA 92612-1073
Tel: (949) 833 - 3000
Fax:(949) 851 - 3277

Serves As:
• Manager, Community Services, Parker Hannifin Corp.

FLONORL, Rose
3610 Hacks Cross Rd.
Memphis, TN 38125
Tel: (901) 434 - 7773
Fax:(901) 434 - 7882

Serves As:
• Manager, Global Community Relations, FedEx Corp.

FLOOD, Jeff
165 Court St.
Rochester, NY 14647
Tel: (315) 671 - 6400

Serves As:
• V. President, External Relations, Utica Region, Exellus Blue Cross Blue Shield

FLORA, Paul J.
1290 Ave. of the Americas
New York, NY 10104
Tel: (212) 554 - 1234
TF: (888) AXA - INFO

Serves As:
• PAC Treasurer, AXA Financial, Inc.

FLORA, Terry
One Riverside Plaza
Columbus, OH 43215-2373
Tel: (614) 883 - 7999
Fax:(614) 223 - 1823

Serves As:
• Public Affairs Contact, (AEP Ohio), American Electric Power Co. Inc.

FLORCZAK, James E.
One CityPlace Dr.
Suite 300
St. Louis, MO 63141
Tel: (314) 994 - 2700
Fax:(314) 994 - 2719

Serves As:
• PAC Treasurer, Arch Coal, Inc.

FLORES, Amy
P.O. Box 10395
Palo Alto, CA 94303-0395
amy_flores@agilent.com
Tel: (650) 752 - 5303
Fax:(650) 752 - 5633

Serves As:
• Manager, Public Relations, Agilent Technologies, Inc.

FLORES, Greg
646 S. Main Ave.
San Antonio, TX 78204
flores.greg@heb.com
Tel: (210) 938 - 8075
Fax:(210) 938 - 8169

Serves As:
• Director, Legislative Affairs, HEB Grocery Co.

FLORES, James C.
700 Milam St.
Suite 3100
Houston, TX 77002
Tel: (832) 239 - 6000

Serves As:
• Chairman of the Board, Plains Resources Inc.

FLORIO, Michael G.
818 Connecticut Ave., Suite 801
Washington, DC 20006
Tel: (202) 955 - 6111
Fax:(202) 955 - 6118

Registered Federal Lobbyist.
Serves As:
• Government Affairs Assistant, Seaboard Corporation

FLORJANCIC, Frederick J.
5400 Legacy Dr., Cluster II, Bldg. 3
Plano, TX 75024
Tel: (972) 265 - 2000
TF: (800) 669 - 5740

Serves As:
• Chief Exec. Officer, Safety-Kleen Systems, Inc.

FLOWER, Will
110 S.E. Sixth St.
28th Floor
Fort Lauderdale, FL 33301
Tel: (954) 769 - 6392
Fax:(954) 769 - 2664

Serves As:
• V. President, Communications, Republic Services, Inc.

FLOWERS, Edsel W.
3330 Cumberland Blvd.
Suite 800
Atlanta, GA 30339
Tel: (678) 742 - 8000

Serves As:
• Senior V. President, Human Resources, Russell Corp.

FLOYD, William R.
1000 Beverly Way
Fort Smith, AR 72919-5273
bill_floyd@beverlycorp.com
Tel: (479) 201 - 2000
Fax:(479) 201 - 1101

Serves As:
• Chairman, President and Chief Exec. Officer, Beverly Enterprises, Inc.

FLUMERFELT, John
Two Atlantic Ave.
Third Floor
Boston, MA 02110
jflumert@calpine.com
Tel: (617) 557 - 5381
Fax:(617) 723 - 7635

Serves As:
• Director, Public Relations, Calpine Corp.

FLUOR, II, J. Robert
One Enterprise Dr.
Aliso Viejo, CA 92656-2606
robert.fluor@fluor.com
Tel: (949) 349 - 7171
Fax:(949) 349 - 5375

Serves As:
• V. President, Global Public Affairs, Fluor Corp.

FLYNN, Bridget
1120 G St. NW
Suite 850
Washington, DC 20005
Tel: (202) 347 - 5910
Fax:(202) 347 - 5916

Serves As:
- Government Affairs Representative, Nationwide

FLYNN, Peter
633 Pennsylvania Ave. NW
Sixth Floor
Washington, DC 20004
Tel: (202) 783 - 7959

Registered Federal Lobbyist.
Serves As:
- Representative, Nat'l Grid USA

FLYNN, Timothy P.
Three Chestnut Ridge Rd.
Montvale, NJ 07645-0435
Tel: (212) 872 - 7925
Fax:(212) 758 - 9819

Serves As:
- Chairman and Chief Exec. Officer, KPMG LLP

FLYNT, III, Roger M.
600 19th St.
Room 28B3
Birmingham, AL 35203
flynt.mayo@bsi.bls.com
Tel: (205) 714 - 0714

Serves As:
- V. President, Regulatory and External Affairs, BellSouth Corp.

FOGARTY, Molly
1101 Pennsylvania Ave. NW
Suite 600
Washington, DC 20004
Tel: (202) 756 - 2299
Fax:(202) 756 - 7556

Registered Federal Lobbyist.
Serves As:
- Government Relations, Nestle USA, Inc.

FOHRER, Alan J.
2244 Walnut Grove Ave.
Rosemead, CA 91770
fohreraj@sce.com
Tel: (626) 302 - 1379
Fax:(626) 302 - 4737

Serves As:
- Chief Exec. Officer, Southern California Edison, an Edison Internat'l Co.

FOLEY, Daniel R.
21001 Van Born Rd.
Taylor, MI 48180
Tel: (313) 792 - 6691
Fax:(313) 792 - 6135

Serves As:
- V. President, Human Resources, Masco Corp.

FOLEY, Michelle
P.O. Box 51609
Indianapolis, IN 46251-0609
Tel: (317) 282 - 2659
Fax:(317) 243 - 4169

Serves As:
- Media Contact, ATA Holdings Corp.

FOLEY, Paul F.
Fifth St. Towers, Suite 1360
150 S. Fifth St.
Minneapolis, MN 55402
foley_paul@mesaba.com
Tel: (612) 333 - 0021
Fax:(612) 337 - 0355

Serves As:
- President and Chief Exec. Officer, MAIR Holdings, Inc.

FOLEY, II, William P.
601 Riverside Ave.
Jacksonville, FL 32204
Tel: (904) 854 - 8100

Serves As:
- Chairman and Chief Exec. Officer, Fidelity Nat'l Financial, Inc.

FOLK, Cassie
8607 Westwood Center Dr.
Vienna, VA 22182
Tel: (703) 448 - 4000
Fax:(703) 448 - 4100

Registered Federal Lobbyist.
Serves As:
- Manager, Government Relations, Feld Entertainment, Inc.

FOLKERTS, Brian
101 Constitution Ave. NW
Suite 400 West
Washington, DC 20001
brian.folkerts@altria.com
Tel: (202) 354 - 1500
Fax:(202) 354 - 1505

Registered Federal Lobbyist.
Serves As:
- V. President, Government Affairs - Food, Altria Group, Inc.
- Director, Federal Government Affairs, Kraft Foods, Inc.

FOLMNSBEE, Anna
P.O. Box 660606
M/S 490
Dallas, TX 75266-0606
afolmns@greyhound.com
Tel: (972) 789 - 7206
Fax:(972) 789 - 7234

Serves As:
- Communications Specialist, Greyhound Lines, Inc.

FOLTA, Carl D.
1515 Broadway
52nd Floor
New York, NY 10036
Tel: (212) 258 - 6352
Fax:(212) 846 - 1727

Serves As:
- Exec V. President, Corporate Relations, Viacom Inc./CBS Corp.

FOLTZ, James
P.O. Box 58090
M/S G2-397
Santa Clara, CA 95052-8090
james.foltz@nsc.com
Tel: (408) 721 - 5693
Fax:(408) 721 - 7254

Serves As:
- Treasurer and Director, Financial Relations, Nat'l Semiconductor Corp.

Responsibilities include investor relations.

FOLTZ, Sharon B.
P.O. Box 711
UE 102
Tucson, AZ 85702
sfoltz@tep.com
Tel: (520) 884 - 3740
Fax:(520) 884 - 3606
TF: (800) 328 - 8853

Serves As:
- Director, Community Relations, UniSource Energy Corp.

FONES, Linda L.
555 12th St. NW
Suite 620 North
Washington, DC 20004
Tel: (202) 223 - 8290
Fax:(202) 293 - 2913

Serves As:
- Adminstrative Coordinator and Grassroots Manager, Ashland Inc.

FONTAINE, David
4411 E. Jones Bridge Rd.
Norcross, GA 30092-1615
Tel: (678) 375 - 1682
Fax:(678) 375 - 3304

Serves As:
- Media Relations Director, CheckFree Corp.

FONTANA, Donna
175 Crossways Park West
Woodbury, NY 11797
Tel: (516) 390 - 1452
Fax:(516) 390 - 1390

Serves As:
- V. President, Public Relations, Weight Watchers Internat'l

FONTENOT, M. L.
507 W. Tenth St.
West Point, GA 31833
Tel: (706) 645 - 4000
Fax:(706) 645 - 4121

Serves As:
- President and Chief Exec. Officer, WestPoint Stevens Inc.

FONTES, Brian F.
1818 N St. NW
Suite 800
Washington, DC 20036
brian.fontes@cingular.com
Tel: (202) 419 - 3000
Ext: 3010
Fax:(202) 419 - 3030

Registered Federal Lobbyist.
Serves As:
- V. President, Federal Relations, Cingular Wireless

FOOSANER, Robert S.
401 Ninth St. NW
Suite 400
Washington, DC 20004
Tel: (202) 585 - 1900
Fax:(202) 585 - 1899

Registered Federal Lobbyist.
Serves As:
- Senior V. President, Government Affairs and Chief Regulatory Officer, Sprint Nextel

FOOTE, William C.
P.O. Box 6721
Chicago, IL 60680-6721
Tel: (312) 606 - 4000
Fax:(312) 606 - 5598

Serves As:
- Chairman and Chief Exec. Officer, USG Corp.

FOOTE-HUDSON, Marilyn
P.O. Box 13398
Research Triangle Park, NC 27709
Tel: (919) 483 - 2588
Fax:(919) 315 - 3015

Serves As:
- Director, GlaxoSmithKline Foundation, GlaxoSmithKline Research and Development

FORBES, Steve
60 Fifth Ave.
New York, NY 10010
Tel: (212) 620 - 2200
Fax:(212) 620 - 2245

Serves As:
- Chief Exec. Officer, Forbes, Inc.

FORBIS, Jeanne
710 Medtronic Pkwy.
Minneapolis, MN 55432-5604
jeanne.forbis@medtronic.com
Tel: (763) 505 - 2814
Fax:(763) 514 - 4879
TF: (800) 328 - 2518

Serves As:
- V. President, Public Relations, Medtronic, Inc.

Responsibilities include corporate philanthropy.

FORD, Allyn
P.O. Box 1088
Roseburg, OR 97470-0252
Tel: (541) 679 - 3311
Fax:(541) 679 - 9543
TF: (800) 245 - 1115

Serves As:
- Chairman, President and Chief Exec. Officer, Roseburg Forest Products Co.

FORD, Joe T.
One Allied Dr.
Little Rock, AR 72202
joe.t.ford@alltel.com
Tel: (501) 905 - 8000

Serves As:
- Chairman of the Board, ALLTEL

FORD, Judy
P.O. Box 2047
Omaha, NE 68103-2047
Tel: (402) 496 - 7809
Fax:(402) 498 - 5548
TF: (800) 247 - 1345

Serves As:
- Senior V. President, Human Resources, AG Processing Inc

Responsibilities include political action.

FORD, Manley
12025 Tech Center Dr.
Livonia, MI 48150
manley.l.ford@trw.com
Tel: (734) 855 - 2616
Fax:(734) 855 - 2696

Serves As:
- Director, Public Relations and Communications, TRW Automotive

FORD, Scott T.
One Allied Dr.
Little Rock, AR 72202
scott.t.ford@alltel.com
Tel: (501) 905 - 8000

Serves As:
- President and Chief Exec. Officer, ALLTEL

FORD, Jr., William Clay
One American Rd.
Dearborn, MI 48126
Tel: (313) 322 - 3000
TF: (800) 555 - 5259

Serves As:
- Chairman and Chief Exec. Officer, Ford Motor Co.

FOREHAND, Joe W.
1345 Ave. of the Americas
New York, NY 10105
Tel: (917) 452 - 4400
Fax:(917) 527 - 9915

Serves As:
- Chairman of the Board, Accenture

FOREMAN, Donald D.
1201 F St. NW
Suite 1000
Washington, DC 20004
Tel: (202) 626 - 7200
Fax:(202) 626 - 7208

Serves As:
- Director, Federal Government Affairs, (R. J. Reynolds Tobacco Co.), Reynolds American Inc.

FOREMAN, Robert B.
13515 Ballantyne Corp. Pl.
Charlotte, NC 28277
Tel: (704) 752 - 4400

Serves As:
- V. President, Human Resources, SPX Corp.

FORESTI, Rob
1345 Ave. of the Americas
New York, NY 10020
Tel: (212) 282 - 5320
Fax:(212) 282 - 6035

Serves As:
- Investor Relations Contact, Avon Products, Inc.

FORKEL, Vicki
P.O. Box 4011
Schaumburg, IL 60168-4011
vforkel@lnc.com
Tel: (847) 466 - 8585

Serves As:
- Charitable Giving Contact (Schaumburg, IL), Lincoln Financial Group

FORREST, Martin
4560 Horton St.
Emeryville, CA 94608-2916
Tel: (510) 655 - 8730
Fax:(510) 655 - 9910

Serves As:
- V. President, Corporate Communications and Investor Relations, Chiron Corp.

FORSBERG, Bruce
1350 I St. NW
Suite 400
Washington, DC 20005-3306
Tel: (202) 371 - 6900
Fax:(202) 842 - 3578

Serves As:
- PAC Treasurer, Motorola, Inc.

FORSEE, Gary D.
2001 Edmund Halley Dr.
Reston, VA 20191
Tel: (703) 433 - 4000

Serves As:
- President and Chief Exec. Officer, Sprint Nextel

FORSLUND, Scott
7001 220th S.W.
Bldg. 3 M/S 308
Mountlake Terrace, WA 98043-2124
scott.forslund@premera.com
Tel: (425) 918 - 5090
Fax:(425) 918 - 5575
TF: (800) 422 - 0032

Serves As:
- Director, Communications, Premera Blue Cross

FORSYTH, John D.
636 Grand Ave.
Des Moines, IA 50309
forsythjd@wellmark.com
Tel: (515) 245 - 4548
Fax:(515) 245 - 5090

Serves As:
- Chairman and Chief Exec. Officer, Wellmark, Inc.

FORSYTH, Stephen
281 Tresser Blvd.
Two Stamford Plaza
Stamford, CT 06901-3238
stephen.forsyth@hexcel.com
Tel: (203) 969 - 0666
Fax:(203) 358 - 3977

Serves As:
- Exec. V. President and Chief Financial Officer, Hexcel Corp.

Responsibilities include corporate philanthropy.

FORSYTHE, John G. "Jack"
Ecolab Center
370 N. Wabasha St.
St. Paul, MN 55102
jack.forsythe@ecolabl.com
Tel: (651) 293 - 2642
Fax:(651) 225 - 2092

Serves As:
- Senior V. President, Tax and Public Affairs, Ecolab Inc.

FORSYTHE, Thomas M.
One General Mills Blvd.
Minneapolis, MN 55426
Tel: (763) 764 - 3103
Fax:(763) 764 - 3734

Serves As:
- V. President, Corporate Communications, General Mills

FORT, Robert C.
Three Commercial Pl.
Norfolk, VA 23510-2191
Tel: (757) 629 - 2710
Fax:(757) 629 - 2822

Serves As:
- V. President, Public Relations, Norfolk Southern Corp.

FORTE, Kathleen H.
1007 Market St.
D-11030
Wilmington, DE 19898
kathleen.h.forte@usa.dupont.com
Tel: (302) 773 - 4418
Fax:(302) 773 - 0188
TF: (800) 441 - 7515

Serves As:
- V. President, DuPont Global Public Affairs, DuPont

FORTE, Mary L.
901 W. Walnut Hill Ln.
Irving, TX 75038-1003
Tel: (972) 580 - 4000
Fax:(972) 580 - 5523

Serves As:
- President and Chief Exec. Officer, Zale Corp.

FORTH, Rodney D.
One Busch Pl.
St. Louis, MO 63118-1852
Tel: (314) 577 - 4618
Fax:(314) 765 - 9190

Serves As:
- Region V. President, Government Affairs, Anheuser-Busch Cos., Inc.

FORTIER, Alison
1550 Crystal Dr.
Crystal Square 2, Suite 300
Arlington, VA 22202
Tel: (703) 413 - 5979
Fax:(703) 413 - 5617

Serves As:
- V. President, Space and Strategic Missile Legislative Affairs, Lockheed Martin Corp.

FOSS, Lisa K.
1900 W. Field Ct.
Lake Forest, IL 60045
lfoss@pactiv.com
Tel: (847) 482 - 2704
Fax:(847) 482 - 3360
TF: (888) 828 - 2850

Serves As:
- V. President, Communications, Pactiv Corp.

FOSSENIER, Patrick
3240 Hillview Ave.
Palo Alto, CA 94304
fossenier.patrick@cnf.com
Tel: (650) 813 - 5353
Fax:(650) 813 - 0160

Serves As:
- Director, Investor Relations, CNF Inc.

FOSTER, Andrew
2101 City West Blvd.
Houston, TX 77042-2827
Tel: (650) 930 - 5550
Fax:(713) 918 - 8000
TF: (800) 841 - 2031

Serves As:
- Director, Public Relations, BMC Software

FOSTER, Bruce C.
601 Van Ness Ave., Suite 2040
San Francisco, CA 94102
fosterbc@sce.com
Tel: (415) 775 - 1856
Fax:(415) 474 - 3080

Serves As:
- V. President, San Francisco Region, Southern California Edison, an Edison Internat'l Co.

Responsibilities include government relations.

FOSTER, Catherine H.
One Infinite Loop
Cupertino, CA 95014
Tel: (408) 996 - 1010
Fax:(408) 996 - 0275

Registered Federal Lobbyist.
Serves As:
- Director, Government Affairs, Apple Computer, Inc.

FOSTER, Jr., Charles H.
Gateway One
101 Gateway Centre Pkwy.
Richmond, VA 23235
Tel: (804) 267 - 8000
Fax:(804) 267 - 8836
TF: (800) 446 - 7086

Serves As:
- Chairman of the Board, LandAmerica Financial Group, Inc.

FOSTER, David
801 Pennsylvania Ave. NW
Suite 710
Washington, DC 20004
david_foster@biogen.com
Tel: (202) 383 - 1440

Serves As:
- V. President, Government Affairs, Biogen Idec Inc.

FOSTER, Debora S.
P.O. Box 57
Pittsburgh, PA 15230-0057
Tel: (412) 456 - 5778
Fax:(412) 456 - 7883

Serves As:
- V. President, Corporate Communications, H. J. Heinz Co.

FOSTER, Emily Diedrich
601 Pennsylvania Ave. NW
North Bldg., Suite 625
Washington, DC 20004
Tel: (202) 393 - 8585
Ext: `
Fax:(202) 393 - 8111

Registered Federal Lobbyist.
Serves As:
- Washington Representative, Cummins, Inc.

FOSTER, Karen
P.O. Box 10100
Reno, NV 89520-0026
karenfoster@sppc.com
Tel: (775) 834 - 5741
Fax:(775) 834 - 4339
TF: (800) 962 - 0399

Serves As:
- Manager, Community Relations, (Sierra Pacific Power Co.), Sierra Pacific Resources

FOSTER, Kent
425 W. Capitol Ave.
P.O. Box 551
Little Rock, AR 72203
Tel: (501) 377 - 3525

Serves As:
- V. President, System Regulatory Affairs and Affiliate Rule Compliance, Entergy Corp.

FOSTER, Kent B.
1600 E. St. Andrews Pl.
Santa Ana, CA 92705
kent.foster@ingrammicro.com
Tel: (714) 566 - 1000
Fax:(714) 566 - 7900

Serves As:
- Chairman of the Board, Ingram Micro, Inc.

FOSTER, Kyna
P.O. Box 1330
Salisbury, NC 28145-1330
Tel: (704) 633 - 8250
Fax:(704) 633 - 8250

Serves As:
- Community Affairs Manager, Food Lion LLC

FOSTER, II, Lee B.
415 Holiday Dr.
Pittsburgh, PA 15220-2793
lfoster@lbfosterco.com
Tel: (412) 928 - 3417
Fax:(412) 928 - 7891
TF: (800) 255 - 4500

Serves As:
- Chairman of the Board, L. B. Foster Co.

FOSTER, Paul
1895 J W Foster Blvd.
Canton, MA 02021
paul.foster@reebok.com
Tel: (781) 401 - 7396
Fax:(781) 401 - 4806

Serves As:
- V. President, Foundation and Trade Relations, Reebok Internat'l Ltd.

FOSTER, Robert G.
2244 Walnut Grove Ave.
Rosemead, CA 91770
fosterrg@sce.com
Tel: (626) 302 - 9210
Fax:(626) 302 - 9213

Serves As:
- President, Southern California Edison, an Edison Internat'l Co.

Responsibilities include regulatory affairs, public affairs, and communications.

FOSTER, Sara E.
8000 Forsyth Blvd.
Clayton, MO 63105
Tel: (314) 746 - 8542

Serves As:
- Senior V. President, Human Resources, Commerce Bancshares Inc.

FOSTER, Scarlett Lee
800 N. Lindbergh Blvd.
St. Louis, MO 63167
slfost@monsanto.com
Tel: (314) 694 - 2883

Serves As:
- Director, Investor Relations, Monsanto Co.

FOSTON, Barbara
1155 Peachtree St. NE
7H08 Campanile
Atlanta, GA 30309-3610
barbara.foston@bellsouth.com
Tel: (404) 249 - 2417
Fax:(404) 249 - 5696

Serves As:
- Specialist, Corporate Contributions Program, BellSouth Corp.

FOTE, Charlie
6200 S. Quebec St.
Greenwood Village, CO 80111
Tel: (303) 488 - 8000
Fax:(303) 967 - 6705

Serves As:
- Chairman and Chief Exec. Officer, First Data

FOTHERGILL, James E.
500 Volvo Pkwy.
Chesapeake, VA 23320
Tel: (757) 321 - 5000
Fax:(757) 321 - 5292

Serves As:
- Chief People Officer, Dollar Tree Stores, Inc.

FOTJIK, Brian J.
2640 White Oak Circle, Suite E
Aurora, IL 60504
Tel: (630) 692 - 6060
Fax:(630) 692 - 6062

Serves As:
- Regional Manager, State Government Relations/Great Lakes, UST Inc.

FOUGHNER, Beth
2455 Paces Ferry Rd.
Atlanta, GA 30339-4024
Tel: (770) 433 - 8211
Fax:(770) 384 - 2356

Serves As:
- Manager, Government Relations, The Home Depot, Inc.

FOUNTAIN, W. Frank
1000 Chrysler Dr.
CIMS 485-10-96
Auburn Hills, MI 48326-2766
wff3@daimlerchrysler.com
Tel: (248) 512 - 4218
Fax:(248) 512 - 1762
TF: (800) 992 - 1997

Serves As:
- Senior V. President, Internal Affairs and Public Policy, DaimlerChrysler Corp.

FOUQUET, Douglas M.
3550 General Atomics Ct.
San Diego, CA 92121
Tel: (858) 455 - 3000
Ext: 2173
Fax:(858) 455 - 3545

Serves As:
- Coordinator, Community Public Relations, General Atomics

FOWLER, Bonny
1500 E. Main St.
Newark, OH 43055
bfowler1@longaberger.com
Tel: (740) 322 - 5257
Fax:(740) 322 - 5240

Serves As:
- Public Relations Representative, The Longaberger Co.

FOWLER, Michael L.
47 State Circle, Suite 403
Annapolis, MD 21401
michael.l.fowler@constellation.com
Tel: (410) 269 - 5279
Fax:(410) 269 - 5289
TF: (888) 460 - 2002

Serves As:
- Senior Government Relations Representative, Constellation Energy

FOWLER, Peggy
121 SW Salmon St.
Portland, OR 97204
peggy_fowler@pgn.com
Tel: (503) 464 - 8000
Fax:(503) 464 - 2354
TF: (800) 542 - 8818

Serves As:
- President and Chief Exec. Officer, Portland General Electric Co.

FOWLER, Richard G.
101 Montgomery St.
San Francisco, CA 94104
Tel: (415) 636 - 9869
TF: (800) 435 - 4000

Serves As:
- Senior V. President, Investor Relations, The Charles Schwab Corp.

FOWLER-MCFADDEN, Kay
901 N. Tatnall St., Second Floor
Wilmington, DE 19801
Tel: (302) 571 - 1571
Fax:(302) 777 - 0491

Serves As:
- Director, External Affairs and Community Relations, Verizon Delaware Inc.

FOWLIE, Mary M.
2600 W. Big Beaver Rd.
Troy, MI 48084
Tel: (248) 643 - 9600
Fax:(248) 637 - 5016
TF: (800) 643 - 9600

Serves As:
- Group Senior V. President, Regulatory Affairs and Compliance, Standard Federal Bank

FOX, Barbara
401 Ninth St., NW
Suite 600
M/S 600
Washington, DC 20004
barbara_fox@freddiemac.com
Tel: (202) 434 - 8618
Fax:(202) 434 - 8626

Registered Federal Lobbyist.
Serves As:
- Director, Government Relations, Freddie Mac

FOX, Denise
2000 Galloping Hill Rd.
Kenilworth, NJ 07033
Tel: (908) 298 - 7616

Serves As:
- Manager, Global Product Communications and Advocacy Development, Schering-Plough Corporation

FOX, Douglas A.
333 Corporate Woods Pkwy.
Vernon Hills, IL 60061-3109
dfox@zebra.com
Tel: (847) 793 - 6735
Fax:(847) 821 - 2545
TF: (800) 423 - 0422

Serves As:
- Director, Investor Relations, Zebra Technologies Corp.

FOX, Edward Z.
P.O. Box 53999
M/S 9085
Phoenix, AZ 85072-3999
edward.fox@pinnaclewest.com
Tel: (602) 250 - 2916
Fax:(605) 250 - 3002

Serves As:
- V. President, Communications, Environment and Safety, Pinnacle West Capital Corp.

FOX, Eric V.
P.O. Box 748
Fort Worth, TX 76101
eric.v.fox@lmcoc.com
Tel: (817) 777 - 8585
Fax:(817) 777 - 2115

Serves As:
- Director, Government Relations, Lockheed Martin Aeronautics Co.

FOX, Jr., Jerome E.
One Invacare Way
Elyria, OH 44035
jfox@invacare.com
Tel: (440) 329 - 6000
Fax:(440) 366 - 9008
TF: (800) 333 - 6900

Serves As:
- Treasurer, Inva PAC; Secretary-Treasurer, Foundation, Invacare Corp.

FOX, Linster
15378 Ave. of Science
San Diego, CA 92128
lfox@anacomp.com
Tel: (858) 716 - 3400
Fax:(858) 716 - 3775
TF: (800) 350 - 3044

Serves As:
- Chief Financial Officer, Anacomp, Inc.

FOX, Susan
1150 17th St. NW
Suite 400
Washington, DC 20036
susan.fox@corp.disney.com
Tel: (202) 222 - 4700

Registered Federal Lobbyist.
Serves As:
- V. President, Government Relations, The Walt Disney Company

FOX, William J.
One Learjet Way
Wichita, KS 67209
Tel: (316) 946 - 2000

Serves As:
- Senior V. President, Public Affairs, Bombardier

FOXHALL, Irene E. "Nene"
P.O. Box 4607
Houston, TX 77210-4607
nfoxha@coair.com
Tel: (713) 324 - 5140
Fax:(713) 324 - 6329

Serves As:
- V. President, State and Civic Affairs, Continental Airlines

FRABLE, Anna
One Health Plaza
East Hanover, NJ 07936
anna.frable@pharma.novartis.com
Tel: (862) 778 - 5388
Fax:(862) 644 - 8585

Serves As:
- Exec. Director, Public Relations, (Novartis Pharmaceuticals Corp.), Novartis Corporation

FRADIN, Russell P.
90 Park Ave.
Tenth Floor
New York, NY 10016-1301
Tel: (212) 907 - 6000
Fax:(212) 907 - 6014

Serves As:
- President and Chief Exec. Officer, The BISYS Group, Inc.

FRANCESCONI, Michael
316 Pennsylvania Ave. SE
Suite 300
Washington, DC 20003
Tel: (202) 675 - 4220
Fax:(202) 675 - 4230

Serves As:
- Manager, Public Affairs, United Parcel Service (UPS)

FRANCIS, Jo
7887 Washington Village Dr.
Dayton, OH 45459
jo.francis@amcast.com
Tel: (937) 291 - 7023
Fax:(937) 291 - 7007

Serves As:
- Exec. Secretary, Amcast Industrial Corporation

Responsibilities include corporate philanthropy.

FRANCIS, Peter
2000 K St., NW
Suite 710
Washington, DC 20006
Tel: (202) 862 - 0200
Fax:(202) 862 - 0267

Serves As:
- Senior International Advisor, Europe, Eurasia, and the Caspian, Exxon Mobil Corp.

FRANCIS, Philip L.
19601 N. 27th Ave.
Phoenix, AZ 85027
pfrancis@ssg.petsmart.com
Tel: (623) 580 - 6100
Fax:(623) 580 - 6508

Serves As:
- Chairman and Chief Exec. Officer, PETsMART, Inc.

FRANCISCO, Terry
Bank of America Corporate Center
100 N. Tryon St.
Charlotte, NC 28255-0001
Tel: (704) 386 - 4343
Fax:(704) 386 - 6699

Serves As:
- Media Contact, Bank of America Corp.

FRANCY, John C.
2090 Florence Ave.
Cincinnati, OH 45206
Tel: (513) 487 - 5912
Fax:(513) 487 - 5586

Serves As:
- V. President and Treasurer; Secretary, Milacron Foundation, Milacron Inc.

FRANK, Peter M.
1667 K St. NW
Suite 250
Washington, DC 20006
Tel: (202) 728 - 9600
Fax:(202) 728 - 9587

Registered Federal Lobbyist.
Serves As:
- V. President, Public Affairs, Kerr-McGee Corp.

FRANKLIN, George A.
P.O. Box 3599
Battle Creek, MI 49016-3599
george.franklin@kellogg.com
Tel: (269) 961 - 2820
Fax:(269) 961 - 6646
TF: (800) 535 - 5644

Registered Federal Lobbyist.
Serves As:
- V. President, Worldwide Government Relations, Kellogg Co.

FRANKLIN, Larry
P.O. Box 269
San Antonio, TX 78291
Tel: (210) 829 - 9000
Fax:(210) 829 - 9403

Serves As:
- Chairman of the Board, Harte-Hanks, Inc.

FRANKLIN, Martin E.
555 Theodore Fremd Ave.
Rye, NY 10580-1455
Tel: (914) 967 - 9400
Fax:(914) 967 - 9405

Serves As:
- Chairman and Chief Exec. Officer, Jarden Corp.

FRANKS, Martin D.
1501 M St. NW
Suite 1100
Washington, DC 20005
Tel: (202) 785 - 7300
Fax:(202) 785 - 6360

Serves As:
- Exec. V. President, Policy and Government Relations, CBS Corp., Viacom Inc./CBS Corp.

FRANSON, Timothy
Lilly Corporate Center
Indianapolis, IN 46285
Tel: (317) 276 - 2000
Fax:(317) 277 - 6579

Serves As:
- V. President, Global Regulatory Affairs, Eli Lilly and Company

FRANTTI, Amy B.
800 Nicollet Mall
BCMNH23K
Minneapolis, MN 55402
amy.frantti@usbank.com
Tel: (612) 303 - 0733
Fax:(612) 303 - 0735

Serves As:
- Assistant V. President, Media Relations, U.S. Bancorp

FRANTZ, Francis X.
One Allied Dr.
Little Rock, AR 72202
Tel: (501) 905 - 5615

Serves As:
- Exec. V. President, External Affairs, General Counsel and Secretary, ALLTEL

Responsibilities include federal and state government affairs and corporate communications.

FRANZ, Liesyl
1331 Pennsylvania Ave. NW
Suite 1300 North
Washington, DC 20004
liesyl.franz@eds.com
Tel: (202) 637 - 6722
Fax:(202) 637 - 6759

Serves As:
- Director, Financial Industry Policy, EDS Corp.

FRASER, James H.
1300 N. 17th St.
Suite 1400
Arlington, VA 22209
Tel: (703) 907 - 8200
Fax:(703) 907 - 8300

Serves As:
- Director, Government Affairs, BAE Systems North America

FRASER, Lori
P.O. Box 58090
Santa Clara, CA 95052-8090
lori.fraser@nsc.com
Tel: (408) 721 - 5000
Fax:(408) 739 - 9803

Serves As:
- Director, Employee Communications, Nat'l Semiconductor Corp.

FRAUTSCHI, Deanna L.
P.O. Box 2020
Bloomington, IL 61701-2020

Serves As:
- Senior V. President, Communications and Human Resources, Country Insurance and Financial Services

FRAZIER, Mell Meredith
1716 Locust St.
Des Moines, IA 50309-3023
Tel: (515) 284 - 2656
Fax:(515) 284 - 3153

Serves As:
- Director, Corporate Planning; V. President, The Meredith Foundation, Meredith Corp.

FRAZIER, Thomas H.
5800 Tennyson Pkwy.
Plano, TX 75024
Tel: (214) 473 - 7000
Ext: 3735

Serves As:
- Senior V. President, Administration, Triad Hospitals, Inc.

Responsibilities include human resources and public affairs.

FREDERIC, Christy
P.O. Box 5000
Pineville, LA 71361-5000
christy.frederic@cleco.com
Tel: (318) 484 - 7400
Fax:(318) 484 - 7465

Serves As:
- General Manager, Safety and Public Affairs, Cleco Corp.

FREDERICK, Christy
12221 Plaza Dr.
Parma, OH 44130
Tel: (216) 535 - 3357
Fax:(216) 676 - 8689

Serves As:
- Director, Public Relations and Government Affairs, Cox Enterprises, Inc.

FREDERICKSEN, Jay A.
50 N. Laura St., Suite 1900
Jacksonville, FL 32202-3638
jay.fredericksen@rayonier.com
Tel: (904) 357 - 9100
Fax:(904) 357 - 9101

Serves As:
- V. President, Corporate Relations, Rayonier Inc.

FREDERICKSON, Mark
P.O. Box 9103
Hopkinton, MA 01748
Tel: (508) 435 - 1000
Ext: 77137
Fax:(508) 435 - 7954
TF: (800) 424 - 3622

Serves As:
- V. President, Corporate Communications, EMC Corp.

FREDRIKSEN, Katharine A.
601 13th St. NW
Suite 850N
Washington, DC 20005
kathy.fredriksen@mirant.com
Tel: (202) 585 - 3832
Fax:(202) 585 - 3806

Serves As:
- Director, Federal Affairs, Mirant Corp.

FREE, Brant
One Massachusetts Ave. NW
Suite 350
Washington, DC 20001
bfree@chubb.com
Tel: (202) 408 - 8123
Ext: 114
Fax:(202) 296 - 7683

Serves As:
- Senior V. President, International External Affairs, The Chubb Corp.

FREECE, Robert A.
63 Lincoln Hwy.
Malvern, PA 19355-2120
bob.freece@vishay.com
Tel: (610) 251 - 5252
Fax:(610) 889 - 9349

Serves As:
- Exec. V. President, Vishay Intertechnology, Inc.

Responsibilities include investor relations.

FREEDMAN, Alan M.
One Blue Hill Plaza
Lobby Level
Pearl River, NY 10965
Tel: (845) 577 - 2922
Fax:(845) 577 - 6913

Serves As:
- Director, Public Affairs, (Rockland Electric Co.), Orange and Rockland Utilities, Inc.

FREEDMAN, Jodi S.
The Mountain
Framingham, MA 01701-9168
jodi_freedman@bose.com
Tel: (508) 766 - 7051
Fax:(508) 620 - 5523

Serves As:
- Senior Communications Specialist, Bose Corp.

FREEDMAN, Joel
Hartford Plaza
HO-1-11
Hartford, CT 06115
jfreedman@thehartford.com
Tel: (860) 547 - 5480
Fax:(860) 547 - 6551

Registered Federal Lobbyist.
Serves As:
- Senior V. President and Director, Government Affairs, The Hartford Financial Services Group Inc.

FREEDMAN, Judy K.
One Campbell Pl.
Camden, NJ 08103-1701
judy_freedman@campbellsoup.com
Tel: (856) 342 - 3892
Fax:(856) 541 - 8185
TF: (800) 257 - 8443

Serves As:
- Group Director, Public Affairs, Campbell Soup Co.

FREEH, Louis J.
1100 N. King St.
0127
Wilmington, DE 19880-127
Tel: (302) 432 - 0956
Fax:(302) 432 - 0039
TF: (800) 441 - 7048

Serves As:
- PAC Treasurer, MBNA Corp.

FREEMAN, Angie
8100 Mitchell Rd.
Eden Prairie, MN 55344
angie.freeman@chrobinson.com
Tel: (952) 937 - 7847
Fax:(952) 937 - 6740

Serves As:
- Director, Investor Relations and Marketing Communications, C.H. Robinson Worldwide, Inc.

FREEMAN, Erin K.
353 Sacramento St.
Suite 1600
San Francisco, CA 94111
Tel: (415) 277 - 1595

Serves As:
- Director, Public Relations, U.S. Bancorp Piper Jaffray Inc.

FREEMAN, James W.
P.O. Box 368
Indianapolis, IN 46206-0368
jim_freeman@aul.com
Tel: (317) 285 - 1609
Fax:(317) 285 - 1979

Serves As:
- V. President, Community Affairs, American United Life Insurance Co.

FREEMAN, Jan H.
300 Exelon Way
Kennett Square, PA 19348
jan.freeman@exeloncorp.com
Tel: (610) 765 - 6906
Fax:(610) 765 - 6902

Serves As:
- V. President, Public Affairs, Exelon Corp.

FREEMAN, Kenneth W.
One Malcolm Ave.
Teterboro, NJ 07608
Tel: (201) 393 - 5000
Fax:(201) 393 - 4755
TF: (800) 222 - 0446

Serves As:
- Chairman of the Board, Quest Diagnostics Inc.

FREEMAN, Phil
5700 Sixth Ave.
Altoona, PA 16602
Tel: (814) 946 - 3611
Fax:(814) 946 - 4375
TF: (800) 487 - 5444

Serves As:
- V. President, Human Resources, Sheetz, Inc.

FREER, Paula D.
700 13th St., NW
Suite 950
Washington, DC 20005
pdfreer@marathonoil.com
Tel: (202) 654 - 4499
Fax:(202) 654 - 4493

Registered Federal Lobbyist.
Serves As:
- Director, Federal Government Affairs, Marathon Oil Corp.

FREIBERT, David
One Quality St.
Lexington, KY 40507
Tel: (859) 367 - 1271
Fax:(859) 367 - 1197

Serves As:
- Director, External Affairs, Kentucky Utilities Company

FREITES, Kristen
4201 Wilson Blvd.
Suite 110-492
Arlington, VA 22203
Tel: (703) 243 - 0973
Fax:(703) 243 - 5790

Registered Federal Lobbyist.
Serves As:
- Senior Government Affairs Specialist, American Medical Security Group, Inc.

FRENCH, Barry
P.O. Box 66100
Chicago, IL 60666
Tel: (847) 700 - 4000
Fax:(847) 700 - 4899

Serves As:
- V. President, Corporate Communications, United Airlines

FRENCH, David D.
2901 Via Fortuna
Austin, TX 78746
Tel: (512) 851 - 4000
TF: (800) 888 - 5016

Serves As:
- President and Chief Exec. Officer, Cirrus Logic, Inc.

FRENCH, Michelle
100 Park Ave., Suite 2705
New York, NY 10017
m.french@ericsson.com

Serves As:
- Director, Media and Industry Analyst Relations, Ericsson Inc.

FRENKEL, Orit
1299 Pennsylvania Ave. NW
11th Floor West
Washington, DC 20004-2407
orit.frenkel@corporate.ge.com
Tel: (202) 637 - 4000
Fax:(202) 637 - 4006

Registered Federal Lobbyist.
Serves As:
- Senior Manager, International Law and Policy, General Electric Co.

FRESCOLN, Leonard D.
4600 Arrowhead Dr.
Ann Arbor, MI 48105
Tel: (734) 622 - 6000
Fax:(734) 622 - 6131

Serves As:
- Chief Executive Officer, Flint Ink Corp.

FRESE, Elizabeth Norris
1501 M St. NW
Suite 1100
Washington, DC 20005
Tel: (202) 785 - 7300
Fax:(202) 785 - 6360

Serves As:
- Office Manager, Government Affairs, Viacom Inc./CBS Corp.

FRESHWATER, Amy H.
4201 Marsh Ln.
Carrolton, TX 75007
afreshwater@crww.com
Tel: (972) 662 - 5549
Fax:(972) 307 - 2811

Serves As:
- Senior Director, Public Relations, (Friday's Hospitality Worldwide), Carlson Companies

FRETZ, Thelma
155 S. Limerick Rd.
Limerick, PA 19468
foundation@teleflex.com
Tel: (610) 948 - 5100
Fax:(610) 948 - 2859

Serves As:
- Contact, Teleflex Foundation, Teleflex Inc.

FREUDMANN, Axel I.
70 Pine St.
New York, NY 10270
Tel: (212) 770 - 7000
Fax:(212) 742 - 2115

Serves As:
- Senior V. President, Human Resources, American Internat'l Group, Inc.

FREY, Erin
The ARAMARK Tower
1101 Market St.
Philadelphia, PA 19107
Tel: (215) 238 - 3000
Fax:(215) 238 - 3333
TF: (800) 999 - 8989

Serves As:
- PAC Contact, ARAMARK

FRIAR, Rick
200 Carillon Pkwy.
St. Petersburg, FL 33716
rick.friar@catalinamarketing.com
Tel: (727) 579 - 5218
Fax:(727) 556 - 2700

Serves As:
- Exec. V. President and Chief Finacial Officer, Catalina Marketing Corp.

FRIBOURG, Paul J.
277 Park Ave.
New York, NY 10172
paul.fribourg@conti.com
Tel: (212) 207 - 5100
Fax:(212) 207 - 5181

Serves As:
- Chairman and Chief Exec. Officer, ContiGroup Companies, Inc.

FRICK, Joseph A.
1901 Market St.
38th Floor
Philadelphia, PA 19103-1480
Tel: (215) 636 - 9559
Fax:(215) 241 - 0403
TF: (800) 555 - 1514

Serves As:
- Chief Exec. Officer, Independence Blue Cross (Pennsylvania)

FRICKE, Howard R.
One Security Benefit Pl.
Topeka, KS 66636-0001
Tel: (785) 438 - 3000
TF: (800) 888 - 2461

Serves As:
- Chairman of the Board, Security Benefit Life Insurance Co.

FRIED, Joanne
2727 N. Central Ave.
P.O. Box 21502
Phoenix, AZ 85004
Tel: (602) 263 - 6194
Fax:(602) 263 - 6772

Serves As:
- Director, Media and Public Relations, (U-Haul Internat'l, Inc.), AMERCO

FRIEDELL, Andrew
601 Pennsylvania Ave. NW
Suite 700
Washington, DC 20004
Tel: (202) 639 - 1881

Registered Federal Lobbyist.
Serves As:
- Manager, Policy and Analysis, Medco Health Solutions, Inc.

FRIEDMAN, Alan J.
404 Wyman St.
Suite 500
Waltham, MA 02451
alan.friedman@novell.com
Tel: (781) 464 - 8000
Fax:(781) 464 - 8100

Serves As:
- Senior V. President, People, Novell, Inc.

FRIEDMANN, Peter
1201 Pennsylvania Ave. NW
Suite 315
Washington, DC 20004
Tel: (202) 783 - 3333
Fax:(202) 783 - 4422

Serves As:
- Director, International Trade Policy and Government Affairs, Reebok Internat'l Ltd.

FRIEL, Kristin
200 Park Ave.
New York, NY 10166
Tel: (212) 412 - 7521

Serves As:
- Corporate Communications Contact, Barclays Capital

FRIERSON, Daniel K.
P.O. Box 25107
Chattanooga, TN 37422-5107
Tel: (423) 510 - 7000
Fax:(423) 510 - 7015
TF: (866) 606 - 7475

Serves As:
- Chairman and Chief Exec. Officer, The Dixie Group, Inc.

FRIOU, Phillip J. "Jack
1932 Wynnton Rd.
Columbus, GA 31999
Tel: (706) 323 - 3431
Fax:(706) 660 - 7333
TF: (800) 992 - 3522

Serves As:
- Senior V. President, Governmental Relations, AFLAC Incorporated

FRISBIE, Bruce
1295 State St.
Springfield, MA 01111-0001
Tel: (413) 744 - 2422
Fax:(413) 744 - 6005
TF: (800) 767 - 1000

Serves As:
- Treasurer, Massachusetts Mutual Life Insurance Co. Political Action Committee, MassMutual Financial Group

FRISCHMANN, Donald E.
20330 Stevens Creek Blvd.
Cupertino, CA 95014-2132
Tel: (408) 517 - 7983
Fax:(408) 517 - 7801

Serves As:
- Senior V. President, Communications and Brand Management, Symantec Corp.

Responsibilities include investor relations.

FRISS, Karen
Lilly Corporate Center
Indianapolis, IN 46285
Tel: (317) 276 - 2000
Fax:(317) 277 - 6579

Serves As:
- Director, Public Policy Planning and Development, Eli Lilly and Company

FRISSORA, Mark P.
500 N. Field Dr.
Lake Forest, IL 60045
mark.frissora@tenneco-automotive.com
Tel: (847) 482 - 5080
Fax:(847) 482 - 5049

Serves As:
- Chairman and Chief Exec. Officer, Tenneco Automotive

FRITTER, Lynne E.
One Tower Sq.
Hartford, CT 06183
Tel: (860) 277 - 5476
Fax:(860) 277 - 2808

Serves As:
- Counsel, Personal Lines, Government Relations, St. Paul Travelers Cos., Inc.

FRITTS, Robert
One Corporate Way
Lansing, MI 48951
Tel: (517) 381 - 5500
Fax:(517) 706 - 5517
TF: (800) 644 - 4565

Serves As:
- PAC Treasurer, Jackson Nat'l Life Insurance Co.

FRITZ, Ron
P.O. Box 368
Indianapolis, IN 46206-0368
Tel: (317) 285 - 1877
Fax:(317) 285 - 1979

Serves As:
- PAC Contact, American United Life Insurance Co.

FRIZZELL, Roger
P.O. Box 619616
Dallas-Fort Worth Airport, TX 75261
Tel: (817) 963 - 1234
Fax:(817) 967 - 2523

Serves As:
- V. President, Corporate Communications, (American Airlines, Inc.), AMR Corp.

FROCLICH, Sara
1020 19th St., NW
Suite 550
Washington, DC 20036
Tel: (202) 296 - 3280
Fax:(202) 296 - 3411

Registered Federal Lobbyist.
Serves As:
- V. President, Government Relations, Genzyme Corp.

FROEHLICH, Melissa
One Marriott Dr.
Washington, DC 20058
Tel: (301) 380 - 3000
Fax:(301) 380 - 8957

Serves As:
- Director, Legislative Affairs, Marriott Internat'l, Inc.

FROH, Richard B.
1333 H St. NW
Suite 300 West
Washington, DC 20005
Tel: (202) 296 - 1314
Fax:(202) 296 - 4067

Registered Federal Lobbyist.
Serves As:
- V. President, Government Relations, Kaiser Permanente

FROMEN, Peter
P.O. Box 10395
Palo Alto, CA 94303-0395
Tel: (650) 752 - 5300
Fax:(650) 752 - 5633

Serves As:
- Investor Relations Associate, Agilent Technologies, Inc.

FROMM, Ronald A.
P.O. Box 29
St. Louis, MO 63166-0029
rfromm@brownshoe.com
Tel: (314) 854 - 4101
Fax:(314) 854 - 4274

Serves As:
- Chairman and Chief Exec. Officer, Brown Shoe Co., Inc.

FRONSKE, Joan
1 Sybase Dr.
Dublin, CA 94568
joan.fronske@sybase.com
Tel: (925) 236 - 4893

Serves As:
- Community Relations and International Public Relations Liaison, Sybase, Inc.

FROST, Richard W.
414 Union St.
Suite 2000
Nashville, TN 37219

Serves As:
- Chief Exec. Officer, Louisiana-Pacific Corporation

FRY, Amy
900 Ridgebury Rd.
P.O. Box 368
Ridgefield, CT 06877
Tel: (203) 798 - 9988
Fax:(203) 791 - 6234

Serves As:
- Corporate Director, Communications and Public Relations, Boehringer Ingelheim Corp.

FRY, Amy M.
2000 Hopmeadow
Simsbury, CT 06079
Tel: (860) 843 - 8820
Fax:(860) 843 - 3390

Serves As:
- V. President, Corporate Relations/Life, The Hartford Financial Services Group Inc.

FU, Cary T.
3000 Technology Dr.
Angleton, TX 77515
Tel: (979) 849 - 6550
Fax:(979) 848 - 5270

Serves As:
- President and Chief Exec. Officer, Benchmark Electronics

FUCHS, Daniel
1301 Pennsylvania
Suite 900
Denver, CO 80203
Tel: (303) 831 - 6268
Fax:(303) 831 - 9214

Serves As:
- Regional Manager, State Government Relations/Rocky Mountain, UST Inc.

FUENTES, Joseph J.
One StorageTek Dr.
Louisville, CO 80028-4377
joe_fuentes@storagetek.com
Tel: (303) 661 - 2523

Serves As:
- Press Contact, Community Issues, StorageTek

FUENTES, Patricia
8200 Jones Branch Dr.
McLean, VA 22102
Tel: (703) 903 - 2000
Fax:(703) 903 - 2447
TF: (800) 373 - 3343

Serves As:
- Manager, Public Relations, Freddie Mac

FUGATE, Karen
3150 Sabre Dr.
Southlake, TX 76092
karen.fugate@sabre-holdings.com
Tel: (682) 605 - 2343
Fax:(682) 264 - 8343

Serves As:
- V. President, Investor Relations, Sabre Holdings Corp.

FUJII, Stacey
161 St. Anthony St.
Suite 815
St. Paul, MN 55103
Tel: (651) 222 - 4314
Fax:(651) 222 - 4372

Serves As:
- Legislative Services - Minnesota/Michigan, Aquila, Inc.

FUJIMOTO, Toshihiko
One Sharp Plaza
Mahwah, NJ 07430-2135
Tel: (201) 529 - 8200
Fax:(201) 529 - 8819

Serves As:
- Chairman and Chief Exec. Officer, Sharp Electronics Corp.

FULD, Jr., Richard S.
745 Seventh Ave.
New York, NY 10019
Tel: (212) 526 - 7000

Serves As:
- Chairman and Chief Exec. Officer, Lehman Brothers

FULGENZI, Marianne
World Headquarters
One Elmcroft Rd.
MSC 63-15
Stamford, CT 06926-0700
marianne.fulgenzi@pb.com
Tel: (203) 351 - 6974
Fax:(203) 351 - 6303

Serves As:
- Director, External Affairs, Pitney Bowes Inc.

FULLER, Joseph H.
8923 Eighth Ave., N.E.
Seattle, WA 98115
joe.fuller@astrazeneca.com
Tel: (206) 526 - 5195
Fax:(206) 526 - 5196
TF: (800) 822 - 9209
Ext: 60024

Serves As:
- Director, State Government Affairs, AstraZeneca Pharmaceuticals

FULLER, Julia P.
1341 W. Mockingbird Ln.
Dallas, TX 75247
jfuller@txi.com
Tel: (972) 647 - 6700
Fax:(972) 647 - 3878

Serves As:
- Assistant Treasurer, Texas Industries Inc. Political Action Committee, Texas Industries, Inc.

FULLER, Neal
SAFECO Plaza
Seattle, WA 98185
Tel: (206) 545 - 5537

Serves As:
- Contact, Investor Relations and SAFECO-PAC, SAFECO Corp.

FULLER, S. Marce
1155 Perimeter Center West
Atlanta, GA 30338
marce.fuller@mirant.com
Tel: (678) 579 - 5000
Fax:(678) 579 - 5001

Serves As:
- President and Chief Exec. Officer, Mirant Corp.

FULLER, Stephen A.
One Massachusetts Ave. NW
Suite 350
Washington, DC 20001
sfuller@chubb.com
Tel: (202) 408 - 8123
Fax:(202) 296 - 7683

Serves As:
- V. President, International External Affairs, The Chubb Corp.

FULLER DICKSESKI, Ms. Jerri
4101 Washington Ave.
Newport News, VA 23607-2770
Tel: (757) 380 - 2341
Fax:(757) 380 - 3867

Serves As:
- Director, Communications, Northrop Grumman Newport News

FULLERTON, Rhonda
P.O. Box 7706
Wichita, KS 67277-7706
Tel: (316) 517 - 1602
Fax:(316) 517 - 7812

Serves As:
- Manager, Community and Corporate Affairs, Cessna Aircraft Co.

FULP, Carol
P.O. Box 111
T-58
Boston, MA 02117
Tel: (617) 572 - 0451
Fax:(617) 572 - 6290

Serves As:
- V. President, Community Relations, John Hancock Financial Services

FULTON, B. Keith
1300 I St. NW
Suite 400 West
Washington, DC 20005
Tel: (202) 515 - 2400

Serves As:
- V. President, Strategic Alliances, Verizon Communications Inc.

FULTON, Kathryn
1299 Pennsylvania Ave. NW
11th Floor West
Washington, DC 20004-2407
kathryn.fulton@corporate.ge.com
Tel: (202) 637 - 4222
Fax:(202) 637 - 4066

Registered Federal Lobbyist.
Serves As:
- Manager, Government Relations, General Electric Co.

FULTON, Paul
3525 Fairystone Park Hwy.
Bassett, VA 24055
Tel: (276) 629 - 6000
Fax:(276) 629 - 6333

Serves As:
- Chairman of the Board, Bassett Furniture Industries, Inc.

FUREY, Tracy
P.O. Box 4000
Princeton, NJ 08543
tracy.furey@bms.com
Tel: (609) 252 - 3208
Fax:(609) 252 - 7830

Serves As:
- V. President, Corporate Affairs, Bristol-Myers Squibb Co.

FURTKEVIC, William
3111 W. Allegheny Ave.
Philadelphia, PA 19132
bill_furtkevic@pepboys.com
Tel: (215) 430 - 9676
Fax:(215) 430 - 3660

Serves As:
- Director, Marketing Communications, The Pep Boys-Manny, Moe & Jack

FUSCO, Joseph A.
725 Fifth Ave.
18th Floor
New York, NY 10022
Tel: (212) 891 - 1500
Fax:(212) 935 - 0141

Serves As:
- Exec. V. President, Government Relations and Regulatory Affairs, Trump Hotels and Casino Resorts, Inc.

FUSON, Jr., Harold W.
P.O. Box 1530
La Jolla, CA 92038-1530
Tel: (858) 454 - 0411

Serves As:
- V. President and Chief Legal Officer, The Copley Press, Inc.

FYNTRILAKIS, Nicholas
140 Garden St.
Hartford, CT 06154
Tel: (860) 987 - 3283
Fax:(860) 987 - 6532

Serves As:
- Communications Consultant, MassMutual Financial Group

GAAL, Elizabeth K.
500 Post Rd. East
Suite 320
Westport, CT 06880
Tel: (203) 222 - 5942
Fax:(203) 222 - 0130

Serves As:
- Investor Relations Associate, Terex Corp.

GABALY, Mike
6801 Rockledge Dr.
Bethesda, MD 20817-1877
Tel: (301) 897 - 6455
Fax:(301) 897 - 6919

Serves As:
- Director, Investor Relations, Lockheed Martin Corp.

GABBIANELLI, Rose
One Mellon Center
500 Grant St.
Pittsburgh, PA 15258-0001
gabbianelli.r@mellon.com
Tel: (412) 234 - 4003
Fax:(412) 236 - 1662

Serves As:
- Senior V. President, Corporate Affairs, Mellon Financial Corp.

GABEL, DeAnne
P.O. Box 4607
Houston, TX 77210-4607
Tel: (713) 324 - 5152
Fax:(713) 324 - 2637

Serves As:
- Investor Relations Contact, Continental Airlines

GABERT, Charla
600 Riverpark Dr.
N. Reading, MA 01864
Tel: (978) 370 - 6225

Serves As:
• Manager, Worldwide Marketing and Communications, Teradyne, Inc.

GABLE, Deborah N.
4411 E. Jones Bridge Rd.
Norcross, GA 30092-1615
Tel: (678) 375 - 3000
Fax:(678) 375 - 1477

Serves As:
• Senior V. President, Human Resources, CheckFree Corp.

GABLE, Greg
101 Montgomery St.
San Francisco, CA 94104
greg.gable@schwab.com
Tel: (415) 636 - 5454
Fax:(415) 636 - 5970
TF: (800) 435 - 4000

Serves As:
• Senior V. President, Corporate Public Relations, The Charles Schwab Corp.

GABRIELE, Eileen
1221 Ave. of the Americas
47th Floor
New York, NY 10020-1095
eileen_gabriele@mcgraw-hill.com
Tel: (212) 512 - 3852
Fax:(212) 512 - 3611

Serves As:
• V. President, Corporate Affairs, The McGraw-Hill Companies, Inc.

GADBAW, R. Michael
1299 Pennsylvania Ave. NW
11th Floor West
Washington, DC 20004-2407
michael.gadbaw@corporate.ge.com
Tel: (202) 637 - 4000
Fax:(202) 637 - 4006

Registered Federal Lobbyist.
Serves As:
• V. President and Senior Counsel, International Law and Policy, General Electric Co.

GADEK, Stanley
9955 Airtran Blvd.
Orlando, FL 32827-5330
Tel: (407) 251 - 5600
Fax:(407) 251 - 5727

Serves As:
• Senior V. President, Finance; Chief Financial Officer; and PAC Treasurer, AirTran Airways

GADOSIK, Barbara L.
101 Prospect Ave. NW
Cleveland, OH 44115
Tel: (216) 566 - 2511
Fax:(216) 566 - 3312

Serves As:
• Director, Corporate Contributions, Sherwin-Williams Co.

GADSBY, Margaret
Two T.W. Alexander Dr.
P.O. Box 12
Research Triangle Park, NC 27009
Tel: (919) 549 - 2000

Serves As:
• Director, Public and Government Affairs, Communications, and Stewardship, Bayer CropScience

GAFFEN, Eileen
P.O. Box 419580
Kansas City, MO 64141-6580
Tel: (816) 274 - 4673
Fax:(816) 274 - 5061

Serves As:
• Manager, Public Relations, Hallmark Cards, Inc.

GAFFORD, Ronald J.
P.O. Box 1590
Dallas, TX 75221-1590
Tel: (214) 443 - 5500

Serves As:
• President and Chief Exec. Officer, Austin Industries

GAGLIARDI, Bill
P.O. Box 994
Midland, MI 48686-0994
bill.gagliardi@dowcorning.com
Tel: (989) 496 - 6393
Fax:(989) 496 - 8240

Serves As:
• Manager, Environmental Health and Safety Communications, Dow Corning Corp.

GAHLON, Dan E.
3M Center
Bldg. 225-15-15
St. Paul, MN 55144-1000
Tel: (651) 733 - 1880
Fax:(651) 737 - 2901

Serves As:
• V. President, Public Relations and Corporate Communications, 3M Company

GAIDAMAK, Donna
1430 Waukegan Rd.
McGaw Park, IL 60085
Tel: (847) 578 - 4434
Fax:(847) 578 - 4438

Serves As:
• Manager, Media Relations, (Cardinal Health Medical Products and Services), Cardinal Health Inc.

GAINER, Bill
225 W. Randolph St.
27 B
Chicago, IL 60606
Tel: (312) 727 - 7569
Fax:(312) 727 - 3722
TF: (800) 327 - 9346

Serves As:
• Director, Government Relations, SBC Illinois

GAINES, Phil J.
10990 Roe Ave.
Overland Park, KS 66211
phil.gaines@yellowroadway.com
Tel: (913) 696 - 6100
Fax:(913) 696 - 6116

Serves As:
• Senior V. President, Investor Relations, Government Relations and Corporate Development, Yellow Roadway Corporation

GAISFORD, Lisa A.
Commonwealth Towers
1300 Wilson Blvd., Suite 200
Arlington, VA 22209-2307
Tel: (703) 516 - 8220
Fax:(703) 516 - 8295

Registered Federal Lobbyist.
Serves As:
• Representative, Rockwell Collins, Inc

GAITHER, John S.
P.O. Box 13582
Research Triangle Park, NC 27709
Tel: (919) 990 - 7500
Fax:(919) 990 - 7711
TF: (800) 448 - 3482

Serves As:
• President and Chief Exec. Officer, Reichhold, Inc.

GAITLIN, John
Prudential Tower Bldg.
Boston, MA 02199-8004
Tel: (617) 421 - 7000
Fax:(617) 421 - 7123

Serves As:
• PAC Treasurer, The Gillette Company

GALA, Ed
100 S. Clinton Ave.
M/S XRX2-004
Rochester, NY 14644
ed.gala@xerox.com
Tel: (585) 423 - 5230
Fax:(585) 423 - 4272

Serves As:
• V. President, Products/Solutions/Services Public Relations, Xerox Corp.

GALANIS, Gary
Six Landmark Sq.
Stamford, CT 06901
Tel: (203) 359 - 7100

Serves As:
• Director, Media Relations and External Affairs, Diageo North America

GALBRAITH, Russ
P.O. Box 8204
Little Rock, AR 72221-8204
Tel: (501) 227 - 0553

Serves As:
• Legislative Representative, Farmers Group, Inc.

GALE, Brent
666 Grand Ave.
P.O. Box 657
Des Moines, IA 50303-0657
Tel: (515) 242 - 4002
Fax:(515) 242 - 4080
TF: (888) 427 - 5632

Serves As:
• V. President, Legislation and Regulation Affairs, MidAmerican Energy Holdings Co.

GALEF, Andrew A.
10900 Wilshire Blvd.
Suite 850
Los Angeles, CA 90024
agalef@magnetek.com
Tel: (310) 208 - 1980
Fax:(310) 208 - 6133

Serves As:
• Chairman of the Board, Magnetek, Inc.

GALINDO, Lucia
2244 Walnut Grove Ave.
Rosemead, CA 91770
galindle@sce.com
Tel: (626) 302 - 2313
Fax:(626) 302 - 8114

Serves As:
• Manager, Community Involvement, Southern California Edison, an Edison Internat'l Co.

GALLAGHER, Charles E.
P.O. Box 119
Maumee, OH 43537
Tel: (419) 893 - 5050
Fax:(419) 891 - 6655

Serves As:
• V. President, Human Resources, The Andersons, Inc.

GALLAGHER, Donna
101 Wood Ave.
Iselin, NJ 08830
Tel: (732) 205 - 5000
Fax:(732) 632 - 9253
TF: (800) 631 - 9505

Serves As:
• Corporate Communications Specialist, Engelhard Corp.

GALLAGHER, Jr., J. Patrick
The Gallagher Center
Two Pierce Pl.
Itasca, IL 60143-3141
Tel: (630) 773 - 3800
Fax:(630) 285 - 4000

Serves As:
- President and Chief Exec. Officer, Arthur J. Gallagher & Co.

Responsibilities include corporate philanthropy.

GALLAGHER, Joan M.
211 Commerce St.
Suite 800
Nashville, TN 37201
Tel: (615) 743 - 6600

Serves As:
- Senior V. President, Corporate Communications, Caremark Rx, Inc.

GALLAGHER, Robert C.
1200 Hansen Rd.
Green Bay, WI 54304
Tel: (920) 491 - 7000
Fax:(920) 491 - 7090
TF: (800) 236 - 2722

Serves As:
- Chairman of the Board, Associated Banc-Corp.

GALLAGHER, Robert E.
The Gallagher Center
Two Pierce Pl.
Itasca, IL 60143-3141
Tel: (630) 773 - 3800
Fax:(630) 285 - 4000

Serves As:
- Chairman of the Board, Arthur J. Gallagher & Co.

GALLAGHER, Shawn
1399 New York Ave. NW
Suite 900
Washington, DC 20005
Tel: (202) 585 - 5800
Fax:(202) 585 - 5820

Registered Federal Lobbyist.
Serves As:
- Representative, American Internat'l Group, Inc.

GALLAGHER, Susan
P.O. Box 66149
M/S 100
St. Louis, MO 63166-6149
Tel: (314) 554 - 2175
Fax:(314) 554 - 2888
TF: (800) 552 - 7583

Serves As:
- Director, Corporate Communications, Ameren Corp.

GALLAGHER, Thomas C.
2999 Circle 75 Pkwy.
Atlanta, GA 30339
tom_gallagher@genpt.com
Tel: (770) 953 - 1700
Fax:(770) 956 - 2211

Serves As:
- Chief Exec. Officer, Genuine Parts Co.

GALLAGHER, Tim J.
Carnival Pl.
3655 N.W. 87th Ave.
Miami, FL 33178-2428
tgallagher@carnival.com
Tel: (305) 599 - 2600
Ext: 16000
Fax:(305) 406 - 8630

Serves As:
- V. President, Public Relations, (Carnival Cruise Lines), Carnival Corp.

GALLAHER, Candy M.
1800 Center St.
Camp Hill, PA 17089
Tel: (717) 302 - 3982
Fax:(717) 302 - 3980

Serves As:
- Director, Regulatory Affairs, Highmark Inc.

GALLAND, Brad
414 Union St.
Suite 2000
Nashville, TN 37219
TF: (800) 547 - 6331

Serves As:
- PAC Treasurer, Louisiana-Pacific Corporation

GALLANT, Ann T.
10455 Mill Run Circle
Owings Mills, MD 21117
Tel: (410) 998 - 6001
Fax:(410) 998 - 5351

Serves As:
- V. President, Corporate Communications, CareFirst BlueCross and BlueShield

GALLANT, Michael
P.O. Box 9103
Hopkinton, MA 01748
gallant_michael@emc.com
Tel: (508) 435 - 1000
Ext: 76357
Fax:(508) 435 - 7954
TF: (800) 424 - 3622

Serves As:
- Director, Public Relations, EMC Corp.

GALLEGO, Delores
P.O. Box 20706
Dept. 976
Atlanta, GA 30320-6001
Tel: (404) 715 - 2458
Fax:(404) 715 - 4779

Serves As:
- General Manager, Public Affairs; PAC Treasurer, Delta Air Lines, Inc.

GALLEGOS, Lisa
One Franklin Pkwy.
San Mateo, CA 94403-1906
lgallegos@frk.com
Tel: (650) 312 - 3395
Fax:(650) 574 - 5012
TF: (800) 342 - 5236

Serves As:
- Manager, Corporate Communications, Franklin Templeton Investments

GALLEGOS, Merlinda
3600 Las Vegas Blvd. S.
Las Vegas, NV 89109
Tel: (702) 650 - 7415
Fax:(702) 650 - 7401

Serves As:
- Contact, The MGM MIRAGE Voice Foundation, MGM MIRAGE

GALLENTINE, Mike
1375 Peachtree St.
Atlanta, GA 30309
Tel: (404) 748 - 7153
Fax:(404) 815 - 8805

Serves As:
- V. President, Investor Relations, Earthlink, Inc.

GALLI, Jr., Joseph
Ten B Glenlake Pkwy.
Suite 600
Alpharetta, GA 30328
Tel: (770) 407 - 3805

Serves As:
- Chief Exec. Officer, Newell Rubbermaid Inc.

GALLIGAN, William H.
427 W. 12th St.
Kansas City, MO 64105
william.h.galligan@kcsr.com
Tel: (816) 983 - 1551
Fax:(816) 983 - 1640
TF: (800) 282 - 8700

Serves As:
- Assistant V. President, Investor Relations, Kansas City Southern

GALLIVAN, Karen
P.O. Box 1441
Minneapolis, MN 55440-1441
Tel: (612) 623 - 6000
Fax:(612) 623 - 6640
TF: (800) 328 - 0211

Serves As:
- V. President, Human Resources, Graco Inc.

GALLO, Ernest
P.O. Box 1130
Modesto, CA 95353
Tel: (209) 341 - 3111
Fax:(209) 341 - 8993

Serves As:
- Chairman of the Board, Ernest and Julio Gallo Winery

GALLO, Joseph E.
P.O. Box 1130
Modesto, CA 95353
Tel: (209) 341 - 3111
Fax:(209) 341 - 3569

Serves As:
- Chief Exec. Officer, Ernest and Julio Gallo Winery

GALLOWAY, David A.
111 W. Monroe St.
Chicago, IL 60603-4095
Tel: (312) 461 - 2121
Fax:(312) 461 - 6640

Serves As:
- Chairman of the Board, Harris Bank

GALLUP, Patricia
730 Milford Rd.
Route 101A
Merrimack, NH 03054-4631
pgallup@pcconnection.com
Tel: (603) 683 - 2000
Fax:(603) 683 - 2041

Serves As:
- Chairman, President and Chief Exec. Officer, PC Connection, Inc.

GALOW, Geoffrey G.
1900 W. Loop South
Suite 1500
Houston, TX 77027
Tel: (713) 877 - 5327
Fax:(713) 877 - 5333
TF: (800) 231 - 8176

Serves As:
- V. President, Investor Relations, Quanex Corp.

GALPIN, Jr., Stephen K.
2000 Galloping Hill Rd.
Kenilworth, NJ 07033
Tel: (908) 298 - 7415
Fax:(908) 298 - 7653

Serves As:
- Staff V. President, Corporate Communications, Schering-Plough Corporation

GALVIN, Tom
1666 K St., NW
Suite 410
Washington, DC 20006
Tel: (202) 973 - 6610
Fax:(202) 466 - 9103

Serves As:
- V. President, Government Relations, VeriSign, Inc.

GAMEZ, Cynthia
P.O. Box 982
El Paso, TX 79960
cgamez1@epelectric.com
Tel: (915) 543 - 2213
Fax:(915) 543 - 2299
TF: (800) 351 - 1621

Serves As:
• Manager, Investor Relations, El Paso Electric Co.

GAMMON, Jeanne
P.O. Box 68900
Seattle, WA 98168-0947
jeanne.gammon@alaskaair.com
Tel: (206) 433 - 3200

Serves As:
• Administrator, Corporate Affairs, (Alaska Airlines, Inc.), Alaska Air Group, Inc.

GAMS, Ed
1303 E. Algonquin Rd.
Schaumburg, IL 60196
Tel: (847) 576 - 6873
Fax:(847) 576 - 5611
TF: (800) 262 - 8509

Serves As:
• Senior V. President and Director, Investor Relations, Motorola, Inc.

GAMSIN, Sharon
2000 Purchase St.
Purchase, NY 10577-2509
sgamsin@mastercard.com
Tel: (914) 249 - 5622
Fax:(914) 249 - 4207

Serves As:
• V. President, Global Communications, MasterCard Internat'l

GANDARA, Marilda L.
151 Farmington Ave.
Hartford, CT 06156
Tel: (860) 273 - 4770
Fax:(860) 273 - 4764

Serves As:
• President, Aetna Foundation, Aetna Inc.

GANDOLFO, Thomas J.
One State St. Plaza
New York, NY 10004
tgandolfo@ambac.com
Tel: (212) 208 - 3349
Fax:(212) 509 - 9190
TF: (800) 221 - 1854

Serves As:
• Senior V. President and Chief Financial Officer, Ambac Financial Group, Inc.
Responsibilities include investor relations.

GANGEMI, Hilary A.
1401 I St. NW
Suite 520
Washington, DC 20005
Tel: (202) 466 - 3561
Fax:(202) 466 - 3583

Serves As:
• Coordinator, Legislative and Political Affairs, HSBC North America Holdings Inc.

GANN, Peggy
1415 Roselle Rd.
Palatine, IL 60067
Tel: (847) 397 - 2600
Fax:(847) 925 - 7500

Serves As:
• V. President, Human Resources and Administration, Square D/Schneider Electric

GANN, Tom
1776 I St. NW
Suite 900
Washington, DC 20006
tgann@siebel.com
Tel: (703) 796 - 9429
Fax:(703) 796 - 7227

Serves As:
• Vice President and General Manager, Public Sector and Homeland Security, Siebel Systems, Inc.
Responsibilities include government relations.

GANNON, Laurie
17901 Von Karman Ave.
Irvine, CA 92614
Tel: (949) 863 - 4500

Serves As:
• Manager, Public Relations, (Taco Bell Corp.), YUM! Brands, Inc.

GANZI, Victor F.
959 Eighth Ave.
New York, NY 10019
Tel: (212) 649 - 2103
Fax:(212) 246 - 3630

Serves As:
• President and Chief Exec. Officer, The Hearst Corp.

GARAVAGLIA, Burt
4680 Wilshire Blvd.
Los Angeles, CA 90010
Tel: (323) 930 - 4016
Fax:(323) 964 - 8095

Serves As:
• Director, Government Affairs, Farmers Group, Inc.

GARAVAGLIA, James M.
P.O. Box 75000
mc 3352
Detroit, MI 48275
Tel: (313) 222 - 3688
Fax:(313) 222 - 8720
TF: (800) 521 - 1190

Serves As:
• Senior V. President, Public Affairs, Comerica Incorporated

GARAY, Fernando
P.O. Box 4689
Houston, TX 77210
Tel: (832) 486 - 1489
Fax:(832) 486 - 1843

Serves As:
• Manager, Public Affairs, CITGO Petroleum Corporation
Responsibilities include investor relations.

GARBERTH, Deisha
1375 Peachtree St.
Atlanta, GA 30309
Tel: (404) 815 - 0770
Fax:(404) 815 - 8805

Serves As:
• Media Relations Contact, Earthlink, Inc.

GARCIA, Elisa D.
P.O. Box 997
Ann Arbor, MI 48106-0997
garciae@dominos.com
Tel: (734) 930 - 3678
Fax:(734) 930 - 4346

Serves As:
• Exec. V. President and General Counsel, Domino's Pizza, LLC
Responsibilties include legal and government affairs.

GARCIA, Lillian D.
P.O. Box 2353
Orlando, FL 32802-2353
lilliangarcia@tupperware.com
Tel: (407) 826 - 8224
Fax:(407) 826 - 4525
TF: (800) 366 - 3800

Serves As:
• Senior V. President, Human Resources-Worldwide, Tupperware Corp.

GARD, Jeff
631 S. Richland Ave.
York, PA 17403
jeff.gard@york.com
Tel: (717) 771 - 7890
Fax:(717) 771 - 7381

Serves As:
• Corporate V. President, Human Resources, York Internat'l Corp.

GARDEPE, William M.
2941 Fairview Park Dr.
Falls Church, VA 22042-4513
Tel: (703) 876 - 3494
Fax:(703) 876 - 3600

Serves As:
• Staff V. President, Legislative Affairs, General Dynamics Corporation

GARDINER, Erin
One Baxter Pkwy.
Deerfield, IL 60015-4633
erin_gardiner@baxter.com
Tel: (847) 948 - 4210
Fax:(847) 948 - 2016

Serves As:
• Manager, External Communications, Baxter Internat'l Inc.

GARDNER, Angela
7000 Cardinal Pl.
Dublin, OH 43017
Tel: (614) 757 - 5000
Fax:(614) 757 - 6000
TF: (800) 234 - 8701

Serves As:
• Manager, Media Relations, Cardinal Health Inc.

GARDNER, Colette
56 Top Gallant Rd.
Stamford, CT 06904
colette.gardner@gartner.com
Tel: (203) 316 - 6994
Fax:(203) 316 - 6488

Serves As:
• Senior V. President, Human Resources, Gartner, Inc.

GARDNER, Gary E.
1101 Third St. South
Minneapolis, MN 55415
ggardner@valspar.com
Tel: (612) 375 - 7737
Fax:(612) 375 - 7723

Serves As:
• V. President, Human Resources and Public Relations, Valspar Corp.

GARDNER, Ph.D., James R.
235 E. 42nd St.
New York, NY 10017-5755
Tel: (212) 573 - 2668
Fax:(212) 808 - 8617

Serves As:
• V. President, Investor Relations, Pfizer Inc.

GARDNER, Thomas R.
1301 Pennsylvania Ave. NW
Suite 1030
Washington, DC 20004
Tel: (202) 824 - 0404
Fax:(202) 347 - 0132

Registered Federal Lobbyist.
Serves As:
• Representative, Allegheny Energy Inc.

GAREY, Daniel T.
6035 Parkland Blvd.
Cleveland, OH 44124-4141
Tel: (216) 896 - 3000
Fax:(216) 896 - 4000
TF: (800) 272 - 7537

Serves As:
• V. President, Human Resources, Parker Hannifin Corp.

GARGARO, Jr., Eugene A.
21001 Van Born Rd.
Taylor, MI 48180
Tel: (313) 792 - 6261
Fax:(313) 792 - 6135

Serves As:
- Vice President and Secretary; Treasurer, Masco Political Action Committee, Masco Corp.

GARIBALDI, Alvin
P.O. Box 61000
New Orleans, LA 70161
Tel: (504) 576 - 4000
Fax:(504) 576 - 4001

Serves As:
- Governmental Affairs Executive, Customer Service, Entergy New Orleans

GARLAND, Janet E.
200 Park Ave.
New York, NY 10166
Tel: (212) 878 - 4072

Serves As:
- Program Administrator, Mitsui USA Foundation, Mitsui and Co. (U.S.A.), Inc.

GARLAND, Patricia
2301 Patriot Blvd.
Glenview, IL 60025-8020
Tel: (224) 521 - 8000

Serves As:
- Director, Human Resources, Anixter Internat'l, Inc.

GARNICK, Ph.D., Robert
One DNA Way
San Francisco, CA 94080-4990
rgarnick@gene.com
Tel: (650) 225 - 1000
Fax:(650) 225 - 6000

Serves As:
- Senior V. President, Regulatory, Quality and Compliance, Genentech, Inc.

GARNIER, Jean-Pierre
P.O. Box 13398
Research Triangle Park, NC 27709
Tel: (919) 483 - 2100
Fax:(919) 315 - 6049

Serves As:
- Chief Exec. Officer, GlaxoSmithKline Research and Development

GAROFALO, Donald L.
100 Fourth Ave. North
Bayport, MN 55003-1096
Tel: (651) 264 - 5150

Serves As:
- Chairman of the Board, Andersen Corp.

GARRARD, Jane
P.O. Box 2353
Orlando, FL 32802-2353
finrel@tupperware.com
Tel: (407) 826 - 8266
Fax:(407) 826 - 4510
TF: (800) 366 - 3800

Serves As:
- V. President, Investor and Media Relations, Tupperware Corp.

GARRARD, Julie
1789 Norwood Ave.
Itasca, IL 60143-1095
jgarrard@fellowes.com
Tel: (630) 893 - 1600
Ext: 2563
Fax:(630) 893 - 1683
TF: (800) 955 - 0959

Serves As:
- Corporate Marketing Manager, Fellowes Manufacturing Co.

Responsibilities include public relations.

GARRAUX, James D.
600 Grant St.
Pittsburgh, PA 15219-2800
Tel: (412) 433 - 1121

Serves As:
- V. President, Labor Relations, United States Steel Corporation

GARREN, Robert "Bob"
804 Green Valley Rd.
Greensboro, NC 27408
Tel: (336) 379 - 2000
Fax:(336) 349 - 6287

Serves As:
- V. President, Human Resources, Internat'l Textiles Group

GARREN, Ruth
P.O. Box 750
Collegedale, TN 37315-0750
Tel: (423) 238 - 7111
Fax:(423) 238 - 7101

Serves As:
- Manager, Corporate Communications and Public Relations, McKee Foods Corp.

GARRETT, J. Patrick
P.O. Box 5000
Pineville, LA 71361-5000
Tel: (318) 484 - 7400
Fax:(318) 484 - 7465

Serves As:
- Chairman of the Board, Cleco Corp.

GARRETT, Kenneth R.
1735 Market St.
Philadelphia, PA 19103
Tel: (215) 299 - 6021
Fax:(215) 299 - 6568

Serves As:
- V. President, Human Resources and Corporate Communications, FMC Corp.

GARRETT, Michael D.
241 Ralph McGill Blvd. NE
Atlanta, GA 30308-3374
Tel: (404) 506 - 6526
Fax:(404) 506 - 3771

Serves As:
- President and Chief Exec. Officer, Georgia Power Co.

GARRETT, Scott
P.O. Box 3100
Fullerton, CA 92834
Tel: (714) 871 - 4848
Fax:(714) 773 - 8283
TF: (800) 742 - 2345

Serves As:
- Chief Executive Officer, Beckman Coulter, Inc.

GARRISON, Lynne G.
P.O. Box 2291
M/S HQ4
Durham, NC 27702-2291
lynne.garrison@bcbsnc.com
Tel: (919) 765 - 7256
Fax:(919) 765 - 4837

Serves As:
- V. President, Corporate Communications, Blue Cross and Blue Shield of North Carolina

GARRISON, Walter R.
1717 Arch St.
35th Floor
Philadelphia, PA 19103-2768
Tel: (215) 569 - 2200
Fax:(215) 569 - 1452

Serves As:
- Chairman of the Board, CDI Corp.

GARRISON, Wayne
615 J.B. Hunt Corporate Dr.
P.O. Box 130
Lowell, AR 72745
Tel: (479) 820 - 0000
Fax:(479) 820 - 8397
TF: (800) 643 - 3622

Serves As:
- Chairman of the Board, J. B. Hunt Transport Services, Inc.

GARRY, Daniel B.
3M Center
Bldg. 225-1S-05
St. Paul, MN 55144-1000
Tel: (651) 736 - 6198
Fax:(651) 736 - 2133

Serves As:
- Manager, Public Issues, 3M Company

GARVEY, Jane
201 E. Fourth St.
Cincinnati, OH 45202
Tel: (513) 723 - 7000
Fax:(513) 458 - 1315
TF: (800) 344 - 3000

Serves As:
- V. President, Corporate Communications, Convergys Corp.

GARVEY, Ph.D., Patricia L.
One Edwards Way
Irvine, CA 92614-5688
Tel: (949) 250 - 2500
Fax:(949) 250 - 2525
TF: (800) 424 - 3278

Serves As:
- Corporate V. President, Regulatory, Quality and Clinical Affairs, Edwards Lifesciences Corp.

GARVEY, Stephen J.
P.O. Box One, 161 St. Anthony St.
St. Paul, MN 55103
sgarvey@mnpower.com
Tel: (612) 225 - 1009
Fax:(612) 224 - 1004

Serves As:
- Manager, State Legislative Affairs, (Minnesota Power), ALLETE

GARVIN, Lana
601 Pennsylvania Ave. NW
North Bldg. Suite 1200
Washington, DC 20004
Tel: (202) 638 - 4170
Fax:(202) 638 - 3670

Serves As:
- Treasurer, Merck and Co. Inc, PAC, Merck & Co., Inc.

GARVIS, Nathan Keller
1000 Nicollet Mall
Minneapolis, MN 55403
Tel: (612) 304 - 6073

Serves As:
- V. President, Government Affairs, Target Corp.

GARY, Tim
3200 West End Ave.
Suite 102
Nashville, TN 37203-1332
Tel: (615) 386 - 8524
Fax:(615) 386 - 8509

Serves As:
- General Counsel, VSHP, Inc./Chief Compliance and Risk Officer, Governmental Programs, Blue Cross and Blue Shield of Tennessee

GARY, W. Bradford
2201 N St. NW
Suite 113
Washington, DC 20037
gary_brad@allergan.com
Tel: (202) 822 - 0982

Registered Federal Lobbyist.
Serves As:
- V. President, Government Operations, Allergan Inc.

GARYN, Hal
13220 California St.
Omaha, NE 68154
Tel: (402) 554 - 5336
Fax:(402) 514 - 5487
TF: (800) 228 - 5023

Serves As:
- Director, Audit, Risk Management, and Investor Relations, Commercial Federal Corp.

GARZA, Belinda
575 Seventh St. NW
Terrell Bldg.
Washington, DC 20004
Tel: (202) 737 - 5523
Fax:(202) 737 - 6069

Registered Federal Lobbyist.
Serves As:
- Office Manager, National Government Relations, Wal-Mart Stores

GARZA, Patricia
Three Lakes Dr.
Northfield, IL 60093-2753
pgarza@kraft.com
Tel: (847) 646 - 3082
Fax:(847) 646 - 6005

Serves As:
- Manager, Corporate Contributions, Kraft Foods, Inc.

GASBARRO, Eric
444 Westminster St.
Providence, RI 02903-3279
gasbarro.e@bcbsri.org
Tel: (401) 459 - 5169
Fax:(401) 455 - 6990
TF: (800) 637 - 3718

Serves As:
- Assistant V. President, Human Resources, Blue Cross & Blue Shield of Rhode Island

GASCON, Toby M.
251 Florida St.
Suite 407
Baton Rouge, LA 70801

Serves As:
- Treasurer, Omega-PAC, Omega Protein Corporation

Responsibilities include media relations

GASPARD, M. Scott
P.O. Box 834
Seattle, WA 98101
Tel: (206) 461 - 2000
Fax:(206) 554 - 4807
TF: (800) 756 - 8000

Registered Federal Lobbyist.
Serves As:
- Senior V. President, Government and Industry Relations, Washington Mutual, Inc.

GASPER, Barbara L.
One American Rd.
Dearborn, MI 48126
Tel: (313) 322 - 3000
TF: (800) 555 - 5259

Serves As:
- V. President, Investor Relations, Ford Motor Co.

GASSER, Michael J.
425 Winter Rd.
Delaware, OH 43015
Tel: (740) 549 - 6000
Fax:(740) 549 - 6100

Serves As:
- Chairman and Chief Exec. Officer, Greif, Inc.

GASTON, Patrick R.
1095 Ave. of the Americas
New York, NY 10036
patrick.g.gaston@verizon.com
Tel: (212) 395 - 2121
Fax:(212) 840 - 6988
TF: (800) 621 - 9900

Serves As:
- President, Verizon Foundation, Verizon Communications Inc.

GATES, III, William H.
One Microsoft Way
Redmond, WA 98052-6399
Tel: (425) 882 - 8080
Fax:(425) 936 - 7329

Serves As:
- Chairman of the Board and Chief Software Architect, Microsoft Corporation

GATTEN, Nathan
3900 Wisconsin Ave. NW
Washington, DC 20016
Tel: (202) 752 - 7000
Fax:(202) 752 - 6099

Registered Federal Lobbyist.
Serves As:
- V. President, Government and Industry Relations, Fannie Mae

GATTINELLA, Wayne T.
669 River Dr.
Elmwood Park, NJ 07407
Tel: (201) 703 - 3400
Fax:(201) 703 - 3401

Serves As:
- President and Chief Exec. Officer, WebMD Corp.

GAUGLER, Bonita
355 Maple Ave.
Harleysville, PA 19438-2297
bgaugler@harleysvillegroup.com
Tel: (215) 256 - 5013
Fax:(215) 256 - 5008
TF: (800) 523 - 6344

Serves As:
- Director, Corporate Affairs and Assistant V. President, Harleysville Group

GAULT, Polly L.
555 12th St. NW
Suite 640
Washington, DC 20004-1200
gaultpl@sce.com
Tel: (202) 393 - 3075
Fax:(202) 393 - 1497

Serves As:
- Regional V. President, Washington D.C., Southern California Edison, an Edison Internat'l Co.
- V. President, Public Affairs, Edison Internat'l

GAUPER, Larry L.
4510 13th Ave. SW
Fargo, ND 58121-0001
larry.gauper@noridian.com
Tel: (701) 282 - 1160
Fax:(701) 282 - 1469
TF: (800) 342 - 4718

Serves As:
- V. President, Communications, Blue Cross and Blue Shield of North Dakota

GAVIN, Anne
1401 I St., NW
Suite 500
Washington, DC 20005
Tel: (202) 263 - 5900
Fax:(202) 263 - 5902

Serves As:
- Manager, State Government Affairs - Northeast Region, Microsoft Corporation

GAVIN, John F.
151 University Ave.
Westwood, MA 02090
Tel: (781) 441 - 8338
Fax:(781) 441 - 8013

Serves As:
- Manager, Investor Relations, NSTAR

GAVIN, Mark
730 Milford Rd.
Route 101A
Merrimack, NH 03054-4631
mgavin@pcconnection.com
Tel: (603) 683 - 2000
Fax:(603) 683 - 2041

Serves As:
- Senior V. President, Finance, Chief Financial Officer and Director, Investor Relations, PC Connection, Inc.

GEANACOPOULOS, David
1300 Pennsylvania Ave. NW
Suite 860
Washington, DC 20004
Tel: (202) 842 - 5800
Fax:(202) 842 - 8612

Registered Federal Lobbyist.
Serves As:
- Director, Industry-Government Relations, Volkswagen of America, Inc.

GEBBEN, Phyllis
P.O. Box 1967
CH4E
Grand Rapids, MI 49501-1967
pgebben@steelcase.com
Tel: (616) 246 - 9860
Fax:(616) 475 - 2200

Serves As:
- Coordinator, Steelcase Foundation Donations, Steelcase Inc.

GEBEL, Riva
P.O. Box 6006
LCO1-322
Cypress, CA 90630
riva.gebel@phs.com
Tel: (714) 825 - 5126
Fax:(714) 825 - 5028

Serves As:
- Director, PacifiCare Health Systems Foundation, PacifiCare Health Systems, Inc.

GEE, Jim
P.O. Box 1411
Tyler, TX 75710-1411
jimgee@brookshires.com
Tel: (903) 534 - 3000
Fax:(903) 534 - 2198

Serves As:
- Manager, Public Relations, Brookshire Grocery Co.

GEERS, James H.
P.O. Box 550
Findlay, OH 45839-0550
jhgeers@coopertire.com
Tel: (419) 423 - 1321
Fax:(419) 424 - 4108

Serves As:
- V. President, Human Resources, Cooper Tire & Rubber Company

GEHLHAART, Donna
1101 Pennsylvania Ave. NW
Suite 200
Washington, DC 20004
donna.gehlhaart@ipaper.com
Tel: (202) 628 - 1223
Ext: 20
Fax:(202) 628 - 1368

Registered Federal Lobbyist.
Serves As:
- Washington Representative, Internat'l Paper

GEIB, Sally L.
Four Colesium Center
2730 W. Tyvola Rd.
Charlotte, NC 28217
sally.geib@goodrich.com
Tel: (704) 423 - 7000
Fax:(704) 423 - 7100

Serves As:
- V. President, Associate General Counsel and Secretary, Goodrich Corporation

Responsibilities include political action.

GEISINGER, Ethel
113 King St.
Armonk, NY 10504
ethel.geisinger@mbia.com
Tel: (914) 273 - 4545
Fax:(914) 765 - 3163

Serves As:
- V. President, Government Relations, MBIA, Inc.

GEISSMAN, Greg
P.O. Box 6482
1600 Faraday Ave.
Carlsbad, CA 92008
gergory.geissman@invitrogen.com
Tel: (760) 476 - 7032
Fax:(760) 602 - 6500
TF: (800) 955 - 6288

Serves As:
- Manager, Public Relations, Invitrogen Corp.

GELLERT, Jay M.
21650 Oxnard St.
Woodland Hills, CA 91367
jay.m.gellert@healthnet.com
Tel: (818) 676 - 6000
Fax:(818) 676 - 6616
TF: (800) 474 - 6676

Serves As:
- President and Chief Exec. Officer, Health Net, Inc.

GELMAN, Matt
1401 I St., NW
Suite 500
Washington, DC 20005
Tel: (202) 263 - 5900
Fax:(202) 263 - 5902

Serves As:
- Manager, Federal Government Affairs, Microsoft Corporation

GELSTON, Tom
500 Post Rd. East
Suite 320
Westport, CT 06880
Tel: (203) 222 - 5943
Fax:(203) 222 - 0130

Serves As:
- Director, Investor Relations and Corporate Communications, Terex Corp.

GEMEINHARDT, Elise A.
1225 New York Ave. NW
Suite 475
Washington, DC 20005
Tel: (202) 371 - 1303
Fax:(202) 371 - 5569

Registered Federal Lobbyist.
Serves As:
- V. President, Federal Affairs, UnitedHealth Group

GEMUNDER, Joel F.
1600 River Center II
100 E. River Center Blvd.
Covington, KY 41011
Tel: (859) 392 - 3300
Fax:(859) 392 - 3333

Serves As:
- President and Chief Exec. Officer, Omnicare, Inc.

GENADER, Robert J.
One State St. Plaza
New York, NY 10004
Tel: (212) 668 - 0340
Fax:(212) 509 - 9190
TF: (800) 221 - 1854

Serves As:
- President and Chief Exec. Officer, Ambac Financial Group, Inc.

GENCUR, Kimberly
P.O. Box 13287
Kansas City, MO 64199-3287
kimberly.gencur@aquila.com
Tel: (816) 467 - 3411
Fax:(816) 467 - 9411

Serves As:
- Legislative Services-Colorado/Kansas, Aquila, Inc.

GENDER, Robert A.
70 Pine St.
19th Floor
New York, NY 10270
Tel: (212) 770 - 7000
Fax:(212) 509 - 9705

Serves As:
- PAC Treasurer, AIG American General Corp.
- PAC Treasurer, American Internat'l Group, Inc.

GENECZKO, Robert M.
Two N. Ninth St.
Allentown, PA 18101-1179
rmgeneczko@pplweb.com
Tel: (484) 634 - 3248
Fax:(610) 774 - 5281
TF: (800) 345 - 3085

Serves As:
- V. President, Customer Services, PPL Corp.

GENNARELLI, David
20330 Stevens Creek Blvd.
Cupertino, CA 95014-2132
david_gennarelli@symantec.com
Tel: (408) 517 - 5272
Fax:(408) 517 - 8186

Serves As:
- Director, Investor Relations, Symantec Corp.

GENO, Patricia
P.O. Box 61000
New Orleans, LA 70161
pgeno@entergy.com
Tel: (504) 576 - 2364
Fax:(504) 576 - 4428

Serves As:
- Director, Employee Communications and Special Services, Entergy Corp.

GENOSI, Courtney
555 12th St. NW
Suite 500
Washington, DC 20004
Tel: (202) 879 - 5978
Fax:(202) 638 - 7857

Registered Federal Lobbyist.
Serves As:
- Manager, Deloitte & Touche LLP

Responsibilities include government affairs.

GENOVESI, Jacqueline
701 Pennsylvania Ave. NW
Suite 520
Washington, DC 20004-2604
Tel: (202) 393 - 3400
Fax:(202) 393 - 4606

Registered Federal Lobbyist.
Serves As:
- Legislative Assistant, The Procter & Gamble Company

GENTILE-SACHS, Valerie
5555 Darrow Rd.
Hudson, OH 44236
Tel: (330) 656 - 2600
Fax:(330) 463 - 6675

Serves As:
- Exec. V. President and General Counsel, Jo-Ann Stores, Inc.

GENTRY, Barbara
9800 Fredericksburg Rd.
San Antonio, TX 78288-0122
Tel: (210) 498 - 1225
Fax:(210) 498 - 8216

Serves As:
- Senior V. President, Community Affairs, United Services Automobile Ass'n (USAA)

GENTRY, Boyd P.
One Ravinia Dr.
Suite 1500
Atlanta, GA 30346
bgentry@marinerhealthcare.com
Tel: (678) 443 - 6872
Fax:(678) 443 - 6874

Serves As:
- Senior V. President, Investor Relations and Treasurer, Sava Senior Care LLC

GENTZ, Robin M.
P.O. Box 24305
Oakland, CA 94623-1305
robin.gentz@clorox.com
Tel: (510) 271 - 7081
Fax:(510) 271 - 6583

Serves As:
- Manager, Government Affairs Issues, The Clorox Co.

GEOGHEGAN, J. Ronald
601 W. Chestnut St.
Louisville, KY 40203
ron.geoghegan@bellsouth.com
Tel: (502) 582 - 3156
Fax:(502) 875 - 6517

Serves As:
- Exec. Director, Regulatory and External Affairs, BellSouth Corp.

GEORGE, Deborah
3499 Blazer Pkwy.
Lexington, KY 40509
Tel: (859) 357 - 3409

Serves As:
- Contact, Corporate Giving, Ashland Inc.

GERACE, James J.
1095 Ave. of the Americas
New York, NY 10036
james.gerace@verizonwireless.com
Tel: (212) 395 - 2121
Fax:(212) 869 - 3265

Serves As:
- V. President, Corporate Communications, Verizon Wireless

GERARD, Valerie L.
1211 Avenue of the Americas
New York, NY 10036
Tel: (212) 422 - 3284
Fax:(212) 536 - 1912

Serves As:
- Senior V. President, Investor Relations, The CIT Group, Inc.

GERBER, Murry S.
One Oxford Center, Suite 3300
Pittsburgh, PA 15219
Tel: (412) 553 - 5700
Fax:(412) 553 - 5757

Serves As:
• Chairman, President and Chief Exec. Officer, Equitable Resources, Inc.

GERBER, William K.
999 W. Big Beaver Rd.
Troy, MI 48084-4782
Tel: (248) 362 - 4444
Fax:(248) 244 - 7572

Serves As:
• Exec. V. President and Chief Operating Officer, Kelly Services, Inc.

GERKE, Scott A.
1001 G St., NW
Suite 950
Washington, DC 20001
scott_gerke@hna.honda.com
Tel: (202) 661 - 4400
Fax:(202) 661 - 4459

Registered Federal Lobbyist.
Serves As:
• Senior Analyst, Government Relations, (Honda North America, Inc.), American Honda Motor Co., Inc.

GERKENS, Henry H.
13410 Sutton Park Dr. South
Jacksonville, FL 32224
Tel: (904) 398 - 9400
Fax:(904) 390 - 1437
TF: (800) 872 - 9400

Serves As:
• President and Chief Exec. Officer, Landstar System, Inc.

GERMAN, Brad
8200 Jones Branch Dr.
M/S 409
McLean, VA 22102
brad_german@freddiemac.com
Tel: (703) 903 - 2437
Fax:(703) 903 - 2447
TF: (800) 373 - 3343

Serves As:
• Manager, Public Relations, Freddie Mac

GERN, Ronald
110 N. Wacker Dr.
Chicago, IL 60606-1511
Tel: (312) 960 - 5000
Fax:(312) 960 - 5475

Serves As:
• Treasurer, General Growth Properties Inc. PAC, General Growth Properties Inc.

GERSBACH, Jim
500 N.E. Multnomah St.
Suite 100
Portland, OR 97232-2099
jim.n.gersbach@kp.org
Tel: (503) 813 - 4827
Fax:(503) 813 - 4235

Serves As:
• Communications and Community Relations Contact-Northwest Region, Kaiser Permanente

GERSTENKORN, Margaret
5301 N. Ironwood Rd.
Milwaukee, WI 53217
Tel: (414) 906 - 6336
Fax:(414) 961 - 7985

Serves As:
• Director, Public Relations, Manpower Inc.

GESCHKE, Dr. Charles M.
345 Park Ave.
San Jose, CA 95110-2704
Tel: (408) 536 - 6000
Fax:(408) 537 - 6000

Serves As:
• Co-Chairman of the Board, Adobe Systems Inc.

GFELLER, Jr., Robert J.
1000 Lowes Blvd.
Moorsville, NC 28117
robert.j.gfeller@lowes.com
Tel: (704) 758 - 100
Fax:(336) 658 - 4766
TF: (800) 445 - 6937

Serves As:
• Senior V. President, Marketing Communications and Advertising, Lowe's Companies, Inc.

GHERTY, James E.
P.O. Box 64101
St. Paul, MN 55164-0101
jegherty@landolakes.com
Tel: (651) 481 - 2222
Fax:(651) 481 - 2000
TF: (800) 328 - 4155

Serves As:
• Chief Exec. Officer, Land O'Lakes, Inc.

GHOSN, Carlos
P.O. Box 191
Gardena, CA 90248-0191
Tel: (310) 771 - 3111
Fax:(310) 516 - 7967

Serves As:
• Chief Exec. Officer, Nissan North America, Inc.

GIAMFORTONE, Joseph Edward
418 Plantain Terrace
Peachtree City, GA 30269
Tel: (770) 486 - 0584

Serves As:
• Senior Government Affairs Manager, Schering-Plough Corporation

GIAMPA, Robin
200 Domain Dr.
Stratham, NH 03885
Tel: (603) 773 - 1174
Fax:(603) 773 - 1251

Serves As:
• Manager, Corporate Communications, The Timberland Co.

GIANELLI, Silvia
2100 Logic Dr.
San Jose, CA 95124-3400
silvia.gianelli@xilinx.com
Tel: (408) 626 - 4328
Fax:(408) 317 - 4926
TF: (800) 836 - 4002

Serves As:
• Manager, Worldwide Corporate Public Relations, Xilinx, Inc.

GIANGRASSO, Chris
2000 Market St.
Philadelphia, PA 19103-9000
Tel: (215) 419 - 7714
Fax:(215) 419 - 7591
TF: (800) 225 - 7788

Serves As:
• V. President, Human Resources and Communications, ATOFINA Chemicals, Inc.

GIANNINI, Thomas
1000 Wilson Blvd., Suite 2300
Arlington, VA 22209
Tel: (703) 875 - 8400

Registered Federal Lobbyist.
Serves As:
• Representative, Northrop Grumman Corp.

GIARALDI, Dominick
P.O. Box 99
Pleasanton, CA 94566-0009
Tel: (925) 467 - 3000

Serves As:
• PAC Treasurer, Safeway Inc.

GIBBENS, Dale
4111 E. 37th St., North
Wichita, KS 67220
Tel: (316) 828 - 5606
Fax:(316) 828 - 5739

Serves As:
• V. President, Human Resources, Koch Industries, Inc.

GIBBONS, David T.
515 Eastern Ave.
Allegan, MI 49010-9070
Tel: (269) 673 - 8451
Fax:(269) 673 - 9128

Serves As:
• Chairman, President and Chief Exec. Officer, Perrigo Co.

GIBBONS, Jr., Joseph F.
2060 E. Ninth St.
Cleveland, OH 44115
joseph.gibbons@mmoh.com
Tel: (216) 687 - 7656
Fax:(216) 687 - 2623

Serves As:
• Director, Government Relations, Medical Mutual of Ohio

GIBBONS, Thomas E.
P.O. Box 193575
San Francisco, CA 94119-3575
Tel: (415) 247 - 3382
Fax:(415) 247 - 3565

Serves As:
• Senior V. President and Treasurer, Del Monte Foods
Responsibilities include investor relations.

GIBBS, James R.
10000 Memorial Dr.
Suite 600
Houston, TX 77024-3341
jgibbs@frontieroil.com
Tel: (713) 688 - 9600
Fax:(713) 688 - 0616

Serves As:
• Chairman, President and Chief Exec. Officer, Frontier Oil Corp.

GIBLIN, Vincent
Three Penn Plaza East
PP-15V
Newark, NJ 07105-2200
Tel: (973) 466 - 4000
Fax:(973) 466 - 7077

Serves As:
• Chairman of the Board, Horizon Blue Cross Blue Shield of New Jersey

GIBSON, David W.
P.O. Box 127
Joplin, MO 64802-0127
Tel: (417) 625 - 5100
Fax:(417) 625 - 5155
TF: (800) 206 - 2300

Serves As:
• V. President, Regulatory and General Services, Empire District Electric Co.

GIBSON, F. Daniel
1111 Westchester Ave.
White Plains, NY 10604
Tel: (914) 640 - 8175
Fax:(914) 640 - 8310
TF: (877) 443 - 4585

Serves As:
• Senior V. President, Corporate Affairs, Starwood Hotels and Resorts Worldwide, Inc.
Responsibilities include investor relations.

GIBSON, Jean H.
77 Grove St.
Rutland, VT 05701
jgibson@cvps.com
Tel: (802) 747 - 5435
Fax:(802) 747 - 2199
TF: (800) 649 - 2877

Serves As:
- Senior V. President, Chief Financial Officer and Treasurer, Central Vermont Public Service Corp.

Responsibilities include investor relations.

GIBSON, Jon R.
1621 Barber Ln.
Milpitas, CA 95035
Tel: (408) 433 - 8000
Fax:(408) 954 - 3220
TF: (866) 574 - 5741

Serves As:
- V. President, Human Resources, LSI Logic Corp.

GIBSON, Phil
P.O. Box 58090
M/S G1-120
Santa Clara, CA 95052-8090
phil.gibson@nsc.com
Tel: (408) 721 - 5000
Fax:(408) 739 - 9803

Serves As:
- V. President, Corporate Marketing and Communications and Web Business, Nat'l Semiconductor Corp.

GIBSON, Sherryl
4615 E. Elwood St.
Phoenix, AZ 85040-1958
Tel: (480) 966 - 5394
Fax:(480) 379 - 3503
TF: (800) 990 - APOL

Serves As:
- PAC Treasurer, Apollo Group, Inc.

GIBSON-BRADY, Holly E.
One Franklin Pkwy.
San Mateo, CA 94403-1906
hgibson@frk.com
Tel: (650) 312 - 4701
Fax:(650) 574 - 5012
TF: (800) 342 - 5236

Serves As:
- V. President, Corporate Communications, Franklin Templeton Investments

GIENKO, Glenn A.
1303 E. Algonquin Rd.
Schaumburg, IL 60196
Tel: (847) 576 - 5260
Fax:(847) 538 - 5191
TF: (800) 262 - 8509

Serves As:
- Exec. V. President and Director, Human Resources, Motorola, Inc.

GIERER, Jr., Vincent A.
100 W. Putnam Ave.
Greenwich, CT 06830
Tel: (203) 661 - 1100
Fax:(203) 863 - 7250

Serves As:
- Chairman, President and Chief Exec. Officer, UST Inc.

GIESE, Jean
4000 Dain Rauscher Plaza
60 S. Sixth St.
Minneapolis, MN 55402
Tel: (612) 661 - 3718

Serves As:
- Director, Investor and Shareholder Relations, PepsiAmericas, Inc.

GIESSELMAN, Janet
9330 Zionsville Rd.
Indianapolis, IN 46268
jgiesselman@dow.com
Tel: (317) 337 - 3000
Fax:(317) 337 - 4880

Serves As:
- V. President, Corporate Affairs, Dow AgroSciences LLC

GIFFORD, Dale
100 Half Day Rd.
Lincolnshire, IL 60069
Tel: (847) 295 - 5000
Fax:(847) 295 - 7634

Serves As:
- Chief Exec. Officer and Chairman, Hewitt Associates Inc.

GIFFORD, John F.
120 San Gabriel Dr.
Sunnyvale, CA 94086
jgifford@maxim-ic.com
Tel: (408) 737 - 7600
Fax:(408) 737 - 7194
TF: (800) 998 - 9872

Serves As:
- Chairman, President and Chief Exec. Officer, Maxim Integrated Products

GIFFORD, Paul S.
Four Colesium Center
2730 W. Tyvola Rd.
Charlotte, NC 28217
paul.gifford@goodrich.com
Tel: (704) 423 - 5517
Fax:(704) 423 - 5516

Serves As:
- V. President, Investor Relations, Goodrich Corporation

GIFFT, John
Commonwealth Towers
1300 Wilson Blvd., Suite 200
Arlington, VA 22209-2307
Tel: (703) 516 - 8220
Fax:(703) 516 - 8295

Serves As:
- Manager, Govermental and Regulatory Affairs, Rockwell Collins, Inc

GILBANE, Jr., Thomas F.
Seven Jackson Walkway
Providence, RI 02903
Tel: (401) 456 - 5800
Fax:(401) 456 - 5404
TF: (800) 445 - 2263

Serves As:
- Chairman and Chief Exec. Officer, Gilbane Building Co.

GILBERT, David M.
101 Constitution Ave., NW
Suite 980 East
Washington, DC 20001
Tel: (202) 942 - 9840
Fax:(202) 942 - 9847
TF: (888) 460 - 2002

Registered Federal Lobbyist.
Serves As:
- Managing Director, Federal Affairs, Constellation Energy

GILBERT, H. Steven
One Enterprise Dr.
Aliso Viejo, CA 92656-2606
Tel: (949) 349 - 2000
Fax:(949) 349 - 2585

Serves As:
- Senior V. President, Human Resources and Administration, Fluor Corp.

GILBERT, H. Vaughn
P.O. Box 355
Pittsburgh, PA 15230-0355
gilberthv@westinghouse.com
Tel: (412) 374 - 3896
Fax:(412) 374 - 3272

Serves As:
- Manager, Public Relations, Westinghouse Electric Company LLC

GILBERT, John R.
One E. Pratt St.
M/S 8E
Baltimore, MD 21202
john.r.gilbert@verizon.com
Tel: (410) 393 - 4178
Fax:(410) 234 - 0320
TF: (800) 621 - 9900

Serves As:
- V. President, Regulatory Affairs/Issues Analysis, Verizon Maryland Inc.

GILBERT, Terry L.
P.O. Box 1530
La Jolla, CA 92038-1530
Tel: (858) 454 - 0411
Fax:(858) 729 - 7672

Serves As:
- Foundation Administrator, The Copley Press, Inc.

GILBERT, William
One Canon Plaza
Lake Success, NY 11042-1198
Tel: (516) 488 - 6700
Fax:(516) 328 - 5069

Serves As:
- Senior V. President, Human Resources, Canon U.S.A., Inc.

GILDART, Kevin P.
700 Washington St.
Bath, ME 04530
Tel: (207) 442 - 2025
Fax:(207) 442 - 5592

Serves As:
- V. President, Human Resources, Bath Iron Works Corp.

GILES, Betsy
1005 Congress Ave.
Suite 850
Austin, TX 78702
Tel: (512) 478 - 3394
Fax:(512) 478 - 0657

Serves As:
- Regional Director, State Government Affairs, (Altria Corporate Services, Inc.), Altria Group, Inc.

GILES, Charlene
P.O. Box 1220
Indianapolis, IN 46206
charlene.giles@veoliawaterna.com
Tel: (317) 639 - 1431
Fax:(317) 263 - 6414

Serves As:
- Director, Human Resources, Veolia Water Indianapolis, LLC

GILES, Chris
P.O. Box 418679
Kansas City, MO 64141-9679
Tel: (816) 556 - 2200
Fax:(816) 556 - 2975

Serves As:
- V. President, Regulatory Affairs, Great Plains Energy, Inc.

GILES, Glenn
1410 Spring Hill Rd., Suite 500
McLean, VA 22102
Tel: (703) 848 - 7200
Fax:(703) 848 - 7600

Serves As:
- V. President, Keane, Inc.

GILES, Tom
701 Pennsylvania Ave. NW
Suite 725
Washington, DC 20004
Tel: (202) 638 - 7429
Fax:(202) 628 - 4763

Serves As:
• Exec. Director, Federal Government Relations, Novartis Corporation

GILL, Emily
P.O. Box 35985
Tulsa, OK 74153-0985
egill@dollar.com
Tel: (918) 669 - 2949
Fax:(918) 669 - 2934

Serves As:
• Staff Manager, Public Relations, (Dollar Rent A Car, Inc.), Dollar Thrifty Automotive Group, Inc.

GILL, James W.
14850 Conference Center Dr.
Chantilly, VA 20151
Tel: (703) 834 - 1700
Fax:(703) 709 - 6087

Serves As:
• Exec. V. President, Human Resources, Rolls-Royce North America Inc.

GILL, Jr., Ruland J.
P.O. Box 45433
Salt Lake City, UT 84145-0433
ruland.gill@questar.com
Tel: (801) 324 - 5212
Fax:(801) 324 - 5483

Serves As:
• V. President, Government Relations, Questar Corporation

GILLEN, Denise
650 Madison Ave.
New York, NY 10022
Tel: (212) 318 - 7516
Fax:(212) 888 - 5780
TF: (800) 377 - 7656

Serves As:
• Investor Relations Contact, Polo Ralph Lauren

GILLESPIE, Karen Sue
950 E. Paces Ferry Rd., Suite 2003
Atlanta, GA 30326
karen.gillespie@bms.com
Tel: (404) 231 - 6460
Fax:(404) 231 - 6464

Serves As:
• Associate Director, State Government Affairs, Bristol-Myers Squibb Co.

GILLEY, Kyle
P.O. Box 799900
Dallas, TX 75379-9900
Tel: (972) 497 - 6218
Fax:(972) 497 - 5268

Serves As:
• Contact, Lennox Employee Advocacy Program, Lennox Internat'l

GILLIAM, Scott A.
P.O. Box 145496
Cincinnati, OH 45250
scott_gilliam@cinfin.com
Tel: (513) 870 - 2000
Fax:(513) 870 - 2985

Serves As:
• Assistant V. President and Government Relations Officer, Cincinnati Financial Corp.

GILLIAM, Thomas
320 Park Ave.
New York, NY 10022
Tel: (212) 224 - 1147
Fax:(212) 224 - 2500

Serves As:
• Contact, Mutual of America Foundation, Mutual of America Life Insurance Co.

GILLIGAN, Rich
P.O. Box 6014
Cypress, CA 90630-0014
Tel: (714) 372 - 6000
Fax:(714) 373 - 1020

Serves As:
• President and Chief Exec. Officer, Mitsubishi Motors North America, Inc.

GILLILAND, Sam
3150 Sabre Dr.
Southlake, TX 76092
Tel: (682) 605 - 1000
Fax:(682) 264 - 9000

Serves As:
• Chairman, President and Chief Exec. Officer, Sabre Holdings Corp.

GILLINGS, Ph.D., Dennis
P.O. Box 13979
Research Triangle Park, NC 27709-3979
Tel: (919) 998 - 2000
Fax:(919) 998 - 2098

Serves As:
• Chairman and Chief Exec. Officer, Quintiles Transnat'l Corp.

GILLISPIE, Toni Perry
300 W. First St.
Dayton, OH 45402
latonia.s.perry@sbc.com
Tel: (937) 227 - 7578
Fax:(937) 227 - 4099

Serves As:
• Director, External Affairs, SBC Ohio

GILLUM, Roderick D.
P.O. Box 300
Detroit, MI 48265-1000
Tel: (313) 556 - 5000
Fax:(248) 696 - 7300

Serves As:
• V. President, Corporate Responsibility and Diversity, General Motors Corp.

GILLUND, Laura
8100 Mitchell Rd.
Eden Prairie, MN 55344
Tel: (952) 937 - 8500
Fax:(952) 937 - 6740

Serves As:
• V. President, Human Resources, C.H. Robinson Worldwide, Inc.

GILMAN, Kenneth B.
622 Third Ave., 37th Floor
New York, NY 10017
Tel: (212) 885 - 2500

Serves As:
• President and Chief Exec. Officer, Asbury Automotive Group

GILMORE, Kristi
One Healthsouth Pkwy.
Birmingham, AL 35243
kristi.gilmore@healthsouth.com
Tel: (205) 967 - 7116
Fax:(205) 969 - 6889
TF: (888) 476 - 8849

Serves As:
• V. President, Corporate Public Relations, HealthSouth Corp.

GILPIN, Don
5200 Sheila St.
Commerce, CA 90040
Tel: (323) 264 - 5200
Ext: 8643
Fax:(323) 265 - 4261

Serves As:
• V. President, Human Resources, Unified Western Grocers, Inc.

GIMBEL, Tod I.
101 Constitution Ave. NW
Suite 400 West
Washington, DC 20001
tod.gimbel@altria.com
Tel: (202) 354 - 1500
Fax:(202) 354 - 1505

Serves As:
• Regional Director, East, Altria Group, Inc.

GINSBERG, Gary
1211 Ave. of the Americas
New York, NY 10036
gginsberg@newscorp.com
Tel: (212) 852 - 7000

Serves As:
• Exec. V. President, Investor Relations and Corporate Communications, News Corporation Ltd.

GINSBERG, Meryl
3100 Hansen Way
Palo Alto, CA 94304-1030
meryl.ginsberg@varian.com
Tel: (650) 424 - 6444
Fax:(650) 842 - 5196

Serves As:
• Manager, Public Relations, Varian Medical Systems, Inc.

GIOIA, Justin J.
One N. Jefferson Ave.
St. Louis, MO 63103
Tel: (314) 955 - 2379
Fax:(314) 955 - 5913
TF: (877) 835 - 7877

Serves As:
• Associate V. President and Director of Investor Relations, A. G. Edwards, Inc.
Responsibilities include corporate philanthropy.

GIPSON, Bill
P.O. Box 127
Joplin, MO 64802-0127
bgipson@empiredistrict.com
Tel: (417) 625 - 5100
Fax:(417) 625 - 5155
TF: (800) 206 - 2300

Registered Federal Lobbyist.
Serves As:
• President and Chief Exec. Officer, Empire District Electric Co.

GIPSON, Kelley J.
1211 Avenue of the Americas
New York, NY 10036
Tel: (212) 536 - 1390
Fax:(212) 536 - 1912

Serves As:
• Exec. V. President, Marketing and Corporate Communications, The CIT Group, Inc.

GIROUARD, Marvin J.
100 Pier 1 Place
Fort Worth, TX 76102
Tel: (817) 252 - 8000

Serves As:
• Chairman and Chief Exec. Officer, Pier 1 Imports

GIULIANO, Tony
One GBC Plaza
Northbrook, IL 60062
tgiuliano@gbc.com
Tel: (847) 291 - 5451
Fax:(847) 291 - 6371

Serves As:
• Treasurer and Director, Investor Relations, General Binding Corp.

GIULIANO, Vincent
One Targeting Centre
Windsor, CT 06095
Tel: (860) 285 - 6126
Fax:(860) 285 - 6230
TF: (800) 559 - 2386

Serves As:
• Senior V. President, Government Relations, Advo Inc.
Responsibilities include political action.

GIVNER, Elaine
70 Maxess Rd.
Melville, NY 11747
egivner@nuhorizons.com
Tel: (631) 396 - 5000
Fax:(631) 696 - 5050

Serves As:
• V. President, Human Resources and Training Development, Nu Horizons Electronics Corp.

GLADER, Paul
6500 N. Mineral Dr., Suite 200
Coeur d'Alene, ID 83815-9408
Tel: (208) 769 - 4100
Fax:(208) 769 - 4122

Serves As:
• Manager, Environmental Services, Hecla Mining Co.

GLADNEY, Carrie L.
111 S. Wacker Dr.
Chicago, IL 60606
carrie.gladney@rrd.com
Tel: (312) 326 - 8031
Fax:(312) 326 - 8494

Serves As:
• Coordinator, Government Relations, R R Donnelley

GLASER, Nancy
1345 Ave. of the Americas
New York, NY 10020
Tel: (212) 282 - 7000
Fax:(212) 282 - 6220

Serves As:
• Senior V. President, Communications, Avon Products, Inc.

GLASGOW, Karin
1025 Connecticut Ave. NW
Suite 1210
Washington, DC 20036
karin.glasgow@united.com
Tel: (202) 296 - 1712
Fax:(202) 296 - 2873

Serves As:
• Manager, Government Affairs, United Airlines

GLASS, Dennis R.
P.O. Box 21008
Greensboro, NC 27420
Tel: (336) 691 - 3000
Fax:(336) 691 - 3938

Serves As:
• President and Chief Exec. Officer, Jefferson-Pilot Corp.

GLASS, Holly P.
14241 Clubhouse Rd.
Gainesville, VA 20155
Tel: (703) 754 - 2848
Fax:(703) 754 - 7889

Registered Federal Lobbyist.
Serves As:
• V. President, Government and Public Relations, C. R. Bard, Inc.

GLASS, J. Kenneth
165 Madison Ave.
Memphis, TN 38103
Tel: (901) 523 - 4444

Serves As:
• Chairman, President and Chief Exec. Officer, First Horizon Nat'l Corp.

GLASSCOCK, Larry C.
120 Monument Circle
Indianapolis, IN 46204
Tel: (317) 532 - 6000

Serves As:
• President and Chief Exec. Officer, Wellpoint, Inc.

GLAUBERMAN, Stu
Two Waterfront Plaza
Suite 500
Honolulu, HI 96813
sglauberman@alohaairlines.com
Tel: (808) 539 - 5947
Fax:(808) 836 - 0303

Serves As:
• Director, Corporate Communications, Aloha Airlines, Inc.

GLAZER, Avram A.
1717 St. James Pl., Suite 550
Houston, TX 77056
Tel: (713) 623 - 0060
Fax:(713) 940 - 6122

Serves As:
• Chairman of the Board, Omega Protein Corporation

GLAZER, Charles T.
3250 Interstate Dr.
Richfield, OH 44286
cglazer@intlsteel.com
Tel: (330) 659 - 9121
Fax:(330) 659 - 9135

Serves As:
• Manager, Communications and Public Relations, Internat'l Steel Group Inc.

GLAZERMAN, Ellen L.
1285 Ave. of the Americas
New York, NY 10019
ellen.glazerman@ey.com
Tel: (212) 773 - 5686

Serves As:
• Contact, Ernst & Young Foundation, Ernst & Young LLP

GLEASON, Donna
1200 Wilson Blvd.
Arlington, VA 22209-2305
Tel: (703) 465 - 3263
Fax:(703) 465 - 3004

Registered Federal Lobbyist.
Serves As:
• Director, Corporate Legislation, The Boeing Co.

GLEASON, Jeffrey
P.O. Box B
Jacksonville, FL 32203-0297
Tel: (904) 783 - 5000
Fax:(904) 783 - 5294

Serves As:
• PAC Treasurer, Winn-Dixie Stores

GLEESON, John
200 Wilmot Rd.
Deerfield, IL 60015-4616
Tel: (847) 914 - 2500
Fax:(847) 914 - 3417

Serves As:
• Corporate V. President and Treasurer, Walgreen Co.
Responsibilities include investor relations.

GLENN, J. Thomas
2200 Kensington Ct.
Oak Brook, IL 60523-2100
Tel: (423) 899 - 6306
Ext: 20
Fax:(423) 892 - 1744

Serves As:
• Chairman of the Board, Ace Hardware Corp.

GLENN, Sara
1401 I St. NW, Suite 1030
Washington, DC 20005
sara.glenn@shell.com
Tel: (202) 466 - 1400
Fax:(202) 466 - 1498

Registered Federal Lobbyist.
Serves As:
• Washington Counsel, Shell Oil Co.

GLENN, T. Michael
942 S. Shady Grove Rd.
Memphis, TN 38120
Tel: (901) 369 - 3600
TF: (800) 238 - 5355

Serves As:
• Exec. V. President, Market Development and Corporate Communications, FedEx Corp.

GLICK, Rich
555 11th St. NW
Sixth Floor
Washington, DC 20004
rich.glick@pacificorp.com
Tel: (202) 508 - 3490
Fax:(202) 639 - 9464

Registered Federal Lobbyist.
Serves As:
• Director, Government Affairs, PacifiCorp

GLOVER, Jerry P.
800 N. Lindbergh Blvd.
St. Louis, MO 63167
Jerry.P.Glover@monsanto.com
Tel: (314) 694 - 3133
Fax:(314) 694 - 4228

Serves As:
• V. President, External Affairs, Monsanto Co.

GLOVER, Lisa
One Centennial Ave.
PO Box 6820
Piscataway, NJ 08854
lglover@americanstandard.com
Tel: (732) 980 - 6048
Fax:(732) 980 - 3335

Serves As:
• Director, Media Relations, American Standard Companies Inc.

GLOVER, Tom
Four W. Red Oak Ln.
White Plains, NY 10604
tom.glover@itt.com
Tel: (914) 641 - 2160
Fax:(914) 696 - 2977

Serves As:
• Director, Public Relations, ITT Industries

GLOWIAK, Brian G.
1000 Chrysler Dr.
CIMS 485-10-94
Auburn Hills, MI 48326-2766
Tel: (248) 512 - 2500
Fax:(248) 512 - 2503
TF: (800) 992 - 1997

Serves As:
• Senior Manager, DaimlerChrysler Corp. Fund, DaimlerChrysler Corp.

GLUECK, Kenneth
1015 15th St. NW
Suite 200
Washington, DC 20005-2605
kenneth.glueck@oracle.com
Tel: (202) 721 - 4815
Fax:(202) 467 - 4250

Registered Federal Lobbyist.
Serves As:
- V. President, Government Affairs, Oracle Corporation

GLYNN, Carolyn R.
340 Kingsland St.
#85, Fourth Fl.
Nutley, NJ 07110-1199
Tel: (973) 562 - 2213
Fax:(973) 562 - 2205

Serves As:
- V. President, Public Affairs, Hoffmann-La Roche Inc. (Roche)

GLYNN, Lynne
2030 Dow Center
Midland, MI 48674-0001
Tel: (989) 636 - 9846
Fax:(989) 638 - 1727

Serves As:
- Foundation Contact, The Dow Chemical Company

GLYNN, Martin J. G.
452 Fifth Ave.
New York, NY 10018
Tel: (212) 525 - 5000
TF: (800) 975 - 4722

Serves As:
- President and Chief Exec. Officer, HSBC USA, Inc.

GLYNN, William C.
P.O. Box 7608
Boise, ID 83707
Tel: (208) 377 - 6840
Fax:(208) 377 - 6097

Serves As:
- President, Intermountain Gas Co.

GMACH, David
Four Irving Pl.
New York, NY 10003
Tel: (212) 460 - 6427
Fax:(212) 614 - 1453

Serves As:
- Director, Public Affairs (Manhattan), Consolidated Edison Co. of New York, Inc.

GNIADEK, Sarah
2200 Kensington Ct.
Oak Brook, IL 60523-2100
Tel: (630) 990 - 6523
Fax:(630) 990 - 1742

Serves As:
- Coordinator Ace Hardware Foundation, Ace Hardware Corp.

GOCHNAUER, Richard W.
2200 E. Golf Rd.
Des Plaines, IL 60016-1267
Tel: (847) 699 - 5000
Fax:(847) 699 - 8046

Serves As:
- President and Chief Exec. Officer, United Stationers Inc.

GODDARD, Kevin
P.O. Box 186
Montpelier, VT 05601
goddardk@bcbsvt.com
Tel: (802) 223 - 6131
Fax:(802) 223 - 4229
TF: (800) 255 - 4550

Serves As:
- V. President, External Affairs, Blue Cross and Blue Shield of Vermont

GODFREY, John
1667 K St. NW
Suite 200
Washington, DC 20006
Tel: (202) 429 - 3652

Registered Federal Lobbyist.
Serves As:
- Representative, (Sony Electronics Inc.), Sony Corp. of America

GODKIN, Lynda
Hartford Plaza
T-12-56
Hartford, CT 06115
lynda.godkin@thehartford.com
Tel: (860) 547 - 4993
Fax:(860) 547 - 6393

Serves As:
- Senior V. President, State and Community Relations, The Hartford Financial Services Group Inc.

Responsibilities include corporate philanthropy.

GODLOVE, Jim
1776 I St. NW
Suite 700
Washington, DC 20006
jwgodlo@ppco.com
Fax:(202) 785 - 0639

Registered Federal Lobbyist.
Serves As:
- Manager, Federal Affairs - International, ConocoPhillips

GOEBEL, Maureen
101 Gordon Dr.
Lionville, PA 19341
Tel: (610) 594 - 2900
Fax:(610) 594 - 3000
TF: (800) 345 - 9800

Serves As:
- Administrator, Herman O. West Foundation, West Pharmaceutical Services

GOEBEL, Summer
P.O. Box 321
M/C 506
Oklahoma City, OK 73101-0321
Tel: (405) 553 - 3523

Serves As:
- Manager, Environment Health and Safety, OGE Energy Corp.

GOEHLER, David
515 Prince St.
Alexandria, VA 22314-3115
dave.goehler@jeppesen.com
Tel: (703) 519 - 5295
Fax:(703) 519 - 5296

Serves As:
- Director, Washington Office, Jeppesen

GOELLER-JOHNSON, Kim
5929 College Ave.
Oakland, CA 94618
kagvelle@dreyers.com
Tel: (510) 601 - 4211
Fax:(510) 601 - 4400

Serves As:
- Manager, Public Relations--Premium Brands, Dreyer's Grand Ice Cream Holdings, Inc.

GOERKE, Brian E.
249 Fifth Ave.
Pittsburgh, PA 15222-2707
brian.goerke@pnc.com
Tel: (412) 762 - 4304
Fax:(412) 762 - 3463

Serves As:
- V. President and Manager, Public Relations, PNC Financial Services Group

GOETTEL, Lisa
3250 Lacey Rd., Suite 600
Downers Grove, IL 60515
lisa.gottel@servicemaster.com
Tel: (901) 681 - 1852
Fax:(901) 766 - 1107

Serves As:
- Senior V. President, Human Resources, The ServiceMaster Co.

GOETZ, Julie
5501 American Blvd. West
Minneapolis, MN 55437
julie.goetz@jostens.com
Tel: (952) 830 - 3332
Fax:(952) 830 - 3293

Serves As:
- Manager, Communications, Jostens, Inc.

GOFF, Alisha
P.O. Box 500
Beaverton, OR 97077
alisha.goff@tektronix.com
Tel: (503) 627 - 7075
Fax:(503) 567 - 3449
TF: (800) 835 - 9433

Serves As:
- Manager, Corporate Communications, Tektronix, Inc.

GOFF, Cynthia
3535 Blue Cross Rd.
MS 3-27
Eagan, MN 55122--115
cynthia.goff@bluecrossmn.com
Tel: (651) 662 - 2872
Fax:(651) 662 - 6201
TF: (800) 382 - 2000

Serves As:
- Director, Public Policy, Blue Cross and Blue Shield of Minnesota

GOFF, Donald G.
1200 Wilson Blvd.
Arlington, VA 22209-2305
Tel: (703) 465 - 3218
Fax:(703) 465 - 3004

Registered Federal Lobbyist.
Serves As:
- Director, Legislative Affairs, Corporate Programs, The Boeing Co.

GOFORTH, Jenifer M.
P.O. Box 10247
Birmingham, AL 35202
jenifer.goforth@regions.com
Tel: (205) 244 - 2823
Fax:(205) 326 - 7784
TF: (800) 734 - 4667

Serves As:
- Senior V. President and Director, Investor Relations, Regions Financial Corp.

GOINGS, E. V. "Rick"
P.O. Box 2353
Orlando, FL 32802-2353
Tel: (407) 826 - 5050
Fax:(407) 826 - 4525
TF: (800) 366 - 3800

Serves As:
- Chairman and Chief Exec. Officer, Tupperware Corp.

GOLD, Clifford D.
636 Grand Ave.
Des Moines, IA 50309
goldcd@wellmark.com
Tel: (515) 245 - 4842
Fax:(515) 245 - 5090

Serves As:
- Group V. President, Marketing and External Relations, Wellmark, Inc.

GOLD, David
4000 E. Union Pacific Ave.
City of Commerce, CA 90023
Tel: (323) 980 - 8145
Fax:(323) 980 - 8160

Serves As:
- Chairman and Chief Exec. Officer, 99 Cents Only Stores

GOLD, Nick
P.O. Box 4569
Atlanta, GA 30302-4569
ngold@aglresources.com
Tel: (404) 584 - 3457
Fax:(404) 584 - 3479

Serves As:
- Director, Media Relations, AGL Resources, Inc.

GOLDBERG, Edward
151 West 34th St.
New York, NY 10001
Tel: (212) 494 - 5568

Serves As:
- V. President, Government Affairs, (Macy's East), Federated Department Stores, Inc.

GOLDBERG, Glenn S.
1221 Ave. of the Americas
49th Floor
New York, NY 10020-1095
glenn_goldberg@mcgraw-hill.com
Tel: (212) 512 - 3724
Fax:(212) 512 - 2048

Serves As:
- Senior V. President, Corporate Affairs and Assistant to the Chairman and Chief Exec. Officer, The McGraw-Hill Companies, Inc.

GOLDBERG, Joel
40 Landsdowne St.
Cambridge, MA 02139
Tel: (617) 679 - 7000
Fax:(617) 374 - 7788
TF: (800) 390 - 5663

Serves As:
- PAC Treasurer, Millennium Pharmaceuticals, Inc.

GOLDBERG, Steve
P.O. Box 391
Madison, WI 53701
steven.goldberg@cunamutual.com
Tel: (608) 231 - 7755
Fax:(608) 236 - 775
TF: (800) 356 - 2644

Serves As:
- Exec. Director, CUNA Mutual Foundation, CUNA Mutual Group

GOLDBERG, Steven J.
100 Campus Dr.
Florham Park, NJ 07932
goldbes@basf-corp.com
Tel: (973) 245 - 6057
Fax:(973) 245 - 6002

Registered Federal Lobbyist.
Serves As:
- V. President and Associate General Counsel, Regulatory Law and Government Affairs, BASF Corporation

GOLDEN, Frank
Metro Center
One Station Pl.
Stamford, CT 06902
frank.golden@thomson.com
Tel: (203) 539 - 8470
Fax:(203) 539 - 7709
TF: (800) 969 - 9974

Serves As:
- V. President, Investor Relations, The Thomson Corporation

GOLDEN, John E.
1500 MacCorkle Ave. SE
Charleston, WV 25314
john.e.golden@verizon.com
Tel: (304) 344 - 7223

Serves As:
- Manager, External Affairs, Verizon West Virginia Inc.

GOLDEN, Kenneth B.
One John Deere Pl.
Moline, IL 61265-8098
Tel: (309) 765 - 5678
Fax:(309) 765 - 5682

Serves As:
- Manager, Public Relations, Deere & Company

GOLDEN, Nan
6820 LBJ Fwy.
Dallas, TX 75240
nan.golden@brinker.com
Tel: (972) 770 - 9510

Serves As:
- Director, Public Affairs, Brinker Internat'l, Inc.

Responsibilities include government affairs.

GOLDFARB, Nancy L.
Lever House, 390 Park Ave.
New York, NY 10022-4698
nancy.goldfarb@unilever.com
Tel: (212) 888 - 1260
Fax:(212) 906 - 4666

Serves As:
- Director, Public Relations, Unilever United States, Inc.

GOLDING, Ben
1445 Ross at Field
Suite 1400
Dallas, TX 75202-2785
Tel: (214) 978 - 8260
Fax:(214) 978 - 8888

Serves As:
- Treasurer, Hunt Oil Co. Political Action Committee, Hunt Oil Co.

GOLDMAN, Andrew
Three Times Square
New York, NY 10036
Tel: (212) 231 - 5047
Fax:(646) 223 - 9054
TF: (800) 225 - 5008

Serves As:
- Exec. V. President, Global Marketing and Communications, Instinet Group Inc.

GOLDMAN, Cindy
P.O. Box 4030
M/S NH335
Golden, CO 80401-0030
Tel: (303) 277 - 3002
Fax:(303) 277 - 7373

Serves As:
- Director and Assistant General Counsel, Coors Brewing Co.

GOLDMAN, Kenneth A.
2207 Bridgepoint Pkwy.
San Mateo, CA 94404
kgoldman@siebel.com
Tel: (650) 295 - 5000
Fax:(650) 295 - 5111
TF: (800) 356 - 3321

Serves As:
- Senior V. President, Finance and Adminstration and Chief Financial Officer, Siebel Systems, Inc.

Responsibilities include investor relations.

GOLDMAN, Rachel
270 Park Ave.
34th Floor
New York, NY 10017-2070
rachel.goldman@jpmorganchase.com
Tel: (212) 270 - 9906
Fax:(212) 270 - 1648

Serves As:
- Senior V. President, Corporate Internal Communications, J. P. Morgan Chase & Co.

GOLDSHEIN, Steven M.
11 Harbor Park Dr.
Port Washington, NY 11050
Tel: (516) 608 - 7000
Fax:(516) 625 - 4072

Serves As:
- Investor Relations Contact, Systemax Inc.

GOLDSMITH, Bram
City National Center
400 N. Roxbury Dr.
Beverly Hills, CA 90210
TF: (800) 773 - 7100

Serves As:
- Chairman of the Board, City Nat'l Corp.

GOLDSMITH, Russell
City National Center
400 N. Roxbury Dr.
Beverly Hills, CA 90210
TF: (800) 773 - 7100

Serves As:
- President and Chief Exec. Officer, City Nat'l Corp.

GOLDSTEIN, I. Steven
730 Third Ave.
New York, NY 10017-3206
sgoldstein@tiaa-cref.org
Tel: (212) 490 - 9000
Fax:(212) 916 - 4840

Serves As:
- Exec. V. President, Public Affairs, TIAA/CREF

GOLDSTEIN, James
1350 I St. NW
Suite 400
Washington, DC 20005-3306
Tel: (202) 371 - 6900
Fax:(202) 842 - 3578

Registered Federal Lobbyist.
Serves As:
- Director, Government Acquisition Policy, Motorola, Inc.

GOLDSTEIN, Jim
2001 Edmund Halley Dr.
Reston, VA 20191
Tel: (703) 433 - 4000

Registered Federal Lobbyist.
Serves As:
- Representative, Sprint Nextel

GOLDSTEIN, L. Steven
730 Third Ave.
New York, NY 10017-3206
Tel: (212) 490 - 9000
Fax:(212) 916 - 5952

Serves As:
- Exec. V. President, Public Affairs, TIAA/CREF

GOLDSTEIN, Lewis
900 King St.
Rye Brook, NY 10573
Tel: (914) 612 - 4000
Fax:(914) 612 - 4100
TF: (800) 426 - 4891

Serves As:
- Corporate Communications Contact, Mott's Inc.

GOLDSTEIN, Richard A.
521 W. 57th St.
New York, NY 10019
Tel: (212) 765 - 5500
Fax:(212) 708 - 7132

Serves As:
- Chairman and Chief Exec. Officer, Internat'l Flavors and Fragrances

GOLDSTEIN, Stuart Z.
55 Water St.
49th Floor
New York, NY 10041-0099
sgoldstein@dtcc.com
Tel: (212) 855 - 5470
Fax:(212) 785 - 9681

Serves As:
- Managing Director, Corporate Communications, The Depository Trust & Clearing Corp.

GOLLEHER, Jan
P.O. Box 54143
Los Angeles, CA 90054
jgolleher@ralphs.com
Tel: (310) 884 - 6210
Fax:(310) 884 - 2569

Serves As:
- Director, Community Relations, Ralphs Grocery Co.

GOLUB, Harvey
One Campbell Pl.
Camden, NJ 08103-1701
harvey_golub@campbellsoup.com
Tel: (856) 342 - 4800
Fax:(856) 342 - 3878
TF: (800) 257 - 8443

Serves As:
- Chairman of the Board, Campbell Soup Co.

GOLUB, Lewis
P.O. Box 1074
Schenectady, NY 12301
Tel: (518) 355 - 5000
Fax:(518) 379 - 3515

Serves As:
- Chairman of the Board, Golub Corp.

GOLUB, Mona
P.O. Box 1074
Schenectady, NY 12301
Tel: (518) 355 - 5000
Fax:(518) 379 - 3515

Serves As:
- Director, Public Relations and Consumer Services, Golub Corp.

GOLUB, Neil M.
P.O. Box 1074
Schenectady, NY 12301
Tel: (518) 355 - 5000
Fax:(518) 379 - 3515

Serves As:
- President and Chief Exec. Officer, Golub Corp.

GOMEZ, Bert
1201 F St. NW
Suite 1000
Washington, DC 20004
Tel: (202) 626 - 7200
Fax:(202) 626 - 7208

Serves As:
- Manager, Federal Government Affairs, (R. J. Reynolds Tobacco Co.), Reynolds American Inc.

GOMEZ, Henry
2145 Hamilton Ave.
San Jose, CA 95125
Tel: (408) 558 - 7400
Fax:(408) 558 - 7401
TF: (800) 322 - 9266

Serves As:
- Senior V. President, Corporate Communications and Government Relations, eBay, Inc.

GONRING, Matthew P.
1201 S. Second St.
Milwaukee, WI 43204-2496
mpgonring@corp.rockwell.com
Tel: (414) 382 - 5575
Fax:(414) 382 - 4444

Serves As:
- V. President, Global Marketing and Communications, Rockwell Automation

GONZALES, David
700 Anderson Hill Rd.
Purchase, NY 10577-1444
david.gonzales@pepsi.com
Tel: (914) 253 - 2000
Fax:(914) 253 - 2070

Serves As:
- V. President, Community Affairs, PepsiCo, Inc.

GONZALES, Jacob
1717 Main St.
Dallas, TX 75201

Serves As:
- Treasurer, Power and Energy PAC of TXU Corp., TXU

GONZALEZ, Emilio
1300 I St. NW
Suite 400 West
Washington, DC 20005
Tel: (202) 515 - 2400

Serves As:
- Director, Public Policy and Strategic Outreach, Verizon Communications Inc.

GONZALEZ PALMER, Anna-Maria
P.O. Box 126
Hunt Valley, MD 21030-0126
Tel: (410) 628 - 8550
Fax:(410) 628 - 8661
TF: (800) 626 - 2616

Serves As:
- V. President, Human Resources, AAI Corp.

GONZALEZ-JOSEPH, Jessica
One Campbell Pl.
Camden, NJ 08103-1701
jessica_gonzalez@campbellsoup.com
Tel: (856) 342 - 3789
Fax:(856) 541 - 8185
TF: (800) 257 - 8443

Serves As:
- Manager, Community Relations, Campbell Soup Co.

GOOD, Ms. Kyle
557 Broadway
New York, NY 10012
Tel: (212) 343 - 6100
Fax:(212) 343 - 6736

Serves As:
- V. President, Corporate Communications and Media Relations, Scholastic, Inc.

GOODALE, Jennifer
120 Park Ave.
New York, NY 10017
Tel: (917) 663 - 2081
Fax:(917) 663 - 5396

Serves As:
- V. President, Corporate Contributions, Altria Group, Inc.

GOODE, David R.
Three Commercial Pl.
Norfolk, VA 23510-2191
Tel: (757) 629 - 2600
Fax:(757) 629 - 2822

Serves As:
- Chairman, President and Chief Exec. Officer, Norfolk Southern Corp.

GOODE, Kimberly Crews
P.O. Box 3599
Battle Creek, MI 49016-3599
Tel: (269) 961 - 2000
Fax:(269) 961 - 2871
TF: (800) 535 - 5644

Serves As:
- V. President, Worldwide Communications, Kellogg Co.

GOODELL, Jeffrey
1101 17th St. NW
Suite 602
Washington, DC 20036
Tel: (202) 467 - 8208
Fax:(202) 467 - 8204

Registered Federal Lobbyist.
Serves As:
- V. President, Government Affairs, Sabre Holdings Corp.

GOODMAN, Andy
One Computer Associates Plaza
Islandia, NY 11749
Tel: (631) 342 - 6000
Fax:(631) 342 - 4295
TF: (800) 225 - 5224

Serves As:
- Exec. V. President, Human Resources, Computer Associates Internat'l, Inc.

GOODMAN, Charles H.
270 Peachtree St. NW
Atlanta, GA 30303
Tel: (404) 257 - 6325
Fax:(404) 506 - 0662

Serves As:
- Senior V. President, Research and Environmental Affairs, Southern Company

GOODMAN, David
P.O. Box 844
Spring House, PA 19477-0844
AdvantaCommunications@advanta.com
Tel: (215) 444 - 5073
Fax:(215) 444 - 5075

Serves As:
- Director, Communications, Advanta Corp.

GOODMAN, Gayle A.
P.O. Box 199000
Dallas, TX 75219-9000
ggoodman@centex.com
Tel: (214) 981 - 6034
Fax:(214) 981 - 6859

Serves As:
- Public Relations Manager, Centex Corporation

GOODMAN, Milda C.
P.O. Box 9000
Newport Beach, CA 92658-9030
mgoodman@pacificlife.com
Tel: (949) 219 - 3469
Fax:(949) 219 - 7614
TF: (800) 800 - 7646

Serves As:
- Assistant V. President, Public Relations and Advertising, Pacific Life Insurance Co.

GOODMAN, Susan
P.O. Box 36611
HDQ-KA
Dallas, TX 75235-1611
Tel: (214) 792 - 7944
Fax:(214) 792 - 6703

Serves As:
- Director, Legislative Awareness Department, Southwest Airlines Co.

GOODNIGHT, Dr. James H.
SAS Campus Dr.
Cary, NC 27513-2414
jim.goodnight@sas.com
Tel: (919) 677 - 8000
Fax:(919) 677 - 4444

Serves As:
- Chairman and Chief Exec. Officer, SAS Institute, Inc.

GOODRICH, David R.
100 W. Walnut St.
Pasadena, CA 91124
Tel: (626) 440 - 2000
Fax:(626) 440 - 2630

Serves As:
- V. President, Human Resources, Parsons Corp.

GOODSTEIN, Richard
1101 Pennsylvania Ave. NW
Suite 510
Washington, DC 20004
goodstrf@airproducts.com
Tel: (202) 659 - 1324
Fax:(202) 659 - 1328

Serves As:
- Federal Relations Representative, Air Products and Chemicals, Inc.

GOODWIN, Jerry H.
1050 Connecticut Ave. NW
Suite 1200
Washington, DC 20036
Tel: (202) 857 - 2411
Fax:(202) 857 - 1737

Serves As:
- PAC Contact, Smithfield Foods, Inc.

GORDON, Howard R.
26950 Agoura Rd.
Calabasas Hills, CA 91301-5335
Tel: (818) 871 - 3000
Fax:(818) 871 - 3100

Serves As:
- Senior V. President, Public Relations and Marketing, Cheesecake Factory Inc.

GORDON, John E. "Ted"
Crystal Gateway 3, 1215 S. Clark St.
Suite 1510
Arlington, VA 22202
Tel: (703) 412 - 5961
Fax:(703) 412 - 5970

Registered Federal Lobbyist.
Serves As:
- V. President, Washington Operations, Alliant Techsystems

GORDON, Karen
40 Westminster St.
Providence, RI 02903-2525
kgordon@textron.com
Tel: (401) 457 - 2362
Fax:(401) 457 - 3598

Serves As:
- Manager, Corporate Communications and Media Relations, Textron Inc.

GORDON, Marsha L.
P.O. Box 256
Dublin, OH 43017
Tel: (614) 764 - 3109
Fax:(614) 764 - 3775

Serves As:
- Investor and Shareholder Relations Specialist, Wendy's Internat'l, Inc.

GORDON, Mary
101 Constitution Ave. NW
Suite 325 East
Washington, DC 20001
mgordon@nortel.com
Tel: (202) 312 - 8060

Registered Federal Lobbyist.
Serves As:
- V. President, Global Government Relations-Congressional Affairs, Nortel Networks

GORDON, Robert
One Computer Associates Plaza
Islandia, NY 11749
bobg@ca.com
Tel: (631) 342 - 2391
Fax:(631) 342 - 4295
TF: (800) 225 - 5224

Serves As:
- Business Unit V. President, Public Relations, Computer Associates Internat'l, Inc.

GORDON, Tina
One Johnson & Johnson Plaza
New Brunswick, NJ 08933-7204
tgordon@corus.jnj.com
Tel: (732) 524 - 3540
Fax:(732) 524 - 3564
TF: (800) 635 - 6789

Serves As:
- Exec. Director, Corporate Communications, Johnson & Johnson

GORDON, Vicki
Three Ravinia Dr., Suite 100
Atlanta, GA 30346
Tel: (770) 604 - 2284
Fax:(770) 604 - 8588

Serves As:
- Senior V. President, Corporate Affairs, InterContinental Hotels Group

GORE, Susan Szita
39 Old Ridgebury Rd.
Danbury, CT 06810-5113
susan_szita-gore@praxair.com
Tel: (203) 837 - 2311
Fax:(203) 837 - 2454
TF: (800) 772 - 9247

Serves As:
- Associate Director, Communications, Praxair, Inc.

GOREL, Michelle
2211 S. 47th St.
Phoenix, AZ 85034
michelle.gorel@avnet.com
Tel: (480) 794 - 6943

Serves As:
- Director, Communications, (Avnet Technology Solutions), Avnet Inc.

GORES, Tom T.
360 N. Crescent Dr., S. Bldg.
Beverly Hills, CA 90210
Tel: (310) 712 - 1850
Fax:(310) 712 - 1848

Serves As:
- Chairman and Chief Exec. Officer, Platinum Equity, LLC

GORGA, Joseph L.
804 Green Valley Rd.
Greensboro, NC 27408
Tel: (336) 379 - 2000
Fax:(336) 379 - 4504

Serves As:
- President and Chief Exec. Officer, Internat'l Textiles Group

GORKEN, Stephen S.
300 Park Ave.
New York, NY 10022
Tel: (212) 310 - 2000
Fax:(212) 310 - 2475

Serves As:
- V. President, Global Labor Relations, Colgate-Palmolive Co.

GORMAN, Leon A.
One Casco St.
Freeport, ME 04033
Tel: (207) 865 - 4761
Fax:(207) 552 - 6821
TF: (800) 221 - 4221

Serves As:
- Chairman of the Board, L. L. Bean, Inc.

GORMAN, Stephen E.
P.O. Box 660606
M/S 490
Dallas, TX 75266-0606
Tel: (972) 789 - 7000
Fax:(972) 789 - 7234

Serves As:
- President and Chief Exec. Officer, Greyhound Lines, Inc.

GORMLEY, Aidan
5960 Heisley Rd.
Mentor, OH 44060-1834
aidan_gormley@steris.com
Tel: (440) 392 - 7607
Fax:(440) 639 - 4450
TF: (800) 548 - 4873

Serves As:
- Senior Director, Corporate Communications and Investor Relations, STERIS Corp.

GORRIE, Ph.D., Thomas M.
One Johnson & Johnson Plaza
WT701
New Brunswick, NJ 08933-7204
Tel: (732) 524 - 6730
Fax:(732) 524 - 5310
TF: (800) 635 - 6789

Serves As:
- V. President, Government Affairs and Policy, Johnson & Johnson

GORSKI, Lori
81 Wyman St.
Waltham, MA 02454-9046
lori.gorski@thermo.com
Tel: (781) 622 - 1242
Fax:(781) 622 - 1207

Serves As:
- Manager, Public Relations, Thermo Electron Corp.

GOSDECK, Sharon
1818 Market St.
Philadelphia, PA 19103
Tel: (215) 299 - 8000
Fax:(215) 299 - 8033
TF: (800) 523 - 0786

Serves As:
- V. President, Corporate Communications, Day & Zimmerman

GOSIER, Ann M.
1310 G St. NW
Suite 770
Washington, DC 20005
Tel: (202) 508 - 0800
Fax:(202) 508 - 0818

Registered Federal Lobbyist.
Serves As:
- V. President, Government Affairs, Guidant Corp.

GOSLEE, Barbara
P.O. Box 587
Warsaw, IN 46581-0587
Tel: (574) 372 - 1514
Fax:(574) 267 - 8137

Serves As:
- Manager, Corporate Communications, Biomet Inc.

GOSPO, Nancy
3200 Highland Ave.
Downers Grove, IL 60515-1223
nancygospo@firsthealth.com
Tel: (630) 737 - 8557
Fax:(630) 737 - 7856
TF: (800) 445 - 1425

Serves As:
- Director, Advertising and Public Relations, First Health

GOTLIEB, Lawrence B.
10990 Wilshire Blvd.
Seventh Floor
Los Angeles, CA 90024
lgotlieb@kbhome.com
Tel: (310) 231 - 4000
Fax:(310) 231 - 4222
Serves As:
- V. President, Government and Public Affairs; and Associate Corporate Counsel, KB HOME

GOTTSCHALK, John
World-Herald Square
Omaha, NE 68102
Tel: (402) 444 - 1000
Fax:(402) 348 - 1828
Serves As:
- Chairman and Chief Exec. Officer, Omaha World-Herald Co.

GOTTSCHALK, Thomas A.
P.O. Box 300
Detroit, MI 48265-1000
Tel: (313) 556 - 5000
Fax:(248) 696 - 7300
Serves As:
- Exec. V. President, Law and Public Policy, General Motors Corp.

GOTTSPONER, Jr., Louis C.
P.O. Box 2020
Springdale, AR 72765-2020
louis.gottsponer@tyson.com
Tel: (479) 290 - 4826
Fax:(479) 290 - 4061
TF: (800) 643 - 3410
Serves As:
- Assistant Secretary and Director, Investor Relations, Tyson Foods, Inc.

GOTTUNG, lizanne C.
DWF Airport Station, P.O. Box 619100
Dallas, TX 75261-9100
Tel: (972) 281 - 1200
Fax:(972) 281 - 1490
TF: (800) 639 - 1352
Serves As:
- Senior V. President, Human Resources, Kimberly-Clark Corp.

GOTTWALD, Bruce C.
P.O. Box 2189
Richmond, VA 23218-2189
Tel: (804) 788 - 5000
Fax:(804) 788 - 5688
TF: (800) 535 - 3030
Serves As:
- Chairman of the Board, NewMarket Corp.

GOTTWALD, John D.
1100 Boulders Pkwy.
Richmond, VA 23225-4035
Tel: (804) 330 - 1000
Fax:(804) 330 - 1177
Serves As:
- Chairman of the Board, Tredegar Corp.

GOTTWALD, Thomas E.
P.O. Box 2189
Richmond, VA 23218-2189
Tel: (804) 788 - 5000
Fax:(804) 788 - 5688
TF: (800) 535 - 3030
Serves As:
- President and Chief Exec. Officer, NewMarket Corp.

GOTTWALD, M.D., William M.
330 S. Fourth St.
Richmond, VA 23219
bill_gottwald@albemarle.com
Tel: (804) 788 - 6000
Fax:(804) 788 - 6094
Serves As:
- Chairman of the Board, Albemarle Corp.

GOULD, Andrew
153 E. 53rd St., 57th Floor
New York, NY 10022-4624
Tel: (212) 350 - 9400
Fax:(212) 350 - 9564
Serves As:
- President and Chief Operating Officer; Chairman and Chief Exec. Officer, Schlumberger Limited

GOULD, Becca
1225 I St. NW
Suite 920
Washington, DC 20005
becca_gould@dell.com
Tel: (202) 408 - 3355
Fax:(202) 408 - 7664
Registered Federal Lobbyist.
Serves As:
- V. President, Government Relations; and PAC Treasurer, Dell Inc.

GOULD, Gerard J.
1000 Stanley Dr.
New Britain, CT 06053
ggould@stanleyworks.com
Tel: (860) 827 - 3833
Fax:(860) 827 - 3895
Serves As:
- V. President, Investor Relations, The Stanley Works

GOULD, Harriet E.
135 Morrissey Blvd.
Boston, MA 02107
hgould@globe.com
Tel: (617) 929 - 2000
Fax:(617) 929 - 3220
Serves As:
- V. President, Employee Relations, Globe Newspaper Co.

GOULD, Michael
1000 Third Ave.
New York, NY 10022
Tel: (212) 705 - 2000
Fax:(212) 705 - 2805
Serves As:
- Chairman and Chief Exec. Officer, Bloomingdale's

GOULD, Robert L.
750 E. Pratt St.
#200, Candler
Baltimore, MD 21202
rob.gould@constellation.com
Tel: (410) 230 - 9840
Fax:(410) 230 - 9849
TF: (888) 460 - 2002
Serves As:
- Managing Director, Corporate Communications, Constellation Energy

GOULD, S. Leland
23733 N. Scottsdale Rd.
Scottsdale, AZ 85255
Tel: (480) 585 - 8888
Fax:(480) 585 - 8893
TF: (800) 937 - 4937
Registered Federal Lobbyist.
Serves As:
- Exec. V. President, Governmental Affairs and Real Estate, (Giant Industries Arizona, Inc.), Giant Industries, Inc.

GOULDTHORPE, Jr., Hugh F.
P.O. Box 27626
Richmond, VA 23261-7626
Tel: (804) 747 - 9794
Fax:(804) 965 - 1907
Serves As:
- V. President, Quality and Communications, Owens & Minor, Inc.

Responsibilities include corporate philanthropy.

GOUSSETIS, Harry A.
200 Old Wilson Bridge Rd.
Columbus, OH 43085
Tel: (614) 438 - 3210
Fax:(614) 438 - 3136
Serves As:
- V. President, Human Resources, Worthington Industries

GOW, Roland
P.O. Box 45433
Salt Lake City, UT 84145-0433
roland.gow@questar.com
Tel: (801) 324 - 5594
Fax:(801) 324 - 5131
Serves As:
- Manager, Environmental Affairs, Questar Corporation

GRABIAK, Terri J.
1301 Pennsylvania Ave. NW
Suite 1030
Washington, DC 20004
Tel: (202) 824 - 0404
Fax:(202) 347 - 0132
Registered Federal Lobbyist.
Serves As:
- Representative, Allegheny Energy Inc.

GRABINSKI, Tim
666 Grand Ave.
P.O. Box 657
Des Moines, IA 50303-0657
tdgrabinski@midamerican.com
Tel: (515) 281 - 2343
Fax:(515) 242 - 4236
TF: (888) 427 - 5632
Serves As:
- Director, Communications Services, MidAmerican Energy Holdings Co.

GRABOW, Karen
P.O. Box 64101
St. Paul, MN 55164-0101
kmgrabow@landolakes.com
Tel: (651) 481 - 2222
Fax:(651) 481 - 2000
TF: (800) 328 - 4155
Serves As:
- V. President, Human Resources, Land O'Lakes, Inc.

GRACE, Karyn
15710 John F. Kennedy Blvd.
Houston, TX 77032
karyn.grace@total.com
Tel: (281) 227 - 5466
Fax:(281) 227 - 5455
Serves As:
- Manager, Public Affairs and Corporate Communications, Total Petrochemicals USA, Inc.

GRADDICK, Joan
I-20 at Alpine Rd.
AX-215
Columbia, SC 29219-0001
joan.graddick@bcbssc.com
Tel: (803) 264 - 3452
Fax:(803) 264 - 5520
TF: (800) 288 - 2227
Ext: 43452
Serves As:
- Senior Public Affairs Specialist, BlueCross BlueShield of South Carolina

GRADDICK-WEIR, Mirian M.
One AT&T Way
4353K2
Bedminster, NJ 07921-0752
mgraddick@att.com
Tel: (908) 234 - 3020
Serves As:
- Exec. V. President, Human Resources, AT&T

GRADLER, Geoffrey
555 12th St., NW
Suite 740 North
Washington, DC 20004
geof.gradler@schwab.com
Tel: (202) 638 - 3752

Registered Federal Lobbyist.
Serves As:
• Senior V. President and Head, Government Affairs, The Charles Schwab Corp.

GRAEFE, Fred
600 Cameron St.
Suite 402
Alexandria, VA 22314
Tel: (440) 329 - 6226

Registered Federal Lobbyist.
Serves As:
• Representative, Invacare Corp.

GRAF, Ronald P.
601 Pennsylvania Ave. NW
Suite 900, South Bldg.
Washington, DC 20004
rgraf@hersheys.com
Tel: (202) 434 - 8278
Fax:(202) 434 - 8258

Registered Federal Lobbyist.
Serves As:
• Senior Director, Government Relations, The Hershey Company

GRAF, Tom
711 High St.
Des Moines, IA 50392-0150
Tel: (515) 235 - 5491
Fax:(515) 246 - 5475
TF: (800) 986 - 3343

Serves As:
• Senior V. President, Investor Relations, The Principal Financial Group

GRAHAM, Alan
P.O. Box 799
Toledo, OH 43695
Tel: (419) 247 - 3731
Fax:(419) 247 - 3821

Serves As:
• V. President, Legal and Corporate Affairs, Pilkington North America

GRAHAM, Allister P.
7600 France Ave. South
Edina, MN 55435
Tel: (952) 832 - 0534
Fax:(952) 844 - 1234

Serves As:
• Chairman of the Board, Nash Finch Company

GRAHAM, David W.
2030 Dow Center
Midland, MI 48674-0001
dwgraham@dow.com
Tel: (989) 636 - 1000
Fax:(989) 636 - 0389

Serves As:
• Global V. President, Environment, Health and Safety, The Dow Chemical Company

GRAHAM, Donald E.
1150 15th St. NW
Washington, DC 20071
Tel: (202) 334 - 6000
Fax:(202) 334 - 4536

Serves As:
• Chairman and Chief Exec. Officer, The Washington Post Co.

GRAHAM, Edward J.
One S. Jersey Plaza
Folsom, NJ 08037
Tel: (609) 561 - 9000
Fax:(609) 561 - 8225

Serves As:
• Chief Exec. Officer, South Jersey Gas Co.

GRAHAM, Margaret
One Bausch & Lomb Pl.
Rochester, NY 14604-0054
mgraham@bausch.com
Tel: (585) 338 - 5469
Fax:(585) 338 - 8551
TF: (800) 344 - 8815

Serves As:
• Director, Corporate Communications, Bausch & Lomb

GRAHAM, Ron
1311 Granite Creek Dr.
Bluesprings, MO 64015
Tel: (816) 228 - 5741
Fax:(816) 224 - 0393

Serves As:
• Manager, Business Relations, (Novartis Pharmaceuticals Corp.), Novartis Corporation

GRAHAM, Rudolph H.
Three Concord Farms
575 Virginia Rd.
Concord, MA 01742
Tel: (978) 371 - 1000
Fax:(978) 371 - 3860

Serves As:
• Chairman of the Board, Welch's

GRAHAM, Suzanne
8005 SW Boeckman Rd.
Wilsonville, OR 97070-7777
suzanne_graham@mentor.com
Tel: (503) 685 - 7789
Fax:(503) 685 - 7704
TF: (800) 547 - 3000

Serves As:
• Media Contact, Mentor Graphics Corp.

GRAHAM-EASLER, Doretha
P.O. Box 98910
Las Vegas, NV 89151-0001
Tel: (702) 367 - 5741
Fax:(702) 579 - 0801
TF: (800) 331 - 3103

Serves As:
• Manager, Community Relations, Nevada Power Co.

GRAHAM-WEAVER, Judy
9955 Airtran Blvd.
Orlando, FL 32827-5330
judy.graham-weave@airtran.com
Tel: (407) 254 - 7448
Fax:(407) 251 - 5727

Serves As:
• Manager, Public Relations, AirTran Airways

GRANADO, Alejandro
P.O. Box 4689
Houston, TX 77210
Tel: (832) 486 - 4000
Fax:(832) 486 - 1814

Serves As:
• Chairman of the Board, CITGO Petroleum Corporation

GRANDJEAN, Sherry
1401 I St. NW
Suite 600
Washington, DC 20005
Tel: (202) 336 - 7400
Fax:(202) 336 - 7515

Registered Federal Lobbyist.
Serves As:
• Congressional Relations Representative, United Technologies Corp.

GRANDQUIST, Deborah
P.O. Box 186
Montpelier, VT 05601
Tel: (802) 223 - 6131
Fax:(802) 223 - 4229
TF: (800) 255 - 4550

Serves As:
• Chairman of the Board, Blue Cross and Blue Shield of Vermont

GRANT, Bruce
851 W. Cypress Creek Rd.
Fort Lauderdale, FL 33309
Tel: (954) 267 - 3000
Fax:(954) 267 - 9319
TF: (800) 424 - 8749

Serves As:
• V. President, Human Resources, Citrix Systems, Inc.

GRANT, Eric
1150 15th St. NW
Washington, DC 20071
Tel: (202) 334 - 6466
Fax:(202) 334 - 5609

Serves As:
• Director, Public Relations and Contributions, The Washington Post Co.

GRANT, Gary J.
7628 Thorndike Rd.
Greensboro, NC 27409-9421
Tel: (336) 664 - 1233
Fax:(336) 931 - 7454

Serves As:
• V. President, Quality, RF Micro Devices, Inc.

GRANT, Hugh
800 N. Lindbergh Blvd.
St. Louis, MO 63167
Tel: (314) 694 - 1000

Serves As:
• Chairman, President and Chief Exec. Officer, Monsanto Co.

GRANT, James
100 Throckmorton St.
Suite 1800
Fort Worth, TX 76102
james.grant@radioshack.com
Tel: (817) 415 - 7833
Fax:(817) 415 - 2335

Serves As:
• Senior Director, Investor Relations, Radio Shack Corporation

GRANT, Jeremy
11419 Sunset Hills Rd.
Reston, VA 20190-5207
Tel: (703) 251 - 8500
Fax:(703) 251 - 8240
TF: (888) 368 - 2152

Registered Federal Lobbyist.
Serves As:
• V. President, MAXIMUS, Inc.

GRANZOW, Paul H.
P.O. Box 1167
Dayton, OH 45401-1167
Tel: (937) 221 - 1000
Fax:(937) 221 - 1239
TF: (800) 755 - 6405

Serves As:
• Chairman of the Board, Standard Register Co.

GRAUER, Peter T.
499 Park Ave.
New York, NY 10022
Tel: (212) 318 - 2000
Fax:(917) 369 - 5000

Serves As:
- Chairman of the Board, Bloomberg L.P.

GRAUL, Faye
7105 Park Point Ct.
Fairfax Station, VA 22039
faye.graul@dowcorning.com
Tel: (703) 440 - 4071
Fax:(703) 440 - 4072

Registered Federal Lobbyist.
Serves As:
- V. President, Government Relations - U.S. Area, Dow Corning Corp.

GRAVEN, T. J.
850 Dixie Hwy.
Louisville, KY 40210
Tel: (502) 585 - 7442
Fax:(502) 774 - 6633

Serves As:
- Assistant V. President and Director, Investor Relations, Brown-Forman Corp.

GRAVES, Angelica
700 13th St., NW
Suite 950
Washington, DC 20005
Tel: (202) 654 - 4499
Fax:(202) 654 - 4493

Serves As:
- Director, Public and State Government Affairs, Marathon Oil Corp.

GRAVES, Chuck
P.O. Box 27626
Richmond, VA 23261-7626
Tel: (804) 488 - 8850
Fax:(804) 270 - 7281

Serves As:
- Shareholder Services, Owens & Minor, Inc.

GRAY, Carrie L. P.
One Dauch Dr.
Detroit, MI 48211
grayc@aam.com
Tel: (313) 758 - 4880
Fax:(313) 758 - 3929

Serves As:
- Director, Corporate Relations, American Axle and Manufacturing, Inc.

GRAY, Curt
1601 Research Blvd.
Rockville, MD 20850
Tel: (301) 838 - 6000
Fax:(301) 838 - 6925

Serves As:
- Senior V. President, Human Resources, BAE Systems North America

GRAY, Ellen
111 Center St.
Little Rock, AR 72201
Tel: (501) 377 - 2000
Fax:(501) 377 - 2666
TF: (800) 643 - 9691

Serves As:
- Senior V. President, Human Resources, Stephens Inc.

GRAY, Jeffrey
5673 Airport Rd.
Roanoke, VA 24012
Tel: (540) 362 - 4911

Serves As:
- Exec. V. President and Chief Financial Officer, Advance Auto Parts, Inc.

Responsibilities include investor relations.

GRAY, John
5995 Barfield Rd.
Atlanta, GA 30328
Tel: (404) 256 - 4900
Fax:(404) 256 - 7277

Serves As:
- Senior V. President, Corporate Communications and Public Relations, The RTM Restaurant Group

GRAY, Robert
145 Hunter Dr.
Wilmington, OH 45177
Tel: (937) 382 - 5591
Fax:(937) 382 - 0896

Serves As:
- PAC Contact, ABX Air, Inc.

GRAY, Steve
Avid Technology Park
One Park West
Tewksbury, MA 01876
Tel: (978) 640 - 6789
Fax:(978) 640 - 1366

Serves As:
- V. President, Corporate and Marketing Communications, Avid Technology, Inc.

GRAYSON, Jon
P.O. Box 550
Nashville, TN 37202
jon.grayson@hcahealthcare.com
Tel: (615) 344 - 2709
Fax:(615) 344 - 1128

Serves As:
- Director, Government Relations, HCA

GREAVES, Roger F.
21650 Oxnard St.
Woodland Hills, CA 91367
Tel: (818) 676 - 6000
Fax:(818) 676 - 8591
TF: (800) 291 - 6911

Serves As:
- Chairman of the Board, Health Net, Inc.

GREBE, Pat
P.O. Box 13979
Research Triangle Park, NC 27709-3979
pat.grebe@quintiles.com
Tel: (919) 998 - 2000
Fax:(919) 998 - 2046

Serves As:
- V. President, Corporate Communication, Quintiles Transnat'l Corp.

GRECO, Anthony D.
P.O. Box 355
Pittsburgh, PA 15230-0355
Tel: (412) 374 - 4111

Serves As:
- Senior V. President, Human Resources and Corporate Relations, Westinghouse Electric Company LLC

GRECZYN, Mary Anne
198 Van Buren St.
Suite 300
Herndon, VA 20170
Tel: (703) 834 - 3400
Fax:(703) 834 - 3340

Serves As:
- Manager, Communications, Airbus North America Holdings, Inc.

GRECZYN, Robert J.
P.O. Box 2291
Durham, NC 27702-2291
Tel: (919) 489 - 7431
Fax:(919) 765 - 4837

Serves As:
- President and Chief Exec. Officer, Blue Cross and Blue Shield of North Carolina

GREEHEY, William E.
P.O. Box 500
San Antonio, TX 78249-112
Tel: (210) 345 - 2000
Fax:(210) 345 - 2646
TF: (800) 531 - 7911

Serves As:
- Chairman and Chief Exec. Officer, Valero Energy Corp.

GREELEY, Marty
145 Pleasant Hill Rd.
Scarborough, ME 04074
Tel: (207) 883 - 2911
Fax:(207) 885 - 3165

Serves As:
- V. President, Government Relations, Hannaford Bros. Co.

GREEN, Carl J.
1900 K St. NW
Suite 800
Washington, DC 20006
carl.green@hal.hitachi.com
Tel: (202) 828 - 9272
Fax:(202) 828 - 9277

Serves As:
- Deputy Senior Representative, Hitachi America, Ltd.

GREEN, Cathy Obriotti
P.O. Box 240130
San Antonio, TX 78224-0130
Tel: (210) 475 - 8000
Fax:(210) 475 - 8060

Serves As:
- V. President, Community Relations, Zachry Construction Corporation

GREEN, Dana I.
200 Wilmot Rd.
Deerfield, IL 60015-4616
dana.green@walgreens.com
Tel: (847) 914 - 3010
Fax:(847) 914 - 3962

Serves As:
- General Counsel, Walgreen Co.

GREEN, James E.
501 Fifth St.
Bristol, TN 37620
Tel: (423) 989 - 8125
Fax:(423) 274 - 8677

Serves As:
- Exec. V. President, Corporate Affairs, King Pharmaceuticals, Inc.

GREEN, Lorraine A.
60 Massachusetts Ave. NE
Washington, DC 20002
Tel: (202) 906 - 3000
Fax:(202) 906 - 3865

Serves As:
- V. President, Human Resources, Amtrak

GREEN, Marc
300 Somerset Corporate Blvd.
Bridgewater, NJ 08807-2854
Tel: (212) 551 - 4000

Serves As:
- Media Relations Contact, Sanofi-Aventis Inc.

GREEN, Richard
P.O. Box 660606
M/S 490
Dallas, TX 75266-0606
Tel: (972) 789 - 7000
Fax:(972) 789 - 7234

Serves As:
- Assistant Treasurer, Greyhound Lines, Inc.

GREEN, Richard C.
P.O. Box 13287
Kansas City, MO 64199-3287
Tel: (816) 421 - 6600
Fax:(816) 467 - 3005

Serves As:
• Chairman, President and Chief Exec. Officer, Aquila, Inc.

GREEN, Ron
Two Democracy Center
6903 Rockledge Dr.
Bethesda, MD 20817-1818
Tel: (301) 564 - 3200
Fax:(301) 564 - 3201

Registered Federal Lobbyist.
Serves As:
• Representative, USEC Inc.

GREEN, William D. "Bill"
1345 Ave. of the Americas
New York, NY 10105
Tel: (917) 452 - 4400
Fax:(917) 527 - 9915

Serves As:
• Chief Exec. Officer, Accenture

GREENBERG, Glenn
175 Berkeley St.
Boston, MA 02116
glenn.greenberg@libertymutual.com
Tel: (617) 574 - 5874
Fax:(617) 350 - 7648

Serves As:
• Consultant, Public Relations, Liberty Mutual Insurance Co.

GREENBERG, Lon R.
P.O. Box 858
Valley Forge, PA 19482
greenbergl@ugicorp.com
Tel: (610) 337 - 1000
Fax:(610) 992 - 3254

Serves As:
• Chairman and Chief Exec. Officer, UGI Corp.

GREENBERG, Mark
P.O. Box 1615
Warren, NJ 07061-1615
mgreenberg@chubb.com
Tel: (908) 903 - 2682
Fax:(908) 903 - 3134

Serves As:
• Senior V. President, Corporate Communications, The Chubb Corp.

GREENBERG, Robert
228 Manhattan Beach Blvd.
Manhattan Beach, CA 90266
Tel: (310) 318 - 3100

Serves As:
• Chairman and Chief Exec. Officer, Skechers U.S.A., Inc.

GREENE, Margaret H.
BellSouth Center
675 W. Peachtree St. NE
Room 4516
Atlanta, GA 30375
margaret.greene@bellsouth.com
Tel: (404) 335 - 0851
Fax:(404) 524 - 1937

Serves As:
• President, Regulatory and External Affairs, BellSouth Corp.

GREENER, Charles V. "Chuck"
3900 Wisconsin Ave. NW
Washington, DC 20016
Tel: (202) 752 - 7000
Fax:(202) 752 - 6099

Serves As:
• Senior V. President, Communications, Fannie Mae

GREENFIELD, Dan
1000 Six PPG Pl.
Pittsburgh, PA 15222-5479
Tel: (412) 394 - 3004
Fax:(412) 394 - 3034

Serves As:
• Director, Investor Relations and Corporate Communications, Allegheny Technologies Incorporated

GREENFIELD, Daniel
1375 Peachtree St.
Atlanta, GA 30309
Tel: (404) 815 - 0770
Fax:(404) 815 - 8805

Serves As:
• V. President, Corporate Communications, Earthlink, Inc.

GREENWALD, Taylor
201 E. Fourth St.
Cincinnati, OH 45202
taylor.greenwald@convergys.com
Tel: (513) 723 - 3961
Fax:(513) 458 - 1315
TF: (800) 344 - 3000

Serves As:
• Director, Investor Relations, Convergys Corp.

GREENWAY, Mark
615 J.B. Hunt Corporate Dr.
P.O. Box 130
Lowell, AR 72745
Tel: (479) 820 - 8240
Fax:(479) 820 - 8397
TF: (800) 643 - 3622

Serves As:
• V. President, Human Resources, J. B. Hunt Transport Services, Inc.

GREENWOOD, Jim
P.O. Box 500
San Antonio, TX 78249-112
jim.greenwood@valero.com
Tel: (210) 345 - 2016
Fax:(210) 345 - 2646
TF: (800) 531 - 7911

Registered Federal Lobbyist.
Serves As:
• V. President, Government Affairs, Valero Energy Corp.

GREER, Carson
330 S. Fourth St.
Richmond, VA 23219
carson_greer@albemarle.com
Tel: (804) 788 - 6092
Fax:(804) 788 - 5688

Serves As:
• Manager, Corporate Communications, Albemarle Corp.

GREER, Curtis
300 U.S. Hwy. One
Newark, NJ 07114
Tel: (973) 424 - 5341
Fax:(973) 994 - 2286

Serves As:
• Region Director, Government Affairs, Anheuser-Busch Cos., Inc.

GREESON, Jennifer
1634 I St. NW
Suite 300
Washington, DC 20006-4021
Tel: (202) 628 - 3838
Fax:(202) 628 - 2525

Serves As:
• Representative, Intel Corp.

GREGG, Sarah M.
1501 K St. NW
Suite 375
Washington, DC 20005
greggs@baxter.com
Tel: (202) 508 - 8206
Fax:(202) 296 - 7177

Registered Federal Lobbyist.
Serves As:
• V. President, Federal Legislative Affairs and Payment Planning, (Baxter Healthcare Corp.), Baxter Internat'l Inc.

GREGG, Vicky B.
801 Pine St.
Chattanooga, TN 37402-2555
Tel: (423) 755 - 5600
TF: (800) 565 - 9140

Serves As:
• Chief Exec. Officer, Blue Cross and Blue Shield of Tennessee

GREGORY, Peter S.
Two Seaport Ln.
Suite 1300
Boston, MA 02210-2019
peter_gregory@cabot-corp.com
Tel: (617) 342 - 6105
Fax:(617) 342 - 6159

Serves As:
• Managing Director, Corporate Giving, Cabot Corp.

GREMER, John F.
104 Wilmot Rd.
mail stop 1444
Deerfield, IL 60015
Tel: (847) 315 - 2856
Fax:(847) 315 - 4417

Serves As:
• Foundation Contact, Walgreen Co.

GRETHER, C. Heidi
435 Mill St.
Williamston, MI 48895
Tel: (517) 371 - 4560
Fax:(517) 485 - 8856

Serves As:
• Director, Government Affairs, BP

GREV, Jason
7601 Penn Ave. South
Richfield, MN 55423
jason.grev@bestbuy.com
Tel: (612) 291 - 1000
Fax:(612) 292 - 4001

Serves As:
• Senior Government Relations Specialist, Best Buy Co., Inc.

GREY, Robin
1025 Eldorado Blvd.
Broomfield, CO 80021
Tel: (720) 888 - 2518
Fax:(720) 888 - 5085
TF: (877) 585 - 8266

Serves As:
• Senior V. President, Investor Relations, Level 3 Communications, Inc.

GRIEB, Patsy
P.O. Box 909700
Kansas City, MO 64190-9700
Tel: (816) 801 - 6488
Fax:(816) 801 - 6590

Serves As:
• Coordinator, Public and Media Relations, Dairy Farmers of America, Inc.

GRIEHS, Leonard F.
One Campbell Pl.
Camden, NJ 08103-1701
len_griehs@campbellsoup.com
Tel: (856) 342 - 6428
Fax:(856) 342 - 3878
TF: (800) 257 - 8443

Serves As:
• V. President, Investor Relations, Campbell Soup Co.

GRIER, Marjorie N.
P.O. Box 26532
Richmond, VA 23261
marjorie_grier@dom.com
Tel: (804) 819 - 2578
Fax:(804) 819 - 2217

Serves As:
• Director, Corporate Philanthropy, Dominion Resources, Inc.

GRIESER, Thomas
P.O. Box 14000
Juno Beach, FL 33408-0420
Tel: (561) 694 - 4000
Fax:(561) 694 - 4620

Serves As:
• PAC Treasurer, FPL Group, Inc.

GRIFFIN, Brian
1001 Pennsylvania Ave. NW
Suite 700 South
Washington, DC 20004
Tel: (202) 662 - 2650
Fax:(202) 662 - 2674

Serves As:
• Director, Government Relations, Honeywell Internat'l, Inc.

GRIFFIN, Janet
636 Grand Ave.
Des Moines, IA 50309
griffinj@wellmark.com
Tel: (515) 248 - 5388
Fax:(515) 245 - 5090

Serves As:
• V. President, Public Policy and Government Relations, Wellmark, Inc.

GRIFFIN, Leslie
1501 K St. NW
Suite 575
Washington, DC 20005
Tel: (202) 654 - 2940

Registered Federal Lobbyist.
Serves As:
• Representative, New York Life Insurance Co.

GRIFFIN, Mary
95 Columbia St.
Albany, NY 12210
griffinm@citi.com
Tel: (518) 432 - 1286

Serves As:
• V. President, New York Region - State and Local Government Relations, Citigroup, Inc.

GRIFFIN, Therese
1426 Main St.
Columbia, SC 29218
tgriffin@scana.com
Tel: (803) 217 - 7240

Serves As:
• Manager, Corporate Communications, (South Carolina Electric and Gas Co.), SCANA Corp.

GRIFFITH, III, G. Sanders
P.O. Box 120
Columbus, GA 31902-0120
Tel: (706) 649 - 2311
Fax:(706) 641 - 6555

Serves As:
• Senior Exec. V. President, General Counsel and Secretary, Synovus Financial Corp.

Responsibilities include governmental and regulatory affairs and strategic planning.

GRIFFITH, Greg
127 Public Square
1500 Key Tower
Cleveland, OH 44114-1221
Tel: (216) 263 - 7455
Fax:(216) 781 - 1502
TF: (800) 519 - 0083

Serves As:
• Director, Investor Relations, OM Group, Inc.

Responsibilities include corporate communications.

GRIFFITH, James M. "Jim"
1000 Beverly Way
Fort Smith, AR 72919-5273
Tel: (479) 201 - 5273
Fax:(479) 201 - 1101

Serves As:
• Senior V. President, Investor Relations and Corporate Communications, Beverly Enterprises, Inc.

GRIFFITH, James W.
1835 Dueber Ave. SW
GNE-17
Canton, OH 44706
james.griffith@timken.com
Tel: (330) 438 - 3000
Fax:(330) 471 - 4041
TF: (800) 223 - 1954

Serves As:
• President and Chief Exec. Officer, The Timken Co.

GRIFFITH, John J.
13220 California St.
Omaha, NE 68154
Tel: (402) 514 - 5445
Fax:(402) 514 - 5484
TF: (800) 228 - 5023

Serves As:
• Director, Human Resources, Commercial Federal Corp.

GRIFFITH, Julie
251 N. Illinois St., Suite 1600
Indianapolis, IN 46204
Tel: (317) 488 - 3507
Fax:(317) 588 - 3519

Serves As:
• General Manager, Government Affairs - Indiana, Cinergy Corp.

GRIFFITH, Ray A.
2200 Kensington Ct.
Oak Brook, IL 60523-2100
rgriff@acehardware.com
Tel: (630) 990 - 6635
Fax:(630) 571 - 0573

Serves As:
• President and Chief Exec. Officer, Ace Hardware Corp.

GRIFFITH, Susan Patricia
6300 Wilson Mills Rd.
Mayfield Village, OH 44143
Tel: (440) 461 - 5000
Fax:(440) 446 - 7168
TF: (800) 776 - 4737

Serves As:
• Chief Human Resources Officer, The Progressive Corporation

GRIFFITHS, Constance A.
20511 Lake Forest Dr.
Lake Forest, CA 92630-7741
constance.griffiths@wdc.com
Tel: (949) 672 - 7891
Fax:(949) 672 - 5408

Serves As:
• Senior Press Relations Specialist, Western Digital Corp.

GRIFFITHS, Jill
151 Farmington Ave.
Hartford, CT 06156
griffithsjb@aetna.com
Tel: (860) 273 - 8162
TF: (800) 872 - 3862

Serves As:
• V. President, Business Communications, (Aetna U.S. Healthcare, Inc.), Aetna Inc.

GRIFFITHS, William C.
2701 Cambridge Ct.
Suite 300
Auburn Hills, MI 48326
Tel: (248) 340 - 9090
Fax:(248) 340 - 9345

Serves As:
• President and Chief Exec. Officer, Champion Enterprises, Inc.

GRILL, Philip M.
1735 New York Ave., N.W.
Suite 500
Washington, DC 20006
pgrill@mindspring.com
Tel: (202) 662 - 8455
Fax:(202) 331 - 1024

Registered Federal Lobbyist.
Serves As:
• V. President, Government Relations, Matson Navigation Company, Inc.

GRIM, Diane E.
18 Loveton Circle
Sparks, MD 21152-6000
diane_grim@mccormick.com
Tel: (410) 771 - 7301
Fax:(410) 527 - 8289

Serves As:
• Treasurer, McCormick & Co., Inc. PAC, McCormick & Company, Inc.

GRIMESTAD, Dwight E.
P.O. Box 1470
Decatur, IL 62525
Tel: (217) 424 - 5200
Fax:(217) 424 - 5839

Serves As:
• V. President, Investor Relations, Archer Daniels Midland Co. (ADM)

GRIMM, Donna
World-Herald Square
Omaha, NE 68102
grimm@owh.com
Tel: (402) 444 - 1000
Fax:(402) 348 - 1828

Serves As:
• Administrator, Omaha World-Herald Foundation, Omaha World-Herald Co.

GRIMMETT, Gail
P.O. Box 20706
Atlanta, GA 30320-6001
Tel: (404) 715 - 2600
Fax:(404) 715 - 2731

Serves As:
• V. President, Revenue and Investor Relations, Delta Air Lines, Inc.

GRINDATTO, Jami
4100 Sara Rd. SE
Rio Rancho, NM 87124
Tel: (505) 893 - 3750
Fax:(505) 893 - 3116

Serves As:
• Manager, Public Affairs, Intel Corp.

GRINGERI, Darris
One HSN Dr.
St. Petersburg, FL 33729
gringerid@hsn.net
Tel: (727) 872 - 1000
Fax:(727) 872 - 7406

Serves As:
• Director, Public Relations, HSN, Inc.

GRINNEY, Jay
One Healthsouth Pkwy.
Birmingham, AL 35243
Tel: (205) 967 - 7116
Fax:(205) 969 - 6889
TF: (888) 476 - 8849

Serves As:
• Chief Exec. Officer and President, HealthSouth Corp.

GRINSTEIN, Gerald
P.O. Box 20706
Atlanta, GA 30320-6001
Tel: (404) 715 - 2600
Fax:(404) 715 - 2731

Serves As:
• Chief Exec. Officer, Delta Air Lines, Inc.

GRISCHOW, Patricia A.
1835 Dueber Ave. SW
GNE 01
Canton, OH 44706
pat.grischow@timken.com
Tel: (330) 471 - 4255
Fax:(330) 471 - 3541
TF: (800) 223 - 1954

Registered Federal Lobbyist.
Serves As:
• Senior Government Affairs Specialist, The Timken Co.

GRISHAM, Marlene
2791 Research Dr.
Rochester Hills, MI 48309-3575
Tel: (248) 299 - 7500
Fax:(248) 299 - 7501

Serves As:
• Marketing, Dura Automotive Systems, Inc.
Responsibilities include corporate communications.

GRISSO, Susan
50 Beale St.
San Francisco, CA 94105-1895
Tel: (415) 768 - 1234
Fax:(415) 768 - 9038

Serves As:
• Foundation Manager, Bechtel Group, Inc.

GRISSOM, Ron
One Energy Pl.
Pensacola, FL 32520
Tel: (850) 444 - 6111
Fax:(850) 444 - 6448
TF: (800) 225 - 5797

Serves As:
• PAC Treasurer, Gulf Power Co.

GRISWELL, J. Barry
711 High St.
Des Moines, IA 50392-0150
griswell.barry@principal.com
Tel: (515) 247 - 5111
Fax:(515) 246 - 5475
TF: (800) 986 - 3343

Serves As:
• Chairman, President and Chief Exec. Officer, The Principal Financial Group

GRIVNER, Carl J.
11111 Sunset Hills Dr.
Reston, VA 20190-5339
Tel: (703) 547 - 2000
Fax:(703) 547 - 2881

Serves As:
• Chief Exec. Officer, XO Communications, Inc.

GRIZZAFFI, Elizabeth M. "Betty"
120 Park Ave.
25th Floor
New York, NY 10017
Tel: (917) 663 - 3544
Fax:(917) 663 - 5739

Serves As:
• Supervisor, Internal Communications, (Altria Corporate Services, Inc.), Altria Group, Inc.

GRIZZLE, Sam
86 S. Cobb Dr.
Marietta, GA 30063-0226
Tel: (770) 494 - 3211
Fax:(770) 494 - 0146

Serves As:
• Director, Program Communications and Trade Relations, Lockheed Martin Aeronautics Co.

GROBAN, M.D., Mark D.
Four Taft Ct.
Rockville, MD 20850
Tel: (301) 762 - 8205
Fax:(301) 838 - 5682

Serves As:
• Chairman of the Board, Mid Atlantic Medical Services Inc.

GROEBE, Peggy
Fifth St. Towers, Suite 1360
150 S. Fifth St.
Minneapolis, MN 55402
groebe_peggy@mesaba.com
Tel: (612) 333 - 0021
Fax:(651) 367 - 5392

Serves As:
• Director, Human Resources, (Mesaba Airlines), MAIR Holdings, Inc.

GROFF, Keralyn
1200 Willow Lake Blvd.
P.O. Box 64683
St. Paul, MN 55164-0683
Keralyn.Groff@hbfuller.com
Tel: (651) 236 - 5104
Fax:(651) 236 - 5056
TF: (800) 214 - 2523

Serves As:
• Director, Public Relations, H. B. Fuller Co.

GROGAN, John D.
P.O. Box 2641
Birmingham, AL 35291
Tel: (205) 257 - 1000
Fax:(205) 257 - 1860

Serves As:
• Manager, Environmental Compliance, Alabama Power Co.

GRONBACH, Tyler
1801 California St.
50th Floor
Denver, CO 80202
tyler.gronbach@qwest.com
Tel: (303) 992 - 2155
Fax:(303) 896 - 3489
TF: (800) 899 - 7780

Serves As:
• V. President, Corporate Communications, Qwest Communications

GROSS, Connie
P.O. Box 6675
Radnor, PA 19087-8675
connie.gross@airgas.com
Tel: (610) 902 - 6240
Fax:(610) 687 - 1058
TF: (800) 255 - 2165

Serves As:
• Administrator, McCausland Foundation, Airgas, Inc.

GROSSMAN, Marc A.
9336 Civic Center Dr.
Beverly Hills, CA 90210
marc_grossman@hilton.com
Tel: (310) 205 - 4030
Fax:(310) 205 - 7686

Serves As:
• Senior V. President, Corporate Affairs, Hilton Hotels Corp.
Responsibilities include investor relations.

GROSSMAN, Steven D.
340 Kingsland St.
Nutley, NJ 07110-1199
Tel: (973) 235 - 5000
Fax:(973) 235 - 7605

Serves As:
• V. President, Human Resources, Hoffmann-La Roche Inc. (Roche)

GROSVENOR, Gilbert
P.O. Box 98199
Washington, DC 20090-8199
Tel: (202) 857 - 7000
Fax:(202) 828 - 6679
TF: (800) 647 - 5463

Serves As:
• Chairman, Board of Trustees, Nat'l Geographic Soc.

GROTHAUS, Chuck
P.O. Box 1101
Minneapolis, MN 55440-1101
chuck.grothaus@adc.com
Tel: (952) 917 - 0306
Fax:(952) 917 - 0647

Serves As:
• Director, Corporate Public Relations, ADC

GROTHUES, Arnold
100 Throckmorton St.
Suite 1800
Fort Worth, TX 76102
arnold.grothues@radioshack.com
Tel: (817) 415 - 3011
Fax:(817) 415 - 2335

Serves As:
• V. President, Industry and Government Affairs, Radio Shack Corporation

GROVER, Jay
4560 Horton St.
Emeryville, CA 94608-2916
Tel: (510) 655 - 8730
Fax:(510) 655 - 9910

Serves As:
• Director, Government and Community Relations, Chiron Corp.
Responsibilities include corporate philanthropy.

GROVES, Tim
100 Dunbar St.
Spartanburg, SC 29306
Tel: (864) 573 - 1600
Fax:(864) 573 - 1695

Serves As:
• Media Relations, Extended Stay America, Inc.

GROWCOCK, Terry D.
P.O. Box 66
Manitowoc, WI 54221-0066
Tel: (920) 684 - 4410
Fax:(920) 652 - 9778

Serves As:
• Chairman and Chief Exec. Officer, The Manitowoc Co., Inc.

GRUBBS, Robert W.
2301 Patriot Blvd.
Glenview, IL 60025-8020
Tel: (224) 521 - 8000

Serves As:
• President and Chief Exec. Officer, Anixter Internat'l, Inc.

GRUBBS, Wendy
1101 Pennsylvania Ave. NW
Suite 1000
Washington, DC 20004
Tel: (202) 879 - 6871
Fax:(202) 783 - 4460

Registered Federal Lobbyist.
Serves As:
• V. President, Federal Government Affairs, Global Consumer Investment Bank, Citigroup, Inc.

GRUBER, Andrea
P.O. Box 20850
Fountain Valley, CA 92728-0850
Tel: (714) 965 - 3000
Fax:(714) 965 - 3837

Serves As:
- Contact, Hyundai Motor America Corporate Contributions Program, Hyundai Motor America

GRUENDL, Ron
One Mellon Center
500 Grant St.
Room 1840
Pittsburgh, PA 15258-0001
gruendl.rr@mellon.com
Tel: (412) 234 - 7157
Fax:(412) 236 - 1662

Serves As:
- Manager, Media Relations, Mellon Financial Corp.

GRUMBACHER, Tim
P.O. Box 2821
York, PA 17405-2821
Tel: (717) 757 - 7660
Fax:(717) 751 - 3196

Serves As:
- Chairman of the Board, The Bon Ton Stores, Inc.

GRUPP, Robert W.
41 Moores Rd.
Frazer, PA 19355
rgrupp@cephalon.com
Tel: (610) 738 - 6402
Fax:(610) 344 - 0981

Serves As:
- V. President, Public Affairs; PAC Treasurer, Cephalon, Inc.

GUARDINO, Leslee
847 Gibraltar Dr.
Bldg. 5
Milpitas, CA 95035
lesleecoleman@ca.slr.com
Tel: (408) 586 - 4232
Fax:(408) 956 - 7699

Registered Federal Lobbyist.
Serves As:
- Senior Director, Government and Community Relations, Solectron Corp.

GUARDUCCI, Mara
555 13th St. NW
Suite 600 West
Washington, DC 20004
Tel: (202) 585 - 9610

Registered Federal Lobbyist.
Serves As:
- Director, Government Affairs, Amgen Inc.

GUARISCO, Annette J.
1660 L St. NW
Fourth Floor
Washington, DC 20036
Tel: (202) 775 - 5080
Fax:(202) 775 - 5045

Registered Federal Lobbyist.
Serves As:
- Deputy Director, Washington Office, General Motors Corp.

GUCK, Susan
Dain Rauscher Plaza
60 S. Sixth St., 19th Floor
Minneapolis, MN 55402-4422
susan.guck@rbcdain.com
Tel: (612) 371 - 7750
Fax:(612) 371 - 2960

Serves As:
- Director, Corporate Communications, RBC Dain Rauscher Corp.

GUDBRANSON, Robert K.
One Invacare Way
Elyria, OH 44035
Tel: (440) 329 - 6001
Fax:(440) 366 - 9008
TF: (800) 333 - 6900

Serves As:
- Director, Investor Relations, Invacare Corp.

GUENIN, Steve
12 E. Armour Blvd.
Kansas City, MO 64111
Tel: (816) 502 - 4000
Fax:(816) 502 - 4155

Serves As:
- Director, Environmental Affairs, Interstate Bakeries Corp.

GUENTHER, Bob
100 Campus Dr.
Florham Park, NJ 07932
guenthr@basf-corp.com
Tel: (973) 245 - 6013
Fax:(973) 245 - 6715

Serves As:
- Media Relations Contact, BASF Corporation

GUENTHER, Cynthia S.
150 N. Orange Grove Blvd.
Pasadena, CA 91103
Tel: (626) 304 - 2204
Fax:(626) 792 - 7312

Serves As:
- Investor Relations Contact, Avery Dennison Corp.

GUERRIERO, Chuck
555 12th St. NW
Suite 650
Washington, DC 20004-1205
Tel: (202) 393 - 7950
Fax:(202) 393 - 7960

Serves As:
- Manager, Advocacy Relations, Eli Lilly and Company

GUERTIN, Shawn M.
6705 Rockledge Dr.
Suite 100
Bethesda, MD 20817
Tel: (301) 581 - 5701
Fax:(301) 493 - 0705

Serves As:
- Exec. V. President and Chief Financial Officer, Coventry Health Care
Responsibilities include investor relations.

GUIDA, Arthur S.
80 Park Plaza
M/S T10C
Newark, NJ 07102-0570
arthur.guida@pseg.com
Tel: (973) 430 - 7135
Fax:(973) 622 - 4261

Serves As:
- Director, Regional Public Affairs PSE&G, PSE&G

GUIDERA, Bill
1401 I St., NW
Suite 500
Washington, DC 20005
Tel: (202) 263 - 5900
Fax:(202) 263 - 5902

Registered Federal Lobbyist.
Serves As:
- Federal Government Affairs Manager, Microsoft Corporation

GUIDRY, Jr., George H.
One American Pl.
Suite 1840
Baton Rouge, LA 70825-2400
Tel: (225) 388 - 9061
Ext: 101
Fax:(225) 383 - 6218

Serves As:
- Regional Manager, Government Affairs, Georgia-Pacific Corp.

GUIDRY, Jerene B.
P.O. Box 51777
New Orleans, LA 70151
Tel: (504) 582 - 4000
Fax:(504) 582 - 1847
TF: (800) 535 - 7094

Serves As:
- Assistant PAC Treasurer; and Projects Coordinator, Communications, Freeport-McMoRan Copper and Gold Inc.

GUILES, Edwin A.
P.O. Box 513249
Los Angeles, CA 90051-1249
Tel: (213) 244 - 1200
Fax:(213) 244 - 8292

Serves As:
- Chairman and Chief Exec. Officer, Southern California Gas Co.

GUILLET, Edward E.
Prudential Tower Bldg.
Boston, MA 02199-8004
ed_guillet@gillette.com
Tel: (617) 421 - 7000
Fax:(617) 421 - 7123

Serves As:
- Senior V. President, Human Resources, The Gillette Company

GUINN, Joe
6200 Northwest Pkwy.
San Antonio, TX 78249
joe.guinn@phs.com
Tel: (210) 478 - 4500
Fax:(210) 478 - 4504

Registered Federal Lobbyist.
Serves As:
- V. President, Public Affairs, PacifiCare Health Systems, Inc.

GUINN, Vicki E.
500 N.E. Multnomah St.
Suite 100
Portland, OR 97232-2099
Tel: (503) 813 - 4823
Fax:(503) 813 - 4576

Serves As:
- Communications and External Affairs, Kaiser Permanente

GUINNESSEY, Kathleen M.
103 JFK Pkwy.
Short Hills, NJ 07078
guinnesseyk@dnb.com
Tel: (973) 921 - 5665

Serves As:
- Vice President, Treasury and Investor Relations, The Dun & Bradstreet Corp.

GULIASI, Les
77 Beale St.
MC B10C
San Francisco, CA 94105
Tel: (415) 973 - 7000

Serves As:
- Director, State Agency Relations, (Pacific Gas and Electric Co.), PG & E Corp.

GULIS, Jr., Stephen L.
9341 Courtland Dr. NE
Rockford, MI 49351
Tel: (616) 866 - 5570
Fax:(616) 866 - 0257

Serves As:
- Exec. V. President and Chief Financial Officer, Wolverine World Wide, Inc.

Responsibilities include investor relations.

GULLETT, Natasha
Three Ravinia Dr., Suite 100
Atlanta, GA 30346
natasha.gullett@ichotelsgroup.com
Tel: (770) 604 - 5597
Fax:(770) 604 - 2059

Serves As:
- Senior Manager, Public Relations, InterContinental Hotels Group

GULMERT, Gustav
1000 Wilson Blvd., Suite 2300
Arlington, VA 22209
gus.gulmert@nge.com
Tel: (703) 875 - 8450
Fax:(703) 243 - 3190

Serves As:
- Manager, Corporate Public Affairs and International Communications, Northrop Grumman Corp.

GUMM, Arlene
5757 N. Green Bay Ave.
Milwaukee, WI 53201-0591
arlene.gumm@jci.com
Tel: (414) 524 - 2363
Fax:(414) 524 - 0118

Serves As:
- Corporate Administrator, Shareholder Relations, Johnson Controls, Inc.

GUNN, David L.
60 Massachusetts Ave. NE
Washington, DC 20002
Tel: (202) 906 - 3960
Fax:(202) 906 - 3865

Serves As:
- President and Chief Exec. Officer, Amtrak

GUNN, Sherrian
1730 Briercroft Ct.
Carrollton, TX 75006
sgunn@cellstar.com
Tel: (972) 466 - 5031
Fax:(972) 466 - 0288
TF: (800) 723 - 9040

Serves As:
- Director, Investor Relations and Corporate Communications, CellStar Corp.

GUPTA, Raj L.
100 Independence Mall West
Philadelphia, PA 19106-2399
Tel: (215) 592 - 3000
Fax:(215) 592 - 3377

Serves As:
- Chairman, Chief Exec. Officer, and President, Rohm and Haas Co.

GUTHRIE, Drew
One Chase Manhattan Plaza
41st Floor
New York, NY 10005
drew.guthrie@assurant.com
Tel: (212) 859 - 7002
Fax:(212) 859 - 7010

Serves As:
- Manager, Communications and Media Relations, Assurant

GUTHRIE, Paul S.
One Reynolds Way
Kettering, OH 45430
paul_guthrie@reyrey.com
Tel: (937) 485 - 8104
Fax:(937) 485 - 8980

Serves As:
- V. President, Corporate Communications, Reynolds and Reynolds Co.

GUTIERREZ, Hugo
5555 San Felipe Rd.
Houston, TX 77056
Tel: (713) 629 - 6600
Fax:(713) 296 - 2952

Serves As:
- Manager, State Government Affairs, Marathon Oil Corp.

GUTMAN, Harvey M.
200 Milik St.
Carteret, NJ 07008-1194
Tel: (732) 499 - 4327
Fax:(732) 499 - 3100

Serves As:
- Senior V. President, Retail Development, Pathmark Stores Inc.

Responsibilities include investor relations.

GUTTAS, Mike
P.O. Box 6014
Cypress, CA 90630-0014
Tel: (714) 372 - 6000
Fax:(714) 373 - 1020

Serves As:
- V. President, Human Resources, (MMNA Manufacturing), Mitsubishi Motors North America, Inc.

GUYETTE, James M.
14850 Conference Center Dr.
Chantilly, VA 20151
Tel: (703) 834 - 1700
Fax:(703) 709 - 6086

Serves As:
- President and Chief Exec. Officer, Rolls-Royce North America Inc.

GUYTON, Louise G.
P.O. Box 75000
mc 3352
Detroit, MI 48275
Tel: (313) 222 - 8620
Fax:(313) 222 - 8720
TF: (800) 521 - 1190

Serves As:
- V. President, Public Affairs, Comerica Incorporated

GYMBURCH, David
163-181 Kenwood Ave.
Oneida, NY 13421
Tel: (315) 361 - 3000
Fax:(315) 361 - 3655

Serves As:
- Manager, Public Relations, Oneida Ltd.

HA, Dr. Joseph M.
One Bowerman Dr.
Beaverton, OR 97005
Tel: (503) 671 - 6453
Fax:(503) 671 - 6300

Serves As:
- V. President, International Business and Government Relations, Nike, Inc.

HAAG, Dan
P.O. Box 710
Minneapolis, MN 54400-0710
Tel: (763) 522 - 2100
Fax:(763) 287 - 5430

Serves As:
- V. President, Human Resources, M. A. Mortenson Company

HAAG, Natalie
One Security Benefit Pl.
Topeka, KS 66636-0001
Tel: (785) 438 - 3000
TF: (800) 888 - 2461

Serves As:
- PAC Contact, Security Benefit Life Insurance Co.

HAAK, Arnie
9955 Airtran Blvd.
Orlando, FL 32827-5330
Tel: (407) 251 - 3618
Fax:(407) 251 - 5727

Serves As:
- Director, Financial Analysis, AirTran Airways

Responsibilities include investor relations.

HAARER, Mark
101 Ash St.
hq08d
San Diego, CA 92101-3017
mhaarer@sempra.com
Tel: (619) 696 - 2035
Fax:(619) 696 - 4379
TF: (877) 736 - 7721

Serves As:
- Manager, Governent Affairs, Sempra Energy

HAAS, Lawrence J.
Two Lafayette Center
1133 21st St., NW, Suite 300
Washington, DC 20036
Tel: (202) 467 - 6600
Fax:(202) 467 - 5187

Serves As:
- Director, Public Affairs, (Manning Selvage & Lee), Leo Burnett Worldwide

HAAS, Robert D.
1155 Battery St.
San Francisco, CA 94111
Tel: (415) 501 - 6000
Fax:(415) 501 - 7112
TF: (800) 872 - 5384

Serves As:
- Chairman of the Board, Levi Strauss and Co.

HAAS, Rosemary T.
1399 New York Ave. NW
Suite 200
Washington, DC 20005
Tel: (202) 378 - 2020
Fax:(202) 783 - 6631

Registered Federal Lobbyist.
Serves As:
- Senior Director, Federal Government Affairs, Abbott Laboratories

HAASE, Bonnie K.
440 Lincoln St.
Worcester, MA 01653
Tel: (508) 855 - 1000

Serves As:
- V. President an Chief Human Resources Officer, Allmerica Property & Casualty Companies, Inc.

HABER, Louis
1221 Ave. of the Americas
47th Floor
New York, NY 10020-1095
louis_haber@mcgraw-hill.com
Tel: (212) 512 - 3203
Fax:(212) 512 - 2703

Serves As:
- Director, Issues Management, The McGraw-Hill Companies, Inc.

HABIG, Douglas
1600 Royal St.
Jasper, IN 47549-1001
Tel: (812) 482 - 1600
Fax:(812) 482 - 8300
TF: (800) 482 - 1616

Serves As:
- Chairman of the Board, Kimball International, Inc.

Responsibilities include corporate philanthropy.

HACHIGIAN, Kirk S.
P.O. Box 4446 Tel: (713) 209 - 8400
Houston, TX 77210-4446 Fax:(713) 209 - 8995

Serves As:
- President and Chief Exec. Officer, Cooper Industries

HACK, Bruce
6060 Center Dr., Fifth Floor Tel: (310) 431 - 4000
Los Angeles, CA 90045 Fax:(310) 342 - 0533

Serves As:
- Chief Exec. Officer, Vivendi Universal Games

HACKETT, James P.
P.O. Box 1967 Tel: (616) 247 - 2710
Grand Rapids, MI 49501-1967 Fax:(616) 473 - 2200

Serves As:
- President, Chief Exec. Officer and Director, Steelcase Inc.

HACKETT, James T.
1201 Lake Robbins Dr. Tel: (832) 636 - 1000
The Woodlands, TX 77380

Serves As:
- President and Chief Exec. Officer, Anadarko Petroleum Corp.

HACKMAN, Timothy B.
1301 K St. NW Tel: (202) 515 - 5115
Suite 1200 Fax:(202) 515 - 4943
Washington, DC 20005
thackman@us.ibm.com

Registered Federal Lobbyist.
Serves As:
- Director, Public Affairs, Science and Technology, Internat'l Business Machines Corp. (IBM)

HACKNEY, Catherine
1201 K St., Suite 1810 Tel: (916) 441 - 3966
Sacramento, CA 95814 Fax:(916) 441 - 4047
hacknece@sce.com

Serves As:
- Manager, Public Affairs - Sacramento, Southern California Edison, an Edison Internat'l Co.

HACKNEY, Ronald D.
150 N. Michigan Ave. Tel: (312) 346 - 6600
Suite 1700 Fax:(312) 580 - 4919
Chicago, IL 60601-7568

Serves As:
- Senior V. President, Human Resources, Smurfit-Stone Container

HACKWORTH, Michael L.
2901 Via Fortuna Tel: (512) 851 - 4000
Austin, TX 78746 TF: (800) 888 - 5016

Serves As:
- Chairman of the Board, Cirrus Logic, Inc.

HADDEN, Jacalyn Hart
124 W. Allegan St. Tel: (517) 702 - 2820
Suite 1900
Lansing, MI 48933
jhhadden@cmsenergy.com

Serves As:
- Director, State Governmental Affairs, (Consumers Energy Co.), CMS Energy Corp.

HADDEN, Laura L.
100 Independence Mall West Tel: (215) 592 - 3054
Philadelphia, PA 19106-2399 Fax:(215) 592 - 6808

Serves As:
- Manager, Marketing Communications, Rohm and Haas Co.

HADDOCK, Robert M.
2390 E. Camelback Rd. Tel: (602) 381 - 4100
Suite 400 Fax:(602) 381 - 4107
Phoenix, AZ 85016-3452

Serves As:
- Chairman and Chief Exec. Officer, Aztar Corp.

HADDOCK, Ron
5400 Legacy Dr., Cluster II, Bldg. 3 Tel: (972) 265 - 2000
Plano, TX 75024 TF: (800) 669 - 5740

Serves As:
- Chairman of the Board, Safety-Kleen Systems, Inc.

HADDRILL, Richard
6601 Bermuda Rd. Tel: (702) 270 - 7600
Las Vegas, NV 89119-3605 Fax:(702) 270 - 7699

Serves As:
- President and Chief Exec. Officer, Alliance Gaming Corp.

HADEED, Rebecca
601 Poydras St. Tel: (504) 568 - 1010
Suite 1900 Fax:(504) 566 - 4580
New Orleans, LA 70130
rhadeed@tdw.com

Serves As:
- Manager, Public Affairs and Corporate Communications, Tidewater Inc.

HADENFELDT, Jerry L.
1716 Locust St. Tel: (515) 284 - 2780
Des Moines, IA 50309-3023 Fax:(515) 284 - 2511

Registered Federal Lobbyist.
Serves As:
- Director, Government Relations, Meredith Corp.

HADFIELD, Judi A.
One Marriott Dr. Tel: (301) 380 - 7430
Washington, DC 20058 Fax:(301) 380 - 2843
judi.hadfield@marriott.com

Serves As:
- V. President, Community Relations and Corporate Projects, Marriott Internat'l, Inc.

HADLEY, Debra
7000 Cardinal Pl. Tel: (614) 757 - 7481
Dublin, OH 43017 Fax:(614) 757 - 8450
debra.hadley@cardinal.com TF: (800) 234 - 8701

Serves As:
- Exec. Director, Cardinal Health Foundation, Cardinal Health Inc.

HADULCO, Ray
170 W. Tasman Dr. Tel: (408) 853 - 6054
San Jose, CA 95134-1706 Fax:(408) 526 - 4100
rayh@cisco.com TF: (800) 553 - 6387

Serves As:
- Media Contact, Public Affairs, Cisco Systems, Inc.

HAEFNER, Michael
3150 Sabre Dr. Tel: (682) 605 - 7031
Southlake, TX 76092 Fax:(682) 264 - 7029

Serves As:
- Senior V. President, Human Resources, Sabre Holdings Corp.

HAEG, Lawrence P.
420 Montgomery St. Tel: (415) 396 - 3070
M/S A0163-029 TF: (800) 411 - 4932
San Francisco, CA 94104

Serves As:
- Exec. V. President and Director, Corporate Communications, Wells Fargo & Co.

HAGAN, Daniel B.
P.O. Box 619616 Tel: (817) 967 - 2340
MD 5575 Fax:(817) 967 - 1477
Dallas-Fort Worth Airport, TX 75261
dan.hagan@aa.com

Serves As:
- Managing Director, Corporate Affairs, AMR Corp.

HAGAR, Rick
15710 John F. Kennedy Blvd. Tel: (281) 227 - 5432
Houston, TX 77032 Fax:(281) 227 - 5466
rick.hagar@total.com

Serves As:
- Public Affairs Advisor, Total Petrochemicals USA, Inc.

HAGEDORN, Jim
14111 Scottslawn Rd. Tel: (937) 644 - 0011
Marysville, OH 43041 Fax:(937) 644 - 7184
jim.hagedorn@scottsco.com TF: (800) 543 - 8873

Serves As:
- Chairman, President and Chief Exec. Officer, The Scotts Company

HAGELIN, David
One Riverside Plaza Tel: (614) 223 - 1938
Columbus, OH 43215-2373 Fax:(614) 223 - 1823

Serves As:
- Corporate Media Relations, American Electric Power Co. Inc.

HAGEN, Sue
One Dole Dr. Tel: (818) 879 - 6600
Westlake Village, CA 91362-7300 Fax:(818) 879 - 6890

Serves As:
- V. President, Human Resources, Dole Food Company, Inc.

HAGER, Jr., George V.
101 E. State St. Tel: (610) 444 - 6350
Kennett Square, PA 19348 Fax:(610) 925 - 4000
info@genesishcc.com

Serves As:
- Chairman and Chief Exec. Officer, Genesis HealthCare Corp.

HAGER, Janice
P.O. Box 1244 Tel: (704) 382 - 6963
EC12H Fax:(704) 382 - 3588
Charlotte, NC 28201-1244
jdhager@duke-energy.com

Serves As:
- V. President, Rates and Regulatory Affairs, Duke Energy Corp.

HAGGE, Stephen
475 W. Terra Cotta Ave. Tel: (815) 477 - 0424
Suite E Fax:(815) 477 - 0481
Crystal Lake, IL 60014-9695

Serves As:
- Chief Financial Officer, AptarGroup, Inc.

Responsibilities include investor relations.

HAGGERTY, Terry
P.O. Box 27131 Tel: (919) 716 - 7459
Raleigh, NC 27611 Fax:(919) 716 - 7074

Serves As:
- Manager, Internal Communications, First Citizens BancShares

HAGMEIER, Katherine L.
3M Center Tel: (651) 575 - 4368
Bldg. 225-1S-15 Fax:(651) 737 - 2901
St. Paul, MN 55144-1000

Registered Federal Lobbyist.
Serves As:
- Media Representative, 3M Company

HAHN, Richard L.
P.O. Box 70 Tel: (208) 388 - 2513
Boise, ID 83707 Fax:(208) 388 - 6955
rhahn@idahopower.com

Serves As:
- Senior Legislative Affairs Representative, (Idaho Power Co.), IDACORP, Inc.

HAINES, Jr., James S.
P.O. Box 889 Tel: (785) 575 - 6300
Topeka, KS 66601-0889 Fax:(785) 575 - 8182

Serves As:
- President and Chief Exec. Officer, Westar Energy, Inc.

HAINES, Robert W.
2000 K St., NW Tel: (202) 862 - 0222
Suite 710 Fax:(202) 862 - 0267
Washington, DC 20006

Registered Federal Lobbyist.
Serves As:
- Deputy Manager, International Relations, Exxon Mobil Corp.

HAIRSTON, III, W. G. (George)
P.O. Box 1295 Tel: (205) 992 - 5752
Birmingham, AL 35201 Fax:(205) 992 - 5363

Serves As:
- Chairman of the Board, Southern Nuclear Operating Co.

HAKE, Kevin
Ten Hwy. 35 Tel: (732) 747 - 7800
Red Bank, NJ 07701-5902 Fax:(732) 747 - 6835

Serves As:
- Senior V. President, Finance and Treasurer, Hovnanian Enterprises, Inc.

Responsibilities include investor relations.

HAKE, Ralph F.
P.O. Box 39 Tel: (641) 792 - 7000
Newton, IA 50208-0039 Fax:(641) 787 - 8376
rhake@maytag.com

Serves As:
- Chairman and Chief Exec. Officer, Maytag Corp.

HAKIM, M.D., Ph.d., Raymond H.
2525 West End Ave., Suite 600 Tel: (615) 345 - 5577
Nashville, TN 37203 Fax:(615) 345 - 5505

Serves As:
- PAC Contact, Renal Care Group, Inc.

HALATA, Paul
One Mercedes Dr.
Montvale, NJ 07645

Serves As:
- President and Chief Exec. Officer, Mercedes-Benz USA, LLC

HALDEMAN, Genevieve L.
20330 Stevens Creek Blvd. Tel: (408) 517 - 7642
Cupertino, CA 95014-2132 Fax:(408) 517 - 8152
glhaldeman@symantec.com

Serves As:
- Director, Corporate Public Relations, Symantec Corp.

HALE, Ellen
450 W. 33rd St. Tel: (212) 621 - 1500
New York, NY 10001 Fax:(212) 621 - 5447

Serves As:
- Director, Corporate Communications, Associated Press

HALE, Jr., J. Joseph
P.O. Box 960 Tel: (513) 287 - 2410
Cincinnati, OH 45201-0960 Fax:(513) 287 - 4030

Serves As:
- V. President, Corporate Communications; and President, Cinergy Foundation, Cinergy Corp.

HALE, John A.
P.O. Box 757 Tel: (417) 358 - 8131
Carthage, MO 64836-0757 Ext: 3000
john.hale@leggett.com Fax:(417) 358 - 5840

Serves As:
- V. President, Human Resources, Leggett & Platt, Inc.

HALE, Rick
P.O. Box 1043 Tel: (601) 932 - 3704
Jackson, MS 39215-1043 Fax:(601) 939 - 7035
TF: (800) 222 - 8046

Serves As:
- President and Chief Exec. Officer, Blue Cross and Blue Shield of Mississippi

HALE, Timothy G.
2280 N. Greenville Ave. Tel: (972) 699 - 6807
Richardson, TX 75082 Fax:(972) 234 - 4669
thale@fossil.com

Serves As:
- Senior V. President and Image Director, Fossil Inc.

HALEY, Glen
1110 American Parkway NE Tel: (610) 712 - 1747
Allentown, PA 18109-3229 Fax:(610) 712 - 4106
glenhaley@agere.com

Serves As:
- Media Relations Contact, Agere Systems Inc.

HALEY, Mariellen
625 Fourth Ave. South Tel: (612) 340 - 8352
Minneapolis, MN 55415 Fax:(612) 340 - 7373
mariellen.haley@thrivent.com

Serves As:
- Media Relations Administrator, Thrivent Financial for Lutherans

HALEY, Roy W.
225 W. Station Square Dr. Tel: (412) 454 - 2200
suite 700 Fax:(412) 454 - 2505
Pittsburgh, PA 15219
rhaley@wescodist.com

Serves As:
- Chairman, President and Chief Exec. Officer, WESCO Internat'l, Inc.

HALIM, Raouf Y.
4000 MacArthur Blvd. Tel: (949) 579 - 3000
Newport Beach, CA 92660 Fax:(949) 579 - 3200

Serves As:
- Chief Exec. Officer and Director, Mindspeed Technologies, Inc.

HALL, Barbara
Administrative Center Tel: (269) 923 - 5000
2000 N. M-63 Fax:(269) 923 - 5443
Benton Harbor, MI 49022-2692

Serves As:
- Contact, Whirlpool Foundation, Whirlpool Corp.

HALL, Barbara
635 Massachusetts Ave. NW Tel: (202) 513 - 2073
Washington, DC 20001 Fax:(202) 513 - 3329

Serves As:
- V. President, Development and Exec. Director, NPR Foundation, Nat'l Public Radio

HALL, Derrick
10990 Wilshire Blvd. Tel: (310) 231 - 4000
Seventh Floor Fax:(310) 231 - 4222
Los Angeles, CA 90024
pr@kbhome.com

Serves As:
- V. President, Communications, KB HOME

HALL, Jr., Donald J.
P.O. Box 419580 Tel: (816) 274 - 5111
Kansas City, MO 64141-6580 Fax:(816) 274 - 5061

Serves As:
- President and Chief Exec. Officer/Vice Chairman, Hallmark Cards, Inc.

HALL, Sr., Donald J.
P.O. Box 419580
Kansas City, MO 64141-6580
Tel: (816) 274 - 5111
Fax:(816) 274 - 5061

Serves As:
• Chairman of the Board, Hallmark Cards, Inc.

HALL, Gene
56 Top Gallant Rd.
Stamford, CT 06904
Tel: (203) 964 - 0096
Fax:(203) 316 - 6488

Serves As:
• Chief Exec. Officer, Gartner, Inc.

HALL, Joseph M.
1201 E. Abingdon Dr.
Suite 300
Alexandria, VA 22314
jhall04@harris.com
Tel: (703) 739 - 1937
Fax:(703) 739 - 2775

Registered Federal Lobbyist.
Serves As:
• V. President, Congressional Relations, Harris Corp.

HALL, Karla
2000 Second Ave.
Detroit, MI 48226
Tel: (313) 235 - 9271
Fax:(313) 235 - 0285

Serves As:
• V. President and Foundation Secretary, DTE Energy Co.

HALL, Kristy
One Chase Manhattan Plaza
41st Floor
New York, NY 10005
Tel: (212) 859 - 7026
Fax:(212) 859 - 7010

Serves As:
• Foundation Administrator, Assurant

HALL, Mary Jane
1201 S. Second St.
Milwaukee, WI 43204-2496
Tel: (414) 382 - 2000
Fax:(414) 382 - 4444

Serves As:
• Senior V. President, Human Resources, Rockwell Automation

HALL, Matthew T.
8400 Maryland Ave.
Clayton, MO 63105
Tel: (314) 259 - 7223
Fax:(314) 259 - 7036
TF: (800) 449 - 4284

Serves As:
• V. President, Public Relations, (Sara Lee Bakery Group), Sara Lee Corp.

HALL, Richard C.
1900 Prairie City Rd.
Folsom, CA 95630
richard.c.hall@intel.com
Tel: (916) 356 - 6122
Fax:(916) 356 - 8070

Serves As:
• Manager, Government Affairs, Intel Corp.

HALL, III, Robert P.
655 15th St. NW
Suite 445
Washington, DC 20005
Tel: (202) 879 - 8515
Fax:(202) 737 - 8111

Registered Federal Lobbyist.
Serves As:
• Director, Government Affairs, (INVISTA), Koch Industries, Inc.

HALL, Terry L.
P.O. Box 537012
Sacramento, CA 95853-7012
Tel: (916) 355 - 4000
Fax:(916) 351 - 8668

Serves As:
• Chairman, President, and Chief Exec. Officer, GenCorp

HALL, Jr., William C.
P.O. Box 26532
Richmond, VA 23261
Tel: (804) 819 - 2040
Fax:(804) 819 - 2233

Serves As:
• V. President, External Affairs and Corporate Communications, Dominion Resources, Inc.

HALLA, Brian L.
P.O. Box 58090
Santa Clara, CA 95052-8090
brian.halla@nsc.com
Tel: (408) 721 - 5000
Fax:(408) 739 - 9803

Serves As:
• Chairman, President and Chief Exec. Officer, Nat'l Semiconductor Corp.

HALLER, Sarah E.
701 Pennsylvania Ave. NW
Suite 725
Washington, DC 20004
tracy.haller@group.novartis.com
Tel: (202) 638 - 7429
Fax:(202) 628 - 4763

Registered Federal Lobbyist.
Serves As:
• Exec. Director, International and Public Affairs, Novartis Corporation

HALLETT BERNARD, Mia
Two PNC Plaza, 34th Floor
Pittsburgh, PA 15222
Tel: (412) 762 - 7076

Serves As:
• V. President and Manager, PNC Foundation, PNC Financial Services Group

HALLMAN, Dwayne D.
One Horace Mann Plaza
Springfield, IL 62715-0001
Tel: (217) 788 - 5708
Fax:(217) 788 - 5161

Serves As:
• Senior V. President, Finance, Horace Mann Educators Corp.
Responsibilities include investor relations.

HALLOCK, Richard W.
10889 Wilshire Blvd.
Los Angeles, CA 90024
Tel: (310) 443 - 6537
Fax:(310) 443 - 6690

Serves As:
• Exec. V. President, Human Resources, Occidental Petroleum Corp.

HALLORAN, Jean M.
P.O. Box 10395
Palo Alto, CA 94303-0395
jean_halloran@agilent.com
Tel: (650) 752 - 5000
Fax:(650) 752 - 5633

Serves As:
• Senior V. President, Human Resources, Agilent Technologies, Inc.

HALLOWELL, Bryce
5050 Lincoln Dr.
Edina, MN 55436
bryce.hallowell@atk.com
Tel: (952) 351 - 3087
Fax:(952) 351 - 3009

Serves As:
• Director, External Communications, Alliant Techsystems

HALLUMS, Tammera
One Village Dr.
Van Buren Township, MI 48111
thallums@visteon.com
Tel: (313) 755 - 0998
Fax:(313) 557 - 983
TF: (800) VIS - TEON

Serves As:
• Manager, U.S. Employee Communications, Visteon Corp.

HALME, Matthew P.
2202 N. Westshore Blvd.
Fifth Floor
Tampa, FL 33607
matthewhalme@outback.com
Tel: (813) 282 - 1225
Fax:(813) 281 - 2114

Registered Federal Lobbyist.
Serves As:
• Director, Government Relations, Outback Steakhouse, Inc.

HALPERN, Cheryl
401 Ninth St. NW
Washington, DC 20004-2129
Tel: (202) 879 - 9600
Fax:(202) 879 - 9700

Serves As:
• Chairman of the Board, Corporation for Public Broadcasting

HALPIN, Carol
P.O. Box 834
Valley Forge, PA 19482-0834
chalpin@ikon.com
Tel: (610) 296 - 8000
Fax:(610) 408 - 7025
TF: (888) 275 - 4566

Serves As:
• Contact, Ikon Office Solutions Foundations, Ikon Office Solutions, Inc.

HALPIN, Janet
26555 Northwestern Hwy.
Southfield, MI 48034
janet_halpin@fmo.com
Tel: (248) 354 - 8847
Fax:(248) 354 - 8950

Serves As:
• Director, Investor Relations, Federal-Mogul Corp.

HALVORSEN, Jerald V.
101 Constitution Ave., NW
Suite 200 East
Washington, DC 20001
Tel: (202) 530 - 7300
Fax:(202) 530 - 7350

Registered Federal Lobbyist.
Serves As:
• V. President, Federal Government Affairs, Entergy Corp.
• V. President, Federal Government Affairs, Entergy Services, Inc.

HALVORSON, George
Ordway Bldg.
One Kaiser Plaza
Oakland, CA 94612
Tel: (510) 271 - 5910
Fax:(510) 271 - 6493

Serves As:
• Chairman and Chief Exec. Officer, Kaiser Permanente

HAMANO, Shinya
750 17th St. NW
Suite 400
Washington, DC 20006
Tel: (202) 861 - 0660
Fax:(202) 861 - 0437

Serves As:
• General Manager, Washington Office, Mitsui and Co. (U.S.A.), Inc.
Responsibilities include government relations.

HAMBRICK, James L.
29400 Lakeland Blvd.
Wickliffe, OH 44092-2298
Tel: (440) 943 - 4200
Fax:(440) 943 - 5337

Serves As:
- Chairman, Chief Exec. Officer and President, The Lubrizol Corp.

HAMBURG, Marc D.
1440 Kiewit Plaza
Omaha, NE 68131
Tel: (402) 346 - 1400
Fax:(402) 346 - 3375

Serves As:
- V. President, Chief Financial Officer and Treasurer, Berkshire Hathaway

Responsibilities include investor relations and corporate philanthropy.

HAMER, Jr., J. William
2801 Hwy. 280 South
P.O. Box 2606
Birmingham, AL 35223
Tel: (205) 268 - 1000

Serves As:
- Senior V. President and Chief Human Resources Officer, Protective Life Corp.

HAMERSLY, Bill
200 E. Basse Rd.
San Antonio, TX 78209
billhamersly@clearchannel.com
Tel: (210) 822 - 2828
Fax:(210) 822 - 2299

Serves As:
- Senior V. President, Human Resources, Clear Channel Communications

HAMILTON, Jonathon
100 Abbott Park Rd.
Abbott Park, IL 60064-3500
Tel: (847) 937 - 8646

Serves As:
- Senior Manager, External Communications, Abbott Laboratories

HAMILTON, Jonna K.
701 Brazos
Suite 1500
Austin, TX 78701
Tel: (512) 472 - 1361
Fax:(512) 472 - 1304

Serves As:
- Area Legislative Affairs Representative, Nationwide

HAMILTON, Lawrence W.
5350 Tech Data Dr.
Clearwater, FL 33760
lawrence.hamilton@techdata.com
Tel: (727) 539 - 7429
Ext: 77013
TF: (800) 237 - 8931

Serves As:
- Senior V. President, Human Resources, Tech Data Corp.

HAMILTON, Paul W.
215 S. Monroe St.
Suite 810
Tallahassee, FL 32301-1888
Tel: (850) 224 - 7517
Fax:(850) 224 - 7197

Serves As:
- V. President, State Legislative Affairs, (Florida Power & Light Company), FPL Group, Inc.

HAMLIN, Garry
9330 Zionsville Rd.
Indianapolis, IN 46268
Tel: (317) 337 - 4799

Serves As:
- Manager, Public Policy Resources, Dow AgroSciences LLC

HAMLING, James L.
3000 Centre Square West
1500 Market St.
Philadelphia, PA 19102
Tel: (215) 563 - 2800
Fax:(215) 575 - 2314

Serves As:
- President and Chief Exec. Officer, Berwind Group

HAMMACK, Steve
1801 California St.
50th Floor
Denver, CO 80202
steve.hammack@qwest.com
Tel: (303) 896 - 3030
Fax:(303) 965 - 3050
TF: (800) 899 - 7780

Serves As:
- Senior Director, Corporate Communications, Qwest Communications

HAMMARLUND, Jennifer
National City Center
1900 E. Ninth St.
Cleveland, OH 44114-3484
Tel: (216) 222 - 2000
Fax:(216) 575 - 2353
TF: (800) 622 - 6736

Serves As:
- V. President and Manager, Investor Relations, Nat'l City Corp.

HAMMER, Jeannine M.
1301 Pennsylvania Ave. NW
Suite 1030
Washington, DC 20004
Tel: (202) 824 - 0404
Fax:(202) 347 - 0132

Registered Federal Lobbyist.
Serves As:
- Representative, Allegheny Energy Inc.

HAMMERGREN, John H.
One Post St.
San Francisco, CA 94104-5296
Tel: (415) 983 - 8300
Fax:(415) 983 - 7160

Serves As:
- Chairman and Chief Exec. Officer, McKesson Corp.

HAMMOND, Elizabeth
I-20 at Alpine Rd.
Columbia, SC 29219-0001
Tel: (803) 264 - 4626
Fax:(803) 264 - 5520
TF: (800) 288 - 2227

Serves As:
- Media Contact, BlueCross BlueShield of South Carolina

HAMMOND, Pat
P.O. Box 2286
Houston, TX 77252-2286
Tel: (713) 497 - 7723
Fax:(713) 488 - 5925
TF: (866) 872 - 6656

Serves As:
- Manager, Media Relations, Reliant Resources

HAMMONDS, Bruce L.
1100 N. King St.
Wilmington, DE 19880-127
Fax:(302) 456 - 8541
TF: (800) 441 - 7048

Serves As:
- President and Chief Exec. Officer, MBNA Corp.

HAMOOD, Al
5400 Legacy Dr.
Plano, TX 75024-3199
Tel: (972) 605 - 6001
Fax:(972) 605 - 6841

Serves As:
- V. President, Investor Relations, EDS Corp.

HAMPTON, Stephanie L.
One Marriott Dr.
Washington, DC 20058
stephanie.hampton@marriott.com
Tel: (301) 380 - 1217
Fax:(301) 897 - 9014

Serves As:
- Senior Director, Media Relations, Marriott Internat'l, Inc.

HAMRAH, Charlene M.
70 Pine St.
New York, NY 10270
Tel: (212) 770 - 7070
Fax:(212) 425 - 3499

Serves As:
- V. President and Director, Investor Relations, American Internat'l Group, Inc.

HAMWAY, Lisa
444 Michigan Ave.
Room 1700
Detroit, MI 48226
Tel: (517) 334 - 3400
TF: (800) 257 - 0902

Serves As:
- Director, Corporate Contributions and External Affairs, SBC Michigan

HANAFEE, Susan
P.O. Box 3005
Columbus, IN 47202-3005
Tel: (317) 610 - 2494
Fax:(812) 377 - 3334

Serves As:
- Exec. Director, Communications and Information, Cummins, Inc.

HANBURY, Trey
2001 Edmund Halley Dr.
Reston, VA 20191
Tel: (703) 433 - 4000

Registered Federal Lobbyist.
Serves As:
- Representative, Sprint Nextel

HANDLY, David J.
P.O. Box 1295
Birmingham, AL 35201
Tel: (205) 992 - 5752
Fax:(205) 992 - 5363

Serves As:
- Treasurer, Southern Nuclear Operating Inc. PAC, Southern Nuclear Operating Co.

HANKIN, Christopher
1300 I St. NW
Suite 420 East
WAS02
Washington, DC 20005
christopher.hankin@sun.com
Tel: (202) 326 - 7520
Fax:(202) 326 - 7525

Serves As:
- Director, U.S. Federal Policy, Sun Microsystems, Inc.

HANKINS, Mary Anne
1200 State Fair Blvd.
Syracuse, NY 13221-4737
Tel: (315) 453 - 8619
Fax:(315) 453 - 8672

Serves As:
- Director, Consumer and Public Affairs, The Penn Traffic Co.

Responsibilities include corporate philanthropy.

HANKS, Stephen G.
P.O. Box 73
Boise, ID 83729
Tel: (208) 386 - 5000
Fax:(208) 386 - 7186

Serves As:
- President and Chief Exec. Officer, Washington Group Internat'l

HANLEY, Colleen
2135 W. Maple Rd.
Troy, MI 48084
colleen.hanley@arvinmeritor.com
Tel: (248) 435 - 1417
Fax:(313) 551 - 2894
TF: (800) 535 - 5560

Serves As:
- Senior Director, Global Marketing Communications, ArvinMeritor

HANLEY, Mark
3201 C St.
Suite 603
Anchorage, AK 99503
Tel: (907) 273 - 6310

Serves As:
- Manager, Public Affairs - Alaska, Anadarko Petroleum Corp.

HANLEY, Marylee
1284 Soldiers Field Rd.
Boston, MA 02135
mhanley@duke-energy.com
Tel: (617) 560 - 1573

Serves As:
- Manager, Government and Public Affairs, DEGT/Maritimes, Duke Energy Corp.

HANLON, Karen
P.O. Box 66360
Scotts Valley, CA 95067-0360
karen.hanlon@seagate.com
Tel: (831) 439 - 2485
Fax:(831) 438 - 0558

Serves As:
- Senior V. President, Worldwide Human Resources, Seagate Technology

HANLON, Tim
420 Montgomery St.
M/S A0112-073
San Francisco, CA 94104
Tel: (415) 396 - 3567
TF: (800) 411 - 4932

Serves As:
- V. President, Wells Fargo Foundation and Manager, Community Support Programs, Wells Fargo & Co.

HANMAN, Gary E.
P.O. Box 909700
Kansas City, MO 64190-9700
ghanman@dfamilk.com
Tel: (816) 801 - 6455
Fax:(816) 801 - 6590

Serves As:
- President and Chief Exec. Officer, Dairy Farmers of America, Inc.

HANNA, Christine E.
1200 Wilson Blvd.
Arlington, VA 22209-2305
Tel: (703) 465 - 3213
Fax:(703) 465 - 3003

Registered Federal Lobbyist.
Serves As:
- Manager, Legislative Affairs, International Programs, The Boeing Co.

HANNA, Elizabeth
1200 Wilson Blvd.
Arlington, VA 22209-2305
Tel: (703) 465 - 3500

Serves As:
- Representative, The Boeing Co.

HANNA, Tania
1201 E. Abingdon Dr.
Suite 300
Alexandria, VA 22314
Tel: (703) 739 - 1946
Fax:(703) 739 - 2775

Serves As:
- Director, Government Relations, Harris Corp.

HANNAH, David H.
350 S. Grand Ave., Suite 5100
Los Angeles, CA 90071
dhannah@rsac.com
Tel: (213) 687 - 7700
Fax:(213) 687 - 8792

Serves As:
- Chief Exec. Officer, Reliance Steel & Aluminum Co.

HANNAY, Lori
50 Minuteman Rd.
Andover, MA 01810
Tel: (978) 684 - 1000
Fax:(978) 684 - 1658

Serves As:
- V. President, Human Resources, Enterasys Networks

HANNEMAN, Christine
1900 W. Field Ct.
Lake Forest, IL 60045
channeman@pactiv.com
Tel: (847) 482 - 2429
Fax:(847) 482 - 3360
TF: (888) 828 - 2850

Serves As:
- Investor Relations Contact, Pactiv Corp.

HANNON, Richard M.
P.O. Box 13466
Phoenix, AZ 85002-3466
Tel: (602) 864 - 4418
Fax:(602) 864 - 4242
TF: (800) 232 - 2345

Serves As:
- Senior V. President, Marketing and Provider Affairs, Blue Cross and Blue Shield of Arizona

HANONIK, Francoise
Reader's Digest Rd.
Pleasantville, NY 10570-7000
Tel: (914) 238 - 1000
Fax:(914) 238 - 4559
TF: (800) 234 - 9000

Serves As:
- Chief Human Resources Officer; V. President, Human Resources North America, Reader's Digest Ass'n, Inc.

HANRAHAN, Paul T.
4300 Wilson Blvd.
11th Floor
Arlington, VA 22203
Tel: (703) 522 - 1315
Fax:(703) 528 - 4510

Serves As:
- President and Chief Exec. Officer, The AES Corp.

HANS, Rick J.
200 Wilmot Rd.
Deerfield, IL 60015-4616
rick.hans@walgreens.com
Tel: (847) 914 - 2385
Fax:(847) 914 - 2678

Serves As:
- Assistant Treasurer and Director, Finance, Walgreen Co.

Responsibilities include investor relations.

HANSEN, Jake
444 N. Capitol St. NW
Suite 722
Washington, DC 20001
jhansen@barrlabs.com
Tel: (202) 393 - 6599
Fax:(202) 638 - 3386

Registered Federal Lobbyist.
Serves As:
- V. President, Government Affairs, (Barr Laboratories, Inc.), Barr Pharmaceuticals, Inc.

HANSEN, Kip L.
1755 S. Clark St.
Suite 1100
Arlington, VA 22202
khansen@drs-esg.com
Tel: (703) 416 - 8000
Fax:(703) 416 - 8010

Registered Federal Lobbyist.
Serves As:
- V. President, Government Relations, DRS Technologies, Inc.

HANSEN, Steven M.
2244 Walnut Grove Ave.
Rosemead, CA 91770
hansensm@sce.com
Tel: (626) 302 - 7969
Fax:(626) 302 - 8066

Serves As:
- Communications Specialist, Southern California Edison, an Edison Internat'l Co.

HANSEN, William
1550 Crystal Dr.
Crystal Square 2, Suite 300
Arlington, VA 22202
Tel: (703) 413 - 5601
Fax:(703) 413 - 5636

Serves As:
- V.P., Army Programs, Civil Agencies SI, & Tech. Serv., Lockheed Martin Corp.

HANSON, Charles R.
10400 W. Higgins
Suite 600
Rosemont, IL 60018
Tel: (847) 298 - 9000
Fax:(847) 298 - 9018
TF: (800) 826 - 4449

Serves As:
- V. President, Environmental Health and Safety, Velsicol Chemical Corp.

HANSON, Debra
P.O. Box 64235
St. Paul, MN 55164-0235
debra.hanson@deluxe.com
Tel: (651) 483 - 7111
Ext: 7367
Fax:(651) 481 - 4477

Serves As:
- Senior Communications Specialist, Deluxe Corp.

HANSON, Henry A.
17845 E. Hwy. 10
Elk River, MN 55330
Tel: (763) 441 - 3121
Fax:(763) 241 - 2366

Serves As:
- Chairman of the Board, Great River Energy

HANSON, John Nils
P.O. Box 554
Milwaukee, WI 53201
Tel: (414) 319 - 8500
Fax:(414) 319 - 8510

Serves As:
- Chairman, President and Chief Exec. Officer, Joy Global Inc.

HANSON, Mark D.
2207 Bridgepoint Pkwy.
San Mateo, CA 94404
Tel: (650) 295 - 5000
Fax:(650) 295 - 5111
TF: (800) 356 - 3321

Serves As:
- Senior V. President, Coporate Development and Investor Relations, Siebel Systems, Inc.

HANSON, Michael J.
125 S. Dakota Ave.
Sioux Falls, SD 57104-6403
mike.hanson@northwestern.com
Tel: (605) 978 - 2908
Fax:(605) 978 - 2840

Serves As:
- Chief Exec. Officer, NorthWestern Corp.

HANSON, Peggy
30 W. Superior St.
Duluth, MN 55802
phanson@mnpower.com
Tel: (218) 722 - 2641
Fax:(218) 279 - 5050

Serves As:
- Community Relations Representative, ALLETE

Responsibilities include corporate contributions.

HANVIK, Bob N.
710 Medtronic Pkwy.
Minneapolis, MN 55432-5604
robert.n.hanvik@medtronic.com
Tel: (763) 505 - 2635
Fax:(763) 514 - 4879
TF: (800) 328 - 2518

Serves As:
- Director, Global Public and Media Relations, Medtronic, Inc.

HANWAY, H. Edward
One Liberty Pl.
1650 Market St.
Philadelphia, PA 19192
Tel: (215) 761 - 1000

Serves As:
- Chairman and Chief Exec. Officer, CIGNA Corp.

HAPNER, DeAnn
One Market
Spear Tower, Suite 2400
San Francisco, CA 94105
Tel: (415) 267 - 7000
Fax:(415) 267 - 7268

Serves As:
- V. President, Federal Regulatory Policy and Rates, (Pacific Gas and Electric Co.), PG & E Corp.

HAPPEL, Branden
Dain Rauscher Plaza
60 S. Sixth St., 19th Floor
Minneapolis, MN 55402-4422
branden.happel@rbcdain.com
Tel: (612) 371 - 2239
Fax:(612) 371 - 2960

Serves As:
- Senior Public Relations Specialist, RBC Dain Rauscher Corp.

HARA, Michael
2701 San Tomas Exwy.
Santa Clara, CA 95050
mhara@nvidia.com
Tel: (408) 486 - 2511
Fax:(408) 486 - 2200

Serves As:
- V. President, Investor Relations and Communications, NVIDIA Corp.

HARBERT, Sophie
8900 Amberglen Blvd.
Austin, TX 78729-1110
Tel: (512) 918 - 5887

Serves As:
- Assistant Manager, Public Affairs Communications, State Farm Insurance Cos.

HARDAGE, Ginger C.
P.O. Box 36611
Dallas, TX 75235-1611
Tel: (214) 792 - 4524

Serves As:
- Senior V. President, Corporate Communications, Southwest Airlines Co.

HARDIN, Jr., Edward L.
211 Commerce St.
Suite 800
Nashville, TN 37201
Tel: (615) 743 - 6600

Serves As:
- Exec. V. President and General Counsel, Caremark Rx, Inc.

Responsibilities include government affairs.

HARDIN, III, Henry T.
One Fountain Square
Chattanooga, TN 37402
hhardiniii@unumprovident.com
Tel: (423) 294 - 1810

Serves As:
- Senior Counsel, UnumProvident Corp.

Responsibilities include TN political action.

HARDING, Anthony J.
200 Old Hook Rd.
Harrington Park, NJ 07640
Tel: (201) 767 - 9300
Fax:(201) 767 - 2892
TF: (800) 230 - 2685

Serves As:
- V. Chairman and Chief Exec. Officer, United Water Resources

HARDING, Scott
One Targeting Centre
Windsor, CT 06095
Tel: (860) 285 - 6100
Fax:(860) 285 - 1567
TF: (800) 559 - 2386

Serves As:
- Chief Exec. Officer, Advo Inc.

HARDMAN, Beth
P.O. Box 8171
Portland, OR 97207
Tel: (503) 228 - 9161
Fax:(503) 220 - 2722

Serves As:
- Director, Human Resources, Pope & Talbot, Inc.

HARDS, Michelle
Box 1000
Toledo, OH 43697-1000
Tel: (419) 535 - 4500
Fax:(419) 535 - 4756

Serves As:
- Director, Investor Relations, Dana Corp.

HARDWICK, Charles A. "Chuck"
235 E. 42nd St.
New York, NY 10017-5755
chardwick@pfizer.com
Tel: (212) 573 - 7833
Fax:(212) 808 - 8880

Registered Federal Lobbyist.
Serves As:
- Senior V. President, Worldwide Gov't Relations, Comm., Media Relations, and Public Policy ; Pres. and Exec. Director, The Pfizer Foundation, Pfizer Inc.

HARDWIG, Brenda
P.O. Box 9000
Newport Beach, CA 92658-9030
Tel: (949) 219 - 3787
Fax:(949) 219 - 7614
TF: (800) 800 - 7646

Serves As:
- Community Relations Coordinator, Pacific Life Insurance Co.

HARDY, Charles
P.O. Box 1590
Dallas, TX 75221-1590
Tel: (214) 443 - 5500
Ext: 575
Fax:(214) 443 - 5516

Serves As:
- Corporate Attorney; PAC Treasurer, Austin Industries

HARDY, Eva S.
P.O. Box 26666
Richmond, VA 23261-6666
eva_s_hardy@dom.com
Tel: (804) 771 - 4741

Serves As:
- Senior V. President, External Affairs and Corporate Communications, Dominion Resources, Inc.

HARDY, Lowell
P.O. Box 30825
Salt Lake City, UT 84130-0825
Tel: (801) 524 - 2700
Fax:(801) 526 - 3000

Serves As:
- Director, Human Resources, Sinclair Oil Corp.

HARGATE, Arthur
150 Innovation Dr.
Elyria, OH 44035
ahargate@rossenvironmental.com
Tel: (440) 366 - 2000

Serves As:
- V. President, Finance and Administration, Ross Environmental Services, Inc.

Responsibilities include government affairs.

HARGEST, Connie
800 LaSalle Ave.
Minneapolis, MN 55402-2006
Tel: (612) 372 - 4664
Fax:(612) 321 - 5137

Serves As:
- Senior Specialist, Local Government Relations, (CenterPoint Energy Minnegasco), CenterPoint Energy

HARGETT, Katina
10000 Richmond Ave.
Fourth Floor
Houston, TX 77042-4200
Tel: (713) 346 - 7766
Fax:(713) 435 - 2195

Serves As:
- Assistant, Investor Relations, Nat'l Oilwell, Inc.

HARGRAVES, Richard N.
720 Olive St.
Room 800
St. Louis, MO 63101
Tel: (314) 342 - 0652
Fax:(314) 436 - 3166

Serves As:
- Director, Corporate Communications, The Laclede Group

HARKEMA, Kathy
102 Main St.
Pella, IA 50219
krafka-harkemakk@pella.com
Tel: (641) 621 - 6971
Fax:(641) 628 - 6070

Serves As:
- Public Affairs Specialist, Pella Corp.

HARKER, Brian J.
512 Bridge St.
Danville, VA 24541
Tel: (434) 792 - 7511
Fax:(434) 791 - 0415

Serves As:
- Chairman and Chief Exec. Officer, Alliance One Internat'l Inc.

HARKIN, Ruth R.
1401 I St. NW
Suite 600
Washington, DC 20005
Tel: (202) 336 - 7463
Fax:(202) 336 - 7515

Serves As:
- Senior V. President, International Affairs and Government Relations, United Technologies Corp.

HARKINS, Katharin R.
One Sun Life Executive Park
Wellesley Hills, MA 02481
Tel: (781) 237 - 6030
Fax:(781) 304 - 5383
TF: (800) 225 - 3950

Serves As:
- V. President, Public Relations and Communications, Sun Life Financial

HARLING, Bernd
980 Hammond Dr. NE
Suite 1000
Atlanta, GA 30328-5313
Tel: (770) 290 - 3500
Fax:(770) 290 - 3700

Serves As:
- General Manager, Public Relations, Porsche Cars North America, Inc.

HARMAN, Charles E.
3350 Peachtree Rd. NE
Atlanta, GA 30326
charman@bcbsga.com
Tel: (404) 842 - 8980
Fax:(404) 842 - 8451

Registered Federal Lobbyist.
Serves As:
- V. President, Public Affairs, Blue Cross Blue Shield of Georgia

HARMAN, Philip
333 Ravenswood Ave.
Menlo Park, CA 94025-3493
Tel: (650) 859 - 2000
Fax:(650) 326 - 5512

Registered Federal Lobbyist.
Serves As:
- Director, Congressional Relations, SRI International

HARMS, Luke
701 Pennsylvania Ave. NW
Suite 750
Washington, DC 20004
Tel: (202) 639 - 9420
Fax:(202) 639 - 9421

Registered Federal Lobbyist.
Serves As:
- Government Affairs Representative, Maytag Corp.

HARMSEN, Dan
P.O. Box 661
Milwaukee, WI 53201-0661
Tel: (414) 224 - 2099
Fax:(414) 224 - 2469

Serves As:
- V. President, Human Resources, Journal Communications, Inc.

HARNETT, Gordon D.
17876 St. Clair Ave.
Cleveland, OH 44110
Tel: (216) 486 - 4200
Fax:(216) 383 - 4091
TF: (800) 321 - 2076

Serves As:
- Chairman, President and Chief Exec. Officer, Brush Engineered Materials Inc.

HARPER, Diane
1000 Wilson Blvd., Suite 2300
Arlington, VA 22209
Tel: (703) 875 - 8400
Fax:(703) 276 - 0711

Registered Federal Lobbyist.
Serves As:
- Manager, Legislative Affairs, Northrop Grumman Corp.

HARPER, Edwin L.
1101 Pennsylvania Ave. NW
Washington, DC 20004
ed.harper@assurant.com
Tel: (202) 756 - 2225

Registered Federal Lobbyist.
Serves As:
- Senior V. President, Public Affairs/Government Relations, Assurant

HARPER, Nick
600 Grant St.
Pittsburgh, PA 15219-2800
Tel: (412) 433 - 1184
Fax:(412) 433 - 1167

Serves As:
- Manager, Investor Relations, United States Steel Corporation

HARPER, Paul D.
3402 E. University Dr.
Phoenix, AZ 85034
Tel: (602) 794 - 9600
Fax:(602) 794 - 9601

Serves As:
- Director, Environmental Affairs and Safety, Eagle-Picher Industries, Inc.

HARPER, Ronald R.
1717 E. Interstate Ave.
Bismarck, ND 58503
rharper@bepc.com
Tel: (701) 223 - 0441
Fax:(701) 224 - 5336

Serves As:
- Chief Exec. Officer, Basin Electric Power Cooperative

HARPER, Stephen F.
1634 I St. NW
Suite 300
Washington, DC 20006-4021
Tel: (202) 628 - 3838
Fax:(202) 628 - 2525

Registered Federal Lobbyist.
Serves As:
- Director, Environmental Health and Safety, Intel Corp.

HARPOLE, David A.
One Houston Center
1221 McKinney Ave.
Houston, TX 77010
david.harpole@lyondell.com
Tel: (713) 652 - 4125
Fax:(713) 652 - 4151

Serves As:
- Manager, Public Affairs, Lyondell Chemical Co.

HARRELL, III, Joel E.
185 Spring St. SW
Atlanta, GA 30303-3703
Tel: (404) 897 - 313
Fax:(404) 527 - 2773

Serves As:
- Resident V. President, Norfolk Southern Corp.

Responsibilities include corporate government relations and lobbying.

HARRINGTON, Deborah
1633 Broadway
New York, NY 10019
Tel: (212) 489 - 1600
Fax:(212) 489 - 1687

Serves As:
- Director, Public Relations, (Deloitte Services LP), Deloitte & Touche LLP

HARRINGTON, Michael
40 Westminster St.
Providence, RI 02903-2525
Tel: (401) 421 - 2800
Fax:(401) 457 - 3598

Serves As:
- Treasurer, Textron Inc. Political Action Committee, Textron Inc.

HARRINGTON, Richard J.
Metro Center
One Station Pl.
Stamford, CT 06902
Tel: (203) 539 - 8000
Fax:(203) 539 - 7734
TF: (800) 969 - 9974

Serves As:
- President and Chief Exec. Officer, The Thomson Corporation

HARRINGTON, Toni
1001 G St., NW
Suite 950
Washington, DC 20001
toni_harrington@hna.honda.com
Tel: (202) 661 - 4400
Fax:(202) 661 - 4459

Registered Federal Lobbyist.
Serves As:
- Assistant V. President, Government and Industry Relations, (Honda North America, Inc.), American Honda Motor Co., Inc.

HARRINGTON, W. Brendan
1250 H St. NW
Suite 800
Washington, DC 20005
brendan.harrington@kodak.com
Tel: (202) 857 - 3400
Fax:(202) 857 - 3401

Serves As:
- Director, International Trade Relations, Eastman Kodak Company

HARRIS, Carl L.
P.O. Box 482
Fort Worth, TX 76101
Tel: (817) 280 - 2425
Fax:(817) 280 - 8221

Serves As:
- Director, Public Affairs and Advertising, Bell Helicopter Textron

HARRIS, E. Lee
P.O. Box 10566
Birmingham, AL 35296
lee.harris@compassbnk.com
Tel: (205) 297 - 3466
Fax:(205) 297 - 3336
TF: (800) 239 - 2265

Serves As:
- Exec. V. President, Human Resources, (Compass Bank), Compass Bancshares, Inc.

HARRIS, Kimberly
P.O. Box 97034
Bellevue, WA 98009-9734
Tel: (425) 452 - 1234
Fax:(425) 462 - 3301

Serves As:
- V. President, Governmental and Regulatory Affairs, Puget Sound Energy

HARRIS, King
475 W. Terra Cotta Ave.
Suite E
Crystal Lake, IL 60014-9695
Tel: (815) 477 - 0424
Fax:(815) 477 - 0481

Serves As:
- Chairman of the Board, AptarGroup, Inc.

HARRIS, Ph.D., Marilyn A.
700 13th St., NW
Suite 950
Washington, DC 20005
maharris@marathonoil.com
Tel: (202) 654 - 4480
Fax:(202) 654 - 4493

Registered Federal Lobbyist.
Serves As:
- V. President, Federal Government Affairs, Marathon Oil Corp.

HARRIS, Richard W.
Three Commercial Pl.
Norfolk, VA 23510-2191
Tel: (757) 629 - 2718
Fax:(757) 629 - 2822

Serves As:
- Director, Corporate Communications, Norfolk Southern Corp.

HARRIS, Robert L.
77 Beale St.
MC B32
San Francisco, CA 94105
Tel: (415) 973 - 3833
Fax:(415) 973 - 1359

Serves As:
- V. President, Environmental Affairs, (Pacific Gas and Electric Co.), PG & E Corp.

HARRIS, Rullie
1412 Eatonton
Madison, GA 31068
rullie.harris@weyerhaeuser.com
Tel: (706) 342 - 3306
Fax:(706) 343 - 1895

Serves As:
- Manager, Government Affairs - Georgia, Weyerhaeuser Co.

HARRIS, Sandy
P.O. Box 511
Kingsport, TN 37662-5075
eastman1@eastman.com
Tel: (423) 229 - 2196
Fax:(423) 224 - 0323
TF: (800) 327 - 8626

Serves As:
- Corporate Information Center, Eastman Chemical Co.

HARRIS, III, W. S.
65 E. State St., Suite 1000
Columbus, OH 43215
Tel: (614) 460 - 3510
Fax:(614) 464 - 1466

Serves As:
- Resident V. President, Public Affairs, Norfolk Southern Corp.

HARRISON, Brian
7575 Fulton St. East
M/S 78-2G
Ada, MI 49355-0001
Tel: (616) 787 - 7560
Fax:(616) 787 - 5624

Serves As:
- Government Affairs Specialist, Alticor Inc.

HARRISON, C. Richard
140 Kendrick St.
Needham, MA 02494
Tel: (781) 370 - 5000
Fax:(781) 370 - 6000
TF: (800) 782 - 3776

Serves As:
- President and Chief Exec. Officer, PTC

HARRISON, David D.
5500 Wayzata Blvd.
Suite 800
Golden Valley, MN 55416-1259
Tel: (763) 545 - 1730

Serves As:
- Exec. V. President and Chief Financial Officer, Pentair, Inc.

Responsibilities include investor relations.

HARRISON, Fran
82 Running Hill Rd.
South Portland, ME 04106-6020
Tel: (207) 775 - 8100
Fax:(207) 761 - 8161
TF: (800) 341 - 0392

Serves As:
- Director, Corporate Communications and Governmental Relations, Fairchild Semiconductor Internat'l, Inc.

HARRISON, III, J. Frank
4100 Coca-Cola Plaza
Charlotte, NC 28211
Tel: (704) 551 - 4400
Fax:(704) 551 - 4646

Serves As:
- Chairman and Chief Exec. Officer, Coca-Cola Bottling Co. Consolidated

HARRISON, Jackie
P.O. Box 227097
Dallas, TX 75222-7097
jackie.harrison@txu.com
Tel: (214) 812 - 4715
Fax:(214) 812 - 7077

Serves As:
- Manager, Shareholder Services, TXU

HARRISON, Kelly B.
P.O. Box 889
Topeka, KS 66601-0889
Tel: (785) 575 - 1636
Fax:(785) 575 - 6427

Serves As:
- V. President, Regulatory, Westar Energy, Inc.

HARRISON, Laurie
4800 Hampden Ln.
Suite 1100
Bethesda, MD 20814
Tel: (301) 841 - 1600
Fax:(301) 841 - 1611

Registered Federal Lobbyist.
Serves As:
- V. President, Government Relations, AREVA Enterprises, Inc.

HARRISON, Monroe
One Hughes Way
Orlando, FL 32805-2205
Tel: (407) 841 - 4755
Fax:(407) 649 - 1670

Serves As:
- Manager, Corporate Citizenship, Hughes Supply, Inc.

HARRISON, Jr., William B.
270 Park Ave.
New York, NY 10017-2070
william.harrison@jpmorganchase.com
Tel: (212) 270 - 6000
Fax:(212) 270 - 1648

Serves As:
- Chairman and Chief Exec. Officer, J. P. Morgan Chase & Co.

HARRMANN, Terry O.
321 E. Walnut, Suite 373
Des Moines, IA 50309
terryharrmann@alliant-energy.com
Tel: (515) 284 - 5699
Fax:(515) 284 - 7130

Serves As:
- Manager, Public Affairs, Alliant Energy Corp.

HARROW, Donald F.
P.O. Box 33068
Charlotte, NC 28233
Tel: (704) 731 - 4318
Fax:(704) 365 - 8515

Serves As:
- V. President, Governmental Relations, Piedmont Natural Gas Co.

Serves as the senior public affairs executive at company headquarters.

HARRY, L. Ray
601 Pennsylvania Ave. NW
Suite 800
Washington, DC 20004
Tel: (202) 261 - 5000
Fax:(202) 296 - 7937

Registered Federal Lobbyist.
Serves As:
- Director, Environmental Issues, Southern Company

HARSANYI, Dr. Fruzsina M.
122 C St. NW
Suite 520
Washington, DC 20001
Tel: (202) 393 - 5100
Fax:(202) 393 - 5110

Registered Federal Lobbyist.
Serves As:
- V. President, Public Affairs, Tyco Internat'l (U.S.), Inc.

HARSH, Jack P.
330 S. Fourth St.
Richmond, VA 23219
jack_harsh@albemarle.com
Tel: (804) 788 - 6000
Fax:(804) 788 - 6094

Serves As:
- V. President, Human Resources, Albemarle Corp.

HARSHMAN, Richard J.
1000 Six PPG Pl.
Pittsburgh, PA 15222-5479
rharshman@alleghenytechnologies.com
Tel: (412) 394 - 2861
Fax:(412) 394 - 3034

Serves As:
- Senior V. President, Finance and Chief Financial Officer, Allegheny Technologies Incorporated

Responsibilities include investor relations.

HART, Angela S.
1932 Wynnton Rd.
Columbus, GA 31999
Tel: (706) 323 - 3431
Fax:(706) 660 - 7333
TF: (800) 992 - 3522

Serves As:
- Senior V. President, Community Relations, AFLAC Incorporated

HART, Janet
P.O. Box 3165
Harrisburg, PA 17105
Tel: (717) 975 - 5758
Fax:(717) 975 - 3760

Serves As:
- Manager, Government Affairs, Rite Aid Corp.

HART, Sandra
220 NW Second Ave.
Portland, OR 97209-3991
Tel: (503) 226 - 4211
Fax:(503) 721 - 2508

Serves As:
- Director, Environmental Services, NW Natural

HARTELL, Steve
2011 Crystal Dr., Crystal Park I
Suite 907
Arlington, VA 22202
Tel: (703) 892 - 0120
Fax:(703) 892 - 0091

Registered Federal Lobbyist.
Serves As:
- Manager, Government Relations, EMC Corp.

HARTIN, Erin
500 McCarthy Blvd.
Milpitas, CA 95035
erin_hartin@maxtor.com
Tel: (408) 678 - 2022
Fax:(408) 952 - 3600
TF: (800) 262 - 9867

Serves As:
- Manager, Public Relations, Maxtor Corp.

HARTJE, Keith
666 Grand Ave.
P.O. Box 657
Des Moines, IA 50303-0657
Tel: (515) 281 - 2575
Fax:(515) 242 - 4080
TF: (888) 427 - 5632

Serves As:
- Senior V. President, Corporate Communications, MidAmerican Energy Holdings Co.

HARTLEY, Thomas Y.
P.O. Box 98510
Las Vegas, NV 89193-8510
Tel: (702) 876 - 7247
Fax:(702) 364 - 3444

Serves As:
- Chairman of the Board, Southwest Gas Corp.

HARTMAN, Donna
P.O. Box 68900
Seattle, WA 98168-0947
donna.hartman@alaskaair.com
Tel: (206) 392 - 5383
Fax:(206) 431 - 5558

Serves As:
- Corporate Contributions Administrator, (Alaska Airlines, Inc.), Alaska Air Group, Inc.

Responsibilities include corporate philanthropy.

HARTMAN, Jennifer
7001 Tower Rd.
Denver, CO 80249-7312
Tel: (720) 374 - 4375
TF: (800) 265 - 5505

Serves As:
- Community Relations Contact, Frontier Airlines, Inc.

HARTMAN, Kathy
P.O. Box 19001
Green Bay, WI 54307-9001
khartma@wpsc.com
Tel: (920) 433 - 1248
Fax:(920) 433 - 1693
TF: (800) 450 - 7260

Serves As:
- Foundation Contact, Wisconsin Public Service Corp.

HARTMAN, Richard M.
2424 Pioneer Ave., Suite 301
Cheyenne, WY 82001
Tel: (307) 778 - 3359
Fax:(307) 778 - 3385

Serves As:
- Special Representative - Cheyenne, (Union Pacific Railroad Co.), Union Pacific Corp.

HARTMAN, William C.
Eaton Center
1111 Superior Ave.
Cleveland, OH 44114-2584
WilliamHartman@eaton.com
Tel: (216) 523 - 4501
Fax:(216) 479 - 7020

Serves As:
- V. President, Investor Relations, Eaton Corp.

HARTMAN KING, Kris
1500 Corporate Dr.
Suite 400
Canonsburg, PA 15317
kking@mylan.com
Tel: (724) 514 - 1800

Serves As:
- Director, Investor Relations, Mylan Laboratories Inc.

HARTOUGH, James B.
P.O. Box 18100
Richmond, VA 23226-8100
Tel: (804) 289 - 9645
Fax:(804) 289 - 9753

Serves As:
- V. President, Corporate Finance and Treasurer; Treasurer, Brink's Co. Political Action Committee, The Brink's Co.

HARTSELL, Charles R.
450 Riverchase Pkwy. East
Birmingham, AL 35244
chartsell@bcbsal.org
Tel: (205) 988 - 2126
Fax:(205) 220 - 4841

Registered Federal Lobbyist.
Serves As:
- Senior V. President, Government Programs, Claims and Public Affairs, Blue Cross and Blue Shield of Alabama

HARTSOE, Joseph R.
801 Pennsylvania Ave. NW
Suite 320
Washington, DC 20004
Tel: (202) 383 - 3430
Fax:(202) 383 - 3459

Registered Federal Lobbyist.
Serves As:
- V. President and Associate General Counsel, Federal Policy, American Electric Power Co. Inc.

HARTVIGSEN, Rich M.
One Nu Skin Plaza
75 W. Center St.
Provo, UT 84601
Tel: (801) 345 - 1000
Fax:(801) 345 - 2799

Serves As:
- V. President, Global Regulatory Affairs, Nu Skin Enterprises

HARTWELL, John
570 Lexington Ave.
20th Floor
New York, NY 10022
john.hartwell@volvo.com
Tel: (212) 418 - 7432

Serves As:
- Director, Investor Relations, North America, Volvo Group North America, Inc.

HARTZ, Phillip M.
2555 Telegraph Rd.
Bloomfield Hills, MI 48302-0954
Tel: (248) 648 - 2500
Fax:(248) 648 - 2525

Serves As:
- Senior V. President, Manufacturer Relations and Corporate Communications, United Auto Group, Inc.

HARVEY, Dane
414 Union St.
Suite 2000
Nashville, TN 37219
Tel: (615) 986 - 5600

Serves As:
- V. President, Environmental Affairs, Louisiana-Pacific Corporation

HARVEY, David R.
3050 Spruce St.
St. Louis, MO 63103
dharvey@sial.com
Tel: (314) 771 - 5765
Fax:(800) 325 - 5052
TF: (800) 325 - 3010

Serves As:
- Chairman, President, and Chief Exec. Officer, Sigma-Aldrich Corp.

HARVEY, Gerald
1550 Crystal Dr.
Crystal Square 2, Suite 300
Arlington, VA 22202
Tel: (703) 413 - 5859
Fax:(703) 413 - 5749

Serves As:
- V. President, Legislative Affairs, Technology Services, Lockheed Martin Corp.

HARVEY, J. Brett
Consol Plaza
1800 Washington Rd.
Pittsburgh, PA 15241-1421
Tel: (412) 831 - 4000
Fax:(412) 831 - 4103

Serves As:
- President and Chief Exec. Officer, CONSOL Energy Inc.

HARVEY, William D.

P.O. Box 77007 Tel: (608) 458 - 3311
Madison, WI 53707-1007 Fax:(608) 458 - 4820

Serves As:
- President and Chief Exec. Officer, Alliant Energy Corp.

HARVILL, Karla

P.O. Box 2210 Tel: (770) 393 - 5091
Atlanta, GA 30301-2210 Fax:(770) 393 - 5347
karla.harvill@goldkist.com

Serves As:
- Manager, Public Relations, Gold Kist Inc.

HARWARD, Floyce M.

2321 Concord Pkwy., South Tel: (704) 788 - 5133
P.O. Box 1098 Fax:(704) 788 - 5139
Concord, NC 28026-1098

Serves As:
- Community Affairs Specialist, Communications and Programs, Philip Morris U.S.A.

HARWELL, Tom

4111 E. 37th St., North Tel: (316) 828 - 7082
Wichita, KS 67220 Fax:(316) 828 - 5739

Serves As:
- Director, Community Outreach, Koch Industries, Inc.

HARWOOD, Joseph E.

P.O. Box 1244 Tel: (704) 382 - 8194
M/S PB05D Fax:(704) 382 - 3588
Charlotte, NC 28201-1244
jharwood@duke-energy.com

Serves As:
- V. President, State Government Affairs, Duke Energy Corp.

HARWOOD, Kevin

370 Woodcliff Dr. Tel: (585) 218 - 3600
Suite 300 TF: (888) 724 - 2169
Fairport, NY 14450
kevin.harwood@cbrands.com

Serves As:
- Manager, Corporate Communications, Constellation Brands, Inc.

HASEK, William J.

500 W. Monroe St. Tel: (312) 621 - 6200
Chicago, IL 60661 Fax:(312) 621 - 6648
TF: (800) 428 - 8161

Serves As:
- PAC Treasurer, GATX Corp.

HASHEM, Peg

One Hamilton Rd. Tel: (860) 654 - 3469
Windsor Locks, CT 06096-1010 Fax:(860) 654 - 5060

Serves As:
- Manager, Public Relations, Hamilton Sundstrand

HASKELL, Robert G.

P.O. Box 9000 Tel: (949) 219 - 3022
Newport Beach, CA 92658-9030 Fax:(949) 219 - 5130
TF: (800) 800 - 7646

Serves As:
- Senior V. President, Public Affairs, Pacific Life Insurance Co.

Responsibilities include corporate philanthropy.

HASKIN, Greg

700 Anderson Hill Rd. Tel: (949) 643 - 5762
Purchase, NY 10577-1444 Fax:(949) 425 - 8220
greg.haskin@pepsi.com

Serves As:
- Manager, Government Affairs, (Pepsi-Cola North America), PepsiCo, Inc.

HASMAN, Glenn R.

P.O. Box 777 Tel: (330) 273 - 8820
Medina, OH 44258 Fax:(330) 225 - 8743
ghasman@rpminc.com

Serves As:
- V. President, Finance and Communications, RPM Internat'l Inc.

Responsibilities include investor relations.

HASSAN, Fred

2000 Galloping Hill Rd. Tel: (908) 298 - 7340
Kenilworth, NJ 07033

Serves As:
- Chairman and Chief Exec. Officer, Schering-Plough Corporation

HASSELBUSCH, Stan L.

415 Holiday Dr. Tel: (412) 928 - 3417
Pittsburgh, PA 15220-2793 Fax:(412) 928 - 7891
shasselbusch@lbfosterco.com TF: (800) 255 - 4500

Serves As:
- President and Chief Exec. Officer, L. B. Foster Co.

HASSELL, John D.

1100 New York Ave. NW Tel: (202) 378 - 2500
Suite 600W Fax:(202) 378 - 2550
Washington, DC 20005
john.hassell@hp.com

Registered Federal Lobbyist.
Serves As:
- Director, Federal and State Government Affairs, Hewlett-Packard Co.

HASSENFELD, Alan G.

P.O. Box 1059 Tel: (401) 431 - 8697
Pawtucket, RI 02862 Fax:(401) 431 - 8535

Serves As:
- Chairman of the Board, Hasbro Inc.

HASSETT, Jace

1717 Pennsylvania Ave. NW Tel: (202) 857 - 3047
Suite 400 Fax:(202) 857 - 3070
Washington, DC 20006
jace_hassett@oxy.com

Registered Federal Lobbyist.
Serves As:
- V. President, Government Affairs-Chemicals, Occidental Internat'l
- V. President, Government Affairs, Occidental Chemical Corp.

HASSEY, L. Patrick

1000 Six PPG Pl. Tel: (412) 394 - 2800
Pittsburgh, PA 15222-5479 Fax:(412) 394 - 2805

Serves As:
- Chairman, President and Chief Exec. Officer, Allegheny Technologies Incorporated

HASTINGS, Robert

1601 Research Blvd. Tel: (301) 838 - 6712
Rockville, MD 20850 Fax:(301) 838 - 6925
robert.hastings@baesystems.com

Serves As:
- V. President, Public Affairs and Communications, BAE Systems North America

HASTINGS, T. Kay

P.O. Box Nine Tel: (281) 491 - 9181
Sugar Land, TX 77487 Fax:(281) 490 - 9584
TF: (800) 727 - 8427

Serves As:
- Senior V. President, Human Resources, Imperial Sugar Co.

Responsibilities include investor and media relations.

HASYCHAK, Michael C.

17876 St. Clair Ave. Tel: (216) 383 - 6823
Cleveland, OH 44110 Fax:(216) 383 - 4091
TF: (800) 321 - 2076

Serves As:
- V. President, Treasurer and Secretary, Brush Engineered Materials Inc.

Responsibilities include investor relations.

HATCHER, Dotti

Two Folsom St. Tel: (650) 952 - 4400
San Francisco, CA 94105 Fax:(415) 427 - 2553
TF: (800) 333 - 7899

Serves As:
- Senior Director, Gap Inc. Community Relations, Gap Inc.

HATCHER, Sandy

1900 W. Loop South Tel: (713) 961 - 4600
Suite 1500 Fax:(713) 877 - 5333
Houston, TX 77027 TF: (800) 231 - 8176
shatcher@quanex.com

Serves As:
- Manager, Human Resources Services, Quanex Corp.

Responsibilities include corporate philanthropy.

HATELEY, J. Michael

1840 Century Park East Tel: (310) 201 - 3043
Los Angeles, CA 90067-2199 Fax:(310) 556 - 4519
hatelmi@mail.northgrum.com

Serves As:
- Corporate V. President and Chief Human Resources and Administrative Officer, Northrop Grumman Corp.

HATHAWAY, Derek C.

P.O. Box 8888 Tel: (717) 763 - 7064
Camp Hill, PA 17001-8888 Fax:(717) 763 - 6424
dhathaway@harsco.com

Serves As:
- Chairman, President and Chief Exec. Officer, Harsco Corp.

HATHCOAT, Lisa
2202 N. Westshore Blvd.
Fifth Floor
Tampa, FL 33607
Tel: (813) 282 - 1225
Fax:(813) 282 - 1209

Serves As:
- Manager, Investor Relations, Outback Steakhouse, Inc.

HATHCOCK, Bonnie
P.O. Box 1438
Louisville, KY 40201-1438
bhathcock@humana.com
Tel: (502) 580 - 1000
Ext: 3575
Fax:(502) 580 - 3677
TF: (800) 486 - 2620

Serves As:
- Senior V. President and Chief Human Resources Officer, Humana Inc.

HATHCOCK, C. Don
1522 BellSouth Plaza
300 S. Brevard St.
Charlotte, NC 28202
don.hathcock@bellsouth.com
Tel: (704) 417 - 8764

Serves As:
- V. President, Legislative Affairs, BellSouth Corp.

HAUB, Christian
Two Paragon Dr.
Montvale, NJ 07645
Tel: (201) 571 - 4240
Fax:(201) 571 - 4445

Serves As:
- Chairman of the Board, The Great Atlantic and Pacific Tea Co.

HAUBRICH, Joel
231 W. Michigan St.
P346
Milwaukee, WI 53201
joel.haubrich@we-energies.com
Tel: (414) 221 - 4102
Fax:(414) 221 - 3814

Serves As:
- Manager, State Government Affairs, Wisconsin Energy Corp.

HAUDRICH, John
8182 Maryland Ave.
Clayton, MO 63105
Tel: (314) 746 - 1266

Serves As:
- Investor Relations Contact, Smurfit-Stone Container

HAUGE, Marilyn I.
2020 Santa Monica Blvd., Suite 600
Santa Monica, CA 90404-2208
mhauge@fmt.com
Tel: (310) 315 - 5500
Fax:(310) 315 - 5599

Serves As:
- Assistant Secretary and Director, Corporate Compliance and Investor Relations, Fremont General Corp.

HAUGHT, Mel
102 Main St.
Pella, IA 50219
Tel: (641) 621 - 1000
Fax:(641) 628 - 6070

Serves As:
- President and Chief Exec. Officer, Pella Corp.

HAULTER, Robert J.
500 Water St.
Jacksonville, FL 32203
Tel: (904) 359 - 3200
Fax:(904) 359 - 1899

Serves As:
- Senior V. President, Human Resources and Labor Relations, CSX Corp.

HAUSER, David L..
P.O. Box 1244
EC3XF
Charlotte, NC 28201-1244
dhauser@duke-energy.com
Tel: (704) 382 - 5963
Fax:(704) 382 - 3588

Serves As:
- Chief Financial Officer, Duke Energy Corp.

HAUSMAN, Tom
1025 W. NASA Blvd.
Melbourne, FL 32919-0001
thausm01@harris.com
Tel: (321) 727 - 9131
Fax:(321) 727 - 9646
TF: (800) 442 - 7747

Serves As:
- Director, Media and Public Relations, Harris Corp.

HAUSSER, Marsha
100 NE Adams St.
Peoria, IL 61629-1465
Tel: (309) 675 - 1307
Fax:(309) 675 - 5588

Serves As:
- Senior Public Information Representative, Caterpillar Inc.

HAVERTY, Michael R.
427 W. 12th St.
Kansas City, MO 64105
Tel: (816) 983 - 1303
Fax:(816) 983 - 1124
TF: (800) 468 - 6740

Serves As:
- Chairman, President, and Chief Exec. Officer, Kansas City Southern

HAVILAND, Bryan
One Nationwide Plaza
Columbus, OH 43215-2220
havilab@nationwide.com
Tel: (614) 249 - 7111
Fax:(614) 249 - 3073

Serves As:
- Officer, Public Relations, Nationwide

HAWKINS, Candace
1000 Corporate Dr.
Fort Lauderdale, FL 33334
Tel: (954) 351 - 5100
Fax:(954) 351 - 5390

Serves As:
- Foundation Contact, (Arby's, Inc.), Triarc Companies, Inc.

HAWKINS, Donald
401 E. Liberty
Ann Arbor, MI 48104-2298
Tel: (734) 669 - 5084
Fax:(734) 930 - 6750

Serves As:
- Senior V. President, Community Affairs, TCF Bank

HAWKINS, J. Michael
1201 K St., Suite 1850
Sacramento, CA 95814
Tel: (916) 448 - 6512
Fax:(916) 973 - 6476

Serves As:
- Senior Legislative Counsel, Kaiser Permanente

HAWKINS, John T. W.
265 Davidson Ave.
Suite 300
Somerset, NJ 08873-4120
jhawkins@medpointepharma.com
Tel: (732) 564 - 2233
Fax:(732) 564 - 2223

Serves As:
- Exec. V. President, Corporate Development and External Affairs, (MedPointe Pharmaceuticals), MedPointe Inc.

HAWKINS, Neil C.
2030 Dow Center
Midland, MI 48674-0001
nchawkins@dow.com
Tel: (989) 636 - 1000
Fax:(989) 636 - 3518

Serves As:
- Director, Issues Management, The Dow Chemical Company

HAWKINS, Wendy
5300 NE Elam Young Pkwy.
Hillsboro, OR 97123-6497
Tel: (503) 456 - 1539
Fax:(503) 696 - 8179

Serves As:
- Intel Foundation Contact, Intel Corp.

HAWKS, Lisa
7601 Penn Ave. South
Richfield, MN 55423
lisa.hawks@bestbuy.com
Tel: (612) 292 - 4000
Fax:(612) 292 - 4001

Serves As:
- Director, Consumer Public Relations, Best Buy Co., Inc.

HAWORTH, Richard G.
One Haworth Center
Holland, MI 49423
Tel: (616) 393 - 1144
Fax:(616) 393 - 1570
TF: (800) 344 - 2600

Serves As:
- Chairman of the Board, Haworth Inc.

HAY, David
999 W. Big Beaver Rd.
Troy, MI 48084-4782
Tel: (248) 362 - 4522
Fax:(248) 244 - 7572

Serves As:
- Senior Director, Government Affairs, Kelly Services, Inc.

HAY, III, Lewis
P.O. Box 14000
Juno Beach, FL 33408-0420
lew_hay@fpl.com
Tel: (561) 694 - 4705
Fax:(561) 694 - 4620

Serves As:
- FPL Group, Chairman, President and Chief Exec. Officer, FPL Group, Inc.

HAYAT, Suzanne
Three Chestnut Ridge Rd.
Montvale, NJ 07645-0435
Tel: (212) 909 - 5000
Fax:(212) 909 - 5299

Serves As:
- Director, International Public Relations, KPMG LLP

HAYDEN, Kathryn
3150 Sabre Dr.
Southlake, TX 76092
kathryn.hayden@sabre-holdings.com
Tel: (682) 605 - 2252
Fax:(682) 264 - 0502

Serves As:
- Senior Manager, Public Relations, (Sabre Airline Solutions), Sabre Holdings Corp.

HAYDEN, Kerry
1365 S. Gilbert Rd.
Floor 1-A
Mesa, AZ 85204
Tel: (480) 926 - 0891
Fax:(480) 926 - 8951

Serves As:
- Legislative Representative, Farmers Group, Inc.

HAYDEN, Ludwig
1401 I St. NW
Suite 1200
Washington, DC 20005-2225
Tel: (202) 408 - 5800
Fax:(202) 408 - 5845

Registered Federal Lobbyist.
Serves As:
- Manager, Federal Relations, Chevron Corp.

HAYES, Brad
358 S. Main St.
Burlington, NC 27215
Tel: (336) 229 - 1127
Fax:(336) 436 - 1205
TF: (800) 334 - 5261

Serves As:
- Senior V. President, Investor Relations, Laboratory Corp. of America Holdings

HAYES, Daniel K.
201 N. Harrison St.
Davenport, IA 52801-1939
Tel: (563) 383 - 2100

Serves As:
- V. President, Communications, Lee Enterprises

HAYES, Michael D.
2030 Dow Center
Midland, MI 48674-0001
mdhayes@dow.com
Tel: (989) 636 - 1000
Fax:(989) 638 - 1727

Serves As:
- Global V. President, Public Affairs, Public Policy and Advocacy, The Dow Chemical Company

HAYES, Michael J.
4300 New Getwell Rd.
Memphis, TN 38118-6801
Tel: (901) 365 - 8880
Fax:(901) 328 - 0354
TF: (800) 374 - 7417

Serves As:
- Chief Exec. Officer, Fred's Inc.

HAYES, Noreen J.
400 Broadway
Cincinnati, OH 45202
Tel: (513) 629 - 1905
Fax:(513) 629 - 1050
TF: (800) 936 - 1212

Serves As:
- Senior V. President, Human Resources, Western and Southern Life Insurance Co.

HAYES, Perry G.
847 Gibraltar Dr.
Milpitas, CA 95035
Tel: (408) 957 - 8500

Serves As:
- Treasurer and V. President, Investor Relations, Solectron Corp.

HAYES, Rodney
18 Loveton Circle
Sparks, MD 21152-6000
rodney_hayes@mccormick.com
Tel: (410) 771 - 7301
Fax:(410) 771 - 7462

Serves As:
- Regulatory Specialist, McCormick & Company, Inc.

HAYES, Susan
9900 Bren Rd. East
Minneapolis, MN 55343
Tel: (952) 936 - 1300
Fax:(952) 936 - 0044
TF: (800) 328 - 5979

Serves As:
- Associate Director, Foundation, UnitedHealth Group

HAYES, Susan
1095 Ave. of the Americas
New York, NY 10036
Tel: (212) 395 - 2121
TF: (800) 621 - 9900

Serves As:
- Director, Public Affairs Programs, Verizon Communications Inc.

HAYES, Thomas F.
P.O. Box 1464
Wall, NJ 07719
Tel: (732) 938 - 1000
Fax:(732) 938 - 2620

Serves As:
- Director, Consumer Community Relations, (New Jersey Natural Gas Co.), New Jersey Resources Corp.

HAYES, Tom
56 Top Gallant Rd.
Stamford, CT 06904
tom.hayes@gartner.com
Tel: (203) 316 - 6835
Fax:(203) 316 - 6488

Serves As:
- Group V. President, Public Relations, Gartner, Inc.

HAYLING, Crystal
50 Beale St.
San Francisco, CA 94105-1808
Tel: (415) 229 - 5000
Fax:(415) 229 - 5070
TF: (800) 200 - 3242

Serves As:
- President and Chief Exec. Officer, Blue Shield of California Foundation, Blue Shield of California

HAYMAKER, Jr., George T.
27422 Portola Pkwy
Suite 350
Foothill Ranch, CA 92610-2831
Tel: (949) 614 - 1740
Fax:(949) 614 - 1930

Serves As:
- Chairman of the Board, Kaiser Aluminum & Chemical Corp.

HAYNES, Mark
1899 Pennsylvania Ave., NW
Suite 300
Washington, DC 20006
haynes@ga.radix.net
Tel: (202) 496 - 8200
Fax:(202) 659 - 1110

Registered Federal Lobbyist.
Serves As:
- V. President, Washington Operations, General Atomics

HAYNES, Mildred W.
1425 K St. NW
Suite 300
Washington, DC 20005
mwhaynes@mmm.com
Tel: (202) 414 - 3000
Fax:(202) 414 - 3037

Registered Federal Lobbyist.
Serves As:
- Manager, Government Relations, 3M Company

HAYON, Beverly
Ordway Bldg.
One Kaiser Plaza
Oakland, CA 94612
beverly.hayon@kp.org
Tel: (510) 271 - 5953
Fax:(510) 271 - 6493

Serves As:
- Director, National Media Relations, Kaiser Permanente

HAYWOOD, Michael S.
401 Ninth St. NW
Suite 1100
Washington, DC 20004
mshaywood@duke-energy.com
Tel: (202) 331 - 8090
Fax:(202) 331 - 1181

Serves As:
- Director, Federal Government Affairs, Duke Energy Corp.

HAZELBAKER, Duane
220 N. Meridian St.
Indianapolis, IN 46204
Tel: (317) 265 - 5266
Fax:(317) 265 - 3995
TF: (800) 257 - 0902

Serves As:
- Director, Corporate Affairs, SBC Indiana

HAZELGROVE, Bruce
P.O. Box 2189
Richmond, VA 23218-2189
Tel: (804) 788 - 5000
Fax:(804) 788 - 5688
TF: (800) 535 - 3030

Serves As:
- Contact, NewMarket Services Contributions Program; and PAC Treasurer, NewMarket Corp.

HAZERA, Ramona B.
1200 Wilson Blvd.
Arlington, VA 22209-2305
Tel: (703) 465 - 3312

Serves As:
- Director, Export-Import Management and Compliance, The Boeing Co.

HEADEN, Sonya
P.O. Box 98910
Las Vegas, NV 89151-0001
Tel: (702) 367 - 5222
Fax:(702) 367 - 5092
TF: (800) 331 - 3103

Serves As:
- Media Contact, Nevada Power Co.

HEALEY, Kate
40 Monument Circle
Suite 700
Indianapolis, IN 46204
kate@emmis.com
Tel: (317) 684 - 6576
Fax:(317) 631 - 3750

Serves As:
- Director, Investor Relations and Media Relations, Emmis Communications Corp.

HEALY, Karen L.
5725 Delphi Dr.
M/S 483-400-501
Troy, MI 48098-2815
Tel: (248) 813 - 2529
Fax:(248) 813 - 2530

Serves As:
- V. President, Corporate Affairs, Marketing Communications, and Facilities, Delphi Corp.

HEALY, Sean
5400 Legacy Dr.
Plano, TX 75024-3199
shealy@eds.com
Tel: (972) 605 - 8173
Fax:(972) 605 - 6841

Serves As:
- Director, Corporate Public Relations, EDS Corp.

HEANEY, Susan Arnot
1345 Ave. of the Americas
New York, NY 10020
susan.heaney@avonfoundation.com
Tel: (212) 282 - 5668
Fax:(212) 282 - 6220

Serves As:
- Foundation Contact, Avon Products, Inc.

HEANY, Sandra K.
101 N. Washington Square
mc 7816
Lansing, MI 48933
Tel: (517) 342 - 5765
Fax:(517) 342 - 5969
TF: (800) 521 - 1190

Serves As:
- Assistant V. President and CRA Coordinator, Community Affairs, Comerica Incorporated

HEARN, Gary
One Goodyear Blvd.
Lawton, OK 73505
gary.hearn@goodyear.com
Tel: (405) 531 - 5842
Fax:(405) 531 - 5899

Serves As:
- Manager, Communications, The Goodyear Tire & Rubber Company

HEARST, Edward
1 Sybase Dr.
Dublin, CA 94568
Tel: (925) 236 - 7515

Registered Federal Lobbyist.
Serves As:
- Government Affairs, Sybase, Inc.

HEARST, Jr., George R.
959 Eighth Ave.
New York, NY 10019
Tel: (212) 649 - 2000
Fax:(212) 765 - 3528

Serves As:
- Chairman of the Board, The Hearst Corp.

HEASLIP, Steven J.
521 W. 57th St.
New York, NY 10019
Tel: (212) 765 - 5500
Fax:(212) 708 - 7132

Serves As:
- Senior V. President, Human Resources, Internat'l Flavors and Fragrances

HEATH, Robert
P.O. Box 702
Milwaukee, WI 53201-0702
Tel: (414) 259 - 5333
Fax:(414) 479 - 1245

Serves As:
- Secretary and Treasurer, Briggs and Stratton Corp. Foundation, Briggs and Stratton Corp.

HEATWOLE, Mike
P.O. Box 196660
MS 542
Anchorage, AK 99519-6660
Tel: (907) 787 - 8870
Fax:(907) 787 - 8240

Serves As:
- Manager, Corporate Communications, Alyeska Pipeline Service Co.

HEBERT, Curtis L.
P.O. Box 61000
New Orleans, LA 70161
cheber7@entergy.com
Tel: (504) 576 - 4743
Fax:(504) 576 - 4428

Serves As:
- Exec. V. President, External Affairs, Entergy Corp.

HEBRON, Anthony
Three Limited Pkwy.
Columbus, OH 43230
Tel: (614) 415 - 7072
Fax:(614) 415 - 1144

Serves As:
- V. President, External Communications, The Limited Brands

HECHT, William F.
Two N. Ninth St.
Allentown, PA 18101-1179
Tel: (610) 774 - 5151
Fax:(610) 774 - 5281
TF: (800) 345 - 3085

Serves As:
- Chairman, President and Chief Exec. Officer, PPL Corp.

HECKMAN, Margaret
P.O. Box 431
Easton, PA 18044-0431
Tel: (610) 559 - 6660

Serves As:
- Corporate Contributions Contact, Binney and Smith Inc.

HECKNER, Kedron L. "Larry"
102 Balzac Court
Cary, NC 27511
Tel: (919) 468 - 0066

Serves As:
- Regional Director/Team Leader, State Government Relations, HSBC North America Holdings Inc.

HEDRICK, Gary R.
P.O. Box 982
El Paso, TX 79960
ghedrick@epelectric.com
Tel: (915) 543 - 5711
Fax:(915) 521 - 4766
TF: (800) 351 - 1621

Serves As:
- President and Chief Exec. Officer, El Paso Electric Co.

HEETER, Charles P.
555 12th St. NW
Suite 500
Washington, DC 20004
Tel: (202) 879 - 5978
Fax:(202) 638 - 7857

Registered Federal Lobbyist.
Serves As:
- Principal, Deloitte & Touche LLP

Responsibilities include government affairs.

HEFFERNAN, Barbara D.
1401 I St. NW
Suite 200
Washington, DC 20005
Tel: (202) 293 - 9494
Fax:(202) 223 - 9594

Registered Federal Lobbyist.
Serves As:
- Director, National Government Affairs, Anheuser-Busch Cos., Inc.

HEFFLER, Mava
301 Merritt Seven
Sixth Floor
Norwalk, CT 06851
Tel: (203) 849 - 7800
Fax:(203) 849 - 7870

Serves As:
- V. President, Marketing and Communications, EMCOR Group, Inc.

HEFNER, Christie
680 N. Lake Shore Dr.
Chicago, IL 60611
Tel: (312) 751 - 8000
Fax:(312) 337 - 0271

Serves As:
- Chairman and Chief Exec. Officer, Playboy Enterprises, Inc.

HEGI, Jr., Frederick B.
2200 E. Golf Rd.
Des Plaines, IL 60016-1267
Tel: (847) 699 - 5000
Fax:(847) 699 - 8046

Serves As:
- Chairman of the Board, United Stationers Inc.

HEHN, Joye
P.O. Box 10566
Birmingham, AL 35296
Tel: (205) 297 - 3554
Fax:(205) 297 - 3043
TF: (800) 239 - 2265

Serves As:
- Contact, Compass Bank Foundation, Compass Bancshares, Inc.

HEIBERG, Danielle Dowling
2000 Pennsylvania Ave. NW
Suite 4200
Washington, DC 20006
Tel: (202) 887 - 6932
Fax:(202) 887 - 6933

Serves As:
- Manager, Legislative Affairs, Yahoo! Inc.

HEID, Werner T.
10955 Vista Sorrento Pkwy.
San Diego, CA 92130
heid@iomega.com
Tel: (858) 314 - 7000
Fax:(858) 314 - 7001

Serves As:
- President and Chief Exec. Officer, Iomega Corp.

HEIDBREDER, Warren W.
Bandag Center
2905 N. Hwy. 61
Muscatine, IA 52761-5886
Tel: (563) 262 - 1260
Fax:(563) 262 - 1263

Serves As:
- V. President, Chief Financial Officer and Corporate Secretary, Bandag, Inc.

Responsibilities include investor relations.

HEIDEMANN, Lyle
8600 W. Bryn Mawr Ave.
Chicago, IL 60631-3505
Tel: (773) 695 - 5000

Serves As:
- President and Chief Exec. Officer, True Value Company

HEILIG, Paul T.
1200 Wilson Blvd.
Arlington, VA 22209-2305
Tel: (703) 465 - 3666
Fax:(703) 465 - 3004

Registered Federal Lobbyist.
Serves As:
- Manager, Legislative Affairs, Homeland Security, Phantom Works, The Boeing Co.

HEILMAN, Janet B.
P.O. Box 115
Austell, GA 30168-0115
Tel: (770) 948 - 3101
Ext: 3779
Fax:(770) 732 - 3401

Serves As:
- Investor Relations Contact, Caraustar Industries, Inc.

HEIMERT, Chrystie
30 Community Dr.
South Burlington, VT 05403-6828
chrystieh@benjerry.com
Tel: (802) 846 - 1500
Ext: 7700
Fax:(802) 846 - 1536

Serves As:
- Director, Public Relations, Ben & Jerry's Homemade Inc.

HEINE, Kevin
One Wall St.
New York, NY 10286
kheine@bankofny.com
Tel: (212) 635 - 1569
Fax:(212) 635 - 1799

Serves As:
- V. President, Corporate Communications, The Bank of New York Co., Inc.

HEINEMAN, Jr., Ben W.
3135 Easton Tpk.
Bldg. E2E
Fairfield, CT 06431
Tel: (203) 373 - 2211
Fax:(203) 373 - 3131

Serves As:
- Senior V. President, Law and Public Affairs, General Electric Co.

HEINONEN, Cheryl
900 Metro Center Blvd.
Foster City, CA 94404-2172
Tel: (650) 432 - 4671
Fax:(650) 432 - 3631

Serves As:
- Media Contact, Visa U.S.A. Inc.

HEINRICH, Daniel J.
P.O. Box 24305
Oakland, CA 94623-1305
heinrich@clorox.com
Tel: (510) 271 - 7377
Fax:(510) 832 - 1463

Serves As:
- Senior V. President and Chief Financial Officer, The Clorox Co.

Responsibilities include investor relations.

HEINRICH, Tim
P.O. Box 77007
Madison, WI 53707-1007
timheinrich@alliantenergy.com
Tel: (608) 458 - 3221
Fax:(608) 458 - 0133

Serves As:
- Director, Community Affairs, Alliant Energy Corp.

HEINZ, Jeffrey R.
12061 Bluemont Way
Reston, VA 20190
Tel: (703) 810 - 7743
Fax:(703) 810 - 7053

Serves As:
- Assistant V. President, Investor Relations, SLM Corp.

HEINZE, Rina
2700 Coast Ave.
Mountain View, CA 94043
Tel: (650) 944 - 6000

Serves As:
- PAC Treasurer, Intuit Inc.

HEISLER, Karen M.
225 City Line Ave.
Suite 200
Bala Cynwyd, PA 19004
Tel: (610) 934 - 7000
Fax:(610) 934 - 7054
TF: (888) 438 - 7488

Serves As:
- Senior V. President, Human Resources and Administrative Services, Pegasus Communications Corp.

HEITMANN, Scott K.
2600 W. Big Beaver Rd.
Troy, MI 48084
Tel: (248) 643 - 9600
Fax:(248) 637 - 2749
TF: (800) 643 - 9600

Serves As:
- Chairman, President, and Chief Exec. Officer, Standard Federal Bank

HELBACH, David W.
P.O. Box 77007
Madison, WI 53707-1007
davidhelbach@alliantenergy.com
Tel: (608) 458 - 5718
Fax:(608) 458 - 3481

Serves As:
- Director, Corporate Public Affairs, Alliant Energy Corp.

HELDRETH, Nick E.
1025 W. NASA Blvd.
Melbourne, FL 32919-0001
Tel: (321) 727 - 9314
Fax:(321) 727 - 9344
TF: (800) 442 - 7747

Serves As:
- V. President, Corporate Relations and Human Resources; Secretary, Harris Corp. Foundation, Harris Corp.

HELLER, Lauren M.
1100 Wilson Blvd.
Suite 1500
Arlington, VA 22209
Tel: (703) 841 - 5700
Fax:(703) 841 - 5792

Registered Federal Lobbyist.
Serves As:
- Director, Government Relations, Raytheon Co.

HELLIER, Richard G.
1401 I St. NW
Suite 600
Washington, DC 20005
Tel: (202) 336 - 7400
Fax:(202) 336 - 7515

Registered Federal Lobbyist.
Serves As:
- Representative, United Technologies Corp.

HELLIWELL, Geoffrey
290 Concord Rd.
Billerica, MA 01821
geoffrey_helliwell@millipore.com
Tel: (978) 715 - 1041

Serves As:
- Treasurer and Director, Investor Relations, Millipore Corp.

HELLMANN, Dennis
130 N. Erie St.
Room 114
Toledo, OH 43624
dennis.j.hellmann@sbc.com
Tel: (419) 245 - 7112
Fax:(419) 245 - 7240

Serves As:
- Director, External Affairs, SBC Ohio

HELM, Robert W.
1000 Wilson Blvd., Suite 2300
Arlington, VA 22209
Tel: (703) 875 - 8500
Fax:(703) 276 - 0711

Registered Federal Lobbyist.
Serves As:
- Corporate V. President, Government Relations, Northrop Grumman Corp.

HELMSTETTER, Dave
44 S. Washington St.
New Bremen, OH 45869
dave.helmstetter@crown.com
Tel: (419) 629 - 2311
Fax:(419) 629 - 3067

Serves As:
- Publicity Administrator, Crown Equipment Corp.

HELSING, Craig R.
The Executive Tower
1399 New York Ave. NW, Suite 425
Washington, DC 20005
Tel: (202) 393 - 2150
Fax:(202) 393 - 2151

Serves As:
- V. President, Government Relations, BMW (U.S.) Holding Corp.

Responsibilities include corporate public affairs.

HEMEYER, Terry
1929 Allen Pkwy.
Houston, TX 77019
terry.hemeyer@sci-us.com
Tel: (713) 525 - 5497
Fax:(713) 525 - 2800

Serves As:
- Managing Director, Corporate Communications, Service Corp. Internat'l

HEMLEPP, Pat D.
One Riverside Plaza
Columbus, OH 43215-2373
Tel: (614) 223 - 1620
Fax:(614) 223 - 1823

Serves As:
- Director, Corporate Media Relations, American Electric Power Co. Inc.

HENDERSON, Bruce A.
One Imation Place
Oakdale, MN 55128-3414
Tel: (651) 704 - 4000
Fax:(651) 704 - 4200
TF: (888) 466 - 3456

Serves As:
- Chairman and Chief Exec. Officer, Imation Corp.

HENDERSON, Colleen
231 W. Michigan
Milwaukee, WI 53203
colleen.henderson@we-energies.com
Tel: (414) 221 - 3152
Fax:(414) 221 - 2594

Serves As:
- Manager of Strategic Planning and Investor Relations, We Energies

HENDERSON, Jay
One Williams Center
Tulsa, OK 74172
jay.henderson@williams.com
Tel: (918) 573 - 2000
TF: (800) 945 - 5426

Serves As:
- V. President, Investor Relations, Williams

HENDERSON, Lisa
One Campbell Pl.
Camden, NJ 08103-1701
lisa_henderson@campbellsoup.com
Tel: (856) 968 - 5891
Fax:(856) 541 - 8185
TF: (800) 257 - 8443

Serves As:
- Director, Organization Communications, Campbell Soup Co.

HENDERSON, Michael J.
One Telecordia Dr.
Piscataway, NJ 08854-4157
Tel: (732) 699 - 2000

Serves As:
- President, Global Communication Solutions, Telcordia Technologies, Inc.

HENDERSON, Susan
410 N. Michigan Ave.
Chicago, IL 60611
Tel: (312) 644 - 2121
Fax:(312) 644 - 0015

Serves As:
- V. President, Corporate Communications, Wm. Wrigley Jr. Co.

HENDERSON-HAWKINS, Amy C.
700 13th St. NW
Suite 220
Washington, DC 20005
amy.hawkins@bnsf.com
Tel: (202) 347 - 8662
Fax:(202) 347 - 8675

Serves As:
- Assistant V. President, Federal Government Affairs, Burlington Northern Santa Fe Corporation

HENDRICKS, Anne
P.O. Box 699030
Miami, FL 33269-9030
anne.hendricks@publix.com
Tel: (305) 652 - 2411
Ext: 3816
Fax:(305) 770 - 3309

Serves As:
- Manager, Media and Community Relations, Publix Super Markets, Inc.

HENDRICKS, Dave
Strawberry Square, Fourth Floor
Harrisburg, PA 17101
david.r.hendricks@verizon.com
Tel: (717) 777 - 4183

Serves As:
- Director, External Affairs, Verizon Pennsylvania Inc.

HENDRICKS, Jr., James R.
P.O. Box 1244
M/S EC12ZA
Charlotte, NC 28201-1244
jhendricks@duke-energy.com
Tel: (704) 382 - 8203
Fax:(704) 382 - 3588

Serves As:
- V. President, Corporate Environment, Health, and Safety, Duke Energy Corp.

HENDRICKS, Steven
1303 E. Algonquin Rd.
Schaumburg, IL 60196
steven.hendricks@motorola.com
Tel: (847) 632 - 6537
Fax:(847) 435 - 8735
TF: (800) 262 - 8509

Serves As:
- Director, Communications and Public Affairs, Global Telecom Solutions Sector, Motorola, Inc.

HENDRICKSON, Arnold
800 LaSalle Ave.
Minneapolis, MN 55402-2006
Tel: (612) 372 - 4664
Fax:(612) 321 - 5137

Serves As:
- Senior Specialist, Local Government Relations, (CenterPoint Energy Minnegasco), CenterPoint Energy

HENDRICKSON, Carey P.
P.O. Box 655237
Dallas, TX 75265-5237
chendrickson@belo.com
Tel: (214) 977 - 6626
Fax:(214) 977 - 7051

Serves As:
- V. President/Investor Relations and Corporate Communications, Belo Corp.

HENDRICKSON, Thomas T.
1050 W. Hampden Ave.
Englewood, CO 80110
Tel: (303) 200 - 5050
Fax:(303) 863 - 2240

Serves As:
- V. Chairman, Chief Accounting Officer, Chief Financial Officer and Treasurer, The Sports Authority, Inc.

Responsibilities include investor relations.

HENDRIKSEN, Roger S.
P.O. Box 550
Findlay, OH 45839-0550
rshendriksen@coopertire.com
Tel: (419) 427 - 4768
Fax:(419) 424 - 4108

Serves As:
- Director, Investor Relations, Cooper Tire & Rubber Company

HENDRIX, Daniel T.
2859 Paces Ferry Rd., Suite 2000
Atlanta, GA 30339
Tel: (770) 437 - 6840
Fax:(770) 437 - 6887

Serves As:
- President and Chief Exec. Officer, Interface Inc.

Responsibilities include corporate communications, corporate philanthropy, and investor relations.

HENINGER, Lynn W.
Crystal Gateway 3, 1215 S. Clark St.
Suite 1510
Arlington, VA 22202
Tel: (703) 412 - 5960
Fax:(703) 412 - 5970

Registered Federal Lobbyist.
Serves As:
- Director, Legislative Liaison, Space, Alliant Techsystems

Responsibilities include political action.

HENKELS, Paul M.
985 Jolly Rd.
Blue Bell, PA 19422-0900
Tel: (215) 283 - 7600
Fax:(215) 283 - 7659

Serves As:
- Chairman of the Board, Henkels & McCoy, Inc.

HENKELS, T. Roderick
985 Jolly Rd.
Blue Bell, PA 19422-0900
Tel: (215) 283 - 7600
Fax:(215) 283 - 7659

Serves As:
- President and Chief Exec. Officer, Henkels & McCoy, Inc.

HENLEY, Jeff
500 Oracle Pkwy.
Redwood Shores, CA 94065
Tel: (650) 506 - 7000
Fax:(650) 633 - 1269
TF: (800) 672 - 2531

Serves As:
- Chairman of the Board, Oracle Corporation

HENLEY, Maria
411 Seventh Ave.
Pittsburgh, PA 15219
Tel: (412) 393 - 1405
Fax:(412) 393 - 6110

Serves As:
- Public Involvement Specialist, Duquesne Light Holdings

HENNEBERRY, Brian
1401 H St. NW
Suite 510
Washington, DC 20005
Tel: (202) 589 - 0909
Fax:(202) 589 - 0922

Registered Federal Lobbyist.
Serves As:
- Representative, Calpine Corp.

HENNEMANN, Carol
One Busch Pl.
St. Louis, MO 63118-1852
Tel: (314) 577 - 2000
Fax:(314) 577 - 2900

Serves As:
- Contact, Charitable Contributions, Anheuser-Busch Cos., Inc.

HENNESSY, Kelly
40 Landsdowne St.
Cambridge, MA 02139
pr@mlnm.com
Tel: (617) 444 - 3221
Fax:(617) 374 - 7788
TF: (800) 390 - 5663

Serves As:
- Manager, Communications and Corporate Public Affairs, Millennium Pharmaceuticals, Inc.

HENNESY, Dale
P.O. Box 321
M/C 1000
Oklahoma City, OK 73101-0321
Tel: (405) 553 - 3484

Serves As:
- Director, Human Resources, OGE Energy Corp.

HENNICK, Michael
P.O. Box 482
Milwaukee, WI 53201-0482
mhennick@mbco.com
Tel: (414) 931 - 4536
Fax:(414) 931 - 6352

Serves As:
- Director, Marketing Communications, Miller Brewing Co.

HENNING, Richard
200 Old Hook Rd.
Harrington Park, NJ 07640
rich.henning@unitedwater.com
Tel: (201) 767 - 2869
Fax:(201) 767 - 2892
TF: (800) 230 - 2685

Serves As:
- Assistant V. President, Communications, United Water Resources

HENNINGS, Janice
3535 Blue Cross Rd. Tel: (651) 662 - 6139
Eagan, MN 55122--115 TF: (800) 382 - 2000

Serves As:
- Policy and Legislative Affairs Media Contact, Blue Cross and Blue Shield of Minnesota

HENNINGSEN, Anker B.
100 NE Adams St. Tel: (309) 578 - 9889
Peoria, IL 61629-1465 Fax:(309) 675 - 6155

Serves As:
- Manager, Marketing Communications, Caterpillar Inc.

HENRICHSEN, Laurie
One American Rd. Tel: (216) 252 - 4943
Cleveland, OH 44144-2398 Fax:(216) 252 - 6778
laurie.henrichsen@amgreetings.com

Serves As:
- Consumer Media and Public Relations, American Greetings Corp.

HENRIKSSON, Ulf
33 Commercial St. Tel: (508) 549 - 2424
Foxboro, MA 02035 Fax:(508) 549 - 4999
TF: (866) 746 - 6477

Serves As:
- Chief Executive, Invensys Systems, Inc.

HENRY, Debra M.
P.O. Box 7408 Tel: (208) 345 - 4550
Boise, ID 83707 Fax:(208) 331 - 7311
dhenry@bcidaho.com

Serves As:
- V. President, Human Resources and Administrative Services, Blue Cross of Idaho

HENRY, Jack
P.O. Box 7840 Tel: (413) 784 - 0600
Springfield, MA 01102 Fax:(413) 732 - 7350
jhenry@bigy.com

Serves As:
- V. President, Human Resources, Big Y Foods Inc.

HENRY, Janice K.
2710 Wycliff Rd. Tel: (919) 781 - 4550
Raleigh, NC 27607-3033 Fax:(919) 783 - 4695

Serves As:
- Senior V. President, Chief Financial Officer and Treasurer, Martin Marietta Materials, Inc.

Responsibilities include investor relations.

HENRY, Kevin A.
4100 Coca-Cola Plaza Tel: (704) 551 - 4400
Charlotte, NC 28211 Fax:(704) 551 - 4646

Serves As:
- V. President, Human Resources, Coca-Cola Bottling Co. Consolidated

HENRY, Marion
701 Pennsylvania Ave. NW Tel: (202) 434 - 4800
Suite 720 Fax:(202) 347 - 4015
Washington, DC 20004

Registered Federal Lobbyist.
Serves As:
- Representative, Siemens Corp.

HENRY, Melissa
P.O. Box 5000 Tel: (318) 484 - 7400
Pineville, LA 71361-5000 Fax:(318) 484 - 7465

Serves As:
- Treasurer, United Employees' PAC, Cleco Corp.

HENSLEY, William L.
1667 K St. NW Tel: (202) 466 - 3866
Suite 430 Fax:(202) 466 - 3886
Washington, DC 20006

Registered Federal Lobbyist.
Serves As:
- Manager, Federal Government Relations, Alyeska Pipeline Service Co.

HENSON, Chris L.
200 W. Second St. Tel: (336) 733 - 2000
Winston-Salem, NC 27101

Serves As:
- Senior Exec. V. President and Chief Financial Officer, BB&T Corp.

Responsibilities include political action and investor relations.

HENSON, Tom
1840 Century Park East Tel: (310) 201 - 3458
Los Angeles, CA 90067-2199 Fax:(310) 556 - 4561
thomas.henson@ngc.com

Serves As:
- Manager, Media Relations, Northrop Grumman Corp.

HERBERT, Allen
2291 Wood Oak Dr. Tel: (703) 709 - 4621
Herndon, VA 20171

Registered Federal Lobbyist.
Serves As:
- Director, Government Affairs, Computer Associates Internat'l, Inc.

HERBERT, C. Theodore
30 N. LaSalle St. Tel: (312) 630 - 1900
Suite 4000 Fax:(312) 630 - 1908
Chicago, IL 60602-2507
ted.herbert@teldta.com

Serves As:
- V. President, Human Resources, Telephone and Data Systems, Inc.

HERBERT, Kathy
250 E. Parkcenter Blvd. Tel: (208) 395 - 6200
Boise, ID 83706 Fax:(208) 395 - 6631

Serves As:
- Exec. V. President, Human Resources, Albertson's, Inc.

HERBSTREIT, Carol
P.O. Box 571 Tel: (414) 438 - 6882
Milwaukee, WI 53201-0571 Fax:(414) 358 - 6798

Serves As:
- Manager, Corporate Communications, Brady Corp.

HERDERT, Jeanie D.
P.O. Box 3100 Tel: (714) 773 - 8762
C-30-B Fax:(714) 773 - 7743
Fullerton, CA 92834 TF: (800) 742 - 2345
jdherbert@beckman.com

Serves As:
- Director, Investor Relations, Beckman Coulter, Inc.

HERGERT, Carolyn
Three Ravinia Dr., Suite 100 Tel: (770) 604 - 8248
Atlanta, GA 30346 Fax:(770) 604 - 2059
carolyn.hegert@ichotelsgroup.com

Serves As:
- Director, Corporate Communications, InterContinental Hotels Group

HERGLOTZ, Kevin
P.O. Box 99 Tel: (925) 467 - 3000
Pleasanton, CA 94566-0009

Serves As:
- V. President, Government Relations and Legislative Affairs, Safeway Inc.

HERIN, Janet
2100 E. Grand Ave. Tel: (310) 615 - 1693
El Segundo, CA 90245 Fax:(310) 615 - 1699
jherin@csc.com

Serves As:
- Senior Media Relations Representative, Computer Sciences Corp.

HERMAN, Cindy
P.O. Box 300 Tel: (920) 231 - 8800
Oshkosh, WI 54903-0300 Fax:(920) 231 - 8621
TF: (800) 282 - 4674

Serves As:
- Corporate Director, Advertising, Public Relations and Promotions, Oshkosh B'Gosh, Inc.

HERMANCE, Frank S.
37 N. Valley Rd., Bldg. Four Tel: (610) 647 - 2121
P.O. Box 1764 Fax:(610) 323 - 9337
Paoli, PA 19301 TF: (800) 473 - 1286

Serves As:
- Chairman and Chief Exec. Officer, Ametek, Inc.

HERMANDORFER, Wayne
1550 Crystal Dr. Tel: (703) 413 - 5777
Crystal Square 2, Suite 300 Fax:(703) 413 - 5617
Arlington, VA 22202
wayne.hermandorfer@lmco.com

Registered Federal Lobbyist.
Serves As:
- Director, Aeronautical Legislative Affairs, Lockheed Martin Corp.

HERNANDEZ, Mary A.
Lever House, 390 Park Ave. Tel: (212) 888 - 1260
New York, NY 10022-4698 Fax:(212) 906 - 4666
mary.hernandez@unilever.com

Serves As:
- Public Affairs Coordinator, Unilever United States, Inc.

HERNDON, Allison
30 Hwy. 90 East Tel: (228) 466 - 4221
Bay St. Louis, MS 39520 Fax:(228) 466 - 4214

Serves As:
- Treasurer, Mississippi Power Co. Federal PAC, Mississippi Power Co.

HERNDON, Heather
1818 N St. NW
Suite 800
Washington, DC 20036
Tel: (202) 419 - 3000
Fax:(202) 419 - 3030

Registered Federal Lobbyist.
Serves As:
- Manager, Congressional Affairs, Cingular Wireless

HERNDON, Wanda
P.O. Box 34067
S-CM1
Seattle, WA 98124-1067
Tel: (206) 447 - 1575
Ext: 88191
Fax:(206) 447 - 9866

Serves As:
- Senior V. President, Worldwide Communications and Public Affairs, Starbucks Corp.

HEROLD, Richard
1776 I St. NW
Suite 1000
Washington, DC 20006-3707
heroldra@bp.com
Tel: (202) 785 - 4888
Fax:(202) 457 - 6597

Registered Federal Lobbyist.
Serves As:
- Director, International Affairs, BP

HERREID, Beth S.
34 N. Meramec Ave.
St. Louis, MO 63105
Tel: (314) 512 - 9200
Fax:(314) 573 - 9455
TF: (800) 470 - 9227

Serves As:
- Director, Corporate Communications and Media Relations, Graybar Electric Co., Inc.

HERRICK, Bill
585 Broadway
Redwood City, CA 94063
Tel: (650) 542 - 3865
Fax:(650) 542 - 5900

Serves As:
- Investor and Media Relations Contact, BroadVision, Inc.

HERRING, Joseph
210 Carnegie Center
Princeton, NJ 08540-6233
Tel: (609) 452 - 4440
Fax:(609) 452 - 9375
TF: (800) 621 - 8901

Serves As:
- President and Chief Exec. Officer, Covance, Inc.

HERRINGTON, Checky
P.O. Box 1640
Jackson, MS 39215-1640
Tel: (601) 368 - 5000
Fax:(601) 964 - 2400

Serves As:
- Manager, Communications, Entergy Mississippi

HERRMANN, Arthur F.
50 W. State St., Suite 1116
Trenton, NJ 08608
art.herrman@prudential.com
Tel: (609) 989 - 7070
Fax:(609) 989 - 7045

Serves As:
- V. President, Government Affairs, Prudential Financial

HERRON, Jesse
Ten B Glenlake Pkwy.
Suite 600
Alpharetta, GA 30328
Tel: (770) 407 - 3800

Serves As:
- V. President, Investor Relations, Newell Rubbermaid Inc.

HERRON, Winnell
646 S. Main Ave.
San Antonio, TX 78204
herron.winnell@heb.com
Tel: (210) 938 - 8000
Fax:(210) 938 - 8169

Serves As:
- Group V. President, Public Affairs and Diversity, HEB Grocery Co.

HERSHFIELD, Lawrence S.
P.O. Box 30008
Honolulu, HI 96820
Tel: (808) 835 - 3700
Fax:(808) 835 - 6735

Serves As:
- Chairman of the Board, Hawaiian Holdings, Inc.

HERTEL, Michael M.
2244 Walnut Grove Ave.
Rosemead, CA 91770
hertelmm@sce.com
Tel: (626) 302 - 9456
Fax:(626) 302 - 9730

Serves As:
- Director, Environmental Affairs, Southern California Edison, an Edison Internat'l Co.

HERTZKE, Bruce D.
P.O. Box 152
Forest City, IA 50436-0152
Tel: (641) 585 - 3535
Fax:(641) 585 - 6966

Serves As:
- Chairman and Chief Exec. Officer, Winnebago Industries, Inc.

HERTZOG, Brian
One Market
Spear Tower, Suite 2400
San Francisco, CA 94105
Tel: (415) 267 - 7205
Fax:(415) 267 - 7262

Serves As:
- Director, Corporate Communications, PG & E Corp.

HERWEG, Darlynn
1400 Douglas St.
Omaha, NE 68179
Tel: (402) 544 - 5034

Serves As:
- Director, Contributions, Union Pacific Corp.

HERZ, Ken
One Mellon Center
500 Grant St.
Room 1840
Pittsburgh, PA 15258-0001
herz.kb@mellon.com
Tel: (412) 234 - 0850
Fax:(412) 236 - 1662

Serves As:
- First V. President and Director, Corporate Communications, Mellon Financial Corp.

HERZBERG, Steven M.
530 Walnut St.
Philadelphia, PA 19172

Serves As:
- Treasurer, Penn Mutual Political Action Committee, The Penn Mutual Life Insurance Co.

HERZFELD, Shannon
P.O. Box 1470
Decatur, IL 62525
Tel: (217) 424 - 5200
TF: (800) 637 - 5843

Serves As:
- V. President, Government Relations, Archer Daniels Midland Co. (ADM)

HESKETT, John
500 Huntsman Way
Salt Lake City, UT 84108
john_heskett@huntsman.com
Tel: (801) 584 - 5768
Fax:(801) 584 - 5781

Serves As:
- V. President, Corporate Development and Investor Relations, Huntsman Corp.

HESS, Christopher D.
Eaton Center
1111 Superior Ave.
Cleveland, OH 44114-2584
christopherdhess@eatonm.com
Tel: (216) 523 - 4198
Fax:(216) 479 - 7013

Serves As:
- Manager, Public Affairs, Eaton Corp.

HESS, John B.
1185 Ave. of the Americas
New York, NY 10036
Tel: (212) 997 - 8500
Fax:(212) 536 - 8390

Serves As:
- Chairman and Chief Exec. Officer, Amerada Hess Corp.

HESS, Robert S.
220 NW Second Ave.
Portland, OR 97209-3991
Tel: (503) 226 - 4211
Fax:(503) 721 - 2508

Serves As:
- Director, Investor Relations, NW Natural

HESTERBERG, Earl J.
950 Echo Lane, Suite 100
Houston, TX 77024
Tel: (713) 647 - 5700
Fax:(713) 647 - 5800

Serves As:
- President and Chief Exec. Officer, Group 1 Automotive, Inc.

HESTERMANN, Dean
1023 Cherry Rd.
Memphis, TN 38117
dhesterman@harrahs.com
Tel: (901) 762 - 8787
Fax:(901) 762 - 8914

Serves As:
- Government Relations, Harrah's Entertainment, Inc.

HETE, Joe
145 Hunter Dr.
Wilmington, OH 45177
Tel: (937) 382 - 5591
Fax:(937) 382 - 0896

Serves As:
- President and Chief Exec. Officer, ABX Air, Inc.

HETRICK, Roger L.
1500 DeKoven Ave.
Racine, WI 53403-2552
Tel: (262) 636 - 1200
Fax:(262) 636 - 1424

Serves As:
- V. President, Human Resources, Modine Manufacturing Company

HEUBERGER, Mark
P.O. Box 430
Memphis, TN 30103
mheuberger@mlgw.org
Tel: (901) 528 - 4491
Fax:(901) 528 - 4086

Serves As:
- Manager, Corporate Communications, Memphis Light, Gas and Water Division

HEUER, Maxine
P.O. Box 2181
320 W. Capitol
Little Rock, AR 72203-2181
Tel: (501) 378 - 2000

Serves As:
- Manager, Public Policy Issues Analysis, Arkansas Blue Cross and Blue Shield

HEULE, Amber
2727 N. Central Ave.
P.O. Box 21502
Phoenix, AZ 85004
Tel: (602) 263 - 6815
Fax:(602) 263 - 6889

Serves As:
- Media and Public Relations Specialist, AMERCO

HEWITT, G. Douglas
P.O. Box 418679
Kansas City, MO 64141-9679
Tel: (816) 556 - 2200
Fax:(816) 556 - 2992

Serves As:
- Pac Treasurer, Great Plains Energy, Inc.

HEWITT, Timothy M.
P.O. Box 1220
Indianapolis, IN 46206
Tel: (317) 639 - 1431
Fax:(317) 263 - 6414

Serves As:
- President and Operations Manager, Veolia Water Indianapolis, LLC

HEYER, Steven J.
1111 Westchester Ave.
White Plains, NY 10604
Tel: (914) 640 - 8200
Fax:(914) 640 - 8310
TF: (877) 443 - 4585

Serves As:
- Chief Exec. Officer, Starwood Hotels and Resorts Worldwide, Inc.

HEYMAN, Steve
901 E St. NW
Fourth Floor
Washington, DC 20004-2037
Tel: (202) 969 - 8000
Fax:(202) 969 - 8031

Registered Federal Lobbyist.
Serves As:
- Representative, SLM Corp.

HIATTE, Patrick D.
P.O. Box 961057
Fort Worth, TX 76161-2830
patrick.hiatte@bnsf.com
Tel: (817) 867 - 6418
Fax:(817) 352 - 7924

Serves As:
- General Director, Corporate Communications, Burlington Northern Santa Fe Corporation

HICKCOX, Charlotte
50 W. Broad St.
Suite 3600
Columbus, OH 43215

Serves As:
- Treasurer, Sprint/United Telephone Co. of Ohio Political Leadership Program PAC, Sprint Nextel

HICKERSON, David B.
8600 W. Bryn Mawr Ave.
Suite 800 South
Chicago, IL 60631
david.hickerson@kodak.com
Tel: (773) 867 - 3570
Fax:(773) 867 - 3571

Serves As:
- Manager, State and Local Government Relations - Midwest Region, Eastman Kodak Company

HICKEY, James J.
1818 Market St.
Philadelphia, PA 19103
Tel: (215) 299 - 8000
Fax:(215) 299 - 8030
TF: (800) 523 - 0786

Serves As:
- V. President, Government Affairs, Day & Zimmerman

HICKEY, Nancy W.
P.O. Box 1967
CH4E
Grand Rapids, MI 49501-1967
nhickey@steelcase.com
Tel: (616) 248 - 7292
Fax:(616) 248 - 7400

Serves As:
- Senior V. President, Global Human Resources; and Chief Administrative Officer, Steelcase Inc.

HICKEY, William V.
Park 80 East
Saddle Brook, NJ 07663-5291
Tel: (201) 791 - 7600
Fax:(201) 703 - 4205

Serves As:
- President and Chief Exec. Officer, Sealed Air Corp.

HICKMAN, Jan
343 State St.
Rochester, NY 14650-0516
jan.hickman@kodak.com
Tel: (585) 724 - 4408
Fax:(585) 724 - 9610

Serves As:
- Director, Employee Communications, Eastman Kodak Company

HICKMAN, Rebecca L.
P.O. Box 53999
M/S 9998
Phoenix, AZ 85072-3999
rebecca.hickman@pinnaclewest.com
Tel: (602) 250 - 5668
Fax:(602) 250 - 2789

Serves As:
- Director, Investor Relations, Pinnacle West Capital Corp.

HICKMAN, Sue
4650 Cushing Pkwy.
Fremont, CA 94538-6470
sue.hickman@lamrc.com
Tel: (510) 572 - 5910
Fax:(510) 572 - 6454

Serves As:
- Administrator, Investor Relations, Lam Research Corp.

HICKMAN, Terri
P.O. Box 105366
One CNN Center
Atlanta, GA 30348-5366
Tel: (404) 827 - 3149
Fax:(404) 827 - 2024

Serves As:
- Director, Community Relations, (Atlanta Thrashers), Turner Broadcasting System, Inc.

HICKS, Carolyn
1660 L St. NW
Fourth Floor
Washington, DC 20036
Tel: (202) 775 - 5027
Fax:(202) 775 - 5045

Serves As:
- Manager, Legislative and Regulatory Affairs - Health, General Motors Corp.

HICKS, Daniel J.
P.O. Box 32260
Louisville, KY 40232
Tel: (502) 448 - 5200

Serves As:
- Manager, Public Affairs, (Rohm and Haas Kentucky Inc.), Rohm and Haas Co.

HICKS, Michael
175 Ghent Rd.
Fairlawn, OH 44333-3330
Tel: (330) 869 - 4411
Fax:(330) 869 - 4288

Serves As:
- Senior V. President and Chief Financial Officer, OMNOVA Solutions Inc.

Responsibilities include investor relations.

HICKS, Robin Y.
5151 E. Raines Rd.
Memphis, TN 38118
Tel: (901) 375 - 2086
Fax:(901) 375 - 2848

Serves As:
- Guest Relations Supervisor, Coors Brewing Co.

HICKS, Uchenna
229 W. 43rd St.
New York, NY 10036
hicksul@nytimes.com
Tel: (212) 556 - 1757

Serves As:
- Project Coordinator, Community Affairs and Media Relations, New York Times Co.

HICKSON, Richard G.
P.O. Box 291
Jackson, MS 39205-0291
Tel: (601) 208 - 5111

Serves As:
- Chairman and Chief Exec. Officer, Trustmark Nat'l Bank

HIER, Mark B.
400 Robert St. North
St. Paul, MN 55101
mark.hier@minnesotamutual.com
Tel: (651) 665 - 3672
Fax:(651) 665 - 4128

Serves As:
- Second V. President, Communications and Research, Minnesota Life Insurance Co.

HIER-KING, Jan
101 Montgomery St.
San Francisco, CA 94104
Tel: (415) 627 - 7000
TF: (800) 435 - 4000

Serves As:
- Exec. V. President, Human Resources, The Charles Schwab Corp.

HIGGINBOTTOM, Q. Steve

P.O. Box 1295
Birmingham, AL 35201
qshiggin@southernco.com
Tel: (205) 992 - 5752
Fax:(205) 992 - 5363

Serves As:

- Manager, Corporate Communications, Southern Nuclear Operating Co.

HIGGINS, David

2000 Post Oak Blvd., Suite 100
Houston, TX 77056-4400
david.higgins@apachecorp.com
Tel: (713) 296 - 6690
Fax:(713) 296 - 6480
TF: (800) 874 - 3262

Serves As:

- Director, Strategic Communications, Apache Corp.

HIGGINS, Grainne

2000 Galloping Hill Rd.
Kenilworth, NJ 07033
Tel: (908) 298 - 4000

Serves As:

- Exec. Director, Global Human Resources, Schering-Plough Corporation

HIGGINS, Kathy

P.O. Box 2291
M/S HQ4
Durham, NC 27702-2291
kathy.higgins@bcbsnc.com
Tel: (919) 765 - 4104
Fax:(919) 765 - 4837

Serves As:

- V. President and V. Chairman, BCBSNC Foundation, Blue Cross and Blue Shield of North Carolina

HIGGINS, Michael R.

7887 Washington Village Dr.
Dayton, OH 45459
michael.higgins@amcast.com
Tel: (937) 291 - 7015
Fax:(937) 291 - 7005

Serves As:

- Treasurer, Amcast Industrial Corporation

Responsibilities include investor relations.

HIGGINS, III, Walter M.

P.O. Box 98910
Las Vegas, NV 89151-0001
Tel: (702) 367 - 5000
Fax:(702) 367 - 5092
TF: (800) 331 - 3103

Serves As:

- Chairman, President and Chief Exec. Officer, Nevada Power Co.
- Chairman, President and Chief Exec. Officer, Sierra Pacific Resources

HIGGINSON, Connie

Three World Financial Center
200 Vesey St.
New York, NY 10285
connie.higgenson@aexp.com
Tel: (212) 640 - 4649
Fax:(212) 640 - 0325

Serves As:

- President, American Express Philanthropic Program and Foundation, American Express Co.

HIGGS, Kira

P.O. Box 711
P2A
Portland, OR 97207
Tel: (503) 321 - 6418
Fax:(503) 321 - 6776

Serves As:

- Assistant V. President, Public Affairs and Communications, Standard Insurance Co.

HIGHLAND, Nick

P.O. Box 1518
Bellevue, WA 98009
nhighland@paccar.com
Tel: (425) 468 - 7400
Fax:(425) 468 - 8216

Serves As:

- Exec. Director, Corporate Human Resources, PACCAR Inc.

HIGHLANDER, Bill

50 W. San Fernando St.
San Jose, CA 95113
highlander@calpine.com
Tel: (408) 792 - 1244
Fax:(408) 297 - 9688
TF: (800) 359 - 5115

Serves As:

- V. President, Public Relations, Calpine Corp.

HIGHTMAN, Carrie

225 W. Randolph St.
27 B
Chicago, IL 60606
Tel: (312) 727 - 4000
TF: (800) 327 - 9346

Serves As:

- President, SBC Illinois

Serves as the company's senior public affairs executive at the headquarters.

HIGHTOWER, Michael R.

4800 Deerwood Campus Pkwy.
Jacksonville, FL 32246-8273
Tel: (904) 905 - 6072
Fax:(904) 905 - 4486
TF: (800) 477 - 3736

Registered Federal Lobbyist.

Serves As:

- V. President, Governmental and Legislative Relations, Blue Cross and Blue Shield of Florida

HILGERT, Kassie

7201 Hamilton Blvd.
Allentown, PA 18195-1501
hilgerk@airproducts.com
Tel: (610) 481 - 8527
Fax:(610) 841 - 5900

Serves As:

- Manager, Community Relations and Philanthropy, Air Products and Chemicals, Inc.

HILL, Alan J.

P.O. Box 4446
Houston, TX 77210-4446
hilla@cooperindustries.com
Tel: (713) 209 - 8414
Fax:(713) 209 - 8983

Serves As:

- V. President and Treasurer, Cooper Industries

Responsibilities include political action.

HILL, Anne

4560 Horton St.
Emeryville, CA 94608-2916
Tel: (510) 655 - 8730
Fax:(510) 655 - 9910

Serves As:

- V. President, Human Resources, Chiron Corp.

HILL, Jr., B. Eugene

1400 Holcomb Bridge Rd.
Roswell, GA 30076
Tel: (770) 587 - 8636
Fax:(770) 587 - 7199

Serves As:

- Senior Director, Government Relations, Kimberly-Clark Corp.

HILL, Charlie W.

P.O. Box 449
Norfolk, VA 23510-0449
Tel: (757) 446 - 2010
Fax:(757) 446 - 2489

Serves As:

- Exec. V. President, Human Resources, Landmark Communications, Inc.

HILL, Daryl R.

1717 E. Interstate Ave.
Bismarck, ND 58503
dhill@bepc.com
Tel: (701) 223 - 0441
Fax:(701) 224 - 5315

Serves As:

- Coordinator, News Media, Basin Electric Power Cooperative

HILL, David Anthony

1710 H St. NW
Tenth Floor
Washington, DC 20006
Tel: (202) 392 - 9900
Fax:(202) 546 - 5111

Serves As:

- V. President and General Counsel, Verizon Washington D.C. Inc.

Reponsibilities include regulatory affairs.

HILL, E. Lynn

700 Milam St.
Suite 3100
Houston, TX 77002
Tel: (832) 239 - 6000

Serves As:

- Chief Accounting Officer, Plains Resources Inc.

Responsibilities include media and investor relations.

HILL, Edward J.

730 15th St. NW
DCI-701-05-11
Washington, DC 20005
edward.j.hill@bankofamerica.com
Tel: (202) 624 - 4134
Ext: 85
Fax:(202) 383 - 3475

Registered Federal Lobbyist.

Serves As:

- V. President, Government Relations, Bank of America Corp.

HILL, Frederick W.

270 Park Ave.
New York, NY 10017-2070
Tel: (212) 270 - 6000
Fax:(212) 270 - 1648

Serves As:

- Exec. V. President; and Head, Marketing and Communications, J. P. Morgan Chase & Co.

HILL, Janet

2600 Colorado Ave.
Santa Monica, CA 90404
Tel: (310) 752 - 8073

Serves As:

- Head, West Cost Communications, (MTV Networks), Viacom Inc./CBS Corp.

HILL, Jim
126 C St. NW
Suite Three
Washington, DC 20001
Tel: (202) 347 - 7390

Serves As:
- Treasurer, Amazon.com Holdings Inc. Separate Segregated Fund, Amazon.com, Inc.

HILL, Julie
200 E. Basse Rd.
San Antonio, TX 78209
juliehill@clearchannel.com
Tel: (210) 822 - 2828
Fax:(210) 822 - 2299

Serves As:
- Senior V. President, Finance and Strategic Development, Clear Channel Communications

HILL, Karen
101 Constitution Ave., NW
Suite 400 East
Washington, DC 20001
Tel: (202) 347 - 7500
Fax:(202) 347 - 7501

Serves As:
- V. President and Director, Federal Regulatory Affairs, Exelon Corp.

HILL, Kevin N.
165 Court St.
Rochester, NY 14647
Tel: (585) 454 - 1700
Fax:(585) 238 - 4233

Serves As:
- Chief Exec. Officer, Exellus Blue Cross Blue Shield

HILL, Lloyd L.
4551 W. 107th St.
Overland Park, KS 66207-4037
Tel: (913) 967 - 4000
Fax:(913) 341 - 1694

Serves As:
- Chairman and Chief Exec. Officer, Applebee's Internat'l, Inc.

HILL, Norman J.
305 Hartman Dr.
Lebanon, TN 37088
Tel: (615) 444 - 5533
Fax:(615) 443 - 9511

Serves As:
- Senior V. President, Human Resources, (Cracker Barrel Old Country Store, Inc.), CBRL Group, Inc.

HILL, Sandra
3900 Wisconsin Ave. NW
Washington, DC 20016
Tel: (202) 752 - 7000
Fax:(202) 752 - 6099

Registered Federal Lobbyist.
Serves As:
- Representative, Fannie Mae

HILLBACK, Elliott D.
500 Kendall St.
Cambridge, MA 02142
Tel: (617) 252 - 7500
Fax:(617) 374 - 7368

Serves As:
- Senior V. President, Corporate Affairs, Genzyme Corp.

HILLEGONDS, Paul
2000 Second Ave.
2476WCB
Detroit, MI 48226
Tel: (313) 235 - 8000

Serves As:
- Senior V. President, Corporate Affairs and Communications, DTE Energy Co.

HILLENBRAND, Ray J.
700 State Route 46 East
Batesville, IN 47006-8835
Tel: (812) 934 - 7000
Fax:(812) 934 - 7371

Serves As:
- Chairman of the Board, Hillenbrand Industries, Inc.

HILLIARD, Herb
165 Madison Ave.
Memphis, TN 38103
Tel: (901) 523 - 4826
Fax:(901) 523 - 4934

Registered Federal Lobbyist.
Serves As:
- Exec. V. President, Risk Management, First Horizon Nat'l Corp.

Responsibilities include government relations.

HILLIARD, R. Glenn
11825 N. Pennsylvania St.
Carmel, IN 46032
Tel: (317) 817 - 6100
TF: (800) 888 - 4918

Serves As:
- Chairman of the Board, Conseco, Inc.

HILSEN, Louise
1101 Pennsylvania Ave. NW
Suite 600
Washington, DC 20004
louise.hilsen@us.nestle.com
Tel: (202) 756 - 2299
Fax:(202) 756 - 7556

Registered Federal Lobbyist.
Serves As:
- V. President, Government Relations, Nestle USA, Inc.

HILT, Meredith
One Tellabs Center
1415 W. Diehl Rd.
MS 10
Naperville, IL 60563
meredith.hilt@tellabs.com
Tel: (630) 798 - 2506
Fax:(630) 798 - 4778

Serves As:
- Exec. Director, Tellabs Foundation, Tellabs

HILTABRAND, Leslie
1221 Lamar
Suite 1600
Houston, TX 77010
Tel: (713) 853 - 5670

Serves As:
- Public Relations Contact, Enron Corp.

HILTNER, Mike
7601 Penn Ave. South
Richfield, MN 55423
Tel: (612) 291 - 1000
Fax:(612) 292 - 4001

Serves As:
- Senior Government Relations Specialist, Best Buy Co., Inc.

HILTON, Barron
9336 Civic Center Dr.
Beverly Hills, CA 90210
Tel: (310) 278 - 4321

Serves As:
- Co-Chairman of the Board, Hilton Hotels Corp.

HIMES, Kathryn S.
818 Connecticut Ave. NW
Suite 600
Washington, DC 20006-2702
Tel: (202) 466 - 0683
Fax:(202) 466 - 0684

Serves As:
- Manager, Government Affairs, Caterpillar Inc.

HINCKLEY, Clark B.
Kennecott Bldg.
One S. Main St., Suite 1380
M/S KC11 066
Salt Lake City, UT 84111
chinckley@zionsbank.com
Tel: (801) 524 - 4787

Serves As:
- Senior V. President, Investor Relations, Zions Bancorporation

HINDMAN, John
P.O. Box 19534
Irvine, CA 92623-9534
hindman_jim@allergan.com
Tel: (714) 246 - 4636
Fax:(714) 246 - 4971
TF: (800) 347 - 4500

Serves As:
- Senior V. President, Treasury and Investor Relations, Allergan Inc.

HINDS, Clifford L.
55 Glenlake Pkwy. NE
Atlanta, GA 30328
Tel: (404) 828 - 6000
Fax:(404) 828 - 6619

Serves As:
- PAC Treasurer, United Parcel Service (UPS)

HINDS, Susanna
One Exeter Plaza
15 Floor
Boston, MA 02116
susanna_hinds@idg.com
Tel: (617) 534 - 4200
Fax:(617) 423 - 0240

Serves As:
- Manager, Communications, Internat'l Data Group

HINE, C. Clarkson
300 Tower Pkwy.
Lincolnshire, IL 60069
clarkson_hine@fortunebrands.com
Tel: (847) 484 - 4400
Fax:(847) 484 - 4497

Serves As:
- V. President, Corporate Communications, Fortune Brands, Inc.

HINES, Gregory
847 Gibraltar Dr.
Bldg. 5
Milpitas, CA 95035
Tel: (408) 586 - 4232
Fax:(408) 956 - 7699

Registered Federal Lobbyist.
Serves As:
- Representative, Solectron Corp.

HINES, Terri
P.O. Box 191
Gardena, CA 90248-0191
Tel: (310) 771 - 3111
Fax:(310) 516 - 7967

Serves As:
- Senior Manager, Lifestyle and Corporate Communications, Nissan North America, Inc.

HININGER, Damon
444 N. Capitol St. NW
Suite 545
Washington, DC 20001
Tel: (202) 347 - 8717
Registered Federal Lobbyist.
Serves As:
• Representative, Corrections Corp. of America

HINRICHS, Charles A.
150 N. Michigan Ave.
Suite 1700
Chicago, IL 60601-7568
Tel: (312) 346 - 6600
Fax:(312) 580 - 4919
Serves As:
• Senior V. President and Chief Financial Officer, Smurfit-Stone Container
Responsibilities include political action.

HINSON, Chuck
101 N. Monroe St.
Suite 1060
Tallahassee, FL 32301
Serves As:
• V. President, State Governmental Affairs, TECO Energy, Inc./Tampa Electric Co.

HINZMAN, Josh
1015 15th St. NW
Suite 200
Washington, DC 20005-2605
Tel: (202) 835 - 7360
Fax:(202) 467 - 4250
Registered Federal Lobbyist.
Serves As:
• Director, Federal Affairs, Oracle Corporation

HIPP, W. Hayne
P.O. Box 502
Greenville, SC 29602
Tel: (864) 241 - 5400
Fax:(864) 241 - 5401
Serves As:
• Chairman and Chief Exec. Officer, Liberty Corp.

HIPPLER, Kimberly E.
1660 L St. NW
Fourth Floor
Washington, DC 20036
kimberly.hippler@gm.com
Tel: (202) 775 - 5015
Fax:(202) 775 - 5049
Serves As:
• Manager, Government Policy and Technology Communications, General Motors Corp.

HIPWELL, Art
P.O. Box 1438
Louisville, KY 40201-1438
ahipwell@humana.com
Tel: (502) 580 - 1000
Fax:(502) 580 - 3677
TF: (800) 486 - 2620
Serves As:
• Senior V. President, Regulatory Affairs and General Counsel, Humana Inc.

HIRABAYASHI, Shinichi
200 Park Ave.
New York, NY 10166
Tel: (212) 878 - 4068
Serves As:
• President, Mitsui USA Foundation, Mitsui and Co. (U.S.A.), Inc.

HIRCHAK, James J.
P.O. Box 7100
Westchester, IL 60154
Tel: (708) 551 - 2600
Fax:(708) 551 - 2700
Serves As:
• V. President, Human Resources, Corn Products Internat'l, Inc.

HIRD, Andrea
3200 Highland Ave.
Downers Grove, IL 60515-1223
communications@firsthealth.com
Tel: (630) 737 - 7900
Fax:(630) 737 - 7856
TF: (800) 445 - 1425
Serves As:
• Director, Communications, First Health

HIRSCH, Elizabeth T.
39 Old Ridgebury Rd.
Danbury, CT 06810-5113
liz_hirsch@praxair.com
Tel: (203) 837 - 2354
Fax:(203) 837 - 2505
TF: (800) 772 - 9247
Serves As:
• Director, Investor Relations, Praxair, Inc.

HIRSCH, Rebecca
2775 Sanders Rd.
Northbrook, IL 60062-6127
Tel: (847) 402 - 5000
Fax:(847) 326 - 7519
TF: (800) 574 - 3553
Serves As:
• National Media Contact, Allstate Insurance Co.

HIRSCH, Susan
P.O. Box 4607
Houston, TX 77210-4607
Tel: (713) 324 - 5080
Fax:(713) 324 - 2087
Serves As:
• Director, Community Affairs, Continental Airlines

HIRST, Fritz
1301 Pennsylvania Ave. NW
Suite 1030
Washington, DC 20004
fhirst@tecoenergy.com
Tel: (202) 824 - 0414
Fax:(202) 824 - 0651
Registered Federal Lobbyist.
Serves As:
• Director, Federal Relations, TECO Energy, Inc./Tampa Electric Co.

HIRT, F. William
100 Erie Insurance Pl.
Erie, PA 16530
Tel: (814) 870 - 2270
Fax:(814) 870 - 3126
Serves As:
• Chairman of the Board, Erie Indeminity Co.

HIRTLE, Richard C.
One Beacon St.
Boston, MA 02108
Tel: (617) 725 - 6000
Serves As:
• PAC Treasurer, OneBeacon Insurance

HISADA, Masao
2000 Sierra Point Pkwy.
Brisbane, CA 94005
Tel: (650) 589 - 8300
Fax:(650) 244 - 7920
TF: (800) 448 - 2244
Serves As:
• Chief Exec. Officer, Hitachi America, Ltd.

HITCHERY, Regina M.
201 Isabella St.
Pittsburgh, PA 15212-5858
Tel: (412) 553 - 4545
Fax:(412) 553 - 4498
Serves As:
• V. President, Human Resources, Alcoa Inc.

HIXON, James A.
Three Commercial Pl.
Norfolk, VA 23510-2191
Tel: (757) 629 - 2600
Fax:(757) 629 - 2822
Serves As:
• Exec. V. President, Finance and Public Affairs, Norfolk Southern Corp.

HLOBIK, Lawrence S.
P.O. Box 27
Boise, ID 83707
lhlobik@simplot.com
Tel: (208) 336 - 2110
Fax:(208) 389 - 7515
Serves As:
• President and Chief Exec. Officer, J. R. Simplot Co.

HO, Claire
N63 W23075 State Hwy. 74
Sussex, WI 53089-2827
Tel: (414) 466 - 2955
TF: (888) 782 - 3226
Serves As:
• Manager, Communications, Quad/Graphics, Inc.

HOADLEY, Douglas
12800 Whitewater Dr.
Minnetonka, MN 55343
Tel: (952) 984 - 0234
Fax:(952) 984 - 0032
Serves As:
• Investor Relations Contact, Mosaic Co.

HOADLEY, Russell S.
5718 Westheimer St.
Houston, TX 77057
rhoadley@hibernia.com
Tel: (504) 533 - 2028
Fax:(504) 533 - 5841
TF: (800) 562 - 9007
Serves As:
• Exec. V. President and Chief Public Affairs, (Hibernia Nat'l Bank), Hibernia Corp.

HOAG, Kim
1111 S. Arroyo Pkwy.
P.O. Box 7084
Pasadena, CA 91105
Tel: (626) 578 - 6808
Fax:(626) 578 - 6875
Serves As:
• V. President, Federal Programs, Jacobs Engineering Group Inc.

HOAG, Rick
1015 15th St. NW
Suite 200
Washington, DC 20005-2605
Tel: (202) 835 - 7360
Fax:(202) 467 - 4250
Registered Federal Lobbyist.
Serves As:
• V. President, Tax Policy, Oracle Corporation

HOAGLIN, Thomas E.
41 S. High St.
Columbus, OH 43287
Tel: (614) 480 - 5533
Fax:(614) 480 - 4973
Serves As:
• Chairman and Chief Exec. Officer, Huntington Bancshares Inc.

HOBBIE, Lynn
P.O. Box 1231
Madison, WI 53701-1231
lhobbie@mge.com
Tel: (608) 252 - 7000
Fax:(608) 252 - 7098
TF: (800) 356 - 6423

Serves As:
• Senior V. President, Marketing, Madison Gas and Electric Co.
Responsibilities include corporate philanthropy.

HOBBS, John
999 Third Ave.
Suite 4300
Seattle, WA 98104
Tel: (206) 467 - 3600
Fax:(206) 467 - 3795

Serves As:
• Director, Investor Relations, Plum Creek Timber Co. Inc.

HOBBS, Laura E.
P.O. Box 98510
Las Vegas, NV 89193-8510
Tel: (702) 364 - 3534
Fax:(702) 367 - 3304

Serves As:
• Director, Human Resources, Southwest Gas Corp.

HOBEL, Candace
40 Fountain Plaza
Buffalo, NY 14202
chobel@dncinc.com
Tel: (716) 858 - 5503
Fax:(716) 858 - 5125

Serves As:
• Coordinator, Public Relations, Delaware North Companies

HOBOR, Nancy A.
100 Grainger Pkwy.
Lake Forest, IL 60045-5201
nancy.hobor@grainger.com
Tel: (847) 535 - 0065
Fax:(847) 535 - 0878

Serves As:
• Senior V. President, Communications and Investor Relations, W. W. Grainger, Inc.

HOBSON, Tom
400 Collins Rd. NE
Cedar Rapids, IA 52498
Tel: (319) 295 - 1000
Fax:(319) 295 - 5429

Serves As:
• Manager, Government Relations, Rockwell Collins, Inc

HOCHHAUSER, Richard M.
P.O. Box 269
San Antonio, TX 78291
Tel: (210) 829 - 9000
Fax:(210) 829 - 9403

Serves As:
• President and Chief Exec. Officer, Harte-Hanks, Inc.

HOCHHAUSER, Steven B.
P.O. Box 5108
Denver, CO 80217-5108
Tel: (303) 978 - 2000
Fax:(303) 978 - 2318
TF: (800) 654 - 3103

Serves As:
• Chairman, President and Chief Exec. Officer, Johns Manville Corp.

HOCK, Doug
1700 Lincoln St.
Denver, CO 80203
Tel: (303) 837 - 5812
Fax:(303) 837 - 6034

Serves As:
• Director, Public Affairs and Communications, Newmont Mining Corp.

HOCKEMA, Jack A.
27422 Portola Pkwy
Suite 350
Foothill Ranch, CA 92610-2831
Tel: (949) 614 - 1740
Fax:(949) 614 - 1930

Serves As:
• President and Chief Exec. Officer, Kaiser Aluminum & Chemical Corp.

HOCKENBROCHT, David W.
2400 E. Ganson
Jackson, MI 49202
dhockenbrocht@sparton.com
Tel: (517) 787 - 8600
Fax:(517) 787 - 1822
TF: (800) 248 - 9579

Serves As:
• President and Chief Exec. Officer, Sparton Corp.
Responsibilities include corporate philanthropy.

HOCKLANDER, Neal C.
P.O. Box 2900
Honolulu, HI 96846
Tel: (808) 537 - 8366
Fax:(808) 537 - 8063
TF: (888) 643 - 3888

Serves As:
• V. Chairman, Human Resources and Security, Bank of Hawaii Corp.

HOCKMAN, Dr. Deborah C.
1601 W. Diehl Rd.
Naperville, IL 60563-1198
Tel: (630) 305 - 1000
Fax:(630) 305 - 2900

Serves As:
• V. President, Safety, Health and Environment and Global Analytical Services, Nalco Co.

HOCKMEYER, Ph.D, Wayne T.
One MedImmune Way
Gaithersburg, MD 20878
Tel: (301) 398 - 0000
Fax:(301) 398 - 9000
TF: (877) 633 - 4411

Serves As:
• Chairman of the Board, MedImmune, Inc.

HODAS, Jo
7001 Tower Rd.
Denver, CO 80249-7312
Tel: (720) 374 - 4504
Fax:(720) 374 - 4375
TF: (800) 265 - 5505

Serves As:
• Senior Manager, Corporate Communications, Frontier Airlines, Inc.

HODEL, Joyce
Three Lakes Dr.
Northfield, IL 60093-2753
jhodel@kraft.com
Tel: (847) 646 - 6938
Fax:(847) 646 - 6005

Serves As:
• Senior Manager, Internal Communications, Kraft Foods, Inc.

HODGE, Richard
801 Pennsylvania Ave. NW
Suite 725
Washington, DC 20004
richard.hodge@sanofi-aventis.com
Tel: (202) 628 - 0500
Fax:(202) 682 - 0538

Registered Federal Lobbyist.
Serves As:
• Senior Manager, Federal Relations and Public Policy, Sanofi-Aventis Inc.
Responsibilities include political action.

HODGE, Ronald
145 Pleasant Hill Rd.
Scarborough, ME 04074
rhodge@hannaford.com
Tel: (207) 883 - 2911
Fax:(207) 885 - 3165

Serves As:
• President and Chief Exec. Officer, Hannaford Bros. Co.

HODGE, Tommy
920 Milliken Rd.
Spartanburg, SC 29304
Tel: (864) 503 - 2020
Fax:(864) 503 - 2100

Serves As:
• V. President, Human Resources, Milliken & Co.

HODGEN, Roy
1101 Pennsylvania Ave., NW
Suite 515
Washington, DC 20004
Tel: (202) 434 - 8938
Fax:(202) 434 - 4585

Registered Federal Lobbyist.
Serves As:
• Manager, Federal Government Affairs, Lyondell Chemical Co.

HODGES, Charles
100 Throckmorton St.
Suite 1800
Fort Worth, TX 76102
charles.hodges@radioshack.com
Tel: (817) 415 - 3300
Fax:(817) 415 - 2335

Serves As:
• Director, Media Relations, Radio Shack Corporation

HODGES, Cheryl D.
1600 River Center II
100 E. River Center Blvd.
Covington, KY 41011
Tel: (859) 392 - 3331
Fax:(859) 392 - 3333

Serves As:
• Senior V. President, Secretary, Investor Relations, Omnicare, Inc.

HODNIK, Margaret L.
30 W. Superior St.
Duluth, MN 55802
Tel: (218) 723 - 3966
Fax:(218) 723 - 3966

Serves As:
• Director, Public Affairs, ALLETE

HOEBERLING, James
1375 Peachtree St.
Atlanta, GA 30309
Tel: (404) 815 - 0770
Fax:(404) 815 - 8805

Serves As:
• Contact, Earthlink, Inc. PAC, Earthlink, Inc.

HOEBERLING, James
5565 Glenridge Connector
Atlanta, GA 30342
Tel: (404) 236 - 6000
Fax:(866) 246 - 4852
TF: (800) 331 - 0500

Serves As:
• Treasurer, Cingular Wireless LLC Employee PAC, Cingular Wireless

HOECH, Stephen L.
P.O. Box 240130
San Antonio, TX 78224-0130
Tel: (210) 475 - 8000
Fax:(210) 475 - 8060

Serves As:
• V. President, Employee Relations, Zachry Construction Corporation

HOEKSEMA, Renze

601 Pennsylvania Ave. NW
Suite 350, North Bldg.
Washington, DC 20004-3613
Tel: (202) 347 - 8420
Fax:(202) 347 - 8423

Registered Federal Lobbyist.
Serves As:
- Director, Federal Affairs, DTE Energy Co.

HOEL, John

101 Constitution Ave. NW
Suite 400 West
Washington, DC 20001
Tel: (202) 354 - 1500
Fax:(202) 354 - 1505

Registered Federal Lobbyist.
Serves As:
- V. President, Federal Government Affairs- Tobacco, Altria Group, Inc.

HOELTER, Timothy K.

3700 W. Juneau Ave.
Milwaukee, WI 53208
Tel: (414) 342 - 4680
Fax:(414) 343 - 8230

Serves As:
- V. President, International Trade Regulatory Affairs; and PAC Treasurer, Harley-Davidson Motor Company

HOEWING, C. Lincoln "Link"

1300 I St. NW
Suite 400 West
Washington, DC 20005
Tel: (202) 515 - 2420
Fax:(202) 336 - 7923

Serves As:
- Assistant V. President, Internet and Technology Policy, Verizon Communications Inc.

HOEY, John P.

185 Franklin St.
Boston, MA 02110
john.p.hoey@verizon.com
Tel: (617) 743 - 4760

Serves As:
- Director, Northeast Bureau Media Relations, Verizon Communications Inc.

HOEY, Richard

200 Park Ave.
New York, NY 10166
Tel: (212) 922 - 6000
Fax:(212) 922 - 6038

Serves As:
- Chief Economist and Chief Investment Strategist, The Dreyfus Corp.

Responsibilities include investor relations.

HOFENSPERGER, Amy

550 Bowie St.
Austin, TX 78703
Tel: (512) 542 - 0380
Fax:(512) 477 - 1069

Serves As:
- Manager, National Public Relations, Whole Foods Market, Inc.

HOFF, Jud

2725 Fairfield Rd.
Kalamazoo, MI 49002
Tel: (616) 385 - 2600
Fax:(616) 385 - 1062

Serves As:
- V. President, Regulatory Affairs and Quality Assurance, Stryker Corp.

HOFF, Susan S.

7601 Penn Ave. South
Richfield, MN 55423
susan.hoff@bestbuy.com
Tel: (612) 291 - 6100
Fax:(612) 292 - 4001

Serves As:
- Senior V. President and Chief Communication Officer, Best Buy Co., Inc.

Responsibilities also include corporate contributions and government affairs.

HOFFMAN, Barry

19975 Victor Pkwy.
Livonia, MI 48152-7001
hoffman@valassis.com
Tel: (734) 591 - 3000
Ext: 16386
Fax:(734) 591 - 4503
TF: (800) 437 - 0479

Serves As:
- Exec. V. President and General Counsel, Valassis Communications, Inc.

Serves as the company's senior public affairs officer.

HOFFMAN, Frederick W.

1000 Chrysler Dr.
CIMS 485-10-95
Auburn Hills, MI 48326-2766
Tel: (248) 512 - 3352
Fax:(248) 512 - 3919
TF: (800) 992 - 1997

Serves As:
- Director, State Relations, DaimlerChrysler Corp.

HOFFMAN, Gordon

1551 Wewatta St.
Denver, CO 80202-6173
ghoffman@gates.com
Tel: (303) 744 - 1911
Ext: 4595
Fax:(303) 744 - 4443

Serves As:
- Manager, Public Relations, Gates Rubber Co.

HOFFMAN, Ian

P.O. Box 240000
170 Graphics Dr.
Huntsville, AL 35758
ian.hoffman@intergraph.com
Tel: (256) 730 - 2604
Fax:(256) 730 - 2048
TF: (800) 345 - 4856

Serves As:
- V. President, Marketing and Communications, Intergraph Corp.

HOFFMAN, Michael J.

8111 Lyndale Ave. South
Bloomington, MN 55420-1196
Tel: (952) 888 - 8801
Fax:(952) 887 - 7961

Serves As:
- President and Chief Exec. Officer, The Toro Co.

HOFFMAN, Richard J.

P.O. Box 4577
Houston, TX 77210-4577
rhoffman@gsfdrill.com
Tel: (281) 925 - 6000
Fax:(281) 925 - 6010

Serves As:
- V. President, Investor Relations, GlobalSantaFe Corp.

HOFFMAN, Robert

1015 15th St. NW
Suite 200
Washington, DC 20005-2605
robert.hoffman@oracle.com
Tel: (202) 721 - 4814
Fax:(202) 467 - 4250

Registered Federal Lobbyist.
Serves As:
- Vice President, Congressional and Legislative Affairs, Oracle Corporation

HOFFMAN, Shelly

One Nationwide Plaza
M/S 1-22-08
Columbus, OH 43215-2220
hoffmas2@nationwide.com
Tel: (614) 677 - 3551
Fax:(614) 249 - 6794

Serves As:
- Director, Corporate Public Relations, Nationwide

HOFFMAN, Thomas F.

Consol Plaza
1800 Washington Rd.
Pittsburgh, PA 15241-1421
Tel: (412) 831 - 4060
Fax:(412) 831 - 4103

Serves As:
- V. President, External Affairs, CONSOL Energy Inc.

HOFFMANN, John

801 Cherry St.
Suite 3900
Fort Worth, TX 76102-6803
john.hoffmann@americredit.com
Tel: (817) 302 - 7627
Fax:(817) 302 - 7479
TF: (800) 644 - 2297

Serves As:
- V. President, Public Relations and Communication, AmeriCredit Corp.

HOFFMEIER, Donna

1225 New York Ave. NW
Suite 475
Washington, DC 20005
Tel: (202) 371 - 1303
Fax:(202) 371 - 5569

Registered Federal Lobbyist.
Serves As:
- V. President, Government Affairs and Strategic Policy, UnitedHealth Group

HOFGARD, Jefferson F.

1200 Wilson Blvd.
Arlington, VA 22209-2305
Tel: (703) 465 - 3219
Fax:(703) 465 - 3041

Serves As:
- Director, International Operations Policy, The Boeing Co.

HOFMANN, Angie M.

575 Seventh St. NW
Terrell Bldg.
Washington, DC 20004
Tel: (202) 737 - 5523
Fax:(202) 737 - 6069

Registered Federal Lobbyist.
Serves As:
- Director, International Trade, Wal-Mart Stores

HOGAN, Gerald F.

1401 I St. NW
Suite 1100
Washington, DC 20005
Tel: (202) 326 - 8815
Fax:(202) 408 - 4797

Registered Federal Lobbyist.
Serves As:
- Exec. Director, Federal Relations, SBC Communications Inc.

HOGAN, Liz

1133 19th St. NW
Washington, DC 20036
Tel: (202) 887 - 3830
Fax:(202) 887 - 3123

Registered Federal Lobbyist.
Serves As:
- Senior Policy Advisor, Government Relations, MCI, Inc.

HOGAN, Randall J.
5500 Wayzata Blvd.
Suite 800
Golden Valley, MN 55416-1259
Tel: (763) 545 - 1730

Serves As:
- Chairman and Chief Exec. Officer, Pentair, Inc.

HOGAN, Timothy R.
P.O. Box 227097
Dallas, TX 75222-7097
thogan@txu.com
Tel: (214) 875 - 9275

Serves As:
- Director, Investor Relations, TXU

HOGARTH, Judy
100 Crystal A Dr.
P.O. Box 810
Hershey, PA 17033
Tel: (717) 534 - 7631
Fax:(717) 534 - 7015

Serves As:
- Public Relations Contact, The Hershey Company

HOHL, Doreen W.
One Riverside Plaza
Columbus, OH 43215-2373
Tel: (614) 223 - 1000
Fax:(614) 223 - 1823

Serves As:
- PAC Treasurer, American Electric Power Co. Inc.

HOKE, John Greg
1342 Trailwood Village Dr.
Kingwood, TX 77339
hokeg@wyeth.com
Tel: (281) 359 - 2905

Serves As:
- Associate Director, State Government Affairs, Wyeth Pharmaceuticals

HOKIN, Richard
P.O. Box 7608
Boise, ID 83707
Tel: (208) 377 - 6840
Fax:(208) 377 - 6097

Serves As:
- Chairman of the Board, Intermountain Gas Co.

HOLCOMBE, Ed
241 Ralph McGill Blvd. NE
BIN 10230
Atlanta, GA 30308-3374
Tel: (404) 506 - 6929
Fax:(404) 506 - 3771

Registered Federal Lobbyist.
Serves As:
- V. President, Governmental and Regulatory Affairs, Georgia Power Co.

HOLDEN, Lee
30 Community Dr.
South Burlington, VT 05403-6828
lee@benjerry.com
Tel: (802) 846 - 1500
Ext: 7701
Fax:(802) 846 - 1536

Serves As:
- Senior Public Relations Specialist, Ben & Jerry's Homemade Inc.

HOLDEN, LuAnn
310 S. St. Mary's
Suite 2400
San Antonio, TX 78205
holdenl@zachry.com
Tel: (210) 258 - 2664
Fax:(210) 258 - 2699

Serves As:
- Manager, Public Affairs, Zachry Construction Corporation

HOLDEN, Richard
P.O. Box 300
Princeton, NJ 08543
richard.holden@dowjones.com
Tel: (609) 520 - 5930

Serves As:
- Exec. Director, Dow Jones Newspaper Fund, Dow Jones and Co.

HOLDING, R. Earl
P.O. Box 30825
Salt Lake City, UT 84130-0825
Tel: (801) 524 - 2700
Fax:(801) 524 - 2848

Serves As:
- Chief Exec. Officer, Sinclair Oil Corp.

HOLEVAS, Christine
One Bank One Plaza
Chicago, IL 60670
Tel: (312) 732 - 4000

Serves As:
- First V. President, Internal Retail Communications, J. P. Morgan Chase & Co.

HOLIDAY, Sue
One American Rd.
Cleveland, OH 44144-2398
Tel: (800) 777 - 4891
Fax:(216) 252 - 6778

Serves As:
- Manager, Consumer Relations, American Greetings Corp.

HOLLAND, Betsy
P.O. Box 105366
One CNN Center
Atlanta, GA 30348-5366
betsy.humphries@turner.com
Tel: (404) 827 - 1170
Fax:(404) 827 - 2437

Serves As:
- Manager, Community Relations, Turner Broadcasting System, Inc.

HOLLAND, Beverly J.
917 E. 11th St.
Tacoma, WA 98421
bhollan@simpson.com
Tel: (253) 779 - 6400
Fax:(253) 280 - 9000

Serves As:
- Manager, Public Affairs, Simpson Investment Co.

HOLLAND, Carter
Avid Technology Park
One Park West
Tewksbury, MA 01876
carter_holland@avid.com
Tel: (978) 640 - 3172
Fax:(978) 640 - 1366

Serves As:
- Director, Corporate Communications, Avid Technology, Inc.

HOLLAND, Larry V.
557 Broadway
New York, NY 10012
lholland@scholastic.com
Tel: (212) 343 - 6100
Fax:(212) 343 - 4876

Serves As:
- Senior V. President, Corporate Human Resources and Employee Services, Scholastic, Inc.

HOLLERAN, Charles B.
One American Rd.
Dearborn, MI 48126
chollera@ford.com
Tel: (313) 322 - 3000
TF: (800) 555 - 5259

Serves As:
- V. President, Public Affairs; and Chief Communications Officer, Ford Motor Co.

HOLLERBACH, Paul
701 First Ave.
Sunnyvale, CA 94089
paulh@yahoo-inc.com
Tel: (408) 349 - 3598
Fax:(408) 616 - 3301

Serves As:
- V. President, Investor Relations, Yahoo! Inc.

HOLLERN, Karen
505 King Ave.
Columbus, OH 43201-2693
Tel: (614) 424 - 7361
Fax:(614) 424 - 3301
TF: (800) 201 - 2011

Serves As:
- Director, Corporate Community Relations, Battelle

HOLLEY, Caroline E.
3350 Peachtree Rd. NE
Atlanta, GA 30326
caroline.holley@bcbsga.com
Tel: (404) 842 - 8207
Fax:(404) 842 - 8287

Serves As:
- Legislative Affairs Specialist, Blue Cross Blue Shield of Georgia

HOLLEY, Rick
999 Third Ave.
Suite 4300
Seattle, WA 98104
Tel: (206) 467 - 3600
Fax:(206) 467 - 3795

Serves As:
- President and Chief Exec. Officer, Plum Creek Timber Co. Inc.

HOLLIDAY, Jr., Charles O.
1007 Market St.
Wilmington, DE 19898
Tel: (302) 773 - 2495
Fax:(302) 773 - 2919
TF: (800) 441 - 7515

Serves As:
- Chairman and Chief Exec. Officer, DuPont

HOLLIDAY, Roger
3330 Cumberland Blvd.
Suite 800
Atlanta, GA 30339
hollidayroger@russellcorp.com
Tel: (678) 742 - 8000

Serves As:
- V. President, Investor Relations, Russell Corp.

HOLLIE, Paul
SAFECO Plaza
Seattle, WA 98185
Tel: (206) 545 - 3048

Serves As:
- Media Relations Contact, SAFECO Corp.

HOLLIMAN, W. G. "Mickey"
101 S. Hanley Rd.
St. Louis, MO 63105-3493
Tel: (314) 863 - 1100
Fax:(314) 863 - 5306

Serves As:
- Chairman and Chief Exec. Officer, Furniture Brands Internat'l, Inc.

HOLLING, Henry W.

100 NE Adams St.
Peoria, IL 61629-1465
Tel: (309) 675 - 4418
Fax:(309) 675 - 5815

Serves As:

- Manager, Community and Corporate Support; V. President and Manager, Foundation, Caterpillar Inc.

HOLLINGER, Fred

23733 N. Scottsdale Rd.
Scottsdale, AZ 85255
Tel: (480) 585 - 8888
Fax:(480) 585 - 8893
TF: (800) 937 - 4937

Serves As:

- Chairman and Chief Exec. Officer, Giant Industries, Inc.

HOLLINGER, Suzy A.P.

P.O. Box 730
Honolulu, HI 96808-0730
shollinger@hei.com
Tel: (808) 543 - 7385
Fax:(808) 543 - 7966

Serves As:

- Manager, Investor Relations, Hawaiian Electric Industries, Inc.

HOLLINGSHEAD, Leslie

6060 Center Dr., Fifth Floor
Los Angeles, CA 90045
Tel: (310) 431 - 4533
Fax:(310) 342 - 0533

Serves As:

- V. President, Corporate Communications, Vivendi Universal Games

HOLLINSHEAD, John

One Houston Center
1221 McKinney Ave.
Houston, TX 77010
Tel: (713) 652 - 7200

Serves As:

- V. President, Human Resources, Lyondell Chemical Co.

HOLLIS, Candace

9336 Civic Center Dr.
Beverly Hills, CA 90210
candace_hollis@hilton.com
Tel: (310) 205 - 8640
Fax:(310) 861 - 5958

Serves As:

- Senior Manager, Corporate Communications, Hilton Hotels Corp.

HOLLIS, Jr., M. Clayton

P.O. Box 407
Lakeland, FL 33802-0407
clayton.hollis@publix.com
Tel: (863) 284 - 5586
Fax:(863) 284 - 5532

Serves As:

- V. President, Public Affairs, Publix Super Markets, Inc.

HOLLOWAY, Jerry

One Enterprise Dr.
Aliso Viejo, CA 92656-2606
jerry.holloway@fluor.com
Tel: (949) 349 - 7411
Fax:(949) 349 - 5981

Serves As:

- Director, Media Relations, Fluor Corp.

HOLLOWAY, Laura

2001 Edmund Halley Dr.
Reston, VA 20191
Tel: (703) 433 - 4000

Registered Federal Lobbyist.
Serves As:

- Representative, Sprint Nextel

HOLMAN, Pamela

701 Ninth St. NW
Washington, DC 20068
Tel: (202) 872 - 3488

Serves As:

- Coordinator, Contributions and Membership Committee, Pepco Holdings, Inc.

HOLMES, Diane

403 E. Capitol St. SE
Washington, DC 20003
diane.holmes@fluor.com
Tel: (202) 548 - 5800
Fax:(202) 548 - 5810

Registered Federal Lobbyist.
Serves As:

- Senior Washington Representative, Fluor Corp.

HOLMES, Janie

P.O. Box 53999
M/S 8508
Phoenix, AZ 85072-3999
janie.holmes@aps.com
Tel: (602) 250 - 2896
Fax:(602) 250 - 2430

Serves As:

- Leader, Internal Communications Department, (Arizona Public Service Co.), Pinnacle West Capital Corp.

HOLMES, Richard

241 Ralph McGill Blvd. NE
Atlanta, GA 30308-3374
Tel: (404) 506 - 3701
Fax:(404) 506 - 3771

Serves As:

- Senior V. President, Employee and Corporate Relations, Georgia Power Co.

HOLSTEIN, Dawn

111 McInnis Pkwy.
San Rafael, CA 94903
dawn.holstein@autodesk.com
Tel: (415) 507 - 6554
Fax:(415) 507 - 5100

Serves As:

- Global Communications Contact, Autodesk Inc.

HOLT, Jack

Consol Plaza
1800 Washington Rd.
Pittsburgh, PA 15241-1421
Tel: (412) 831 - 4053
Fax:(412) 831 - 4004

Serves As:

- Senior V. President, Safety, CONSOL Energy Inc.

HOLT, Terry

Two N. Riverside Plaza
Suite 2100
Chicago, IL 60606
terry_holt@equityoffice.com
Tel: (312) 466 - 3102
Fax:(312) 559 - 3102

Serves As:

- V. President, Public Relations, Equity Office Properties Trust

HOLT, Timothy J.

7201 Hamilton Blvd.
Allentown, PA 18195-1501
holttj@airproducts.com
Tel: (610) 481 - 4453
Fax:(610) 841 - 5900

Serves As:

- Director, Corporate Relations, Air Products and Chemicals, Inc.

HOLWILL, Richard N.

214 Massachusetts Ave. NE
Suite 210
Washington, DC 20002
Tel: (202) 547 - 0300
Fax:(202) 547 - 5008

Serves As:

- V. President, Public Policy, (Amway Corp.), Alticor Inc.

Responsibilities include worldwide government affairs.

HOLYFIELD, Jeff

One Energy Plaza
Jackson, MI 49201
Tel: (517) 788 - 2396

Serves As:

- Director, News and Information, CMS Energy Corp.

HONEYCUTT, Van B.

2100 E. Grand Ave.
El Segundo, CA 90245
vhoneycutt@csc.com
Tel: (310) 615 - 1726

Serves As:

- Chairman and Chief Exec. Officer, Computer Sciences Corp.

HOOD, Charles H.

133 Peachtree St., N.E.
Atlanta, GA 30303
Tel: (404) 652 - 6483
Fax:(404) 584 - 1470

Serves As:

- V. President, State Governmental Affairs, Georgia-Pacific Corp.

HOOD, William L.

9525 W. Bryn Mawr Ave.
Suite 700
Rosemont, IL 60018
bill.hood@aa.com
Tel: (847) 928 - 5437
Fax:(847) 928 - 5695

Serves As:

- Managing Director, Corporate Affairs, (American Airlines, Inc.), AMR Corp.

HOOLEY, Jim

1776 I St. NW
Suite 900
Washington, DC 20006
jhooley@siebel.com
Tel: (202) 756 - 1413
Fax:(202) 756 - 1414

Registered Federal Lobbyist.
Serves As:

- Exec. Director, U.S. Government Affairs, Siebel Systems, Inc.

HOOTKIN, Pamela N.

200 Madison Ave.
New York, NY 10016
Tel: (212) 381 - 3500
Fax:(212) 381 - 3959

Serves As:

- V. President, Treasurer and Investor Relations, Phillips-Van Heusen Corp.

HOOVER, R. David

P.O. Box 5000
Broomfield, CO 80038-5000
Tel: (303) 469 - 3131
Fax:(303) 460 - 2127

Serves As:

- Chairman, President and Chief Exec. Officer, Ball Corp.

HOOVER, Rose
600 Grant St., Suite 4600
Pittsburgh, PA 15219
rhoover@ampcopgh.com
Tel: (412) 456 - 4418
Fax:(412) 456 - 4404

Serves As:
- V. President and Corporate Secretary, Ampco-Pittsburgh Corp.

Responsibilities include corporate philanthropy.

HOPE, Doreen C.
101 Constitution Ave. NW
Washington, DC 20080-
dhope@washgas.com
Tel: (703) 750 - 2000
Fax:(703) 750 - 4574

Registered Federal Lobbyist.
Serves As:
- Director, Federal Affairs, Washington Gas

HOPKINS, Denny
6363 Main St.
Williamsville, NY 14221
Tel: (716) 635 - 5000
Fax:(716) 633 - 0898
TF: (800) 522 - 2522

Serves As:
- V. President, Advertising and Public Relations, Tops Markets LLC

HOPKINS, Douglas W.
P.O. Box 1734
USA 19
Atlanta, GA 30301
dhopkins@na.ko.com
Tel: (404) 676 - 7733
Fax:(404) 515 - 2272

Serves As:
- Manager, Corporate Affairs, Finance, and Administration, The Coca-Cola Co.

HOPKINS, Frank
5205 N. O'Connor Blvd.
Suite 900
Irving, TX 75039
Tel: (972) 444 - 9001
Fax:(972) 969 - 3516

Serves As:
- V. President, Investor Relations, Pioneer Natural Resources Co.

HOPKINS, Gary
P.O. Box 31907
Santa Barbara, CA 93130
gary.hopkins@tenethealth.com
Tel: (805) 563 - 7000
Ext: 6885
Fax:(805) 563 - 6840

Serves As:
- Senior Director, Corporate Communciations, Tenet Healthcare Corp.

HOPKINS, Madeline
680 E. Swedesford Rd.
Wayne, PA 19087
madeline.hopkins@sungard.com
Tel: (484) 582 - 5506
Fax:(484) 225 - 1120

Serves As:
- V. President, Investor Relations, SunGard Data Systems, Inc.

HOPKINS, Mark D.
1401 I St. NW
Suite 1200
Washington, DC 20005-2225
Tel: (202) 408 - 5800
Fax:(202) 408 - 5845

Registered Federal Lobbyist.
Serves As:
- Manager, Federal Relations, Chevron Corp.

HOPKINS, Thomas E.
101 Prospect Ave. NW
Cleveland, OH 44115
Tel: (216) 566 - 2071
Fax:(216) 566 - 3312

Serves As:
- Senior V. President, Human Resources, Sherwin-Williams Co.

HOPP, Daniel F.
Administrative Center
2000 N. M-63
Benton Harbor, MI 49022-2692
daniel_f_hopp@email.whirlpool.com
Tel: (269) 923 - 5000
Fax:(269) 923 - 5443

Serves As:
- Senior V. President, Corporate Affairs and General Counsel, Whirlpool Corp.

HOPPE, Marge
1551 Wewatta St.
Denver, CO 80202-6173
Tel: (303) 744 - 1911
Fax:(303) 744 - 4443

Serves As:
- Contact, Gates Corporate Giving Program, Gates Rubber Co.

HOPPER, Gary
1899 Pennsylvania Ave., NW
Suite 300
Washington, DC 20006
Tel: (202) 496 - 8200
Fax:(202) 659 - 1110

Registered Federal Lobbyist.
Serves As:
- V. President, Washington Operations, General Atomics

HORDER-KOOP, Robin
7575 Fulton St. East
M/S 78-1M
Ada, MI 49355-0001
Tel: (616) 787 - 7717
Fax:(616) 787 - 6177

Serves As:
- V. President, Worldwide Human Resources, Alticor Inc.

HORI, Tetsuro
1900 K St. NW
Suite 800
Washington, DC 20006
Tel: (202) 828 - 9272
Fax:(202) 828 - 9277

Serves As:
- Liaison Manager for International Relations, Hitachi America, Ltd.

HORN, Randall C. "Randy"
P.O. Box 1365
Columbia, SC 29202
Tel: (803) 798 - 7000
TF: (800) 325 - 4368

Serves As:
- President and Chief Exec. Officer, Colonial Life & Accident Insurance Co.

HORNBACHER, Mickey
700 13th St. NW
Suite 220
Washington, DC 20005
Tel: (202) 347 - 8662
Fax:(202) 347 - 8675

Serves As:
- Manager, Government Affairs, (BNSF Railway Company), Burlington Northern Santa Fe Corporation

HORNBUCKLE, Mertroe B.
One John Deere Pl.
Moline, IL 61265-8098
Tel: (309) 765 - 4252
Fax:(309) 765 - 5066

Serves As:
- V. President, Human Resources, Deere & Company

HORNE, W. Scott
211 Mount Airy Rd.
Basking Ridge, NJ 07920
horne@avaya.com
Tel: (908) 953 - 3476
Fax:(908) 953 - 7609

Serves As:
- Corporate Communications Contact, Avaya Inc.

HORNER, Leigh
434 Fayetteville St. Mall
Suite 1610
Raleigh, NC 27601
Tel: (919) 465 - 3712

Serves As:
- Director, Public Affairs, Sprint Nextel

HORNING, Bill
201 Mission St.
San Francisco, CA 94105
Tel: (415) 278 - 4602
Fax:(415) 278 - 6028

Serves As:
- Investor Relations Contact, Providian Financial Corp.

HORSTMAN, Joseph P.
539 S. Main St.
Room 2635
Findlay, OH 45840

Serves As:
- PAC Treasurer, Marathon Oil Corp.

HORSTMAN, Mary Alice
2775 Sanders Rd.
Northbrook, IL 60062-6127
Tel: (847) 402 - 5000
Fax:(847) 326 - 7519
TF: (800) 574 - 3553

Serves As:
- Director, Corporate Relations, Allstate Insurance Co.

HORTON, Donald R.
301 Commerce St.
Suite 500
Fort Worth, TX 76006
dhorton@drhorton.com
Tel: (817) 390 - 8200
Fax:(817) 390 - 1715

Serves As:
- Chairman of the Board, D. R. Horton, Inc.

HORVATH, James
101 N. Third St.
Moorhead, MN 56560-1990
jhorvath@crystalsugar.com
Tel: (218) 236 - 4400
Fax:(218) 236 - 4718

Serves As:
- Chief Exec. Officer, American Crystal Sugar Co.

HORVATH, Jane
601 Pennsylvania Ave. NW
North Bldg. Suite 1200
Washington, DC 20004
Tel: (202) 638 - 4170
Fax:(202) 638 - 3670

Serves As:
- Director, Public Policy, Merck & Co., Inc.

HORWITZ, Steve
2325 Orchard Pkwy.
San Jose, CA 95131
shorowitz@atmel.com
Tel: (408) 487 - 2677
Fax:(408) 436 - 4200

Serves As:
- Director, Investor Relations, Atmel Corp.

HOSFORD, Chris L.
P.O. Box 20850
Fountain Valley, CA 92728-0850
chosford@hmausa.com
Tel: (714) 965 - 3000

Serves As:
- V. President, Communications, Hyundai Motor America

HOSKINS, Adriana
9000 W. 67th St.
Shawnee Mission, KS 66202
adriana_hoskins@seaboardcorp.com
Tel: (913) 676 - 8800
Fax:(913) 676 - 8976

Serves As:
- Manager, Treasury, Seaboard Corporation

Responsibilities include investor relations.

HOSTETTER, Carl
1100 N. Market St.
Wilmington, DE 19890
Tel: (302) 651 - 1000
Fax:(302) 651 - 8937
TF: (800) 441 - 7120

Serves As:
- PAC Contact, Wilmington Trust Co.

HOSTETTER, Jerry
499 Park Ave.
New York, NY 10022
Tel: (212) 758 - 8568
Fax:(212) 758 - 8421

Serves As:
- V. President, Investor Relations and Corporate Communications, Smithfield Foods, Inc.

Responsibilities also include government relations.

HOTARD, John
P.O. Box 619616
MD 5575
Dallas-Fort Worth Airport, TX 75261
john.hotard@aa.com
Tel: (817) 967 - 1577
Fax:(817) 967 - 3816

Serves As:
- Manager, Corporate Communications, AMR Corp.

HOTSENPILLER, Susan
1235 S. Clark St.
Suite 1100
Arlington, VA 22202
hotsenps@aaicorp.com
Tel: (703) 412 - 4170
Fax:(703) 416 - 4820

Registered Federal Lobbyist.
Serves As:
- Director, Legislative Affairs, AAI Corp.

HOUGHTON, James R.
One Riverfront Plaza
Corning, NY 14831-0001
houghtonjr@corning.com
Tel: (607) 974 - 8668
Fax:(607) 974 - 8444

Serves As:
- Chairman of the Board, Corning Incorporated

HOUPT, Mary
111 W. Monroe St.
Chicago, IL 60603-4095
Tel: (312) 461 - 6661
Fax:(312) 461 - 4702

Serves As:
- V. President, Community Affairs, Harris Bank

Responsibilities include corporate philanthropy.

HOURIGAN, John
1700 S. Patterson Blvd.
Dayton, OH 45479
john.hourigan@ncr.com
Tel: (937) 445 - 2078
Fax:(937) 445 - 1847

Serves As:
- Director, Corporate Media Relations, NCR Corporation

HOUSER, Susan
711 High St.
Des Moines, IA 50392-0150
houser.susan@principal.com
Tel: (515) 248 - 2268
Fax:(515) 246 - 5475
TF: (800) 986 - 3343

Serves As:
- Media Relations Contact, The Principal Financial Group

Responsibilities include investor relations.

HOUSTON, J. Wayne
P.O. Box 385014
Birmingham, AL 35238-5014
houstonw@vmcmail.com
Tel: (205) 298 - 3171
Fax:(205) 298 - 2960

Serves As:
- V. President, Human Resources, Vulcan Materials Co.

HOUTON, Jamie
1401 I St., NW
Suite 500
Washington, DC 20005
Tel: (202) 263 - 5900
Fax:(202) 263 - 5902

Registered Federal Lobbyist.
Serves As:
- Manager, Federal Government Affairs, Microsoft Corporation

HOVNANIAN, Ara K.
Ten Hwy. 35
Red Bank, NJ 07701-5902
Tel: (732) 747 - 7800
Fax:(732) 747 - 6835

Serves As:
- President and Chief Exec. Officer, Hovnanian Enterprises, Inc.

HOVNANIAN, Kevork S.
Ten Hwy. 35
Red Bank, NJ 07701-5902
Tel: (732) 747 - 7800
Fax:(732) 747 - 6835

Serves As:
- Chairman of the Board, Hovnanian Enterprises, Inc.

HOWARD, Amber
22301 Foothill Blvd.
Hayward, CA 94541
Tel: (510) 727 - 3000
Fax:(510) 727 - 2300

Serves As:
- Manager, Internal Communications, Mervyn's

HOWARD, David
P.O. Box 2959
Winston-Salem, NC 27102
Tel: (336) 741 - 3489
Fax:(336) 741 - 7220

Serves As:
- Public Relations Representative, (R. J. Reynolds Tobacco Co.), Reynolds American Inc.

HOWARD, Jane A.
1015 15th St. NW
Suite 700
Washington, DC 20005-2605
jahoward@bechtel.com
Tel: (202) 828 - 5200
Fax:(202) 785 - 2645

Registered Federal Lobbyist.
Serves As:
- Manager, Global Market Access - BCorp, Bechtel Group, Inc.

HOWARD, Jaren J.
20 N. Broadway, Suite 1500
Oklahoma City, OK 73102
Tel: (405) 235 - 3611
Fax:(405) 552 - 4667

Registered Federal Lobbyist.
Serves As:
- Representative, Devon Energy Corp.

HOWARD, Jeanne
8000 Forsyth Blvd.
Clayton, MO 63105
jeanne.howard@commercebank.com
TF: (800) 892 - 7100

Serves As:
- Director, Regional Marketing, Commerce Bancshares Inc.

Responsibilities include media relations.

HOWARD, Jerry
5555 San Felipe Rd.
Houston, TX 77056
Tel: (713) 629 - 6600
Fax:(713) 296 - 2952

Serves As:
- Senior V. President, Corporate Affairs, Marathon Oil Corp.

Responsibilities include government affairs.

HOWARD, Kay
10707 Clay Rd.
P.O. Box 2863
Houston, TX 77252
Tel: (713) 877 - 2363

Serves As:
- Director, Communications, Lennar Corp.

HOWARD, Robert J.
415 Holiday Dr.
Pittsburgh, PA 15220-2793
rhoward@lbfosterco.com
Tel: (412) 928 - 3417
Fax:(412) 928 - 3422
TF: (800) 255 - 4500

Serves As:
- V. President, Human Resources, L. B. Foster Co.

HOWARD, Roger W.
3253 E. Chestnut Epwy.
Springfield, MO 65802
roger.howard@bnsf.com
Tel: (417) 829 - 4902
Fax:(417) 829 - 4903

Serves As:
- Director, Government Affairs, Burlington Northern Santa Fe Corporation

HOWARD, Stan
2000 Market St.
Philadelphia, PA 19103-9000
Tel: (215) 419 - 7027
Fax:(215) 419 - 7591
TF: (800) 225 - 7788

Serves As:
- Senior Communications Manager, ATOFINA Chemicals, Inc.

HOWE, Deirdre
555 13th St. NW Tel: (202) 637 - 7228
Suite 3 - East Fax:(202) 637 - 8715
Washington, DC 20004
deirdre.howe@vitas.com

Serves As:
- Exec. V. President, VITAS Healthcare Corporation

HOWE, Linda
P.O. Box 3440 Tel: (808) 525 - 6642
Honolulu, HI 96801-3440 Fax:(808) 525 - 6677
lhowe@abinc.com

Serves As:
- Manager, Community Relations; and V. President, Alexander & Baldwin Foundation, Alexander & Baldwin, Inc.

HOWELL, Adrienne
P.O. Box 52075 Tel: (602) 395 - 4045
Phoenix, AZ 85072-2075

Serves As:
- Administrator, Consumer Affairs, Southwest Gas Corp.

HOWELL, Cynthia
925 L St., Suite 650 Tel: (916) 492 - 4243
Sacramento, CA 95814 Fax:(916) 443 - 2994
crhowell@sempra.com

Serves As:
- Manager, Governmental Affairs- State Agency Affairs, Sempra Energy

HOWELL, III, Joseph M.
1025 Eldorado Blvd. Tel: (720) 888 - 2517
Broomfield, CO 80021 Fax:(720) 888 - 5085

Serves As:
- Group V. President, Corporate Marketing, Level 3 Communications, Inc.

Responsibilities include media relations.

HOWELL, Mary L.
1101 Pennsylvania Ave. NW Tel: (202) 637 - 3802
Suite 400 Fax:(202) 637 - 3860
Washington, DC 20004-2504

Registered Federal Lobbyist.
Serves As:
- Exec. V. President, Government, International Investor Relations, and Corporate Communications, Textron Inc.

HOWELL, Sarah
1776 I St. NW Tel: (202) 457 - 6603
Suite 1000 Fax:(202) 457 - 6597
Washington, DC 20006-3707

Serves As:
- Director, Environmental and Corporate Communications, BP

HOWELL, Steve
435 N. Michigan Ave. Tel: (312) 222 - 5650
Chicago, IL 60611 Fax:(312) 222 - 1573
showell@tribune.com

Serves As:
- V. President, Safety and Security Services, Tribune Co.

HOWLETT, Steven
1299 Pennsylvania Ave. NW Tel: (202) 637 - 4000
11th Floor West Fax:(202) 637 - 4006
Washington, DC 20004-2407

Registered Federal Lobbyist.
Serves As:
- Representative, General Electric Co.

HOWORTH, Charles
333 Commerce St. Tel: (615) 214 - 6520
Suite 2104
Nashville, TN 37201
charles.howorth@bellsouth.com

Serves As:
- V. President, Regulatory Affairs, BellSouth Corp.

HOYDYSH, Dan
11720 Plaza America Dr. Tel: (703) 439 - 5000
Tower 3 Fax:(703) 439 - 5172
Reston, VA 20190
dan.hoydysh@unisys.com

Registered Federal Lobbyist.
Serves As:
- Director, Washington Office, Unisys Corp.

HOYT, Susan S.
500 Staples Dr. Tel: (508) 253 - 7234
Framingham, MA 01702 Ext: 37231
susan.hoyt@staples.com Fax:(508) 253 - 8955

Serves As:
- Exec. V. President, Human Resources, Staples, Inc.

HRABCHAK, Dennis
P.O. Box 1564 Tel: (203) 499 - 2000
New Haven, CT 06506-0901 Fax:(203) 499 - 3626
TF: (800) 722 - 5584

Serves As:
- V. President, Corporate Affairs, The United Illuminating Company

HRABUSA, John
P.O. Box 407 Tel: (863) 688 - 1188
Lakeland, FL 33802-0407 Ext: 53281
Fax:(863) 616 - 5693

Serves As:
- Senior V. President, Publix Super Markets, Inc.

Responsibilities include human resources and public affairs.

HRAPKIEWICZ, Steve
One Corporate Way Tel: (517) 381 - 5500
Lansing, MI 48951 Fax:(517) 706 - 5517
TF: (800) 644 - 4565

Serves As:
- Senior V. President, Human Resources, Jackson Nat'l Life Insurance Co.

HREVNACK, Linda A.
730 Central Ave. Tel: (908) 277 - 8182
Murray Hill, NJ 07974 Fax:(908) 277 - 8098
linda.hrevnack@crbard.com TF: (800) 367 - 2273

Serves As:
- Manager, Community Affairs and Contributions, C. R. Bard, Inc.

HRYBENKO, Elizabeth
1111 Stewart Ave. Tel: (516) 803 - 2300
Bethpage, NY 11714-3581 Fax:(516) 803 - 1186
ehrybenk@cablevision.com

Serves As:
- Director, Investor Relations, Cablevision Systems Corp.

HUANG, Albert
160 Rio Robles Tel: (408) 875 - 3000
San Jose, CA 95134 Fax:(408) 875 - 4144
albert.huang@kla-tencor.com

Serves As:
- Manager, Investor Relations, KLA-Tencor

HUANG, Jen-Hsun
2701 San Tomas Exwy. Tel: (408) 486 - 2000
Santa Clara, CA 95050 Fax:(408) 486 - 2200

Serves As:
- Chief Exec. Officer, President and Co-Founder, NVIDIA Corp.

HUBBARD, Craig K.
109 Northpark Blvd. Tel: (985) 801 - 5117
Covington, LA 70433-5001 Ext: 5117
craig.hubbard@scppool.com Fax:(985) 809 - 1045

Serves As:
- Treasurer and Secretary, SCP Pool Corp.

Responsibilities include investor relations.

HUBBARD, Sherry L.
1225 19th St. NW Tel: (202) 296 - 4933
Suite 450 Fax:(202) 296 - 4951
Washington, DC 20036
sherry.hubbard@cox.com

Registered Federal Lobbyist.
Serves As:
- Director, Operations, Cox Enterprises, Inc.

HUBBLE, Don W.
424 S. Woods Mill Rd. Tel: (314) 854 - 3800
Chesterfield, MO 63017 Fax:(314) 854 - 3890

Serves As:
- Chairman of the Board, Angelica Corp.

HUBER, Beth
145 Hunter Dr. Tel: (937) 382 - 5591
2061 G Ext: 2536
Wilmington, OH 45177 Fax:(937) 382 - 0896
beth.huber@abxair.com

Serves As:
- Supervisor, Community Relations, ABX Air, Inc.

Responsibilities include media relations and investor relations.

HUDSON, Betty
P.O. Box 98199 Tel: (202) 857 - 7000
Washington, DC 20090-8199 Fax:(202) 828 - 6679
TF: (800) 647 - 5463

Serves As:
- Senior V. President, Communications, Nat'l Geographic Soc.

HUDSON, C. B.
P.O. Box 2612 — Tel: (205) 325 - 4200
Birmingham, AL 35202 — Fax:(205) 325 - 4198

Serves As:
- Chairman and Chief Exec. Officer, Torchmark Corp.

HUDSON, David
P.O. Box 871 — Tel: (918) 588 - 7000
Tulsa, OK 74102-0871 — Fax:(918) 588 - 7960

Serves As:
- PAC Treasurer, ONEOK, Inc.

HUDSON, Douglas K
220 S. Ridgewood Ave. — Tel: (352) 732 - 6522
Daytona Beach, FL 32114 — TF: (800) 877 - 2769
dhudson@bbinsurance.com

Serves As:
- Director, Communications and Investor Relations, Brown & Brown, Inc.

HUDSON, Katherine M.
100 S. Saunders Rd. — Tel: (847) 735 - 9200
Lake Forest, IL 60045

Serves As:
- Chairman of the Board, Case New Holland Inc.

HUDSON, Laura C.
1150 Connecticut Ave. NW — Tel: (202) 367 - 2760
Suite 1025 — Fax:(202) 367 - 2790
Washington, DC 20036
lhudson@unocal.com

Registered Federal Lobbyist.
Serves As:
- Government Relations Specialist, International and Federal Affairs, UNOCAL Corp.

HUDSON, Margaret R. "Peggy"
1776 I St. NW — Tel: (202) 785 - 6581
Suite 1000 — Fax:(202) 457 - 6597
Washington, DC 20006-3707
hudspr@bp.com

Registered Federal Lobbyist.
Serves As:
- V. President, Federal and International Affairs, BP

HUDSON, Sherrill W.
TECO Plaza — Tel: (813) 228 - 4111
702 N. Franklin St. — Fax:(813) 228 - 4811
Tampa, FL 33602

Serves As:
- Chairman and Chief Exec. Officer, TECO Energy, Inc./Tampa Electric Co.

HUETT, Linda
175 Crossways Park West — Tel: (516) 390 - 1400
Woodbury, NY 11797 — Fax:(516) 390 - 1302

Serves As:
- President and Chief Exec. Officer, Weight Watchers Internat'l

HUFF, Dale
444 Westminster St. — Tel: (401) 459 - 1232
Providence, RI 02903-3279 — Fax:(401) 459 - 1333
huff.d@bcbsri.org — TF: (800) 637 - 3718

Serves As:
- Chief Communications Officer, Blue Cross & Blue Shield of Rhode Island

HUFFER, Russell
7900 Xerxes Ave. South — Tel: (952) 835 - 1874
Suite 1800 — Fax:(952) 835 - 3196
Minneapolis, MN 55431-1159

Serves As:
- Chairman, President and Chief Exec. Officer, Apogee Enterprises, Inc.

HUFFMAN, Kenneth J.
1230 Ave. of the Americas — Tel: (212) 603 - 8111
New York, NY 10020
investorrelations_newyork@oxy.com

Serves As:
- V. President, Investor Relations, Occidental Petroleum Corp.

HUGE, Arthur
1645 Bergstrom Rd. — Tel: (920) 751 - 1000
Neenah, WI 54956 — Fax:(920) 951 - 1236
TF: (800) 558 - 5073

Serves As:
- President and Chief Exec. Officer, Menasha Corporation

HUGER, Gregory F.
1150 Connecticut Ave. NW — Tel: (202) 367 - 2760
Suite 1025 — Fax:(202) 367 - 2790
Washington, DC 20036
ghuger@unocal.com

Serves As:
- Director, Corporate Responsibility, UNOCAL Corp.

HUGGINS, Nancy
P.O. Box 1074 — Tel: (518) 355 - 5000
Schenectady, NY 12301 — Fax:(518) 379 - 3515

Serves As:
- Contact, Golub Foundation, Golub Corp.

HUGHES, Bill
1499 Post Rd. — Tel: (203) 319 - 4700
Fairfield, CT 06824 — Fax:(203) 319 - 4701

Serves As:
- V. President, Global Communications, IMS Health, Inc.

HUGHES, Caressa F.
1929 Allen Pkwy. — Tel: (713) 525 - 5230
Houston, TX 77019 — Fax:(713) 525 - 7674
caressa.hughes@sci-us.com

Serves As:
- Managing Director, Governmental Affairs, Service Corp. Internat'l

HUGHES, Celeste
1221 Ave. of the Americas — Tel: (212) 512 - 2192
48th Floor — Fax:(212) 512 - 3840
New York, NY 10020-1095
celeste_hughes@mcgraw-hill.com

Serves As:
- Manager, Communications and Investor Relations, The McGraw-Hill Companies, Inc.

HUGHES, Coleen R.
P.O. Box 75000 — Tel: (313) 222 - 8618
mc 3352 — Fax:(313) 222 - 8720
Detroit, MI 48275 — TF: (800) 521 - 1190

Serves As:
- CRA Coordinator, Public Affairs, Comerica Incorporated

HUGHES, David H.
One Hughes Way — Tel: (407) 841 - 4755
Orlando, FL 32805-2205 — Fax:(407) 649 - 1670
dhughes@hughessupply.com

Serves As:
- Chairman of the Board, Hughes Supply, Inc.

HUGHES, Gerald
222 Berkeley St. — Tel: (617) 351 - 5000
Boston, MA 02116 — Fax:(617) 351 - 1100

Serves As:
- Senior V. President, Human Resources, Houghton Mifflin Co.

HUGHES, Gerald F.
101 Constitution Ave., NW — Tel: (202) 218 - 3800
Suite 801 East
Washington, DC 20001

Registered Federal Lobbyist.
Serves As:
- Representative, FedEx Corp.

HUGHES, Ivan
P.O. Box 4065 — Tel: (318) 388 - 9000
Monroe, LA 71211-4065 — Fax:(318) 388 - 9799
ivan.hughes@centurytel.com

Serves As:
- V. President, Human Resources, CenturyTel, Inc.

HUGHES, John P.
601 Van Ness Ave., Suite 2040 — Tel: (415) 775 - 1856
San Francisco, CA 94102 — Fax:(415) 474 - 3080
hughesjp@sce.com

Serves As:
- Manager, Regulatory Affairs, Southern California Edison, an Edison Internat'l Co.

HUGHES, Kristin
1100 New York Ave. NW — Tel: (202) 378 - 2500
Suite 600W — Fax:(202) 378 - 2550
Washington, DC 20005
kristin_hughes@hp.com

Registered Federal Lobbyist.
Serves As:
- Manager, Federal and International Public Policy, Hewlett-Packard Co.

HUGHES, Louise S.
P.O. Box 599 — Tel: (513) 983 - 6357
Cincinnati, OH 45201-0599
hughes.ls@pg.com

Serves As:
- Associate Director, Ohio Government Relations, The Procter & Gamble Company

HUGHES, Paul
345 Park Ave.
San Jose, CA 95110-2704
Tel: (408) 536 - 6000
Fax:(408) 537 - 6000

Registered Federal Lobbyist.
Serves As:
• Public Policy Advisor, Adobe Systems Inc.

HUGHES, R. Douglas
1100 Wilson Blvd.
Suite 1500
Arlington, VA 22209
Tel: (703) 841 - 5700
Fax:(703) 841 - 5792

Serves As:
• Senior Director, Government Relations, Raytheon Co.

HUGHES, Rodney
200 W. Second St.
Winston-Salem, NC 27101
Tel: (336) 733 - 2000

Serves As:
• Contact, BB&T Contributions Committee, BB&T Corp.

HUGHES, Shirley
3311 E. Old Shakopee Rd.
Minneapolis, MN 55425-1640
Tel: (952) 853 - 3301
Fax:(952) 853 - 7272

Serves As:
• Senior V. President, Human Resources, Ceridian Corp.

HUGHES, Vickie
P.O. Box 511
Kingsport, TN 37662-5075
vhughes@eastman.com
Tel: (423) 229 - 1302
Fax:(423) 229 - 1679
TF: (800) 327 - 8626

Serves As:
• Senior Exec. Assistant, Communications and Public Affairs, Eastman Chemical Co.

HUIZENGA, H. Wayne
100 Dunbar St.
Spartanburg, SC 29306
Tel: (864) 573 - 1600
Fax:(864) 573 - 1695

Serves As:
• Chairman of the Board, Extended Stay America, Inc.

HULEWICZ, Geoffrey M.
850 Lagoon Dr.
Chula Vista, CA 91910-2098
Tel: (619) 691 - 3635
Fax:(619) 691 - 2584

Serves As:
• Senior Employee Communications Specialist, Goodrich Corp. - Aerostructures

HULING, Charles H.
241 Ralph McGill Blvd. NE
Atlanta, GA 30308-3374
Tel: (404) 506 - 7716
Fax:(404) 506 - 3771

Serves As:
• Director, Environmental Affairs, Georgia Power Co.

HULL, Jeffrey S.
555 12th St.
Eighth Floor
Oakland, CA 94607
jhull@matson.com
Tel: (510) 628 - 4534
Fax:(510) 628 - 7359

Serves As:
• Manager, Public Relations, Matson Navigation Company, Inc.

HULLIN, Tod
World Headquarters
100 N. Riverside
Chicago, IL 60606-1596
Tel: (312) 544 - 2002
Fax:(312) 544 - 2082

Serves As:
• Senior V. President, Communications, The Boeing Co.

HUMANN, L. Phillip
P.O. Box 4410
Atlanta, GA 30302
phil.humann@suntrust.com
Tel: (404) 588 - 7711
Fax:(404) 581 - 1664

Serves As:
• Chairman and Chief Exec. Officer, SunTrust Banks, Inc.

HUMENESKY, Greg
100 Pier 1 Place
Fort Worth, TX 76102
Tel: (817) 252 - 8000

Serves As:
• Exec. V. President, Human Resources, Pier 1 Imports

HUMPHREY, David
P.O. Box 10048
Fort Smith, AR 72917
Tel: (479) 785 - 6200
Fax:(479) 785 - 6004

Serves As:
• Director, Investor Relations, Arkansas Best Corporation

HUMPHREY, James E.
100 Fourth Ave. North
Bayport, MN 55003-1096
Tel: (651) 264 - 5150

Serves As:
• President and Chief Exec. Officer, Andersen Corp.

HUMPHREY, Megan
One Health Plaza
East Hanover, NJ 07936
Tel: (862) 778 - 6724
Fax:(862) 644 - 8585

Serves As:
• Associate Director, Public Relations, (Novartis Pharmaceuticals Corp.), Novartis Corporation

HUMPHREY, Perry
300 Willbrook Office Park
Fairport, NY 14450
Tel: (585) 218 - 3600

Serves As:
• PAC Treasurer, Constellation Brands, Inc.

HUMPHREYS, Mary
2941 Fairview Park Dr.
Falls Church, VA 22042-4513
Tel: (703) 876 - 3389
Fax:(703) 876 - 3555

Serves As:
• Manager, Public Affairs, General Dynamics Corporation

HUMPHRIES, Fred
One Microsoft Way
Redmond, WA 98052-6399
Tel: (425) 882 - 8080
Fax:(425) 936 - 7329

Serves As:
• Director, State Government Affairs, Microsoft Corporation

HUMPHRIES, John
1401 I St. NW
Suite 600
Washington, DC 20005
Tel: (202) 336 - 7400
Fax:(202) 336 - 7515

Serves As:
• PAC Treasurer, United Technologies Corp.

HUMPHRIES, John M.
1401 I St. NW
Suite 600
Washington, DC 20005
jack.humphries@utc.com
Tel: (202) 336 - 7474
Fax:(202) 336 - 7515

Registered Federal Lobbyist.
Serves As:
• V. President, Government Relations and PAC Chair, United Technologies Corp.

HUNT, Bob
1185 Sanctuary Pkwy.
Suite 250
Alpharetta, GA 30004
Tel: (678) 393 - 2563
Fax:(678) 393 - 9631

Serves As:
• Manager, Government Affairs (Southern Region), Coors Brewing Co.

HUNT, Kevin J.
P.O. Box 618
St. Louis, MO 63188-0618
Tel: (314) 877 - 7990
Fax:(314) 877 - 7667

Serves As:
• Co-Chief Exec. Officer and President, Ralcorp Holdings, Inc.

HUNT, M. Truman
One Nu Skin Plaza
75 W. Center St.
Provo, UT 84601
Tel: (801) 345 - 1000
Fax:(801) 345 - 2799

Serves As:
• President and Chief Exec. Officer, Nu Skin Enterprises

HUNT, Ray L.
1445 Ross at Field
Suite 1400
Dallas, TX 75202-2785
Tel: (214) 978 - 8000
Fax:(214) 978 - 8888

Serves As:
• Chief Exec. Officer, Hunt Oil Co.

HUNT, Rod
P.O. Box 73
Boise, ID 83729
rod.hunt@wgint.com
Tel: (208) 386 - 5254
Fax:(208) 386 - 5065

Serves As:
• Director, Corporate Communications, Washington Group Internat'l

HUNT, Sue
901 S. Central Exwy.
Richardson, TX 75080
Tel: (972) 766 - 6900
Fax:(972) 766 - 5298

Serves As:
• V. President, Human Resources, Blue Cross and Blue Shield of Texas, Inc.

HUNT, Tim
14 Cambridge Center
Cambridge, MA 02142
Tel: (617) 914 - 6524
Fax:(617) 679 - 2617

Serves As:
• Senior Director, Public Affairs, Biogen Idec Inc.

HUNTER, Adolph
2655 Seely Ave.
Bldg. 8
San Jose, CA 95134
adolph@cadence.com
Tel: (408) 948 - 1234
Fax:(408) 944 - 0747
TF: (800) 862 - 4522

Serves As:
- Director, Corporate Communications, Cadence Design Systems, Inc.

HUNTER, Gerald R.
P.O. Box 650205
Dallas, TX 75265-0205
gerald.hunter@atmosenergy.com
Tel: (972) 855 - 3116
Fax:(972) 855 - 3040
TF: (800) 382 - 8667

Serves As:
- Director, Corporate Communications, Atmos Energy Corp.

HUNTER, Kelli A.
50606 AXP Financial Center
Minneapolis, MN 55474
Tel: (612) 671 - 3131
Fax:(612) 671 - 2741
TF: (800) 328 - 8300

Serves As:
- Exec. V. President, Human Resources, Ameriprise Financial Services Inc.

HUNTER, Thom
800 N. Harvey, Room 399
Oklahoma City, OK 73102
Tel: (405) 291 - 6078
Fax:(405) 278 - 4628

Serves As:
- Area Manager, Corporate Communications, (Southwestern Bell Telephone Co.), SBC Communications Inc.

HUNTER, Yvonne
P.O. Box 53999
M/S 9988
Phoenix, AZ 85072-3999
yvonne.hunter@pinnaclewest.com
Tel: (602) 250 - 4520
Fax:(602) 250 - 3887

Serves As:
- Senior Public Affairs Representative, Pinnacle West Capital Corp.

HUNTER-PERKINS, Paula
301 Commerce St.
Suite 500
Fort Worth, TX 76006
Tel: (817) 390 - 8200
Fax:(817) 390 - 1715

Serves As:
- V. President and Director, Human Resources, D. R. Horton, Inc.

HUNTER-TURNER, Kimberly
101 Constitution Ave. NW
Suite 800
Washington, DC 20001
Tel: (202) 742 - 4270
Fax:(202) 742 - 4271

Registered Federal Lobbyist.
Serves As:
- V. President, Government Relations, Cendant Corp.

HUNTINGTON, Erin B.
555 12th St. NW
Suite 650
Washington, DC 20004-1205
Tel: (202) 393 - 7950
Fax:(202) 393 - 7960

Registered Federal Lobbyist.
Serves As:
- Manager, International and Public Government Relations, Eli Lilly and Company

HUNTINGTON, Michael E.
P.O. Box 7608
Boise, ID 83707
Tel: (208) 377 - 6840
Fax:(208) 377 - 6097

Serves As:
- V. President, Marketing and External Affairs, Intermountain Gas Co.

HUNTSMAN, Jon M.
500 Huntsman Way
Salt Lake City, UT 84108
Tel: (801) 584 - 5700
Fax:(801) 584 - 5781

Serves As:
- Chairman of the Board, Huntsman Corp.

HUNTSMAN, Peter
3040 Post Oak Blvd.
Houston, TX 77056
peter_huntsman@huntsman.com
Tel: (713) 235 - 6000

Serves As:
- President and Chief Exec. Officer, Huntsman Corp.

HUNZIKER, Leslie
500 N. Field Dr.
Lake Forest, IL 60045
leslie.hunziker@tenneco-automotive.com
Tel: (847) 482 - 5042
Fax:(847) 482 - 5049

Serves As:
- Director, Investor Relations, Tenneco Automotive

HURD, Michael V.
3000 Hanover St.
Palo Alto, CA 94304
Tel: (650) 857 - 1501
Fax:(650) 857 - 5518
TF: (800) 752 - 0900

Serves As:
- President and Chief Exec. Officer, Hewlett-Packard Co.

HURLEY, Bill
One AMD Pl.
P.O. Box 3453
Sunnyvale, CA 94088
Tel: (408) 749 - 4000
TF: (800) 538 - 8450

Serves As:
- Assistant General Counsel and Director, Government Relations, Advanced Micro Devices, Inc.

HURLEY, Bob
P.O. Box 3100
Fullerton, CA 92834
Tel: (714) 773 - 7987
Fax:(714) 773 - 7743
TF: (800) 742 - 2345

Serves As:
- V. President, Human Resources and Corporate Communications, Beckman Coulter, Inc.

HURLEY, John R.
Seven Hanover Square
M/S H-26-E
New York, NY 10004-2616
Tel: (212) 598 - 8000
Fax:(212) 949 - 2170

Serves As:
- PAC Treasurer, Guardian Life Insurance Co. of America

HURLEY, Terence
340 Kingsland St.
Nutley, NJ 07110-1199
terence_j.hurley@roche.com
Tel: (973) 562 - 2882
Fax:(973) 562 - 5589

Serves As:
- Director, Product Public Affairs - Metabolic Disease, Anti-infectives, Hoffmann-La Roche Inc. (Roche)

HURLOW, Randy
P.O. Box 1938
Sumner, WA 98390-0800
rhurlow@rei.com
Tel: (253) 395 - 5877
Fax:(253) 395 - 8135

Serves As:
- Manager, Public Relations, Recreational Equipment, Inc.

HURT, Michael
1200 Wilson Blvd.
Arlington, VA 22209-2305
Tel: (703) 465 - 3500

Serves As:
- Representative, The Boeing Co.

HURWITZ, Charles E.
1330 post Oak Blvd.
Suite 2000
Houston, TX 77056
Tel: (713) 975 - 7600
Fax:(713) 267 - 3701

Serves As:
- Chairman and Chief Exec. Officer, MAXXAM Inc.

HURWITZ, Geoffrey B.
1300 Wilson Blvd.
Arlington, VA 22209
Tel: (703) 741 - 5881
Fax:(703) 741 - 5884

Registered Federal Lobbyist.
Serves As:
- Director, Government Relations, Rohm and Haas Co.

HUSKEY, Teresa
13737 Noel Rd.
Dallas, TX 75240
teresa.huskey@tenethealth.com
Tel: (469) 893 - 2293
Fax:(469) 893 - 8637

Serves As:
- Senior Director, Government Relations, Tenet Healthcare Corp.

HUSSEY, Terry A.
P.O. Box 2601
Troy, MI 48007-2601
Tel: (248) 643 - 3500
Fax:(248) 643 - 3687

Serves As:
- V. President, Human Resources, Thyssenkrupp Budd Company

HUTCHESON, Randy
1101 Pennsylvania Ave. NW
Suite 400
Washington, DC 20004-2504
Tel: (202) 637 - 3800
Fax:(202) 637 - 3860

Registered Federal Lobbyist.
Serves As:
- Representative, Textron Inc.

HUTCHESON, Stewart
10307 Pacific Center Ct.
San Diego, CA 92121
Tel: (858) 882 - 6000
Fax:(858) 882 - 6010

Serves As:
- Chief Exec. Officer, Leap Wireless International, Inc.

HUTCHESON, Tad
9955 Airtran Blvd.
Orlando, FL 32827-5330
tad.hutcheson@airtran.com
Tel: (407) 254 - 7442
Fax:(407) 251 - 5727

Serves As:
- Director, Corporte Communications, AirTran Airways

Responsibilities include corporate giving.

HUTCHINSON, John L.
One Energy Pl.
Pensacola, FL 32520
jlhutchi@southernco.com
Tel: (850) 444 - 6750
Fax:(850) 444 - 6448
TF: (800) 225 - 5797

Serves As:
- Manager, Public Affairs, Gulf Power Co.

HUTCHINSON, Libby
P.O. Box 834
WMT 0735
Seattle, WA 98101
libby.hutchinson@wamu.net
Tel: (206) 461 - 2484
Fax:(206) 554 - 4807
TF: (800) 756 - 8000

Serves As:
- First V. President and Manager, Corporate Public Relations, Washington Mutual, Inc.

HUTCHINSON, Phil
P.O. Box 4100
M/S 2278
St. Louis, MO 63136-8506
Tel: (314) 553 - 3420
Fax:(314) 553 - 3527

Serves As:
- V. President, Human Resources, Emerson

HUTCHISON, Barry
1401 I St. NW
Suite 1100
Washington, DC 20005
Tel: (202) 326 - 8836
Fax:(202) 289 - 3699

Registered Federal Lobbyist.
Serves As:
- Exec. Director, Federal Relations, SBC Communications Inc.

HUTTER, Christopher T.
One Targeting Centre
Windsor, CT 06095
cthutter@advo.com
Tel: (860) 285 - 6424
Fax:(860) 285 - 6245
TF: (800) 559 - 2386

Serves As:
- V. President, Investor Relations; and Treasurer, Advo Inc.

HUTTERLY, Jane M.
1525 Howe St.
Racine, WI 53403
Tel: (262) 260 - 2000
Fax:(262) 260 - 6004

Serves As:
- Exec. V. President, Worldwide Corporate and Environmental Affairs, SC Johnson

HUTTON, Edward L.
2600 Chemed Center
255 E. Fifth St.
Cincinnati, OH 45202-4726
Tel: (513) 762 - 6900
Fax:(513) 762 - 6919

Serves As:
- Chairman of the Board, The Chemed Corporation

HUTTON, Helena
1425 K St. NW
Suite 300
Washington, DC 20005
Tel: (202) 414 - 3000
Fax:(202) 414 - 3037

Registered Federal Lobbyist.
Serves As:
- Manager, Government Relations, 3M Company

HUTTON, Michael S.
4800 Deerwood Campus Pkwy.
Jacksonville, FL 32246-8273
michael.hutton@bcbsfl.com
Tel: (904) 791 - 6111
Fax:(904) 905 - 4486
TF: (800) 477 - 3736

Serves As:
- Grants Manager, Blue Cross and Blue Shield of Florida

HUTTON, Randall L.
P.O. Box B
Jacksonville, FL 32203-0297
randyhutton@winndixie.com
Tel: (904) 783 - 5408
Fax:(904) 783 - 5294

Serves As:
- V. President/Director, Government Relations, Winn-Dixie Stores

HUTTON, Ron
1000 Alfred Nobel Dr.
Hercules, CA 94547-1811
ron_hutton@bio-rad.com
Tel: (510) 741 - 6142
Fax:(510) 741 - 5817
TF: (800) 424 - 6723

Serves As:
- Treasurer and Manager, Investor Relations, Bio-Rad Laboratories, Inc.

HWANG, Dr. Li-San
3475 East Foothill Blvd.
Pasadena, CA 91107
Tel: (626) 351 - 4664
Fax:(626) 351 - 5291

Serves As:
- Chairman and Chief Exec. Officer, Tetra Tech, Inc.

HYDE, Douglas W.
P.O. Box 300
Oshkosh, WI 54903-0300
Tel: (920) 231 - 8800
Fax:(920) 231 - 8621
TF: (800) 282 - 4674

Serves As:
- Chairman and Chief Exec. Officer, Oshkosh B'Gosh, Inc.

HYDE, Karen
1225 17th St.
Denver, CO 80202
Tel: (303) 571 - 7511
Fax:(303) 294 - 8120

Serves As:
- Xcel Energy Employee PAC (XPAC), Xcel Energy, Inc.

HYDE, Marcia
19975 Victor Pkwy.
Livonia, MI 48152-7001
hydem@valassis.com
Tel: (734) 591 - 3000
Ext: 16343
Fax:(734) 591 - 4503
TF: (800) 437 - 0479

Serves As:
- V. President, Human Resources and Communications Center, Valassis Communications, Inc.

HYDE, Richard W.
401 Ninth St. NW
Suite 1100
Washington, DC 20004
rwhyde@duke-energy.com
Tel: (202) 331 - 8090
Fax:(202) 331 - 1181

Serves As:
- Director, Federal Governmental Affairs-Washington, Duke Energy Corp.

HYDE, Thomas D.
702 SW Eighth St.
Bentonville, AR 72716
Tel: (479) 273 - 4000
Fax:(479) 273 - 4053

Serves As:
- Exec. V. President, Legal and Corporate Affairs and Secretary, Wal-Mart Stores

HYNCIK, Sarah
Three Penn Plaza East
PP-15V
M/S PP-16H
Newark, NJ 07105-2200
Tel: (973) 466 - 8546
Fax:(973) 466 - 7077

Serves As:
- Government Affairs Associate, Horizon Blue Cross Blue Shield of New Jersey

IACO, Steve
200 Park Ave.
New York, NY 10166
Tel: (212) 984 - 6535

Serves As:
- Senior Managing Director, Corporate Communications, CB Richard Ellis Services, Inc.

IANNUCCI, Patricia J.
25 Harbor Park Dr.
Port Washington, NY 11050
pat_iannucci@pall.com
Tel: (516) 801 - 9100
Fax:(516) 484 - 3649
TF: (800) 876 - 7255

Serves As:
- V. President, Corporate Communications, Pall Corp.

IANNUZI, Salvatore
One Symbol Plaza
Holtsville, NY 11742-1300
Tel: (631) 738 - 2400
Fax:(631) 738 - 5990
TF: (800) 722 - 6234

Serves As:
- Interim President and Chief Exec. Officer, Symbol Technologies, Inc.

IARROBINO, Paul
1200 Wilson Blvd.
Arlington, VA 22209-2305
Tel: (703) 465 - 3304

Registered Federal Lobbyist.
Serves As:
- Manager, Legislative Affairs, Missile Defense, The Boeing Co.

IBRAHIM, S.A.
1601 Market St.
12th Floor
Philadelphia, PA 19103
Tel: (215) 564 - 6600

Serves As:
- Chief Exec. Officer, Radian Group, Inc.

IBSEN, Marlene
One Tower Sq. — Tel: (860) 277 - 9039
Hartford, CT 06183 — Fax:(860) 954 - 8497

Serves As:
- President, St. Paul's Travelers Connecticut Foundation, St. Paul Travelers Cos., Inc.

ICAHN, Charles
11111 Sunset Hills Dr. — Tel: (703) 547 - 2000
Reston, VA 20190-5339 — Fax:(703) 547 - 2881

Serves As:
- Chairman of the Board, XO Communications, Inc.

ICHIOKA, Sam
Five Dedrick Pl. — Tel: (973) 882 - 2000
West Caldwell, NJ 07006-6398 — Fax:(973) 808 - 7555

Serves As:
- Chairman and Chief Exec. Officer, Ricoh Corp.

ICHORD, J. William
1150 Connecticut Ave. NW — Tel: (202) 367 - 2773
Suite 1025 — Fax:(202) 367 - 2790
Washington, DC 20036
wichord@unocal.com

Registered Federal Lobbyist.
Serves As:
- V. President, Government and International Relations, UNOCAL Corp.

IDESON, D. Scott
P.O. Box 30270 — Tel: (801) 333 - 2100
Salt Lake City, UT 84130-0270

Serves As:
- President and Chief Exec. Officer, Regence BlueCross BlueShield of Utah

Responsibilities include corporate philanthropy.

IKEDA, Donna
One Franklin Pkwy. — Tel: (650) 312 - 2000
San Mateo, CA 94403-1906 — Fax:(650) 312 - 3655
dikeda@frk.com — TF: (800) 342 - 5236

Serves As:
- Senior V. President, Human Resources International, Franklin Templeton Investments

ILES, Thom
2000 John Deere Run — Tel: (919) 804 - 2795
Raleigh, NC 27513

Serves As:
- Director, Public Affairs, Deere & Company

ILLOBRE, Nick
One Blue Hill Plaza — Tel: (845) 577 - 2752
Pearl River, NY 10965 — Fax:(845) 577 - 2958

Serves As:
- Director, Human Resources, Orange and Rockland Utilities, Inc.

ILTCH, Michael
Fox Office Center — Tel: (313) 983 - 6000
2211 Woodward Ave. — Fax:(313) 983 - 6197
Detroit, MI 48201-3400

Serves As:
- Chairman and Chief Exec. Officer, Little Caesar Enterprises

IMHOF, Hugh
P.O. Box 3727 — Tel: (509) 495 - 4264
Spokane, WA 99220-3727 — Fax:(509) 495 - 8725
hugh.imhof@avistacorp.com — TF: (800) 727 - 9170

Serves As:
- Manager, Media and Information, Avista Corp.

IMMELT, Jeffrey R.
3135 Easton Tpk. — Tel: (203) 373 - 2211
Bldg. E2E — Fax:(203) 373 - 3131
Fairfield, CT 06431
jeffrey.immelt@corporate.ge.com

Serves As:
- Chairman and Chief Exec. Officer, General Electric Co.

INFANTE, Dominick
P.O. Box 6000 — Tel: (856) 488 - 8500
Cherry Hill, NJ 08034-6000 — Fax:(856) 488 - 0485

Serves As:
- Manager, Product Public Relations, Subaru of America, Inc.

ING, Charles E.
1850 M St. NW — Tel: (202) 775 - 1700
Suite 600 — Fax:(202) 822 - 0928
Washington, DC 20036

Registered Federal Lobbyist.
Serves As:
- Director, Government Affairs, Toyota Motor North America, Inc.

INGALLS, Donald R.
1901 Main St. — Tel: (716) 887 - 6900
Buffalo, NY 14208-0080 — Fax:(716) 887 - 8981
TF: (888) 249 - 2583

Serves As:
- V. President, Government Affairs and Community Relations, HealthNow New York Inc.

INGLE, Don
P.O. Box 190 — Tel: (630) 983 - 8676
Aurora, IL 60507-0190 — Ext: 2939
dingle@nicor.com — Fax:(630) 983 - 9183

Serves As:
- Director, Corporate Communications, (NICOR Gas), Nicor, Inc.

INGLE, Ed
1401 I St., NW — Tel: (202) 263 - 5900
Suite 500 — Fax:(202) 263 - 5902
Washington, DC 20005

Registered Federal Lobbyist.
Serves As:
- Senior Director, Legislative Affairs, Microsoft Corporation

INGLE, Molly
P.O. Box 81226 — Tel: (206) 266 - 1000
Seattle, WA 98108-1226 — Fax:(206) 266 - 1821
ingle@amazon.com

Serves As:
- Media Contact, Amazon.com, Inc.

INGLE, II, Robert P.
P.O. Box 6676 — Tel: (828) 669 - 2941
Asheville, NC 28816 — Fax:(828) 669 - 3667
ringle@ingles-markets.com

Serves As:
- Chairman and Chief Exec. Officer, Ingles Markets, Inc.

INGLEE, William
1550 Crystal Dr. — Tel: (703) 413 - 5984
Crystal Square 2, Suite 300 — Fax:(703) 413 - 5617
Arlington, VA 22202

Registered Federal Lobbyist.
Serves As:
- V. President, Legislative Affairs, Lockheed Martin Corp.

INGRAHAM, Tricia
1144 E. Market St. — Tel: (330) 796 - 8517
Akron, OH 44316-0001 — Fax:(330) 796 - 1817
tricia_ingraham@goodyear.com

Serves As:
- Manager, Business and Financial Communications, The Goodyear Tire & Rubber Company

INGRAM, Dale
One Information Way — Tel: (501) 342 - 4346
Little Rock, AR 72202 — Fax:(501) 342 - 3913
TF: (888) 322 - 9466

Serves As:
- Public Relations Leader, Acxiom Corporation

INISS, Laura
11111 Sunset Hills Dr. — Tel: (703) 547 - 2000
Reston, VA 20190-5339 — Fax:(703) 547 - 2881

Serves As:
- Financial Analyst and PAC Treasurer, XO Communications, Inc.

INOSANTO, Judith
55 Water St. — Tel: (212) 855 - 5479
49th Floor — Fax:(212) 855 - 5424
New York, NY 10041-0099
jinosanto@dtcc.com

Serves As:
- Director, Corporate Communications, The Depository Trust & Clearing Corp.

INOUYE, Wayne
7565 Irvine Center Dr. — Tel: (949) 471 - 7000
Irvine, CA 92618 — Fax:(949) 471 - 7041

Serves As:
- President and Chief Exec. Officer, Gateway, Inc.

IOACHIM, Jackie
1515 Broadway — Tel: (212) 708 - 1600
New York, NY 10036

Serves As:
- V. President, Consumer Public Relations- Movies, (Showtime Networks Inc.), Viacom Inc./CBS Corp.

IOVINO, Charlyn A.
1331 F St. NW — Tel: (202) 419 - 7047
Suite 450 — Fax:(202) 223 - 4424
Washington, DC 20004
iovinoca@aetna.com

Registered Federal Lobbyist.
Serves As:
- V. President and Counsel, Aetna Inc.

IRANI, Dr. Ray R.
10889 Wilshire Blvd. — Tel: (310) 208 - 8800
Los Angeles, CA 90024 — Fax:(310) 443 - 6690

Serves As:
- Chairman and Chief Exec. Officer, Occidental Petroleum Corp.

IRVIN, Carolin
One State Farm Dr. — Tel: (610) 358 - 8320
Concordville, PA 19339 — Fax:(610) 358 - 7698

Serves As:
- Manager, Public Affairs, State Farm Insurance Cos.

IRVIN, Donna
The ARAMARK Tower — Tel: (215) 238 - 3271
1101 Market St. — TF: (800) 999 - 8989
Philadelphia, PA 19107

Serves As:
- Exec. Director, Corporate Contributions, ARAMARK

IRVIN, Rodney D.
1300 Wilson Blvd. — Tel: (703) 524 - 7647
Suite 900 — Fax:(703) 524 - 7707
Arlington, VA 22209-2307
rodirvin@eastman.com

Registered Federal Lobbyist.
Serves As:
- Director, Government Relations, Eastman Chemical Co.

IRVING, George C.
3110 Glenn Knolls Ct. — Tel: (770) 664 - 7151
Alpharetta, GA 30022 — Fax:(770) 751 - 7485

Serves As:
- Director, State Government Affairs, Johnson & Johnson

IRVING, Mark
One Davis Ave. — Tel: (718) 390 - 6368
Staten Island, NY 10310 — Fax:(718) 720 - 3802

Serves As:
- Director, Public Affairs (Staten Island), Consolidated Edison Co. of New York, Inc.

IRWIN, William T.
1401 I St. NW — Tel: (202) 408 - 5800
Suite 1200 — Fax:(202) 408 - 5845
Washington, DC 20005-2225

Registered Federal Lobbyist.
Serves As:
- Manager, International Relations, Chevron Corp.

ISAACS, David
1100 New York Ave. NW — Tel: (202) 378 - 2500
Suite 600W — Fax:(202) 378 - 2550
Washington, DC 20005
david_isaacs@hp.com

Registered Federal Lobbyist.
Serves As:
- Director, Government and Public Policy, Hewlett-Packard Co.

ISAKOW, Selwyn
2701 Cambridge Ct. — Tel: (248) 340 - 9090
Suite 300 — Fax:(248) 340 - 9345
Auburn Hills, MI 48326

Serves As:
- Chairman of the Board, Champion Enterprises, Inc.

ISDELL, E. Neville
P.O. Box 1734 — Tel: (404) 676 - 2121
Atlanta, GA 30301 — Fax:(404) 676 - 6792

Serves As:
- Chairman and Chief Exec. Officer, The Coca-Cola Co.

ISENBERG, Eugene M.
515 W. Greens Rd. — Tel: (281) 874 - 0035
Suite 1200 — Fax:(281) 872 - 5205
Houston, TX 77067-4525
eisenberg@nabors.com

Serves As:
- Chairman and Chief Exec. Officer, Nabors Industries, Ltd.

ISERMAN, Katrina M.
280 Beacon St. — Tel: (617) 266 - 3112
Boston, MA 02116
isermank@wyeth.com

Serves As:
- Associate Director, State Government Affairs, Wyeth Pharmaceuticals

ISHIGAMI, Kunio
P.O. Box 6000 — Tel: (856) 488 - 8500
Cherry Hill, NJ 08034-6000 — Fax:(856) 488 - 0485
kishigami@subaru.com

Serves As:
- Chairman, President, and Chief Exec. Officer, Subaru of America, Inc.

ISIP, Laurene
210 Carnegie Center — Tel: (609) 452 - 4440
Princeton, NJ 08540-6233 — Fax:(609) 452 - 9375
TF: (800) 621 - 8901

Serves As:
- Senior Director, Corporate Communications, Covance, Inc.

ISLER, Micaela
1401 I St. NW — Tel: (202) 466 - 3561
Suite 520 — Fax:(202) 466 - 3583
Washington, DC 20005

Serves As:
- PAC Director, HSBC North America Holdings Inc.

ISOM, W. Howard
P.O. Box 1768 — Tel: (916) 442 - 0771
Sacramento, CA 95812-1768 — Fax:(916) 325 - 2880
hisom@bdgrowers.com

Serves As:
- Chairman of the Board, Blue Diamond Growers

ITEIL, Linda
11401 Lamar Ave. — Tel: (913) 458 - 4629
Overland Park, KS 66211 — Fax:(913) 458 - 2934

Serves As:
- Communications Specialist, Black & Veatch

ITKIN, Laurie
10307 Pacific Center Ct. — Tel: (858) 882 - 6000
San Diego, CA 92121 — Fax:(858) 882 - 6010

Serves As:
- Director, Government Affairs, Leap Wireless International, Inc.

IVERSON, Betty
3100 S. Sheridan — Tel: (303) 909 - 0304
IC-339
Denver, CO 80227
iversonb@wyeth.com

Serves As:
- Associate Director, State Government Affairs, Wyeth Pharmaceuticals

IVEY, Susan
P.O. Box 2990 — Tel: (336) 741 - 5500
Winston-Salem, NC 27102 — Fax:(336) 741 - 5511

Serves As:
- Chairman, President and Chief Exec. Officer, Reynolds American Inc.

IVY, Conway G.
101 Prospect Ave. NW — Tel: (216) 566 - 2140
Cleveland, OH 44115 — Fax:(216) 566 - 2947

Serves As:
- Senior V. President, Corporate Planning and Development, Sherwin-Williams Co.

Responsibilities include corporate communications and public relations and development.

IYER, Suzanne
P.O. Box 24305 — Tel: (510) 271 - 7739
Oakland, CA 94623-1305 — Fax:(510) 271 - 6583
suzanne.iyer@clorox.com

Serves As:
- Government Affairs Issues Manager, The Clorox Co.

JABBONSKY, Larry
700 Anderson Hill Rd. — Tel: (914) 253 - 2647
Purchase, NY 10577-1444 — Fax:(914) 249 - 8202
larry.jabbonsky@pepsi.com

Serves As:
- Public Relations, (Pepsi-Cola North America), PepsiCo, Inc.

JACHINO, Laura
Metro Center — Tel: (203) 539 - 8000
One Station Pl. — Fax:(203) 539 - 7734
Stamford, CT 06902 — TF: (800) 969 - 9974

Serves As:
- Manager, Corporate Giving, The Thomson Corporation

JACKO, Jr., John H.
5215 N. O'Connor Blvd.
Suite 2300
Irving, TX 75039
Tel: (972) 443 - 6500
Fax:(972) 443 - 6800

Serves As:
- V. President, Marketing and Communications, Flowserve Corp.

JACKSON, Blair
1000 Beverly Way
Fort Smith, AR 72919-5273
Tel: (479) 201 - 5263
Fax:(479) 201 - 1101

Serves As:
- V. President, Corporate Communications, Beverly Enterprises, Inc.

JACKSON, Dan
650 N.E. Holladay, Suite 1400
Portland, OR 97232
Tel: (503) 872 - 1300
Fax:(503) 872 - 1349
TF: (800) 633 - 1488

Serves As:
- Exec. V. President and Chief Financial Officer, KinderCare Learning Centers, Inc.

Responsibilities include investor relations.

JACKSON, Debbie
P.O. Box 2486
Birmingham, AL 35201-2486
Tel: (205) 940 - 9400
Fax:(205) 912 - 4628

Serves As:
- Senior V. President, Human Resources, Bruno's Inc.

JACKSON, Eric
The Scoular Bldg.
2027 Dodge St.
Omaha, NE 68102
ejackson@scoular.com
Tel: (402) 342 - 3500
Fax:(402) 342 - 5568
TF: (800) 488 - 3500

Serves As:
- Senior V. President and Media Contact, The Scoular Co.

JACKSON, Glenn F.
1627 I St. NW
Suite 900
Washington, DC 20006
glenn.jackson@williams.com
Tel: (202) 833 - 8994
Fax:(202) 835 - 0707

Registered Federal Lobbyist.
Serves As:
- Director, Government Affairs, Williams

JACKSON, Jennifer
12950 Worldgate Dr.
Suite 600
Herndon, VA 20170
jennifer.jackson@lafarge-na.com
Tel: (703) 480 - 3600
Fax:(703) 796 - 2214

Serves As:
- Coordinator, Public Affairs, Lafarge North America, Inc.

JACKSON, Joleen
333 Continental Blvd.
El Segundo, CA 90245-5012
Tel: (310) 252 - 2000
Fax:(310) 252 - 2180

Serves As:
- Director, Investor Relations, Mattel, Inc.

JACKSON, Kathleen
635 Massachusetts Ave. NW
Washington, DC 20001
Tel: (202) 513 - 2000
Fax:(202) 513 - 3329

Serves As:
- V. President, Human Resources, Nat'l Public Radio

JACKSON, Keith
5005 E. McDowell Rd.
Phoenix, AZ 85008
Tel: (602) 244 - 6600
Fax:(602) 244 - 4830

Serves As:
- President and Chief Exec. Officer, ON Semiconductor Corp.

JACKSON, Laura J.
636 Grand Ave.
Des Moines, IA 50309
jacksonlj@wellmark.com
Tel: (515) 235 - 4473
Fax:(515) 248 - 5528

Serves As:
- Senior V. President, Human Resources, Wellmark, Inc.

JACKSON, Laura Min
One Edwards Way
Irvine, CA 92614-5688
laura_jackson@edwards.com
Tel: (949) 250 - 2500
Ext: 6804
Fax:(949) 250 - 2525
TF: (800) 424 - 3278

Serves As:
- V. President, Global Communications, Edwards Lifesciences Corp.

JACKSON, Lisa
700 13th St., N.W., Suite 700
Washington, DC 20005-3960
Tel: (202) 508 - 6303
Fax:(202) 508 - 6305

Registered Federal Lobbyist.
Serves As:
- Washington Representative, Emerson

JACKSON, Lorie D.
2000 K St., NW
Suite 710
Washington, DC 20006
Tel: (202) 862 - 0200
Fax:(202) 862 - 0267

Serves As:
- Washington Representative, Senate, Exxon Mobil Corp.

JACKSON, Marianne
50 Beale St.
San Francisco, CA 94105-1808
Tel: (415) 229 - 5000
Fax:(415) 229 - 5070
TF: (800) 200 - 3242

Serves As:
- Senior V. President, Human Resources, Blue Shield of California

JACKSON, Mary Ann
7900 Xerxes Ave. South
Suite 1800
Minneapolis, MN 55431-1159
mjackson@apog.com
Tel: (952) 487 - 7538
Fax:(952) 835 - 3196

Serves As:
- Director, Investor Relations, Apogee Enterprises, Inc.

Responsibilities include media relations.

JACKSON, Mary L.
Cash America Bldg.
1600 W. Seventh St.
Fort Worth, TX 76102-2599
mjackson@casham.com
Tel: (817) 570 - 1616
Fax:(817) 570 - 1645

Serves As:
- V. President, Public and Government Relations, Cash America Internat'l, Inc.

JACKSON, Michael
AutoNation Tower
110 SE Sixth St.
Fort Lauderdale, FL 33301
jacksonm@autonation.com
Tel: (954) 769 - 7200
Fax:(954) 769 - 6494

Serves As:
- Chairman and Chief Exec. Officer, AutoNation, Inc.

JACKSON, Neal
635 Massachusetts Ave. NW
Washington, DC 20001
Tel: (202) 513 - 2000
Fax:(202) 513 - 3329

Serves As:
- V. President, Legal Affairs, General Counsel and Secretary, Nat'l Public Radio

Responsibilities include legislative affairs.

JACKSON, Paul A.
444 N. Capitol St., N.W., Suite 740
Washington, DC 20001
Tel: (202) 824 - 6500
Fax:(202) 824 - 6510

Serves As:
- Director, Government Relations, News Corporation Ltd.

JACKSON, Roger A.
21557 Telegraph Rd.
Southfield, MI 48034
rjackson@lear.com
Tel: (248) 447 - 1562
Fax:(248) 447 - 1722

Serves As:
- Senior V. President, Human Resources and Corporate Relations, Lear Corporation

JACKSON, Russell M.
77 Beale St.
San Francisco, CA 94105
Tel: (415) 267 - 7136
Fax:(415) 267 - 7258

Serves As:
- Senior V. President, Human Resources, (Pacific Gas and Electric Co.), PG & E Corp.

JACKSON, Selina
316 Pennsylvania Ave. SE
Suite 300
Washington, DC 20003
Tel: (202) 675 - 4220
Fax:(202) 675 - 4230

Serves As:
- Manager, Public Affairs, United Parcel Service (UPS)

JACKSON, Tami S.
601 Pennsylvania Ave. NW
North Bldg., Suite 325
Washington, DC 20004
tami.s.jackson@usa.dupont.com
Tel: (202) 728 - 3645
Fax:(202) 728 - 3649

Serves As:
- Manager, State Government and Public Affairs, DuPont

JACKSON, Yvonne
235 E. 42nd St.
New York, NY 10017-5755
Tel: (212) 733 - 2323
Fax:(212) 573 - 1853

Serves As:
- Senior V. President and Head, Human Resources, Pfizer Inc.

JACOB, Bernard
One Energy Pl.
Pensacola, FL 32520
Tel: (850) 444 - 6111
Fax:(850) 444 - 6448
TF: (800) 225 - 5797

Serves As:
• V. President, External Affairs and Corporate Services, Gulf Power Co.

JACOB, John E.
One Busch Pl.
St. Louis, MO 63118-1852
Tel: (314) 577 - 2000
Fax:(314) 577 - 2900

Serves As:
• Exec. V. President, Global Communications, Anheuser-Busch Cos., Inc.

JACOBS, Bryan
101 Constitution Ave., NW
Suite 800 West
Washington, DC 20001
Tel: (202) 772 - 2497
Fax:(202) 772 - 2496

Registered Federal Lobbyist.
Serves As:
• Director, Government Relations, The Home Depot, Inc.

JACOBS, Irwin
5775 Morehouse Dr.
San Diego, CA 92121-2779
Tel: (858) 587 - 1121
Fax:(858) 658 - 2100

Serves As:
• Chairman of the Board, Qualcomm Inc.

JACOBS, Sr., Jeremy J.
40 Fountain Plaza
Buffalo, NY 14202
Tel: (716) 858 - 5000
Fax:(716) 858 - 5125

Serves As:
• Chairman and Chief Exec. Officer, Delaware North Companies

JACOBS, Libby
711 High St.
Des Moines, IA 50392-0150
jacobs.libby@principal.com
Tel: (515) 248 - 3641
Fax:(515) 246 - 5475
TF: (800) 986 - 3343

Serves As:
• Assistant Director, Community Relations, The Principal Financial Group

JACOBS, Lynn
1140 Connecticut Ave. NW
Suite 510
Washington, DC 20036
Tel: (202) 327 - 5240
Fax:(202) 327 - 5249

Registered Federal Lobbyist.
Serves As:
• V. President, Government Affairs, Prudential Financial

JACOBS, Paul
5775 Morehouse Dr.
San Diego, CA 92121-2779
Tel: (858) 587 - 1121
Fax:(858) 658 - 2100

Serves As:
• Chief Exec. Officer, Qualcomm Inc.

JACOBSEN, Jennifer
800 Connecticut Ave. NW
Suite 800
Washington, DC 20006
Tel: (202) 457 - 8582
Fax:(202) 457 - 8861

Registered Federal Lobbyist.
Serves As:
• Director, Domestic Public Policy, Time Warner Inc.

JACOBSON, Debra
P.O. Box 98510
Las Vegas, NV 89193-8510
Tel: (702) 876 - 7163
Fax:(702) 873 - 3820

Serves As:
• Senior Manager, State Regulatory Affairs, Southwest Gas Corp.
Responsibilities include political action.

JACOBSON, Michael R.
2145 Hamilton Ave.
San Jose, CA 95125
mjacobson@ebay.com
Tel: (408) 558 - 7400
Fax:(408) 558 - 7401
TF: (800) 322 - 9266

Serves As:
• V. President, Legal Affairs, General Counsel and Secretary, eBay, Inc.

JACOBSON, Paul
5619 DTC Pkwy.
Greenwood, CO 80111
paul.jacobson@adelphia.com
Tel: (303) 268 - 6426

Serves As:
• V. President, Corporate Communications, Adelphia Communications Corp.

JACOBSON, Sybil
One MetLife Plaza
Long Island City, NY 11101

Serves As:
• Contact, MetLife Foundation, MetLife, Inc.

JACOBUS, Pattie
1001 Trout Brook Crossing
Rocky Hill, CT 06067
patti.jacobus@henkel.com
Tel: (860) 571 - 5100

Serves As:
• V. President, Corporate Communications, Henkel Corp.

JACOBY, Peter G.
1120 20th St. NW
Suite 1000
Washington, DC 20036-3406
pgjacoby@att.com
Tel: (202) 457 - 3810
Fax:(202) 457 - 2267

Registered Federal Lobbyist.
Serves As:
• V. President and Director, Congressional Relations, AT&T

JACQUET, Richard J. "Dick"
1941 Ringwood Ave.
San Jose, CA 95131-1721
Tel: (408) 451 - 9400
Fax:(408) 451 - 1632

Serves As:
• Senior V. President, Human Resources, Bell Microproducts, Inc.

JAEHNERT, Frank M.
P.O. Box 571
Milwaukee, WI 53201-0571
Tel: (414) 358 - 6600
Fax:(800) 292 - 2289

Serves As:
• President and Chief Exec. Officer, Brady Corp.

JAENKE, Norma
3925 N. Hastings Way
Eau Claire, WI 54703-3703
Tel: (715) 839 - 2121
Fax:(715) 839 - 2122

Serves As:
• Exec. Director, Presto Foundation, Nat'l Presto Industries, Inc.

JAHR, Dale T.
P.O. Box 1400
Rapid City, SD 57709-1400
djahr@bh-corp.com
Tel: (605) 721 - 2326
Fax:(605) 721 - 2568

Serves As:
• Investor Relations Director, Black Hills Corp.

JAKSICH, Mark C.
One Valmont Plaza
Omaha, NE 68154-5215
Tel: (402) 963 - 1000
Fax:(402) 963 - 1095

Serves As:
• Treasurer, Valmont Industries PAC, Valmont Industries, Inc.

JAKUBIK, Chris
Prudential Tower Bldg.
Boston, MA 02199-8004
chris_jakubik@gillette.com
Tel: (617) 421 - 7000
Fax:(617) 421 - 7123

Serves As:
• V. President, Corporate Public Relations, The Gillette Company

JALENAK, Jr., C.R.
P.O. Box 430
Memphis, TN 30103
Tel: (901) 528 - 4011
Fax:(901) 528 - 4758

Serves As:
• Chairman of the Board, Memphis Light, Gas and Water Division

JAMES, Cynthia
40650 Encyclopedia Circle
Fremont, CA 94538-2453
cjames@tmw.com
Tel: (510) 723 - 8621

Serves As:
• Director, Corporate Giving, Men's Wearhouse, Inc.

JAMES, Donald M.
P.O. Box 385014
Birmingham, AL 35238-5014
Tel: (205) 298 - 3000
Fax:(205) 298 - 2960

Serves As:
• Chairman and Chief Exec. Officer, Vulcan Materials Co.

JAMES, Elizabeth
113 King St.
Armonk, NY 10504
elizabeth.james@mbia.com
Tel: (914) 765 - 3889
Fax:(914) 765 - 3898

Serves As:
• V. President, Corporate Communications, MBIA, Inc.

JAMES, Thomas A.
880 Carillon Pkwy.
St. Petersburg, FL 33716
Tel: (727) 567 - 1000

Serves As:
• Chairman and Chief Exec. Officer, Raymond James Financial, Inc.

JAMES-COPELAND, Margot
127 Public Square
Cleveland, OH 44114
margot_copeland@keybank.com
Tel: (216) 689 - 4724
Fax:(216) 689 - 3865

Serves As:
- Exec. V. President, Civic Affairs and Corporate Diversity; Chairman, KeyCorp Foundation, KeyCorp

JAMESON, Booth
1331 Pennsylvania Ave. NW
Suite 1300 North
Washington, DC 20004
booth.jameson@eds.com
Tel: (202) 637 - 6741
Fax:(202) 637 - 6759

Registered Federal Lobbyist.
Serves As:
- Director, Global Government Affairs, EDS Corp.

JAMISON, III, George H.
United Technologies Bldg.
One Financial Plaza
Hartford, CT 06101
Tel: (860) 728 - 7000
Fax:(860) 728 - 6494

Serves As:
- V. President, Communications, United Technologies Corp.

JAMISON, Wendy
1100 N. King St.
0127
Wilmington, DE 19880-127
wendy.jamison@mbna.com
Tel: (302) 432 - 0956
Fax:(302) 432 - 0039
TF: (800) 441 - 7048

Serves As:
- First V. President, Government Affairs, MBNA Corp.

JAMISON, Jr., Zean
8600 South Blvd.
Charlotte, NC 28273
Tel: (704) 554 - 1421
Fax:(704) 554 - 5562
TF: (800) 438 - 1880

Serves As:
- Director, Foundation, Lance, Inc.

JANASZ, Kathleen
710 Medtronic Pkwy.
Minneapolis, MN 55432-5604
Tel: (763) 505 - 2634
Fax:(763) 514 - 4879
TF: (800) 328 - 2518

Serves As:
- Manager, Public Relations, Medtronic, Inc.

JANEWAY, Barbara
P.O. Box 54143
Los Angeles, CA 90054
bjaneway@ralphs.com
Tel: (310) 884 - 2993
Fax:(310) 884 - 2632

Serves As:
- Public Relations Coordinator, Ralphs Grocery Co.

JANJIGIAN, Janet
10250 Constellation Blvd.
Los Angeles, CA 90067-6241
Tel: (310) 449 - 3660
Fax:(310) 449 - 8757

Serves As:
- Senior V. President, Corporate Communications, Metro-Goldwyn-Mayer Inc.

JANKE, Jr., Kenneth S.
1932 Wynnton Rd.
Columbus, GA 31999
Tel: (706) 323 - 3431
Fax:(706) 660 - 7333
TF: (800) 992 - 3522

Serves As:
- Senior V. President, Investor Relations, AFLAC Incorporated

JANNAZO, Frank
333 N. Summit St.
16th Floor.
Toledo, OH 43604-2617
Tel: (419) 252 - 5500
Fax:(419) 252 - 5554

Serves As:
- PAC Treasurer, Manor Care, Inc.

JANNING, James C.
1415 W. 22nd St.
Suite 1100
Oak Brook, IL 60523
Tel: (630) 954 - 2000

Serves As:
- Chairman of the Board, Federal Signal Corp.

JANS, Megan C.
1200 Wilson Blvd.
Arlington, VA 22209-2305
Tel: (703) 465 - 3687
Fax:(703) 465 - 3004

Registered Federal Lobbyist.
Serves As:
- Manager, Legislative Affairs, Army Programs, The Boeing Co.

JANSON, Dan
82 Running Hill Rd.
South Portland, ME 04106-6020
Tel: (207) 775 - 8660
Fax:(207) 761 - 3415
TF: (800) 341 - 0392

Serves As:
- Senior Director, Investor Relations, Fairchild Semiconductor Internat'l, Inc.

JANUSHKOWSKY, Vera
1201 K St., Suite 1010
Sacramento, CA 95814
vjanushkowsky@pfizer.com
Tel: (916) 557 - 1177
Ext: 7504
Fax:(916) 557 - 1175

Serves As:
- Director, Government Relations, Pfizer Inc.

JANZEN, Margaret
One MetroTech Center
Brooklyn, NY 11201
Tel: (718) 403 - 8592
Fax:(718) 488 - 1763

Serves As:
- Investor Relations Contact, KeySpan Corp.

JAQUOTOT, Baldomero Falcones
2000 Purchase St.
Purchase, NY 10577-2509
Tel: (914) 249 - 2000
Fax:(914) 249 - 4206

Serves As:
- Chairman, MasterCard Internat'l

JARDOT, Leo C.
1667 K St. NW
Suite 1270
Washington, DC 20036
jardotl@wyeth.com
Tel: (202) 659 - 8320
Fax:(202) 659 - 2158

Registered Federal Lobbyist.
Serves As:
- V. President, Government Relations, Wyeth
- V. President, Government Relations, Wyeth Pharmaceuticals

JARK, Heidi B.
38 Fountain Square
Cincinnati, OH 45263
Tel: (513) 579 - 5300
Fax:(513) 579 - 5226
TF: (800) 972 - 3030

Serves As:
- Foundation Contact, Fifth Third Bancorp.

JARMAN, Richard B.
1250 H St. NW
Suite 800
Washington, DC 20005
richard.jarman@kodak.com
Tel: (202) 857 - 3400
Fax:(202) 857 - 3401

Registered Federal Lobbyist.
Serves As:
- Director, Advanced Manufacturing Affairs, Eastman Kodak Company

JARVIS, Chris
7001 220th S.W.
Bldg. 3 M/S 308
Mountlake Terrace, WA 98043-2124
chris.jarvis@premera.com
Tel: (425) 918 - 3368
Fax:(425) 918 - 5575
TF: (800) 422 - 0032

Serves As:
- Manager, Communications, Premera Blue Cross

JARVIS, Debbi L.
701 Ninth St. NW
Washington, DC 20068
dljarvis@pepco.com
Tel: (202) 872 - 2680
Fax:(202) 331 - 4857

Serves As:
- Manager, Media Relations, Pepco Holdings, Inc.

JARVIS, Mary Beth
4111 E. 37th St., North
Wichita, KS 67220
jarvism@kochind.com
Tel: (316) 828 - 3756
Fax:(316) 828 - 6997

Serves As:
- Director, Communication, Koch Industries, Inc.

JASINOWSKI, Isabel H.
1420 New York Ave. NW
Suite 200
Washington, DC 20005
ihjasinowski@goodyear.com
Tel: (202) 682 - 9250
Fax:(202) 682 - 1533

Registered Federal Lobbyist.
Serves As:
- V. President, Government Relations and Head of Washington, DC Office, The Goodyear Tire & Rubber Company

JASKOSKI, Peter J.
P.O. Box 2511
Houston, TX 77252-2511
Tel: (713) 420 - 2600
Fax:(713) 420 - 4993

Serves As:
- Director, Government Affairs, El Paso Corp.

JASNOFF, Jeffrey M.
7902 Westpark Dr.
McLean, VA 22102
Tel: (703) 273 - 7500
Fax:(703) 744 - 1601
TF: (888) 434 - 4648

Serves As:
- Senior V. President, Human Resources, Sunrise Assisted Living, Inc.

JASPER, Carl W.
120 San Gabriel Dr.
Sunnyvale, CA 94086
Tel: (408) 737 - 7600
Fax:(408) 737 - 7194
TF: (800) 998 - 9872

Serves As:
- V. President, Maxim Integrated Products

JASTROW, II, Kenneth M.
P.O. Box 40
Austin, TX 78767
Tel: (512) 434 - 5800

Serves As:
- Chairman and Chief Exec. Officer, Temple-Inland Inc.

JAY, Martin
33 Commercial St.
Foxboro, MA 02035
Tel: (508) 549 - 2424
Fax:(508) 549 - 4999
TF: (866) 746 - 6477

Serves As:
- Chairman of the Board, Invensys Systems, Inc.

JAYO, David
P.O. Box 1938
Sumner, WA 98390-0800
djayo@rei.com
Tel: (253) 395 - 5928
Fax:(253) 395 - 8135

Serves As:
- Manager, Corporate Giving, Recreational Equipment, Inc.

JEAN, Raymond A.
1900 W. Loop South
Suite 1500
Houston, TX 77027
rjean@quanex.com
Tel: (713) 961 - 4600
Fax:(713) 439 - 1016
TF: (800) 231 - 8176

Serves As:
- Chairman, President and Chief Exec. Officer, Quanex Corp.

JEANSONNE, Clay
P.O. Box 2504
Houston, TX 77252-2504
Tel: (713) 297 - 5000
Fax:(713) 297 - 5100

Serves As:
- Director, Investor Relations, Pogo Producing Co.

JEFFERS, Paul
680 E. Swedesford Rd.
Wayne, PA 19087
paul.jeffers@sungard.com
Tel: (484) 582 - 5506
Fax:(484) 225 - 1120

Serves As:
- V. President, Human Resources, SunGard Data Systems, Inc.

JEFFERS, Tom
700 State Route 46 East
Batesville, IN 47006-8835
Tel: (812) 934 - 7000
Fax:(812) 934 - 7371

Serves As:
- Contact, HI PAC, Hillenbrand Industries, Inc.

JEFFREY, Bob
466 Lexington Ave.
New York, NY 10017
Tel: (212) 210 - 7000
Fax:(212) 210 - 7770

Serves As:
- Chairman and Chief Exec. Officer, J. Walter Thompson Co.

JEFFRIES, Michael S.
6301 Fitch Path
New Albany, OH 43054
Tel: (614) 283 - 6500
Fax:(614) 283 - 6710

Serves As:
- Chairman and Chief Exec. Officer, Abercrombie & Fitch Co.

JEFFRIES, Jr., Russ E.
301 S. College St., Suite 4000
One Wachovia Center
Charlotte, NC 28288-0370
Tel: (704) 374 - 3488
Fax:(704) 374 - 7021
TF: (800) 275 - 3862

Serves As:
- PAC Contact, Wachovia Corp.

JENKINS, Jr., Charlie
P.O. Box 407
Lakeland, FL 33802-0407
charlie.jenkins@publix.com
Tel: (863) 688 - 7407
Ext: 52227
Fax:(863) 284 - 5532

Serves As:
- Chief Exec. Officer, Publix Super Markets, Inc.

JENKINS, Francis P.
1251 Ave. of the Americas, Suite 900
New York, NY 10020
fjenkins@roysterclark.com
Tel: (212) 332 - 2965
Fax:(212) 332 - 2999

Serves As:
- Chairman and Chief Exec. Officer, Royster-Clark, Inc.

JENKINS, Howard M.
P.O. Box 407
Lakeland, FL 33802-0407
howard.jenkins@publix.com
Tel: (863) 688 - 7407
Fax:(863) 284 - 5532

Serves As:
- Chairman of the Board, Publix Super Markets, Inc.

JENKINS, Lawanda
10455 Mill Run Circle
Owings Mills, MD 21117
Tel: (410) 998 - 6010
Fax:(410) 998 - 5351

Serves As:
- Manager, Community Relations, CareFirst BlueCross and BlueShield

JENKINS, LuAnn
P.O. Box 58090
Santa Clara, CA 95052-8090
Tel: (408) 721 - 5000
Fax:(408) 739 - 9803

Serves As:
- Manager, Exec. Communications, Nat'l Semiconductor Corp.

JENKINS, Jr., Maynard
645 E. Missouri Ave., Suite 400
Phoenix, AZ 85012
Tel: (602) 265 - 9200
Fax:(602) 631 - 7321

Serves As:
- Chairman and Chief Exec. Officer, CSK Auto, Inc.

JENKINS, Rosalie
55 Water St.
49th Floor
New York, NY 10041-0099
rjenkins@dtcc.com
Tel: (212) 855 - 5468
Fax:(212) 908 - 2327

Serves As:
- Director, Corporate Communications, The Depository Trust & Clearing Corp.

JENKINSON, Rick
Liberty Ln.
Hampton, NH 03842
Tel: (603) 926 - 5911
Fax:(603) 929 - 2379

Serves As:
- V. President, Government Affairs and Public Relations, Fisher Scientific Internat'l Inc.

JENNESS, James M.
P.O. Box 3599
Battle Creek, MI 49016-3599
Tel: (269) 961 - 2000
Fax:(269) 961 - 2871
TF: (800) 962 - 1413

Serves As:
- Chairman abd Chief Exec. Officer, Kellogg Co.

JENNINGS, Donna N.
10400 W. Higgins
Suite 600
Rosemont, IL 60018
Tel: (847) 298 - 9000
Ext: 3474
Fax:(847) 298 - 9018
TF: (800) 826 - 4449

Serves As:
- V. President, Human Resources and Communications, Velsicol Chemical Corp.

JENNINGS, James B.
1445 Ross at Field
Suite 1400
Dallas, TX 75202-2785
Tel: (214) 978 - 8000
Fax:(214) 978 - 8888

Serves As:
- Chairman of the Board, Hunt Oil Co.

JENNINGS, Karen E.
P.O. Box 2933
San Antonio, TX 78299-2933
Tel: (210) 821 - 4105
Fax:(210) 351 - 2198
TF: (800) 351 - 7221

Serves As:
- Senior Exec. V. President, Human Resources and Communications, SBC Communications Inc.

JENNINGS, Mary
4345 Southpoint Blvd.
Jacksonville, FL 32216
Tel: (904) 332 - 3000

Serves As:
- V. President, Compliance and Tax, PSS World Medical, Inc.

JENNINGS, Michael A.
701 San Marco Blvd.
12th Floor
Jacksonville, FL 32207
mike.jennings@prudential.com
Tel: (904) 313 - 3269
Fax:(904) 313 - 7884

Serves As:
- V. President, Government Affairs, Prudential Financial

JENNINGS, Roberta R.
38 Fountain Square
Cincinnati, OH 45263
Tel: (513) 579 - 4153
Fax:(513) 579 - 5226
TF: (800) 972 - 3030

Serves As:
- V. President and Corporate Director, Fifth Third Bancorp.

JENNINGS, Thomas
2929 Allen Pkwy.
Houston, TX 77019
Tel: (713) 342 - 7489
Fax:(713) 523 - 8531

Serves As:
- Director, State Government Relations, AIG American General Corp.

JENSEN, Brad
211 N. Church St., Floor 3
Rockford, IL 61108
Tel: (815) 987 - 3697
Fax:(815) 987 - 3420

Serves As:
- Area Manager, External Affairs, SBC Illinois

JENSEN, Conway W.
400 N. Ashley Dr.
Tampa, FL 33602
conway.jensen@sykes.com
Tel: (813) 274 - 1000
Fax:(813) 273 - 0148

Serves As:
- V. President, Public Relations and Corporate Administration, Sykes Enterprises, Inc.

JENSEN, Margaret "Maggie"
400 Robert St. North
St. Paul, MN 55101
margaret.jensen@minnesotalife.com
Tel: (651) 665 - 7558
Fax:(651) 665 - 4128

Serves As:
- Consultant, Media Relations, Minnesota Life Insurance Co.

JENSEN, Thomas F.
316 Pennsylvania Ave. SE
Suite 300
Washington, DC 20003
tjensen@ups.com
Tel: (202) 675 - 4220
Fax:(202) 675 - 4230

Registered Federal Lobbyist.
Serves As:
- Manager, Public Affairs, United Parcel Service (UPS)

JENSO, Randall L.
P.O. Box 30008
Honolulu, HI 96820
Tel: (808) 835 - 3700
Fax:(808) 835 - 3690

Serves As:
- Treasurer and Secretary, Hawaiian Holdings, Inc.

JERZYK, Tim
P.O. Box 32070
Louisville, KY 40232
Tel: (502) 874 - 8300

Serves As:
- V. President, Investor Relations, YUM! Brands, Inc.

JESANIS, Mike
25 Research Dr.
Westborough, MA 01582
Tel: (508) 389 - 2000
Fax:(508) 389 - 2605

Serves As:
- President and Chief Exec. Officer, Nat'l Grid USA

JESTER, Chad
One Nationwide Plaza
Columbus, OH 43215-2220
Tel: (614) 249 - 7111
Fax:(614) 249 - 3073

Serves As:
- V. President, Corporate Public Involvement, Nationwide

JEWELL, Sally
P.O. Box 1938
Sumner, WA 98390-0800
sjewell@rei.com
Tel: (253) 395 - 3780
Fax:(253) 395 - 4368

Serves As:
- President and Chief Exec. Officer, Recreational Equipment, Inc.

JEWS, William L.
10455 Mill Run Circle
Owings Mills, MD 21117
Tel: (410) 581 - 3000

Serves As:
- President and Chief Exec. Officer, CareFirst BlueCross and BlueShield

JIMENEZ, Carlos A.
Reader's Digest Rd.
Pleasantville, NY 10570-7000
carlos.jimenez@rd.com
Tel: (914) 244 - 5308
Fax:(914) 238 - 4559
TF: (800) 234 - 9000

Serves As:
- Associate Director, Investor Relations, Reader's Digest Ass'n, Inc.

JIMENEZ, Roberto I.
6205 Peachtree Dunwoody Rd.
Atlanta, GA 30328
Tel: (678) 645 - 0000

Serves As:
- V. President, Corporate Communications and Public Affairs, Cox Enterprises, Inc.

JIRSA, Robert J.
999 Third Ave.
Suite 4300
Seattle, WA 98104
Tel: (206) 467 - 3600
Fax:(206) 467 - 3795

Serves As:
- Director, Corporate Affairs, Plum Creek Timber Co. Inc.

Responsibilities include political action.

JIWANLAL, Rich
P.O. Box 85
Wichita, KS 67201-0085
Tel: (316) 676 - 7111
Fax:(316) 676 - 8286

Serves As:
- V. President, Human Resources, Raytheon Aircraft Company

JOB, Judy
231 W. Michigan St.
P346
Milwaukee, WI 53201
judy.job@@we-energies.com
Tel: (414) 221 - 2348
Fax:(414) 221 - 3814

Serves As:
- PAC Administrator, Wisconsin Energy Corp.

JOBS, Steve
One Infinite Loop
Cupertino, CA 95014
Tel: (408) 996 - 1010
Fax:(408) 996 - 0275

Serves As:
- Chief Exec. Officer, Apple Computer, Inc.

JODREY, Darrel Cox
1350 I St. NW
Suite 1210
M/S 1006
Washington, DC 20005-3305
Tel: (202) 589 - 1000
Fax:(202) 589 - 1001

Registered Federal Lobbyist.
Serves As:
- Executive Director, Federal Affairs, Johnson & Johnson

JOERRES, Jeffrey A.
5301 N. Ironwood Rd.
Milwaukee, WI 53217
Tel: (414) 961 - 1000
Fax:(414) 961 - 7081

Serves As:
- Chairman and Chief Exec. Officer, Manpower Inc.

JOHANNPETER, Jorge Gerard
P.O. Box 31328
Tampa, FL 33631-3328
Tel: (813) 286 - 8383
Fax:(813) 207 - 2251

Serves As:
- Chairman of the Board, Gerdau Ameristeel Corp.

JOHANNS, Stephanie
601 Pennsylvania Ave. NW
Suite 720
Washington, DC 20004
Tel: (202) 783 - 3970
Fax:(202) 783 - 3982

Serves As:
- Senior V. President, Federal Regulatory Affairs, ALLTEL

JOHANSEN, Judi
825 N.E. Multnomah
Suite 2000
Portland, OR 97232
Tel: (503) 813 - 5000
Fax:(503) 813 - 7247
TF: (888) 221 - 7070

Serves As:
- President and Chief Exec. Officer, PacifiCorp

JOHANSEN, Renee
1345 Ave. of the Americas
New York, NY 10020
Tel: (212) 282 - 5320
Fax:(212) 282 - 6035

Serves As:
- V. President, Investor Relations, Avon Products, Inc.

JOHANSON, Bonnie L.
47 State Circle, Suite 403
Annapolis, MD 21401
bonnie.l.johansen@constellation.com
Tel: (410) 269 - 5282
Fax:(410) 269 - 5289
TF: (888) 460 - 2002

Serves As:
- Senior Government Relations Representative, Constellation Energy

JOHANSSON, Kurt J.
P.O. Box 810
Amherst, NY 14226
Tel: (716) 689 - 4972
Fax:(716) 568 - 6098

Serves As:
- Chairman, Mark IV Industries, Inc.

JOHN, Mike
1645 Bergstrom Rd.
Neenah, WI 54956
Tel: (920) 751 - 1000
Fax:(920) 951 - 1236
TF: (800) 558 - 5073

Serves As:
• Director, Communications, Menasha Corporation

JOHNANNES, Mary P.
1350 I St. NW
Suite 1000
Washington, DC 20005
mjohnannes@ford.com
Tel: (202) 962 - 5384
Fax:(202) 336 - 7223

Registered Federal Lobbyist.
Serves As:
• Legislative Manager, Financial Services, Ford Motor Co.

JOHNS, John D.
2801 Hwy. 280 South
P.O. Box 2606
Birmingham, AL 35223
Tel: (205) 268 - 1000

Serves As:
• Chairman, President, and Chief Exec. Officer, Protective Life Corp.

JOHNSEY, Walter F.
P.O. Box 10246
Birmingham, AL 35202
Tel: (205) 945 - 6300
Fax:(205) 945 - 6570

Serves As:
• Senior Exec. V. President, External Affairs, Drummond Co., Inc.

JOHNSON, Alison
11 Madison Ave.
New York, NY 10010-3629
alison.johnson@csfb.com
Tel: (212) 325 - 2000
Fax:(212) 538 - 4633

Serves As:
• Contact, CSFB Foundation, Credit Suisse First Boston

JOHNSON, Barbara P.
Bridgeport Center
850 Main St.
Bridgeport, CT 06604-4913
barbara.johnson@peoples.com
Tel: (203) 338 - 7171

Serves As:
• Senior V. President, Community Relations, People's Bank

JOHNSON, Broderick D.
1120 20th St. NW
Suite 1000
Washington, DC 20036-3406
broderickdjohns@att.com
Tel: (202) 457 - 3810
Fax:(202) 457 - 2267

Serves As:
• V. President, Congressional Relations, AT&T

JOHNSON, Bruce C.
200 Domain Dr.
Stratham, NH 03885
Tel: (603) 772 - 9500
Fax:(603) 773 - 1251

Serves As:
• Senior V. President, Human Resources, The Timberland Co.

JOHNSON, Charleen
290 Concord Rd.
Billerica, MA 01821
Charleen_Johnson@millipore.com
Tel: (978) 715 - 1268
Fax:(978) 715 - 1385

Serves As:
• Exec. Director, Millipore Foundation, Millipore Corp.

JOHNSON, Charles B.
One Franklin Pkwy.
San Mateo, CA 94403-1906
Tel: (650) 312 - 3001
TF: (800) 342 - 5236

Serves As:
• Chairman of the Board, Franklin Templeton Investments

JOHNSON, Cheryl A.
One Seagate
Toledo, OH 43666
cheryl.johnson@us.o-i.com
Tel: (419) 247 - 1386
Fax:(419) 247 - 2839

Serves As:
• Contributions Administrator, Owens-Illinois, Inc.

JOHNSON, Clark
4345 Southpoint Blvd.
Jacksonville, FL 32216
Tel: (904) 332 - 3000

Serves As:
• Chairman of the Board, PSS World Medical, Inc.

JOHNSON, Colleen A.
100 Independence Mall West
Philadelphia, PA 19106-2399
Tel: (215) 592 - 3000
Fax:(215) 592 - 3377

Serves As:
• PAC Treasurer, Rohm and Haas Co.

JOHNSON, Craig M.
700 N.W. 107th Ave.
Miami, FL 33172
Tel: (305) 559 - 4000
Fax:(305) 229 - 6453
TF: (800) 741 - 4663

Serves As:
• V. President, Community Development, Lennar Corp.

JOHNSON, Cynthia K.
1455 Pennsylvania Ave. NW
Suite 375
MS 4072
Washington, DC 20004
ckjohnson@ti.com
Tel: (202) 628 - 3133
Fax:(202) 628 - 2980

Registered Federal Lobbyist.
Serves As:
• Director, Government Relations-International Trade, Texas Instruments Incorporated

JOHNSON, Dana
700 Central Ave.
Louisville, KY 40208
Tel: (502) 636 - 4400
Fax:(502) 636 - 4430
TF: (800) 283 - 3729

Serves As:
• Director, Community Relations, Churchill Downs, Inc.

JOHNSON, Daniel S.
3535 Blue Cross Rd.
Eagan, MN 55122--115
Tel: (651) 662 - 1580
Fax:(651) 662 - 1570
TF: (800) 382 - 2000

Serves As:
• Exec. Director, Blue Cross and Blue Shield of Minnesota Foundation and Community Affairs, Blue Cross and Blue Shield of Minnesota

JOHNSON, Darrell
P.O. Box 1330
Salisbury, NC 28145-1330
Tel: (704) 633 - 8250
Ext: 3064
Fax:(704) 633 - 8250

Serves As:
• Senior V. President, Human Resources, Food Lion LLC

JOHNSON, David J.
650 N.E. Holladay, Suite 1400
Portland, OR 97232
Tel: (503) 872 - 1300
Fax:(503) 872 - 1349
TF: (800) 633 - 1488

Serves As:
• Chairman and Chief Exec. Officer, KinderCare Learning Centers, Inc.

JOHNSON, Dee
7701 Forsyth Blvd.
Suite 800
St. Louis, MO 63105-1861
Tel: (314) 854 - 8045
Fax:(314) 854 - 8003

Serves As:
• Director, Investor Relations, Belden CDT Inc.
Responsibilities include public affairs.

JOHNSON, Derrick
28601 Clemens Rd.
Westlake, OH 44145
Tel: (440) 892 - 1580
Fax:(440) 892 - 9507

Serves As:
• Director, Corporate Public Relations, Nordson Corp.

JOHNSON, Don T.
1400 Opus Place
Suite 600
Downers Grove, IL 60515
Tel: (630) 271 - 8100

Serves As:
• Chairman, President and Chief Exec. Officer, Aftermarket Technology Corp.

JOHNSON, Edna Boone
5505 Blue Lagoon Dr.
Miami, FL 33126
Tel: (305) 378 - 3000
Fax:(305) 378 - 7910

Serves As:
• Senior V. President, Global Communications, Burger King Corporation

JOHNSON, III, Edward C.
82 Devonshire St.
Boston, MA 02109-3614
Tel: (617) 563 - 7000
Fax:(617) 476 - 6150

Serves As:
• Chairman and Chief Exec. Officer, FMR Corp.

JOHNSON, Erin
466 Lexington Ave.
New York, NY 10017
erin.johnson@jwt.com
Tel: (212) 210 - 7243
Fax:(212) 210 - 7770

Serves As:
• Director, Corporate Communications, J. Walter Thompson Co.

JOHNSON, Jr., George D.
100 Dunbar St.
Spartanburg, SC 29306
Tel: (864) 573 - 1600
Fax:(864) 573 - 1695

Serves As:
- Chief Exec. Officer, Extended Stay America, Inc.

JOHNSON, George L.
I-20 at Alpine Rd.
AX-210
Columbia, SC 29219-0001
george.johnson@bcbssc.com
Tel: (803) 264 - 2021
Fax:(803) 264 - 5522
TF: (800) 288 - 2227
Ext: 42021

Serves As:
- V. President, Corporate Communications and Public Affairs, BlueCross BlueShield of South Carolina

JOHNSON, Greogory E.
One Franklin Pkwy.
San Mateo, CA 94403-1906
Tel: (650) 312 - 2000
Fax:(650) 312 - 5606
TF: (800) 632 - 2350

Serves As:
- President and Chief Exec. Officer, Franklin Templeton Investments

JOHNSON, Dr. H. Fisk
1525 Howe St.
Racine, WI 53403
Tel: (262) 260 - 2000
Fax:(262) 260 - 6004

Serves As:
- Chairman and Chief Exec. Officer, SC Johnson

JOHNSON, Hope
11911 Freedom Dr.
Suite 600
Reston, VA 20190
johnsonhe@worldkitchen.com
Tel: (607) 377 - 5258
Fax:(607) 377 - 8962
TF: (800) 999 - 3436

Serves As:
- Media Relations, World Kitchen, Inc.

JOHNSON, Ivan D.
1550 W. Deer Valley Rd.
Phoenix, AZ 85027
ivan.johnson@cox.com
Tel: (623) 328 - 3250
Fax:(623) 328 - 3580

Serves As:
- V. President, Community Relations/Televideo, (Cox Communications, Inc.), Cox Enterprises, Inc.

JOHNSON, James C.
World Headquarters
100 N. Riverside
Chicago, IL 60606-1596
Tel: (312) 544 - 2000
Fax:(312) 544 - 2829

Serves As:
- V. President, Associate General Counsel and Corporate Secretary, The Boeing Co.

Responsibilities include investor relations.

JOHNSON, Jane L.
P.O. Box 19109
Greensboro, NC 27419-9109
Tel: (336) 294 - 4410
Fax:(336) 294 - 5422

Serves As:
- Director, Governmental Affairs, Unifi, Inc.

JOHNSON, Jay
P.O. Box 13979
Research Triangle Park, NC 27709-3979
jay.johnson@quintiles.com
Tel: (919) 998 - 2066
Fax:(919) 998 - 2098

Serves As:
- Senior Director, Corporate Communication, Quintiles Transnat'l Corp.

JOHNSON, Joel W.
One Hormel Pl.
Austin, MN 55912-3680
Tel: (507) 437 - 5611

Serves As:
- Chairman and Chief Exec. Officer, Hormel Foods Corp.

JOHNSON, John D.
P.O. Box 64089
St. Paul, MN 55164-0089
Tel: (651) 355 - 6000
Fax:(651) 355 - 6432
TF: (800) 232 - 3639

Serves As:
- President and Chief Exec. Officer, CHS Inc.

JOHNSON, Karl D.
2941 Fairview Park Dr.
Falls Church, VA 22042-4513
Tel: (703) 876 - 3172
Fax:(703) 876 - 3555

Serves As:
- Director, Public Affairs, General Dynamics Corporation

JOHNSON, Kathryn
200 E. Basse Rd.
San Antonio, TX 78209
kathrynmaysjohnson@clearchannel.com
Tel: (210) 822 - 2828
Fax:(210) 822 - 2299

Serves As:
- Senior V. President, Corporate Relations, Clear Channel Communications

JOHNSON, Kerrick
P.O. Box 39
Montpelier, VT 05601-0039
Tel: (802) 229 - 9448
Fax:(802) 229 - 9541

Serves As:
- Director, Governmental Affairs, Central Vermont Public Service Corp.

JOHNSON, L. Oakley
1399 New York Ave. NW
Suite 900
Washington, DC 20005
Tel: (202) 585 - 5800
Fax:(202) 585 - 5820

Registered Federal Lobbyist.
Serves As:
- Senior V. President, Corporate Affairs, American Internat'l Group, Inc.

JOHNSON, Leah
399 Park Ave.
New York, NY 10043
Tel: (212) 559 - 9446
Fax:(212) 793 - 3946
TF: (800) 285 - 3000

Serves As:
- Director, Public Affairs, Citigroup, Inc.

JOHNSON, Linda
2100 E. Grand Ave.
El Segundo, CA 90245
ljohnson@csc.com
Tel: (310) 615 - 1722
Fax:(310) 322 - 9805

Serves As:
- Senior Manager, Corporate Communications and Marketing, Computer Sciences Corp.

Responsibilities also include corporate philanthropy.

JOHNSON, Linda
1000 Louisiana St.
Suite 5800
Houston, TX 77002-5050
Tel: (713) 507 - 6400
Fax:(713) 507 - 3871

Serves As:
- V. President, Human Resources, Dynegy, Inc.

JOHNSON, Lionel
1101 Pennsylvania Ave. NW
Suite 1000
Washington, DC 20004
johnsonli@citi.com
Tel: (202) 879 - 6855
Fax:(202) 783 - 4460

Registered Federal Lobbyist.
Serves As:
- V. President, International Government Relations, Citigroup, Inc.

JOHNSON, Lori
P.O. Box 5625
MS25
Minneapolis, MN 55440-5625
Tel: (952) 742 - 6194
Fax:(952) 742 - 6208

Serves As:
- Public Affairs Counselor, Cargill, Incorporated

JOHNSON, Marlys
610 Gateway Dr.
North Sioux City, SD 57049-2000
marlys.johnson@gateway.com
Tel: (800) 846 - 4503
Fax:(605) 232 - 2757

Serves As:
- Manager, Investor Relations, Gateway, Inc.

JOHNSON, Martha C.
P.O. Box 391
Covington, KY 41012-0391
mcjohnson@ashland.com
Tel: (859) 815 - 3333
Fax:(859) 815 - 4795

Serves As:
- V. President, Communications and Corporate Affairs, Ashland Inc.

JOHNSON, Melinda
1666 K St. NW
Suite 500
Washington, DC 20006
Tel: (202) 887 - 1469

Registered Federal Lobbyist.
Serves As:
- Director, Government Affairs, AmeriSource Bergen Corp.

JOHNSON, Nancie S.
601 Pennsylvania Ave. NW
North Bldg., Suite 325
Washington, DC 20004
nancie.s.johnson@usa.dupont.com
Tel: (202) 728 - 3645
Fax:(202) 728 - 3649

Serves As:
- V. President, Government Affairs, DuPont

JOHNSON, Paul
50606 AXP Financial Center
Minneapolis, MN 55474
paul.w.johnson@ameriprise.com
Tel: (612) 671 - 0625
Fax:(612) 671 - 5112
TF: (800) 328 - 8300

Serves As:
- Director, Public Affairs and Communications, Ameriprise Financial Services Inc.

JOHNSON, Philip R.
622 Third Ave., 37th Floor
New York, NY 10017
Tel: (212) 885 - 2500

Serves As:
- V. President, Human Resources, Asbury Automotive Group

JOHNSON, Preston
1111 Louisiana St.
Houston, TX 77002
Tel: (713) 207 - 1111

Serves As:
- Senior V. President, Human Resources and Shared Services, CenterPoint Energy

JOHNSON, Rachel
1050 W. Hampden Ave.
Englewood, CO 80110
rachel_vargas@sportsauthority.com
Tel: (303) 200 - 5050
Fax:(303) 863 - 2240

Serves As:
- Administrative Assistant, Advertising, The Sports Authority, Inc.

Responsibilities include corporate philanthropy.

JOHNSON, Randy
1350 I St. NW
Suite 400
Washington, DC 20005-3306
Tel: (202) 371 - 6900
Fax:(202) 842 - 3578

Registered Federal Lobbyist.
Serves As:
- Director, U.S. Human Resources and Legislative Affairs, Motorola, Inc.

JOHNSON, Rhonda S.
500 W. Monroe St.
Chicago, IL 60661
rhonda.johnson@gatx.com
Tel: (312) 621 - 6200
Fax:(312) 621 - 6648
TF: (800) 428 - 8161

Serves As:
- Director, Inverstor Relations, GATX Corp.

JOHNSON, Robbin S.
P.O. Box 9300
Minneapolis, MN 55440-9300
robbin_johnson@cargill.com
Tel: (952) 742 - 6206
Fax:(952) 742 - 7209

Serves As:
- Senior V. President and Director, Corporate Affairs, Cargill, Incorporated

JOHNSON, Robert J.
1200 Hansen Rd.
Green Bay, WI 54304
Tel: (920) 491 - 7170
Fax:(920) 491 - 7090
TF: (800) 236 - 2722

Serves As:
- Director, Human Resources, Associated Banc-Corp.

JOHNSON, S. A. "Tony"
27175 Haggerty Rd.
Novi, MI 48377
Tel: (248) 675 - 6000
Fax:(248) 675 - 6200

Serves As:
- Chairman of the Board, Tower Automotive, Inc.

JOHNSON, Stephen L.
400 California St.
17th Floor
San Francisco, CA 94104
stephen.johnson@uboc.com
Tel: (415) 765 - 3252
Fax:(415) 765 - 3257

Serves As:
- Senior V. President and Director, Public Relations and Government Affairs, Union Bank of California

JOHNSON, Steven C.
7421 W. 129th St., Suite 300
Overland Park, KS 66213
sjohnson@kgas.com
Tel: (913) 319 - 8604
Fax:(913) 319 - 8606

Serves As:
- Manager, Government Affairs -- Kansas, ONEOK, Inc.

JOHNSON, Susan
Seneca St. at Jamison Rd.
East Aurora, NY 14052
sjohnson@moog.com
Tel: (716) 687 - 4225
Fax:(716) 687 - 4595

Serves As:
- Manager, Shareholder Relations, Moog Inc.

JOHNSON, Susan M.
One Pershing Square
2301 Main St.
Kansas City, MO 64108
susan.johnson@bcbskc.com
Tel: (816) 395 - 3566

Serves As:
- Director, Corporate Communications, Blue Cross and Blue Shield of Kansas City

JOHNSON, Thomas H.
1021 E. Cary St.
Richmond, VA 23217
Tel: (804) 697 - 1000
Fax:(804) 697 - 1199

Serves As:
- Chairman and Chief Exec. Officer, Chesapeake Corp.

JOHNSON, Timothy A.
300 Phillipi Rd.
Columbus, OH 43228-5311
Tel: (614) 278 - 6622
Fax:(614) 278 - 6666

Serves As:
- V. President, Strategic Planning and Investor Relations, Big Lots Inc.

JOHNSON, Todd M.
710 E. 24th St.
M. R. 43400
Minneapolis, MN 55404
todd.johnson@allina.com
Tel: (612) 775 - 9658
Fax:(612) 775 - 9634

Serves As:
- V. President, Government Affairs, Allina Hospitals and Clinics

JOHNSON, William B.
P.O. Box 2641
Birmingham, AL 35291
Tel: (205) 257 - 1000
Fax:(205) 257 - 1860

Serves As:
- President, Alabama Power Foundation, Inc., Alabama Power Co.

JOHNSON, William D.
P.O. Box 1551
Peb 1212
Raleigh, NC 27602-1551
Tel: (919) 546 - 6463
Fax:(919) 546 - 5245

Serves As:
- Group President, Progress Energy

Responsibilities include public affairs.

JOHNSON, William R.
P.O. Box 57
Pittsburgh, PA 15230-0057
Tel: (412) 456 - 5700
Fax:(412) 456 - 6128

Serves As:
- Chairman, President and Chief Exec. Officer, H. J. Heinz Co.

JOHNSON-DAVIS, Sara L.
560 Bloomfield Ave.
Bloomfield, CT 06002
Tel: (860) 286 - 0042
Fax:(860) 286 - 8926

Serves As:
- Associate Director, State Government Affairs, (Novartis Pharmaceuticals Corp.), Novartis Corporation

JOHNSON-OBEY, Kristen
401 Ninth St., NW
Suite 600
M/S 600
Washington, DC 20004
Tel: (202) 434 - 8613
Fax:(202) 434 - 8626

Serves As:
- Senior Director, Government Relations, Freddie Mac

JOHNSTON, Ann A.
P.O. Box 2990
Winston-Salem, NC 27102
Tel: (336) 741 - 5000

Serves As:
- Exec. V. President, Human Resources, Reynolds American Inc.

JOHNSTON, Gerald E. "Jerry"
P.O. Box 24305
Oakland, CA 94623-1305
Tel: (510) 271 - 7000
Fax:(510) 832 - 1463

Serves As:
- Chairman, Chief Exec. Officer, and President, The Clorox Co.

JOHNSTON, Mr. Kelly D.
One Campbell Pl.
Camden, NJ 08103-1701
kelly_johnston@campbellsoup.com
Tel: (856) 968 - 4367
Fax:(856) 342 - 3889
TF: (800) 257 - 8443

Serves As:
- V. President, Government Relations, Campbell Soup Co.

JOHNSTON, Lawrence R.
250 E. Parkcenter Blvd.
Boise, ID 83706
Tel: (208) 395 - 6200
Fax:(208) 395 - 6631

Serves As:
- Chairman and Chief Exec. Officer, Albertson's, Inc.

JOHNSTON, Michael F.
One Village Dr.
Van Buren Township, MI 48111
Tel: (313) 755 - 2800
TF: (800) VIS - TEON

Serves As:
- Chairman, President and Chief Exec. Officer, Visteon Corp.

JOHNSTON, Stacey
One Franklin Pkwy.
San Mateo, CA 94403-1906
sjohnst@frk.com
Tel: (650) 525 - 7558
TF: (800) 342 - 5236

Serves As:
- Senior Coordinator, Public Relations, Franklin Templeton Investments

JOHNSTON, William P.
2525 West End Ave., Suite 600
Nashville, TN 37203
Tel: (615) 345 - 5500
Fax:(615) 345 - 5505

Serves As:
- Chairman of the Board, Renal Care Group, Inc.

JOHNSTONE, Brian
86 S. Cobb Dr.
Marietta, GA 30063-0226
brian.johnstone@lmco.com
Tel: (770) 494 - 4124
Fax:(770) 494 - 0146

Serves As:
- Director, Public Affairs, Lockheed Martin Aeronautics Co.

JOHNSTONE, Tom
1111 Adams Ave.
Norristown, PA 19403-2403
Tel: (610) 630 - 2800
Fax:(610) 630 - 2801

Serves As:
- President and Chief Exec. Officer, SKF USA, Inc.

JOINT, David
P.O. Box 51777
New Orleans, LA 70151
Tel: (504) 582 - 4000
Fax:(504) 582 - 1847
TF: (800) 535 - 7094

Serves As:
- Manager, Investor Relations, Freeport-McMoRan Copper and Gold Inc.

JOLLIVETTE, Cyrus
4800 Deerwood Campus Pkwy.
Jacksonville, FL 32246-8273
Tel: (904) 791 - 6111
Fax:(904) 905 - 4486
TF: (800) 477 - 3736

Registered Federal Lobbyist.
Serves As:
- Senior V. President, Public Affairs, Blue Cross and Blue Shield of Florida

JONAS, Eric A.
9950 Mayland Dr.
Richmond, VA 23233
Tel: (804) 527 - 4000
Fax:(804) 527 - 4164

Serves As:
- Senior V. President, Human Resources, Circuit City Stores, Inc.

JONES, Adrienne
130 E. Randolph Dr.
24th Floor
Chicago, IL 60601
a.jones@pecorp.com
Tel: (312) 240 - 3750
Fax:(312) 240 - 4389

Serves As:
- Director, Government Relations, Peoples Energy Corp.

JONES, Alison
1350 I St. NW
Suite 1000
Washington, DC 20005
Tel: (202) 962 - 5400
Fax:(202) 336 - 7223

Serves As:
- Legislative Manager, Ford Motor Co.

JONES, Art
122 C St. NW
Suite 520
Washington, DC 20001
Tel: (202) 393 - 5100
Fax:(202) 393 - 5110

Registered Federal Lobbyist.
Serves As:
- Representative, Tyco Internat'l (U.S.), Inc.

JONES, Barbara
1150 18th St. NW
Suite 200
Washington, DC 20036
barbara.jones1@halliburton.com
Tel: (202) 223 - 0820
Fax:(202) 223 - 2385

Registered Federal Lobbyist.
Serves As:
- Director, Government Affairs, Halliburton Company

JONES, Boland T.
The Lenox Bldg., Suite 700
3399 Peachtree Rd. NE
Atlanta, GA 30326
boland.jones@premiereglobal.com
Tel: (404) 262 - 8400

Serves As:
- Chairman and Chief Exec. Officer, Premiere Global Services, Inc.

JONES, Brenda C.
4411 E. Jones Bridge Rd.
Norcross, GA 30092-1615
Tel: (678) 375 - 3430
Fax:(678) 375 - 2025

Serves As:
- Director, Government Affairs; and PAC Treasurer, CheckFree Corp.

JONES, Jr., Carl E.
P.O. Box 10247
Birmingham, AL 35202
Tel: (205) 326 - 7273
Fax:(205) 326 - 7818
TF: (800) 734 - 4667

Serves As:
- Chairman and Chief Exec. Officer, Regions Financial Corp.

JONES, Chris
P.O. Box 2511
Houston, TX 77252-2511
Tel: (713) 420 - 4136
Fax:(713) 420 - 4417

Serves As:
- Manager, Investor Relations, El Paso Corp.

JONES, Christopher
1166 Ave. of the Americas
New York, NY 10036
christopher.r.jones@marsh.com
Tel: (212) 345 - 3683
Fax:(212) 345 - 2309

Serves As:
- Assistant V. President, Media Relations, Marsh Inc.

JONES, Chuck
1000 Alderman Dr.
Alpharetta, GA 30005-4101
chuck.jones@choicepoint.com
Tel: (770) 752 - 3594
Fax:(770) 752 - 6062

Serves As:
- Director, External Affairs, ChoicePoint Inc.

JONES, Clayton M.
400 Collins Rd. NE
Cedar Rapids, IA 52498
Tel: (319) 295 - 1000
Fax:(319) 295 - 5429

Serves As:
- Chairman, President and Chief Exec. Officer, Rockwell Collins, Inc

JONES, D. Paul
P.O. Box 10566
Birmingham, AL 35296
paul.jones@compassbnk.com
Tel: (205) 297 - 3529
TF: (800) 239 - 2265

Serves As:
- Chairman and Chief Exec. Officer, Compass Bancshares, Inc.

JONES, D. Randall
1341 W. Mockingbird Ln.
Dallas, TX 75247
rjones@txi.com
Tel: (972) 647 - 6701
Fax:(972) 647 - 3355

Serves As:
- V. President, Corporate Communications and Government Affairs, Texas Industries, Inc.

JONES, David
P.O. Box 1438
Louisville, KY 40201-1438
djones@humana.com
Tel: (502) 580 - 1000
Fax:(502) 580 - 3677
TF: (800) 486 - 2620

Serves As:
- Chairman of the Board, Humana Inc.

JONES, David
851 W. Cypress Creek Rd.
Fort Lauderdale, FL 33309
Tel: (954) 267 - 3000
Fax:(954) 267 - 9319
TF: (800) 424 - 8749

Serves As:
- Corporate V. President, Business Development and Corporate Affairs, Citrix Systems, Inc.

JONES, David A.
Six Concourse Pkwy.
Suite 3300
Atlanta, GA 30328
Tel: (770) 829 - 6200

Serves As:
- Chairman and Chief Exec. Officer, Sprectrum Brands

JONES, Diana
600 Lafayette East
M/S 0250
Detroit, MI 48226
djones@bcbsm.com
Tel: (313) 225 - 7230
Fax:(313) 225 - 9693

Serves As:
- V. President, Community Affairs, Blue Cross Blue Shield of Michigan

JONES, Diane R.
1250 H St. NW
Suite 800
Washington, DC 20005
diane.jones@kodak.com
Tel: (202) 857 - 3462
Fax:(202) 857 - 3401

Registered Federal Lobbyist.
Serves As:
- Director, Public Affairs - Health Imaging, Eastman Kodak Company

JONES, Diane S.
Two N. Cascade Ave. Tel: (719) 448 - 5814
14th Floor Fax:(719) 448 - 5824
Colorado Springs, CO 80903
diane.jones@westmoreland.com

Serves As:
- V. President, Corporate Relations, Westmoreland Coal Co.

JONES, Earl F.
AP2-225 Tel: (502) 452 - 3164
Louisville, KY 40225

Serves As:
- Senior Counsel, Government Relations, (GE Consumer Products), General Electric Co.

JONES, Glenn R.
9697 E. Mineral Ave. Tel: (303) 792 - 3111
Englewood, CO 80112 Fax:(303) 792 - 8211

Serves As:
- President and Chief Exec. Officer, Jones Internat'l, Ltd.

JONES, Greg
P.O. Box 1349 Tel: (770) 270 - 7890
Tucker, GA 30085-1349 Fax:(770) 270 - 7080
TF: (800) 241 - 5374

Serves As:
- Director, Public Relations, Oglethorpe Power Corp.

JONES, Ingrid Saunders
P.O. Box 1734 Tel: (404) 676 - 2121
Atlanta, GA 30301 Fax:(404) 676 - 6792
ijones@na.ko.com

Serves As:
- Senior V. President, Corporate External Affairs, The Coca-Cola Co.

JONES, Jake
1401 H St. NW Tel: (202) 414 - 6746
Suite 700 Fax:(202) 414 - 6743
Washington, DC 20005
jj91@daimlerchrysler.com

Registered Federal Lobbyist.
Serves As:
- Senior Manager, Legislative Affairs, DaimlerChrysler Corp.

JONES, Jan
P.O. Box 98905 Tel: (702) 407 - 6387
Las Vegas, NV 89193-8905 Fax:(702) 407 - 6388

Serves As:
- Senior V. President, Communications and Government Relations, Harrah's Entertainment, Inc.

JONES, Jane D.
1929 Allen Pkwy. Tel: (713) 522 - 5141
Houston, TX 77019 Fax:(713) 525 - 2800

Serves As:
- V. President, Human Resources, Service Corp. Internat'l

JONES, John
P.O. Box 4065 Tel: (318) 362 - 1583
Monroe, LA 71211-4065 Fax:(318) 388 - 9602
john.jones@centurytel.com

Serves As:
- V. President, Federal Government Relations, CenturyTel, Inc.

JONES, III, John P.
7201 Hamilton Blvd. Tel: (610) 481 - 4911
Allentown, PA 18195-1501 Fax:(610) 841 - 5900

Serves As:
- Chairman, President and Chief Exec. Officer, Air Products and Chemicals, Inc.

JONES, Krista
P.O. Box 772531 Tel: (717) 541 - 6768
Harrisburg, PA 17177-2531 Fax:(717) 541 - 6696

Serves As:
- Marketing Communications Specialist, Capital BlueCross (Pennsylvania)

JONES, Larry
400 W. 15th St. Tel: (512) 391 - 2970
Suite 1500 Fax:(512) 391 - 2965
Austin, TX 78701

Serves As:
- Public Affairs Contact, (AEP Texas), American Electric Power Co. Inc.

JONES, Mark
601 Pennsylvania Ave. NW Tel: (202) 347 - 8420
Suite 350, North Bldg. Fax:(202) 347 - 8423
Washington, DC 20004-3613

Serves As:
- Regional Manager, Federal Affairs, DTE Energy Co.

JONES, Mary S.
1400 Douglas St. Tel: (402) 544 - 6111
Omaha, NE 68179

Serves As:
- V. President and Treasurer, Union Pacific Corp.

Responsibilities include investor relations.

JONES, Marya
24025 Park Sorrento Tel: (818) 223 - 7591
Suite 400 Fax:(818) 223 - 7667
Calabasas, CA 91302 TF: (800) 267 - 0998

Serves As:
- Director, Communications, The Ryland Group, Inc.

JONES, Melis
One i2 Pl. Tel: (469) 357 - 1000
11701 Luna Rd. Fax:(469) 357 - 1798
Dallas, TX 75234

Serves As:
- Foundation Contact, i2 Technologies, Inc.

JONES, Michelle
32605 W. Twelve Mile Rd. Tel: (248) 848 - 2269
Farmington Hills, MI 48334-3339 Fax:(248) 488 - 2089
mjones@covansys.com TF: (800) 688 - 2088

Serves As:
- V. President, Marketing, Covansys

Responsibilities include corporate communications.

JONES, Patricia
710 E. 24th St. Tel: (612) 775 - 9727
M. R. 43303
Minneapolis, MN 55404
patricia.jones@allina.com

Serves As:
- Exec. V. President, Human Resources, Allina Hospitals and Clinics

JONES, Robert D.
P.O. Box 26666 Tel: (412) 497 - 6578
Richmond, PA 23261-2666
robert_d_jones@dom.com

Serves As:
- Senior External Affairs Manager - PA, Dominion Peoples

JONES, Robert W.
100 W. Walnut St. Tel: (626) 440 - 2000
Pasadena, CA 91124 Fax:(626) 440 - 2630

Serves As:
- PAC Treasurer, Parsons Corp.

JONES, Russell H.
1332 Blue Hills Ave. Tel: (860) 243 - 6307
P.O. Box 1 Fax:(860) 243 - 6365
Bloomfield, CT 06002-0001
rhj-corp@kaman.com

Serves As:
- Senior V. President, Chief Investment Officer and Treasurer, Kaman Corp.

Responsibilities include public relations and corporate contributions.

JONES, Sandie
P.O. Box 53999 Tel: (602) 250 - 2257
M/S 8010
Phoenix, AZ 85072-3999
sandie.jones@pinnaclewest.com

Serves As:
- Contributions Coordinator, Pinnacle West Capital Corp.

JONES, Sheldon
608 Fifth Ave. Tel: (212) 830 - 2457
New York, NY 10020 Fax:(212) 246 - 0185
sheldon.jones@group.novartis.com

Serves As:
- V. President, Corporate Communications, Novartis Corporation

JONES, Stella
800/850 Ridgeview Dr. Tel: (610) 651 - 6000
Horsham, PA 19044 Fax:(610) 651 - 6100

Serves As:
- V. President, Regulatory Affairs, Centocor, Inc.

JONES, Tiffany
20330 Stevens Creek Blvd. Tel: (408) 517 - 8000
Cupertino, CA 95014-2132 Fax:(408) 517 - 8186

Registered Federal Lobbyist.
Serves As:
- Representative, Symantec Corp.

JONES, Tom
One Health Plaza
East Hanover, NJ 07936
tom.jones@pharma.novartis.com
Tel: (862) 778 - 3772
Fax:(862) 644 - 8585

Serves As:
- Exec. Director, Public Relations, (Novartis Pharmaceuticals Corp.), Novartis Corporation

JONES, Victoria
P.O. Box 24305
Oakland, CA 94623-1305
victoria.jones@clorox.com
Tel: (510) 271 - 2971
Fax:(510) 271 - 6583

Registered Federal Lobbyist.
Serves As:
- Director, Government Affairs and Community Relations, The Clorox Co.

JONES, Virginia Walker
P.O. Box 2006
Birmingham, AL 35201

Serves As:
- Treasurer, Coca-Cola Bottling Co. United Inc. Committee for Good Government, Coca-Cola Bottling Co. Consolidated

JONES, William H.
11420 Lackland Rd.
St. Louis, MO 63146-6928
Tel: (314) 994 - 9900

Serves As:
- V. President, Human Resources, Schnuck Markets, Inc.

JONES TURNER, Marta
1919 Flowers Circle
Thomasville, GA 31757
Tel: (229) 227 - 2317
Fax:(229) 225 - 3806

Serves As:
- Senior V. President, Corporate Relations, Flowers Foods

Responsibilities include corporate philianthropy.

JONTA, David L.
P.O. Box 92957
Los Angeles, CA 90009-2957
dave.l.jonta@aero.org
Tel: (310) 336 - 5041
Fax:(310) 336 - 7055

Serves As:
- Media Relations Specialist, The Aerospace Corp.

JOOS, David W.
One Energy Plaza
Jackson, MI 49201
Tel: (517) 788 - 0550

Serves As:
- President and Chief Exec. Officer, CMS Energy Corp.

JORDAHL, William
P.O. Box 77007
Madison, WI 53707-1007
billjordahl@alliantenergy.com
Tel: (608) 458 - 4814
Fax:(608) 458 - 3481

Registered Federal Lobbyist.
Serves As:
- Manager, Public Affairs, Alliant Energy Corp.

JORDAN, Blake
One Citizens Plaza
Providence, RI 02903
Tel: (617) 725 - 5841
Fax:(617) 725 - 5807

Serves As:
- Senior V. President; and Director, Corporate Giving, Citizens Financial Group, Inc.

JORDAN, Jennifer
2655 Seely Ave.
San Jose, CA 95134
Tel: (408) 943 - 1234
Fax:(408) 943 - 0513
TF: (800) 862 - 4522

Serves As:
- Corporate V. President, Investor Relations, Cadence Design Systems, Inc.

JORDAN, Kimberley
P.O. Box 1000
Montville, NJ 07045
TF: (800) 237 - 5392

Serves As:
- Manager, Product Public Relations, Berlex, Inc.

JORDAN, Lani
P.O. Box 64089
St. Paul, MN 55164-0089
lani.jordan@chsinc.com
Tel: (651) 355 - 6000
Fax:(651) 355 - 6432
TF: (800) 232 - 3639

Serves As:
- Director, Corporate Communications, CHS Inc.

JORDAN, Michael H.
5400 Legacy Dr.
Plano, TX 75024-3199
Tel: (972) 604 - 6000
Fax:(972) 605 - 6841

Serves As:
- Chairman and Chief Exec. Officer, EDS Corp.

JORDAN, Peter
1401 I St. NW
Suite 600
Washington, DC 20005
Tel: (202) 336 - 7400
Fax:(202) 336 - 7515

Registered Federal Lobbyist.
Serves As:
- Representative, United Technologies Corp.

JORDAN, Raymond
One Johnson & Johnson Plaza
New Brunswick, NJ 08933-7204
Tel: (732) 524 - 0400
Ext: 3535
Fax:(732) 524 - 3564
TF: (800) 635 - 6789

Serves As:
- V. President, Corporate Communications, Johnson & Johnson

JORDAN, Walt
P.O. Box 227097
Suite 37-024
Dallas, TX 75222-7097
Tel: (214) 812 - 2660
Fax:(214) 812 - 3455

Serves As:
- Director, Policy Campaign, TXU

JORDAN, William
1200 G St. NW
Suite 900
Washington, DC 20005-3802
Tel: (202) 383 - 3705
Fax:(202) 383 - 3718

Registered Federal Lobbyist.
Serves As:
- Director, Government Affairs and Communications, The McGraw-Hill Companies, Inc.

JORGENSEN, Kelly
P.O. Box 2047
Omaha, NE 68103-2047
Tel: (402) 496 - 7809
Fax:(402) 498 - 2208

Serves As:
- Director, Environmental Affairs, AG Processing Inc

JORGENSON, James A.
One Hormel Pl.
Austin, MN 55912-3680
Tel: (507) 437 - 5611

Serves As:
- Senior V. President, Human Resources, Hormel Foods Corp.

JORLING, Thomas C.
400 Atlantic St.
Stamford, CT 06921
thomas.jorling@ipaper.com
Tel: (203) 541 - 8649
Fax:(203) 541 - 8257
TF: (800) 223 - 1268

Serves As:
- V. President, Environmental Affairs, Internat'l Paper

JOSEFOWICZ, Gregory P.
100 Phoenix Dr.
Ann Arbor, MI 48108
gjosefow@bordersgroupinc.com
Tel: (734) 477 - 1100
Fax:(734) 477 - 1901

Serves As:
- Chairman, President and Chief Exec. Officer, Borders Group, Inc.

JOSEPH, Gayle
2300 Harmon Rd.
Auburn Hills, MI 48326-1714
Tel: (248) 340 - 1800
Fax:(248) 340 - 2395

Serves As:
- Director, Communications, Guardian Industries Corp.

JOSEPH, Roger D.
600 Kellwood Pkwy.
Chesterfield, MO 63017
roger_joseph@kellwood.com
Tel: (314) 576 - 3437
Fax:(314) 576 - 3460

Serves As:
- V. President, Investor Relations and Treasurer, Kellwood Co.

JOSEPH, Rosalind
1290 Ave. of the Americas
New York, NY 10104
rosalind.joseph@axa-financial.com
Tel: (212) 314 - 4295
TF: (888) AXA - INFO

Serves As:
- Manager, AXA Group Communications and Media Relations, AXA Financial, Inc.

JOUSTRA, Jana
P.O. Box 550
Nashville, TN 37202
Tel: (615) 344 - 9551
Fax:(615) 344 - 5722

Serves As:
- V. Preisdent, Communications, HCA

JOYA, Munehiko
1900 K St. NW
Suite 800
Washington, DC 20006
Tel: (202) 828 - 9272
Fax:(202) 828 - 9277

Serves As:
- Manager, Government and Public Affairs, Hitachi America, Ltd.

JOYCE, Robert
200 Milik St.
Carteret, NJ 07008-1194
Tel: (732) 499 - 3500
Fax:(732) 499 - 6872

Serves As:
- Exec. V. President, Human Resources, Pathmark Stores Inc.

JOYCE, Tom
12061 Bluemont Way
Reston, VA 20190
tom.joyce@slma.com
Tel: (703) 984 - 5610
Fax:(703) 810 - 7053

Serves As:
- V. President, Corporate Communications, SLM Corp.

JOYCE, William H.
1601 W. Diehl Rd.
Naperville, IL 60563-1198
Tel: (630) 305 - 1000
Fax:(630) 305 - 2900

Serves As:
- Chairman and Chief Exec. Officer, Nalco Co.

JOYNER, Michael
106 E. College Ave., Suite 800
Tallahassee, FL 32301

Serves As:
- Manager, State Public Affairs -Florida, Progress Energy

JUDGE, Dolly
325 Seventh St. NW
Suite 1200
Washington, DC 20004-1007
Tel: (202) 783 - 7070
Fax:(202) 347 - 2044

Registered Federal Lobbyist.
Serves As:
- Senior Director, Federal Relations, Pfizer Inc.

JUHNKE, Richard
401 Ninth St. NW
Suite 400
Washington, DC 20004
Tel: (202) 585 - 1912
Fax:(202) 585 - 1899

Serves As:
- V. President, Federal Regulatory -- LDD, Sprint Nextel

JULASON, Kristin P.
601 Pennsylvania Ave. NW
Suite 500 South Bldg.
Washington, DC 20004
kristin.julason@cigna.com
Tel: (202) 861 - 1451
Fax:(202) 296 - 2521

Registered Federal Lobbyist.
Serves As:
- V. President, Federal Affairs Communications, CIGNA Corp.

JULIAN, Ken D.
P.O. Box 8888
Camp Hill, PA 17001-8888
kjulian@harsco.com
Tel: (717) 763 - 7064
Fax:(717) 763 - 6402

Serves As:
- Director, Corporate Communications, Harsco Corp.

JUMPER, Steven
101 Constitution Ave. NW
Washington, DC 20080
sjumper@washgas.com
Tel: (703) 750 - 2000
Fax:(703) 750 - 4574

Registered Federal Lobbyist.
Serves As:
- Director, DC and Maryland Public Affairs, Washington Gas

Responsibilities include corporate contributions.

JUNCK, Mary E.
201 N. Harrison St.
Davenport, IA 52801-1939
Tel: (563) 383 - 2100

Serves As:
- Chairman, President and Chief Exec. Officer, Lee Enterprises

JUNG, Andrea
1345 Ave. of the Americas
New York, NY 10020
Tel: (212) 282 - 5000
Fax:(212) 282 - 6220

Serves As:
- Chairman and Chief Exec. Officer, Avon Products, Inc.

JURAN, Tim
P.O. Box 2765
Houston, TX 77255-2765
Tel: (713) 232 - 7500
Fax:(713) 232 - 7031

Serves As:
- V. President, Human Resources, Transocean Inc.

JURCY, Jan
2211 S. 47th St.
Phoenix, AZ 85034
jan.jurcy@avnet.com
Tel: (480) 643 - 7642
Fax:(480) 643 - 7415

Serves As:
- V. President, Public Relations, Avnet Inc.

JUREK, Richard
50 S. LaSalle St.
Chicago, IL 60675
Tel: (312) 444 - 5218
TF: (888) 289 - 6542

Serves As:
- V. President, Public Relations, Northern Trust Co.

JUREK, Steve
1815 Capitol Ave.
Omaha, NE 68102
steve.jurek@aquila.com
Tel: (402) 221 - 2262
Fax:(402) 221 - 2501

Serves As:
- V. President, Regulatory Services-Gas, Aquila, Inc.

JURGENS, Richard N.
5820 Westown Pkwy.
West Des Moines, IA 50266-8223
Tel: (515) 267 - 2800
Fax:(515) 267 - 2817

Serves As:
- President, Chief Exec. Officer and Chief Operating Officer, Hy-Vee, Inc.

JURGENSEN, William G.
One Nationwide Plaza
Columbus, OH 43215-2220
Tel: (614) 249 - 7111
Fax:(614) 249 - 3073

Serves As:
- Chief Exec. Officer, Nationwide

JURKOWSKY, Tom
6801 Rockledge Dr.
Bethesda, MD 20817-1877
Tel: (301) 897 - 6352
Fax:(301) 897 - 6289

Serves As:
- V. President, Media Relations, Lockheed Martin Corp.

JUVES, Jose
14 Cambridge Center
Cambridge, MA 02142
Tel: (617) 914 - 6524
Fax:(617) 679 - 2617

Serves As:
- Associate Director, Public Affairs, Biogen Idec Inc.

KABEISEMAN, Margaret M.
1300 Connecticut Ave. NW
Suite 900
Washington, DC 20036
mmuskett@visa.com
Tel: (202) 296 - 9230
Fax:(202) 862 - 5498

Registered Federal Lobbyist.
Serves As:
- Legislative Manager, Visa U.S.A. Inc.

KADEN, Ellen O.
One Campbell Pl.
Camden, NJ 08103-1701
ellen_kaden@campbellsoup.com
Tel: (856) 342 - 6125
Fax:(856) 342 - 5216
TF: (800) 257 - 8443

Serves As:
- Senior V. President, Law and Government Affairs, Campbell Soup Co.

KADOW, Joseph J.
2202 N. Westshore Blvd.
Fifth Floor
Tampa, FL 33607
Tel: (813) 282 - 1225
Fax:(813) 282 - 1209

Serves As:
- Treasurer, Outback Steakhouse PAC, Outback Steakhouse, Inc.

KAEHLER, Norma H.
1101 17th St. NW
Suite 600
Washington, DC 20036
Tel: (202) 496 - 5654
Fax:(202) 496 - 5660

Registered Federal Lobbyist.
Serves As:
- Managing Director, Government Affairs and Contact, American Airlines PAC, (American Airlines, Inc.), AMR Corp.

KAFERLE, Dan
One Computer Associates Plaza
Islandia, NY 11749
daniel.kaferle@ca.com
Tel: (631) 342 - 2111
Fax:(631) 342 - 4295
TF: (800) 225 - 5224

Serves As:
- Senior V. President, Corporate Communications, Computer Associates Internat'l, Inc.

KAGEL, Kris
1285 Ave. of the Americas
New York, NY 10019-6028
Tel: (212) 713 - 8703
Fax:(212) 713 - 1087

Serves As:
- Contact, Community Affairs, UBS Financial Services Inc.

KAHN, Becky
P.O. Box 1299
Minneapolis, MN 55440-1299
Tel: (952) 887 - 3131
Fax:(952) 887 - 3155
TF: (800) 887 - 3131

Serves As:
- Manager, Corporate Communications, Donaldson Company, Inc.

KAHN, Claudia
Four World Financial Center
250 Vesey St.
New York, NY 10080
Tel: (212) 449 - 1000

Serves As:
• Senior V. President, Public Policy, Merrill Lynch & Co., Inc.

KAHN, Joshua E.
667 Madison Ave.
New York, NY 10021-8087
jkahn@loews.com
Tel: (212) 521 - 2788
Fax:(212) 521 - 2714

Serves As:
• Manager, Investor Relations, Loews Corporation

KAHN, Melissa
1620 L St. NW
Suite 800
Washington, DC 20036-5617
Tel: (202) 659 - 3575
Fax:(202) 659 - 1026

Serves As:
• V. President, Government and Industry Relations, MetLife, Inc.

KAHN, Susan
1000 Nicollet Mall
Minneapolis, MN 55403
investor.relations@target.com
Tel: (612) 304 - 6073

Serves As:
• V. President, Investor Relations, Target Corp.

KAHRS, Kenneth L.
100 Universal City Plaza
Universal City, CA 91608
Tel: (818) 777 - 1000
Fax:(818) 866 - 3363

Serves As:
• Exec. V. President, Human Resources, NBC Universal

KAIGLER, Denise
1895 J W Foster Blvd.
Canton, MA 02021
denise.kaigler@reebok.com
Tel: (781) 401 - 7869
Fax:(781) 401 - 4000

Serves As:
• Corporate V. President, Global Communicaitons, Reebok Internat'l Ltd.

KAIN, Peter B.
P.O. Box 66100
Chicago, IL 60666
Tel: (847) 700 - 4000
Fax:(847) 700 - 4899

Serves As:
• Vice President, Labor Relations, United Airlines

KAINE, Mike
540 Broad St.
Newark, NJ 07101
Tel: (973) 649 - 9900
Fax:(973) 643 - 5106

Serves As:
• Manager, Communications, Verizon New Jersey, Inc.

KAISER, George B.
P.O. Box 2300
Tulsa, OK 74192
Tel: (918) 588 - 6000
Fax:(918) 588 - 6300

Serves As:
• Chairman of the Board, BOK Financial Corp.

KAISER, Robert A.
1730 Briercroft Ct.
Carrollton, TX 75006
Tel: (972) 466 - 5000
TF: (800) 723 - 9040

Serves As:
• Chief Exec. Officer, CellStar Corp.

KALETA, Edward
1776 I St. NW
Suite 890
Washington, DC 20006
Tel: (202) 467 - 5821
Fax:(202) 467 - 5825

Serves As:
• Pac Treasurer, Humana Inc.

KALINKA, John T.
P.O. Box 2450
Grand Rapids, MI 49501
kalinka@foremost.com
Tel: (616) 942 - 3000
Fax:(616) 956 - 2093

Serves As:
• Assistant V. President, Corporate Communications, Foremost Corp. of America

KALLET, Peter J.
163-181 Kenwood Ave.
Oneida, NY 13421
Tel: (315) 361 - 3000

Serves As:
• Chairman, President and Chief Exec. Officer, Oneida Ltd.

KAMERSCHEN, Robert W.
1000 Alderman Dr.
Alpharetta, GA 30005-4101
Tel: (770) 752 - 6000
Fax:(770) 752 - 5939

Serves As:
• V. President, Law and Public Policy, ChoicePoint Inc.

KAMINSKI, Robert M.
901 E. 233rd St.
Carson, CA 90745-6204
Tel: (310) 835 - 8400
Fax:(310) 952 - 7760

Serves As:
• Chief Exec. Officer, Leiner Health Products, Inc.

KAMINSKY, Marci N.
P.O. Box 6721
Chicago, IL 60680-6721
mkaminsky@usg.com
Tel: (312) 606 - 4124
Fax:(312) 606 - 5301

Serves As:
• Senior V. President, Communications, USG Corp.

KAMMER, Randy M.
4800 Deerwood Campus Pkwy.
Jacksonville, FL 32246-8273
Tel: (904) 905 - 6661
Fax:(904) 905 - 4486
TF: (800) 477 - 3736

Serves As:
• V. President, Regulatory Affairs and Public Policy, Blue Cross and Blue Shield of Florida

KAMPF, Lisa
Three Times Square
New York, NY 10036
lisa.kampf@instinet.com
Tel: (212) 231 - 5022
Fax:(646) 223 - 9054
TF: (800) 225 - 5008

Serves As:
• Exec. V. President, Investor Relations, Instinet Group Inc.

KAMPFER, Tom
10955 Vista Sorrento Pkwy.
San Diego, CA 92130
Tel: (858) 314 - 7000
Fax:(858) 314 - 7001

Serves As:
• Exec. V. President, Business Solutions, Iomega Corp.

KANDEL, David L.
150 E. Gay St.
Room 4-A
Columbus, OH 43215
david.l.kandel@sbc.com
Tel: (614) 223 - 5652
Fax:(614) 223 - 6296

Serves As:
• Director, External Affairs, SBC Ohio

KANDERS, Emily
667 Madison Ave.
New York, NY 10021-8087
ekanders@loews.com
Tel: (212) 521 - 2833
Fax:(212) 521 - 2379

Serves As:
• Director, Public Relations, (Loews Hotels), Loews Corporation

KANDES, Carrie
5995 Mayfair Rd.
P.O. Box 3077
North Canton, OH 44720-8077
Tel: (330) 490 - 4000
Fax:(330) 490 - 3794

Serves As:
• Manager, Media Relations, Diebold, Inc.

KANE, Doniele
427 W. 12th St.
Kansas City, MO 64105
doniele.c.kane@kcsr.com
Tel: (816) 983 - 1372
Fax:(816) 983 - 1124
TF: (800) 468 - 6740

Serves As:
• Director, Corporate Communications, Kansas City Southern

KANE, Jacqueline P.
P.O. Box 24305
Oakland, CA 94623-1305
Tel: (510) 271 - 7503
Fax:(510) 208 - 1556

Serves As:
• Senior V. President, Human Resources, The Clorox Co.

KANE, Laura
1932 Wynnton Rd.
Columbus, GA 31999
lkane@aflac.com
Tel: (706) 596 - 3493
Fax:(706) 660 - 7333
TF: (800) 992 - 3522

Serves As:
• Manager, Corporate Communications, AFLAC Incorporated

KANE, Mark M.
TECO Plaza
702 N. Franklin St.
Tampa, FL 33602
mmkane@tecoenergy.com
Tel: (813) 228 - 4111
Fax:(813) 228 - 4262

Serves As:
• Director, Investor Relations, TECO Energy, Inc./Tampa Electric Co.

KANEB, John A.
90 Everett Ave.
Chelsea, MA 02150-2301
Tel: (617) 887 - 3000
Fax:(617) 887 - 8484

Serves As:
• Chairman, President and Chief Exec. Officer, H. P. Hood Inc.

KANGAS, Edward A.
P.O. Box 31907 Tel: (805) 563 - 7000
Santa Barbara, CA 93130 Fax:(805) 563 - 7070

Serves As:
• Chairman of the Board, Tenet Healthcare Corp.

KANGAS, Nancy
P.O. Box 496 Tel: (218) 739 - 8200
215 S. Cascade St. S. Fax:(218) 739 - 8218
Fergus Falls, MN 56538-0496 TF: (866) 410 - 8780

Serves As:
• Director, Human Resources, IT and Safety, Otter Tail Power Co.

KANN, Peter R.
World Financial Center Tel: (212) 416 - 3055
200 Liberty St.
New York, NY 10281
peter.kann@dowjones.com

Serves As:
• Chairman and Chief Exec. Officer, Dow Jones and Co.

KANNAPPAN, S. Kenneth
345 Encinal St. Tel: (831) 426 - 5858
Santa Cruz, CA 95060 Ext: 7741
Fax:(831) 426 - 6098
TF: (800) 544 - 4660

Serves As:
• President and Chief Exec. Officer, Plantronics, Inc.

KANOFSKY, Gordon R.
3773 Howard Hughes Pkwy. Tel: (702) 567 - 7000
Suite 490 Fax:(702) 369 - 8860
Las Vegas, NV 89109-0949

Serves As:
• Exec. V. President, Ameristar Casinos, Inc.
Responsibilities include government and legal affairs.

KANOY, Erin J.
2001 M St. NW Tel: (202) 533 - 5256
Washington, DC 20036-3310 Fax:(202) 533 - 8500

Registered Federal Lobbyist.
Serves As:
• Senior Legislative Analyst, Government Affairs, KPMG LLP

KANTOR, Gregg
220 NW Second Ave. Tel: (503) 220 - 2425
Portland, OR 97209-3991 Fax:(503) 220 - 2584

Serves As:
• Senior V. President, Public Affairs and Communication, NW Natural

KANTRO, Ms. Gayle
200 E. Randolph St. Tel: (312) 782 - 5800
Chicago, IL 60601-6436 Fax:(312) 782 - 4339

Serves As:
• Director, Public Relations, Jones Lang LaSalle Inc.

KAPLAN, Edward L.
333 Corporate Woods Pkwy. Tel: (847) 634 - 6700
Vernon Hills, IL 60061-3109 Fax:(847) 913 - 8766
ekaplan@zebra.com TF: (800) 423 - 0422

Serves As:
• Chairman and Chief Exec. Officer, Zebra Technologies Corp.

KAPLAN, James
1333 H St., NW Tel: (202) 898 - 8343
Suite 410
Washington, DC 20005

Serves As:
• V. President, Government Relations, Instinet Group Inc.

KAPLAN, Martin A.
1768 Automation Pkwy. Tel: (408) 546 - 5000
San Jose, CA 95131 Fax:(408) 954 - 0760

Serves As:
• Chairman of the Board, JDS Uniphase Corp.

KAPLAN, Philip E.
100 Campus Dr. Tel: (973) 245 - 6000
Florham Park, NJ 07932 Fax:(973) 245 - 6002

Serves As:
• PAC Treasurer, BASF Corporation

KAPOR, Ana
850 Lincoln Center Dr. Tel: (650) 638 - 6227
Foster City, CA 94404-1128 Fax:(650) 554 - 2920
kapora1@appliedbiosystems.com

Serves As:
• Manager, Corporate Communications and Investor Relations, Applera Corp.

KAPPELMAN, Pete
P.O. Box 64101 Tel: (651) 481 - 2222
St. Paul, MN 55164-0101 Fax:(651) 481 - 2000
TF: (800) 328 - 4155

Serves As:
• Chairman of the Board, Land O'Lakes, Inc.

KAPPES, Susan C.
P.O. Box 650205 Tel: (972) 855 - 3729
Dallas, TX 75265-0205 Fax:(972) 855 - 3030
TF: (800) 382 - 8667

Serves As:
• V. President, Investor Relations and Corporate Communications, Atmos Energy Corp.

KAPPLAHN, Mike
P.O. Box 1074 Tel: (253) 857 - 8801
Gig Harbor, WA 98335 Fax:(253) 857 - 8816

Serves As:
• Legislative Representative, Farmers Group, Inc.

KAPTAIN, Donna L.
2180 Rutherford Rd. Tel: (760) 931 - 1771
Carlsbad, CA 92008-7328 Fax:(760) 930 - 5015
TF: (800) 228 - 2767

Serves As:
• Senior V. President, Human Resources, Callaway Golf Co.

KAPUSTA, Susan M.
600 Grant St. Tel: (412) 433 - 1121
Pittsburgh, PA 15219-2800

Serves As:
• General Manager, United States Steel Foundation, Inc., United States Steel Corporation

KARAKANTAS, Paul T.
89 East Ave.
Rochester, NY 14649

Serves As:
• Treasurer, Energy East PAC, Energy East Corp.

KARATZ, Bruce
10990 Wilshire Blvd. Tel: (310) 231 - 4000
Seventh Floor Fax:(310) 231 - 4222
Los Angeles, CA 90024
bkaratz@kbhome.com

Serves As:
• Chairman and Chief Exec. Officer, KB HOME

KARBOWIAK, Christine
535 Marriott Dr. Tel: (615) 937 - 0088
Nashville, TN 37214-8900 Fax:(615) 937 - 1414

Serves As:
• V. President, Public Affairs, Bridgestone Americas Holding, Inc.

KARCH, Paul J.
P.O. Box 359 Tel: (920) 734 - 9841
Appleton, WI 54912-0359 Fax:(920) 991 - 8080
TF: (800) 558 - 8390

Serves As:
• V. President, Human Resources and Law; Secretary; and General Counsel, Appleton

KARDELL, Lisa R.
601 Pennsylvania Ave. NW Tel: (202) 628 - 3500
North Bldg. Suite 300 Fax:(202) 628 - 0400
Washington, DC 20004
lkardell@wm.com

Serves As:
• Manager, Federal and State Government Affairs, Waste Management, Inc.

KARMANOS, Jr., Peter
One Campus Martius Tel: (313) 227 - 7300
Detroit, MI 48226 Fax:(313) 227 - 7555
TF: (800) 292 - 7432

Serves As:
• Chairman and Chief Exec. Officer, Compuware Corp.

KAROL, Kathryn Dickey
555 12th St. NW Tel: (202) 393 - 7950
Suite 650 Fax:(202) 393 - 7960
Washington, DC 20004-1205

Registered Federal Lobbyist.
Serves As:
• Director, International and Public Government Affairs, Eli Lilly and Company

KARP, Roberta
1441 Broadway Tel: (212) 625 - 3408
New York, NY 10018

Serves As:
• Senior V. President, Corporate Affairs, and General Counsel, Liz Claiborne Inc.

KARR, Doyle
P.O. Box 14453
Des Moines, IA 50306-3453
doyle.karr@pioneer.com
Tel: (515) 248 - 4800
Fax:(515) 270 - 4112
TF: (800) 247 - 6803

Serves As:
- Diretor, Communications, Pioneer Hi-Bred Internat'l, Inc.

KARTSOTIS, Kosta N.
2280 N. Greenville Ave.
Richardson, TX 75082
kkartsotis@fossil.com
Tel: (972) 234 - 2525
Fax:(972) 234 - 4669

Serves As:
- President and Chief Exec. Officer, Fossil Inc.

KARTSOTIS, Tom
2280 N. Greenville Ave.
Richardson, TX 75082
tkartsotis@fossil.com
Tel: (972) 234 - 2525
Fax:(972) 234 - 4669

Serves As:
- Chairman of the Board, Fossil Inc.

KASPER-GWYN, Laurie
P.O. Box 513249
Los Angeles, CA 90051-1249
Tel: (213) 244 - 2580
Fax:(213) 244 - 4997

Serves As:
- Manager, Policy and Strategy, Southern California Gas Co.

KASPEREK, Robert W.
600 Lafayette East
M/S 2028
Detroit, MI 48226
rkasperek@bcbsm.com
Tel: (313) 225 - 8135
Fax:(313) 225 - 8020

Serves As:
- V. President, Regulatory Affairs, Blue Cross Blue Shield of Michigan

KASSEBAUM, Jim
9125 Rehco Rd.
San Diego, CA 92121-2270
Tel: (858) 453 - 7845
Fax:(858) 677 - 3489

Serves As:
- V. President, Corporate Communications, PETCO Animal Supplies, Inc.

KASSEL, Terry
Four World Financial Center
250 Vesey St.
New York, NY 10080
Tel: (212) 236 - 1000

Serves As:
- Senior V. President, Leadership and Development, Merrill Lynch & Co., Inc.

KASSLING, William E.
1001 Air Brake Ave.
Wilmerding, PA 15148-1036
Tel: (412) 825 - 1000
Fax:(412) 825 - 1019

Serves As:
- Chairman, President and Chief Exec. Officer, Westinghouse Air Brake Technologies Corp.

KASTE, Mary
P.O. Box 64089
St. Paul, MN 55164-0089
mary.kaste@chsinc.com
Tel: (651) 355 - 6000
Fax:(651) 355 - 6432
TF: (800) 232 - 3639

Serves As:
- Manager, Corporate Contributions; and Manager, CHS Cooperative Foundation, CHS Inc.

KATCHMAN, Don
1000 Lakeside Ave.
Cleveland, OH 44114-7000
katchman@ferro.com
Tel: (216) 875 - 6241
Fax:(216) 875 - 7237

Serves As:
- V. President, Ferro Foundation; and Corporate Risk Manager, Ferro Corp.

KATHWARI, M. Farooq
Ethan Allen Dr.
P.O. Box 1966
Danbury, CT 06813-2966
Tel: (203) 743 - 8500
Fax:(203) 743 - 8298

Serves As:
- Chairman, President and Chief Exec. Officer, Ethan Allen Interiors Inc.

KATOPODIS, Louis
5235 Katy Fwy.
Houston, TX 77007
Tel: (713) 869 - 5060
Fax:(713) 869 - 6197

Serves As:
- President and Chief Exec. Officer, Fiesta Mart Inc.

KATZ, Francine I.
One Busch Pl.
St. Louis, MO 63118-1852
Tel: (314) 577 - 9744
Fax:(314) 577 - 3194

Serves As:
- V. President, Communications and Consumer Affairs, Anheuser-Busch Cos., Inc.

KATZ, Gina
P.O. Box 66360
Scotts Valley, CA 95067-0360
gina.katz@seagate.com
Tel: (831) 439 - 2691
Fax:(831) 438 - 4127

Serves As:
- Manager, Corporate Communications, Seagate Technology

Responsibilities include corporate philanthropy.

KATZ, Marcia
25 Harbor Park Dr.
Port Washington, NY 11050
marcia_katz@pall.com
Tel: (516) 801 - 9128
Fax:(516) 484 - 3649
TF: (800) 876 - 7255

Serves As:
- Director, Public Relations, Pall Corp.

KATZENBACH, Nicholas
22001 Loudoun County Pkwy.
Ashburn, VA 20147
Tel: (703) 886 - 5600
TF: (877) MCI - 1000

Serves As:
- Chairman of the Board, MCI, Inc.

KATZENMEYER, Tom
Three Limited Pkwy.
Columbus, OH 43230
Tel: (614) 415 - 7000
Fax:(614) 415 - 7079

Serves As:
- V. President, Investor Relations, The Limited Brands

KAUCIC, Louis A.
4551 W. 107th St.
Overland Park, KS 66207-4037
Tel: (913) 967 - 4000
Fax:(913) 341 - 1694

Serves As:
- Exec. V. President and Chief People Officer, Applebee's Internat'l, Inc.

KAUFMAN, Adrianne
175 Berkeley St.
Boston, MA 02116
adrianne.kaufman@libertymutual.com
Tel: (617) 574 - 5983
Fax:(617) 350 - 7648

Serves As:
- Senior Public Relations Specialist, Liberty Mutual Insurance Co.

KAUFMAN, Andrea J.
800 Nicollet Mall
BCMNH210
Minneapolis, MN 55402
Tel: (612) 303 - 7824
Fax:(612) 303 - 7884

Serves As:
- Treasurer, U.S. Bancorp Political Participation Program, U.S. Bancorp

KAUFMAN, Emma Jo
100 Mission Ridge
Goodlettsville, TN 37072
ekauffman@dollargeneral.com
Tel: (615) 855 - 5525

Serves As:
- Senior Director, Investor Relations, Dollar General Corp.

KAUFMAN, Lisi
1401 I St. NW
Suite 600
Washington, DC 20005
Tel: (202) 336 - 7400
Fax:(202) 336 - 7515

Serves As:
- Senior V. President, Government and International Affairs, United Technologies Corp.

KAUFMANN, B. W.
3M Center
St. Paul, MN 55144-1000
Tel: (651) 733 - 1110
Fax:(651) 733 - 9973

Serves As:
- Manager, Contributions and Community Affairs, 3M Company

KAUFMANN, Robert
1120 G St. NW
Suite 1050
Washington, DC 20005-3801
Tel: (202) 347 - 4446
Fax:(202) 347 - 7058

Registered Federal Lobbyist.
Serves As:
- Representative, Georgia-Pacific Corp.

KAVANAGH, Anthony P.
801 Pennsylvania Ave. NW
Suite 320
Washington, DC 20004
Tel: (202) 383 - 3430
Fax:(202) 628 - 4276

Registered Federal Lobbyist.
Serves As:
- V. President, Governmental Affairs, American Electric Power Co. Inc.

KAVANAGH, K. C.
1111 Westchester Ave.
White Plains, NY 10604
kc.kavanagh@starwoodhotels.com
Tel: (914) 640 - 8339
Fax:(914) 640 - 8310
TF: (877) 443 - 4585

Serves As:
- V. President, Public Relations, Cross Branded Programs/Lead National Publicist, Starwood Hotels and Resorts Worldwide, Inc.

KAVANAUGH, Kathleen
1401 I St. NW Tel: (202) 326 - 8836
Suite 1100 Fax:(202) 289 - 3699
Washington, DC 20005

Serves As:
- Associate Director, SBC Communications Inc.

KAWULOK, Donald W.
216 16th St. Mall Tel: (303) 825 - 7661
Suite 860 Fax:(303) 825 - 4629
Denver, CO 80202

Serves As:
- Manager, Government Affairs, Coors Brewing Co.

KAY, Christopher K.
One Geoffrey Way Tel: (973) 617 - 3500
Wayne, NJ 07470-2030

Serves As:
- Exec. V. President, Operations, General Counsel and Corporate Secretary, Toys "R" Us, Inc.

Responsibilities include corporate communications and corporate philanthropy.

KAYE, Alan
333 Continental Blvd. Tel: (310) 252 - 2000
El Segundo, CA 90245-5012 Fax:(310) 252 - 2180

Serves As:
- Senior V. President, Human Resources, Mattel, Inc.

KAYE, Bronwen A.
1667 K St. NW Tel: (202) 659 - 8320
Suite 1270 Fax:(202) 659 - 2158
Washington, DC 20036
kayeb@wyeth.com

Registered Federal Lobbyist.
Serves As:
- Senior Director, Government Relations, Wyeth

KAZEMIER, Jeanie A.
7575 Fulton St. East Tel: (616) 787 - 8584
M/S 78-2G Fax:(616) 787 - 5624
Ada, MI 49355-0001

Serves As:
- Senior Legislative Analyst, Alticor Inc.

KAZMIERCZAK, Theresa
One M & T Plaza Tel: (716) 842 - 5445
Buffalo, NY 14203 Fax:(716) 842 - 5839
TF: (800) 836 - 1500

Serves As:
- Manager, Corporate and Community Affairs, M&T Bank Corporation

KEAN, Michael H.
1200 G St. NW Tel: (202) 383 - 3700
Suite 900 Fax:(202) 383 - 3718
Washington, DC 20005-3802

Registered Federal Lobbyist.
Serves As:
- Representative, The McGraw-Hill Companies, Inc.

KEANE, Brian T.
100 City Square Tel: (617) 241 - 9200
Boston, MA 02129 Fax:(617) 241 - 8027
brian_t_keane@keane.com

Serves As:
- President and Chief Exec. Officer, Keane, Inc.

KEANE, John F.
100 City Square Tel: (617) 241 - 9200
Boston, MA 02129 Fax:(617) 241 - 8027
john_f_keane@keane.com

Serves As:
- Chairman of the Board, Keane, Inc.

KEANEY, David
1300 I St. NW Tel: (202) 962 - 8640
Suite 1090 Fax:(202) 289 - 6819
Washington, DC 20005

Registered Federal Lobbyist.
Serves As:
- Representative, Chiron Corp.

KEARNS, Dennis A.
1001 Congress, Suite 250 Tel: (512) 473 - 2823
Austin, TX 78701 Fax:(512) 473 - 8570
dennis.kearns@bnsf.com

Serves As:
- Legislative Counsel and Exec. Director, Government Affairs, Burlington Northern Santa Fe Corporation

KEATING, Anne
1000 Third Ave. Tel: (212) 705 - 2434
New York, NY 10022 Fax:(212) 705 - 2805

Serves As:
- Senior V. President, Public Relations, Bloomingdale's

Responsibilities include corporate philanthropy.

KEATING, Brian G.
P.O. Box 2301 Tel: (513) 397 - 9900
Cincinnati, OH 45201-2301 Fax:(513) 723 - 9815

Serves As:
- V. President, Human Resources and Administration, Cincinnati Bell Inc.

KEATING, David
110 N. Wacker Dr. Tel: (312) 960 - 6325
Chicago, IL 60606-1511 Fax:(312) 960 - 5475

Serves As:
- Senior Manager, Media Relations, General Growth Properties Inc.

KEATING, Mary Ellen
122 Fifth Ave. Tel: (212) 633 - 3323
New York, NY 10011 Fax:(212) 807 - 6033

Serves As:
- Senior V. President, Corporate Communications and Public Affairs, Barnes & Noble, Inc.

KEATING, Mary Jo
P.O. Box 270 Tel: (860) 665 - 5181
M/S BMN 1 Fax:(860) 665 - 5262
Hartford, CT 06141-0270 TF: (800) 286 - 2000
KeatiMJ@nu.com

Serves As:
- V. President, Corporate Communications, (Northeast Utilities Service Co.), Northeast Utilities

KEATING, Timothy
1001 Pennsylvania Ave. NW Tel: (202) 662 - 2650
Suite 700 South Fax:(202) 662 - 2674
Washington, DC 20004

Serves As:
- Senior V. President, Government Relations, Honeywell Internat'l, Inc.

KEATON, Dan
1134 Market St. Tel: (304) 234 - 2400
Wheeling, WV 26003 Fax:(304) 234 - 2261

Serves As:
- V. President, Human Resources, Wheeling-Pittsburgh Steel Corp.

Responsibilities include political action.

KECK, Patty
9191 S. Jamaica St. Tel: (720) 286 - 2596
Englewood, CO 80112 Fax:(720) 286 - 9250
patty.keck@ch2m.com

Serves As:
- Manager, Public Relations, CH2M Hill Companies, Inc.

KEEBLER, Jack
Seneca St. at Jamison Rd. Tel: (716) 652 - 2000
East Aurora, NY 14052 Fax:(716) 687 - 4457
jack.keebler@moog.com

Serves As:
- Manager, Human Resources, Moog Inc.

KEEFE, Kenneth
490 L'Enfant Plaza SW Tel: (202) 378 - 2373
Suite 511 Fax:(202) 220 - 7093
Washington, DC 20024
klkeefe@avaya.com

Registered Federal Lobbyist.
Serves As:
- Director, Government Affairs, Federal/State, Avaya Inc.

KEEFE, Susan
26877 Tourney Rd. Tel: (661) 287 - 5484
Valencia, CA 91355 Fax:(661) 287 - 5495
susan.keefe@borax.com

Serves As:
- Manager, Global Public Affairs, U.S. Borax Inc.

KEEGAN, Brendan M.
One Marriott Dr. Tel: (301) 380 - 1010
Washington, DC 20058 Fax:(301) 380 - 4055
brendan.keegan@marriott.com

Serves As:
- Exec. V. President, Human Resources, Marriott Internat'l, Inc.

KEEGAN, Diana
1399 New York Ave. NW
Suite 900
Washington, DC 20005
Tel: (202) 585 - 5800
Fax:(202) 585 - 5820

Registered Federal Lobbyist.
Serves As:
• Representative, American Internat'l Group, Inc.

KEEGAN, Mark
655 Third Ave.
New York, NY 10017
mark.keegan@mitsubishicorp.com
Tel: (212) 605 - 2000
Fax:(212) 605 - 1908

Serves As:
• Manager, Corporate Communications, Mitsubishi International Corporation

KEEGAN, Robert J.
1144 E. Market St.
Akron, OH 44316-0001
Tel: (330) 796 - 2121
Fax:(330) 796 - 2222

Serves As:
• Chairman of the Board, Chief Exec. Officer and President, The Goodyear Tire & Rubber Company

KEEL, Clarence
200 W. Second St.
Winston-Salem, NC 27101
Tel: (336) 733 - 2000

Serves As:
• V. President, Shareholder Relations, BB&T Corp.

KEELING, Chip
P.O. Box 32010
Louisville, KY 40232-2010
chip.keeling@lgeenergy.com
Tel: (502) 627 - 2502

Serves As:
• V. President, U.S. Communications, LG&E Energy LLC

KEENAN, Melanie
560 Lexington Ave.
20th Floor
New York, NY 10022
melanie.keenan@cbre.com
Tel: (212) 284 - 8073

Serves As:
• Director, Communications, CB Richard Ellis Services, Inc.

KEENAN, Vince
2211 S. 47th St.
Phoenix, AZ 85034
Tel: (480) 643 - 7053
Fax:(480) 643 - 7370

Serves As:
• V. President and Director, Investor Relations, Avnet Inc.

KEENE, Linda L.
101 Ash St.
San Diego, CA 92101-3017
Tel: (619) 696 - 2063
Fax:(619) 696 - 4838
TF: (877) 736 - 7721

Serves As:
• Treasurer, Sempra Energy Employee PAC and Legal Support Supervisor, Sempra Energy

KEEVIL, Julian
P.O. Box 25099
Richmond, VA 23260
Tel: (804) 359 - 9311
Fax:(804) 254 - 3541

Serves As:
• V. President; and Foundation Contact, (Universal Leaf Tobacco Co., Inc.), Universal Corp.

KEHOE, Michael E.
150 E. Gay St., Room 4A
Columbus, OH 43215
michael.kehoe@sbc.com
Tel: (614) 223 - 8236
Fax:(614) 223 - 6296

Serves As:
• V. President, External Affairs, SBC Ohio

KEIM, Patrick C.
139 N. Last Chance Gulch
Helena, MT 59601
patrick.keim@bnsf.com
Tel: (406) 447 - 2301
Fax:(406) 449 - 8610

Serves As:
• Director, Government Affairs, Burlington Northern Santa Fe Corporation

KEIR, Gerry
P.O. Box 3200
Honolulu, HI 96847
Tel: (808) 525 - 7086
Fax:(808) 557 - 086

Serves As:
• Exec. V. President, Corporate Communications, BancWest Corp.

KEITH, Erbin
101 Ash St.
hq17
San Diego, CA 92101-3017
ekeith@sempra.com
Tel: (619) 696 - 4676
Fax:(619) 696 - 4656
TF: (877) 736 - 7721

Serves As:
• V. President, Global Regulatory Affairs and Administration, Sempra Energy

KEITH, Robert E.
800 The Safeguard Bldg.
435 Devon Park Dr.
Wayne, PA 19087-1945
Tel: (610) 293 - 0600
Fax:(610) 293 - 0601
TF: (888) 733 - 1200

Serves As:
• Chairman of the Board, Safeguard Scientifics, Inc.

KELASH, Paul
625 Fourth Ave. South
Minneapolis, MN 55415
paul.kelash@thrivent.com
Tel: (612) 340 - 4274
Fax:(612) 340 - 4070

Serves As:
• Director, Media Relations, Thrivent Financial for Lutherans

KELCH, Margaret
35716 Royalton Rd.
Grafton, OH 44044
mkelch@rossenvironmental.com
Tel: (440) 366 - 2000
Fax:(440) 748 - 2200

Serves As:
• Manager, Community Relations, Ross Environmental Services, Inc.

KELLEHER, Edward C.
55 Water St.
49th Floor
New York, NY 10041-0099
eckelleher@dtcc.com
Tel: (212) 855 - 5301
Fax:(212) 785 - 9681

Serves As:
• Director, Corporate Communications, The Depository Trust & Clearing Corp.

KELLEHER, Herbert D.
P.O. Box 36611
Dallas, TX 75235-1611
Tel: (214) 792 - 4000
TF: (800) 435 - 9792

Serves As:
• Chairman of the Board, Southwest Airlines Co.

KELLEHER, Lawrence J.
P.O. Box 14000
Juno Beach, FL 33408-0420
Tel: (561) 694 - 4642
Fax:(561) 694 - 4620

Serves As:
• V. President, Human Resources, FPL Group, Inc.

KELLER, Dennis J.
One Tower Ln.
Suite 1000
Oakbrook Terrace, IL 60181-4624
Tel: (630) 571 - 7700
Fax:(630) 571 - 0317
TF: (800) 225 - 8000

Serves As:
• Chairman of the Board, DeVry Inc.

KELLER, James A.
401 Ninth St. NW
Suite 640
Washington, DC 20004
Tel: (202) 585 - 8930

Registered Federal Lobbyist.
Serves As:
• Federal Government Relations Respresentative, J. P. Morgan Chase & Co.

KELLER, Robert G.
175 E. Old Country Rd.
Hicksville, NY 11801
Tel: (516) 545 - 5147
Fax:(516) 545 - 8193

Serves As:
• Exec. Director, KeySpan Foundation, KeySpan Corp.

KELLER, Thomas C.
P.O. Box 513338
Los Angeles, CA 90051-1338
Tel: (626) 821 - 7000
Fax:(626) 821 - 7933

Serves As:
• President and Chief Exec. Officer, Vons

KELLEY, Barbara M.
One Bausch & Lomb Pl.
Rochester, NY 14604-0054
barbara_m_kelley@bausch.com
Tel: (585) 338 - 5386
Fax:(585) 338 - 8551
TF: (800) 344 - 8815

Serves As:
• V. President, Communications and Investor Relations, Bausch & Lomb

KELLEY, Brian P.
700 Oakmont Lane
Westmont, IL 60559
Tel: (630) 570 - 3000
Fax:(630) 570 - 3606

Serves As:
• President and Chief Exec. Officer, SIRVA, Inc.

KELLEY, John B.
P.O. Box 3440
Honolulu, HI 96801-3440
jkelley@abinc.com
Tel: (808) 525 - 8422
Fax:(808) 525 - 6651

Serves As:
• V. President, Investor Relations, Alexander & Baldwin, Inc.

KELLEY, Joseph B.
555 12th St. NW
Suite 650
Washington, DC 20004-1205
Tel: (202) 393 - 7950
Fax:(202) 393 - 7960

Serves As:
- V. President, Government Relations and Public Affairs, Eli Lilly and Company

KELLEY, Kevin
2244 Walnut Grove Ave.
Rosemead, CA 91770
kevin.kelley@edisonintl.com
Tel: (626) 302 - 1033

Serves As:
- Manager, Media Relations, Edison Internat'l

KELLEY, Mike
10990 Roe Ave.
Overland Park, KS 66211
Tel: (913) 696 - 6121
Fax:(913) 323 - 9710

Serves As:
- V. President, Government Relations, Yellow Roadway Corporation

KELLEY, Winston R.
P.O. Box 1244
M/S EC12B
Charlotte, NC 28201-1244
wrkelley@duke-energy.com
Tel: (704) 382 - 5783
Fax:(704) 382 - 3264

Serves As:
- V. President, Government and Business Relations/Duke Power, Duke Energy Corp.

KELLOGG, Allison Cooke
114 W. 47th St.
New York, NY 10036
Tel: (212) 852 - 1127
Fax:(212) 852 - 1140

Serves As:
- Senior V. President, Public Relations, U.S. Trust Corp.

KELLOGG, Fernanda M.
727 Fifth Ave.
New York, NY 10022
Tel: (212) 230 - 5343
Fax:(212) 230 - 6734

Serves As:
- Senior V. President, Public Relations, Tiffany & Co.

KELLY, Alex
2000 Galloping Hill Rd.
Kenilworth, NJ 07033
Tel: (908) 298 - 7450

Serves As:
- V. President, Investor Relations, Schering-Plough Corporation

KELLY, Allison
5775 Morehouse Dr.
San Diego, CA 92121-2779
Tel: (858) 587 - 1121
Fax:(858) 651 - 3255

Serves As:
- Corporate Giving Contact, Qualcomm Inc.

KELLY, Anastasia D.
22001 Loudoun County Pkwy.
Ashburn, VA 20147
Tel: (703) 886 - 5600
TF: (877) MCI - 1000

Serves As:
- General Counsel and Exec. V. President, MCI, Inc.

Responsibilities include legal, regulatory and legislative affairs.

KELLY, Brian
2001 Pennsylvania Ave. NW
Suite 500
Washington, DC 20006
Tel: (202) 379 - 7100
Fax:(202) 466 - 7718

Registered Federal Lobbyist.
Serves As:
- Senior Director, Government Affairs, Comcast Corporation

KELLY, Brian G.
3100 Ocean Park Blvd.
Santa Monica, CA 90405-3032
Tel: (310) 255 - 2000
Fax:(310) 255 - 2100

Serves As:
- Co-Chairman of the Board, Activision, Inc.

KELLY, Bronwen K.
730 Central Ave.
Murray Hill, NJ 07974
Tel: (908) 277 - 8000
Fax:(908) 277 - 8078
TF: (800) 367 - 2273

Serves As:
- V. President, Human Resources, C. R. Bard, Inc.

KELLY, Dan
P.O. Box 1410
Sanford, NC 27330
Tel: (919) 774 - 6700
Fax:(919) 774 - 3329

Serves As:
- V. President, Chief Financial Officer and Secretary, The Pantry, Inc.

Responsibilities include media relations

KELLY, Edmund F.
175 Berkeley St.
Boston, MA 02116
Tel: (617) 357 - 9500
Fax:(617) 350 - 7648

Serves As:
- Chairman, President, and Chief Exec. Officer, Liberty Mutual Insurance Co.

KELLY, III, Edward J.
P.O. Box 1477
Baltimore, MD 21203
Tel: (410) 237 - 5900
Fax:(410) 237 - 5364

Serves As:
- Chairman and Chief Exec. Officer, Mercantile Bankshares Corporation

KELLY, Gary C.
P.O. Box 36611
Dallas, TX 75235-1611
Tel: (214) 792 - 4000
TF: (800) 435 - 9792

Serves As:
- V. Chairman and Chief Exec. Officer, Southwest Airlines Co.

KELLY, Henry P.
1325 Airmotive Way, Suite 100
Reno, NV 89502-3239
Tel: (775) 688 - 6300
Fax:(775) 688 - 6338

Serves As:
- V. President, Human Resources, AMERCO

KELLY, John T.
P.O. Box 60219
New Orleans, LA 70160
Tel: (504) 566 - 1300
TF: (877) 989 - 4550

Serves As:
- Chairman and Interim Chief Exec. Officer, Pan American Life Insurance Co.

KELLY, Kimberly A.
One BET Plaza
1900 W Pl. NE
Washington, DC 20018
kimberly.kelly@bet.net
Tel: (202) 608 - 2000
Fax:(202) 608 - 2595

Serves As:
- Counsel, Government Affairs and Affiliate Regulations, (BET), Viacom Inc./CBS Corp.

KELLY, Maria
355 Maple Ave.
Harleysville, PA 19438-2297
Tel: (215) 256 - 5022
Fax:(215) 256 - 5799
TF: (800) 523 - 6344

Serves As:
- Government Affairs Counsel, Harleysville Group

KELLY, Maureen
1000 Wilson Blvd., Suite 2300
Arlington, VA 22209
Tel: (703) 875 - 8400

Registered Federal Lobbyist.
Serves As:
- Representative, Northrop Grumman Corp.

KELLY, Mike
5445 Corporate Dr.
Suite 200
Troy, MI 48098-2683
mkelly@intermet.com
Tel: (248) 952 - 2546
Fax:(248) 952 - 2501

Serves As:
- Director, Communications, Intermet Corp.

KELLY, Molly A.
200 E. Randolph St.
Chicago, IL 60601-6436
Tel: (312) 782 - 5800
Fax:(312) 782 - 4339

Serves As:
- Chief Marketing and Communications Officer, Jones Lang LaSalle Inc.

KELLY, Rex E.
P.O. Box 4079
Gulfport, MS 39502
Tel: (228) 865 - 5778
Fax:(228) 865 - 5771

Serves As:
- Director, Corporate Communications, Mississippi Power Co.

KELLY, Richard C.
414 Nicollet Mall
Minneapolis, MN 55401-1927
Tel: (612) 330 - 5500
Fax:(612) 330 - 6947
TF: (800) 328 - 8226

Serves As:
- Chief Exec. Officer, Xcel Energy, Inc.

KELLY, Thomas A.
One Bank One Plaza
Chicago, IL 60670
Tel: (312) 732 - 4000

Serves As:
- Senior V. President, Regional and Retail Media Relations, J. P. Morgan Chase & Co.

KELLY, Vincent D.
6677 Richmond Hwy.
Alexandria, VA 22306
Tel: (703) 660 - 6677
Fax:(703) 768 - 9622

Serves As:
- President and Chief Exec. Officer, USA Mobility, Inc.

KELLY, William P.
One American Rd.
Dearborn, MI 48126
Tel: (313) 323 - 9223
Fax:(313) 248 - 3514
TF: (800) 555 - 5259

Serves As:
- Director, International Governmental Affairs, Ford Motor Co.

KELLY-DOBAY, Pamela
40 Landsdowne St.
Cambridge, MA 02139
Tel: (617) 679 - 7323
Fax:(617) 374 - 7788
TF: (800) 390 - 5663

Serves As:
- Administrative Coordinator, Global Corporate Affairs, Millennium Pharmaceuticals, Inc.

Responsibilities include investor and media relations.

KELLY-JUDD, Virginia
P.O. Box 1438
Louisville, KY 40201-1438
Tel: (502) 580 - 3041
Fax:(502) 580 - 3677
TF: (800) 486 - 2620

Serves As:
- Exec. Director, Humana Foundation, Humana Inc.

KELSAY, Brendan
1401 I St., NW
Suite 401
Washington, DC 20005
brendankelsay@clearchannel.com
Tel: (202) 289 - 3230
Fax:(202) 289 - 0050

Registered Federal Lobbyist.
Serves As:
- Director, Government Affairs, Clear Channel Communications

KELSO, Alan W.
1390 Enclave Pkwy.
Houston, TX 77077-2099
Tel: (281) 584 - 1759
Fax:(281) 584 - 2721

Serves As:
- Assistant V. President, Safety and Labor Relations, Sysco Corp.

KELSO, Karen
550 Madison Ave.
New York, NY 10022-3211
karen_kelso@sonyusa.com
Tel: (212) 833 - 6033
Fax:(212) 833 - 6997

Serves As:
- Senior Director, Public Affairs, Sony Corp. of America

KEMERER, Russ
201 Stanwix St.
Second Floor
Pittsburgh, PA 15222
Tel: (412) 633 - 3248

Serves As:
- Director, External Relations, Verizon Pennsylvania Inc.

KEMMER, Mark L.
1660 L St. NW
Fourth Floor
Washington, DC 20036
Tel: (202) 775 - 5066
Fax:(202) 775 - 5024

Registered Federal Lobbyist.
Serves As:
- Director, Legislative and Regulatory Affairs/Energy, General Motors Corp.

KEMMISH, Sandra
1300 S. Clinton St.
Fort Wayne, IN 46801-8863
skemmish@lnc.com
Tel: (260) 455 - 389

Serves As:
- Charitable Giving Contact (Fort Wayne, IN), Lincoln Financial Group

KEMP, Steve B.
5005 LBJ Fwy.
Dallas, TX 75244
Tel: (972) 404 - 3800
Fax:(972) 404 - 3669
TF: (800) 578 - 8880

Serves As:
- V. President, Health Environment and Safety, Occidental Chemical Corp.

KEMPER, Christopher
National City Center
1900 E. Ninth St.
Cleveland, OH 44114-3484
christopher.kemper@nationalcity.com
Tel: (513) 455 - 9228
Fax:(226) 575 - 2353
TF: (800) 622 - 6736

Serves As:
- Media Contact, Nat'l City Corp.

Media contact for Greater Cincinnati, Northern Kentucky and Missouri.

KEMPER, David W.
8000 Forsyth Blvd.
Clayton, MO 63105
Fax:(314) 746 - 8514
TF: (800) 892 - 7100

Serves As:
- Chairman, President, and Chief Exec. Officer, Commerce Bancshares Inc.

KEMPER, J. Mariner
P.O. Box 419226
Kansas City, MO 64141-6226
Tel: (816) 860 - 7000
Fax:(816) 860 - 5675

Serves As:
- Chairman and Chief Exec. Officer, UMB Financial Corp.

KENDALL, Sara
P.O. Box 9777
M/S EC2-2C1
Federal Way, WA 98063-9777
sara.kendall@weyerhaeuser.com
Tel: (253) 924 - 3290
Fax:(253) 924 - 2013
TF: (800) 525 - 5440

Serves As:
- V. President, Office of the Environment, Weyerhaeuser Co.

KENEALY, Pat
One Exeter Plaza
15 Floor
Boston, MA 02116
Tel: (617) 534 - 4200
Fax:(617) 423 - 0240

Serves As:
- Chief Exec. Officer, Internat'l Data Group

KENKEL, Mary
1301 Pennsylvania Ave., N.W., Suite 1030
Washington, DC 20004
Tel: (202) 824 - 0400
Fax:(202) 824 - 0418

Registered Federal Lobbyist.
Serves As:
- General Manager, Federal Government Affairs and National Media, Cinergy Corp.

KENNEDY, Bernard
185 Central Ave.
Bethpage, NY 11714
bkennedy@kingkullen.com
Tel: (516) 733 - 7100
Fax:(516) 827 - 6262

Serves As:
- Chairman and Chief Exec. Officer, King Kullen Grocery Co.

Responsibilities include corporate philanthropy.

KENNEDY, Daniel E.
1015 15th St. NW
Suite 700
Washington, DC 20005-2605
Tel: (202) 828 - 5200
Fax:(202) 785 - 2645

Registered Federal Lobbyist.
Serves As:
- V. President and Manager, Government Affairs, (Bechtel National, Inc.), Bechtel Group, Inc.

KENNEDY, Elizabeth
5100 Harding Hwy.
Mays Landing, NJ 08330
betty.kennedy@conectiv.com
Tel: (609) 625 - 5567
Fax:(609) 625 - 6944

Serves As:
- Senior Public Affairs Consultant - NJ, (Atlantic City Electric), Conectiv

KENNEDY, Heather
101 Constitution Ave., NW
Suite 800 West
Washington, DC 20001
Tel: (202) 772 - 2497
Fax:(202) 772 - 2496

Serves As:
- PAC Contact, The Home Depot, Inc.

KENNEDY, James C.
6205 Peachtree Dunwoody Rd.
Atlanta, GA 30328
Tel: (678) 645 - 0000

Serves As:
- Chairman and Chief Exec. Officer, Cox Enterprises, Inc.

KENNEDY, Jeanne
10455 Mill Run Circle
Owings Mills, MD 21117
Tel: (410) 581 - 3000
Fax:(410) 998 - 5351

Serves As:
- V. President, Business Risk Management, CareFirst BlueCross and BlueShield

KENNEDY, John
P.O. Box 20706
Atlanta, GA 30320-6001
Tel: (404) 715 - 2600
Fax:(404) 715 - 2731

Serves As:
- General Manager, Media Relations, Delta Air Lines, Inc.

KENNEDY, John P.
5757 N. Green Bay Ave.
Milwaukee, WI 53201-0591
Tel: (414) 524 - 1200
Fax:(414) 524 - 2077

Serves As:
- Senior V. President, Secretary and General Counsel; PAC Contact, Johnson Controls, Inc.

KENNEDY, Kevin J.
1768 Automation Pkwy.
San Jose, CA 95131
Tel: (408) 546 - 5000
Fax:(408) 546 - 4300

Serves As:
- Chief Exec. Officer, JDS Uniphase Corp.

KENNEDY, Lisa
300 Somerset Corporate Blvd.
Bridgewater, NJ 08807-2854
Tel: (908) 243 - 6361
Fax:(908) 231 - 3614
TF: (800) 981 - 2491

Serves As:
- Product and Scientific Communications, Sanofi-Aventis Inc.

KENNEDY, Michael D.
1350 I St. NW
Suite 400
Washington, DC 20005-3306
Tel: (202) 371 - 6900
Fax:(202) 842 - 3578

Registered Federal Lobbyist.
Serves As:
- Senior V. President and Director, Global Government Relations Organization, Motorola, Inc.

KENNEDY, Parker S.
One First American Way
Santa Ana, CA 92707
Tel: (714) 800 - 3000
Fax:(714) 800 - 4790

Serves As:
- Chairman, President and Chief Exec. Officer, The First American Corp.

KENNEDY, Sean
1401 I St. NW
Suite 1100
Washington, DC 20005
Tel: (202) 326 - 8913
Fax:(202) 289 - 3699

Serves As:
- Exec. Director, Federal Relations, SBC Communications Inc.

KENNEDY, Sharlene D.
1275 K St. NW
Suite 1200
Washington, DC 20005
sharlene.kennedy@delta.com
Tel: (202) 216 - 0700
Fax:(202) 216 - 0824

Registered Federal Lobbyist.
Serves As:
- Manager, Government Affairs, Delta Air Lines, Inc.

KENNEDY, Jr., Dr. W. Keith
3240 Hillview Ave.
Palo Alto, CA 94304
Tel: (650) 494 - 2900
Fax:(650) 813 - 0160

Serves As:
- Chairman of the Board, CNF Inc.

KENNETT, Doug
1200 Wilson Blvd.
Arlington, VA 22209-2305
Tel: (703) 465 - 3532
Fax:(703) 465 - 3033

Serves As:
- Director, Communications, The Boeing Co.

KENNEY, Brian A.
500 W. Monroe St.
Chicago, IL 60661
Tel: (312) 621 - 6200
Fax:(312) 621 - 6648
TF: (800) 428 - 8161

Serves As:
- President and Chief Executive Officer, GATX Corp.

KENNEY, Ryan
P.O. Box 1271
Portland, OR 97207-1271
Tel: (503) 225 - 5336
Fax:(503) 225 - 5283

Serves As:
- Director, Human Resources, Regence BlueCross BlueShield of Oregon

KENNY, Gregory B.
Four Tesseneer Dr.
Highland Heights, KY 41076
Tel: (859) 572 - 8000
Fax:(859) 572 - 8458

Serves As:
- President and Chief Exec. Officer, General Cable Corp.

KENNY, Katharine W.
Four N. Fourth St.
Richmond, VA 23219-2230
katharine.kenny@masseyenergyco.com
Tel: (804) 788 - 1824
Fax:(804) 788 - 1870

Serves As:
- V. President, Investor Relations, Massey Energy Co.

KENT, Jr., J. Gaston
1840 Century Park East
Los Angeles, CA 90067-2199
Tel: (310) 553 - 6262
Fax:(310) 201 - 3023

Serves As:
- V. President, Investor Relations, Northrop Grumman Corp.

KENT, Philip I.
P.O. Box 105366
One CNN Center
Atlanta, GA 30348-5366
Tel: (404) 827 - 1700
Fax:(404) 827 - 2024

Serves As:
- Chairman and Chief Exec. Officer, Turner Broadcasting System, Inc.

KEOGH, Frank
4510 13th Ave. SW
Fargo, ND 58121-0001
Tel: (701) 282 - 1100
Fax:(701) 282 - 1469
TF: (800) 342 - 4718

Serves As:
- Chairman of the Board, Blue Cross and Blue Shield of North Dakota

KEOUGH, Kim
444 Westminster St.
Providence, RI 02903-3279
keough.k@bcbsri.org
Tel: (401) 459 - 5601
Fax:(401) 459 - 1333
TF: (800) 637 - 3718

Serves As:
- Assistant V. President, Public Relations, Blue Cross & Blue Shield of Rhode Island

KEOUGH, Michael J.
P.O. Box 115
Austell, GA 30168-0115
Tel: (770) 948 - 3101
Fax:(770) 732 - 3401

Serves As:
- President and Chief Exec. Officer, Caraustar Industries, Inc.

KERLEY, Bobby
P.O. Box 4079
Gulfport, MS 39502
Tel: (228) 864 - 1211
Fax:(228) 865 - 5616

Serves As:
- V. President, Customer Services and Marketing, Mississippi Power Co.

KERLEY, Greg D.
2350 N. Sam Houston Pkwy. East
Suite 300
Houston, TX 77032
Tel: (281) 618 - 4700
Fax:(281) 618 - 4820

Serves As:
- Exec. V. President and Chief Financial Officer, Southwestern Energy Co.

Responsibilities include investor relations.

KERMAN, Neil
1895 J W Foster Blvd.
Canton, MA 02021
neil.kerman@reebok.com
Tel: (781) 401 - 7152
Fax:(781) 401 - 4422

Serves As:
- V. President, Corporate Finance, Reebok Internat'l Ltd.

Responsibilities include investor relations.

KERN, Michael J.
3040 Post Oak Blvd.
Houston, TX 77056
mike_kern@huntsman.com
Tel: (713) 235 - 6000

Serves As:
- Senior V. President, Environmental, Health, and Safety, Huntsman Corp.

KERN, Ms. Terri
18831 Von Karman, Suite 400
Irvine, CA 92612
terri.kern@sunh.com
Tel: (949) 255 - 7100
Fax:(949) 255 - 7054
TF: (800) 509 - 4340

Serves As:
- Senior V. President, Communications and Business Develoment, Sun Healthcare Group, Inc.

KERNS, Kim
1111 Stewart Ave.
Bethpage, NY 11714-3581
Tel: (516) 803 - 2300
Fax:(516) 803 - 1186

Serves As:
- V. President, Corporate Communications, Cablevision Systems Corp.

KERR, Barbara J.
850 Lincoln Center Dr.
Foster City, CA 94404-1128
kerrbj@appliedbiosystems.com
Tel: (650) 638 - 6310

Serves As:
- V. President, Human Resources, Applera Corp.

KERR, Eleanor
701 Pennsylvania Ave. NW
Suite 720
Washington, DC 20004
eleanor.kerr@sc.siemens.com
Tel: (202) 434 - 4800
Fax:(202) 347 - 4015

Registered Federal Lobbyist.
Serves As:
- Director, Legislative Affairs -- Healthcare Appropriations, Siemens Corp.

KERR, Guy H.
P.O. Box 655237 Tel: (214) 977 - 6606
Dallas, TX 75265-5237 Fax:(214) 977 - 6603

Registered Federal Lobbyist.
Serves As:
• Senior V. President, Law and Government, Belo Corp.

KERR, James B.
Unisys Way Tel: (215) 986 - 5795
M/S A2-17 Ext: 4386
Blue Bell, PA 19424 Fax:(215) 986 - 2312
james.kerr@unn.unisys.com

Serves As:
• Director, Investor Relations, Unisys Corp.

KERR, Mary
P.O. Box 2821 Tel: (717) 751 - 3071
York, PA 17405-2821 Fax:(717) 751 - 3037

Serves As:
• V. President, Corporate Communications, The Bon Ton Stores, Inc.

KERR, William T.
1716 Locust St. Tel: (515) 284 - 3000
Des Moines, IA 50309-3023 Fax:(515) 284 - 3806
bkerr@mdp.com

Serves As:
• Chairman and Chief Exec. Officer, Meredith Corp.

KERRIDGE, Ike
3900 Essex Ln., Suite 1200 Tel: (713) 439 - 8662
Houston, TX 77027-5177 Fax:(713) 439 - 8699

Serves As:
• Exec. Director, Baker Hughes Foundation, Baker Hughes Inc.

KERRIGAN, Kenneth
Five Times Square Tel: (212) 773 - 3000
New York, NY 10036 Fax:(212) 773 - 6350

Serves As:
• Deputy Director, Public Relations, Ernst & Young LLP

KERSTIN, Jeff
27175 Haggerty Rd. Tel: (248) 675 - 6000
Novi, MI 48377 Fax:(248) 675 - 6200

Serves As:
• Manager, Investor Relations, Tower Automotive, Inc.

KESSLER, Debbie
30 Community Dr. Tel: (802) 846 - 1500
South Burlington, VT 05403-6828

Serves As:
• Foundation Contact, Ben & Jerry's Homemade Inc.

KESSLER, Ellen
One MetroTech Center Tel: (718) 403 - 6977
Brooklyn, NY 11201 Fax:(718) 488 - 1763

Serves As:
• Investor Relations Contact, KeySpan Corp.

KESSLER, Lorie
2000 Second Ave. Tel: (313) 235 - 5555
Detroit, MI 48226
kesslerl@dteenergy.com

Serves As:
• Director, Media Relations, DTE Energy Co.

KESSLER, Susan
100 Grainger Pkwy. Tel: (847) 535 - 1543
Lake Forest, IL 60045-5201
susie.kessler@grainger.com

Serves As:
• Manager, Public Affairs, W. W. Grainger, Inc.
Responsibilities include corporate philanthropy.

KESTER, Steven J.
5204 E. Ben White Blvd.
M/S 500
Austin, TX 78741

Registered Federal Lobbyist.
Serves As:
• Representative, Advanced Micro Devices, Inc.
• Contact, Advanced Micro Devices Inc. PAC

KETAY, Julie
Three First National Plaza Tel: (312) 558 - 8727
70 W. Madison St. Fax:(312) 558 - 8653
Chicago, IL 60602-4260 TF: (800) 727 - 2533

Serves As:
• Exec. Director, Corporate Media Relations, Sara Lee Corp.

KETCHEL, Kim
9697 E. Mineral Ave. Tel: (303) 792 - 3111
Englewood, CO 80112 Fax:(303) 784 - 8508

Serves As:
• V. President, Marketing and Communications, Jones Internat'l, Ltd.

KETCHEN, Valerie C.
1800 Center St. Tel: (717) 302 - 3974
Camp Hill, PA 17089 Fax:(717) 302 - 3969

Registered Federal Lobbyist.
Serves As:
• Senior Representative, Government Affairs, (Clarity Vision, Inc., Highmark Life and Casualty Group, Inc., United Concordia Cos., Inc.), Highmark Inc.

KETTLER, Jr., William H.
P.O. Box 650283 Tel: (972) 699 - 4000
Dallas, TX 75265-0283 Fax:(972) 699 - 4025

Serves As:
• V. President, Human Resources, Xanser Corp.

KEWITSCH, Kris
800 Nicollet Mall Tel: (612) 303 - 6000
Suite 800
J13S25
Minneapolis, MN 55402
kristin.k.kewitsch@pjc.com

Serves As:
• Manager, Community Relations, U.S. Bancorp Piper Jaffray Inc.

KEYES, James M.
2711 N. Haskell Ave. Tel: (214) 828 - 7011
Dallas, TX 75204 Fax:(214) 828 - 7090

Serves As:
• Chairman, President and Chief Exec. Officer, 7-Eleven, Inc.

KEYES, Steve
3800 Hamlin Rd. Tel: (248) 754 - 5054
Auburn Hills, MI 48326 Fax:(248) 754 - 4930

Serves As:
• Director, Corporate Communications, Volkswagen of America, Inc.

KEYMER, Kenneth L.
555 Glenridge Connector NE Tel: (404) 459 - 4450
Suite 300
Atlanta, GA 30342

Serves As:
• Chief Exec. Officer, AFC Enterprises

KEYSER, Richard L.
100 Grainger Pkwy. Tel: (847) 535 - 1000
Lake Forest, IL 60045-5201
keyser.r@grainger.com

Serves As:
• Chairman and Chief Exec. Officer, W. W. Grainger, Inc.

KHAIL, Steve
P.O. Box 66 Tel: (920) 652 - 1713
Manitowoc, WI 54221-0066 Fax:(920) 652 - 9778

Serves As:
• Director, Investor Relations and Corporate Communications, The Manitowoc Co., Inc.

KHOURY, Jennifer
1500 Market St. Tel: (215) 320 - 7408
Philadelphia, PA 19102 Fax:(215) 981 - 7790

Serves As:
• Senior Director, Corporate Communications, Comcast Corporation

KIDO, Veronica
100 City Square Tel: (617) 241 - 9200
Boston, MA 02129 Ext: 1390
vkido@keane.com Fax:(617) 241 - 8027

Serves As:
• Director, Marketing Communications, Keane, Inc.

KIECKHEFER, Robert
300 E. Randolph St. Tel: (312) 653 - 6629
Chicago, IL 60601 Fax:(312) 819 - 1220

Serves As:
• V. President, Public Affairs, Health Care Service Corp.

KIEDAISCH, Gary A.
3600 N. Hydraulic Tel: (316) 832 - 2700
Wichita, KS 67219

Serves As:
• President and Chief Exec. Officer, The Coleman Company, Inc.

KIENER, Ashlie
3800 Mueller Rd. Tel: (636) 443 - 6150
St. Charles, MO 63301 Fax:(636) 443 - 7208

Serves As:
- Director, Public Affairs, (Central States Coca-Cola Bottling Co.), Coca-Cola Enterprises Inc.

KIERLIN, Robert A.
P.O. Box 978 Tel: (507) 454 - 5374
Winona, MN 55987 Fax:(507) 453 - 8049

Serves As:
- Founder and Chairman, Fastenal Co.

KIGER, Lundy
P.O. Box 1740 Tel: (918) 962 - 9451
Panama, OK 74951

Serves As:
- PAC Treasurer, The AES Corp.

KIGHT, Peter J.
4411 E. Jones Bridge Rd. Tel: (678) 375 - 3000
Norcross, GA 30092-1615 Fax:(678) 375 - 1477

Serves As:
- Chairman and Chief Exec. Officer, CheckFree Corp.

KIGUCHI, Stafford
P.O. Box 2900 Tel: (808) 537 - 8246
Honolulu, HI 96846 Fax:(808) 537 - 8440
skiguchi@boh.com TF: (888) 643 - 3888

Serves As:
- Senior V. President and Manager, Corporate Communications, Bank of Hawaii Corp.

KILBY, Don
P.O. Box 321 Tel: (405) 553 - 3211
Oklahoma City, OK 73101-0321

Serves As:
- Coordinator, Shareowner Relations, OGE Energy Corp.

KILGANNON, Susan B.
One Penn Plaza Tel: (212) 330 - 1998
New York, NY 10119 Fax:(212) 947 - 6975

Serves As:
- V. President, Communications, URS Corp.

KILGORE, Gregory
401 Ninth St. NW Tel: (202) 585 - 1930
Suite 400 Fax:(202) 585 - 1899
Washington, DC 20004

Registered Federal Lobbyist.
Serves As:
- Director, Government Affairs, Sprint Nextel

KILIAN, Thomas J.
17800 Royalton Rd. Tel: (440) 572 - 2400
Cleveland, OH 44136-5149 Fax:(440) 878 - 2959
TF: (800) 321 - 3997

Serves As:
- President and Chief Exec. Officer, Ceres Group, Inc.

KILIC, Michelle
1700 E. Putnam Ave. Tel: (203) 698 - 5921
Suite 400 Fax:(203) 698 - 7925
Greenwich, CT 06370

Serves As:
- Manager, Investor Relations, Premcor Inc.

KILLEEN, John J. "Jay"
1919 Pennsylvania Ave. NW Tel: (202) 530 - 8905
Suite 650 Fax:(202) 530 - 5641
Washington, DC 20006
killeenj@saic.com

Registered Federal Lobbyist.
Serves As:
- Senior V. President, Government Affairs, Science Applications Internat'l Corp.

KILLINGER, Kerry
P.O. Box 834 Tel: (206) 461 - 2000
Seattle, WA 98101 Fax:(206) 554 - 4807
kerry.killinger@wamu.net TF: (800) 756 - 8000

Serves As:
- Chairman, President and Chief Exec. Officer, Washington Mutual, Inc.

KILLINGSWORTH, Cleve
401 Park Dr. Tel: (617) 246 - 5000
Boston, MA 02215 TF: (800) 325 - 2583

Serves As:
- President and Chief Exec. Officer, Blue Cross and Blue Shield of Massachusetts

KILPATRIC, Mike N.
1300 Morris Dr. Tel: (610) 727 - 7118
Suite 100 Fax:(610) 727 - 3603
Chesterbrook, PA 19087-5594 TF: (800) 829 - 3132
mkilpatric@amerisourcebergen.com

Serves As:
- V. President, Corporate and Investor Relations, AmeriSource Bergen Corp.

KILTS, James M.
Prudential Tower Bldg. Tel: (617) 421 - 7000
Boston, MA 02199-8004 Fax:(617) 421 - 7123
james_kilts@gillette.com

Serves As:
- Chairman, President and Chief Exec. Officer, The Gillette Company

KIM, James J.
1900 S. Price Rd. Tel: (480) 821 - 5000
Chandler, AZ 85248-1604 Fax:(480) 821 - 8276

Serves As:
- Chairman and Chief Exec. Officer, Amkor Technology, Inc.

KIMBLE, Jenifer
9487 Regency Square Blvd. Tel: (904) 727 - 2513
Jacksonville, FL 32225
jenifer.kimble@crowley.com

Serves As:
- Senior Specialist, Corporate Communications, Crowley Maritime Corp.

KIMBRO, Kenneth J.
P.O. Box 2020 Tel: (479) 290 - 4000
Springdale, AR 72765-2020 TF: (800) 424 - 4253
ken.kimbro@tyson.com

Serves As:
- Senior V. President, Human Resources, Tyson Foods, Inc.

KIMBROUGH, Reed
72 Marietta St. NW Tel: (404) 526 - 5151
Atlanta, GA 30303 Fax:(404) 526 - 5199

Serves As:
- V. President, Community Affairs and Workforce Diversity, Atlanta Journal Constitution

Responsibilities include corporate philanthropy.

KIMMEL, Max
P.O. Box 1088 Tel: (541) 679 - 3311
Roseburg, OR 97470-0252 Fax:(541) 679 - 9543
TF: (800) 245 - 1115

Serves As:
- Manager, Environmental Affairs, Roseburg Forest Products Co.

KIMMEL, Sydney
250 Rittenhouse Circle Tel: (215) 785 - 4000
Bristol, PA 19007 Fax:(215) 785 - 1228

Serves As:
- Chairman of the Board and Director, Jones Apparel Group

KIMMET, Pamela
600 Mountain Ave. Tel: (908) 582 - 8500
Murray Hill, NJ 07974-0636 Fax:(908) 508 - 2576
TF: (888) 458 - 2368

Serves As:
- Senior V. President, Human Resources, Lucent Technologies

KIMMINS, Jr., William E.
One Busch Pl. Tel: (314) 577 - 2329
St. Louis, MO 63118-1852 Fax:(314) 577 - 7622

Serves As:
- V. President and Treasurer, Anheuser-Busch Cos., Inc.

Responsibilities include political action.

KIMMITT, Jay
1300 N. 17th St. Tel: (703) 525 - 8400
Suite 1040 Fax:(703) 525 - 8408
Arlington, VA 22209

Serves As:
- Senior V. President, Government Operations, Oshkosh Truck Corp.

KIMMITT, Robert M.
800 Connecticut Ave. NW Tel: (202) 457 - 8582
Suite 800 Fax:(202) 457 - 8861
Washington, DC 20006
robert.kimmett@timewarner.com

Registered Federal Lobbyist.
Serves As:
- Exec. V. President, Global Public Policy, Time Warner Inc.

KINARD, Judy
P.O. Box 5660 Tel: (303) 626 - 8213
Denver, CO 80217 Fax:(303) 626 - 8228
jkinard@transmontaigne.com

Serves As:
- Director, Corporate Communications, TransMontaigne, Inc.

KINCAID, Richard D.
Two N. Riverside Plaza
Suite 2100
Chicago, IL 60606
Tel: (312) 466 - 3300
Fax:(312) 454 - 0332

Serves As:
- President and Chief Exec. Officer, Equity Office Properties Trust

KINCAID, Tracey
P.O. Box 6006
Cypress, CA 90630
tracy.kincaid@phs.com
Tel: (714) 226 - 3084
Fax:(714) 226 - 3581

Serves As:
- V. President, Corporate Communications, PacifiCare Health Systems, Inc.

KINDER, Richard D.
500 Dallas St., Suite 1000
Houston, TX 77002
Tel: (713) 369 - 9000
Fax:(713) 369 - 9100
TF: (800) 324 - 2900

Serves As:
- Chairman, President and Chief Exec. Officer, Kinder Morgan, Inc.

KINDLE, Fred
501 Merritt Seven
Norwalk, CT 06851
Tel: (203) 750 - 2200
Fax:(203) 750 - 2263
TF: (800) 626 - 4999

Serves As:
- Chief Exec. Officer Designate, ABB Inc.

KINDLE, Jo Ann T.
600 Corporate Park Dr.
St. Louis, MO 63105
jkindle@erac.com
Tel: (314) 512 - 2754
Fax:(314) 512 - 4706

Serves As:
- President, Enterprise Rent-A-Car Foundation, Enterprise Rent-A-Car Co.

KING, Allen B.
P.O. Box 25099
Richmond, VA 23260
Tel: (804) 359 - 9311
Fax:(804) 254 - 3584

Serves As:
- Chairman, President and Chief Exec. Officer, Universal Corp.

KING, Anne
P.O. Box 1000
Montville, NJ 07045
anne_king@berlex.com
Fax:(973) 487 - 2005
TF: (800) 237 - 5392

Serves As:
- Manager, Public Affairs, Berlex, Inc.

KING, Barbara T.
3120 Breckinridge Blvd.
Duluth, GA 30099-0001
Tel: (770) 381 - 1000
Fax:(770) 564 - 6110

Serves As:
- Exec. V. President, Field Communications, Primerica Financial Services, Inc.

KING, Brandy
P.O. Box 36611
Dallas, TX 75235-1611
Tel: (214) 792 - 5138
Fax:(214) 792 - 4200

Serves As:
- Regional Manager, Public Relations, Southwest Airlines Co.

KING, J. Joseph
2222 Wellington Ct.
Lisle, IL 60532
Tel: (630) 969 - 4550
Fax:(630) 969 - 1352
TF: (800) 786 - 6539

Serves As:
- V. Chairman and Chief Exec. Officer, Molex Incorporated

KING, Jim
14111 Scottslawn Rd.
Marysville, OH 43041
jim.king@scottsco.com
Tel: (937) 578 - 5622
Fax:(937) 644 - 7184
TF: (800) 543 - 8873

Serves As:
- Senior Director, Investor Relations and Corporate Communications, The Scotts Company

KING, Joshua
Hartford Plaza
Hartford, CT 06115
Tel: (860) 547 - 2293
Fax:(860) 547 - 3799

Serves As:
- V. President, Media Relations, The Hartford Financial Services Group Inc.

KING, Julie
P.O. Box 4607
Houston, TX 77210-4607
jking05@coair.com
Tel: (713) 324 - 5080
Fax:(713) 324 - 2087

Serves As:
- Manager, Public Relations, Continental Airlines

KING, Karol
P.O. Box 960
Cincinnati, OH 45201-0960
Tel: (513) 287 - 1251
Fax:(513) 651 - 9196

Serves As:
- Manager, Cinergy Foundation, Cinergy Corp.

KING, Kate
One Health Plaza
East Hanover, NJ 07936
kate.king@pharma.novartis.com
Tel: (862) 778 - 5588
Fax:(862) 644 - 8585

Serves As:
- Associate Director, Public Relations, (Novartis Pharmaceuticals Corp.), Novartis Corporation

KING, Larry
4600 Arrowhead Dr.
Ann Arbor, MI 48105
Tel: (734) 622 - 6000
Fax:(734) 622 - 6141

Serves As:
- General Counsel, Flint Ink Corp.

KING, Michelle
130 Royall St.
Canton, MA 02021
michelle.king@dunkinbrands.com
Tel: (781) 737 - 3585
Fax:(781) 986 - 6987

Serves As:
- Media Contact, Dunkin' Brands

KING, Ron
P.O. Box 3283
Tulsa, OK 74102-3283
Tel: (918) 560 - 3500
Fax:(918) 592 - 9492

Serves As:
- Chairman, President and Chief Exec. Officer, BlueCross BlueShield of Oklahoma

KING, Steven Dale
100 Half Day Rd.
Lincolnshire, IL 60069
Tel: (847) 295 - 5000
Fax:(847) 295 - 7634

Serves As:
- Chief Human Resources Officer, Hewitt Associates Inc.

KING, Thomas A.
Lilly Corporate Center
Indianapolis, IN 46285
Tel: (317) 276 - 2000
Fax:(317) 277 - 6579

Serves As:
- Manager, Community Relations; President, Foundation, Eli Lilly and Company

KING, Thomas A.
6300 Wilson Mills Rd.
Mayfield Village, OH 44143
Tel: (440) 461 - 5000
Fax:(440) 446 - 7168
TF: (800) 776 - 4737

Serves As:
- V. President and Treasurer, The Progressive Corporation

Responsibilities include investor relations.

KING, Thomas B.
One Market
Spear Tower, Suite 2400
San Francisco, CA 94105
Tel: (415) 267 - 7000
Fax:(415) 267 - 7268

Serves As:
- President and Chief Exec. Officer, (Pacific Gas and Electric Co.), PG & E Corp.

KING, W. Russell
P.O. Box 51777
New Orleans, LA 70151
Tel: (504) 582 - 4000
Fax:(504) 582 - 1847
TF: (800) 535 - 7094

Serves As:
- Senior V. President, International Relations and Federal Government Relations, Freeport-McMoRan Copper and Gold Inc.

KINGSCOTT, Kathleen N.
1301 K St. NW
Suite 1200
Washington, DC 20005
Tel: (202) 515 - 5193
Fax:(202) 515 - 4943

Registered Federal Lobbyist.

Serves As:
- Director, Public Policy Programs, Internat'l Business Machines Corp. (IBM)

KINNAW, Kevin J.
19001 S. Western Ave.
M/S A107
Torrance, CA 90509
Tel: (310) 468 - 3938
Fax:(310) 468 - 7808

Serves As:
- Manager, National State Government Affairs, (Toyota Motor Sales - USA), Toyota Motor North America, Inc.

KINNEY, Janie Ann
1500 K St. NW
Suite 650
Washington, DC 20005
Tel: (202) 715 - 1000
Fax:(202) 715 - 1001

Registered Federal Lobbyist.
Serves As:
- V. President, Federal Government Relations and Public Policy, GlaxoSmithKline Research and Development

KINNEY, Michael
P.O. Box 1468
Wall, NJ 07719
Tel: (732) 938 - 1031
Fax:(732) 938 - 3154

Serves As:
- Media Contact, New Jersey Resources Corp.

KINNEY, Mike
414 Union St.
Suite 2000
Nashville, TN 37219
Tel: (615) 986 - 5600
TF: (877) 744 - 5600

Serves As:
- Investor Relations Contact, Louisiana-Pacific Corporation

KINSALL, Kevin R.
One N. Central Ave.
Phoenix, AZ 85004-3014
kkinsall@phelpsdodge.com
Tel: (602) 366 - 8100
Fax:(602) 234 - 8337
TF: (800) 528 - 1182

Serves As:
- Director, State and Local Governmental Relations, Phelps Dodge Corp.

KINZEL, Will C.
1001 G St. NW
Suite 100 East
Washington, DC 20001
Tel: (202) 737 - 7575
Fax:(202) 737 - 9090

Registered Federal Lobbyist.
Serves As:
- Manager, Government Affairs, Case New Holland Inc.

KINZEY, Ruth
P.O. Box 1330
Salisbury, NC 28145-1330
Tel: (704) 633 - 8250
Ext: 2892
Fax:(704) 633 - 8250

Serves As:
- Corporate Communications Director, Food Lion LLC

KIRBY, Sue
P.O. Box 500
Beaverton, OR 97077
Tel: (503) 627 - 7111
Fax:(503) 567 - 3449
TF: (800) 835 - 9433

Serves As:
- V. President, Human Resources, Tektronix, Inc.

KIRCHER, Christopher P.
One ConAgra Dr.
Omaha, NE 68102-5001
Tel: (402) 595 - 4000

Serves As:
- V. President, Communications, ConAgra Foods, Inc.

KIRCHNER, Audrey
222 S. Ninth St.
Suite 2300
Minneapolis, MN 55402-4099
Tel: (612) 376 - 3007
Fax:(612) 376 - 3150

Serves As:
- Administrative Assistant, Bemis Company, Inc.

Responsibilities include corporate contributions.

KIRCHOFFNER, Don
P.O. Box A-3005
Chicago, IL 60690-3005
Tel: (312) 394 - 3001
Fax:(312) 394 - 2995

Serves As:
- V. President, Corporate Communications, Exelon Corp.

KIRINCIC, Paul E.
One Post St.
San Francisco, CA 94104-5296
Tel: (415) 983 - 8300
Fax:(415) 983 - 7160

Serves As:
- Senior V. President, Human Resources, McKesson Corp.

KIRKBRIDE, Jean
P.O. Box 8700
Grand Rapids, MI 49518
jean_kirkbride@spartanstores.com
Tel: (616) 878 - 8319
Fax:(616) 878 - 2775

Serves As:
- Exec. Assistant, Spartan Stores Inc.

Responsibilities include investor relations.

KIRKHAM, Brandan
700 13th St., NW
Suite 950
Washington, DC 20005
Tel: (202) 654 - 4499
Fax:(202) 654 - 4493

Registered Federal Lobbyist.
Serves As:
- Representative, Federal Government Affairs, Marathon Oil Corp.

KIRKHORN, Erik
201 E. Fourth St.
Cincinnati, OH 45202
erik.kirkhorn@convergys.com
Tel: (513) 723 - 4900
Fax:(513) 421 - 8624
TF: (800) 344 - 3000

Serves As:
- Director, Government Relations, Convergys Corp.

KIRKISH, Sara
1350 I St. NW
Suite 1000
Washington, DC 20005
Tel: (202) 962 - 5379
Fax:(202) 336 - 7228

Registered Federal Lobbyist.
Serves As:
- Regulatory Manager, Safety and Energy, Ford Motor Co.

KIRKPATRICK, Linda
2000 Purchase St.
Purchase, NY 10577-2509
Tel: (914) 249 - 2000
Fax:(914) 249 - 4206

Serves As:
- Treasurer, Mastercard Internat'l Employees PAC, MasterCard Internat'l

KIRKPATRICK, Robert K.
300 Park Ave.
New York, NY 10022
Tel: (212) 310 - 2000
Fax:(212) 310 - 3284

Serves As:
- V. President, Global Media, Colgate-Palmolive Co.

KIRKPATRICK, Ron
19001 S. Western Ave.
Torrance, CA 90509
Tel: (310) 468 - 7802
Fax:(310) 468 - 7800

Serves As:
- National Manager, Internal Communications, Toyota Motor North America, Inc.

KIRKUS, Sandra L.
P.O. Box 502
Greenville, SC 29602
Tel: (864) 241 - 5400
Fax:(864) 241 - 5401

Serves As:
- Treasurer, Libety Corp. Federal PAC, Liberty Corp.

KIRSCH, William S.
11825 N. Pennsylvania St.
Carmel, IN 46032
Tel: (317) 817 - 6100
TF: (800) 888 - 4918

Serves As:
- President and Chief Exec. Officer, Conseco, Inc.

KIRTLAND, Jennifer
500 McCarthy Blvd.
Milpitas, CA 95035
investor_relations@maxtor.com
Tel: (408) 324 - 7056
Fax:(408) 952 - 3600
TF: (800) 262 - 9867

Serves As:
- Senior Director, Investor Relations, Maxtor Corp.

KIRTMAN, Deanna M.
1550 Crystal Dr.
Crystal Square 2, Suite 300
Arlington, VA 22202
Tel: (703) 413 - 5911
Fax:(703) 413 - 5888

Registered Federal Lobbyist.
Serves As:
- Director, Legislative Affairs, Navy Programs, Lockheed Martin Corp.

KISER, David
343 State St.
Rochester, NY 14650-0516
david.kiser@kodak.com
Tel: (585) 724 - 4000
Fax:(585) 724 - 1724

Serves As:
- V. President and Director, Corporate Health, Safety and Environment, Eastman Kodak Company

KISSAM, IV, Luther
330 S. Fourth St.
Richmond, VA 23219
Tel: (804) 788 - 6000
Fax:(804) 788 - 5688

Serves As:
- PAC Treasurer, Albemarle Corp.

KISSEL, Marie
1401 H St. NW
Suite 700
Washington, DC 20005
Tel: (202) 414 - 6732
Fax:(202) 414 - 6741

Registered Federal Lobbyist.
Serves As:
- Senior Manager, Trade Policy, DaimlerChrysler Corp.

KISSELL, Felise G.
555 Glenridge Connector NE
Suite 300
Atlanta, GA 30342
fkissell@afce.com
Tel: (404) 459 - 4450

Serves As:
- V. President, Investor Relations and Finance, AFC Enterprises

KISSINGER, Jim
2001 Edmund Halley Dr.
Reston, VA 20191
Tel: (703) 433 - 4000

Serves As:
- Senior V. President, Human Resources, Sprint Nextel

KISTLER, Brenda Peters
RR 1, Box 88A
Tallula, IL 62688
brenda-kistler@worldnet.att.net
Tel: (217) 632 - 2691
Fax:(217) 632 - 2710

Serves As:
- Government Affairs Advocate, Farmers Group, Inc.

KITCHEL, Gretchen S.
P.O. Box 53999
M/S 9988
Phoenix, AZ 85072-3999
gretchen.kitchel@pinnaclewest.com
Tel: (602) 250 - 2832

Serves As:
- Senior Public Affairs Representative, Pinnacle West Capital Corp.

KITCHEN, Charles A.
1200 N. Nash St.
Suite 1150
Arlington, VA 22209
ckitchen@ato.com
Tel: (703) 527 - 2099
Fax:(703) 527 - 2092

Registered Federal Lobbyist.
Serves As:
- Director, Government Relations, ATOFINA Chemicals, Inc.

KITCHENS, John L.
P.O. Box 029100
Miami, FL 33102
john_kitchens@fpl.com
Tel: (305) 552 - 4806
Fax:(305) 552 - 2144

Serves As:
- Corporate Contributions Administrator, (Florida Power & Light Company), FPL Group, Inc.

KITEI, Lisa
100 Jim Moran Blvd.
Deerfield Beach, FL 33442
Tel: (954) 429 - 2000
Fax:(954) 429 - 2300

Serves As:
- V. President, Corporate Communications, JM Family Enterprises, Inc.

KITTNER, Bert
3900 Paramount Pkwy.
Morrisville, NC 27560
bert.kittner@rtp.ppdi.com
Tel: (919) 462 - 5509
Fax:(919) 462 - 4274

Serves As:
- Manager, Corporate Communications, Pharmaceutical Product Development, Inc.

KITTREDGE, Francine
745 Seventh Ave.
New York, NY 10019
Tel: (212) 526 - 7000

Serves As:
- Managing Director, Lehman Brothers Philanthropy, Lehman Brothers

KIVETT, Melissa
One Chase Manhattan Plaza
41st Floor
New York, NY 10005
melissa.kivett@assurant.com
Tel: (212) 859 - 7029
Fax:(212) 859 - 7010

Serves As:
- V. President, Investor Relations, Assurant

KLAASSEN, Paul J.
7902 Westpark Dr.
McLean, VA 22102
Tel: (703) 273 - 7500
Fax:(703) 744 - 1601
TF: (888) 434 - 4648

Serves As:
- Founder, Chairman, and Chief Exec. Officer, Sunrise Assisted Living, Inc.

Also serves as Chairman, Sunrise Assisted Living Foundation, Inc.

KLAASSEN, Teresa M.
7902 Westpark Dr.
McLean, VA 22102
Tel: (703) 273 - 7500
Fax:(703) 744 - 1601
TF: (888) 434 - 4648

Serves As:
- Secretary, Sunrise Assisted Living Foundation, Inc., Sunrise Assisted Living, Inc.

KLAPPA, Gale E.
231 W. Michigan
Milwaukee, WI 53203
Tel: (414) 221 - 4525
Fax:(414) 221 - 4519

Serves As:
- Chairman and Chief Exec. Officer, We Energies
- Chairman, President and Chief Exec. Officer, Wisconsin Energy Corp.

KLATSKY, Bruce J.
200 Madison Ave.
New York, NY 10016
Tel: (212) 381 - 3500
Fax:(212) 381 - 3959

Serves As:
- Chairman and Chief Exec. Officer, Phillips-Van Heusen Corp.

Responsibilities include corporate philanthropy.

KLEBE, Elizabeth L.
7201 Hamilton Blvd.
Allentown, PA 18195-1501
klebeel@airproducts.com
Tel: (610) 481 - 4697
Fax:(610) 841 - 5900

Serves As:
- V. President, Corporate Communications, Air Products and Chemicals, Inc.

KLEEMEIER, Judith
Ten Finderne Ave.
Bridgewater, NJ 08807
Tel: (908) 203 - 2800
Fax:(908) 203 - 2918

Serves As:
- Director, Human Resources, ICI American Holdings, Inc.

Responsibilities include corporate philanthropy.

KLEIN, Alex
2001 Edmund Halley Dr.
Reston, VA 20191
Tel: (703) 433 - 4000

Registered Federal Lobbyist.
Serves As:
- Representative, Sprint Nextel

KLEIN, David H.
165 Court St.
Rochester, NY 14647
Tel: (585) 454 - 1700
Fax:(585) 238 - 4233

Serves As:
- Chief Exec. Officer, The Lifetime Healthcare Companies

KLEIN, Jeff
P.O. Box 1000
Charlotte, NC 28201-1000
Tel: (704) 522 - 2000
Fax:(704) 522 - 2055

Serves As:
- PAC Contact, Royal & SunAlliance USA Inc.

KLEIN, John
Bridgeport Center
850 Main St.
Bridgeport, CT 06604-4913
john.klein@peoples.com
Tel: (203) 338 - 7171

Serves As:
- Chairman, Chief Exec. Officer and President, People's Bank

KLEIN, Jonathan
3135 Easton Tpk.
Bldg. E2E
Fairfield, CT 06431
jonathan.klein@ge.com
Tel: (203) 373 - 2241
Fax:(203) 373 - 3131

Serves As:
- Corporate Communications Contact, General Electric Co.

KLEIN, Kenneth H.
1401 H St. NW
Suite 200
Washington, DC 20005
Tel: (202) 414 - 1287
Fax:(202) 414 - 1217

Registered Federal Lobbyist.
Serves As:
- Director, International External Affairs, Xerox Corp.

KLEIN, Mark
P.O. Box 5625
Minneapolis, MN 55440-5625
mark_klein@cargill.com
Tel: (952) 742 - 6211
Fax:(952) 742 - 7393

Serves As:
- Public Affairs Counselor, Cargill, Incorporated

KLEIN, Mary
P.O Box 19002
Green Bay, WI 54307-9002
mklein@wpsr.com
Tel: (920) 433 - 5522
Fax:(920) 433 - 5741

Serves As:
- Foundation Contact, Wisconsin Public Service Corp.

KLEIN, Paul N.
2244 Walnut Grove Ave.
Rosemead, CA 91770
kleinpn@sce.com
Tel: (626) 302 - 7935
Fax: (626) 302 - 8066

Serves As:
• Manager, Corporate Communications, Southern California Edison, an Edison Internat'l Co.

KLEIN, Scott W.
150 N. Clinton St.
Chicago, IL 60661
Tel: (312) 726 - 1221
Fax: (312) 726 - 0360
TF: (800) 317 - 6245

Serves As:
• President and Chief Exec. Officer, Information Resources, Inc.

KLEIN, Starr T.
P.O. Box 25107
Chattanooga, TN 37422-5107
Tel: (423) 510 - 7005
Fax: (423) 510 - 7015
TF: (866) 695 - 2470

Serves As:
• Secretary, The Dixie Group, Inc.
Responsibilities include corporate philanthropy.

KLEIN, Ward
533 Maryville University Dr.
St. Louis, MO 63141
Tel: (314) 985 - 2000
Fax: (314) 982 - 2201
TF: (800) 383 - 7328

Serves As:
• Chief Exec. Officer, Energizer Holdings Inc.

KLEINER, Amy
8000 S. Federal Way
Boise, ID 83707
Tel: (208) 368 - 4000
Fax: (208) 368 - 2536

Registered Federal Lobbyist.
Serves As:
• Representative, Micron Technology, Inc.

KLEPPE, Roger
3535 Blue Cross Rd.
Eagan, MN 55122--115
Tel: (651) 662 - 8000
TF: (800) 382 - 2000

Serves As:
• Senior V. President, Human Resources, Blue Cross and Blue Shield of Minnesota

KLEVEN, C. F.
3M Center
St. Paul, MN 55144-1000
Tel: (651) 733 - 1110
Fax: (651) 733 - 9973

Serves As:
• Manager, Contributions and Secretary, 3M Foundation, 3M Company

KLIMEK, Mary
5501 American Blvd. West
Minneapolis, MN 55437
Tel: (952) 830 - 3235

Serves As:
• Foundation Director, Jostens, Inc.

KLIMSTRA, Cindy T.
200 N. Milwaukee Ave.
Vernon Hills, IL 60061
cklimstra@cdw.com
Tel: (847) 968 - 0268
Fax: (847) 465 - 3444
TF: (800) 800 - 4239

Serves As:
• Director, Investor Relations, CDW Corp.

KLINE, Deb
211 Mount Airy Rd.
Basking Ridge, NJ 07920
klined@avaya.com
Tel: (908) 953 - 6179
Fax: (908) 953 - 7609

Serves As:
• Corporate Communications, Eastern North America and Canada, Avaya Inc.

KLINE, Douglas E.
101 Ash St.
HQ15A
San Diego, CA 92101-3017
dkline@sempra.com
Tel: (619) 696 - 4866
Fax: (619) 696 - 4379
TF: (877) 736 - 7721

Serves As:
• Director, Public Relations, Sempra Energy

KLINE, Lowry F.
P.O. Box 723040
Atlanta, GA 31139-0040
Tel: (770) 989 - 3000
Fax: (770) 989 - 3363

Serves As:
• Chairman of the Board, Coca-Cola Enterprises Inc.

KLINE, Riddi
5555 Darrow Rd.
Hudson, OH 44236
Tel: (330) 463 - 6915
Fax: (330) 463 - 6675

Serves As:
• Public Relations Contact, Jo-Ann Stores, Inc.

KLINE, Steven L.
900 Seventh St. NW, Suite 950
Washington, DC 20001-3886
Tel: (202) 638 - 3500
Fax: (202) 638 - 3522

Registered Federal Lobbyist.
Serves As:
• V. President, Federal Governmental and Regulatory Relations, (Pacific Gas and Electric Co.), PG & E Corp.

KLINE, Thomas E.
Administrative Center
2000 N. M-63
Benton Harbor, MI 49022-2692
thomas_e_kline@email.whirlpool.com
Tel: (269) 923 - 3738
Fax: (269) 923 - 5443

Serves As:
• Director, External Communications, Whirlpool Corp.

KLINEFELTER, Chris W.
One ConAgra Dr.
Omaha, NE 68102-5001
Tel: (402) 595 - 4154
Fax: (402) 595 - 4083

Serves As:
• V. President, Investor Relations, ConAgra Foods, Inc.

KLINESTIVER, John
500 McCarthy Blvd.
Milpitas, CA 95035
Tel: (408) 894 - 5000
Fax: (408) 952 - 3600
TF: (800) 262 - 9867

Serves As:
• Senior V. President, Human Resources, Maxtor Corp.

KLINETOB, Sametta
1275 K St. NW
Suite 1200
Washington, DC 20005
Tel: (202) 216 - 0700
Fax: (202) 216 - 0824

Serves As:
• Director, Government Affairs, Delta Air Lines, Inc.

KLING, Cris
P.O. Box 496
215 S. Cascade St. S.
Fergus Falls, MN 56538-0496
ckling@otpco.com
Tel: (218) 739 - 8297
Fax: (218) 739 - 8762
TF: (866) 410 - 8780

Serves As:
• Director, Public Relations, Otter Tail Power Co.

KLINGLESMITH, Candace
One Energy Pl.
Pensacola, FL 32520
Tel: (850) 444 - 6806
Fax: (850) 444 - 6448
TF: (800) 225 - 5797

Serves As:
• Corporate Services Specialist; and Foundation Contact, Gulf Power Co.

KLOOSTERBOER, Jay
4300 Wilson Blvd.
11th Floor
Arlington, VA 22203
Tel: (703) 522 - 1315
Fax: (703) 528 - 4510

Serves As:
• V. President and Chief Human Resources Officer, The AES Corp.

KLOPFENSTEIN, Vaughn M.
P.O. Box 6000
Sioux City, IA 51102-6000
Tel: (712) 277 - 1340
Fax: (712) 277 - 7383

Serves As:
• Treasurer, Terra Industries Inc. PAC, Terra Industries Inc.

KLOSE, Kevin
635 Massachusetts Ave. NW
Washington, DC 20001
kklose@npr.org
Tel: (202) 513 - 2000
Fax: (202) 513 - 3329

Serves As:
• President and Chief Exec. Officer, Nat'l Public Radio

KLUCSIK, David
259 Prospect Plains Rd.
Cranbury, NJ 08512
Tel: (609) 860 - 3616
Fax: (609) 409 - 8652

Serves As:
• Director, Communications, Rhodia, Inc.

KLUG, Jonathan P.
P.O. Box 2933
San Antonio, TX 78299-2933
Tel: (210) 821 - 4105
TF: (800) 351 - 7221

Serves As:
• Treasurer, SBC Communications Inc. Employee Federal PAC, SBC Communications Inc.

KLUMPYAN, Julie K.
P.O. Box 500
San Antonio, TX 78249-112
Tel: (210) 345 - 2435
Fax: (210) 345 - 2646
TF: (800) 531 - 7911

Serves As:
• Manager, Government Affairs, Valero Energy Corp.

KMETKO, Christy
5875 Landerbrook Dr.
Suite 300
Cleveland, OH 44124-4017
ir@naccoind.com
Tel: (440) 449 - 9669
Fax:(440) 449 - 9607

Serves As:
- Investor Relations and Media Contact, NACCO Industries

KMIECIK, Tom
1100 Terminal Tower
50 Public Square
Cleveland, OH 44113-2203
tomkmiecik@forestcity.net
Tel: (216) 416 - 3215
Fax:(216) 263 - 4808

Serves As:
- Assistant Treasurer, Forest City Enterprises, Inc.

Responsibilities include investor relations.

KNAACK-ESBECK, Jane
5820 Westown Pkwy.
West Des Moines, IA 50266-8223
Tel: (515) 267 - 2840
Fax:(515) 267 - 2817

Serves As:
- V. President, Human Resources, Hy-Vee, Inc.

KNAPP, Rick
59 Route Ten
Bldg. 404/306
East Hanover, NJ 07936
Tel: (862) 778 - 8421

Serves As:
- Head, State Government Affairs and Health Policy, Novartis Corporation

KNAPPEN, Ted
1101 14th St., NW
Washington, DC 20005
tknappe@peyser.com
Tel: (202) 638 - 3490
Fax:(202) 638 - 3516

Serves As:
- Consultant, Government Affairs, Greyhound Lines, Inc.

KNELL, Gary E.
One Lincoln Plaza
New York, NY 10023
Tel: (212) 595 - 3456
Fax:(212) 875 - 6088

Serves As:
- President and Chief Exec. Officer, Sesame Workshop

KNICKEL, Carin S.
P.O. Box 2197
Houston, TX 77252-2197
Tel: (281) 293 - 1000
Fax:(281) 293 - 1440

Serves As:
- V. President, Human Resources, ConocoPhillips

KNIGHT, Philip H.
One Bowerman Dr.
Beaverton, OR 97005
Tel: (503) 671 - 6453
Fax:(503) 671 - 6300

Serves As:
- Chairman of the Board, Nike, Inc.

KNIK, Bernadette
115 W. College Dr.
Marshall, MN 56258
Tel: (507) 532 - 3274
Fax:(507) 537 - 8224
TF: (800) 533 - 5290

Serves As:
- Senior V. President, Human Resources, The Schwan Food Co.

KNISELY, Anne
P.O. Box 2463
Houston, TX 77252-2463
Tel: (713) 241 - 6161
Fax:(713) 241 - 6988

Serves As:
- Manager, Media Relations, Shell Oil Co.

KNOEBEL, Cindy
P.O. Box 21488
Greensboro, NC 27420-1488
cindy_knoebel@vfc.com
Tel: (336) 424 - 6189
Fax:(336) 424 - 7631

Serves As:
- V. President, Financial and Corporate Communications, V. F. Corporation

Responsibilities include investor relations.

KNOLL, Albert B.
1130 Connecticut Ave. NW
Suite 710
Washington, DC 20036
abknoll@sunocoinc.com
Tel: (202) 628 - 1010
Fax:(202) 628 - 1041

Registered Federal Lobbyist.
Serves As:
- Director, Federal Government Relations, Sunoco, Inc.

KNOTT, Kerry
2001 Pennsylvania Ave. NW
Suite 500
Washington, DC 20006
kerry_knott@comcast.com
Tel: (202) 379 - 7105
Fax:(202) 466 - 7718

Registered Federal Lobbyist.
Serves As:
- V. President, Federal Government Affairs, Comcast Corporation

KNOWLTON, Timothy S.
P.O. Box 3599
Battle Creek, MI 49016-3599
Tel: (269) 961 - 2837
Fax:(269) 961 - 6646
TF: (800) 535 - 5644

Serves As:
- V. President, Corporate Social Responsibility, Kellogg Co.

KNOX, Mark A.
P.O. Box 3014
Naperville, IL 60566-7014
mknox@nicor.com
Tel: (630) 305 - 9500
Ext: 2529
Fax:(630) 357 - 7534
TF: (888) 642 - 6748

Serves As:
- Director, Investor Relations, Nicor, Inc.

KNUDSEN, Nancy
1835 Dueber Ave. SW
Canton, OH 44706
Tel: (330) 438 - 3000
Fax:(330) 471 - 3810
TF: (800) 223 - 1954

Serves As:
- Program Director, Timken Foundation of Canton, The Timken Co.

KNUPP, Ralph
7628 Thorndike Rd.
Greensboro, NC 27409-9421
Tel: (336) 664 - 1233
Fax:(336) 931 - 7454

Serves As:
- V. President, Human Resources, RF Micro Devices, Inc.

Responsibilities include corporate philanthropy.

KNUTH, Kathy S.
Three Lakes Dr.
Northfield, IL 60093-2753
kknuth@kraft.com
Tel: (847) 646 - 2666
Fax:(847) 646 - 6005

Serves As:
- Senior Director, Corporate Affairs, North America Commercial, Kraft Foods, Inc.

KNUTSON, Kent
101 Constitution Ave., NW
Suite 800 West
Washington, DC 20001
kent_knutson@homedepot.com
Tel: (202) 772 - 2497
Fax:(202) 772 - 2496

Registered Federal Lobbyist.
Serves As:
- V. President, Government Relations, The Home Depot, Inc.

KNUTSON, Marlys
2100 Hwy. 55
Medina, MN 55340
marlys.knutson@polarisind.com
Tel: (763) 417 - 8650
Fax:(763) 542 - 0599

Serves As:
- Manager, Corporate Communications, Polaris Industries Inc.

KOBAYASHI, Todd
P.O. Box 418679
Kansas City, MO 64141-9679
Tel: (816) 556 - 2904
Fax:(816) 556 - 2992

Serves As:
- V. President, Strategy and Investor Relations, Great Plains Energy, Inc.

KOBER, Lori Ann
112 W. 34th St.
New York, NY 10120
lkober@footlocker-inc.com
Tel: (212) 720 - 3700
Fax:(212) 720 - 4397

Serves As:
- V. President, Public Relations, Footlocker Inc.

KOBERLE, Roseanne
P.O. Box 1468
Wall, NJ 07719
Tel: (732) 938 - 1112
Fax:(732) 938 - 3154

Serves As:
- Manager, Corporate Communications, New Jersey Resources Corp.

KOCH, Charles G.
4111 E. 37th St., North
Wichita, KS 67220
Tel: (316) 828 - 5500
Fax:(316) 828 - 5739

Serves As:
- Chairman and Chief Exec. Officer, Koch Industries, Inc.

KOCH, Craig R.
225 Brae Blvd.
Park Ridge, NJ 07656
Tel: (201) 307 - 2600
Fax:(201) 307 - 2644

Serves As:
- Chairman and Chief Exec. Officer, Hertz Corp.

KOCH, Douglas
P.O. Box 29
St. Louis, MO 63166-0029
dkoch@brownshoe.com
Tel: (314) 854 - 4120
Fax:(314) 854 - 4274

Serves As:
• Senior V. President, Human Resources, Brown Shoe Co., Inc.

KOCH, Kevin
4747 McLane Pkwy.
Temple, TX 76504
Tel: (254) 771 - 7500
Fax:(254) 771 - 7244

Serves As:
• Treasurer, McLane Company Inc. Federal PAC, McLane Company, Inc.

KOCHMAN, Ron
560 Lexington Ave.
15th Floor
New York, NY 10022
rkochman@volt.com
Tel: (212) 704 - 2490
Fax:(212) 704 - 2424
TF: (800) 533 - 2401

Serves As:
• V. President, Investor Relations and Corporate Communicatons, Volt Information Sciences, Inc.

KOCKLER, Kimberly
19 N. Main St.
Wilkes-Barre, PA 18711-0302
Tel: (570) 200 - 6300

Serves As:
• Director, Policy Management, Blue Cross of Northeastern Pennsylvania
Responsibilities include political action.

KOEHLER, Susan
9197 S. Peoria St.
Englewood, CO 80112-5833
Tel: (303) 397 - 8313
Fax:(303) 397 - 8199
TF: (800) 835 - 3832

Serves As:
• Media Relations, TeleTech Holdings, Inc.

KOENIG, Bob
P.O. Box 321
Oklahoma City, OK 73101-0321
Tel: (405) 553 - 3358

Serves As:
• Manager, Regulatory Affairs, OGE Energy Corp.

KOENIG, Brian C.
5030 Sugarloaf Pkwy.
Lawrenceville, GA 30042-2869
brian.koenig@sciatl.com
Tel: (770) 236 - 5000
Fax:(770) 236 - 4775
TF: (800) 236 - 5000

Serves As:
• Senior V. President, Human Resources, Scientific-Atlanta, Inc.

KOENIG, Julie
700 Central Ave.
Louisville, KY 40208
Tel: (502) 636 - 4502
Fax:(502) 636 - 4430
TF: (800) 283 - 3729

Serves As:
• Director, Communications, Churchill Downs, Inc.

KOESTLER, Ph.D., Thomas P.
2000 Galloping Hill Rd.
Kenilworth, NJ 07033
Tel: (908) 740 - 2204

Serves As:
• Exec. V. President, Global Regulatory Affairs and Global Project Management, Schering-Plough Corporation

KOFFEL, Martin M.
600 Montgomery St.
26th Floor
San Francisco, CA 94111-2728
Tel: (415) 774 - 2700
Fax:(415) 398 - 1904

Serves As:
• Chairman, President and Chief Exec. Officer, URS Corp.

KOFOL, Milan
One Boston Scientific Pl.
Natick, MA 01760-1537
kofolm@bsci.com
Tel: (508) 650 - 8595
Fax:(508) 647 - 2200

Serves As:
• V. President, Investor Relations and Treasurer, Boston Scientific Corp.

KOGA, Nobuyuki
Two World Financial Center
Building B
New York, NY 10028-1198
Tel: (212) 667 - 9300
Fax:(212) 667 - 1058

Serves As:
• President and Chief Exec. Officer, Nomura Securities Internat'l, Inc.

KOHLBERGER, Richard A.
100 W. Putnam Ave.
Greenwich, CT 06830
Tel: (203) 622 - 3674
Fax:(203) 863 - 7250

Serves As:
• Senior V. President, Human Resources and Corporate Administration, General Counsel and Corporate Secretary, UST Inc.

KOHLER, Jr., Herbert V.
444 Highland Dr.
Kohler, WI 53044
herbert.kohler@kohler.com
Tel: (920) 457 - 4441
Fax:(920) 457 - 1271

Serves As:
• Chairman, President and Chief Exec. Officer, Kohler Co.

KOHLER, Laura
444 Highland Dr.
Kohler, WI 53044
laura.kohler@kohler.com
Tel: (920) 457 - 4441
Ext: 72607
Fax:(920) 459 - 1839

Serves As:
• Senior V. President, Human Resources, Kohler Co.

KOHNER, Phil
One North Dale Mabry, Suite 950
Tampa, FL 33609
Tel: (813) 877 - 2726
Fax:(813) 739 - 0204

Serves As:
• Manager, Human Resources, Masonite Internat'l Corp.

KOHRT, Carl F.
505 King Ave.
Columbus, OH 43201-2693
Tel: (614) 424 - 6424
Fax:(614) 424 - 3260
TF: (800) 201 - 2011

Serves As:
• President and Chief Exec. Officer, Battelle

KOIRTYOHANN, Barbara J.
P.O. Box 419580
Mail Drop 288
Kansas City, MO 64141-6580
bkoirt2@hallmark.com
Tel: (816) 274 - 5244
Fax:(816) 274 - 5061

Serves As:
• Director, Public Affairs, Hallmark Cards, Inc.

KOLBE, Peter
Gateway One
101 Gateway Centre Pkwy.
Richmond, VA 23235
Tel: (804) 267 - 8000
Fax:(804) 267 - 8836
TF: (800) 446 - 7086

Serves As:
• V. President, Government Relations, LandAmerica Financial Group, Inc.

KOLEGA, Andra
920 Main St.
Kansas City, MO 64105-2017
Tel: (816) 221 - 4000
Fax:(816) 480 - 4617

Serves As:
• V. President, Community Relations, AMC Entertainment Inc.

KOLESNIKOFF, Nicholai
413 New Jersey Ave., SE
Washington, DC 20003
Tel: (202) 543 - 1749
Fax:(202) 543 - 1680

Registered Federal Lobbyist.
Serves As:
• V. President, Government Relations, Jacobs Engineering Group Inc.

KOLING, Barry R.
919 E. Main St.
Richmond, VA 23219
barry.koling@suntrust.com
Tel: (804) 782 - 5000
Fax:(804) 782 - 7064

Serves As:
• First V. President and Director, Corporate Communications, SunTrust Banks, Inc.

KOLKMANN, Richard J.
414 Nicollet Mall
Minneapolis, MN 55401-1927
dick.kolkmann@xcelenergy.com
Tel: (612) 215 - 4559

Serves As:
• Managing Director, Investor Relations, Xcel Energy, Inc.

KOLLEDA, Leslie
1481 S. Nova Rd.
Daytona Beach, FL 32114
Tel: (386) 947 - 5158
Fax:(386) 258 - 7939

Serves As:
• Manager, Public Relations, The Progressive Corporation

KOMINEK, Anne G.
1300 I St. NW
Suite 420 East
Washington, DC 20005
Tel: (202) 789 - 6525
Fax:(202) 789 - 6593

Serves As:
• PAC Contact, Ceridian Corp.

KONDO, Koichi
1919 Torrance Blvd.
Torrance, CA 90501-2746
Tel: (310) 783 - 2000
Fax:(310) 783 - 3900

Serves As:
• President and Chief Exec. Officer, American Honda Motor Co., Inc.

KONG, David
6201 N. 24th Pkwy. Tel: (602) 957 - 4200
Phoenix, AZ 85016-2023 TF: (800) 528 - 1234

Serves As:
• President and Chief Exec. Officer, Best Western Internat'l

KOOKESH, Albert M.
One Sealaska Plaza, Suite 400 Tel: (907) 586 - 1512
Juneau, AK 99801-1276 Fax:(907) 586 - 2304

Serves As:
• Chairman of the Board, Sealaska Corp.

KOON, Barbara
P.O. Box 99 Tel: (925) 467 - 3135
Pleasanton, CA 94566-0009

Serves As:
• Coordinator, Safeway Foundation, Safeway Inc.

KOON, Tracy
2200 Mission College Blvd. Tel: (408) 765 - 5609
RN5-56 Fax:(408) 765 - 5101
Santa Clara, CA 95052-8119 TF: (800) 628 - 8686
Tracy.Koon@intel.com

Serves As:
• Manager, Corporate Affairs, Intel Corp.

KOONCE, Neil W.
804 Green Valley Rd.
Greensboro, NC 27415

Serves As:
• Treasurer, Cone Mills PAC, Internat'l Textiles Group

KOONCE, Thomas
800 Connecticut Ave. NW Tel: (202) 533 - 1100
Suite 600 Fax:(202) 533 - 1134
Washington, DC 20006

Registered Federal Lobbyist.
Serves As:
• Representative, Accenture

KOPCZICK, Elise M.
100 First Stamford Pl. Tel: (203) 363 - 7349
Stamford, CT 06902 Fax:(203) 363 - 7295
ekopczick@craneco.com

Serves As:
• V. President, Human Resources, Crane Co.

KOPECKY, Sr., John J.
1401 I St. NW Tel: (202) 336 - 7400
Suite 600 Fax:(202) 336 - 7515
Washington, DC 20005

Registered Federal Lobbyist.
Serves As:
• Representative, United Technologies Corp.

KOPPEL, Robert
1133 19th St. NW Tel: (202) 887 - 3830
Washington, DC 20036 Fax:(202) 887 - 3123

Registered Federal Lobbyist.
Serves As:
• V. President, Regulatory, MCI, Inc.

KOPPERUD, Steve
818 Connecticut Ave. NW Tel: (202) 776 - 0071
Suite 225
Washington, DC 20006

Registered Federal Lobbyist.
Serves As:
• Contact, Government Affairs, Nestle Purina PetCare Co.

KOPPY, Brian D.
P.O. Box 489 Tel: (860) 973 - 2126
Bristol, CT 06011-0489 Fax:(860) 589 - 3507

Serves As:
• Investor Relations Contact, Barnes Group Inc.

KORDA, William
2621 W. 15th Place Tel: (773) 788 - 3358
Chicago, IL 60608 Fax:(773) 762 - 2194
william.korda@ryersontull.com

Serves As:
• V. President, Human Resources, Ryerson Tull

KORDASIEWICZ, Gloria
6363 Main St. Tel: (716) 857 - 7705
Williamsville, NY 14221 Fax:(716) 857 - 7439
kordasiewiczg@natfuel.com TF: (800) 365 - 3234

Serves As:
• Contact, Nat'l Fuel Political Action Committee, Nat'l Fuel Gas Co.

KORELL, Harold M.
2350 N. Sam Houston Pkwy. East Tel: (281) 618 - 4700
Suite 300 Fax:(281) 618 - 4820
Houston, TX 77032

Serves As:
• Chairman, President and Chief Exec. Officer, Southwestern Energy Co.

KORKUCH, Marylu
One Massachusetts Ave. NW Tel: (202) 408 - 8123
Suite 350 Fax:(202) 296 - 7683
Washington, DC 20001
mkorkuch@chubb.com

Registered Federal Lobbyist.
Serves As:
• V. President and Director, Government Affairs, The Chubb Corp.

KOROPEY, Lesia
One Mercedes Dr. Tel: (201) 573 - 4709
Montvale, NJ 07645 Fax:(201) 573 - 4370
TF: (800) 367 - 6372

Serves As:
• Community and Social Affairs, Mercedes-Benz USA, LLC

KORSTANGE, Jason
200 Lake St. E. Tel: (952) 745 - 2755
Wayzata, MN 55391 Fax:(952) 745 - 2775

Serves As:
• President, TCF Foundation, TCF Financial Corp.
Responsibilities include corporate communications.

KOSAIAN, Rebecca
P.O. Box 75000 Tel: (313) 222 - 7300
mc 3350 Fax:(313) 222 - 6040
Detroit, MI 48275 TF: (800) 521 - 1190

Serves As:
• Employee Communications Representative, Comerica Incorporated

KOSCHE, Peter C.
190 Carondelet Plaza Tel: (314) 480 - 1400
Suite 1530
Clayton, MO 63105-3443
pckosche@corp.olin.com

Serves As:
• Senior V. President, Corporate Affairs, Olin Corp.

KOSH, Mitchell A.
650 Madison Ave. Tel: (212) 318 - 7000
New York, NY 10022 Fax:(212) 888 - 5780

Serves As:
• Senior V. President, Human Resources, Polo Ralph Lauren

KOSOWSKI, James "Jim"
1134 Market St. Tel: (304) 234 - 2440
Wheeling, WV 26003 Fax:(304) 234 - 2442

Serves As:
• PAC Contact, Wheeling-Pittsburgh Steel Corp.

KOSTER, Sherry
Dain Rauscher Plaza Tel: (612) 371 - 2765
60 S. Sixth St., 19th Floor Fax:(612) 371 - 7933
Minneapolis, MN 55402-4422
sherry.koster@rbcdain.com

Serves As:
• Program Manager, RBC Dain Rauscher Foundation, RBC Dain Rauscher Corp.

KOSTERMAN, Gayle P.
1525 Howe St. Tel: (262) 260 - 2000
Racine, WI 53403 Fax:(262) 260 - 6004

Serves As:
• Exec. V. President, Worldwide Human Resources, SC Johnson

KOTHMANN, Cindy
P.O. Box 35167 Tel: (713) 667 - 5601
Houston, TX 77235 Fax:(713) 295 - 5486
ckothmann@stagestores.com TF: (800) 324 - 3244

Serves As:
• Community Relations Contact, Stage Stores, Inc.

KOTICK, Robert A.
3100 Ocean Park Blvd. Tel: (310) 255 - 2000
Santa Monica, CA 90405-3032 Fax:(310) 255 - 2100

Serves As:
• Chairman, Chief Exec. Officer and Director, Activision, Inc.

KOTKE, Connie
8111 Lyndale Ave. South Tel: (952) 887 - 8984
Bloomington, MN 55420-1196 Fax:(952) 887 - 7961
pr@toro.com

Serves As:
• Media Relations Contact, The Toro Co.

KOTKIN, Jeffrey R.
P.O. Box 270
M/S BMW 1
Hartford, CT 06141-0270
Tel: (860) 665 - 5154
Fax:(860) 665 - 5457
TF: (800) 286 - 2000

Serves As:
- V. President, Investor Relations, (Northeast Utilities Service Co.), Northeast Utilities

KOURAKOS, Jessica
2632 Marine Way
Mountain View, CA 94043
Tel: (650) 944 - 6000
Fax:(650) 944 - 3699

Serves As:
- V. President, Investor Relations, Intuit Inc.

KOUROUPAS, Paul
200 Park Ave.
Suite 300
Florham Park, NJ 07932
Tel: (973) 937 - 0100
Fax:(973) 360 - 0148
TF: (800) 336 - 7000

Serves As:
- V. President, and Senior Counsel (Regulatory Affairs), Global Crossing Ltd.

KOURY, Frederick S.
5500 Wayzata Blvd.
Suite 800
Golden Valley, MN 55416-1259
Tel: (763) 545 - 1730

Serves As:
- Senior V. President, Human Resources, Pentair, Inc.

KOUTSKY, Lori J.
400 Robert St. North
St. Paul, MN 55101
lori.koutsky@minnesotamutual.com
Tel: (651) 665 - 3501
Fax:(651) 665 - 4488

Serves As:
- Manager, Community Relations and Foundation, Minnesota Life Insurance Co.

KOVACEVICH, Kathy
9330 Balboa Ave.
San Diego, CA 92123-1516
Tel: (858) 571 - 2544
Fax:(858) 571 - 4064

Serves As:
- Contact, Jack in the Box Foundation, Jack in the Box Inc.

KOVACEVICH, Richard M.
420 Montgomery St.
San Francisco, CA 94104
Tel: (415) 396 - 6408
TF: (800) 411 - 4932

Serves As:
- Chairman, President and Chief Exec. Officer, Wells Fargo & Co.

KOVACS, Patricia
One Imation Place
Oakdale, MN 55128-3414
Tel: (651) 704 - 4762
Fax:(651) 704 - 4200

Serves As:
- Manager, Corporate Communications and Community Affairs, Imation Corp.

Responsibilities include corporate contributions.

KOVAR, Mike L.
2280 N. Greenville Ave.
Richardson, TX 75082
mkovar@fossil.com
Tel: (972) 699 - 2229
Fax:(972) 498 - 9448

Serves As:
- Senior V. President, Chief Financial Officer, and Treasurer, Fossil Inc.

Responsibilities include investor relations.

KOWAL, Katria N.
Ten Penn Center
1801 Market St.
Philadelphia, PA 19103-1699
Tel: (215) 977 - 3000
Fax:(215) 977 - 3409

Serves As:
- PAC Treasurer, Sunoco, Inc.

KOWALSKI, Michael J.
727 Fifth Ave.
New York, NY 10022
Tel: (212) 755 - 8000
Fax:(212) 230 - 6734

Serves As:
- Chairman, President and Chief Exec. Officer, Tiffany & Co.

KOWALSKI, Tom
P.O. Box 300
Detroit, MI 48265-1000
Tel: (313) 556 - 5000
Fax:(248) 696 - 7300

Serves As:
- V. President, Global Communications, General Motors Corp.

KOZAK, Tina
47659 Halyard Dr.
Plymouth, MI 48170
tinadoher@metaldyne.com
Tel: (734) 207 - 6713
Fax:(734) 207 - 6696

Serves As:
- Public Relations Specialist, Metaldyne Corp.

KOZAKEWICZ, Raymond
P.O. Box 85333
Richmond, VA 23293-0001
kozakewicz@mediageneral.com
Tel: (804) 649 - 6748
Fax:(804) 649 - 6865

Serves As:
- Media Contact, Media General Inc.

KOZEL, David F.
200 Madison Ave.
New York, NY 10016
Tel: (212) 381 - 3500
Fax:(212) 381 - 3959

Serves As:
- V. President, Human Resources, Phillips-Van Heusen Corp.

KOZLOWSKI, Elizabeth P.
1295 State St.
Springfield, MA 01111-0001
Tel: (413) 744 - 5633
Fax:(413) 744 - 6005
TF: (800) 767 - 1000

Registered Federal Lobbyist.
Serves As:
- Manager, Grassroots and Communications, MassMutual Financial Group

KOZLOWSKI, Patrice M.
200 Park Ave.
New York, NY 10166
kozlowski.pm@dreyfus.com
Tel: (212) 922 - 6030
Fax:(212) 922 - 6585

Serves As:
- Senior V. President, Corporate Communications, The Dreyfus Corp.

KRABILL, Connie
One Owens Corning Pkwy.
Toledo, OH 43659
Tel: (419) 248 - 8000
Fax:(419) 248 - 6227
TF: (800) 438 - 7465

Serves As:
- Foundation Contact, Owens Corning

KRAHE, Ph.D., Michael J.
100 Erie Insurance Pl.
Erie, PA 16530
Tel: (814) 870 - 2850
Fax:(814) 870 - 2444

Serves As:
- Exec. V. President, Human Development and Leadership, Erie Indeminity Co.

KRAHULEC, James E.
P.O. Box 3165
Harrisburg, PA 17105
Tel: (717) 975 - 5710
Fax:(717) 975 - 3760

Serves As:
- V. President, Government and Trade Relations, Rite Aid Corp.

KRAKOWSKI, Capt. Henry P.
P.O. Box 66100
Chicago, IL 60666
Tel: (847) 700 - 4000
Fax:(847) 700 - 4899

Serves As:
- Vice President, Corporate Safety and Quality Assurance, United Airlines

KRAKOWSKY, Philippe
1114 Ave. of the Americas
New York, NY 10036
pkrakowsky@interpublic.com
Tel: (212) 704 - 1328

Serves As:
- Senior V. President and Director, Corporate Communications, The Interpublic Group of Companies

KRALL, David A.
Avid Technology Park
One Park West
Tewksbury, MA 01876
Tel: (978) 640 - 6789
Fax:(978) 640 - 1366

Serves As:
- President and Chief Exec. Officer, Avid Technology, Inc.

KRAMER, Jack
One CVS Dr.
Woonsocket, RI 02895
Tel: (401) 765 - 1500
Ext: 3005
Fax:(401) 769 - 6012

Serves As:
- Senior V. President, Governmental Affairs and Corporate Relations, CVS

KRAMER, Mindy
2200 Old Germantown Rd.
Delray Beach, FL 33445
Tel: (561) 438 - 4800
Fax:(561) 438 - 4400

Serves As:
- Manager, Public Relations, Office Depot, Inc.

KRAMER, Walter
2000 Market St.
Philadelphia, PA 19103-9000
Tel: (215) 419 - 7149
Fax:(215) 419 - 7591
TF: (800) 225 - 7788

Serves As:
- Manager, Community Relations, ATOFINA Chemicals, Inc.

KRAMUNE, Bruce
1101 Pennsylvania Ave. NW
Suite 400
Washington, DC 20004-2504
Tel: (202) 637 - 3800
Fax:(202) 637 - 3860

Registered Federal Lobbyist.
Serves As:
- Representative, Textron Inc.

KRANE, David
1600 Amphitheatre Pkwy.
Mountain View, CA 94043
david@google.com
Tel: (650) 623 - 4096
Fax:(650) 618 - 1499

Serves As:
- Corporate Public Relations Contact, Google Inc.

KRASNOFF, Eric
25 Harbor Park Dr.
Port Washington, NY 11050
eric_krasnoff@pall.com
Tel: (516) 484 - 5400
Fax:(516) 484 - 5228
TF: (800) 876 - 7255

Serves As:
- Chairman and Chief Exec. Officer, Pall Corp.
Responsibilities include corporate philanthropy.

KRATOVIL, Edward D.
100 W. Putnam Ave.
Greenwich, CT 06830
Tel: (203) 622 - 3667
Fax:(203) 622 - 3315

Registered Federal Lobbyist.
Serves As:
- Senior V. President, Worldwide Government Relations, UST Inc.

KRAUS, Eric A.
Prudential Tower Bldg.
Boston, MA 02199-8004
eric_kraus@gillette.com
Tel: (617) 421 - 7194
Fax:(617) 421 - 7123

Serves As:
- V. President, Corporate Communications, The Gillette Company

KRAUS, Steve
P.O. Box 1231
Madison, WI 53701-1231
skraus@mge.com
Tel: (608) 252 - 7907
Fax:(608) 252 - 7098
TF: (800) 356 - 6423

Serves As:
- Manager, Media Relations, Madison Gas and Electric Co.

KRAUSE, David W.
P.O. Box 7888
Van Nuys, CA 91409-7888
Tel: (818) 986 - 4800
Fax:(818) 379 - 7381

Serves As:
- Chairman of the Board, Sunkist Growers

KRAUSE, Kristin
101 Constitution Ave., NW
Suite 801 East
Washington, DC 20001
kristin.krause@fedex.com
Tel: (202) 218 - 3800
Fax:(202) 218 - 3803

Serves As:
- Senior Communications Specialist, FedEx Corp.

KRAUSE, Robert A.
250 Stephenson Hwy.
Troy, MI 48083
robert.krause@colaik.com
Tel: (248) 733 - 4355

Serves As:
- V. President, Treasurer; and Head, Investor Relations, Collins & Aikman Corp.

KRAUSE, Roy G.
2050 Spectrum Blvd.
Fort Lauderdale, FL 33309
Tel: (954) 308 - 7600
Fax:(954) 938 - 7790

Serves As:
- President and Chief Operating Officer, Spherion Corp.

KRAUSS, Mark
1600 N.W. 163rd St.
Miami, FL 33169
Tel: (305) 625 - 4171
Fax:(305) 625 - 2790

Serves As:
- National Director, Human Resources, Southern Wine & Spirits of America

KRAVETZ, Carolyn
130 Royall St.
Canton, MA 02021
Tel: (781) 737 - 3602
Fax:(781) 986 - 6987

Serves As:
- Media Contact, Dunkin' Brands

KREH, Kent
5770 Fleet St.
Carlsbad, CA 92008
Tel: (760) 696 - 4000
Fax:(760) 696 - 4009
TF: (800) 597 - 5366

Serves As:
- Chairman of the Board, Jenny Craig, Inc.

KREHBIEL, Frederick A.
2222 Wellington Ct.
Lisle, IL 60532
Tel: (630) 969 - 4550
Fax:(630) 969 - 1352
TF: (800) 786 - 6539

Serves As:
- Co-Chairman of the Board, Molex Incorporated

KREHBIEL, Jr., John H.
2222 Wellington Ct.
Lisle, IL 60532
Tel: (630) 969 - 4550
Fax:(630) 969 - 1352
TF: (800) 786 - 6539

Serves As:
- Co-Chairman of the Board, Molex Incorporated

KREIZENBECK, Jason B.
8000 S. Federal Way
Boise, ID 83707
Tel: (208) 368 - 4400
Fax:(208) 368 - 2536

Registered Federal Lobbyist.
Serves As:
- Manager, Government Affairs, Micron Technology, Inc.

KRELL, Joanne K.
P.O. Box 300
Detroit, MI 48265-1000
joanne.k.krell@gm.com
Tel: (313) 665 - 2443
Fax:(248) 696 - 7300

Serves As:
- Manager, Energy/Environment Communciations, General Motors Corp.
- Contact, Corporate Contributions, General Motors Acceptance Corp. (GMAC)

KREMA, Lawrence J.
Two N. Riverside Plaza
Suite 2100
Chicago, IL 60606
lawrence_krema@equityoffice.com
Tel: (312) 466 - 3300
Fax:(312) 454 - 0332

Serves As:
- Senior V. President, Human Resources and Communications, Equity Office Properties Trust

KRESLER, Tisha
200 Park Ave.
Suite 300
Florham Park, NJ 07932
Tel: (973) 937 - 0146
Fax:(973) 360 - 0148
TF: (800) 336 - 7000

Serves As:
- Media Relations Contact, Global Crossing Ltd.

KRESS, John
1700 N. Webster Ct.
Green Bay, WI 54307-9017
Tel: (920) 433 - 5111
Fax:(920) 433 - 5471
TF: (800) 236 - 8400

Serves As:
- Secretary, George Kress Foundation, Green Bay Packaging Inc.

KRESS, William F.
1700 N. Webster Ct.
Green Bay, WI 54307-9017
Tel: (920) 433 - 5111
Fax:(920) 433 - 5471
TF: (800) 236 - 8400

Serves As:
- President, Green Bay Packaging Inc.

KREVOR, Lawrence R.
2001 Edmund Halley Dr.
Reston, VA 20191
Tel: (703) 433 - 4000

Registered Federal Lobbyist.
Serves As:
- V. President, Government Affairs, Sprint Nextel

KRIENS, Scott
1194 N. Mathilda Ave.
Sunnyvale, CA 94089-1206
skriens@juniper.net
Tel: (408) 745 - 2000

Serves As:
- Chairman and Chief Exec. Officer, Juniper Networks, Inc.

KRIER, Mary
1919 Flowers Circle
Thomasville, GA 31757
Tel: (229) 227 - 2333
Fax:(229) 225 - 3806

Serves As:
- V. President, Communications, Flowers Foods

KRIKAVA, Steven
P.O. Box 64101
St. Paul, MN 55164-0101
spkrikava@landolakes.com
Tel: (651) 481 - 2222
Fax:(651) 481 - 2000
TF: (800) 328 - 4155

Serves As:
- Director, Government Relations, Land O'Lakes, Inc.

KRINER, Michael
800 Cabin Hill Dr.
Greensburg, PA 15601
Tel: (724) 837 - 3000

Serves As:
- Treasurer, Allegheny Energy Inc. Federal PAC, Allegheny Energy Inc.

KRISTAN, Stephen M.
2933 Salt Springs Rd. Tel: (330) 797 - 2750
Youngstown, OH 44509 Fax:(330) 797 - 2753
stephen.m.kristan@sbc.com

Serves As:
• Director, External Affairs, SBC Ohio

KRISTIANSEN, Lars B.
1997 Annapolis Exchange Pkwy. Tel: (410) 972 - 2803
Suite 410 Fax:(410) 972 - 2940
Annapolis, MD 21401

Serves As:
• Representative, Legislative Affairs, Nationwide

KRISTOFF, John
5995 Mayfair Rd. Tel: (330) 490 - 5900
P.O. Box 3077 Fax:(330) 490 - 3794
North Canton, OH 44720-8077
kristoj@diebold.com

Serves As:
• V. President, Global Communication and Investor Relations, Diebold, Inc.

KRIVORUCHKA, Mark
P.O. Box 39 Tel: (641) 792 - 7000
Newton, IA 50208-0039 Fax:(641) 787 - 8376
mkrivo@maytag.com

Serves As:
• Senior V. President, Human Resources, Maytag Corp.

KROC, Rochelle
One Hormel Pl. Tel: (507) 437 - 5611
Austin, MN 55912-3680

Serves As:
• Manager, Consumer Affairs, Hormel Foods Corp.

KROLL, Dave
One AMD Pl. Tel: (408) 749 - 4000
P.O. Box 3453 TF: (800) 538 - 8450
Sunnyvale, CA 94088

Serves As:
• Director, Corporate Communications, Advanced Micro Devices, Inc.

KROMER, Mary Lou
P.O. Box 14000 Tel: (561) 694 - 6464
Juno Beach, FL 33408-0420 Fax:(561) 694 - 4620

Serves As:
• V. President, Corporate Communications, (Florida Power & Light Company), FPL Group, Inc.

KROMHOLZ, Steve
1645 Bergstrom Rd. Tel: (920) 751 - 1000
Neenah, WI 54956 Fax:(920) 951 - 1236
TF: (800) 558 - 5073

Serves As:
• President, Menasha Corp. Foundation, Menasha Corporation

KROMIDAS, Larry P.
427 N. Shamrock Tel: (618) 258 - 3206
East Alton, IL 62024

Serves As:
• Director, Investor and Media Relations, Olin Corp.

KRUGER, Dan
P.O. Box 15645 Tel: (702) 242 - 7000
Las Vegas, NV 89114-5645 Fax:(702) 242 - 1531

Serves As:
• V. President, Human Resources, Sierra Health Services, Inc.

KRULAK, Allan C.
1100 Terminal Tower Tel: (216) 621 - 6060
50 Public Square Fax:(216) 263 - 4808
Cleveland, OH 44113-2203

Serves As:
• V. President and Director, Community Affairs, Forest City Enterprises, Inc.

KRULEWITCH, Deborah
767 Fifth Ave. Tel: (212) 572 - 4200
New York, NY 10153-0023 Fax:(212) 572 - 6633
dkrulewitch@estee.com

Serves As:
• Assistant to Chairman and V. President, Corporate Administration, Estee Lauder Companies, Inc.
Responsibilities include corporate philanthropy.

KRUMHOLTZ, Jack
1401 I St., NW Tel: (202) 263 - 5910
Suite 500 Fax:(202) 263 - 5902
Washington, DC 20005

Registered Federal Lobbyist.
Serves As:
• Associate General Counsel and Director, Federal Affairs, Microsoft Corporation

KRYGIER, Edward J.
501 Merritt Seven Tel: (203) 750 - 3000
Norwalk, CT 06856-4500
ejkrygier@corp.olin.com

Serves As:
• Treasurer, Olin Corp. Good Government Fund, Olin Corp.

KSANSNAK, James
2801 Hunting Park Ave. Tel: (215) 221 - 8500
Philadelphia, PA 19129 Fax:(215) 228 - 3970
TF: (800) 248 - 2789

Serves As:
• Chairman of the Board, Tasty Baking Co.

KUBASA, Julie
P.O. Box 482 Tel: (414) 931 - 4208
Milwaukee, WI 53201-0482 Fax:(414) 931 - 6352
jkubasa@mbco.com

Serves As:
• Manager, Corporate Affairs, Miller Brewing Co.

KUBERA, Dan
One N. Field Ct. Tel: (847) 735 - 4617
Lake Forest, IL 60045-4811 Fax:(847) 735 - 4750
daniel.kubera@brunswick.com

Serves As:
• Director, Public and Financial Relations, Brunswick Corp.

KUBIK, Rob
1350 I St. NW Tel: (202) 371 - 6900
Suite 400 Fax:(202) 842 - 3578
Washington, DC 20005-3306

Registered Federal Lobbyist.
Serves As:
• Manager, Spectrum and Regulatory Policy, Motorola, Inc.

KUCHLING, Ginny
29400 Lakeland Blvd. Tel: (440) 347 - 1241
Wickliffe, OH 44092-2298 Fax:(440) 347 - 1858

Serves As:
• Community Relations Specialist, The Lubrizol Corp.
Responsibilities include corporate philanthropy.

KUDWA, Amy
2345 Crystal Dr. Tel: (703) 872 - 5182
Arlington, VA 22227 Fax:(703) 872 - 5104
akudwa@usairways.com

Serves As:
• Manager, Public Relations, US Airways Group, Inc.

KUEBLER, Christopher A.
210 Carnegie Center Tel: (609) 452 - 4440
Princeton, NJ 08540-6233 Fax:(609) 452 - 9375
TF: (800) 621 - 8901

Serves As:
• Chairman of the Board, Covance, Inc.

KUEHN, Ronald L.
P.O. Box 2511 Tel: (713) 420 - 2131
Houston, TX 77252-2511 Fax:(713) 420 - 4993

Serves As:
• Chairman of the Board, El Paso Corp.

KUESTER, Dennis J.
770 N. Water St. Tel: (414) 765 - 7700
Milwaukee, WI 53202 Fax:(414) 765 - 7899

Serves As:
• Chairman of the Board and Chief Exec. Officer, Marshall & Ilsley Corp.

KUFLICK, Terry
375 Hudson St. Tel: (212) 229 - 6379
New York, NY 10014 Fax:(212) 229 - 6390
tkuflik@tcco.com

Serves As:
• Director, Public Relations, The Turner Corp.

KUHLMAN, Erin
100 W. Walnut St. Tel: (626) 440 - 4590
Pasadena, CA 91124 Fax:(626) 440 - 2630
erin.kuhlman@parsons.com

Serves As:
• V. President, Corporate Relations, Parsons Corp.

KUHLMANN, David
P.O. Box 834 Tel: (206) 377 - 4072
Seattle, WA 98101 Fax:(206) 554 - 4807
david.kuhlman@wamu.net TF: (800) 756 - 8000

Serves As:
• Corporate Public Relations, Washington Mutual, Inc.

KUHN, Edward P.

24601 Center Ridge Rd.
Suite 200
Westlake, OH 44145-5639

Tel: (440) 808 - 9100
Fax:(440) 808 - 4458
TF: (800) 961 - 2961

Serves As:
- Chairman of the Board, TravelCenters of America, Inc.

KUHN, Paul R.

1332 Blue Hills Ave.
P.O. Box 1
Bloomfield, CT 06002-0001

Tel: (860) 243 - 7100
Fax:(860) 243 - 6101

Serves As:
- Chairman, President and Chief Exec. Officer, Kaman Corp.

KUIPER, Joost

135 S. LaSalle St.
Chicago, IL 60603

Tel: (312) 904 - 2000
Fax:(312) 904 - 6521

Serves As:
- Chairman of the Board, LaSalle Bank N.A.

KULA, William R.

600 Hidden Ridge
Irving, TX 75015-2092

Tel: (972) 718 - 6924

Serves As:
- Director, Western Bureau Media Relations, Verizon Communications Inc.

KULESHER, Kate M.

7430 Birch Creek Pl.
Lincoln, NE 68516
kuleshk@wyeth.com

Tel: (402) 420 - 2445
Fax:(402) 420 - 2737

Serves As:
- Associate Director, State Government Affairs, Wyeth Pharmaceuticals

KULLMAN, Mary C.

720 Olive St.
Room 1527
St. Louis, MO 63101

Tel: (314) 342 - 0531
Fax:(314) 421 - 1979

Serves As:
- Secretary and Associate General Counsel, The Laclede Group

Responsibilities include corporate philanthropy.

KULLMAN, Timothy E.

19601 N. 27th Ave.
Phoenix, AZ 85027

Tel: (623) 580 - 6100
Fax:(623) 580 - 6508

Serves As:
- Senior V. President and Chief Financial Officer, PETsMART, Inc.

Responsibilities include investor relations.

KULOW, Lynn

444 Highland Dr.
Kohler, WI 53044

Tel: (920) 457 - 4441
Fax:(920) 457 - 9064

Serves As:
- Senior Communications Specialist - Corporate Giving and Civic Services, Kohler Co.

KUMAR, Subhaash

400 N. Ashley Dr.
Tampa, FL 33602

Tel: (813) 274 - 1000
Fax:(813) 273 - 0148

Serves As:
- Senior Director, Investor Relations, Sykes Enterprises, Inc.

KUMMER, Randy L.

1100 Superior Ave.
Cleveland, OH 44114-2589
rlkummer@cleveland-cliffs.com

Tel: (216) 694 - 5700
Fax:(216) 694 - 4880

Serves As:
- Senior V. President, Human Resources, Cleveland-Cliffs Inc

KUNDERT, Glen A.

270 Peachtree St. NW
Atlanta, GA 30303

Tel: (404) 506 - 5135

Serves As:
- Director, Investor Relations, Southern Company

KUNERT, Kathryn

666 Grand Ave.
P.O. Box 657
Des Moines, IA 50303-0657

Tel: (515) 281 - 2287
Fax:(515) 242 - 4398
TF: (888) 427 - 5632

Serves As:
- V. President, Community Relations and Legislative Projects, (MidAmerican Energy Co.), MidAmerican Energy Holdings Co.

KUNIANSKY, Max

800 Cabin Hill Dr.
Greensburg, PA 15601

Tel: (724) 838 - 6895

Serves As:
- Director, Investor Relations, Allegheny Energy Inc.

KUNICKI, Walter

231 W. Michigan
P446
Milwaukee, WI 53203
walter.kunicki@we-energies.com

Tel: (414) 221 - 3414
Fax:(414) 221 - 4655

Serves As:
- V. President, Customer Relations, We Energies

KUNKLE, Jr., Gary

P.O. Box 872
York, PA 17405-0872

Tel: (717) 845 - 7511
Fax:(717) 849 - 4762
TF: (800) 877 - 0020

Serves As:
- Chairman and Chief Exec. Officer, Dentsply Internat'l

KUNTZ, Edward L.

680 S. Fourth Ave.
Louisville, KY 40202-2412

Tel: (502) 596 - 7300
Fax:(502) 596 - 4099

Serves As:
- Chairman of the Board, Kindred Healthcare, Inc.

KURAITIS, Vytenis P.

201 N. Harrison St.
Davenport, IA 52801-1939

Tel: (563) 383 - 2100

Serves As:
- V. President, Human Resources, Lee Enterprises

KURNATH, M.D., Joseph F.

165 Court St.
Rochester, NY 14647

Tel: (585) 454 - 1700
Fax:(585) 238 - 4233

Serves As:
- Chairman of the Board, The Lifetime Healthcare Companies

KURTZ, Larry

One Post St.
31st Floor
San Francisco, CA 94104-5296
larry.kurtz@mckesson.com

Tel: (415) 983 - 8418
Fax:(415) 983 - 7160

Serves As:
- V. President, Investor Relations, McKesson Corp.

KURTZ, Ronald

501 Merritt Seven
Norwalk, CT 06851

Tel: (203) 750 - 2407
Fax:(203) 750 - 7788
TF: (800) 626 - 4999

Serves As:
- Director, Media Relations, ABB Inc.

KUSER, William

199 Benson Rd.
Middlebury, VT 06749

Tel: (203) 573 - 2213
Fax:(203) 573 - 3711

Serves As:
- Investor Relations Contact, Chemtura

KUSH, Donna

4211 S. 102nd St.
Omaha, NE 68127-1031
dkush@ameritrade.com

Tel: (402) 827 - 8931
Fax:(402) 597 - 7789
TF: (800) 237 - 8692

Serves As:
- Managing Director, Corporate Communications, Ameritrade Holding Corp.

KUSHNER, Stephanie K.

1415 W. 22nd St.
Suite 1100
Oak Brook, IL 60523

Tel: (630) 954 - 2020

Serves As:
- V. President and Chief Financial Officer, Federal Signal Corp.

Responsibilities include investor relations.

KUSIN, Gary

Three Galleria Tower
13155 Noel Rd., Suite 1600
Dallas, TX 75240

Tel: (214) 550 - 7000

Serves As:
- President and Chief Exec. Officer, FedEx Kinko's Office and Print Services

KUTCHER, Kenneth

P.O. Box 70
Fort Mill, SC 29716

Tel: (803) 547 - 1500

Serves As:
- Exec. V. President and Chief Financial Officer, Springs Industries, Inc.

KWALWASSER, Marsha H.

1840 Century Park East
Los Angeles, CA 90067-2199

Tel: (310) 201 - 3398
Fax:(310) 556 - 4595

Registered Federal Lobbyist.

Serves As:
- Director, Government Relations, Northrop Grumman Corp.

KWAPIS, Jennifer
700 Tower Dr. Tel: (248) 650 - 0390
Troy, MI 48098
jennifer.kwapis@eds.com

Serves As:
- Mid-Atlantic and Midwest Regional Director, State Government, EDS Corp.

KWONG, Linda K.
500 Bic Dr. Tel: (203) 783 - 2049
Milford, CT 06460 Fax:(203) 783 - 2684

Serves As:
- Director, Corporate Communications, BIC Corp.

KYD, Margot A.
8326 Century Park Tel: (619) 696 - 2000
San Diego, CA 92123 Fax:(619) 696 - 1814

Serves As:
- Senior V. President and Chief Administrative Officer, Human Resources, San Diego Gas and Electric Co.

KYLE, David L.
P.O. Box 871 Tel: (918) 588 - 7930
Tulsa, OK 74102-0871 Fax:(918) 588 - 7960
dkyle@oneok.com

Serves As:
- Chairman, President and Chief Exec. Officer, ONEOK, Inc.

Also serves as President and Exec. Director of the ONEOK Foundation, Inc.

KYRIAKOU, Linda G.
200 Park Ave. Tel: (212) 986 - 5500
New York, NY 10166 Ext: 5253
linda_kyriakou@sequa.com Fax:(212) 370 - 1969

Serves As:
- V. President, Corporate Communications, Sequa Corp.

Responsibilities include investor relations.

KYTE, John
5400 Legacy Dr., Cluster II, Bldg. 3 Tel: (972) 265 - 2030
Plano, TX 75024 TF: (800) 669 - 5740
john_kyte@was.bm.com

Serves As:
- Director, Corporate Communications and Government Relations, Safety-Kleen Systems, Inc.

LA BARGE, Susan
9341 Courtland Dr. NE Tel: (616) 866 - 5500
hb2l1 Fax:(616) 866 - 0257
Rockford, MI 49351

Serves As:
- Foundation Contact, Wolverine World Wide, Inc.

LA BRUNA, Stanley
80 Park Plaza Tel: (973) 430 - 7380
M/S T17A Fax:(973) 623 - 7758
Newark, NJ 07102-0570
stanley.labruna@pseg.com

Serves As:
- V. President, Environment, Health and Safety, PSE&G

LA PLANTE, Bobbi
2325 Orchard Pkwy. Tel: (408) 441 - 0311
San Jose, CA 95131 Fax:(408) 436 - 4200
blaplante@atmel.com

Serves As:
- V. President, Global Human Resources, Atmel Corp.

LA RUE, Mary
3000 Centre Square West Tel: (215) 563 - 2800
1500 Market St. Fax:(215) 575 - 2314
Philadelphia, PA 19102

Serves As:
- Chairperson, Corporate Contributions, Berwind Group

LAAKE, Karen
2001 Pennsylvania Ave. NW Tel: (202) 263 - 0000
Suite 650 Fax:(202) 263 - 0010
Washington, DC 20006

Serves As:
- PAC Contact, Qualcomm Inc.

LAATSCH, Tim
P.O. Box 8050 Tel: (715) 422 - 4023
Wisconsin Rapids, WI 54495-8050 Fax:(715) 422 - 3882

Serves As:
- Senior V. President, Communications, Stora Enso North America

LABAR, Susan
915 Secaucus Rd. Tel: (201) 453 - 6955
Secaucus, NJ 07094 TF: (800) 527 - 5355

Serves As:
- Director, Investor Relations, The Children's Place Retail Stores, Inc.

LABEAU, Bill
1299 Pennsylvania Ave. NW Tel: (202) 898 - 6406
Suite 1100W Fax:(202) 637 - 4531
Washington, DC 20004

Serves As:
- Senior Regulatory Counsel, NBC Universal

LABELLE, Diane
2700 Post Oak Blvd. Tel: (713) 624 - 8000
Suite 1800 Fax:(713) 624 - 8085
Houston, TX 77056 TF: (877) 820 - 2522

Serves As:
- Director, Corporate Communications, Air Liquide America Corp.

LABERGE, Alfred
151 Farmington Ave. Tel: (860) 273 - 4788
MS RWAK Fax:(860) 273 - 6675
Hartford, CT 06156
labergear@aetna.com

Serves As:
- Assistant V. President, Corporate Public Relations, Aetna Inc.

LABOMBARD, Susan
101 Constitution Ave. NW Tel: (202) 742 - 4459
Suite 800 Fax:(202) 742 - 4458
Washington, DC 20001

Registered Federal Lobbyist.
Serves As:
- Manager, Federal Legislative Affairs, Ameren Corp.

LABUSKES, Richard
One Mellon Center Tel: (412) 234 - 4948
500 Grant St. Fax:(412) 236 - 5150
Room 2850
Pittsburgh, PA 15258-0001
labuskes.r@mellon.com

Serves As:
- First V. President, Government Affairs, Mellon Financial Corp.

LABUTKA, Carolyn E.
200 E.Randolph St. Tel: (312) 381 - 3549
Chicago, IL 60601 Fax:(312) 381 - 0240

Serves As:
- V. President and Exec. Director, Aon Foundation, Aon Corp.

LACANNE, Therese
17845 E. Hwy. 10 Tel: (763) 241 - 2280
Elk River, MN 55330 Fax:(763) 241 - 2366
tlacanne@grenergy.com

Serves As:
- Media Contact, Great River Energy

LACEY, Jamie
One MedImmune Way Tel: (301) 398 - 4035
Gaithersburg, MD 20878 Fax:(301) 398 - 9000
TF: (877) 633 - 4411

Serves As:
- Director, Public Relations, MedImmune, Inc.

LACEY, Jim
1295 State St. Tel: (413) 744 - 2365
Springfield, MA 01111-0001 Fax:(413) 744 - 6005
TF: (800) 767 - 1000

Serves As:
- Assistant V. President, Media and Public Relations, MassMutual Financial Group

LACKEY, Dave
82 Devonshire St. Tel: (617) 563 - 7000
Boston, MA 02109-3614 Fax:(617) 476 - 6150

Serves As:
- Director, Public Relations, FMR Corp.

LACKEY, Stephen
One Mellon Center Tel: (412) 234 - 5601
500 Grant St. Fax:(412) 236 - 5461
Room 0370
Pittsburgh, PA 15258-0001
lackey.s@mellon.com

Serves As:
- First V. President, Investor Relations, Mellon Financial Corp.

LACKEY, William "Bill"
2100 E. Grand Ave. Tel: (310) 615 - 1700
El Segundo, CA 90245 Fax:(310) 647 - 1801
blackey3@csc.com

Serves As:
- Director, Investor Relations, Computer Sciences Corp.

LACY, Alan J.
3333 Beverly Rd.
Hoffman Estates, IL 60179-0001
Tel: (847) 286 - 2500
Fax:(847) 286 - 7881
TF: (800) 732 - 7780

Serves As:
- V. Chairman and Chief Exec. Officer, Sears Holding Corp.

LADD, Thomas E.
One Marriott Dr.
Washington, DC 20058
thomas.ladd@marriott.com
Tel: (301) 380 - 1236
Fax:(301) 380 - 8957

Registered Federal Lobbyist.
Serves As:
- Senior V. President, Government Affairs, Marriott Internat'l, Inc.

LAFFOON, IV, Polk
50 W. San Fernando St.
15th Floor
San Jose, CA 95113
Tel: (408) 938 - 7838
Fax:(408) 938 - 7766

Serves As:
- V. President, Corporate Relations, Knight Ridder

Responsibilities include corporate contributions.

LAFLEY, Alan G.
P.O. Box 599
Cincinnati, OH 45201-0599
lafley.ag@pg.com
Tel: (513) 983 - 1100
Fax:(513) 983 - 9181

Serves As:
- Chairman, President and Chief Exec. Officer, The Procter & Gamble Company

LAGRECA, Celia A.
7261 Mercy Rd.
P.O. Box 3248
Omaha, NE 68180
Tel: (402) 390 - 1838
Fax:(402) 398 - 3736

Serves As:
- Senior V. President, Corporate Communications, Blue Cross and Blue Shield of Nebraska

LAIDLAW, Meg
717 Texas Ave.
Houston, TX 77002
mlaidlaw@calpine.com
Tel: (713) 830 - 8655

Serves As:
- Director, Public Relations, Calpine Corp.

LAKEFIELD, Bruce R.
2345 Crystal Dr.
Arlington, VA 22227
Tel: (703) 872 - 7000
Fax:(703) 872 - 7093

Serves As:
- President and Chief Exec. Officer, US Airways Group, Inc.

LAKES, Sharon
2300 W. Plano Pkwy.
Plano, TX 75075
sharon.lakes@ps.net
Tel: (972) 577 - 6012

Serves As:
- Manager, Media Relations (Healthcare), Perot Systems Corp.

LALLY, Pamela K.
P.O. Box 1271
MS E12A
Portland, OR 97207-1271
pklally@regence.com
Tel: (503) 225 - 6982
Fax:(503) 225 - 5283

Registered Federal Lobbyist.
Serves As:
- Manager, Legislative Affairs, Regence BlueCross BlueShield of Oregon

LALOR, Angela
3M Center
St. Paul, MN 55144-1000
Tel: (651) 733 - 1110
Fax:(651) 733 - 9973

Serves As:
- Exec. Director, Human Resources, 3M Company

LAMAND, Richard A.
2050 Spectrum Blvd.
Fort Lauderdale, FL 33309
Tel: (954) 308 - 7600
Fax:(954) 938 - 7790

Serves As:
- Senior V. President and Chief Human Resources Officer, Spherion Corp.

LAMARCA, Louis
325 Seventh St. NW
Suite 1200
Washington, DC 20004-1007
Tel: (202) 783 - 7070
Fax:(202) 347 - 2044

Registered Federal Lobbyist.
Serves As:
- Director, Federal Relations, Pfizer Inc.

LAMB, Michele
One S. Jersey Plaza
Folsom, NJ 08037
Tel: (609) 561 - 9000
Ext: 4171
Fax:(609) 561 - 8225

Serves As:
- Communications Specialist, South Jersey Gas Co.

LAMB, Jr., Thomas F.
249 Fifth Ave.
Pittsburgh, PA 15222-2707
Tel: (412) 762 - 7558
Fax:(412) 762 - 2784

Registered Federal Lobbyist.
Serves As:
- Senior V. President, Government Affairs, PNC Financial Services Group

LAMB, W. Scott
27422 Portola Pkwy
Suite 350
Foothill Ranch, CA 92610-2831
scott.lamb@kaiseral.com
Tel: (949) 614 - 1740
Fax:(949) 614 - 1930

Serves As:
- V. President, Investor Relations and Corporate Communications, Kaiser Aluminum & Chemical Corp.

LAMBERGMAN, Barry
1350 I St. NW
Suite 400
Washington, DC 20005-3306
Tel: (202) 371 - 6900
Fax:(202) 842 - 3578

Registered Federal Lobbyist.
Serves As:
- Director, Government Relations and Regulatory Affairs, Motorola, Inc.

LAMBERT, Betsy H.
1100 CommScope Pl. SE
Hickory, NC 28603
blambert@commscope.com
Tel: (828) 323 - 4873
Fax:(828) 982 - 1708

Serves As:
- Manager, Corporate Communications and Media Relations, CommScope

LAMBERT, Cheryl Ann
3333 Beverly Rd.
Hoffman Estates, IL 60179-0001
clambe4@sears.com
Tel: (847) 286 - 4714
Fax:(847) 286 - 7881
TF: (800) 732 - 7780

Serves As:
- Contact Contributions, Sears Holding Corp.

LAMBERT, Janet Lynch
1455 Pennsylvania Ave. NW
Suite 100
Washington, DC 20004
Tel: (202) 756 - 0184

Registered Federal Lobbyist.
Serves As:
- Director, Government Relations, Invitrogen Corp.

LAMBERT, William M.
P.O. Box 426
Pittsburgh, PA 15230
Tel: (412) 967 - 3194
Fax:(412) 967 - 3477
TF: (800) 672 - 2222

Serves As:
- Chairman, Mine Safety Appliances Co. PAC, Mine Safety Appliances Co. (MSA)

LAMBOURNE, Gordon
One Marriott Dr.
Washington, DC 20058
gordon.lambourne@marriott.com
Tel: (301) 380 - 1368
Fax:(301) 897 - 9014

Serves As:
- V. President Brand Public Relations, Marriott Internat'l, Inc.

LAMBRIGHT, Stephen K.
One Busch Pl.
St. Louis, MO 63118-1852
Tel: (314) 577 - 2000
Fax:(314) 577 - 2900

Serves As:
- Group V. President and Senior Counsel, Anheuser-Busch Cos., Inc.

Responsibilities include public affairs.

LAMMARTINO, Nicholas
4400 Main St.
Kansas City, MO 64111
Tel: (816) 753 - 6900
Fax:(816) 753 - 5346
TF: (800) 829 - 7733

Serves As:
- Director, Communications, H & R Block, Inc.

LAMPARD, Brenda S.
10802 Bower Ave.
Williamsport, MD 21795

Serves As:
- Treasurer, Allegheny Energy Inc. PAC, Allegheny Energy Inc.

LAMPE, Anna Carol
P.O. Box 419580
M/S 203
Kansas City, MO 64141-6580
Tel: (816) 274 - 3589
Fax:(816) 274 - 7397

Serves As:
- Research Project Leader, Hallmark Cards, Inc.

LAMPE, Kathy
120 Park Ave.
New York, NY 10017
Tel: (917) 663 - 3044
Fax:(917) 663 - 2167

Serves As:
- Assistant Corporate Secretary, Altria Group, Inc.

Responsibilities include investor relations.

LAMPERT, Edward S.
3333 Beverly Rd.
Hoffman Estates, IL 60179-0001
Tel: (847) 286 - 2500
Fax:(847) 286 - 7881
TF: (800) 732 - 7780

Serves As:
- Chairman of the Board, Sears Holding Corp.

LAMPERT, Steven B.
P.O. Box 15437
FOC 3C/W
Wilmington, DE 19850-5437
steve.lampert@astrazeneca.com
Tel: (302) 886 - 7862
Fax:(302) 886 - 3119
TF: (800) 456 - 3669

Serves As:
- Exec. Director, Brand Communications, AstraZeneca Pharmaceuticals

LAMPL, John W.
7520 Astoria Blvd.
Jackson Heights, NY 11370
Tel: (347) 418 - 4729
Fax:(347) 397 - 4204

Serves As:
- V. President, Corporate Communications (The Americas), British Airways

LANCASTER, Rick
17845 E. Hwy. 10
Elk River, MN 55330
Tel: (763) 241 - 2428
Fax:(763) 241 - 6285

Serves As:
- V. President, Public Affairs, Great River Energy

LANCASTER, Ronnie B.
1101 Pennsylvania Ave. NW
Washington, DC 20004
Tel: (202) 756 - 2469

Serves As:
- Senior V. President, Federal Government Relations, Assurant

LANCE, Howard L.
1025 W. NASA Blvd.
Melbourne, FL 32919-0001
Tel: (321) 727 - 9100
Fax:(321) 727 - 9646
TF: (800) 442 - 7747

Serves As:
- Chairman, President and Chief Exec. Officer, Harris Corp.

LANCEFORD, Michael L.
P.O. Box 799045
Dallas, TX 75379-9045
Tel: (972) 687 - 5332
Fax:(972) 387 - 1611
TF: (800) 627 - 9529

Serves As:
- Manager, Media Relations, Mary Kay Inc.

LAND, Mark
P.O. Box 3005
Columbus, IN 47202-3005
mark.d.land@cummins.com
Tel: (317) 610 - 2456
Fax:(812) 377 - 3613

Serves As:
- Director, Public Relations, Cummins, Inc.

LANDE, Jae
P.O. Box 85587
San Diego, CA 92186-5587
Tel: (858) 277 - 6780
Fax:(858) 505 - 1523

Serves As:
- Director, Public Relations, Cubic Corp.

LANDERS, Cindy
P.O. Box 4427
Houston, TX 77210-4427
Tel: (713) 546 - 6272
Fax:(713) 546 - 4041

Serves As:
- Director, Alliance and Identity, Jiffy Lube Internat'l, Inc.

Responsibilities include public relations.

LANDERS, David M.
1201 F St. NW
Suite 450
Washington, DC 20004
Tel: (202) 626 - 3301

Registered Federal Lobbyist.
Serves As:
- Representative, Credit Suisse First Boston

LANDIS, Jeff
One Sun Life Executive Park
SC 2132
Wellesley Hills, MA 02481
jeff_Landis@sunlife.com
Tel: (781) 446 - 1955
Fax:(781) 304 - 5383
TF: (800) 225 - 3950

Serves As:
- Manager, Community and Creative Services, Sun Life Financial

LANDKAMER, Jason
801 Cherry St.
Suite 3900
Fort Worth, TX 76102-6803
Tel: (817) 302 - 7811
Fax:(817) 302 - 7479
TF: (800) 644 - 2297

Serves As:
- Assistant V. President, Investor Relations, AmeriCredit Corp.

LANDON, Allan R.
P.O. Box 2900
Honolulu, HI 96846
Fax:(808) 537 - 8440
TF: (888) 643 - 3888

Serves As:
- Chairman, Chief Exec. Officer, and President, Bank of Hawaii Corp.

LANDY, Christine
One Health Plaza
East Hanover, NJ 07936
christine.landy@pharma.novartis.com
Tel: (862) 778 - 8026
Fax:(862) 644 - 8585

Serves As:
- Associate Director, Public Relations, (Novartis Pharmaceuticals Corp.), Novartis Corporation

LANE, Andrew
601 Jefferson St.
Houston, TX 77002
Tel: (713) 759 - 2600
Fax:(713) 753 - 5353

Serves As:
- Chief Operating Officer, Kellogg Brown and Root

LANE, Barry
2141 Rosecrans Ave., Suite 4000
El Segundo, CA 90245
blane@unocal.com
Tel: (310) 726 - 7731

Serves As:
- Manager, Public Relations, UNOCAL Corp.

LANE, Carol
2200 Clarendon Blvd., Suite 1202
Arlington, VA 22201
Tel: (703) 284 - 5400
Fax:(703) 284 - 5449

Serves As:
- V. President, Washington Operations, (Ball Aerospace & Technologies), Ball Corp.

LANE, Jeffrey A.
P.O. Box 599
Cincinnati, OH 45201-0599
lane.ja@pg.com

Serves As:
- V. President, State and Local Government Relations, The Procter & Gamble Company

LANE, Joyce L.
P.O. Box 8080
McKinney, TX 75070
jlane@torchmarkco.com
Tel: (972) 569 - 3627
Fax:(972) 569 - 3696

Serves As:
- V. President, Investor Relations, Torchmark Corp.

LANE, Kenneth F.
1301 K St. NW
Suite 1000 East Tower
Washington, DC 20005
Tel: (202) 715 - 1118
Fax:(202) 715 - 1114

Serves As:
- V. President, State Government Relations, Diageo North America

LANE, Laura
800 Connecticut Ave. NW
Suite 800
Washington, DC 20006
Tel: (202) 457 - 8582
Fax:(202) 457 - 8861

Registered Federal Lobbyist.
Serves As:
- Representative, Time Warner Inc.

LANE, Laurence F.
101 E. State St.
Kennett Square, PA 19348
laurence.lane@genesishcc.com
Tel: (610) 444 - 8430
Fax:(610) 925 - 4242

Serves As:
- V. President, Government Relations, Genesis HealthCare Corp.

LANE, Rick
444 N. Capitol St., N.W., Suite 740
Washington, DC 20001
rlane@newscorp.com
Tel: (202) 824 - 6500
Fax:(202) 824 - 6510

Registered Federal Lobbyist.
Serves As:
• V. President, Government Relations, News Corporation Ltd.

LANE, Robert W.
One John Deere Pl.
Moline, IL 61265-8098
Tel: (309) 765 - 4114
Fax:(309) 765 - 5772

Serves As:
• Chairman and Chief Exec. Officer, Deere & Company

LANE, William C.
818 Connecticut Ave. NW
Suite 600
Washington, DC 20006-2702
Tel: (202) 466 - 0672
Fax:(202) 466 - 0684

Registered Federal Lobbyist.
Serves As:
• Washington Director, Governmental Affairs, Caterpillar Inc.

LANEY, David M.
60 Massachusetts Ave. NE
Washington, DC 20002
Tel: (202) 906 - 3000
Fax:(202) 906 - 3865

Serves As:
• Chairman of the Board, Amtrak

LANEY, Sandra E.
2600 Chemed Center
255 E. Fifth St.
Cincinnati, OH 45202-4726
Tel: (513) 762 - 6900
Fax:(513) 762 - 6919

Serves As:
• President, The Chemed Foundation, The Chemed Corporation

LANFANT, Katya
1111 Stewart Ave.
Bethpage, NY 11714-3581
Tel: (516) 803 - 2539
Fax:(516) 803 - 2368

Serves As:
• Manager, Corporate Communications, Cablevision Systems Corp.

LANG, III, Edward A.
110 S.E. Sixth St.
28th Floor
Fort Lauderdale, FL 33301
Tel: (954) 769 - 3591
Fax:(954) 769 - 6407

Serves As:
• V. President, Finance and Treasurer, Republic Services, Inc.
Responsibilities include shareholder relations.

LANG, Gregory S.
6024 Silver Creek Valley Rd.
San Jose, CA 95138
gregory.lang@idt.com
Tel: (408) 284 - 8200

Serves As:
• President and Chief Exec. Officer, Integrated Device Technology, Inc.

LANG, James
711 High St.
Des Moines, IA 50392-0150
Tel: (515) 247 - 5111
Fax:(515) 246 - 5475
TF: (800) 986 - 3343

Serves As:
• Treasurer, Principal Life Insurance Co. PAC, The Principal Financial Group

LANG, Nancy
4800 Hampden Ln.
Suite 1100
Bethesda, MD 20814
Tel: (301) 841 - 1693
Fax:(301) 841 - 1611

Serves As:
• Public Relations Contact, AREVA Enterprises, Inc.

LANG, Ray
525 W. Van Buren St.
Chicago, IL 60607
Tel: (312) 880 - 5233
Fax:(312) 880 - 5167

Serves As:
• Director, Government Affairs - Midwest, Amtrak

LANG, Sherry
770 Cochituate Rd.
Framingham, MA 01701
Tel: (508) 390 - 2323
Fax:(508) 390 - 2091

Serves As:
• V. President, Investor and Public Relations, The TJX Companies, Inc.

LANGAN, Thomas P.
816 Connecticut Ave. NW
Seventh Floor
Washington, DC 20006-2705
Tel: (202) 828 - 1010
Fax:(202) 828 - 4550

Registered Federal Lobbyist.
Serves As:
• Manager, Government Affairs, Unilever United States, Inc.

LANGDON, Jerry J.
P.O. Box 2286
Houston, TX 77252-2286
Tel: (281) 866 - 1167
Fax:(713) 488 - 5925
TF: (866) 872 - 6656

Serves As:
• Exec. V. President, Public and Regulatory Affairs, Reliant Resources

LANGDON, Steve
1600 Amphitheatre Pkwy.
Mountain View, CA 94043
slangdon@google.com
Tel: (650) 623 - 4950
Fax:(650) 618 - 1499

Serves As:
• Manager,Public Relations, Google Inc.

LANGE, Deborah
1015 15th St. NW
Suite 200
Washington, DC 20005-2605
Tel: (202) 835 - 7360
Fax:(202) 467 - 4250

Registered Federal Lobbyist.
Serves As:
• PAC Contact, Oracle Corporation

LANGE, Tom
8182 Maryland Ave.
Clayton, MO 63105
Tel: (314) 746 - 1236
Fax:(314) 746 - 1437

Serves As:
• Director, Public Relations, Smurfit-Stone Container

LANGEL, Kurt O.
McLeod USA Technology Park
6400 C St., SW
Cedar Rapids, IA 52406
Tel: (319) 364 - 0000
Fax:(319) 790 - 7767
TF: (800) 896 - 8330

Serves As:
• V. President, Human Resources, McLeod USA Inc.

LANGHORST, Rosemary
600 Corporate Park Dr.
St. Louis, MO 63105
rlanghorst@erac.com
Tel: (314) 512 - 5000
Fax:(314) 512 - 4706

Serves As:
• Treasurer, Enterprise Rent-A-Car Co. PAC, Enterprise Rent-A-Car Co.

LANGKNECHT, John M.
1000 Wilson Blvd., Suite 2300
Arlington, VA 22209
Tel: (703) 875 - 8400

Registered Federal Lobbyist.
Serves As:
• Representative, Northrop Grumman Corp.

LANGLEY, Kelly
P.O. Box 10100
Reno, NV 89520-0026
Tel: (775) 834 - 5723
Fax:(775) 834 - 5462
TF: (800) 962 - 0399

Serves As:
• Investor Relations Contact, Sierra Pacific Resources

LANIER, Elizabeth K.
2345 Crystal Dr.
Arlington, VA 22227
liz_lanier@usairways.com
Tel: (703) 872 - 7000
Fax:(703) 872 - 5208

Serves As:
• Exec. V. President, Corporate Affairs; General Counsel, US Airways Group, Inc.

LANIER, Hope
P.O. Box 33068
Charlotte, NC 28233
Tel: (704) 731 - 4308

Serves As:
• Manager, Government Relations, Piedmont Natural Gas Co.

LANIER, Jr., Joseph L.
P.O. Box 261
Danville, VA 24543
Tel: (434) 799 - 7000
Fax:(434) 799 - 7276

Serves As:
• Chairman and Chief Exec. Officer, Dan River, Inc.

LANSINGER, Jr., William C.
1399 New York Ave. NW
Suite 350
Washington, DC 20005
Tel: (202) 662 - 1700
Fax:(202) 293 - 2887

Registered Federal Lobbyist.
Serves As:
• Director, FERC Relations, Sempra Energy

LANT, Steven V.
284 South Ave.
Poughkeepsie, NY 12601-4879
Tel: (845) 452 - 2000
Fax:(845) 486 - 5465
TF: (800) 527 - 2714

Serves As:
• Chairman, President and Chief Exec. Officer, CH Energy Group, Inc.

LANZ, Robert J. "Bob"
Three Skyline Dr.
Hawthorne, NY 10532
Tel: (914) 789 - 1193
Fax:(914) 345 - 3944

Serves As:
- V. President, Public Affairs, (Coca-Cola Bottling Co. of New York, Inc., The), Coca-Cola Enterprises Inc.

LANZA, Frank C.
600 Third Ave
New York, NY 10016
Tel: (212) 697 - 1111
Fax:(212) 867 - 5249
TF: (866) 463 - 6555

Serves As:
- Chairman and Chief Exec. Officer, L-3 Communications Corp.

LAPENTA, Robert
1830 Route 130
Burlington, NJ 08016
bob.lapenta@coat.com
Tel: (609) 387 - 7800
Ext: 1216
Fax:(609) 239 - 8242

Serves As:
- Chief Financial Officer, Burlington Coat Factory Warehouse Corp.

Responsibilities include investor relations.

LAPHAM, Elise
One Sun Life Executive Park
Wellesley Hills, MA 02481
elise_lapham@sunlife.com
Tel: (781) 237 - 6030
Fax:(781) 304 - 5383
TF: (800) 225 - 3950

Serves As:
- Communications Officer, Sun Life Financial

LAPIERRE, Shannon
One Computer Associates Plaza
Islandia, NY 11749
shannon.lapierr@ca.com
Tel: (631) 342 - 3839
Fax:(631) 342 - 4295
TF: (800) 225 - 5224

Serves As:
- V. President, Corporate Media Relations, Computer Associates Internat'l, Inc.

LAPIERRE, Steven N.
1331 Pennsylvania Ave. NW
Suite 550 South
Washington, DC 20004
Tel: (202) 637 - 8020
Fax:(202) 637 - 8028

Registered Federal Lobbyist.
Serves As:
- Director, Legislative Affairs, Boston Scientific Corp.

LAPP, Robert J.
1835 Dueber Ave. SW
GNE-01
Canton, OH 44706
robert_lapp@timken.com
Tel: (330) 471 - 4275
Fax:(330) 471 - 3541
TF: (800) 223 - 1954

Registered Federal Lobbyist.
Serves As:
- V. President, Government Affairs, The Timken Co.

LAPRIORE, Cheryl
440 Lincoln St.
Worcester, MA 01653
Tel: (508) 855 - 1000

Serves As:
- V. President, Corporate Community Relations, Allmerica Property & Casualty Companies, Inc.

LARAIA, Mary
135 S. LaSalle St.
Chicago, IL 60603
Tel: (312) 904 - 6038
Fax:(312) 904 - 4050

Serves As:
- Group Senior V. President, Civic and Community Development, LaSalle Bank N.A.

LARANCE, Charles L.
700 Market St.
St. Louis, MO 63101
Tel: (314) 843 - 8700
Fax:(314) 444 - 0681

Serves As:
- V. President, Corporate Relations, GenAmerica Financial Corp.

LARCHET, Patricia A.
5770 Fleet St.
Carlsbad, CA 92008
Tel: (760) 696 - 4000
Fax:(760) 696 - 4009
TF: (800) 597 - 5366

Serves As:
- Vice Chairman and Chief Exec. Officer, Jenny Craig, Inc.

LARCOM, M. Kay
1776 I St. NW
Suite 700
Washington, DC 20006
m.kay.larcom@conoco.com
Fax:(202) 785 - 0639

Registered Federal Lobbyist.
Serves As:
- Director, Federal Affairs - International, ConocoPhillips

LARE, James J.
One State Farm Dr.
Concordville, PA 19339-0001
Tel: (610) 358 - 7009
Fax:(610) 358 - 7698

Serves As:
- Director, Government Relations, State Farm Insurance Cos.

LARKIN, Courtney
One Tower Sq.
Hartford, CT 06183
Tel: (860) 654 - 7869
Fax:(860) 277 - 2808

Serves As:
- Counsel, Personal Lines, Government Relations, St. Paul Travelers Cos., Inc.

LARKIN, James
One Post St.
San Francisco, CA 94104-5296
james.larkin@mckesson.com
Tel: (415) 983 - 8300
Fax:(415) 983 - 7160

Serves As:
- Director, Corporate Communications, McKesson Corp.

LARKIN, Lyle N.
3125 Myers St.
Riverside, CA 92503
Tel: (909) 351 - 3535
Fax:(909) 351 - 3931

Serves As:
- V. President, Treasurer and Assistant Secretary, Fleetwood Enterprises

Responsibilities include corporate philanthropy, communications, and investor relations.

LAROSA, Paul
P.O. Box 61000
New Orleans, LA 70161
plarosa@entergy.com
Tel: (504) 576 - 4878
Fax:(504) 576 - 4428

Serves As:
- Director, Investor Relations, Entergy Corp.

LARSEN, David
P.O. Box 9777
Federal Way, WA 98063-9777
Tel: (253) 924 - 3456
Fax:(253) 924 - 3685
TF: (800) 525 - 5440

Serves As:
- V. President, Corporate Communications, Weyerhaeuser Co.

LARSEN, Jennifer
1375 N. Highway Dr.
Fenton, MO 63099
jennifer.larsen@maritz.com
Tel: (636) 827 - 1523
Fax:(636) 827 - 8605

Serves As:
- Director, Public Relations, Maritz Inc.

LARSEN, Marshall O.
Four Colesium Center
2730 W. Tyvola Rd.
Charlotte, NC 28217
Tel: (704) 423 - 7000
Fax:(704) 423 - 7100

Serves As:
- Chairman, President and Chief Exec. Officer, Goodrich Corporation

LARSON, Art
101 Ash St.
hq15a
San Diego, CA 92101-3017
alarson@sempra.com
Tel: (619) 696 - 4307
Fax:(619) 696 - 4379
TF: (877) 736 - 7721

Serves As:
- Manager, Public Relations, Sempra Energy

LARSON, Daniel M.
1455 Pennsylvania Ave. NW
Suite 375
MS 4072
Washington, DC 20004
danlarson@ti.com
Tel: (202) 628 - 3133
Fax:(202) 628 - 2980

Registered Federal Lobbyist.
Serves As:
- Director, Government and Media Relations, Texas Instruments Incorporated

LARSON, David R.
1201 Lake Robbins Dr.
The Woodlands, TX 77380
david_larson@anadarko.com
Tel: (832) 636 - 3265

Serves As:
- V. President, Investor Relations, Anadarko Petroleum Corp.

LARSON, Erik
14850 Conference Center Dr.
Chantilly, VA 20151
Tel: (703) 407 - 5720
Fax:(703) 621 - 9140

Serves As:
- Manager, Communications and Planning, Rolls-Royce North America Inc.

LARSON, Greg
6903 Rockledge Dr.
Suite 1500
Bethesda, MD 20817
greg.larson@hostmarriott.com
Tel: (240) 744 - 5800

Serves As:
- Treasurer and Senior V. President, Investor Relations, Host Marriott Corp.

LARSON, Tom

P.O. Box 64089
St. Paul, MN 55164-0089
tlarson@cenexharveststates.com
Tel: (651) 355 - 6000
Fax:(651) 355 - 6432
TF: (800) 232 - 3639

Serves As:
- Exec. V. President, Public Affairs and Chief Operating Officer, CHS Inc.
Responsibilities include communications, public and government affairs and the CHS Foundation.

LARSON, William B.

6565 N. MacArthur Blvd.
Suite 800
Irving, TX 75039
Tel: (214) 689 - 4325
Fax:(214) 689 - 4326

Serves As:
- V. President and Chief Financial Officer, Commercial Metals Co.
Responsibilities include corporate contributions and investor relations.

LASERSON, Frances G.

99 Church St.
New York, NY 10007-2707
fran.laserson@moodys.com
Tel: (212) 553 - 7758
Fax:(212) 553 - 4820

Serves As:
- Senior V. President, Corporate Communications, Moody's Corp.

LASKARIS, George

One MetroTech Center
Brooklyn, NY 11201
Tel: (718) 403 - 2526
Fax:(718) 488 - 1763

Serves As:
- Director, Investor Relations, KeySpan Corp.

LASKY, William M.

One JLG Dr.
McConnellsburg, PA 17233-9533
Tel: (717) 485 - 5161
Fax:(717) 485 - 6417
TF: (877) 534 - 5438

Serves As:
- Chairman, President and Chief Exec. Officer, JLG Industries, Inc.

LASRSON, Randall J.

P.O. Box 5660
Denver, CO 80217
rlarson@transmontaigne.com
Tel: (303) 626 - 8200
Fax:(303) 626 - 8228

Serves As:
- Exec. V. President and Chief Financial Officer, TransMontaigne, Inc.
Responsibilities include investor relations.

LASS, Holly B.

801 Pennsylvania Ave. NW
Suite 620
Washington, DC 20004-2615
Tel: (202) 783 - 7220
Fax:(202) 783 - 8127

Registered Federal Lobbyist.
Serves As:
- Manager, Federal Relations, Reliant Resources

LASSITER, Phillip B.

One State St. Plaza
New York, NY 10004
plassiter@ambac.com
Tel: (212) 668 - 0340
Fax:(212) 509 - 9190
TF: (800) 221 - 1854

Serves As:
- Chairman of the Board, Ambac Financial Group, Inc.

LATAIF, Maryanne

3100 Ocean Park Blvd.
Santa Monica, CA 90405-3032
Tel: (310) 255 - 2704
Fax:(310) 255 - 2100

Serves As:
- V. President, Corporate Communications, Activision, Inc.

LAUBER, Gwyn

3965 Freedom Circle
Santa Clara, CA 95054
gwyn_lauber@mcafee.com
Tel: (408) 346 - 5358
Fax:(408) 346 - 3459
TF: (800) 338 - 8754

Serves As:
- Director, Investor Relations, McAfee, Inc.

LAUDENSLAGER, John

411 Seventh Ave.
Pittsburgh, PA 15219
jlaudenslager@dqe.com
Tel: (412) 393 - 1502
Fax:(412) 393 - 5517

Serves As:
- Senior Manager, Media and Government Relations, Duquesne Light Holdings

LAUDER, Leonard A.

767 Fifth Ave.
New York, NY 10153-0023
Tel: (212) 572 - 4200
Fax:(212) 572 - 6633

Serves As:
- Chairman of the Board, Estee Lauder Companies, Inc.

LAUDER, William P.

767 Fifth Ave.
New York, NY 10153-0023
Tel: (212) 572 - 4200
Fax:(212) 572 - 6633

Serves As:
- President and Chief Exec. Officer, Estee Lauder Companies, Inc.

LAUDERBACK, Sherry

19975 Victor Pkwy.
Livonia, MI 48152-7001
lauderbacks@valassis.com
Tel: (734) 591 - 7374
Ext: 17374
Fax:(734) 591 - 4503
TF: (800) 437 - 0479

Serves As:
- Director, Investor Relations and Communications Center, Valassis Communications, Inc.

LAUDIEN, Lori E.

101 Constitution Ave. NW
Suite 1000 East
Washington, DC 20001
Tel: (202) 637 - 3700
Fax:(202) 637 - 3773

Serves As:
- V. President, Government Affairs, Goldman, Sachs and Co.

LAUDIN, Jeff

One Valmont Plaza
Omaha, NE 68154-5215
jsl1@valmont.com
Tel: (402) 963 - 1158
Fax:(402) 963 - 1197

Serves As:
- Manager, Investor Relations, Valmont Industries, Inc.

LAUDISIO, Glenda

101 Wolf Dr.
Thorofare, NJ 08086
glenda.laudisio@checkpt.com
Tel: (856) 384 - 2411
Fax:(856) 384 - 1480
TF: (800) 257 - 5540

Serves As:
- Director, Corporate Communications, Checkpoint Systems, Inc.

LAUGHLIN, Andrea J.

249 Fifth Ave.
Pittsburgh, PA 15222-2707
Tel: (412) 762 - 2728
Fax:(412) 762 - 3463

Serves As:
- V. President and District Manager, Corporate Relations, PNC Financial Services Group

LAUREN, Ralph

650 Madison Ave.
New York, NY 10022
Tel: (212) 318 - 7000
Fax:(212) 888 - 5780

Serves As:
- Chairman and Chief Exec. Officer, Polo Ralph Lauren

LAURINO, Carl J.

P.O. Box 66
Manitowoc, WI 54221-0066
Tel: (920) 652 - 1720
Fax:(920) 652 - 9778

Serves As:
- Senior V. President and Chief Financial Officer; PAC Treasurer, The Manitowoc Co., Inc.

LAUSSADE, Denise

P.O. Box 261
Danville, VA 24543
Tel: (434) 799 - 4113
Fax:(434) 799 - 7276

Serves As:
- V. President, Finance, Dan River, Inc.
Responsibilities include investor relations.

LAUSTEN, Connie L.

633 Pennsylvania Ave. NW
Sixth Floor
Washington, DC 20004
connie.lausten@us.ngrid.com
Tel: (202) 783 - 7959

Registered Federal Lobbyist.
Serves As:
- Manager, Federal Regulatory Affairs, Nat'l Grid USA

LAVECCHIA, Jean

P.O. Box 270
Hartford, CT 06141-0270
Tel: (860) 665 - 3560
Fax:(860) 665 - 5078
TF: (800) 286 - 2000

Serves As:
- V. President, Human Resources and Environmental Services, (Northeast Utilities Service Co.), Northeast Utilities

LAVELL, Jennifer

P.O. Box 300
Oshkosh, WI 54903-0300
Tel: (920) 231 - 8800
Fax:(920) 231 - 8621
TF: (800) 282 - 4674

Serves As:
- Public Relations Specialist, Oshkosh B'Gosh, Inc.

LAVENDA, Len

Discovery Dr.
Swiftwater, PA 18370
len.lavenda@sanofipasteur.com
Tel: (570) 839 - 4446
Fax:(570) 839 - 5415

Serves As:
- U.S. Media Relations, Sanofi Pasteur, Inc.

LAVERTY, Bob
One Health Plaza
East Hanover, NJ 07936
bob.laverty@pharma.novartis.com
Tel: (862) 778 - 3564
Fax:(862) 644 - 8585

Serves As:
- V. President, Communications, (Novartis Pharmaceuticals Corp.), Novartis Corporation

LAVIN, Cathy
101 Ash St.
Hq. 15E
San Diego, CA 92101-3017
Tel: (619) 696 - 2069
Fax:(619) 696 - 1868
TF: (877) 736 - 7721

Serves As:
- Program Administrator, Corporate Community Relations, Sempra Energy

LAWLER, Kathleen A.
3700 W. Juneau Ave.
Milwaukee, WI 53208
kathleen.lawler@harley-davidson.com
Tel: (414) 342 - 4680
Fax:(414) 343 - 8230

Serves As:
- V. President, Communications, Harley-Davidson Motor Company

LAWLESS, Bridget
230 Park Ave.
New York, NY 10017
bridget.lawless@jpmorganchase.com
Tel: (212) 622 - 3306

Serves As:
- J. P. Morgan Chase & Co. Federal and State PACs Treasurer, J. P. Morgan Chase & Co.

LAWLESS, Robert J.
18 Loveton Circle
Sparks, MD 21152-6000
Tel: (410) 771 - 7301
Fax:(410) 771 - 7462

Serves As:
- Chairman, President, and Chief Exec. Officer, McCormick & Company, Inc.

LAWRENCE, Deborah B.
1627 I St. NW
Suite 900
Washington, DC 20006
deborah.lawrence@williams.com
Tel: (202) 833 - 8994
Fax:(202) 835 - 0707

Serves As:
- V. President, Government Affairs, Williams

LAWRENCE, H. Adam
601 Pennsylvania Ave. NW
Suite 800
Washington, DC 20004
halawrence@southernco.com
Tel: (202) 261 - 5000
Fax:(202) 296 - 7937

Registered Federal Lobbyist.
Serves As:
- Director, Federal Legislative Affairs, Southern Company

LAWRENCE, J. Rodney
100 Pier 1 Place
Fort Worth, TX 76102
Tel: (817) 252 - 8000

Serves As:
- Exec. V. President, Legal Affairs and Corporate Secretary; PAC Treasurer, Pier 1 Imports

LAWRENCE, Jeffrey D.
P.O. Box 997
Ann Arbor, MI 48106-0997
lawrenj@dominos.com
Tel: (734) 930 - 3030
Fax:(734) 930 - 4346

Serves As:
- Contact, Domino's Pizza PAC, Domino's Pizza, LLC

LAWRENCE, Megan
1201 Pennsylvania Ave. NW
Washington, DC 20004
Tel: (202) 626 - 6781

Serves As:
- Director, Government Affairs, Alaska Air Group, Inc.

LAWRENCE, Robert W.
11 W. 42nd St.
New York, NY 10035
Tel: (212) 476 - 1000
Fax:(212) 476 - 1281

Serves As:
- Senior V. President, Human Resources, Empire Blue Cross and Blue Shield

LAWRENCE, Stewart
1201 Lake Robbins Dr.
The Woodlands, TX 77380
stewart_lawrence@anadarko.com
Tel: (832) 636 - 3326

Serves As:
- Manager, Investor Relations, Anadarko Petroleum Corp.

LAWRENCE, Ted
1025 Lenox Park Blvd.
Suite 6B648
Atlanta, GA 30319
Tel: (404) 986 - 1738

Serves As:
- Exec. Director, Regulatory and External Affairs, BellSouth Corp.

LAWSON, David
800 Connecticut Ave. NW
Suite 950
Washington, DC 20006
Tel: (202) 533 - 2100

Serves As:
- Managing Director, J. P. Morgan Chase & Co.

LAWSON, Libby
P.O. Box 2020
Springdale, AR 72765-2020
libby.lawson@tyson.com
Tel: (479) 290 - 3486
Fax:(479) 290 - 7984
TF: (800) 424 - 4253

Serves As:
- V. President, Public and Community Relations, Tyson Foods, Inc.

LAWSON, Lisa B.
Four Tesseneer Dr.
Highland Heights, KY 41076
Tel: (859) 572 - 8000
Fax:(859) 572 - 8458

Serves As:
- V. President, Corporate Communications, General Cable Corp.

LAWSON, Martha G.
P.O. Box 511
Kingsport, TN 37662-5075
mglawson@eastman.com
Tel: (423) 229 - 6574
Fax:(423) 229 - 1008
TF: (800) 327 - 8626

Serves As:
- Director, Communications and Brand Management, Eastman Chemical Co.

LAWSON, Richard C.
1350 I St., N.W., Suite 1030
Washington, DC 20005-3305
Tel: (202) 682 - 1280
Fax:(202) 682 - 1412

Registered Federal Lobbyist.
Serves As:
- V. President, Federal Government Relations, The Principal Financial Group

LAWTON, Alison
500 Kendall St.
Cambridge, MA 02142
Tel: (617) 252 - 7500
Fax:(617) 374 - 7368

Serves As:
- Senior V. President, Regulatory Affairs and Corporate Quality Systems, Genzyme Corp.

LAY, Robert
P.O. Box 419248
Kansas City, MO 64141-6248
Tel: (816) 234 - 2000
TF: (800) 892 - 7100

Serves As:
- Treasurer, Commerce Bancs PAC, Commerce Bancshares Inc.

LAYMAN, Nancy
211 Schilling Circle
Hunt Valley, MD 21031
Tel: (410) 527 - 6278

Serves As:
- Manager, Trade Communications, McCormick & Company, Inc.

LAYMON, Joe W.
One American Rd.
Dearborn, MI 48126
Tel: (313) 322 - 3000
TF: (800) 555 - 5259

Serves As:
- Group V. President, Corporate Human Resources, Ford Motor Co.

LAZENBY, Mark
P.O. Box 26532
Richmond, VA 23261
mark_lazenby@dom.com
Tel: (804) 819 - 2042
Fax:(804) 819 - 2233

Serves As:
- Corporate Communications, Dominion Resources, Inc.

LAZER, Bob
45 Knightsbridge Rd.
Piscataway, NJ 08854
Tel: (732) 699 - 5955
Fax:(732) 336 - 3433

Serves As:
- Contact, Telecordia Corporate Giving, Telcordia Technologies, Inc.

LAZIO, Rick
One Bank One Plaza
Chicago, IL 60670
Tel: (312) 732 - 4000

Serves As:
- Exec. V. President, Global Government Relations and Public Policy, J. P. Morgan Chase & Co.

LE, Jaime Leigh
495 E. Java Dr.
Sunnyvale, CA 94089
jaime.le@netapp.com
Tel: (408) 822 - 3761
Fax:(408) 822 - 4501

Serves As:
- Senior Program Manager, Public Relations, Network Appliance, Inc.

LE FEBVRE, Jarred
5350 Tech Data Dr.
Clearwater, FL 33760
jarred.lefebvre@techdata.com
Tel: (727) 539 - 7429
Fax:(727) 538 - 5866
TF: (800) 237 - 8931

Serves As:
- Communications Specialist, Tech Data Corp.

LE HENAFF, Thierry
2000 Market St.
Philadelphia, PA 19103-9000
Tel: (215) 419 - 7000
Fax:(215) 419 - 7591
TF: (800) 225 - 7788

Serves As:
- Chairman and Chief Exec. Officer, ATOFINA Chemicals, Inc.

LE POCHAT, Joe
1101 17th St. NW
Suite 600
Washington, DC 20036
Tel: (202) 496 - 5654
Fax:(202) 496 - 5660

Registered Federal Lobbyist.
Serves As:
- Managing Director, International and Government Affairs, (American Airlines, Inc.), AMR Corp.

LEA, DeDe
1501 M St. NW
Suite 1100
Washington, DC 20005
Tel: (202) 785 - 7300
Fax:(202) 785 - 6360

Serves As:
- Senior V. President, Government Relations, Viacom Inc., Viacom Inc./CBS Corp.

LEAHY, Susan
401 Park Dr.
Boston, MA 02215
susan.leahy-schuh@bcbsma.com
Tel: (617) 246 - 4823
TF: (800) 325 - 2583

Serves As:
- Director, Public Relations and Media, Blue Cross and Blue Shield of Massachusetts

LEAKE, Earl D.
8600 South Blvd.
Charlotte, NC 28273
Tel: (704) 554 - 1421
Fax:(704) 554 - 5562
TF: (800) 438 - 1880

Serves As:
- V. President, Human Resources, Lance, Inc.

LEAMER, Marybeth H.
6205 Peachtree Dunwoody Rd.
Atlanta, GA 30328
marybeth.leamer@cox.com
Tel: (678) 645 - 0000

Serves As:
- V. President, Human Resources, Cox Enterprises, Inc.

LEAR, Nancy
2711 N. Haskell Ave.
Dallas, TX 75204
Tel: (214) 828 - 7480
Fax:(214) 828 - 7090

Serves As:
- Manager, Community Affairs, 7-Eleven, Inc.

LEARY, John P.
United Technologies Bldg.
One Financial Plaza
Hartford, CT 06101
Tel: (860) 728 - 7000
Fax:(860) 728 - 6494

Serves As:
- V. President, Employee Relations, United Technologies Corp.

LEASK, Janie
P.O. Box 196660
MS 542
Anchorage, AK 99519-6660
Tel: (907) 787 - 8870
Fax:(907) 787 - 8240

Serves As:
- Manager, Community Relations, Alyeska Pipeline Service Co.

LEAVENWORTH, Elaine
1399 New York Ave. NW
Suite 200
Washington, DC 20005
Tel: (202) 378 - 2020
Fax:(202) 783 - 6631

Registered Federal Lobbyist.
Serves As:
- V. President, Government Affairs, Abbott Laboratories

LEBLANC, Richard A.
500 N. Akard St.
Suite 4300
Dallas, TX 75201-3331
rleblanc@enscous.com
Tel: (214) 397 - 3011
Fax:(214) 397 - 3370
TF: (800) 423 - 8006

Serves As:
- V. President, Investor Relations, ENSCO Internat'l Inc.

LECHLEITER, Richard A.
680 S. Fourth Ave.
Louisville, KY 40202-2412
rich_lechleiter@kindredhealthcare.com
Tel: (502) 596 - 7734
Fax:(502) 596 - 4063

Serves As:
- Senior V. President and Chief Financial Officer, Kindred Healthcare, Inc.

Responsibilities include investor relations.

LEDBETTER, Nancy
P.O. Box 618
St. Louis, MO 63188-0618
Tel: (314) 877 - 7854
Fax:(314) 877 - 7667

Serves As:
- Contributions Contact, Ralcorp Holdings, Inc.

LEDER, Bob
P.O. Box 482
Fort Worth, TX 76101
bleder@bellhelicopter.textron.com
Tel: (817) 280 - 6440
Fax:(817) 280 - 8221

Serves As:
- Manager, Communications Operations, Bell Helicopter Textron

LEDFORD, Nancy
P.O. Box 511
Kingsport, TN 37662-5075
nledford@eastman.com
Tel: (423) 229 - 5264
Fax:(423) 229 - 1008
TF: (800) 327 - 8626

Serves As:
- Manager, Disclosure Communications, Eastman Chemical Co.

LEDOUX, Marque I.
1500 K St. NW
Suite 375
Washington, DC 20005
Tel: (202) 383 - 4166
Fax:(202) 383 - 4018

Serves As:
- Assistant V. President, Public Affairs, Norfolk Southern Corp.

LEDUC, Michael R.
One Sun Life Executive Park
Wellesley Hills, MA 02481
Tel: (781) 237 - 6030
Fax:(781) 304 - 5383
TF: (800) 225 - 3950

Serves As:
- V. President, Industry and Government Affairs, Sun Life Financial

LEDWICK, Tim
3191 Broadbridge Ave.
Stratford, CT 06614-2559
tim.ledwick@dictaphone.com
Tel: (203) 381 - 7000

Serves As:
- Financial Information Contact, Dictaphone Corp.

LEE, Albert
4000 E. Union Pacific Ave.
City of Commerce, CA 90023
Tel: (323) 980 - 8145
Fax:(323) 980 - 8160

Serves As:
- Secretary to the President and Manager, Investor Relations, 99 Cents Only Stores

LEE, Celeste Reid
401 Park Dr.
Boston, MA 02215
celeste.lee@bcbsmafoundation.org
Tel: (617) 246 - 5000
TF: (800) 325 - 2583

Serves As:
- Director, Community Partnerships, Blue Cross and Blue Shield of Massachusetts

LEE, Daniel
1155 Battery St.
San Francisco, CA 94111
Tel: (415) 501 - 6000
Fax:(415) 501 - 7112
TF: (800) 872 - 5384

Serves As:
- Manager, Community Affairs and Corporate Affairs, Levi Strauss and Co.

LEE, Daniel R.
3800 Howard Hughes Prkwy.
Las Vegas, NV 89109
Tel: (702) 784 - 7777

Serves As:
- Chairman and Chief Exec. Officer, Pinnacle Entertainment, Inc.

LEE, Edmund
70 Pine St.
New York, NY 10270
Tel: (212) 770 - 6698
Fax:(212) 770 - 6786

Registered Federal Lobbyist.
Serves As:
- Assistant V. President, International and Corporate Affairs, American Internat'l Group, Inc.

LEE, J. Terrence
165 Madison Ave.
Memphis, TN 38103
Tel: (901) 523 - 4380
Fax:(901) 523 - 4354

Serves As:
- Senior V. President, Corporate Communications, First Horizon Nat'l Corp.

LEE, Joe R.
P.O. Box 593330
Orlando, FL 32859
Tel: (407) 245 - 4000
Fax:(407) 245 - 4462

Serves As:
- Chairman, Darden Restaurants, Inc.

LEE, Jonathan
39 Old Ridgebury Rd.
Danbury, CT 06810-5113
jon_lee@praxair.com
Tel: (203) 837 - 2039
Fax:(203) 837 - 2505
TF: (800) 772 - 9247

Serves As:
- Media Contact, Praxair, Inc.

LEE, III, Joseph
P.O. Box 430
Memphis, TN 30103
Tel: (901) 528 - 4011

Serves As:
- President and Chief Exec. Officer, Memphis Light, Gas and Water Division

Responsibilities include corporate philanthropy.

LEE, Misha
1800 N. Point Dr.
Stevens Point, WI 54481
Tel: (715) 346 - 6000
Fax:(715) 346 - 6346

Serves As:
- Manager, Government Relations, Sentry Insurance

LEE, Roberta
13410 Sutton Park Dr. South
Jacksonville, FL 32224
Tel: (904) 398 - 9400
Fax:(904) 390 - 1437
TF: (800) 872 - 9400

Serves As:
- Contact, Landstar Scholarship Fund, Landstar System, Inc.

LEE, Robin
2020 Santa Monica Blvd., Suite 600
Santa Monica, CA 90404-2208
rlee@fmt.com
Tel: (310) 315 - 5500
Fax:(310) 315 - 5599

Serves As:
- Director, Human Resources, Fremont General Corp.

LEE, William J.
1100 Wilson Blvd.
Suite 1500
Arlington, VA 22209
william_j_lee@raytheon.com
Tel: (703) 841 - 5700
Fax:(703) 841 - 5792

Registered Federal Lobbyist.
Serves As:
- Director, Government Relations, Raytheon Co.

LEEDS, Candace
667 Madison Ave.
New York, NY 10021-8087
cleeds@loews.com
Tel: (212) 521 - 2416
Fax:(212) 521 - 2860

Serves As:
- V. President, Public Affairs, (Loews Hotels), Loews Corporation

Responsibilities include corporate communications and corporate philanthropy.

LEEDS, Richard
11 Harbor Park Dr.
Port Washington, NY 11050
service@globalindustrial.com
Tel: (516) 608 - 7000
Fax:(516) 625 - 0038

Serves As:
- Chairman and Chief Exec. Officer, Systemax Inc.

Responsibilities include corporate communications.

LEER, Steven F.
One CityPlace Dr.
Suite 300
St. Louis, MO 63141
Tel: (314) 994 - 2700
Fax:(314) 994 - 2719

Serves As:
- President and Chief Exec. Officer, Arch Coal, Inc.

LEFEBVRE, Laurel
500 Staples Dr.
Framingham, MA 01702
laurel.lefebvre@staples.com
Tel: (508) 253 - 5000
Ext: 34080
Fax:(508) 253 - 8955

Serves As:
- V. President, Investor Relations, Staples, Inc.

LEFORT, G. Neil
2222 Wellington Ct.
Lisle, IL 60532
nlefort@molex.com
Tel: (630) 527 - 4344
Fax:(630) 969 - 1352
TF: (800) 786 - 6539

Serves As:
- V. President, Investor Relations, Molex Incorporated

LEFRANCOIS, Ronald J.
1501 K St. NW
Suite 575
Washington, DC 20005
Tel: (202) 654 - 2943
Fax:(202) 654 - 2945

Registered Federal Lobbyist.
Serves As:
- V. President, Governmental Affairs, New York Life Insurance Co.

LEFTWICH, Gary
P.O. Box 1000
Carrollton, GA 30119
gary_leftwich@southwire.com
Tel: (770) 832 - 4884
Fax:(770) 832 - 4584
TF: (800) 444 - 1700

Serves As:
- Senior Communications Specialist, Southwire Co.

Responsibilities include corporate philanthropy.

LEGERE, John
200 Park Ave.
Suite 300
Florham Park, NJ 07932
Tel: (973) 937 - 0100
Fax:(973) 360 - 0148
TF: (800) 336 - 7000

Serves As:
- Chief Exec. Officer, Global Crossing Ltd.

LEGERE, Mr. Marc
1007 Market St.
Room D-11078
Wilmington, DE 19898
Tel: (302) 774 - 1000
Fax:(302) 773 - 2919
TF: (800) 441 - 7515

Serves As:
- PAC Treasurer, DuPont

LEGREVES, Frederique
P.O. Box 191
Gardena, CA 90248-0191
Tel: (310) 771 - 3111
Fax:(310) 771 - 5656

Serves As:
- V. President, Corporate Communications, Nissan North America, Inc.

LEHMAN, Alice L.
301 S. College St., Suite 4000
One Wachovia Center
NC 0206
Charlotte, NC 28288-0370
alice.lehman@wachovia.com
Tel: (704) 374 - 6565
Fax:(704) 374 - 3425
TF: (800) 275 - 3862

Serves As:
- Senior V. President and Managing Director, Investor Relations, Wachovia Corp.

LEHR, Jr., William
P.O. Box 772531
Harrisburg, PA 17177-2531
Tel: (717) 541 - 7000
Fax:(717) 541 - 6072

Serves As:
- Chairman of the Board, Capital BlueCross (Pennsylvania)

LEI, Dr. Wayne
121 SW Salmon St.
1WTC-0303
Portland, OR 97204
wayne_lei@pgn.com
Tel: (503) 464 - 8000
Fax:(503) 464 - 2354

Serves As:
- Director, Environmental Policy Programs, Portland General Electric Co.

LEINWEAVER, Jeff
P.O. Box 81226
Seattle, WA 98108-1226
Tel: (206) 266 - 1000
Fax:(206) 266 - 1821

Serves As:
- Coordinator, Public Relations, Amazon.com, Inc.

LEMARCHAND-WOOD, Flavie
800 Third Ave., Fourth Floor
New York, NY 10022
Tel: (212) 572 - 1118

Serves As:
- Director, Corporate Communications, Vivendi Universal

LEMBO, Philip J.
One NSTAR Way
Westwood, MA 02090
philip_lembo@nstaronline.com
Tel: (617) 424 - 3562
Fax:(617) 424 - 4032

Serves As:
- Assistant Treasurer, Corporate Finance and Investor Relations, NSTAR

LEMKE, Karmen
P.O. Box 19001
M/S A2
Green Bay, WI 54307-9001
klemke@wpsc.com
Tel: (920) 433 - 1433
Fax:(920) 433 - 1693
TF: (800) 450 - 7260

Serves As:
- Leader, Community Relations, Wisconsin Public Service Corp.

LEMMON, David L.
P.O. Box 1624
Alpharetta, GA 30009-9934
Fax:(678) 762 - 2883
TF: (800) 275 - 3004

Serves As:
- President and Chief Exec. Officer, Colonial Pipeline Co.

LEMSON, Steve D.
Three World Financial Center
200 Vesey St.
New York, NY 10285
steve.lemson@aexp.com
Tel: (212) 640 - 5028

Serves As:
- V. President, State Government Affairs, American Express Co.

LENAHAN, Joan O.
P.O. Box 1438
Louisville, KY 40201-1438
jlenahan@humana.com
Tel: (502) 580 - 3778
Fax:(502) 580 - 3677
TF: (800) 486 - 2620

Serves As:
- Corporate Secretary, Humana Inc.

Responsibilities include investor relations.

LENHART, William G.
P.O. Box 3300
Elkhart, IN 46515
blenhart@coachmen.com
Tel: (574) 262 - 0123
Fax:(574) 262 - 8823

Serves As:
- Senior V. President, Human Resources, Coachmen Industries, Inc.

Responsibilities also include corporate philanthropy.

LENNON, Frank T.
P.O. Box 18100
Richmond, VA 23226-8100
Tel: (804) 289 - 9660
Fax:(804) 289 - 9753

Serves As:
- V. President and Chief Administrative Officer, The Brink's Co.

Responsibilities include corporate philanthropy.

LENNOX, Thomas D.
6301 Fitch Path
New Albany, OH 43054
tom_lennox@abercrombie.com
Tel: (614) 283 - 6751
Fax:(614) 283 - 6710

Serves As:
- Director, Investor Relations and Corporate Communications, Abercrombie & Fitch Co.

LENNY, Richard H.
100 Crystal A Dr.
P.O. Box 810
Hershey, PA 17033
Tel: (717) 534 - 4200
Fax:(717) 534 - 7015

Serves As:
- Chairman, President and Chief Exec. Officer, The Hershey Company

LENOVER, Susan
1300 N. 17th St.
Suite 1400
Arlington, VA 22209
Tel: (703) 907 - 8200
Fax:(703) 907 - 8300

Serves As:
- Assistant to the V. President, Coporate Communications, BAE Systems North America

LENTINI, Jr., Anthony R.
2000 Post Oak Blvd., Suite 100
Houston, TX 77056-4400
tony.lentini@apachecorp.com
Tel: (713) 296 - 6107
Fax:(713) 296 - 6480
TF: (800) 874 - 3262

Serves As:
- V. President, Public and International Affairs, Apache Corp.

LEONARD, J. Wayne
P.O. Box 61000
New Orleans, LA 70161
jleonard@entergy.com
Tel: (504) 576 - 4000

Serves As:
- Chairman and Chief Exec. Officer, Entergy Services, Inc.
- Chief Exec. Officer, Entergy Corp.

LEONARD, Jan
P.O. Box 419226
Kansas City, MO 64141-6226
Tel: (816) 860 - 7000
Fax:(816) 860 - 5675

Serves As:
- Managing Director, Charitable Trust, UMB Financial Corp.

Responsibilites include corporate philanthropy.

LEONARD, Joseph B.
9955 Airtran Blvd.
Orlando, FL 32827-5330
Tel: (407) 251 - 5600
Fax:(407) 251 - 5727

Serves As:
- Chairman and Chief Exec. Officer, AirTran Airways

LEONARD, K.
1201 Lake Robbins Dr.
The Woodlands, TX 77380
Tel: (832) 636 - 3594

Serves As:
- Senior Corporate Communications Advisor, Anadarko Petroleum Corp.

LEONARD, Mary
One John Deere Pl.
Moline, IL 61265-8098
Tel: (309) 765 - 4106
Fax:(309) 765 - 5682

Serves As:
- Communications Manager, Public Relations, Deere & Company

LEONARD, Scott
60 Massachusetts Ave. NE
Washington, DC 20002
Tel: (202) 906 - 3000
Fax:(202) 906 - 3865

Serves As:
- Government Affairs Specialist, Amtrak

LEONI, Nanette
2244 Walnut Grove Ave.
Rosemead, CA 91770
nanette.leoni@edisonintl.com
Tel: (626) 302 - 3680

Serves As:
- Manager, Investor Relations, Edison Internat'l

LEPPERT, Thomas C.
375 Hudson St.
New York, NY 10014
Tel: (212) 229 - 6000
Fax:(212) 229 - 6390

Serves As:
- Chairman and Chief Exec. Officer, The Turner Corp.

LEPPETITO, Caroline
1499 Post Rd.
Fairfield, CT 06824
Tel: (610) 834 - 5716

Serves As:
- Director, Public Relations, IMS Health, Inc.

LEPRI, Sandy
1001 Air Brake Ave.
Wilmerding, PA 15148-1036
Tel: (412) 825 - 1000
Fax:(412) 825 - 1019

Serves As:
- Manager, Public Relations, Westinghouse Air Brake Technologies Corp.

LERCH, Marie
8283 Greensboro Dr.
McLean, VA 22102-3802
lerch_marie@bah.com
Tel: (703) 902 - 5559
Fax:(703) 902 - 3323

Serves As:
- Senior Director, Marketing and Communications, Booz Allen Hamilton Inc.

LERETTE, Susan
300 Concord Plaza Dr.
San Antonio, TX 78216
Tel: (210) 283 - 2001
Fax:(210) 283 - 2003
TF: (800) 837 - 8768

Serves As:
- V. President, Human Resources, Tesoro Petroleum Corp.

LERNER, Mark
6601 Bermuda Rd.
Las Vegas, NV 89119-3605
Tel: (702) 270 - 7600
Fax:(702) 270 - 7699

Serves As:
- Senior V. President, Law and Government; General Counsel and Secretary, Alliance Gaming Corp.

LERNER, Randolph D.
1100 N. King St.
Wilmington, DE 19880-127
Fax:(302) 456 - 8541
TF: (800) 441 - 7048

Serves As:
- Chairman of the Board, MBNA Corp.

LESAR, David J.
601 Jefferson St.
Houston, TX 77002
Tel: (713) 753 - 2000
Fax:(713) 753 - 5353

Serves As:
- Chairman and Chief Exec. Officer, Kellogg Brown and Root

LESHER, Michelle
P.O. Box 100
Whitehouse Station, NJ 08889-0100
Tel: (908) 423 - 4111
Fax:(908) 735 - 1181
TF: (800) 423 - 1000

Serves As:
- Coordinator, Public Policy Research and Analysis, Merck & Co., Inc.

LESHNE, Jerry
1114 Ave. of the Americas
New York, NY 10036
Tel: (212) 704 - 1439

Serves As:
- V. President, Financial Planning and Analysis and Investor Relations, The Interpublic Group of Companies

LESKO, Dirk A.
700 Washington St.
Bath, ME 04530
dirk.lesko@gdbiw.com
Tel: (207) 442 - 2072
Fax:(207) 442 - 1009

Serves As:
• Director, Strategic Planning and Communications, Bath Iron Works Corp.

LESLEY, Robert
P.O. Box 1640
Jackson, MS 39215-1640
rlesley@entergy.com
Tel: (601) 368 - 5000
Fax:(601) 964 - 2400

Serves As:
• Coordinator, Media Relations, Entergy Mississippi

LESSER, Jill A.
800 Connecticut Ave. NW
Suite 800
Washington, DC 20006
Tel: (202) 457 - 8582
Fax:(202) 457 - 8861

Registered Federal Lobbyist.
Serves As:
• Senior Policy Advisor, Time Warner Inc.

LESSTRANG, David
2011 Crystal Dr., Crystal Park I
Suite 907
Arlington, VA 22202
lesstrang_david@emc.com
Tel: (703) 769 - 6202
Fax:(703) 892 - 0091

Registered Federal Lobbyist.
Serves As:
• Manager, Government Affairs, EMC Corp.

LESTELLE, James F.
5718 Westheimer St.
Houston, TX 77057
jlestelle@hibernia.com
Tel: (504) 533 - 5482
Fax:(504) 533 - 5841
TF: (800) 562 - 9007

Serves As:
• Senior V. President, Corporate Communications, Hibernia Corp.

LESTER, W. Howard
3250 Van Ness Ave.
San Francisco, CA 94109
Tel: (415) 421 - 7900
Fax:(415) 616 - 8463

Serves As:
• Chairman of the Board, Williams-Sonoma, Inc.

LETHAM, Dennis J.
2301 Patriot Blvd.
Glenview, IL 60025-8020
Tel: (224) 521 - 8601

Serves As:
• Chief Financial Officer and Senior V. President, Finance, Anixter Internat'l, Inc.
Responsibilities include investor relations.

LETKIEWICZ, James D.
770 N. Water St.
Eighth Floor
Milwaukee, WI 53202
Tel: (414) 765 - 7700
Fax:(414) 765 - 7899

Serves As:
• V. President, Human Resources, Marshall & Ilsley Corp.

LETTIERI, Lisa D.
2701 Cambridge Ct.
Suite 300
Auburn Hills, MI 48326
llettieri@championhomes.net
Tel: (248) 340 - 7731
Fax:(248) 340 - 9345

Serves As:
• V. President, Investor Relations, Champion Enterprises, Inc.

LETZLER, Steve
55 Water St.
49th Floor
New York, NY 10041-0099
sletzler@dtcc.com
Tel: (212) 855 - 5469
Fax:(212) 908 - 2366

Serves As:
• Director, Corporate Communications, The Depository Trust & Clearing Corp.

LEULIETTE, Timothy D.
47659 Halyard Dr.
Plymouth, MI 48170
Tel: (734) 207 - 6200
Fax:(734) 207 - 6500

Serves As:
• Chairman, President and Chief Exec. Officer, Metaldyne Corp.

LEVEN, Stephen H.
P.O. Box 660199
M/S 8658
Dallas, TX 75266-0199
s-leven@ti.com
Tel: (214) 480 - 4700
Fax:(214) 480 - 1977
TF: (800) 336 - 5236

Serves As:
• Senior V. President, Human Resources, Texas Instruments Incorporated

LEVENSON, Allen
622 Third Ave., 37th Floor
New York, NY 10017
Tel: (212) 885 - 2500

Serves As:
• V. President, Sales and Marketing, Asbury Automotive Group
Responsibilities include public relations.

LEVENSON, Nancy R.
1133 Connecticut Ave. NW
Suite 650
Washington, DC 20036
Tel: (202) 331 - 1186
Fax:(202) 659 - 2338

Registered Federal Lobbyist.
Serves As:
• Director, U.S. Federal Government Relations, SC Johnson

LEVENSON, Sam
Nine W. 57th St.
37th Floor
New York, NY 10019
sam.levenson@cendant.com
Tel: (212) 413 - 1834

Serves As:
• Senior V. President, Investor Relations, Cendant Corp.

LEVESQUE, Gerald R. "Gerry"
19 Sugar Maple Dr.
Coventry, RI 02816
gerard.levesque@az.com
Tel: (401) 827 - 0558
Fax:(401) 827 - 0574
TF: (800) 822 - 9209
Ext: 69022

Serves As:
• Associate Director, State Government Affairs, AstraZeneca Pharmaceuticals

LEVETZOW, Pam
3520 Broadway
Kansas City, MO 64111
Tel: (816) 360 - 5753

Serves As:
• Director, Public Affairs, Southern Union Company

LEVEY, Jeffrey R.
1101 Pennsylvania Ave. NW
Suite 1000
Washington, DC 20004
jeffrey.levey@citicorp.com
Tel: (202) 879 - 6818
Fax:(202) 783 - 1873

Registered Federal Lobbyist.
Serves As:
• V. President, Tax Legislation, Citigroup, Inc.

LEVIN, Andrew W.
1401 I St., NW
Suite 401
Washington, DC 20005
Tel: (202) 289 - 3230
Fax:(202) 289 - 0050

Registered Federal Lobbyist.
Serves As:
• Representative, Clear Channel Communications
• Contact, Clear Channel Communications Inc. Political Action Committee
Responsibilities include political action.

LEVIN, Robert
3900 Wisconsin Ave. NW
Washington, DC 20016
Tel: (202) 752 - 7000
Fax:(202) 752 - 6099

Serves As:
• Exec. V. President, Housing and Community Development, Fannie Mae

LEVINE, Brian
2200 Old Germantown Rd.
Delray Beach, FL 33445
Tel: (561) 438 - 2895
Fax:(561) 438 - 4400

Serves As:
• Director, Public Relations, Office Depot, Inc.

LEVINE, Howard R.
P.O. Box 1017
Charlotte, NC 28201-1017
hlevine@familydollar.com
Tel: (704) 847 - 6961
Fax:(704) 847 - 0189

Serves As:
• Chairman and Chief Exec. Officer, Family Dollar Stores, Inc.

LEVINE, Michelle
1194 N. Mathilda Ave.
Sunnyvale, CA 94089-1206
Tel: (408) 936 - 2775
Fax:(408) 745 - 2100

Serves As:
• Senior Manager, Investor Relations, Juniper Networks, Inc.

LEVINE, Norman M.
One Tower Ln.
Suite 1000
Oakbrook Terrace, IL 60181-4624
Tel: (630) 571 - 7700
Fax:(630) 571 - 0317
TF: (800) 225 - 8000

Serves As:
• Senior V. President,PAC Treasurer, DeVry Inc.

LEVINSON, Arthur D.
One DNA Way
San Francisco, CA 94080-4990
alevinson@gene.com
Tel: (650) 225 - 1000
Fax:(650) 225 - 6000

Serves As:
• Chairman and Chief Exec. Officer, Genentech, Inc.

LEVITAN, Mickey
40 Monument Circle
Suite 700
Indianapolis, IN 46204
Tel: (317) 266 - 0100
Fax:(317) 631 - 3750

Serves As:
• Senior V. President, Human Resources, Emmis Communications Corp.

LEVY, Beverly
310 Orange St.
New Haven, CT 06510
Tel: (203) 771 - 4474

Serves As:
• Company Spokesperson, Media and External Affairs, SBC SNET

LEVY, Jean-Bernard
800 Third Ave., Fourth Floor
New York, NY 10022
Tel: (212) 572 - 7000

Serves As:
• Chairman and Chief Exec. Officer, Vivendi Universal

LEVY, Kenneth
160 Rio Robles
San Jose, CA 95134
Tel: (408) 875 - 3000
Fax:(408) 875 - 4266

Serves As:
• Chairman of the Board, KLA-Tencor

LEVY, Michael
401 Ninth St. NW
Washington, DC 20004-2129
Tel: (202) 879 - 9758
Fax:(202) 879 - 9700

Serves As:
• Corporate and Public Affairs Contact, Corporation for Public Broadcasting

LEVY, Richard M.
3100 Hansen Way
Palo Alto, CA 94304-1030
Tel: (650) 493 - 4000
Fax:(650) 842 - 5196

Serves As:
• Chairman, President and Chief Exec. Officer, Varian Medical Systems, Inc.

LEVY, Susan M.
111 S. Wacker Dr.
Chicago, IL 60606
susan.levy@rrd.com
Tel: (312) 326 - 8102
Fax:(312) 326 - 8262

Serves As:
• Director, Community Relations, R R Donnelley

LEVY-BUENO, Crystal
55 Water St.
49th Floor
New York, NY 10041-0099
clevy-bueno@dtcc.com
Tel: (212) 855 - 5473
Fax:(212) 908 - 2224

Serves As:
• Director, Corporate Communications, The Depository Trust & Clearing Corp.

LEWEKE, Richard A.
201 Mission St.
San Francisco, CA 94105
Tel: (415) 543 - 0404
Fax:(415) 278 - 6028

Serves As:
• V. Chairman and Chief Human Resources Officer, Providian Financial Corp.

LEWELLEN, Michael
One BET Plaza
1235 W Pl., N.E.
Washington, DC 20018
Tel: (202) 608 - 2003
Fax:(202) 608 - 2518

Serves As:
• V. President, Communications, (BET), Viacom Inc./CBS Corp.

LEWENT, Judy C.
P.O. Box 100
Whitehouse Station, NJ 08889-0100
Tel: (908) 423 - 5244
Fax:(908) 735 - 1270
TF: (800) 423 - 1000

Serves As:
• Exec. V. President, Chief Financial Officer; and President, Human Health Asia, Merck & Co., Inc.
Responsibilities include investor relations.

LEWIN, Luis E.
435 N. Michigan Ave.
Chicago, IL 60611
llewin@tribune.com
Tel: (312) 222 - 4581
Fax:(312) 222 - 1573

Serves As:
• Senior V. President, Human Resources, Tribune Co.

LEWIN, Rene R.
Five Giralda Farms
Madison, NJ 07940
Tel: (973) 660 - 5258
Fax:(973) 660 - 5771

Serves As:
• Senior V. President, Human Resources, Wyeth

LEWIS, Alex
203 E. Main St.
Spartanburg, SC 29319-0001
Tel: (877) 784 - 7167
Fax:(864) 597 - 8216

Serves As:
• Assistant Treasurer and Director, Investor Relations, Denny's Corp.

LEWIS, Buford
2000 K St., NW
Suite 710
Washington, DC 20006
Tel: (202) 862 - 0200
Fax:(202) 862 - 0267

Serves As:
• Washington Representative - U.S. Senate, Exxon Mobil Corp.

LEWIS, Cathy
P.O. Box 834
Valley Forge, PA 19482-0834
clewis@ikon.com
Tel: (610) 296 - 8000
Fax:(610) 408 - 7025
TF: (888) 275 - 4566

Serves As:
• Senior V. President, Marketing, Ikon Office Solutions, Inc.
Responsibilities include corporate communications and contributions.

LEWIS, Chris
201 Mission St.
San Francisco, CA 94105
chris_lewis@providian.com
Tel: (415) 543 - 0404
Fax:(415) 278 - 6028

Serves As:
• V. President, Corporate Affairs, Providian Financial Corp.

LEWIS, D. Scott
P.O. Box 190
Aurora, IL 60507-0190
slewis@nicor.com
Tel: (630) 983 - 8676
Ext: 3147
Fax:(630) 548 - 3574

Serves As:
• Assistant V. President, Government Relations, (NICOR Gas), Nicor, Inc.

LEWIS, David F.
P.O. Box 799900
Dallas, TX 75379-9900
Tel: (972) 497 - 5316
Fax:(972) 497 - 5268

Serves As:
• V. President, Government Affairs, Lennox Internat'l

LEWIS, Diana D.
Ecolab Center
370 N. Wabasha St.
St. Paul, MN 55102
diana.lewis@ecolab.com
Tel: (651) 293 - 2344
Fax:(651) 225 - 2092

Serves As:
• V. President, Human Resources, Ecolab Inc.

LEWIS, Greg
635 Massachusetts Ave. NW
Washington, DC 20001
Tel: (202) 513 - 2000
Fax:(202) 513 - 3329

Registered Federal Lobbyist.
Serves As:
• Legal Counsel, Nat'l Public Radio

LEWIS, H. Craig
2001 Market St., Suite 29
Philadelphia, PA 19103
Tel: (215) 209 - 4284
Fax:(215) 209 - 4286

Serves As:
• V. President, Corporate Affairs, Norfolk Southern Corp.

LEWIS, Hallie
601 Pennsylvania Ave. NW
Suite 700
Washington, DC 20004
Tel: (202) 639 - 1881

Registered Federal Lobbyist.
Serves As:
• Manager, Government Affairs, Medco Health Solutions, Inc.

LEWIS, Jaye
One American Rd.
Cleveland, OH 44144-2398
Tel: (216) 252 - 7300
Fax:(216) 252 - 6778

Serves As:
• Trade Media and Public Relations Contact, American Greetings Corp.

LEWIS, Karen
P.O. Box 10395
Palo Alto, CA 94303-0395
karen_lewis@agilent.com
Tel: (650) 752 - 5153
Fax:(650) 752 - 5633

Serves As:
• Exec. Director, Agilent Foundation, Agilent Technologies, Inc.

LEWIS, Kenneth D.
Bank of America Corporate Center
100 N. Tryon St.
Charlotte, NC 28255-0001
Tel: (704) 386 - 4343
Fax:(704) 386 - 6699

Serves As:
- Chairman, President and Chief Exec. Officer, Bank of America Corp.

LEWIS, Maris
20330 Stevens Creek Blvd.
Cupertino, CA 95014-2132
marisa_lewis@symantec.com
Tel: (408) 517 - 8239
Fax:(408) 517 - 8186

Serves As:
- Manager, Investor Relations, Symantec Corp.

LEWIS, Nicholas
316 Pennsylvania Ave. SE
Suite 300
Washington, DC 20003
nlewis@ups.com
Tel: (202) 675 - 4222
Fax:(202) 675 - 4230

Registered Federal Lobbyist.
Serves As:
- Manager, Public Affairs, United Parcel Service (UPS)

LEWIS, Peter B.
6300 Wilson Mills Rd.
Mayfield Village, OH 44143
Tel: (440) 461 - 5000
Fax:(440) 446 - 7168
TF: (800) 876 - 6327

Serves As:
- Chairman of the Board, The Progressive Corporation

LEWIS, Philip G.
100 Independence Mall West
Philadelphia, PA 19106-2399
Tel: (215) 785 - 7421
Fax:(215) 592 - 3377

Serves As:
- V. President and Director, Environmental Health and Safety, Rohm and Haas Co.

LEWIS, Ray
2941 Fairview Park Dr.
Falls Church, VA 22042-4513
Tel: (703) 876 - 3195
Fax:(703) 876 - 3186

Serves As:
- Staff V. President, Investor Relations, General Dynamics Corporation

LEWIS, Richard A.
1201 Lake Robbins Dr.
The Woodlands, TX 77380
richard_lewis@anadarko.com
Tel: (832) 636 - 1000

Serves As:
- V. President, Human Resources, Anadarko Petroleum Corp.

LEWIS, Roderic W.
8000 S. Federal Way
Boise, ID 83707
Tel: (208) 368 - 4000
Fax:(208) 368 - 2536

Registered Federal Lobbyist.
Serves As:
- V. President, Legal Affairs/General Counsel, and Corporate Secretary, Micron Technology, Inc.

Responsibilities include investor relations.

LEWIS, Roger L.
13220 California St.
Omaha, NE 68154
Tel: (402) 514 - 5306
Fax:(402) 514 - 5486
TF: (800) 228 - 5023

Serves As:
- Senior V. President and Director, Marketing, Commercial Federal Corp.

Responsibilities include corporate philanthropy.

LEWIS, Scott
2100 Logic Dr.
San Jose, CA 95124-3400
scottl@xilinx.com
Tel: (408) 879 - 4556
Fax:(408) 371 - 4926
TF: (800) 836 - 4002

Serves As:
- Director, Corporate Communications, Xilinx, Inc.

LEWIS-CLAPPER, Caskie
6950 Columbia Gateway Dr.
Columbia, MD 21046
Tel: (410) 953 - 1000
Fax:(410) 953 - 5200

Serves As:
- Chief Human Resources Officer, Magellan Health Services, Inc.

LEZMAN, Steve
555W. Monroe St.
Chicago, IL 60661
Tel: (941) 742 - 2578
Fax:(941) 749 - 3966

Serves As:
- Director, Government Affairs, (Tropicana Products), PepsiCo, Inc.

LEZY, Normand G.
575 Seventh St. NW
Terrell Bldg.
Washington, DC 20004
nlezy@wal-mart.com
Tel: (202) 737 - 5523
Fax:(202) 737 - 6069

Registered Federal Lobbyist.
Serves As:
- V. President, National Government Relations, Wal-Mart Stores

LIBERATORE, Robert G.
1401 H St. NW
Suite 700
Washington, DC 20005
Tel: (202) 414 - 6747
Fax:(202) 414 - 6716

Registered Federal Lobbyist.
Serves As:
- Senior V. President, External Affairs and Public Policy, DaimlerChrysler Corp.

LIBONATI, John J.
1401 K St. NW
Suite 702
Washington, DC 20005
john.libonati@owenscorning.com
Tel: (202) 216 - 1080

Registered Federal Lobbyist.
Serves As:
- Vice President, Government and Public Affairs, Owens Corning

LIBRO, William J.
122 C St. NW
Suite 840
Washington, DC 20001
blibro@exchange1.mnpower.com
Tel: (202) 638 - 7707
Fax:(202) 638 - 7710

Registered Federal Lobbyist.
Serves As:
- Director, Federal Affairs, ALLETE

LIDDLE, Jack W.
Crystal Gateway One, Suite 1102
1235 S. Clark St.
Arlington, VA 22202
jack.liddle@cubic.com
Tel: (703) 415 - 1600
Fax:(703) 415 - 1608

Registered Federal Lobbyist.
Serves As:
- V. President, Legislative Affairs, (Cubic Defense Systems), Cubic Corp.

LIDDLE, Lynn M.
P.O. Box 997
Ann Arbor, MI 48106-0997
Tel: (734) 930 - 3563
Fax:(734) 668 - 1946

Serves As:
- Executive V. President, Corporate Communications and Investor Relations, Domino's Pizza, LLC

LIDDY, Edward M.
2775 Sanders Rd.
Northbrook, IL 60062-6127
eliddy@allstate.com
Tel: (847) 402 - 5000
Fax:(847) 402 - 5448
TF: (800) 574 - 3553

Serves As:
- Chairman, President and Chief Exec. Officer, Allstate Insurance Co.

LIDELL, Steve
P.O. Box 1408
Fayetteville, AR 72702-1408

Serves As:
- Manager, Environmental Affairs, Southwestern Energy Co.

LIDEN, Barry
One Edwards Way
Irvine, CA 92614-5688
Tel: (949) 250 - 6881
Fax:(949) 250 - 2733
TF: (800) 424 - 3278

Serves As:
- Director, Global Communications, Edwards Lifesciences Corp.

LIEBER, Michele
1660 L St. NW
Fourth Floor
Washington, DC 20036
Tel: (202) 775 - 5027
Fax:(202) 775 - 5045

Serves As:
- Director, Legislative and Regulatory Policy, Financial Services, General Motors Corp.
- Director, Legislative and Regulatory Affairs, Financial Services, General Motors Acceptance Corp. (GMAC)

LIEBERMAN, Ross J.
1233 20th St., NW
Suite 701
Washington, DC 20036
Tel: (202) 293 - 0981
Fax:(202) 293 - 0984

Registered Federal Lobbyist.
Serves As:
- Government Relations, EchoStar Communications Corp.

LIEBMAN, Jeanette
3050 Bowers Ave.
P.O. Box 58039
Santa Clara, CA 95054-3299
Tel: (408) 727 - 5555
Fax:(408) 748 - 9943

Serves As:
- Group V. President, Global Human Resources, Applied Materials, Inc.

LIEFELD, Gwen
4900 IDS Center
80 S. Eighth St.
Minneapolis, MN 55402
Tel: (612) 337 - 5903
Fax:(612) 337 - 5904

Serves As:
- Manager, Valspar Foundation, Valspar Corp.

LIETEAU, Michael P.
225 W. Randolph St.
27 B
Chicago, IL 60606
Tel: (312) 727 - 6105
Fax:(312) 727 - 3722
TF: (800) 327 - 9346

Serves As:
- Director, Government Relations, SBC Illinois

LIFSON, Arthur
601 Pennsylvania Ave. NW
Suite 500 South Bldg.
Washington, DC 20004
arthur.lifson@cigna.com
Tel: (202) 296 - 7174
Ext: 689
Fax:(202) 296 - 2521

Serves As:
- V. President, Federal Affairs, CIGNA Corp.

LIGOCKI, Kathleen
27175 Haggerty Rd.
Novi, MI 48377
Tel: (248) 675 - 6000
Fax:(248) 675 - 6200

Serves As:
- President and Chief Exec. Officer, Tower Automotive, Inc.

LIGON, Duke
20 N. Broadway, Suite 1500
Oklahoma City, OK 73102
Tel: (405) 552 - 4604
Fax:(405) 552 - 4667

Serves As:
- Senior V. President, General Counsel; and PAC Contact, Devon Energy Corp.

LILBURN, Tom
1275 Pennsylvania Ave. NW
Suite 801
Washington, DC 20004-2404
Tel: (202) 737 - 8900
Fax:(202) 737 - 8909

Serves As:
- Director, Federal Government Relations, Healthcare, Bayer Corporation

LILIENTHAL, Stephen W.
CNA Center
333 S. Wabash Ave.
Chicago, IL 60685
Tel: (312) 822 - 5000
Fax:(312) 822 - 6419

Serves As:
- Chairman and Chief Exec. Officer, CNA Financial Corp.

LILLARD, Judith
One Penn Plaza
New York, NY 10119
Tel: (212) 736 - 4444
Fax:(212) 947 - 6975

Serves As:
- Corporate Communications Contact, URS Corp.

LILLBACK, David
300 Somerset Corporate Blvd.
Bridgewater, NJ 08807-2854
Tel: (908) 243 - 6000
Fax:(908) 231 - 3614
TF: (800) 981 - 2491

Serves As:
- V. President, Human Resources, Sanofi-Aventis Inc.

LILLEY, David
Five Garret Mountain Plaza
West Paterson, NJ 07424
david_lilley@gm.cytec.com
Tel: (973) 357 - 3100
Fax:(973) 357 - 3054
TF: (800) 652 - 6013

Serves As:
- Chairman, President and Chief Exec. Officer, Cytec Industries Inc.

LILLY, Diane P.
Wells Fargo Center
Sixth & Marquette
M/S N9305-171
Minneapolis, MN 55479
Tel: (612) 667 - 8308
Fax:(612) 667 - 9403

Registered Federal Lobbyist.
Serves As:
- Senior V. President and Manager, Government Relations, Wells Fargo & Co.

LILLY, Jeff
851 W. Cypress Creek Rd.
Fort Lauderdale, FL 33309
jeff.lilly@citrix.com
Tel: (954) 267 - 2886
Fax:(954) 267 - 3101
TF: (800) 424 - 8749

Serves As:
- Manager, Investor Relations, Citrix Systems, Inc.

LILYGREN, Sara J.
601 Pennsylvania Ave., NW
Suite 750 South
Washington, DC 20004
sara.lilygren@tyson.com
Tel: (202) 393 - 3921
Fax:(202) 393 - 3922

Serves As:
- Director, Federal Government Affairs, Tyson Foods, Inc.

LIN, Kenneth
101 Constitution Ave. NW
Suite 800
Washington, DC 20001
Tel: (202) 742 - 4270
Fax:(202) 742 - 4271

Serves As:
- Policy and Information Analysis, Cendant Corp.

LINCOLN, Rose
SAFECO Plaza
Seattle, WA 98185
Tel: (206) 545 - 5000

Serves As:
- Manager, Corporate Contributions, SAFECO Corp.

LIND, Valerie L.
710 Medtronic Pkwy.
Minneapolis, MN 55432-5604
valerie.l.lind@medtronic.com
Tel: (763) 505 - 2631
Fax:(763) 514 - 4879
TF: (800) 328 - 2518

Serves As:
- Manager, Public Relations, Medtronic, Inc.

LINDBLOOM, Chad M.
8100 Mitchell Rd.
Eden Prairie, MN 55344
Tel: (952) 937 - 7779
Fax:(952) 937 - 6740

Serves As:
- V. President and Chief Financial Officer, C.H. Robinson Worldwide, Inc.

Responsibilities include investor relations.

LINDEMAN, Martha O.
680 N. Lake Shore Dr.
Chicago, IL 60611
Tel: (312) 373 - 2430
Fax:(312) 266 - 8506

Serves As:
- Senior V. President, Corporate Communications and Investor Relations, Playboy Enterprises, Inc.

LINDEMANN, Ellen
270 Peachtree St. NW
Atlanta, GA 30303
Tel: (404) 506 - 5000

Serves As:
- Senior V. President, Human Resources, Southern Company

LINDEMANN, George L.
417Lackawanna Ave.
Scranton, PA 18503

Serves As:
- Chairman and Chief Exec. Officer, Southern Union Company

LINDENBERG, Keith
1633 Broadway
New York, NY 10019
Tel: (212) 489 - 2000
Fax:(212) 489 - 1687

Serves As:
- National Director, Deloitte & Touche LLP

LINDER, Mary C.
2700 Lone Oak Pkwy.
M/S A1300
Eagan, MN 55121
Tel: (612) 726 - 2111
Fax:(612) 726 - 3942
TF: (800) 225 - 2525

Serves As:
- Senior V. President, Corporate and Brand Communications, Northwest Airlines, Inc.

LINDER-SCHOLER, Bill
P.O. Box 1101
Minneapolis, MN 55440-1101
bill.linder-scholer@adc.com
Tel: (952) 915 - 0580
Fax:(952) 917 - 0965

Serves As:
- Exec. Director, ADC Foundation, ADC

LINDLEY, Mark C.
P.O. Box 7100
Westchester, IL 60154
Tel: (708) 551 - 2602
Fax:(708) 551 - 2601

Serves As:
- Director, Corporate Communications, Corn Products Internat'l, Inc.

LINDMAN, Mary Jane
P.O. Box 3283
Tulsa, OK 74102-3283
Tel: (918) 592 - 9484
Fax:(918) 592 - 9492

Serves As:
- Contact, Blue Cross and Blue Shield of Oklahoma Caring Program for Children, BlueCross BlueShield of Oklahoma

LINDNER, Carl H.
One E. Fourth St. Tel: (513) 579 - 2121
Cincinnati, OH 45202 Fax:(513) 579 - 2580

Serves As:
- Chairman of the Board, American Financial Group Inc.

LINDNER, III, Carl H.
One E. Fourth St. Tel: (513) 579 - 2121
Cincinnati, OH 45202 Fax:(513) 579 - 2580

Serves As:
- Co-Chief Exec. Officer, American Financial Group Inc.

LINDNER, S. Craig
One E. Fourth St. Tel: (513) 579 - 2121
Cincinnati, OH 45202 Fax:(513) 579 - 2580

Serves As:
- Co-Chief Exec. Officer, American Financial Group Inc.

LINDSAY, Mark
9900 Bren Rd. East Tel: (952) 992 - 4297
Minneapolis, MN 55343 Fax:(952) 936 - 0044
TF: (800) 328 - 5979

Serves As:
- Director, Public Communications and Strategy, UnitedHealth Group

LINDSAY, Stewart
50 Main St. Tel: (914) 684 - 3369
Sixth Floor
White Plains, NY 10606-1901
stewart.lindsay@binge.com

Serves As:
- Media Contact, Bunge Ltd.

LINDSEY, Mark E.
1221 Lamar Tel: (713) 853 - 6161
Suite 1600
Houston, TX 77010

Serves As:
- PAC Treasurer, Enron Corp.

LINDSTROM, Alan H.
2655 Seely Ave. Tel: (408) 943 - 1234
Bldg. 5 Fax:(408) 943 - 0513
San Jose, CA 95134

Serves As:
- Senior Manager, Investor Relations, Cadence Design Systems, Inc.

LINN, Myron
102 Main St. Tel: (641) 621 - 6045
Pella, IA 50219 Fax:(641) 628 - 6070

Serves As:
- Manager, Government Affairs, Pella Corp.

LINNEHAN, Ann M.
409 12th St., S.W., Suite 701 Tel: (202) 488 - 4464
Washington, DC 20024-2191 Fax:(202) 488 - 4396

Registered Federal Lobbyist.
Serves As:
- Representative, Pitney Bowes Inc.

LINNELL, Norman C.
P.O. Box 1299 Tel: (952) 703 - 4999
MS 101 Fax:(952) 887 - 3005
Minneapolis, MN 55440-1299 TF: (800) 887 - 3131
donaldsonfoundation@mail.donaldson.com

Serves As:
- President, The Donaldson Foundation, Donaldson Company, Inc.

LINNERT, Terrence G.
Four Colesium Center Tel: (704) 423 - 7000
2730 W. Tyvola Rd. Fax:(704) 423 - 7100
Charlotte, NC 28217

Serves As:
- Exec. V. President, Administration and General Counsel, Goodrich Corporation

LINSCOTT, John
Cash America Bldg. Tel: (817) 335 - 1100
1600 W. Seventh St. Fax:(817) 570 - 1645
Fort Worth, TX 76102-2599

Serves As:
- PAC Treasurer, Cash America Internat'l, Inc.

LINTHICUM, Kimberly
555 13th St. NW Tel: (202) 585 - 9610
Suite 600 West
Washington, DC 20004

Registered Federal Lobbyist.
Serves As:
- Representative, Amgen Inc.

LINTNER, Nancy L.
United Technologies Bldg. Tel: (860) 728 - 7000
One Financial Plaza Fax:(860) 728 - 6494
Hartford, CT 06101

Serves As:
- V. President, Communications, United Technologies Corp.

LINTNER, Nancy T.
One Carrier Pl. Tel: (860) 674 - 3000
Farmington, CT 06034-4015 Fax:(860) 674 - 3193

Serves As:
- V. Presiden, Community Affairs, Carrier Corp.

LINVILLE, Randal L.
9401 Indian Creek Pkwy. Tel: (913) 338 - 1474
Bldg. 40, Suite 850 Fax:(913) 338 - 2999
Overland Park, KS 66210
rlinville@scoular.com

Serves As:
- President and Chief Exec. Officer, The Scoular Co.

LINVILLE, Richard A.
P.O. Box 33068 Tel: (704) 364 - 3120
Charlotte, NC 28233

Serves As:
- V. President, Human Resources, Piedmont Natural Gas Co.

LIPP, Kathy
P.O. Box 77007 Tel: (608) 458 - 4812
Madison, WI 53707-1007

Serves As:
- Chief Environmental, Health and Safety Officer, Alliant Energy Corp.

LIPP, Robert I.
One Tower Sq. Tel: (860) 954 - 3273
Hartford, CT 06183 Fax:(860) 954 - 1161

Serves As:
- Chairman of the Board, St. Paul Travelers Cos., Inc.

LIPTON, Steven D.
225 Byers Rd. Tel: (937) 866 - 6251
Miamisburg, OH 45342 Fax:(937) 865 - 5470

Serves As:
- Chief Financial Officer, Huffy Corp.

LIPTROT, Martin
942 S. Shady Grove Rd. Tel: (901) 369 - 3600
Memphis, TN 38120 TF: (800) 238 - 5355

Serves As:
- Managing Director, Global Communications, FedEx Corp.

LISKEY, Anita
20 S. Wacker Dr. Tel: (312) 466 - 4613
Chicago, IL 60606-7499 Fax:(312) 930 - 3439
aliskey@cme.com

Serves As:
- Director, Corporate Communications, Chicago Mercantile Exchange Inc.

LITTEN, Brian J.
Three Penn Plaza East Tel: (973) 466 - 8753
PP-15V Fax:(973) 466 - 7077
M/S PP-16H
Newark, NJ 07105-2200

Serves As:
- Director, Government Affairs, Horizon Blue Cross Blue Shield of New Jersey
Responsibilities include political action.

LITTLE, Barbara A.
1155 15th St., N.W., Suite 611 Tel: (202) 223 - 4411
Washington, DC 20005 Fax:(202) 223 - 1849

Registered Federal Lobbyist.
Serves As:
- V. President, Government Relations, NewMarket Corp.
- V. President, Government Relations, Albemarle Corp.

LITTLE, Brian
P.O. Box 4569 Tel: (404) 584 - 4414
Atlanta, GA 30302-4569 Fax:(404) 584 - 3479
blittle@aglresources.com

Serves As:
- Director, Investor Relations, AGL Resources, Inc.

LITTLE, Brian K.
Corporate Communications Dept. Tel: (336) 436 - 5005
430 S. Spring St.
Burlington, NC 27215
media@labcorp.com

Serves As:
- Manager, Corporate Communications, Laboratory Corp. of America Holdings

LITTLEJOHN, Steve
13900 Riverport Dr.
M/S STL2IN
Maryland Heights, MO 63043
slittlejohn@express-scripts.com
Tel: (314) 702 - 7556
Fax:(314) 702 - 7059

Serves As:
- V. President, Public Relations, Express Scripts, Inc.

LITTRELL, Dee
Cash America Bldg.
1600 W. Seventh St.
Fort Worth, TX 76102-2599
dlittrell@casham.com
Tel: (817) 335 - 1100
Fax:(817) 570 - 1645

Serves As:
- Manager, Investor Relations, Cash America Internat'l, Inc.

LITTRELL, Ph.D., R.N., Kathee
One DNA Way
San Francisco, CA 94080-4990
Tel: (650) 225 - 1034
Fax:(650) 225 - 6000

Serves As:
- Director, Investor Relations, Genentech, Inc.

LITZ, Jodie L.
175 Ghent Rd.
Fairlawn, OH 44333-3330
Tel: (330) 869 - 4200
Fax:(330) 869 - 4288

Serves As:
- Treasurer, OMNOVA Solutions Inc. PAC, OMNOVA Solutions Inc.

LIU, Margaret C.
3900 Wisconsin Ave. NW
Washington, DC 20016
Tel: (202) 752 - 7000
Fax:(202) 752 - 6099

Serves As:
- V. President, Government and Industry Relations, Fannie Mae

LIUTKUS, Tom
24601 Center Ridge Rd.
Suite 200
Westlake, OH 44145-5639
liutkus.tom@tatravelcenters.com
Tel: (440) 808 - 7364
Fax:(440) 808 - 4458
TF: (800) 961 - 2961

Serves As:
- Director, Advertising and Public Relations, TravelCenters of America, Inc.

LIVELY, Robert W.
1130 Connecticut Ave. NW
Suite 500
Washington, DC 20036
Tel: (202) 463 - 7372
Fax:(202) 463 - 8809

Registered Federal Lobbyist.
Serves As:
- Staff V. President, Federal Government Affairs, Schering-Plough Corporation

LIVERETT, Deborah
50 S. LaSalle St.
Chicago, IL 60675
Tel: (312) 630 - 0679
Fax:(312) 630 - 1809

Serves As:
- Contact, Northern Trust Co. Charitable Trust and Corp. Contributions, Northern Trust Co.

LIVERS-POWERS, Crystal
P.O. Box 1595
Indianapolis, IN 46206-1595
crystal.liverspowers@aes.com
Tel: (317) 261 - 8423
Fax:(317) 630 - 5726

Serves As:
- Director, Media Relations, IPL (an AES Company)

LIVINGSTON, Bob
3001 Douglas Blvd.
Suite 200
Roseville, CA 95661
Tel: (916) 786 - 2666
Fax:(916) 786 - 9396

Serves As:
- Manager, Government Affairs (Western Region), Coors Brewing Co.

LIVINGSTON, Liesl
P.O. Box 66760
St. Louis, MO 63166-6760
lmlivi@solutia.com
Tel: (314) 674 - 7777
Fax:(314) 674 - 2899

Serves As:
- Director, Investor Relations, Solutia Inc.

LLANAS, Gil
720 E. Wisconsin Ave.
Milwaukee, WI 53202-4797
Tel: (414) 271 - 1444
Fax:(414) 665 - 2463
TF: (800) 323 - 7033

Serves As:
- Foundation Contact, Northwestern Mutual Financial Network

LLOYD, Richard W.
One Johnson & Johnson Plaza
New Brunswick, NJ 08933-7204
rlloyd@corus.jnj.com
Tel: (732) 524 - 3726
Fax:(732) 524 - 3005
TF: (800) 635 - 6789

Serves As:
- Executive Director, Government Affairs, Johnson & Johnson

LOBBE, Klaus Peter
100 Campus Dr.
Florham Park, NJ 07932
Tel: (973) 245 - 6000
Fax:(973) 245 - 6002

Serves As:
- Chairman and Chief Exec. Officer, BASF Corporation

LOCANTRO, Karen
P.O. Box 19925
Metairie, LA 70179-0925
Tel: (504) 837 - 5880
Fax:(504) 849 - 2307
TF: (800) 535 - 6017

Serves As:
- Manager, External Communications, Stewart Enterprises, Inc.

LOCK, Andrew
P.O. Box 302
Zeeland, MI 49464-0302
Tel: (616) 654 - 3000
Fax:(616) 654 - 5234

Serves As:
- Senior V. President, Human Resources, Herman Miller Inc.

LOCKARD, Richard A.
101 S. Hanley Rd.
St. Louis, MO 63105-3493
rlockard@furniturebrands.com
Tel: (314) 863 - 1100
Fax:(314) 863 - 5306

Serves As:
- Director, Employee Benefits and Risk Management, Furniture Brands Internat'l, Inc.

LOCKE, David R.
3200 West End Ave.
Suite 102
Nashville, TN 37203-1332
Tel: (615) 386 - 8524
Fax:(615) 386 - 8509

Serves As:
- Director, State Government Relations, Blue Cross and Blue Shield of Tennessee

LOCKHART, Michael D.
P.O. Box 3001
Lancaster, PA 17604-3001
mdlockhart@armstrong.com
Tel: (717) 397 - 3371

Serves As:
- Chairman and Chief Exec. Officer, Armstrong Holdings, Inc.

LOCKHART, Sandie
2222 Wellington Ct.
Lisle, IL 60532
Tel: (630) 969 - 4550
Fax:(630) 969 - 1352
TF: (800) 786 - 6539

Serves As:
- Contact, Molex Incorporated Corporate Contributions Program, Molex Incorporated

LOCKHART, Stan
8000 S. Federal Way
Boise, ID 83707
Tel: (208) 368 - 4000
Fax:(208) 368 - 2536

Registered Federal Lobbyist.
Serves As:
- Representative, Micron Technology, Inc.

LOCKLEY, Jr., Elmore
Dominion Tower
625 Liberty Ave.
Pittsburgh, PA 15222
elmore_lockley@dom.com
Tel: (412) 497 - 6742

Serves As:
- Manager, Media Relations - PA, Dominion Peoples

LOCKRIDGE, B. Russell
One N. Field Ct.
Lake Forest, IL 60045-4811
russell.lockridge@brunswick.com
Tel: (847) 735 - 4214
Fax:(847) 735 - 4050

Serves As:
- V. President and Chief Human Resources Officer, Brunswick Corp.

LOCKWOOD, Ken
One Enterprise Dr.
Aliso Viejo, CA 92656-2606
Tel: (949) 349 - 3909
Fax:(949) 349 - 5375

Serves As:
- V. President, Investor Relations, Fluor Corp.

LODER, Christopher
P.O. Box 100
Whitehouse Station, NJ 08889-0100
Tel: (908) 423 - 3786
Fax:(908) 735 - 1181
TF: (800) 423 - 1000

Serves As:
- Media Contact, Merck & Co., Inc.

LODGE, Ted S.
225 City Line Ave.
Suite 200
Bala Cynwyd, PA 19004
Tel: (610) 934 - 7000
Fax:(610) 934 - 7054
TF: (888) 438 - 7488

Serves As:
- President and Chief Operating Officer, Pegasus Communications Corp.

Responsibilities include political action.

LOEPP, Dan
600 Lafayette East
M/S 2003
Detroit, MI 48226
dloepp@bcbsm.com
Tel: (313) 225 - 6841
Fax:(313) 225 - 6250

Serves As:
- Senior V. President and Chief of Staff, Blue Cross Blue Shield of Michigan

Responsibilities include governmental affairs and political action.

LOEWENBERG, Stephen M.
870 Winter St.
Waltham, MA 02451
Tel: (781) 522 - 3000

Serves As:
- PAC Treasurer, Raytheon Co.

LOFRUMENTO, Peter
1755 Broadway
New York, NY 10019
Tel: (212) 841 - 8000

Serves As:
- Senior V. President, Corporate Communications, Universal Music Group

LOFTUS, Jo-Ann
11 Wall St.
6th Floor
New York, NY 10005
Tel: (212) 656 - 3367
Fax:(212) 656 - 5605

Serves As:
- Manager, Public Affairs, New York Stock Exchange, Inc.

LOFTUS, Terry E.
P.O. Box 599
Cincinnati, OH 45201-0599
loftus.te@pg.com
Tel: (513) 983 - 9736
Fax:(513) 983 - 0669

Serves As:
- Associate Director, External Relations/Corporate Communications, The Procter & Gamble Company

LOGAN, James A.
601 Madison St.
Suite 200
Alexandria, VA 22314
Tel: (703) 549 - 9266
Fax:(703) 549 - 9268

Serves As:
- Director, Washington Operations, (Allison Transmission Division), General Motors Corp.

LOGUE, Ronald E.
225 Franklin St.
Boston, MA 02110
Tel: (617) 786 - 3000
Fax:(617) 664 - 4999

Serves As:
- Chairman and Chief Exec. Officer, State Street Corp.

LOIS, James E.
One Blue Hill Plaza
Pearl River, NY 10965
jelois@oru.com
Tel: (845) 577 - 2941
Fax:(845) 577 - 6913

Serves As:
- Manager, Corporate Communications, Orange and Rockland Utilities, Inc.

LOKE, Su
14111 Scottslawn Rd.
Marysville, OH 43041
su.lok@scotts.com
Tel: (937) 578 - 5169
Fax:(937) 644 - 7184
TF: (800) 543 - 8873

Serves As:
- Manager, Public Relations, The Scotts Company

LOMBARD, Tanya
101 Constitution Ave. NW
Suite 400 West
Washington, DC 20001
tanya.lombard@altria.com
Tel: (202) 354 - 1500
Fax:(202) 354 - 1505

Serves As:
- Director, Government Affairs- Tobacco, Altria Group, Inc.

LOMBARDI, Christopher J.
1100 Wilson Blvd.
Suite 1500
Arlington, VA 22209
Tel: (703) 841 - 5700
Fax:(703) 841 - 5792

Registered Federal Lobbyist.
Serves As:
- Manager, Government Relations, Raytheon Co.

LONDON, Dr. J. P.
1100 N. Glebe Rd.
Arlington, VA 22201-4798
Tel: (703) 841 - 7800
Fax:(703) 841 - 7882

Serves As:
- Chairman, President and Chief Exec. Officer, CACI Internat'l Inc.

LONDON, Kevin B.
82 Running Hill Rd.
South Portland, ME 04106-6020
Tel: (207) 775 - 8100
Fax:(207) 761 - 6020
TF: (800) 341 - 0392

Serves As:
- Senior V. President, Human Resources, Fairchild Semiconductor Internat'l, Inc.

LONDON, MaryAnne
525 S. Eighth St.
Minneapolis, MN 55404
Tel: (612) 332 - 7281
Fax:(612) 332 - 0217

Serves As:
- Senior V. President, Public Relations, (Kraus-Anderson Communications Group), Kraus-Anderson Cos. Inc.

LONDON, Shelly J.
One Centennial Ave.
PO Box 6820
Piscataway, NJ 08854
slondon@americanstandard.com
Tel: (732) 980 - 6175
Fax:(732) 980 - 3335

Serves As:
- V. President and Chief Communications Officer, American Standard Companies Inc.

LONDRA, Kathy
37 N. Valley Rd., Bldg. Four
P.O. Box 1764
Paoli, PA 19301
kathy.londra@ametek.com
Tel: (610) 647 - 2121
Fax:(610) 323 - 9337
TF: (800) 473 - 1286

Serves As:
- Administrator, The Ametek Foundation, Ametek, Inc.

LONERGAN, Robert
100 Independence Mall West
Philadelphia, PA 19106-2399
Tel: (215) 592 - 3000
Fax:(215) 592 - 3377

Serves As:
- V. President, General Counsel; Secretary, Rohm and Haas Co.

Responsibilities include regulatory and environmental affairs.

LONG, Carrie
1850 N. Central Ave.
Suite 800
Phoenix, AZ 85004-4545
clong@viad.com
Tel: (602) 207 - 4000
Ext: 2681

Serves As:
- Director, Investor Relations, Viad Corp

LONG, Deborah J.
2801 Hwy. 280 South
P.O. Box 2606
Birmingham, AL 35223
Tel: (205) 268 - 1000

Serves As:
- Senior V. President, Secretary and General Counsel, Protective Life Corp.

Responsibilities include government relations.

LONG, Joe B.
1500 MacCorkle Ave. SE
Charleston, WV 25314
joseph.b.long@verizon.com
Tel: (304) 344 - 7267
Fax:(304) 344 - 6397

Serves As:
- Manager, Corporate Communications and External Affairs, Verizon West Virginia Inc.

LONG, Joel
World-Herald Square
Omaha, NE 68102
Tel: (402) 444 - 1493
Fax:(402) 348 - 1828

Serves As:
- Director, Public Relations, Omaha World-Herald Co.

LONG, John C.
100 Crystal A Dr.
P.O. Box 810
Hershey, PA 17033
jlong@hersheys.com
Tel: (717) 534 - 3237
Fax:(717) 534 - 7015

Serves As:
- V. President, Public Affairs, The Hershey Company

LONG, Lynn
P.O. Box 441
Trexlertown, PA 18087
longl@airproducts.com

Serves As:
- Treasurer, Air Products and Chemicals Inc. Political Action Committee, Air Products and Chemicals, Inc.

LONG, Margaret
822 Salem Dr.
Ballston Spa, NY 12020
Tel: (518) 885 - 8415
Fax:(518) 884 - 8045

Serves As:
- Director, Government Affairs, Novartis Corporation

LONG, Robert L.
P.O. Box 2765
Houston, TX 77255-2765
Tel: (713) 232 - 7500
Fax:(713) 232 - 7031

Serves As:
- President and Chief Exec. Officer, Transocean Inc.

LONGABERGER, Rachel
1500 E. Main St.
Newark, OH 43055
rlongaberger@longaberger.com
Tel: (740) 322 - 5000
Fax:(740) 322 - 5240

Serves As:
- President, Longaberger Foundation, The Longaberger Co.

LONGABERGER, Tami
1500 E. Main St.
Newark, OH 43055
tlongaberger@longaberger.com
Tel: (740) 322 - 5000
Fax:(740) 322 - 5240

Serves As:
- President and Chief Exec. Officer, The Longaberger Co.

LONGFELLOW, David
1110 American Parkway NE
Allentown, PA 18109-3229
Tel: (610) 712 - 6011
Fax:(610) 712 - 4106

Serves As:
- V. President, Investor and Government Relations, Agere Systems Inc.

LONGFORD, Bernadette L.
500 S. Buena Vista St.
Burbank, CA 91521
Tel: (818) 560 - 1000
Fax:(818) 560 - 1930

Serves As:
- Manager, Corporate Community Relations, The Walt Disney Company

LONGSTREET, John H.
3030 LBJ Frwy.
Suite 700
Dallas, TX 75234
Tel: (972) 243 - 6191
Fax:(972) 888 - 7555

Serves As:
- Senior V. President, Human Resources, ClubCorp Internat'l Inc.

LONGWELL, Lance
1499 Post Rd.
Fairfield, CT 06824
Tel: (203) 319 - 4700
Fax:(203) 319 - 4701

Serves As:
- Manager, Public Realtions, IMS Health, Inc.

LONNEGREN, Paul
1025 Eldorado Blvd.
Broomfield, CO 80021
Tel: (720) 888 - 6099
Fax:(720) 888 - 5085

Serves As:
- Director, Marketing Communications and Public Relations, Level 3 Communications, Inc.

LOOF, Per-Olef
P.O. Box 5928
Greenville, SC 29606
Tel: (864) 963 - 6300
Fax:(864) 963 - 6322

Serves As:
- President and Chief Exec. Officer, KEMET Corp.

LOONEY, Robert J.
1745 S. Clark St., Suite 404
Arlington, VA 22202
bob.looney@chsinc.com
Tel: (703) 413 - 9620
Fax:(703) 413 - 9626

Serves As:
- Director, Federal Affairs, CHS Inc.

LOOYENGA, Roger
6101 Anacapri Blvd.
Lansing, MI 48917
Tel: (517) 323 - 1200
Fax:(517) 323 - 8796

Serves As:
- Chief Exec. Officer, Auto-Owners Insurance Group

LOPEZ, Johann
1401 I St. NW
Suite 200
Washington, DC 20005
Tel: (202) 293 - 9494
Fax:(202) 223 - 9594

Serves As:
- Region Director, Government Affairs, Anheuser-Busch Cos., Inc.

LOPEZ-BAFFO, Minnie
P.O. Box 513249
Los Angeles, CA 90051-1249
Tel: (213) 244 - 2523
Fax:(213) 244 - 4997

Serves As:
- Project Manager, Regional Affairs, Southern California Gas Co.

LOPORCHIO, Vincent
82 Devonshire St.
Boston, MA 02109-3614
Tel: (617) 563 - 5800
Fax:(617) 476 - 6150

Serves As:
- V. President, Media Relations, FMR Corp.

LORANGER, Steven R.
Four W. Red Oak Ln.
White Plains, NY 10604
Tel: (914) 641 - 2000
Fax:(914) 696 - 2950

Serves As:
- Chairman and Chief Exec. Officer, ITT Industries

LORBERBAUM, Jeffrey S.
P.O. Box 12069
Calhoun, GA 30703
jeff_lorberbaum@mohawkind.com
Tel: (706) 629 - 7721
Fax:(706) 629 - 3851
TF: (800) 241 - 4494

Serves As:
- Chairman, President and Chief Exec. Officer, Mohawk Industries, Inc.

LORD, Albert L.
12061 Bluemont Way
Reston, VA 20190
Tel: (703) 810 - 3000
Fax:(703) 810 - 7053

Serves As:
- Chairman of the Board, SLM Corp.

LORD, Curtis
4800 Deerwood Campus Pkwy.
Jacksonville, FL 32246-8273
Tel: (904) 791 - 6111
Fax:(904) 905 - 4486
TF: (800) 477 - 3736

Registered Federal Lobbyist.
Serves As:
- Representative, Blue Cross and Blue Shield of Florida

LORD, Nat
1300 Morris Dr.
Suite 100
Chesterbrook, PA 19087-5594
Tel: (610) 727 - 7000
Fax:(610) 727 - 3600
TF: (800) 829 - 3132

Serves As:
- Director, Legislative Government Affairs, AmeriSource Bergen Corp.

LORD, Wayne
P.O. Box 2210
Atlanta, GA 30301-2210
wayne.lord@goldkist.com
Tel: (770) 393 - 5312
Fax:(770) 393 - 5347

Serves As:
- V. President, Corporate Relations, Gold Kist Inc.

Responsibilities include political action and corporate philanthropy.

LORENZ, Lad
8326 Century Park
San Diego, CA 92123
Tel: (619) 696 - 2000
Fax:(619) 696 - 1868

Serves As:
- V. President, Regulatory Affairs, San Diego Gas and Electric Co.

LORETO, Marty
P.O. Box 26500
Tucson, AZ 85726-6500
Tel: (520) 794 - 6416

Serves As:
- Administrator, Consumer Affairs, Southwest Gas Corp.

LORION, Mike
400 N. McCarthy Blvd.
Milpitas, CA 95035
Tel: (408) 503 - 7000
Fax:(408) 503 - 2750

Serves As:
- V. President, Education, palmOne, Inc.

LOSCOCCO, Peter F.
180 E. Broad St.
Columbus, OH 43215-3799
peter.loscocco@hexionchem.com
Tel: (614) 225 - 4127

Serves As:
- V. President, Public Affairs, Hexion Specialty Chemicals, Inc.

Responsibilities include investor relations.

LOTSBERG, Warren K.
600 Market St. West
Huron, SD 57350
warren.lotsberg@northwestern.com
Tel: (605) 353 - 8240
Fax:(605) 353 - 8286

Serves As:
- Director, South Dakota Government Relations, NorthWestern Corp.

LOTT, Cherie Nanette
115 Perimeter Center Place, N.E.
Suite 650
Atlanta, GA 30346
Tel: (770) 399 - 5916

Serves As:
- Manager, Regulatory Legislation, Humana Inc.

LOUDA, Dale
1331 Pennsylvania Ave. NW
Suite 512
Washington, DC 20004
Tel: (202) 662 - 8750
Fax:(202) 662 - 8749

Serves As:
- Manager, Federal Government Relations, PPL Corp.

LOUDERMILK, Joey M.
1932 Wynnton Rd.
Columbus, GA 31999
Tel: (706) 323 - 3431
Fax:(706) 660 - 7333
TF: (800) 992 - 3522

Serves As:
- Exec. V. President, General Counsel and Corporate Secretary, AFLAC Incorporated

Responsibilities include political action.

LOUGEE, Jr., Robert W.
1800 W. Park Dr.
Suite 250
Westborough, MA 01581-3989
bob.lougee@usamobility.com
Tel: (508) 870 - 6771
Fax:(508) 366 - 8966

Serves As:
- Contact, Public Relations and Investor Relations, USA Mobility, Inc.

LOUGHLIN, Denise
1717 Arch St., 17th Floor
Philadelphia, PA 19103
denise.g.loughlin@verizon.com
Tel: (215) 466 - 3351
Fax:(215) 466 - 5931

Serves As:
- Director, External Affairs, Verizon Pennsylvania Inc.

LOUGHLIN, Larry
P.O. Box 780
Warren, PA 16365
Tel: (814) 723 - 1500
Fax:(814) 726 - 4602

Serves As:
- V. President, Human Resources, United Refining Co.

LOUGHNOT, Katie
4440 Rosewood Dr.
Pleasanton, CA 94588
katie.loughnot@ros.com
Tel: (925) 965 - 4509
TF: (800) 945 - 7677

Serves As:
- V. President, Investor and Media Relations, Ross Stores, Inc.

LOUIS, Andrew R.
Three Lincoln Center
5430 LBJ Fwy., Suite 1700
Dallas, TX 75240-2697
Tel: (972) 450 - 4243
Fax:(972) 448 - 1445

Serves As:
- Secretary, Valhi, Inc.

Responsibilities include investor relations.

LOUISON, Deborah
1225 I St. NW
Washington, DC 20005
Tel: (202) 661 - 6189
Fax:(202) 464 - 0431

Serves As:
- V. President, Government Affairs, Cadbury Schweppes Americas Beverages

LOUREIRO, Paulo
153 E. 53rd St., 57th Floor
New York, NY 10022-4624
Tel: (212) 350 - 9400
Fax:(212) 350 - 9564

Serves As:
- Manager, Investor Relations, Schlumberger Limited

LOVE, Cathy B.
1426 Main St.
Columbia, SC 29218
clove@scana.com
Tel: (803) 217 - 7777

Serves As:
- General Manager, Public Affairs, SCANA Corp.

LOVE, Daryl
3499 Blazer Pkwy.
Lexington, KY 40509
Tel: (859) 357 - 3136

Serves As:
- Community Relations Manager, Ashland Inc.

LOVELAND, Darcy
Three Rockledge Rd.
Laguna Beach, CA 92651
Tel: (949) 497 - 2907
Fax:(949) 497 - 2927

Serves As:
- Counsel, Government Relations, (Kaiser Foundation Health Plan, Inc.), Kaiser Permanente

LOVEMAN, Gary
P.O. Box 98905
Las Vegas, NV 89193-8905
Tel: (702) 407 - 6000

Serves As:
- Chairman of the Board, President and Chief Exec. Officer, Harrah's Entertainment, Inc.

LOVENG, Jeff
801 Pennsylvania Ave. NW
Suite 310
Washington, DC 20004
Tel: (202) 434 - 8150
Fax:(202) 434 - 8156

Registered Federal Lobbyist.
Serves As:
- Manager, Federal Government Affairs, FirstEnergy Corp.

LOWAN, Ted
101 Wood Ave.
Iselin, NJ 08830
Tel: (732) 205 - 6360
Fax:(732) 321 - 1161
TF: (800) 631 - 9505

Serves As:
- Director, Corporate Communications, Engelhard Corp.

LOWDER, Robert E.
Colonial Financial Center
One Commerce St.
Montgomery, AL 36104
Tel: (334) 240 - 5000
TF: (800) 285 - 5886

Serves As:
- Chairman and Chief Exec. Officer, The Colonial Bancgroup, Inc.

LOWE, Carol P.
13925 Ballantyne Corp. Pl., Suite 400
Charlotte, NC 28277
Tel: (704) 501 - 1100
Fax:(704) 501 - 1191

Serves As:
- V. President and Chief Financial Officer, Carlisle Companies Inc.

LOWE, Cathey S.
24025 Park Sorrento
Suite 400
Calabasas, CA 91302
clowe@ryland.com
Tel: (818) 223 - 7530
Fax:(818) 223 - 7667
TF: (800) 267 - 0998

Serves As:
- Senior V. President, Finance, The Ryland Group, Inc.

Responsibilities include investor relations.

LOWE, D. Fred
P.O. Box 5108
Denver, CO 80217-5108
Tel: (303) 978 - 2000
Fax:(303) 978 - 2318
TF: (800) 654 - 3103

Serves As:
- V. President, Human Resources, Johns Manville Corp.

LOWE, John E.
P.O. Box 2197
Houston, TX 77252-2197
Tel: (281) 293 - 1000
Fax:(281) 293 - 1440

Serves As:
- Exec. V. President, Planning Strategy and Corporate Affairs, ConocoPhillips

LOWE, Kenneth W.
312 Walnut St.
2800 Scripps Center
Cincinnati, OH 45202
lowe@scripps.com
Tel: (513) 977 - 3000
Fax:(513) 977 - 3721

Serves As:
- President and Chief Exec. Officer, E. W. Scripps Co.

LOWE, Leticia
1111 Louisiana St.
Houston, TX 77002
Tel: (713) 207 - 7702

Serves As:
- Manager, Media Relations, CenterPoint Energy

LOWE, Michael B.
111 W. Monroe St.
Chicago, IL 60603-4095
Tel: (312) 461 - 2121
Fax:(312) 461 - 6640

Serves As:
- Executive V. President, Human Resources, Harris Bank

LOWE, Jr., William M.
P.O. Box 19109
Greensboro, NC 27419-9109
Tel: (336) 316 - 5664
Fax:(336) 294 - 5422

Serves As:
- Chief Operating Officer and Chief Financial Officer, Unifi, Inc.

Responsibilities include investor relations.

LOWELL, Judy K.
6000 American Pkwy.
Madison, WI 53783
jpowell@amfam.com
Tel: (608) 242 - 4100
Fax:(608) 243 - 4928

Serves As:
- Manager, Community Relations, American Family Insurance Group

LOWENTHAL, Rob
3325 Paddocks Pkwy.
Suite 100
Suwanee, Ga 30024-6060
Tel: (678) 455 - 2320

Serves As:
- Manager, Public Affairs, State Farm Insurance Cos.

LOWER, II, Louis G.
One Horace Mann Plaza
Springfield, IL 62715-0001
Tel: (217) 789 - 2500
Fax:(217) 788 - 5161

Serves As:
- President and Chief Exec. Officer, Horace Mann Educators Corp.

LOWERY, Elizabeth A.
P.O. Box 300
Detroit, MI 48265-1000
Tel: (313) 556 - 5000
Fax:(248) 696 - 7300

Serves As:
- V. President, Environment and Energy, General Motors Corp.

LOWERY, Kate
550 Bowie St.
Austin, TX 78703
Tel: (512) 477 - 4455

Serves As:
- National Director, Public Relations, Whole Foods Market, Inc.

LOWERY, Kevin G.
201 Isabella St.
Pittsburgh, PA 15212-5858
kevin.lowery@alcoa.com
Tel: (412) 553 - 1424
Fax:(412) 553 - 4498

Serves As:
- Director, Corporate Communications, Alcoa Inc.

LOWREY, Carmen Guzman
3900 Wisconsin Ave. NW
Washington, DC 20016
Tel: (202) 752 - 7000
Fax:(202) 752 - 6099

Registered Federal Lobbyist.
Serves As:
- Representative, Fannie Mae

LOWREY, Lon
16606 Jamestown Forest Dr.
Florissant, MO 63034
Tel: (314) 355 - 9631
Fax:(314) 355 - 9635

Serves As:
- Director, Government Affairs, Novartis Corporation

LOWRIMORE, Lawrence
475 W. Terra Cotta Ave.
Suite E
Crystal Lake, IL 60014-9695
Tel: (815) 477 - 0424
Fax:(815) 477 - 0481

Serves As:
- V. President, Human Resources, AptarGroup, Inc.

LOWRY, Bruce
2211 N. First St.
San Jose, CA 95131
blowry@novell.com
Tel: (415) 383 - 8408

Serves As:
- Director, Global Public Relations, Novell, Inc.

LOWRY, Ph.D., David
P.O. Box 51777
New Orleans, LA 70151
david_lowry@fmi.com
Tel: (504) 582 - 1803
Fax:(504) 582 - 1847
TF: (800) 535 - 7094

Serves As:
- President and Exec. Director, Freeport-McMoRan Foundation, Freeport-McMoRan Copper and Gold Inc.

LOWRY, Joanna
11800 Wilshire Blvd.
Los Angeles, CA 90025
Tel: (310) 575 - 7080
Fax:(310) 575 - 7280

Serves As:
- Senior V. President, Media Relations, (UPN), Viacom Inc./CBS Corp.

LOYA, Brian D.
P.O. Box 85587
San Diego, CA 92186-5587
Tel: (858) 277 - 6780
Fax:(858) 505 - 1523

Serves As:
- PAC Treasurer, Cubic Corp.

LOYD, Janey
Metro Center
One Station Pl.
Stamford, CT 06902
janey.loyd@thomson.com
Tel: (203) 539 - 8000
Fax:(203) 539 - 7734
TF: (800) 969 - 9974

Serves As:
- V. President, Corporate Communications, The Thomson Corporation

LOYND, Mike
101 S. Hanley Rd.
St. Louis, MO 63105-3493
Tel: (314) 863 - 1100
Fax:(314) 863 - 7047

Serves As:
- Administrator, Charitable Trust, Furniture Brands Internat'l, Inc.

LOZANO, Joe J.
P.O. Box 240130
San Antonio, TX 78224-0130
Tel: (210) 475 - 8000
Ext: 8019
Fax:(210) 475 - 8602

Serves As:
- Senior V. President/Controller, Zachry Construction Corporation

Responsibilities include political action.

LUBBERS, Tim
405 Water St.
P.O. Box 5026
Port Huron, MI 48061-5026
Tel: (810) 987 - 7900
Fax:(810) 989 - 4098

Serves As:
- Director, Marketing and Corporate Communications, SEMCO ENERGY, Inc.

LUBER, Eldridge H.
P.O. Box 401
Oklahoma City, OK 73101-0401
eluber@oneok.com
Tel: (405) 551 - 6706
Fax:(405) 551 - 6801

Serves As:
- Manager, Governmental Affairs - Oklahoma, ONEOK, Inc.

LUBIN, Joel
1120 20th St. NW
Suite 1000
Washington, DC 20036-3406
lubin@att.com
Tel: (202) 457 - 3810
Fax:(202) 457 - 2545

Registered Federal Lobbyist.
Serves As:
- V. President, Federal Public Policy, AT&T

LUBY, Ellen
11270 W. Park Place
Milwaukee, WI 53224-9510
Tel: (414) 359 - 4128
Fax:(414) 359 - 4198

Serves As:
- Manager, Human Resources, A. O. Smith Corp.

LUCAS, Barbara B.
701 E. Joppa Rd.
Towson, MD 21286
barbara.lucas@bdk.com
Tel: (410) 716 - 2980
Fax:(410) 716 - 2933

Serves As:
- Senior V. President, Public Affairs; and Corporate Secretary, The Black & Decker Corp.

Responsibilities include corporate philanthropy.

LUCAS, Jamie
360 Hamilton Ave., Suite 1103
White Plains, NY 10601-1841
jlucas@heinekenusa.com
Tel: (914) 681 - 4114
Fax:(914) 989 - 1003

Serves As:
- Director, Corporate Communications, Heineken USA Inc.

LUCAS, Paul
P.O. Box 482
Milwaukee, WI 53201-0482
Tel: (414) 931 - 3129
Fax:(414) 931 - 3183

Serves As:
- Director, State Government Affairs, Miller Brewing Co.

LUCAS, Ron
P.O. Box 35167
Houston, TX 77235
rlucas@stagestoresinc.com
Tel: (713) 667 - 5601
Fax:(713) 295 - 5486
TF: (800) 324 - 3244

Serves As:
- Exec. V. President, Human Resources, Stage Stores, Inc.

LUCAS, Steven S.
591 Redwood Hwy.
Building 4000
Mill Valley, CA 94941

Serves As:
- PAC Treasurer, MGM MIRAGE

LUCCI, Jerry
411 Seventh Ave.
Pittsburgh, PA 15219
jlucci@dqe.com
Tel: (412) 393 - 1258
Fax:(412) 393 - 1412

Serves As:
- General Manager, Corporate Communications, Duquesne Light Holdings

LUCEY, Anne C.
1501 M St. NW
Suite 1100
Washington, DC 20005
Tel: (202) 785 - 7300
Fax:(202) 785 - 6360

Registered Federal Lobbyist.
Serves As:
- Senior V. President, Regulatory Policy, CBS Corp., Viacom Inc./CBS Corp.

LUCIEN, Arthur
643 W. 43rd St., Eighth Floor
New York, NY 10036
alucien@ups.com
Tel: (212) 631 - 6565

Serves As:
- Manager, Public Affairs, United Parcel Service (UPS)

LUCIER, Gergory T.
P.O. Box 6482
1600 Faraday Ave.
Carlsbad, CA 92008
Tel: (760) 603 - 7200
Fax:(760) 602 - 6500
TF: (800) 955 - 6288

Serves As:
- Chairman and Chief Exec. Officer, Invitrogen Corp.

LUCKI, Anthony
222 Berkeley St.
Boston, MA 02116
Tel: (617) 351 - 5000
Fax:(617) 351 - 1100

Serves As:
- President and Chief Exec. Officer, Houghton Mifflin Co.

LUCKOW, Ericka
720 E. Wisconsin Ave.
Milwaukee, WI 53202-4797
erikaluckow@northwsternmutual.com
Tel: (414) 271 - 1444
Fax:(414) 665 - 2463
TF: (800) 323 - 7033

Serves As:
- Media Contact, Northwestern Mutual Financial Network

LUCORE, Rebecca
100 Bayer Rd.
Pittsburgh, PA 15205-9741
Tel: (412) 777 - 5791
Fax:(412) 778 - 4432
TF: (800) 662 - 2927

Serves As:
- Exec. Director, Bayer Foundation, Bayer Corporation

LUCZO, Stephen J.
P.O. Box 66360
Scotts Valley, CA 95067-0360
Tel: (831) 438 - 6550
Fax:(831) 438 - 0558

Serves As:
- Chairman of the Board, Seagate Technology

LUDECKE, Kristin
One Massachusetts Ave. NW
Suite 360
Washington, DC 20001
Tel: (202) 408 - 0183
Fax:(202) 408 - 0214

Serves As:
- Manager, Government and Public Affairs, PSE&G

LUDROF, Jeffrey A.
100 Erie Insurance Pl.
Erie, PA 16530
Tel: (814) 870 - 2507
Fax:(814) 870 - 3126

Serves As:
- President and Chief Exec. Officer, Erie Indeminity Co.

LUDWIG, Edward J.
One Becton Dr.
Franklin Lakes, NJ 07417-1880
edward_ludwig@bd.com
Tel: (201) 847 - 6800
Fax:(201) 847 - 6475

Serves As:
- Chairman, President and Chief Exec. Officer, Becton, Dickinson and Co.

LUDWIG, Jim
P.O. Box 889
Topeka, KS 66601-0889
Tel: (785) 575 - 6300
Fax:(785) 575 - 8182

Serves As:
- V. President, Public Affairs, Westar Energy, Inc.

LUEDER, Laura
P.O. Box 5650
Bismarck, ND 58506-5650
laura.lueder@mduresources.com
Tel: (701) 222 - 7874
Fax:(701) 222 - 7865
TF: (800) 437 - 8000

Serves As:
- Senior Public Information Representative, MDU Resources Group, Inc.

LUEGER, Susan A.
720 E. Wisconsin Ave.
Milwaukee, WI 53202-4797
Tel: (414) 665 - 7197
Fax:(414) 665 - 2463
TF: (800) 323 - 7033

Serves As:
- V. President, Human Resources, Northwestern Mutual Financial Network

LUFANO, Dr. Robert
4800 Deerwood Campus Pkwy.
Jacksonville, FL 32246-8273
Tel: (904) 791 - 6111
Fax:(904) 905 - 4486
TF: (800) 477 - 3736

Serves As:
- Chairman and Chief Exec. Officer, Blue Cross and Blue Shield of Florida

LUFF, David C.
76 S. Main St.
Akron, OH 44308-1890
Tel: (330) 384 - 5798
Fax:(330) 761 - 4204
TF: (800) 633 - 4766

Serves As:
- V. President, State Government Affairs, FirstEnergy Corp.

LUFF, Paula
235 E. 42nd St.
New York, NY 10017-5755
paula.luff@pfizer.com
Tel: (212) 573 - 2932
Fax:(212) 573 - 2883

Serves As:
- Director, International Philanthropy Programs, Pfizer Inc.

LUFT, Robert V.D. "Bob"
P.O. Box 61000
New Orleans, LA 70161
Tel: (504) 576 - 4000
Fax:(504) 576 - 4428

Serves As:
- Chairman of the Board, Entergy Corp.

LUFTGLASS, Rick
235 E. 42nd St.
New York, NY 10017-5755
rich.luftglass@pfizer.com
Tel: (212) 573 - 7491
Fax:(212) 573 - 2883

Serves As:
- Director, U.S. Philanthropy, Pfizer Inc.

LUGAR, Ellen Goldberg
One General Mills Blvd.
Minneapolis, MN 55426
Tel: (763) 764 - 7600
Fax:(763) 764 - 7384

Serves As:
- Exec. Director, General Mills Foundation, General Mills

LUGAR, Kelly
1133 19th St. NW
Washington, DC 20036
Tel: (202) 887 - 3830
Fax:(202) 887 - 3123

Registered Federal Lobbyist.
Serves As:
- Representative, MCI, Inc.

LUGINBILL, Kerry
2750 S. Priest Dr.
Tempe, AZ 85282
Tel: (480) 929 - 8014
Fax:(480) 894 - 4176

Serves As:
- Director, Public Affairs, Safeway Inc.

LUGINBILL, Mark
198 Van Buren St.
Suite 300
Herndon, VA 20170
Tel: (703) 834 - 3400
Fax:(703) 834 - 3340

Serves As:
- Manager, Communications, Airbus North America Holdings, Inc.

LUKACH, Carol
1007 Market St.
Wilmington, DE 19898
Tel: (302) 774 - 0583
Fax:(302) 774 - 7321
TF: (800) 441 - 7515

Serves As:
- V. President, Investor Relations, DuPont

LUKE, Jr., John A.
One High Ridge Park
Stamford, CT 06905-1322
jaluke@meadwestvaco.com
Tel: (203) 461 - 7400

Serves As:
- Chairman and Chief Exec. Officer, MeadWestvaco Corp.

LUKENS, Max L.
P.O. Box 1637
Houston, TX 77251-1637
m.lukens@ssss.com
Tel: (713) 868 - 7605
Fax:(713) 426 - 1331

Serves As:
- President and Chief Exec. Officer, Stewart & Stevenson Services, Inc.

LUKIEWSKI, Carolyn
21557 Telegraph Rd.
Southfield, MI 48034
clukiewski@lear.com
Tel: (248) 447 - 1684
Fax:(248) 447 - 1722

Serves As:
- Investor Relations Contact, Lear Corporation

LUMME, Dale A.
Crystal Gateway 3, 1215 S. Clark St.
Suite 1510
Arlington, VA 22202
Tel: (703) 412 - 5977
Fax:(703) 412 - 5970

Registered Federal Lobbyist.
Serves As:
- Representative, Alliant Techsystems

LUMPKIN, Marc
9601 S. Meridian Blvd.
Englewood, CO 80112
marc.lumpkin@echostar.com
Tel: (303) 723 - 2020
Fax:(303) 723 - 1399

Serves As:
- Director, Communications, EchoStar Communications Corp.

Contractor

LUMPKINS, Robert L.
12800 Whitewater Dr.
Minnetonka, MN 55343
Tel: (800) 918 - 8270
Fax:(952) 984 - 0032

Serves As:
- Chairman of the Board, Mosaic Co.

LUNCEFORD, Michael L.
P.O. Box 799045
Dallas, TX 75379-9045
lunceforddm@marykay.com
Tel: (972) 687 - 6300
Fax:(972) 387 - 1611
TF: (800) 627 - 9529

Registered Federal Lobbyist.
Serves As:
- Senior V. President, Government Relations, Mary Kay Inc.

LUND, Peter
40 Monument Circle
Suite 700
Indianapolis, IN 46204
Tel: (317) 266 - 0100
Fax:(317) 631 - 3750

Serves As:
- Media Consultant, Emmis Communications Corp.

LUND, Rolf
800 LaSalle Ave.
Minneapolis, MN 55402-2006
Tel: (612) 372 - 4664
Fax:(612) 321 - 5137

Serves As:
- Manager, Public Relations, (CenterPoint Energy Minnegasco), CenterPoint Energy

LUNDGREN, John F.
1000 Stanley Dr.
New Britain, CT 06053
Tel: (860) 225 - 5111
Fax:(860) 827 - 3937

Serves As:
- Chairman and Chief Exec. Officer, The Stanley Works

LUNDGREN, Terry
Seven W. Seventh St.
Cincinnati, OH 45202
Tel: (513) 579 - 7000
Fax:(513) 579 - 7555
TF: (800) 261 - 5385

Serves As:
- Chairman, President and Chief Exec. Officer, Federated Department Stores, Inc.

LUPIEN, Pam
One MedImmune Way
Gaithersburg, MD 20878
Tel: (301) 398 - 0000
Fax:(301) 398 - 9000
TF: (877) 633 - 4411

Serves As:
- V. President, Human Resources, MedImmune, Inc.

LUPINACCI, Catherine
Four W. Red Oak Ln.
White Plains, NY 10604
Tel: (914) 641 - 2000
Fax:(914) 696 - 2950

Serves As:
- PAC Treasurer, ITT Industries

LUPTON, Margaret "Peg"
Ethan Allen Dr.
P.O. Box 1966
Danbury, CT 06813-2966
plupton@ethanalleninc.com
Tel: (203) 743 - 8234
Fax:(203) 743 - 8298

Serves As:
- Director, Investor Relations; and Assistant Secretary, Ethan Allen Interiors Inc.

LURAY, Jennifer M.
1399 New York Ave. NW
Suite 200
Washington, DC 20005
Tel: (202) 378 - 2020
Fax:(202) 783 - 6631

Serves As:
- Senior Director, Government Affairs and Policy, Abbott Laboratories

LURIA, Robert S.
12 Spruce Run
East Greenbush, NY 12061-9611
Tel: (518) 477 - 2581

Serves As:
- State Government Affairs, GlaxoSmithKline Research and Development

LUSCOMB, Brian
9330 Balboa Ave.
San Diego, CA 92123-1516
Tel: (858) 571 - 2121
Fax:(858) 571 - 2225

Serves As:
- Div. V. President, Corporate Communications, Jack in the Box Inc.

LUSK, Doug
2200 Mission College Blvd.
Santa Clara, CA 95052-8119
Tel: (408) 765 - 1679
Fax:(408) 765 - 1966
TF: (800) 628 - 8686

Serves As:
- Director, Investor Relations, Intel Corp.

LUSK, Jerry E.
P.O. Box 4309
Helena, MT 59604-4309
Tel: (406) 444 - 8200
Fax:(406) 447 - 3454
TF: (800) 447 - 7828

Serves As:
- Chairman of the Board, Blue Cross and Blue Shield of Montana

LUSSIER, Kathy
P.O. Box B
Jacksonville, FL 32203-0297
kathylussier@winn-dixie.com
Tel: (904) 370 - 6025
Fax:(904) 783 - 5294

Serves As:
- Senior Director, Communications, Winn-Dixie Stores

LUSTIG, David Vernon
816 Connecticut Ave. NW
Seventh Floor
Washington, DC 20006-2705
david.lustig@unilever.com
Tel: (202) 828 - 1010
Fax:(202) 828 - 4550

Registered Federal Lobbyist.
Serves As:
- Director, Government Relations, Unilever United States, Inc.
- Director, Government Relations, Unilever Home & Personal Care - North America

LUTER, III, Joseph W.
200 Commerce St.
Smithfield, VA 23430
Tel: (757) 365 - 3000
Fax:(757) 365 - 3017
TF: (888) 366 - 6767

Serves As:
- Chairman and Chief Exec. Officer, Smithfield Foods, Inc.

LUTH, Jeff
1900 S. Price Rd.
Chandler, AZ 85248-1604
jluth@amkor.com
Tel: (480) 821 - 2408
Ext: 5130
Fax:(480) 821 - 1713

Serves As:
- V. President, Corporate Communications, Amkor Technology, Inc.

Responsibilities include investor relations.

LUTHER, Jon
130 Royall St.
Canton, MA 02021
Tel: (781) 737 - 5200
Fax:(781) 986 - 6987

Serves As:
- Chief Exec. Officer, Dunkin' Brands

LUTHER, Lisa Acheson
4800 Deerwood Campus Pkwy.
Jacksonville, FL 32246-8273
Tel: (904) 905 - 3402
Fax:(904) 905 - 4486
TF: (800) 477 - 3736

Serves As:
- Senior Consultant, Public Relations, Blue Cross and Blue Shield of Florida

LUTHIN, James C.
2211 Sanders Rd.
Northbrook, IL 60062

Serves As:
- PAC Treasurer, Caremark Rx, Inc.

LUTHRINGER, Paul
959 Eighth Ave.
New York, NY 10019
Tel: (212) 649 - 2000
Fax:(212) 765 - 3528

Serves As:
- Exec. Director, Corporate Communications, The Hearst Corp.

LUX, Julie
2000 Galloping Hill Rd.
Kenilworth, NJ 07033
Tel: (908) 298 - 4774

Serves As:
- Director, Global Product Communications and Advocacy Development, Schering-Plough Corporation

LUZZI, Richard D.
101 Gordon Dr.
Lionville, PA 19341
Tel: (610) 594 - 2900
Fax:(610) 594 - 3000
TF: (800) 345 - 9800

Serves As:
- V. President, Human Resources, West Pharmaceutical Services

LYBARGER, Stanley A.
P.O. Box 2300
Tulsa, OK 74192
Tel: (918) 588 - 6000
Fax:(918) 588 - 6300

Serves As:
- President and Chief Exec. Officer, BOK Financial Corp.

LYMAN, Kevin
One AMD Pl.
P.O. Box 3453
Sunnyvale, CA 94088
Tel: (408) 749 - 4000
TF: (800) 538 - 8450

Serves As:
- Senior V. President, Human Resources, Advanced Micro Devices, Inc.

LYNCH, David
601 Pennsylvania Ave. NW
South Bldg., Suite 850
Washington, DC 20004
dlynch1@txu.com
Tel: (202) 628 - 2748
Fax:(202) 628 - 1007

Serves As:
- Director, Federal Advocacy, TXU

LYNCH, David H.
401 Ninth St., NW
Suite 600
Washington, DC 20004
Tel: (202) 434 - 8609
Fax:(202) 434 - 8626

Serves As:
- Director, Government Relations, Freddie Mac

LYNCH, Dennis L.
P.O. Box 256
Dublin, OH 43017
Tel: (614) 764 - 3553
Fax:(614) 764 - 3459

Serves As:
- Senior V. President, Communications, Wendy's Internat'l, Inc.

LYNCH, Kevin
45 Erieview Plaza
Room 1500
Cleveland, OH 44114
kl1652@sbc.com
Tel: (216) 822 - 7283
Fax:(216) 822 - 1791

Serves As:
- Director, External Affairs, SBC Ohio

LYNCH, Kevin A.
825 N.E. Multnomah
Suite 2000
Portland, OR 97232
kevin.lynch@pacificorp.com
Tel: (503) 813 - 5678
Fax:(503) 813 - 5272
TF: (888) 221 - 7070

Registered Federal Lobbyist.
Serves As:
- V. President, Government Affairs, PacifiCorp

LYNCH, Michael J.
3600 W. Lake Ave.
Glenview, IL 60025-5811
Tel: (847) 657 - 4232
Fax:(847) 657 - 7892

Serves As:
- V. President, Government Affairs; and PAC Treasurer, Illinois Tool Works Inc.

LYNCH, Patrick C.
2859 Paces Ferry Rd., Suite 2000
Atlanta, GA 30339
patrick.lynch@us.interfaceinc.com
Tel: (770) 437 - 6800
Fax:(770) 437 - 6809

Serves As:
- Chief Financial Officer, Interface Inc.

Responsibilities include corporate communications, corporate philanthropy, and investor relations.

LYNCH, Peter L.
P.O. Box B
Jacksonville, FL 32203-0297
Tel: (904) 783 - 5000
Fax:(904) 783 - 5294

Serves As:
- President and Chief Exec Officer, Winn-Dixie Stores

LYNCH, Philip J.
850 Dixie Hwy.
Louisville, KY 40210
Tel: (502) 774 - 7928
Fax:(502) 774 - 7185

Serves As:
- V. President and Director, Corporate Communications, Brown-Forman Corp.

LYNCH, Richard G.
211 Riverside Dr.
Evansville, IN 47708-1251
Tel: (812) 491 - 4000
Fax:(812) 491 - 4078
TF: (800) 227 - 1376

Serves As:
- Senior V. President, Human Resources and Administration, Vectren Corp.

LYNCH, Robin Abruzere
505 King Ave.
Columbus, OH 43201-2693
Tel: (614) 424 - 6424
Fax:(614) 424 - 3260
TF: (800) 201 - 2011

Registered Federal Lobbyist.
Serves As:
- Representative, Battelle

LYNCH, Shawn
4650 Cushing Pkwy.
Fremont, CA 94538-6470
shawn.lynch@lamrc.com
Tel: (510) 572 - 1776
Fax:(510) 572 - 2935

Serves As:
- Manager, Corporate Relations, Lam Research Corp.

LYNN, James N.
18 Loveton Circle
Sparks, MD 21152-6000
jim_lynn@mccormick.com
Tel: (410) 771 - 7301
Fax:(410) 771 - 7462

Serves As:
- Manager, Print Communications, McCormick & Company, Inc.

LYNN, Jim
One McDonald's Plaza
Oak Brook, IL 60523
jim.lynn@mcd.com
Tel: (630) 623 - 3387
Fax:(630) 623 - 4999

Serves As:
- V. President, Communication Services, McDonald's Corp.

LYNN, Karen J.
P.O. Box 39
Newton, IA 50208-0039
Tel: (641) 792 - 7000
Fax:(641) 787 - 8376

Serves As:
- V. President, Corporate Communications, Maytag Corp.

LYNN, Steve
P.O. Box 711
Tucson, AZ 85702
slynn@tep.com
Tel: (520) 884 - 3629
Fax:(520) 884 - 3606
TF: (800) 328 - 8853

Serves As:
- Senior V. President, Communications and Government Relations, UniSource Energy Corp.

LYNN, William J.
1100 Wilson Blvd.
Suite 1500
Arlington, VA 22209
Tel: (703) 841 - 5700
Fax:(703) 841 - 5792

Registered Federal Lobbyist.
Serves As:
- Senior V. President, Government Operations, Raytheon Co.

LYON, John
2300 W. Plano Pkwy.
Plano, TX 75075
invest@ps.net
Tel: (972) 577 - 0000
Fax:(972) 577 - 6790

Serves As:
- Director, Investor Relations, Perot Systems Corp.

LYON, Sydelle
1300 N. 17th St.
Suite 1400
Arlington, VA 22209
Tel: (703) 907 - 8200
Fax:(703) 907 - 8300

Serves As:
- PAC Manager, BAE Systems North America

LYONS, Daniel M.
P.O. Box 593330
Orlando, FL 32859
dlyons@darden.com
Tel: (407) 245 - 5217
Fax:(407) 245 - 5114

Serves As:
- Senior V. President, Human Resources, Darden Restaurants, Inc.

LYONS, John F.
1350 I St. NW
Suite 400
Washington, DC 20005-3306
Tel: (202) 371 - 6900
Fax:(202) 842 - 3578

Registered Federal Lobbyist.
Serves As:
- Director, Telecommunications Regulation, Motorola, Inc.

LYONS, Kelly
One State Farm Plaza
Bloomington, IL 61710-0001
Tel: (309) 766 - 1115

Serves As:
- Director, Public Affairs, (State Farm Mutual Automobile Insurance Co.), State Farm Insurance Cos.

LYONS, Laurie S.
4360 Brownsboro Rd.
Suite 300
Louisville, KY 40207
llyons@thomasind.com
Tel: (502) 893 - 4600
Fax:(502) 895 - 6618
TF: (800) 626 - 2847

Serves As:
- V. President, Corporate Communications, Thomas Industries Inc.

LYONS, Melanie
1440 Broadway
New York, NY 10018
Tel: (212) 626 - 5704
Fax:(212) 626 - 5304

Serves As:
- Foundation Contact, Liz Claiborne Inc.

LYONS, William M.
4500 Main St.
Kansas City, MO 64111
Tel: (816) 531 - 5575
Fax:(816) 340 - 7962
TF: (800) 345 - 2021

Serves As:
- President and Chief Exec. Officer, American Century Cos., Inc.

LYTLE, Gary R.
607 14th St. NW
Suite 950
Washington, DC 20005
Tel: (202) 429 - 0303
Fax:(202) 293 - 0561

Registered Federal Lobbyist.
Serves As:
- Senior V. President, Federal Relations, Qwest Communications

LYTTLE, Cathy
200 Old Wilson Bridge Rd.
Columbus, OH 43085
cmlyttle@worthingtonindustries.com
Tel: (614) 438 - 3077
Fax:(614) 840 - 4150

Serves As:
- V. President, Corporate Communications, Worthington Industries

LYTTLE, Mr. Kim E.
20 Stanwix St.
14th Floor
Pittsburgh, PA 15222-4802
Tel: (412) 644 - 7710
Fax:(412) 644 - 7723

Serves As:
- V. President, Public Affairs, (Nat'l City Bank, Pennsylvania), Nat'l City Corp.

MAAG, Allen
2211 S. 47th St.
Phoenix, AZ 85034
al.maag@avnet.com
Tel: (480) 643 - 7651
Fax:(480) 643 - 7240

Serves As:
- Chief Communications Officer, Avnet Inc.

Responsibilities include corporate communications public affairs and community relations.

MAAS, Norman H.
100 Campus Dr.
Florham Park, NJ 07932
Tel: (973) 245 - 6000
Fax:(973) 245 - 6002

Serves As:
- Senior V. President, Human Resources, BASF Corporation

MAAS, Suzanne W.
135 Morrissey Blvd.
Boston, MA 02107
Tel: (617) 929 - 2041
Fax:(617) 929 - 2010

Serves As:
- Exec. Director, Boston Globe Foundation, Globe Newspaper Co.

MABUS, Raymond E.
1000 Columbia Ave.
Linwood, PA 19061-3998
Tel: (610) 859 - 3000
Fax:(610) 859 - 3035
TF: (800) 776 - 3626

Serves As:
- Chairman of the Board, Foamex Internat'l Inc.

MACALUS, Sam
P.O. Box 59159
Minneapolis, MN 55459-8212
smacalus@carlson.com
Tel: (763) 212 - 2477
Fax:(763) 212 - 2219

Serves As:
- Director, Public Relations, Carlson Companies

MACARTHUR, Kip
655 15th St. NW
Suite 425
Washington, DC 20005
Tel: (202) 628 - 7840
Fax:(202) 638 - 1096

Serves As:
- Director, Legislative Affairs, Wellpoint, Inc.

MACAUDA, Michele
310 Orange St.
New Haven, CT 06510
Tel: (203) 771 - 5200
Fax:(203) 497 - 9184

Serves As:
- President and Chief Exec. Officer, SBC SNET

MACAULAY, William E.
5847 San Felipe, Suite 3300
Houston, TX 77057
Tel: (713) 789 - 1400
Fax:(713) 789 - 1430

Serves As:
- Chairman of the Board, Pride Internat'l, Inc.

MACCARTHY, Mark
1300 Connecticut Ave. NW
Suite 900
Washington, DC 20036
mmaccarthy@visa.com
Tel: (202) 296 - 9230
Fax:(202) 862 - 5498

Registered Federal Lobbyist.
Serves As:
- Contact, VISA USA Political Action Committee, Visa U.S.A. Inc.

MACCAUL, Cathy
One Microsoft Way
Redmond, WA 98052-6399
Tel: (425) 882 - 8080
Fax:(425) 936 - 7329

Serves As:
- Manager, Communications, Microsoft Corporation

MACDONALD, Carey
1801 California St.
50th Floor
Denver, CO 80202
Tel: (303) 896 - 5386
TF: (800) 899 - 7780

Serves As:
- Contact, Qwest Foundation, Qwest Communications

MACDONALD, Kelley S.
225 Franklin St.
Boston, MA 02110
Tel: (617) 786 - 3000
Fax:(617) 664 - 4999

Serves As:
- Senior V. President, Investor Relations, State Street Corp.

MACDONALD, Laurie
800 N. Brand Blvd.
Glendale, CA 91203
laurie.macdonald@us.nestle.com
Tel: (818) 549 - 7131
Fax:(818) 549 - 5884
TF: (800) 225 - 2270

Serves As:
- V. President, Corporate and Brand Affairs, Nestle USA, Inc.

MACENCZAK, Lee
P.O. Box 20706
Atlanta, GA 30320-6001
Tel: (404) 715 - 2600
Fax:(404) 715 - 2731

Serves As:
- Executive V. President and Chief Human Resources Officer, Delta Air Lines, Inc.

MACFADYEN, Jr., Alex G.
P.O. Box 27131
Raleigh, NC 27611
Tel: (919) 716 - 3127
Fax:(919) 716 - 7074

Serves As:
- Group V. President and Director, Government Affairs, (First Citizens Bank), First Citizens BancShares

MACFARLANE, John C.
P.O. Box 496
215 S. Cascade St. S.
Fergus Falls, MN 56538-0496
jmacfarlane@otpco.com
Tel: (218) 739 - 8200
Fax:(218) 739 - 8218
TF: (866) 410 - 8780

Serves As:
- Chairman of the Board, Otter Tail Power Co.

Responsibilities include corporate philanthropy.

MACHATTON, Doug
6201 South Fwy.
Fort Worth, TX 76134
Tel: (817) 293 - 0450
Fax:(817) 551 - 4615

Serves As:
- V. President, Investor Relations and Strategic Corporate Communications, Alcon Inc.

MACHOTA, John J.
1400 Opus Place
Suite 600
Downers Grove, IL 60515
Tel: (630) 271 - 8100

Serves As:
- V. President, Human Resources, Aftermarket Technology Corp.

MACHUT, Marlene
800 High St.
Hackettstown, NJ 07840
Tel: (908) 852 - 1000

Serves As:
- Director, External Affairs, Mars, Inc.

MACINNIS, Frank
301 Merritt Seven
Sixth Floor
Norwalk, CT 06851
frank_macinnis@emcorgroup.com
Tel: (203) 849 - 7800
Fax:(203) 849 - 7850

Serves As:
- Chairman and Chief Exec. Officer, EMCOR Group, Inc.

MACINTOSH, Wendy W.
111 Trumbull St.
Hartford, CT 06103
Tel: (860) 947 - 7033

Serves As:
- Director, Legislative Affairs, SBC SNET

MACINTYRE, Michael
281 Tresser Blvd.
Two Stamford Plaza
Stamford, CT 06901-3238
Tel: (203) 969 - 0666
Fax:(203) 358 - 3977

Serves As:
- PAC Treasurer, Hexcel Corp.

MACK, David J.
165 Court St.
Rochester, NY 14647
Tel: (585) 454 - 1700
Fax:(585) 238 - 4233

Serves As:
• Senior V. President, Corporate Affairs, The Lifetime Healthcare Companies

MACK, John J.
1585 Broadway
New York, NY 10036
Tel: (212) 761 - 4000
Fax:(212) 761 - 0086

Serves As:
• Chairman and Chief Exec. Officer, Morgan Stanley

MACK, Michelle D.
6625 W. 78th St.
M/S BL0220
Bloomington, MN 55439
Tel: (952) 820 - 7000
Fax:(952) 837 - 7103

Serves As:
• Government Affairs Analyst, Express Scripts, Inc.

MACKAY, Chris B.
1133 19th St. NW
Washington, DC 20036
Tel: (202) 887 - 3830
Fax:(202) 887 - 3123

Registered Federal Lobbyist.
Serves As:
• PAC Treasurer, MCI, Inc.

MACKAY, William L.
P.O. Box 68900
Seattle, WA 98168-0947
Tel: (206) 433 - 3200
Fax:(206) 431 - 5558

Serves As:
• V. President, Public and Government Affairs, (Alaska Airlines, Inc.), Alaska Air Group, Inc.
Responsibilities include corporate philanthropy, corporate communications, and political action.

MACKENZIE, Tod J.
700 Anderson Hill Rd.
Purchase, NY 10577-1444
tod.mackenzie@pepsi.com
Tel: (914) 253 - 2000

Serves As:
• Senior V. President, Corporate Communications, PepsiCo, Inc.

MACKEY, John P.
550 Bowie St.
Austin, TX 78703
Tel: (512) 477 - 4455
Fax:(512) 477 - 1069

Serves As:
• Chairman and Chief Exec. Officer, Whole Foods Market, Inc.

MACKEY, Rachel
1500 E. Main St.
Newark, OH 43055
rmackey@longaberger.com
Tel: (740) 322 - 5414
Fax:(740) 322 - 5240

Serves As:
• Public Relations Representative, The Longaberger Co.

MACKIN, Ginny
301 S. College St., Suite 4000
One Wachovia Center
NC 0570
Charlotte, NC 28288-0370
ginny.mackin@wachovia.com
Tel: (704) 374 - 6565
Fax:(704) 374 - 3425
TF: (800) 275 - 3862

Serves As:
• Senior V. President and Director, Corporate Communications, Wachovia Corp.

MACKINNON, Gail G.
1501 M St. NW
Suite 1100
Washington, DC 20005
Tel: (202) 785 - 7300
Fax:(202) 785 - 6360

Registered Federal Lobbyist.
Serves As:
• Senior V. President, Washington, CBS Corp., Viacom Inc./CBS Corp.

MACLEAY, Thomas H.
One Nat'l Life Dr.
Montpelier, VT 05604
Tel: (802) 229 - 3333
Fax:(802) 229 - 9281
TF: (800) 732 - 8939

Serves As:
• Chairman, President and Chief Exec. Officer, Nat'l Life Insurance Co.

MACMAHON, Mark R.
Three Commercial Pl.
Norfolk, VA 23510-2191
Tel: (757) 629 - 2615
Fax:(757) 629 - 2822

Serves As:
• V. President, Labor Relations, Norfolk Southern Corp.

MACMAHON, Thomas P.
Corporate Communications Dept.
430 S. Spring St.
Burlington, NC 27215

Serves As:
• Chairman and Chief Exec. Officer, Laboratory Corp. of America Holdings

MACOMBER, Debbie
1120 20th St. NW
Suite 1000
Washington, DC 20036-3406
Tel: (202) 457 - 3810
Fax:(202) 457 - 2008

Serves As:
• Staff Manager, Federal Government Affairs, AT&T

MACRAE, Bruce
25201 Paseo de Alicia
Suite 200
Laguna Hills, CA 12653
bmacrae@ups.com
Tel: (949) 452 - 2082
Fax:(949) 452 - 2040

Serves As:
• Manager, Public Affairs, United Parcel Service (UPS)

MACRIDES, Foster G.
777 Dedham St.
Canton, MA 02021
Tel: (781) 828 - 4900
Ext: 5266
Fax:(781) 828 - 9012
TF: (800) 225 - 9702

Serves As:
• V. President, Human Resources, Cumberland Farms, Inc.
Responsibilities also include corporate communications.

MACTAS, Mark
One Stamford Plaza
263 Tresser Blvd.
Stamford, CT 06901
mactasm@towers.com
Tel: (203) 326 - 5400
Fax:(203) 326 - 5499

Serves As:
• Chairman and Chief Exec. Officer, Towers Perrin

MADDEN, Kathryn
400 California St.
San Francisco, CA 94104
Tel: (415) 765 - 0400
Fax:(415) 765 - 3257

Serves As:
• Manager, Media Relations and Vice President, Public Relations, Union Bank of California

MADDEN, Kevin P.
P.O. Box 4569
Atlanta, GA 30302-4569
Tel: (404) 584 - 4000
Fax:(404) 584 - 3479

Serves As:
• Exec. V. President, Distribution Operations and External Affairs, AGL Resources, Inc.

MADEIRA, Rebecca W.
700 Anderson Hill Rd.
Purchase, NY 10577-1444
rebecca.madeira@pepsi.com
Tel: (914) 253 - 2000
Fax:(914) 767 - 7214

Serves As:
• Senior V. President, Public Affairs, (Pepsi-Cola North America), PepsiCo, Inc.

MADER, Kelly F.
701 Market St.
St. Louis, MO 63101-1826
Tel: (314) 342 - 7564
Fax:(314) 342 - 7799

Serves As:
• V. President, State Government Affairs, Peabody Energy

MADISON, M. Emily
1330 post Oak Blvd.
Suite 2000
Houston, TX 77056
Tel: (713) 975 - 7600
Fax:(713) 267 - 3701

Serves As:
• V. President, Finance, MAXXAM Inc.

MADOUS, Martin
290 Concord Rd.
Billerica, MA 01821
Tel: (978) 715 - 4321
Fax:(978) 715 - 1393
TF: (800) 645 - 5476

Serves As:
• Chairman, Chief Exec. Officer and President, Millipore Corp.

MADSEN, Jeffrey
1303 E. Algonquin Rd.
Schaumburg, IL 60196
jeffrey.madsen@motorola.com
Tel: (847) 862 - 0035
Fax:(847) 341 - 4462
TF: (800) 262 - 8509

Serves As:
• Director, Communications and Public Affairs, Integrated Electronic Systems Sector, Motorola, Inc.

MAESTRI, Bruno
1500 K St. NW
Suite 375
Washington, DC 20005
Tel: (202) 383 - 4425
Fax:(202) 383 - 4018

Serves As:
• V. President, Public Affairs, Norfolk Southern Corp.

MAGINN, Marjorie
120 Monument Circle
Indianapolis, IN 46204
Tel: (317) 488 - 6032

Serves As:
- V. President, Industry and Political Affairs, Wellpoint, Inc.

MAGINNIS, Jr., John H.
P.O. Box 98029
Baton Rouge, LA 70898-9029
Tel: (225) 295 - 2405
Fax:(225) 295 - 2583
TF: (800) 599 - 2583

Serves As:
- V. President, Corporate Communications, Blue Cross and Blue Shield of Louisiana

MAGLEBY, Curtis N.
1350 I St. NW
Suite 1000
Washington, DC 20005
Tel: (202) 962 - 5367
Fax:(202) 336 - 7223

Registered Federal Lobbyist.
Serves As:
- Legislative Manager, Clean Air and Fuels, Ford Motor Co.

MAGRONE, James
745 Fifth Ave.
New York, NY 10151
Tel: (212) 745 - 0100
Fax:(212) 745 - 0121

Serves As:
- Senior V. President, Investor Relations, Primedia Inc.

MAGUIRE, Andrew G.
One PPG Pl.
Pittsburgh, PA 15272
amaguire@ppg.com
Tel: (412) 434 - 2316
Fax:(412) 434 - 4666

Serves As:
- General Manager, Marketing and Communications, PPG Industries Inc.

MAHAN, Marsha J.
625 Fourth Ave. South
Minneapolis, MN 55415
marsha.mahan@thrivent.com
Tel: (612) 340 - 7000
Fax:(612) 340 - 7373

Serves As:
- PAC Treasurer, Thrivent Financial for Lutherans

MAHERAS, John
Three Lakes Dr.
Northfield, IL 60093-2753
Tel: (847) 646 - 2472
Fax:(847) 646 - 6005

Serves As:
- Government Affairs Liaison, Kraft Foods, Inc.

MAHLOCH, Jeffrey G.
P.O. Box 702
Milwaukee, WI 53201-0702
Tel: (414) 259 - 5333
Fax:(414) 479 - 1245

Serves As:
- V. President, Human Resources, Briggs and Stratton Corp.

MAHONEY, Jr., George R.
P.O. Box 1017
Charlotte, NC 28201-1017
gmahoney@familydollar.com
Tel: (704) 814 - 3252
Fax:(704) 841 - 1401

Serves As:
- Director, Family Dollar Stores, Inc.

Responsibilities include investor relations and corporate communications.

MAHONEY, James V.
1065 Woodman Dr.
Dayton, OH 45432
Tel: (937) 224 - 6000
Fax:(937) 259 - 7813

Serves As:
- President and Chief Exec. Officer, DPL Inc.

MAHONEY, John
One Targeting Centre
Windsor, CT 06095
Tel: (860) 285 - 6100
Fax:(860) 285 - 1567
TF: (800) 559 - 2386

Serves As:
- Chairman of the Board, Advo Inc.

MAHONEY, John J.
500 Staples Dr.
Framingham, MA 01702
john.mahoney@staples.com
Tel: (508) 253 - 8969
Ext: 37298
Fax:(508) 253 - 8955

Serves As:
- Exec. V. President, Chief Administrative Officer and Chief Financial Officer, Staples, Inc.

Responsibilities include government affairs.

MAI, Vincent A.
One Lincoln Plaza
New York, NY 10023
Tel: (212) 595 - 3456
Fax:(212) 875 - 6088

Serves As:
- Chairman of the Board, Sesame Workshop

MAIMAN, Seth E.
1133 19th St. NW
Washington, DC 20036
Tel: (202) 887 - 3830
Fax:(202) 887 - 3123

Registered Federal Lobbyist.
Serves As:
- Representative, MCI, Inc.

MAIN, Timothy L.
10560 Dr. Martin Luther King Jr. St. North
St. Petersburg, FL 33716
time_maine@jabil.com
Tel: (727) 577 - 9749
Fax:(727) 579 - 8529

Serves As:
- President and Chief Exec. Officer, Jabil Circuit, Inc.

MAITLAND, Peter K.
P.O. Box 6721
Chicago, IL 60680-6721
pmaitland@usg.com
Tel: (312) 606 - 4024
Fax:(312) 606 - 3872

Serves As:
- V. President, Compensation, Benefits, and Administration, USG Corp.

Responsibilities include corporate philanthropy.

MAJESKI, Glenn
100 Campus Dr.
M/S 3-045
Florham Park, NJ 07932
majeskg@basf-corp.com
Tel: (973) 245 - 6070
Fax:(973) 245 - 6714

Serves As:
- Manager, Corporate Donations, BASF Corporation

MAJESKIE, Dennis
180 Jo Ray Ct.
Mankato, MN 56001
majeskd@wyeth.com
Tel: (507) 344 - 4393
Fax:(507) 344 - 4394

Serves As:
- Director State Government Affairs, Wyeth Pharmaceuticals

MAJOR-SOSIAS, Mari Angeles
Two Democracy Center
6903 Rockledge Dr.
Bethesda, MD 20817-1818
Tel: (301) 564 - 3200
Fax:(301) 564 - 3201

Serves As:
- Manager, Investor Relations, USEC Inc.

MAKRAKIS, Kathleen
One Executive Dr.
Fort Lee, NJ 07024
investorrelations@alpharma.com
Tel: (201) 228 - 5085
Fax:(201) 947 - 5541
TF: (800) 445 - 4216

Serves As:
- V. President, Investor Relations, Alpharma Inc.

MALASPINA, Rick
Ordway Bldg.
One Kaiser Plaza
Oakland, CA 94612
rick.malaspina@kp.org
Tel: (510) 987 - 3900
Fax:(510) 873 - 5345

Serves As:
- Media Director - Northern California Region, Kaiser Permanente

MALCOLM, Steven J.
One Williams Center
Tulsa, OK 74172
Tel: (918) 573 - 2000
TF: (800) 945 - 5426

Serves As:
- Chairman and Chief Exec. Officer, Williams

MALECEK, Thomas G.
P.O. Box 29
St. Louis, MO 63166-0029
tmalecek@brownshoe.com
Tel: (314) 854 - 4084
Fax:(314) 854 - 2016

Serves As:
- Director, Security; and Contact, Brown Shoe Charitable Trust, Brown Shoe Co., Inc.

MALLAHAN, Mary Ann
3600 W. Lake Ave.
Glenview, IL 60025-5811
Tel: (847) 657 - 4092
Fax:(847) 657 - 4505

Serves As:
- Manager, Community Relations, Illinois Tool Works Inc.

MALLARD, Daren
5030 Sugarloaf Pkwy.
Lawrenceville, GA 30042-2869
daren.mallard@sciatl.com
Tel: (770) 236 - 4770
Fax:(770) 236 - 4775
TF: (800) 236 - 5000

Serves As:
- Manager, Investor Relations, Scientific-Atlanta, Inc.

MALLETT, Robert L.
235 E. 42nd St.
New York, NY 10017-5755
robert.mallett@pfizer.com
Tel: (212) 733 - 0922
Fax:(212) 573 - 2883

Serves As:
- Senior V. President, Corporate Affairs, Pfizer Inc.

MALLEY, Bonnie J.
One American Row
Hartford, CT 06102
Tel: (860) 403 - 5000
Fax:(860) 403 - 5755

Serves As:
- Senior V. President, Human Resources and Corporate Services, The Phoenix Companies, Inc.

MALNAK, Brian P.
1401 I St. NW, Suite 1030
Washington, DC 20005
Tel: (202) 466 - 1405
Fax:(202) 466 - 1498

Serves As:
- V. President, Government Affairs, Shell Oil Co.

MALONE, Harry
1550 Crystal Dr.
Crystal Square 2, Suite 300
Arlington, VA 22202
harry.malone@lmco.com
Tel: (703) 413 - 5753
Fax:(703) 413 - 5617

Registered Federal Lobbyist.
Serves As:
- Director, Legislative Affairs, Army Programs, Lockheed Martin Corp.

MALONE, John C.
12300 Liberty Blvd.
Englewood, CO 80112
Tel: (720) 875 - 5400
Fax:(720) 875 - 5401

Serves As:
- Chairman and Chief Exec. Officer, Liberty Media Corp.

MALONE STANCAVAGE, Kerry L.
One Williams Center
47th Floor
Tulsa, OK 74172
kerry.malone@williams.com
Tel: (918) 573 - 2110
Fax:(918) 573 - 6714
TF: (800) 945 - 5426

Serves As:
- Director, Corporate Communications, Williams

MALONEY, Cathleen M.
One Mercer Rd.
Natick, MA 01760
cmaloney@bjs.com
Tel: (508) 651 - 6650
Fax:(508) 651 - 6167
TF: (800) 257 - 2582

Serves As:
- V. President and Manager, Investor Relations, BJ's Wholesale Club, Inc.

MALONEY, Robert H.
3900 Wisconsin Ave. NW
Washington, DC 20016
robert_h_maloney@fanniemae.com
Tel: (202) 752 - 7958
Fax:(202) 752 - 6014

Registered Federal Lobbyist.
Serves As:
- V. President, Government and Industry Relations, Fannie Mae

MALZAHN, Dan
7601 Lewinsville Rd., Suite 300
McLean, VA 22102
Tel: (703) 761 - 2137
Fax:(703) 761 - 2030

Serves As:
- Investor Relations Contact, NVR, Inc.

MANASSAH, Edward E.
P.O. Box 740031
Louisville, KY 40201-7431
emanassa@louisvil.gannett.com
Tel: (502) 582 - 4101
TF: (800) 765 - 4011

Serves As:
- President and Publisher, The Courier-Journal

MANCINI, Paul
P.O. Box 2933
San Antonio, TX 78299-2933
Tel: (210) 821 - 4105
TF: (800) 351 - 7221

Serves As:
- V. President, External Affairs, SBC Communications Inc.

MANCINO, Joseph L.
615 Merrick Ave.
Westbury, NY 11590
Tel: (516) 683 - 4100

Serves As:
- Co-Chairman of the Board, New York Community Bancorp, Inc.

MANDEVILLE, James
P.O. Box 6936
Jacksonville, FL 32236

Serves As:
- Treasurer, Florida Health Political Action Committee, Blue Cross and Blue Shield of Florida

MANDT, David
8720 Red Oak Blvd.
Suite 315
Charlotte, NC 28217
Tel: (704) 587 - 9051

Serves As:
- Director, Marketing/Communications, (Paramount Parks), Viacom Inc./CBS Corp.

MANDYCK, John M.
One Carrier Pl.
Farmington, CT 06034-4015
john.mandyck@carrier.utc.com
Tel: (860) 674 - 3006
Fax:(860) 674 - 3193

Serves As:
- V. President, Government and International Relations, Carrier Corp.

MANEKI, Freya
One Dole Dr.
Westlake Village, CA 91362-7300
Tel: (818) 879 - 6600
Fax:(818) 879 - 6890

Serves As:
- Corporate Communications, Dole Food Company, Inc.

Responsibilities include investor relations.

MANERI, K. Peter
2100 E. Grand Ave.
El Segundo, CA 90245
pmaneri@csc.com
Tel: (310) 615 - 1783

Serves As:
- V. President, Corporate Communications and Marketing, Computer Sciences Corp.

MANERO, Joseph
CNA Center
333 S. Wabash Ave.
Chicago, IL 60685
Tel: (312) 822 - 2894
Fax:(312) 822 - 1186

Serves As:
- Director, State Government Relations, CNA Financial Corp.

MANERO, Linda
355 Maple Ave.
Harleysville, PA 19438-2297
lmanero@harleysvillegroup.com
Tel: (215) 256 - 5061
Fax:(215) 256 - 5799
TF: (800) 523 - 6344

Serves As:
- Manager, Marketing Communications, Harleysville Group

MANES, Julie
601 Pennsylvania Ave. NW
North Bldg. Suite 325
Washington, DC 20004
julie.manes@pioneer.com
Tel: (202) 728 - 3613
Fax:(202) 728 - 3649

Serves As:
- Washington Representative, Pioneer Hi-Bred Internat'l, Inc.

MANESS, Alan D.
1900 M St. NW
Suite 730
Washington, DC 20036
Tel: (202) 263 - 4400
Fax:(202) 263 - 4435

Registered Federal Lobbyist.
Serves As:
- Associate General Counsel, State Farm Insurance Cos.

MANESS, Katherine W.
600 13th St. NW
Suite 340 West
Washington, DC 20005
Tel: (202) 662 - 0140
Fax:(202) 662 - 0199

Registered Federal Lobbyist.
Serves As:
- Director, Political Affairs, Union Pacific Corp.

MANFREDI, John F.
Prudential Tower Bldg.
Boston, MA 02199-8004
john_manfredi@gillette.com
Tel: (617) 421 - 7000
Fax:(617) 421 - 7123

Serves As:
- Senior V. President, Corporate Affairs, The Gillette Company

Responsibilities include corporate communications and investor relations.

MANGAN, Terrence K.
Webster Plaza
145 Bank St.
MO 315
Waterbury, CT 06702
tmangan@websterbank.com
Tel: (203) 578 - 2318
TF: (800) 325 - 2424

Serves As:
- Senior V. President, Investor Relations, Webster Financial Corp.

MANGANELLO, Timothy M.
3850 Hamlin Rd.
Auburn Hills, MI 48326
Tel: (248) 754 - 9200

Serves As:
- Chairman and Chief Exec. Officer, BorgWarner Inc.

MANGINELLI, Gail
5770 Fleet St.
Carlsbad, CA 92008
gail@jennycraig.com
Tel: (760) 696 - 4000
Fax:(760) 696 - 4009
TF: (800) 597 - 5366

Serves As:
- Communications, Jenny Craig, Inc.

MANGINO, Gohn
385 Washington St.
St. Paul, MN 55102
Tel: (860) 277 - 0406

Serves As:
- PAC Treasurer, St. Paul Travelers Cos., Inc.

MANISCALO, Tim
9330 Zionsville Rd.
Indianapolis, IN 46268
tmmaniscalo@dow.com
Tel: (317) 337 - 4359
Fax:(317) 337 - 4880

Serves As:
- Manager, Corporate Contributions, Dow AgroSciences LLC

MANKE, Dave
1401 I St. NW
Suite 600
Washington, DC 20005
Tel: (202) 336 - 7400
Fax:(202) 336 - 7515

Serves As:
- Interim Sr. V. President, Gov. Rels. and Int'l Affairs, United Technologies Corp.

MANN, Cathy
Five Houston Center
1401 McKinney, Suite 2400
Houston, TX 77010
cathy.mann@halliburton.com
Tel: (713) 759 - 2605

Serves As:
- Director, Public Relations, Halliburton Company

MANN, James L.
680 E. Swedesford Rd.
Wayne, PA 19087
james.mann@sungard.com
Tel: (484) 582 - 5506
Fax:(484) 225 - 1120

Serves As:
- Chairman of the Board, SunGard Data Systems, Inc.

MANN, Larry E.
P.O. Box 468
Donaldsonville, LA 70346
Tel: (504) 473 - 8291
Fax:(504) 473 - 1864

Serves As:
- Manager, Industrial Relations, C F Industries, Inc.

MANN, Marie
2801 Hunting Park Ave.
Philadelphia, PA 19129
Tel: (215) 221 - 8500
Ext: 8573
Fax:(215) 228 - 3970
TF: (800) 248 - 2789

Serves As:
- Contact, Tasty Baking Foundation, Tasty Baking Co.

MANN, Mary M.
1101 Pennsylvania Ave. NW
Suite 200
Washington, DC 20004
mary.mann@ipaper.com
Tel: (202) 628 - 1223
Ext: 19
Fax:(202) 628 - 1368

Registered Federal Lobbyist.
Serves As:
- Washington Representative, Internat'l Paper

MANN, Michelle
151 Almaden Blvd.
M/S A11
San Jose, CA 95110-2704
Tel: (408) 536 - 3993
Fax:(408) 537 - 6313

Serves As:
- Group Manager, Corporate Affairs/Community Relations, Adobe Systems Inc.

MANN, Steve
N56 W17000 Ridgewood Dr.
Menomonee Falls, WI 53051
Tel: (262) 703 - 6397
Fax:(262) 703 - 6143

Serves As:
- Coordinator, Public Relations, Kohl's Corp.

MANN, Susan O.
1401 I St., NW
Suite 500
Washington, DC 20005
Tel: (202) 263 - 5900
Fax:(202) 263 - 5902

Registered Federal Lobbyist.
Serves As:
- Manager, Federal Affairs, Microsoft Corporation

MANNE, Kenneth W.
600 Third Ave
New York, NY 10016
Tel: (212) 697 - 1111
Fax:(212) 867 - 5249
TF: (866) 463 - 6555

Serves As:
- V. President, Human Resources, L-3 Communications Corp.

MANNING, Clark P.
One Corporate Way
Lansing, MI 48951
Tel: (517) 381 - 5500
Fax:(517) 706 - 5517
TF: (800) 644 - 4565

Serves As:
- President and Chief Exec. Officer, Jackson Nat'l Life Insurance Co.

MANNING, David J.
One MetroTech Center
Brooklyn, NY 11201
Tel: (718) 403 - 2000
Fax:(718) 488 - 1763

Serves As:
- Senior V. President, Corporate Affairs, KeySpan Corp.

Responsibilities include corporate communications and community and government affairs.

MANNING, Dennis J.
Seven Hanover Square
M/S H-26-E
New York, NY 10004-2616
Tel: (212) 598 - 8000
Fax:(212) 949 - 2170

Serves As:
- President and Chief Exec. Officer, Guardian Life Insurance Co. of America

MANNING, Kenneth P.
777 E. Wisconsin Ave., 11th Floor
Milwaukee, WI 53202-5304
kenneth.manning@sensient-tech.com
Tel: (414) 271 - 6755
Fax:(414) 347 - 3785

Serves As:
- Chairman, President and Chief Exec. Officer, Sensient Technology Corp.

MANNING, Lori
One State Farm Plaza
Bloomington, IL 61710-0001
Tel: (309) 766 - 9739

Serves As:
- Director, Public Affairs; Contact, State Farm Companies Foundation, State Farm Insurance Cos.

MANNING, Tim
One NSTAR Way
Westwood, MA 02090
Tel: (617) 424 - 2000
Fax:(617) 424 - 2523

Serves As:
- Senior V. President, Human Resources, NSTAR

MANNION, Eileen
172 W. State St.
Trenton, NJ 08608
Tel: (609) 989 - 9906
Fax:(609) 599 - 2189

Serves As:
- Director, State Government Affairs, Verizon New Jersey, Inc.

MANNION, Sean
One Research Court
Suite 350
Rockville, MD 20850-3221
Tel: (301) 977 - 6717
Fax:(301) 977 - 6907

Serves As:
- V. President and Washington Contact, Mutual of America Life Insurance Co.

MANNO, Sue
P.O. Box 799900
Dallas, TX 75379-9900
Tel: (972) 497 - 5094
Fax:(972) 497 - 5299

Serves As:
- Foundation Contact, Lennox Internat'l

MANOOGIAN, Richard A.
21001 Van Born Rd.
Taylor, MI 48180
Tel: (313) 274 - 7400
Fax:(313) 792 - 6135

Serves As:
- Chairman and Chief Exec. Officer, Masco Corp.

MANOS, Kim
333 Continental Blvd.
El Segundo, CA 90245-5012
Tel: (310) 252 - 2908
Fax:(310) 252 - 4443

Serves As:
- Administrator, Mattel Children's Foundation, Mattel, Inc.

MANSELL, Kevin B.
N56 W17000 Ridgewood Dr.
Menomonee Falls, WI 53051
Tel: (262) 703 - 7000
Fax:(262) 703 - 6143

Serves As:
- President, Kohl's Corp.

MANSFIELD, Teresa
358 S. Main St.
Burlington, NC 27215
Tel: (336) 229 - 1127
Fax:(336) 436 - 1205
TF: (800) 334 - 5261

Serves As:
• Community Affairs Contact, Laboratory Corp. of America Holdings
Responsibilities include corporate philanthropy.

MANSFIELD, William L.
1101 Third St. South
Minneapolis, MN 55415
Tel: (612) 332 - 7371
Fax:(612) 375 - 7723

Serves As:
• President and Chief Exec. Officer, Valspar Corp.

MANSON, Craig G.
3311 E. Old Shakopee Rd.
Minneapolis, MN 55425-1640
Tel: (952) 853 - 6022
Fax:(952) 853 - 7272

Serves As:
• V. President, Investor Relations, Ceridian Corp.

MANSOURKIA, Maggie
1133 19th St. NW
Washington, DC 20036
Tel: (202) 887 - 3830
Fax:(202) 887 - 3123

Registered Federal Lobbyist.
Serves As:
• Representative, MCI, Inc.

MANSSON, Fabian
15010 NE 36th St.
Redmond, WA 98052
Tel: (425) 755 - 6100
Fax:(425) 755 - 7696

Serves As:
• President and Chief Exec. Officer, Eddie Bauer, Inc.

MANTELLI, Lucille M.
9952 Eastman Park Dr.
Windsor, CO 80551-1334
lucille.mantelli@kodak.com
Tel: (970) 686 - 4102
Fax:(970) 686 - 4154

Serves As:
• Director, Communications and Public Affairs (Kodak Division), Eastman Kodak Company

MANUEL, Gordon R.
P.O. Box 1028
Greenville, SC 29602
Tel: (864) 282 - 9448
Fax:(864) 282 - 9594

Serves As:
• Director, Government Affairs, Bowater Incorporated
Responsibilities include corporate contributions and communications.

MANZ, Richard W.
Financial Center
695 E. Main St.
Stamford, CT 06901
Tel: (203) 328 - 5000
Ext: 5661
Fax:(203) 328 - 6423
TF: (800) 431 - 9994

Serves As:
• Contributions Contact, General Re Corp.

MANZELLA, Michael
111 S. Wacker Dr.
Chicago, IL 60606
michael.manzella@rrd.com
Tel: (312) 326 - 8038
Fax:(630) 322 - 6711

Serves As:
• V. President, Environmental Affairs, R R Donnelley

MANZULLI, Michael F.
615 Merrick Ave.
Westbury, NY 11590
Tel: (516) 683 - 4100

Serves As:
• Co-Chairman of the Board, New York Community Bancorp, Inc.

MARAGHY, Susan
1550 Crystal Dr.
Crystal Square 2, Suite 300
Arlington, VA 22202
Tel: (703) 413 - 5601
Fax:(703) 413 - 5636

Serves As:
• V. President, Homeland Security and Information Technology, Lockheed Martin Corp.

MARANELL, Mike
P.O. Box 2047
Omaha, NE 68103-2047
Tel: (402) 496 - 2279
Fax:(402) 498 - 5552

Serves As:
• Senior V. President, Corporate and Member Relations, AG Processing Inc

MARCELA, Paul
P.O. Box 994
Midland, MI 48686-0994
paul.marcela@dowcorning.com
Tel: (989) 496 - 6365
Fax:(989) 496 - 1709

Serves As:
• Chairman, Dow Corning Legislative Action Team, Dow Corning Corp.

MARCHANT, Ross H.
P.O. Box 17357
Salt Lake City, UT 84117
Tel: (801) 272 - 8081

Serves As:
• Legislative Representative, Farmers Group, Inc.

MARCHETTA, Russell
Five Dedrick Pl.
West Caldwell, NJ 07006-6398
russell.marchetta@ricoh-usa.com
Tel: (973) 882 - 2075
Fax:(973) 882 - 2506

Serves As:
• Manager, Public Relations, Ricoh Corp.
Responsibilities include corporate philanthropy.

MARCHETTI, Robert
111 Monument Circle
29th Floor
Indianapolis, IN 46204-5129
Tel: (317) 971 - 2000
Fax:(317) 971 - 2040

Serves As:
• V. President, Human Resources, Guidant Corp.

MARCHETTI, Tina
711 High St.
Des Moines, IA 50392-0150
marchetti.tina@principal.com
Tel: (515) 248 - 0065
Fax:(515) 246 - 5475
TF: (800) 986 - 3343

Serves As:
• Media Relations Contact, Financial Communications, The Principal Financial Group

MARCHIOLI, Nelson J.
203 E. Main St.
Spartanburg, SC 29319-0001
Tel: (864) 597 - 8000

Serves As:
• Chief Exec. Officer and President, Denny's Corp.

MARCHON, Theresa M.
51 Madison Ave.
New York, NY 10010
theresa_m_marchon@newyorklife.com
Tel: (212) 576 - 5624
Fax:(212) 576 - 8145

Serves As:
• Media Representative, New York Life Insurance Co.

MARCIN, Robert H.
One Village Dr.
Van Buren Township, MI 48111
Tel: (313) 755 - 2800
TF: (800) VIS - TEON

Serves As:
• Senior V. President, Corporate Relations, Visteon Corp.

MARCUS, Richard C.
901 W. Walnut Hill Ln.
Irving, TX 75038-1003
Tel: (972) 580 - 4000
Fax:(972) 580 - 5523

Serves As:
• Chairman of the Board, Zale Corp.

MARDER, Thomas O.
One Marriott Dr.
Washington, DC 20058
thomas.marder@marriott.com
Tel: (301) 380 - 2553
Fax:(301) 897 - 9014

Serves As:
• V. President, Corporate Relations, Marriott Internat'l, Inc.

MARENTETTE, Charles
5725 Delphi Dr.
Troy, MI 48098-2815
Tel: (248) 813 - 2495
Fax:(248) 813 - 2670

Serves As:
• Director, Investor Relations, Delphi Corp.

MARGARITIS, Bill
942 S. Shady Grove Rd.
Memphis, TN 38120
wgmargaritis@fedex.com
Tel: (901) 818 - 7090
TF: (800) 238 - 5355

Serves As:
• Corporate V. President, Worldwide Corporate Communications and Investor Relations, FedEx Corp.

MARGOLIS, Laura
2775 Sanders Rd.
Northbrook, IL 60062-6127
Tel: (847) 402 - 5000
Fax:(847) 326 - 7519
TF: (800) 574 - 3553

Serves As:
• National Media Contact, Allstate Insurance Co.

MARGOLIS, Lawrence A.
11450 Technology Circle
Duluth, GA 30097

Serves As:
• PAC Treasurer, Anixter Internat'l, Inc.

MARGULIS, Heidi
P.O. Box 1438
Louisville, KY 40201-1438
hmargulis@humana.com
Tel: (502) 580 - 1854
Fax:(502) 580 - 3677
TF: (800) 486 - 2620

Registered Federal Lobbyist.
Serves As:
• Senior V. President, Government Relations, Humana Inc.

MARIETTA, Sally Scott
1301 K St. NW
Suite 1200
Washington, DC 20005
Tel: (202) 515 - 5013

Serves As:
• Corporate Community Relations Manager, Internat'l Business Machines Corp. (IBM)

MARILLEY, Leanne D.
Three Commercial Pl.
Norfolk, VA 23510-2191
Tel: (757) 629 - 2861

Serves As:
• Director, Investor Relations, Norfolk Southern Corp.

MARINEAU, Philip A.
1155 Battery St.
San Francisco, CA 94111
Tel: (415) 501 - 6000
Fax:(415) 501 - 7112
TF: (800) 872 - 5384

Serves As:
• President and Chief Exec. Officer, Levi Strauss and Co.

MARINO, John
1235 S. Clark St.
Suite 708
Arlington, VA 22202
john.marino@flightsafety.com
Tel: (703) 414 - 5501
Fax:(703) 414 - 5504

Serves As:
• V. President, Government Relations, FlightSafety Internat'l

MARINO, William J.
Three Penn Plaza East
PP-15V
M/S PP-16A
Newark, NJ 07105-2200
Tel: (973) 466 - 4000
Fax:(973) 466 - 7077

Serves As:
• President and Chief Exec. Officer, Horizon Blue Cross Blue Shield of New Jersey

MARION, Joanne
P.O. Box 1000
Montville, NJ 07045
TF: (800) 237 - 5392

Serves As:
• Director, Investor Relations, Berlex, Inc.

MARITATO, Anna Maria
284 State St., Second Floor
Albany, NY 12210
amaritato@pfizer.com
Tel: (518) 463 - 9133

Serves As:
• Director, Government Relations, Pfizer Inc.

MARITZ, Steve
1375 N. Highway Dr.
Fenton, MO 63099
Tel: (636) 827 - 4000
Fax:(636) 827 - 2089

Serves As:
• Chairman and Chief Exec. Officer, Maritz Inc.

MARK, Larry
P.O. Box 1734
Atlanta, GA 30301
lmark@na.ko.com
Tel: (404) 676 - 2121
Fax:(404) 676 - 6792

Serves As:
• Director, Investor Relations, The Coca-Cola Co.

MARK, Reuben
300 Park Ave.
New York, NY 10022
Tel: (212) 310 - 2000
Fax:(212) 310 - 3284

Serves As:
• Chairman and Chief Exec. Officer, Colgate-Palmolive Co.

MARKEE, Richard L.
One Geoffrey Way
Wayne, NJ 07470-2030
Tel: (973) 617 - 3500

Serves As:
• Interim Chief Exec. Officer, Toys "R" Us, Inc.

MARKER, Mike
220 N. Meridian St.
Indianapolis, IN 46204
Tel: (317) 265 - 4020
TF: (800) 257 - 0902

Serves As:
• Media Relations Contact, SBC Indiana

MARKIEWICZ, Stephanie J.
1120 20th St. NW
Suite 1000
Washington, DC 20036-3406
smarkiewicz@att.com
Tel: (202) 457 - 3810
Fax:(202) 263 - 2640

Registered Federal Lobbyist.
Serves As:
• V. President, Congressional Relations, AT&T

MARKISON, Brian A.
501 Fifth St.
Bristol, TN 37620
Tel: (423) 989 - 8000
Fax:(423) 274 - 8677

Serves As:
• President and Chief Exec. Officer, King Pharmaceuticals, Inc.

MARKLEY, Christopher D.
P.O. Box 2361
Harrisburg, PA 17105-2361
Tel: (717) 234 - 4941
Ext: 6895
Fax:(717) 257 - 6911
TF: (800) 388 - 4764

Serves As:
• V. President, Corporate Communications, Penn Nat'l Insurance

MARKLEY, Lynn
P.O. Box 660634
Dallas, TX 75266-0634
Tel: (972) 334 - 2404
Fax:(972) 334 - 2045

Serves As:
• Senior V. President, Public Relations, Frito-Lay, Inc.

MARKLEY, III, William C.
1111 S. Arroyo Pkwy.
P.O. Box 7084
Pasadena, CA 91105
Tel: (626) 578 - 6855
Fax:(626) 578 - 6837

Serves As:
• V. President, Law; PAC Treasurer, Jacobs Engineering Group Inc.

MARKOFF, Ph.D., Richard
P.O. Box 7033
Indianapolis, IN 46207
rmarkoff@simon.com
Tel: (317) 263 - 2361
Fax:(317) 263 - 2318

Serves As:
• Exec. Director, Simon Youth Foundation, Simon Property Group

MARKS, Alan
Two Folsom St.
San Francisco, CA 94105
Tel: (650) 952 - 4400
Fax:(415) 427 - 2553
TF: (800) 333 - 7899

Serves As:
• V. President, Corporate Communications, Gap Inc.

MARKS, Dawn
2301 Patriot Blvd.
Glenview, IL 60025-8020
Tel: (224) 521 - 8484

Serves As:
• Media Relations Contact, Anixter Internat'l, Inc.

MARKS, Debra
1301 K St. NW
Suite 1200
Washington, DC 20005
Tel: (202) 515 - 5184

Serves As:
• Government Relations, Internat'l Business Machines Corp. (IBM)

MARKS, Jeffrey
1401 I St. NW
Suite 600
Washington, DC 20005
Tel: (202) 336 - 7400
Fax:(202) 336 - 7515

Serves As:
• Manager and Counsel, Environment and Energy, United Technologies Corp.

MARKS, John
One Medline Place
Mundelein, IL 60060
jmarks@medline.com
Tel: (847) 949 - 5500
Fax:(800) 351 - 1512
TF: (800) 633 - 5463

Serves As:
• Director, Corporate Communications, Medline Industries, Inc.

MARKS, Robert E.
203 E. Main St.
Spartanburg, SC 29319-0001
Tel: (864) 597 - 8000

Serves As:
• Chairman of the Board, Denny's Corp.

MARKUS, John
One Healthsouth Pkwy.
Birmingham, AL 35243
Tel: (205) 967 - 7116
Fax:(205) 969 - 6889
TF: (888) 476 - 8849

Serves As:
• Exec. V. President and Chief Compliance Officer, HealthSouth Corp.
Responsibilities include government affairs.

MARLO, Stephen M.
1717 Pennsylvania Ave. NW Tel: (202) 261 - 1909
Suite 900 Fax:(202) 261 - 1949
Washington, DC 20006

Registered Federal Lobbyist.
Serves As:
- Manager, Washington Operations, (Stone & Webster Engineering), Stone & Webster, Inc.
- V. President, Government Affairs, The Shaw Group Inc.

MARLON, M.D., Anthony M.
P.O. Box 15645 Tel: (702) 242 - 7000
Las Vegas, NV 89114-5645 Fax:(702) 242 - 1531

Serves As:
- Chairman and Chief Exec. Officer, Sierra Health Services, Inc.

MARMER, Ms. Lynn
1014 Vine St. Tel: (513) 762 - 4441
Cincinnati, OH 45202-1100 Fax:(513) 762 - 1295

Registered Federal Lobbyist.
Serves As:
- Group V. President, Corporate Affairs, The Kroger Co.

MAROHN, William
Ten B Glenlake Pkwy. Tel: (770) 407 - 3800
Suite 600
Alpharetta, GA 30328

Serves As:
- Chairman of the Board, Newell Rubbermaid Inc.

MAROSITS, Joseph E.
Five Garret Mountain Plaza Tel: (973) 357 - 3290
West Paterson, NJ 07424 Fax:(973) 357 - 3060
joseph_marosits@gm.cytec.com TF: (800) 652 - 6013

Serves As:
- V. President, Human Resources, Cytec Industries Inc.

MAROTTA, Kim
P.O. Box 482 Tel: (414) 931 - 2817
Milwaukee, WI 53201-0482 Fax:(414) 931 - 6352

Serves As:
- Contact, Miller Brewing Co. Corporate Giving Program, Miller Brewing Co.

MARQUES, Jose
400 Broadway Tel: (513) 629 - 1448
Cincinnati, OH 45202 Fax:(513) 629 - 1220
TF: (800) 936 - 1212

Serves As:
- Manager, Media Relations, Western and Southern Life Insurance Co.

MARRINAN, Susan F.
P.O. Box 1430 Tel: (414) 656 - 5550
Kenosha, WI 53141-1430 Fax:(414) 656 - 5577
susan.marrinan@snapon.com

Serves As:
- V. President, Secretary and General Counsel, Snap-on Incorporated

Responsibilities include government affairs.

MARRIOTT, Jr., J. W.
One Marriott Dr. Tel: (301) 380 - 3000
Washington, DC 20058 Fax:(301) 380 - 8957

Serves As:
- Chairman and Chief Exec. Officer, Marriott Internat'l, Inc.

MARRIOTT, Richard
6903 Rockledge Dr. Tel: (240) 744 - 1000
Suite 1500
Bethesda, MD 20817
richard.marriott@hostmarriott.com

Serves As:
- Chairman of the Board, Host Marriott Corp.

MARS, John Franklyn
6885 Elm St. Tel: (703) 821 - 4900
McLean, VA 22101 Fax:(703) 448 - 9678

Serves As:
- Chairman of the Board, Mars, Inc.

MARSH, Don E.
9800 Crosspoint Blvd. Tel: (317) 594 - 2100
Indianapolis, IN 46256 Fax:(317) 594 - 2704

Serves As:
- Chairman and Chief Exec. Officer, Marsh Supermarkets, Inc.

MARSH, Joan M.
1120 20th St. NW Tel: (202) 457 - 3810
Suite 1000 Fax:(202) 457 - 2716
Washington, DC 20036-3406
joanmariemarsh@att.com

Serves As:
- V. President, Federal Regulatory Affairs, AT&T

MARSH, Jodi
9800 Crosspoint Blvd. Tel: (317) 594 - 2640
Indianapolis, IN 46256 Fax:(317) 594 - 2705

Serves As:
- V. President, Community Relations, Marsh Supermarkets, Inc.

Responsibilities include corporate philanthropy.

MARSH, Laurie
1601 W. Diehl Rd. Tel: (630) 305 - 1753
Naperville, IL 60563-1198 Fax:(630) 305 - 2893

Serves As:
- President, Nalco Foundation, Nalco Co.

MARSH, Tom
1600 River Center II Tel: (859) 392 - 3300
100 E. River Center Blvd. Fax:(859) 392 - 3333
Covington, KY 41011

Serves As:
- PAC Treasurer, Omnicare, Inc.

MARSHALL, Beverly K.
401 Ninth St. NW Tel: (202) 331 - 8090
Suite 1100 Fax:(202) 331 - 1181
Washington, DC 20004
bkmarshall@duke-energy.com

Serves As:
- V. President, Federal Government Affairs, Duke Energy Corp.

MARSHALL, Jon A.
P.O. Box 4577 Tel: (281) 925 - 6000
Houston, TX 77210-4577 Fax:(281) 925 - 6010

Serves As:
- President and Chief Exec. Officer, GlobalSantaFe Corp.

MARSHALL, Patricia Warr
730 15th St. NW Tel: (202) 624 - 4134
Washington, DC 20005 Fax:(202) 383 - 3475

Serves As:
- Senior V. President, State Government Relations, Bank of America Corp.

MARSHALL, Richard N.
417Lackawanna Ave.
Scranton, PA 18503

Serves As:
- V. President and Treasurer, Southern Union Company

Responsibilities include investor relations.

MARSHALL, Ron
7600 France Ave. South Tel: (952) 832 - 0534
Edina, MN 55435 Fax:(952) 844 - 1234
rmarshall@nashfinch.com

Serves As:
- Chief Exec. Officer, Nash Finch Company

MARSHALL, Siri S.
One General Mills Blvd. Tel: (763) 764 - 7600
Minneapolis, MN 55426

Serves As:
- Senior V. President, General Counsel, and Chief Governance and Compliance Officer, General Mills

MARSHALL-BLAKE, Lorina L.
1901 Market St. Tel: (215) 636 - 9559
38th Floor Fax:(215) 241 - 0403
Philadelphia, PA 19103-1480 TF: (800) 555 - 1514
lorina.marshall@ibx.com

Serves As:
- V. President, Government Relations, Independence Blue Cross (Pennsylvania)

MARSHALL-HOWARTH, Rebecca
33 Commercial St. Tel: (508) 549 - 2424
Foxboro, MA 02035 Fax:(508) 549 - 4999
rebecca.marshall-howarth@invensys.com TF: (866) 746 - 6477

Serves As:
- Manager, Marketing Communications, Invensys Systems, Inc.

MARSHO, Kim M.
1301 K St. NW Tel: (202) 515 - 4522
Suite 1200
Washington, DC 20005

Serves As:
- Program Manager, Market Access/Trade, Internat'l Business Machines Corp. (IBM)

MARSOCCI, Bob
P.O. Box 956 Tel: (310) 964 - 0700
El Segundo, CA 90245-0956 Fax:(310) 535 - 5225

Serves As:
- Senior Director, Public Relations, The DIRECTV Group, Inc.

MARSTELLER, Helen
631 S. Richland Ave.
York, PA 17403
Tel: (717) 771 - 7890
Fax:(717) 771 - 7381

Serves As:
- V. President, Investor Relations, York Internat'l Corp.

MARTENSTEIN, Lynn
1050 Caribbean Way
Miami, FL 33132-3203
Tel: (305) 539 - 6000
Fax:(305) 375 - 0711

Serves As:
- V. President, Corporate Communications, Royal Caribbean Internat'l

MARTIN, Alisa
1445 Ross at Field
Suite 1400
Dallas, TX 75202-2785
Tel: (214) 978 - 8060
Fax:(214) 978 - 8888

Serves As:
- Director, Corporate Communications, Hunt Oil Co.

MARTIN, Andrea
100 Mission Ridge
Goodlettsville, TN 37072
amartin@dollargeneral.com
Tel: (615) 855 - 4228

Serves As:
- Media Contact, Dollar General Corp.

MARTIN, Beth
231 W. Michigan
Milwaukee, WI 53203
Tel: (414) 221 - 3687
Fax:(414) 221 - 2821

Serves As:
- Communications Specialist, We Energies

MARTIN, Brian T.
Metro Center
One Station Pl.
Stamford, CT 06902
Tel: (203) 539 - 8000
Fax:(203) 539 - 7734
TF: (800) 969 - 9974

Serves As:
- Senior V. President, Corporate Affairs, The Thomson Corporation

MARTIN, C. Alan
P.O. Box 2641
Birmingham, AL 35291
Tel: (205) 257 - 1000
Fax:(205) 257 - 1860

Serves As:
- Exec. V. President, Customer Service and Satisfaction, Alabama Power Co.

MARTIN, David
P.O. Box 127
Joplin, MO 64802-0127
dmartin@empiredistrict.com
Tel: (417) 625 - 6107
Fax:(417) 625 - 5155
TF: (800) 206 - 2300

Registered Federal Lobbyist.
Serves As:
- Manager, Governmental Relations, Empire District Electric Co.

Responsibilities include political action.

MARTIN, Dennis
One GBC Plaza
Northbrook, IL 60062
Tel: (847) 272 - 3700
Fax:(847) 272 - 3723

Serves As:
- Chairman and Chief Exec. Officer, General Binding Corp.

MARTIN, Donna
P.O. Box 66149
MC 500
St. Louis, MO 63166-6149
Tel: (314) 554 - 2454
Fax:(314) 992 - 6693
TF: (800) 552 - 7583

Serves As:
- Senior V. President and Chief Human Resources Officer, Ameren Corp.

MARTIN, Elizabeth
165 Court St.
Rochester, NY 14647
emartin@bcbscny.org
Tel: (315) 671 - 6408
Fax:(315) 448 - 3939

Serves As:
- V. President, Communications, Central New York Region, Exellus Blue Cross Blue Shield

MARTIN, Fran
P.O. Box 70
Boise, ID 83707
fmartin@idahopower.com
Tel: (208) 388 - 2530
Fax:(208) 388 - 6955

Serves As:
- Contact, Corporate Contributions and Ida-PAC, (Idaho Power Co.), IDACORP, Inc.

MARTIN, Jeffrey C.
750 Lakeshore Pkwy.
Birmingham, AL 35211
Tel: (205) 940 - 4000

Registered Federal Lobbyist.
Serves As:
- Senior V. President, Compliance and Government Affairs, Saks, Inc.

MARTIN, Jeffrey L.
818 S. Kansas Ave.
Topeka, KS 66601
Tel: (785) 575 - 6300
Fax:(785) 575 - 1796

Serves As:
- PAC Treasurer, Westar Energy, Inc.

MARTIN, Jennifer
P.O. Box 6006
Cypress, CA 90630
jennifer.martim@phs.com
Tel: (714) 226 - 2725
Fax:(714) 226 - 3653

Registered Federal Lobbyist.
Serves As:
- Manager, Public Policy, PacifiCare Health Systems, Inc.

MARTIN, PhD, Jennifer H.
625 Fourth Ave. South
Minneapolis, MN 55415
Tel: (612) 340 - 7000
Fax:(612) 340 - 7373

Serves As:
- Senior V. President, Human Resources, Thrivent Financial for Lutherans

MARTIN, John K.
One Time Warner Center
New York, NY 10019
Tel: (212) 484 - 8000
Fax:(212) 489 - 6183

Serves As:
- V. President, Investor Relations, Time Warner Inc.

MARTIN, Larry
P.O. Box 1130
Modesto, CA 95353
Tel: (209) 341 - 3016
Fax:(209) 341 - 3208

Serves As:
- V. President, Government Affairs, Ernest and Julio Gallo Winery

MARTIN, Michael A.
370 Woodcliff Dr.
Suite 300
Fairport, NY 14450
mike.martin@cbrands.com
Tel: (585) 218 - 3669
TF: (888) 724 - 2169

Serves As:
- V. President, Corporate Communications, Constellation Brands, Inc.

MARTIN, R. Brad
750 Lakeshore Pkwy.
Birmingham, AL 35211
brad_martin@saksinc.com
Tel: (205) 940 - 4000

Serves As:
- Chairman and Chief Exec. Officer, Saks, Inc.

MARTIN, Randy
1200 State Fair Blvd.
Syracuse, NY 13221-4737
rmartin@penntraffic.com
Tel: (315) 453 - 2423
Fax:(315) 461 - 2645

Serves As:
- V. President and Chief Administrative Officer, The Penn Traffic Co.

Responsibilities include investor relations.

MARTIN, Robert J.
P.O. Box M
Allentown, PA 18105-5000
Tel: (610) 709 - 2670
Fax:(610) 709 - 3308

Serves As:
- Senior Manager, Communications, Mack Trucks, Inc.

MARTIN, Jr., Rodney O.
2929 Allen Pkwy.
Houston, TX 77019
Tel: (713) 831 - 8500
Fax:(713) 523 - 8531

Serves As:
- President and Chief Exec. Officer, AIG American General Corp.

MARTIN, Steven S.
7261 Mercy Rd.
P.O. Box 3248
Omaha, NE 68180
Tel: (402) 390 - 1800
Fax:(402) 398 - 3736

Serves As:
- President and Chief Exec. Officer, Blue Cross and Blue Shield of Nebraska

MARTIN, Thomas R.
Four W. Red Oak Ln.
White Plains, NY 10604
tom.martin@itt.com
Tel: (914) 641 - 2157
Fax:(914) 696 - 2977

Serves As:
- Senior V. President and Director, Corporate Relations, ITT Industries

Responsibilities include corporate philanthropy, community relations and domestic government affairs.

MARTIN, Tracie
P.O. Box 36611
Dallas, TX 75235-1611
Tel: (214) 792 - 4103

Serves As:
- Manager, Civic and Charitable Contributions, Southwest Airlines Co.

MARTINEAU PLANKENTON, Maria
P.O. Box 31907
Santa Barbara, CA 93130
Tel: (805) 563 - 7000
Fax:(805) 563 - 7070

Serves As:
- Exec. Director, Foundation, Tenet Healthcare Corp.

MARTINEZ, Andrew G.
111-B S. Monroe St.
Tallahassee, FL 32301-1583
Tel: (850) 222 - 6200
Fax:(850) 222 - 6205

Serves As:
- Representative, Area Legislative Affairs, Nationwide

MARTINEZ, Annette
P.O. Box 3014
Naperville, IL 60566-7014
amartinez@nicor.com
Tel: (630) 388 - 2781
Fax:(630) 357 - 7534
TF: (888) 642 - 6748

Serves As:
- Manager, Media Relations, Nicor, Inc.

MARTINSEN, Dan
1515 Broadway
New York, NY 10036
Tel: (212) 258 - 6000
Ext: 8116
Fax:(212) 258 - 1773

Serves As:
- Senior V. President, Communications, (Nickelodeon/Nick at Nite), Viacom Inc./CBS Corp.

MARTINY, Mary Ann
3700 W. Juneau Ave.
Milwaukee, WI 53208
Tel: (414) 342 - 4680
Fax:(414) 343 - 8230

Serves As:
- Manager, Harley-Davidson Foundation, Harley-Davidson Motor Company

MARTODAM, Katen K.
3M Center
St. Paul, MN 55144-1000
Tel: (651) 733 - 1110
Fax:(651) 733 - 9973

Serves As:
- PAC Treasurer, 3M Company

MARTORE, Gracia C.
7950 Jones Branch Dr.
McLean, VA 22107
gmartore@gannett.com
Tel: (703) 854 - 6918
Fax:(703) 276 - 2046

Serves As:
- Senior V. President and Chief Financial Officer, Gannett Co., Inc.

Responsibilities include investor relations.

MARUCCO, Albert M.
575 Seventh St. NW
Suite 600
Ninth Floor
Washington, DC 20004

Serves As:
- PAC Treasurer, Crowley Maritime Corp.

MARULLO, Larry
1201 Walnut St.
Kansas City, MO 64106
Tel: (816) 556 - 2897
Fax:(816) 556 - 2995

Serves As:
- Director, Government Affairs and Community Relations, (Kansas City Power and Light Co.), Great Plains Energy, Inc.

MARVENTANO, David
403 E. Capitol St. SE
Washington, DC 20003
Tel: (202) 548 - 5800
Fax:(202) 548 - 5810

Registered Federal Lobbyist.
Serves As:
- Senior V. President, Government Relations, Fluor Corp.

MARVENTANO, Jessica Wallace
1401 I St., NW
Suite 401
Washington, DC 20005
jessicaamarventano@clearchannel.com
Tel: (202) 289 - 3224
Fax:(202) 289 - 0050

Registered Federal Lobbyist.
Serves As:
- Senior V. President, Government Affairs, Clear Channel Communications

Responsibilities include political action.

MARYMEE, Mark
100 Bloomfield Hills Pkwy., Suite 300
Bloomfield Hills, MI 48304-2946
Tel: (248) 433 - 4648
Fax:(248) 433 - 4598
TF: (800) 777 - 8583

Serves As:
- Public Relations Contact, Pulte Homes, Inc.

MARZOCCHI, Robert A.
P.O. Box 1615
Warren, NJ 07061-1615
Tel: (908) 903 - 2000
Fax:(908) 903 - 2027

Serves As:
- PAC Treasurer, The Chubb Corp.

MAS, Russ
P.O. Box 834
Valley Forge, PA 19482-0834
rmas@ikon.com
Tel: (610) 408 - 7220
Fax:(610) 408 - 7025
TF: (888) 275 - 4566

Serves As:
- Manager, Public Relations, Ikon Office Solutions, Inc.

MASCH, Donald
Crystal Gateway 3, 1215 S. Clark St.
Suite 1510
Arlington, VA 22202
donald_masch@atk.com
Tel: (703) 412 - 5977
Fax:(703) 412 - 5970

Registered Federal Lobbyist.
Serves As:
- Director, Government Relations, Alliant Techsystems

MASCIO, Judy
1830 Route 130
Burlington, NJ 08016
judy.mascio@coat.com
Tel: (609) 387 - 7800
Ext: 2217
Fax:(609) 239 - 8242

Serves As:
- Director, Human Resources, Burlington Coat Factory Warehouse Corp.

MASKREY, Judith F.
One PPG Pl.
Pittsburgh, PA 15272
Tel: (412) 434 - 2476
Fax:(412) 434 - 4666

Serves As:
- Director, Government Affairs, PPG Industries Inc.

MASON, Chris
One AAR Pl.
1100 N. Wood Dale Rd.
Wood Dale, IL 60191
chris.mason@aarcorp.com
Tel: (630) 227 - 2062
Fax:(630) 227 - 2019

Serves As:
- Director, Corporate Communications, AAR Corp.

MASON, David W.
101 Sun Ave. NE
Albuquerque, NM 87109
Fax:(505) 468 - 4023

Serves As:
- PAC Contact, Sun Healthcare Group, Inc.

MASON, Don E.
P.O. Box 4079
Gulfport, MS 39502
Tel: (228) 865 - 5339
Fax:(228) 865 - 5616

Serves As:
- V. President, External Affairs and Corporate Services, Mississippi Power Co.

MASON, Jr., James A.
241 Ralph McGill Blvd.
Atlanta, GA 30308
Tel: (404) 506 - 7750

Serves As:
- Contact, Southern Company Employees PAC, Southern Company

MASON, Jay
68 State Circle
Annapolis, MD 21401
Tel: (410) 268 - 0858
Fax:(410) 268 - 0506

Serves As:
- Manager, State Governmental Affairs (MD), Allegheny Energy Inc.

MASON, Marcus
60 Massachusetts Ave. NE
Washington, DC 20002
Tel: (202) 906 - 3000
Fax:(202) 906 - 3865

Serves As:
- Senior Director, Government Affairs - House, Amtrak

MASON, Mike
2525 Stemmons Fwy.
Dallas, TX 75207-2401
mike.mason@trin.net
Tel: (214) 631 - 4420
Fax:(214) 689 - 0501

Serves As:
- PAC Treasurer, Trinity Industries, Inc.

MASON, Paul
P.O. Box 21008
Greensboro, NC 27420
paul.mason@jpfinancial.com
Tel: (336) 691 - 3313
Fax:(336) 691 - 3311

Serves As:
- V. President, Corporate Affairs, Jefferson-Pilot Corp.

MASON, Tyler
P.O. Box 6006
C420-583
Cypress, CA 90630
tyler.mason@phs.com
Tel: (714) 226 - 3530
Fax:(714) 226 - 3018

Serves As:
- V. President, Public Relations, PacifiCare Health Systems, Inc.

MASSARONI, Kenneth M.

5030 Sugarloaf Pkwy.
Lawrenceville, GA 30042-2869
Tel: (770) 236 - 5000
Fax:(770) 236 - 4775
TF: (800) 236 - 5000

Serves As:
- Treasurer, Scientific-Atlantic PAC, Scientific-Atlanta, Inc.

MASSEE, Ned W.

One High Ridge Park
Stamford, CT 06905-1322
Tel: (203) 461 - 7577
Fax:(203) 461 - 7521

Serves As:
- V. President, Corporate Affairs, MeadWestvaco Corp.

MASSENGILL, Matthew E.

20511 Lake Forest Dr.
Lake Forest, CA 92630-7741
Tel: (949) 672 - 7000
Fax:(949) 672 - 5408

Serves As:
- Chairman and Chief Exec. Officer, Western Digital Corp.

MASSENGILL, R. Scott

One Centennial Ave.
PO Box 6820
Piscataway, NJ 08854
Tel: (732) 980 - 6000
Fax:(732) 980 - 3340

Serves As:
- V. President, Treasurer and Contact, Corporate Foundation, American Standard Companies Inc.

MASSETH, Michael D.

DWF Airport Station, P.O. Box 619100
Dallas, TX 75261-9100
mmasseth@kcc.com
Tel: (972) 281 - 1478
Fax:(972) 281 - 1490
TF: (800) 639 - 1352

Serves As:
- V. President, Investor Relations, Kimberly-Clark Corp.

MASSEY, Jr., Marvin S.

P.O. Box 1411
Tyler, TX 75710-1411
Tel: (903) 534 - 3000
Fax:(903) 534 - 2206

Serves As:
- Chairman and Chief. Exec. Officer, Brookshire Grocery Co.

MASSEY, Sheryl R.

1717 E. Interstate Ave.
Bismarck, ND 58503
smassey@bepc.com
Tel: (701) 223 - 0441
Fax:(701) 224 - 5336

Serves As:
- Treasurer, Basin Electric PAC, (Basin Cooperative Serivces, Basin Telecommunication, Inc., Dakota Coal Co., Dakota Gasification Co.), Basin Electric Power Cooperative

MASSIMO, Mary

237 Park Ave.
New York, NY 10017
Tel: (212) 527 - 4915

Serves As:
- Exec. V. President, Human Resources, Revlon, Inc.

MASSINGILL, Teena

P.O. Box 99
Pleasanton, CA 94566-0009
Tel: (925) 467 - 3361

Serves As:
- Northern California Public Affairs, Safeway Inc.

MASTER-PARKER, Linda

600 Galleria Pkwy.
Suite 100
Atlanta, GA 30339
lindamaster-parker@prgx.com
Tel: (770) 779 - 3295
Fax:(770) 779 - 3133
TF: (800) 752 - 5894

Serves As:
- Corporate Communications Contact, PRG-Schultz Internat'l, Inc.

MASTERN, Susan

Ten B Glenlake Pkwy.
Suite 600
Alpharetta, GA 30328
Tel: (770) 407 - 3817
Fax:(770) 407 - 3983

Serves As:
- Director, Public Relations, Newell Rubbermaid Inc.

MASTERS, Janet

601 Rayovac Dr.
Madison, WI 53711-2460
janet.masters@spectrumbrands.com
Tel: (608) 275 - 4967
Fax:(608) 275 - 4967

Serves As:
- Director, Corporate Communications, Sprectrum Brands

MASTERSON, Keith

1600 Royal St.
Jasper, IN 47549
Tel: (812) 634 - 3234
Fax:(812) 634 - 3060

Serves As:
- Environmental Manager, Kimball International, Inc.

MASTERSON, Ken

101 Constitution Ave., NW
Suite 801 East
Washington, DC 20001
Tel: (202) 218 - 3800

Registered Federal Lobbyist.
Serves As:
- Executive Vice President, FedEx Corp.

MASTRO, Thomas J.

One Wall St.
Tenth Floor
New York, NY 10286
Tel: (212) 495 - 1784
Fax:(212) 635 - 1799

Serves As:
- Comptroller and PAC Treasurer, The Bank of New York Co., Inc.

MASUDA, Kelly

10990 Wilshire Blvd.
Seventh Floor
Los Angeles, CA 90024
kmasuda@kbhome.com
Tel: (310) 231 - 4184
Fax:(310) 388 - 1470

Serves As:
- V. President and Investor Relations Contact, KB HOME

MATEUS, Lois

850 Dixie Hwy.
Louisville, KY 40210
lois_mateus@b-f.com
Tel: (502) 774 - 7682
Fax:(502) 774 - 7185

Serves As:
- Senior V. President, Corporate Communications and Services, Brown-Forman Corp.

Responsibilities include corporate philanthropy.

MATHENY, Kenneth L.

5555 San Felipe Rd.
Houston, TX 77056
klmatheny@marathonoil.com
Tel: (713) 296 - 4114
Fax:(713) 296 - 2952

Serves As:
- V. President, Investor Relations and Public Affairs, Marathon Oil Corp.

MATHER, M. Gay

10000 Richmond Ave.
Fourth Floor
Houston, TX 77042-4200
Tel: (713) 346 - 7775
Fax:(713) 435 - 2195

Serves As:
- Director, Communications, Nat'l Oilwell, Inc.

Responsibilities include investor relations.

MATHERS, Kim

P.O. Box 6000
Sioux City, IA 51102-6000
kmathers@terraindustries.com
Tel: (712) 233 - 6411
Fax:(712) 277 - 7383

Serves As:
- Manager, Communications, Terra Industries Inc.

MATHEWS, Dan

1050 Caribbean Way
Miami, FL 33132-3203
Tel: (305) 539 - 6153
Fax:(305) 539 - 0562

Serves As:
- Manager, Investor Relations, Royal Caribbean Internat'l

MATHEWS, Julie

30 N. LaSalle St.
Suite 4000
Chicago, IL 60602-2507
julie.mathews@teldta.com
Tel: (312) 592 - 5341
Fax:(312) 630 - 1908

Serves As:
- Manager, Investor Relations, Telephone and Data Systems, Inc.

MATHIAS, Charles B.

1100 New York Ave. NW
Washington, DC 20005
Tel: (202) 669 - 8368

Registered Federal Lobbyist.
Serves As:
- Representative, Lucent Technologies

MATHIEU, Mark J.

1000 Stanley Dr.
New Britain, CT 06053
mmathieu@stanleyworks.com
Tel: (860) 827 - 3818
Fax:(860) 827 - 3809

Serves As:
- V. President, Human Resources, The Stanley Works

MATHIOT, Lawrence K.

150 Fayetteville St. Mall
Suite 2810
Raleigh, NC 27601

Serves As:
- Treasurer, Sprint Nextel Corp. Mid-Atlantic Region Telecom PAC, Sprint Nextel

MATHIS, Catherine J.
229 W. 43rd St.
New York, NY 10036
mathicj@nytimes.com
Tel: (212) 556 - 1981
Fax:(212) 556 - 7389

Serves As:
• V. President, Corporate Communications, New York Times Co.
Responsibilities include investor relations.

MATHUR, Punam N.
3260 Industrial Rd.
Las Vegas, NV 89109
punam@mirage.com
Tel: (702) 650 - 7406
Fax:(702) 650 - 7401

Serves As:
• V. President, Community Affairs, MGM MIRAGE
Responsibilities include political action, corporate philanthropy, and government affairs.

MATLEY, Diana L.
1621 Barber Ln.
Milpitas, CA 95035
Tel: (408) 433 - 8000
Fax:(408) 954 - 3220
TF: (866) 574 - 5741

Serves As:
• V. President, Investor Relations, LSI Logic Corp.

MATROS, Richard K.
18831 Von Karman, Suite 400
Irvine, CA 92612
Tel: (949) 255 - 7100
Fax:(949) 255 - 7054
TF: (800) 509 - 4340

Serves As:
• Chairman and Chief Exec. Officer, Sun Healthcare Group, Inc.

MATSUI, Connie L.
14 Cambridge Center
Cambridge, MA 02142
Tel: (617) 679 - 2000
Fax:(617) 679 - 2617

Serves As:
• Exec. V. President, Corporate Strategy and Communications, Biogen Idec Inc.

MATTERA, Paul
175 Berkeley St.
MS 07E
Boston, MA 02116
Tel: (617) 574 - 5679
Fax:(617) 350 - 7648

Registered Federal Lobbyist.
Serves As:
• Senior V. President and Chief Public Affairs Officer, Liberty Mutual Insurance Co.

MATTERN, John M.
111 W. Monroe St.
Chicago, IL 60603-4095
Tel: (312) 461 - 3295
Fax:(312) 293 - 5811

Serves As:
• V. President, Harris Bank
Responsibilities include government relations.

MATTESON, Jr., Richard A.
One Energy Plaza
Jackson, MI 49201
rmatteson@cmsenergy.com
Tel: (517) 788 - 2258
Fax:(517) 788 - 0940

Serves As:
• Director, Corporate Communications, CMS Energy Corp.

MATTHEWS, Caz
3350 Peachtree Rd. NE
Atlanta, GA 30326
Tel: (404) 842 - 8000
Fax:(404) 842 - 8801

Serves As:
• President and Chief Exec. Officer, Blue Cross Blue Shield of Georgia

MATTHEWS, Frank
10707 Clay Rd.
P.O. Box 2863
Houston, TX 77252
frank.matthews@ushome.com
Tel: (713) 877 - 2348

Serves As:
• Director, Human Resources, Lennar Corp.

MATTHEWS, Jim
115 Perimeter Center Pl.
Suite 460
Atlanta, GA 30346
Tel: (770) 395 - 4577
Fax:(770) 395 - 4529

Serves As:
• V. President, Finance and Chief Financial Officer, Georgia Gulf Corp.
Responsibilities include investor relations.

MATTHEWS, John
999 Lake Dr.
Issaquah, WA 98027
Tel: (425) 313 - 8100
Fax:(425) 313 - 6593

Serves As:
• Senior V. President, Human Resources and Risk Management, Costco Wholesale Corp.

MATTHEWS, Odonna
6300 Sheriff Rd.
Landover, MD 20785
Tel: (301) 341 - 4365
Fax:(301) 618 - 4968

Serves As:
• V. President, Consumer Affairs, Giant Food LLC

MATTHEWS, T. J.
P.O. Box 10580
Reno, NV 89510-0580
Tel: (775) 448 - 7777

Serves As:
• Chairman and Chief Exec. Officer, Internat'l Game Technology

MATTHEWS, Ted S.
P.O. Box 70
Fort Mill, SC 29716
ted.matthews@springs.com
Tel: (803) 547 - 1500
Fax:(803) 547 - 1636

Serves As:
• V. President, Corporate Communications, Springs Industries, Inc.
Responsibilities also include corporate philanthropy.

MATTIA, Tom
5400 Legacy Dr.
Plano, TX 75024-3199
tom.mattia@eds.com
Tel: (972) 604 - 6000
Fax:(972) 605 - 6841

Serves As:
• V. President, Global Corporate Communications, EDS Corp.

MATTISON, Robert M.
P.O. Box 1441
Minneapolis, MN 55440-1441
Tel: (612) 623 - 6000
Fax:(612) 623 - 6944
TF: (800) 328 - 0211

Serves As:
• President, The Graco Foundation, Graco Inc.

MATTON, Mike
1200 Wilson Blvd.
Arlington, VA 22209-2305
Tel: (703) 465 - 3625
Fax:(703) 465 - 3002

Registered Federal Lobbyist.
Serves As:
• V. President, Legislative Affairs, The Boeing Co.

MATTOX, Michael M.
1133 S.W. Topeka Blvd.
Topeka, KS 66629
mike.mattox@bcbsks.com
Tel: (785) 291 - 8700
Fax:(785) 291 - 8216

Serves As:
• President and Chief Exec. Officer, Blue Cross and Blue Shield of Kansas, Inc.

MATUSCHEK, Jennifer
5251 DTC Pkwy.
Suite 1400
Greenwood Village, CO 80111-2742
jmatuschek@ciber.com
Tel: (303) 220 - 0100
Fax:(303) 220 - 7100
TF: (800) 242 - 3799

Serves As:
• V. President, Investor Relations, CIBER, Inc.

MATUSZAK, S. J.
130 E. Randolph Dr.
24th Floor
Chicago, IL 60601
Tel: (312) 240 - 4100
Fax:(312) 240 - 4082

Serves As:
• Director, Environmental Affairs, Peoples Energy Corp.

MATZ, R. Kevin
301 Merritt Seven
Sixth Floor
Norwalk, CT 06851
kevin_matz@emcorgroup.com
Tel: (203) 849 - 7800
Fax:(203) 849 - 7810

Serves As:
• Senior V. President, Shared Services, EMCOR Group, Inc.

MAUNOIR, Peter F.
P.O. Box 60219
New Orleans, LA 70160
Tel: (504) 566 - 3774

Serves As:
• Second V. President, Government Relations, Pan American Life Insurance Co.

MAURANO, Richard "Rick" V.
3900 Wisconsin Ave. NW
Washington, DC 20016
Tel: (202) 752 - 7000
Fax:(202) 752 - 6099

Registered Federal Lobbyist.
Serves As:
• Director, Government and Industry Relations, Fannie Mae

MAURER, Jack
100 Campus Dr.
Florham Park, NJ 07932
maurerjl@basf.com
Tel: (973) 245 - 6072
Fax:(973) 245 - 6714

Serves As:
• Manager, Media Relations, BASF Corporation

MAURER, James
722 N. Broadway
18th Floor
Milwaukee, WI 53202
TF: (800) 257 - 0902

Serves As:
- V. President, SBC Wisconsin

Responsibilities include public affairs.

MAURY, Nicole F.
2020 Santa Monica Blvd., Suite 600
Santa Monica, CA 90404-2208
nmaury@fmt.com
Tel: (310) 315 - 5508
Fax:(310) 315 - 5599

Serves As:
- Director, Corporate Communications, Fremont General Corp.

MAUS, Julie
P.O. Box 127
Joplin, MO 64802-0127
jmaus@empiredistrict.com
Tel: (417) 625 - 5101
Fax:(417) 625 - 5155
TF: (800) 206 - 2300

Serves As:
- Communications Specialist, Empire District Electric Co.

MAXEY, Catherine C.
2030 Dow Center
Midland, MI 48674-0001
ccmaxey@dow.com
Tel: (989) 636 - 1000
Fax:(989) 638 - 1727

Serves As:
- Public Affairs Director, Chemicals and Intermediates and Performance Chemicals and Thermosets, The Dow Chemical Company

MAXFIELD, Melissa
2001 Pennsylvania Ave. NW
Suite 500
Washington, DC 20006
Tel: (202) 379 - 7100
Fax:(202) 466 - 7718

Registered Federal Lobbyist.
Serves As:
- Senior Director, Federal Government Affairs, Comcast Corporation

MAXWELL, William A.
1100 New York Ave. NW
Suite 600W
Washington, DC 20005
wmaxwell@hp.com
Tel: (202) 378 - 2500
Fax:(202) 378 - 2550

Registered Federal Lobbyist.
Serves As:
- Director, International Development and Finance, Hewlett-Packard Co.

MAY, Darwin
101 W. Washington
Indianapolis, IN 46255
Tel: (317) 267 - 7000
Fax:(317) 267 - 3957

Serves As:
- V. President, Community Relations, Nat'l City Corp.

MAY, Karen J.
One Baxter Pkwy.
Deerfield, IL 60015-4633
Tel: (847) 948 - 2025
Fax:(847) 948 - 3642

Serves As:
- Corporate V. President, Human Resources, Baxter Internat'l Inc.

MAY, Robert P.
One Healthsouth Pkwy.
Birmingham, AL 35243
Tel: (205) 967 - 7116
Fax:(205) 969 - 6889
TF: (888) 476 - 8849

Serves As:
- Chairman of the Board, HealthSouth Corp.

MAY, Steven L.
601 Pennsylvania Ave. NW
North Bldg., Suite 625
Washington, DC 20004
steven.may@cummins.com
Tel: (202) 393 - 8585
Fax:(202) 393 - 8111

Registered Federal Lobbyist.
Serves As:
- V. President, Government Relations, Cummins, Inc.

MAY, Thomas J.
One NSTAR Way
Westwood, MA 02090
Tel: (617) 424 - 2000
Fax:(617) 424 - 2523

Serves As:
- Chairman, President and Chief Exec. Officer, NSTAR

MAYBERRY, Michael
277 Park Ave.
New York, NY 10172
michael.mayberry@conti.com
Tel: (212) 207 - 5100
Fax:(212) 207 - 5181

Serves As:
- Treasurer, ContiGroup Companies Political Action Committee, ContiGroup Companies, Inc.

MAYER, Jerome
8607 Westwood Center Dr.
Vienna, VA 22182
Tel: (703) 448 - 4000
Fax:(703) 448 - 4100

Registered Federal Lobbyist.
Serves As:
- Legislative Representative, Feld Entertainment, Inc.

MAYER, Vicky
P.O. Box 599
Cincinnati, OH 45201-0599
Tel: (513) 983 - 1100
Fax:(513) 983 - 9369

Serves As:
- Corporate Communications, The Procter & Gamble Company

MAYES, Ms. Gray
P.O. Box 660199
M/S 8656
Dallas, TX 75266-0199
gmayes@ti.com
Tel: (214) 480 - 6870
Fax:(214) 480 - 6820
TF: (800) 336 - 5236

Registered Federal Lobbyist.
Serves As:
- Director, Public Affairs and Manager, State and Community Affairs, Texas Instruments Incorporated

Responsibilities include political action.

MAYES, Jonathan O.
P.O. Box 99
Pleasanton, CA 94566-0009
Tel: (925) 467 - 3070
Fax:(925) 467 - 3323

Serves As:
- V. President, Government Relations, Safeway Inc.

MAYNARD, Ray
1550 Crystal Dr.
Crystal Square 2, Suite 300
Arlington, VA 22202
Tel: (703) 413 - 5607
Fax:(703) 413 - 5636

Serves As:
- Director, Legislative Affairs, Space Systems, Lockheed Martin Corp.

MAYO, Joseph
2250 Corporate Park Dr.
Suite 300
Herndon, VA 20171-4835
Tel: (703) 673 - 5000
Fax:(703) 673 - 5001

Registered Federal Lobbyist.
Serves As:
- Director, Public Affairs, Triple Canopy, Inc.

MAYO, Will
P.O. Box 1640
Jackson, MS 39215-1640
Tel: (601) 368 - 5000
Fax:(601) 964 - 2400

Serves As:
- V. President, Government Affairs -- Mississippi, Entergy Mississippi

MAYS, Alfred
One Johnson & Johnson Plaza
New Brunswick, NJ 08933-7204
amays@corus.jnj.com
Tel: (732) 524 - 3372
Fax:(732) 214 - 0334
TF: (800) 635 - 6789

Serves As:
- V. President, Corporate Contributions, Johnson & Johnson

MAYS, Lowry
200 E. Basse Rd.
San Antonio, TX 78209
llowrymays@clearchannel.com
Tel: (210) 822 - 2828
Fax:(210) 822 - 2299

Serves As:
- Chairman of the Board, Clear Channel Communications

MAYS, Mark
200 E. Basse Rd.
San Antonio, TX 78209
markpmays@clearchannel.com
Tel: (210) 822 - 2828
Fax:(210) 822 - 2299

Serves As:
- President and Chief Exec. Officer, Clear Channel Communications

Responsibilities include political action.

MAYS, Thomas
P.O. Box 9000
Newport Beach, CA 92658-9030
Tel: (949) 219 - 3639
Fax:(949) 219 - 7614
TF: (800) 800 - 7646

Serves As:
- V. President, Government Relations, Pacific Life Insurance Co.

MAYUGA, Ann Marie
700 Market St.
St. Louis, MO 63101
ammayuga@genam.com
Tel: (314) 843 - 8700
Fax:(314) 444 - 0681

Serves As:
- Media Contact, GenAmerica Financial Corp.

MAYZEL, Michael
1600 Amphitheatre Pkwy.
Mountain View, CA 94043
Tel: (650) 623 - 4000
Fax:(650) 618 - 1499

Serves As:
- Manager, Advertising, Google Inc.

MAZER, Brian K.
34 Maple St.
Milford, MA 01757
Tel: (508) 478 - 2000
Fax:(508) 872 - 1990
TF: (800) 252 - 4752

Serves As:
- Seniot V. President, Human Resources, Investor Relations, Waters Corp.

MAZZOLA, Jim
7000 Cardinal Pl.
Dublin, OH 43017
jim.mazzola@cardinal.com
Tel: (614) 757 - 5000
Fax:(614) 757 - 6000
TF: (800) 234 - 8701

Serves As:
- V. President, Public Relations and Corporate Communications, Cardinal Health Inc.

MCADAM, Robert "Bob"
702 SW Eighth St.
M/S 0150
Bentonville, AR 72716
Tel: (479) 277 - 0284
Fax:(479) 277 - 2473

Serves As:
- V. President, State and Local Government Affairs, Wal-Mart Stores

MCALEXANDER, Gayle
5350 Tech Data Dr.
MS D1-10
Clearwater, FL 33760
gayle.mcalexander@techdata.com
Tel: (727) 539 - 7429
Ext: 85013
TF: (800) 237 - 8931

Serves As:
- Coordinator, Human Resources, Tech Data Corp.

Responsibilities include corporate contributions.

MCALISTER, John W.
P.O. Box 1244
M/S PB05D
Charlotte, NC 28201-1244
jwmcalister@duke-energy.com
Tel: (704) 382 - 8346
Fax:(704) 382 - 3588

Serves As:
- Regional Director, North Carolina Governmental Affairs, Duke Energy Corp.

MCALISTER, Maurice L.
P.O. Box 6000
Newport Beach, CA 92658-6000
Tel: (949) 854 - 3100
Fax:(949) 854 - 8162

Serves As:
- Chairman of the Board, Downey Savings and Loan Ass'n, F.A.

MCALISTER, Sheryl
Bank of America Corporate Center
100 N. Tryon St.
Charlotte, NC 28255-0001
sheryl.mcalister@bankofamerica.com
Tel: (704) 386 - 4343
Fax:(704) 386 - 6699

Serves As:
- Public Relations, Bank of America Corp.

MCANDREW, Kelly
One Pepsi Way
Somers, NY 10589-2201
kelly.mcandrew@pepsi.com
Tel: (914) 767 - 7690
Fax:(914) 767 - 1264

Serves As:
- Director, Public Relations, The Pepsi Bottling Group

MCANDREW, Mark S.
P.O. Box 2612
Birmingham, AL 35202
Tel: (205) 325 - 4200
Fax:(205) 325 - 4198

Serves As:
- Chief Exec. Officer, Torchmark Corp.

MCANDREWS, Brian
One Post St.
San Francisco, CA 94104-5296
brian.mcandrews@mckesson.com
Tel: (415) 983 - 8656
Fax:(415) 983 - 7160

Serves As:
- Director, Corporate Affairs, McKesson Corp.

MCANDREWS, Colleen C.
1441 Fourth St.
Santa Monica, CA 90401
Tel: (310) 458 - 1405

Serves As:
- PAC Treasurer, Global Crossing Ltd.

MCANUFF, Stacie
19975 Victor Pkwy.
Livonia, MI 48152-7001
mcanuffs@valassis.com
Tel: (734) 591 - 7375
Ext: 17375
Fax:(734) 591 - 4503
TF: (800) 437 - 0479

Serves As:
- Communications Center Supervisor, Valassis Communications, Inc.

MCARDLE, Frank
2401 Pennsylvania Ave. NW
Suite 450
Washington, DC 20037
Tel: (202) 331 - 155

Serves As:
- Washington Representative, Hewitt Associates Inc.

MCARDLE, Kevin J.
355 Maple Ave.
Harleysville, PA 19438-2297
kmcardle@harleysvillegroup.com
Tel: (215) 256 - 5279
Fax:(215) 256 - 5799
TF: (800) 523 - 6344

Serves As:
- V. President, Communications, Harleysville Group

MCARTHUR, John R.
410 S. Wilmington St.
PEB 13
Raleigh, NC 27601-1551
Tel: (919) 546 - 4070
Fax:(919) 546 - 5474

Serves As:
- Senior V. President, Corporate Relations, (Progress Energy Service Co., LLC), Progress Energy

MCARTOR, T. Allen
198 Van Buren St.
Suite 300
Herndon, VA 20170
Tel: (703) 834 - 3400
Fax:(703) 834 - 3567

Serves As:
- Chairman of the Board, Airbus North America Holdings, Inc.

MCAULAY, William A.
P.O. Box 1349
Raleigh, NC 27602-1349
Tel: (919) 836 - 2327
Fax:(919) 836 - 2343

Serves As:
- Director, Legislative and Regulatory Relations, (Public Service Co. of North Carolina), SCANA Corp.

MCAULEY, Kathryn F.
P.O. Box 9777
M/S CH1C32
Federal Way, WA 98063-9777
kathy.mcauley@weyerhaeuser.com
Tel: (253) 924 - 2058
Fax:(253) 924 - 3870
TF: (800) 525 - 5440

Serves As:
- V. President, Investor Relations, Weyerhaeuser Co.

MCAULIFFE, Mary E.
600 13th St. NW
Suite 340 West
Washington, DC 20005
Tel: (202) 662 - 0100
Fax:(202) 662 - 0199

Registered Federal Lobbyist.
Serves As:
- V. President, External Relations, Union Pacific Corp.

MCBRIDE, Paul F.
701 E. Joppa Rd.
Towson, MD 21286
Tel: (410) 716 - 3900
Fax:(410) 716 - 2933

Serves As:
- Senior V. President, Human Resources and Corporate Initiatives, The Black & Decker Corp.

MCBRIDE, Sharon
228 S. Washington St., Suite 115
Alexandria, VA 22314

Registered Federal Lobbyist.
Serves As:
- PAC Director, eBay, Inc.

MCBROOM, Marty
801 Pennsylvania Ave. NW
Suite 320
Washington, DC 20004
Tel: (202) 383 - 3430
Fax:(202) 383 - 3459

Registered Federal Lobbyist.
Serves As:
- Director, Federal Environmental Affairs, American Electric Power Co. Inc.

MCBURNEY, Thomas R.
1101 Third St. South
Minneapolis, MN 55415
Tel: (612) 332 - 7371
Fax:(612) 375 - 7723

Serves As:
- Chairman of the Board, Valspar Corp.

MCCABE, E. James
2775 Sanders Rd.
Suite A3
Northbrook, IL 60062-6127
Tel: (847) 402 - 5889
Fax:(847) 326 - 7524

Serves As:
- Manager, Government Relations, Allstate Insurance Co.

MCCABE, Patrick
4800 Deerwood Campus Pkwy.
Jacksonville, FL 32246-8273
Tel: (904) 905 - 6123
Fax:(904) 905 - 4486
TF: (800) 477 - 3736

Serves As:
• V. President, Corporate Communications, Blue Cross and Blue Shield of Florida

MCCAFFREY, Diane
P.O. Box 419580
Kansas City, MO 64141-6580
Tel: (816) 274 - 7926
Fax:(816) 274 - 5061

Serves As:
• Manager, Business Communications, Hallmark Cards, Inc.

MCCAIN, Jeanelle Medlin
1201 Main St.
Suite 1850
Columbia, SC 29201
Tel: (803) 252 - 6830
Fax:(803) 252 - 6269

Serves As:
• Manager, Public Affairs - SC, Progress Energy

MCCALL, Claire S.
Genesco Park, Suite 490
P.O. Box 731
Nashville, TN 37202-0731
Tel: (615) 367 - 8283
Fax:(615) 367 - 8278

Serves As:
• Director, Corporate Relations, Genesco
Responsibilities include corporate contributions.

MCCALL-LINK, Susan
Ten N. Martin Luther King Jr. Ave, Floor One
Waukegan, IL 60085
Tel: (847) 244 - 9977
Fax:(847) 336 - 5808

Serves As:
• Area Manager, External Affairs, SBC Illinois

MCCALLISTER, Michael B.
P.O. Box 1438
Louisville, KY 40201-1438
mmccallister@humana.com
Tel: (502) 580 - 1000
Fax:(502) 580 - 3677
TF: (800) 486 - 2620

Serves As:
• President and Chief Exec. Officer, Humana Inc.

MCCANN, Cynthia M.
550 Bowie St.
Austin, TX 78703
Tel: (512) 477 - 4455
Fax:(512) 477 - 1069

Serves As:
• V. President, Investor Relations, Whole Foods Market, Inc.

MCCANN, Nancy
1100 Terminal Tower
50 Public Square
Cleveland, OH 44113-2203
nancymccann@forestcity.net
Tel: (216) 416 - 3004
Fax:(216) 263 - 4808

Serves As:
• V. President, Marketing, Forest City Enterprises, Inc.
Responsibilities include media relations.

MCCANN, Steven F.
141 N. Civic Dr.
Walnut Creek, CA 94596
Tel: (925) 937 - 1170
Fax:(925) 210 - 6886

Serves As:
• Exec. V. President, Chief Financial Officer, and Treasurer, Longs Drug Stores Corp.

MCCANN, Vonya B.
401 Ninth St. NW
Suite 400
Washington, DC 20004
Tel: (202) 585 - 1902
Fax:(202) 585 - 1899

Serves As:
• Senior V. President, External Affairs, Sprint Nextel

MCCARGO, William
5030 Sugarloaf Pkwy.
Lawrenceville, GA 30042-2869
Tel: (770) 236 - 4607
Fax:(770) 236 - 4751
TF: (800) 236 - 5000

Serves As:
• Director, Community Affairs, Scientific-Atlanta, Inc.
Responsibilities include corporate philanthropy.

MCCARRON, Suzanne
5959 Las Colinas Blvd.
Irving, TX 75039-2298
Tel: (972) 444 - 1125
Fax:(972) 444 - 1139

Serves As:
• Manager, Communications, Exxon Mobil Corp.

MCCARTHY, Daniel J.
Two N. Ninth St.
Allentown, PA 18101-1179
djmccarthy@pplweb.com
Tel: (610) 774 - 5758
Fax:(610) 774 - 5281
TF: (800) 345 - 3085

Serves As:
• Director, Corporate Communications, PPL Corp.

MCCARTHY, Daniel M.
1401 I St. NW
Suite 200
Washington, DC 20005
Tel: (202) 293 - 9494
Fax:(202) 223 - 9594

Registered Federal Lobbyist.
Serves As:
• Director, National Government Affairs, Anheuser-Busch Cos., Inc.

MCCARTHY, James R.
701 Pennsylvania Ave. NW
Suite 520
Washington, DC 20004-2604
mccarthy.jr@pg.com
Tel: (202) 393 - 3400
Fax:(202) 393 - 4606

Registered Federal Lobbyist.
Serves As:
• Director, National Government Relations, The Procter & Gamble Company

MCCARTHY, John
600 Third Ave.
36th Floor
New York, NY 10016
Tel: (212) 697 - 1105
Fax:(212) 338 - 5662

Serves As:
• Director, Communications, Loral Space & Communications

MCCARTHY, Joseph L.
198 Champion Ct.
San Jose, CA 95134
jmy@cypress.com
Tel: (408) 943 - 2902
Fax:(408) 456 - 1910

Serves As:
• V. President, Corporate Communications, Cypress Semiconductor Corp.

MCCARTHY, Justin J.
325 Seventh St. NW
Suite 1200
Washington, DC 20004-1007
Tel: (202) 783 - 7070
Fax:(202) 347 - 2044

Registered Federal Lobbyist.
Serves As:
• Director, Government Relations, Pfizer Inc.

MCCARTHY, Kathleen
175 Berkeley St.
Boston, MA 02116
kathleen.mccarthy@libertymutual.com
Tel: (617) 654 - 3022
Fax:(617) 350 - 7648

Serves As:
• Public Affairs Associate, Liberty Mutual Insurance Co.

MCCARTNEY, Mary S.
Four Irving Pl.
New York, NY 10003
Tel: (212) 460 - 4571
Fax:(212) 614 - 1821

Serves As:
• Director, Corporate Communications, Consolidated Edison Co. of New York, Inc.

MCCARTY, Kevin Patrick
6001 36th Ave. West
Everett, WA 98203-9280
Tel: (425) 265 - 2490
Fax:(425) 356 - 3549

Serves As:
• Director, Corporate Public Relations and Investor Relations, UNOVA, Inc.

MCCARTY, Melissa D.
2350 N. Sam Houston Pkwy. East
Suite 300
Houston, TX 77032
Tel: (281) 618 - 4700
Fax:(281) 618 - 4820

Serves As:
• Treasurer, Southwestern Energy Co. PAC, Southwestern Energy Co.

MCCARTY, Michael P.
P.O. Box 7033
Indianapolis, IN 46207
mimccarty@simon.com
Tel: (317) 263 - 2925
Fax:(317) 263 - 2318

Serves As:
• Senior V. President, Research and Corporate Communications, Simon Property Group

MCCARTY, S. Scott
P.O. Box 5000
Broomfield, CO 80038-5000
smccarty@ball.com
Tel: (303) 460 - 2103
Fax:(303) 460 - 2663

Serves As:
• Director, Corporate Relations, Ball Corp.

MCCARTY, Todd
P.O. Box 3165
Harrisburg, PA 17105
Tel: (717) 761 - 2633

Serves As:
• Senior V. President, Human Resources, Rite Aid Corp.

MCCARVEL, Cynthia
P.O. Box 889
Topeka, KS 66601-0889
Tel: (785) 575 - 1544
Fax:(785) 575 - 6399

Serves As:
• Contact, Westar Energy Foundation, Westar Energy, Inc.

MCCASKEY, Raymond
300 E. Randolph St.
Chicago, IL 60601
mccaskeyr@bcbsil.com
Tel: (312) 653 - 6000
Fax:(312) 819 - 1220

Serves As:
- President and Chief Exec. Officer, Health Care Service Corp.

MCCASLIN, Teresa E.
277 Park Ave.
New York, NY 10172
Tel: (212) 207 - 5560
Fax:(212) 207 - 5043

Serves As:
- Exec. V. President, Human Resources and Information Systems, ContiGroup Companies, Inc.

MCCAUGHEY, Eileen
1133 21st St. NW
Suite 900
Washington, DC 20036
Tel: (202) 463 - 4100
Fax:(202) 463 - 4141

Registered Federal Lobbyist.
Serves As:
- Director, Planning and Political Operations, BellSouth Corp.

MCCAULLEY, Sharyn L.
P.O. Box 351
Barberton, OH 44203
slmccaulley@babcock.com
Tel: (330) 860 - 1326
Fax:(330) 860 - 6362

Serves As:
- Manager, Communications, The Babcock & Wilcox Company

MCCAUSLAND, Peter
P.O. Box 6675
Radnor, PA 19087-8675
Tel: (610) 687 - 5253
Fax:(610) 687 - 1052
TF: (800) 255 - 2165

Serves As:
- President, Chairman and Chief Exec. Officer, Airgas, Inc.

MCCAY, Mike
P.O. Box 4410
Atlanta, GA 30302
michael.mccay@suntrust.com
Tel: (404) 588 - 7230
Fax:(404) 581 - 1664

Serves As:
- Media Relations Officer, SunTrust Banks, Inc.

MCCLAIN, John
Six Sylvan Way
Parsippany, NJ 07054
Tel: (973) 428 - 9700

Serves As:
- Treasurer, Cendant Corp. PAC, Cendant Corp.

MCCLAIN, Thomas E.
505 King Ave.
Columbus, OH 43201-2693
Tel: (614) 424 - 7728
Fax:(614) 424 - 3260
TF: (800) 201 - 2011

Serves As:
- V. President, Corporate Communications, Battelle

MCCLAINE, James E.
1001 Air Brake Ave.
Wilmerding, PA 15148-1036
Tel: (412) 825 - 1000
Fax:(412) 825 - 1019

Serves As:
- V. President, Railroad Sevice; Treasurer, Wabtec Corp. PAC, Westinghouse Air Brake Technologies Corp.

MCCLANAHAN, David M.
1111 Louisiana St.
Houston, TX 77002
Tel: (713) 207 - 1111

Serves As:
- President and Chief Exec. Officer, CenterPoint Energy

MCCLEAN, Scott D.
1550 Crystal Dr.
Crystal Square 2, Suite 300
Arlington, VA 22202
scott.mcclean@lmco.com
Tel: (703) 413 - 5955
Fax:(703) 413 - 5617

Registered Federal Lobbyist.
Serves As:
- Director, Aeronautical Legislative Affairs, Lockheed Martin Corp.

MCCLELLAN, Brette
6201 South Fwy.
Fort Worth, TX 76134
Tel: (817) 293 - 0450
Fax:(817) 551 - 4615

Serves As:
- Director, Governmental Relations, Alcon Inc.

Responsibilities include political action.

MCCLELLAN, Jr., Donald W.
707 D St. NW
Washington, DC 20004
donald.mcclellan@gateway.com
Tel: (202) 737 - 2000
Fax:(202) 737 - 2688

Registered Federal Lobbyist.
Serves As:
- V. President, Government Relations, Gateway, Inc.

MCCLELLAND, Sue
P.O. Box 1130
Modesto, CA 95353
Tel: (209) 341 - 3188
Fax:(209) 341 - 8993

Serves As:
- V. President, Media, Ernest and Julio Gallo Winery

MCCLELLAND, Valorie A.
850 Lagoon Dr.
Chula Vista, CA 91910-2098
Tel: (619) 691 - 3688
Fax:(619) 691 - 2584

Serves As:
- Manager, Communications, Goodrich Corp. - Aerostructures

MCCLERKIN, Hayes C.
P.O. Box 2181
320 W. Capitol
Little Rock, AR 72203-2181
Tel: (501) 378 - 2000

Serves As:
- Chairman of the Board, Arkansas Blue Cross and Blue Shield

MCCLOSKEY, William J.
1133 21st St. NW
Suite 900
Washington, DC 20036
bill.mccloskey@bellsouth.com
Tel: (202) 463 - 4129
Fax:(202) 463 - 4612

Serves As:
- Director, Media Relations, BellSouth Corp.

MCCLURE, Charles G. "Chip"
2135 W. Maple Rd.
Troy, MI 48084
Tel: (248) 435 - 1000
Fax:(248) 435 - 1393
TF: (800) 535 - 5560

Serves As:
- Chairman, Chief Exec. Officer and President, ArvinMeritor

MCCLURE, Jennifer
One Tower Ln.
Suite 1000
Oakbrook Terrace, IL 60181-4624
Tel: (630) 706 - 3118
TF: (800) 225 - 8000

Serves As:
- Director, Government and Association Relations, DeVry Inc.

MCCLURE, Krista
2135 W. Maple Rd.
Troy, MI 48084
krista.mclure@arvinmeritor.com
Tel: (248) 435 - 7115
Fax:(248) 435 - 1031
TF: (800) 535 - 5560

Serves As:
- Senior Director, Corporate Communications and Media Relations, ArvinMeritor

MCCOLLOUGH, W. Alan
9950 Mayland Dr.
Richmond, VA 23233
alan_mccollough@circuitcity.com
Tel: (804) 527 - 4000
Fax:(804) 527 - 4164

Serves As:
- Chairman and Chief Exec. Officer, Circuit City Stores, Inc.

MCCOLLUM, David
P.O. Box 4689
Houston, TX 77210
Tel: (832) 486 - 4260
Fax:(832) 486 - 1843

Serves As:
- Investor Relations Contact, CITGO Petroleum Corporation

MCCOLLUM, Lauren M.
1100 Wilson Blvd.
Suite 1500
Arlington, VA 22209
Tel: (703) 841 - 5700
Fax:(703) 841 - 5792

Registered Federal Lobbyist.
Serves As:
- Manager, Government Relations (Air Force Programs), Raytheon Co.

MCCONKEY, Judy
1440 Granville Rd.
Newark, OH 43055-1519
Tel: (740) 364 - 5400
Fax:(740) 364 - 5410

Serves As:
- Assistant Manager, Public Affairs, State Farm Insurance Cos.

MCCONNELL, Clay
198 Van Buren St.
Suite 300
Herndon, VA 20170
Tel: (703) 834 - 3400
Fax:(703) 834 - 3567

Serves As:
- V. President, Communications, Airbus North America Holdings, Inc.

MCCONNELL, John P.
200 Old Wilson Bridge Rd.
Columbus, OH 43085
Tel: (614) 438 - 3210
Fax:(614) 438 - 3136

Serves As:
- Chairman and Chief Exec. Officer, Worthington Industries

MCCOOL, Jr., James M.
1130 Connecticut Ave. NW, Suite 830
Washington, DC 20036
Tel: (202) 261 - 5000
Fax:(202) 296 - 7937

Registered Federal Lobbyist.
Serves As:
- Federal Legislative Affairs Director, Georgia Power Co.
- Director, Government Affairs, Southern Company
- Washington Representative, Alabama Power Co.

MCCOOL, Rody Woischke
One Riverside Plaza
Columbus, OH 43215-2373
Tel: (614) 223 - 1697
Fax:(614) 223 - 1682

Serves As:
- Contributions Administrator, American Electric Power Co. Inc.

MCCORKINDALE, Douglas H.
7950 Jones Branch Dr.
McLean, VA 22107
Tel: (703) 854 - 6000
Ext: 6046
Fax:(703) 276 - 2046

Serves As:
- Chairman of the Board, Gannett Co., Inc.

MCCORMICK, Andy
235 E. 42nd St.
New York, NY 10017-5755
amccormick@pfizer.com
Tel: (212) 573 - 1226
Fax:(212) 808 - 8799

Serves As:
- V. President, Media Relations, Pfizer Inc.

MCCORMICK, Chris
One Casco St.
Freeport, ME 04033
Tel: (207) 865 - 4761
Fax:(207) 552 - 6821
TF: (800) 221 - 4221

Serves As:
- Chief Exec. Officer, L. L. Bean, Inc.

MCCORMICK, Ellen
P.O. Box 1222
Sacramento, CA 95812
ellen.mccormick@astrazeneca.com
Tel: (916) 457 - 3703
Fax:(916) 457 - 3413
TF: (800) 893 - 0390
Ext: 41981

Serves As:
- Manager, State Government Affairs, AstraZeneca Pharmaceuticals

MCCORMICK, Fione
Ten Finderne Ave.
Bridgewater, NJ 08807-3300
Tel: (908) 685 - 5000
Fax:(609) 409 - 5699
TF: (800) 797 - 4992

Serves As:
- Senior V. President, Human Resources, Nat'l Starch and Chemical Co.

MCCORMICK, Linda
6211 N. Ann Arbor Rd.
P.O. Box 122
Dundee, MI 48131
linda.mccormick@holcim.com
Tel: (734) 529 - 2411
Fax:(734) 529 - 5268
TF: (800) 854 - 4656

Serves As:
- Administrator, Public Affairs, Holcim (US) Inc.

Responsibilities include corporate philanthropy.

MCCOURT, Marion EE.
701 Pennsylvania Ave. NW
Suite 500
Washington, DC 20004
Tel: (202) 350 - 5571
Fax:(202) 350 - 5510

Serves As:
- V. President, Government, Policy and Managed Markets, AstraZeneca Pharmaceuticals

MCCOWN, Lynn
P.O. Box 858
Valley Forge, PA 19482
Tel: (610) 337 - 1000
Fax:(610) 992 - 3259

Serves As:
- V. President, Human Resources, UGI Corp.

MCCOY, Alan H.
703 Curtis St.
Middletown, OH 45043
Tel: (513) 425 - 2826
Fax:(513) 425 - 2676

Serves As:
- V. President, Government and Public Relations, AK Steel Corp.

MCCOY, Carol A.
P.O. Box 2612
Birmingham, AL 35202
Tel: (205) 325 - 4200
Fax:(205) 325 - 4198

Serves As:
- V. President, Associate General Counsel and Secretary, Torchmark Corp.

MCCOY, Michael J.
One Hormel Pl.
Austin, MN 55912-3680
Tel: (507) 437 - 5611
Fax:(507) 437 - 5129

Serves As:
- Senior V. President and Chief Financial Officer, Hormel Foods Corp.

Responsibilities include political action and investor relations.

MCCOY, Susan R.
P.O. Box 757
Carthage, MO 64836-0757
Tel: (417) 358 - 8131

Serves As:
- Director, Investor Relations, Leggett & Platt, Inc.

MCCRACKEN, Larry
World Headquarters
100 N. Riverside
Chicago, IL 60606-1596
Tel: (312) 544 - 2002
Fax:(312) 544 - 2955

Serves As:
- V. President, Corporate Communications, The Boeing Co.

MCCRACKEN, Steven R.
One Seagate
Toledo, OH 43666
steven.mccracken@us.o-i.com
Tel: (419) 247 - 5000
Fax:(419) 247 - 2839

Serves As:
- Chairman, President and Chief Exec. Officer, Owens-Illinois, Inc.

MCCRAGUE, Cynthia
P.O. Box 1734
Atlanta, GA 30301
Tel: (404) 676 - 2121
Fax:(404) 676 - 6792

Serves As:
- Senior V. President and Director, Human Resources, The Coca-Cola Co.

MCCRANIE, J. Daniel
5005 E. McDowell Rd.
Phoenix, AZ 85008
Tel: (602) 244 - 6600
Fax:(602) 244 - 4830

Serves As:
- Chairman of the Board, ON Semiconductor Corp.

MCCRARY, Charles D.
P.O. Box 2641
Birmingham, AL 35291
Tel: (205) 257 - 1000
Fax:(205) 257 - 5100

Serves As:
- President and Chief Exec. Officer, Alabama Power Co.

MCCRAY, Ronald D.
DWF Airport Station, P.O. Box 619100
Dallas, TX 75261-9100
Tel: (972) 281 - 1215
Fax:(972) 281 - 1492
TF: (800) 639 - 1352

Serves As:
- Senior V. President, Law and Government Affairs, Kimberly-Clark Corp.

MCCRODDEN, Bruce A.
National City Center
1900 E. Ninth St.
M/S 01-2157
Cleveland, OH 44114-3484
bruce.mccrodden@nationalcity.com
Tel: (216) 222 - 2994
Fax:(216) 222 - 2670
TF: (800) 622 - 6736

Registered Federal Lobbyist.
Serves As:
- Senior V. President, Corporate Public Affairs, Nat'l City Corp.

Responsibilities include political action.

MCCUE, Thomas A.
3210 Watling St.
East Chicago, IN 46312
thomas.mccue@ispat.com
Tel: (219) 399 - 5166
Fax:(219) 399 - 1898

Serves As:
- Treasurer, Ispat Inland Inc.

Responsibilities include political action.

MCCULLOCH, Ned
1301 K St. NW
Suite 1200
Washington, DC 20005
nmcculloch@us.ibm.com
Tel: (202) 515 - 4019
Fax:(202) 515 - 5194

Serves As:
- Governmental Programs Executive, Internat'l Business Machines Corp. (IBM)

MCCURVILL, John
172 W. State St.
Trenton, NJ 08608

Serves As:
- Director, State Government Affairs, Verizon New Jersey, Inc.

MCDANIEL, Dennis E.
9450 Seward Rd.
Fairfield, OH 45014
dennis.mcdaniel@ocas.com
Tel: (513) 603 - 2197
Fax:(513) 609 - 7900
TF: (800) 843 - 6446

Serves As:
- V. President, Strategic Planning and Investor Relations, The Ohio Casualty Group

MCDANIEL, Jr., Raymond W.

99 Church St.
New York, NY 10007-2707
Tel: (212) 553 - 0300
Fax:(212) 553 - 4820

Serves As:
- Chairman and Chief Exec. Officer, Moody's Corp.

MCDEDE, David

340 Kingsland St.
Nutley, NJ 07110-1199
Tel: (973) 235 - 5000
Fax:(973) 235 - 7605

Serves As:
- PAC Treasurer, Hoffmann-La Roche Inc. (Roche)

MCDERMOTT, Daniel J.

1050 Connecticut Ave. NW, Suite 1000
Washington, DC 20036
Dan_McDermott@providian.com
Tel: (202) 772 - 1101
Fax:(202) 772 - 3367

Registered Federal Lobbyist.
Serves As:
- Senior V. President, Government Relations, Providian Financial Corp.

MCDERMOTT, John

120 Fifth Ave. Pl.
Suite 2628
Pittsburgh, PA 15222
Tel: (412) 544 - 8247
Fax:(412) 544 - 5318

Serves As:
- V. President, Corporate Communications, Highmark Inc.

MCDONALD, Catherine E.

7201 Hamilton Blvd.
Allentown, PA 18195-1501
mcdonace@airproducts.com
Tel: (610) 481 - 3673
Fax:(610) 481 - 6642

Serves As:
- Manager, Financial Communications, Air Products and Chemicals, Inc.

MCDONALD, Gwen

495 E. Java Dr.
Sunnyvale, CA 94089
Tel: (408) 822 - 6000
Fax:(408) 822 - 4501

Serves As:
- Senior V. President, Human Resources, Network Appliance, Inc.

MCDONALD, Harry T.

P.O. Box 2210
Atlanta, GA 30301-2210
harry.mcdonald@goldkist.com
Tel: (770) 206 - 6918
Fax:(770) 393 - 5347

Serves As:
- V. President, Human Resources, Gold Kist Inc.

MCDONALD, Hugh

425 W. Capitol, 40th Floor
Little Rock, AR 72201
Tel: (501) 377 - 4000
TF: (800) 377 - 4448

Serves As:
- Chief Exec. Officer, Entergy Arkansas, Inc.

MCDONALD, Jack A.

1250 H St. NW, Suite 555
Washington, DC 20005
jack_mcdonald@beverlycorp.org
Tel: (202) 393 - 2800
Fax:(202) 783 - 5411

Registered Federal Lobbyist.
Serves As:
- Senior V. President, Government Relations, Beverly Enterprises, Inc.

MCDONALD, James E.

P.O. Box 52034
M/S 7602
Phoenix, AZ 85072-2034
james.mcdonald@aps.com
Tel: (602) 250 - 3704

Serves As:
- Nuclear Communications, (Arizona Public Service Co.), Pinnacle West Capital Corp.

MCDONALD, James F.

5030 Sugarloaf Pkwy.
Lawrenceville, GA 30042-2869
Tel: (770) 236 - 5000
Fax:(770) 236 - 4775
TF: (800) 236 - 5000

Serves As:
- Chairman, President and Chief Exec. Officer, Scientific-Atlanta, Inc.

MCDONALD, James P.

One Mellon Center
500 Grant St.
Room 1830
Pittsburgh, PA 15258-0001
Tel: (412) 234 - 2732
Fax:(412) 234 - 0831

Serves As:
- First V. President and Director, Community Affairs, Mellon Financial Corp.

MCDONALD, Mackey J.

P.O. Box 21488
Greensboro, NC 27420-1488
mackey_mcdonald@vfc.com
Tel: (336) 424 - 6000
Fax:(336) 424 - 7631

Serves As:
- Chairman, President, and Chief Exec. Officer, V. F. Corporation

MCDONALD, Michael K.

Commonwealth Towers
1300 Wilson Blvd., Suite 200
Arlington, VA 22209-2307
mkmcdona@collins.rockwell.com
Tel: (703) 516 - 8220
Fax:(703) 516 - 8298

Registered Federal Lobbyist.
Serves As:
- V. President, Government Operations, Rockwell Collins, Inc
- Representative, Rockwell Automation

MCDONALD, Robert D.

700 13th St., N.W., Suite 700
Washington, DC 20005-3960
Tel: (202) 508 - 6303
Fax:(202) 508 - 6305

Registered Federal Lobbyist.
Serves As:
- V. President, Government Affairs, Emerson

MCDONALD, Sammantha

8326 Century Park
San Diego, CA 92123
smcdonald@semprautilities.com
Tel: (619) 696 - 2000
Fax:(619) 696 - 1868

Serves As:
- Manager, Corporate Community Relations, San Diego Gas and Electric Co.

MCDONALD, Sidney

P.O. Box 240000
170 Graphics Dr.
Huntsville, AL 35758
Tel: (256) 730 - 2000
TF: (800) 345 - 4856

Serves As:
- Chairman of the Board, Intergraph Corp.

MCDONNELL, Thomas A.

333 W. 11th St.
Kansas City, MO 64105
Tel: (816) 435 - 1000
Fax:(816) 435 - 8630
TF: (888) 378 - 4636

Serves As:
- President and Chief Exec. Officer, DST Systems, Inc.

MCDONOUGH, John L.

440 Lincoln St.
Worcester, MA 01653
Tel: (508) 855 - 1000

Serves As:
- Treasurer, First Allmerica Financial Life Insurance Co. PAC, Allmerica Property & Casualty Companies, Inc.

MCDONOUGH, Maureen

100 Fourth Ave. North
Bayport, MN 55003-1096
maureen.mcdonough@andersencorp.com
Tel: (651) 264 - 5287

Serves As:
- Director, Corporate Communications, Andersen Corp.

MCDONOUGH, Thomas

75 Fountain St.
Providence, RI 02902-0050
Tel: (401) 277 - 7000
Fax:(401) 277 - 7461

Serves As:
- Director, Human Resources, The Providence Journal Co.

MCDOUGAL, Ted

3333 Beverly Rd.
Hoffman Estates, IL 60179-0001
Tel: (847) 286 - 2500
Fax:(847) 286 - 7881
TF: (800) 732 - 7780

Serves As:
- V. President, Public Relations, Sears Holding Corp.

MCDOUGALD, Grace E.

P.O. Box 1624
Alpharetta, GA 30009-9934
Fax:(678) 762 - 2315
TF: (800) 275 - 3004

Serves As:
- Manager, Community Relations, Colonial Pipeline Co.

MCDOUGALL, Linda M.

4400 Main St.
Kansas City, MO 64111
lmcdougall@hrblock.com
Tel: (816) 932 - 7542
Fax:(816) 753 - 8628
TF: (800) 829 - 7733

Serves As:
- V. President, Corporate Communications, H & R Block, Inc.

MCDOWELL, Julie

155 S. Limerick Rd.
Limerick, PA 19468
Tel: (610) 948 - 5100
Fax:(610) 948 - 0811

Serves As:
- V. President, Corporate Communications, Teleflex Inc.

MCDOWELL, Marian E.

1401 I St. NW
Suite 1100
Washington, DC 20005
Tel: (202) 326 - 8861
Fax:(202) 408 - 7817

Registered Federal Lobbyist.
Serves As:
- Exec. Director, Federal Relations, SBC Communications Inc.

MCELROY, Jerel
10350 E. Dakota Ave. Tel: (303) 344 - 7245
Denver, CO 80231-1314

Serves As:
- Community and Government Relations Representative, Kaiser Permanente

MCEWAN, Julie
P.O. Box 1167 Tel: (937) 221 - 1825
Dayton, OH 45401-1167 Fax:(937) 221 - 1486
julie.mcewan@standardregister.com TF: (800) 755 - 6405

Serves As:
- Manager, Public Relations, Standard Register Co.

MCFADDEN, Charles B.
1426 Main St. Tel: (803) 217 - 9247
Columbia, SC 29218
cmcfadden@scana.com

Serves As:
- Senior V. President, Governmental Affairs and Economic Development, SCANA Corp.

MCFADDEN, Ernest
360 Hamilton Ave., Suite 1103 Tel: (914) 286 - 4757
White Plains, NY 10601-1841 Fax:(914) 286 - 4727
emcfadden@heinekenusa.com TF: (800) 811 - 4966

Serves As:
- Manager, Industry and Government Affairs/Southeast, Heineken USA Inc.

MCFADDEN, Jeanmarie
11 Madison Ave. Tel: (212) 325 - 2000
New York, NY 10010-3629 Fax:(212) 538 - 4633

Serves As:
- Director, Corporate Communications, Credit Suisse First Boston

MCFADDEN, Nancy
One Market Tel: (415) 267 - 7000
Spear Tower, Suite 2400 Fax:(415) 267 - 7268
San Francisco, CA 94105

Serves As:
- V. President, Governmental Relations, (Pacific Gas and Electric Co.), PG & E Corp.

MCFARLAND, Andrew
50 Beale St. Tel: (415) 229 - 5000
San Francisco, CA 94105-1808 Fax:(415) 229 - 5070
andrew.mcfarland@blueshieldfoundation.org TF: (800) 200 - 3242

Serves As:
- Grants Administrator, Blue Shield of California

MCFARLAND, Cliff
15710 John F. Kennedy Blvd. Tel: (281) 227 - 5000
Houston, TX 77032 Fax:(281) 227 - 5455

Serves As:
- PAC Treasurer, Total Petrochemicals USA, Inc.

MCFARLAND, Richard P.
1100 Wilson Blvd. Tel: (703) 841 - 5700
Suite 1500 Fax:(703) 841 - 5792
Arlington, VA 22209

Registered Federal Lobbyist.
Serves As:
- Director, Government Relations, Raytheon Co.

MCFAYDEN, Shannon
301 S. College St., Suite 4000 Tel: (704) 374 - 6565
One Wachovia Center Fax:(704) 374 - 3425
Charlotte, NC 28288-0370 TF: (800) 275 - 3862

Serves As:
- Head of Human Resources and Corporate Relations, Wachovia Corp.

MCGAGIN, Nancy
500 W. Capitol Ave. Tel: (916) 373 - 3333
West Sacramento, CA 95605 Fax:(916) 371 - 1323
nmcgagin@raleys.com

Serves As:
- Manager, Corporate Consumer Affairs, Raley's

MCGAVICK, Mike
SAFECO Plaza Tel: (206) 545 - 5000
Seattle, WA 98185

Serves As:
- Chairman, President, and Chief Exec. Officer, SAFECO Corp.

MCGEE, Karesh
2315 N. First St. Tel: (408) 570 - 8288
San Jose, CA 95131 Fax:(408) 570 - 8901

Serves As:
- Public Relations Contact, BEA Systems, Inc.

MCGEE, Kate
1015 15th St. NW Tel: (202) 721 - 4813
Suite 200 Fax:(202) 467 - 4250
Washington, DC 20005-2605
kate.mcgee@oracle.com

Registered Federal Lobbyist.
Serves As:
- V. President, Corporate Affairs, Oracle Corporation

MCGEE, Robert M.
1717 Pennsylvania Ave., N.W., Suite 400 Tel: (202) 857 - 3011
Washington, DC 20006 Fax:(202) 857 - 3030

Registered Federal Lobbyist.
Serves As:
- President, Occidental Petroleum Corp.
- Vice President, Occidental Internat'l

MCGEHEE, Robert
P.O. Box 1551 Tel: (919) 546 - 7371
Raleigh, NC 27602-1551 Fax:(919) 546 - 7536

Serves As:
- Chairman and Chief Exec. Officer, Progress Energy

MCGILLEN, Linda
P.O. Box 4309 Tel: (406) 444 - 8931
Helena, MT 59604-4309 Fax:(406) 447 - 3454
lmcgillen@bcbsmt.com TF: (800) 447 - 7828

Serves As:
- Director, Corporate Communications, Blue Cross and Blue Shield of Montana

MCGILLICUDDY, John
11 W. 42nd St. Tel: (212) 476 - 1000
New York, NY 10035 Fax:(212) 476 - 1281

Serves As:
- Chairman of the Board, Empire Blue Cross and Blue Shield

MCGINNIS, W. Patrick
Checkerboard Square Tel: (314) 982 - 1000
St. Louis, MO 63164 Fax:(314) 982 - 2752

Serves As:
- President and Chief Exec. Officer, Nestle Purina PetCare Co.

MCGIVERN, Timothy
1401 I St. NW Tel: (202) 326 - 8877
Suite 1100 Fax:(202) 408 - 4796
Washington, DC 20005

Registered Federal Lobbyist.
Serves As:
- Exec. Director, Federal Relations, SBC Communications Inc.

MCGLOCKLIN, Bill
1111 Adams Ave. Tel: (610) 630 - 2800
Norristown, PA 19403-2403 Fax:(610) 630 - 2801
bill.mcglocklin@skf.com

Serves As:
- Director, Environmental Affairs, SKF USA, Inc.

MCGOUGH, Dennis
190 Carondelet Plaza Tel: (314) 480 - 1400
Suite 1530
Clayton, MO 63105-3443

Serves As:
- V. President, Human Resources, Olin Corp.

MCGOVERN, Patrick J.
One Exeter Plaza Tel: (617) 534 - 4200
15 Floor Fax:(617) 423 - 0240
Boston, MA 02116
patrick_mcgovern@idg.com

Serves As:
- Founder and Chairman, Internat'l Data Group

MCGRADY, James
3241 Westerville Rd. Tel: (614) 478 - 2208
Columbus, OH 43224 Fax:(614) 473 - 2721

Serves As:
- Chief Financial Officer, Retail Ventures, Inc.

Responsibilities include corporate communications and investor relations.

MCGRAIL, Kelly
410 N. Michigan Ave. Tel: (312) 645 - 4754
Chicago, IL 60611 Fax:(312) 644 - 0015
kmcgrail@wrigley.com

Serves As:
- Director, Investor and Public Relations, Wm. Wrigley Jr. Co.

MCGRANE, Mary
1020 19th St., NW
Suite 550
Washington, DC 20036
Tel: (202) 296 - 3280
Fax:(202) 296 - 3411

Registered Federal Lobbyist.
Serves As:
- Senior V. President, Genzyme Corp.

MCGRATH, Con
1375 N. Highway Dr.
Fenton, MO 63099
Tel: (636) 827 - 4000
Fax:(636) 827 - 2089

Serves As:
- V. President, People and Organizational Development, Maritz Inc.

MCGRATH, Don
100 Campus Dr.
Florham Park, NJ 07932
Tel: (973) 245 - 6000
Fax:(973) 245 - 6002

Serves As:
- V. President, Corporate Communications, BASF Corporation

MCGRATH, Don J.
P.O. Box 3200
Honolulu, HI 96847
Tel: (808) 525 - 7000
Fax:(808) 557 - 086

Serves As:
- Chief Exec. Officer, BancWest Corp.

MCGRATH, Eugene R.
Four Irving Pl.
New York, NY 10003
Tel: (212) 460 - 4600
Fax:(212) 677 - 0734

Serves As:
- Chairman of the Board, Consolidated Edison Co. of New York, Inc.

MCGRATH, Joseph W.
Unisys Way
Blue Bell, PA 19424
Tel: (215) 986 - 4011
Fax:(215) 986 - 6850

Serves As:
- President and Chief Exec. Officer, Unisys Corp.

MCGRATH, Michael E.
One i2 Pl.
11701 Luna Rd.
Dallas, TX 75234
Tel: (469) 357 - 1000
Fax:(469) 357 - 1798

Serves As:
- Chief Exec. Officer and President, i2 Technologies, Inc.

MCGRATH, Robert
200 Park Ave.
New York, NY 10166
robert.mcgrath@cbre.com
Tel: (212) 984 - 8267
Fax:(212) 984 - 8207

Serves As:
- Senior Director, Corporate Communications, CB Richard Ellis Services, Inc.

MCGRAW, III, Harold
1221 Ave. of the Americas
New York, NY 10020-1095
Tel: (212) 512 - 2000

Serves As:
- Chairman, President and Chief Exec. Officer, The McGraw-Hill Companies, Inc.

MCGREGOR, Scott A.
P.O. Box 57013
Irvine, CA 92619-7013
Tel: (949) 450 - 8700
Fax:(949) 450 - 8710

Serves As:
- President and Chief Executive Officer, Broadcom Corp.

MCGREGOR, Wynn D.
P.O. Box 650205
Dallas, TX 75265-0205
wynn.mcgregor@atmosenergy.com
Tel: (972) 934 - 9227
Fax:(972) 855 - 3030
TF: (800) 382 - 8667

Serves As:
- V. President, Human Resources, Atmos Energy Corp.

MCGUINN, Martin G.
One Mellon Center
500 Grant St.
Pittsburgh, PA 15258-0001
Tel: (412) 234 - 5000
Fax:(412) 236 - 1662

Serves As:
- Chairman and Chief Exec. Officer, Mellon Financial Corp.

MCGUIRE, Alice
2135 W. Maple Rd.
Troy, MI 48084
alice.mcguire@arvinmeritor.com
Tel: (248) 655 - 2159
Fax:(248) 435 - 1189
TF: (800) 535 - 5560

Serves As:
- V. President, Investor Relations, ArvinMeritor

MCGUIRE, Mark
1101 Pennsylvania Ave. NW
Suite 200
Washington, DC 20004
Tel: (202) 628 - 1223
Fax:(202) 628 - 1368

Serves As:
- V. President and Deputy General Counsel, Legal and External Affairs, Internat'l Paper

MCGUIRE, Mike
One CVS Dr.
Woonsocket, RI 02895
Tel: (401) 765 - 1500
Fax:(401) 769 - 4488

Serves As:
- Director, Investor Relations, CVS

MCGUIRE, William W.
9900 Bren Rd. East
Minneapolis, MN 55343
Tel: (952) 936 - 1300
Fax:(952) 936 - 0044
TF: (800) 328 - 5979

Serves As:
- Chairman and Chief Exec. Officer, UnitedHealth Group

MCGUIRE-HECKMAN, Laura
P.O. Box 1642
M/S W0-9C60
Houston, TX 77251-1642
lmcguireheckman@duke-energy.com
Tel: (713) 627 - 4332
Fax:(713) 989 - 3076

Serves As:
- Regional Director, State Governmental Affairs, Duke Energy Corp.

MCGUIRL, Tom
P.O. Box 300
Princeton, NJ 08543
tom.mcguirl@dowjones.com
Tel: (609) 520 - 5143
Fax:(609) 520 - 5180

Serves As:
- Administrative Officer, Dow Jones Foundation, Treasurer, Dow Jones and Co., Dow Jones and Co.

MCGURL, Maureen K.
P.O. Box 55888
Boston, MA 02205-5888
Tel: (781) 380 - 8000
Fax:(781) 770 - 6416
TF: (800) 767 - 7772

Serves As:
- Exec. V. President, Human Resources and Support Services, The Stop & Shop Supermarket Co.

MCHALE, David R.
P.O. Box 270
Hartford, CT 06141-0270
Tel: (860) 665 - 5601
Fax:(860) 665 - 3177
TF: (800) 286 - 2000

Serves As:
- V. President and Treasurer, Northeast Utilities

Responsibilities include investor relations.

MCHALE, Erin
4800 Hampden Ln.
Suite 1100
Bethesda, MD 20814
Tel: (301) 841 - 1600
Fax:(301) 841 - 1611

Registered Federal Lobbyist.
Serves As:
- Manager, Federal Affairs, AREVA Enterprises, Inc.

MCHALE, Jack F.
Unisys Way
Blue Bell, PA 19424
jack.mchale@unisys.com
Tel: (215) 986 - 6999
Fax:(215) 986 - 2312

Serves As:
- Corporate V. President, Investor Relations, Unisys Corp.

MCHALE, Michael
300 Chestnut Ridge Rd
Woodcliff Lake, NJ 07677
Tel: (201) 307 - 3814
Fax:(201) 573 - 8416

Serves As:
- Group Communications Manager, BMW (U.S.) Holding Corp.

MCHALE, Sharon
8200 Jones Branch Dr.
McLean, VA 22102
sharon_mchale@freddiemac.com
Tel: (703) 903 - 2438
Fax:(703) 903 - 2447
TF: (800) 373 - 3343

Serves As:
- Director, Public Relations, Freddie Mac

MCHENRY, Melissa
One Riverside Plaza
Columbus, OH 43215-2373
Tel: (614) 716 - 1120
Fax:(614) 223 - 1823

Serves As:
- Corporate Media Relations Contact, American Electric Power Co. Inc.

MCHUGH, Joseph H.
60 Massachusetts Ave. NE
Washington, DC 20002
Tel: (202) 906 - 3867
Fax:(202) 906 - 3865

Serves As:
- V. President, Government Affairs and Policy, Amtrak

MCINDOE, John
150 N. Clinton St.
Chicago, IL 60661
john.mcindow@infores.com
Tel: (312) 474 - 7862
Fax:(312) 474 - 2542
TF: (800) 317 - 6245

Serves As:
- Director, Public Relations, Information Resources, Inc.

MCINERNEY, Anne
14850 Conference Center Dr.
Chantilly, VA 20151
anne.mcinerney@rolls-royce.com
Tel: (703) 621 - 2871
Fax:(703) 709 - 6086

Registered Federal Lobbyist.
Serves As:
- Director, Legislative Affairs, Rolls-Royce North America Inc.

MCINERNEY, Thomas J.
One HSN Dr.
St. Petersburg, FL 33729
Tel: (727) 872 - 1000
Fax:(727) 872 - 6615

Serves As:
- Chief Exec. Officer, HSN, Inc.

MCINNIS, Ellen
Wells Fargo Center
Sixth & Marquette
M/S N9305-171
Minneapolis, MN 55479
Tel: (612) 667 - 7618
Fax:(612) 667 - 9403

Serves As:
- Director, Local and Minnesota Government Relations, Wells Fargo & Co.

MCINTIRE, James D.
999 W. Big Beaver Rd.
Troy, MI 48084-4782
james_mcintire@kellyservices.com
Tel: (248) 244 - 5370
Fax:(248) 244 - 5497

Serves As:
- V. President, Public Affairs, Kelly Services, Inc.

Responsibilities include political action.

MCINTYRE, Carolyn
925 L St., Suite 650
Sacramento, CA 95814
cmcintyre@sempra.com
Tel: (916) 492 - 4245
Fax:(916) 443 - 2994

Serves As:
- Regional V. President, State Government Affairs, Sempra Energy

MCINTYRE, Diane
5929 College Ave.
Oakland, CA 94618
dmmcinty@dreyers.com
Tel: (510) 652 - 4338
Fax:(510) 450 - 4592

Serves As:
- Manager, Public Relations--Superpremium Brands, Dreyer's Grand Ice Cream Holdings, Inc.

MCINTYRE, James A.
2020 Santa Monica Blvd., Suite 600
Santa Monica, CA 90404-2208
jmcintyre@fmt.com
Tel: (310) 315 - 5500
Fax:(310) 315 - 5599

Serves As:
- Chairman of the Board, Fremont General Corp.

MCINTYRE, Pamela
P.O. Box 98029
Baton Rouge, LA 70898-9029
Tel: (225) 295 - 3307
Fax:(225) 295 - 2054
TF: (800) 599 - 2583

Serves As:
- Interim V. President, Human Resources, Blue Cross and Blue Shield of Louisiana

MCINTYRE, Susan
277 Park Ave.
New York, NY 10172
susan.mcintyre@conti.com
Tel: (212) 207 - 5879
Fax:(212) 207 - 5043

Serves As:
- Assistant Secretary, ContiGroup Companies Foundation, ContiGroup Companies, Inc.

MCINTYRE, Yvonne A.
1401 H St. NW
Suite 510
Washington, DC 20005
Tel: (202) 589 - 0909
Fax:(202) 589 - 0922

Registered Federal Lobbyist.
Serves As:
- Representative, Calpine Corp.

MCKAY, Barbara S.
801 E. 86th Ave.
Merrillville, IN 46410
Tel: (219) 647 - 6200
Fax:(219) 647 - 6225
TF: (877) 647 - 5990

Serves As:
- V. President, Communictions, NiSource Inc.

MCKAY, Bernard F.
601 Pennsylvania Ave. NW
North Bldg., Suite 200
Washington, DC 20004
Tel: (202) 484 - 1490

Serves As:
- V. President, Government Affairs, Intuit Inc.

MCKAY, Bruce
444 N. Capitol St. NW
Suite 729
Washington, DC 20001
bruce_mckay@dom.com
Tel: (202) 585 - 4207
Fax:(202) 737 - 3874

Serves As:
- Manager, Federal Policy, Dominion Resources, Inc.

MCKAY, Eugenie M.
6101 Anacapri Blvd.
Lansing, MI 48917
Tel: (517) 323 - 1200
Fax:(517) 323 - 8796

Serves As:
- Director, Corporate Communications, Auto-Owners Insurance Group

MCKAY, Kelly
1000 Third Ave.
New York, NY 10022
kelly.mckay@fds.com
Tel: (212) 705 - 2443
Fax:(212) 705 - 2805

Serves As:
- Press Contact, Bloomingdale's

MCKAY, Tod
P.O. Box 7408
Boise, ID 83707
tmckay@bcidaho.com
Tel: (208) 331 - 7465
Fax:(208) 331 - 7335

Serves As:
- Corporate and Media Relations Specialist, Blue Cross of Idaho

MCKEE, Jack C.
P.O. Box 750
Collegedale, TN 37315-0750
Tel: (423) 238 - 7111
Fax:(423) 238 - 7101

Serves As:
- Chief Exec. Officer, McKee Foods Corp.

MCKEE, Lynn B.
The ARAMARK Tower
1101 Market St.
Philadelphia, PA 19107
Tel: (215) 238 - 3000
Fax:(215) 238 - 3333
TF: (800) 999 - 8989

Serves As:
- Exec. V. President, Human Resources, ARAMARK

MCKEE, Mike
P.O. Box 750
Collegedale, TN 37315-0750
Tel: (423) 238 - 7111
Fax:(423) 238 - 7101

Serves As:
- President, McKee Foods Corp.

MCKELVEY, Andrew J.
622 Third Ave.
39th Floor
New York, NY 10017
andrew.mckelvey@tmp.com
Tel: (212) 351 - 7000

Serves As:
- Chairman and Chief Exec. Officer, Monster Worldwide, Inc.

MCKELVEY, Stephen J.
P.O. Box 489
Bristol, CT 06011-0489
Tel: (860) 973 - 2132
Fax:(860) 585 - 7795

Serves As:
- Associate Director, Corporate Communications, Barnes Group Inc.

MCKENNA, Christina
One NSTAR Way
Westwood, MA 02090
christina_mckenna@nstaronline.com
Tel: (617) 424 - 2107
Fax:(617) 424 - 2523

Serves As:
- Media Contact, NSTAR

MCKENNA, Marty
Two N. Riverside Plaza
Suite 400
Chicago, IL 60606
Tel: (312) 928 - 1901
Fax:(312) 454 - 0614

Serves As:
- Assistant V. President, Investor Relations and Public Relations, Equity Residential

Responsibilities include corporate philanthropy.

MCKENNA, Tim
150 N. Michigan Ave.
Suite 1700
Chicago, IL 60601-7568
Tel: (312) 580 - 4637
Fax:(312) 580 - 4919

Serves As:
- Senior V. President, Investor Relations and Communications, Smurfit-Stone Container

MCKENNA, W. Andrew
123 S. Front St.
Memphis, TN 38103
Tel: (901) 495 - 6500
Fax:(901) 495 - 8300

Serves As:
- Chairman of the Board, AutoZone, Inc.

MCKENZIE, Katherine F.
One Citizens Plaza
Providence, RI 02903
Tel: (401) 456 - 7000
Fax:(401) 456 - 7819

Serves As:
- Group Exec. V. President, Human Resources, Citizens Financial Group, Inc.

MCKENZIE, Sandra L.
P.O. Box 554
Milwaukee, WI 53201
Tel: (414) 319 - 8500
Fax:(414) 319 - 8510

Serves As:
- Contact, Joy Global Foundation, Joy Global Inc.

Responsibilities include investor relations.

MCKENZIE, Sherry
6101 Anacapri Blvd.
Lansing, MI 48917
Tel: (517) 323 - 1200
Fax:(517) 323 - 8796

Serves As:
- Manager, Education and Training, Auto-Owners Insurance Group

MCKENZIE-SWARTS, Molly
9336 Civic Center Dr.
Beverly Hills, CA 90210
molly_mckenzie-swarts@hilton.com
Tel: (310) 205 - 4084

Serves As:
- Senior V. President, Human Resources and Administration, Hilton Hotels Corp.

MCKEOGH, John F.
100 Independence Mall West
Philadelphia, PA 19106-2399
Tel: (215) 592 - 2740
Fax:(215) 592 - 3738

Serves As:
- V. President, Public Affairs, Rohm and Haas Co.

MCKEOWN, James
101 E. State St.
Kennett Square, PA 19348
info@genesishcc.com
Tel: (610) 444 - 6350
Fax:(610) 925 - 4000

Serves As:
- Chief Financial Officer, Genesis HealthCare Corp.

Responsibilities include investor relations.

MCKINLEY, James P.
37 N. Valley Rd., Bldg. Four
P.O. Box 1764
Paoli, PA 19301
jim.mckinley@ametek.com
Tel: (610) 889 - 5234
Fax:(610) 323 - 9337
TF: (800) 473 - 1286

Serves As:
- Manager, Corporate Communications, Ametek, Inc.

MCKINLEY, Martha
300 Chestnut Ridge Rd
Woodcliff Lake, NJ 07677
Tel: (201) 307 - 3786
Fax:(201) 307 - 3607

Serves As:
- Manager, Business Communications, BMW (U.S.) Holding Corp.

MCKINNELL, Ph.D., Henry A.
235 E. 42nd St.
New York, NY 10017-5755
Tel: (212) 573 - 2323
Fax:(212) 573 - 1853

Serves As:
- Chairman and Chief Exec. Officer, Pfizer Inc.

MCKINNEY, Joyce E.
755 Crossover Ln.
Memphis, TN 38117
joyce_mckinney@hilton.com
Tel: (901) 374 - 5000
Ext: 6309
Fax:(901) 374 - 5935

Serves As:
- Senior Manager, Corporate Communications, Hilton Hotels Corp.

MCKINNEY, Mr. Kris A.
231 W. Michigan St.
A231
Milwaukee, WI 53201
kris.mckinney@we-energies.com
Tel: (414) 221 - 2157
Fax:(414) 221 - 2169

Serves As:
- Manager, Environmental Strategy, Wisconsin Energy Corp.

MCKINNEY, Lewis P.
One Busch Pl.
St. Louis, MO 63118-1852
Tel: (314) 577 - 7066
Fax:(314) 577 - 7616

Serves As:
- Region Director, Government Affairs, Anheuser-Busch Cos., Inc.

MCKINNEY, Myron W.
P.O. Box 127
Joplin, MO 64802-0127
mmckinney@empiredistrict.com
Tel: (417) 625 - 5100
Fax:(417) 625 - 5155
TF: (800) 206 - 2300

Serves As:
- Chairman of the Board, Empire District Electric Co.

MCKINNEY, Rachel P.
P.O. Box 872
York, PA 17405-0872
Tel: (717) 845 - 7511
Fax:(717) 849 - 4762
TF: (800) 877 - 0020

Serves As:
- Corporate V. President, Human Resources, Dentsply Internat'l

MCKINNISH, Richmond
13925 Ballantyne Corp. Pl., Suite 400
Charlotte, NC 28277
Tel: (704) 501 - 1100
Fax:(704) 501 - 1190

Serves As:
- Chief Exec. Officer, Carlisle Companies Inc.

MCKINNON, Paul
One Dell Way
Round Rock, TX 78682
Tel: (512) 338 - 4400
Fax:(512) 728 - 3653
TF: (800) 289 - 3355

Serves As:
- Senior V. President, Human Resources, Dell Inc.

MCKITTRICK, Beverly E.
101 Constitution Ave. NW
Suite 400 West
Washington, DC 20001
beverly.mckittrick@altria.com
Tel: (202) 354 - 1500
Fax:(202) 354 - 1505

Registered Federal Lobbyist.
Serves As:
- Director, Federal Policy- Tobacco, (Altria Corporate Services, Inc.), Altria Group, Inc.

MCKONE, Timothy P.
1401 I St. NW
Suite 1100
Washington, DC 20005
Tel: (202) 326 - 8820
Fax:(202) 408 - 4808

Registered Federal Lobbyist.
Serves As:
- V. President, Federal Relations, SBC Communications Inc.

MCLAIN, Patrick M.
1500 K St. NW
Suite 650
Washington, DC 20005
Tel: (202) 715 - 1000
Fax:(202) 715 - 1001

Registered Federal Lobbyist.
Serves As:
- Federal Government Relations, GlaxoSmithKline Research and Development

MCLARE, Rachael
535 Madison Ave.
New York, NY 10022
Tel: (212) 421 - 5010
Fax:(212) 421 - 5084

Serves As:
- Director, Investor Relations, BP

MCLAREN, K. Louise
One Sun Life Executive Park
Wellesley Hills, MA 02481
Tel: (781) 237 - 6030
Fax:(781) 304 - 5383
TF: (800) 225 - 3950

Serves As:
- V. President, Human Resources, Sun Life Financial

MCLAUCHLAN, Michael D.
P.O. Box 75000
mc 3352
Detroit, MI 48275
Tel: (313) 222 - 7496
Fax:(313) 222 - 8720
TF: (800) 521 - 1190

Serves As:
- First V. President, Government Relations, Comerica Incorporated

MCLAUGHLIN, Elizabeth J.
P.O. Box 1000
Charlotte, NC 28201-1000
Tel: (704) 522 - 3064
Fax:(704) 522 - 2055

Serves As:
- V. President, Corporate Communications and Corporate Citizenship, Royal & SunAlliance USA Inc.

MCLAUGHLIN, Susan
One Geoffrey Way
Wayne, NJ 07470-2030
Tel: (973) 617 - 5900

Serves As:
• Manager, Public Relations, Toys "R" Us, Inc.

MCLEAN, Leah
401 River Oaks Pkwy.
San Jose, CA 95134
leah.mclean@wj.com
Tel: (408) 577 - 6200
Fax:(408) 577 - 6620

Serves As:
• Media Relations, WJ Communications

MCLERNON, Kevin
1300 I St. NW
Suite 400 West
Washington, DC 20005
Tel: (202) 515 - 2400

Serves As:
• Exec. Director, Political Operations, Verizon Communications Inc.

MCLOUGHLIN, Peter C.
One Busch Pl.
St. Louis, MO 63118-1852
Tel: (314) 577 - 2000
Fax:(314) 577 - 2900

Serves As:
• V. President, Corporate Media, Anheuser-Busch Cos., Inc.

MCLUCAS, Scott
2001 M St. NW
Washington, DC 20036-3310
Tel: (202) 533 - 3000
Fax:(202) 533 - 8500

Serves As:
• Manager, Government Affairs, KPMG LLP

MCMAHON, John
One Blue Hill Plaza
Pearl River, NY 10965
Tel: (845) 352 - 6000
Fax:(845) 577 - 6913
TF: (877) 434 - 4100

Serves As:
• President and Chief Exec. Officer, Orange and Rockland Utilities, Inc.

MCMAHON, Kevin
1100 Wilson Blvd.
Suite 1225
Arlington, VA 22209
Tel: (703) 224 - 0931

Registered Federal Lobbyist.
Serves As:
• V. President, Government Relations, TRW Automotive
Responsiblities include political action and government affairs.

MCMANUS, Brian
1090 Vermont Ave. NW
Suite 1290
Washington, DC 20005
Tel: (202) 589 - 0088

Registered Federal Lobbyist.
Serves As:
• V. President, Federal Affairs, Golden Rule Insurance Co.

MCMASTER, Helen
555 13th St. NW
Suite 3 - East
Washington, DC 20004
helen.mcmaster@vitas.com
Tel: (202) 637 - 7228
Fax:(202) 637 - 8715

Serves As:
• Corporate Administrator, VITAS Healthcare Corporation

MCMASTERS, Beth
300 Phillipi Rd.
Columbus, OH 43228-5311
Tel: (614) 278 - 6974
Fax:(614) 278 - 6676

Serves As:
• Public Relations Contact, Big Lots Inc.

MCMILLAN, C. Steven
Three First National Plaza
70 W. Madison St.
Chicago, IL 60602-4260
Tel: (312) 726 - 2600
Fax:(312) 726 - 3712
TF: (800) 727 - 2533

Serves As:
• Chairman, President and Chief Exec. Officer, Sara Lee Corp.

MCMILLAN, David
30 W. Superior St.
Duluth, MN 55802
dmcmillan@mnpower.com
Tel: (218) 279 - 5000
Fax:(218) 279 - 5050

Serves As:
• Senior V. President, Marketing and Public Affairs, (Minnesota Power), ALLETE

MCMILLAN, Gail
511 Theodore Fremd
Bldg. 21
Bronx, NY 10580
Tel: (718) 904 - 4841
Fax:(718) 904 - 4860

Serves As:
• Director, Public Affairs (Bronx), Consolidated Edison Co. of New York, Inc.

MCMILLAN, Stephen
701 Pennsylvania Ave. NW
Suite 500
Washington, DC 20004
stephen.s.d.mcmillan@astrazeneca.com
Tel: (202) 350 - 5577
Fax:(202) 350 - 5510

Registered Federal Lobbyist.
Serves As:
• Director, Pharmaceutical Federal Government Affairs, AstraZeneca Pharmaceuticals

MCMILLEN, Mary Ellen
500 N. Third St., Suite 500
Harrisburg, PA 17101
maryellen.mcmillen@ibx.com
Tel: (717) 233 - 6464
Fax:(717) 233 - 6773

Serves As:
• V. President, Legislative Policy, Independence Blue Cross (Pennsylvania)

MCMULLAN, M.D., J. Bart
P.O. Box 1271
Portland, OR 97207-1271
Tel: (503) 225 - 5336
Fax:(503) 225 - 5283

Serves As:
• President and Chief Exec. Officer, Regence BlueCross BlueShield of Oregon

MCMULLEN, Kevin M.
175 Ghent Rd.
Fairlawn, OH 44333-3330
Tel: (330) 869 - 4200
Fax:(330) 869 - 4288

Serves As:
• Chairman, President and Chief Exec. Officer, OMNOVA Solutions Inc.

MCMULLEN, Melinda
One Bank One Plaza
Chicago, IL 60670
Tel: (312) 732 - 4000

Serves As:
• President, Communications for Regional and Retail, J. P. Morgan Chase & Co.

MCMULLIAN, Amos R.
1919 Flowers Circle
Thomasville, GA 31757
Tel: (229) 226 - 9110
Fax:(229) 225 - 3806

Serves As:
• Chairman of the Board, Flowers Foods

MCMURPHY, Michael A.
4800 Hampden Ln.
Suite 1100
Bethesda, MD 20814
Tel: (301) 841 - 1600
Fax:(301) 841 - 1611

Serves As:
• Co-Chief Exec. Officer, AREVA Enterprises, Inc.

MCMURRAY, Charles
P.O. Box 1299
Minneapolis, MN 55440-1299
Tel: (952) 887 - 3131
Fax:(952) 887 - 3155
TF: (800) 887 - 3131

Serves As:
• V. President, Human Resources, Donaldson Company, Inc.

MCMURRAY, Sharon R.
P.O. Box 75000
mc 3350
Detroit, MI 48275
Tel: (313) 222 - 4881
Fax:(313) 222 - 3240
TF: (800) 521 - 1190

Serves As:
• Senior V. President, Corporate Communications, Comerica Incorporated

MCMURTRY, Dana
120 Monument Circle
Indianapolis, IN 46204
dana.mcmurtry@wellpoint.com
Tel: (317) 532 - 6000

Serves As:
• V. President, Health Policy and Analysis, Wellpoint, Inc.

MCNAIR, Jr., Robert E.
1301 Gervais St., Suite 516
Columbia, SC 29201
Tel: (803) 254 - 7765

Serves As:
• Regional Manager, Government Affairs, Georgia-Pacific Corp.

MCNAMARA, Joe
2300 W. Plano Pkwy.
Plano, TX 75075
joe.mcnamara@ps.net
Tel: (972) 577 - 6165

Serves As:
• Director, Communications, Perot Systems Corp.

MCNAMARA, Kathleen
120 Park Ave.
17th Floor
New York, NY 10017
Tel: (917) 663 - 3046
Fax:(917) 663 - 5475

Serves As:
• Manager, Contributions Programs, (Altria Corporate Services, Inc.), Altria Group, Inc.

MCNAMARA, Kevin J.
2600 Chemed Center
255 E. Fifth St.
Cincinnati, OH 45202-4726
Tel: (513) 762 - 6900
Fax:(513) 762 - 6919

Serves As:
- President and Chief Exec. Officer, The Chemed Corporation
- Chairman of the Board, VITAS Healthcare Corporation

MCNAMARA, Michael D.
175 King St.
Armonk, NY 10504
Tel: (212) 317 - 5663

Serves As:
- Corporate Communications Contact, Swiss Re America Corp.

MCNAMARA, Will
101 Ash St.
hq13f
San Diego, CA 92101-3017
wmcnamara@sempra.com
Tel: (619) 696 - 2006
Fax:(619) 696 - 4266
TF: (877) 736 - 7721

Serves As:
- Manager, Legislative Policy and Analysis, Sempra Energy

MCNAMEE, Brian
One Amgen Center Dr.
Thousand Oaks, CA 91320-1799
brianm@amgen.com
Tel: (805) 447 - 1000
Fax:(805) 499 - 3507

Serves As:
- Senior V. President, Human Resources, Amgen Inc.

MCNEAL, Edward C.
Box 1000
Toledo, OH 43697-1000
Tel: (419) 535 - 4662
Fax:(419) 535 - 4756

Serves As:
- V. President, Government Relations, Dana Corp.

Responsibilities also include corporate philanthropy.

MCNEALY, Scott
4150 Network Circle
Santa Clara, CA 95054
scott.mcnealy@sun.com
Tel: (650) 786 - 8843
TF: (800) 555 - 9786

Serves As:
- Chairman and Chief Exec. Officer, Sun Microsystems, Inc.

MCNEASE, D. F.
2800 Post Oak Blvd., Suite 5450
Houston, TX 77056-6196
Tel: (713) 621 - 7800
Fax:(713) 960 - 7560

Serves As:
- Chairman, President and Chief Exec. Officer, Rowan Companies, Inc.

MCNEEL, Richard L.
111 Lord Dr.
Cary, NC 27511
Tel: (919) 468 - 5979
Fax:(919) 469 - 5777

Serves As:
- President and Chief Exec. Officer, LORD Corporation

MCNEELEY, Robert D.
300 N. Meridian St., Suite 1500
Indianapolis, IN 46204-1763
Tel: (317) 247 - 8141
Fax:(317) 248 - 6472

Serves As:
- President and Chief Exec. Officer, Reilly Industries, Inc.

MCNEIL, Jr., Chris E.
One Sealaska Plaza, Suite 400
Juneau, AK 99801-1276
Tel: (907) 586 - 1512
Fax:(907) 586 - 2304

Serves As:
- President and Chief Exec. Officer, Sealaska Corp.

MCNEILL, Dana W.
636 Grand Ave.
Des Moines, IA 50309
mcneilldw@wellmark.com
Tel: (515) 235 - 4178
Fax:(515) 248 - 5382

Serves As:
- V. President, Corporate and Marketing Communications, Wellmark, Inc.

MCNEILL, Laura
601 Pennsylvania Ave. NW
South Bldg., Suite 850
Washington, DC 20004
Tel: (202) 628 - 2749
Fax:(202) 628 - 1007

Serves As:
- Manager, Federal Advocacy, TXU

MCNERNEY, Jr., W. James
3M Center
St. Paul, MN 55144-1000
Tel: (651) 733 - 1110
Fax:(651) 733 - 9973

Serves As:
- Chairman and Chief Exec. Officer, 3M Company

MCNEW, Patti
231 W. Michigan St.
Milwaukee, WI 53201
patti.mcnew@we-energies.com
Tel: (414) 221 - 2107
Fax:(414) 221 - 2412

Serves As:
- Administrator, Wisconsin Energy Corp. Foundation, Wisconsin Energy Corp.

MCNULTY, Barry J.
231 W. Michigan St.
P346
Milwaukee, WI 53201
barry.mcnulty@we-energies.com
Tel: (414) 221 - 2235
Fax:(414) 221 - 2395

Serves As:
- Director, PTF Public Affairs, Wisconsin Energy Corp.

MCNULTY, Diane
229 W. 43rd St.
New York, NY 10036
mcnuldc@nytimes.com
Tel: (212) 556 - 5244

Serves As:
- Group Director, Community Affairs and Media Relations, New York Times Co.

MCNULTY, James F.
100 W. Walnut St.
Pasadena, CA 91124
Tel: (626) 440 - 2000
Fax:(626) 440 - 2630

Serves As:
- Chairman and Chief Exec. Officer, Parsons Corp.

MCNUTT, Rob
P.O. Box 50
Boise, ID 83728-0001
Tel: (208) 384 - 7023
Fax:(208) 384 - 4841

Serves As:
- Investor Relations Contact, Boise Cascade Corp.

MCPEAK, Brian
100 Independence Mall West
Philadelphia, PA 19106-2399
Tel: (215) 592 - 2741
Fax:(215) 592 - 6808

Serves As:
- Director, Corporate Communications, Rohm and Haas Co.

MCPHEE, Gerald T.
1717 Pennsylvania Ave. NW
Suite 400
Washington, DC 20006
jerry_mcphee@oxy.com
Tel: (202) 857 - 3038
Fax:(202) 857 - 3014

Registered Federal Lobbyist.
Serves As:
- Senior V. President, Federal Relations, Occidental Internat'l
- Senior V. President, Federal Relations, Occidental Petroleum Corp.

MCPHEE, Jessica
Six Landmark Sq.
Stamford, CT 06901
Tel: (203) 359 - 7100

Serves As:
- Manager, Corporate Communications, Diageo North America

MCPHERSON, Samuel N.
P.O. Box 1017
Charlotte, NC 28201-1017
smcpherson@familydollar.com
Tel: (704) 814 - 3518
Fax:(704) 847 - 0189

Serves As:
- Senior V. President, Human Resources, Family Dollar Stores, Inc.

MCRAE, Jack
7001 220th S.W.
MS 355
Mountlake Terrace, WA 98043-2124
jack.mcrae@premera.com
Tel: (425) 918 - 5757
Fax:(425) 918 - 5635

Serves As:
- Senior V. President, Legislative and Congressional Affairs, Premera Blue Cross

MCRAE, Larry
6201 N. 24th Pkwy.
Phoenix, AZ 85016-2023
Tel: (602) 957 - 4200
TF: (800) 528 - 1234

Serves As:
- Chairman of the Board, Best Western Internat'l

MCSHANE, Michael A.
10455 Mill Run Circle
Owings Mills, MD 21117
Tel: (410) 581 - 3000

Serves As:
- V. President, Human Resources, CareFirst BlueCross and BlueShield

MCSHEPARD, Randell
P.O. Box 777
Medina, OH 44258
Tel: (330) 273 - 8857
Fax:(330) 225 - 8743

Serves As:
- Contributions Contact, RPM Internat'l Inc.

MCSKIMMING, Jen
P.O. Box 68900
Seattle, WA 98168-0947
jen.mcskimming@horizonair.com
Tel: (206) 431 - 4672
Fax:(206) 431 - 5558

Serves As:
- Manager, Media Relations, (Horizon Air Industries), Alaska Air Group, Inc.

MCSWEENEY, Denny
1840 Century Park East
Los Angeles, CA 90067-2199
Tel: (310) 229 - 1311
Fax:(310) 201 - 3023

Serves As:
- Director, Investor Relations, Northrop Grumman Corp.

MCSWEENEY, Diana
2000 Purchase St.
Purchase, NY 10577-2509
Tel: (914) 249 - 6224
Fax:(914) 249 - 4206

Serves As:
- Contact, MasterCard Philanthropy Program, MasterCard Internat'l

MCSWEENY, Thomas
1200 Wilson Blvd.
Arlington, VA 22209-2305
Tel: (703) 465 - 3500

Registered Federal Lobbyist.
Serves As:
- Representative, The Boeing Co.

MCVICKER, Melissa
2200 Mission College Blvd.
Santa Clara, CA 95052-8119
Tel: (408) 765 - 8080
Fax:(408) 765 - 9904
TF: (800) 628 - 8686

Serves As:
- Co-Director, Worldwide Press Relations, Intel Corp.

MCWILLIAMS, John
7733 Forsyth Blvd.
Suite 2300
St. Louis, MO 63105
Tel: (314) 863 - 7422
Fax:(314) 863 - 0769
TF: (800) 677 - 1238

Serves As:
- Senior V. President and Chief Human Resources Officer, RehabCare Group, Inc.

MEAD, Donald T.
P.O. Box 1109
Muscatine, IA 52761-0071
Tel: (563) 264 - 7400
Fax:(563) 264 - 7217

Serves As:
- V. President, Member and Community Relations, HNI Corp.

MEADE, Peter
401 Park Dr.
Boston, MA 02215
Tel: (617) 246 - 5000
TF: (800) 325 - 2583

Serves As:
- Exec. V. President, Corporate Affairs, Blue Cross and Blue Shield of Massachusetts

MEADE, Sharon
850 Dixie Hwy.
Louisville, KY 40210
sharon_meade@b-f.com
Tel: (502) 585 - 1100
Fax:(502) 774 - 6633

Serves As:
- Manager, Internal Strategic Communications, Brown-Forman Corp.

MEADOWS, Amy
P.O. Box 655237
Dallas, TX 75265-5237
Tel: (214) 977 - 6661
Fax:(214) 977 - 6620

Serves As:
- Exec. Director, Belo Foundation, Belo Corp.

MEADOWS, Steve
P.O. Box 2197
Houston, TX 77252-2197
Tel: (281) 293 - 1000
Fax:(281) 293 - 1440

Serves As:
- V. President, State Government Affairs, ConocoPhillips

MEALS, Simeon
2000 K St., NW
Suite 710
Washington, DC 20006
Tel: (202) 862 - 0200
Fax:(202) 862 - 0267

Serves As:
- International Advisor, Africa, Exxon Mobil Corp.

MEANS, Paul
425 W. Capitol, 40th Floor
Little Rock, AR 72201
pmeans@entergy.com
Tel: (501) 377 - 4000
TF: (800) 377 - 4448

Serves As:
- Manager, State Government Affairs, Entergy Arkansas, Inc.

MEANY, Dennis M.
521 W. 57th St.
New York, NY 10019
Tel: (212) 708 - 7243
Fax:(212) 708 - 7191

Serves As:
- Senior V. President, General Counsel and Secretary, Internat'l Flavors and Fragrances

Responsibilities include government relations.

MEASELL, John H.
1300 N. 17th St.
Suite 1400
Arlington, VA 22209
john.h.measell@baesystems.com
Tel: (703) 907 - 8261
Fax:(703) 465 - 0329

Serves As:
- Director, Public Relations, BAE Systems North America

MEDICI, Christopher J.
100 Weybosset St.
Providence, RI 02903
cmedici@negasco.com
Tel: (401) 574 - 2068
Fax:(401) 273 - 4243

Serves As:
- Director, Communications, (New England Gas Co.), Southern Union Company

MEEK, Pamela
SAS Campus Dr.
Cary, NC 27513-2414
pamela.meek@sas.com
Tel: (919) 531 - 7883
Fax:(919) 677 - 4444

Serves As:
- Director, Global Public Relations, SAS Institute, Inc.

MEEKER, Thomas H.
700 Central Ave.
Louisville, KY 40208
Tel: (502) 636 - 4400
Fax:(502) 636 - 4430
TF: (800) 283 - 3729

Serves As:
- President and Chief Exec. Officer, Churchill Downs, Inc.

MEGELA, Anne-Marie
600 301 Blvd. West
Bradenton, FL 34205
annemarie.megela@gevityhr.com
Tel: (941) 741 - 4672
Fax:(941) 744 - 8030
TF: (800) 243 - 8489

Serves As:
- Senior Director, Investor Relations, Gevity HR, Inc.

MEHTA, Siddarth N.
2700 Sanders Rd.
Prospect Heights, IL 60070
Tel: (847) 564 - 5000
Fax:(847) 805 - 7452

Serves As:
- Chairman and Chief Exec. Officer, HSBC North America Holdings Inc.

MEIER, Cherry
13309 Chasewood Cove
Austin, TX 78727
cherry.meier@vitas.com
Tel: (512) 252 - 2843
Fax:(512) 252 - 2847

Serves As:
- Senior Director, Public Affairs, VITAS Healthcare Corporation

MEIHOFF, Darcie
401 Harbor Isles Blvd.
Klamath Falls, OR 97601
Tel: (541) 882 - 3451
Fax:(541) 855 - 7454
TF: (800) 535 - 3936

Serves As:
- Director, Public Affairs, JELD-WEN, Inc.

MEIJER, Doug
2929 Walker Ave. NW
Grand Rapids, MI 49544-1307
Tel: (616) 453 - 6711
Fax:(616) 791 - 2886

Serves As:
- Co-Chairman, Meijer, Inc.

MEIJER, Hendrik G. "Hank"
2929 Walker Ave. NW
Grand Rapids, MI 49544-1307
Tel: (616) 453 - 6711
Fax:(616) 791 - 2886

Serves As:
- Co-Chairman and Chief Exec. Officer, Meijer, Inc.

MEINTZER, Kip E.
1240 Crossman Ave.
Sunnyvale, CA 94089-1116
kip.meintzer@palmsource.com
Tel: (408) 400 - 1909
Fax:(408) 400 - 1580

Serves As:
- Director, Investor Relations, PalmSource, Inc.

MEINZ, Thomas P.
P.O Box 19002
Green Bay, WI 54307-9002
tmeinz@wpsr.com
Tel: (920) 433 - 1293
Fax:(920) 433 - 5741

Serves As:
- Exec. V. President, Public Affairs; PAC Treasurer, Wisconsin Public Service Corp.
- Senior V. President, Public Affairs, WPS Resources Corp.

Responsibilities include government affairs.

MEISTER, Mark W.
29400 Lakeland Blvd.
Wickliffe, OH 44092-2298
mwm@lubrizol.com
Tel: (440) 347 - 5641
Fax:(440) 347 - 1858

Serves As:
- V. President, Human Resources, The Lubrizol Corp.

MEKELBURG, Andrew
1300 I St. NW
Suite 400 West
Washington, DC 20005
Tel: (202) 515 - 2400

Registered Federal Lobbyist.
Serves As:
- Assistant V. President, Federal Government Relations, Verizon Communications Inc.

MELAMED, Carol
1150 15th St. NW
Washington, DC 20071
Tel: (202) 334 - 6000

Serves As:
- V. President, Government Relations, The Washington Post Co.

MELANI, M.D., Ken
120 Fifth Ave. Pl.
Suite 3111
Pittsburgh, PA 15222
Tel: (412) 544 - 7245
Fax:(412) 544 - 8240

Serves As:
- Chief Exec. Officer and President, Highmark Inc.

MELCHERT, Karen E.
CNA Center
333 S. Wabash Ave.
43rd Floor
Chicago, IL 60685
Tel: (312) 822 - 2718
Fax:(312) 822 - 1186

Serves As:
- Director, State Government Relations, (CNA Insurance Cos.), CNA Financial Corp.

MELCHIONNI, III, William
125 State St.
Albany, NY 12207
Tel: (518) 455 - 8930
Fax:(518) 426 - 5891

Serves As:
- Area Representative, Legislative Affairs, Nationwide

MELLANDER, William
2775 Sanders Rd.
Northbrook, IL 60062-6127
Tel: (847) 402 - 5000
Fax:(847) 326 - 7519
TF: (800) 574 - 3553

Serves As:
- National Media Contact, Allstate Insurance Co.

MELLEY, Maura L.
One American Row
Hartford, CT 06102
maura.melley@phoenixwm.com
Tel: (860) 403 - 5025
Fax:(860) 403 - 5755

Serves As:
- Senior Advisor, Public Affairs, The Phoenix Companies, Inc.

MELLION, Donna
13410 Sutton Park Dr. South
Jacksonville, FL 32224
dmellion@landstar.com
Tel: (904) 398 - 9400
Fax:(904) 390 - 1437
TF: (800) 872 - 9400

Serves As:
- V. President, Corporate Communications, Landstar System, Inc.

MELLODY, Kathleen
1620 L St. NW
Suite 800
Washington, DC 20036-5617
kmellody@metlife.com
Tel: (202) 659 - 3575
Fax:(202) 659 - 1026

Registered Federal Lobbyist.
Serves As:
- Counsel, Government Relations, MetLife, Inc.

MELLON, Bill
2700 Lone Oak Pkwy.
M/S A1310
Eagan, MN 55121
Tel: (612) 726 - 2331
Fax:(612) 727 - 4408

Serves As:
- Managing Director, Corporate Communications, Northwest Airlines, Inc.

MELLOR, James R.
Two Democracy Center
6903 Rockledge Dr.
Bethesda, MD 20817-1818
mellorjr@usec.com
Tel: (301) 564 - 3200
Fax:(301) 564 - 3201

Serves As:
- Chairman, President and Chief Exec. Officer, USEC Inc.

MELONE, Joseph J.
One Horace Mann Plaza
Springfield, IL 62715-0001
Tel: (217) 789 - 2500
Fax:(217) 788 - 5161

Serves As:
- Chairman of the Board, Horace Mann Educators Corp.

MELROSE, Kendrick B.
8111 Lyndale Ave. South
Bloomington, MN 55420-1196
Tel: (952) 888 - 8801
Fax:(952) 887 - 7961

Serves As:
- Chairman of the Board, The Toro Co.

MELSOP, J. William
6095 Parkland Blvd.
Cleveland, OH 44124
Tel: (440) 544 - 2600
Fax:(440) 544 - 2616

Serves As:
- Chairman and Chief Exec. Officer, The Austin Co.

MELTON, Jerry L.
P.O. Box 12069
Calhoun, GA 30703
Tel: (706) 629 - 7721
Fax:(706) 629 - 3851
TF: (800) 241 - 4494

Serves As:
- V. President, Human Resources, Mohawk Industries, Inc.

Responsibilities also include public relations and communicatons.

MELTSNER, James R.
1000 Wilson Blvd., Suite 2300
Arlington, VA 22209
jim.meltsner@ngc.com
Tel: (703) 875 - 5846
Fax:(703) 276 - 0711

Registered Federal Lobbyist.
Serves As:
- Manager, Legislative Affairs, Northrop Grumman Corp.

MELUSKY, Linda M.
P.O. Box 772531
Harrisburg, PA 17177-2531
Tel: (717) 541 - 6135
Fax:(717) 541 - 6696

Serves As:
- Government Relations Representative/ PAC, Capital BlueCross (Pennsylvania)

MENAKER, Howard M.
1015 15th St. NW
Suite 700
Washington, DC 20005-2605
Tel: (202) 828 - 5200
Fax:(202) 785 - 2645

Serves As:
- Manager, Public Affairs, (Bechtel Systems and Infrastructure), Bechtel Group, Inc.

MENDELSSOHN, Irwin A.
50 S. LaSalle St.
Chicago, IL 60675
Tel: (312) 557 - 7218
TF: (888) 289 - 6542

Serves As:
- Treasurer, North Trust Co. Political Action Committee, Northern Trust Co.

MENDEZ, Ivette
540 Broad St.
18th Floor
Newark, NJ 07102
ivette.mendez@verizon.com
Tel: (973) 649 - 4834
TF: (800) 621 - 9900

Serves As:
- Director, International Media Relations, Verizon Communications Inc.

MENDOLA, Meredith
140 Kendrick St.
Needham, MA 02494
mmendola@ptc.com
Tel: (781) 370 - 6151
Fax:(781) 370 - 5225
TF: (800) 782 - 3776

Serves As:
- V. President, Corporate Communications, PTC

Responsibilities include investor relations.

MENGEBIER, David G.
One Energy Plaza
Jackson, MI 49201
Tel: (517) 788 - 1818
Fax:(517) 788 - 0953

Registered Federal Lobbyist.
Serves As:
- Senior V. President, Governmental and Public Affairs/Community Services, CMS Energy Corp.

MENGEL, Phillip
700 E. Butterfield Rd.
Suite 250
Lombard, IL 60148
Tel: (630) 678 - 8000
Fax:(630) 678 - 8131

Serves As:
- Chief Exec. Officer, U.S. Can Corp.

MENNE, Mike
P.O. Box 66149
St. Louis, MO 63166-6149
Tel: (314) 554 - 2816
Fax:(314) 554 - 4182
TF: (800) 552 - 7583

Serves As:
- V. President, Environmental Safety and Health, Ameren Corp.

MENOGAN, Annita
P.O. Box 4030
Golden, CO 80401-0030
Tel: (303) 277 - 5919
Fax:(303) 277 - 2601

Serves As:
- V. President and Corporate Secretary, Coors Brewing Co.

Responsibilities include investor relations.

MENTA, Chet
Liberty Ln.
Hampton, NH 03842
chet.menta@fishersci.com
Tel: (603) 929 - 2381
Fax:(603) 929 - 2260

Serves As:
- V. President and Treasurer, Fisher Scientific Internat'l Inc.

MENTESANA, Beth K.
7201 Hamilton Blvd.
Allentown, PA 18195-1501
mentesbk@airproducts.com
Tel: (610) 481 - 2459
Fax:(610) 841 - 5900

Serves As:
- Manager, Corporate Public Relations, Air Products and Chemicals, Inc.

MENTESANA, Carolyn
DWF Airport Station, P.O. Box 619100
Dallas, TX 75261-9100
Tel: (972) 281 - 1485
Fax:(972) 281 - 1490
TF: (800) 639 - 1352

Serves As:
- V. President, Kimberly-Clark Foundation, Kimberly-Clark Corp.

MEOLI, Marie
1600 E. St. Andrews Pl.
Santa Ana, CA 92705
marie.meoli@ingrammicro.com
Tel: (714) 382 - 2190
Fax:(714) 566 - 7900

Serves As:
- Senior Manager, Public Relations, Ingram Micro, Inc.

MERBER, Selig S.
1299 Pennsylvania Ave. NW
11th Floor West
Washington, DC 20004-2407
Tel: (202) 637 - 4116
Fax:(202) 637 - 4006

Registered Federal Lobbyist.
Serves As:
- Counsel, International Trade Regulation, General Electric Co.

MERCER, D. Scott
691 S. Milpitas Blvd.
Milpitas, CA 95035-5473
Tel: (408) 945 - 8600
Fax:(408) 262 - 2533

Serves As:
- Interim Chief Exec. Officer, Adaptec, Inc.

MERCER, Howard
100 Jericho Quadrangle
Jericho, NY 11753
Tel: (516) 938 - 5544
Fax:(516) 938 - 5644

Serves As:
- Director, Public Relations, Griffon Corp.

Responsibilities also include investor relations.

MERCER, Robert
P.O. Box 956
El Segundo, CA 90245-0956
Tel: (310) 726 - 4683
Fax:(310) 535 - 5225

Serves As:
- Director, Public Relations, The DIRECTV Group, Inc.

MERIAGE, Lawrence P.
10889 Wilshire Blvd.
Los Angeles, CA 90024
Tel: (310) 443 - 6562
Fax:(310) 443 - 6246

Serves As:
- V. President, Corporate Communications and Public Affairs, (Occidental Oil and Gas Corp.), Occidental Petroleum Corp.

MERKELLIBERTORE, Karen
1901 Main St.
Buffalo, NY 14208-0080
Tel: (716) 887 - 6900
Ext: 8811
Fax:(716) 887 - 8981
TF: (888) 249 - 2583

Serves As:
- Media Relations Contact, HealthNow New York Inc.

MERRIAM, Laura
One Lillehei Plaza
St. Paul, MN 55117-9983
lmerriam@sjm.com
Tel: (651) 766 - 3029
Fax:(651) 766 - 3045

Serves As:
- Director, Investor Relations, St. Jude Medical, Inc.

MERRILL, Geoff
1201 Pennsylvania Ave. NW
Suite 300
Washington, DC 20004
geoff.merrill@volvo.com
Tel: (202) 661 - 4770
Fax:(202) 661 - 4771

Registered Federal Lobbyist.
Serves As:
- V. President, Government Relations and Public Affairs, Volvo Group North America, Inc.

MERRITT, Liz
P.O. Drawer F
Scottsdale, AZ 85252
Tel: (480) 660 - 3337
Fax:(480) 606 - 3328
TF: (800) 421 - 5718

Serves As:
- Director, Public Relations, Rural Metro Corp.

MERRITT, Robert S. "Chip"
41 Moores Rd.
Frazer, PA 19355
cmerritt@cephalon.com
Tel: (610) 738 - 6376
Fax:(610) 344 - 0981

Serves As:
- Senior Director, Investor Relations, Cephalon, Inc.

MERRIWETHER, John C.
5811 Pelican Bay Blvd., Suite 500
Naples, FL 34108-2710
John.Merriwether@hma.com
Tel: (239) 598 - 3104
Fax:(239) 597 - 5794

Serves As:
- V. President, Financial Relations, Health Management Associates, Inc.

Responsibilities include investor relations and corporate communications.

MERSKI, Richard P.
1399 New York Ave. NW
Suite 900
Washington, DC 20005
Tel: (202) 585 - 5807
Fax:(202) 585 - 5820

Registered Federal Lobbyist.
Serves As:
- V. President, Corporate Affairs, American Internat'l Group, Inc.

MERSON, Michael
10455 Mill Run Circle
Owings Mills, MD 21117
Tel: (410) 581 - 3000
Fax:(410) 998 - 5351

Serves As:
- Chairman of the Board, CareFirst BlueCross and BlueShield

MESLOH, James C.
Dominion Tower
625 Liberty Ave.
Pittsburgh, PA 15222
james_mesloh@dom.com
Tel: (412) 690 - 1200

Serves As:
- Foundation Contact, Dominion Peoples

MESSINA, Cynthia
P.O. Box 98510
Las Vegas, NV 89193-8510
Tel: (702) 876 - 7011
Fax:(702) 220 - 4736

Serves As:
- Administrator, Communications, Southwest Gas Corp.

MESSINA, Raymond A.
401 Ninth St., NW, Suite 650
Washington, DC 20004
Tel: (202) 654 - 2000
Fax:(202) 654 - 2100

Registered Federal Lobbyist.
Serves As:
- Exec. Director, Government Affairs, Morgan Stanley

MESSING, David J.
P.O. Box 4607
Houston, TX 77210-4607
dmessi@coair.com
Tel: (713) 324 - 5080
Fax:(713) 324 - 2087

Serves As:
- Managing Director, Public Relations, Continental Airlines

MESSINGER, Matt
8700 W. Bryn Mawr Ave.
Chicago, IL 60631
mmessinger@ballyfitness.com
Tel: (773) 380 - 3000
Fax:(773) 399 - 0476

Serves As:
- Senior Director, Public Director, Bally Total Fitness Holding Corp.

MESSMAN, Jack L.
404 Wyman St.
Suite 500
Waltham, MA 02451
Tel: (781) 464 - 8000
Fax:(781) 464 - 8100
TF: (800) 861 - 7000

Serves As:
- Chairman and Chief Exec. Officer, Novell, Inc.

MESSMER, Jr., Harold M.
2884 Sand Hill Rd. Tel: (650) 234 - 6000
Suite 200 Fax:(650) 234 - 6999
Menlo Park, CA 94025

Serves As:
- Chairman and Chief Exec. Officer, Robert Half International Inc.

MESSURI, Mari-Louise
25 Research Dr. Tel: (508) 389 - 2000
Westborough, MA 01582 Fax:(508) 389 - 2605

Serves As:
- Treasurer, National Grid USA PAC, Nat'l Grid USA

METCALF, Wendy
645 E. Missouri Ave., Suite 400 Tel: (602) 265 - 9200
Phoenix, AZ 85012 Fax:(602) 631 - 7321

Serves As:
- Director, Media, CSK Auto, Inc.

METZ, Bonnie
901 N. Tatnall St., Second Floor Tel: (302) 571 - 1571
Wilmington, DE 19801 Fax:(302) 576 - 1132

Serves As:
- Chief Lobbyist, State Affairs, Verizon Delaware Inc.

METZ, Craig
2011 Crystal Dr., Crystal Park 1 Tel: (703) 769 - 6202
Suite 907 Fax:(703) 892 - 0091
Arlington, VA 22202
metz_craig@emc.com

Registered Federal Lobbyist.
Serves As:
- Manager, Government Affairs, EMC Corp.

METZGER, William
One N. Field Ct. Tel: (847) 735 - 4700
Lake Forest, IL 60045-4811 Fax:(847) 735 - 4765

Serves As:
- PAC Treasurer, Brunswick Corp.

METZLER, Jill
333 W. 11th St. Tel: (816) 843 - 9087
Kansas City, MO 64105 Fax:(816) 843 - 9245
jdmetzler@dstsystems.com TF: (888) 378 - 4636

Serves As:
- Media Relations Contact, DST Systems, Inc.

MEUNIER, Louis
50 O'Farrell St. Tel: (415) 954 - 6406
San Francisco, CA 94108 Fax:(415) 984 - 7137

Serves As:
- Exec. V. President, External Affairs, (Macy's West), Federated Department Stores, Inc.

MEYER, Armin
540 White Plains Rd. Tel: (914) 785 - 2000
Tarrytown, NY 10591-2005 Fax:(914) 785 - 2211
TF: (800) 431 - 1900

Serves As:
- Chairman and Chief Exec. Officer, Ciba Specialty Chemicals

MEYER, Arthur G. "Art"
1065 Woodman Dr. Tel: (937) 259 - 7208
Dayton, OH 45432 Fax:(937) 259 - 7386

Serves As:
- V. President and Corporate Secretary, (Dayton Power and Light Co.), DPL Inc.

Responsibilities include legal and corporate affairs.

MEYER, Carol
1345 Ave. of the Americas Tel: (917) 452 - 4400
New York, NY 10105 Fax:(917) 527 - 9915

Serves As:
- Managing Partner, Investor Relations, Accenture

MEYER, David J.
P.O. Box 3727 Tel: (509) 489 - 0500
Spokane, WA 99220-3727 Fax:(509) 495 - 8725
TF: (800) 727 - 9170

Serves As:
- V. President and Chief Counsel, Regulatory and Government Affairs, Avista Corp.

MEYER, Edward H.
777 Third Ave. Tel: (212) 546 - 2000
New York, NY 10017 Fax:(212) 546 - 1495

Serves As:
- Chairman, Chief Exec. Officer and President, Grey Global Group Inc.

MEYER, III, Henry
127 Public Square Tel: (216) 689 - 3000
Cleveland, OH 44114 Fax:(216) 689 - 8710

Serves As:
- Chairman and Chief Exec. Officer, KeyCorp

MEYER, Jennifer
224 W. 30th St. Tel: (212) 624 - 3912
New York, NY 10001 Fax:(212) 624 - 3881
jmeyer@webmd.net

Serves As:
- V. President, Communications, WebMD Corp.

MEYER, Katie
71 S. wacker Dr Tel: (312) 750 - 1234
Chicago, IL 60606 Fax:(312) 750 - 8550

Serves As:
- V. President, Communications, Global Hyatt Corp.

MEYER, Laurie L.
200 Wilmot Rd. Tel: (847) 914 - 2920
Deerfield, IL 60015-4616 Fax:(847) 914 - 3086
laurie.meyer@walgreens.com

Serves As:
- Divisional V. President, Corporate Communications, Walgreen Co.

MEYER, Jr., Richard W.
P.O. Box 51609 Tel: (317) 247 - 4000
Indianapolis, IN 46251-0609 Fax:(317) 243 - 4169

Serves As:
- Senior V. President, Employee Relations, ATA Holdings Corp.

MEYER, Jr., Russell W.
P.O. Box 7706 Tel: (316) 517 - 6000
Wichita, KS 67277-7706 Fax:(316) 517 - 6640

Serves As:
- Chairman Emeritus, Cessna Aircraft Co.

MEYER, Timothy B.
48 Monroe Tpk. Tel: (203) 459 - 7271
Trumbull, CT 06611 Fax:(203) 452 - 4610
tmeyer@oxfordhealth.com TF: (800) 889 - 7658

Registered Federal Lobbyist.
Serves As:
- V. President, Government Relations, Oxford Health Plans Inc.

MEYER, Vance
500 Water St. Tel: (904) 359 - 3161
Jacksonville, FL 32203 Fax:(904) 359 - 1899

Serves As:
- V. President, Corporate Communications, CSX Corp.

MEYERS, David W.
P.O. Box 70 Tel: (208) 383 - 2728
Boise, ID 83707 Fax:(208) 388 - 6955

Serves As:
- General Manager, Relicensing and Environmental Affairs, (Idaho Power Co.), IDACORP, Inc.

MICALI, James
P.O. Box 19001 Tel: (864) 458 - 5000
Greenville, SC 29602 Fax:(864) 458 - 6359
TF: (800) 847 - 3435

Serves As:
- Chairman and President, Michelin North America, Inc.

MICHAELS, Paul S.
6885 Elm St. Tel: (703) 821 - 4900
McLean, VA 22101 Fax:(703) 448 - 9678

Serves As:
- President, Mars, Inc.

MICHALSKI, Jeanne
P.O. Box 961057 Tel: (817) 352 - 6460
Fort Worth, TX 76161-2830 Fax:(817) 352 - 7924
jeanne.michalski@bnsf.com

Serves As:
- V. President, Human Resources, Burlington Northern Santa Fe Corporation

MICHEL, Geoffrey S.
400 Robert St. North Tel: (651) 665 - 3500
St. Paul, MN 55101 Fax:(651) 665 - 3853
geoffrey.michel@minnesotamutual.com

Serves As:
- Director, Government Affairs, Minnesota Life Insurance Co.

MICHEL, Laurie L.
601 Pennsylvania Ave. NW
North Bldg. Suite 1200
Washington, DC 20004
Tel: (202) 638 - 4170
Fax:(202) 638 - 3670

Registered Federal Lobbyist.
Serves As:
• Senior Director, Counsel, Federal Policy and Government Relations, Merck & Co., Inc.

MICHELMAN, Douglas
900 Metro Center Blvd.
Foster City, CA 94404-2172
Tel: (650) 432 - 3200
Fax:(650) 432 - 3631

Serves As:
• Exec. V. President, Corporate Relations, Visa U.S.A. Inc.

MICKELSON, Gary R.
P.O. Box 2020
Springdale, AR 72765-2020
gary.mickelson@tyson.com
Tel: (479) 290 - 4000
Fax:(479) 290 - 7984
TF: (800) 424 - 4253

Serves As:
• Director, Corporate Media Relations, Tyson Foods, Inc.

MICKNA, Karl
One Haworth Center
Holland, MI 49423
Tel: (616) 393 - 1865
Fax:(616) 393 - 1570
TF: (800) 344 - 2600

Serves As:
• Media Specialist, Haworth Inc.

MICLOT, Stephanie
17666 Fitch
Irvine, CA 92614
Tel: (949) 253 - 2339
Fax:(949) 474 - 7675

Serves As:
• Director, Corporate Communications and Marketing, Freedom Communications Inc.

MIDDELBURG, Suzanne J.
2244 Walnut Grove Ave.
Rosemead, CA 91770
middelsj@sce.com
Tel: (626) 302 - 2433
Fax:(626) 302 - 8003

Serves As:
• Manager, Consumer Affairs, Southern California Edison, an Edison Internat'l Co.

MIDDLETON, John J.
Five Jillian Way
Mt. Laurel, NJ 08054
middletj@wyeth.com
Tel: (856) 802 - 0074

Serves As:
• Director, State Government Affairs, Wyeth Pharmaceuticals

MIELKE, Wayne J.
P.O. Box 75000
mc 3350
Detroit, MI 48275
Tel: (313) 222 - 4732
Fax:(313) 222 - 3240
TF: (800) 521 - 1190

Serves As:
• V. President, Corporate Communications, Comerica Incorporated

MIES, John
P.O. Box M
Allentown, PA 18105-5000
Tel: (610) 709 - 3011
Fax:(610) 709 - 3308

Serves As:
• V. President, Communications, Mack Trucks, Inc.

MIHALSKI, Edmund J.
555 12th St. NW
Suite 650
Washington, DC 20004-1205
Tel: (202) 393 - 7950
Fax:(202) 393 - 7960

Registered Federal Lobbyist.
Serves As:
• Director, Federal Affairs, Eli Lilly and Company

MIKALAUSKAS, Kenneth
1500 Market St.
Philadelphia, PA 19102
Tel: (215) 665 - 1700
Fax:(215) 981 - 7712

Serves As:
• Treasurer, Comcast Corp. Political Action Committee, Comcast Corporation

MIKEL, John
701 Pennsylvania Ave. NW
Suite 720
Washington, DC 20004
Tel: (202) 434 - 4800
Fax:(202) 347 - 4015

Registered Federal Lobbyist.
Serves As:
• Director, Legislative Affairs, Siemens Corp.

MIKELLS, Kathryn
P.O. Box 66100
Chicago, IL 60666
Tel: (847) 700 - 4000
Fax:(847) 700 - 4899

Serves As:
• PAC Treasurer, United Airlines

MIKELSONS, J. George
P.O. Box 51609
Indianapolis, IN 46251-0609
Tel: (317) 247 - 4000
Fax:(317) 243 - 4169

Serves As:
• Chairman, President and Chief Exec. Officer, ATA Holdings Corp.

MIKOLS, Elizabeth H.
7660 Imperial Way
Allentown, PA 18195-1040
emikols@lehighcement.com
Tel: (610) 366 - 4753
Fax:(610) 366 - 4684
TF: (800) 523 - 5488

Serves As:
• Manager, Public Affairs, Lehigh Cement Company

MIKULA, Jim I.
P.O. Box 53999
M/S 8376
Phoenix, AZ 85072-3999
jim.mikula@pinnaclewest.com
Tel: (602) 250 - 2232

Serves As:
• Consultant, Environment, Pinnacle West Capital Corp.

MIKULINA, David
71 S. wacker Dr
Chicago, IL 60606
dmikulin@corphq.hyatt.com
Tel: (312) 750 - 8264
Fax:(312) 750 - 8550

Serves As:
• Assistant V. President, Risk Management, Global Hyatt Corp.

MILANESE, Wendy
One Campbell Pl.
Camden, NJ 08103-1701
wendy_milanese@campbellsoup.com
Tel: (856) 342 - 6423
Fax:(856) 541 - 8185
TF: (800) 257 - 8443

Serves As:
• Grant Administrator, Campbell Soup Foundation, Campbell Soup Co.

MILANO, Ann Marie
1090 Vermont Ave. NW
Suite 1290
Washington, DC 20005
Tel: (202) 589 - 0400

Registered Federal Lobbyist.
Serves As:
• Representative, Golden Rule Insurance Co.

MILANO, Bernard J.
Three Chestnut Ridge Rd.
Montvale, NJ 07645-0435
Tel: (201) 505 - 3400
Fax:(201) 505 - 3404

Serves As:
• President, KPMG LLP
Responsibilities include corporate philanthropy.

MILCHOVICH, Raymond J.
Perryville Corporate Park
Clinton, NJ 08809-4000
Tel: (908) 730 - 4000
Fax:(908) 730 - 5315

Serves As:
• Chairman and Chief Exec. Officer, Foster Wheeler Ltd.

MILES, David
4400 Main St.
Kansas City, MO 64111
davmiles@hrblock.com
Tel: (816) 932 - 4821
Fax:(816) 753 - 1585
TF: (800) 829 - 7733

Serves As:
• President, H&R Block Foundation, H & R Block, Inc.

MILES, II, John C.
P.O. Box 872
York, PA 17405-0872
jmiles@dentsply.com
Tel: (717) 845 - 7511
Fax:(717) 849 - 4762
TF: (800) 877 - 0020

Serves As:
• Director, Dentsply Internat'l

MILES, Lisa
11419 Sunset Hills Rd.
Reston, VA 20190-5207
lisamiles@maximus.com
Tel: (703) 251 - 8500
Fax:(703) 251 - 8240
TF: (888) 368 - 2152

Serves As:
• Director, Investor Relations, MAXIMUS, Inc.

MILETTI, John D.
One Tower Sq.
Hartford, CT 06183
Tel: (860) 277 - 0459
Fax:(860) 277 - 2808

Serves As:
• V. President, Personal Lines, Government Relations, St. Paul Travelers Cos., Inc.

MILEVOJ, Andy
122 Fifth Ave.
New York, NY 10011
amilevoj@bn.com
Tel: (212) 633 - 3489
Fax:(212) 675 - 0413

Serves As:
• Manager, Investor Relations, Barnes & Noble, Inc.

MILEWSKI, Dennis
One State St.
Hartford, CT 06103
dennis_milewski@hsb.com
Tel: (860) 722 - 5567

Serves As:
- Manager, Media Relations, Hartford Steam Boiler Inspection and Insurance Co.

MILLAN, Jacqueline R.
700 Anderson Hill Rd.
Purchase, NY 10577-1444
Tel: (914) 253 - 3153
Fax:(914) 253 - 3553

Serves As:
- Director, Corporate Contributions, PepsiCo, Inc.

MILLARD, Howard
P.O. Box 1537
Salisbury, MD 21802-1537
howard.millard@perdue.com
Tel: (410) 543 - 3000
Fax:(410) 543 - 3884

Serves As:
- Foundation Contact, Perdue Farms

MILLER, Alan B.
P.O. Box 61558
King of Prussia, PA 19406-0958
Tel: (610) 768 - 3300
Fax:(610) 768 - 3312

Serves As:
- Chairman and Chief Exec. Officer, Universal Health Services, Inc.

MILLER, Alan D.
1555 Promontery Circle
Greeley, CO 80638-0001
Tel: (970) 351 - 5350
Fax:(970) 351 - 5424

Serves As:
- Assistant Manager, Public Affairs, State Farm Insurance Cos.

MILLER, Andrew M.
840 Gessner
Suite 1400
Houston, TX 77024
Tel: (713) 650 - 6200
Fax:(713) 653 - 6815

Serves As:
- Exec. V. President, Human Resources, Cemex USA

MILLER, Bonnie R.
216 16th St. Mall, Suite 860
Denver, CO 80202
Tel: (303) 825 - 7661
Fax:(303) 825 - 4629

Serves As:
- Manager, Colorado Government Affairs, Coors Brewing Co.

MILLER, Brian
P.O. Box 42308
Portland, OR 97242
Tel: (503) 888 - 7765

Serves As:
- Legislative Representative, (Farmers Insurance Group of Companies), Farmers Group, Inc.

MILLER, Brian W.
1776 I St. NW
Suite 1000
Washington, DC 20006-3707
millerbw@bp.com
Tel: (202) 785 - 4888
Fax:(202) 457 - 6597

Registered Federal Lobbyist.
Serves As:
- Director, U.S. Government and International Affairs, BP

MILLER, Christine M.
P.O. Box 672
Deer Park, TX 77536
Tel: (713) 476 - 8109

Serves As:
- Manager, Public Affairs, (Rohm and Haas Texas Inc.), Rohm and Haas Co.

MILLER, Chuck
5350 Tech Data Dr.
Clearwater, FL 33760
chuck.miller@techdata.com
Tel: (727) 571 - 9305
Fax:(727) 571 - 9140
TF: (800) 237 - 8931

Serves As:
- Director, Corporate Communications, Tech Data Corp.

MILLER, D. James
P.O. Box 51777
New Orleans, LA 70151
Tel: (504) 582 - 4239
Fax:(504) 582 - 1847
TF: (800) 535 - 7094

Serves As:
- V. President, Environmental Affairs and Safety, Freeport-McMoRan Copper and Gold Inc.

MILLER, Ph.D., Dane A.
P.O. Box 587
Warsaw, IN 46581-0587
dane.miller@biometmail.com
Tel: (574) 267 - 6639
Fax:(574) 267 - 8137

Serves As:
- President and Chief Exec. Officer, Biomet Inc.

MILLER, David
3050 Bowers Ave.
P.O. Box 58039
Santa Clara, CA 95054-3299
david_miller@appliedmaterials.com
Tel: (408) 563 - 9582
Fax:(408) 986 - 7115

Serves As:
- Senior Manager, Worldwide Media Relations, Applied Materials, Inc.

MILLER, David N.
2700 Watt Ave.
P.O. Box 15038
Sacramento, CA 95851
Tel: (916) 972 - 4545
Fax:(916) 979 - 1388

Serves As:
- Exec. Director, External Affairs, (SBC Pacific Bell), SBC Communications Inc.

MILLER, Debra L.
1835 Dueber Ave. SW
GNE-20
Canton, OH 44706
deb.miller@timken.com
Tel: (330) 438 - 3000
Fax:(330) 471 - 4041
TF: (800) 223 - 1954

Serves As:
- Senior V. President, Communications and Community Affairs, The Timken Co.

MILLER, Ed
24000 Honda Pkwy.
Marysville, OH 43040
Tel: (937) 645 - 8789
Fax:(937) 645 - 8787

Serves As:
- Manager, Corporate Communications, Government Trade and Community, (Honda of America Manufacturing, Inc.), American Honda Motor Co., Inc.

MILLER, Forrest E.
P.O. Box 2933
San Antonio, TX 78299-2933
Tel: (210) 821 - 4105
TF: (800) 351 - 7221

Serves As:
- Group President, External Affairs and Planning, SBC Communications Inc.

MILLER, Gregory A.
698 12th St., S.E., Suite 220
Salem, OR 97301
Tel: (503) 588 - 0311

Serves As:
- Manager, Government Affairs (Oregon), Weyerhaeuser Co.

MILLER, Heather K.
P.O. Box 419226
Kansas City, MO 64141-6226
Tel: (816) 860 - 7000
Fax:(816) 860 - 5675

Serves As:
- Senior V. President, Marketing Communications, UMB Financial Corp.

MILLER, Howard
115 W. College Dr.
Marshall, MN 56258
Tel: (507) 532 - 8700
Fax:(507) 537 - 8794
TF: (800) 533 - 5290

Serves As:
- V. President, Corporate Relations, The Schwan Food Co.

MILLER, Irving
19001 S. Western Ave.
Torrance, CA 90509
Tel: (310) 468 - 5030
Fax:(310) 468 - 7809

Serves As:
- Group V. President, Corporate Communications, (Toyota Motor Sales - USA), Toyota Motor North America, Inc.

MILLER, Janice
2211 S. 47th St.
Phoenix, AZ 85034
janice.miller@avnet.com
Tel: (480) 643 - 2000

Serves As:
- V. President, Organizational Development and Human Resources, Avnet Inc.

MILLER, Jean
50606 AXP Financial Center
Minneapolis, MN 55474
jean.m.miller@ameriprise.com
Tel: (612) 671 - 1933
Fax:(612) 671 - 5112
TF: (800) 328 - 8300

Serves As:
- Manager, Public Affairs and Communications, Ameriprise Financial Services Inc.

MILLER, John
50 W. San Fernando St.
San Jose, CA 95113
Tel: (408) 995 - 5115
Fax:(408) 297 - 9688
TF: (800) 359 - 5115

Serves As:
- Senior V. President, Human Resources and Safety, Calpine Corp.

MILLER, Jon H.
P.O. Box 70
Boise, ID 83707
Fax:(208) 388 - 6955

Serves As:
- Chairman of the Board, IDACORP, Inc.

MILLER, Joseph A. "Buzz"
601 Pennsylvania Ave. NW
Suite 800
Washington, DC 20004
Tel: (202) 261 - 5000
Fax:(202) 296 - 7937

Registered Federal Lobbyist.
Serves As:
- V. President, Governmental Relations, Southern Company
- V. President, Government Relations, Alabama Power Co.

MILLER, Karla
P.O. Box 1470
Decatur, IL 62525
Tel: (217) 424 - 5200
Fax:(217) 424 - 5839

Serves As:
- V. President, Public Relations, Archer Daniels Midland Co. (ADM)

Responsibilities include investor relations.

MILLER, Kristine B.
1200 Wilson Blvd.
Arlington, VA 22209-2305
Tel: (703) 465 - 3232
Fax:(703) 465 - 3362

Registered Federal Lobbyist.
Serves As:
- PAC Manager, The Boeing Co.

MILLER, Larry C.
1540 Genesee St.
Kansas City, MO 64102
lcmiller@butlermfg.org
Tel: (816) 968 - 3216
Fax:(816) 968 - 6503

Serves As:
- Chief Financial Officer and V. President, Finance, Butler Manufacturing Co.

Responsibilities include corporate communications and investor relations.

MILLER, Lorraine D.
Prominence in Buckhead, 3475 Piedmont Rd.
North East
Suite 1420
Atlanta, GA 30305
miller.lorraine@wpstv.com
Tel: (404) 378 - 0491

Serves As:
- Senior V. President, Finance and External Communications, WestPoint Stevens Inc.

Responsibilities include investor relations.

MILLER, Mark
211 Riverside Dr.
Evansville, IN 47708-1251
mmiller@vectren.com
Tel: (812) 491 - 4000
Fax:(812) 491 - 4078
TF: (800) 227 - 1376

Serves As:
- Foundation Contact, Vectren Corp.

MILLER, Mark
9487 Regency Square Blvd.
Jacksonville, FL 32225
mark.miller@crowley.com
Tel: (904) 727 - 4295

Serves As:
- Director, Corporate Communications, Crowley Maritime Corp.

MILLER, Mark S.
2926 Piper Dr.
Vero Beach, FL 32960
m.miller@newpiper.com
Tel: (772) 299 - 2900
Fax:(772) 978 - 5697

Serves As:
- Director, Corporate Communications, The New Piper Aircraft Inc.

MILLER, Melanie E. R.
222 S. Ninth St.
Suite 2300
Minneapolis, MN 55402-4099
Tel: (612) 376 - 3000

Serves As:
- V. President and Treasurer, Bemis Company, Inc.

Responsibilities include investor relations.

MILLER, Melissa
731 Market St.
Suite 410
San Francisco, CA 94103
mmiller2@tmw.com
Tel: (510) 723 - 8402

Serves As:
- Public Relations Coordinator, Men's Wearhouse, Inc.

MILLER, Jr., Merrill A. "Pete"
10000 Richmond Ave.
Fourth Floor
Houston, TX 77042-4200
Tel: (713) 346 - 7500
Fax:(713) 435 - 2195

Serves As:
- Chairman, President and Chief Exec. Officer, Nat'l Oilwell, Inc.

MILLER, Paul
33 Commercial St.
Foxboro, MA 02035
paul.miller@ivensys.com
Tel: (508) 549 - 6240
Fax:(508) 549 - 4834
TF: (866) 746 - 6477

Serves As:
- Manager, Public Relations, (Invensys Process Systems), Invensys Systems, Inc.

MILLER, R. Scott
701 Pennsylvania Ave. NW
Suite 520
Washington, DC 20004-2604
miller.rs@pg.com
Tel: (202) 393 - 3404
Fax:(202) 393 - 4606

Registered Federal Lobbyist.
Serves As:
- Director, National Government Relations, The Procter & Gamble Company

MILLER, Ralph R.
P.O. Box 51777
New Orleans, LA 70151
ralph_miller@fmi.com
Tel: (504) 582 - 4711
Fax:(504) 582 - 1847
TF: (800) 535 - 7094

Serves As:
- V. President, State Government Relations, Freeport-McMoRan Copper and Gold Inc.

MILLER, Robert A.
3375 Mitchell Lane
Boulder, CO 80301
Tel: (303) 440 - 5220
Fax:(303) 928 - 0022
TF: (800) 494 - 9453

Serves As:
- Chairman of the Board, Wild Oats Markets, Inc.

MILLER, Robert G.
P.O. Box 3165
Harrisburg, PA 17105
Tel: (717) 761 - 2633

Serves As:
- Chairman of the Board, Rite Aid Corp.

MILLER, Rodney K.
1401 S. Carpenter Ave.
Iron Mountain, MI 49801
rod.miller@we-energies.com
Tel: (906) 779 - 2478
Fax:(906) 779 - 2488

Serves As:
- Principal Representative, State Relations - Michigan, Wisconsin Energy Corp.

MILLER, Rodney S. "Steve"
5725 Delphi Dr.
Troy, MI 48098-2815
Tel: (248) 813 - 2000
Fax:(248) 813 - 2670

Serves As:
- Chairman and Chief Exec. Officer, Delphi Corp.

MILLER, Russell H.
20 Park Rd., Suite E
Burlingame, CA 94010

Serves As:
- Treasurer, Applied Materials Inc. PAC, Applied Materials, Inc.

MILLER, Samuel H.
1100 Terminal Tower
50 Public Square
Cleveland, OH 44113-2203
Tel: (216) 621 - 6060
Fax:(216) 263 - 4808

Serves As:
- Co-Chairman of the Board, Forest City Enterprises, Inc.

MILLER, Samuel V.
PO Box 19032
Green Bay, WI 54307
Tel: (920) 661 - 1111
Fax:(920) 661 - 2222
TF: (800) 232 - 5432

Serves As:
- Chairman, President and Chief Exec. Officer, American Medical Security Group, Inc.

MILLER, Sandra
511 Theodore Fremd Ave.
Rye, NY 10580
Tel: (914) 925 - 6047
Fax:(914) 921 - 3758

Serves As:
- Director, Public Affairs (Westchester), Consolidated Edison Co. of New York, Inc.

MILLER, Sharon
P.O. Box 407
Lakeland, FL 33802-0407
Tel: (863) 688 - 1188
Fax:(863) 616 - 5755

Serves As:
- Executive Director, Publix Super Markets Charities, Inc., Publix Super Markets, Inc.

MILLER, Stuart A.
700 N.W. 107th Ave.
Miami, FL 33172
Tel: (305) 559 - 4000
Fax:(305) 229 - 6453
TF: (800) 741 - 4663

Serves As:
- President and Chief Exec. Officer, Lennar Corp.

MILLER, T. Michael
One Beacon St.
Boston, MA 02108
Tel: (617) 725 - 6000

Serves As:
- President and Chief Exec. Officer, OneBeacon Insurance

MILLER, Teri L.
2050 Spectrum Blvd. Tel: (954) 308 - 7600
Fort Lauderdale, FL 33309 Fax:(954) 351 - 8117
terilmiller@sherion.com

Serves As:
- Director, Strategic Analysis, Spherion Corp.

Responsibilities include shareholder relations.

MILLIGAN, Rene
451 Florida St. Tel: (225) 288 - 7106
Baton Rouge, LA 70801-1765 Fax:(225) 388 - 7848
rene_milligan@albemarle.com

Serves As:
- Marketing Communications Representative, Albemarle Corp.

MILLIKEN, Roger
920 Milliken Rd. Tel: (864) 503 - 2020
Spartanburg, SC 29304 Fax:(864) 503 - 2100

Serves As:
- Chairman and Chief Exec. Officer, Milliken & Co.

MILLS, Andy
One Medline Place Tel: (847) 949 - 5500
Mundelein, IL 60060 Fax:(800) 351 - 1512
TF: (800) 633 - 5463

Serves As:
- President, Medline Industries, Inc.

MILLS, Bytha
5445 Corporate Dr. Tel: (248) 952 - 2500
Suite 200 Fax:(248) 952 - 2501
Troy, MI 48098-2683
bmills@intermet.com

Serves As:
- Vice President, Administration, Intermet Corp.

Responsibilities include public affairs.

MILLS, Charles A.
500 N. Akard St. Tel: (214) 397 - 3000
Suite 4300 Fax:(214) 397 - 3376
Dallas, TX 75201-3331 TF: (800) 423 - 8006

Serves As:
- V. President, Human Resources and Security, ENSCO Internat'l Inc.

MILLS, Charles S.
One Medline Place Tel: (847) 949 - 5500
Mundelein, IL 60060 Fax:(800) 351 - 1512
TF: (800) 633 - 5463

Serves As:
- Chief Exec. Officer, Medline Industries, Inc.

MILLS, Fred
P.O. Box 1595 Tel: (317) 261 - 8261
Indianapolis, IN 46206-1595 Fax:(317) 630 - 5726

Serves As:
- Director, Government Affairs, IPL (an AES Company)

MILLS, Gerald T.
3402 E. University Dr. Tel: (602) 794 - 9600
Phoenix, AZ 85034 Fax:(602) 794 - 9601

Serves As:
- Senior V. President, Human Resources, Eagle-Picher Industries, Inc.

MILLS, Gordon R. "Pete"
1717 Pennsylvania Ave. NW Tel: (202) 293 - 8550
Suite 700 Fax:(202) 974 - 1128
Washington, DC 20006
pete_mills@countrywide.com

Serves As:
- Senior V. President, Legislative/Regulatory Affairs, Countrywide Home Loans Inc.

MILLS, Josephine
1345 Ave. of the Americas Tel: (212) 282 - 5609
27th Floor Fax:(212) 282 - 6086
New York, NY 10020

Serves As:
- Director, Global Government Affairs, Avon Products, Inc.

Responsibilities include political action.

MILLS, Kelli A.
1425 K St. NW Tel: (202) 408 - 0090
Suite 650 Fax:(202) 408 - 1750
Washington, DC 20005
kelli.mills@roche.com

Registered Federal Lobbyist.
Serves As:
- Assistant Director, Federal Government Affairs, Hoffmann-La Roche Inc. (Roche)

MILLS, Steven R.
P.O. Box 1470 Tel: (217) 424 - 5200
Decatur, IL 62525 TF: (800) 637 - 5843

Serves As:
- PAC Treasurer, Archer Daniels Midland Co. (ADM)

MILLS, Vonda
P.O. Box 4030 Tel: (303) 277 - 5816
M/S NH345 Fax:(303) 277 - 6082
Golden, CO 80401-0030

Serves As:
- Chief People Officer, Coors Brewing Co.

MILLS, William R.
P.O. Box 471 Tel: (570) 286 - 3229
Sunbury, PA 17801 Fax:(570) 286 - 3625

Serves As:
- Senior V. President, Finance; and Treasurer, Weis Markets, Inc.

Responsibilities include shareholder relations.

MILNES, William R.
P.O. Box 186 Tel: (802) 223 - 6131
Montpelier, VT 05601 Fax:(802) 223 - 4229
milnesw@bcbsvt.com TF: (800) 255 - 4550

Serves As:
- President and Chief Exec. Officer, Blue Cross and Blue Shield of Vermont

MILO, Yori
7001 220th S.W. Tel: (425) 918 - 5900
Mountlake Terrace, WA 98043-2124 Fax:(425) 918 - 5635
TF: (800) 422 - 0032

Serves As:
- Exec. V. President, Chief Legal and Public Policy Officer, Premera Blue Cross

MILSTEIN, Monroe G.
1830 Route 130 Tel: (609) 387 - 7800
Burlington, NJ 08016 Ext: 1201
monroe.milstein@coat.com Fax:(609) 239 - 8242

Serves As:
- Chairman, President and Chief Exec. Officer, Burlington Coat Factory Warehouse Corp.

Responsibilities include corporate philanthropy.

MILTON, Jr., John D.
P.O. Box 4667 Tel: (904) 355 - 1781
Jacksonville, FL 32201 Fax:(904) 355 - 0817

Serves As:
- Exec. V. President, Treasurer and Chief Financial Officer, Florida Rock Industries, Inc.

Responsibilities include political action and corporate philanthropy.

MINARDI, Samuel A.
Seven Greenbrier St. Tel: (304) 345 - 4695
Charleston, WV 25311 Fax:(304) 345 - 4571

Serves As:
- Manager, State Government Affairs (WV), Allegheny Energy Inc.

MINDE, Kathy
P.O. Box 799900 Tel: (972) 497 - 5000
Dallas, TX 75379-9900 Fax:(972) 497 - 5292

Serves As:
- Treasurer, Lennox Employee Advocacy Program, Lennox Internat'l

MINEHART, Paul
340 Kingsland St. Tel: (973) 562 - 6595
Nutley, NJ 07110-1199 Fax:(973) 562 - 2208
paul.minehart@roche.com

Serves As:
- Director, Corporate and Business Communications, Hoffmann-La Roche Inc. (Roche)

MINELLA, Lynn C.
7201 Hamilton Blvd. Tel: (610) 481 - 6667
Allentown, PA 18195-1501 Fax:(610) 841 - 5900
minelllc@airproducts.com

Serves As:
- V. President, Human Resouces, Air Products and Chemicals, Inc.

MINEO, John
6363 Main St. Tel: (716) 635 - 5000
Williamsville, NY 14221 Fax:(716) 633 - 0898
TF: (800) 522 - 2522

Serves As:
- V. President, General Counsel and Corporate Secretary, Tops Markets LLC

Responsibilities include government relations.

MINOR, Bill
198 Champion Ct. Tel: (408) 943 - 2600
San Jose, CA 95134 Fax:(408) 943 - 4730

Serves As:
- V. President, Human Resources, Cypress Semiconductor Corp.

MINOR, III, G. Gilmore
P.O. Box 27626 Tel: (804) 747 - 9794
Richmond, VA 23261-7626 Fax:(804) 270 - 7281

Serves As:
- Chairman of the Board, Owens & Minor, Inc.

MINOTT, Darrell
1100 N. King St. Fax:(302) 432 - 0705
0127 TF: (302) 432 - 0039
Wilmington, DE 19880-127
darrell.minott@mbna.com

Registered Federal Lobbyist.
Serves As:
- Exec. V. President, Federal Government Affairs, MBNA Corp.

MINSHALL, Janice
One GEICO Plaza Tel: (301) 986 - 3000
Washington, DC 20076 Fax:(301) 986 - 2068

Serves As:
- Assistant V. President, Communications, GEICO Corp.

MINTER, George A.
P.O. Box 13287 Tel: (816) 467 - 3772
Kansas City, MO 64199-3287 Fax:(816) 467 - 3005
george.minter@aquila.com

Serves As:
- V. President, Corporate Communications, Aquila, Inc.

MINTZ, Bill
2000 Post Oak Blvd., Suite 100 Tel: (713) 296 - 7276
Houston, TX 77056-4400 Fax:(713) 296 - 6452
bill.mintz@apachecorp.com TF: (800) 874 - 3262

Serves As:
- Director, Public and International Affairs, Apache Corp.

MINTZ, Robert
12015 115th Ave. NE Tel: (425) 605 - 6165
Building E, Suite 220 Fax:(425) 914 - 2967
Kirkland, WA 98034

Serves As:
- Manager, Public Relations, DHL Holdings (USA), Inc.

MIRE, Evelyn M.
601 Jefferson St. Tel: (713) 753 - 2633
Houston, TX 77002 Fax:(713) 759 - 5353

Serves As:
- V. President, Investor Relations, Kellogg Brown and Root

MIRE, Weldon J.
601 Jefferson St. Tel: (713) 753 - 2000
Houston, TX 77002 Fax:(713) 753 - 5353

Serves As:
- V. President, Human Resources, Kellogg Brown and Root

MISENER, Paul E.
126 C St. NW Tel: (202) 347 - 7390
Suite Three
Washington, DC 20001

Registered Federal Lobbyist.
Serves As:
- V. President, Global Public Policy, Amazon.com, Inc.

MITAU, Lee R.
P.O. Box 1441 Tel: (612) 623 - 6000
Minneapolis, MN 55440-1441 Fax:(612) 623 - 6777
TF: (800) 328 - 0211

Serves As:
- Chairman of the Board, Graco Inc.

MITCHELL, David F.
401 Ninth St. NW Tel: (202) 331 - 8090
Suite 1100 Fax:(202) 331 - 1181
Washington, DC 20004
dmitchel@duke-energy.com

Serves As:
- Director, EHS Federal Government Affairs, Duke Energy Corp.

MITCHELL, Eileen
225 W. Randolph St. Tel: (312) 220 - 2377
27 B Fax:(312) 727 - 3722
Chicago, IL 60606 TF: (800) 327 - 9346

Serves As:
- Senior V. President, SBC Illinois

MITCHELL, George J.
500 S. Buena Vista St. Tel: (818) 560 - 1000
Burbank, CA 91521 Fax:(818) 560 - 1930

Serves As:
- Chairman of the Board, The Walt Disney Company

MITCHELL, Harry J.
1500 MacCorckle Ave., S.E. Tel: (304) 344 - 7562
Charleston, WV 25314
harry.j.mitchell@verizon.com

Serves As:
- Director, Mid-Atlantic Bureau Media Relations, Verizon Communications Inc.

MITCHELL, Janet D.
9125 Rehco Rd. Tel: (858) 453 - 7845
San Diego, CA 92121-2270 Fax:(858) 677 - 3489

Serves As:
- Senior V. President, Human Resources and Administration, PETCO Animal Supplies, Inc.

MITCHELL, Jeanne
2000 K St., NW Tel: (202) 862 - 0200
Suite 710 Fax:(202) 862 - 0269
Washington, DC 20006

Registered Federal Lobbyist.
Serves As:
- Washington Representative, House of Representatives, Exxon Mobil Corp.

MITCHELL, Jill
1803 Gears Rd. Tel: (281) 591 - 4166
Houston, TX 60601 Fax:(281) 591 - 4134
jille.mitchell@fmcti.com

Serves As:
- Supervisor, Communications Projects and Programs, FMC Technologies, Inc.

MITCHELL, Michael
250 E. Fifth St. Tel: (513) 784 - 8959
Cincinnati, OH 45202 Fax:(513) 784 - 8030
mmitchell@chiquita.com

Serves As:
- Director, Corporate Communications, Chiquita Brands Internat'l, Inc.

MITCHELL, Michael
655 15th St., NW Tel: (202) 638 - 6890
Suite 410 Fax:(202) 220 - 3619
Washington, DC 20005

Serves As:
- Representative, UST Inc.

MITCHELL, Mike
1550 Crystal Dr. Tel: (703) 413 - 5601
Crystal Square 2, Suite 300 Fax:(703) 413 - 5636
Arlington, VA 22202

Serves As:
- Representative, Lockheed Martin Corp.

MITCHELL, Robert D.
300 Chestnut Ridge Rd Tel: (201) 307 - 3701
Woodcliff Lake, NJ 07677 Fax:(201) 307 - 3607

Serves As:
- Manager, Corporate Communications, BMW (U.S.) Holding Corp.

MITCHELL, Ruth
5820 Westown Pkwy. Tel: (515) 267 - 2893
West Des Moines, IA 50266-8223 Fax:(515) 267 - 2362

Serves As:
- Assistant V. President, Communications, Hy-Vee, Inc.

MITCHELL, Steven A.
3901 Elmswick Ct. Tel: (919) 662 - 3889
Apex, NC 27502 Fax:(919) 662 - 3217

Serves As:
- Associate Director, Government Affairs, (Novartis Pharmaceuticals Corp.), Novartis Corporation

MITCHELL, Susan P.
1211 Avenue of the Americas Tel: (212) 536 - 1390
New York, NY 10036 Fax:(212) 536 - 1912
susan.mitchell@cit.com

Serves As:
- Exec. V. President, Human Resources, The CIT Group, Inc.

MITCHELL, Suzanne
One Owens Corning Pkwy. Tel: (419) 248 - 6255
Toledo, OH 43659 Fax:(419) 248 - 6227
suzanne.mitchell@owenscorning.com TF: (800) 438 - 7465

Serves As:
- Business Media Relations Senior Specialist, Owens Corning

MITCHELL, William
50 Marcus Dr. Tel: (631) 847 - 2000
Melville, NY 11747

Serves As:
- Chief Exec. Officer, Arrow Electronics, Inc.

MITCHELSON, Randy K.
607 E. Adams St.
Springfield, IL 62739
Tel: (217) 535 - 5059
Fax:(217) 535 - 5095

Serves As:
• Director, Government Relations, (AmerenCIPS), Ameren Corp.

MIX, Douglas
P.O. Box 35920
Cleveland, OH 44135-0920
Tel: (216) 898 - 1800
Fax:(216) 898 - 2393

Serves As:
• V. President, Regulatory Affairs, Electrolux North America, Inc.

MIXON, III, A Malachi
One Invacare Way
Elyria, OH 44035
Tel: (440) 329 - 6000
Fax:(440) 366 - 9008
TF: (800) 333 - 6900

Serves As:
• Chairman and Chief Exec. Officer, Invacare Corp.

MIZE, Gregory
P.O. Box 7045
Troy, MI 48007-7045
Tel: (248) 362 - 4400
Ext: 211
Fax:(248) 362 - 0718

Serves As:
• V. President, Investor Relations, Handleman Company
Responsibilities also include corporate communications.

MLYNARCZYK, Mark
1658 N. Milwaukee
M/S PMB293
Chicago, IL 60647-5412
mark.mlynarczyk@roche.com
Tel: (312) 492 - 9691
Fax:(312) 492 - 9693

Serves As:
• Manager, Regional Government Affairs, Hoffmann-La Roche Inc. (Roche)

MOCHA, Jeff
U.S. Bank Plaza
505 N. Seventh St. Ste 2000
St. Louis, MO 63101
Tel: (314) 259 - 6200
Fax:(314) 621 - 1778

Serves As:
• Manager, Public Relations, Hardee's Food Systems, Inc.

MOCK, Kathleen A.
3535 Blue Cross Rd.
Eagan, MN 55122--115
Tel: (651) 662 - 2580
Fax:(651) 662 - 6201
TF: (800) 382 - 2000

Serves As:
• V. President, Policy and Legislative Affairs, Blue Cross and Blue Shield of Minnesota

MODI, David T.
1501 Lee Hwy.
Suite 140
Arlington, VA 22209-1109
Tel: (703) 525 - 4015
Fax:(703) 525 - 0327

Registered Federal Lobbyist.
Serves As:
• V. President, Government and Public Affairs, American Standard Companies Inc.

MODJTABAI, Avid
420 Montgomery St.
San Francisco, CA 94104
Tel: (415) 396 - 3612
TF: (800) 411 - 4932

Serves As:
• Exec. V. President, Human Resources, Wells Fargo & Co.

MODLIN, Kathleen
21001 Van Born Rd.
Taylor, MI 48180
Tel: (313) 792 - 6382
Fax:(313) 792 - 6666

Serves As:
• Director, Corporate Communications, Masco Corp.

MODUGNO, Al
1166 Ave. of the Americas
New York, NY 10036
alfred.j.modugno@marsh.com
Tel: (212) 345 - 2448
Fax:(212) 345 - 2309

Serves As:
• Senior V. President, Media Relations, Marsh Inc.

MOEHLE, Mary Jo
12405 Powerscourt Dr.
St. Louis, MO 63131
mmoehle@chartercom.com
Tel: (314) 543 - 2397
Fax:(314) 965 - 0571

Serves As:
• Senior Director, Investor Relations, Charter Communications, Inc.

MOELLER, Phil
Market Square, 801 Pennsylvania Ave., NW
Suite 640, West Tower
Washington, DC 20004-2615
philmoeller@alliantenergy.com
Tel: (202) 347 - 8132
Fax:(202) 347 - 8136

Registered Federal Lobbyist.
Serves As:
• Washington Representative and PAC Contact, Alliant Energy Corp.

MOERKE, Audrey
P.O. Box 482
Milwaukee, WI 53201-0482
amoerke@mbco.com
Tel: (414) 931 - 3365
Fax:(414) 931 - 6352

Serves As:
• Senior Communication Programs Producer, Miller Brewing Co.

MOERSDORF, Wolfram
P.O. Box 2601
Troy, MI 48007-2601
Tel: (248) 643 - 3500
Fax:(248) 643 - 3687

Serves As:
• Chairman of the Board, Thyssenkrupp Budd Company

MOFFET, Barbara S.
P.O. Box 98199
Washington, DC 20090-8199
bmoffett@ngs.org
Tel: (202) 857 - 7756
Fax:(202) 828 - 6679

Serves As:
• Director, Media Relations, Nat'l Geographic Soc.

MOFFETT, James R.
P.O. Box 51777
New Orleans, LA 70151
Tel: (504) 582 - 4000
Fax:(504) 582 - 1847
TF: (800) 535 - 7094

Serves As:
• Chairman of the Board, Freeport-McMoRan Copper and Gold Inc.

MOFFITT, Gus
1095 Morris Ave.
Union, NJ 07083

Serves As:
• V. President, Global Safety and Environmental Affairs, Schering-Plough Corporation

MOGLIA, Joseph H.
4211 S. 102nd St.
Omaha, NE 68127-1031
Tel: (402) 597 - 5658
Fax:(402) 597 - 7789
TF: (800) 237 - 8692

Serves As:
• Chief Exec. Officer, Ameritrade Holding Corp.

MOHAPATRA, Surya N.
One Malcolm Ave.
Teterboro, NJ 07608
Tel: (201) 393 - 5000
Fax:(201) 393 - 4755
TF: (800) 222 - 0446

Serves As:
• President and Chief Exec. Officer, Quest Diagnostics Inc.

MOHNEY, Mike
P.O. Box 2020
Springdale, AR 72765-2020
mike.mohney@tyson.com
Tel: (479) 290 - 4000
Fax:(479) 290 - 7984
TF: (800) 643 - 3410

Serves As:
• Director, Internal Communications, Tyson Foods, Inc.

MOHR, Marshall
691 S. Milpitas Blvd.
Milpitas, CA 95035-5473
marshall_mohr@adaptec.com
Tel: (408) 957 - 6773
Fax:(408) 262 - 2533

Serves As:
• Chief Financial Officer, Adaptec, Inc.
Responsibilities include investor relations.

MOHRBACHER, James A.
P.O. Box 1231
Madison, WI 53701-1231
jmohrbacher@mge.com
Tel: (608) 252 - 7000
Fax:(608) 252 - 7098
TF: (800) 356 - 6423

Serves As:
• Manager, Government and Business Relations, Madison Gas and Electric Co.

MOLENDORP, Dayton H.
P.O. Box 368
Indianapolis, IN 46206-0368
Tel: (317) 285 - 1370
Fax:(317) 285 - 1979

Serves As:
• President and Chief Exec. Officer, American United Life Insurance Co.

MOLER, Elizabeth A. "Betsy"
101 Constitution Ave., NW
Suite 400 East
Washington, DC 20001
elizabeth.moler@exeloncorp.com
Tel: (202) 347 - 7500
Fax:(202) 347 - 7501

Registered Federal Lobbyist.
Serves As:
- Exec. V. President, Government and Environmental Affairs and Public Policy, Exelon Corp.

MOLETTERI, Patrick
One AT&T Way
Bedminster, NJ 07921-0752
Tel: (908) 234 - 3020

Serves As:
- Treasurer, AT&T PAC, AT&T

MOLINARO, Peter A.
1776 I St. NW
Suite 1050
Washington, DC 20006
Tel: (202) 429 - 3400
Fax:(202) 429 - 3467

Registered Federal Lobbyist.
Serves As:
- V. President, Federal and State Government Affairs, The Dow Chemical Company

Responsibilities include political action.

MOLINO, Patricia
One Johnson & Johnson Plaza
New Brunswick, NJ 08933-7204
pmolino@corus.jnj.com
Tel: (908) 524 - 3373
Fax:(908) 524 - 3621
TF: (800) 635 - 6789

Serves As:
- V. President, Corporate Communications, Johnson & Johnson

MOLLEN, John T. "Jack"
P.O. Box 9103
Hopkinton, MA 01748
Tel: (508) 435 - 1000
Fax:(508) 497 - 6912
TF: (800) 424 - 3622

Serves As:
- Senior V. President, Human Resources, EMC Corp.

MOLNAR, Dr. Attila
100 Bayer Rd.
Pittsburgh, PA 15205-9741
Tel: (412) 777 - 2000
TF: (800) 662 - 2927

Serves As:
- President and Chief Exec. Officer, Bayer Corporation

MOLONEY, John M.
1200 Wilson Blvd.
Arlington, VA 22209-2305
Tel: (703) 465 - 3500

Serves As:
- Director, Legislative Affairs, The Boeing Co.

MOLTNER, Bill
P.O. Box 799900
Dallas, TX 75379-9900
bill.moltner@lennoxintl.com
Tel: (972) 497 - 6670
Fax:(972) 497 - 5292

Serves As:
- V. President, Investor Relations, Lennox Internat'l

MOMEYER, Alan
667 Madison Ave.
New York, NY 10021-8087
amomeyer@loews.com
Tel: (212) 521 - 2500
Fax:(212) 521 - 2466

Serves As:
- V. President, Human Resources, Loews Corporation

MONAHAN, Michael
4211 W. Boyscout Blvd.
Tampa, FL 33607
Tel: (813) 871 - 4132
Fax:(813) 871 - 4399

Serves As:
- Director, Corporate Communications, Walter Industries, Inc.

MONAHAN, Michael J.
Ecolab Center
370 N. Wabasha St.
St. Paul, MN 55102
michael.monahan@ecolab.com
Tel: (651) 293 - 2809
Fax:(651) 225 - 3123

Serves As:
- V. President, External Relations, Ecolab Inc.

Responsibilities include corporate contributions and investor relations.

MONBERG, Kirsten
One i2 Pl.
11701 Luna Rd.
Dallas, TX 75234
kirsten_monberg@i2.com
Tel: (469) 357 - 4966
Fax:(469) 357 - 3677

Serves As:
- Senior Specialist, Public Relations, i2 Technologies, Inc.

MONCHEIN, Minta A.
1100 Terminal Tower
50 Public Square
Cleveland, OH 44113-2203
Tel: (216) 621 - 6060
Fax:(216) 263 - 4808

Serves As:
- V. President and Director, Human Resources, Forest City Enterprises, Inc.

MONFRE, Katie
270 E. Kilbourn
Milwaukee, WI 53202
Tel: (414) 347 - 6480
Fax:(414) 347 - 6696
TF: (800) 558 - 9900

Serves As:
- Director, Corporate Relations, Mortgage Guaranty Insurance Corp. (MGIC)

MONFRIED, David M.
200 Park Ave.
New York, NY 10166
Tel: (212) 578 - 2211
TF: (800) 638 - 5433

Serves As:
- Senior V. President, Corporate Communications, MetLife, Inc.

MONFRIED, Martha J.
P.O. Box 4569
Atlanta, GA 30302-4569
Tel: (404) 584 - 4000
Fax:(404) 584 - 3479

Serves As:
- Director, Public Affairs, AGL Resources, Inc.

MONGAN, Adrienne
Centre Square, West Tower
1500 Market St., Suite 3900
Philadelphia, PA 19102-2112
amongan@lfg.com
Tel: (215) 448 - 1400
Fax:(215) 448 - 3962
TF: (877) 275 - 5462

Serves As:
- Manager, Strategic Communications, Lincoln Financial Group

MONGELLI, John M.
1000 Alderman Dr.
Alpharetta, GA 30005-4101
Tel: (770) 752 - 6000
Fax:(770) 752 - 6167

Serves As:
- V. President, Corporate Investor Relations, ChoicePoint Inc.

MONROE, Joanna
P.O. Box 2910
Tacoma, WA 98401-2910
Tel: (253) 383 - 9101
TF: (800) 610 - 8920

Serves As:
- V. President, Legal and Governmental Affairs, Labor Ready, Inc.

MONROE, Michael J.
127 Public Square
Cleveland, OH 44114
michael_monroe@keybank.com
Tel: (216) 689 - 3509
Fax:(216) 689 - 0848

Serves As:
- Exec. V. President, Public Affairs, KeyCorp

MONROY, Woody
P.O. Box 66360
Scotts Valley, CA 95067-0360
woody_monroy@seagate.com
Tel: (831) 439 - 2838
Fax:(831) 438 - 4127

Serves As:
- Exec. Director, Corporate Communications, Seagate Technology

MONSEAU, Marc
One Johnson & Johnson Plaza
New Brunswick, NJ 08933-7204
mmonseau@corus.jnj.com
Tel: (732) 524 - 1130
Fax:(732) 214 - 0334
TF: (800) 635 - 6789

Serves As:
- Assistant Director, Corporate Communications, Johnson & Johnson

MONTAGUE, Karen
P.O. Box 500
Beaverton, OR 97077
Tel: (503) 627 - 7111
Fax:(503) 567 - 3449
TF: (800) 835 - 9433

Serves As:
- Contact, Tektronix Foundation, Tektronix, Inc.

MONTAGUE, Tonda A.
P.O. Box 36611
Dallas, TX 75235-1611
Tel: (214) 792 - 4362

Serves As:
- Director, Employee Communications, Southwest Airlines Co.

MONTAGUE, William P.
P.O. Box 810
Amherst, NY 14226
Tel: (716) 689 - 4972
Fax:(716) 568 - 6098

Serves As:
- Chief Exec. Officer, Mark IV Industries, Inc.

MONTELEONE, Robert
40 Lane Rd.
Fairfield, NJ 07004
Tel: (973) 882 - 9000

Serves As:
- V. President, Human Resources, Covanta Energy Corp.

MONTER, Cathy
P.O. Box 351
Barberton, OH 44203
Tel: (330) 860 - 2620
Fax:(330) 860 - 1886

Serves As:
- Manager, Human Resources, The Babcock & Wilcox Company

MONTGOMERY, Glenn A.
P.O. Box 1615
Warren, NJ 07061-1615
gmontgomery@chubb.com
Tel: (908) 903 - 2365
Fax:(908) 903 - 2027

Serves As:
- Financial Information Contact, The Chubb Corp.

MONTGOMERY, Jacque
10350 E. Dakota Ave.
Denver, CO 80231-1314
jacque.montgomery@kp.org
Tel: (303) 344 - 7410

Serves As:
- Media Representative - Colorado Region, Kaiser Permanente

MONTGOMERY, Larry
N56 W17000 Ridgewood Dr.
Menomonee Falls, WI 53051
Tel: (262) 703 - 7000
Fax:(262) 703 - 6143

Serves As:
- Chairman and Chief Exec. Officer, Kohl's Corp.

MONTGOMERY, Paul
P.O. Box 431
Kingsport, TN 37662
pmontgomery@eastman.com
Tel: (423) 229 - 1413
Fax:(423) 229 - 8280

Serves As:
- Director, Community Relations and Corporate Travel, Eastman Chemical Co.

Responsibilities include corporate philanthropy.

MONTGOMERY, Paul
Four Tesseneer Dr.
Highland Heights, KY 41076
Tel: (859) 572 - 8684
Fax:(859) 572 - 8458

Serves As:
- Director, Finance and Investor Relations, General Cable Corp.

MONTGOMERY, Robin
1426 Main St.
Columbia, SC 29218
rmontgomery@scana.com
Tel: (803) 576 - 8649
Fax:(803) 217 - 8825

Serves As:
- Manager, Public Affairs, SCANA Corp.

MONTRONE, Paul M.
Liberty Ln.
Hampton, NH 03842
Tel: (603) 929 - 5911
Fax:(603) 929 - 2379

Serves As:
- Chairman and Chief Exec. Officer, Fisher Scientific Internat'l Inc.

MOODY, Dave
310 E. Daphne Rd.
Fox Point, WI 53217
moodyd2@wyeth.com
Tel: (414) 352 - 1016

Serves As:
- Director, State Government Affairs, Wyeth Pharmaceuticals

MOODY, Jr., James L.
200 Milik St.
Carteret, NJ 07008-1194
Tel: (732) 499 - 3000
Fax:(732) 499 - 6872

Serves As:
- Chairman of the Board, Pathmark Stores Inc.

MOODY, Nancy
101 S. Washington Square, Suite 700
Lansing, MI 48933-1708
Tel: (517) 371 - 2350
Fax:(517) 371 - 1016

Serves As:
- Director, State Government Affairs, DTE Energy Co.

MOODY, Robert L.
One Moody Plaza
Galveston, TX 77550-7999
Tel: (409) 763 - 4661
Fax:(409) 766 - 6933
TF: (800) 899 - 6502

Serves As:
- Chairman and Chief Exec. Officer, American Nat'l Insurance Co.

MOONEY, James P.
127 Public Square
1500 Key Tower
Cleveland, OH 44114-1221
Tel: (216) 781 - 0083
Fax:(216) 781 - 1502
TF: (800) 519 - 0083

Serves As:
- Chief Exec. Officer, OM Group, Inc.

MOONVES, Leslie
7800 Beverly Blvd.
Los Angeles, CA 90036
Tel: (323) 575 - 2345

Serves As:
- Chairman, President and Chief Exec. Officer, (CBS Television), Viacom Inc./CBS Corp.

MOOR, Karl P.
601 Pennsylvania Ave. NW
Suite 800
Washington, DC 20004
Tel: (202) 261 - 5000
Fax:(202) 296 - 7937

Registered Federal Lobbyist.
Serves As:
- Representative, Southern Company

MOORE, Bill
7001 220th S.W.
MS 354
Mountlake Terrace, WA 98043-2124
bill.moore@premera.com
Tel: (425) 918 - 4720

Serves As:
- Manager, Legislative Policy, Premera Blue Cross

MOORE, Cheryl
P.O. Box 29269
Richmond, VA 23242-9269
Tel: (804) 484 - 6273
Fax:(804) 484 - 7701

Serves As:
- Director, Corporate Communications, Performance Food Group Co.

MOORE, Dennis M.
469 N. Harrison St.
Princeton, NJ 08543-5297
Tel: (609) 683 - 5900
Fax:(609) 497 - 7269

Serves As:
- V. President, Human Resources, Church & Dwight Co., Inc.

MOORE, Erin
650 Madison Ave.
New York, NY 10022
Tel: (212) 318 - 7402
Fax:(212) 888 - 5780
TF: (800) 377 - 7656

Serves As:
- Media Contact, Polo Ralph Lauren

MOORE, Frank
1840 Century Park East
Los Angeles, CA 90067-2199
f.moore@ngc.com
Tel: (310) 201 - 3335
Fax:(310) 556 - 4561

Serves As:
- Director, Media Relations, Northrop Grumman Corp.

MOORE, Ian
1211 Ave. of the Americas
New York, NY 10036
Tel: (212) 852 - 7000

Serves As:
- Exec. V. President, Human Resources, News Corporation Ltd.

MOORE, Jay S.
3525 Fairystone Park Hwy.
Bassett, VA 24055
jsmoore@bassettfurniture.com
Tel: (276) 629 - 6450
Fax:(276) 629 - 6418

Serves As:
- Director, Corporate and Community Affairs, Bassett Furniture Industries, Inc.

MOORE, Jessica
1150 17th St. NW
Suite 400
Washington, DC 20036
jessica.moore@disney.com
Tel: (202) 222 - 4735
Fax:(202) 222 - 4799

Serves As:
- Manager, Government Relations, The Walt Disney Company

MOORE, John R.
3125 Myers St.
Riverside, CA 92503
Tel: (909) 351 - 3500
Fax:(909) 351 - 3931

Serves As:
- V. President, Human Resources, Fleetwood Enterprises

MOORE, John W.
2700 Lone Oak Pkwy.
M/S MEM 1150
Eagan, MN 55121
john.moore@nwa.com
Tel: (901) 922 - 0382
Fax:(901) 922 - 0375

Serves As:
- Managing Director, State and Local Affairs, Northwest Airlines, Inc.

MOORE, Julie
4650 Cushing Pkwy.
Fremont, CA 94538-6470
Tel: (510) 572 - 0200
Fax:(510) 572 - 6454

Serves As:
- Corporate Contributions Contact, Lam Research Corp.

MOORE, Julie W.
604 W. 14th St.
Austin, TX 78701
julie_moore@oxy.com
Tel: (512) 476 - 2245
Fax:(512) 473 - 8476

Serves As:
- Manager - Texas State Government Affairs, Occidental Chemical Corp.

MOORE, Kevin
P.O. Box 1564
New Haven, CT 06506-0901
Tel: (203) 499 - 2000
Fax:(203) 499 - 3626
TF: (800) 722 - 5584

Serves As:
- Director, Communications, The United Illuminating Company

MOORE, Laura K.
100 Throckmorton St.
Suite 1800
Fort Worth, TX 76102
laura.moore@radioshack.com
Tel: (817) 415 - 3327
Fax:(817) 415 - 2335

Serves As:
- Senior V. President and Chief Communications Officer, Radio Shack Corporation

MOORE, Linda
415 Holiday Dr.
Pittsburgh, PA 15220-2793
lmoore@lbfosterco.com
Tel: (412) 928 - 3417
Fax:(412) 928 - 7891
TF: (800) 255 - 4500

Serves As:
- Contact, L.B. Foster Charitable Trust, L. B. Foster Co.

MOORE, Lynn
1201 Winterson Rd.
Linthicum, MD 21090
Tel: (410) 694 - 5700
Fax:(410) 694 - 5750

Serves As:
- V. President, Global Human Resources, CIENA Corp.

MOORE, Patrick J.
150 N. Michigan Ave.
Suite 1700
Chicago, IL 60601-7568
Tel: (312) 346 - 6600
Fax:(312) 580 - 4919

Serves As:
- Chairman and Chief Exec. Officer, Smurfit-Stone Container

MOORE, Richard
P.O. Box 4569
Atlanta, GA 30302-4569
rmoore@aglresources.com
Tel: (404) 584 - 9470
Fax:(404) 584 - 3479

Serves As:
- Director, Government Affairs and Economic Development, AGL Resources, Inc.

MOORE, Rosemary
P.O. Box 66100
Chicago, IL 60666
Tel: (847) 700 - 4000
Fax:(847) 700 - 4899

Serves As:
- Senior Vice President, Corporate and Gov. Affairs, United Airlines

MOORE, Steve E.
P.O. Box 321
M/C 1100
Oklahoma City, OK 73101-0321
Tel: (405) 553 - 3203
Fax:(405) 553 - 3760

Serves As:
- Chairman, Chief Exec. Officer and President, OGE Energy Corp.

MOORE, Susan F.
1120 G St. NW
Suite 1050
Washington, DC 20005-3801
Tel: (202) 347 - 4446
Fax:(202) 347 - 7058

Serves As:
- V. President, Environmental Affairs, Georgia-Pacific Corp.

MOORE, Tiffany M.
1725 I St. NW
Suite 300
Washington, DC 20006
tiffany.moore@kellogg.com
Tel: (202) 349 - 3788
Fax:(202) 349 - 3789

Registered Federal Lobbyist.
Serves As:
- Associate Director, Government Relations, Kellogg Co.

MOORE, Walter K.
808 17th St. NW
Suite 250
Washington, DC 20006
wmoore@gene.com
Tel: (202) 296 - 7272
Fax:(202) 296 - 7290

Registered Federal Lobbyist.
Serves As:
- V. President, Government Affairs, Genentech, Inc.

MOORHEAD, Randall B.
1300 I St. NW
Suite 1070 East
Washington, DC 20005
Tel: (202) 962 - 8550
Fax:(202) 962 - 8560

Registered Federal Lobbyist.
Serves As:
- V. President, Government Affairs, Philips Electronics North America

MORABITO, John S.
2001 Pennsylvania Ave. NW
Suite 500
Washington, DC 20006
Tel: (202) 379 - 7100
Fax:(202) 466 - 7718

Registered Federal Lobbyist.
Serves As:
- Senior Director and Policy Counsel, Federal Affairs, Comcast Corporation

MORALES, Vincent
One PPG Pl.
Pittsburgh, PA 15272
Tel: (412) 434 - 3740
Fax:(412) 434 - 4666

Serves As:
- Director, Investor Relations, PPG Industries Inc.

MORALI, Philippe
400 N. McCarthy Blvd.
Milpitas, CA 95035
Tel: (408) 503 - 7000
Fax:(408) 503 - 2750

Serves As:
- Interim Chief Financial Officer, palmOne, Inc.

Responsibilities include investor relations.

MORAN, Jan
100 Jim Moran Blvd.
Deerfield Beach, FL 33442
Tel: (954) 429 - 2000
Fax:(954) 429 - 2300

Serves As:
- V. President, Community Relations and Marine Departments, JM Family Enterprises, Inc.

MORAN, Jim
SAFECO Plaza
Seattle, WA 98185
Tel: (206) 545 - 5291

Serves As:
- Representative, Community Relations, SAFECO Corp.

MORAN, Mike
1350 I St. NW
Suite 1000
Washington, DC 20005
mmoran@ford.com
Tel: (202) 962 - 5416
Fax:(202) 962 - 5417

Serves As:
- Director, Washington Regional Officer, Ford Motor Co.

MORAN, Patricia
100 Jim Moran Blvd.
Deerfield Beach, FL 33442
Tel: (954) 429 - 2000
Fax:(954) 429 - 2300

Serves As:
- Chairman of the Board, JM Family Enterprises, Inc.

MORAN, Thomas J.
320 Park Ave.
New York, NY 10022
Tel: (212) 224 - 1600
Fax:(212) 224 - 2518

Serves As:
- Chairman of the Board, President, and Chief Exec. Officer, Mutual of America Life Insurance Co.

MORAN, Tom
610 Opperman Dr.
Eagan, MN 55123-1340
thomas.moran@thomson.com
Tel: (651) 687 - 7000
Fax:(651) 687 - 7302
TF: (800) 328 - 9352

Serves As:
- Senior V. President, Human Resources, Thomson West

MORAN, Tracy
P.O. Box 34067
Seattle, WA 98124-1067
Tel: (206) 318 - 7806
Fax:(206) 318 - 0635

Serves As:
- Director, Investor Relations, Starbucks Corp.

MORAN, Ursula H.
One Geoffrey Way
Wayne, NJ 07470-2030
Tel: (973) 617 - 5756

Serves As:
- V. President, Investor Relations, Toys "R" Us, Inc.

MORANDE, Thomas
200 E. Randolph St.
Chicago, IL 60601-6436
Tel: (312) 782 - 5800
Fax:(312) 782 - 4339

Serves As:
- Treasurer, Jones Lang LaSalle Americas Inc. PAC, Jones Lang LaSalle Inc.

MOREAN, William D.
10560 Dr. Martin Luther King Jr. St. North
St. Petersburg, FL 33716
Tel: (727) 577 - 9749
Fax:(727) 579 - 8529

Serves As:
- Chairman of the Board, Jabil Circuit, Inc.

MOREAU, Andrew
One Allied Dr.
Little Rock, AR 72202
andrew.moreau@alltel.com
Tel: (501) 905 - 7962
Fax:(501) 905 - 6018

Serves As:
- V. President, Corporate Communications, ALLTEL

MOREL, Jr., Donald E.
101 Gordon Dr.
Lionville, PA 19341
Tel: (610) 594 - 2900
Fax:(610) 594 - 3000
TF: (800) 345 - 9800

Serves As:
- Chairman, President, and Chief Exec. Officer, West Pharmaceutical Services

MORELAND, Jeffrey R.
P.O. Box 961057
Fort Worth, TX 76161-2830
jeffrey.moreland@bnsf.com
Tel: (817) 352 - 1350
Fax:(817) 352 - 7111
TF: (800) 795 - 2673

Serves As:
- Exec. V. President, Law and Government Affairs and Secretary, Burlington Northern Santa Fe Corporation

MORELAND, Myra
47659 Halyard Dr.
Plymouth, MI 48170
Tel: (734) 207 - 6762
Fax:(734) 207 - 6500

Serves As:
- V. President, Corporate Affairs, Metaldyne Corp.

MORELLI, Carla A.
Ecolab Center
370 N. Wabasha St.
St. Paul, MN 55102
carla.morelli@ecolab.com
Tel: (651) 293 - 2148
Fax:(651) 225 - 3274

Serves As:
- Administrative Assistant, Ecolab Inc.

Responsibilities include government affairs.

MORETON, Mary
50 Beale St.
San Francisco, CA 94105-1895
Tel: (415) 768 - 1234
Fax:(415) 768 - 9038

Serves As:
- Manager, Human Resources, Bechtel Group, Inc.

MORFOGEN, Ann L.
550 Madison Ave.
New York, NY 10022-3211
ann_morfogen@sonyusa.com
Tel: (212) 833 - 6873
Fax:(212) 833 - 6862

Serves As:
- Senior V. President, Communications and Public Affairs; President, Sony USA Foundation, Sony Corp. of America

MORGAN, Charles D.
One Information Way
Little Rock, AR 72202
Tel: (501) 342 - 6161
Fax:(501) 342 - 3913

Serves As:
- Chairman and Company Leader, Acxiom Corporation

MORGAN, Eileen
40 Fountain Plaza
Buffalo, NY 14202
Tel: (716) 858 - 5000
Fax:(716) 858 - 5125

Serves As:
- V. President, Human Resources, Delaware North Companies

MORGAN, Gina
One Health Plaza
East Hanover, NJ 07936
Tel: (862) 778 - 5567
Fax:(862) 644 - 8585

Serves As:
- Exec. Director, Public Relations, (Novartis Pharmaceuticals Corp.), Novartis Corporation

MORGAN, J. Railton
1350 I St. NW
Suite 1000
Washington, DC 20005
Tel: (202) 962 - 5400
Fax:(202) 336 - 7223

Registered Federal Lobbyist.
Serves As:
- Legislative Manager; Energy, Environment, and Safety, Ford Motor Co.

MORGAN, James C.
3050 Bowers Ave.
P.O. Box 58039
Santa Clara, CA 95054-3299
Tel: (408) 727 - 5555
Fax:(408) 748 - 5119

Serves As:
- Chairman of the Board, Applied Materials, Inc.

MORGAN, Jason
One Gaylord Dr.
Nashville, TN 37214
Tel: (615) 316 - 6561
Fax:(615) 316 - 6751

Serves As:
- V. President, Strategic Planning and Investor Relations, Gaylord Entertainment Co.

MORGAN, Jeanette
P.O. Box 58090
M/S G2-129
Santa Clara, CA 95052-8090
jeanette.morgan@nsc.com
Tel: (408) 721 - 7874
Fax:(408) 739 - 9803

Serves As:
- Director, Worldwide Government Affairs, Nat'l Semiconductor Corp.

MORGAN, Jim
1121 L St., Suite 211
Sacramento, CA 95814
Tel: (916) 442 - 7288
Fax:(916) 442 - 7293

Serves As:
- Senior Associate Director, Government Affairs, Novartis Corporation

MORGAN, Joseph P.
P.O. Box 1167
Dayton, OH 45401-1167
joe.morgan@standardregister.com
Tel: (937) 913 - 6377
Fax:(937) 221 - 1239
TF: (800) 755 - 6405

Serves As:
- V. President and Chief Technology Officer, Standard Register Co.

Responsibilities include public affairs.

MORGAN, Marsha K.
P.O. Box 961057
Fort Worth, TX 76161-2830
marsha.morgan@bnsf.com
Tel: (817) 352 - 6452
Fax:(817) 352 - 7171

Serves As:
- V. President, Investor Relations, Burlington Northern Santa Fe Corporation

MORGAN, Michael K.
4111 E. 37th St., North
Wichita, KS 67220
Tel: (316) 828 - 5274
Fax:(316) 828 - 5739

Serves As:
- Director, Government and Public Affairs, Koch Industries, Inc.

MORGAN, Thomas I.
One Hughes Way
Orlando, FL 32805-2205
Tel: (407) 841 - 4755
Fax:(407) 649 - 1670

Serves As:
- Chief Exec. Officer, Hughes Supply, Inc.

MORGAN, Thomas Todd
P.O. Box 40
Austin, TX 78767
Tel: (512) 615 - 1108

Serves As:
- PAC Treasurer, Temple-Inland Inc.

MORGENSTERN, William E.
One Rentway Place
Erie, PA 16505
wmorgenstern@rentway.com
Tel: (814) 455 - 5378
Fax:(814) 461 - 5400
TF: (800) 736 - 8929

Serves As:
- Chairman and Chief Exec. Officer, Rent-Way, Inc.

MORGRIDGE, John P.
170 W. Tasman Dr.
San Jose, CA 95134-1706
jmorgridge@cisco.com
Tel: (408) 526 - 4000
Fax:(408) 526 - 4100
TF: (800) 553 - 6387

Serves As:
- Chairman of the Board, Cisco Systems, Inc.

MORIMURA, Takashi
400 California St.
San Francisco, CA 94104
Tel: (415) 765 - 0400
Fax:(415) 765 - 3257

Serves As:
- President and Chief Exec. Officer, Union Bank of California

MORIN, William G.
1400 I St. NW
Suite 540
Washington, DC 20005
william_morin@amat.com
Tel: (202) 638 - 4434

Registered Federal Lobbyist.
Serves As:
- Director, Government Affairs, Applied Materials, Inc.

MORITZ, Gloria
P.O. Box 2511
Houston, TX 77252-2511
Tel: (713) 420 - 2600
Fax:(713) 420 - 4993

Serves As:
- Coordinator, Community Relations, El Paso Corp.

MORLEY, Patricia
P.O. Box 2463
Houston, TX 77252-2463
Tel: (713) 241 - 0494
Fax:(713) 241 - 6988

Serves As:
- Manager, Corporate Communications, Shell Oil Co.

MOROVICH, Nancy C.
P.O. Box 61000
New Orleans, LA 70161
nmorovi@entergy.com
Tel: (504) 576 - 5506
Fax:(504) 576 - 4428

Serves As:
- V. President, Investor Relations, Entergy Corp.

MORRELL, Adrienne B.
2107 Wilson Blvd.
Arlington, VA 22201
adrienne.b.morrell@healthnet.com
Tel: (571) 227 - 6561
Fax:(571) 227 - 6709

Serves As:
- V. President, Government Relations; Contact Health Net Inc. PAC, Health Net, Inc.

MORRILL, James A.
1455 Pennsylvania Ave., N.W., Suite 1260
Washington, DC 20004
Tel: (202) 783 - 0350
Fax:(202) 783 - 3332

Registered Federal Lobbyist.
Serves As:
- V. President and Director, Federal Relations, Legislative and Regulatory Management, Lincoln Financial Group

MORRIS, Barry
250 E. Fifth St.
Cincinnati, OH 45202
bmorris@chiquita.com
Tel: (513) 784 - 8000
Fax:(513) 784 - 8030

Serves As:
- V. President, Human Resources, Chiquita Brands Internat'l, Inc.

MORRIS, Jr., Clifton H.
801 Cherry St.
Suite 3900
Fort Worth, TX 76102-6803
Tel: (817) 302 - 7000
Fax:(817) 302 - 7479
TF: (800) 644 - 2297

Serves As:
- Chairman and Chief Exec. Officer, AmeriCredit Corp.

MORRIS, Doug
1755 Broadway
New York, NY 10019
Tel: (212) 841 - 8000

Serves As:
- Chairman and Chief Exec. Officer, Universal Music Group

MORRIS, Ed
21700 Atlantic Blvd.
Dulles, VA 20166
Tel: (703) 406 - 5000
Fax:(703) 406 - 5572

Registered Federal Lobbyist.
Serves As:
- Representative, Orbital Sciences Corp.

MORRIS, JoAnna H.
3135 Easton Tpk.
Bldg. E2E
Fairfield, CT 06431
Tel: (203) 373 - 2211
Fax:(203) 373 - 3131

Serves As:
- Director, Corporate Investor Communicatons, General Electric Co.

MORRIS, Les
P.O. Box 7033
Indianapolis, IN 46207
Tel: (317) 263 - 7711
Fax:(317) 263 - 2318

Serves As:
- Manager, Corporate Public Affairs, Simon Property Group

MORRIS, Mark E.
443 Shaker Rd.
East Longmeadow, MA 01028-3101
mmorris@hasbro.com
Tel: (413) 525 - 6411
Fax:(413) 525 - 4365

Serves As:
- Director, Public Relations, (Hasbro Games), Hasbro Inc.

MORRIS, Michael G.
One Riverside Plaza
Columbus, OH 43215-2373
Tel: (614) 223 - 1000
Fax:(614) 223 - 1823

Serves As:
- Chairman, President and Chief Exec. Officer, American Electric Power Co. Inc.

MORRIS, Renea
201 E. Fourth St.
Cincinnati, OH 45202
Tel: (513) 723 - 7000
Fax:(513) 458 - 1315
TF: (800) 344 - 3000

Serves As:
- Director, Public Relations, Convergys Corp.

MORRIS, Unique
126 C St. NW
Suite Three
Washington, DC 20001
morris@amazon.com
Tel: (202) 347 - 7389

Serves As:
- Coordinator, Public Policy, Amazon.com, Inc.

MORRIS, Valencia Y.
21557 Telegraph Rd.
Southfield, MI 48034
vmorris@lear.com
Tel: (248) 447 - 5938
Fax:(248) 447 - 1722

Serves As:
- Manager, Community Relations, Lear Corporation

Responsibilities include corporate philanthropy.

MORRISEY, Stephen
1025 Connecticut Ave. NW
Suite 1210
Washington, DC 20036
Tel: (202) 296 - 2733
Fax:(202) 296 - 2873

Registered Federal Lobbyist.
Serves As:
- Senior Director, Governmental Affairs, United Airlines

MORRISON, Andrew F.
120 Monument Circle
IN 13A-312
Indianapolis, IN 46204
andrew.morrison@wellpoint.com
Tel: (317) 488 - 6296
Fax:(317) 488 - 6896

Serves As:
- Senior V. President, Public Affairs, Wellpoint, Inc.

MORRISON, Craig D.
180 E. Broad St.
Columbus, OH 43215-3799
Tel: (614) 225 - 4000

Serves As:
- President and Chief Exec. Officer, Hexion Specialty Chemicals, Inc.

MORRISON, Gary L.
6363 Main St.
Williamsville, NY 14221
morrisong@natfuel.com
Tel: (716) 857 - 7179
Fax:(716) 857 - 7439
TF: (800) 365 - 3234

Registered Federal Lobbyist.
Serves As:
- General Manager, Government Affairs, Nat'l Fuel Gas Co.

MORRISON, Kathleen A.
2700 Sanders Rd.
Prospect Heights, IL 60070
kamorrison@household.com
Tel: (847) 564 - 6111
Fax:(847) 205 - 7490

Serves As:
- Director, Public Relations, HSBC North America Holdings Inc.

MORRISON, Kelly
100 Abbott Park Rd.
Abbott Park, IL 60064-3500
Tel: (847) 937 - 3802

Serves As:
- Manager, External Communications, Abbott Laboratories

MORRISON, Mark
1800 Honda Dr.
Lincoln, AL 35096
Tel: (205) 355 - 5000
Fax:(205) 355 - 5020

Serves As:
- Manager, Corporate Affairs and Communications, (Honda Manufacturing of Alabama LLC), American Honda Motor Co., Inc.

MORRISON, Maryann
100 NE Adams St.
Peoria, IL 61629-1465
Tel: (309) 675 - 4464
Fax:(309) 675 - 6155

Serves As:
- Corporate Contributions, Caterpillar Inc.

MORRISSEY, Karen M.
Two Seaport Ln.
Suite 1300
Boston, MA 02210-2019
Tel: (617) 342 - 6221
Fax:(617) 342 - 6312

Serves As:
- V. President, Corporate Affairs, Cabot Corp.

Responsibilities include corporate communications.

MORROW, Christina A.
701 Market St.
St. Louis, MO 63101-1826
Tel: (314) 342 - 7651
Fax:(314) 342 - 7799

Serves As:
- Director, Investor Relations and Assistant Treasurer, Peabody Energy

MORROW, Roy L.
22801 St. Clair Ave.
Cleveland, OH 44117-1199
Roy_Morrow@lincolnelectric.com
Tel: (216) 383 - 4893
Fax:(216) 383 - 8220

Serves As:
- Director, Corporate Relations, Lincoln Electric Holdings, Inc.

Responsibilities include corporate philanthropy, public relations, and investor relations.

MORSE, Carole
121 SW Salmon St.
1WTC-0303
Portland, OR 97204
carole_morse@pgn.com
Tel: (503) 464 - 8000
Fax:(503) 464 - 2354

Serves As:
- Consultant, Corporate Contributions and Community Affairs, Portland General Electric Co.

MORSE, Jr., John B.
1150 15th St. NW
Washington, DC 20071
morsej@washpost.com
Tel: (202) 334 - 6662
Fax:(202) 334 - 1031

Serves As:
- Chief Financial Officer and V. President, Finance, The Washington Post Co.

Responsibilities include investor relations.

MORTENSON, Alice
P.O. Box 710
Minneapolis, MN 54400-0710
Tel: (763) 522 - 2100
Fax:(763) 287 - 5430

Serves As:
- Director, Community Relations, M. A. Mortenson Company

MORTENSON, Jr., M. A.
P.O. Box 710
Minneapolis, MN 54400-0710
Tel: (763) 522 - 2100
Fax:(763) 287 - 5430

Serves As:
- Chairman and Chief Exec. Officer, M. A. Mortenson Company

MORTIMER, Michael
P.O. Box 13979
Research Triangle Park, NC 27709-3979
Tel: (919) 998 - 2000
Fax:(919) 998 - 2098

Serves As:
- Senior V. President, Human Resources, Quintiles Transnat'l Corp.

MORTON, Faye
804 Green Valley Rd.
Greensboro, NC 27408
Tel: (336) 379 - 2000
Fax:(336) 379 - 4504

Serves As:
- Treasurer, Burlington Industries Good Government Committee, Internat'l Textiles Group

MORTON, Gregg F.
1133 21st St. NW
Suite 900
Washington, DC 20036
Tel: (202) 463 - 4100
Fax:(202) 463 - 4141

Registered Federal Lobbyist.
Serves As:
- Representative, BellSouth Corp.

MORTON, John Douglas
1050 W. Hampden Ave.
Englewood, CO 80110
Tel: (303) 200 - 5050
Fax:(303) 863 - 2240

Serves As:
- Chairman, President and Chief Exec. Officer, The Sports Authority, Inc.

MORTON, Margaret L.
P.O. Box 270
M/S BMW 2
Hartford, CT 06141-0270
MortoML@nu.com
Tel: (860) 665 - 5000
Fax:(860) 665 - 3177
TF: (800) 286 - 2000

Serves As:
- V. President, Government Affairs, (Northeast Utilities Service Co.), Northeast Utilities

MOSBY-WILLIAMS, Carolyn
P.O. Box 1220
Indianapolis, IN 46206
carolyn.mosby-williams@veoliawaterna.com
Tel: (317) 639 - 1431
Fax:(317) 263 - 6414

Serves As:
- V. President, Communications and Community Relations, Veolia Water Indianapolis, LLC

MOSELEY, Colin
917 E. 11th St.
Tacoma, WA 98421
Tel: (253) 779 - 6400
Fax:(253) 280 - 9000

Serves As:
- Chairman and Chief Exec. Officer, Simpson Investment Co.

MOSER, Mike
P.O. Box 50
Boise, ID 83728-0001
Tel: (208) 384 - 6016
Fax:(208) 384 - 4841

Serves As:
- Media Contact, Boise Cascade Corp.

MOSES, Glenn
1235 S. Clark St.
Suite 708
Arlington, VA 22202
glenn.moses@flightsafety.com
Tel: (703) 414 - 5502
Fax:(703) 414 - 5504

Serves As:
- Director, Government Relations, FlightSafety Internat'l

MOSKOWITZ, Louise A.
P.O. Box 53999
M/S 8010
Phoenix, AZ 85072-3999
louise.moskowitz@pinnaclewest.com
Tel: (602) 250 - 2291
Fax:(602) 250 - 2419

Serves As:
- Coordinator, Corporate Events (CR/ED Consultant), Pinnacle West Capital Corp.

Responsibilities include community affairs.

MOSLEY, Vanessa
6000 American Pkwy.
Madison, WI 53783
Tel: (608) 249 - 2111
Fax:(608) 245 - 8619

Serves As:
- Director, Consumer Affairs, American Family Insurance Group

MOSNER, Lawrence J.
P.O. Box 64235
St. Paul, MN 55164-0235
Tel: (651) 483 - 7111
Fax:(651) 481 - 4163

Serves As:
- Chairman and Chief Exec. Officer, Deluxe Corp.

MOSS, Karen
100 Mission Ridge
Goodlettsville, TN 37072
kmoss@dollargeneral.com
Tel: (615) 855 - 5210
Fax:(615) 855 - 5527

Serves As:
- Director, Corporate Communications, Dollar General Corp.

MOSS, Kevin A.
P.O. Box 1464
Wall, NJ 07719
Tel: (732) 938 - 1214
Fax:(732) 938 - 2620

Serves As:
- Senior V. President, Regulatory Affairs, (New Jersey Natural Gas Co.), New Jersey Resources Corp.

MOSS, Ralph L.
818 Connecticut Ave., Suite 801
Washington, DC 20006
ralph_moss@seaboardcorp.com
Tel: (202) 452 - 7960
Fax:(202) 452 - 7942

Registered Federal Lobbyist.
Serves As:
- V. President, Government Affairs, Seaboard Corporation

MOSS, Susan E.
680 S. Fourth Ave.
Louisville, KY 40202-2412
Tel: (502) 596 - 7296
Fax:(502) 596 - 4099

Serves As:
- V. President, Corporate Communications, Kindred Healthcare, Inc.

MOSS, William
Two Paragon Dr.
Montvale, NJ 07645
Tel: (201) 571 - 4019
Fax:(201) 571 - 8719

Serves As:
- V. President and Treasurer, The Great Atlantic and Pacific Tea Co.

Responsibilities include investor relations.

MOSSLER, Diane L.
2941 Fairview Park Dr.
Falls Church, VA 22042-4513
Tel: (703) 876 - 3000
Fax:(703) 876 - 3125

Serves As:
- PAC Treasurer, General Dynamics Corporation

MOSTROM, Joel K.
1021 E. Cary St.
Richmond, VA 23217
joel.mostrom@cskcorp.com
Tel: (804) 697 - 1147
Fax:(804) 697 - 1199

Serves As:
- Senior V. President and Chief Financial Officer, Chesapeake Corp.

Responsibilities include investor relations.

MOTT, David M.
One MedImmune Way
Gaithersburg, MD 20878
mottd@medimmune.com
Tel: (301) 398 - 0000
Fax:(301) 398 - 9000
TF: (877) 633 - 4411

Serves As:
- V. Chairman, President and Chief Exec. Officer, MedImmune, Inc.

MOTT, Rodney B.
3250 Interstate Dr.
Richfield, OH 44286
Fax:(330) 659 - 9135

Serves As:
- Chief Exec. Officer and President, Internat'l Steel Group Inc.

MOTT, Roger
1300 I St. NW
Suite 400 West
Washington, DC 20005
Tel: (202) 515 - 2400

Registered Federal Lobbyist.
Serves As:
- V. President, Federal Government Relations, Verizon Communications Inc.

MOUNTAIN, Janet
One Dell Way
Round Rock, TX 78682
Tel: (512) 338 - 4400
Fax:(512) 728 - 3653
TF: (800) 289 - 3355

Serves As:
- Exec. Director, Foundation, Dell Inc.

MOUNTCASTLE, Laura L.
One Energy Plaza
Jackson, MI 49201
llmountc@cmsenergy.com
Tel: (517) 788 - 0123
Fax:(517) 788 - 1006

Serves As:
- V. President, Investor Relations and Treasurer, CMS Energy Corp.

MOUSSEAU, Brad
730 Milford Rd.
Route 101A
Merrimack, NH 03054-4631
bmousseau@pcconnection.com
Tel: (603) 683 - 2000
Fax:(603) 683 - 5748

Serves As:
- V. President, Human Resources, PC Connection, Inc.

MOXLEY, Jodie
198 Van Buren St.
Suite 300
Herndon, VA 20170
Tel: (703) 834 - 3400
Fax:(703) 834 - 3567

Registered Federal Lobbyist.
Serves As:
- Government Affairs, Airbus North America Holdings, Inc.

MOYER, Jenni
1500 Market St.
Philadelphia, PA 19102
Tel: (215) 851 - 3311
Fax:(215) 981 - 7790

Serves As:
- Director, Corporate Communications, Comcast Corporation

MOYER, Matthew G.
P.O. Box 199000
Dallas, TX 75219-9000
Tel: (214) 981 - 5000
Fax:(214) 981 - 6859

Serves As:
- V. President, Investor Relations, Centex Corporation

MOZDINIEWICZ, Nathalie
100 Park Ave., Suite 2705
New York, NY 10017

Serves As:
- Investor Relations Program Coordinator, Ericsson Inc.

MOZILO, Angelo R.
4500 Park Granada
Calabasas, CA 91302
Tel: (818) 225 - 3000
TF: (800) 556 - 9568

Serves As:
- Chairman and Chief Exec. Officer, Countrywide Home Loans Inc.

MUCHA, Zenia
500 S. Buena Vista St.
Burbank, CA 91521
zenia.mucha@corp.disney.com
Tel: (818) 560 - 1000
Fax:(818) 560 - 1930

Serves As:
- Senior V. President, Corporate Communications, The Walt Disney Company

MUCHOW, Debi
2655 Seely Ave.
San Jose, CA 95134
Tel: (408) 943 - 1234
Fax:(408) 943 - 0513
TF: (800) 862 - 4522

Serves As:
- Corporate V. President, Human Resources and Organizational Development, Cadence Design Systems, Inc.

MUDD, Michael
Three Lakes Dr.
Northfield, IL 60093-2753
Tel: (847) 646 - 2868
Fax:(847) 646 - 6005

Serves As:
- Exec. V. President, Global Corporate Affairs, Kraft Foods, Inc.

MUELLER, Carl
175 Berkeley St.
Boston, MA 02116
Tel: (617) 357 - 9500
Fax:(617) 350 - 7648

Serves As:
- Manager, Internal Communications, Liberty Mutual Insurance Co.

MUELLER, Edward A.
3250 Van Ness Ave.
San Francisco, CA 94109
Tel: (415) 421 - 7900
Fax:(415) 616 - 8463

Serves As:
- Chief Exec. Officer, Williams-Sonoma, Inc.

MUELLER, Kathleen
1200 Willow Lake Blvd.
P.O. Box 64683
St. Paul, MN 55164-0683
kathy.mueller@hbfuller.com
Tel: (651) 236 - 5161
Fax:(651) 236 - 5165
TF: (800) 214 - 2523

Serves As:
- Manager, Corporate Communications, H. B. Fuller Co.

MUENZMAIER, Marty
1101 15th St. NW
Suite 1000
Washington, DC 20005
Tel: (202) 530 - 8160
Fax:(202) 530 - 8180

Registered Federal Lobbyist.
Serves As:
- Representative, Cargill, Incorporated

MUHLBERG, Judith A.
2001 Edmund Halley Dr.
Reston, VA 20191
Tel: (703) 433 - 4000

Serves As:
- Senior V. President, Corporate Communications, Sprint Nextel

MUIR, Nigel D.
39 Old Ridgebury Rd.
Danbury, CT 06810-5113
nigel_muir@praxair.com
Tel: (203) 837 - 2240
Fax:(203) 837 - 2555
TF: (800) 772 - 9247

Serves As:
- V. President, Communications and Public Relations; President, Praxair Foundation Inc., Praxair, Inc.

MUIR, William F.
200 Renaissance Center
Detroit, MI 48265
Tel: (313) 556 - 5000
Fax:(313) 556 - 5108
TF: (800) 200 - 4622

Serves As:
- President, General Motors Acceptance Corp. (GMAC)

MUKHERJEE, Malay
3210 Watling St.
East Chicago, IN 46312
Tel: (219) 399 - 1200
Fax:(219) 399 - 5544

Serves As:
- Chief Exec. Officer, Ispat Inland Inc.

MULCAHY, Anne M.
800 Long Ridge Rd.
Stamford, CT 06904
Tel: (203) 968 - 3000
TF: (800) 275 - 9376

Serves As:
- Chairman and Chief Exec. Officer, Xerox Corp.

MULDER, David M.
1955 Field Ct.
Lake Forest, IL 60045
Tel: (847) 803 - 4600
Fax:(847) 803 - 5629
TF: (800) 272 - 5629

Serves As:
- Exec. V. President, Chief Administrative Officer, and Senior Financial Officer, Salton, Inc.

Responsibilities include investor relations.

MULLALLY, Kathleen
320 Park Ave.
New York, NY 10022
Tel: (212) 224 - 1643
Fax:(212) 224 - 2529

Serves As:
- V. President, Corporate Communications, Mutual of America Life Insurance Co.

MULLEN, Dennis M.
P.O. Box 20670
Rochester, NY 14602-0670
dmullen@birdseyefoods.com
Tel: (585) 383 - 1850
Fax:(585) 385 - 2857
TF: (800) 999 - 5044

Serves As:
- Chairman, President and Chief Exec. Officer, Birds Eye Foods

MULLEN, James C.
14 Cambridge Center
Cambridge, MA 02142
Tel: (617) 679 - 2000
Fax:(617) 679 - 2617

Serves As:
- President and Chief Exec. Officer, Biogen Idec Inc.

MULLEN, John
1200 S. Pine Island Rd.
Suite 61000
Plantation, FL 33324
Tel: (954) 888 - 7000
Fax:(954) 888 - 7310

Serves As:
- Chief Exec. Officer, DHL Holdings (USA), Inc.

MULLEN, Susan
P.O. Box 1564
New Haven, CT 06506-0901
Tel: (203) 499 - 2000
Fax:(203) 499 - 3626
TF: (800) 722 - 5584

Serves As:
- Senior Human Resources Exec., The United Illuminating Company

MULLER, Karen P.
1200 Willow Lake Blvd.
P.O. Box 64683
St. Paul, MN 55164-0683
karen.muller@hbfuller.com
Tel: (651) 236 - 5207
Fax:(651) 236 - 5056
TF: (800) 214 - 2523

Serves As:
- Exec. Director, Foundation, H. B. Fuller Co.

MULLER, Trudy
209 Redwood Shores Pkwy.
Redwood City, CA 94065-1175
Tel: (650) 628 - 1500
Fax:(650) 628 - 1415

Serves As:
- Senior Manager, Corporate Communications, Electronic Arts Inc.

MULLET, Mark S.
1300 I St. NW
Suite 400 West
Washington, DC 20005
mark.s.mullet@verizon.com
Tel: (202) 515 - 2553

Registered Federal Lobbyist.
Serves As:
- V. President, Federal Government Relations, Verizon Communications Inc.

MULLETT, Charles
3240 Hillview Ave.
Palo Alto, CA 94304
Tel: (650) 494 - 2900
Fax:(650) 813 - 0160

Registered Federal Lobbyist.
Serves As:
- Representative, CNF Inc.

MULLIGAN, Robert J.
One Massachusetts Ave. NW
Suite 350
Washington, DC 20001
rmulligan@chubb.com
Tel: (202) 408 - 8123
Fax:(202) 296 - 7683

Registered Federal Lobbyist.
Serves As:
- V. President, International External Affairs, The Chubb Corp.

MULLINS, Mike
1101 15th St. NW
Suite 1000
Washington, DC 20005
mike_mullins@cargill.com
Tel: (202) 530 - 8160
Fax:(202) 530 - 8180

Registered Federal Lobbyist.
Serves As:
- Assistant V. President, Public Affairs, Cargill, Incorporated

MULLINS-GRISSOM, Janet
1350 I St. NW
Suite 1000
Washington, DC 20005
Tel: (202) 962 - 5377
Fax:(202) 962 - 5377

Registered Federal Lobbyist.
Serves As:
- V. President, Washington Affairs, Ford Motor Co.

MULVA, James J. "Jim"
P.O. Box 2197
Houston, TX 77252-2197
Tel: (281) 293 - 1000

Serves As:
- Chairman and Chief Exec. Officer, ConocoPhillips

MULVEHILL, Joseph J.
8100 Mitchell Rd.
Eden Prairie, MN 55344
mulvjoe@chrobinson.com
Tel: (952) 937 - 8500
Fax:(952) 937 - 6740

Serves As:
- V. President, International, C.H. Robinson Worldwide, Inc.

MULVEY, Kevin C. W.
1399 New York Ave. NW
Suite 900
Washington, DC 20005
Tel: (202) 585 - 5800
Fax:(202) 585 - 5820

Registered Federal Lobbyist.
Serves As:
- Assistant V. President, International Government Affairs, American Internat'l Group, Inc.

MULVIHILL SOUTHEY, Kristen
3100 Ocean Park Blvd.
Santa Monica, CA 90405-3032
kmulvihill@activision.com
Tel: (310) 255 - 2635
Fax:(310) 255 - 2100

Serves As:
- V. President, Investor Relations, Activision, Inc.

MUMA, Leslie M.
P.O. Box 979
Brookfield, WI 53008-0979
Tel: (262) 879 - 5000
TF: (800) 872 - 7882

Serves As:
- President and Chief Exec. Officer, Fiserv, Inc.

MUNDKUR, Christine
400 Chesnut Ridge Rd.
Woodcliff Lake, NJ 07677
Tel: (201) 930 - 3300
Fax:(201) 930 - 3330
TF: (800) 222 - 0190

Serves As:
- Senior V. President, Quality and Regulatory Counsel, (Barr Laboratories, Inc.), Barr Pharmaceuticals, Inc.

MUNDY, Donna T.
2211 Congress St.
M/S B128
Portland, ME 04122-0545
dmundy@unumprovident.com
Tel: (207) 575 - 4354
Fax:(207) 575 - 4304

Registered Federal Lobbyist.
Serves As:
- Senior V. President, Government Relations, UnumProvident Corp.

MUNGER, Kitty
P.O. Box 256
Dublin, OH 43017
kitty_munger@wendys.com
Tel: (614) 764 - 3241
Ext: 3241
Fax:(614) 764 - 6707

Serves As:
- Manager, Communications, Wendy's Internat'l, Inc.

MUNGUIA, Roberto F.
201 N. Seventh St.
Lincoln, NE 68508-1309
roberto.munguia@bnsf.com
Tel: (402) 458 - 7738
Fax:(402) 458 - 7739

Serves As:
- Director, Government Affairs, Burlington Northern Santa Fe Corporation

MUNIZ-BANDONI, Katharyn O.
2244 Walnut Grove Ave.
Rosemead, CA 91770
munizbko@sce.com
Tel: (626) 302 - 3503
Fax:(626) 302 - 3007

Serves As:
- Employee Contributions Chair, Southern California Edison, an Edison Internat'l Co.

MUNOZ, Sandra
942 S. Shady Grove Rd.
Memphis, TN 38120
smunoz@fedex.com
Tel: (901) 434 - 7781
TF: (800) 238 - 5355

Serves As:
- Government Affairs and International Media Relations Contact, FedEx Corp.

MUNROE, J. Brian
1401 H St., NW
Suite 650
Washington, DC 20005
Tel: (202) 289 - 6598
Fax:(202) 289 - 7257

Registered Federal Lobbyist.
Serves As:
- V. President, Government Relations and Public Policy, Millennium Pharmaceuticals, Inc.

MUNSON, Kathy
3125 Myers St.
Riverside, CA 92503
kathy.munson@fleetwood.com
Tel: (909) 351 - 3650
Fax:(909) 351 - 3931

Serves As:
- Director, Investor Relations, Fleetwood Enterprises

MURABITO, John M.
One Liberty Pl.
1650 Market St.
Philadelphia, PA 19192
Tel: (215) 761 - 1000

Serves As:
- Exec. V. President, Human Resources, CIGNA Corp.

MURANO, Ph.D., Genesio
One DNA Way
San Francisco, CA 94080-4990
Tel: (650) 225 - 1000
Fax:(650) 225 - 6000

Serves As:
- V. President, Regulatory Affairs, Genentech, Inc.

MURAT, Corinne
333 Continental Blvd.
MI-1418
El Segundo, CA 90245-5012
corinne.murat@mattel.com
Tel: (310) 252 - 6628
Fax:(310) 252 - 4443

Registered Federal Lobbyist.
Serves As:
- Senor Manager, Government Affairs, Mattel, Inc.

MURDOCH, K. Rupert
1211 Ave. of the Americas
New York, NY 10036
Tel: (212) 852 - 7000

Serves As:
- Chairman and Chief Exec. Officer, News Corporation Ltd.
- Chairman of the Board, The DIRECTV Group, Inc.

MURDOCK, David H.
One Dole Dr.
Westlake Village, CA 91362-7300
Tel: (818) 879 - 6600
Fax:(818) 879 - 6890

Serves As:
- Chairman and Chief Exec. Officer, Dole Food Company, Inc.

MURDOCK, Leslie
1111 Lockheed Martin Way
Bldg. 157
Sunnyvale, CA 94089
Tel: (408) 742 - 5605
Fax:(408) 743 - 2239

Serves As:
- Manager, Community Relations, Lockheed Martin Space Systems Company

MURDY, Wayne W.
1700 Lincoln St.
Denver, CO 80203
Tel: (303) 863 - 7414
Fax:(303) 837 - 5837

Serves As:
- Chairman and Chief Exec. Officer, Newmont Mining Corp.

MURPHEY, Lynn
6601 Hawkinsville Rd.
Macon, GA 31297-0278
lynn.murphey@cox.com
Tel: (478) 784 - 5106
Fax:(478) 784 - 5100

Serves As:
- Director, Public Relations, (Cox Communications, Inc.), Cox Enterprises, Inc.

MURPHY, Barry
One Microsoft Way
Redmond, WA 98052-6399
Tel: (425) 882 - 8080
Fax:(425) 703 - 7329

Serves As:
- Senior Manager, State Government Affairs, Microsoft Corporation

MURPHY, Bernie
5235 Katy Fwy.
Houston, TX 77007
Tel: (713) 869 - 5060
Ext: 243
Fax:(713) 869 - 6197

Serves As:
- Director, Public Affairs, Fiesta Mart Inc.

MURPHY, Brian J.
34 Maple St.
Milford, MA 01757
brian_j_murphy@waters.com
Tel: (508) 478 - 2614
Fax:(508) 872 - 1990
TF: (800) 252 - 4752

Serves As:
- Manager, Corporate Communications, Waters Corp.

MURPHY, Dan
P.O. Box 834
Valley Forge, PA 19482-0834
Tel: (610) 408 - 7196
Fax:(610) 408 - 7025
TF: (888) 275 - 4566

Serves As:
- Director, Investor Realtions, Ikon Office Solutions, Inc.

MURPHY, Dan K.
601 Riverside Ave.
Jacksonville, FL 32204
dkmurphy@fnf.com
Tel: (904) 854 - 8120
Fax:(904) 357 - 1023

Serves As:
- Senior V. President, Finance and Investor Relations, Fidelity Nat'l Financial, Inc.

Responsibilities include media relations.

MURPHY, Daniel J.
5050 Lincoln Dr.
Edina, MN 55436
Tel: (952) 351 - 3000
Fax:(952) 351 - 3009

Serves As:
- Chairman and Chief Exec. Officer, Alliant Techsystems

MURPHY, David L.
1221 Ave. of the Americas
New York, NY 10020-1095
Tel: (212) 512 - 2000

Serves As:
- Exec. V. President, Human Resources, The McGraw-Hill Companies, Inc.

MURPHY, Edward H.
1100 N. King St.
Wilmington, DE 19880-127
Tel: (302) 456 - 8541
Fax:(302) 456 - 8541
TF: (800) 441 - 7048

Serves As:
- Director, Investor Relations, MBNA Corp.

MURPHY, James E.
1345 Ave. of the Americas
New York, NY 10105
Tel: (917) 452 - 4400
Fax:(917) 527 - 9915

Serves As:
- Global Managing Director, Marketing and Communications, Accenture

MURPHY, Jeanne-Marie
730 15th St. NW
DC1-701-05-11
Washington, DC 20005
jeanne-marie.murphy@bankofamerica.com
Tel: (202) 624 - 4134
Fax:(202) 383 - 3475

Registered Federal Lobbyist.
Serves As:
- Senior V. President, Federal Government Relations, Bank of America Corp.

Responsibilities include political action.

MURPHY, John P.
175 Berkeley St.
Boston, MA 02116
Tel: (617) 357 - 9500
Fax:(617) 350 - 7648

Serves As:
- Legislative Counsel, Liberty Mutual Insurance Co.

MURPHY, Joseph F.
One Wall St.
New York, NY 10286
jfmurphy@bankofny.com
Tel: (212) 635 - 7740
Fax:(212) 635 - 1799

Serves As:
- Managing Director, Investor Relations, The Bank of New York Co., Inc.

MURPHY, Judith T.
800 Nicollet Mall
BCMNH23K
Minneapolis, MN 55402
judith.murphy@usbank.com
Tel: (612) 303 - 0783
Fax:(612) 303 - 0782

Serves As:
- V. President, Investor Relations, U.S. Bancorp

MURPHY, Julie
345 Encinal St.
Santa Cruz, CA 95060
julie.murphy@plantronics.com
Tel: (831) 426 - 5858
Ext: 7864
Fax:(831) 426 - 6098
TF: (800) 544 - 4660

Serves As:
- V. President, Human Resources, Plantronics, Inc.

MURPHY, Kathleen
P.O. Box 30270
Salt Lake City, UT 84130-0270
kathleen.murphy@regence.com
Tel: (801) 333 - 5756

Serves As:
- Assistant Director, Corporate Communications, Regence BlueCross BlueShield of Utah

MURPHY, Mark
P.O. Box 9300
MS 50
Minneapolis, MN 55440-9300
mark_murphy@cargill.com
Tel: (952) 742 - 2792
Fax:(952) 742 - 7224

Serves As:
- Exec. Director, Cargill Foundation; and Manager, Stakeholder Relations, Cargill, Incorporated

Responsibilities include corporate communications.

MURPHY, Michelle
5500 Wayzata Blvd.
Suite 800
Golden Valley, MN 55416-1259
Tel: (763) 545 - 1730

Serves As:
- Manager, Pentair Foundation, Pentair, Inc.

MURPHY, Patricia A.
700 13th St. NW
Suite 220
Washington, DC 20005
Tel: (202) 347 - 8662
Fax:(202) 347 - 8675

Serves As:
- PAC Contact, Burlington Northern Santa Fe Corporation

MURPHY, Patrick T.
Webster Plaza
145 Bank St.
MO 405
Waterbury, CT 06702
ptmurphy@websterbank.com
Tel: (203) 578 - 2273
Fax:(203) 755 - 5539

Serves As:
- Exec. V. President, Human Resources, Webster Financial Corp.

MURPHY, Paul M.
999 Waterside Dr.
Eighth Floor
Norfolk, VA 23510
pmmurphy@roysterclark.com
Tel: (757) 222 - 9513

Serves As:
- Director, Public Relations, Royster-Clark, Inc.

MURPHY, Peter
United Technologies Bldg.
One Financial Plaza
Hartford, CT 06101
Tel: (860) 728 - 7977
Fax:(860) 728 - 6255

Serves As:
- Director, Worldwide Public Relations, United Technologies Corp.

MURPHY, Sean
2001 Pennsylvania Ave. NW
Suite 650
Washington, DC 20006
Tel: (202) 263 - 0000
Fax:(202) 263 - 0010

Registered Federal Lobbyist.
Serves As:
- Director, International Trade and Technology Policy, Qualcomm Inc.

MURPHY, Thomas E.
2001 Edmund Halley Dr.
Reston, VA 20191
Tel: (703) 433 - 4000

Serves As:
- Senior V. President, Corporate Communications and Brand Management, Sprint Nextel

MURRAY, Alice
72 Marietta St. NW
Atlanta, GA 30303
Tel: (404) 526 - 5151
Fax:(404) 526 - 5199

Serves As:
- Director of Marketing Administration, Atlanta Journal Constitution

Responsibilities include corporate communications.

MURRAY, Mark
One Microsoft Way
Redmond, WA 98052-6399
Tel: (425) 882 - 8080
Fax:(425) 936 - 7329

Serves As:
- Director, Corporate Public Relations, Microsoft Corporation

MURRAY, Michael W.
1803 Gears Rd.
Houston, TX 60601
michael.murray@fmcti.com
Tel: (281) 591 - 4556
Fax:(281) 591 - 4102

Serves As:
- V. President, Human Resources, FMC Technologies, Inc.

MURRAY, Mike
101 Ash St.
hq13f
San Diego, CA 92101-3017
mmurray@sempra.com
Tel: (619) 696 - 2320
Fax:(619) 696 - 4266
TF: (877) 736 - 7721

Serves As:
- Director, Legislative Policy and Analysis, Sempra Energy

MURRAY, Nancy
650 Madison Ave.
New York, NY 10022
Tel: (212) 318 - 7862
Fax:(212) 888 - 5780

Serves As:
- V. President, Investor Relations, Polo Ralph Lauren

MURRAY, Patricia
2200 Mission College Blvd.
Santa Clara, CA 95052-8119
Tel: (408) 765 - 8080
Fax:(408) 765 - 9904
TF: (800) 628 - 8686

Serves As:
- Senior V. President and Director, Human Resources, Intel Corp.

MURRAY, Paul
P.O. Box 302
Zeeland, MI 49464-0302
paul_murray@hermanmiller.com
Tel: (616) 654 - 3000
Fax:(616) 654 - 5234

Serves As:
- Manager, Environmental Affairs, Herman Miller Inc.

MURRAY, Robert W.
10900 Wilshire Blvd.
Suite 850
Los Angeles, CA 90024
bmurray@magnetek.com
Tel: (310) 208 - 1980
Fax:(310) 208 - 6133

Serves As:
- V. President, Communications and Public Relations, Magnetek, Inc.

MURRAY, Rosemary G.
2345 Crystal Dr.
Arlington, VA 22227
rosemary_murray@usairways.com
Tel: (703) 872 - 5140
Fax:(703) 872 - 5109

Registered Federal Lobbyist.
Serves As:
- V. President, Government Affairs, US Airways Group, Inc.

MURRAY, Stephen D.
P.O. Box 13287
Kansas City, MO 64199-3287
steve.murray@aquila.com
Tel: (816) 467 - 3434
Fax:(816) 467 - 9434

Serves As:
- Legislative Services - Missouri, Aquila, Inc.

MURRILL, Tom
1050 Caribbean Way
Miami, FL 33132-3203
Tel: (305) 539 - 6000
Fax:(305) 375 - 0711

Serves As:
- Chief Officer, Human Resources, Royal Caribbean Internat'l

MURTLOW, Ann D.
P.O. Box 1595
Indianapolis, IN 46206-1595
Tel: (317) 261 - 8261
Fax:(317) 630 - 5726

Serves As:
- Chairman and Chief Exec. Officer, IPL (an AES Company)

MUSACCHIA, Mary U.
SAS Campus Dr.
Cary, NC 27513-2414
mary.musacchia@sas.com
Tel: (919) 677 - 8000
Fax:(919) 677 - 4444

Registered Federal Lobbyist.
Serves As:
- Counsel to the President/Chief Exec. Officer, Government Affairs, SAS Institute, Inc.

MUSARRA, Gerald
1550 Crystal Dr.
Crystal Square 2, Suite 300
Arlington, VA 22202
Tel: (703) 413 - 5791
Fax:(703) 413 - 5908

Serves As:
- V. President, Trade and Regulatory Affairs, Lockheed Martin Corp.

MUSIAL, Thomas G.
P.O. Box 66
Manitowoc, WI 54221-0066
Tel: (920) 684 - 4410
Fax:(920) 652 - 9778

Serves As:
- Senior V. President, Human Resources and Administration, The Manitowoc Co., Inc.

MUSIL, Ruthellyn
435 N. Michigan Ave.
Chicago, IL 60611
rmusil@tribune.com
Tel: (312) 222 - 3787
Fax:(312) 222 - 1573

Serves As:
- Senior V. President, Corporate Relations, Tribune Co.

Responsibilities include investor relations.

MUSKOVICH, John A.
225 Byers Rd.
Miamisburg, OH 45342
Tel: (937) 866 - 6251
Fax:(937) 865 - 5470

Serves As:
- Chief Exec. Officer, Huffy Corp.

MUSSALLEM, Michael A.
One Edwards Way
Irvine, CA 92614-5688
Tel: (949) 250 - 2500
Fax:(949) 250 - 2525
TF: (800) 424 - 3278

Serves As:
- Chairman and Chief Exec. Officer, Edwards Lifesciences Corp.

MUSTAIN, Christopher
1301 K St. NW
Suite 1200
Washington, DC 20005
Tel: (202) 515 - 5000

Registered Federal Lobbyist.
Serves As:
- Governmental Programs Executive, Internat'l Business Machines Corp. (IBM)

MUTALIK, Sujata
440 Lincoln St.
Worcester, MA 01653
smutalik@allmerica.com
Tel: (508) 855 - 3457

Serves As:
- V. President, Investor Relations, Allmerica Property & Casualty Companies, Inc.

MUTCH, Krista
1099 18th St.
Suite 1200
Denver, CO 80202
kmutch@westerngas.com
Tel: (303) 252 - 6094
Fax:(303) 457 - 8482
TF: (800) 933 - 5603

Serves As:
- Manager, Government Relations, Western Gas Resources, Inc.

MUTH, Ken
6000 American Pkwy.
Madison, WI 53783
Tel: (608) 242 - 4100
Fax:(608) 243 - 4921

Serves As:
- Director, Media Relations, American Family Insurance Group

MYATT, Tom
8309 W. 3595 S
P.O. Box 6333
Magna, UT 84044-6333
Tel: (801) 569 - 6000
Fax:(801) 569 - 6045

Serves As:
- Treasurer, Kennecott Holdings Corp. PAC, Kennecott Utah Copper

MYERS, A. Maurice
1001 Fannin St., Suite 4000
Houston, TX 77002
Tel: (713) 512 - 6200
Fax:(713) 512 - 6299

Serves As:
- Chairman of the Board, Waste Management, Inc.

MYERS, Bret
152 W. 57th St.
42nd Floor
New York, NY 10019
Tel: (212) 314 - 7300
Fax:(212) 314 - 7309

Serves As:
- PAC Treasurer, IAC/InterActiveCorp

MYERS, C. David
631 S. Richland Ave.
York, PA 17403
Tel: (717) 771 - 7890
Fax:(717) 771 - 6473

Serves As:
- Chief Exec. Officer, York Internat'l Corp.

MYERS, Cherie
1121 124th NE
Bellevue, WA 98005

Serves As:
- Director, Public Affairs, Safeway Inc.

MYERS, David
13900 Riverport Dr.
Maryland Heights, MO 63043
Tel: (314) 702 - 7173
Fax:(314) 702 - 7037

Serves As:
- V. President, Investor Relations, Express Scripts, Inc.

MYERS, David
7201 Hamilton Blvd.
Allentown, PA 18195-1501
myersdj@airproducts.com
Tel: (610) 481 - 8185
Fax:(610) 841 - 5900

Serves As:
- Manager, Government Relations, Air Products and Chemicals, Inc.

MYERS, James M.
9125 Rehco Rd.
San Diego, CA 92121-2270
Tel: (858) 453 - 7845
Fax:(858) 677 - 3489

Serves As:
- Chief Exec. Officer, PETCO Animal Supplies, Inc.

MYERS, Jim
645 E. Missouri Ave., Suite 400
Phoenix, AZ 85012
Tel: (602) 265 - 9200
Fax:(602) 631 - 7321

Serves As:
- Director, Creative/Broadcast Production and Public Relations, CSK Auto, Inc.

MYERS, Karen Magee
1331 Pennsylvania Ave. NW
Suite 1300 North
Washington, DC 20004
karen.myers@eds.com
Tel: (202) 637 - 6720
Fax:(202) 637 - 6759

Registered Federal Lobbyist.
Serves As:
- Director, Tax and Treasury Policy, EDS Corp.

MYERS, Larry L.
P.O. Box 73
Boise, ID 83729
Tel: (208) 386 - 5000
Fax:(208) 386 - 7186

Serves As:
- Senior V. President, Human Resources, Washington Group Internat'l

MYERS, Robert
1895 J W Foster Blvd.
Canton, MA 02021
Tel: (781) 401 - 5000
Fax:(781) 401 - 4000

Serves As:
- Senior V. President and Chief Human Resources Officer, Reebok Internat'l Ltd.

MYERS, Stephen E.
1293 S. Main St.
Akron, OH 44301
Tel: (330) 253 - 5592
Fax:(330) 761 - 6156

Serves As:
- Chairman of the Board, Myers Industries, Inc.

MYRES, Albert H.
1401 I St. NW, Suite 1030
Washington, DC 20005
albert.myres@shell.com
Tel: (202) 466 - 1474
Fax:(202) 466 - 1498

Registered Federal Lobbyist.
Serves As:
- Senior Advisor, (Shell Chemical Co.), Shell Oil Co.

MYSEL, Amy
8600 W. Bryn Mawr Ave.
Chicago, IL 60631-3505
Tel: (773) 695 - 5000

Serves As:
- Senior V. President, Human Resources and Communications, True Value Company

MYSLIWY, Allie
SAFECO Plaza
Seattle, WA 98185
Tel: (206) 545 - 5000

Serves As:
- Exec. V. President, Human Resources, SAFECO Corp.

MYSZKA, Michele
P.O. Box 9000
Newport Beach, CA 92658-9030
Tel: (949) 219 - 3214
Fax:(949) 219 - 7614
TF: (800) 800 - 7646

Serves As:
- Director, Community Relations, Pacific Life Insurance Co.

MYTYCH, Jerome
2004 Miner St.
Des Plaines, IL 60016
Tel: (847) 759 - 5261
Fax:(847) 759 - 5263

Serves As:
- Area Manager, External Affairs, SBC Illinois

NABHAN, Lou Anne
P.O. Box 85333
Richmond, VA 23293-0001
lnabhan@mediageneral.com
Tel: (804) 649 - 6103
Fax:(804) 649 - 6865

Serves As:
- V. President, Corporate Communications, Media General Inc.

NADATA, Arthur
70 Maxess Rd.
Melville, NY 11747
anadata@nuhorizons.com
Tel: (631) 396 - 5000
Fax:(631) 696 - 5050

Serves As:
- Chairman, President and Chief Exec. Officer, Nu Horizons Electronics Corp.

NADEAU, Dan
700 Washington St.
Bath, ME 04530
dan.nadeau@gdbiw.com
Tel: (207) 442 - 1635
Fax:(207) 442 - 3356

Serves As:
- Director, Environmental Health and Safety, Bath Iron Works Corp.

NADHERNY, Steven T.
1001 G St. NW
Suite 100 East
Washington, DC 20001
Tel: (202) 737 - 7575
Fax:(202) 737 - 9090

Registered Federal Lobbyist.
Serves As:
- Director, Government Affairs, Case New Holland Inc.

NAGEL, David
1240 Crossman Ave.
Sunnyvale, CA 94089-1116
Tel: (408) 400 - 3000
Fax:(408) 400 - 1500

Serves As:
- President and Chief Exec. Officer, PalmSource, Inc.

NAGY, Susan
One Wellpoint Way
Thousand Oak, CA 91362-5035
Tel: (805) 557 - 6788
Fax:(805) 557 - 6831

Serves As:
- Contact, Wellpoint, Inc. Corporate Contributions Program, Wellpoint, Inc.

NAKAISHI, Drake
541 Colonel Dewees Rd.
Wayne, PA 19087
drake.nakaishi@astrazeneca.com
Tel: (610) 688 - 2345
Fax:(610) 989 - 0109
TF: (866) 672 - 6155
Ext: 70212

Serves As:
- Director, State Government Affairs Operation, AstraZeneca Pharmaceuticals

NAKAJIMA, Leslie M.
1 Sybase Dr. Tel: (925) 236 - 8650
Dublin, CA 94568
leslien@sybase.com

Serves As:
- Contact, Corporate and International Public Relations, Sybase, Inc.

NAKAMURA, Kent
2001 Edmund Halley Dr. Tel: (703) 433 - 4000
Reston, VA 20191

Registered Federal Lobbyist.
Serves As:
- Representative, Sprint Nextel

NAKANELUA-RICHARDS, Debbie
P.O. Box 30008 Tel: (808) 835 - 3700
Honolulu, HI 96820 Fax:(808) 838 - 6746

Serves As:
- Senior Manager, Government and Community Relations, Hawaiian Holdings, Inc.

NAKANISHI, Greg
3900 Essex Ln., Suite 1200 Tel: (713) 439 - 8737
Houston, TX 77027-5177 Fax:(713) 439 - 8699

Serves As:
- V. President, Human Resources, Baker Hughes Inc.

NAKU, Rolf D.
Ten Penn Center Tel: (215) 977 - 3000
1801 Market St. Fax:(215) 977 - 3409
Philadelphia, PA 19103-1699

Serves As:
- Senior V. President, Human Resouces and Public Affairs, Sunoco, Inc.

NALBACH, Kay C.
101 N. Wacker Dr. Tel: (312) 357 - 5331
Chicago, IL 60606 Fax:(312) 444 - 2710
knalbach@hartmarx.com

Serves As:
- President, Hartmarx Charitable Foundation, Hartmarx

NAMES, Christine
301 Merritt Seven Tel: (203) 849 - 7800
Sixth Floor Fax:(203) 849 - 7900
Norwalk, CT 06851

Serves As:
- V. President, Human Resources, EMCOR Group, Inc.

NANDA, Jyoti
24025 Park Sorrento Tel: (818) 223 - 7615
Suite 400 Fax:(818) 223 - 7667
Calabasas, CA 91302 TF: (800) 267 - 0998
jnanda@ryland.com

Serves As:
- Manager, Communications, The Ryland Group, Inc.

NANGREAVE, Richard
165 Court St. Tel: (585) 454 - 1700
Rochester, NY 14647 Fax:(585) 238 - 4233

Serves As:
- V. President, Human Resources, The Lifetime Healthcare Companies

NAPHIN, Lucie F.
111 S. Wacker Dr. Tel: (312) 326 - 8030
Chicago, IL 60606 Fax:(312) 326 - 8494
lucie.naphin@rrd.com

Registered Federal Lobbyist.
Serves As:
- V. President, Government Relations, R R Donnelley

Responsibilities include political action.

NARDELLI, Robert L.
2455 Paces Ferry Rd. Tel: (770) 433 - 8211
Atlanta, GA 30339-4024 Fax:(770) 384 - 2356

Serves As:
- Chairman, President and Chief Exec. Officer, The Home Depot, Inc.

NASH, Jr., John F.
910 16th St. NW Tel: (202) 775 - 0084
Suite 402 Fax:(202) 775 - 0784
Washington, DC 20006

Registered Federal Lobbyist.
Serves As:
- Washington Counsel, Milliken & Co.

NASH, Julie
8000 S. Federal Way Tel: (208) 368 - 4400
Boise, ID 83707 Fax:(208) 368 - 2536
jnash@micron.com

Serves As:
- Manager, Strategic Communications, Micron Technology, Inc.

NASH, Mr. Kelly
6565 N. MacArthur Blvd. Tel: (214) 689 - 4300
Suite 800 Fax:(214) 689 - 5886
Irving, TX 75039

Serves As:
- Manager, Environment, Commercial Metals Co.

NASH, Paul
1300 I St. NW Tel: (202) 515 - 2400
Suite 400 West
Washington, DC 20005

Registered Federal Lobbyist.
Serves As:
- Director, Federal Relations, Verizon Wireless

NASSEF, David T.
2151 Jamieson Ave. Tel: (703) 566 - 2307
Alexandria, VA 22314 Fax:(703) 566 - 2311
dtnassef@aol.com

Registered Federal Lobbyist.
Serves As:
- V. President, Federal Relations, Pitney Bowes Inc.

NASSETTA, Christopher J.
6903 Rockledge Dr. Tel: (240) 744 - 1000
Suite 1500
Bethesda, MD 20817
christopher.nassetta@hostmarriott.com

Serves As:
- Chief Exec. Officer and President, Host Marriott Corp.

NAU, Charles
1350 I St. NW Tel: (202) 589 - 1000
Suite 1210 Fax:(202) 408 - 9490
Washington, DC 20005-3305

Registered Federal Lobbyist.
Serves As:
- Director, Federal Affairs, Johnson & Johnson

NAUSER, Debbie
11501 Northeast Exwy. Tel: (405) 475 - 2500
Oklahoma City, OK 73131-6499 Fax:(405) 475 - 2558

Serves As:
- V. President, Public Relations, Six Flags, Inc.

NAVARRE, Richard A.
701 Market St. Tel: (314) 342 - 7708
St. Louis, MO 63101-1826 Fax:(314) 342 - 7597
rnavarre@peabodyenergy.com

Serves As:
- Exec. V. President and Chief Financial Officer, Peabody Energy

Responsibilities include public affairs.

NAY, Gale Dudley
P.O. Box 3005 Tel: (812) 377 - 3114
Columbus, IN 47202-3005 Fax:(812) 377 - 7897

Serves As:
- Foundation Contact, Cummins, Inc.

NAYDEN, Hank
One GEICO Plaza Tel: (301) 986 - 3000
Washington, DC 20076 Fax:(301) 986 - 2888

Serves As:
- V. President and Legislative Counsel, GEICO Corp.

NEAL, Erin
Crystal Gateway 3, 1215 S. Clark St. Tel: (703) 412 - 5977
Suite 1510 Fax:(703) 412 - 5970
Arlington, VA 22202

Registered Federal Lobbyist.
Serves As:
- Senior Manager, Congressional Relations, Alliant Techsystems

NEAL, Jerry D.
7628 Thorndike Rd. Tel: (336) 664 - 1233
Greensboro, NC 27409-9421 Fax:(336) 931 - 7454

Serves As:
- Exec. V. President, Marketing and Strategic Development, RF Micro Devices, Inc.

Responsibilities include corporate communications.

NEAL, Philip M.
150 N. Orange Grove Blvd. Tel: (626) 304 - 2000
Pasadena, CA 91103 Fax:(626) 792 - 7312

Serves As:
- Chairman of the Board, Avery Dennison Corp.

NEALE, Gary L.
801 E. 86th Ave.
Merrillville, IN 46410
Tel: (219) 647 - 5990
Fax:(219) 647 - 6225
TF: (877) 647 - 5990

Serves As:
• Chairman of the Board, NiSource Inc.

NEALE, Karen
1101 Pennsylvania Ave. NW
Suite 200
Washington, DC 20004
karen.neale@ipaper.com
Tel: (202) 628 - 1223
Ext: 34
Fax:(202) 628 - 1368

Registered Federal Lobbyist.
Serves As:
• Washington Representative, Internat'l Paper

NEALIS, Jim
12950 Worldgate Dr.
Suite 600
Herndon, VA 20170
jim.nealis@lafargecorp.com
Tel: (703) 480 - 3600
Fax:(703) 796 - 2214

Serves As:
• Senior V. President, Human Resources, Lafarge North America, Inc.

NEARY, Daniel P.
Mutual of Omaha Plaza
Omaha, NE 68175-0001
Tel: (402) 342 - 7600
Fax:(402) 351 - 2775

Serves As:
• Chairman and Chief Exec. Officer, Mutual of Omaha Insurance Co.

NEEDHAM, III, Victor
P.O. Box 960
M/S 28AT
Cincinnati, OH 45201-0960
Tel: (513) 287 - 2609

Serves As:
• Manager, Regional Government Affairs, Cinergy Corp.

NEELY, Anthony
P.O. Box 300
Detroit, MI 48265-1000
anthony.neely@gm.com
Tel: (313) 665 - 9536
Fax:(248) 696 - 7300

Serves As:
• Manager, External Communications, General Motors Corp.

NEFF, Marie A.
600 Galleria Pkwy.
Suite 100
Atlanta, GA 30339
marie.neff@prgx.com
Tel: (770) 779 - 3900
Fax:(770) 779 - 3042

Serves As:
• Exec. V. President, Human Resources, PRG-Schultz Internat'l, Inc.

NEIHARDT, Jonas
2001 Pennsylvania Ave. NW
Suite 650
Washington, DC 20006
jonasn@qualcomm.com
Tel: (202) 263 - 0000
Fax:(202) 263 - 0010

Registered Federal Lobbyist.
Serves As:
• V. President, Government Relations, Qualcomm Inc.

NEIKIRK, Christopher R.
Three Commercial Pl.
Norfolk, VA 23510-2191
Tel: (757) 533 - 4960
Fax:(757) 629 - 2822

Serves As:
• Contact, Norfolk Southern Corp. Good Government Fund, Norfolk Southern Corp.

NEIL, Steven E.
P.O. Box 2300
Tulsa, OK 74192
Tel: (918) 588 - 6752
Fax:(918) 588 - 6300

Serves As:
• Investor Relations Contact, BOK Financial Corp.

NEILS, Michelle
225 Wilmington
Suite 500
Chadds Ford, PA 19317-9039
Tel: (610) 361 - 4115

Serves As:
• Manager, Government Affairs, State Farm Insurance Cos.

NEILSEN, Craig H.
3773 Howard Hughes Pkwy.
Suite 490
Las Vegas, NV 89109-0949
Tel: (702) 567 - 7000
Fax:(702) 369 - 8860

Serves As:
• Chairman, President, and Chief Exec. Officer, Ameristar Casinos, Inc.

NEISES, Kenneth J.
720 Olive St.
St. Louis, MO 63101
Tel: (314) 342 - 0601
Fax:(314) 421 - 1979

Serves As:
• Exec. V. President, Energy and Administration Services, The Laclede Group
Responsibilities include regulatory affairs.

NEKOLA, Kathleen
120 Park Ave.
New York, NY 10017
Tel: (917) 663 - 3686
Fax:(917) 663 - 5513

Serves As:
• Director, Corporate Affairs Planning, Altria Group, Inc.

NELSON, Carl A.
1101 17th St. NW
Suite 600
Washington, DC 20036
Tel: (202) 496 - 5654
Fax:(202) 496 - 5660

Serves As:
• Associate General Counsel, AMR Corp.

NELSON, David
600 Montgomery St.
26th Floor
San Francisco, CA 94111-2728
Tel: (415) 774 - 2700
Fax:(415) 398 - 1905

Serves As:
• Investor Relations Contact, URS Corp.

NELSON, Dean B.
745 Fifth Ave.
New York, NY 10151
Tel: (212) 745 - 0100
Fax:(212) 745 - 0121

Serves As:
• Chairman of the Board, Primedia Inc.

NELSON, Jr., Donald M.
101 Constitution Ave. NW
Suite 400 West
Washington, DC 20001
donald.nelson@altria.com
Tel: (202) 354 - 1500
Fax:(202) 354 - 1505

Registered Federal Lobbyist.
Serves As:
• V. President, International Business Relations, (Altria Corporate Services, Inc.), Altria Group, Inc.

NELSON, Jeffrey
1095 Ave. of the Americas
New York, NY 10036
jeffrey.nelson@verizonwireless.com
Tel: (212) 395 - 2121
Fax:(212) 869 - 3265

Serves As:
• Exec. Director, Media Relations and Public Policy, Verizon Wireless

NELSON, Jenna R.
400 N. Ashley Dr.
Tampa, FL 33602
jenna.nelson@sykes.com
Tel: (813) 274 - 1000
Fax:(813) 273 - 0148

Serves As:
• Group Executive and Senior V. President, Human Resources and Administration, Sykes Enterprises, Inc.

NELSON, Joanie
Fox Office Center
2211 Woodward Ave.
Detroit, MI 48201-3400
Tel: (313) 983 - 6000
Fax:(313) 983 - 6390

Serves As:
• V. President, Human Resources, Little Caesar Enterprises

NELSON, Karlyn
35 W. Wacker Dr.
Chicago, IL 60601
karlyn.nelson@chi.leoburnett.com
Tel: (312) 220 - 3921
Fax:(312) 220 - 3299

Serves As:
• Associate Manager, Corporate Public Relations, Leo Burnett Worldwide

NELSON, L. L.
9191 S. Jamaica St.
Englewood, CO 80112
Tel: (303) 771 - 0900
Fax:(720) 286 - 9250

Serves As:
• Treasurer, Foundation; PAC Treasurer, CH2M Hill Companies, Inc.

NELSON, Laura
1515 Broadway
20th Floor
New York, NY 10036
Tel: (212) 846 - 7920
Fax:(212) 258 - 7705

Serves As:
• Senior V. President, Corporate Communications, (VH-1), Viacom Inc./CBS Corp.

NELSON, Lisa
800 Connecticut Ave. NW
Suite 800
Washington, DC 20006
Tel: (202) 457 - 8582
Fax:(202) 457 - 8861

Registered Federal Lobbyist.
Serves As:
• V. President, External Relations, Time Warner Inc.

NELSON, R. D. "Dan"
2000 K St., NW
Suite 710
Washington, DC 20006
Tel: (202) 862 - 0200
Fax:(202) 862 - 0267

Registered Federal Lobbyist.
Serves As:
• V. President, Washington Office, Exxon Mobil Corp.

NELSON, Robert E.
999 Lake Dr.
Issaquah, WA 98027
Tel: (425) 313 - 8255
Fax:(425) 313 - 6430

Serves As:
• V. President, Financial Planning and Investor Relations, Costco Wholesale Corp.

NELSON, Sally
425 Portland Ave.
Minneapolis, MN 55415
Tel: (612) 673 - 7771
Fax:(612) 673 - 4835
TF: (800) 829 - 8742

Serves As:
• Director, Communications and Community Affairs, Star Tribune

NELSON, Steven C.
3250 Van Ness Ave.
San Francisco, CA 94109
Tel: (415) 616 - 8754
Fax:(415) 616 - 8463

Serves As:
• Director, Investor Relations, Williams-Sonoma, Inc.

NELSON, Thomas C.
2001 Rexford Rd.
Charlotte, NC 28211
Tel: (704) 365 - 7300
Fax:(704) 329 - 6421

Serves As:
• Chairman, President and Chief Exec. Officer, National Gypsum Co.

NELSON, Tim
Two International Plaza, Suite 240
Philadelphia, PA 19113
Tel: (610) 595 - 7079
Fax:(610) 595 - 7002

Serves As:
• Manager, Public Affairs, United Parcel Service (UPS)

NELSON, Todd S.
4615 E. Elwood St.
Phoenix, AZ 85040-1958
todd.nelson@apollogrp.edu
Tel: (480) 966 - 5394
Fax:(480) 379 - 3503
TF: (800) 990 - APOL

Serves As:
• Chairman, Chief Exec. Officer and President, Apollo Group, Inc.

NELSON, Virginia
770 Cochituate Rd.
Framingham, MA 01701
Tel: (508) 390 - 1000
Ext: 2467

Serves As:
• Assistant V. President, Community Relations, The TJX Companies, Inc.

NELSON, W. Mark
101 Ash St.
hq08d
San Diego, CA 92101-3017
wmnelson@sempraglobal.com
Tel: (619) 696 - 2060
Fax:(619) 696 - 2500
TF: (877) 736 - 7721

Serves As:
• Director, Governmental Affairs, Sempra Energy

NELSON, William M.
3M Center
Bldg. 225-1S-15
St. Paul, MN 55144-1000
wmnelson@mmm.com
Tel: (651) 733 - 6516
Fax:(651) 737 - 2901

Serves As:
• Regional Manager, State Government Affairs, 3M Company

NEMEROFF, Anne-Beth
100 Jim Moran Blvd.
Deerfield Beach, FL 33442
anne-beth.nemeroff@jmfamily.com
Tel: (954) 429 - 2387
Fax:(954) 429 - 2300

Serves As:
• Director, Corporate Communications, JM Family Enterprises, Inc.

NEMIRE, Laura B.
One Seagate
Toledo, OH 43666
laura.nemire@us.o-i.com
Tel: (419) 247 - 8053
Fax:(419) 247 - 2839

Serves As:
• Human Resources Specialist, Owens-Illinois, Inc.

NEMIROW, Arnold M.
P.O. Box 1028
Greenville, SC 29602
Tel: (864) 271 - 7733
Fax:(864) 282 - 9482

Serves As:
• Chairman, President and Chief Exec. Officer, Bowater Incorporated

NEMITZ, Bryce E.
McLeod USA Technology Park
6400 C St., SW
Cedar Rapids, IA 52406
Tel: (319) 364 - 0000
Fax:(319) 364 - 7800
TF: (800) 896 - 8330

Serves As:
• V. President, Corporate Communications and Investor Relations, McLeod USA Inc.

NEPERENY, David
100 Brodhead Rd.
Suite 230
Bethlehem, PA 18017
Tel: (610) 866 - 4400
Fax:(610) 866 - 9430

Serves As:
• President and Chief Exec. Officer, Buzzi Unicem USA

NERREN, Evonne
P.O. Box 40
Austin, TX 78767
Tel: (936) 829 - 1721

Serves As:
• Secretary - Treasurer, Temple-Inland Foundation, Temple-Inland Inc.

NESS, Judith L.
10700 E. 350 Hwy.
Kansas City, MO 64138
judy.ness@aquila.com
Tel: (816) 737 - 7528
Fax:(816) 737 - 7921

Serves As:
• Director, Community Services-Missouri, Aquila, Inc.

NESSELHOFF, Gayle
P.O. Box 599
Cincinnati, OH 45201-0599
Tel: (513) 945 - 8454
Fax:(513) 845 - 8979

Serves As:
• Contact, Procter and Gamble Fund, The Procter & Gamble Company

NESSER, Anita
P.O. Box 199000
Dallas, TX 75219-9000
Tel: (214) 981 - 5000
Fax:(214) 981 - 6859

Serves As:
• PAC Treasurer, Centex Corporation

NESSL, Sarah
4300 N. Harbor Blvd.
c-30-b
Fullerton, CA 92835
Tel: (714) 773 - 8763
Fax:(714) 773 - 7743
TF: (800) 742 - 2345

Serves As:
• Community Relations, Beckman Coulter, Inc.
Responsibilities include corporate philanthropy.

NESTER, Chris
3150 Sabre Dr.
Southlake, TX 76092
Tel: (682) 605 - 1000
Fax:(682) 264 - 9000

Serves As:
• Manager, Investor Relations, Sabre Holdings Corp.

NESTOR, David L.
1301 Ave. of the Americas
New York, NY 10019
david.nestor@us.pwc.com
Tel: (646) 471 - 4855
Fax:(646) 394 - 5355

Serves As:
• Head, Public Relations, PriceWaterhouseCoopers LLP

NETCHVOLODOFF, Alexander V.
1225 19th St. NW
Suite 450
Washington, DC 20036
alexander.netchvolodoff@cox.com
Tel: (202) 296 - 4933
Fax:(202) 296 - 4951

Registered Federal Lobbyist.
Serves As:
• Senior V. President, Public Policy, Cox Enterprises, Inc.

NETHERLAND, Joseph H.
1803 Gears Rd.
Houston, TX 60601
Tel: (281) 591 - 4100
Fax:(281) 591 - 4102

Serves As:
• Chariman, President and Chief Exec. Officer, FMC Technologies, Inc.

NETHERY, Regina
P.O. Box 1438
Louisville, KY 40201-1438
rnethery@humana.com
Tel: (502) 580 - 3644
Fax:(502) 580 - 3677
TF: (800) 486 - 2620

Serves As:
• V. President, Investor Relations, Humana Inc.

NETTLES, Patrick H.
1201 Winterson Rd.
Linthicum, MD 21090
pnettles@ciena.com
Tel: (410) 694 - 5700
Fax:(410) 694 - 5750

Serves As:
• Exec. Chairman of the Board, CIENA Corp.

NEUBAUER, Joseph
The ARAMARK Tower
1101 Market St.
Philadelphia, PA 19107
Tel: (215) 238 - 3000
Fax:(215) 238 - 3333
TF: (800) 999 - 8989

Serves As:
- Chairman and Chief Exec. Officer, ARAMARK

NEUMANN, E. John
Two Democracy Center
6903 Rockledge Dr.
Bethesda, MD 20817-1818
Tel: (301) 564 - 3200
Fax:(301) 564 - 3201

Registered Federal Lobbyist.
Serves As:
- V. President, Government Relations, USEC Inc.

NEUMANN, Larry
1331 Pennsylvania Ave. NW
Suite 550 South
Washington, DC 20004
Tel: (202) 637 - 8020
Fax:(202) 637 - 8028

Registered Federal Lobbyist.
Serves As:
- Representative, Boston Scientific Corp.

NEUMANN, Susan
250 E. Parkcenter Blvd.
Boise, ID 83706
Tel: (208) 395 - 6200
Fax:(208) 395 - 6631
TF: (877) 932 - 7948

Serves As:
- Senior V. President, Education, Communications and Public Affairs, Albertson's, Inc.

NEVADOMSKI, Stacie
33 Benedict Pl.
Greenwich, CT 06830
Tel: (203) 625 - 1101
Fax:(203) 625 - 2142
TF: (800) 366 - 4011

Serves As:
- Director, Corporate Affairs, Unilever Home & Personal Care - North America

Responsibilities include corporate philanthropy.

NEWBERRY, Steven
4650 Cushing Pkwy.
Fremont, CA 94538-6470
Tel: (510) 572 - 0200
Fax:(510) 572 - 2935

Serves As:
- President and Chief Exec. Officer, Lam Research Corp.

NEWBOE, Betty
3050 Bowers Ave.
P.O. Box 58039
Santa Clara, CA 95054-3299
betty_x_newboe@appliedmaterials.com
Tel: (408) 563 - 0647
Fax:(408) 986 - 2855

Serves As:
- Director, Product Public Relations, Applied Materials, Inc.

NEWCOMB, Sharon
One Ocean Spray Dr.
Lakeville-Middleboro, MA 02349
snewcomb@oceanspray.com
Tel: (508) 946 - 7185
Fax:(508) 946 - 7704
TF: (800) 662 - 3263

Serves As:
- Public Relations Specialist, Marketing Public Relations, Ocean Spray Cranberries, Inc.

NEWGARD, Amy
501 W. Michigan St.
Milwaukee, WI 53201
Tel: (414) 299 - 7722
Fax:(414) 299 - 6168

Serves As:
- Treasurer, Assurant Political Action Committee, Assurant

NEWMAN, Andrea Fischer
901 15th St. NW
Suite 310
M/S WAS 1150
Washington, DC 20005
Tel: (202) 842 - 3193
Fax:(202) 289 - 6834

Serves As:
- Senior V. President, Government Affairs, Northwest Airlines, Inc.

NEWMAN, Cindy C.
2030 Dow Center
Midland, MI 48674-0001
ccnewman@dow.com
Tel: (989) 636 - 1000
Fax:(989) 636 - 3518

Serves As:
- Director, Corporate Communications, The Dow Chemical Company

NEWMAN, Gary
150 N. Clinton St.
Chicago, IL 60661
Tel: (312) 726 - 1221
Fax:(312) 726 - 0360
TF: (800) 317 - 6245

Serves As:
- Exec. V. President, Chief People Officer, Human Resources, Information Resources, Inc.

NEWMAN, Lynn
211 Mount Airy Rd.
Basking Ridge, NJ 07920
lynnnewman@avaya.com
Tel: (908) 953 - 8692
Fax:(908) 953 - 7609

Serves As:
- Financial Media and Corporate Issues, Avaya Inc.

NEWMAN, Mark S.
Five Sylvan Way
Parsippany, NJ 07054
msn@drs.com
Tel: (973) 898 - 1500
Fax:(973) 898 - 4730

Serves As:
- Chairman, President and Chief Exec. Officer, DRS Technologies, Inc.

NEWMAN, Melissa
607 14th St. NW
Suite 950
Washington, DC 20005
Tel: (202) 429 - 3100
Fax:(202) 293 - 0561

Serves As:
- V. President, Federal Regulatory, Qwest Communications

NEWMAN, Neilly
209 Redwood Shores Pkwy.
Redwood City, CA 94065-1175
Tel: (650) 628 - 1500
Fax:(650) 628 - 1415

Serves As:
- Assistant V. President, Corporate Communications, Electronic Arts Inc.

NEWMAN, Ron
41 S. High St.
Columbus, OH 43287
ron.newman@huntington.com
Tel: (614) 480 - 8300
Fax:(614) 480 - 746

Serves As:
- Media Contact, Huntington Bancshares Inc.

NEWMAN, Steven L.
P.O. Box 2765
Houston, TX 77255-2765
Tel: (713) 232 - 7500
Fax:(713) 232 - 7031

Serves As:
- V. President, Human Resources, Transocean Inc.

NEWMAN, Jr., Thomas B.
321 Harrison Ave.
Boston, MA 02118-2238
Tel: (617) 482 - 2425
Fax:(617) 422 - 2910

Serves As:
- V. President, Corporate Relations, Teradyne, Inc.

Responsibilities include investor relations.

NEWPERSON, Deborah Cundy
P.O. Box 59159
Minneapolis, MN 55459-8212
Tel: (763) 212 - 1000
Fax:(763) 212 - 2219

Serves As:
- V. President, Community Affairs, Carlson Companies

NEWPORT, Janet G.
P.O. Box 6006
C420-536
Cypress, CA 90630
janet.newport@phs.com
Tel: (714) 226 - 3707
Fax:(714) 226 - 3653

Registered Federal Lobbyist.
Serves As:
- V. President, Public Policy, PacifiCare Health Systems, Inc.

NEWSOME, Susan
27175 Haggerty Rd.
Novi, MI 48377
Tel: (248) 675 - 6000
Fax:(248) 675 - 6200

Serves As:
- Leader, Human Resources, Tower Automotive, Inc.

NEWTON, Donna
350 S. Grand Ave., Suite 5100
Los Angeles, CA 90071
dnewton@rsac.com
Tel: (213) 687 - 7700
Fax:(213) 687 - 8792

Serves As:
- V. President, Human Resources, Reliance Steel & Aluminum Co.

NEWTON, Jo Ann
2244 Walnut Grove Ave.
Rosemead, CA 91770
joann.newton@edisonintl.com
Tel: (626) 302 - 2515

Serves As:
- V. President, Investor Relations, Edison Internat'l

NGHE, Quan V.
P.O. Box 32070
Louisville, KY 40232
Tel: (502) 874 - 8300

Serves As:
- Director, Investor Relations, YUM! Brands, Inc.

NIBLING, Kenneth L.
10000 Richmond Ave.
Fourth Floor
Houston, TX 77042-4200
Tel: (713) 346 - 7500
Fax:(713) 435 - 2195

Serves As:
• V. President, Human Resources, Nat'l Oilwell, Inc.

NIBLOCK, Robert A.
1000 Lowes Blvd.
Moorsville, NC 28117
Tel: (704) 758 - 100
Fax:(336) 658 - 4766
TF: (800) 445 - 6937

Serves As:
• Chairman and Chief Exec. Officer, Lowe's Companies, Inc.

NICELY, Olza M.
One GEICO Plaza
Washington, DC 20076
Tel: (301) 986 - 3000
Fax:(301) 986 - 2888

Serves As:
• Chairman and Chief Exec. Officer, GEICO Corp.

NICHOLAS, Charles R.
10500 W. 153rd St.
Orland Park, IL 60462
Tel: (708) 349 - 3300
Fax:(708) 349 - 5444

Serves As:
• Chairman of the Board, Andrew Corp.

NICHOLS, Craig J.
110 S.E. Sixth St.
28th Floor
Fort Lauderdale, FL 33301
Tel: (954) 769 - 2400
Fax:(954) 769 - 2664

Serves As:
• V. President, Human Resources, Republic Services, Inc.

NICHOLS, David
1425 K St. NW
Suite 650
Washington, DC 20005
david.nichols@roche.com
Tel: (202) 408 - 0090
Fax:(202) 408 - 1750

Registered Federal Lobbyist.
Serves As:
• Director, Federal Government Affairs, Hoffmann-La Roche Inc. (Roche)

NICHOLS, J. Larry
20 N. Broadway, Suite 1500
Oklahoma City, OK 73102
nicholsl@dvn.com
Tel: (405) 235 - 3611
Fax:(405) 552 - 4667

Serves As:
• Chairman and Chief Exec. Officer, Devon Energy Corp.

NICHOLS, John D.
225 W. Washington St.
Chicago, IL 60606-3418
Tel: (312) 372 - 9500
Fax:(312) 845 - 5305

Serves As:
• President and Chief Exec. Officer, The Marmon Group, Inc.

NICHOLS, Michael C.
1390 Enclave Pkwy.
Houston, TX 77077-2099
Tel: (281) 584 - 1390
Fax:(281) 584 - 2721

Serves As:
• V. President, General Counsel, Corp. Secretary; and PAC Treasurer, Sysco Corp.

NICHOLSON, Bruce J.
625 Fourth Ave. South
Minneapolis, MN 55415
bruce.nicholson@thrivent.com
Tel: (612) 340 - 7000
Fax:(612) 340 - 7373

Serves As:
• Chairman, President and Chief Exec. Officer, Thrivent Financial for Lutherans

NICHOLSON, Ed
P.O. Box 2020
Springdale, AR 72765-2020
ed.nicholson@tyson.com
Tel: (479) 290 - 4591
Fax:(479) 290 - 7984
TF: (800) 643 - 3410

Serves As:
• Director, Corporate Community Relations, Tyson Foods, Inc.

NICHOLSON, Jon R.
515 Post Oak Blvd., Suite 600
Houston, TX 77027-3415
Tel: (713) 693 - 4194
Fax:(713) 693 - 4323
TF: (800) 257 - 3826

Serves As:
• Senior V. President, Human Resources, Weatherford Internat'l Ltd.

NICHOLSON, Marlene
1501 K St., NW
Suite 500
Washington, DC 20005
marlene.nicholson@barcap.com
Tel: (202) 736 - 8653

Registered Federal Lobbyist.
Serves As:
• Director, Government Relations, Barclays Capital

NICHOLSON, Thomas
2700 Sanders Rd.
Prospect Heights, IL 60070
Tel: (847) 564 - 5000
Fax:(847) 805 - 7452

Serves As:
• Public Affairs, HSBC North America Holdings Inc.

NICHOLSON, Jr., Thomas A.
200 W. Second St.
Winston-Salem, NC 27101
Tel: (336) 733 - 3058

Serves As:
• Exec. V. President, Investor Relations, BB&T Corp.

NICKELS, Janet
One S. Jersey Plaza
Folsom, NJ 08037
Tel: (609) 561 - 9000
Fax:(609) 561 - 8225

Serves As:
• Sr. Vice President, Corporate Comm. and Admin. Services, South Jersey Gas Co.

NICKLES, J. David
400 Perimeter Center Terrace, Suite 1000
Atlanta, GA 30346
david.nickles@pfizer.com
Tel: (770) 551 - 5174
Fax:(770) 804 - 1783

Serves As:
• Senior Government Relations Manager--Florida, Pfizer Inc.

NICOLI, David P.
P.O. Box 15437
Wilmington, DE 19850-5437
Tel: (302) 886 - 3771
Fax:(302) 886 - 3029
TF: (800) 456 - 3669

Serves As:
• V. President, Communications and External Relations, AstraZeneca Pharmaceuticals

NICOLL, Edward J.
Three Times Square
New York, NY 10036
Tel: (212) 310 - 9500
Fax:(646) 223 - 9054
TF: (800) 225 - 5008

Serves As:
• Chief Exec. Officer, Instinet Group Inc.

NIEHAUS, Fred
6200 S. Quebec St.
Greenwood Village, CO 80111
Tel: (303) 967 - 8000
Fax:(303) 967 - 6705

Serves As:
• Senior V. President, Public Affairs, First Data

NIEKAMP, Randy
44 S. Washington St.
New Bremen, OH 45869
randy.niekamp@crown.com
Tel: (419) 629 - 2311
Fax:(419) 629 - 3796

Serves As:
• V. President, Human Resources, Crown Equipment Corp.

NIELSEN, John A.
3210 Watling St.
East Chicago, IN 46312
john.nielsen@ispat.com
Tel: (219) 399 - 6631
Fax:(219) 399 - 6637

Serves As:
• Director, Government and Public Affairs, Ispat Inland Inc.

NIELSON, Caroline
60 Massachusetts Ave. NE
Washington, DC 20002
Tel: (202) 906 - 3000
Fax:(202) 906 - 3865

Serves As:
• Senior Director, Government Affairs - Senate, Amtrak

NIEMI, Dennis L.
30 W. Superior St.
Duluth, MN 55802
dniemi@mnpower.com
Tel: (218) 723 - 3945
Fax:(218) 279 - 5050

Serves As:
• Director, Environmental Services, ALLETE

NIEMIEC, Richard
3535 Blue Cross Rd.
Eagan, MN 55122--115
Tel: (651) 662 - 8550
Fax:(651) 662 - 1989
TF: (800) 382 - 2000

Serves As:
• Senior V. President, Corporate Affairs, Blue Cross and Blue Shield of Minnesota

NIEMIER, Charles E.
P.O. Box 587
Warsaw, IN 46581-0587
charles.niemier@biometmail.com
Tel: (574) 267 - 6639
Fax:(574) 267 - 8137

Serves As:
• Senior V. President, International Operations, Biomet Inc.

NIENABER, Kelli
7565 Irvine Center Dr.
Irvine, CA 92618
Tel: (949) 471 - 7000
Fax:(949) 471 - 7041

Registered Federal Lobbyist.
Serves As:
- Manager, Government Relations, Gateway, Inc.

NIFFENEGGER, Jonelle
One Tower Ln.
Suite 1000
Oakbrook Terrace, IL 60181-4624
Tel: (630) 571 - 7700
Fax:(630) 571 - 0317
TF: (800) 225 - 8000

Serves As:
- Director, Public Relations, DeVry Inc.

NIGBOR, Donald E.
3000 Technology Dr.
Angleton, TX 77515
Tel: (979) 849 - 6550
Fax:(979) 848 - 5270

Serves As:
- Chairman of the Board, Benchmark Electronics

NIGRO, Melissa B.
P.O. Box 6675
Radnor, PA 19087-8675
melissa.nigro@airgas.com
Tel: (610) 902 - 6206
Fax:(610) 687 - 1052
TF: (800) 255 - 2165

Serves As:
- Director, Investor Relations, Airgas, Inc.

NIKITAS, Ariana
One Tellabs Center
1415 W. Diehl Rd.
Naperville, IL 60563
ariana.nikitas@tellabs.com
Tel: (630) 798 - 2532
Fax:(630) 798 - 2000

Serves As:
- Manager, Public Relations, Tellabs

NIKOLAI, Jim T.
800 Nicollet Mall
Minneapolis, MN 55402
Tel: (612) 303 - 7860
Fax:(612) 303 - 0788

Serves As:
- PAC Contact, U.S. Bancorp

NIKOLIS, William G.
P.O. Box 2521
Houston, TX 77252-2521
wnikolis@teppco.com
Tel: (713) 759 - 3636
Fax:(713) 759 - 3645
TF: (800) 877 - 3636

Registered Federal Lobbyist.
Serves As:
- Director, Government and Public Affairs, Texas Eastern Products Pipeline Company, LLC (TEPPCO)

NINES, Chris
P.O. Box 40
Austin, TX 78767
chrisnines@templeinland.com
Tel: (512) 434 - 5587
Fax:(512) 434 - 3750

Serves As:
- Director, Investor Relations, Temple-Inland Inc.

Responsibilities include corporate communications.

NIX, Jerry
2999 Circle 75 Pkwy.
Atlanta, GA 30339
jerry_nix@genpt.com
Tel: (770) 953 - 1700
Fax:(770) 956 - 2211

Serves As:
- Executive V. President, Finance, Genuine Parts Co.

Responsibilities include investor relations and corporate contributions and communications.

NIXON, Michael
One S. Jersey Plaza
Folsom, NJ 08037
Tel: (609) 561 - 9000
Ext: 4464
Fax:(609) 561 - 8225

Serves As:
- Supervisor, Corporate Communications, South Jersey Gas Co.

NOAH, Sandi
175 Ghent Rd.
Fairlawn, OH 44333-3330
Tel: (330) 869 - 4292
Fax:(330) 869 - 4288

Serves As:
- Director, Communications, OMNOVA Solutions Inc.

NOBLES, Anne
Lilly Corporate Center
Indianapolis, IN 46285
Tel: (317) 276 - 2000
Fax:(317) 277 - 6579

Serves As:
- V. President, Corporate Affairs, Eli Lilly and Company

NOBLITT, Niles L.
P.O. Box 587
Warsaw, IN 46581-0587
niles.noblitt@biometmail.com
Tel: (574) 267 - 6639
Fax:(574) 267 - 8137

Serves As:
- Chairman of the Board, Biomet Inc.

NOCERA, Barbara
1025 Connecticut Ave., N.W., Suite 910
Washington, DC 20036
bnocera@mazdausa.com
Tel: (202) 467 - 5096

Registered Federal Lobbyist.
Serves As:
- Director, Government and Public Affairs, Mazda North American Operations

NODDLE, Jeff
P.O. Box 990
Minneapolis, MN 55440
Tel: (952) 828 - 4000
Fax:(952) 828 - 8998

Serves As:
- Chairman, President and Chief Exec. Officer, Supervalu Inc.

NOEL, Jeff
Administrative Center
2000 N. M-63
Benton Harbor, MI 49022-2692
Tel: (269) 923 - 5000
Fax:(269) 923 - 5443

Serves As:
- V. President, Communications and Public Affairs, Whirlpool Corp.

NOGUCHI, Phil
555 13th St. NW
Suite 600 West
Washington, DC 20004
Tel: (202) 585 - 9610

Serves As:
- Director, Regulatory Development, Amgen Inc.

NOKES, Sara
1101 Pennsylvania Ave. NW
Suite 1000
Washington, DC 20004
nokess@citigroup.com
Tel: (202) 879 - 6849
Fax:(202) 783 - 4460

Registered Federal Lobbyist.
Serves As:
- Manager, Political and External Affairs, Citigroup, Inc.

NOLAN, George
2775 Sanders Rd.
Northbrook, IL 60062-6127
Tel: (847) 402 - 5000
Fax:(847) 326 - 7519
TF: (800) 574 - 3553

Serves As:
- National Media Contact, Allstate Insurance Co.

NOLAN, George C.
153 E. 53rd St.
56th Floor
New York, NY 10022-4611
Tel: (212) 258 - 4000
Fax:(212) 767 - 0580
TF: (800) 743 - 6367

Serves As:
- Chief Exec.Officer, Siemens Corp.

NOLAN, James P.
Mutual of Omaha Plaza
Omaha, NE 68175-0001
jim.nolan@mutualofomaha.com
Tel: (402) 351 - 2944
Fax:(402) 351 - 2407

Serves As:
- First V. President, Corporate Communications, Mutual of Omaha Insurance Co.

NOLAN, Jr., Joseph R.
One NSTAR Way
M/S P1700
Westwood, MA 02090
joseph_nolan@nstaronline.com
Tel: (617) 424 - 2446
Fax:(617) 424 - 2523

Serves As:
- Senior V. President, Customer and Corporate Relations, NSTAR

NOLAN, William C.
P.O. Box 7000
El Dorado, AR 71731-7000
Tel: (870) 862 - 6411
Fax:(870) 864 - 6373

Serves As:
- Chairman of the Board, Murphy Oil Corp.

NOLAND, Thomas
P.O. Box 1438
Louisville, KY 40201-1438
Tel: (502) 580 - 3674
Fax:(502) 580 - 3677
TF: (800) 486 - 2620

Serves As:
- Senior V. President, Corporate Communications, Humana Inc.

NOLLEN, Margaret R.
P.O. Box 105605
Atlanta, GA 30348
Tel: (404) 652 - 4000
Fax:(404) 654 - 4789
TF: (800) 519 - 3111

Serves As:
- V. President, Investor Relations, Georgia-Pacific Corp.

NOLTE, Reed

1211 Ave. of the Americas
New York, NY 10036
rnolte@newscorp.com
Tel: (212) 852 - 7092
Fax:(212) 852 - 7145

Serves As:
- Senior V. President, Investor Relations, News Corporation Ltd.

NORAT, Cecelia

70 Pine St.
New York, NY 10270
Tel: (212) 770 - 7000
Fax:(212) 770 - 7821

Serves As:
- V. President, State Relations, American Internat'l Group, Inc.

NORCROSS, Jeanne

P.O. Box 8700
Grand Rapids, MI 49518
jeanne_norcross@spartanstores.com
Tel: (616) 878 - 2830
Fax:(616) 878 - 2775

Serves As:
- Director, Public Relations, Spartan Stores Inc.

NORDEN, Jed L.

3241 Westerville Rd.
Columbus, OH 43224
Tel: (614) 237 - 7100
Fax:(614) 238 - 5774

Serves As:
- Exec. V. President, Human Resources, Retail Ventures, Inc.

NORDSTROM, Bruce A.

1617 Sixth Ave.
Suite 700
Seattle, WA 98101
bruce.nordstrom@nordstrom.com
Tel: (206) 628 - 2111
Fax:(206) 628 - 1795

Serves As:
- Chairman of the Board, Nordstrom, Inc.

NORMAN, Brian

502 Beach St., Room 119C
Flint, MI 48502
Tel: (810) 768 - 0394
Fax:(810) 768 - 0386

Serves As:
- Manager, External Affairs, SBC Michigan

NORRIS, Cathy J.

P.O. Box 260317
Littleton, CO 80163
cathy.norris@bnsf.com
Tel: (303) 480 - 7406
Fax:(303) 480 - 7407

Serves As:
- Director, Government Affairs, Burlington Northern Santa Fe Corporation

NORRIS, Diane

P.O. Box 7608
Boise, ID 83707
Tel: (208) 377 - 6840
Fax:(208) 377 - 6097

Serves As:
- Assistant to the President, Intermountain Gas Co.

Responsibilities include corporate philanthropy.

NORRIS, Frances

101 Constitution Ave. NW, Suite 400W
Washington, DC 20001
Tel: (202) 354 - 1554
Fax:(202) 354 - 1505

Registered Federal Lobbyist.
Serves As:
- V. President, Federal Government Affairs - Food, Kraft Foods, Inc.

NORRIS, Jr., John W.

P.O. Box 799900
Dallas, TX 75379-9900
john.norris@lennoxintl.com
Tel: (972) 497 - 5000
Fax:(972) 497 - 5299

Serves As:
- Chairman of the Board, Lennox Internat'l

NORRIS, Paul J.

7500 Grace Dr.
Columbia, MD 21044
Tel: (410) 531 - 4000
Fax:(410) 531 - 4367

Serves As:
- Chairman of the Board, W. R. Grace & Co.

NORTHAM, Donna

P.O. Box 1365
Columbia, SC 29202
Tel: (803) 213 - 5634
Fax:(803) 213 - 7461
TF: (800) 325 - 4368

Serves As:
- Assistant V. President, Corporate and External Communications, Colonial Life & Accident Insurance Co.

Responsibilities include community affairs.

NORTHCUTT, Scott M.

1200 S. Pine Island Rd.
Suite 61000
Plantation, FL 33324
Tel: (954) 888 - 7000
Fax:(954) 888 - 7310

Serves As:
- Exec. V. President, Human Resources, DHL Holdings (USA), Inc.

NORTON, David K.

1111 Westchester Ave.
White Plains, NY 10604
david.norton@starwoodhotels.com
Tel: (914) 640 - 5253
Fax:(914) 640 - 8310
TF: (877) 443 - 4585

Serves As:
- Exec. V. President, Human Resources, Starwood Hotels and Resorts Worldwide, Inc.

NORTON, JoAnne

17666 Fitch
Irvine, CA 92614
Tel: (949) 253 - 2300
Fax:(949) 474 - 7675

Serves As:
- V. President, Shareholder Relations, Freedom Communications Inc.

NORTON, Joe

70 Pine St.
New York, NY 10270
Tel: (212) 770 - 3144
Fax:(212) 770 - 7821

Serves As:
- Director, Public Relations, American Internat'l Group, Inc.

NORTON, Margaret

800 Boylston St.
Boston, MA 02199-8003
margaret_norton@nstaronline.com
Tel: (617) 424 - 2490
Fax:(617) 424 - 2736

Serves As:
- Director, Corporate Communications, NSTAR

NORTON, Marshall N.

P.O. Box 85333
Richmond, VA 23293-0001
Tel: (804) 649 - 6000
Fax:(804) 649 - 6865

Serves As:
- Chief Exec.Officer, Media General Inc.

NORTON, Mary

55 Technology Way
West Greenwich, RI 02817
mary.norton@gtech.com
Tel: (401) 392 - 7603
Fax:(401) 392 - 0315

Serves As:
- Director, Investor Relations, GTECH Corp.

NORTON, Nancy T.

1100 Wilson Blvd.
Suite 1500
Arlington, VA 22209
Tel: (703) 841 - 5700
Fax:(703) 841 - 5792

Registered Federal Lobbyist.
Serves As:
- Director, Government Relations, Raytheon Co.

NORTON, Patrick H.

1284 N. Telegraph Rd.
Monroe, MI 48162
Tel: (734) 242 - 1444
Fax:(734) 457 - 4910

Serves As:
- Chairman of the Board, La-Z-Boy Incorporated

NORTON, Reginald J.

One PPG Pl.
Pittsburgh, PA 15272
rnorton@ppg.com
Tel: (412) 434 - 2398

Serves As:
- Global Director, Environment, Health and Safety, PPG Industries Inc.

NORTON, Rita

1666 K St. NW
Suite 500
Washington, DC 20006
Tel: (202) 887 - 1469

Registered Federal Lobbyist.
Serves As:
- V. President, Government Affairs, AmeriSource Bergen Corp.

NORVE, Joan

13410 Sutton Park Dr. South
Jacksonville, FL 32224
jnorve@landstar.com
Tel: (904) 390 - 1516
Fax:(904) 390 - 1216
TF: (800) 872 - 9400

Serves As:
- V. President, Human Resources, Landstar System, Inc.

NORVELLE, James W.

P.O. Box 26532
Richmond, VA 23261
Jim_Norvelle@dom.com
Tel: (804) 771 - 6115
Fax:(804) 771 - 3054

Serves As:
- Director, Media Relations (Electric), Dominion Resources, Inc.

NORWITZ, Steven E.

100 E. Pratt St.
Baltimore, MD 21202
steve_norwitz@troweprice.com
Tel: (410) 345 - 2124
Fax:(410) 345 - 4661
TF: (800) 638 - 7890

Serves As:
- V. President, Public Relations, T. Rowe Price Associates

NOSBUSCH, Keith
1201 S. Second St.
Milwaukee, WI 43204-2496
Tel: (414) 382 - 2000
Fax:(414) 382 - 4444

Serves As:
• Chairman and Chief Exec. Officer, Rockwell Automation

NOTEBAERT, Richard C.
1801 California St.
50th Floor
Denver, CO 80202
Tel: (303) 992 - 1414
Fax:(303) 296 - 4097
TF: (800) 899 - 7780

Serves As:
• Chairman and Chief Exec. Officer, Qwest Communications

NOVAK, David C.
P.O. Box 32070
Louisville, KY 40232
Tel: (502) 874 - 8300

Serves As:
• Chairman and Chief Exec. Officer, YUM! Brands, Inc.

NOVAK, Richard E.
6001 W. Market St.
Greensboro, NC 27409
rnovak@gfd.com
Tel: (336) 316 - 4000
Fax:(336) 316 - 4057

Serves As:
• V. President, Human Resources, Guilford Mills, Inc.
Responsibilities include communications.

NOVICH, Neil S.
2621 W. 15th Place
Chicago, IL 60608
neil.novich@ryersontull.com
Tel: (773) 762 - 2121
Fax:(773) 762 - 3311

Serves As:
• Chairman, President and Chief Exec. Officer, Ryerson Tull

NOVIELLO, Nick
101 Columbia Rd.
Morristown, NJ 07962-4658
Tel: (973) 455 - 2222
Fax:(973) 455 - 4807

Serves As:
• Director, Investor Relations, Honeywell Internat'l, Inc.

NOWICKI, Joe
P.O. Box 302
Zeeland, MI 49464-0302
Tel: (616) 654 - 3000
Fax:(616) 654 - 3632

Serves As:
• V. President, Investor Relations, Herman Miller Inc.

NOWICKI, Paul E.
547 W. Jackson Blvd., Suite 1509
Chicago, IL 60661-5717
paul.nowicki@bnsf.com
Tel: (312) 850 - 5678
Fax:(312) 850 - 5677

Serves As:
• Assistant V. President, Government and Public Policy, Burlington Northern Santa Fe Corporation

NOWLAN, Kelly
47 State Circle
Suite 402
Annapolis, MD 21401
kelly.nowlan@constellation.com
Tel: (410) 269 - 5195
Fax:(410) 269 - 5289
TF: (888) 460 - 2002

Serves As:
• Government Relations Administrator, Constellation Energy

NOYES, Chris
4643 S. Ulster St.
Suite 1300
Denver, CO 80237-2868
Tel: (303) 220 - 6693
Fax:(303) 220 - 6662

Serves As:
• Investor Relations- Denver, UnitedGlobalCom, Inc.

NUGENT, Jeffrey L.
2701 Cambridge Ct.
Suite 300
Auburn Hills, MI 48326
Tel: (248) 340 - 9090
Fax:(248) 340 - 9345

Serves As:
• V. President, Human Resources, Champion Enterprises, Inc.

NUGENT, Robert J.
9330 Balboa Ave.
San Diego, CA 92123-1516
Tel: (858) 571 - 2121
Fax:(858) 571 - 2225

Serves As:
• Chairman and Chief Exec. Officer, Jack in the Box Inc.

NUMAINVILLE, Brian
7600 France Ave. South
Edina, MN 55435
brian.numainville@nashfinch.com
Tel: (952) 832 - 0534
Fax:(952) 844 - 1234

Serves As:
• Senior Director, Research and Public Relations, Nash Finch Company

NUNAN, William C.
1901 Harrison St.
Oakland, CA 94612
Tel: (510) 446 - 3614
Fax:(510) 446 - 4259

Serves As:
• Group Senior V. President, Golden West Financial Corp.

NUNEZ, Alexander G.
47 State Circle, Suite 403
Annapolis, MD 21401
alexander.g.nunez@constellation.com
Tel: (410) 269 - 5193
Fax:(410) 269 - 5289
TF: (888) 460 - 2002

Serves As:
• Senior Public Affairs Representative and Annapolis Counsel, Constellation Energy

NUSBAUM, Edward E.
175 W. Jackson Blvd.
20th Floor
Chicago, IL 60604
edward.nusbaum@gt.com
Tel: (312) 856 - 0001
Fax:(312) 861 - 1340

Serves As:
• Chief Exec. Officer, Grant Thornton LLP

NUSBAUM, Sandra
4200 Wackenhut Dr.
Palm Beach Gardens, FL 33410-4243
snusbaum@wackenhut.com
Tel: (561) 622 - 5656
Fax:(561) 691 - 6738
TF: (800) 922 - 6488

Serves As:
• Senior V. President, Human Resources, The Wackenhut Corporation

NUSSBAUM, Bennett L.
P.O. Box B
Jacksonville, FL 32203-0297
bennettnussbaum@winn-dixie.com
Tel: (904) 370 - 6655
Fax:(904) 783 - 5294

Serves As:
• Senior V. President and Chief Financial Officer, Winn-Dixie Stores
Responsibilities include investor relations.

NUTI, William R. (Bill)
1700 S. Patterson Blvd.
Dayton, OH 45479
Tel: (937) 445 - 5000
Fax:(937) 445 - 1847

Serves As:
• President and Chief Exec. Officer, NCR Corporation

NUTTER, W. L.
50 N. Laura St., Suite 1900
Jacksonville, FL 32202-3638
Tel: (904) 357 - 9100
Fax:(904) 357 - 9101

Serves As:
• Chairman and Chief Exec. Officer, Rayonier Inc.

NUTTING, Lisa
2000 Post Oak Blvd., Suite 100
Houston, TX 77056-4400
lisa.nutting@apachecorp.com
Tel: (713) 296 - 7279
Fax:(713) 296 - 6480
TF: (800) 874 - 3262

Serves As:
• Manager, Corporate Communications, Apache Corp.

NUXOLL, Erin
P.O. Box 50
Boise, ID 83728-0001
Tel: (208) 384 - 394
Fax:(208) 384 - 4841

Serves As:
• V. President, Human Resources, Boise Cascade Corp.

O'BRIEN, Christine Davis
4205 Lonesome Valley Ct.
Austin, TX 78731
christine.daviso'brien@astrazeneca.com
Tel: (512) 419 - 0455
Fax:(512) 419 - 0456
TF: (800) 822 - 9209
Ext: 60012

Serves As:
• Director, State Government Affairs, AstraZeneca Pharmaceuticals

O'BRIEN, Dan
607 E. Adams St.
Springfield, IL 62739
Tel: (217) 535 - 5489
Fax:(217) 535 - 5095

Serves As:
• Public Affairs Representative, (AmerenCIPS), Ameren Corp.

O'BRIEN, David
120 Fifth Ave. Pl.
Suite 3124
Pittsburgh, PA 15222
Tel: (412) 544 - 5250
Fax:(412) 544 - 8054

Serves As:
• Exec. V. President, Government Services, Highmark Inc.

O'BRIEN, Dermot J.
730 Third Ave.
New York, NY 10017-3206
Tel: (212) 490 - 9000
Fax:(212) 916 - 5952

Serves As:
• Exec. V. President, Human Resources, TIAA/CREF

O'BRIEN, Gary
100 Independence Mall West
Philadelphia, PA 19106-2399
Tel: (215) 592 - 3409
Fax:(215) 592 - 3377

Serves As:
- Director, Investor Relations, Rohm and Haas Co.

O'BRIEN, James J.
P.O. Box 391
Covington, KY 41012-0391
Tel: (859) 815 - 3333
Fax:(859) 815 - 4795

Serves As:
- Chairman and Chief Exec. Officer, Ashland Inc.

O'BRIEN, Kevin
One Nationwide Plaza
Columbus, OH 43215-2220
obrienk1@nationwide.com
Tel: (614) 677 - 5331
Fax:(614) 249 - 3073

Serves As:
- V. President, Investor Relations, Nationwide

O'BRIEN, Morgan K.
411 Seventh Ave.
Pittsburgh, PA 15219
mobrien@dqe.com
Tel: (412) 393 - 6000
Fax:(412) 393 - 6448

Serves As:
- President and Chief Exec. Officer, Duquesne Light Holdings

O'BRIEN, Polly
World Headquarters
One Elmcroft Rd.
63-15
Stamford, CT 06926-0700
polly.obrien@pb.com
Tel: (203) 351 - 6669
Fax:(203) 351 - 6303

Serves As:
- Director, Community Affairs, Pitney Bowes Inc.

Responsibilities include corporate philanthropy.

O'BRIEN, Roseanne
1840 Century Park East
Los Angeles, CA 90067-2199
Tel: (310) 201 - 3333
Fax:(310) 201 - 3023

Serves As:
- Corporate V. President, Communications, Northrop Grumman Corp.

O'BRIEN, Rosemary
1515 Broadway
New York, NY 10036
Tel: (212) 258 - 6000
Fax:(212) 258 - 7705

Serves As:
- V. President, Communications, (Nickelodeon/Nick at Nite), Viacom Inc./CBS Corp.

O'BRIEN, Rosemary L.
1401 I St., N.W., Suite 340
Washington, DC 20005-2225
Tel: (202) 371 - 9279
Fax:(202) 371 - 9169

Registered Federal Lobbyist.
Serves As:
- V. President, Public Affairs, C F Industries, Inc.

O'BRIEN, Sean P.
The Lenox Bldg., Suite 700
3399 Peachtree Rd. NE
Atlanta, GA 30326
sean.obrien@premiereglobal.com
Tel: (404) 262 - 8462
Fax:(866) 825 - 7082

Serves As:
- Senior V. President, Strategic Planning and Investor Relations, Premiere Global Services, Inc.

O'BRIEN, Timothy J.
One American Rd.
Dearborn, MI 48126
Tel: (313) 322 - 3000
TF: (800) 555 - 5259

Serves As:
- V. President, Corporate Relations, Ford Motor Co.

O'BRIEN, III, Urban F. "Obie"
2000 Post Oak Blvd., Suite 100
Houston, TX 77056-4400
obie.obrien@apachecorp.com
Tel: (713) 296 - 6150
Fax:(713) 296 - 6480
TF: (800) 874 - 3262

Serves As:
- Director, Governmental, Regulatory and Community Affairs, Apache Corp.

O'BRIEN, William
50 Minuteman Rd.
Andover, MA 01810
Tel: (978) 684 - 1000
Fax:(978) 684 - 1658

Serves As:
- Executive Chairman of the Board, Enterasys Networks

O'CONNELL, Cronan
607 14th St. NW
Suite 950
Washington, DC 20005
Tel: (202) 429 - 3100
Fax:(202) 293 - 0561

Serves As:
- V. President, Federal Regulatory, Qwest Communications

O'CONNELL, James J.
1300 I St. NW
Suite 420 East
Washington, DC 20005
james.j.oconnell@ceridian.com
Tel: (202) 789 - 6525
Fax:(202) 789 - 6593

Registered Federal Lobbyist.
Serves As:
- V. President, Government Relations and HR Policy, Ceridian Corp.

O'CONNELL, Maureen A.
444 N. Capitol St., N.W., Suite 740
Washington, DC 20001
moconnell@newscorp.com
Tel: (202) 824 - 6503
Fax:(202) 824 - 6510

Registered Federal Lobbyist.
Serves As:
- V. President, Regulatory and Government Affairs, News Corporation Ltd.

O'CONNOR, Ann M.
100 Universal City Plaza
Universal City, CA 91608
Tel: (818) 777 - 9632
Fax:(818) 866 - 3363

Serves As:
- V. President, Governmental Relations, NBC Universal

O'CONNOR, Edward J.
11270 W. Park Place
Milwaukee, WI 53224-9510
Tel: (414) 359 - 4101
Fax:(414) 359 - 4198

Serves As:
- Foundation Contact, A. O. Smith Corp.

Responsibilities also include corporate philanthropy.

O'CONNOR, James E.
110 S.E. Sixth St.
28th Floor
Fort Lauderdale, FL 33301
Tel: (954) 769 - 2400
Fax:(954) 769 - 2664

Serves As:
- Chairman and Chief Exec. Officer, Republic Services, Inc.

O'CONNOR, Kevin
847 Gibraltar Dr.
Milpitas, CA 95035
Tel: (408) 957 - 8500

Serves As:
- Exec. V. President, Human Resources, Solectron Corp.

O'CONNOR, Patrick
300 E. Randolph St.
Chicago, IL 60601
Tel: (312) 653 - 6000
Fax:(312) 819 - 1220

Serves As:
- Senior V. President, Human Resources Business, Health Care Service Corp.

O'CONNOR, Teresa
1350 I St. NW
Suite 400
Washington, DC 20005-3306
Tel: (202) 371 - 6900
Fax:(202) 842 - 3578

Registered Federal Lobbyist.
Serves As:
- Director, Global Regulatory Relations, Motorola, Inc.

O'DELL, Julie
P.O. Box 419580
Kansas City, MO 64141-6580
jodell1@hallmark.com
Tel: (816) 274 - 5961
Fax:(816) 274 - 5061

Serves As:
- Director, Public Relations, Hallmark Cards, Inc.

O'DELL, Susan
One Targeting Centre
Windsor, CT 06095
Tel: (860) 285 - 6100
Fax:(860) 285 - 1567
TF: (800) 559 - 2386

Serves As:
- Contact, Advo-System Inc. Corporate Giving Program, Advo Inc.

O'DELL, Waldon W.
5995 Mayfair Rd.
P.O. Box 3077
North Canton, OH 44720-8077
odellw@diebold.com
Tel: (330) 490 - 4000
Fax:(330) 490 - 3794

Serves As:
- Chairman and Chief Exec. Officer, Diebold, Inc.

O'DONNELL, Carol
Brighton Landing, 20 Guest St.
Boston, MA 02135-2088
Tel: (617) 783 - 4000
Ext: 2351
Fax:(617) 783 - 5152
TF: (800) 343 - 1395

Serves As:
- V. President, Human Resources, New Balance Athletic Shoe, Inc.

O'DONNELL, John A.
801 Pennsylvania Ave. NW
Suite 212
Washington, DC 20004
john.a.odonnell@xcelenergy.com
Tel: (202) 783 - 5505
Fax:(202) 783 - 6873

Registered Federal Lobbyist.
Serves As:
- Director, Federal Public Affairs, Xcel Energy, Inc.

O'DONNELL, Kathy
One Citizens Plaza
Providence, RI 02903
kathy.o'donnell@citizensbank.com
Tel: (401) 455 - 5507
Fax:(401) 456 - 7819

Serves As:
- V. President and Director, Public Relations, Citizens Financial Group, Inc.

O'DONNELL, Nancy
Six Concourse Pkwy.
Suite 3300
Atlanta, GA 30328
Tel: (770) 289 - 6208

Serves As:
- V. President, Investor Relations, Sprectrum Brands

O'DONOVAN, Timothy J.
9341 Courtland Dr. NE
Rockford, MI 49351
Tel: (616) 866 - 5500
Fax:(616) 866 - 0257

Serves As:
- President, Chief Exec. Officer and Chairman of the Board, Wolverine World Wide, Inc.

O'FARRELL, Michael K.
3050 Bowers Ave.
P.O. Box 58039
Santa Clara, CA 95054-3299
Tel: (408) 727 - 5555
Fax:(408) 748 - 5119

Serves As:
- V. President, Community and University Relations, Applied Materials, Inc.

O'HARA, Stephen M.
424 S. Woods Mill Rd.
Chesterfield, MO 63017
Tel: (314) 854 - 3800
Fax:(314) 854 - 3890

Serves As:
- Chief Exec. Officer, Angelica Corp.

O'HOLLAREN, Sean B.
1001 Pennsylvania Ave. NW
Suite 700 South
Washington, DC 20004
Tel: (202) 662 - 2650
Fax:(202) 662 - 2674

Serves As:
- Senior Director, Government Relations, Honeywell Internat'l, Inc.

O'KEEFE, Jeffrey
Ten Hwy. 35
Red Bank, NJ 07701-5902
Tel: (732) 747 - 7800
Fax:(732) 747 - 6835

Serves As:
- Director, Investor Relations, Hovnanian Enterprises, Inc.

O'KEEFE, Rush
101 Constitution Ave., NW
Suite 801 East
Washington, DC 20001
Tel: (202) 218 - 3800

Registered Federal Lobbyist.
Serves As:
- V. President, Regulatory, FedEx Corp.

O'KEEFE, Sean M.
P.O. Box 3440
Honolulu, HI 96801-3440
Tel: (808) 877 - 0081
Fax:(808) 871 - 7663

Serves As:
- Director, Environmental Affairs, Alexander & Baldwin, Inc.

O'LEARY, David
225 Franklin St.
Boston, MA 02110
Tel: (617) 786 - 3000
Fax:(617) 664 - 4999

Serves As:
- Exec. V. President, Global Human Resources, State Street Corp.

O'LEARY, Kevin
340 Kingsland St.
Nutley, NJ 07110-1199
Tel: (973) 235 - 5000

Serves As:
- V. President, Business Policy and State Government Affairs, Hoffmann-La Roche Inc. (Roche)

O'LOONEY, Michael
Four World Financial Center
250 Vesey St.
New York, NY 10080
Tel: (212) 449 - 1000

Serves As:
- First V. President, Corporate Communications, Merrill Lynch & Co., Inc.

O'MALLEY, Thomas D.
1700 E. Putnam Ave.
Suite 400
Greenwich, CT 06370
Tel: (203) 698 - 7500
Fax:(203) 698 - 7925

Serves As:
- Chairman and Chief Exec. Officer, Premcor Inc.

O'MEARA, John M.
One Pierce Place
Suite 1500
Itasca, IL 60143
Tel: (630) 875 - 7201
Fax:(630) 875 - 7393

Serves As:
- President and Chief Exec. Officer, First Midwest Bancorp, Inc.

O'MEARA, Robert P.
One Pierce Place
Suite 1500
Itasca, IL 60143
Tel: (630) 875 - 7450
Fax:(630) 875 - 7369

Serves As:
- Chairman of the Board, First Midwest Bancorp, Inc.

O'NEAL, Al
P.O. Box 98512
Las Vegas, NV 89193-8512
Tel: (702) 365 - 2076

Serves As:
- Administrator, Consumer Affairs, Southwest Gas Corp.

O'NEAL, Denise
30003 Bainbridge Rd.
Solon, OH 44139
Tel: (440) 498 - 7733

Serves As:
- Treasurer, Nestle USA PAC, Nestle USA, Inc.

O'NEAL, E. Stanley
Four World Financial Center
250 Vesey St.
New York, NY 10080
Tel: (212) 236 - 1000

Serves As:
- Chairman, Chief Exec. Officer, and President, Merrill Lynch & Co., Inc.

O'NEIL, Terry M.
P.O. Box 54143
Los Angeles, CA 90054
toneil@ralphs.com
Tel: (310) 884 - 4680
Fax:(310) 884 - 2632

Serves As:
- Director, Public Relations, Ralphs Grocery Co.

O'NEIL, Jr., William B.
3010 Stonehurst Dr.
Emmitsburg, MD 21727
william.oneil@bcbssc.com
Tel: (301) 447 - 1926
Fax:(301) 447 - 1928

Registered Federal Lobbyist.
Serves As:
- Federal Affairs Representative, BlueCross BlueShield of South Carolina

O'NEIL-WHITE, Alphonso
1901 Main St.
Buffalo, NY 14208-0080
Tel: (716) 887 - 6900
Fax:(716) 887 - 8981
TF: (888) 249 - 2583

Serves As:
- President and Chief Exec. Officer, HealthNow New York Inc.

O'NEILL, Finbarr
One Reynolds Way
Kettering, OH 45430
finbarr_oneill@reyrey.com
Tel: (937) 485 - 2000
Fax:(937) 485 - 1800

Serves As:
- President and Chief Exec. Officer, Reynolds and Reynolds Co.

O'NEILL, Marion C.
80 Park Plaza
M/S T10C
Newark, NJ 07102-0570
marion.oneill@pseg.com
Tel: (973) 430 - 7842
Fax:(973) 297 - 1480

Serves As:
- Manager, Corporate Contributions, PSE&G

O'NEILL, Martin
Two Seaport Ln.
Suite 1300
Boston, MA 02210-2019
Tel: (617) 345 - 0100
Fax:(617) 342 - 6103

Serves As:
- V. President, Safety, Health and Environmental Affairs, Cabot Corp.

O'NEILL, Mary Lynn
383 Madison Ave.
New York, NY 10179
Tel: (212) 272 - 2000
Fax:(212) 272 - 5143
TF: (800) 417 - 2327

Registered Federal Lobbyist.
Serves As:
- PAC Administrator and Managing Director, Equity Research, Bear, Stearns and Co. Inc.

O'NEILL, Peter
P.O. Box 15645 Tel: (702) 242 - 7000
Las Vegas, NV 89114-5645 Fax:(702) 242 - 1531

Serves As:
• V. President, Public and Investor Relations, Sierra Health Services, Inc.

O'NEILL, Rita
P.O. Box 5650 Tel: (701) 222 - 7834
Bismarck, ND 58506-5650 Fax:(701) 222 - 7859
rita.oneill@mduresources.com TF: (800) 437 - 8000

Serves As:
• Contact, MDUResources Group Good Government Fund, MDU Resources Group, Inc.

O'NEILL, Thomas J.
One Penn Plaza Tel: (212) 465 - 5000
Second Floor Fax:(212) 465 - 5096
New York, NY 10119

Serves As:
• Chairman and Chief Exec. Officer, Parsons Brinckerhoff

O'NEILL, William S.
401 Ninth St. NW Tel: (202) 585 - 1933
Suite 400 Fax:(202) 585 - 1899
Washington, DC 20004

Registered Federal Lobbyist.
Serves As:
• Director, Government Affairs, Sprint Nextel

O'REILLY, Bill
1800 N. Point Dr. Tel: (715) 346 - 6000
Stevens Point, WI 54481 Fax:(715) 346 - 6346

Serves As:
• V. President, General Counsel, and Corporate Secretary, Sentry Insurance
Responsibilities include public affairs.

O'REILLY, David J.
6001 Bollinger Canyon Rd. Tel: (925) 842 - 1000
San Ramon, CA 94583

Serves As:
• Chairman and Chief Exec. Officer, Chevron Corp.

O'ROURKE, Sr., James V.
1717 Arch St., 17th Floor Tel: (215) 466 - 9900
Philadelphia, PA 19103

Serves As:
• President and Chief Exec. Officer, Verizon Pennsylvania Inc.

O'ROURKE, Raymond J.
1585 Broadway Tel: (212) 761 - 4262
New York, NY 10036 Fax:(212) 761 - 0086

Serves As:
• Managing Director, Corporate Affairs, Morgan Stanley
Responsibilities include media relations

O'SHAUGHNESSY, Brian
487 E. Middlefield Rd. Tel: (650) 961 - 7500
Mountian View, CA 94043-4047 Fax:(650) 961 - 7300

Serves As:
• Director, Public Affairs, VeriSign, Inc.

O'SHEA, Denis
One State St. Tel: (860) 722 - 5313
Hartford, CT 06103 Fax:(860) 722 - 5106
denis_o'shea@hsb.com

Serves As:
• V. President, Communications, Hartford Steam Boiler Inspection and Insurance Co.

O'SHEA, Karen
P.O. Box 799900 Tel: (972) 497 - 5172
Dallas, TX 75379-9900 Fax:(972) 497 - 5292
karen.oshea@lennoxintl.com

Serves As:
• V. President, Communications and Public Relations, Lennox Internat'l

O'SULLIVAN, James J.
P.O. Box 19734 Tel: (949) 727 - 1990
Irvine, CA 92623-9734 Fax:(949) 727 - 6101
TF: (800) 222 - 5500

Serves As:
• President and Chief Exec. Officer; Chairman, Mazda Foundation (USA) Inc., Mazda North American Operations

O'SULLIVAN, Patrick
P.O. Box 2181 Tel: (501) 378 - 2221
320 W. Capitol Fax:(501) 378 - 2969
Little Rock, AR 72203-2181

Serves As:
• V. President, Advertising and Communications, Arkansas Blue Cross and Blue Shield

O'TOOLE, J. Denis
1401 I St. NW Tel: (202) 466 - 3561
Suite 520 Fax:(202) 466 - 3583
Washington, DC 20005

Registered Federal Lobbyist.
Serves As:
• Senior V. President, Government Relations, (Household Financial Group Ltd.), HSBC North America Holdings Inc.

O'TOOLE, Nancy
2801 Hunting Park Ave. Tel: (215) 221 - 8500
Philadelphia, PA 19129 Ext: 8593
nancy.otoole@tastykake.com Fax:(215) 228 - 3288
TF: (800) 248 - 2789

Serves As:
• V. President, Human Resources, Tasty Baking Co.

O'TOOLE, Robert J.
11270 W. Park Place Tel: (414) 359 - 4000
Milwaukee, WI 53224-9510 Fax:(414) 359 - 4064

Serves As:
• Chairman and Chief Exec. Officer, A. O. Smith Corp.

O'TOOLE, Stephen E.
1660 L St. NW Tel: (202) 775 - 5056
Fourth Floor Fax:(202) 775 - 5045
Washington, DC 20036

Registered Federal Lobbyist.
Serves As:
• Director, Legislative and Regulatory Affairs/Safety, General Motors Corp.

O'TOOLE, Timothy
100 S. Biscayne Blvd., Suite 1500 Tel: (305) 374 - 4143
Miami, FL 33131
tim.otoole@vitas.com

Serves As:
• Chief Exec. Officer, VITAS Healthcare Corporation

O.NEILL, Mike
Three World Financial Center Tel: (212) 640 - 5951
200 Vesey St. Fax:(212) 640 - 0332
New York, NY 10285

Serves As:
• Senior V. President, Corporate and Financial Public Relations, American Express Co.

OAKES, Dennis
151 Farmington Ave. Tel: (860) 273 - 6184
RW3H Fax:(860) 372 - 3971
Hartford, CT 06156 TF: (800) 872 - 3862
oakesd@aetna.com

Serves As:
• V. President, Public Policy, Aetna Inc.

OBERLE, Mark
1601 W. LBJ Fwy. Tel: (972) 443 - 4464
Dallas, TX 75234 Fax:(972) 332 - 9373
mark.oberle@celanese.com

Serves As:
• Investor Relations Contact, Celanese

OBERTON, Willard D.
P.O. Box 978 Tel: (507) 454 - 5374
Winona, MN 55987 Fax:(507) 453 - 8049

Serves As:
• Chief Exec. Officer and President, Fastenal Co.

OBITS, Catherine A.
447 W. 48th St. Tel: (231) 924 - 3175
Suite 153
Fremont, MI 49412

Serves As:
• Program Manager, Gerber Foundation, Gerber Products Co.

ODAK, Perry D.
3375 Mitchell Lane Tel: (303) 440 - 5220
Boulder, CO 80301 Fax:(303) 928 - 0022
TF: (800) 494 - 9453

Serves As:
• President and Chief Exec. Officer, Wild Oats Markets, Inc.

ODDY, Sharon
One Telecordia Dr. Tel: (732) 699 - 4203
Piscataway, NJ 08854-4157
oddys@telcordia.com

Serves As:
• Senior Specialist, Communications, Telcordia Technologies, Inc.

ODEEN, Philip
One Reynolds Way
Kettering, OH 45430
Tel: (937) 485 - 2000
Fax:(937) 485 - 8980
Serves As:
• Chairman of the Board, Reynolds and Reynolds Co.

ODELL, Nina
P.O. Box 97034
Bellevue, WA 98009-9734
Tel: (425) 462 - 3330
Fax:(425) 462 - 3301
Serves As:
• Director, Government and Community Affairs, Puget Sound Energy

ODENTHAL, Susan M.
One Johnson & Johnson Plaza
New Brunswick, NJ 08933-7204
sodente@corus.jnj.com
Tel: (732) 524 - 0400
Fax:(732) 214 - 0334
TF: (800) 635 - 6789
Serves As:
• V. President, Corporate Communications, Johnson & Johnson

ODLAND, Steve
2200 Old Germantown Rd.
Delray Beach, FL 33445
Tel: (561) 438 - 4800
Fax:(561) 438 - 4400
Serves As:
• Chairman and Chief Exec. Officer, Office Depot, Inc.

ODOM, Amy M.
3350 Peachtree Rd. NE
Atlanta, GA 30326
amy.odom@bcbsga.com
Tel: (404) 842 - 8132
Fax:(404) 842 - 8801
Registered Federal Lobbyist.
Serves As:
• Director, Public Affairs, Blue Cross Blue Shield of Georgia

ODOM, Kevin
3000 Technology Dr.
Angleton, TX 77515
kevin.odom@bench.com
Tel: (979) 849 - 6550
Ext: 1360
Fax:(979) 848 - 5270
Serves As:
• Corporate Communications Contact, Benchmark Electronics

ODOM, Melanie
P.O. Box 75000
MC 3352
Detroit, MI 48275
Tel: (313) 222 - 4105
TF: (800) 521 - 1190
Serves As:
• V. President, Public Affairs, Comerica Incorporated

OEHRIG, Susan
One State St. Plaza
New York, NY 10004
Tel: (212) 668 - 0340
Fax:(212) 509 - 9190
TF: (800) 221 - 1854
Serves As:
• Chairman, Contributions Committee, Ambac Financial Group, Inc.

OEI, Gia L.
Liberty Ln.
Hampton, NH 03842
gia.oei@fishersci.com
Tel: (603) 929 - 2489
Fax:(603) 929 - 2449
Serves As:
• Director, Coporate Communications, Fisher Scientific Internat'l Inc.

OESTREICH, Karl W.
3535 Blue Cross Rd.
Route 4-59
Eagan, MN 55122--115
karl_w_oestreich@bluecrossmn.com
Tel: (651) 662 - 1502
Fax:(651) 662 - 1570
TF: (800) 382 - 2000
Serves As:
• Director, Media and Public Relations, Blue Cross and Blue Shield of Minnesota

OESTRIECHER, Anne
5718 Westheimer St.
Houston, TX 77057
Tel: (713) 789 - 7879
TF: (800) 562 - 9007
Serves As:
• Pac Treasurer, Hibernia Corp.

OFF, George W.
101 Wolf Dr.
Thorofare, NJ 08086
Tel: (856) 848 - 1800
Fax:(856) 848 - 0937
TF: (800) 257 - 5540
Serves As:
• Chief Exec. Officer, Checkpoint Systems, Inc.

OFMAN, Joshua J.
555 13th St. NW
Suite 600 West
Washington, DC 20004
Tel: (202) 585 - 9610
Registered Federal Lobbyist.
Serves As:
• V. President, Reimbursement and Payment Policy, Amgen Inc.

OGLESBY, Tony E.
One Ravinia Dr.
Suite 1500
Atlanta, GA 30346
Tel: (678) 443 - 7000
Fax:(678) 393 - 8054
TF: (800) 929 - 4762
Serves As:
• Chief Exec. Officer, Sava Senior Care LLC

OGURA-HUERTA, Michie
1700 Lincoln St.
Denver, CO 80203
Tel: (303) 863 - 7414
Fax:(303) 837 - 5837
Serves As:
• Administrator, Contributions, Newmont Mining Corp.

OHDE, Takashi
1900 K St. NW
Suite 800
Washington, DC 20006
Tel: (202) 828 - 9272
Fax:(202) 828 - 9277
Registered Federal Lobbyist.
Serves As:
• Senior Representative, Hitachi America, Ltd.

OJAKLI, Ziad S.
1350 I St. NW
Suite 1000
Washington, DC 20005
Tel: (202) 962 - 5400
Fax:(202) 336 - 7223
Registered Federal Lobbyist.
Serves As:
• Group V. President, Corporate Affairs, Ford Motor Co.

OKLE, Debbie L.
P.O. Box 1046
Dallas, TX 75221-1046
dokle@commercialmetals.com
Tel: (214) 689 - 4354
Fax:(214) 689 - 5886
Serves As:
• Director, Public Relations, Commercial Metals Co.

OKUN, B. Robert
1299 Pennsylvania Ave. NW
11th Floor West
Washington, DC 20004-2407
Tel: (202) 637 - 4532
Fax:(202) 637 - 4006
Registered Federal Lobbyist.
Serves As:
• V. President, NBC Universal Washington, General Electric Co.
• V. President, Government Relations, NBC Universal

OKUYAMA, Hirofumi
Eight Corporate Center Dr.
Melville, NY 11747
Tel: (631) 753 - 7000
Fax:(631) 753 - 7041
Serves As:
• President and Chief Exec. Officer, NEC USA, Inc.

OLDHAM, Steven D.
5847 San Felipe, Suite 3300
Houston, TX 77057
soldham@prideinternational.com
Tel: (713) 789 - 1400
Fax:(713) 789 - 1430
Serves As:
• V. President, Treasury and Investor Relations, Pride Internat'l, Inc.

OLERICH, Shirley
691 S. Milpitas Blvd.
Milpitas, CA 95035-5473
Tel: (408) 945 - 8600
Fax:(408) 262 - 2533
Serves As:
• V. President, Human Resources, Adaptec, Inc.

OLIGER, Michael
Checkerboard Square
St. Louis, MO 63164
Tel: (314) 982 - 1000
Fax:(314) 982 - 2752
Serves As:
• PAC Treasurer, Nestle Purina PetCare Co.

OLIS, Dennis
1303 E. Algonquin Rd.
Schaumburg, IL 60196
Tel: (847) 576 - 4995
Fax:(847) 576 - 5372
TF: (800) 262 - 8509
Serves As:
• Director, Investor Relations, Motorola, Inc.

OLIVER, John V.
One Casco St.
Freeport, ME 04033
Tel: (207) 552 - 6006
Fax:(207) 552 - 6821
TF: (800) 221 - 4221
Serves As:
• V. President, Public Affairs, L. L. Bean, Inc.

OLIVER, Michael O.
P.O. Box 571
Milwaukee, WI 53201-0571
Tel: (414) 358 - 6600
Fax:(800) 292 - 2289
Serves As:
• Senior V. President, Human Resources, Brady Corp.

OLIVER, Sandra
400 Morgan Ln. Tel: (203) 812 - 3804
West Haven, CT 06516 Fax:(203) 812 - 6570

Serves As:
- Director, Public Policy and State Government Affairs, (Bayer Corporation Pharmaceutical Division), Bayer Corporation

OLIVER, Walter M.
2941 Fairview Park Dr. Tel: (703) 876 - 3000
Falls Church, VA 22042-4513 Fax:(703) 876 - 3125

Serves As:
- V. President, Human Resources, General Dynamics Corporation

OLIVER, William H.
One AT&T Way Tel: (908) 234 - 5090
Room 5B210 Fax:(908) 532 - 1332
Bedminster, NJ 07921-0752
wholiver@att.com

Serves As:
- V. President, Public Affairs, AT&T

OLIVERA, Chris
100 Throckmorton St. Tel: (817) 415 - 3011
Suite 1800 Fax:(817) 415 - 2335
Fort Worth, TX 76102

Serves As:
- Contributions Program Contact, Radio Shack Corporation

OLIVERIO, Tamara
19975 Victor Pkwy. Tel: (734) 591 - 3000
Livonia, MI 48152-7001 Ext: 14955
oliverit@valassis.com Fax:(734) 591 - 4503
TF: (800) 437 - 0479

Serves As:
- Public Relations Specialist, Valassis Communications, Inc.

OLIVIER, Robert
3170 Fairview Park Dr. Tel: (703) 876 - 1000
Falls Church, VA 22042 Fax:(703) 849 - 1005

Serves As:
- Senior Director, Corporate Communications, Computer Sciences Corp.

OLLIS, Patricia
2926 Piper Dr. Tel: (772) 567 - 4361
Vero Beach, FL 32960 Fax:(772) 978 - 6584
p.ollis@newpiper.com

Serves As:
- Exec. Assistant to the President, The New Piper Aircraft Inc.

Responsibilities include corporate philanthropy.

OLMSTED, Peter J.
Four Tesseneer Dr. Tel: (859) 572 - 8000
Highland Heights, KY 41076 Fax:(859) 572 - 8458

Serves As:
- Senior V. President, Human Resources, General Cable Corp.

OLOFFSON, Cathy
P.O. Box 2020 Tel: (309) 821 - 2171
Bloomington, IL 61701-2020

Serves As:
- Media Relations Coordinator, Country Insurance and Financial Services

OLSEN, Don H.
10003 Woodloch Forest Dr. Tel: (281) 719 - 4175
The Woodlands, TX 77380
don_olsen@huntsman.com

Serves As:
- Senior V. President, Public Affairs, Huntsman Corp.

OLSEN, Kandace
17845 E. Hwy. 10 Tel: (763) 241 - 2293
Elk River, MN 55330 Fax:(763) 241 - 2366
kolsen@grenergy.com

Serves As:
- Manager, Communications, Great River Energy

OLSEN, Lynnea
11115 11th St., Suite 205 Tel: (916) 321 - 5529
Sacramento, CA 95814
olsenl@citigroup.com

Serves As:
- V. President and Counsel, West Region - State and Local Government Relations, Citigroup, Inc.

OLSEN, Scott
555 13th St. NW Tel: (202) 585 - 9610
Suite 600 West
Washington, DC 20004

Registered Federal Lobbyist.
Serves As:
- Director, Government Affairs, Amgen Inc.

OLSON, David W.
21650 Oxnard St. Tel: (818) 676 - 6978
Woodland Hills, CA 91367 Fax:(818) 676 - 8591
david.w.olson@healthnet.com TF: (800) 474 - 6676

Serves As:
- Senior V. President, Corporate Communications, Health Net, Inc.

OLSON, Don
2060 E. Ninth St. Tel: (216) 687 - 2899
Cleveland, OH 44115 Fax:(216) 687 - 6164

Serves As:
- Manager, Media Relations, Medical Mutual of Ohio

OLSON, Don D.
1800 N. Point Dr. Tel: (715) 346 - 6000
Stevens Point, WI 54481 Fax:(715) 346 - 6346

Serves As:
- V. President, Human Resources, Sentry Insurance

OLSON, Kathleen P.
Mutual of Omaha Plaza Tel: (402) 351 - 2192
Omaha, NE 68175-0001 Fax:(402) 351 - 2407
kathy.olson@mutualofomaha.com

Serves As:
- V. President, Communications and Public Relations, Mutual of Omaha Insurance Co.

OLSON, Patty
82 Running Hill Rd. Tel: (207) 775 - 8728
South Portland, ME 04106-6020 Fax:(207) 761 - 6020
TF: (800) 341 - 0392

Serves As:
- Media Relations, Fairchild Semiconductor Internat'l, Inc.

OLSON, Rick
1680 Capital One Dr. Tel: (703) 875 - 1000
12th Floor
McLean, VA 22102

Registered Federal Lobbyist.
Serves As:
- Representative, Capital One Financial Corp.

OLSON, Tim
1211 W. Myrtle St. Tel: (208) 336 - 2420
Boise, ID 83702 Fax:(208) 333 - 7896
tolson.id@regence.com

Serves As:
- V. President, Community and Public Affairs, Regence BlueShield of Idaho

Responsibilities include political action.

OLSON-GOUDE, Jennifer A.
800 Nicollet Mall Tel: (612) 303 - 6277
Suite 800
Minneapolis, MN 55402
jennifer.a.olson-goude@pjc.com

Serves As:
- Director, Communications and Investor Relations, U.S. Bancorp Piper Jaffray Inc.

OLVANY, Karen
Seven Hanover Square Tel: (212) 598 - 8000
M/S H-26-E Fax:(212) 949 - 2170
New York, NY 10004-2616

Serves As:
- Contributions Contact, Guardian Life Insurance Co. of America

OMIDYAR, Pierre M.
2145 Hamilton Ave. Tel: (408) 558 - 7400
San Jose, CA 95125 Fax:(408) 558 - 7401
pomidyar@ebay.com TF: (800) 322 - 9266

Serves As:
- Founder and Chairman, eBay, Inc.

OPACIC, George
77 Beale St. Tel: (415) 973 - 7000
MC B29H Fax:(415) 972 - 5105
San Francisco, CA 94105

Serves As:
- Manager, Political Contributions, PG & E Corp.

OPLINGER, William F.
390 Park Ave. Tel: (212) 826 - 2674
New York, NY 10022

Serves As:
- Director, Investor Relations, Alcoa Inc.

OPPERMAN, Jeffrey
501 Merritt Seven Tel: (203) 750 - 2448
Norwalk, CT 06851 Fax:(203) 750 - 7788
TF: (800) 626 - 4999

Serves As:
- Manager, Corporate Communications, ABB Inc.

OPPERMAN, Sarah R.
2030 Dow Center
Midland, MI 48674-0001
sropperman@dow.com
Tel: (989) 636 - 1000
Fax:(989) 638 - 1727

Serves As:
- Global V. President, Public Affairs, Communications and Reputation, The Dow Chemical Company

ORBUCH, David B.
710 E. 24th St.
M. R. 43202
Minneapolis, MN 55404
david.orbuch@allina.com
Tel: (612) 775 - 5819
Fax:(612) 775 - 9739

Serves As:
- Exec. V. President, Corporate Responsibility and Community Relations, Allina Hospitals and Clinics

ORDMAN, Marty
One Dole Dr.
Westlake Village, CA 91362-7300
Tel: (818) 879 - 6600
Fax:(818) 879 - 6890

Serves As:
- V. President, Marketing Services, Dole Food Company, Inc.

Responsibilities include corporate contributions.

ORENDORFF, Al
200 E.Randolph St.
Chicago, IL 60601
al_orendorff@aon.com
Tel: (312) 381 - 3153
Fax:(312) 381 - 0240

Serves As:
- Director, Public Relations, Aon Corp.

ORESON, Keith
5673 Airport Rd.
Roanoke, VA 24012
Tel: (540) 362 - 4911

Serves As:
- Senior V. President, Human Resources and Benefits, Advance Auto Parts, Inc.

ORLANDELLA, Frank
1666 K St. NW
Suite 420
Washington, DC 20006
frank_orlandella@agilent.com
Tel: (202) 416 - 6210
Fax:(202) 416 - 6253

Registered Federal Lobbyist.
Serves As:
- Director, Federal Public Policy, Agilent Technologies, Inc.

ORLANDO, Anthony J.
40 Lane Rd.
Fairfield, NJ 07004
Tel: (973) 882 - 9000

Serves As:
- Director, President and Chief Exec. Officer, Covanta Energy Corp.

ORLOWSKY, Martin L.
P.O. Box 10529
Greensboro, NC 27404-0529
Tel: (336) 335 - 7000
Fax:(336) 335 - 7550
TF: (888) 278 - 1133

Serves As:
- Chairman and Chief Exec. Officer, Lorillard Tobacco Co.

ORMOND, Paul A.
333 N. Summit St.
16th Floor.
Toledo, OH 43604-2617
Tel: (419) 252 - 5535
Fax:(419) 252 - 5564

Serves As:
- Chairman, President and Chief Exec. Officer, Manor Care, Inc.

OROZCO, Bernie
925 L St.
Suite 650
Sacramento, CA 95814
borozco@sempra.com
Tel: (916) 492 - 4244

Serves As:
- Manager, Governmental Affairs- State Agency Affairs, Sempra Energy

ORR, Deano
Five W. Haggett St., Suite 914
Raleigh, NC 27601
deano.orr@ipaper.com
Tel: (919) 831 - 4764

Serves As:
- Regional Public Affairs Manager, Internat'l Paper

ORR, James F.
201 E. Fourth St.
Cincinnati, OH 45202
Tel: (513) 723 - 7000
Fax:(513) 458 - 1315
TF: (800) 344 - 3000

Serves As:
- Chairman, President, and Chief Exec. Officer, Convergys Corp.

ORR, John C.
1293 S. Main St.
Akron, OH 44301
Tel: (330) 253 - 5592
Fax:(330) 761 - 6156

Serves As:
- Chief Exec. Officer, Myers Industries, Inc.

ORR, Scott
241 Ralph McGill Blvd. NE
Atlanta, GA 30308-3374
Tel: (404) 506 - 1366
Fax:(404) 506 - 3771

Registered Federal Lobbyist.
Serves As:
- Federal Legislative Affairs Coordinator, Georgia Power Co.

ORSINO, Philip S.
One North Dale Mabry, Suite 950
Tampa, FL 33609
Tel: (813) 877 - 2726
Fax:(813) 739 - 0204

Serves As:
- Chairman of the Board, President and Chief Exec. Officer, Masonite Internat'l Corp.

ORTEGA, Jennifer
500 W. Capitol Ave.
West Sacramento, CA 95605
jortega@raleys.com
Tel: (916) 373 - 6019
Fax:(916) 371 - 1323

Serves As:
- Media Contact, Raley's

ORTINO, Hector R.
1000 Lakeside Ave.
Cleveland, OH 44114-7000
Tel: (216) 641 - 8580

Serves As:
- Chairman and Chief Exec. Officer, Ferro Corp.

ORTIZ, Carlos
One CVS Dr.
Woonsocket, RI 02895
Tel: (401) 765 - 1500
Fax:(401) 762 - 9227

Serves As:
- V. President, Governmental Affairs, CVS

ORTIZ, Carmen
Ten Finderne Ave.
Bridgewater, NJ 08807-3300
carmen.ortiz@nstarch.com
Tel: (908) 685 - 5000
Fax:(908) 685 - 5096
TF: (800) 797 - 4992

Serves As:
- Foundation Financial Specialist, Nat'l Starch and Chemical Co.

OSBORN, William A.
50 S. LaSalle St.
Chicago, IL 60675
Tel: (312) 630 - 6000
TF: (888) 289 - 6542

Serves As:
- Chairman, President and Chief Exec. Officer, Northern Trust Co.

OSBORNE, Burl
450 W. 33rd St.
New York, NY 10001
Tel: (212) 621 - 1500
Fax:(212) 621 - 5447

Serves As:
- Chairman of the Board, Associated Press

OSBORNE, Richard J.
P.O. Box 1244
M/S EC3XG
Charlotte, NC 28201-1244
rosborne@duke-energy.com
Tel: (704) 382 - 5159

Serves As:
- Group V. President, Public and Regulatory Policy, Duke Energy Corp.

OSBORNE, Virginia
Three Ravinia Dr., Suite 100
Atlanta, GA 30346
virginia.osborne@ichotelsgroup.com
Tel: (770) 604 - 2037
Fax:(770) 604 - 2059

Serves As:
- Senior Manager, Public Relations, InterContinental Hotels Group

OSHIRO, Paul T.
P.O. Box 3440
Honolulu, HI 96801-3440
Tel: (808) 525 - 6611
Fax:(808) 525 - 6652

Serves As:
- Treasurer, A&B FEDPAC, Alexander & Baldwin, Inc.

OSKISON, Kathrine L.
P.O. Box 419580
Kansas City, MO 64141-6580
Tel: (816) 274 - 3920
Fax:(816) 274 - 5061
TF: (800) 425 - 5627

Serves As:
- Public Relations Assistant, Hallmark Cards, Inc.

OSORIO, Macky
P.O. Box 4607
Houston, TX 77210-4607
mosori@coair.com
Tel: (713) 324 - 5080
Fax:(713) 324 - 2087

Serves As:
- Manager, Public Relations, Continental Airlines

OSTERMANN, Marc
P.O. Box 708
Warsaw, IN 46581-0708
Tel: (574) 267 - 6131
Fax:(574) 372 - 4988
TF: (800) 613 - 6131

Serves As:
- Manager, Investor Relations, Zimmer Holdings, Inc.

OSTRANDER, Jane
500 N. Field Dr.
Lake Forest, IL 60045
jane.ostrander@tenneco-automotive.com
Tel: (847) 482 - 5607
Fax:(847) 482 - 5049

Serves As:
- Director, Corporate Communications, Tenneco Automotive

OSTRONIC, John
101 Constitution Ave. NW
Suite 400 West
Washington, DC 20001
john.ostronic@altria.com
Tel: (202) 354 - 1500
Fax:(202) 354 - 1505

Serves As:
- Manager, Political Outreach, Altria Group, Inc.

OSTRONIC, Judith M.
601 Pennsylvania Ave. NW
Suite 620
Washington, DC 20004
Tel: (202) 508 - 5301
Fax:(202) 508 - 5304

Serves As:
- PAC Treasurer, Northeast Utilities

OSWALD, J. William "Bill"
701 Brazos St., Suite 495
Austin, TX 78701
Tel: (512) 476 - 4795
Ext: 6722
Fax:(512) 477 - 3586

Serves As:
- Director, Government Affairs, Koch Industries, Inc.

OTAKA, Hideaki (Harry)
Nine W. 57th St.
Suite 4900
New York, NY 10019
Tel: (212) 223 - 0303
Fax:(212) 750 - 3564

Serves As:
- President and Chief Exec. Officer, Toyota Motor North America, Inc.

OTELLINI, Paul S.
2200 Mission College Blvd.
Santa Clara, CA 95052-8119
Tel: (408) 765 - 8080
Fax:(408) 765 - 9904
TF: (800) 628 - 8686

Serves As:
- Chief Exec. Officer, Intel Corp.

OTIS, Clarence
P.O. Box 593330
Orlando, FL 32859
Tel: (407) 245 - 4000
Fax:(407) 245 - 4462

Serves As:
- Chief Exec. Officer, Darden Restaurants, Inc.

OTT, Kathleen
1000 Wilson Blvd., Suite 2300
Arlington, VA 22209
Tel: (703) 525 - 6767
Fax:(703) 276 - 0711

Serves As:
- Manager, Legislative Affairs, Northrop Grumman Corp.

OTTO, Billie
P.O. Box 2910
Tacoma, WA 98401-2910
Tel: (253) 383 - 9101
TF: (800) 610 - 8920

Serves As:
- V. President and Controller/Chief Information Officer, Labor Ready, Inc.

OTTO, Charlotte R.
P.O. Box 599
Cincinnati, OH 45201-0599
otto.cr@pg.com
Tel: (513) 983 - 1100
Fax:(513) 983 - 8240

Serves As:
- Global External Relations Officer, The Procter & Gamble Company

OTTO, Lori
1401 I St., NW
Suite 500
Washington, DC 20005
Tel: (202) 263 - 5900
Fax:(202) 263 - 5902

Registered Federal Lobbyist.
Serves As:
- Manager, Federal Government Affairs, Microsoft Corporation

OTTOSEN, Karl J.
6916 Wolf Run Shoals
Fairfax Station, VA 22309
Tel: (703) 978 - 8038
Fax:(703) 978 - 8039

Serves As:
- V. President, Government Affairs, (N L Industries, Inc.), Valhi, Inc.

OUCHI, Dawn
34 N. Meramec Ave.
St. Louis, MO 63105
Tel: (314) 512 - 9200
Fax:(314) 573 - 9455
TF: (800) 470 - 9227

Serves As:
- Manager, Public and Media Relations, Graybar Electric Co., Inc.

OVELMAN, Karen
1700 E. Putnam Ave.
Suite 400
Greenwich, CT 06370
Tel: (203) 698 - 5669
Fax:(203) 698 - 7925

Serves As:
- V. President, Investor Relations and External Reporting, Premcor Inc.

Responsibilities also include media relations.

OVER, Clive
2325 Orchard Pkwy.
San Jose, CA 95131
cliveover@atmel.com
Tel: (408) 441 - 0311
Fax:(408) 436 - 4200

Serves As:
- Corporate Communications Contact, Atmel Corp.

OVERBY, Paul
1501 Lebanon Church Rd
Pittsbugh, PA 15236

Serves As:
- Treasurer, Bombardier Transportation Holdings USA Employee Political Fund, Bombardier

OVERSTREET, Jack C.
1550 Crystal Dr.
Crystal Square 2, Suite 300
Arlington, VA 22202
Tel: (703) 413 - 5634
Fax:(703) 413 - 5737

Registered Federal Lobbyist.
Serves As:
- V. President, Aeronautical Legislative Affairs, Lockheed Martin Corp.

OVERTON, David
26950 Agoura Rd.
Calabasas Hills, CA 91301-5335
Tel: (818) 871 - 3000
Fax:(818) 871 - 3100

Serves As:
- Chairman, President and Chief Exec. Officer, Cheesecake Factory Inc.

Responsibilities include corporate philanthropy.

OWEN, Allen E.
1000 Broad St.
Phenix City, AL 36867
aeo@meadwestvaco.com
Tel: (334) 448 - 6356
Fax:(334) 448 - 6508

Serves As:
- Manager, Regional State Government Relations, MeadWestvaco Corp.

OWEN, Clay
5565 Glenridge Connector
Atlanta, GA 30342
clay.owen@cingular.com
Tel: (404) 236 - 6153
Fax:(866) 246 - 4852
TF: (800) 331 - 0500

Serves As:
- Senior Director, Media Relations, Cingular Wireless

OWEN, Laura N.
P.O. Box 1101
Minneapolis, MN 55440-1101
laura.owen@adc.com
Tel: (952) 914 - 6188
Fax:(952) 946 - 3292

Serves As:
- V. President, Human Resources, ADC

OWEN, Lori
2100 Logic Dr.
San Jose, CA 95124-3400
lori.owen@xilinx.com
Tel: (408) 559 - 7778
Fax:(408) 559 - 7114
TF: (800) 836 - 4002

Serves As:
- Investor Relations Analyst, Xilinx, Inc.

OWEN, Steve
10 Burton Hills Blvd.
Nashville, TN 37215
steve.owen@correctionscorp.com
Tel: (615) 263 - 3107
Fax:(615) 263 - 3140
TF: (800) 624 - 2931

Serves As:
- Director, Marketing and Communications, Corrections Corp. of America

OWENS, James W.
100 NE Adams St.
Peoria, IL 61629-1465
Tel: (309) 675 - 1000
Fax:(309) 675 - 6155

Serves As:
- Chairman and Chief Exec. Officer, Caterpillar Inc.

OWENS, Michelle L.
Mutual of Omaha Plaza
Omaha, NE 68175-0001
michelle.owens@mutualofomaha.com
Tel: (402) 351 - 4610
Fax:(402) 351 - 2775

Serves As:
- First V. President, Legislative Issues Management, Mutual of Omaha Insurance Co.

OWENS, Sharon
1111 Louisiana St.
Houston, TX 77002
Tel: (713) 207 - 1111

Serves As:
- V. President, Community Relations, CenterPoint Energy

OXLEY, Terry
3130 S. 38th St.
Tacoma, WA 98409
Tel: (253) 476 - 6334
Fax:(253) 476 - 6415

Serves As:
- Director, Community Services, Puget Sound Energy

OZANNE, Colleen K.
P.O. Box 82542
Lincoln, NE 68501
Tel: (402) 327 - 5677

Serves As:
- Public Affairs Specialist, State Farm Insurance Cos.

PABLO, Christopher G.
1441 Kapiolani Blvd., 17th Floor
Honolulu, HI 96814-4407
Tel: (808) 983 - 4982

Serves As:
- Director, Government and Community Affairs, Kaiser Permanente

PACE, Amanda
P.O. Box 1734
Atlanta, GA 30301
apace@na.ko.com
Tel: (404) 676 - 2121
Fax:(404) 676 - 6792

Serves As:
- Director, Consumer Affairs, The Coca-Cola Co.

PACE, Anne
P.O. Box 9103
Hopkinton, MA 01748
pace_anne@emc.com
Tel: (508) 435 - 1000
Ext: 77932
Fax:(508) 435 - 7954
TF: (800) 424 - 3622

Serves As:
- Corporate Public Relations Manager, EMC Corp.

PACE, Charles D.
P.O. Box 1043
Jackson, MS 39215-1043
cpace@bcbsms.com
Tel: (601) 644 - 5026
Fax:(601) 939 - 7035
TF: (800) 222 - 8046

Registered Federal Lobbyist.
Serves As:
- Governmental Affairs and Compliance, Blue Cross and Blue Shield of Mississippi

PACE, Joanne
11 Madison Ave.
New York, NY 10010-3629
Tel: (212) 325 - 2000
Fax:(212) 538 - 4633

Serves As:
- Global Head, Human Resources, Credit Suisse First Boston

PACHECO, John
414 Nicollet Mall
Minneapolis, MN 55401-1927
Tel: (612) 330 - 5500
Fax:(612) 330 - 6947
TF: (800) 328 - 8226

Serves As:
- Director, Xcel Energy Foundation, Xcel Energy, Inc.

PACHTNER, John
1111 Broadway
Oakland, CA 94607-5500
john.pachtner@apl.com
Tel: (510) 272 - 8000
Fax:(510) 272 - 7421

Serves As:
- Community Affairs Contact, APL Americas

PACK, Nicole
111 McInnis Pkwy.
San Rafael, CA 94903
nicole.pack@autodesk.com
Tel: (415) 507 - 6282
Fax:(415) 507 - 5100

Serves As:
- Corporate Communications Contact, Autodesk Inc.

PACKER, Daniel F.
P.O. Box 61000
New Orleans, LA 70161
Tel: (504) 576 - 4000
Fax:(504) 576 - 4001

Serves As:
- President and Chief Exec. Officer, Entergy New Orleans

PACKWOOD, Jan B.
P.O. Box 70
Boise, ID 83707
jpackwood@idahopower.com
Tel: (208) 388 - 2200
Fax:(208) 388 - 6955

Serves As:
- President and Chief Exec. Officer, IDACORP, Inc.

PACOTTI, Linda
777 Scuddersmill Rd.
Plainsboro, NJ 08536
linda.pacotti@bms.com
Tel: (609) 897 - 5214

Serves As:
- Associate Director, Government Affairs, Bristol-Myers Squibb Co.

PADDEN, Preston R.
1150 17th St. NW
Suite 400
Washington, DC 20036
preston.padden@corp.disney.com
Tel: (202) 222 - 4700

Registered Federal Lobbyist.
Serves As:
- Exec. V. President, Government Relations, The Walt Disney Company

PADGETT, Pamela
1025 W. NASA Blvd.
Melbourne, FL 32919-0001
Tel: (321) 727 - 9383
Fax:(321) 727 - 9222
TF: (800) 442 - 7747

Serves As:
- V. President, Investor Relations, Harris Corp.

PADOT, Tim
One Corporate Way
Lansing, MI 48951
Tel: (517) 702 - 2425
Fax:(517) 706 - 5517
TF: (800) 644 - 4565

Serves As:
- Director, Corporate Communications, Jackson Nat'l Life Insurance Co.

PAGAN, Cheryl
404 Wyman St.
Suite 500
Waltham, MA 02451
Tel: (781) 464 - 8000
Fax:(781) 464 - 8100

Serves As:
- Foundation Contact, Novell, Inc.

PAGE, Barbara
P.O. Box 1074
Schenectady, NY 12301
Tel: (518) 355 - 5000
Fax:(518) 379 - 3515

Serves As:
- Promotions and Special Events Manager, Golub Corp.

Responsibilities include public relations.

PAGEL, Craig R.
30 W. Superior St.
Duluth, MN 55802
cpagel@mnpower.com
Tel: (218) 722 - 5642
Ext: 3759
Fax:(218) 279 - 5050

Serves As:
- Senior Government Affairs Representative, (Minnesota Power), ALLETE

PAGLIARO, Kara
14 Cambridge Center
Cambridge, MA 02142
Tel: (617) 914 - 6524
Fax:(617) 679 - 2617

Serves As:
- Associate, Public Affairs, Biogen Idec Inc.

PAGON, Marshall W.
225 City Line Ave.
Suite 200
Bala Cynwyd, PA 19004
Tel: (610) 934 - 7000
Fax:(610) 934 - 7054
TF: (888) 438 - 7488

Serves As:
- Chairman and Chief Exec. Officer, Pegasus Communications Corp.

PAI CHIN, Vivian
One Johnson & Johnson Plaza
New Brunswick, NJ 08933-7204
Tel: (732) 524 - 0400
Fax:(732) 214 - 0334
TF: (800) 635 - 6789

Serves As:
- Director, Environmental Regulatory Affairs, Johnson & Johnson

PAIGE, Bennie F.
P.O. Box 1640
Jackson, MS 39215-1640
bpaige@entergy.com
Tel: (601) 969 - 2455
Fax:(601) 964 - 2400

Serves As:
- Director, State Governmental Affairs, Entergy Mississippi

PAINE, III, W. Dexter
401 River Oaks Pkwy.
San Jose, CA 95134
dexter.paine@wj.com
Tel: (408) 577 - 6200
Fax:(408) 577 - 6620

Serves As:
- Chairman of the Board, WJ Communications

PAJOR, Charlie
1601 W. Diehl Rd.
Naperville, IL 60563-1198
Tel: (630) 305 - 1556
Fax:(630) 305 - 1973

Serves As:
- Senior Manager, Communications, Nalco Co.

PAK, Shannon
8607 Westwood Center Dr.
Vienna, VA 22182
Tel: (703) 448 - 4000
Fax:(703) 448 - 4100

Serves As:
- Contact, Public Relations, Feld Entertainment, Inc.

PALADINO, Dr. Albert E.
7628 Thorndike Rd.
Greensboro, NC 27409-9421
Tel: (336) 664 - 1233
Fax:(336) 931 - 7454

Serves As:
- Chairman of the Board, RF Micro Devices, Inc.

PALADINO, Amy
Avid Technology Park
One Park West
Tewksbury, MA 01876
amy_paladino@avid.com
Tel: (978) 640 - 3051
Fax:(978) 640 - 1366

Serves As:
- Manager, Public Relations, Avid Technology, Inc.

PALADINO, Steven
135 Duryea Rd.
Melville, NY 11747
Tel: (631) 843 - 5500
Fax:(631) 843 - 5979

Serves As:
- Exec. V. President and Chief Financial Officer, Henry Schein, Inc.

PALAZZO, Marc
4111 E. 37th St., North
Wichita, KS 67220
Tel: (316) 828 - 5500
Fax:(316) 828 - 5739

Serves As:
- Director, Public Affairs, Koch Industries, Inc.

PALEN, Gregory R.
2100 Hwy. 55
Medina, MN 55340
Tel: (763) 417 - 8650
Fax:(763) 542 - 0599

Serves As:
- Chairman of the Board, Polaris Industries Inc.

PALENSKE, Fred
1133 S.W. Topeka Blvd.
Topeka, KS 66629
fred.palenske@bcbsks.com
Tel: (785) 291 - 7810
Fax:(785) 291 - 8216

Serves As:
- Director, Legislative and Regulatory Relations, Blue Cross and Blue Shield of Kansas, Inc.

PALERMO, Liza Fiore
2050 Spectrum Blvd.
Fort Lauderdale, FL 33309
lizapalermo@spherion.com
Tel: (954) 308 - 7600
Fax:(954) 938 - 7790

Serves As:
- V. President, Corporate Communications, Spherion Corp.

PALEY, Liz
650 Madison Ave.
New York, NY 10022
Tel: (212) 318 - 7000
Fax:(212) 888 - 5780

Serves As:
- V. President, Ralph Lauren Advertising, Polo Ralph Lauren

PALIZZA, John M.
1390 Enclave Pkwy.
Houston, TX 77077-2099
Tel: (281) 584 - 1390
Fax:(281) 584 - 2721

Serves As:
- Assistant Treasurer, Sysco Corp.

Responsibilities include investor relations.

PALMER, Mr. Cass
2950 Industrial Rd.
Las Vegas, NV 89109-1100
Tel: (702) 792 - 7200
Fax:(702) 792 - 7266
TF: (800) 695 - 2455

Serves As:
- V. President, Human Resources, Boyd Gaming Corp.

PALMER, Elaine
700 Anderson Hill Rd.
Purchase, NY 10577-1444
elaine.palmer@pepsi.com
Tel: (914) 253 - 3122
Fax:(914) 253 - 2203

Serves As:
- Director, External Affairs, PepsiCo, Inc.

PALMER, Frederick D.
701 Market St.
St. Louis, MO 63101-1826
fpalmer@peabodyenergy.com
Tel: (314) 342 - 7624
Fax:(314) 342 - 7614

Registered Federal Lobbyist.
Serves As:
- Exec. V. President, Government Affairs, Peabody Energy

Responsibilities include corporate philanthropy.

PALMER, Randy
200 E. Basse Rd.
San Antonio, TX 78209
randypalmer@clearchannel.com
Tel: (210) 822 - 2828
Fax:(210) 822 - 2299

Serves As:
- V. President, Investor Relations, Clear Channel Communications

PALMER, Roy
1225 17th St.
Denver, CO 80202
Tel: (303) 294 - 2808
Fax:(303) 294 - 8120

Serves As:
- Interim Director, State Government Affairs, Xcel Energy, Inc.

PALMER, Susan
711 High St.
Des Moines, IA 50392-0150
Tel: (515) 247 - 5111
Fax:(515) 246 - 5475
TF: (800) 986 - 3343

Registered Federal Lobbyist.
Serves As:
- Director, Government Relations, The Principal Financial Group

PALMER, Susan K.
1818 N St. NW
Suite 800
Washington, DC 20036
susan.k.palmer@cingular.com
Tel: (202) 419 - 3000
Ext: 3009

Serves As:
- Manager, Regulatory Affairs, Cingular Wireless

PALMIERI, Anita
2000 Market St.
Philadelphia, PA 19103-9000
Tel: (215) 419 - 5013
Fax:(215) 419 - 7591
TF: (800) 225 - 7788

Serves As:
- Senior Communications Manager, ATOFINA Chemicals, Inc.

PALMISANO, Samuel J.
New Orchard Rd.
Armonk, NY 10504
Tel: (914) 499 - 1900
Fax:(914) 499 - 7382
TF: (800) 426 - 4968

Serves As:
- Chairman, President and Chief Exec. Officer, Internat'l Business Machines Corp. (IBM)

PALMS, John Michael
One Chase Manhattan Plaza
41st Floor
New York, NY 10005
Tel: (212) 859 - 7000
Fax:(212) 859 - 7010

Serves As:
- Chairman of the Board, Assurant

PALOMBI, David R.
8200 Jones Branch Dr.
M/S 407
McLean, VA 22102
david_palombi@freddiemac.com
Tel: (703) 903 - 2512
Fax:(703) 903 - 2447
TF: (800) 373 - 3343

Serves As:
- V. President, Corporate Communications and Marketing Department, Freddie Mac

PANCAKE, R. Robbins
1666 K St. NW
Suite 420
Washington, DC 20006
Tel: (202) 416 - 6210
Fax:(202) 416 - 6253

Registered Federal Lobbyist.
Serves As:
- Representative, Agilent Technologies, Inc.

PANEGA, Andrew
111 S. Wacker Dr.
Chicago, IL 60606
Tel: (312) 326 - 8990
Fax:(312) 326 - 7660

Serves As:
- Senior V. President, Human Resources, R R Donnelley

PANELAS, Tom
Britannica Centre
310 S. Michigan Ave.
Chicago, IL 60604
tpanelas@us.britannica.com
Tel: (312) 347 - 7309
Fax:(312) 294 - 2158

Serves As:
- Director, Public Relations, Encyclopaedia Britannica, Inc.

PANG, Laurinda
200 Park Ave.
Suite 300
Florham Park, NJ 07932
glbc@globalcrossing.com
Tel: (973) 937 - 0100
Fax:(973) 360 - 0148
TF: (800) 336 - 7000

Serves As:
- V. President, Investor Relations, Global Crossing Ltd.

PANG, Sarah
CNA Center
333 S. Wabash Ave.
Chicago, IL 60685
Tel: (312) 822 - 6394
Fax:(312) 817 - 2042

Serves As:
- Foundation Executive Director, CNA Financial Corp.

PANIGEL, Michael
153 E. 53rd St.
56th Floor
New York, NY 10022-4611
Tel: (212) 258 - 4000
Fax:(212) 767 - 0580
TF: (800) 743 - 6367

Serves As:
- Senior V. President, Human Resources, Siemens Corp.

PANTALEONI, Anthony D.
100 First Stamford Pl.
Stamford, CT 06902
apantaleoni@craneco.com
Tel: (203) 363 - 7214
Fax:(203) 363 - 7295

Serves As:
- V. President, Environment, Health and Safety, Crane Co.

PANTER, Gregory W.
P.O. Box 70
Boise, ID 83707
Tel: (208) 388 - 2200
Fax:(208) 388 - 6955

Serves As:
- V. President, Public Affairs, IDACORP, Inc.

PANUS, Mark
One Campus Dr.
Parsippany, NJ 07054
mark.panus@cendant.com
Tel: (973) 496 - 7215

Serves As:
- V. President, Communications and Public Affairs, Cendant Corp.

PANZER, Carolyn
1301 K St. NW
Suite 1000 East Tower
Washington, DC 20005
Tel: (202) 715 - 1105
Fax:(202) 715 - 1114

Serves As:
- Senior V. President, Public Policy, Diageo North America

PAONE, Jon
51 Madison Ave.
New York, NY 10010
Tel: (212) 576 - 7842
Fax:(212) 576 - 8145

Serves As:
- Corporate V. President, Governmental Affairs, New York Life Insurance Co.

Responsibilities include political action.

PAPADELLIS, Randy C.
One Ocean Spray Dr.
Lakeville-Middleboro, MA 02349
Tel: (508) 946 - 1000
Fax:(508) 946 - 7704
TF: (800) 662 - 3263

Serves As:
- Chief Exec. Officer, Ocean Spray Cranberries, Inc.

PAPEN, Harold
P.O. Box 909700
Kansas City, MO 64190-9700
hpapen@dfamilk.com
Tel: (816) 801 - 6490
Fax:(816) 801 - 6590

Serves As:
- Corporate V. President, Human Resources and Administration, Dairy Farmers of America, Inc.

PAPILLON, Scott
710 Medtronic Pkwy.
Minneapolis, MN 55432-5604
scott.papillon@medtronic.com
Tel: (763) 505 - 2632
Fax:(763) 514 - 4879
TF: (800) 328 - 2518

Serves As:
- Senior Public Relations Manager, Medtronic, Inc.

PAPOVITCH, Dale
1350 I St. NW
Suite 400
Washington, DC 20005-3306
Tel: (202) 371 - 6900
Fax:(202) 842 - 3578

Serves As:
- Director, International Regulatory Affairs, Motorola, Inc.

PAPPAS, Dean T.
1615 L St. NW
Suite 650
Washington, DC 20036
Tel: (202) 626 - 8240
Fax:(202) 626 - 8575

Registered Federal Lobbyist.
Serves As:
- Counsel, Allstate Insurance Co.

PARADOSSI, Pete
2400 W. Lloyd Exwy.
Evansville, IN 47721
pete.paradossi@bms.com
Tel: (812) 429 - 7413
Fax:(812) 429 - 8994

Serves As:
- Associate Director, Public Affairs and Communications, (Mead Johnson Nutritionals), Bristol-Myers Squibb Co.

PARANDIAN, Chris
601 Pennsylvania Ave. NW
Suite 720
Washington, DC 20004
Tel: (202) 783 - 3970
Fax:(202) 783 - 3982

Registered Federal Lobbyist.
Serves As:
- V. President, Federal Legislative Affairs, ALLTEL

PARANICAS, Dean J.
One Becton Dr.
Franklin Lakes, NJ 07417-1880
paranicas@bd.com
Tel: (201) 847 - 6800
Fax:(201) 847 - 6475

Serves As:
- V. President, Corporate Secretary and Public Policy, Becton, Dickinson and Co.

PARENTE, Joseph A.
17800 Royalton Rd.
Cleveland, OH 44136-5149
Tel: (440) 572 - 2400
Fax:(440) 878 - 2959
TF: (800) 321 - 3997

Serves As:
- V. President and Director, Consumer Relations, Ceres Group, Inc.

PARIS, Gordon
350 N. Orleans
Chicago, IL 60654
Tel: (312) 321 - 3000

Serves As:
- Chairman of the Board, Chicago Sun-Times

PARIS, Leslie
P.O. Box 2300
Tulsa, OK 74192
Tel: (918) 588 - 6000
Fax:(918) 588 - 6853

Serves As:
- V. President, Community Relations, BOK Financial Corp.

PARISH, Rhonda
203 E. Main St.
Spartanburg, SC 29319-0001
Tel: (864) 597 - 8000

Serves As:
- Senior V. President, Human Resources, Denny's Corp.

PARK, Dr. Chong Sup
500 McCarthy Blvd.
Milpitas, CA 95035
Tel: (408) 894 - 5000
Fax:(408) 952 - 3600
TF: (800) 262 - 9867

Serves As:
- Chairman and Chief Exec. Officer, Maxtor Corp.

PARK, Chris
600 Mountain Ave.
Murray Hill, NJ 07974-0636
Tel: (908) 582 - 8500
Fax:(908) 508 - 2576
TF: (888) 458 - 2368

Serves As:
- President, Lucent Technologies Foundation, Lucent Technologies

PARK, Kathy
229 W. 43rd St.
New York, NY 10036
parkk@nytimes.com
Tel: (212) 556 - 4059
Fax:(212) 556 - 7389

Serves As:
- Manager, Public Relations, New York Times Co.

PARK, Laure
One Malcolm Ave.
Teterboro, NJ 07608
Tel: (201) 393 - 5030
Fax:(201) 393 - 4755
TF: (800) 222 - 0446

Serves As:
- Corporate V. President, Investor Relations, Quest Diagnostics Inc.

PARKE, Bill
1303 E. Algonquin Rd.
Schaumburg, IL 60196
william.parke@motorola.com
Tel: (847) 576 - 4525
Fax:(847) 576 - 4554
TF: (800) 262 - 8509

Serves As:
- Director, Financial Communication, Motorola, Inc.

PARKE, Brian R.
P.O. Box 19109
Greensboro, NC 27419-9109
Tel: (336) 294 - 4410
Fax:(336) 294 - 5422

Serves As:
- Chairman, President and Chief Exec. Officer, Unifi, Inc.

PARKER, Allison
P.O. Box 7000 — Tel: (870) 864 - 6385
El Dorado, AR 71731-7000 — Fax:(870) 864 - 6373
aparker@murphyoilcorp.com

Serves As:
- Manager, Community and Public Relations, Murphy Oil Corp.

PARKER, Dave
250 E. Parkcenter Blvd. — Tel: (208) 395 - 6622
Boise, ID 83706 — Fax:(208) 395 - 6631
david.parker@albertsons.com — TF: (877) 932 - 7948

Serves As:
- V. President, Investor Relations, Albertson's, Inc.

PARKER, David T.
8000 S. Federal Way — Tel: (208) 368 - 4400
M/S 407 — Fax:(208) 368 - 2536
Boise, ID 83707
dtparker@micron.com

Serves As:
- Director, Corporate Communications, Micron Technology, Inc.

PARKER, Gary
P.O. Box 834 — Tel: (206) 461 - 2000
Seattle, WA 98101 — Fax:(206) 554 - 4807
TF: (800) 756 - 8000

Registered Federal Lobbyist.
Serves As:
- Representative, Washington Mutual, Inc.

PARKER, Virginia M.
942 S. Shady Grove Rd. — Tel: (901) 818 - 7443
Memphis, TN 38120 — Fax:(901) 818 - 7194
TF: (800) 238 - 5355

Serves As:
- Administrator, Government Affairs, FedEx Corp.

PARKER, Wendy
1300 I St. NW — Tel: (202) 772 - 3500
Suite 525 West — Fax:(202) 772 - 3535
Washington, DC 20005

Registered Federal Lobbyist.
Serves As:
- V. President, Federal Affairs, Caremark Rx, Inc.

PARKIN, Jerry D.
666 Grand Ave. — Tel: (515) 244 - 9377
Suite 1707
Des Moines, IA 50309

Serves As:
- Director, State Public Affairs, Deere & Company

PARKINSON, Jr., Robert L.
One Baxter Pkwy. — Tel: (847) 948 - 2025
Deerfield, IL 60015-4633 — Fax:(847) 948 - 3642

Serves As:
- Chairman and Chief Exec. Officer, Baxter Internat'l Inc.

PARKS, Michael
800/850 Ridgeview Dr. — Tel: (215) 983 - 8000
Horsham, PA 19044 — Fax:(610) 651 - 6100

Serves As:
- Media and Public Relations Contact, Centocor, Inc.

PARNES, Andrew H.
15326 Alton Pkwy. — Tel: (949) 789 - 1600
Irvine, CA 92618 — Fax:(949) 789 - 1609

Serves As:
- Exec. V. President, Finance/Chief Financial Officer, Standard Pacific Corp.

PARR, Marlena J.
P.O. Box 1400 — Tel: (605) 721 - 1700
Rapid City, SD 57709-1400 — Fax:(605) 721 - 2599
mparr@bh-corp.com

Serves As:
- PAC Treasurer, Black Hills Corp.

PARR, Michael
601 Pennsylvania Ave. NW — Tel: (202) 728 - 3661
North Bldg., Suite 325 — Fax:(202) 728 - 3649
Washington, DC 20004

Serves As:
- Sr.Manager, Government Affairs, DuPont

PARRISH, Harlan
Colonial Financial Center — Tel: (334) 240 - 5000
One Commerce St. — TF: (800) 285 - 5886
Montgomery, AL 36104

Serves As:
- PAC Treasurer, The Colonial Bancgroup, Inc.

PARRISH, Laura
5235 Katy Fwy. — Tel: (713) 869 - 5060
Houston, TX 77007 — Fax:(713) 869 - 6197

Serves As:
- Human Resources Contact, Fiesta Mart Inc.

PARRISH, Steven C.
120 Park Ave. — Tel: (917) 663 - 3074
22nd Floor — Fax:(917) 663 - 2395
New York, NY 10017

Serves As:
- Senior V. President, Corporate Affairs, Altria Group, Inc.

PARROTT, Joseph R.
5825 Glenridge Dr. — Tel: (404) 250 - 3599
Bldg. Three, Suite 101
Atlanta, GA 30328
joe.parrott@rayonier.com

Serves As:
- Manager, Government Relations, Rayonier Inc.

PARROTT, Sharon Thomas
One Tower Ln. — Tel: (630) 571 - 7700
Suite 1000 — Fax:(630) 571 - 1991
Oakbrook Terrace, IL 60181-4624 — TF: (800) 225 - 8000

Serves As:
- Senior V. President, Chief Compliance Officer, DeVry Inc.

PARRY, Kathy
P.O. Box 186 — Tel: (802) 371 - 3205
Montpelier, VT 05601 — Fax:(802) 223 - 4229
parryk@bcbsvt.com — TF: (800) 255 - 4550

Serves As:
- Coordinator, External Affairs, Blue Cross and Blue Shield of Vermont

PARSKY, Barbara J.
2244 Walnut Grove Ave. — Tel: (626) 302 - 2204
Rosemead, CA 91770
barbara.parsky@edisonintl.com

Serves As:
- V. President, Corporate Communications, Edison Internat'l
- V. President, Corporate Communications, Southern California Edison, an Edison Internat'l Co.

PARSONS, Eric E.
P.O. Box 711 — Tel: (503) 321 - 7000
Portland, OR 97207 — Fax:(503) 321 - 7935

Serves As:
- Chairman, President and Chief Exec. Officer, Standard Insurance Co.

PARSONS, Richard D.
One Time Warner Center — Tel: (212) 484 - 8000
New York, NY 10019 — Fax:(212) 489 - 6183

Serves As:
- Chairman and Chief Exec. Officer, Time Warner Inc.

PARTRIDGE, Kathleen S.
11690 Northwest 105 St. — Tel: (305) 500 - 3726
Miami, FL 33178 — Fax:(305) 500 - 4129

Serves As:
- Treasurer, Ryder Employees PAC, Ryder System, Inc.

PASCHAL, Annelle
700 E. Butterfield Rd. — Tel: (630) 678 - 8022
Suite 250 — Fax:(630) 678 - 8131
Lombard, IL 60148

Serves As:
- Director, Corporate Professional Relations, U.S. Can Corp.

Responsibilities include corporate communications.

PASCO, Gina
P.O. Box 191 — Tel: (310) 771 - 3111
Gardena, CA 90248-0191 — Fax:(310) 516 - 7967

Serves As:
- Manager, Corporate Communications, Nissan North America, Inc.

PASINSKI, Janess
4615 E. Elwood St. — Tel: (480) 966 - 5394
Phoenix, AZ 85040-1958 — Fax:(480) 379 - 3503
janess.pasinski@apollogrp.edu — TF: (800) 990 - APOL

Serves As:
- Manager, Investor Relations, Apollo Group, Inc.

PASSMAN, Pamela
One Microsoft Way — Tel: (425) 882 - 8080
Redmond, WA 98052-6399 — Fax:(425) 936 - 7329

Registered Federal Lobbyist.
Serves As:
- Acting Director, Community Affairs; and Head, Corporate Affairs, Microsoft Corporation

PASSMORE-MCLAUGHLIN, Cynthia
225 Windsor Dr.
Itasca, IL 60143
Tel: (630) 875 - 5300
Fax:(630) 875 - 5858
TF: (800) 436 - 3726

Serves As:
- Chief Exec. Officer, Enesco Group, Inc.

PASSOV, Richard A.
235 E. 42nd St.
New York, NY 10017-5755
Tel: (212) 573 - 2323
Fax:(212) 573 - 1853

Serves As:
- PAC Treasurer, Pfizer Inc.

PASTRE, Peter
1620 L St. NW
Suite 800
Washington, DC 20036-5617
Tel: (202) 659 - 3575
Fax:(202) 659 - 1026

Registered Federal Lobbyist.
Serves As:
- V. President, MetLife, Inc.

PASTUSZEK, Lydia
25 Research Dr.
Westborough, MA 01582
Tel: (508) 389 - 3600
Fax:(508) 366 - 5498

Serves As:
- Senior V. President, Human Resources, Nat'l Grid USA

PATE, William C.
1155 Peachtree St. NE
1915 Campanile
Atlanta, GA 30309-3610
william.pate@bellsouth.com
Tel: (404) 249 - 2400
Fax:(404) 249 - 2866

Serves As:
- V. President, Advertising and Public Relations, BellSouth Corp.

PATEL, Hami B.
101 N. Wacker Dr.
Chicago, IL 60606
Tel: (312) 372 - 5200
Fax:(312) 444 - 2710

Serves As:
- Chairman and Chief Exec. Officer, Hartmarx

PATIENT, William F.
33587 Walker Rd.
Avon Lake, OH 44093-0175
Tel: (440) 930 - 1000
Fax:(440) 930 - 1750

Serves As:
- Chairman of the Board, PolyOne Corp.

PATINEAU, Paula J.
5050 Lincoln Dr.
Edina, MN 55436
paula_patineau@atk.com
Tel: (952) 351 - 3000
Fax:(952) 351 - 3053

Serves As:
- Senior V. President, Human Resources and Administrative Services, Alliant Techsystems

Responsibilities include corporate philanthropy.

PATINO, Edgar
P.O. Box 98910
Las Vegas, NV 89151-0001
Tel: (702) 367 - 5747
Fax:(702) 367 - 5092
TF: (800) 331 - 3103

Serves As:
- Government Affairs, Nevada Power Co.

PATMOR, Roxanne I.
2244 Walnut Grove Ave.
Rosemead, CA 91770
patmorri@sce.com
Tel: (626) 302 - 7982
Fax:(626) 302 - 6262

Serves As:
- Manager, Strategic Communications, Southern California Edison, an Edison Internat'l Co.

PATRICK, Michael W.
P.O. Box 391
Columbus, GA 31902-0391
Tel: (706) 576 - 3400
Fax:(706) 576 - 2812
TF: (800) 241 - 0431

Serves As:
- Chairman, President and Chief Exec. Officer, Carmike Cinemas, Inc.

PATRICK, Thomas M.
130 E. Randolph Dr.
24th Floor
Chicago, IL 60601
t.patrick@pecorp.com
Tel: (312) 240 - 4403
Fax:(312) 240 - 4541

Serves As:
- Chairman, President and Chief Exec. Officer, Peoples Energy Corp.

PATSKY, Deborah
Five Dedrick Pl.
West Caldwell, NJ 07006-6398
Tel: (973) 882 - 2000
Fax:(973) 808 - 7555

Serves As:
- V. President, Human Resources, Ricoh Corp.

PATTERSON, Chris
4747 N. Channel Ave.
Portland, OR 97217
Tel: (503) 745 - 8000
Fax:(503) 745 - 8921

Serves As:
- President and Chief Exec. Officer, Freightliner LLC

PATTERSON, Deborah
800 N. Lindbergh Blvd.
St. Louis, MO 63167
Tel: (314) 694 - 4596
Fax:(314) 694 - 7658

Serves As:
- President and Chairman, Monsanto Fund, Monsanto Co.

PATTERSON, Kenneth E.
14850 Conference Center Dr.
Chantilly, VA 20151
ken.patterson@rolls-royce.com
Tel: (703) 834 - 1700
Fax:(703) 709 - 6086

Serves As:
- Corporate Financial Controller, Rolls-Royce North America Inc.

Responsibilities include corporate philanthropy.

PATTERSON, Mark
101 Constitution Ave. NW
Suite 1000 East
Washington, DC 20001
Tel: (202) 637 - 3700
Fax:(202) 637 - 3773

Serves As:
- V. President, Governmental Affairs, Goldman, Sachs and Co.

PATTERSON, Shawn
3535 Blue Cross Rd.
Eagan, MN 55122--115
Tel: (651) 662 - 8766
Fax:(651) 662 - 1570
TF: (800) 382 - 2000

Serves As:
- V. President, Marketing and Communications, Blue Cross and Blue Shield of Minnesota

PATTON, Thomas B.
1300 I St. NW
Suite 1070 East
Washington, DC 20005
tom.patton@phillips.com
Tel: (202) 962 - 8550
Fax:(202) 962 - 8560

Registered Federal Lobbyist.
Serves As:
- V. President, Government Relations, Philips Electronics North America

PAUGH, Laura E.
One Marriott Dr.
Washington, DC 20058
laura.paugh@marriott.com
Tel: (301) 380 - 7418
Fax:(301) 380 - 5067

Serves As:
- Senior V. President, Investor Relations, Marriott Internat'l, Inc.

PAUKOVITS, Timothy J.
Two N. Ninth St.
Allentown, PA 18101-1179
tjpaukovits@pplweb.com
Tel: (610) 774 - 4124
Fax:(610) 774 - 5106
TF: (800) 345 - 3085

Serves As:
- Manager, Investor Relations, PPL Corp.

PAUL, Gerald
63 Lincoln Hwy.
Malvern, PA 19355-2120
Tel: (610) 644 - 1300
Fax:(610) 889 - 9349

Serves As:
- President and Chief Exec. Officer, Vishay Intertechnology, Inc.

PAUL, Patricia J.
6363 Main St.
Williamsville, NY 14221
paulp@natfuel.com
Tel: (716) 857 - 7780
Fax:(716) 857 - 7439
TF: (800) 365 - 3234

Serves As:
- Manager, Government Affairs, Nat'l Fuel Gas Co.

PAUL, Robert
7601 Lewinsville Rd., Suite 300
McLean, VA 22102
Tel: (703) 761 - 2251
Fax:(703) 761 - 2030

Serves As:
- Senior V. President, Human Resources, NVR, Inc.

PAUL, Robert A.
600 Grant St., Suite 4600
Pittsburgh, PA 15219
rpaul@ampcopgh.com
Tel: (412) 456 - 4453
Fax:(412) 456 - 4404

Serves As:
- Chairman and Chief Exec. Officer, Ampco-Pittsburgh Corp.

PAULENICH, Fred
1155 Battery St.
San Francisco, CA 94111
Tel: (415) 501 - 6000
Fax:(415) 501 - 7112
TF: (800) 872 - 5384

Serves As:
- Senior V. President, Worldwide Human Resources, Levi Strauss and Co.

PAULEY, Dennis
635 18th St.
Rock Island, IL 61201
Tel: (309) 788 - 7312
Fax:(309) 793 - 5410

Serves As:
• Area Manager, External Affairs, SBC Illinois

PAULI, Christel
10889 Wilshire Blvd.
Los Angeles, CA 90024
Tel: (310) 208 - 8800
Fax:(310) 443 - 6690

Serves As:
• Assistant Secretary, Occidental Petroleum Corp. Social Responsibility, Occidental Petroleum Corp.

PAULL, Lindy
1900 K St. NW
Suite 900
Washington, DC 20006
Tel: (202) 822 - 4000
Fax:(202) 822 - 5640

Registered Federal Lobbyist.
Serves As:
• Representative, PriceWaterhouseCoopers LLP

PAULSEN, Marianne
1111 Louisiana St.
Houston, TX 77002
Tel: (713) 207 - 6500

Serves As:
• Investor Relations Contact, CenterPoint Energy

PAULSON, Jr., Henry M.
85 Broad St.
New York, NY 10004
Tel: (212) 902 - 1000
Fax:(212) 902 - 3000

Serves As:
• Chairman and Chief Exec. Officer, Goldman, Sachs and Co.

PAULSON, Kerry L.
2640 White Oak Circle
Suite E
Aurora, IL 60504
Tel: (630) 692 - 6060
Fax:(630) 692 - 6062

Serves As:
• Director, State Government Relations/West, UST Inc.

PAULSON, Nancy
3600 N. Hydraulic
Wichita, KS 67219
Tel: (316) 832 - 2700

Serves As:
• Senior V. President, Global Human Resources, The Coleman Company, Inc.

PAULY, Jennifer
229 W. 43rd St.
New York, NY 10036
paulyj@nytimes.com
Tel: (212) 556 - 1718

Serves As:
• Assistant Director, Community Affairs and Media Relations, New York Times Co.

PAVLICEK, Steve
One Moody Plaza
Galveston, TX 77550-7999
Tel: (409) 766 - 6447
Fax:(409) 766 - 6933
TF: (800) 899 - 6502

Serves As:
• Senior V. President and Controller, American Nat'l Insurance Co.
Responsibilities include investor relations.

PAVLIK, Paul J.
800 Cabin Hill Dr.
Greensburg, PA 15601
ppavlik@alleghenyenergy.com
Tel: (724) 837 - 3000

Serves As:
• Manager, State Governmental Affairs, Allegheny Energy Inc.

PAVLOVIC, Dejan
1015 15th St. NW
Suite 200
Washington, DC 20005-2605
dejan.pavlovic@oracle.com
Tel: (202) 721 - 4809
Fax:(202) 467 - 4250

Registered Federal Lobbyist.
Serves As:
• Director, Regulatory Affairs and Development, Oracle Corporation

PAVLOVICH, Steve
3000 Hanover St.
Palo Alto, CA 94304
Tel: (650) 857 - 3950
Fax:(650) 857 - 5518
TF: (800) 752 - 0900

Serves As:
• Director, Investor Relations, Hewlett-Packard Co.

PAXTON, Gary L.
P.O. Box 35985
Tulsa, OK 74153-0985
Tel: (918) 660 - 7700
Fax:(918) 669 - 2934

Serves As:
• President and Chief Exec. Officer, Dollar Thrifty Automotive Group, Inc.

PAXTON, Nancy
One Infinite Loop
Cupertino, CA 95014
paxton1@apple.com
Tel: (408) 996 - 1010
Fax:(408) 996 - 0275

Serves As:
• Director, Investor Relations, Apple Computer, Inc.

PAYETTE, Michael W.
101 N. Wacker Dr., Suite 1910
Chicago, IL 60606
Tel: (312) 853 - 8402
Fax:(312) 853 - 8420

Serves As:
• Government Affairs, Union Pacific Corp.

PAYNE, Charles
P.O. Box 2601
Troy, MI 48007-2601
Tel: (248) 643 - 3500
Fax:(248) 643 - 3687

Serves As:
• Corporate Manager, Environmental Affairs, Thyssenkrupp Budd Company

PAYNE, Christopher
P.O. Box 35985
Tulsa, OK 74153-0985
chris.payne@thrifty.com
Tel: (918) 660 - 7700
Fax:(918) 669 - 2934

Serves As:
• Manager, Corporate Communications, (Thrifty Inc.), Dollar Thrifty Automotive Group, Inc.

PAYNE, Christopher
751 Broad St.
Newark, NJ 07102-3777
Tel: (973) 802 - 6000
Fax:(973) 802 - 3128
TF: (800) THE - ROCK

Registered Federal Lobbyist.
Serves As:
• Project Manager, Government Affairs, Prudential Financial

PAYNE, John H.
Two N. Jackson St.
Montgomery, AL 36104
Tel: (334) 223 - 5446

Serves As:
• Manager, State Legislative Affairs, Alabama Power Co.

PAYNE, Maura
P.O. Box 2990
Winston-Salem, NC 27102
paynem@rjrt.com
Tel: (336) 741 - 5000
Fax:(336) 741 - 5607

Serves As:
• V. President, Communications, Reynolds American Inc.

PAYNE, Tara Ford
300 Concord Plaza Dr.
San Antonio, TX 78216
tford@tesoropetroleum.com
Tel: (210) 283 - 2676
Fax:(210) 283 - 2003
TF: (800) 837 - 8768

Serves As:
• Director, Public Relations and Corporate Communications, Tesoro Petroleum Corp.

PAYNE, Tommy J.
P.O. Box 2990
Winston-Salem, NC 27102
Tel: (336) 741 - 5000
Fax:(336) 741 - 7975

Serves As:
• Exec. V. President, External Relations, Reynolds American Inc.

PAZ, George
13900 Riverport Dr.
Maryland Heights, MO 63043
Tel: (314) 770 - 1666
Fax:(314) 702 - 7037
TF: (800) 332 - 5455

Serves As:
• President and Chief Exec. Officer, Express Scripts, Inc.

PEACE, Chris
1401 I St. NW
Suite 600
Washington, DC 20005
Tel: (202) 336 - 7400
Fax:(202) 336 - 7515

Registered Federal Lobbyist.
Serves As:
• Congressional Relations Representative, United Technologies Corp.

PEACOCK, Jr., Robert B.
P.O. Box 482
Milwaukee, WI 53201-0482
Tel: (414) 931 - 3443
Fax:(414) 931 - 6352

Serves As:
• Manager, Employee Communications, Miller Brewing Co.

PEACOCK, Tracy
P.O. Box 2910
Tacoma, WA 98401-2910
Tel: (253) 383 - 9101
TF: (800) 610 - 8920

Serves As:
• Contact, Community Involvement Fund, Labor Ready, Inc.

PEARCE, David F.
401 Ninth St., NW, Suite 650
Washington, DC 20004
Tel: (202) 654 - 2000
Fax:(202) 654 - 2100

Registered Federal Lobbyist.
Serves As:
• Exec. Director, Government Affairs, Morgan Stanley

PEARCE, Harry
101 Constitution Ave. NW
Suite 325 East
Washington, DC 20001
Tel: (202) 312 - 8060

Serves As:
• Chairman of the Board, Nortel Networks

PEARL, Barry
P.O. Box 2521
Houston, TX 77252-2521
Tel: (713) 759 - 3636
Fax:(713) 759 - 3957
TF: (800) 877 - 3636

Serves As:
• President and Chief Exec. Officer, Texas Eastern Products Pipeline Company, LLC (TEPPCO)

PEARL, Suzanne
1850 N. Central Ave.
Suite 800
Phoenix, AZ 85004-4545
spearl@viad.com
Tel: (602) 207 - 2817
Fax:(602) 207 - 5455

Serves As:
• V. President, Human Resources, Viad Corp

PEARSON, Mary Frances
1225 Connecticut Ave. NW
Washington, DC 20036
maryfrances.pearson@ey.com
Tel: (202) 327 - 6000

Registered Federal Lobbyist.
Serves As:
• Partner; National Director, Government Relations, Ernst & Young LLP

PEARSON, Ronald D.
5820 Westown Pkwy.
West Des Moines, IA 50266-8223
Tel: (515) 267 - 2800
Fax:(515) 267 - 2817

Serves As:
• Chairman of the Board, Hy-Vee, Inc.

PEASE, Edward A.
14850 Conference Center Dr.
Chantilly, VA 20151
Tel: (703) 621 - 2797
Fax:(703) 621 - 4989

Registered Federal Lobbyist.
Serves As:
• Senior V. President, Government Relations, Rolls-Royce North America Inc.

PEASE, Kendell
2941 Fairview Park Dr.
Falls Church, VA 22042-4513
Tel: (703) 876 - 3093
Fax:(703) 876 - 3555

Serves As:
• V. President, Communications, General Dynamics Corporation

PECK, Nancy
One ConAgra Dr.
Omaha, NE 68102-5001
Tel: (402) 595 - 4215
Fax:(402) 595 - 4595

Serves As:
• Contact, ConAgra Foods Foundation, ConAgra Foods, Inc.

PECK, Pamela S.
P.O. Box 35985
Tulsa, OK 74153-0985
Tel: (918) 660 - 7700
Fax:(918) 669 - 2934

Serves As:
• PAC Treasurer, Dollar Thrifty Automotive Group, Inc.

PECKHAM, Katie
P.O. Box 4844
Syracuse, NY 13221-4844
Tel: (315) 433 - 0100
Ext: 5594
Fax:(315) 433 - 2345
TF: (800) 654 - 8838

Serves As:
• Communications Contact, Dairylea Cooperative Inc.

PEDEN, Keith
870 Winter St.
Waltham, MA 02451
keith.peden@raytheon.com
Tel: (781) 522 - 3000

Serves As:
• Senior V. President, Human Resources, Raytheon Co.

PEDERSON, Merle
711 High St.
Des Moines, IA 50392-0150
pederson.merle@principal.com
Tel: (515) 248 - 2186
TF: (800) 986 - 3343

Serves As:
• V. President, Government Relations, The Principal Financial Group

PEDERSON, Patty
800 LaSalle Ave.
Minneapolis, MN 55402-2006
Tel: (612) 372 - 4664
Fax:(612) 321 - 5137

Serves As:
• Associate Director, Public Relations, (CenterPoint Energy Minnegasco), CenterPoint Energy

PEDRI, Melissa
1200 G St. NW
Suite 900
Washington, DC 20005-3802
Tel: (202) 383 - 3700
Fax:(202) 383 - 3718

Registered Federal Lobbyist.
Serves As:
• Representative, The McGraw-Hill Companies, Inc.

PEEK, Jeffrey M.
1211 Avenue of the Americas
New York, NY 10036
Tel: (212) 536 - 1390
Fax:(212) 536 - 1912

Serves As:
• Chairman, President and Chief Exec. Officer, The CIT Group, Inc.

PEEL, Michael A.
One General Mills Blvd.
Minneapolis, MN 55426
Tel: (763) 764 - 7600

Serves As:
• Senior V. President, Human Resources and Corporate Services, General Mills

PEERMAN, Allyson
One AMD Pl.
P.O. Box 3453
Sunnyvale, CA 94088
Tel: (408) 749 - 4000
TF: (800) 538 - 8450

Serves As:
• Manager, Corporate Community Affairs, Advanced Micro Devices, Inc.

PEETS, Terry R.
11911 Freedom Dr.
Suite 600
Reston, VA 20190
Tel: (703) 456 - 4700
Fax:(607) 377 - 8962
TF: (800) 999 - 3436

Serves As:
• Chairman of the Board, World Kitchen, Inc.

PEEVY, Mary
1100 N. Glebe Rd.
Arlington, VA 22201-4798
mpeevy@caci.com
Tel: (703) 841 - 3719
Fax:(703) 841 - 7882

Serves As:
• Coordinator, Investor Relations, CACI Internat'l Inc.

PEGAU, Sharon
601 W. Riverside Ave.
Suite 1100
Spokane, WA 99201
Tel: (509) 835 - 1515
Fax:(509) 835 - 1555

Serves As:
• Contact, Potlatch Foundation for Higher Education, Potlatch Corp.

PEGO, Margaret
80 Park Plaza
M/S T21A
Newark, NJ 07102-0570
margaret.pego@pseg.com
Tel: (973) 430 - 7243
Fax:(973) 642 - 1689

Serves As:
• V. President, Human Resources, PSE&G

PEISER, Robert A.
P.O. Box Nine
Sugar Land, TX 77487
Tel: (281) 491 - 9181
Fax:(281) 490 - 9584
TF: (800) 727 - 8427

Serves As:
• President and Chief Exec. Officer, Imperial Sugar Co.

PEISNER, Jonathan
250 Stephenson Hwy.
Troy, MI 48083
Tel: (248) 824 - 2500

Serves As:
• PAC Treasurer, Collins & Aikman Corp.

PEKNY, Anthony
411 Seventh Ave.
Pittsburgh, PA 15219
Tel: (412) 393 - 6000
Fax:(412) 393 - 6448

Serves As:
• PAC Treasurer, Duquesne Light Holdings

PELLETIER, Eric
1299 Pennsylvania Ave. NW
11th Floor West
Washington, DC 20004-2407
Tel: (202) 637 - 4000
Fax:(202) 637 - 4006

Serves As:
• Senior Manager, Government Relations, General Electric Co.

PELTON, Jack J.
P.O. Box 7706 Tel: (316) 517 - 6000
Wichita, KS 67277-7706 Fax:(316) 517 - 6640

Serves As:
- President, Chief Exec. Officer and Chairman of the Board, Cessna Aircraft Co.

PELTZ, Nelson
280 Park Ave. Tel: (212) 451 - 3000
New York, NY 10017 Fax:(212) 451 - 3134

Serves As:
- Chairman and Chief Exec. Officer, Triarc Companies, Inc.

PEMBERTON, John L.
601 Pennsylvania Ave. NW Tel: (202) 261 - 5000
Suite 800 Fax:(202) 296 - 7937
Washington, DC 20004

Registered Federal Lobbyist.
Serves As:
- Director, Federal Affairs, Southern Company

PENCE, Greg
P.O. Box 868 Tel: (812) 464 - 9800
Evansville, IN 47705-0868 Fax:(812) 464 - 9825
TF: (800) 467 - 1928

Serves As:
- Media Relations Contact, Integra Bank N.A.

PENCE, Robin
4300 Wilson Blvd. Tel: (703) 682 - 6552
11th Floor Fax:(703) 528 - 4510
Arlington, VA 22203

Serves As:
- V. President, Communications, The AES Corp.

PENDELL-LEAVITT, Cami
602 W. Ionia Tel: (517) 371 - 7905
Lansing, MI 48933 Fax:(517) 372 - 7979

Serves As:
- Manager, Executive Branch Relations and Legislative Affairs, Blue Cross Blue Shield of Michigan

PENDER, Annemarie
1025 Connecticut Ave., N.W., Suite 910 Tel: (202) 467 - 5088
Washington, DC 20036
apender@mazdausa.com

Registered Federal Lobbyist.
Serves As:
- Government and East Coast Public Affairs Representative, Mazda North American Operations

PENN, Oren
1900 K St. NW Tel: (202) 822 - 4000
Suite 900 Fax:(202) 822 - 5640
Washington, DC 20006

Registered Federal Lobbyist.
Serves As:
- Representative, PriceWaterhouseCoopers LLP

PENNINGTON, D. Mike
2135 W. Maple Rd. Tel: (248) 435 - 1933
Troy, MI 48084 Fax:(248) 435 - 9946
david.pennington@arvinmeritor.com TF: (800) 535 - 5560

Serves As:
- Senior Director, Global Marketing Communications, ArvinMeritor

PENNINGTON, Hal N.
Genesco Park, Suite 490 Tel: (615) 367 - 7000
P.O. Box 731 Fax:(615) 367 - 8278
Nashville, TN 37202-0731

Serves As:
- Chairman of the Board, President and Chief Exec. Officer, Genesco

PENNINGTON, Kevin P.
1110 American Parkway NE Tel: (610) 712 - 4323
Allentown, PA 18109-3229 Fax:(610) 712 - 4106

Serves As:
- Senior V. President, Human Resources and Real Estate, Agere Systems Inc.

PENROSE, Sheila A.
200 E. Randolph St. Tel: (312) 782 - 5800
Chicago, IL 60601-6436 Fax:(312) 782 - 4339

Serves As:
- Chairman of the Board, Jones Lang LaSalle Inc.

PENSABENE, Gregory M.
800 Connecticut Ave. NW Tel: (202) 861 - 5918
Suite 700 Fax:(202) 861 - 8065
Washington, DC 20006

Registered Federal Lobbyist.
Serves As:
- V. President, Government Relations, Anadarko Petroleum Corp.

PENSEC, John
P.O. Box 105250 Tel: (770) 593 - 5443
Atlanta, GA 30348 Fax:(770) 593 - 5367
jpensec@harland.net TF: (800) 723 - 3690

Serves As:
- Director, Corporate Communications and Community Relations, John H. Harland Co.

PENSHORN, John S.
9900 Bren Rd. East Tel: (952) 936 - 7214
Minneapolis, MN 55343 Fax:(952) 936 - 0044
TF: (800) 328 - 5979

Serves As:
- Senior V. President, UnitedHealth Group

Responsibilities include investor relations.

PENSKE, Roger S.
2555 Telegraph Rd. Tel: (248) 648 - 2500
Bloomfield Hills, MI 48302-0954 Fax:(248) 648 - 2525

Serves As:
- Chairman and Chief Exec. Officer, United Auto Group, Inc.
- Chairman and Chief Exec. Officer, Penske Truck Leasing Co. LP

PERALTA, Jesus
1401 I St., N.W., Suite 340 Tel: (202) 371 - 9279
Washington, DC 20005-2225 Fax:(202) 371 - 9169

Serves As:
- Policy Manager, C F Industries, Inc.

PERDUE, David A.
100 Mission Ridge Tel: (615) 855 - 4000
Goodlettsville, TN 37072

Serves As:
- Chairman and Chief Exec. Officer, Dollar General Corp.

PERDUE, James A.
P.O. Box 1537 Tel: (410) 543 - 3000
Salisbury, MD 21802-1537 Fax:(410) 543 - 3884

Serves As:
- Chairman and Chief Exec. Officer, Perdue Farms

PERELMAN, Ronald O.
237 Park Ave. Tel: (212) 572 - 5000
New York, NY 10017

Serves As:
- Chairman of the Board, Revlon, Inc.

PEREZ, Antonio
343 State St. Tel: (585) 724 - 4000
Rochester, NY 14650-0516 Fax:(585) 724 - 1724

Serves As:
- Chief Exec. Officer and President, Eastman Kodak Company

PEREZ, Derek
2701 San Tomas Exwy. Tel: (408) 486 - 2512
Santa Clara, CA 95050 Fax:(408) 486 - 4512
dperez@nvidia.com

Serves As:
- Director, Public Relations, NVIDIA Corp.

PEREZ, Gilberto
840 Gessner Tel: (713) 650 - 6200
Suite 1400 Fax:(713) 653 - 6815
Houston, TX 77024

Serves As:
- President and Chief Exec. Officer, Cemex USA

PEREZ, Katherine C.
P.O. Box 1642 Tel: (713) 627 - 6527
Houston, TX 77251-1642 Fax:(713) 627 - 5767
kperez@duke-energy.com

Serves As:
- Director, Public Affairs/DENA, Duke Energy Corp.

PEREZ, William D. "Bill"
One Bowerman Dr. Tel: (503) 671 - 6453
Beaverton, OR 97005 Fax:(503) 671 - 6300

Serves As:
- President and Chief Exec. Officer, Nike, Inc.

PEREZ DE LA MESA, Manuel J.
109 Northpark Blvd. Tel: (985) 892 - 5521
Covington, LA 70433-5001 Fax:(985) 892 - 1657

Serves As:
- President and Chief Exec. Officer, SCP Pool Corp.

PERIBERE, Jerome
9330 Zionsville Rd. Tel: (317) 337 - 3000
Indianapolis, IN 46268

Serves As:
• President and Chief Exec. Officer, Dow AgroSciences LLC
Serves as the main headquarters Senior Public Affairs Executive.

PERILLE, Christopher J.
410 N. Michigan Ave. Tel: (312) 645 - 4077
Chicago, IL 60611 Fax:(312) 644 - 0015
cperille@wrigley.com

Serves As:
• Senior Director, Corporate Communications, Wm. Wrigley Jr. Co.
Responsibilities include government affairs.

PERKINS, Charlie
Five Times Square Tel: (212) 773 - 2418
New York, NY 10036 Fax:(212) 773 - 7982

Serves As:
• Director, Public Relations, Ernst & Young LLP

PERKINS, Peter
1000 Wilson Blvd., Suite 2300 Tel: (703) 525 - 6767
Arlington, VA 22209 Fax:(703) 276 - 0711

Registered Federal Lobbyist.
Serves As:
• Manager, Legislative Affairs, Northrop Grumman Corp.

PERKINS, Vicki
120 Monument Circle Tel: (317) 488 - 6216
Indianapolis, IN 46204

Serves As:
• Exec. Director, Anthem Blue Cross and Blue Shield Foundation, Wellpoint, Inc.

PERLEGOS, George
2325 Orchard Pkwy. Tel: (408) 441 - 0311
San Jose, CA 95131 Fax:(408) 436 - 4200
gperlegos@atmel.com

Serves As:
• Chairman, President and Chief Exec. Officer, Atmel Corp.

PERLMUTTER, Barbara
1166 Ave. of The Americas Tel: (212) 345 - 5585
New York, NY 10036-2774 Fax:(212) 345 - 4838
barbara.perlmutter@mmc.com

Serves As:
• Senior V. President, Public Affairs, Marsh & McLennan Companies, Inc.

PERLMUTTER, Shira
800 Connecticut Ave. NW Tel: (202) 457 - 8582
Suite 800 Fax:(202) 457 - 8861
Washington, DC 20006

Registered Federal Lobbyist.
Serves As:
• Representative, Time Warner Inc.

PERNIE, Chris
655 15th St. NW Tel: (202) 783 - 0900
Suite 300 Fax:(202) 783 - 2308
Washington, DC 20005

Registered Federal Lobbyist.
Serves As:
• Representative, Bristol-Myers Squibb Co.

PERNOTTO, Steve
2801 W. Tyvola Rd. Tel: (704) 426 - 1890
Charlotte, NC 28217-4500 Fax:(704) 357 - 1876
steve_pernotto@belk.com

Serves As:
• Exec. V. President, Human Resources, Belk, Inc.
Responsibilities include corporate communications.

PERNU, Cathy
Three Lakes Dr. Tel: (847) 646 - 3946
Northfield, IL 60093-2753 Fax:(847) 646 - 6005

Serves As:
• Senior Manager, Corporate Communications, Kraft Foods, Inc.

PEROT, H. Ross
2300 W. Plano Pkwy. Tel: (972) 577 - 0000
Plano, TX 75075

Serves As:
• Chairman of the Board, Perot Systems Corp.

PEROT, Jr., H. Ross
2300 W. Plano Pkwy. Tel: (972) 577 - 0000
Plano, TX 75075

Serves As:
• President and Chief Exec. Officer, Perot Systems Corp.

PERROS, Georgette
1455 F St. NW Tel: (202) 628 - 6442
Suite 420 Fax:(202) 628 - 6537
Washington, DC 20004

Registered Federal Lobbyist.
Serves As:
• Representative, United Services Automobile Ass'n (USAA)

PERRY, Barry W.
101 Wood Ave. Tel: (732) 205 - 5000
Iselin, NJ 08830 Fax:(732) 632 - 9253
TF: (800) 631 - 9505

Serves As:
• Chairman and Chief Exec. Officer, Engelhard Corp.

PERRY, Beverly L.
701 Ninth St. NW Tel: (202) 872 - 2373
Washington, DC 20068
blperry@pepco.com

Registered Federal Lobbyist.
Serves As:
• Senior V. President, Government Affairs and Public Policy, Pepco Holdings, Inc.

PERRY, Bill
55 Glenlake Pkwy. NE Tel: (404) 828 - 4184
Atlanta, GA 30328 Fax:(404) 828 - 6971
bperry@ups.com

Serves As:
• Manager, Communications, United Parcel Service (UPS)

PERRY, Denise
One Ocean Spray Dr. Tel: (508) 946 - 7634
Lakeville-Middleboro, MA 02349 Fax:(508) 946 - 7704
dperry@oceanspray.com TF: (800) 662 - 3263

Serves As:
• Corporate Communications Contact, Ocean Spray Cranberries, Inc.

PERRY, Earnestine
3495 Piedmont Rd. NE Tel: (404) 364 - 4754
Atlanta, GA 30305-1736
earnestine.perry@kp.org

Serves As:
• Media Representative - Georgia Region, Kaiser Permanente

PERRY, Edmund F.
1301 K St. NW Tel: (202) 515 - 5039
Suite 1200 Fax:(202) 515 - 5906
Washington, DC 20005

Registered Federal Lobbyist.
Serves As:
• Director, Political Programs, Internat'l Business Machines Corp. (IBM)

PERRY, Teresa
1099 18th St. Tel: (303) 252 - 6087
Suite 1200 Fax:(303) 457 - 8482
Denver, CO 80202 TF: (800) 933 - 5603
tmassaro@westerngas.com

Serves As:
• Director, Corporate Communications and Services, Western Gas Resources, Inc.
Responsibilities also include corporate philanthropy.

PERRY, Tim C.
1667 K St. NW Tel: (202) 496 - 2482
Suite 400 Fax:(202) 775 - 8427
Washington, DC 20006

Registered Federal Lobbyist.
Serves As:
• Trade and Regulatory Afffairs, APL Americas

PESCE, William J.
111 River St. Tel: (201) 748 - 6000
M/S 7-02 Fax:(201) 748 - 6008
Hoboken, NJ 07030-5774

Serves As:
• President and Chief Exec. Officer, John Wiley & Sons, Inc.

PESKE, Sherry E.
12950 Worldgate Dr. Tel: (703) 480 - 3600
Suite 600 Fax:(703) 796 - 2214
Herndon, VA 20170
sherry.peske@lafarge-na.com

Serves As:
• V. President, Corporate Communications and Public Affairs, Lafarge North America, Inc.

PESSNER, Kirk Alan
20 Park Rd., Suite E Tel: (650) 401 - 8735
Burlingame, CA 94010 Fax:(650) 401 - 8739
kirk.pessner@sun.com

Serves As:
• PAC Treasurer, Sun Microsystems, Inc.

PETERMAN, Donna C.
249 Fifth Ave.
Pittsburgh, PA 15222-2707
Tel: (412) 762 - 2000

Serves As:
- Senior V. President and Director, Corporate Communications, PNC Financial Services Group

PETERS, Brenda J.
P.O. Box 2521
Houston, TX 77252-2521
bpeters@teppco.com
Tel: (713) 759 - 3954
Fax:(713) 759 - 3957
TF: (800) 877 - 3636

Serves As:
- Director, Investor Relations, Texas Eastern Products Pipeline Company, LLC (TEPPCO)

PETERS, Brian
Dain Rauscher Plaza
60 S. Sixth St., 19th Floor
Minneapolis, MN 55402-4422
Tel: (612) 371 - 7750
Fax:(612) 371 - 2960

Serves As:
- President and Chief Exec. Officer, RBC Dain Rauscher Corp.

PETERS, Jeffrey R.
Cranberry Court, Suite 101
212 N. Third St.
Harrisburg, PA 17101
Tel: (717) 232 - 5634
Fax:(717) 232 - 0691

Serves As:
- Director, Government Affairs and Media Relations, Sunoco, Inc.

PETERS, Linda
One MedImmune Way
Gaithersburg, MD 20878
Tel: (301) 398 - 0000
Fax:(301) 398 - 9000
TF: (877) 633 - 4411

Serves As:
- Senior V. President, Regulatory Affairs, MedImmune, Inc.

PETERS, Mark
10475 Park Meadows Dr.
Littleton, CO 80124

Serves As:
- Treasurer, Time Warner Telecom Inc. PAC, Time Warner Inc.

PETERS, Mary O.
700 Milam St.
Suite 3100
Houston, TX 77002
Tel: (832) 239 - 6000

Serves As:
- V. President, Administration and Human Resources, Plains Resources Inc.

PETERSEN, Gail L.
Five Garret Mountain Plaza
West Paterson, NJ 07424
Tel: (973) 357 - 3100
Fax:(973) 357 - 3065
TF: (800) 652 - 6013

Serves As:
- Director, Communications and Public Affairs, Cytec Industries Inc.

PETERSEN, John
One Nu Skin Plaza
75 W. Center St.
Provo, UT 84601
jpeterse@nuskin.com
Tel: (801) 345 - 2104
Fax:(801) 345 - 2799

Serves As:
- Director, Public Relations, Nu Skin Enterprises

Responsibilities include corporate contributions.

PETERSEN, LeeAnn M.
1201 Pennsylvania Ave. NW
Suite 300
Washington, DC 20004
leeann.peterson@volvo.com
Tel: (202) 661 - 4770
Fax:(202) 661 - 4771

Registered Federal Lobbyist.
Serves As:
- Manager, Government Relations and Public Affairs, Volvo Group North America, Inc.

PETERSEN, Tom
200 First St. SE
Cedar Rapids, IA 52401
tompetersen@alliantenergy.com
Tel: (319) 786 - 4490
Fax:(319) 786 - 4796

Serves As:
- Director, Corporate Communications, Alliant Energy Corp.

PETERSON, Allen L.
400 Robert St. North
St. Paul, MN 55101
Tel: (651) 665 - 3500
Fax:(651) 665 - 4488

Serves As:
- PAC Treasurer, Minnesota Life Insurance Co.

PETERSON, Brian
P.O. Box 1470
Decatur, IL 62525
Tel: (217) 424 - 5413
Fax:(217) 424 - 5839
TF: (800) 637 - 5843

Serves As:
- Senior V. President, Corporate Affairs, Archer Daniels Midland Co. (ADM)

PETERSON, Coleman
702 SW Eighth St.
M/S 0200
Bentonville, AR 72716
Tel: (479) 273 - 4000
Fax:(479) 273 - 4053

Serves As:
- Exec. V. President, Human Resources, Wal-Mart Stores

PETERSON, Deborah S.
One Rentway Place
Erie, PA 16505
dpeterson@rentway.com
Tel: (814) 455 - 1511
Ext: 5225
Fax:(814) 461 - 5837
TF: (800) 736 - 8929

Serves As:
- Manager, Investor Relations, Rent-Way, Inc.

PETERSON, Dennis
One Bowerman Dr.
Beaverton, OR 97005
Tel: (503) 671 - 6453
Fax:(503) 671 - 6300

Serves As:
- Treasurer, Nike Inc. Federal PAC, Nike, Inc.

PETERSON, Donald K.
211 Mount Airy Rd.
Basking Ridge, NJ 07920
dpeterson@avaya.com
Tel: (908) 953 - 6000
Fax:(908) 953 - 7609

Serves As:
- Chairman and Chief Exec. Officer, Avaya Inc.

PETERSON, Heather
1 Sybase Dr.
Dublin, CA 94568
heather.peterson@sybase.com
Tel: (925) 236 - 6517

Serves As:
- Corporate and International Public Relations Contact, Sybase, Inc.

PETERSON, Jeffrey K.
Ecolab Center
370 N. Wabasha St.
St. Paul, MN 55102
jeff.k.peterson@ecolab.com
Tel: (651) 293 - 2557
Fax:(651) 225 - 3274

Serves As:
- Director, Government Relations; and PAC Administrator, Ecolab Inc.

PETERSON, Mark W.
P.O. Box 2301
Cincinnati, OH 45201-2301
Tel: (513) 397 - 9900
Fax:(513) 723 - 9815

Serves As:
- V. President and Treasurer; PAC Treasurer, Cincinnati Bell Inc.

PETERSON, Ralph R.
9191 S. Jamaica St.
Englewood, CO 80112
Tel: (303) 771 - 0900
Fax:(720) 286 - 9250

Serves As:
- Chairman, President and Chief Exec. Officer, CH2M Hill Companies, Inc.

PETERSON, Sheila
33 Commercial St.
Foxboro, MA 02035
speterson@foxboro.com
Tel: (508) 549 - 3218
Fax:(508) 549 - 2626
TF: (866) 746 - 6477

Serves As:
- Manager, Community Relations (Public Affairs), Invensys Systems, Inc.

PETERSON, Timothy A.
Commonwealth Towers
1300 Wilson Blvd., Suite 200
Arlington, VA 22209-2307
Tel: (703) 516 - 8220
Fax:(703) 516 - 8295

Registered Federal Lobbyist.
Serves As:
- Director, Congressional Relations-Government Programs, Rockwell Collins, Inc

PETITO, Joseph P.
1900 K St. NW
Suite 900
Washington, DC 20006
Tel: (202) 822 - 5812
Fax:(202) 822 - 5640

Serves As:
- Partner, Professional and Regulatory Activities, PriceWaterhouseCoopers LLP

Responsibilities include government affairs.

PETITT, Douglas
211 Riverside Dr.
Evansville, IN 47708-1251
Tel: (812) 491 - 4000
Fax:(812) 491 - 4078
TF: (800) 227 - 1376

Serves As:
- V. President, Government Affairs, Vectren Corp.

PETKUS, Douglas
500 Arcola Rd.
Collegeville, PA 19426
petkusd@wyeth.com
Tel: (484) 865 - 5000

Serves As:
- V. President, Global Public Relations, Wyeth Pharmaceuticals

PETRACRA, Mark
11270 W. Park Place
Milwaukee, WI 53224-9510
Tel: (414) 359 - 4000
Fax:(414) 359 - 4064

Serves As:
- V. President, Human Resources and Public Affairs, A. O. Smith Corp.

PETRATIS, David D.
1415 Roselle Rd.
Palatine, IL 60067
Tel: (847) 397 - 2600
Fax:(847) 925 - 7500

Serves As:
- President and Chief Exec. Officer, Square D/Schneider Electric

PETRELLI, Charlene
One Oxford Center, Suite 3300
Pittsburgh, PA 15219
Tel: (412) 553 - 5712
Fax:(412) 553 - 5732

Serves As:
- V. President, Human Resources, Equitable Resources, Inc.

PETRUCCI, Laurie J.
112 W. 34th St.
New York, NY 10120
Tel: (212) 720 - 3700
Fax:(212) 720 - 4397

Serves As:
- Senior V. President, Human Resources, Footlocker Inc.

PETRY, May
2315 N. First St.
San Jose, CA 95131
may.petry@bea.com
Tel: (408) 570 - 8704
Fax:(408) 570 - 8901

Serves As:
- Public Relations Contact, BEA Systems, Inc.

PETTERS, C. Michael
4101 Washington Ave.
Newport News, VA 23607-2770
Tel: (757) 380 - 2000
Fax:(757) 380 - 3875

Serves As:
- V. President, Human Resources, Administration and Trades, Northrop Grumman Newport News

PETTERS, Thomas J.
1265 Main St.
Bldg. W. Three
Waltham, MA 02451
Tel: (781) 386 - 2000

Serves As:
- Chairman of the Board, Polaroid Corp.

PETTINGILL, Richard
710 E. 24th St.
M.R. 43303
Minneapolis, MN 55404
dick.pettingill@allina.com
Tel: (612) 775 - 9732
Fax:(612) 775 - 9723

Serves As:
- President and Chief Exec. Officer, Allina Hospitals and Clinics

PETZ, Carl
11401 Lamar Ave.
Overland Park, KS 66211
Tel: (913) 458 - 4685
Fax:(913) 458 - 2934

Serves As:
- Director, Corporate Communications, Black & Veatch

PEURYE, Celene
One Baxter Pkwy.
Deerfield, IL 60015-4633
Tel: (847) 948 - 4604
Fax:(847) 948 - 4026

Serves As:
- Exec. Director, Foundation, Baxter Internat'l Inc.

PFANNER, Jennifer
P.O. Box 1768
Sacramento, CA 95812-1768
jpfanner@bdgrowers.com
Tel: (916) 325 - 2859
Fax:(916) 325 - 2880

Serves As:
- Media Relations Contact, Blue Diamond Growers

PFEFFER, Gerald S.
1000 Kiewit Plaza
Omaha, NE 68131
Tel: (402) 342 - 2052
Fax:(402) 271 - 2939

Serves As:
- V. President, Marketing, Peter Kiewit Sons', Inc.

Responsibilities include corporate communications.

PFEIFER-HARMS, Bev
U.S. Bank Plaza
505 N. Seventh St. Ste 2000
Suite 3610
St. Louis, MO 63101
Tel: (314) 259 - 6315
Fax:(314) 621 - 1778

Serves As:
- Manager, Public Relations, Hardee's Food Systems, Inc.

Responsibilities include corporate philanthropy.

PFERDEHIRT, Dough
153 E. 53rd St., 57th Floor
New York, NY 10022-4624
Tel: (212) 350 - 9400
Fax:(212) 350 - 9564

Serves As:
- V. President, Communications and Investor Relations, Schlumberger Limited

PFISTER, Barbara
3210 Watling St.
East Chicago, IN 46312
barbara.pfister@ispat.com
Tel: (219) 399 - 7873
Fax:(219) 399 - 6637

Serves As:
- Legislative Assistant, Government and Public Affairs, Ispat Inland Inc.

PFORZHEIMER, Harry
2632 Marine Way
Mountain View, CA 94043
Tel: (650) 944 - 6000
Fax:(650) 944 - 3699

Serves As:
- V. President, Communications, Intuit Inc.

PFUND, William H.
P.O. Box 1430
Kenosha, WI 53141-1430
Tel: (414) 656 - 6488
Fax:(414) 656 - 5577

Serves As:
- V. President, Investor Relations, Snap-on Incorporated

PHAN, Stacie
400 Morgan Ln.
West Haven, CT 06516
Tel: (203) 812 - 3804
Fax:(203) 812 - 6570

Serves As:
- Manager, Public Policy and Communications, Pharmaceutical Division, Bayer Corporation

PHANSTIEL, Howard G.
P.O. Box 6006
Cypress, CA 90630
Tel: (714) 227 - 3000
Fax:(714) 226 - 3653

Serves As:
- Chairman and Chief Exec. Officer, PacifiCare Health Systems, Inc.

PHELIZON, Jean-Francois
P.O. Box 860
Valley Forge, PA 19482
Tel: (610) 341 - 7000
Fax:(610) 341 - 7777

Serves As:
- Chief Exec. Officer, Saint-Gobain Corp.

PHENIX, Amy
710 E. 24th St.
M. R. 43202
Minneapolis, MN 55404
amy.phenix@allina.com
Tel: (612) 775 - 9767
Fax:(612) 775 - 9739

Serves As:
- V. President, Communications, Allina Hospitals and Clinics

PHIFER, Cozette
5770 Fleet St.
Carlsbad, CA 92008
cphifer@jennycraig.com
Tel: (760) 696 - 4000
Fax:(760) 696 - 4009
TF: (800) 597 - 5366

Serves As:
- Director, Public Relations, Jenny Craig, Inc.

PHILLIPS, Carrie
P.O. Box 1295
Birmingham, AL 35201
Tel: (205) 992 - 5168
Fax:(205) 992 - 6165

Registered Federal Lobbyist.
Serves As:
- Manager, Government Relations, Southern Nuclear Operating Co.

PHILLIPS, Christopher R.
One Ocean Spray Dr.
Lakeville-Middleboro, MA 02349
cphillips@oceanspray.com
Tel: (508) 946 - 7318
Fax:(508) 947 - 9791
TF: (800) 662 - 3263

Serves As:
- Manager, Corporate Communications and Public Affairs, Ocean Spray Cranberries, Inc.

PHILLIPS, David E.
6801 Rockledge Dr.
Bethesda, MD 20817-1877
david.phillips@lmco.com
Tel: (301) 897 - 6292
Fax:(301) 897 - 6252

Serves As:
- Manager, Lockheed Martin Foundation, Lockheed Martin Corp.

PHILLIPS, Dean
325 Pennsylvania Ave. SE
P.O. Box 280
Washington, DC 20003

Serves As:
• Pac Treasurer, Exxon Mobil Corp.

PHILLIPS, Debra
1715 Aaron Brenner Dr. Tel: (901) 434 - 3122
Renaissance Center, Suite 600 Fax:(901) 434 - 3155
Memphis, TN 38120
debra.phillips@fedex.com

Serves As:
• Managing Director, Communications, FedEx Freight

PHILLIPS, Diana
1334 York Ave. Tel: (212) 606 - 7176
New York, NY 10021 Fax:(212) 606 - 7107
diana.phillips@sothebys.com

Serves As:
• Senior V. President, Corporate Affairs, Sotheby's Holdings, Inc.

PHILLIPS, G. Patrick
900 Metro Center Blvd. Tel: (650) 432 - 3200
Foster City, CA 94404-2172 Fax:(650) 432 - 3631

Serves As:
• Chairman of the Board, Visa U.S.A. Inc.

PHILLIPS, Jeanne
1445 Ross at Field Tel: (214) 978 - 8534
Suite 1400 Fax:(214) 978 - 8888
Dallas, TX 75202-2785

Serves As:
• Public Affairs, Hunt Oil Co.

PHILLIPS, Karen Borlaug
601 Pennsylvania Ave. NW, Suite 500 Tel: (202) 347 - 7816
Washington, DC 20004 Fax:(202) 347 - 8237
karen.phillips@cn.ca

Registered Federal Lobbyist.
Serves As:
• V. President, North American Public and Government Affairs, Canadian Nat'l / Illinois Central

PHILLIPS, Karen Kraus
100 Erie Insurance Pl. Tel: (814) 870 - 4665
Erie, PA 16530 Fax:(814) 870 - 3126

Serves As:
• Manager and V. President, Corporate Communications and Investor Relations, Erie Indeminity Co.

PHILLIPS, Marilyn
600 Third Ave. Tel: (212) 878 - 5007
28th Fl. Fax:(212) 878 - 5079
New York, NY 10017-4085

Serves As:
• Director, Corporate Contributions, Wyeth

PHILLIPS, Paula
6501 Legacy Dr. Tel: (972) 431 - 1250
Plano, TX 75024-3698 Fax:(972) 431 - 1362
TF: (800) 222 - 6161

Serves As:
• Senior Government Relations Coordinator, J. C. Penney Co., Inc.

PHILLIPS, Robert W. "Bob"
1334 S. Central Ave. Tel: (213) 744 - 8653
Los Angeles, CA 90021 Fax:(213) 744 - 8903

Serves As:
• V. President, Public Affairs, (BCI Coca-Cola Bottling Co. of Los Angeles), Coca-Cola Enterprises Inc.

PHILLIPS, Susan A.
101 Constitution Ave. NW Tel: (202) 312 - 8060
Suite 325 East
Washington, DC 20001
aphillip@nortel.com

Registered Federal Lobbyist.
Serves As:
• V. President, Global Government Relations, Nortel Networks

PHILLIPS, Tom
701 Pennsylvania Ave. NW Tel: (202) 434 - 4800
Suite 720 Fax:(202) 347 - 4015
Washington, DC 20004

Registered Federal Lobbyist.
Serves As:
• Representative, Siemens Corp.

PHILPOTT, Fred
1194 N. Mathilda Ave. Tel: (408) 745 - 2000
Sunnyvale, CA 94089-1206 Fax:(408) 745 - 2100
TF: (888) 584 - 737

Serves As:
• V. President, Human Resources, Juniper Networks, Inc.

PHILPOTT, Joy
12405 Powerscourt Dr. Tel: (770) 754 - 5275
St. Louis, MO 63131
jphilpott1@charter.com

Serves As:
• V. President, Government Affairs and Franchise Relations, Charter Communications, Inc.

PHOENIX, Angela
1850 N. Central Ave. Tel: (602) 207 - 5608
Suite 800 Fax:(602) 207 - 5900
Phoenix, AZ 85004-4545
aphoenix@viad.com

Serves As:
• Manager, Corporate Communications, Viad Corp

PIANO, Phyllis J.
One Amgen Center Dr. Tel: (805) 447 - 1000
Thousand Oaks, CA 91320-1799 Fax:(805) 447 - 1010

Serves As:
• V. President, Corporate Communications and Philanthropy, Amgen Inc.

PICCININI, Robert M.
P.O. Box 4278 Tel: (209) 574 - 6210
Modesto, CA 95352 Fax:(209) 577 - 3845

Serves As:
• Chairman and Chief Exec. Officer, Save Mart Supermarkets

PICCOLO, Joann
1350 I St. NW Tel: (202) 371 - 6942
Suite 400 Fax:(202) 842 - 3578
Washington, DC 20005-3306

Registered Federal Lobbyist.
Serves As:
• Corporate V. President and Director, U.S. Government Relations, Motorola, Inc.

PICKAR, Joy Keyser
1555 Promontery Circle Tel: (970) 395 - 5150
Greeley, CO 80638-0001

Serves As:
• Assistant Manager, Public Affairs, (State Farm Mutual Automobile Insurance Co.), State Farm Insurance Cos.

PICKARD, Mary E.
385 Washington St. Tel: (651) 310 - 7359
St. Paul, MN 55102 Fax:(651) 310 - 2327

Serves As:
• President, St. Paul Travelers Cos., Inc. Foundation and V. President Community Affairs, St. Paul Travelers Cos., Inc.

PICKART, George A.
1016 16th St. NW Tel: (202) 293 - 5794
Suite 500 Fax:(202) 223 - 6178
Washington, DC 20036

Registered Federal Lobbyist.
Serves As:
• Director, International Affairs, CMS Energy Corp.

PICKEL, Bryan
751 Broad St. Tel: (973) 802 - 6000
Newark, NJ 07102-3777 Fax:(973) 802 - 3128
TF: (800) THE - ROCK

Registered Federal Lobbyist.
Serves As:
• Lobbyist, Prudential Financial

PICKERING, Brian
7261 Mercy Rd. Tel: (402) 398 - 3694
P.O. Box 3248 Fax:(402) 398 - 3736
Omaha, NE 68180
brian.pickering@bcbsne.com

Serves As:
• Manager, Public Relations and Communications, Blue Cross and Blue Shield of Nebraska

PICKERING, Thomas R.
1200 Wilson Blvd. Tel: (703) 465 - 3471
Arlington, VA 22209-2305

Serves As:
• Senior V. President, International Relations, The Boeing Co.

PIDCOCK, Paulette C.
1331 Pennsylvania Ave. NW
Suite 512
Washington, DC 20004
Tel: (202) 662 - 8750
Fax:(202) 662 - 8749

Serves As:
- V. President, Federal Government Relations, PPL Corp.

PIEN, Howard
4560 Horton St.
Emeryville, CA 94608-2916
Tel: (510) 655 - 8730
Fax:(510) 655 - 9910

Serves As:
- Chairman, President and Chief Exec. Officer, Chiron Corp.

PIEPER, James
2700 Sanders Rd.
Prospect Heights, IL 60070
Tel: (847) 564 - 5000
Fax:(847) 805 - 7452

Serves As:
- Manager, Public Affairs, HSBC North America Holdings Inc.

PIERCE, Darryl
Four Park St.
Concord, NH 03301
Tel: (603) 226 - 1550
Fax:(603) 225 - 9861

Serves As:
- Director, Public Affairs Programs, Verizon Communications Inc.

PIERCE, Harvey R.
6000 American Pkwy.
Madison, WI 53783
Tel: (608) 249 - 4100
Ext: 30451
Fax:(608) 243 - 4928

Serves As:
- Chairman and Chief Exec. Officer, American Family Insurance Group

PIERCE, Larry
500 Dallas St., Suite 1000
Houston, TX 77002
Tel: (713) 369 - 9000
Fax:(713) 369 - 9100
TF: (800) 324 - 2900

Serves As:
- Director, Corporate Communications, Kinder Morgan, Inc.

PIERCE, Michael G.
6095 Parkland Blvd.
Cleveland, OH 44124
Tel: (440) 544 - 2600
Fax:(440) 544 - 2616

Serves As:
- Manager, Marketing and Communication Services, The Austin Co.

PIERGROSSI, Michael N.
7500 Grace Dr.
Columbia, MD 21044
Tel: (410) 531 - 4000
Fax:(410) 531 - 4367

Serves As:
- V. President, Leadership and Organization Development, W. R. Grace & Co.

Responsibilities include human resources.

PIETAK, Carole L.
3111 W. Allegheny Ave.
Philadelphia, PA 19132
Tel: (215) 430 - 9095
Fax:(215) 430 - 9533

Serves As:
- V. President, Human Resources, The Pep Boys-Manny, Moe & Jack

PIETRUSKO, Robert
40 Landsdowne St.
Cambridge, MA 02139
pietrusko@mpi.com
Tel: (617) 679 - 7000
Fax:(617) 374 - 7788
TF: (800) 390 - 5663

Serves As:
- V. President, Worldwide Regulatory Affairs, Millennium Pharmaceuticals, Inc.

Responsibilities include government relations.

PIETSCH, Brian
801 Pennsylvania Ave. NW
Suite 650
Unit 53
Washington, DC 20004
Tel: (202) 624 - 0761
Fax:(202) 624 - 0775

Serves As:
- V. President, State Government Relations, Ameriprise Financial Services Inc.

Responsibilities include political action.

PIGNATELLI, James S.
P.O. Box 711
Tucson, AZ 85702
jpignatelli@tep.com
Tel: (520) 884 - 3623
TF: (800) 328 - 8853

Serves As:
- Chairman, President, and Chief Exec. Officer, UniSource Energy Corp.

PIGOTT, Mark C.
P.O. Box 1518
Bellevue, WA 98009
Tel: (425) 468 - 7400
Fax:(425) 468 - 8216

Serves As:
- Chairman and Chief Exec. Officer, PACCAR Inc.

PIKE, Doug
One Houston Center
1221 McKinney Ave.
Houston, TX 77010
Tel: (713) 652 - 4590

Serves As:
- Director, Investor Relations, Lyondell Chemical Co.

PIKE, William
1585 Broadway
New York, NY 10036
Tel: (212) 761 - 4000
Fax:(212) 761 - 0086

Serves As:
- Managing Director, Finance and Investor Relations, Morgan Stanley

PILAND, Julius L. "Bud"
McDermott Internat'l / Babcock & Wilcox
1820 N. Fort Myer Dr., Suite 804
Arlington, VA 22209
Tel: (703) 351 - 6304
Fax:(703) 351 - 6417

Serves As:
- Manager, Government Programs, The Babcock & Wilcox Company

PILCICKI, Mary
155 S. Limerick Rd.
Limerick, PA 19468
mpilcicki@teleflex.com
Tel: (610) 948 - 2850
Fax:(610) 948 - 1055

Serves As:
- Project Manager, Teleflex Inc.

PILEGGI, Dominic J.
8155 T & B Blvd.
Memphis, TN 38125
Tel: (901) 252 - 5000

Serves As:
- Chief Exec. Officer, Thomas & Betts Corp.

PILGRIM, Lonnie "Bo"
P.O. Box 93
Pittsburg, TX 75686
Tel: (903) 855 - 1000
TF: (800) 824 - 1159

Serves As:
- Chairman of the Board, Pilgrim's Pride Corp.

PILON, Lawrence J.
100 Grainger Pkwy.
Lake Forest, IL 60045-5201
Tel: (847) 535 - 1000

Serves As:
- Senior V. President, Human Resources, W. W. Grainger, Inc.

PILON, M. C. Belk
2801 W. Tyvola Rd.
Charlotte, NC 28217-4500
m_c_belk@belk.com
Tel: (704) 426 - 8396
Fax:(704) 357 - 1876

Serves As:
- Foundation Administrator, Belk, Inc.

PILOT, Krista
United Technologies Bldg.
One Financial Plaza
Hartford, CT 06101
Tel: (860) 728 - 7000
Fax:(860) 728 - 6494

Serves As:
- Director, Corporate Giving and Community Relations, United Technologies Corp.

PINE, Linda K.
40 Landsdowne St.
Cambridge, MA 02139
pine@mpi.com
Tel: (617) 679 - 7000
Fax:(617) 374 - 7788
TF: (800) 390 - 5663

Serves As:
- Senior V. President, Human Resources, Millennium Pharmaceuticals, Inc.

PINEDA, Kimberly
500 Oracle Pkwy.
Redwood Shores, CA 94065
kimberly.pineda@oracle.com
Tel: (650) 506 - 8831
Fax:(650) 506 - 7200
TF: (800) 672 - 2531

Serves As:
- Corporate Community Relations Contact, Oracle Corporation

PINEDA, Patricia
Nine W. 57th St.
Suite 4900
New York, NY 10019
Tel: (212) 223 - 0303
Fax:(212) 750 - 3564

Serves As:
- Group V. President, Corporate Communications and General Counsel, Toyota Motor North America, Inc.

PIPPIN, M. Lenny
115 W. College Dr.
Marshall, MN 56258
Tel: (507) 532 - 3274
Fax:(507) 537 - 8224
TF: (800) 533 - 5290

Serves As:
- President and Chief Exec. Officer, The Schwan Food Co.

PIRAINO, Jr., Thomas A.
6035 Parkland Blvd.
Cleveland, OH 44124-4141
Tel: (216) 896 - 3000
Fax:(216) 896 - 4000
TF: (800) 272 - 7537

Serves As:
- V. President, Secretary and General Counsel; Secretary, Parker Hannifin Foundation, Parker Hannifin Corp.

Responsibilities include investor relations.

PIRKEY, Herbert L.
11270 W. Park Place
Milwaukee, WI 53224-9510
Tel: (414) 359 - 4126
Fax:(414) 359 - 4064

Serves As:
- Director, Safety, Health and Environment, A. O. Smith Corp.

PIRRI, Sue
111 McInnis Pkwy.
San Rafael, CA 94903
sue.pirri@autodesk.com
Tel: (415) 507 - 6705
Fax:(415) 507 - 6129

Serves As:
- V. President, Investor Relations, Autodesk Inc.

PISCHKE, Peggy
5301 N. Ironwood Rd.
Milwaukee, WI 53217
Tel: (414) 961 - 1000
Fax:(414) 961 - 7985

Serves As:
- Contact, Manpower Foundation, Manpower Inc.

PISTACCHIO, Lisa
1500 Crittenden Lane
Mountain View, CA 94043
Tel: (650) 933 - 5683
Fax:(650) 933 - 0283

Serves As:
- Corporate Public Relations Contact, SGI

PISTELL, Timothy K.
6035 Parkland Blvd.
Cleveland, OH 44124-4141
Tel: (216) 896 - 3000
Fax:(216) 896 - 4000
TF: (800) 272 - 7537

Serves As:
- Treasurer, Parker Hannifin Corp.

Responsibilities include political action.

PITCHER, Jed
P.O. Box 30270
Salt Lake City, UT 84130-0270
Tel: (801) 333 - 2000

Serves As:
- Chairman of the Board, Regence BlueCross BlueShield of Utah

PITCHER, Kathleen
P.O. Box 30270
Salt Lake City, UT 84130-0270
Tel: (801) 333 - 2100

Serves As:
- Exec. Director, Caring Foundation for Children, Regence BlueCross BlueShield of Utah

PITCHER, Thomas B.
3125 Myers St.
Riverside, CA 92503
Tel: (909) 351 - 3500
Fax:(909) 351 - 3931

Serves As:
- Chairman of the Board, Fleetwood Enterprises

PITCHFORD, Barbara F.
P.O. Box 26532
Richmond, VA 23261
barbara_pitchford@dom.com
Tel: (804) 819 - 2000
Fax:(804) 819 - 2233

Serves As:
- Assistant Corporate Secretary, Dominion Resources, Inc.

Responsibilities include investor relations.

PITSCH, Peter K.
1634 I St. NW
Suite 300
Washington, DC 20006-4021
Tel: (202) 626 - 4383
Fax:(202) 628 - 2525

Serves As:
- Director, Communications Policy, Intel Corp.

PITTMAN, J.
1155 Peachtree St. NE
14D03
Atlanta, GA 30309-3610
Tel: (404) 249 - 2000
Fax:(404) 249 - 2071

Serves As:
- Treasurer, BellSouth Corp. Employees' Federal PAC, BellSouth Corp.

PITTMAN, Lee
501 Woodlane St., Suite 103
Little Rock, AR 72201
lee.pittman@ipaper.com
Tel: (501) 374 - 8927
Fax:(501) 374 - 7118

Serves As:
- Manager, Public Affairs, Internat'l Paper

PITTON, Kathleen A.
P.O. Box 75000
mc 3350
Detroit, MI 48275
Tel: (313) 222 - 4916
Fax:(313) 222 - 3240
TF: (800) 521 - 1190

Serves As:
- V. President, Corporate Communications, Comerica Incorporated

PIZARRO, Anne
One Campbell Pl.
Camden, NJ 08103-1701
anne_pizarro@campbellsoup.com
Tel: (856) 342 - 6390
Fax:(856) 968 - 2976
TF: (800) 257 - 8443

Serves As:
- Director, Campbell's Labels for Education Program, Campbell Soup Co.

PIZZI, Charles P.
2801 Hunting Park Ave.
Philadelphia, PA 19129
Tel: (215) 221 - 8500
Ext: 8696
Fax:(215) 228 - 3970
TF: (800) 248 - 2789

Serves As:
- President and Chief Exec. Officer, Tasty Baking Co.

PLAISANCE, Melissa C.
P.O. Box 99
Pleasanton, CA 94566-0009
Tel: (925) 467 - 3000

Serves As:
- Senior V. President, Finance and Investor Relations, Safeway Inc.

PLAMANN, Alfred A.
5200 Sheila St.
Commerce, CA 90040
Tel: (323) 264 - 5200
Ext: 4268
Fax:(323) 265 - 4261

Serves As:
- President and Chief Exec. Officer, Unified Western Grocers, Inc.

PLANK, Raymond
2000 Post Oak Blvd., Suite 100
Houston, TX 77056-4400
raymond.plank@apachecorp.com
Tel: (713) 296 - 6000
Fax:(713) 296 - 6480
TF: (800) 874 - 3262

Serves As:
- Chairman of the Board, Apache Corp.

PLANT, Christopher K.
3800 Howard Hughes Prkwy.
Las Vegas, NV 89109
Tel: (702) 784 - 7777

Serves As:
- V. President, Investor Relations and Treasurer, Pinnacle Entertainment, Inc.

PLANT, John C.
12025 Tech Center Dr.
Livonia, MI 48150
Tel: (734) 855 - 2600
Fax:(734) 855 - 2473

Serves As:
- President and Chief Exec. Officer, TRW Automotive

PLANTE, Gerald
P.O. Box 6000
Cherry Hill, NJ 08034-6000
gplante@subaru.com
Tel: (856) 488 - 8500
Fax:(856) 488 - 0485

Serves As:
- General Manager, Governmental Affairs, Subaru of America, Inc.

PLASKETT, Kim
P.O. Box 660606
M/S 490
Dallas, TX 75266-0606
kplaske@greyhound.com
Tel: (972) 789 - 7204
Fax:(972) 789 - 7234

Serves As:
- Director, Corporate Commununications, Greyhound Lines, Inc.

PLATANIA, Lynn M.
100 Throckmorton St.
Suite 1800
TC2-14
Fort Worth, TX 76102
lynn.platania@radioshack.com
Tel: (817) 415 - 3011
Fax:(817) 415 - 2335

Serves As:
- Director, Community Relations, Radio Shack Corporation

Responsibilities include corporate philanthropy.

PLATT, Lewis E.
World Headquarters
100 N. Riverside
Chicago, IL 60606-1596
Tel: (312) 544 - 2000
Fax:(312) 544 - 2082

Serves As:
- Chairman of the Board, The Boeing Co.

PLATT, Melanie M.
P.O. Box 4569
Atlanta, GA 30302-4569
Tel: (404) 584 - 4000
Fax:(404) 584 - 3479

Serves As:
- Senior V. President, Human Resources, AGL Resources, Inc.

PLATT, Shawn M.
135 S. LaSalle St.
Chicago, IL 60603
shawn.platt@abnamro.com
Tel: (312) 904 - 7240
Fax:(312) 904 - 6521

Serves As:
• Director, Communications, LaSalle Bank N.A.

PLECS, Scott
1100 Wilson Blvd.
Suite 1500
Arlington, VA 22209
Tel: (703) 841 - 5700
Fax:(703) 841 - 5792

Registered Federal Lobbyist.
Serves As:
• Director, Government Relations, Raytheon Co.

PLEDGER, Gary L.
600 19th St. North
Birmingham, AL 35203
gary.pledger@bellsouth.com
Tel: (205) 714 - 0222
Fax:(205) 321 - 2699

Serves As:
• Director, Corporate and External Affairs, BellSouth Corp.
Responsibilities include state government relations.

PLEHN, Pamela
One HSBC Center
Buffalo, NY 14203
pamela.plehn@us.hsbc.com
Tel: (716) 841 - 5003

Serves As:
• V. President, Group Public Affairs Media Relations, HSBC USA, Inc.

PLEISS, Dave
4211 S. 102nd St.
Omaha, NE 68127-1031
dpleiss@ameritrade.com
Tel: (402) 597 - 5658
Fax:(402) 597 - 7789
TF: (800) 237 - 8692

Serves As:
• Director, Investor Relations, Ameritrade Holding Corp.

PLEPLER, Andrew
Bank of America Corporate Center
100 N. Tryon St.
Charlotte, NC 28255-0001
Tel: (704) 386 - 4343
Fax:(704) 386 - 6699

Serves As:
• President, Foundation, Bank of America Corp.

PLEPLER, Richard L.
1100 Ave. of the Americas
New York, NY 10036
richard.plepler@hbo.com
Tel: (212) 512 - 1960
Fax:(212) 512 - 1182

Serves As:
• Exec. V. President, Corporate Communications, Home Box Office (HBO)

PLESCIA, Frank
800 N. Lindbergh Blvd.
St. Louis, MO 63167
Tel: (314) 694 - 6096

Serves As:
• Director, State and Local Government Affairs, Monsanto Co.

PLESSALA DUPERIER, Laurie
101 Constitution Ave. NW
Suite 400 West
Washington, DC 20001
Tel: (202) 354 - 1500
Fax:(202) 354 - 1505

Serves As:
• V. President and Associate General Counsel, Government Affairs, Altria Group, Inc.

PLEWS, Andy
111 W. Monroe St.
Chicago, IL 60603-4095
Tel: (312) 461 - 6623
Fax:(312) 461 - 7869

Serves As:
• V. President, Corporate Communications, Harris Bank

PLITT, Domenica L.
P.O. Box 4079
Gulfport, MS 39502
Tel: (228) 865 - 5904
Fax:(228) 865 - 5876

Serves As:
• Exec. Director, Mississippi Power Education Foundation, Mississippi Power Co.

PLOHOROS, Tony
345 Park Ave.
New York, NY 10154-0037
tony.plohoros@bms.com
Tel: (212) 546 - 4379
Fax:(212) 546 - 9711

Serves As:
• Corporate and Business Communications Contact, Bristol-Myers Squibb Co.

PLOTT, Todd
13737 Noel Rd.
Dallas, TX 75240

Serves As:
• PAC Treasurer, Tenet Healthcare Corp.

PLUES, Patrick
Five Giralda Farms
Madison, NJ 07940
Tel: (484) 865 - -516
Fax:(484) 865 - 6420

Serves As:
• Contact, Wyeth Good Government Fund, Wyeth

PLUHOWSKI, John E.
2929 Allen Pkwy.
Houston, TX 77019-2155
Tel: (713) 522 - 1111
Fax:(713) 523 - 8531

Serves As:
• V. President, Corporate Communications, AIG SunAmerica Inc.

PLUMB, Priscilla
20555 State Hwy. # 249
Houston, TX 77070-2698
priscilla.plumb@hp.com
Tel: (281) 514 - 5160
Fax:(281) 518 - 7491

Serves As:
• Director, Public Affairs, Hewlett-Packard Co.

POCOCK, J. Michael
1265 Main St.
Bldg. W. Three
Waltham, MA 02451
Tel: (781) 386 - 2000

Serves As:
• President and Chief Exec. Officer, Polaroid Corp.

POEPPELMEIER, David C.
76 S. Main St.
Akron, OH 44308-1890
Tel: (330) 384 - 5813
Fax:(330) 384 - 4539
TF: (800) 633 - 4766

Serves As:
• Director, Employee Communications, FirstEnergy Corp.

POHLAD, Robert C.
3501 Algonquin Rd.
Rolling Meadows, IL 60008
robert.pohlad@pepsiamericas.com
Tel: (847) 818 - 5000
Fax:(847) 847 - 6880

Serves As:
• Chairman and Chief Exec. Officer, PepsiAmericas, Inc.

POHLAND, Carl R.
Fifth St. Towers, Suite 1360
150 S. Fifth St.
Minneapolis, MN 55402
Tel: (612) 333 - 0021
Fax:(612) 337 - 0355

Serves As:
• Chairman of the Board, MAIR Holdings, Inc.

POHLMAN, Ray
123 S. Front St.
Memphis, TN 38103
ray.pohlman@autozone.com
Tel: (901) 495 - 7962
Fax:(901) 495 - 8300

Serves As:
• Director, Government Affairs and Media Contact, AutoZone, Inc.
Responsibilities include political action.

POILLON, Peter R.
One State St. Plaza
New York, NY 10004
ppoillon@ambac.com
Tel: (212) 208 - 3333
Fax:(212) 208 - 3108
TF: (800) 221 - 1854

Serves As:
• Managing Director, Investor Relations and Media Contact, Ambac Financial Group, Inc.

POLACK, Rob
300 N. Meridian St., Suite 1500
Indianapolis, IN 46204-1763
Tel: (317) 247 - 8141
Fax:(317) 248 - 6472

Serves As:
• Public Affairs, Reilly Industries, Inc.

POLAK, Stephanie
1110 American Parkway NE
Allentown, PA 18109-3229
spolak@agere.com
Tel: (610) 712 - 7292
Fax:(610) 712 - 4106

Serves As:
• Contact, Lehigh Valley Community Involvement Council, Agere Systems Inc.

POLEHNA, James
999 W. Big Beaver Rd.
Troy, MI 48084-4782
james_polehna@kellyservices.com
Tel: (248) 244 - 4586
Fax:(248) 244 - 5515

Serves As:
• Director, Investor Relations, Kelly Services, Inc.

POLEN, Dallas A.
P.O. Box 219139
Kansas City, MO 64121-9139
Tel: (816) 753 - 7000
Ext: 8713
Fax:(816) 753 - 4902

Serves As:
• Director, Governmental Affairs, Kansas City Life Insurance Co.
Responsibilities include corporate philanthropy.

POLEY, Paul R.
20 N. Broadway, Suite 1500 Tel: (405) 235 - 3611
Oklahoma City, OK 73102 Fax:(405) 552 - 4667

Serves As:
- V. President, Human Resources, Devon Energy Corp.

POLGAR, Thomas C.
122 C St. NW Tel: (202) 393 - 5100
Suite 520 Fax:(202) 393 - 5110
Washington, DC 20001

Serves As:
- Senior V. President, Public Affairs, Tyco Internat'l (U.S.), Inc.

POLIDORE, Mary Jo
P.O. Box 748 Tel: (817) 777 - 6736
Fort Worth, TX 76101 Fax:(817) 777 - 2115
mary.jo.polidore@lmco.com

Serves As:
- V. President, Communications, Lockheed Martin Aeronautics Co.

POLING, Fletcher H.
1717 E. Interstate Ave. Tel: (701) 223 - 0441
Bismarck, ND 58503 Fax:(701) 224 - 5336
fpoling@bepc.com

Serves As:
- Legislative Representative, (Basin Cooperative Serivces, Basin Telecommunication, Inc., Dakota Coal Co., Dakota Gasification Co.), Basin Electric Power Cooperative

POLING, Mike
701 Pennsylvania Ave. NW Tel: (202) 742 - 4519
Suite 300 Fax:(202) 742 - 4644
Washington, DC 20004

Serves As:
- Manager, Federal Government Affairs, (Kansas City Power and Light Co.), Great Plains Energy, Inc.

POLK, David
Nine Roszel Rd. Tel: (609) 720 - 4387
Princeton, NJ 08540 Fax:(609) 720 - 4208
dpolk@tyco.com

Serves As:
- Media Contact, Tyco Internat'l (U.S.), Inc.

POLK, Stephen
26955 Northwestern Hwy. Tel: (248) 728 - 7000
Southfield, MI 48034 Fax:(248) 728 - 7777

Serves As:
- Chairman and Chief Exec. Officer, R.L. Polk & Co.

POLK, Terry
P.O. Box 990 Tel: (952) 828 - 4000
Minneapolis, MN 55440 Fax:(952) 828 - 8998

Serves As:
- Contact, Supervalu Foundation, Supervalu Inc.

POLLACK, Irwin
225 Brae Blvd. Tel: (201) 307 - 2619
Park Ridge, NJ 07656 Fax:(201) 307 - 2644

Serves As:
- Senior V. President, Employee Relations, Hertz Corp.

POLLARD, C. William
2211 Congress St. Tel: (207) 575 - 2211
Portland, ME 04122-0545

Serves As:
- Chairman of the Board, UnumProvident Corp.

POLLARD, Carl F.
700 Central Ave. Tel: (502) 636 - 4400
Louisville, KY 40208 Fax:(502) 636 - 4430
TF: (800) 283 - 3729

Serves As:
- Chairman of the Board, Churchill Downs, Inc.

POLLEY, Greg
555 12th St., NW Tel: (202) 638 - 3750
Suite 740 North
Washington, DC 20004

Registered Federal Lobbyist.
Serves As:
- Representative, The Charles Schwab Corp.

POLOVINA, Gina B.
2950 Industrial Rd. Tel: (702) 792 - 7200
Las Vegas, NV 89109-1100 Fax:(702) 792 - 7266
TF: (800) 695 - 2455

Serves As:
- V. President, Government and Community Affairs, Boyd Gaming Corp.

POLSKI, Thomas J.
P.O. Box 59159 Tel: (763) 212 - 5616
Minneapolis, MN 55459-8212 Fax:(763) 212 - 3400
tpolski@carlson.com

Serves As:
- V. President, Public Relations and Communications (Hospitality Group), Carlson Companies

POLTRONIERI, Jeanine
1350 I St. NW Tel: (202) 371 - 6900
Suite 400 Fax:(202) 842 - 3578
Washington, DC 20005-3306

Registered Federal Lobbyist.
Serves As:
- Director, Telecom Strategy and Regulation, Motorola, Inc.

POLZIN, Mark
P.O. Box 4100 Tel: (314) 982 - 1758
St. Louis, MO 63136-8506 Fax:(314) 982 - 9100

Serves As:
- Media Relations Contact, Emerson

POLZIN, Michael
200 Wilmot Rd. Tel: (847) 914 - 2925
M/S #2166 Fax:(847) 914 - 3086
Deerfield, IL 60015-4616
michael.polzin@walgreens.com

Serves As:
- Manager, External Communications, Walgreen Co.

POMA, John M.
Four N. Fourth St. Tel: (804) 788 - 1800
Richmond, VA 23219-2230 Fax:(804) 788 - 1870

Serves As:
- V. President, Human Resources, Massey Energy Co.

POMERLEAU, Mark F.
One High Ridge Park Tel: (203) 461 - 7616
Stamford, CT 06905-1322
mfp@meadwestvaco.com

Serves As:
- Director, Investor Relations, MeadWestvaco Corp.

POMEROY, Glenn
1299 Pennsylvania Ave. NW Tel: (202) 637 - 4000
11th Floor West Fax:(202) 637 - 4006
Washington, DC 20004-2407

Registered Federal Lobbyist.
Serves As:
- Representative, General Electric Co.

POMEROY, Jill
1201 E. Abingdon Dr. Tel: (703) 739 - 1946
Suite 300 Fax:(703) 739 - 2775
Alexandria, VA 22314
jpomeroy@harris.com

Serves As:
- Manager, Government Relations, Harris Corp.

POMFRET, Jacqueline M.
701 Pennsylvania Ave. NW Tel: (202) 350 - 5578
Suite 500 Fax:(202) 350 - 5510
Washington, DC 20004

Registered Federal Lobbyist.
Serves As:
- Senior Manager, Federal Government Affairs, AstraZeneca Pharmaceuticals

POMYKAL, Elizabeth Ann
P.O. Box 660199 Tel: (214) 480 - 6873
MS 8656 Fax:(214) 480 - 6820
Dallas, TX 75266-0199 TF: (800) 336 - 5236
annpomykal@ti.com

Serves As:
- Director, Public Affairs and Contributions Manager, Texas Instruments Incorporated

PON, Joe
3050 Bowers Ave. Tel: (408) 748 - 5508
P.O. Box 58039 Fax:(408) 986 - 7115
MS 2710
Santa Clara, CA 95054-3299
joe_pon@appliedmaterials.com

Serves As:
- Director, Corporate and Government Affairs, Applied Materials, Inc.

PONCZAK, Glen
5757 N. Green Bay Ave. Tel: (414) 524 - 2375
Milwaukee, WI 53201-0591 Fax:(414) 524 - 2077
glen.l.ponczak@jci.com

Serves As:
- Director, External Communications, Johnson Controls, Inc.

POND, Jr., Byron O.
7887 Washington Village Dr.
Dayton, OH 45459
byron.pond@amcast.com
Tel: (937) 291 - 7000
Fax:(937) 291 - 7007

Serves As:
- Chairman, President and Chief Exec. Officer, Amcast Industrial Corporation

POND, Kirk P.
82 Running Hill Rd.
South Portland, ME 04106-6020
Tel: (207) 775 - 8100
Fax:(207) 761 - 6020
TF: (800) 341 - 0392

Serves As:
- Chairman of the Board, Fairchild Semiconductor Internat'l, Inc.

POND, Peter B.
11419 Sunset Hills Rd.
Reston, VA 20190-5207
Tel: (703) 251 - 8500
Fax:(703) 251 - 8240
TF: (888) 368 - 2152

Serves As:
- Chairman of the Board, MAXIMUS, Inc.

PONITZ, Cathy
One Reynolds Way
Kettering, OH 45430
catherine_ponitz@reyrey.com
Tel: (937) 485 - 8140
Fax:(937) 485 - 0941

Serves As:
- Director, Community Relations, Reynolds and Reynolds Co.

PONTIUS, Stanley N.
9450 Seward Rd.
Fairfield, OH 45014
stanley.pontius@ocas.com
Tel: (513) 603 - 2600
Fax:(513) 609 - 7900
TF: (800) 843 - 6446

Serves As:
- Chairman of the Board, The Ohio Casualty Group

POOL, Lesley
2828 N. Haskell Ave.
Dallas, TX 75204
Tel: (214) 841 - 6111

Serves As:
- Senior V. President and Chief Marketing Officer, Affiliated Computer Services, Inc. (ACS)

Responsibilities include media relations.

POOLE, Jay
615 Maury St.
Richmond, VA 23224
Tel: (804) 484 - 2313

Serves As:
- V. President, Agricultural Policy and Programs, Altria Group, Inc.

POPE, Gail
P.O. Box 33068
Charlotte, NC 28233
Tel: (704) 731 - 4683

Serves As:
- Community Relations Representative, Piedmont Natural Gas Co.

POPE, Gary Philip
450 Riverchase Pkwy. East
Birmingham, AL 35244
Tel: (205) 220 - 2100
Fax:(205) 220 - 4841

Serves As:
- President and Chief Exec. Officer, Blue Cross and Blue Shield of Alabama

POPLAR, David D.
P.O. Box 256
Dublin, OH 43017
Tel: (614) 764 - 3100
Fax:(614) 764 - 7335

Serves As:
- Director, Investor Relations, Wendy's Internat'l, Inc.

POPPEN, Joel
8000 S. Federal Way
Boise, ID 83707
Tel: (208) 368 - 4000
Fax:(208) 368 - 2536

Registered Federal Lobbyist.
Serves As:
- Representative, Micron Technology, Inc.

PORDON, Anthony R.
2555 Telegraph Rd.
Bloomfield Hills, MI 48302-0954
tony.pordon@unitedauto.com
Tel: (248) 648 - 2500
Fax:(248) 648 - 2600

Serves As:
- V. President, Investor Relations, United Auto Group, Inc.

PORTER, Catherine
1666 K St. NW
Suite 420
Washington, DC 20006
Tel: (202) 416 - 6210
Fax:(202) 416 - 6253

Registered Federal Lobbyist.
Serves As:
- Representative, Agilent Technologies, Inc.

PORTER, Daragh
P.O. Box 391
Covington, KY 41012-0391
Tel: (859) 815 - 3825
Fax:(859) 815 - 5056

Serves As:
- V. President, Finance and Treasurer, Ashland Inc.

PORTER, J. Benson
P.O. Box 834
WMT 1706
Seattle, WA 98101
benson.porter@wamu.net
Tel: (206) 461 - 8854
Fax:(206) 554 - 4807
TF: (800) 756 - 8000

Serves As:
- Senior V. President, Community and External Affairs, (Washington Mutual Bank), Washington Mutual, Inc.

PORTER, Jim
P.O. Box 59159
Minneapolis, MN 55459-8212
Tel: (763) 212 - 1915
Fax:(763) 212 - 2219

Serves As:
- Exec. V. President, Human Resources, Carlson Companies

PORTER, Michael C.
2000 Second Ave.
Detroit, MI 48226
Tel: (313) 235 - 8850

Serves As:
- V. President, Corporate Communications, DTE Energy Co.

PORTER, Orson C.
507 Second St. NE
Washington, DC 20002
Tel: (202) 543 - 6453
Fax:(202) 544 - 6453

Registered Federal Lobbyist.
Serves As:
- Representative, Nike, Inc.

PORTER, Pam
One Riverfront Plaza
Corning, NY 14831-0001
Tel: (607) 974 - 9000
Fax:(607) 974 - 8551

Serves As:
- Director, Corporate Media Relations, Corning Incorporated

PORTER, Tammy
500 N. Akard St.
Suite 12-045
Dallas, TX 75201
Tel: (214) 812 - 4600

Serves As:
- Treasurer, Electrical Delivery PAC of TXU Corp., TXU

PORTNOY, James
101 Constitution Ave. NW
Suite 400 West
Washington, DC 20001
james.portnoy@altria.com
Tel: (202) 354 - 1500
Fax:(202) 354 - 1505

Serves As:
- Senior Legislative Counsel, Altria Group, Inc.

PORZIG, Ullrich
3231 S.E. Sixth St.
Topeka, KS 66607
Tel: (785) 233 - 5171
Fax:(785) 295 - 6866

Serves As:
- PAC Treasurer, Payless ShoeSource

POSES, Frederic M.
One Centennial Ave.
PO Box 6820
Piscataway, NJ 08854
Tel: (732) 980 - 6000
Fax:(732) 980 - 3340

Serves As:
- Chairman and Chief Exec. Officer, American Standard Companies Inc.

POSSNER, Karen B.
1133 21st St. NW
Suite 900
Washington, DC 20036
karen.possner@bellsouth.com
Tel: (202) 463 - 4100
Fax:(202) 463 - 4637

Registered Federal Lobbyist.
Serves As:
- V. President, National Security and Strategic Policy, BellSouth Corp.

POST, Andrew
63 Lincoln Hwy.
Malvern, PA 19355-2120
andrew.post@vishay.com
Tel: (610) 251 - 5287
Fax:(610) 889 - 9349

Serves As:
- Manager, Global Communications, Vishay Intertechnology, Inc.

POST, III, Glen F.
P.O. Box 4065
Monroe, LA 71211-4065
Tel: (318) 388 - 9000
Fax:(318) 340 - 5520

Serves As:
- Chairman and Chief Exec. Officer, CenturyTel, Inc.

POST, Jeff
P.O. Box 391
Madison, WI 53701
Tel: (608) 238 - 5851
Fax:(608) 238 - 0830
TF: (800) 356 - 2644

Serves As:
- Chief Exec. Officer, CUNA Mutual Group

POST, William J.
P.O. Box 53999
M/S 9036
Phoenix, AZ 85072-3999
william.post@pinnaclewest.com
Tel: (602) 250 - 1000
Ext: 2588
Fax:(602) 250 - 3002

Serves As:
- Chairman and Chief Exec. Officer, Pinnacle West Capital Corp.

POSTERNEK, Noel G.
140 Kendrick St.
Needham, MA 02494
Tel: (781) 370 - 5000
Fax:(781) 370 - 6000
TF: (800) 782 - 3776

Serves As:
- Chairman of the Board, PTC

POTILLO, Beth
One Dole Dr.
Westlake Village, CA 91362-7300
Tel: (818) 879 - 6600
Fax:(818) 879 - 6628

Serves As:
- Treasurer, Dole Food Co. Inc. PAC, Dole Food Company, Inc.

POTTER, Jeff S.
7001 Tower Rd.
Denver, CO 80249-7312
jpotter@flyfrontier.com
Tel: (720) 374 - 4200
Fax:(720) 374 - 4375
TF: (800) 265 - 5505

Serves As:
- President and Chief Exec. Officer, Frontier Airlines, Inc.

POTTER, Katherine
50 W. San Fernando St.
San Jose, CA 95113
katherip@calpine.com
Tel: (408) 792 - 1168
Fax:(408) 297 - 9688
TF: (800) 359 - 5115

Serves As:
- Manager, Public Relations, Calpine Corp.

POTTER, Wendell
Two Liberty Pl.
1601 Chestnut St.
Philadelphia, PA 19192-1553
wendell.potter@cigna.com
Tel: (215) 761 - 4450
Fax:(215) 761 - 5351

Serves As:
- V. President, Corporate and Executive Communications, CIGNA Corp.

POTTS, James S.
701 Ninth St. NW
Washington, DC 20068
Tel: (202) 872 - 2000

Serves As:
- PAC Contact, Pepco Holdings, Inc.

POTTS, Roy
1661 W. Hill St.
Louisville, KY 40210
Tel: (502) 775 - 4692
Fax:(502) 775 - 4691

Serves As:
- Manager, Public Affairs, (Coca-Cola Bottling Co. of Kentucky), Coca-Cola Enterprises Inc.

POWELL, Anita W.
P.O. Box 26666
20th Floor
Richmond, VA 23261-6666
Anita_Powell@dom.com
Tel: (804) 771 - 4442
Fax:(804) 771 - 3643

Serves As:
- PAC and Grassroots Manager, Dominion Resources, Inc.

POWELL, Aquila
1250 H St. NW
Suite 800
Washington, DC 20005
aquila.powell@kodak.com
Tel: (202) 857 - 3465
Fax:(202) 857 - 3401

Serves As:
- Director, Workforce Policy, Eastman Kodak Company

POWELL, Nigel
One Bowerman Dr.
Beaverton, OR 97005
Tel: (503) 671 - 6453
Fax:(503) 671 - 6300

Serves As:
- Director, Corporate Communications, Nike, Inc.

POWELL, Stephen
220 N. Meridian St.
Indianapolis, IN 46204
Tel: (317) 265 - 5965
Fax:(317) 265 - 3995
TF: (800) 257 - 0902

Serves As:
- Director, External Affairs - City Government, SBC Indiana

POWELL, Susanne
P.O. Box 2291
M/S HQ4
Durham, NC 27702-2291
susanne.powell@bcbsnc.com
Tel: (919) 765 - 4897
Fax:(919) 765 - 4837

Serves As:
- Director, Corporate Communications, Blue Cross and Blue Shield of North Carolina

POWELL, William H.
Ten Finderne Ave.
Bridgewater, NJ 08807-3300
Tel: (908) 685 - 5000
Fax:(609) 409 - 5699
TF: (800) 797 - 4992

Serves As:
- Chairman and Chief Exec. Officer, Nat'l Starch and Chemical Co.

POWERS, Edward
25 Research Dr.
Westborough, MA 01582
Tel: (508) 389 - 3568
Fax:(508) 389 - 3198

Serves As:
- Director, Corporate Communications, Nat'l Grid USA

POWERS, Linda M.
CNA Center
333 S. Wabash Ave.
43 South
Chicago, IL 60685
Tel: (312) 822 - 4212
Fax:(312) 822 - 1186

Serves As:
- Director, State Government Relations, CNA Financial Corp.

POWERS, Robert
Four W. Red Oak Ln.
White Plains, NY 10604
robert.powers@itt.com
Tel: (914) 641 - 2030
Fax:(914) 696 - 2960

Serves As:
- V. President, Investor Relations, ITT Industries

POWERS, Timothy H.
584 Derby Milford Rd.
Orange, CT 06477
Tel: (203) 799 - 4100
Fax:(203) 799 - 4223

Serves As:
- Chairman, President and Chief Exec. Officer, Hubbell Incorporated

Responsibilities include corporate philanthropy.

PRABHU, Krish A.
One Tellabs Center
1415 W. Diehl Rd.
Naperville, IL 60563
Tel: (630) 798 - 8800
Fax:(630) 798 - 2000

Serves As:
- President and Chief Exec. Officer, Tellabs

PRAHL, Paula J.
P.O. Box 9312
Minneaplois, MN 55440-9312
paula.prahl@bestbuy.com
Tel: (612) 291 - 6120
Fax:(612) 292 - 4001

Serves As:
- V. President, Public Affairs; PAC Treasurer, Best Buy Co., Inc.

PRASAD, Sanjay
1015 15th St. NW
Suite 200
Washington, DC 20005-2605
Tel: (202) 835 - 7360
Fax:(202) 467 - 4250

Registered Federal Lobbyist.
Serves As:
- Chief Patent Counsel, Oracle Corporation

PRASSER, Kelly
101 Ash St.
HQ15G
San Diego, CA 92101-3017
kprasser@sempra.com
Tel: (619) 696 - 4230
Fax:(619) 696 - 2500
TF: (877) 736 - 7721

Serves As:
- Manager, Community Relations and Events, Sempra Energy

PRATT, John
201 E. Fourth St.
Cincinnati, OH 45202
john.pratt@convergys.com
Tel: (513) 723 - 3333
Fax:(513) 458 - 1315
TF: (800) 344 - 3000

Serves As:
- Corporate Public Relations, Convergys Corp.

PREISS, Jeremy
1401 I St. NW
Suite 600
Washington, DC 20005
Tel: (202) 336 - 7400
Fax:(202) 336 - 7515

Registered Federal Lobbyist.
Serves As:
- Chief International Trade Counsel, United Technologies Corp.

PRESNELL, Florie
P.O. Box 6676
Asheville, NC 28816
Tel: (828) 669 - 2941
Fax:(828) 669 - 3678

Serves As:
- Controller, Ingles Markets, Inc.

Responsibilities include corporate communications and investor relations.

PRESSLER, Paul S.
Two Folsom St.
San Francisco, CA 94105
Tel: (650) 952 - 4400
Fax:(415) 427 - 2553
TF: (800) 333 - 7899

Serves As:
- President and Chief Exec. Officer, Gap Inc.

PRESTON, Alan
6001 Bollinger Canyon Rd.
San Ramon, CA 94583
Tel: (925) 842 - 1000

Serves As:
- V. President, Human Resources, Chevron Corp.

PRESTON, Margaret
P.O. Box 2257
Baltimore, MD 21203
Tel: (410) 237 - 5862

Serves As:
- Secretary, Foundation, Deutsche Banc Alex.Brown

PREUSS, J. Christopher
1660 L St. NW
Fourth Floor
Washington, DC 20036
jchristopher.preuss@gm.com
Tel: (202) 775 - 5008
Fax:(202) 775 - 5045

Serves As:
- Staff Director, Washington and Advanced Technology Communications, General Motors Corp.

PREUX, Patrick
One Carrier Pl.
Farmington, CT 06034-4015
Tel: (860) 674 - 3000
Fax:(860) 674 - 3193

Serves As:
- V. President, Human Resources, Carrier Corp.

PREZZANO, Wilbur J.
8600 South Blvd.
Charlotte, NC 28273
Tel: (704) 554 - 1421
Fax:(704) 554 - 5562
TF: (800) 438 - 1880

Serves As:
- Chairman of the Board, Lance, Inc.

PRIADKA, Nicholas
P.O. Box 1299
Minneapolis, MN 55440-1299
Tel: (952) 887 - 3131
Fax:(952) 887 - 3155
TF: (800) 887 - 3131

Serves As:
- Senior V. President, International, Donaldson Company, Inc.

PRIBYL, James C.
1025 Eldorado Blvd.
Broomfield, CO 80021
james.pribyl@level3.com
Tel: (720) 888 - 1000
Fax:(720) 888 - 5085

Registered Federal Lobbyist.
Serves As:
- Director, Government Affairs; and PAC Treasurer, Level 3 Communications, Inc.

PRICE, Barbara T.
28601 Clemens Rd.
Westlake, OH 44145
bprice@nordson.com
Tel: (440) 414 - 5344
Fax:(440) 892 - 9507

Serves As:
- Manager, Shareholder Services, Nordson Corp.

PRICE, Corinn
19001 Crescent Springs Dr.
Kingwood, TX 77339-3802
corinn_price@administaff.com
Tel: (281) 348 - 3893
TF: (800) 237 - 3170

Serves As:
- Director, Community Relations, Administaff, Inc.

PRICE, Keith J.
1144 E. Market St.
Akron, OH 44316-0001
kprice@goodyear.com
Tel: (330) 796 - 1863
Fax:(330) 796 - 1817

Serves As:
- Director, Corporate Communications Programs, The Goodyear Tire & Rubber Company

PRICE, Kevin S.
50 F St., NW
Suite 900
Washington, DC 20001
kprice@crystalsugar.com
Tel: (202) 879 - 0804
Fax:(202) 626 - 8896

Registered Federal Lobbyist.
Serves As:
- Director, Government Affairs, American Crystal Sugar Co.

PRICE, Leslie A.
3150 Sabre Dr.
Southlake, TX 76092
leslie.price@sabre-holdings.com
Tel: (682) 605 - 2267
Fax:(682) 264 - 8267

Serves As:
- Senior V. President, Corporate Communications, Sabre Holdings Corp.

PRICE, Robert
Hartford Plaza
Hartford, CT 06115
Tel: (860) 547 - 5000
Fax:(860) 547 - 3799

Serves As:
- PAC Treasurer, The Hartford Financial Services Group Inc.

PRICE, Walter
301 S. College St., Suite 4000
One Wachovia Center
Charlotte, NC 28288-0370
Tel: (704) 374 - 6565
Fax:(704) 374 - 3425
TF: (800) 275 - 3862

Registered Federal Lobbyist.
Serves As:
- Representative, Wachovia Corp.

PRICE-EDWARDS, Tonsa
15501 N. Dial Blvd.
Scottsdale, AZ 85260
Tel: (480) 754 - 3425
Fax:(480) 754 - 1098

Serves As:
- Director, Human Resources International and Employment Services, The Dial Corporation

PRICHARD, David A.
1500 DeKoven Ave.
Racine, WI 53403-2552
d.a.pritchard@na.modine.com
Tel: (262) 636 - 8434
Fax:(262) 636 - 1424

Serves As:
- Director, Investor Relations and Corporate Communications, Modine Manufacturing Company

PRIDE, Ann L.
101 Constitution Ave. NW
Suite 200 East
Washington, DC 20001
apride@entergy.com
Tel: (202) 530 - 7300
Fax:(202) 530 - 7350

Registered Federal Lobbyist.
Serves As:
- Director, Public Affairs Policy and Strategy, Entergy Services, Inc.
- Director, Public Affairs Policy and Strategy, Entergy Corp.

PRINCE, III, Charles O.
399 Park Ave.
New York, NY 10043
Tel: (212) 559 - 1000
Fax:(212) 793 - 3946
TF: (800) 285 - 3000

Serves As:
- Chief Exec. Officer, Citigroup, Inc.

PRINCE, Sharon
Five Giralda Farms
Madison, NJ 07940
princes@wyeth.com
Tel: (973) 660 - 5034

Serves As:
- Assistant V. President, Corporate Communications, Wyeth

PRINCIPE, Jeanne
511 Fifth Ave.
New York, NY 10017
Tel: (212) 953 - 4100
Fax:(212) 578 - 1832

Serves As:
- Foundation Contact, Overseas Shipholding Group, Inc.

PRINCIPI, Anthony J.
325 Seventh St. NW
Suite 1200
Washington, DC 20004-1007
Tel: (202) 783 - 7070
Fax:(202) 347 - 2044

Serves As:
- V. President, Government Relations, Pfizer Inc.

PRINCIVALLE, Karin
100 Parsons Pond Dr.
Franklin Lakes, NJ 07417
Tel: (201) 269 - 3400

Serves As:
- Senior V. President, Human Resources, Medco Health Solutions, Inc.

PRINGLE, David L.
1932 Wynnton Rd.
Columbus, GA 31999
Tel: (706) 596 - 3985
Fax:(706) 660 - 7333
TF: (800) 992 - 3522

Registered Federal Lobbyist.
Serves As:
- V. President, Federal Relations, AFLAC Incorporated

PRINTZ, Peter
P.O. Box 385014
Birmingham, AL 35238-5014
printzp@vmcmail.com
Tel: (205) 298 - 3000
Fax:(205) 298 - 2960

Serves As:
- V. President, Safety, Health, and Environment, Vulcan Materials Co.

PRITCHARD, Bill
One Panasonic Way
Secaucus, NJ 07094
pritchardw@us.panasonic.com
Tel: (201) 348 - 7182
Fax:(201) 392 - 6007
TF: (888) 275 - 2995

Serves As:
- Public Relations, Matsushita Electric Corp. of America

PRITZKER, Thomas J.
71 S. wacker Dr
Chicago, IL 60606
Tel: (312) 750 - 1234
Fax:(312) 750 - 8550

Serves As:
- Chairman and Chief Exec. Officer, Global Hyatt Corp.

PROBST, III, Lawrence F.
209 Redwood Shores Pkwy.
Redwood City, CA 94065-1175
Tel: (650) 628 - 1500
Fax:(650) 628 - 1415

Serves As:
- Chairman and Chief Exec. Officer, Electronic Arts Inc.

PROCHNOW, James
PO Box 19032
Green Bay, WI 54307
Tel: (920) 661 - 1353
Fax:(920) 661 - 2025
TF: (800) 232 - 5432

Serves As:
- PAC Treasurer, American Medical Security Group, Inc.

PROCTOR, Danielle
3550 General Atomics Ct.
San Diego, CA 92121
Tel: (858) 455 - 3000
Fax:(858) 455 - 3545

Serves As:
- PAC Treasurer, General Atomics

PROCTOR, Karen
557 Broadway
New York, NY 10012
kproctor@scholastic.com
Tel: (212) 343 - 6157

Serves As:
- V. President, Community Affairs and Government Relations, Scholastic, Inc.

Responsibilities include corporate philanthropy.

PROFFER, Phyllis J.
141 N. Civic Dr.
Walnut Creek, CA 94596
pproffer@longs.com
Tel: (925) 979 - 3979
Fax:(925) 210 - 6400

Serves As:
- V. President, Investor Relations and Corporate Communications, Longs Drug Stores Corp.

PROSPERI, David P.
20 S. Wacker Dr.
Chicago, IL 60606-7499
dprosper@cme.com
Tel: (312) 634 - 8770
Fax:(312) 930 - 3439

Serves As:
- Director, Public Relations, Chicago Mercantile Exchange Inc.

PROSSER, Jr., John W.
1111 S. Arroyo Pkwy.
P.O. Box 7084
Pasadena, CA 91105
Tel: (626) 578 - 6803
Fax:(626) 578 - 6875

Serves As:
- Senior V. President, Finance and Administration, Jacobs Engineering Group Inc.

Responsibilities include corporate philanthropy and investor relations.

PROTZ, William
200 Carillon Pkwy.
St. Petersburg, FL 33716
bill.protz@catalinamarketing.com
Tel: (727) 579 - 5069
Fax:(727) 556 - 2700

Serves As:
- Exec. Director, Community Relations, Catalina Marketing Corp.

Responsibilities include corporate philanthropy.

PROULX, Damian
Ten Finderne Ave.
Bridgewater, NJ 08807-3300
damian.proulx@nstarch.com
Tel: (908) 685 - 5148
Fax:(609) 409 - 5699
TF: (800) 797 - 4992

Serves As:
- Employee Communications Editor, Nat'l Starch and Chemical Co.

PROUT, Gerald R.
1667 K St. NW
Suite 460
Washington, DC 20006
jerry_prout@fmc.com
Tel: (202) 956 - 5200
Fax:(202) 956 - 5235

Registered Federal Lobbyist.
Serves As:
- V. President, Government and Public Affairs, FMC Corp.

PROVEAUX, Terry
2525 West End Ave., Suite 600
Nashville, TN 37203
Tel: (615) 345 - 5577
Fax:(615) 345 - 5505

Serves As:
- Director, Corporate Communications and Investor Relations, Renal Care Group, Inc.

PROVINE, William C.
2800 Post Oak Blvd., Suite 5450
Houston, TX 77056-6196
Tel: (713) 960 - 7575
Fax:(713) 960 - 7560

Serves As:
- V. President, Investor Relations, Rowan Companies, Inc.

PROWITT, Peter D.
1299 Pennsylvania Ave. NW
11th Floor West
Washington, DC 20004-2407
peter.prowitt@corporate.ge.com
Tel: (202) 637 - 4000
Fax:(202) 637 - 4006

Registered Federal Lobbyist.
Serves As:
- Manager, Federal Government Relations, General Electric Co.

PRUITT, Claudia
5803 Glenmont Dr.
Houston, TX 77081-1701
capruitt@tmw.com
Tel: (713) 592 - 7322
Fax:(713) 592 - 7075
TF: (800) 776 - 7848

Serves As:
- V. President and Assistant Treasurer, Men's Wearhouse, Inc.

Responsibilities include investor relations.

PRUITT, Gary E.
P.O. Box 34325
Seattle, WA 98124-1325
Tel: (425) 889 - 3400
Fax:(425) 889 - 4100

Serves As:
- Chairman and Chief Exec. Officer, Univar USA, Inc.

PRUSHER, Craig S.
5505 Blue Lagoon Dr.
Miami, FL 33126
cprusher@whopper.com
Tel: (305) 378 - 3066
Fax:(305) 378 - 7910

Serves As:
- V. President, Assistant General Counsel; PAC Treasurer, Burger King Corporation

PRUSKY, Andrew R.
1000 Columbia Ave.
Linwood, PA 19061-3998
Tel: (610) 859 - 3000
Fax:(610) 859 - 3035
TF: (800) 776 - 3626

Serves As:
- Assistant General Counsel, Foamex Internat'l Inc.

Responsibilities include investor relations.

PRYOR, Jr., David
101 Constitution Ave., NW
Suite 801 East
Washington, DC 20001
Tel: (202) 218 - 3800

Registered Federal Lobbyist.
Serves As:
- Senior Federal Affairs Representative, FedEx Corp.

PTAK, Alan C.
2250 Corporate Park Dr.
Suite 300
Herndon, VA 20171-4835
Tel: (703) 673 - 5000
Fax:(703) 673 - 5001

Serves As:
- V. President, Government Relations, Triple Canopy, Inc.

PUCHALSKI, Philip J.
165 Court St.
Rochester, NY 14647
Tel: (585) 238 - 4367
Fax:(585) 238 - 4233

Serves As:
- Corporate V. President, Corporate Communications, The Lifetime Healthcare Companies

PUCHALSKY, Andrea

21557 Telegraph Rd.
Southfield, MI 48034
apuchalsky@lear.com
Tel: (248) 447 - 1651
Fax:(248) 447 - 1722

Serves As:
- Director, Corporate Communications, Lear Corporation

PUCKETT, Marlene

P.O. Box 73
Boise, ID 83729
marlene.puckett@wgint.com
Tel: (208) 386 - 5201
Fax:(208) 386 - 6166

Serves As:
- Administrator, Director, and Secretary, Washington Internat'l Group Inc. Foundation, Washington Group Internat'l

PUGH, David L.

One Applied Plaza
Cleveland, OH 44115
dpugh@applied.com
Tel: (216) 426 - 4000
Ext: 4447
Fax:(216) 426 - 4804
TF: (877) 279 - 2799

Serves As:
- Chairman and Chief Exec. Officer, Applied Industrial Technologies

PUGLIESE, Jr., Frank P.

601 Pennsylvania Ave. NW
North Bldg., Suite 325
Washington, DC 20004
Tel: (202) 728 - 3600
Fax:(202) 728 - 3649

Registered Federal Lobbyist.
Serves As:
- Managing Director, Government Affairs, DuPont

PUGLIESE, Ronald J.

213 Millville Ave.
Naugatuck, CT 06770
Tel: (203) 720 - 1614

Serves As:
- Regional Director/Team Leader, State Government Relations, HSBC North America Holdings Inc.

PUGNETTI, Wendy J.

50 N. Laura St., Suite 1900
Jacksonville, FL 32202-3638
wendy.pugnetti@rayonier.com
Tel: (904) 357 - 9181
Fax:(904) 357 - 9918

Serves As:
- Director, Corporate Relations, Rayonier Inc.

PULATIE, David L.

One N. Central Ave.
Phoenix, AZ 85004-3014
dpulatie@phelpsdodge.com
Tel: (602) 366 - 8100
Fax:(602) 234 - 8337
TF: (800) 528 - 1182

Serves As:
- Senior V. President, Human Resources, Phelps Dodge Corp.

PULLEY, Cassandra M.

Three First National Plaza
70 W. Madison St.
Chicago, IL 60602-4260
Tel: (312) 726 - 2600
Fax:(312) 726 - 3712
TF: (800) 727 - 2533

Serves As:
- V. President, Public Responsibility, Sara Lee Corp.

PULLING, Wendy

77 Beale St.
MC B24A
San Francisco, CA 94105
Tel: (415) 973 - 7000
Fax:(415) 973 - 0230

Serves As:
- Director, Environmental Services, (Pacific Gas and Electric Co.), PG & E Corp.

PULTE, William

100 Bloomfield Hills Pkwy., Suite 300
Bloomfield Hills, MI 48304-2946
Tel: (248) 647 - 2750
Fax:(248) 433 - 4598
TF: (800) 777 - 8583

Serves As:
- Chairman of the Board, Pulte Homes, Inc.

PULVER, Kenneth C.

P.O. Box 1907
Albany, NY 12201-1907
Tel: (518) 445 - 2214
Fax:(518) 447 - 6343

Serves As:
- V. President, Global Marketing and Communications, Albany Internat'l Corp.

Responsibilities include government relations.

PUMA, Dennis R.

P.O. Box 1468
Wall, NJ 07719
Tel: (732) 938 - 1229
Fax:(732) 938 - 3154

Serves As:
- Manager, Treasury Services, New Jersey Resources Corp.

Responsibilities include investor relations.

PUNARO, Arnold L.

10260 Campus Point Dr.
San Diego, CA 92121
Tel: (858) 826 - 6000
Fax:(858) 826 - 6634

Serves As:
- Exec. V. President, Government Affairs and Communications, Science Applications Internat'l Corp.

PUNGELLO, Dr. Elizabeth

P.O. Box 571
Milwaukee, WI 53201-0571
Tel: (414) 358 - 6600
Fax:(800) 292 - 2289

Serves As:
- President, Foundation, Brady Corp.

PURCELL, James E.

444 Westminster St.
Providence, RI 02903-3279
purcell.j@bcbsri.org
Tel: (401) 459 - 2500
Fax:(401) 459 - 1290
TF: (800) 637 - 3718

Serves As:
- Acting President and Chief Exec. Officer, Blue Cross & Blue Shield of Rhode Island

PURCELL, W. Riker

Gateway One
101 Gateway Centre Pkwy.
Richmond, VA 23235
Tel: (804) 267 - 8330
Fax:(804) 267 - 8836
TF: (800) 446 - 7086

Serves As:
- Secretary, LandAmerica Foundation, LandAmerica Financial Group, Inc.

PURVES, Tom

300 Chestnut Ridge Rd
Woodcliff Lake, NJ 07677
Tel: (201) 307 - 3501

Serves As:
- Chairman and Chief Exec. Officer, BMW (U.S.) Holding Corp.

PURYEAR, Gus

444 N. Capitol St. NW
Suite 545
Washington, DC 20001
Tel: (202) 347 - 8717

Registered Federal Lobbyist.
Serves As:
- Representative, Corrections Corp. of America
- Contact, Corrections Corp. of American PAC

PUSKAR, Milan

1500 Corporate Dr.
Suite 400
Canonsburg, PA 15317
Tel: (724) 514 - 1800

Serves As:
- Chairman of the Board, Mylan Laboratories Inc.

PYHEL, Nicole C.

P.O. Box 300
Princeton, NJ 08543
nicole.pyhel@dowjones.com
Tel: (609) 520 - 4057

Serves As:
- Director, Corporate Communications, Dow Jones and Co.

PYLE, Tom

655 15th St. NW
Suite 445
Washington, DC 20005
Tel: (202) 737 - 1977
Fax:(202) 737 - 8111

Registered Federal Lobbyist.
Serves As:
- Director, Government Affairs, Koch Industries, Inc.

PYOTT, David E. I.

P.O. Box 19534
Irvine, CA 92623-9534
Tel: (714) 246 - 4500
Fax:(714) 246 - 4971
TF: (800) 347 - 4500

Serves As:
- Chairman, President and Chief Exec. Officer, Allergan Inc.

QAMAR, Robert K.

3191 Broadbridge Ave.
Stratford, CT 06614-2559
Tel: (203) 381 - 7000

Serves As:
- Representative, Dictaphone Corp.

Responsibilities include public relations.

QUADRACCI, Thomas

N63 W23075 State Hwy. 74
Sussex, WI 53089-2827
Tel: (414) 566 - 6000
TF: (888) 782 - 3226

Serves As:
- Chief Exec. Officer, Quad/Graphics, Inc.

QUARTA, Elizabeth

1000 Third Ave.
New York, NY 10022
elizabethquarta@fdw.com
Tel: (212) 705 - 2349
Fax:(212) 705 - 2805

Serves As:
- Press Contact, Bloomingdale's

QUEALY, Patricia A.
1133 21st St. NW
Suite 450
Washington, DC 20036
Tel: (202) 872 - 0556
Fax:(202) 872 - 0908

Registered Federal Lobbyist.
Serves As:
- V. President, Government Affairs, First Health

QUESNEL, Paul A.
P.O. Box 196612
Anchorage, AK 99519-6612
Tel: (907) 564 - 5585

Serves As:
- Director, Government Affairs, (BP Exploration - Alaska, Inc.), BP

QUICK, Kate
P.O. Box 21488
Greensboro, NC 27420-1488
kate_quick@vfc.com
Tel: (336) 424 - 7747
Fax:(336) 424 - 7631

Serves As:
- Specialist, Human Resources, V. F. Corporation

Responsibilities include corporate contributions.

QUIGLEY, Dan
77 Beale St.
MC B32
San Francisco, CA 94105
Tel: (415) 973 - 1636
Fax:(415) 973 - 8239

Serves As:
- Director, Corporate Contributions, (Pacific Gas and Electric Co.), PG & E Corp.

QUIGLEY, James H.
1633 Broadway
New York, NY 10019
Tel: (212) 489 - 1600
Fax:(212) 489 - 1687

Serves As:
- Chief Exec. Officer, Deloitte & Touche LLP

QUILES, Marissa
2775 Sanders Rd.
Northbrook, IL 60062-6127
Tel: (847) 402 - 5000
Fax:(847) 326 - 7519
TF: (800) 574 - 3553

Serves As:
- National Media Contact, Allstate Insurance Co.

QUILLARD, Maria
2100 Logic Dr.
San Jose, CA 95124-3400
maria.quillard@xilinx.com
Tel: (408) 879 - 4988
Fax:(408) 559 - 7114
TF: (800) 836 - 4002

Serves As:
- Manager, Investor Relations, Xilinx, Inc.

QUINLAN, Mike
444 N. Capitol St. NW
Suite 545
Washington, DC 20001
Tel: (202) 347 - 8717

Registered Federal Lobbyist.
Serves As:
- Representative, Corrections Corp. of America

QUINN, Eva S.
711 High St.
Des Moines, IA 50392-0150
quinn.eva@principal.com
Tel: (515) 247 - 7468
TF: (800) 986 - 3343

Serves As:
- Second V. President, Corporate Relations, The Principal Financial Group

QUINN, Jack
1300 Morris Dr.
Suite 100
Chesterbrook, PA 19087-5594
Tel: (610) 727 - 7000
Fax:(610) 727 - 3600
TF: (800) 829 - 3132

Serves As:
- PAC Treasurer, AmeriSource Bergen Corp.

QUINN, Jeffry N.
P.O. Box 66760
St. Louis, MO 63166-6760
Tel: (314) 674 - 1000
Fax:(314) 674 - 1585

Serves As:
- President and Chief Exec. Officer, Solutia Inc.

QUINN, John
65 W. Webster St.
Joliet, IL 60432
Tel: (815) 727 - 0424
Fax:(815) 727 - 0426

Serves As:
- Area Manager, External Affairs, SBC Illinois

QUINN, Lucia
One Boston Scientific Pl.
Natick, MA 01760-1537
Tel: (508) 650 - 8000
Fax:(508) 647 - 2200

Serves As:
- Senior V. President, Human Resources, Boston Scientific Corp.

QUINN, Margaret
7050 Camp Hill Rd.
Fort Washington, PA 19034
Tel: (215) 273 - 7759
Fax:(215) 273 - 4145

Serves As:
- Manager, Government Affairs and Policy, (McNeil Consumer & Specialty Pharmaceuticals), Johnson & Johnson

QUINN, Matthew C.
P.O. Box 4569
Atlanta, GA 30302-4569
mcquinn@aglresources.com
Tel: (404) 584 - 3192
Fax:(404) 584 - 3479

Serves As:
- Planning Director, Investor Relations, AGL Resources, Inc.

QUINN, Robert W.
1120 20th St. NW
Suite 1000
Washington, DC 20036-3406
rquinn@att.com
Tel: (202) 457 - 3810
Fax:(202) 263 - 2655

Registered Federal Lobbyist.
Serves As:
- V. President and Director Federal Regulatory Affairs, AT&T

QUINN-QUINTIN, Karen A.
10500 W. 153rd St.
Orland Park, IL 60462
Tel: (708) 349 - 3300
Fax:(708) 349 - 5444

Serves As:
- V. President and Chief Human Resources Officer, Andrew Corp.

QUINT, C. Robert
1601 Market St.
12th Floor
Philadelphia, PA 19103
Tel: (215) 564 - 6600

Serves As:
- President and Chief Operating Officer; PAC Treasurer, Radian Group, Inc.

QUINTANA, Jr., Henry
P.O. Box 982
El Paso, TX 79960
hquintan@epelectric.com
Tel: (915) 543 - 5824
Fax:(915) 521 - 4766
TF: (800) 351 - 1621

Serves As:
- Manager, Public Relations, El Paso Electric Co.

QUIRAMA, Luis
1345 Ave. of the Americas
New York, NY 10020
Tel: (212) 282 - 7000
Fax:(212) 282 - 6220

Serves As:
- Shareholder Relations Contact, Avon Products, Inc.

QUISH, Kimberly M.
555 12th St., NW
Suite 740 North
Washington, DC 20004
Tel: (202) 638 - 3757
Fax:(202) 638 - 3823

Registered Federal Lobbyist.
Serves As:
- V. President, Government Affairs, The Charles Schwab Corp.

QUIST, Earl C.
1850 M St. NW
Suite 600
Washington, DC 20036
Tel: (202) 775 - 1700
Fax:(202) 822 - 0928

Registered Federal Lobbyist.
Serves As:
- Director, Industry Affairs, Toyota Motor North America, Inc.

RAASCH, Robert L.
100 City Square
Boston, MA 02129
robert_l_raasch@keane.com
Tel: (617) 241 - 9200
Fax:(617) 241 - 8027

Registered Federal Lobbyist.
Serves As:
- Director, Government Affairs, (Keane Federal Systems, Inc.), Keane, Inc.

RABE, Eric W.
1717 Arch St.
Philadelphia, PA 19103
Tel: (215) 963 - 6531

Serves As:
- V. President, Telecom Media Relations, Verizon Communications Inc.

RABIN, Glenn S.
601 Pennsylvania Ave. NW
Suite 720
Washington, DC 20004
glenn.rabin@alltel.com
Tel: (202) 783 - 3973
Fax:(202) 783 - 3982

Registered Federal Lobbyist.
Serves As:
- V. President, Federal Communications Counsel, ALLTEL

RABIN, Stanley A.
6565 N. MacArthur Blvd.
Suite 800
Irving, TX 75039
Tel: (214) 689 - 4300
Fax:(214) 689 - 5886

Serves As:
• Chairman and Chief Exec. Officer, Commercial Metals Co.

RABINOWITZ, Julie M.
1667 K St. NW
Suite 1270
Washington, DC 20036
Tel: (202) 659 - 8320
Fax:(202) 659 - 2158

Registered Federal Lobbyist.
Serves As:
• Senior Director and Counsel, Government Relations, Wyeth

RABITEAU, Marsha
1101 Connecticut Ave. NW
Suite 401
Washington, DC 20036
Tel: (202) 296 - 7513
Fax:(202) 296 - 7514

Registered Federal Lobbyist.
Serves As:
• Representative, The Hartford Financial Services Group Inc.

RABOLD, Robert E. H.
3776 S. High St.
Columbus, OH 43207-0863
Tel: (614) 491 - 2225
Fax:(614) 492 - 4949
TF: (800) 272 - 7675

Serves As:
• Chairman of the Board, Bob Evans Farms, Inc.

RACHESKY, Mark H.
10307 Pacific Center Ct.
San Diego, CA 92121
Tel: (858) 882 - 6000
Fax:(858) 882 - 6010

Serves As:
• Chairman of the Board, Leap Wireless International, Inc.

RACKLEY, Eugene M. "Gene"
P.O. Box 723040
Atlanta, GA 31139-0040
Tel: (770) 989 - 3000
Fax:(770) 989 - 3788

Serves As:
• Corporate Manager, Government Relations, Coca-Cola Enterprises Inc.

RACKLYEFT, Jamie
100 Phoenix Dr.
Ann Arbor, MI 48108
jracklye@bordersgroupinc.com
Tel: (734) 477 - 1622
Fax:(734) 477 - 4730

Serves As:
• Manager, Corporate Communications, Borders Group, Inc.

RADCLIFFE, Sunny
121 SW Salmon St.
MTC-0301
Portland, OR 97204
sania_radcliffe@pgn.com
Tel: (503) 464 - 8000
Fax:(503) 464 - 2354

Serves As:
• PAC Treasurer; Public Affairs, Portland General Electric Co.

RADIGAN, Patrick
2001 Rexford Rd.
Charlotte, NC 28211
Tel: (704) 365 - 7300
Fax:(704) 365 - 7406

Serves As:
• Director, Environmental Service, National Gypsum Co.

RADKE, Steven M.
720 E. Wisconsin Ave.
Milwaukee, WI 53202-4797
Tel: (414) 271 - 1444
Fax:(414) 665 - 2463
TF: (800) 323 - 7033

Registered Federal Lobbyist.
Serves As:
• Representative, Northwestern Mutual Financial Network

RADOSEVICH, Teri
2211 S. 47th St.
Phoenix, AZ 85034
teri.radosevich@avnet.com
Tel: (480) 643 - 2000

Serves As:
• Director, Community Relations, Avnet Inc.
Responsibilities include government affairs.

RAGAN, Debbie
Kerr-McGee Center, Box 25861
Oklahoma City, OK 73125
Tel: (405) 270 - 1313
Fax:(405) 270 - 3029
TF: (800) 786 - 2556

Serves As:
• Communications Specialist, Kerr-McGee Corp.

RAGAN, Robert H.
1015 15th St. NW
Suite 700
Washington, DC 20005-2605
Tel: (202) 828 - 5200
Fax:(202) 785 - 2645

Registered Federal Lobbyist.
Serves As:
• Principal V. President and Manager, (Bechtel Systems and Infrastructure), Bechtel Group, Inc.

RAGETH, Jeffrey K.
3M Center
Bldg. 225-1S-15
St. Paul, MN 55144-1000
jkrageth@mmm.com
Tel: (651) 575 - 3556

Serves As:
• National Manager, State Government Affairs, 3M Company

RAHN, Stephen E.
1300 S. Clinton St.
Fort Wayne, IN 46801-8863
Tel: (260) 455 - 3140

Serves As:
• V. President and Associate General Director, State Relations, (Lincoln Nat'l Life Insurance Co., The), Lincoln Financial Group

RAINES, Franklin D.
3900 Wisconsin Ave. NW
Washington, DC 20016
Tel: (202) 752 - 7000
Fax:(202) 752 - 6014

Serves As:
• Chairman and Chief Exec. Officer, Fannie Mae

RAINES, Mel
101 Constitution Ave. NW
Suite 400 West
Washington, DC 20001
Tel: (202) 354 - 1500
Fax:(202) 354 - 1505

Serves As:
• Director, GA Outreach and Communications, Altria Group, Inc.

RAINEY, John
615 Maury St.
Richmond, VA 23224
Tel: (804) 484 - 6292
Fax:(804) 274 - 2841

Serves As:
• Regional Director, State Government Affairs, Altria Group, Inc.

RAINWATER, Gary L.
P.O. Box 66149
St. Louis, MO 63166-6149
Tel: (314) 621 - 3222
Fax:(314) 554 - 3066
TF: (800) 552 - 7583

Serves As:
• Chairman and Chief Exec. Officer, Ameren Corp.

RAK, Adam
20330 Stevens Creek Blvd.
Cupertino, CA 95014-2132
Tel: (408) 517 - 8231
Fax:(408) 517 - 8186

Registered Federal Lobbyist.
Serves As:
• Director, Government Relations, Symantec Corp.

RAKOCZY, Mary
P.O. Box 3608
MS 140-10
Harrisburg, PA 17105-3608
mjrakoczy@tycoelectronic.com
Tel: (717) 592 - 4869
Fax:(717) 592 - 4022

Serves As:
• Contact, Tyco Electronics Foundation, Tyco Electronics Corp.

RAKOW, Jay
10250 Constellation Blvd.
Los Angeles, CA 90067-6241
Tel: (310) 449 - 3000
Fax:(310) 449 - 8757

Serves As:
• Senior Exec. V. President and General Counsel, Metro-Goldwyn-Mayer Inc.
Responsibilities include public affairs.

RALES, Steven M.
2099 Pennsylvania Ave. NW
Washington, DC 20006
Tel: (202) 828 - 0850
Fax:(202) 828 - 0860

Serves As:
• Chairman of the Board, Danaher Corp.

RAMAGANO, Cheryl K.
P.O. Box 61558
King of Prussia, PA 19406-0958
Tel: (610) 768 - 3402
Fax:(610) 382 - 4407

Serves As:
• Treasurer and PAC Contact, Universal Health Services, Inc.
Responsibilities include shareholder relations.

RAMPINO, Louis J.
2020 Santa Monica Blvd., Suite 600
Santa Monica, CA 90404-2208
Tel: (310) 315 - 5500
Fax:(310) 315 - 5599

Serves As:
• Chief Exec. Officer, Fremont General Corp.

RAMPY, Stacey
601 Pennsylvania Ave. NW
North Bldg. Suite 1200
Washington, DC 20004
Tel: (202) 638 - 4170
Fax:(202) 638 - 3670
Registered Federal Lobbyist.
Serves As:
- Director, Government Relations, Merck & Co., Inc.

RAMSEY, Carol
870 Winter St.
Waltham, MA 02451
Tel: (781) 522 - 3000
Serves As:
- Director, Corporate Contributions, Raytheon Co.

RAMSEY, Craig R.
920 Main St.
Kansas City, MO 64105-2017
Tel: (816) 221 - 4000
Fax:(816) 480 - 4617
Serves As:
- Chief Financial Officer, AMC Entertainment Inc.

Responsibilities include investor relations.

RAMSEY, Lynne F.
12405 Powerscourt Dr.
St. Louis, MO 63131
lramsey@chartercom.com
Tel: (314) 543 - 5687
Fax:(314) 965 - 5761
Serves As:
- Senior V. President, Human Resources, Charter Communications, Inc.

RAMSEYER, Roger
4111 E. 37th St., North
Wichita, KS 67220
Tel: (316) 828 - 1525
Fax:(316) 828 - 1121
Serves As:
- Director, Public Affairs, (INVISTA), Koch Industries, Inc.

RAND, Kathryn
101 Constitution Ave., NW
Suite 801 East
Washington, DC 20001
Tel: (202) 218 - 3800
Registered Federal Lobbyist.
Serves As:
- Manager; PAC Treasurer, FedEx Corp.

RANDALL, Kathleen A.
P.O. Box 369
Summerville, SC 39484
Tel: (843) 871 - 1543
Serves As:
- Government Affairs Representative, BP

RANDAZZO, Richard P.
26555 Northwestern Hwy.
Southfield, MI 48034
richard_randazzo@fmo.com
Tel: (248) 354 - 4380
Fax:(248) 354 - 8950
Serves As:
- Senior V. President, Human Resources, Federal-Mogul Corp.

Responsibilities include corporate contributions.

RANDEL, Jane
1441 Broadway
New York, NY 10018
Tel: (212) 625 - 3408
Fax:(212) 626 - 5813
Serves As:
- V. President, Public Relations, Liz Claiborne Inc.

RANDLETT, Tamsin S.
Two Folsom St.
San Francisco, CA 94105
Tel: (650) 952 - 4400
Fax:(415) 427 - 2553
TF: (800) 333 - 7899
Serves As:
- Senior Director, Government Affairs, Gap Inc.

RANDOLPH, Beverly
P.O. Box 24305
Oakland, CA 94623-1305
beverly.randolph@clorox.com
Tel: (510) 271 - 7283
Fax:(510) 208 - 2682
Serves As:
- Consumer Services Manager, The Clorox Co.

RANERI, Lewis S.
One Computer Associates Plaza
Islandia, NY 11749
Tel: (631) 342 - 6000
Fax:(631) 342 - 4295
TF: (800) 225 - 5224
Serves As:
- Chairman of the Board, Computer Associates Internat'l, Inc.

RANKIN, Jr., Alfred M.
5875 Landerbrook Dr.
Suite 300
Cleveland, OH 44124-4017
Tel: (440) 449 - 9600
Fax:(440) 449 - 9607
Serves As:
- Chairman, President and Chief Exec. Officer, NACCO Industries

RANKINE, Debbie
1835 Dueber Ave. SW
BLC-24
Canton, OH 44706
debbie.rankine@timken.com
Tel: (330) 438 - 3000
Fax:(330) 471 - 6633
TF: (800) 223 - 1954
Serves As:
- Contact, Timken Co. Educational Fund, The Timken Co.

RANNINGER, Rebecca A.
20330 Stevens Creek Blvd.
Cupertino, CA 95014-2132
branninger@symantec.com
Tel: (408) 517 - 8280
Fax:(408) 517 - 8186
Serves As:
- Senior V. President, Human Resources, Symantec Corp.

RANTON, James D.
Seven Hanover Square
M/S H-26-E
New York, NY 10004-2616
Tel: (212) 598 - 8000
Fax:(212) 949 - 2170
Serves As:
- Senior V. President, Human Resources, Guardian Life Insurance Co. of America

RAPHAEL, Joanne H.
Two N. Ninth St.
Allentown, PA 18101-1179
jhraphael@pplweb.com
Tel: (610) 774 - 5372
Fax:(610) 774 - 4751
TF: (800) 345 - 3085
Serves As:
- V. President, External Affairs, PPL Corp.

RAQUE, Bruce
P.O. Box 32010
Louisville, KY 40232-2010
bruce.raque@lgeenergy.com
Tel: (502) 627 - 4846
Fax:(502) 217 - 2654
Serves As:
- Treasurer, FEDLOUPAC, LG&E Energy LLC

RAQUET, Bonnie
P.O. Box 5625
MS25
Minneapolis, MN 55440-5625
bonnie_raquet@cargill.com
Tel: (952) 742 - 5215
Fax:(952) 742 - 7209
Serves As:
- Corporate V. President, Public Affairs, Cargill, Incorporated

RASMUSSEN, B. J.
1201 Third Ave.
Seattle, WA 98101-3044
Tel: (206) 621 - 3211
Fax:(206) 621 - 3151
Serves As:
- Manager, Western Communications, RBC Dain Rauscher Corp.

RASMUSSEN, Edward J.
Four Irving Pl.
New York, NY 10003
Tel: (212) 460 - 4600
Fax:(212) 677 - 0734
Serves As:
- PAC Treasurer, Consolidated Edison Co. of New York, Inc.

RASTETTER, Ph.D., William H.
14 Cambridge Center
Cambridge, MA 02142
Tel: (617) 679 - 2000
Fax:(617) 679 - 2617
Serves As:
- Exec. Chairman of the Board, Biogen Idec Inc.

RATCLIFFE, David M.
270 Peachtree St. NW
Atlanta, GA 30303
Tel: (404) 506 - 5000
Serves As:
- Chairman, President and Chief Exec. Officer, Southern Company

RATLIFF, Robert J.
4205 River Green Pkwy.
Duluth, GA 30096-2568
Tel: (770) 813 - 9200
Fax:(770) 813 - 6118
Serves As:
- Chairman of the Board, AGCO Corp.

RATNER, Albert B.
1100 Terminal Tower
50 Public Square
Cleveland, OH 44113-2203
Tel: (216) 621 - 6060
Fax:(216) 263 - 4808
Serves As:
- Co-Chairman of the Board, Forest City Enterprises, Inc.

RATNER, Charles A.
1100 Terminal Tower
50 Public Square
Cleveland, OH 44113-2203
Tel: (216) 621 - 6060
Fax:(216) 263 - 4808
Serves As:
- President and Chief Exec. Officer, Forest City Enterprises, Inc.

RATTIE, Keith O.
P.O. Box 45433 Tel: (801) 324 - 5132
Salt Lake City, UT 84145-0433 Fax:(801) 324 - 5483

Serves As:
- Chairman, President, Chief Exec. Officer, Questar Corporation

RATTRAY, Paula
72 Marietta St. NW Tel: (404) 526 - 5151
Atlanta, GA 30303 Fax:(404) 526 - 5199
prattray@ajc.com

Serves As:
- V. President, Marketing, Atlanta Journal Constitution

Responsibilities include public affairs.

RAUBER, Jr., John W.
1808 I St. NW Tel: (202) 223 - 4817
Eighth Floor Fax:(202) 296 - 0011
Washington, DC 20006

Registered Federal Lobbyist.
Serves As:
- Director, Washington Public Affairs, Deere & Company

RAY, Dick
6201 South Fwy. Tel: (817) 293 - 0450
M/S AM-16 Fax:(817) 551 - 4615
Fort Worth, TX 76134

Serves As:
- Director, Safety and Environmental Affairs, Alcon Inc.

RAY, Gary A.
10990 Wilshire Blvd. Tel: (310) 231 - 4000
Seventh Floor Fax:(310) 231 - 4222
Los Angeles, CA 90024
gray@kbhome.com

Serves As:
- Senior V. President, Human Resources, KB HOME

RAY, Gene W.
3033 Science Park Rd. Tel: (858) 552 - 9500
San Diego, CA 92121-1199 Fax:(858) 552 - 9645
gray@titan.com

Serves As:
- Chairman, President and Chief Exec. Officer, L-3 Communications Titan Group

RAY, Glenn
One American Rd. Tel: (313) 594 - 4410
Dearborn, MI 48126 Fax:(313) 845 - 0570
gray2@ford.com TF: (800) 555 - 5259

Serves As:
- Manager, Corporate Communications, Ford Motor Co.

RAY, Katherine
P.O. Box 120 Tel: (706) 649 - 2267
Columbus, GA 31902-0120 Fax:(706) 641 - 6555

Serves As:
- Contact, Synovus Financial Corp. Committee for Good Leadership, Synovus Financial Corp.

RAY, Robert T.
950 Echo Lane, Suite 100 Tel: (713) 647 - 5700
Houston, TX 77024 Fax:(713) 647 - 5888

Serves As:
- Senior V. President, Chief Financial Officer and Treasurer, Group 1 Automotive, Inc.

Responsibilities include investor relations.

RAYBURN, David B.
1500 DeKoven Ave. Tel: (262) 636 - 1200
Racine, WI 53403-2552 Fax:(262) 636 - 1424

Serves As:
- President and Chief Exec. Officer, Modine Manufacturing Company

RAYDEN, Michael W.
3885 Morse Rd. Tel: (614) 775 - 3500
Columbus, OH 43219 Ext: 3510
mrayden@limitedtoo.com Fax:(614) 479 - 3619

Serves As:
- Chairman, President and Chief Exec. Officer, Too, Inc.

RAYMENT, Cary
6201 South Fwy. Tel: (817) 293 - 0450
Fort Worth, TX 76134 Fax:(817) 551 - 4615

Serves As:
- Chairman, President and Chief Exec. Officer, Alcon Inc.

RAYMOND, Brian J.
1301 K St. NW Tel: (202) 515 - 5434
Suite 1200 Fax:(202) 515 - 5906
Washington, DC 20005
braymond@us.ibm.com

Registered Federal Lobbyist.
Serves As:
- Program Manager, Grassroots and Political Programs, Internat'l Business Machines Corp. (IBM)

RAYMOND, John T.
700 Milam St. Tel: (832) 239 - 6000
Suite 3100
Houston, TX 77002

Serves As:
- Chief Exec. Officer and President, Plains Resources Inc.

RAYMOND, Katharine
One Information Way Tel: (501) 342 - 3545
Little Rock, AR 72202 Fax:(501) 342 - 3913
TF: (888) 322 - 9466

Serves As:
- Investor Relations Coordinator, Acxiom Corporation

RAYMOND, Lee R.
5959 Las Colinas Blvd. Tel: (972) 444 - 1000
Irving, TX 75039-2298 Fax:(972) 444 - 1350

Serves As:
- Chairman and Chief Exec. Officer, Exxon Mobil Corp.

RAYMOND, Louise
1221 Ave. of the Americas Tel: (212) 512 - 2001
47th Floor Fax:(212) 512 - 3611
New York, NY 10020-1095
louise_raymond@mcgraw-hill.com

Serves As:
- Director, Global Corporate Social Responsibility, The McGraw-Hill Companies, Inc.

RAYMONT, Scott V.
17876 St. Clair Ave. Tel: (216) 486 - 4200
Cleveland, OH 44110 Fax:(216) 383 - 4091
TF: (800) 321 - 2076

Serves As:
- Treasurer, Brush Wellman Good Government Fund, Brush Engineered Materials Inc.

RAYMUND, Steven A.
5350 Tech Data Dr. Tel: (727) 539 - 7429
Clearwater, FL 33760 Fax:(727) 538 - 5866
steve.raymund@techdata.com TF: (800) 237 - 8931

Serves As:
- Chairman and Chief Exec. Officer, Tech Data Corp.

RAYNOR, Michael S.
150 S. Monroe St., Suite 400 Tel: (850) 577 - 5500
Tallahassee, FL 32301-1556
michael.raynor@bellsouth.com

Serves As:
- V. President, Public Affairs, BellSouth Corp.

RAZEE, Sher
P.O. Box 4030 Tel: (303) 277 - 2813
M/S NH280 Fax:(303) 277 - 5723
Golden, CO 80401-0030

Serves As:
- Government Affairs, Coors Brewing Co.

RAZI, Nazneen
200 E. Randolph St. Tel: (312) 782 - 5800
Chicago, IL 60601-6436 Fax:(312) 782 - 4339

Serves As:
- Chief Human Resources Officer, Jones Lang LaSalle Inc.

READ, Joslyn
P.O. Box 956 Tel: (310) 964 - 0700
El Segundo, CA 90245-0956 Fax:(310) 647 - 6212

Registered Federal Lobbyist.
Serves As:
- Representative, The DIRECTV Group, Inc.

READ, William
2200 Renaissance Blvd., Suite 200 Tel: (610) 270 - 8100
Gulph Mills, PA 19406-2755 Fax:(610) 270 - 8104

Serves As:
- V. President, Human Resources, Henkel Corp.

REAGAN, Marty P.
P.O. Box 2047
Omaha, NE 68103-2047
Tel: (402) 496 - 7809
Fax:(402) 498 - 2215
TF: (800) 247 - 1345

Serves As:
- Chief Exec. Officer, AG Processing Inc

REAGAN, Paul
111 W. Monroe St.
Chicago, IL 60603-4095
Tel: (312) 461 - 3167

Serves As:
- Contact, Harris Government Affairs Fund, Harris Bank

REAL, Bill
Alvarado Square
Albuquerque, NM 87158
Tel: (505) 241 - 2700
Fax:(505) 241 - 2355
TF: (800) 545 - 4425

Serves As:
- Senior V. President, Public Policy, Public Service Co. of New Mexico

REAMY, Jeff M.
1776 I St. NW
Suite 700
Washington, DC 20006
jmreamy@ppco.com
Tel: (202) 833 - 0922
Fax:(202) 785 - 0639

Registered Federal Lobbyist.
Serves As:
- Manager, Federal Affairs - Downstream, ConocoPhillips

REARDON, Nancy A.
One Campbell Pl.
Camden, NJ 08103-1701
nancy_reardon@cambellsoup.com
Tel: (856) 342 - 6440
Fax:(856) 342 - 4782
TF: (800) 257 - 8443

Serves As:
- Senior V. President; Chief Human Resources and Communications Officer, Campbell Soup Co.

REARDON, Susan
1350 I St. NW
Suite 1210
Washington, DC 20005-3305
Tel: (202) 408 - 9482
Fax:(202) 408 - 9490

Serves As:
- Director, Federal Affairs, Johnson & Johnson

REARDON, William E.
P.O. Box 872
York, PA 17405-0872
wreardon@dentsply.com
Tel: (717) 845 - 7511
Fax:(717) 849 - 4762
TF: (800) 877 - 0020

Serves As:
- Corporate Treasurer, Dentsply Internat'l Foundation, Dentsply Internat'l

REAVIS, Kirk
300 Somerset Corporate Blvd.
Bridgewater, NJ 08807-2854
Tel: (908) 243 - 6000
Fax:(908) 231 - 3614
TF: (800) 981 - 2491

Serves As:
- V. President, Industrial Relations, Sanofi-Aventis Inc.

REAVY, Dan
1717 Arch St., 17th Floor
Philadelphia, PA 19103
daniel.j.reavy@verizon.com
Tel: (215) 362 - 1900
Fax:(215) 466 - 5931

Serves As:
- Director, External Affairs, Verizon Pennsylvania Inc.

REBEL, Jerry P.
9330 Balboa Ave.
San Diego, CA 92123-1516
Tel: (858) 571 - 2121
Fax:(858) 571 - 2225

Serves As:
- Senior V. President and Chief Financial Officer, Jack in the Box Inc.

Responsibilities include investor relations.

REDDEN, David M.
9800 Crosspoint Blvd.
Indianapolis, IN 46256
Tel: (317) 594 - 2101
Fax:(317) 594 - 2704

Serves As:
- Senior V. President, Human Resources, Marsh Supermarkets, Inc.

REDDING, Cindy
P.O. Box 5650
Bismarck, ND 58506-5650
cindy.redding@mduresources.com
Tel: (701) 222 - 7795
Fax:(701) 222 - 7867
TF: (800) 437 - 8000

Serves As:
- V. President, Human Resources, MDU Resources Group, Inc.

REDDING, E. J.
704 Maynard Rd.
Helena, MT 59602
e.j.redding@mduresources.com
Tel: (406) 431 - 0962
Fax:(406) 458 - 6091

Serves As:
- Governmental Affairs Representative, MDU Resources Group, Inc.

REDENBAUGH, Mike A.
P.O. Box 482
Fort Worth, TX 76101
Tel: (817) 280 - 5000
Fax:(817) 280 - 3299

Serves As:
- Chief Exec. Officer, Bell Helicopter Textron

REDIFER, Paul
1301 K St. NW
Suite 1200
Washington, DC 20005
rediferp@us.ibm.com
Tel: (202) 515 - 5081

Serves As:
- Regional Manager, Government Relations, Internat'l Business Machines Corp. (IBM)

REDIKER, Dennis L.
P.O. Box 1167
Dayton, OH 45401-1167
Tel: (937) 221 - 1000
Fax:(937) 221 - 1239
TF: (800) 755 - 6405

Serves As:
- Chief Exec. Officer, Standard Register Co.

REDMOND, James
165 Court St.
Rochester, NY 14647
Tel: (585) 238 - 4579
Fax:(585) 238 - 4233

Serves As:
- Regional V. President, Communications, The Lifetime Healthcare Companies

REDMOND, Leo
460 Point San Bruno Blvd.
San Francisco, CA 94080

Serves As:
- PAC Treasurer; and Foundation Contact, Genentech, Inc.

REDMOND, Nancy
595 Westport Ave.
Norwalk, CT 06851
nancy_redmond@pepperidgefarm.com
Tel: (203) 846 - 7395
Fax:(203) 846 - 7130

Serves As:
- Director, Corporate and Brand Communications, (Pepperidge Farm, Inc.), Campbell Soup Co.

REDMOND, Wynona
711 Jorie Blvd
Oak Brook, IL 60523
Tel: (630) 891 - 5175
Fax:(630) 891 - 5180

Serves As:
- Director, Public Affairs, Dominick's Finer Foods, Inc.

REDSTONE, Sumner
1515 Broadway
New York, NY 10036
Tel: (212) 258 - 6000

Serves As:
- Chairman and Chief Exec. Officer, Viacom Inc./CBS Corp.

REECE, Gary
1299 Pennsylvania Ave. NW
11th Floor West
Washington, DC 20004-2407
Tel: (202) 637 - 4000
Fax:(202) 637 - 4006

Registered Federal Lobbyist.
Serves As:
- Representative, General Electric Co.

REED, Colin V.
One Gaylord Dr.
Nashville, TN 37214
creed@gaylordentertainment.com
Tel: (615) 316 - 6000
Fax:(615) 316 - 6060

Serves As:
- Chairman, and Chief Exec. Officer, Gaylord Entertainment Co.

REED, Jim
1717 Arch St., 17th Floor
Philadelphia, PA 19103
james.a.reed@verizon.com
Tel: (215) 466 - 4838
Fax:(215) 466 - 5931

Serves As:
- Director, External Affairs, Verizon Pennsylvania Inc.

REED, Jr., John G.
P.O. Box 1470
Decatur, IL 62525
Tel: (217) 424 - 5200
TF: (800) 637 - 5843

Serves As:
- V. President, Governmental Affairs, Archer Daniels Midland Co. (ADM)

REED, Marc C.
1095 Ave. of the Americas
New York, NY 10036
Tel: (212) 395 - 2121
TF: (800) 621 - 9900

Serves As:
- Exec. V. President, Human Resources, Verizon Communications Inc.

REED, Mark L.
One NSTAR Way
Westwood, MA 02090
mark_reed@nstaronline.com
Tel: (617) 424 - 2000
Fax:(617) 424 - 2736

Serves As:
- Director, Public Affairs, NSTAR

REED, William L.
8326 Century Park
San Diego, CA 92123
wreed@semprautilities.com
Tel: (858) 650 - 4093
Fax:(858) 650 - 6145

Serves As:
- Senior V. President, Regulatory Affairs and Strategic Planning, San Diego Gas and Electric Co.

REESE, David K.
1200 Wilson Blvd.
Arlington, VA 22209-2305
Tel: (703) 465 - 3500

Serves As:
- Representative, The Boeing Co.

REESE, Donald W.
Two N. Jackson St.
Montgomery, AL 36104
Tel: (334) 223 - 5440

Serves As:
- V. President, State Relations, Alabama Power Co.

REESE, Stuart H.
1295 State St.
Springfield, MA 01111-0001
Tel: (413) 744 - 8411
Fax:(413) 744 - 6005
TF: (800) 767 - 1000

Serves As:
- President and Chief Exec. Officer, MassMutual Financial Group

REEVES, Eddie
2300 W. Plano Pkwy.
Plano, TX 75075
Tel: (972) 577 - 0000

Serves As:
- V. President, Corporate Communications, Perot Systems Corp.

REEVES, Robert K.
1201 Lake Robbins Dr.
The Woodlands, TX 77380
Tel: (832) 636 - 1000

Serves As:
- Senior V. President, Corporate Affairs and Law, Anadarko Petroleum Corp.

REGAL, Kelly
P.O. Box 105366
One CNN Center
Atlanta, GA 30348-5366
Tel: (404) 827 - 1700
Fax:(404) 827 - 2024

Serves As:
- Exec. V. President, Human Resources and Corporate Communications, Turner Broadcasting System, Inc.

REGAN, Frank J.
77 Beale St.
MC B32
San Francisco, CA 94105
Tel: (415) 973 - 6587
Fax:(415) 972 - 5529

Serves As:
- V. President, Governmental Relations, (Pacific Gas and Electric Co.), PG & E Corp.

REGAN, Mary Pat
225 W. Randolph St.
27 B
Chicago, IL 60606
Tel: (312) 220 - 2345
Fax:(312) 727 - 3722
TF: (800) 327 - 9346

Serves As:
- V. President, Regulatory Affairs, SBC Illinois

REGAN, Jr., Michael
444 N. Capitol St., N.W., Suite 740
Washington, DC 20001
mregan@newscorp.com
Tel: (202) 824 - 6502
Fax:(202) 824 - 6510

Registered Federal Lobbyist.
Serves As:
- Senior V. President, Regulatory and Government Affairs, News Corporation Ltd.

REGAN, Timothy J.
1350 I St. NW
Suite 500
Washington, DC 20005-3305
regantj@corning.com
Tel: (202) 682 - 3140
Fax:(202) 682 - 3130

Registered Federal Lobbyist.
Serves As:
- Senior V. President, Government Affairs, Corning Incorporated

Responsibilities include political action.

REGAS, Kathi M.
2222 Wellington Ct.
Lisle, IL 60532
Tel: (630) 527 - 4593
Fax:(630) 969 - 1352
TF: (800) 786 - 6539

Serves As:
- V. President, Human Resources, Molex Incorporated

REGELBRUGGE, Laurie
1150 Connecticut Ave. NW
Suite 1025
Washington, DC 20036
lregelbrugge@unocal.com
Tel: (202) 367 - 2760
Fax:(202) 367 - 2790

Serves As:
- Manager, UNOCAL Foundation, UNOCAL Corp.

REGENSTREIF, Isaac
825 N.E. Multnomah
Suite 2000
Portland, OR 97232
isaac.regenstreif@pacificorp.com
Tel: (503) 813 - 7257
Fax:(503) 813 - 7249
TF: (888) 221 - 7070

Serves As:
- Exec. Director, PacifiCorp Foundation for Learning, PacifiCorp

REICHERTS, Elizabeth "Liz"
1776 I St. NW
Suite 1000
Washington, DC 20006-3707
reicheea@bp.com
Tel: (202) 785 - 4888
Fax:(202) 457 - 6597

Registered Federal Lobbyist.
Serves As:
- Director,US Government and International Affairs, BP

REID, Brenda
2600 Delk Rd.
Marietta, GA 30067-6202
brenda.reid@publix.com
Tel: (770) 952 - 6601
Ext: 3649
Fax:(770) 618 - 2581

Serves As:
- Manager, Community Affairs, Publix Super Markets, Inc.

REID, Dale G.
1000 Six PPG Pl.
Pittsburgh, PA 15222-5479
dreid@alleghenytechnologies.com
Tel: (412) 394 - 2800
Fax:(412) 394 - 3034

Serves As:
- V. President, Controller, Chief Accounting Officer and Treasurer, Allegheny Technologies Incorporated

Responsibilities include political action.

REID, Gregory A.
10990 Roe Ave.
Overland Park, KS 66211
Tel: (913) 696 - 6100
Ext: 6193
Fax:(913) 696 - 6128

Serves As:
- Senior V. President and Chief Marketing Officer, Yellow Roadway Corporation

REID, Harland
196 Van Buren St., Suite 450
Herndon, VA 20170-5337
Tel: (703) 456 - 2553
Fax:(703) 456 - 2551

Registered Federal Lobbyist.
Serves As:
- Senior Director, Government Affairs, Nissan North America, Inc.

REID, Jim
3600 N. Hydraulic
Wichita, KS 67219
Tel: (316) 832 - 2700

Serves As:
- Senior Director, Public Relations, The Coleman Company, Inc.

REID, Kathryn A.
P.O. Box 75000
mc 3352
Detroit, MI 48275
Tel: (313) 222 - 7276
Fax:(313) 222 - 8720
TF: (800) 521 - 1190

Serves As:
- First V. President, Affiliate CRA/Public Affairs, Comerica Incorporated

REID, Lynnann
P.O. Box 355
Pittsburgh, PA 15230-0355
reid1ls@westinghouse.com
Tel: (412) 374 - 6824
Fax:(412) 374 - 3272

Serves As:
- Manager, Employee Communications and Community Relations, Westinghouse Electric Company LLC

REID, Robin
300 N. Meridian St., Suite 1500
Indianapolis, IN 46204-1763
rreid@reillyind.com
Tel: (317) 247 - 8141
Fax:(317) 248 - 6472

Serves As:
- Communications Specialist, Reilly Industries, Inc.

REID, Thomas G.
One Sun Life Executive Park
Wellesley Hills, MA 02481
Tel: (781) 237 - 6030
Fax:(781) 304 - 5383
TF: (800) 225 - 3950

Serves As:
• V. President, Investor Relations, Sun Life Financial

REID, Tim H.
555 12th St.
Eighth Floor
Oakland, CA 94607
treid@matson.com
Tel: (510) 628 - 4000
Fax:(510) 628 - 7359

Serves As:
• PAC Treasurer, Matson Navigation Company, Inc.

REID, Timothy J.
3231 S.E. Sixth St.
Topeka, KS 66607
Tel: (785) 295 - 6695
Fax:(785) 295 - 6866

Serves As:
• Director, Corporate Communications and Investor Relations, Payless ShoeSource

REIGLE, Thomas
1525 Howe St.
Racine, WI 53403
Tel: (262) 260 - 4440
Fax:(262) 260 - 2652

Serves As:
• Director, Community Leadership, SC Johnson

REILLEY, Dennis H.
39 Old Ridgebury Rd.
Danbury, CT 06810-5113
Tel: (203) 837 - 2000
Fax:(203) 837 - 2505
TF: (800) 772 - 9247

Serves As:
• Chairman, President and Chief Exec. Officer, Praxair, Inc.

REILLY, Lawrence J.
25 Research Dr.
Westborough, MA 01582
Tel: (508) 389 - 9000
Fax:(508) 389 - 2605

Serves As:
• Senior V. President, General Counsel, and Corporate Secretary, Nat'l Grid USA
Responsibilities include legal and external affairs; federal affairs; and regulatory research.

REIMERS, Jean D.
1275 Pennsylvania Ave. NW
Suite 801
Washington, DC 20004
Tel: (202) 756 - 3779
Fax:(202) 737 - 8909

Registered Federal Lobbyist.
Serves As:
• Director, Government Relations, Bayer CropScience
• Director, Federal Government Relations, Bayer Corporation

REINDL, Robert C.
One Edwards Way
Irvine, CA 92614-5688
Tel: (949) 250 - 2500
Fax:(949) 250 - 2525
TF: (800) 424 - 3278

Serves As:
• V. President, Human Resources, Edwards Lifesciences Corp.

REINEMUND, Steven S
700 Anderson Hill Rd.
Purchase, NY 10577-1444
Tel: (914) 253 - 2000
Fax:(914) 253 - 2070

Serves As:
• Chairman and Chief Exec. Officer, PepsiCo, Inc.

REINHARD, P. J.
700 N. Adams St.
Green Bay, WI 54301
Tel: (920) 433 - 4901
Fax:(920) 433 - 1526

Serves As:
• Foundation Contact, WPS Resources Corp.

REINHART, Tony
1350 I St. NW
Suite 1000
Washington, DC 20005
Tel: (202) 962 - 5400
Fax:(202) 336 - 7223

Serves As:
• Legislative Manager, Ford Motor Co.

REINKE, Melissa
3135 Easton Tpk.
Bldg. E2E
Fairfield, CT 06431
Tel: (203) 749 - 2227
Fax:(203) 373 - 3131

Serves As:
• Manager, Corporate Relations, General Electric Co.

REISENWEBER, Richard L.
P.O. Box 40
Austin, TX 78767
Tel: (512) 434 - 5800

Serves As:
• V. President, Environmental Affairs, Temple-Inland Inc.

REISTER, Lisa
Alvarado Square
Albuquerque, NM 87158
Tel: (505) 241 - 2787
Fax:(505) 241 - 2355
TF: (800) 545 - 4425

Serves As:
• Exec. Director, Investor Relations, Public Service Co. of New Mexico

REITER, Jeff
435 N. Michigan Ave.
Chicago, IL 60611
jreiter@tribune.com
Tel: (312) 222 - 3303
Fax:(312) 222 - 1573

Serves As:
• Director, Corporate Communications, Tribune Co.

REITHEMEYER, Betsy
702 SW Eighth St.
M/S 0150
Bentonville, AR 72716
Tel: (479) 277 - 0357
Fax:(479) 273 - 6850

Serves As:
• Director, Wal-Mart Foundation, Wal-Mart Stores

REITINGER, Phil
1401 I St., NW
Suite 500
Washington, DC 20005
Tel: (202) 263 - 5900
Fax:(202) 263 - 5902

Serves As:
• Senior Security Strategist, Microsoft Corporation

REMBOULIS, Marie
26555 Northwestern Hwy.
Southfield, MI 48034
Tel: (248) 354 - 9809
Fax:(248) 354 - 7060

Serves As:
• V. President, Corporate Communications, Federal-Mogul Corp.

REMMERS, Chrys A.
TECO Plaza
702 N. Franklin St.
Tampa, FL 33602
Tel: (813) 228 - 4111
Fax:(813) 228 - 4811

Serves As:
• PAC Treasurer, TECO Energy, Inc./Tampa Electric Co.

RENARD, Paul
770 N. Water St.
Eighth Floor
Milwaukee, WI 53202
Tel: (414) 765 - 7700
Fax:(414) 765 - 7899

Serves As:
• Senior V. President, Corporate Human Resources, Marshall & Ilsley Corp.

RENDA, Larree M.
P.O. Box 99
Pleasanton, CA 94566-0009
Tel: (925) 467 - 3000

Serves As:
• Exec. V. President, Retail Operations, Human Resources, Public Affairs, Labor and Government Relations, Reengineering and Communications, Safeway Inc.

RENDER, Cecelia
28601 Clemens Rd.
Westlake, OH 44145
Tel: (440) 892 - 1580
Fax:(440) 892 - 9507

Serves As:
• Acting Director, Nordson Corp. Foundation, Nordson Corp.

RENFRO, John M.
500 S. Buena Vista St.
Burbank, CA 91521
Tel: (818) 560 - 1000
Fax:(818) 560 - 1930

Serves As:
• Senior V. President and Chief Human Resources Officer, The Walt Disney Company

RENFRO, Norman L.
P.O. Box 500
San Antonio, TX 78249-112
renfron@valero.com
Tel: (210) 345 - 2069
Fax:(210) 345 - 2646
TF: (800) 531 - 7911

Serves As:
• V. President, Health, Safety and Environmental, Valero Energy Corp.

RENFROW, Paul
P.O. Box 321
M/C 1111
Oklahoma City, OK 73101-0321
Tel: (405) 553 - 3287
Fax:(405) 553 - 3760

Serves As:
• V. President, Public Affairs, OGE Energy Corp.

RENJEL, Louis E.
601 Pennsylvania Ave. NW
North Bldg., Suite 625
Washington, DC 20004
Tel: (202) 393 - 8585
Ext: `
Fax:(202) 393 - 8111

Registered Federal Lobbyist.
Serves As:
• Director, Legislative and Regulatory Affairs, Cummins, Inc.

RENNER, Stacey A.
284 South Ave.
Poughkeepsie, NY 12601-4879
srenner@cenhud.com
Tel: (845) 486 - 5730
Fax:(845) 486 - 5465
TF: (800) 527 - 2714

Serves As:
• Assistant Treasurer, Investor Relations, CH Energy Group, Inc.

RENTON, George
265 Davidson Ave.
Suite 300
Somerset, NJ 08873-4120
Tel: (732) 564 - 2200
Fax:(732) 564 - 2223

Serves As:
• V. President, Human Resources, MedPointe Inc.

RENWICK, Glenn M.
6300 Wilson Mills Rd.
Mayfield Village, OH 44143
Tel: (440) 461 - 5000
Fax:(440) 446 - 7168
TF: (800) 876 - 6327

Serves As:
• President and Chief Exec. Officer, The Progressive Corporation

RENWICK, IV, John P.
P.O. Box 3599
Battle Creek, MI 49016-3599
john.renwick@kellogg.com
Tel: (269) 961 - 6365
Fax:(269) 961 - 2871
TF: (800) 535 - 5644

Serves As:
• V. President, Investor Relations and Corporate Planning, Kellogg Co.

RENYI, Thomas A.
One Wall St.
New York, NY 10286
Tel: (212) 495 - 1784
Fax:(212) 635 - 1799

Serves As:
• Chairman and Chief Exec. Officer, The Bank of New York Co., Inc.

RENZULLI, Carmine
2700 N. First St.
San Jose, CA 95134
Tel: (408) 964 - 3500
Fax:(408) 964 - 3636

Serves As:
• Senior V. President, Global Human Resources, Sanmina-SCI Corp.

RESER, Galen J.
101 Constitution Ave. NW
Suite 900
Washington, DC 20001
galen.reser@pepsi.com
Tel: (202) 742 - 4408
Fax:(202) 742 - 4422

Registered Federal Lobbyist.
Serves As:
• V. President, North America Government Affairs, PepsiCo, Inc.

RESHESKE, Frances A.
Four Irving Pl.
New York, NY 10003
resheskef@coned.com
Tel: (212) 460 - 3882
Fax:(212) 353 - 2501

Serves As:
• Senior V. President, Public Affairs, Consolidated Edison Co. of New York, Inc.

RESLER, Barclay T.
800 Connecticut Ave. NW
Suite 711
Washington, DC 20006
bresler@na.ko.com
Tel: (202) 973 - 2660
Fax:(202) 466 - 2262

Registered Federal Lobbyist.
Serves As:
• V. President, Governmental Relations, The Coca-Cola Co.

RESMAN, Cindy
One Baxter Pkwy.
Deerfield, IL 60015-4633
cindy_resman@baxter.com
Tel: (847) 948 - 2815
Fax:(847) 948 - 2016

Serves As:
• Director, External Communications, Baxter Internat'l Inc.

RESNICK, Alice R.
333 Ravenswood Ave.
Menlo Park, CA 94025-3493
inquiry.line@sri.com
Tel: (650) 859 - 2000
Fax:(650) 326 - 5512

Serves As:
• V. President, Corporate and Marketing Communications, SRI International

REUM, W. Robert
180 N. Stetson St.
Suite 1800
Chicago, IL 60601
Tel: (312) 645 - 1700
Fax:(312) 819 - 8420

Serves As:
• Chairman, President, and Chief Exec. Officer, Amsted Industries Inc.

REUSCH, Jami
P.O. Box 1349
Tucker, GA 30085-1349
Tel: (770) 270 - 7600
Fax:(770) 270 - 7872
TF: (800) 241 - 5374

Serves As:
• V. President, Human Resources, Oglethorpe Power Corp.

REUTER, Joanne
Alvarado Square
Albuquerque, NM 87158
Tel: (505) 241 - 2700
Fax:(505) 241 - 2355
TF: (800) 545 - 4425

Serves As:
• V. President, Regulatory Affairs, Public Service Co. of New Mexico

REWINKEL, Melissa S.
1700 Pennsylvania Ave. NW
Suite 500
Washington, DC 20006-4771
melissa.rewinkel@mutualofomaha.com
Tel: (202) 393 - 6205
Fax:(202) 639 - 8808

Registered Federal Lobbyist.
Serves As:
• V. President, Government Affairs, Mutual of Omaha Insurance Co.

REYNARD, Richard
1755 S. Clark St.
Suite 1100
Arlington, VA 22202
Tel: (703) 416 - 8000
Fax:(703) 416 - 8010

Registered Federal Lobbyist.
Serves As:
• V. President, DRS Technologies, Inc.

REYNICK, Marilyn
32 Ave. of the Americas, Room S606
New York, NY 10013-2412

Serves As:
• Director, AT&T Foundation, AT&T

REYNOLDS, Dudley C.
605 Richard Arrington Jr. Blvd. North
Birmingham, AL 35203-2707
Tel: (205) 326 - 2700
Fax:(205) 322 - 6895
TF: (800) 654 - 3206

Serves As:
• PAC Treasurer, Energen Corp.

REYNOLDS, Glenn
1133 21st St. NW
Suite 900
Washington, DC 20036
glenn.reynolds@bellsouth.com
Tel: (202) 463 - 4100
Fax:(202) 463 - 4142

Serves As:
• V. President, Federal Regulatory, BellSouth Corp.

REYNOLDS, Jeanne
P.O. Box 1365
Columbia, SC 29202
jdreynolds@unum.com
Tel: (803) 213 - 6274
Fax:(803) 213 - 7433
TF: (800) 325 - 4368

Serves As:
• Media Relations, Colonial Life & Accident Insurance Co.

REYNOLDS, Patrick A.
P.O. Box 120
Columbus, GA 31902-0120
SNVIR@synovus.com
Tel: (706) 649 - 5216
Fax:(706) 644 - 8065

Serves As:
• Senior V. President and Director, Investor Relations, Synovus Financial Corp.

REYNOLDS, Paul
P.O. Box 53999
M/S 8516
Phoenix, AZ 85072-3999
paul.reynolds@pinnaclewest.com
Tel: (602) 250 - 5656
Fax:(602) 250 - 2772

Serves As:
• Director, Corporate Communications, Pinnacle West Capital Corp.

REYNOLDS, Paula
P.O. Box 4569
Atlanta, GA 30302-4569
Tel: (404) 584 - 9470
Fax:(404) 584 - 3479

Serves As:
• Chairman, President and Chief Exec. Officer, AGL Resources, Inc.

REYNOLDS, Rob
45 Erieview Plaza
Room 1600
Cleveland, OH 44114
rob.x.reynolds@sbc.com
Tel: (216) 822 - 1178
Fax:(216) 822 - 8220

Serves As:
• Senior Director, External Affairs, SBC Ohio

REYNOLDS, Rob
901 E. 233rd St.
Carson, CA 90745-6204
Tel: (310) 952 - 1511
Fax:(310) 952 - 7760

Serves As:
• Chief Financial Officer, Leiner Health Products, Inc.
Responsibilities include investor relations.

REYNOLDS, Jr., Robert A.
34 N. Meramec Ave.
St. Louis, MO 63105
Tel: (314) 512 - 9200
Fax:(314) 573 - 9455
TF: (800) 470 - 9227

Serves As:
- Chairman, President and Chief Exec. Officer, Graybar Electric Co., Inc.

REYNOLDS, Jr., William G.
2859 Paces Ferry Rd., Suite 2000
Atlanta, GA 30339
Tel: (770) 437 - 6880
Fax:(770) 319 - 0070

Serves As:
- Manager, Human Resources, Interface Inc.

RHEIN, Arthur
6065 Parkland Blvd.
Cleveland, OH 44124
arthur.rhein@agilysys.com
Tel: (440) 720 - 8500
Fax:(440) 720 - 8501
TF: (800) 422 - 2400

Serves As:
- Chairman, President and Chief Exec. Officer, Agilysys, Inc.

RHINEHART, M. K.
P.O. Box 5108
Denver, CO 80217-5108
Tel: (303) 978 - 2000
Fax:(303) 978 - 2318
TF: (800) 654 - 3103

Serves As:
- President, Foundation, Johns Manville Corp.

RHINES, Walden C.
8005 SW Boeckman Rd.
Wilsonville, OR 97070-7777
Tel: (503) 685 - 7000
Fax:(503) 685 - 7704
TF: (800) 547 - 3000

Serves As:
- Chairman and Chief Exec. Officer, Mentor Graphics Corp.

RHOADS, James D.
414 Nicollet Mall
Minneapolis, MN 55401-1927
Tel: (612) 330 - 5500
Fax:(612) 330 - 6947
TF: (800) 328 - 8226

Serves As:
- Contributions Specialist, Xcel Energy Foundation, Xcel Energy, Inc.

RHOADS, Jeff
One Quality St.
Lexington, KY 40507
Tel: (859) 367 - 5517
Fax:(859) 367 - 1185

Serves As:
- Communications Specialist, Kentucky Utilities Company

RHODES, Gary
1014 Vine St.
Cincinnati, OH 45202-1100
Tel: (513) 762 - 1304
Fax:(513) 762 - 1295

Serves As:
- Director, Corporate Communications, The Kroger Co.

RHODES, Gene
145 Hunter Dr.
Wilmington, OH 45177
Tel: (937) 382 - 5591
Fax:(937) 382 - 0896

Serves As:
- V. President, Human Resources, ABX Air, Inc.

RHODES, George R.
P.O. Box 872
York, PA 17405-0872
grhodes@dentsply.com
Tel: (717) 845 - 7511
Fax:(717) 849 - 4762
TF: (800) 877 - 0020

Serves As:
- V. President, Professional Relations and Corporate Communications, Dentsply Internat'l

RHODES, John H.
P.O. Box 2361
Harrisburg, PA 17105-2361
Tel: (717) 234 - 4941
Fax:(717) 255 - 6850
TF: (800) 388 - 4764

Serves As:
- Chairman of the Board, Penn Nat'l Insurance

RHODES, William C.
123 S. Front St.
Memphis, TN 38103
Tel: (901) 495 - 6500
Fax:(901) 495 - 8300

Serves As:
- President and Chief Exec. Officer, AutoZone, Inc.

RHONE, Adrienne G.
1301 K St. NW
Suite 1200
Washington, DC 20005
Tel: (202) 515 - 5103
Fax:(202) 515 - 5906

Registered Federal Lobbyist.
Serves As:
- Director, Government Relations, Internat'l Business Machines Corp. (IBM)

RHUDY, Marily
Five Giralda Farms
Madison, NJ 07940
rhudym@wyeth.com
Tel: (973) 660 - 5141
Fax:(973) 660 - 7322

Serves As:
- Senior V. President, Public Affairs, Wyeth
- V. President, Public Affairs, Wyeth Pharmaceuticals

RHYNE, Lisa A.
P.O. Box 1244
Charlotte, NC 28201-1244
Tel: (704) 382 - 8357
Fax:(704) 382 - 3558

Serves As:
- PAC Contact, Duke Energy Corp.

RHYNE, Mary Anne
P.O. Box 13398
Research Triangle Park, NC 27709
Tel: (919) 483 - 2839
Fax:(919) 549 - 7459

Serves As:
- Director, Media Relations, GlaxoSmithKline Research and Development

RIABOV, Darelle L
P.O. Box 1991
One Brandywine Gateway
Wilmington, DE 19899-1991
Tel: (302) 421 - 3300
Fax:(302) 421 - 2592

Serves As:
- Director, Corporate Communications, Blue Cross and Blue Shield of Delaware

RICCI, James
Six Landmark Sq.
Stamford, CT 06901
Tel: (203) 359 - 7100

Serves As:
- PAC Treasurer, Diageo North America

RICCIARDI, David K.
P.O. Box 1564
New Haven, CT 06506-0901
Tel: (203) 499 - 2000
Fax:(203) 499 - 3626
TF: (800) 722 - 5584

Serves As:
- Treasurer, Electric Employees Committee of The United Illuminating Co., The United Illuminating Company

RICCIARDI, Mike
P.O. Box 1231
Madison, WI 53701-1231
Tel: (608) 252 - 7000
Fax:(608) 252 - 7098
TF: (800) 356 - 6423

Serves As:
- Director, Safety and Environmental Affairs, Madison Gas and Electric Co.

RICE, Charles L.
600 Grant St.
Pittsburgh, PA 15219-2800
Tel: (412) 433 - 1121

Serves As:
- General Manager, Public Affairs, United States Steel Corporation

RICE, Cherie C.
1001 Fannin St., Suite 4000
Houston, TX 77002
crice@wm.com
Tel: (713) 512 - 6574
Fax:(713) 512 - 6299

Serves As:
- V. President, Investor Relations, Waste Management, Inc.

RICE, Fred B.
1100 Superior Ave.
Cleveland, OH 44114-2589
fbrice@cleveland-cliffs.com
Tel: (216) 694 - 5459
Fax:(216) 694 - 6741

Serves As:
- Director, Investor Relations, Cleveland-Cliffs Inc

RICE, Jeff
100 Mission Ridge
Goodlettsville, TN 37072
Tel: (615) 855 - 4000

Serves As:
- V. President, Human Resources, Dollar General Corp.

RICE, Marc
270 Peachtree St. NW
Atlanta, GA 30303
Tel: (404) 506 - 5333

Serves As:
- Media Relations, Southern Company

RICE, Thomas
P.O. Box 31907
Santa Barbara, CA 93130
thomas.rice@tenethealth.com
Tel: (805) 563 - 6883
Fax:(805) 563 - 6877

Serves As:
- Senior V. President, Investor Relations, Tenet Healthcare Corp.

RICE, Thomas P.
4955 Orange Dr.
Davie, FL 33314
Tel: (954) 584 - 0300
Fax:(954) 792 - 1034
TF: (800) 621 - 7143

Serves As:
- Chief Exec. Officer and Director, Andrx Corp.

RICE, Timothy G.
1065 Woodman Dr.
Dayton, OH 45432
Tel: (937) 224 - 6000
Fax:(937) 259 - 7813

Serves As:
- PAC Treasurer, DPL Inc.

RICH, Carol
710 Medtronic Pkwy.
Minneapolis, MN 55432-5604
Tel: (763) 514 - 4000
Fax:(763) 514 - 4879
TF: (800) 328 - 2518

Serves As:
- Manager, Communications, Medtronic, Inc.

RICH, Jr., James E.
1401 I St. NW, Suite 1030
Washington, DC 20005
james.rich@shell.com
Tel: (202) 466 - 1425
Fax:(202) 466 - 1498

Registered Federal Lobbyist.
Serves As:
- Senior Washington Counsel, Shell Oil Co.

RICH, Jeffrey A.
2828 N. Haskell Ave.
Dallas, TX 75204
jeff.rich@acs-inc.com
Tel: (214) 841 - 6111

Serves As:
- Chief Exec. Officer, Affiliated Computer Services, Inc. (ACS)

RICH, Karen
4000 House Ave.
Cheyenne, WY 82001
Tel: (307) 432 - 2829
Fax:(307) 638 - 6927

Serves As:
- Contact, Caring Program for Children, Blue Cross and Blue Shield of Wyoming

RICH, Linda D.
801 Pennsylvania Ave. NW
Suite 630
Washington, DC 20004
Tel: (202) 347 - 4300
Fax:(202) 347 - 4370

Registered Federal Lobbyist.
Serves As:
- Senior V. President, Government Relations, New York Stock Exchange, Inc.

RICH, Norman S.
P.O. Box 471
Sunbury, PA 17801
Tel: (570) 286 - 4571
Fax:(570) 286 - 3286

Serves As:
- President and Chief Exec. Officer, Weis Markets, Inc.

RICHARD, Cheryl
P.O. Box 4577
Houston, TX 77210-4577
Tel: (281) 925 - 6000
Fax:(281) 925 - 6010

Serves As:
- Senior V. President, Human Resources, GlobalSantaFe Corp.

RICHARD, Jr., Daniel D.
One Market
Spear Tower, Suite 2400
San Francisco, CA 94105
Tel: (415) 267 - 7130
Fax:(415) 267 - 7255

Serves As:
- Senior V. President, Public Policy and Government Affairs, PG & E Corp.

RICHARDS, Allan
Two Paragon Dr.
Montvale, NJ 07645
Tel: (201) 571 - 4240
Fax:(201) 571 - 8719

Serves As:
- Senior V. President, Human Resources, Labor Relations and Legal Services, The Great Atlantic and Pacific Tea Co.

RICHARDS, John
255 N. Admiral Byrd Rd.
Salt Lake City, UT 84116

Serves As:
- Treasurer, Zions Bancorporation PAC, Zions Bancorporation

RICHARDS, Joyce
2323 Grand
Kansas City, MO 64108
Tel: (816) 474 - 2314

Serves As:
- Community Relations Contact, Assurant

RICHARDS, Mark R.
P.O. Box 359
Appleton, WI 54912-0359
Tel: (920) 734 - 9841
Fax:(920) 991 - 8080
TF: (800) 558 - 8390

Serves As:
- President and Chief Exec. Officer, Appleton

RICHARDS, Patricia M.
700 13th St., NW
Suite 950
Washington, DC 20005
pmrichards@marathonoil.com
Tel: (202) 654 - 4499
Fax:(202) 654 - 4493

Registered Federal Lobbyist.
Serves As:
- Director, Federal Government Affairs, Marathon Oil Corp.

RICHARDS, Randy
6001 Bollinger Canyon Rd.
San Ramon, CA 94583
Tel: (925) 842 - 3523

Serves As:
- Manager, Investor Relations, Chevron Corp.

RICHARDS, Shawna
1150 15th St. NW
Washington, DC 20071
richardss@washpost.com
Tel: (202) 334 - 6632
Fax:(202) 334 - 4536

Serves As:
- Coordinator, Corporate Affairs, The Washington Post Co.

RICHARDS, Steven
P.O. Box 486
Little Rock, AR 72203
Tel: (501) 376 - 5550
Fax:(501) 376 - 5885
TF: (800) 643 - 8274

Serves As:
- Manager, Communications, Dillard's Inc.

RICHARDS, Timothy J.
1299 Pennsylvania Ave. NW
11th Floor West
Washington, DC 20004-2407
timothy.richards@corporate.ge.com
Tel: (202) 637 - 4000
Fax:(202) 637 - 4006

Registered Federal Lobbyist.
Serves As:
- Senior Manager, International Trade and Investment, General Electric Co.

RICHARDSON, Joseph H.
1301 Pennsylvania Ave. NW
Suite 1030
Washington, DC 20004
Tel: (202) 824 - 0404
Fax:(202) 347 - 0132

Registered Federal Lobbyist.
Serves As:
- Representative, Allegheny Energy Inc.

RICHARDSON, Kevin C.
3250 Lacey Rd., Suite 600
Downers Grove, IL 60515
kevin.richardson@servicemaster.com
Tel: (630) 663 - 2025
Fax:(630) 663 - 2023

Serves As:
- Senior V. President, Government Affairs, The ServiceMaster Co.

RICHARDSON, Susan
5555 San Felipe Rd.
Houston, TX 77056
slrichardson@marathonoil.com
Tel: (713) 296 - 3915
Fax:(713) 296 - 2952

Serves As:
- External Affairs Coordinator, Marathon Oil Corp.

RICHENHAGEN, Martin
4205 River Green Pkwy.
Duluth, GA 30096-2568
Tel: (770) 813 - 6101
Fax:(770) 813 - 6118

Serves As:
- President and Chief Exec. Officer, AGCO Corp.

RICHEY, Albert L.
1201 Lake Robbins Dr.
The Woodlands, TX 77380
Tel: (832) 636 - 1000

Serves As:
- V. President and Treasurer; Treasurer, Anadarko Petroleum Corp. Political Action Committee, Anadarko Petroleum Corp.

RICHMOND, Marty
101 S. Hanley Rd.
St. Louis, MO 63105-3493
mrichmond@furniturebrands.com
Tel: (314) 862 - 7133
Fax:(314) 863 - 7047

Serves As:
- Manager, Corporate Communications, Furniture Brands Internat'l, Inc.

RICHNER, BSN, MPH, Ms. Randel
One Boston Scientific Pl.
Natick, MA 01760-1537
Tel: (508) 650 - 7410
Fax:(508) 647 - 5348

Registered Federal Lobbyist.
Serves As:
- V. President, Federal Affairs, Reimbursement and Outcomes Planning, Boston Scientific Corp.

RICHTER, Kirk A.
3050 Spruce St.
St. Louis, MO 63103
Tel: (314) 286 - 8004
Fax:(314) 286 - 7874
TF: (800) 325 - 3010

Serves As:
- Treasurer, Sigma-Aldrich Corp.

Responsibilities include corporate philanthropy and investor relations.

RICKETTS, J. Joe
4211 S. 102nd St.
Omaha, NE 68127-1031
Tel: (402) 597 - 5658
Fax:(402) 597 - 7789
TF: (800) 237 - 8692

Serves As:
- Chairman of the Board, Ameritrade Holding Corp.

Also is the founder of the company.

RICKS, Ron
P.O. Box 36611
Dallas, TX 75235-1611
Tel: (214) 792 - 4174

Serves As:
- Senior V. President, Law, Airports and Public Affairs, Southwest Airlines Co.

RIDDER, P. Anthony
50 W. San Fernando St.
15th Floor
San Jose, CA 95113
Tel: (408) 938 - 7700
Fax:(408) 938 - 7766

Serves As:
- Chairman and Chief Exec. Officer, Knight Ridder

RIDDIFORD, David
15501 N. Dial Blvd.
Scottsdale, AZ 85260
Tel: (480) 754 - 3425
Fax:(480) 754 - 1098

Serves As:
- PAC Treasurer, The Dial Corporation

RIDDLE, Gregory A.
P.O. Box 511
Kingsport, TN 37662-5075
griddle@eastman.com
Tel: (423) 229 - 8692
Fax:(423) 229 - 1351
TF: (800) 327 - 8626

Serves As:
- Director, Investor Relations, Eastman Chemical Co.

RIDDLE, R. Lucia
1350 I St., N.W., Suite 1030
Washington, DC 20005-3305
riddle.lucia@principal.com
Tel: (202) 682 - 1280
Fax:(202) 682 - 1412

Registered Federal Lobbyist.
Serves As:
- V. President, Government Relations, The Principal Financial Group

RIDDLE-BARGER, Donna
P.O. Box 61000
New Orleans, LA 70161
Tel: (504) 576 - 4000
Fax:(504) 576 - 4001

Serves As:
- Director, Corporate Contributions, Entergy New Orleans

RIDDLE-BARGER, Patty
425 W. Capitol Ave.
P.O. Box 551
Little Rock, AR 72203

Serves As:
- Director, Corporate Contributions, Entergy Corp.

RIDEOUT, Dana
P.O. Box 1551
Raleigh, NC 27602-1551
Tel: (919) 546 - 7984

Serves As:
- Secretary-Treasurer, Federal and State PACs, Progress Energy

RIDGE, Robert A.
P.O. Box 2197
Houston, TX 77252-2197
Tel: (281) 293 - 1000

Serves As:
- V. President, Health, Safety and Environment, ConocoPhillips

RIDLON, Dean
Avid Technology Park
One Park West
Tewksbury, MA 01876
investor_relations@avid.com
Tel: (978) 640 - 5309
Fax:(978) 640 - 3166

Serves As:
- Director, Investor Relations, Avid Technology, Inc.

RIENDEAU, Brian
P.O. Box 32070
Louisville, KY 40232
brian.riendeau@yum.com
Tel: (502) 874 - 8434
Fax:(502) 456 - 8662

Registered Federal Lobbyist.
Serves As:
- V. President, Government Affairs, YUM! Brands, Inc.

RIETH, Andy
111 Monument Circle
29th Floor
Indianapolis, IN 46204-5129
arieth@guidant.com
Tel: (317) 971 - 2061
Fax:(317) 971 - 2045

Serves As:
- Director, Investor Relations, Guidant Corp.

RIFE, Gayle
P.O. Box 3165
Harrisburg, PA 17105
Tel: (717) 972 - 3940
Fax:(717) 731 - 4737

Serves As:
- Coordinator, Contributions, Rite Aid Corp.

RIFKIN, Cynthia
One Ravinia Dr.
Suite 1500
Atlanta, GA 30346
Tel: (678) 443 - 7000
Fax:(678) 393 - 8054
TF: (800) 929 - 4762

Serves As:
- Pac Treasurer, Sava Senior Care LLC

RIGBY, Gina J.
1932 Wynnton Rd.
Columbus, GA 31999
Tel: (706) 323 - 3431
Fax:(706) 660 - 7333
TF: (800) 992 - 3522

Registered Federal Lobbyist.
Serves As:
- Director, Federal Relations, AFLAC Incorporated

RIGGINS, William
P.O. Box 418679
Kansas City, MO 64141-9679
Tel: (816) 556 - 2200
Fax:(816) 556 - 2975

Serves As:
- V. President, Legal and Environmental Affairs, (Kansas City Power and Light Co.), Great Plains Energy, Inc.

RIGGIO, Leonard
122 Fifth Ave.
New York, NY 10011
Tel: (212) 633 - 3333
Fax:(212) 366 - 5186

Serves As:
- Chairman, Barnes & Noble, Inc.

RIGGIO, Stephen
122 Fifth Ave.
New York, NY 10011
Tel: (212) 633 - 3444
Fax:(212) 675 - 0413

Serves As:
- Chief Exec. Officer, Barnes & Noble, Inc.

RIGGLEMAN, David L.
1310 Fairmont Ave.
Fairmont, WV 26551-0392
driggle@alleghenyenergy.com
Tel: (304) 367 - 3430
Fax:(304) 367 - 3156

Serves As:
- Director, State Affairs (WV), Allegheny Energy Inc.

RIGGS, Andrea
152 W. 57th St.
42nd Floor
New York, NY 10019
Tel: (212) 314 - 7280
Fax:(212) 314 - 7309

Serves As:
- Director, Corporate Communications, IAC/InterActiveCorp

RIGGS, Greg
P.O. Box 20706
Atlanta, GA 30320-6001
Tel: (404) 715 - 2600
Fax:(404) 715 - 2731

Serves As:
- Senior V. President, General Counsel and Chief Corporate Affairs Officer, Delta Air Lines, Inc.

Responsibilities include corporate communications and government affairs.

RIGSBEE, Teresa
231 Maple Ave.
Burlington, NC 27215
Tel: (336) 584 - 5171

Serves As:
- PAC Treasurer, Laboratory Corp. of America Holdings

RIITH, Michael J.
601 Pennsylvania Ave. NW
Suite 800
Washington, DC 20004
Tel: (202) 261 - 5000
Fax:(202) 296 - 7937

Registered Federal Lobbyist.
Serves As:
- Manager, Federal Legislative Affairs, Southern Company

RIKER, Sue
P.O. Box 20670
Rochester, NY 14602-0670
sriker@birdseyefoods.com
Tel: (585) 264 - 3155
Fax:(585) 383 - 1606
TF: (800) 999 - 5044

Serves As:
- Contact, Birds Eye Foods Foundation, Birds Eye Foods

RIKER, Walt
One McDonald's Plaza
Oak Brook, IL 60523
walt.riker@mcd.com
Tel: (630) 623 - 7318
Fax:(630) 623 - 8843

Serves As:
- Corp. V. President, Corporate Communications, McDonald's Corp.

RIKSEN, Michael R.
635 Massachusetts Ave. NW
Washington, DC 20001
mriksen@npr.org
Tel: (202) 513 - 2741
Fax:(202) 513 - 3329

Registered Federal Lobbyist.
Serves As:
- V. President, Government Relations, Nat'l Public Radio

RILEY, Beth
P.O. Box 3001
Lancaster, PA 17604-3001
Tel: (717) 396 - 6354

Serves As:
- Director, Investor Relations, Armstrong Holdings, Inc.

RILEY, Carey J.
2941 Fairview Park Dr.
Falls Church, VA 22042-4513
Tel: (703) 876 - 3309
Fax:(703) 876 - 3600

Registered Federal Lobbyist.
Serves As:
- Staff V. President, Government Relations, General Dynamics Corporation

RILEY, Dan
3450 S. 344th Way
Suite 201
Auburn, WA 98001
Tel: (253) 896 - 7300

Serves As:
- Manager, Government Affairs, Tesoro Petroleum Corp.

RILEY, Dawn
9755 Patuxent Woods Dr.
Columbia, MD 21046
Tel: (410) 312 - 7100
Fax:(410) 312 - 7167

Serves As:
- Public Relations Contact, U.S. Foodservice

RILEY, Emily
1601 Market St.
12th Floor
Philadelphia, PA 19103
emily.riley@radian.biz
Tel: (215) 231 - 1328

Serves As:
- Public Relations, (Radian Guaranty), Radian Group, Inc.

RILEY, Jr., H. John
P.O. Box 4446
Houston, TX 77210-4446
riley@cooperindustries.com
Tel: (713) 209 - 8401
Fax:(713) 209 - 8977

Serves As:
- Chairman of the Board, Cooper Industries

RILEY, James R.
5959 Las Colinas Blvd.
Suite 2380
Irving, TX 75039-2298
Tel: (972) 444 - 1190
Fax:(972) 444 - 1168

Serves As:
- Operations Manager, Public Affairs, Exxon Mobil Corp.

RILEY, John S.
1313 N. Market St.
Wilmington, DE 19894-0001
jriley@herc.com
Tel: (302) 594 - 6025
Fax:(302) 594 - 6909

Serves As:
- Director, Public Affairs, Hercules Incorporated

RIMO, Patricia A.
1100 New York Ave. NW
Washington, DC 20005
primo@lucent.com
Tel: (202) 669 - 8368

Registered Federal Lobbyist.
Serves As:
- V. President, Global Government Affairs, Lucent Technologies

RINARD, David
P.O. Box 1967
PS
Grand Rapids, MI 49501-1967
drinard@steelcase.com
Tel: (616) 247 - 2996
Fax:(616) 246 - 9191

Serves As:
- Director, Corporate Environmental Quality, Steelcase Inc.

RINDSKOPF, Steven P.
1284 N. Telegraph Rd.
Monroe, MI 48162
Tel: (734) 241 - 2888
Fax:(734) 241 - 3452

Serves As:
- V. President, Human Resources, La-Z-Boy Incorporated

RING, Audrey
AutoNation Tower
110 SE Sixth St.
20th Floor
Fort Lauderdale, FL 33301
ringa@autonation.com
Tel: (954) 769 - 4687
Fax:(954) 769 - 6389

Serves As:
- Director, Corporate Communications, AutoNation, Inc.

RING, Russell C.
1300 I St. NW
Suite 525 West
Washington, DC 20005
Tel: (202) 772 - 3500
Fax:(202) 772 - 3535

Registered Federal Lobbyist.
Serves As:
- Senior V. President, Government Relations, Caremark Rx, Inc.

RING, Timothy M.
730 Central Ave.
Murray Hill, NJ 07974
Tel: (908) 277 - 8000
Fax:(908) 277 - 8078
TF: (800) 367 - 2273

Registered Federal Lobbyist.
Serves As:
- Chairman and Chief Exec. Officer, C. R. Bard, Inc.

RINGEL, Grant
P.O. Box 97034
Bellevue, WA 98009-9734
Tel: (425) 462 - 3181
Fax:(425) 462 - 3301

Serves As:
- Director, Corporate Communications, Puget Sound Energy

RINGLER, James M. (Jim)
1700 S. Patterson Blvd.
Dayton, OH 45479
Tel: (937) 445 - 5000
Fax:(937) 445 - 1847

Serves As:
- Chairman of the Board, NCR Corporation

RINGLEY, Sharon
126 C St. NW
Suite Three
Washington, DC 20001
Tel: (202) 347 - 7390

Registered Federal Lobbyist.
Serves As:
- Representative, Amazon.com, Inc.

RINGO, D. Scott
P.O. Box 2301
Cincinnati, OH 45201-2301
scott.ringo@cinbell.com
Tel: (513) 397 - 1354
Fax:(513) 723 - 9815

Serves As:
- Government Relations Contact, Cincinnati Bell Inc.

RIORDAN, Robert F.
11401 Lamar Ave.
Overland Park, KS 66211
riordanrf@bv.com
Tel: (913) 458 - 7867
Fax:(913) 458 - 3730

Registered Federal Lobbyist.
Serves As:
- V. President, Government Affairs and PAC Contact, Black & Veatch

RIOS, Sabrina
851 W. Cypress Creek Rd.
Fort Lauderdale, FL 33309
sabrina.rios@citrix.com
Tel: (954) 267 - 2529
Fax:(954) 267 - 2525
TF: (800) 424 - 8749

Serves As:
- Manager, Product Public Relations, Citrix Systems, Inc.

RIPPENGER, Patricia
1667 K St. NW
Suite 460
Washington, DC 20006
Tel: (202) 956 - 5200
Fax:(202) 956 - 5235

Registered Federal Lobbyist.
Serves As:
- Government Affairs Assistant, FMC Corp.

RIS, Jr., William K.
1101 17th St. NW
Suite 600
Washington, DC 20036
Tel: (202) 496 - 5666
Fax:(202) 496 - 5660

Registered Federal Lobbyist.
Serves As:
- Senior V. President, Government Affairs, (American Airlines, Inc.), AMR Corp.

RISCASSI, Robert W.
1215 S. Clark St.
Suite1205
Arlington, VA 22202
Tel: (703) 412 - 7190

Serves As:
• V. President, Washington, DC Operations, L-3 Communications Corp.

RITCHIE, Nicole
P.O. Box 430
Memphis, TN 30103
nritchie@mlgw.org
Tel: (901) 528 - 4557
Fax:(901) 528 - 4758

Serves As:
• Supervisor, Corporate Communications, Memphis Light, Gas and Water Division

RITTER, Douglas
2941 Fairview Park Dr.
Falls Church, VA 22042-4513
Tel: (703) 876 - 3254
Fax:(703) 876 - 3600

Registered Federal Lobbyist.
Serves As:
• Staff V. President, Government Relations, General Dynamics Corporation

RITZ, Daniel L.
One Bausch & Lomb Pl.
Rochester, NY 14604-0054
dritz@bausch.com
Tel: (585) 338 - 5802
Fax:(585) 338 - 8551
TF: (800) 344 - 8815

Serves As:
• Director, Investor Relations, Bausch & Lomb

RITZEL, Joseph
1818 Market St.
22nd Floor
Philadelphia, PA 19103
Tel: (215) 299 - 8000
TF: (800) 523 - 0786

Serves As:
• Chief Financial Officer; Treasurer, DayPAC - Federal, Day & Zimmerman

RIVKIN, Robert S.
200 E.Randolph St.
Chicago, IL 60601
Tel: (312) 381 - 1000
Fax:(312) 381 - 0240

Serves As:
• V. President, Deputy General Counsel, Litigation and Government Affairs, Aon Corp.

RIZK, Mo
P.O. Box 34325
Seattle, WA 98124-1325
Tel: (425) 889 - 3400
Fax:(425) 889 - 4100

Serves As:
• Manager, Regulatory Affairs, Univar USA, Inc.

RIZVI, Ken
5005 E. McDowell Rd.
Phoenix, AZ 85008
Tel: (602) 244 - 6600
Fax:(602) 244 - 4830

Serves As:
• Director, Investor Relations, ON Semiconductor Corp.

RIZZI, Deborah
200 Old Hook Rd.
Harrington Park, NJ 07640
deborah.rizzi@unitedwater.com
Tel: (201) 767 - 2867
Fax:(201) 767 - 2892
TF: (800) 230 - 2685

Serves As:
• Director, Corporate Communications, United Water Resources

RIZZO, Eric
1201 F St., NW
Washington, DC 20004
Tel: (202) 737 - 1445

Registered Federal Lobbyist.
Serves As:
• Director, Federal Affairs, (Farmers Insurance Group of Companies), Farmers Group, Inc.

RIZZO YOUNG, Kathleen
One HSBC Center
Buffalo, NY 14203
kathleen.rizzo.young@us.hsbc.com
Tel: (716) 841 - 5003

Serves As:
• First V. President, Group Public Affairs Media Relations, HSBC USA, Inc.

ROALSTAD, Steve
1225 17th St.
Denver, CO 80202
steve.roalstad@xcelenergy.com
Tel: (303) 294 - 2000
Fax:(303) 294 - 8120

Serves As:
• Director, Media Relations, Xcel Energy, Inc.

ROANE, Michael L.
425 Winter Rd.
Delaware, OH 43015
Tel: (740) 549 - 6000
Fax:(740) 549 - 6100

Serves As:
• Senior V. President, Human Resources and Communications, Greif, Inc.

ROB, Sally
1710 SAIC Dr.
McLean, VA 22102
sally.d.rob@saic.com
Tel: (703) 676 - 4343
Fax:(703) 676 - 7732

Serves As:
• Contact, Corporate Giving Program, Science Applications Internat'l Corp.

ROBARE, Margaret A.
30 W. Superior St.
Duluth, MN 55802
mrobare@mnpower.com
Tel: (218) 722 - 5642
Ext: 3654
Fax:(218) 279 - 5050

Serves As:
• Government Relations Representative, ALLETE

ROBB, Erica
500 Volvo Pkwy.
Chesapeake, VA 23320
Tel: (757) 321 - 5000
Fax:(757) 321 - 5292

Serves As:
• Director, Investor Relations, Dollar Tree Stores, Inc.

ROBB, Floyd
1717 E. Interstate Ave.
Bismarck, ND 58503
frobb@bepc.com
Tel: (701) 223 - 0441
Fax:(701) 255 - 5142

Serves As:
• V. President, Communications and Marketing Support, Basin Electric Power Cooperative

ROBBINS, Kris
One Security Benefit Pl.
Topeka, KS 66636-0001
Tel: (785) 438 - 3000
TF: (800) 888 - 2461

Serves As:
• President and Chief Exec. Officer, Security Benefit Life Insurance Co.

ROBBINS, Michelle E.
1550 Crystal Dr.
Crystal Square 2, Suite 300
Arlington, VA 22202
Tel: (703) 413 - 5612
Fax:(703) 413 - 5819

Registered Federal Lobbyist.
Serves As:
• Director, Space Legislative Affairs, NASA Programs, Lockheed Martin Corp.

ROBBINS, Norman B.
P.O. Box 748
Fort Worth, TX 76101
Tel: (817) 777 - 8294
Fax:(817) 777 - 2115

Serves As:
• Manager, Community Relations, Lockheed Martin Aeronautics Co.

ROBERTS, Beth
Carnival Pl.
3655 N.W. 87th Ave.
Miami, FL 33178-2428
Tel: (305) 406 - 5539
Fax:(305) 406 - 4700

Serves As:
• V. President, Investor Relations, Carnival Corp.

ROBERTS, Brian L.
1500 Market St.
Philadelphia, PA 19102
Tel: (215) 665 - 1700
Fax:(215) 981 - 7790

Serves As:
• Chairman and Chief Exec. Officer, Comcast Corporation

ROBERTS, Cate
40 Westminster St.
Providence, RI 02903-2525
Tel: (401) 457 - 3172
Fax:(401) 457 - 3598

Serves As:
• Director, Community Affairs, Textron Inc.

ROBERTS, David A.
P.O. Box 1441
Minneapolis, MN 55440-1441
Tel: (612) 623 - 6000
Fax:(612) 623 - 6944
TF: (800) 328 - 0211

Serves As:
• Chief Exec. Officer and President, Graco Inc.

ROBERTS, David G.
801 Pennsylvania Ave. NW
North Bldg., Suite 250
Washington, DC 20004
Tel: (202) 783 - 5530
Fax:(202) 783 - 5569

Registered Federal Lobbyist.
Serves As:
• Director, Public Affairs-Federal, Progress Energy

ROBERTS, Denton C.
2001 Edmund Halley Dr.
Reston, VA 20191
Tel: (703) 433 - 4000

Serves As:
• V. President and Chief State External Affairs Officer, Sprint Nextel

ROBERTS, Ellen J.
1100 N. Market St.
Wilmington, DE 19890
eroberts@wilmingtontrust.com
Tel: (302) 651 - 8069
Fax:(302) 651 - 8937
TF: (800) 441 - 7120

Serves As:
- V. President, Investor Relations, Wilmington Trust Co.

ROBERTS, J. Michael
1600 River Center II
100 E. River Center Blvd.
Covington, KY 41011
Tel: (859) 392 - 3300
Fax:(859) 392 - 3333

Serves As:
- V. President, Human Resources, Omnicare, Inc.

ROBERTS, Jeff
50 Marcus Dr.
Melville, NY 11747
Tel: (631) 847 - 2000

Serves As:
- Director, Media Relations, Arrow Electronics, Inc.

ROBERTS, Judy
20 N. Broadway, Suite 1500
Oklahoma City, OK 73102
judy.roberts@dvn.com
Tel: (405) 235 - 3611
Fax:(405) 552 - 7818

Serves As:
- Shareholder Services Administrator, Devon Energy Corp.

ROBERTS, Leonard H.
100 Throckmorton St.
Suite 1800
Fort Worth, TX 76102
Tel: (817) 415 - 3011
Fax:(817) 415 - 2335

Serves As:
- Chairman and Chief Exec. Officer, Radio Shack Corporation

ROBERTS, Leslie
P.O. Box 799045
Dallas, TX 75379-9045
Tel: (972) 687 - 6300
Fax:(972) 387 - 1611
TF: (800) 627 - 9529

Registered Federal Lobbyist.
Serves As:
- Representative, Mary Kay Inc.

ROBERTS, Perry A.
P.O. Box 4100
M/S 3289
St. Louis, MO 63136-8506
perry.roberts@emrsn.com
Tel: (314) 553 - 3289
Fax:(314) 553 - 3414

Registered Federal Lobbyist.
Serves As:
- V. President, Public Affairs, Emerson

Responsibilities include political action.

ROBERTS, Roselee N.
1200 Wilson Blvd.
Arlington, VA 22209-2305
Tel: (703) 465 - 3681

Registered Federal Lobbyist.
Serves As:
- Director, Legislative Affairs -- Space and Legislation, The Boeing Co.

ROBERTS, S. Randy
P.O. Box 407
Lakeland, FL 33802-0407
Tel: (863) 688 - 7407
Ext: 58978
Fax:(863) 284 - 5532

Serves As:
- Director, Government Relations, Publix Super Markets, Inc.

ROBERTS-MYERS, Tammy M.
3776 S. High St.
Columbus, OH 43207-0863
Tel: (614) 492 - 4954
Fax:(614) 497 - 4330
TF: (800) 272 - 7675

Serves As:
- Director, Corporate Communications, Bob Evans Farms, Inc.

ROBERTS-SMITH, Jodie
P.O. Box 1398
Gastonia, NC 28053-1398
jroberts-smith@scana.com
Tel: (704) 834 - 6427

Serves As:
- Public Affairs Coordinator, (Public Service Co. of North Carolina), SCANA Corp.

ROBERTSON, Dave
121 SW Salmon St.
Portland, OR 97204
dave_robertson@pgn.com
Tel: (503) 464 - 8000
Fax:(503) 464 - 2354

Serves As:
- Director, Government Policy, Portland General Electric Co.

ROBERTSON, Jerry E.
5960 Heisley Rd.
Mentor, OH 44060-1834
Tel: (440) 354 - 2600
Fax:(440) 639 - 4450
TF: (800) 548 - 4873

Serves As:
- Chairman of the Board, STERIS Corp.

ROBERTSON, John
300 Concord Plaza Dr.
San Antonio, TX 78216
jrobertson@@tesoropetroleum.com
Tel: (210) 283 - 2001
Fax:(210) 283 - 2003
TF: (800) 837 - 8768

Serves As:
- Director, Investor Relations, Tesoro Petroleum Corp.

ROBERTSON, Kent
50 W. San Fernando St.
San Jose, CA 95113
kentr@calpine.com
Tel: (408) 794 - 2416
Fax:(408) 297 - 9688
TF: (800) 359 - 5115

Serves As:
- Manager, Public Relations, Calpine Corp.

ROBERTSON, Pamela
942 S. Shady Grove Rd.
Memphis, TN 38120
pam.robertson@fedex.com
Tel: (901) 434 - 7048
TF: (800) 238 - 5355

Serves As:
- Community Relations Contact, FedEx Corp.

ROBERTSON, Stephen W.
11825 N. Pennsylvania St.
Carmel, IN 46032
steve_robertson@conseco.com
Tel: (317) 817 - 3539
TF: (800) 888 - 4918

Registered Federal Lobbyist.
Serves As:
- Senior V. President, Chief Compliance and Regulatory Affairs Officer, Conseco, Inc.

Responsibilities include political action.

ROBEY, Elinore
101 Montgomery St.
San Francisco, CA 94104
Tel: (877) 408 - 5438
Fax:(415) 636 - 3262

Serves As:
- Contact, Charles Schwab Corp. Foundation, The Charles Schwab Corp.

ROBEY, Tom
5030 Sugarloaf Pkwy.
Lawrenceville, GA 30042-2869
tom.robey@sciatl.com
Tel: (770) 236 - 4608
Fax:(770) 236 - 4775
TF: (800) 236 - 5000

Serves As:
- V. President, Investor Relations, Scientific-Atlanta, Inc.

ROBINETTE, Lee
P.O. Box 1060
Hot Springs, AR 71902-1060
Tel: (501) 624 - 8138

Serves As:
- Communications Director, Southern Region, Weyerhaeuser Co.

ROBINS, Brian
680 E. Swedesford Rd.
Wayne, PA 19087
Tel: (484) 582 - 5468
Fax:(484) 225 - 1120

Serves As:
- Press Contact, SunGard Data Systems, Inc.

ROBINSON, Carole
1515 Broadway
New York, NY 10036
Tel: (212) 258 - 6000
Ext: 8760
Fax:(212) 258 - 8100

Serves As:
- Exec. V. President, Press Relations, (MTV Networks), Viacom Inc./CBS Corp.

ROBINSON, Hank
680 S. Fourth Ave.
Louisville, KY 40202-2412
Tel: (502) 596 - 7300
Fax:(502) 596 - 4099

Serves As:
- Treasurer, Kindred Healthcare, Inc. PAC, Kindred Healthcare, Inc.

ROBINSON, Heather
1025 Eldorado Blvd.
Broomfield, CO 80021
Tel: (720) 888 - 2097
Fax:(720) 888 - 5085

Serves As:
- Manager, Corporate Communications, Level 3 Communications, Inc.

ROBINSON, Janet L.
229 W. 43rd St.
New York, NY 10036
Tel: (212) 556 - 1234

Serves As:
- President and Chief Exec. Officer, New York Times Co.

ROBINSON, Ken
One Citizens Plaza
Providence, RI 02903
Tel: (401) 455 - 5934
Fax:(401) 456 - 7644

Serves As:
- Senior V. President and Manager, Government Relations, Citizens Financial Group, Inc.

ROBINSON, Mal
One Security Benefit Pl.
Topeka, KS 66636-0001
Tel: (785) 438 - 3000
TF: (800) 888 - 2461

Serves As:
- Contact, Security Benefit Life Insurance Co. Charitable Trust, Security Benefit Life Insurance Co.

ROBINSON, Pat
P.O. Box 98029
Baton Rouge, LA 70898-9029
Tel: (225) 295 - 2206
Fax:(225) 298 - 1812
TF: (800) 599 - 2583

Serves As:
- Foundation Contact, Blue Cross and Blue Shield of Louisiana

ROBINSON, Richard
557 Broadway
New York, NY 10012
rrobinson@scholastic.com
Tel: (212) 343 - 6100
Fax:(212) 343 - 6736

Serves As:
- Chairman and Chief Exec. Officer, Scholastic, Inc.

ROBINSON, Ronn
101A Enterprise Dr.
P.O. Box 5190
Frankfort, KY 40602
Tel: (502) 696 - 7003

Serves As:
- Manager, Corporate Communications, (Kentucky Power), American Electric Power Co. Inc.

ROBINSON, Susan
Seven W. Seventh St.
Cincinnati, OH 45202
Tel: (513) 579 - 7778
Fax:(513) 579 - 7393
TF: (800) 261 - 5385

Serves As:
- Operating V. President, Investor Relations, Federated Department Stores, Inc.

ROBINSON, Susannah
Two Seaport Ln.
Suite 1300
Boston, MA 02210-2019
Tel: (617) 345 - 0100
Fax:(617) 342 - 6103

Serves As:
- Director, Investor Relations, Cabot Corp.

ROBINSON, Tom
P.O. Box 418679
Kansas City, MO 64141-9679
Tel: (816) 556 - 2365
Fax:(816) 556 - 2222

Serves As:
- Media Contact, Great Plains Energy, Inc.

ROBINSON, Warren L.
P.O. Box 5650
Bismarck, ND 58506-5650
warren.robinson@mduresources.com
Tel: (701) 222 - 7991
Fax:(701) 222 - 7607
TF: (800) 437 - 8000

Serves As:
- Exec. V. President and Chief Financial Officer, MDU Resources Group, Inc.

Responsibilities include investor relations.

ROBITAILLE, Rick
P.O. Box 50648
Casper, WY 82605
Tel: (307) 232 - 9505

Serves As:
- Manager, Public Affairs - Western Division, Anadarko Petroleum Corp.

ROBLES, Jr, Jose
9800 Fredericksburg Rd.
San Antonio, TX 78288-0122
Tel: (210) 456 - 1800
Fax:(210) 498 - 9940

Serves As:
- Exec. V. President, Chief Financial Officer and Corporate Treasurer, United Services Automobile Ass'n (USAA)

Responsibilities include political action.

ROBY, Carolyn
Wells Fargo Center
Sixth & Marquette
Minneapolis, MN 55479
Tel: (612) 667 - 7860
Fax:(612) 667 - 8283

Serves As:
- V. President, Wells Fargo Foundation Minnesota, Wells Fargo & Co.

ROCH, Elizabeth
P.O. Box 66100
Chicago, IL 60666
elizabeth.a.roch@ual.com
Tel: (847) 700 - 6564
Fax:(847) 700 - 4081

Serves As:
- Director, Communications Services, United Airlines

ROCHE, Cathy S.
P.O. Box 1244
M/S EC06G
Charlotte, NC 28201-1244
csroche@duke-energy.com
Tel: (704) 373 - 4860
Fax:(704) 382 - 8375

Serves As:
- V. President, Corporate Communications, Duke Energy Corp.

ROCHE, George
100 E. Pratt St.
Baltimore, MD 21202
groche@troweprice.com
Tel: (410) 345 - 2000
Fax:(410) 345 - 4661
TF: (800) 638 - 7890

Serves As:
- Chairman and President, T. Rowe Price Associates

ROCHE, Mark A.
300 Tower Pkwy.
Lincolnshire, IL 60069
mark_roche@fortunebrands.com
Tel: (847) 484 - 4400
Fax:(847) 484 - 4490

Serves As:
- Senior V. President, General Counsel and Secretary, Fortune Brands, Inc.

ROCHE, Martin J. "Frank"
15378 Ave. of Science
San Diego, CA 92128
Tel: (858) 716 - 3400
Fax:(858) 716 - 3775
TF: (800) 350 - 3044

Serves As:
- Exec. V. President and General Manager, International, Anacomp, Inc.

ROCHE, Michael F.
1401 I St. NW
Suite 200
Washington, DC 20005
Tel: (202) 293 - 9494
Fax:(202) 223 - 9594

Registered Federal Lobbyist.
Serves As:
- V. President, National Affairs, Anheuser-Busch Cos., Inc.

ROCHELEAU, Dale A.
77 Grove St.
Rutland, VT 05701
Tel: (802) 773 - 2711
Fax:(802) 747 - 2199
TF: (800) 649 - 2877

Serves As:
- Senior V. President, Legal and Public Affairs; and Corporate Secretary, Central Vermont Public Service Corp.

ROCHKIND, Jennifer
Nine W. 57th St.
Suite 4900
New York, NY 10019
Tel: (212) 223 - 0303
Fax:(212) 750 - 3564

Serves As:
- Contact, Toyota USA Foundation, Toyota Motor North America, Inc.

ROCK, Doug
P.O. Box 60068
Houston, TX 77205-0068
Tel: (281) 443 - 3370
TF: (800) 877 - 6484

Serves As:
- Chairman and Chief Exec. Officer, Smith Internat'l, Inc.

ROCK, Michael A.
600 13th St. NW
Suite 340 West
Washington, DC 20005
Tel: (202) 662 - 0130
Fax:(202) 662 - 0199

Registered Federal Lobbyist.
Serves As:
- Assistant V. President, External Affairs, Union Pacific Corp.

ROCKWOOD, Stephen D.
10260 Campus Point Dr.
San Diego, CA 92121
Tel: (858) 826 - 6000
Fax:(858) 826 - 6634

Serves As:
- Director, Employee Relations, Science Applications Internat'l Corp.

RODENBOUGH, Dean T.
P.O. Box 419580
Kansas City, MO 64141-6580
Tel: (816) 274 - 5111
Fax:(816) 274 - 5061

Serves As:
- Director, Corporate Communications, Hallmark Cards, Inc.

RODGERS, Richard F.
101 Constitution Ave., NW
Suite 801 East
Washington, DC 20001
Tel: (202) 218 - 3800

Serves As:
- Staff V. President, Government Affairs, FedEx Corp.

RODGERS, Susan
9487 Regency Square Blvd.
Jacksonville, FL 32225
susan.rodgers@crowley.com
Tel: (904) 727 - 2291

Serves As:
- V. President, Human Resources, Crowley Maritime Corp.

RODGERS, T. J.
198 Champion Ct.
San Jose, CA 95134
Tel: (408) 943 - 2600
Fax:(408) 943 - 4730

Serves As:
- President and Chief Exec. Officer, Cypress Semiconductor Corp.

RODKEY, Jane
1800 Center St.
Camp Hill, PA 17089
Tel: (717) 302 - 3977
Fax:(717) 302 - 3969

Serves As:
- Government Affairs Coordinator, Highmark Inc.

RODMAN, Len C.
11401 Lamar Ave.
Overland Park, KS 66211
rodmanlc@bv.com
Tel: (913) 458 - 2000
Fax:(913) 458 - 3730

Serves As:
- Chairman, President and Chief Exec. Officer, Black & Veatch

RODONO, Nick
2001 Rexford Rd.
Charlotte, NC 28211
Tel: (704) 365 - 7300
Fax:(704) 365 - 7218

Serves As:
- V. President, Human Resources, National Gypsum Co.

RODRIGUEZ, Adrian
P.O. Box 834
Seattle, WA 98101
adrian.rodriguez@wamu.net
Tel: (206) 377 - 3268
Fax:(206) 554 - 4807
TF: (800) 756 - 8000

Serves As:
- Manager, Corporate Public Relations, Washington Mutual, Inc.

RODRIGUEZ, Joseph L.
P.O. Box 6482
1600 Faraday Ave.
Carlsbad, CA 92008
Tel: (760) 603 - 7200
Fax:(760) 602 - 6500
TF: (800) 955 - 6288

Serves As:
- Senior V. President, Human Resources, Invitrogen Corp.

RODRIGUEZ, Monique
5775 Morehouse Dr.
San Diego, CA 92121-2779
Tel: (858) 587 - 1121
Fax:(858) 658 - 2100

Serves As:
- Government Relations, Qualcomm Inc.

RODRIGUEZ, Raymund
P.O. Box 982
El Paso, TX 79960
rrodrigu@epelectric.com
Tel: (915) 543 - 4156
Fax:(915) 543 - 2299
TF: (800) 351 - 1621

Registered Federal Lobbyist.
Serves As:
- Governmental Affairs Representative, El Paso Electric Co.

ROEDEL, Richard
622 Broadway
New York, NY 10012
Tel: (646) 536 - 2842

Serves As:
- Chairman and Chief Exec. Officer, Take-Two Interactive Software, Inc.

ROEDER, Susan
100 Fourth Ave. North
Bayport, MN 55003-1096
susan.roeder@andersencorp.com
Tel: (651) 264 - 7432

Serves As:
- Manager, Community Relations and Public Affairs, Andersen Corp.

ROEHR, Mary
201 N. Washington Square, Suite 920
Lansing, MI 48933
Tel: (517) 334 - 3412
Fax:(517) 334 - 3429

Serves As:
- Manager, External Affairs, SBC Michigan

ROELANDTS, Willem P.
2100 Logic Dr.
San Jose, CA 95124-3400
Tel: (408) 559 - 7778
Fax:(408) 559 - 7114
TF: (800) 836 - 4002

Serves As:
- Chairman, President and Chief Exec. Officer, Xilinx, Inc.

ROESSER, Tom
1401 I St., NW
Suite 500
Washington, DC 20005
Tel: (202) 263 - 5900
Fax:(202) 263 - 5902

Registered Federal Lobbyist.
Serves As:
- Director, Tax Affairs, Microsoft Corporation

ROGEL, Steven R.
P.O. Box 9777
Federal Way, WA 98063-9777
Tel: (253) 924 - 3456
Fax:(253) 924 - 3685
TF: (800) 525 - 5440

Serves As:
- Chairman, President, and Chief Exec. Officer, Weyerhaeuser Co.

ROGERO, Larry
Three Galleria Tower
13155 Noel Rd., Suite 1600
Dallas, TX 75240
Tel: (214) 550 - 7000

Serves As:
- Director, Environmental Affairs, FedEx Kinko's Office and Print Services

ROGERS, James E.
P.O. Box 960
Cincinnati, OH 45201-0960
Tel: (513) 421 - 9500
Fax:(513) 651 - 9196

Serves As:
- Chairman, President and Chief Exec. Officer, Cinergy Corp.

ROGERS, James E.
P.O. Box 115
Austell, GA 30168-0115
Fax:(770) 732 - 3401

Serves As:
- Chairman of the Board, Caraustar Industries, Inc.

ROGERS, James S.
P.O. Box 31328
Tampa, FL 33631-3328
jrogers@gerdauameristeel.com
Tel: (813) 286 - 8383
Fax:(813) 207 - 2251

Serves As:
- V. President, Human Resources, Gerdau Ameristeel Corp.

ROGERS, Kathie M.
P.O. Box 777
Medina, OH 44258
Tel: (330) 776 - 4488
Fax:(330) 220 - 8636

Serves As:
- Manager, Investor Relations, RPM Internat'l Inc.

ROGERS, Michael T.
P.O. Box 2951
Beaumont, TX 77704
Tel: (409) 838 - 6631

Serves As:
- Communications Specialist, Entergy Texas

ROGERS, Millie D.
1650 Tysons Blvd.
Suite 1700
McLean, VA 22201
millie.rogers@itt.com
Tel: (703) 790 - 6300
Fax:(703) 790 - 6365

Serves As:
- Director, Marketing Communications and Public Relations, ITT Industries

ROGERS, Jr., Ralph L.
120 Park Ave.
New York, NY 10017
Tel: (917) 663 - 2206
Fax:(917) 663 - 5431

Serves As:
- Director, Corporate Responsibility Planning, (Altria Corporate Services, Inc.), Altria Group, Inc.

ROGERS, Richard R.
P.O. Box 799045
Dallas, TX 75379-9045
rogersr@marykay.com
Tel: (972) 687 - 6300
Fax:(972) 387 - 1611
TF: (800) 627 - 9529

Serves As:
- Chairman and Chief Exec. Officer, Mary Kay Inc.

ROGERS, Robert D.
1341 W. Mockingbird Ln.
Dallas, TX 75247
Tel: (972) 647 - 6700
Fax:(972) 647 - 3878

Serves As:
- Chairman of the Board, Texas Industries, Inc.

ROGERS, Steve
220 N. Meridian St.
Indianapolis, IN 46204
Tel: (317) 265 - 3903
Fax:(317) 265 - 4354
TF: (800) 257 - 0902

Serves As:
- Director, Government Affairs, SBC Indiana

ROGERS, Sue
22301 Foothill Blvd.
M/S 4790
Hayward, CA 94541
Tel: (510) 727 - 5669
Fax:(510) 727 - 2300

Serves As:
- Grants Administrator, Mervyn's

ROGERS, Susan
1776 I St. NW
Suite 1000
Washington, DC 20006-3707
rogerssl@bp.com
Tel: (202) 785 - 4888
Fax:(202) 457 - 6597

Registered Federal Lobbyist.
Serves As:
- Director, Tax Policy, BP

ROGERS, T. Gary
5929 College Ave.
Oakland, CA 94618
Tel: (510) 652 - 8187

Serves As:
- Chairman and Chief Exec. Officer, Dreyer's Grand Ice Cream Holdings, Inc.

ROGERS, Terence R.
2621 W. 15th Place
Chicago, IL 60608
terence.rogers@ryersontull.com
Tel: (773) 762 - 2153
Ext: 3720
Fax:(773) 762 - 3311

Serves As:
- V. President, Finance; and Treasurer, Ryerson Tull

Responsibilities include investor relations

ROGERSON, Craig A.
1313 N. Market St.
Wilmington, DE 19894-0001
Tel: (302) 594 - 5000
Fax:(302) 594 - 5400

Serves As:
- President and Chief Exec. Officer, Hercules Incorporated

ROHR, James E.
249 Fifth Ave.
Pittsburgh, PA 15222-2707
Tel: (412) 762 - 2000

Serves As:
- Chairman and Chief Exec. Officer, PNC Financial Services Group

ROHR, Mark C.
330 S. Fourth St.
Richmond, VA 23219
Tel: (804) 788 - 6000
Fax:(804) 788 - 5688

Serves As:
- President and Chief Exec. Officer, Albemarle Corp.

ROHRBACH, Kate
One Post St.
32nd Floor
San Francisco, CA 94104-5296
kate.rohrbach@mckesson.com
Tel: (415) 983 - 8300
Fax:(415) 983 - 7160

Serves As:
- V. President, Corporate Communications, McKesson Corp.

ROHRKASTE, Michael
P.O. Box 2566
Oshkosh, WI 54903-2566
mrohrkaste@oshtruck.com
Tel: (920) 235 - 9150
Fax:(920) 233 - 9268

Serves As:
- V. President, Human Resources, Oshkosh Truck Corp.

ROJAS, Ernesto J.
409 12th St., S.W., Suite 701
Washington, DC 20024-2191
ernie.rojas@pb.com
Tel: (202) 488 - 4464
Fax:(202) 488 - 4396

Serves As:
- Director, Regulatory Affairs, Pitney Bowes Inc.

ROLFE, Christopher C.
P.O. Box 1244
M/S PB04M
Charlotte, NC 28201-1244
crolfe@duke-energy.com
Tel: (704) 382 - 4343
Fax:(704) 382 - 3588

Serves As:
- V. President, Human Resources, Duke Energy Corp.

ROLFS, Stephen J.
777 E. Wisconsin Ave., 11th Floor
Milwaukee, WI 53202-5304
stephen.rolfs@sensient-tech.com
Tel: (414) 347 - 3743
Fax:(414) 347 - 3785

Serves As:
- V. President, Controller and Chief Accounting Officer, Sensient Technology Corp.

Responsibilities include investor relations.

ROLLI, Nicholas M.
120 Park Ave.
New York, NY 10017
Tel: (917) 663 - 4000
Fax:(917) 663 - 5430

Serves As:
- V. President, Investor Relations and Financial Communications, (Altria Corporate Services, Inc.), Altria Group, Inc.

ROLLIER, Philippe R.
12950 Worldgate Dr.
Suite 600
Herndon, VA 20170
Tel: (703) 480 - 3600
Fax:(703) 796 - 2214

Serves As:
- President and Chief Exec. Officer, Lafarge North America, Inc.

ROLLINS, Gary
2170 Piedmont Road, N.E.
Atlanta, GA 30324
Tel: (404) 888 - 2000

Serves As:
- Chief Exec. Officer, President and Chief Operating Officer, Rollins, Inc.

ROLLINS, Kevin B.
One Dell Way
Round Rock, TX 78682
Tel: (512) 338 - 4400
Fax:(512) 728 - 3653
TF: (800) 289 - 3355

Serves As:
- President and Chief Exec. Officer, Dell Inc.

ROLLINS, R. Randall
2170 Piedmont Road, N.E.
Atlanta, GA 30324
Tel: (404) 888 - 2000

Serves As:
- Chairman of the Board, Rollins, Inc.

ROLLISON, Kelly
P.O. Box 15437
Wilmington, DE 19850-5437
Tel: (302) 886 - 3000
Fax:(302) 886 - 2972
TF: (800) 456 - 3669

Serves As:
- Treasurer, Zeneca Inc. Political Action Committee, AstraZeneca Pharmaceuticals

ROMAN, Anne
100 Phoenix Dr.
Ann Arbor, MI 48108
aroman@bordersgroupinc.com
Tel: (734) 477 - 1392
Fax:(734) 477 - 1517

Serves As:
- Director, Public Relations, Borders Group, Inc.

ROMAN, George C.
1200 Wilson Blvd.
Arlington, VA 22209-2305
Tel: (703) 465 - 3434
Fax:(703) 465 - 3134

Serves As:
- V. President and Chief of Staff, Washington Operations, The Boeing Co.

ROMINE, Francine
One American Rd.
Dearborn, MI 48126
fromine@ford.com
Tel: (313) 322 - 1185
TF: (800) 555 - 5259

Serves As:
- Strategic Communications Manager, National Communications, Ford Motor Co.

ROMINSKI, Kathryn Hubbard
3415 University Ave.
St. Paul, MN 55114
Tel: (651) 642 - 4305
Fax:(651) 642 - 4103

Serves As:
- Exec. Director, Hubbard Foundation, Hubbard Broadcasting, Inc.

ROMITO, Mark
P.O. Box 2301
Cincinnati, OH 45201-2301
mark.romito@cinbell.com
Tel: (513) 397 - 1366
Fax:(513) 723 - 9815

Serves As:
- Federal and State Regulatory Affairs, Cincinnati Bell Inc.

ROMOSER, Chris
10955 Vista Sorrento Pkwy.
San Diego, CA 92130
romoser@iomega.com
Tel: (858) 314 - 7180
Fax:(858) 314 - 7001

Serves As:
- Director, Corporate Communications and Public Relations, Iomega Corp.

RONALD, Mark
1601 Research Blvd.
Rockville, MD 20850
Tel: (301) 838 - 6000

Serves As:
- President and Chief Exec. Officer, BAE Systems North America

RONAN, Jr., Joseph E.
50 W. San Fernando St.
San Jose, CA 95113
joer@calpine.com
Tel: (408) 794 - 2607
Fax:(408) 975 - 4648
TF: (800) 359 - 5115

Serves As:
- Senior V. President, Government and Regulatory Affairs, Calpine Corp.

Responsibilities include political action.

RONEY, Blake M.
One Nu Skin Plaza
75 W. Center St.
Provo, UT 84601
broney@nuskin.net
Tel: (801) 345 - 1000
Fax:(801) 345 - 1099

Serves As:
- Chairman of the Board, Nu Skin Enterprises

ROOF, Donald C.
P.O. Box 554
Milwaukee, WI 53201
Tel: (414) 319 - 8500
Fax:(414) 319 - 8510

Serves As:
- Exec. V. President and Chief Financial Officer, Joy Global Inc.

Responsibilities include investor relations.

ROOKS, John M.
622 Third Ave., 37th Floor
New York, NY 10017
Tel: (203) 356 - 4400

Serves As:
- V. President, Risk Management, Asbury Automotive Group

ROONEY, Pat
1090 Vermont Ave. NW
Suite 1290
Washington, DC 20005
Tel: (202) 589 - 0088

Registered Federal Lobbyist.
Serves As:
- Representative, Golden Rule Insurance Co.

ROONEY, Therese
712 11th St
Lawrence, IL 62439
Tel: (317) 943 - 8000
Fax:(618) 943 - 8031

Serves As:
- Chairman of the Board, Golden Rule Insurance Co.

ROOS, David E.
111 Washington Ave., Suite 706
Albany, NY 12210-2213
droos@att.com
Tel: (518) 463 - 3107
Fax:(518) 463 - 5943

Serves As:
- State Director, Government Affairs, AT&T

ROOSA, Bryan R.
1660 L St. NW
Fourth Floor
Washington, DC 20036
Tel: (202) 775 - 5086
Fax:(202) 775 - 5024

Registered Federal Lobbyist.
Serves As:
- Director, State Government Relations, General Motors Corp.

ROOU, Tammy
720 E. Wisconsin Ave.
Milwaukee, WI 53202-4797
Tel: (414) 271 - 1444
Fax:(414) 665 - 2463
TF: (800) 323 - 7033

Serves As:
- PAC Treasurer, Northwestern Mutual Financial Network

ROPER, Bart
1899 Pennsylvania Ave., NW
Suite 300
Washington, DC 20006
Tel: (202) 496 - 8200
Fax:(202) 659 - 1110

Registered Federal Lobbyist.
Serves As:
- V. President, Washington Operations, (General Atomics Aeronautical Systems, Inc.), General Atomics

ROSA, David
622 Third Ave.
39th Floor
New York, NY 10017
david.rosa@tmp.com
Tel: (212) 351 - 7067

Serves As:
- Senior V. President and Global Brand Manager, Monster Worldwide, Inc.

Responsibilities include corporate communications and political action.

ROSADO, Mary
601 Pennsylvania Ave. NW
Washington, DC
Tel: (202) 756 - 7219
Fax:(202) 207 - 3623

Serves As:
- V. President, Federal Government Affairs, Express Scripts, Inc.

ROSBE, Jr., Robert L.
One Ocean Spray Dr.
Lakeville-Middleboro, MA 02349
Tel: (508) 946 - 1000
Fax:(508) 946 - 7704
TF: (800) 662 - 3263

Serves As:
- Chairman of the Board, Ocean Spray Cranberries, Inc.

ROSE, Amy
P.O. Box 100
Whitehouse Station, NJ 08889-0100
Tel: (908) 423 - 6537
Fax:(908) 735 - 1181
TF: (800) 423 - 1000

Serves As:
- Media Contact, Merck & Co., Inc.

ROSE, David
1634 I St. NW
Suite 300
Washington, DC 20006-4021
david.rose@intel.com
Tel: (202) 626 - 4390
Fax:(202) 628 - 2525

Registered Federal Lobbyist.
Serves As:
- Director, Export/Import/InfoSec Affairs, Intel Corp.

ROSE, George P.
One Executive Dr.
Fort Lee, NJ 07024
Tel: (201) 947 - 7774
Fax:(201) 947 - 5541
TF: (800) 445 - 4216

Serves As:
- Exec. V. President, Human Resources and Communications, Alpharma Inc.

ROSE, Matthew K.
P.O. Box 961057
Fort Worth, TX 76161-2830
Tel: (817) 867 - 6100
Fax:(817) 352 - 7924

Serves As:
- Chairman, President, and Chief Exec. Officer, Burlington Northern Santa Fe Corporation

ROSE, Melissa L.
6950 Columbia Gateway Dr.
Columbia, MD 21046
TF: (877) 645 - 6464

Serves As:
- Senior V. President, Investor Relations, Magellan Health Services, Inc.

ROSE, Michael L.
P.O. Box 650283
Dallas, TX 75265-0283
Tel: (972) 699 - 4000
Fax:(972) 699 - 4025

Serves As:
- President and Chief Operating Officer, Xanser Corp.

ROSE, Michael M.
6363 Main St.
Williamsville, NY 14221
rosem@natfuel.com
Tel: (716) 857 - 7438
Fax:(716) 857 - 7439
TF: (800) 365 - 3234

Serves As:
- Manager, Government Affairs, Nat'l Fuel Gas Co.

ROSE, Mitch F.
1150 17th St. NW
Suite 400
Washington, DC 20036
Tel: (202) 222 - 4700

Registered Federal Lobbyist.
Serves As:
- V. President, Government Relations, The Walt Disney Company

ROSE, Robert E.
P.O. Box 4577
Houston, TX 77210-4577
rrose@gsfdrill.com
Tel: (281) 925 - 6000
Fax:(281) 925 - 6010

Serves As:
- Chairman of the Board, GlobalSantaFe Corp.

ROSE, Tom
P.O. Box 227097
Suite 37-054
Dallas, TX 75222-7097
tom.rose@txu.com
Tel: (214) 812 - 3247
Fax:(214) 812 - 3455

Serves As:
- Director, Public Policy, TXU

ROSEN, Andrew M.
P.O. Box 29
St. Louis, MO 63166-0029
arosen@brownshoe.com
Tel: (314) 854 - 4124
Fax:(314) 854 - 4274

Serves As:
- Senior V. President, Treasurer and Chief Financial Officer, Brown Shoe Co., Inc.

Responsibilities include investor relations.

ROSEN, Brian
One MedImmune Way
Gaithersburg, MD 20878
Tel: (301) 398 - 0000
Fax:(301) 398 - 9000
TF: (877) 633 - 4411

Serves As:
- Treasurer, MedImmune Inc. Employee Political Awareness Committee, MedImmune, Inc.

ROSEN, Hugh
12061 Bluemont Way
Reston, VA 20190
hugh.rosen@slma.com
Tel: (703) 984 - 6227
Fax:(703) 810 - 7053

Serves As:
- Press Contact, Sallie Mae Fund, SLM Corp.

ROSEN, James A.
Route 10 - Green Hills
P.O. Box 563
Reading, PA 19603
james.rosen@penske.com
Tel: (610) 775 - 6325

Registered Federal Lobbyist.
Serves As:
- V. President, Government Relations, Penske Truck Leasing Co. LP

Responsibilities include political action.

ROSENBERG, R.A.
1710 SAIC Dr.
McLean, VA 22102
rosenbergr@saic.com
Tel: (703) 676 - 4343
Fax:(703) 676 - 7732

Serves As:
- Exec. V. President, Washington Operations, Science Applications Internat'l Corp.

ROSENBLATT, David
111 Eighth Ave.
Tenth Floor
New York, NY 10011
Tel: (212) 683 - 0001
Fax:(212) 287 - 1203

Serves As:
- Chief Exec. Officer, DoubleClick, Inc.

ROSENBLUM, Jay E.
1225 Connecticut Ave. NW
Washington, DC 20036
jay.rosemblum@ey.com
Tel: (202) 327 - 6000

Serves As:
- Director, Government Relations, Ernst & Young LLP

ROSENBLUM, Lisa
1111 Stewart Ave.
Bethpage, NY 11714-3581
lrosenbl@cablevision.com
Tel: (516) 803 - 2580
Fax:(516) 803 - 1186

Serves As:
- Senior V. President, Government Relations and Education, Cablevision Systems Corp.

Responsibilities include political action.

ROSENBURY, W. Mark
P.O. Box 6000
Sioux City, IA 51102-6000
mrosenbury@terraindustries.com
Tel: (712) 279 - 8756
Fax:(712) 294 - 1130

Serves As:
- Senior V. President and Chief Administrative Officer, Terra Industries Inc.

Responsibilities include corporate communications and investor relations.

ROSENE, Lars
5215 N. O'Connor Blvd.
Suite 2300
Irving, TX 75039
lrosene@flowserve.com
Tel: (972) 443 - 6500
Fax:(972) 443 - 6800

Serves As:
- Director, Public Affairs, Flowserve Corp.

ROSENFELD, Irene B.
P.O. Box 660634
Dallas, TX 75266-0634
Tel: (972) 334 - 7000
Fax:(972) 334 - 2019

Serves As:
- Chairman and Chief Exec. Officer, Frito-Lay, Inc.

ROSENSHIN, Allen
1285 Ave. of the Americas
New York, NY 10019-6095
Tel: (212) 459 - 5000
Fax:(212) 459 - 6645

Serves As:
- Chief Exec. Officer, BBDO New York

ROSENSTEELE, James
11825 N. Pennsylvania St.
Carmel, IN 46032
james_rosensteele@conseco.com
Tel: (317) 817 - 4418
TF: (800) 888 - 4918

Serves As:
- Senior V. President, Marketing Communications, Conseco, Inc.

Responsibilities include public affairs.

ROSENSTOCK, John
One State Farm Plaza
(B-4)
Bloomington, IL 61710-0001
Tel: (309) 766 - 3379

Serves As:
- Director, Public Affairs, State Farm Insurance Cos.

ROSENSTOCK, Shelley
340 Kingsland St.
Nutley, NJ 07110-1199
shelley.rosenstock@roche.com
Tel: (973) 562 - 2373
Fax:(973) 562 - 2333

Serves As:
- Director, Product Public Affairs - Oncology and Dermatology, Hoffmann-La Roche Inc. (Roche)

ROSENTHAL, Daniel D.
P.O. Box 6000
Newport Beach, CA 92658-6000
Tel: (949) 854 - 3100
Fax:(949) 854 - 8162

Serves As:
- President and Chief Executive Officer, Downey Savings and Loan Ass'n, F.A.

ROSENTHAL, Jack
229 W. 43rd St.
New York, NY 10036
Tel: (212) 556 - 1234

Serves As:
- President, New York Times Co. Foundation, New York Times Co.

ROSIA, Megan
901 15th St. NW
Suite 310
M/S WAS 1150
Washington, DC 20005
Tel: (202) 842 - 3193
Fax:(202) 289 - 6834

Serves As:
- Managing Director, Government Affairs and Associate General Counsel, Northwest Airlines, Inc.

ROSIER, W. Grady
4747 McLane Pkwy.
Temple, TX 76504
Tel: (254) 771 - 7500
Fax:(254) 771 - 2284

Serves As:
- President and Chief Exec. Officer, McLane Company, Inc.

ROSNER, William E.
249 Fifth Ave.
Pittsburgh, PA 15222-2707
Tel: (412) 762 - 2000

Serves As:
- Chief Human Resources Officer, PNC Financial Services Group

ROSS, Gary
200 N. Milwaukee Ave.
Vernon Hills, IL 60061
Tel: (847) 371 - 5048
Fax:(847) 465 - 3444
TF: (800) 800 - 4239

Serves As:
- General Manager, Corporate Communications, CDW Corp.

ROSS, Jacquie
1768 Automation Pkwy.
San Jose, CA 95131
Tel: (408) 546 - 5000
Fax:(408) 546 - 4300

Serves As:
- Investor Relations Contact, JDS Uniphase Corp.

ROSS, Louise
560 Lexington Ave.
15th Floor
New York, NY 10022
lross@volt.com
Tel: (212) 704 - 2458
Fax:(212) 704 - 2424
TF: (800) 533 - 2401

Serves As:
- V. President, Human Resources, Volt Information Sciences, Inc.

ROSS, Thomas E.
411 Seventh Ave.
Pittsburgh, PA 15219
tross@dqe.com
Tel: (412) 393 - 1191
Fax:(412) 393 - 1263

Serves As:
- Manager, Shareholder Relations, Duquesne Light Holdings

ROSS, Tommy
1201 K St., Suite 1810
Sacramento, CA 95814
rosst@sce.com
Tel: (916) 441 - 3966
Fax:(916) 441 - 4047

Serves As:
- V. President, Public Affairs - Sacramento Region, Southern California Edison, an Edison Internat'l Co.

ROSS, Jr., Wilbur L.
3250 Interstate Dr.
Richfield, OH 44286
Fax:(330) 659 - 9135

Serves As:
- Chairman of the Board, Internat'l Steel Group Inc.
- Chairman of the Board, Internat'l Textiles Group

ROSS-RINGER, Cindy
One State Farm Plaza
(B-4)
Bloomington, IL 61710-0001
Tel: (309) 763 - 5906
Fax:(309) 766 - 2670

Serves As:
- Director, Public Affairs, State Farm Insurance Cos.

ROSSITER, Greg
One Gaylord Dr.
Nashville, TN 37214
grossiter@gaylordentertainment.com
Tel: (615) 316 - 6000
Fax:(615) 316 - 6060

Serves As:
- V. President, Corporate Communications, Gaylord Entertainment Co.

ROSSITER, Robert E.
21557 Telegraph Rd.
Southfield, MI 48034
Tel: (248) 447 - 1500

Serves As:
- Chairman and Chief Exec. Officer, Lear Corporation

ROSSKAMM, Alan
5555 Darrow Rd.
Hudson, OH 44236
Tel: (330) 656 - 2600
Fax:(330) 463 - 6675

Serves As:
- Chairman, President and Chief Exec. Officer, Jo-Ann Stores, Inc.

ROSSKAMM, Betty
5555 Darrow Rd.
Hudson, OH 44236
Tel: (330) 656 - 2600
Fax:(330) 463 - 6675

Serves As:
- Senior V. President, Jo-Ann Stores, Inc.

Responsibilities include corporate philanthropy.

ROSSMAN, Patricia
540 White Plains Rd.
Tarrytown, NY 10591-2005
pat.rossman@cibase.com
Tel: (914) 785 - 2000
Fax:(914) 785 - 2211
TF: (800) 431 - 1900

Serves As:
- Head, Corporate Communications, Ciba Specialty Chemicals

ROST, Rynthia M.
One GEICO Plaza
Washington, DC 20076
Tel: (301) 986 - 3839
Fax:(301) 986 - 2888

Serves As:
- V. President, Public Affairs, GEICO Corp.

ROSTOW, Victoria P. "Penny"
401 Ninth St. NW
Suite 640
Washington, DC 20004
Tel: (202) 585 - 8930

Registered Federal Lobbyist.
Serves As:
- Senior V. President and Director, Federal Government Relations, J. P. Morgan Chase & Co.

ROSTRON, Paul
2711 N. Haskell Ave.
Dallas, TX 75204
Tel: (214) 828 - 7011
Fax:(214) 828 - 7090

Serves As:
- Senior V. President, Human Resources, 7-Eleven, Inc.

ROTH, Brenda
4101 Washington Ave.
Newport News, VA 23607-2770
brenda.roth@ngc.com
Tel: (757) 380 - 3011

Serves As:
- Community Relations Representative, Northrop Grumman Newport News

ROTH, David E.
P.O. Box 871
Tulsa, OK 74102-0871
droth@oneok.com
Tel: (918) 588 - 7924
Fax:(918) 588 - 7960

Serves As:
- V. President, Human Resources, ONEOK, Inc.

ROTH, Deborah
152 W. 57th St.
42nd Floor
New York, NY 10019
Tel: (212) 314 - 7254
Fax:(212) 314 - 7309

Serves As:
- V. President, Corporate Communications, IAC/InterActiveCorp

ROTH, Mary Jo
17845 E. Hwy. 10
Elk River, MN 55330
Tel: (763) 441 - 3121
Fax:(763) 241 - 2366

Serves As:
- Manager, Environmental Services, Great River Energy

ROTH, Michael I.
1114 Ave. of the Americas
New York, NY 10036
Tel: (212) 704 - 1200

Serves As:
- Chairman of the Board and Chief Executive Officer, The Interpublic Group of Companies

ROTH, Paul R.
5565 Glenridge Connector
Atlanta, GA 30342
Tel: (404) 236 - 6000
Fax:(866) 246 - 4852
TF: (800) 331 - 0500

Serves As:
- Exec. V. President, External Affairs and Public Relations, Cingular Wireless

ROTH, Royal
316 Pennsylvania Ave. SE
Suite 300
Washington, DC 20003
Tel: (202) 675 - 4220
Fax:(202) 675 - 4230

Serves As:
- PAC Contact, United Parcel Service (UPS)

ROTHBERG, Adam
1230 Ave. of the Americas
New York, NY 20020
Tel: (212) 698 - 1132
Fax:(212) 698 - 7297

Serves As:
- V. President, Communications, (Simon & Schuster Inc.), Viacom Inc./CBS Corp.

ROTHLEITNER, Mark M.
701 E. Joppa Rd.
Towson, MD 21286
mark.rothleitner@bdk.com
Tel: (410) 716 - 3076
Fax:(410) 716 - 2933

Serves As:
- V. President, Investor Relations and Treasurer, The Black & Decker Corp.

ROTHROCK-HARKE, Jill
2345 Crystal Dr.
Suite 708
Arlington, VA 22202
Tel: (703) 236 - 2751
Fax:(703) 236 - 1931

Registered Federal Lobbyist.
Serves As:
- Manager, Government Affairs, Washington Group Internat'l

ROTHWELL, Sharon
21001 Van Born Rd.
Taylor, MI 48180
Tel: (313) 792 - 6028
Fax:(313) 792 - 6135

Serves As:
- V. President, Corporate Affairs, Masco Corp.

ROTHWELL, Tim
300 Somerset Corporate Blvd.
Bridgewater, NJ 08807-2854
Tel: (908) 243 - 6000
Fax:(908) 231 - 3614
TF: (800) 981 - 2491

Serves As:
- President and Chief Exec. Officer, Sanofi-Aventis Inc.

ROTTY, Sharron
8005 SW Boeckman Rd.
Wilsonville, OR 97070-7777
Tel: (503) 685 - 7000
Fax:(503) 685 - 7704
TF: (800) 547 - 3000

Serves As:
- V. President, Human Resources, Mentor Graphics Corp.

ROUCH, Jeffrey D.
1120 G St. NW
Suite 850
Washington, DC 20005
Tel: (202) 347 - 5910
Fax:(202) 347 - 5916

Serves As:
- V. President, Federal Relations, Nationwide

ROUECHE, Jay
757 N. Eldridge
Houston, TX 77079
jroueche@mcdermott.com
Tel: (281) 870 - 5011

Serves As:
- Director, Investor Relations and Communications, McDermott Internat'l, Inc.

ROULEAU, R. Michael
8000 Bent Branch Dr.
Irving, TX 75063
Tel: (972) 409 - 1300
Fax:(972) 409 - 1556

Serves As:
- President and Chief Exec. Officer, Michaels Stores, Inc.

ROUNDS, Becky
2244 Walnut Grove Ave.
Rosemead, CA 91770
roundsra@sce.com
Tel: (626) 302 - 7953
Fax:(626) 302 - 8066

Serves As:
- Manager, Corporate Communications, Southern California Edison, an Edison Internat'l Co.

ROUSE, III, Charles F.
300 Somerset Corporate Blvd.
M/S SC3-835A
Bridgewater, NJ 08807-2854
charles.rouse@sanofi-aventis.com
Tel: (908) 243 - 6050
Fax:(908) 231 - 3614
TF: (800) 981 - 2491

Serves As:
- V. President, Communications and Corporate Affairs, Sanofi-Aventis Inc.

ROUSSEL, Jerry
1350 I St. NW
Suite 1000
Washington, DC 20005
jroussel@ford.com
Tel: (202) 962 - 5386
Fax:(202) 336 - 7226

Registered Federal Lobbyist.
Serves As:
• Regulatory Manager, Environment, Ford Motor Co.

ROWAN, Vernon C.
6625 W. 78th St.
Bloomington, MN 55439
rowenc@express-scripts.com
Tel: (952) 837 - 5136
Fax:(952) 837 - 7103

Serves As:
• V. President, Government Affairs, Express Scripts, Inc.

ROWE, Dennis C.
P.O. Box 2361
Harrisburg, PA 17105-2361
Tel: (717) 234 - 4941
Fax:(717) 255 - 6850
TF: (800) 388 - 4764

Serves As:
• President and Chief Exec. Officer, Penn Nat'l Insurance

ROWE, M.D., John W.
151 Farmington Ave.
Hartford, CT 06156
Tel: (860) 273 - 0123
TF: (800) 872 - 3862

Serves As:
• Chairman and Chief Exec. Officer, Aetna Inc.

ROWE, John W.
P.O. Box A-3005
Chicago, IL 60690-3005
Tel: (312) 394 - 5725

Serves As:
• Chairman and Chief Exec. Officer, Exelon Corp.

ROWE, Michael
3100 Ocean Park Blvd.
Santa Monica, CA 90405-3032
Tel: (310) 255 - 2000
Fax:(310) 255 - 2100

Serves As:
• Exec. V. President, Human Resources, Activision, Inc.

ROWE, Scott
4000 Warner Blvd.
Burbank, CA 91522
scott.rowe@warnerbros.com
Tel: (818) 954 - 5806

Serves As:
• V. President, Corporate Communications, (Warner Brothers Entertainment), Time Warner Inc.

ROWE, William E.
P.O. Box 19925
Metairie, LA 70179-0925
Tel: (504) 837 - 5880
Fax:(504) 849 - 2307
TF: (800) 535 - 6017

Serves As:
• Chairman of the Board, Stewart Enterprises, Inc.

ROWE-GRAVES, Erin L.
7575 Fulton St. East
M/S 49-2N
Ada, MI 49355-0001
Tel: (616) 787 - 7144
Fax:(616) 787 - 4764

Serves As:
• Manager, Industry and Community Affairs, Alticor Inc.

ROWELL, Susan M.
1133 S.W. Topeka Blvd.
MS 502
Topeka, KS 66629
susan.rowell@bcbsks.com
Tel: (785) 291 - 8698
Fax:(785) 291 - 7664

Serves As:
• Manager, Communications, Blue Cross and Blue Shield of Kansas, Inc.

ROWEN, Michael
1680 Capital One Dr.
12th Floor
McLean, VA 22102
Tel: (703) 720 - 2455

Serves As:
• Investor Relations Contact, Capital One Financial Corp.

ROWLAND, Juna
13224 Fountainhead Plaza
Hagerstown, MD 21742
ir@jlg.com
Tel: (240) 313 - 1816

Serves As:
• V. President, Corporate and Investor Relations, JLG Industries, Inc.

ROWLAND, Rachael
11419 Sunset Hills Rd.
Reston, VA 20190-5207
rrowland@maximus.com
Tel: (703) 251 - 8500
Fax:(703) 251 - 8240
TF: (888) 368 - 2152

Serves As:
• V. President, Public and Media Relations, MAXIMUS, Inc.

ROWLAND, Robert O.
1101 Pennsylvania Ave. NW
Suite 400
Washington, DC 20004-2504
Tel: (202) 637 - 3800
Fax:(202) 637 - 3862

Registered Federal Lobbyist.
Serves As:
• V. President, Government Affairs, Textron Inc.

ROWTEN, Michael J.
Kerr-McGee Center, Box 25861
Oklahoma City, OK 73125
Tel: (405) 270 - 3199
Fax:(405) 270 - 3029
TF: (800) 786 - 2556

Serves As:
• Director, Community Relations, Kerr-McGee Corp.

ROY, Alex D.
130 E. Randolph Dr.
24th Floor
Chicago, IL 60601
a.roy@pecorp.com
Tel: (312) 240 - 7800
Fax:(312) 240 - 4220

Serves As:
• Manager, Financial and Shareholder Services, Peoples Energy Corp.

ROYCE, Susan M.
284 South Ave.
Poughkeepsie, NY 12601-4879
Tel: (845) 452 - 2000
Fax:(845) 486 - 5465
TF: (800) 527 - 2714

Serves As:
• Director, Community Outreach, CH Energy Group, Inc.

ROYER, Mark
4680 Wilshire Blvd.
Los Angeles, CA 90010
mark.royer@farmersinsurance.com
Tel: (323) 964 - 8020
Fax:(323) 964 - 8095

Serves As:
• Director, Political Action and Administration, Farmers Group, Inc.

ROZANSKI, Horacio
8283 Greensboro Dr.
McLean, VA 22102-3802
Tel: (703) 902 - 5000
Fax:(703) 902 - 3333

Serves As:
• V. President and Chief Human Resources Officer, Booz Allen Hamilton Inc.

ROZELLE, Mark A.
100 W. Putnam Ave.
Greenwich, CT 06830
Tel: (203) 622 - 3520
Fax:(203) 622 - 3561

Serves As:
• V. President, Investor Relations and Corporate Communications, UST Inc.

ROZSA, Bette Jo
One Riverside Plaza
Columbus, OH 43215-2373
bjrozsa@aep.com
Tel: (614) 223 - 2840
Fax:(614) 223 - 2807

Serves As:
• Managing Director, Investor Relations, American Electric Power Co. Inc.

ROZZELL, Scott
1111 Louisiana St.
Houston, TX 77002
Tel: (713) 207 - 1111

Serves As:
• Exec. V. President and General Counsel, CenterPoint Energy
Responsibilities include legislative and regulatory affairs and corporate communications.

RUANE, Robert W.
320 Park Ave.
New York, NY 10022
Tel: (212) 224 - 1641
Fax:(212) 224 - 2529

Serves As:
• Senior V. President, Corporate Communications, Mutual of America Life Insurance Co.

RUANO, Jose
P.O. Box 482
Milwaukee, WI 53201-0482
jruano@mbco.com
Tel: (414) 931 - 4568
Fax:(414) 931 - 6312

Serves As:
• Manager, Corporate Relations, Miller Brewing Co.

RUBIN, Donald S.
1221 Ave. of the Americas
48th Floor
New York, NY 10020-1095
donald_rubin@mcgraw-hill.com
Tel: (212) 512 - 4321
Fax:(212) 512 - 3840

Serves As:
• Senior V. President, Investor Relations, The McGraw-Hill Companies, Inc.

RUBIN, Elizabeth
555 12th St. NW
Suite 650
Washington, DC 20004-1205
Tel: (202) 393 - 7950
Fax:(202) 393 - 7960

Serves As:
• Senior Associate, Advocacy Relations, Eli Lilly and Company

RUBIN, Joe
1401 I St. NW
Suite 240
Washington, DC 20005-2225
Tel: (202) 414 - 8000
Fax:(202) 414 - 8010

Serves As:
- V. President, Government Affairs, MasterCard Internat'l

RUBIN, Michael
607 14th St. NW
Suite 950
Washington, DC 20005
Tel: (202) 429 - 0303
Fax:(202) 293 - 0561

Registered Federal Lobbyist.
Serves As:
- Vice President, Congressional Affairs, Qwest Communications

Responsibilities also include political action.

RUBINGER, David
1550 Peachtree St., N.W.
Atlanta, GA 30309
david.rubinger@equifax.com
Tel: (404) 885 - 8555
Fax:(404) 885 - 8078

Serves As:
- V. President, Communications, Equifax Inc.

RUBINO, Thomas
Three Penn Plaza East
PP-15V
Newark, NJ 07105-2200
Thomas_Rubino@horizonblue.com
Tel: (973) 466 - 8755
Fax:(973) 466 - 8762

Serves As:
- Director, Public Affairs, Horizon Blue Cross Blue Shield of New Jersey

RUBINSTEIN, Ira
1401 I St., NW
Suite 500
Washington, DC 20005
Tel: (202) 263 - 5900
Fax:(202) 263 - 5902

Registered Federal Lobbyist.
Serves As:
- Representative, Microsoft Corporation

RUBIO, Lea
Ordway Bldg.
One Kaiser Plaza
Oakland, CA 94612
Tel: (510) 987 - 3900
Fax:(510) 873 - 5345

Serves As:
- Senior Media Representative - Northern California Region, Kaiser Permanente

RUDD, Dana R.
1776 I St. NW
Suite 700
Washington, DC 20006
drrudd@ppco.com
Tel: (202) 833 - 0914
Fax:(202) 785 - 0639

Registered Federal Lobbyist.
Serves As:
- Manager, Federal Affairs - Upstream, ConocoPhillips

RUDE, Michael W.
2725 Fairfield Rd.
Kalamazoo, MI 49002
Tel: (616) 385 - 2600
Fax:(616) 385 - 1062

Serves As:
- V. President, Human Resources, Stryker Corp.

RUDELL, Jeanne
48 Monroe Tpk.
Trumbull, CT 06611
jrudell@oxhp.com
Tel: (203) 459 - 6000
Fax:(203) 452 - 4884
TF: (800) 889 - 7658

Serves As:
- V. President, Human Resources, Oxford Health Plans Inc.

RUDICH, Yvette
103 JFK Pkwy.
Short Hills, NJ 07078
Tel: (973) 921 - 5986

Serves As:
- Leader, Global External Communications, The Dun & Bradstreet Corp.

RUDIWITZ, Irv
7520 Astoria Blvd.
Jackson Heights, NY 11370
Tel: (347) 418 - 4000
Fax:(347) 397 - 4204

Serves As:
- Senior V. President, Human Resources, British Airways

RUDNAY, D'Arcy
1500 Market St.
Philadelphia, PA 19102
Tel: (215) 981 - 8582
Fax:(215) 981 - 7790

Serves As:
- V. President, Corporate Communications, Comcast Corporation

RUDOLPH, Deborah
1100 Ave. of the Americas
New York, NY 10036
Tel: (212) 512 - 5119
Fax:(212) 512 - 1182

Serves As:
- Contact, Corporate Giving Program, Home Box Office (HBO)

RUDOLPH, Frank W.
P.O. Box 8003
Menasha, WI 54952-8003
Tel: (920) 751 - 7777
Fax:(920) 751 - 7790

Serves As:
- V. President, Human Resources, Banta Corp.

Also serves as President, Banta Foundation.

RUDOLPH, Heidi
3333 Beverly Rd.
BC-113A
Hoffman Estates, IL 60179-0001
Tel: (847) 286 - 2500
Fax:(847) 286 - 7881
TF: (800) 732 - 7780

Serves As:
- Treasurer, Sears Holdings Corp. PAC, Sears Holding Corp.

RUDY, Suzanne B.
7628 Thorndike Rd.
Greensboro, NC 27409-9421
Tel: (336) 664 - 1233
Fax:(336) 931 - 7454

Serves As:
- V. President and Corporate Treasurer, RF Micro Devices, Inc.

Responsibilities include government relations.

RUEBEL, Thomas J.
38 Fountain Square
Cincinnati, OH 45263
Tel: (513) 579 - 5300
Fax:(513) 579 - 5226
TF: (800) 972 - 3030

Registered Federal Lobbyist.
Serves As:
- Director, Government Affairs, Fifth Third Bancorp.

RUED, Scott D.
2791 Research Dr.
Rochester Hills, MI 48309-3575
Tel: (248) 299 - 7500
Fax:(248) 299 - 7501

Serves As:
- Chairman of the Board, Dura Automotive Systems, Inc.

RUEFF, Jr., J. Russell
209 Redwood Shores Pkwy.
Redwood City, CA 94065-1175
Tel: (650) 628 - 1500
Fax:(650) 628 - 1415

Serves As:
- Exec. V. President, Human Resources, Electronic Arts Inc.

RUEHLING, Michael J.
1331 Pennsylvania Ave. NW
Suite 560
Washington, DC 20004
mike_ruehling@csx.com
Tel: (202) 783 - 8124
Fax:(202) 783 - 5929

Registered Federal Lobbyist.
Serves As:
- Senior V. President, Federal Legislation, CSX Corp.

RUETTGERS, Mike
P.O. Box 9103
Hopkinton, MA 01748
Tel: (508) 435 - 1000
Fax:(508) 435 - 7954
TF: (800) 424 - 3622

Serves As:
- Chairman of the Board, EMC Corp.

RUFE, Ellen
6130 Stoneridge Mall Rd., Suite 150
Pleasanton, CA 94588
erufe@volt.com
Tel: (925) 463 - 2871
Fax:(925) 463 - 2807

Serves As:
- Director, Marketing Communications, Volt Information Sciences, Inc.

RUFF, Gary F.
5445 Corporate Dr.
Suite 200
Troy, MI 48098-2683
Tel: (248) 952 - 2500
Fax:(248) 952 - 2501

Serves As:
- Chairman and Chief Executive Officer, Intermet Corp.

RUFFATTO, Karen
One Horace Mann Plaza
Springfield, IL 62715-0001
Tel: (217) 788 - 5707
Fax:(217) 788 - 5161

Serves As:
- Investor Relations Administrator, Horace Mann Educators Corp.

RUGEN, Karen
P.O. Box 3165
Harrisburg, PA 17105
Tel: (717) 730 - 7766
Fax:(717) 731 - 4737

Serves As:
- Senior V. President, Corporate Communications and Public Affairs, Rite Aid Corp.

RUH, William J.
17800 Royalton Rd.
Cleveland, OH 44136-5149
Tel: (440) 572 - 2400
Fax:(440) 878 - 2959
TF: (800) 321 - 3997

Serves As:
- Chairman of the Board, Ceres Group, Inc.

RUHLEN, Stephen S.
800 Connecticut Ave. NW Tel: (202) 533 - 2100
Suite 950
Washington, DC 20006
Serves As:
• V. President and Director, Government Affairs, J. P. Morgan Chase & Co.

RUIZ, Angel
6300 Legacy Dr. Tel: (972) 583 - 0000
Plano, TX 75024 Fax:(972) 889 - 9846
Serves As:
• President and Chief Exec. Officer, Ericsson Inc.

RUIZ, Art
1900 M St. NW Tel: (202) 263 - 4400
Suite 730 Fax:(202) 263 - 4435
Washington, DC 20036
Serves As:
• Director, Federal Affairs, State Farm Insurance Cos.

RUIZ, Ph.D., Hector de J.
One AMD Pl. Tel: (408) 749 - 4000
P.O. Box 3453 TF: (800) 538 - 8450
Sunnyvale, CA 94088
Serves As:
• Chairman, President and Chief Exec. Officer, Advanced Micro Devices, Inc.

RUIZ, Laura M.
330 S. Fourth St. Tel: (804) 778 - 6005
Richmond, VA 23219 Fax:(804) 788 - 5688
laura_ruiz@albemarle.com
Serves As:
• Corporate Director, Investor Relations and Consumer Advocacy, Albemarle Corp.

RUMP, Rick
333 N. Summit St. Tel: (419) 252 - 5981
16th Floor. Fax:(419) 252 - 5596
Toledo, OH 43604-2617
rrump@hcr-manorcare.com
Serves As:
• Director, Corporate Communications, Manor Care, Inc.

RUNCIS, Veronica M.
Eaton Center Tel: (216) 523 - 4835
1111 Superior Ave. Fax:(216) 479 - 7013
Cleveland, OH 44114-2584
veronicaruncis@eaton.com
Serves As:
• Manager, Corporate Contributions, Eaton Corp.

RUNCK, Elise
Two World Financial Center Tel: (212) 667 - 9300
Building B Fax:(212) 667 - 1058
New York, NY 10028-1198
Serves As:
• Director, Human Resources, Nomura Securities Internat'l, Inc.

RUNDALL, Scott
1716 Locust St. Tel: (515) 284 - 2325
Des Moines, IA 50309-3023 Fax:(515) 284 - 3806
scott.rundall@meredith.com
Serves As:
• V. President, Human Resources, Meredith Corp.

RUNDE, James A.
1585 Broadway Tel: (212) 761 - 8413
New York, NY 10036 Fax:(212) 761 - 0086
Serves As:
• PAC Treasurer, Morgan Stanley

RUNGE, Lisa
2100 E. Grand Ave. Tel: (310) 615 - 1680
El Segundo, CA 90245 Fax:(310) 647 - 1801
lrunge@csc.com
Serves As:
• Manager, Investor Relations, Computer Sciences Corp.

RUNKEL, Jack
P.O. Box 57 Tel: (412) 456 - 6034
Pittsburgh, PA 15230-0057 Fax:(412) 456 - 6128
Serves As:
• V. President, Investor Relations; Chairman, H. J. Heinz Co. Foundation, H. J. Heinz Co.

RUNYAN, John C.
1101 Pennsylvania Ave. NW Tel: (202) 628 - 1223
Suite 200 Ext: 30
Washington, DC 20004 Fax:(202) 628 - 1368
john.runyan@ipaper.com
Registered Federal Lobbyist.
Serves As:
• Washington Representative, Internat'l Paper

RUPINSKI, Walter F.
1200 Wilson Blvd. Tel: (703) 465 - 3500
Arlington, VA 22209-2305
Serves As:
• V. President, Export Management and Compliance, The Boeing Co.

RUPP, Joseph D.
190 Carondelet Plaza Tel: (314) 480 - 1400
Suite 1530
Clayton, MO 63105-3443
Serves As:
• Chairman, President and Chief Exec. Officer, Olin Corp.

RUPPEL, Jim
P.O. Box 36611 Tel: (214) 792 - 4000
Dallas, TX 75235-1611 Fax:(214) 792 - 5099
Serves As:
• V. President, Customer Relations and Rapid Rewards, Southwest Airlines Co.

RUPRECHT, William
1334 York Ave. Tel: (212) 606 - 7000
New York, NY 10021 Fax:(212) 606 - 7107
Serves As:
• President and Chief Exec. Officer, Sotheby's Holdings, Inc.

RUSERT, Beth
1375 N. Highway Dr. Tel: (636) 827 - 2949
Fenton, MO 63099 Fax:(636) 827 - 8605
beth.rusert@maritz.com
Serves As:
• V. President, Public Relations and Corporate Communications Communications, Maritz Inc.

RUSH, Jerry
2135 W. Maple Rd. Tel: (248) 435 - 7907
Troy, MI 48084 Fax:(248) 435 - 1031
jerry.rush@arvinmeritor.com TF: (800) 535 - 5560
Serves As:
• Senior Director, Government Affairs and Community Relations, ArvinMeritor

RUSH, Jimmie
444 N. Capitol St., N.W., Suite 740 Tel: (202) 824 - 6504
Washington, DC 20001 Fax:(202) 824 - 6510
jrush@newscorp.com
Serves As:
• Manager, Government Relations, News Corporation Ltd.

RUSSACK, Richard A.
P.O. Box 961057 Tel: (817) 867 - 6425
Fort Worth, TX 76161-2830 Fax:(817) 352 - 7924
richard.russack@bnsf.com
Serves As:
• V. President, Corporate Relations; and President, Burlington Northern Santa Fe Foundation, Burlington Northern Santa Fe Corporation

RUSSELL, Alison
1441 Kapiolani Blvd. Tel: (808) 432 - 4983
17th Floor
Honolulu, HI 96814-4407
alison.x.russell@kp.org
Serves As:
• Media Representative - Hawaii Region, Kaiser Permanente

RUSSELL, Cheryl
1200 Wilson Blvd. Tel: (703) 465 - 3610
Arlington, VA 22209-2305
Serves As:
• Director, EXIM, OMB and Federal Affairs, The Boeing Co.

RUSSELL, Gene
P.O. Box 13287 Tel: (816) 467 - 3865
Kansas City, MO 64199-3287 Fax:(816) 467 - 9865
gene.russell@aquila.com
Serves As:
• Director, Environmental Services, Aquila, Inc.

RUSSELL, Jr., George A.
225 Franklin St. Tel: (617) 664 - 3866
Boston, MA 02110 Fax:(617) 451 - 6315
garussell@statestreet.com
Serves As:
• Exec. V. President, Community Affairs, State Street Corp.

RUSSELL, Judy
P.O. Box 391 Tel: (706) 576 - 2737
Columbus, GA 31902-0391 Fax:(775) 310 - 5435
TF: (800) 241 - 0431
Serves As:
• Director, Investor and Public Relations, Carmike Cinemas, Inc.

RUSSELL, Richard G.
100 Crystal A Dr.
P.O. Box 810
Hershey, PA 17033
rickrussell@hersheys.com
Tel: (717) 534 - 7547
Fax:(717) 534 - 7038

Serves As:
• Director, State and Local Government Relations, The Hershey Company

RUSSELL, Theresa A.
1101 Pennsylvania Ave. NW
Suite 1000
Washington, DC 20004
Tel: (202) 879 - 6871
Fax:(202) 783 - 4460

Serves As:
• Treasurer, Citigroup Inc. Federal/State PAC, Citigroup, Inc.

RUSSINOFF, Paul
800 Connecticut Ave. NW
Suite 800
Washington, DC 20006
Tel: (202) 457 - 8582
Fax:(202) 457 - 8861

Serves As:
• Director, State Policy, Time Warner Inc.

RUSSO, Dan
P.O. Box 68900
Seattle, WA 98168-0947
Tel: (206) 431 - 4513
Fax:(206) 431 - 5558

Serves As:
• Director, Marketing and Communications, (Horizon Air Industries), Alaska Air Group, Inc.

RUSSO, Jeanne
1500 Market St.
Philadelphia, PA 19102
Tel: (215) 981 - 8552
Fax:(215) 981 - 7790

Serves As:
• Director, Corporate Communications, Comcast Corporation

RUSSO, Patricia F.
600 Mountain Ave.
Murray Hill, NJ 07974-0636
Tel: (908) 582 - 8500
Fax:(908) 508 - 2576
TF: (888) 458 - 2368

Serves As:
• Chairman and Chief Exec. Officer, Lucent Technologies

RUSSO, Tony
550 Newport Center Dr.
Newport Beach, CA 92660
Tel: (949) 720 - 2471
Fax:(949) 720 - 2450

Serves As:
• PAC Contact, The Irvine Company

RUSSOM, Mary S.
P.O. Box 385014
Birmingham, AL 35238-5014
russomm@vmcmail.com
Tel: (205) 298 - 3229
Fax:(205) 298 - 2960

Serves As:
• Manager, Community Programs, Vulcan Materials Co.

RUST, Jr., Edward B.
One State Farm Plaza
Bloomington, IL 61710-0001
Tel: (309) 766 - 2871

Serves As:
• Chairman and Chief Exec. Officer, State Farm Insurance Cos.

RUSTAD, Dave
625 Fourth Ave. South
Minneapolis, MN 55415
dave.rustad@thrivent.com
Tel: (612) 340 - 7037
Fax:(612) 340 - 7373

Serves As:
• Senior Media Relations Specialist, Thrivent Financial for Lutherans

RUSZIN, Jr., Thomas E.
750 E. Pratt St.
16th Floor
Baltimore, MD 21202
thomas.e.ruszin@constellation.com
Tel: (410) 783 - 3610
Fax:(410) 783 - 3610
TF: (888) 460 - 2002

Serves As:
• V. President, Total Rewards and HR Services, Constellation Energy
Responsibilities include investor relations.

RUTER, Philip E.
1200 Wilson Blvd.
Arlington, VA 22209-2305
Tel: (703) 465 - 3665

Registered Federal Lobbyist.
Serves As:
• Deputy Legislative Affairs Director, The Boeing Co.

RUTHERFORD, Linda
P.O. Box 36611
Dallas, TX 75235-1611
Tel: (214) 792 - 4625

Serves As:
• Director, Public Relations, Southwest Airlines Co.

RUTT, Sheila M.
5995 Mayfair Rd.
P.O. Box 3077
North Canton, OH 44720-8077
Tel: (330) 490 - 4000
Fax:(330) 490 - 3794

Serves As:
• V. President, Chief Human Resources Officer, Diebold, Inc.

RUTTMAN, David C.
P.O. Box 3283
Tulsa, OK 74102-3283
Tel: (918) 560 - 3500
Fax:(918) 592 - 9492

Serves As:
• V. President, Human Resources, BlueCross BlueShield of Oklahoma

RYAN, Amy
14 Cambridge Center
Cambridge, MA 02142
Tel: (617) 914 - 6524
Fax:(617) 679 - 2617

Serves As:
• Associate Director, Public Affairs, Biogen Idec Inc.

RYAN, Arthur F.
751 Broad St.
Floor 24
Newark, NJ 07102-3777
Tel: (973) 802 - 6000
Fax:(973) 802 - 3128
TF: (800) THE - ROCK

Serves As:
• Chairman, President and Chief Exec. Officer, Prudential Financial

RYAN, Dan
1025 Connecticut Ave., N.W., Suite 910
Washington, DC 20036
Tel: (202) 467 - 5088

Registered Federal Lobbyist.
Serves As:
• Manager, Government and Safety Affairs, Mazda North American Operations

RYAN, Holly
P.O. Box 997
Ann Arbor, MI 48106-0997
ryanh@dominos.com
Tel: (734) 930 - 3030
Fax:(734) 930 - 4346

Serves As:
• Manager, Public Relations, Domino's Pizza, LLC
Responsibilities also include corporate philanthropy.

RYAN, James R.
6801 Rockledge Dr.
Bethesda, MD 20817-1877
Tel: (301) 897 - 6584
Fax:(301) 897 - 6919

Serves As:
• V. President, Investor Relations, Lockheed Martin Corp.

RYAN, Jimmy
1101 Pennsylvania Ave. NW
Suite 1000
Washington, DC 20004
Tel: (202) 879 - 6871
Fax:(202) 783 - 4460

Registered Federal Lobbyist.
Serves As:
• V. President, Federal Government Relations, Citigroup, Inc.

RYAN, John G.
655 15th St. NW
Suite 300
Washington, DC 20005
john.ryan@bms.com
Tel: (202) 783 - 0900
Fax:(202) 783 - 2308

Registered Federal Lobbyist.
Serves As:
• Senior Counsel and Director, Government Affairs, Bristol-Myers Squibb Co.

RYAN, John J.
One Penn Plaza
Second Floor
New York, NY 10119
Tel: (212) 465 - 5000
Fax:(212) 465 - 5096

Serves As:
• Senior V. President/Director, Human Resources, Parsons Brinckerhoff

RYAN, III, John T.
P.O. Box 426
Pittsburgh, PA 15230
john.ryan@msanet.com
Tel: (412) 967 - 3000
Fax:(412) 967 - 3452
TF: (800) 672 - 2222

Serves As:
• Chairman and Chief Exec. Officer, Mine Safety Appliances Co. (MSA)

RYAN, Mark
100 Bayer Rd.
Pittsburgh, PA 15205-9741
Tel: (412) 777 - 2000
TF: (800) 662 - 2927

Serves As:
• Senior V. President, Communications, Bayer Corporation

RYAN, Mary E. "Beth"
103 The Mayfair, 625 S. 14th St.
Lincoln, NE 68508

Serves As:
• Legislative Representative, Union Pacific Corp.

RYAN, Mary T.
1400 Opus Place
Suite 600
Downers Grove, IL 60515
maryan@corpatc.com
Tel: (630) 663 - 8283

Serves As:
• V. President, Communications and Investor Relations, Aftermarket Technology Corp.

RYAN, Patrick G.
200 E.Randolph St.
Chicago, IL 60601
Tel: (312) 381 - 1000
Fax:(312) 381 - 0240

Serves As:
• Executive Chairman, Aon Corp.

RYAN, Paul T.
82 Devonshire St.
Boston, MA 02109-3614
Tel: (617) 563 - 7000
Fax:(617) 476 - 6150

Serves As:
• PACs' Treasurer, FMR Corp.

RYAN, Thomas M.
One CVS Dr.
Woonsocket, RI 02895
Tel: (401) 765 - 1500
Fax:(401) 769 - 4488

Serves As:
• Chairman, President and Chief Exec. Officer, CVS

RYBARCZYK, Mark J.
90 Park Ave.
Tenth Floor
New York, NY 10016-1301
Tel: (212) 907 - 6000
Fax:(212) 907 - 6001

Serves As:
• Exec. V. President, Human Resources, The BISYS Group, Inc.

RYBKA, Stephen J.
P.O. Box 1464
Wall, NJ 07719
Tel: (732) 938 - 1280
Fax:(732) 938 - 2620

Serves As:
• Manager, Public Affairs, (New Jersey Natural Gas Co.), New Jersey Resources Corp.

RYDER, Beverly P.
2244 Walnut Grove Ave.
Rosemead, CA 91770
beverly.ryder@sce.com
Tel: (626) 302 - 2204
Fax:(626) 302 - 2240

Serves As:
• V. President, Community Involvement and Secretary, Edison Internat'l

RYDER, Thomas
Reader's Digest Rd.
Pleasantville, NY 10570-7000
thomas_ryder@rd.com
Tel: (914) 238 - 1000
Fax:(914) 238 - 4559
TF: (800) 234 - 9000

Serves As:
• Chairman and Chief Exec. Officer, Reader's Digest Ass'n, Inc.

RYERSE, Malcolm A. "Mac"
601 W. Riverside Ave.
Suite 1100
Spokane, WA 99201
Tel: (509) 835 - 1512
Fax:(509) 835 - 1566

Serves As:
• Secretary, Potlatch Corp.
Responsibilities include shareholder relations.

RYLAND, Julie S.
605 Richard Arrington Jr. Blvd. North
Birmingham, AL 35203-2707
Tel: (205) 326 - 8421
Fax:(205) 322 - 6895
TF: (800) 654 - 3206

Serves As:
• V. President, Investor Relations, Energen Corp.

RYMER, Gail
6801 Rockledge Dr.
Bethesda, MD 20817-1877
Tel: (301) 897 - 6293
Fax:(301) 897 - 6252

Serves As:
• Director, Corporate Affairs, Lockheed Martin Corp.
Responsibilities include corporate philanthropy.

RYND, John T.
13135 S. Dairy Ashford
Suite 800
Sugar Land, TX 77478
Tel: (281) 276 - 6100
Fax:(281) 491 - 2092

Serves As:
• V. President, Investor Relations, Noble Drilling Corp.

SA, Ph.D., Sophie
One Panasonic Way
Panazip 3G-7A
Secaucus, NJ 07094
Tel: (201) 392 - 4132
Fax:(201) 392 - 6910
TF: (888) 275 - 2995

Serves As:
• Exec. Director, The Panasonic Foundation, Matsushita Electric Corp. of America

SABIN, David C.
1955 Field Ct.
Lake Forest, IL 60045
Tel: (847) 803 - 4600
Fax:(847) 803 - 5629
TF: (800) 272 - 5629

Serves As:
• Chairman and Secretary, Salton, Inc.

SABIN, Joshua
60 Massachusetts Ave. NE
Washington, DC 20002
Tel: (202) 906 - 3000
Fax:(202) 906 - 3865

Serves As:
• Senior Government Affairs Officer-Midwest, Amtrak

SABLO, Thomas A. "Tony"
P.O. Box 98199
Washington, DC 20090-8199
Tel: (202) 857 - 7000
Fax:(202) 828 - 6679
TF: (800) 647 - 5463

Serves As:
• Senior V. President, Human Resources, Nat'l Geographic Soc.

SABO, Douglas
1908 New Hampshire Ave., NW
Washington, DC 20009
dsabo@nai.com
Tel: (202) 462 - 1976

Serves As:
• Director, Government and Community Relations, McAfee, Inc.
Responsibilities include corporate philanthropy.

SACHS, Lowell
1300 I St. NW
Suite 420 East
WAS02
Washington, DC 20005
lowell.sachs@sun.com
Tel: (202) 326 - 7520
Fax:(202) 326 - 7525

Registered Federal Lobbyist.
Serves As:
• Manager, Government Affairs, Sun Microsystems, Inc.

SACKS, Barbara
1133 19th St. NW
Washington, DC 20036
Tel: (202) 887 - 3830
Fax:(202) 887 - 3123

Registered Federal Lobbyist.
Serves As:
• Representative, MCI, Inc.

SADLER, Linda C.
Commonwealth Towers
1300 Wilson Blvd., Suite 200
Arlington, VA 22209-2307
lcsadler@collins.rockwell.com
Tel: (703) 516 - 8220
Fax:(703) 516 - 8295

Registered Federal Lobbyist.
Serves As:
• Director, Governmental and Regulatory Affairs, Rockwell Collins, Inc
• Representative, Rockwell Automation

SADLER, Jr., Robert E.
One M & T Plaza
Buffalo, NY 14203
Tel: (716) 842 - 5445
Fax:(716) 842 - 5839
TF: (800) 836 - 1500

Serves As:
• President and Chief Exec. Officer, M&T Bank Corporation

SADOWSKI, Peter T.
601 Riverside Ave.
Suite 220
Jacksonville, FL 32204
ptsadowski@fnf.com
Tel: (904) 854 - 8100

Serves As:
• Treasurer, Fidelity Nat'l Financial Inc. Political Action Committee, Fidelity Nat'l Financial, Inc.

SAFER, Will
One Panasonic Way
Secaucus, NJ 07094
saferw@us.panasonic.com
Tel: (201) 392 - 6124
Fax:(201) 392 - 6007
TF: (888) 275 - 2995

Serves As:
• Public Relations, Matsushita Electric Corp. of America

SAFFELL, Michelle A.
20511 Lake Forest Dr.
Lake Forest, CA 92630-7741
michelle.a.saffell@wdc.com
Tel: (949) 672 - 7908
Fax:(949) 672 - 5408

Serves As:
• Coordinator, Investor Relations, Western Digital Corp.

SAFRA, Jacob E.
Britannica Centre
310 S. Michigan Ave.
Chicago, IL 60604
Tel: (312) 347 - 7000
Fax:(312) 294 - 2158

Serves As:
• Chairman of the Board, Encyclopaedia Britannica, Inc.

SAFRIT, Barry
3525 Fairystone Park Hwy. Tel: (276) 629 - 6757
Bassett, VA 24055 Fax:(276) 629 - 6332

Serves As:
- V. President and Chief Financial Officer, Bassett Furniture Industries, Inc.

Responsibilities include investor relations.

SAGEHORN, Dave
P.O. Box 2566 Tel: (920) 235 - 9150
Oshkosh, WI 54903-2566 Fax:(920) 233 - 9251

Serves As:
- V. President, Business Development, Oshkosh Truck Corp.

Responsibilities include political action.

SAHLMAN, Rachel
P.O. Box 53999 Tel: (602) 250 - 2192
M/S 8585
Phoenix, AZ 85072-3999
rachel.sahlman@aps.com

Serves As:
- Leader, E-Business Communications, (Arizona Public Service Co.), Pinnacle West Capital Corp.

SAKS, Larry
333 Corporate Woods Pkwy. Tel: (847) 793 - 6909
Vernon Hills, IL 60061-3109 Fax:(847) 913 - 8766
lsaks@zebra.com TF: (800) 423 - 0422

Serves As:
- Director, Human Resources, Zebra Technologies Corp.

SAKURAI, Motoatsu
655 Third Ave. Tel: (212) 605 - 2000
New York, NY 10017 Fax:(212) 605 - 2597
motoatsu.sakurai@mitsubishicorp.com

Serves As:
- President and Chief Exec. Officer, Mitsubishi International Corporation

SALAMIDO, Gary J.
P.O. Box 13398 Tel: (919) 363 - 7853
Research Triangle Park, NC 27709 Fax:(919) 315 - 6049

Serves As:
- PAC Treasurer, GlaxoSmithKline Research and Development

SALAMON, Lisa
101 E. State St. Tel: (610) 444 - 8433
Kennett Square, PA 19348 Fax:(610) 925 - 4242
lisa.salamon@genesishcc.com

Serves As:
- Director, Public Relations, Genesis HealthCare Corp.

SALAVANTIS, Peter J.
1560 Wilson Blvd. Tel: (703) 276 - 3519
Suite 1175 Fax:(703) 276 - 8168
Suite 1175
Arlington, VA 22209
pater.salavantis@meus.mea.com

Serves As:
- V. President, Public Affairs, Mitsubishi Electric & Electronics USA

SALEM, Richard
P.O. Box 1000 Fax:(973) 487 - 2052
Montville, NJ 07045 TF: (800) 237 - 5392
richard_salem@berlex.com

Serves As:
- V. President, Public Relations and Marketing Services, Berlex, Inc.

SALEMI, Hank
11501 Northeast Exwy. Tel: (405) 475 - 2500
Oklahoma City, OK 73131-6499 Fax:(405) 475 - 2558

Serves As:
- Senior V. President, Marketing, Six Flags, Inc.

Responsibilities include public relations.

SALETTA, Jill
Three Lakes Dr. Tel: (847) 646 - 5808
Northfield, IL 60093-2753 Fax:(847) 646 - 6005

Serves As:
- Senior Manager, Corporate Affairs, Kraft Foods, Inc.

SALINAS, Susan
155 S. Limerick Rd. Tel: (610) 948 - 5100
Limerick, PA 19468 Fax:(610) 948 - 0811

Serves As:
- Director, Safety and Environmental Affairs, Teleflex Inc.

SALINGER, Frank M.
1301 Pennsylvania Ave. NW Tel: (202) 347 - 1289
Suite 500 Fax:(202) 347 - 6876
M/S DCC
Washington, DC 20004-1701
fsalinger@advanta.com

Serves As:
- V. President, Government Relations, Advanta Corp.

SALISBURY, Keith
2011 Crystal Dr., Crystal Park 1 Tel: (703) 769 - 6202
Suite 907 Fax:(703) 892 - 0091
Arlington, VA 22202
salisbury_keith@emc.com

Registered Federal Lobbyist.
Serves As:
- Director, Government Affairs, EMC Corp.

SALISBURY, Randy
The Lenox Bldg., Suite 700 Tel: (404) 262 - 8461
3399 Peachtree Rd. NE
Atlanta, GA 30326
randy.salisbury@premiereglobal.com

Serves As:
- Exec. V. President and Chief Marketing Officer, Premiere Global Services, Inc.

Reponsibilities include media relations.

SALMON, Scott R.
1101 Pennsylvania Ave. NW Tel: (202) 783 - 6797
Suite 510 Fax:(202) 783 - 6309
Washington, DC 20004

Registered Federal Lobbyist.
Serves As:
- Managing Director, Government Affairs--Europe, United States Steel Corporation

SALMON, Shannon
1350 I St. NW Tel: (202) 589 - 1000
Suite 1210 Fax:(202) 408 - 9490
Washington, DC 20005-3305
ssalmon@corus.jnj.com

Registered Federal Lobbyist.
Serves As:
- V. President, Federal Affairs, Johnson & Johnson

SALOMON, Catherine
Two N. Riverside Plaza Tel: (312) 928 - 1282
Suite 400 Fax:(312) 454 - 9588
Chicago, IL 60606

Serves As:
- Director, Corporate Human Resources, Equity Residential

SALOP, Mike A.
333 Continental Blvd. Tel: (310) 252 - 2000
El Segundo, CA 90245-5012 Fax:(310) 252 - 2180

Serves As:
- V. President, Investor Relations, Mattel, Inc.

SALTZMAN, Joyce
201 Isabella St. Tel: (412) 553 - 4467
Pittsburgh, PA 15212-5858 Fax:(412) 553 - 4498
joyce.saltzman@alcoa.com

Serves As:
- Media Contact, Alcoa Inc.

SALVAS, Betty
P.O. Box 593330 Tel: (407) 245 - 6734
Orlando, FL 32859 Fax:(407) 245 - 4462
bsalvas@darden.com

Serves As:
- Corporate Relations Representative, Darden Restaurants, Inc.

SAMBATARO, Jr., Joseph P.
P.O. Box 2910 Tel: (253) 383 - 9101
Tacoma, WA 98401-2910 TF: (800) 610 - 8920

Serves As:
- Chief Exec. Officer, Labor Ready, Inc.

SAMENUK, George
3965 Freedom Circle Tel: (408) 346 - 5101
Santa Clara, CA 95054 TF: (800) 338 - 8754
gsamenuk@mcafee.com

Serves As:
- Chairman and Chief Exec. Officer, McAfee, Inc.

SAMMIS, Elizabeth
Four Taft Ct. Tel: (301) 838 - 5638
Rockville, MD 20850 Fax:(301) 545 - 5972
bsammis@mamsi.com

Serves As:
- Senior V. President, Corporate Communications, Mid Atlantic Medical Services Inc.

SAMMONS, Christopher D.
4171 Essen Lane
Baton Rouge, LA 70809
Tel: (225) 932 - 2546
Fax:(225) 932 - 2661
TF: (800) 747 - 3322

Serves As:
- V. President, Investor Relations and Corporate Communications, The Shaw Group Inc.

SAMMONS, Mary
P.O. Box 3165
Harrisburg, PA 17105
Tel: (717) 761 - 2633

Serves As:
- President and Chief Exec. Officer, Rite Aid Corp.

SAMOLUK, Thomas E.
P.O. Box 111
Boston, MA 02117
Tel: (617) 572 - 1300
Fax:(617) 572 - 1545

Serves As:
- V. President, Government Relations, John Hancock Financial Services

SAMORA, Jr., Joseph E.
1001 G St. NW
Suite 100 East
Washington, DC 20001
Tel: (202) 737 - 7575
Fax:(202) 737 - 9090

Registered Federal Lobbyist.
Serves As:
- Senior V. President; PAC Treasurer, Case New Holland Inc.

SAMPLE, Bill
1401 I St., NW
Suite 500
Washington, DC 20005
Tel: (202) 263 - 5900
Fax:(202) 263 - 5902

Registered Federal Lobbyist.
Serves As:
- Representative, Microsoft Corporation

SAMPSON, John
1401 I St., NW
Suite 500
Washington, DC 20005
Tel: (202) 263 - 5900
Fax:(202) 263 - 5902

Registered Federal Lobbyist.
Serves As:
- Manager, Federal Government Affairs, Microsoft Corporation

SAMUEL, Joe
6200 S. Quebec St.
Greenwood Village, CO 80111
Tel: (303) 967 - 7195
Fax:(303) 967 - 6705

Registered Federal Lobbyist.
Serves As:
- V. President, Government Relations, First Data

SAMUELI, Ph.D., Henry
P.O. Box 57013
Irvine, CA 92619-7013
Tel: (949) 450 - 8700
Fax:(949) 450 - 8710

Serves As:
- Chairman of the Board, Broadcom Corp.

SAMUELS, Alexandra
100 Independence Mall West
Philadelphia, PA 19106-2399
Tel: (215) 592 - 3644
Fax:(215) 592 - 6808

Serves As:
- Manager, Rohm and Haas Corporate Social Investment, Rohm and Haas Co.

SAMUELS, Gary
One Malcolm Ave.
Teterboro, NJ 07608
media@questdiagnostics.com
Tel: (201) 393 - 8363
Fax:(201) 393 - 4755
TF: (800) 222 - 0446

Serves As:
- V. President, External Communications, Quest Diagnostics Inc.

SANBORN, Sally
P.O. Box 4278
Modesto, CA 95352
ssanborn@savemart.com
Tel: (209) 574 - 6226
Fax:(209) 577 - 3845

Serves As:
- Director, Marketing, Save Mart Supermarkets

Responsibilities include corporate communications and government affairs.

SANCHEZ, Jose L.
1155 Westmoreland, Suite 234
El Paso, TX 79925
Tel: (915) 771 - 8856

Serves As:
- Director, Governmental Affairs, Southwest Airlines Co.

SANCHEZ, Judy
111 Ponce de Leon Ave.
Clewiston, FL 33440
Tel: (863) 983 - 8121
Fax:(863) 983 - 9827

Serves As:
- Director, Corporate Communications, United States Sugar Corp.

SANDER, Raymond J.
1501 K St. NW
Suite 575
Washington, DC 20005
Tel: (202) 654 - 2950
Fax:(202) 654 - 2955

Registered Federal Lobbyist.
Serves As:
- Senior V. President, N.Y. Life International, New York Life Insurance Co.

SANDERS, Allison
200 Old Wilson Bridge Rd.
Columbus, OH 43085
Tel: (614) 438 - 3133
Fax:(614) 438 - 3136

Serves As:
- Manager, Investor Relations, Worthington Industries

SANDERS, Gary A.
4200 Wackenhut Dr.
Palm Beach Gardens, FL 33410-4243
Tel: (561) 622 - 5656
Fax:(561) 691 - 6738
TF: (800) 922 - 6488

Serves As:
- Chairman and Chief Exec. Officer, The Wackenhut Corporation

SANDERS, Greg
1776 I St. NW
Suite 1000
Washington, DC 20006-3707
Tel: (202) 785 - 4888
Fax:(202) 457 - 6597

Serves As:
- Director, International Affairs, BP

SANDERS, Joshua
2436 Pennsylvania Ave.
Suite 4
Weirton, WV 26062
Tel: (304) 723 - 1016
Fax:(304) 723 - 4377

Serves As:
- Regional Manager, State Government Relations/Mid-Atlantic, UST Inc.

SANDERS, Leslie D.
Two N. Jackson St.
Montgomery, AL 36104
Tel: (334) 223 - 5405

Serves As:
- Director, Constituency Relations, Alabama Power Co.

SANDERS, Manda
120 Fifth Ave. Pl.
Suite 2628
Pittsburgh, PA 15222
Tel: (412) 544 - 8030
Fax:(412) 544 - 5318

Serves As:
- Government Affairs Representative, (Clarity Vision, Inc., Highmark Life and Casualty Group, Inc., United Concordia Cos., Inc.), Highmark Inc.

SANDHERR, Cynthia C.
1808 I St. NW
Eighth Floor
Washington, DC 20006
Tel: (202) 223 - 4817
Fax:(202) 296 - 0011

Registered Federal Lobbyist.
Serves As:
- Director, Washington Public Affairs, Deere & Company

SANDLER, Herbert M.
1901 Harrison St.
Oakland, CA 94612
Tel: (510) 446 - 3420
Fax:(510) 446 - 4259

Serves As:
- Co-Chairman and Co-Chief Exec. Officer, Golden West Financial Corp.

SANDLER, Marion O.
1901 Harrison St.
Oakland, CA 94612
Tel: (510) 446 - 3420
Fax:(510) 446 - 4259

Serves As:
- Co-Chairman and Co-Chief Exec. Officer, Golden West Financial Corp.

SANDLIN, Scott
P.O. Drawer 2128
Dalton, GA 30722-2128
Tel: (706) 278 - 3812
Fax:(706) 275 - 1719

Serves As:
- V. President, Marketing and Communications, Shaw Industries

SANDS, Richard
370 Woodcliff Dr.
Suite 300
Fairport, NY 14450
richard.sands@cbrands.com
Tel: (585) 218 - 3669
TF: (888) 724 - 2169

Serves As:
- Chairman and Chief Exec. Officer, Constellation Brands, Inc.

SANFORD, Daniel
201 Mission St.
San Francisco, CA 94105
Tel: (415) 543 - 0404
Fax:(415) 278 - 6028

Serves As:
- Senior V. President; PAC Treasurer, Providian Financial Corp.

SANFORD, Jill
1801 California St.
50th Floor
Denver, CO 80202
Tel: (303) 992 - 1400
Fax:(303) 992 - 1724
TF: (800) 899 - 7780

Serves As:
- Chief Human Resources Officer, Qwest Communications

SANGER, Stephen W.
One General Mills Blvd.
Minneapolis, MN 55426
Tel: (763) 764 - 7600

Serves As:
- Chairman and Chief Exec. Officer, General Mills

SANNINO, Louis J.
757 N. Eldridge
Houston, TX 77079
Tel: (281) 870 - 5011
Fax:(281) 870 - 5045

Serves As:
- Senior V. President, Human Resources and Corporate Compliance Officer, McDermott Internat'l, Inc.

SANSOT, Karen
209 Redwood Shores Pkwy.
Redwood City, CA 94065-1175
Tel: (650) 628 - 5597
Fax:(650) 628 - 1415

Serves As:
- Director, Investor Relations, Electronic Arts Inc.

SANSOUCIE, Lori
N56 W17000 Ridgewood Dr.
Menomonee Falls, WI 53051
Tel: (262) 703 - 6572
Fax:(262) 703 - 6501

Serves As:
- Manager, Public Relations, Kohl's Corp.

SANTANASTO, James A.
Two N. Ninth St.
Allentown, PA 18101-1179
jasantanasto@pplweb.com
Tel: (610) 774 - 5910
Fax:(610) 774 - 5281
TF: (800) 345 - 3085

Serves As:
- Manager, Employee and Marketing Communications, PPL Corp.

SANTINI, Gino
Lilly Corporate Center
Indianapolis, IN 46285
Tel: (317) 276 - 2000
Fax:(317) 277 - 6579

Serves As:
- Senior V. President, Corporate Strategy and Policy, Eli Lilly and Company

SANTOS, Barbara J.
555 12th St. NW
Suite 640
Washington, DC 20004-1200
santosbj@sce.com
Tel: (202) 393 - 3075
Fax:(202) 393 - 1497

Serves As:
- Government Relations Assistant, Southern California Edison, an Edison Internat'l Co.
- Government Relations Assistant, Edison Internat'l

SANTOS, Jerry
200 Park Ave.
Suite 300
Florham Park, NJ 07932
jerry.santos@globalcrossing.com
Tel: (973) 937 - 0100
Fax:(973) 360 - 0148
TF: (800) 336 - 7000

Serves As:
- Senior V. President, Corporate Communications, Global Crossing Ltd.

SAPADIN, Glenn
100 Park Ave., Suite 2705
New York, NY 10017
Tel: (212) 685 - 4030
Fax:(212) 213 - 0159

Serves As:
- Manager, Investor Relations, Ericsson Inc.

SAPERSTEIN, Steve
26877 Tourney Rd.
Valencia, CA 91355
steve.saperstein@borax.com
Tel: (661) 287 - 5400
Fax:(661) 287 - 5495

Serves As:
- Chief Human Resources Officer, U.S. Borax Inc.

SARGEANT, Timothy J.
101 Constitution Ave. NW
Washington, DC 20080
tsargeant@washgas.com
Tel: (703) 750 - 2000
Fax:(703) 750 - 4574

Serves As:
- Media Spokesperson, Washington Gas

SARGENT, Ronald L.
500 Staples Dr.
Framingham, MA 01702
ron.sargent@staples.com
Tel: (508) 253 - 5000
Ext: 37510

Serves As:
- Chief Exec. Officer and Chairman of the Board, Staples, Inc.

SARGIS, Donna
1133 19th St. NW
Washington, DC 20036
Tel: (202) 887 - 3830
Fax:(202) 887 - 3123

Serves As:
- Regulatory Affairs, MCI, Inc.

SARTAIN, Libby
701 First Ave.
Sunnyvale, CA 94089
Tel: (408) 731 - 3300
Fax:(408) 616 - 3301

Serves As:
- Senior V. President, Human Resources, Yahoo! Inc.

SARVADI, Paul J.
19001 Crescent Springs Dr.
Kingwood, TX 77339-3802
Tel: (281) 358 - 8986
TF: (800) 237 - 3170

Serves As:
- Chairman and Chief Exec. Officer, Administaff, Inc.

SASSER, Bob
500 Volvo Pkwy.
Chesapeake, VA 23320
Tel: (757) 321 - 5000
Fax:(757) 321 - 5292

Serves As:
- Chief Exec. Officer, Dollar Tree Stores, Inc.

SASSO, Greg W.
P.O. Box 587
Warsaw, IN 46581-0587
greg.sasso@biometmail.com
Tel: (574) 372 - 1528
Fax:(574) 267 - 8137

Serves As:
- V. President, Corporate Development and Communications, Biomet Inc.

SATO, Peggy A.
528 Cottage St., N.E., Suite 1B
Salem, OR 97301
Tel: (503) 378 - 1576

Serves As:
- Regional Manager, Government Affairs, Georgia-Pacific Corp.

SATTLER, Ryan J.
P.O. Box 2821
York, PA 17405-2821
Tel: (717) 757 - 7660
Fax:(717) 751 - 3196

Serves As:
- Senior V. President, Human Resources, The Bon Ton Stores, Inc.

Responsibilities include corporate philanthropy.

SAUCIER, Christine
9555 Delegates Row
Indianapolis, IN 46240
Tel: (317) 581 - 3400

Serves As:
- Legislative Representative, Farmers Group, Inc.

SAUER, Ann E.
1550 Crystal Dr.
Crystal Square 2, Suite 300
Arlington, VA 22202
Tel: (703) 413 - 5601
Fax:(703) 413 - 5636

Serves As:
- V. President, Navy, Marine Corps, Coast Guard and Air Force, SI Programs, Lockheed Martin Corp.

SAUER, Matthew A.
1600 E. St. Andrews Pl.
Santa Ana, CA 92705
Tel: (714) 566 - 1000
Fax:(714) 566 - 7900

Serves As:
- Senior V. President, Human Resources, Ingram Micro, Inc.

SAUER, Nancy L.
14141 Southwest Fwy.
Sugar Land, TX 77478-3435
nsauer@unocal.com
Tel: (281) 287 - 5826
Fax:(281) 287 - 5162

Serves As:
- State Government Relations Director, UNOCAL Corp.

SAUNDERS, Joseph
201 Mission St.
San Francisco, CA 94105
Tel: (415) 543 - 0404
Fax:(415) 278 - 6028

Serves As:
- Chairman, President and Chief Exec. Officer, Providian Financial Corp.

SAUVE, Kathleen A.
P.O. Box 2521
Houston, TX 77252-2521
kasauve@teppco.com
Tel: (713) 759 - 3635
Fax:(713) 759 - 3957
TF: (800) 877 - 3636

Serves As:
- Director, Public and Media Relations, Texas Eastern Products Pipeline Company, LLC (TEPPCO)

SAVERCOOL, John
1501 K St. NW
Suite 1100
Washington, DC 20005
Tel: (202) 585 - 4000

Registered Federal Lobbyist.
Serves As:
- Exec. Director and Senior Lobbyist, UBS Americas, UBS Financial Services Inc.

SAVILLE, Paul C.
7601 Lewinsville Rd., Suite 300
McLean, VA 22102
Tel: (703) 761 - 2000
Fax:(703) 761 - 2030

Serves As:
- Chief Exec. Officer, NVR, Inc.

SAVNER, David
2941 Fairview Park Dr.
Falls Church, VA 22042-4513
Tel: (703) 876 - 3000
Fax:(703) 876 - 3125

Serves As:
- Senior V. President and General Counsel, General Dynamics Corporation

SAVNER, Richard
200 Milik St.
Carteret, NJ 07008-1194
Tel: (732) 499 - 4327
Fax:(732) 499 - 3072

Serves As:
- Director, Public Affairs, Pathmark Stores Inc.

Responsibilities include corporate communications, government affairs, and corporate philanthropy.

SAVOIA, Sally A.
39 Old Ridgebury Rd.
Danbury, CT 06810-5113
Tel: (203) 837 - 2000
Fax:(203) 837 - 2505
TF: (800) 772 - 9247

Serves As:
- V. President, Human Resources, Praxair, Inc.

SAWYER, Chris
P.O. Box 10247
Birmingham, AL 35202
Tel: (205) 326 - 7100
Fax:(205) 244 - 2897
TF: (800) 734 - 4667

Serves As:
- Treasurer, Regions Financial Corp. Political Action Committee, Regions Financial Corp.

SAYE-ARMIJO, Stephanie
DWF Airport Station, P.O. Box 619100
Dallas, TX 75261-9100
sarmijo@kcc.com
Tel: (972) 281 - 1443
Fax:(972) 281 - 1490
TF: (800) 639 - 1352

Serves As:
- Corporate Communications Contact, Kimberly-Clark Corp.

SAYEGH, Eli
1941 Ringwood Ave.
San Jose, CA 95131-1721
Tel: (408) 451 - 1865
Fax:(408) 451 - 1694

Serves As:
- Director, Investor Relations, Bell Microproducts, Inc.

SAYERS, Richard
6065 Parkland Blvd.
Cleveland, OH 44124
rick.sayers@agilysys.com
Tel: (440) 720 - 8675
Fax:(440) 720 - 8501
TF: (800) 422 - 2400

Serves As:
- Exec. V. President, Chief Human Resources Officer, Agilysys, Inc.

SAYLES, Helen E. R.
175 Berkeley St.
Boston, MA 02116
Tel: (617) 357 - 9500
Fax:(617) 350 - 7648

Serves As:
- Senior V. President, Human Resources and Administration, Liberty Mutual Insurance Co.

SAYLES, Thomas S.
101 Ash St.
HQ18
San Diego, CA 92101-3017
tsayles@sempra.com
Tel: (619) 696 - 4614
Fax:(619) 696 - 9202
TF: (877) 736 - 7721

Serves As:
- V. President, Governmental and Community Affairs, Sempra Energy

SAYNOR, Joan
P.O. Box 199000
Dallas, TX 75219-9000
jsaynor@centex.com
Tel: (214) 981 - 6636
Fax:(214) 981 - 6859

Serves As:
- Manager, Community Relations, Centex Corporation

SAYRE, Peter B.
751 Broad St.
Third Floor
Newark, NJ 07102-3777
peter.sayre@prudential.com
Tel: (973) 802 - 6000
Fax:(973) 802 - 6303
TF: (800) THE - ROCK

Serves As:
- Treasurer, Prudential Financial Inc. PAC, Prudential Financial

SAZAWAL, Vijay
Two Democracy Center
6903 Rockledge Dr.
Bethesda, MD 20817-1818
Tel: (301) 564 - 3200
Fax:(301) 564 - 3201

Registered Federal Lobbyist.
Serves As:
- Representative, USEC Inc.

SCADUTO, James A.
P.O. Box 300
Princeton, NJ 08543
Tel: (609) 520 - 4701

Serves As:
- V. President, Human Resources, Dow Jones and Co.

SCALERA, Ciro
540 Broad St.
Newark, NJ 07101
Tel: (973) 649 - 3186
Fax:(973) 624 - 7410

Serves As:
- Director, Public Affairs, Verizon New Jersey, Inc.

SCAMINACE, Joseph M. "Joe"
127 Public Square
1500 Key Tower
Cleveland, OH 44114-1221
Tel: (216) 781 - 0083
Fax:(216) 781 - 1502
TF: (800) 519 - 0083

Serves As:
- Chairman of the Board, OM Group, Inc.

SCARBOROUGH, Dean A.
150 N. Orange Grove Blvd.
Pasadena, CA 91103
Tel: (626) 304 - 2000
Fax:(626) 792 - 7312

Serves As:
- President and Chief Exec. Officer, Avery Dennison Corp.

SCARBOROUGH, Jim
P.O. Box 35167
Houston, TX 77235
jscarborough@stagestoresinc.com
Tel: (713) 667 - 5601
Fax:(713) 295 - 5486
TF: (800) 324 - 3244

Serves As:
- Chairman, President and Chief Exec. Officer, Stage Stores, Inc.

SCARBOROUGH, Stephen J.
15326 Alton Pkwy.
Irvine, CA 92618
Tel: (949) 789 - 1600
Fax:(949) 789 - 1609

Serves As:
- Chairman and Chief Exec. Officer, Standard Pacific Corp.

SCARDINO, Kim
1133 19th St. NW
Washington, DC 20036
Tel: (202) 736 - 6478
Fax:(202) 887 - 3123

Serves As:
- Director, Federal Regulatory Affairs, MCI, Inc.

SCARDOELLI, Harley
P.O. Box 31328
Tampa, FL 33631-3328
hscardoe@gerdauameristeel.com
Tel: (813) 207 - 2372
Fax:(813) 207 - 2251

Serves As:
- Investment Relations Contact, Gerdau Ameristeel Corp.

SCARRY, Robert D.
750 First St. NE
suite 1070
Washington, DC 20002
Tel: (202) 216 - 1780

Serves As:
- PAC Treasurer, Bunge Ltd.

SCARTH, Victoria
33 Commercial St.
Foxboro, MA 02035
Tel: (508) 549 - 2424
Fax:(508) 549 - 4999
TF: (866) 746 - 6477

Serves As:
- Senior V. President, Group Marketing and Communications, Invensys Systems, Inc.

SCATURRO, Peter K.
114 W. 47th St.
New York, NY 10036
Tel: (212) 852 - 1000
Fax:(212) 852 - 1140

Serves As:
- Chairman and Chief Exec. Officer, U.S. Trust Corp.

SCEPPAGUERCIO, Maria A.

237 Park Ave.
New York, NY 10017
Tel: (212) 527 - 5230

Serves As:
- Senior V. President, Investor Relations, Revlon, Inc.

SCHAAF, Steve

P.O. Box 14453
Des Moines, IA 50306-3453
Tel: (515) 248 - 4800
Fax:(515) 248 - 4842
TF: (800) 247 - 6803

Serves As:
- Program Manager, Community Investment, Pioneer Hi-Bred Internat'l, Inc.

SCHACHER, Alden

101 California St.
10th Floor
San Francisco, CA 94111
alden.schacher@eds.com
Tel: (415) 912 - 5250
Fax:(415) 912 - 5399

Serves As:
- Regional Director, State Government Affairs, West, EDS Corp.

SCHAEFER, Barbara W.

1400 Douglas St.
Omaha, NE 68179
Tel: (402) 544 - 5747

Serves As:
- Senior V. President, Human Resources, Union Pacific Corp.

SCHAEFER, Jr., George A.

38 Fountain Square
Cincinnati, OH 45263
Tel: (513) 579 - 5300
Fax:(513) 579 - 5226
TF: (800) 972 - 3030

Serves As:
- President and Chief Exec. Officer, Fifth Third Bancorp.

SCHAEFFER, Leonard D.

120 Monument Circle
Indianapolis, IN 46204
Tel: (317) 532 - 6000

Serves As:
- Chairman of the Board, Wellpoint, Inc.

SCHAFER, Agnes

P.O. Box 909700
Kansas City, MO 64190-9700
Tel: (816) 801 - 6455
Fax:(816) 801 - 6590

Serves As:
- V. President, Communications and Public Relations, Dairy Farmers of America, Inc.

SCHAFER, Dan A.

P.O. Box 1734
Atlanta, GA 30301
Tel: (404) 676 - 2121
Fax:(404) 676 - 6792

Serves As:
- Director, North American Communications, The Coca-Cola Co.

SCHAFFER, Amy E.

1100 Connecticut Ave. NW
Suite 530
Washington, DC 20036
Tel: (202) 293 - 7222
Fax:(202) 293 - 2955

Registered Federal Lobbyist.
Serves As:
- Manager, Federal Regulatory Affairs, Weyerhaeuser Co.

SCHAFFER, III, Archie

P.O. Box 2020
Springdale, AR 72765-2020
archie.schffer@tyson.com
Tel: (479) 290 - 7232
Fax:(479) 290 - 7984
TF: (800) 643 - 3410

Serves As:
- Senior V. President, External Relations, Tyson Foods, Inc.

Responsibilities include corporate contributions.

SCHAFFER, Laurie

555 12th St., NW
Suite 740 North
Washington, DC 20004
Tel: (202) 638 - 3750

Registered Federal Lobbyist.
Serves As:
- Representative, The Charles Schwab Corp.

SCHAFFER, Quentin M.

1100 Ave. of the Americas
New York, NY 10036
quentin.schaffer@hbo.com
Tel: (212) 512 - 1329
Fax:(212) 512 - 1182

Serves As:
- Senior V. President, Corporate Communications, Home Box Office (HBO)

SCHAFFNER, Tom

5200 Sheila St.
Commerce, CA 90040
Tel: (323) 264 - 5200
Ext: 4150
Fax:(323) 265 - 4261

Serves As:
- Contact Communications, Unified Western Grocers, Inc.

SCHALK, Bill

110 E. Wayne St.
Fort Wayne, IN 46802
Tel: (269) 465 - 6101

Serves As:
- Public Affairs Contact, (Indiana Michigan Power Co.), American Electric Power Co. Inc.

SCHANTZ, Victoria

750 First St. NE
suite 1070
Washington, DC 20002
Tel: (202) 216 - 1780

Registered Federal Lobbyist.
Serves As:
- Representative, Bunge Ltd.

SCHAR, Dwight C.

7601 Lewinsville Rd., Suite 300
McLean, VA 22102
Tel: (703) 761 - 2000
Fax:(703) 761 - 2030

Serves As:
- Chairman of the Board, NVR, Inc.

SCHARP, Anders

1111 Adams Ave.
Norristown, PA 19403-2403
anders.scharp@skf.com
Tel: (610) 630 - 2800
Fax:(610) 630 - 2801

Serves As:
- Chairman of the Board, SKF USA, Inc.

SCHARTON, Yolanda M.

P.O. Box 990
Minneapolis, MN 55440
Tel: (952) 828 - 4000
Fax:(952) 828 - 8998

Serves As:
- V. President, Investor Relations and Corporate Communications, Supervalu Inc.

SCHAUB, Patricia A.

800 Cabin Hill Dr.
Greensburg, PA 15601
pschaub@alleghenyenergy.com
Tel: (724) 837 - 3000

Registered Federal Lobbyist.
Serves As:
- V. President, External Affairs, Allegheny Energy Inc.

SCHAUER, Robert

One AT&T Way
2347H3
Bedminster, NJ 07921-0752
rschauer@att.com
Tel: (908) 234 - 3020

Serves As:
- V. President, Public Relations - Public Policy, AT&T

SCHAVIEN, Lee

8326 Century Park
San Diego, CA 92123
Tel: (619) 696 - 2000
Fax:(619) 696 - 1868

Serves As:
- V. President, Regulatory Affairs, San Diego Gas and Electric Co.

SCHEIBEL, John

2000 Pennsylvania Ave. NW
Suite 4200
Washington, DC 20006
scheibel@yahoo-inc.com
Tel: (202) 887 - 6932
Fax:(202) 887 - 6933

Registered Federal Lobbyist.
Serves As:
- V. President, Public Policy, Yahoo! Inc.

Responsibilities also include political action.

SCHEID, Jay

435 N. Michigan Ave.
Chicago, IL 60611
jscheid@tribune.com
Tel: (312) 222 - 4567

Serves As:
- Director, Environmental Safety and Risk Management, Tribune Co.

SCHEIN, Chris

P.O. Box 227097
Dallas, TX 75222-7097
Tel: (214) 812 - 5338
Fax:(214) 812 - 3176

Serves As:
- Director, Media and Public Relations, TXU

SCHEIN, Steve M.

211 Riverside Dr.
Evansville, IN 47708-1251
sschein@vectren.com
Tel: (812) 491 - 4000
Fax:(812) 491 - 4078
TF: (800) 227 - 1376

Serves As:
- V. President, Investor Relations, Vectren Corp.

SCHELLHAS, Robert
1101 Pennsylvania Ave. NW
Suite 1000
Washington, DC 20004
Tel: (202) 879 - 6814
Fax:(202) 783 - 4460

Registered Federal Lobbyist.
Serves As:
- V. President, Federal Government Affairs, Citigroup, Inc.

SCHENK, Ernest J.
515 Eastern Ave.
Allegan, MI 49010-9070
eschenk@perrigo.com
Tel: (269) 673 - 9212
Fax:(269) 673 - 9128

Serves As:
- Manager, Investor Relations and Communications, Perrigo Co.

SCHER, Barry F.
6300 Sheriff Rd.
Landover, MD 20785
bscher@aholdusa.com
Tel: (301) 341 - 4710
Fax:(301) 618 - 4967

Serves As:
- V. President, Public Affairs, Giant Food LLC

SCHER, Norman A.
1100 Boulders Pkwy.
Richmond, VA 23225-4035
Tel: (804) 330 - 1000
Fax:(804) 330 - 1177

Serves As:
- President and Chief Exec. Officer, Tredegar Corp.

SCHERER, Rachel
710 Medtronic Pkwy.
Minneapolis, MN 55432-5604
Tel: (763) 505 - 2694
Fax:(763) 514 - 6272
TF: (800) 328 - 2518

Serves As:
- Director, Investor Relations, Medtronic, Inc.

SCHERER, Skip
1144 E. Market St.
Akron, OH 44316-0001
wkscherer@goodyear.com
Tel: (330) 796 - 1054
Fax:(330) 796 - 1817

Serves As:
- Manager, Communications, Engineered and Chemical Products, The Goodyear Tire & Rubber Company

SCHERMERHORN, Todd C.
730 Central Ave.
Murray Hill, NJ 07974
todd.schermerhorn@crbard.com
Tel: (908) 277 - 8139
Fax:(908) 277 - 8078
TF: (800) 367 - 2273

Serves As:
- Senior V. President and Chief Financial Officer, C. R. Bard, Inc.

Responsibilities include corporate communications, investor relations, and political action.

SCHEV, Meg
500 Water St.
Jacksonville, FL 32203
Tel: (904) 366 - 2949

Serves As:
- Regional Media Contact, CSX Corp.

SCHEXNAYDER, Alexandra
P.O. Box 26234
Richmond, VA 23260-6234
alexandra.schexnayder@sscoop.com
Tel: (804) 281 - 1368
Fax:(804) 281 - 1119

Serves As:
- Manager, Corporate Communications, Southern States Cooperative

SCHEXNAYDER, Todd G.
P.O. Box 60219
New Orleans, LA 70160
Tel: (504) 566 - 1300
TF: (877) 989 - 4550

Serves As:
- Senior V. President, Human Resources and Corporate Services, Pan American Life Insurance Co.

SCHIANO, Anthony
6363 Main St.
Williamsville, NY 14221
Tel: (716) 635 - 5000
Fax:(716) 633 - 0898
TF: (800) 522 - 2522

Serves As:
- President and Chief Exec. Officer, Tops Markets LLC

SCHIFF, Jr., John J.
P.O. Box 145496
Cincinnati, OH 45250
Tel: (513) 870 - 2000
Fax:(513) 870 - 2935

Serves As:
- Chairman, President and Chief Exec. Officer, Cincinnati Financial Corp.

SCHILLACE, Kim
P.O. Box 1000
Montville, NJ 07045
kimberly_schillace@berlex.com
TF: (800) 237 - 5392

Serves As:
- Manager, Product Public Relations, Berlex, Inc.

SCHILLING, John
196 Van Buren St., Suite 450
Herndon, VA 20170-5337
Tel: (703) 456 - 2553
Fax:(703) 456 - 2551

Serves As:
- Manager, Corporate Communications, Nissan North America, Inc.

SCHINDLER, David L.
One GEICO Plaza
Washington, DC 20076
dschindler@geico.com
Tel: (301) 986 - 3000
Fax:(301) 986 - 2068

Serves As:
- Senior V. President, Human Resources, GEICO Corp.

SCHINDLER, Ellyn
Discovery Dr.
Swiftwater, PA 18370
ellyn.schindler@sanofipasteur.com
Tel: (570) 895 - 2689
Fax:(570) 839 - 7235

Serves As:
- U.S. Media Relations, Sanofi Pasteur, Inc.

SCHINTZIUS, David
One Post St.
San Francisco, CA 94104-5296
Tel: (415) 983 - 8300
Fax:(415) 983 - 7160

Serves As:
- PAC Treasurer, McKesson Corp.

SCHJERVEN, Robert E.
P.O. Box 799900
Dallas, TX 75379-9900
Tel: (972) 497 - 5000
Fax:(972) 497 - 5299

Serves As:
- Chief Exec. Officer, Lennox Internat'l

SCHLAISS, Karl-Heinz
1401 H St. NW
Suite 700
Washington, DC 20005
Tel: (202) 414 - 6744
Fax:(202) 414 - 6738

Serves As:
- Senior Manager, Corporate Relations, DaimlerChrysler Corp.

SCHLAPP, Matt
655 15th St. NW
Suite 445
Washington, DC 20005
Tel: (202) 737 - 1977
Fax:(202) 737 - 8111

Serves As:
- Exec. Director, Federal Affairs, Koch Industries, Inc.

SCHLATTER, Julie A.
333 W. 11th St.
Kansas City, MO 64105
Tel: (816) 435 - 1000
Fax:(816) 435 - 8630
TF: (888) 378 - 4636

Serves As:
- Director, Corporate Marketing and Technology Communications, DST Systems, Inc.

SCHLEGEL, Nancy
1550 Crystal Dr.
Crystal Square 2, Suite 300
Arlington, VA 22202
Tel: (703) 413 - 5680
Fax:(703) 413 - 5908

Serves As:
- Director, International Relations and Trade, Lockheed Martin Corp.

SCHLEIN, Michael
399 Park Ave.
New York, NY 10043
schleinm@citi.com
Tel: (212) 793 - 0141
Fax:(212) 793 - 3946
TF: (800) 285 - 3000

Serves As:
- Senior V. President, Global Corporate Affairs, Human Resources and Business Practices, Citigroup, Inc.

SCHLEYER, William T.
5619 DTC Pkwy.
Greenwood, CO 80111
Tel: (303) 268 - 6300

Serves As:
- Chairman and Chief Exec. Officer, Adelphia Communications Corp.

SCHLOESSER, Lynn L.
1300 Wilson Blvd.
Suite 900
Arlington, VA 22209-2307
Tel: (703) 524 - 7661
Fax:(703) 524 - 7707

Registered Federal Lobbyist.
Serves As:
- Manager, Federal Government Relations, Eastman Chemical Co.

SCHLUTER, Kathleen H.
720 E. Wisconsin Ave.
Milwaukee, WI 53202-4797
Tel: (414) 271 - 1444
Fax:(414) 665 - 2463
TF: (800) 323 - 7033

Registered Federal Lobbyist.
Serves As:
- Representative, Northwestern Mutual Financial Network

SCHMALTZ, Heather Dahlberg
Three Limited Pkwy.
Columbus, OH 43230
Tel: (614) 415 - 7282
Fax:(614) 415 - 7080

Serves As:
- Government Affairs Manager, The Limited Brands

SCHMEIDER, Robert
P.O. Box 471
Sunbury, PA 17801
Tel: (570) 286 - 4571
Fax:(570) 286 - 3286

Serves As:
- Director, Quality Control, Weis Markets, Inc.

SCHMELER, Frank R.
P.O. Box 1907
Albany, NY 12201-1907
Tel: (518) 445 - 2200
Fax:(518) 445 - 2265

Serves As:
- Chairman and Chief Exec. Officer, Albany Internat'l Corp.

SCHMIDT, Dr. Eric E.
1600 Amphitheatre Pkwy.
Mountain View, CA 94043
Tel: (650) 623 - 4000
Fax:(650) 618 - 1499

Serves As:
- Chairman and Chief Exec. Officer, Google Inc.

SCHMIDT, Kurt T.
200 Kimball Dr.
Parsippany, NJ 07054
Tel: (973) 503 - 8000
Fax:(973) 503 - 8400
TF: (800) 443 - 7237

Serves As:
- President, Gerber Products Co.

SCHMIDT, Lynne D.
One PPG Pl.
40 East
Pittsburgh, PA 15272
Tel: (412) 434 - 4397
Fax:(412) 434 - 4666

Serves As:
- V. President, Government and Community Affairs; Exec. Director, PPG Industries Foundation, PPG Industries Inc.

SCHMIEDT, Robert
3259 Eagle Watch Dr.
Woodstock, GA 30189
robert.schmiedt@roche.com
Tel: (770) 591 - 4460
Fax:(770) 591 - 6747

Serves As:
- Senior Regional Manager, State Government Affairs, (HLR Service Corp.), Hoffmann-La Roche Inc. (Roche)

SCHMITT, Edward A.
115 Perimeter Center Pl.
Suite 460
Atlanta, GA 30346
Tel: (770) 395 - 4500
Fax:(770) 395 - 4529

Serves As:
- Chairman, President and Chief Exec. Officer, Georgia Gulf Corp.

SCHMITT, Glenda
P.O. Box 1101
Minneapolis, MN 55440-1101
glenda.schmitt@adc.com
Tel: (952) 917 - 0445
Fax:(952) 917 - 0965
TF: (800) 366 - 3889

Serves As:
- Community Relations Specialist, ADC

SCHMITT, Jane C.
1333 West Loop South
Suite 1700
Houston, TX 77027
Tel: (713) 513 - 3300
Fax:(713) 513 - 3456

Serves As:
- V. President, Human Resources, Cooper Cameron Corp.

SCHNABEL, Andrew G.
1100 Wilson Blvd.
Suite 1500
Arlington, VA 22209
Tel: (703) 841 - 5700
Fax:(703) 841 - 5792

Registered Federal Lobbyist.
Serves As:
- Director, Government Relations, Raytheon Co.

SCHNABEL, Maria
5565 Glenridge Connector
Atlanta, GA 30342
maria.schnabel@cingular.com
Tel: (404) 236 - 6432
Fax:(866) 246 - 4852
TF: (800) 331 - 0500

Serves As:
- Director, Hispanic Public Relations, Cingular Wireless

SCHNATTER, John H.
P.O. Box 99900
Louisville, KY 40269-0900
Tel: (502) 261 - 7272
Fax:(502) 261 - 4315

Serves As:
- Chairman and Chief Exec. Officer, Papa John's Internat'l Inc.

SCHNECK, Kara L.
One Nu Skin Plaza
75 W. Center St.
Provo, UT 84601
kschneck@nuskin.net
Tel: (801) 345 - 2116
Fax:(801) 345 - 2199

Serves As:
- Senior Director, Global Public Relations, Nu Skin Enterprises

SCHNEIDER, Anna-Maria
1560 Wilson Blvd.
Suite 1200
Arlington, VA 22209
aschneider@mmsa.com
Tel: (703) 525 - 4800

Registered Federal Lobbyist.
Serves As:
- Exec. Director, Government Relations, U.S. Operations, Mitsubishi Motors North America, Inc.

SCHNEIDER, Carrie
One Energy Plaza
Jackson, MI 49201
Tel: (517) 788 - 2322
Fax:(517) 788 - 1315

Serves As:
- Contact, Consumers Energy Co. Employees for Better Employment, CMS Energy Corp.

SCHNEIDER, Richard A.
Five Sylvan Way
Parsippany, NJ 07054
Tel: (973) 898 - 1500
Fax:(973) 898 - 4730

Serves As:
- Exec. V. President and Chief Financial Officer, DRS Technologies, Inc.

Also serves as PAC contact.

SCHNEIDER, Russell P.
1300 I St. NW
Suite 450 East
Washington, DC 20005-7211
russell.p.schneider@monsanto.com
Tel: (202) 783 - 2460
Fax:(202) 789 - 1819

Registered Federal Lobbyist.
Serves As:
- Director, Agricultural Regulation, Monsanto Co.

SCHNEIER, Craig Eric
14 Cambridge Center
Cambridge, MA 02142
Tel: (617) 679 - 2000
Fax:(617) 679 - 2617

Serves As:
- Exec. V. President, Human Resources, Biogen Idec Inc.

SCHNELL, Bill
2901 Via Fortuna
Austin, TX 78746
bill.schnell@cirrus.com
Tel: (512) 851 - 4000
TF: (800) 888 - 5016

Serves As:
- Manager, Public Relations, Cirrus Logic, Inc.

SCHNIEDER, Bryan
104 Wilmot Rd.
mail stop 1444
Deerfield, IL 60015
Tel: (847) 315 - 4440
Fax:(847) 315 - 4660

Serves As:
- PAC Contact, Walgreen Co.

SCHNIEDERS, Richard J.
1390 Enclave Pkwy.
Houston, TX 77077-2099
Tel: (281) 584 - 1390
Fax:(281) 584 - 2721

Serves As:
- Chairman and Chief Exec. Officer, Sysco Corp.

SCHNOOR, Candace
One John Deere Pl.
Moline, IL 61265-8098
Tel: (309) 765 - 8000
Fax:(309) 765 - 5772

Serves As:
- PAC Treasurer, Deere & Company

SCHNORR, Lisa
370 Woodcliff Dr.
Suite 300
Fairport, NY 14450
lisa.schnorr@cbrands.com
Tel: (585) 218 - 3677
TF: (888) 724 - 2169

Serves As:
- V. President, Investor Relations, Constellation Brands, Inc.

SCHNUCK, Craig D.
11420 Lackland Rd.
St. Louis, MO 63146-6928
Tel: (314) 994 - 9900
Fax:(314) 994 - 4465

Serves As:
- Chairman and Chief Exec. Officer, Schnuck Markets, Inc.

SCHNUCK, Todd
11420 Lackland Rd. Tel: (314) 944 - 9900
St. Louis, MO 63146-6928

Serves As:
- Corporate V. President and Chief Financial Officer, Schnuck Markets, Inc.
Responsibilities include investor relations.

SCHOEN, John
1601 W. Diehl Rd. Tel: (630) 305 - 1147
Naperville, IL 60563-1198 Fax:(630) 305 - 1973

Serves As:
- Manager, Communications, Nalco Co.

SCHOEN, William J.
5811 Pelican Bay Blvd., Suite 500 Tel: (239) 598 - 3175
Naples, FL 34108-2710 Fax:(239) 596 - 1426

Serves As:
- Chairman of the Board, Health Management Associates, Inc.

SCHOENBAUM, John A.
401 Park Dr. Tel: (617) 246 - 4356
Boston, MA 02215 TF: (800) 325 - 2583
Schoenbaum_John_A/bos1_bcbsma@bcbsma.com

Serves As:
- V. President, Corporate Affairs, Blue Cross and Blue Shield of Massachusetts

SCHOENBERG, Allan
20 S. Wacker Dr. Tel: (312) 930 - 8189
Chicago, IL 60606-7499 Fax:(312) 930 - 3439
aschoenb@cme.com

Serves As:
- Associate Director, Technology Communications, Chicago Mercantile Exchange Inc.

SCHOENBERGER, Douglas
1120 20th St. NW Tel: (202) 457 - 3810
Suite 1000 Fax:(202) 457 - 2008
Washington, DC 20036-3406

Registered Federal Lobbyist.
Serves As:
- V. President, International Government Affairs, AT&T

SCHOENBERGER, Jeff
1776 I St. NW Tel: (202) 429 - 3400
Suite 1050 Fax:(202) 429 - 3467
Washington, DC 20006

Serves As:
- Legislative Assistant, The Dow Chemical Company

SCHOENBORN, Jeffrey
345 Park Ave. Tel: (212) 546 - 2846
New York, NY 10154-0037 Fax:(212) 546 - 4020
jeffrey@schoenborn@bms.com

Serves As:
- Corporate Communications Contact, Bristol-Myers Squibb Co.

SCHOENIG, Vince
4101 Washington Ave. Tel: (757) 380 - 2000
Newport News, VA 23607-2770 Fax:(757) 380 - 3875

Serves As:
- PAC Treasurer, Northrop Grumman Newport News

SCHOLNICK, Howard D.
1399 New York Ave. NW Tel: (202) 378 - 2020
Suite 200 Fax:(202) 783 - 6631
Washington, DC 20005

Serves As:
- Director, Federal Government Affairs, Abbott Laboratories

SCHOLTZ, Stacy A.
Mutual of Omaha Plaza Tel: (402) 351 - 4310
Omaha, NE 68175-0001 Fax:(402) 351 - 2651
stacy.scholtz@mutualofomaha.com

Serves As:
- Exec. V. President, Corporate Services, Mutual of Omaha Insurance Co.

SCHOMBURG, Paul
1130 Connecticut Ave. NW Tel: (202) 912 - 3800
Suite 1100
Washington, DC 20036

Registered Federal Lobbyist.
Serves As:
- Manager, Government and Public Affairs, Matsushita Electric Corp. of America

SCHOONYAN, Gary L.
601 Van Ness Ave., Suite 2040 Tel: (415) 775 - 1856
San Francisco, CA 94102 Fax:(415) 474 - 3080
schoongl@sce.com

Serves As:
- Director, Regulatory Policy and Affairs, Southern California Edison, an Edison Internat'l Co.

SCHOPP, Keith M.
Checkerboard Square Tel: (314) 982 - 2577
St. Louis, MO 63164 Fax:(314) 982 - 2752
kschopp@purina.com

Serves As:
- V. President, Public Relations, Nestle Purina PetCare Co.

SCHORR, Todd W.
700 Oakmont Lane Tel: (630) 570 - 3000
Westmont, IL 60559 Fax:(630) 570 - 3606

Serves As:
- Senior V. President, Human Resources, SIRVA, Inc.

SCHOTT, Buzz
8326 Century Park Tel: (619) 696 - 2000
San Diego, CA 92123 Fax:(619) 696 - 1868

Serves As:
- Director, Regional Public Affairs, San Diego Gas and Electric Co.

SCHOTT, Laurence F.
8330 Century Park Ct. Tel: (858) 654 - 6305
San Diego, CA 92123 Fax:(858) 654 - 6301
TF: (877) 736 - 7729

Serves As:
- V. President, Regional Public Affairs, Sempra Energy
San Diego Gas and Electric

SCHOTTENSTEIN, Jay L.
1800 Moler Dr.
Columbus, OH 43207

Serves As:
- Chairman of the Board, Retail Ventures, Inc.

SCHRAMM, Deborah A.
Kerr-McGee Center, Box 25861 Tel: (405) 270 - 2877
Oklahoma City, OK 73125 Fax:(405) 270 - 3029
TF: (800) 786 - 2556

Serves As:
- V. President, Corporate Communications, Kerr-McGee Corp.

SCHRANZ, James E.
P.O. Box 1590 Tel: (214) 443 - 5500
Dallas, TX 75221-1590

Serves As:
- V. President, Human Resources and Treasurer, Austin Industries

SCHREIBER, Jr., George A.
PO Box 5004 Tel: (248) 702 - 6000
Port Huron, MI 48060 Fax:(248) 702 - 6300

Serves As:
- President and Chief Exec. Officer, SEMCO ENERGY, Inc.

SCHREMPP, Jurgen E.
1000 Chrysler Dr. Tel: (248) 576 - 5741
Auburn Hills, MI 48326-2766 Fax:(248) 576 - 4742
TF: (800) 992 - 1997

Serves As:
- Chairman of the Board, DaimlerChrysler Corp.

SCHRICK, Diane
One DNA Way Tel: (650) 225 - 1599
San Francisco, CA 94080-4990 Fax:(650) 225 - 6000

Serves As:
- Manager, Investor Relations, Genentech, Inc.

SCHRIVER, Donald H.
P.O. Box 909700 Tel: (816) 801 - 6470
Kansas City, MO 64190-9700 Fax:(816) 801 - 6471
dschriver@dfamilk.com

Serves As:
- Exec. V. President; Contact, Associated Milk Producers, Inc. Contributions Program, Dairy Farmers of America, Inc.

SCHROEDER, Kenneth L.
160 Rio Robles Tel: (408) 875 - 3000
San Jose, CA 95134 Fax:(408) 875 - 4266

Serves As:
- Chief Exec. Officer, KLA-Tencor

SCHROEDER, Lee
1111 Stewart Ave. Tel: (516) 803 - 2534
Bethpage, NY 11714-3581 Fax:(516) 803 - 1186

Serves As:
- V. President, Government and Regulatory Strategy, Cablevision Systems Corp.

SCHROEDER, Stephen O.
P.O. Box 550
Findlay, OH 45839-0550
soschroeder@coopertire.com
Tel: (419) 423 - 1321
Fax:(419) 424 - 4212

Serves As:
- V. President-Treasurer, Cooper Tire & Rubber Company

Responsibilities include public affairs and political action.

SCHROETER, Lisa
1776 I St. NW
Suite 1050
Washington, DC 20006
Tel: (202) 429 - 3400
Fax:(202) 429 - 3467

Registered Federal Lobbyist.
Serves As:
- Director, International Government Affairs, The Dow Chemical Company

SCHRUM, Roger P.
125 S. Dakota Ave.
Sioux Falls, SD 57104-6403
roger.schrum@northwestern.com
Tel: (605) 978 - 2848
Fax:(605) 978 - 2840

Serves As:
- V. President, Human Resources and Communications, NorthWestern Corp.

Responsibilities include investor relations.

SCHUELER, Charles
1111 Stewart Ave.
Bethpage, NY 11714-3581
cschuele@cablevision.com
Tel: (516) 803 - 1013
Fax:(516) 803 - 1186

Serves As:
- Senior V. President, Media and Community Relations, Cablevision Systems Corp.

SCHUESSLER, John T. "Jack"
P.O. Box 256
Dublin, OH 43017
jack_schuessler@wendys.com
Tel: (614) 764 - 3100
Fax:(614) 764 - 3459

Serves As:
- Chairman and Chief Exec. Officer, Wendy's Internat'l, Inc.

SCHUH, Dale R.
1800 N. Point Dr.
Stevens Point, WI 54481
Tel: (715) 346 - 6000
Fax:(715) 346 - 6346

Serves As:
- Chairman and Chief Exec. Officer, Sentry Insurance

SCHUITEMA, George
130 E. Randolph Dr.
24th Floor
Chicago, IL 60601
g.schuitema@pecorp.com
Tel: (312) 240 - 4544
Fax:(312) 240 - 4937

Serves As:
- Manager, Risk Management, Peoples Energy Corp.

SCHULER, J. Terry
150 N. Orange Grove Blvd.
Pasadena, CA 91103
terry.schuler@averydennison.com
Tel: (626) 304 - 2000
Fax:(626) 792 - 7312

Serves As:
- Senior V. President, Human Resources, Avery Dennison Corp.

SCHULTE, Robert L.
111 Center St.
Little Rock, AR 72201
Tel: (501) 377 - 2000
Fax:(501) 377 - 2666
TF: (800) 643 - 9691

Serves As:
- PAC Treasurer, Stephens Inc.

SCHULTZ, Alan F.
19975 Victor Pkwy.
Livonia, MI 48152-7001
schultza@valassis.com
Tel: (734) 591 - 3000
Ext: 17326
Fax:(734) 591 - 4503
TF: (800) 437 - 0479

Serves As:
- Chairman, President and Chief Exec. Officer, Valassis Communications, Inc.

SCHULTZ, Howard
P.O. Box 34067
Seattle, WA 98124-1067
Tel: (206) 447 - 1575
Fax:(206) 682 - 9051

Serves As:
- Chairman and Chief Global Strategist, Starbucks Corp.

SCHULTZ, Robert F.
600 Grant St., Suite 4600
Pittsburgh, PA 15219
rschultz@ampcopgh.com
Tel: (412) 456 - 4491
Fax:(412) 456 - 4404

Serves As:
- V. President, Industrial Relations; and Senior Counsel, Ampco-Pittsburgh Corp.

SCHULTZ, Steven
315 Second St. SE
P.O. Box 2220
Jamestown, ND 58402

Serves As:
- PAC Treasurer, Otter Tail Power Co.

SCHULWOLF, Francie
Three Ravinia Dr., Suite 100
Atlanta, GA 30346
fschulwolf@ichotelsgroup.com
Tel: (770) 604 - 2906
Fax:(770) 604 - 2059

Serves As:
- V. President, Corporate Communications, InterContinental Hotels Group

SCHULZ, William
60 Massachusetts Ave. NE
Washington, DC 20002
Tel: (202) 906 - 3000
Fax:(202) 906 - 3865

Serves As:
- Chief, Corporate Communications, Amtrak

SCHULZE, Richard M.
7601 Penn Ave. South
Richfield, MN 55423
richard.schulze@bestbuy.com
Tel: (612) 291 - 1000

Serves As:
- Chairman of the Board, Best Buy Co., Inc.

SCHUMAN, Allan L.
Ecolab Center
370 N. Wabasha St.
St. Paul, MN 55102
Tel: (651) 293 - 2233
Fax:(651) 225 - 2092

Serves As:
- Chairman of the Board, Ecolab Inc.

SCHURGER, Marc
P.O. Box 511
Kingsport, TN 37662-5075
Tel: (423) 229 - 5921
Fax:(423) 224 - 0208
TF: (800) 327 - 8626

Serves As:
- Director, Product Safety and Health, Eastman Chemical Co.

Responsibilities include environmental affairs.

SCHURMAN, Mark W.
P.O. Box 302
Zeeland, MI 49464-0302
mark_schurman@hermanmiller.com
Tel: (616) 654 - 5498
Fax:(616) 654 - 5234

Serves As:
- Director, Corporate External Communications, Herman Miller Inc.

SCHUSSEL, Mark
P.O. Box 1615
Warren, NJ 07061-1615
mschussel@chubb.com
Tel: (908) 903 - 2107
Fax:(908) 903 - 2027

Serves As:
- Manager, Public Relations, The Chubb Corp.

SCHUSTER, James E.
P.O. Box 85
Wichita, KS 67201-0085
Tel: (316) 676 - 7111
Fax:(316) 676 - 8286

Serves As:
- Chairman and Chief Exec. Officer, Raytheon Aircraft Company

SCHUTZMAN, David
1633 Broadway
New York, NY 10019
Tel: (212) 489 - 1600
Fax:(212) 489 - 1687

Serves As:
- Director, Public Relations Industries and Functions, (Deloitte Services LP), Deloitte & Touche LLP

SCHUYLER, William J.
1500 K St. NW
Suite 650
Washington, DC 20005
Tel: (202) 715 - 1000
Fax:(202) 715 - 1001

Registered Federal Lobbyist.
Serves As:
- Director, Federal Government Relations, GlaxoSmithKline Research and Development

SCHWAB, Charles R.
101 Montgomery St.
San Francisco, CA 94104
charles.schwab@schwab.com
Tel: (415) 627 - 7000
TF: (800) 435 - 4000

Serves As:
- Chairman and Chief Exec. Officer, The Charles Schwab Corp.

SCHWAB, Cindy
100 Abbott Park Rd.
Abbott Park, IL 60064-3500
Tel: (847) 937 - 7075
Fax:(847) 935 - 5051

Serves As:
- V. President, Abbott Fund, Abbott Laboratories

SCHWAB, Mark J.
P.O. Box 431
Easton, PA 18044-0431
Tel: (610) 253 - 6271
Fax:(610) 250 - 5768

Serves As:
• President and Chief Exec. Officer, Binney and Smith Inc.

SCHWAB, Richard F.
1200 Wilson Blvd.
Arlington, VA 22209-2305
Tel: (703) 465 - 3686

Registered Federal Lobbyist.
Serves As:
• Legislative Affairs, Navy and USMC Programs, The Boeing Co.

SCHWAGER, Rob
3191 Broadbridge Ave.
Stratford, CT 06614-2559
Tel: (203) 381 - 7000

Serves As:
• Chairman and Chief Exec. Officer, Dictaphone Corp.

SCHWAN, Alfred
115 W. College Dr.
Marshall, MN 56258
Tel: (507) 532 - 3274
Fax:(507) 537 - 8224
TF: (800) 533 - 5290

Serves As:
• Chairman of the Board, The Schwan Food Co.

SCHWANZ, Donald K.
905 West Blvd., North
Elkhart, IN 46514
dschwanz@ctscorp.com
Tel: (574) 293 - 7511
Fax:(574) 293 - 6146

Serves As:
• President and Chief Exec. Officer, CTS Corp.

SCHWARK, Ryerson
8005 SW Boeckman Rd.
Wilsonville, OR 97070-7777
ry_schwark@mentor.com
Tel: (503) 685 - 1462
Fax:(503) 685 - 7704
TF: (800) 547 - 3000

Serves As:
• Director, Public Relations and Investor Relations, Mentor Graphics Corp.

SCHWARTZ, Bernard L.
600 Third Ave.
36th Floor
New York, NY 10016
bernard.schwartz@hq.loral.com
Tel: (212) 697 - 1105
Fax:(212) 338 - 5662

Serves As:
• Chairman and Chief Exec. Officer, Loral Space & Communications
Responsibilities include corporate philanthropy.

SCHWARTZ, David
1000 Alfred Nobel Dr.
Hercules, CA 94547-1811
Tel: (510) 724 - 7000
Fax:(510) 741 - 5817
TF: (800) 424 - 6723

Serves As:
• Chairman of the Board, Bio-Rad Laboratories, Inc.

SCHWARTZ, Elizabeth Nash
1200 Wilson Blvd.
Arlington, VA 22209-2305
Tel: (703) 465 - 3668

Registered Federal Lobbyist.
Serves As:
• Director, Legislative Affairs, The Boeing Co.

SCHWARTZ, John
114 N. Division, Room G2
Grand Rapids, MI 49503
Tel: (616) 732 - 1966
Fax:(616) 776 - 6595

Serves As:
• Manager, External Affairs, SBC Michigan

SCHWARTZ, Lew
56 Top Gallant Rd.
Stamford, CT 06904
Tel: (203) 316 - 6311
Fax:(203) 316 - 6488

Serves As:
• Senior V. President and General Counsel, Gartner, Inc.
Responsibilities include public affairs.

SCHWARTZ, Mordecai
Two Liberty Pl.
1601 Chestnut St.
Philadelphia, PA 19192
Tel: (215) 761 - 1000

Serves As:
• PAC Treasurer, CIGNA Corp.

SCHWARTZ, Norman
1000 Alfred Nobel Dr.
Hercules, CA 94547-1811
Tel: (510) 724 - 7000
Fax:(510) 741 - 5817
TF: (800) 424 - 6723

Serves As:
• President and Chief Exec. Officer, Bio-Rad Laboratories, Inc.

SCHWARTZ, Paula
229 W. 43rd St.
New York, NY 10036
Tel: (212) 556 - 5224

Serves As:
• Manager, Investor Relations and Online Communications, New York Times Co.

SCHWARZENBAUER, Peter
980 Hammond Dr. NE
Suite 1000
Atlanta, GA 30328-5313
Tel: (770) 290 - 3500
Fax:(770) 290 - 3700

Serves As:
• President and Chief Exec. Officer, Porsche Cars North America, Inc.

SCHWEDER, J. Michael
One AT&T Way
3161C3
Bedminster, NJ 07921-0752
schweder@att.com
Tel: (908) 234 - 3020

Registered Federal Lobbyist.
Serves As:
• Director, Government Relations Regional, AT&T

SCHWEINFURTH, Lynn
6820 LBJ Fwy.
Dallas, TX 75240
Tel: (972) 770 - 7228
Fax:(972) 770 - 8815

Serves As:
• V. President, Investor Relations, Brinker Internat'l, Inc.

SCHWEITZER, Jeff
101 N. Third St.
Moorhead, MN 56560-1990
Tel: (218) 236 - 4400
Ext: 4492
Fax:(218) 236 - 4718

Serves As:
• Manager, Public Relations, American Crystal Sugar Co.
Responsibilities include corporate philanthropy.

SCHWER, William F.
P.O. Box Nine
Sugar Land, TX 77487
Tel: (281) 490 - 9795
Fax:(281) 490 - 9584

Serves As:
• Senior V. President, Secretary and General Counsel, Imperial Sugar Co.
Responsibilities include corporate communications and corporate philanthropy.

SCIBARRAS, Don
3333 Beverly Rd.
Hoffman Estates, IL 60179-0001
Tel: (847) 286 - 0324
Fax:(847) 286 - 7881
TF: (800) 732 - 7780

Registered Federal Lobbyist.
Serves As:
• Government Affairs, Sears Holding Corp.

SCIPPA, Raymond A.
757 N. Eldridge
Houston, TX 77079
rscippa@mcdermott.com
Tel: (281) 870 - 5025
Fax:(281) 870 - 5045

Serves As:
• Director, Public Relations, (J. Ray McDermott, SA), McDermott Internat'l, Inc.

SCLAVOS, Stratton D.
487 E. Middlefield Rd.
Mountian View, CA 94043-4047
Tel: (650) 961 - 7500
Fax:(650) 961 - 7300

Serves As:
• Chairman and Chief Exec. Officer, VeriSign, Inc.

SCOTT, Ann
P.O. Box 5000
Broomfield, CO 80038-5000
ascott@ball.com
Tel: (303) 460 - 3537
Fax:(303) 460 - 2127

Serves As:
• Manager, Investor Relations and Pension Plans, Ball Corp.

SCOTT, Beverly
631 S. Richland Ave.
York, PA 17403
Tel: (717) 771 - 7000
Fax:(717) 771 - 7252

Serves As:
• Contact, Corporate Giving, York Internat'l Corp.

SCOTT, Billie
P.O. Box 7033
Indianapolis, IN 46207
bscott@simon.com
Tel: (317) 263 - 7148
Fax:(317) 263 - 2318

Serves As:
• Director, Public Relations, Simon Property Group

SCOTT, Cameron
608 Fifth Ave.
New York, NY 10020
Tel: (212) 830 - 2431
Fax:(212) 246 - 0185

Serves As:
• Foundation Contact, Novartis Corporation

SCOTT, Carl
Mutual of Omaha Plaza
Omaha, NE 68175-0001
carl.scott@mutualofomaha.com
Tel: (402) 351 - 8208
Fax:(402) 351 - 5710

Serves As:
- Contact, Mutual of Omaha Cos. General Managers PAC, Mutual of Omaha Insurance Co.

SCOTT, Cathy N.
20511 Lake Forest Dr.
Lake Forest, CA 92630-7741
Tel: (949) 672 - 7000
Fax:(949) 672 - 5408

Serves As:
- V. President, Marketing Communications, Western Digital Corp.

SCOTT, Dennis
Two Democracy Center
6903 Rockledge Dr.
Bethesda, MD 20817-1818
Tel: (301) 564 - 3200
Fax:(301) 564 - 3201

Registered Federal Lobbyist.
Serves As:
- Representative, USEC Inc.

SCOTT, Eileen R.
200 Milik St.
Carteret, NJ 07008-1194
Tel: (732) 499 - 3500
Fax:(732) 499 - 6872

Serves As:
- Chief Exec. Officer, Pathmark Stores Inc.

SCOTT, Gregory R.
101 Constitution Ave. NW
Suite 400 West
Washington, DC 20001
gregory.scott@altria.com
Tel: (202) 354 - 1500
Fax:(202) 354 - 1505

Registered Federal Lobbyist.
Serves As:
- Director, Federal Affairs - Tobacco, (Altria Corporate Services, Inc.), Altria Group, Inc.

SCOTT, H. Lee
702 SW Eighth St.
M/S 0105
Bentonville, AR 72716
Tel: (479) 273 - 4000
Fax:(479) 273 - 4053

Serves As:
- President and Chief Exec. Officer, Wal-Mart Stores

SCOTT, Joan
P.O. Box 58090
M/S G2-129
Santa Clara, CA 95052-8090
joan.p.scott@nsc.com
Tel: (408) 721 - 5000
Fax:(408) 739 - 9803

Serves As:
- Director, Community Relations and Nat'l Semiconductor Foundation, Nat'l Semiconductor Corp.

SCOTT, Kathy A.
P.O. Box 029100
Miami, FL 33102
kathy_scott@fpl.com
Tel: (305) 552 - 2368
Fax:(305) 552 - 2144

Serves As:
- Media Relations, FPL Group, Inc.

SCOTT, Lars W.
701 Market St.
St. Louis, MO 63101-1826
lscott@peabodyenergy.com
Tel: (314) 342 - 7594
Fax:(314) 342 - 7799

Registered Federal Lobbyist.
Serves As:
- Director, Coal Technology Development, Peabody Energy

Responsibilities include environmental affairs.

SCOTT, Ron
11111 Sunset Hills Dr.
Reston, VA 20190-5339
Tel: (703) 547 - 2000
Fax:(703) 547 - 2881

Serves As:
- Senior V. President, XO Communications, XO Communications, Inc.

SCOTT, III, Samuel C.
P.O. Box 7100
Westchester, IL 60154
Tel: (708) 551 - 2600
Fax:(708) 551 - 2700

Serves As:
- Chairman, President and Chief Exec. Officer, Corn Products Internat'l, Inc.

SCOTT, Jr., Walter
1025 Eldorado Blvd.
Broomfield, CO 80021
Tel: (720) 888 - 1000
Fax:(720) 888 - 5085

Serves As:
- Chairman of the Board, Level 3 Communications, Inc.

SCOTTINO, Tom
One Tellabs Center
1415 W. Diehl Rd.
Naperville, IL 60563
tom.scottino@tellabs.com
Tel: (630) 798 - 3602
Fax:(630) 798 - 3333

Serves As:
- Manager, Investor Relations, Tellabs

SCRANTON, III, William W.
355 Maple Ave.
Harleysville, PA 19438-2297
Tel: (215) 256 - 5000
Fax:(215) 256 - 5799
TF: (800) 523 - 6344

Serves As:
- Chairman of the Board, Harleysville Group

SCRIBNER, Thomas R.
P.O. Box 26234
Richmond, VA 23260-6234
tom.scribner@sscoop.com
Tel: (804) 281 - 1000
Fax:(804) 281 - 1119

Serves As:
- President and Chief Exec. Officer, Southern States Cooperative

SCRIVANO, David
Fox Office Center
2211 Woodward Ave.
Detroit, MI 48201-3400
Tel: (313) 983 - 6000
Fax:(313) 983 - 6390

Serves As:
- President, Little Caesar Enterprises

SCRUGGS, Frank
2200 Old Germantown Rd.
Delray Beach, FL 33445
Tel: (561) 438 - 4800
Fax:(561) 438 - 4400

Serves As:
- Exec. V. President, Human Resources, Office Depot, Inc.

SCRUGGS, John F.
101 Constitution Ave. NW
Suite 400 West
Washington, DC 20001
john.scruggs@altria.com
Tel: (202) 354 - 1500
Fax:(202) 354 - 1505

Registered Federal Lobbyist.
Serves As:
- V. President, Government Affairs, Altria Group, Inc.

SCULLY, James H.
750 Lakeshore Pkwy.
Birmingham, AL 35211
Tel: (205) 940 - 4000

Serves As:
- PAC Treasurer, Saks, Inc.

SCULLY, John
135 S. LaSalle St.
Chicago, IL 60603
Tel: (312) 904 - 2000
Fax:(312) 904 - 6521

Serves As:
- Senior V. President, Human Resources, LaSalle Bank N.A.

SCULLY, Jr., Timothy H.
655 15th St.NW
Washington, DC 20005
Tel: (202) 661 - 8631

Registered Federal Lobbyist.
Serves As:
- V. President, Government Affairs, Miller Brewing Co.

SCZUDLO, Rebecca T.
Ten G St. NE, Suite 580
Washington, DC 20002
Tel: (202) 216 - 9760
Fax:(202) 216 - 9785

Serves As:
- V. President, Federal Government Affairs, (NiSource Corporate Services), NiSource Inc.

SEASE, Gary T.
500 Water St.
Jacksonville, FL 32203
gary_sease@csx.com
Tel: (904) 359 - 1719
Fax:(904) 359 - 1899

Serves As:
- Managing Director, Employee Communications, CSX Corp.

SEBASTIAN, Tina
111 Lord Dr.
Cary, NC 27511
tina_sebastian@lord.com
Tel: (919) 468 - 5979
Fax:(919) 469 - 5777

Serves As:
- Manager, Employee Relations, LORD Corporation

SEBITS, Trent
4111 E. 37th St., North
Wichita, KS 67220
Tel: (316) 828 - 8896
Fax:(316) 828 - 5739

Serves As:
- Manager, Government and Public Affairs, Koch Industries, Inc.

SECCHIA, Peter F.

2801 E. Beltline NE
Grand Rapids, MI 49525
psecchia@ufpi.com
Tel: (616) 364 - 6161
Fax:(616) 364 - 5558

Serves As:
- Chairman of the Board, Universal Forest Products, Inc.

Responsibilities include corporate philanthropy.

SECHRIST, Steve

220 NW Second Ave.
Portland, OR 97209-3991
sms@nwnatural.com
Tel: (503) 226 - 4211
Ext: 3517
Fax:(503) 721 - 2508

Serves As:
- Senior Specialist, Public Relations, NW Natural

SECOR, Ph.D., Jacob

9330 Zionsville Rd.
Indianapolis, IN 46268
jsecor@dow.com
Tel: (317) 337 - 4751
Fax:(317) 337 - 4880

Serves As:
- Leader, State Government and Public Affairs, Midwest and South, Dow AgroSciences LLC

SECOR, Richard M.

P.O. Box 1430
Kenosha, WI 53141-1430
richard.secor@snapon.com
Tel: (414) 656 - 5561
Fax:(414) 656 - 5577

Serves As:
- Director, Corporate Communications, Snap-on Incorporated

SEDNEY, Diana

1401 I St. NW
Suite 1200
Washington, DC 20005-2225
Tel: (202) 408 - 5800
Fax:(202) 408 - 5845

Registered Federal Lobbyist.
Serves As:
- Manager, International Relations, Chevron Corp.

SEEGER, Christopher C.

1455 F St. NW
Suite 420
Washington, DC 20004
chris.seeger@usaa.com
Tel: (202) 528 - 6442
Fax:(202) 628 - 6537

Registered Federal Lobbyist.
Serves As:
- Senior V. President, Federal Government Relations, United Services Automobile Ass'n (USAA)

SEGAL, Susan A.

Centre Square, West Tower
1500 Market St., Suite 3900
Philadelphia, PA 19102-2112
sasegal@lfg.com
Tel: (215) 448 - 1400
Fax:(215) 448 - 3962
TF: (877) 275 - 5462

Serves As:
- Charitable Giving Contact (Philadelphia, PA), Lincoln Financial Group

SEGLEM, Christopher K.

Two N. Cascade Ave.
14th Floor
Colorado Springs, CO 80903
Tel: (719) 442 - 2600
Fax:(719) 448 - 5824

Serves As:
- Chairman, President, and Chief Exec. Officer, Westmoreland Coal Co.

SEIBERLICH, William C.

P.O. Box 860
Valley Forge, PA 19482
Tel: (610) 341 - 7187
Fax:(610) 341 - 7777

Serves As:
- Manager, Communications, Saint-Gobain Corp.

SEIDEL, Joseph L.

1201 F St. NW
Suite 450
Washington, DC 20004
Tel: (202) 626 - 3301

Registered Federal Lobbyist.
Serves As:
- Director, Credit Suisse First Boston

SEIDENBERG, Ivan G.

1095 Ave. of the Americas
New York, NY 10036
ivan.seidenberg@verizon.com
Tel: (212) 395 - 2121
TF: (800) 621 - 9900

Serves As:
- Chairman and Chief Exec. Officer, Verizon Communications Inc.

SEIDLITS, Curtis

P.O. Box 227097
Dallas, TX 75222-7097
cseidlits@txu.com
Tel: (214) 812 - 4600
Fax:(214) 812 - 4758

Serves As:
- Senior V. President, Governmental Advocacy, TXU

SEIFERT, David P.

P.O. Box 419580
Kansas City, MO 64141-6580
Tel: (816) 274 - 3761
Fax:(816) 274 - 5061

Serves As:
- Manager, Strategic Communications International, Hallmark Cards, Inc.

SEINES, James

10307 Pacific Center Ct.
San Diego, CA 92121
jseines@leapwireless.com
Tel: (858) 882 - 6000
Fax:(858) 882 - 6030

Serves As:
- Director, Public Affairs and Investor Relations, Leap Wireless International, Inc.

SEITZ, Andrew

Two T.W. Alexander Dr.
P.O. Box 12
Research Triangle Park, NC 27009
andrew.seitz@bayercropscience.com
Tel: (919) 549 - 2000

Serves As:
- Media Contact, Bayer CropScience

SEITZ, Carol

P.O. Box 98199
Washington, DC 20090-8199
cseitz@ngs.org
Tel: (202) 857 - 6678
Fax:(202) 828 - 6679
TF: (800) 647 - 5463

Serves As:
- Director, Media Relations, Nat'l Geographic Soc.

SELANDER, Robert W.

2000 Purchase St.
Purchase, NY 10577-2509
Tel: (914) 249 - 2000
Fax:(914) 249 - 4206

Serves As:
- President and Chief Exec. Officer, MasterCard Internat'l

SELCKE, Stephen F.

225 W. Randolph St.
27 B
Chicago, IL 60606
Tel: (312) 220 - 8717
Fax:(312) 727 - 3722
TF: (800) 327 - 9346

Serves As:
- V. President, External Affairs, SBC Illinois

Responsibilities include political action.

SELF, W. David

605 Richard Arrington Jr. Blvd. North
Birmingham, AL 35203-2707
Tel: (205) 326 - 8100
Fax:(205) 326 - 2704
TF: (800) 654 - 3206

Serves As:
- V. President, Human Resources and Administration, Energen Corp.

SELIGMAN, Scott D.

1401 I St. NW
Suite 600
Washington, DC 20005
Tel: (202) 336 - 7400
Fax:(202) 336 - 7530

Serves As:
- Director, Public Relations, United Technologies Corp.

SELL, Angela

71 S. wacker Dr
Chicago, IL 60606
asell@corphq.hyatt.com
Tel: (312) 920 - 2325
Fax:(312) 750 - 8550

Serves As:
- Manager, Public Relations, (Hyatt Hotels Corp.), Global Hyatt Corp.

SELLERS, Mary

P.O. Box 1438
Louisville, KY 40201-1438
msellers1@humana.com
Tel: (502) 580 - 3689
Fax:(502) 580 - 3677
TF: (800) 486 - 2620

Serves As:
- Manager, Media Relations, Humana Inc.

SELLERS, Nick

P.O. Box 2641
Birmingham, AL 35291
Tel: (205) 257 - 3111
Fax:(205) 257 - 2622

Serves As:
- Director, Federal Legislative Relations, Alabama Power Co.

SELLMAN, Patricia

3250 Van Ness Ave.
San Francisco, CA 94109
Tel: (415) 733 - 3168
Fax:(415) 616 - 8463

Serves As:
- V. President, Public Relations, Williams-Sonoma, Inc.

SELNER, Joseph B.

1200 Hansen Rd.
Green Bay, WI 54304
joe.selner@associatedbank.com
Tel: (920) 491 - 7120
Fax:(920) 491 - 7090
TF: (800) 236 - 2722

Serves As:
- Exec. V. President and Chief Financial Officer, Associated Banc-Corp.

Responsibilities include shareholder relations.

SEMEL, Terry
701 First Ave.
Sunnyvale, CA 94089
terry@yahoo-inc.com
Tel: (408) 731 - 3300
Fax:(408) 616 - 3301

Serves As:
• Chairman and Chief Exec. Officer, Yahoo! Inc.

SEMIK, Chris
6035 Parkland Blvd.
Cleveland, OH 44124-4141
csemik@parker.com
Tel: (216) 896 - 3000
Fax:(216) 896 - 4000
TF: (800) 272 - 7537

Serves As:
• Contact, Parker Hannifin Foundation, Parker Hannifin Corp.

SEMLER, Jerry D.
P.O. Box 368
Indianapolis, IN 46206-0368
Tel: (317) 285 - 1877
Fax:(317) 285 - 1979

Serves As:
• Chairman of the Board, American United Life Insurance Co.
Also is the president of the OneAmerica Foundation.

SEMRAU, Kelly M.
1525 Howe St.
Racine, WI 53403
Tel: (262) 260 - 2000
Fax:(262) 260 - 6004

Serves As:
• V. President, Global Public Affairs and Communication, SC Johnson

SENA, Janet L.
1301 Pennsylvania Ave. NW
Suite 1030
Washington, DC 20004
jlsena@tecoenergy.com
Tel: (202) 824 - 0411
Fax:(202) 824 - 0651

Registered Federal Lobbyist.
Serves As:
• V. President, Federal Affairs, TECO Energy, Inc./Tampa Electric Co.

SENCHAK, Dennis E.
801 E. 86th Ave.
Merrillville, IN 46410
Tel: (219) 647 - 6200
Fax:(219) 647 - 6225
TF: (877) 647 - 5990

Serves As:
• V. President, Investor Relations, Assistant Treasurer and Assistant Secretary, NiSource Inc.

SENG, Mark
26555 Northwestern Hwy.
Southfield, MI 48034
Tel: (248) 354 - 7700
Fax:(248) 354 - 8950

Serves As:
• PAC Treasurer, Federal-Mogul Corp.

SENN, W. Edward
1300 I St. NW
Suite 400 West
Washington, DC 20005
Tel: (202) 515 - 2400

Registered Federal Lobbyist.
Serves As:
• V. President, Government Affairs - House, Verizon Communications Inc.

SENSEMAN, Kathryn
P.O. Box 52075
Phoenix, AZ 85072
Tel: (602) 395 - 4045

Serves As:
• Government Affairs Specialist, Southwest Gas Corp.

SENSIBAUGH, Cynthia B.
1399 New York Ave. NW
Suite 200
Washington, DC 20005
Tel: (202) 378 - 2020
Fax:(202) 783 - 6631

Registered Federal Lobbyist.
Serves As:
• Senior Director, Federal Government Affairs, Abbott Laboratories

SENTY, James A.
1099 18th St.
Suite 1200
Denver, CO 80202
Tel: (303) 452 - 5603
Fax:(303) 457 - 8482
TF: (800) 933 - 5603

Serves As:
• Chairman of the Board, Western Gas Resources, Inc.

SENWICK, Lex
499 Park Ave.
New York, NY 10022
Tel: (212) 318 - 2000
Fax:(917) 369 - 5000

Serves As:
• Chief Exec. Officer, Bloomberg L.P.

SEOMIN, Denise
6201 N. 24th Pkwy.
Phoenix, AZ 85016-2023
denise.seomin@bestwestern.com
Tel: (602) 957 - 5668
Fax:(602) 957 - 5641
TF: (800) 528 - 1234

Serves As:
• Manager, Consumer Media Relations, Best Western Internat'l

SERBY, Gary
P.O. Box 1059
Pawtucket, RI 02862
gserby@hasbro.com
Tel: (401) 727 - 5582
Fax:(401) 431 - 8535

Serves As:
• V. President, Public Relations, Hasbro Inc.

SERKES, Jeffrey D.
1301 Pennsylvania Ave. NW
Suite 1030
Washington, DC 20004
Tel: (202) 824 - 0404
Fax:(202) 347 - 0132

Registered Federal Lobbyist.
Serves As:
• Representative, Allegheny Energy Inc.

SERMERSHEIM, Ronald J.
1600 Royal St.
Jasper, IN 47549-1001
Tel: (812) 482 - 1600
Fax:(812) 482 - 8300
TF: (800) 482 - 1616

Serves As:
• V. President, Environmental Health and Safety, Kimball International, Inc.

SERRA, Matthew D.
112 W. 34th St.
New York, NY 10120
mserra@footlocker-inc.com
Tel: (212) 720 - 3700
Fax:(212) 720 - 4397

Serves As:
• Chairman, President and Chief Exec. Officer, Footlocker Inc.

SERRANO, Socorro L.
393 E. Walnut St.
Pasadena, CA 91188
Tel: (626) 405 - 3004
Fax:(626) 405 - 3176

Serves As:
• Senior Media Representative - Southern Califonia Region, Kaiser Permanente

SERVIDEA, Philip D.
555 12th St. NW, Suite 610
Washington, DC 20004
philip.d.servidea@ncr.com
Tel: (202) 347 - 6745
Fax:(202) 347 - 6884

Registered Federal Lobbyist.
Serves As:
• V. President, Government Affairs, NCR Corporation

SETTELMYER, Scott
601 Pennsylvania Ave. NW
Suite 720
Washington, DC 20004
Tel: (202) 783 - 3970
Fax:(202) 783 - 3982

Serves As:
• PAC Treasurer, ALLTEL

SETTINO, Mary Winn
One Pepsi Way
Somers, NY 10589-2201
marwinn.settino@pepsi.com
Tel: (914) 767 - 7216
Fax:(914) 767 - 1813

Serves As:
• Director, Investor Relations, The Pepsi Bottling Group

SETZEPFANDT, R.Ph., Scott
10330 Upper 196th Way West
Lakeville, MN 55044
Tel: (952) 469 - 5452
Fax:(952) 469 - 5453

Serves As:
• Senior Regional Manager, State Government Affairs, (HLR Service Corp.), Hoffmann-La Roche Inc. (Roche)

SEUTTER, Susan
P.O. Box 58090
M/S W-105
Santa Clara, CA 95052-8090
susan.seutter@nsc.com
Tel: (408) 721 - 5000
Fax:(408) 739 - 9803

Serves As:
• Director, Corporate Environmental, Health and Safety, Nat'l Semiconductor Corp.

SEWALL, Frank B.
P.O. Box 2181
320 W. Capitol
Little Rock, AR 72203-2181
Tel: (501) 378 - 3297

Serves As:
• Senior Counsel, Regulatory, Arkansas Blue Cross and Blue Shield

SEWELL, John
P.O. Box 1043
Jackson, MS 39215-1043
Tel: (601) 932 - 3704
Fax:(601) 939 - 7035
TF: (800) 222 - 8046

Serves As:
• Contact, Blue Cross and Blue Shield of Missisippi Foundation, Blue Cross and Blue Shield of Mississippi

SEWELL, Susan
77 W. 66th St.
New York, NY 10023
sewells@abc.com
Tel: (212) 456 - 7777
Fax:(212) 456 - 7909
TF: (800) 221 - 7386

Serves As:
- V. President, Media Relations-Network Communications, (ABC Television Network), ABC, Inc.

SEXTON, Beth R.
P.O. Box 834
Valley Forge, PA 19482-0834
bsexton@ikon.com
Tel: (610) 408 - 7224
Fax:(610) 408 - 7025
TF: (888) 275 - 4566

Serves As:
- Senior V. President, Human Resources, Ikon Office Solutions, Inc.

SEXTON, Wilson B.
109 Northpark Blvd.
Covington, LA 70433-5001
Tel: (985) 892 - 5521
Fax:(985) 892 - 1657

Serves As:
- Chairman of the Board, SCP Pool Corp.

SEYER, Sheryl A.
909 Hidden Ridge, Suite 600
Irving, TX 75038
sheryl.seyer@laquinta.com
Tel: (214) 492 - 6689
Fax:(214) 596 - 6013

Serves As:
- Manager, Investor Relations, La Quinta Inns

SEYMOUR TOWERY, Anne
6501 Legacy Dr.
Plano, TX 75024-3698
Tel: (972) 431 - 4147
Fax:(972) 431 - 1362
TF: (800) 222 - 6161

Serves As:
- V. President and Director, Company Communications, J. C. Penney Co., Inc.

SHACKOULS, Bobby S.
717 Texas Ave.
Suite 2100
Houston, TX 77002-2712
Tel: (713) 624 - 9000
Fax:(713) 624 - 9645
TF: (800) 262 - 3456

Serves As:
- Chairman, President, Chief Exec. Officer, Burlington Resources Inc.

SHAFFER, Fred
351 Phelps Dr.
Irving, TX 75038
fshaffer@kcc.com
Tel: (920) 721 - 3117

Registered Federal Lobbyist.
Serves As:
- Senior Director, Government Relations, Kimberly-Clark Corp.

SHAFFER, James W.
424 S. Woods Mill Rd.
Chesterfield, MO 63017
Tel: (314) 854 - 3800
Fax:(314) 854 - 3890

Serves As:
- V. President and Chief Financial Officer, Angelica Corp.

Serves as the senior public affairs executive at company headquarters.

SHAFFER, Teresa
P.O. Box 511
Kingsport, TN 37662-5075
shaffert@eastman.com
Tel: (423) 229 - 6962
Fax:(423) 224 - 0847
TF: (800) 327 - 8626

Serves As:
- Community Relations Representative, Eastman Chemical Co.

SHAH, Atish
9336 Civic Center Dr.
Beverly Hills, CA 90210
atish_shah@hilton.com
Tel: (310) 205 - 8664

Serves As:
- V. President, Investor Relations, Hilton Hotels Corp.

SHAH, Nimish
1425 K St. NW
Suite 650
Washington, DC 20005
nimish.shah@roche.com
Tel: (202) 408 - 0090
Fax:(202) 408 - 1750

Registered Federal Lobbyist.
Serves As:
- Manager, Public Policy, Hoffmann-La Roche Inc. (Roche)

SHAHEEN, George T.
2207 Bridgepoint Pkwy.
San Mateo, CA 94404
Tel: (650) 295 - 5000
Fax:(650) 295 - 5111
TF: (800) 356 - 3321

Serves As:
- Chief Exec. Officer, Siebel Systems, Inc.

SHALMY, Donald L. "Pat"
P.O. Box 98910
Las Vegas, NV 89151-0001
Tel: (702) 367 - 5000
Fax:(702) 367 - 5092
TF: (800) 331 - 3103

Serves As:
- President, Nevada Power Co.

Responsibilities include corporate philanthropy.

SHAMION, Vicki
N56 W17000 Ridgewood Dr.
Menomonee Falls, WI 53051
Tel: (262) 703 - 1464
Fax:(262) 703 - 7115

Serves As:
- Director, Public Relations, Kohl's Corp.

SHAMLEY, Mark W.
P.O. Box 2353
Orlando, FL 32802-2353
markshamley@tupperware.com
Tel: (407) 826 - 8755
Fax:(407) 826 - 4525

Serves As:
- Director, Global Corporate Citizenship, Tupperware Corp.

SHANHOLTZ, Beth
1111 Westchester Ave.
White Plains, NY 10604
beth.shanholtz@starwoodhotels.com
Tel: (914) 640 - 8112
Fax:(914) 640 - 8310
TF: (877) 443 - 4585

Serves As:
- Executive, Starwood Foundation, Starwood Hotels and Resorts Worldwide, Inc.

SHANK, Brian
104 Mancino Ct.
Cary, NC 27519
brian.shank@az.com
Tel: (919) 462 - 1847
Fax:(919) 462 - 1856
TF: (877) 893 - 0390
Ext: 43428

Serves As:
- Associate Director, State Government Affairs, AstraZeneca Pharmaceuticals

SHANKS, Carolyn C.
P.O. Box 1640
Jackson, MS 39215-1640
cshanks@entergy.com
Tel: (601) 368 - 5000
Fax:(601) 964 - 2400

Serves As:
- President and Chief Exec. Officer, Entergy Mississippi

SHAPIRO, Jeffrey Alan
601 13th St. NW
Suite 510 South
Washington, DC 20005
Tel: (202) 737 - 8200
Fax:(202) 638 - 4914

Registered Federal Lobbyist.
Serves As:
- Washington Representative, General Mills

SHAPIRO, Marc
4200 Wackenhut Dr.
Palm Beach Gardens, FL 33410-4243
Tel: (561) 622 - 5656
Fax:(561) 691 - 6738
TF: (800) 922 - 6488

Serves As:
- V. President, Strategic Partnerships, The Wackenhut Corporation

Responsibilities include investor relations.

SHAPIRO, Richard
840 Gessner
Suite 1400
Houston, TX 77024
Tel: (713) 650 - 6200
Fax:(713) 653 - 6815

Serves As:
- Exec. V. President, Public Affairs and Marketing, Cemex USA

SHAPIRO, Steven H.
One Pierce Place
Suite 1500
Itasca, IL 60143
Tel: (630) 875 - 7345
Fax:(630) 875 - 7360

Serves As:
- Exec. V. President and Corporate Secretary, First Midwest Bancorp, Inc.

Responsibilities include investor and media relations.

SHARER, Kevin
One Amgen Center Dr.
Thousand Oaks, CA 91320-1799
kevins@amgen.com
Tel: (805) 447 - 1000
Fax:(805) 499 - 3507

Serves As:
- Chairman, President and Chief Exec. Officer, Amgen Inc.

SHARKEY, Steve
1350 I St. NW
Suite 400
Washington, DC 20005-3306
Tel: (202) 371 - 6900
Fax:(202) 842 - 3578

Registered Federal Lobbyist.
Serves As:
- Director, Spectrum and Standards Strategy, Motorola, Inc.

SHARMAN, James A.
11911 Freedom Dr.
Suite 600
Reston, VA 20190
Tel: (703) 456 - 4700
Fax:(607) 377 - 8962
TF: (800) 999 - 3436

Serves As:
- President and Chief Exec. Officer, World Kitchen, Inc.

SHARMAN, Leslie
4201 Marsh Ln.
Carrolton, TX 75007
Tel: (972) 662 - 4621
Fax:(972) 662 - 5588

Serves As:
- Treasurer, Carlson Restaurants Worldwide Political Action Committee, Carlson Companies

SHARP, Douglas S.
19001 Crescent Springs Dr.
Kingwood, TX 77339-3802
douglas_sharp@administaff.com
Tel: (281) 348 - 3232
TF: (800) 237 - 3170

Serves As:
- V. President, Finance and Chief Financial Officer, Administaff, Inc.

Responsibilities include investor relations.

SHARP, Mark
1130 Connecticut Ave. NW
Suite 1100
Washington, DC 20036
Tel: (202) 912 - 3800

Registered Federal Lobbyist.
Serves As:
- General Manager, Corporate Environmental Department, Matsushita Electric Corp. of America

SHATTUCK, III, Mayo A.
750 E. Pratt St.
18th Floor
Baltimore, MD 21202
Tel: (410) 783 - 2800
TF: (888) 460 - 2002

Serves As:
- Chairman, President and Chief Exec. Officer, Constellation Energy

SHATTUCK, Steve
20511 Lake Forest Dr.
Lake Forest, CA 92630-7741
steve.shattuck@wdc.com
Tel: (949) 672 - 7817
Fax:(949) 672 - 5408

Serves As:
- Director, Public Relations, Western Digital Corp.

SHAUGHNESSY, John
610 Opperman Dr.
Eagan, MN 55123-1340
john.shaughnessy@thomson.com
Tel: (651) 687 - 4749
Fax:(651) 687 - 5388
TF: (800) 328 - 9352

Serves As:
- Corporate Communications, Thomson West

SHAULTS, Donna
225 Windsor Dr.
Itasca, IL 60143
Tel: (630) 875 - 5300
Ext: 5464
Fax:(630) 875 - 5858
TF: (800) 436 - 3726

Serves As:
- Director, Corporate Communications, Enesco Group, Inc.

SHAW, Brad
2455 Paces Ferry Rd.
Atlanta, GA 30339-4024
Tel: (770) 433 - 8211
Fax:(770) 384 - 2356

Serves As:
- Senior V. President, Communications and External Affairs, The Home Depot, Inc.

SHAW, Ellie
101 Constitution Ave., NW
Suite 400 East
Washington, DC 20001
ellie.shaw@exeloncorp.com
Tel: (202) 347 - 7500
Fax:(202) 347 - 7501

Serves As:
- Manager, Public Affairs, Exelon Corp.

SHAW, Jeffrey W.
P.O. Box 98510
Las Vegas, NV 89193-8510
Tel: (702) 876 - 7011
Fax:(702) 364 - 3444

Serves As:
- Chief Exec. Officer, Southwest Gas Corp.

SHAW, Julius
P.O. Drawer 2128
Dalton, GA 30722-2128
Tel: (706) 278 - 3812
Fax:(706) 275 - 1719

Serves As:
- Exec. V. President, Shaw Industries

Responsibilities include external communications.

SHAW, Mary Kay
One McDonald's Plaza
Oak Brook, IL 60523
Tel: (630) 623 - 7559
Fax:(630) 623 - 5004

Serves As:
- V. President, Investor Relations and Financial Communications, McDonald's Corp.

SHAW, Michiele
P.O. Box 5000
Pineville, LA 71361-5000
Tel: (318) 484 - 7400
Fax:(318) 484 - 7465

Serves As:
- V. President, Human Resources, Communications and Ethics, Cleco Corp.

SHAW, Richard C.
One Applied Plaza
Cleveland, OH 44115
rshaw@applied.com
Tel: (216) 426 - 4343
Fax:(216) 426 - 4808
TF: (877) 279 - 2799

Serves As:
- V. President, Communications and Learning, Applied Industrial Technologies

SHAW, Robert E.
P.O. Drawer 2128
Dalton, GA 30722-2128
Tel: (706) 278 - 3812
Fax:(706) 275 - 1719

Serves As:
- Chairman and Chief Exec. Officer, Shaw Industries

SHAW, Scott
P.O. Box 355
Pittsburgh, PA 15230-0355
shawsa@westinghouse.com
Tel: (412) 374 - 6737
Fax:(412) 374 - 3244

Serves As:
- Communications Specialist, Westinghouse Electric Company LLC

SHAW, Steve
10250 Constellation Blvd.
Los Angeles, CA 90067-6241
sshaw@mgm.com
Tel: (310) 449 - 3000
Fax:(310) 449 - 8757

Serves As:
- Senior V. President, Human Resources, Metro-Goldwyn-Mayer Inc.

SHAW, William
560 Lexington Ave.
15th Floor
New York, NY 10022
wshaw@volt.com
Tel: (212) 704 - 2400
Fax:(212) 704 - 2411
TF: (800) 533 - 2401

Serves As:
- Chairman, President, and Chief Exec. Officer, Volt Information Sciences, Inc.

SHAWMEKER, Mary Ann
Seven W. Seventh St.
Cincinnati, OH 45202
Tel: (513) 579 - 7292
Fax:(513) 579 - 7185
TF: (800) 261 - 5385

Serves As:
- Operations V. President, Corporate Communications, Federated Department Stores, Inc.

SHAY, Jr., Paul E.
2244 Walnut Grove Ave.
Rosemead, CA 91770
shaype@sce.com
Tel: (626) 302 - 1984
Fax:(626) 302 - 6315

Serves As:
- Director, Corporate Public Affairs, Southern California Edison, an Edison Internat'l Co.
- PAC Treasurer, Edison Internat'l

SHEA, Barry F.
P.O. Box 261
Danville, VA 24543
Tel: (434) 799 - 7000
Fax:(434) 799 - 7276

Serves As:
- Treasurer, Dan River Foundation, Dan River, Inc.

SHEA, Christina S.
One General Mills Blvd.
Minneapolis, MN 55426
Tel: (763) 764 - 3413

Serves As:
- Senior V. President, External Relations and President, General Mills Foundation, General Mills

SHEA, Martin M.
1515 Broadway
New York, NY 10036
Tel: (212) 846 - 6515
Fax:(212) 258 - 1705

Serves As:
- Exec. V. President, Investor Relations, Viacom Inc./CBS Corp.

SHEAHAN, Laurie
P.O. Box 618
St. Louis, MO 63188-0618
Tel: (314) 877 - 7994
Fax:(314) 877 - 7667

Serves As:
- Investor and Public Relations Contact, Ralcorp Holdings, Inc.

SHEEHAN, Kevin
5215 N. O'Connor Blvd.
Suite 2300
Irving, TX 75039
Tel: (972) 443 - 6500
Fax:(972) 443 - 6800

Serves As:
- Interim Chief Executive Officer, Flowserve Corp.

SHEEHAN, Shaun M.
1501 K St. NW
Suite 550
Washington, DC 20005
ssheehan@tribune.com
Tel: (202) 775 - 7750
Fax:(202) 223 - 3844

Registered Federal Lobbyist.
Serves As:
- V. President, Washington Affairs, (Tribune Broadcasting Co.), Tribune Co.

SHEEHAN, Stephen G.
81 Wyman St.
Waltham, MA 02454-9046
stephen.sheehan@thermo.com
Tel: (781) 622 - 1000
Fax:(781) 622 - 1207

Serves As:
- V. President, Human Resources, Thermo Electron Corp.

SHEEHY, Pat
305 Hartman Dr.
Lebanon, TN 37088
Tel: (615) 444 - 5533
Fax:(615) 443 - 9511

Serves As:
- Manager, Government Relations, (Cracker Barrel Old Country Store, Inc.), CBRL Group, Inc.

SHEEHY, Timothy J.
1301 K St. NW
Suite 1200
Washington, DC 20005
Tel: (202) 515 - 5077
Fax:(202) 515 - 5078

Registered Federal Lobbyist.
Serves As:
- Director, Networked Economy, Internat'l Business Machines Corp. (IBM)

SHEETZ, Stanton R.
5700 Sixth Ave.
Altoona, PA 16602
Tel: (814) 946 - 3611
Fax:(814) 946 - 4375
TF: (800) 487 - 5444

Serves As:
- President and Chief Exec. Officer, Sheetz, Inc.

Responsibilities include political action.

SHEETZ, Stephen G.
5700 Sixth Ave.
Altoona, PA 16602
Tel: (814) 946 - 3611
Fax:(814) 946 - 4375
TF: (800) 487 - 5444

Serves As:
- Chairman of the Board, Sheetz, Inc.

SHEFFER, Gary
3135 Easton Tpk.
Bldg. E2E
Fairfield, CT 06431
gary.sheffer@ge.com
Tel: (203) 373 - 2211
Fax:(203) 373 - 3131

Serves As:
- Exec. Director, Communications and Public Affairs, General Electric Co.

SHEFFER, Rich
P.O. Box 1299
Minneapolis, MN 55440-1299
rscheffer@mail.donaldson.com
Tel: (952) 887 - 3753
Fax:(952) 887 - 3005
TF: (800) 887 - 3131

Serves As:
- Assistant Treasurer and Director, Investor Relations, Donaldson Company, Inc.

SHEFFIELD, Peter
P.O. Box 1244
M/S ECO6G
Charlotte, NC 28201-1244
pysheffield@duke-energy.com
Tel: (704) 373 - 4503
Fax:(704) 382 - 8375

Serves As:
- Manager, Media, Duke Energy Corp.

SHEFFIELD, Scott D.
5205 N. O'Connor Blvd.
Suite 900
Irving, TX 75039
Tel: (972) 444 - 9001
Fax:(972) 969 - 3516

Serves As:
- Chairman, President and Chief Exec. Officer, Pioneer Natural Resources Co.

SHEIL, David R.
P.O. Box 4446
Houston, TX 77210-4446
sheil@cooperindustries.com
Tel: (713) 209 - 8418
Fax:(713) 209 - 8989

Serves As:
- Senior V. President, Human Resources, Cooper Industries

SHEIRE, James B.
1300 I St. NW
Suite 1070 East
Washington, DC 20005
Tel: (202) 962 - 8550
Fax:(202) 962 - 8560

Registered Federal Lobbyist.
Serves As:
- Manager, Legislative and Regulatory Affairs, Philips Electronics North America

SHEKHOAR, Alexander
48 Monroe Tpk.
Trumbull, CT 06611
Tel: (203) 459 - 6000
Fax:(203) 459 - 6464
TF: (800) 889 - 7658

Registered Federal Lobbyist.
Serves As:
- Representative, Oxford Health Plans Inc.

SHELBY, Melanie M.
900 Seventh St. NW, Suite 950
Washington, DC 20001-3886
Tel: (202) 638 - 3500
Fax:(202) 638 - 3522

Serves As:
- Manager, Federal Governmental Relations, PG & E Corp.

SHELL, Fred
2000 Second Ave.
Detroit, MI 48226
Tel: (313) 235 - 8000

Serves As:
- V. President, Corporate and Governmental Affairs, DTE Energy Co.

SHELL, Terri
711 High St.
Des Moines, IA 50392-0150
shell.terri@principal.com
Tel: (515) 283 - 8858
Fax:(515) 246 - 5475
TF: (800) 986 - 3343

Serves As:
- Media Relations Contact, The Principal Financial Group

SHELTON, Bridget A.
P.O. Box 9239
Newark, DE 19714-9239
Tel: (302) 283 - 5808
Fax:(302) 283 - 6015

Serves As:
- Public Affairs Coordinator, (Delmarva Power), Conectiv

SHELTON, James D.
5800 Tennyson Pkwy.
Plano, TX 75024
Tel: (214) 473 - 7000

Serves As:
- Chairman and Chief Exec. Officer, Triad Hospitals, Inc.

SHELTON, Stephanie
P.O. Box 31328
Tampa, FL 33631-3328
sshelton@gerdauameristeel.com
Tel: (813) 207 - 2257
Fax:(813) 207 - 2280

Serves As:
- Manager, Corporate Communications, Gerdau Ameristeel Corp.

SHEPARD, Ethel
Two Seaport Ln.
Suite 1300
Boston, MA 02210-2019
Tel: (617) 342 - 6254
Fax:(617) 342 - 6312

Serves As:
- Manager, Corporate Communications, Cabot Corp.

SHEPARD, Katherine L.
Brighton Landing, 20 Guest St.
Boston, MA 02135-2088
Tel: (617) 783 - 4000
Ext: 2240
Fax:(617) 746 - 6240
TF: (800) 343 - 4648

Serves As:
- Senior Manager, Corporate Communications, New Balance Athletic Shoe, Inc.

SHEPARD, Kathy
9336 Civic Center Dr.
Beverly Hills, CA 90210
kathy_shepard@hilton.com
Tel: (310) 205 - 7676
Fax:(310) 205 - 7678

Serves As:
- V. President, Corporate Communications, Hilton Hotels Corp.

Responsibilities include corporate contributions and government affairs.

SHEPARD, Krista
870 Winter St.
Waltham, MA 02451
krista_shepard@raytheon.com
Tel: (781) 522 - 3000

Serves As:
- Director, Communications, Raytheon Co.

SHEPARD, Stacey
413 New Jersey Ave., SE
Washington, DC 20003
Tel: (202) 543 - 3486
Fax:(202) 543 - 1680

Registered Federal Lobbyist.
Serves As:
- Director, Government Affairs, Jacobs Engineering Group Inc.

SHEPHARD, Donald C. "Buzz"
1645 Bergstrom Rd.
Neenah, WI 54956
Tel: (920) 751 - 1000
Fax:(920) 951 - 1236
TF: (800) 558 - 5073

Serves As:
- Chairman of the Board, Menasha Corporation

SHEPHERD, Michael
P.O. Box 3200
Honolulu, HI 96847
Tel: (808) 525 - 7000
Fax:(808) 557 - 086

Serves As:
- Exec. V. President and General Counsel, BancWest Corp.

SHEPPARD, George N.
607 E. Adams St.
Springfield, IL 62739
Tel: (618) 993 - 4628
Fax:(618) 993 - 4610

Serves As:
- Public Affairs Representative, (AmerenCIPS), Ameren Corp.

SHEPPARD, Kristen
50 Minuteman Rd.
Andover, MA 01810
ksheppar@enterasys.com
Tel: (978) 684 - 1000
Fax:(978) 684 - 1658

Serves As:
- V. President, Investor Relations and Corporate Affairs, Enterasys Networks

SHERBIN, Bob
7565 Irvine Center Dr.
Irvine, CA 92618
Tel: (949) 471 - 7000
Fax:(949) 471 - 7041

Serves As:
- Director, Corporate Communications, Gateway, Inc.

SHERIDAN, John P.
890 Winter St., Suite 300
Waltham, MA 02451
jpsheridan@duke-energy.com
Tel: (617) 560 - 1444
Fax:(617) 560 - 1580

Serves As:
- Regional Director, Public and Government Relations, Algonquin Gas Transmission, LLC/Duke Energy
- Regional Director, State Governmental Affairs, Duke Energy Corp.

SHERMAN, Karen
P.O. Box 99900
Louisville, KY 40269-0900
karen_sherman@papajohns.com
Tel: (502) 261 - 4987
Fax:(502) 261 - 4315

Serves As:
- V. President, Communications, Papa John's Internat'l Inc.

SHERMAN, Rachel
635 Massachusetts Ave. NW
Washington, DC 20001
Tel: (202) 513 - 2000
Fax:(202) 513 - 3329

Serves As:
- Manager, Government Relations, Nat'l Public Radio

SHERMAN, Roger L.
P.O. Box 577
Rupert, WI 25984
Tel: (304) 392 - 6373

Serves As:
- Public Affairs Forester, MeadWestvaco Corp.

SHERMAN, Susan D.
P.O. Box 2463
Houston, TX 77252-2463
Tel: (713) 241 - 6161
Fax:(713) 241 - 4044

Serves As:
- PAC Treasurer, Shell Oil Co.

SHERMAN, Zach
1550 Crystal Dr.
Crystal Square 2, Suite 300
Arlington, VA 22202
Tel: (703) 413 - 5915
Fax:(703) 413 - 5636

Serves As:
- Political Programs Manager, Lockheed Martin Employees Political Action Committee, Lockheed Martin Corp.

SHERMER, Angie M.
45200 Business Ct.
Suite 100
Dulles, VA 20166-6715
Tel: (703) 650 - 6000
Fax:(703) 650 - 6299

Serves As:
- V. President, Employee Services, FLYi, Inc.

SHERRARD, Rachel
825 N.E. Multnomah
Suite 2000
Portland, OR 97232
rachel.sherrard@pacificorp.com
Tel: (503) 813 - 5688
Fax:(503) 813 - 5378
TF: (888) 221 - 7070

Serves As:
- V. President, External Communications, PacifiCorp

SHERRILL, Parker
310 25th Ave. North, Suite 101
Nashville, TN 37203
parker.sherrill@hcahealthcare.com
Tel: (615) 320 - 9028
Fax:(615) 963 - 3841

Serves As:
- Consultant, Government Relations, HCA

SHERRY, Don E.
Box 401
Oklahoma City, OK 73101-0401
dsherry@oneok.com
Tel: (405) 551 - 6738
Fax:(405) 551 - 6779

Serves As:
- Manager, Communications, (Oklahoma Natural Gas Co.), ONEOK, Inc.

SHERWIN, R. Lawrence
720 Olive St.
St. Louis, MO 63101
Tel: (314) 342 - 0500
Fax:(314) 421 - 1979

Serves As:
- Assistant V. President, Regulatory Administration, The Laclede Group

SHERWOOD, Amy
P.O. Box 32070
Louisville, KY 40232
Tel: (502) 874 - 8200
Fax:(502) 874 - 8324

Serves As:
- V. President, Public Relations and Consumer Affairs, YUM! Brands, Inc.

SHESTAK, David A.
1201 K St., Suite 815
Sacramento, CA 95814
dshestak@corus.jnj.com
Tel: (916) 443 - 2010
Fax:(916) 446 - 6896

Serves As:
- Director, State Government Affairs, Johnson & Johnson

SHEVCHIK, Joan O.
P.O. Box 145496
Cincinnati, OH 45250
Tel: (513) 870 - 2198
Fax:(513) 870 - 2935

Serves As:
- Senior V. President, Corporate Communications, Cincinnati Financial Corp.

SHEW, Archie R.
956 Woodsedge Ln.
Westerville, OH 43081
archie.shew@roche.com
Tel: (614) 523 - 3921
Fax:(614) 523 - 3941

Serves As:
- Senior Regional Manager, State Government Affairs, (HLR Service Corp.), Hoffmann-La Roche Inc. (Roche)

SHIELDS, Jerry
2455 Paces Ferry Rd.
\
Atlanta, GA 30339-4024
jerry_shields@homedepot.com
Tel: (770) 384 - 2741
Fax:(770) 384 - 2685

Serves As:
- Senior Manager, Public Relations, The Home Depot, Inc.

SHIELDS, R. Eugene
P.O. Box 1438
Louisville, KY 40201-1438
Tel: (502) 580 - 1000
Fax:(502) 580 - 3677
TF: (800) 486 - 2620

Serves As:
- Senior V. President, Government Programs, Humana Inc.

SHIELY, John S.
P.O. Box 702
Milwaukee, WI 53201-0702
Tel: (414) 259 - 5333
Fax:(414) 479 - 1245

Serves As:
- Chairman, President and Chief Exec. Officer, Briggs and Stratton Corp.

SHILLABER, James
P.O. Box 1000
Montville, NJ 07045
Fax:(973) 487 - 2003
TF: (800) 237 - 5392

Serves As:
- Director, Human Resources, Berlex, Inc.

SHILOBRIT, Tracy
5301 N. Ironwood Rd.
Milwaukee, WI 53217
tracy.shilobrit@manpower.com
Tel: (414) 906 - 6088
Fax:(414) 961 - 8780

Serves As:
- Director, Corporate and Global Communications, Manpower Inc.

SHIMURA, Tetsuo
400 California St.
San Francisco, CA 94104
Tel: (415) 765 - 0400
Fax:(415) 765 - 3257

Serves As:
- Chairman of the Board, Union Bank of California

SHIN, Hyun Kyu "Frank"
1667 K St., NW
Suite 1210
Washington, DC 20006
hyunkyushin@hyundai-motor.co
Tel: (202) 296 - 5550
Fax:(202) 296 - 6436

Serves As:
• Representative, Hyundai Motor America
Serves as the senior public affairs officer.

SHIPP, Catherine
5400 Legacy Dr., Cluster II, Bldg. 3
Plano, TX 75024
Tel: (972) 265 - 2000
TF: (800) 669 - 5740

Serves As:
• PAC Treasurer, Safety-Kleen Systems, Inc.

SHIPPAR, Donald J.
30 W. Superior St.
Duluth, MN 55802
Tel: (218) 279 - 5000
Fax:(218) 279 - 5050

Serves As:
• President and Chief Exec. Officer, ALLETE

SHIVEL, John
One Fruit of the Loom Dr.
Bowling Green, KY 42102
Tel: (270) 781 - 6400
Fax:(270) 781 - 6588

Serves As:
• V. President, Advertising and Corporate Communications, (Fruit of the Loom, Inc.), Berkshire Hathaway

SHIVERY, Charles W.
P.O. Box 270
Hartford, CT 06141-0270
Tel: (860) 665 - 5000
Fax:(860) 665 - 3177
TF: (800) 286 - 2000

Serves As:
• Chairman, President and Chief Exec. Officer, Northeast Utilities

SHOBE, Debbie
P.O. Box 32010
Louisville, KY 40232-2010
debbie.shobe@lgeenergy.com
Tel: (502) 627 - 4793

Serves As:
• Associate Community Relations Specialist, (Louisville Gas & Electric Co.), LG&E Energy LLC

SHOCKLEY, Larry G.
1133 15th St. NW
Suite 800
Washington, DC 20005-2701
Tel: (202) 775 - 3300
Fax:(202) 775 - 3422

Serves As:
• V. President, Government Relations, Parsons Corp.

SHOEN, Edward "Joe"
1325 Airmotive Way, Suite 100
Reno, NV 89502-3239
Tel: (775) 688 - 6300
Fax:(775) 688 - 6338

Serves As:
• Chairman and President, AMERCO

SHOLKIN, Howie
One Exeter Plaza
15 Floor
Boston, MA 02116
howard_sholkin@idg.com
Tel: (617) 534 - 4200
Fax:(617) 423 - 0240

Serves As:
• Director, Corporate Communications, Internat'l Data Group

SHOLL, James
P.O. Box 3599
Battle Creek, MI 49016-3599
Tel: (269) 961 - 2000
Fax:(269) 961 - 2871
TF: (800) 535 - 5644

Serves As:
• Treasurer, Kellogg Better Government Committee, Kellogg Co.

SHOOP, Neil
2525 Stemmons Fwy.
Dallas, TX 75207-2401
neil.shoop@trin.net
Tel: (214) 631 - 4420
Fax:(214) 689 - 0501

Serves As:
• Director, Investor Relations, Trinity Industries, Inc.

SHOPTAW, Robert L.
P.O. Box 2181
320 W. Capitol
Little Rock, AR 72203-2181
Tel: (501) 378 - 2000

Serves As:
• Chief Exec. Officer, Arkansas Blue Cross and Blue Shield

SHORE, Jerry A.
4300 New Getwell Rd.
Memphis, TN 38118-6801
Tel: (901) 365 - 3733
Ext: 2217
Fax:(901) 328 - 0354
TF: (800) 374 - 7417

Serves As:
• Chief Financial Officer and Exec. V. President, Fred's Inc.
Responsibilities include investor relations.

SHORE, William A.
P.O. Box 13398
Research Triangle Park, NC 27709
Tel: (919) 483 - 2719
Fax:(919) 483 - 8765

Serves As:
• Director, Corporate Community Affairs, GlaxoSmithKline Research and Development

SHORT, Hellen F.
One Johnson & Johnson Plaza
New Brunswick, NJ 08933-7204
Tel: (732) 524 - 6491
Fax:(732) 214 - 0334
TF: (800) 635 - 6789

Serves As:
• V. President, Investor Relations, Johnson & Johnson

SHORT, John H.
7733 Forsyth Blvd.
Suite 2300
St. Louis, MO 63105
Tel: (314) 863 - 7422
Fax:(314) 863 - 0769
TF: (800) 677 - 1238

Serves As:
• Chief Exec. Officer, RehabCare Group, Inc.

SHORT, Joseph A.
6363 Main St.
Williamsville, NY 14221
shortj@natfuel.com
Tel: (716) 857 - 7842
Fax:(716) 857 - 7439
TF: (800) 365 - 3234

Serves As:
• Treasurer, Nat'l Fuel Political Action Committee, Nat'l Fuel Gas Co.

SHORTELL, Alan
1501 K St. NW
Suite 575
Washington, DC 20005
Tel: (202) 654 - 2940

Registered Federal Lobbyist.
Serves As:
• Representative, New York Life Insurance Co.

SHOTWELL, James P.
555 12th St. NW
Suite 640
Washington, DC 20004-2505
Tel: (202) 393 - 3075
Fax:(202) 393 - 1497

Serves As:
• Director, Federal Regulatory Affairs, Edison Internat'l

SHRADER, Patricia B.
One Becton Dr.
Franklin Lakes, NJ 07417-1880
patricia_shrader@bd.com
Tel: (201) 847 - 7429
Fax:(201) 847 - 6475

Serves As:
• V. President, Corporate Regulatory, Public Policy and Communications, Becton, Dickinson and Co.

SHRADER, Ralph W.
8283 Greensboro Dr.
McLean, VA 22102-3802
Tel: (703) 902 - 5000
Fax:(703) 902 - 3333

Serves As:
• Chairman and Chief Exec. Officer, Booz Allen Hamilton Inc.

SHRIVER, Debra
959 Eighth Ave.
New York, NY 10019
Tel: (212) 649 - 2461
Fax:(212) 765 - 3528

Serves As:
• V. President and Chief Communications Officer, The Hearst Corp.

SHRIVER, Michael
1100 N. King St.
Wilmington, DE 19880-127
Tel: (302) 453 - 9930
Fax:(302) 456 - 8541
TF: (800) 441 - 7048

Serves As:
• Contact, MBNA Foundation, MBNA Corp.

SHUDTZ, Peter J.
1331 Pennsylvania Ave. NW
Suite 560
Washington, DC 20004
peter_shudtz@csx.com
Tel: (202) 783 - 1343
Fax:(202) 783 - 5929

Registered Federal Lobbyist.
Serves As:
• Senior V. President, Regulatory Affairs and Washington Counsel, CSX Corp.

SHULMAN, Steven J.
55 Nod Rd
Avon, CT 06001
Tel: (860) 507 - 1900
Fax:(860) 507 - 1990
TF: (800) 410 - 8312

Serves As:
- Chairman and Chief Exec. Officer, Magellan Health Services, Inc.

SHULTZ, Ed
P.O. Box 12646
Reading, PA 19612
eshultz1@sovereignbank.com
Tel: (610) 378 - 6159
Fax:(610) 378 - 6155

Serves As:
- Vice President and Director, Public Relations, Sovereign Bancorp, Inc.

SHULTZ, Gary
P.O. Box 6014
Cypress, CA 90630-0014
Tel: (714) 372 - 6000
Fax:(714) 373 - 1020

Serves As:
- V. President, Legal and Government Affairs and General Counsel, (MMNA Manufacturing), Mitsubishi Motors North America, Inc.

SHULTZ, Martin L.
P.O. Box 53999
Phoenix, AZ 85072-3999
martin.shultz@pinnaclewest.com
Tel: (602) 250 - 2866
Fax:(602) 250 - 3902

Serves As:
- V. President, Government Affairs, Pinnacle West Capital Corp.

SHURDUT, Bradley A.
1776 I St. NW
Suite 1050
Washington, DC 20006
bshurdut@dow.com
Tel: (202) 429 - 3434
Fax:(202) 429 - 3467

Registered Federal Lobbyist.
Serves As:
- Global Leader, Government and Regulatory Affairs, Biotechnology, Dow AgroSciences LLC

SHYDLO, Maria Gordon
48 Monroe Tpk.
Trumbull, CT 06611
mshydlo@oxhp.com
Tel: (203) 459 - 7674
Fax:(203) 452 - 4644
TF: (800) 889 - 7658

Serves As:
- Director, Public and Community Relations, Oxford Health Plans Inc.

SIAS, Spencer
3100 Hansen Way
Palo Alto, CA 94304-1030
spencer.sias@varian.com
Tel: (650) 424 - 5782
Fax:(650) 842 - 5196

Serves As:
- Director, Corporate Communications and Investor Relations, Varian Medical Systems, Inc.

SIAS, Thelma
231 W. Michigan
Milwaukee, WI 53203
thelma.sias@we-energies.com
Tel: (414) 221 - 3651
Fax:(414) 221 - 3853

Serves As:
- V. President, Local Affairs, We Energies
- V. President, Local Affairs, Wisconsin Energy Corp.

SIBBERNSEN, Richard D.
1155 Peachtree St. NE
Atlanta, GA 30309-3610
Tel: (404) 249 - 2000
Fax:(404) 249 - 2071

Serves As:
- V. President, Human Resources, BellSouth Corp.

SIBERT, Rich
2515 McKinney Ave., Suite 1200
Dallas, TX 75201
Tel: (214) 303 - 3400
Fax:(214) 303 - 3499

Serves As:
- Director,Investor Relations, Dean Foods Company

SIBLEY, Beth
950 Echo Lane, Suite 100
Houston, TX 77024
bsibley@group1auto.com
Tel: (713) 647 - 5700
Fax:(713) 647 - 5869

Serves As:
- PAC Treasurer, Group 1 Automotive, Inc.

SIBOLD, Jr., Robert G.
2700 N. First St.
San Jose, CA 95134
Tel: (408) 964 - 3500
Fax:(408) 964 - 3636

Serves As:
- Treasurer, SCI Systems PAC, Sanmina-SCI Corp.

SICKELS, Linda S.
316 W. 12th St.
Suite 102
Austin, TX 78701
linda.sickels@trin.net
Tel: (512) 478 - 4844

Registered Federal Lobbyist.
Serves As:
- V. President, Government Relations, Trinity Industries, Inc.

SICREE, Joseph R.
3103 Philmont Ave.
Huntingdon Valley, PA 19006
jsicree@tollbrothersinc.com
Tel: (215) 938 - 8045
Fax:(215) 938 - 8010

Serves As:
- V. President, Chief Accounting Officer and Director, Investor Relations, Toll Brothers, Inc.

SIDES, Delores
804 Green Valley Rd.
Greensboro, NC 27408
Tel: (336) 379 - 2903
Fax:(336) 379 - 4504

Serves As:
- Director, Corporate Communications, Internat'l Textiles Group

SIDHU, Jay
P.O. Box 12646
Reading, PA 19612
Tel: (610) 320 - 8400
Fax:(610) 320 - 8448

Serves As:
- Chairman and Chief Exec. Officer, Sovereign Bancorp, Inc.

SIDHU, Sanjiv S.
One i2 Pl.
11701 Luna Rd.
Dallas, TX 75234
Tel: (469) 357 - 1000
Fax:(469) 357 - 1798

Serves As:
- Chairman of the Board, i2 Technologies, Inc.

SIEBEL, Carl A.
475 W. Terra Cotta Ave.
Suite E
Crystal Lake, IL 60014-9695
Tel: (815) 477 - 0424
Fax:(815) 477 - 0481

Serves As:
- President and Chief Exec. Officer, AptarGroup, Inc.

SIEBEL, Thomas M.
2207 Bridgepoint Pkwy.
San Mateo, CA 94404
tsiebel@siebel.com
Tel: (650) 295 - 5000
Fax:(650) 295 - 5111
TF: (800) 356 - 3321

Serves As:
- Chairman of the Board, Siebel Systems, Inc.

SIEBER, Rich
411 Seventh Ave.
Pittsburgh, PA 15219
rsieber@dqe.com
Tel: (412) 393 - 6393
Fax:(412) 393 - 6825

Serves As:
- Manager, Marketing Communications, (Duquesne Light Co.), Duquesne Light Holdings

SIEGAL, L. Pendleton
601 W. Riverside Ave.
Suite 1100
Spokane, WA 99201
Tel: (509) 835 - 1500
Fax:(509) 835 - 1555

Serves As:
- Chairman and Chief Exec. Officer, Potlatch Corp.

SIEGEL, Jeannette
6501 Legacy Dr.
Plano, TX 75024-3698
Tel: (972) 431 - 1000
Fax:(972) 431 - 1362
TF: (800) 222 - 6161

Serves As:
- V. President, Foundations, J. C. Penney Co., Inc.

SIEGEL, Kenneth S.
1111 Westchester Ave.
White Plains, NY 10604
kenneth.siegel@starwoodhotels.com
Tel: (914) 640 - 8200
Fax:(914) 640 - 8310
TF: (877) 443 - 4585

Serves As:
- Exec. V. President, General Counsel and Secretary, Starwood Hotels and Resorts Worldwide, Inc.

Responsibilities include government affairs.

SIEGEL, Laurie
Nine Roszel Rd.
Princeton, NJ 08540
Tel: (609) 720 - 4200
Fax:(609) 720 - 4208

Serves As:
- Senior V. President, Human Resources, Tyco Internat'l (U.S.), Inc.

SIEGEL, Mark
5565 Glenridge Connector
Atlanta, GA 30342
mark.a.siegel@cingular.com
Tel: (404) 236 - 6312
Fax:(866) 246 - 4852
TF: (800) 331 - 0500

Serves As:
• Exec. Director, Media Relations, Cingular Wireless

SIEGEL, Susan
P.O. Box 1907
Albany, NY 12201-1907
Tel: (518) 445 - 2284
Fax:(518) 447 - 6343

Serves As:
• Manager, Corporate Communications, Albany Internat'l Corp.

SIEGEL, Wendy
124 W. Allegan, Suite 800
Lansing, MI 48933

Serves As:
• PAC Treasurer, ArvinMeritor

SIEGER, Daniel
25 Atlantic Ave.
Erlanger, KY 41018
Tel: (859) 372 - 3871
Fax:(859) 746 - 4569

Serves As:
• Manager, Media Relations, (Toyota Motor Manufacturing North America), Toyota Motor North America, Inc.

SIELUFF, Courtney
P.O. Box 98905
Las Vegas, NV 89193-8905
Tel: (702) 407 - 6000

Serves As:
• PAC Treasurer, Harrah's Entertainment, Inc.

SIEMENS, Jr., George R.
P.O. Box 32010
Louisville, KY 40232-2010
george.siemens@lgeenergy.com
Tel: (502) 627 - 2323
Fax:(502) 217 - 2654

Serves As:
• V. President, External Affairs, LG&E Energy LLC

SIERRA, Rodrigo
130 E. Randolph Dr.
18th Floor
Chicago, IL 60601
r.sierra@pecorp.com
Tel: (312) 240 - 4380
Fax:(312) 240 - 4389

Serves As:
• V. President, Communications and Government Relations, Peoples Energy Corp.

SIEWERT, Richard L. "Jake"
390 Park Ave.
New York, NY 10022
jake.siewert@alcoa.com
Tel: (212) 836 - 2733

Serves As:
• V. President, Environment, Health and Safety and Global Communications and Public Strategy, Alcoa Inc.

SIGALOS, George P.
1550 Wilson Blvd.
Suite 200
Arlington, VA 22209
Tel: (703) 526 - 7500
Fax:(703) 526 - 7585

Registered Federal Lobbyist.
Serves As:
• Director, Government Relations, Kellogg Brown and Root

SIGEL, Arthur R.
10400 W. Higgins
Suite 600
Rosemont, IL 60018
Tel: (847) 298 - 9000
Fax:(847) 298 - 9018
TF: (800) 826 - 4449

Serves As:
• Chairman, President and Chief Exec. Officer, Velsicol Chemical Corp.

SIGLE, Marc
1285 Ave. of the Americas
New York, NY 10019-6095
Tel: (212) 459 - 5000
Fax:(212) 459 - 6645

Serves As:
• Exec. V. President and Treasurer, BBDO New York
Responsibilities include corporate giving.

SIGMAN, Stanley T.
5565 Glenridge Connector
Atlanta, GA 30342
Tel: (404) 236 - 6000
Fax:(866) 246 - 4852
TF: (800) 331 - 0500

Serves As:
• President and Chief Exec. Officer, Cingular Wireless

SIGMON, Scott
8846 Walter Ct. SW
Olympia, WA 98512
Tel: (360) 943 - 3466

Serves As:
• Government Affairs Executive, Schering-Plough Corporation

SILINSKY-KEPHART, Linda
225 Schlumberger Dr.
Sugarland, TX 77478
Tel: (281) 285 - 4270

Serves As:
• Manager, Public Affairs, Schlumberger Limited

SILVER, Lawrence A.
880 Carillon Pkwy.
St. Petersburg, FL 33716
Tel: (727) 567 - 1000

Serves As:
• Senior V. President, Investor Relations, Raymond James Financial, Inc.
Responsibilities include public relations.

SILVER, Steven G.
1301 Ave. of the Americas
New York, NY 10019
steven.g.silber@us.pwc.com
Tel: (646) 471 - 4059
Fax:(646) 394 - 5355

Serves As:
• Corporate Public Relations Contact, PriceWaterhouseCoopers LLP

SILVERMAN, Henry R.
Nine W. 57th St.
37th Floor
New York, NY 10019
henry.silverman@cendant.com
Tel: (212) 413 - 1800

Serves As:
• Chairman, President and Chief Exec. Officer, Cendant Corp.

SILVERTHORNE, Scott
1680 Capital One Dr.
12th Floor
McLean, VA 22102
Tel: (703) 875 - 1000

Registered Federal Lobbyist.
Serves As:
• Director, Government Relations, Capital One Financial Corp.
Responsibilities include political action.

SIMEK, Jeffrey
100 Parsons Pond Dr.
Franklin Lakes, NJ 07417
Tel: (201) 269 - 6400

Serves As:
• V. President, Public Affairs, Medco Health Solutions, Inc.

SIMI, Lawrence J.
77 Beale St.
MC B29H
San Francisco, CA 94105
Tel: (415) 973 - 3032
Fax:(415) 973 - 1718

Serves As:
• Director, Regional Governmental Relations, (Pacific Gas and Electric Co.), PG & E Corp.

SIMMERMAN, Ed
P.O. Box 7608
Boise, ID 83707
Tel: (208) 377 - 6840
Fax:(208) 377 - 6097

Serves As:
• Assistant Corporate Treasurer, Intermountain Gas Co.
Responsibilities include corporate philanthropy.

SIMMONS, Harold C.
Three Lincoln Center
5430 LBJ Fwy., Suite 1700
Dallas, TX 75240-2697
Tel: (972) 233 - 1700
Fax:(972) 448 - 1445

Serves As:
• Chairman of the Board, Valhi, Inc.

SIMMONS, Harris H.
Kennecott Bldg.
One S. Main St., Suite 1380
Salt Lake City, UT 84111
Tel: (801) 524 - 4730

Serves As:
• Chairman, President and Chief Exec. Officer, Zions Bancorporation
Responsibilities include corporate philanthropy.

SIMMONS, Irina
P.O. Box 9103
Hopkinton, MA 01748
Tel: (508) 435 - 1000
Fax:(508) 435 - 7954
TF: (800) 424 - 3622

Serves As:
• Senior V. President and PAC Treasurer, EMC Corp.

SIMMS, Kristine D.
101 Constitution Ave. NW
Suite 200 East
Washington, DC 20001
ksimms@entergy.com
Tel: (202) 530 - 7300
Fax:(202) 530 - 7350

Registered Federal Lobbyist.
Serves As:
• Director, Federal Government Affairs, Entergy Services, Inc.

SIMOCK, Debbie
P.O. Box 3727
Spokane, WA 99220-3727
Tel: (509) 489 - 0500
Fax:(509) 495 - 8725
TF: (800) 727 - 9170

Serves As:
- Foundation Contact, Avista Corp.

SIMON, Cosette R.
175 King St.
Armonk, NY 10504
Tel: (914) 828 - 8000
Fax:(914) 828 - 7000
TF: (888) 794 - 7773

Registered Federal Lobbyist.
Serves As:
- Senior V. President, Swiss Re America Corp.

SIMON, Darryl A.
1850 K St. NW
Suite 500
Washington, DC 20006-2213
Tel: (202) 729 - 1700
Fax:(202) 729 - 1150
TF: (800) 417 - 2277

Serves As:
- Senior V. President, Human Resources and Risk Management, CarrAmerica Realty Corp.

SIMON, David
P.O. Box 7033
Indianapolis, IN 46207
Tel: (317) 636 - 1600
Fax:(317) 263 - 2318

Serves As:
- Chief Exec. Officer, Simon Property Group

SIMON, Geoff
P.O. Box 5650
Bismarck, ND 58506-5650
geoff.simon@mduresources.com
Tel: (701) 222 - 7830
Fax:(701) 222 - 7859
TF: (800) 437 - 8000

Serves As:
- Director, State Governmental Affairs, MDU Resources Group, Inc.

SIMON, Herbert
P.O. Box 7033
Indianapolis, IN 46207
Tel: (317) 636 - 1600
Fax:(317) 263 - 2318

Serves As:
- Co-Chairman of the Board, Simon Property Group

SIMON, Jim
One Nationwide Plaza
Columbus, OH 43215-2220
Tel: (614) 249 - 7111
Fax:(614) 249 - 3073

Serves As:
- V. President, Corporate Communications, Nationwide

SIMON, John R.
9197 S. Peoria St.
Englewood, CO 80112-5833
john.simon@teletech.com
Tel: (303) 397 - 8100
Fax:(303) 397 - 8199
TF: (800) 835 - 3832

Serves As:
- Senior V. President, Human Resources, TeleTech Holdings, Inc.

SIMON, Melvin
P.O. Box 7033
Indianapolis, IN 46207
Tel: (317) 636 - 1600
Fax:(317) 263 - 2318

Serves As:
- Co-Chairman of the Board, Simon Property Group

SIMON, Susan Whyte
2101 E. Jefferson St.
Rockville, MD 20852
susan.whyte.simon@kp.org
Tel: (301) 816 - 6264

Serves As:
- Media Representative - MidAtlantic Region, Kaiser Permanente

SIMONE, Frank S.
1120 20th St. NW
Suite 1000
Washington, DC 20036-3406
fsimone@att.com
Tel: (202) 457 - 3810
Fax:(202) 457 - 2545

Serves As:
- V. President, Federal Regulatory Affairs, AT&T

SIMONETTI, Arthur J.
1001 Pennsylvania Ave. NW
Suite 700 South
Washington, DC 20004
Tel: (202) 662 - 2671
Fax:(202) 662 - 2674

Registered Federal Lobbyist.
Serves As:
- Manager, Trade Legislation and Regulation, Honeywell Internat'l, Inc.

SIMONETTI, Ms. Toni
767 Fifth Ave.
New York, NY 10153
Tel: (212) 418 - 6380

Serves As:
- V. President, Communications and Public Policy, General Motors Acceptance Corp. (GMAC)

SIMONS, Ann
1106 Villanova St. NE
Olympia, WA 98516
simonsa@wyeth.com
Tel: (360) 789 - 7699

Serves As:
- Director, State Government Affairs, Wyeth Pharmaceuticals

SIMONTON, Kay
206 W. 13th St.
Austin, TX 78701
Tel: (512) 472 - 2721
Fax:(512) 472 - 3256

Serves As:
- Government Relations Representative, Blue Cross and Blue Shield of Texas, Inc.

SIMPKINS, Maurice M.
6011 University Blvd.
Suite 260
Ellicott City, MD 21043
msimpkins@ryland.com
Tel: (410) 712 - 7012

Serves As:
- V. President, Public Affairs, The Ryland Group, Inc.

SIMPLOT, Scott R.
P.O. Box 27
Boise, ID 83707
Tel: (208) 336 - 2110
Fax:(208) 389 - 7515

Serves As:
- Chairman of the Board, J. R. Simplot Co.

SIMPSON, Irma E.
7950 Jones Branch Dr.
McLean, VA 22107
Tel: (703) 854 - 6000
Ext: 6046
Fax:(703) 276 - 2046

Serves As:
- Manager, Gannett Foundation, Gannett Co., Inc.

SIMPSON, James P.
P.O. Box 708
Warsaw, IN 46581-0708
Tel: (574) 267 - 6131
Fax:(574) 372 - 4988
TF: (800) 613 - 6131

Serves As:
- V. President, Quality Regulatory and Government Affairs, Zimmer Holdings, Inc.

SIMPSON, Sarah S.
300 Concord Plaza Dr.
San Antonio, TX 78216
Tel: (210) 828 - 8484
Fax:(210) 283 - 2003
TF: (800) 837 - 8768

Serves As:
- V. President, Corporate Communications, Tesoro Petroleum Corp.

SIMS, Don
P.O. Box 30150
Reno, NV 89520
Tel: (775) 834 - 3616

Serves As:
- Manager, Shareholder Relations, Nevada Power Co.

SIMS, Julia
P.O. Box 1271
MSE7C
Portland, OR 97207-1271
Tel: (503) 273 - 4682
Fax:(503) 225 - 5283

Serves As:
- Community Relations Coordinator, Regence BlueCross BlueShield of Oregon

SIMS, Roberta W.
101 Constitution Ave. NW
Washington, DC 20080
rsims@washgas.com
Tel: (703) 750 - 2000
Fax:(703) 750 - 4574

Serves As:
- V. President, Corporate Relations, Washington Gas

SINCLAIR, Charles L.
1144 E. Market St.
Akron, OH 44316-0001
Tel: (330) 796 - 2154
Fax:(330) 796 - 9112

Serves As:
- Senior V. President, Global Communications, The Goodyear Tire & Rubber Company

SINEGAL, James D.
999 Lake Dr.
Issaquah, WA 98027
Tel: (425) 313 - 8100
Fax:(425) 313 - 6593

Serves As:
- President, Chief Exec. Officer, Costco Wholesale Corp.

Also serves on the board of directors.

SINGER, David V.
8600 South Blvd.
Charlotte, NC 28273
Tel: (704) 554 - 1421
Fax:(704) 554 - 5562
TF: (800) 438 - 1880

Serves As:
• President and Chief Exec. Officer, Lance, Inc.

SINGER, Jim
870 Winter St.
Waltham, MA 02451
Tel: (781) 522 - 5136

Serves As:
• Manger, Investor Relations, Raytheon Co.

SIRLOUIS, Jacque
III Cascade Plaza
Akron, OH 44308-1103
Tel: (330) 846 - 8877
Fax:(330) 384 - 7008

Serves As:
• Director, Public Relations, FirstMerit Corporation

SIROLA, Bill
1201 K St., Suite 920
Greater California-Corporate Law West
Sacramento, CA 95814
Tel: (916) 321 - 6927
Fax:(916) 321 - 6902

Serves As:
• Manager, Public Affairs, State Farm Insurance Cos.

SISCO, Robby D.
Two Seaport Ln.
Suite 1300
Boston, MA 02210-2019
Tel: (617) 342 - 6004
Fax:(617) 342 - 6089

Serves As:
• V. President, Human Resources, Cabot Corp.

SISK, Mark D.
740 W. New Circle Rd.
Lexington, KY 40550
sisk@lexmark.com
Tel: (859) 232 - 5934
Fax:(859) 232 - 7529
TF: (800) 539 - 6275

Serves As:
• V. President, Investor Relations, Lexmark Internat'l, Inc.

SISKA, Nancy P.
P.O. Box 9300
Minneapolis, MN 55440-9300
nancy_siska@cargill.com
Tel: (952) 742 - 5172
Fax:(952) 742 - 6215

Serves As:
• Corporate V. President, Human Resources, Cargill, Incorporated

SISSENER, Einar W.
One Executive Dr.
Fort Lee, NJ 07024
Tel: (201) 947 - 7774
Fax:(201) 947 - 5541
TF: (800) 445 - 4216

Serves As:
• Chairman of the Board, Alpharma Inc.

SITKIEWICZ, Donna M.
Three Lakes Dr.
Northfield, IL 60093-2753
Tel: (847) 646 - 5770
Fax:(847) 646 - 6005

Serves As:
• Director, Corporate Affairs, Kraft Foods, Inc.

SIVEIRA, Mike
P.O. Box 4278
Modesto, CA 95352
mike@savemartcorp.com
Tel: (209) 577 - 6303
Fax:(209) 577 - 3857

Serves As:
• V. President, Human Resources and Law, Save Mart Supermarkets
Responsibilities also include government relations.

SIVINSKI, Tina
5400 Legacy Dr.
Plano, TX 75024-3199
Tel: (972) 605 - 6000
Fax:(972) 605 - 6841

Serves As:
• Exec. V. President, Human Resources, EDS Corp.

SKAALRUD, Nancy
P.O. Box 1441
Minneapolis, MN 55440-1441
Tel: (612) 623 - 6684
Fax:(612) 623 - 6944
TF: (800) 328 - 0211

Serves As:
• Secretary, The Graco Foundation, Graco Inc.

SKAFIDAS, Mary
1221 Ave. of the Americas
47th Floor
New York, NY 10020-1095
mary_skafidas@mcgraw-hill.com
Tel: (212) 512 - 2826
Fax:(212) 512 - 2703

Serves As:
• Manager, Corporate Communications, The McGraw-Hill Companies, Inc.

SKAGGS, Jr., Robert C.
801 E. 86th Ave.
Merrillville, IN 46410
Tel: (219) 647 - 6200
Fax:(219) 647 - 6225
TF: (877) 647 - 5990

Serves As:
• Chief Exec. Officer, NiSource Inc.

SKAINS, Thomas E.
P.O. Box 33068
Charlotte, NC 28233
Tel: (704) 364 - 3120

Serves As:
• Chairman, President and Chief Exec. Officer, Piedmont Natural Gas Co.

SKARIE, David P.
P.O. Box 618
St. Louis, MO 63188-0618
Tel: (314) 877 - 7711
Fax:(314) 877 - 7663

Serves As:
• Co-Chief Exec. Officer and President, Ralcorp Holdings, Inc.

SKEEN, Kerry B.
45200 Business Ct.
Suite 100
Dulles, VA 20166-6715
Tel: (703) 650 - 6000
Fax:(703) 650 - 6299

Serves As:
• Chairman and Chief Exec. Officer, FLYi, Inc.

SKELTON, H. Jay
P.O. Box B
Jacksonville, FL 32203-0297
Tel: (904) 783 - 5000
Fax:(904) 783 - 5294

Serves As:
• Chairman of the Board, Winn-Dixie Stores

SKERNOLIS, Edmund J.
601 Pennsylvania Ave. NW
North Bldg. Suite 300
Washington, DC 20004
eskernolis@wm.com
Tel: (202) 628 - 3500
Fax:(202) 628 - 0400

Serves As:
• Director, Government Affairs, Waste Management, Inc.

SKIDMORE, Brenda L.
919 E. Main St.
Richmond, VA 23219
brenda.skidmore@suntrust.com
Tel: (804) 782 - 5000
Fax:(804) 782 - 7064

Registered Federal Lobbyist.
Serves As:
• Senior V. President, Government Relations, SunTrust Banks, Inc.

SKIDMORE, Janet
P.O. Box 100
Whitehouse Station, NJ 08889-0100
Tel: (908) 423 - 3046
Fax:(908) 735 - 1181
TF: (800) 423 - 1000

Serves As:
• Media Contact, Merck & Co., Inc.

SKINNELL, Christopher E.
591 Redwood Hwy.
Bldg. 4000
Mill Valley, CA 94941

Serves As:
• Treasurer, Pinnacle Entertainment Inc. PAC, Pinnacle Entertainment, Inc.

SKINNER, Claire C.
P.O. Box 3300
Elkhart, IN 46515
cskinner@coachmen.com
Tel: (574) 262 - 0123
Fax:(574) 262 - 8823

Serves As:
• Chairman and Chief Exec. Officer, Coachmen Industries, Inc.

SKINNER, James A.
One McDonald's Plaza
Oak Brook, IL 60523
Tel: (630) 623 - 3000
Fax:(630) 623 - 5004

Serves As:
• Chairman and Chief Exec. Officer, McDonald's Corp.

SKINNER, Jr., Robert
600 Kellwood Pkwy.
Chesterfield, MO 63017
Tel: (314) 576 - 3100
Fax:(314) 576 - 3460

Serves As:
• President and Chief Exec. Officer, Kellwood Co.

SKINNER, Samantha
P.O. Box 1106
Lewiston, ID 83501
Tel: (208) 798 - 2247
Fax:(208) 798 - 2087

Serves As:
• Contact, Team Regence, Regence BlueShield of Idaho

SKIPPER, Misty
500 Water St.
Jacksonville, FL 32203
Tel: (904) 366 - 2949

Serves As:
• Regional Media Contact, CSX Corp.

SKOCH, Daniel A.
17876 St. Clair Ave.
Cleveland, OH 44110
Tel: (216) 486 - 4200
Fax:(216) 383 - 4091
TF: (800) 321 - 2076

Serves As:
- Senior V. President, Administration and Human Resources, Brush Engineered Materials Inc.

Responsibilities include corporate philanthropy.

SKOGLUND, Cynthia
P.O. Box 3100
Fullerton, CA 92834
Tel: (714) 773 - 8213
Fax:(714) 773 - 8111
TF: (800) 742 - 2345

Serves As:
- Investor Relations Specialist, Beckman Coulter, Inc.

SKORNIAK, Kim
500 Water St.
Jacksonville, FL 32203
Tel: (904) 366 - 2949

Serves As:
- Regional Media Contact, CSX Corp.

SKOTAK, Theresa L.
2791 Research Dr.
Rochester Hills, MI 48309-3575
Tel: (248) 299 - 7500
Fax:(248) 299 - 7501

Serves As:
- V. President, Human Resources, Dura Automotive Systems, Inc.

SKWAREK, Daniel
901 15th St. NW
Suite 310
M/S WAS 1150
Washington, DC 20005
Tel: (202) 842 - 3193
Fax:(202) 289 - 6834

Serves As:
- Director, International and Regulatory Affairs, Northwest Airlines, Inc.

SKYBA, Kirsten
P.O. Box 2566
Oshkosh, WI 54903-2566
kskyba@oshtruck.com
Tel: (920) 233 - 9621
Fax:(920) 233 - 9251

Serves As:
- V. President, Marketing Communications, Oshkosh Truck Corp.

SLACK, Henry R.
P.O. Box 6000
Sioux City, IA 51102-6000

Serves As:
- Chairman of the Board, Terra Industries Inc.

SLAGEL, Gary E.
Consol Plaza
1800 Washington Rd.
Pittsburgh, PA 15241-1421
Tel: (412) 831 - 4532
Fax:(412) 831 - 4574

Serves As:
- Director, Government Affairs, CONSOL Energy Inc.

SLAGGIE, Stephen M.
P.O. Box 978
Winona, MN 55987
smslaggi@fastenal.com
Tel: (507) 453 - 8212
Fax:(507) 453 - 8049

Serves As:
- Secretary, Fastenal Co.

Responsibilities include corporate philanthropy and investor relations.

SLARK, Martin P.
2222 Wellington Ct.
Lisle, IL 60532
Tel: (630) 969 - 4550
Fax:(630) 969 - 1352
TF: (800) 786 - 6539

Serves As:
- Chief Exec. Officer, Molex Incorporated

SLATE, David L.
3240 Hillview Ave.
Palo Alto, CA 94304
Tel: (650) 494 - 2900
Fax:(650) 813 - 0160

Serves As:
- V. President, Human Resources and Deputy General Counsel, CNF Inc.

SLAUGHTER, Stacey C.
9697 E. Mineral Ave.
Englewood, CO 80112
Tel: (303) 792 - 3111
Fax:(303) 784 - 8508

Serves As:
- Assistant Treasurer, Jones Internat'l, Ltd.

SLAVIN, Stephanie
P.O. Box 2286
Houston, TX 77252-2286
sslavin@reliant.com
Tel: (713) 497 - 6983
Fax:(713) 488 - 5925
TF: (866) 872 - 6656

Serves As:
- Director, Investor Relations and Communications, Reliant Resources

SLEDD, Robert C.
P.O. Box 29269
Richmond, VA 23242-9269
bsledd@pfgc.com
Tel: (804) 285 - 7340
Fax:(804) 484 - 7701

Serves As:
- Chairman, President and Chief Exec. Officer, Performance Food Group Co.

SLEEMAN, Donald G.
375 Hudson St.
New York, NY 10014
dsleeman@tcco.com
Tel: (212) 229 - 6000
Fax:(212) 229 - 6390

Serves As:
- Exec. V. President and Chief Financial Officer, The Turner Corp.

Responsibilities include investor relations.

SLESINGER, Arthur E.
900 Ridgebury Rd.
P.O. Box 368
Ridgefield, CT 06877
Tel: (203) 798 - 5075
Fax:(203) 791 - 6476

Serves As:
- Corporate Director, Environmental Affairs/Health Safety, Boehringer Ingelheim Corp.

SLINGERLEND, Mac J.
5251 DTC Pkwy.
Suite 1400
Greenwood Village, CO 80111-2742
Tel: (303) 220 - 0100
Fax:(303) 220 - 7100
TF: (800) 242 - 3799

Serves As:
- President and Chief Exec. Officer, CIBER, Inc.

SLIZEWSKI, Beatrice B.
P.O. Box 20670
Rochester, NY 14602-0670
bslizewski@birdseyefoods.com
Tel: (585) 264 - 3189
Fax:(585) 383 - 5609
TF: (800) 999 - 5044

Serves As:
- V. President, Corporate Communications, Birds Eye Foods

Responsibilities include corporate contributions.

SLOAN, John
2200 E. Golf Rd.
Des Plaines, IL 60016-1267
Tel: (847) 699 - 5000
Fax:(847) 699 - 8046

Serves As:
- Senior V. President, Human Resources, United Stationers Inc.

SLOAN, Patricia
437 Madison Ave.
Ninth Floor
New York, NY 10022
pat.sloan@ddb.com
Tel: (212) 415 - 2109
Fax:(212) 415 - 3414

Serves As:
- Senior V. President and Corporate Director, Public Affairs, Omnicom Group Inc.

SLOAT, Julie
One Riverside Plaza
Columbus, OH 43215-2373
Tel: (614) 716 - 2885
Fax:(614) 223 - 1823

Serves As:
- V. President, Investor Relations, American Electric Power Co. Inc.

SLOATE, Gregg
P.O. Box 34325
Seattle, WA 98124-1325
gregg.sloate@univarcorp.com
Tel: (425) 638 - 4911
Fax:(425) 638 - 4953

Serves As:
- Director, Investor Relations, Univar USA, Inc.

SLONE, Deck S.
One CityPlace Dr.
Suite 300
St. Louis, MO 63141
Tel: (314) 994 - 2700
Fax:(314) 994 - 2719

Serves As:
- V. President, Investor Relations and Public Affairs, Arch Coal, Inc.

SLONE, Peter B.
1420 New York Ave. NW
Suite 600
Washington, DC 20005
Tel: (202) 393 - 6444
Fax:(202) 289 - 9222

Serves As:
- V. President, Government Affairs, Medtronic, Inc.

SLUDER, Rick
P.O. Box 13398
Research Triangle Park, NC 27709
Tel: (919) 483 - 2839
Fax:(919) 549 - 7459

Serves As:
- V. President, U.S. Pharmaceuticals Communications, GlaxoSmithKline Research and Development

SLUSARK, Arthur J. "Art"
1716 Locust St. | Tel: (515) 284 - 3404
Des Moines, IA 50309-3023 | Fax:(515) 284 - 2511
art.slusark@meredith.com

Serves As:
- V. President, Corporate Communications and Government Relations, Meredith Corp.

SLUSS, Jessica
7601 Penn Ave. South | Tel: (612) 291 - 6108
Richfield, MN 55423 | Fax:(612) 292 - 4001

Serves As:
- Community Relations Specialist, Best Buy Co., Inc.

SMALL, Malinda B.
750 E. Pratt St. | Tel: (410) 783 - 3266
Fifth Floor | Fax:(410) 783 - 3279
Baltimore, MD 21202 | TF: (888) 460 - 2002
malinda.b.small@constellation.com

Serves As:
- Managing Director, Brand Implementation, Constellation Energy

Responsibilities include corporate philanthropy.

SMALLENBERGER, James A.
699 Walnut St. | Tel: (515) 362 - 3600
Des Moines, IA 50309

Serves As:
- Contact, Political Action, AmerUs Group

SMALLING, Laurie
575 Seventh St. NW | Tel: (202) 737 - 5523
Terrell Bldg. | Fax:(202) 737 - 6069
Washington, DC 20004

Registered Federal Lobbyist.
Serves As:
- Manager, Corporate Affairs, Wal-Mart Stores

SMARR, Karen J.
1200 Columbia Ave. | Tel: (909) 781 - 5690
Riverside, CA 92507-2114 | Fax:(909) 781 - 5006

Serves As:
- Secretary-Treasurer, Foundation, Bourns, Inc.

SMART, Jill
1345 Ave. of the Americas | Tel: (917) 452 - 4400
New York, NY 10105 | Fax:(917) 527 - 9915

Serves As:
- Managing Partner, Human Resources, Accenture

SMEDSTAD, Barry
P.O. Box 115 | Tel: (770) 948 - 3101
Austell, GA 30168-0115 | Fax:(770) 732 - 3401

Serves As:
- V. President, Human Resources and Public Relations, Caraustar Industries, Inc.

SMELTZER, Judy H.
1735 Market St. | Tel: (215) 299 - 6710
Philadelphia, PA 19103 | Fax:(215) 299 - 6274

Serves As:
- Director, State Government Relations, FMC Corp.

SMERKO, Barbara K.
Four Taft Ct. | Tel: (301) 838 - 5613
Rockville, MD 20850 | Fax:(301) 545 - 5972

Serves As:
- Exec. Director, MAMSI Children's Foundation, Inc., Mid Atlantic Medical Services Inc.

SMIT, Neil
12405 Powerscourt Dr. | Tel: (314) 965 - 0555
St. Louis, MO 63131 | Fax:(314) 965 - 9745

Serves As:
- President and Chief Exec. Officer, Charter Communications, Inc.

SMITH, Andrea
P.O. Box 98910 | Tel: (702) 367 - 5843
M/S 15 | Fax:(702) 367 - 5092
Las Vegas, NV 89151-0001 | TF: (800) 331 - 3103
asmith@nevp.com

Serves As:
- Director, Corporate Communications, Nevada Power Co.

SMITH, Andrew
225 City Line Ave. | Tel: (610) 934 - 7000
Suite 200 | Fax:(610) 934 - 7054
Bala Cynwyd, PA 19004 | TF: (888) 438 - 7488
andrew.smith@pgtv.com

Serves As:
- Investor Relations Contact, Pegasus Communications Corp.

SMITH, Anita M.
P.O. Box 772531 | Tel: (717) 541 - 7000
Harrisburg, PA 17177-2531 | Fax:(717) 541 - 6072

Serves As:
- President and Chief Exec. Officer, Capital BlueCross (Pennsylvania)

SMITH, Ann
100 Parsons Pond Dr. | Tel: (201) 269 - 5984
Franklin Lakes, NJ 07417

Serves As:
- Director, Public Affairs, Medco Health Solutions, Inc.

SMITH, B. J.
3935 Northpointe Dr. | Tel: (740) 454 - 3471
Zanesville, OH 43701 | Fax:(740) 454 - 3478
bj.smith@sbc.com

Serves As:
- Director, External Affairs, SBC Ohio

SMITH, Bill
404 Wyman St. | Tel: (781) 464 - 8052
Suite 500 | Fax:(781) 464 - 8100
Waltham, MA 02451
wsmith@novell.com

Serves As:
- V. President, Investor Relations, Novell, Inc.

SMITH, Bradford L.
One Microsoft Way | Tel: (425) 882 - 8080
Redmond, WA 98052-6399 | Fax:(425) 936 - 7329

Serves As:
- Senior V. President, Law and Corporate Affairs, Microsoft Corporation

SMITH, Bradford T.
Corporate Communications Dept.
430 S. Spring St.
M/S 65050
Burlington, NC 27215

Serves As:
- Exec. V. President, Public Affairs, Law and Compliance, Laboratory Corp. of America Holdings

SMITH, Brandee
P.O. Box 13287 | Tel: (816) 467 - 3304
Kansas City, MO 64199-3287 | Fax:(816) 467 - 3005
brandee.smith@aquila.com

Serves As:
- Communications Coordinator, Aquila, Inc.

SMITH, Brenda
900 Old River Rd. | Tel: (661) 663 - 2771
Bakersfield, CA 93311-6000 | Fax:(661) 663 - 2799

Serves As:
- Manager, Public Affairs - California, State Farm Insurance Cos.

SMITH, Brian
401 Ninth St., NW | Tel: (202) 434 - 8637
Suite 600 | Fax:(202) 434 - 8626
M/S 600
Washington, DC 20004
brian_smith@freddiemac.com

Serves As:
- Director, Government Relations, Freddie Mac

SMITH, Brian
P.O. Box 500 | Tel: (503) 627 - 7111
Beaverton, OR 97077 | Fax:(503) 567 - 3449
TF: (800) 835 - 9433

Serves As:
- Manager, Investor Relations, Tektronix, Inc.

SMITH, Brigid M.
Three High Ridge Park | Tel: (203) 614 - 5600
Stamford, CT 06905 | Fax:(203) 614 - 4602
bsmith@czn.com

Serves As:
- Assistant V. President, Corporate Communications, Citizens Communications Co.

SMITH, Bruce A.
300 Concord Plaza Dr. | Tel: (210) 283 - 2001
San Antonio, TX 78216 | Fax:(210) 283 - 2003
TF: (800) 837 - 8768

Serves As:
- Chairman, President, and Chief Exec. Officer, Tesoro Petroleum Corp.

SMITH, Claire H.
P.O. Box 7888 | Tel: (818) 379 - 7455
Van Nuys, CA 91409-7888 | Fax:(818) 379 - 7141
csmith@sunistgrowers.com

Serves As:
- Director, Corporate Communications, Sunkist Growers

SMITH, Corrine
11401 Lamar Ave.
Overland Park, KS 66211
smithco@bv.com
Tel: (913) 458 - 3500

Serves As:
- V. President, Brand Management and Communications, Black & Veatch

SMITH, Craig R.
P.O. Box 27626
Richmond, VA 23261-7626
Tel: (804) 747 - 9794
Fax:(804) 270 - 7281

Serves As:
- Chief Exec. Officer, Owens & Minor, Inc.

SMITH, Dan
333 N. Point Center East
Suite 15
Alpharetta, GA 30022
Tel: (678) 297 - 9365
Fax:(678) 297 - 9393

Serves As:
- Regional Director, State Government Affairs, Altria Group, Inc.

SMITH, Dan
100 Phoenix Dr.
Ann Arbor, MI 48108
dsmith@bordersgroupinc.com
Tel: (734) 477 - 1798
Fax:(734) 477 - 1899

Serves As:
- Senior V. President, Human Resources, Borders Group, Inc.

SMITH, Dan
6400 Seven States Blvd.
San Antonio, TX 78244
Tel: (972) 788 - 7707
Fax:(972) 788 - 7795

Serves As:
- Manager, Public Affairs, United Parcel Service (UPS)

SMITH, Dan F.
One Houston Center
1221 McKinney Ave.
Houston, TX 77010
Tel: (713) 652 - 7200

Serves As:
- President and Chief Exec. Officer, Lyondell Chemical Co.

SMITH, David A.
4345 Southpoint Blvd.
Jacksonville, FL 32216
Tel: (904) 332 - 3000

Serves As:
- Chief Exec. Officer, PSS World Medical, Inc.

SMITH, David H.
1455 Pennsylvania Ave. NW
Suite 100
Washington, DC 20004
Tel: (202) 756 - 0184

Serves As:
- PAC Treasurer, Invitrogen Corp.

SMITH, Dennis A.
515 W. Greens Rd.
Suite 1200
Houston, TX 77067-4525
dsmith@nabors.com
Tel: (281) 775 - 8038
Fax:(281) 872 - 5205

Serves As:
- Director, Corporate Development, Nabors Industries, Ltd.

Responsibilities include corporate communications and investor relations.

SMITH, Derek V.
1000 Alderman Dr.
Alpharetta, GA 30005-4101
Tel: (770) 752 - 6000
Fax:(770) 752 - 6005

Serves As:
- Chairman and Chief Exec. Officer, ChoicePoint Inc.

SMITH, Donald N.
1855 Boston Rd.
Wilbraham, MA 01095
Tel: (413) 543 - 2400
Fax:(413) 543 - 9355
TF: (800) 966 - 9970

Serves As:
- Chairman of the Board, Friendly Ice Cream Corp.

SMITH, Dorothy Brown
P.O. Box 3001
Lancaster, PA 17604-3001
Tel: (717) 396 - 5696

Serves As:
- V. President, Corporate Communications and Diversity, Armstrong Holdings, Inc.

SMITH, Elden L.
3125 Myers St.
Riverside, CA 92503
Tel: (909) 351 - 3500
Fax:(909) 351 - 3931

Serves As:
- President and Chief Exec. Officer, Fleetwood Enterprises

SMITH, Eleanor
980 Hammond Dr. NE
Suite 1000
Atlanta, GA 30328-5313
esmith@porschecars.com
Tel: (770) 290 - 3626
Fax:(770) 290 - 3706

Serves As:
- Public Relations Specialist, Porsche Cars North America, Inc.

SMITH, Frederick W.
942 S. Shady Grove Rd.
Memphis, TN 38120
Tel: (901) 369 - 3600
TF: (800) 238 - 5355

Serves As:
- Chairman, President and Chief Exec. Officer, FedEx Corp.

SMITH, Gary B.
1201 Winterson Rd.
Linthicum, MD 21090
Tel: (410) 694 - 5700
Fax:(410) 694 - 5750

Serves As:
- President and Chief Exec. Officer, CIENA Corp.

SMITH, Gary L.
P.O. Box 119
Maumee, OH 43537
gary_smith@andersonsinc.com
Tel: (419) 891 - 6417
Fax:(419) 891 - 6655

Serves As:
- V. President, Finance and Treasurer, Anderson Foundation, The Andersons, Inc.

Responsibilities include investor relations.

SMITH, Gavin H.
717 Texas Ave.
Suite 2100
Houston, TX 77002-2712
gsmith@br-inc.com
Tel: (713) 624 - 9898
Fax:(713) 624 - 9955
TF: (800) 262 - 3456

Serves As:
- V. President, Corporate Affairs; President, Burlington Resources/Meridian Oil Foundation; BRPAC Director and Treasurer, (Burlington Resources Oil & Gas Co.), Burlington Resources Inc.

Responsibilities include government affairs.

SMITH, Greg
870 Winter St.
Waltham, MA 02451
Tel: (781) 522 - 5141

Serves As:
- V. President, Investor Relations, Raytheon Co.

SMITH, Guy
Six Landmark Sq.
Stamford, CT 06901
Tel: (203) 359 - 7100

Serves As:
- Exec. V. President, External Affairs and Corporate Strategy, Diageo North America

SMITH, J. Brian
80 Park Plaza
M/S T6B
Newark, NJ 07102-0570
Tel: (973) 430 - 6564
Fax:(973) 624 - 7491

Serves As:
- Director, Investor Relations, PSE&G

SMITH, James C.
Webster Plaza
145 Bank St.
Waterbury, CT 06702
jsmith@websterbank.com
Tel: (800) 325 - 2424

Serves As:
- Chairman and Chief Exec. Officer, Webster Financial Corp.

SMITH, James C.
56 Top Gallant Rd.
Stamford, CT 06904
Tel: (203) 964 - 0096
Fax:(203) 316 - 6488

Serves As:
- Chairman of the Board, Gartner, Inc.

SMITH, James C.
1401 I St. NW
Suite 1100
Washington, DC 20005
Tel: (202) 326 - 8800
Fax:(202) 408 - 4796

Serves As:
- Senior V. President, FCC, SBC Communications Inc.

SMITH, Janet
P.O. Box 10395
Palo Alto, CA 94303-0395
janet_smith@agilent.com
Tel: (970) 679 - 5397

Serves As:
- Media Relations Contact, Agilent Technologies, Inc.

SMITH, Janis
3900 Wisconsin Ave. NW
Washington, DC 20016
Tel: (202) 752 - 6673
Fax:(202) 752 - 7044

Serves As:
- Director, Financial Communications, Fannie Mae

SMITH, Jeffrey A.
1919 Torrance Blvd. Tel: (310) 781 - 5062
100-3C-2A Fax:(310) 787 - 4417
Torrance, CA 90501-2746
jeffrey_smith@ahm.honda.com

Serves As:
- Assistant V. President, Corporate Affairs and Communications, American Honda Motor Co., Inc.

SMITH, Jeffrey R.
2700 Lone Oak Pkwy. Tel: (612) 726 - 2331
M/S A1310 Fax:(612) 726 - 3942
Eagan, MN 55121

Serves As:
- Director, Internal Communications, Northwest Airlines, Inc.

SMITH, Jim
P.O. Box 860 Tel: (610) 341 - 7000
Valley Forge, PA 19482 Fax:(610) 341 - 7777

Serves As:
- Director, Environmental Affairs, Saint-Gobain Corp.

SMITH, Joe
P.O. Box 593330 Tel: (407) 245 - 5530
Orlando, FL 32859 Fax:(407) 245 - 4325
jsmith@darden.com

Serves As:
- Director, Communications and Travel Services, Darden Restaurants, Inc.

SMITH, Joe
P.O. Box 711 Tel: (520) 884 - 3650
Tucson, AZ 85702 Fax:(520) 884 - 3606
josmith@uns.com TF: (800) 328 - 8853

Serves As:
- Director, Investor Relations, UniSource Energy Corp.

SMITH, Joel
101 N. Third St. Tel: (218) 236 - 4400
Moorhead, MN 56560-1990 Ext: 4347
jsmith@crystalsugar.com Fax:(218) 236 - 4388

Serves As:
- Manager, Regulatory Affairs, American Crystal Sugar Co.

SMITH, John F.
P.O. Box 20706 Tel: (404) 715 - 2600
Atlanta, GA 30320-6001 Fax:(404) 715 - 2731

Serves As:
- Non-Exec. Chairman of the Board, Delta Air Lines, Inc.

SMITH, Jr., Julian H.
P.O. Box 2641 Tel: (205) 257 - 2187
Birmingham, AL 35291 Fax:(205) 257 - 2622

Serves As:
- V. President, Corporate Relations, Alabama Power Co.

SMITH, Karen A.
P.O. Box 599 Tel: (513) 983 - 1100
Cincinnati, OH 45201-0599
smith.ka@pg.com

Serves As:
- Associate Director, State and Local Government Relations, The Procter & Gamble Company

SMITH, Keith
1401 I St. NW Tel: (202) 336 - 7400
Suite 600 Fax:(202) 336 - 7515
Washington, DC 20005

Registered Federal Lobbyist.
Serves As:
- Senior Manager, International Trade and Tax Policy, United Technologies Corp.

SMITH, Kent
P.O. Box 6000 Tel: (949) 854 - 3100
Newport Beach, CA 92658-6000 Fax:(949) 854 - 4560

Serves As:
- Contact, Downey Savings and Loan Ass'n PAC, Downey Savings and Loan Ass'n, F.A.

SMITH, Kirsten
999 Third Ave. Tel: (206) 467 - 3600
Suite 4300 Fax:(206) 467 - 3795
Seattle, WA 98104

Serves As:
- Corporate Affairs, Plum Creek Timber Co. Inc.

SMITH, Lem
1667 K St. NW Tel: (202) 728 - 9600
Suite 250 Fax:(202) 728 - 9587
Washington, DC 20006

Serves As:
- Director, Federal Relations, Kerr-McGee Corp.

SMITH, Leslie
600 14th St. NW Tel: (202) 585 - 4100
Suite 400
Washington, DC 20005

Serves As:
- Managing Director, Washington Office, U.S. Trust Corp.

SMITH, Loretta G.
P.O. Box 75000 Tel: (313) 222 - 6987
mc 3352 Fax:(313) 222 - 8720
Detroit, MI 48275 TF: (800) 521 - 1190

Serves As:
- V. President, Community Relations, Comerica Incorporated

SMITH, Mark
P.O. Box 55888 Tel: (781) 380 - 8000
Boston, MA 02205-5888 Fax:(781) 770 - 6416
TF: (800) 767 - 7772

Serves As:
- President and Chief Exec. Officer, The Stop & Shop Supermarket Co.

SMITH, Mark H.
850 Dixie Hwy. Tel: (502) 774 - 7152
Louisville, KY 40210 Fax:(502) 774 - 6720
mark_smith@b-f.com

Serves As:
- V. President/Director, Government Relations and Public Policy, Brown-Forman Corp.

SMITH, Michelle
122 Fifth Ave. Tel: (212) 633 - 3280
New York, NY 10011 Fax:(212) 645 - 1828
msmith@bn.com

Serves As:
- V. President, Human Resources, Barnes & Noble, Inc.

SMITH, O. Bruton
6415 Idlewild Rd., Suite 109 Tel: (704) 566 - 2400
Charlotte, NC 28212 Fax:(704) 536 - 4668

Serves As:
- Chairman and Chief Exec. Officer, Sonic Automotive, Inc.

SMITH, Orin C.
P.O. Box 34067 Tel: (206) 447 - 1575
Seattle, WA 98124-1067 Fax:(206) 682 - 9051

Serves As:
- President and Chief Exec. Officer, Starbucks Corp.

SMITH, Perry L.
535 Marriott Dr. Tel: (615) 937 - 0088
Nashville, TN 37214-8900 Fax:(615) 937 - 3612

Serves As:
- Community and Public Relations Coordinator, Bridgestone Americas Holding, Inc.

SMITH, Peter C.
5505 Blue Lagoon Dr. Tel: (305) 378 - 3000
Miami, FL 33126 Fax:(305) 378 - 7910

Serves As:
- Chief Human Resources Officer, Burger King Corporation

SMITH, Richard M.
251 W. 57th St. Tel: (212) 445 - 4000
22nd Floor Fax:(212) 445 - 4757
New York, NY 10019 TF: (800) 631 - 1040

Serves As:
- Chairman of the Board and Editor in Chief, Newsweek, Inc.

SMITH, Richard P.
P.O. Box 4844 Tel: (315) 433 - 0100
Syracuse, NY 13221-4844 Fax:(315) 433 - 2345
TF: (800) 654 - 8838

Serves As:
- Chief Exec. Officer, Dairylea Cooperative Inc.

SMITH, Robert
Lilly Corporate Center Tel: (317) 276 - 2000
Indianapolis, IN 46285 Fax:(317) 277 - 6579

Serves As:
- Director, Corporate Communications/Public Affairs, Eli Lilly and Company

SMITH, Robert J.
20 Greenfield St. Tel: (617) 725 - 8801
Brockton, MA 02401 Fax:(617) 725 - 1002
SmithRJ@nu.com

Serves As:
- Director, State Governmental Affairs, Northeast Utilities

SMITH, Rodney A.
1401 I St. NW
Suite 1100
Washington, DC 20005
Tel: (202) 326 - 8818
Fax:(202) 408 - 4796
Registered Federal Lobbyist.
Serves As:
- Exec. Director, Federal Relations, SBC Communications Inc.

SMITH, Roger S.
11270 W. Park Place
Milwaukee, WI 53224-9510
Tel: (414) 359 - 4129
Fax:(414) 359 - 4064
Serves As:
- Manager, Corporate Advertising and Public Affairs, A. O. Smith Corp.
Responsibilities include government affairs.

SMITH, S. Marijke
1300 Pennsylvania Ave. NW
Suite 860
Washington, DC 20004
Tel: (202) 842 - 5800
Fax:(202) 842 - 8612
Serves As:
- Government Relations Assistant, Volkswagen of America, Inc.

SMITH, Stephen J.
One American Rd.
Cleveland, OH 44144-2398
Tel: (216) 252 - 4864
Fax:(216) 252 - 6778
Serves As:
- V. President, Treasurer and Investor Relations, American Greetings Corp.

SMITH, Steven D.
4800 Deerwood Campus Pkwy.
DCC3-4
Jacksonville, FL 32246-8273
Tel: (904) 905 - 6742
Fax:(904) 905 - 4486
TF: (800) 477 - 3736
Serves As:
- Director, State Government/Legislation Relations, Blue Cross and Blue Shield of Florida

SMITH, Steven J.
P.O. Box 661
Milwaukee, WI 53201-0661
Tel: (414) 224 - 2000
Fax:(414) 224 - 2469
Serves As:
- Chairman and Chief Exec. Officer, Journal Communications, Inc.

SMITH, Thomas A.
P.O. Box 1349
Tucker, GA 30085-1349
Tel: (770) 270 - 7600
Fax:(770) 270 - 7077
TF: (800) 241 - 5374
Serves As:
- President and Chief Exec. Officer, Oglethorpe Power Corp.

SMITH, W. Lamar
1300 Connecticut Ave. NW
Suite 900
Washington, DC 20036
lsmith@visa.com
Tel: (202) 296 - 9230
Fax:(202) 862 - 5498
Registered Federal Lobbyist.
Serves As:
- Senior V. President, Government Relations, Visa U.S.A. Inc.

SMITH, Zeke W.
P.O. Box 2641
Birmingham, AL 35291
Tel: (205) 257 - 2167
Fax:(205) 257 - 1860
Serves As:
- Director, Regulatory and Pricing, Alabama Power Co.

SMITH-CALLAHAN, Deborah Ann
400 Perimeter Center Terrace, Suite 1000
Atlanta, GA 30346
dsmith-callahan@pfizer.com
Tel: (770) 551 - 5173
Fax:(770) 804 - 1783
Serves As:
- Director, Government Relations, Pfizer Inc.

SMITH-JANIS, Megan
77 Beale St.
San Francisco, CA 94105
Tel: (415) 973 - 8190
Fax:(415) 973 - 7666
Serves As:
- Director, Governmental Relations, PG & E Corp.

SMOTER, Jennifer
100 Abbott Park Rd.
Abbott Park, IL 60064-3500
Tel: (847) 935 - 8865
Fax:(847) 937 - 9555
Serves As:
- Director, External Communications, Abbott Laboratories

SMUCKER, Richard K.
Strawberry Lane
Orrville, OH 44667-0280
Tel: (330) 682 - 3000
Fax:(330) 684 - 6410
TF: (888) 550 - 9555
Serves As:
- President, Co-Chief Exec. Officer and Chief Financial Officer, The J. M. Smucker Company

SMUCKER, Timothy P.
Strawberry Lane
Orrville, OH 44667-0280
Tel: (330) 682 - 3000
Fax:(330) 684 - 6410
TF: (888) 550 - 9555
Serves As:
- Chairman and Co-Chief Exec. Officer, The J. M. Smucker Company

SMULYAN, Jeffrey H.
40 Monument Circle
Suite 700
Indianapolis, IN 46204
Tel: (317) 266 - 0100
Fax:(317) 631 - 3750
Serves As:
- Chairman, President and Chief Exec. Officer, Emmis Communications Corp.

SMYRE, Calvin
P.O. Box 120
Columbus, GA 31902-0120
Tel: (706) 649 - 2243
Fax:(706) 641 - 6555
Serves As:
- Exec. V. President, Corporate Affairs, Synovus Financial Corp.

SMYTH, D. Edward I. "Ted"
P.O. Box 57
Pittsburgh, PA 15230-0057
ted.smyth@hjheinz.com
Tel: (412) 456 - 5780
Fax:(412) 456 - 6025
Serves As:
- Chief Administrative Officer; and Senior V. President, Corporate and Government Affairs, H. J. Heinz Co.

SNADER, Kristofer
1000 Nationwide Dr.
Harrisburg, PA 17110-2655
Tel: (717) 657 - 6763
Fax:(717) 657 - 6601
Serves As:
- Area Legislative Affairs Representative, Nationwide

SNEAD, Michael C.
750 E. Pratt St.
Baltimore, MD 21202
Tel: (410) 234 - 6302
Fax:(410) 234 - 5487
TF: (888) 460 - 2002
Serves As:
- Manager, Occupational Health and Environmental Management, Constellation Energy

SNEED, Jan
777 Third Ave.
New York, NY 10017
Tel: (212) 546 - 2000
Fax:(212) 546 - 1495
Serves As:
- Senior V. President, Corporate Affairs, Grey Global Group Inc.
Responsibilities include corporate communications.

SNEED, Norris P.
P.O. Box 511
Kingsport, TN 37662-5075
npsneed@eastman.com
Tel: (423) 229 - 8498
Fax:(423) 229 - 1679
TF: (800) 327 - 8626
Serves As:
- Senior V. President, Communications, Public Affairs, Human Resources and Organizational Effectiveness, Eastman Chemical Co.

SNEERINGER, Thomas M.
1101 Pennsylvania Ave. NW
Suite 510
Washington, DC 20004
Tel: (202) 783 - 6333
Fax:(202) 783 - 6309
Registered Federal Lobbyist.
Serves As:
- Director, Governmental Affairs, United States Steel Corporation

SNIDER, Paul
3420 Broadway
Kansas City, MO 64111-2404
Fax:(816) 360 - 5541
Serves As:
- Public Affairs Specialist, (Missouri Gas Energy), Southern Union Company

SNOW, Jr., David B.
100 Parsons Pond Dr.
Franklin Lakes, NJ 07417
Tel: (201) 269 - 3400
Serves As:
- Chairman, President and Chief Exec. Officer, Medco Health Solutions, Inc.

SNOW, Hank
P.O. Box 1088
Roseburg, OR 97470-0252
Tel: (541) 679 - 3311
Fax:(541) 679 - 2646
TF: (800) 245 - 1115
Serves As:
- V. President, Human Resources, Roseburg Forest Products Co.

SNOW, Terry Wilson
P.O. Box 35985
Tulsa, OK 74153-0985
tsnow@dtag.com
Tel: (918) 660 - 7700
Fax:(918) 669 - 2934
Serves As:
- Exec. Director, Corporate Communications, Dollar Thrifty Automotive Group, Inc.

SNOWDEN, David
9800 Fredericksburg Rd.
D-3-E
San Antonio, TX 78288-0122
Tel: (210) 456 - 1800
Fax:(210) 498 - 9940

Serves As:
• Exec. Director, Property and Casualty Communications, United Services Automobile Ass'n (USAA)

SNOWHITE, Larry S.
1156 15th St.
Suite 1005
Washington, DC 20005
Tel: (202) 467 - 5350

Registered Federal Lobbyist.
Serves As:
• V. President, Government Relations, Houghton Mifflin Co.

SNYDER, Bob
5335 Triangle Pkwy.
Suite 500
Norcross, GA 30092-2556
Tel: (770) 417 - 2104

Serves As:
• Manager, Public Affairs, United Parcel Service (UPS)

SNYDER, Cameron
100 Fourth Ave. North
Bayport, MN 55003-1096
cameron.snyder@andersencorp.com
Tel: (651) 264 - 5881

Serves As:
• Manager, Brand Public Relations, Andersen Corp.

SNYDER, Donna
301 Carlson Pkwy., Suite 100
Plymouth, MN 55447
dds@carlson.com
Tel: (952) 404 - 5051
Fax:(952) 404 - 5601

Serves As:
• Contact, Curtis L. Carlson Family Foundation, Carlson Companies

SNYDER, Gerard
19 N. Main St.
Wilkes-Barre, PA 18711-0302
gerard.snyder@bcnepa.com
Tel: (570) 200 - 6310
Fax:(570) 200 - 6699

Serves As:
• Manager, Public Relations, Blue Cross of Northeastern Pennsylvania

SNYDER, Jeffrey
77 W. 66th St.
New York, NY 10023
Tel: (212) 456 - 7777
TF: (800) 221 - 7386

Serves As:
• V. President, ABC News--Media Relations, ABC, Inc.

SNYDER, Peter L.
7201 Hamilton Blvd.
Allentown, PA 18195-1501
snyderpl@airproducts.com
Tel: (610) 481 - 3278
Fax:(610) 841 - 5900

Serves As:
• Manager, Government Relations, Air Products and Chemicals, Inc.

SNYDER, Richard D.
7565 Irvine Center Dr.
Irvine, CA 92618
Tel: (949) 471 - 7000
Fax:(949) 471 - 7041

Serves As:
• Chairman of the Board, Gateway, Inc.

SNYDER, Timothy C.
16 E. Broad St.
Suite 301
Columbus, OH 43215
Tel: (502) 580 - 3580

Serves As:
• Director, Regional Legislative Affairs, Midwest Region, Humana Inc.

SOARDS, Bill
220 N. Meridian St.
Indianapolis, IN 46204
Tel: (317) 265 - 2707
Fax:(317) 265 - 4354
TF: (800) 257 - 0902

Serves As:
• Director, Government Affairs, SBC Indiana

SODINI, Peter J.
P.O. Box 1410
Sanford, NC 27330
Tel: (919) 774 - 6700
Fax:(919) 774 - 3329

Serves As:
• President and Chief Exec. Officer, The Pantry, Inc.

SOHN, Harold L.
P.O. Box 5000
Broomfield, CO 80038-5000
hsohn@ball.com
Tel: (303) 460 - 2126
Fax:(303) 460 - 2127

Serves As:
• V. President, Corporate Relations, Ball Corp.
Responsibilities include government relations, corporate communications, corporate philanthropy, and political action.

SOKOL, David L.
666 Grand Ave.
P.O. Box 657
Des Moines, IA 50303-0657
Tel: (515) 242 - 4300
Fax:(515) 242 - 4080
TF: (888) 427 - 5632

Serves As:
• Chairman and Chief Exec. Officer, MidAmerican Energy Holdings Co.

SOLA, Jure
2700 N. First St.
San Jose, CA 95134
jure.sola@sanmina-sci.com
Tel: (408) 964 - 3500
Fax:(408) 964 - 3636

Serves As:
• Chairman and Chief Exec. Officer, Sanmina-SCI Corp.

SOLCHER, Steve
2101 City West Blvd.
Houston, TX 77042-2827
Tel: (713) 918 - 8800
Fax:(713) 918 - 8000
TF: (800) 841 - 2031

Serves As:
• Investor Relations Contact, BMC Software

SOLDO, Marie H.
P.O. Box 15645
Las Vegas, NV 89114-5645
Tel: (702) 242 - 7000
Fax:(702) 242 - 1531

Serves As:
• Exec. V. President, Government Affairs and Special Projects, Sierra Health Services, Inc.
Responsibilities include political action.

SOLOMON, Fred
800 Cabin Hill Dr.
Greensburg, PA 15601
fsolomo@alleghenyenergy.com
Tel: (724) 838 - 6650

Serves As:
• Media Contact, Allegheny Energy Inc.

SOLOMON, Howard
909 Third Ave.
New York, NY 10022
Tel: (212) 421 - 7850
Fax:(212) 750 - 9152
TF: (800) 947 - 5227

Serves As:
• Chairman and Chief Exec. Officer, Forest Laboratories, Inc.

SOLOMON, Larry
P.O. Box 2933
San Antonio, TX 78299-2933
lary.solomon@sbc.com
Tel: (210) 351 - 3990
TF: (800) 351 - 7221

Serves As:
• Press Contact, Corporate/Financial Issues, SBC Communications Inc.

SOLOMON, Maura
1101 Pennsylvania Ave. NW
Suite 1000
Washington, DC 20004
solomonma@citigroup.com
Tel: (202) 879 - 6820
Fax:(202) 783 - 4460

Registered Federal Lobbyist.
Serves As:
• V. President and Counsel, Federal Government Relations, Citigroup, Inc.

SOLOMON, William T.
P.O. Box 1590
Dallas, TX 75221-1590
Tel: (214) 443 - 5500

Serves As:
• Chairman of the Board, Austin Industries

SOLSO, Theodore M. "Tim"
P.O. Box 3005
Columbus, IN 47202-3005
tim.m.solso@cummins.com
Tel: (812) 377 - 5000
Fax:(812) 342 - 9288

Serves As:
• Chairman and Chief Exec. Officer, Cummins, Inc.

SOMERS, Erin S.
6950 Columbia Gateway Dr.
Columbia, MD 21046
essomers@magellanhealth.com
Tel: (410) 953 - 1000
Fax:(410) 953 - 5200

Serves As:
• V. President, Public Relations and Communications, Magellan Health Services, Inc.

SOMMER, Judah C.
101 Constitution Ave. NW
Suite 1000 East
Washington, DC 20001
Tel: (202) 637 - 3700
Fax:(202) 637 - 3773

Serves As:
• PAC Treasurer, Goldman, Sachs and Co.

SOMMER, Ron

One Mellon Center
500 Grant St.
Pittsburgh, PA 15258-0001
sommer.rw@mellon.com
Tel: (412) 236 - 0082
Fax:(412) 236 - 1662

Serves As:
- V. President, Media Relations, Mellon Financial Corp.

SOMPOLSKI, Timothy A.

1114 Ave. of the Americas
New York, NY 10036
Tel: (212) 704 - 1200

Serves As:
- Exec. V. President and Chief Human Resources Officer, The Interpublic Group of Companies

SOMSAK, Marlene

400 N. McCarthy Blvd.
Milpitas, CA 95035
Tel: (408) 503 - 7000
Fax:(408) 503 - 2750

Serves As:
- V. President, Corporate Communications, palmOne, Inc.

SON, Christopher M.

One Dauch Dr.
Detroit, MI 48211
chris.son@aam.com
Tel: (313) 758 - 4814
Fax:(313) 758 - 3929

Serves As:
- Director, Investor Relations, American Axle and Manufacturing, Inc.

SONNICHSEN, Ethan A.

1501 M St. NW
Suite 1100
Washington, DC 20005
Tel: (202) 785 - 7300
Fax:(202) 785 - 6360

Serves As:
- Legislative Assistant, Viacom Inc./CBS Corp.

SOOD, Arvind

One Amgen Center Dr.
Thousand Oaks, CA 91320-1799
Tel: (805) 447 - 1060
Fax:(805) 447 - 1010

Serves As:
- V. President, Investor Relations, Amgen Inc.

SOOS, Paula C.

40 Lane Rd.
Fairfield, NJ 07004
Tel: (973) 882 - 7081
Fax:(973) 882 - 7251

Serves As:
- Senior Director, Government Relations, Covanta Energy Corp.

SORDS, David

9600 Burnet Rd.
Austin, TX 78758
Tel: (512) 832 - 2518

Serves As:
- Director, Public Affairs, Coca-Cola Enterprises Inc.

SORELL, C.F.A., Thomas G.

Seven Hanover Square
M/S H-26-E
New York, NY 10004-2616
Tel: (212) 598 - 8000
Fax:(212) 949 - 2170

Serves As:
- Exec. V. President and Chief Investment Officer, Guardian Life Insurance Co. of America

SORENSEN, Jim

4510 13th Ave. SW
Fargo, ND 58121-0001
jim.sorensen@noridian.com
Tel: (701) 282 - 1485
Fax:(701) 282 - 1469
TF: (800) 342 - 4718

Serves As:
- Assistant V. President, Communications, Blue Cross and Blue Shield of North Dakota

SORENSEN, Rick

P.O. Box 10580
Reno, NV 89510-0580
Tel: (775) 448 - 7777
Fax:(775) 448 - 0960

Serves As:
- Manager, Public Relations, Internat'l Game Technology

SORONEN, Rita

P.O. Box 256
Dublin, OH 43017
rita_soronen@wendys.com
Tel: (614) 764 - 8482
Fax:(614) 766 - 3871

Serves As:
- Exec. Director, Dave Thomas Foundation for Adoption, Wendy's Internat'l, Inc.

SORRELLS, J. Charles

P.O. Box 511
Kingsport, TN 37662-5075
Tel: (423) 229 - 8111
Fax:(423) 229 - 8280
TF: (800) 327 - 8626

Serves As:
- Government Relations Fellow, Eastman Chemical Co.

SORRELLS, John

101 Constitution Ave. NW
Suite 400 West
Washington, DC 20001
john.sorrells@altria.com
Tel: (202) 354 - 1500
Fax:(202) 354 - 1505

Serves As:
- Director, Corporate Communications, (Altria Corporate Services, Inc.), Altria Group, Inc.

SORTINO, Gus C.

1111 Adams Ave.
Norristown, PA 19403-2403
gus.c.sortino@skf.com
Tel: (610) 630 - 2800
Fax:(610) 630 - 2801

Serves As:
- Director, Communications, SKF USA, Inc.

SOSA, Jose F.

One Johnson & Johnson Plaza
New Brunswick, NJ 08933-7204
jsosa@corus.jnj.com
Tel: (732) 524 - 3070
Fax:(732) 524 - 3005
TF: (800) 635 - 6789

Serves As:
- Director, External Affairs, Johnson & Johnson

SOTAK, Sonya D.

555 12th St. NW
Suite 650
Washington, DC 20004-1205
Tel: (202) 393 - 7950
Fax:(202) 393 - 7960

Serves As:
- Manager, Government Affairs, Eli Lilly and Company

SOULLIERE, Anne-Marie

82 Devonshire St.
Boston, MA 02109-3614
Tel: (617) 563 - 7000
Fax:(617) 476 - 6150

Serves As:
- Senior V. President, Foundation, FMR Corp.

SOUPATA, Lea

55 Glenlake Pkwy. NE
Atlanta, GA 30328
lsoupata@ups.com
Tel: (404) 828 - 6000
Fax:(404) 828 - 6619

Serves As:
- Senior V. President, Human Resources, United Parcel Service (UPS)

SOUSA, John

1000 Louisiana St.
Suite 5800
Houston, TX 77002-5050
john.sousa@dynegy.com
Tel: (713) 507 - 6400
Fax:(713) 507 - 3871

Serves As:
- V. President, Public Relations, Dynegy, Inc.

Responsibilities include corporate philanthropy.

SOUTHERLAND, Kenneth L.

One Sealaska Plaza, Suite 400
Juneau, AK 99801-1276
Tel: (907) 586 - 1512
Fax:(907) 586 - 2304

Serves As:
- Manager, Human Resources, Sealaska Corp.

SOUTTER, Anne

3120 Breckinridge Blvd.
Duluth, GA 30099-0001
Tel: (770) 381 - 1000
Fax:(770) 564 - 6110

Serves As:
- Contact, PFS Local Contributions Program, Primerica Financial Services, Inc.

SOUTUS, Sonya

P.O. Box 1734
Atlanta, GA 30301
ssoutus@na.ko.com
Tel: (404) 676 - 2121
Fax:(404) 515 - 6428

Serves As:
- Assistant V. President and Director, Media Relations, The Coca-Cola Co.

SOUZA, Stephen M.

600 Third Ave
New York, NY 10016
Tel: (212) 697 - 1111
Fax:(212) 867 - 5249
TF: (866) 463 - 6555

Serves As:
- V. President and Treasurer, L-3 Communications Corp. PAC, L-3 Communications Corp.

SOUZA, Teresa

P.O. Box 982
El Paso, TX 79960
Tel: (915) 543 - 5823
Fax:(915) 521 - 4766
TF: (800) 351 - 1621

Serves As:
- News and Public Information Representative, El Paso Electric Co.

SOWTON, Tim

26955 Northwestern Hwy.
Southfield, MI 48034
Tel: (248) 728 - 7000
Fax:(248) 728 - 7777

Serves As:
- Regional Director, Government Relations, R.L. Polk & Co.

SPAGNOL, Tracy
100 Bayer Rd.
Pittsburgh, PA 15205-9741
Tel: (412) 777 - 2000
TF: (800) 662 - 2927

Serves As:
- Treasurer, Bayer Corp. PAC, Bayer Corporation

SPAGNOLI, Julie
1275 Pennsylvania Ave. NW
Suite 801
Washington, DC 20004-2404
Tel: (202) 737 - 8900
Fax:(202) 737 - 8909

Serves As:
- Director, Federal Government Relations, Bayer Corporation

SPAK, Deborah G.
One Baxter Pkwy.
Deerfield, IL 60015-4633
deborah_spak@baxter.com
Tel: (847) 948 - 2349
Fax:(847) 948 - 2016

Serves As:
- Director, External Communications, Baxter Internat'l Inc.

SPANGLER, Dan
8000 S. Federal Way
Boise, ID 83707
Tel: (208) 363 - 3675
Fax:(208) 368 - 2536

Serves As:
- Corporate Contributions Contact - University Relations, Micron Technology, Inc.

SPANGLER, James K.
500 N. Field Dr.
Lake Forest, IL 60045
james.spangler@tenneco-automotive.com
Tel: (847) 482 - 5810
Fax:(847) 482 - 5049

Serves As:
- V. President, Global Communications, Tenneco Automotive

SPARBY, David M.
414 Nicollet Mall
Minneapolis, MN 55401-1927
Tel: (612) 330 - 7752

Serves As:
- V. President, Regulatory and Government Affairs, Xcel Energy, Inc.

SPARKS-BEDDOE, Angela M.
P.O. Box 12904
Albany, NY 12212-2904
amsparks@energyeast.com
Tel: (518) 434 - 6002

Registered Federal Lobbyist.
Serves As:
- V. President, Public Affairs, Energy East Corp.

Responsibilities include government affairs.

SPATHAKIS, Andrew
550 U.S. Hwy. 202/206
Suite 310
Bedminster, NJ 07921

Serves As:
- PAC Treasurer, Celanese

SPATZ, Ian D.
601 Pennsylvania Ave. NW
North Bldg. Suite 1200
Washington, DC 20004
Tel: (202) 638 - 4170
Fax:(202) 638 - 3670

Registered Federal Lobbyist.
Serves As:
- V. President, Public Policy, Merck & Co., Inc.

SPEAR, Jonathan B.
One Amgen Center Dr.
Thousand Oaks, CA 91320-1799
Tel: (805) 447 - 1000
Fax:(805) 447 - 1010

Serves As:
- V. President, Public Policy, Amgen Inc.

SPEARS, James B.
333 Commerce St., Suite 2102
Nashville, TN 37201-3300
jim.spears@bellsouth.com
Tel: (615) 214 - 3800

Serves As:
- Exec. Director, Regulatory and External Affairs, BellSouth Corp.

SPEECHLY, David
1401 Harbor Bay Pkwy.
Alameda, CA 94502
david.speechly@celera.com
Tel: (510) 749 - 7853
Fax:(510) 749 - 6200

Serves As:
- Senior Director, Investor Relations and Corporate Communications, (Celara Genomics), Applera Corp.

SPEER, David
3600 W. Lake Ave.
Glenview, IL 60025-5811
Tel: (847) 724 - 7500
Fax:(847) 657 - 4268

Serves As:
- Chief Executive Officer, Illinois Tool Works Inc.

SPEESE, Mark E.
5700 Tennyson Pkwy., Third Floor
Plano, TX 75024
mspeese@racenter.com
Tel: (972) 801 - 1199
Fax:(972) 943 - 0116
TF: (800) 275 - 2696

Serves As:
- Chairman and Chief Exec. Officer, Rent-A-Center, Inc.

SPELICH, John W.
500 S. Buena Vista St.
Burbank, CA 91521
Tel: (818) 560 - 8543
Fax:(818) 560 - 1930

Serves As:
- Corporate Communications, The Walt Disney Company

SPELTZ, Robert
One Bowerman Dr.
Beaverton, OR 97005
robert.speltz@nike.com
Tel: (503) 671 - 6453
Fax:(503) 671 - 6300

Serves As:
- Director, Global Community Affairs, Nike, Inc.

SPENCER, Adriane
7516 Jeannette St.
New Orleans, LA 70118
adriane.spencer2@astrazeneca.com
Tel: (504) 866 - 0990
Fax:(504) 866 - 3991
TF: (800) 822 - 9209
Ext: 60886

Serves As:
- Director, State Government Affairs, AstraZeneca Pharmaceuticals

SPENCER, Gaylord
2999 Circle 75 Pkwy.
Atlanta, GA 30339
gaylord_spencer@genpt.com
Tel: (770) 953 - 1700
Fax:(770) 956 - 2211

Serves As:
- V. President, Marketing Strategy, Genuine Parts Co.

Responsibilities include corporate communications.

SPENCER, Lawrence F.
P.O. Box 70
Boise, ID 83707
lspencer@idahopower.com
Tel: (208) 388 - 2664
Fax:(208) 388 - 6955
TF: (800) 635 - 5406

Serves As:
- Director, Investor Relations, IDACORP, Inc.

SPENCER, Steve R.
P.O. Box 2641
Birmingham, AL 35291
Tel: (205) 257 - 1000
Fax:(205) 257 - 2176

Serves As:
- Exec. V. President, External Affairs, Alabama Power Co.

SPENGLER, Bob
P.O. Box 4278
Modesto, CA 95352
Tel: (209) 577 - 1600
Fax:(209) 577 - 3845

Serves As:
- President and Chief Operating Officer, Save Mart Supermarkets

SPERLICH, Harold K.
2902 Enterprise Dr.
Anderson, IN 46013
Tel: (765) 778 - 6499
Fax:(765) 778 - 6404
TF: (800) 372 - 5131

Serves As:
- Chairman of the Board, Delco Remy Internat'l Inc.

SPEROS, James
Five Times Square
New York, NY 10036
james.speros@ey.com
Tel: (212) 773 - 3000
Fax:(212) 773 - 6350

Serves As:
- Director, Marketing Communications, Ernst & Young LLP

SPERRY, Sam R.
P.O. Box 68900
Seattle, WA 98168-0947
Tel: (206) 392 - 5038
Fax:(206) 431 - 5558

Serves As:
- Director, Corporate Communications, (Alaska Airlines, Inc.), Alaska Air Group, Inc.

SPIEGELBERG, Laurie A.
P.O. Box 73
Boise, ID 83729
Tel: (208) 386 - 5255
Fax:(208) 386 - 7186

Serves As:
- V. President, Communications, Washington Group Internat'l

SPIERKEL, Gregory M.E.
1600 E. St. Andrews Pl.
Santa Ana, CA 92705
Tel: (714) 566 - 1000
Fax:(714) 566 - 7900

Serves As:
- Chief Exec. Officer, Ingram Micro, Inc.

SPIGELMYER, Sharon
800 Connecticut Ave. NW
Suite 600
Washington, DC 20006
Tel: (202) 533 - 1100
Fax:(202) 533 - 1134

Registered Federal Lobbyist.
Serves As:
- Associate, Government Relations, Accenture

SPIGELMYER, Toni R.
1390 Enclave Pkwy.
Houston, TX 77077-2099
Tel: (281) 554 - 1458
Fax:(281) 584 - 2721

Serves As:
- Media Contact, Sysco Corp.

SPILLMAN, Robert
3525 Fairystone Park Hwy.
Bassett, VA 24055
rspillman@bassettfurniture.com
Tel: (276) 629 - 6000
Fax:(276) 629 - 6332

Serves As:
- President and Chief Exec. Officer, Bassett Furniture Industries, Inc.

SPINDLER, Laurie
1240 Crossman Ave.
Sunnyvale, CA 94089-1116
laurie.spindler@palmsource.com
Tel: (408) 400 - 1924
Fax:(408) 400 - 1500

Serves As:
- Public Relations Specialist, PalmSource, Inc.

SPINELLA, Patricia A.
One Becton Dr.
Franklin Lakes, NJ 07417-1880
Tel: (201) 847 - 5453
Fax:(201) 847 - 6475

Serves As:
- Investor Relations Contact, Becton, Dickinson and Co.

SPIRES, William J.
63 Lincoln Hwy.
Malvern, PA 19355-2120
william.spires@vishay.com
Tel: (610) 251 - 5255
Fax:(610) 296 - 0657

Serves As:
- Senior V. President and Secretary, Vishay Intertechnology, Inc.

Responsibilities include corporate contributions.

SPITLER, Todd M.
P.O. Box 2950
Los Angeles, CA 90051
spitlert@vmcmail.com
Tel: (323) 474 - 3208
Fax:(323) 258 - 3289

Serves As:
- Manager, Community Outreach, Vulcan Materials Co.

SPITZA, Anne
5005 E. McDowell Rd.
Phoenix, AZ 85008
anne.spitza@onsemi.com
Tel: (602) 244 - 6398
Fax:(602) 244 - 4830

Serves As:
- Manager, Media Relations, ON Semiconductor Corp.

SPITZBERG, Marian
P.O. Box 655237
Dallas, TX 75265-5237
mspitzberg@belo.com
Tel: (214) 977 - 6627
Fax:(214) 977 - 6603

Serves As:
- Senior V. President, Human Resources, Belo Corp.

SPIZZO, Allen A.
1313 N. Market St.
Wilmington, DE 19894-0001
aspizzo@herc.com
Tel: (302) 594 - 6491
Fax:(302) 594 - 5400

Serves As:
- V. Presidentand Chief Financial Officer, Hercules Incorporated

Responsibilities include investor relations.

SPLINTER, Michael R.
3050 Bowers Ave.
P.O. Box 58039
Santa Clara, CA 95054-3299
Tel: (408) 727 - 5555
Fax:(408) 748 - 9943

Serves As:
- President and Chief Exec. Officer, Applied Materials, Inc.

SPONSLER, Linda L.
P.O. Box 3283
Tulsa, OK 74102-3283
Tel: (918) 560 - 3500
Fax:(918) 592 - 9492

Serves As:
- V. President, Advertising and Public Communications; and V. President and Director, Caring Program, BlueCross BlueShield of Oklahoma

SPORKIN, Andi
635 Massachusetts Ave. NW
Washington, DC 20001
Tel: (202) 513 - 2000
Fax:(202) 513 - 3329

Serves As:
- V. President, Communications, Nat'l Public Radio

SPRADLIN, Diane
5400 Legacy Dr.
Plano, TX 75024-3199
Tel: (972) 605 - 6000
Fax:(972) 605 - 6841

Serves As:
- Exec. Director, Foundation, EDS Corp.

SPRAGUE, Joseph
1201 Pennsylvania Ave. NW
Washington, DC 20004
joe.sprague@alaskaair.com
Tel: (202) 626 - 6781

Registered Federal Lobbyist.
Serves As:
- Senior V. President, Public and Government Affairs, (Alaska Airlines, Inc.), Alaska Air Group, Inc.

SPRAGUE, K. Collins
Savings League Bldg., Suite 101
1501 S. Capitol Way
Olympia, WA 98501
csprague@hctc.com
Tel: (360) 956 - 7436
Fax:(360) 754 - 7465

Serves As:
- Director, State Government Relations-WA, Avista Corp.

SPRAGUE, Lisa
P.O. Box 50085
Watsonville, CA 95077-5085
Tel: (831) 724 - 1011
Fax:(831) 722 - 9657
TF: (800) 482 - 1518

Serves As:
- PAC Treasurer, Granite Construction Inc.

SPRATLEN, Susan A.
5205 N. O'Connor Blvd.
Suite 900
Irving, TX 75039
Tel: (972) 444 - 9001
Fax:(972) 969 - 3576

Serves As:
- V. President, Investor Relations and Communications, Pioneer Natural Resources Co.

SPRAUVE, Anthony
P.O. Box 34067
Seattle, WA 98124-1067
Tel: (206) 447 - 1575
Fax:(206) 682 - 9051

Serves As:
- V. President, Worldwide Public Affairs, Starbucks Corp.

SPRECK, Nicole
110 N. Wacker Dr.
Chicago, IL 60606-1511
Tel: (312) 960 - 6386
Fax:(312) 960 - 5475

Serves As:
- Manager, Corporate Communications, General Growth Properties Inc.

SPRINGER, Anna
Two World Financial Center
Building B
New York, NY 10028-1198
Tel: (212) 667 - 9300
Fax:(212) 667 - 1058

Serves As:
- Director, Corporate Communications, Nomura Securities Internat'l, Inc.

SPROGER, Philip C.
7201 Hamilton Blvd.
Allentown, PA 18195-1501
sprogepc@airproducts.com
Tel: (610) 481 - 7461
Fax:(610) 841 - 5900

Serves As:
- Director, Investor Relations, Air Products and Chemicals, Inc.

SPROLES, Joseph D.
508 Michigan National Tower
124 West Allegan
Lansing, MI 48933
Tel: (517) 377 - 6906
Fax:(517) 377 - 5369

Serves As:
- Regional Director, Lansing, General Motors Corp.

SPROW, Frank B.
5959 Las Colinas Blvd.
Irving, TX 75039-2298
Tel: (972) 444 - 1677
Fax:(972) 444 - 1350

Serves As:
- V. President, Safety, Health and Environment, Exxon Mobil Corp.

SPURLOCK, Nancy H.
2001 Rexford Rd.
Charlotte, NC 28211
nhspurlock@nationalgypsum.com
Tel: (704) 365 - 7556
Fax:(704) 329 - 6421

Serves As:
- Director, Corporate Communications, National Gypsum Co.

ST. AMAND, Janet G.
1401 I St. NW
Suite 520
Washington, DC 20005
Tel: (202) 466 - 3561
Fax:(202) 466 - 3583

Registered Federal Lobbyist.
Serves As:
- Director/Counsel, Federal Governmental Relations, HSBC North America Holdings Inc.

ST. DENIS, Kelly
101 Innovation Dr.
San Jose, CA 95134-1941
Tel: (408) 544 - 6397
Fax:(408) 544 - 7740

Serves As:
- Media Relations Contact, Altera Corp.

STADLER, Gerry
One United Dr.
Fenton, MO 63026
Tel: (636) 326 - 3100
Fax:(636) 326 - 1106

Serves As:
- Chairman and Chief Exec. Officer, UniGroup, Inc.

STADLER, John W.
600 E. Main St.
Richmond, VA 23219
Tel: (804) 772 - 1534
Fax:(804) 772 - 1539

Serves As:
- Director, Government Relations, Verizon Communications Inc.

STADSTAD, G. Terry
101 N. Third St.
Moorhead, MN 56560-1990
Tel: (218) 236 - 4400
Fax:(218) 236 - 4485

Serves As:
- Chairman of the Board, American Crystal Sugar Co.

STAFF, Joel V.
P.O. Box 2286
Houston, TX 77252-2286
Tel: (281) 866 - 1167
Fax:(713) 488 - 5925
TF: (866) 872 - 6656

Serves As:
- Chairman, President and Chief Exec. Officer, Reliant Resources

STAFFIERI, Victor A.
One Quality St.
Lexington, KY 40507
Tel: (859) 255 - 2100
Fax:(502) 627 - 3609
TF: (800) 331 - 7370

Serves As:
- Chairman and Chief Exec. Officer, Kentucky Utilities Company

STAFFORD, Bill
1560 Johnston St.
Wheatland, WY 82201
bstafford@bepc.com
Tel: (307) 322 - 9121
Fax:(307) 322 - 3823

Serves As:
- Director, Government Relations, Basin Electric Power Cooperative

STAFFORD, Lori
1500 DeKoven Ave.
Racine, WI 53403-2552
l.stafford@na.modine.com
Tel: (262) 636 - 1001
Fax:(262) 636 - 1424

Serves As:
- Manager, Corporate Communications, Modine Manufacturing Company

STAFFORD, Sherri
544 Westheimer Rd.
Houston, TX 77056
Tel: (713) 989 - 7652

Serves As:
- Corporate Affairs Representative, Southern Union Company

STAGGS, Philip W.
11720 Borman Dr.
St. Louis, MO 63146
Tel: (314) 292 - 2000

Serves As:
- V. President, Human Resources; and V. President, Foundation, Bunge Ltd.

STAHL, Jack L.
237 Park Ave.
New York, NY 10017
Tel: (212) 527 - 4000

Serves As:
- President and Chief Exec. Officer, Revlon, Inc.

STALBOERGER, Philip G.
3535 Blue Cross Rd.
MS 3-27
Eagan, MN 55122--115
Tel: (651) 662 - 2151
Fax:(651) 662 - 6201
TF: (800) 382 - 2000

Registered Federal Lobbyist.
Serves As:
- Director, Legislative Affairs, Blue Cross and Blue Shield of Minnesota

STALEY, Warren R.
P.O. Box 9300
Minneapolis, MN 55440-9300
warren_staley@cargill.com
Tel: (952) 742 - 7575
Fax:(952) 742 - 7393

Serves As:
- Chairman and Chief Exec. Officer, Cargill, Incorporated

STALL, Nancy
444 Highland Dr.
Kohler, WI 53044
Tel: (920) 457 - 4441
Fax:(920) 459 - 1623

Serves As:
- Manager, Public Affairs, Kohler Co.

STALNAKER, Buddy
P.O. Box 13297
Richmond, VA 23225
Tel: (804) 302 - 1700
Fax:(804) 302 - 1760

Serves As:
- V. President, Human Resources and Administration, Swedish Match North America Inc.

STAMBAUGH, Dana
1441 Broadway
New York, NY 10018
Tel: (212) 626 - 3491

Serves As:
- Media Contact, Liz Claiborne Inc.

STAMP, Jr., Charles R.
1808 I St. NW
Eighth Floor
Washington, DC 20006
Tel: (202) 223 - 4817
Fax:(202) 296 - 0011

Registered Federal Lobbyist.
Serves As:
- V. President, Public Affairs Worldwide, (Global AgServices), Deere & Company

STANDISH, Fred
P.O. Box 191
Gardena, CA 90248-0191
Tel: (310) 771 - 3111
Fax:(310) 516 - 7967

Serves As:
- Director, Corporate Communications, (Nissan Technical Center North America), Nissan North America, Inc.

STANFORD, Janna
200 Old Wilson Bridge Rd.
Columbus, OH 43085
Tel: (614) 840 - 3498
Fax:(614) 840 - 4150

Serves As:
- PAC Contact, Worthington Industries

STANGARONE, Bob
P.O. Box 7706
Wichita, KS 67277-7706
Tel: (316) 517 - 6131
Fax:(316) 517 - 6640

Serves As:
- V. President, Communications, Cessna Aircraft Co.

STANGES, Milly C.
1101 Pennsylvania Ave., NW
Suite 800
Washington, DC 20004
mstanges@tiaa-cref.org
Tel: (202) 637 - 8925
Fax:(202) 637 - 8930

Serves As:
- V. President, Federal Relations, TIAA/CREF

STANTON, Matt
1301 K St. NW
Suite 250 West Tower
Washington, DC 20005
Tel: (202) 962 - 0551
Fax:(202) 962 - 0561

Registered Federal Lobbyist.
Serves As:
- Director, Government Affairs, (Jim Beam Brands Worldwide, Inc.), Fortune Brands, Inc.

STANTON, Shanti
655 15th St., NW
Suite 410
Washington, DC 20005
Tel: (202) 638 - 6890
Fax:(202) 220 - 3619

Serves As:
- Representative, UST Inc.

STANZ, Paul L.
1100 N. King St.
Wilmington, DE 19880-127
paul.stanz@mbna.com
Tel: (469) 201 - 5971
Fax:(469) 201 - 4108
TF: (800) 441 - 7048

Serves As:
- First V. President, State Government Affairs, MBNA Corp.

STANZIONE, Robert J.
3871 Lakefield Dr.
Suwanee, GA 30024
Tel: (770) 622 - 8400
Fax:(770) 622 - 8770

Serves As:
- Chairman, President and Chief Exec. Officer, ARRIS Group, Inc.

STAPLES, Cathy
7701 Forsyth Blvd.
Suite 800
St. Louis, MO 63105-1861
Tel: (314) 854 - 8000
Fax:(314) 854 - 8001

Serves As:
- V. President, Human Resources, Belden CDT Inc.

STARCHER, Darlene
2801 W. Tyvola Rd.
Charlotte, NC 28217-4500
darlene_starcher@belk.com
Tel: (704) 357 - 1000
Fax:(704) 357 - 1876

Serves As:
- Director, Communications, Belk, Inc.

STARK, Kenneth J.
P.O. Box 554
Milwaukee, WI 53201
Tel: (414) 319 - 8500
Fax:(414) 319 - 8510

Serves As:
- PAC Contact, Joy Global Inc.

STARKEY, III, James H.
P.O. Box 25099
Richmond, VA 23260
Tel: (804) 359 - 9311
Ext: 724

Serves As:
- V. President, External Affairs, Universal Corp.

STARKEY, Joseph P.
2000 Galloping Hill Rd.
Kenilworth, NJ 07033
Tel: (908) 298 - 7418
Fax:(908) 298 - 7349

Serves As:
- Exec. Director, Public Affairs; and President, Schering-Plough Foundation, Schering-Plough Corporation

STARKS, Daniel J.
One Lillehei Plaza
St. Paul, MN 55117-9983
Tel: (651) 483 - 2000
Fax:(651) 766 - 3045

Serves As:
- Chairman, President, and Chief Exec. Officer, St. Jude Medical, Inc.

STATA, Ray
One Technology Way
P.O. Box 9106
Norwood, MA 02062-9106
Tel: (781) 329 - 4700
Fax:(781) 326 - 8703
TF: (800) 262 - 5643

Serves As:
- Chairman of the Board, Analog Devices, Inc.

STATEN, Reesa M.
2884 Sand Hill Rd.
Suite 200
Menlo Park, CA 94025
Tel: (650) 234 - 6242
Fax:(650) 234 - 6998

Serves As:
- V. President, Corporate Communications, Robert Half International Inc.

STATEN, Theresa Hopkins
P.O. Box 270
M/S NUE 2
Hartford, CT 06141-0270
hopkit@nu.com
Tel: (860) 721 - 4063
Fax:(860) 721 - 4331
TF: (800) 286 - 2000

Serves As:
- Chairman and President, Northeast Utilities Foundation, Northeast Utilities

STAUTBERG, Timothy E.
312 Walnut St.
2800 Scripps Center
Cincinnati, OH 45202
stautberg@scripps.com
Tel: (513) 977 - 3826
Fax:(513) 977 - 3721

Serves As:
- V. President, Communications and Investor Relations, E. W. Scripps Co.

STAVINOHA, Katie
4111 E. 37th St., North
Wichita, KS 67220
Tel: (316) 828 - 3621
Fax:(316) 828 - 5739

Serves As:
- Manager, Communication, Koch Industries, Inc.

STAVROPOULOS, William S.
2030 Dow Center
Midland, MI 48674-0001
Tel: (989) 636 - 1000
Fax:(989) 638 - 1740

Serves As:
- Chairman and Chief Exec. Officer, The Dow Chemical Company

STAWSBURG, Steve
P.O. Box 2990
Winston-Salem, NC 27102
Tel: (336) 741 - 5500
Fax:(336) 741 - 5511

Serves As:
- Foundation Contact, Reynolds American Inc.

STEAD, Justin
2280 N. Greenville Ave.
Richardson, TX 75082
Tel: (972) 234 - 2525
Fax:(972) 234 - 4669

Serves As:
- V. President, National Sales Manager and Marketing, Fossil Inc.

Responsibilities include corporate philanthropy.

STEAD, Tatiana
1680 Capital One Dr.
Suite 1300
McLean, VA 22102
Tel: (703) 720 - 2352
Fax:(703) 720 - 2315

Serves As:
- Director, Corporate Media, Capital One Financial Corp.

STEADMAN, Jr., Eugene
1331 Pennsylvania Ave. NW
Suite 600
Washington, DC 20004-1790
esteadman@celanese.com
Tel: (703) 637 - 3468
Fax:(972) 443 - 8684

Registered Federal Lobbyist.
Serves As:
- Director, Governmental Relations, Celanese

STEARN, Geoffrey
2001 Edmund Halley Dr.
Reston, VA 20191
Tel: (703) 433 - 4000

Registered Federal Lobbyist.
Serves As:
- Representative, Sprint Nextel

STEBBINS, Michele
One Tower Sq.
Hartford, CT 06183
Tel: (860) 277 - 2894
Fax:(860) 277 - 4563

Serves As:
- Second V. President, Commercial Lines Government Relations, St. Paul Travelers Cos., Inc.

STEBEL, Eric
One Houston Center
1221 McKinney Ave.
Houston, TX 77010
eric.stebel@lyondell.com
Tel: (713) 309 - 3987

Serves As:
- Manager, Marketing Communications, Lyondell Chemical Co.

STECHER, Don
3826 Rivers Edge Dr.
Lake Oswego, OR 97034
Tel: (503) 638 - 5101
Fax:(503) 638 - 5202

Serves As:
- Manager, Government Affairs, (Novartis Pharmaceuticals Corp.), Novartis Corporation

STEEL, Elisa
495 E. Java Dr.
Sunnyvale, CA 94089
Tel: (408) 822 - 6000
Fax:(408) 822 - 4501

Serves As:
- V. President, Corporate Communications, Network Appliance, Inc.

STEELE, Lauren C.
4100 Coca-Cola Plaza
Charlotte, NC 28211
Tel: (704) 551 - 4551
Fax:(704) 551 - 4646

Serves As:
- V. President, Corporate Affairs, Coca-Cola Bottling Co. Consolidated

Responsibilities include corporate communications.

STEELE, Mary
P.O. Box 4410
Atlanta, GA 30302
Tel: (404) 588 - 7711
Fax:(404) 581 - 1664

Serves As:
- Director, Human Resources, SunTrust Banks, Inc.

STEELE, Robert
P.O. Box 1349
Tucker, GA 30085-1349
Tel: (770) 270 - 7600
Fax:(770) 270 - 7080
TF: (800) 241 - 5374

Registered Federal Lobbyist.
Serves As:
- V. President, External Affairs, Oglethorpe Power Corp.

Responsibilities include regulatory affairs.

STEEN, Daniel K.
1155 21st St. NW
Suite 310
Washington, DC 20036
daniel.steen@us.o-i.com
Tel: (202) 785 - 3559
Fax:(202) 785 - 8534

Registered Federal Lobbyist.
Serves As:
- Director, Public Affairs, Owens-Illinois, Inc.

STEEN, Daniel V.
76 S. Main St.
Akron, OH 44308-1890
Tel: (330) 384 - 3704
Fax:(330) 384 - 5433
TF: (800) 633 - 4766

Serves As:
- V. President, Environmental, FirstEnergy Corp.

STEEN, William
P.O. Box 60219
New Orleans, LA 70160
wsteen@wewill4u.com
Tel: (504) 566 - 1300

Serves As:
- Corporate Secretary and Senior V. President, Government Relations, Pan American Life Insurance Co.

STEENLAND, Doug
2700 Lone Oak Pkwy.
Eagan, MN 55121
Tel: (612) 726 - 2111
Fax:(612) 726 - 0776
TF: (800) 225 - 2525

Serves As:
- Chief Exec. Officer, Northwest Airlines, Inc.

STEERS, Bill
6415 Idlewild Rd., Suite 109
Charlotte, NC 28212
Tel: (704) 566 - 2400
Fax:(704) 536 - 4668

Serves As:
- Manager, Media Relations, Sonic Automotive, Inc.

STEFFEN, Todd
P.O. Box 19001
M/S A2
Green Bay, WI 54307-9001
tsteffe@wpsr.com
Tel: (920) 433 - 1617
Fax:(920) 433 - 5741
TF: (800) 450 - 7260

Serves As:
- Director, Corporate Communications, Wisconsin Public Service Corp.

STEFFL, Jerry
655 15th St. NW
Suite 425
Washington, DC 20005
Tel: (202) 628 - 7840
Fax:(202) 638 - 1096

Serves As:
- Director, Legislative Affairs, Wellpoint, Inc.

STEFL, Allan
800 N. Brand Blvd.
Glendale, CA 91203
allan.stefl@us.nestle.com
Tel: (818) 549 - 6000
Fax:(818) 549 - 5884
TF: (800) 225 - 2270

Serves As:
- Senior V. President, Communications, Nestle USA, Inc.

STEGEMAN, Mark A.
1284 N. Telegraph Rd.
Monroe, MI 48162
Tel: (734) 242 - 4418
Fax:(734) 457 - 2005

Serves As:
- V. President and Treasurer, La-Z-Boy Incorporated

Responsibilities include investor relations.

STEGEMANN, Robert S.
99 Washington Ave., Suite 1950
Albany, NY 12207
robert.stegemann@ipaper.com
Tel: (518) 465 - 5600
Ext: 3103
Fax:(518) 465 - 5618

Serves As:
- Manager, Public Affairs, Internat'l Paper

STEIL, Robert J.
PO Box 19032
Green Bay, WI 54307
Tel: (920) 661 - 1353
Fax:(920) 661 - 2025
TF: (800) 232 - 5432

Registered Federal Lobbyist.
Serves As:
- National Director, Government Affairs, American Medical Security Group, Inc.

STEIN, Christine
100 E. Pratt St.
Baltimore, MD 21202
cstein@troweprice.com
Tel: (410) 345 - 2000
Ext: 3603
Fax:(410) 345 - 4661
TF: (800) 638 - 7890

Serves As:
- Program Officer, T. Rowe Price Associates Foundation, T. Rowe Price Associates

STEIN, Larry
1680 Capital One Dr.
12th Floor
McLean, VA 22102
Tel: (703) 875 - 1000

Registered Federal Lobbyist.
Serves As:
- Representative, Capital One Financial Corp.

STEIN, Mary
P.O. Box 619810
DFW Airport, TX 76261
Tel: (972) 453 - 7016
Fax:(972) 453 - 7413

Serves As:
- Director, Public Affairs Programs, (Verizon Information Services Inc.), Verizon Communications Inc.

STEIN, Michael J.
401 Ninth St., NW, Suite 650
Washington, DC 20004
Tel: (202) 654 - 2000
Fax:(202) 654 - 2100

Registered Federal Lobbyist.
Serves As:
- Exec.Director, Government Affairs, Morgan Stanley

STEINBAUER, Tom
3773 Howard Hughes Pkwy.
Suite 490
Las Vegas, NV 89109-0949
Tel: (702) 567 - 7000
Fax:(702) 369 - 8860

Serves As:
- Senior V. President, Finance and Chief Financial Officer, Ameristar Casinos, Inc.

Responsibilities include investor relations.

STEINBLITZ, David H.
901 W. Walnut Hill Ln.
Irving, TX 75038-1003
Tel: (972) 580 - 4000
Fax:(972) 580 - 5523

Serves As:
- V. President and Treasurer, Zale Corp.

Responsibilities include investor and media relations.

STEINER, David P.
1001 Fannin St., Suite 4000
Houston, TX 77002
Tel: (713) 512 - 6200
Fax:(713) 512 - 6299

Serves As:
- Chief Exec. Officer, Waste Management, Inc.

STEINER, David P.
701 Pennsylvania Ave. NW
Suite 750
Washington, DC 20004
Tel: (202) 639 - 9420
Fax:(202) 639 - 9421

Registered Federal Lobbyist.
Serves As:
- V. President, Government Affairs, Maytag Corp.

STEINER, Jennifer
333 N. Summit St.
16th Floor.
Toledo, OH 43604-2617
jsteiner@hcr-manorcare.com
Tel: (419) 252 - 5989
Fax:(419) 252 - 5521

Serves As:
- Exec. Director, HCR Manor Care Foundation, Manor Care, Inc.

STEINKRAUSS, Mark A.
30 N. LaSalle St.
Suite 4000
Chicago, IL 60602-2507
mark.steinkrauss@teldta.com
Tel: (312) 592 - 5384
Fax:(312) 630 - 1908

Serves As:
- V. President, Corporate Relations, Telephone and Data Systems, Inc.

STELLMON, John
P.O. Box 1106
Lewiston, ID 83501
Tel: (208) 746 - 2671
Fax:(208) 798 - 2087

Serves As:
- President and Chief Exec. Officer, Regence BlueShield of Idaho

STEMME, Brian
Lilly Corporate Center
Indianapolis, IN 46285
Tel: (317) 276 - 2000
Fax:(317) 277 - 6579

Serves As:
- Government Relations Associate, Eli Lilly and Company

STENDER, Bruce W.
30 W. Superior St.
Duluth, MN 55802
Tel: (218) 279 - 5000
Fax:(218) 279 - 5050

Serves As:
- Chairman of the Board, ALLETE

STENITZER, George
One Tellabs Center
1415 W. Diehl Rd.
Naperville, IL 60563
george.stenitzer@tellabs.com
Tel: (630) 798 - 3800
Fax:(630) 798 - 4776

Serves As:
- V. President, Corporate Communications, Tellabs

STEPHENS, Bess
3000 Hanover St.
Palo Alto, CA 94304
bess_stephens@hp.com
Tel: (650) 857 - 2857
Fax:(650) 857 - 5518
TF: (800) 752 - 0900

Serves As:
- V. President, Philanthropy and Education, Hewlett-Packard Co.

STEPHENS, Donna
3102 Riverwalk Dr.
Annapolis, MD 21403
Tel: (410) 263 - 8756

Serves As:
- Manager, State Government Affairs, Bayer Corporation

STEPHENS, J. T.
P.O. Box 1943
Birmingham, AL 35201-1943
Tel: (205) 991 - 6600
Fax:(205) 995 - 1517

Serves As:
- Chairman of the Board, EBSCO Industries, Inc.

STEPHENS, Leonard C.
10307 Pacific Center Ct.
San Diego, CA 92121
Tel: (858) 882 - 6000
Fax:(858) 882 - 6010

Serves As:
- Senior V. President, Human Resources, Leap Wireless International, Inc.

STEPHENS, Melvin
21557 Telegraph Rd.
Southfield, MI 48034
Tel: (248) 447 - 1500
Fax:(248) 447 - 1722

Serves As:
- V. President, Investor Relations and Corporate Communications, Lear Corporation

STEPHENS, Tom D.
P.O. Box 650205
Dallas, TX 75265-0205
Tom.Stephens@atmosenergy.com
Tel: (972) 855 - 3789
Fax:(972) 855 - 3030
TF: (800) 382 - 8667

Serves As:
- Director, Governmental Affairs, Atmos Energy Corp.

Responsibilities include political action.

STEPHENS, W. Thomas
P.O. Box 50
Boise, ID 83728-0001
Tel: (208) 384 - 6161
Fax:(208) 384 - 4841

Serves As:
- Chairman and Chief Exec. Officer, Boise Cascade Corp.

STEPHENS, Warren A.
111 Center St.
Little Rock, AR 72201
Tel: (501) 377 - 2000
Fax:(501) 377 - 2666
TF: (800) 643 - 9691

Serves As:
- Chairman, President, and Chief Exec. Officer, Stephens Inc.

STEPP, J. Michael
P.O. Box 32665
Charlotte, NC 28232-2665
Tel: (704) 547 - 8500
Fax:(704) 547 - 2360

Serves As:
- President, Foundation, Collins & Aikman Corp.

STERBA, Jeff
Alvarado Square
Albuquerque, NM 87158
Tel: (505) 241 - 2700
Fax:(505) 241 - 2355
TF: (800) 545 - 4425

Serves As:
- Chairman, President and Chief Exec. Officer, Public Service Co. of New Mexico

STERGIO, Gerald
700 Washington St.
Bath, ME 04530
Tel: (207) 443 - 3311
Fax:(207) 442 - 1567

Serves As:
- Director, Labor Relations, Bath Iron Works Corp.

STERLING, Charlotte B.
One Marriott Dr.
Washington, DC 20058
charlotte.sterling@marriott.com
Tel: (301) 380 - 7406
Fax:(301) 897 - 9014

Serves As:
- Exec. V. President, Communications, Marriott Internat'l, Inc.

STERLING, Thomas W.
600 Grant St.
Pittsburgh, PA 15219-2800
Tel: (412) 433 - 1121

Serves As:
- Senior V. President, Human Resources and Business Services, United States Steel Corporation

STERN, Michael
CNA Center
333 S. Wabash Ave.
Chicago, IL 60685
Tel: (312) 822 - 4641
Fax:(312) 822 - 1186

Serves As:
- Director, State Government Relations, CNA Financial Corp.

STERNAD, Kenneth B.
55 Glenlake Pkwy. NE
Atlanta, GA 30328
ksternad@ups.com
Tel: (404) 828 - 7123
Fax:(404) 828 - 6593

Serves As:
- V. President, Public Relations, United Parcel Service (UPS)

STERNBERG, Seymour
51 Madison Ave.
New York, NY 10010
Tel: (212) 576 - 7000
Fax:(212) 576 - 8145

Serves As:
- Chairman, President and Chief Exec. Officer, New York Life Insurance Co.

STERNLICHT, Barry S.
1111 Westchester Ave.
White Plains, NY 10604
barry.sternlicht@starwoodhotels.com
Tel: (914) 640 - 8200
Fax:(914) 640 - 8310
TF: (877) 443 - 4585

Serves As:
- Exec. Chairman and Chief Design Officer, Starwood Hotels and Resorts Worldwide, Inc.

STETSON, Karl
8383 158th Ave. Northeast
Redmond, WA 98052
kstetson@us.ibm.com
Tel: (425) 497 - 4065

Serves As:
- Manager, Public Relations, (Rational Software), Internat'l Business Machines Corp. (IBM)

STEVENS, Cindy M.
555 12th St. NW
Suite 500
Washington, DC 20004
Tel: (202) 879 - 5978
Fax:(202) 638 - 7845

Registered Federal Lobbyist.
Serves As:
- Director, Federal Programs, Deloitte & Touche LLP

STEVENS, Dwaine
P.O. Box 2226-F
Jacksonville, FL 32231-0084
dwaine.stevens@publix.com
Tel: (904) 693 - 6107
Fax:(904) 693 - 6111

Serves As:
- Manager, Media and Community Relations, Publix Super Markets, Inc.

STEVENS, Jonathan
901 E St. NW
Fourth Floor
Washington, DC 20004-2037
Tel: (202) 969 - 8000
Fax:(202) 969 - 8031

Registered Federal Lobbyist.
Serves As:
- Representative, SLM Corp.

STEVENS, Robert J.
6801 Rockledge Dr.
Bethesda, MD 20817-1877
Tel: (301) 897 - 6000
Fax:(301) 897 - 6083

Serves As:
- President, Chief Exec. Officer, and Chairman of the Board, Lockheed Martin Corp.

STEVENS-EDOUARD, Sylvia
401 Park Dr.
Boston, MA 02215
Tel: (617) 246 - 4845
TF: (800) 325 - 2583

Serves As:
- Director, Community Relations, Blue Cross and Blue Shield of Massachusetts

STEVENSON, Bobby G.
5251 DTC Pkwy.
Suite 1400
Greenwood Village, CO 80111-2742
Tel: (303) 220 - 0100
Fax:(303) 220 - 7100
TF: (800) 242 - 3799

Serves As:
- Chairman of the Board, CIBER, Inc.

STEVENSON, Lawrence N.
3111 W. Allegheny Ave.
Philadelphia, PA 19132
Tel: (215) 430 - 9095
Fax:(215) 430 - 9533

Serves As:
- Chairman and Chief Exec. Officer, The Pep Boys-Manny, Moe & Jack

STEWARD, William R.
1401 I St. NW
Suite 520
Washington, DC 20005
Tel: (202) 466 - 3561
Fax:(202) 466 - 3583

Serves As:
- Director, Governmental Relations, HSBC North America Holdings Inc.

STEWART, Amy Watson
605 Richard Arrington Jr. Blvd. North
Birmingham, AL 35203-2707
Tel: (205) 326 - 8144
Fax:(205) 326 - 8140
TF: (800) 654 - 3206

Serves As:
- V. President, Rates and Regulations, (Alabama Gas. Corp.), Energen Corp.

STEWART, Barbara L.
One Bank One Plaza
Chicago, IL 60670
Tel: (312) 732 - 4000

Serves As:
- Senior V. President and Director, State and Local Government Relations, J. P. Morgan Chase & Co.

STEWART, Carolyn
P.O. Box 4689
Houston, TX 77210
Tel: (832) 486 - 4000
Fax:(832) 486 - 1814

Serves As:
- Corporate Contributions Contact, CITGO Petroleum Corporation

STEWART, Donald A.
One Sun Life Executive Park
Wellesley Hills, MA 02481
donald_stewart@sunlife.com
Tel: (781) 237 - 6030
Fax:(781) 304 - 5383
TF: (800) 225 - 3950

Serves As:
- Chief Exec. Officer, Sun Life Financial

STEWART, Edward L.
P.O. Box 36611
Dallas, TX 75235-1611
Tel: (214) 792 - 4187

Serves As:
- Senior Director, Public Relations, Southwest Airlines Co.

STEWART, Faith
1144 E. Market St.
Akron, OH 44316-0001
Tel: (330) 796 - 8928
Fax:(330) 796 - 2806

Serves As:
- Director, Community Involvement, The Goodyear Tire & Rubber Company

STEWART, Homer
One N. Field Ct.
Lake Forest, IL 60045-4811
homer.stewart@brunswick.com
Tel: (847) 735 - 4214
Fax:(847) 735 - 4765

Serves As:
- President, Brunswick Foundation; Manager, Human Resources, Brunswick Corp.

STEWART, J. W.
P.O. Box 4442
Houston, TX 77210-4442
Tel: (713) 462 - 4239
Fax:(713) 895 - 5851

Serves As:
- Chairman, President and Chief Exec. Officer, BJ Services Co.

STEWART, Janice M.
50 W. San Fernando St.
San Jose, CA 95113
Tel: (408) 792 - 1180
Fax:(408) 975 - 4648

Serves As:
- President and Chief Exec. Officer, Calpine Foundation, Calpine Corp.

STEWART, Jason
Metro Center
One Station Pl.
Stamford, CT 06902
jason.stewart@thomson.com
Tel: (203) 539 - 8339
Fax:(203) 539 - 7734
TF: (800) 969 - 9974

Serves As:
- V. President, Media Relations, The Thomson Corporation

STEWART, Jonathan T.
2710 Wycliff Rd.
Raleigh, NC 27607-3033
Tel: (919) 781 - 4550
Fax:(919) 783 - 4695

Serves As:
- Senior V. President, Human Resources, Martin Marietta Materials, Inc.

STEWART, Joyce
Consol Plaza
1800 Washington Rd.
Pittsburgh, PA 15241-1421
Tel: (412) 831 - 4068
Fax:(412) 831 - 4103

Serves As:
- Coordinator, Public Relations, CONSOL Energy Inc.

STEWART, LeAnne M.
7600 France Ave. South
Edina, MN 55435
lstewart@nashfinch.com
Tel: (952) 844 - 1060
Fax:(952) 844 - 1239

Serves As:
- Senior V. President, Chief Financial Officer and Treasurer, Nash Finch Company

Responsibilities include investor relations.

STEWART, Marise R.
1101 Pennsylvania Ave. NW
Suite 400
Washington, DC 20004-2504
Tel: (202) 637 - 3818
Fax:(202) 637 - 3863

Registered Federal Lobbyist.
Serves As:
- Director, Government Affairs, Textron Inc.

STEWART, Steve W.
1301 K St. NW
Suite 1200
Washington, DC 20005
stewarts@us.ibm.com
Tel: (202) 515 - 5054
Fax:(202) 515 - 4943

Registered Federal Lobbyist.
Serves As:
- Director, Market Access/Trade/Telecom, Internat'l Business Machines Corp. (IBM)

STICKLER, Bob
Bank of America Corporate Center
100 N. Tryon St.
Charlotte, NC 28255-0001
Tel: (704) 386 - 4343
Fax:(704) 386 - 6699

Serves As:
- Investor Communications, Bank of America Corp.

STIEFEL, Toni
One MedImmune Way
Gaithersburg, MD 20878
Tel: (301) 398 - 0000
Fax:(301) 398 - 9000
TF: (877) 633 - 4411

Serves As:
- Contact, Corporate Contributions, MedImmune, Inc.

STIFFLER-CLAUS, Vanessa
555 11th St. NW
Suite 525
Washington, DC 20004
Tel: (202) 393 - 2426
Fax:(202) 783 - 8410

Serves As:
- Federal Affairs Associate, CH2M Hill Companies, Inc.

STILL, Julie A.
P.O. Box 66360
Scotts Valley, CA 95067-0360
julie_still@seagate.com
Tel: (831) 439 - 2276
Fax:(831) 438 - 4127

Serves As:
- V. President, Corporate Communications, Seagate Technology

STILL, Stephen W.
P.O. Box 2612
Birmingham, AL 35202
Tel: (205) 325 - 4200
Fax:(205) 325 - 4198

Serves As:
- Treasurer, Torchmark Corp. PAC, Torchmark Corp.

STILLWELL, Arlene
P.O. Box 5650
Bismarck, ND 58506-5650
arlene.stillwell@mduresources.com
Tel: (701) 222 - 7900
Fax:(701) 222 - 7801
TF: (800) 437 - 8000

Serves As:
- Investor Relations Specialist, MDU Resources Group, Inc.

STILLWELL, Robert D.
2950 Industrial Rd.
Las Vegas, NV 89109-1100
Tel: (702) 792 - 7200
Fax:(702) 792 - 7266
TF: (800) 695 - 2455

Serves As:
- V. President, Corporate Communications, Boyd Gaming Corp.

STINGER, Cynthia M.
2345 Crystal Dr.
Suite 708
Arlington, VA 22202
cynthia.stinger@wgint.com
Tel: (703) 236 - 2740
Fax:(703) 236 - 1930

Registered Federal Lobbyist.
Serves As:
- V. President, Government Affairs, Washington Group Internat'l

STINNEFORD, Mark
P.O. Box 2291
M/S HQ4
Durham, NC 27702-2291
mark.stinneford@bcbsnc.com
Tel: (919) 765 - 3745
Fax:(919) 765 - 4837

Serves As:
- Manager, Public Affairs, Blue Cross and Blue Shield of North Carolina

STINSON, Kenneth E.
1000 Kiewit Plaza
Omaha, NE 68131
Tel: (402) 342 - 2052
Fax:(402) 271 - 2939

Serves As:
- Chairman and Chief Exec. Officer, Peter Kiewit Sons', Inc.

STINSON, Mary Ann
P.O. Box 740031
Louisville, KY 40201-7431
Tel: (502) 582 - 4011
Fax:(502) 582 - 4066
TF: (800) 765 - 4011

Serves As:
- Exec. Assistant to the Publisher, The Courier-Journal

Responsibilities include corporate philanthropy.

STINSON, William W.
One Sun Life Executive Park
Wellesley Hills, MA 02481
Tel: (781) 237 - 6030
Fax:(781) 304 - 5383
TF: (800) 225 - 3950

Serves As:
- Chairman of the Board, Sun Life Financial

STIRITZ, William
533 Maryville University Dr.
St. Louis, MO 63141
Tel: (314) 985 - 2000
Fax:(314) 982 - 2201
TF: (800) 383 - 7328

Serves As:
- Chairman of the Board, Energizer Holdings Inc.

STITES, Thomas A.
4000 MacArthur Blvd.
Newport Beach, CA 92660
thomas.stites@mindspeed.com
Tel: (949) 579 - 3650
Fax:(949) 579 - 3200

Serves As:
- Senior V. President, Communications, Mindspeed Technologies, Inc.

STITT, Emily A.
Eaton Center
1111 Superior Ave.
Cleveland, OH 44114-2584
emmystitt@eaton.com
Tel: (216) 523 - 4450
Fax:(216) 479 - 7013

Serves As:
- Administrator, Matching Gifts, Eaton Corp.

STITT, Kevin
Bank of America Corporate Center
100 N. Tryon St.
Charlotte, NC 28255-0001
kevin.stitt@bankofamerica.com
Tel: (704) 386 - 4343
Fax:(704) 386 - 6699

Serves As:
- Investor Relations Executive, Bank of America Corp.

STITZER, Todd
P.O. Box 869077
Plano, TX 75086-9077
Tel: (972) 673 - 7000
Fax:(972) 673 - 7980
TF: (800) 696 - 5891

Serves As:
- Chief Exec. Officer, Cadbury Schweppes Americas Beverages

STIX, Louise A.
P.O. Box 10270
Stamford, CT 06904-2270
Tel: (203) 967 - 5194
Fax:(203) 967 - 5229

Serves As:
- Senior Manager, Advertising, Branding and Communications, Savin Corp.

STOCK, Bill
77 Beale St.
MC B10C
San Francisco, CA 94105
Tel: (415) 973 - 7000
Fax:(415) 973 - 7226

Serves As:
- Manager, Regulatory Relations, (Pacific Gas and Electric Co.), PG & E Corp.

STOCKER, Lisa
P.O. Box 390
Warren, AR 71671
Tel: (870) 226 - 1114
Fax:(870) 226 - 6367

Serves As:
- Director, Public Affairs, Potlatch Corp.

STOCKER, M.D., Michael A.
11 W. 42nd St.
New York, NY 10035
Tel: (212) 476 - 1000
Fax:(212) 476 - 1281

Serves As:
- President and Chief Exec. Officer, Empire Blue Cross and Blue Shield

STOCKHOLM, Charles M.
P.O. Box 3440
Honolulu, HI 96801-3440
Tel: (808) 525 - 6611
Fax:(808) 525 - 6652

Serves As:
- Chairman of the Board, Alexander & Baldwin, Inc.
- Chairman of the Board, Matson Navigation Company, Inc.

STOCKMAN, David A.
250 Stephenson Hwy.
Troy, MI 48083
Tel: (248) 824 - 2500

Serves As:
- Chairman and Chief Exec. Officer, Collins & Aikman Corp.

STOCKTON, Chris
2800 Post Oak Blvd.
Box 1396
Houston, TX 77056
Tel: (713) 215 - 2010
Fax:(713) 215 - 4154

Serves As:
- Coordinator, External Communications, (Williams Gas Pipelines-Transco), Williams

STOCKTON, Robert
1717 St. James Pl., Suite 550
Houston, TX 77056
Tel: (713) 623 - 0060
Fax:(713) 940 - 6122

Serves As:
- Exec. V. President, Chief Financial Officer and Secretary, Omega Protein Corporation

Responsibilities include media relations.

STODDARD, Alexander S.
1401 I St. NW
Suite 345
Washington, DC 20005
ahstodd@meadwestvaco.com
Tel: (202) 289 - 0802
Fax:(202) 289 - 8815

Serves As:
- Manager, Federal Relations, MeadWestvaco Corp.

Responsibilities include political action.

STODDART, Ms. Sandy
9950 Mayland Dr.
Richmond, VA 23233
sandy_stoddart@circuitcity.com
Tel: (804) 527 - 4000
Fax:(804) 527 - 4164

Serves As:
- Exec. Director, Circuit City Foundation, Circuit City Stores, Inc.

STODNICK, Gregory
1293 S. Main St.
Akron, OH 44301
Tel: (330) 253 - 5592
Fax:(330) 761 - 6156

Serves As:
- V. President, Finance and Chief Financial Officer, Myers Industries, Inc.

Responsibilities include investor relations.

STOEBE, Rich
5501 American Blvd. West
Minneapolis, MN 55437
richard.stoebe@jostens.com
Tel: (952) 830 - 3300
Fax:(952) 897 - 4116

Serves As:
- Director, Communications, Jostens, Inc.

STOECKEL, Howard B.
260 Baltimore Pike
Wawa, PA 19063
Tel: (610) 358 - 8000
Fax:(610) 358 - 8878
TF: (800) 283 - 9292

Serves As:
- Chief Exec. Officer, Wawa, Inc.

STOHLER, Thom
12061 Bluemont Way
Reston, VA 20190
thom.stohler@slma.com
Tel: (703) 984 - 5586
Fax:(703) 810 - 7053

Serves As:
- Press Contact, Government Relations and Policy, SLM Corp.

STOJIC, Helen
600 Lafayette East
M/S 0221
Detroit, MI 48226
hstojic@bcbsm.com
Tel: (313) 225 - 8113
Fax:(313) 225 - 6764

Serves As:
- Director, Media Relations, Blue Cross Blue Shield of Michigan

STOKE, Sheila A.
P.O. Box 868
Evansville, IN 47705-0868
Tel: (812) 464 - 9677
Fax:(812) 464 - 9825
TF: (800) 467 - 1928

Serves As:
- Senior V. President and Controller, Integra Bank N.A.

STOKER, Penny
P.O. Box 15437
Wilmington, DE 19850-5437
Tel: (302) 886 - 3000
Fax:(302) 886 - 2972
TF: (800) 456 - 3669

Serves As:
- V. President, Human Resources, AstraZeneca Pharmaceuticals

STOKES, Jack
450 W. 33rd St.
New York, NY 10001
Tel: (212) 621 - 1720
Fax:(212) 621 - 5447

Serves As:
- Director, Media Relations, Associated Press

STOKES, Patrick T.
One Busch Pl.
St. Louis, MO 63118-1852
Tel: (314) 577 - 2000
Fax:(314) 577 - 2900

Serves As:
- President and Chief Exec. Officer, Anheuser-Busch Cos., Inc.

STOKEY, Judy
P.O. Box 98910
M/S 29
Las Vegas, NV 89151-0001
jstokey@nevp.com
Tel: (702) 367 - 5000
Fax:(702) 579 - 0608
TF: (800) 331 - 3103

Serves As:
- Executive, Government Affairs, Nevada Power Co.

STOLTENBERG, Jessica
Five Giralda Farms
Madison, NJ 07940
stoltj@wyeth.com
Tel: (973) 660 - 5000
Fax:(973) 660 - 6900

Serves As:
- V. President, Corporate Communications, Wyeth

STONE, Daniel B.
2525 Armitage Ave.
Melrose Park, IL 60160
dstone@alberto.com
Tel: (708) 450 - 3005
Fax:(708) 450 - 3435

Serves As:
- V. President, Corporate Communications, Alberto-Culver Co.

Responsibilities include corporate philanthropy.

STONE, Gloria
One Health Plaza
East Hanover, NJ 07936
Tel: (862) 778 - 5587
Fax:(862) 644 - 8585

Serves As:
- Director, Global Public Relations, (Novartis Pharmaceuticals Corp.), Novartis Corporation

STONE, J. Sam
P.O. Box 909700
Kansas City, MO 64190-9700
Tel: (816) 801 - 6455
Fax:(816) 801 - 6590

Registered Federal Lobbyist.
Serves As:
- V. President, Government and Member Relations; PAC Treasurer, Dairy Farmers of America, Inc.

STONECIPHER, David A.
P.O. Box 21008
Greensboro, NC 27420
david.stonecipher@jpfinancial.com
Tel: (336) 691 - 3000
Fax:(336) 691 - 3938

Serves As:
- Chairman of the Board, Jefferson-Pilot Corp.

STONER, Diane
5251 DTC Pkwy.
Suite 1400
Greenwood Village, CO 80111-2742
dstoner@ciber.com
Tel: (303) 874 - 2112
Fax:(303) 220 - 7100
TF: (800) 242 - 3799

Serves As:
- Manager, Public Relations/Marketing Communications, CIBER, Inc.

STORCH, David P.
One AAR Pl.
1100 N. Wood Dale Rd.
Wood Dale, IL 60191
aarceo@aarcorp.com
Tel: (630) 227 - 2000
Fax:(630) 227 - 2019

Serves As:
- President and Chief Exec. Officer, AAR Corp.

STORK, Frank J.
636 Grand Ave.
Des Moines, IA 50309
storkfj@wellmark.com
Tel: (515) 248 - 5388
Fax:(515) 245 - 5090
TF: (800) 362 - 1697

Registered Federal Lobbyist.
Serves As:
- Treasurer, Wellmark Inc. PAC, Wellmark, Inc.

STORY, Jeremy
One StorageTek Dr.
Louisville, CO 80028-4377
jeremy_story@storagetek.com
Tel: (303) 661 - 6169

Serves As:
- Press Contact, Corporate and Legal Issues, StorageTek

STORY, Susan N.
One Energy Pl.
Pensacola, FL 32520
Tel: (850) 444 - 6111
Fax:(850) 444 - 6448
TF: (800) 225 - 5797

Serves As:
- President and Chief Exec. Officer, Gulf Power Co.

STOTLAR, Douglas
3240 Hillview Ave.
Palo Alto, CA 94304
Tel: (650) 494 - 2900
Fax:(650) 813 - 0160

Serves As:
- President and Chief Exec. Officer, CNF Inc.

STOUT, Joe W.
P.O. Box 748
Fort Worth, TX 76101
joe.w.stout@lmco.com
Tel: (817) 763 - 4086
Fax:(817) 777 - 2115

Serves As:
- Director, Communications, Lockheed Martin Aeronautics Co.

STOUT, Robert R.
Marine Air Terminal, LaGuardia Airport
Flushing, NY 11371
Tel: (718) 565 - 4774
Fax:(718) 565 - 4134

Serves As:
- Corporate Director, Human Resources, FlightSafety Internat'l

STOUT, Stan
555 Glenridge Connector NE
Suite 300
Atlanta, GA 30342
Tel: (404) 459 - 4450

Serves As:
- V. President and Chief People Services Officer, AFC Enterprises

STOVALL, Ronald
Three World Financial Center
200 Vesey St.
New York, NY 10285
ronald.stovall@aexp.com
Tel: (212) 640 - 5574

Serves As:
- Senior V. President, Investor Relations, American Express Co.

STOWE, Paige
175 E. Capitol St.
P.O. Box 811
Jackson, MS 39205
paige.stowe@bellsouth.net
Tel: (601) 961 - 3800
Fax:(601) 961 - 0415

Serves As:
- V. President, Regulatory, BellSouth Corp.

STOWELL, John L.
P.O. Box 960
Suite 2801
Cincinnati, OH 45201-0960
jstowell@cinergy.com
Tel: (513) 287 - 3540
Fax:(513) 287 - 3412

Serves As:
- V. President, Environmental Strategy, Federal Affairs and Sustainability, Cinergy Corp.

STOWERS, III, James E.
4500 Main St.
Kansas City, MO 64111
Tel: (816) 531 - 5575
Fax:(816) 340 - 7962
TF: (800) 345 - 2021

Serves As:
- Chairman of the Board, American Century Cos., Inc.

STRACHAN, Ian
Three Times Square
New York, NY 10036
Tel: (212) 310 - 9500
Fax:(646) 223 - 9054
TF: (800) 225 - 5008

Serves As:
- Chairman of the Board, Instinet Group Inc.

STRACHAN, Linda
1300 I St. NW
Suite 450 East
Washington, DC 20005-7211
Tel: (202) 783 - 2460
Fax:(202) 789 - 1819

Serves As:
- PAC Contact, Monsanto Co.

STRADER, Frederick M.
P.O. Box 126
Hunt Valley, MD 21030-0126
Tel: (410) 666 - 1400
TF: (800) 626 - 2616

Serves As:
- President and Chief Exec. Officer, AAI Corp.

STRAHL, David
2000 SBC Center Dr.
4B03B
Hoffman Estates, IL 60196
Tel: (847) 248 - 8616
Fax:(847) 248 - 2277

Serves As:
- Area Manager, External Affairs, SBC Illinois

STRAIT, Melissa
5995 Barfield Rd.
Atlanta, GA 30328
Tel: (404) 256 - 4900
Fax:(404) 256 - 7277

Serves As:
- Senior V. President, Human Resources Training and Development, The RTM Restaurant Group

STRANSKY, Paul
5600 Beech Tree Ln.
Caledonia, MI 49316
Tel: (616) 956 - 4096

Serves As:
- Director, Government Affairs, (Farmers Insurance Group of Companies), Farmers Group, Inc.

STRASSBURGER, Raymond
101 Constitution Ave. NW
Suite 325 East
Washington, DC 20001
rlstrass@nortel.com
Tel: (202) 312 - 8060

Registered Federal Lobbyist.
Serves As:
- Senior Washington Counsel, Nortel Networks

STRAUB, Terrence D.
1101 Pennsylvania Ave. NW
Suite 510
Washington, DC 20004
Tel: (202) 783 - 6331
Fax:(202) 783 - 6309

Registered Federal Lobbyist.
Serves As:
- Senior V. President, Public Policy and Governmental Affairs, United States Steel Corporation

STRAUBE, David
1345 Ave. of the Americas
New York, NY 10105
Tel: (917) 452 - 2349
Fax:(917) 527 - 9915

Serves As:
- Director, Investor Relations (New York), Accenture

STRAUSBURG, Ginny
1065 Woodman Dr.
Dayton, OH 45432
Tel: (937) 259 - 7924
Fax:(937) 259 - 7923

Serves As:
- Exec. Director, Dayton Power & Light Foundation, DPL Inc.

STRAUSS, Catherine B.
355 Maple Ave.
Harleysville, PA 19438-2297
cstrauss@harleysvillegroup.com
Tel: (215) 256 - 5000
Fax:(215) 256 - 5602
TF: (800) 523 - 6344

Serves As:
- Exec. V. President, Human Resources, Harleysville Group

STRAUTMAN, Alex
P.O. Box 219139
Kansas City, MO 64121-9139
Tel: (816) 753 - 7299
Ext: 8825
Fax:(816) 753 - 0138

Serves As:
- Director, Communications and Public Information, Kansas City Life Insurance Co.

STRAWN, Kathryn A.
Courthouse Plaza NE
Dayton, OH 45463
kas@meadwestvaco.com
Tel: (937) 495 - 3031
Fax:(937) 495 - 4103

Serves As:
- Manager, Corporate Contributions, MeadWestvaco Corp.

STRAYER, Jaqueline F.
50 Marcus Dr.
Melville, NY 11747
Tel: (631) 847 - 2000

Serves As:
- V. President, Corporate Communications, Arrow Electronics, Inc.

STREEM, Craig A.
200 E.Randolph St.
Chicago, IL 60601
Tel: (312) 381 - 1000
Fax:(312) 381 - 0240

Serves As:
- V. President, Investor Relations, Aon Corp.

STREET, James E.
500 Dallas St., Suite 1000
Houston, TX 77002
Tel: (713) 369 - 9000
Fax:(713) 369 - 9100
TF: (800) 324 - 2900

Serves As:
- V. President, Human Resources, Kinder Morgan, Inc.

STREETER, Stephanie A.
P.O. Box 8003
Menasha, WI 54952-8003
Tel: (920) 751 - 7777
Fax:(920) 751 - 7790

Serves As:
- Chairman, President and Chief Exec. Officer, Banta Corp.

STRICKLAND, Carol A.
114 W. 47th St.
New York, NY 10036
Tel: (212) 852 - 1400
Fax:(212) 852 - 1341

Serves As:
- Managing Director, Corporate Secretary, U.S. Trust Corp.

Responsibilities include corporate philanthropy.

STRICKLAND, Christine
770 Cochituate Rd.
Framingham, MA 01701
Tel: (508) 390 - 3199
Fax:(508) 390 - 2091

Serves As:
- Manager, TJX Foundation, The TJX Companies, Inc.

STRICKLAND, Robert S.
420 Montgomery St.
M/S A0163-024
San Francisco, CA 94104
Tel: (415) 396 - 0523
TF: (800) 411 - 4932

Serves As:
- Manager, Investor Relations, Wells Fargo & Co.

STRICKLAND, Steve
425 W. Capitol, 40th Floor
Little Rock, AR 72201
Tel: (501) 377 - 4000
TF: (800) 377 - 4448

Serves As:
- V. President, Regulatory Affairs, Entergy Arkansas, Inc.

STRIGL, Dennis F.
1095 Ave. of the Americas
New York, NY 10036
Tel: (212) 395 - 2121
Fax:(212) 869 - 3265

Serves As:
- Chairman, President and Chief Exec. Officer, Verizon Wireless

STRINGER, Howard
550 Madison Ave.
New York, NY 10022-3211
Tel: (212) 833 - 6800
Fax:(212) 833 - 6932

Serves As:
- Chairman and Chief Exec. Officer, Sony Corp. of America

STROBEL, Russ M.
P.O. Box 3014
Naperville, IL 60566-7014
Tel: (630) 305 - 9500
Fax:(630) 357 - 7534
TF: (888) 642 - 6748

Serves As:
- Chief Exec. Officer, Nicor, Inc.

STROH, Jeff
6900 S. Yosemite
Englewood, CO 80112-1412

Serves As:
- Director, Public Affairs, Safeway Inc.

STROHM, Jason
7000 Cardinal Pl.
Dublin, OH 43017
jason.strohm@cardinal.com
Tel: (614) 757 - 5000
Fax:(614) 757 - 6000
TF: (800) 234 - 8701

Serves As:
- V. President, Investor Relations, Cardinal Health Inc.

STROHMAIER, Debra
425 Winter Rd.
Delaware, OH 43015
Tel: (740) 549 - 6000
Fax:(740) 549 - 6100

Serves As:
- Director, Communications, Greif, Inc.

Responsibilities include government and investor relations.

STROM, Monika
3535 Blue Cross Rd.
Eagan, MN 55122--115
monika_strom@bluecrossmn.com
Tel: (651) 662 - 6889
TF: (800) 382 - 2000

Serves As:
- Community Affairs, Media Contact, Blue Cross and Blue Shield of Minnesota

STROME, Stephen
P.O. Box 7045
Troy, MI 48007-7045
Tel: (248) 362 - 4400
Fax:(248) 362 - 6409

Serves As:
- Chairman and Chief Exec. Officer, Handleman Company

STROMQUIST, Jeri
740 W. New Circle Rd.
Lexington, KY 40550
Tel: (859) 232 - 2000
Fax:(859) 232 - 2403
TF: (800) 539 - 6275

Serves As:
- V. President, Human Resources, Lexmark Internat'l, Inc.

STRONG, Wendi I.
9800 Fredericksburg Rd.
San Antonio, TX 78288-0122
Tel: (210) 456 - 1800
Fax:(210) 498 - 9940

Serves As:
- Exec. V. President, Corporate Communications, United Services Automobile Ass'n (USAA)

STROPKI, Jr., John M.
22801 St. Clair Ave.
Cleveland, OH 44117-1199
Tel: (216) 481 - 8100
Fax:(216) 486 - 1751

Serves As:
- Chairman and Chief Exec. Officer, Lincoln Electric Holdings, Inc.

STROUCKEN, Albert P. L.
1200 Willow Lake Blvd.
P.O. Box 64683
St. Paul, MN 55164-0683
Tel: (651) 236 - 5900
Fax:(651) 236 - 5165
TF: (800) 214 - 2523

Serves As:
- Chairman, President, and Chief Exec. Officer, H. B. Fuller Co.

STROUD, Matthew
P.O. Box 593330
Orlando, FL 32859
mstroud@darden.com
Tel: (407) 245 - 5144
Fax:(407) 245 - 5510

Serves As:
- V. President, Investor Relations, Darden Restaurants, Inc.

STROW, David
P.O. Box 98905
Las Vegas, NV 89193-8905
dstrow@harrahs.com
Tel: (702) 407 - 6000
Fax:(702) 407 - 6530

Serves As:
- Assistant Director, Communications, Harrah's Entertainment, Inc.

STRUCK, Richard M.
One Blue Hill Plaza
Pearl River, NY 10965
Tel: (845) 577 - 2498
Fax:(845) 577 - 6913

Serves As:
- Director, Public Policy and Economic Development, Orange and Rockland Utilities, Inc.

STRUDLER, Robert J.
700 N.W. 107th Ave.
Miami, FL 33172
Tel: (305) 559 - 4000
Fax:(305) 229 - 6453
TF: (800) 741 - 4663

Serves As:
- Chairman of the Board, Lennar Corp.

STRUMWASSER, Ph.D., Ira
600 Lafayette East
M/S X520
Detroit, MI 48226
istrumwasser@bcbsm.com
Tel: (313) 225 - 6399
Fax:(313) 225 - 7730

Serves As:
- Exec. Director, Blue Cross Blue Shield of Michigan Foundation, Blue Cross Blue Shield of Michigan

STRYKER, David
100 Campus Dr.
Florham Park, NJ 07932
Tel: (973) 245 - 6000
Fax:(973) 245 - 6002

Serves As:
- Senior V. President and General Counsel, BASF Corporation

Responsibilities include legal and government affairs.

STRYKER-LUFTIG, Linda
452 Fifth Ave.
Seventh Fl.
New York, NY 10018
linda.stryker-luftig@us.hsbc.com
Tel: (212) 525 - 5000
TF: (800) 975 - 4722

Serves As:
- Exec. V. President, Group Public Affairs, HSBC USA, Inc.

STUART, Alyson B.
1800 Center St.
Camp Hill, PA 17089
Tel: (717) 302 - 3978
Fax:(717) 302 - 3969

Serves As:
- Government Affairs, Exec. Secretary, Highmark Inc.

STUART, Ph.D., Bryan
P.O. Box 2710
Carmichael, CA 95609-2710
blstuart@dow.com
Tel: (916) 944 - 0278
Fax:(916) 791 - 6800

Serves As:
- Leader, State Government and Public Affairs, Western States, Dow AgroSciences LLC

STUART, John
140 Kendrick St.
Needham, MA 02494
Tel: (781) 370 - 5979
Fax:(781) 370 - 5536
TF: (800) 782 - 3776

Serves As:
- Contact, PTC Partnership for Innovative Learning, PTC

STUART, John H.
5005 LBJ Fwy.
Dallas, TX 75244
john_stuart@oxy.com
Tel: (972) 404 - 3800
Fax:(972) 404 - 3669
TF: (800) 578 - 8880

Serves As:
- V. President, Public and Government Affairs, Occidental Chemical Corp.

STUCKLE, Elizabeth
Two Democracy Center
6903 Rockledge Dr.
Bethesda, MD 20817-1818
stucklee@usec.com
Tel: (301) 564 - 3200
Fax:(301) 564 - 3201

Serves As:
- Director, Corporate Communications, USEC Inc.

STUEBER, Frederick
22801 St. Clair Ave.
Cleveland, OH 44117-1199
Tel: (216) 481 - 8100
Fax:(216) 486 - 1751

Serves As:
- Senior V. President, Secreatary and General Counsel, Lincoln Electric Holdings, Inc.

Serves as the Senior Public Affairs Exec. at headquarters.

STUECKER, Phillip J.
4360 Brownsboro Rd.
Suite 300
Louisville, KY 40207
pstuecker@thomasind.com
Tel: (502) 893 - 4600
Fax:(502) 895 - 6618
TF: (800) 626 - 2847

Serves As:
- V. President; Chief Financial Officer and Secretary, Thomas Industries Inc.

Responsibilities include corporate philanthropy.

STULL, Eric
5619 DTC Pkwy.
Greenwood, CO 80111
erica.stull@adelphia.com
Tel: (303) 268 - 6502
TF: (877) 496 - 6704

Serves As:
- Director, External Communications, Adelphia Communications Corp.

STULL, Gail B.
P.O. Box 57
Pittsburgh, PA 15230-0057
gail.stull@hjheinz.com
Tel: (412) 456 - 5782
Fax:(412) 456 - 7883

Serves As:
- Manager, On-Line Media, H. J. Heinz Co.

STUMP, Denise S.
14111 Scottslawn Rd.
Marysville, OH 43041
Tel: (937) 644 - 0011
Fax:(937) 644 - 7184
TF: (800) 543 - 8873

Serves As:
- Exec. V. President, Global Human Resources, The Scotts Company

STURGEON, Edward J.
One CVS Dr.
Woonsocket, RI 02895
Tel: (401) 765 - 1500
Fax:(401) 769 - 4488

Serves As:
- PAC Treasurer, CVS

STURKEN, Craig C.
P.O. Box 8700
Grand Rapids, MI 49518
Tel: (616) 878 - 2000
Fax:(616) 878 - 2775

Serves As:
- Chairman, President and Chief Exec. Officer, Spartan Stores Inc.

STURMAN, Steven
50 Beale St.
San Francisco, CA 94105-1808
Tel: (415) 229 - 5000
Fax:(415) 229 - 5070
TF: (800) 200 - 3242

Serves As:
- PAC Treasurer, Blue Shield of California

STUTTS, Mary
One DNA Way
San Francisco, CA 94080-4990
Tel: (650) 225 - 5759
Fax:(650) 225 - 6000

Serves As:
- Director, Corporate Relations, Genentech, Inc.

STUTZENSTEIN, Sara
5030 Sugarloaf Pkwy.
Lawrenceville, GA 30042-2869
sara.stutzenstein@sciatl.com
Tel: (770) 236 - 2181
Fax:(770) 236 - 3088
TF: (800) 236 - 5000

Serves As:
- Manager, Public Relations, Scientific-Atlanta, Inc.

SU'A, Kelly
5929 College Ave.
Oakland, CA 94618
Tel: (510) 652 - 8187
Fax:(510) 601 - 4400

Serves As:
- Secretary-Treasurer, Charitable Foundation, Dreyer's Grand Ice Cream Holdings, Inc.

SUAREZ, Aquiles
3900 Wisconsin Ave. NW
Washington, DC 20016
Tel: (202) 752 - 7000
Fax:(202) 752 - 6099

Registered Federal Lobbyist.
Serves As:
- Representative, Fannie Mae

SUBRAMANIAM, Uma
160 Rio Robles
San Jose, CA 95134
uma.subramaniam@kla-tencor.com
Tel: (408) 875 - 5473
Fax:(408) 875 - 4144

Serves As:
- Senior MarCom Manager, KLA-Tencor

SUDBURY, David M.
6565 N. MacArthur Blvd.
Suite 800
Irving, TX 75039
dsudbury@commercialmetals.com
Tel: (214) 689 - 4367
Fax:(214) 689 - 5886

Serves As:
- V. President, General Counsel and Secretary, Commercial Metals Co.

Responsibilities include shareholder relations.

SUGAR, Ronald D.
1840 Century Park East
Los Angeles, CA 90067-2199
Tel: (310) 553 - 6262
Fax:(310) 201 - 3023

Serves As:
- Chairman, President and Chief Exec. Officer, Northrop Grumman Corp.

SULLENBARGER, Daniel T.
5555 San Felipe Rd.
Houston, TX 77056
Tel: (713) 629 - 6600
Fax:(713) 296 - 2952

Serves As:
- V. President, Health, Environment and Safety, Marathon Oil Corp.

SULLIVAN, Chris T.
2202 N. Westshore Blvd.
Fifth Floor
Tampa, FL 33607
Tel: (813) 282 - 1225
Fax:(813) 282 - 1209

Serves As:
- Chairman and Chief Exec. Officer, Outback Steakhouse, Inc.

SULLIVAN, Francis
Five Giralda Farms
Madison, NJ 07940
Tel: (973) 660 - 6923
Fax:(973) 660 - 5771

Serves As:
- Director, Public Affairs, (Wyeth Consumer Healthcare), Wyeth

SULLIVAN, Frank C.
P.O. Box 777
Medina, OH 44258
Tel: (330) 273 - 5090
Fax:(330) 225 - 8743

Serves As:
- President and Chief Exec. Officer, RPM Internat'l Inc.

SULLIVAN, Gary
200 E.Randolph St.
Chicago, IL 60601
Tel: (312) 381 - 1000
Fax:(312) 381 - 0240

Serves As:
- V. President, Corporate Communications, Aon Corp.

SULLIVAN, Marcia
1005 Congress Ave.
Suite 850
Austin, TX 78702
Tel: (800) 525 - 5680
Fax:(512) 478 - 0647

Serves As:
- Director, Public Affairs, (Altria Corporate Services, Inc.), Altria Group, Inc.

SULLIVAN, Mark P.
400 Main St.
East Hartford, CT 06108
Tel: (860) 565 - 9600
Fax:(860) 565 - 8896

Serves As:
- Director, Media Relations, Pratt & Whitney

SULLIVAN, Martin J.
70 Pine St.
New York, NY 10270
Tel: (212) 770 - 7000
Fax:(212) 770 - 7821

Serves As:
- President and Chief Executive Officer, American Internat'l Group, Inc.
- President and Chief Exec. Officer, AIG American General Corp.

SULLIVAN, Michael D.
601 W. Riverside Ave.
Suite 1100
Spokane, WA 99201
miked.sullivan@potlatchcorp.com
Tel: (509) 835 - 1516
Fax:(509) 835 - 1559

Serves As:
- Director, Corporate Communications, Potlatch Corp.

SULLIVAN, Michael T.
607 E. Adams St.
Springfield, IL 62739
Tel: (217) 535 - 5489
Fax:(217) 535 - 5095

Serves As:
- Manager, Govenmental Relations, Ameren Corp.

SULLIVAN, Patty
14841 Dallas Pkwy.
Dallas, TX 75254
patty.sullivan@pizzahut.com
Tel: (972) 338 - 7700
Fax:(972) 338 - 6869

Serves As:
- Public Relations Contact, (Pizza Hut, Inc.), YUM! Brands, Inc.

SULLIVAN, Peg
1800 N. Point Dr.
Stevens Point, WI 54481
Tel: (715) 346 - 6000
Fax:(715) 346 - 6346

Serves As:
- Exec. Director, Sentry Foundation, Sentry Insurance

SULLIVAN, Robert J.
P.O. Box 2910
Tacoma, WA 98401-2910
Tel: (253) 383 - 9101
TF: (800) 610 - 8920

Serves As:
- Chairman of the Board, Labor Ready, Inc.

SULLIVAN, Robert T.
2001 Market St.
Philadelphia, PA 19101
robert_sullivan@csx.com
Tel: (215) 209 - 4580

Serves As:
- Director, Media Relations and Public Affairs, (CSX Transportation), CSX Corp.

SULLIVAN, Steve R.
2244 Walnut Grove Ave.
Rosemead, CA 91770
sullivsr@sce.com
Tel: (626) 302 - 1951
Fax:(626) 302 - 1959

Serves As:
- Regional V. President, Southern California Edison, an Edison Internat'l Co.

Serves as the company's senior public affairs official.

SULLIVAN, Thomas C.
225 Byers Rd.
Miamisburg, OH 45342
Tel: (937) 866 - 6251
Fax:(937) 865 - 5470

Serves As:
- Chairman of the Board, Huffy Corp.
- Chairman of the Board, RPM Internat'l Inc.

SULLIVAN, Tonya
P.O. Box 419580
Kansas City, MO 64141-6580
Tel: (816) 274 - 5220
Fax:(816) 274 - 5061

Serves As:
- Assistant, Public Affairs, Hallmark Cards, Inc.

SULLIVAN, Veronica
11 Wall St.
New York, NY 10005
Tel: (212) 656 - 3000
Fax:(212) 656 - 2347

Registered Federal Lobbyist.
Serves As:
- Director, State and City Government Relations, New York Stock Exchange, Inc.

SULLIVAN, William P.
P.O. Box 10395
Palo Alto, CA 94303-0395
Tel: (650) 752 - 5300
Fax:(650) 752 - 5633

Serves As:
- President and Chief Exec. Officer, Agilent Technologies, Inc.

SULZBERGER, Jr., Arthur O.
229 W. 43rd St.
New York, NY 10036
Tel: (212) 556 - 1234

Serves As:
- Chairman and Publisher, New York Times Co.

SUMME, Gregory L.
45 William St., Third Floor
Wellesley Hills, MA 02481-4078
Tel: (781) 237 - 5100
Fax:(781) 431 - 4255

Serves As:
- Chairman, Chief Exec. Officer and President, PerkinElmer, Inc.

SUMMERS, Michael H.
1401 I St. NW
Suite 600
Washington, DC 20005
Tel: (202) 336 - 7427

Serves As:
- Director, Washington Operations, Pratt & Whitney

SUMMERS, Von
220 NW Second Ave.
Portland, OR 97209-3991
Tel: (503) 226 - 4211
Ext: 2348
Fax:(503) 721 - 2508

Serves As:
- Contact, NW Natural Philanthropy Program, NW Natural

SUMPTER-JOHNSON, Mary
655 15th St. NW
Suite 300
Washington, DC 20005
Tel: (202) 783 - 0900
Fax:(202) 783 - 2308

Registered Federal Lobbyist.
Serves As:
• Manager, Government Affairs, Bristol-Myers Squibb Co.

SUNDAY, Delena M.
1617 Sixth Ave.
Suite 700
Seattle, WA 98101
delena.sunday@nordstrom.com
Tel: (206) 628 - 2111
Fax:(206) 628 - 1795

Serves As:
• Exec. V. President, Human Resources and Diversity Affairs, Nordstrom, Inc.

SUNSERI, Patricia A.
1500 Corporate Dr.
Suite 400
Canonsburg, PA 15317
Tel: (724) 514 - 1825

Serves As:
• Senior V. President, Mylan Laboratories Inc.
Responsibilities include corporate contributions.

SUPIC, Mark L.
3120 Breckinridge Blvd.
Duluth, GA 30099-0001
Tel: (770) 564 - 6328
Fax:(770) 564 - 6110

Serves As:
• Senior V. President, Corporate Relations, Primerica Financial Services, Inc.

SUPPLE, Phil
One State Farm Plaza
Bloomington, IL 61710-0001
Tel: (309) 766 - 9921

Serves As:
• Director, Public Affairs, State Farm Insurance Cos.

SURDEZ, Paul
210 Carnegie Center
Princeton, NJ 08540-6233
Tel: (609) 452 - 4440
Fax:(609) 452 - 9375
TF: (800) 621 - 8901

Serves As:
• Director, Investor Relations, Covance, Inc.

SURMA, Jr., John P.
600 Grant St.
Pittsburgh, PA 15219-2800
Tel: (412) 433 - 1121

Serves As:
• President and Chief Exec. Officer, United States Steel Corporation

SURRATT, Anthony
6205 Peachtree Dunwoody Rd.
Atlanta, GA 30328
anthony.surratt@cox.com
Tel: (678) 645 - 0000

Serves As:
• Exec. Director, Public Relations, (Cox Communications, Inc.), Cox Enterprises, Inc.

SUSMAN, Sally
767 Fifth Ave.
New York, NY 10153-0023
ssussman@estee.com
Tel: (212) 572 - 4200
Fax:(212) 572 - 6633

Serves As:
• Senior V. President, Global Communications, Estee Lauder Companies, Inc.

SUTHERBY, Dan
45 William St., Third Floor
Wellesley Hills, MA 02481-4078
Tel: (781) 431 - 4306
Fax:(781) 431 - 4255

Serves As:
• Investor and Media Relations Contact, PerkinElmer, Inc.

SUTHERLAND, Frank A.
P.O. Box 21008
Greensboro, NC 27420
Tel: (336) 691 - 3469
Fax:(336) 691 - 3938

Serves As:
• V. President, Legal, (Jefferson-Pilot Life Insurance Co.), Jefferson-Pilot Corp.
Responsibilities include political action.

SUTHERLAND, P. D.
535 Madison Ave.
New York, NY 10022
Tel: (212) 421 - 5010
Fax:(212) 421 - 5084

Serves As:
• Chairman of the Board, BP

SUTLIVE, Charles
P.O. Box 1734
USA 645
Atlanta, GA 30301
csutlive@na.ko.com
Tel: (404) 676 - 5451
Fax:(404) 676 - 8265

Serves As:
• Manager, State Government Relations, The Coca-Cola Co.

SUTO, Margaret M.
6363 Main St.
Williamsville, NY 14221
sutom@natfuel.com
Tel: (716) 857 - 6987
Fax:(716) 857 - 7439
TF: (800) 365 - 3234

Serves As:
• Director, Investor Relations, Nat'l Fuel Gas Co.

SUTPHEN, David
1501 M St. NW
Suite 1100
Washington, DC 20005
Tel: (202) 785 - 7300
Fax:(202) 785 - 6360

Serves As:
• V. President, Government Affairs, Viacom Inc./CBS Corp.

SUTTER, Thomas
2937 Tipperary Dr.
Tallahassee, FL 32309
suttert@wyeth.com
Tel: (850) 385 - 8877

Serves As:
• Associate Director, State Government Affairs, Wyeth Pharmaceuticals

SUTTMEIER, Catherine H.
163-181 Kenwood Ave.
Oneida, NY 13421
Tel: (315) 361 - 3000
Fax:(315) 361 - 3700

Serves As:
• Corporate V. President, General Counsel and Secretary, Oneida Ltd.
Responsibilities include political action.

SUTTON, Beth
701 Market St.
St. Louis, MO 63101-1826
bsutton@peabodyenergy.com
Tel: (505) 287 - 2636
Fax:(505) 287 - 5516

Serves As:
• Manager, Public Affairs, Peabody Energy

SUTTON, Howard G.
75 Fountain St.
Providence, RI 02902-0050
Tel: (401) 277 - 7000
Fax:(401) 277 - 7461

Serves As:
• Chairman, Publisher and Chief Exec. Officer, The Providence Journal Co.
Responsibilities include corporate philanthropy.

SUTTON, Neal S.
P.O. Box 60068
Houston, TX 77205-0068
nsutton@smith.com
Tel: (281) 443 - 3370
TF: (800) 877 - 6484

Serves As:
• Senior V. President, Administration, General Counsel and Secretary, Smith Internat'l, Inc.
Responsibilities include corporate philanthropy.

SUTTON, Stephen L.
1000 Wilson Blvd., Suite 2300
Arlington, VA 22209
Tel: (703) 875 - 8400
Fax:(703) 276 - 0711

Registered Federal Lobbyist.
Serves As:
• Manager, Legislative Affairs, Northrop Grumman Corp.

SUTTON, Thomas C.
P.O. Box 9000
Newport Beach, CA 92658-9030
Tel: (949) 219 - 3011
Fax:(949) 219 - 5130
TF: (800) 800 - 7646

Serves As:
• Chairman and Chief Exec. Officer, Pacific Life Insurance Co.

SUZUKI, Cynthia
2000 Galloping Hill Rd.
Kenilworth, NJ 07033
Tel: (908) 298 - 4000

Serves As:
• Director, Government Affairs, Schering-Plough Corporation

SVEC, Victor P.
701 Market St.
St. Louis, MO 63101-1826
vsvec@peabodyenergy.com
Tel: (314) 342 - 7768
Fax:(314) 342 - 7799

Serves As:
• V. President, Public and Investor Relations, Peabody Energy

SWAIN, Cynthia
600 Third Ave
New York, NY 10016
Tel: (212) 697 - 1111
Fax:(212) 867 - 5249
TF: (866) 463 - 6555

Serves As:
• V. President, Corporate Communications, L-3 Communications Corp.

SWAIN, Kristin A.
One Riverfront Plaza
MP-LB-C
Corning, NY 14831-0001
swainka@corning.com
Tel: (607) 974 - 8722
Fax:(607) 974 - 8551

Serves As:
- President, Corning Foundation, Corning Incorporated

SWAINSON, John
One Computer Associates Plaza
Islandia, NY 11749
Tel: (631) 342 - 6000
Fax:(631) 342 - 6800
TF: (800) 225 - 5224

Serves As:
- President and Chief Exec. Officer, Computer Associates Internat'l, Inc.

SWALES, Larry D.
5959 Las Colinas Blvd.
Irving, TX 75039-2298
Tel: (972) 444 - 1000
Fax:(972) 444 - 1350

Serves As:
- Issues Advisor, Public Affairs, Exxon Mobil Corp.

SWAN, Alex
3871 Lakefield Dr.
Suwanee, GA 30024
alex.swan@arrisi.com
Tel: (770) 622 - 8400
Fax:(770) 622 - 8770

Serves As:
- Director, Media Relations, ARRIS Group, Inc.

SWAN, Kelly
One Williams Center
Tulsa, OK 74172
Tel: (918) 573 - 6932
TF: (800) 945 - 5426

Serves As:
- Manager, Public Relations, Williams

SWANGER, Jr., Russel S.
P.O. Box 8888
Camp Hill, PA 17001-8888
Tel: (717) 763 - 7064
Fax:(717) 763 - 6424

Serves As:
- Senior Counsel and Director, Government Affairs, Harsco Corp.

SWANK, Darrell
P.O. Box Nine
Sugar Land, TX 77487
dswank@imperialsugar.com
Tel: (281) 491 - 9181
Fax:(281) 490 - 9584

Serves As:
- Exec. V. President and Chief Financial Officer, Imperial Sugar Co.
Responsibilities include coporate communications.

SWANK, William E.
P.O. Box 029100
Miami, FL 33102
bill_swank@fpl.com
Tel: (305) 552 - 3231
Fax:(305) 552 - 2144

Serves As:
- Media Relations, (Florida Power & Light Company), FPL Group, Inc.

SWANN, Lance B.
3170 Fairview Park Dr.
Falls Church, VA 22042
lswann@csc.com
Tel: (703) 876 - 1000
Fax:(703) 849 - 1005

Serves As:
- V. President, Government Relations, Computer Sciences Corp.

SWANSON, Gregory E.
Bank of America Plaza
600 Peachtree St. NE
Atlanta, GA 30308
Tel: (404) 607 - 5267

Serves As:
- Treasurer, Bank of America Corp. State and Federal PAC, Bank of America Corp.

SWANSON, William H.
870 Winter St.
Waltham, MA 02451
Tel: (781) 522 - 3000

Serves As:
- Chairman and Chief Exec. Officer, Raytheon Co.

SWANTEK, Rosemary V.
P.O. Box 994
#C02100
Midland, MI 48686-0994
Tel: (989) 496 - 4000
Fax:(989) 496 - 8240

Serves As:
- Manager, Internal Communications, Dow Corning Corp.

SWARENS, Greg C.
P.O. Box 419580
MD 288
Kansas City, MO 64141-6580
Tel: (816) 274 - 7457
Fax:(816) 274 - 5061

Serves As:
- Manager, Public Affairs, Hallmark Cards, Inc.

SWARTZ, Carole
1144 E. Market St.
Akron, OH 44316-0001
cswartz@goodyear.com
Tel: (330) 796 - 2936
Fax:(330) 796 - 1237

Serves As:
- Manager, Racing Public Relations, The Goodyear Tire & Rubber Company

SWARTZ, Jeffrey B.
200 Domain Dr.
Stratham, NH 03885
Tel: (603) 772 - 9500
Fax:(603) 773 - 1251

Serves As:
- President and Chief Exec. Officer, The Timberland Co.

SWARTZ, Sidney W.
200 Domain Dr.
Stratham, NH 03885
Tel: (603) 772 - 9500
Fax:(603) 773 - 1251

Serves As:
- Chairman of the Board, The Timberland Co.

SWEARINGEN, Gregg
1700 S. Patterson Blvd.
Dayton, OH 45479
gregg.swearingen@ncr.com
Tel: (937) 445 - 4700
Fax:(937) 445 - 5541

Serves As:
- V. President, Investor Relations, NCR Corporation

SWEENEY, Brian J.
325 Cedar St., Suite 620
St. Paul, MN 55101
brian.sweeney@bnsf.com
Tel: (651) 298 - 2458
Fax:(651) 298 - 7352

Serves As:
- Legislative Counsel and Exec. Director, Government Affairs, Burlington Northern Santa Fe Corporation

SWEENEY, Edward
P.O. Box 58090
M/S C1-128
Santa Clara, CA 95052-8090
eddie.sweeney@nsc.com
Tel: (408) 721 - 6101
Fax:(408) 739 - 9803

Serves As:
- Senior V. President, Worldwide Human Resources, Nat'l Semiconductor Corp.

SWEENEY, Laurel
1300 I St. NW
Suite 1070 East
Washington, DC 20005
Tel: (202) 962 - 8550
Fax:(202) 962 - 8560

Registered Federal Lobbyist.
Serves As:
- Representative, Philips Electronics North America

SWEENEY, Robert
1101 Pennsylvania Ave. NW
Suite 1000
Washington, DC 20004
sweeneyr@citi.com
Tel: (202) 879 - 6871
Fax:(202) 783 - 4460

Serves As:
- V. President, Mid-Atlantic Region, State and Local Government Relations, Citigroup, Inc.

SWEENEY, Jr., William R.
1331 Pennsylvania Ave. NW
Suite 1300 North
Washington, DC 20004
bill.sweeney@eds.com
Tel: (202) 637 - 6751
Fax:(202) 637 - 4974

Registered Federal Lobbyist.
Serves As:
- V. President, Global Government Affairs, EDS Corp.

SWEERS, Nick
2001 Edmund Halley Dr.
Reston, VA 20191
nicholas.sweers@sprint.com
Tel: (703) 433 - 4000

Serves As:
- National Media Contact, Sprint Nextel

SWEET, Frederic H.
720 E. Wisconsin Ave.
Milwaukee, WI 53202-4797
Tel: (414) 271 - 1444
Fax:(414) 665 - 2463
TF: (800) 323 - 7033

Serves As:
- Senior V. President, Government Relations, Northwestern Mutual Financial Network

SWEET, James
Ten B Glenlake Pkwy.
Suite 600
Alpharetta, GA 30328
Tel: (770) 407 - 3800

Serves As:
- V. President, Human Resources, Newell Rubbermaid Inc.

SWEITZER, Don R.
55 Technology Way
West Greenwich, RI 02817
Tel: (401) 392 - 1000
Fax:(401) 392 - 1234

Serves As:
- Senior V. President, Global Business Development and Public Affairs, GTECH Corp.

SWENSON, Curtis A.
9301 W. 55th St.
LaGrange, IL 60525
curt.swenson@gm.com
Tel: (708) 387 - 6264
Fax:(708) 387 - 3944

Serves As:
- Director, Marketing and ebusiness, General Motors Corp.

SWIENTON, Gregory T.
11690 Northwest 105 St.
Miami, FL 33178
gregory_swienton@ryder.com
Tel: (305) 500 - 4440
Fax:(305) 500 - 4490

Serves As:
- Chairman, President and Chief Exec. Officer, Ryder System, Inc.

SWIFT, Al
815 Connecticut Ave. NW
Suite 330
Washington, DC 20006
Tel: (202) 263 - 6260
Fax:(202) 728 - 0338

Registered Federal Lobbyist.
Serves As:
- Representative, Quest Diagnostics Inc.

SWIGER, Holly
41625 Thornton Ave.
Hemet, CA 92544
holly.swiger@vitas.com
Tel: (951) 791 - 8623
Fax:(951) 203 - 9600

Serves As:
- Senior Director, Public Affairs, VITAS Healthcare Corporation

SWINDELLS, William
1000 SW Broadway
Suite 2200
Portland, OR 97205
Tel: (503) 223 - 9228
Fax:(503) 240 - 5232
TF: (800) 831 - 2187

Serves As:
- Chairman of the Board, Oregon Steel Mills Inc.

SWINDLE, Jack E.
P.O. Box 660199
M/S 8656
Dallas, TX 75266-0199
tifoundation@ti.com
Tel: (214) 480 - 3221
Fax:(214) 480 - 6820
TF: (800) 336 - 5236

Serves As:
- President, Texas Instruments Foundation, Texas Instruments Incorporated

SWINK, Philip
700 Anderson Hill Rd.
Purchase, NY 10577-1444
Tel: (914) 253 - 2613
Fax:(914) 249 - 8201

Registered Federal Lobbyist.
Serves As:
- V. President, Government Affairs, (Pepsi-Cola North America), PepsiCo, Inc.

SWINNEY, Carol
1303 E. Algonquin Rd.
Schaumburg, IL 60196
Tel: (847) 576 - 6200
Fax:(847) 576 - 5611
TF: (800) 262 - 8509

Serves As:
- Manager, Community Relations and Motorola Foundation, Motorola, Inc.

SWINTEK, Albert
800 LaSalle Ave.
Minneapolis, MN 55402-2006
Tel: (612) 372 - 4664
Fax:(612) 321 - 5137

Serves As:
- Manager, Local Government Relations, (CenterPoint Energy Minnegasco), CenterPoint Energy

SWIRE, Andrew
555 13th St. NW
Suite 600 West
Washington, DC 20004
Tel: (202) 585 - 9610

Registered Federal Lobbyist.
Serves As:
- Associate Director, Government Relations, Amgen Inc.

SWITZ, Robert E.
P.O. Box 1101
Minneapolis, MN 55440-1101
Tel: (952) 938 - 8080
Fax:(952) 917 - 1717

Serves As:
- President and Chief Exec. Officer, ADC

SWOVERLAND, Gary
P.O. Box 64101
St. Paul, MN 55164-0101
gaswoverland@landolakes.com
Tel: (651) 481 - 2222
Fax:(651) 481 - 2000
TF: (800) 328 - 4155

Serves As:
- Director, Corporate Risk, Land O'Lakes, Inc.

SY. WRBA, John
Three Lincoln Center
5430 LBJ Fwy., Suite 1700
Dallas, TX 75240-2697
Tel: (972) 233 - 1700
Fax:(972) 448 - 1445

Serves As:
- PAC Treasurer, Valhi, Inc.

SYERS, Doc
1650 Tysons Blvd.
Suite 1700
McLean, VA 22201
Tel: (703) 790 - 6328
Fax:(703) 790 - 6365

Registered Federal Lobbyist.
Serves As:
- Director, Congressional Relations, ITT Industries

SYKES, Charles E.
400 N. Ashley Dr.
Tampa, FL 33602
Tel: (813) 274 - 1000
Fax:(813) 273 - 0148

Serves As:
- President and Chief Exec. Officer, Sykes Enterprises, Inc.

SYKES, James A.
260 Interstate N. Circle NW
Atlanta, GA 30339
james.sykes@assurant.com
Tel: (770) 763 - 1015
Fax:(770) 859 - 4325

Serves As:
- Director, Corporate Communications, (Assurant Solutions), Assurant

SYKES, Ronald
3885 Morse Rd.
Columbus, OH 43219
rsykes@limitedtoo.com
Tel: (614) 775 - 3500
Ext: 3810
Fax:(614) 479 - 3619

Serves As:
- Senior V. President, Human Resources, Too, Inc.

Responsibilities also include corporate philanthropy.

SYLVESTER, Brad
2350 N. Sam Houston Pkwy. East
Suite 300
Houston, TX 77032
Tel: (281) 618 - 4700
Fax:(281) 618 - 4820

Serves As:
- Investor Relations Coordinator, Southwestern Energy Co.

SYMANOSKIE, Chris
1001 Fleet St.
Baltimore, MD 21202-4346
chris.symanoskie@laureate-inc.com
Tel: (410) 843 - 6394
Fax:(410) 843 - 8065

Serves As:
- Director, Investor Relations and Corporate Communications, Laureate Education, Inc.

SYNOWICKI, Robert E.
P.O. Box 37308
Omaha, NE 68137
Tel: (402) 895 - 6640
Fax:(402) 894 - 3990
TF: (800) 228 - 2240

Serves As:
- Exec. V. President, Werner Enterprises, Inc.

Responsibilities include political action.

SYRON, Richard F.
8200 Jones Branch Dr.
M/S 431
McLean, VA 22102
Tel: (703) 903 - 3000
Fax:(703) 903 - 3495
TF: (800) 373 - 3343

Serves As:
- Chairman and Chief Exec. Officer, Freddie Mac

SZCZESNY, Jeff
500 W. Capitol Ave.
West Sacramento, CA 95605
Tel: (916) 373 - 3333
Fax:(916) 371 - 1323

Serves As:
- Senior V. President, Human Resources, Raley's

SZCZUPAKIEWICZ, Kathy
5757 N. Green Bay Ave.
Milwaukee, WI 53201-0591
Tel: (414) 524 - 1200
Fax:(414) 524 - 2077

Serves As:
- Foundation Administrator, Johnson Controls Foundation, Johnson Controls, Inc.

SZEWS, Charlie
P.O. Box 2566
Oshkosh, WI 54903-2566
Tel: (920) 235 - 9151
Ext: 2332
Fax:(920) 233 - 9251

Serves As:
- Exec. V. President and Chief Financial Officer, Oshkosh Truck Corp.

Responsibilities include investor relations.

SZMURLO, F. L.
1601 W. Diehl Rd.
Naperville, IL 60563-1198
Tel: (630) 305 - 1000
Fax:(630) 305 - 2944

Serves As:
- Director, Insurance and Risk Management, Nalco Co.

SZYMANCZYK, Michael
6601 W. Broad St.
Richmond, VA 23230
Tel: (804) 274 - 2000
Fax:(804) 484 - 8231

Serves As:
- Chairman, President and Chief Exec. Officer, Philip Morris U.S.A.

SZYMANSKI, Nancy
2655 Seely Ave.
Bldg. 8
San Jose, CA 95134
nancy@cadence.com
Tel: (408) 473 - 8382
Fax:(408) 944 - 0747
TF: (800) 862 - 4522

Serves As:
- Senior Manager, Corporate Public Relations, Cadence Design Systems, Inc.

TABAK, James W.
101 E. State St.
Kennett Square, PA 19348
james.tabak@genesishcc.com
Tel: (610) 444 - 6350
Fax:(610) 925 - 4352

Serves As:
- Senior V. President, Human Resources, Genesis HealthCare Corp.

TACKETT, Bruce
2000 K St., NW
Suite 710
Washington, DC 20006
Tel: (202) 862 - 0275
Fax:(202) 862 - 0267

Registered Federal Lobbyist.
Serves As:
- Washington Representative, Government Agencies, Exxon Mobil Corp.

TACKETT, Everett
5005 E. McDowell Rd.
Phoenix, AZ 85008
everett.tackett@onsemi.com
Tel: (602) 244 - 4534
Fax:(602) 244 - 4830

Serves As:
- Director, Internal Communications, ON Semiconductor Corp.

TAGARIELLO, Alayna
Seven Hanover Square
M/S H-26-E
New York, NY 10004-2616
alayna_tagariello@glic.com
Tel: (212) 598 - 8329
Fax:(212) 949 - 2170

Serves As:
- Media Contact, Guardian Life Insurance Co. of America

TAGGART, David M.
P.O. Box 1734
Atlanta, GA 30301
dtaggart@na.ko.com
Tel: (404) 676 - 2121
Fax:(404) 676 - 6792

Serves As:
- Treasurer, Coca-Cola Co. Non-Partisan Committee for Good Government, The Coca-Cola Co.

TAGGART, Richard
P.O. Box 9777
M/S CH1C32
Federal Way, WA 98063-9777
Tel: (253) 924 - 3892
Fax:(253) 924 - 3543
TF: (800) 525 - 5440

Serves As:
- Exec. V. President and Chief Financial Officer, Weyerhaeuser Co.

TAGLIAFERRO, Maria
One Technology Way
P.O. Box 9106
Norwood, MA 02062-9106
maria.tagliaferra@analog.com
Tel: (781) 461 - 3282
Fax:(781) 461 - 3638
TF: (800) 262 - 5643

Serves As:
- Director, Corporate Communications, Analog Devices, Inc.

TAICH, Adam S.
P.O. Box 6482
1600 Faraday Ave.
Carlsbad, CA 92008
Tel: (760) 603 - 7200
Fax:(760) 602 - 6500
TF: (800) 955 - 6288

Serves As:
- V. President, Investor Relations, Invitrogen Corp.

TAKAHASHI, Matt
2000 Sierra Point Pkwy.
Brisbane, CA 94005
masahiro.takahashi@hal.hitachi.com
Tel: (650) 244 - 7902
Fax:(650) 244 - 7920
TF: (800) 448 - 2244

Serves As:
- Assistant Manager, Investor and Public Relations, Hitachi America, Ltd.

TALBERT, J. Michael
P.O. Box 2765
Houston, TX 77255-2765
Tel: (713) 232 - 7500
Fax:(713) 232 - 7031

Serves As:
- Chairman of the Board, Transocean Inc.

TALBOT, Andrea
P.O. Box 772531
Harrisburg, PA 17177-2531
Tel: (717) 703 - 8574
Fax:(717) 651 - 4325

Serves As:
- Senior Consultant, Health Education, Capital BlueCross (Pennsylvania)

TALLEY, Bruce B.
1455 Pennsylvania Ave. NW
Suite 210
Washington, DC 20004
Tel: (202) 639 - 4062
Fax:(202) 737 - 1311

Registered Federal Lobbyist.
Serves As:
- V. President, Government Affairs, ABB Inc.
Responsibilities include political action.

TALLEY, Drew J.
One Giralda Farms
Madison, NJ 07940
Tel: (973) 822 - 7390
Fax:(973) 822 - 7048

Serves As:
- Staff V. President, Risk Management and Insurance, Schering-Plough Corporation

TALTON, Jim
1100 Terminal Tower
50 Public Square
Cleveland, OH 44113-2203
Tel: (216) 621 - 6060
Fax:(216) 263 - 4808

Serves As:
- Exec. V. President, Human Resources, Forest City Enterprises, Inc.

TALWALKAR, Abhijit Y.
1621 Barber Ln.
Milpitas, CA 95035
Tel: (408) 433 - 8000
Fax:(408) 954 - 3220
TF: (866) 574 - 5741

Serves As:
- Chief Exec. Officer, LSI Logic Corp.

TALWAR, Marie
1299 Pennsylvania Ave. NW
11th Floor West
Washington, DC 20004-2407
Tel: (202) 637 - 4000
Fax:(202) 637 - 4006

Serves As:
- PAC Treasurer, General Electric Co.

TAMBAKERAS, Markos I.
P.O. Box 231
Latrobe, PA 15650
Tel: (724) 539 - 5000
Fax:(724) 539 - 4710

Serves As:
- Chairman, President, and Chief Exec. Officer, Kennametal Inc.

TAMIR, Ronen
608 Fifth Ave.
New York, NY 10020
Tel: (212) 830 - 2433
Fax:(212) 830 - 2405

Serves As:
- V. President, Investor Relations, Novartis Corporation

TAN, Hock E.
6024 Silver Creek Valley Rd.
San Jose, CA 95138
Tel: (408) 284 - 8200

Serves As:
- Chairman of the Board, Integrated Device Technology, Inc.

TANAKA, Lance N.
P.O. Box 2900
Honolulu, HI 96846
Tel: (808) 537 - 8351
Fax:(808) 537 - 8440
TF: (888) 643 - 3888

Serves As:
- V. President and Manager, Government Affairs, Bank of Hawaii Corp.

TANIELIAN, Matthew
601 Pennsylvania Ave. NW
Suite 520, N. Bldg.
Washington, DC 20004
Tel: (202) 661 - 4000
Fax:(202) 661 - 4041

Registered Federal Lobbyist.
Serves As:
- Senior Policy Counsel, Cisco Systems, Inc.

TANII, Akahiro
1130 Connecticut Ave. NW
Suite 1100
Washington, DC 20036
Tel: (202) 912 - 3800

Registered Federal Lobbyist.
Serves As:
- Senior Representative, (Matsushita Electrical Industrial Co.), Matsushita Electric Corp. of America

TANSKI, Ronald J.
6363 Main St.
Williamsville, NY 14221
Tel: (716) 857 - 6904
Fax:(716) 857 - 1856
TF: (800) 365 - 3234

Serves As:
- Treasurer, Investor Relations Officer, Nat'l Fuel Gas Co.

TANTILLO, Auggie
910 16th St. NW
Suite 402
Washington, DC 20006
Tel: (202) 775 - 0084
Fax:(202) 775 - 0784

Registered Federal Lobbyist.
Serves As:
- Representative, Milliken & Co.

TANZBERGER, Eric D.
1929 Allen Pkwy.
Houston, TX 77019
Tel: (713) 522 - 5141
Fax:(713) 525 - 2800

Serves As:
- V. President and Corporate Controller, Service Corp. Internat'l

Responsibilities include investor relations.

TAPP, Jim
1000 Wilson Blvd., Suite 2300
Arlington, VA 22209
Tel: (703) 875 - 8400

Registered Federal Lobbyist.
Serves As:
- Representative, Northrop Grumman Corp.

TAPPAN, Joan S.
1200 Wilson Blvd.
Arlington, VA 22209-2305
Tel: (703) 465 - 3258
Fax:(703) 465 - 3045

Serves As:
- Director, Constituent Relations, The Boeing Co.

TARANTOLA, Bob
2840 E. Yellowstone Hwy.
Casper, WY 82602
robert.tarantola@pacificorp.com
Tel: (307) 577 - 6901

Serves As:
- V. President, Wyoming, PacifiCorp

Responsibilities include public affairs.

TARBELL, Anne A.
280 Park Ave.
New York, NY 10017
atarbell@triarc.com
Tel: (212) 451 - 3030
Fax:(212) 451 - 3134

Serves As:
- Senior V. President, Corporate Communications and Investor Relations, Triarc Companies, Inc.

TARBOX, Amy
40 Landsdowne St.
Cambridge, MA 02139
info@mlmn.com
Tel: (617) 551 - 5879
Fax:(617) 374 - 7788
TF: (800) 390 - 5663

Serves As:
- Associate, Global Corporate Affairs, Millennium Pharmaceuticals, Inc.

TARDANICO, Susan
40 Westminster St.
Providence, RI 02903-2525
stardanico@textron.com
Tel: (401) 457 - 2354
Fax:(401) 457 - 3598

Serves As:
- Exec. Director, Corporate Communications, Textron Inc.

TARDY, Warren
310 25th Ave. North
Suite 101
Nashville, TN 37203
warren.tardy@hcahealthcare.com
Tel: (615) 320 - 8797
Fax:(615) 963 - 3841

Serves As:
- Consultant, Government Relations, HCA

TART, Wallace L.
5301 Wisconsin Ave. NW
Suite 400
Washington, DC 20015
Tel: (202) 364 - 1600
Fax:(202) 537 - 4876

Serves As:
- Manager, DC Office, A. G. Edwards, Inc.

TASAKA, Diane
4680 Wilshire Blvd.
Los Angeles, CA 90010
Tel: (323) 932 - 3018

Serves As:
- Director, Corporate Communications, Farmers Group, Inc.

TASAKI, Akira
5665 Plaza Drive
Cypress, CA 90630-0007
Tel: (714) 220 - 2500
Fax:(714) 229 - 3898

Serves As:
- President and Chief Exec. Officer, Mitsubishi Electric & Electronics USA

TASHER, Steven A.
Five Giralda Farms
Madison, NJ 07940
Tel: (973) 660 - 5210
Fax:(973) 660 - 5771

Serves As:
- V. President, Environmental Affairs, Facilities Operations and Associate General Counsel, Wyeth

TASHJIAN, Lee
One Enterprise Dr.
Aliso Viejo, CA 92656-2606
Tel: (949) 349 - 2000
Fax:(949) 349 - 2585

Serves As:
- V. President, Corporate Communications, Fluor Corp.

TASSOT, Beatrice M.
600 Mountain Ave.
Room 6F418
Murray Hill, NJ 07974-0636
bmtassot@lucent.com
Tel: (908) 582 - 8500
Fax:(908) 508 - 2576
TF: (888) 458 - 2368

Serves As:
- Director, Corporate Contributions, Lucent Technologies

TATE, Amanda
9950 Mayland Dr.
Richmond, VA 23233
Tel: (804) 418 - 8298
Fax:(804) 527 - 4164

Serves As:
- Senior Public Relations Representative, Circuit City Stores, Inc.

TATE, Brenda K.
63 Lincoln Hwy.
Malvern, PA 19355-2120
brenda.tate@vishay.com
Tel: (610) 644 - 1300
Fax:(610) 889 - 9349

Serves As:
- Corporate Investor Relations Contact, Vishay Intertechnology, Inc.

TATHAM, Tom
1065 Woodman Dr.
Dayton, OH 45432
Tel: (937) 259 - 7347
Fax:(937) 259 - 7813

Serves As:
- Manager, Corporate Communications and Community Relations, (Dayton Power and Light Co.), DPL Inc.

TATKO, Mike
P.O. Box 1106
Lewiston, ID 83501
mtatko.id@regence.com
Tel: (208) 798 - 2221
Fax:(208) 798 - 2087

Serves As:
- Strategic Communications, Regence BlueShield of Idaho

TAUKE, Hon. Thomas J.
1300 I St. NW
Suite 400 West
Washington, DC 20005
thomas.j.tauke@verizon.com
Tel: (202) 515 - 2400
Fax:(202) 336 - 7921

Registered Federal Lobbyist.
Serves As:
- Exec. V. President, Public Affairs and Communications, Verizon Communications Inc.

TAULBEE, Richard
400 Broadway
Cincinnati, OH 45202
Tel: (513) 629 - 1905
Fax:(513) 629 - 1220
TF: (800) 936 - 1212

Serves As:
- Contact, Corporate Giving, Western and Southern Life Insurance Co.

TAUNTON, Michael J.
One MetroTech Center
Brooklyn, NY 11201
Tel: (718) 403 - 3265
Fax:(718) 488 - 1763

Serves As:
- V. President and Treasurer, KeySpan Corp.

Responsibilities include investor relations.

TAUREL, Sidney
Lilly Corporate Center
Indianapolis, IN 46285
Tel: (317) 276 - 2000
Fax:(317) 277 - 6579

Serves As:
- Chairman, President and Chief Exec. Officer, Eli Lilly and Company

TAYLOR, Andre
605 Richard Arrington Jr. Blvd. North
Birmingham, AL 35203-2707
Tel: (205) 326 - 1613
Fax:(205) 714 - 5039
TF: (800) 654 - 3206

Serves As:
- V. President, Communications, (Alabama Gas. Corp.), Energen Corp.

Responsibilities include coporate philanthropy.

TAYLOR, Andrew C.
600 Corporate Park Dr.
St. Louis, MO 63105
Tel: (314) 512 - 5000
Fax:(314) 512 - 4706

Serves As:
- Chairman and Chief Exec. Officer, Enterprise Rent-A-Car Co.

TAYLOR, Ann
801 Pennsylvania Ave. NW
Suite 725
Washington, DC 20004
ann.taylor@sanofi-aventis.com
Tel: (202) 628 - 0500
Fax:(202) 682 - 0538

Registered Federal Lobbyist.
Serves As:
- Director, Health Policy and Pharmaceutical Programs, Sanofi-Aventis Inc.

TAYLOR, Ben
425 Portland Ave.
Minneapolis, MN 55415
Tel: (612) 673 - 7457
Fax:(612) 673 - 4835
TF: (800) 829 - 8742

Serves As:
- Senior V. President, Communications, Star Tribune

TAYLOR, Bill
One Valmont Plaza
Omaha, NE 68154-5215
wrt@valmont.com
Tel: (402) 359 - 2201
Fax:(402) 359 - 2848

Serves As:
- Director, Environmental Affairs, Valmont Industries, Inc.

TAYLOR, Chuck
3170 Fairview Park Dr.
Falls Church, VA 22042
ctaylor@csc.com
Tel: (703) 641 - 3430

Serves As:
- Director, Communications Federal Sector, Computer Sciences Corp.

TAYLOR, Corina
600 Kellwood Pkwy.
Chesterfield, MO 63017
corina.taylor@kellwood.com
Tel: (314) 576 - 3391
Fax:(314) 576 - 3460

Serves As:
- Director, Corporate Communications, Kellwood Co.

TAYLOR, Dean E.
601 Poydras St.
Suite 1900
New Orleans, LA 70130
Tel: (504) 568 - 1010
Fax:(504) 566 - 4580

Serves As:
- Chairman, President, and Chief Exec. Officer, Tidewater Inc.

TAYLOR, Geoffrey E.
165 Court St.
Rochester, NY 14647
Tel: (585) 454 - 1700
Fax:(585) 238 - 4233

Serves As:
- Senior V. President, Corporate Communications, The Lifetime Healthcare Companies

TAYLOR, Gina A.
544 Westheimer Rd.
Houston, TX 77056
Tel: (713) 989 - 7557

Serves As:
- Director, Internal Affairs, Southern Union Company

TAYLOR, Goldie
10151 Carver Rd.
Cincinnati, OH 45242
Tel: (513) 936 - 2001
Fax:(513) 936 - 2020

Serves As:
- Director, Communications and Public Relations, (Sara Lee Foods), Sara Lee Corp.

TAYLOR, Greg D.
2208 Joyce Bridge Ct.
Chesterfield, MO 63017
Tel: (636) 530 - 6350

Serves As:
- Regional Director, State Government Relations, HSBC North America Holdings Inc.

TAYLOR, Jeff
444 Westminster St.
Providence, RI 02903-3279
taylor.j@bcbsri.org
Tel: (401) 459 - 1241
Fax:(401) 459 - 1333
TF: (800) 637 - 3718

Serves As:
- Director, Legislative Affairs, Blue Cross & Blue Shield of Rhode Island

TAYLOR, Jim
305 Hartman Dr.
Lebanon, TN 37088
Tel: (615) 444 - 5533
Fax:(615) 443 - 9322

Serves As:
- Manager, Communications, (Cracker Barrel Old Country Store, Inc.), CBRL Group, Inc.

TAYLOR, Joan
11420 Lackland Rd.
St. Louis, MO 63146-6928
jtaylor@schnucks.com
Tel: (314) 944 - 9900

Serves As:
- Director, Consumer Relations, Schnuck Markets, Inc.

TAYLOR, Joe
6820 LBJ Fwy.
Dallas, TX 75240
Tel: (972) 980 - 9917
Fax:(972) 770 - 9400

Serves As:
- V. President Corporate Affairs and PAC Contact, Brinker Internat'l, Inc.

TAYLOR, III, John
1399 New York Ave. NW
Suite 200
Washington, DC 20005
Tel: (202) 378 - 2020
Fax:(202) 783 - 6631

Serves As:
- Divisional V. President, Federal Government Affairs, Abbott Laboratories

TAYLOR, John I.
2000 Millbrook Dr.
Lincolnshire, IL 60069
john.taylor@zenith.com
Tel: (847) 391 - 8181
Fax:(847) 391 - 8177

Serves As:
- V. President, Public Affairs and Communications, Zenith Electronics Corp.

TAYLOR, Julie M.
P.O. Box 7408
Boise, ID 83707
jtaylor@bcidaho.com
Tel: (208) 331 - 7357
Fax:(208) 331 - 7320

Serves As:
- Director, Governmental Affairs, Blue Cross of Idaho

TAYLOR, Karen D.
P.O. Box 2286
Houston, TX 77252-2286
Tel: (281) 866 - 1167
Fax:(713) 488 - 5925
TF: (866) 872 - 6656

Serves As:
- Senior V. President, Human Resources and Administration, Reliant Resources

TAYLOR, Kris
Ecolab Center
370 N. Wabasha St.
St. Paul, MN 55102
Tel: (651) 293 - 2259
Fax:(651) 225 - 2092

Serves As:
- Director, Community Relations, Ecolab Inc.

TAYLOR, Kristina
1101 Pennsylvania Ave., NW
Suite 515
Washington, DC 20004
Tel: (202) 639 - 0750

Serves As:
- Coordinator, Government Affairs, Lyondell Chemical Co.

TAYLOR, Lonnie
2001 Edmund Halley Dr.
Reston, VA 20191
Tel: (703) 433 - 4000

Registered Federal Lobbyist.
Serves As:
- V. President, State and Federal Relations, Sprint Nextel

TAYLOR, Mary
1290 Ave. of the Americas
New York, NY 10104
Tel: (212) 314 - 5845
TF: (888) AXA - INFO

Serves As:
- Corporate Communications Contact, AXA Financial, Inc.

TAYLOR, Norman
2570 Hunter Green Ct. SE
Grand Rapids, MI 49546
Tel: (616) 954 - 1738
Fax:(616) 954 - 1879

Serves As:
- Associate Director, Government Affairs, Novartis Corporation

TAYLOR, Penny R.
P.O. Box 52075
Phoenix, AZ 85072-2075
Tel: (602) 395 - 4085

Serves As:
- Specialist, Government Relations, Southwest Gas Corp.

TAYLOR, Ronald
901 S. Central Exwy.
Richardson, TX 75080
Tel: (972) 766 - 6900
Fax:(972) 766 - 5298

Serves As:
- V. President and General Counsel, Legal and Government Affairs, Blue Cross and Blue Shield of Texas, Inc.

TAYLOR, Ronald L.
One Tower Ln.
Suite 1000
Oakbrook Terrace, IL 60181-4624
Tel: (630) 571 - 7700
Fax:(630) 571 - 0317
TF: (800) 225 - 8000

Serves As:
- Chief Exec. Officer, DeVry Inc.

TAYLOR, Roxanne
1345 Ave. of the Americas
New York, NY 10105
roxanne.taylor@accenture.com
Tel: (917) 452 - 5106
Fax:(917) 527 - 9915

Serves As:
- Managing Partner, Corporate Communications, Accenture

TAYLOR, Steve
3050 Bowers Ave.
P.O. Box 58039
Santa Clara, CA 95054-3299
steve_taylor@appliedmaterials.com
Tel: (512) 272 - 2120
Fax:(512) 272 - 3041

Serves As:
- Director, North American Corporate Affairs, Applied Materials, Inc.

TAYLOR, Sue
6001 36th Ave. West
Everett, WA 98203-9280
Tel: (425) 265 - 2400
Fax:(425) 265 - 2425

Serves As:
- Chief Information Officer and V. President, Human Resources, UNOVA, Inc.

TAYLOR, Teresa H.
P.O. Box 4079
Gulfport, MS 39502
Tel: (228) 865 - 5468
Fax:(228) 865 - 5771

Serves As:
- Supervisor, Employee Communications, Mississippi Power Co.

TAYLOR, Tiarzha
P.O. Box 191
Gardena, CA 90248-0191
Tel: (310) 771 - 3330
Fax:(310) 516 - 7967

Serves As:
- Manager, Corporate Relations, Nissan North America, Inc.

TEARNO, T. Daniel
360 Hamilton Ave., Suite 1103
White Plains, NY 10601-1841
Tel: (914) 681 - 4113
Fax:(914) 989 - 1003

Serves As:
- V. President, Corporate Affairs and Chairman, Heineken USA Good Government Fund, Heineken USA Inc.

Also serves as the Washington Representative.

TECHAR, Frank J.
111 W. Monroe St.
Chicago, IL 60603-4095
Tel: (312) 461 - 3500
Fax:(312) 461 - 6640

Serves As:
- President and Chief Exec. Officer, Harris Bank

TECK, Kristin
11505 W. Dodge Rd.
Omaha, NE 68154
Tel: (402) 934 - 0256
Fax:(402) 933 - 0010

Serves As:
- V. President, Government and Public Affairs, Cox Enterprises, Inc.

TEEL, Jim
500 W. Capitol Ave.
West Sacramento, CA 95605
jteel@raleys.com
Tel: (916) 373 - 3333
Fax:(916) 371 - 1323

Serves As:
- Co-Chairman of the Board, Raley's

TEEL, Joyce Raley
500 W. Capitol Ave.
West Sacramento, CA 95605
jrteel@raleys.com
Tel: (916) 373 - 3333
Fax:(916) 371 - 1323

Serves As:
- Co-Chairman of the Board, Raley's

TEETER, Geoff
One DNA Way
San Francisco, CA 94080-4990
Tel: (650) 225 - 8171
Fax:(650) 225 - 6000

Serves As:
- Director, Employee/Community Relations, Genentech, Inc.

TEETS, Robert
P.O. Box 4446
Houston, TX 77210-4446
teets@cooperindustries.com
Tel: (713) 209 - 8635
Fax:(713) 209 - 8990

Serves As:
- V. President, Environmental Affairs and Risk Management, Cooper Industries

TEETS, Robin
P.O. Box 57
Pittsburgh, PA 15230-0057
robin.teets@hjheinz.com
Tel: (412) 456 - 3562
Fax:(412) 456 - 5776

Serves As:
- Senior Manager, Communications, Heinz North America, H. J. Heinz Co.

TEHEL, Megan
711 High St.
Des Moines, IA 50392-0150
tehel.megan@principal.com
Tel: (515) 246 - 4907
Fax:(515) 246 - 5475
TF: (800) 986 - 3343

Serves As:
- Community Involvement Contact, The Principal Financial Group

TEJERO-DECOLLI, Aida
250 Rittenhouse Circle
Bristol, PA 19007
Tel: (215) 785 - 4000
Fax:(215) 785 - 1795

Serves As:
- Senior V. President, Human Resources, Jones Apparel Group

TELLALIAN, Christina
1667 K St. NW
Suite 200
Washington, DC 20006
christina.tellalian@am.sony.com
Tel: (202) 429 - 3652
Fax:(202) 429 - 3663

Registered Federal Lobbyist.
Serves As:
- Senior Manager, Public and Government Affairs, (Sony Electronics Inc.), Sony Corp. of America

TELLE, Jim
One N. Central Ave.
Phoenix, AZ 85004-3014
jtelle@phelpsdodge.com
Tel: (602) 366 - 7963
Fax:(602) 234 - 8337
TF: (800) 528 - 1182

Serves As:
- Manager, Corporate Communications, Phelps Dodge Corp.

TEMARES, Steven H.
650 Liberty Ave.
Union, NJ 07083
Tel: (908) 688 - 0888
Fax:(908) 688 - 6483

Serves As:
- President and Chief Exec. Officer, Bed Bath & Beyond Inc.

TEMENAK, James M.
2941 Fairview Park Dr.
Falls Church, VA 22042-4513
Tel: (703) 876 - 3000
Fax:(703) 876 - 3600

Registered Federal Lobbyist.
Serves As:
- Staff V. President, Marine Systems, General Dynamics Corporation

TEMMINS, Amy
60 S. Market St.
Suite 1000
San Jose, CA 95113

Serves As:
- Program Coordinator, eBay Foundation, eBay, Inc.

TEMPLE, Nancy H.
P.O. Box 1551
Raleigh, NC 27602-1551
Tel: (919) 546 - 4550
Fax:(919) 546 - 6615

Serves As:
- V. President, Corporate Communications, Progress Energy

TEMPLETON, Mark B.
851 W. Cypress Creek Rd.
Fort Lauderdale, FL 33309
mark.templeton@citrix.com
Tel: (954) 267 - 3000
Fax:(954) 267 - 3100
TF: (800) 424 - 8749

Serves As:
- President and Chief Exec. Officer, Citrix Systems, Inc.

TEMPLETON, Richard K.
P.O. Box 660199
Dallas, TX 75266-0199
Tel: (214) 995 - 2011
Fax:(214) 995 - 5150
TF: (800) 336 - 5236

Serves As:
- President and Chief Exec. Officer, Texas Instruments Incorporated

TEN EYCK, Greg
4551 Forbes Blvd.
Lanham, MD 20706
greg.teneyck@safeway.com
Tel: (301) 918 - 6500

Serves As:
- Director, Public Affairs, Safeway Inc.

TENNILLE, Lacye E.
655 15th St. NW
Suite 445
Washington, DC 20005
Tel: (202) 737 - 1977
Fax:(202) 737 - 8111

Serves As:
- Pac Treasurer, Koch Industries, Inc.

TENUTA, Joshua P.
One Infinite Loop
Cupertino, CA 95014
Tel: (408) 996 - 1010
Fax:(408) 996 - 0275

Registered Federal Lobbyist.
Serves As:
- Attorney, Apple Computer, Inc.

TEPLITZ, Steven N.
800 Connecticut Ave. NW
Suite 800
Washington, DC 20006
Tel: (202) 457 - 8582
Fax:(202) 457 - 8861

Registered Federal Lobbyist.
Serves As:
- V. President and Associate General Counsel, Time Warner Inc.

TER-JUNG, Susie
50 Main St.
Sixth Floor
White Plains, NY 10606-1901
susie.ter-jung@bunge.com
Tel: (914) 684 - 3398

Serves As:
- Communications and Investor Relations Contact, Bunge Ltd.

TERESZCUK, Alexis
100 Universal City Plaza
Universal City, CA 91608
Tel: (818) 777 - 8053
Fax:(818) 866 - 8053

Serves As:
- Manager, Government Relations, NBC Universal

TERMEER, Henri A.
500 Kendall St.
Cambridge, MA 02142
Tel: (617) 252 - 7500
Fax:(617) 252 - 7600

Serves As:
- Chairman, President and Chief Exec. Officer, Genzyme Corp.

TERPAY, Susan M.
Three Commercial Pl.
Norfolk, VA 23510-2191
Tel: (757) 823 - 5204
Fax:(757) 629 - 2822

Serves As:
- Director, Public Relations, Norfolk Southern Corp.

TERRELL, Todd A.
270 Peachtree St. NW
Bin 908A
Atlanta, GA 30303
Tel: (404) 506 - 0566
Fax:(404) 506 - 0584

Serves As:
- Director, Corporate Communications, Southern Company

TERRY, Hilliard
P.O. Box 10395
Palo Alto, CA 94303-0395
Tel: (650) 752 - 5300
Fax:(650) 752 - 5633

Serves As:
- Director, Investor Relations, Agilent Technologies, Inc.

TESKA, Liz
Five Giralda Farms
Madison, NJ 07940
Tel: (973) 660 - 5000
Fax:(973) 660 - 5771

Serves As:
- Corporate Public Affairs, Wyeth

TESORIERO, Jean
One MetroTech Center
Brooklyn, NY 11201
Tel: (718) 403 - 2000
Fax:(718) 488 - 1763

Serves As:
- Grant Analyst, KeySpan Foundation, KeySpan Corp.

TETREAULT, Kristin S.
48 Monroe Tpk.
Trumbull, CT 06611
ktetreau@oxhp.com
Tel: (203) 459 - 6000
Fax:(203) 452 - 4884
TF: (800) 889 - 7658

Serves As:
- Director, Internal Communications, Oxford Health Plans Inc.

TEUTSCH, Nancy
One Haworth Center
Holland, MI 49423
Tel: (616) 393 - 1304
Fax:(616) 393 - 1570
TF: (800) 344 - 2600

Serves As:
- V. President, Global Human Resources, Haworth Inc.

TEW, W. Scott
540 White Plains Rd.
Tarrytown, NY 10591-2005
scott.tew@cibase.com
Tel: (914) 785 - 4578
Fax:(914) 785 - 2211
TF: (800) 431 - 1900

Serves As:
- Head, Public Affairs, Ciba Specialty Chemicals

TEWS, Shane
1666 K St., NW
Suite 410
Washington, DC 20006
Tel: (202) 973 - 6603
Fax:(202) 466 - 9103

Serves As:
- Director, Government Relations; and PAC Director, VeriSign, Inc.

THACHER, Michael W.
2141 Rosecrans Ave., Suite 4000
El Segundo, CA 90245
mthacher@unocal.com
Tel: (310) 726 - 7734

Serves As:
- General Manager, Public Relations and Communications, UNOCAL Corp.

THACKER, Michael
2315 N. First St.
San Jose, CA 95131
Tel: (408) 570 - 8040
Fax:(408) 570 - 8901

Serves As:
- Public Relations Contact, BEA Systems, Inc.

THAIN, John A.
11 Wall St.
New York, NY 10005
Tel: (212) 656 - 3000
Fax:(212) 656 - 2347

Serves As:
- Chief Exec. Officer, New York Stock Exchange, Inc.

THAMAN, Michael H.
One Owens Corning Pkwy.
Toledo, OH 43659
mike.thaman@owenscorning.com
Tel: (419) 248 - 7098
Fax:(419) 248 - 6227
TF: (800) 438 - 7465

Serves As:
- Chairman, Senior V. President and Chief Financial Officer, Owens Corning

Also serves as Chairman, Owens Corning Foundation.

THAMERT, Thomas E.
One Oxford Center, Suite 3300
Pittsburgh, PA 15219
Tel: (412) 553 - 7712
Fax:(412) 553 - 5757

Serves As:
- Manager, Government Affairs, Equitable Resources, Inc.

THAMES, John E.
P.O. Box 14662
Reading, PA 19612-4662
Tel: (610) 208 - 2000
Fax:(610) 208 - 3716

Serves As:
- V. President, Human Resources, Carpenter Technology Corp.

THARP, Christina
1835 Dueber Ave. SW
GNW-37
Canton, OH 44706
christina.tharp@timken.com
Tel: (330) 471 - 3294
Fax:(330) 471 - 7032
TF: (800) 223 - 1954

Serves As:
- Manager, Marketing Communications, The Timken Co.

THARPE, Ray
2200 Old Germantown Rd.
Delray Beach, FL 33445
rthorpe@officedepot.com
Tel: (561) 438 - 4800
Fax:(561) 438 - 4400

Serves As:
- Director, Investor Relations, Office Depot, Inc.

THAXTON, Alysia
910 16th St. NW
Suite 402
Washington, DC 20006
Tel: (202) 775 - 0084
Fax:(202) 775 - 0784

Serves As:
- Legislative Assistant, Milliken & Co.

THEDFORD, Joyce
201 Robert S. Kerr Ave.
Mezzanine
Oklahoma City, OK 73102

Serves As:
- PAC Treasurer, BOK Financial Corp.

THEILLMAN, Michael
6501 Legacy Dr.
Plano, TX 75024-3698
Tel: (972) 431 - 1000
Fax:(972) 431 - 1362
TF: (800) 222 - 6161

Serves As:
- Executive V. President, Chief Human resources and Administrative Officer, J. C. Penney Co., Inc.

THELEN, Dan
6101 Anacapri Blvd.
Lansing, MI 48917
Tel: (517) 323 - 1200
Fax:(517) 323 - 8796

Serves As:
- V. President, Personnel, Auto-Owners Insurance Group

THEVENET, Philip M.
1500 K St. NW
Suite 650
Washington, DC 20005
Tel: (202) 715 - 1000
Fax:(202) 715 - 1001

Registered Federal Lobbyist.
Serves As:
- Federal Government Relations, GlaxoSmithKline Research and Development

THIBAU, Janelle C. M.
1455 Pennsylvania Ave. NW
Suite 950
Washington, DC 20004-1087
janelle_thibau@ml.com
Tel: (202) 661 - 7100
Fax:(202) 661 - 7110

Registered Federal Lobbyist.
Serves As:
- V. President, Government Relations, Merrill Lynch & Co., Inc.

THIBDAUE, Lisa J.
P.O. Box 270
Hartford, CT 06141-0270
Tel: (860) 665 - 5883
Fax:(860) 665 - 4853
TF: (800) 286 - 2000

Serves As:
- V. President, Rates, Regulatory Affairs, and Compliance, (Northeast Utilities Service Co.), Northeast Utilities

THICKPENNY, Mark C.
3240 Hillview Ave.
Palo Alto, CA 94304
Tel: (650) 494 - 2900
Fax:(650) 813 - 0160

Serves As:
- V. President and Treasurer, CNF Inc.

Responsibilities include political action.

THIELE, E. E.
2800 Post Oak Blvd., Suite 5450
Houston, TX 77056-6196
Tel: (713) 621 - 7800
Fax:(713) 960 - 7560

Serves As:
- Senior V. President, Finance, Administration and Treasurer, Rowan Companies, Inc.

Responsibilities include corporate philanthropy.

THIELE, Mary
211 Mount Airy Rd.
Basking Ridge, NJ 07920
mthiele@avaya.com
Tel: (908) 953 - 6152
Fax:(908) 953 - 7609

Serves As:
- Corporate Communications, Western North America, Avaya Inc.

THIERWECHTER, Douglas E.
5555 San Felipe Rd.
Houston, TX 77056
dethierwechter@marathonoil.com
Tel: (713) 629 - 3918
Fax:(713) 296 - 3394

Serves As:
- Manager, State Government Affairs, Marathon Oil Corp.

THIES, Gregory A.
601 13th St. NW
Suite 200 North
Washington, DC 20005
thiesg@basf-corp.com
Tel: (202) 414 - 6337
Fax:(202) 682 - 9459

Registered Federal Lobbyist.
Serves As:
- Director, Government Affairs, BASF Corporation

THILL, Howard S.
5555 San Felipe Rd.
Houston, TX 77056
hjthill@marathonoil.com
Tel: (713) 629 - 4140
Fax:(713) 296 - 2952

Serves As:
- Manager, Investor Relations, Marathon Oil Corp.

THILL, Maggie
Three Galleria Tower
13155 Noel Rd., Suite 1600
Dallas, TX 75240
maggie.thill@fedexkinkos.com
Tel: (214) 550 - 7026
Fax:(214) 550 - 7217

Serves As:
- Corporate Communications, FedEx Kinko's Office and Print Services

THIRSTRUP-ZAR, Barbara
P.O. Box 1400
Rapid City, SD 57709-1400
bthirstrup@bh-corp.com
Tel: (605) 721 - 1700
Fax:(605) 721 - 2568

Serves As:
- Manager, Governmental and Public Affairs, Black Hills Corp.

THIRY, Kent J.
601 Hawaii St.
El Segundo, CA 90245
Tel: (310) 536 - 2400

Serves As:
- Chairman and Chief Exec. Officer, DaVita, Inc.
- Chairman of the Board, Oxford Health Plans Inc.

THOM, Ms. Edlu J.
1101 Pennsylvania Ave., NW
Suite 515
Washington, DC 20004
ejthom@cais.com
Tel: (202) 434 - 8938
Fax:(202) 434 - 4585

Registered Federal Lobbyist.
Serves As:
- Director, Government Affairs; and PAC Treasurer, Lyondell Chemical Co.

THOMAS, Beverly
3495 Piedmont Rd. NE
Atlanta, GA 30305-1736
Tel: (404) 364 - 4713
Fax:(404) 364 - 4794

Serves As:
- V. President, Communications and Public Affairs, Kaiser Permanente

THOMAS, Bruce
4000 MacArthur Blvd.
Newport Beach, CA 92660
Tel: (949) 483 - 2698

Serves As:
- Director, Investor Relations, Conexant Systems, Inc.

THOMAS, Curtis
P.O. Box 196660
MS 815
Anchorage, AK 99519-6660
Tel: (907) 450 - 5857
Fax:(907) 450 - 5894

Serves As:
- Manager, Fairbanks Communications, Alyeska Pipeline Service Co.

THOMAS, Dale
9501 Shea Blvd.
Scottsdale, AZ 85260
Tel: (480) 614 - 7212

Serves As:
- Manager, Public Relations, Caremark Rx, Inc.

THOMAS, David M.
1499 Post Rd.
Fairfield, CT 06824
dthomas@imshealth.com
Tel: (203) 319 - 4700
Fax:(203) 319 - 4701

Serves As:
- Chairman of the Board, IMS Health, Inc.

THOMAS, Frank
111 Center St.
Little Rock, AR 72201
Tel: (501) 377 - 2000
Fax:(501) 377 - 3453
TF: (800) 643 - 9691

Serves As:
- V. President, Media and Government Relations, Stephens Inc.

THOMAS, Gary C.
100 Jim Moran Blvd.
Deerfield Beach, FL 33442
gary.thomas@jmfamily.com
Tel: (954) 429 - 2603
Fax:(954) 429 - 2300

Serves As:
- Exec. V. President, Human Resources, JM Family Enterprises, Inc.

THOMAS, Glen
P.O. Box 430
Memphis, TN 30103
Tel: (901) 528 - 4557
Fax:(901) 528 - 4758

Serves As:
- Senior Communications Specialist, Memphis Light, Gas and Water Division

THOMAS, Gordon M.
1101 Pennsylvania Ave. NW
Suite 400
Washington, DC 20004-2504
gthomas@dc.textron.com
Tel: (202) 637 - 3821
Fax:(202) 637 - 3863

Registered Federal Lobbyist.
Serves As:
- Director, Government Affairs, Textron Inc.

THOMAS, Gregory M.
340 Kingsland St.
Nutley, NJ 07110-1199
greg.thomas@roche.com
Tel: (973) 562 - 2198
Fax:(973) 562 - 2666

Serves As:
- Director, State Government Affairs, (HLR Service Corp.), Hoffmann-La Roche Inc. (Roche)

THOMAS, Headen B.
P.O. Box 33068
Charlotte, NC 28233
headen.thomas@piedmontng.com
Tel: (704) 731 - 4438
Fax:(704) 764 - 1395

Serves As:
- Director, Investor Relations, Piedmont Natural Gas Co.

THOMAS, Kurt
270 E. Kilbourn
Milwaukee, WI 53202
Tel: (414) 347 - 6480
Fax:(414) 347 - 6696
TF: (800) 558 - 9900

Serves As:
- V. President, Mortgage Guaranty Insurance Corp. (MGIC)

Responsibilities also include corporate philanthropy.

THOMAS, Larry
550 Newport Center Dr.
Newport Beach, CA 92660
Tel: (949) 720 - 3232
Fax:(949) 720 - 2501

Serves As:
- Group Senior V. President, Corporate Communications, The Irvine Company

THOMAS, Lee M.
P.O. Box 105605
Atlanta, GA 30348
Tel: (404) 652 - 4000
Fax:(404) 654 - 4789
TF: (800) 519 - 3111

Serves As:
- President and Chief Operating Officer, Georgia-Pacific Corp.

THOMAS, Michael L.
P.O. Box 50085
Watsonville, CA 95077-5085
Tel: (831) 761 - 4709
Fax:(831) 722 - 9657
TF: (800) 482 - 1518

Serves As:
- V. President, Human Resources, Granite Construction Inc.

Responsibilities include corporate philanthropy.

THOMAS, Pat
316 Pennsylvania Ave. SE
Suite 300
Washington, DC 20003
Tel: (202) 675 - 4220
Fax:(202) 675 - 4230

Serves As:
- Manager, Public Affairs, United Parcel Service (UPS)

THOMAS, R. Lindsay
P.O. Box 4569
Atlanta, GA 30302-4569
Tel: (404) 584 - 4000
Fax:(404) 584 - 3479

Serves As:
- Senior V. President, Governmental Affairs, AGL Resources, Inc.

THOMAS, Sandi
1825 Barrett Lakes Blvd. NW
Suite 400
Kennesaw, GA 30144
thomass@wyeth.com
Tel: (678) 355 - 5642

Serves As:
- Director, State Government Affairs, Wyeth Pharmaceuticals

THOMAS, W. Dennis
400 Atlantic St.
Stamford, CT 06921
dennis.thomas@ipaper.com
Tel: (203) 541 - 8000
Fax:(203) 541 - 8200
TF: (800) 223 - 1268

Serves As:
- Senior V. President, Public Affairs and Communications, Internat'l Paper

Responsibilities include corporate contributions.

THOMASON, Rick
5800 Tennyson Pkwy.
Plano, TX 75024
Tel: (214) 473 - 7000

Serves As:
- V. President, Human Resouces, Triad Hospitals, Inc.

THOMPSON, Alicia
555 Glenridge Connector NE
Suite 300
Atlanta, GA 30342
Tel: (404) 459 - 4572

Serves As:
- V. President, Communications and Public Relations, (Popeyes Chicken & Biscuits), AFC Enterprises

THOMPSON, Barbara W.
P.O. Box 27131
Raleigh, NC 27611
Tel: (919) 716 - 2716
Fax:(919) 716 - 7074

Serves As:
- Senior V. President and Public Relations Manager, First Citizens BancShares

Responsibilities include corporate philanthropy.

THOMPSON, Bina H.
300 Park Ave.
New York, NY 10022
Tel: (212) 310 - 3072
Fax:(212) 310 - 3302

Serves As:
- V. President, Investor Relations, Colgate-Palmolive Co.

THOMPSON, Jr., Bruce E.
1455 Pennsylvania Ave. NW
Suite 950
Washington, DC 20004-1087
Tel: (202) 661 - 7100
Fax:(202) 661 - 7110

Serves As:
- First V. President and Director, Government Relations, Merrill Lynch & Co., Inc.

Responsibilities include political action.

THOMPSON, Charles P.
P.O. Box 53999
M/S 8010
Phoenix, AZ 85072-3999
charles.thompson@aps.com
Tel: (602) 250 - 2888
Fax:(602) 250 - 2113

Serves As:
- Manager, Rural Community Development, (Arizona Public Service Co.), Pinnacle West Capital Corp.

THOMPSON, David
1155 Perimeter Center West
Atlanta, GA 30338
Tel: (678) 579 - 5298
Fax:(678) 579 - 5001

Serves As:
- Manager, Media Relations and Corporate Communications, Mirant Corp.

THOMPSON, David W.
21839 Atlantic Blvd.
Dulles, VA 20166
thompson.david@orbital.com
Tel: (703) 406 - 5000
Fax:(703) 406 - 5572

Serves As:
- Chairman and Chief Exec. Officer, Orbital Sciences Corp.

THOMPSON, Deborah
2345 Crystal Dr.
Arlington, VA 22227
Tel: (703) 872 - 5100
Fax:(703) 872 - 5134

Serves As:
- Corporate Contributions Contact, US Airways Group, Inc.

THOMPSON, Denise Love
41 S. High St.
Columbus, OH 43287
Tel: (614) 480 - 8300
Fax:(614) 480 - 4723

Serves As:
- Treasurer, HBI-PAC, Huntington Bancshares Inc.

THOMPSON, Diane
4615 E. Elwood St.
Phoenix, AZ 85040-1958
Tel: (480) 966 - 5394
Fax:(480) 379 - 3503
TF: (800) 990 - APOL

Serves As:
- V. President/Counsel, Human Resources, Apollo Group, Inc.

THOMPSON, Eric
1101 Connecticut Ave. NW
Suite 401
Washington, DC 20036
ethompson@thehartford.com
Tel: (202) 296 - 7513
Fax:(202) 296 - 7514

Registered Federal Lobbyist.
Serves As:
- V. President, Federal Affairs, The Hartford Financial Services Group Inc.

THOMPSON, G. Kennedy
301 S. College St., Suite 4000
One Wachovia Center
NC 0005
Charlotte, NC 28288-0370
ken.thompson@wachovia.com
Tel: (704) 374 - 6565
Fax:(704) 374 - 3425
TF: (800) 275 - 3862

Serves As:
- Chairman, President and Chief Exec. Officer, Wachovia Corp.

THOMPSON, III, George R.
P.O. Box 702
Milwaukee, WI 53201-0702
Tel: (414) 259 - 5333
Fax:(414) 479 - 1245

Serves As:
- V. President, Community Relations and Corporate Communications, Briggs and Stratton Corp.

THOMPSON, J. Kirk
615 J.B. Hunt Corporate Dr.
P.O. Box 130
Lowell, AR 72745
kirk-thompson@jbhunt.com
Tel: (479) 820 - 8110
Fax:(479) 820 - 8397
TF: (800) 643 - 3622

Serves As:
- President and Chief Exec. Officer, J. B. Hunt Transport Services, Inc.

Responsibilities include shareholder relations.

THOMPSON, James E.
McLeod USA Technology Park
6400 C St., SW
Cedar Rapids, IA 52406
Tel: (319) 364 - 0000
Fax:(319) 790 - 7767
TF: (800) 896 - 8330

Serves As:
- Group V. President, General Counsel and Secretary, McLeod USA Inc.

Responsibilities include government and regulatory affairs.

THOMPSON, Jenifer
4747 Willow Rd.
Pleasanton, CA 94588
jthompson@shaklee.com
Tel: (925) 924 - 2004
Fax:(925) 924 - 2280

Serves As:
- Manager, Corporate Relations, Shaklee Corp.

THOMPSON, John
P.O. Box 1943
Birmingham, AL 35201-1943
jthompson@ebsco.com
Tel: (205) 991 - 6600
Ext: 1100
Fax:(205) 995 - 1517

Serves As:
- Director, Human Resources, EBSCO Industries, Inc.

THOMPSON, John W.
20330 Stevens Creek Blvd. Tel: (408) 517 - 8000
Cupertino, CA 95014-2132 Fax:(408) 517 - 8186
jthompson@symantec.com

Serves As:
- Chairman and Chief Exec. Officer, Symantec Corp.

THOMPSON, Julie
35 W. Wacker Dr. Tel: (312) 220 - 5995
Chicago, IL 60601 Fax:(312) 220 - 6599
julie.thompson@chi.leoburnett.com

Serves As:
- Senior V. President and Director, Corporate Communications, Leo Burnett Worldwide

THOMPSON, Katherine
135 S. LaSalle St. Tel: (312) 904 - 2000
Chicago, IL 60603 Fax:(312) 904 - 6521

Serves As:
- Pac Treasurer, LaSalle Bank N.A.

THOMPSON, Kirby A.
1550 Peachtree St., N.W. Tel: (404) 885 - 8360
Atlanta, GA 30309 Fax:(404) 885 - 8215
kirby.thompson@equifax.com

Registered Federal Lobbyist.
Serves As:
- V. President, Legislative Affairs and Community Affairs, Equifax Inc.

THOMPSON, Linda
691 S. Milpitas Blvd. Tel: (408) 945 - 8600
Milpitas, CA 95035-5473 Fax:(408) 262 - 2533

Serves As:
- Foundation Contact, Adaptec, Inc.

THOMPSON, Linda L.
12 E. Armour Blvd. Tel: (816) 502 - 4230
Kansas City, MO 64111 Fax:(816) 502 - 4155
thompson_linda@interstatebrands.com

Serves As:
- Director, Stockholder Relations and Assistant Corporate Secretary, Interstate Bakeries Corp.

THOMPSON, Martk S.
82 Running Hill Rd. Tel: (207) 775 - 8100
South Portland, ME 04106-6020 Fax:(207) 761 - 6020
TF: (800) 341 - 0392

Serves As:
- Chief Exec. Officer, Fairchild Semiconductor Internat'l, Inc.

THOMPSON, Michael
3900 Wisconsin Ave. NW Tel: (202) 752 - 7000
Washington, DC 20016 Fax:(202) 752 - 6099

Registered Federal Lobbyist.
Serves As:
- Representative, Fannie Mae

THOMPSON, Michael A.
P.O. Box 26666 OJRP 20 Tel: (804) 771 - 3655
Richmond, VA 23261-6666
Michael_Thompson@dom.com

Serves As:
- Manager, State Government Affairs, North Carolina and Ohio, Dominion Resources, Inc.

THOMPSON, Patricia L.
One Massachusetts Ave. NW Tel: (202) 408 - 0183
Suite 360 Fax:(202) 408 - 0214
Washington, DC 20001
patricia.thompson@pseg.com

Registered Federal Lobbyist.
Serves As:
- General Manager, Federal Affairs, PSE&G

THOMPSON, Paul B.
2180 Rutherford Rd. Tel: (760) 931 - 1771
Carlsbad, CA 92008-7328 Fax:(760) 930 - 5015
TF: (800) 228 - 2767

Serves As:
- Exec. Director, Foundation, Callaway Golf Co.

THOMPSON, Richard L.
655 15th St. NW Tel: (202) 783 - 8618
Suite 300 Fax:(202) 638 - 3709
Washington, DC 20005
dick.thompson@bms.com

Registered Federal Lobbyist.
Serves As:
- Senior V. President, Policy and Government Affairs, Bristol-Myers Squibb Co.

THOMPSON, Rosalind
5555 Darrow Rd. Tel: (330) 463 - 3489
Hudson, OH 44236 Fax:(330) 463 - 6675

Serves As:
- Exec. V. President, Human Resources, Jo-Ann Stores, Inc.

THOMPSON, Sheri C.
P.O. Box 1943 Tel: (205) 991 - 1278
Birmingham, AL 35201-1943 Fax:(205) 995 - 1636
scthompson@ebsco.com

Serves As:
- Manager, Public Relations, EBSCO Industries, Inc.

THOMPSON, Wendy
2325 Orchard Pkwy. Tel: (408) 441 - 0311
San Jose, CA 95131 Fax:(408) 436 - 4200
wthompson@atmel.com

Serves As:
- Corporate Communications Contact, Atmel Corp.

THOMSON, David K. R.
Metro Center Tel: (203) 539 - 8000
One Station Pl. Fax:(203) 539 - 7734
Stamford, CT 06902 TF: (800) 969 - 9974

Serves As:
- Chairman of the Board, The Thomson Corporation

THOMSON, Lynn Harding
1299 Pennsylvania Ave. NW Tel: (202) 637 - 4022
11th Floor West Fax:(202) 637 - 4006
Washington, DC 20004-2407
lynn.thomson@corporate.ge.com

Registered Federal Lobbyist.
Serves As:
- Manager, Federal Government Relations, General Electric Co.

THONIS, Peter
1095 Ave. of the Americas Tel: (212) 395 - 2355
New York, NY 10036 Fax:(212) 730 - 0901
peter.thonis@verizon.com TF: (800) 621 - 9900

Serves As:
- Senior V. President, Public Affairs, Verizon Communications Inc.

THORN, Stu
P.O. Box 1000 Tel: (770) 832 - 4242
Carrollton, GA 30119 Fax:(770) 832 - 4584
TF: (800) 444 - 1700

Serves As:
- President and Chief Exec. Officer, Southwire Co.

THORNE, Carl F.
500 N. Akard St. Tel: (214) 397 - 3000
Suite 4300 Fax:(214) 397 - 3379
Dallas, TX 75201-3331 TF: (800) 423 - 8006

Serves As:
- Chairman and Chief Exec. Officer, ENSCO Internat'l Inc.

THORNE, Donna M.
I-20 at Alpine Rd. Tel: (803) 264 - 2437
AX-210 Fax:(803) 264 - 5522
Columbia, SC 29219-0001 TF: (800) 288 - 2227
donna.thorne@bcbssc.com Ext: 42437

Serves As:
- Director, Corporate Communications, BlueCross BlueShield of South Carolina

THORNE, Mike
8445 Freeport Pkwy.
Suite 400
Irving, TX 75063

Serves As:
- Treasurer, DIPAC, Computer Sciences Corp.

THORNTON, Jr., Billy F.
P.O. Box 4079 Tel: (228) 865 - 5295
Gulfport, MS 39502 Fax:(228) 865 - 5616

Serves As:
- Manager, Regulatory and Federal Legislative Affairs, Mississippi Power Co.

THORNTON, Lora
5400 Legacy Dr. Tel: (972) 605 - 6818
Plano, TX 75024-3199 Fax:(972) 605 - 6841
lora.thornton@eds.com

Serves As:
- Manager, Global Community Affairs and Corporate Contributions, EDS Corp.

THORP, Timothy J.
30 W. Superior St. Tel: (218) 279 - 5000
Duluth, MN 55802 Fax:(218) 279 - 5050
tthorp@allete.com

Serves As:
- V. President, Investor Relations, ALLETE

THORSGAARD, Marybeth
One General Mills Blvd. Tel: (763) 764 - 6364
Minneapolis, MN 55426 Fax:(763) 764 - 3734

Serves As:
- Director, Corporate Relations, General Mills

THRASH, James E.
1133 15th St. NW Tel: (202) 775 - 3300
Suite 800 Fax:(202) 775 - 3422
Washington, DC 20005-2701

Serves As:
- Senior V. President, Government Relations, Parsons Corp.

THRASHER, Linda K.
12800 Whitewater Dr. Tel: (952) 984 - 0350
Minnetonka, MN 55343 Fax:(952) 984 - 0032

Serves As:
- V. President, Public Affairs, Mosaic Co.

THRASHER, Rex C.
301 Merritt Seven Tel: (203) 849 - 7800
Sixth Floor Fax:(203) 849 - 7840
Norwalk, CT 06851
rex_thrasher@emcorgroup.com

Serves As:
- V. President, Risk Management, EMCOR Group, Inc.

THYEN, James C.
1600 Royal St. Tel: (812) 482 - 1600
Jasper, IN 47549-1001 Fax:(812) 482 - 8300
TF: (800) 482 - 1616

Serves As:
- Chief Exec. Officer, Kimball International, Inc.

TIBOLLO, Colleen
P.O. Box 810 Tel: (716) 689 - 4972
Amherst, NY 14226 Fax:(716) 568 - 6098
colleen_tibollo@mark-iv.com

Serves As:
- Director, Corporate Communications, Mark IV Industries, Inc.

TICK, Susan
10202 W. Washington Blvd. Tel: (310) 244 - 6660
Thalberg 1131 Fax:(310) 244 - 0177
Culver City, CA 90232
susan_tick@spe.sony.com

Serves As:
- Senior V. President, Corporate Communications, (Sony Pictures Entertainment), Sony Corp. of America

TIDDY, Michael E.
1100 New York Ave. NW Tel: (202) 669 - 8368
Washington, DC 20005

Registered Federal Lobbyist.
Serves As:
- Pac Treasurer, Lucent Technologies

TIELINEN, Roberta
P.O. Box 9740 Tel: (207) 842 - 9461
Portland, ME 04104-5001
rtielinen@lnc.com

Serves As:
- Charitable Giving Contact (Portland, ME), Lincoln Financial Group

TIEMANN, Bruce
McLeod USA Technology Park Tel: (319) 364 - 0000
6400 C St., SW Fax:(319) 790 - 7767
Cedar Rapids, IA 52406 TF: (800) 896 - 8330

Serves As:
- Manager, Corporate Communications, McLeod USA Inc.

TIGHE, John
P.O. Box 1000 Tel: (704) 522 - 2000
Charlotte, NC 28201-1000 Fax:(704) 522 - 2055

Serves As:
- President and Chief Exec. Officer, Royal & SunAlliance USA Inc.

TILDEN, Bradley
P.O. Box 68900 Tel: (206) 433 - 3200
Seattle, WA 98168-0947 Fax:(206) 431 - 5558

Serves As:
- Divisional Exec. V. President and Chief Financial Officer, Alaska Air Group, Inc.

Responsibilities include political action.

TILDESLEY, Arthur
399 Park Ave. Tel: (212) 559 - 1000
New York, NY 10043 Fax:(212) 793 - 3946
TF: (800) 285 - 3000

Serves As:
- Director, Investor Relations, Citigroup, Inc.

TILLER, Thomas C.
2100 Hwy. 55 Tel: (763) 417 - 8650
Medina, MN 55340 Fax:(763) 542 - 0599

Serves As:
- President and Chief Exec. Officer, Polaris Industries Inc.

TILLMAN, Audrey B.
1932 Wynnton Rd. Tel: (706) 323 - 3431
Columbus, GA 31999 Fax:(706) 660 - 7333
TF: (800) 992 - 3522

Serves As:
- Senior V. President; and Director, Human Resources, Facilities and Health Services, AFLAC Incorporated

TILTON, Glenn F.
P.O. Box 66100 Tel: (847) 700 - 4000
Chicago, IL 60666 Fax:(847) 700 - 4899

Serves As:
- Chairman, President and Chief Exec. Officer, United Airlines

TIMKEN, Jr., W. R. "Tim"
1835 Dueber Ave. SW Tel: (330) 438 - 3000
GME-15 Fax:(330) 471 - 4041
Canton, OH 44706 TF: (800) 223 - 1954

Serves As:
- Chairman of the Board, The Timken Co.

TIMMENY, Michael
601 Pennsylvania Ave. NW Tel: (202) 661 - 4040
Suite 520, N. Bldg. Fax:(202) 661 - 4041
Washington, DC 20004
mtimmeny@cisco.com

Registered Federal Lobbyist.
Serves As:
- Director, Federal Government Affairs, Cisco Systems, Inc.

TIMMERMAN, William B.
1426 Main St. Tel: (803) 748 - 3000
Columbia, SC 29218 Fax:(803) 217 - 8825

Serves As:
- Chairman, President, and Chief Exec. Officer, SCANA Corp.

TIMOTHY, Alan R.
P.O. Box 4030 Tel: (303) 277 - 6240
M/S NH280 Fax:(303) 277 - 5723
Golden, CO 80401-0030

Serves As:
- V. President, Government Affairs, Coors Brewing Co.

TINDAL, Mike
SAS Campus Dr. Tel: (919) 531 - 0789
Cary, NC 27513-2414 Fax:(919) 677 - 4444
mike.tindal@sas.com

Serves As:
- Senior Director, Global Corporate Communications, SAS Institute, Inc.

TINKLEPAUGH, Bill
2111 Wilson Blvd., Suite 700 Tel: (703) 351 - 5022
Arlington, VA 22201 Fax:(703) 351 - 9772

Registered Federal Lobbyist.
Serves As:
- Senior V. President, Government and Industry Relations, Dean Foods Company

TINNELL, Greg L.
250 Stephenson Hwy. Tel: (248) 824 - 1629
Troy, MI 48083
greg.tinnell@colaik.com

Serves As:
- Senior V. President, Human Resources, Collins & Aikman Corp.

TIPPL, Thomas
P.O. Box 599 Tel: (513) 983 - 1100
Cincinnati, OH 45201-0599 Fax:(513) 983 - 9369

Serves As:
- Director, Investor Relations and Shareholder Services, The Procter & Gamble Company

TIPSON, Fred
1401 I St., NW Tel: (202) 263 - 5900
Suite 500 Fax:(202) 263 - 5902
Washington, DC 20005

Registered Federal Lobbyist.
Serves As:
- Director, International Trade and Development and Senior Policy Counsel, Microsoft Corporation

TISCH, James S.
667 Madison Ave. Tel: (212) 521 - 2000
New York, NY 10021-8087 Fax:(212) 521 - 2416

Serves As:
- President and Chief Exec. Officer, Loews Corporation

TISCH, Preston Robert
667 Madison Ave.
New York, NY 10021-8087
btisch@loews.com
Tel: (212) 521 - 2000
Fax:(212) 521 - 2416

Serves As:
• Chairman of the Board, Loews Corporation

TITZMAN, Donna
P.O. Box 500
San Antonio, TX 78249-112
titzmand@valero.com
Tel: (210) 345 - 2000
Fax:(210) 345 - 2646

Serves As:
• Treasurer, Valero Energy Corp. Political Action Committee, Valero Energy Corp.

TOAN, Barrett A.
13900 Riverport Dr.
Maryland Heights, MO 63043
Tel: (314) 770 - 1666
Fax:(314) 702 - 7037
TF: (800) 332 - 5455

Serves As:
• Chairman of the Board, Express Scripts, Inc.

TOBACK, Andrea
Britannica Centre
310 S. Michigan Ave.
Chicago, IL 60604
Tel: (312) 347 - 7000
Fax:(312) 294 - 2158

Serves As:
• Exec. Director, Human Resources and Benefits, Encyclopaedia Britannica, Inc.

TOBACK, Paul A.
8700 W. Bryn Mawr Ave.
Chicago, IL 60631
Tel: (773) 380 - 3000
Fax:(773) 399 - 0476

Serves As:
• Chairman and Chief Exec. Officer, Bally Total Fitness Holding Corp.

TOBIAS, Maura C.
1855 Boston Rd.
Wilbraham, MA 01095
Tel: (413) 543 - 2400
Ext: 2814
Fax:(413) 543 - 3966
TF: (800) 966 - 9970

Serves As:
• Director, Corporate Public Affairs, Friendly Ice Cream Corp.

TOBIN, James R.
One Boston Scientific Pl.
Natick, MA 01760-1537
Tel: (508) 650 - 8000
Fax:(508) 647 - 2200

Serves As:
• President and Chief Exec. Officer, Boston Scientific Corp.

TODD, Stephen K.
600 Grant St.
Pittsburgh, PA 15219-2800
Tel: (412) 433 - 1121

Serves As:
• V. President, Law and Environmental Affairs, United States Steel Corporation

TOFFERI, Mr. Leigh J.
P.O. Box 186
Montpelier, VT 05601
tofferil@bcbsvt.com
Tel: (802) 371 - 3205
Fax:(802) 223 - 4229
TF: (800) 255 - 4550

Serves As:
• Director, Government, Public and Community Relations, Blue Cross and Blue Shield of Vermont

TOGNERI, Gabriel B.
One Market
Spear Tower, Suite 2400
San Francisco, CA 94105
Tel: (415) 267 - 7100
Fax:(415) 267 - 7262

Serves As:
• V. President, Investor Relations, PG & E Corp.

TOKER, Mary Catherine
601 13th St. NW
Suite 510 South
Washington, DC 20005
Tel: (202) 737 - 8200
Fax:(202) 638 - 4914

Registered Federal Lobbyist.
Serves As:
• V. President, Government Relations, General Mills

TOKISH, Jr., Timothy J.
200 Civic Center Dr.
Columbus, OH 43215
Tel: (614) 460 - 4207

Serves As:
• PAC Treasurer, NiSource Inc.

TOLBERT, J. David
555 Theodore Fremd Ave.
Rye, NY 10580-1455
Tel: (914) 967 - 9400
Fax:(914) 967 - 9405

Serves As:
• Senior V. President, Human Resources and Corporate Risk, Jarden Corp.

TOLEDANO, Gabrielle
2207 Bridgepoint Pkwy.
San Mateo, CA 94404
Tel: (650) 295 - 5000
Fax:(650) 295 - 5111
TF: (800) 356 - 3321

Serves As:
• V. President, Human Resources, Siebel Systems, Inc.

TOLER, Mary M.
901 D St. SW
Suite 900
Washington, DC 20024
Tel: (202) 646 - 5255
Fax:(202) 646 - 5271

Registered Federal Lobbyist.
Serves As:
• Assistant Director, Congressional Affairs, Battelle

TOLL, Robert I.
3103 Philmont Ave.
Huntingdon Valley, PA 19006
rtoll@tollbrothersinc.com
Tel: (215) 938 - 8000
Fax:(215) 938 - 8019

Serves As:
• Chairman and Chief Exec. Officer, Toll Brothers, Inc.

TOLMAN, Gareth W.
One Moody Plaza
Galveston, TX 77550-7999
gary.tolman@anico.com
Tel: (409) 766 - 6560
Fax:(409) 766 - 6663
TF: (800) 899 - 6502

Serves As:
• Senior V. President, Corporate Affairs, American Nat'l Insurance Co.
Responsibilities include political action.

TOLVIN, Jeff
1290 Ave. of the Americas
New York, NY 10104
jeffrey.tolvin@axa-financial.com
Tel: (212) 314 - 2811
TF: (888) AXA - INFO

Serves As:
• Assistant V. President, Public Relations, AXA Financial, Inc.

TOMA, Al
1919 S. Broadway
Green Bay, WI 54304
Tel: (920) 438 - 2475

Serves As:
• Regional Manager, Government Affairs, Georgia-Pacific Corp.

TOMALSKI, Sarah
51 Madison Ave.
New York, NY 10010
sarah_tomalski@newyorklife.com
Tel: (212) 576 - 5897
Fax:(212) 576 - 8145

Serves As:
• Media Representative, New York Life Insurance Co.

TOMASELLI, Marlene
One M & T Plaza
Buffalo, NY 14203
Tel: (716) 842 - 5445
Fax:(716) 842 - 5839
TF: (800) 836 - 1500

Serves As:
• Treasurer, Manufacturers and Traders Trust Co. PAC, M&T Bank Corporation

TOMCALA, Karen A.
77 Beale St.
San Francisco, CA 94105
Tel: (415) 973 - 7000
Fax:(415) 972 - 5625

Serves As:
• V. President, Regulatory Relations, PG & E Corp.

TOMEK, Allison
8151 Peters Rd.
Fourth Floor
Plantation, FL 33324
allison.tomek@andrx.com
Tel: (954) 382 - 7696
Fax:(954) 382 - 7729

Serves As:
• Manager, Investor Relations, Andrx Corp.
Responsibilities include media relations.

TOMINOVICH, Kathryn "K.C."
1225 Connecticut Ave. NW
Washington, DC 20036
kathryn.tominovich@ey.com

Registered Federal Lobbyist.
Serves As:
• Political and Legislative Director, Ernst & Young LLP

TOMNITZ, Donald J.
301 Commerce St.
Suite 500
Fort Worth, TX 76006
dtomnitz@drhorton.com
Tel: (817) 390 - 8200
Fax:(817) 390 - 1715

Serves As:
• V. Chairman, President and Chief Exec. Officer, D. R. Horton, Inc.

TOMOFF, Donald
5555 Darrow Rd.
Hudson, OH 44236
Tel: (330) 656 - 2600
Fax:(330) 463 - 6675

Serves As:
- V. President, Finance, Jo-Ann Stores, Inc.

Responsibilities include investor and media relations.

TOMPSON, Randolph C.
P.O. Box 718
Winston-Salem, NC 27102
tompsor@rjrt.com
Tel: (336) 741 - 7287
Fax:(336) 741 - 1205

Serves As:
- Senior Director, Legislative Support, Reynolds American Inc.

TONES, Frank
1401 I St., NW
Suite 500
Washington, DC 20005
Tel: (202) 263 - 5900
Fax:(202) 263 - 5902

Registered Federal Lobbyist.
Serves As:
- Representative, Microsoft Corporation

TONGE, Charles R.
111 W. Monroe St.
Chicago, IL 60603-4095
Tel: (312) 461 - 3911
Fax:(312) 461 - 5454

Serves As:
- Exec. V. President, Community Banks, Harris Bank

TOOHEY, Mark
4680 Wilshire Blvd.
Los Angeles, CA 90010
Tel: (323) 930 - 6397
Fax:(323) 964 - 8095

Serves As:
- Assistant V. President, Government Affairs, Farmers Group, Inc.

TOOHEY, Michael J.
555 12th St. NW
Suite 620 North
Washington, DC 20004
mjtoohey@ashland.com
Tel: (202) 223 - 8290
Fax:(202) 293 - 2913

Registered Federal Lobbyist.
Serves As:
- Director, Government Relations, Ashland Inc.

TOOMAN, Jr., Lee D.
712 11th St
Lawrence, IL 62439
Tel: (317) 943 - 8000
Fax:(618) 943 - 8031

Serves As:
- V. President, Government Relations, Golden Rule Insurance Co.

TOPAZI, Anthony
P.O. Box 4079
Gulfport, MS 39502
Tel: (228) 864 - 1211
Fax:(228) 865 - 5616

Serves As:
- President and Chief Exec. Officer, Mississippi Power Co.

TOPODAS, Jonathan M.
1331 F St. NW
Suite 450
Washington, DC 20004
jonathan.topodas@aetna.com
Tel: (202) 419 - 7042
Fax:(202) 223 - 4424

Registered Federal Lobbyist.
Serves As:
- V. President and Counsel; PAC Treasurer, Aetna Inc.

TOPOLEWSKI, Jen
2775 Sanders Rd.
Northbrook, IL 60062-6127
Tel: (847) 402 - 5000
Fax:(847) 326 - 7519
TF: (800) 574 - 3553

Serves As:
- National Media Contact, Allstate Insurance Co.

TORANGO, Angie
P.O. Box 997
Ann Arbor, MI 48106-0997
Tel: (734) 930 - 3565
Fax:(734) 930 - 4346

Serves As:
- Domino's Pizza Community Relations Program Contact, Domino's Pizza, LLC

TORBERT, Martin
Ten Finderne Ave.
Bridgewater, NJ 08807-3300
martin.torbert@nstarch.com
Tel: (908) 685 - 5185
Fax:(908) 685 - 5096
TF: (800) 797 - 4992

Serves As:
- Director, Marketing Communications and Public Relations, Nat'l Starch and Chemical Co.

TORCOLINI, Robert J.
P.O. Box 14662
Reading, PA 19612-4662
Tel: (610) 208 - 2000
Fax:(610) 208 - 3716

Serves As:
- Chairman, President and Chief Exec. Officer, Carpenter Technology Corp.

TORGERSON, William T.
701 Ninth St. NW
Washington, DC 20068
Tel: (202) 872 - 2000

Serves As:
- Vice Chairman and General Counsel, Pepco Holdings, Inc.

TORNQUIST, Alice
2001 Pennsylvania Ave. NW
Suite 650
Washington, DC 20006
Tel: (202) 263 - 0000
Fax:(202) 263 - 0010

Registered Federal Lobbyist.
Serves As:
- Director, Government Affairs, Qualcomm Inc.

TORO, Ralph
100 Seaview Dr.
Secaucus, NJ 07096
rafael.toro@goya.com
Tel: (201) 348 - 4900
Ext: 2238
Fax:(201) 348 - 6609

Serves As:
- Director, Public Relations, Goya Foods, Inc.

TORR, Denine
100 Mission Ridge
Goodlettsville, TN 37072
dtorr@dollargeneral.com
Tel: (615) 855 - 4000

Serves As:
- Coordinator, Charitable Contributions, Dollar General Corp.

TORRES, Frank
1401 I St., NW
Suite 500
Washington, DC 20005
Tel: (202) 263 - 5900
Fax:(202) 263 - 5902

Registered Federal Lobbyist.
Serves As:
- Representative, Microsoft Corporation

TORSONE, Johnna G.
World Headquarters
One Elmcroft Rd.
Stamford, CT 06926-0700
Tel: (203) 356 - 5000
Fax:(203) 351 - 6303

Serves As:
- Senior V. President and Chief Human Resources Officer, Pitney Bowes Inc.

TORTELLI, Ronald C.
P.O. Box 990
Minneapolis, MN 55440
Tel: (952) 828 - 4201
Fax:(952) 828 - 8998

Serves As:
- Senior V. President, Human Resources, Supervalu Inc.

TOSCH, Gay G.
200 Renaissance Center
Detroit, MI 48265
Tel: (313) 556 - 5000
Fax:(313) 556 - 5108
TF: (800) 200 - 4622

Serves As:
- V. President, Human Resources, General Motors Acceptance Corp. (GMAC)

TOTARO, David J.
7733 Forsyth Blvd.
Suite 2300
St. Louis, MO 63105
djtotaro@rehabcare.com
Tel: (314) 659 - 2115
Fax:(314) 863 - 0769
TF: (800) 677 - 1238

Serves As:
- Senior V. President, Marketing and Communications, RehabCare Group, Inc.

TOVELLO, Pam
P.O. Box 66100
Chicago, IL 60666
pam.tovello@ual.com
Tel: (847) 700 - 4000
Fax:(847) 700 - 4899

Serves As:
- Worldwide Communications, United Airlines

TOWELL, Jean
720 E. Wisconsin Ave.
Milwaukee, WI 53202-4797
jeantowell@northwesternmutual.com
Tel: (414) 271 - 1444
Fax:(414) 665 - 2463
TF: (800) 323 - 7033

Serves As:
- Media Contact, Northwestern Mutual Financial Network

TOWLER, Susan
4800 Deerwood Campus Pkwy.
Jacksonville, FL 32246-8273
Tel: (904) 905 - 6803
Fax:(904) 905 - 4486
TF: (800) 477 - 3736

Serves As:
- V. President, Community Relations, Blue Cross and Blue Shield of Florida

TOWNS, Jessic
1201 Winterson Rd.
Linthicum, MD 21090
Tel: (410) 694 - 5700
Fax:(410) 694 - 5750

Serves As:
- Investor Relations Contact, CIENA Corp.

TOWNSEND, Angie D.

P.O. Box 1349 | Tel: (919) 836 - 2321
Raleigh, NC 27602-1349 | Fax:(919) 836 - 2343
adtownsend@scana.com

Serves As:
• Communications Specialist, (Public Service Co. of North Carolina), SCANA Corp.

TOWNSEND, Michael T.

555 12th St., NW | Tel: (202) 638 - 3755
Suite 740 North | Fax:(202) 638 - 3823
Washington, DC 20004
michael.townsend@schwab.com

Registered Federal Lobbyist.
Serves As:
• V. President, Public Policy, The Charles Schwab Corp.

TOWNSEND, Dr. Rod

7250 NW 62nd Ave. | Tel: (515) 270 - 4146
Johnston, IA 50131 | Fax:(515) 334 - 4478
rod.townsend@pioneer.com

Serves As:
• Director, Regulatory Science, Pioneer Hi-Bred Internat'l, Inc.

TOWNSHEND-ZELLNER, Heidi

2244 Walnut Grove Ave. | Tel: (626) 302 - 1453
Rosemead, CA 91770
heidi.townshend@edisonintl.com

Serves As:
• Manager, Shareholder Services, Edison Internat'l

TOWNSLEY, Theresa

345 Park Ave. | Tel: (408) 536 - 6000
San Jose, CA 95110-2704 | Fax:(408) 537 - 6000

Serves As:
• Senior V. President, Human Resources, Adobe Systems Inc.

TRACY, Mike

P.O. Box 10246 | Tel: (205) 945 - 6518
Birmingham, AL 35202 | Fax:(205) 945 - 6522

Serves As:
• Manager, Public Relations; President, Mining Division, Drummond Co., Inc.

TRACY, W. Michael

1501 S. Capitol Way, Suite 204 | Tel: (360) 943 - 9115
Olympia, WA 98501 | Fax:(360) 786 - 5925

Serves As:
• Director, State Government Relations, Puget Sound Energy

TRAGASH, Steven

111 Monument Circle | Tel: (317) 971 - 2031
29th Floor | Fax:(317) 971 - 2040
Indianapolis, IN 46204-5129
stragash@guidant.com

Serves As:
• Director, Corporate Communications, Guidant Corp.

TRAINOR, Jim

700 Oakmont Lane | Tel: (630) 570 - 4828
Westmont, IL 60559 | Fax:(630) 570 - 3606

Serves As:
• V. President, Corporate Communications, SIRVA, Inc.

TRAMUTO, James A.

900 Seventh St. NW, Suite 950 | Tel: (202) 638 - 3500
Washington, DC 20001-3886 | Fax:(202) 638 - 3522

Serves As:
• V. President, Governmental Relations, PG & E Corp.

TRANTER, G. Thomas

1350 I St. NW | Tel: (202) 682 - 3200
Suite 500 | Fax:(202) 682 - 3130
Washington, DC 20005-3305

Registered Federal Lobbyist.
Serves As:
• Representative, Corning Incorporated

TRATNIK, Janis

100 Grainger Pkwy. | Tel: (847) 535 - 4339
Lake Forest, IL 60045-5201
jan.tratnik@grainger.com

Serves As:
• Director, Corporate Communications and Public Affairs, W. W. Grainger, Inc.

TRAUB, Tom

P.O. Box 64089 | Tel: (651) 355 - 6000
St. Paul, MN 55164-0089 | Fax:(651) 355 - 6432
TF: (800) 232 - 3639

Serves As:
• V. President, Human Resources, CHS Inc.

TRAVIS, Jim

1300 I St. NW | Tel: (202) 783 - 2460
Suite 450 East | Fax:(202) 789 - 1819
Washington, DC 20005-7211

Serves As:
• Director, Federal Government Affairs, Monsanto Co.

TRAYNHAM, David

1200 Wilson Blvd. | Tel: (703) 465 - 3652
Arlington, VA 22209-2305

Serves As:
• Director, Strategy and Policy, Commercial Airplane Programs, The Boeing Co.

TREACY, Dennis H.

200 Commerce St. | Tel: (757) 365 - 3000
Smithfield, VA 23430 | Fax:(757) 365 - 3017
TF: (888) 366 - 6767

Serves As:
• V. President, Environmental and Government Affairs, Smithfield Foods, Inc.

TREFTS, Al

100 S. Saunders Rd. | Tel: (847) 955 - 3821
Lake Forest, IL 60045 | Fax:(847) 955 - 3961

Serves As:
• Senior Director, Investor Relations and Corporate Finance, Case New Holland Inc.

TREITLER, Betsy

One SunAmerica Center | Tel: (310) 772 - 6000
Los Angeles, CA 90067-6022 | TF: (800) 871 - 2000

Serves As:
• V. President, Marketing/Communications, AIG SunAmerica Inc.

TREMBLAY, Victor

25 Research Dr. | Tel: (508) 389 - 3709
Westborough, MA 01582 | Fax:(508) 836 - 5487

Serves As:
• Contact, Matching Gifts Program, Nat'l Grid USA

TREML, Bernard J.

700 N. Adams St. | Tel: (920) 433 - 4901
Green Bay, WI 54301 | Fax:(920) 433 - 1526
btreml@wpsr.com

Serves As:
• V. President, Human Resources, WPS Resources Corp.

TRENT, Grace Chen

22001 Loudoun County Pkwy. | Tel: (703) 886 - 5600
Ashburn, VA 20147 | TF: (877) MCI - 1000

Serves As:
• Senior V. President, Communications and Chief of Staff, MCI, Inc.

TREON, Julie C.

P.O. Box 391 | Tel: (859) 815 - 3333
Covington, KY 41012-0391 | Fax:(859) 815 - 4795

Serves As:
• Director, Communications, Ashland Inc.

TRETIAK, Stan

1001 E. Broad St., 230 Old City Hall | Tel: (804) 782 - 9441
Richmond, VA 23219 | Fax:(804) 225 - 8356

Serves As:
• Manager, Government Affairs, Eastern Region, Coors Brewing Co.

TREVINO, J. Michael

5555 San Felipe Rd. | Tel: (713) 629 - 6600
Houston, TX 77056 | Fax:(713) 296 - 3394
mjtrevino@marathonoil.com

Serves As:
• General Manager, Public Affairs, Marathon Oil Corp.

TREVINO, Michael

2775 Sanders Rd. | Tel: (847) 402 - 5000
Northbrook, IL 60062-6127 | Fax:(847) 326 - 7519
TF: (800) 574 - 3553

Serves As:
• National Media Contact, Allstate Insurance Co.

TRIANO, Charles E.

909 Third Ave. | Tel: (212) 246 - 714
New York, NY 10022 | Fax:(212) 750 - 9152
TF: (800) 947 - 5227

Serves As:
• V. President, Investor Relations, Forest Laboratories, Inc.
Responsibilities also include corporate communications.

TRICE, Fran
P.O. Box Nine
Sugar Land, TX 77487
ftrice@imperialsugar.com
Tel: (281) 491 - 9181
Fax:(281) 490 - 9584

Serves As:
- Manager, Investor Relations, Imperial Sugar Co.

TRICE, Patzetta M.
P.O. Box 894
Indianapolis, IN 46206
patzetta.trice@gm.com
Tel: (317) 242 - 2615
Fax:(317) 242 - 0193

Serves As:
- Director, Communications and Public Affairs, (Allison Transmission Division), General Motors Corp.

TRIMBLE, Christine
5775 Morehouse Dr.
San Diego, CA 92121-2779
Tel: (858) 587 - 1121
Fax:(858) 658 - 2100

Serves As:
- Senior Director, Corporate Public Relations and Communications, Qualcomm Inc.

TRITCH, Stephen R.
P.O. Box 355
Pittsburgh, PA 15230-0355
Tel: (412) 374 - 4111

Serves As:
- President and Chief Exec. Officer, Westinghouse Electric Company LLC

TROMBLEY OAKES, Martha
One Nat'l Life Dr.
Montpelier, VT 05604
Tel: (802) 229 - 7214
Fax:(802) 229 - 9281
TF: (800) 732 - 8939

Serves As:
- Corporate Contributions Contact, Nat'l Life Insurance Co.

Responsibilities include media relations.

TRON, Dionn M.
400 Main St.
East Hartford, CT 06108
Tel: (860) 565 - 4321

Serves As:
- V. President, Communications, Pratt & Whitney

TROUBA, James S.
32605 W. Twelve Mile Rd.
Farmington Hills, MI 48334-3339
Tel: (248) 848 - 2267
Fax:(248) 488 - 2089
TF: (800) 688 - 2088

Serves As:
- Chief Financial Officer and Investor Relations Contact, Covansys

TROY, Gregory T.
175 Ghent Rd.
Fairlawn, OH 44333-3330
Tel: (330) 869 - 4200
Fax:(330) 869 - 4288

Serves As:
- Senior V. President, Human Resources, OMNOVA Solutions Inc.

TROY, Joe
4211 W. Boyscout Blvd.
Tampa, FL 33607
Tel: (813) 871 - 4404
Fax:(813) 871 - 4420

Serves As:
- Senior V. President, Financial Services, Walter Industries, Inc.

Responsibilities include investor relations.

TRUDELL, Tracy
P.O. Box 4844
Syracuse, NY 13221-4844
Tel: (315) 433 - 0100
Ext: 5598
Fax:(315) 433 - 2345
TF: (800) 654 - 8838

Serves As:
- Communications Contact, Dairylea Cooperative Inc.

TRUDGEON, Jon
Kerr-McGee Center, Box 25861
Oklahoma City, OK 73125
Tel: (405) 270 - 1313
Fax:(405) 270 - 3029
TF: (800) 786 - 2556

Serves As:
- Administrator, Corporate Relations and Contributions, Kerr-McGee Corp.

TRUEBA, Jr., Humberto
3800 Howard Hughes Prkwy.
Las Vegas, NV 89109
Tel: (702) 784 - 7777

Serves As:
- Senior V. President, Human Resources, Pinnacle Entertainment, Inc.

TRUELL, Peter
200 Park Ave.
New York, NY 10166
Tel: (212) 412 - 7576

Serves As:
- Corporate Communications Contaact, Barclays Capital

TRUETT, Eugene M.
P.O. Box 8888
Camp Hill, PA 17001-8888
etruett@harsco.com
Tel: (717) 763 - 5677
Fax:(717) 763 - 6402

Serves As:
- Director, Investor Relations, Credit and Specialized Finance, Harsco Corp.

TRUMBLE, David
6201 N. 24th Pkwy.
Phoenix, AZ 85016-2023
david.trumble@bestwestern.com
Tel: (602) 957 - 5753
Fax:(602) 957 - 5641
TF: (800) 528 - 1234

Serves As:
- Director, External Communications, Best Western Internat'l

TRUMP, Donald J.
725 Fifth Ave.
18th Floor
New York, NY 10022
Tel: (212) 832 - 2000
Fax:(212) 935 - 0141

Serves As:
- Chairman, President, and Chief Exec. Officer, Trump Hotels and Casino Resorts, Inc.

TRUSHEIM, H. Edwin
7733 Forsyth Blvd.
Suite 2300
St. Louis, MO 63105
Tel: (314) 863 - 7422
Fax:(314) 863 - 0769
TF: (800) 677 - 1238

Serves As:
- Chairman of the Board, RehabCare Group, Inc.

TRUSTY, David L.
P.O. Box 33068
Charlotte, NC 28233
Tel: (704) 364 - 3120

Serves As:
- V. President, Corporate Communications, Piedmont Natural Gas Co.

TRYKA, Jeffrey
P.O. Box 3300
Elkhart, IN 46515
jtryka@coachmen.com
Tel: (574) 262 - 0123
Fax:(574) 262 - 8823

Serves As:
- Director, Planning and Investor Relations, Coachmen Industries, Inc.

Responsibilities include media relations.

TRYLOFF, Robin S.
Three First National Plaza
70 W. Madison St.
Chicago, IL 60602-4260
Tel: (312) 558 - 8448
Fax:(312) 419 - 3192
TF: (800) 727 - 2533

Serves As:
- Director, Community Relations and Exec. Director, Sara Lee Foundation, Sara Lee Corp.

TSCHIEGG, Steven D.
1835 Dueber Ave. SW
GNE-26
Canton, OH 44706
steve.tschiegg@timken.com
Tel: (330) 471 - 7446
Fax:(330) 471 - 2797
TF: (800) 223 - 1954

Serves As:
- Manager, Investor Relations, The Timken Co.

TSCHUDY, Phil
P.O. Box 391
Madison, WI 53701
philip.tschudy@cunamutual.com
Tel: (608) 231 - 7188
Fax:(608) 236 - 7188
TF: (800) 356 - 2644

Serves As:
- Manager, Media Relations, CUNA Mutual Group

TSEU, Marvin
345 Encinal St.
Santa Cruz, CA 95060
Tel: (831) 426 - 5858
Fax:(831) 426 - 6098
TF: (800) 544 - 4660

Serves As:
- Chairman of the Board, Plantronics, Inc.

TSIEN, Robert
8200 Jones Branch Dr.
McLean, VA 22102
Tel: (703) 903 - 2000
Fax:(703) 903 - 2447
TF: (800) 373 - 3343

Serves As:
- PAC Contact, Freddie Mac

TSUNEKAWA, Yasuji
P.O. Box 13582
Research Triangle Park, NC 27709
Tel: (919) 990 - 7500
Fax:(919) 990 - 7711
TF: (800) 448 - 3482

Serves As:
- Chairman of the Board, Reichhold, Inc.

TUCCI, Joseph
P.O. Box 9103
Hopkinton, MA 01748
Tel: (508) 435 - 1000
Fax:(508) 435 - 7954
TF: (800) 424 - 3622

Serves As:
- President and Chief Exec. Officer, EMC Corp.

TUCHMAN, Kenneth
9197 S. Peoria St.
Englewood, CO 80112-5833
ken.tuchman@teletech.com
Tel: (303) 397 - 8100
Fax:(303) 397 - 8199
TF: (800) 835 - 3832

Serves As:
- Chairman and Chief Exec. Officer, TeleTech Holdings, Inc.

TUCKER, Chris
P.O. Box 4100
M/S 1068
St. Louis, MO 63136-8506
Tel: (314) 553 - 2197
Fax:(314) 553 - 1213

Serves As:
- Director, Investor Relations, Emerson

Responsibilites include corporate communications.

TUCKER, Debi
P.O. Box 550
Nashville, TN 37202
debi.tucker@hcahealthcare.com
Tel: (615) 963 - 3830
Fax:(615) 963 - 3841

Serves As:
- Manager, Government Relations, HCA

TUCKER, Gregory
1111 N. Charles St.
Baltimore, MD 21201
gtucker@aegonusa.com
Tel: (410) 576 - 4751
Fax:(410) 374 - 8685

Serves As:
- Public Relations Officer, AEGON USA, Inc.

TUCKER, Susan
P.O. Box 431
Easton, PA 18044-0431
Tel: (610) 253 - 6272
Ext: 4293
Fax:(610) 250 - 5768

Serves As:
- Media Contact, Binney and Smith Inc.

TUFF, Tim
P.O. Box 105250
Atlanta, GA 30348
ttuff@harland.net
Tel: (770) 981 - 9460
Fax:(770) 593 - 5367
TF: (800) 723 - 3690

Serves As:
- Chairman and Chief Exec. Officer, John H. Harland Co.

TUGGLE, Clyde C.
P.O. Box 1734
Atlanta, GA 30301
ctuggle@na.ko.com
Tel: (404) 676 - 2121
Fax:(404) 676 - 6792

Serves As:
- Senior V. President and Director, Worldwide Public Affairs and Communications, The Coca-Cola Co.

TUITELE, Sonja
3375 Mitchell Lane
Boulder, CO 80301
Tel: (303) 440 - 5220
Fax:(303) 928 - 0022
TF: (800) 494 - 9453

Serves As:
- Director, Corporate Communications, Wild Oats Markets, Inc.

TULLY, John
P.O. Box 19001
Greenville, SC 29602
Tel: (864) 458 - 5000
Fax:(864) 458 - 6359
TF: (800) 847 - 3435

Serves As:
- Director, Community Relations, Michelin North America, Inc.

TULLY, Nancy
One Symbol Plaza
Holtsville, NY 11742-1300
tullyn@symbol.com
Tel: (631) 738 - 5050
Fax:(631) 738 - 4645
TF: (800) 722 - 6234

Serves As:
- V. President, Corporate Communications, Symbol Technologies, Inc.

Responsibilities include investor relations.

TUOSTO, Michael R.
80 Park Plaza
M/S T-10
Newark, NJ 07102-0570
michael.tuosto@pseg.com
Tel: (973) 430 - 6414
Fax:(973) 623 - 8711

Serves As:
- General Manager, Public Affairs; Contact, Public Service Electric and Gas Co. PAC, PSE&G

TURBES, Susan M.
800 LaSalle Ave.
FL 14
Minneapolis, MN 55402-2006
Tel: (612) 321 - 4850
Fax:(612) 321 - 5137

Serves As:
- Associate Director, State Government Relations, (CenterPoint Energy Minnegasco), CenterPoint Energy

TURLEY, James S.
Five Times Square
New York, NY 10036
james.turley@ey.com
Tel: (212) 773 - 3000
Fax:(212) 773 - 6350

Serves As:
- Chairman and Chief Exec. Officer, Ernst & Young LLP

TURNER, Betty
Bank of America Corporate Center
100 N. Tryon St.
Charlotte, NC 28255-0001
Tel: (704) 386 - 4343
Fax:(704) 386 - 6699

Serves As:
- V. President, State/Local Lobbyist and State Government Relations, Bank of America Corp.

TURNER, Beverly
385 Washington St.
St. Paul, MN 55102
Tel: (651) 310 - 5890
Fax:(651) 310 - 6306

Serves As:
- V. President, Specialty Commercial Government Relations, St. Paul Travelers Cos., Inc.

TURNER, Bob
1400 Douglas St.
Omaha, NE 68179
Tel: (402) 544 - 5255

Serves As:
- President, Union Pacific Foundation; and Senior V. President, Corporate Relations, Union Pacific Corp.

TURNER, Charles H. "Cary"
100 Pier 1 Place
Fort Worth, TX 76102
Tel: (817) 252 - 8000

Serves As:
- Exec. V. President, Chief Financial Officer and Treasurer, Pier 1 Imports

Responsibilities include investor relations.

TURNER, Henry
101 Constitution Ave. NW
Suite 400 West
Washington, DC 20001
henry.turner@altria.com
Tel: (202) 354 - 1500
Fax:(202) 354 - 1505

Serves As:
- V. President, State Government Affairs, Altria Group, Inc.

TURNER, Richard B.
130 E. Randolph Dr.
18th Floor
Chicago, IL 60601
Tel: (312) 240 - 7516
Fax:(312) 240 - 4389

Serves As:
- Manager, Corporate Contributions, Peoples Energy Corp.

TURNER, Ronald L.
3311 E. Old Shakopee Rd.
Minneapolis, MN 55425-1640
Tel: (952) 853 - 8100
Fax:(952) 853 - 7272

Serves As:
- Chairman, President and Chief Exec. Officer, Ceridian Corp.

TURNER, Sheila
P.O. Box 650283
Dallas, TX 75265-0283
Tel: (972) 699 - 4000
Fax:(972) 699 - 4025

Serves As:
- Investor Relations, Xanser Corp.

TURNER, W. Bruce
55 Technology Way
West Greenwich, RI 02817
Tel: (401) 392 - 1000
Fax:(401) 392 - 1234

Serves As:
- President and Chief Exec. Officer, GTECH Corp.

TUROSKY, Kurt
76 S. Main St.
Akron, OH 44308-1890
Tel: (330) 384 - 5500
Fax:(330) 384 - 5902

Serves As:
- Director, Investor Relations, FirstEnergy Corp.

TUSHINGHAM, Julie
P.O. Box 4577
Houston, TX 77210-4577
julie.tushingham@gsfdrill.com
Tel: (281) 925 - 6443
Fax:(281) 925 - 6010

Serves As:
- Manager, Media and Corporate Communications, GlobalSantaFe Corp.

TUTTLE, Gayle
P.O. Box 2291 Tel: (919) 765 - 3747
Durham, NC 27702-2291 Fax:(919) 765 - 4837
Serves As:
• Media Contact, Blue Cross and Blue Shield of North Carolina

TUTTLE, Susan C.
1301 K St. NW Tel: (202) 515 - 5503
Suite 1200 Fax:(202) 515 - 5078
Washington, DC 20005
stuttle@us.ibm.com
Registered Federal Lobbyist.
Serves As:
• Program Manager, Public Affairs, Trade and Investment, Internat'l Business Machines Corp. (IBM)

TUTUNDGY, Carol S.
400 Atlantic St. Tel: (203) 541 - 8000
Stamford, CT 06921 Fax:(203) 541 - 8200
carol.tutundgy@ipaper.com TF: (800) 223 - 1268
Serves As:
• V. President, Investor Relations, Internat'l Paper

TUTWILER, Margaret
11 Wall St. Tel: (212) 656 - 3000
New York, NY 10005 Fax:(212) 656 - 2347
Serves As:
• Exec. V. President, Communications and Government Relations, New York Stock Exchange, Inc.

TWILLEY, Jr., Wm. Edward
P.O. Box 118005 Tel: (803) 745 - 3024
Charleston, SC 29423
Serves As:
• Manager, Regional State Government Relations, MeadWestvaco Corp.

TWIST, Steven J.
1850 N. Central Ave. Tel: (602) 207 - 2940
Suite 800
Phoenix, AZ 85004-4545
stwist@viad.com
Serves As:
• Assistant General Counsel, Viad Corp
Responsibilities include political action.

TWOMEY, Kevin
P.O. Box 3165 Tel: (717) 761 - 2633
Harrisburg, PA 17105
Serves As:
• Senior V. President and Chief Financial Officer, Rite Aid Corp.
Responsibilities include investor relations.

TYCOCKI, Elaine S.
216 N. Chestnut St. Tel: (517) 482 - 8026
Lansing, MI 48933-1021 Fax:(517) 482 - 8064
Serves As:
• Director, Government Affairs, SEMCO ENERGY, Inc.

TYCZKOWSKI, Sue
501 W. Michigan St. Tel: (414) 299 - 7722
Milwaukee, WI 53201 Fax:(414) 299 - 6168
Serves As:
• Contact, Assurant Political Action Committee, Assurant

TYNER, Kay
P.O. Box 2504 Tel: (713) 297 - 5000
Houston, TX 77252-2504 Fax:(713) 297 - 5100
Serves As:
• Contact, Pogo Producing Co. Corporate Contributions, Pogo Producing Co.

TYREE, Larry D.
Three Commercial Pl. Tel: (757) 533 - 4810
Norfolk, VA 23510-2191 Fax:(757) 533 - 4917
Serves As:
• Assistant Corporate Secretary, Stockholder Records, Norfolk Southern Corp.
Responsibilities include investor relations.

TYRRELL, Thomas
550 Madison Ave. Tel: (212) 833 - 7907
New York, NY 10022-3211 Fax:(212) 833 - 7888
thomas_tyrrell@sonymusic.com
Registered Federal Lobbyist.
Serves As:
• Exec. V. President, External and Governmental Affairs, (Sony BMG Music Entertainment, Inc.), Sony Corp. of America

TYSARCZYK, Michael
249 Fifth Ave. Tel: (412) 762 - 8148
28th Floor Fax:(412) 762 - 3463
Pittsburgh, PA 15222-2707
Serves As:
• V. President, Corporate Communications, PNC Financial Services Group

TYSON, John H.
P.O. Box 2020 Tel: (479) 290 - 4000
Springdale, AR 72765-2020 Fax:(479) 290 - 7849
john.tyson@tyson.com TF: (800) 643 - 3410
Serves As:
• Chairman and Chief Exec. Officer, Tyson Foods, Inc.

TYSON, Lynn A.
One Dell Way Tel: (512) 723 - 1130
M/S 9006 Fax:(512) 728 - 4238
Round Rock, TX 78682 TF: (800) 289 - 3355
lynn_tyson@dell.com
Serves As:
• V. President, Investor Relations and Corporate Communications, Dell Inc.

UDOUJ, Marsha
425 W. Capitol, 40th Floor Tel: (501) 377 - 3522
Little Rock, AR 72201 TF: (800) 377 - 4448
mudouj@entergy.com
Serves As:
• Corporate Contributions Coordinator, Entergy Arkansas, Inc.

UGOL, Marc L.
750 E. Pratt St. Tel: (410) 783 - 2800
Fifth Floor TF: (888) 460 - 2002
Baltimore, MD 21202
Serves As:
• V. President, CEG Human Resources, Constellation Energy

UHLIG, Ken
1375 Peachtree St. Tel: (404) 815 - 0770
Atlanta, GA 30309 Fax:(404) 815 - 8805
Serves As:
• Chief People Officer, Earthlink, Inc.

UHLMANN, Rick
P.O. Box 391 Tel: (608) 231 - 8940
Madison, WI 53701 Fax:(608) 236 - 8940
rick.uhlmann@cunamutual.com TF: (800) 356 - 2644
Serves As:
• Senior Manager, Media Relations, CUNA Mutual Group

UHRICH, Marie A.
625 Fourth Ave. South Tel: (612) 340 - 7000
Minneapolis, MN 55415 Fax:(612) 340 - 7373
Serves As:
• Senior V. President, Communications, Thrivent Financial for Lutherans

ULBRANTT, Laura
315 Park Ave. South Tel: (212) 460 - 1900
New York, NY 10010 Fax:(212) 598 - 4869
Serves As:
• Corporate Secretary, Leucadia Nat'l Corp.
Responsibilities include investor relations and corporate philanthropy.

ULLMAN, III, Myron E.
6501 Legacy Dr. Tel: (972) 431 - 1000
Plano, TX 75024-3698 Fax:(972) 431 - 1362
TF: (800) 222 - 6161
Serves As:
• Chairman and Chief Exec. Officer, J. C. Penney Co., Inc.

ULLSTROM, Galen F.
Mutual of Omaha Plaza Tel: (402) 351 - 5235
Omaha, NE 68175-0001 Fax:(402) 351 - 5710
galen.ullstrom@mutualofomaha.com
Serves As:
• Senior V. President, State Government Relations, Mutual of Omaha Insurance Co.

ULMER, Daniel P.
107 W. Main St. Tel: (701) 223 - 6348
P.O. Box 2657 Fax:(701) 255 - 5595
Bismarck, ND 58501
Serves As:
• Director, Government Relations, Blue Cross and Blue Shield of North Dakota

ULRICH, Garrett J.
1855 Boston Rd. Tel: (413) 543 - 2400
Wilbraham, MA 01095 Fax:(413) 543 - 9355
TF: (800) 966 - 9970
Serves As:
• V. President, Human Resources, Friendly Ice Cream Corp.

ULRICH, Robert J.
1000 Nicollet Mall Tel: (612) 304 - 6073
Minneapolis, MN 55403
Serves As:
• Chairman and Chief Exec. Officer, Target Corp.

ULSH, Sandy
One American Rd.
Room 335
Dearborn, MI 48126
sulsh@ford.com
Tel: (313) 845 - 8711
Fax:(313) 337 - 6680
TF: (800) 555 - 5259

Serves As:
- President, Ford Fund, Ford Motor Co.

UMPHENOUR, Jr., Russell
5995 Barfield Rd.
Atlanta, GA 30328
Tel: (404) 256 - 4900
Fax:(404) 256 - 7277

Serves As:
- Chief Exec. Officer, The RTM Restaurant Group

UNANNE, Robert I.
100 Seaview Dr.
Secaucus, NJ 07096
Tel: (201) 348 - 4900
Fax:(201) 348 - 6609

Serves As:
- President, Goya Foods, Inc.

UNDERDOWN, Jacqueline
P.O. Box 50085
Watsonville, CA 95077-5085
jaque.underdown@gcinc.com
Tel: (831) 761 - 4741
Fax:(831) 761 - 7871
TF: (800) 482 - 1518

Serves As:
- Manager, Investor Relations, Granite Construction Inc.

UNDERWOOD, Brian C.
One N. Jefferson Ave.
St. Louis, MO 63103
Tel: (314) 955 - 3711
Fax:(314) 955 - 4308
TF: (877) 835 - 7877

Serves As:
- V. President, Director of Compliance, A. G. Edwards, Inc.

UNDERWOOD, Shawn
9125 Rehco Rd.
San Diego, CA 92121-2270
shawnu@petco.com
Tel: (858) 453 - 7845
Ext: 3571
Fax:(858) 677 - 3489

Serves As:
- Communications Representative, PETCO Animal Supplies, Inc.

UNDERWOOD, Tracy
19001 S. Western Ave.
Torrance, CA 90509
Tel: (310) 468 - 5278
Fax:(310) 468 - 7809

Serves As:
- Contact, Toyota Motor Sales, U.S.A.. Corporate Giving Program and Toyota USA Foundation, (Toyota Motor Sales - USA), Toyota Motor North America, Inc.

UNEMORI, Lynne
P.O. Box 2750
Honolulu, HI 96840-0001
lynne.unemori@heco.com
Tel: (808) 543 - 7972
Fax:(808) 543 - 7790

Serves As:
- Director, Corporate Communications, (Hawaiian Electric Co., Inc.), Hawaiian Electric Industries, Inc.

UNGER, John
P.O. Box 1477
Baltimore, MD 21203
Tel: (410) 237 - 5900
Fax:(410) 237 - 5437

Serves As:
- Exec. V. President, General Counsel and Secretary, (Mercantile-Safe Deposit and Trust Co.), Mercantile Bankshares Corporation

Responsibilities include political action.

UNHJEM, Michael B.
4510 13th Ave. SW
Fargo, ND 58121-0001
Tel: (701) 282 - 1100
Fax:(701) 282 - 1469
TF: (800) 342 - 4718

Serves As:
- President and Chief Exec. Officer, Blue Cross and Blue Shield of North Dakota

UPBIN, Hal J.
600 Kellwood Pkwy.
Chesterfield, MO 63017
hju@kellwood.com
Tel: (314) 576 - 3100
Fax:(314) 576 - 3460

Serves As:
- Chairman of the Board, Kellwood Co.

UPCHURCH, Gene
P.O. Box 1551
Raleigh, NC 27602-1551
Tel: (919) 546 - 3302
Fax:(919) 546 - 7536

Serves As:
- V. President, State Public Affairs, Progress Energy

UPSHUR, Annis
1100 Connecticut Ave. NW
Suite 530
M/S CH1M31
Washington, DC 20036
annis.upshur@weyerhaeuser.com
Tel: (202) 293 - 7222
Fax:(202) 293 - 2955

Serves As:
- Treasurer, Weyerhaeuser Co. PAC, Weyerhaeuser Co.

URBANI, Joseph
2000 Market St.
Philadelphia, PA 19103-9000
Tel: (215) 419 - 7000
Fax:(215) 419 - 7591
TF: (800) 225 - 7788

Serves As:
- Treasurer, ATOFINA PAC, ATOFINA Chemicals, Inc.

URBAS, Carrie
One Health Plaza
East Hanover, NJ 07936
Tel: (862) 778 - 7062
Fax:(862) 644 - 8585

Serves As:
- Associate Director, Public Relations, (Novartis Pharmaceuticals Corp.), Novartis Corporation

URLIS, Allan
666 Grand Ave.
P.O. Box 657
Des Moines, IA 50303-0657
agurlis@midamerican.com
Tel: (515) 281 - 2785
Fax:(515) 242 - 4236
TF: (888) 427 - 5632

Serves As:
- Director, Media Relations, MidAmerican Energy Holdings Co.

USAJ, Joseph
One Invacare Way
Elyria, OH 44035
Tel: (440) 329 - 6000
Fax:(440) 366 - 9008
TF: (800) 333 - 6900

Serves As:
- Senior V. President, Human Resources, Invacare Corp.

USHER, Thomas J.
600 Grant St.
Pittsburgh, PA 15219-2800
Tel: (412) 433 - 1101

Serves As:
- Chairman of the Board, United States Steel Corporation

USHER, William
717 Texas Ave.
Suite 2100
Houston, TX 77002-2712
wusher@br-inc.com
Tel: (713) 624 - 9500
Fax:(713) 624 - 9645
TF: (800) 262 - 3456

Serves As:
- V. President, Human Resources and Administration, Burlington Resources Inc.

USNIK, Toby
229 W. 43rd St.
New York, NY 10036
usnikt@nytimes.com
Tel: (212) 556 - 4425

Serves As:
- Director, Public Relations, New York Times Co.

USTIAN, Daniel C.
P.O. Box 1488
4201 Winfield Rd.
Warrenfield, IL 60555
Tel: (630) 753 - 5000

Serves As:
- Chairman, President and Chief Exec. Officer, Navistar Internat'l Corp.

UTLEY, Kort
5295 S. 300 West
Suite 475
Murray, UT 84107
kort.utley@kennecott.com
Tel: (801) 743 - 4624
Fax:(801) 743 - 4659

Serves As:
- Manager, Community Relations, Kennecott Land

UTLEY, Lorna
300 Renaissance Center
Detroit, MI 48265-3000
Tel: (313) 556 - 5000
Fax:(313) 665 - 0746

Serves As:
- President, General Motors Foundation, General Motors Corp.

UTTERBACK, Rob
700 State Route 46 East
Batesville, IN 47006-8835
rob_utterback@hillenbrand.com
Tel: (812) 934 - 7359
Fax:(812) 934 - 7371

Serves As:
- Communications Coordinator, Hillenbrand Industries, Inc.

VACHON, Brian
One Nat'l Life Dr.
Montpelier, VT 05604
bvachon@nationallife.com
Tel: (802) 229 - 3333
Fax:(802) 229 - 9281
TF: (800) 732 - 8939

Serves As:
- V. President, Communications, Nat'l Life Insurance Co.

VAGI, Joseph C.
1021 E. Cary St.
Richmond, VA 23217
joe.vaggi@cskcorp.com
Tel: (804) 697 - 1110
Fax:(804) 697 - 1197

Serves As:
- Manager, Corporate Communications, Chesapeake Corp.

VALAURI, Susan R.
4401 Creedmoor Rd.
P.O. Box 25458
Raleigh, NC 27611-1003
Tel: (919) 571 - 3747
Fax:(919) 571 - 3732

Serves As:
- Director, Government Relations - North Carolina, Nationwide

VALE, Larry M.
100 City Square
Boston, MA 02129
larry_m_vale@keane.com
Tel: (617) 241 - 9200
Ext: 1290
Fax:(617) 241 - 8027

Serves As:
- V. President, Investor Relations, Keane, Inc.

VALENTINE, Wanda
P.O. Box 511
Kingsport, TN 37662-5075
wandav@eastman.com
Tel: (423) 229 - 4406
Fax:(423) 229 - 8280
TF: (800) 327 - 8626

Serves As:
- Community Relations Associate, Eastman Chemical Co.

VALINE, Jade
P.O. Box 956
El Segundo, CA 90245-0956
Tel: (310) 964 - 3429
Fax:(310) 535 - 5225

Serves As:
- Public Relations Specialist, The DIRECTV Group, Inc.

VALLAIRE, Jane
26950 Agoura Rd.
Calabasas Hills, CA 91301-5335
Tel: (818) 871 - 3000
Fax:(818) 871 - 3100

Serves As:
- Manager, Investor Relations, Cheesecake Factory Inc.
Responsibilities include media relations.

VALLEE, Roy
2211 S. 47th St.
Phoenix, AZ 85034
roy.vallee@avnet.com
Tel: (480) 463 - 2000

Serves As:
- Chairman and Chief Exec. Officer, Avnet Inc.

VAN, Kristin
150 N. Clinton St.
Chicago, IL 60661
Tel: (312) 726 - 1221
Fax:(312) 726 - 0360
TF: (800) 317 - 6245

Serves As:
- V. President, Corporate Communications, Information Resources, Inc.

VAN BERKEL, Jack
4400 MacArthur Blvd.
Suite 600
Newport Beach, CA 92660
jack.vanberkel@cbre.com
Tel: (949) 809 - 4229
Fax:(949) 809 - 4799

Serves As:
- Senior V. President, Human Resources, CB Richard Ellis Services, Inc.

VAN DE WALLE, Dave
200 E.Randolph St.
Chicago, IL 60601
dave_vandewalle@aon.com
Tel: (312) 381 - 5028
Fax:(312) 381 - 0240

Serves As:
- V. President, Global Public Relations, Aon Corp.

VAN DEN BRANDT, Bill
P.O. Box 359
Appleton, WI 54912-0359
bvandenbrandt@appletonpapers.com
Tel: (920) 991 - 8613
Fax:(920) 991 - 8506
TF: (800) 558 - 8390

Serves As:
- Manager, Corporate Communications, Appleton

VAN DEN HOOGEN, Ingrid
4150 Network Circle
Santa Clara, CA 95054
Tel: (650) 960 - 1300
TF: (800) 555 - 9786

Serves As:
- V. President, Global Communications, Sun Microsystems, Inc.

VAN DER MINNE, Frans
360 Hamilton Ave., Suite 1103
White Plains, NY 10601-1841
Tel: (914) 681 - 4111
Fax:(914) 681 - 1900

Serves As:
- President and Chief Exec. Officer, Heineken USA Inc.

VAN DER VEER, Jeroen
P.O. Box 2463
Houston, TX 77252-2463
Tel: (713) 241 - 6161
Fax:(713) 241 - 4044

Serves As:
- Chairman of the Board, Shell Oil Co.

VAN DOORN, John E.
1040 Baumock Burn Dr.
Worthington, OH 43235
Tel: (614) 888 - 8891

Serves As:
- Regional Director, State Government Relations, HSBC North America Holdings Inc.

VAN DUYNE, Nancy H.
1350 I St. NW
Suite 1250
Washington, DC 20005
nvandu@coair.com
Tel: (202) 289 - 6060
Fax:(202) 289 - 1546

Registered Federal Lobbyist.
Serves As:
- Staff V. President, Congressional Affairs, Continental Airlines

VAN DYK, Deborah
P.O. Box 19010
Green Bay, WI 54307-9010
Tel: (920) 437 - 7601
Fax:(920) 437 - 1617

Serves As:
- V. President, Industry and Regulatory Affairs, Schreiber Foods, Inc.

VAN DYKE, Concetta
650 Liberty Ave.
Union, NJ 07083
Tel: (908) 688 - 0888
Fax:(908) 688 - 6483

Serves As:
- V. President, Human Resources, Bed Bath & Beyond Inc.

VAN DYKE, Jeff A.
121 W. Morgan St.
First Floor
Raleigh, NC 27601
jeff.vandyke@bellsouth.com
Tel: (919) 821 - 6016

Serves As:
- Exec. Director, Regulatory and External Affairs, BellSouth Corp.

VAN DYKE, William G.
P.O. Box 1299
Minneapolis, MN 55440-1299
Tel: (952) 887 - 3131
Fax:(952) 887 - 3005
TF: (800) 887 - 3131

Serves As:
- Chairman of the Board, Donaldson Company, Inc.

VAN EGMOND, Juliane H.
1275 Pennsylvania Ave. NW
Suite 801
Washington, DC 20004-2404
Tel: (202) 737 - 8900
Fax:(202) 737 - 8909

Registered Federal Lobbyist.
Serves As:
- Director, Federal Government Relations, Bayer Corporation

VAN EPPES, Jim
17845 E. Hwy. 10
Elk River, MN 55330
Tel: (763) 441 - 3121
Fax:(763) 241 - 2366

Serves As:
- President and Chief Exec. Officer, Great River Energy

VAN ETTEN, Laura
3900 Wisconsin Ave. NW
Washington, DC 20016
Tel: (202) 752 - 1442
Fax:(202) 752 - 6099

Registered Federal Lobbyist.
Serves As:
- Director, Government and Industry Relations, Fannie Mae

VAN GORDER, Jan R.
100 Erie Insurance Pl.
Erie, PA 16530
Tel: (814) 870 - 2000
Fax:(814) 870 - 3126

Serves As:
- PAC Treasurer, Erie Indeminity Co.

VAN HERIK, Ed
8326 Century Park
San Diego, CA 92123
Tel: (619) 696 - 2000
Fax:(619) 696 - 1868

Serves As:
- Manager, Communications, San Diego Gas and Electric Co.

VAN HISE, David W.
21001 Van Born Rd. Tel: (313) 792 - 6961
Taylor, MI 48180 Fax:(313) 792 - 6135

Serves As:
- V. President, International, Masco Corp.

VAN HOUTEN, Pamela
340 Kingsland St. Tel: (973) 562 - 2231
Nutley, NJ 07110-1199
pamela.vanhoute@roche.com

Serves As:
- Director, Product Public Relations - Virology, Primary Care, Hoffmann-La Roche Inc. (Roche)

VAN HOVE, Caroline
P.O. Box 19534 Tel: (714) 245 - 5134
Irvine, CA 92623-9534 Fax:(714) 246 - 4971
TF: (800) 347 - 4500

Serves As:
- Media Contact, Allergan Inc.

VAN LEEUWEN, Mitzi
P.O. Box 13582 Tel: (919) 990 - 7500
Research Triangle Park, NC 27709 Fax:(919) 990 - 7711
mitzi.vanleeuwen@reichhold.com TF: (800) 448 - 3482

Serves As:
- Senior V. President, Corporate Services, Reichhold, Inc.

VAN MERKENSTEIJN, James
1501 K St. NW Tel: (202) 654 - 2940
Suite 575
Washington, DC 20005

Registered Federal Lobbyist.
Serves As:
- Representative, New York Life Insurance Co.

VAN NESS, Heather
340 Kingsland St. Tel: (973) 562 - 2203
Nutley, NJ 07110-1199
heather.vanness@roche.com

Serves As:
- Director, Product Public Relations - HIV, Transplant, Hoffmann-La Roche Inc. (Roche)

VAN NESS, Jana
P.O. Box 53999 Tel: (602) 250 - 2310
M/S 9905 Fax:(602) 250 - 3399
Phoenix, AZ 85072-3999
jana.vanness@aps.com

Serves As:
- State Regulatory Group Leader, Pinnacle West Capital Corp.

VAN NIEUWBURG, Eric M.
3164 Gold Camp Dr. Tel: (916) 631 - 0282
Suite B-230 Fax:(916) 853 - 9067
Rancho Cordova, CA 95670

Serves As:
- Regional Manager, State Government Relations/Pacific, UST Inc.

VAN PAASSCHEN, Frits
P.O. Box 4030 Tel: (303) 279 - 6565
Golden, CO 80401-0030

Serves As:
- President and Chief Exec. Officer, Coors Brewing Co.

VAN PELT, Jack F.
34 N. Meramec Ave. Tel: (314) 512 - 9200
St. Louis, MO 63105 Fax:(314) 573 - 9455
TF: (800) 470 - 9227

Serves As:
- V. President, Human Resources, Graybar Electric Co., Inc.

VAN PELT, Jason
601 Pennsylvania Ave. NW Tel: (202) 638 - 4170
North Bldg. Suite 1200 Fax:(202) 638 - 3670
Washington, DC 20004

Registered Federal Lobbyist.
Serves As:
- Director, Goverment Relations, Merck & Co., Inc.

VAN PELT, Nessa
P.O. Box 269 Tel: (210) 829 - 9000
San Antonio, TX 78291 Fax:(210) 829 - 9403

Serves As:
- Administrative Assistant, Harte-Hanks, Inc.

Responsibilities include public affairs.

VAN SICKLE, Rebecca
850 Third Ave. Tel: (212) 559 - 9163
13th Floor
New York, NY 10022-6211

Serves As:
- Grants Manager, Citigroup Foundation, Citigroup, Inc.

VAN STEDUM, Edward J.
2999 Circle 75 Pkwy. Tel: (770) 953 - 1700
Atlanta, GA 30339 Fax:(770) 956 - 2211
edward_vanstedum@genpt.com

Serves As:
- Senior V. President, Human Resources, Genuine Parts Co.

VAN VALKENBURGH, Lee H.
P.O. Box 772531 Tel: (717) 541 - 6137
Dept. 2531 Fax:(717) 541 - 6696
Harrisburg, PA 17177-2531

Serves As:
- V. President, Corporate Services, Capital BlueCross (Pennsylvania)

VAN VLIERBERGEN, Brian
300 E. Randolph St. Tel: (312) 653 - 6000
Chicago, IL 60601 Fax:(312) 819 - 1220

Serves As:
- PAC Treasurer, (Blue Cross and Blue Shield of Illinois), Health Care Service Corp.

VAN WACHEM, Lodewijk Christiaan
200 Park Ave. Tel: (973) 937 - 0100
Suite 300 Fax:(973) 360 - 0148
Florham Park, NJ 07932 TF: (800) 336 - 7000

Serves As:
- Chairman of the Board, Global Crossing Ltd.

VAN WAGENEN, Paul G.
P.O. Box 2504 Tel: (713) 297 - 5000
Houston, TX 77252-2504 Fax:(713) 297 - 5100

Serves As:
- Chairman, President and Chief Exec. Officer, Pogo Producing Co.

VAN WAY, Catherine
601 Pennsylvania Ave. NW Tel: (202) 393 - 8585
North Bldg., Suite 625 Fax:(202) 393 - 8111
Washington, DC 20004

Registered Federal Lobbyist.
Serves As:
- Director, Legislative and Regulatory Affairs, Cummins, Inc.

Responsibilities also include political action.

VAN ZANTE, Mary
102 Main St. Tel: (641) 621 - 6224
Pella, IA 50219 Fax:(641) 628 - 6070

Serves As:
- Director, Pella Rolscreen Foundation, Pella Corp.

VANANDEL, Steve
7575 Fulton St. East Tel: (616) 787 - 6000
Ada, MI 49355-0001 Fax:(616) 787 - 6177

Serves As:
- Chairman of the Board, Alticor Inc.

VANBUREN, Denise Doring
284 South Ave. Tel: (845) 452 - 2000
Poughkeepsie, NY 12601-4879 Fax:(845) 471 - 8323
TF: (800) 527 - 2714

Serves As:
- V. President, Corporate Communications and Community Relations, CH Energy Group, Inc.

Responsibilities include corporate philanthropy.

VANCE, Sylvia
P.O. Box 757 Tel: (417) 358 - 8131
Carthage, MO 64836-0757
svance@leggett.com

Serves As:
- Contact, Leggett & Platt Corporate Contributions, Leggett & Platt, Inc.

VANCIL, Jennifer
One Seagate Tel: (419) 247 - 5000
Toledo, OH 43666 Fax:(419) 247 - 2839
jennifer.vancil@us.o-i.com

Serves As:
- PAC Contact, Owens-Illinois, Inc.

Responsibilities include government affairs.

VANDERHAVEN, Paul

333 Clay St.
Suite 3600
Houston, TX 70002-4109

Tel: (713) 650 - 3700
Fax:(713) 654 - 9552

Serves As:
- Senior V. President, Finance and Chief Financial Officer, Sterling Chemicals, Inc.

VANDERLINDE, Daisy L.

123 S. Front St.
Memphis, TN 38103

Tel: (901) 495 - 6500
Fax:(901) 495 - 8300

Serves As:
- Senior V. President, Human Resources and Loss Prevention, AutoZone, Inc.

VANDERVOORT, Richard M.

P.O. Box 7100
Westchester, IL 60154
ir@cornproducts.com

Tel: (708) 551 - 2595
Fax:(708) 551 - 2700

Serves As:
- V. P., Strategic Business Dev., Investor Relations, and Gov. and Regulatory Affairs, Corn Products Internat'l, Inc.

VANDERWOUDE, Michael

P.O. Box 2301
Cincinnati, OH 45201-2301

Tel: (513) 397 - 9900
Fax:(513) 723 - 9815

Serves As:
- V. President, Investor Relations and Corporate Communications, Cincinnati Bell Inc.

VANDEVEER, Michael D.

2400 W. Lloyd Exwy.
M/S B216
Evansville, IN 47711-0001
michael.vandeveer@bms.com

Tel: (812) 429 - 7418

Serves As:
- Associate Director, State Government Affairs, Bristol-Myers Squibb Co.

VANDRISSE, Peg

50606 AXP Financial Center
Minneapolis, MN 55474

Tel: (612) 671 - 3541
Fax:(612) 671 - 2741
TF: (800) 328 - 8300

Serves As:
- Manager, Regulatory Affairs, Ameriprise Financial Services Inc.

VANLANDINGHAM, Mark D.

Kerr-McGee Center, Box 25861
Oklahoma City, OK 73125

Tel: (405) 270 - 2028
Fax:(405) 270 - 3029
TF: (800) 786 - 2556

Registered Federal Lobbyist.
Serves As:
- Manager, State Relations, Kerr-McGee Corp.

VARELA, Vicki

5295 S. 300 West
Suite 475
Murray, UT 84107
vicki.varela@kennecott.com

Tel: (801) 743 - 4624
Fax:(801) 743 - 4659

Serves As:
- V. President, Public Policy, Kennecott Land

VARETTONI, Robert A.

1095 Ave. of the Americas
New York, NY 10036
robert.a.varettoni@verizon.com

Tel: (212) 395 - 7726
TF: (800) 621 - 9900

Serves As:
- Exec. Director, Financial Media Relations, Verizon Communications Inc.

VARGAS, Cesar

915 L St., Suite 1410
Sacramento, CA 95814

Tel: (916) 441 - 2288
Fax:(916) 441 - 2897

Serves As:
- Regional Director, State Government Affairs, Altria Group, Inc.

VARGAS, James F.

P.O. Box 1530
La Jolla, CA 92038-1530

Tel: (858) 454 - 0411

Serves As:
- V. President and Chief Human Resources Officer, The Copley Press, Inc.

VARGAS, Nelson

401 E. Jackson St., Suite 3300
Tampa, FL 33602

Tel: (813) 276 - 4600
Fax:(813) 242 - 7447
TF: (800) 242 - 7447

Serves As:
- Manager, Public Relations and Advertising, Lykes Lines Limited

VARGO, Carlee J.

600 Grant St.
Room 685
Pittsburgh, PA 15219-2800

Tel: (412) 433 - 6777
Fax:(412) 433 - 6847

Serves As:
- Public Affairs Representative, United States Steel Corporation

VARLEY, Robert W.

1201 E. 55th St.
Cleveland, OH 44103
robert_w_varley@dom.com

Tel: (216) 736 - 6207

Serves As:
- Director, State and Local Affairs, Dominion Resources, Inc.

VARMA, Gale H.

450 Winks Ln.
Bensalem, PA 19020

Tel: (215) 245 - 9100
Fax:(215) 638 - 6759

Serves As:
- Exec. V. President, Human Resources, Charming Shoppes, Inc.

VARMECKY, Ronald E.

249 Fifth Ave.
Pittsburgh, PA 15222-2707

Tel: (412) 762 - 2000

Serves As:
- PAC Treasurer, PNC Financial Services Group

VASAN, Regina M. "Jenny"

6801 Rockledge Dr.
Bethesda, MD 20817-1877

Tel: (301) 897 - 6290
Fax:(301) 897 - 6252

Serves As:
- V. President, Management Communications, Lockheed Martin Corp.

VASQUEZ, Jaime

P.O. Box 14662
Reading, PA 19612-4662
jvasquez@cartech.com

Tel: (610) 208 - 2165
Fax:(610) 208 - 2989

Serves As:
- V. President and Treasurer, Investor Relations, Carpenter Technology Corp.

Responsibilities include communications.

VASSALLO, Susan

135 Duryea Rd.
Melville, NY 11747
susan.vassallo@henryschein.com

Tel: (631) 843 - 5611
Fax:(631) 843 - 5562

Serves As:
- Director, Corporate Communications, Henry Schein, Inc.

VATTIKUTI, Rejendra B.

32605 W. Twelve Mile Rd.
Farmington Hills, MI 48334-3339

Tel: (248) 488 - 2088
Fax:(248) 488 - 2089
TF: (800) 688 - 2088

Serves As:
- Chairman, President and Chief Exec. Officer, Covansys

VAUGHN, Ken

One N. Central Ave.
Phoenix, AZ 85004-3014
kvaughn@phelpsdodge.com

Tel: (602) 366 - 8318
Fax:(602) 234 - 8337
TF: (800) 528 - 1182

Serves As:
- Manager, Mining Communications, Phelps Dodge Corp.

VAUGHN, Philip

403 E. Capitol St. SE
Washington, DC 20003
philip.vaughn@fluor.com

Tel: (202) 548 - 5800
Fax:(202) 548 - 5810

Registered Federal Lobbyist.
Serves As:
- Senior Director, Government Relations, Fluor Corp.

VAUGHT, Martin W.

1600 Royal St.
Jasper, IN 47549-1001

Tel: (812) 482 - 8255
Fax:(812) 482 - 8300
TF: (800) 482 - 1616

Serves As:
- Director, Public Relations, Kimball International, Inc.

VAVRINA, Jr., Robert T.

P.O. Box 2291
Durham, NC 27702-2291

Tel: (919) 489 - 7431
Fax:(919) 765 - 4837

Serves As:
- Senior V. President, Human Resources, Blue Cross and Blue Shield of North Carolina

VAZQUEZ, Carlos M.

P.O. Box 1564
New Haven, CT 06506-0901
carlos.vazquez@uinet.com

Tel: (203) 499 - 2825
Fax:(203) 499 - 3626
TF: (800) 722 - 5584

Registered Federal Lobbyist.
Serves As:
- Director,Government Affairs, The United Illuminating Company

VEA, Michael T.

P.O. Box 868
Evansville, IN 47705-0868

Tel: (812) 464 - 9800
Fax:(812) 464 - 9825
TF: (800) 467 - 1928

Serves As:
- Chairman, President and Chief Exec. Officer, Integra Bank N.A.

VEGA, Louis A.
1776 I St. NW
Suite 1050
Washington, DC 20006
Tel: (202) 429 - 3400
Fax:(202) 429 - 3467

Registered Federal Lobbyist.
Serves As:
• Director, Federal and State Government Affairs, The Dow Chemical Company

VEGIL, Frank H.
P.O. Box 982
El Paso, TX 79960
Tel: (915) 543 - 5711
Fax:(915) 521 - 4766
TF: (800) 351 - 1621

Serves As:
• PAC Treasurer, El Paso Electric Co.

VEILLEUX, Jennifer
One CVS Dr.
Woonsocket, RI 02895
Tel: (401) 765 - 1500
Fax:(401) 769 - 4488

Serves As:
• Director, Community Relations, CVS

VEITH, Sally
901 15th St. NW
Suite 310
M/S WAS 1150
Washington, DC 20005
Tel: (202) 842 - 3193
Fax:(202) 289 - 6834

Registered Federal Lobbyist.
Serves As:
• Director, Government Affairs, Northwest Airlines, Inc.

VELASQUEZ, Chris
P.O. Box 994
Midland, MI 48686-0994
Tel: (989) 496 - 4000
Fax:(989) 496 - 8240

Serves As:
• PAC Treasurer, Dow Corning Corp.

VELASQUEZ, Michael
1025 Connecticut Ave. NW, Suite 501
Washington, DC 20036
michael.velasquez@aerojet.com
Tel: (202) 828 - 6830
Fax:(202) 828 - 6849

Serves As:
• Director, Congressional Relations, (Aerojet), GenCorp

VELTKAMP, Vicki
6500 N. Mineral Dr., Suite 200
Coeur d'Alene, ID 83815-9408
Tel: (208) 769 - 4100
Fax:(208) 769 - 7612

Serves As:
• V. President, Investor and Public Relations, Hecla Mining Co.

VENEGAS, Nora H.
601 Pennsylvania Ave., NW
Suite 750 South
Washington, DC 20004
Tel: (202) 393 - 3921
Fax:(202) 393 - 3922

Serves As:
• Manager, Federal Government Relations, Tyson Foods, Inc.

VENGLARIK, Cecilia
1717 Arch St.
35th Floor
Philadelphia, PA 19103-2768
Tel: (215) 569 - 2200
Fax:(215) 569 - 1452

Serves As:
• Senior V. President, Human Resources, CDI Corp.

VENN, Rich
2100 E. Grand Ave.
El Segundo, CA 90245
rvenn@csc.com
Tel: (310) 615 - 3926

Serves As:
• Media Relations Representative, Computer Sciences Corp.

VENNETT, David J.
1850 M St. NW
Suite 600
Washington, DC 20036
Tel: (202) 775 - 1700
Fax:(202) 822 - 0928

Serves As:
• National Manager, Government Affairs and Special Projects, Toyota Motor North America, Inc.

VENTIMIGLIA, Ph.D., Peter A.
540 Broad St.
Newark, NJ 07101
Tel: (973) 649 - 9900
Fax:(973) 643 - 5106

Serves As:
• V. President, External Affairs/Statewide Community Relations, Verizon New Jersey, Inc.
Responsibilities include corporate philanthropy.

VENTURA, Elizabeth
383 Madison Ave.
New York, NY 10179
Tel: (212) 272 - 9251
Fax:(212) 272 - 5143
TF: (800) 417 - 2327

Serves As:
• Director, Investor Relations, Bear, Stearns and Co. Inc.

VENTURELLI, Larry
Administrative Center
2000 N. M-63
Benton Harbor, MI 49022-2692
Tel: (269) 923 - 5000
Fax:(269) 923 - 5443

Serves As:
• Director, Investor Relations, Whirlpool Corp.

VERDERY, Jenifer
1634 I St. NW
Suite 300
Washington, DC 20006-4021
Tel: (202) 626 - 4383
Fax:(202) 628 - 2525

Serves As:
• Manager, Human Resources Policy, Intel Corp.

VERDOORN, D. R. "Sid"
8100 Mitchell Rd.
Eden Prairie, MN 55344
Tel: (952) 937 - 8500
Fax:(952) 937 - 6740

Serves As:
• Chairman of the Board, C.H. Robinson Worldwide, Inc.

VERGAS, Sophia G.
P.O. Box 502
Greenville, SC 29602
Tel: (864) 241 - 5496
Fax:(864) 241 - 5401

Serves As:
• Secretary, Liberty Corp. Foundation, Liberty Corp.

VERHAGEN, Timothy J.
P.O. Box 960
Cincinnati, OH 45201-0960
Tel: (513) 421 - 9500

Serves As:
• V. President, Human Resources, Cinergy Corp.

VERHEGGEN, Ted
1776 I St. NW
Suite 1050
Washington, DC 20006
Tel: (202) 429 - 3400
Fax:(202) 429 - 3467

Registered Federal Lobbyist.
Serves As:
• Legislative Counsel, The Dow Chemical Company

VERHEIJ, Richard H.
655 15th St., NW
Suite 410
Washington, DC 20005
Tel: (202) 638 - 6890
Fax:(202) 220 - 3619

Registered Federal Lobbyist.
Serves As:
• Representative, UST Inc.

VERMILLION, Nancy
2555 Telegraph Rd.
Bloomfield Hills, MI 48302-0954
nvermillion@unitedauto.com
Tel: (248) 648 - 2500
Fax:(248) 648 - 2525

Serves As:
• Specialist, Corporate Communications, United Auto Group, Inc.

VERNEY, Steven
2775 Sanders Rd.
Northbrook, IL 60062-6127
Tel: (847) 402 - 5000
Fax:(847) 326 - 7519
TF: (800) 574 - 3553

Serves As:
• PAC Treasurer, Allstate Insurance Co.

VERNON, Kim
200 Madison Ave.
New York, NY 10016
Tel: (212) 381 - 3500
Fax:(212) 381 - 3959

Serves As:
• Senior V. President, Global Advertising and Communications, (Calvin Klein), Phillips-Van Heusen Corp.

VEROSTIC, Joseph R.
P.O. Box 18100
Richmond, VA 23226-8100
Tel: (804) 289 - 9600
Fax:(804) 289 - 9770

Serves As:
• Director, Human Resources, The Brink's Co.
Responsibilities include corporate giving.

VERRECCHIA, Alfred J.
P.O. Box 1059
Pawtucket, RI 02862
Tel: (401) 431 - 8697
Fax:(401) 431 - 8535

Serves As:
• President and Chief Exec. Officer, Hasbro Inc.

VERSAGGI, John D.
655 15th St., NW
Suite 410
Washington, DC 20005
Tel: (202) 638 - 6890
Fax:(202) 220 - 3619

Registered Federal Lobbyist.
Serves As:
• Representative, UST Inc.

VERVILLE, Anne-Lee
225 Windsor Dr.
Itasca, IL 60143
Tel: (630) 875 - 5300
Ext: 5553
Fax:(630) 875 - 5858
TF: (800) 436 - 3726

Serves As:
- Chairman of the Board, Enesco Group, Inc.

VESSELLA, Candace C.
1300 N. 17th St.
Suite 1400
Arlington, VA 22209
Tel: (703) 907 - 8200
Fax:(703) 907 - 8300

Serves As:
- V. President, Government Affairs, BAE Systems North America

Responsibilities include political action.

VEST, Gary L.
100 NE Adams St.
Peoria, IL 61629-1465
Tel: (309) 675 - 1000
Fax:(309) 675 - 6155

Serves As:
- PAC Treasurer, Caterpillar Inc.

VICK, Craig
P.O. Box 27626
Richmond, VA 23261-7626
Tel: (804) 965 - 5889
Fax:(804) 762 - 8589

Serves As:
- Manager, Recruitment and Employee Relations, Owens & Minor, Inc.

VICTOR, Jayne L.
444 N. Capitol St. NW
Suite 729
Washington, DC 20001
Jayne_Victor@dom.com
Tel: (202) 585 - 4203
Fax:(202) 737 - 3874

Serves As:
- Director, Corporate Federal Affairs, Dominion Resources, Inc.

VICTORIA, Justin R.
Five Giralda Farms
Madison, NJ 07940
victorj@wyeth.com
Tel: (973) 660 - 5340
Fax:(973) 660 - 5771

Serves As:
- V. President, Investor Relations, Wyeth

VIETS, Gilbert F.
P.O. Box 51609
Indianapolis, IN 46251-0609
Tel: (317) 247 - 4000
Fax:(317) 243 - 4169

Serves As:
- PAC Treasurer, ATA Holdings Corp.

VIGELAND, John
700 Pilgrim Way
Green Bay, WI 54304
Tel: (920) 429 - 4132
Fax:(920) 429 - 5328

Serves As:
- Director, Corporate Communications, Shopko Stores, Inc.

VIKNER, Paul L.
P.O. Box M
Allentown, PA 18105-5000
Tel: (610) 709 - 3011
Fax:(610) 709 - 3308

Serves As:
- President and Chief Exec. Officer, Mack Trucks, Inc.

VILA, Aracelia
2000 Galloping Hill Rd.
Kenilworth, NJ 07033
Tel: (908) 298 - 4035

Serves As:
- V. President, Public Affairs and Global Marketing, Schering-Plough Corporation

VILHAUER, Robert J.
1200 Wilson Blvd.
Arlington, VA 22209-2305
Tel: (703) 465 - 3671

Serves As:
- Director, Air Traffic Management, The Boeing Co.

VILL, Robert J.
1441 Broadway
New York, NY 10018
Tel: (212) 354 - 4900
Fax:(212) 626 - 3416

Serves As:
- Treasurer and V. President, Investor Relations, Liz Claiborne Inc.

VILLA, Linda D.
One Telecordia Dr.
Piscataway, NJ 08854-4157
Tel: (732) 699 - 2000

Serves As:
- Corporate V. President, Human Resources, Telcordia Technologies, Inc.

VILLARINO, Jose
3000 Hanover St.
Palo Alto, CA 94304
jose_villarino@hp.com
Tel: (650) 857 - 4872
Fax:(650) 857 - 5518
TF: (800) 752 - 0900

Serves As:
- Shareholder Relations, Hewlett-Packard Co.

VILLARRUBIA, Kel P.
5601 Citrus Blvd.
Harahan, LA 70123
Tel: (504) 818 - 7360
Fax:(504) 826 - 7258

Serves As:
- V. President, Public Affairs, (Louisiana Coca-Cola Bottling Co. Ltd.), Coca-Cola Enterprises Inc.

VILLASENOR, Lilia
P.O. Box 6000
Newport Beach, CA 92658-6000
Tel: (949) 854 - 3100
Fax:(949) 823 - 5375

Serves As:
- Manager, Community Development and Investment, Downey Savings and Loan Ass'n, F.A.

Responsibilities include corporate philanthropy.

VILLEGOS, Pedro
101 Ash St.
hqu8d
San Diego, CA 92101-3017
pvillegos@sempra.com
Tel: (619) 696 - 4016
Fax:(619) 696 - 2500
TF: (877) 736 - 7721

Serves As:
- Government Affairs Manager, Sempra Energy

VINCENT, Robert K.
55 Technology Way
West Greenwich, RI 02817
Tel: (401) 392 - 7452
Fax:(401) 392 - 1234

Serves As:
- V. President, Corporate Communications, GTECH Corp.

VINES, Jason
1000 Chrysler Dr.
Auburn Hills, MI 48326-2766
Tel: (248) 576 - 5741
Fax:(248) 576 - 4742
TF: (800) 992 - 1997

Serves As:
- V. President, Corporate Communications, DaimlerChrysler Corp.

VINNEY, Les C.
5960 Heisley Rd.
Mentor, OH 44060-1834
Tel: (440) 354 - 2600
Fax:(440) 639 - 4450
TF: (800) 548 - 4873

Serves As:
- President and Chief Exec. Officer, STERIS Corp.

VIPOND, J. Robert
100 First Stamford Pl.
Stamford, CT 06902
Tel: (203) 363 - 7301
Fax:(203) 363 - 7303

Serves As:
- V. President, Finance and Chief Financial Officer, Crane Co.

VIRGO, John A.
9000 W. 67th St.
Shawnee Mission, KS 66202
john_virgo@seaboardcorp.com
Tel: (913) 676 - 8800
Fax:(913) 676 - 8872

Serves As:
- V. President, Corporate Controller and Chief Accounting Officer, Seaboard Corporation

Responsibilities include corporate philanthropy.

VISCONTI, Diego
1345 Ave. of the Americas
New York, NY 10105
Tel: (917) 452 - 4400
Fax:(917) 527 - 9915

Serves As:
- Group Chief Exec., Communications and High Tech, Accenture

VISHNY, Michael
4000 MacArthur Blvd.
Newport Beach, CA 92660
Tel: (949) 483 - 4600

Serves As:
- Senior V. President, Human Resources, Conexant Systems, Inc.

VITA, John
175 W. Jackson Blvd.
20th Floor
Chicago, IL 60604
john.vita@gt.com
Tel: (312) 602 - 8655
Fax:(312) 861 - 1340

Serves As:
- National Director, Corporate Communications, Grant Thornton LLP

VIZZACCARO, Dina
1301 Pennsylvania Ave. NW
Suite 1030
Washington, DC 20004
dina.vizzaccaro@delphi.com
Tel: (202) 824 - 0412
Fax:(202) 628 - 5815

Registered Federal Lobbyist.
Serves As:
- Director, Federal Relations, Delphi Corp.

VOEGELE, Craig C.
1501 S. Capitol Way, Suite 307
Olympia, WA 98501-2296
Tel: (360) 352 - 5270
Fax:(360) 357 - 3124

Serves As:
- Public Policy Manager - Washington and California, Boise Cascade Corp.

VOEPEL, David
625 S. Second St.
Suite 103B
Springfield, IL 62704
david_voepel@baxter.com
Tel: (217) 753 - 9626
Fax:(217) 753 - 9627

Serves As:
- Director, State Government Affairs, Baxter Internat'l Inc.

VOGEL, Gloria
175 King St.
Armonk, NY 10504
Tel: (914) 828 - 8078
Fax:(914) 828 - 7000
TF: (888) 794 - 7773

Serves As:
- Investor Relations Contact, Swiss Re America Corp.

VOGEL, Vern
5820 Westown Pkwy.
West Des Moines, IA 50266-8223
Tel: (515) 267 - 2848
Fax:(515) 267 - 2817

Serves As:
- Assistant V. President, Risk Management, Hy-Vee, Inc.

VOGT, Terry
One Busch Pl.
St. Louis, MO 63118-1852
Tel: (314) 577 - 2000
Fax:(314) 577 - 2900

Serves As:
- V. President, Communications, Anheuser-Busch Cos., Inc.

VOLKEMA, Michael A.
P.O. Box 302
Zeeland, MI 49464-0302
michael_volkema@hermanmiller.com
Tel: (616) 654 - 3000
Fax:(616) 654 - 5234

Serves As:
- Chairman of the Board, Herman Miller Inc.

VOLKENING, Ronnie R.
2711 N. Haskell Ave.
Dallas, TX 75204
Tel: (214) 841 - 6598
Fax:(214) 841 - 6727

Registered Federal Lobbyist.
Serves As:
- Director, Government Affairs, 7-Eleven, Inc.

VOLKLAND, Leigh
P.O. Box 6006
Cypress, CA 90630
leigh.volkland@phs.com
Tel: (714) 226 - 3211
Fax:(714) 226 - 3653

Serves As:
- Director, Government Relations, PacifiCare Health Systems, Inc.

VOLLRATH, Fred
2100 E. Grand Ave.
El Segundo, CA 90245
fvollrat@csc.com
Tel: (310) 615 - 1785
Fax:(310) 322 - 9767

Serves As:
- V. President, Human Resources, Computer Sciences Corp.

VOLPE, Ralph
1901 Main St.
Buffalo, NY 14208-0080
Tel: (716) 887 - 6900
Fax:(716) 887 - 8981
TF: (888) 249 - 2583

Serves As:
- V. President, Human Resources and Administrative Services, HealthNow New York Inc.

VOLTZ, Sue
113 King St.
Armonk, NY 10504
Tel: (914) 273 - 4545
Fax:(914) 765 - 3163

Serves As:
- MBIA Foundation Contact, MBIA, Inc.

VOLTZ CARLSON, Trisha
5718 Westheimer St.
Houston, TX 77057
tvoltz@hibernia.com
Tel: (504) 533 - 2180
Fax:(504) 533 - 2367
TF: (800) 562 - 9007

Serves As:
- Senior V. President, Investor Relations, Hibernia Corp.

VOLZ, Carl M.
818 Connecticut Ave. NW
Suite 600
Washington, DC 20006-2702
Tel: (202) 466 - 0670
Fax:(202) 466 - 0684

Registered Federal Lobbyist.
Serves As:
- Manager, Government Affairs Issue Analysis, Caterpillar Inc.

VON BARGEN, Christina
11 Madison Ave.
New York, NY 10010-3629
Tel: (212) 325 - 2802
Fax:(212) 538 - 4633

Serves As:
- Media Contact, Credit Suisse First Boston

VON BOSTEL, Sylvia
8283 Greensboro Dr.
McLean, VA 22102-3802
Tel: (703) 902 - 5518
Fax:(703) 902 - 3333

Serves As:
- Manager, Government Relations, Booz Allen Hamilton Inc.

VON ROSENBERG, III, Joseph L.
1717 St. James Pl., Suite 550
Houston, TX 77056
Tel: (713) 623 - 0060
Fax:(713) 940 - 6122

Serves As:
- President and Chief Exec. Officer, Omega Protein Corporation

VONK, Erik
600 301 Blvd. West
Bradenton, FL 34205
erik.vonk@gevityhr.com
Tel: (941) 741 - 4300
Fax:(941) 741 - 4333
TF: (800) 243 - 8489

Serves As:
- Chairman and Chief Exec. Officer, Gevity HR, Inc.

VORDENBAUMEN, Sr., Timothy L.
1600 River Center II
100 E. River Center Blvd.
Covington, KY 41011
Tel: (859) 392 - 3300
Fax:(859) 392 - 3333

Serves As:
- V. President, Government Affairs, Omnicare, Inc.

VOSS, Laura
740 W. New Circle Rd.
Lexington, KY 40550
lvoss@lexmark.com
Tel: (859) 232 - 7551
Fax:(859) 232 - 7529
TF: (800) 539 - 6275

Serves As:
- Director, Community Relations, Lexmark Internat'l, Inc.

Responsibilities include corporate philanthropy and government affairs.

VOSS, Martha
1850 M St. NW
Suite 600
Washington, DC 20036
Tel: (202) 775 - 1700
Fax:(202) 822 - 0928

Serves As:
- Manager, Public Affairs and Issues Communications, Toyota Motor North America, Inc.

VREELAND, Amy
Brighton Landing, 20 Guest St.
Boston, MA 02135-2088
amy.vreeland@newbalance.com
Tel: (617) 746 - 2214
Fax:(617) 787 - 9355
TF: (800) 343 - 1395

Serves As:
- Manager, Corporate Communications, New Balance Athletic Shoe, Inc.

VUCKSON, Joe
350 Campus Dr.
Marlborough, MA 01752-3064
Tel: (508) 323 - 5000
Fax:(508) 323 - 1111

Serves As:
- Manager, Corporate Public Relations, 3Com Corp.

VUJOVICH, Christine M.
601 Pennsylvania Ave. NW
North Bldg., Suite 625
Washington, DC 20004
christine.m.vujovich@cummins.com
Tel: (202) 393 - 8585
Fax:(202) 393 - 8111

Registered Federal Lobbyist.
Serves As:
- V. President, Marketing and Environmental Policy, Cummins, Inc.

VUMBACCO, Joseph V.
5811 Pelican Bay Blvd., Suite 500
Naples, FL 34108-2710
Tel: (239) 597 - 7161
Fax:(239) 597 - 5794

Serves As:
- President and Chief Exec. Officer, Health Management Associates, Inc.

WACHOLTZ, Margaret
P.O. Box 300
Oshkosh, WI 54903-0300
Tel: (920) 231 - 8800
Fax:(920) 231 - 8621
TF: (800) 282 - 4674

Serves As:
- Corporate Grants Contact, Oshkosh B'Gosh, Inc.

WACKERLE, Rex
1140 Connecticut Ave. NW
Suite 510
Washington, DC 20036
rex.wackerle@prudential.com
Tel: (202) 327 - 5240
Fax:(202) 327 - 5249

Registered Federal Lobbyist.
Serves As:
- V. President, Government Relations, Prudential Financial

WACKERMAN, Dorothy C.
P.O. Box 860
Valley Forge, PA 19482
Tel: (610) 341 - 7000
Fax:(610) 341 - 7777

Serves As:
- V. President, Communications, Saint-Gobain Corp.

WADDELL, Greg
1301 K St. NW
Suite 1200
Washington, DC 20005
Tel: (202) 515 - 5446

Serves As:
- Program Manager, Networked Society, Internat'l Business Machines Corp. (IBM)

WADDELL, M. Keith
2884 Sand Hill Rd.
Suite 200
Menlo Park, CA 94025
Tel: (650) 234 - 6000
Fax:(650) 234 - 6999

Serves As:
- V. Chairman and Chief Financial Officer, Robert Half International Inc.

Responsibilities include investor relations.

WADDY, Victoria J.
310 S. St. Mary's
Suite 2400
San Antonio, TX 78205
waddyvj@zachry.com
Tel: (210) 258 - 2662
Fax:(210) 258 - 2688

Serves As:
- Director, Public Affairs, Zachry Construction Corporation

WADE, Chet G.
P.O. Box 2666
Richmond, VA 23261
Chet_Wade@dom.com
Tel: (804) 771 - 5697

Serves As:
- Director Employee Communications, Dominion Resources, Inc.

WADE, Dana H.
345 California St.
Suite 2200
San Francisco, CA 94104
dana.h.wade@pjc.com

Serves As:
- V. President, Public Affairs and Media Relations, U.S. Bancorp Piper Jaffray Inc.

WADE, Dennis
One Healthsouth Pkwy.
Birmingham, AL 35243
dennis.wade@healthsouth.com
Tel: (205) 967 - 7116
Fax:(205) 969 - 6889
TF: (888) 476 - 8849

Serves As:
- Group V. President, Human Resources, HealthSouth Corp.

WADE, Tara
1101 Pennsylvania Ave. NW
Sixth Floor
Washington, DC 20004
Tel: (202) 756 - 7750
Fax:(202) 756 - 7545

Registered Federal Lobbyist.
Serves As:
- Legislative Policy Analyst, E*TRADE Financial Corp.

WADHWANI, Romesh
150 N. Clinton St.
Chicago, IL 60661
Tel: (312) 726 - 1221
Fax:(312) 726 - 0360
TF: (800) 317 - 6245

Serves As:
- Chairman of the Board, Information Resources, Inc.

WADSWORTH, Howard C.
P.O. Box 650283
Dallas, TX 75265-0283
investor@kaneb.com
Tel: (972) 699 - 4055
Fax:(972) 699 - 3524

Serves As:
- Senior V. President, Chief Financial Officer, Treasurer and Secretary, Xanser Corp.

Responsibilities include corporate communications and investor relations.

WAGGONER, Debra
1350 I St. NW
Suite 500
Washington, DC 20005-3305
Tel: (202) 682 - 3200
Fax:(202) 682 - 3130

Registered Federal Lobbyist.
Serves As:
- Director, Public Policy, Corning Incorporated

WAGGONER, James J.
P.O. Box 1518
Bellevue, WA 98009
Tel: (425) 468 - 7400
Fax:(425) 468 - 8216

Serves As:
- V. President and General Manager, PACCAR Foundation, PACCAR Inc.

WAGNER, Anna
P.O. Box 511
Kingsport, TN 37662-5075
awagner@eastman.com
Tel: (423) 229 - 2030
Fax:(423) 229 - 8280
TF: (800) 327 - 8626

Serves As:
- Senior Administrative Assistant, Government Relations, Eastman Chemical Co.

WAGNER, Brian
1200 Wilson Blvd.
Arlington, VA 22209-2305
Tel: (703) 465 - 3241
Fax:(703) 465 - 3003

Registered Federal Lobbyist.
Serves As:
- Legislative Affairs -- Space Issues, The Boeing Co.

WAGNER, Harold A.
1110 American Parkway NE
Allentown, PA 18109-3229
Tel: (610) 712 - 4323
Fax:(610) 712 - 4106

Serves As:
- Chairman of the Board, Agere Systems Inc.

WAGNER, Heidi L.
808 17th St. NW
Suite 250
Washington, DC 20006
Tel: (202) 296 - 7272
Fax:(202) 296 - 7290

Registered Federal Lobbyist.
Serves As:
- Senior Director, Government Affairs, Genentech, Inc.

WAGNER, Kelly J.
National City Center
1900 E. Ninth St.
Cleveland, OH 44114-3484
kelly.j.wagner@nationalcity.com
Tel: (216) 222 - 9514
Fax:(216) 222 - 4221
TF: (800) 622 - 6736

Serves As:
- Media Contact, Nat'l City Corp.

Media contact for Ohio only

WAGNER, Keoni
P.O. Box 30008
Honolulu, HI 96820
Tel: (808) 838 - 6778
Fax:(808) 840 - 8213

Serves As:
- V. President, Corporate Communications, Hawaiian Holdings, Inc.

WAGNER, Mark F.
400 N. Capitol St. NW
Suite 590
Washington, DC 20001
Tel: (202) 393 - 3224
Fax:(202) 393 - 7718

Registered Federal Lobbyist.
Serves As:
- Director, Government Affairs, Johnson Controls, Inc.

WAGNER, Jr., Raymond T.
600 Corporate Park Dr.
St. Louis, MO 63105
rwagner@erac.com
Tel: (314) 512 - 2897
Fax:(314) 512 - 4897

Serves As:
- V. President, Governmental and Legislative Affairs, Enterprise Rent-A-Car Co.

WAGONER, Jr., G. Richard
P.O. Box 300
Detroit, MI 48265-1000
Tel: (313) 556 - 5000
Fax:(248) 696 - 7300

Serves As:
- Chairman and Chief Exec. Officer, General Motors Corp.

WAHL, Fred
1215 S. Clark St.
Suite1205
Arlington, VA 22202
Tel: (703) 412 - 7190

Serves As:
- V. President, Government Affairs, L-3 Communications Corp.

WAHLSTROM, Scott E.
1001 Air Brake Ave.
Wilmerding, PA 15148-1036
Tel: (412) 825 - 1000
Fax:(412) 825 - 1091

Serves As:
- V. President, Human Resources, Westinghouse Air Brake Technologies Corp.

WAI, Sam S. M.
101 N. Third St.
Moorhead, MN 56560-1990
swai@crystalsugar.com
Tel: (218) 236 - 4400
Ext: 4430
Fax:(218) 236 - 4485

Serves As:
- Treasurer, American Crystal PAC, American Crystal Sugar Co.

WAINSCOTT, James L.
703 Curtis St.
Middletown, OH 45043
Tel: (513) 425 - 5392
Fax:(513) 425 - 2676
TF: (800) 331 - 5050

Serves As:
- President and Chief Exec. Officer, AK Steel Corp.

WAINWRIGHT, Joan E.
P.O. Box 100
Whitehouse Station, NJ 08889-0100
Tel: (908) 423 - 5257
Fax:(908) 735 - 1196
TF: (800) 423 - 1000

Serves As:
- V. President, Public Affairs, Merck & Co., Inc.

WAITE, Durga
P.O. Box 97034
PSE12
Bellevue, WA 98009-9734
durga.waite@pse.com
Tel: (425) 462 - 3808
Fax:(425) 462 - 3300

Serves As:
- Director, Investor Relations, Puget Sound Energy

WAJSGRAS, David C.
21557 Telegraph Rd.
Southfield, MI 48034
Tel: (248) 447 - 1500
Fax:(248) 447 - 1722

Serves As:
- Senior V. President and Chief Financial Officer, Lear Corporation

Responsibilities include investor relations.

WAKEFIELD, Tayce A.
300 Renaissance Center
Detroit, MI 48265-3000
tayce.wakefield@gm.com
Tel: (313) 665 - 5000
Fax:(313) 665 - 0746

Serves As:
- Exec. Director, Environment and Energy Public Policy Center, General Motors Corp.

WALAS, Kathleen
1345 Ave. of the Americas
27th Floor
New York, NY 10020
Tel: (212) 282 - 5140

Serves As:
- President, Avon Products Foundation, Avon Products, Inc.

WALCK, Ken M.
7201 Hamilton Blvd.
Allentown, PA 18195-1501
walckkm@airproducts.com
Tel: (610) 481 - 8315
Fax:(610) 481 - 2729

Serves As:
- Manager, Investor Relations, Air Products and Chemicals, Inc.

WALDE, Lewis
6500 N. Mineral Dr., Suite 200
Coeur d'Alene, ID 83815-9408
Tel: (208) 769 - 4100
Fax:(208) 769 - 4107

Serves As:
- PAC Contact, Hecla Mining Co.

WALDEN, Ann
3600 N. Hydraulic
Wichita, KS 67219
Tel: (316) 832 - 2700

Serves As:
- Manager, Public Relations, The Coleman Company, Inc.

WALDEN, John
7601 Penn Ave. South
Richfield, MN 55423
Tel: (612) 291 - 1000

Serves As:
- Representative, Best Buy Co., Inc.

WALDRON, Thomas R.
5780 Powers Ferry Rd. NW
Atlanta, GA 30327
Tel: (770) 980 - 5100
Fax:(770) 980 - 3301

Serves As:
- Exec. V. President, Human Resources, Communications and Administration, ING Americas

WALDROP, Tom
2200 Mission College Blvd.
Santa Clara, CA 95052-8119
tom.waldrop@intel.com
Tel: (408) 765 - 8478
Fax:(408) 765 - 6008
TF: (800) 628 - 8686

Serves As:
- Co-Director, Worldwide Press Relations, Intel Corp.

WALENZ, Nicole
World-Herald Square
Omaha, NE 68102
Tel: (402) 444 - 1121
Fax:(402) 348 - 1828

Serves As:
- Coordinator, Public Relations, Omaha World-Herald Co.

WALKER, Allen
One Chase Manhattan Plaza
41st Floor
New York, NY 10005
allen.walker@assurant.com
Tel: (212) 859 - 7000
Fax:(212) 859 - 7010

Serves As:
- V. President, Development and Corporate Communications, Assurant

WALKER, Brian C.
P.O. Box 302
Zeeland, MI 49464-0302
Tel: (616) 654 - 3000
Fax:(616) 654 - 3632

Serves As:
- President and Chief Exec. Officer, Herman Miller Inc.

WALKER, Cary
606 S. Olive St.
Los Angeles, CA 90014
cary.walker@cnb.com
Tel: (213) 833 - 4715
Fax:(213) 833 - 4702
TF: (800) 773 - 7100

Serves As:
- Senior V. President and Manager, Corporate Public Relations, (City Nat'l Bank), City Nat'l Corp.

WALKER, Cory T.
220 S. Ridgewood Ave.
Daytona Beach, FL 32114
cwalker@bbins.com
Tel: (386) 239 - 7250
Fax:(386) 239 - 7252
TF: (800) 877 - 2769

Serves As:
- Senior V. President, Treasurer and Chief Financial Officer, Brown & Brown, Inc.

Responsibilities include media and investor relations.

WALKER, Crystal
Island Center
2701 N. Rocky Point
Tampa, FL 33607
cwalker@calpine.com
Tel: (813) 637 - 7333

Serves As:
- Manager, Government and Public Affairs, Calpine Corp.

WALKER, Diane
P.O. Box 13287
Kansas City, MO 64199-3287
diane.walker@aquila.com
Tel: (816) 467 - 3686
Fax:(816) 467 - 9686

Serves As:
- Corporate Communications, Aquila, Inc.

WALKER, Donald L.
1835 Dueber Ave. SW
GNE-17
Canton, OH 44706
donald.l.walker@timken.com
Tel: (330) 438 - 3000
Fax:(330) 471 - 4041
TF: (800) 223 - 1954

Serves As:
- Senior V. President, Human Resources and Organizational Advancement, The Timken Co.

WALKER, Doug
P.O. Box 1938
Sumner, WA 98390-0800
Board@rei.com
Tel: (253) 395 - 3780
Fax:(253) 395 - 4368

Serves As:
- Chairman of the Board, Recreational Equipment, Inc.

WALKER, Jerry
P.O. Box 26234
Richmond, VA 23260-6234
jerry.walker@sscoop.com
Tel: (804) 281 - 1000
Fax:(804) 281 - 1119

Serves As:
- V. President, Human Resources, Southern States Cooperative

WALKER, Joan H.
1801 California St.
50th Floor
Denver, CO 80202
Tel: (303) 992 - 1412
Fax:(303) 992 - 1028
TF: (800) 899 - 7780

Serves As:
- Senior V. President, Corporate Communications, Qwest Communications

WALKER, John E. "Ned"
P.O. Box 4607
Houston, TX 77210-4607
nwalke@coair.com
Tel: (713) 324 - 5080
Fax:(713) 324 - 2087

Serves As:
- Senior V. President, Worldwide Corporate Communications, Continental Airlines

WALKER, Lisa
120 Park Ave.
New York, NY 10017
Tel: (917) 663 - 2878
Fax:(917) 663 - 5874

Serves As:
- Director, Corporate Contributions, Altria Group, Inc.

WALKER, Lori A.
1101 Third St. South
Minneapolis, MN 55415
Tel: (612) 332 - 7371
Fax:(612) 375 - 7723

Serves As:
- V. President, Treasurer and Controller, Valspar Corp.

WALKER, Nancy
U.S. Route 202, P.O. Box 300
Raritan, NJ 08869-0602
Tel: (908) 218 - 6636
Fax:(908) 218 - 1416

Serves As:
- V. President, Public Affairs, (Ortho-McNeil Pharmaceutical, Inc.), Johnson & Johnson

WALKER, Renee

999 W. Big Beaver Rd.
Troy, MI 48084-4782
renee_walker@kellyservices.com
Tel: (248) 362 - 4444
Fax:(248) 244 - 7572

Serves As:
• Manager, Public Relations, Kelly Services, Inc.

WALKER, Ruth

P.O. Box 2450
Grand Rapids, MI 49501
walker@foremost.com
Tel: (616) 942 - 3000
Fax:(616) 956 - 2093

Serves As:
• Manager, Public Relations and Corporate Communications, Foremost Corp. of America

WALKER, Samuel D.

P.O. Box 4030
M/S MCCC
Golden, CO 80401-0030
Tel: (303) 277 - 2164
Fax:(303) 277 - 6212

Serves As:
• Global Chief Legal Officer, Coors Brewing Co.

WALKER, Todd A.

655 15th St., NW
Suite 410
Washington, DC 20005
Tel: (202) 638 - 6890
Fax:(202) 220 - 3619

Registered Federal Lobbyist.
Serves As:
• V. President, Federal Government Relations, (UST Public Affairs Inc. (USTPA)), UST Inc.

WALKER, III, William G.

215 S. Monroe St., Suite 810
Tallahassee, FL 32301
Tel: (850) 224 - 7517
Fax:(850) 224 - 7197

Serves As:
• V. President, Regulatory Affairs, (Florida Power & Light Company), FPL Group, Inc.

WALL, Charles T.

200 Old Hook Rd.
Harrington Park, NJ 07640
Tel: (201) 767 - 9300
Fax:(201) 767 - 2892
TF: (800) 230 - 2685

Serves As:
• Senior V. President, Human Resources, United Water Resources

WALL, Merrill S.

11622 El Camino Real
M/S SBTR 0837
San Diego, CA 92130

Serves As:
• Senior V. President, Human Resources, Zions Bancorporation

WALL, Rhonda

6415 Idlewild Rd., Suite 109
Charlotte, NC 28212
rhonda.wall@sonicautomotive.com
Tel: (704) 566 - 2400
Fax:(704) 536 - 4668

Serves As:
• Divisional Human Resources Manager, Northern Region, Sonic Automotive, Inc.

WALLACE, Brad

One State Farm Plaza
M/S (B-4)
Bloomington, IL 61710-0001
Tel: (309) 766 - 9273

Serves As:
• Public Affairs Consultant, State Farm Insurance Cos.

WALLACE, Christine

1700 S. Patterson Blvd.
Dayton, OH 45479
christine.wallace@ncr.com
Tel: (937) 445 - 5000
Fax:(937) 445 - 1847
TF: (800) 225 - 5627

Serves As:
• Senior V. President, Human Resources, NCR Corporation

WALLACE, Edward

16530 Via Esprillo
San Diego, CA 92127
ed.wallace@am.sony.com

Serves As:
• Senior Manager, Community Affairs, (Sony Electronics Inc.), Sony Corp. of America

WALLACE, Jr., Edward B.

GM Fairfax Assembly
3201 Fairfax Trafficway
Kansas City, KS 66115-1307
edward.wallace@gm.com
Tel: (913) 573 - 3994
Fax:(913) 573 - 3996

Serves As:
• Regional Director, Midwest, General Motors Corp.

WALLACE, Richard K.

17666 Fitch
Irvine, CA 92614
Tel: (949) 553 - 9292
Fax:(949) 474 - 7675

Serves As:
• V. President, Corporate Affairs, Freedom Communications Inc.

WALLACE, Rob

1299 Pennsylvania Ave. NW
11th Floor West
Washington, DC 20004-2407
rob.wallace@corporate.ge.com
Tel: (202) 637 - 4000
Fax:(202) 637 - 4006

Registered Federal Lobbyist.
Serves As:
• Manager, Government and Industry Programs, General Electric Co.

WALLACE, Roger

5205 N. O'Connor Blvd.
Suite 900
Irving, TX 75039
Tel: (972) 444 - 9001
Fax:(972) 969 - 3516

Serves As:
• V. President, Government Affairs, Pioneer Natural Resources Co.

WALLACE, Timothy R.

2525 Stemmons Fwy.
Dallas, TX 75207-2401
timothy.wallace@trin.net
Tel: (214) 631 - 4420
Fax:(214) 689 - 0501

Serves As:
• Chairman, President and Chief Exec. Officer, Trinity Industries, Inc.

WALLACE, Tom

555 12th St. NW
Suite 650
Washington, DC 20004-1205
Tel: (202) 393 - 7950
Fax:(202) 393 - 7960

Serves As:
• Director, U.S. Advocacy, Eli Lilly and Company

WALLACE, Tricia Primrose

One Time Warner Center
New York, NY 10019
Tel: (212) 484 - 7450
Fax:(212) 489 - 6183

Serves As:
• V. President, Corporate Communications, Time Warner Inc.

WALLER, Regina T.

P.O. Box 1295
Birmingham, AL 35201
rtwaller@southernco.com
Tel: (205) 992 - 5752
Fax:(205) 992 - 5363

Serves As:
• Communications Specialist, Southern Nuclear Operating Co.

WALLER, Tony

One State Farm Plaza
M/S B-4
Bloomington, IL 61710-0001
Tel: (309) 766 - 9765

Serves As:
• Public Affairs Consultant, State Farm Insurance Cos.

WALLING, Kevin R.

P.O. Box 231
Latrobe, PA 15650
Tel: (724) 539 - 5000
Fax:(724) 539 - 4710

Serves As:
• V. President and Chief Human Resources Officer, Kennametal Inc.

WALLS, Carol

P.O. Box 39
Newton, IA 50208-0039
cwalls@maytag.com
Tel: (641) 792 - 7000
Fax:(641) 787 - 8102

Serves As:
• Coordinator, Shareholder Relations, Maytag Corp.

WALLS, Patricia

750 E. Pratt St.
G&E Bldg., #700
Baltimore, MD 21202
Tel: (410) 234 - 6151
Fax:(410) 234 - 6858
TF: (888) 460 - 2002

Serves As:
• Manager, BGE Human Resources, (BGE), Constellation Energy

WALORSKI, Mitchell J.

905 West Blvd., North
Elkhart, IN 46514
Tel: (574) 293 - 7511
Fax:(574) 293 - 6146

Serves As:
• Director, Investor Relations, CTS Corp.

WALSH, Ann Marie

One NSTAR Way
Westwood, MA 02090
Tel: (617) 424 - 2000
Fax:(617) 424 - 2523

Serves As:
• NSTAR Foundation Contact, NSTAR

WALSH, Jack
1499 Post Rd.
Fairfield, CT 06824
jwalsh@imshealth.com
Tel: (203) 319 - 4700
Fax:(203) 319 - 4701

Serves As:
- V. President, Investor Relations, IMS Health, Inc.

WALSH, Jennifer
P.O. Box 34067
Seattle, WA 98124-1067
Tel: (206) 447 - 1575
Fax:(206) 682 - 9051

Serves As:
- Public Relations Specialist, Starbucks Corp.

WALSH, John F.
417Lackawanna Ave.
Scranton, PA 18503

Serves As:
- Director, Investor Relations, Southern Union Company

WALSH, Kimberly
77 Beale St.
San Francisco, CA 94105
Tel: (415) 973 - 0015
Fax:(415) 973 - 0951

Serves As:
- V. President, Communications, (Pacific Gas and Electric Co.), PG & E Corp.

WALSH, Matt
One Franklin Pkwy.
San Mateo, CA 94403-1906
mwalsh1@frk.com
Tel: (650) 312 - 2245
TF: (800) 342 - 5236

Serves As:
- Senior Coordinator, Public Relations, Franklin Templeton Investments

WALSH, Richard F.
45 William St., Third Floor
Wellesley Hills, MA 02481-4078
Tel: (781) 431 - 4122
Fax:(781) 431 - 4255

Serves As:
- Senior V. President, Human Resources, PerkinElmer, Inc.

WALSH, Richard J.
P.O. Box 593330
Orlando, FL 32859
rwalsh@darden.com
Tel: (407) 245 - 5366
Fax:(407) 245 - 5310

Serves As:
- Senior V. President, Corporate Affairs, Darden Restaurants, Inc.

Responsibilities include government affairs.

WALSH, Sarah J.
1500 K St. NW
Suite 650
Washington, DC 20005
Tel: (202) 715 - 1000
Fax:(202) 715 - 1001

Registered Federal Lobbyist.
Serves As:
- Federal Government Relations, GlaxoSmithKline Research and Development

WALSH, Stephen
1850 K St. NW
Suite 500
Washington, DC 20006-2213
stephen.walsh@carramerica.com
Tel: (202) 729 - 1764
Fax:(202) 729 - 1150
TF: (800) 417 - 2277

Serves As:
- Senior V. President, Capital Markets, CarrAmerica Realty Corp.

Responsibilities include investor relations.

WALSH, Susan M.
1401 I St. NW
Suite 600
Washington, DC 20005
Tel: (202) 336 - 7400
Fax:(202) 336 - 7515

Registered Federal Lobbyist.
Serves As:
- Representative, United Technologies Corp.

WALSH, Jr., William J.
80 Park Plaza
M/S T10C
Newark, NJ 07102-0570
william.walsh3@pseg.com
Tel: (973) 430 - 5763
Fax:(973) 297 - 1480

Serves As:
- Director, Corporate Responsibility, PSE&G

WALSTROM, Michele
P.O. Box 39
Newton, IA 50208-0039
mwalst@maytag.com
Tel: (641) 792 - 7000
Fax:(641) 787 - 8376

Serves As:
- Manager, Community Relations and Foundation, Maytag Corp.

WALTER, Clark
200 N. Milwaukee Ave.
Vernon Hills, IL 60061
cwalter@cdw.com
Tel: (847) 968 - 0728
Fax:(847) 465 - 3444
TF: (800) 800 - 4239

Serves As:
- Senior Program Manager, Investor Relations, CDW Corp.

WALTER, Dale N.
P.O. Box 5204
Norwalk, CT 06856-5204
dnwalter@archchemicals.com
Tel: (203) 229 - 3033
Fax:(203) 229 - 3213
TF: (877) 275 - 6973

Serves As:
- Manager, Corporate Communications, Arch Chemicals, Inc.

WALTER, Eileen M.
1201 S. Second St.
Milwaukee, WI 43204-2496
Tel: (414) 382 - 1548
Fax:(414) 382 - 1442

Serves As:
- Global Community Relations, Rockwell Automation

Responsibilities include corporate philanthropy.

WALTER, Robert D.
7000 Cardinal Pl.
Dublin, OH 43017
Tel: (614) 757 - 5000
Fax:(614) 757 - 6000
TF: (800) 234 - 8701

Serves As:
- Chairman and Chief Exec. Officer, Cardinal Health Inc.

WALTER, Susan J.
2190 N.W. 82nd St., Suite Three
Clive, IA 50325
susan.walter@aquila.com
Tel: (515) 270 - 6336
Fax:(515) 270 - 6384

Serves As:
- Director, Government Affairs-Iowa, Aquila, Inc.

WALTER, William G.
1735 Market St.
Philadelphia, PA 19103
Tel: (215) 299 - 6000

Serves As:
- Chairman, President and Chief Exec. Officer, FMC Corp.

WALTERMIRE, Thomas
33587 Walker Rd.
Avon Lake, OH 44093-0175
Tel: (440) 930 - 1000
Fax:(440) 930 - 1750

Serves As:
- President and Chief Exec. Officer, PolyOne Corp.

WALTERS, Beth A.
10560 Dr. Martin Luther King Jr. St. North
St. Petersburg, FL 33716
beth_walters@jabil.com
Tel: (727) 803 - 3349
Fax:(727) 579 - 8529

Serves As:
- V. President, Communications and Investor Relations, Jabil Circuit, Inc.

WALTERS, Gregory
1550 Crystal Dr.
Crystal Square 2, Suite 300
Arlington, VA 22202
Tel: (703) 413 - 5601
Fax:(703) 413 - 5636

Serves As:
- Representative, Lockheed Martin Corp.

WALTERS, Jim
P.O. Box 7706
Wichita, KS 67277-7706
Tel: (316) 517 - 1287
Fax:(316) 517 - 6640

Serves As:
- Senior V. President, Human Resources, Cessna Aircraft Co.

WALTERS, Peter
2300 Harmon Rd.
Auburn Hills, MI 48326-1714
Tel: (248) 340 - 1800
Fax:(248) 340 - 9988

Serves As:
- Group V. President; and PAC Treasurer, Guardian Industries Corp.

Responsibilities include corporate public affairs.

WALTERS, Thomas P.
600 S. Second St., Suite 101
Springfield, IL 62704
Tel: (217) 753 - 8050
Fax:(217) 753 - 3618

Serves As:
- Illinois Government Affairs Representative, Caterpillar Inc.

WALTON, Aaron
120 Fifth Ave. Pl.
Suite 3110
Pittsburgh, PA 15222
Tel: (412) 544 - 5439
Fax:(412) 544 - 8054

Serves As:
- Senior V. President, Corporate Affairs, Highmark Inc.

WALTON, Jerry W.
615 J.B. Hunt Corporate Dr.
P.O. Box 130
Lowell, AR 72745
jerry-walton@jbhunt.com
Tel: (479) 820 - 8120
Fax:(479) 820 - 8397
TF: (800) 643 - 3622

Serves As:
- Exec. V. President, Finance and Administration; and Chief Financial Officer, J. B. Hunt Transport Services, Inc.

Responsibilities include government affairs.

WALTON, Jon D.
1000 Six PPG Pl.
Pittsburgh, PA 15222-5479
jwalton@alleghenytechnologies.com
Tel: (412) 394 - 2800
Fax:(412) 394 - 3035

Serves As:
- Exec. V. President, Human Resources; Chief Legal and Compliance Officer; General Counsel; and Secretary, Allegheny Technologies Incorporated

Responsibilities include corporate philanthropy.

WALTON, Mia K.
14850 Conference Center Dr.
Chantilly, VA 20151
mia.walton@rolls-royce.com
Tel: (703) 621 - 2709
Fax:(703) 709 - 6086

Serves As:
- V. President, Corporate Communications, Rolls-Royce North America Inc.

WALTON, S. Robson
702 SW Eighth St.
M/S 0105
Bentonville, AR 72716
Tel: (479) 273 - 4000
Fax:(479) 273 - 4053

Serves As:
- Chairman of the Board, Wal-Mart Stores

WALTON, Susan
3700 W. Juneau Ave.
Milwaukee, WI 53208
Tel: (414) 342 - 4680
Fax:(414) 343 - 8230

Serves As:
- Director, Corporate Communications, Harley-Davidson Motor Company

WALTRIP, Robert L.
1929 Allen Pkwy.
Houston, TX 77019
Tel: (713) 522 - 5141
Fax:(713) 525 - 2800

Serves As:
- Chairman and Chief Exec. Officer, Service Corp. Internat'l

WAMBOLD, Richard L.
1900 W. Field Ct.
Lake Forest, IL 60045
rwambold@pactiv.com
Tel: (847) 482 - 2000
TF: (888) 828 - 2850

Serves As:
- Chairman and Chief Exec. Officer, Pactiv Corp.

WANG, Bill
5959 Las Colinas Blvd.
Irving, TX 75039-2298
Tel: (972) 444 - 1000
Fax:(972) 444 - 1350

Serves As:
- Manager, Investor Relations, Exxon Mobil Corp.

WANSTREET, Joanne
29400 Lakeland Blvd.
Wickliffe, OH 44092-2298
Tel: (440) 347 - 5253

Serves As:
- V. President, Global Communications, The Lubrizol Corp.

Responsibilities include investor relations.

WAPPEL, Paul
One Horace Mann Plaza
Springfield, IL 62715-0001
Tel: (217) 789 - 2500
Fax:(217) 788 - 5161

Serves As:
- Assistant V. President, Corporate Communications and Public Relations, Horace Mann Educators Corp.

WARD, Caleb
Two Democracy Center
6903 Rockledge Dr.
Bethesda, MD 20817-1818
Tel: (301) 564 - 3200
Fax:(301) 564 - 3201

Registered Federal Lobbyist.
Serves As:
- Government Relations Associate, USEC Inc.

WARD, Gregg
701 Pennsylvania Ave. NW
Suite 720
Washington, DC 20004
gregg.ward@siemens.com
Tel: (202) 434 - 4800
Fax:(202) 347 - 4015

Serves As:
- Senior V. President, Government Affairs, Siemens Corp.

WARD, John F. "Jack"
3330 Cumberland Blvd.
Suite 800
Atlanta, GA 30339
Tel: (678) 742 - 8000

Serves As:
- Chairman and Chief Exec. Officer, Russell Corp.

WARD, Jonathan P.
3250 Lacey Rd., Suite 600
Downers Grove, IL 60515
jonathan.ward@servicemaster.com
Tel: (630) 663 - 2000
Fax:(630) 663 - 2001

Serves As:
- Chairman and Chief Exec. Officer, The ServiceMaster Co.

WARD, Laysha
1000 Nicollet Mall
Minneapolis, MN 55403
community.relations@target.com
Tel: (612) 304 - 6073

Serves As:
- V. President, Community Relations, Target Corp.

WARD, Melissa
6820 LBJ Fwy.
Dallas, TX 75240
Tel: (972) 980 - 9917
Fax:(972) 770 - 5977

Serves As:
- Community Relations Manager, Brinker International Corporate Giving Program, Brinker Internat'l, Inc.

WARD, Michael J.
500 Water St.
Jacksonville, FL 32203
Tel: (904) 359 - 3200

Serves As:
- Chairman, President, and Chief Exec. Officer, CSX Corp.

WARD, Nancy K.
3135 Easton Tpk.
Bldg. E2E
Fairfield, CT 06431
nancy.ward@corporate.ge.com
Tel: (203) 921 - 2063
Fax:(203) 373 - 3131

Serves As:
- Manager, Government Relations, General Electric Co.

WARD, Paul
1515 Broadway
New York, NY 10036
Tel: (212) 258 - 7704
Fax:(212) 258 - 7705

Serves As:
- Senior V. President, Communications, (Nickelodeon/Nick at Nite), Viacom Inc./CBS Corp.

WARD, Stephen D.
1331 Pennsylvania Ave. NW
Suite 1300 North
Washington, DC 20004
stephen.ward@eds.com
Tel: (202) 637 - 6709
Fax:(202) 637 - 6759

Registered Federal Lobbyist.
Serves As:
- Director, Global Government Affairs, EDS Corp.

WARD, Wilbur
P.O. Box 26234
Richmond, VA 23260-6234
Tel: (804) 281 - 1000
Fax:(804) 281 - 1119

Serves As:
- Chairman of the Board, Southern States Cooperative

WARDE, Anne M.
P.O. Box 3100
Fullerton, CA 92834
amwarde@beckman.com
Tel: (714) 773 - 7655
Fax:(714) 773 - 7743
TF: (800) 742 - 2345

Serves As:
- Manager, Communications, Beckman Coulter, Inc.

WARFEL, Michael G.
1800 Center St.
Camp Hill, PA 17089
Tel: (717) 302 - 3979
Fax:(717) 302 - 3969

Registered Federal Lobbyist.
Serves As:
- V. President, Government Affairs, (Clarity Vision, Inc., Highmark Life and Casualty Group, Inc., United Concordia Cos., Inc.), Highmark Inc.

WARLICK-JARVIE, Lois
P.O. Box 20670
Rochester, NY 14602-0670
Tel: (585) 264 - 3136
Fax:(585) 383 - 1281
TF: (800) 999 - 5044

Serves As:
- V. President, Human Resources, Birds Eye Foods

WARMENHOVEN, Daniel J.
495 E. Java Dr.
Sunnyvale, CA 94089
dwarmenhoven@netapp.com
Tel: (408) 822 - 6000
Fax:(408) 822 - 4501

Serves As:
- Chief Exec. Officer, Network Appliance, Inc.

WARNER, Ann D.
1015 15th St. NW
Suite 700
Washington, DC 20005-2605
Tel: (202) 828 - 5200
Fax:(202) 785 - 2645

Registered Federal Lobbyist.
Serves As:
- V. President, Government Programs, (Bechtel Systems and Infrastructure), Bechtel Group, Inc.

WARNER, Gail K.
Four Colesium Center
2730 W. Tyvola Rd.
Charlotte, NC 28217
gail.warner@goodrich.com
Tel: (704) 423 - 7048
Fax:(704) 423 - 7127

Serves As:
- Director, Media Relations, Goodrich Corporation

WARNER, John R.
P.O. Box 5928
Greenville, SC 29606
investorrelations@kamet.com
Tel: (864) 963 - 6640
Fax:(864) 963 - 6322

Serves As:
- V. President, Strategy and Communications, KEMET Corp.

WARNER, Sherri L.
2600 Chemed Center
255 E. Fifth St.
Cincinnati, OH 45202-4726
Tel: (513) 762 - 6900
Fax:(513) 762 - 6919
TF: (800) 438 - 7686

Serves As:
- Director, Investor Relations, The Chemed Corporation

Responsibilities include media relations.

WARNER, William H.
1301 K St. NW
Suite 1200
Washington, DC 20005
Tel: (202) 515 - 5000

Registered Federal Lobbyist.
Serves As:
- Representative, Internat'l Business Machines Corp. (IBM)

WARNOCK, Dr. John E.
345 Park Ave.
San Jose, CA 95110-2704
Tel: (408) 536 - 6000
Fax:(408) 537 - 6000

Serves As:
- Co-Chairman of the Board, Adobe Systems Inc.

WARNOCK, Lloyd "Aldie"
1155 Perimeter Center West
Atlanta, GA 30338
Tel: (678) 579 - 5145
Fax:(678) 579 - 5001

Serves As:
- Senior V. President, Governmental and Regulatory Affairs, Mirant Corp.

WARR, David E.
655 15th St. NW
Suite 300
Washington, DC 20005
david.warr@bms.com
Tel: (202) 783 - 0900
Fax:(202) 783 - 2308

Registered Federal Lobbyist.
Serves As:
- Director, International Government Affairs, Bristol-Myers Squibb Co.

WARRELL, Andrew
5959 Las Colinas Blvd.
Irving, TX 75039-2298
Tel: (972) 444 - 1000
Fax:(972) 444 - 1350

Serves As:
- Manager, Investor Relations, Exxon Mobil Corp.

WARREN, Bill
One Computer Associates Plaza
Islandia, NY 11749
william.warren@ca.com
Tel: (631) 342 - 6344
Fax:(631) 342 - 4295
TF: (800) 225 - 5224

Serves As:
- Senior V. President, Executive Communications and Public Affairs, Computer Associates Internat'l, Inc.

WARREN, Denise M.
One First American Way
Santa Ana, CA 92707
dwarren@firstam.com
Tel: (714) 800 - 3915
Fax:(714) 800 - 4790

Serves As:
- V. President and Director, Investor Relations, The First American Corp.

WARREN, Diane D.
200 E. Basse Rd.
San Antonio, TX 78209
dianedwarren@clearchannel.com
Tel: (210) 822 - 2828
Fax:(210) 822 - 2299

Serves As:
- Senior V. President, Corporate Affairs, Clear Channel Communications

WARREN, Gregory A.
13858 Bainwick Dr. NW
Pickerington, OH 43147
warreng@wyeth.com
Tel: (740) 927 - 3521
Fax:(740) 927 - 3591

Serves As:
- Director, State Government Affairs, Wyeth Pharmaceuticals

WARREN, Karen A.
P.O. Box 1059
Pawtucket, RI 02862
kwarren@hasbro.com
Tel: (401) 727 - 5401
Fax:(401) 431 - 8535

Serves As:
- Senior V. President, Investor Relations, Hasbro Inc.

WARREN, Mitch
60 Massachusetts Ave. NE
Washington, DC 20002
Tel: (202) 906 - 3000
Fax:(202) 906 - 3865

Serves As:
- Senior Director, National State Relations, Amtrak

WARREN, Jr., William Michael
605 Richard Arrington Jr. Blvd. North
Birmingham, AL 35203-2707
mwarren@energen.com
Tel: (205) 326 - 8166
Fax:(205) 322 - 6895
TF: (800) 654 - 3206

Serves As:
- Chairman and Chief Exec. Officer, Energen Corp.

WARSCHAUER, Bonnie
P.O. Box 32070
Louisville, KY 40232
Tel: (502) 874 - 8300

Serves As:
- Director, Public Relations, (KFC), YUM! Brands, Inc.

WARWICK, Peter
610 Opperman Dr.
Eagan, MN 55123-1340
Tel: (651) 687 - 7000
Fax:(651) 687 - 7302
TF: (800) 328 - 9352

Serves As:
- President and Chief Exec. Officer, Thomson West

WASHBURN, Barbara J.
1660 L St. NW
Fourth Floor
Washington, DC 20036
Tel: (202) 775 - 5026
Fax:(202) 775 - 5097

Registered Federal Lobbyist.
Serves As:
- Director, Legislative and Regulatory Affairs/Tax, General Motors Corp.

WASHINGTON, Dennis R.
P.O. Box 73
Boise, ID 83729
Tel: (208) 386 - 5000
Fax:(208) 386 - 7186

Serves As:
- Chairman of the Board, Washington Group Internat'l

WASHINGTON, Greg J.
1401 I St. NW
Suite 1200
Washington, DC 20005-2225
Tel: (202) 408 - 5800
Fax:(202) 408 - 5845

Registered Federal Lobbyist.
Serves As:
- Manager, Federal Relations, Chevron Corp.

WASHINGTON, Jr., Lawrence J.
2030 Dow Center
Midland, MI 48674-0001
Tel: (989) 636 - 1000

Serves As:
- Corporate V. President, Environment, Health and Safety, Human Resources and Public Affairs, The Dow Chemical Company

WASHINGTON, Lisa
2100 Logic Dr.
San Jose, CA 95124-3400
lisa.washington@xilinx.com
Tel: (408) 626 - 6272

Serves As:
- Director, WW Public Relations, Xilinx, Inc.

WASHINGTON, Shaunise
101 Constitution Ave. NW
Suite 400 West
Washington, DC 20001
shaunise.washington@altria.com
Tel: (202) 354 - 1500
Fax:(202) 354 - 1505

Serves As:
- V. President, Government Affairs Policy Outreach, Altria Group, Inc.
- Treasurer, Kraft Foods Global Inc. PAC, Kraft Foods, Inc.

WASHKEWICZ, Don
6035 Parkland Blvd.
Cleveland, OH 44124-4141
Tel: (216) 896 - 3000
Fax:(216) 896 - 4000
TF: (800) 272 - 7537

Serves As:
- President and Chief Exec. Officer, Parker Hannifin Corp.

WASSERMAN, David S.
1025 W. NASA Blvd.
Melbourne, FL 32919-0001
dwasserman@harris.com
Tel: (321) 727 - 9194
Fax:(321) 727 - 9344
TF: (800) 442 - 7747

Serves As:
- V. President and Treasurer; PAC Treasurer, Harris Corp.

Responsibilities include regulatory affairs.

WATANABE, Kenichi
Two World Financial Center
Building B
New York, NY 10028-1198
Tel: (212) 667 - 9300
Fax:(212) 667 - 1058

Serves As:
- Exec. V. President, Nomura Securities Internat'l, Inc.

Responsibilities include investor relations.

WATERS, Beth
Discovery Dr.
Swiftwater, PA 18370
Tel: (570) 839 - 7187
Fax:(570) 839 - 7235

Serves As:
- Senior V. President, Communications, Sanofi Pasteur, Inc.

WATJEN, Thomas R.
One Fountain Square
Chattanooga, TN 37402
twatjen@unumprovident.com
Tel: (423) 294 - 6866
Fax:(423) 294 - 3194

Serves As:
- President and Chief Exec. Officer, UnumProvident Corp.

WATKINS, Carole S.
7000 Cardinal Pl.
Dublin, OH 43017
Tel: (614) 757 - 5000
Fax:(614) 757 - 6000
TF: (800) 234 - 8701

Serves As:
- Exec. V. President, Human Resources, Cardinal Health Inc.

WATKINS, Ian J.
4955 Orange Dr.
Davie, FL 33314
Tel: (954) 584 - 0300
Fax:(954) 792 - 1034
TF: (800) 621 - 7143

Serves As:
- Senior V. President, Human Resources, Andrx Corp.

WATKINS, James P. "Jim"
Five Giralda Farms
Madison, NJ 07940
watkinj@wyeth.com
Tel: (973) 660 - 5027

Serves As:
- Director, State Government Affairs, Wyeth
- Associate Director, State Government Affairs, Wyeth Pharmaceuticals

WATKINS, Katherine R.
P.O. Box 511
Kingsport, TN 37662-5075
Tel: (423) 229 - 3078
Fax:(423) 229 - 1525
TF: (800) 327 - 8626

Serves As:
- Manager, Marketing Communications, Eastman Chemical Co.

WATKINS, Wendy A.
40 Fountain Plaza
Buffalo, NY 14202
wwatkins@dncinc.com
Tel: (716) 858 - 5092
Fax:(716) 858 - 5125

Serves As:
- V. President, Corporate Communications and Public Relations, Delaware North Companies

WATKINS, William
P.O. Box 66360
Scotts Valley, CA 95067-0360
Tel: (831) 438 - 6550
Fax:(831) 438 - 0558

Serves As:
- Chief Exec. Officer, Seagate Technology

WATKINS, Wynfred C.
6501 Legacy Dr.
Plano, TX 75024-3698
Tel: (972) 431 - 1972
Fax:(972) 431 - 1362
TF: (800) 222 - 6161

Serves As:
- Senior V. President and Director, Communications and Public Affairs, J. C. Penney Co., Inc.

WATSON, Allison
P.O. Box 834
Seattle, WA 98101
Tel: (206) 461 - 2000
Fax:(206) 554 - 4807
TF: (800) 756 - 8000

Registered Federal Lobbyist.
Serves As:
- Representative, Washington Mutual, Inc.

WATSON, Anne N.
One E. Fourth St.
Cincinnati, OH 45202
Tel: (513) 579 - 6652
Fax:(513) 579 - 2580

Serves As:
- V. President, Investor Relations, (Great American Insurance Co.), American Financial Group Inc.

WATSON, Craig
11270 W. Park Place
Milwaukee, WI 53224-9510
cwatson@aosmith.com
Tel: (414) 359 - 4009
Fax:(414) 359 - 4198

Serves As:
- Director, Investor Relations, A. O. Smith Corp.

WATSON, Craig G.
1390 Enclave Pkwy.
Houston, TX 77077-2099
Tel: (281) 584 - 1390
Fax:(281) 584 - 2721

Serves As:
- V. President, Quality Assurance, Sysco Corp.

WATSON, Don W.
645 E. Missouri Ave., Suite 400
Phoenix, AZ 85012
Tel: (602) 631 - 7224
Fax:(602) 631 - 7321

Serves As:
- Senior V. President and Chief Financial Officer, CSK Auto, Inc.

Responsibilities include investor relations.

WATSON, Ellen
8111 Lyndale Ave. South
Bloomington, MN 55420-1196
Tel: (952) 888 - 8801
Fax:(952) 887 - 7961

Serves As:
- Foundation Coordinator, The Toro Co.

WATSON, Karen
One GEICO Plaza
Washington, DC 20076
Tel: (301) 986 - 3000
Ext: 2387
Fax:(301) 986 - 2068

Serves As:
- Administrator, GEICO Philanthropic Foundation, GEICO Corp.

WATSON, Karen E.
1233 20th St., NW
Suite 701
Washington, DC 20036
Tel: (202) 293 - 0981
Fax:(202) 293 - 0984

Registered Federal Lobbyist.
Serves As:
- Director, Government Relations, EchoStar Communications Corp.

WATSON, Noel G.
1111 S. Arroyo Pkwy.
P.O. Box 7084
Pasadena, CA 91105
Tel: (626) 578 - 6801
Fax:(626) 578 - 6875

Serves As:
- Chairman and Chief Exec. Officer, Jacobs Engineering Group Inc.

WATSON, Steven L.
Three Lincoln Center
5430 LBJ Fwy., Suite 1700
Dallas, TX 75240-2697
Tel: (972) 233 - 1700
Fax:(972) 448 - 1445

Serves As:
- President and Chief Exec. Officer, Valhi, Inc.

WATSON, Vicki
2000 Purchase St.
Purchase, NY 10577-2509
Tel: (914) 249 - 2000
Fax:(914) 249 - 4206

Serves As:
- Cordinator, Global Communications, MasterCard Internat'l

WATSON, Weldon L.
P.O. Box 871
Tulsa, OK 74102-0871
wwatson@oneok.com
Tel: (918) 588 - 7158
Fax:(918) 588 - 7971

Serves As:
- V. President, Investor Relations and Communications, ONEOK, Inc.

WATSON, Wendy
P.O. Box 757
Carthage, MO 64836-0757
Tel: (417) 358 - 8131

Serves As:
- Contact, Leggett and Platt Political Involvement Fund, Leggett & Platt, Inc.

WATT, Linda M.
141 N. Civic Dr.
Walnut Creek, CA 94596
lwatt@longs.com
Tel: (925) 937 - 1170
Fax:(925) 210 - 6886

Serves As:
- Senior V. President, Human Resources, Longs Drug Stores Corp.

WATTS, David H.
P.O. Box 50085
Watsonville, CA 95077-5085
Tel: (831) 724 - 1011
Fax:(831) 722 - 9657
TF: (800) 482 - 1518

Serves As:
- Chairman of the Board, Granite Construction Inc.

WAUGH, Seth H.
60 Wall St. Tel: (212) 469 - 8000
New York, NY 10005
Serves As:
• President and Chief Exec. Officer, Deutsche Banc Alex.Brown

WAUN DE RESTREPO, Susan
P.O. Box 300 Tel: (313) 556 - 5000
Detroit, MI 48265-1000 Fax:(248) 696 - 7300
susan.waun@gm.com
Serves As:
• Staff Assistant, Stockholder Relations, General Motors Corp.

WAYMAN, Robert P.
3000 Hanover St. Tel: (650) 857 - 1501
Palo Alto, CA 94304 Fax:(650) 857 - 5518
TF: (800) 752 - 0900
Serves As:
• Chief Financial Officer, Hewlett-Packard Co.

WAZ, Jr., Joseph W.
1500 Market St. Tel: (215) 981 - 7607
Philadelphia, PA 19102 Fax:(215) 981 - 7712
jww@comcast.com
Registered Federal Lobbyist.
Serves As:
• V. President, External Affairs and Public Policy Counsel, Comcast Corporation
Responsibilities include corporate contributions and government affairs.

WEATHERHOLTZ, Karen D.
18 Loveton Circle Tel: (410) 771 - 7193
Sparks, MD 21152-6000 Fax:(410) 771 - 7462
Serves As:
• Senior V. President, Human Resources, McCormick & Company, Inc.

WEATHERS, Frank
304 S. Jackson, Third Floor Tel: (517) 780 - 3846
Jackson, MI 49201 Fax:(517) 780 - 3847
Serves As:
• Director, External Affairs, SBC Michigan

WEAVER, Donna B.
120 W. 45th St. Tel: (212) 329 - 8072
Floor 27 Fax:(212) 329 - 8073
New York, NY 10036
donna.weaver@kellwood.com
Serves As:
• V. President, Corporate Communications, Kellwood Co.

WEAVER, Frank C.
1200 Wilson Blvd. Tel: (703) 465 - 3448
Arlington, VA 22209-2305
Serves As:
• Director, Telecommunications Policy, The Boeing Co.

WEAVER, John
37 N. Valley Rd., Bldg. Four Tel: (610) 647 - 2121
P.O. Box 1764 Fax:(610) 323 - 9337
Paoli, PA 19301 TF: (800) 473 - 1286
john.weaver@ametek.com
Serves As:
• V. President, Human Resources, Ametek, Inc.

WEAVER, Laura
1445 Ross at Field Tel: (214) 978 - 8000
Suite 1400 Fax:(214) 978 - 8888
Dallas, TX 75202-2785
Serves As:
• V. President, Human Resources, Hunt Oil Co.

WEAVER, Philip G.
P.O. Box 550 Tel: (419) 423 - 1321
Findlay, OH 45839-0550 Fax:(419) 424 - 4212
pgweaver@coopertire.com
Serves As:
• V. President and Chief Financial Officer, Cooper Tire & Rubber Company
Responsibilities include corporate philanthropy.

WEBB, Clif
1007 Market St. Tel: (302) 774 - 4005
D-11028-1 Fax:(302) 774 - 9560
Wilmington, DE 19898 TF: (800) 441 - 7515
r-clifton.webb@usa.dupont.com
Serves As:
• Director, Corporate Media Relations, DuPont

WEBB, Diane
4000 Allen Rd., Room 201 Tel: (734) 266 - 4208
Allen Park, MI 48101 Fax:(734) 523 - 2589
Serves As:
• Manager, External Affairs, SBC Michigan

WEBB, Keri
2902 Enterprise Dr. Tel: (765) 778 - 6523
Anderson, IN 46013 Fax:(765) 778 - 6404
TF: (800) 372 - 5131
Serves As:
• Investor Relations Contact, Delco Remy Internat'l Inc.

WEBB, Vincent
1717 Arch St. Tel: (215) 636 - 1240
35th Floor Fax:(215) 569 - 1452
Philadelphia, PA 19103-2768
vince.webb@cdicorp.com
Serves As:
• V. President, Corporate Communications and Marketing, CDI Corp.
Responsibilities include investor relations.

WEBB, Wendy
500 S. Buena Vista St. Tel: (818) 560 - 5758
Burbank, CA 91521 Fax:(818) 560 - 1930
Serves As:
• Senior V. President, Investor Relations, The Walt Disney Company

WEBER, Dwight E.
4650 SW Macadam Ave. Tel: (503) 417 - 4855
Suite 440 Fax:(503) 417 - 4817
Portland, OR 97239-4254
Serves As:
• Director, Communications, Precision Castparts Corp.
Responsibilities include shareholder relations.

WEBER, Greg
1155 Perimeter Center West Tel: (678) 579 - 5000
Atlanta, GA 30338 Fax:(678) 579 - 5001
Serves As:
• Treasurer, Mirant Corp. PAC, Mirant Corp.

WEBER, Gregory M.
1901 Market St. Tel: (215) 636 - 9559
38th Floor Fax:(215) 241 - 0403
Philadelphia, PA 19103-1480 TF: (800) 555 - 1514
gregory.weber@ibx.com
Serves As:
• Communications Specialist, Independence Blue Cross (Pennsylvania)

WEBER, James F.
One Seagate Tel: (419) 247 - 2700
Toledo, OH 43666 Fax:(419) 247 - 1218
james.weber@us.o-i.com
Serves As:
• Director, Investor Relations, Owens-Illinois, Inc.
Responsibilities include investor relations.

WEBER, John H.
3402 E. University Dr. Tel: (602) 794 - 9600
Phoenix, AZ 85034 Fax:(602) 794 - 9601
Serves As:
• President and Chief Exec. Officer, Eagle-Picher Industries, Inc.

WEBER, Mark R.
5725 Delphi Dr. Tel: (248) 813 - 2000
Troy, MI 48098-2815 Fax:(248) 813 - 2670
Serves As:
• Exec. V. President, Operations, Human Resources Management and Corporate Affairs, Delphi Corp.

WEBER-MILLSTEIN, Karen
P.O. Box 34325 Tel: (425) 889 - 3475
Seattle, WA 98124-1325 Fax:(425) 889 - 4138
Serves As:
• Manager, Corporate Communications, Univar USA, Inc.

WEBSTER, David
Three Ravinia Dr., Suite 100 Tel: (770) 604 - 2000
Atlanta, GA 30346
Serves As:
• Chairman of the Board, InterContinental Hotels Group

WEBSTER, Scott
5929 College Ave. Tel: (510) 450 - 4545
Oakland, CA 94618
cswebste@dreyers.com
Serves As:
• Assistant Treasurer, Investor Relations, Dreyer's Grand Ice Cream Holdings, Inc.

WEDGE, Michael T.
One Mercer Rd. Tel: (508) 651 - 7400
Natick, MA 01760 Fax:(508) 651 - 6167
TF: (800) 257 - 2582
Serves As:
• President and Chief Exec. Officer, BJ's Wholesale Club, Inc.

WEEDITZ, Paul
5555 San Felipe Rd.
Houston, TX 77056
peweeditz@marathonoil.com
Tel: (713) 296 - 3910
Fax:(713) 296 - 2952

Serves As:
- Director, External Communications, Marathon Oil Corp.

WEEKLEY, Daniel A.
Rope Ferry Rd.
Waterford, CT 06385
daniel_a_weekley@dom.com
Tel: (860) 444 - 5271
TF: (800) 552 - 4034

Serves As:
- Director, State and Local Affairs, Dominion Resources, Inc.

WEEKS, Wendell P.
One Riverfront Plaza
Corning, NY 14831-0001
Tel: (607) 974 - 9000
Fax:(607) 974 - 8551

Serves As:
- President and Chief Exec. Officer, Corning Incorporated

WEGMANN, Timothy
901 Marquette Ave., # 2300
Minneapolis, MN 55402

Serves As:
- Treasurer, NRG Energy Inc. PAC, Xcel Energy, Inc.

WEHNER, Hilary S.
420 Seventh St. NW
Suite 918
Washington, DC 20004
Tel: (202) 628 - 6515
Fax:(202) 628 - 6947

Registered Federal Lobbyist.
Serves As:
- Manager, Federal Government Affairs, Consolidated Edison Co. of New York, Inc.

WEHRMEISTER, Charles J.
Three Commercial Pl.
Norfolk, VA 23510-2191
Tel: (757) 629 - 2600
Fax:(757) 629 - 2822

Serves As:
- V. President, Safety and Environmental, Norfolk Southern Corp.

WEICKER, Scot B.
100 W. Putnam Ave.
Greenwich, CT 06830
Tel: (203) 622 - 3282
Fax:(203) 863 - 7259

Serves As:
- Director, Corporate Contributions and Events, UST Inc.

WEIDENKOPF, Thomas W.
101 Columbia Rd.
Morristown, NJ 07962-4658
Tel: (973) 455 - 2000
Fax:(973) 455 - 4807

Serves As:
- Senior V. President, Human Resources and Communications, Honeywell Internat'l, Inc.

WEIDERHOLT, James R.
8155 T & B Blvd.
Memphis, TN 38125
Tel: (901) 252 - 5000

Serves As:
- V. President, Communications, Thomas & Betts Corp.

WEIDMAN, David N.
1601 W. LBJ Fwy.
Dallas, TX 75234
Tel: (972) 443 - 4000

Serves As:
- President and Chief Exec. Officer, Celanese

WEIDMAN, Sheila
P.O. Box 105605
Atlanta, GA 30348
Tel: (404) 652 - 4000
Fax:(404) 654 - 4789
TF: (800) 519 - 3111

Serves As:
- V. President, Corporate Communications and Corporate Marketing, Georgia-Pacific Corp.

WEIDNER, Robert K.
1101 30th St. NW
Suite 200
Washington, DC 20007
Tel: (202) 342 - 9240
Fax:(202) 293 - 3484

Serves As:
- Senior DC Office Exec., Questar Corporation

WEIDNER, Tim J.
Eaton Center
1111 Superior Ave.
Cleveland, OH 44114-2584
TimWeidner@eaton.com
Tel: (216) 523 - 4744
Fax:(216) 479 - 7080

Serves As:
- Manager, Digital Communications, Eaton Corp.

WEIGHT, Brian H.
6501 Legacy Dr.
Plano, TX 75024-3698
Tel: (972) 431 - 1000
Fax:(972) 431 - 1362
TF: (800) 222 - 6161

Serves As:
- PAC Treasurer, J. C. Penney Co., Inc.

WEIHOFF, John P.
8100 Mitchell Rd.
Eden Prairie, MN 55344
Tel: (952) 937 - 8500
Fax:(952) 937 - 6740

Serves As:
- Chief Exec. Officer, C.H. Robinson Worldwide, Inc.

WEILL, Sanford I.
399 Park Ave.
New York, NY 10043
Tel: (212) 559 - 1000
Fax:(212) 793 - 3946
TF: (800) 285 - 3000

Serves As:
- Chairman of the Board, Citigroup, Inc.

WEIMAN, Lori
One MedImmune Way
Gaithersburg, MD 20878
weimanl@medimmune.com
Tel: (301) 398 - 0000
Fax:(301) 398 - 9000
TF: (877) 633 - 4411

Serves As:
- V. President, Corporate Communications, MedImmune, Inc.

Responsibilities include investor relations.

WEINBACH, Arthur F.
One ADP Blvd.
Roseland, NJ 07068-1728
arthur_weinbach@adp.com
Tel: (973) 974 - 5000
TF: (800) 225 - 5237

Serves As:
- Chairman and Chief Exec. Officer, Automatic Data Processing, Inc.

WEINBACH, Lawrence A.
Unisys Way
Blue Bell, PA 19424
lawrence.weinbach@unisys.com
Tel: (215) 986 - 4011
Fax:(215) 986 - 6850

Serves As:
- Chairman of the Board, Unisys Corp.

WEINBERG, David
228 Manhattan Beach Blvd.
Manhattan Beach, CA 90266
Tel: (310) 318 - 3100

Serves As:
- Exec. V. President and Chief Financial Officer, Skechers U.S.A., Inc.

Responsibilities include investor relations.

WEINBERG, Tom
601 Hawaii St.
El Segundo, CA 90245
Tel: (202) 393 - 4060

Serves As:
- PAC Treasurer, DaVita, Inc.

WEINBERGER, Caspar
60 Fifth Ave.
New York, NY 10010
Tel: (212) 620 - 2200
Fax:(212) 620 - 2245

Serves As:
- Chairman of the Board, Forbes, Inc.

WEINBERGER, Robert A.
700 13th St. NW
Suite 700
Washington, DC 20005-5922
rweinberger@hrblock.com
Tel: (202) 508 - 6364
Fax:(202) 508 - 6330

Registered Federal Lobbyist.
Serves As:
- V. President, Government Relations, H & R Block, Inc.

WEINE, Ken
251 W. 57th St.
22nd Floor
New York, NY 10019
Tel: (212) 445 - 4000
Fax:(212) 445 - 4757
TF: (800) 631 - 1040

Serves As:
- Director, Corporate Communications, Newsweek, Inc.

WEINER, Faith
P.O. Box 55888
Boston, MA 02205-5888
Tel: (781) 380 - 8000
Fax:(781) 770 - 6416
TF: (800) 767 - 7772

Serves As:
- Senior Director, Government and Public Affairs, The Stop & Shop Supermarket Co.

WEINER, Glen
730 Third Ave.
New York, NY 10017-3206
gweiner@tiaa-cref.org
Tel: (212) 490 - 9000
Ext: 5986
Fax:(212) 916 - 5952

Serves As:
- Media Contact, TIAA/CREF

WEINER, Robert
4345 Southpoint Blvd.
Jacksonville, FL 32216
Tel: (904) 332 - 3000

Serves As:
- V. President, Investor Relations, PSS World Medical, Inc.

WEINSTEIN, David
82 Devonshire St.
Boston, MA 02109-3614
Tel: (617) 563 - 7000
Fax:(617) 476 - 6150

Serves As:
- Chief Administrator, FMR Corp.

Responsibilities include government relations.

WEINSTEIN, Elaine
One MetroTech Center
Brooklyn, NY 11201
Tel: (718) 403 - 2000
Fax:(718) 488 - 1763

Serves As:
- Senior V. President, Human Resources and Chief Diversity Officer, KeySpan Corp.

WEINSTEIN, Dr. Martin
200 Park Ave.
New York, NY 10166
Tel: (212) 986 - 5500
Fax:(212) 370 - 1969

Serves As:
- V. Chairman and Chief Exec. Officer, Sequa Corp.

WEINSTEIN, Michael
120 Fifth Ave. Pl.
Suite 1933
Pittsburgh, PA 15222
Tel: (412) 544 - 7903
Fax:(412) 544 - 5318

Serves As:
- Senior Media and Communications Consultant, Highmark Inc.

WEINSTEIN, Warren
555 12th St. NW
Suite 640
Washington, DC 20004-2505
Tel: (202) 393 - 3075
Fax:(202) 393 - 1497

Serves As:
- Manager, Federal Affairs, Edison Internat'l

WEIR, Jeff
P.O. Box 58090
M/S G1-124
Santa Clara, CA 95052-8090
jeff.weir@nsc.com
Tel: (408) 721 - 5199
Fax:(408) 739 - 9803

Serves As:
- Director, Worldwide Public Relations, Nat'l Semiconductor Corp.

WEIRTZ, Paul
150 E. Gay St.
Suite 4A
Columbus, OH 43215
Tel: (614) 223 - 4145
Fax:(614) 223 - 4017

Serves As:
- Senior Director, Government Affairs, SBC Ohio

WEIS, Robert F.
P.O. Box 471
Sunbury, PA 17801
Tel: (570) 286 - 4571
Fax:(570) 286 - 3286

Serves As:
- Chairman of the Board, Weis Markets, Inc.

WEISGALL, Jonathan M.
1200 New Hampshire Ave. NW
Suite 300
Washington, DC 20036
jmweisgall@midamerican.com
Tel: (202) 828 - 1378
Fax:(202) 828 - 1380

Serves As:
- V. President, Legislative Affairs, MidAmerican Energy Holdings Co.

WEISS, Alison B.
601 Pennsylvania Ave., NW
Suite 420, S. Bldg.
Washington, DC 20004
Tel: (202) 737 - 0440
Fax:(202) 628 - 2313

Registered Federal Lobbyist.
Serves As:
- Director, Government Relations, MassMutual Financial Group

WEISS, Deborah H.
1101 Third St. South
Minneapolis, MN 55415
dweiss@valspar.com
Tel: (612) 375 - 7302
Fax:(612) 375 - 7723

Serves As:
- Director, Public Relations, Valspar Corp.

WEISS, Kathleen
P.O. Box 199000
Dallas, TX 75219-9000
Tel: (214) 981 - 5000
Fax:(214) 981 - 6859

Serves As:
- Director, Government and Public Affairs, Centex Corporation

WEISS, Leven C.
1000 Chrysler Dr.
CIMS 485-10-95
Auburn Hills, MI 48326-2766
Tel: (248) 512 - 3360
Fax:(248) 512 - 3919
TF: (800) 992 - 1997

Serves As:
- Senior Manager, Civic and Community Relations, DaimlerChrysler Corp.

WEISS, Morry
One American Rd.
Cleveland, OH 44144-2398
Tel: (216) 252 - 7300
Fax:(216) 252 - 6778

Serves As:
- Chairman of the Board, American Greetings Corp.

WEISS, Steven H.
1221 Ave. of the Americas
47th Floor
New York, NY 10020-1095
weissh@mcgraw-hill.com
Tel: (212) 512 - 2247
Fax:(212) 512 - 2507

Serves As:
- V. President, Corporate Communications, The McGraw-Hill Companies, Inc.

WEISS, Zev
One American Rd.
Cleveland, OH 44144-2398
Tel: (216) 252 - 7300
Fax:(216) 252 - 6778

Serves As:
- Chief Exec. Officer, American Greetings Corp.

WEISSER, Alberto
50 Main St.
Sixth Floor
White Plains, NY 10606-1901
Tel: (914) 684 - 2800

Serves As:
- Chairman and Chief Exec. Officer, Bunge Ltd.

WEISZ, Terry M.
One Marriott Dr.
Dept. 93527
Washington, DC 20058
terry.weisz@Marriott.com
Tel: (301) 380 - 1033
Fax:(301) 380 - 5764

Serves As:
- V. President, Internal Communications, Marriott Internat'l, Inc.

WEITMAN, Gary
435 N. Michigan Ave.
Chicago, IL 60611
gweitman@tribune.com
Tel: (312) 222 - 3394
Fax:(312) 222 - 1573

Serves As:
- V. President, Communications, Tribune Co.

WEITMAN, Jr., Warren
1334 York Ave.
New York, NY 10021
Tel: (212) 606 - 7000
Fax:(212) 606 - 7107

Serves As:
- Chairman of the Board, Sotheby's Holdings, Inc.

WELCH, Jr., James S.
850 Dixie Hwy.
Louisville, KY 40210
Tel: (502) 774 - 7351
Fax:(502) 774 - 7185

Serves As:
- V. Chairman, Strategy and Human Resources, Brown-Forman Corp.

WELCH, John F.
1350 I St. NW
Suite 400
Washington, DC 20005-3306
Tel: (202) 371 - 6900
Fax:(202) 842 - 3578

Registered Federal Lobbyist.
Serves As:
- V. President and Director, Global EME Government Relations, Motorola, Inc.

WELCH, Kimberly A.
One Village Dr.
Van Buren Township, MI 48111
kwelch5@visteon.com
Tel: (313) 755 - 3537
Fax:(313) 722 - 1658
TF: (800) VIS - TEON

Serves As:
- V. President, Corporate Communications, Visteon Corp.

WELCH, Margaret G.
One N. Jefferson Ave.
St. Louis, MO 63103
Tel: (314) 955 - 5912
Fax:(314) 955 - 5547
TF: (877) 835 - 7877

Serves As:
- Director, Public Relations, A. G. Edwards, Inc.

WELCH, Nicholas
1401 I St. NW, Suite 1030
Washington, DC 20005
nicholas.welch@shell.com
Tel: (202) 466 - 1416
Fax:(202) 466 - 1498

Serves As:
• Advisor, International Relations, Shell Oil Co.

WELDING, Robert D.
1415 W. 22nd St.
Suite 1100
Oak Brook, IL 60523
Tel: (630) 954 - 2000

Serves As:
• President and Chief Exec. Officer, Federal Signal Corp.

WELDON, Amy
7601 Penn Ave. South
Richfield, MN 55423
amy.weldon@bestbuy.com
Tel: (612) 291 - 1000
Fax:(612) 292 - 4001

Serves As:
• Public Affairs Specialist, Best Buy Co., Inc.

WELDON, Dennis
8005 SW Boeckman Rd.
Wilsonville, OR 97070-7777
dennis-weldon@mentor.com
Tel: (503) 685 - 1462
Fax:(503) 685 - 7704
TF: (800) 547 - 3000

Serves As:
• V. President, Investor Relations, Mentor Graphics Corp.

WELDON, William C.
One Johnson & Johnson Plaza
New Brunswick, NJ 08933-7204
Tel: (732) 524 - 0400
Fax:(732) 524 - 5848
TF: (800) 635 - 6789

Serves As:
• Chairman and Chief Exec. Officer, Johnson & Johnson

WELLER, Joe
800 N. Brand Blvd.
Glendale, CA 91203
joe.weller@us.nestle.com
Tel: (818) 549 - 6000
Fax:(818) 549 - 6952
TF: (800) 225 - 2270

Serves As:
• Chairman and Chief Exec. Officer, Nestle USA, Inc.

WELLER, Mary
1800 N. Point Dr.
Stevens Point, WI 54481
Tel: (715) 346 - 6000
Fax:(715) 346 - 6363

Serves As:
• Director, Advertising and Promotions, Sentry Insurance
Responsibilities include public affairs.

WELLING, Brad G.
1399 New York Ave. NW
Suite 900
Washington, DC 20005
Tel: (202) 585 - 5800
Fax:(202) 585 - 5820

Registered Federal Lobbyist.
Serves As:
• Assistant V. President, Federal Government Affairs, American Internat'l Group, Inc.

WELLMAN, Jr., Arnold F.
316 Pennsylvania Ave. SE
Suite 300
Washington, DC 20003
awellman@ups.com
Tel: (202) 675 - 4251
Fax:(202) 675 - 3384

Registered Federal Lobbyist.
Serves As:
• Corporate V. President, Domestic and International Public Affairs, United Parcel Service (UPS)

WELLS, Chris
P.O. Box 1518
Bellevue, WA 98009
Tel: (425) 468 - 7400
Fax:(425) 468 - 8216

Serves As:
• Treasurer, People PAC, PACCAR Inc.

WELLS, Kent M.
1818 N St. NW
Suite 800
800
Washington, DC 20036
kent.wells@cingular.com
Tel: (202) 419 - 3000
Ext: 3025

Registered Federal Lobbyist.
Serves As:
• V. President, Congressional Affairs, Cingular Wireless

WELLS, Robert J.
101 Prospect Ave. NW
Cleveland, OH 44115
Tel: (216) 566 - 2244
Fax:(216) 566 - 3312

Serves As:
• V. President, Corporate Planning and Communications, Sherwin-Williams Co.

WELLS, Sarah E.
1331 Pennsylvania Ave. NW
Suite 550 South
Washington, DC 20004
Tel: (202) 637 - 8020
Fax:(202) 637 - 8028

Registered Federal Lobbyist.
Serves As:
• Director, Health Policy and Payment, Boston Scientific Corp.

WELSH, Charles B.
750 E. Pratt St.
200, Candler
Baltimore, MD 21202
Tel: (410) 230 - 9860
Fax:(410) 783 - 3269
TF: (888) 460 - 2002

Serves As:
• Manager, Marketing Communications and Research, Constellation Energy

WELSH, Nancy K.
400 Collins Rd. NE
Cedar Rapids, IA 52498
nkwelsh@rockwellcollins.com
Tel: (319) 295 - 2123
Fax:(319) 295 - 5429

Serves As:
• Media Relations Contact, Rockwell Collins, Inc

WELSH, Thomas M.
76 S. Main St.
Akron, OH 44308-1890
Tel: (330) 384 - 5804
Fax:(330) 384 - 4539
TF: (800) 633 - 4766

Serves As:
• Senior V. President, External Affairs, FirstEnergy Corp.

WELSH, Walter
Hartford Plaza
Hartford, CT 06115
walter.welsh@hartfordlife.com
Tel: (860) 843 - 6453
Fax:(860) 843 - 6958

Serves As:
• Senior V. President and Director, Government Affairs, The Hartford Financial Services Group Inc.

WELTMANN, Allen J.
1900 K St. NW
Suite 900
Washington, DC 20006
Tel: (202) 822 - 4222
Fax:(202) 822 - 5800

Registered Federal Lobbyist.
Serves As:
• Partner in Charge, Professional and Regulatory Activities, PriceWaterhouseCoopers LLP
Responsibilities include government affairs.

WENDELKEN, Janet T.
P.O. Box 25, Rte. 340 South
Elkton, VA 22827
Tel: (540) 289 - 8211
Fax:(540) 289 - 8405

Serves As:
• Manager, Public Relations (Shenandoah Brewery), Coors Brewing Co.

WENDT, Richard
401 Harbor Isles Blvd.
Klamath Falls, OR 97601
Tel: (541) 882 - 3451
Fax:(541) 855 - 7454
TF: (800) 535 - 3936

Serves As:
• Chairman of the Board, JELD-WEN, Inc.

WENDT, Roderick C.
401 Harbor Isles Blvd.
Klamath Falls, OR 97601
Tel: (541) 882 - 3451
Fax:(541) 855 - 7454
TF: (800) 535 - 3936

Serves As:
• President, JELD-WEN, Inc.
Responsibilities include corporate philanthropy.

WENKER, Kris
One General Mills Blvd.
Minneapolis, MN 55426
Tel: (763) 764 - 2607

Serves As:
• V. President, Investor Relations, General Mills

WENNING, Werner
100 Bayer Rd.
Pittsburgh, PA 15205-9741
Tel: (412) 777 - 2000
TF: (800) 662 - 2927

Serves As:
• Chairman of the Board, Bayer Corporation

WENTWORTH, John A.
5555 Melrose Ave.
Los Angeles, CA 90038
Tel: (323) 956 - 5394

Serves As:
• Exec. V. President, Media Relations, Viacom Inc./CBS Corp.

WENZL, Sharon
27175 Haggerty Rd.
Novi, MI 48377
Tel: (248) 675 - 6000
Fax:(248) 675 - 6200

Serves As:
• Manager, Marketing and Public Relations, Tower Automotive, Inc.

WERFELMAN, William H.
51 Madison Ave. Tel: (212) 576 - 5385
New York, NY 10010 Fax:(212) 447 - 4273
william_werfelman@newyorklife.com

Serves As:
- First V. President, Media Relations, New York Life Insurance Co.

WERNER, Clarence L.
P.O. Box 37308 Tel: (402) 895 - 6640
Omaha, NE 68137 Fax:(402) 894 - 3990
TF: (800) 228 - 2240

Serves As:
- Chairman and Chief Exec. Officer, Werner Enterprises, Inc.

WESLEY, Norman H.
300 Tower Pkwy. Tel: (847) 484 - 4400
Lincolnshire, IL 60069

Serves As:
- Chairman and Chief Exec. Officer, Fortune Brands, Inc.

WESLEY, Timothy R.
1001 Air Brake Ave. Tel: (412) 825 - 1543
Wilmerding, PA 15148-1036 Fax:(412) 825 - 1789

Serves As:
- V. President, Investor Relations and Corporate Communications, Westinghouse Air Brake Technologies Corp.

WESLOW, Norman J.
6501 Legacy Dr. Tel: (972) 431 - 4147
Plano, TX 75024-3698 Fax:(972) 431 - 1362
nweslow@jcpenney.com TF: (800) 222 - 6161

Serves As:
- Senior Government Relations Counsel, J. C. Penney Co., Inc.

WESOLOWSKI, Tim M.
201 E. Fourth St. Tel: (513) 723 - 7000
Cincinnati, OH 45202 Fax:(513) 458 - 1315
TF: (800) 344 - 3000

Serves As:
- PAC Contact, Convergys Corp.

WESSLING, David W.
12800 Whitewater Dr. Tel: (800) 918 - 8270
Minnetonka, MN 55343 Fax:(952) 984 - 0032

Serves As:
- V. President, Human Resources, Mosaic Co.

WEST, Edward
120 Monument Circle Tel: (317) 488 - 6100
Indianapolis, IN 46204
ed.west@wellpoint.com

Serves As:
- Senior V. President, Corporate Communications, Wellpoint, Inc.

WEST, G. Frank
406 First St. SE Tel: (202) 488 - 8562
Third Floor Fax:(202) 488 - 3803
Washington, DC 20003
fwest@oneok.com

Registered Federal Lobbyist.
Serves As:
- Manager, Governmental Affairs - Federal, ONEOK, Inc.

WEST, Heather O.
Administrative Center Tel: (269) 923 - 5000
2000 N. M-63 Fax:(269) 923 - 5443
Benton Harbor, MI 49022-2692

Registered Federal Lobbyist.
Serves As:
- Representative, Whirlpool Corp.

WEST, Mindy
P.O. Box 7000 Tel: (870) 864 - 6315
El Dorado, AR 71731-7000 Fax:(870) 864 - 6373
mwest@murphyoilcorp.com

Serves As:
- Director, Investor Relations, Murphy Oil Corp.

WEST, Pete
1225 17th St. Tel: (303) 571 - 7511
Denver, CO 80202 Fax:(303) 294 - 8120

Serves As:
- Director, Community Services, Xcel Energy, Inc.

WEST, Teresa Lynne
P.O. Box 660199 Tel: (214) 480 - 5030
MS 8657 Fax:(214) 480 - 5025
Dallas, TX 75266-0199 TF: (800) 336 - 5236
t-west@ti.com

Serves As:
- Senior V. President and Manager, Communications and Investor Relations, Texas Instruments Incorporated

WESTERHAUS, James
Ecolab Center Tel: (651) 293 - 2183
370 N. Wabasha St. Fax:(651) 225 - 3274
St. Paul, MN 55102
jim.westerhaus@ecolab.com

Serves As:
- V. President, Government Relations, Ecolab Inc.

WESTERHEIDE, Jeff
P.O. Box 227097 Tel: (214) 812 - 4600
Dallas, TX 75222-7097

Serves As:
- Treasurer, TXU Corp. PAC, TXU

WESTERHOF, Rob
1251 Ave. of the Americas Tel: (212) 536 - 0500
20th Floor Fax:(212) 536 - 0875
New York, NY 10020

Serves As:
- President and Chief Exec. Officer, Philips Electronics North America

WESTFALL, Linda "Tuckie"
101 Constitution Ave. NW Tel: (202) 354 - 1500
Suite 400 West Fax:(202) 354 - 1505
Washington, DC 20001
tuckie.westfall@altria.com

Registered Federal Lobbyist.
Serves As:
- Director, Government Affairs - Food, (Altria Corporate Services, Inc.), Altria Group, Inc.
- Director, Federal Government Affairs, Kraft Foods, Inc.

WESTIN, Sherrie Rollins
One Lincoln Plaza Tel: (212) 595 - 3456
New York, NY 10023 Fax:(212) 875 - 6088

Serves As:
- Exec. V. President, Corporate Affairs, Education and Development, Sesame Workshop

WESTPHAL, Steven
444 Highland Dr. Tel: (920) 457 - 4441
Kohler, WI 53044 Ext: 74740
steven.westphal@kohler.com Fax:(920) 459 - 1583

Serves As:
- Attorney, Kohler Co.

Responsibilities include government affairs.

WETMORE, Douglas J.
521 W. 57th St. Tel: (212) 708 - 7145
New York, NY 10019 Fax:(212) 708 - 7132

Serves As:
- Senior V. President and Chief Financial Officer, Internat'l Flavors and Fragrances

Responsibilities include corporate philanthropy and investor relations.

WETTSTAEDT, Lisa
722 N. Broadway Tel: (414) 270 - 5915
18th Floor Fax:(414) 28- - 5909
Milwaukee, WI 53202 TF: (800) 257 - 0902

Serves As:
- Manager, External Affairs, SBC Wisconsin

WETZ, Philip A.
13501 Katy Fwy. Tel: (281) 870 - 6075
Houston, TX 77079 Fax:(281) 588 - 4772

Serves As:
- Worldwide Manager, Public Affairs, Exxon Mobil Chemical Co.

WEVERSTAD, Alan R.
300 Renaissance Center Tel: (313) 556 - 5000
Detroit, MI 48265-3000 Fax:(313) 665 - 0746
alan.weverstad@gm.com

Serves As:
- Exec. Director, Environment and Energy Public Policy Center - Mobile, General Motors Corp.

WEXNER, Leslie
Three Limited Pkwy. Tel: (614) 415 - 7000
Columbus, OH 43230 Fax:(614) 415 - 7079

Serves As:
- Chairman and Chief Exec. Officer, The Limited Brands

WEYERS, Larry L.
P.O. Box 19001 Tel: (920) 433 - 1334
M/S G6 Fax:(920) 433 - 1693
Green Bay, WI 54307-9001 TF: (800) 450 - 7260
lweyers@wpsr.com

Serves As:
- Chairman and Chief Exec. Officer, Wisconsin Public Service Corp.
- Chairman, President and Chief Exec. Officer, WPS Resources Corp.

WEYRAUCH, Jennifer
1303 E. Algonquin Rd.
Schaumburg, IL 60196
jennifer.weyrauch@motorola.com
Tel: (847) 435 - 5320
Fax:(847) 576 - 4554
TF: (800) 262 - 8509

Serves As:
- Director, Corporate Communications, Motorola, Inc.

WHALEN, Brian B.
P.O. Box 1488
4201 Winfield Rd.
Warrenfield, IL 60555
brian.whalen@nav-international.com
Tel: (630) 753 - 2604
Fax:(630) 753 - 2192

Registered Federal Lobbyist.
Serves As:
- V. President, Public Affairs; President, Navistar Foundation, (Internat'l Truck and Engine Corp.), Navistar Internat'l Corp.

WHALEN, Kevin
847 Gibraltar Dr.
Milpitas, CA 95035
kevinwhalen@ca.slr.com
Tel: (408) 956 - 6854
Fax:(408) 956 - 6075

Serves As:
- V. President, Corporate Communications, Solectron Corp.

WHALEN, Mary Lynne
1201 F St. NW
Suite 450
Washington, DC 20004
mary.whalen@csfb.com
Tel: (202) 626 - 3301

Registered Federal Lobbyist.
Serves As:
- Managing Director, Credit Suisse First Boston

Responsibilities include political action.

WHALEY, Christine G.
P.O. Box 1537
Salisbury, MD 21802-1537
chris.whaley@perdue.com
Tel: (410) 543 - 3000
Fax:(410) 543 - 3884

Serves As:
- Representative, Perdue Farms

WHEARY, Herbert S.
P.O. Box 26666
Richmond, VA 23261-6666
Herbert_Wheary@dom.com
Tel: (804) 771 - 3611

Serves As:
- Public Policy Director, Dominion Resources, Inc.

WHEATLEY, Richard
P.O. Box 2511
Houston, TX 77252-2511
Tel: (713) 420 - 6828
Fax:(713) 420 - 4993

Serves As:
- Manager, Media Relations, El Paso Corp.

WHEELER, Anita L.
One ConAgra Dr.
Omaha, NE 68102-5001
Tel: (402) 595 - 4215
Fax:(402) 595 - 4595

Serves As:
- President, ConAgra Foods Foundation, ConAgra Foods, Inc.

WHEELER, Colin
6200 S. Quebec St.
Greenwood Village, CO 80111
colin.wheeler@firstdatacorp.com
Tel: (303) 967 - 6553
Fax:(303) 967 - 6705

Serves As:
- V. President, Media Relations, First Data

WHEELER, Deb L.
One State Farm Plaza
Bloomington, IL 61710-0001
Tel: (309) 766 - 9580

Serves As:
- Public Affairs Consultant, State Farm Insurance Cos.

WHEELER, Kathy
2655 Seely Ave.
San Jose, CA 95134
Tel: (408) 943 - 1234
Fax:(408) 943 - 0513

Serves As:
- Community Involvement Contact, Cadence Design Systems, Inc.

WHEELESS, Charles Randy
P.O. Box 1244
M/S ECO6G
Charlotte, NC 28201-1244
crwheele@duke-energy.com
Tel: (704) 382 - 8979
Fax:(704) 382 - 8375

Serves As:
- Senior Communications Specialist (General Corporate Info, Human Resources, E-business, IT/IM, Environment), Duke Energy Corp.

WHELAN, John
712 11th St
Lawrence, IL 62439
Tel: (317) 943 - 8000
Fax:(618) 943 - 8031

Serves As:
- President and Chief Exec. Officer, Golden Rule Insurance Co.

WHELAN, Karen M. L.
P.O. Box 25099
Richmond, VA 23260
Tel: (804) 359 - 9311

Serves As:
- V. President and Treasurer, Universal Corp.

Responsibilities include investor relations.

WHELAN, Mike
P.O. Box 6000
Cherry Hill, NJ 08034-6000
Tel: (856) 488 - 8500
Fax:(856) 488 - 0485

Serves As:
- National Manager, Corporate Communications, Subaru of America, Inc.

WHIPPLE, Kenneth
One Energy Plaza
Jackson, MI 49201
Tel: (517) 788 - 0550

Serves As:
- Chairman of the Board, CMS Energy Corp.

WHISLER, J. Steven
One N. Central Ave.
Phoenix, AZ 85004-3014
Tel: (602) 366 - 8100
Fax:(602) 234 - 8337
TF: (800) 528 - 1182

Serves As:
- Chairman and Chief Exec. Officer, Phelps Dodge Corp.

WHITACRE, Jr., Edward E.
P.O. Box 2933
San Antonio, TX 78299-2933
Tel: (210) 821 - 4105
Fax:(210) 351 - 2198
TF: (800) 351 - 7221

Serves As:
- Chairman and Chief Exec. Officer, SBC Communications Inc.

WHITAKER, Michael G.
P.O. Box 66100
Chicago, IL 60666
michael.whitaker@ual.com
Tel: (847) 700 - 3955
Fax:(847) 700 - 4165

Serves As:
- V. President, International and Regulatory Affairs, United Airlines

WHITCHER, Ginger
13410 Sutton Park Dr. South
Jacksonville, FL 32224
gwhitcher@landstar.com
Tel: (904) 398 - 9400
Fax:(904) 390 - 1437
TF: (800) 872 - 9400

Serves As:
- Manager, Corporate Communications, Landstar System, Inc.

WHITCOMB, Gus
702 SW Eighth St.
Bentonville, AR 72716
Tel: (479) 273 - 4314
Fax:(479) 273 - 4053

Serves As:
- Media Relations Contact, Wal-Mart Stores

WHITE, Allison
P.O. Box 1411
Tyler, TX 75710-1411
Tel: (903) 534 - 3000
Fax:(903) 534 - 2206

Serves As:
- Foundation Contact, Brookshire Grocery Co.

WHITE, Barney
4747 McLane Pkwy.
Temple, TX 76504
Tel: (254) 771 - 7500
Fax:(254) 771 - 7486

Serves As:
- Senior Manager, Governmental Affairs and Corporate Communications, McLane Company, Inc.

WHITE, Bill
2001 Edmund Halley Dr.
Reston, VA 20191
bill.white@mail.sprint.com
Tel: (703) 433 - 4000

Serves As:
- V. President, Corporate Communications, Sprint Nextel

WHITE, Brett
100 N. Sepulveda Blvd.
Suite 1050
El Segundo, CA 90245
Tel: (310) 606 - 4720
Fax:(310) 606 - 4701

Serves As:
- Chief Exec. Officer, CB Richard Ellis Services, Inc.

WHITE, Brooke
1617 Sixth Ave. Tel: (206) 373 - 3030
Suite 700 Fax:(206) 373 - 3039
Seattle, WA 98101
brooke.white@nordstrom.com

Serves As:
- V. President, Corporate Communications, Nordstrom, Inc.

WHITE, Colleen T.
One Becton Dr. Tel: (201) 847 - 5369
Franklin Lakes, NJ 07417-1880 Fax:(201) 847 - 6475

Serves As:
- Corporate Communications Contact, Becton, Dickinson and Co.

WHITE, David
2700 N. First St. Tel: (408) 964 - 3500
San Jose, CA 95134 Fax:(408) 964 - 3636

Serves As:
- Exec. V. President and Chief Financial Officer, Sanmina-SCI Corp.

Responsibilities include investor relations.

WHITE, Dawn B.
999 Ponce de Leon Blvd. Tel: (305) 520 - 3233
Suite 610 Fax:(305) 520 - 3404
Coral Gables, FL 33134
dawn.white@aa.com

Serves As:
- Managing Director, Corporate Affairs, (American Airlines, Inc.), AMR Corp.

WHITE, Grover L.
141 N. Civic Dr. Tel: (925) 937 - 1170
Walnut Creek, CA 94596 Fax:(925) 210 - 6886

Serves As:
- Contact,Corporate Giving Program, Longs Drug Stores Corp.

WHITE, J. Randall
Three First National Plaza Tel: (312) 726 - 2600
70 W. Madison St. Fax:(312) 726 - 3712
Chicago, IL 60602-4260 TF: (800) 727 - 2533

Serves As:
- V. President, Public Affairs, Sara Lee Corp.

WHITE, James J.
1399 New York Ave. NW Tel: (202) 378 - 2020
Suite 200 Fax:(202) 783 - 6631
Washington, DC 20005

Serves As:
- Director, Federal Government Affairs, Abbott Laboratories

WHITE, Jane C.
50 Kennedy Plaza Tel: (401) 751 - 1600
Providence, RI 02903 Fax:(401) 751 - 4610

Serves As:
- Director, Human Resources/Administration, Nortek Inc.

WHITE, Kyle D.
P.O. Box 1400 Tel: (605) 721 - 1700
Rapid City, SD 57709-1400 Fax:(605) 721 - 2568

Serves As:
- V. President, Corporate Affairs, Black Hills Corp.

WHITE, Larry D.
One Allied Dr. Tel: (501) 905 - 5590
Little Rock, AR 72202 Fax:(501) 905 - 6018
larry.d.white@alltel.com

Serves As:
- Manager, Corporate Communications, ALLTEL

WHITE, Lynda
One N. Central Ave. Tel: (602) 366 - 8100
Phoenix, AZ 85004-3014 Fax:(602) 234 - 8337
TF: (800) 528 - 1182

Serves As:
- Manager, State and Local Government Relations, Phelps Dodge Corp.

WHITE, Martin A.
P.O. Box 5650 Tel: (701) 222 - 7900
Bismarck, ND 58506-5650 Fax:(701) 222 - 7607
TF: (800) 437 - 8000

Serves As:
- Chairman and Chief Exec. Officer, MDU Resources Group, Inc.

WHITE, Molly
One Bowerman Dr. Tel: (503) 671 - 6453
Beaverton, OR 97005 Fax:(503) 671 - 6300

Serves As:
- Director, U.S. Community Affairs, Nike, Inc.

WHITE, Pamela S.
P.O. Box 961039 Tel: (817) 352 - 2326
Ft. Worth, TX 76161-0039 Fax:(817) 352 - 2392
pamela.white@bnsf.com

Serves As:
- Manager, Government Affairs, Burlington Northern Santa Fe Corporation

WHITE, Jr., Raymon M.
1201 E. Abingdon Dr. Tel: (703) 739 - 1937
Suite 300 Fax:(703) 739 - 2775
Alexandria, VA 22314
rwhite@harris.com

Registered Federal Lobbyist.
Serves As:
- V. President, Washington Operations, Harris Corp.

WHITE, Richard J.
231 W. Michigan St. Tel: (414) 221 - 2555
P453 Fax:(414) 221 - 2310
Milwaukee, WI 53201
rick.white@we-energies.com

Serves As:
- V. President, Communications, Wisconsin Energy Corp.

WHITE, Shannon
6001 W. Market St. Tel: (336) 316 - 4000
Greensboro, NC 27409 Fax:(336) 316 - 4057

Serves As:
- President and Chief Exec. Officer, Guilford Mills, Inc.

WHITE, Thomas A. H.
One Fountain Square Tel: (423) 294 - 8996
Chattanooga, TN 37402 Fax:(423) 294 - 3962
tawhite@unumprovident.com

Serves As:
- V. President, Corporate Relations, UnumProvident Corp.

WHITE, Tony L.
301 Merritt Seven Tel: (203) 840 - 2000
P.O. Box 5435 TF: (800) 761 - 5381
Norwalk, CT 06856-5435

Serves As:
- Chairman, President and Chief Exec. Officer, Applera Corp.

WHITE, Vincent W.
20 N. Broadway, Suite 1500 Tel: (405) 552 - 4505
Oklahoma City, OK 73102 Fax:(405) 552 - 7818

Serves As:
- V. President, Communications and Investor Relations, Devon Energy Corp.

WHITE, W. Ward
720 E. Wisconsin Ave. Tel: (414) 665 - 2075
Milwaukee, WI 53202-4797 Fax:(414) 665 - 2463
TF: (800) 323 - 7033

Serves As:
- V. President, Corporate Relations, Northwestern Mutual Financial Network

WHITE, Walter
1300 I St. NW Tel: (202) 515 - 2400
Suite 400 West
Washington, DC 20005

Serves As:
- V. President, State and Local Government, Verizon Communications Inc.

WHITE, Ward H.
1133 21st St. NW Tel: (202) 463 - 4100
Suite 900 Fax:(202) 463 - 8070
Washington, DC 20036
ward.white@bellsouth.com

Registered Federal Lobbyist.
Serves As:
- V. President, Federal Relations, BellSouth Corp.

WHITE-IVY, Nita C.
1 Sybase Dr. Tel: (925) 236 - 5000
Dublin, CA 94568
nita.white-ivey@sybase.com

Serves As:
- V. President, Human Resources, Sybase, Inc.

WHITEFORD, Stan
P.O. Box 201 Tel: (918) 599 - 2574
Tulsa, OK 74102

Serves As:
- Communications Consultant, (AEP Public Service Co. of Oklahoma), American Electric Power Co. Inc.

WHITEHEAD, Carol
2201 Miller Rd.
Wilson, NC 27893

Serves As:
- Treasurer, Alliance One Internat'l Inc. PAC, Alliance One Internat'l Inc.

WHITEHEAD, Samuel W.
P.O. Box 1624
Alpharetta, GA 30009-9934
Fax:(678) 762 - 2315
TF: (800) 275 - 3004

Serves As:
- Manager, Government Affairs, Colonial Pipeline Co.

WHITEHORN, Kelly M.
P.O. Box 2181
320 W. Capitol
Little Rock, AR 72203-2181
Tel: (501) 378 - 2344
Fax:(501) 378 - 2969

Serves As:
- Communications Coordinator, Arkansas Blue Cross and Blue Shield

WHITEHURST, Calvert S.
1101 Pennsylvania Ave. NW
Suite 400
Washington, DC 20004-2504
Tel: (202) 637 - 3833
Fax:(202) 637 - 3863

Registered Federal Lobbyist.
Serves As:
- Manager, Public Affairs, Textron Inc.

WHITELEY, Sherry
2632 Marine Way
Mountain View, CA 94043
Tel: (650) 944 - 6000
Fax:(650) 944 - 3999

Serves As:
- Senior V. President, Human Resources, Intuit Inc.

WHITESELL, Shirley J.
180 N. Stetson St.
Suite 1800
Chicago, IL 60601
Tel: (312) 819 - 8515
Fax:(312) 819 - 8423

Serves As:
- V. President, People, Amsted Industries Inc.
Responsibilities include corporate philanthropy.

WHITESIDE, Jeffrey W.
211 Riverside Dr.
Evansville, IN 47708-1251
Tel: (812) 491 - 4000
Fax:(812) 491 - 4078
TF: (800) 227 - 1376

Serves As:
- V. President, Corporate Communications and Public Affairs, Vectren Corp.

WHITING, Paul L.
400 N. Ashley Dr.
Tampa, FL 33602
Tel: (813) 274 - 1000
Fax:(813) 273 - 0148

Serves As:
- Chairman of the Board, Sykes Enterprises, Inc.

WHITLOCK, Gary
1111 Louisiana St.
Houston, TX 77002
Tel: (713) 207 - 1111

Serves As:
- Exec. V. President and Chief Financial Officer, CenterPoint Energy
Responsibilities include investor relations.

WHITMAN, Margaret C. "Meg"
2145 Hamilton Ave.
San Jose, CA 95125
mwhitman@ebay.com
Tel: (408) 558 - 7400
Fax:(408) 558 - 7401
TF: (800) 322 - 9266

Serves As:
- President and Chief Exec. Officer, eBay, Inc.

WHITMER, Richard E.
600 Lafayette East
M/S 2001
Detroit, MI 48226
rwhitmer@bcbsm.com
Tel: (313) 225 - 9000
Fax:(313) 225 - 6250

Serves As:
- President and Chief Exec. Officer, Blue Cross Blue Shield of Michigan

WHITMIRE, John
Consol Plaza
1800 Washington Rd.
Pittsburgh, PA 15241-1421
Tel: (412) 831 - 4000
Fax:(412) 831 - 4103

Serves As:
- Chairman of the Board, CONSOL Energy Inc.

WHITMOYER, Heidi A. F.
P.O. Box 13009
Reading, PA 19612

Serves As:
- PAC Treasurer, UGI Corp.

WHITNEY, Lee
6801 Rockledge Dr.
Bethesda, MD 20817-1877
Tel: (301) 897 - 6121
Fax:(301) 897 - 6289

Serves As:
- V. President, Strategy and Marketing Communications, Lockheed Martin Corp.

WHITT, Richard S.
1133 19th St. NW
Washington, DC 20036
Tel: (202) 887 - 3845
Fax:(202) 887 - 3123

Serves As:
- Director, Internet Policy, MCI, Inc.

WHITTAKER, May
P.O. Box 21008
Greensboro, NC 27420
may.whittaker@jpfinancial.com
Tel: (336) 691 - 3039
Fax:(336) 691 - 3311

Serves As:
- Budget and Contributions Assistant, Jefferson-Pilot Corp.

WHITTERS, Joseph H.
3200 Highland Ave.
Downers Grove, IL 60515-1223
Tel: (630) 737 - 7900
Fax:(630) 719 - 0093
TF: (800) 719 - 9701

Serves As:
- V. President, Finance and Chief Financial Officer, First Health
Responsibilities include political action and public affairs.

WHITUS, Ernie
2135 W. Maple Rd.
Troy, MI 48084
Tel: (248) 435 - 1060
Fax:(248) 435 - 1393
TF: (800) 535 - 5560

Serves As:
- Senior V. President, Human Resources, ArvinMeritor

WHYTE, Craig
P.O. Box 190
Aurora, IL 60507-0190

Serves As:
- Director, Community Relations, Nicor, Inc.

WICKMAN, Pamela A.
870 Winter St.
Waltham, MA 02451
Tel: (781) 522 - 3000

Serves As:
- Senior V. President, Corporate Affairs and Communications, Raytheon Co.

WICKS, Judy DeRango
4411 E. Jones Bridge Rd.
Norcross, GA 30092-1615
Tel: (678) 375 - 3000
Fax:(678) 375 - 1477

Serves As:
- V. President, Media Strategy, CheckFree Corp.

WIDERA, Barbara
P.O. Box 1167
Dayton, OH 45401-1167
barbara.widera@standardregister.com
Tel: (937) 221 - 1000
Fax:(937) 221 - 1239
TF: (800) 755 - 6405

Serves As:
- Contact, The Sherman-Standard Register Foundation, Standard Register Co.

WIDMAYER, Karen L.
1850 K St. NW
Suite 500
Washington, DC 20006-2213
karen.widmayer@carramerica.com
Tel: (202) 729 - 1789
Fax:(202) 729 - 1150
TF: (800) 417 - 2277

Serves As:
- Senior V. President, Corporate Communications, CarrAmerica Realty Corp.

WIESE, Jr., Arthur E. F.
P.O. Box 61000
New Orleans, LA 70161
awiese@entergy.com
Tel: (504) 576 - 2547
Fax:(504) 576 - 4428

Serves As:
- V. President, Corporate Communications, Entergy Corp.

WIESE, Nancy
800 Long Ridge Rd.
M/S STHQ
Stamford, CT 06904
nancy.wiese@xerox.com
Tel: (203) 968 - 3374

Serves As:
- V. President, Corporate Advertising/Branding/Sponsorships, Xerox Corp.

WIETIES, Cindy
2929 Allen Pkwy.
Houston, TX 77019
Tel: (713) 522 - 1111
Fax:(713) 523 - 8531

Serves As:
- Director, Community Relations, AIG American General Corp.

WIGGERS, Jr., R. Gray
P.O. Box 291
Jackson, MS 39205-0291
Tel: (601) 208 - 5111

Serves As:
- Senior V. President, Public Affairs, Trustmark Nat'l Bank
Responsibilities include corporate philanthropy.

WIGGINS, Michael
P.O. Box 1000
Carrollton, GA 30119
Tel: (770) 832 - 4242
Ext: 4963
Fax:(770) 832 - 4584
TF: (800) 444 - 1700

Serves As:
- V. President, Human Resources, Southwire Co.

WIGHT, David
P.O. Box 196660
Anchorage, AK 99519-6660
Tel: (907) 787 - 8700
Fax:(907) 787 - 8611

Serves As:
- President and Chief Exec. Officer, Alyeska Pipeline Service Co.

WIGINTON, Joel
1667 K St. NW
Suite 200
Washington, DC 20006
joel.wiginton@am.sony.com
Tel: (202) 429 - 3652
Fax:(202) 429 - 3663

Registered Federal Lobbyist.
Serves As:
- V. President and Senior Counsel, Government Affairs, (Sony Electronics Inc.), Sony Corp. of America

WIIK, Ingrid
One Executive Dr.
Fort Lee, NJ 07024
Tel: (201) 947 - 7774
Fax:(201) 947 - 5541
TF: (800) 445 - 4216

Serves As:
- President and Chief Exec. Officer, Alpharma Inc.

WILANSKY, Heywood
3241 Westerville Rd.
Columbus, OH 43224
Tel: (617) 348 - 7000

Serves As:
- President and Chief Exec. Officer, Retail Ventures, Inc.

WILBURNE, Douglas R.
40 Westminster St.
Providence, RI 02903-2525
Tel: (401) 457 - 3606
Fax:(401) 457 - 3598

Serves As:
- V. President, Communications and Investor Relations, Textron Inc.

WILCOX, Courtney
P.O. Box 4607
Houston, TX 77210-4607
courtney.wilcox@coair.com
Tel: (713) 324 - 5080
Fax:(713) 324 - 2087

Serves As:
- Senior Specialist, Public Relations, Continental Airlines

WILCOX, Peter G.
700 Anderson Hill Rd.
Purchase, NY 10577-1444
peter.wilcox@pepsi.com
Tel: (914) 253 - 2609
Fax:(914) 253 - 8201

Serves As:
- Manager, Government Affairs - East, (Pepsi-Cola North America), PepsiCo, Inc.

WILD, PhD, Anthony H.
265 Davidson Ave.
Suite 300
Somerset, NJ 08873-4120
awild@medpointepharma.com
Tel: (732) 564 - 2222
Fax:(732) 564 - 2223

Serves As:
- Chairman and Chief Exec. Officer, MedPointe Inc.

WILDER, C. John
P.O. Box 227097
Dallas, TX 75222-7097
Tel: (214) 812 - 4447

Serves As:
- Chairman, President and Chief Exec. Officer, TXU

WILDER, Todd
One Infinite Loop
Cupertino, CA 95014
wilder@apple.com
Tel: (408) 974 - 8335
Fax:(408) 996 - 0275

Serves As:
- Education and Government Media Relations, Apple Computer, Inc.

WILDEROTTER, Maggie
Three High Ridge Park
Stamford, CT 06905
Tel: (203) 614 - 5600
Fax:(203) 614 - 4602

Serves As:
- President and Chief Exec. Officer, Citizens Communications Co.

WILDFONG, John
1550 Crystal Dr.
Crystal Square 2, Suite 300
Arlington, VA 22202
Tel: (703) 413 - 5601
Fax:(703) 413 - 5636

Serves As:
- V. President, Fixed Wing Aviation, Lockheed Martin Corp.

WILEY, Deborah E.
111 River St.
M/S 7-01
Hoboken, NJ 07030-5774
Tel: (201) 748 - 6000
Fax:(201) 748 - 6008

Serves As:
- Senior V. President, Corporate Communications, John Wiley & Sons, Inc.

WILEY, Jeremy
444 N. Capitol St. NW
Suite 545
Washington, DC 20001
Tel: (202) 347 - 8717

Registered Federal Lobbyist.
Serves As:
- Legislative Affairs, Corrections Corp. of America

WILEY, Peter B.
111 River St.
M/S 7-02
Hoboken, NJ 07030-5774
Tel: (201) 748 - 6000
Fax:(201) 748 - 6008

Serves As:
- Chairman of the Board, John Wiley & Sons, Inc.

WILEY, Roy
P.O. Box 1488
4201 Winfield Rd.
Warrenfield, IL 60555
roy.wiley@nav-international.com
Tel: (630) 753 - 2627

Serves As:
- Media Relations Contact, Navistar Internat'l Corp.

WILF, Marcia
P.O. Box 844
Spring House, PA 19477-0844
Tel: (215) 657 - 4000
Fax:(215) 444 - 5075

Serves As:
- V. President, Human Resources, Advanta Corp.

WILKERSON, John
12025 Tech Center Dr.
Livonia, MI 48150
john.wilkerson@trw.com
Tel: (734) 855 - 3864
Fax:(734) 855 - 2450

Serves As:
- Senior Manager, Communications - North America, TRW Automotive

WILKIE, Jack
2711 N. Haskell Ave.
Dallas, TX 75204
Tel: (214) 828 - 7011
Fax:(214) 828 - 7090

Serves As:
- V. President, Corporate Communications, 7-Eleven, Inc.

WILKINSON, Andrea
801 Pennsylvania Ave. NW
Suite 725
Washington, DC 20004
Tel: (202) 898 - 3192
Fax:(202) 371 - 1107

Registered Federal Lobbyist.
Serves As:
- Representative, Sanofi Pasteur, Inc.

WILKINSON, Bruce W.
757 N. Eldridge
Houston, TX 77079
Tel: (281) 870 - 4411
Fax:(281) 870 - 5045

Serves As:
- Chairman and Chief Exec. Officer, McDermott Internat'l, Inc.

WILKINSON, Jr., Edward A.
1881 Campus Commons Dr.
Reston, VA 20191
ewilkinson@ingr.com
Tel: (703) 264 - 5644

Serves As:
- Treasurer, Intergraph Corp. PAC, Intergraph Corp.

WILLA, Elizabeth
1901 Market St.
38th Floor
Philadelphia, PA 19103-1480
Tel: (215) 636 - 9559
Fax:(215) 241 - 0403
TF: (800) 555 - 1514

Serves As:
- V. President, Corporate and Public Affairs, Independence Blue Cross (Pennsylvania)

WILLETT, Mark
P.O. Box 31907
Santa Barbara, CA 93130
Tel: (805) 563 - 6863
Fax:(805) 682 - 5462

Serves As:
- V. President, Government Programs, Tenet Healthcare Corp.

WILLIAM, Dennis
10700 E. 350 Hwy.
Kansas City, MO 64138
denny.williams@aquila.com
Tel: (816) 737 - 7857
Fax:(816) 737 - 7505

Serves As:
- V. President, Regulatory Services-Electric, Aquila, Inc.

WILLIAMS, Alexia
6801 Industrial Rd. Tel: (703) 750 - 5637
Springfield, VA 22151
Serves As:
• Virginia Public Affairs Contact, Washington Gas

WILLIAMS, Alison
1701 SAIC Dr. Tel: (703) 676 - 6762
McLean, VA 22102
Serves As:
• Director, Public Affairs, Science Applications Internat'l Corp.

WILLIAMS, Andrew
12950 Worldgate Dr. Tel: (703) 480 - 3600
Suite 600 Fax:(703) 796 - 2214
Herndon, VA 20170
Serves As:
• Manager, Internal and Online Communications, Lafarge North America, Inc.

WILLIAMS, Ather
One Johnson & Johnson Plaza Tel: (732) 524 - 0400
New Brunswick, NJ 08933-7204 Fax:(732) 214 - 0334
TF: (800) 635 - 6789
Serves As:
• V. President, Environmental Affairs, Johnson & Johnson

WILLIAMS, C. Michael
5400 Legacy Dr., Cluster II, Bldg. 3 Tel: (972) 265 - 2000
Plano, TX 75024 TF: (800) 669 - 5740
Serves As:
• Senior V. President, Human Resources, Safety-Kleen Systems, Inc.

WILLIAMS, Carolyn R.
P.O. Box 513249 Tel: (213) 244 - 2555
Los Angeles, CA 90051-1249 Fax:(213) 244 - 8254
crwilliams@semprautilities.com
Serves As:
• Manager, Community Relations, Southern California Gas Co.

WILLIAMS, Christine
P.O. Box 4569 Tel: (404) 584 - 4000
Atlanta, GA 30302-4569 Fax:(404) 584 - 3479
Serves As:
• PAC Treasurer, AGL Resources, Inc.

WILLIAMS, Cindy
633 N. Orange Ave. Tel: (407) 420 - 5591
MP307 Fax:(407) 420 - 6258
Orlando, FL 32801-1349
cwilliams@orlandosentinel.com
Serves As:
• Manager, Family Fund, Orlando Sentinel Communications

WILLIAMS, D. Richard
3120 Breckinridge Blvd. Tel: (770) 381 - 1000
Duluth, GA 30099-0001 Fax:(770) 564 - 6161
Serves As:
• Co-Chief Exec. Officer, Primerica Financial Services, Inc.

WILLIAMS, David
2600 Chemed Center Tel: (513) 762 - 6901
255 E. Fifth St. Fax:(513) 762 - 6919
Cincinnati, OH 45202-4726 TF: (800) 438 - 7686
Serves As:
• Exec. V. President, Chief Financial Officer and Spokesperson, The Chemed Corporation
Responsibilities include investor relations.

WILLIAMS, George
P.O. Box 593330 Tel: (407) 245 - 5312
Orlando, FL 32859 Fax:(407) 245 - 5135
Serves As:
• V. President, Government and Environmental Relations, Darden Restaurants, Inc.

WILLIAMS, George P.
1001 G St. NW Tel: (202) 662 - 1701
Sixth Floor East Fax:(202) 293 - 2887
Washington, DC 20001-4545
gwilliams@sempra.com
Registered Federal Lobbyist.
Serves As:
• Director, Federal Governmental Affairs, Southern California Gas Co.
• Manager, Governmental Affairs, Sempra Energy

WILLIAMS, James D. "Dennie"
P.O. Box 5000 Tel: (318) 484 - 7688
Pineville, LA 71361-5000 Fax:(318) 484 - 7106
dennie.williams@cleco.com
Serves As:
• Director, State and Federal Affairs, Cleco Corp.

WILLIAMS, Jay
P.O. Box 127 Tel: (417) 625 - 5100
Joplin, MO 64802-0127 Fax:(417) 625 - 5155
TF: (800) 206 - 2300
Serves As:
• PAC Treasurer, Empire District Electric Co.

WILLIAMS, Jimmie L.
1717 Pennsylvania Ave. NW Tel: (202) 974 - 1100
Suite 700 Fax:(202) 974 - 1128
Washington, DC 20006
jimmie_williams@countrywide.com
Registered Federal Lobbyist.
Serves As:
• V. President, Legislative/Regulatory Affairs, Countrywide Home Loans Inc.

WILLIAMS, Jr., Junius H.
2700 Cromwell Rd. Tel: (757) 857 - 2690
Norfolk, VA 23501
Junius_Williams@dom.com
Serves As:
• Director, State and Local Affairs, Dominion Resources, Inc.

WILLIAMS, Katherine Crocker
4800 Hampden Ln. Tel: (301) 841 - 1600
Suite 1100 Fax:(301) 841 - 1611
Bethesda, MD 20814
Serves As:
• PAC Treasurer, AREVA Enterprises, Inc.

WILLIAMS, Kimberly A.
1500 K St. NW Tel: (202) 715 - 1000
Suite 650 Fax:(202) 715 - 1001
Washington, DC 20005
Registered Federal Lobbyist.
Serves As:
• Federal Government Relations, GlaxoSmithKline Research and Development

WILLIAMS, Larry
4211 W. Boyscout Blvd. Tel: (813) 871 - 4811
Tampa, FL 33607 Fax:(813) 871 - 4399
Serves As:
• Senior V. President, Human Resources, Walter Industries, Inc.

WILLIAMS, Lisa T.
P.O. Box 188 Tel: (504) 631 - 8609
Morgan City, LA 70381
ltwilliams@mcdermott.com
Serves As:
• Public Relations Supervisor, (J. Ray McDermott, SA), McDermott Internat'l, Inc.

WILLIAMS, Marcus P.
1301 K St. NW Tel: (202) 515 - 5522
Suite 1200 Fax:(202) 515 - 5528
Washington, DC 20005
Serves As:
• Counsel, Governmental Programs, Internat'l Business Machines Corp. (IBM)

WILLIAMS, Margaret
50 W. Bowary Tel: (330) 384 - 3281
Room 457
Akro, OH 44308
margaret.williams@sbc.com
Serves As:
• Director, External Affairs, SBC Ohio

WILLIAMS, Mona
702 SW Eighth St. Tel: (479) 273 - 4314
M/S 0150 Fax:(479) 273 - 4053
Bentonville, AR 72716
Serves As:
• V. President, Corporate Communications, Wal-Mart Stores

WILLIAMS, Nanci
3150 Sabre Dr. Tel: (682) 605 - 2271
Southlake, TX 76092 Fax:(682) 264 - 0502
nanci.williams@sabre-holdings.com
Serves As:
• Senior Manager, Media Relations, (Sabre Travel Network), Sabre Holdings Corp.

WILLIAMS, Peter
3375 Mitchell Lane Tel: (303) 440 - 5220
Boulder, CO 80301 Fax:(303) 928 - 0022
TF: (800) 494 - 9453
Serves As:
• V. President, Human Resources, Wild Oats Markets, Inc.

WILLIAMS, Rachelle
P.O. Box 982
El Paso, TX 79960
rwilli5@epelectric.com
Tel: (915) 543 - 5711
Fax:(915) 521 - 4766
TF: (800) 351 - 1621

Serves As:
- Investor Relations, El Paso Electric Co.

WILLIAMS, Ralph "Wil"
3033 Science Park Rd.
San Diego, CA 92121-1199
Tel: (858) 552 - 9724
Fax:(858) 552 - 9477

Serves As:
- V. President, Corporate Communications, L-3 Communications Titan Group

WILLIAMS, Randy
4500 Main St.
Kansas City, MO 64111
Tel: (816) 531 - 5575
Fax:(816) 340 - 7962
TF: (800) 345 - 2021

Serves As:
- Community Relations, American Century Cos., Inc.

WILLIAMS, Richard
100 Independence Mall West
Philadelphia, PA 19106-2399
Tel: (215) 592 - 2409
Fax:(215) 592 - 6808

Serves As:
- Manager, Financial Communications, Rohm and Haas Co.

WILLIAMS, Robert E.
P.O. Box 6721
Chicago, IL 60680-6721
rewilliams@usg.com
Tel: (312) 606 - 4356
Fax:(312) 606 - 5301

Serves As:
- Director, Corporate Communications, USG Corp.

WILLIAMS, Robin L.
1300 Wilson Blvd.
Arlington, VA 22209
Tel: (703) 741 - 5880
Fax:(703) 741 - 5884

Registered Federal Lobbyist.
Serves As:
- Director, State Government Relations, Rohm and Haas Co.

WILLIAMS, Sheryl
41 Moores Rd.
Frazer, PA 19355
swilliam@cephalon.com
Tel: (610) 738 - 6493
Fax:(610) 344 - 0981

Serves As:
- Senior Director, Public Relations, Cephalon, Inc.

WILLIAMS, Susan L.
P.O. Box 21488
Greensboro, NC 27420-1488
susan_williams@vfc.com
Tel: (336) 424 - 6000
Fax:(336) 424 - 7631

Serves As:
- V. President, Human Resources, V. F. Corporation

WILLIAMS, T. E.
365 Canal St., Suite 3000
New Orleans, LA 70130
tommy.williams@bellsouth.com
Tel: (504) 528 - 2200
Fax:(504) 528 - 7556

Serves As:
- V. President, Regulatory, BellSouth Corp.

WILLIAMS, Terry
50606 AXP Financial Center
Minneapolis, MN 55474
Tel: (612) 671 - 3131
Fax:(612) 671 - 5112
TF: (800) 328 - 8300

Serves As:
- Director, Community Relations Program, Ameriprise Financial Services Inc.

WILLIAMS, Tobhiyah
One Oxford Center, Suite 3300
Pittsburgh, PA 15219
Tel: (412) 553 - 5700
Fax:(412) 553 - 5757

Serves As:
- PAC Treasurer, Equitable Resources, Inc.

WILLIAMS KNOPP, Hellen
P.O. Box 982
El Paso, TX 79960
hknopp@epelectric.com
Tel: (915) 543 - 5711
Fax:(915) 521 - 4766
TF: (800) 351 - 1621

Serves As:
- V. President, Public Affairs, El Paso Electric Co.

WILLIAMSON, Anita
1166 Ave. of the Americas
New York, NY 10036
Tel: (212) 345 - 6000
Fax:(212) 345 - 2309

Serves As:
- Corporate Communications, Marsh Inc.

WILLIAMSON, Bruce A.
1000 Louisiana St.
Suite 5800
Houston, TX 77002-5050
Tel: (713) 507 - 6400
Fax:(713) 507 - 3871

Serves As:
- Chairman, President and Chief Exec. Officer, Dynegy, Inc.

WILLIAMSON, Charles R.
2141 Rosecrans Ave., Suite 4000
El Segundo, CA 90245
cwilliamson@unocal.com
Tel: (310) 726 - 7600

Serves As:
- Chairman and Chief Exec. Officer, UNOCAL Corp.

WILLIAMSON, Dennis A.
P.O. Box 655237
Dallas, TX 75265-5237
Tel: (214) 977 - 6606
Fax:(214) 977 - 6603

Serves As:
- Senior Corporate V. President and Chief Financial Officer, Belo Corp.

WILLIAMSON, Patricia M.
Five Sylvan Way
Parsippany, NJ 07054
p.williamson@drs.com
Tel: (973) 898 - 1500
Ext: 6025
Fax:(973) 898 - 4730

Serves As:
- V. President, Corporate Communications and Investor Relations, DRS Technologies, Inc.

WILLIAMSON, Wendi
20 N. Broadway, Suite 1500
Oklahoma City, OK 73102
wendi.williamson@dvn.com
Tel: (405) 228 - 4494
Fax:(405) 552 - 7818

Serves As:
- Supervisor, Communications, Devon Energy Corp.

WILLIS, Elizabeth "Beth"
414 Nicollet Mall
Minneapolis, MN 55401-1927
Tel: (612) 215 - 5320

Serves As:
- V. President, Corporate Communications, Xcel Energy, Inc.

WILLIS, Lori
11420 Lackland Rd.
St. Louis, MO 63146-6928
lwillis@schnucks.com
Tel: (314) 994 - 4602

Serves As:
- Director, Communications, Schnuck Markets, Inc.

WILLOUGHBY, Jeannine
P.O. Box 120
Columbus, GA 31902-0120
jwilloug@synovusservicecorp.com
Tel: (706) 649 - 5850
Fax:(706) 641 - 6555

Serves As:
- Senior Communications Specialist, Synovus Financial Corp.

WILLS, Richard H.
P.O. Box 500
Beaverton, OR 97077
richard.wills@tek.com
Tel: (503) 627 - 7111
Fax:(503) 567 - 3449
TF: (800) 835 - 9433

Serves As:
- Chairman, President and Chief Exec. Officer, Tektronix, Inc.

WILMERS, Robert G.
One M & T Plaza
Buffalo, NY 14203
Tel: (716) 842 - 5445
Fax:(716) 842 - 5839
TF: (800) 836 - 1500

Serves As:
- Chairman of the Board, M&T Bank Corporation

WILMS, Anne M.
100 Independence Mall West
Philadelphia, PA 19106-2399
Tel: (215) 592 - 3000
Fax:(215) 592 - 3377

Serves As:
- V. President, Chief Information Officer, and Director, Human Resources, Rohm and Haas Co.

WILNER, Carol W.
1120 20th St. NW
Suite 1000
Washington, DC 20036-3406
cwilner@att.com
Tel: (202) 457 - 3810
Fax:(202) 457 - 2258

Registered Federal Lobbyist.
Serves As:
- V. President and Director, Executive Branch Relations, AT&T

WILSON, Adrian D.
7261 Mercy Rd.
P.O. Box 3248
Omaha, NE 68180
Tel: (402) 390 - 1800
Fax:(402) 398 - 3736

Serves As:
- PAC Treasurer, Blue Cross and Blue Shield of Nebraska

WILSON, Alexandra M.
1225 19th St. NW
Suite 450
Washington, DC 20036
alexandra.wilson@cox.com
Tel: (202) 296 - 4933
Fax:(202) 296 - 4951

Registered Federal Lobbyist.
Serves As:
- V. President, Public Policy, Cox Enterprises, Inc.

WILSON, Andy
2099 Pennsylvania Ave. NW
Washington, DC 20006
Tel: (202) 828 - 0850
Fax:(202) 828 - 0860

Serves As:
- V. President, Investor Relations, Danaher Corp.

WILSON, Cleo F.
680 N. Lake Shore Dr.
Chicago, IL 60611
cleow@playboy.com
Tel: (312) 373 - 2435
Fax:(312) 266 - 8506

Serves As:
- V. President, Public Affairs; Exec. Director, Playboy Foundation, Playboy Enterprises, Inc.

WILSON, Darien E.
340 Kingsland St.
Nutley, NJ 07110-1199
darien_e.wilson@roche.com
Tel: (973) 562 - 2232
Fax:(973) 562 - 2206

Serves As:
- Director, Corporate and Business Communications, Hoffmann-La Roche Inc. (Roche)

WILSON, Darrell
1500 K St. NW
Suite 375
Washington, DC 20005
darrell.wilson@nscorp.com
Tel: (202) 383 - 4123
Fax:(202) 383 - 4018

Serves As:
- Director, Public Affairs, Norfolk Southern Corp.

WILSON, Dwight T.
P.O. Box 6675
Radnor, PA 19087-8675
Tel: (610) 687 - 5253
Fax:(610) 687 - 1052
TF: (800) 255 - 2165

Serves As:
- Senior V. President, Human Resources, Airgas, Inc.

WILSON, Gary L.
2700 Lone Oak Pkwy.
Eagan, MN 55121
Tel: (612) 726 - 2111
Fax:(612) 726 - 0776

Serves As:
- Chairman of the Board, Northwest Airlines, Inc.

WILSON, Greg
1776 I St. NW
Suite 1030
Washington, DC 20006
Tel: (202) 822 - 1690
Ext: 12
Fax:(202) 822 - 1693

Registered Federal Lobbyist.
Serves As:
- Director, Federal Affairs, Solutia Inc.

WILSON, Jay R.
1185 Ave. of the Americas
New York, NY 10036
Tel: (212) 536 - 8940
Fax:(212) 536 - 8390

Serves As:
- V. President, Investor Relations, Amerada Hess Corp.

Responsbilities include corporate relations.

WILSON, John K.
1200 Wilson Blvd.
Arlington, VA 22209-2305
Tel: (703) 465 - 3608

Registered Federal Lobbyist.
Serves As:
- Manager, Legislative Affairs, Air Force Programs, The Boeing Co.

WILSON, Larry
P.O. Box 9090
250E
Everett, WA 98206-9090
larry.wilson@fluke.com
Tel: (425) 446 - 5671
Fax:(425) 446 - 5116

Serves As:
- Manager, Public Relations, Fluke Corporation

WILSON, Lynn
P.O. Box 13287
Kansas City, MO 64199-3287
Tel: (816) 467 - 3776
Fax:(816) 467 - 9776

Serves As:
- Contact, Corporate Giving Program, Aquila, Inc.

WILSON, Michael M.
801 Pennsylvania Ave. NW
Suite 220
Washington, DC 20004-2604
michael_m_wilson@fpl.com
Tel: (202) 347 - 7082
Fax:(202) 347 - 7076

Registered Federal Lobbyist.
Serves As:
- V. President, Governmental Affairs, (Florida Power & Light Company), FPL Group, Inc.

WILSON, Michelle
P.O. Box 81226
Seattle, WA 98108-1226
Tel: (206) 266 - 1000
Fax:(206) 266 - 1821

Serves As:
- Senior V. President, Human Resources, General Counsel and Secretary, Amazon.com, Inc.

WILSON, Roy J.
P.O. Box 19534
Irvine, CA 92623-9534
Tel: (714) 246 - 4500
Fax:(714) 246 - 4971
TF: (800) 347 - 4500

Serves As:
- Exec. V. President, Human Resources and Information Technology, Allergan Inc.

WILSON, Sarah
700 13th St. NW
Suite 700
Washington, DC 20005-5922
Tel: (202) 508 - 6363
Fax:(202) 508 - 6330

Serves As:
- Legislative Assistant, H & R Block, Inc.

WILSON, Stephen R.
One Salem Lake Dr.
Long Grove, IL 60047
Tel: (847) 438 - 9500
Fax:(847) 438 - 0211

Serves As:
- President and Chief Exec. Officer, C F Industries, Inc.

WILSON, Terri G.
101 S. Fifth St.
Louisville, KY 40202
terri.wilson@nationalcity.com
Tel: (502) 581 - 4073
Fax:(502) 581 - 7953

Serves As:
- V. President - Media Relations Officer, Nat'l City Corp.

Media contact for Illinois, Indiana and Kentucky.

WILSON, W. Keith
370 Woodcliff Dr.
Suite 300
Fairport, NY 14450
Tel: (585) 218 - 3600
TF: (888) 724 - 2169

Serves As:
- Exec. V. President and Chief Human Resources Officer, Constellation Brands, Inc.

WILSON, Wayne
4680 Wilshire Blvd.
Los Angeles, CA 90010
Tel: (323) 932 - 3177
Fax:(323) 964 - 8095

Serves As:
- V. President, Legislative and Regulatory Affairs, (Farmers Insurance Group of Companies), Farmers Group, Inc.

WILSON, Wendy
700 State Route 46 East
Batesville, IN 47006-8835
Tel: (812) 934 - 7670
Fax:(812) 934 - 7371

Serves As:
- V. President, Investor Relations, Hillenbrand Industries, Inc.

WILT, Peter J.
1000 Louisiana St.
Suite 5800
Houston, TX 77002-5050
Tel: (713) 507 - 6400
Fax:(713) 507 - 3871

Serves As:
- V. President, Investor Relations, Dynegy, Inc.

WINANS, Christopher
70 Pine St.
New York, NY 10270
Tel: (212) 770 - 7000
Fax:(212) 509 - 9705

Serves As:
- V. President, Media Relations, American Internat'l Group, Inc.

WINBORN, Erik
575 Seventh St. NW
Terrell Bldg.
Washington, DC 20004
Tel: (202) 737 - 5523
Fax:(202) 737 - 6069

Registered Federal Lobbyist.
Serves As:
- Director, National Government Relations, Wal-Mart Stores

WINCHALL, Steve
1000 Wilson Blvd., Suite 2300 Tel: (703) 875 - 8400
Arlington, VA 22209
Registered Federal Lobbyist.
Serves As:
- Representative, Northrop Grumman Corp.

WINCHESTER, Judith A.
800 Connecticut Ave. NW Tel: (202) 452 - 4700
Suite 1200 Fax:(202) 452 - 4791
Washington, DC 20006
Registered Federal Lobbyist.
Serves As:
- Managing Director, Government Affairs, Lehman Brothers

WINDHAM, E. Bruce
P.O. Box 10246 Tel: (205) 387 - 0501
Birmingham, AL 35202 Fax:(205) 945 - 6570
Registered Federal Lobbyist.
Serves As:
- Director, Regulatory and Governmental Relations, Drummond Co., Inc.

WINDLE, Timothy J.
1111 Broadway Tel: (510) 272 - 8000
Oakland, CA 94607-5500 Fax:(510) 272 - 7421
timothy_windle@apl.com
Serves As:
- General Counsel and Treasurer, APL Ltd. PAC, APL Americas

WINGATE, Heather
1101 Pennsylvania Ave. NW Tel: (202) 879 - 6845
Suite 1000 Fax:(202) 783 - 4460
Washington, DC 20004
Registered Federal Lobbyist.
Serves As:
- V. President, Global Government Affairs, Citigroup, Inc.

WINGFIELD, Steven
Two Democracy Center Tel: (301) 564 - 3200
6903 Rockledge Dr. Fax:(301) 564 - 3201
Bethesda, MD 20817-1818
wingfieldd@usec.com
Serves As:
- Director, Investor Relations, USEC Inc.

WINGO, Patrick T.
1230 Peachtree St., N.E. Tel: (404) 810 - 4769
Room 400 Fax:(404) 810 - 5901
Atlanta, GA 30309
wingo@att.com
Serves As:
- Director, Law and Government Affairs - Georgia, AT&T

WINGO, William Bruce
325 Old City Hall Tel: (804) 649 - 2485
1001 E. Broad St. Fax:(804) 649 - 3447
Richmond, VA 23219-1908
Serves As:
- Resident V. President, Norfolk Southern Corp.

Responsibilities include corporate public and government affairs.

WINKER, Jeff
P.O. Box 419580 Tel: (816) 274 - 5111
Kansas City, MO 64141-6580 Fax:(816) 274 - 5061
Serves As:
- Communications Strategist, Hallmark Cards, Inc.

WINKLEMAN, Dennis R.
P.O. Box 554 Tel: (414) 319 - 8500
Milwaukee, WI 53201 Fax:(414) 319 - 8510
Serves As:
- Exec. V. President, Human Resources, Joy Global Inc.

WINKLER, Philip
1101 Pennsylvania Ave. NW Tel: (202) 659 - 1324
Suite 510 Fax:(202) 659 - 1328
Washington, DC 20004
Registered Federal Lobbyist.
Serves As:
- Representative, Air Products and Chemicals, Inc.

WINN, III, H. John
1426 Main St. Tel: (803) 217 - 9240
Columbia, SC 29218 Fax:(803) 217 - 8825
jwinn@scana.com
Serves As:
- Manager, Investor Relations and Shareholder Services, SCANA Corp.

WINN, Tracy
120 Monument Circle Tel: (317) 488 - 6134
Indianapolis, IN 46204
Serves As:
- PAC Contact, Wellpoint, Inc.

WINSTON, Jacqueline B.
P.O. Box 1365 Tel: (803) 798 - 7000
Columbia, SC 29202 TF: (800) 325 - 4368
Serves As:
- PAC Treasurer, Colonial Life & Accident Insurance Co.

WINSTON, Michael
2701 San Tomas Exwy. Tel: (408) 486 - 2000
Santa Clara, CA 95050 Fax:(408) 486 - 2200
Serves As:
- V. President, Human Resources, NVIDIA Corp.

WINTE, Jill
Checkerboard Square Tel: (314) 982 - 2929
St. Louis, MO 63164 Fax:(314) 982 - 2752
jwinte@purina.com
Serves As:
- Director, Employee and Corporate Communications, Nestle Purina PetCare Co.

WINTER, David
1021 E. Cary St. Tel: (804) 697 - 1000
Richmond, VA 23217 Fax:(804) 697 - 1199
Serves As:
- Director, Human Resources, Chesapeake Corp.

WINTER, Katie
22301 Foothill Blvd. Tel: (510) 727 - 2634
MS 4050 Fax:(510) 727 - 2300
Hayward, CA 94541
Serves As:
- Senior Manager, Public Relations, Mervyn's

WINTON, Deborah
5780 Powers Ferry Rd. NW Tel: (770) 980 - 5100
Atlanta, GA 30327 Fax:(770) 980 - 3301
Registered Federal Lobbyist.
Serves As:
- Representative, ING Americas

WINTON, Jeffrey A.
2000 Galloping Hill Rd. Tel: (908) 298 - 7662
Kenilworth, NJ 07033
Serves As:
- Group V. President, Global Communications, Schering-Plough Corporation

WINTROB, Jay S.
One SunAmerica Center Tel: (310) 772 - 6000
Los Angeles, CA 90067-6022 TF: (800) 871 - 2000
Serves As:
- President and Chief Exec. Officer, AIG SunAmerica Inc.

WIRCH, John R.
PO Box 19032 Tel: (920) 661 - 1111
Green Bay, WI 54307 Fax:(920) 661 - 2222
TF: (800) 232 - 5432
Serves As:
- V. President, Human Resources, American Medical Security Group, Inc.

WIRTH, Paul G.
Two N. Ninth St. Tel: (610) 774 - 5562
Allentown, PA 18101-1179 Fax:(610) 774 - 5281
pgwirth@pplweb.com TF: (800) 345 - 3085
Serves As:
- Manager, Public Relations, PPL Corp.

WIRTH, Ronald O.
1099 18th St. Tel: (303) 252 - 6090
Suite 1200 Fax:(303) 457 - 8482
Denver, CO 80202 TF: (800) 933 - 5603
rwirth@westerngas.com
Serves As:
- Director, Investor Relations, Western Gas Resources, Inc.

WISCHHUSEN, John
70 Maxess Rd. Tel: (631) 396 - 5000
Melville, NY 11747 Ext: 125
jwischhusen@nuhorizons.com Fax:(631) 396 - 7576
Serves As:
- Director, Marketing Communications, Nu Horizons Electronics Corp.

WISDOM, Jennifer
5700 Tennyson Pkwy., Third Floor
Plano, TX 75024
Tel: (972) 801 - 1100
Fax:(972) 943 - 0112
TF: (800) 275 - 2696

Serves As:
- V. President, Human Resources, Rent-A-Center, Inc.

WISE, Allen F.
6705 Rockledge Dr.
Suite 100
Bethesda, MD 20817
Tel: (301) 581 - 0600
Fax:(301) 493 - 0705

Serves As:
- Chairman of the Board, Coventry Health Care

WISE, Charles W. "Bud"
One PPG Pl.
12 North
Pittsburgh, PA 15272
Tel: (412) 434 - 3715
Fax:(412) 434 - 4666

Serves As:
- V. President, Human Resources, PPG Industries Inc.

WISE, R. Halsey
P.O. Box 240000
170 Graphics Dr.
Huntsville, AL 35758
Tel: (256) 730 - 2000
TF: (800) 345 - 4856

Serves As:
- President and Chief Exec. Officer, Intergraph Corp.

WISE COOK, Judith
801 Pennsylvania Ave. NW
Suite 725
Washington, DC 20004
judy.cook@sanofi-aventis.com
Tel: (202) 883 - 3184
Fax:(202) 682 - 0538

Registered Federal Lobbyist.
Serves As:
- Director, Health Policy and Biotechnology Programs, Sanofi-Aventis Inc.

WISECUP, Reyne K.
P.O. Box 978
Winona, MN 55987
Tel: (507) 453 - 8112
Fax:(507) 453 - 8049

Serves As:
- V. President, Employee Development, Fastenal Co.

WISNER, Frank G.
70 Pine St.
New York, NY 10270
Tel: (212) 770 - 7000
Fax:(212) 770 - 7821

Serves As:
- V. Chairman, External Affairs, American Internat'l Group, Inc.

WISNIEWSKI, Anthony
One MedImmune Way
Gaithersburg, MD 20878
wisniewskia@medimmune.com
Tel: (301) 398 - 0000
Fax:(301) 398 - 9000
TF: (877) 633 - 4411

Serves As:
- Director, Public Policy, MedImmune, Inc.

WISOR, Russell C.
1909 K St. NW
Suite 750
Washington, DC 20006-1171
russell.wisor@alcoa.com
Tel: (202) 956 - 5306
Fax:(202) 956 - 5305

Registered Federal Lobbyist.
Serves As:
- V. President, Government Affairs, Alcoa Inc.

WITENSTEIN, Adele
1399 New York Ave. NW
Suite 200
Washington, DC 20005
Tel: (202) 378 - 2020
Fax:(202) 783 - 6631

Serves As:
- Senior Director, Policy and Government Affairs, Abbott Laboratories

WITORT, Stephen F.
1425 K St. NW
Suite 300
Washington, DC 20005
Tel: (202) 414 - 3000
Fax:(202) 414 - 3037

Registered Federal Lobbyist.
Serves As:
- Director, Public Affairs, 3M Company

WITT, Warren
560 Lexington Ave.
15th Floor
New York, NY 10022
wwitt@volt.com
Tel: (212) 704 - 2400
Fax:(212) 704 - 2417
TF: (800) 533 - 2401

Serves As:
- Director, Risk Management, Volt Information Sciences, Inc.

WITTENBERG, Margaret
550 Bowie St.
Austin, TX 78703
Tel: (512) 477 - 4455
Fax:(512) 477 - 1069

Serves As:
- V. President, Marketing and Public Affairs, Whole Foods Market, Inc.

WITTER, Frank
3800 Hamlin Rd.
Auburn Hills, MI 48326
Tel: (248) 754 - 5000
Fax:(248) 754 - 4930

Serves As:
- President and Chief Exec. Officer, Volkswagen of America, Inc.

WITTIG, Paul
1415 W. 22nd St.
Suite 1100
Oak Brook, IL 60523
Tel: (630) 954 - 2030

Serves As:
- Director, Rish Management, Trade and Finance, Federal Signal Corp.

WOHLT, Judith A.
700 Oakmont Lane
Westmont, IL 60559
Tel: (630) 570 - 3000
Fax:(630) 570 - 3606

Serves As:
- Manager, Corporate Communications, SIRVA, Inc.

WOLAK, Jeanne B.
601 Pennsylvania Ave. NW
Suite 800
Washington, DC 20004
Tel: (202) 261 - 5000
Fax:(202) 296 - 7937

Registered Federal Lobbyist.
Serves As:
- Director, Federal Legislative Affairs, Southern Company

WOLD, Steve
5050 Lincoln Dr.
Edina, MN 55436
steve_wold@atk.com
Tel: (952) 351 - 3056
Fax:(952) 351 - 3009

Serves As:
- V. President, Investor Relations, Alliant Techsystems

WOLF, Dale B.
6705 Rockledge Dr.
Suite 100
Bethesda, MD 20817
Tel: (301) 581 - 0600
Fax:(301) 493 - 0705

Serves As:
- Chief Exec. Officer, Coventry Health Care

WOLF, Ellen
Two Democracy Center
6903 Rockledge Dr.
Bethesda, MD 20817-1818
Tel: (301) 564 - 3200
Fax:(301) 564 - 3201

Serves As:
- Pac Treasurer, USEC Inc.

WOLF, Howard
P.O. Box 1637
Houston, TX 77251-1637
Tel: (713) 868 - 7614
Fax:(713) 426 - 1331

Serves As:
- Chairman of the Board, Stewart & Stevenson Services, Inc.

WOLF, James E.
1501 Lee Hwy.
Suite 140
Arlington, VA 22209-1109
asdwolf@aol.com
Tel: (703) 525 - 4015
Fax:(703) 525 - 0327

Serves As:
- V. President, American Standard Companies Inc.

WOLF, Stephen M.
111 S. Wacker Dr.
Chicago, IL 60606
Tel: (312) 326 - 8000

Serves As:
- Chairman of the Board, R R Donnelley

WOLFCALE, Amy
World Financial Center
200 Liberty St.
New York, NY 10281
Tel: (609) 420 - 4000

Serves As:
- V. President, Corporate Communications, Dow Jones and Co.

WOLFE, John
170 Utopia St.
Manchester, CT 06040-0310
john.wolfe@cox.com
Tel: (860) 432 - 5008
Fax:(860) 512 - 5115

Serves As:
- V. President, Government and Public Affairs, (Cox Communications, Inc.), Cox Enterprises, Inc.

WOLFE, Stephen P.
8111 Lyndale Ave. South
Bloomington, MN 55420-1196
Tel: (952) 888 - 8801
Fax:(952) 887 - 7961

Serves As:
- V. President, Finance, Chief Financial Officer and Treasurer, The Toro Co.
Responsibilities include investor relations.

WOLFF, Stephen
400 Robert St. North
St. Paul, MN 55101
stephen.wolff@minnesotamutual.com
Tel: (651) 665 - 3500
Fax:(651) 665 - 4128

Serves As:
- Director, Communications, Minnesota Life Insurance Co.

WOLFORD, Richard G.
P.O. Box 193575
San Francisco, CA 94119-3575
Tel: (415) 247 - 3000
Fax:(415) 247 - 3565

Serves As:
- Chairman, President and Chief Exec. Officer, Del Monte Foods

WOLKOFF, Neal L.
86 Trinity Pl.
New York, NY 10006
Tel: (212) 306 - 1000
Fax:(212) 306 - 1152

Serves As:
- Chairman and Chief Executive Officer, American Stock Exchange

WOLLENBERG, Richard H.
P.O. Box 639
Longview, WA 98632
Tel: (360) 425 - 1550
Fax:(360) 575 - 5934

Serves As:
- Chairman, President and Chief Exec. Officer, Longview Fibre Co.

WOLLITZ, Jeffry R.
4800 Deerwood Campus Pkwy.
DCC3-4
Jacksonville, FL 32246-8273
Tel: (904) 905 - 6072
Fax:(904) 905 - 4486
TF: (800) 477 - 3736

Registered Federal Lobbyist.
Serves As:
- Director, Federal Government/Legislation Relations, Blue Cross and Blue Shield of Florida

WOLTER, Gary J.
P.O. Box 1231
Madison, WI 53701-1231
Tel: (608) 252 - 7000
Fax:(608) 252 - 7098
TF: (800) 356 - 6423

Serves As:
- Chairman, President, and Chief Exec. Officer, Madison Gas and Electric Co.

WONG, Irene
60 S. Market St.
Suite 1000
San Jose, CA 95113

Serves As:
- Exec. Director, eBay Foundation, eBay, Inc.

WONG, Teresa
1201 Lake Robbins Dr.
The Woodlands, TX 77380
teresa_wong@anadarko.com
Tel: (832) 636 - 1203

Serves As:
- Manager, Public Affairs and Corporate Communications, Anadarko Petroleum Corp.

WONNELL, David
P.O. Box 6721
Chicago, IL 60680-6721
dgwonnel@usg.com
Tel: (312) 606 - 4016
Fax:(312) 606 - 4484

Serves As:
- Director, Environment and Manufacturing Services, USG Corp.

WOOD, Barry
P.O. Box 93
Pittsburg, TX 75686
Tel: (903) 855 - 1000
TF: (800) 824 - 1159

Serves As:
- Director, Media Relations and Communications, Pilgrim's Pride Corp.

WOOD, C. William
P.O. Box 6006
LC05-322
Cypress, CA 90630
bill.wood@phs.com
Tel: (714) 825 - 5125
Fax:(714) 825 - 5028

Serves As:
- V. President, Community Relations; President, PacifiCare Foundation, PacifiCare Health Systems, Inc.

WOOD, Kristin
20 S. Wacker Dr.
Chicago, IL 60606-7499
kwood@cme.com
Tel: (312) 930 - 4510
Fax:(312) 930 - 3439

Serves As:
- Foundation Contact, Chicago Mercantile Exchange Inc.

WOOD, Paul
One American Rd.
M/S 8N/184
Dearborn, MI 48126
pwood@ford.com
Tel: (313) 621 - 2961
Fax:(313) 248 - 9204
TF: (800) 555 - 5259

Registered Federal Lobbyist.
Serves As:
- Manager, Public Affairs, Ford Motor Co.

WOOD, Paul G.
12 West St.
M/S 8N
Annapolis, MD 21401
paul.g.wood@verizon.com
Tel: (410) 269 - 6653
Fax:(410) 269 - 5719

Serves As:
- V. President, Government Affairs, Verizon Maryland Inc.

WOOD, Paul W.
Lever House, 390 Park Ave.
New York, NY 10022-4698
paul.wood@unilever.com
Tel: (212) 888 - 1260
Fax:(212) 688 - 3411

Serves As:
- V. President, Corporate Affairs, Unilever United States, Inc.

WOOD, Jr., Richard D.
260 Baltimore Pike
Wawa, PA 19063
Tel: (610) 358 - 8000
Fax:(610) 358 - 8878
TF: (800) 283 - 9292

Serves As:
- Chairman of the Board, Wawa, Inc.

WOOD, Robert E.
P.O. Box 5650
Bismarck, ND 58506-5650
robert.wood@mduresources.com
Tel: (701) 222 - 7828
Fax:(701) 222 - 7607
TF: (800) 437 - 8000

Serves As:
- Senior V. President, Governmental and Public Affairs, MDU Resources Group, Inc.

WOOD, Robert L.
199 Benson Rd.
Middlebury, VT 06749
Tel: (203) 573 - 2000
Fax:(203) 573 - 3711

Serves As:
- Chairman, President and Chief Exec. Officer, Chemtura

WOOD, Tom
1127 11th St., Suite 747B
Sacramento, CA 95814
woodt@wyeth.com
Tel: (916) 491 - 4051

Serves As:
- Associate Director, State Government Relations, Wyeth Pharmaceuticals

WOODARD, Kimberly
575 Seventh St. NW
Terrell Bldg.
Washington, DC 20004
Tel: (202) 737 - 5523
Fax:(202) 737 - 6069

Registered Federal Lobbyist.
Serves As:
- Director, National Government Relations, Wal-Mart Stores

WOODBURN, Connie R.
7000 Cardinal Pl.
Dublin, OH 43017
connie.woodburn@cardinal.com
Tel: (614) 757 - 7769
Fax:(614) 757 - 5115
TF: (800) 234 - 8701

Registered Federal Lobbyist.
Serves As:
- Senior V. President, Government Relations, Cardinal Health Inc.

WOODHOUSE, Michael A.
305 Hartman Dr.
Lebanon, TN 37088
Tel: (615) 444 - 5533
Fax:(615) 443 - 9511

Serves As:
- Chairman, President and Chief Exec. Officer, CBRL Group, Inc.

WOODLEF, John B.
301 S. Tryon St., Suite 1800
Charlotte, NC 28202
Tel: (704) 372 - 5404
Fax:(704) 372 - 6409

Serves As:
- V. President, Finance and Chief Financial Officer, Ruddick Corp.
Responsibilities include investor relations.

WOODRUFF, Sheri L.
Nine Roszel Rd.
Princeton, NJ 08540
Tel: (609) 720 - 4399
Fax:(609) 720 - 4208

Serves As:
- Media Contact, Tyco Internat'l (U.S.), Inc.

WOODS, Betty

P.O. Box 3100
Fullerton, CA 92834
Tel: (714) 871 - 4848
Fax:(714) 773 - 8283
TF: (800) 742 - 2345

Serves As:
• Chairman of the Board, Beckman Coulter, Inc.

WOODS, David W.

300 Exelon Way
Kennett Square, PA 19348
david.woods@exeloncorp.com
Tel: (610) 765 - 6900
Fax:(610) 765 - 6902

Serves As:
• Senior V. President, Public Affairs, Exelon Corp.
Responsibilities include government affairs.

WOODS, Jerry D.

1000 Wilson Blvd., Suite 2300
Arlington, VA 22209
Tel: (703) 875 - 8400
Fax:(703) 276 - 0711

Registered Federal Lobbyist.
Serves As:
• Manager, Legislative Affairs, Northrop Grumman Corp.

WOODS, Mary

2101 E. Jefferson St.
Rockville, MD 20852
Tel: (301) 816 - 2424
Fax:(301) 816 - 7119

Serves As:
• Corporate Communications, Kaiser Permanente

WOODS, Steven

P.O. Box 431
Easton, PA 18044-0431
Tel: (610) 253 - 6271
Fax:(610) 250 - 5768

Serves As:
• V. President, Human Resources, Binney and Smith Inc.

WOODS, Thomas

5725 Delphi Dr.
483-400-501
Troy, MI 48098-2815
Tel: (248) 813 - 2620
Fax:(248) 813 - 3253

Serves As:
• Regional Director, Government and Community Relations, Delphi Corp.

WOODSON, Nathaniel

P.O. Box 1564
New Haven, CT 06506-0901
nathaniel.woodson@uinet.com
Tel: (203) 499 - 2000
Fax:(203) 499 - 3626
TF: (800) 722 - 5584

Serves As:
• Chairman and Chief Exec. Officer, The United Illuminating Company

WOODSON-BRYANT, Sharon

445 S. Figueroa St.
Los Angeles, CA 90071
sharonw.bryant@uboc.com
Tel: (213) 236 - 4145
Fax:(213) 236 - 4147

Serves As:
• V. President, Corporate Communications, Union Bank of California

WOOLLEY, Howard

1300 I St. NW
Suite 400 West
Washington, DC 20005
howard.woolley@verizonwireless.com
Tel: (202) 589 - 3740

Registered Federal Lobbyist.
Serves As:
• V. President, Federal Relations, Verizon Wireless

WOOLWORTH, Dick

P.O. Box 1271
M/S E15A
Portland, OR 97207-1271
Tel: (503) 225 - 5228
Fax:(503) 225 - 5283

Serves As:
• Chairman of the Board, Regence BlueCross BlueShield of Oregon

WOOLWORTH, Richard

220 NW Second Ave.
Portland, OR 97209-3991
Tel: (503) 226 - 4211
Fax:(503) 721 - 2508

Serves As:
• Chairman of the Board, NW Natural

WOOTTON, Michael J.

P.O. Box 7888
Van Nuys, CA 91409-7888
mwootton@sunkistgrowers.com
Tel: (818) 986 - 4800
Fax:(818) 379 - 7511

Registered Federal Lobbyist.
Serves As:
• V. President, Corporate Relations/Counsel, Sunkist Growers

WORDEN, Jeff

One PPG Pl.
7 South
Pittsburgh, PA 15272
Tel: (412) 434 - 3046
Fax:(412) 434 - 4666

Serves As:
• Manager, Public Relations, PPG Industries Inc.

WORK, Dale

1300 I St. NW
Suite 1070 East
Washington, DC 20005
Tel: (202) 962 - 8550
Fax:(202) 962 - 8560

Registered Federal Lobbyist.
Serves As:
• Vice President, Technology Policy and Industry Affairs, Philips Electronics North America

WORKMAN, Larry E.

P.O. Box 272
Alexander City, AL 35011

Serves As:
• Treasurer, Russell Corp. PAC, Russell Corp.

WORMLEY, Harry J.

P.O. Box 2641
Birmingham, AL 35291
Tel: (205) 257 - 2602
Fax:(205) 257 - 2622

Serves As:
• Director, Corporate Relations, Alabama Power Co.

WORRELL, James

115 Perimeter Center Pl.
Suite 460
Atlanta, GA 30346
Tel: (770) 395 - 4500
Fax:(770) 395 - 4529

Serves As:
• Director, Human Resources, Georgia Gulf Corp.

WORTMAN, Mary

P.O. Box 92957
450
Los Angeles, CA 90009-2957
mary.f.wortman@aero.org
Tel: (310) 336 - 0128
Fax:(310) 336 - 7055

Serves As:
• Director, Internal Communications, The Aerospace Corp.

WRAASE, Dennis R.

701 Ninth St. NW
Washington, DC 20068
Tel: (202) 872 - 2000

Serves As:
• Chairman, President and Chief Executive Officer, Pepco Holdings, Inc.
• Chief Exec. Officer, Conectiv

WRATHER, Janet V.

1111 Lockheed Martin Way
Bldg. 157
Sunnyvale, CA 94089
janet.wrather@lmco.com
Tel: (408) 742 - 6688
Fax:(408) 743 - 2239

Serves As:
• V. President, Communications, Lockheed Martin Space Systems Company

WRAY, Susan

One Haworth Center
Holland, MI 49423
Tel: (616) 393 - 1604
Fax:(616) 393 - 3138
TF: (800) 344 - 2600

Serves As:
• Manager, Public and Member Communications, Haworth Inc.

WREN, John D.

437 Madison Ave.
Ninth Floor
New York, NY 10022
Tel: (212) 415 - 3600
Fax:(212) 415 - 3530

Serves As:
• President and Chief Exec. Officer, Omnicom Group Inc.

WRIGHT, Allen

4111 E. 37th St., North
Wichita, KS 67220
allen.wright@fhr.com
Tel: (316) 828 - 8721
Fax:(316) 828 - 4228

Serves As:
• V. President, Public Affairs, (Flint Hills Resources, LP), Koch Industries, Inc.

WRIGHT, Jr., Arnold W.

Two Liberty Pl.
1601 Chestnut St.
Philadelphia, PA 19192
woodie.wright@cigna.com
Tel: (215) 761 - 6055
Fax:(215) 761 - 5515

Serves As:
• V. President, Contributions and Exec. Director, CIGNA Foundation, CIGNA Corp.

WRIGHT, Belinda

P.O. Box 1410
Sanford, NC 27330
Tel: (919) 774 - 6700
Fax:(919) 774 - 3329

Serves As:
• Investor Relations Contact, The Pantry, Inc.

WRIGHT, Charles S.

11270 W. Park Place
Milwaukee, WI 53224-9510
Tel: (414) 359 - 4104
Fax:(414) 359 - 4064

Serves As:
• Manager, Corporate Communications, A. O. Smith Corp.

WRIGHT, Crystal
1355 Jefferson St. NW
Washington, DC 20011
Tel: (202) 291 - 8481

Serves As:
- V. President, Public Relations, Leiner Health Products, Inc.

WRIGHT, Elease E.
151 Farmington Ave.
Hartford, CT 06156
Tel: (860) 273 - 8371
Fax:(860) 560 - 8721

Serves As:
- Senior V. President, Human Resources, Aetna Inc.

WRIGHT, Felix E.
P.O. Box 757
Carthage, MO 64836-0757
felix.wright@leggett.com
Tel: (417) 358 - 8131
Fax:(417) 358 - 7155

Serves As:
- Chairman and Chief Exec. Officer, Leggett & Platt, Inc.

WRIGHT, James L.
1100 CommScope Pl. SE
Hickory, NC 28603
Tel: (828) 324 - 2200
Fax:(828) 982 - 1708

Serves As:
- Senior V. President, Human Resources and Environment, CommScope

WRIGHT, James T.
P.O. Box 1028
Greenville, SC 29602
Tel: (864) 271 - 7733
Fax:(864) 282 - 9482

Serves As:
- Senior V. President, Human Resources, Bowater Incorporated

WRIGHT, Jason
Four World Financial Center
250 Vesey St.
New York, NY 10080
Tel: (212) 236 - 1000

Serves As:
- Senior V. President, Communications and Public Affairs, Merrill Lynch & Co., Inc.

WRIGHT, John
8111 Lyndale Ave. South
Bloomington, MN 55420-1196
Tel: (952) 887 - 8865
Fax:(952) 887 - 7961

Serves As:
- Director, Investor Relations, The Toro Co.

WRIGHT, Kenneth D.
P.O. Box 2291
M/S HQ4
Durham, NC 27702-2291
ken.wright@bcbsnc.com
Tel: (919) 765 - 7582
Fax:(919) 765 - 4837

Serves As:
- Director, State and Federal Relations, Blue Cross and Blue Shield of North Carolina

WRIGHT, Lee E.
P.O. Box 2910
Shawnee Mission, KS 66201
Tel: (913) 661 - 6300

Serves As:
- Legislative Representative, (Farmers Insurance Group of Companies), Farmers Group, Inc.

WRIGHT, Lori E.
1133 19th St. NW
Washington, DC 20036
Tel: (202) 887 - 3830
Fax:(202) 887 - 3123

Serves As:
- Manager, FCC Regulatory, MCI, Inc.

WRIGHT, Michael J.
5710 Painted Valley Dr.
Austin, TX 78759
michael.wright@roche.com
Tel: (512) 343 - 2915
Fax:(512) 343 - 7811

Serves As:
- Senior Regional Manager, State Government Affairs, (HLR Service Corp.), Hoffmann-La Roche Inc. (Roche)

WRIGHT, Robert E.
2141 Rosecrans Ave., Suite 4000
El Segundo, CA 90245
Tel: (310) 726 - 7665
Fax:(310) 726 - 7818

Serves As:
- V. President, Investor Relations, UNOCAL Corp.

WRIGHT, Samuel H.
101 Constitution Ave. NW
Suite 800
Washington, DC 20001
samuel.wright@cendant.com
Tel: (202) 742 - 4270
Fax:(202) 742 - 4271

Registered Federal Lobbyist.
Serves As:
- Senior V. President, Government Relations, Cendant Corp.

WRIGHT, Usha
Four W. Red Oak Ln.
White Plains, NY 10604
usha.wright@itt.com
Tel: (914) 641 - 2053
Fax:(914) 696 - 2950

Serves As:
- V. President, Associate General Counsel, and Director, Environment, Safety and Health, ITT Industries

WRIGHT, W. Lance
Two Democracy Center
6903 Rockledge Dr.
Bethesda, MD 20817-1818
Tel: (301) 564 - 3200
Fax:(301) 564 - 3201

Serves As:
- V. President, Human Resources and Administration, USEC Inc.

WRIGHT, Yvonne Klemets
41 Moores Rd.
Frazer, PA 19355
ywright@cephalon.com
Tel: (610) 738 - 6340
Fax:(610) 344 - 0981

Serves As:
- Manager, Corporate Communications, Cephalon, Inc.

WRIGHT-VIOLICH, Kimberly
101 Montgomery St.
San Francisco, CA 94104
Tel: (415) 627 - 7000
TF: (800) 435 - 4000

Serves As:
- President, Schwab Fund for Charitable Giving, The Charles Schwab Corp.

WRIGLEY, Robert E.
198 Van Buren St.
Suite 300
Herndon, VA 20170
Tel: (703) 834 - 3400
Fax:(703) 834 - 3567

Registered Federal Lobbyist.
Serves As:
- Director, Governmental Affairs, Airbus North America Holdings, Inc.

WRIGLEY, Jr., William
410 N. Michigan Ave.
Chicago, IL 60611
Tel: (312) 644 - 2121
Ext: 4132
Fax:(312) 644 - 0015

Serves As:
- Chairman, President and Chief Exec. Officer, Wm. Wrigley Jr. Co.

WRISTEN, Edward L.
3200 Highland Ave.
Downers Grove, IL 60515-1223
Tel: (630) 737 - 7900
Fax:(630) 737 - 7856
TF: (800) 445 - 1425

Serves As:
- President and Chief Exec. Officer, First Health

WROBEL, Gene
P.O. Box 240000
170 Graphics Dr.
Huntsville, AL 35758
Tel: (256) 730 - 2000
TF: (800) 345 - 4856

Serves As:
- V. President and Treasurer, Intergraph Corp.

Responsibilities include investor relations.

WROBLESKI, Ann
1101 Pennsylvania Ave. NW
Suite 200
Washington, DC 20004
Tel: (202) 628 - 1223
Fax:(202) 628 - 1368

Serves As:
- V. President, Public Affairs, Internat'l Paper

WU, Jeanne
2315 N. First St.
San Jose, CA 95131
Tel: (408) 570 - 8000
Fax:(408) 570 - 8901

Serves As:
- Senior V. President, Human Resources, BEA Systems, Inc.

WUERST, Jessie
P.O. Box 3727
Spokane, WA 99220-3727
jessie.wuerst@avistacorp.com
Tel: (509) 495 - 8578
Fax:(509) 495 - 8725
TF: (800) 727 - 9170

Serves As:
- Investor Relations Contact, Avista Corp.

WULFF, John K.
1313 N. Market St.
Wilmington, DE 19894-0001
Tel: (302) 594 - 5000
Fax:(302) 594 - 5400

Serves As:
- Chairman of the Board, Hercules Incorporated

WYATT, Jr., E. Lee
6415 Idlewild Rd., Suite 109
Charlotte, NC 28212
Tel: (704) 566 - 2400
Fax:(704) 536 - 4668

Serves As:
- Treasurer, Sonic Automotive Inc. Federal PAC and Sonic Automotive Inc. State PAC, Sonic Automotive, Inc.

WYCHE, Jr., Paul B.
2801 W. Tyvola Rd.
Charlotte, NC 28217-4500
paul_wyche@belk.com
Tel: (704) 426 - 8404
Fax:(704) 357 - 1876

Serves As:
- Senior V. President and Associate Counsel, Belk, Inc.

Responsibilititites include corporate philanthropy.

WYLD, Deborah
P.O. Box 3040
Norfolk, VA 23501
Tel: (757) 629 - 2881
Fax:(757) 629 - 2361

Serves As:
- Exec. Director, Norfolk Southern Foundation, Norfolk Southern Corp.

WYLIE, Scott
101 Innovation Dr.
San Jose, CA 95134-1941
swylie@altera.com
Tel: (408) 544 - 6996
Fax:(408) 544 - 7740

Serves As:
- V. President, Investor Relations, Altera Corp.

WYLY, Jr., Charles J.
8000 Bent Branch Dr.
Irving, TX 75063
Tel: (972) 409 - 1300
Fax:(972) 409 - 1556

Serves As:
- Chairman of the Board, Michaels Stores, Inc.

WYMAN, William
P.O. Box 300
Oshkosh, WI 54903-0300
Tel: (920) 231 - 8800
Fax:(920) 231 - 8621
TF: (800) 282 - 4674

Serves As:
- Corporate Contributions Contact, Oshkosh B'Gosh, Inc.

WYNN, Peg
2100 Logic Dr.
San Jose, CA 95124-3400
peg.wynn@xilinx.com
Tel: (408) 559 - 7778
Ext: 5031
Fax:(408) 559 - 7114
TF: (800) 836 - 4002

Serves As:
- V. President, Worldwide Human Resources, Xilinx, Inc.

WYNNE, Bob
500 Oracle Pkwy.
Redwood Shores, CA 94065
bob.wynne@oracle.com
Tel: (650) 506 - 5834
Fax:(650) 633 - 1269
TF: (800) 672 - 2531

Serves As:
- V. President, Corporate Communications, Oracle Corporation

WYPER, Janet
One Casco St.
Freeport, ME 04033
Tel: (207) 552 - 6038
Fax:(207) 552 - 6821
TF: (800) 221 - 4221

Serves As:
- Manager, Community Relations, L. L. Bean, Inc.

WYRICK, Cindy
P.O. Box 2900
Honolulu, HI 96846
cwyrick@boh.com
Tel: (808) 537 - 8430
Fax:(808) 538 - 4445
TF: (888) 643 - 3888

Serves As:
- Senior V. President, Investor Relations/Corporate Secretary, Bank of Hawaii Corp.

WYZGA, Michael S.
1020 19th St., NW
Suite 550
Washington, DC 20036
Tel: (202) 296 - 3280
Fax:(202) 296 - 3411

Serves As:
- PAC Treasurer, Genzyme Corp.

YABLON, Leonard H.
60 Fifth Ave.
New York, NY 10010
Tel: (212) 620 - 2200
Fax:(212) 620 - 2245

Serves As:
- Secretary/Treasurer, Foundation, Forbes, Inc.

YAEGER, Douglas H.
720 Olive St.
St. Louis, MO 63101
Tel: (314) 342 - 0500
Fax:(314) 421 - 1979

Serves As:
- Chairman and Chief Exec. Officer, The Laclede Group

YAEGER, Lynn
290 Harbor Dr.
Stamford, CT 06902
Tel: (203) 328 - 0600
Fax:(203) 328 - 0690

Serves As:
- Exec. V. President, Corporate Affairs, (Time Warner Cable), Time Warner Inc.

YAGOW, Tim
625 Fourth Ave. South
Minneapolis, MN 55415
Tel: (612) 340 - 5821
Fax:(612) 340 - 7373

Serves As:
- Foundation Contact, Thrivent Financial for Lutherans

YAHIA, Laurence H.S.
175 Berkeley St.
Boston, MA 02116
Tel: (617) 357 - 9500
Fax:(617) 350 - 7648

Serves As:
- Pac Treasurer, Liberty Mutual Insurance Co.

YAMADA, Tadataka
P.O. Box 13398
Research Triangle Park, NC 27709
Tel: (919) 483 - 2100
Fax:(919) 549 - 7459

Serves As:
- Chairman of the Board, GlaxoSmithKline Research and Development

YAMADA, Yoshihiko
One Panasonic Way
Secaucus, NJ 07094
Tel: (201) 348 - 7000
Fax:(201) 392 - 6007
TF: (888) 275 - 2995

Serves As:
- Chairman and Chief Executive Officer, Matsushita Electric Corp. of America

YAMAMOTO, Alan
P.O. Box 730
Honolulu, HI 96808-0730
atyamamoto@hei.com
Tel: (808) 543 - 5662
Fax:(808) 543 - 7966

Serves As:
- Director, Community Relations, Hawaiian Electric Industries, Inc.

YAMANAKA, Ruthann S.
P.O. Box 3440
Honolulu, HI 96801-3440
Tel: (808) 525 - 8425
Fax:(808) 525 - 6611

Serves As:
- V. President, Human Resources, Alexander & Baldwin, Inc.

YAMASAKI, Steven T.
10990 Roe Ave.
Overland Park, KS 66211
Tel: (913) 696 - 6100
Fax:(913) 696 - 6116

Serves As:
- Senior V. President, Human Resources, Yellow Roadway Corporation

YAMASAKI, Vicki
P.O. Box 368
Indianapolis, IN 46206-0368
Tel: (317) 285 - 1877
Fax:(317) 285 - 1979

Serves As:
- V. President, Planning and Communications, American United Life Insurance Co.

YANAWAY, Diane
P.O. Box 227097
Dallas, TX 75222-7097
dyanawa1@txu.com
Tel: (214) 812 - 4905
Fax:(214) 812 - 4974

Serves As:
- Director, Public Advocacy, TXU

YANCEY, Carol B.
2999 Circle 75 Pkwy.
Atlanta, GA 30339
carol_yancey@genpt.com
Tel: (770) 953 - 1700
Fax:(770) 956 - 2211

Serves As:
- V. President and Corporate Secretary, Genuine Parts Co.

Responsibilities include investor relations.

YANCEY, H. Evonne
3495 Piedmont Rd., N.E.
Atlanta, GA 30305
Tel: (404) 364 - 7037
Fax:(404) 364 - 4792

Serves As:
- Director, Government and Community Affairs, (Kaiser Foundation Health Plan of Georgia), Kaiser Permanente

YANCEY, James D.
P.O. Box 120
Columbus, GA 31902-0120
Tel: (706) 649 - 2267
Fax:(706) 641 - 6555

Serves As:
- Chairman of the Board, Synovus Financial Corp.

YANCOSEK, Rosemarie
2000 Galloping Hill Rd.
Kenilworth, NJ 07033
Tel: (908) 298 - 7476

Serves As:
- Exec. Director, Global Communications, Schering-Plough Corporation

YANG, Wendy
1700 Lincoln St.
Denver, CO 80203
wyang@corp.newmont.com
Tel: (303) 863 - 7414
Fax:(303) 837 - 5837

Serves As:
- Director, Investor Relations, Newmont Mining Corp.

YANIS, Glenn
11419 Sunset Hills Rd.
Reston, VA 20190-5207
Tel: (703) 251 - 8500
Fax:(703) 251 - 8240
TF: (888) 368 - 2152

Serves As:
- PAC Contact, MAXIMUS, Inc.

YANO, David Marvin
One Enterprise Dr.
Aliso Viejo, CA 92656-2606
Tel: (949) 349 - 7171
Fax:(949) 349 - 5375

Serves As:
- PAC Contact, Fluor Corp.

YANOWITZ, Harry F.
3111 W. Allegheny Ave.
Philadelphia, PA 19132
Tel: (215) 430 - 9720
Fax:(215) 430 - 9533

Serves As:
- Senior V. President, Strategy and Business Development, The Pep Boys-Manny, Moe & Jack

Responsibilities include investor relations.

YARBROUGH, Dan
P.O. Box 6006
C120-533
Cypress, CA 90630
dan.yarbrough@phs.com
Tel: (714) 226 - 3540
Fax:(714) 226 - 3581

Serves As:
- Director, Investor Relations, PacifiCare Health Systems, Inc.

YARICK, Paul E.
12 E. Armour Blvd.
Kansas City, MO 64111
yarick_paul@interstatebrands.com
Tel: (816) 502 - 4164
Fax:(816) 502 - 4155

Serves As:
- V. President and Treasurer, Interstate Bakeries Corp.

Responsibilities include corporate communications.

YARRINGTON, Patricia E.
6001 Bollinger Canyon Rd.
San Ramon, CA 94583
Tel: (925) 842 - 1000

Serves As:
- V. President, Policy, Government and Public Affairs, Chevron Corp.

YASS, Robert K. "Bob"
Hartford Plaza
HO 1-11
Hartford, CT 06115
ryass@thehartford.com
Tel: (860) 547 - 4963
Fax:(860) 547 - 6551

Serves As:
- V. President, Government Affairs, The Hartford Financial Services Group Inc.

YBARRA, Frank
4551 W. 107th St.
Overland Park, KS 66207-4037
frank.ybarra@applebees.com
Tel: (913) 967 - 4159
Fax:(913) 341 - 1694

Serves As:
- Senior Communications Manager, Applebee's Internat'l, Inc.

YEAMANS, Becky
200 Park Ave.
Suite 300
Florham Park, NJ 07932
becky.yeamans@globalcrossing.com
Tel: (973) 937 - 0155
Fax:(973) 360 - 0148
TF: (800) 336 - 7000

Serves As:
- V. President, Media and Analysts Relations, Global Crossing Ltd.

YEATMAN, C. Perry
33 Benedict Pl.
Greenwich, CT 06830
Tel: (203) 661 - 2000
Fax:(203) 625 - 2370
TF: (800) 366 - 4011

Serves As:
- V. President, Corporate Affairs, Unilever Home & Personal Care - North America

YELVERTON, Todd W.
601 Pennsylvania Ave. NW
Suite 800
Washington, DC 20004
Tel: (202) 261 - 5000
Fax:(202) 296 - 7937

Registered Federal Lobbyist.
Serves As:
- Director, Federal Regulatory Affairs, Southern Company

YEMENIDJIAN, Alex
10250 Constellation Blvd.
Los Angeles, CA 90067-6241
ayemenidjian@mgm.com
Tel: (310) 449 - 3000
Fax:(310) 449 - 8757

Serves As:
- Chairman and Chief Exec. Officer, Metro-Goldwyn-Mayer Inc.

YESKO, Diane M.
120 Park Ave.
25th Floor
New York, NY 10017
Tel: (917) 663 - 3457
Fax:(917) 663 - 5439

Serves As:
- Supervisor, External Communications, (Altria Corporate Services, Inc.), Altria Group, Inc.

YEUTTER, Van
1101 15th St. NW
Suite 1000
Washington, DC 20005
v_yeutter@cargill.com
Tel: (202) 530 - 8160
Fax:(202) 530 - 8180

Serves As:
- Assistant V. President, Public Affiars, Cargill, Incorporated

YINGLING, Bill
P.O. Box 9239
Newark, DE 19714-9239
Tel: (302) 283 - 5811

Serves As:
- Senior Public Relations Consultant - Delmarva Power, Conectiv

YINGST, Tara
1621 Barber Ln.
D-125
Milpitas, CA 95035
tara@lsil.com
Tel: (408) 433 - 8000
Fax:(408) 954 - 3220
TF: (866) 574 - 5741

Serves As:
- Manager, Corporate and Employee Communications, LSI Logic Corp.

YOCHIM, Maryann C.
1100 State St.
Erie, PA 16501
yochimm@natfuel.com
Tel: (814) 871 - 8231

Serves As:
- Manager, Government Affairs, Nat'l Fuel Gas Co.

YOCHUM, Doreen "Dory"
1240 Crossman Ave.
Sunnyvale, CA 94089-1116
Tel: (408) 400 - 3000
Fax:(408) 400 - 1500

Serves As:
- Chief Administrative Officer and Secretary, PalmSource, Inc.

Responsibilities include human resources.

YOCUM, Robert G.
P.O. Box 8888
Camp Hill, PA 17001-8888
ryocum@harsco.com
Tel: (717) 763 - 7064
Fax:(717) 763 - 6424

Serves As:
- Assistant Treasurer and Chairman, Harsco Corp. Fund, Harsco Corp.

YOCUM, Robert H.
300 N. Meridian St., Suite 1500
Indianapolis, IN 46204-1763
Tel: (317) 247 - 8141
Fax:(317) 248 - 6472

Serves As:
- Chairman of the Board, Reilly Industries, Inc.

YODER, Kelly
One Seagate
27th Floor
Toledo, OH 43666
kyoder@o-i.com
Tel: (419) 247 - 5000
Fax:(419) 247 - 2839

Serves As:
- Corporate Communications Supervisor, Owens-Illinois, Inc.

YOH, III, Harold L.
1818 Market St.
Philadelphia, PA 19103
Tel: (215) 299 - 8000
TF: (800) 523 - 0786

Serves As:
- Chairman and Chief Exec. Officer, Day & Zimmerman

YOHE, D. Scott
1275 K St. NW
Suite 1200
Washington, DC 20005
Tel: (202) 296 - 6464
Fax:(202) 466 - 2610

Registered Federal Lobbyist.
Serves As:
- Senior V. President, Government Affairs, Delta Air Lines, Inc.

YOHMAN, Mark
P.O. Box 799900
Dallas, TX 75379-9900
mark.yohman@lennoxintl.com
Tel: (972) 497 - 5069
Fax:(972) 497 - 5299

Serves As:
- Director, Environmental Affairs, Lennox Internat'l

YONKUS, Stacey
622 Third Ave., 37th Floor
New York, NY 10017
syonkus@asburyauto.com
Tel: (212) 885 - 2512

Serves As:
- Director, Investor Relations, Asbury Automotive Group

YOO, Tae
170 W. Tasman Dr.
San Jose, CA 95134-1706
Tel: (408) 526 - 7659
Fax:(408) 526 - 6310
TF: (800) 553 - 6387

Serves As:
- V. President and Contact, Cisco Foundation, Cisco Systems, Inc.

YORK, Caroline
One MedImmune Way
Gaithersburg, MD 20878
yorkc@medimmune.com
Tel: (301) 398 - 0000
Fax:(301) 398 - 9000
TF: (877) 633 - 4411

Serves As:
- V. President, Government Affairs, MedImmune, Inc.

YORK, Elizabeth
1500 K St. NW
Suite 650
Washington, DC 20005
Tel: (202) 715 - 1000
Fax:(202) 715 - 1001

Registered Federal Lobbyist.
Serves As:
- Federal Government Relations, GlaxoSmithKline Research and Development

YOSHIDA, Motokazu
200 Park Ave.
New York, NY 10166
Tel: (212) 878 - 4000

Serves As:
- President and Chief Exec. Officer, Mitsui and Co. (U.S.A.), Inc.

YOST, R. David
1300 Morris Dr.
Suite 100
Chesterbrook, PA 19087-5594
Tel: (610) 727 - 7000
Fax:(610) 727 - 3600
TF: (800) 829 - 3132

Serves As:
- Chief Exec. Officer, AmeriSource Bergen Corp.

YOUNG, Annetta
P.O. Box 2020
Springdale, AR 72765-2020
annetta.young@tyson.com
Tel: (479) 290 - 4000
Fax:(479) 290 - 7984
TF: (800) 424 - 4253

Serves As:
- Administrator, Corporate Giving, Tyson Foods, Inc.

YOUNG, April
4201 Marsh Ln.
Carrolton, TX 75007
Tel: (972) 662 - 5685
Fax:(972) 307 - 2820

Serves As:
- Government Affairs Manager, (Carlson Restaurants Worldwide, Inc.), Carlson Companies

YOUNG, Charles
Nine Roszel Rd.
Princeton, NJ 08540
Tel: (609) 720 - 4200
Fax:(609) 720 - 4208

Serves As:
- Senior V. President, Corporate Marketing and Communications, Tyco Internat'l (U.S.), Inc.

Responsibilities include corporate philanthropy and community relations.

YOUNG, Dan
550 Newport Center Dr.
Newport Beach, CA 92660
Tel: (949) 720 - 2526
Fax:(949) 720 - 2575

Serves As:
- Exec. V. President, Entitlement and Public Affairs, The Irvine Company

YOUNG, Debbie
1929 Allen Pkwy.
Houston, TX 77019
debbie.young@sci-us.com
Tel: (713) 525 - 9088
Fax:(713) 525 - 2800

Serves As:
- Director, Investor Relations, Service Corp. Internat'l

YOUNG, Dona Davis
One American Row
Hartford, CT 06102
Tel: (860) 403 - 5967
Fax:(860) 403 - 5755

Serves As:
- Chairman, President and Chief Exec. Officer, The Phoenix Companies, Inc.

YOUNG, Douglas L.
200 Lake St. E.
Wayzata, MN 55391
Tel: (952) 475 - 7064
Fax:(952) 475 - 7969

Serves As:
- Compliance Officer, Legal Department, TCF Financial Corp.

Responsibilities include political action.

YOUNG, III, Edward D.
1300 I St. NW
Suite 400 West
Washington, DC 20005
edward.d.young@verizon.com
Tel: (202) 515 - 2400

Serves As:
- Senior V. President, Federal Government Relations, Verizon Communications Inc.

YOUNG, J. T.
1350 I St. NW
Suite 1000
Washington, DC 20005
Tel: (202) 962 - 5400
Fax:(202) 336 - 7223

Serves As:
- Legislative Manager, Ford Motor Co.

YOUNG, Julie
6065 Parkland Blvd.
Cleveland, OH 44124
julie.young@agilysys.com
Tel: (440) 720 - 8602
Fax:(440) 720 - 8720
TF: (800) 422 - 2400

Serves As:
- Director, Corporate Communications, Agilysys, Inc.

YOUNG, Kevin
Center Square
1500 Market St.
Philadelphia, PA 19102
Tel: (215) 246 - 6120
Fax:(215) 246 - 4463

Serves As:
- General Counsel, Towers Perrin

Responsibilities include government affairs.

YOUNG, Larry D.
3501 Algonquin Rd.
Rolling Meadows, IL 60008
Tel: (847) 818 - 5000
Fax:(847) 847 - 6880

Serves As:
- Exec. V. President, Corporate Affairs, PepsiAmericas, Inc.

YOUNG, Lisa
615 J.B. Hunt Corporate Dr.
P.O. Box 130
Lowell, AR 72745
lisa-young@jbhunt.com
Tel: (479) 820 - 0000
Fax:(479) 820 - 4241
TF: (800) 643 - 3622

Serves As:
- Manager, Corporate Communications, J. B. Hunt Transport Services, Inc.

YOUNG, Mary Lou
1201 S. Second St.
Milwaukee, WI 43204-2496
Tel: (414) 382 - 2000
Fax:(414) 382 - 4444

Serves As:
- Director, State and Community Relations, Rockwell Automation

YOUNG, Nancy N.
3330 Cumberland Blvd.
Suite 800
Atlanta, GA 30339
youngnancy@russellcorp.com
Tel: (678) 742 - 8118
Fax:(678) 742 - 8514

Serves As:
- V. President, Communications and Community Relations, Russell Corp.

YOUNG, Rich
540 Broad St.
Newark, NJ 07101
Tel: (973) 649 - 9900
Fax:(973) 643 - 5106

Serves As:
- Manager, Media Relations, Verizon New Jersey, Inc.

YOUNG, Robert
77 Grove St.
Rutland, VT 05701
Tel: (802) 773 - 2711
Fax:(802) 747 - 2199
TF: (800) 649 - 2877

Serves As:
- President and Chief Exec. Officer, Central Vermont Public Service Corp.

YOUNG, III, Robert A.
P.O. Box 10048
Fort Smith, AR 72917
Tel: (479) 785 - 6000
Fax:(479) 785 - 6004

Serves As:
- Chairman, President and Chief Exec. Officer, Arkansas Best Corporation

YOUNG, Robert H.
1901 Market St.
38th Floor
Philadelphia, PA 19103-1480
Tel: (215) 636 - 9559
Fax:(215) 241 - 0403
TF: (800) 555 - 1514

Serves As:
- Chairman of the Board, Independence Blue Cross (Pennsylvania)

YOUNG, Sally
One Baxter Pkwy.
Deerfield, IL 60015-4633
sally_young@baxter.com
Tel: (847) 948 - 2304
Fax:(847) 948 - 3216

Serves As:
- V. President, Corporate Communications, Baxter Internat'l Inc.

YOUNG, Shelley
200 Park Ave.
New York, NY 10166
Tel: (212) 984 - 8359

Serves As:
- Director, Investor Relations, CB Richard Ellis Services, Inc.

YOUNG, Stephen G.
Consol Plaza
1800 Washington Rd.
Pittsburgh, PA 15241-1421
Tel: (412) 831 - 4043
Fax:(412) 831 - 4574

Serves As:
• V. President, Government Affairs, CONSOL Energy Inc.

YOUNG, Teross
P.O. Box 1330
Salisbury, NC 28145-1330
Tel: (704) 633 - 8250
Fax:(704) 633 - 8250

Serves As:
• Manager, Government Affairs, Food Lion LLC

YOUNGDAHL, Douglas D.
P.O. Box 1768
Sacramento, CA 95812-1768
dyoungdahl@bdgrowers.com
Tel: (916) 442 - 0771
Fax:(916) 325 - 2880

Serves As:
• President and Chief Exec. Officer, Blue Diamond Growers

YOUNGER, Jennie
P.O. Box 13398
Research Triangle Park, NC 27709
Tel: (919) 483 - 2100
Fax:(919) 315 - 6049

Serves As:
• Senior V. President, Corporate Communications and Community Partnerships, GlaxoSmithKline Research and Development

YOUNGMAN, David
250 Stephenson Hwy.
Troy, MI 48083
david.youngman@colaik.com
Tel: (248) 824 - 1562
Fax:(248) 824 - 1532

Serves As:
• Director, Corporate Communications, Collins & Aikman Corp.

YOUNGMAN, Michael L.
720 E. Wisconsin Ave.
Milwaukee, WI 53202-4797
Tel: (414) 665 - 1891
Fax:(414) 665 - 5756
TF: (800) 323 - 7033

Registered Federal Lobbyist.
Serves As:
• V. President, Government Relations, Northwestern Mutual Financial Network

YU, Shannon
1620 L St. NW
Suite 800
Washington, DC 20036-5617
Tel: (202) 659 - 3575
Fax:(202) 659 - 1026

Serves As:
• Assistant V. President, MetLife, Inc.

YUCKERT, Gregory H.
P.O. Box 9777
Federal Way, WA 98063-9777
greg.yuckert@weyerhaeuser.com
Tel: (253) 924 - 3770
Fax:(253) 924 - 3685
TF: (800) 525 - 5440

Serves As:
• V. President, Labor Relations, Weyerhaeuser Co.

YUDIN, Stephanie
Three Ravinia Dr., Suite 100
Atlanta, GA 30346
stephanie.yudin@ichotelsgroup.com
Tel: (770) 604 - 5083
Fax:(770) 604 - 2059

Serves As:
• Senior Manager, Public Relations, InterContinental Hotels Group

YUDKOFF, Royce R.
6677 Richmond Hwy.
Alexandria, VA 22306
Tel: (703) 660 - 6677
Fax:(703) 768 - 9622

Serves As:
• Chairman of the Board, USA Mobility, Inc.

YUILLE, Antonia
30 Flatbush Ave.
Brooklyn, NY 11217
Tel: (718) 802 - 5066
Fax:(718) 802 - 5554

Serves As:
• Director, Public Affairs (Brooklyn), Consolidated Edison Co. of New York, Inc.

ZABEL, C. Michael
One M & T Plaza
Buffalo, NY 14203
Tel: (716) 842 - 5445
Fax:(716) 842 - 5839
TF: (800) 836 - 1500

Serves As:
• V. President and Manager, Corporate Communications, M&T Bank Corporation

ZABLE, Walter J.
P.O. Box 85587
San Diego, CA 92186-5587
walter.zable@cubic.com
Tel: (858) 277 - 6780
Fax:(858) 505 - 1523

Serves As:
• Chairman, President and Chief Exec. Officer, Cubic Corp.

ZACHRY, Jr., H. B.
P.O. Box 240130
San Antonio, TX 78224-0130
zachryhb@zachry.com
Tel: (210) 475 - 8000
Fax:(210) 475 - 8060

Serves As:
• Chairman of the Board, Zachry Construction Corporation

ZACHRY, John B.
P.O. Box 240130
San Antonio, TX 78224-0130
Tel: (210) 475 - 8000
Fax:(210) 475 - 8060

Serves As:
• Chief Exec. Officer, Zachry Construction Corporation

ZAINEY, Michael S.
5718 Westheimer St.
Houston, TX 77057
Tel: (713) 789 - 7879
TF: (800) 562 - 9007

Serves As:
• Exec. V. President, Human Resources, Hibernia Corp.

ZAKOWICZ, Stefanie
6363 Main St.
Williamsville, NY 14221
Tel: (716) 635 - 5885
Fax:(716) 633 - 0898
TF: (800) 522 - 2522

Serves As:
• Director, Public Relations, Tops Markets LLC

ZAMORANO, Manuel
1201 K St., Suite 1810
Sacramento, CA 95814
zamoram@sce.com
Tel: (916) 441 - 3966
Fax:(916) 441 - 4047

Serves As:
• Corporate Representative, Southern California Edison, an Edison Internat'l Co.

ZAMPA, Mike
1111 Broadway
Oakland, CA 94607-5500
michael_zampa@apl.com
Tel: (510) 272 - 7380
Fax:(510) 272 - 7421

Serves As:
• Director, Corporate Communications, APL Americas

ZANDER, Edward J.
1303 E. Algonquin Rd.
Schaumburg, IL 60196
Tel: (847) 576 - 5000
Fax:(847) 576 - 5372
TF: (800) 262 - 8509

Serves As:
• Chairman and Chief Exec. Officer, Motorola, Inc.

ZANDMAN, Felix
63 Lincoln Hwy.
Malvern, PA 19355-2120
felix.zandman@vishay.com
Tel: (610) 644 - 1300
Fax:(610) 296 - 0657

Serves As:
• Chairman and Chief Business Development Officer, Vishay Intertechnology, Inc.

ZANDONA, Oliver
2000 K St., NW
Suite 710
Washington, DC 20006
Tel: (202) 862 - 0200
Fax:(202) 862 - 0267

Serves As:
• International Advisor, Middle East, Exxon Mobil Corp.

ZANOWIC, Kathleen
1300 I St. NW
Suite 400 West
Washington, DC 20005
Tel: (202) 515 - 2400

Registered Federal Lobbyist.
Serves As:
• Assistant V. President, Federal Government Relations, Verizon Communications Inc.

ZAPLER, Thomas A.
101 N. Wacker Dr., Suite 1910
Chicago, IL 60606
Tel: (312) 853 - 8402
Fax:(312) 853 - 8420

Serves As:
• Government Affairs, Union Pacific Corp.

ZAPS, Dietrich
P.O. Box 2601
Troy, MI 48007-2601
Tel: (248) 643 - 3500
Fax:(248) 643 - 3687

Serves As:
• President and Chief Exec. Officer, Thyssenkrupp Budd Company

ZARB, Frank G.
70 Pine St.
New York, NY 10270
Tel: (212) 770 - 7000
Fax:(212) 509 - 9705

Serves As:
• Interim Chairman of the Board, American Internat'l Group, Inc.

ZARCONE, Michael A.
1620 L St. NW
Suite 800
Washington, DC 20036-5617
Tel: (202) 659 - 3575
Fax:(202) 659 - 1026
Registered Federal Lobbyist.
Serves As:
- Senior V. President, Government and Industry Relations, MetLife, Inc.

ZARKIN, Herbert J.
One Mercer Rd.
Natick, MA 01760
Tel: (508) 651 - 7400
Fax:(508) 651 - 6167
TF: (800) 257 - 2582
Serves As:
- Chairman of the Board, BJ's Wholesale Club, Inc.

ZARRELLA, Ronald L.
One Bausch & Lomb Pl.
Rochester, NY 14604-0054
Tel: (585) 338 - 6000
Fax:(585) 338 - 6007
TF: (800) 344 - 8815
Serves As:
- Chairman and Chief Exec. Officer, Bausch & Lomb

ZARRELLI, Michael J.
214 Massachusetts Ave. NE
Suite 210
Washington, DC 20002
Tel: (202) 547 - 5005
Fax:(202) 547 - 5008
Registered Federal Lobbyist.
Serves As:
- Manager, Federal Affairs, Alticor Inc.

ZASTROW, Katja
1401 I St. NW
Suite 200
Washington, DC 20005
Tel: (202) 293 - 9494
Fax:(202) 223 - 9594
Serves As:
- Region Director, Government Affairs, Anheuser-Busch Cos., Inc.

ZASTUDIL, Thomas M.
29400 Lakeland Blvd.
Wickliffe, OH 44092-2298
tmz@lubrizol.com
Tel: (440) 347 - 1741
Fax:(440) 347 - 5317
Serves As:
- Manager, Human Resources, The Lubrizol Corp.

ZATKIN, Steven R.
Ordway Bldg.
One Kaiser Plaza
Oakland, CA 94612
Tel: (510) 271 - 2626
Fax:(510) 271 - 5917
Serves As:
- Senior V. President, Government Relations, Kaiser Permanente

ZATORSKI, Karen
1515 Broadway
New York, NY 10036
Tel: (212) 258 - 6369
Fax:(212) 258 - 6464
Serves As:
- V. President, Corporate Relations, Viacom Inc./CBS Corp.

ZEBROSKI, Shirley
1660 L St. NW
Fourth Floor
Washington, DC 20036
Tel: (202) 775 - 5082
Fax:(202) 775 - 5097
Registered Federal Lobbyist.
Serves As:
- Director, Legislative and Regulatory Affairs, General Motors Corp.

ZECH, Ronald H.
500 W. Monroe St.
Chicago, IL 60661
Tel: (312) 621 - 6200
Fax:(312) 612 - 6648
TF: (800) 428 - 8161
Serves As:
- Chairman of the Board, GATX Corp.

ZEEHANDELAAR, Mona
1601 Market St.
12th Floor
Philadelphia, PA 19103
Tel: (215) 231 - 1674
Serves As:
- V. President, Investor Relations, Radian Group, Inc.

ZEHNDER, Anthony
11825 N. Pennsylvania St.
Carmel, IN 46032
Tel: (317) 817 - 6100
TF: (800) 888 - 4918
Serves As:
- Exec. V. President, Corporate Communications, Conseco, Inc.

ZEHR, Melinda
P.O. Box 2020
Bloomington, IL 61701-2020
Tel: (309) 821 - 2009
Serves As:
- Manager, Public Relations, Country Insurance and Financial Services

ZEISER, John S.
1716 Locust St.
Des Moines, IA 50309-3023
john.zieser@meredith.com
Tel: (515) 284 - 2780
Fax:(515) 284 - 2511
Serves As:
- V. President, Corporate Development, Meredith Corp.

Responsibilities include public affairs.

ZEITLER, Dennis L.
P.O. Box 426
Pittsburgh, PA 15230
dennis.zeitler@msanet.com
Tel: (412) 967 - 3046
Fax:(412) 967 - 3367
TF: (800) 672 - 2222
Serves As:
- V. President, CFO and Treasurer, Mine Safety Appliances Co. (MSA)

Responsibilities include political action and corporate philanthropy.

ZELENIAK, Nancy
3900 Paramount Pkwy.
Morrisville, NC 27560
Tel: (919) 462 - 4088
Serves As:
- Head, Corporate Communications, Pharmaceutical Product Development, Inc.

ZELL, Samuel
Two N. Riverside Plaza
Suite 2100
Chicago, IL 60606
Tel: (312) 466 - 3300
Fax:(312) 454 - 0332
Serves As:
- Chairman of the Board, Equity Office Properties Trust
- Chairman of the Board, Anixter Internat'l, Inc.
- Chairman of the Board, Equity Residential

ZELNAK, Jr., Stephen P.
2710 Wycliff Rd.
Raleigh, NC 27607-3033
Tel: (919) 781 - 4550
Fax:(919) 783 - 4695
Serves As:
- Chairman, President and Chief Exec. Officer, Martin Marietta Materials, Inc.

ZENTNER, Meg
770 N. Water St.
Sixth Floor
Milwaukee, WI 53202
Tel: (414) 765 - 7700
Fax:(414) 765 - 7899
Serves As:
- Secretary, Marshall & Ilsley Foundation, Marshall & Ilsley Corp.

ZEPEDA VERA, Patricia
3050 Bowers Ave.
P.O. Box 58039
Santa Clara, CA 95054-3299
patricia_zepeda_vera@appliedmaterials.com
Tel: (408) 563 - 8160
Fax:(408) 986 - 7115
Serves As:
- Specialist, Worldwide Media Relations, Applied Materials, Inc.

ZERBE, Julie A.
300 Park Ave.
New York, NY 10022
Tel: (212) 310 - 2000
Fax:(212) 310 - 3284
Serves As:
- V. President, Corporate Communications, Colgate-Palmolive Co.

ZERZA, Fred
P.O. Box 27
Boise, ID 83707
fzerza@simplot.com
Tel: (208) 389 - 7337
Fax:(208) 389 - 7433
Serves As:
- V. President, Public and Government Relations, J. R. Simplot Co.

Responsibilities include corporate philanthropy.

ZETSCHE, Dieter
1000 Chrysler Dr.
Auburn Hills, MI 48326-2766
Tel: (248) 576 - 5741
Fax:(248) 576 - 4742
TF: (800) 992 - 1997
Serves As:
- President and Chief Exec. Officer, DaimlerChrysler Corp.

ZEUMER, James P.
100 Bloomfield Hills Pkwy., Suite 300
Bloomfield Hills, MI 48304-2946
Tel: (248) 647 - 2750
Fax:(248) 433 - 4598
TF: (800) 777 - 8583
Serves As:
- V. President, Investor and Corporate Communications, Pulte Homes, Inc.

ZIEGLER, Gregory J.
P.O. Box 145496
Cincinnati, OH 45250
greg_ziegler@cinfin.com
Tel: (513) 870 - 2000
Fax:(513) 870 - 2911
Serves As:
- V. President and Director, Personnel, Cincinnati Financial Corp.

Responsibilities include corporate philanthropy.

ZIEGLER, Marie Z.
One John Deere Pl. Tel: (309) 765 - 4491
Moline, IL 61265-8098 Fax:(309) 765 - 4663
Serves As:
- V. President, Investor Relations, Deere & Company

ZIEGLER, Pat
300 Phillipi Rd. Tel: (614) 278 - 6820
Columbus, OH 43228-5311 Fax:(614) 278 - 6676
Serves As:
- Public Relations Contact, Big Lots Inc.

ZIEMNICK, Douglas
2000 Second Ave. Tel: (313) 235 - 8000
Detroit, MI 48226 Fax:(313) 235 - 0327
Serves As:
- PAC Treasurer, DTE Energy Co.

ZILLMER, John J.
15880 N. Greenway-Hayden Loop Tel: (480) 627 - 2700
Suite 100 Fax:(480) 627 - 2701
Scottsdale, AZ 85260
Serves As:
- Chairman and Chief Exec. Officer, Allied Waste Industries, Inc.

ZIMMER, George A.
5803 Glenmont Dr. Tel: (713) 592 - 7200
Houston, TX 77081-1701 Fax:(713) 664 - 1957
TF: (800) 776 - 7848
Serves As:
- Chairman and Chief Exec. Officer, Men's Wearhouse, Inc.

ZIMMER, Robert
401 Ninth St., NW Tel: (202) 434 - 8639
Suite 600 Fax:(202) 434 - 8626
Washington, DC 20004
robert_zimmer@freddiemac.com
Serves As:
- V. President, Government Relations, House Relations, Freddie Mac

ZIMMERMAN, John M.
AutoNation Tower Tel: (954) 769 - 6000
110 SE Sixth St. Fax:(954) 769 - 6398
29th Floor
Fort Lauderdale, FL 33301
zimmermanj@autonation.com
Serves As:
- V. President, Investor Relations, AutoNation, Inc.

ZIMMERMAN, Michael J.
270 E. Kilbourn Tel: (414) 347 - 6596
Milwaukee, WI 53202 Fax:(414) 347 - 6696
mike_zimmerman@mgic.com TF: (800) 558 - 9900
Serves As:
- V. President, Investor Relations, Mortgage Guaranty Insurance Corp. (MGIC)

ZIMMERMAN, S. LaNette
801 E. 86th Ave. Tel: (219) 647 - 6200
Merrillville, IN 46410 Fax:(219) 647 - 6225
TF: (877) 647 - 5990
Serves As:
- Exec. V. President, Human Resources and Communications, NiSource Inc.

ZIMPHER, W. Craig
One Nationwide Plaza Tel: (614) 249 - 4795
Columbus, OH 43215-2220 Fax:(614) 249 - 3073
Registered Federal Lobbyist.
Serves As:
- V. President, Government Relations, Nationwide

ZINS, Mary
2100 Hwy. 55 Tel: (763) 417 - 8650
Medina, MN 55340 Fax:(763) 542 - 0599
Serves As:
- Treasurer, Polaris Industries Inc. Political Participation Program, Polaris Industries Inc.

ZINTEK, Arthur
231 W. Michigan St. Tel: (414) 221 - 3149
P456 Fax:(414) 221 - 4608
Milwaukee, WI 53201
arthur.zintek@we-energies.com
Serves As:
- V. President, Human Resources, Wisconsin Energy Corp.

ZIPPERSTEIN, Steve
1095 Ave. of the Americas Tel: (212) 395 - 2121
New York, NY 10036 Fax:(212) 869 - 3265
Serves As:
- V. President, Legal and External Affairs, Verizon Wireless

Responsibilities include regulatory affairs and public policy matters.

ZIRAKPARUAR, Ph.D., Esmail
Two T.W. Alexander Dr. Tel: (919) 549 - 2000
P.O. Box 12
Research Triangle Park, NC 27009
Serves As:
- President and Chief Exec. Officer, Bayer CropScience

ZITLOW, Kelly
100 Half Day Rd. Tel: (847) 442 - 7662
Lincolnshire, IL 60069 Fax:(847) 295 - 7634
kelly.zitlow@hewitt.com
Serves As:
- Manager, Public Relations, Hewitt Associates Inc.

ZITO, Greg A.
31 W. 271 Prairie Ln. Tel: (630) 584 - 1183
Wayne, IL 60184
Serves As:
- Regional Director, State Government Relations, HSBC North America Holdings Inc.

ZITO, Pat
P.O. Box 799 Tel: (419) 247 - 3731
Toledo, OH 43695 Fax:(419) 247 - 3821
Serves As:
- Chairman and Chief Exec. Officer, Pilkington North America

ZITO, Robert T.
345 Park Ave. Tel: (212) 546 - 4000
New York, NY 10154-0037 Fax:(212) 546 - 4020
Serves As:
- Senior V. President, Corporate Affairs, Bristol-Myers Squibb Co.

ZIVANOVIC-SMITH, Maria
1301 K St. NW Tel: (202) 515 - 5109
Suite 1200 Fax:(202) 515 - 4943
Washington, DC 20005
Serves As:
- Senior Professional, Governmental Programs, Internat'l Business Machines Corp. (IBM)

ZIZZO, Lawrence F.
703 Curtis St. Tel: (513) 425 - 5000
Middletown, OH 45043 Fax:(513) 425 - 2676
TF: (800) 331 - 5050
Serves As:
- V. President, Human Resources, AK Steel Corp.

ZOBEL, Bill
101 Ash St. Tel: (619) 696 - 2512
hq13f Fax:(619) 696 - 4266
San Diego, CA 92101-3017 TF: (877) 736 - 7721
Serves As:
- Environmental Legislative Manager, Sempra Energy

ZOGLMAN, Robert R.
900 19th St. NW Tel: (202) 945 - 6405
Suite 350 Fax:(202) 945 - 6404
Washington, DC 20006
Registered Federal Lobbyist.
Serves As:
- V. President, Government and International Affairs, Westinghouse Electric Company LLC

ZOLLARS, Ron
10260 Campus Point Dr. Tel: (858) 826 - 7896
San Diego, CA 92121 Fax:(858) 826 - 6634
zollarsr@saic.com
Serves As:
- Director, Public Affairs, Science Applications Internat'l Corp.

ZOLLARS, William D.
10990 Roe Ave. Tel: (913) 696 - 6100
Overland Park, KS 66211 Ext: 6110
Fax:(913) 696 - 6116
Serves As:
- Chairman, President and Chief Exec. Officer, Yellow Roadway Corporation

ZOMER, Binyamin A.
800 Connecticut Ave. NW Tel: (202) 533 - 1100
Suite 600 Fax:(202) 533 - 1134
Washington, DC 20006
Registered Federal Lobbyist.
Serves As:
- Representative, Accenture

ZORE, Edward J.
720 E. Wisconsin Ave. Tel: (414) 271 - 1444
Milwaukee, WI 53202-4797 Fax:(414) 665 - 2463
TF: (800) 323 - 7033
Serves As:
- President and Chief Exec. Officer, Northwestern Mutual Financial Network

ZORN, Michael
Seven W. Seventh St.
Cincinnati, OH 45202
Tel: (513) 579 - 7000
Fax:(513) 579 - 7555
TF: (800) 261 - 5385

Serves As:
- V. President, Employee Relations, Federated Department Stores, Inc.

ZUEHLKE, Gerald L.
601 W. Riverside Ave.
Suite 1100
Spokane, WA 99201
Tel: (509) 835 - 1550
Fax:(509) 835 - 1555

Serves As:
- Chief Financial Officer, Potlatch Corp.

Responsibilities include investor relations.

ZUKOWSKI, Perry
One GBC Plaza
Northbrook, IL 60062
pzukowski@gbc.com
Tel: (847) 291 - 5456
Fax:(847) 272 - 3723

Serves As:
- V. President, Human Resources, General Binding Corp.

ZUMSTEIN, Ron
451 Florida St.
Baton Rouge, LA 70801-1765
ron_zumstein@albemarle.com
Tel: (225) 388 - 3030
Fax:(225) 388 - 7848

Serves As:
- V. President, Health, Safety and Environment, Albemarle Corp.

ZUMWALT, LeAnne
601 Hawaii St.
El Segundo, CA 90245
Tel: (650) 696 - 8910

Serves As:
- V. President, Investor Relations, DaVita, Inc.

ZUMWINKLE, Michael
P.O. Box 9300
Minneapolis, MN 55440-9300
michael_zumwinkle@cargill.com
Tel: (952) 742 - 2982
Fax:(952) 742 - 7393

Serves As:
- Director, State Government Relations, Cargill, Incorporated

ZUNDEL, Don
One Infinite Loop
Cupertino, CA 95014
Tel: (707) 546 - 7966
Fax:(707) 695 - 1857

Serves As:
- Contact, Apple Education Grants Program, Apple Computer, Inc.

ZURAWSKI, Paul R.
1001 Pennsylvania Ave. NW
Suite 700 South
Washington, DC 20004
Tel: (202) 662 - 2650
Fax:(202) 662 - 2674

Registered Federal Lobbyist.
Serves As:
- Director, Tax and Benefits Policy, Honeywell Internat'l, Inc.

ZUTZ, Denise M.
5757 N. Green Bay Ave.
Milwaukee, WI 53201-0591
denise.zutz@jci.com
Tel: (414) 524 - 3155
Fax:(414) 524 - 2077

Serves As:
- V. President, Corporate Communications and Investor Relations, Johnson Controls, Inc.

ZWECK, Brad L.
P.O. Box 8017
Wausau, WI 54402-8017
brad.zweck@wausau.com
Tel: (715) 842 - 6570
Fax:(715) 847 - 8740
TF: (800) 435 - 4401

Serves As:
- Manager, Communications and Public Affairs, Employers Insurance Co. of Wausau

ZWINGER, Robert
One Rentway Place
Erie, PA 16505
Tel: (814) 455 - 5378
Fax:(814) 461 - 5400
TF: (800) 736 - 8929

Serves As:
- V. President, Advertising and Marketing, Rent-Way, Inc.

Responsibilities include media relations.

ZYGOCKI, Rhonda I.
6001 Bollinger Canyon Rd.
San Ramon, CA 94583
Tel: (925) 842 - 1000

Serves As:
- V. President, Health, Environment and Safety, Chevron Corp.

2006 National Directory of Corporate Public Affairs

Industry Index

Every company in this book has been coded under subject headings that best describe the nature of the company's principal business activity.

Accounting

Deloitte & Touche LLP ... 154
Ernst & Young LLP ... 186
Grant Thornton LLP ... 225
KPMG LLP ... 283
PriceWaterhouseCoopers LLP ... 392
Robert Half International Inc. ... 412

Advertising/Public Relations

Advo Inc. ... 8
Alberto-Culver Co. ... 16
BBDO New York ... 66
Leo Burnett Worldwide ... 95
Clear Channel Communications ... 124
DoubleClick, Inc. ... 163
Grey Global Group Inc. ... 227
Harte-Hanks, Inc. ... 234
Insight Enterprises, Inc. ... 257
Omnicom Group Inc. ... 362
R.L. Polk & Co. ... 388
J. Walter Thompson Co. ... 473
Valassis Communications, Inc. ... 499
Yahoo! Inc. ... 529

Agriculture/Farming

AGCO Corp. ... 11
Alexander & Baldwin, Inc. ... 18
The Andersons, Inc. ... 40
Archer Daniels Midland Co. (ADM) ... 47
Battelle ... 64
Bayer CropScience ... 66
Bunge Ltd. ... 93
Burlington Northern Santa Fe Corporation ... 94
Caterpillar Inc. ... 105
CHS Inc. ... 116
Dairylea Cooperative Inc. ... 150
Deere & Company ... 152
The Dow Chemical Company ... 164
DuPont ... 169
Monsanto Co. ... 331
Pioneer Hi-Bred Internat'l, Inc. ... 385
The Scotts Company ... 430
The Scoular Co. ... 430
J. R. Simplot Co. ... 439
Southern States Cooperative ... 447
Terra Industries Inc. ... 469
United States Sugar Corp. ... 492
Universal Corp. ... 494

Airlines/Air Service

ABX Air, Inc. ... 4
Airbus North America Holdings, Inc. ... 14
AirTran Airways ... 14
Alaska Air Group, Inc. ... 15
Aloha Airlines, Inc. ... 24
AMR Corp. ... 37
ATA Holdings Corp. ... 53
The Brink's Co. ... 89
British Airways ... 91
CNF Inc. ... 126
Continental Airlines ... 138
Delta Air Lines, Inc. ... 155
DHL Holdings (USA), Inc. ... 158
FedEx Corp. ... 192
FLYi, Inc. ... 199
Hawaiian Holdings, Inc. ... 236
MAIR Holdings, Inc. ... 303
Northwest Airlines, Inc. ... 354
Southwest Airlines Co. ... 448
United Airlines ... 489
US Airways Group, Inc. ... 496

Apparel/Clothing

Abercrombie & Fitch Co. ... 4
The Bon Ton Stores, Inc. ... 86
Brown Shoe Co., Inc. ... 92
Burlington Coat Factory Warehouse Corp. ... 94
The Children's Place Retail Stores, Inc. ... 115
Fossil Inc. ... 202
Gap Inc. ... 208
Genesco ... 216
Hartmarx ... 235
J. Crew Group, Inc. ... 266
Jones Apparel Group ... 271
Kellwood Co. ... 276
Kohl's Corp. ... 282
L. L. Bean, Inc. ... 285
Levi Strauss and Co. ... 291
The Limited Brands ... 294
Liz Claiborne Inc. ... 296
Men's Wearhouse, Inc. ... 319
New Balance Athletic Shoe, Inc. ... 344
Nike, Inc. ... 349
Oshkosh B'Gosh, Inc. ... 365
Phillips-Van Heusen Corp. ... 382
Polo Ralph Lauren ... 388
Recreational Equipment, Inc. ... 406
Reebok Internat'l Ltd. ... 406
Ross Stores, Inc. ... 415
Russell Corp. ... 416
Sara Lee Corp. ... 421
Skechers U.S.A., Inc. ... 440
The Stride Rite Corp. ... 459
The Timberland Co. ... 475
The TJX Companies, Inc. ... 476
Too, Inc. ... 477
Unifi, Inc. ... 486
V. F. Corporation ... 505
Wolverine World Wide, Inc. ... 525

Automotive Industry

3M Company ... 1
Advance Auto Parts, Inc. ... 7
Aftermarket Technology Corp. ... 10
ALLETE ... 20
American Axle and Manufacturing, Inc. ... 29
American Honda Motor Co., Inc. ... 32
ArvinMeritor ... 48
Asbury Automotive Group ... 48
AutoNation, Inc. ... 55

AutoZone, Inc. 55
BASF Corporation 63
Battelle 64
Berwind Group 72
BMW (U.S.) Holding Corp. 83
BorgWarner Inc. 87
Coachmen Industries, Inc. 127
Collins & Aikman Corp. 129
Cooper Tire & Rubber Company 139
Crown Equipment Corp. 145
CSK Auto, Inc. 146
CTS Corp. 147
DaimlerChrysler Corp. 149
Dana Corp. 151
Danaher Corp. 151
Delphi Corp. 155
Dollar Thrifty Automotive Group, Inc. 161
DuPont 169
Dura Automotive Systems, Inc. 170
Eagle-Picher Industries, Inc. 171
Eaton Corp. 173
Enterprise Rent-A-Car Co. 184
Federal-Mogul Corp. 191
Fleetwood Enterprises 197
Ford Motor Co. 201
Gates Rubber Co. 209
General Motors Corp. 214
Genuine Parts Co. 216
Group 1 Automotive, Inc. 228
Harley-Davidson Motor Company 232
Hayes Lemmerz Internat'l, Inc. 237
Hertz Corp. 241
Hyundai Motor America 253
Intermet Corp. 259
Jiffy Lube Internat'l, Inc. 268
Johnson Controls, Inc. 271
Lear Corporation 289
LORD Corporation 299
Mack Trucks, Inc. 302
Mazda North American Operations 311
Mercedes-Benz USA, LLC 320
Mitsubishi Motors North America, Inc. 330
Nissan North America, Inc. 350
Oshkosh Truck Corp. 365
PACCAR Inc. 368
The Pep Boys-Manny, Moe & Jack 376
Pilkington North America 384
R.L. Polk & Co. 388
Porsche Cars North America, Inc. 389
Rockwell Automation 412
Safety-Kleen Systems, Inc. 418
Sequa Corp. 434
Snap-on Incorporated 442
Sonic Automotive, Inc. 443
Subaru of America, Inc. 459
Tenneco Automotive 469
Thyssenkrupp Budd Company 474
Tower Automotive, Inc. 478
Toyota Motor North America, Inc. 478
TRW Automotive 481
United Auto Group, Inc. 489
Visteon Corp. 507
Volkswagen of America, Inc. 508
Winnebago Industries, Inc. 524

Aviation/Aerospace

AAR Corp. 3
The Aerospace Corp. 8
Airbus North America Holdings, Inc. 14
Alliant Techsystems 21
Battelle 64
Bell Helicopter Textron 69
The Boeing Co. 84
Bombardier 86
Cessna Aircraft Co. 111
Crane Co. 144
DaimlerChrysler Corp. 149
Eaton Corp. 173
FlightSafety Internat'l 197
Frontier Airlines, Inc. 206
GenCorp 210
General Dynamics Corporation 212
General Motors Corp. 214
Goodrich Corp. - Aerostructures 223
Goodrich Corporation 223
Gulfstream Aerospace Corp. 230
Hexcel Corp. 242
Honeywell Internat'l, Inc. 247
Jeppesen 268
Kaman Corp. 274
Lockheed Martin Aeronautics Co. 296
Lockheed Martin Corp. 296
Lockheed Martin Space Systems Company 297
Loral Space & Communications 298
LORD Corporation 299
Moog Inc. 332
The New Piper Aircraft Inc. 345
Northrop Grumman Corp. 353
Pall Corp. 370
Parker Hannifin Corp. 371
Pratt & Whitney 391
Raytheon Aircraft Company 404
Rockwell Collins, Inc. 413
Rolls-Royce North America Inc. 414
Sequa Corp. 434
Textron Inc. 471
United Technologies Corp. 492

Banking

Associated Banc-Corp. 49
BancWest Corp. 60
Bank of America Corp. 60
Bank of Hawaii Corp. 61
The Bank of New York Co., Inc. 61
BOK Financial Corp. 85
Citigroup, Inc. 122
Citizens Financial Group, Inc. 123
City Nat'l Corp. 124
The Colonial Bancgroup, Inc. 129
Comerica Incorporated 131
Commerce Bancshares Inc. 131
Commercial Federal Corp. 132
Compass Bancshares, Inc. 132
The Depository Trust & Clearing Corp. 157
Deutsche Banc Alex.Brown 157
Fifth Third Bancorp. 194
First Citizens BancShares 194
First Horizon Nat'l Corp. 196
First Midwest Bancorp, Inc. 196
FirstMerit Corporation 197
Frost Nat'l Bank 207
Harris Bank 233
Hibernia Corp. 243
HSBC USA, Inc. 250
Huntington Bancshares Inc. 252
Integra Bank N.A. 257
KeyCorp 278
LaSalle Bank N.A. 288
M&T Bank Corporation 301
Marshall & Ilsley Corp. 306
MBNA Corp. 311
Mellon Financial Corp. 319
Mercantile Bankshares Corporation 320
J. P. Morgan Chase & Co. 332
Nat'l City Corp. 337
New York Community Bancorp, Inc. 345
Northern Trust Co. 353
People's Bank 375
PNC Financial Services Group 387
Providian Financial Corp. 396
Standard Federal Bank 453
State Street Corp. 456
SunTrust Banks, Inc. 462
TCF Bank 465
TCF Financial Corp. 465
Trustmark Nat'l Bank 481
U.S. Trust Corp. 485
Union Bank of California 487
U.S. Bancorp 497
Washington Mutual, Inc. 512
Webster Financial Corp. 515
Wells Fargo & Co. 516
Wilmington Trust Co. 523
Zions Bancorporation 532

Beverage Industry

Anheuser-Busch Cos., Inc. 41

Brown-Forman Corp. 92
Cadbury Schweppes Americas Beverages 97
Coca-Cola Bottling Co. Consolidated 127
The Coca-Cola Co. 127
Coca-Cola Enterprises Inc. 128
Constellation Brands, Inc. 137
Coors Brewing Co. 140
Dairylea Cooperative Inc. 150
Dean Foods Company 152
Diageo North America 158
Fortune Brands, Inc. 202
Ernest and Julio Gallo Winery 208
Heineken USA Inc. 239
Miller Brewing Co. 327
Mott's Inc. 335
Pall Corp. 370
The Pepsi Bottling Group 377
PepsiAmericas, Inc. 377
PepsiCo, Inc. 377
Sara Lee Corp. 421
SKF USA, Inc. 440
Southern Wine & Spirits of America 447
Starbucks Corp. 455
Welch's 515

Biotechnology

Berlex, Inc. 72
Genentech, Inc. 211
SRI International 452

Cemeteries/Funerals

Stewart Enterprises, Inc. 458

Chemical Industry

3M Company 1
ABB Inc. 3
Air Liquide America Corp. 13
Air Products and Chemicals, Inc. 13
Albemarle Corp. 16
Arch Chemicals, Inc. 46
ATOFINA Chemicals, Inc. 54
Avery Dennison Corp. 56
BASF Corporation 63
Battelle 64
Bayer Corporation 65
Bechtel Group, Inc. 67
Berwind Group 72
BP 88
Cabot Corp. 97
Celanese 107
Chemtura 114
Church & Dwight Co., Inc. 117
Ciba Specialty Chemicals 117
ConocoPhillips 135
Cytec Industries Inc. 149
The Dow Chemical Company 164
Dow Corning Corp. 165
Drummond Co., Inc. 167
DuPont 169
Eagle-Picher Industries, Inc. 171
Eastman Chemical Co. 171
Eastman Kodak Company 172
Engelhard Corp. 181
Exxon Mobil Chemical Co. 188
Exxon Mobil Corp. 188
Ferro Corp. 193
Flint Ink Corp. 197
FMC Corp. 199
Foster Wheeler Ltd. 203
Freeport-McMoRan Copper and Gold Inc. 205
H. B. Fuller Co. 207
GenCorp 210
Georgia Gulf Corp. 217
Georgia-Pacific Corp. 217
W. R. Grace & Co. 224
Henkel Corp. 240
Hercules Incorporated 240
Hexion Specialty Chemicals, Inc. 243
Huntsman Corp. 253
ICI American Holdings, Inc. 254
Illinois Tool Works Inc. 255
Internat'l Flavors and Fragrances 261
Invensys Systems, Inc. 264
Invitrogen Corp. 264
Kaiser Aluminum & Chemical Corp. 273
Kerr-McGee Corp. 278
Koch Industries, Inc. 282
The Lubrizol Corp. 300
Lyondell Chemical Co. 301
MeadWestvaco Corp. 316
Milliken & Co. 327
Millipore Corp. 327
Mitsubishi International Corporation 330
Mosaic Co. 334
Nalco Co. 337
Nat'l Starch and Chemical Co. 341
NewMarket Corp. 347
Occidental Chemical Corp. 359
Olin Corp. 361
OM Group, Inc. 361
OMNOVA Solutions Inc. 362
Polaroid Corp. 388
PPG Industries Inc. 390
Praxair, Inc. 391
PSE&G 397
Reichhold, Inc. 408
Reilly Industries, Inc. 408
Rhodia, Inc. 411
Rohm and Haas Co. 413
RPM Internat'l Inc. 416
Sensient Technology Corp. 433
Sequa Corp. 434
Shell Oil Co. 436
Sherwin-Williams Co. 436
Sigma-Aldrich Corp. 438
SRI International 452
Sterling Chemicals, Inc. 457
Terra Industries Inc. 469
Total Petrochemicals USA, Inc. 478
TransMontaigne, Inc. 479
U.S. Borax Inc. 485
Univar USA, Inc. 494
Valhi, Inc. 500
Velsicol Chemical Corp. 501
Vulcan Materials Co. 508

Coal

Arch Coal, Inc. 46
Berwind Group 72
Burlington Northern Santa Fe Corporation 94
Cleveland-Cliffs Inc. 125
CONSOL Energy Inc. 136
Drummond Co., Inc. 167
Exxon Mobil Corp. 188
Kennecott Energy Co. 277
Massey Energy Co. 307
NACCO Industries 337
Peabody Energy 373
Sunoco, Inc. 461
TECO Energy, Inc./Tampa Electric Co. 466
Westmoreland Coal Co. 520

Commodities

Cargill, Incorporated 102
ContiGroup Companies, Inc. 138
Koch Industries, Inc. 282
Sempra Energy 432

Communications

3Com Corp. 1
Adelphia Communications Corp. 6
Advanced Micro Devices, Inc. 7
ALLTEL 23
Anixter Internat'l, Inc. 41
ARRIS Group, Inc. 48
Avnet Inc. 57
Belden CDT Inc. 69
BellSouth Corp. 69
Black Hills Corp. 76
CenturyTel, Inc. 110
Charter Communications, Inc. 112
CIBER, Inc. 118
Cincinnati Bell Inc. 119
Comcast Corporation 130

CommScope ... 132
Computer Sciences Corp. ... 133
Corning Incorporated ... 141
Corporation for Public Broadcasting ... 141
Cox Enterprises, Inc. ... 143
CTS Corp. ... 147
Dictaphone Corp. ... 159
Duquesne Light Holdings ... 170
Earthlink, Inc. ... 171
Eaton Corp. ... 173
EchoStar Communications Corp. ... 174
Ericsson Inc. ... 185
Fellowes Manufacturing Co. ... 193
Gannett Co., Inc. ... 208
Global Crossing Ltd. ... 220
Griffon Corp. ... 228
Harris Corp. ... 233
Henkels & McCoy, Inc. ... 240
Houghton Mifflin Co. ... 249
Intergraph Corp. ... 259
Internat'l Business Machines Corp. (IBM) ... 260
The Interpublic Group of Companies ... 262
Jefferson-Pilot Corp. ... 267
Juniper Networks, Inc. ... 272
L-3 Communications Titan Group ... 284
Landmark Communications, Inc. ... 288
Level 3 Communications, Inc. ... 291
Loral Space & Communications ... 298
Lucent Technologies ... 300
MCI, Inc. ... 314
McLeod USA Inc. ... 315
Media General Inc. ... 317
Monster Worldwide, Inc. ... 331
NEC USA, Inc. ... 343
News Corporation Ltd. ... 347
Nortel Networks ... 352
Northrop Grumman Corp. ... 353
Omnicom Group Inc. ... 362
Orlando Sentinel Communications ... 365
Perot Systems Corp. ... 379
Premiere Global Services, Inc. ... 392
Primedia Inc. ... 393
Questar Corporation ... 401
Qwest Communications ... 402
RF Micro Devices, Inc. ... 411
Rockwell Collins, Inc ... 413
SBC Communications Inc. ... 422
SBC Illinois ... 423
SBC Indiana ... 424
SBC Michigan ... 424
SBC Ohio ... 424
SBC SNET ... 425
SBC Wisconsin ... 425
Science Applications Internat'l Corp. ... 429
Scientific-Atlanta, Inc. ... 429
Siemens Corp. ... 437
Sony Corp. of America ... 444
Sprint Nextel ... 450
Sykes Enterprises, Inc. ... 463
Telcordia Technologies, Inc. ... 467
Tellabs ... 468
Time Warner Inc. ... 475
Turner Broadcasting System, Inc. ... 482
UnitedGlobalCom, Inc. ... 494
Verizon Communications Inc. ... 502
Verizon Delaware Inc. ... 503
Verizon Maryland Inc. ... 503
Verizon New Jersey, Inc. ... 503
Verizon Pennsylvania Inc. ... 503
Verizon Washington D.C. Inc. ... 504
Verizon West Virginia Inc. ... 504
Verizon Wireless ... 504
The Washington Post Co. ... 513
XO Communications, Inc. ... 529
Yahoo! Inc. ... 529

Computers/Software

Activision, Inc. ... 5
Acxiom Corporation ... 5
Adaptec, Inc. ... 5
Adobe Systems Inc. ... 6
Affiliated Computer Services, Inc. (ACS) ... 9
Agere Systems Inc. ... 11
Agilysys, Inc. ... 11
Altera Corp. ... 24
American Power Conversion Corp. ... 33
Analog Devices, Inc. ... 39
Apple Computer, Inc. ... 43
AT&T ... 52
Autodesk Inc. ... 55
Automatic Data Processing, Inc. ... 55
BEA Systems, Inc. ... 67
Bell Microproducts, Inc. ... 69
BMC Software ... 83
Brady Corp. ... 89
BroadVision, Inc. ... 91
CACI Internat'l Inc. ... 97
Cadence Design Systems, Inc. ... 97
CDW Corp. ... 106
Ceridian Corp. ... 111
ChoicePoint Inc. ... 115
Citrix Systems, Inc. ... 123
Computer Associates Internat'l, Inc. ... 133
Computer Sciences Corp. ... 133
Compuware Corp. ... 134
Comverse Technology, Inc. ... 134
Covansys ... 143
CTS Corp. ... 147
Dell Inc. ... 154
DoubleClick, Inc. ... 163
DST Systems, Inc. ... 167
Earthlink, Inc. ... 171
eBay, Inc. ... 173
EDS Corp. ... 175
Electronic Arts Inc. ... 178
EMC Corp. ... 178
Fairchild Semiconductor Internat'l, Inc. ... 189
Fellowes Manufacturing Co. ... 193
First Data ... 195
Fiserv, Inc. ... 197
Gateway, Inc. ... 209
GTECH Corp. ... 228
Hewlett-Packard Co. ... 241
Honeywell Internat'l, Inc. ... 247
i2 Technologies, Inc. ... 254
Information Resources, Inc. ... 256
Ingram Micro, Inc. ... 257
Intel Corp. ... 258
Internat'l Business Machines Corp. (IBM) ... 260
Intuit Inc. ... 263
Iomega Corp. ... 264
Juniper Networks, Inc. ... 272
Keane, Inc. ... 275
KLA-Tencor ... 281
L-3 Communications Titan Group ... 284
Lexmark Internat'l, Inc. ... 292
LSI Logic Corp. ... 300
Maxim Integrated Products ... 309
Maxtor Corp. ... 310
McAfee, Inc. ... 312
Mentor Graphics Corp. ... 320
Micron Technology, Inc. ... 324
Microsoft Corporation ... 325
Monster Worldwide, Inc. ... 331
NCR Corporation ... 342
Network Appliance, Inc. ... 344
Novell, Inc. ... 357
NVIDIA Corp. ... 358
Office Depot, Inc. ... 360
Oracle Corporation ... 364
palmOne, Inc. ... 370
PalmSource, Inc. ... 370
PC Connection, Inc. ... 373
Perot Systems Corp. ... 379
PTC ... 398
Quantum Corporation ... 400
Reynolds and Reynolds Co. ... 411
Safeguard Scientifics, Inc. ... 418
SAS Institute, Inc. ... 422
Savin Corp. ... 422
Science Applications Internat'l Corp. ... 429
Seagate Technology ... 431
SGI ... 435
Siebel Systems, Inc. ... 437
Standard Register Co. ... 454
StorageTek ... 458
Sun Microsystems, Inc. ... 460
SunGard Data Systems, Inc. ... 460
Sybase, Inc. ... 463

Symantec Corp. 463
Symbol Technologies, Inc. 463
Systemax Inc. 464
Take-Two Interactive Software, Inc. 464
Tech Data Corp. 466
Time Warner Inc. 475
United Technologies Corp. 492
UNOVA, Inc. 496
Volt Information Sciences, Inc. 508
Western Digital Corp. 519
Xerox Corp. 528
Xilinx, Inc. 529

Conglomerates

Altria Group, Inc. 25
Berwind Group 72
Carlson Companies 103
Covanta Energy Corp. 143
The Dow Chemical Company 164
Gates Rubber Co. 209
General Dynamics Corporation 212
General Electric Co. 213
W. R. Grace & Co. 224
Hillenbrand Industries, Inc. 244
Ikon Office Solutions, Inc. 255
IPL (an AES Company) 264
Kraft Foods, Inc. 283
Loews Corporation 297
Philips Electronics North America 382
The Procter & Gamble Company 394
Ruddick Corp. 416
E. W. Scripps Co. 430
Viad Corp 506

Construction and Construction Materials

American Standard Companies Inc. 34
The Austin Co. 54
Austin Industries 54
Black & Veatch 75
Boise Cascade Corp. 85
Butler Manufacturing Co. 95
Buzzi Unicem USA 96
Centex Corporation 109
Champion Enterprises, Inc. 112
Day & Zimmerman 152
Deere & Company 152
DuPont 169
EMCOR Group, Inc. 178
Fastenal Co. 191
Fleetwood Enterprises 197
Florida Rock Industries, Inc. 198
Forest City Enterprises, Inc. 202
L. B. Foster Co. 202
Foster Wheeler Ltd. 203
Georgia-Pacific Corp. 217
Gilbane Building Co. 219
Granite Construction Inc. 225
Halliburton Company 230
Harsco Corp. 234
Holcim (US) Inc. 246
The Home Depot, Inc. 246
D. R. Horton, Inc. 248
Hovnanian Enterprises, Inc. 249
Hughes Supply, Inc. 251
Johns Manville Corp. 269
Kellogg Brown and Root 275
Peter Kiewit Sons', Inc. 279
Kraus-Anderson Cos. Inc. 284
Lafarge North America, Inc. 286
Lennar Corp. 290
Martin Marietta Materials, Inc. 306
Masonite Internat'l Corp. 307
MDU Resources Group, Inc. 315
M. A. Mortenson Company 333
National Gypsum Co. 339
Nortek Inc. 352
NVR, Inc. 358
Parsons Corp. 372
The Ryland Group, Inc. 417
Saint-Gobain Corp. 419
The Shaw Group Inc. 435
Standard Pacific Corp. 453
Terex Corp. 469
Texas Industries, Inc. 470
Toll Brothers, Inc. 477
Trinity Industries, Inc. 481
The Turner Corp. 482
URS Corp. 496
USG Corp. 498
Valspar Corp. 500
Vulcan Materials Co. 508
Walter Industries, Inc. 511
Washington Group Internat'l 512
Zachry Construction Corporation 531

Cosmetics/Personal Care/Jewelry

Alberto-Culver Co. 16
AptarGroup, Inc. 45
Avon Products, Inc. 57
BIC Corp. 73
Church & Dwight Co., Inc. 117
Colgate-Palmolive Co. 129
CVS 148
The Dial Corporation 158
Estee Lauder Companies, Inc. 186
The Gillette Company 219
Internat'l Flavors and Fragrances 261
Johnson & Johnson 270
Jostens, Inc. 272
Kimberly-Clark Corp. 280
Mary Kay Inc. 306
Nu Skin Enterprises 357
The Procter & Gamble Company 394
Regis Corporation 408
Revlon, Inc. 410
Sotheby's Holdings, Inc. 444
Tiffany & Co. 474
Unilever Home & Personal Care - North America 486
Unilever United States, Inc. 487
Zale Corp. 531

Defense Industry

AAI Corp. 2
Alliant Techsystems 21
BAE Systems North America 59
Bechtel Group, Inc. 67
The Boeing Co. 84
Cubic Corp. 147
DRS Technologies, Inc. 166
Eaton Corp. 173
GenCorp 210
General Dynamics Corporation 212
General Electric Co. 213
Gulfstream Aerospace Corp. 230
Hamilton Sundstrand 231
Honeywell Internat'l, Inc. 247
Lockheed Martin Aeronautics Co. 296
Lockheed Martin Corp. 296
Lockheed Martin Space Systems Company 297
Loral Space & Communications 298
LORD Corporation 299
Northrop Grumman Corp. 353
Parker Hannifin Corp. 371
Pratt & Whitney 391
Raytheon Co. 404
Science Applications Internat'l Corp. 429
Textron Inc. 471
Unisys Corp. 488
United Technologies Corp. 492

Education

Apollo Group, Inc. 43
DeVry Inc. 157
Laureate Education, Inc. 289
The McGraw-Hill Companies, Inc. 313
The Washington Post Co. 513

Electric Utility

The AES Corp. 8
Alabama Power Co. 15
Allegheny Energy Inc. 18
ALLETE 20
Alliant Energy Corp. 21

Ameren Corp. 28
American Electric Power Co. Inc. 30
Aquila, Inc. 45
Avista Corp. 56
CenterPoint Energy 108
Central Vermont Public Service Corp. 109
CH Energy Group, Inc. 111
Cinergy Corp. 119
Cleco Corp. 124
CMS Energy Corp. 126
Conectiv 134
Conexant Systems, Inc. 135
Consolidated Edison Co. of New York, Inc. 136
Constellation Energy 137
Dominion Resources, Inc. 162
DPL Inc. 166
DTE Energy Co. 167
Duke Energy Corp. 168
Duquesne Light Holdings 170
Dynegy, Inc. 171
El Paso Electric Co. 177
Empire District Electric Co. 179
Energy East Corp. 181
Entergy Arkansas, Inc. 182
Entergy Corp. 182
Entergy Mississippi 183
Entergy New Orleans 183
Entergy Services, Inc. 183
Entergy Texas 184
Exelon Corp. 187
FirstEnergy Corp. 196
Foster Wheeler Ltd. 203
FPL Group, Inc. 203
Georgia Power Co. 218
Great Plains Energy, Inc. 226
Gulf Power Co. 229
Hawaiian Electric Industries, Inc. 236
Henkels & McCoy, Inc. 240
IDACORP, Inc. 254
IPL (an AES Company) 264
Kentucky Utilities Company 278
KeySpan Corp. 279
LG&E Energy LLC 292
Madison Gas and Electric Co. 302
MDU Resources Group, Inc. 315
Memphis Light, Gas and Water Division 319
MidAmerican Energy Holdings Co. 326
Mirant Corp. 329
Mississippi Power Co. 329
Nat'l Grid USA 339
Nevada Power Co. 344
NiSource Inc. 349
Northeast Utilities 352
NorthWestern Corp. 355
NSTAR 357
OGE Energy Corp. 360
Oglethorpe Power Corp. 361
Orange and Rockland Utilities, Inc. 364
Otter Tail Power Co. 366
PacifiCorp 369
Pepco Holdings, Inc. 376
PG & E Corp. 380
Pinnacle West Capital Corp. 384
PNC Financial Services Group 387
Portland General Electric Co. 389
PPL Corp. 390
Progress Energy 395
PSE&G 397
Public Service Co. of New Mexico 398
Puget Sound Energy 399
Reliant Resources 409
San Diego Gas and Electric Co. 420
SCANA Corp. 426
Sempra Energy 432
Sierra Pacific Resources 438
Southern California Edison, an Edison Internat'l Co. 445
Southern Company 446
TECO Energy, Inc./Tampa Electric Co. 466
TXU 482
UGI Corp. 485
UniSource Energy Corp. 488
The United Illuminating Company 489
Vectren Corp. 501
We Energies 514
Westar Energy, Inc. 518
Wisconsin Energy Corp. 524
Wisconsin Public Service Corp. 524
WPS Resources Corp. 526
Xcel Energy, Inc. 528

Electronic/Electrical Components & Equipment

3M Company 1
Advanced Micro Devices, Inc. 7
American Power Conversion Corp. 33
Amkor Technology, Inc. 37
Applied Materials, Inc. 44
Arrow Electronics, Inc. 48
Avnet Inc. 57
Benchmark Electronics 71
Bose Corp. 87
Bourns, Inc. 87
Broadcom Corp. 91
Circuit City Stores, Inc. 120
Cirrus Logic, Inc. 121
Cooper Industries 139
CTS Corp. 147
Cubic Corp. 147
Danaher Corp. 151
Dictaphone Corp. 159
Eaton Corp. 173
EDS Corp. 175
Electrolux North America, Inc. 178
EMCOR Group, Inc. 178
Emerson 179
Energizer Holdings Inc. 181
Engelhard Corp. 181
Fluke Corporation 198
General Dynamics Corporation 212
General Electric Co. 213
Graybar Electric Co., Inc. 225
Griffon Corp. 228
Hewlett-Packard Co. 241
Hitachi America, Ltd. 244
Honeywell Internat'l, Inc. 247
Hubbell Incorporated 250
Hughes Supply, Inc. 251
Imation Corp. 255
Intel Corp. 258
Intergraph Corp. 259
Jabil Circuit, Inc. 266
JDS Uniphase Corp. 267
Joy Global Inc. 272
KEMET Corp. 277
Kimball International, Inc. 280
Lam Research Corp. 287
Lincoln Electric Holdings, Inc. 295
LORD Corporation 299
Magnetek, Inc. 302
Matsushita Electric Corp. of America 309
Mentor Graphics Corp. 320
Micron Technology, Inc. 324
Millipore Corp. 327
Mitsubishi Electric & Electronics USA 329
Molex Incorporated 331
Motorola, Inc. 334
Nat'l Semiconductor Corp. 340
NEC USA, Inc. 343
Northrop Grumman Corp. 353
Nu Horizons Electronics Corp. 357
ON Semiconductor Corp. 362
Pentair, Inc. 375
PerkinElmer, Inc. 378
Philips Electronics North America 382
Plantronics, Inc. 386
Qualcomm Inc. 400
Quantum Corporation 400
Radio Shack Corporation 403
Raytheon Co. 404
RF Micro Devices, Inc. 411
Ricoh Corp. 411
Salton, Inc. 420
Sanmina-SCI Corp. 420
Savin Corp. 422
Schlumberger Limited 427
Sharp Electronics Corp. 435
Siemens Corp. 437
Solectron Corp. 442
Sony Corp. of America 444
Southwire Co. 449

Sparton Corp. 450
Sprectrum Brands 450
Square D/Schneider Electric 452
Sybase, Inc. 463
Symbol Technologies, Inc. 463
Tektronix, Inc. 466
Teleflex Inc. 467
Teradyne, Inc. 469
Texas Instruments Incorporated 471
Thomas & Betts Corp. 472
Thomas Industries Inc. 472
Tyco Electronics Corp. 483
Tyco Internat'l (U.S.), Inc. 483
Unisys Corp. 488
Vishay Intertechnology, Inc. 507
WESCO Internat'l, Inc. 518
Westinghouse Electric Company LLC 519
Whirlpool Corp. 521
WJ Communications 525
Xerox Corp. 528
Zenith Electronics Corp. 531

Emergency and Security Services

Rural Metro Corp. 416
The Wackenhut Corporation 509

Engineering

The Aerospace Corp. 8
Agilent Technologies, Inc. 11
The Austin Co. 54
Bechtel Group, Inc. 67
Black & Veatch 75
CH2M Hill Companies, Inc. 112
Day & Zimmerman 152
Engelhard Corp. 181
Fluor Corp. 198
Foster Wheeler Ltd. 203
Hartford Steam Boiler Inspection and Insurance Co. 235
Henkels & McCoy, Inc. 240
Jacobs Engineering Group Inc. 266
Kellogg Brown and Root 275
LORD Corporation 299
Parsons Brinckerhoff 372
Parsons Corp. 372
The Shaw Group Inc. 435
SRI International 452
Stone & Webster, Inc. 458
Tetra Tech, Inc. 470
Washington Group Internat'l 512

Fertilizers

C F Industries, Inc. 111
Mosaic Co. 334
Rhodia, Inc. 411
Royster-Clark, Inc. 415
The Scotts Company 430
J. R. Simplot Co. 439
Southern States Cooperative 447

Financial Services

ABB Inc. 3
Advanta Corp. 7
AIG American General Corp. 12
AIG SunAmerica Inc. 13
Allmerica Property & Casualty Companies, Inc. 22
Ambac Financial Group, Inc. 27
American Century Cos., Inc. 29
American Express Co. 30
American Financial Group Inc. 31
AmeriCredit Corp. 34
Ameriprise Financial Services Inc. 35
Ameritrade Holding Corp. 36
AXA Financial, Inc. 58
BancWest Corp. 60
Bank of America Corp. 60
Barclays Capital 62
BB&T Corp. 66
Capital One Financial Corp. 100
Cash America Internat'l, Inc. 104
Centex Corporation 109
Ceridian Corp. 111
CheckFree Corp. 113
CHS Inc. 116
The CIT Group, Inc. 121
Citigroup, Inc. 122
Citizens Financial Group, Inc. 123
CNA Financial Corp. 126
Comerica Incorporated 131
Commerce Bancshares Inc. 131
Commercial Federal Corp. 132
Compass Bancshares, Inc. 132
Conseco, Inc. 135
Country Insurance and Financial Services 142
Credit Suisse First Boston 144
CUNA Mutual Group 148
The Depository Trust & Clearing Corp. 157
E*TRADE Financial Corp. 186
Fannie Mae 189
Fifth Third Bancorp. 194
First Citizens BancShares 194
First Data 195
First Horizon Nat'l Corp. 196
FirstMerit Corporation 197
Franklin Templeton Investments 204
Freddie Mac 204
Fremont General Corp. 206
GATX Corp. 209
General Motors Acceptance Corp. (GMAC) 214
Golden West Financial Corp. 222
H & R Block, Inc. 230
John H. Harland Co. 232
Harris Bank 233
Hibernia Corp. 243
HSBC North America Holdings Inc. 249
HSBC USA, Inc. 250
Huntington Bancshares Inc. 252
ING Americas 256
Instinet Group Inc. 257
Integra Bank N.A. 257
Jones Lang LaSalle Inc. 272
KeyCorp 278
Koch Industries, Inc. 282
Lehman Brothers 290
Leucadia Nat'l Corp. 291
Liberty Mutual Insurance Co. 293
Lincoln Financial Group 295
M&T Bank Corporation 301
Marsh & McLennan Companies, Inc. 306
Marshall & Ilsley Corp. 306
MasterCard Internat'l 308
The McGraw-Hill Companies, Inc. 313
Mellon Financial Corp. 319
Mercantile Bankshares Corporation 320
Merrill Lynch & Co., Inc. 322
J. P. Morgan Chase & Co. 332
Morgan Stanley 333
Mortgage Guaranty Insurance Corp. (MGIC) 333
Nat'l City Corp. 337
Nat'l Life Insurance Co. 339
New York Life Insurance Co. 345
Nomura Securities Internat'l, Inc. 350
Northern Trust Co. 353
NVR, Inc. 358
People's Bank 375
PNC Financial Services Group 387
PRG-Schultz Internat'l, Inc. 392
T. Rowe Price Associates 392
Primerica Financial Services, Inc. 393
Prudential Financial 397
Raymond James Financial, Inc. 404
RBC Dain Rauscher Corp. 405
Regions Financial Corp. 407
Robert Half International Inc. 412
Security Benefit Life Insurance Co. 432
SLM Corp. 440
Sovereign Bancorp, Inc. 449
State Street Corp. 456
Sun Life Financial 460
SunGard Data Systems, Inc. 460
SunTrust Banks, Inc. 462
Sykes Enterprises, Inc. 463
Synovus Financial Corp. 464
TCF Financial Corp. 465
Temple-Inland Inc. 468
Thrivent Financial for Lutherans 473

Towers Perrin ... 478
U.S. Bancorp Piper Jaffray Inc. ... 484
U.S. Trust Corp. ... 485
UBS Financial Services Inc. ... 485
UMB Financial Corp. ... 486
Union Bank of California ... 487
United Services Automobile Ass'n (USAA) ... 491
U.S. Bancorp ... 497
Visa U.S.A. Inc. ... 506
Wachovia Corp. ... 509
Washington Mutual, Inc. ... 512
Webster Financial Corp. ... 515

Floor Covering Industry

The Dixie Group, Inc. ... 160
LORD Corporation ... 299

Food Industry

AFC Enterprises ... 9
AG Processing Inc ... 10
Alberto-Culver Co. ... 16
Albertson's, Inc. ... 17
Altria Group, Inc. ... 25
American Crystal Sugar Co. ... 29
American Financial Group Inc. ... 31
Applebee's Internat'l, Inc. ... 43
ARAMARK ... 46
Ben & Jerry's Homemade Inc. ... 71
Berkshire Hathaway ... 71
Birds Eye Foods ... 75
BJ's Wholesale Club, Inc. ... 75
Blue Diamond Growers ... 82
Bob Evans Farms, Inc. ... 84
Brinker Internat'l, Inc. ... 90
Brookshire Grocery Co. ... 91
Bruno's Inc. ... 92
Bunge Ltd ... 93
Burger King Corporation ... 93
Campbell Soup Co. ... 99
CBRL Group, Inc. ... 106
Cheesecake Factory Inc. ... 113
Chiquita Brands Internat'l, Inc. ... 115
The Clorox Co. ... 125
ConAgra Foods, Inc. ... 134
Corn Products Internat'l, Inc. ... 141
Cumberland Farms, Inc. ... 147
Dairy Farmers of America, Inc. ... 150
Dairylea Cooperative Inc. ... 150
Darden Restaurants, Inc. ... 151
Dean Foods Company ... 152
Del Monte Foods ... 153
Delaware North Companies ... 153
Denny's Corp. ... 156
The Dial Corporation ... 158
Dole Food Company, Inc. ... 160
Dominick's Finer Foods, Inc. ... 161
Domino's Pizza, LLC ... 162
Dreyer's Grand Ice Cream Holdings, Inc. ... 166
Dunkin' Brands ... 169
DuPont ... 169
Fiesta Mart Inc. ... 194
Flowers Foods ... 198
FMC Technologies, Inc. ... 199
Food Lion LLC ... 200
Friendly Ice Cream Corp. ... 206
Frito-Lay, Inc. ... 206
General Mills ... 214
Gerber Products Co. ... 218
Giant Food LLC ... 219
Golub Corp. ... 222
Goya Foods, Inc. ... 224
Hardee's Food Systems, Inc. ... 232
HEB Grocery Co. ... 239
H. J. Heinz Co. ... 239
The Hershey Company ... 241
H. P. Hood Inc. ... 248
Hormel Foods Corp. ... 248
Hy-Vee, Inc. ... 253
Imperial Sugar Co. ... 255
Ingles Markets, Inc. ... 257
Interstate Bakeries Corp. ... 262
Invensys Systems, Inc. ... 264
Jack in the Box Inc. ... 266
Kellogg Co. ... 276
King Kullen Grocery Co. ... 281
Kraft Foods, Inc. ... 283
The Kroger Co. ... 284
L-3 Communications Titan Group ... 284
Lance, Inc. ... 287
Land O'Lakes, Inc. ... 287
Little Caesar Enterprises ... 295
The Manitowoc Co., Inc. ... 303
Mars, Inc. ... 305
Marsh Supermarkets, Inc. ... 306
McCormick & Company, Inc. ... 312
McDonald's Corp. ... 313
McKee Foods Corp. ... 314
McLane Company, Inc. ... 315
Meijer, Inc. ... 318
Fred Meyer Stores ... 323
Mitsubishi International Corporation ... 330
Mott's Inc. ... 335
Nash Finch Company ... 337
Nestle Purina PetCare Co. ... 343
Nestle USA, Inc. ... 343
Ocean Spray Cranberries, Inc. ... 360
Omega Protein Corporation ... 362
Outback Steakhouse, Inc. ... 366
Pall Corp. ... 370
Papa John's Internat'l Inc. ... 371
The Penn Traffic Co. ... 374
PepsiCo, Inc. ... 377
Perdue Farms ... 378
Performance Food Group Co. ... 378
Perrigo Co. ... 379
Pilgrim's Pride Corp. ... 383
The Procter & Gamble Company ... 394
Publix Super Markets, Inc. ... 399
Ralcorp Holdings, Inc. ... 403
Raley's ... 403
C.H. Robinson Worldwide, Inc. ... 412
The RTM Restaurant Group ... 416
Ruddick Corp. ... 416
Safeway Inc. ... 418
Sara Lee Corp. ... 421
Schreiber Foods, Inc. ... 428
The Schwan Food Co. ... 428
Seaboard Corporation ... 430
Sensient Technology Corp. ... 433
Shaklee Corp. ... 435
J. R. Simplot Co. ... 439
SKF USA, Inc. ... 440
Smithfield Foods, Inc. ... 441
The J. M. Smucker Company ... 442
Spartan Stores Inc. ... 449
Sunkist Growers ... 460
Supervalu Inc. ... 462
Sysco Corp. ... 464
Tasty Baking Co. ... 465
Tops Markets LLC ... 477
TravelCenters of America, Inc. ... 480
Triarc Companies, Inc. ... 480
Tyson Foods, Inc. ... 484
U.S. Foodservice ... 485
Unified Western Grocers, Inc. ... 486
Unilever United States, Inc. ... 487
United States Sugar Corp. ... 492
Valhi, Inc. ... 500
Vons ... 508
Weis Markets, Inc. ... 515
Welch's ... 515
Wendy's Internat'l, Inc. ... 517
Whole Foods Market, Inc. ... 522
Wild Oats Markets, Inc. ... 522
Winn-Dixie Stores ... 523
Wm. Wrigley Jr. Co. ... 526
YUM! Brands, Inc. ... 530

Forest Products/Paper/Wood

Appleton ... 44
Asplundh Tree Expert Co. ... 49
Avery Dennison Corp. ... 56
Boise Cascade Corp. ... 85
Burlington Northern Santa Fe Corporation ... 94
Caraustar Industries, Inc. ... 100
Cleveland-Cliffs Inc. ... 125
Engelhard Corp. ... 181

Forest City Enterprises, Inc. 202
Georgia-Pacific Corp. 217
Ikon Office Solutions, Inc. 255
Internat'l Paper 261
JELD-WEN, Inc. 267
Kerr-McGee Corp. 278
Kimberly-Clark Corp. 280
Longview Fibre Co. 298
Louisiana-Pacific Corporation 299
MAXXAM Inc. 310
MeadWestvaco Corp. 316
Nat'l Fuel Gas Co. 338
Pella Corp. 374
Plum Creek Timber Co. Inc. 387
Pope & Talbot, Inc. 389
Potlatch Corp. 389
Rayonier Inc. 404
Roseburg Forest Products Co. 414
Sealaska Corp. 431
Simpson Investment Co. 439
SKF USA, Inc. 440
Smurfit-Stone Container 442
Stora Enso North America 458
Temple-Inland Inc. 468
Universal Forest Products, Inc. 495
Valhi, Inc. 500
Weyerhaeuser Co. 520

Furniture/Furnishings/ Plumbing/Household Products

Ace Hardware Corp. 5
Andersen Corp. 40
AptarGroup, Inc. 45
Armstrong Holdings, Inc. 48
Bassett Furniture Industries, Inc. 64
Bed Bath & Beyond Inc. 68
Berkshire Hathaway 71
Big Lots Inc. 73
BJ's Wholesale Club, Inc. 75
The Bon Ton Stores, Inc. 86
The Clorox Co. 125
Colgate-Palmolive Co. 129
The Dial Corporation 158
Duchossois Industries, Inc. 168
Electrolux North America, Inc. 178
Enesco Group, Inc. 181
Ethan Allen Interiors Inc. 186
Fortune Brands, Inc. 202
Furniture Brands Internat'l, Inc. 207
Haworth Inc. 236
Herman Miller Inc. 240
Jarden Corp. 267
Kimball International, Inc. 280
Kohler Co. 282
La-Z-Boy Incorporated 285
Leggett & Platt, Inc. 289
The Longaberger Co. 297
Lowe's Companies, Inc. 299
Masco Corp. 307
Maytag Corp. 310
Michaels Stores, Inc. 324
Mohawk Industries, Inc. 330
Nat'l Presto Industries, Inc. 340
Newell Rubbermaid Inc. 347
OMNOVA Solutions Inc. 362
Oneida Ltd. 363
Pella Corp. 374
SC Johnson 425
Shaw Industries 435
Sherwin-Williams Co. 436
Springs Industries, Inc. 450
Square D/Schneider Electric 452
Steelcase Inc. 456
Unilever United States, Inc. 487
Valspar Corp. 500
Whirlpool Corp. 521
Williams-Sonoma, Inc. 523
World Kitchen, Inc. 525

Gas Utility

AGL Resources, Inc. 12
Algonquin Gas Transmission, LLC/Duke Energy 18
Allegheny Energy Inc. 18
Ameren Corp. 28
Aquila, Inc. 45
Atmos Energy Corp. 53
CenterPoint Energy 108
CH Energy Group, Inc. 111
CMS Energy Corp. 126
Conectiv 134
Consolidated Edison Co. of New York, Inc. 136
Constellation Energy 137
Dominion Peoples 161
Dominion Resources, Inc. 162
DPL Inc. 166
DTE Energy Co. 167
Duquesne Light Holdings 170
Dynegy, Inc. 171
Energen Corp. 180
Energy East Corp. 181
Entergy New Orleans 183
Exelon Corp. 187
Great Plains Energy, Inc. 226
Intermountain Gas Co. 260
Invensys Systems, Inc. 264
IPL (an AES Company) 264
KeySpan Corp. 279
The Laclede Group 286
LG&E Energy LLC 292
Madison Gas and Electric Co. 302
MDU Resources Group, Inc. 315
Memphis Light, Gas and Water Division 319
MidAmerican Energy Holdings Co. 326
Nat'l Fuel Gas Co. 338
New Jersey Resources Corp. 345
Nicor, Inc. 348
NiSource Inc. 349
Northeast Utilities 352
NorthWestern Corp. 355
NW Natural 358
ONEOK, Inc. 363
Orange and Rockland Utilities, Inc. 364
Peoples Energy Corp. 376
Pepco Holdings, Inc. 376
Piedmont Natural Gas Co. 383
PSE&G 397
Public Service Co. of New Mexico 398
Puget Sound Energy 399
Questar Corporation 401
SEMCO ENERGY, Inc. 432
Sempra Energy 432
South Jersey Gas Co. 444
Southern California Gas Co. 445
Southern Union Company 447
Southwest Gas Corp. 448
UGI Corp. 485
Vectren Corp. 501
Washington Gas 511
We Energies 514
Wisconsin Energy Corp. 524
Wisconsin Public Service Corp. 524
Xcel Energy, Inc. 528

Gases (Industrial)

Air Liquide America Corp. 13
Air Products and Chemicals, Inc. 13
Airgas, Inc. 14
Enron Corp. 182
Equitable Resources, Inc. 184
Foster Wheeler Ltd. 203
Harsco Corp. 234

Glass

Apogee Enterprises, Inc. 43
Corning Incorporated 141
Guardian Industries Corp. 228
Owens Corning 367
Owens-Illinois, Inc. 367
Pella Corp. 374
Pilkington North America 384
PPG Industries Inc. 390
Saint-Gobain Corp. 419
World Kitchen, Inc. 525

Heating/Air Conditioning

Carrier Corp. 104

Lennox Internat'l 291
Modine Manufacturing Company 330
Owens Corning 367
Thermo Electron Corp. 472
York Internat'l Corp. 530

Hotels/Motels

Best Western Internat'l 73
Carlson Companies 103
Cendant Corp. 108
Darden Restaurants, Inc. 151
Delaware North Companies 153
The Walt Disney Company 159
Extended Stay America, Inc. 188
Harrah's Entertainment, Inc. 233
Hilton Hotels Corp. 244
Host Marriott Corp. 249
Global Hyatt Corp. 253
InterContinental Hotels Group 259
Kohler Co. 282
La Quinta Inns 285
Loews Corporation 297
Marriott Internat'l, Inc. 305
MGM MIRAGE 324
Nestle USA, Inc. 343

Information Technology

Affiliated Computer Services, Inc. (ACS) 9
Anacomp, Inc. 39
The BISYS Group, Inc. 75
Brady Corp. 89
EBSCO Industries, Inc. 174
Equifax Inc. 184
The First American Corp. 194
Gartner, Inc. 209
Google Inc. 224
Internat'l Data Group 260
Mark IV Industries, Inc. 304
SRI International 452

Insurance

AEGON USA, Inc. 8
Aetna Inc. 9
AFLAC Incorporated 10
AIG American General Corp. 12
AIG SunAmerica Inc. 13
Allmerica Property & Casualty Companies, Inc. 22
Allstate Insurance Co. 23
AMERCO 28
American Family Insurance Group 31
American Internat'l Group, Inc. 32
American Nat'l Insurance Co. 33
American United Life Insurance Co. 34
Aon Corp. 41
Arkansas Blue Cross and Blue Shield 47
Assurant 50
Auto-Owners Insurance Group 54
AXA Financial, Inc. 58
Berkshire Hathaway 71
The BISYS Group, Inc. 75
Blue Cross and Blue Shield of Alabama 76
Blue Cross and Blue Shield of Arizona 76
Blue Cross and Blue Shield of Delaware 77
Blue Cross and Blue Shield of Florida 77
Blue Cross and Blue Shield of Kansas City 77
Blue Cross and Blue Shield of Kansas, Inc. 78
Blue Cross and Blue Shield of Louisiana 78
Blue Cross and Blue Shield of Massachusetts 78
Blue Cross and Blue Shield of Minnesota 78
Blue Cross and Blue Shield of Mississippi 79
Blue Cross and Blue Shield of Montana 79
Blue Cross and Blue Shield of Nebraska 79
Blue Cross and Blue Shield of North Carolina 79
Blue Cross and Blue Shield of North Dakota 80
Blue Cross & Blue Shield of Rhode Island 80
Blue Cross and Blue Shield of Tennessee 80
Blue Cross and Blue Shield of Texas, Inc. 80
Blue Cross and Blue Shield of Vermont 81
Blue Cross and Blue Shield of Wyoming 81
Blue Cross Blue Shield of Georgia 81
Blue Cross Blue Shield of Michigan 81
Blue Cross of Idaho 81
Blue Cross of Northeastern Pennsylvania 82
Blue Shield of California 82
BlueCross BlueShield of Oklahoma 83
BlueCross BlueShield of South Carolina 83
Brown & Brown, Inc. 92
Capital BlueCross (Pennsylvania) 100
CareFirst BlueCross and BlueShield 101
The Chubb Corp. 116
CIGNA Corp. 118
Cincinnati Financial Corp. 119
CNA Financial Corp. 126
Colonial Life & Accident Insurance Co. 129
Conseco, Inc. 135
CUNA Mutual Group 148
Empire Blue Cross and Blue Shield 179
Employers Insurance Co. of Wausau 180
Erie Indeminity Co. 185
Exellus Blue Cross Blue Shield 187
Farmers Group, Inc. 190
Fidelity Nat'l Financial, Inc. 193
The First American Corp. 194
First Midwest Bancorp, Inc. 196
Foremost Corp. of America 202
Arthur J. Gallagher & Co. 207
GEICO Corp. 210
GenAmerica Financial Corp. 210
General Re Corp. 216
Golden Rule Insurance Co. 221
Guardian Life Insurance Co. of America 228
Harleysville Group 232
The Hartford Financial Services Group Inc. 234
Hartford Steam Boiler Inspection and Insurance Co. 235
Health Care Service Corp. 237
HealthNow New York Inc. 238
Highmark Inc. 243
Hillenbrand Industries, Inc. 244
Horace Mann Educators Corp. 248
Horizon Blue Cross Blue Shield of New Jersey 248
HSBC North America Holdings Inc. 249
Humana Inc. 251
Independence Blue Cross (Pennsylvania) 256
Jackson Nat'l Life Insurance Co. 266
Jefferson-Pilot Corp. 267
John Hancock Financial Services 269
Kaiser Permanente 273
Kansas City Life Insurance Co. 274
LandAmerica Financial Group, Inc. 288
Leucadia Nat'l Corp. 291
Liberty Mutual Insurance Co. 293
The Lifetime Healthcare Companies 293
Lincoln Financial Group 295
Loews Corporation 297
Marsh Inc. 306
MassMutual Financial Group 307
MAXIMUS, Inc. 310
MBIA, Inc. 311
Medical Mutual of Ohio 317
MetLife, Inc. 322
Mid Atlantic Medical Services Inc. 325
Minnesota Life Insurance Co. 328
Mountain State Blue Cross Blue Shield 335
Mutual of America Life Insurance Co. 335
Mutual of Omaha Insurance Co. 336
Nat'l Life Insurance Co. 339
Nationwide 341
New York Life Insurance Co. 345
Northwestern Mutual Financial Network 355
The Ohio Casualty Group 361
OneBeacon Insurance 363
Pacific Life Insurance Co. 368
Pan American Life Insurance Co. 371
The Penn Mutual Life Insurance Co. 374
Penn Nat'l Insurance 374
J. C. Penney Co., Inc. 374
The Phoenix Companies, Inc. 383
Premera Blue Cross 392
Primerica Financial Services, Inc. 393
The Principal Financial Group 393
The Progressive Corporation 396
Protective Life Corp. 396
Prudential Financial 397
Radian Group, Inc. 402
Regence BlueCross BlueShield of Oregon 406
Regence BlueCross BlueShield of Utah 406
Regence BlueShield of Idaho 407

Royal & SunAlliance USA Inc. 415
SAFECO Corp. 418
Security Benefit Life Insurance Co. 432
Sentry Insurance 434
Standard Insurance Co. 453
State Farm Insurance Cos. 455
Swiss Re America Corp. 462
TIAA/CREF 474
Tidewater Inc. 474
Torchmark Corp. 477
Towers Perrin 478
Trustmark Nat'l Bank 481
United Services Automobile Ass'n (USAA) 491
UnumProvident Corp. 496
Webster Financial Corp. 515
Wellmark, Inc. 516
Wellpoint, Inc. 516
Western and Southern Life Insurance Co. 518

Investment Industry/Markets

American Stock Exchange 34
Ameritrade Holding Corp. 36
Bear, Stearns and Co. Inc. 67
The BISYS Group, Inc. 75
Chicago Mercantile Exchange Inc. 114
Conseco, Inc. 135
The Dreyfus Corp. 166
A. G. Edwards, Inc. 176
FMR Corp. 200
Goldman, Sachs and Co. 222
Koch Industries, Inc. 282
Lehman Brothers 290
Merrill Lynch & Co., Inc. 322
New York Stock Exchange, Inc. 346
Pioneer Natural Resources Co. 385
T. Rowe Price Associates 392
Raymond James Financial, Inc. 404
Ruddick Corp. 416
The Charles Schwab Corp. 428
Sealaska Corp. 431
Starwood Hotels and Resorts Worldwide, Inc. 455
Stephens Inc. 457
Towers Perrin 478
Trustmark Nat'l Bank 481
U.S. Bancorp Piper Jaffray Inc. 484
UBS Financial Services Inc. 485

Leasing

Bandag, Inc. 60
Equity Residential 185
Leucadia Nat'l Corp. 291

Machinery/Equipment/Industrial Tools

ABB Inc. 3
AGCO Corp. 11
Albany Internat'l Corp. 16
Ametek, Inc. 36
Ampco-Pittsburgh Corp. 37
Amsted Industries Inc. 38
Applied Industrial Technologies 44
The Babcock & Wilcox Company 58
Baker Hughes Inc. 59
Barnes Group Inc. 62
The Black & Decker Corp. 75
Briggs and Stratton Corp. 89
Cargill, Incorporated 102
Case New Holland Inc. 104
Caterpillar Inc. 105
Cooper Industries 139
Crane Co. 144
Crowley Maritime Corp. 145
Crown Holdings, Inc. 145
Cummins, Inc. 147
Delco Remy Internat'l Inc. 153
Diebold, Inc. 159
Donaldson Company, Inc. 163
Eaton Corp. 173
Federal-Mogul Corp. 191
Flowserve Corp. 198
Gates Rubber Co. 209
General Binding Corp. 212
General Electric Co. 213
Goodrich Corporation 223
W. R. Grace & Co. 224
Graco Inc. 225
W. W. Grainger, Inc. 225
Hamilton Sundstrand 231
Harsco Corp. 234
Hillenbrand Industries, Inc. 244
Illinois Tool Works Inc. 255
Intermet Corp. 259
ITT Industries 265
JLG Industries, Inc. 268
Johnson Controls, Inc. 271
Joy Global Inc. 272
Kaman Corp. 274
Kennametal Inc. 277
Lincoln Electric Holdings, Inc. 295
LORD Corporation 299
The Manitowoc Co., Inc. 303
Mark IV Industries, Inc. 304
Milacron Inc. 326
Mine Safety Appliances Co. (MSA) 328
Mitsubishi International Corporation 330
NACCO Industries 337
Navistar Internat'l Corp. 342
Nordson Corp. 350
Northrop Grumman Newport News 354
Pall Corp. 370
Parker Hannifin Corp. 371
Pitney Bowes Inc. 385
Sequa Corp. 434
A. O. Smith Corp. 441
Snap-on Incorporated 442
SPX Corp. 451
The Stanley Works 454
Stewart & Stevenson Services, Inc. 457
Teleflex Inc. 467
Terex Corp. 469
Thomas Industries Inc. 472
Tidewater Inc. 474
The Toro Co. 477
Tyco Internat'l (U.S.), Inc. 483
United States Sugar Corp. 492
Volvo Group North America, Inc. 508
Weatherford Internat'l Ltd. 514
Wheeling-Pittsburgh Steel Corp. 521
Zebra Technologies Corp. 531

Medical and Health Care

3M Company 1
Abbott Laboratories 3
Aetna Inc. 9
Alcon Inc. 17
Allergan Inc. 19
Allina Hospitals and Clinics 22
American Medical Security Group, Inc. 33
Amgen Inc. 36
Angelica Corp. 40
Arkansas Blue Cross and Blue Shield 47
Bausch & Lomb 64
Baxter Internat'l Inc. 65
Bayer Corporation 65
Becton, Dickinson and Co. 68
Beverly Enterprises, Inc. 73
Biomet Inc. 74
Blue Cross and Blue Shield of Alabama 76
Blue Cross and Blue Shield of Arizona 76
Blue Cross and Blue Shield of Delaware 77
Blue Cross and Blue Shield of Florida 77
Blue Cross and Blue Shield of Kansas City 77
Blue Cross and Blue Shield of Kansas, Inc. 78
Blue Cross and Blue Shield of Louisiana 78
Blue Cross and Blue Shield of Massachusetts 78
Blue Cross and Blue Shield of Minnesota 78
Blue Cross and Blue Shield of Mississippi 79
Blue Cross and Blue Shield of Montana 79
Blue Cross and Blue Shield of Nebraska 79
Blue Cross and Blue Shield of North Carolina 79
Blue Cross and Blue Shield of North Dakota 80
Blue Cross & Blue Shield of Rhode Island 80
Blue Cross and Blue Shield of Tennessee 80
Blue Cross and Blue Shield of Texas, Inc. 80
Blue Cross and Blue Shield of Vermont 81
Blue Cross and Blue Shield of Wyoming 81
Blue Cross Blue Shield of Georgia 81

Blue Cross Blue Shield of Michigan 81
Blue Cross of Idaho 81
Blue Cross of Northeastern Pennsylvania 82
Blue Shield of California 82
BlueCross BlueShield of Oklahoma 83
BlueCross BlueShield of South Carolina 83
Boston Scientific Corp. 87
Briggs and Stratton Corp. 89
C. R. Bard, Inc. 96
Capital BlueCross (Pennsylvania) 100
CareFirst BlueCross and BlueShield 101
Coventry Health Care 143
DaVita, Inc. 152
Dentsply Internat'l 156
Edwards Lifesciences Corp. 176
Empire Blue Cross and Blue Shield 179
Exellus Blue Cross Blue Shield 187
Express Scripts, Inc. 187
First Health 195
Genzyme Corp. 217
Guidant Corp. 229
HCA 237
Health Care Service Corp. 237
Health Management Associates, Inc. 237
Health Net, Inc. 238
HealthNow New York Inc. 238
HealthSouth Corp. 238
Henry Schein, Inc. 240
Highmark Inc. 243
Horizon Blue Cross Blue Shield of New Jersey 248
Independence Blue Cross (Pennsylvania) 256
Invacare Corp. 263
Jenny Craig, Inc. 268
Johnson & Johnson 270
Kindred Healthcare, Inc. 281
The Lifetime Healthcare Companies 293
Manor Care, Inc. 303
McKesson Corp. 315
Medco Health Solutions, Inc. 316
MedImmune, Inc. 317
Medline Industries, Inc. 318
Medtronic, Inc. 318
Mid Atlantic Medical Services Inc. 325
Mountain State Blue Cross Blue Shield 335
Omnicare, Inc. 362
Owens & Minor, Inc. 367
Oxford Health Plans Inc. 368
PacifiCare Health Systems, Inc. 369
Pfizer Inc. 379
Premera Blue Cross 392
PSS World Medical, Inc. 398
Quest Diagnostics Inc. 401
Quintiles Transnat'l Corp. 401
Regence BlueCross BlueShield of Oregon 406
Regence BlueCross BlueShield of Utah 406
Regence BlueShield of Idaho 407
RehabCare Group, Inc. 408
Renal Care Group, Inc. 409
Rural Metro Corp. 416
Sanofi Pasteur, Inc. 420
Sava Senior Care LLC 422
Science Applications Internat'l Corp. 429
Sierra Health Services, Inc. 438
St. Jude Medical, Inc. 452
STERIS Corp. 457
Sun Healthcare Group, Inc. 459
Sunrise Assisted Living, Inc. 461
Tenet Healthcare Corp. 468
Triad Hospitals, Inc. 480
UnitedHealth Group 494
Universal Health Services, Inc. 495
Varian Medical Systems, Inc. 501
VITAS Healthcare Corporation 507
WebMD Corp. 515
Wellmark, Inc. 516
Wellpoint, Inc. 516
West Pharmaceutical Services 518
Zimmer Holdings, Inc. 532

Mining

Arch Coal, Inc. 46
Cleveland-Cliffs Inc 125
CONSOL Energy Inc. 136
Freeport-McMoRan Copper and Gold Inc. 205
Hecla Mining Co. 239
Invensys Systems, Inc. 264
Kennecott Energy Co. 277
Kennecott Utah Copper 277
Peter Kiewit Sons', Inc. 279
Newmont Mining Corp. 347
Phelps Dodge Corp. 381
Sealaska Corp. 431
Terex Corp. 469
U.S. Borax Inc. 485

Music/Musical Instruments

Kaman Corp. 274

Non-Ferrous Metals/Metal Working

Alcoa Inc. 17
Amcast Industrial Corporation 27
Bechtel Group, Inc. 67
Brush Engineered Materials Inc. 93
Century Aluminum Co. 110
Duchossois Industries, Inc. 168
Eagle-Picher Industries, Inc. 171
General Cable Corp. 212
Hecla Mining Co. 239
Intermet Corp. 259
Kaiser Aluminum & Chemical Corp. 273
Kohler Co. 282
Metaldyne Corp. 322
Mitsubishi International Corporation 330
Nucor Corp. 358
Phelps Dodge Corp. 381
Precision Castparts Corp. 391
Quanex Corp. 400
Reliance Steel & Aluminum Co. 408
Tredegar Corp. 480
Trinity Industries, Inc. 481

Nuclear Energy

AREVA Enterprises, Inc. 47
General Atomics 211
PPL Corp. 390
USEC Inc. 497

Nutrition/Fitness

Leiner Health Products, Inc. 290
Shaklee Corp. 435
Weight Watchers Internat'l 515

Packaging/Containers

Ball Corp. 59
Bemis Company, Inc. 71
Boise Cascade Corp. 85
Caraustar Industries, Inc. 100
Chesapeake Corp. 114
Crown Holdings, Inc. 145
Green Bay Packaging Inc. 227
Greif, Inc. 227
MeadWestvaco Corp. 316
Menasha Corporation 319
Pactiv Corp. 370
Rockwell Automation 412
Saint-Gobain Corp. 419
Smurfit-Stone Container 442
Sonoco Products Co. 443
Temple-Inland Inc. 468
U.S. Can Corp. 491
West Pharmaceutical Services 518
WestPoint Stevens Inc. 520

Petroleum/Oil/Natural Gas

ABB Inc. 3
Amerada Hess Corp. 27
Anadarko Petroleum Corp. 39
Apache Corp. 42
Ashland Inc. 49
Avista Corp. 56
Baker Hughes Inc. 59
Bechtel Group, Inc. 67

BJ Services Co. 75
Black Hills Corp. 76
BP 88
Burlington Resources Inc. 95
Cemex USA 107
CenterPoint Energy 108
CH Energy Group, Inc. 111
Chemtura 114
Chevron Corp. 114
CITGO Petroleum Corporation 121
CMS Energy Corp. 126
Colonial Pipeline Co. 130
ConocoPhillips 135
CONSOL Energy Inc. 136
Cumberland Farms, Inc. 147
Devon Energy Corp. 157
Dynegy, Inc. 171
El Paso Corp. 177
Energy East Corp. 181
Enron Corp. 182
Equitable Resources, Inc. 184
Exxon Mobil Corp. 188
Foster Wheeler Ltd. 203
Frontier Oil Corp. 207
Giant Industries, Inc. 219
GlobalSantaFe Corp. 221
Halliburton Company 230
Hunt Oil Co. 252
Intermountain Gas Co. 260
Jiffy Lube Internat'l, Inc. 268
Kerr-McGee Corp. 278
Kinder Morgan, Inc. 280
Koch Industries, Inc. 282
Loews Corporation 297
Lyondell Chemical Co. 301
Marathon Oil Corp. 304
McDermott Internat'l, Inc. 312
Murphy Oil Corp. 335
Nabors Industries, Ltd. 337
Nat'l Life Insurance Co. 339
Nat'l Oilwell, Inc. 340
NewMarket Corp. 347
Noble Drilling Corp. 350
Occidental Petroleum Corp. 359
ONEOK, Inc. 363
Pioneer Natural Resources Co. 385
Plains Resources Inc. 386
Pogo Producing Co. 387
Premcor Inc. 392
Progress Energy 395
PSE&G 397
Questar Corporation 401
Rockwell Automation 412
Rowan Companies, Inc. 415
Schlumberger Limited 427
Shell Oil Co. 436
Sinclair Oil Corp. 439
SKF USA, Inc. 440
Southern States Cooperative 447
Southwestern Energy Co. 449
Sunoco, Inc. 461
TECO Energy, Inc./Tampa Electric Co. 466
Tesoro Petroleum Corp. 470
Texas Eastern Products Pipeline Company, LLC (TEPPCO) 470
Total Petrochemicals USA, Inc. 478
TransMontaigne, Inc. 479
UGI Corp. 485
United Refining Co. 491
UNOCAL Corp. 495
Valero Energy Corp. 499
Western Gas Resources, Inc. 519
Williams 522
Xanser Corp. 527

Pharmaceuticals

Abbott Laboratories 3
Alcon Inc. 17
Allergan Inc. 19
Alpharma Inc. 24
AmeriSource Bergen Corp. 35
Andrx Corp. 40
Applera Corp. 43
AstraZeneca Pharmaceuticals 50
Barr Pharmaceuticals, Inc. 62
Battelle 64
Bausch & Lomb 64
Bayer Corporation 65
Berlex, Inc. 72
Berwind Group 72
Boehringer Ingelheim Corp. 84
Bristol-Myers Squibb Co. 90
Caremark Rx, Inc. 101
Cephalon, Inc. 110
Covance, Inc. 143
CVS 148
Forest Laboratories, Inc. 202
Fred's Inc. 204
GenCorp 210
GlaxoSmithKline Research and Development 220
Hoffmann-La Roche Inc. (Roche) 245
ICI American Holdings, Inc. 254
Johnson & Johnson 270
King Pharmaceuticals, Inc. 281
Eli Lilly and Company 293
Longs Drug Stores Corp. 298
McKesson Corp. 315
Medco Health Solutions, Inc. 316
MedPointe Inc. 318
Merck & Co., Inc. 320
Millennium Pharmaceuticals, Inc. 326
Millipore Corp. 327
Mylan Laboratories Inc. 336
Novartis Corporation 355
Omnicare, Inc. 362
Pall Corp. 370
Perrigo Co. 379
Pfizer Inc. 379
Pharmaceutical Product Development, Inc. 381
The Procter & Gamble Company 394
PSS World Medical, Inc. 398
Quintiles Transnat'l Corp. 401
Rockwell Automation 412
Sanofi-Aventis Inc. 421
Schering-Plough Corporation 426
SRI International 452
Stryker Corp. 459
Wyeth 526
Wyeth Pharmaceuticals 527

Photography/Art

Binney and Smith Inc. 74
Canon U.S.A., Inc. 99
Eastman Kodak Company 172
Hallmark Cards, Inc. 231
Polaroid Corp. 388
Ricoh Corp. 411
Sotheby's Holdings, Inc. 444

Pipelines

Algonquin Gas Transmission, LLC/Duke Energy 18
BJ Services Co. 75
CenterPoint Energy 108
Kinder Morgan, Inc. 280
Koch Industries, Inc. 282
MDU Resources Group, Inc. 315
Nat'l Fuel Gas Co. 338
NiSource Inc. 349
OGE Energy Corp. 360
Texas Eastern Products Pipeline Company, LLC (TEPPCO) 470

Plastics

Bridgestone Americas Holding, Inc. 89
The Dow Chemical Company 164
DuPont 169
Hercules Incorporated 240
Huntsman Corp. 253
Myers Industries, Inc. 336
Owens-Illinois, Inc. 367
PolyOne Corp. 388
Reichhold, Inc. 408
Ryerson Tull 417
Saint-Gobain Corp. 419
Tredegar Corp. 480
Tupperware Corp. 482

Pollution/Waste

Bechtel Group, Inc. 67
CH2M Hill Companies, Inc. 112
Donaldson Company, Inc. 163
Ecolab Inc. 174
Engelhard Corp. 181
Koch Industries, Inc. 282
PerkinElmer, Inc. 378
Republic Services, Inc. 410
Rockwell Automation 412
Ross Environmental Services, Inc. 414
Safety-Kleen Systems, Inc. 418
Science Applications Internat'l Corp. 429
Waste Management, Inc. 513

Poultry Processing

Gold Kist Inc. 221

Press/Journalism

Associated Press 50
Atlanta Journal Constitution 53
Chicago Sun-Times 115
The Copley Press, Inc. 140
The Courier-Journal 143
Forbes, Inc. 201
Freedom Communications Inc. 205
Globe Newspaper Co. 221
Harte-Hanks, Inc. 234
The Hearst Corp. 238
Internat'l Data Group 260
Journal Communications, Inc. 272
Knight Ridder 281
Landmark Communications, Inc. 288
Lee Enterprises 289
New York Times Co. 346
News Corporation Ltd. 347
Newsweek, Inc. 348
Omaha World-Herald Co. 361
Orlando Sentinel Communications 365
The Providence Journal Co. 396
E. W. Scripps Co. 430
Star Tribune 454
Tribune Co. 480
The Washington Post Co. 513

Printing

American Greetings Corp. 31
Banta Corp. 61
Deluxe Corp. 156
R R Donnelley 163
FedEx Kinko's Office and Print Services 193
Gannett Co., Inc. 208
Hallmark Cards, Inc. 231
Jostens, Inc. 272
Journal Communications, Inc. 272
Quad/Graphics, Inc. 400

Publishing

American Greetings Corp. 31
Atlanta Journal Constitution 53
Belo Corp. 71
Berkshire Hathaway 71
Bloomberg L.P. 76
Chicago Sun-Times 115
The Copley Press, Inc. 140
The Courier-Journal 143
Dow Jones and Co. 165
The Dun & Bradstreet Corp. 169
Emmis Communications Corp. 179
Encyclopaedia Britannica, Inc. 180
Forbes, Inc. 201
Freedom Communications Inc. 205
Gannett Co., Inc. 208
Globe Newspaper Co. 221
The Hearst Corp. 238
Houghton Mifflin Co. 249
Journal Communications, Inc. 272
Landmark Communications, Inc. 288
Lee Enterprises 289
Meredith Corp. 321
Nat'l Geographic Soc. 339
New York Times Co. 346
News Corporation Ltd. 347
Newsweek, Inc. 348
Omaha World-Herald Co. 361
Playboy Enterprises, Inc. 386
R.L. Polk & Co. 388
The Providence Journal Co. 396
Rand McNally 403
Reader's Digest Ass'n, Inc. 405
Scholastic, Inc. 427
E. W. Scripps Co. 430
Star Tribune 454
Thomson West 473
Time Warner Inc. 475
The Washington Post Co. 513
John Wiley & Sons, Inc. 522

Radio/TV

ABC, Inc. 4
Adelphia Communications Corp. 6
AFLAC Incorporated 10
Avid Technology, Inc. 56
Belo Corp. 71
Bloomberg L.P. 76
Cablevision Systems Corp. 96
Clear Channel Communications 124
Comcast Corporation 130
Corporation for Public Broadcasting 141
Cox Enterprises, Inc. 143
The DIRECTV Group, Inc. 159
The Walt Disney Company 159
Emmis Communications Corp. 179
Gannett Co., Inc. 208
Harte-Hanks, Inc. 234
Home Box Office (HBO) 246
HSN, Inc. 250
Hubbard Broadcasting, Inc. 250
IAC/InterActiveCorp 254
Jefferson-Pilot Corp. 267
Jones Internat'l, Ltd. 271
Journal Communications, Inc. 272
Knight Ridder 281
Landmark Communications, Inc. 288
Liberty Corp. 292
Liberty Media Corp. 293
Media General Inc. 317
Meredith Corp. 321
Nat'l Geographic Soc. 339
Nat'l Public Radio 340
NBC Universal 342
News Corporation Ltd. 347
Orbital Sciences Corp. 364
Scientific-Atlanta, Inc. 429
E. W. Scripps Co. 430
Sesame Workshop 434
Sony Corp. of America 444
Time Warner Inc. 475
Tribune Co. 480
Turner Broadcasting System, Inc. 482
Viacom Inc./CBS Corp. 505
The Washington Post Co. 513

Railroad Industry

Amtrak 38
Burlington Northern Santa Fe Corporation 94
Canadian Nat'l / Illinois Central 99
CSX Corp. 146
Duchossois Industries, Inc. 168
GATX Corp. 209
Kansas City Southern 274
Norfolk Southern Corp. 351
Trinity Industries, Inc. 481
Union Pacific Corp. 487
Westinghouse Air Brake Technologies Corp. 519

Real Estate/Housing

Alexander & Baldwin, Inc. 18
APL Americas 42
Carlson Companies 103
CarrAmerica Realty Corp. 104

CB Richard Ellis Services, Inc. 106
EBSCO Industries, Inc. 174
Equity Office Properties Trust 185
Equity Residential 185
Forest City Enterprises, Inc. 202
The Irvine Company 264
Jones Lang LaSalle Inc. 272
Kohler Co. 282
Kraus-Anderson Cos. Inc. 284
LandAmerica Financial Group, Inc. 288
Leucadia Nat'l Corp. 291
MAXXAM Inc. 310
The Ryland Group, Inc. 417
SAFECO Corp. 418
Simon Property Group 439
Tidewater Inc. 474
Toll Brothers, Inc. 477
Trump Hotels and Casino Resorts, Inc. 481
United Services Automobile Ass'n (USAA) 491

Research

Amgen Inc. 36
The First American Corp. 194
Internat'l Data Group 260
Millipore Corp. 327
Orbital Sciences Corp. 364
Science Applications Internat'l Corp. 429

Retailing

7-Eleven, Inc. 2
99 Cents Only Stores 2
Albertson's, Inc. 17
Amazon.com, Inc. 26
The Andersons, Inc. 40
Barnes & Noble, Inc. 62
Bed Bath & Beyond Inc. 68
Belk, Inc. 69
Berkshire Hathaway 71
Best Buy Co., Inc. 72
Big Lots Inc. 73
Big Y Foods Inc. 73
BJ's Wholesale Club, Inc. 75
Bloomingdale's 76
Borders Group, Inc. 86
Bose Corp. 87
Burlington Coat Factory Warehouse Corp. 94
Checkpoint Systems, Inc. 113
Circuit City Stores, Inc. 120
Costco Wholesale Corp. 142
CSK Auto, Inc. 146
CVS 148
Demoulas Market Basket 156
Dillard's Inc. 159
Dollar General Corp. 161
Dollar Tree Stores, Inc. 161
Dominick's Finer Foods, Inc. 161
Eddie Bauer, Inc. 175
Family Dollar Stores, Inc. 189
Fiesta Mart Inc. 194
Footlocker Inc. 201
Fred's Inc. 204
General Growth Properties Inc. 214
Genesco 216
Giant Food LLC 219
The Great Atlantic and Pacific Tea Co. 226
Group 1 Automotive, Inc. 228
Hannaford Bros. Co. 231
Harte-Hanks, Inc. 234
The Home Depot, Inc. 246
Huffy Corp. 251
J. Crew Group, Inc. 266
JM Family Enterprises, Inc. 269
Jo-Ann Stores, Inc. 269
King Kullen Grocery Co. 281
Kohl's Corp. 282
The Kroger Co. 284
Lowe's Companies, Inc. 299
Meijer, Inc. 318
Men's Wearhouse, Inc. 319
Mervyn's 322
Michaels Stores, Inc. 324
Nash Finch Company 337
Nordstrom, Inc. 351
Office Depot, Inc. 360
The Pantry, Inc. 371
Pathmark Stores Inc. 372
Payless ShoeSource 372
J. C. Penney Co., Inc. 374
PETCO Animal Supplies, Inc. 379
PETsMART, Inc. 379
Phillips-Van Heusen Corp. 382
Pier 1 Imports 383
Polo Ralph Lauren 388
Raley's 403
Ralphs Grocery Co. 403
Retail Ventures, Inc. 410
Rite Aid Corp. 411
Ross Stores, Inc. 415
Ruddick Corp. 416
Safeway Inc. 418
Saks, Inc. 419
Save Mart Supermarkets 422
Schnuck Markets, Inc. 427
Scholastic, Inc. 427
Sears Holding Corp. 431
Shaw's Supermarkets, Inc. 436
Sheetz, Inc. 436
Shopko Stores, Inc. 437
Simon Property Group 439
Stage Stores, Inc. 453
Staples, Inc. 454
Starbucks Corp. 455
The Stop & Shop Supermarket Co. 458
Target Corp. 465
Tesoro Petroleum Corp. 470
Tiffany & Co. 474
The TJX Companies, Inc. 476
TravelCenters of America, Inc. 480
True Value Company 481
United Auto Group, Inc. 489
United Stationers Inc. 492
Wal-Mart Stores 510
Walgreen Co. 511
Wawa, Inc. 514
Winn-Dixie Stores 523

Risk Management

Moody's Corp. 332

Rubber/Tires

Bandag, Inc. 60
Bridgestone Americas Holding, Inc. 89
Cooper Tire & Rubber Company 139
Eagle-Picher Industries, Inc. 171
The Goodyear Tire & Rubber Company 223
Michelin North America, Inc. 324
Myers Industries, Inc. 336

Safety/Security

The Brink's Co. 89
Corrections Corp. of America 141
Day & Zimmerman 152
DuPont 169
Federal Signal Corp. 191
Mark IV Industries, Inc. 304
Mine Safety Appliances Co. (MSA) 328
Science Applications Internat'l Corp. 429
Symantec Corp. 463
Triple Canopy, Inc. 481
The Wackenhut Corporation 509

Savings and Loan

American Financial Group Inc. 31
Downey Savings and Loan Ass'n, F.A. 166
SAFECO Corp. 418
Standard Federal Bank 453

Scientific Instruments

The Aerospace Corp. 8
Amgen Inc. 36
Applera Corp. 43
Beckman Coulter, Inc. 68

Bio-Rad Laboratories, Inc. 74
Bourns, Inc. 87
Cooper Cameron Corp. 139
Cubic Corp. 147
Dentsply Internat'l 156
Edwards Lifesciences Corp. 176
Fisher Scientific Internat'l Inc. 197
Fluke Corporation 198
General Atomics 211
Graco Inc. 225
Eli Lilly and Company 293
Medtronic, Inc. 318
Pall Corp. 370
PerkinElmer, Inc. 378
Raytheon Co. 404
SRI International 452
Tektronix, Inc. 466
Waters Corp. 514

Service Industry

ARAMARK 46
Fluor Corp. 198
Hertz Corp. 241
Hillenbrand Industries, Inc. 244
Jostens, Inc. 272
Kelly Services, Inc. 276
Manpower Inc. 303
Maritz Inc. 304
Marriott Internat'l, Inc. 305
McDonald's Corp. 313
Nordstrom, Inc. 351
Rollins, Inc. 414
Safety-Kleen Systems, Inc. 418
Service Corp. Internat'l 434
The ServiceMaster Co. 434
United Parcel Service (UPS) 490

Shipping/Shipbuilding

Alexander & Baldwin, Inc. 18
APL Americas 42
Bath Iron Works Corp. 64
Carnival Corp. 103
Crowley Maritime Corp. 145
Lykes Lines Limited 301
Matson Navigation Company, Inc. 308
Nicor, Inc. 348
Northrop Grumman Corp. 353
Northrop Grumman Newport News 354
Overseas Shipholding Group, Inc. 366

Sports/Recreation/Entertainment

Activision, Inc. 5
Alliance Gaming Corp. 20
Ameristar Casinos, Inc. 35
Aztar Corp. 58
Bally Total Fitness Holding Corp. 59
Boyd Gaming Corp. 88
Brunswick Corp. 92
Callaway Golf Co. 98
Carmike Cinemas, Inc. 103
Carnival Corp. 103
Churchill Downs, Inc. 117
Clear Channel Communications 124
ClubCorp Internat'l Inc. 125
The Coleman Company, Inc. 129
Delaware North Companies 153
The DIRECTV Group, Inc. 159
The Walt Disney Company 159
Electronic Arts Inc. 178
Feld Entertainment, Inc. 193
Fortune Brands, Inc. 202
Gaylord Entertainment Co. 210
GTECH Corp. 228
Harley-Davidson Motor Company 232
Harrah's Entertainment, Inc. 233
Hasbro Inc. 236
Home Box Office (HBO) 246
Huffy Corp. 251
Liberty Media Corp. 293
Mattel, Inc. 309
Metro-Goldwyn-Mayer Inc. 323
MGM MIRAGE 324
NBC Universal 342
News Corporation Ltd. 347
Nike, Inc. 349
Pinnacle Entertainment, Inc. 384
Playboy Enterprises, Inc. 386
Polaris Industries Inc. 388
Recreational Equipment, Inc. 406
SCP Pool Corp. 430
Six Flags, Inc. 440
Sony Corp. of America 444
The Sports Authority, Inc. 450
Time Warner Inc. 475
Toys "R" Us, Inc. 479
Tribune Co. 480
Turner Broadcasting System, Inc. 482
Universal Music Group 495
Viacom Inc./CBS Corp. 505
Vivendi Universal 507
Vivendi Universal Games 507
Winnebago Industries, Inc. 524

Steel Industry

AK Steel Corp. 14
Allegheny Technologies Incorporated 19
Carpenter Technology Corp. 103
Commercial Metals Co. 132
L. B. Foster Co. 202
Gerdau Ameristeel Corp. 219
Harsco Corp. 234
Internat'l Steel Group Inc. 262
Ispat Inland Inc. 265
Kennametal Inc. 277
Leggett & Platt, Inc. 289
Oregon Steel Mills Inc. 365
Precision Castparts Corp. 391
Quanex Corp. 400
Ryerson Tull 417
SKF USA, Inc. 440
The Timken Co. 476
United States Steel Corporation 491
Valmont Industries, Inc. 500
Wheeling-Pittsburgh Steel Corp. 521
Worthington Industries 525

Tax Services

Grant Thornton LLP 225
H & R Block, Inc. 230

Telephone/Telecommunications Industry

3Com Corp. 1
3M Company 1
ADC 5
Agere Systems Inc. 11
Allegheny Energy Inc. 18
Andrew Corp. 40
AT&T 52
Avaya Inc. 56
BellSouth Corp. 69
Broadcom Corp. 91
Cablevision Systems Corp. 96
CellStar Corp. 107
CenturyTel, Inc. 110
CIENA Corp. 118
Cincinnati Bell Inc. 119
Cingular Wireless 120
Citizens Communications Co. 123
Comverse Technology, Inc. 134
Conexant Systems, Inc. 135
Earthlink, Inc. 171
Enterasys Networks 182
Ericsson Inc. 185
Global Crossing Ltd. 220
Google Inc. 224
IAC/InterActiveCorp 254
Juniper Networks, Inc. 272
Leap Wireless International, Inc. 289
MCI, Inc. 314
Mindspeed Technologies, Inc. 328
Nortel Networks 352
PalmSource, Inc. 370
Pegasus Communications Corp. 373
Pepco Holdings, Inc. 376

Qwest Communications ... 402
SBC Communications Inc. ... 422
SBC Illinois ... 423
SBC Indiana ... 424
SBC Michigan ... 424
SBC Ohio ... 424
SBC SNET ... 425
SBC Wisconsin ... 425
Sparton Corp. ... 450
Sprint Nextel ... 450
Telephone and Data Systems, Inc. ... 467
Tellabs ... 468
USA Mobility, Inc. ... 497
VeriSign, Inc. ... 501
Verizon Communications Inc. ... 502
Verizon Delaware Inc. ... 503
Verizon Maryland Inc. ... 503
Verizon New Jersey, Inc. ... 503
Verizon Pennsylvania Inc. ... 503
Verizon Washington D.C. Inc. ... 504
Verizon West Virginia Inc. ... 504
Verizon Wireless ... 504
Volt Information Sciences, Inc. ... 508
Xcel Energy, Inc. ... 528
XO Communications, Inc. ... 529

Textile Industry

Albany Internat'l Corp. ... 16
Angelica Corp. ... 40
Armstrong Holdings, Inc. ... 48
Berkshire Hathaway ... 71
Dan River, Inc. ... 151
Guilford Mills, Inc. ... 229
Internat'l Textiles Group ... 262
Jo-Ann Stores, Inc. ... 269
Milliken & Co. ... 327
Mitsubishi International Corporation ... 330
OMNOVA Solutions Inc. ... 362
Ruddick Corp. ... 416
Springs Industries, Inc. ... 450
Unifi, Inc. ... 486
WestPoint Stevens Inc. ... 520

Tobacco Industry

Alliance One Internat'l Inc. ... 20
Altria Group, Inc. ... 25
Loews Corporation ... 297
Lorillard Tobacco Co. ... 299
Philip Morris U.S.A. ... 382
Reynolds American Inc. ... 410
Swedish Match North America Inc. ... 462
Universal Corp. ... 494
UST Inc. ... 498

Training and Simulation Systems

AAI Corp. ... 2

Transportation

FMC Technologies, Inc. ... 199
Landstar System, Inc. ... 288
Werner Enterprises, Inc. ... 518
Westinghouse Air Brake Technologies Corp. ... 519
Yellow Roadway Corporation ... 530

Travel Industry

American Express Co. ... 30
Amtrak ... 38
Carlson Companies ... 103
Frontier Airlines, Inc. ... 206
Greyhound Lines, Inc. ... 227
Michelin North America, Inc. ... 324
Sabre Holdings Corp. ... 417

Trucking/Busing

AMERCO ... 28
Arkansas Best Corporation ... 47
CNF Inc. ... 126
FedEx Corp. ... 192
FedEx Freight ... 193
Freightliner LLC ... 206
Greyhound Lines, Inc. ... 227
J. B. Hunt Transport Services, Inc. ... 252
Murphy Oil Corp. ... 335
Penske Truck Leasing Co. LP ... 375
Ryder System, Inc. ... 416
SIRVA, Inc. ... 439
TravelCenters of America, Inc. ... 480
United Parcel Service (UPS) ... 490

Unmanned Aerial Vehicles

AAI Corp. ... 2

Water Utility

Duquesne Light Holdings ... 170
Memphis Light, Gas and Water Division ... 319
Public Service Co. of New Mexico ... 398
TECO Energy, Inc./Tampa Electric Co. ... 466
United Water Resources ... 493
Veolia Water Indianapolis, LLC ... 501

2006 National Directory of Corporate Public Affairs

Geographic Index

All companies are listed here according to the location of their headquarters offices.

- The listings in this index are arranged as follows:
- alphabetically by state
- alphabetically by city within state
- alphabetically by company name within city within state

Alabama

Birmingham

Alabama Power Co. 15
Blue Cross and Blue Shield of Alabama 76
Bruno's Inc. 92
Compass Bancshares, Inc. 132
Drummond Co., Inc. 167
EBSCO Industries, Inc. 174
Energen Corp. 180
HealthSouth Corp. 238
Protective Life Corp. 396
Regions Financial Corp. 407
Saks, Inc. 419
Southern Nuclear Operating Co. 446
Torchmark Corp. 477
Vulcan Materials Co. 508

Huntsville

Intergraph Corp. 259

Montgomery

The Colonial Bancgroup, Inc. 129

Alaska

Anchorage

Alyeska Pipeline Service Co. 26

Juneau

Sealaska Corp. 431

Arizona

Chandler

Amkor Technology, Inc. 37

Phoenix

Apollo Group, Inc. 43
Avnet Inc. 57
Aztar Corp. 58
Best Western Internat'l 73
Blue Cross and Blue Shield of Arizona 76
CSK Auto, Inc. 146
Eagle-Picher Industries, Inc. 171
ON Semiconductor Corp. 362
PETsMART, Inc. 379
Phelps Dodge Corp. 381
Pinnacle West Capital Corp. 384
Viad Corp 506

Scottsdale

Allied Waste Industries, Inc. 22
The Dial Corporation 158
Giant Industries, Inc. 219
Rural Metro Corp. 416

Tempe

Insight Enterprises, Inc. 257

Tucson

UniSource Energy Corp. 488

Arkansas

Bentonville

Wal-Mart Stores 510

El Dorado

Murphy Oil Corp. 335

Fort Smith

Arkansas Best Corporation 47
Beverly Enterprises, Inc. 73

Little Rock

Acxiom Corporation 5
ALLTEL 23
Arkansas Blue Cross and Blue Shield 47
Dillard's Inc. 159
Entergy Arkansas, Inc. 182
Stephens Inc. 457

Lowell

J. B. Hunt Transport Services, Inc. 252

Springdale

Tyson Foods, Inc. 484

California

Aliso Viejo

Fluor Corp. 198

Beverly Hills

City Nat'l Corp. 124
Hilton Hotels Corp. 244
Platinum Equity, LLC 386

Brisbane

Hitachi America, Ltd. 244

Burbank
The Walt Disney Company 159

Calabasas
Countrywide Home Loans Inc. 142
The Ryland Group, Inc. 417

Calabasas Hills
Cheesecake Factory Inc. 113

Carlsbad
Callaway Golf Co. 98
Invitrogen Corp. 264
Jenny Craig, Inc. 268

Carson
Leiner Health Products, Inc. 290

Chula Vista
Goodrich Corp. - Aerostructures 223

City of Commerce
99 Cents Only Stores 2

Commerce
Unified Western Grocers, Inc. 486

Cupertino
Apple Computer, Inc. 43
Symantec Corp. 463

Cypress
Mitsubishi Electric & Electronics USA 329
Mitsubishi Motors North America, Inc. 330
PacifiCare Health Systems, Inc. 369

Dublin
Sybase, Inc. 463

El Segundo
CB Richard Ellis Services, Inc. 106
Computer Sciences Corp. 133
DaVita, Inc. 152
The DIRECTV Group, Inc. 159
Mattel, Inc. 309
UNOCAL Corp. 495

Emeryville
Chiron Corp. 115

Foothill Ranch
Kaiser Aluminum & Chemical Corp. 273

Foster City
Visa U.S.A. Inc. 506

Fountain Valley
Hyundai Motor America 253

Fremont
Lam Research Corp. 287

Fullerton
Beckman Coulter, Inc. 68

Gardena
Nissan North America, Inc. 350

Glendale
Nestle USA, Inc. 343

Hayward
Mervyn's 322

Hercules
Bio-Rad Laboratories, Inc. 74

Irvine
Allergan Inc. 19
Broadcom Corp. 91
Edwards Lifesciences Corp. 176
Freedom Communications Inc. 205
Gateway, Inc. 209
Mazda North American Operations 311
Standard Pacific Corp. 453
Sun Healthcare Group, Inc. 459

La Jolla
The Copley Press, Inc. 140

Lake Forest
Western Digital Corp. 519

Los Angeles
The Aerospace Corp. 8
AIG SunAmerica Inc. 13
Farmers Group, Inc. 190
KB HOME 275
Magnetek, Inc. 302
Metro-Goldwyn-Mayer Inc. 323
Northrop Grumman Corp. 353
Occidental Petroleum Corp. 359
Ralphs Grocery Co. 403
Reliance Steel & Aluminum Co. 408
Southern California Gas Co. 445
Vivendi Universal Games 507
Vons 508

Manhattan Beach
Skechers U.S.A., Inc. 440

Menlo Park
Robert Half International Inc. 412
SRI International 452

Milpitas
Adaptec, Inc. 5
LSI Logic Corp. 300
Maxtor Corp. 310
palmOne, Inc. 370
Quantum Corporation 400
Solectron Corp. 442

Modesto
Ernest and Julio Gallo Winery 208
Save Mart Supermarkets 422

Monterey
Century Aluminum Co. 110

Mountain View
Google Inc. 224
Intuit Inc. 263
SGI 435
VeriSign, Inc. 501

Newport Beach
Conexant Systems, Inc. 135
Downey Savings and Loan Ass'n, F.A. 166
The Irvine Company 264
Mindspeed Technologies, Inc. 328
Pacific Life Insurance Co. 368

Oakland
APL Americas 42
The Clorox Co. 125
Crowley Maritime Corp. 145
Dreyer's Grand Ice Cream Holdings, Inc. 166
Golden West Financial Corp. 222
Kaiser Permanente 273
Matson Navigation Company, Inc. 308

Palo Alto
Agilent Technologies, Inc. 11
CNF Inc. 126
Hewlett-Packard Co. 241
Varian Medical Systems, Inc. 501

Pasadena
Avery Dennison Corp. 56
Jacobs Engineering Group Inc. 266
Parsons Corp. 372
Tetra Tech, Inc. 470

Pleasanton
Ross Stores, Inc. 415
Safeway Inc. 418
Shaklee Corp. 435

Redwood City
BroadVision, Inc. ... 91
Electronic Arts Inc. ... 178

Redwood Shores
Oracle Corporation ... 364

Riverside
Bourns, Inc. ... 87
Fleetwood Enterprises ... 197

Rosemead
Edison Internat'l ... 175
Southern California Edison, an Edison Internat'l Co. ... 445

Sacramento
Blue Diamond Growers ... 82
GenCorp ... 210

San Diego
Anacomp, Inc. ... 39
Cubic Corp. ... 147
General Atomics ... 211
Iomega Corp. ... 264
Jack in the Box Inc. ... 266
L-3 Communications Titan Group ... 284
Leap Wireless International, Inc. ... 289
PETCO Animal Supplies, Inc. ... 379
Qualcomm Inc. ... 400
San Diego Gas and Electric Co. ... 420
Science Applications Internat'l Corp. ... 429
Sempra Energy ... 432

San Francisco
Bechtel Group, Inc. ... 67
Blue Shield of California ... 82
Del Monte Foods ... 153
Gap Inc. ... 208
Genentech, Inc. ... 211
Levi Strauss and Co. ... 291
McKesson Corp. ... 315
PG & E Corp. ... 380
Providian Financial Corp. ... 396
The Charles Schwab Corp. ... 428
Union Bank of California ... 487
URS Corp. ... 496
Wells Fargo & Co. ... 516
Williams-Sonoma, Inc. ... 523

San Jose
Adobe Systems Inc. ... 6
Altera Corp. ... 24
Atmel Corp. ... 53
BEA Systems, Inc. ... 67
Bell Microproducts, Inc. ... 69
Cadence Design Systems, Inc. ... 97
Calpine Corp. ... 98
Cisco Systems, Inc. ... 121
Cypress Semiconductor Corp. ... 149
eBay, Inc. ... 173
Integrated Device Technology, Inc. ... 258
JDS Uniphase Corp. ... 267
KLA-Tencor ... 281
Knight Ridder ... 281
Sanmina-SCI Corp. ... 420
WJ Communications ... 525
Xilinx, Inc. ... 529

San Mateo
Franklin Templeton Investments ... 204
Siebel Systems, Inc. ... 437

San Rafael
Autodesk Inc. ... 55

San Ramon
Chevron Corp. ... 114

Santa Ana
The First American Corp. ... 194
Ingram Micro, Inc. ... 257

Santa Barbara
Tenet Healthcare Corp. ... 468

Santa Clara
Applied Materials, Inc. ... 44
Intel Corp. ... 258
McAfee, Inc. ... 312
Nat'l Semiconductor Corp. ... 340
NVIDIA Corp. ... 358
Sun Microsystems, Inc. ... 460

Santa Cruz
Plantronics, Inc. ... 386

Santa Monica
Activision, Inc. ... 5
Fremont General Corp. ... 206

Scotts Valley
Seagate Technology ... 431

Sunnyvale
Advanced Micro Devices, Inc. ... 7
Juniper Networks, Inc. ... 272
Lockheed Martin Space Systems Company ... 297
Maxim Integrated Products ... 309
Network Appliance, Inc. ... 344
PalmSource, Inc. ... 370
Yahoo! Inc. ... 529

Thousand Oaks
Amgen Inc. ... 36

Torrance
American Honda Motor Co., Inc. ... 32

Universal City
NBC Universal ... 342

Valencia
U.S. Borax Inc. ... 485

Van Nuys
Sunkist Growers ... 460

Walnut Creek
Longs Drug Stores Corp. ... 298

Watsonville
Granite Construction Inc. ... 225

West Sacramento
Raley's ... 403

Westlake Village
Dole Food Company, Inc. ... 160

Woodland Hills
Health Net, Inc. ... 238

Colorado

Boulder
Wild Oats Markets, Inc. ... 522

Broomfield
Ball Corp. ... 59
Level 3 Communications, Inc. ... 291

Colorado Springs
Westmoreland Coal Co. ... 520

Denver
Frontier Airlines, Inc. ... 206
Gates Rubber Co. ... 209
Johns Manville Corp. ... 269
Newmont Mining Corp. ... 347
Qwest Communications ... 402
TransMontaigne, Inc. ... 479
UnitedGlobalCom, Inc. ... 494
Western Gas Resources, Inc. ... 519

Englewood
CH2M Hill Companies, Inc. ... 112
EchoStar Communications Corp. ... 174
Jeppesen ... 268
Jones Internat'l, Ltd. ... 271

Liberty Media Corp. 293
The Sports Authority, Inc. 450
TeleTech Holdings, Inc. 467

Golden
Coors Brewing Co. 140

Greenwood
Adelphia Communications Corp. 6

Greenwood Village
CIBER, Inc. 118
First Data 195

Louisville
StorageTek 458

Connecticut

Avon
Magellan Health Services, Inc 302

Bloomfield
Kaman Corp. 274

Bridgeport
People's Bank 375

Bristol
Barnes Group Inc. 62

Danbury
Ethan Allen Interiors Inc. 186
Praxair, Inc. 391

East Hartford
Pratt & Whitney 391

Fairfield
General Electric Co. 213
IMS Health, Inc. 256

Farmington
Carrier Corp. 104

Greenwich
Premcor Inc. 392
Unilever Home & Personal Care - North America 486
UST Inc. 498

Hartford
Aetna Inc. 9
The Hartford Financial Services Group Inc. 234
Hartford Steam Boiler Inspection and Insurance Co. 235
Northeast Utilities 352
The Phoenix Companies, Inc. 383
United Technologies Corp. 492

Milford
BIC Corp. 73

New Britain
The Stanley Works 454

New Haven
SBC SNET 425
The United Illuminating Company 489

Norwalk
ABB Inc. 3
Applera Corp. 43
Arch Chemicals, Inc. 46
EMCOR Group, Inc. 178

Orange
Hubbell Incorporated 250

Ridgefield
Boehringer Ingelheim Corp. 84

Stamford
Citizens Communications Co. 123
Crane Co. 144
Diageo North America 158
Gartner, Inc. 209
General Re Corp. 216
Hexcel Corp. 242
Internat'l Paper 261
MeadWestvaco Corp. 316
Pitney Bowes Inc. 385
Savin Corp. 422
The Thomson Corporation 473
Towers Perrin 478
Xerox Corp. 528

Stratford
Dictaphone Corp. 159

Trumbull
Oxford Health Plans Inc. 368

Waterbury
Webster Financial Corp. 515

Westport
Terex Corp. 469

Windsor
Advo Inc. 8

Windsor Locks
Hamilton Sundstrand 231

Delaware

Newark
Conectiv 134

Wilmington
AstraZeneca Pharmaceuticals 50
Blue Cross and Blue Shield of Delaware 77
DuPont 169
Hercules Incorporated 240
MBNA Corp. 311
Verizon Delaware Inc. 503
Wilmington Trust Co. 523

Dist. of Col.

Washington
Amtrak 38
Canadian Nat'l / Illinois Central 99
CarrAmerica Realty Corp. 104
Corporation for Public Broadcasting 141
Danaher Corp. 151
Fannie Mae 189
GEICO Corp. 210
Marriott Internat'l, Inc. 305
Nat'l Geographic Soc. 339
Nat'l Public Radio 340
Nortel Networks 352
Occidental Internat'l 359
Pepco Holdings, Inc. 376
Verizon Washington D.C. Inc. 504
Washington Gas 511
The Washington Post Co. 513

Florida

Bradenton
Gevity HR, Inc. 219

Clearwater
Tech Data Corp. 466

Clewiston
United States Sugar Corp. 492

Davie
Andrx Corp. 40

Daytona Beach
Brown & Brown, Inc. 92

Deerfield Beach
JM Family Enterprises, Inc. 269

Delray Beach
Office Depot, Inc. 360

Fort Lauderdale
AutoNation, Inc. 55
Citrix Systems, Inc. 123
Republic Services, Inc. 410
Spherion Corp. 450

Jacksonville
Blue Cross and Blue Shield of Florida 77
CSX Corp. 146
Fidelity Nat'l Financial, Inc. 193
Florida Rock Industries, Inc. 198
Landstar System, Inc. 288
PSS World Medical, Inc. 398
Rayonier Inc. 404
Winn-Dixie Stores 523

Juno Beach
FPL Group, Inc. 203

Lakeland
Publix Super Markets, Inc. 399

Melbourne
Harris Corp. 233

Miami
Burger King Corporation 93
Carnival Corp. 103
Lennar Corp. 290
Royal Caribbean Internat'l 415
Ryder System, Inc. 416
Southern Wine & Spirits of America 447
VITAS Healthcare Corporation 507

Naples
Health Management Associates, Inc. 237

Orlando
AirTran Airways 14
Darden Restaurants, Inc. 151
Hughes Supply, Inc. 251
Orlando Sentinel Communications 365
Tupperware Corp. 482

Palm Beach Gardens
The Wackenhut Corporation 509

Pensacola
Gulf Power Co. 229

Plantation
DHL Holdings (USA), Inc. 158

St. Petersburg
Catalina Marketing Corp. 105
HSN, Inc. 250
Jabil Circuit, Inc. 266
Raymond James Financial, Inc. 404

Tampa
Gerdau Ameristeel Corp. 219
Lykes Lines Limited 301
Masonite Internat'l Corp. 307
Outback Steakhouse, Inc. 366
Sykes Enterprises, Inc. 463
TECO Energy, Inc./Tampa Electric Co. 466
Walter Industries, Inc. 511

Vero Beach
The New Piper Aircraft Inc. 345

West Palm Beach
Jacuzzi Brands, Inc. 267

Georgia

Alpharetta
ChoicePoint Inc. 115
Colonial Pipeline Co. 130
Newell Rubbermaid Inc. 347

Atlanta
AFC Enterprises 9
AGL Resources, Inc. 12
Atlanta Journal Constitution 53
BellSouth Corp. 69
Blue Cross Blue Shield of Georgia 81
Cingular Wireless 120
The Coca-Cola Co. 127
Coca-Cola Enterprises Inc. 128
Cox Enterprises, Inc. 143
Delta Air Lines, Inc. 155
Earthlink, Inc. 171
Equifax Inc. 184
Genuine Parts Co. 216
Georgia Gulf Corp. 217
Georgia-Pacific Corp. 217
Georgia Power Co. 218
Gold Kist Inc. 221
John H. Harland Co. 232
The Home Depot, Inc. 246
ING Americas 256
InterContinental Hotels Group 259
Interface Inc. 259
Mirant Corp. 329
Porsche Cars North America, Inc. 389
Premiere Global Services, Inc. 392
PRG-Schultz Internat'l, Inc. 392
Rollins, Inc. 414
The RTM Restaurant Group 416
Russell Corp. 416
Sava Senior Care LLC 422
Southern Company 446
Sprectrum Brands 450
SunTrust Banks, Inc. 462
Turner Broadcasting System, Inc. 482
United Parcel Service (UPS) 490

Austell
Caraustar Industries, Inc. 100

Calhoun
Mohawk Industries, Inc. 330

Carrollton
Southwire Co. 449

Columbus
AFLAC Incorporated 10
Carmike Cinemas, Inc. 103
Synovus Financial Corp. 464

Dalton
Shaw Industries 435

Duluth
AGCO Corp. 11
Primerica Financial Services, Inc. 393

Lawrenceville
Scientific-Atlanta, Inc. 429

Norcross
CheckFree Corp. 113

Savannah
Gulfstream Aerospace Corp. 230

Suwanee
ARRIS Group, Inc. 48

Thomasville
Flowers Foods 198

Tucker
Oglethorpe Power Corp. 361

West Point
WestPoint Stevens Inc. 520

Hawaii

Honolulu
Alexander & Baldwin, Inc. 18
Aloha Airlines, Inc. 24

BancWest Corp. 60
Bank of Hawaii Corp. 61
Hawaiian Electric Industries, Inc. 236
Hawaiian Holdings, Inc. 236

Idaho

Boise
Albertson's, Inc. 17
Blue Cross of Idaho 81
Boise Cascade Corp. 85
IDACORP, Inc. 254
Intermountain Gas Co. 260
Micron Technology, Inc. 324
J. R. Simplot Co. 439
Washington Group Internat'l 512

Coeur d'Alene
Hecla Mining Co. 239

Lewiston
Regence BlueShield of Idaho 407

Illinois

Abbott Park
Abbott Laboratories 3

Bloomington
Country Insurance and Financial Services 142
State Farm Insurance Cos. 455

Chicago
Amsted Industries Inc. 38
Aon Corp. 41
Bally Total Fitness Holding Corp. 59
The Boeing Co. 84
Leo Burnett Worldwide 95
Chicago Mercantile Exchange Inc. 114
Chicago Sun-Times 115
CNA Financial Corp. 126
R R Donnelley 163
Encyclopaedia Britannica, Inc. 180
Equity Office Properties Trust 185
Equity Residential 185
Exelon Corp. 187
GATX Corp. 209
General Growth Properties Inc. 214
Grant Thornton LLP 225
Harris Bank 233
Hartmarx 235
Health Care Service Corp. 237
Global Hyatt Corp. 253
Information Resources, Inc. 256
Jones Lang LaSalle Inc. 272
LaSalle Bank N.A. 288
The Marmon Group, Inc. 305
Northern Trust Co. 353
Peoples Energy Corp. 376
Playboy Enterprises, Inc. 386
Rand McNally 403
Ryerson Tull 417
Sara Lee Corp. 421
SBC Illinois 423
Smurfit-Stone Container 442
Telephone and Data Systems, Inc. 467
Tribune Co. 480
True Value Company 481
United Airlines 489
USG Corp. 498
Wm. Wrigley Jr. Co. 526

Crystal Lake
AptarGroup, Inc. 45

Decatur
Archer Daniels Midland Co. (ADM) 47

Deerfield
Baxter Internat'l Inc. 65
Walgreen Co. 511

Des Plaines
United Stationers Inc. 492

Downers Grove
Aftermarket Technology Corp. 10
First Health 195
The ServiceMaster Co. 434

Elmhurst
Duchossois Industries, Inc. 168

Glenview
Anixter Internat'l, Inc. 41
Illinois Tool Works Inc. 255

Hoffman Estates
Sears Holding Corp. 431

Itasca
Enesco Group, Inc. 181
Fellowes Manufacturing Co. 193
First Midwest Bancorp, Inc. 196
Arthur J. Gallagher & Co. 207

Lake Forest
Brunswick Corp. 92
Case New Holland Inc. 104
W. W. Grainger, Inc. 225
Pactiv Corp. 370
Salton, Inc. 420
Tenneco Automotive 469

Lawrence
Golden Rule Insurance Co. 221

Lincolnshire
Fortune Brands, Inc. 202
Hewitt Associates Inc. 241
Zenith Electronics Corp. 531

Lisle
Molex Incorporated 331

Lombard
U.S. Can Corp. 491

Long Grove
C F Industries, Inc. 111

Melrose Park
Alberto-Culver Co. 16

Moline
Deere & Company 152

Mundelein
Medline Industries, Inc. 318

Naperville
Nalco Co. 337
Nicor, Inc. 348
Tellabs 468

Northbrook
Allstate Insurance Co. 23
General Binding Corp. 212

Northfield
Kraft Foods, Inc. 283

Oak Brook
Ace Hardware Corp. 5
Dominick's Finer Foods, Inc. 161
Federal Signal Corp. 191
McDonald's Corp. 313

Oakbrook Terrace
DeVry Inc. 157

Orland Park
Andrew Corp. 40

Palatine
Square D/Schneider Electric 452

Peoria
Caterpillar Inc. 105

Prospect Heights
HSBC North America Holdings Inc. 249

Rolling Meadows
PepsiAmericas, Inc. 377

Rosemont
Velsicol Chemical Corp. 501

Schaumburg
Motorola, Inc. 334

Springfield
Horace Mann Educators Corp. 248

Vernon Hills
CDW Corp. 106
Zebra Technologies Corp. 531

Warrenfield
Navistar Internat'l Corp. 342

Westchester
Corn Products Internat'l, Inc. 141

Westmont
SIRVA, Inc. 439

Wood Dale
AAR Corp. 3

Indiana

Anderson
Delco Remy Internat'l Inc. 153

Batesville
Hillenbrand Industries, Inc. 244

Carmel
Conseco, Inc. 135

Columbus
Cummins, Inc. 147

East Chicago
Ispat Inland Inc. 265

Elkhart
Coachmen Industries, Inc. 127
CTS Corp. 147

Evansville
Integra Bank N.A. 257
Vectren Corp. 501

Indianapolis
American United Life Insurance Co. 34
ATA Holdings Corp. 53
Dow AgroSciences LLC 163
Emmis Communications Corp. 179
Guidant Corp. 229
IPL (an AES Company) 264
Eli Lilly and Company 293
Marsh Supermarkets, Inc. 306
Reilly Industries, Inc. 408
SBC Indiana 424
Simon Property Group 439
Veolia Water Indianapolis, LLC 501
Wellpoint, Inc. 516

Jasper
Kimball International, Inc. 280

Merrillville
NiSource Inc. 349

Warsaw
Biomet Inc. 74
Zimmer Holdings, Inc. 532

Iowa

Cedar Rapids
McLeod USA Inc. 315
Rockwell Collins, Inc 413

Davenport
Lee Enterprises 289

Des Moines
AmerUs Group 36
Meredith Corp. 321
MidAmerican Energy Holdings Co. 326
Pioneer Hi-Bred Internat'l, Inc. 385
The Principal Financial Group 393
Wellmark, Inc. 516

Forest City
Winnebago Industries, Inc. 524

Muscatine
Bandag, Inc. 60
HNI Corp. 245

Newton
Maytag Corp. 310

Pella
Pella Corp. 374

Sioux City
Terra Industries Inc. 469

West Des Moines
Hy-Vee, Inc. 253

Kansas

Overland Park
Applebee's Internat'l, Inc. 43
Black & Veatch 75
Yellow Roadway Corporation 530

Shawnee Mission
Seaboard Corporation 430

Topeka
Blue Cross and Blue Shield of Kansas, Inc. 78
Payless ShoeSource 372
Security Benefit Life Insurance Co. 432
Westar Energy, Inc. 518

Wichita
Bombardier 86
Cessna Aircraft Co. 111
The Coleman Company, Inc. 129
Koch Industries, Inc. 282
Raytheon Aircraft Company 404

Kentucky

Covington
Ashland Inc. 49
Omnicare, Inc. 362

Highland Heights
General Cable Corp. 212

Lexington
Kentucky Utilities Company 278
Lexmark Internat'l, Inc. 292

Louisville
Brown-Forman Corp. 92
Churchill Downs, Inc. 117
The Courier-Journal 143
Humana Inc. 251
Kindred Healthcare, Inc. 281
LG&E Energy LLC 292
Papa John's Internat'l Inc. 371
Thomas Industries Inc. 472
YUM! Brands, Inc. 530

Louisiana

Baton Rouge
Albemarle Corp. 16
Blue Cross and Blue Shield of Louisiana 78
The Shaw Group Inc. 435
Stone & Webster, Inc. 458

Covington
SCP Pool Corp. 430

Metairie
Stewart Enterprises, Inc. 458

Monroe
CenturyTel, Inc. 110

New Orleans
Entergy Corp. 182
Entergy New Orleans 183
Entergy Services, Inc. 183
Freeport-McMoRan Copper and Gold Inc. 205
Pan American Life Insurance Co. 371
Tidewater Inc. 474

Pineville
Cleco Corp. 124

Maine

Bath
Bath Iron Works Corp. 64

Freeport
L. L. Bean, Inc. 285

Portland
UnumProvident Corp. 496

Scarborough
Hannaford Bros. Co. 231

South Portland
Fairchild Semiconductor Internat'l, Inc. 189

Maryland

Baltimore
AEGON USA, Inc. 8
Constellation Energy 137
Laureate Education, Inc. 289
Mercantile Bankshares Corporation 320
T. Rowe Price Associates 392
Verizon Maryland Inc. 503

Bethesda
AREVA Enterprises, Inc. 47
Coventry Health Care 143
Host Marriott Corp. 249
Lockheed Martin Corp. 296
USEC Inc. 497

Columbia
W. R. Grace & Co. 224
U.S. Foodservice 485

Gaithersburg
MedImmune, Inc. 317

Hunt Valley
AAI Corp. 2

Landover
Giant Food LLC 219

Linthicum
CIENA Corp. 118

Owings Mills
CareFirst BlueCross and BlueShield 101

Rockville
BAE Systems North America 59
Mid Atlantic Medical Services Inc. 325

Salisbury
Perdue Farms 378

Sparks
McCormick & Company, Inc. 312

Towson
The Black & Decker Corp. 75

Massachusetts

Andover
Enterasys Networks 182

Billerica
Millipore Corp. 327

Boston
Blue Cross and Blue Shield of Massachusetts 78
Cabot Corp. 97
FMR Corp. 200
The Gillette Company 219
Globe Newspaper Co. 221
Houghton Mifflin Co. 249
Internat'l Data Group 260
John Hancock Financial Services 269
Keane, Inc. 275
Liberty Mutual Insurance Co. 293
New Balance Athletic Shoe, Inc. 344
OneBeacon Insurance 363
State Street Corp. 456
The Stop & Shop Supermarket Co. 458
Teradyne, Inc. 469

Cambridge
Biogen Idec Inc. 74
Genzyme Corp. 217
Millennium Pharmaceuticals, Inc. 326

Canton
Cumberland Farms, Inc. 147
Dunkin' Brands 169
Reebok Internat'l Ltd. 406

Chelsea
H. P. Hood Inc. 248

Concord
Welch's 515

Foxboro
Invensys Systems, Inc. 264

Framingham
Bose Corp. 87
Staples, Inc. 454
The TJX Companies, Inc. 476

Hopkinton
EMC Corp. 178

Lakeville-Middleboro
Ocean Spray Cranberries, Inc. 360

Lexington
The Stride Rite Corp. 459

Marlborough
3Com Corp. 1

Milford
Waters Corp. 514

Natick
BJ's Wholesale Club, Inc. 75
Boston Scientific Corp. 87

Needham
PTC 398

Norwood
Analog Devices, Inc. 39

Springfield
Big Y Foods Inc. 73
MassMutual Financial Group 307

Tewksbury
Avid Technology, Inc. 56
Demoulas Market Basket 156

Waltham
Algonquin Gas Transmission, LLC/Duke Energy 18
Novell, Inc. 357
Polaroid Corp. 388
Raytheon Co. 404
Thermo Electron Corp. 472

Wellesley Hills
PerkinElmer, Inc. 378
Sun Life Financial 460

West Bridgewater
Shaw's Supermarkets, Inc. 436

Westborough
Nat'l Grid USA 339

Westwood
NSTAR 357

Wilbraham
Friendly Ice Cream Corp. 206

Worcester
Allmerica Property & Casualty Companies, Inc. 22

Michigan

Ada
Alticor Inc. 24

Allegan
Perrigo Co. 379

Ann Arbor
Borders Group, Inc. 86
Domino's Pizza, LLC 162
Flint Ink Corp. 197
TCF Bank 465

Auburn Hills
BorgWarner Inc. 87
Champion Enterprises, Inc. 112
DaimlerChrysler Corp. 149
Guardian Industries Corp. 228
Volkswagen of America, Inc. 508

Battle Creek
Kellogg Co. 276

Benton Harbor
Whirlpool Corp. 521

Bloomfield Hills
Pulte Homes, Inc. 400
United Auto Group, Inc. 489

Dearborn
Ford Motor Co. 201

Detroit
American Axle and Manufacturing, Inc. 29
Blue Cross Blue Shield of Michigan 81
Comerica Incorporated 131
Compuware Corp. 134
DTE Energy Co. 167
General Motors Acceptance Corp. (GMAC) 214
General Motors Corp. 214
Little Caesar Enterprises 295
SBC Michigan 424

Dundee
Holcim (US) Inc. 246

Farmington Hills
Covansys 143

Grand Rapids
Foremost Corp. of America 202
Meijer, Inc. 318
Spartan Stores Inc. 449
Steelcase Inc. 456
Universal Forest Products, Inc. 495

Holland
Haworth Inc. 236

Jackson
CMS Energy Corp. 126
Sparton Corp. 450

Kalamazoo
Stryker Corp. 459

Lansing
Auto-Owners Insurance Group 54
Jackson Nat'l Life Insurance Co. 266

Livonia
TRW Automotive 481
Valassis Communications, Inc. 499

Midland
The Dow Chemical Company 164
Dow Corning Corp. 165

Monroe
La-Z-Boy Incorporated 285

Northville
Hayes Lemmerz Internat'l, Inc. 237

Novi
Tower Automotive, Inc. 478

Plymouth
Metaldyne Corp. 322

Port Huron
SEMCO ENERGY, Inc. 432

Rochester Hills
Dura Automotive Systems, Inc. 170

Rockford
Wolverine World Wide, Inc. 525

Southfield
Federal-Mogul Corp. 191
Lear Corporation 289
R.L. Polk & Co. 388

Taylor
Masco Corp. 307

Troy
ArvinMeritor 48
Collins & Aikman Corp. 129
Delphi Corp. 155
Handleman Company 231
Intermet Corp. 259
Kelly Services, Inc. 276
Standard Federal Bank 453
Thyssenkrupp Budd Company 474

Van Buren Township
Visteon Corp. 507

Zeeland
Herman Miller Inc. 240

Minnesota

Austin
Hormel Foods Corp. 248

Bayport
Andersen Corp. 40

Bloomington
The Toro Co. 477

Duluth
ALLETE....20

Eagan
Blue Cross and Blue Shield of Minnesota....78
Northwest Airlines, Inc....354
Thomson West....473

Eden Prairie
C.H. Robinson Worldwide, Inc....412

Edina
Alliant Techsystems....21
Nash Finch Company....337

Elk River
Great River Energy....226

Fergus Falls
Otter Tail Power Co....366

Golden Valley
Pentair, Inc....375

Marshall
The Schwan Food Co....428

Medina
Polaris Industries Inc....388

Minneapolis
ADC....5
Allina Hospitals and Clinics....22
Ameriprise Financial Services Inc....35
Apogee Enterprises, Inc....43
Bemis Company, Inc....71
Cargill, Incorporated....102
Carlson Companies....103
Ceridian Corp....111
Donaldson Company, Inc....163
General Mills....214
Graco Inc....225
Jostens, Inc....272
Kraus-Anderson Cos. Inc....284
MAIR Holdings, Inc....303
Medtronic, Inc....318
M. A. Mortenson Company....333
RBC Dain Rauscher Corp....405
Regis Corporation....408
Star Tribune....454
Supervalu Inc....462
Target Corp....465
Thrivent Financial for Lutherans....473
U.S. Bancorp Piper Jaffray Inc....484
UnitedHealth Group....494
U.S. Bancorp....497
Valspar Corp....500
Xcel Energy, Inc....528

Minnetonka
Mosaic Co....334

Moorhead
American Crystal Sugar Co....29

Oakdale
Imation Corp....255

Richfield
Best Buy Co., Inc....72

St. Paul
3M Company....1
CHS Inc....116
Deluxe Corp....156
Ecolab Inc....174
H. B. Fuller Co....207
Hubbard Broadcasting, Inc....250
Land O'Lakes, Inc....287
Minnesota Life Insurance Co....328
St. Jude Medical, Inc....452
St. Paul Travelers Cos., Inc....452

Wayzata
TCF Financial Corp....465

Winona
Fastenal Co....191

Mississippi

Gulfport
Mississippi Power Co....329

Jackson
Blue Cross and Blue Shield of Mississippi....79
Entergy Mississippi....183
Trustmark Nat'l Bank....481

Missouri

Carthage
Leggett & Platt, Inc....289

Chesterfield
Angelica Corp....40
Kellwood Co....276

Clayton
Olin Corp....361

Fenton
Maritz Inc....304
UniGroup, Inc....486

Joplin
Empire District Electric Co....179

Kansas City
AMC Entertainment Inc....27
American Century Cos., Inc....29
Aquila, Inc....45
Blue Cross and Blue Shield of Kansas City....77
Butler Manufacturing Co....95
Commerce Bancshares Inc....131
Dairy Farmers of America, Inc....150
DST Systems, Inc....167
Great Plains Energy, Inc....226
H & R Block, Inc....230
Hallmark Cards, Inc....231
Interstate Bakeries Corp....262
Kansas City Life Insurance Co....274
Kansas City Southern....274
UMB Financial Corp....486

Maryland Heights
Express Scripts, Inc....187

St. Louis
Ameren Corp....28
Anheuser-Busch Cos., Inc....41
Arch Coal, Inc....46
Belden CDT Inc....69
Brown Shoe Co., Inc....92
Charter Communications, Inc....112
A. G. Edwards, Inc....176
Emerson....179
Energizer Holdings Inc....181
Enterprise Rent-A-Car Co....184
Furniture Brands Internat'l, Inc....207
GenAmerica Financial Corp....210
Graybar Electric Co., Inc....225
Hardee's Food Systems, Inc....232
The Laclede Group....286
Monsanto Co....331
Nestle Purina PetCare Co....343
Peabody Energy....373
Ralcorp Holdings, Inc....403
RehabCare Group, Inc....408
Schnuck Markets, Inc....427
Sigma-Aldrich Corp....438
Solutia Inc....443

Montana

Helena
Blue Cross and Blue Shield of Montana....79

Nebraska

Omaha
AG Processing Inc ... 10
Ameritrade Holding Corp. ... 36
Berkshire Hathaway ... 71
Blue Cross and Blue Shield of Nebraska ... 79
Commercial Federal Corp. ... 132
ConAgra Foods, Inc. ... 134
Peter Kiewit Sons', Inc. ... 279
Mutual of Omaha Insurance Co. ... 336
Omaha World-Herald Co. ... 361
The Scoular Co. ... 430
Union Pacific Corp. ... 487
Valmont Industries, Inc. ... 500
Werner Enterprises, Inc. ... 518

Nevada

Las Vegas
Alliance Gaming Corp. ... 20
Ameristar Casinos, Inc. ... 35
Boyd Gaming Corp. ... 88
Harrah's Entertainment, Inc. ... 233
MGM MIRAGE ... 324
Nevada Power Co. ... 344
Pinnacle Entertainment, Inc. ... 384
Sierra Health Services, Inc. ... 438
Southwest Gas Corp. ... 448

Reno
AMERCO ... 28
Internat'l Game Technology ... 261
Sierra Pacific Resources ... 438

New Hampshire

Hampton
Fisher Scientific Internat'l Inc. ... 197

Merrimack
PC Connection, Inc. ... 373

Stratham
The Timberland Co. ... 475

New Jersey

Basking Ridge
Avaya Inc. ... 56

Bedminster
AT&T ... 52

Bridgewater
ICI American Holdings, Inc. ... 254
Nat'l Starch and Chemical Co. ... 341
Sanofi-Aventis Inc. ... 421

Burlington
Burlington Coat Factory Warehouse Corp. ... 94

Camden
Campbell Soup Co. ... 99

Carteret
Pathmark Stores Inc. ... 372

Cherry Hill
Subaru of America, Inc. ... 459

Clinton
Foster Wheeler Ltd. ... 203

Cranbury
Rhodia, Inc. ... 411

Elmwood Park
WebMD Corp. ... 515

Fairfield
Covanta Energy Corp. ... 143

Florham Park
BASF Corporation ... 63
Global Crossing Ltd. ... 220

Folsom
South Jersey Gas Co. ... 444

Fort Lee
Alpharma Inc. ... 24

Franklin Lakes
Becton, Dickinson and Co. ... 68
Medco Health Solutions, Inc. ... 316

Harrington Park
United Water Resources ... 493

Hoboken
John Wiley & Sons, Inc. ... 522

Iselin
Engelhard Corp. ... 181

Kenilworth
Schering-Plough Corporation ... 426

Madison
Wyeth ... 526

Mahwah
Sharp Electronics Corp. ... 435

Montvale
The Great Atlantic and Pacific Tea Co. ... 226
KPMG LLP ... 283
Mercedes-Benz USA, LLC ... 320

Montville
Berlex, Inc. ... 72

Morristown
Honeywell Internat'l, Inc. ... 247

Murray Hill
C. R. Bard, Inc. ... 96
Lucent Technologies ... 300

New Brunswick
Johnson & Johnson ... 270

Newark
Horizon Blue Cross Blue Shield of New Jersey ... 248
Prudential Financial ... 397
PSE&G ... 397
Verizon New Jersey, Inc. ... 503

Nutley
Hoffmann-La Roche Inc. (Roche) ... 245

Park Ridge
Hertz Corp. ... 241

Parsippany
DRS Technologies, Inc. ... 166
Gerber Products Co. ... 218

Piscataway
American Standard Companies Inc. ... 34
Telcordia Technologies, Inc. ... 467

Princeton
Church & Dwight Co., Inc. ... 117
Covance, Inc. ... 143
Tyco Internat'l (U.S.), Inc. ... 483

Red Bank
Hovnanian Enterprises, Inc. ... 249

Roseland
Automatic Data Processing, Inc. ... 55

Saddle Brook
Sealed Air Corp. ... 431

Secaucus
The Children's Place Retail Stores, Inc. ... 115
Goya Foods, Inc. ... 224
Matsushita Electric Corp. of America ... 309

Short Hills
The Dun & Bradstreet Corp. ... 169

Somerset
MedPointe Inc. ... 318

Teterboro
Quest Diagnostics Inc. ... 401

Thorofare
Checkpoint Systems, Inc. ... 113

Union
Bed Bath & Beyond Inc. ... 68

Wall
New Jersey Resources Corp. ... 345

Warren
The Chubb Corp. ... 116

Wayne
Toys "R" Us, Inc. ... 479

West Caldwell
Ricoh Corp. ... 411

West Paterson
Cytec Industries Inc. ... 149

Whitehouse Station
Merck & Co., Inc. ... 320

Woodcliff Lake
Barr Pharmaceuticals, Inc. ... 62
BMW (U.S.) Holding Corp. ... 83

New Mexico

Albuquerque
Public Service Co. of New Mexico ... 398

New York

Albany
Albany Internat'l Corp. ... 16
Energy East Corp. ... 181

Amherst
Mark IV Industries, Inc. ... 304

Armonk
Internat'l Business Machines Corp. (IBM) ... 260
MBIA, Inc. ... 311
Swiss Re America Corp. ... 462

Bethpage
Cablevision Systems Corp. ... 96
King Kullen Grocery Co. ... 281

Brooklyn
KeySpan Corp. ... 279

Buffalo
Delaware North Companies ... 153
HealthNow New York Inc. ... 238
M&T Bank Corporation ... 301

Corning
Corning Incorporated ... 141

East Aurora
Moog Inc. ... 332

Fairport
Constellation Brands, Inc. ... 137

Flushing
FlightSafety Internat'l ... 197

Holtsville
Symbol Technologies, Inc. ... 463

Islandia
Computer Associates Internat'l, Inc. ... 133

Jackson Heights
British Airways ... 91

Jericho
Griffon Corp. ... 228

Lake Success
Canon U.S.A., Inc. ... 99

Melville
Arrow Electronics, Inc. ... 48
Henry Schein, Inc. ... 240
NEC USA, Inc. ... 343
Nu Horizons Electronics Corp. ... 357

New York
ABC, Inc. ... 4
Accenture ... 4
Altria Group, Inc. ... 25
Ambac Financial Group, Inc. ... 27
Amerada Hess Corp. ... 27
American Express Co. ... 30
American Internat'l Group, Inc. ... 32
American Stock Exchange ... 34
Asbury Automotive Group ... 48
Associated Press ... 50
Assurant ... 50
Avon Products, Inc. ... 57
AXA Financial, Inc. ... 58
The Bank of New York Co., Inc. ... 61
Barclays Capital ... 62
Barnes & Noble, Inc. ... 62
BBDO New York ... 66
Bear, Stearns and Co. Inc. ... 67
The BISYS Group, Inc. ... 75
Bloomberg L.P. ... 76
Bloomingdale's ... 76
BP ... 88
Bristol-Myers Squibb Co. ... 90
Cendant Corp. ... 108
The CIT Group, Inc. ... 121
Citigroup, Inc. ... 122
Colgate-Palmolive Co. ... 129
Consolidated Edison Co. of New York, Inc. ... 136
ContiGroup Companies, Inc. ... 138
Credit Suisse First Boston ... 144
Deloitte & Touche LLP ... 154
The Depository Trust & Clearing Corp. ... 157
Deutsche Banc Alex.Brown ... 157
DoubleClick, Inc. ... 163
Dow Jones and Co. ... 165
The Dreyfus Corp. ... 166
Empire Blue Cross and Blue Shield ... 179
Ernst & Young LLP ... 186
Estee Lauder Companies, Inc. ... 186
E*TRADE Financial Corp. ... 186
Footlocker Inc. ... 201
Forbes, Inc. ... 201
Forest Laboratories, Inc. ... 202
Goldman, Sachs and Co. ... 222
Grey Global Group Inc. ... 227
Guardian Life Insurance Co. of America ... 228
The Hearst Corp. ... 238
Home Box Office (HBO) ... 246
HSBC USA, Inc. ... 250
IAC/InterActiveCorp ... 254
Instinet Group Inc. ... 257
Internat'l Flavors and Fragrances ... 261
The Interpublic Group of Companies ... 262
J. Crew Group, Inc. ... 266
L-3 Communications Corp. ... 284
Lehman Brothers ... 290
Leucadia Nat'l Corp. ... 291
Liz Claiborne Inc. ... 296
Loews Corporation ... 297
Loral Space & Communications ... 298

Marsh & McLennan Companies, Inc. 306
Marsh Inc. 306
The McGraw-Hill Companies, Inc. 313
Merrill Lynch & Co., Inc. 322
MetLife, Inc. 322
Mitsubishi International Corporation 330
Mitsui and Co. (U.S.A.), Inc. 330
Monster Worldwide, Inc. 331
Moody's Corp. 332
J. P. Morgan Chase & Co. 332
Morgan Stanley 333
Mutual of America Life Insurance Co. 335
New York Life Insurance Co. 345
New York Stock Exchange, Inc. 346
New York Times Co. 346
News Corporation Ltd. 347
Newsweek, Inc. 348
Nomura Securities Internat'l, Inc. 350
Novartis Corporation 355
Omnicom Group Inc. 362
Overseas Shipholding Group, Inc. 366
Parsons Brinckerhoff 372
Pfizer Inc. 379
Philips Electronics North America 382
Phillips-Van Heusen Corp. 382
Polo Ralph Lauren 388
PriceWaterhouseCoopers LLP 392
Primedia Inc. 393
Revlon, Inc. 410
Royster-Clark, Inc. 415
Schlumberger Limited 427
Scholastic, Inc. 427
Sequa Corp. 434
Sesame Workshop 434
Siemens Corp. 437
Sony Corp. of America 444
Sotheby's Holdings, Inc. 444
Take-Two Interactive Software, Inc. 464
J. Walter Thompson Co. 473
TIAA/CREF 474
Tiffany & Co. 474
Time Warner Inc. 475
Toyota Motor North America, Inc. 478
Triarc Companies, Inc. 480
Trump Hotels and Casino Resorts, Inc. 481
The Turner Corp. 482
U.S. Trust Corp. 485
UBS Financial Services Inc. 485
Unilever United States, Inc. 487
Universal Music Group 495
Verizon Communications Inc. 502
Verizon Wireless 504
Viacom Inc./CBS Corp. 505
Vivendi Universal 507
Volt Information Sciences, Inc. 508
Volvo Group North America, Inc. 508

Oneida
Oneida Ltd. 363

Pearl River
Orange and Rockland Utilities, Inc. 364

Pleasantville
Reader's Digest Ass'n, Inc. 405

Port Washington
Pall Corp. 370
Systemax Inc. 464

Poughkeepsie
CH Energy Group, Inc. 111

Purchase
MasterCard Internat'l 308
PepsiCo, Inc. 377

Rochester
Bausch & Lomb 64
Birds Eye Foods 75
Eastman Kodak Company 172
Exellus Blue Cross Blue Shield 187
The Lifetime Healthcare Companies 293

Rye
Jarden Corp. 267

Rye Brook
Mott's Inc. 335

Schenectady
Golub Corp. 222

Somers
The Pepsi Bottling Group 377

Syracuse
Dairylea Cooperative Inc. 150
The Penn Traffic Co. 374

Tarrytown
Ciba Specialty Chemicals 117

Westbury
New York Community Bancorp, Inc. 345

White Plains
Bunge Ltd. 93
Heineken USA Inc. 239
ITT Industries 265
Starwood Hotels and Resorts Worldwide, Inc. 455

Williamsville
Nat'l Fuel Gas Co. 338
Tops Markets LLC 477

Woodbury
Comverse Technology, Inc. 134
Weight Watchers Internat'l 515

North Carolina

Asheville
Ingles Markets, Inc. 257

Burlington
Laboratory Corp. of America Holdings 286

Cary
LORD Corporation 299
SAS Institute, Inc. 422

Charlotte
Bank of America Corp. 60
Belk, Inc. 69
Carlisle Companies Inc. 103
Coca-Cola Bottling Co. Consolidated 127
Duke Energy Corp. 168
Family Dollar Stores, Inc. 189
Goodrich Corporation 223
Lance, Inc. 287
National Gypsum Co. 339
Nucor Corp. 358
Piedmont Natural Gas Co. 383
Royal & SunAlliance USA Inc. 415
Ruddick Corp. 416
Sonic Automotive, Inc. 443
SPX Corp. 451
Wachovia Corp. 509

Durham
Blue Cross and Blue Shield of North Carolina 79

Greensboro
Guilford Mills, Inc. 229
Internat'l Textiles Group 262
Jefferson-Pilot Corp. 267
Lorillard Tobacco Co. 299
RF Micro Devices, Inc. 411
Unifi, Inc. 486
V. F. Corporation 505

Hickory
CommScope 132

Moorsville
Lowe's Companies, Inc. 299

Raleigh
First Citizens BancShares....194
Martin Marietta Materials, Inc....306
Progress Energy....395

Research Triangle Park
Bayer CropScience....66
GlaxoSmithKline Research and Development....220
Quintiles Transnat'l Corp....401
Reichhold, Inc....408

Salisbury
Food Lion LLC....200

Sanford
The Pantry, Inc....371

Wilmington
Pharmaceutical Product Development, Inc....381

Winston-Salem
BB&T Corp....66
Reynolds American Inc....410

North Dakota

Bismarck
Basin Electric Power Cooperative....63
MDU Resources Group, Inc....315

Fargo
Blue Cross and Blue Shield of North Dakota....80

Ohio

Akron
FirstEnergy Corp....196
FirstMerit Corporation....197
The Goodyear Tire & Rubber Company....223
Myers Industries, Inc....336

Avon Lake
PolyOne Corp....388

Barberton
The Babcock & Wilcox Company....58

Canton
The Timken Co....476

Cincinnati
American Financial Group Inc....31
The Chemed Corporation....113
Chiquita Brands Internat'l, Inc....115
Cincinnati Bell Inc....119
Cincinnati Financial Corp....119
Cinergy Corp....119
Convergys Corp....138
Federated Department Stores, Inc....191
Fifth Third Bancorp....194
The Kroger Co....284
Milacron Inc....326
The Procter & Gamble Company....394
E. W. Scripps Co....430
Western and Southern Life Insurance Co....518

Cleveland
Agilysys, Inc....11
American Greetings Corp....31
Applied Industrial Technologies....44
The Austin Co....54
Brush Engineered Materials Inc....93
Ceres Group, Inc....110
Cleveland-Cliffs Inc....125
Eaton Corp....173
Electrolux North America, Inc....178
Ferro Corp....193
Forest City Enterprises, Inc....202
KeyCorp....278
Lincoln Electric Holdings, Inc....295
Medical Mutual of Ohio....317
NACCO Industries....337
Nat'l City Corp....337
OM Group, Inc....361
Parker Hannifin Corp....371
SBC Ohio....424
Sherwin-Williams Co....436

Columbus
American Electric Power Co. Inc....30
Battelle....64
Big Lots Inc....73
Bob Evans Farms, Inc....84
Hexion Specialty Chemicals, Inc....243
Huntington Bancshares Inc....252
The Limited Brands....294
Nationwide....341
Retail Ventures, Inc....410
Too, Inc....477
Worthington Industries....525

Dayton
Amcast Industrial Corporation....27
DPL Inc....166
NCR Corporation....342
Standard Register Co....454

Delaware
Greif, Inc....227

Dublin
Cardinal Health Inc....100
Wendy's Internat'l, Inc....517

Elyria
Invacare Corp....263
Ross Environmental Services, Inc....414

Fairfield
The Ohio Casualty Group....361

Fairlawn
OMNOVA Solutions Inc....362

Findlay
Cooper Tire & Rubber Company....139

Hudson
Jo-Ann Stores, Inc....269

Kettering
Reynolds and Reynolds Co....411

Marysville
The Scotts Company....430

Maumee
The Andersons, Inc....40

Mayfield Village
The Progressive Corporation....396

Medina
RPM Internat'l Inc....416

Mentor
STERIS Corp....457

Miamisburg
Huffy Corp....251

Middletown
AK Steel Corp....14

New Albany
Abercrombie & Fitch Co....4

New Bremen
Crown Equipment Corp....145

Newark
The Longaberger Co....297

North Canton
Diebold, Inc....159

Orrville
The J. M. Smucker Company....442

Richfield
Internat'l Steel Group Inc. 262

Toledo
Dana Corp. 151
Manor Care, Inc. 303
Owens Corning 367
Owens-Illinois, Inc. 367
Pilkington North America 384

Westlake
Nordson Corp. 350
TravelCenters of America, Inc. 480

Wickliffe
The Lubrizol Corp. 300

Wilmington
ABX Air, Inc. 4

Oklahoma

Oklahoma City
Devon Energy Corp. 157
Kerr-McGee Corp. 278
OGE Energy Corp. 360
Six Flags, Inc. 440

Tulsa
BlueCross BlueShield of Oklahoma 83
BOK Financial Corp. 85
Dollar Thrifty Automotive Group, Inc. 161
ONEOK, Inc. 363
Williams 522

Oregon

Beaverton
Nike, Inc. 349
Tektronix, Inc. 466

Klamath Falls
JELD-WEN, Inc. 267

Portland
Freightliner LLC 206
KinderCare Learning Centers, Inc. 280
Fred Meyer Stores 323
NW Natural 358
Oregon Steel Mills Inc. 365
PacifiCorp 369
Pope & Talbot, Inc. 389
Portland General Electric Co. 389
Precision Castparts Corp. 391
Regence BlueCross BlueShield of Oregon 406
Standard Insurance Co. 453

Roseburg
Roseburg Forest Products Co. 414

Wilsonville
Mentor Graphics Corp. 320

Pennsylvania

Allentown
Agere Systems Inc. 11
Air Products and Chemicals, Inc. 13
Lehigh Cement Company 290
Mack Trucks, Inc. 302
PPL Corp. 390

Altoona
Sheetz, Inc. 436

Bala Cynwyd
Pegasus Communications Corp. 373

Bensalem
Charming Shoppes, Inc. 112

Bethlehem
Buzzi Unicem USA 96

Blue Bell
Henkels & McCoy, Inc. 240
Unisys Corp. 488

Bristol
Jones Apparel Group 271

Camp Hill
Harsco Corp. 234
Highmark Inc. 243

Canonsburg
Mylan Laboratories Inc. 336

Chesterbrook
AmeriSource Bergen Corp. 35

Collegeville
Wyeth Pharmaceuticals 527

Easton
Binney and Smith Inc. 74

Erie
Erie Indeminity Co. 185
Rent-Way, Inc. 409

Frazer
Cephalon, Inc. 110

Greensburg
Allegheny Energy Inc. 18

Gulph Mills
Henkel Corp. 240

Harleysville
Harleysville Group 232

Harrisburg
Capital BlueCross (Pennsylvania) 100
Penn Nat'l Insurance 374
Rite Aid Corp. 411
Tyco Electronics Corp. 483

Hershey
The Hershey Company 241

Horsham
Centocor, Inc. 109
The Penn Mutual Life Insurance Co. 374

Huntingdon Valley
Toll Brothers, Inc. 477

Kennett Square
Genesis HealthCare Corp. 216

King of Prussia
Universal Health Services, Inc. 495

Lancaster
Armstrong Holdings, Inc. 48

Latrobe
Kennametal Inc. 277

Limerick
Teleflex Inc. 467

Linwood
Foamex Internat'l Inc. 200

Lionville
West Pharmaceutical Services 518

Malvern
Vishay Intertechnology, Inc. 507

McConnellsburg
JLG Industries, Inc. 268

Norristown
SKF USA, Inc. 440

Paoli
Ametek, Inc. 36

Philadelphia
ARAMARK 46
ATOFINA Chemicals, Inc. 54
Berwind Group 72
CDI Corp. 106
CIGNA Corp. 118
Comcast Corporation 130
Crown Holdings, Inc. 145
Day & Zimmerman 152
FMC Corp. 199
Independence Blue Cross (Pennsylvania) 256
Lincoln Financial Group 295
The Pep Boys-Manny, Moe & Jack 376
Radian Group, Inc. 402
Rohm and Haas Co. 413
Sunoco, Inc. 461
Tasty Baking Co. 465
Verizon Pennsylvania Inc. 503

Pittsburgh
Alcoa Inc. 17
Allegheny Technologies Incorporated 19
Ampco-Pittsburgh Corp. 37
Bayer Corporation 65
CONSOL Energy Inc. 136
Duquesne Light Holdings 170
Equitable Resources, Inc. 184
L. B. Foster Co. 202
H. J. Heinz Co. 239
Mellon Financial Corp. 319
Mine Safety Appliances Co. (MSA) 328
PNC Financial Services Group 387
PPG Industries Inc. 390
United States Steel Corporation 491
WESCO Internat'l, Inc. 518
Westinghouse Electric Company LLC 519

Radnor
Airgas, Inc. 14

Reading
Carpenter Technology Corp. 103
Penske Truck Leasing Co. LP 375
Sovereign Bancorp, Inc. 449

Richmond
Dominion Peoples 161

Scranton
Southern Union Company 447

Spring House
Advanta Corp. 7

Sunbury
Weis Markets, Inc. 515

Swiftwater
Sanofi Pasteur, Inc. 420

Valley Forge
Ikon Office Solutions, Inc. 255
Saint-Gobain Corp. 419
UGI Corp. 485

Warren
United Refining Co. 491

Wawa
Wawa, Inc. 514

Wayne
Safeguard Scientifics, Inc. 418
SunGard Data Systems, Inc. 460

Wilkes-Barre
Blue Cross of Northeastern Pennsylvania 82

Willow Grove
Asplundh Tree Expert Co. 49

Wilmerding
Westinghouse Air Brake Technologies Corp. 519

York
The Bon Ton Stores, Inc. 86
Dentsply Internat'l. 156
York Internat'l Corp. 530

Rhode Island

Pawtucket
Hasbro Inc. 236

Providence
Blue Cross & Blue Shield of Rhode Island 80
Citizens Financial Group, Inc. 123
Gilbane Building Co. 219
Nortek Inc. 352
The Providence Journal Co. 396
Textron Inc. 471

West Greenwich
GTECH Corp. 228

West Kingston
American Power Conversion Corp. 33

Woonsocket
CVS 148

South Carolina

Columbia
BlueCross BlueShield of South Carolina 83
Colonial Life & Accident Insurance Co. 129
SCANA Corp. 426

Fort Mill
Springs Industries, Inc. 450

Greenville
Bowater Incorporated 88
KEMET Corp. 277
Liberty Corp. 292
Michelin North America, Inc. 324

Hartsville
Sonoco Products Co. 443

Spartanburg
Denny's Corp. 156
Extended Stay America, Inc. 188
Milliken & Co. 327

South Dakota

Rapid City
Black Hills Corp. 76

Sioux Falls
NorthWestern Corp. 355

Tennessee

Bristol
King Pharmaceuticals, Inc. 281

Chattanooga
Blue Cross and Blue Shield of Tennessee 80
The Dixie Group, Inc. 160

Collegedale
McKee Foods Corp. 314

Goodlettsville
Dollar General Corp. 161

Kingsport
Eastman Chemical Co. 171

Lebanon
CBRL Group, Inc. 106

Memphis
AutoZone, Inc. 55
FedEx Corp. 192
FedEx Freight 193
First Horizon Nat'l Corp. 196
Fred's Inc. 204
Memphis Light, Gas and Water Division 319
Thomas & Betts Corp. 472

Nashville
Bridgestone Americas Holding, Inc. 89
Caremark Rx, Inc. 101
Corrections Corp. of America 141
Gaylord Entertainment Co. 210
Genesco 216
HCA 237
Louisiana-Pacific Corporation 299
Renal Care Group, Inc. 409

Texas

Angleton
Benchmark Electronics 71

Austin
Cirrus Logic, Inc. 121
Temple-Inland Inc. 468
Whole Foods Market, Inc. 522

Beaumont
Entergy Texas 184

Carrollton
CellStar Corp 107

Dallas
7-Eleven, Inc. 2
Affiliated Computer Services, Inc. (ACS) 9
Atmos Energy Corp. 53
Austin Industries 54
Belo Corp. 71
Brinker Internat'l, Inc. 90
Celanese 107
Centex Corporation 109
ClubCorp Internat'l Inc. 125
Dean Foods Company 152
ENSCO Internat'l Inc. 182
FedEx Kinko's Office and Print Services 193
Frito-Lay, Inc. 206
Greyhound Lines, Inc. 227
Hunt Oil Co. 252
i2 Technologies, Inc. 254
Kimberly-Clark Corp. 280
Lennox Internat'l 291
Mary Kay Inc. 306
Occidental Chemical Corp. 359
Southwest Airlines Co. 448
Texas Industries, Inc. 470
Texas Instruments Incorporated 471
Trinity Industries, Inc. 481
TXU 482
Valhi, Inc. 500
Xanser Corp. 527

Dallas-Fort Worth Airport
AMR Corp. 37

El Paso
El Paso Electric Co. 177

Fort Worth
Alcon Inc. 17
AmeriCredit Corp. 34
Bell Helicopter Textron 69
Burlington Northern Santa Fe Corporation 94
Cash America Internat'l, Inc. 104
D. R. Horton, Inc. 248
Lockheed Martin Aeronautics Co. 296
Pier 1 Imports 383
Radio Shack Corporation 403

Galveston
American Nat'l Insurance Co. 33

Houston
AIG American General Corp. 12
Air Liquide America Corp. 13
Apache Corp. 42
Baker Hughes Inc. 59
BJ Services Co. 75
BMC Software 83
Burlington Resources Inc. 95
Cemex USA 107
CenterPoint Energy 108
CITGO Petroleum Corporation 121
ConocoPhillips 135
Continental Airlines 138
Cooper Cameron Corp. 139
Cooper Industries 139
Dynegy, Inc. 171
El Paso Corp. 177
Enron Corp. 182
Exxon Mobil Chemical Co. 188
Fiesta Mart Inc. 194
FMC Technologies, Inc. 199
Frontier Oil Corp. 207
GlobalSantaFe Corp. 221
Group 1 Automotive, Inc. 228
Halliburton Company 230
Hibernia Corp. 243
Jiffy Lube Internat'l, Inc. 268
Kellogg Brown and Root 275
Kinder Morgan, Inc. 280
Lyondell Chemical Co. 301
Marathon Oil Corp. 304
MAXXAM Inc. 310
McDermott Internat'l, Inc. 312
Men's Wearhouse, Inc. 319
Nabors Industries, Ltd. 337
Nat'l Oilwell, Inc. 340
Omega Protein Corporation 362
Plains Resources Inc. 386
Pogo Producing Co. 387
Pride Internat'l, Inc. 393
Quanex Corp. 400
Reliant Resources 409
Rowan Companies, Inc. 415
Service Corp. Internat'l 434
Shell Oil Co. 436
Smith Internat'l, Inc. 441
Southwestern Energy Co. 449
Stage Stores, Inc. 453
Sterling Chemicals, Inc. 457
Stewart & Stevenson Services, Inc. 457
Sysco Corp. 464
Texas Eastern Products Pipeline Company, LLC (TEPPCO) 470
Total Petrochemicals USA, Inc. 478
Transocean Inc. 479
Waste Management, Inc. 513
Weatherford Internat'l Ltd. 514

Irving
Commercial Metals Co. 132
Exxon Mobil Corp. 188
Flowserve Corp. 198
La Quinta Inns 285
Michaels Stores, Inc. 324
Pioneer Natural Resources Co. 385
Zale Corp. 531

Kingwood
Administaff, Inc. 6

Pittsburg
Pilgrim's Pride Corp. 383

Plano
Cadbury Schweppes Americas Beverages 97
EDS Corp. 175
Ericsson Inc. 185
J. C. Penney Co., Inc. 374
Perot Systems Corp. 379
Rent-A-Center, Inc. 409
Safety-Kleen Systems, Inc. 418
Triad Hospitals, Inc. 480

Richardson
Blue Cross and Blue Shield of Texas, Inc. 80
Fossil Inc. 202

Round Rock
Dell Inc. 154

San Antonio
Clear Channel Communications 124
Frost Nat'l Bank 207
Harte-Hanks, Inc. 234
HEB Grocery Co. 239
SBC Communications Inc. 422
Tesoro Petroleum Corp. 470
United Services Automobile Ass'n (USAA) 491
Valero Energy Corp. 499
Zachry Construction Corporation 531

Southlake
Sabre Holdings Corp. 417

Sugar Land
Imperial Sugar Co. 255
Noble Drilling Corp. 350

Temple
McLane Company, Inc. 315

The Woodlands
Anadarko Petroleum Corp. 39

Tyler
Brookshire Grocery Co. 91

Utah

Magna
Kennecott Utah Copper 277

Murray
Kennecott Land 277

Provo
Nu Skin Enterprises 357

Salt Lake City
Huntsman Corp. 253
Questar Corporation 401
Regence BlueCross BlueShield of Utah 406
Sinclair Oil Corp. 439
Zions Bancorporation 532

Vermont

Middlebury
Chemtura 114

Montpelier
Blue Cross and Blue Shield of Vermont 81
Nat'l Life Insurance Co. 339

Rutland
Central Vermont Public Service Corp. 109

South Burlington
Ben & Jerry's Homemade Inc. 71

Virginia

Alexandria
USA Mobility, Inc. 497

Arlington
The AES Corp. 8
CACI Internat'l Inc. 97
US Airways Group, Inc. 496

Ashburn
MCI, Inc. 314

Bassett
Bassett Furniture Industries, Inc. 64

Chantilly
Rolls-Royce North America Inc. 414

Chesapeake
Dollar Tree Stores, Inc. 161

Danville
Alliance One Internat'l Inc. 20
Dan River, Inc. 151

Dulles
FLYi, Inc. 199
Orbital Sciences Corp. 364

Falls Church
General Dynamics Corporation 212

Herndon
Airbus North America Holdings, Inc. 14
Lafarge North America, Inc. 286
Triple Canopy, Inc. 481

McLean
Booz Allen Hamilton Inc. 86
Capital One Financial Corp. 100
Freddie Mac 204
Gannett Co., Inc. 208
Mars, Inc. 305
NVR, Inc. 358
Sunrise Assisted Living, Inc. 461

Newport News
Northrop Grumman Newport News 354

Norfolk
Landmark Communications, Inc. 288
Norfolk Southern Corp. 351

Reston
MAXIMUS, Inc. 310
SLM Corp. 440
Sprint Nextel 450
World Kitchen, Inc. 525
XO Communications, Inc. 529

Richmond
The Brink's Co. 89
Chesapeake Corp. 114
Circuit City Stores, Inc. 120
Dominion Resources, Inc. 162
LandAmerica Financial Group, Inc. 288
Massey Energy Co. 307
Media General Inc. 317
NewMarket Corp. 347
Owens & Minor, Inc. 367
Performance Food Group Co. 378
Philip Morris U.S.A. 382
Southern States Cooperative 447
Swedish Match North America Inc. 462
Tredegar Corp. 480
Universal Corp. 494

Roanoke
Advance Auto Parts, Inc. 7

Smithfield
Smithfield Foods, Inc. 441

Vienna
Feld Entertainment, Inc. 193

Washington

Bellevue
PACCAR Inc. 368
Puget Sound Energy 399

Everett
Fluke Corporation 198
UNOVA, Inc. 496

Federal Way
Weyerhaeuser Co. 520

Issaquah
Costco Wholesale Corp. 142

Longview

Longview Fibre Co. ... 298

Mountlake Terrace

Premera Blue Cross ... 392

Redmond

Eddie Bauer, Inc. ... 175
Microsoft Corporation ... 325

Seattle

Alaska Air Group, Inc. ... 15
Amazon.com, Inc. ... 26
Nordstrom, Inc. ... 351
Plum Creek Timber Co. Inc. ... 387
SAFECO Corp. ... 418
Starbucks Corp. ... 455
Univar USA, Inc. ... 494
Washington Mutual, Inc. ... 512

Spokane

Avista Corp. ... 56
Potlatch Corp. ... 389

Sumner

Recreational Equipment, Inc. ... 406

Tacoma

Labor Ready, Inc. ... 285
Simpson Investment Co. ... 439

West Virginia

Charleston

Verizon West Virginia Inc. ... 504

Wheeling

Mountain State Blue Cross Blue Shield ... 335
Wheeling-Pittsburgh Steel Corp. ... 521

Wisconsin

Appleton

Appleton ... 44

Brookfield

Fiserv, Inc. ... 197

Eau Claire

Nat'l Presto Industries, Inc. ... 340

Green Bay

American Medical Security Group, Inc. ... 33
Associated Banc-Corp. ... 49
Green Bay Packaging Inc. ... 227
Schreiber Foods, Inc. ... 428
Shopko Stores, Inc. ... 437
Wisconsin Public Service Corp. ... 524
WPS Resources Corp. ... 526

Kenosha

Snap-on Incorporated ... 442

Kohler

Kohler Co. ... 282

Madison

Alliant Energy Corp. ... 21
American Family Insurance Group ... 31
CUNA Mutual Group ... 148
Madison Gas and Electric Co. ... 302

Manitowoc

The Manitowoc Co., Inc. ... 303

Menasha

Banta Corp. ... 61

Menomonee Falls

Kohl's Corp. ... 282

Milwaukee

Brady Corp. ... 89
Briggs and Stratton Corp. ... 89
Harley-Davidson Motor Company ... 232
Johnson Controls, Inc. ... 271
Journal Communications, Inc. ... 272
Joy Global Inc. ... 272
Manpower Inc. ... 303
Marshall & Ilsley Corp. ... 306
Miller Brewing Co. ... 327
Mortgage Guaranty Insurance Corp. (MGIC) ... 333
Northwestern Mutual Financial Network ... 355
Rockwell Automation ... 412
SBC Wisconsin ... 425
Sensient Technology Corp. ... 433
A. O. Smith Corp. ... 441
We Energies ... 514
Wisconsin Energy Corp. ... 524

Neenah

Menasha Corporation ... 319

Oshkosh

Oshkosh B'Gosh, Inc. ... 365
Oshkosh Truck Corp. ... 365

Racine

Modine Manufacturing Company ... 330
SC Johnson ... 425

Stevens Point

Sentry Insurance ... 434

Sussex

Quad/Graphics, Inc. ... 400

Wausau

Employers Insurance Co. of Wausau ... 180

Wisconsin Rapids

Stora Enso North America ... 458

Wyoming

Cheyenne

Blue Cross and Blue Shield of Wyoming ... 81

Gillette

Kennecott Energy Co. ... 277

Public Affairs Council Section Introduction

THE PUBLIC AFFAIRS COUNCIL: MAKING YOUR CONNECTIONS

The pace of public affairs is accelerating rapidly. Complex issues take more time to analyze, but a crisis demands a quick response. All politics is local, but public affairs is becoming increasingly global. Staffs are smaller, but expectations are higher.

To keep up with this changing world, corporate public affairs departments – and the consultants and associations that serve them – need a highly effective information network. That network exists in the Public Affairs Council.

The Public Affairs Council is the premier professional association for public affairs executives. It provides unique information, training and other resources to its members to support their effective participation in government, community and public relations activities at all levels. Its over 550 corporate, association and consultant members work together to enhance the value and professionalism of the public affairs practice, and to provide thoughtful leadership as corporate citizens.

Launched in 1954 at the urging of President Dwight D. Eisenhower, the Council has a long-standing reputation for anticipating public affairs professionals' needs. Thousands of member company employees take advantage of its programs and services each year.

Member companies belong to the Public Affairs Council for many reasons. Some organizations integrate the Council's training programs and services into their day-to-day operations; others regularly call the Council staff for expert advice. But all members know that they are more than customers – they are investors in an organization that provides exceptional returns.

The Council provides many important benefits to members, including:

I. Information Central

This is our customized service that provides immediate answers to the most difficult public affairs questions. Members can access information about effective grassroots programs, crisis management, campaign finance laws, software applications, public interest groups, PAC solicitations, ethics laws, use of the Internet, international public affairs, benchmarking and a host of other subjects.

We can tell members everything they need to know about a public affairs issue, plus the names and phone numbers of other professionals who have dealt successfully with the same problem. We can identify consultants who specialize in the area in which members are seeking assistance.

Staff from the Council and its affiliate, the Foundation for Public Affairs, regularly receive more than 1,600 calls each year from members seeking assistance.

2. Conferences and Workshops

The Council's reputation has been built on effective and timely seminars covering key public affairs topics. Each year, more than 30 major conferences are held, including:

National Grassroots Conference
The nation's largest forum for corporate and trade association professionals working to build or improve their grassroots political programs.

Public Affairs Institute
A week-long mind-stretching program for public affairs fast-trackers eager to explore ideas that shape the world and discuss issues with major opinion-makers on the faculty.

National Political Action Committee Conference
The premier meeting for PAC administrators who want to refine their solicitation strategies, allocate dollars wisely and evaluate the effectiveness of their programs.

Public Affairs Management Series
Innovative workshops on critical topics such as information technology, strategic planning and managing external resources.

State Workshops
These programs offer participants the dos and don'ts of working with individual state governments. Legislative leaders, local lobbyists and political reporters are featured speakers.

Public Affairs Council members receive a substantial discount on all conference registration fees. Visit our website at www.pac.org to view our conference calendar.

3. Research and Analysis

Through ongoing surveys, statistical reports and issue analysis, the Public Affairs Council staff identifies trends in the profession and helps companies measure their own performance. The Council's major research study, *The State of Corporate Public Affairs*, examines how companies organize and manage the function. Areas analyzed include public affairs budgets, staffing, federal and state government relations, and management-related interests. Other studies analyze public affairs compensation, PAC and grassroots programs, and state and federal lobbying activities.

Through the Council's Center for Public Affairs Management, members can receive customized benchmarking reports.

4. Communications

Every month, all members receive *Impact*, the association's newsletter about public affairs news and trends. *Impact* has received numerous national awards for excellence.

The Council also produces an electronic news service called *Public Affairs Monitor*. This biweekly service provides summaries of major national news stories dealing with public affairs issues. It is delivered via e-mail directly to Council members.

Other Council publications are available for purchase, including books on benchmarking, strategic planning and political action committees. Members receive substantial discounts on all publications.

5. Information Retrieval Services

Looking for public affairs job descriptions? Looking for a new issues management system? When companies belong to the Council, they can access the only comprehensive library on public affairs programs. Members frequently visit the Council's headquarters to check out our files or to meet with staff to discuss a particular information need. The Council's Web site gives members an electronic link to the expertise of both staff and thousands of other public affairs professionals.

6. Professional Network

The Council operates online discussion groups for members with an interest in PACs, federal government relations, state government relations, grassroots, international affairs, public relations, community affairs, issues management and Washington office administration.

Members of the Council also work together on many projects to advance the profession, including task forces, management roundtables and the development of new programs. When they sit at the table with top executives from leading companies, members are learning from the best – and they are establishing their own reputations as public affairs leaders. As a part of this network, members have unmatched opportunities for professional growth.

Who Belongs to the Public Affairs Council?

The Council's membership is composed of more than 550 corporations and trade associations with public affairs departments, plus public affairs consultancies. While individual executives often benefit from programs and services, the membership is held by the organization. All employees of that organization qualify to receive member benefits.

Every major industry sector is represented in the Council, including manufacturing, utilities, retailing, transportation, banking, insurance and diversified service companies.

Within member companies and associations, programs and services are designed for employees in the following fields:

- Public affairs management
- Government affairs
- Issues management
- Community relations
- Political action committees
- Corporate communications
- Grassroots
- Corporate philanthropy
- International affairs
- Other related fields

Public Affairs Council
2033 K Street, N.W.
Suite 700
Washington, D.C. 20006
(202) 872-1790 (Phone)
(202) 835-8343 (FAX)
http://www.pac.org

Public Affairs Council Membership Directory

7-Eleven Inc.
2711 North Haskell Avenue — Tel: (214) 841-6598
Dallas, TX 75204 — Fax: (214) 841-6727
Contact: Mr. Ronnie R. Volkening
Director, Government Affairs

AAA
607 14th Street, NW — Tel: (202) 942-2080
Suite 200 — Fax: (202) 783-4788
Washington, DC 20005
Contact: Ms. Kathleen F. Marvaso
Managing Director, Government Relations

AAA Auto Club South
1515 N. Westshore Boulevard — Tel: (813) 289-5057
Tampa, FL 33607 — Fax: (813) 289-1340
Contact: Mr. Kevin Bakewell
Vice President, Public & Government Relations

AARP
601 E Street, NW — Tel: (202) 434-3381
Room A6130 — Fax: (202) 434-6432
Washington, DC 20049
Contact: Mr. Christopher W. Hansen
Associate Executive Director for State and National Issues

ABB Inc.
1455 Pennsylvania, NW — Tel: (202) 639-4062
Willard Building, Suite 210 — Fax: (202) 737-1311
Washington, DC 20004
Contact: Mr. Bruce B. Talley
Vice President, Government Affairs

ACA International
4040 West 70th Street — Tel: (952) 926-6547
Minneapolis, MN 55435 — Fax: (952) 915-3922
Contact: Ms. Jenifer Loon
Director, Government Affairs

Academy of Managed Care Pharmacy
100 North Pitt Street — Tel: (703) 683-8416
Suite 400 — Fax: (703) 683-8417
Alexandria, VA 22314
Contact: Ms. Melissa James
Legislative Analyst

AdVanced Advocacy
4000 Abermarle Street, NW — Tel: (202) 244-4866
Suite 302 — Fax: (800) 883-0513
Washington, DC 20016
Contact: Ms. Stephanie Vance
Advocacy Guru

Aegon USA, INC
1111 N. Charles Street — Tel: (410) 576-4529
MS #17 — Fax: (410) 347-8621
Baltimore, MD 21201
Contact: Ms. Jeanne De Cervens
Assistant General Counsel & Director of Government Relations

AES Corporation, The
4300 Wilson Boulevard — Tel: (703) 682-6484
Arlington, VA 22203 — Fax: (703) 682-6587
Contact: Ms. Teresa Mullett Ressel
Vice President

Affiliated Computer Services, Inc.
1200 K Street, NW — Tel: (202) 414-3720
12th Floor — Fax: (202) 289-8274
Washington, DC 20005
Contact: Ms. Audrey Rowe
Senior Vice President, Public Affairs

Affinity Health Plan
2500 Halsey Street — Tel: (718) 794-7696
Bronx, NY 10461 — Fax: (718) 794-7800
Contact: Ms. Abenaa Abboa-Offei
Vice President of Public Affairs

Air Conditioning Refrigeration Institute
4100 N. Fairfax Drive — Tel: (703) 524-8800
Arlington, VA 22203 — Fax: (703) 528-3816
Contact: Ms. Deborah E. Miller
Vice President, Government and International Affairs

Air Products and Chemicals, Inc.
7201 Hamilton Boulevard — Tel: (610) 481-4453
Allentown, PA 18195-1501 — Fax: (610) 706-6088
Contact: Mr. Timothy J. Holt
Director, Corporate Relations

Alcoa, Inc.
P.O. Box 10 — Tel: (812) 853-1695
Newburgh, IN 47629 — Fax: (812) 853-1086
Contact: Mr. Michael E. Belwood
Manager, North American Public Strategies

Allegheny Energy, Inc.
800 Cabin Hill Drive — Tel: (724) 838-6530
Greensburg, PA 15601 — Fax: (724) 853-3609
Contact: Mr. Paul J. Pavlik
Manager, State Government Affairs

Allergan, Inc.
16825 Burnet Court — Tel: (262) 782-2186
Brookfield, WI 53005 — Fax: (262) 782-5561
Contact: Mr. Bruce W. Stevenson
Director, State Government Affairs

Alliance of Automobile Manufacturers
1401 Eye Street, NW — Tel: (202) 326-5500
Suite 900 — Fax: (202) 326-5598
Washington, DC 20005
Contact: Mr. Kenneth Gear
Vice President, State Affairs

Alliant Energy Corporation
4902 N. Biltmore Lane — Tel: (608) 458-5718
P.O. Box 77007 — Fax: (608) 458-3481
Madison, WI 53707-1007
Contact: Mr. David W. Helbach
Director, Corporate Public Affairs

Allianz Life Insurance Company of North America
5701 Golden Hills Drive Tel: (763) 765-5500
Minneapolis, MN 55416 Fax: (763) 765-7229
Contact: Ms. Elizabeth A. Malkerson
Senior Vice President, Corporate Marketing & Communication

Allstate Insurance Company
2775 Sanders Road Tel: (847) 402-5889
Suite A3 Fax: (847) 326-7524
Northbrook, IL 600626-127
Contact: Mr. E. James McCabe
Manager, Government Relations

Altria Group, Inc.
120 Park Avenue Tel: (917) 663-3924
17th Floor Fax: (917) 663-5464
New York, NY 10017
Contact: Mr. Thomas J. Collamore
Vice President, Public Affairs

America's Health Insurance Plans
601 Pennsylvania Avenue, NW Tel: (202) 778-8473
South Building Suite 500 Fax: (202) 778-8479
Washington, DC 20036-3421
Contact: Mr. T. Anthony Lamb
Director of Political Affairs

American Academy of Pediatrics
601 13th Street, N.W. Tel: (202) 347-8600
Suite 400 North Fax: (202) 393-6137
Washington, DC 20005
Contact: Ms. Marjorie Tharp
Public Affairs Manager

American Association of Nurse Anesthetists
412 First Street, Southeast Tel: (202) 484-8400
Suite 12 Fax: (202) 484-8408
Washington, DC 20003
Contact: Mr. Frank Purcell
Director

American Association of Oral and Maxillofacial Surgeons
9700 West Bryn Mawr Avenue Tel: (847) 233-4321
Rosemont, IL 60018-5701 Fax: (847) 678-4619
Contact: Ms. Jeanne Tuerk
Manager, Governmental Affairs

American Association of Orthopaedic Surgeons
317 Massachusetts Avenue, NE Tel: (202) 546-4430
Suite 100 Fax: (202) 546-5051
Washington, DC 20002
Contact: Mr. David A. Lovett
Director, Washington Office

American Bankers Association
1120 Connecticut Avenue, NW Tel: (202) 663-5113
Washington, DC 20036 Fax: (202) 663-7544
Contact: Mr. Gary Fields
BankPAC Treasurer & Director of State Association Division

American Beverage Association
1101 16th Street NW Tel: (202) 463-6706
Washington, DC 20036 Fax: (202) 463-8178
Contact: Ms. Susan K. Neely
President

American Cancer Society
900 E Street, NW Tel: (202) 661-5700
Suite 650 Fax: (202) 661-5750
Washington, DC 20004
Contact: Mr. Daniel E. Smith
National Vice President, Federal and State Government Relations

American Century Investments
P.O. Box 418210 Tel: (816) 340-4066
4500 Main Street Fax: (816) 340-7790
Kansas City, MO 64141-9210
Contact: Mr. William B. Bates
Vice President, Government Affairs

American Chemistry Council
1300 Wilson Boulevard Tel: (703) 741-5000
Arlington, VA 22209 Fax: (703) 741-6000
Contact: Mr. Charlie Van Vlack
Executive Vice President

American Chiropractic Association
1701 Clarendon Boulevard Tel: (703) 276-8800
Arlington, VA 22209 Fax: (703) 243-2593
Contact: Ms. Kimberly Krocker
Senior Manager for Political Affairs

American College of Cardiology
9111 Old Georgetown Road Tel: (301) 493-2374
Bethesda, MD 20814-1699 Fax: (301) 897-8757
Contact: Ms. Dana Langley Birdsong
Director, Political Action Committee & Grassroots

American College of Emergency Physicians
2121 K Street, NW Tel: (202) 728-0610
Suite 325 Fax: (202) 728-0617
Washington, DC 20037-1801
Contact: Ms. Jeanne Slade
Political Action Director

American College of Radiology
1701 Pennsylvania Avenue, NW Tel: (703) 648-8974
Suite 610 Fax: (703) 262-9312
Washington, DC 20006
Contact: Ms. Heng Diep
Project Specialist, Political Outreach & Development

American Council of Life Insurers
101 Constitution Avenue, NW Tel: (202) 624-2155
Suite 700 Fax: (202) 624-2319
Washington, DC 20001-2133
Contact: Mr. Dan Mahoney
Senior Vice President, Public Affairs & Publishing

American Crystal Sugar Company
50 F Street, NW Tel: (202) 879-0804
Suite 900 Fax: (202) 626-8896
Washington, DC 20001
Contact: Mr. Kevin S. Price
Director of Government Affairs

American Dental Association
1111 14th Street, NW Tel: (202) 789-5171
Suite 1100 Fax: (202) 898-2437
Washington, DC 20005
Contact: Mr. Francis X. McLaughlin, Jr.
Director of Political Affairs/ADPAC

American Electric Power (AEP)
1 Riverside Plaza Tel: (614) 716-1640
Columbus, OH 43215-2373 Fax: (614) 716-1682
Contact: Mr. Christopher Amatos
Public Affairs & PAC Manager

American Express Company
801 Pennsylvania Avenue, NW Tel: (202) 434-0156
Suite 650 Fax: (202) 624-0775
Washington, DC 20004
Contact: Mr. Robert B. Thomson, III
Vice President, Government Affairs

American Family Insurance
6000 American Parkway Tel: (608) 249-2111
Madison, WI 53783 Fax: (608) 245-8619
Contact: Ms. Heidi Krumenauer
Political Action Director

American Forest and Paper Association
1111 19th Street, NW Tel: (202) 463-2430
Suite 800 Fax: (202) 463-2424
Washington, DC 20036
Contact: Mr. Patrick Rita
Vice President, State Government Affairs

American Gas Association
400 N. Capitol Street, NW — Tel: (202) 824-7210
Washington, DC 20001-1511 — Fax: (202) 824-7092
Contact: Mr. Richard D. Shelby
Executive Vice President, Public Affairs

American Heart Association
1150 Connecticut Ave. NW — Tel: (202) 785-7903
Suite 300 — Fax: (202) 785-7950
Washington, DC 20036
Contact: Ms. Suzanne Pechilio Polis
Grassroots Advocacy Director

American Institute of Architects, The
1735 New York Avenue, NW — Tel: (202) 626-7383
Washington, DC 20006 — Fax: (202) 626-7583
Contact: Mr. Adam Melis
Manager, Political Programs

American International Group, Inc.
70 Pine Street — Tel: (212) 770-7887
New York, NY 10270 — Fax: (212) 770-6786
Contact: Mr. Edward T. Cloonan
Vice President, Corporate Affairs

American Lung Association of Pennsylvania
3001 Old Gettysburg Road — Tel: (717) 541-5864
Camp Hill, PA 17011 — Fax: (717) 541-8828
Contact: Ms. Kristin Davis
Director of Community Outreach & Special Projects

American Medical Association
1101 Vermont Avenue, NW — Tel: (202) 789-7467
Washington, DC 20005 — Fax: (202) 789-7469
Contact: Mr. Kevin Walker
Vice President of Political Affairs

American Nurses Association
8515 Georgia Avenue — Tel: (301) 628-5096
Suite 400 — Fax: (301) 628-5348
Silver Spring, MD 20910
Contact: Ms. Shari Dexter
ANA-PAC Administrator

American Petroleum Institute
1220 L Street, NW — Tel: (202) 682-8120
Washington, DC 20005-8029 — Fax: (202) 682-8115
Contact: Mr. Jim C. Craig
Group Director

American Podiatric Medical Association
9312 Old Georgetown Road — Tel: (301) 581-9232
Bethesda, MD 20814-1621 — Fax: (301) 571-4905
Contact: Ms. Faye B. Frankfort
Director, Legislative Advocacy

American Senior Housing Association
5100 Wisconsin Avenue, NW — Tel: (202) 885-5561
Suite 307 — Fax: (202) 885-1616
Washington, DC 20016
Contact: Mr. Stephen Denis
Director

American Traffic Safety Services Association
15 Riverside Parkway — Tel: (540) 368-1701
Suite 100 — Fax: (540) 368-1717
Fredericksburg, VA 22406-1022
Contact: Mr. Robert N. Dingess
Director, Government Relations

American Trucking Associations, Inc.
2200 Mill Road — Tel: (703) 838-1759
Alexandria, VA 22314 — Fax: (703) 836-2023
Contact: Ms. Crystal C. Reid
Vice President, Strategic Outreach

Americans for the Arts
1000 Vermont Avenue, NW — Tel: (202) 371-2830
6th Floor — Fax: (202) 371-0424
Washington, DC 20005
Contact: Mr. Jay H. Dick
Director of State Arts Policy

AmerisourceBergen -PharMerica Inc.
3625 Queen Palm Drive — Tel: (877) 975-2273
Tampa, FL 33619 — Fax: (813) 628-8871
Contact: Mr. Jon B. Rawlson
Vice President of Government Affairs

Anheuser-Busch Companies, Inc.
One Busch Place — Tel: (314) 577-4594
202-8N — Fax: (314) 577-1773
St. Louis, MO 63118-1852
Contact: Mr. Bernard J. Fullenkamp
Director, Industry & Government Affairs Administration

APCO Worldwide
700 12th Street, NW — Tel: (202) 778-1010
Suite 800 — Fax: (202) 861-0525
Washington, DC 20005
Contact: Ms. Margery Kraus
President and CEO

Apple Computer, Inc.
1 Infinite Loop — Tel: (408) 974-5800
MS 81-2CF — Fax: (408) 974-5870
Cupertino, CA 95014
Contact: Ms. Catherine H. Foster
Director, Worldwide Government Affairs

Applied Materials, Inc.
3050 Bowers Avenue, MS 0104 — Tel: (408) 748-5508
P.O. Box 58039 — Fax: (408) 748-5510
Santa Clara, CA 95054
Contact: Mr. Joe Pon
Managing Director, Corporate Affairs

Aqua Pennsylvania Inc.
762 West Lancaster Avenue — Tel: (610) 645-1081
Bryn Mawr, PA 19010 — Fax: (610) 645-1061
Contact: Mr. Christopher Franklin
Vice President, Corporate & Public Affairs

Aquila, Inc.
161 St. Anthony Avenue — Tel: (651) 222-4314
Suite 815 — Fax: (651) 222-4372
St. Paul, MN 55103
Contact: Ms. Stacey S. Fujii
Director of Government Services

Arch Chemicals, Inc.
1200 Lower River Road — Tel: (423) 238-5922
PO Box 800 — Fax: (423) 780-2505
Charleston, TN 37310
Contact: Ms. Laura B. Tew
Director, Stakeholder Relations

Archer Daniels Midland Co.
4666 Faries Parkway — Tel: (217) 451-8150
Decatur, IL 62526 — Fax: (217) 451-8166
Contact: Mr. Gregory Webb
Vice President, Public Affairs

Aristotle, Inc.
1640 India Hook Road — Tel: (803) 909-2331
Rock Hill, SC 29732 — Fax: (803) 909-2335
Contact: Mr. Jeff Ashe
Executive Vice President, PAC & Grassroots Development

Ashland Inc.
3499 Blazer Parkway — Tel: (859) 357-3101
Lexington, KY 40509 — Fax: (859) 357-3100
Contact: Ms. Martha C. Johnson
Vice President, Communication & Corporate Affairs

Associated Builders and Contractors, Inc.
4250 North Fairfax Drive — Tel: (703) 812-2005
9th Floor — Fax: (703) 812-8202
Arlington, VA 22203
Contact: Ms. Meredith Nethercutt
Grassroots Coordinator

Association for Supervision and Curriculum Development
1703 N Beauregard Street — Tel: (703) 578-9600
Alexandria, VA 22311-1714 — Fax: (703) 575-5402
Contact: Ms. Kathleen M. Welling
Regional Director

Association of American Medical Colleges
2450 N Street, NW — Tel: (202) 828-0459
Washington, DC 20037-1126 — Fax: (202) 828-1123
Contact: Ms. Elisa K. Siegel
Senior Vice President, Office of Communications

Association of American Railroads
50 F Street, NW — Tel: (202) 639-2537
Suite 1250 — Fax: (202) 639-2526
Washington, DC 20001
Contact: Mr. H.K. Obie O'Bannon
Senior Vice President, Government Affairs

Association of Fundraising Professionals
1101 King Street — Tel: (703) 519-8455
Suite 700 — Fax: (703) 684-0540
Alexandria, VA 22314-2967
Contact: Mr. Walter Sczudlo
Executive Vice President & General Counsel

Association of PeriOperative Registered Nurses
2170 South Parker Road — Tel: (303) 755-6304
Suite 300 — Fax: (303) 338-5165
Denver, CO 80231-5711
Contact: Ms. Cathy Sparkman
Director of State Public Affairs

Association of Public Television Stations, The
666 11th Street, NW — Tel: (202) 654-4221
Suite 1100 — Fax: (202) 654-4236
Washington, DC 20001
Contact: Ms. Debra Tica Sanchez
Grassroots Coordinator

AstraZeneca
701 Pennsylvania Avenue, NW — Tel: (202) 350-5571
Suite 500 — Fax: (202) 350-5510
Washington, DC 20004
Contact: Mr. Richard Buckley
Vice President, Federal Government Affairs

AT&T
One AT&T Way — Tel: (908) 234-5090
Room 5B210 — Fax: (908) 532-1332
Bedminster, NJ 07921
Contact: Mr. William H. Oliver
Vice President, Public Relations

Atlantic Health Systems Inc.
325 Columbia Turnpike — Tel: (973) 660-3260
Florham Park, NJ 07932 — Fax: (973) 660-9116
Contact: Ms. Madeline Ferraro, Esq.
Vice President, Government & Public Affairs

Atmos Energy Corporation
P.O. Box 650205 — Tel: (972) 934-9227
5430 LBJ Freeway, Suite 1800 — Fax: (972) 855-3040
Dallas, TX 75265-0205
Contact: Mr. Gerald R. Hunter
Director, Corporate Communications

Auto Club Group, The
1 Auto Club Drive — Tel: (313) 336-1170
Dearborn, MI 48126 — Fax: (313) 336-0993
Contact: Ms. Kathryn B. Harrison
Vice President & Chief Public Affairs Officer

Automobile Club of Southern California
3333 Fairview Road — Tel: (714) 885-1253
A131 — Fax: (714) 885-1279
Costa Mesa, CA 92626
Contact: Ms. Alice Bisno
Vice President, Legislative and Regulatory Affairs

AutoZone
PO Box 2198 — Tel: (901) 495-7862
Memphis, TN 38101-9842 — Fax: (901) 495-8300
Contact: Mr. Ray Pohlman
Director, Government Affairs

Avon Products, Inc.
1345 Avenue of the Americas — Tel: (212) 282-5609
27th Floor — Fax: (212) 282-6086
New York, NY 10105-0196
Contact: Ms. Josephine Mills
Executive Director, Global Government

BAE Systems
1300 N. 17th Street — Tel: (703) 907-8259
Suite 1400 — Fax: (703) 907-8300
Arlington, VA 22209
Contact: Ms. Susan Lenover
Assistant To the Vice President

Bank of America Corporation
730 15th Street, NW — Tel: (202) 624-4134
Mail Code DC1-701-05-11 — Fax: (202) 383-3475
Washington, DC 20005
Contact: Ms. Jeanne-Marie Murphy
Senior Vice President, Federal Government Relations

Barrick Gold North America
136 E South Temple — Tel: (801) 560-7084
Ste. 1300 — Fax: (801) 539-0665
Salt Lake City, UT 84111
Contact: Ms. Be Be Adams
Manager, Community Relations and Government Affairs

Bausch & Lomb
One Bausch & Lomb Place — Tel: (585) 338-5386
Rochester, NY 14604-0054 — Fax: (585) 338-8551
Contact: Ms. Barbara M. Kelley
Vice President, Public Affairs

Baxter Healthcare Corporation
1501 K Street, NW — Tel: (202) 508-8206
Suite 375 — Fax: (202) 508-8201
Washington, DC 20005
Contact: Ms. Sarah M. Gregg
Vice President, Federal Legislative Affairs

Bayer Corporation Pharmaceutical Division
400 Morgan Lane — Tel: (203) 812-3804
West Haven, CT 6516 — Fax: (203) 812-6570
Contact: Ms. Sandra Oliver
Director, Public Policy & State Government Affairs

Becton Dickinson and Company
One Becton Drive — Tel: (201) 847-7429
MC 084 — Fax: (201) 847-6295
Franklin Lakes, NJ 07417-1880
Contact: Ms. Patricia Shrader
Vice President, Corporate Regulatory Public Policy and Communication

BellSouth Corporation
1133 21st Street, NW — Tel: (202) 463-4101
Suite 900 — Fax: (202) 463-4141
Washington, DC 20036
Contact: Mr. Herschel L. Abbott, Jr.
Vice President of Governmental Affairs

Berkeley Lab
One Cyclotron Road — Tel: (510) 486-6601
MS 65-0013 — Fax: (510) 486-4553
Berkeley, CA 94720
Contact: Mr. Reid A. Edwards, III
Head, Public Affairs Department

Berlex Laboratories
P.O. Box 1000 — Tel: (973) 487-2246
Montville, NJ 07045 — Fax: (973) 487-2005
Contact: Ms. Jane A. Kramer
Vice President, Public Affairs

Best Buy Co., Inc.
7601 Penn Avenue South — Tel: (612) 291-6120
Richfield, MN 55423 — Fax: (612) 292-4001
Contact: Ms. Paula J. Prahl
Vice President, Public Affairs

Biegel Group, Inc., The
1133 21st Street, NW — Tel: (202) 659-0279
3rd Floor — Fax: (202) 659-0282
Washington, DC 20036
Contact: Mr. Len Biegel
President

Blue Cross Blue Shield Association
1310 G Street, NW — Tel: (202) 626-8624
12th Floor — Fax: (202) 626-4833
Washington, DC 20009
Contact: Mr. Dan Bradfield
National Advocacy Director

Blue Cross Blue Shield of Arizona
8220 N. 23rd Avenue — Tel: (602) 864-5653
MS C300 — Fax: (602) 864-4184
Phoenix, AZ 85021
Contact: Ms. Lyn B. McKay
Public Policy and Education Director

Blue Shield of California
50 Beale St. — Tel: (415) 229-5110
San Francisco, CA 94105
Contact: Mr. Tom Epstein
Vice President, Public Affairs

BlueCross and BlueShield of Minnesota
3535 Blue Cross Road — Tel: (651) 662-1502
Eagan, MN 55122 — Fax: (651) 662-1570
Contact: Mr. Karl W. Oestreich
Director, Media and Public Relations

BlueCross BlueShield of Oklahoma
3401 NW 63rd Street — Tel: (405) 841-9503
Oklahoma City, OK 73116 — Fax: (405) 841-9663
Contact: Ms. Beverly Binkowski
Manager, Public Affairs

BlueCross BlueShield of South Carolina
I-20 Alpine Road — Tel: (803) 264-3452
MC AA-G08 — Fax: (803) 264-5520
Columbia, SC 29219
Contact: Ms. Joan Graddick
Senior Public Affairs Specialist

Boeing Company, The
100 North Riverside Plaza — Tel: (312) 544-2265
MC 5002-9012 — Fax: (312) 544-2074
Chicago, IL 60606-1596
Contact: Ms. Sarah Nava Garvey
Director, Government Relations

Boston Scientific Corporation
One Boston Scientific Place — Tel: (508) 652-7410
Natick, MA 01760 — Fax: (508) 647-5348
Contact: Ms. Randel Richner, BSN, MPH
Vice President, Federal Affairs, Reimbursement and Outcomes Planning

BP
1776 I St., NW — Tel: (202) 457-6573
Suite 1000 — Fax: (202) 457-6597
Washington, DC 20006
Contact: Mr. Michael P. Brien
Chief of Staff, US Gov't & Public Affairs

Bravo Group, Inc.
20 N. Market Square — Tel: (717) 214-2200
Suite 800 — Fax: (717) 214-2205
Harrisburg, PA 17101
Contact: Ms. Shannon Graham
Director, Public Affairs

Brick Industry Association
11490 Commerce Park — Tel: (703) 674-1545
Reston, VA 20191 — Fax: (703) 620-3928
Contact: Mr. Joseph S. Casper
Vice President

Broadcast Music, Inc.
320 West 57th Street — Tel: (212) 830-3882
New York, NY 10019-3790 — Fax: (212) 830-8340
Contact: Mr. Fred Cannon
Sr. Vice President, Government Relations

Brookhaven National Laboratory
Building 134 — Tel: (631) 344-4747
Upton, NY 11973 — Fax: (631) 344-5004
Contact: Ms. Margaret Lynch
Assistant Laboratory Director

Brown-Forman Corporation
850 Dixie Highway — Tel: (502) 774-7152
Louisville, KY 40210 — Fax: (502) 774-6720
Contact: Mr. Mark Smith
Vice President, Director of Government Relations and Public Policy

Brush Engineered Materials Inc.
17876 St. Clair Avenue — Tel: (216) 383-6835
Cleveland, OH 44110 — Fax: (216) 481-2523
Contact: Mr. Patrick Carpenter
Director, Corporate Communications

Burlington Northern Santa Fe Corporation
700 13th Street NW — Tel: (202) 347-8662
Ste 220 — Fax: (202) 347-8675
Washington, DC 20005
Contact: Ms. Patti Murphy
Mannager, Legislative Affairs

Burson-Marsteller
1801 K Street, NW — Tel: (202) 530-4555
Suite 1000-L — Fax: (202) 530-4681
Washington, DC 20006
Contact: Mr. Richard I. Mintz
Chairman, U.S. Public Affairs

Business Software Alliance
1150 18th Street, NW — Tel: (202) 530-5136
Suite 700 — Fax: (202) 872-5501
Washington, DC 20036
Contact: Ms. Diane Smiroldo
Vice President, Public Affairs

C.R. Bard, Inc.
14241 Clubhouse Road — Tel: (703) 754-2848
Gainesville, VA 20155 — Fax: (703) 754-7889
Contact: Ms. Holly P. Glass
Vice President, Government and Public Relations

California Business Roundtable
1215 K Street — Tel: (916) 553-4093
Suite 1570 — Fax: (916) 553-4097
Sacramento, CA 95814
Contact: Mr. Bill Hauck
President

California Chamber of Commerce
1215 K Street — Tel: (916) 444-6670
Suite 1400 — Fax: (916) 325-1284
Sacramento, CA 95814
Contact: Ms. Michele Zschau
Vice President, Public Affairs

Calpine Corporation
50 West San Fernando Street — Tel: (408) 794-2607
San Jose, CA 95113 — Fax: (408) 975-4648
Contact: Mr. Joseph E. Ronan, Jr.
Senior Vice President-Government & Regulatory Affairs

Canadian Institute of Chartered Accountants, The
277 Wellington Street West — Tel: (416) 204-3296
Toronto, ON M5V 3H2 — Fax: (416) 204-3424
Canada
Contact: Mr. J. Scott Allinson
Manager, Government Relations & Communications

Capital BlueCross
P.O. Box 772531 Tel: (717) 541-6134
Harrisburg, PA 17177-2531 Fax: (717) 541-2407
Contact: Mr. Aji Abraham
Director, Government Liaison

Capitol Advantage
P.O. Box 2018 Tel: (703) 289-4670
Merrifield, VA 22116 Fax: (703) 289-4678
Contact: Mr. Robert Hansan
President

CAPSTRAT INC.
1201 Edwards Mill Road Tel: (919) 882-1969
Suite 102 Fax: (919) 834-7959
Raleigh, NC 27607
Contact: Ms. April White
Account Executive

CAPTEL
300 Fifth Street, NE Tel: (202) 546-6874
Washington, DC 20002 Fax: (202) 546-3871
Contact: Mr. Philip S. Smith
President & CEO

Cardinal Health, Inc.
7000 Cardinal Place Tel: (614) 757-7769
Dublin, OH 43017 Fax: (614) 757-5115
Contact: Ms. Connie R. Woodburn
Senior Vice President, Government Relations

Caremark Rx, Inc.
1300 I Street, NW Tel: (202) 772-3501
Suite 525 West Fax: (202) 772-3535
Washington, DC 20005
Contact: Mr. Russell C. Ring
Senior Vice President, Government Relations

Cargill Incorporated
P.O. Box 5724 Tel: (952) 742-5215
Minneapolis, MN 55440-5724 Fax: (952) 742-7209
Contact: Ms. Bonnie Raquet
Corporate Vice President, Public Affairs

Carlson Restaurants
4201 Marsh Lane Tel: (972) 662-5685
Carrollton, TX 75007 Fax: (972) 307-2820
Contact: Ms. April Young
Government Affairs Manager

Cash America International Inc.
1600 West 7th Street Tel: (817) 570-1616
Fort Worth, TX 76102 Fax: (817) 570-1645
Contact: Ms. Mary L. Jackson
Vice President, Public and Government Relations

Caterpillar Inc.
100 NE Adams Street Tel: (309) 675-4872
Peoria, IL 61629-1465 Fax: (309) 675-5815
Contact: Mr. Timothy L. Elder
Director, Corporate Public Affairs

CBRL Group, Inc.
P.O. Box 787 Tel: (615) 235-4161
Lebanon, TN 37088-0787 Fax: (615) 235-4066
Contact: Mr. Patrick Sheehy
Director, Government Relations

Centene Corporation
1233 20th Street, NW Tel: (202) 223-8010
Suite 200 Fax: (202) 223-8162
Washington, DC 20036
Contact: Ms. Marie Glancy
Vice President, Government Relations

Center for Corporate Citizenship At Boston College
36 College Road Tel: (617) 552-4545
Chestnut Hill, MA 02167 Fax: (617) 552-8499
Contact: Mr. Bradley Googins
Executive Director

CenterPoint Energy
P.O. Box 4567 Tel: (713) 207-3471
Houston, TX 77210 Fax: (713) 207-9819
Contact: Ms. Diane Hasell
Director, Regulatory & Governmental Affairs

Centre for Corporate Public Affairs
128 Exhibition Street Tel: 011-61-3-9650-1
4th Floor Fax: 011-61-3-9650-1
Melbourne, VI 3000
Australia
Contact: Mr. Geoff D. Allen
Chairman

Cephalon, Inc.
145 Brandywine Parkway Tel: (610) 738-6402
West Chester, PA 19380-4245 Fax: (610) 344-0981
Contact: Mr. Robert W. Grupp
Vice President, Corporate Communications

CF Industries, Inc.
1401 Eye Street, NW Tel: (202) 371-9279
Suite 340 Fax: (202) 371-9169
Washington, DC 20005-2225
Contact: Ms. Rosemary L. O'Brien
Vice President, Public Affairs

CH2M Hill, Inc.
555 11th Street, NW Tel: (202) 393-2426
Suite 525 Fax: (202) 783-8410
Washington, DC 20004
Contact: Mr. Richard L. Corrigan
Senior Vice President, Governmental Affairs

Charleston/Orwig, Inc.
515 W. North Shore Drive Tel: (262) 563-5100
Hartland, WI 53029 Fax: (262) 563-5101
Contact: Ms. Elizabeth A. Andersen
Vice President, Account Group Director

CheckFree Corporation
4411 E. Jones Bridge Road Tel: (678) 375-3430
Norcross, GA 30092 Fax: (678) 375-2025
Contact: Ms. Brenda C. Jones
Director of Government Affairs

Chevron Corp.
1401 I Street, NW Tel: (202) 408-5865
Washington, DC 20005 Fax: (202) 408-5845
Contact: Ms. Lisa Barry
Vice President and General Manager, Government Affairs

Chicago Board of Trade
1455 Pennsylvania Avenue, NW Tel: (202) 783-1190
Suite 1225 Fax: (202) 347-5835
Washington, DC 20004
Contact: Ms. Julie Bauer
Vice President, Government Relations

Chicago Mercantile Exchange
701 Pennsylvania Avenue, NW Tel: 202-638-3838
#01 Fax: 202-638-5799
Washington, DC 20004
Contact: Ms. Lanae Clarke
Associate Director, Government & Political Affairs

Chiron Corporation
1300 Eye Street, NW Tel: (202) 962-8653
Suite 1090 E Fax: (202) 289-6819
Washington, DC 20005
Contact: Ms. Shannon C. Steward
Office Director, PAC Administrator

Ciba Specialty Chemicals
540 White Plains Road Tel: (914) 785-2692
Tarrytown, NY 10591 Fax: (914) 785-2211
Contact: Mr. Kevin Bryla
Vice President, Communications and Public Affairs

Cincinnati Bell Telephone Co.
201 East 4th Street — Tel: (513) 397-7540
102-890 — Fax: (513) 723-9815
Cincinnati, OH 45202
Contact: Mr. Christopher S. Colwell
Vice President, Government Relations

Cinergy Corp.
139 East Fourth Street — Tel: (513) 287-3540
Suite 2801 — Fax: (513) 287-3412
Cincinnati, OH 45202
Contact: Mr. John L. Stowell
V.P., Fed. Leg. Affairs, Env. Strategy & Sustainability

Cisco Systems Inc.
170 West Tasman Drive — Tel: (408) 526-6650
San Jose, CA 95134-1706 — Fax: (408) 853-1598
Contact: Ms. Laura Ipsen
Vice President, Worldwide Government Affairs

Citizens' Educational Foundation
513 Capitol Street, NW — Tel: (202) 546-3060
Suite 200 — Fax: (202) 546-3380
Washington, DC 20002
Contact: Ms. Marisol Strong
Executive Manager

Clarian Health Partners
950 N. Meridian Street — Tel: (317) 962-4526
Suite 1200 — Fax: (317) 962-4533
Indianapolis, IN 46204
Contact: Mr. Jon Mills
Sr. Public Relations Coordinator

CLECO
2030 Donahue Ferry Road — Tel: (318) 484-7688
PO Box 5000 — Fax: (318) 484-7106
Pineville, LA 71361-5000
Contact: Mr. James D. Williams
Director, State & Federal Affairs

Clorox Company, The
1221 Broadway — Tel: (510) 271-2971
Oakland, CA 94612-1837 — Fax: (510) 271-6583
Contact: Ms. Victoria Jones
Director, Government Affairs and Community Relations

CNA Insurance Association
CNA Center — Tel: (312) 822-1740
43 South — Fax: (312) 822-1186
Chicago, IL 60685
Contact: Ms. Heather E. Davis
Vice President

CNA Surety
P.O. Box 5077 — Tel: (605) 977-7715
Sioux Falls, SD 57117-5077 — Fax: (605) 330-7401
Contact: Mr. William G. Peterson
Public Affairs Officer

CoBank
P.O. Box 5110 — Tel: (303) 740-4362
Denver, CO 80217 — Fax: (303) 224-2732
Contact: Mr. Jack Cassidy
Senior Vice President Manager, Corporate & Board Relations

Coca-Cola Company, The
One Coca-Cola Plaza — Tel: (404) 676-2914
Atlanta, GA 30281 — Fax: (404) 598-2914
Contact: Ms. Sheryl Albright
PAC Coordinator

Coca-Cola Enterprises Inc.
2500 Windy Ridge Parkway — Tel: (770) 989-3775
Atlanta, GA 30339 — Fax: (770) 989-3781
Contact: Mr. John H. Downs
Senior Vice President, Public Affairs

College of American Pathologists
1350 I Street, NW — Tel: (202) 354-7106
Suite 590 — Fax: (202) 354-7155
Washington, DC 20005-3305
Contact: Ms. Denise J. Bell
Director, Federal & State Legislative Affairs

Collegiate Funding Services
1300 Connecticut Avenue, NW — Tel: (202) 659-1042
Suite 905 — Fax: (202) 659-4648
Washington, DC 20036
Contact: Mr. James R. Newell
Vice President, Government Relations

Colorado Springs Utilities
P.O. Box 1103 — Tel: (719) 668-8020
M/C 950 — Fax: (719) 668-8020
Colorado Springs, CO 80947
Contact: Ms. Lisa Mills
Business Affairs & Issues Manager

Comerica Bank
3551 Hamlin Road — Tel: (248) 371-7270
Auburn Hills, MI 48326 — Fax: (248) 371-7272
Contact: Ms. Kerri L. Gursinski
Institutional Trust Officer

Computing Technology Industry Association, The
4350 N. Fairfax Drive — Tel: (703) 812-1333
Suite 440 — Fax: (703) 812-1337
Arlington, VA 22213
Contact: Mr. Roger J. Cochetti
Group Director, US Public Policy

ConocoPhillips
1776 Eye Street, NW — Tel: (202) 833-0907
Suite 700 — Fax: (202) 785-0639
Washington, DC 20006
Contact: Mr. Don R. Duncan
Vice President, Federal & International Affairs

Consolidated Edison Co. of New York, Inc.
4 Irving Place — Tel: (212) 460-4277
Room 1650-S — Fax: (212) 460-3730
New York, NY 10003
Contact: Ms. Marie C. Smith
Director of Strategic Partnerships

Constellation Brands, Inc.
370 Woodcliff Drive — Tel: (585) 218-3638
Fairport, NY 14450 — Fax: (585) 218-3607
Contact: Ms. Virginia Clark
Vice President, External Affairs

Constellation Energy
47 State Circle — Tel: (410) 269-5281
Suite 403 — Fax: (410) 269-5288
Annapolis, MD 21401
Contact: Ms. Mary E. Dempsey
Manager, Public Affairs

Consumer Electronics Association
2500 Wilson Boulevard — Tel: (703) 907-7577
Arlington, VA 22201-3834 — Fax: (703) 907-7693
Contact: Ms. Veronica O'Connell
Director of Government Affairs

Convergys Corporation
201 E. Fourth Street — Tel: (513) 784-2141
Room 102-1870 — Fax: (513) 723-6815
Cincinnati, OH 45202-2301
Contact: Mr. Matt Davis
Senior Associate, Government Relations

Convio
11921 N. Mopac Expressway — Tel: (514) 652-2684
Suite 200
Austin, TX 78759
Contact: Ms. Lori Mize
Marketing/Sales Coordinator

Cooper Industries, Inc.
P.O. Box 4446 Tel: (713) 209-8835
Houston, TX 77210-4446 Fax: (713) 209-8982
Contact: Mr. John S. Breed
Director, Media & Government Relations

Coors Brewing Company
P.O. Box 4030 Tel: (303) 277-6240
Mail Stop NH 280 Fax: (303) 277-5723
Golden, CO 80401-0030
Contact: Mr. Alan R. Timothy
Vice President, Public Affairs

Cornerstone Government Affairs, LLC
300 Independence Avenue, SE Tel: (202) 448-9512
Washington, DC 20003 Fax: (202) 448-9501
Contact: Ms. Dana C. Stewart
Vice President

Countrywide Financial Corporation
1717 Pennsylvania Avenue, NW Tel: (202) 223-7850
Suite 625 Fax: (202) 974-1128
Washington, DC 20006
Contact: Mr. Pete Mills
Senior Vice President, Legislative & Regulatory Affairs

Credit Suisse First Boston Corporation
1201 F Street, NW Tel: (202) 626-3303
Suite 450 Fax: (202) 626-3310
Washington, DC 20004
Contact: Ms. Mary Lynne Whalen
Managing Director

Credit Union National Association, Inc.
601 Pennsylvania Avenue, NW Tel: (202) 638-5777
Suite 600, South Building Fax: (202) 638-7751
Washington, DC 20004
Contact: Mr. Richard Gose
Vice President, Political Affairs

Crompton Corp.
199 Benson Road Tel: (203) 573-2227
Middlebury, CT 06749 Fax: (203) 573-4430
Contact: Mr. Lloyd N. Moon
Vice President, Government and Industry Affairs

CSX Corporation
1331 Pennsylvania Avenue, NW Tel: (202) 626-4922
National Place, Suite 560 South Fax: (202) 783-5929
Washington, DC 20004
Contact: Mr. Michael J. Ruehling
Vice President, Federal Legislation

CTIA - The Wireless Association
1400 16th Street, NW Tel: (202) 736-2997
Suite 600 Fax: (202) 776-0540
Washington, DC 20036
Contact: Ms. Shannon B. Howard
Director, Government Affairs

Cummins-Allison Corporation
891 Feehanville Drive Tel: (847) 493-6603
Mt. Prospect, IL 60056 Fax: (847) 299-4940
Contact: Mr. Tim Minor
Vice President, Government Relations

DaimlerChrysler AG
1000 Chrysler Drive Tel: (248) 512-4218
CIMS 485-10-96 Fax: (248) 512-1762
Auburn Hills, MI 48326-2766
Contact: Mr. W. Frank Fountain
Senior VP, External Affairs and Public Policy (Auburn Hills)

Dana Corporation
P.O. Box 1000 Tel: (419) 535-4662
Toledo, OH 43697 Fax: (419) 535-4756
Contact: Mr. Edward C. McNeal
Vice President, Government Relations

Darden Restaurants, Inc.
P.O. Box 593330 Tel: (407) 245-5366
5900 Lake Ellenor Drive Fax: (407) 245-5310
Orlando, FL 32859
Contact: Mr. Richard J. Walsh
Senior Vice President, Corporate Affairs

DCI Group, L.L.C.
Two Lafayette Centre Tel: (202) 546-4242
1133 21st Street, NW, Suite M100 Fax: (202) 546-4243
Washington, DC 20036
Contact: Ms. Heather Lauer
Vice President of Operations and Administration

Deere & Company
1808 I Street, NW Tel: (202) 223-4817
Washington, DC 20006 Fax: (202) 296-0011
Contact: Mr. John W. Rauber, Jr.
Director, International Affairs

Dell, Inc.
One Dell Way Tel: (512) 728-7347
M38045 Fax: (512) 728-4238
Round Rock, TX 78682
Contact: Ms. Cathie Hargett
Director, Corporate Communications

Democracy Data & Communications, L.L.C.
1029 North Royal Street Tel: (703) 684-1282
Suite 200 Fax: (703) 683-9626
Alexandria, VA 22314
Contact: Mr. Bernard R. McConnon
President

Detroit Regional Chamber
P.O. Box 33840 Tel: (313) 964-4000
Detroit, MI 48232-0840 Fax: (303) 964-0037
Contact: Ms. Karen Batchelor
Senior Vice President, Public Affairs

Diageo North America
1301 K Street, NW Tel: (202) 715-1118
East Tower, Suite 1000E Fax: (202) 715-1114
Washington, DC 20005
Contact: Mr. Kenneth F. Lane
Vice President, State Government Relations

DigitalGlobe
1317 F Street, NW Tel: (202) 662-3734
Suite 600 Fax: (202) 347-8910
Washington, DC 20004
Contact: Ms. Dawn Sienicki
Director, Washington DC Operations

Direct Impact Company, The
99 Canal Center Plaza Tel: (703) 684-1245
Suite 400 Fax: (703) 684-1249
Alexandria, VA 22314
Contact: Ms. Mary Beth Bloomberg
Senior Vice President

Dittus Communications
1150 17th Street, NW Tel: (202) 715-1550
Suite 701 Fax: (202) 775-1404
Washington, DC 20036
Contact: Ms. Gloria Story Dittus
President and Chief Executive Officer

Dominion Resources, Inc.
P.O. Box 26666 Tel: (804) 771-4442
20th Floor Fax: (804) 771-3643
Richmond, VA 23261
Contact: Ms. Anita Powell
Political Affairs Coordinator

Dow Chemical Company, The
2030 Dow Center Tel: (989) 636-4746
Midland, MI 48674 Fax: (989) 636-6239
Contact: Mr. Michael D. Hayes
Vice President, Public Policy and Advocacy

Dow Corning Corporation
7105 Park Point Court
Fairfax Station, VA 22039
Tel: (703) 440-4071
Fax: (703) 440-4072
Contact: Ms. Faye A. Graul
U.S. Area Vice President, Government Relations

DTE Energy Co.
601 Pennsylvania Avenue, NW
Suite 350, North Building
Washington, DC 20004
Tel: (202) 347-8420
Fax: (202) 347-8423
Contact: Mr. Renze L. Hoeksema
Director, Federal Government Affairs

Duane Morris Government Affairs LLC
4200 One Liberty Place
Philadelphia, PA 19103-7396
Tel: (215) 979-1370
Fax: (215) 979-1372
Contact: Mr. Kenneth E. Davis
Managing Director

Duke Energy Corporation
422 South Church Street
Mail Code PB05D
Charlotte, NC 28202
Tel: (704) 382-8194
Fax: (704) 382-3588
Contact: Mr. Joseph E. Harwood
Vice President, State Government Affairs

Dunn & Associates, Inc., Michael E.
1700 North Moore Street
Suite 2225
Arlington, VA 22209
Tel: (703) 527-6644
Fax: (703) 527-8040
Contact: Mr. Michael E. Dunn
President

DuPont & Company
601 Pennsylvania Ave., NW
Suite 325 - North Building
Washington, DC 20004
Tel: (202) 728-3645
Fax: (202) 728-3649
Contact: Ms. Nancie S. Johnson
Vice President, Government Affairs

E-Advocates
901 Fifteenth St NW
Suite 1020
Washington, DC 20005
Tel: (202) 962-3955
Fax: (202) 962-0995
Contact: Ms. Pam Fielding
President

Easter Seals, Inc.
700 13th Street, NW
Suite 200
Washington, DC 20005
Tel: (202) 347-3066
Fax: (202) 737-7914
Contact: Mr. Joseph D. Romer
Executive Vice President, Public Affairs

Eastman Chemical Company
200 S. Wilcox Drive
Kingsport, TN 37662
Tel: (423) 229-2030
Fax: (423) 229-8280
Contact: Mr. Rodney D. Irvin
Vice President, Government Relations

Eastman Kodak Company
1250 H St, N.W.
Ste 800
Washington, DC 20005
Tel: (202) 857-3474
Fax: (202) 857-3401
Contact: Mr. Stephen J. Ciccone
Vice President, Public Affairs

Eaton Corporation
1111 Superior Avenue
Eaton Center
Cleveland, OH 44114-2584
Tel: (216) 523-4664
Fax: (216) 479-7013
Contact: Mr. William B. Doggett
Vice President, Public & Community Affairs

Edelman
1875 Eye St, NW
Suite 900
Washington, DC 20006
Tel: (202) 326-1759
Fax: (202) 789-0598
Contact: Mr. J. Peter Segall
General Manager

Edison Electric Institute
701 Pennsylvania Avenue, NW
Washington, DC 20004-2696
Tel: (202) 508-5569
Fax: (202) 508-5403
Contact: Mr. Morry B. Markowitz
Senior Director Exeternal Affairs

Edison Group, The
1708 Peachtree Street
Suite 100
Atlanta, GA 30309
Tel: (404) 885-9596
Fax: (404) 885-9558
Contact: Ms. Joanne Martin-Sanders
Director, Marketing and Business Development

Edward Howard & Co.
50 W. Broad Street
Suite 2200
Columbus, OH 43215
Tel: (614) 224-4600
Fax: (614) 224-8740
Contact: Ms. Marilyn J. Tomasi
Sr. Vice President & Columbus Office Manager

Edwards Lifesciences, LLC
One Edwards Way
M/S 98
Irvine, CA 92614
Contact: Ms. Neleen Eisinger
Vice President, Government Affairs

ElectriCities of North Carolina, Inc.
P.O. Box 29513
Raleigh, NC 27626-0513
Tel: (919) 760-6336
Fax: (919) 760-6050
Contact: Ms. Jeanne Milliken Bonds
Director, Political Action and Communications

Enbridge Energy Company, Inc.
1100 Louisiana
Suite 3300
Houston, TX 77002
Tel: (713) 821-2236
Fax: (713) 821-2230
Contact: Mr. Larry Springer
Public Affairs Manager

Energy East Corporation
601 13th Street, NW
Suite 720 South
Washington, DC 20005
Tel: (202) 783-5521
Fax: (202) 783-5117
Contact: Ms. Angela M. Sparks-Beddoe
Vice President, Public Affairs

Entergy Corporation
101 Constitution Avenue, NW
Suite 200 East
Washington, DC 20001
Tel: (202) 530-7325
Fax: (202) 530-7350
Contact: Mr. Arthur E.F. Wiese, Jr.
Vice President, Corporate Communications

Executive Communications Services
911 Main Street
2201 Commerce Tower
Kansas City, MO 64105
Tel: (816) 471-5225
Fax: (816) 221-6201
Contact: Mr. Charles W. Hucker
President

Executive Communications, Inc.
10355 Linn Station Road
Louisville, KY 40223
Tel: (502) 544-0532
Fax: (502) 412-5454
Contact: Ms. Elizabeth J. Welsh
President

Exelon Corporation
101 Constitution Avenue, NW
Suite 400 East
Washington, DC 20001
Tel: (202) 347-0808
Fax: (202) 347-7501
Contact: Mr. David C. Brown
Vice President, Congressional Affairs

Express Scripts, Inc.
6625 West 78th Street
Mail Route BL0220
Bloomington, MN 55439
Tel: (952) 837-5103
Fax: (952) 837-7103
Contact: Ms. Michelle D. Mack
Government Affairs Analyst

Exxon Mobil Corporation
5959 Las Colinas Blvd — Tel: (972) 444-1190
Suite 2380 — Fax: (972) 444-1168
Irving, TX 75039-2298
Contact: Mr. James R. Riley
Public Affairs Operations Manager

Fannie Mae
3900 Wisconsin Avenue, NW — Tel: (202) 752-7180
Washington, DC 20016 — Fax: (202) 752-6099
Contact: Ms. Jessica Erickson
Manager, Political Action Committee

Farmers Insurance Group of Companies
4680 Wilshire Boulevard — Tel: (323) 932-3177
Los Angeles, CA 90010 — Fax: (323) 964-8095
Contact: Mr. Wayne Wilson
Vice President, Legislative and Regulatory Affairs

Federal Home Loan Bank of Pittsburgh
601 Grant Avenue — Tel: (412) 288-5142
Pittsburgh, PA 15219-4455 — Fax: (412) 288-7315
Contact: Mr. Bill Miller
Manager, Government Relations

FedEx Corporation
942 S. Shady Grove Rd. — Tel: (901) 818-7443
Memphis, TN 38120 — Fax: (901) 818-7194
Contact: Ms. Virginia M. Parker
Administrator Government Affairs

Fidelity Investments
82 Devonshire Street — Tel: (617) 392-2658
F5E — Fax: (617) 476-5120
Boston, MA 02109
Contact: Mr. Davis Lackey
Vice President, Public Policy

First Health
1133 21 Street, NW — Tel: (202) 872-0555
Suite 450 — Fax: (202) 223-0120
Washington, DC 20036
Contact: Ms. Melissa Dodson Schooley
Vice President, Government Relations

Fleishman Hillard Inc.
1615 L Street, NW — Tel: (202) 828-8889
Suite 1000 — Fax: (202) 296-3977
Washington, DC 20036
Contact: Mr. William Black
Senior Vice President & Partner

Flint Hills Resources, LP
4111 East 37th Street North — Tel: (316) 828-8721
Wichita, KS 67201 — Fax: (316) 828-4228
Contact: Mr. Allen Wright
Vice President, Public Affairs

Florida Power & Light Company
801 Pennsylvania Avenue, NW — Tel: (202) 347-7082
Suite 220 — Fax: (202) 347-7076
Washington, DC 20004-2604
Contact: Mr. Michael M. Wilson
Vice President, Governmental Affairs

Florida Retail Federation
227 S. Adams St. — Tel: (850) 222-4082
Tallahassee, FL 32301 — Fax: (850) 561-6625
Contact: Mr. Keith M. Wemm
Program Director

Flowserve Corporation
5215 N. O'Connor Boulevard — Tel: (972) 443-6684
Suite 2300 — Fax: (972) 443-6984
Irving, TX 75039
Contact: Ms. Amy Callender
Public Affairs Specialist

Fluor Corporation
One Enterprise Drive — Tel: (949) 349-7171
Aliso Viejo, CA 92656-2606 — Fax: (949) 349-5375
Contact: Mr. J. Robert Fluor, II
Vice President, Corporate and Public Affairs

FMC Corporation
1735 Market Street — Tel: (215) 299-6710
Philadelphia, PA 19103-7501 — Fax: (215) 299-6274
Contact: Ms. Judith H. Smeltzer
Director, State Government Relations

Ford Motor Company
One American Road — Tel: (313) 337-6180
Suite 338 — Fax: (313) 323-2683
Dearborn, MI 48126
Contact: Mr. Raymond Byers
Director, U.S. State and Local Government Relations

Forum Strategies, LLC
770 Broadway — Tel: (212) 653-8726
2nd Floor — Fax: (646) 495-6002
New York, NY 10003
Contact: Mr. David G. Laufer
President

GE Consumer Finance
1600 Summer St — Tel: (203) 585-6323
Stamford, CT 10598 — Fax: (203) 585-6338
Contact: Ms. Virginia N. Stache
Legislative Affairs Manager

Gen-Probe Incorporated
10210 Genetic Center Drive — Tel: (858) 410-8758
San Diego, CA 92121 — Fax: (858) 410-8191
Contact: Ms. Linda Ivor
Associate Director, Government Affairs

Genentech, Inc.
1399 New York Avenue — Tel: (202) 296-7272
Suite 300 — Fax: (202) 296-7290
Washington, DC 20005
Contact: Mr. Walter K. Moore
Vice President, Government Affairs

General Mills, Inc.
601 13th Street, NW — Tel: (202) 737-8200
Suite 510 South — Fax: (202) 638-4914
Washington, DC 20005
Contact: Ms. Mary Catherine Toker
Vice President, Government Relations

General Motors Corporation
1660 L Street, NW — Tel: (202) 775-5068
Suite 401 — Fax: (202) 775-5077
Washington, DC 20036
Contact: Ms. Deborah I. Dingell
Executive Director, Community and Government Relations

GetActive Software, Inc.
2855 Telegraph Avenue — Tel: (510) 540-6060
Suite 600 — Fax: (202) 659-7733
Berkeley, CA 94705
Contact: Mr. Sheeraz Haji
CEO & President

Goff + Associates
2025 North Summit Avenue — Tel: (414) 277-0606
Suite 107 — Fax: (414) 277-0630
Milwaukee, WI 53202
Contact: Mr. Mark Goff
President

GolinHarris Communications
2200 Clarendon Blvd. — Tel: (703) 741-7500
Suite 1100 — Fax: (703) 741-7501
Arlington, VA 22201
Contact: Mr. Michael Fulton
Executive Vice President

Goodrich Corporation
1100 Wilson Boulevard — Tel: (703) 558-8230
Suite 900 — Fax: (703) 558-8262
Arlington, VA 22209-2297
Contact: Ms. Gerrie Bjornson
Vice President, Government Relations

Grange Mutual Casualty Company
650 South Front Street — Tel: (614) 445-2607
Columbus, OH 43206-1049 — Fax: (614) 445-2428
Contact: Ms. Christine L. Lowe
Corporate Paralegal

Great River Energy
PO Box 800 — Tel: (763) 241-2428
Elk River, MN 55330-0800 — Fax: (763) 241-6285
Contact: Mr. Rick Lancaster
Vice President, Public Affairs

Great West Life & Annuity Insurance Company
8525 E. Orchard Road — Tel: (303) 737-4649
2T3 — Fax: (303) 737-3827
Greenwood Village, CO 80111
Contact: Mr. Richard G. Schultz
Vice President, Counsel & Associate Secretary

Guidant Corporation
1310 G Street, NW — Tel: (202) 508-0800
Suite 770 — Fax: (202) 508-0818
Washington, DC 20005
Contact: Ms. Ann M. Gosier
Vice President, Government Affairs

Gulf States Paper Corporation
P.O. Box 48999 — Tel: (205) 562-5419
Tuscaloosa, AL 35404-8999 — Fax: (205) 562-5012
Contact: Mr. Dan Meissner
Director, Government & Community Relations

Haggerty Group, The
9915 Hillridge Drive — Tel: (301) 942-1996
Kensington, MD 20895-3230 — Fax: (301) 942-9740
Contact: Mr. Patrick B. Haggerty
President

Hallmark Cards, Inc.
P.O. Box 419580 — Tel: (816) 274-5244
MD 288 — Fax: (816) 274-5061
Kansas City, MO 64141
Contact: Ms. Barbara Koirtyohann
Director, Public Affairs

Harley-Davidson Motor Company
3700 W. Juneau Avenue — Tel: (414) 343-8246
Milwaukee, WI 53208 — Fax: (414) 343-4990
Contact: Mr. Wayne T. Curtin
Director, Government Affairs

Harrah's Entertainment, Inc.
One Harrah's Court — Tel: (702) 407-6387
Las Vegas, NV 89119 — Fax: (702) 407-6388
Contact: Ms. Jan L. Jones
Senior Vice President, Communications & Government Relations

Hartford Financial Services Group, The
Hartford Plaza — Tel: (860) 547-5480
Hartford, CT 06115 — Fax: (860) 547-6551
Contact: Mr. Joel Freedman
Senior Vice President/Director, Government Affairs

HBSC - North America
1401 Eye Street, NW — Tel: (202) 466-3561
Suite 520 — Fax: (202) 466-3583
Washington, DC 20005
Contact: Mr. J. Denis O'Toole
Senior Vice President, Government Relations

HCA, Inc.
310 25th Avenue North — Tel: (615) 320-9028
Suite 101 — Fax: (615) 963-3841
Nashville, TN 37203
Contact: Mr. Parker Sherrill
Consultant, Government Relations

Health Net Federal Services
2107 Wilson Boulevard — Tel: (571) 227-6561
Arlington, VA 22201 — Fax: (571) 227-6714
Contact: Ms. Adrienne B. Morrell
Vice President, Government Relations

Healthcare Distribution Management Association
901 North Glebe Road — Tel: (703) 885-0233
Suite 1000 — Fax: (202) 312-5005
Arlington, VA 22203
Contact: Mr. Scott M. Melville
Senior Vice President, Government Relations

Heineken U.S.A., Inc.
1001 G Street NW — Tel: (202) 737-5090
700 East — Fax: (202) 737-5095
Washington, DC 20001
Contact: Mr. T. Daniel Tearno
Vice President, Corporate Affairs

Hercules Incorporated
1313 N. Market Street — Tel: (302) 594-5252
Wilmington, DE 19894-0001 — Fax: (302) 594-6909
Contact: Mr. John Riley
Director, Public Affairs

Hershey Company, The
601 Pennsylvania Avenue, NW — Tel: (202) 434-8278
Suite 900, South Building — Fax: (202) 434-8258
Washington, DC 20036
Contact: Mr. Ronald P. Graf
Director, Federal Government Relations

Hewlett-Packard Company
3000 Hanover Street — Tel: (650) 857-4321
MS 20BU — Fax: (650) 857-7594
Palo Alto, CA 94304
Contact: Mr. Gary P. Fazzino
Vice President, Government & Public Affairs

Hibernia Corporation
P.O. Box 61540 — Tel: (504) 533-2545
New Orleans, LA 70161 — Fax: (504) 533-2367
Contact: Mr. Patrick Bell
Vice President, Government Relations

Highmark Inc.
1800 Center Street — Tel: (717) 302-3979
Camp Hill, PA 17089 — Fax: (717) 302-3969
Contact: Mr. Michael G. Warfel
Vice President, Government Affairs

Himle Horner Incorporated
8500 Normandale Lake Boulevard — Tel: (952) 831-3200
Suite 720 — Fax: (952) 831-5116
Bloomington, MN 55437
Contact: Mr. John Himle
President

Hoewing/Consulting
23800 Whites Ferry Road — Tel: (301) 972-8599
Dickerson, MD 20842 — Fax: (301) 972-8599
Contact: Mr. Raymond L. Hoewing
President

Hoffmann-La Roche Inc.
340 Kingsland Street — Tel: (973) 562-2213
Bld #85 /6 — Fax: (973) 562-2205
Nutley, NJ 7110-1199
Contact: Ms. Carolyn R. Glynn
Vice President, Public Affairs

Holcim (US) Inc.
201 Jones Road — Tel: (781) 647-2521
Waltham, MA 02451 — Fax: (781) 647-2516
Contact: Mr. Thomas A. Chizmadia
Vice President, Communications and Public Affairs

Home Depot, The
2455 Paces Ferry Road — Tel: (770) 384-3274
Atlanta, GA 30339-4024 — Fax: (770) 384-2775
Contact: Ms. Beth Foughner
Manager, Government Relations

Honda North America, Inc.
1001 G Street, NW
Suite 950
Washington, DC 20001
Tel: (202) 441-6600
Fax: (202) 661-4459
Contact: Ms. Ember A. Brillhart
State Legislative Coordinator

Horizon Blue Cross Blue Shield of New Jersey
3 Penn Plaza
PP16H
Newark, NJ 7105-2200
Tel: (973) 466-8754
Fax: (973) 466-7077
Contact: Mr. Patrick DeDeo
Senior Manager, Government Affairs

Hormel Foods Corporation
One Hormel Place
Austin, MN 55912-3680
Tel: (507) 437-5640
Fax: (507) 437-5135
Contact: Mr. Joe C. Swedberg
VP, Legislative Affairs & Marketing Services

Human Genome Sciences, Inc.
14200 Shady Grove Road
Rockville, MD 20850
Tel: (301) 309-8504
Fax: (301) 309-0092
Contact: Mr. Jerry Parrott
Vice President, Corporate Communications & Public Policy

Hunt Oil Company
1445 Ross Avenue
Suite 1500
Dallas, TX 75202-2785
Tel: (214) 978-8534
Fax: (214) 855-6726
Contact: Hon. Jeanne L. Phillips
Government and Public Affairs

Hutchinson Cancer Research Center, Fred
823 Yale Avenue N.
J5-300
Seattle, WA 98109-1024
Tel: (206) 667-2856
Fax: (202) 667-4382
Contact: Ms. Linda Gainer
Vice President of External Affairs and Communications

IBM Corporation
1301 K Street, NW
Suite 1200
Washington, DC 20005
Tel: (202) 515-5800
Fax: (202) 515-5906
Contact: Mr. Christopher Caine
Vice President, Governmental Programs

Illinois Association of School Boards
2921 Baker Drive
Springfield, IL 62703-5929
Tel: (217) 528-9688
Fax: (217) 528-1442
Contact: Mr. Ben Schwarm
Associate Executive Director

Impact Texas
2038 Winged Foot Court
Reston, VA 20191
Tel: (202) 744-9805
Fax: (512) 257-1468
Contact: Mr. Richard D. Stone
Partner

InfoCision Management Corporation
250 N. Cleveland-Massillon Road
Akron, OH 44333
Tel: (330) 670-5130
Fax: (330) 670-6397
Contact: Mr. Steve Brubaker
Senior Vice President, Corporate Affairs

ING Americas
601 13th Street, NW
Suite 550 N
Washington, DC 20005
Tel: (202) 879-8116
Fax: (202) 393-2308
Contact: Ms. Deborah Winston
Vice President, Federal Government Affairs

Insurance Federation of Minnesota
400 Robert Street North
Suite 208
St. Paul, MN 55101-2015
Tel: (651) 292-1099
Fax: (651) 228-7369
Contact: Mr. Alvin L. Parsons
President & CEO

Intel Corporation
1900 Prairie City Road, FM6-03
Folsom, CA 95630
Tel: (916) 356-6122
Fax: (916) 356-2392
Contact: Mr. Richard C. Hall
Director, Corporate Government Affairs

InterActiveCorp
1275 Pennsylvania Avenue, NW
9th Floor
Washington, DC 20004
Tel: (202) 661-6374
Fax: (202) 783-4512
Contact: Mr. Brent Thompson
Director of Government Affairs

InterGen Energy, Inc.
15 Wayside Road
Burlington, MA 01803
Tel: (781) 993-3170
Fax: (781) 564-5251
Contact: Mr. Robert J. Morris
Vice President, Public Affairs

International Council of Shopping Centers
1399 New York Avenue, NW
Suite 720
Washington, DC 20005
Tel: (202) 626-1400
Fax: (202) 626-1418
Contact: Mr. Herbert L. Tyson
Staff Vice President, Government Relations

International Health Racquet & Sportsclub Association
263 Summer Street
Boston, MA 02210
Tel: (617) 951-0055
Fax: (617) 951-0056
Contact: Ms. Helen Durkin
Director of Public Policy

International Paper
1101 Pennsylvania Avenue, NW
#200
Washington, DC 20004
Tel: (202) 628-1223
Fax: (202) 628-1368
Contact: Ms. Lyn M. Withey
Vice President, Public Affairs

International Sign Association
707 N. Saint Asaph Street
Alexandria, VA 22314-1911
Tel: (703) 836-4014
Fax: (703) 836-8353
Contact: Ms. Lori M. Anderson
President & CEO

International Speedway Corp.
1801 W. International Speedway Boulevard
Daytona Beach, FL 32114
Tel: (386) 947-6624
Fax: (386) 947-6796
Contact: Ms. Sue Santa
Senior Director, Public and Legal Affairs

International Truck & Engine Corporation
P.O. Box 1488.
Warrenville, IL 60555-7488
Tel: (312) 836-3932
Fax: (312) 836-3937
Contact: Mr. Thomas L. Trueblood
Manager, Green Diesel Technology Public Affairs

Intuit
55 Airport Road
Dudley, MA 01571
Tel: (508) 943-2636
Fax: (508) 943-1393
Contact: Mr. Jim Ruda
Senior Policy Advisor

Investment Company Institute
1401 H Street, NW
Suite 1200
Washington, DC 20005-2148
Tel: (202) 326-5800
Contact: Ms. Vivian Lausevic
Director, Political Affairs

Invitrogen Corp.
1455 Pennsylvania Avenue, NW
Suite 100
Washington, DC 20004
Tel: (202) 349-4065
Fax: (202) 349-4099
Contact: Ms. Janet Lynch Lambert
Director, Government Relations

Ispat Inland Inc.
3210 Watling Street
East Chicago, IN 46312
Tel: (219) 399-6631
Fax: (219) 399-6637
Contact: Mr. John Nielsen
Director, Government & Public Affairs

Issue Dynamics Inc.
919 18th St., NW
10th Floor
Washington, DC 20006
Tel: (202) 263-2910
Fax: (202) 263-2960
Contact: Mr. Ken Deutsch
Executive Vice President

Jasculca/Terman and Associates
730 N. Franklin Street
Suite 510
Chicago, IL 60610
Tel: (312) 573-5508
Fax: (312) 337-8189
Contact: Ms. Jennifer Solomon
Account Supervisor

JK Group, Inc.
P.O. Box 7174
Princeton, NJ 08543
Tel: (609) 799-7830
Fax: (609) 799-9528
Contact: Ms. Rita Kusler
Chief Organizational Officer

JM Family Enterprises, Inc.
111 NW 12th Avenue
Deerfield Beach, FL 33442
Tel: (954) 429-2000
Fax: (954) 429-2677
Contact: Mr. Jay Allison
Vice President, Government Relations

Johnson & Johnson
One Johnson and Johnson Plaza
WT204
New Brunswick, NJ 08933
Tel: (732) 524-3373
Contact: Ms. Patricia Molino
Vice President, Group Issues & Communications Manager

Jones Day
901 Lakeside Avenue
North Point
Cleveland, OH 44114-1190
Tel: (216) 586-7349
Fax: (216) 579-0212
Contact: Mr. Dennis M. Lafferty
Executive Assistant to the Managing Partner

JPMorgan Chase & Co.
402 W. Broadway
AZ1-4005 - Suite 1790
San Diego, CA 92101
Tel: (619) 702-0831
Fax: (619) 702-0820
Contact: Mr. Brian Finch
Corporate Relations Manager

Kansas City Power & Light
1201 Walnut
Kansas City, MO 64106
Tel: (816) 556-2897
Fax: (816) 556-2975
Contact: Mr. Larry Marullo
Director of Government Affairs & Community Relations

KCI
8023 Vantage Drive
San Antonio, TX 78230
Tel: (210) 255-6220
Fax: (210) 255-6031
Contact: Ms. Susan Morris
Vice President, Health Policy

Kelly Services, Inc.
999 West Big Beaver Road
Troy, MI 48084
Tel: (248) 244-5370
Fax: (248) 244-5497
Contact: Mr. James McIntire
Vice President, Public Affairs

Ketchum
1285 Avenue of the Americas
New York, NY 10019
Tel: (646) 935-4139
Fax: (646) 935-4468
Contact: Mr. Christopher Nelson
Senior Vice President/Director, Issues & Crisis Management

KeySpan Energy Delivery
175 East Old Country Road
Hicksville, NY 11801
Tel: (516) 545-4405
Fax: (516) 545-5065
Contact: Mr. Edward Carr
Government Relations Manager

Keystone Automotive Industries, Inc.
11701 NW 101st Road
Suite #1
Medley, FL 33178
Tel: (305) 863-7564
Fax: (305) 863-7567
Contact: Ms. Eileen A. Sottile
Director, Government Relations

Kintera, Inc.
9605 Scranton Road
#200
San Diego, CA 92121
Tel: (858) 795-3000
Fax: (858) 795-3010
Contact: Ms. Debra Signer
Senior Marketing Manager

Koch Industries, Inc.
655 15th St., NW
Washington, DC 20005
Tel: (202) 737-1977
Fax: (202) 879-8111
Contact: Ms. Lacye Tennille
PAC Director

KPMG LLP
2001 M Street, NW
Washington, DC 20036
Tel: (202) 533-3126
Fax: (202) 533-8516
Contact: Mr. Stephen Allis
Partner in Charge of Government Affairs

L.L. Bean
Casco Street
Freeport, ME 04033
Tel: (207) 552-6006
Fax: (207) 552-2220
Contact: Mr. John V. Oliver
Vice President of Public Affairs

Labor Ready, Inc.
1015 A Street
PO Box 2910
Tacoma, WA 98401
Tel: (253) 680-8473
Fax: (253) 502-5799
Contact: Ms. Natalie McNair-Huff
Paralegal & PAC Administrator

Land O' Lakes, Inc.
P.O. Box 64101
Mail Stop 2025
St. Paul, MN 55164-0101
Tel: (651) 481-2269
Fax: (651) 481-2000
Contact: Mr. Steven Krikava
Director, Government Relations

Leggett & Platt Incorporated
1 Leggett Road
P.O. Box 757
Carthage, MO 64836
Tel: (417) 358-8131x
Fax: (417) 358-6045
Contact: Dr. Lance G. Beshore, Ph.D.
Vice President, Public Affairs & Government Relations

Legislative Demographic Services
3975 Fair Ridge Drive
50 West Corporate Center, Suite 100 S.
Fairfax, VA 22033-2924
Tel: (703) 259-5237
Fax: (703) 259-5226
Contact: Mr. Edward A. Grefe
Vice President and Chief Political Consultant

Lennox International, Inc.
2140 Lake Park Blvd.
Richardson, TX 75080
Tel: (972) 497-5316
Fax: (972) 497-5268
Contact: Mr. David F. Lewis
Vice President, Government Affairs

LensCrafters, Inc.
4000 Luxotica Place
Mason, OH 45040
Contact: Mr. Joseph B. Neville
Associate Vice President, Regulatory Services

Liberty Mutual Insurance Company
175 Berkeley Street
Mail Stop 07E
Boston, MA 02117-0140
Tel: (617) 574-5679
Fax: (617) 574-5783
Contact: Mr. Paul Mattera
Senior Vice President

Ligand Pharmaceuticals
10275 Science Center Drive
San Diego, CA 92121-1117
Tel: (858) 550-7569
Fax: (858) 550-1845
Contact: Ms. Terese M. Ghio
Vice President, Government Affairs

Limited Brands, The
Three Limited Parkway
Columbus, OH 43230
Tel: (614) 415-7282
Fax: (614) 415-7080
Contact: Ms. Heather Dahlberg Schmaltz
Government Affairs Specialist

Lincoln National Corporation
1455 Pennsylvania Avenue, NW
Suite 1260
Washington, DC 20004
Tel: (202) 783-0350
Fax: (202) 783-3332
Contact: Mr. James A. Morrill
Vice President and Director of Federal Relations

Lockheed Martin Corp.
1550 Crystal Drive
Suite 300
Arlington, VA 22202-4127
Tel: (703) 413-5996
Fax: (703) 413-5846
Contact: Mr. Stephen E. Chaudet
Vice President, State & Local Government Affairs & PAC

Louisiana Pacific Corp.
414 Union Street
Suite 2000
Nashville, TN 37219
Tel: (903) 520-2229
Fax: (866) 947-1411
Contact: Mr. David Hudnall
Forest Resource Environmental Manager

Lucent Technologies, Inc.
1100 New York Avenue, NW
Suite 640 W. Tower
Washington, DC 20005
Tel: (202) 312-5902
Fax: (202) 312-5904
Contact: Mr. Charles Mathias
Director, Government/Regulatory Affairs

Main Line Health
130 S. Bryn Mawr Avenue
1st Floor, D Wing
Bryn Mawr, PA 19010
Tel: (610) 526-8310
Fax: (610) 526-3769
Contact: Mr. Richard Wells
Vice President, Public Affairs

Mary Kay Cosmetics, Inc.
16251 N. Dallas Parkway
Addison, TX 75001
Tel: (972) 687-6756
Fax: (972) 687-1674
Contact: Mr. Kerry Tassopolous
Director, Government Relations

MasterCard International, Inc.
2000 Purchase Street
Purchase, NY 10577-2509
Tel: (914) 249-6189
Fax: (914) 249-3648
Contact: Ms. Heidi Davidson
Vice President, Public Policy

Mattel, Inc.
333 Continental Boulevard
M1-1418
El Segundo, CA 90245
Tel: (310) 252-6628
Fax: (310) 252-4443
Contact: Ms. Corinne Murat
Senior Manager, Government Affairs

May Department Stores Company
611 Olive Street
#1750
St. Louis, MO 63101
Tel: (314) 342-6725
Fax: (314) 342-3066
Contact: Mr. Richard A. Cohen
Vice President of Public Affairs & Senior Counsel

Mayo Clinic
200 First Street, SW
Rochester, MN 55905
Tel: (507) 284-2430
Fax: (507) 284-8713
Contact: Mr. Chris Gade
Chair, Division of External Relations

MBNA
1100 North King Street
MS 0127
Wilmington, DE 19884-0127
Tel: (302) 432-0956
Fax: (302) 432-0304
Contact: Ms. Wendy Y. Jamison
First Vice President, Government Affairs

McCormick Company
1000 S. Adams
Amarillo, TX 79101
Tel: (806) 374-5333
Fax: (806) 372-7040
Contact: Ms. Kathy Cornett
Chairman

McDonald's Corporation
One Kroc Drive
Oak Brook, IL 60523
Tel: (630) 623-7096
Contact: Mr. Timothy Peters
Director of Public Affairs

McGuire Communications
520 North Kenmore Street
Arlington, VA 22201-1728
Tel: (703) 522-8636
Contact: Mr. Jake McGuire
President

McKesson Corporation
One Post Street
Suite 3200
San Francisco, CA 94104
Tel: (415) 983-8494
Fax: (415) 732-2694
Contact: Ms. Ann Richardson Berkey
Vice President, Public Affairs

McLane Company Inc.
4747 McLane Parkway
Temple, TX 76503
Tel: (254) 771-7431
Fax: (254) 771-7486
Contact: Mr. Bernard H. White
Senior Government Affairs Manager

MDU Resources Group, Inc.
918 E Divide Avenue
Bismarck, ND 58501
Tel: (701) 222-7828
Fax: (701) 222-7607
Contact: Mr. Robert E. Wood
Senior VP, Governmental & Public Affairs

MeadWestvaco Corporation
One High Ridge Park
Stamford, CT 06905-1322
Tel: (203) 461-7577
Fax: (203) 461-7521
Contact: Mr. Ned W. Massee
Vice President, Corporate Affairs

Memorial Hermann Healthcare System
9401 Southwest Freeway
Suite 1223
Houston, TX 77074
Tel: (713) 448-6717
Contact: Mr. Tim Schauer
Director of Government Relations

Merck & Co., Inc.
One Merck Drive
P.O. Box 100
Whitehouse Station, NJ 08889-0100
Tel: (908) 423-5257
Fax: (908) 735-1196
Contact: Ms. Joan E. Wainwright
Vice President, Public Affairs

Meredith Corporation
1716 Locust Street
Des Moines, IA 50309-3023
Tel: (515) 284-2780
Fax: (515) 284-2511
Contact: Mr. Jerry L. Hadenfeldt
Director, Government Relations

Methodist Hospital, The
6565 Fannin
Suite D200
Houston, TX 77030
Tel: (713) 441-2920
Fax: (713) 790-2605
Contact: Ms. Carolyn J. Belk
Vice President, Government Relations

Metropolitan Transit Authority
P.O. Box 61429
Houston, TX 77208
Tel: (713) 739-4980
Fax: (713) 739-3815
Contact: Ms. Karen Marshall
Director, Community Outreach & Government Affairs

Michelin North America, Inc.
1 Parkway South
Greenville, SC 29615
Tel: (864)458-5080
Fax: (864)458-6359
Contact: Mr. Steve Evered
Director, Government Affairs

Microsoft Corporation
1401 I Street, NW
Suite 500
Washington, DC 20005
Tel: (202) 263-5910
Fax: (202) 263-5902
Contact: Mr. Jack Krumholtz
Associate General Counsel & Federal Affairs Director

MidAmerican Energy Company
P.O. Box 657 Tel: (515) 281-2287
Des Moines, IA 50303-0657 Fax: (515) 242-4395
Contact: Ms. Kathryn Marie Kunert
V.P., Community Relations and Legislative Projects

Miller Brewing Company
3939 West Highland Boulevard Tel: (414) 931-3129
Milwaukee, WI 53208 Fax: (414) 931-3183
Contact: Mr. Paul J. Lucas
Regional Director, State Government Affairs

Mindshare Interactive Campaigns, L.L.C.
1025 Vermont Avenue, NW Tel: (202) 654-0800
Suite 1200 Fax: (202) 654-0839
Washington, DC 20005
Contact: Mr. Dan Solomon
CEO

Minnesota Business Partnership
80 South 8th Street Tel: (612) 370-0840
Suite 3610 Fax: (612) 334-3086
Minneapolis, MN 55402-2213
Contact: Mr. Charlie Weaver
Executive Director

Morgan & Myers
N16 W23233 Stone Ridge Drive Tel: (262) 650-7260
Suite 200 Fax: (262) 650-7261
Waukesha, WI 53188
Contact: Mr. Matt Hamrin
Counselor

Mortgage Bankers Association
1919 Pennsylvania Avenue, NW Tel: (202) 557-2858
Suite 800 Fax: (202) 721-0248
Washington, DC 20006
Contact: Mr. Paul L. Hilliar, III
Manager

Motorola, Inc.
1350 I Street, NW Tel: (202) 371-6942
Suite 400 Fax: (202) 842-3578
Washington, DC 20005
Contact: Ms. Joann Piccolo
Corporate Vice President, U.S. Government Relations

MSHC Partners, Inc.
1101 14th Street, NW Tel: (202) 478-7905
Suite 300 Fax: (202) 223-1280
Washington, DC 20005
Contact: Ms. Trish Hoppey
Partner

MultiState Associates Incorporated
11 Grace Avenue Tel: (516) 466-0266
Suite 112 Fax: (516) 487-9679
Great Neck, NY 11021
Contact: Mr. Steven Markowitz
Principal

Mutual of Omaha Insurance Company
1700 Pennsylvania Avenue, NW Tel: (202) 393-6200
Suite 500 Fax: (202) 639-8808
Washington, DC 20007
Contact: Mr. William C. Mattox
Executive Vice President, Federal Government Affairs

MWH Capitol Management, Inc.
180 W. Washington Tel: (312) 960-2215
Suite 1100 Fax: (312) 960-2220
Chicago, IL 60602
Contact: Mr. Gary J. LaPaille
President

MWW Group
One Meadowlands Plaza Tel: (201) 507-9500
6th Floor Fax: (201) 460-9404
East Rutherford, NJ 07073-2137
Contact: Mr. Robert G. Sommer
Executive Vice President

Mylan Laboratories Inc.
1500 Corporate Drive Tel: (724) 514-1800
Suite 400 Fax: (724) 514-1873
Canonsburg, PA 15317
Contact: Mr. Rich Wheland
Government Relations Specialist

National Apartment Association
201 North Union Street Tel: (703) 518-6141
Suite 200 Fax: (703) 518-6191
Alexandria, VA 22314
Contact: Ms. Barbara Vassallo
Director, State & Local Policy

National Association of Broadcasters
1771 N Street, NW Tel: (202) 429-5308
Washington, DC 20036 Fax: (202) 775-2157
Contact: Mr. John Orlando
Executive Vice President, Government Relations

National Association of Chain Drug Stores
413 North Lee Street Tel: (703) 837-4104
Alexandria, VA 22314 Fax: (703) 836-2182
Contact: Mr. Lee Verstandig
Senior Vice President, Government Affairs

National Association of Children's Hospitals
401 Wythe Street Tel: (703) 797-6005
Alexandria, VA 22314 Fax: (703) 684-1589
Contact: Ms. Lisa M. Tate
Vice President, Public Affairs

National Association of Federal Credit Unions
3138 10th Street North Tel: (703) 522-4770
Arlington, VA 22201 Fax: (703) 522-0594
Contact: Ms. Erica Anderson
Associate Director of Political Affairs

National Association of Home Builders
1201 15th St, NW Tel: (202) 266-8470
Washington, DC 20005-2800 Fax: (202) 266-8572
Contact: Ms. Bhauna Pandit
Director of Finance, BUILD-PAC

National Association of Manufacturers
1331 Pennsylvania Avenue, NW Tel: (202) 637-3118
Suite 600 Fax: (202) 637-3182
Washington, DC 20004-1790
Contact: Ms. Tiffany N. Adams
Vice President, Public Affairs

National Association of Mutual Insurance Companies
P.O. Box 68700 Tel: 202.628.1558
Indianapolis, IN 46268 Fax: (202) 628-1601
Contact: Ms. Christina L. Kendall
Political Director

National Association of Real Estate Investment Trusts
1875 Eye St, NW Tel: (202) 739-9411
Suite 600 Fax: (202) 739-9401
Washington, DC 20006
Contact: Mr. Martin DePoy
Vice President for Government Relations

National Association of Realtors
500 New Jersey Avenue, NW Tel: (800) 874-6500
Washington, DC 20001
Contact: Mr. Gregory Knopp
Managing Director, Political Programs

National Athletic Trainers' Association
2952 Stemmons Freeway Tel: (214) 637-6282
Suite 200 Fax: (214) 637-2206
Dallas, TX 75247
Contact: Ms. Teresa Foster Welch
Assistant Executive Director

National Federation of Independent Business
1201 F Street, NW Tel: (202) 314-2010
Suite 200 Fax: (202) 484-9267
Washington, DC 20004
Contact: Ms. Sharon Wolff Sussin
National Political Director

National Field Resource Network
407 S. Dearborn Street
Suite 600
Chicago, IL 60605
Tel: (312) 654-8817
Fax: (312) 291-0250
Contact: Mr. Tim Smith
President

National Governors Association
444 N. Capitol St. NW
Suite 267
Washington, DC 20001-1512
Tel: (202) 624-5300
Fax: (202) 624-5313
Contact: Mr. David Quam
Director, State & Federal Relations

National Lumber and Building Materials Dealers Association
900 2nd Street, NE
Suite 305
Washington, DC 20002
Tel: (202) 547-2230
Fax: (202) 547-7640
Contact: Ms. Colleen Rocha Levine
Director, Legislative Affairs and LUDPAC

National Marine Manufacturers Association
444 N. Capitol Street, NW
Suite 645
Washington, DC 20001
Tel: (202) 737-9762
Fax: (202) 628-4716
Contact: Mr. Nick Tindall
PAC Manager

National Mining Association
101 Constitution Avenue, NW
Suite 500 East
Washington, DC 20001
Tel: (202) 463-2664
Fax: (202) 463-2666
Contact: Mr. Marc A. Ross
Director, Grassroots

National Multi Housing Council
1850 M Street, NW
Suite 540
Washington, DC 20036
Tel: (202) 974-2334
Fax: (202) 775-0112
Contact: Ms. Michele Cherry
Manager of Legislative Operations

National Nutritional Foods Association
1220 19th Street, NW
Suite 400
Washington, DC 20036
Tel: (202) 223-0101
Fax: (202) 223-0250
Contact: Ms. Tracy A. Taylor
Vice President of Public Affairs & Communication

National Pork Producers Council
122 C Street, NW
Suite 875
Washington, DC 20001
Tel: (202) 347-3600
Fax: (202) 347-5265
Contact: Mr. Kirk Ferrell
Vice President, Public Affairs

National Restaurant Association
1200 17th Street, NW
Washington, DC 20036-3097
Tel: (202) 331-5904
Fax: (202) 973-5374
Contact: Mr. Tom Foulkes
Director, State Relations

National Semiconductor Corporation
3689 Kifer Road
M/S G1-129
Santa Clara, CA 95051
Tel: (408) 721-7874
Fax: (408) 721-1212
Contact: Ms. Jeanette E. Morgan
Senior Director, Worldwide Government Affairs

National Write Your Congressman, Inc.
9696 Skillman
Founders Building
Dallas, TX 75243
Tel: (214) 280-4040
Fax: (214) 342-9186
Contact: Mr. David J. Berry
President - Corporate Division

Nationwide Insurance Companies
One Nationwide Plaza
1-36-18
Columbus, OH 43215-2220
Tel: (614) 677-4069
Fax: (614) 677-4099
Contact: Mr. Gregory S. Lashutka
Senior Vice President, Corporate Relations

Nebraska Public Power District
1414 15th Street
Columbus, NE 68601
Tel: (402) 563-5773
Fax: (402) 563-5145
Contact: Mr. John C. McClure
Vice President, Government and Public Affairs

New Century Mortgage Corporation
18400 Von Karman Avenue
Suite 1000
Irvine, CA 92612
Tel: (949) 224-5721
Fax: (949) 862-7922
Contact: Ms. Dinesa D. Thomas, MPP
AVP, Government Relations & Public Affairs

New York Life Insurance Company
1501 K Street, NW
Suite 117M
Washington, DC 20005
Tel: (202) 654-2941
Fax: (202) 654-2945
Contact: Ms. Jessie M. Colgate
Senior Vice President, Governmental Affairs

New York Power Authority
30 South Pearl Street
10th Floor
Albany, NY 12207
Tel: (518) 433-6748
Fax: (518) 433-6781
Contact: Mr. Frederick E. Chase
Director, Community Relations

NiSource Corporate Services
10 G Street, NE
Suite 580
Washington, DC 20002
Tel: (202) 216-9770
Fax: (202) 216-9785
Contact: Ms. Rebecca T. Sczudlo
Vice President, Federal Government Affairs

NORCAL Mutual Insurance Company
560 Davis Street
2nd Floor
San Francisco, CA 94111-1902
Tel: (415) 835-0816
Fax: (415) 835-9819
Contact: Mr. Philip Hinderberger
Senior Vice President and General Counsel

Nortel
101 Constitution Ave., NW
Suite 325 East
Washington, DC 20001
Tel: (202) 312-8086
Fax: (202) 312-8066
Contact: Ms. Susan Phillips
Vice President, Global Government Relations

North Carolina Electric Membership Corporation
P.O. Box 27306
3400 Summer Boulevard
Raleigh, NC 27611-7306
Tel: (919) 875-3079
Fax: (919) 878-3970
Contact: Ms. Nelle P. Hotchkiss
Sr. VP., Corporate Relations

Northeast Utilities
601Pennsylvania Avenue, NW
Suite 620, South Building
Washington, DC 20004
Tel: (202) 368-1146
Fax: (202) 374-7064
Contact: Mr. Todd Lavin
Executive Director, Federal Governmental Affairs

Northrop Grumman Corporation
1840 Century Park East
Los Angeles, CA 90067
Tel: (310) 201-3398
Fax: (310) 556-4595
Contact: Ms. Marsha H. Kwalwasser
Director, Government Relations

Northwestern Mutual
720 East Wisconsin Avenue
Milwaukee, WI 53202
Tel: (414) 665-1891
Fax: (414) 625-3838
Contact: Mr. Michael L. Youngman
Vice President

NOVA Chemicals Inc.
1550 Coraopolis Heights Road
Westponte Center
Moon Township, PA 15108
Tel: (412) 490-4062
Fax: (412) 490-4002
Contact: Mr. Greg Wilkinson
Vice President, Public Affairs

Novartis Corporation
701 Pennsylvania Avenue, NW — Tel: (202) 638-7429
Suite 725 — Fax: (202) 628-4764
Washington, DC 20004
Contact: Mr. David Drake
Executive Director, Federal Government Relations

NRG Energy, Inc.
PO Box 1001 — Tel: (860) 343-6967
1866 River Road — Fax: (860) 343-6968
Middletown, CT 06457
Contact: Mr. Raymond G. Long
Director, Government Affairs

Nuclear Energy Institute
1776 I Street, NW — Tel: (202) 739-8031
Suite 400 — Fax: (202) 293-3056
Washington, DC 20006
Contact: Ms. Angelina S. Howard
Exec. Vice President, Member Relations & External Affairs

Office Depot, Inc.
2200 Old Germantown Road — Tel: (561) 438-78626
Delray Beach, FL 33445 — Fax: (561) 438 3601
Contact: Ms. Mary Wong
Director, Community Relations

Ohio Health
1087 Dennison Avenue — Tel: (614) 544-5034
Columbus, OH 43201 — Fax: (614) 544-5936
Contact: Ms. Karen Morrison
Director of Public Affairs

OnPoint Advocacy
1029 North Royal Street
Suite 250
Alexandria, VA 22314
Contact: Mr. Thomas Benjamin
Principal

Option One Mortgage Corporation
3 ADA — Tel: (949) 790-8142
Irvine, CA 92618-2304 — Fax: (949) 790-7510
Contact: Mr. James Gazdecki
Vice President of Government Relations

Oracle USA, Inc.
1015 15th Street, NW — Tel: (202) 721-4807
Suite 200 — Fax: (202) 467-4250
Washington, DC 20005
Contact: Ms. Janie O'Connor
Manager of Political Programs & Compliance

Orange & Rockland Utilities
One Blue Hill Plaza — Tel: (845) 577-2922
Lobby Level — Fax: (845) 577-6913
Pearl River, NY 10968
Contact: Mr. Alan M. Freedman
Director, Public Affairs

Pacific Life Insurance Company
700 Newport Center Drive — Tel: (949) 219-3022
Newport Beach, CA 92660-6397 — Fax: (949) 219-5130
Contact: Mr. Robert G. Haskell
Senior Vice President, Public Affairs

PacifiCare Health Systems Inc.
5995 Plaza Drive — Tel: (714) 226-3707
M/S CY20-536 — Fax: (714) 226-3653
Cypress, CA 90630
Contact: Ms. Janet Newport
Vice President, Public Policy

Paramount Strategic Advocacy
3615 22nd Street — Tel: (916) 930-0457
Sacramento, CA 95818 — Fax: (916) 405-4012
Contact: Mr. Peter Gambee
President & CEO

Penn National Insurance
Two North Second Street — Tel: (717) 255-6336
Harrisburg, PA 17101 — Fax: (717) 255-6317
Contact: Ms. Lisa C. Katterman
Associate Counsel and Director, Government Relations

PEPCO Holdings, Inc.
701 9th Street, NW — Tel: (202) 872-2128
Washington, DC 20068 — Fax: (202) 872-7967
Contact: Ms. Christine Wilson
Administrative Associate & PAC Administrator

PepsiCo, Inc.
101 Constitution Avenue, NW — Tel: (202) 742-4408
Suite 4263 — Fax: (202) 742-4863
Washington, DC 20001
Contact: Mr. Galen Reser
Vice President, North America Government Affairs

PG&E Corporation
900 7th St, NW — Tel: (202) 638-3517
Suite 950 — Fax: (202) 638-3522
Washington, DC 20001-3886
Contact: Mr. Steven L. Kline
Vice President, Federal Governmental & Regulatory Relations

Pharmaceutical Research and Manufacturers of America
1100 15th Street, NW — Tel: (202) 835-3510
9th Floor — Fax: (202) 728-3932
Washington, DC 20005
Contact: Mr. Russ Bantham
Chief Operating Officer

Phillips International, Inc.
1 Massachusetts Avenue, NW — Tel: (202) 842-2002
Washington, DC 20001 — Fax: (202) 216-9188
Contact: Mr. Jeff Hollingsworth
Vice President for Government Relations

Piedmont Natural Gas
P.O. Box 33068 — Tel: (704) 731-4318
1915 Rexford Road — Fax: (704) 365-8515
Charlotte, NC 28233
Contact: Mr. Donald F. Harrow
Vice President, Governmental Relations

Pinnacle West Capital Corporation
801 Pennsylvania Avenue, NW — Tel: (202) 293-2655
Suite 214 — Fax: (202) 293-2666
Washington, DC 20004
Contact: Mr. Robert S. Aiken
Vice President, Federal Affairs

Pitney Bowes Inc.
One Elmcroft Road — Tel: (203) 351-6263
MSC: 64-23 — Fax: (203) 961-0291
Stamford, CT 06926-0700
Contact: Mr. Joseph M. Ercolano
V.P., Government Affairs-State & Local

Porter Novelli Public Affairs
1909 K Street, NW — Tel: (202) 955-6200
Suite 400 — Fax: (202) 955-6215
Washington, DC 20006
Contact: Ms. Carolyn Tieger
Partner

Portland General Electric Company
121 S.W. Salmon Street — Tel: (503) 464-7329
1WTC0301 — Fax: (503) 464-2354
Portland, OR 97204-2901
Contact: Ms. Sania Radcliffe
PAC Treasurer

Potlatch Corporation
805 Mill Road — Tel: (208) 799-1781
Lewiston, ID 83501 — Fax: (208) 799-1918
Contact: Mr. Mark J. Benson
Director, Public Affairs

PPG Industries, Inc.
One PPG Place Tel: (412) 434-4397
40 South Fax: (412) 434-4666
Pittsburgh, PA 15272
Contact: Ms. Lynne D. Schmidt
Vice President, Government and Community Affairs

PPL Corporation
Two North Ninth Street Tel: (610) 774-5372
Allentown, PA 18101 Fax: (610) 774-4751
Contact: Ms. Joanne H. Raphael
Vice President, External Affairs

Praxair, Inc.
39 Old Ridgebury Road Tel: (203) 794-3000
M-1
Danbury, CT 06810-5113
Contact: Ms. Valerie K. King
Director, Government Affairs

Premera Blue Cross
7001 220th Street, SW Tel: (425) 918-5070
Building 3, M/S 308 Fax: (425) 918-5575
Mountlake Terrace, WA 98043
Contact: Mr. Scott Forslund
Communications Director

Princeton Public Affairs Group
160 West State Street Tel: (609) 396-8838
Trenton, NJ 08608 Fax: (609) 989-7491
Contact: Mr. David Smith

Principal Financial Group
1350 I Street, NW Tel: (202) 682-1280
Suite 880 Fax: (202) 682-1412
Washington, DC 20005-3305
Contact: Ms. R. Lucia Riddle
Vice President, Federal Government Relations

Procter & Gamble Company, The
Procter & Gamble Plaza Tel: (513) 983-5168
C-6 Fax: (513) 983-8984
Cincinnati, OH 45201-0599
Contact: Mr. Jeffrey A. Lane
Vice President, Legislative & Regulatory Relations

Progress Energy
410 S. Wilmington Street Tel: (919) 546-6463
PEB 1505 Fax: (919) 546-5245
Raleigh, NC 27602-1551
Contact: Mr. Pender E. Upchurch, III
Vice President, State Public Affairs & Executive Development

Prudential Financial
1140 Connecticut Avenue, NW Tel: (202) 327-5240
Suite 510 Fax: (202) 327-5249
Washington, DC 20036
Contact: Mr. Rex B. Wackerle
Vice President

PSE&G
P.O. Box 570 Tel: (973) 430-5763
80 Park Plaza Fax: (973) 297-1480
Newark, NJ 07102-0570
Contact: Ms. Maria B. Pinho
Director, Corporate Responsibility

Public Affairs Support Services
1020 N. Fairfax Street Tel: (703) 684-2915
5th Floor Fax: (703) 684-7121
Alexandria, VA 22314
Contact: Ms. Mary P. O'Reilly
Vice President, Marketing

Publix Super Markets, Inc.
3300 Publix Corporate Parkway Tel: (863) 680-5384
Lakeland, FL 33811 Fax: (863) 284-5534
Contact: Mr. S. Randy Roberts
Director of Government Relations

Puget Sound Energy
10885 NE 4th Street Tel: (425) 462-3448
Mail Stop: PSE-12 Fax: (425) 462-3300
Bellevue, WA 98004-5591
Contact: Mr. Philip K. Bussey
Vice President, Regional & Public Affairs

Qorvis Communications
1201 Connecticut Avenue, NW Tel: (202) 496-1000
Suite 300 Fax: (202) 496-1300
Washington, DC 20036
Contact: Mr. Eric Lundberg
Managing Director

Quest Diagnostics Incorporated
815 Connecticut Avenue, NW Tel: (202) 263-6263
Suite 330 Fax: (202) 728-0338
Washington, DC 20006
Contact: Ms. Kristen Cusick
Director, Government Affairs

Randstad North America
2015 South Park Place Tel: (770) 937-7165
Atlanta, GA 30339 Fax: (770) 937-7206
Contact: Ms. Karen Carlisle
Director, Government & Public Affairs

Rayonier Inc.
50 N. Laura St. Tel: (904) 357-9106
Suite 1900 Fax: (904) 357-9101
Jacksonville, FL 32202-3638
Contact: Mr. Jay A. Fredericksen
Vice President, Corporate Relations

Reckitt Benckiser Inc.
176 CR 418 Tel: (254) 546-0298
P.O. Box 140 Fax: (254) 546-0299
Satin, TX 76685
Contact: Ms. Janet Wengler
Director, Government Affairs

Retail Industry Leaders Association
1700 North Moore Street Tel: (703) 841-2300
Suite 2250
Arlington, VA 22209
Contact: Mr. Paul Kelly
Sr. Vice President, Federal & State Government Affairs

Rinker Group Limited
P.O. Box 5697 Tel: 011.612.9412.66
West Chatswood, NSW 1515 Fax: 011.612.9412.66
Australia
Contact: Ms. Debra Stirling
Vice President, Corporate Affairs & Investor Relations

Rockwell Collins
1,300 Wilson Boulevard Tel: (703) 516-8230
Suite 200 Fax: (703) 516-8298
Arlington, VA 22209-2307
Contact: Mr. Michael McDonald
Vice President, Government Operations

Rohm and Haas Company
1300 Wilson Boulevard Tel: (703) 741-5881
Arlington, VA 22209 Fax: (703) 741-5884
Contact: Mr. Geoffrey B. Hurwitz
Director, Government Relations

RPMc Communications, Inc.
160 Lazy Laurel Chase Tel: (770) 552-0983
Roswell, GA 30076 Fax: (770) 552-8132
Contact: Mr. Roy McAllister
President

RR Donnelley
111 South Wacker Drive Tel: (312) 326-8031
Chicago, IL 60606-4301 Fax: (312) 326-8494
Contact: Ms. Carrie L. Gladney
Coordinator, Government Relations

Russell Williams, LLC
1133 21st Street — Tel: (202) 528-2446
Suite 300
Washington, D. 20036
Contact: Mr. Scott Williams
President

S.C. Johnson & Son, Inc.
1133 Connecticut Avenue, NW — Tel: (202) 331-1186
Suite 650 — Fax: (202) 659-2338
Washington, DC 20036
Contact: Ms. Nancy R. Levenson
Director of U.S. Federal Government Relations

Safeway Inc.
5918 Stoneridge Mall Road — Tel: (925) 467-2957
Pleasanton, CA 94588-3229 — Fax: (925) 467-3323
Contact: Mr. Kevin Herglotz
Vice President, Government Relations and Legislative Affairs

Sallie Mae
901 E Street, NW — Tel: (202) 969-8020
Suite 410 — Fax: (202) 969-8031
Washington, DC 20004-2037
Contact: Ms. Rose DiNapoli
Vice President, Government & Industry Relations

Salt River Project
P.O. Box 52025 — Tel: (602) 236-2645
Mail Station PAB 230 — Fax: (602) 236-2556
Phoenix, AZ 85072-2025
Contact: Mr. D. Michael Rappoport
Associate General Manager

Sankyo Pharma
120 Boxelder Lane — Tel: (770) 649-0541
Roswell, GA 30076 — Fax: (770) 649-4817
Contact: Ms. Elizabeth Brewer
Manager, Government Affairs

Sanofi-Aventis Pharmaceuticals Group
801 Pennsylvania Avenue, NW — Tel: (202) 898-3191
Suite 725 — Fax: (202) 682-0538
Washington, DC 20004
Contact: Mr. Richard M. Hodge
Director, Federal Government Relations

SAP America, Inc.
1300 Pennsylvania Avenue, NW — Tel: (202) 312-3635
Suite 500/North Tower/Gray — Fax: (202) 312-3501
Washington, DC 20004
Contact: Ms. Mary Arnold
Vice President, Government Relations

School of Management At The University of Texas At Dallas, The
P.O. Box 830688 — Tel: (972) 883-2741
SM 42 — Fax: (972) 883-4095
Richardson, TX 75083-0688
Contact: Dr. Diane S. McNulty, Ph.D.
Associate Dean for External Affairs and Corporate Development

SCI Management Corp.
1929 Allen Parkway — Tel: (713) 525-5230
Houston, TX 77019 — Fax: (713) 525-7674
Contact: Ms. Caressa Hughes
Managing Director, Governmental Affairs

Sealed Air Corporation
Park 80 East — Tel: (201) 791-7600
Saddle Brook, NJ 07663 — Fax: (201) 703-4152
Contact: Ms. Mary Coventry
Vice President, Communications and Government Affairs

Seattle, Port of
2711 Alaskan Way — Tel: (206) 728-3383
P.O. Box 1209 — Fax: (206) 728-3413
Seattle, WA 98111-1209
Contact: Ms. Jane L. Kilburn
Director, Public Affairs

Securities Industry Association
120 Broadway — Tel: (212) 618-0533
35th Floor — Fax: (212) 968-0703
New York, NY 102710080
Contact: Ms. Nancy Donohoe-Lancia
Vice President and Director, State Government Affairs

Semiconductor Equipment & Materials International (SEMI)
1401 K Street, NW — Tel: (202) 289-0440
Suite 601 — Fax: (202) 289-0441
Washington, DC 20005
Contact: Ms. Victoria Hadfield
President, SEMI North America & Global Industry Advocacy

Sempra Energy Utilities
8330 Century Park Court — Tel: (858) 654-6305
San Diego, CA 92123 — Fax: (858) 654-6301
Contact: Mr. Laurence F. Schott
Vice President, Regional Public Affairs

Siemens Corporation
701 Pennsylvania Avenue, NW — Tel: (202) 434-4834
Suite 720 — Fax: (202) 347-4015
Washington, DC 20004
Contact: Ms. Gayle Pitts
Director, Political Affairs

Sierra Health Services, Inc.
PO Box 15645 — Tel: (702) 242-7191
Las Vegas, NV 89114-5645 — Fax: (702) 242-7931
Contact: Ms. Ann Tinker
Manager, Government Affairs

Sierra Pacific Resources
6226 W. Sahara Avenue — Tel: (702) 367-5622
P.O. Box 98910 — Fax: (702) 579-0608
Las Vegas, NV 89150-0011
Contact: Ms. Judy Stokey
Director, Government Affairs

Skadden, Arps, Slate, Meagher & Flom
1440 New York Avenue, NW — Tel: (202) 371-7007
Washington, DC 20005-2111 — Fax: (202) 371-7956
Contact: Mr. Kenneth A. Gross
Partner

Slevin Group, Inc., The
525 East College Avenue — Tel: (850) 906-9888
Tallahassee, FL 32301 — Fax: (850) 906-0888
Contact: Mr. Patrick Slevin
Public Relations Consultant

Soap and Detergent Association, The
1500 K Street, NW — Tel: (202) 662-2518
Suite 300 — Fax: (202) 347-4110
Washington, DC 20005
Contact: Mr. Dennis Griesing
Vice President of Government Affairs

Society for Human Resource Management, The
1800 Duke Street — Tel: (703) 535-6042
Alexandria, VA 22314 — Fax: (703) 535-6492
Contact: Ms. Kathron A. Compton
Chief External Affairs Officer

Soft Edge Inc., The
P.O. Box 460 — Tel: (703) 442-8353
1617 Carlin Lane — Fax: (703) 790-9630
McLean, VA 22101
Contact: Mr. Robert Zehnder
President

Solvay Pharmaceuticals
901 Sawyer Road — Tel: (770) 578-5581
Marietta, GA 30062 — Fax: (770) 578-2003
Contact: Ms. Jan Reusse
Government & Public Affairs

SonoSite, Inc
21919 30th Drive, SE — Tel: (425) 951-1430
Bothell, WA 98021 — Fax: (425) 984-9607
Contact: Ms. Shannon Atchison
Senior Paralegal

South Central Connecticut Regional Water Authority
90 Sargent Dr. Tel: (203) 401-2605
New Haven, CT 06511 Fax: (203) 603-4814
Contact: Ms. Carlene E. Kulisch
Government Relations Administrator

Southern California Edison
2244 Walnut Grove Avenue Tel: (626) 302-1984
Rosemead, CA 91770 Fax: (626) 302-6315
Contact: Mr. Paul E. Shay, Jr.
Director, Public Affairs

Southern Company
601 Pennsylvania Avenue, NW Tel: (202) 261-5000
Suite 800 Fax: (202) 296-7937
Washington, DC 20004
Contact: Ms. Jolie K. Luu
Administrative Assistant

Spartanburg Regional Healthcare System
101 E. Wood Street Tel: (864) 560-6705
Spartanburg, SC 29303 Fax: (864) 560-7327
Contact: Mr. Matthew A. Van Patton
Director of Government Relations

Specialty Equipment Market Association (SEMA)
1707 Evelyn Drive Tel: (202) 783-4032
Rockville, MD 20852 Fax: (301) 231-7696
Contact: Ms. Linda Spencer
Director, International and Government Relations

Sprint Nextel Communications
6450 Sprint Parkway Tel: (913) 315-9104
Mailstop: KSOPHN0212-2A153 Fax: (913) 523-9844
Overland Park, KS 66251
Contact: Ms. Sheryl A. Wright
Vice President, Government Affairs

St. Jude Medical, Inc.
One Lillehei Plaza Tel: (651) 481-7790
St. Paul, MN 55117 Fax: (651) 490-4344
Contact: Mr. Peter L. Gove
Vice President, Corporate Relations

Starbucks Coffee Company
2401 Utah Avenue South Tel: (206) 318-6065
Seattle, WA 98134 Fax: (206) 318-0806
Contact: Ms. Sandra E. Taylor
Senior Vice President, Corporate Social Responsibility

State and Federal Communications, Inc.
80 South Summit Street Tel: (330) 761-9960
Suite 100 Fax: (330) 761-9965
Akron, OH 44308
Contact: Ms. Elizabeth Z. Bartz
President & CEO

State Farm Insurance Companies
One State Farm Plaza B-4 Tel: (309) 766-0457
Bloomington, IL 61710 Fax: (309) 766-0860
Contact: Ms. Barbara Kirchgasler
Vice President, Corporate Communications & External Relations

Stateside Associates
2300 Clarendon Boulevard Tel: (703) 525-7466
Suite 407 Fax: (703) 525-7057
Arlington, VA 22201-3367
Contact: Ms. Constance Campanella
President and CEO

Steel, Hector & Davis LLP
215 S. Monroe Street Tel: (850) 222-2300
Suite 601 Fax: (850) 222-8410
Tallahassee, FL 32301
Contact: Mr. Sean Stafford
Governmental Consultant

StorageTek
One Storage Tek Dr. Tel: (303) 661-6169
Louisville, CO 80028-4307 Fax: (303) 661-2541
Contact: Mr. Jeremy Story
Director, Corporate Communications

Sullivan & LeShane, Inc.
287 Capitol Avenue Tel: (860) 560-0000
Hartford, CT 06106 Fax: (860) 548-9984
Contact: Ms. Patricia LeShane
CEO

Suncor Energy
P.O. Box 38 Tel: (403) 269-8703
112 4th Avenue, SW Fax: (403) 269-6217
Calgary, Alberta, T2P 2V5
Canada
Contact: Ms. Patricia O'Reilly
Vice President, Communications & Public Affairs

Sunoco, Inc.
212 North Third Street Tel: (717) 232-5634
Suite 101 Fax: (717) 232-0691
Harrisburg, PA 17101
Contact: Mr. Jeffrey R. Peters
Director, Government Affairs & Media Relations

Susan Davis International
1000 Vermont Avenue, NW Tel: (202) 408-0808
Suite 700 Fax: (202) 408-1231
Washington, DC 20005
Contact: Ms. Susan Davis

Symantec Corporation
20330 Stevens Creek Blvd. Tel: (408) 517-8231
Cupertino, CA 95014 Fax: (408) 517-7749
Contact: Mr. Adam Rak
Director, Government Relations

Syngenta
1399 New York Avenue, NW Tel: (202) 347-8758
Suite 750 Fax: (202) 347-8758
Washington, DC 20004
Contact: Ms. Sarah Hull
Vice President of Public Affairs

Synopsys, Inc.
700 E. Middle Field Road Tel: (650) 584-4396
Mountain View, CA 94043 Fax: (650) 584-1510
Contact: Ms. Erin Brennock
Manager, Community Relations & Government Affairs

Synthetic Organic Chemical Manufacturers Association
1850 M Street, NW Tel: (202) 721-4122
7th Floor Fax: (202) 296-8120
Washington, DC 20036
Contact: Mr. Robert D. McArver
Director of Government Relations

Takeda Pharmaceuticals America, Inc.
475 Half Day Road Tel: (847) 383-7847
Lincolnshire, IL 60069 Fax: (847) 383-3901
Contact: Mr. Steven M. Kermisch
Director, State Government Affairs

Target Corporation
1000 Nicollet Mall Tel: (612) 696-6866
TPS 3275 Fax: (612) 696-5500
Minneapolis, MN 55403-2467
Contact: Mr. Nathan Keller Garvis
Vice President, Government Affairs

Tenaska, Inc.
1044 N. 115th Street Tel: (402) 691-9595
Suite 400 Fax: (402) 691-9575
Omaha, NE 68154
Contact: Ms. Jana Martin
Director of Public & Government Affairs

Tesoro Petroleum Companies, Inc.
300 Concord Plaza Drive Tel: (210) 283-2578
San Antonio, TX 78216 Fax: (210) 283-2207
Contact: Mr. Gene Burden
Senior Vice President, Human Resources and Government Affairs

Texas Association for Home Care
3737 Executive Center Drive — Tel: (512) 338-9293
Suite 268 — Fax: (512) 338-9496
Austin, TX 78731
Contact: Ms. Jan Orr
Membership and PAC Development Coordinator

Texas Health Resources
611 Ryan Plaza Drive — Tel: (817) 462-7937
Suite 900 — Fax: (817) 462-7886
Arlington, TX 76011
Contact: Mr. David J. Tesmer
Vice President, Government & Community Affairs

Texas Instruments
P.O. Box 660199 — Tel: (214) 480-6873
MS 8656 — Fax: (214) 480-6820
Dallas, TX 75266
Contact: Ms. Elizabeth Ann Pomykal
Dir. of Corporate & Foundation Giving

Textron Inc.
1101 Pennsylvania Avenue, NW — Tel: (202) 637-3821
Suite 400 — Fax: (202) 637-3863
Washington, DC 20004-2504
Contact: Mr. Gordon M. Thomas
Executive Director, Government Affairs

ThedaCare and Touchpoint Health Plan
122 E. College Avenue — Tel: (920) 830-5846
P.O. Box 8025 — Fax: (920) 830-5853
Appleton, WI 54912-8025
Contact: Mr. John F. Gillespie
Manager, Public & Government Relations

Thomson West
610 Opperman Drive — Tel: (612) 687-4015
Eagan, MN 55123 — Fax: (612) 687-5581
Contact: Ms. Ruth Orrick
Sr. Vice President, Corporate Communications

Thrivent Financial for Lutherans
4321 North Ballard Road — Tel: (920) 628-3738
Appleton, WI 54919 — Fax: (920) 628-3711
Contact: Mr. Brian Casey
Manager, State and Political Affairs

Timken Company, The
1835 Dueber Avenue, SW — Tel: (330) 471-4275
GNE-01 — Fax: (330) 471-3541
Canton, OH 44706-0928
Contact: Mr. Robert J. Lapp
Vice President, Government Affairs

Toyota Motor Sales U.S.A., Inc.
19001 South Western Avenue — Tel: (310) 468-3938
Legal Dept., A107 — Fax: (310) 468-7808
Torrance, CA 90509
Contact: Mr. Kevin Kinnaw
National State Government Affairs Manager

Trammell Group, The
P. O. Box 124 — Tel: (717) 534-0803
Hershey, PA 17033 — Fax: (717) 533-0705
Contact: Mr. James M. Trammell, II
Principal

Treated Wood Council
1111 19th Street, NW — Tel: (202) 463-2045
Suite 800 — Fax: (202) 463-2059
Washington, DC 20036
Contact: Mr. Jeff T. Miller
Executive Director

Triad Communication
1915 I Street, NW — Tel: (202) 332-3800
Suite 200 — Fax: (202) 332-5195
Washington, DC 20006-2116
Contact: Mr. Mike Malik
President

Trion Communications
235 Promenade Street — Tel: (401) 453-3100
Suite 600 — Fax: (401) 453-6690
Providence, RI 02908
Contact: Mr. Francis X. McMahon, Esq.
Partner

TrustMark Insurance Co
400 Field Drive — Tel: (847) 283-4020
Lake Forest, IL 60045 — Fax: (847) 615-3872
Contact: Mr. Sean McManamy
Second Vice President of Government Affairs

Turner Government and Public Affairs
1025 Connecticut Avenue — Tel: (202) 466-2511
Suite 1012 — Fax: (202) 466-3114
Washington, DC 20036
Contact: Ms. Caren Turner
CEO

Two Men and A Truck, International
3400 Belle Chase Way — Tel: (517) 394-7210
Lansing, MI 48911 — Fax: (517) 394-7432
Contact: Mr. Matt Cutler
Director of Corporate and Government Relations

TXU
1601 Bryan Street — Tel: (214) 812-2660
Suite 37-024 — Fax: (214) 812-3455
Dallas, TX 75201-3411
Contact: Mr. Walt Jordan
Governmental Director

Tyco International (US) Inc.
607 14th Street, NW — Tel: (202) 350-6903
Suite 550 — Fax: (202) 393-5110
Washington, DC 20005
Contact: Ms. Maria Penna
Executive Administrator

U.S. Bancorp
800 Nicollet Mall — Tel: (612) 303-7860
Mail Code BC-MN-H210 — Fax: (612) 303-0788
Minneapolis, MN 55402
Contact: Mr. Jim Nikolai
Government Relations Specialist

U.S. Chamber of Commerce
1615 H Street, NW — Tel: (202) 463-5965
Washington, DC 20062 — Fax: (202) 463-3190
Contact: Mr. Chad Mitchell
Executive Director, Grassroots and Advocacy Programs

Underwriters Laboratories, Inc.
1850 M Street, NW — Tel: (202) 296-1435
Suite 1000 — Fax: (202) 872-1576
Washington, DC 20036
Contact: Mrs. Ann Weeks
Director, Government, Industry & International Affairs

Unilever
816 Connecticut Avenue, NW — Tel: (202) 828-1010
Suite 700 — Fax: (202) 828-4550
Washington, DC 20006-2705
Contact: Mr. David Vernon Lustig
Director, Government Relations and Public Affairs

Union Pacific Corporation
600 13th Street, NW — Tel: (202) 662-0140
Suite 340 — Fax: (202) 662-0199
Washington, DC 20005
Contact: Ms. Katie W. Maness
Director for Washington Affairs

Unisys Corporation
Unisys Way — Tel: (215) 986-6656
M/S A2-7 — Fax: (215) 986-0526
Blue Bell, PA 19424
Contact: Mr. David H. Pingree
Vice President, Government Relations

United Health Group
701 Pennsylvania Avenue, NW
Suite 530
Washington, DC 20004
Tel: (202) 383-6400
Fax: (202) 383-6412
Contact: Ms. Elise A. Gemeinhardt
Vice President, Federal Affairs

United Parcel Service
316 Pennsylvania Avenue, SE
Suite 300
Washington, DC 20003
Tel: (202) 675-4251
Fax: (202) 675-3384
Contact: Mr. Arnold F. Wellman
Corporate Vice President, Domestic & International Public Affairs

Unocal Corporation
14141 Southwest Freeway
Sugar Land, TX 77478
Tel: (281) 287-5826
Fax: (281) 287-5162
Contact: Ms. Nancy L. Sauer
State Government Relations Director

UnumProvident Corporation
2211 Congress Street
M351
Portland, ME 04122-0545
Tel: (207) 575-4354
Fax: (207) 575-4304
Contact: Ms. Donna T. Mundy
Senior Vice President, Government Relations

USAA
9800 Fredericksburg Road
F3E
San Antonio, TX 78288-4501
Tel: (210) 498-2743
Fax: (210) 498-0883
Contact: Mr. William H. McCartney
Sr. Vice President, Govt. & Industry Relations

UST Inc.
100 West Putnam Avenue
Greenwich, CT 06830
Tel: (203) 622-3669
Fax: (203) 863-7250
Contact: Ms. Lynda M. LaMonte
Manager, Issue Management

Vanguard Group, The
100 Vanguard Boulevard
Malvern, PA 19355
Tel: (610) 669-6219
Fax: (610) 669-6840
Contact: Mr. Brian Mattes
Principal & Director of Government Relations

Verizon
1300 I Street, NW
Suite 400 West
Washington, DC 20005
Tel: (202) 515-2420
Fax: (202) 336-7923
Contact: Mr. Lincoln Hoewing
Assistant Vice President, Internet & Technology Policy

Verizon - New Jersey, Inc.
540 Broad Street, 17th Floor
Newark, NJ 07101
Tel: (973) 649-3186
Fax: (973) 624-7410
Contact: Mr. Ciro Scalera
Director of Public Affairs

Visa U.S.A. Inc.
1300 Connecticut Avenue, NW
#900
Washington, DC 20036
Tel: (703) 287-4503
Fax: (202) 862-5498
Contact: Ms. Lisa Nelson
Director, Domestic Public Policy

Visteon Corporation
One Village Center Drive
Van Buren Township, MI 48111-5711
Tel: (734) 710-4661
Fax: (734) 736-5560
Contact: Ms. Lydia R. Allen
Communications/Special Proj. Government Affairs

Vocus, Inc.
4296 Forbes Boulevard
Lanham, MD 20706-4856
Tel: (301) 459-6079
Fax: (301) 459-2827
Contact: Ms. Erin Sweeney
Marketing and Events Manager

Vulcan Materials Company
1200 Urban Center Drive
Birmingham, AL 35242
Tel: (205) 298-3229
Fax: (205) 298-2960
Contact: Ms. Mary S. Russom
Manager, Community Programs

Wachovia Corporation
301 S. College Street
NC0024 - 22nd Floor
Charlotte, NC 28288
Tel: (704) 383-7865
Fax: (704) 383-7867
Contact: Mr. Vincent Randazzo
SVP - Director of Public Policy

Waggener Edstrom
225 108th Avenue, NE
#700
Bellevue, WA 98004
Tel: (425) 638-7151
Fax: (425) 638-7001
Contact: Ms. Diane Aboulafia-D'Jaen
Senior Vice President

Waggener Edstrom Worldwide
1401 K Street, NW
Suite 401
Washington, DC 20005
Tel: (202) 326-0780
Fax: (202) 326-0781
Contact: Mr. Torod B. Neptune
Senior Vice President & U.S. Public Affairs Practice Director

Walgreen Co.
PO Box 9510
Alexandria, VA 22304
Tel: (703) 461-3132
Fax: (703) 461-3172
Contact: Ms. Debbie B. Garza
Director, Government and Community Relations

Washington Gas
101 Constitution Avenue, NW
Washington, DC 20080
Tel: (202) 624-6696
Fax: (202) 624-6010
Contact: Mr. Steven Jumper
Director, DC/ MD Public Affairs

Washington Group International
2345 Crystal Drive
Suite 708
Arlington, VA 22202
Tel: (703) 236-2740
Fax: (703) 236-1931
Contact: Ms. Cynthia Stinger
Vice President, Government Affairs

Washington Mutual Bank
1215 4th Avenue
16th Floor - MS: FCB 1620
Seattle, WA 98161
Tel: (206) 377-4081
Fax: (206) 554-5098
Contact: Ms. Suzanne Dale Estey
Vice President, Government & Industry Relations

We Energies
231 West Michigan
P346
Milwaukee, WI 53203
Tel: (414) 221-2348
Fax: (414) 221-3814
Contact: Ms. Judy Job
PAC Administrator

Weber Shandwick Worldwide
676 N. St. Clair
Chicago, IL 60611
Tel: (312) 988-2326
Fax: (312) 988-2489
Contact: Mr. Bryan K. Specht
Senior Vice President, Director, Corporate Affairs

WellChoice, Inc.
11 West 42nd Street
18th Floor
New York, NY 10036
Tel: (212) 476-1000
Fax: (212) 476-1430
Contact: Ms. Deborah Bohren
Senior Vice President, Public Affairs

Wellington Management Company
75 State Street
Boston, MA 02109
Tel: (617) 790-7746
Fax: (617) 790-7255
Contact: Ms. Sara Lou Sherman
Vice President & Counsel

WellPoint, Inc.
One WellPoint Way
T2-1A6
Thousand Oaks, CA 91362-5035
Tel: (805) 557-6776
Fax: (805) 557-6828
Contact: Mr. Andrew F. Morrison
Senior Vice President, Public Affairs

Wells Fargo & Company
Wells Fargo Center/ N9305-084
6th & Marquette
Minneapolis, MN 55479
Tel: (612) 667-6891
Fax: (612) 667-9403
Contact: Mr. William N. Kelly
Vice President, Government Relations

Wendy's International, Inc.
4288 W. Dublin Granville Road
Dublin, OH 43017
Tel: (614) 764-3437
Fax: (614) 764-3330
Contact: Ms. Mary A. Schell
Vice President, Government Relations

Werth Associates Inc., Paul
88 East Broad Street
Suite 2070
Columbus, OH 43215
Tel: (614) 224-8114
Fax: (614) 224-8509
Contact: Ms. Sandra W. Harbrecht, APR
President

West NetScan-a Thomson Business
803 West Broad Street
Fourth Floor
Falls Church, VA 22046
Tel: (703) 531-1228
Fax: (703) 533-0020
Contact: Ms. Sheryl Bell
Vice President

Western Corporate Federal Credit Union
924 Overland Court
San Dimas, CA 91773-1750
Tel: (909) 394-6472
Fax: (909) 592-4545
Contact: Ms. Sheri Ledbetter
Director, Public Affairs

Weyerhaeuser Company
PO Box 9777
CH1M31
Federal Way, WA 98063-9777
Tel: (253) 924-3770
Fax: (253) 924-4652
Contact: Ms. Creigh H. Agnew
Vice President, Government Affairs & Corporate Contributions

Whipple and Associates, John R.
1301 Mountain Laurel Circle
Harrisburg, PA 17110
Tel: (717) 234-4633
Fax: (717) 234-4634
Contact: Mr. John R. Whipple
President

Whirlpool Corporation
Administrative Center
2000 North M-63/ MD 3005
Benton Harbor, MI 49022
Tel: (269) 923-4645
Fax: (269) 923-4652
Contact: Mr. Thomas F. Catania, Jr.
Vice President, Government Relations

Wilmington Trust Company
1100 North Market Street
Wilmington, DE 19890-0001
Tel: (302) 651-8702
Fax: (302) 651-1145
Contact: Mr. Carl E. Hostetter
Vice President

Winthrop & Weinstine, P.A.
225 South 5th Street
Suite 3500
Minneapolis, MN 55402-4629
Tel: (612) 604-6404
Fax: (612) 604-6804
Contact: Mr. John Knapp
Attorney

World Wrestling Entertainment, Inc.
1241 East Main Street
Stamford, CT 06902
Tel: (203) 353-5066
Fax: (203) 328-2560
Contact: Mr. Gary Davis
Vice President, Corporate Communications

Wyeth
5 Giralda Farms
Madison, NJ 07940
Tel: (973) 660-5013
Fax: (973) 660-7322
Contact: Mr. Lowell Weiner
Assistant Vice President, Public Relations

Yellow Roadway Corporation
10990 Roe Avenue
Overland Park, KS 66211
Tel: (913) 696-6121
Fax: (913) 323-9710
Contact: Mr. Mike Kelley
Vice President, Government Relations

Zachry Construction Corporation
310 South St. Mary's Street
Suite 2400
San Antonio, TX 78205
Tel: (210) 258-2662
Fax: (210) 258-2688
Contact: Ms. Victoria J. Waddy
Director, Public Affairs

TELL YOUR FRIENDS about this goldmine of information on the corporate public affairs industry. Nowhere else will they find **CURRENT, ACCURATE DATA** on the key players in corporate communications, public relations, government affairs, philanthropy, policy-making, political action, and environmental and regulatory affairs.

There are plenty of up-to-date contacts, facts, and figures to go around. So go ahead and share these order cards with your friends and colleagues, or use them to **ORDER YOUR OWN** personal desk copy.

Better still . . . **PUT YOURSELF ON STANDING ORDER** to receive each edition as it is published every December! You'll stay updated on all the latest developments without the hassle of purchase orders and renewal forms.

JUST MAIL one of these cards TODAY!

For **ONLINE ORDERING** or information on our other directories, visit us at:

http://www.columbiabooks.com

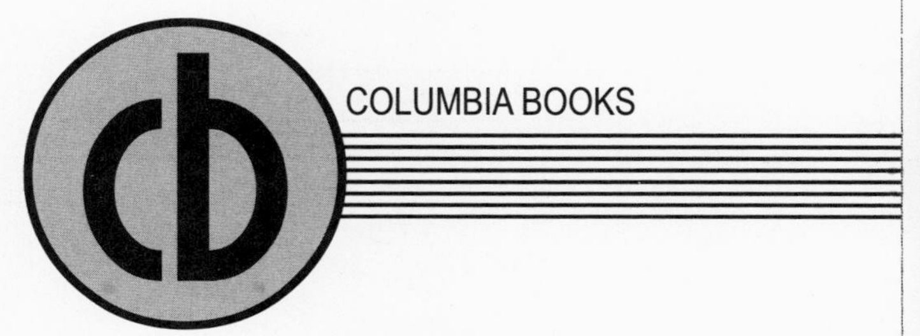

ORDER CARD

Please enter my order for the ***Nat'l Directory of Corporate Public Affairs***

☐ Twenty-fourth Edition (2006) $199.00

DC residents add 5.75% sales tax

☐ Put me on Standing Order for this and all future editions (at a 10% reduction).

☐ **Check enclosed**

☐ **Credit Card** ☐ MasterCard ☐ Visa ☐ AMEX

CREDIT CARD # ____________________

EXPIRATION DATE ____________________

SIGNATURE (required) ____________________

NAME ____________________

ORGANIZATION ____________________

ADDRESS ____________________

CITY/STATE/ZIP ____________________ PHONE (required) ____________________

SIGNATURE (required) ____________________ DATE ____________________

B406

ORDER CARD

Please enter my order for the ***Nat'l Directory of Corporate Public Affairs***

☐ Twenty-fourth Edition (2006) $199.00

DC residents add 5.75% sales tax

☐ Put me on Standing Order for this and all future editions (at a 10% reduction).

☐ **Check enclosed**

☐ **Credit Card** ☐ MasterCard ☐ Visa ☐ AMEX

CREDIT CARD # ____________________

EXPIRATION DATE ____________________

SIGNATURE (required) ____________________

NAME ____________________

ORGANIZATION ____________________

ADDRESS ____________________

CITY/STATE/ZIP ____________________ PHONE (required) ____________________

SIGNATURE (required) ____________________ DATE ____________________

B406

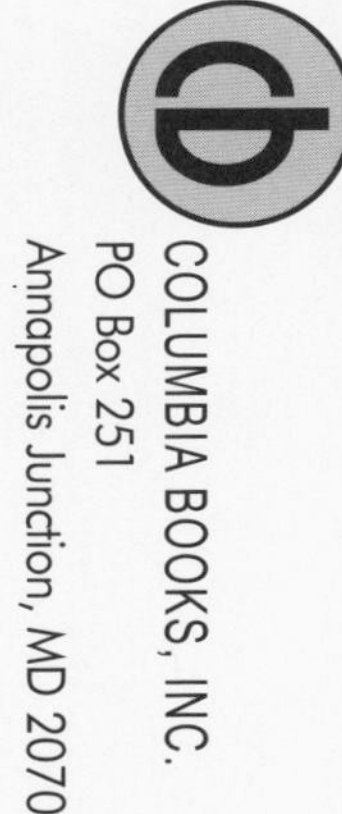

COLUMBIA BOOKS, INC.
PO Box 251
Annapolis Junction, MD 20701-0251

Place
Stamp
Here

COLUMBIA BOOKS, INC.
PO Box 251
Annapolis Junction, MD 20701-0251

Place
Stamp
Here

MAIL one of these cards TODAY

This directory is available through subscription. Just tear out one of these cards and mail it today to receive the most recent edition.

Put yourself on **STANDING ORDER**, and you'll receive EACH annual edition as soon as it is published—without the hassle of having to re-order every year—and you'll get it at a **10% DISCOUNT.**

Tell your friends and colleagues about us. Better still, pass along one of these tear-out cards so that they can benefit from this valuable reference tool!

We also take phone orders, so if you have any questions about the ***National Directory of Corporate Public Affairs*** or any of our other reference books, or if you would like to place an order, please call us at (888) 265-0600. We'll be happy to assist you!

Be sure to visit our web site at
http://www.columbiabooks.com

And be sure to sample our online products. ***Washington Representatives*** is available online at **www.lobbyists.info**, and both ***National Trade and Professional Associations*** and ***State and Regional Associations*** are available online at
www.associationexecs.com

Visit these sites for free demos!

DON'T DELAY!